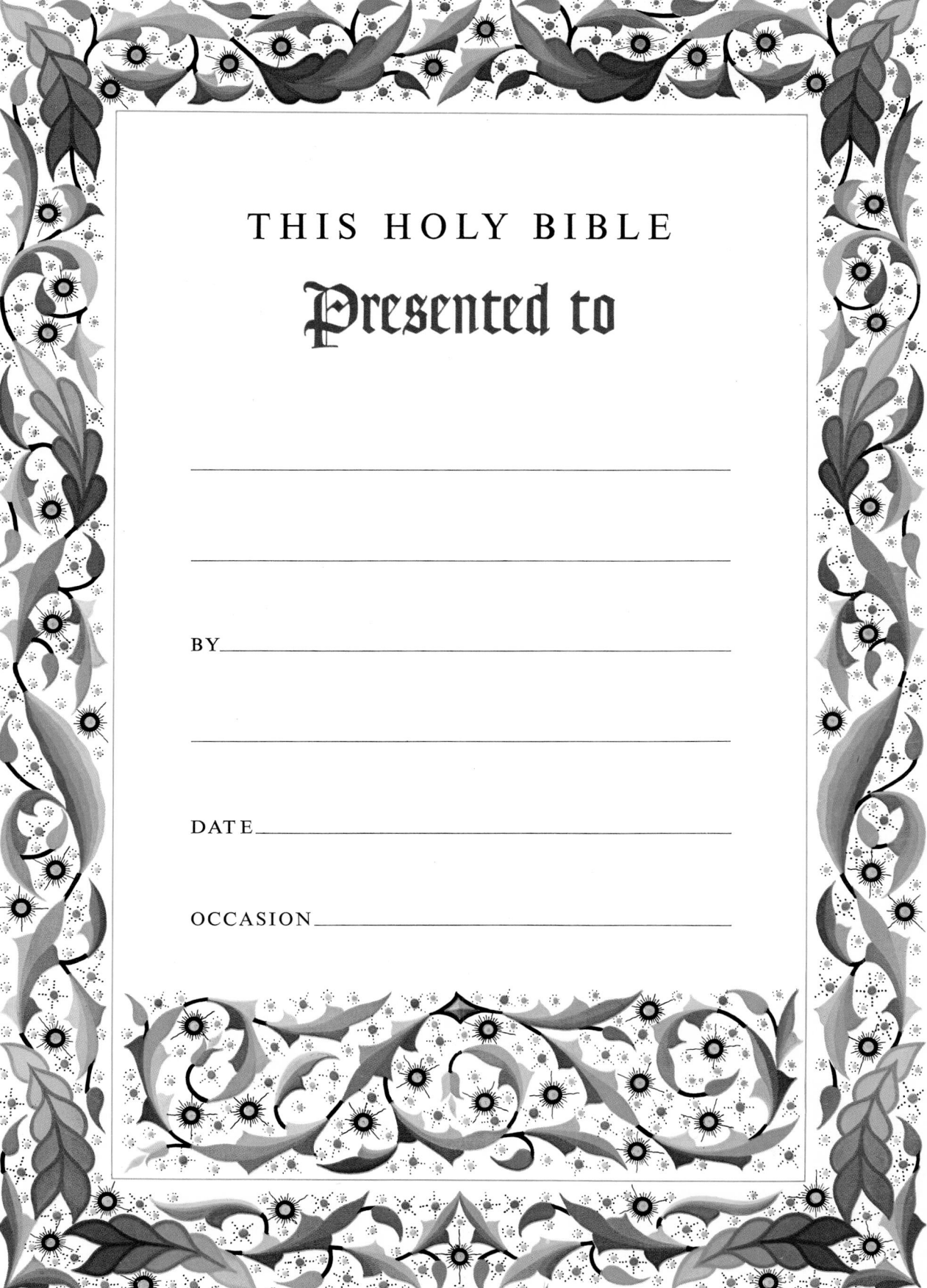

THIS HOLY BIBLE

Presented to

_____

_____

BY_____

_____

DATE_____

OCCASION_____

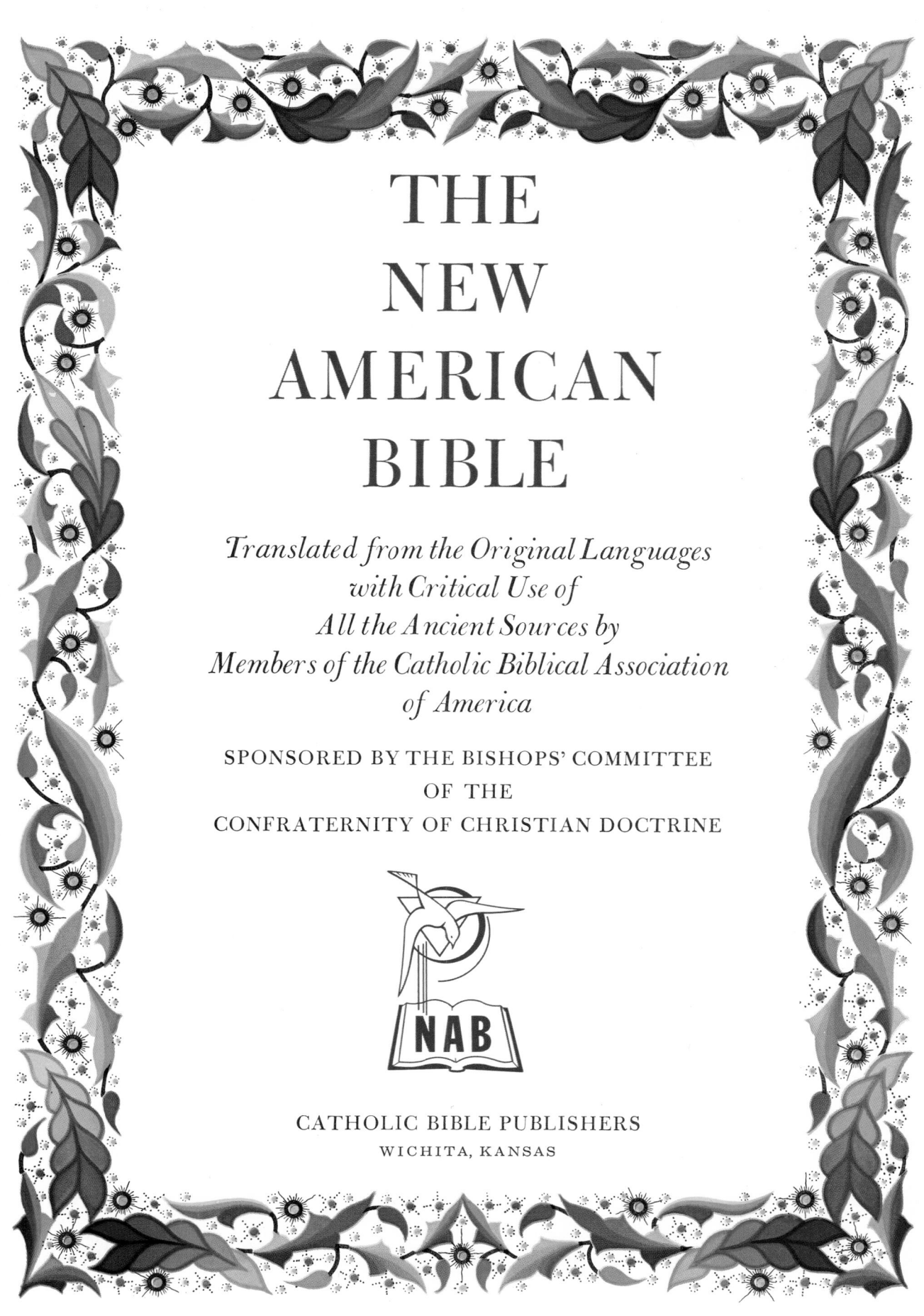

THE
NEW
AMERICAN
BIBLE

Translated from the Original Languages
with Critical Use of
All the Ancient Sources by
Members of the Catholic Biblical Association
of America

SPONSORED BY THE BISHOPS' COMMITTEE
OF THE
CONFRATERNITY OF CHRISTIAN DOCTRINE

CATHOLIC BIBLE PUBLISHERS
WICHITA, KANSAS

NIHIL OBSTAT

STEPHEN J. HARTDEGEN, O.F.M., S.S.L.
CHRISTIAN P. CEROKE, O.Carm., S.T.D.

IMPRIMATUR

✠PATRICK CARDINAL O'BOYLE, D.D.
Archbishop of Washington

PRINTED IN THE UNITED STATES OF AMERICA

1972-1973 EDITION

Pope Paul VI
AND
THE VATICAN

Pope Paul VI

MEETING in secret conclave, the College of Cardinals on June 19, 1963, elected a new Pope to succeed the late Pope John XXIII. Their selection was His Eminence Giovanni Battista Cardinal Montini, Archbishop of Milan, who at once accepted the position and immediately became the Supreme Pontiff, the 263rd successor of St. Peter. His coronation took place June 30 at which time he took the name of Paul VI.

The second of three sons, Pope Paul was born on Sept. 26, 1897, at Concesio, near the city of Brescia, in the foothills of the Italian Alps. He was ordained when 23 and after a short period spent in parish work, continued his studies and received degrees in civil and canon law, theology, and philosophy. He was named an attache of the nunciature at Warsaw, but served for less than a year, returning to Rome because of his health. In 1933 he became a clerk in the Vatican Secretariat of State. In 1936 he was appointed Undersecretary to the Papal Secretary of State, and in 1944 was named Vatican Substitute Secretary of State and then Pro-Secretary of State for Ordinary Affairs in 1952. He was consecrated Archbishop of Milan on Dec. 12, 1954, and created Cardinal by Pope John XXIII on Dec. 15, 1958. He visited the United States in 1951 and again in 1960 when Notre Dame University awarded him an honorary degree.

The Succession of Popes

St. Peter (-67)
St. Linus (67-76)
St. Anacletus (76-88)
St. Clement (88-97)
St. Evaristus (97-105)
St. Alexander I (105-115)
St. Sixtus I (115-125)
St. Telesphorus (125-136)
St. Hyginus (136-140)
St. Pius I (140-155)
St. Anicetus (155-166)
St. Soter (166-175)
St. Eleutherius (175-189)
St. Victor I (189-199)
St. Zephyrinus (199-217)
St. Callistus I (217-222)
St. Urban I (222-230)
St. Pontian (230-235)
St. Anterus (235-236)
St. Fabian (236-250)
St. Cornelius (251-253)
St. Lucius I (253-254)
St. Stephen I (254-257)
St. Sixtus II (257-258)
St. Dionysius (259-268)
St. Felix I (269-274)
St. Eutychian (275-283)
St. Caius (283-296)
St. Marcellinus (296-304)
St. Marcellus I (308-309)
St. Eusebius (309?-310?)
St. Meltiades (311-314)
St. Sylvester I (314-335)
St. Marcus (336-336)
St. Julius I (337-352)
Liberius (352-366)
St. Damasus I (366-384)
St. Siricius (384-399)
St. Anastasius I (399-401)
St. Innocent I (401-417)
St. Zozimus (417-418)
St. Boniface I (418-422)
St. Celestine I (422-432)
St. Sixtus III (432-440)
St. Leo I (440-461)
St. Hilary (461-468)
St. Simplicius (468-483)
St. Felix III (II) (483-492)
St. Gelasius I (492-496)
Anastasius II (496-498)
St. Symmachus (498-514)
St. Hormisdas (514-523)
St. John I (523-526)

St. Felix IV (III) (526-530)
Boniface II (530-532)
John II (533-535)
St. Agapitus I (535-536)
St. Silverius (536-537)
Vigilius (537-555)
Pelagius I (556-561)
John III (561-574)
Benedict I (575-579)
Pelagius II (579-590)
St. Gregory I (590-604)
Sabinianus (604-606)
Boniface III (607-607)
St. Boniface IV (608-615)
St. Deusdedit (Adeodatus I) (615-618)
Boniface V (619-625)
Honorius I (625-638)
Severinus (640-640)
John IV (640-642)
Theodore I (642-649)
St. Martin I (649-655)
St. Eugene I (654-657)
St. Vitalian (657-672)
Adeodatus II (672-676)
Donus (676-678)
St. Agatho (678-681)
St. Leo II (682-683)
St. Benedict II (684-685)
John V (685-686)
Conon (686-687)
St. Sergius I (687-701)
John VI (701-705)
John VII (705-707)
Sisinnius (708-708)
Constantine (708-715)
St. Gregory II (715-731)
St. Gregory III (731-741)
St. Zachary (741-752)
St. Stephen II (752-752)
Stephen II (III) (752-757)
St. Paul I (757-767)
Stephen III (IV) (768-772)
Adrian I (772-795)
St. Leo III (795-816)
Stephen IV (V) (816-817)
St. Paschal I (817-824)
Eugene II (824-827)
Valentine (827-827)
Gregory IV (827-844)
Sergius II (844-847)
St. Leo IV (847-855)
Benedict III (855-858)

St. Nicholas I (858-867)
Adrian II (867-872)
John VIII (872-882)
Marinus I (882-884)
St. Adrian III (884-885)
Stephen V (VI) (885-891)
Formosus (891-896)
Boniface VI (896-896)
Stephen VI (VII) (896-897)
Romanus (897-897)
Theodore II (897-897)
John IX (898-900)
Benedict IV (900-903)
Leo V (903-903)
Sergius III (904-911)
Anastasius III (911-913)
Landus (913-914)
John X (914-928)
Leo VI (928-928)
Stephen VII (VIII) (928-931)
John XI (931-935)
Leo VII (936-939)
Stephen VIII (IX) (939-942)
Marinus II (942-946)
Agapitus II (946-955)
John XII (955-964)
Leo VIII (963-965)
Benedict V (964-966)
John XIII (965-972)
Benedict VI (973-974)
Benedict VII (974-983)
John XIV (983-984)
John XV (985-996)
Gregory V (996-999)
Sylvester II (999-1003)
John XVII (1003-1003)
John XVIII (1004-1009)
Sergius IV (1009-1012)
Benedict VIII (1012-1024)
John XIX (1024-1032)
Benedict IX (1032-1044)
Sylvester III (1045-1045)
Benedict IX (1045-1045)
Gregory VI (1045-1046)
Clement II (1046-1047)
Benedict IX (1047-1048)
Damasus II (1048-1048)
St. Leo IX (1049-1054)
Victor II (1055-1057)
Stephen IX (X) (1057-1058)
Nicholas II (1059-1061)
Alexander II (1061-1073)
St. Gregory VII (1073-1085)

Bl. Victor III (1086-1087)
Bl. Urban II (1088-1099)
Paschal II (1099-1118)
Gelasius II (1118-1119)
Callistus II (1119-1124)
Honorius II (1124-1130)
Innocent II (1130-1143)
Celestine II (1143-1144)
Lucius II (1144-1145)
Bl. Eugene III (1145-1153)
Anastasius IV (1153-1154)
Adrian IV (1154-1159)
Alexander III (1159-1181)
Lucius III (1181-1185)
Urban III (1185-1187)
Gregory VIII (1187-1187)
Clement III (1187-1191)
Celestine III (1191-1198)
Innocent III (1198-1216)
Honorius III (1216-1227)
Gregory IX (1227-1241)
Celestine IV (1241-1241)
Innocent IV (1243-1254)
Alexander IV (1254-1261)
Urban IV (1261-1264)
Clement IV (1265-1268)
Bl. Gregory X (1271-1276)
Bl. Innocent V (1276-1276)
Adrian V (1276-1276)
John XXI (1276-1277)
Nicholas III (1277-1280)
Martin IV (1281-1285)
Honorius IV (1285-1287)
Nicholas IV (1288-1292)
St. Celestine V (1294-1294)
Boniface VIII (1294-1303)
Bl. Benedict XI (1303-1304)
Clement V (1305-1314)
John XXII (1316-1334)
Benedict XII (1334-1342)
Clement VI (1342-1352)
Innocent VI (1352-1362)
Bl. Urban V (1362-1370)
Gregory XI (1370-1378)
Urban VI (1378-1389)
Boniface IX (1389-1404)
Innocent VII (1404-1406)
Gregory XII (1406-1415)
Martin V (1417-1431)
Eugene IV (1431-1447)
Nicholas V (1447-1455)
Callistus III (1455-1458)
Pius II (1458-1464)

Paul II (1464-1471)
Sixtus IV (1471-1484)
Innocent VIII (1484-1492)
Alexander VI (1492-1503)
Pius III (1503-1503)
Julius II (1503-1513)
Leo X (1513-1521)
Adrian VI (1522-1523)
Clement VII (1523-1534)
Paul III (1534-1549)
Julius III (1550-1555)
Marcellus II (1555-1555)
Paul IV (1555-1559)
Pius IV (1559-1565)
St. Pius V (1566-1572)
Gregory XIII (1572-1585)
Sixtus V (1585-1590)
Urban VII (1590-1590)
Gregory XIV (1590-1591)
Innocent IX (1591-1591)
Clement VIII (1592-1605)
Leo XI (1605-1605)
Paul V (1605-1621)
Gregory XV (1621-1623)
Urban VIII (1623-1644)
Innocent X (1644-1655)
Alexander VII (1655-1667)
Clement IX (1667-1669)
Clement X (1670-1676)
Bl. Innocent XI (1676-1689)
Alexander VIII (1689-1691)
Innocent XII (1691-1700)
Clement XI (1700-1721)
Innocent XIII (1721-1724)
Benedict XIII (1724-1730)
Clement XII (1730-1740)
Benedict XIV (1740-1758)
Clement XIII (1758-1769)
Clement XIV (1769-1774)
Pius VI (1775-1799)
Pius VII (1800-1823)
Leo XII (1823-1829)
Pius VIII (1829-1830)
Gregory XVI (1831-1846)
Pius IX (1846-1878)
Leo XIII (1878-1903)
St. Pius X (1903-1914)
Benedict XV (1914-1922)
Pius XI (1922-1939)
Pius XII (1939-1958)
John XXIII (1958-1963)
Paul VI (1963-   )

The Swiss Guards in St. Peter's Church piazza

THE VATICAN

THE VATICAN CITY STATE is the smallest sovereign state in the world and the territorial seat of the Papacy. It embraces an area of 108.7 acres and is located on one of the original seven hills of Rome, where it is now completely surrounded by the City of Rome. From here the Pope administers to over 600,000,000 Catholics spread throughout the world. About half of the area comprises the Vatican Gardens, while the rest contains the Vatican Palace where the Pope resides, St. Peter's Basilica, museums, art galleries, a radio station, stores and offices, and apartments for over 1,000 permanent residents. Most of these residents are priests and religious in Vatican service; the rest are engaged in secretarial, domestic, trade, and service occupations.

In addition to Vatican City proper, the extra-territorial rights of the Vatican extend to thirteen buildings in Rome, including the major basilicas and office buildings of various Congregations of the Roman Curia, and to the Villa of Castel Gandolfo, fifteen miles southeast of Rome, which is the summer home of the Pope.

The government of Vatican City is in the hands of the Pope, who entrusts its functions to the Pontifical Commission, which he appoints. The Vatican has a Secretary of State and maintains diplomatic relations with other nations, and most nations are, in turn, represented at the Papal Court.

During the Middle Ages the Pope controlled a much greater land area; as late as the Nineteenth Century, he ruled 16,000 square miles of Papal State across the middle of Italy with a population of over 3,000,000. This was lost to the Kingdom of Italy, under King Emmanuel II, who seized Rome in 1870. The Popes then remained virtual prisoners within Vatican City until the Lateran Treaty of 1929, in which the Church recognized the Kingdom of Italy, and in turn, the Kingdom of Italy recognized the Vatican as a free and independent state.

THE SWISS GUARDS

The Vatican maintains its own armed forces, which consists of two professional and three honorary bodies. One of these is the famous Swiss Guards, which dates back to 1506. Members of the Guard are all of noble descent. They are Catholics with a height of 5 feet 11 inches or more, bachelors, and they are accepted between the ages of eighteen and twenty-five. They are eligible for pensions after ten years. It is practically a hereditary occupation, as the same families are represented through the years.

The Guards dress in colorful Renaissance uniforms reputedly designed by Michelangelo. Their duties are to protect the personal safety of the Pope and to guard the main gates of the Vatican.

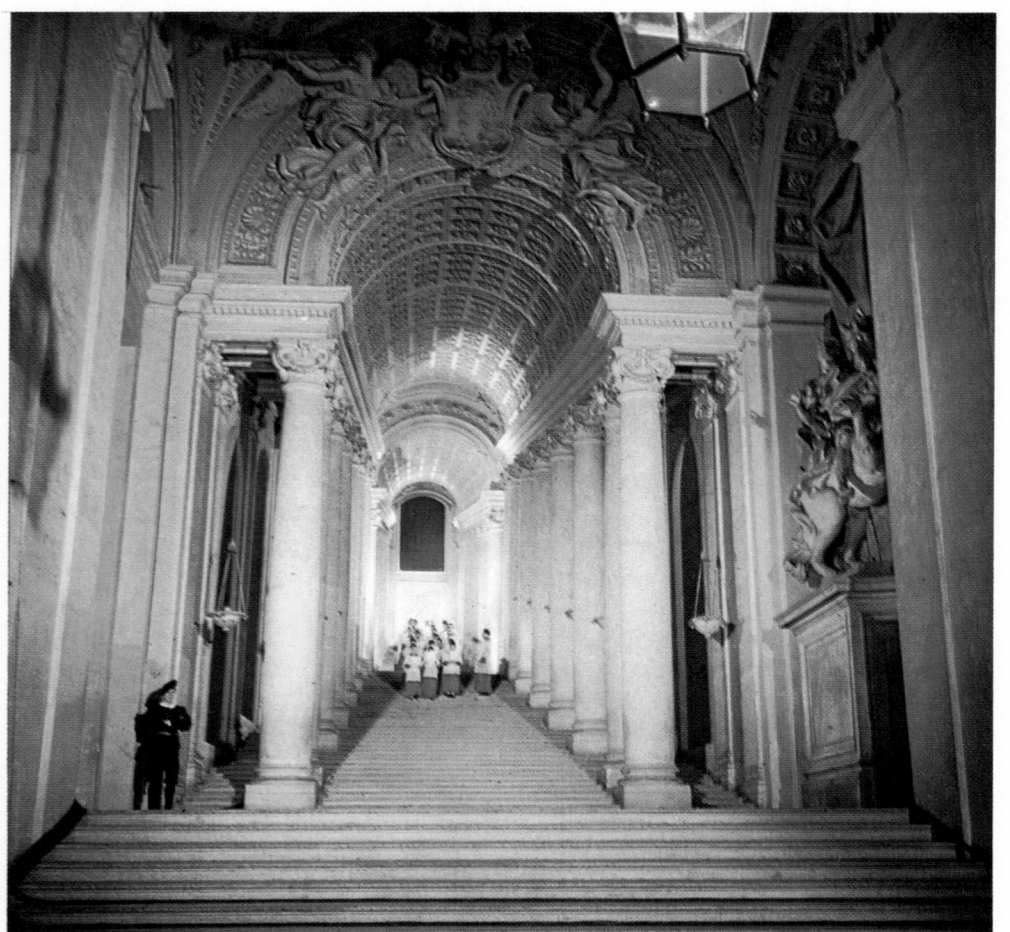

*The Sistine Choir
descending a staircase*

*The Faithful gather
to see and hear the Pope*

The Papal Gendarmes are the official police of Vatican City. Serving as attendants in the Papal chambers and on civil occasions are the Noble Guards, Palatine Guards, and Gentlemen of his Holiness.

THE BASILICA OF ST. PETER'S

St. Peter's Church is the largest and greatest church in Christendom. The area on which the Church stands was originally a cemetery; it was the burial place of St. Peter and many of the early Popes and martyrs. The Roman Emperor Constantine first erected a basilica over St. Peter's tomb in the Fourth Century, and a succession of Popes added to it. When the Church fell into decay, a new Church of St. Peter's

*The Council Fathers meet
in St. Peter's Church*

*St. Peter's high altar
and canopy,
designed by Bernini*

was conceived by Pope Nicholas V (1447–1455), and building began under Pope Julius II in 1506. The work was continued under a succession of Popes, and the Church was finally dedicated one hundred twenty years later by Pope Urban VIII in 1626.

St. Peter's Church is 694 feet long, and its transepts are 451 feet wide. The summit of the dome is 435 feet from the ground, and the dome's diameter is 138 feet. The whole building comprises an area of 163,182 square feet. The first architect was Leon Alberti, and he was followed by G. da Sangallo, Bramonte, and A. da Sangallo. Michelangelo was also one of the chief architects and designed the dome. Raphael was involved in the architecture and also painted the tremendous murals that decorate the Borgia Apartments and the Logge. Another important contributor was Bernini, who executed the bronze canopy and high altar in St. Peter's Church, and also the colonnades surrounding the great piazza in front of the Church.

THE SISTINE CHAPEL AND CHOIR

The exquisite Sistine Chapel is renowned no less for its choir than for its paintings. It was built by Pope Sixtus IV in 1477, and Raphael, Michelangelo, and other famous artists contributed to its decorations. A vast fresco of Michelangelo, which covers the vaulted ceiling, is undoubtedly the most famous painting in the world. Working while lying on his back on the high scaffolding, it took him four years to complete.

It is here that the College of Cardinals gather from all parts of the world to elect a new Pope upon the death of the reigning one. They remain "locked up" until a new Pope is elected. The shortest election was that of Pius XII, which lasted twenty hours. The longest occurred in 1268, when it took the Cardinals two years, nine months, and two days before naming Pope Gregory X.

THE VATICAN GARDENS

Beautiful formal gardens form about half of Vatican City. They are situated on the highest point of Vatican City and look down on a portion of the city of Rome. During the years 1870 to 1929, the Popes, as "Prisoners of the Vatican," confined their outside walks entirely to this area. Consequently, the various Popes showed an interest in gardening by helping lay out the flower gardens, the fountains, and the irrigation system which keeps the gardens almost perpetually green. The garden is a perfect place for viewing the dome of St. Peter's Church.

TREASURES OF THE VATICAN

The Vatican is undoubtedly the richest depository in the world of art, antiquities, books, and statues. From the year 1367, Vatican City was the regular palace and residence of the Popes, who one after the other gradually enriched it. In an age when all the world was Catholic, the great artists flocked to Rome to contribute to the Church's glory.

The Vatican Palace is the home of the Pope and it alone contains about 10,000 rooms and 1,000 staircases. The Vatican Library dates back 1,500 years; it contains

THE LAST JUDGMENT *mural in the Sistine Chapel, by Michelangelo*

THE PIETÀ, *a sculpture by Michelangelo, in St. Peter's Church*

over 70,000 manuscripts and 7,500 incunabula, and also more contemporary books. The Vatican is filled with priceless statues found beneath the ruins of ancient Rome, some 70,000 of which were excavated. The Museums are filled with masterpieces of Raphael, Michelangelo, Botticelli, Ghirlandaio, Montegna, Perugino, Fra Angelo, and untold others of every age. There are medals, curios, and antiquities of every description. Almost half the area of Vatican City contains three and four-story buildings, which are packed with invaluable treasures of classical antiquities of Greek, Egyptian, and Etruscan origin. Much of this material is available to serious students and scholars, who come here from all over the world to study.

Pope Pius XII began the updating of the Vatican Library and installed a modern reference system. Most of the important items in the Library have been micro-filmed for the Pius XII Memorial Library at St. Louis University, St. Louis, Missouri.

At the special request of Cardinal Spellman of New York, the Pope permitted Michelangelo's statue, the *Pietà*, to be shipped to New York for exhibition in the Catholic Pavilion at the New York City's World's Fair in 1965, where millions of people were able to view it.

Table of Contents

1

Acknowledgments

SINCE the making of any reference type of publication such as this edition of THE NEW AMERICAN BIBLE of necessity involves a great number of people, the publisher wishes to acknowledge and thank here those who have contributed importantly to this publication and without whose assistance this work would not have been possible.

To the Bishops' Committee of the Confraternity of Christian Doctrine, editors in chief and associate editors and translators of THE NEW AMERICAN BIBLE for the years of exhaustive labor which this dedicated group has given to make possible THE NEW AMERICAN BIBLE.

To Reverend William M. Carr, A.B., Director of Education, Wichita, Kansas, for his invaluable help and guidance toward the editorial and research work necessary in publishing this edition of the Bible.

To Reverend Lawrence E. Pierce, M.Lit., pastor of St. John's Catholic Church, Herington, Kansas, for editing, updating and writing many of the articles appearing in the "Catholic Encyclopedic Dictionary and Biblical Reference Guide," the "Synchronous History of the Nations" and the "Origin, Inspiration and History of the Bible."

To the Rev. Robert J. Willmes, S.J., and the Rev. Jerome V. Jacobsen, S.J., of Loyola University, Chicago, Illinois, and to the Jesuit fathers—theologians and biblical scholars—at West Baden College, West Baden Springs, Indiana, for their critical review of the "Catholic Encyclopedic Dictionary and Biblical Reference Guide" and other material in this Bible.

To Rev. James J. Close of St. John Brebeuf Church, Niles, Illinois, for posing for the color pictures of the Mass, and for making valuable suggestions for producing the Mass section. To Daniel Leddy, John LeCluz, Lawrence M. Lenahan and Thomas Tietz for acting as servers. To Henry Green for acting as leader and to Thomas L. Barrett for acting as lector. To Mrs. Geraldine Green, Miss Kathleen Green and Howard E. Reichardt for posing in the Communion scene. Also to Rt. Rev. Msgr. John Flanagan, pastor of St. John Brebeuf Church, for permission to use his church for the photographs of the Mass.

To Harry O. Lytle for his dedication and untiring energy necessary for the complete proofreading and editing of this edition of THE NEW AMERICAN BIBLE and all reference work and supplemental material contained in this edition.

To St. Anthony Guild Press, Paterson, New Jersey, for permission to adapt and reproduce the charts, "A Harmony of the Gospels—Outline of Chronology," from the book, A Chronological Harmony of the Gospels, by Rev. Stephen Hartdegen, O.F.M., S.Scr.L.

To Mrs. George Ember for planning and supervising the writing of the "Catholic Encyclopedic Dictionary and Biblical Reference Guide."

To Michael Stancik as art director and designer, for the design, layout, line drawings, and the many typographic specifications. To Curt Mundstock for his border designs.

To Dominick Franco for furnishing the Kodachromes and granting permission to use the pictures of The Vatican.

To Camera Clix, Three Lions, Inc., and Midland Publishers for furnishing many of the Kodachromes of the art masterpieces used to illustrate this Bible. To Felici, Official Vatican Photographer, for furnishing Kodachromes of Pope Paul VI. To Nowell Ward, Glencoe, Illinois, for taking the pictures of the Mass.

3

Bishops' Committee of
The Confraternity of Christian Doctrine

Most Rev. John J. Dougherty, S.T.L., S.S.D., past Regent of Institute of Judaeo-Christian Studies; Auxiliary Bishop of Newark.

Rev. William A. Dowd, S.J., S.T.D., S.S.L., Professor of Theology at Xavier University, Cincinnati, Ohio.

Rev. Joseph A. Fitzmyer, S.J., M.A., S.T.L., S.S.L., Ph.D., Professor Near Eastern Languages and Literature—University of Chicago.

Prof. David Noel Freedman, Ph.D., Dean of Faculty—San Francisco Theological Seminary, San Anselmo, California.

Rev. Michael J. Gruenthaner, S.J., S.T.D., S.S.D. (✝1962)

Rev. Thomas P. Halton, M.A., Ph.D., Associate Professor of Greek at Catholic University of America.

Rev. Hilary Hayden, O.S.B., M.A., S.T.L., former President of Classical Association of the Atlantic States; Chairman of the Northeast Conference on Teaching Languages; Instructor at St. Anselm's Abbey School, Washington, D.C.

Rev. Msgr. Maurice A. Hofer, S.S.L., Professor of Scripture, Pontifical College Josephinum, Worthington, Ohio.

Rev. John Knox, Ph.D., S.T.D., Professor of New Testament—Episcopal Theological Seminary of the Southwest.

Rev. Justin Krellner, O.S.B., S.T.D. (✝1949)

Rev. Richard Kugelman, C.P., M.A., S.T.L., S.S.L., Professor of Scripture, St. John's University, New York.

Rev. Joseph L. Lilly, C.M., S.T.D., S.S.L. (✝1952)

Rev. Roderick F. MacKenzie, S.J., M.A., S.S.D., Professor of Scripture—Pontifical Biblical Institute, Rome; Consultor Pontifical Biblical Commission.

Rev. Edward A. Mangan, C.SS.R., S.S.L. (✝1955)

Rev. Daniel W. Martin, C.M., S.T.L., S.S.L.—contributed to work on Old Testament.

Rev. William H. McClellan, S.J. (✝1951)

Rev. James M. McGlinchey, C.M., S.T.D. (✝1961)

Rev. Frederick Moriarty, S.J., S.S.L., S.T.D., Professor of Scripture—Pontifical Gregorian University, Rome.

Rev. Richard T. Murphy, O.P., S.T.D., S.S.D., Professor of Religious Knowledge at King's College.

Rev. Roland E. Murphy, O. Carm., M.A., S.T.D., S.S.L., Professor of Scripture—Catholic University of America; Visiting Professor at Yale and Duke Universities.

Rev. Msgr. William L. Newton, M.S., S.S.D.,—Pastor in Cleveland, Ohio—Retired.

Rev. Eberhard Olinger, O.S.B. (✝1967)

Rev. Msgr. Charles H. Pickar, O.S.A., S.T.L., S.S.L., longtime Professor of New Testament at Augustinian College in Washington, D.C.

Rev. Jerome D. Quinn, M.A., S.T.L., S.S.L., Professor of Scripture, St. Paul Seminary, St. Paul, Minn.

Rev. Christopher Rehwinkel, O.F.M., S.T.D., S.S.Lect. Gen., Professor of Scripture, Quincy College, Illinois.

Rev. Msgr. John R. Rowan, S.T.D., S.S.L. (✝1953)

Prof. James A. Sanders, Ph.D., Professor of Old Testament Scripture, Union Theological Seminary, N.Y.

Rev. Raymond Schoeder, S.J., Ph.D., Professor of Sacred Scripture, De Paul University.

Rev. Edward F. Siegman, C.PP.S., S.T.D., S.S.L. (✝1967)

Rev. David M. Stanley, S.J., S.T.L., S.S.D., Professor of Scripture, Regis College—Toronto

Rev. Msgr. Matthew P. Stapleton, S.T.D., S.S.L., longtime Professor of Scripture at St. John's Seminary, Brighton, Mass.

Rev. Msgr. John E. Steinmueller, S.T.D., S.S.L., Consultor, Pontifical Biblical Commission.

Rev. John Ujlaki, O.S.B., S.T.D., Litt. D. (✝1964)

Rev. Bruce Vawter, C.M., S.T.L., S.S.D., Professor of Scripture, De Paul University.

Rev. John B. Weisengoff, S.T.D., S.S.L., Professor of Scripture, De Paul University.

Preface To

THE NEW AMERICAN BIBLE

HIS HOLINESS POPE PIUS XII issued his now famous encyclical on Scripture studies, *Divino afflante Spiritu* on September 30, 1943. He wrote: "We ought to explain the original text which was written by the inspired author himself and has more authority and greater weight than any, even the very best, translation whether ancient or modern. This can be done all the more easily and fruitfully if to the knowledge of languages be joined a real skill in literary criticism of the same text."

Early in 1944, in conformity with the spirit of the encyclical, and with the encouragement of Archbishop Cicognani, Apostolic Delegate to the United States, the Bishops' Committee of the Confraternity of Christian Doctrine requested members of the Catholic Biblical Association of America to translate the Sacred Scriptures from the original languages or from the oldest extant form of the text, and to present the sense of the biblical text in as correct a form as possible.

The first English Catholic version of the Bible, the Douay-Rheims (1582–1609/10), and its revision by Bishop Challoner (1750) were based on the Latin Vulgate. In view of the relative certainties more recently attained by textual and higher criticism, it has become increasingly desirable that contemporary translations of the sacred books into English be prepared in which due reverence for the text and strict observance of the rules of criticism would be combined.

THE NEW AMERICAN BIBLE has accomplished this in response to the need of the church in America today. It is the achievement of some fifty biblical scholars, the greater number of whom, though not all, are Catholics. In particular, the editors-in-chief have devoted twenty-five years to this work. The collaboration of scholars who are not Catholic fulfills the directive of the Second Vatican Council, not only that "correct translations be made into different languages especially from the original texts of the sacred books," but that, "with the approval of the church authority, these translations be produced in cooperation with separated brothers" so that "all Christians may be able to use them."

The text of the books contained in THE NEW AMERICAN BIBLE is a completely new translation throughout. From the original and the oldest available texts of the sacred books, it aims to convey as directly as possible the thought and individual style of the inspired writers. The better understanding of Hebrew and Greek, and the steady development of the science of textual criticism, the fruit of patient study since the time of St. Jerome, have allowed the translators and editors in their use of all available materials to approach more closely than ever before the sense of what the sacred authors actually wrote.

Where the translation supposes the received text—Hebrew, Aramaic, or Greek, as the case may be—ordinarily contained in the best-known editions, as the original or the oldest extant form, no additional remarks are necessary. But for those who are happily able to study the original text of the Scriptures at firsthand, a supplementary series of textual notes pertaining to the Old Testament is added in an appendix to the typical edition published by the St. Anthony Guild Press. These furnish a guide in those cases in which the editorial board judges that the manuscripts in the original languages, or the evidence of the ancient versions, or some similar source, furnish the correct reading of a passage, or at least a reading more true to the original than that customarily printed in the available editions.

The Massoretic text of 1 and 2 Samuel has in numerous instances been corrected by the more ancient manuscripts Samuel a, b, and c from Cave 4 of Qumran, with the aid of important evidence from the Septuagint in both its oldest form and its Lucianic recension. Fragments of the lost Book of Tobit in Aramaic and in Hebrew, recovered from Cave 4 of Qumran, are in substantial agreement with the Sinaiticus Greek recension used for the translation of this book. The lost original Hebrew text of 1 Maccabees is replaced by its oldest extant form in Greek. Judith, 2 Maccabees, and parts of Esther are also translated from the Greek.

The basic text for the Psalms is not the Massoretic but one which the editors considered closer to the original inspired form, namely the Hebrew text underlying the new Latin Psalter of the Church, the *Liber Psalmorum* (1944,[1] 1945 [2]). Nevertheless they retained full liberty to establish the reading of the original text on sound critical principles.

The translation of Sirach, based on the original Hebrew as far as it is preserved and corrected from the ancient versions, is often interpreted in the light of the traditional Greek text. In the Book of Baruch the basic text is the Greek of the Septuagint, with some readings derived from an underlying Hebrew form no longer extant. In the deuterocanonical sections of Daniel (3, 24–90; 13, 1–14, 42), the basic text is the Greek text of Theodotion, occasionally revised according to the Greek text of the Septuagint.

In some instances in the Book of Job, in Proverbs, Sirach, Isaiah, Jeremiah, Ezekiel, Hosea, Amos, Micah, Nahum, Habakkuk, and Zechariah there is good reason to believe that the original order of lines was accidentally disturbed in the transmission of the text. The verse numbers given in such cases are always those of the current Hebrew text, though the arrangement differs. In these instances the textual notes advise the reader of the difficulty. Cases of exceptional dislocation are called to the reader's attention by footnotes.

The Books of *Genesis to Ruth* were first published in 1952; the Wisdom Books, *Job to Sirach*, in 1955; the Prophetic Books, *Isaiah to Malachi*, in 1961; and the Books of *Samuel to Maccabees*, in 1969. In the present edition of *Genesis to Ruth* there are certain new features: a general introduction to the Pentateuch, a retranslation of the text of Genesis with an introduction, cross-references, and revised textual notes, besides new and expanded exegetical notes which take into consideration the various sources or literary traditions.

The revision of *Job to Sirach* includes changes in strophe division in Job and Proverbs and in titles of principal parts and sections of Wisdom and Ecclesiastes. Corrections in the text of Sirach are made in 39, 27–44, 17 on the basis of the Masada text, and in 51, 13–30 on the basis of the occurrence of this canticle in the Psalms scroll from Qumran Cave 11. In the typical edition published by St. Anthony Guild Press, new corrections are reflected in the textual notes of Job, Proverbs, Wisdom, and Sirach. In the Psalms, the enumeration found in the Hebrew text is followed instead of the double enumeration, according to both the Hebrew and the Latin Vulgate texts, contained in the previous edition of this book.

In the Prophetic Books *Isaiah to Malachi,* only minor revisions have been made in the structure and wording of the texts, and in the textual notes.

The spelling of proper names in THE NEW AMERICAN BIBLE follows the customary forms found in most English Bibles since the Authorized Version.

* * * * *

The New Testament translation has been approached with essentially the same fidelity to the thought and individual style of the biblical writers as was applied in the Old Testament. In some cases, however, the problem of marked literary peculiarities

must be met. What by any Western standard are the limited vocabularies and stylistic infelicities of the evangelists cannot be retained in the exact form in which they appear in the originals without displeasing the modern ear. A compromise is here attempted whereby some measure of the poverty of the evangelists' expression is kept and placed at the service of their message in its richness. Similarly, the syntactical shortcomings of Paul, his frequent lapses into anacoluthon, and the like, are rendered as they occur in his epistles rather than "smoothed out." Only thus, the translators suppose, will contemporary readers have some adequate idea of the kind of writing they have before them. When the prose of the original flows more smoothly, as in Luke, Acts, and Hebrews, it is reflected in the translation.

The Gospel according to John comprises a special case. Absolute fidelity to his technique of reiterated phrasing would result in an assault on the English ear, yet the softening of the vocal effect by substitution of other words and phrases would destroy the effectiveness of his poetry. Again, resort is had to compromise. This is not an easy matter when the very repetitiousness which the author deliberately employed is at the same time regarded by those who read and speak English to be a serious stylistic defect. Only those familiar with the Greek originals can know what a relentless tattoo Johannine poetry can produce. A similar observation could be made regarding other New Testament books as well. Matthew and Mark are given to identical phrasing twice and three times in the same sentence. As for the rhetorical overgrowth and mixed figures of speech in the letters of Peter, James, and Jude, the translator must resist a powerful compulsion to tidy them up if only to enable him to render these epistles intelligibly.

Without seeking refuge in complaints against the inspired authors, however, the translators of THE NEW AMERICAN BIBLE here state that what they have attempted is a translation rather than a paraphrase. To be sure, all translation can be called paraphrase by definition. Any striving for complete fidelity will shortly end in infidelity. Nonetheless, it must be pointed out that the temptation to improve overladen sentences by the consolidation or elimination of multiplied adjectives, or the simplification of clumsy hendiadys, has been resisted here. For the most part, rhetorically ineffective words and phrases are retained in this translation in some form, even when it is clear that a Western contemporary writer would never have employed them.

One other matter should be mentioned. Despite the arbitrary character of the divisions into numbered verses (a scheme which in its present form is only four centuries old), the translators have made a constant effort to keep within an English verse the whole verbal content of the Greek verse. At times the effort has not seemed worth the result since it often does violence to the original author's flow of expression, which preceded it by so many centuries. If this translation had been prepared for purposes of public reading only, the editors would have foregone the effort at an early stage. But since they never departed from the three-fold objective of preparing a translation suitable for liturgical use, private reading, and the purposes of students, the last-named consideration prevailed. Those familiar with Greek should be able to discover how the translators of the New Testament have rendered any given original verse of Scripture, if their exegetical or theological tasks require them to know this. At the same time, the fact should be set down here that the editors did not commit themselves in the synoptic gospels to rendering repeated words or phrases identically.

This leads to a final consideration: the text used by the translators of the New Testament. Here, punctuation and verse division are at least as important as variant readings. In general, Nestle-Aland's *Novum Testamentum Graece* (25th edition, 1963) was followed. Additional help was derived from *The Greek New Testament* (editors Aland, Black, Metzger, Wikgren), produced for the use of translators by the United Bible Societies in 1966. However, the editors did not confine themselves strictly to these texts; at times, they inclined toward readings otherwise attested. The omission of alternative translations does not mean that the translators think them without merit, but only that in every case they had to make a choice.

Poorly attested readings do not occur in this translation. Doubtful readings of some merit appear within brackets; public readers may include such words or phrases, or omit them entirely without any damage to sense. Parentheses are used, as ordinarily in English, as a punctuation device. Material they enclose is in no sense textually doubtful. It is simply thought to be parenthetical in the intention of the biblical author, even though there is no such punctuation mark in Greek. The difficulty in dealing with quotation marks is well known. Since they do not appear in any form in the original text, wherever they occur here they constitute an editorial decision.

The work of translating the Bible has been characterized as "the sacred and apostolic work of interpreting the word of God and of presenting it to the laity in translations as clear as the difficulty of the matter and the limitations of human knowledge permit" (A. G. Cicognani, Apostolic Delegate, in *The Catholic Biblical Quarterly*, 6, [1944], 389f). In the appraisal of the present work, it is hoped that the words of the encyclical *Divino afflante Spiritu* will serve as a guide: "Let all the sons of the church bear in mind that the efforts of these resolute laborers in the vineyard of the Lord should be judged not only with equity and justice but also with the greatest charity; all moreover should abhor that intemperate zeal which imagines that whatever is new should for that very reason be opposed or suspected."

Conscious of their personal limitations for the task thus defined, those who have prepared this text cannot expect that it will be considered perfect; but they can hope that it may deepen in its readers "the right understanding of the divinely given Scriptures," and awaken in them "that piety by which it behooves us to be grateful to the God of all providence, who from the throne of his majesty has sent these books as so many personal letters to his own children" (*Divino afflante Spiritu*).

Origin
Inspiration, and History
of the Bible

Origin of the Bible

NO BOOK in the history of the world has wielded as much influence on civilization as the Holy Bible. The Bible is unique in that it had God as its Author, while all other books were composed by human beings. It is indeed, the Book of Books.

THE DEPOSIT OF FAITH

The Catholic Church derives all of its teaching authority from its tradition, the doctrine which has come down to it from Christ. This tradition is preserved in written form in the "Bible" which contains the principle truths of faith taught to the Apostles by Christ.

Inspired men were moved by the Spirit of God to commit these matters to writing in the early church. Only a short time after Christ's Ascension, perhaps within twenty years, the need to preserve these truths in a permanent form was recognized. Before any book was accepted as "authentic" however, the authority of an Apostle was demanded by the early Christian communities. Mark's Gospel was accepted because he was Peter's companion. Similarly, though Luke was a man who had not seen Christ, his book gained acceptance through St. Paul's authority.

The Church has protected and guarded these books which contained the revelations of Christ to His disciples and their testimony concerning Him.

THE BIBLE DEFINED

The other source of supernatural knowledge is the Bible. In the words of the Council of Trent, which enumerated the books of the Bible under their proper titles, the Church declares that she receives: "All the books of the Testaments, Old and New, since the one God is the Author of both." The Vatican Council is more explicit: "The Church holds those books as sacred and canonical, not because, having been composed by human industry, they were afterwards approved by her authority, nor merely because they contain revelation without error, but because having been written under the inspiration of the Holy Spirit, they have God as their Author."

The word "Bible" comes from the Greek *biblion* meaning "the book;" the plural is *ta biblia,* "the books." In the Greek the word is a neuter, but later on the word *biblia* was taken for a feminine singular, "the book." Taken in this sense, it refers to all the books of both Testaments. The Bible is the Book par excellence.

THE BIBLE NEEDS AN INTERPRETER

The Bible is extremely difficult to understand, even by Bible scholars. It was written in languages long dead, and in the manner and idiom of the time. To interpret the Bible, it is not only necessary to understand the languages in which the Bible was written, but to understand the meanings that the words of the Bible had at the time they were written. The Bible, therefore, has to be interpreted to be understood, and for Catholics, the Church, guided by the Holy Spirit, is the official guardian and infallible interpreter of the Bible.

CANON OF THE BIBLE

The Bible contains 72 books (or 73, depending on whether the Book of Lamentations is listed as a separate book and not as a part of Jeremiah), varying in length from a few hundred words to many thousands. Together, these books comprise the official list or canon of the Bible. Of these books, 45 were written before the time of Christ and are called the books of the Old Testament. The other 27 books were written after the time of Christ and are called the books of the New Testament.

MEANING OF THE WORD "TESTAMENT"

The meaning of the word "testament" as used here is that of a pact, an agreement, or a covenant. The Old

Testament is the pact or alliance that God made first with the Patriarchs and then with the Jewish people through Moses; a Saviour is promised and a Law is proclaimed, and salvation is through the Law.

The New Testament is the covenant or the alliance that God made with all men whereby, through the mediatorship of His Son, Jesus Christ, all men can be saved.

DETERMINATION OF THE BIBLE CANON

At the time the books of the New Testament were written, many other pious stories and legends relating to Christ and His times were also widely circulated. As a result, in the early centuries of the Church, there was some confusion and doubt as to which books were inspired and biblical, and which were not. As far as is known, it was the Council of Hippo in A.D. 393 which first determined which books were inspired and were to be included in the Bible canon, a canon in every respect identical with the canon of the Council of Trent. Subsequent Councils confirmed this decision, and the Council of Trent, in 1546, formally canonized all the traditional books of the Bible. These books comprise the Old and the New Testaments, and it is a matter of faith for Catholics to believe that all passages of all books are equally inspired.

THE APOCRYPHA

Those books which were rejected by the Council of Hippo as being non-biblical belong to what is called the Apocrypha. These books treat largely of the incidents and events during the life of Christ not related in the books of the Bible. They are often well worth reading, as they offer much historical information not otherwise available. However, some of these stories have slightly heretical tendencies.

The Catholic use of the word "Apocrypha," as defined above, should be distinguished from the incorrect Protestant use of the word. Protestants use this term to designate the seven books of the Bible included in the Catholic Bible canon, but not accepted or found in Protestant Bibles. These seven books are: Tobit, Judith, Wisdom, Sirach, Baruch, 1 and 2 Maccabees, and parts of Esther and Daniel. Protestants call the books found in the Catholic Apocrypha the Pseudepigraphal books.

HISTORY OF THE PROTESTANT CANON

The difference in the Catholic and Protestant Bibles arose in the following manner. The Jews living in the few centuries before Christ were divided into two groups—the Jews dwelling in Palestine and speaking Hebrew, and the large number of Jews scattered throughout the Roman Empire and speaking the Greek language, a consequence of the conquest of Alexander the Great of Greece.

CRITERIA OF THE JEWISH CANON

In the several centuries before the coming of Christ, the Jews in Palestine re-examined and eliminated some of the books from the existing collection as not in harmony with the Law of Moses and as of doubtful inspiration. The Pharisees set up four criteria which their sacred books had to pass in order to be included in the revised Jewish canon: (1) They had to be in harmony with the Pentateuch (Torah or Law); (2) They had to have been written before the time of Ezra; (3) They had to be written in Hebrew; (4) They had to have been written in Palestine.

BIBLE BOOKS ELIMINATED BY THE JEWS

The application of these arbitrary criteria eliminated Judith, probably written in Aramaic; Wisdom and 2 Maccabees, written in Greek; Tobit and parts of Daniel and Esther, written in Aramaic and probably outside of Palestine; Baruch, written outside of Palestine; and Sirach and 1 Maccabees, written after the time of Ezra. By the 1st Century after Christ, this revised canon was generally accepted by all Jews.

THE CHURCH RECOGNIZES THE ALEXANDRINE CANON

From the earliest times, the Christian Church recognized the Jewish canon of the Greek-Roman tradition, or Alexandrine canon, as being the true Bible. Jesus Himself quoted from this Bible, and not until the Reformation was this canon seriously challenged.

These seven disputed books are also called the deuterocanonical books, while the rest of the books of the Old Testament comprise the protocanonical books. By protocanonical books is meant the "books of the first canon," books of the Old Testament accepted by both Christians and Jews. The deuterocanonical books, "books of the second canon," are those seven books found only in the Catholic canon.

Luther rejected the deuterocanonical books of the Old Testament. At one time he also eliminated Hebrews, James, Jude, and the Apocalypse from the New Testament, but later Protestants reinserted them. Today the Catholic and Protestant New Testament books are identical.

LANGUAGES OF THE BIBLE

The books of the Bible were originally written in three languages: Hebrew, Aramaic, and Greek. Aramaic is a branch of the Semitic languages, and was the language used in Palestine in the time of Christ. It is the language Christ spoke. Hebrew is a Semitic language which originated in Chanaan and which was passed on by Abraham and his descendants, reaching its greatest glory in the reigns of David and Solomon. It was the language of the Holy Land until about the 3rd Century B.C., when it was supplanted by Aramaic.

The Greek language as used in the Bible is not the classical Greek as we know it today, but a dialect spread throughout the known world of the time by conquests of Alexander the Great.

Most of the books of the Old Testament were written in Hebrew, while all of the New Testament, excepting Matthew, was written in Greek. The Book of Wisdom and 2 Maccabees were also written in Greek. Portions of the Book of Daniel, Ezra, Jeremiah, and Esther, and all of Tobit, Judith, and the Gospel of St. Matthew were written in Aramaic.

TEXTUAL DIVISION OF THE BIBLE

The Bible as originally set down was not divided into chapter and verse as we know it today. Stephen Langton, Archbishop of Canterbury in the 13th Century, first divided the Bible text into Chapters. Santes Pagninus divided the Old Testament chapters into verses in 1528, and Robert Etienne, a printer in Paris, did the same for the New Testament in 1551.

THE OLD TESTAMENT

In the past we have tended to think of the books of the Bible as historical (such as Genesis, Exodus, Kings, and Maccabees); legal (Leviticus, Deuteronomy, etc.); prophetic (predicting the future); and so on.

An appreciation of the Jewish method of dividing the books (given on the previous page) may be a more helpful method. The first five books of the Bible (Genesis, Exodus, Leviticus, Numbers and Deuteronomy) were considered the books central to their faith. They were called Torah in Hebrew. The word Torah means an "instruction" not just a lesson but the kind of instruction a parent gives to a child when he wants him to obey.

Many of the books which we think of as historical (Joshua, Judges, Samuel and Kings) were considered "prophetic" by the Jews. By prophetic they meant an inspired sermon. These books recounted events from their history in order to moralize. They were sermons from history. In these books we may find prophets appearing but they are prophets who act. They leave us no long sermons. They are part of the rough and tumble of life. Important Kings may hardly be mentioned simply because they offered few examples to be imitated. Unimportant kings may receive more attention because they were good men. This is not our modern way of writing history, of course. Even for them it was not primarily history. It was rather religious editorializing. We may err by thinking of them as history. They are that but they are much more. The Jews called them the "former" prophets not because they came earlier in time but because they were bound into the Bible first.

The Prophetical books, the "latter prophets," whether written by the prophet himself or by a disciple, are inspired sermons. A prophet is a man who speaks for God and to his own times. He is a man concerned about his own world. He sometimes predicts the future. More frequently it is the immediate future. When he does so he is exercising a power that is not, strictly speaking, prophetic. It is an additional power from God. We tend to be led astray if we think of them primarily as predictors of the future.

The "Writings" are a catch-all for other books. Chronicles, which we think of as history, is a many-faceted book. To call it history is to miss many of its qualities. The poetry of Psalms and Wisdom-literature such as Proverbs is also included in this section. Daniel, which is a special kind of literature known as "apocalyptic" is included here though in the past we thought of it as among the Prophetic books.

Those books accepted by the Septuagint or Greek version of the Hebrew Bible but which the Jews rejected after the time of Christ are called "Deutero-Canonical" books. They, together with parts of Daniel and Esther, are not accepted as part of the Bible by Protestants or Jews. Catholics have always revered them as such since the earliest days of the church.

THE NEW TESTAMENT

In the New Testament we think of the "four gospels" of Matthew, Mark, Luke and John. These are the Gospels (or "good news") of Jesus Christ. But Acts of Apostles is the same kind of book. It is the "gospel of the Holy Spirit" and depicts the work of Christ continued in the early Church.

Though none of the "four gospels" are a "Life of Christ" for they tell us very little about most of His life, they do use incidents from the life of Christ to illustrate His teaching. Primarily then, the Gospels and Acts (also written by Luke) present us with the message, mission, and works of Christ. Every man who saw Christ saw him from a unique perspective. These four men we call Evangelists saw him from their own particular points of view.

"Epistles" are letters of various kinds. Some are like "letters to the editor" that were intended to be widely circulated, not only in the church to which they were sent but throughout the territory. Others were quite private. Charming little "Philemon" is a short note of Paul to a convert. Still others were written in the style of a letter as a style of literature. The Epistles of James and Peter are really treatises on doctrine.

The last book of the Bible, "Revelations" (or Apocalypse) is the only New Testament book written in a very popular style of the day. As with Daniel and Ezekiel in the Old Testament it was written in a kind of code to persecuted members of God's people recounting God's saving acts in the past in the face of present trials. They look forward, also, to saving acts in the future based on their faith in Him.

Inspiration of the Bible

THE BOOKS of the Bible have as their principal author the Holy Spirit, although He Himself did not write them. The Holy Spirit inspired the human authors of the Bible to write down in their own words, and in the manner and style of the day, what He wanted them to write, and He guided them to the extent that they wrote faithfully what they had been taught. This working together of God and man in the writing of the Bible is called inspiration. This inspiration covers not only matters of faith and morals, but extends as well to the facts of history as related, and to the whole Bible.

BIBLICAL INSPIRATION DEFINED

Pope Leo XIII, in his encyclical *Providentissimus Deus*, explains how inspiration affected the biblical writers. "By supernatural power God so moved and impelled them to write, He was so present to them, that they first rightly understood, then willed faithfully to write down, and finally expressed in apt words and with infallible truth the things which He ordered, and those only."

BIBLICAL REFERENCES TO ITS INSPIRATION

Besides the infallible teaching of the Church as to the inspiration of the Bible, we have reliable historical evidence as well. Many indirect passages in the Old Testament refer to its inspiration (Isaiah 8, 1; Wisdom 7, 15), and in the New Testament St. Paul refers to it in 2 Peter 1, 20-21.

TRADITION CONFIRMS BIBLICAL INSPIRATION

Tradition, too, provides overwhelming proof that from the earliest days of the Church it was believed that the Bible was inspired. The Fathers of the Church allude to it in many passages, stating variously that the books were inspired, that God is the Author of the Bible, and that the sacred writers were the instruments of God. Throughout its history, the Church has made many official pronouncements in ecclesiastical documents reaffirming the fact of inspiration.

EXTENT OF INSPIRATION

The Council of Trent on April 8, 1546, decreed that "those entire books with all their parts as have been accustomed to be read in the Catholic Church" must be considered as sacred and canonical. This was reaffirmed by the Council of the Vatican in 1870. In the centuries since this decree, Catholic theologians differed on two points of interpretation, as to whether matters of faith and morals alone were to be considered inspired or to whether inspiration extended just to important matters. These questions were settled by Pope Leo XIII in his encyclical *Providentissimus Deus*, in which he reaffirmed the decisions of the Council of Trent and emphasized that the Bible in all its parts was inspired and that a stated fact must be accepted as falling under inspiration, down to the most insignificant item; that is, *the whole Bible is the Word of God.*

History of the Bible

NO ORIGINAL MANUSCRIPTS of the Bible have come down to us, due to the perishable material upon which they were written and the fact that the Roman emperors decreed the destruction of the manuscripts during the Christian persecutions. While none of the original manuscripts are known to exist, some very ancient transcriptions have survived the years.

ANCIENT MANUSCRIPTS OF THE BIBLE

The oldest Hebrew manuscript known is a copy of the Book of Isaiah, written in Hebrew in the 2nd Century. It was found in 1947 in a cave near Jericho. The oldest Greek fragment known to exist is in the John Ryland Library in Manchester, England. This fragment is from the 2nd Century A.D. Several thousand other ancient Greek manuscripts have been found, the three most complete and important being the Codex Sinaiticus, Codex Vaticanus, and the Codex Alexandrinus, all probably of the 4th and 5th Century after Christ. The Codex Vaticanus is in the Vatican library.

EARLY TRANSLATIONS OF THE BIBLE

The most important early translations of the Bible were the Septuagint and the Vulgate. The Septuagint, a Greek translation of the Old Testament, was begun about 250 B.C. and completed about 100 B.C. This translation was made for the Jews of Egypt so that they could read their sacred books in Greek, the only language that most of them understood at that time. Before long, the Septuagint was widely used in Palestine and distributed throughout the Greek-speaking peoples of the Mediterranean world during the time of Christ and for the 1st Century or longer of the Christian era. The Apostles of Christ used this translation in their teaching.

THE BIBLE IN THE FIRST TWO CENTURIES AFTER CHRIST

In the early days of the Church, the Scriptures were read at divine services in Greek. An early translation from Greek to Latin was needed for many of the Christians in the West could not understand Greek. Such translations, gathered together, made up the first Latin Bible. Prepared by so many different people of varying education, the translations were uneven and inaccurate. By the 2nd Century, there were a number of Latin translations, the most widely circulated being the *Old Latin,* or *Itala.*

ST. JEROME AND THE VULGATE TRANSLATION

Because of the numerous variant readings of the *Itala,* due to the copyists, revisers, or translators, Pope Damasus requested St. Jerome to revise and correct the New Testament. St. Jerome began his revision with the four Gospels and then revised the remaining books of the New Testament, but more hurriedly. The work was completed at Rome about A.D. 383-4. After the death of Pope Damasus, St. Jerome went to the Holy Land. He spent 34 years there, devoting his time to revising the Bible, to exegetical works, but mainly to the great work of his life—the translation of the protocanonical books of the Old Testament from Hebrew into Latin. This work extended over a period of fifteen years and it was a prodigious task, for the modern Vulgate is made up of: (a) the protocanonical books of the Old Testament, with the exception of the Psalter, translated from the Hebrew by St. Jerome; (b) the deuterocanonical books of Tobit and Judith from the Aramaic by St. Jerome; (c) the deuterocanonical books of Wisdom, Sirach, Baruch, and 1 and 2 Maccabees from the Old Latin unrevised by St. Jerome; (d) the deuterocanonical parts of Daniel from the Greek of Theodotion and of Esther from the Septuagint; and (e) the New Testament revised from the Old Latin by St. Jerome.

THE VULGATE SUPERSEDES ALL OTHER VERSIONS

As St. Jerome's work on the Old Testament was a work of private enterprise, it met great opposition. He was accused of changing the text of the Bible, which was familiar to the people in the *Itala* or Old Latin. However, as time went on the great merits of his work were recognized. By the 9th Century, Jerome's version was universally accepted. In view of its general adoption, it gradually assumed the name of "Vulgate," the "disseminated" or people's Bible.

THE CHURCH APPROVES THE VULGATE

On April 8, 1546, the Church, in the Council of Trent, designated the Vulgate as the official Church translation. To this day the Vulgate remains the official version of the Church, and translations of it are found in practically every language in the world. However, it does not mean that it is to be preferred over the Septuagint or over original manuscripts, or that it was entirely free from error. On the contrary, the Church recognized certain limitations in the translation from the beginning, and ordered a revision. This revised version was published in 1592 under Pope Clement VIII.

THE VULGATE FROM JEROME TO GUTENBERG

Jerome's text suffered many vicissitudes throughout the ages. In assembling a complete Bible, copyists would take some of their readings, by misadventure, from the old Latin texts and some from the Vulgate; both texts were in circulation. A monk might have memorized several passages from the old version in school, then, in writing a copy of the Vulgate, subconsciously lapse into the old phrasing so familiar to him. Some of the transcribers were not exercising a critical sense and would incorporate texts from other manuscripts, parallel passages, and texts from the liturgy.

The invention of printing only multiplied these problems for a time, but eventually scholars were able to print a text near to the text as it came from the hands of St. Jerome. While the Vulgate became the official version of the Western Church, it did not prevent other translations from being made. A Coptic version appeared in the 2nd Century; Ulfilas, an Arian bishop, made a Gothic translation in the 4th Century, and there were numerous Syrian, Armenian, Georgian, Arabic, and Slavonic versions in the early centuries.

GUTENBERG AND THE FIRST PRINTED BIBLE

The invention and development of a practical printing process by Gutenberg in the 15th Century did more to revolutionize and modernize the world than any other invention. Prior to this, all manuscripts and books had to be copied by hand and only the very wealthy could ever afford to have one. At once the tedious work of the professional copyist was ended. Not only did it do away with the copyist, it eliminated the many human errors made in copying.

By 1450 Gutenberg had developed the art of printing so well that he was ready to print his first book; the first book printed was the Bible, in the Latin Vulgate translation. About two years were spent in printing and binding the Bible, and it was completed in 1452. Over 200 copies were printed in the first edition.

THE BIBLE IN PRINT

With the invention of printing, the Bible ran through edition after edition—124 in the first 50 years, all sponsored by the Catholic Church. By the time Luther's New Testament appeared in 1522 there were 14 complete editions in German. Parallel with this in time was the appearance of 11 Italian translations, 10 French, 2 Bohemian, one Flemish, and one Russian.

THE BIBLE IN ENGLISH

The first complete English translation of the Bible appeared relatively late, probably not until the 14th Century. However, the English people were not without the Bible in those early years, as the Latin Vulgate was widely disseminated and in daily use. In addition, numerous paraphrases, translations, and commentaries of various Bible stories were well known through scop and gleeman, the popular storytellers of their day.

EARLY HISTORY NOT DEFINITELY KNOWN

Much of the earlier history of the Bible in English still remains a mystery. Tradition holds that Aidan, Bishop of Landisfarne, who died in 651, encouraged his followers to read the Scriptures in their own tongue. Aldhelm, Bishop of Sherborne until his death in 709, is said to have translated the Psalms into the Saxon language. Between 721 and 901 various writers, including the Venerable Bede, Eadfrith, Alcuin, and King Alfred, are believed to have translated parts or all of the Bible stories into Old English. In the 10th Century, a translation of the first seven books of the Bible and the Book of Job made by Aelfric, Archbishop of Canterbury from 994 to 1005, was in circulation.

During the time between the death of Aelfric and the reputed work of Wyclif in 1380, other translations are reported to have existed. However, this was a period of great transition in the English language, and practically nothing remains of these writings. It was not until the 15th Century that English as we know it today emerged as a definite language.

WYCLIF'S TRANSLATION

The next important English version is the so-called Wyclif translation, of which over 150 manuscripts are extant. It is taken indirectly from the Vulgate. Much doubt has been cast recently on the theory that Wyclif was responsible for this pre-Reformation Bible in recent years, since the translation is largely Catholic in tone and diction and since most of the manuscripts of this version were found in the possession of notably Catholic families.

THE DOUAY-RHEIMS TRANSLATION

The first complete and printed Catholic English translation that is definitely known appeared rather late, at the turn of the 16th Century. This is known as the Douay-Rheims version. It was a translation of the Latin Vulgate and was produced in France by English scholars who had fled the Catholic persecutions in England. The New Testament was published in Rheims in 1582 and the Old Testament in Douay in 1610.

Since the Douay-Rheims translation, the English language has undergone continuous changes. It was necessary, therefore, to revise and bring the Bible up to date from time to time. Bishop Challoner of England undertook and published a complete revision of the Douay-Rheims in 1750, and several less successful revisions appeared between that time and the 20th Century.

PROTESTANT BIBLICAL SCHOLARSHIP

Besides the Catholic versions of the Bible mentioned above, numerous Protestant versions of the Bible in English have appeared since the Reformation. William Tyndale (1484-1536) was one of the first Protestant translators of the Bible. His translation is especially noteworthy because he translated from the original Greek versions then available to him rather than from the traditional Vulgate.

Miles Coverdale translated and printed a complete English Bible in 1535. Coverdale's translation was the first English edition of the Bible to separate the deuterocanonical books from the protocanonical books. The deuterocanonical books were put in the back of the regular Bible text.

Between the publication of Coverdale's Bible and the King James or Authorized version, other less important translations took place. Noteworthy among these were the Taverner's Bible, the Great Bible, Cranmer's Bible, the Geneva Bible, and the Bishop's Bible.

THE KING JAMES BIBLE

When James I ascended the throne of England in 1603, numerous and variant Protestant Bibles were in circulation. In 1604 preparations were, therefore, made to undertake a revision of the Protestant Bible. A group of scholars was organized, and using the Bishop's Bible as the basis for their new translation, produced the King James version, which was published in 1611.

While of great literary merit, Protestants themselves recognized many serious defects in the translation. In 1881-1885 a revision was made, and this is popularly known as the Revised Version. Many other modern versions are also published today, the most important, perhaps, being the Revised Standard Version published in 1952. More recently the New English Version, among others have been published.

PRESENT CATHOLIC BIBLICAL SCHOLARSHIP

Pope Leo XIII gave the modern impetus to Bible study when he issued his famous encyclical, *Providentissimus Deus*, which set up standards for all future Bible scholarship. In addition, he established the Biblical Commission in 1902 to study and to give answers to biblical questions. In 1890 M. J. Lagrange, O. P., founded the Ecole Biblique at Jerusalem and also established the periodical, *Revue Biblique*. The Biblical Institute was established in Rome in 1908 by Pius X to give advanced training to biblical scholars.

In 1907 the Biblical Commission asked the Benedictine Order to undertake the task of revising the Vulgate, and this translation is still in process. Under the direction of the English Jesuit, Reverend Cuthbert Lattey, English and American scholars produced the Westminster edition of the Sacred Scriptures directly from the Greek and Hebrew texts. Other modern versions include a translation of the New Testament from the original languages by Fr. F. Spencer, O. P., and this was published in 1937. A complete translation of the Bible was made by Msgr. Ronald Knox of England in 1950 and has attained wide popularity because of the modernness and clarity of its language.

CONFRATERNITY TRANSLATION OF THE BIBLE

In the United States in the last 40 years, there has been a general revival of religion and the hierarchy felt a great need for an accurate modern translation of the Bible. Out of this has developed a new translation of the Bible by American Scripture scholars, sponsored by the Confraternity of Christian Doctrine.

The first task of this group was to prepare a modern edition of the Challoner revision of the Douay-Rheims English translation of the Bible. Proceeding with this, they published the New Testament in 1941, and then began the translation of the Old Testament. However, Pope Pius XII issued his Encyclical, *Divino Afflante Spiritu,* in 1943 which dealt with, among other things, the need for a new translation of the Bible directly from the original languages of the sacred authors. For this reason, the further revision of the Challoner-Douay-Rheims version was abandoned.

The Confraternity then began the new translation of the Old Testament directly from the original Hebrew and of the New Testament from the original languages. The New American Bible is a culmination of their efforts.

A Harmony of The Gospels
Outline of Chronology

	MATTHEW	MARK	LUKE	JOHN
PROLOGUE				
The Gospel is history			1, 1-4	
The Word				1, 1-18
PART I. BIRTH AND EARLY LIFE OF CHRIST				
Annunciations				
Annunciation of the Baptizer			1, 5-25	
Annunciation of the Saviour			1, 26-38	
Jesus is the Messiah	1, 1-17		†3, 23-38	
Mary visits Elizabeth: Mary's Canticle			1, 39-56	
Birth of the Baptizer and of the Messiah				
Birth of the Baptizer: The name John			1, 57-66	
The Canticle of Zechariah: (Benedictus)			1, 67-80	
Joseph learns of the Incarnation	1, 18-25a			
Birth of the Messiah			2, 1-7	
The shepherds at the crib			2, 8-20	
The Infant Saviour				
Circumcision of Jesus	1, 25b		2, 21	
His Presentation			2, 22-38	
The Magi adore Jesus	2, 1-12			
The Holy Family in Egypt	2, 13-15			
Massacre of the Innocents	2, 16-18			
The return from Egypt	2, 19-21			
The Hidden Christ				
Christ's childhood at Nazareth	2, 22-23		2, 39-40	
The Child Jesus in the Temple			2, 41-50	
The hidden life			2, 51-52	
PART II. BEGINNING OF CHRIST'S PUBLIC MINISTRY				
John Prepares the Way				
The voice in the desert	3, 1-6	1, 1-6a	3, 1-6	
The preacher of repentance	3, 7-10		3, 7-9	
The guide of sincere souls			3, 10-14	
Witnesses to the Arrival of the Saviour				
The Baptizer proclaims the Saviour's arrival	3, 11-12	1, 6b-8	3, 15-18	
Baptism of Christ: The Father's witness	3, 13-17	1, 9-11	3, 21-22	
Jesus is tempted	4, 1-11	1, 12-13	4, 1-13	
John answers the Sanhedrin delegates				1, 19-28
The Baptizer points out the Christ				1, 29-34
Springtime of Faith in Christ				
Andrew, John, and Peter				1, 35-42
Philip and Nathanael				1, 43-51
Jesus' first miracle				2, 1-11
His brief stay in Capernaum				2, 12
PART III. EARLY MINISTRY IN JUDEA				
Christ in Jerusalem for a Passover				
Jesus cleanses the Temple				2, 13-17
He vindicates His authority				2, 18-22

Since The Gospels are not intended to be biographies, and since each was written for a specific group with a catechetical purpose, this Harmony is necessarily approximate and tentative.

	MATTHEW	MARK	LUKE	JOHN
Imperfect faith of many hearers				2, 23-25
Christ discourses with Nicodemus				3, 1-15
The necessity of faith in Christ				3, 16-21

Ministry outside Jerusalem

Christ evangelizes in Judea				3, 22-24
The Baptizer's last witness to Christ				3, 25-30
Jesus is the revelation of the Father				3, 31-36
John is imprisoned	14, 3-5	6, 17-20	†3, 19-20	

Christ in Samaria

Jesus leaves Judea for Galilee	4, 12	1, 14a	4, 14a	4, 1-3
The Samaritan woman				4, 4-30
Jesus instructs His disciples				4, 31-38
Fruits of the Gospel in Sychar				4, 39-42

PART IV. EARLY GALILEAN MINISTRY

Inauguration of the Kingdom by Miracles and Preaching

Jesus is received in Galilee				4, 43-45
Second miracle at Cana				4, 46-54
He preaches repentance and the kingdom of God	4, 17	1, 14b-15	4, 14b-15	
His first preaching at Nazareth			4, 16-22a	
Capernaum, His own city	4, 13-16	1, 21	4, 31	
Christ preaches with power and authority	7, 28b-29	1, 22	4, 32	
The draft of fishes: Call of Simon, Andrew, James, and John	4, 18-22	1, 16-20	†5, 1-11	
Jesus cures a demoniac in the synagogue of Capernaum		1, 23-28	4, 33-37	
He heals Peter's mother-in-law	8, 14-15	1, 29-31	4, 38-39	
He cures many others on the same day	8, 16-17	1, 32-34	4, 40-41	
Jesus leaves Capernaum to spread the Gospel	4, 23	1, 35-39	4, 42-44	
He cures a leper	8, 1-4	1, 40-45	5, 12-16	

Hostility of the Scribes and Pharisees

Jesus cures a paralytic at Capernaum	9, 1-8	2, 1-12	5, 17-26	
The call of Matthew	9, 9-13	2, 13-17	5, 27-32	
The question of fasting	9, 14-17	2, 18-22	5, 33-39	
The Sabbath: The ears of grain	12, 1-8	2, 23-28	6, 1-5	
The man with a withered hand	12, 9-13	3, 1-5	6, 6-10	
The first plot to kill Christ	12, 14	3, 6	6, 11	

Forming the Kingdom of God

SERMON ON THE MOUNT

Jesus chooses the Twelve Apostles	10, 1-4	3, 13-19	6, 12-16	
Large crowds gather to hear Him	12, 15-21; 4, 24-25	3, 7-12	6, 17-19	

INTRODUCTION TO THE SERMON

Christ, the divine teacher	5, 1-2		6, 20a	
Beatitudes and maledictions	5, 3-12		6, 20b-26	
The Apostles, salt and light	5, 13-16			

THE OLD LAW AND THE NEW

Christ relates the New Law to the Old	5, 17-20			
Anger	5, 21-24; *5, 25-26			
Adultery	5, 27-30			
Divorce	5, 31-32		†16, 18	
Oaths	5, 33-37			
Retaliation	5, 38-42		†6, 29-30	
The love of enemies	5, 43-48		6, 27-28; 6, 32-36	

GOOD WORKS

Avoid hypocrisy and do all for God	6, 1			
Almsgiving	6, 2-4			
Prayer	6, 5-8; *6, 9-15		*11, 1-4	
Fasting	6, 16-18			
Detachment from earthly things	*6, 19-21		*12, 33-34	
Purity of intention	*6, 22-23		*11, 34-36	
Undivided service	*6, 24		*16, 13	
Trust in God's Providence	*6, 25-34		*12, 22-31	
Rash judgment	7, 1-5		6, 37-42	
Profanation of holy things	7, 6			
The power of prayer	*7, 7-11		*11, 9-13	
The perfect way	7, 12		†6, 31	

EXHORTATION TO VIGILANCE

The narrow path	7, 13-14		*13, 24	
False prophets	7, 15-20		6, 43-45	
Self-deception	7, 21-23		6, 46	
Conclusion: solid virtue	7, 24-27		6, 47-49	

	MATTHEW	MARK	LUKE	JOHN
Contrary Reactions to Christ's Preaching and Miracles				
The centurion's servant	7, 28a; 8, 5-13	....	7, 1-10	....
The widow's son at Naim	....	....	7, 11-17	....
John's messengers to Christ	11, 2-6	....	7, 18-23	....
Christ gives witness concerning the Baptist	11, 7-19	....	7, 24-35; †16, 16	....
A penitent woman anoints the feet of Jesus	....	....	7, 36-50	....
Holy women administer to Christ and His Apostles	....	....	8, 1-3	....
Christ's relatives disquiet themselves concerning Him	....	3, 20-21	....	....
The true kinsmen of Christ	12, 46-50	3, 31-35	†8, 19-21	....
Teaching in Parables				
The sower and the seed	13, 1-9	4, 1-9	8, 4-8	....
Why Christ taught in parables	13, 10-11; 13, 13-15	4, 10-12	8, 9-10	....
He explains the parable of the sower	13, 18-23	4, 13-20	8, 11-15	....
The mystery of the kingdom must be made manifest	13, 12	4, 21-25	8, 16-18	....
Parable of the growth of the seed	....	4, 26-29	....	....
The wheat and the weeds	13, 24-30	....	....	....
The mustard seed	13, 31-32	4, 30-32	†13, 18-19	....
The leaven	13, 33	....	†13, 20-21	....
Christ's teaching in parables fulfills a prophecy	13, 34-35	4, 33-34	....	....
Explanation of the wheat and the weeds	13, 36-43	....	....	....
The treasure and the pearl	13, 44-46	....	....	....
The net	13, 47-50	....	....	....
Conclusion	13, 51-52	....	....	....
Miracles Wrought on and near the Lake of Gennesaret				
The storm on the lake	13, 53; 8, 18; 8, 23-27	4, 35-40	8, 22-25	....
The exorcism in Gadarene	8, 28-34	5, 1-20	8, 26-39	....
The hemorrhage victim and the daughter of Jairus	9, 1; 9, 18-26	5, 21-43	8, 40-56	....
Two blind men and a dumb demoniac	9, 27-34	....	....	....
Jesus is rejected and threatened at Nazareth	13, 54-58	6, 1-6a	†4, 22b-30	....
The Mission of the Apostles				
The need of shepherds	9, 35-38; 10, 1	6, 6b-7	9, 1-2	....
Instructions for the apostolate	10, 5-16; 11, 1	6, 8-13	9, 3-6	....
Martyrdom of the Baptist	14, 6-12	6, 21-29	....	....
Various opinions concerning Christ	14, 1-2	6, 14-16	9, 7-9	....
Return of the Apostles	....	6, 30	9, 10a	....
The Bread of Life				
Multiplication of the loaves	14, 13-21	6, 31-44	9, 10b-17	†6, 1-15
Jesus walks on the water	14, 22-33	6, 45-52	....	†6, 16-21
Other miracles	14, 34-36	6, 53-56	....	....
DISCOURSE ON THE BREAD OF LIFE				
Introduction	....	....	....	†6, 22-25
Material bread and the Bread of Life	....	....	....	†6, 26-34
Jesus is the Bread of Life given through faith	....	....	....	†6, 35-47
The Body and Blood of Christ	....	....	....	†6, 48-59
The test of faith	....	....	....	†6, 60-72

PART V. MINISTRY OF CHRIST CHIEFLY OUTSIDE GALILEE

	MATTHEW	MARK	LUKE	JOHN
The Second Passover				
The cure at the pool of Bethesda	....	....	....	5, 1-15
Renewed persecution of Christ	....	....	....	5, 16-18
Christ's claim to divinity	....	....	....	5, 19-30
His Father's witness	....	....	....	5, 31-47
Retirement to Northern Galilee: More Intimate Training of the Disciples				
Jesus and the Pharisees	15, 1-20	7, 1-23	....	7, 1
The Canaanite woman	15, 21-28	7, 24-30	....	....
Jesus heals the suffering	15, 29-31	7, 31-37	....	....
Second multiplication of loaves	15, 32-39	8, 1-10	....	....
The Pharisees and Sadducees ask a sign	16, 1-4	8, 11-13	....	....
The leaven of the Pharisees	16, 5-12	8, 14-21	....	....
A blind man at Bethesda	....	8, 22-26	....	....
Peter's confession: His primacy in the Church	16, 13-20	8, 27-30	9, 18-21	....
First prediction of Christ's Passion and Resurrection	16, 21-23	8, 31-33	9, 22	....
The doctrine of the Cross	16, 24-27	8, 34-38	9, 23-26	....
The kingdom of God is near	16, 28	8, 39	9, 27	....
Jesus is transfigured	17, 1-8	9, 1-7	9, 28-36	....
The coming of Elijah	17, 9-13	9, 8-12	....	....
A possessed boy	17, 14-20	9, 13-28	9, 37-44a	....
Second prediction of the Passion	17, 21-22	9, 29-31	9, 44b-45	....
The Temple tax	17, 23-26	....	....	....
PREACHINGS OF CHRIST				
Humility	18, 1-5	9, 32-36	9, 46-48	....

	MATTHEW	MARK	LUKE	JOHN
Tolerance		9, 37-39	9, 49-50	
Reward of charity to Christ's disciples	10, 41-42	9, 40		
Avoiding scandal	18, 6-7	9, 41	†17, 1-2	
Value of the human soul	18, 10-14			
On avoiding the occasions of sin	18, 8-9	9, 42-49		
Fraternal correction	18, 15-18; 18, 21-22		†17, 3-4	
Power of united prayer	18, 19-20			
The unmerciful servant	18, 23-35			

The Journey to Jerusalem for the Feast of Tabernacles

	MATTHEW	MARK	LUKE	JOHN
Jesus goes privately to the Feast of Tabernacles				7, 2-13
Departure from Galilee			9, 51	
The hostile Samaritans			9, 52-56	
Sacrifice to follow Christ	8, 19-22		9, 57-62	
Mission of the seventy-two disciples			10, 1-12	
The impenitent towns	11, 20-24; 10, 40		10, 13-16	
Return of the disciples			10, 17-20	
Revelation of the Father and the Son	11, 25-27		10, 21-22	
The yoke of Christ	11, 28-30			
The privilege of seeing and hearing Christ	13, 16-17		10, 23-24	
The good Samaritan			10, 25-37	
Martha and Mary			10, 38-42	

The Feast of Tabernacles

	MATTHEW	MARK	LUKE	JOHN
The source of Christ's teachings				7, 14-24
Christ's divine origin				7, 25-29
His enemies order His arrest				7, 30-32
Christ's future state				7, 33-36
Jesus, fountain of supernatural life				7, 37-39
Dissension concerning Christ				7, 40-53
The adulteress				8, 1-11
The light of the world				8, 12-20
Punishment of unbelief				8, 21-30
The children of Abraham				8, 31-47
Christ and Abraham				8, 48-59
The man born blind				9, 1-41
The good shepherd				10, 1-18
Good and bad faith				10, 19-21

From the Feast of Tabernacles to the Feast of the Dedication

	MATTHEW	MARK	LUKE	JOHN
The Our Father	6, 9-15		11, 1-4	
The importunate friend			11, 5-8	
Prayer is always heard	7, 7-11		11, 9-13	
Blasphemy of the Pharisees	12, 22-37	3, 22-30	11, 14-23; †12, 10	
Satan's return	12, 43-45		11, 24-26	
The praise of Mary			11, 27-28	
The sign of Jonah	12, 38-42		11, 29-32	
Light of man and light of the world	6, 22-23		11, 33-36	
Denunciation of the Pharisees			11, 37-52	
Snares against Christ			11, 53-54	
Warning against hypocrisy: Courage in persecution	10, 24-33		12, 1-9	
Assurance of divine assistance			12, 11-12	
Warning against avarice			12, 13-21	
Trust in divine Providence	6, 25-34; 6, 19-21		12, 22-34	
The watchful servants	24, 43-44		12, 35-40	
Accountability to God	24, 45-51		12, 41-48	
For or against Christ	10, 34-36		12, 49-53	
Blindness of Christ's enemies	5, 25-26		12, 54-59	
The necessity of repentance			13, 1-5	
The barren fig tree			13, 6-9	
Cure of the stooped woman on the Sabbath			13, 10-17	
The narrow gate			13, 22-30	
Jesus and Herod			13, 31-33	

Feast of the Dedication

	MATTHEW	MARK	LUKE	JOHN
Jesus and the Father are one				10, 22-30
The Jews attempt to stone Christ				10, 31-39

From the Feast of the Dedication to Christ's Withdrawal to Ephraim

	MATTHEW	MARK	LUKE	JOHN
Jesus in Perea	19, 1-2	10, 1		10, 40-42
A man with dropsy			14, 1-6	
The last seat			14, 7-11	
Lowly guests			14, 12-14	
Parable of the great supper			14, 15-24	
Following of Christ	10, 37-39		14, 25-35	

GOD'S MERCY TOWARDS SINNERS

	MATTHEW	MARK	LUKE	JOHN
The lost sheep			15, 1-7	
The lost coin			15, 8-10	
The prodigal son			15, 11-32	

	MATTHEW	MARK	LUKE	JOHN
FOUR LESSONS FOR THE USE OF WEALTH				
The unjust steward.........................			16, 1-12	
God and mammon...........................	6, 24		16, 13	
Pretenses of the Pharisees.................			16, 14-17	
The rich man and Lazarus..................			16, 19-31	
Faith and service..........................			17, 5-10	
Onward to Jerusalem.......................			17, 11	
The ten lepers.............................			17, 12-19	
Coming of the kingdom of God..............	24, 26-28; 24, 37-41		17, 20-37	
The godless judge..........................			18, 1-8	
The Pharisee and the publican.............			18, 9-14	
Marriage and divorce......................	19, 3-9	10, 2-12		
Religious celibacy	19, 10-12			
Jesus blesses the children.................	19, 13-15	10, 13-16	18, 15-17	
The rich young man: Danger of riches......	19, 16-26	10, 17-27	18, 18-27	
Reward of poverty practised for Christ......	19, 27-30	10, 28-31	18, 28-30	
The laborers in the vineyard..............	20, 1-16			
The raising of Lazarus.....................				11, 1-44
The Sanhedrin conspires to kill Christ......				11, 45-53
Jesus retires to Ephraim...................				11, 54-56
Last Journey to Jerusalem				
Third prediction of the Passion and Resurrection...	20, 17-19	10, 32-34	18, 31-34	
Ambition of the mother of James and John........	20, 20-28	10, 35-45		
The blind men at Jericho...................	20, 29-34	10, 46-52	18, 35-43	
Jesus and Zacchaeus.......................			19, 1-10	
Parable of the gold pieces.................			19, 11-28	
The anointing at Bethany..................	26, 6-13	14, 3-9		12, 1-11

PART VI. FINAL MINISTRY IN JERUSALEM

Palm Sunday

The Messiah's triumphal entry into Jerusalem.....	21, 1-11; 21, 14-16	11, 1-11a	19, 29-44	12, 12-19
Christ's last words to the people.............				12, 20-36
He retires to Bethany for the night..........	21, 17	11, 11b		

Monday in Holy Week

Jesus curses a fig tree......................	21, 18-19a	11, 12-14		
Jesus cleanses the Temple a second time.........	21, 12-13	11, 15-18	19, 45-48	
Return to Bethany.........................		11, 19		

Tuesday in Holy Week

The withered fig tree......................	21, 19b-22	11, 20-26		
The authority of Jesus.....................	21, 23-27	11, 27-33	20, 1-8	
The two sons..............................	21, 28-32			
The vine-dressers	21, 33-46	12, 1-12	20, 9-19	
The marriage feast........................	22, 1-14			
Tribute to Caesar.........................	22, 15-22	12, 13-17	20, 20-26	
The Sadducees and the Resurrection........	22, 23-33	12, 18-27	20, 27-39	
The great commandment...................	22, 34-40	12, 28-34a		
Son and Lord of David.....................	22, 41-46	12, 34b-37	20, 40-44	
Hypocrisy of the Scribes and Pharisees......	23, 1-36	12, 38-40	20, 45-47	
Lament over Jerusalem.....................	23, 37-39		†13, 34-35	
The widow's mite..........................		12, 41-44	21, 1-4	
The Jews reject the Messiah................				12, 37-50
Jesus foretells the destruction of Jerusalem and the Temple	24, 1-20; 10, 17-23	13, 1-18	21, 5-24	
The end of the world and the coming of the Son of Man	24, 21-25; 24, 29-31	13, 19-27	21, 25-27	
The time of the destruction of Jerusalem......	24, 32-35	13, 28-31	21, 28-33	
The Son of Man shall come suddenly...........	24, 36; 24, 42	13, 32-37	21, 34-36	
The ten virgins............................	25, 1-13			
Parable of the talents.....................	25, 14-30			
The last judgment.........................	25, 31-46			
How Christ Spent His last nights...........			21, 37-38	
Wednesday: The council and the betrayal........	26, 1-5; 26, 14-16	14, 1-2; 14, 10-11	22, 1-6	

Maundy Thursday

Preparation for the Passover................	26, 17-19	14, 12-16	22, 7-13	
The Last Supper...........................	26, 20; 26, 29	14, 17; 14, 25	22, 14-18	
The quarrel over precedence...............			22, 24-30	
Jesus washes His disciples' feet.............				13, 1-20
The betrayer	26, 21-25	14, 18-21	†22, 21-23	13, 21-30
Institution of the Eucharist and the Priesthood.....	26, 26-28	14, 22-24	22, 19-20	(1 Cor. 11, 23-25)
The new commandment....................				13, 31-35
Peter's denials foretold....................	26, 31-35	14, 27-31	22, 31-34a	13, 36-38
Dangers and hardships shall try the Apostles......			22, 34b-38	
Words of comfort: Promise of the Holy Spirit......				14, 1-31
Union with Christ.........................				15, 1-17
The world's hatred........................				15, 18-27

	MATTHEW	MARK	LUKE	JOHN
Persecution foretold				16, 1-5
The role of the Advocate: Necessity of Christ's departure: Joy after sorrow				16, 6-33
Christ's priestly prayer				17, 1-26

PART VII. THE PASSION AND DEATH OF JESUS

Gethsemani

	MATTHEW	MARK	LUKE	JOHN
Christ enters the garden with His Apostles	26, 30	14, 26	22, 39	18, 1
His agony and bloody sweat	26, 36-46	14, 32-42	22, 40-46	
The kiss of Judas: The arrest	26, 47-56	14, 43-52	22, 47-53	18, 2-12

The Trial of Christ

	MATTHEW	MARK	LUKE	JOHN
Jesus before Annas				18, 13
Jesus before the Sanhedrin: The charge of blasphemy	26, 57-66	14, 53-64	22, 54-55	
Peter's denials	26, 69-75	14, 66-72	22, 56-62	18, 14-27
Jesus is mocked and maltreated	26, 67-68	14, 65	22, 63-65	
Second hearing before the Sanhedrin: Jesus is condemned	27, 1	15, 1a	22, 66-71	
Despair and suicide of Judas	27, 3-10			(Acts 1, 15-20)
Jesus before Pilate	27, 2	15, 1b	23, 1	18, 28
The Jews accuse Christ: The questioning and indecision of Pilate	27, 11-14	15, 2-5	23, 2-5	18, 29-38
Jesus before Herod			23, 6-12	
Pilate declares Christ's innocence			23, 13-16	
Christ or Barabbas	27, 15-23	15, 6-15a	23, 17-23	18, 39-40
Jesus is scourged and crowned with thorns	27, 26-30	15, 15b-19		19, 1-3
Pilate's last resistance	27, 24-25			19, 4-15
Jesus is condemned to be crucified	27, 26; 27, 31a	15, 15b; 15, 20a	23, 24-25	19, 16a

Crucifixion and Death of Christ

	MATTHEW	MARK	LUKE	JOHN
The Way of the Cross	27, 31b-32	15, 20b-21	23, 26-32	19, 16b-17a
Christ is crucified	27, 33-35a	15, 22-24a; 15, 25	23, 33a	19, 17b-18a
The two thieves	27, 38	15, 27-28	23, 33b	19, 18b
The title on the cross	27, 37	15, 26	†23, 38	19, 19-22
The first word: forgiveness			23, 34a	
Christ's garments are divided	27, 35b-36	15, 24b	23, 34b	19, 23-24
The insults of the Jews and soldiers	27, 39-43	15, 29-32	23, 35-37	
The second word: a promise of paradise	27, 44		23, 39-43	
The third word: Jesus bequeaths His Mother				19, 25-27
The fourth word: a plea for divine assistance	27, 45-47	15, 33-35	23, 44-45a	
The fifth word: a cry of thirst	27, 48-49	15, 36		19, 28-29
The sixth word: consummation				19, 30a
The seventh word: abandonment to God			23, 46a	
The death of Christ	27, 50	15, 37	23, 46b	19, 30b
Miracles that accompanied the death of Christ	27, 51-56	15, 38-41	†23, 45b; 23, 47-49	
The pierced heart				19, 31-37
The burial of Christ	27, 57-61	15, 42-47	23, 50-56a	19, 38-42
The Sabbath rest			23, 56b	
The watch at the sepulchre	27, 62-66			

PART VIII. THE RISEN CHRIST

The Day of the Resurrection

	MATTHEW	MARK	LUKE	JOHN
The women at the grave	28, 1-4	16, 1-4	24, 1-2	20, 1
Mary Magdalene				20, 2
Angels appear to the holy women	28, 5-7	16, 5-8	24, 3-8	
The women inform the Apostles	28, 8		24, 9-11	
Peter and John			24, 12	20, 3-10
Jesus appears to Mary Magdalene, then to the other women	28, 9-10	16, 9-11		20, 11-18
The guards and the chief priests	28, 11-15			
The disciples at Emmaus		16, 12	24, 13-32	
Their report to the Apostles in Jerusalem		16, 13	24, 33-35	
Jesus appears to the Apostles in the absence of Thomas			24, 36-43	20, 19-23

Other Appearances of the Risen Saviour

	MATTHEW	MARK	LUKE	JOHN
Jesus again appears to the Eleven in Jerusalem		16, 14		20, 24-29
The appearance in Galilee: Jesus found His Apostolic Church				21, 1-23
Commission of the Apostles	28, 16-20	16, 15-18		
The last instructions of Jesus			24, 44-49	
Jesus ascends into heaven		16, 19-20	24, 50-53	(Acts 1, 9-12)

EPILOGUE

	MATTHEW	MARK	LUKE	JOHN
Epilogue by St. John				20, 30-31; 21, 24-25

Passages which appear in the proper order of time but outside their context are marked with a cross (†); if they are not in their proper order of occurrence, they are marked with an asterisk (°).

The letters "a" and "b" refer to the first or second part of a verse, respectively. This table is reproduced and adapted from the book, *A Chronological Harmony of the Gospels*, by Stephen J. Hartdegen, with permission St. Anthony's Guild, Paterson, New Jersey. Copyright 1942 and 1945.

Synchronous

History of the Nations

Showing Their Origin, Chief Events, Changes or Extinction, from the Earliest Period Through New Testament Period

The earliest history of mankind, so far as we know, begins with the peoples known as Sumerians. The mountainous region North and Northeast of Mesopotamia is generally accepted as their primitive home. Issuing thence, they conquered or settled Babylonia, and through amalgamations with the native races (about some of which we know very little) became the earliest known inhabitants of Babylonia. These were succeeded by the Semites—progenitors of the Hebrews of the Old Testament.

I. FROM THE EARLIEST HISTORIC RECORDS TO 2200 B. C.

Earliest fixed date in Egyptian records. The migration of Sumerians from the mountains north and northeast and settlement in Babylonia, where they gradually absorbed the native races. The First Dynasty of Ur.

B. C.	Babylonis	Border Peoples (East of Babylonia)	Egypt (*Heb.* Mizraim)	Border Peoples (Between Egypt and Babylonia)	Greeks (Cretans and Mycenæans)
5000	**I. Pre-History** 5000. Government in Babylonia had reached the form known as the city-state; the southern group of cities (known collectively as Sumer) comprised the area occupied by Eridu, Lagash (Shirpurla), Ur, Larsa, Uruk (Erech) and Isin; the northern group known as Accad or Akkad, Sippar, Nippur, Kutha and later Babylon. **II. Sumerians and Semites** 4500. The earliest history of mankind, so far as we now know, begins with the natives found in Mesopotamia by the Sumerians, who migrated down into that valley from the mountains North and Northeast of it. They settled there with some degree of civilization and built up such city-states as Eridu, Erech, Lagash, Ur, Larsa and Isin. They had a system of picture writing which developed into the cuneiform script. Some Semites were probably already there, as some Semitic words and gods occur in their inscriptions. Their culture appears in the excavations at Ur (in its first dynasty). 　While Sumer (South Babylonia) was controlled by Sumerian city-states, Akkad (North Babylonia) was early ruled by Semites—Akkadians.	Out of these tribes developed the Elamites, Medes, Persians, and Hindus. 4500. There are traces of Mongol influence in these early inhabitants suggesting migration possibly from the region of Turkestan. At the same time there is evidence of Semitic influence especially in the region of Elam from which place there seems to be a continuous trace of Semites northwestward to Lydia. Early migrations brought people from Central Asia into this area.	**1. Prehistoric Period** Egyptian records name the gods as the earliest rulers and kings, who were descendants of gods, succeeded them. Actual history begins by revealing, in the Nile valley, a number of districts or nomes held together chiefly by a religious bond. 4241. Earliest fixed date marking the introduction of the calendar. (Breasted.) 4000. Pre-dynastic kingdoms flourish in Upper and Lower Egypt. 3800-3600. Pre-dynastic kings Ka-ap and Ro are placed within these dates according to recent interpretations of tombs and vases.	A variety of tribes and peoples dwelt on the ill-defined borders of Egypt and Babylonia. We come to know their names later through their attacks upon the various states. These tribes and other migratory peoples from the older Semitic centers became the founders of the Syrian states and Asia Minor. 4500. The primitive peoples in this area possessed a palæolithic culture similar to that of North African peoples as is shown by the implements from Sinai, Palestine and Phœnicia. They developed domesticated animals such as the goat, camel and ass and led a pastoral life.	**I. Prehistoric Period** Extensive excavations in Crete reveal a prehistoric civilization before the Bronze Age. 4500. Archæology has unearthed many evidences of a very early culture in the form of clay figures, a characteristic black-ware and, what is known as red-ware, similar to materials found in pre-dynastic Egypt. This culture seems to be similar to what was found in other parts of the Eastern Mediterranean for this same period. 3500. Beginning of the Bronze Age in Crete. 3500. Early Minoan Civilization begins. 3100. Second Minoan Age begins.
4000	4000. Semitic dynasty of Kish. This is the legendary period of Babylonian history. Kings and gods are frequently confused in the records of this period. 3638. Third dynasty of Kish. Contemporary records begin. This makes historical reckoning much more reliable. 3200. Dynasty of Akshak, which constitutes a short period when the Sumerians were rulers. 3100. Urnina, first known ruler of Lagash, a city-state near the confluence of the Tigris and Euphrates rivers. 3089. Fourth dynasty of Kish. Semitic influence felt. 3000. Eannatum of Lagash overthrows Kish and commemorates the event in the "Stele of the Vultures."	3260-3200. A Sumerian people set up a rule at Awan east of the Tigris River. 3000. A Sumerian civilization in Susa is evidenced by archæological remains.	**II. The Old Kingdom** (Includes Dynasties 1 to 10) 3400. Accession of MENES and beginning of dynasties. Under Menes the kingdoms were unified.	3000-2500. Tribes which later developed into Syrians, Phœnicians, Hebrews and Moabites, gathered in the region along the east shore of the Mediterranean.	3000-2500. Rising civilization on coasts and islands of the Aegean Sea, and in Crete.
3000					
	2800. Lugal-zaggisi of Erech was the first great conqueror whose campaigns went West to the Mediterranean Sea, and North into Akkad. 2750. Sargon I. and his son, Naram-Sin, of Akkad, conquered Armenia, Elam, parts of Arabia, and reached the Mediterranean Sea. 　Sumerians and Semites began to amalgamate, especially in Akkad. 2737. Shargali-sharri subdues the Amorites and makes war on Gutium, whose wild tribes threaten to overthrow Chaldean Civilization. 2474. Sumerian revival under Ur-Engur, author of the Sumerian law code. 2450. Gudea of Lagash, priest-king, powerful ruler, built palaces, temples, and set up bronze statues. 　Rivalry and strife current between the chief cities of Sumer (S. Babylonia). 2400. Zariku, King of Assyria, made tributary to Sumerians. 2300. Brief Sumerian Revival. 2225. First Babylonian dynasty. The South lost its political power and the city of Babylon became for the first time the seat of government. 2225-1926. First Babylonian dynasty opened a new era. Sumer was defeated by Hammurabi (2123-2081), sixth king of the dynasty, who compiled a code of laws, revealing notable advances in culture. Many resemble the laws of Moses.	2300. Assyria (Asshur) founded by a colony from Babylonia. Nineveh also in existence. 2100. Chedorlaomer, king of Elam, invades South Babylonia.	3350. Second Dynasty. Semitic type of names indicate migrations from Asia. 3200. Third Dynasty. Zoser built the "step-pyramid" of Sakkarah. 3100-3000. Fourth Dynasty built the great pyramids of Gizeh, Cheops, etc. Copper and wheel pottery were in use, the Capital was located at Memphis. 3000-2900. Fifth Dynasty. The worship of the sun-god, Ra, was prominent in this period. 2590-2570. Primitive sea-voyages made to Palestine. Government centralized at Memphis.	2700. The Phœnicians settle on the Sidonion coast and build Aradus (Arvad); later Tyre and Byblos. 2500. Semitic migrations into Syria and Palestine, about Jerusalem. 2100. Bedouins appeared in the desert of North Arabia. These were a nomadic race concerning whom very little is known at this early date.	2930. Copper Age begins in Cyprus. 2870. First settlement of Troy. 2700. Chalcolithic Age in Thessaly. 2600. Third Minoan Age begins. 2500. The cities of Mycenæ and Tiryns already founded. 2200. First period of the Bronze Age begins in Cyprus.
2000					

[1] Dates earlier than 893 B. C. are largely conjectural.

II. FROM THE AGE OF ABRAHAM TO THE RISE OF ASSYRIA, 2200 — 1120 B. C.

Abraham became first great leader of the Hebrews. Sumerians gradually absorbed by Semites in Babylonian Valley. Assyrians settled on upper Tigris river. Hittites of Asia Minor clash with Babylonia, Assyria, and Egypt. Egypt expels Shepherd kings from the Nile Valley. New Egyptian Empire. Assyrians conquer their southern neighbors—Babylonia. Hebrews enslaved in Egypt escape under Moses.

B. C.	Semites and Hebrews	Babylonia—Assyria	Egypt	Greeks
2200	**2. Semites and Hebrews**	**III. Early Babylonian Empire**	2445-2160. Kings resided at Heracleopolis; numerous struggles with Thebes to which seat of government was finally moved.	2000-1000. Achæans and Greeks settle in Greece proper, and Ionians in Asia Minor.
1850	1850. Abraham migrated from Ur of the Chaldees to Harran, in upper Mesopotamia thence to Canaan (Gen. 11:31-12:9), and settled there. He tried Egypt but was glad to return to Canaan. Amraphel (Hammurabi) and three kings of the East subdued five rebellious kings of the West, and carried off Lot, whom Abraham rescued (Gen. 14).	2225-1760	2250. Rise and triumph of Thebes.	
	The episode of Abraham and Hagar was not a social anomaly in that day (Gen. 16). Circumcision adopted as mark of covenant between the Lord and his people. Isaac, the promised heir, allayed Abraham's fears (Gen. 21). Abraham's loyalty to Jehovah led to an attempted sacrifice of Isaac, as was done in Babylonia at that day (Gen. 22).	2123-2081. H A M M U R A B I (Amraphel), great ruler and law-giver, united the whole of Babylonia. His code of laws one of the most important oriental discoveries. Under him Babylon reached a high degree of culture.	**III. Middle Kingdom** (Includes Dynasties 12 to 17) 2000-1788. This period reached its highest development in the Twelfth dynasty, which was Theban. Obelisks, public works, regulation of Nile, Lake Mœris, and the Labyrinth belong to this period.	2100-1500. The third, fourth and fifth settlements of ancient Troy were made during this period. The occupants, however, did not exercise any political power or influence. There was possibly some trade between Troy and Thrace and the Danube Basin.
	Death of Abraham, buried in the cave of Machpelah, bought from a Hittite (Gen. 23). Esau married Hittite women (Gen. 26:34). Jacob deceived Isaac, buncoed Esau out of his birthright, and fled to Paddan-Aram on the Euphrates River. Married Aramæan kinsfolk (Gen. 27-29). Prospered, returned after 20 years with family, flocks and herds (Gen. 30 and 31). Jacob calmed down Esau's wrath (Gen. 32), and was victor in wrestling with the angel (Gen. 32:24-30).	1926. Hittite raid on Akkad. End of First dynasty of Babylon.		
1750	Over the Jordan they crossed into Western Canaan. His sons naturally were shepherds and cowherds. Joseph was a dreamer who with adolescent assurance told his dreams, and nettled his brothers. They sold him to a Midianite caravan on the road to Egypt. Potiphar, Egyptian official, bought him as a slave (Gen. 37:28-36).			
1725	**3. Hebrews in Egypt and the Desert**	1800-1500. Assyria ruled by patesis or governors. **IV. Kassite Period** (1760-1185)		1800-1600. "Golden Age" of Cretan civilization. Great palace at Knossos completed.
	Joseph in Potiphar's house, maligned and imprisoned; and later released (Gen. 39 and 40). Made premier of all Egypt (Gen. 41). Stored surplus grain. Famine drove Joseph's brothers to buy grain in Egypt (Gen. 42-44). Joseph plays role of an actor, identifies himself to his brothers. Jacob and his clan migrate to Egypt, settle in Goshen (Gen. 45-47).	1760. Third, or Kassite, dynasty of foreign kings in power. 1746. Kassites under Gandash conquer Babylonia and hold it for about 600 years.	1788-1580. The HYKSOS, or Shepherd Kings, conquer Egypt and rule about 200 years. The invaders introduce the horse into Egypt. Period of comparative obscurity.	The priest kings of Knossus exercised suzerainty over a considerable empire. The cultural and political influence of Crete was supreme in the Eastern Mediterranean.
	1893. Jacob died in Egypt, buried in Machpelah (Gen. 50). Joseph also died there and was later buried in Canaan (Josh. 24:32). Their posterity lived, worked and multiplied among the Egyptians. During the Hyksos period there was free communication between Canaan and Egypt over 200 years.	1700. Assyria gains overlordship over the Semites of the Middle Euphrates Valley.		
1500	1580. Hebrews were apparently undisturbed in the expulsion of the Hyksos rulers.	1561-1537. Agum II., a great Kassite king, who conquered much territory and built up his kingdom.	**IV. The Egyptian Empire** (Includes Dynasties 18-20e)	1500. Rise of Trojan power.
	The *Habiri* of the Tel el-Amarua age who savagely attacked Egyptian authority in Canaan may have been Hebrews sympathetic with the Hyksos, or roving bandits.		1580. After the expulsion of the Hyksos, Egypt was organized as a military state. Syria was conquered and made tributary by 1500.	
1300	Birth of Moses. His dramatic rescue, and education in the royal court of Egypt (cf. Acts 7:22). On an inspection tour of the Hebrews, he saw an Egyptian beating a Hebrew. Moses was furious and then and there slew the Egyptian and covered him with sand. Next day he learned it was out, and fled to the desert (Ex. 2:11-15) and became a shepherd. After a desert education of forty years God sent him back to Egypt (Ex. 3) to rescue his people. He and Aaron faced the Pharaoh and requested Israel's release. The Pharaoh scornfully refused (Ex. 7-10). Ten plagues finally clubbed his obstinacy into submission, and he shouted "Begone" (Ex. 12:29-32).		1479-1447. Thutmose III. 1414-1379. AMENHOTEP III., Great king, called the "Magnificent." 1380-1362. AMENHOTEP IV. 1360. Tutenkhaton changes name to Tutenkhamon. 1321-1300. SETI I. 1300-1234. R A M S E S II., the Great.	1400. Probable Mycenæan invasion destroyed Cretan civilization. 1400-1300. B l o o m of the Aegean and Mycenæan civilization. After 1400 B. C., we know nothing of the political history of Crete. The destruction had been complete, but it is clear that the cultural history of Crete followed closely the development of Greece and the other islands of the same period.
1250	Feast of Passover established (Ex. 12:1-28)—in memory of Israel's salvation from death of firstborn. Hebrews mobilized towards Red Sea, with their flocks, herds, and "borrowed" jewels (Ex. 12:33-39). Pharaoh rescinded his orders to Israel, but too late. Pursued them with 600 choice chariots (Ex. 14:1-20). Israel protected by a cloud-screen in the rear. Sea driven back by wind all night, Israel passed through on the dry sand, Egyptians following were caught in the backwash of waves, mired and sunk (Ex. 14:5-31). Israel now in the desert, lacked water (Ex. 15:22-27), food (Ex. 16:13-36), and proper shelter. Encamped at Sinai, where God gave Moses laws and religious ordinances (Ex. 19-23). The tabernacle and priesthood were ordained to meet Israel's religious needs (Ex. 24-40). But Israel "murmured," hankered for the "flesh-pots of Egypt" (Ex. 16:3; Num. 11:4). For their constant complaining Israel was penalized to wander in the desert forty years, until the bones of the grumblers should be left to bleach in the desert (Num. 14:26-25). The survivors should be only bedouin shepherds about the oasis, Kadesh-Barnea (Num. 20:1-14).	1380. BURNABURIASH, greatest of Kassite kings, established political relations with Egypt, settled boundary with Assyria. See Tel-el-Amarna Letters. 1350. Great expansion of Assyria; capital removed from Asshur to Calah (Nineveh). **V. Period of Decline** (1300-745) 1300. Kassites absorbed into the Semitic population of Babylonia. 1275. Continuous struggle between Assyria and Babylonia. 1250. King of Assyria conquers Babylon and rules seven years. 1250-1210. Decline of Babylonian power and rise of Assyria. 1200. Rise of Phœnician maritime power, founding of Tyre.	1240. Movement from Thebes to Delta where Syrian influence increases. Growth of Priesthood. 1234-1214. Merneptah drove out foreign invaders. Supposed Pharaoh of the Exodus. 1201-1171. RAMSES III., greatest king in twentieth dynasty. Built temples at Karnak and Medinet Habu. Great naval battle at Pelusium.	1240. Rise of the Achæans in Greece. 1200. Dorian invasion ended the grand prehistoric age of Greece.
1200	Israel entered the back-door into Canaan, through Edom and the East Jordan peoples, after forcing their passage (Num. 21:21-22:1). Balaam and his traducers (Num. 25, 26, 31). East Jordan was partitioned among two and one-half tribes (Num. 32). Moses views the land, dies and is buried on Mt. Nebo (Deut. 34). Joshua the new leader (Num. 27:18-23).			1193-1184. TROJAN WAR.
	After several fatal episodes with neighboring peoples, Israel crossed the Jordan and captured Jericho (Josh. 1:1-6), getting a foothold on West Jordan territory. Ai, after fatal repulses to Israel, taken by strategy (Josh. 7, 8). Military campaigns both to the North and South gave Israel general political mastery of the land (Josh. 9-12). West Jordan was apportioned out to the remaining nine and one-half tribes (Josh. 13-21).			

III. FROM THE RISE OF ASSYRIA TO THE

Hebrews reach the acme of their national power. Appearance of the Medo-Sea. Homeric age in Greece. Assyria reaches the zenith of her power. Medes, and Egyptians. Babylonia under Nebuchadrezzar reached her apex of

B. C.	4. Israel under Judges	Babylonia-Assyria	Egypt
1200	1180. Israel settled among the Canaanites with all their customs, manners, and appealing religious rituals. Jehovah-worship lost its glow, and local shrines caught the weaker devotees (Judg. 3:1-6). So far did they fall into an idolatrous abyss, that God sent neighboring peoples to punish their apostasy (Judg. 2:13). Judges were the leaders who pulled them out of their shocking plight; pledged to return to Jehovah.	1210-1150. The Hittite power having been destroyed and Egypt having withdrawn from the competition for empire in Syria and the region to the North, the field was left fairly clear for Assyrian expansion, which began to take place in real earnest in the first half of the twelfth century B.C.	1170. Ramses IV. Egypt stopped work on the mines of Sinai.
	The first lash of Jehovah's whip was a raid by the Aramæans from way up on the Euphrates River, which lasted eight years. Othniel (first judge), kin of good Caleb, broke their hold, and gave Israel peace 40 years (Judg. 3:7-11). The Moabites and allies East of Jordan balanced their grudge against Israel by crossing that river, and setting up their king Eglon in old restored Jericho. For 18 years he exacted heavy tribute from his old foe, until Ehud (second judge) by an act of treachery, assassinated Eglon, mobilized an army, routed, pursued and defeated the enemy, and gave the land rest "eighty years" (Judg. 3:12-30). The Philistines' grip on Israel was broken by the valor and skill of Shamgar (Judg. 3:31). The most tragic clash of this period was that with the Canaanites, when Deborah (fourth judge), Barak, Sisera and Jael were the actors—celebrated in the earliest poem of the Old Testament (Judg. 5). The Midianites East of the Jordan made annual foraging raids into the West, reducing Israel almost to starvation, until God raised up that dramatic character Gideon (fifth judge), who saved the day by real strategy (Judg. 6-8). The Ammonites, on the edge of the desert, tyrannized over Israel until that border ruffian Jephthah (sixth judge) shattered their power (Judg. 10:1-12:7).	Following the death of Tiglath-Pileser I, Assyria entered a period of decided decline. The glory of the first empire was utterly obscured. Records conveying reliable information are very few in number. 1146. Nebuchadnezzar I defeated Elam but was in turn subdued by Assyria.	**V. Decay of the Empire** (1150-525) 1145. Ramses IX. Valley of Tombs looted.
	The persistent encroachments of the Philistines down on the seaboard were checkmated by that acrobatic Samson (seventh judge) for twenty years (Judg. 12:8-16:31).	1120. Tiglath-Pileser I took Babylon and ruled it. 1115. Tiglath-Pileser I campaigned to Phœnicia and received tribute and gifts from Egypt.	1118. Ramses XI.
	The migration of the Danites to Laish (or Dan) raises the curtain on the religious decline and degeneracy of that day (Judg. 17 and 18), which resulted in a tribal protest and slaughter of 600 Benjaminites.	1107. Babylonian raid on Assyria with conquest and period of relapse in Assyria.	
1100	The Book of Ruth is a refreshing oasis in the bleak desert-waste of Judges (Ruth).	1100-930. History of Babylon of little importance until 600 B. C. Assyria the great power of Western Asia till the rise of the New Babylonian Empire after the destruction of Nineveh in 612 B. C.	1100-980. A dynasty of priest kings, founded by Her-Hor. The latter part of this period is contemporary with David and Solomon. Began building the temple about 967.
1100	1050. A glance at the life of judge Eli's day reveals sharp contrasts between Eli's sons and Samuel's parents (I. Sam. 1:1-3:21). Samuel, the chosen leader (1 Sam. 3). The Philistine victory and capture of the Ark (1 Sam. 4:1-7:2).	1060-1020. Babylonia revolted against Assyrian rule and put an end to the First Assyrian Empire.	1091. At beginning of the twenty-first dynasty two lines of kings: one at Thebes and another at Tanis. Power of Tanis established and great wall built.
	5. The Kingdom of Israel Israel demands a king (1 Sam. 8-9), Saul is chosen and anointed (1 Sam. 10 and 11). Saul put to the test, in routing the Ammonites (chap. 11). Saul vested with all authority by Samuel, and charged to keep the covenant—the Lord confirmed his counsel (1 Sam. 12). Saul rescued Israel from the Philistines' yoke, and clashed with Samuel (1 Sam. 13-15). Saul meets David, who became an outlaw before Saul's jealousy (1 Sam. 16-20). David, hunted like a partridge—fled to Philistia (1 Sam. 26:20). In a final great battle between Israel and Philistia at Mt. Gilboa, Saul and his sons were slain (1 Sam. 28 and 31; 1 Chron. 10).	1050-1000. Aramæan invasions of the Fertile Crescent were recommenced with greater intensity than ever before. With centers at Aleppo and Damascus, right on the trade routes from the Mediterranean to the Euphrates they prospered greatly.	This wall was eighty feet thick and enclosed the great temple at Tanis. The rulers of this place show very little initiative in other directions, however, and during the century and a half in which they maintained themselves in power there was a steady industrial and economic decline.
	1010. Saul's death left the land in the hands of the Philistines. But David, anointed king at Hebron (2 Sam. 1:1-2:7), gave heart to Israel. Remnants of Saul's house dispatched, David was anointed king over all Israel at Hebron (2 Sam. 5).		
	Jerusalem made capital of the kingdom, and the ark put there. (2 Sam. 5:6-10; 6). David organized an army (2 Sam. 21:15-22; 23:8-39), and an administration (2 Sam. 8:16-18; 20:23-26). Neighboring peoples alarmed, challenged the new king, only to be defeated in battle. David's zenith soon reached. Power and privilege entrapped him (2 Sam. 11:1-12:31), stained his character; and Nathan the prophet pierced his conscience. The fruits of his deeds appeared in his family; Absalom slew his half-brother Amnon, Absalom rebelled and was slain in battle, and sorrows never left David.		*A very complex and obscure period.*
1000		1000-950. Assyrian revival. Expansion from the Caspian Sea to the Persian Gulf and Westward to Cappadocia.	
930	971. By an intrigue of royal officials Solomon sat on the throne (1 Kgs. 1). He savagely wiped out with the sword all rivals to the throne (1 Kgs. 2:12-46). Made a wise choice in a vision (1 Kgs. 3:4-15). Organized an elaborate government (1 Kgs. 4). Sealed foreign relations by marrying foreign wives and princesses. Built his palace and the temple on an extravagant scale (1 Kgs. 5-7). His dedication prayer (1 Kgs. 8). His revenues immense, from domestic and foreign trade, including marine, failed to balance his budget (1 Kgs. 9-10). Solomon's wisdom proverbial, widespread, acute, as in case of the two mothers (1 Kgs. 3:16-28). He is credited with the Book of Proverbs and two Psalms (72, 127). Visitors came from many lands to hear his wisdom, even the queen of Sheba (1 Kgs. 10:1-10). But rebellions were smoldering in Egypt. In spite of wealth, wisdom, reputation, military power, the leprosy of polygamy ate out his vital moral and religious character to the near-destruction of his realm—a doubtful heritage to his successor. He passed out in the dim twilight of his career.	950. The Kingdom of Van with its capital at Tuspas rose to prominence on the Northern borders of Assyria. Assyrians sometimes refer to it as Urartu.	One of Solomon's vessels joined with Egyptian trading ships to make a journey to Tarshish. 987-952. Pasebkhanu II. King Solomon married one of his daughters.

FALL OF BABYLON, 1120 — 538 B. C.

Persian people. Phœnicians control the maritime trade of the Mediterranean
Phœnician cities began to decline. Assyria declined and fell before Babylonians,
glory. Waned under Nabonidus and fell to Cyrus the Persian.

Phœnicia-Lydia Phrygia	Greeks	Rome	Persians	China, Japan, India	B. C.
1175. Asia Minor was opened up after the fall of Troy. 1173. The Hittite power was overthrown at Boghaz Keui. 1170. Tubal, Meshech and other tribes made their appearance. 1150. A post-Hittite culture made its appearance in Northern Syria with its center at Carchemish. 1150-1100. Aramæans who were Semitic nomads, concentrated in the Syrian desert, being checked in their expansion northward by the Assyrians, or possibly also by a general advance of foreign tribes from Asia Minor.	1183. Troy's capture, an important event in connection with the Greek settlements in Asia Minor. 1150. The vanguard of a larger migration of later date made its appearance in Greece. Both Dorian and Achæan elements were present. 1115. The Pelopid dynasty in Argos and Mycenæ in the Peloponnesus came to an end.	Traces of men have been discovered in Italy as far back as the Old Stone Age, while remains of the late stone age are abundant. The bronze age is preceded by the copper age in which copper implements were used side by side with those of stone or flint. The first invasion of Italy of which we have clear evidence came at the beginning of the bronze age. The new-comers came from central Europe and are distinguishable from earlier inhabitants of Italy by their burial customs. These late comers practiced cremation whereas the former buried their dead.	The original territory of Persia proper seems to have corresponded roughly to the modern province of Iran. Its length was about 450 miles and its average width 250 miles. It was first occupied by people from Bactria or possibly Turkestan. This was at a very early period and information concerning these people is very uncertain.		1200
				China: 1150-770. T h e Chou Dynasty. This is an era of the conventionalization of culture. The great books of household and court ritual and social economy appeared: Chou Li, I Li and Li Chi. China: 1122-1100. Chou Kung, brother of Wu Wang, founder of the Chou dynasty exerted tremendous influence as a humanistic standardizer of custom. Democracy and free speech prevailed and there were even experiments in state socialism.	
1100. Tyre attains first rank among Phœnician seacoast towns.	1100. The Mycenæan Empire was broken up. Outside tribes and influences made their appearance. **II. Formation of Greek States** (1100-500) 1100-950. Great migrations in Greece of Dorians and Thessalians. Ionic colonies founded in Asia Minor.	1100. The Etruscans already in central Italy. 1100-753. This period is obscure because of the absence of a key to the written language of the Etruscans.	1100. Formation of a powerful empire in Bactria. Deeds of kings celebrated in the Shahnameh of Firdusi.		1100
	1075-1000. The period of the great Dorian invasion into the Peloponnesus by way of Attica and the Isthmus of Corinth. 1068. Codrus, last king of Athens. Beginning of rule of archons.	Successive waves of immigrants moved southward, entering into and occupying the entire Padus Valley.	While Aryan tribes in the West were being extirpated in many wars with the Egyptians, Hittites and Assyrians, or were being absorbed by the native population, the great highland of Iran was being occupied by the Iranians. They were divided into numerous tribes and these again were subdivided into many minor tribes and clans. Thirteen main divisions are recognized in the Avesta, the most important of which were the Medes, Persians and Parthians.	China: 1078-1053, the reign of K'ang who consolidated the empire. All the feudal princes acknowledged their allegiance to the ruling house of Chou, but there followed speedily a marked degeneracy in the characters of the ruling kings. Lawlessness spread far and wide.	
1050-970. King of Tyre ruled over Cyprus. A period of trade and colonization. 970-930. The King of Tyre got certain villages in the northern part of the Hebrew kingdom in return for trade facilities. He also made a treaty of alliance with Solomon.	1050-950. Large migrating groups of different customs and speech came to Greece. The Aeolian Group occupied Thessaly and Bœotia and some islands like Lesbos. The Ionians came to Attica and the Cyclades while the Dorians occupied Crete, Milos, Thera and islands off the southwest coast of Asia Minor, besides the Peloponnesus where they had come earlier.	1000. Original Italic stock was scattered through the hills and valleys of Central Italy by this date or earlier. These people lived in huts protecting themselves as best they could. Rome itself began in such a collection of huts, the site being occupied by the year 1000 B.C.	1000. Period of ZOROASTER and Zoroastrianism, was chief of the Magi, a priestly tribe of Media. His faith became the leading religious belief of the Persians.	China: 1000. Artesan and trade guilds made their appearance.	1000
Phœnician workmen were sent to Jerusalem to aid in the artistic decoration of the temple and palace. Most of the cedar wood which was used in the construction was imported from Phœnicia. This is a period of great foreign trade.	950-900. Migrations of Ionians into Asia Minor continued. The colonists carried with them into the new Greece beyond the Aegean, their social traditions of the old civilization which in the mother country was being overwhelmed by the Dorian invaders. These traditions helped to produce the luxurious Ionian civilization of later years.	950-900. The Etruscans who no doubt entered Italy shortly after the Trojan War were gradually consolidating their position. Coming as pirates their successive settlements extended over a considerable period of years somewhat like those of the Danes and Saxons in England.	The name of Zoroaster is connected with so much of unreliable tradition that it is difficult to determine what are actually the facts concerning him. According to one account he was a king who conquered Babylon in 2458. According to other accounts it would seem that he lived even later than the date here given. 950. Persians made their appearance in Southwestern Armenia where they were in close contact with the Medes.	China: 1000-947, the reign of Mu Wang, a great traveler who, with his charioteer went westward as far as it was possible to penetrate. Out into the desert he went, he may have gone as far as Persia or India.	930

B. C.	6. The Dual Kingdoms		Babylonia-Assyria	Egypt
	Judah	Israel		
930				950-750. This is a period of rival Pharaohs and internal strife in which the Ethiopians became dominant at the beginning and later were driven out only to be succeeded by other foreigners, notably, the Assyrians. At different times during this period Egypt exercised an overlordship over Palestine, Phœnicia and other peoples of the Syrian coast of the Mediterranean.
	931. 1. *Rehoboam* [17], son of Solomon, made King at Jerusalem; went to Shechem to have it confirmed. Asked for his policy, he endorsed his father's, with ominous increases. Forced to flee to Jerusalem. Shemaiah prophet rebuked him (1 Kgs 12:1-24).	1. *Jeroboam* [22] son of Nebat, made king of ten tribes at Shechem. Established calf worship as counter to Jehovah at Jerusalem (1 Kgs. 12:25-33). Politically a strong ruler, religiously "made Israel to sin."	930-640. *Brilliant epoch of Assyria. A period of conquest, expansion, architecture, sculpture and literary activity.* Assyria had as a neighbor to the North a Caucasian people who occupied the kingdom of Van, which embraced the greater part of modern Armenia. They were a people of considerable importance during all of this time when Assyria was in the ascendancy.	
	926. Shishak, King of Egypt, invaded land and looted Jerusalem (2 Chron. 12).		950-900. The Babylonians had a great order of priests known as Baru or diviners, who traced the origin of their profession back through many centuries. They said that all human knowledge had been written upon tablets before the flood and buried in Sippar. The prophets could divine future events it was claimed. Direct oracles such as the Delphic oracle in Greece were not known.	*Twenty-second dynasty* of Egypt. 945—
	914. 2. *Abijam* [3], son of Rehoboam, fought Israel—defeated.			945-924. Sheshonq (Shishak of the Bible), married to sister of the wife of King Solomon. Great conquests in Syria. (926) Capture of Jerusalem.
	912. 3. *Asa* [41], son of Abijam, made Judah prosperous. Promoted religious and political reforms. Had a great army. Warred with Baasha. Bribed Benhadad to fight Baasha (1 Kgs. 15:16-22). Defeated Zerah the Ethiopian (2 Chron. 14:9-15). Asa sharply rebuked by prophets.	Death of Jeroboam, his son, 2. *Nadab* [2] on throne. Slain by 3. *Baasha* [24], usurper. Wipes out house of Jeroboam, warred against Asa of Judah.	884-860. Ashurnasirpal. One of the greatest Assyrian kings. Extended the empire. Moved the government to Calah (Nimrud) from Ashur. Built a palace there.	
900	885. Jehu, son of Hanani (of Israel), Azariah (of Judah), Oded (of Israel). Locked up Hanani (2 Chron. 16:7-10).	Death of Baasha, his son 4. *Elah* [2], slain by 5. *Zimri* [7 days], usurper. 6. Tibni and *Omri* [12], four years of civil war. Omri put capital at Samaria. Trade pacts with Phœnicia.	He crossed the Euphrates and reached the Orontes, Lebanon and finally the Mediterranean. He captured many prisoners and slew numerous others. If the records be true he surpassed all other Oriental despots in cruelty and ferocity; for he flayed, impaled and otherwise barbarously put to death countless foes and captives.	900-800. The Pharaohs of this period contended with rivals and invaders, chief of whom were the Ethiopians who had risen to a position of great importance at Napata on the Upper Nile. They extended their power at last over the whole of Egypt. This Ethiopian domination lasted for two-thirds of a century, until the great Assyrian invasion of a later date broke and drove these southern people back to their original homes.
	874. Asa's sickness and death (2 Chron. 16:11-14).	7. *Ahab* [22], son of Omri, married Jezebel of Sidon. Baal cult became state religion of Israel. Famine of three and one-half years. Test on Carmel between Elijah and 450 prophets of Baal (1 Kgs. 18:20-40).		
	871. 4. *Jehoshaphat* [25], son of Asa, a religious and political reformer. Taught the law of God (2 Chron. 17:1-9).	Elijah fled to Mt. Horeb. The "still small voice" (1 Kgs. 19:1-14).		895. Takelot I. succeeded his father Osorkon I. at Bubastis. After his death he was succeeded by his son Osorkon II. who regained control of Thebes and repaired the Luxor Temple after a great flood. This family was rent by feuds and revolts. Powerful mercenary commanders feeling themselves aggrieved sought time and again to improve their position by force of arms.
	Jehoshaphat, popular, prosperous ruler, received tribute from Philistines and Edomites (2 Chron. 17:10-19).	Elisha made Elijah's successor. Victor over Syrians at Samaria and Aphek (1 Kgs. 20). Episode of Naboth's vineyard (1 Kgs. 21).		
	Jehoshaphat visits Ahab, forms a league (1 Kgs. 22:1-4). Prophets consulted (1 Kgs. 22:5-36). Jehoram, his son, regent (2 Kgs. 1:17; 3:1), married Athaliah, daughter of Ahab (2 Kgs. 11:1).	Ahab in a league against Assyria at Karkar. 8. *Ahaziah* [2], regent with his father Ahab.	860-825. Shalmaneser III. Ceaseless wars made him master of Western Asia. First contact with Israelites. Jehu, King of Israel, among those who sent tribute. Built palace at Calah (Nimrud). Protectorate over Babylon. In the thirty-five years of his rule he is credited with no less than thirty-two expeditions. He intervened in Mesopotamia and thus made Babylon a vassal kingdom. In Northern Syria he consolidated his father's conquests and began the invasion of central Syria but without results. Allied forces of contingents from Phœnicia, Syria and Aramæan principalities successfully barred his southward progress.	860. Takelot II. succeeded to the throne.
	849. 5. *Jehoram* [8] son of Jehoshaphat, became king, his father still living (2 Kgs. 8:16). Jehoshaphat died. Jehoram slew his brethren (2 Chron. 21:4).	Ahab slain in battle at Ramothgilead (1 Kgs. 22:29-40). On Ahaziah's death, his son 9. *Jehoram* [12] joins Jehoshaphat against Moab. Jehoram wounded in battle, slain by		850. The high priest Osorkon began a series of annals on the walls of the Temple of Karnak recording his deeds and his gifts to the temple. He was driven out of the city, however, by a revolt which spread and finally developed into civil war.
	841. 6. *Ahaziah* [1], son of Jehoram, slain by Jehu near Jezreel (2 Chron. 22:5-9).	10. *Jehu* [28], usurper, wiped out house of Omri, and Baal worshippers; retained calf-worship (2 Kgs. 9 and 10). Paid tribute to Shalmaneser III. of Assyria.		
	Athaliah [6], his mother, usurps throne of Judah—destroys seed royal.		850-800. Astrology was highly developed in this period. This was an attempt at divination by planets and constellations and atmospheric conditions. It had one good by-product in an astonishingly accurate knowledge of astronomy. Many of the planets had been identified. Eclipses were observed to the point where they could be foretold.	
	836. 7. *Jehoash* [40], son of Ahaziah, secretly crowned as a child. Athaliah slain (2 Kgs. 11:4-20). Priest Jehoiada his pilot (2 Chron. 23:16-24:15). After death of Jehoiada, reforms waned, idolatry won out (2 Chron. 24:17-24).	Jehu loses E. Jordan to Hazael of Damascus. 11. *Jehoahaz* [17], son of Jehu, captured by Hazael of Syria (2 Kgs. 13:22-25).		
	Hazael's army before Jerusalem, bought off (2 Kgs. 12:17, 18).	Maintained the record — "made Israel to sin."	825-812. Shamsi-Adad IV of Assyria.	
	Zechariah priest, son of Jehoiada, rebuked Jehoash and was stoned (2 Chron. 24:20-24).	12. *Jehoash* [16], son of Jehoahaz, regent two years. Defeated Syria three times.	812-782. Adad-nirari III. captured Damascus. Married Babylonian princess Semiramis.	
	Amaziah regent with his father Jehoash, who was slain at Millo.	Jeroboam (II.) regent with his father. Death of Jehoash of Israel.		
800				

OF BABYLON, 1120 — 538 B. C.—Continued

Phœnicia-Lydia Phrygia	Greeks	Rome	Persians	China, Japan, India	B. C.
					930
970. King Hiram sent material for Solomon's Temple and built the causeway connecting Tyre with the mainland, so that the city was no longer located on an island but on a peninsula.	950-900. Bards or Rhapsodes, forerunners of Homer, exercised their art at the courts of Mycenæan and Minoan chieftains. They composed hymns in honor of the gods or narrative poems recounting heroic deeds of valor of some leader, presumably an ancestor of the chief whose guest the minstrel was. 900. Period of *HOMER*. Poems of Homer reflect the Mycenæan and Aegean period of the Greeks.	900-850. This still is a period of many migrations of barbaric and semi-barbaric tribes from Central Europe, possibly from beyond the Danube. For the most part they occupied Northern Italy, there being few if any traces of them south of the Apennines. The inhabitants of this region developed their own Bronze Age civilization. The latter part of this period witnesses the introduction of iron implements and weapons. These people cremated their dead and used burial urns of a distinctive type placed in well tombs. The name most commonly given to these people who came from Central Europe is Umbrian. At one time they lived on both sides of the Apennines.	900. Indo-European people migrated apparently from Scythia into Armenia. Finding the Kingdom of Van too strong to be conquered or overrun, they moved southeastward to the Iranian plateau. They are known to historians as the Medes. They were a pastoral people. There were six tribes of them with a strictly patriarchal organization. The clans lived more or less independently warring among themselves, but when they came into conflict with a people like the Assyrians they stood together for mutual protection	China: 946-934. Kung Wang. This is the period of feudalism in China. The great landlords of the country did not see why they should obey the king. They felt that they were like kings on their own land. They could do as they liked and would not need to serve the king.	
					900
	900-850. Society of this period is strongly aristocratic. The nobles alone got attention in the literature of the period. The rest of the population was taken for granted as is also the institution of slavery. Slaves, male and female, were found on the large domains or in the palaces. 875-850. The Greek fringe on the West coast of Asia Minor was being completed. Only here and there were any difficulties in the way such as the Lycians who were not a folk of Aryan speech. These people held the territory between Doris and Pamphylia as an insuperable barrier to real unity of the Greeks in this region.		900-850. There appeared certain nomadic people who were known as "Turan" or "Turanian." The origin of the word is obscure being derived perhaps from some obsolete tribal name. It is found repeatedly in the Avesta under the form "Tura" and seems to date back to Zoroaster himself where these people are represented as faithful adherents of the prophet. **I. Ancient Persian Period** (836-640)	China: 878-842. Li Wang. The principles of justice and law were established by Duke of Shao. The Duke of Shao was also a man of literary talents. He wrote an ode which remains in the Shih Ching in which, under the guise of an address to a former tyrant, he gives a solemn warning to the reigning monarch. That the warning was needed is indicated by the fact that the emperor, Li, soon after had to flee from a rebellion which he had aroused.	
855. Phœnicia joined with Syria and various Aramæan princes to stem the tide of Assyrian invasions into Syria and the Eastern Mediterranean area. 850-800. This was a period of colonization. The typical Phœnician colony was only a trading station inhabited by traders who had not ceased to be counted as citizens of the mother country. In Phœnicia itself the main interest was in the maintenance and extension of foreign trade. The government encouraged such ventures because of the profits which resulted. Phœnician traders were everywhere first in the field and it was very easy to keep first place because their barbarous customers that all others were dangerous.		850-800. The origin and development of alphabets in early Italy seem to link early settlements of Greeks in Italy with the founding of Cumæ. Greek traditions represent this as a colony from Chalcis in Eubœa in the 11th century B. C. Objections are raised, however, to a date so early because of the limitation of sea transport at so early an epoch. But after all the discount has been allowed which such objections interpose, it would still seem quite certain that the settlement was made sometime within the period here indicated.	850-740. The Persians were a people on the outside of the Assyrian Empire to the Northeast. At first they appeared in Southwestern Armenia and then migrated to the district North and Northeast of Susiana.		
			825-812. Media and Persia were invaded by Shamshi-Adad IV of Assyria and were compelled to pay tribute.	China: 827-781. Suan Wang. A period of great drought and famine. The Tartars also entered his kingdom and he could not defeat them. He grew discouraged and careless. It was his wife, a woman of unusual sagacity, who urged and persuaded him to save his kingdom.	
846-814. Carthage founded by the Phœnicians, supposedly under the leadership of Elissa (Dido of the Aeneid). 845-840. Repeated attacks of the Assyrians on Phœnicia finally led to the payment of an annual tribute to Assyria, as the price of peace. 800. Phrygia an independent monarchy.	820. Legislation of Lycurgus founded the stability of Sparta. 800. Development of music in the Grecian colonies of Asia Minor.	800. More Etruscan settlements in Italy.		India: 800: Brahmanic period of Vedic literature.	800

B. C.	Kingdoms of Judah	Israel	Babylonia-Assyria	Egypt
800	797. 8. *Amaziah* [29], slew slayers of his father. Defeated Edom, adopted its idols (2 Chron. 25: 14-16).		825-782. The last years of the great kings of Assyria, Shalmaneser III, Shamsi-Adad IV. (825-812) and Adad-nirari III. (812-782). Shalmaneser III. had a great deal of trouble with his northern neighbors in the kingdom of Van. It was all he could do to prevent their actually invading his own kingdom. In the last year or two of his reign he saw a large part of his work undone. One of his sons rebelled and that led to a partitioning of the empire, only half remaining faithful to Shalmaneser.	800-780. This was a period of strife and internal dissension. The high priest at Thebes was forced to flee and when he finally gained the support of his father's followers he returned to Thebes amid great rejoicing. With a long fleet of ships he approached the city. He returned to the temple from which Amon came forth in gorgeous procession. Nevertheless the gods delivered an oracle exempting the Thebans from punishment.
790	"A prophet" rebuked Amaziah; a "Man of God" barred alliance with Israel (2 Chron. 25:7-10).			
787	Uzziah (Azariah) regent with his father Amaziah.			
785	Amaziah challenged Joash of Israel; was defeated, captured, and Jerusalem plundered (2 Chron. 25:17-24).			
	Amaziah slain by his servants at Lachish (2 Kgs. 14:17-22). Uzziah succeeds him.	13. *Jeroboam II.* [41], son of Jehoash; great army officer. Israel's former boundaries restored.	*Shalmaneser IV.* (782-773) of Assyria was fighting desperately to bring the old empire of his father under his own sway, a united domain.	
	782. 9. *Uzziah* (*Azariah*) [52] began to rule alone. Prophet Zechariah his teacher—and he prospered (2 Chron. 26:5). Recovered former limits of Judah, fortified country — all prospered (2 Chron. 26:1-15).	Amos (of Judah), prophet, who arraigned Israel for her crimes, idolatries, and debaucheries. Hosea (of Israel) charges people and King with alienation from Jehovah.	Ashur-dan (773-755) of Assyria ruled in a period of dynastic disputes in which the lack of authority in the dependencies led to their breaking away in some instances.	780. Rise of independent kingdom in Nubia. 775-740. An Ethiopian power of considerable importance developed in the Southern territory of the Upper Nile. Its influence gradually extended over the whole of Egypt.
	Uzziah's presumption, sacrilege, and leprosy (2 Chron. 26:16-23).	Jeroboam II. died. Anarchy in Israel.	Ashur-nirari II. (755-746) of Assyria.	The king of the Nubian or Ethiopian conquering host bore all the titles of the old Pharaohs. He called himself Lord of the Two Lands, as if he governed all Egypt. If he was known by an Egyptian name at the beginning he dropped it soon and later gave forth his personal name of pure Nubian origin. He built temples and decorated them with reliefs as the Egyptians had done. The ritual depicted on the walls of the temples is the same as that in use in Thebes.
	750. 10. *Jotham* [16], regent in place of Uzziah, a leper (2 Kgs. 15:5)—a reasonably good king.			
742	Ahaz regent with Jotham his father (2 Kgs. 17:1), his grandfather Uzziah being a leper, in an infirmary.	14. *Zechariah* [6 mos.], slain by 15. *Shallum* [1 mo.], First year of *Pekah* [20], East of Jordan, second year (2 Kgs. 15:32). Shallum slain by 16. *Menahem* [10], usurper. Tribute paid to Pul of Assyria (2 Kgs. 15:17-22).	745-727. Tiglath-Pileser III. (identical with the king Pul of the Bible) made Babylonia subject to Assyria. Extended his empire into Egypt on the West and to the Indus on the East. 741. Tiglath-Pileser III. listed Hiram of Tyre among those from whom he collected tribute. It is quite evident from the reference, however, that Hiram II. was not only king of Tyre, as the Assyrians called him, but also king of Sidon and possibly of the colony in Cyprus.	745. The twenty-second dynasty came to an end. One of the delta lords named Pedibast, gained the dominant position among his rivals and founded a new house, the twenty-third dynasty. 731. Pedibast forced to share his throne with king Yewepet, a dynast of the Eastern delta. This is also a period of many feuds and civil wars.
738		17. *Pekahiah* [2], son of Menahem, slain by		
736	Uzziah's death in a leper's house.	18. *Pekah* [20], with a long prior reign East of the Jordan. This is his first year in Samaria, 16th from his beginning in Gilead.	735. Ahaz became tributary to Assyria. ISAIAH denounced the alliance.	734-732. Tiglath-Pileser III. devastated the West down to the frontier of Egypt. But the kings of the delta were too involved in their own complicated and petty wars to render any assistance to the Hebrews. This foreshadowed for Egypt the ultimate loss of Palestine.
734	Sixteenth and death year of Jotham, seventh of regency of Uzziah.	Pekah and Rezin of Damascus defeat Ahaz.		
	732. 11. *Ahaz* [16], his son. Facing Pekah and Rezin he appeals to Assyria for help (2 Kgs. 16: 7-16). Meets King of Assyria in Damascus. Imports Syrian altar to Jerusalem (2 Kgs. 16: 10-16).	Hoshea slew Pekah (20th year from his beginning to reign East of Jordan in 750 B.C. (2 Kgs. 15:30).	Damascus falls to Assyria.	
732	"Twentieth year" — from the beginning of Jotham's regency —old method of dating still in use (2 Kgs. 15:30).	19. *Hoshea* [9], first full year (2 Kgs. 17:1).	730-728. Tiglath-Pileser III conquered and annexed all of Transjordania, deporting a large part of the population.	
730	Prophet Micah in Judah countering Ahaz's sacrileges and desecrations. A. adopted religion of kings of Israel. Shut up the house of the Lord. Isaiah reprimanded and denounced King Ahaz.		727-722. Shalmaneser V. suppressed the revolt of the Phœnician cities and the Kingdom of Israel.	
728	Hezekiah regent with Ahaz his father.	Coquetted with Egypt, withheld usual tribute from Assyria, whose army came west to enforce collection. Hoshea taken, imprisoned, by Assyria.		
	727. 12. *Hezekiah* [29], first full year. Made drastic religious reforms — observed passover, restored temple services — reenforced by Isaiah the prophet.	Seventh year of Hoshea (old dating, though Hoshea was in prison) Samaria began to be besieged by Shalmaneser V. "Ninth year" from beginning of Hoshea's reign—though a captive.		
724	"Fourth Year" of Hezekiah (2 Kgs. 18:9).	Samaria capitulated to Sargon II. 28,290 persons carried into captivity. Foreigners imported to fill the vacancies in the land.	722-705. SARGON II. conquered Samaria and destroyed the kingdom of Israel. He received tribute from Arabia, Egypt, and Cyprus; suppressed revolts in Armenia, Media and Babylonia, and united the latter with Assyria.	(722-654) 722. Egypt lost Palestine to Assyria.
722	"Sixth year" of Hezekiah (2 Kgs. 18:10).			

OF BABYLONIA, 1120 — 538 B. C.—Continued

Phœnicia-Lydia Phrygia	Greeks	Rome	Persians	China, Japan, India	B. C.
800-750. Military expeditions of the Assyrians reached South Syria and Phœnicia, whose independence seems to have been lost. Whether this submission was continuous is not clear, but the Assyrian records make it plain that tribute was paid and there is no evidence of revolt or even resistance.	800-750. Largely a legendary period when the mythology of Greece seems to have had its origin. 8C0-750. The Greek cities were passing through a process of political, constitutional and economic evolution. The mass of the people exercised very little political influence. The upper classes in the cities, being a small minority, held the political power, while the peasants outside the cities turned to the governing class only as a last resort.	800. The Etruscans, a new and racially quite distinct people, were in the height of their power in the territory of Central Italy north of the Tiber. For four centuries they were the most powerful state in the peninsula. That they were a people with an advanced material civilization is evidenced by the wall-paintings, the vases and metal-work, extant to this day. Their earlier home seems to have been on the Eastern shores of the Mediterranean.	812-782. During the time of Adad-nirari of Assyria numerous Assyrian expeditions were made into Media. The Medes and Persians in that early day were proving themselves rather troublesome neighbors and the Assyrians' desire for their territory did not improve the prospect for peace. 800-750. It must be borne in mind that the region of Persia was filled with people who had been compelled to move out of the territory which they had previously occupied, either by severity of climate or because the pressure of other more savage tribes upon them. Thus the Medes had come in from the Northwest and the Iranians or Persians proper, from the Northeast through Bactria. It was in connection with this migration that the horse was introduced into Western Asia. When the Assyrians resisted them as they moved farther and farther toward Assyrian territory there was begun a long struggle which finally ended in Persian supremacy. 740. Western Iran (Media and Persia) subject to Assyria. The conquest of the Medes by Tiglath-Pileser III seems to have been facilitated by the lack of union in the Median tribes. This was contrary to the usual solidarity of the Medes in the face of a common foe. Tiglath-Pileser claimed to have brought back many prisoners and much spoil in the form of horses and cattle. 730-720. The Medes were not content to sit and passively admit the overlordship of the Assyrians. Time and time again they revolted. They made alliances with barbarian tribes from the outside, notably the Cimmerians and the Ashguza (perhaps the Scythians) who had invaded Asia Minor and Armenia. Their efforts were however of little avail and they remained in the hands of the Assyrians at least during the reigns of three successive Assyrian kings.	China: 789. The army of Suan Wang was defeated in a battle against certain Tangutan tribes. China: 780-700. Constant struggles between central power and feudal states. China: 770-720. P'ing Wang. This was the period in which the Chou Dynasty declined and was finally overthrown. The government was transferred to the city of Lo-Yang in the province of Honan and for the rest of the period the dynasty is known as that of the Eastern Chou. This is eloquent testimony of the pressure of the barbarians in the West. The dukes of the several states were furthermore taking possession of entire provinces and governing without reference to imperial edicts. When P'ing died, his poverty was such that there was not enough money in the treasury to bury him decently, nor did there seem to be any duke or prince who cared enough to provide the burial. India: 750-700. Aryan tribes occupied a large part of Northern India. They were at that early date acquainted with metals. They had blacksmiths, coppersmiths and goldsmiths among them, besides carpenters, barbers and other artisans. They fought from chariots and used the horse although the elephant had not yet come into use. This is the period in which they were leaving their nomadic ways and building cattle pens to keep in their cattle, which were still their chief form of wealth. They had learned to build ships and were carrying on a little commerce.	800 790 787 785 742 738 736 734 732 730 728 724 722
750-600. Greek colonies were being established on the Lydian coast of Asia Minor.	776. FIRST OLYMPIAD, cr first year the Olympian victor was recorded. 754-753. Origin of the ephorate in Sparta. 750-700. The age of Aristocracies. 750-550. Colonizing period of the Greeks.	**I. Mythical Period of the Kings** (753-510) 753-716. Romulus. 753. ROME founded. 750. Sabines incorporated with Romans. 750. The Greeks made settlements in Sicily and the Western Mediterranean as the foundations of a rival civilization were laid on the banks of the Tiber.			
743. The Phœnicians were no longer passively submissive to Assyrian rule as they had been. From this time until the fall of Nineveh frequent efforts were made to establish Phœnician independence.	743-724. FIRST MESSENIAN WAR between Messenia and Sparta. A gradual change was going on in the government of Attica (Athens). At first the government was monarchic in form but step by step the nobles encroached on the royal power and diminished; first, by changing the rule from a hereditary to an elective monarchy, and second, by gradually reducing the tenure of power, first to ten years and later to a shorter period until finally it was made but one year. At the same time they drastically reduced the duties of the office.	750-725. The city of Rome was gradually being built up on the Seven Hills, a place which was chosen because it could be so easily defended. It was situated some distance from the sea and thus was protected from raids by pirates, at the same time the Tiber made trade with the outside world possible, and finally because of an island in the river at that point, crossing from the north to the south banks of the river was not so difficult.			
728. Midas of Phrygia foments rebellion against rule of Sargon in Northern Syria.	740-725. The object of the Spartans in conquering the Messenians was to increase the number of lots of land for their citizens, at the same time reducing the Messenians to the condition of helots. As helots they had to pay their conquerors and masters one half of the produce of the land which they cultivated. Hard as this was, however, it was not as bad as the condition of similar classes in Attica at the same time, where the amount was five-sixths of the produce for the overlord.	750-725. In this period of early beginnings a fortress was built and the city of Rome was governed as an elective monarchy with the tenure of office for life, similar to that which was to be found in the early years of Venetian history. It grew into a flourishing center of commerce and industry and increased its territory by force of arms. This natural impulse to grow was favored by prudent laws. Thus the city attracted immigrants from neighboring peoples. These people were easily assimilated. Most of them came from the Sabines and Etruscans.			
725. Eulæus IX (Assyrian, Luli) ruled under the name of Pylas as king of Tyre, Sidon and other cities in the region. His country was invaded by Shalmaneser IV.	725. Appearance of Oriental influence in Greek Art, beginning of Greek architecture in stone.				

B. C.	7. Judah Alone	Babylonia-Assyria	Persia
720	720. Isaiah the prophet urged on Hezekiah in his radical religious reforms. 713. Hezekiah's sickness brought him to himself—humiliated him. Isaiah predicted Hezekiah's death—his penitence postponed it (Isa. 38). 712. Embassy of Merodach-Baladan from Babylon to Hezekiah (2 Kgs. 20:12-19). Isaiah scored his pride in showing M.-B. his war strength (Isa. 39). 701. Southwest Palestine invaded by Sennacherib on way to Egypt. Hezekiah, guilty of joining rebels, heavily penalized (2 Kgs. 18:14-16). Two feints against Jerusalem failed to cause capitulation (Isa. 36-37; 35). Summary disaster to the Assyrian troops (Isa. 37:36, 37).	722-705. Sargon II, king of Assyria. He defeated the Egyptians at Raphia, captured the Hittite stronghold at Carchemish (717) in the Euphrates Valley, and drove the Chaldeans out of Babylon. Sargon II.'s Tartan took Ashdod (Isa. 20:1). 705. Sargon slain in battle, succeeded by his son *Sennacherib* (705-681). Rebellion in Southwest Palestine target of Sennacherib's aim. Claimed victory over Egyptians at Eltekeh—Tirhakah being their general.	720-710. A gradual process of unification was going on in Media. Thus were laid the foundations for future imperial greatness. 708-655. Deioces was unanimously accepted as head of the Medes and assumed royal station. He fixed his capital at Ecbatana in the heart of the Zagros hills. It was a natural fortress on top of which stood the royal palace.
700	Good King Hezekiah passed on, succeeded by his son 698. 13. *Manasseh* [55]. A recoil against Jehovah worship, prophets killed, temple violated, foreign gods popular (2 Kgs. 21:1-16). Manasseh paid tribute to Esarhaddon. 670. Manasseh training Judah to be anti-Jehovah worshippers. 648. Manasseh coquetted with Egypt, carried captive to Babylon. On repenting was restored to his throne (2 Chron. 33:11-13). Reversed his former religious policy, fortified Jerusalem. Death of Manasseh, succeeded by his son 642. 14. *Amon* [2], rank idolater, as his father formerly was. Slain in an uprising (2 Kgs. 21:19-26). Succeeded by his son 639. 15. *Josiah* [31], reared by reactionists against Manasseh's disloyalty to Jehovah. Josiah, on good advice, purged the temple and land of idols, of idol-worshippers, and other evil symbols. Huldah the prophetess with him in it all (2 Kgs. 22:1-23:25). 626. Jeremiah began to prophesy (Jer. 1:1, 2). 625. Zephaniah pushed reforms with his prophecy (Zeph). 621. "Book of the law" found in the rubbish of the temple (2 Kgs. 22:8-20; King and people renew covenant. Reforms reach to Bethel and Samaria. Passover again celebrated (2 Kgs. 23:21-23). 612. Prophet Nahum's tragic picture of Nineveh's crash—Nahum. Josiah slain at Megiddo by Egyptians (2 Kgs. 23:29, 30). The people crown 608. 16. *Jehoahaz* [3 mos.] his son. Ousted from throne, carried to Egypt (2 Kgs. 23:30-34). 17. *Jehoiakim* [11] a brother, enthroned by Necho; headstrong defiant youth (2 Kgs. 23:34-24:6). 604. Jerusalem subject to Nebuchadnezzar. Daniel and companions carried to Babylon (Dan. 1:1). 602. Jehoiakim threw off yoke of Babylon (2 Kgs. 24:1). Neighboring troops of Babylon raided him (2 Kgs. 24:2).	681. Sennacherib killed by his sons, *Esarhaddon* (681-668) his son, his successor (2 Kgs. 19:37). Esarhaddon conquered Egypt—Tirhakah escaping into Ethiopia. 668. Death of Esarhaddon, succeeded by *Ashurbanipal* (668-626) his son. Re-captured Egypt, razing Memphis and No Amon (Thebes). (Nah. 3:8-10). Ashurbanipal overthrew the Elamites, and looted Susa. Cyaxares founded Empire of Media. Possible Scythian invasion from the North. 626. Assyrian power declining at death of Ashurbanipal. NABOPOLASSAR, governor of Babylon, makes the latter independent, and wars against Assyria. 612. Fall of Nineveh, capital of the ASSYRIAN EMPIRE. In 605 Nebuchadnezzar defeated Necho at Carchemish and drove the Egyptians out of Asia and annexed Syria to the Babylonian Empire. Then he succeeded his father to the throne and began to make Babylon one of the wonders of the world. Temples were erected to the gods and great walls were constructed around the city and a strong fortress was erected. Canals were dug throughout the country and a great reservoir was excavated near the capital. It was a splendid reign. 604-561. NEBUCHADNEZZAR II. makes Babylonia the leading nation of the East. Conquered Jerusalem (586) and subdued Tyre (585). *Splendid architectural era at Babylon.*	640. Medes revolt from Assyria and establish the Median Empire (640-558.) 624-584. CYAXARES, with Nabopolassar of Babylonia, capture Nineveh (612) and destroy the Assyrian Empire (604). Cyaxares remodeled the army on the basis of Assyrian military organization, but he gave special care to the cavalry, training it so thoroughly that it was the strongest branch of the service. 614. Cyaxares entered Assyria, taking Ashur and leveling it to the ground.
600	598. Chaldean army seized Jerusalem and dispatched Jehoiakim (2 Chron. 36:6; Jer. 22:19; 36:30). 597. 18. *Jehoiachin* [3 mos.] son, carried captive to Babylon (first proper captivity), and all the best citizens of Jerusalem, including Ezekiel. 19. *Zedekiah* [11], son of Josiah. Suspected of intriguing with Egypt. Went to Babylon to assure Nebuchadnezzar of his loyalty. 592. Ezekiel began to prophesy in Babylonia to the Jewish exiles, predicting their future, condemning evils in Jerusalem (Ezek. 6-8). 588. Zedekiah, finally traitor to Babylon, in favor of Egypt. Jerusalem besieged by Babylonian army (2 Kgs. 24:18-20). Egyptian allies met and defeated by Babylonians (Jer. 37:5-7). Jeremiah enmeshed in all the events of the siege (Jer. 37 and 38). 586. Jerusalem broken into, captured, looted, burnt, razed, Jews carried captive to Babylon—except poor folks (Jer. 39:1-10). Jeremiah chose to stay with peasants (Jer. 39:11-14). Gedaliah made governor of remnant left in the land. Slain by treachery (Jer. 39:14-41:18). Jeremiah carried to Egypt (42:1-43:7). Obadiah the prophet condemned the Edomites (Obadiah). 585. Jeremiah found colony of idolatrous Jews in Egypt (Jer. 44). **8. Jews in Exile in Babylonia** 581. Supplemental captivity by Nebuzaradan (Jer. 52:30). Ezekiel, the priest-prophet, the first Jewish citizen of the exile. Foretold fate of the other nations, and the ideal future of Israel as a god-fearing nation (Ezek. 40-48). 561. Jehoiachin, imprisoned Jewish king, released, honored by Evil-Merodach (Jer. 52:31-34). 558. Jews lived under favorable conditions, became merchants and tradesmen in Babylonia. Scribes were active in preserving their old records.	Nebuchadnezzar's death—*Evil-Merodach* (561-559), his son, king. Slain by and succeeded by a brother-in-law *Neriglissar* (559-555), a general at siege of Jerusalem-Nergal-shar-ezer (Jer. 39:3). Cyrus overthrew Astyages of Media, and ruled the realm. 555-538. NABONIDUS, father of the Biblical Belshazzar, great builder and restorer of temples. Cyrus conquered Crœsus of Lydia—Asia Minor. Turned to Babylonia. Babylon opened its gates, welcomed him. Took over its government for two years.	590. Median advance northwestward, reached the River Halys. This brought the Medes in conflict with the Lydians. For five years the war continued when the war ended in a stalemate and Cyaxares came to terms with Alyattes of Lydia. 585. Cyaxares subdued the nomads of Armenia and annexed the plateau. Gradually the remainder of Armenia was brought under the control of the Persians. 584-558. Astyages, last King of Medes. Cyrus revolted, deposed the king, became king of Persia and master of the East. 558-529. CYRUS, emperor. Conquered Crœsus, King of Lydia.
538			

OF BABYLON, 1120 — 538 B. C.—Continued

Egypt	Phœnicia-Lydia Phrygia	Greeks	Rome	China, Japan, India	B. C.
So (*Sibe*) of Egypt.	720. Coined money made its appearance in Lydia.		This is the period in Roman history which is generally considered legendary. Doubtless some of the general traditions were correct, but they were too overladen with legend and myth to be accepted as they stand.	720-700. This was another period of Tartar invasions. These Tartars were trained to fight and they loved war. Though they raised no crops, they thought they had a right to sweep down on the farm lands and carry off the harvests of other people. Their attack was fierce and sudden. If they did not succeed they ran away and would be sure to return later. When they conquered they plundered and killed without mercy.	720
		705. Owing to a domestic revolution whose cause is uncertain, a Lacedaemonian colony was begun at Taras in Southern Italy.			
		700. Beginnings of Greek architecture in stone.	700. Etruscan bucchero ware appeared.		700
Tirhakah (688–663) Ethiopian ruler over Egypt.				China: 685-643. The age of the great sages, Duke Huan of Ch'i, Duke Siang of Sung, Duke Wen of Ch'in, Mu of Ch'in and Chuang of Ch'u.	
653-610. PSAMTIK I. re-united Egypt. In alliance with Gyges, King of Lydia, made Egypt independent of Assyria. Built a magnificent palace at Sais, the new capital. *Revival of art, religion and literature.*	675. Cimmerians invaded Asia Minor and captured Sardis.
636. Last Assyrian governor of Phœnicia.	675. Homeric *Hymn to Demeter* and *Hymn to Apollo.*
650. Rise of tyrannies in the Isthmus states.
645-628. SECOND MESSENIAN WAR. Sparta victorious.	660-500. Etruscan dominance in Italy.
641-616. Ancus Marcius. Capture of Ostia. War with Latins.	Japan: 660-585. Jimmu Tenno, first Mikado. Largely legendary.
This emperor is said to have lived to the ripe old age of 127 or 137 years. His tomb remains in the conquered province of Yamato and is visited annually on April 3rd by imperial envoys.	
609-594. NECHO II. crosses Palestine to help Assyria, but is vanquished at Carchemish by Nebuchadnezzar. II. of Babylonia (604).	610. Alyattes, King of Lydia, battles with Cyaxares of Media. Erected magnificent buildings at Sardis.	625. Corinth at its zenith. PERIANDER, tyrant.
621. LAWS OF DRACO at Athens.
Draco was the first legislator at Athen to formulate a written code of the laws. The law abolished the old blood feuds and established a regular procedure for the trial of homicide.	616-578. Tarquinius Priscus. Treaty with Latins. Temple of Jupiter on the capitol. *Important advance in power and civilization.*	China: 604. The great philosopher Lao Tze was born. He was the founder of Taoism.	
		600-590. FIRST SACRED WAR.	600. Spread of the Greek alphabet in Italy.		600
594-589. Psamtik II.
589-569. Pharaoh-Hophra.
580-560. The theocratic character of the government was becoming more and more pronounced until the king was but a puppet in the hands of the priests, who could even command him to take his own life and make way for another weakling chosen by these same priests.
560. The Nubian kings occupied their own capital at Meroë. This placed a difficult cataract between them and the invaders from the North and saved the kingdom along the Upper Nile for them for a number of years.
570-526. AAHMES II. Encouraged Greek settlement. Magnificent buildings at Naucratis and Sais.	585. Alyattes made a pact with Cyaxares, the Mede.
580. Alyattes made a pact with the Ionians.
573. Tyre besieged by Nebuchadnezzar.
560. CRŒSUS, son of Alyattes, subdued all the Grecian cities of the coast.
546. SARDIS CAPTURED and Lydia absorbed into Persian Empire.
538. Phœnicia became a Persian province.
530. CARTHAGE becomes independent.
Phœnicia: through its influence the whole country is allowed to carry on its trade as usual, under the authority and protection of the king of Persia.
508. Carthage makes its first commercial treaty with Rome.
500. Carthage trades with the Greeks.
Carthage effects an alliance with the Persians against Sicily.	594. SOLON, archon of Athens. *Laws and reforms.*
590. Amphictyony at Delphi.
560-527. PISISTRATUS, tyrant of Athens. Ionia and Greek cities of Asia conquered by Cyrus of Persia.
The Rise of Athens
510. Athenian democracy fully established.	590. Etruscan invasion of the Po Valley.
At the same time their influence seems to have extended south across the Tiber into Latium and Campania. It is quite likely that this Etruscan influence was operative in the founding of cities of prominent significance later, viz., Capua and Nola.
578-534. Servius Tullius. Rome consolidated. Rise of patricians and plebeians.
534-510. Tarquinius Superbus. End of the Kings. Rome a Republic with two Consuls.	Japan: 581-549. Suizei, second emperor of Japan.
China: 551. CONFUCIUS born. Greatest figure in Chinese history.
This great Chinese philosopher introduces a new religion, opposed to that of Fohi, and boldly inveighs against the vice and immorality of the times.	538

31

IV. FROM THE FALL OF BABYLON TO THE

Babylon welcomed her new ruler, Cyrus. Cyrus released the Hebrew exiles,
second temple. Queen Esther. Xerxes' campaigns against Greece. A Jewish
Palestine under Persian sway. Overrun

B. C.	9. Jews in Dispersion and Returning	The Persian Empire	Egypt
538	537-536. Cyrus' edict released Jews to return to Jerusalem and to build the temple. First return under Zerubbabel. Began to build the temple. Samaritans frustrated it.	539-538. War of Cyrus against the Babylonians. Babylon captured. The Babylonian Empire incorporated with the Persian. Cyrus' edict for all captives, who wished to return to their native land. 529-522. CAMBYSES conquered Egypt by his victory at Pelusium. Cambyses committed suicide, succeeded by *Darius I. Hystaspes* (521–485) of Persia. Exacted heavy tribute of Egypt.	Death of Cyrus, succeeded by his son, *Cambyses* (529–522). Invaded Egypt, defeated Psamtik III. and captured Thebes, but was repulsed by Ethiopians. 525. Psamtik III. defeated by Cambyses at Pelusium. Egypt a Persian province.
	520-516. Prophets Haggai and Zechariah urged the Jews to build the temple. Darius being favorable, it was completed and dedicated (Ezra 5-7).	521–485. *Darius has special interest because he was first to extend Persian authority into Europe, and thus paved the way for the subsequent invasion of Greece.* 518. Revolt of Babylon, and destruction of that city after a twenty months' siege. Indian campaign, in which the countries north of the Indus become subject to Persia. Indus the boundary of the empire. 513. (?). Unsuccessful expedition of Darius against the Scythians with a land force of 700,000 men. Macedonia and Thrace tributary. 500-494. The Ionian colonies rebel, and are assisted by the Athenians, which gives rise to the Perso-Grecian wars and the national hatred between the two countries.	520. Capture of Thebes (Luxor), and transplantation of 6000 Egyptians to Susiana. The Persian kings exact a large tribute. The fisheries of Lake Mœris, etc.
500	494. Colony of Jews at Elephantine, island in Nile river, at foot of first cataract in Egypt. Aramaic papyri describe their life. Had a temple to Yahu.	499. Sardis burnt by the Ionians. **Grecian wars** follow. 494. The Greeks and their allies defeated in naval engagement at the Island of Lade. 493-490. War of Darius against the European Greeks. Revolt among the Egyptians. 492. First expedition, under Mardonius, unsuccessful. 490. Second expedition, defeated at Marathon by Miltiades. 486. Egypt revolts and is not reduced to subjection until 484.	486. Revolts, but is again subdued by Xerxes. The tribute increased. Death of Darius, successor was *Xerxes I.* (485–464). Egypt rebelled, but failed.
	485. Ahasuerus of Esther was Xerxes I. of Persia.	485. Death of Darius. He was succeeded by his son XERXES I. (485–465). Revolt of Babylon against Persian rule. This together with the revolt of Egypt complicated things for Xerxes, who was planning his expedition into Greece.	486–405. Rawlinson says that "Egypt became now for a full generation the obsequious slave of Persia and gave no more trouble to her subjugator than the weakest, or the most contented, of the provinces." The Persian kings from Cambyses to Darius II are sometimes listed as the twenty-seventh dynasty. On the whole it was a period of prosperity.
	457? Second return of Jews, under Ezra, priest and scribe "to teach in Israel statutes and ordinances" (Ezra 7:10). Had superlative authority from Artaxerxes (Ezra 7:26). Attempted moral reforms amid adverse conditions (Ezra 9:1-10:17).	480. Xerxes invaded Greece, Thermopylæ, Salamis. Elaborated great palace at Persepolis, Hypostyle Hall, fine bull-capitals, good bas-reliefs with invocations to Ahura Mazda. Propylæa, winged human-headed bulls. Hanging draperies.	
	444? Nehemiah, cup-bearer to king of Persia, given leave of absence, passports and commissions to return to Jerusalem, to build the walls, to enforce economic and religious reforms on basis of law (Neh. 1:1-2:8). Work done, returned to Persia (Neh. 2:9-12:47).	Fourth Persian campaign against Greeks—defeated at Platæa and Mykale. 479. Persians expelled from Greece.	
	432? Nehemiah's second trip to Jerusalem, to complete reforms. Jerusalem put under governorship of his brother Hanani (Neh. 7:2). Jerusalem a self-respecting colony under Persian overlordship.	Xerxes and his eldest son murdered. Successor *Artaxerxes Longimanus* (464-424). 462-455. Second revolt of the Egyptians.	
	424. Malachi depicts social and religious defects which Neh. found in Jerusalem. Also foretells a new future for Israel, for the pious and faithful.	424. Xerxes II. murdered by his brother Sogdianus same year. 412. Sparta recognized Persian rule in Asia Minor.	
	415? Death(!) of Nehemiah. High-priests rule Jerusalem under Persian authority.	405. Egypt declared its independence. 404. ARTAXERXES II. Revolt of his younger brother Cyrus, aided by Greeks.	404. Egypt independent of Persia for short period.
400	407? Governor of Jerusalem (17th year of Darius II.) ordered temple of Yahu, destroyed by Persians, to be rebuilt on its former site on Elephantine; and "meat-offerings and incense let them offer upon this altar just as it was formerly done."	401. Cyrus defeated at Cunaxa and slain. "Retreat of the Ten Thousand."	
		398. Artaxerxes II. War with Greece. Egypt and Cyprus assisted Greece.	
		394. Persian fleet defeated the Spartans at Cnidus.	378. Last dynasty of native Egyptian kings begins its rule.
		389. Cyprus revolts against Persia, aided by Athens and Achoris.	361. Treaty with Sparta vs. Persians.
		370-363. Renewed revolts in Asia Minor. Egypt joined the rebels and invaded Syria.	359-342. Persian invasions of Egypt. Nectanebo II. last native king.
	350. Chronicler (1 Chron. 3:19-24) gives 6th generation of Zerubbabel—indicating about the date of this part of the compilation of Chronicles.	358. Artaxerxes III. seized the throne. Persians defeated in Egypt. 340. CONQUEST OF EGYPT.	
	350. The Jews in the Jerusalem colony, and in Babylonia enjoyed liberal policies under Persian overlords. They paid their regular taxes, served in the army, and stood by their imperial oath of fealty. Their scribes compiled, copied, and preserved their ancient records. The priests measurably observed the ordinances and laws of the past—all under the supervision of a high priest—head of the colony, accountable to the Persian government.	337. MITHRADATES I. of Pontus became independent of Persia. 335. Darius III. ascended the throne.	334-323. Alexander the Great overthrows Persians, and is master of Egypt. Greek domination. Alexandria founded.
334	The Samaritan community stood alone. Had its own rival temple and ritual. Being only partly Jewish it was a liberalizing influence on all neighbors—in sharp contrast with the narrow restricted Judaism centered at Jerusalem.	334-332. Alexander the Great defeated Darius at Granicus and Issus.	EUCLID (Alexandria), (fl. 325).

RISE OF ALEXANDER THE GREAT, 538 — 334 B. C.

who returned to Palestine. Established a colony about Jerusalem. Built the colony in Egypt. Ezra and Nehemiah reforming the Jewish colony in Palestine. by armies of contending nations.

Carthage	The Greeks	Rome	China, Japan, India	B. C.
536. The Carthaginians led by Malchus, had conquered almost all of Sicily and in 536 defeated the Phocians and the Massaliotes on the Corsican coast. But Malchus having failed in Sardinia, was banished. He then laid siege to Carthage itself and entered the city as victor, but he was put to death by the very parties which had supported him.	**III. Persian Wars** (500-449) See under Persia. 500. Reorganization of the Athenian army, which became significant in the Persian wars. 498. Athens sends help to Ionian cities in Asia Minor and thus attracts the wrath of Persia. 492. Themistocles elected archon at Athens.	**II. The Republic to the Beginning of the Punic Wars** (510-264) Struggle between patricians and plebians and development of Roman consolidation. 509. First commercial treaty with Carthage. According to this treaty Rome gave up the right to sail or trade on the Eastern Mediterranean, and the Carthaginians agreed not to attack or damage any of the cities in Latium whether subject to Rome or not. This willingness on the part of Rome to abandon a career of commerce without a struggle can be accounted for only by the fact that Rome became involved almost immediately in a war with Etruria, in which, in fact, she sustained a rather serious defeat.	Japan: 548-511. Annei ruled as emperor. India: 521. Darius, son of Hystaspes, having consolidated his power as master of the Persian Empire began an invasion of India. He sent an explorer ahead, who explored the Punjab region. It was then that Darius attacked and annexed the provinces west of the Indus. Japan: 510-477. Rule of Itoku.	538
520. Mago, son of Hanno, of the powerful house of Barca, succeeded Malchus. He conquered Sardinia and the Balearic Islands, where he founded Port Mahon. 509. The first commercial treaty with Rome was negotiated. It assigned Italy to Rome and the African waters to Carthage. Sicily was to be neutral.	485. Revolt of Babylon against Persian rule. This together with the revolt of Egypt complicated things for Xerxes, who was planning his expedition into Greece. 506. Aegina, the strongest naval power in the Aegean Sea, began an attack upon Athens and Thebes after a long period of hostile feeling. Athens called upon Sparta for help and Aegina was forced to give up her threats.			500

480. Carthaginians invaded Sicily; defeated at Himera by Gela.	490. MARATHON. The Athenians under Miltiades defeated the Persians under Datis. Free government and Greek civilization saved. *Athens mistress of the sea.*
	 489. Miltiades attacks Poros and fails. His condemnation and death follow.
	 485. Gela, master of Syracuse.
	         ÆSCHYLUS (525-456)
	 481-480. Third expedition of the Persians against Greece, under Xerxes.
	 480. Battle of the Greeks under Leonidas, at Thermopylæ. Naval battle of Salamis saved Athens.
	 479. Fourth expedition of the Persians against Greece. Greek victories at Platæa and Mycale. Persian army destroyed.
	         SOPHOCLES (495-406).
	 465. Battle of the Eurymedon.
	 464-456. THIRD MESSENIAN WAR.
	 457-445. War of the Spartans and Bœotians against Athens.
	 451. Five-year Truce between Sparta and Athens.
	 449. Battle of Salamis in Cyprus.
	       HERODOTUS (484-425).
	       EURIPIDES (480-407).
	 445. End of Persian war. Thirty years' peace between Athens and Sparta.
	       PERICLES (490-429).
	 444-429. Athens under the administration of Pericles, reached the zenith of its greatness.
	       PHIDIAS (500-440).
	 431-404. PELOPONNESIAN WAR—between Athens and Sparta.
	       SOCRATES (469-399).
	 421. ALCIBIADES in power at Athens.
	       THUCYDIDES (471-399).
		498. First Dictator.
		 First struggle, on account of the oppression of the debtors.
		 493. Tribunes of the people.
		 491. Comitia Tributa, in which the people have the preponderance.
		 Second struggle, respecting the division of lands.
		 486. First Agrarian law.
		 Continual wars against the neighboring states.
		
		 481-475. Wars with Veii.
		
		 471. First Publilian Laws.
		
		 467. Death of Hiero, Tyrant of Syracuse.
		
		 451-449. The Decemvirate.
		 450. The Twelve Tables.
		
		 448. Valerian and Horatian Laws.
		
		 445. Canuleian Laws.
		
		 444. Consular Tribunes.
			India: 487. Death of Gautama Buddha.
			
			 478. China: Death of Confucius. China distracted by internal wars.
			
			 Japan: 475-393. Rule of Kosho.
			
			 450. India: Brick and stone buildings in existence.	

410. HANNIBAL and Hamilcar invade Sicily. 405. Treaty between Carthage and Syracuse. Landed aristocracy created at Carthage.	415-413. Expedition of the Athenians against Syracuse. Greek defeat. Decline of Athenian power. 405. LYSANDER of Sparta destroyed Athenian fleet. 404. Surrender of Athens and end of Peloponnesian War. Sparta supreme in Greece. 404. The rule of the Thirty Tyrants in Athens, Death of Alcibiades.			400

360. Carthaginians form settlements in Spain.
 	
 343. Greek cities of Sicily freed from Carthage.
 	
 340. The Carthaginians were defeated by Timoleon at Crimissus.
	399-394. War between the Spartans and Persians. Fall of Spartan power in Asia.
	       PLATO (429-347).
	 396. Revolt of Rhodes against Sparta.
	 394. The long walls of Athens are rebuilt.
	 379-362. War between Thebes and Sparta. Thebes freed.
	 378. Thebes makes alliance with Athens.
	 375. Athenian naval victory over Sparta at Naxos.
	 359. Rise of the Macedonian power. PHILIP OF MACEDON.
	       DEMOSTHENES (382-322).
	 357-355. The Social War.
	 355-346. Second Sacred War against the Phocians, who seized Delphi.
	       ARISTOTLE (384-322).
	
	 V. The Macedonian Period
	 (338-146)
	 339-338. THIRD SACRED WAR. Macedonians against Athens and Thebes.
	 338. Macedonia supreme under PHILIP II.
	 336. Philip assassinated.
	 336-323. ALEXANDER THE GREAT, King of Macedonia. Great extension of power.
	 334-328. WARS OF ALEXANDER IN ASIA.
	 334. Battle at Granicus.
	 333. Founded Alexandria in Egypt. Occupied Babylon, subdued Persia and Darius III. Invaded India in 327.
		392. Dionysius, tyrant of Syracuse, successfully opposes the Carthaginians under Mago.
		
		 390. GAUL'S INVASION OF ITALY. Rome burned.
		 377-367. Licinian Laws.
		
		 366. First Plebeian Consul.
		
		 348. Treaty of commerce with Carthage.
		
		 343-341. FIRST SAMNITE WAR.
		
		 340-338. Great Latin War.
		
		 The Latins were conquered. They gave to the Romans their cities, their worship, their laws, and their lands. They were put in a cruel position. One of the consuls finally advised clemency unless Rome wished to be surrounded by a desert. The Latins were then given Roman citizenship.
			372. China: MENCIUS born.
			
			 326. India: Alexander's invasion.
			
			 Alexander invaded the Punjab, defeated the ruler, Porus, and received his submission. After marching on further into the interior, word reached him of revolt at home and he **decided** that it would be inexpedient to go farther. He returned by way of the Indus River, the Indian Ocean and the Persian Gulf.	

				334

V. FROM THE RISE OF ALEXANDER THE GREAT TO

Persian supremacy shattered at battle of Issus (333 B. C.). Tyre besieged
Egypt becomes Greek territory. All Persia falls to Alexander. Alexander's death
Jewish communities in Palestine suffer under heels of clashing armies. Antiochus

B. C.	10. The Jews Under Greek Overlords	Greeks Invade Asia	Carthage	The Immense Greek Empire
335		Alexander plunged into Asia-Minor—victorious at Granicus.	330. Carthage became more and more interested in the Greek colonies in Sicily and Southern Italy. After the death of Timoleon, Syracuse, distracted by internal factional strife, was exposed to Carthaginian aggression.	
	332. Jews under Alexander and Greek rule. High-priest Jaddua named in Neh. 12:11.	Routed and defeated Darius and the royal Persian army at Issus.		
		Tyre besieged, captured, destroyed, Mediterranean fleet sunk.		
		Egypt fell a prey to Alexander.		
		Alexander formally took over the Persian Empire.		323. Death of Alexander at Babylon. His empire split up brother and his posthumous son. Antipater and Craterus Antigonus, Pamphylia, Phrygia and Lycia; Eumenes, Alex-the Hellespont.
		Alexander's death in Babylon, June 13, 323.		323-301. WARS OF ALEXANDER'S SUCCESSORS for his ASIATIC before peace was concluded between the contending claimants.
	323. Jews in Palestine nominally under the Ptolemies of Egypt.	*Ptolemy Soter I*, son of Lagus, annexed Palestine to Phœnicia and Syria.		*KINGDOMS AND STATES which arose upon the DIVISION*

				Carthage rises in wealth and political importance.	Macedonia	Greece	Thrace
	320. Ptolemy Lagi formally took over Jerusalem by strategy, and carried great numbers of Jews to Egypt.	Alexander's real contribution to Asia was the Greek culture and ideals. Methods of warfare, planned city building, homes of comfort, artistic surroundings—all lifted the level of life and living.		317. Carthage and Syracuse at war.	323. Perdiccas appointed regent: slain 321.	323-322. L a m i a n War: Phocian at head of affairs. Death of Demosthenes.	323. LYSIMACHUS is appointed governor of Thrace.
	311-301. Jerusalem subject to Antigonus of Phrygia.			312. Carthage again invades Sicily.	319. Polysperchon succeeds Antipater, and proclaims liberty to the Grecian cities.	321. Antipater, regent of the empire.	
	312. Strong colony of Jews in Alexandria, Egypt.	Seleucid kings begin rule in Syria.		310. Agathocles invades Carthaginian territory in Africa.		317. Phocion put to death by the Athenians. Demetrius Phalereus governs Athens.	
		Golden age of the Ptolemies follows.		306. Peace with Syracuse.		315. Cassander rebuilds Thebes.	
				In this peace Agathocles was compelled to submit to Carthage. Sicily was divided nearly equally between Agathocles and Carthage. Agathocles, however, was not entirely discouraged. He made diplomatic and marriage alliances with the sovereigns of Alexander's Empire and held on firmly to the purpose to drive the Carthaginians out of the island.		314. Freedom of Greek cities proclaimed by Antigonus.	
						303. D e m e t r i u s Poliorcetes, general of the Grecia states, opposes Cassander.	307. Lysimachus seizes the throne.
300	301. Palestine fell to Ptolemies at death of Antigonus in the battle of Ipsus.				302. CASSANDER, king of Macedonia.		302. Invades Asia.

	299. Simon I. The Just, High Priest.		305-280. After the death of Agathocles the Carthaginians re-established their supremacy in Sicily. Mago even offered assistance to Rome against Pyrrhus.	301. AFTER THE BATTLE OF IPSUS ALEXANDER'S	

				Macedonia	Greek States
	The Greek language and culture planted in Palestine by Alexander's successors won the favor of many Jews. Greeks imported and settled in Palestine introduced the intimate customs and manners of the Greek ritual and worship—that is, Hellenism.			296. Death of Cassander. Quarrels of his two sons, Antipater and Alexander.	
	The Jews dispersed in Asia Minor, in Egypt and in the East did not throw overboard their religious faith in its entirety. Too many of them commingled Judaism and Hellenism.			287. Demetrius expelled by Pyrrhus. Lysimachus drives Pyrrhus out of Macedonia.	287. Athens revolts from Demetrius.
	In Palestine the high-priest was still their religious head, and in the earlier years under the Ptolemies had a measure of religious freedom.			283. Death of Demetrius.	
	The Jews carried to Egypt, and those who went voluntarily, soon made it their home, settling largely in Alexandria, the thrifty city founded by Alexander. There Jew and Greek mingled freely and soon made the city a literary center. The Jew worshipped the God of his fathers and spoke Greek.		279. Carthage encourages Rome against Pyrrhus and then Rome's success arouses the jealousy of Carthage.	281. Lysimachus defeated and slain by Seleucus.	281. The ACHÆAN LEAGUE created.
				280. Sosthenes ascends the throne and liberates his country; but falls, 278.	Lysimachus defeated and slain by Seleucus in the battle of Korupedion.
			277. Pyrrhus crossed to Sicily thus threatening Carthage. He even planned to sail to Africa but was compelled to return to Italy.	277. ANTIGONUS GONATAS, King of Macedonia, descendant of one of Alexander's generals, master of all Greece except Sparta.	
					274. Pyrrhus invades Macedon, defeats Antigonus, and is proclaimed king.
			275-264. Carthage claimed the monopoly of the Mediterranean waters and seized every foreign ship found between Sardinia and Gibraltar.		272. Pyrrhus besieges Sparta and Argos—is slain, and Antigonus is restored.
275					266. The Chremonidean War. Athens and Sparta allied in revolt against Macedonia.

MACCABÆAN REVOLT, 334 — 167 B. C.

and captured by Alexander. Palestine and the Jews yield to the Greek conqueror.
(323 B. C.). Contests between Alexander's officers for shares of his kingdom.
Epiphanes tried to force Greek worship and custom on the Jews.

of Alexander The Great	Rome	China-Japan-India	B. C.
	334. The cities of Campania concluded an alliance with Rome. They retained their independence but arrayed themselves on the side of Rome against their common foes.	China: 333. The new kingdom of Ch'in arose and threatened the union of Chinese states. But Su Ch'in formed a league against this up-start power. He managed for a while by moving his capital from place to place but in 317 he was stabbed to death and his efforts came to naught.	335

among his generals after his death. Perdiccas became regent in Asia for Alexander's half shared the regency of the west. The other generals received lieutenancies: Ptolemæus, Egypt; ander's secretary, Paphlagonia and Cappadocia; and Cassander, Caria; Leonnatus, Phrygia on

DOMINIONS. The first partition of the empire was made 322, but twenty-two years elapsed

OF THE MACEDONIAN EMPIRE AT THE DEATH OF ALEXANDER THE GREAT.

				Rome	China-Japan-India
				326-304. SECOND SAMNITE WAR.	325-315. India. MAURYA DYNASTY, most brilliant of old Hindu dynasties.
				321. The Samnites defeat the Romans at the Caudine Forks and send them under the yoke.	China: 314-256. The reign of Nan Wang, the last of the Chou emperors. His reign was followed by a brief period of anarchy and then the dynasty of Ch'in stepped into power.

Egypt	Palestine	Phrygia, Lycia Pamphylia	Syria	Rome	China-Japan-India
323. Ptolemy I. Soter, the son of Lagus.	323. Annexed with Phœnicia to Syria.	320. Phrygia, Lycia, Pamphylia fell to the share of Antigonus, who defeats Eumenes and makes himself master of all Asia Minor.	321. The Kingdom of the Seleucidæ founded by SELEUCUS NICATOR, who received Babylon as his province.		
320. Ptolemy makes himself master of Cyprus and Syria.					
313. Revolt in Cyprus crushed by Ptolemy.	312. Capture of Jerusalem by Ptolemy. Colony of Jews in Alexandria.	315. Formation of a league against Antigonus by Ptolemy, Cassander, Seleucus, and Lysimachus.	312. Syria ruled by Seleucus Nicator; he takes Babylon. Era of the Seleucidæ.	309. Fabius Maximus defeats the Etrurians at the Vadimonian Lake.	312-306. India: Seleucus attempts to recover provinces of Alexander.
305. Ptolemy assumes the regal title of Egypt.	311-301. Subject to Antigonus.			308. The Umbri, the Maesi, the Peligni and some of the Hernici seized the opportunity presented by the difficulties with which Rome was confronted to attempt to recover their independence. The leading influence among these enemies, however, was the Umbrian Confederation. After a few initial successes their lack of discipline proved their undoing and Rome again triumphed.	
Alexandria begins a great period.					
					300. India: Brahmanic system of caste instituted.
	301. Again under Egypt.	301. Battle of Ipsus. Antigonus killed.	301. After the battle of Ipsus, Seleucus gains the provinces of Syria, Cappadocia, Mesopotamia, and Armenia.	307. The Carthaginians defeat Agathocles and besiege Syracuse.	

EMPIRE WAS AGAIN DIVIDED INTO FOUR CHIEF PARTS.

Egypt	Palestine	Seleucid Kingdom	Rome	China-Japan-India
The empire of the Ptolemies extended over Egypt, Libya, Cyrene, Arabia Petræa, Judæa, Phœnicia, Damascus, and Cyprus. Golden age of the Ptolemies.	300. Canon of Old Testament, under Simon the Just.	299. Seleucus built or improved a great number of cities, including Antioch, Seleucia, Apamea, and Laodicea.	298-290. THIRD SAMNITE WAR. *These wars pave the way to the subjugation of Italy, and the future greatness of Rome.*	
	284. The *Septuagint* translation of the *Old Testament,* begun at Alexandria, by order of Ptolemy Philadelphus.	287. Seleucus defeats Demetrius Poliorcetes and keeps him prisoner.	286. LAW OF HORTENSIUS, by which the decrees of the Plebs are made absolute in the state. The end of the long struggle between Patricians and Plebeians.	China: 289. The death of Mencius. This great sage did for Confucius what Plato did for Socrates; he gathered up his sayings and brought them out in the form of the Nine Confucian Classics, the Five Ching and the Four Shu, constituting what have sometimes been called the Old and the New Testaments of Confucianism.
283-247. PTOLEMY II. Philadelphus, the most magnificent of the Egyptian kings, is associated by his father in the kingdom. Canal of Arsinöe. Obelisk.		280. Antiochus I. succeeds Seleucus.	283. Defeat of the Etruscans at Lake Vadimo.	
			282-272. ROMAN WAR WITH TARENTUM. Tarentum seeks the aid of PYRRHUS, king of Epirus.	
		278-250. Nicodemedes I.	278. Pyrrhus lands in Sicily, and makes himself master of all the Carthaginian towns.	
		277. Gauls (Galatia) invaded Asia Minor.	275. Defeat of Pyrrhus at Beneventum.	
		277-244. Antiochus carried on wars with Ptolemy of Egypt and Antigonus of Macedonia. He did not go directly into Europe but he enlarged his domains in Asia Minor. However, he had continual difficulty with Cappadocia, Pontus and Armenia, while the Eastern parts of his kingdom in the region of Bactria fell almost entirely away.	266. Roman subjugation of Italy is completed. Contest over Sicily.	264. India: ASOKA descendant of Chandragupta, reigns in Magadha; he is a friend of Buddhism.
273. Ambassadors sent to Rome.				
272. Roman embassy sent to Egypt.				275

B. C.	Jewish History			Macedonia	Greek States	Parthia
275	283-247 Ptolemy II. Philadelphus inaugurated a translation of the Hebrew Old Testament into Greek (285-130 B. C.). This translation was begun in Alexandria about 285 B. C. and was continued under different scholars for about 150 years —until completed. It is called the *Septuagint* or *LXX*, from the traditional number of translators who carried out the project. This first Greek version of the Hebrew Old Testament was adopted by the Hellenistic Jews everywhere. Even in Palestine it soon commanded the attention of the Greek-speaking Jews. So that down in Christian times the Greek language became the language of the New Testament. 247-222. Ptolemy III. Euergetes. Jews in Palestine trampled under feet of the armies of Ptolemies of Egypt and Seleucids of Asia—see-sawing over Palestine. The first three Ptolemies (283-222) gave the Jews of Egypt and Palestine their golden age of these fateful centuries. Indeed, comparative peace and prosperity regaled their daily life. But the accession of Ptolemy IV. Philopator (222-204) gives us another picture. Antiochus III. the Great, king of Syria, seized Tyre and Ptolemais, and advanced to the frontiers of Egypt. Philopator arose to meet the challenge and in 217 B.C. soundly defeated Antiochus at Raphia. But in his profligate life he neglected the government, and his subordinates reversed the policy of the earlier Ptolemies toward the Jews, who now felt the sting of oppression. Ptolemy V, Epiphanes (204-181 B.C.) was forced to submit to the dismemberment of his realm. Antiochus (203 B.C.) invaded Palestine and, finding the Jews mainly on his side, granted favors to their temple and their city. Soon, thereafter, Antiochus being occupied elsewhere, General Scopas was sent from Egypt to recover Syria and occupy Jerusalem. He overran Judea, destroyed fortified places, and slew numbers of the Jews. In 198 B.C. Antiochus returned, routed Scopas at Paneas near Mt. Hermon, and swept the country clear of the enemy until he reached Jerusalem. He was met by a food-laden grateful people, who accepted their new ruler with gratitude. Antiochus would have invaded Egypt if word had not reached him that Rome had taken the young Ptolemy under its aegis. Antiochus countered this move by proposing a marriage of his daughter to the Egyptian king, promising at the same time to grant her a dowry of Cœle-Syria, Phœnicia, and Palestine. The pact was concluded, and Palestine and its population were incorporated into the kingdom of the Seleucidæ. 198. The Jews assist Antiochus in expelling Scopas and the Egyptian troops from Jerusalem; final establishment of the Syrian power in Palestine. 196. Organization of a dissenting religious party or sect at Damascus: called the Covenanters or the Zadokites. They believed in the law and the prophets.	**Old Testament Literature** 200. The Book of Ecclesiastes. Late sections such as chapters 1-9 of the Book of Proverbs.	**Extra Canonical: Jewish Literature** 200. The Book of Tobit. Somewhat similar to Esther.	275. A horde of Celtic warriors from the Danube lands crossed over into Asia Minor after a series of devastating forays in Macedonia and Greece. They took possession of the Central Plateau and forced a federation of tribal kingdoms, known as Galatia. 262. Antigonus took Athens. End of its independence and political importance. 227. War between Cleomenes, King of Sparta, and the Ætolian league. 226 Athens freed from Macedonia allied with Rome. 211. Alliance of Rome the Ætolians, Spartans, Eleans and Illyria. 204. General peace. 203. Philip wages war against Attalus and the Rhodians. 200-197. SECOND MACEDONIAN WAR. 197. Philip V. defeated at Cynoscephalæ by the Romans under Flaminius. 196. Macedonian Greece declared free by the Romans.	255. Antigonus liberates Athens. Athens joins the Achæan League. 227. Revolution in Sparta. 211. The Ætolians secure the alliance of Rome against the Achæans and the Macedonians. 207. Battle of Mantinea: Philopœmen, the general of the Achæan League, defeats the Spartans. 198. The Achæans and Spartans join the Romans against Macedonia.	255. Diodotus made himself king of Bactria and tried to expand his dominions. The chieftain of a tribe of Iranian nomads fled before him into Parthia out of the region East of the Caspian. This chieftain was Arsaces, later king of Parthia. 250-248. Arsaces I. founds the kingdom of Parthia, having killed Agathocles, and expelled the Macedonians. 250-227. Parthia and Bactria win their independence from the empire of the Seleucids. 248-238. Troubles between Syria and Egypt enabled Arsaces, not only to maintain himself in Parthia, but also to conquer Hyrcania. He was constantly in danger from Bactria, however. 238. Seleucus marched against Parthia and Arsaces fled. Seleucus II was soon recalled and then Arsaces returned. The day of this victory is celebrated by the Parthians as the beginning of their independence. 216. Arsaces III. King of Parthia. 212-205 Parthia was engaged in a seven-years war with Antiochus of the Seleucid kingdom who tried to maintain his supremacy over this area, a thing which Parthia was determined to prevent. In the end Antiochus because of other difficulties was forced to recognize the independence of Parthia. Parthia then began to grow in power and influence and in extent of territory until it was a powerful rival of all Asiatic powers of the time. 196. Arsaces IV., King of Parthia. 209. Conquest of certain Parthian and Hyrcanian towns by Antiochus III.
200						

MACCABÆAN REVOLT, 334 — 167 B. C.—Continued

Egypt	Seleucid Empire	Carthage	Rome	China, India, Japan	B. C.
			III. Epoch of the Punic Wars, and Beginning of the Universal Rule of Rome (264-146)		275
	261. Revolt of Parthians from Seleucid rule. Parthian kingdom formed.	264-241. FIRST PUNIC WAR. of Hannibal.	Carthaginians led by Hamilcar, father		
			260. First Roman fleet built. Victory at sea.		
258. Battle of Cos, End of Egypt's sea command.	261-246. Antiochus II. This ruler made an attempt to get a footing in Thrace, but did not succeed.	256. Regulus invades Africa, and is defeated by Xanthippus, a Spartan general.	Scipio Africanus. ARCHIMEDES (287-212). 255. Roman fleet wrecked off Pachynus.	China: 249. The founding of the Ch'in dynasty under Chuang Hsiang Wang, who had the services of a very astute minister, Lü P'u Wei, who was a great scholar and literary light.	
247-230. Ptolemy III., Euergetes. Extended his empire by conquests in Mesopotamia, Babylonia, Persia, Susiana, and Media, and extends his influence as far as Thrace and Macedonia.	250. Antiochus concluded a treaty with Ptolemy II, repudiating his wife Laodice to marry Ptolemy's daughter, Berenice.	241. Peace with Carthage. The ceded parts of Sicily formed the first Roman province there. 241. The Roman fleet under Catulus defeats the Carthaginians off the Ægatian Islands.			
	246. Antiochus left Berenice to live again with Laodice, but she poisoned him and proclaimed her son as king.	238. Hamilcar begins establishment of Carthaginian power in Spain.	240. Reform of the Centuriate Assembly.		
	246-227. Seleucus II. Laodice having put her son on the throne, had her partisans at Antioch kill Berenice and her son, which brought an invasion from Berenice's brother Ptolemy III.	HANNIBAL (247-183). 221. Hannibal succeeds Asdrubal in the command.	228. Rome sets up a protectorate over the Illyrian Coast. 224. The Romans first cross the Po.	221-210. China: Chi-Huang-Ti, first universal emperor. GREAT WALL BUILT. Besides this great wall the emperor had many roads, canals and bridges built. If the empire was to be one country under one ruler nothing was more necessary than to have good roads. The emperor loved to travel. He went from one end of China to the other with a great crowd of chariots and attendants following him. Everywhere he left inscriptions carved on stone pillars, telling the world what a great man he was and what he had done.	
This man was a great conqueror. He extended the kingdom into the East to such an extent that his influence in that section was said to be second only to Alexander the Great.	223. Antiochus III., the Great, ruled Syria, Phœnicia to Egypt. 217. Antiochus III. defeated by Ptolemy Philopator in the battle of Raphia.	218-201. SECOND PUNIC WAR.	219. Hannibal takes Saguntum and crosses the Alps. Hannibal crossed the Alps. 217. Romans defeated at Lake Trasimene. 216. Romans at Cannæ totally defeated by Hannibal. Fabius Maximus, Dictator.		
230-205. This is the period of the rule of Ptolemy IV. This is a lamentable instance of decay in a great family. The tables were turned on Syria with its active and mature rulers was more than a match for the infant who succeeded to the Egyptian throne. He posed as a patron of Greek letters but did very little even in that endeavor.	212-206. Campaigns in Upper Asia against the Parthians and Bactrians. 209. Antiochus III invaded Parthia, occupying the capital, Hecatompylus, and pushing forward into Hyrcania.	204. Scipio carries the war into Africa. 203. Hearing that Scipio had taken Utica and defeated Hasdrubal and Syphax, king of Numidia, Hannibal returned from Italy to attempt to save Carthage.	215. Treaty between Hannibal and Philip V. of Macedonia. 214-205. FIRST WAR WITH MACEDONIA. 212. Syracuse taken by Marcellus. Archimedes killed. 211. Capua taken by the Romans. 209. Publius Scipio takes New Carthage.	China: 215. Chi-Huang Ti made a vain attempt to destroy the Confucian classics. He ordered all copies burned in order that no record earlier than the record of his own great deeds should exist. Various copies were hidden in defiance of this order and thus the sayings of the great sage were preserved.	
205. Ptolemy V., Epiphanes. Lost most of the cities of Palestine and Phœnicia to Antiochus, and the cities of the Hellespont to Philip V. of Macedon. Egypt assisted by Rome.	205-204. Antiochus led a short expedition from Seleucia on the Tigris down the Persian Gulf against the Gerrhæans on the Arabian coast. In the same year he concluded a treaty with Philip of Macedon for the partition of the Ptolemaic possessions.	202. Hannibal, with a hastily levied army, was defeated.	207. Nero and Livy defeat Hasdrubal at the Metaurus—Hasdrubal killed. Here it was decided that the civilization of the world was to be Roman rather than Carthaginian. 206. The Carthaginians defeated in the battle of Ilipa and driven out of Spain. 206. Scipio is elected consul.	206. China: The dynasty of Han founded; it lasts until 221 A. D. One of the most brilliant periods in the history of China.	
Roman influence prevails from this time.		202. Flight of Hannibal. Carthage conquered. Battle of Zama. End of Punic War.			
200-196. This was the period of the great native revolt against Epiphanes which affected the whole country. Down to 186 B. C. Harmakhis and Ankhmakhis, native kings supported by the Ethiopians, reigned in succession at Thebes. Trouble in lower Egypt was continuous for even a longer period of time. Thebes lost everything except its religious importance under the Ptolemies. The civilization of Egypt was a decadent civilization and the country was an easy prey to any enterprising warlike people who might wish to take it.	198. Antiochus defeats the Egyptians under Scopas in a great battle in Palestine. 195. Hannibal flees to Antiochus III. 192. Syria at war with Rome. 190. Scipio Asiaticus defeats Antiochus III., at Magnesia and compels him to cede all of Asia Minor excepting Cilicia.	196. Hannibal joins Antiochus, whom he urges to carry on war against the Romans. 193. Massinissa, King of Numidia, harasses the Carthaginians, and injures their commerce.	195. Cato in Spain. 192-190. War with Antiochus of Syria, who is totally defeated at Magnesia by Scipio Asiaticus. 190. The vanquished Antiochus surrendered all of Asia to Rome as far as the Taurus River and promised to pay fifteen thousand talents as indemnity over a period of twelve years, to reduce his fleet and to keep no more war elephants. Rome kept the indemnity for herself but distributed all her territories to her allies. At the same time she liberated the Greek cities in Asia Minor.	199-138. India: So-called "Greek Kings."	
					200

VI. FROM THE MACCABÆAN REVOLT

B. C.	Jewish History	Old Testament Literature	Extra Canonical: Jewish Literature	Egypt	Parthia	Seleucid Empire
190			180. The Book of Ecclesiasticus. (Ben Sira.) Similar to the Book of Proverbs.	187. Ptolemy renews his alliance with the Achæans. 181-146. Ptolemy VI. (Philometor).	181-174. Arsaces V., conquers the Mardians on the Caspian.	189. ARMENIA revolts from the Seleucid rule and establishes its independence. 187. Antiochus III. killed; succeeded by Seleucus IV. Philopator. 182. Death of Hannibal in Bithynia.
180	175. Jason bought outright the high priesthood, deposing Onias III. 172. Menelaus outbid Jason and was ordained high priest. Jason robbed the Temple. 170. Antiochus Epiphanes invaded Jerusalem and plundered the Temple. Many acts of persecution.		170. The Book of Enoch chapters 1-36; 106, 7. Apocalyptic literature similar to Daniel.	171-168. War with Antiochus Epiphanes.	174-136. Mithradates I., raises Parthia to an exalted rank. Mithradates had to fight hard with the Greeks of Bactria, especially the Eucratides, but at last he was able to conquer the greater part of Eastern Iran.	175-164. Antiochus IV. Epiphanes. Universally hated and despised. 171. Invades Egypt, and gains a victory at Pelusium. 170. Another victory. Subjugation of Egypt as far as Alexandria.
170	168. Forces of Antiochus Epiphanes desecrated the Temple. Daily sacrifice discontinued. Altar to Zeus erected in the Temple. 167. Maccabæan Revolt under Mattathias and his five sons. Started as a struggle for religious freedom and rallied to its side many of the finest spirits in Jewish life. 166-161. Judas Maccabæus, son of Mattathias, leader. Syrian armies repeatedly defeated by the smaller forces of the Maccabæans. Temple rededicated December 25, 165 B. C. Judas secured religious liberty from Syrians but was killed in battle, 161. 161-142. Jonathan, younger brother of Judas, ruler. Period of intrigue and diplomacy.	165. The Book of Daniel. A few Psalms as for example Psalm 110.	165. The Book of Enoch, chapters 83-90. Apocalyptic literature similar to Daniel.	169. War between Egypt and Syria. 164. Partition of the kingdom. Physcon receives Cyrene and Libya.	165-150. Mithradates I expanded his empire in conquest until it covered almost the whole territory of the earlier Persian Empire excepting in Asia Minor and Syria. 163. Mithradates conquered Media, where he refounded the town of Rhagae, near Teheran, under the name of Arsacia.	164. Dies on his way to Babylon. Loss of Babylonia, Persia, and all the countries between the Euphrates and Indus. 161-150. Demetrius I. Soter.
160	Continued struggle of the Jews, in defence of their civil and religious rights to 130. 153. Jonathan appointed high priest. Office remained vacant 160-153 B. C.	150. The Book Esther. Some scribal additions made in some of the late Old Testament books.	150. The Book of Judith. Story of a Jewess similar to Esther.			153-152. Alexander Balas Occupies Ptolemais. 150. Demetrius killed in battle. 150-125. Demetrius II. Nicator, regains his father's kingdom by the aid of Ptolemy Philometor.
150	143-135. Simon, older brother of Judas, ruler. Largely period of peace and prosperity. Friendly relations with Rome. 142. Simon made king and high priest. 141. First coinage of money in Judaism. This fact represented the assumption of kingly rights by Simon. 135-105. John Hyrcanus, son of Simon, ruler. Period of great expansion, great building operations. 133. Peace with Syria. 130. Samaritan Temple destroyed. 129. Edom conquered and compelled to acknowledge Jewish Law. 130. John Hyrcanus, aided by the Parthians, asserts his entire independence. 110. Hyrcanus joins the Sadducees.		125. Testaments of the Twelve Patriarchs. Apocalyptic literature containing some of the highest ethical standards in Judaism. 125. The Book of Enoch, chapters 72-82. 110. The Book of Jubilees, a rewriting of Genesis.	146-117. Ptolemy VII. (Euergetes II.), a cruel and odious tyrant. 143. Embassy of Scipio Africanus to Alexandria. 130. The Alexandrines rebel. The king flees to Cyprus. 117-81. Ptolemy VIII. (Soter II.) Cleopatra and her younger son, Alexander, jointly reign in Egypt.	141. The Parthians invaded Babylonia. 138. The invasion of Demetrius II. of Syria. 128. Invasion of Antiochus. Parthian empire is henceforward freed from the attacks of the Syrian kings. 124-87. Mithradates II., restores tranquillity to the East after a long succession of bloody wars. He meets with a powerful rival in Tigranes I. King of Armenia.	137-128. Antiochus VI. Sidetes, marries Cleopatra. 129. War with Parthia, in which Antiochus is slain, 126. The succeeding history of the Seleucidæ is a horrid picture of civil wars, family feuds, and deeds of violence. 111. Conclusion of war by a partition of territory. Syria and Phœnicia are the only provinces that acknowledge the sway of the king of Syria.
110						

TO THE BEGINNING OF ROMAN RULE IN PALESTINE, 167-63 B. C.

Carthage	Rome	Macedonia	Greek States	China, India, Japan	B. C.
The dangers which threaten Carthage are much increased by the rising jealousy of Rome, the daring hostilities of Massinissa, and the factious spirit of her own citizens.	*Rome the Arbitress of Nations, from the Atlantic to the Euphrates.* 184. Censorship of Cato.	181. Demetrius is put to death by his father.	189. The Ætolian League crushed by the Romans. 188. Philopœmen abrogates the laws of Lycurgus in Sparta. 183. Philopœmen is taken prisoner and put to death by the Messenians. *Decline of the Achæan League.*	China: 187-179. The reign of Lü Hou, the first woman to rule in China.	190 180
174. Raids of Massinissa against Carthage are begun. They form many an excuse for the Romans to intervene. 170-155: Continued raids and depredations by Massinissa of Numidia which seemed calculated to arouse resistance on the part of Carthage so as to justify an attack by Rome.	177. Istria subdued. **171-168. THIRD MACEDONIAN WAR.** This war in its first stages was not so favorable to Rome. In the legions were many soldiers who went to war attended by their slaves. They refused to obey orders when it was inconvenient. Their object was booty rather than victory. Owing to the lack of discipline and the ineptitude of the Roman generals, the Romans suffered several serious reverses. The prestige of Rome in the East was shaken. Friends and allies began to waver. But when the Roman people really became alarmed, they could remedy such situations as the Battle of Pydna showed.	179. Death of Philip. 171-148. Macedonia fell into difficulties with Rome time and time again. After a series of wars in which the Roman net was gradually tightened, Macedonia like the neighboring states fell into the hands of the Romans.	172. The Romans effect the dissolution of the Bœotian confederacy.	China: 179-156. Wen Ti, a ruler of very attractive personality, much beloved by the people. His unselfishness and moderation are illustrated by his giving up the building of a projected Dew Tower when he found it would cost one hundred bars of gold. He refused to spend on one building what would furnish ten households with a fortune.	170
Carthage tried desperately to regain some of her former commerce and prosperity, but her success, small as it was, only raised the suspicions and jealousy of Rome, while the continual harrassing of Massinissa made any improvement almost impossible.	168. Decisive battle of **Pydna**, and overthrow of the kingdom of Macedon. 167. The tributum or property tax was discontinued because the wealth which was flowing into Rome from her eastern conquests was ample to take care of the expenses of government and conquest. This sudden influx of wealth led to extravagance and the lowering of standards of honor in regard to public money.	168, June 22. The Battle of Pydna. 20,000 Macedonians were slain and 11,000 taken prisoners, while the Romans lost scarcely 100 men. Perseus attempted flight, but soon had to give himself up and was sent to Rome.	168. Battle of Pydna. For the time being Rome did not organize any provinces in this part of the world but extended her protectorate from the Adriatic to Mt. Taurus. Although the more brutal side of Roman nature revealed itself in Greek affairs, the inability of the Greeks to combine was fatal to their interests. In every state there existed a Romanizing party which constantly provoked and invited interference. On the slightest pretext an army would be brought into Greece.	166. China: Tartar invasion. India: 165-150. This was a period of Greek influence. Traces of their science of astronomy and their beautiful sculptures and their coins are left and can still be found in the museums of India.	160
152. Massinissa's party expelled from Carthage, which leads to a war. Massinissa defeats the Carthaginians. *Carthage at this time contained 700,000 inhabitants.*	*The Romans aspire to universal empire. Increased patronage of literature and the arts. Grecian system of education adopted at Rome.* 159. The law against bribery is enacted. 155-150. SPANISH WAR. The Roman arms unsuccessful in Spain.		155. Meander invaded India and laid waste the country as far as Saketa and Rajaputana. 155. Embassy of Diogenes, Carniades, and Critolaus to Rome. 150. Dissensions between the Spartans and Achæans.		150
149-146. THIRD PUNIC WAR. 146. P. Scipio Æmilianus takes and destroys Carthage. *A Roman province.*	149-8. FOURTH MACEDONIAN WAR. *Cato's continual harangue "Delenda est Carthago."*	148. Macedon reduced to a *Roman province.*	146. Fall of Corinth. *Roman province of Achæa.*	China: 140-87. The rule of Wu Ti, whose reign of fifty-four years is one of the most splendid in Chinese history. He fought against the Huns, patronized literature and extended the imperial authority over a larger area. Wu Ti was a Taoist, which faith he followed with great devotion.	

IV. Epoch of the Civil Wars

AFFAIRS IN THE WEST	AFFAIRS AND CIVIL WARS IN ROME	AFFAIRS IN THE EAST	China, India, Japan	
146-140. War with Viriathus, the gallant leader of the Lusitani, who maintains a six years' war with Rome. 145. Æmilianus is sent against Viriathus. 143-133. NUMANTINE WAR of ten years. 140. Viriathus is treacherously murdered, and Lusitania becomes a Roman province. 128. Flaccus reduces the Transalpine Ligurians. *Increase of Roman power in Transalpine Gaul.* 122. Aix, the first Roman colony in Gaul. *Gaul a Roman province.*	A struggle arises between the aristocracy (the nobiles and optimates, or rich families of senators and magistrates) and the plebs, or common people. 142. The first stone bridge over the Tiber. 139. The Gabinian Law is enacted. 133-121. CIVIL TROUBLES UNDER THE GRACCHI. 130. The Tribunes obtain a seat and the right of voting in the senate. 123. Tribunate of CAIUS GRACCHUS. Renewal of the Agrarian Law. 121. General struggle in the city, C. Gracchus and 3000 citizens killed. *Triumph of the aristocracy.*	133. Pergamus bequeathed to Rome by Attalus III. 118. Death of Micipsa, King of Numidia, and assassination of Hiempsal by Jugurtha.	140. China: VOUTI, Emperor, Great Ruler, invasion of Huns. China: 104. Li Kuang-li, military leader of the Chinese, carried Chinese banners as far west as the land of the Parthians.	110

VI. FROM THE MACCABEAN REVOLT

B. C.	Jewish History	Old Testament Literature	Extra Canonical: Jewish Literature	Egypt	Parthia	Seleucid Empire
110	108. Destruction of Samaria. 105. Death of John Hyrcanus. The first mention of Pharisees as a religious party or sect. 104-78. Alexander Jannaeus. Energetic military leader, ruthless and overbearing. No regard for priestly functions. Period of unrest and civil war. Sadducees in power. Many acts of party cruelty. 97. Capture of Gaza. 94. Moab and Ammon conquered.	100. Old Testament practically closed. Greek Translation (Septuagint) of the Old Testament practically completed.	100. Sibylline Oracles Book III Semi-Apocalyptic literature; I and II Maccabees History of the Maccabean Revolt; III Maccabees Stories of the early Maccabean Martyrs; Prayer of Manasses, a prayer of repentance; Prayer of Azariah and the Song of the Three Children, one of the additions to Daniel; Bel and Dragon, exposure of idolatry; Susanna, another addition to Daniel; Epistle of Jeremy, elaboration of Jeremiah's letter to exiles; Additions to Esther; Letter of Aristeas, story of the Greek translation of the Old Testament.	108. Cleopatra Kokke called her son, Alexander, to Egypt and Soter fled to Cyprus taking his brother's place and holding the island against his mother's forces. 104-3. Soter and Cleopatra made various attempts to gain predominance in Palestine, but they had no success. 102. Alexander shook off the yoke of Cleopatra and married Soter's daughter, Berenice. 101. Cleopatra Kokke died. 101-89. The rule of Alexander I as sole ruler in Egypt.	100-95. Mithradates II, the Great, defeated Artavasdes, the king of Great Armenia. His son, Tigranes, who was a hostage in the hands of the Parthians, was redeemed only by the cession of seventy valleys. When Tigranes attempted to seize Cappadocia, the Roman praetor, Sulla, advanced against him.	110-80. A period of intrigue and civil strife full of assassinations. 96-95. Seleucus VI. 95. Antiochus XI. 95-88. Demetrius III.
100				89. Alexander I expelled by popular uprising. 88. Soter was recalled and made king over Egypt and Cyprus, ruling in association with his daughter Berenice. 82. Revolt and three years' siege of Thebes, which is captured and destroyed. This period of Egyptian history is very obscure, being characterized by internal strife and family intrigue. All the while Roman influence is growing.		88-83. Philip I. SYRIA 83. Tigranes, King of Armenia, is invited by the Syrians to assume the crown.
	78-68. Alexandra, wife of Alexander Jannaeus, ruler. No military campaigns. Pharisees in power, often called the golden age of the Pharisees. First elementary school system established in connection with the synagogue. Temple tax of a half shekel imposed on every adult Israelite. 63. Coming of Pompey and Roman rule in Palestine.		75f. The Book of Enoch, chapters 37-71; 91-105; 108. Apocalyptic literature containing beliefs in a coming Messiah, the Son of Man. 50. The Book of the Wisdom of Solomon, a treatment of problem of immortality, wisdom, and evils of idolatry. 50. Psalms of Solomon, similar to some of the Psalms in the Old Testament; IV Maccabees, a lecture on certain phases of martyrdom. Zadokite Fragments. Parts of the Covenant of the religious party organized in Damascus 196 B. C.	80. On the death of Soter, Berenice assumed charge of the government, but a son of Alexander I, Ptolemy X entered Alexandria under Roman patronage, married and quickly assassinated Berenice. 80-51. Ptolemy XI, Auletes, the flute-player, ruled as king, but with a very doubtful right. In the first place, he was an illegitimate heir, and in the next place, the Romans contended that Alexander II had bequeathed the kingdom to the Roman people. 58. Rome took Cyprus from Egypt. 58-53. Auletes in Exile. 51. On the death of Auletes, the rule of Egypt was left to Ptolemy XII, Philopater, and his sister Cleopatra.	92. First public transactions between *Rome and Parthia*. 88-63. Wars with MITHRADATES THE GREAT, KING OF PONTUS. 68-60. Arsaces XII. contemporary with the third Mithradatic War. 54. First war with Rome caused by the invasion of Crassus. 52-51. The Parthians invade Syria.	74. Bithynia bequeathed to Rome by King Nicomedes III. 69. He is expelled by Lucullus 65-62. Antiochus Asiaticus is expelled by Pompey, who reduces Syria to a Roman province. By the absorption of Syria, Rome comes into touch with the Parthian power. The aggressiveness of the Parthians necessitated many expeditions by Roman generals over a long period of years before the disturbance was brought under control. 52. Parthians overrun Syria and threaten Antioch.
50	47-43. Antipater appointed proconsul of Judea. Native of Edom (Idumea). 40. Parthian invasion and capture of Jerusalem. 40-37. Herod, son of Antipater, appointed king of Judea. 37-4. Herod the Great made king of Judea. A period of internal expansion, great building operations, excessive taxation, unemployment, and civil strife.		30f. Schools of Hillel and Shammai active. 20-40 A. D.? Philo of Alexandria, Philosopher. Did much to popularize the Jewish Scriptures in the Greek World.	48. ALEXANDRINE WAR. Ptolemy perishes in the contest, and the crown falls to CLEOPATRA, who reigns jointly with Ptolemy II. 44. Cleopatra removes her brother by poison. 36. Cleopatra obtains from Antony grant of Phœnicia, Cyrene and Cyprus. 30. Dies by her own hand. *A Roman province.*	50-25. The Parthian army had undergone a thorough reorganization so that it was possible for the general, Surenas, to put at the king's disposal over 1000 mailed horsemen and a standing army of 10,000 men, including the train which also composed his attendants and the harem. 38. Arsaces XV. 36. Defeats Antony.	40. Parthians invade Syria, take Antioch and Sidon, plunder Jerusalem, and advance as far as the Mediterranean.
25	25. Samaria rebuilt.					

TO THE BEGINNING OF ROMAN RULE IN PALESTINE 167-63 B. C.

Rome		Rome	China, India, Japan	B. C.
AFFAIRS IN THE WEST	AFFAIRS AND CIVIL WARS IN ROME	AFFAIRS IN THE EAST		110
113-101. CIMBRIAN WAR. The Cimbrians and Teutones migrate along the Danube to the boundaries of Illyria.	100. Marius suffered from his successes in a towering ambition for more power. In spite of the fact that he had violated the constitution by his five consulships, he was determined to have a sixth term and leagued himself with ambitious demagogues to gain his end. He even resorted to violence to carry the elections	111-106. JUGURTHINE WAR. Mummius and Metellus take part in it; and Marius ends it by the capture of Jugurtha, 106. Marius then returned to Rome and staged a big triumph. Jugurtha, after gracing his victor's triumph, died in a Roman dungeon.		
			China: 100. Szu-ma Ch'ien, historian in the period of the Han Dynasty, the "Herodotus of China."	100
91-88. MARSIAN OR SOCIAL WAR, which cost the lives of 300,000 men; and ends in the concession of the rights and privileges of Roman citizenship to the Italian states.		96. Cyrene bequeathed to the Romans by Apion. 92. Sulla settles the affairs of Asia Minor.	97-30. Japan: Sujin, Mikado. Important reforms. Sujin was called "the Great Civilizer." He was connected with a great many reforms. He is said to have established a system of taxation based on the arrow notches of the men and the finger tips of the women, that is to say, on the products of the chase and the loom. A great pestilence swept over Japan in his reign. He built a great many shrines and temples.	
83-72. Sertorius, the opponent of Sulla, goes into Spain, becomes general of the Lusitani.	88-82. FIRST ROMAN CIVIL WAR OF MARIUS AND SULLA. Sulla obtains the command against Mithradates. Marius by an alliance with Sulpicius and the people. Sulla is created perpetual dictator. *CICERO (106-43).*			
78. War with Rome.	79-78. Abdication and death of Sulla. *Rising splendor of Rome. Marble theater of Saurus for 80,000 spectators. Magnificent houses of the Roman nobles. Library of Lucullus.*	66. Pompey in Asia, about the Caucasus, 65, in Syria, 64. Settles the affairs of Asia, 63.		
72. The Helvetii and other tribes, under Ariovistus, advance into Gaul, but are defeated by JULIUS CÆSAR, 58.	73-71. WAR WITH SPARTACUS the gladiator, at the head of 70,000 slaves in Italy. Concluded by Crassus and Pompey.	54-53. Parthian War, in which Crassus is slain.		
			86. Death of Emperor Wu Ti.	
	65-62. Catiline's conspiracy suppressed by the vigilance of Cicero. 60. FIRST TRIUMVIRATE: Cæsar, Pompey and Crassus.	Crassus made a short incursion into Mesopotamia and then withdrew into Syria in 54. The next year he again crossed the Euphrates intending to penetrate deeply into the enemy's country. But he underestimated the strength of the Parthians and was surrounded near Carrhae and his force was cut to pieces. Crassus himself was enticed into a conference and treacherously killed.	86-73. Rule of Chao Ti.	
58-51. GALLIC WAR. Cæsar's eight campaigns in Gaul—he arrests the invasion of the Helvetii and expels the Germans. 55. First invasion of Britain, and expedition into Germany. 54. Second invasion of Britain. 54-53. Cæsar crosses the Rhine, but is unsuccessful in his attack upon the Germans.			73-48. Rule Hsuan Ti.	50
49-31. SECOND ROMAN CIVIL WAR between Cæsar and Pompey: Cæsar crosses the Rubicon with 6,000 men, and in sixty days makes himself master of Italy. Cæsar marches into Spain, and forces Pompey's troops to surrender.			48-32. Rule of Yuan Ti.	
	48. Cæsar gains the decisive victory of **Pharsalla** over Pompey, who flees into Egypt and is there slain. *VIRGIL (70-19).* 47. Cæsar in Asia. War with Pharnaces, King of Bosporus, ("veni, vidi, vici"). 46. AFRICAN WAR: defeat of Scipio and Juba at Thapsus. Cato kills himself at Utica. Cæsar returns to Rome. Dictator for ten years.		40. India: Trade with Greece, Rome, Egypt, China, and the East. Period of Hindu power.	
45. War in Spain; defeat of Pompey's two sons at Munda—Cæsar returns to Rome—Perpetual dictator, and Consul for ten years.	44. Plans an expedition against the Parthians, but is assassinated in the senate house by Brutus, Cassius, and other conspirators, on the ides of March. Antony and Octavianus (Cæsar's heir) obtain the upper hand in Rome. SECOND TRIUMVIRATE: Antony, Octavianus, and Lepidus. 42. Civil war of the triumvirate against the republicans—Philippi—death of Brutus and Cassius. 41-30. Quarrels of the Oligarchy.	36. Antony, without waiting for his army which he had sent through the Valley of the Araxes with the siege train, invaded Parthia. Phraates, king of Parthia, attacked the other Roman army almost destroying it. This left Antony in a serious position. He attempted a siege with inadequate resources, from which he had to retreat later on mid great hardships, having accomplished nothing.		
	36. Defeat and death of Pompey.		China: 36. Steady trade relations were set up with the Roman Empire.	
	33-30. Civil war between Octavianus and Antony.			
	31. Defeat of Antony at Actium. Cæsar gains his fleet and army—death of Antony. OCTAVIANUS CÆSAR sole master of the republic. Political indifference of the masses has given ambitious military men the opportunity to seize power. At first it was in the form of a triple dictatorship known as a triumvirate, where each of the three generals was held in check by the other two, but after the defeat of Anthony the check on the power of one man was brushed aside and a real monarchy was being set up.		30. Japan: Sujin, the great civilizer, died. 27. India: Andhra kingdom very powerful.	
30. PERIOD OF THE ROMAN EMPIRE BEGINS. HISTORY OF THE EMPIRE IS NOW PRACTICALLY THAT OF THE CIVILIZED WORLD, DIVIDED INTO LATIN, GREEK, AND ORIENTAL PROVINCES.				25

VII. ROMAN RULE IN

B. C.	Jewish and Christian History	New Testament Literature	Extra Canonical Jewish Literature	Parthia	China, India, Japan
25	17. Herod's Temple started—still in process of construction during the ministry of Jesus. 5. Birth of Jesus Christ, date uncertain. 4. Death of Herod. 4 B. C.-6 A. D. Archelaus, son of Herod, king of Judea. Deposed in 6 A. D. and Judea placed directly under Roman rule. 4 B. C.-39 A. D. Herod Antipas, son of Herod, tetrarch of Galilee and Perea. Part of the trial of Jesus was before Herod Antipas, because Jesus was from Galilee.			25. Tiridates aspires to the sovereignty, but is defeated and takes refuge at the court of Augustus. 20 Phraates restores the standards taken from Crassus. 18. Sends his sons as hostages to Rome. *Gradual decline of the Parthian Kingdom.*	India: 25 B. C. The Sunga dynasty, after lasting 112 years was succeeded by the Kanva dynasty, which soon came to an end in 25 B. C., being overthrown by an unknown king of the Andhra dynasty of the Satavahanas, whose power originated in the deltas of the Godovan and Kistna Rivers.
4	4 B. C.-34 A. D. Philip son of Herod, tetrarch of the northeastern districts of Palestine.			*Series of struggles for succession to the throne for over one hundred years.*	

A. D.					
1			6-27. The Book of the Assumption of Moses. Apocalyptic literature similar to Mark 13.	1-50 A. D. A decided change was going on in Parthia. The reign of Vologaeses I, which immediately follows this period, reflects a decided advance toward Hellenism. The line of Arsacids, which came to the throne in the person of Artabanus in 10 A. D., stood in open opposition to the old kings with their leaning toward the Romans. The new regime laid much more stress on the Oriental character of their state.	
	18-36. Caiaphas high priest.				21. India: Gondophares, King of Kabul and Punjab.
	25-26. Mission of John the Baptist. 26-36. Pontius Pilate, Roman procurator. 29-30. Crucifixion of Jesus Christ.				India: 40-78 A. D. The Yueh-chi, nomads from Central Asia, had crossed the Hindu Kush into Northwestern India. They were originally divided into five tribes, which were united under the rule of Kadhpises I (40-78), the founder of the Kushan dynasty. He conquered the Kabul Valley and annihilated whatever remained of Greek domination, and swept away the petty Indo-Greek and Indo-Parthian principalities on The Indus. His successors completed the conquest, thus opening a channel for commerce with the Roman Empire.
	37-38. St. Paul converted to Christianity. 30-40. Gamaliel I. 41-44. Short reign of Herod Agrippa I. 44. Theudas: Messianic claims, insurrection against Rome. 49. Council of the Apostles at Jerusalem.	48-52. St. Paul's earlier Epistles.			
	50f. St. Paul's Missions. 52. Period of rebellions against Rome. 55. St. Paul arrested in Jerusalem.		50. The Book of II Enoch. Semi-apocalyptic literature of Greek origin. 50-90. The Book of II Baruch. Apocalyptic literature bearing some similarities to St. Paul's Epistles.	50. Vologeses I. 52. War against Rome for the possession of Armenia Minor.	58. China: Ming-Ti introduces Buddhism.
	64. First traditional persecution of the Christians by Nero. 66. Declaration of war against Rome.	62-64? St. Paul's later Epistles. 65-90. Gospels of Mark, Matthew, and Luke. The Books of Acts.	37-100? Josephus, Jewish Historian, writer of the Jewish Wars, etc.	65. Terminated at the death of Tigranes, when Tiridates accepts the crown of Armenia from Nero.	
	70. Destruction of Jerusalem and the Temple by Titus.		70f. The Book of IV Ezra. Apocalyptic literature with many points of similarity to the Book of Revelation.		71-130. Japan: Keiko and Yamato-Dake make large conquests. China: 90 A.D. The publication of the historical records of the Han Dynasty. Books multiplied. The annals of the Han dynasty tell us that the imperial library possessed 3,123 volumes of the classics, 2,705 volumes of philosophy, 1,318 of poetry, 790 on warfare, 2,538 on mathematics and 868 on medicine. One of the great literary lights of the period was a woman, P'au Chao.
	90. Council of Jamnia. Jamnia was center of Judaism shortly after 70 A. D. Old Testament Canon fixed. 95. Second traditional persecution of the Christians by Domitian.	60- 100. Books of Hebrews; James; I Peter; Revelation; Jude, and Gospel of John. Books of I, II, and III John; I and II Timothy, and Titus. Book of II Peter.	90. Death of Vologeses. Arsaces XXIV. in alliance with the Romans, embellishes Ctesiphon. 100. Books of I Baruch similar to parts of Jeremiah; Martyrdom of Isaiah, story of death of Isaiah; Sibylline Oracles IV and V, Semi-apocalyptic material; Adam and Eve, Semi-apocalyptic material.	107. Chosroes (Arsaces XXV.), implicated in a war with Trajan on account of Armenia	109. China: Conquest of Korea.
125	112-113. Third traditional persecution of the Christians by Trajan.			117. Chosroes restored. 121. Vologeses II., (Arsaces XXVI.)	125. India: Nagar-Juna, great apostle of Buddhism.

PALESTINE, 63 B. C.—100 A. D.

The Roman Empire—In Europe, Asia, and Africa—Under Augustus Cæsar, Emperor		The Roman Empire	B. C.
			25

31-34. Cæsar Octavianus Augustus. The surname Augustus (the Illustrious, the Sublime), which was given Octavianus by the Senate in 27 B. C., is the name by which he was known as sole ruler of the Roman world.

Countries Subject to Roman Dominion	Age of Augustus	The Roman Empire
In Europe:—*Spain, Gaul, Britain, Italy, Rhætia, Vindelicia, Noricum, Pannonia, Illyria, Greece, Macedonia, Thrace, Mœsia, Dacia.* In Asia:—*Asia Minor, Syria, Phœnicia, Palestine, the northern and eastern coasts of the Black Sea, Armenia, Mesopotamia, Assyria.* In Africa:—*Egypt, and the whole of the northern coast.* Its distant territories were *Scandia, Sarmatia, India, Æthiopia,* and *Galatia;* Rome itself being the common center of the whole.	27-25. Expedition of Augustus against the Cantabri and Astures. 25. Expedition to Arabia, without results, conducted by C. Ælius Gallus, prefect of Egypt. 22-21. Successful war against the Ethiopians, by Petronius, the successor of Gallus in Egypt. 20. Campaign of Augustus against the Parthians. Tigranes was reinstated in the kingdom of Armenia. 19. Subjugation of Spain completed. 15. Rhætia made a Roman province, along with Vindelicia (now Augsburg) and Noricum. 12-9. Drusus undertook four campaigns in Germany proper.	30. Augustus bestows increase of territory on Herod. 29. Herod kills his wife, Mariamne. 25. Herod begins extensive building operations in Judea; rebuilds Samaria, reconstructs temple at Jerusalem, 20-19. 4. Birth of **Jesus Christ.** Date now generally accepted though not actually certain.

B. C. 4 | A. D. 1

German Nations		The Christian Church	A. D.
6-9. Varus, in his camp on the Weser, governs Lower Germany as a Roman province. 9. Hermann, or Arminius defeats Varus at **Winfeld-Lippe.** Teutonic independence established by the defeat of the Roman legions. The line drawn between the Germanic and Latin races. 14-17. Expedition of Germanicus.	4-6. Campaigns of Tiberius in Germany. 7. Germanicus is sent into Germany. 14-37. Tiberius (Claudius Nero), step-son of Augustus.	6. Judea made a Roman province under a procurator.	1
The Romans from this time maintain military power on the right bank of the Rhine and from the Maine to the Danube.	37-41. Caligula (properly, Gaius Cæsar Germanicus), youngest son of Germanicus.	26. Pontius Pilate becomes procurator of Judea. 28-29. Baptism of Jesus Christ and beginning of His public work. 30. Crucifixion of Jesus Christ. 35-36. ST. PAUL converted to Christianity.	
	41-54. Claudius (Tiberius Claudius Nero), son of Drusus, influenced largely by 1, the shameless Messalina; 2, the ambitious Agrippina. 43. Commencement of the conquest of Britain.	42. St. Peter, the Apostle, after filling the see of Antioch seven years, goes to Rome. 49. Council of the Apostles at Jerusalem.	
50. Colony of Claudius. Agrippa (Cologne) founded.	54-68. Nero (Nero Claudius Cæsar Augustus Germanicus). Destroys Britannicus and all the Julian family. 59-62. Murders his wife and mother.	56. Paul arrested in Jerusalem. 59. Paul arrives in Rome.	
	64. Fire at Rome, followed, 65. by the persecution of the Christians. 68. Death of Nero, and extinction of the house of Cæsar. 69-79. Vespasianus, (Titus Flavius Vespasianus), one of the best of Roman princes. Eruption of Vesuvius and destruction of Herculaneum, Pompeii and Stabiæ.	64. First traditional persecution of Christians, by Nero. 66. Outbreak of Jewish war. 67. Pope Linus. Vespasian despatched against the Jews.	
69-70. Revolt of the Batavians in Belgian Gaul.		70. The destruction of Jerusalem by Titus. 72. Conquest of Judea completed.	
	86-107. DACIAN WARS.	95. Second traditional persecution of the Christians, by Domitian.	
			125

Prayer to the Holy Spirit

To be recited before reading Holy Scripture

Come, Holy Spirit, fill the hearts of your faithful people and kindle in them the fire of your love.

V. Send forth your spirit and they shall be created.

R. And you will renew the face of the earth.

LET US PRAY: O God, you instructed the hearts of the faithful by the light of the Holy Spirit: grant that in the same Spirit we may be truly wise, and ever rejoice in His consolation. Through Christ our Lord. Amen.

Prayer of St. Bede the Venerable

To be recited after reading Holy Scripture

Let me not, O Lord, be puffed up with worldly wisdom, which passes away, but grant me that love which never ceases, that I may not choose to know anything among men but Jesus, and Him crucified. I pray Thee, dear Jesus, that he upon whom Thou hast graciously given the sweet savor of the words of Thy knowledge, may also possess Thee, Font of all wisdom, and shine forever before thy countenance. Amen.

The Old Testament

The Pentateuch

THE PENTATEUCH, which consists of the first five books of the Bible (Genesis, Exodus, Leviticus, Numbers, Deuteronomy), enjoys particular prestige among the Jews as the "Law," or "Torah," the concrete expression of God's will in their regard. It is more than a body of legal doctrine, even though such material occupies many chapters, for it contains the story of the formation of the People of God: Abraham and the patriarchs, Moses and the oppressed Hebrews in Egypt, the birth of Israel in the Sinai covenant, the journey to the threshold of the Promised Land, and the "discourses" of Moses.

The grandeur of this historic sweep is the result of a careful and complex joining of several historical traditions, or sources. These are primarily four: the so-called Yahwist, Elohist, Priestly and Deuteronomic strands that run through the Pentateuch. (They are conveniently abbreviated as J, E, P and D.) Each brings to the Torah its own characteristics, its own theological viewpoint—a rich variety of interpretation that the sensitive reader will take pains to appreciate. A superficial difference between two of these sources is responsible for their names: the Yahwist prefers the name *Yahweh* (represented in translation as LORD) by which God revealed himself to Israel; the Elohist prefers the generic name for God, *Elohim*. The Yahwist is concrete, imaginative, using many anthropomorphisms in its theological approach, as seen, e. g., in the narrative of creation in Gn 2, compared with the Priestly version in Gn 1. The Elohist is more sober, moralistic. The Priestly strand, which emphasizes genealogies, is more severely theological in tone. The Deuteronomic approach is characterized by the intense hortatory style of Dt 5–11, and by certain principles from which it works, such as the centralization of worship in the Jerusalem temple.

However, even this analysis of the Pentateuch is an oversimplification, for it is not always possible to distinguish with certainty among the various sources. The fact is that each of these individual traditions incorporates much older material. The Yahwist was himself a collector and adapter. His narrative is made up of many disparate stories that have been reoriented, and given a meaning within the context in which they now stand; e. g., the story of Abraham and Isaac in Gn 22. Within the J and P traditions one has to reckon with many individual units; these had their own history and life-setting before they were brought together into the present more or less connected narrative.

This is not to deny the role of Moses in the development of the Pentateuch. It is true we do not conceive of him as the author of the books in the modern sense. But there is no reason to doubt that, in the events described in these traditions, he had a uniquely important role, especially as lawgiver. Even the later laws that have been added in P and D are presented as a Mosaic heritage. Moses is the lawgiver *par excellence*, and all later legislation is conceived in his spirit, and therefore attributed to him. Hence, the reader is not held to undeviating literalness in interpreting the words, "the Lord said to Moses." One must keep in mind that the Pentateuch is the crystallization of Israel's age-old relationship with God.

In presenting the story of the birth of the People of God, the Pentateuch looks back to the promises made to the patriarchs, and forward to the continuing fulfillment of these promises in later books of the Bible. The promises find their classic expression in Gn 12, 1ff. The "God of the Fathers" challenges Abraham to believe: the patriarch is to receive a people, a land, and through him the nations will somehow be blessed.

The mysterious and tortuous way in which this people is brought into being is described: Despite Sarah's sterility, Isaac is finally born—to be offered in sacrifice! The promises are renewed to him eventually, and to the devious Jacob, as if to show that the divine design will be effected, with or without human cunning. The magnificent story of Joseph is highlighted by the theme of Providence; the promise of a people is taking shape.

Israel is not formed in a vacuum, but amid the age-old civilizations of Mesopotamia and the Nile. Oppression in Egypt provokes a striking intervention of God.

Yahweh reveals himself to Moses as a savior, and the epic story of deliverance is told in Exodus. This book also tells of the Sinai covenant, which is rightfully regarded as the key to the Old Testament. Through the covenant Israel becomes Yahweh's people, and Yahweh becomes Israel's God. This act of grace marks the fulfillment of the first promise: that Abraham will be the father of a great nation, God's special possession. The laws in Exodus and Leviticus (P tradition) are both early and late. They spell out the proper relationship of the federation of the twelve tribes with the Lord. He is a jealous God, demanding exclusive allegiance; he cannot be imaged; he takes vengeance upon the wicked, and shows mercy to the good. Slowly the Lord reveals himself to his people; with remarkable honesty, Israel records the unsteady response—the murmurings and rebellions and infidelities through the desert wanderings up to the plains of Moab.

This sacred history was formed within the bosom of early Israel, guided by the spirit of God. It was sung beside the desert campfires; it was commemorated in the liturgical feasts, such as Passover; it was transmitted by word of mouth from generation to generation—until all was brought together in writing, about the sixth century B.C., when the literary formation of the Pentateuch came to an end.

The Book of Deuteronomy has a history quite peculiar to itself. Its old traditions and law code (12—26) are put forth in the form of "discourses" of Moses before his death. The extraordinarily intense and hortatory tone fits the mood of a discourse. The book contains possibly the preaching of the Levites in the northern kingdom of Israel before its fall in 721 B.C. If this book is situated in its proper historical perspective, its true impact is more vividly appreciated. It is the blueprint of the great "Deuteronomic" reform under King Josiah (640-609 B.C.). This was an attempt to galvanize the people into a wholehearted commitment to the covenant ideals, into an obedience motivated by the great commandment of love (Dt 6, 4ff). Israel has yet another chance, if it obeys. The people are poised between life and death; and they are exhorted to choose life—today (26, 16-19; 30, 15-20).

The Book of Genesis

Introduction

Genesis, the first book of the Bible, opens with the Hebrew word *bereshit,* which means "in the beginning." The title "Genesis" was given to the Septuagint (Greek) translation of the book because of its concern with the origin of the world (Gn 1, 1; 2, 4), of the human race, and, in particular, of the Hebrew people.

Eleven structural units (*toledoth*), of unequal length and importance, present the unity and purpose of the book in terms of God's universal sovereignty, his dealings with men, and his choice and formation of a special people to be the instrument of his plan of salvation.

The tracing of the direct descendance from Adam to Jacob constitutes the major part of the book, while the genealogical tables of lateral branches are not so developed nor of such interest as those that pertain to the story of the Israelite people. In fact, these lateral branches gradually disappear from the narrative. And with the introduction of Abraham and his covenant with God, the history of humanity as such becomes contracted to the story of the descendants of Abraham through Isaac and Jacob—the chosen people.

Despite its unity of plan and purpose, the book is a complex work, not to be attributed to a single original author. Several sources, or literary traditions, that the final redactor used in his composition are discernible. These are the Yahwist (J), Elohist (E) and Priestly (P) sources, which in turn reflect older oral traditions (see Introduction to the Pentateuch).

In Genesis, the Yahwist source is the most important by reason of its teaching, its antiquity, and the continuity it gives the book. It constitutes a sacred history, continually drawing attention to the working out of God's design through his interventions in the affairs of men. The Elohist source, less well preserved, is found in fragmentary form only, depicting God's manifestations through visions and dreams rather than theophanies. Angels are God's intermediaries with men. Moreover, there is a solicitude for the divine transcendence and greater sensitivity toward the moral order. The Priestly source contains those elements—chronological data, lists, genealogies—that construct the framework of Genesis and bind its contents together. To the J and E sources it adds such legal institutions as the sabbath rest, circumcision, and the alliances between God and Noah and God and Abraham.

The interpreter of Genesis will recognize at once the distinct object that sets chapters 1—11 apart: the recounting of the origin of the world and of man (primeval history). To make the truths contained in these chapters intelligible to the Israelite people destined to preserve them, they needed to be expressed through elements prevailing among that people at that time. For this reason, the truths themselves must therefore be clearly distinguished from their literary garb.

With the story of the patriarchs Abraham, Isaac and Jacob (11, 27—50, 26), the character of the narrative changes. While we do not view the account of the patriarchs as history in the strict sense, nevertheless certain of the matters recounted from the time of Abraham onward can be placed in the actual historical and social framework of the Near East in the early part of the second millennium B. C. (2000-1500), and documented by non-biblical sources.

Genesis contains many religious teachings of basic importance: the pre-existence and transcendence of God, his wisdom and goodness, his power through which all things are made and on which they all depend; the special creation of man in God's image and likeness, and of woman from the substance of man; the institution of marriage as the union of one man with one woman; man's original state of innocence; man's sin of pride and disobedience; its consequences for the proto-parents and their posterity. Despite the severity of their punishment, hope of reconciliation is offered by God through the first as well as the subsequent promises of salvation and blessing. Abraham is blessed for his faith and obedience, and he is to be a blessing for all nations through his offspring, Isaac, Jacob, and Jacob's sons (Gn 12, 3; 18, 18; 22, 18), of whom the Messiah, mankind's greatest blessing, will eventually be born (Gal 3, 8).

Frequent references to Genesis are found in the New Testament. Christ becomes the antithesis of Adam: sin and death come to mankind through Adam, justification and life through Jesus Christ (Rom 5, 12.17ff). Noah's ark becomes the symbol of the Church, by which men are saved from destruction through the waters of baptism (1 Pt 3, 20ff); Abraham's faith is the model for all believers; the sacrifice of his son Isaac typifies the sacrifice of Christ, Son of the Father. The Liturgy, too, relates the persons of Abel, Abraham and Melchizedek to Christ in his act of sacrifice.

The Book of Genesis is divided as follows:

I: THE PRIMEVAL HISTORY

First Story of Creation

1 ¹*†IN THE BEGINNING, when God created the heavens and the earth, ²*†the earth was a formless wasteland, and darkness covered the abyss, while a mighty wind swept over the waters.

³*Then God said, "Let there be light," and there was light. ⁴God saw how good the light was. God then separated the light from the darkness. ⁵†God called the light "day," and the darkness he called "night." Thus evening came, and morning followed—the first day.

⁶Then God said, "Let there be a dome in the middle of the waters, to separate one body of water from the other." And so it happened: ⁷*God made the dome, and it separated the water above the dome from the water below it. ⁸God called the dome "the sky." Evening came, and morning followed—the second day.

⁹*Then God said, "Let the water under the sky be gathered into a single basin, so that the dry land may appear." And so it happened: the water under the sky was gathered into its basin, and the dry land appeared. ¹⁰God called the dry land "the earth," and the basin of the water he called "the sea." God saw how good it was. ¹¹*Then God said, "Let the earth bring forth vegetation: every kind of plant that bears seed and every kind of fruit tree on earth that bears fruit with its seed in it." And so it happened: ¹²the earth brought forth every kind of plant that bears seed and every kind of fruit tree on earth that bears fruit with its seed in it. God saw how good it was. ¹³Evening came, and morning followed—the third day.

¹⁴*Then God said: "Let there be lights in the dome of the sky, to separate day from night. Let them mark the fixed times, the days and the years, ¹⁵and serve as luminaries in the dome of the sky, to shed light upon the earth." And so it happened: ¹⁶*God made the two great lights, the greater one to govern the day, and the lesser one to govern the night; and he made the stars. ¹⁷God set them in the dome of the sky, to shed light upon the earth, ¹⁸to govern the day and the night, and to separate the light from the darkness. God saw how good it was. ¹⁹Evening came, and morning followed—the fourth day.

²⁰*Then God said, "Let the water teem with an abundance of living creatures, and on the earth let birds fly beneath the dome of the sky." And so it happened: ²¹God created the great sea monsters and all kinds of swimming creatures with which the water teems, and all kinds of winged birds. God saw how good it was, ²²*and God blessed them, saying, "Be fertile, multiply, and fill the water of the seas; and let the birds multiply on the earth." ²³Evening came, and morning followed—the fifth day.

²⁴*Then God said, "Let the earth bring forth all kinds of living creatures: cattle, creeping things, and wild animals of all kinds." And so it happened: ²⁵God made all kinds of wild animals, all kinds of cattle, and all kinds of creeping things of the earth. God saw how good it was. ²⁶*†Then God said: "Let us make man in our image, after our likeness. Let them have dominion over the fish of the sea, the birds of the air, and the cattle, and over all the wild animals and all the creatures that crawl on the ground."

²⁷God created man in his image;
    in the divine image he created him;
    male and female he created them.

²⁸*God blessed them, saying: "Be fertile and multiply; fill the earth and subdue it. Have dominion over the fish of the sea, the birds of the air, and all the living things that move on the earth." ²⁹*God also said: "See, I give you every seed-bearing plant all over the earth and every tree that has seed-bearing fruit on it to be your food; ³⁰and to all the animals of the land, all the birds of the air, and all the living creatures that crawl on the ground, I give all the green plants for food." And so it happened. ³¹*God looked at everything he had made, and he found it very good. Evening came, and morning followed—the sixth day.

2 ¹*THUS the heavens and the earth and all their array were completed. ²*Since on the seventh day God was finished with the work he had been doing, he rested on the seventh day from all the work he had undertaken. ³*So God blessed the seventh day

---

＊

1/1: 2, 1.4; Pss 8, 4;
    38–39; 90, 2;
    Wis 11, 17; Sir 16, 24;
    Jer 10, 12; 2 Mc 7, 28;
    Acts 14, 15; Col 1, 16f;
    Heb 1, 2f; 3, 4; 11, 3;
    Rv 4, 11.
2: Jer 4, 23.
3: 2 Cor 4, 6.
7: Prv 8, 27f; 2 Pt 3, 5.
9: Jb 38, 8; Ps 33, 7;
    Jer 5, 22.
11: Ps 104, 14.
14: Jb 26, 10; Ps 19, 1f;
    Bar 3, 33.
16: Dt 4, 19; Ps 136, 7ff;
    Wis 13, 2ff; Jer 31, 35.
20: Jb 12, 7-10.

22: 8, 17.
24: Sir 16, 27f; Bar 3, 32.
26f: 5, 1.3; 9, 6; Ps 8, 5f;
    Wis 2, 23; 10, 2;
    Sir 17, 1.3f; Jas 3, 7;
    1 Cor 11, 7; Eph 4, 24;
    Col 3, 10; Mt 19, 4;
    Mk 10,6.
28: 8, 17; 9, 1; Pss 8, 6-9;
    115, 16; Wis 9, 2.
29f: 9, 3; Ps 104, 14f.
31: 1 Tm 4, 4.
2/1: Is 45, 12; Jn 1, 3.
2: Ex 20, 9ff; 31, 17;
    Heb 4.10.
3: Ex 20, 11; Dt 5, 14;
    Neh 9, 14.

---

† 1, 1–2, 4a: This section introduces the whole Pentateuch. It shows how God brought an orderly universe out of primordial chaos.

1, 2: *The abyss:* the primordial ocean according to the ancient Semitic cosmogony. After God's creative activity, part of this vast body forms the salt-water seas (vv 9f); part of it is the fresh water under the earth (Ps 33, 7; Ez 31, 4), which wells forth on the earth as springs and fountains (Gn 7, 11; 8, 2; Prv 3, 20). Part of it, "the upper water" (Ps 148, 4; Dn 3, 60), is held up by the dome of the sky (Gn 1, 6f), from which rain descends on the earth (Gn 7, 11; 2 Kgs 7, 2.19; Ps 104, 13). *A mighty wind:* literally, "a wind of God," or "a spirit of God"; cf Gn 8, 1.

1, 5: In ancient Israel a day was considered to begin at sunset. According to the highly artificial literary structure of Gn 1, 1–2, 4a, God's creative activity is divided into six days to teach the sacredness of the sabbath rest on the seventh day in the Israelite religion (2, 2f).

1, 26: Man is here presented as the climax of God's creative activity; he resembles God primarily because of the dominion God gives him over the rest of creation.

and made it holy, because on it he rested from all the work he had done in creation.

4†Such is the story of the heavens and the earth at their creation.

Second Story of Creation

At the time when the Lord God made the earth and the heavens—**5**while as yet there was no field shrub on earth and no grass of the field had sprouted, for the Lord God had sent no rain upon the earth and there was no man to till the soil, **6**but a stream was welling up out of the earth and was watering all the surface of the ground—**7***†the Lord God formed man out of the clay of the ground and blew into his nostrils the breath of life, and so man became a living being.

8*†Then the Lord God planted a garden in Eden, in the east, and he placed there the man whom he had formed. **9***Out of the ground the Lord God made various trees grow that were delightful to look at and good for food, with the tree of life in the middle of the garden and the tree of the knowledge of good and bad.

10†A river rises in Eden to water the garden; beyond there it divides and becomes four branches. **11**The name of the first is the Pishon; it is the one that winds through the whole land of Havilah, where there is gold. **12**The gold of that land is excellent; bdellium and lapis lazuli are also there. **13***The name of the second river is the Gihon; it is the one that winds all through the land of Cush. **14**The name of the third river is the Tigris; it is the one that flows east of Asshur. The fourth river is the Euphrates.

15*The Lord God then took the man and settled him in the garden of Eden, to cultivate and care for it. **16***The Lord God gave man this order: "You are free to eat from any of the trees of the garden **17***except the tree of the knowledge of good and bad. From that tree you shall not eat; the moment you eat from it you are surely doomed to die."

18*The Lord God said: "It is not good for the man to be alone. I will make a suitable partner for him." **19**So the Lord God formed out of the ground various wild animals and various birds of the air, and he brought them to the man to see what he would call them; whatever the man called each of them would be its name. **20**The man gave names to all the cattle, all the birds of the air, and all the wild animals; but none proved to be the suitable partner for the man.

21*So the Lord God cast a deep sleep on the man, and while he was asleep, he took out one of his ribs and closed up its place with flesh. **22**The Lord God then built up into a woman the rib that he had taken

from the man. When he brought her to the man, **23**†the man said:

"This one, at last, is bone of my bones
    and flesh of my flesh;
This one shall be called 'woman,'
    for out of 'her man' this one has been taken."

24*†That is why a man leaves his father and mother and clings to his wife, and the two of them become one body.

25The man and his wife were both naked, yet they felt no shame.

The Fall of Man

3 **1**Now the serpent was the most cunning of all the animals that the Lord God had made. The serpent asked the woman, "Did God really tell you not to eat from any of the trees in the garden?" **2**The woman answered the serpent: "We may eat of the fruit of the trees in the garden; **3***it is only about the fruit of the tree in the middle of the garden that God said, 'You shall not eat it or even touch it, lest you die.'" **4***But the serpent said to the woman: "You certainly will not die! **5**No, God knows well that the moment you eat of it your eyes will be opened and know what is good and what is bad." **6***The woman saw that the tree was good for food, pleasing to the eyes, and desirable for gaining wisdom. So she took some of its fruit and ate it; and she also gave some to her husband, who was with her, and he ate it. **7**Then the eyes of both of them were opened, and they realized that they were naked; so they sewed fig leaves together and made loincloths for themselves.

8*†When they heard the sound of the Lord God moving about in the garden at the breezy time of the

---

† 2, 4b-25: This section is chiefly concerned with the creation of man. It is much older than the narrative of 1, 1—2, 4a. Here God is depicted as creating man before the rest of his creatures, which are made for man's sake.

2, 7: God is portrayed as a potter molding man's body out of clay. There is a play on words in Hebrew between *adam* ("man") and *adama* ("ground"). *Being:* literally, "soul."

2, 8: *Eden:* used here as the name of a region in southern Mesopotamia; the term is derived from the Sumerian word *eden,* "fertile plain." A similar-sounding Hebrew word means "delight"; the *garden in Eden* could therefore be understood as the "garden of delight," so that, through the Greek version, it is now known also as "paradise," literally, a "pleasure park."

2, 10-14: *Rises:* in flood to overflow its banks. *Beyond there:* as one travels upstream. *Branches:* literally, "heads," i. e., upper courses. Eden is near the head of the Persian Gulf, where the Tigris and the Euphrates join with two other streams to form a single river. *The land of Cush* here and in 10, 8, is not Ethiopia (Nubia) as elsewhere, but the region of the Kassites, east of Mesopotamia.

2, 23: There is a play on the similar-sounding Hebrew words *ishsha* ("woman") and *ishah* ("her man, her husband").

2, 24: *One body:* literally "one flesh"; classical Hebrew has no specific word for "body." The sacred writer stresses the fact that conjugal union is willed by God.

3, 5: *Like gods who know:* or "like God who knows."

3, 8: *The breezy time of the day:* literally "the wind of the day." On most days in Palestine a cooling breeze blows from the sea shortly before sunset.

  7: 3,19; 18, 27; Tb 8,6;   18: Tb 8, 6; Sir 36, 24;
     Jb 34, 15; Pss 103, 14;   1 Cor 11, 9; 1 Tm 2, 13.
     104, 29; Eccl 3,20;   21: Sir 17, 1; 1 Cor 11, 8f;
     12,7; Wis 7, 1; Sir 33,   1 Tm 2, 13.
     10; 1 Cor 15, 45.   24: Mt 19, 5; Mk 10, 7;
  8: Is 51, 3; Ez 31, 9.   1 Cor 7, 10f; Eph 5, 31.
  9: 3, 22; Prv 3, 18;   3/3: 2, 17; Rom 6, 23.
     Rv 2, 7; 22, 2.14.   4f: Wis 2, 24; Sir 25, 14
 13: Sir 24, 25.   Is 14, 14; Jn 8, 44;
 15: Sir 7, 15.   2 Cor 11, 3.
 16: Ps 104, 14.   6: 3, 22; 1 Tm 2, 14.
 17: 3, 2f; Rom 6, 23.   8: Jer 23, 24.

day, the man and his wife hid themselves from the LORD God among the trees of the garden. [9]The LORD God then called to the man and asked him, "Where are you?" [10]He answered, "I heard you in the garden; but I was afraid, because I was naked, so I hid myself." [11]Then he asked, "Who told you that you were naked? You have eaten, then, from the tree of which I had forbidden you to eat!" [12]The man replied, "The woman whom you put here with me—she gave me fruit from the tree, and so I ate it." [13]*The LORD God then asked the woman, "Why did you do such a thing?" The woman answered, "The serpent tricked me into it, so I ate it."

[14]*Then the LORD God said to the serpent:

"Because you have done this, you shall be banned
    from all the animals
    and from all the wild creatures;
On your belly shall you crawl,
    and dirt shall you eat
    all the days of your life.
[15]*†I will put enmity between you and the woman,
    and between your offspring and hers;
He will strike at your head,
    while you strike at his heel."

[16]*To the woman he said:

"I will intensify the pangs of your childbearing;
    in pain shall you bring forth children.
Yet your urge shall be for your husband,
    and he shall be your master."

[17]*To the man he said: "Because you listened to your wife and ate from the tree of which I had forbidden you to eat,

"Cursed be the ground because of you!
    In toil shall you eat its yield
    all the days of your life.
[18]Thorns and thistles shall it bring forth to you,
    as you eat of the plants of the field.
[19]*By the sweat of your face
    shall you get bread to eat,
Until you return to the ground,
    from which you were taken;
For you are dirt,
    and to dirt you shall return."

[20]†The man called his wife Eve, because she became the mother of all the living.

[21]For the man and his wife the LORD God made leather garments, with which he clothed them. [22]*Then the LORD God said: "See! The man has become like one of us, knowing what is good and what is bad! Therefore, he must not be allowed to put out his hand to take fruit from the tree of life also, and thus eat of it and live forever." [23]The LORD God therefore banished him from the garden of Eden, to till the ground from which he had been taken. [24]†When he expelled the man, he settled him east of the garden of Eden; and he stationed the cherubim and the fiery revolving sword, to guard the way to the tree of life.

Cain and Abel

4 [1]†THE man had relations with his wife Eve, and she conceived and bore Cain, saying, "I have produced a man with the help of the LORD." [2]Next she bore his brother Abel. Abel became a keeper of flocks, and Cain a tiller of the soil. [3]In the course of time Cain brought an offering to the LORD from the fruit of the soil, [4]*while Abel, for his part, brought one of the best firstlings of his flock. The LORD looked with favor on Abel and his offering, [5]but on Cain and his offering he did not. Cain greatly resented this and was crestfallen. [6]So the LORD said to Cain: "Why are you so resentful and crestfallen? [7]*†If you do well, you can hold up your head; but if not, sin is a demon lurking at the door: his urge is toward you, yet you can be his master."

[8]*Cain said to his brother Abel, "Let us go out in the field." When they were in the field, Cain attacked his brother Abel and killed him. [9]Then the LORD asked Cain, "Where is your brother Abel?" He answered, "I do not know. Am I my brother's keeper?" [10]The LORD then said: "What have you done! Listen: your brother's blood cries out to me from the soil! [11]*Therefore you shall be banned from the soil that opened its mouth to receive your brother's blood from your hand. [12]If you till the soil, it shall no longer give you its produce. You shall become a restless wanderer on the earth." [13]Cain said to the LORD: "My punishment is too great to bear. [14]Since you have now banished me from the soil, and I must avoid your presence and be-

---

† 3, 15: *He will strike . . . at his heel:* since the antecedent for *he* and *his* is the collective noun *offspring,* i. e., all the descendants of the woman, a more exact rendering of the sacred writer's words would be, "They will strike . . . at their heels." However, later theology saw in this passage more than unending hostility between snakes and men. The serpent was regarded as the devil (Wis 2, 24; Jn 8, 44; Rv 12, 9; 20, 2), whose eventual defeat seems implied in the contrast between *head* and *heel.* Because "the Son of God appeared that he might destroy the works of the devil" (1 Jn 3, 8), the passage can be understood as the first promise of a Redeemer for fallen mankind. The woman's offspring then is primarily Jesus Christ.

3, 20: This verse seems to be out of place; it would fit better after v 24. The Hebrew name *hawwa* ("Eve") is related to the Hebrew word *hay* ("living").

3, 24: The above rendering is based on the ancient Greek version; that of the current Hebrew is, When he expelled the man, he settled, east of the garden of Eden, the cherubim. . . .

4, 1: The Hebrew name *qayin* ("Cain") and the term *qaniti* ("I have produced") present another play on words.

4, 7: *Demon lurking:* in Hebrew, *robes,* literally "croucher," is used here, like the similar Akkadian term *rabisu,* to designate a certain kind of evil spirit.

13: 2 Cor 11, 3.
14: Is 65, 25; Mi 7, 17; Rv 12, 9.
15: Is 7, 14; 9, 5; Rom 16, 20; 1 Jn 3, 8; Rv 12, 17.
16: 1 Cor 11, 3; Eph 5, 22f; 1 Tm 2, 12.
17: 5, 29; Rom 5, 12; 8, 20; Heb 6, 8.
19: 2, 7; Jb 10, 9: 34, 15; Pss 90, 3; 103, 14;
Eccl 3, 20; 12, 7; Wis 15, 8; Sir 10,9; 17, 2; Rom 5, 12; 1 Cor 15, 21; Heb 9, 27.
22: 2, 9; Rv 22, 2.14.
4/4: Ex 34, 19; Heb 11, 4.
7: Sir 7, 1; Jude 11.
8: Wis 10, 3; Mt 23, 35; Lk 11, 51; 1 Jn 3, 12; Jude 11.
11: Dt 27, 24.

come a restless wanderer on the earth, anyone may kill me at sight." **15**†"Not so!" the Lord said to him. "If anyone kills Cain, Cain shall be avenged sevenfold." So the Lord put a mark on Cain, lest anyone should kill him at sight. **16**†Cain then left the Lord's presence and settled in the land of Nod, east of Eden.

Descendants of Cain and Seth

17†Cain had relations with his wife, and she conceived and bore Enoch. Cain also became the founder of a city, which he named after his son Enoch. **18**To Enoch was born Irad, and Irad became the father of Mehujael; Mehujael became the father of Methusael, and Methusael became the father of Lamech. **19**Lamech took two wives; the name of the first was Adah, and the name of the second Zillah. **20**Adah gave birth to Jabal, the ancestor of all who dwell in tents and keep cattle. **21**His brother's name was Jubal; he was the ancestor of all who play the lyre and the pipe. **22**Zillah, on her part, gave birth to Tubalcain, the ancestor of all who forge instruments of bronze and iron. The sister of Tubalcain was Naamah.

23Lamech said to his wives:

"Adah and Zillah, hear my voice;
    wives of Lamech, listen to my utterance:
I have killed a man for wounding me,
    a boy for bruising me.
24If Cain is avenged sevenfold,
    then Lamech seventy-sevenfold."

25†Adam again had relations with his wife, and she gave birth to a son whom she called Seth. "God has granted me more offspring in place of Abel," she said, "because Cain slew him." **26***To Seth, in turn, a son was born, and he named him Enosh.

At that time men began to invoke the Lord by name.

Generations: Adam to Noah

5 **1***†THIS is the record of the descendants of Adam. When God created man, he made him in the likeness of God; **2**he created them male and female. When they were created, he blessed them and named them "man."

3*Adam was one hundred and thirty years old when he begot a son in his likeness, after his image; and he named him Seth. **4**Adam lived eight hundred years after the birth of Seth, and he had other sons and daughters. **5**The whole lifetime of Adam was nine hundred and thirty years; then he died.

6When Seth was one hundred and five years old, he became the father of Enosh. **7**Seth lived eight hundred and seven years after the birth of Enosh, and he had other sons and daughters. **8**The whole lifetime of Seth was nine hundred and twelve years; then he died.

9When Enosh was ninety years old, he became the father of Kenan. **10**Enosh lived eight hundred and fif-

teen years after the birth of Kenan, and he had other sons and daughters. **11**The whole lifetime of Enosh was nine hundred and five years; then he died.

12When Kenan was seventy years old, he became the father of Mahalalel. **13**Kenan lived eight hundred and forty years after the birth of Mahalalel, and he had other sons and daughters. **14**The whole lifetime of Kenan was nine hundred and ten years; then he died.

15When Mahalalel was sixty-five years old, he became the father of Jared. **16**Mahalalel lived eight hundred and thirty years after the birth of Jared, and he had other sons and daughters. **17**The whole lifetime of Mahalalel was eight hundred and ninety-five years; then he died.

18When Jared was one hundred and sixty-two years old, he became the father of Enoch. **19**Jared lived eight hundred years after the birth of Enoch, and he had other sons and daughters. **20**The whole lifetime of Jared was nine hundred and sixty-two years; then he died.

21When Enoch was sixty-five years old, he became the father of Methuselah. **22**Enoch lived three hundred years after the birth of Methuselah, and he had other sons and daughters. **23**The whole lifetime of Enoch was three hundred and sixty-five years. **24***†Then Enoch walked with God, and he was no longer here, for God took him.

25When Methuselah was one hundred and eighty-seven years old, he became the father of Lamech. **26**Methuselah lived seven hundred and eighty-two

---

† 4, 15: *A mark:* probably a tattoo. The use of tattooing for tribal marks has always been common among the nomads of the Near Eastern deserts.

4, 16: *The land of Nod:* not a definite geographic region. The term merely means "the land of nomads."

4, 17-22: In vv 12-16 Cain was presented as the archetype of nomadic peoples. The sacred author in this section follows another ancient tradition that makes Cain the prototype of sedentary peoples with higher material culture.

4, 25f: *Has granted:* Hebrew *shat,* a wordplay on the name *shet* ("Seth"). *Enosh:* in Hebrew, a synonym of *adam* ("man"). *At that time . . . name:* men began to call God by his personal name, Yahweh, rendered as "the Lord" in this version of the Bible. The ancient, so-called Yahwist, source used here employs the name Yahweh long before the time of Moses. Another ancient source, the Elohist (from its use of the term *Elohim,* "God," instead of *Yahweh,* "Lord," for the pre-Mosaic period), makes Moses the first to use Yahweh as the proper name of Israel's God, previously known by other names as well; cf Ex 3, 13ff.

5, 1-32: Although this chapter, with its highly schematic form, belongs to the relatively late "Priestly document," it is based on very ancient traditions. Together with 11, 10-26, its primary purpose is to bridge the genealogical gap between Adam and Abraham. Adam's line is traced through Seth, but several names in the series are the same as, or similar to, certain names in Cain's line (4, 17ff). The long lifespans attributed to these ten antediluvian patriarchs have a symbolic rather than a historical value. Babylonian tradition also recorded ten kings with fantastically high ages who reigned successively before the flood.

5, 24: In place of the usual formula, *Then he died,* the change to *Enoch walked with God* clearly implies that he did not die, but like Elijah (2 Kgs 2, 11f) was taken alive to God's abode.

26: 1 Chr 1, 1; Lk 3, 38.
5/1: 1, 27; Wis 2, 23; Sir 17, 1; 1 Cor 11, 7; Jas 3, 9.
3: 4, 25.
3-32: 1 Chr 1, 1-4; Lk 3, 36ff.
24: Wis 4, 10f; Sir 44, 16; 49, 14; Heb 11, 5.

years after the birth of Lamech, and he had other sons and daughters. **27**The whole lifetime of Methuselah was nine hundred and sixty-nine years; then he died.

28When Lamech was one hundred and eighty-two years old, he begot a son **29***†and named him Noah, saying, "Out of the very ground that the Lord has put under a curse, this one shall bring us relief from our work and the toil of our hands." **30**Lamech lived five hundred and ninety-five years after the birth of Noah, and he had other sons and daughters. **31**The whole lifetime of Lamech was seven hundred and seventy-seven years; then he died.

32*When Noah was five hundred years old, he became the father of Shem, Ham, and Japheth.

Origin of the Nephilim

6 **1**†when men began to multiply on earth and daughters were born to them, **2***†the sons of heaven saw how beautiful the daughters of man were, and so they took for their wives as many of them as they chose. **3**†Then the Lord said: "My spirit shall not remain in man forever, since he is but flesh. His days shall comprise one hundred and twenty years."

4*†At that time the Nephilim appeared on earth (as well as later), after the sons of heaven had intercourse with the daughters of man, who bore them sons. They were the heroes of old, the men of renown.

Warning of the Flood

5*†When the Lord saw how great was man's wickedness on earth, and how no desire that his heart conceived was ever anything but evil, **6**he regretted that he had made man on the earth, and his heart was grieved.

7So the Lord said: "I will wipe out from the earth the men whom I have created, and not only the men, but also the beasts and the creeping things and the birds of the air, for I am sorry that I made them." **8**But Noah found favor with the Lord.

9*These are the descendants of Noah. Noah, a good man and blameless in that age, **10**for he walked with God, begot three sons: Shem, Ham, and Japheth.

11*In the eyes of God the earth was corrupt and full of lawlessness. **12***When God saw how corrupt the earth had become, since all mortals led depraved lives on earth, **13***he said to Noah: "I have decided to put an end to all mortals on earth; the earth is full of lawlessness because of them. So I will destroy them and all life on earth.

Preparation for the Flood

14†"Make yourself an ark of gopherwood, put various compartments in it, and cover it inside and out with pitch. **15**†This is how you shall build it: the length

of the ark shall be three hundred cubits, its width fifty cubits, and its height thirty cubits. **16**†Make an opening for daylight in the ark, and finish the ark a cubit above it. Put an entrance in the side of the ark, which you shall make with bottom, second and third decks. **17***I, on my part, am about to bring the flood [waters] on the earth, to destroy everywhere all creatures in which there is the breath of life; everything on earth shall perish. **18***But with you I will establish my covenant; you and your sons, your wife and your sons' wives, shall go into the ark. **19**Of all other living creatures you shall bring two into the ark, one male and one female, that you may keep them alive with you. **20**Of all kinds of birds, of all kinds of beasts, and of all kinds of creeping things, two of each shall come into

---

† 5, 29: There is a similarity in sound between the Hebrew word *noah,* "Noah," and the verbal phrase *yenahamenu,* "he will bring us relief"; this latter refers both to the curse put on the soil because of the fall of man (3, 17ff) and to Noah's success in agriculture, especially in raising grapes for wine (9, 20f).

6, 1-4: This is apparently a fragment of an old legend that had borrowed much from ancient mythology. The sacred author incorporates it here, not only in order to account for the prehistoric giants of Palestine, whom the Israelites called *the Nephilim,* but also to introduce the story of the flood with a moral orientation—the constantly increasing wickedness of mankind.

6, 2: *The sons of heaven:* literally "the sons of the gods" or "the sons of God," i. e., the celestial beings of mythology.

6, 3: *My spirit:* the breath of life referred to in 2, 7. *His days . . . years:* probably the time God would still let men live on earth before destroying them with the flood, rather than the maximum span of life God would allot to individual men in the future.

6, 4: *As well as later:* According to Nm 13, 33, when the Israelites invaded Palestine and found there the tall aboriginal Anakim, they likened them to *the Nephilim;* cf Dt 2, 10f. Perhaps the huge megalithic structures in Palestine were thought to have been built by a race of giants, whose superhuman strength was attributed to semi-divine origin. *The heroes of old:* the legendary worthies of ancient mythology.

6, 5—8, 22: The story of the great flood here recorded is a composite narrative based on two separate sources interwoven into an intricate patchwork. To the Yahwist source, with some later editorial additions, are usually assigned 6, 5-8; 7, 1-5.7-10.12.16b.17b. 22-23; 8, 2b-3a.6-12.13b.20-22. The other sections come from the "Priestly document." The combination of the two sources produced certain duplications (e. g., 6, 13-22 of the Yahwist source, beside 7, 1-5 of the Priestly source); also certain inconsistencies, such as the number of the various animals taken into the ark (6, 19f; 7, 14f of the Priestly source, beside 7, 2f of the Yahwist source), and the timetable of the flood (8, 3-5.13f of the Priestly source, beside 7, 4.10.12.17b; 8, 6.10.12 of the Yahwist source). Both biblical sources go back ultimately to an ancient Mesopotamian story of a great flood, preserved in the eleventh tablet of the Gilgamesh Epic. The latter account, in some respects remarkably similar to the biblical account, is in others very different from it.

6, 14: *Gopherwood:* an unidentified wood not mentioned elsewhere; *gopher* is merely the Hebrew word for it.

6, 15: The dimensions of Noah's ark were approximately 440x73x44 feet, a foot and a half to the cubit. The ark of the Babylonian flood story was an exact cube, 120 cubits in length, width and height.

6, 16: *Opening for daylight:* a conjectural rendering of the Hebrew word *sohar,* occurring only here. The reference is probably to an open space on all sides near the top of the ark to admit light and air. The ark also had a window or hatch, which could be opened and closed (8, 6).

❋
29: 3, 17ff.
32: 6, 10; 10, 1.
6/2: Mt 24, 38; Lk 17, 26f.
4: Wis 14, 6; Bar 3, 26.
5: Ps 14, 2f.
9: Wis 10, 4; Sir 44, 17.
11: Jb 22, 15ff.
12: Ps 14, 2.
13: Sir 40, 9f; 44, 17; Mt 24, 37ff.
17: 7, 4.21; 2 Pt 2, 5.
18: 9, 9; Wis 14, 6; Heb 11, 7; 1 Pt 3, 20.

the ark with you, to stay alive. **21**Moreover, you are to provide yourself with all the food that is to be eaten, and store it away, that it may serve as provisions for you and for them." **22**This Noah did; he carried out all the commands that God gave him.

7 **1***THEN the LORD said to Noah: "Go into the ark, you and all your household, for you alone in this age have I found to be truly just. **2**Of every clean animal, take with you seven pairs, a male and its mate; and of the unclean animals, one pair, a male and its mate; **3**likewise, of every clean bird of the air, seven pairs, a male and a female, and of all the unclean birds, one pair, a male and a female. Thus you will keep their issue alive over all the earth. **4***Seven days from now I will bring rain down on the earth for forty days and forty nights, and so I will wipe out from the surface of the earth every moving creature that I have made." **5**Noah did just as the LORD had commanded him.

The Great Flood

6Noah was six hundred years old when the flood waters came upon the earth. **7***Together with his sons, his wife, and his sons' wives, Noah went into the ark because of the waters of the flood. **8**Of the clean animals and the unclean, of the birds, and of everything that creeps on the ground, **9***[two by two,] male and female entered the ark with Noah, just as the LORD had commanded him. **10**As soon as the seven days were over, the waters of the flood came upon the earth.

11†In the six hundredth year of Noah's life, in the second month, on the seventeenth day of the month: it was on that day that

All the fountains of the great abyss burst forth,
    and the floodgates of the sky were opened.

12For forty days and forty nights heavy rain poured down on the earth.

13On the precise day named, Noah and his sons Shem, Ham, and Japheth, and Noah's wife, and the three wives of Noah's sons had entered the ark, **14**together with every kind of wild beast, every kind of domestic animal, every kind of creeping thing of the earth, and every kind of bird. **15**Pairs of all creatures in which there was the breath of life entered the ark with Noah. **16**Those that entered were male and female, and of all species they came, as God had commanded Noah. Then the LORD shut him in.

17The flood continued upon the earth for forty days. As the waters increased, they lifted the ark, so that it rose above the earth. **18**The swelling waters increased greatly, but the ark floated on the surface of the waters. **19**Higher and higher above the earth rose the waters, until all the highest mountains everywhere were submerged, **20**the crest rising fifteen cubits higher than the submerged mountains. **21***All creatures that stirred on earth perished: birds, cattle, wild animals, and all that swarmed on the earth, as well as all mankind. **22**Everything on dry land with the faintest breath of life in its nostrils died out. **23**The LORD wiped out every living thing on earth: man and cattle, the creeping things and the birds of the air; all were wiped out from the earth. Only Noah and those with him in the ark were left. **24**The waters maintained their crest over the earth for one hundred and fifty days,

8 **1**and then God remembered Noah and all the animals, wild and tame, that were with him in the ark. So God made a wind sweep over the earth, and the waters began to subside. **2**The fountains of the abyss and the floodgates of the sky were closed, and the downpour from the sky was held back. **3**Gradually the waters receded from the earth. At the end of one hundred and fifty days, the waters had so diminished **4**†that, in the seventh month, on the seventeenth day of the month, the ark came to rest on the mountains of Ararat. **5**The waters continued to diminish until the tenth month, and on the first day of the tenth month the tops of the mountains appeared.

6†At the end of forty days Noah opened the hatch he had made in the ark, **7**and he sent out a raven, to see if the waters had lessened on the earth. It flew back and forth until the waters dried off from the earth. **8**Then he sent out a dove, to see if the waters had lessened on the earth. **9**But the dove could find no place to alight and perch, and it returned to him in the ark, for there was water all over the earth. Putting out his hand, he caught the dove and drew it back to him inside the ark. **10**He waited seven days more and again sent the dove out from the ark. **11**In the evening the dove came back to him, and there in its bill was a plucked-off olive leaf! So Noah knew that the waters had lessened on the earth. **12**He waited still another seven days and then released the dove once more; and this time it did not come back.

13In the six hundred and first year of Noah's life, in the first month, on the first day of the month, the water began to dry up on the earth. Noah then removed the covering of the ark and saw that the surface of the ground was drying up. In the second month, on the twenty-seventh day of the month, the earth was dry.

15Then God said to Noah: **16**"Go out of the ark, together with your wife and your sons and your sons' wives. **17***Bring out with you every living thing that is with you—all bodily creatures, be they birds or animals or creeping things of the earth—and let them abound on the earth, breeding and multiplying on it."

---

†   7, 11: *Abyss:* the subterranean ocean; see note on 1, 2.

8, 4: *Ararat:* ancient Urartu, north of the Mesopotamian plain, part of modern Armenia.

8, 6: In the original Yahwist source, from which this verse is taken, the forty days refer to the full period of the flood itself (cf 7, 4.17); in the present context, however, they seem to refer to a period following the date just given in v 5 from the Priestly source.

❋
    7/1: Wis 10, 4; Sir 44, 17;   9: 6, 19.
         2 Pt 2, 5.   21ff: Jb 22, 16; Mt 24, 39;
      4: 6, 17; 2 Pt 2, 5.   Lk 17, 27; 2 Pt 3, 6.
      7: Wis 14, 6; 1 Pt 3, 20;   8/17: 1, 22.28.
         2 Pt 2, 5.

¹⁸So Noah came out, together with his wife and his sons and his sons' wives; ¹⁹and all the animals, wild and tame, all the birds, and all the creeping creatures of the earth left the ark, one kind after another.

²⁰Then Noah built an altar to the LORD, and choosing from every clean animal and every clean bird, he offered holocausts on the altar. ²¹*†When the LORD smelled the sweet odor, he said to himself: "Never again will I doom the earth because of man, since the desires of man's heart are evil from the start; nor will I ever again strike down all living beings, as I have done.

²²*As long as the earth lasts,
    seedtime and harvest,
    cold and heat,
Summer and winter,
    and day and night
    shall not cease."

Covenant with Noah

9 ¹*GOD blessed Noah and his sons and said to them: "Be fertile and multiply and fill the earth. ²Dread fear of you shall come upon all the animals of the earth and all the birds of the air, upon all the creatures that move about on the ground and all the fishes of the sea; into your power they are delivered. ³*†Every creature that is alive shall be yours to eat; I give them all to you as I did the green plants. ⁴*†Only flesh with its lifeblood still in it you shall not eat. ⁵*For your own lifeblood, too, I will demand an accounting: from every animal I will demand it, and from man in regard to his fellow man I will demand an accounting for human life.

⁶*If anyone sheds the blood of man,
    by man shall his blood be shed;
For in the image of God
    has man been made.

⁷*Be fertile, then, and multiply; abound on earth and subdue it."

⁸God said to Noah and to his sons with him: ⁹*"See, I am now establishing my covenant with you and your descendants after you ¹⁰and with every living creature that was with you: all the birds, and the various tame and wild animals that were with you and came out of the ark. ¹¹*I will establish my covenant with you, that never again shall all bodily creatures be destroyed by the waters of a flood; there shall not be another flood to devastate the earth." ¹²God added: "This is the sign that I am giving for all ages to come, of the covenant between me and you and every living creature with you: ¹³*I set my bow in the clouds to serve as a sign of the covenant between me and the earth. ¹⁴When I bring clouds over the earth, and the bow appears in the clouds, ¹⁵*I will recall the covenant I have made between me and you and all living beings, so that the waters shall never again become a flood to destroy all mortal beings. ¹⁶As the bow appears in the clouds, I will see it and recall the everlasting covenant that I have established between God and all living beings— all mortal creatures that are on earth." ¹⁷God told Noah: "This is the sign of the covenant I have established between me and all mortal creatures that are on earth."

Noah and His Sons

¹⁸*†The sons of Noah who came out of the ark were Shem, Ham, and Japheth. (Ham was the father of Canaan.) ¹⁹These three were the sons of Noah, and from them the whole earth was peopled.

²⁰Now Noah, a man of the soil, was the first to plant a vineyard. ²¹*When he drank some of the wine, he became drunk and lay naked inside his tent. ²²Ham, the father of Canaan, saw his father's nakedness, and he told his two brothers outside about it. ²³Shem and Japheth, however, took a robe, and holding it on their backs, they walked backward and covered their father's nakedness; since their faces were turned the other way, they did not see their father's nakedness. ²⁴When Noah woke up from his drunkenness and learned what his youngest son had done to him, ²⁵*he said:

"Cursed be Canaan!
    The lowest of slaves
    shall he be to his brothers."

²⁶†He also said:

"Blessed be the LORD, the God of Shem!
    Let Canaan be his slave.

✱

21: Sir 44, 18; Is 54, 9; Rom 7, 18.
22: Jer 33, 20.25.
9/1: 1, 22.28; 8, 17; Jas 3, 7.
3: 1, 29f; Dt 12, 15.
4: Lv 7, 26f; 17, 4; Dt 12, 16.23; 1 Sm 14, 33; Acts 15, 20.
5: 4, 10f; Ex 21, 12.
6: 1, 26f; Lv 24, 17; Nm 35, 33; Jas 3, 9.
7: 1, 28; 8, 17; 9, 2.
9: 6, 18.
11: Sir 44, 18; Is 54, 9.
13: Sir 43, 12.
15: Is 54, 9.
18: 5, 32; 10, 1.
21: Lam 4, 21; Heb 2, 15.
25: Dt 27, 16; Wis 12, 11.

---

† 8, 21: *From the start:* literally "from his youth." It is uncertain whether this means from the beginning of the human race or from the early years of the individual.

9, 3: Antediluvian creatures, including man, are depicted as vegetarians (1, 29f), becoming carnivorous only after the flood.

9, 4: Because a living being dies when it loses most of its blood, the ancients regarded blood as the seat of life, and therefore as sacred. Although in itself the prohibition against eating meat with blood in it is comparable to the ritual laws of the Mosaic code, the Jews considered it binding on all men, because it was given by God to Noah, the new ancestor of all mankind; therefore the early Christian Church retained it for a time (Acts 15, 20.29).

9, 18-27: This story seems to be a composite of two earlier accounts; in the one, Ham was guilty, whereas in the other, it was Canaan. One purpose of the story is to justify the Israelites' enslavement of the Canaanites because of certain indecent sexual practices in the Canaanite religion. Obviously the story offers no justification for enslaving African Negroes, even though Canaan is presented as a "son" of Ham because the land of Canaan belonged to Hamitic Egypt at the time of the Israelite invasion.

9, 26: *Blessed . . . Shem:* Perhaps the text read originally, "Blessed of the LORD be Shem," which would be expected in the context.

27†May God expand Japheth,
so that he dwells among the tents of Shem;
and let Canaan be his slave."

28Noah lived three hundred and fifty years after the flood. **29**The whole lifetime of Noah was nine hundred and fifty years; then he died.

Table of the Nations

10 **1**†THESE are the descendants of Noah's sons, Shem, Ham, and Japheth, to whom sons were born after the flood.

2*†The descendants of Japheth:
Gomer, Magog, Madai, Javan, Tubal, Meshech, and Tiras.
3†The descendants of Gomer:
Ashkenaz, Riphath, and Togarmah.
4†The descendants of Javan:
Elishah, Tarshish, the Kittim, and the Rodanim.

5These are the descendants of Japheth, and from them sprang the maritime nations, in their respective lands—each with its own language—by their clans within their nations.

6†The descendants of Ham:
Cush, Mizraim, Put, and Canaan.
7The descendants of Cush:
Seba, Havilah, Sabtah, Raamah, and Sabteca.
The descendants of Raamah:
Sheba and Dedan.

8†Cush became the father of Nimrod, who was the first potentate on earth. **9**He was a mighty hunter by the grace of the LORD; hence the saying, "Like Nimrod, a mighty hunter by the grace of the LORD." **10**†The chief cities of his kingdom were Babylon, Erech, and Accad, all of them in the land of Shinar. **11**†From that land he went forth to Asshur, where he built Nineveh, Rehoboth-Ir, and Calah, **12**†as well as Resen, between Nineveh and Calah, the latter being the principal city.

13*Mizraim became the father of the Ludim, the Anamim, the Lehabim, the Naphtuhim, **14**†the Pathrusim, the Casluhim, and the Caphtorim from whom the Philistines sprang.

15†Canaan became the father of Sidon, his first-born, and of Heth; **16**also of the Jebusites, the Amorites, the Girgashites, **17**the Hivites, the Arkites, the Sinites, **18**the Arvadites, the Zemarites, and the Hamathites. Afterward, the clans of the Canaanites spread out, **19**†so that the Canaanite borders extended from Sidon all the way to Gerar, near Gaza, and all the way to Sodom, Gomorrah, Admah, and Zeboiim, near Lasha.

20These are the descendants of Ham, according to their clans and languages, by their lands and nations.

21To Shem also, Japheth's oldest brother and the ancestor of all the children of Eber, sons were born.

22*The descendants of Shem:
Elam, Asshur, Arpachshad, Lud, and Aram.
23The descendants of Aram:
Uz, Hul, Gether, and Mash.

24Arpachshad became the father of Shelah, and Shelah became the father of Eber. **25**†To Eber two sons were born: the name of the first was Peleg, for in his time the world was divided; and the name of his brother was Joktan.

26Joktan became the father of Almodad, Sheleph, Hazarmaveth, Jerah, **27**Hadoram, Uzal, Diklah, **28**Obal, Abimael, Sheba, **29**Ophir, Havilah, and Jobab. All these were descendants of Joktan. **30**Their settlements extended all the way to Sephar, the eastern hill country.

31These are the descendants of Shem, according to their clans and languages, by their lands and nations.

---

† 9, 27: In the Hebrew text there is a play on the words *yapt* ("expand") and *yepet* ("Japheth").

10, 1-32: This chapter presents a remarkably good classification of the various peoples known to the ancient Israelites; it is theologically important as stressing the basic family unity of all men on earth. The relationship between the various peoples is based partly on linguistic, partly on geographic, partly on political grounds *according to their . . . languages, . . . lands and nations* (v 31). In general, *the descendants of Japheth* (vv 2-5) are the peoples of the Indo-European languages to the north and west of Mesopotamia and Syria; *the descendants of Ham* (vv 6-20) are the Hamitic-speaking peoples of northern Africa; and *the descendants of Shem* (vv 21-31) are the Semitic-speaking peoples of Mesopotamia, Syria and Arabia. But there are many exceptions to this rule; the Semitic-speaking peoples of Canaan, for instance, are considered descendants of Ham, because at the time they were subject to Hamitic Egypt (vv 6.15-19). This chapter is a composite from the Yahwist source (vv 8-19.21.24-30) of about the ninth century B. C., and the Priestly source (vv 1-7.20.22f.31f) of a few centuries later. That is why certain tribes of Arabia are listed under both Ham (v 7) and Shem (vv 26ff).

10, 2: *Gomer:* the Cimmerians; *Madai:* the Medes; *Javan:* the Greeks.

10, 3: *Ashkenaz:* the Scythians.

10, 4: *Elishah:* Cyprus; *the Kittim:* certain inhabitants of Cyprus; *the Rodanim:* the inhabitants of Rhodes.

10, 6: *Cush:* Biblical Ethiopia, modern Nubia; *Mizraim:* Egypt; *Put:* either Punt in East Africa or Libya.

10, 8: *Cush:* here, the Kassites; see note on 2, 10-14. *Nimrod:* probably Tukulti-Ninurta I (thirteenth century B. C.), the first Assyrian conqueror of Babylonia and a famous city-builder at home.

10, 10: *Shinar:* ancient Sumer in southern Mesopotamia, mentioned also in 11, 2; 14, 1.

10, 11: *Asshur:* Assyria. *Rehoboth-Ir:* literally "wide-streets city," was probably not the name of another city, but an epithet of Nineveh; cf Jon 3, 3.

10, 12: *Calah:* Assyrian Kalhu, the capital of Assyria in the ninth century B. C.

10, 14: *The Pathrusim:* the people of upper (southern) Egypt; cf Is 11, 11; Jer 44, 1; Ez 29, 14; 30, 14. *Caphtorim:* Crete; for Caphtor as the place of origin of the Philistines, cf Dt 2, 23; Am 9, 7; Jer 47, 4.

10, 15: *Heth:* the biblical Hittites; see note on Gn 23, 3.

10, 19: *Lasha:* the reading of this name is uncertain; perhaps it should be "Bela"; cf 14, 2.

10, 25: In the Hebrew text there is a play on the name *Peleg* and the word *niplega*, "was divided."

---

* 10/2-8: 1 Chr 1, 5-10.   13-18: 1 Chr 1, 11-16.
    2: Ez 38, 2.   22-29: 1 Chr 1, 17-23.

³²These are the groupings of Noah's sons, according to their origins and by their nations. From these the other nations of the earth branched out after the flood.

The Tower of Babel

11 ¹†THE whole world spoke the same language, using the same words. ²†While men were migrating in the east, they came upon a valley in the land of Shinar and settled there. ³They said to one another, "Come, let us mold bricks and harden them with fire." They used bricks for stone, and bitumen for mortar. ⁴†Then they said, "Come, let us build ourselves a city and a tower with its top in the sky, and so make a name for ourselves; otherwise we shall be scattered all over the earth."

⁵The Lord came down to see the city and the tower that the men had built. ⁶Then the Lord said: "If now, while they are one people, all speaking the same language, they have started to do this, nothing will later stop them from doing whatever they presume to do. ⁷Let us then go down and there confuse their language, so that one will not understand what another says." ⁸Thus the Lord scattered them from there all over the earth, and they stopped building the city. ⁹†That is why it was called Babel, because there the Lord confused the speech of all the world. It was from that place that he scattered them all over the earth.

The Line from Shem to Abraham

¹⁰⁑†This is the record of the descendants of Shem. When Shem was one hundred years old, he became the father of Arpachshad, two years after the flood. ¹¹Shem lived five hundred years after the birth of Arpachshad, and he had other sons and daughters.

¹²†When Arpachshad was thirty-five years old, he became the father of Shelah. ¹³Arpachshad lived four hundred and three years after the birth of Shelah, and he had other sons and daughters.

¹⁴When Shelah was thirty years old, he became the father of Eber. ¹⁵Shelah lived four hundred and three years after the birth of Eber, and he had other sons and daughters.

¹⁶†When Eber was thirty-four years old, he became the father of Peleg. ¹⁷Eber lived four hundred and thirty years after the birth of Peleg, and he had other sons and daughters.

¹⁸When Peleg was thirty years old, he became the father of Reu. ¹⁹Peleg lived two hundred and nine years after the birth of Reu, and he had other sons and daughters.

²⁰When Reu was thirty-two years old, he became the father of Serug. ²¹Reu lived two hundred and seven years after the birth of Serug, and he had other sons and daughters.

²²When Serug was thirty years old, he became the father of Nahor. ²³Serug lived two hundred years after the birth of Nahor, and he had other sons and daughters.

²⁴When Nahor was twenty-nine years old, he became the father of Terah. ²⁵Nahor lived one hundred and nineteen years after the birth of Terah, and he had other sons and daughters.

²⁶⁑When Terah was seventy years old, he became the father of Abram, Nahor and Haran.

II: THE PATRIARCH ABRAHAM

Terah

²⁷THIS IS THE RECORD of the descendants of Terah. Terah became the father of Abram, Nahor, and Haran, and Haran became the father of Lot. ²⁸†Haran died before his father Terah, in his native land, in Ur of the Chaldeans. ²⁹⁑Abram and Nahor took wives; the name of Abram's wife was Sarai, and the name of Nahor's wife was Milcah, daughter of Haran, the father of Milcah and Iscah. ³⁰Sarai was barren; she had no child.

³¹⁑†Terah took his son Abram, his grandson Lot, son of Haran, and his daughter-in-law Sarai, the wife of his son Abram, and brought them out of Ur of the

11, 1-9: This story, based on traditions about the temple towers or ziggurats of Babylonia, is used by the sacred writer primarily to illustrate man's increasing wickedness, shown here in his presumptuous effort to create an urban culture apart from God. The secondary motive in the story is to present an imaginative origin of the diversity of languages among the various peoples inhabiting the earth, as well as an artificial explanation of the name "Babylon."

11, 2: Shinar: see note on 10, 10.

11, 4: Tower with its top in the sky: a direct reference to the chief ziggurat of Babylon, the E-sag-ila, signifying "the house that raises high its head." Babylonian ziggurats were the earliest skyscrapers.

11, 9: Babel: the Hebrew form of the name "Babylon"; the native name, Bab-ili, means "gate of the gods." The Hebrew word balil, "he confused," has a similar sound. Apparently the name referred originally only to a certain part of the city, the district near the gate that led to the temple area.

11, 10-26: This section is a continuation of the genealogical record given in 5, 1-32; see note there. Although the ages of the patriarchs in this list are much lower than those of the antediluvian patriarchs, they are still artificial and devoid of historical value. The ages given here are from the current Hebrew text; the Samaritan and Greek texts have divergent sets of numbers in most cases.

11, 12: The Greek text has a certain Kenan (cf 5, 9f) between Arpachshad and Shelah. This text is followed in Lk 3, 36.

11, 16: Eber: the eponymous ancestor of the Hebrews, "descendants of Eber" (10, 21.24-30); see note on 14, 13.

11, 28: Ur of the Chaldeans: Ur was an extremely ancient city of the Sumerians (later, of the Babylonians) in southern Mesopotamia. The Greek text has "the land of the Chaldeans." In either case, the term Chaldeans is an anachronism, because the Chaldeans were not known to history until approximately a thousand years after Abraham's time.

11, 31: The Samaritan and Greek texts include Nahor and his wife in Terah's migration to Haran. Although this is probably due to scribal harmonization, Nahor's family actually did migrate to Haran; cf 24, 10; 27, 43.

11/10-26: 1 Chr 1, 24-27; Lk 3, 34ff.
26: Jos 24, 2; 1 Chr 1, 27.
29: 17, 15; 20, 12.
31: Jos 24, 3; Neh 9, 7; Jdt 5, 6-9; Acts 7, 4.

Chaldeans, to go to the land of Canaan. But when they reached Haran, they settled there. **32**†The lifetime of Terah was two hundred and five years; then Terah died in Haran.

Abram's Call and Migration

12 **1***THE LORD said to Abram: "Go forth from the land of your kinsfolk and from your father's house to a land that I will show you.

2*"I will make of you a great nation,
    and I will bless you;
I will make your name great,
    so that you will be a blessing.
3*†I will bless those who bless you
    and curse those who curse you.
All the communities of the earth
    shall find blessing in you."

4*Abram went as the LORD directed him, and Lot went with him. Abram was seventy-five years old when he left Haran. **5**†Abram took his wife Sarai, his brother's son Lot, all the possessions that they had accumulated, and the persons they had acquired in Haran, and they set out for the land of Canaan. When they came to the land of Canaan, **6**Abram passed through the land as far as the sacred place at Shechem, by the terebinth of Moreh. (The Canaanites were then in the land.)
7*The LORD appeared to Abram and said, "To your descendants I will give this land." So Abram built an altar there to the LORD who had appeared to him. **8**From there he moved on to the hill country east of Bethel, pitching his tent with Bethel to the west and Ai to the east. He built an altar there to the LORD and invoked the LORD by name. **9**†Then Abram journeyed on by stages to the Negeb.

Abram and Sarai in Egypt

10*There was famine in the land; so Abram went down to Egypt to sojourn there, since the famine in the land was severe. **11**When he was about to enter Egypt, he said to his wife Sarai: "I know well how beautiful a woman you are. **12**When the Egyptians see you, they will say, 'She is his wife'; then they will kill me, but let you live. **13***†Please say, therefore, that you are my sister, so that it may go well with me on your account and my life may be spared for your sake." **14**When Abram came to Egypt, the Egyptians saw how beautiful the woman was; **15**and when Pharaoh's courtiers saw her, they praised her to Pharaoh. So she was taken into Pharaoh's palace. **16**†On her account it went very well with Abram, and he received flocks and herds, male and female slaves, male and female asses, and camels.

17*But the LORD struck Pharaoh and his household with severe plagues because of Abram's wife Sarai. **18**Then Pharaoh summoned Abram and said to him: "How could you do this to me! Why didn't you tell me she was your wife? **19**Why did you say, 'She is my sister,' so that I took her for my wife? Here, then, is your wife. Take her and be gone!" **20**Then Pharaoh gave men orders concerning him, and they sent him on his way, with his wife and all that belonged to him.

Abram and Lot Part

13 **1***FROM Egypt Abram went up to the Negeb with his wife and all that belonged to him, and Lot accompanied him. **2***Now Abram was very rich in livestock, silver, and gold. **3**From the Negeb he traveled by stages toward Bethel, to the place between Bethel and Ai where his tent had formerly stood, **4***the site where he had first built the altar; and there he invoked the LORD by name.

5Lot, who went with Abram, also had flocks and herds and tents, **6**so that the land could not support them if they stayed together; their possessions were so great that they could not dwell together. **7**There were quarrels between the herdsmen of Abram's livestock and those of Lot's. (At this time the Canaanites and the Perizzites were occupying the land.)

8So Abram said to Lot: "Let there be no strife between you and me, or between your herdsmen and mine, for we are kinsmen. **9**Is not the whole land at your disposal? Please separate from me. If you prefer

---

† 11, 32: Since Terah was seventy years old when his son Abraham was born (v 26), and Abraham was seventy-five when he left Haran (12, 4), Terah lived in Haran for sixty years after Abraham's departure. According to the tradition in the Samaritan text, Terah died when he was one hundred and forty-five years old, therefore, in the same year in which Abraham left Haran. This is the tradition followed in St. Stephen's speech: Abraham left Haran "after his father's death" (Acts 7, 4).

12, 3: *Shall find blessing in you:* the sense of the Hebrew expression is probably reflexive, "shall bless themselves through you" (i. e., in giving a blessing they shall say, "May you be as blessed as Abraham"), rather than passive, "shall be blessed in you." Since the term is understood in a passive sense in the New Testament (Acts 3, 25; Gal. 3, 8), it is rendered here by a neutral expression that admits of both meanings. So also in the blessings given by God to Isaac (26, 4) and Jacob (28, 14).

12, 5: *Persons:* slaves and retainers that formed the social aggregate under the leadership of Abraham; cf 14, 14.

12, 9: *The Negeb:* the semidesert land of southern Palestine.

12, 13: *You are my sister:* although Abraham's deceit may not be fully defensible, his statement was at least a half-truth; Sarah was indeed his relative, called "a sister" in Hebrew; cf 20, 12. Moreover, the ancient traditions on which this story and the parallel ones in 20, 1-18 and 26, 6-11 are based, probably come from the Hurrian custom of wife-sister marriage. Among the Hurrians, with whom Abraham's clan lived in close contact at Haran, a man could adopt his wife as his sister and thus give her higher status.

12, 16: *Camels:* domesticated camels probably did not come into common use in the ancient Near East until the end of the second millennium B. C. Thus the mention of camels at the time of the patriarchs (24, 11-64; 30, 43; 31, 17.34; 32, 8.16; 37, 25) is seemingly an anachronism.

❋
12/1: Acts 7, 3; Heb 11, 8.
  2: 17, 6; Sir 44, 20;
    Rom 4, 17-22.
  3: 18, 18; 22, 18;
    Acts 3, 25; Gal 3, 8.
  4f: 11, 31; Jos 24, 3;
    Acts 7, 4.

  7: Ex 33, 1; Dt 34, 4;
    Acts 7, 5.
  10: 26, 1.
  13: 20, 12f; 26, 7.
  17: Ps 105, 14.
13/1: 12, 9.
  2: Ps 112, 1ff; Prv 10, 22.
  4: 12, 8.

the left, I will go to the right; if you prefer the right, I will go to the left." ¹⁰Lot looked about and saw how well watered the whole Jordan Plain was as far as Zoar, like the Lord's own garden, or like Egypt. (This was before the Lord had destroyed Sodom and Gomorrah.) ¹¹Lot, therefore, chose for himself the whole Jordan Plain and set out eastward. Thus they separated from each other; ¹²Abram stayed in the land of Canaan, while Lot settled among the cities of the Plain, pitching his tents near Sodom. ¹³*Now the inhabitants of Sodom were very wicked in the sins they committed against the Lord.

¹⁴*After Lot had left, the Lord said to Abram: "Look about you, and from where you are, gaze to the north and south, east and west; ¹⁵*all the land that you see I will give to you and your descendants forever. ¹⁶*I will make your descendants like the dust of the earth; if anyone could count the dust of the earth, your descendants too might be counted. ¹⁷Set forth and walk about in the land, through its length and breadth, for to you I will give it." ¹⁸*Abram moved his tents and went on to settle near the terebinth of Mamre, which is at Hebron. There he built an altar to the Lord.

The Four Kings

14 ¹†IN the days of . . . , Amraphel king of Shinar, Arioch king of Ellasar, Chedorlaomer king of Elam, and Tidal king of Goiim ²made war on Bera king of Sodom, Birsha king of Gomorrah, Shinab king of Admah, Shemeber king of Zeboiim, and the king of Bela (that is, Zoar). ³†All the latter kings joined forces in the Valley of Siddim (that is, the Salt Sea). ⁴For twelve years they had been subject to Chedorlaomer, but in the thirteenth year they rebelled. ⁵†In the fourteenth year Chedorlaomer and the kings allied with him came and defeated the Rephaim in Ashteroth-karnaim, the Zuzim in Ham, the Emim in Shaveh-kiriathaim, ⁶*and the Horites in the hill country of Seir, as far as El-paran, close by the wilderness. ⁷They then turned back and came to Enmishpat (that is, Kadesh), and they subdued the whole country both of the Amalekites and of the Amorites who dwelt in Hazazon-tamar. ⁸Thereupon the king of Sodom, the king of Gomorrah, the king of Admah, the king of Zeboiim, and the king of Bela (that is, Zoar) marched out, and in the Valley of Siddim they went into battle against them: ⁹against Chedorlaomer king of Elam, Tidal king of Goiim, Amraphel king of Shinar, and Arioch king of Ellasar—four kings against five. ¹⁰Now the Valley of Siddim was full of bitumen pits; and as the kings of Sodom and Gomorrah fled, they fell into these, while the rest fled to the mountains. ¹¹The victors seized all the possessions and food supplies of Sodom and Gomorrah and then went their way,

¹²*taking with them Abram's nephew Lot, who had been living in Sodom, as well as his possessions.

¹³†A fugitive came and brought the news to Abram the Hebrew, who was camping at the terebinth of Mamre the Amorite, a kinsman of Eshcol and Aner; these were in league with Abram. ¹⁴When Abram heard that his nephew had been captured, he mustered three hundred and eighteen of his retainers, born in his house, and went in pursuit as far as Dan. ¹⁵He and his party deployed against them at night, defeated them, and pursued them as far as Hobah, which is north of Damascus. ¹⁶He recovered all the possessions, besides bringing back his kinsman Lot and his possessions, along with the women and the other captives.

¹⁷When Abram returned from his victory over Chedorlaomer and the kings who were allied with him, the king of Sodom went out to greet him in the Valley of Shaveh (that is, the King's Valley). ¹⁸*†Melchizedek, king of Salem, brought out bread and wine, and being a priest of God Most High, he blessed Abram with these words:

¹⁹†"Blessed be Abram by God Most High,
        the creator of heaven and earth;
²⁰†And blessed be God Most High,
        who delivered your foes into your hand."

Then Abram gave him a tenth of everything.

²¹The king of Sodom said to Abram, "Give me the people; the goods you may keep." ²²But Abram replied to the king of Sodom: "I have sworn to the Lord, God Most High, the creator of heaven and earth, ²³that I would not take so much as a thread or a sandal strap

---

† 14, 1: *In the days of . . . :* the personal name by which the event is dated has not been preserved.

14, 3: *The Salt Sea:* now known as the Dead Sea.

14, 5f: The five kings came from north to south through the land east of the Jordan.

14, 13: *Abram the Hebrew:* elsewhere in the Old Testament, until the last pre-Christian centuries, the term "Hebrew" is used only by non-Israelites, or by Israelites in speaking to foreigners, since it evidently had a disparaging connotation—something like "immigrant." The account in this chapter may, therefore, have been taken originally from a non-Israelite source, in which Abraham, a warlike sheik of Palestine, appears as a truly historical figure of profane history.

14, 18: *Salem:* traditionally identified with Jerusalem (Ps 76, 3), but the Hebrew text is not certain; instead of the present *melek shalem* ("king of Salem"), the original may have been *melek shelomo* ("a king allied to him"). In Heb 7, 2, "king of Salem" is interpreted as "king of peace" (*shalom*).

14, 19: *God Most High:* in Hebrew, *el-elyon.* In Canaanite texts, each element may occur separately as the name of a specific deity, or they may be applied together to a single deity, as is done here by the Canaanite priest Melchizedek. For the Israelites, *el* became a poetic synonym for *elohim* ("God"); *elyon* ("Most High") became one of the titles of their God Yahweh.

14, 20: *Abram gave him:* literally "he gave him"; but *Abram* is to be understood as the subject of the sentence, for the tithes were the tenth part assigned to priests; cf Heb 7, 4-10.

14, 22: Abraham uses the name of the Canaanite god *el-elyon* ("God the Most High") in apposition to the name of his God, *yahweh* ("the Lord").

✼ 13: 18, 20; Ez 16, 49;
        2 Pt 2, 6ff; Jude 1, 7.
14: 28, 14.
15: 12, 7; Mt 5, 4;
        Lk 1, 55; Acts 7, 5;
        Gal 3, 16.
16: 22, 17; Nm 23, 10.
18: 14, 13.
14/6: Dt 2, 12.
12: 13, 10ff.
18: Ps 110, 4; Heb 5,
        6.10; 7, 1.

from anything that is yours, lest you should say, 'I made Abram rich.' ²⁴Nothing for me except what my servants have used up and the share that is due to the men who joined me—Aner, Eshcol and Mamre; let them take their share."

The Covenant with Abram

15 ¹SOME time after these events, this word of the LORD came to Abram in a vision:

"Fear not, Abram!
I am your shield;
I will make your reward very great."

²But Abram said, 'O Lord GOD, what good will your gifts be, if I keep on being childless and have as my heir the steward of my house, Eliezer?" ³Abram continued, "See, you have given me no offspring, and so one of my servants will be my heir." ⁴*Then the word of the LORD came to him: "No, that one shall not be your heir; your own issue shall be your heir." ⁵*He took him outside and said: "Look up at the sky and count the stars, if you can. Just so," he added, "shall your descendants be." ⁶*†Abram put his faith in the LORD, who credited it to him as an act of righteousness.

⁷*He then said to him, "I am the LORD who brought you from Ur of the Chaldeans to give you this land as a possession." ⁸"O Lord GOD," he asked, "how am I to know that I shall possess it?" ⁹*†He answered him, "Bring me a three-year-old heifer, a three-year-old she-goat, a three-year-old ram, a turtledove, and a young pigeon." ¹⁰He brought him all these, split them in two, and placed each half opposite the other; but the birds he did not cut up. ¹¹Birds of prey swooped down on the carcasses, but Abram stayed with them. ¹²As the sun was about to set, a trance fell upon Abram, and a deep, terrifying darkness enveloped him.

¹³*Then the LORD said to Abram: "Know for certain that your descendants shall be aliens in a land not their own, where they shall be enslaved and oppressed for four hundred years. ¹⁴*But I will bring judgment on the nation they must serve, and in the end they will depart with great wealth. ¹⁵You, however, shall join your forefathers in peace; you shall be buried at a contented old age. ¹⁶*†In the fourth time-span the others shall come back here; the wickedness of the Amorites will not have reached its full measure until then."

¹⁷†When the sun had set and it was dark, there appeared a smoking brazier and a flaming torch, which passed between those pieces. ¹⁸*†It was on that occasion that the LORD made a covenant with Abram, saying: "To your descendants I give this land, from the Wadi of Egypt to the Great River [the Euphrates], ¹⁹*the land of the Kenites, the Kenizzites, the Kadmonites, ²⁰the Hittites, the Perizzites, the Rephaim, ²¹the Amorites, the Canaanites, the Girgashites, and the Jebusites."

Birth of Ishmael

16 ¹*†ABRAM's wife Sarai had borne him no children. She had, however, an Egyptian maidservant named Hagar. ²*Sarai said to Abram: "The LORD has kept me from bearing children. Have intercourse, then, with my maid; perhaps I shall have sons through her." Abram heeded Sarai's request. ³Thus, after Abram had lived ten years in the land of Canaan, his wife Sarai took her maid, Hagar the Egyptian, and gave her to her husband Abram to be his concubine. ⁴*He had intercourse with her, and she became pregnant. When she became aware of her pregnancy, she looked on her mistress with disdain. ⁵*So Sarai said to Abram: "You are responsible for this outrage against me. I myself gave my maid to your embrace; but ever since she became aware of her pregnancy, she has been looking on me with disdain. May the LORD decide between you and me!" ⁶Abram told Sarai: "Your maid is in your power. Do to her whatever you please." Sarai then abused her so much that Hagar ran away from her.

⁷*†The LORD's messenger found her by a spring in the wilderness, the spring on the road to Shur, ⁸and he asked, "Hagar, maid of Sarai, where have you come from and where are you going?" She answered, "I am running away from my mistress, Sarai." ⁹But the LORD's messenger told her: "Go back to your mistress and submit to her abusive treatment. ¹⁰*I will make your descendants so numerous," added the LORD's messen-

---

⁑	
15/4: 17, 16.	Acts 13, 20; Gal 3, 17.
5: 22, 17; 28, 14;	14: Ex 32, 13; Dt 1, 10;
Ex 32, 13; Dt 1, 10;	16: 1 Kgs 21, 26.
Sir 44, 21; Rom 4, 18;	18: Ex 32, 13; Neh 9, 8;
Heb 11, 12.	Ps 105, 11; Sir 44, 21.
6: 1 Mc 2, 52;	19f: Dt 7, 1.
Rom 4, 3.9.22;	16/1: 11, 30.
Gal 3, 6f; Jas 2, 23.	2: 21, 8f; Gal 4, 22.
7: 11, 31; 12, 1;	4: Sm 1, 6; Prv 30, 23.
Ex 32, 13; Neh 9, 7f;	5-16: 21, 10-19.
Acts 7, 2f.	7: Ex 15, 22.
9: Lv 1, 14.	10: 17, 20; 21, 13.18;
13: Ex 12, 40; Nm 20, 15;	25, 12-18.
Jdt 5, 9f; Is 52, 4;	

---

†   15, 6: Abraham's *faith* in God's promises was regarded as *an act of righteousness,* i. e., as expressing the "right" attitude of man toward God. In turn, God credited this to Abraham, i. e., gave him title to the fulfillment of God's promises. St. Paul (Rom 4, 1-25; Gal 3, 6-9) makes Abraham's faith a model for that of Christians.

15, 9: *Three-year-old:* ritually mature.

15, 16: *Time-span:* the Hebrew term *dor* is commonly rendered as "generation," but it may signify a period of varying length. Neither this passage nor the statement about the four hundred years has any value for determining how long the Israelites were in Egypt.

15, 17: *Brazier:* literally "oven"; a portable one is meant here. The smoke and fire represent God's presence. Although the text does not mention it, Abraham no doubt also walked between the split carcasses. For the meaning of this strange ceremony, see note on Jer 38, 18ff.

15, 18: *Made a covenant:* literally "cut a covenant"; the expression derives from the ceremony of cutting the animals in two.

16, 1-6: Sarah's actions are all in keeping with the laws of the time, as known from ancient extra-biblical sources.

16, 7: *The Lord's messenger:* a manifestation of God in human form; therefore in v 13 the messenger is identified with the Lord himself.

ger, "that they will be too many to count. ¹¹†Besides," the LORD's messenger said to her:

"You are now pregnant and shall bear a son;
  you shall name him Ishmael,
For the LORD has heard you,
  God has answered you,
¹²*He shall be a wild ass of a man,
  his hand against everyone,
  and everyone's hand against him;
In opposition to all his kin
  shall he encamp."

¹³*†To the LORD who spoke to her she gave a name, saying, "You are the God of Vision"; she meant, "Have I really seen God and remained alive after my vision?" ¹⁴†That is why the well is called Beer-lahai-roi. It is between Kadesh and Bered.

¹⁵*Hagar bore Abram a son, and Abram named the son whom Hagar bore him Ishmael. ¹⁶Abram was eighty-six years old when Hagar bore him Ishmael.

Covenant of Circumcision

17 ¹*†WHEN Abram was ninety-nine years old, the LORD appeared to him and said: "I am God the Almighty. Walk in my presence and be blameless. ²*Between you and me I will establish my covenant, and I will multiply you exceedingly."

³When Abram prostrated himself, God continued to speak to him: ⁴*"My covenant with you is this: you are to become the father of a host of nations. ⁵*†No longer shall you be called Abram; your name shall be Abraham, for I am making you the father of a host of nations. ⁶I will render you exceedingly fertile; I will make nations of you; kings shall stem from you. ⁷*I will maintain my covenant with you and your descendants after you throughout the ages as an everlasting pact, to be your God and the God of your descendants after you. ⁸*I will give to you and to your descendants after you the land in which you are now staying, the whole land of Canaan, as a permanent possession; and I will be their God."

⁹God also said to Abraham: "On your part, you and your descendants after you must keep my covenant throughout the ages. ¹⁰*This is my covenant with you and your descendants after you that you must keep: every male among you shall be circumcised. ¹¹*Circumcise the flesh of your foreskin, and that shall be the mark of the covenant between you and me. ¹²*Throughout the ages, every male among you, when he is eight days old, shall be circumcised, including

houseborn slaves and those acquired with money from any foreigner who is not of your blood. ¹³Yes, both the houseborn slaves and those acquired with money must be circumcised. Thus my covenant shall be in your flesh as an everlasting pact. ¹⁴If a male is uncircumcised, that is, if the flesh of his foreskin has not been cut away, such a one shall be cut off from his people; he has broken my covenant."

¹⁵†God further said to Abraham: "As for your wife Sarai, do not call her Sarai; her name shall be Sarah. ¹⁶*I will bless her, and I will give you a son by her. Him also will I bless; he shall give rise to nations, and rulers of peoples shall issue from him." ¹⁷*†Abraham prostrated himself and laughed as he said to himself, "Can a child be born to a man who is a hundred years old? Or can Sarah give birth at ninety?" ¹⁸Then Abraham said to God, "Let but Ishmael live on by your favor!" ¹⁹*God replied: "Nevertheless, your wife Sarah is to bear you a son, and you shall call him Isaac. I will maintain my covenant with him as an everlasting pact, to be his God and the God of his descendants after him. ²⁰*As for Ishmael, I am heeding you: I hereby bless him. I will make him fertile and will multiply him exceedingly. He shall become the father of twelve chieftains, and I will make of him a great nation. ²¹*But my covenant I will maintain with Isaac, whom Sarah shall bear to you by this time next year." ²²When he had finished speaking with him, God departed from Abraham.

²³Then Abraham took his son Ishmael and all his slaves, whether born in his house or acquired with his money—every male among the members of Abraham's household—and he circumcised the flesh of their foreskins on that same day, as God had told him to do. ²⁴*Abraham was ninety-nine years old when the flesh of his foreskin was circumcised, ²⁵and his son Ishmael was thirteen years old when the flesh of his foreskin was circumcised. ²⁶Thus, on that same day Abraham and his son Ishmael were circumcised; ²⁷and all the male members of his household, including the slaves born in his house or acquired with his money from foreigners, were circumcised with him.

---

† 16, 11: *Ishmael:* in Hebrew the name means "God has heard."

16, 13: *The God of Vision:* in Hebrew, *el-roi;* hence the name of the spring. *Remained alive:* for the ancient notion that a person died on seeing God, cf 32, 31; Ex 20, 19; Dt 4, 33; Jgs 13, 22.

16, 14: *Beer-lahai-roi:* probably "the well of living sight," i. e., the well where one can see (God) and yet live.

17, 1: *The Almighty:* traditional but incorrect rendering of the divine title *shaddai,* of uncertain meaning.

17, 5: *Abram* and *Abraham* are merely two forms of the same name, both meaning, "the father is exalted"; another variant form is Abiram (Nm 16, 1; 1 Kgs 16, 34). The additional *-ha-* in the form Abraham is explained by folk etymology as coming from *ab-hamon goyim,* "father of a host of nations."

17, 15: *Sarai* and *Sarah* are variant forms of the same name, both meaning "princess."

17, 17: *Laughed: yishaq,* which is the Hebrew form of the name "Isaac"; other similar explanations of the name are given in 18, 12 and 21, 6.

✶
12: 21, 20; 25, 18.
13: 24, 62.
15: 16, 2; Gal 4, 22.
17/1: 35, 11; Ex 6, 3.
2: 12, 2; 13, 16;
    Ex 32, 13.
4: Sir 44, 21; Rom 4, 17.
5: Neh 9, 7.
7: Ps 105, 42; Lk 1, 72f;
    Gal 3, 16.
8: Ex 32, 13; Dt 1, 8;
    14, 2; Lk 1, 55;
    Acts 7, 5.

10: Jn 7, 22; Acts 7, 8;
    Rom 4, 11.
11: Sir 44, 21.
12: Lv 12, 3;
    Lk 1, 59; 2, 21.
16: 18, 10; Gal 4, 23.
17: Rom 4, 19; Heb 11, 11f.
19: 11, 30; 21, 2; Ex 32,
    13; Sir 44, 22.
20: 16, 10; 21, 13.18;
    25, 12-16.
21: 18, 14; 21, 2; 26, 2-5;
    Rom 9, 7.
24: 17, 10; Rom 4, 11.

Abraham's Visitors

18 ¹THE LORD appeared to Abraham by the terebinth of Mamre, as he sat in the entrance of his tent, while the day was growing hot. ²*Looking up, he saw three men standing nearby. When he saw them, he ran from the entrance of the tent to greet them; and bowing to the ground, ³†he said: "Sir, if I may ask you this favor, please do not go on past your servant. ⁴Let some water be brought, that you may bathe your feet, and then rest yourselves under the tree. ⁵Now that you have come this close to your servant, let me bring you a little food, that you may refresh yourselves; and afterward you may go on your way." "Very well," they replied, "do as you have said."

⁶†Abraham hastened into the tent and told Sarah, "Quick, three seahs of fine flour! Knead it and make rolls." ⁷He ran to the herd, picked out a tender, choice steer, and gave it to a servant, who quickly prepared it. ⁸†Then he got some curds and milk, as well as the steer that had been prepared, and set these before them; and he waited on them under the tree while they ate.

⁹"Where is your wife Sarah?" they asked him. "There in the tent," he replied. ¹⁰*†One of them said, "I will surely return to you about this time next year, and Sarah will then have a son." Sarah was listening at the entrance of the tent, just behind him. ¹¹*Now Abraham and Sarah were old, advanced in years, and Sarah had stopped having her womanly periods. ¹²†So Sarah laughed to herself and said, "Now that I am so withered and my husband is so old, am I still to have sexual pleasure?" ¹³But the LORD said to Abraham: "Why did Sarah laugh and say, 'Shall I really bear a child, old as I am?' ¹⁴*Is anything too marvelous for the LORD to do? At the appointed time, about this time next year, I will return to you, and Sarah will have a son." ¹⁵Because she was afraid, Sarah dissembled, saying, "I didn't laugh." But he said, "Yes you did."

Abraham Intercedes for Sodom

¹⁶The men set out from there and looked down toward Sodom; Abraham was walking with them, to see them on their way. ¹⁷The LORD reflected: "Shall I hide from Abraham what I am about to do, ¹⁸*now that he is to become a great and populous nation, and all the nations of the earth are to find blessing in him? ¹⁹Indeed, I have singled him out that he may direct his sons and his posterity to keep the way of the LORD by doing what is right and just, so that the LORD may carry into effect for Abraham the promises he made

about him." ²⁰*†Then the LORD said: "The outcry against Sodom and Gomorrah is so great, and their sin so grave, ²¹that I must go down and see whether or not their actions fully correspond to the cry against them that comes to me. I mean to find out."

²²While the two men walked on farther toward Sodom, the LORD remained standing before Abraham. ²³Then Abraham drew nearer to him and said: "Will you sweep away the innocent with the guilty? ²⁴Suppose there were fifty innocent people in the city; would you wipe out the place, rather than spare it for the sake of the fifty innocent people within it? ²⁵*Far be it from you to do such a thing, to make the innocent die with the guilty, so that the innocent and the guilty would be treated alike! Should not the judge of all the world act with justice?" ²⁶The LORD replied, "If I find fifty innocent people in the city of Sodom, I will spare the whole place for their sake." ²⁷*Abraham spoke up again: "See how I am presuming to speak to my Lord, though I am but dust and ashes! ²⁸What if there are five less than fifty innocent people? Will you destroy the whole city because of those five?" "I will not destroy it," he answered, "if I find forty-five there." ²⁹But Abraham persisted, saying, "What if only forty are found there?" He replied, "I will forbear doing it for the sake of the forty." ³⁰Then he said, "Let not my Lord grow impatient if I go on. What if only thirty are found there?" He replied, "I will forbear doing it if I can find but thirty there." ³¹Still he went on, "Since I have thus dared to speak to my Lord, what if there are no more than twenty?" "I will not destroy it," he answered, "for the sake of the twenty." ³²*But he still persisted: "Please, let not my Lord grow angry if I speak up this last time. What if there are at least ten there?" "For the sake of those ten," he replied, "I will not destroy it."

³³The LORD departed as soon as he had finished speaking with Abraham, and Abraham returned home.

---

† 18, 3: Abraham addresses the leader of the group, whom he does not yet recognize as Yahweh; in the next two verses he speaks to all *three men*. The other two are later (19, 1) identified as messengers.

18, 6: *Three seahs:* one ephah, about half a bushel.

18, 8: *Curds:* a type of soft cheese or yoghurt.

18, 10: *One of them:* i. e., the Lord. Abraham now realizes this for the first time when he hears the prediction of a miraculous birth. *About this time next year:* literally "when the time becomes alive," i. e., at the time when birth is due after the period of gestation; the conception is understood as taking place soon after the prediction.

18, 12: *Sarah laughed:* see note on 17, 17.

18, 20: Israelite tradition was unanimous in ascribing the destruction of Sodom and Gomorrah to the wickedness of these cities, but tradition varied in regard to the nature of this wickedness. According to the present account of the Yahwist, the sin of Sodom was homosexuality (19, 4f), which is therefore also known as sodomy; but according to Isaiah (1, 9f; 3, 9), it was a lack of social justice; Ezekiel (16, 46-51) described it as a disregard for the poor, whereas Jeremiah (23, 14) saw it as general immorality.

✻ 18/2: Heb 13, 1f.
10: 17, 19; 21, 1;
2 Kgs 4, 16; Rom 9, 9.
11: 17, 17; Rom 4, 19;
Heb 11, 11f.
14: Mt 19, 26; Mk 10, 27;
Lk 1, 37; 18, 27;
Rom 4, 21.

18: Lk 1, 55.
20: 19, 13; Is 3, 9;
Lk 17, 28; Jude 1, 7.
25: Dt 32, 4; Jb 8, 3.20;
Wis 12, 15.
27: Sir 10, 9; 17, 27.
32: Jer 5, 1; Ez 22, 30.

Destruction of Sodom and Gomorrah

19 ¹THE two angels reached Sodom in the evening, as Lot was sitting at the gate of Sodom. When Lot saw them, he got up to greet them; and bowing down with his face to the ground, ²*†he said, "Please, gentlemen, come aside into your servant's house for the night, and bathe your feet; you can get up early to continue your journey." But they replied, "No, we shall pass the night in the town square." ³He urged them so strongly, however, that they turned aside to his place and entered his house. He prepared a meal for them, baking cakes without leaven, and they dined.

⁴*Before they went to bed, all the townsmen of Sodom, both young and old—all the people to the last man—closed in on the house. ⁵They called to Lot and said to him, "Where are the men who came to your house tonight? Bring them out to us that we may have intimacies with them." ⁶Lot went out to meet them at the entrance. When he had shut the door behind him, ⁷he said, "I beg you, my brothers, not to do this wicked thing. ⁸I have two daughters who have never had intercourse with men. Let me bring them out to you, and you may do to them as you please. But don't do anything to these men, for you know they have come under the shelter of my roof." ⁹*They replied, "Stand back! This fellow," they sneered, "came here as an immigrant, and now he dares to give orders! We'll treat you worse than them!" With that, they pressed hard against Lot, moving in closer to break down the door. ¹⁰But his guests put out their hands, pulled Lot inside with them, and closed the door; ¹¹†at the same time they struck the men at the entrance of the house, one and all, with such a blinding light that they were utterly unable to reach the doorway.

¹²*†Then the angels said to Lot: "Who else belongs to you here? Your sons [sons-in-law] and your daughters and all who belong to you in the city—take them away from it! ¹³*We are about to destroy this place, for the outcry reaching the LORD against those in the city is so great that he has sent us to destroy it." ¹⁴†So Lot went out and spoke to his sons-in-law, who had contracted marriage with his daughters. "Get up and leave this place," he told them; "the LORD is about to destroy the city." But his sons-in-law thought he was joking.

¹⁵As dawn was breaking, the angels urged Lot on, saying, "On your way! Take with you your wife and your two daughters who are here, or you will be swept away in the punishment of the city." ¹⁶When he hesitated, the men, by the LORD's mercy, seized his hand and the hands of his wife and his two daughters and led them to safety outside the city. ¹⁷*As soon as they had been brought outside, he was told: "Flee for your life! Don't look back or stop anywhere on the Plain. Get off to the hills at once, or you will be swept away." ¹⁸"Oh, no, my lord!" replied Lot. ¹⁹"You have already thought enough of your servant to do me the great kindness of intervening to save my life. But I cannot flee to the hills to keep the disaster from overtaking me, and so I shall die. ²⁰†Look, this town ahead is near enough to escape to. It's only a small place. Let me flee there—it's a small place, isn't it?—that my life may be saved." ²¹"Well, then," he replied, "I will also grant you the favor you now ask. I will not overthrow the town you speak of. ²²*Hurry, escape there! I cannot do anything until you arrive there." That is why the town is called Zoar.

²³*The sun was just rising over the earth as Lot arrived in Zoar; ²⁴*at the same time the LORD rained down sulphurous fire upon Sodom and Gomorrah [from the LORD out of heaven]. ²⁵*†He overthrew those cities and the whole Plain, together with the inhabitants of the cities and the produce of the soil. ²⁶*But Lot's wife looked back, and she was turned into a pillar of salt.

²⁷Early the next morning Abraham went to the place where he had stood in the LORD's presence. ²⁸*†As he looked down toward Sodom and Gomorrah and the whole region of the Plain, he saw dense smoke over the land rising like fumes from a furnace.

²⁹Thus it came to pass: when God destroyed the Cities of the Plain, he was mindful of Abraham by sending Lot away from the upheaval by which God overthrew the cities where Lot had been living.

Moabites and Ammonites

³⁰†Since Lot was afraid to stay in Zoar, he and his two daughters went up from Zoar and settled in the

---

† 19, 2: *Gentlemen:* Lot does not yet know that the distinguished-looking men are God's messengers; cf 18, 3.

19, 11: *Blinding light:* a preternatural flash that temporarily dazed the wicked men and revealed to Lot the true nature of his guests.

19, 12: Since Lot apparently had no *sons,* a glossator interpreted the term to mean *sons-in-law.*

19, 14: It is uncertain whether Lot's *sons-in-law* were fully married to his daughters or only "engaged" to them (Israelite "engagement" was the first part of the marriage ceremony), or even whether the daughters involved were the same as, or different from, the two daughters who were still in their father's house.

19, 20: *A small place:* the Hebrew word *misar,* literally "a little thing," has the same root consonants as the name of the town *Zoar* in v 22.

19, 25: *Overthrew:* The consistent use of this term, literally "turned upside down," to describe the destruction of the Cities of the Plain seems to imply that their upheaval (v 29) was caused primarily by an earthquake; this would naturally be accompanied by a disastrous fire, especially in a region containing bitumen (14, 10) and its accompanying gases.

19, 28f: From the height east of Hebron, Abraham could easily see the region at the southern end of the Dead Sea, where the *Cities of the Plain* were probably located.

19, 30-38: This Israelite tale about the origin of Israel's neighbors east of the Jordan and the Dead Sea was told partly in the

✿
19/2: Wis 10, 6; Sir 16, 8;
     Ez 16, 50; Heb 13, 1f.
4-9: Jgs 19, 22-25;
     Jude 1, 7.
9: 13, 12; 2 Pt 2, 7f.
12: 2 Pt 7, 9.
13: Is 1, 7.9; Zep 2, 9;
     Lk 17, 29.
17: Wis 10, 6.

22: Wis 10, 6.
23: Pss 9, 6; 11, 6; 107, 34.
24: Wis 10, 7; Is 1, 9;
     13, 19; Lam 4, 6;
     17, 29; 2 Pt 2, 6.
25: Dt 29, 22; Jer 50, 40;
     Am 4, 11.
26: Wis 10, 7; Lk 17, 32.
28: Rv 9, 2; 14, 10f.

hill country, where he lived with his two daughters in a cave. [31]The older one said to the younger: "Our father is getting old, and there is not a man on earth to unite with us as was the custom everywhere. [32]Come, let us ply our father with wine and then lie with him, that we may have offspring by our father." [33]So that night they plied their father with wine, and the older one went in and lay with her father; but he was not aware of her lying down or her getting up.

[34]Next day the older one said to the younger: "Last night it was I who lay with my father. Let us ply him with wine again tonight, and then you go in and lie with him, that we may both have offspring by our father." [35]So that night, too, they plied their father with wine, and then the younger one went in and lay with him; but again he was not aware of her lying down or her getting up.

[36]Thus both of Lot's daughters became pregnant by their father. [37]*†The older one gave birth to a son whom she named Moab, saying, "From my father." He is the ancestor of the Moabites of today. [38]*†The younger one, too, gave birth to a son, and she named him Ammon, saying, "The son of my kin." He is the ancestor of the Ammonites of today.

Abraham at Gerar

20 [1]†ABRAHAM journeyed on to the region of the Negeb, where he settled between Kadesh and Shur. While he stayed in Gerar, [2]he said of his wife Sarah, "She is my sister." So Abimelech, king of Gerar, sent and took Sarah. [3]But God came to Abimelech in a dream one night and said to him, "You are about to die because of the woman you have taken, for she has a husband." [4]Abimelech, who had not approached her, said: "O Lord, would you slay a man even though he is innocent? [5]He himself told me, 'She is my sister,' and she herself also stated, 'He is my brother.' I did it in good faith and with clean hands." [6]God answered him in the dream: "Yes, I know you did it in good faith. In fact, it was I who kept you from sinning against me; that is why I did not let you touch her. [7]†Therefore, return the man's wife—as a spokesman he will intercede for you—that your life may be saved. If you do not return her, you can be sure that you and all who are yours will certainly die."

[8]Early the next morning Abimelech called all his court officials and informed them of everything that had happened, and the men were horrified. [9]Then Abimelech summoned Abraham and said to him: "How could you do this to us! What wrong did I do to you that you should have brought such monstrous guilt on me and my kingdom? You have treated me in an intolerable way. [10]What were you afraid of," he asked him, "that you should have done such a thing?" [11]"I was afraid," answered Abraham, "because I thought there would surely be no fear of God in this place, and so they would kill me on account of my wife. [12]*Besides, she is in truth my sister, but only my father's daughter, not my mother's; and so she became my wife. [13]When God sent me wandering from my father's house, I asked her: 'Would you do me this favor? In whatever place we come to, say that I am your brother.'"

[14]Then Abimelech took flocks and herds and male and female slaves and gave them to Abraham; and after he restored his wife Sarah to him, [15]he said, "Here, my land lies at your disposal; settle wherever you please." [16]†To Sarah he said: "See, I have given your brother a thousand shekels of silver. Let that serve you as a vindication before all who are with you; your honor has been preserved with everyone." [17]Abraham then interceded with God, and God restored health to Abimelech, that is, to his wife and his maidservants, so that they could bear children; [18]for God had tightly closed every womb in Abimelech's household on account of Abraham's wife Sarah.

Birth of Isaac

21 [1]*THE LORD took note of Sarah as he had said he would; he did for her as he had promised. [2]*Sarah became pregnant and bore Abraham a son in his old age, at the set time that God had stated. [3]*Abraham gave the name Isaac to this son of his whom Sarah bore him. [4]*When his son Isaac was eight days old, Abraham circumcised him, as God had commanded. [5]Abraham was a hundred years old when his son Isaac was born to him. [6]*Sarah then said, "God has given me cause to laugh, and all who hear of it will laugh with me. [7]Who would have told Abraham," she added, "that Sarah would nurse children! Yet I have borne him a son in his old age." [8]Isaac grew, and on the day of the child's weaning, Abraham held a great feast.

[9]†Sarah noticed the son whom Hagar the Egyptian had borne to Abraham playing with her son Isaac; [10]*so she demanded of Abraham: "Drive out that slave and her son! No son of that slave is going to share the inheritance with my son Isaac!" [11]Abraham was greatly distressed, especially on account of his son

---

† to ridicule these racially related but rival nations and partly to give folk etymologies for their names.

19, 37: *From my father:* in Hebrew, *meabi,* similar in sound to the name "Moab."

19, 38: *The son of my kin:* in Hebrew, *ben-ammi,* similar in sound to the name "Ammonites."

20, 1-18: This story from the Elohist source (see note on 4, 25) combines elements found in the two very similar but distinct stories of the Yahwist source, in 12, 10-20 and 26, 6-11.

20, 7: *Spokesman:* the Hebrew term *nabi* used here is regularly translated as "prophet," but it simply means "one who speaks on behalf of another," whether the latter is God, as in almost all cases, or another man, as in Ex 4, 16.

20, 16: *A thousand shekels of silver:* not a gift distinct from that of the animals and the slaves (v 14), but the monetary value of these.

21, 9-19: This story of Hagar's expulsion, in the Elohist source, is in general a duplicate of the one from the Yahwist source in 16, 5-14; but the two stories differ greatly in detail.

---

*
37: Dt 2, 9.
38: Dt 2, 19.
20/12: 12, 13.
21/1: 17, 19; 18, 10.
2: Gal 4, 23; Heb 11, 11.

3: Mt 1, 2; Lk 3, 34.
4: 17, 10ff; Acts 7, 8.
6: 17, 17.
10: Jgs 11, 2; Gal 4, 30.

Ishmael. **12***But God said to Abraham: "Do not be distressed about the boy or about your slave woman. Heed the demands of Sarah, no matter what she is asking of you; for it is through Isaac that descendants shall bear your name. **13**As for the son of the slave woman, I will make a great nation of him also, since he too is your offspring."

14†Early the next morning Abraham got some bread and a skin of water and gave them to Hagar. Then, placing the child on her back, he sent her away. As she roamed aimlessly in the wilderness of Beer-sheba, **15**the water in the skin was used up. So she put the child down under a shrub, **16**and then went and sat down opposite him, about a bowshot away; for she said to herself, "Let me not watch the child die." As she sat opposite him, he began to cry. **17***God heard the boy's cry, and God's messenger called to Hagar from heaven: "What is the matter, Hagar? Don't be afraid; God has heard the boy's cry in this plight of his. **18**Arise, lift up the boy and hold him by the hand; for I will make of him a great nation." **19**Then God opened her eyes, and she saw a well of water. She went and filled the skin with water, and then let the boy drink.

20God was with the boy as he grew up. He lived in the wilderness and became an expert bowman, **21**with his home in the wilderness of Paran. His mother got a wife for him from the land of Egypt.

The Pact at Beer-sheba

22†About that time Abimelech, accompanied by Phicol, the commander of his army, said to Abraham: "God is with you in everything you do. **23**†Therefore, swear to me by God at this place that you will not deal falsely with me or with my progeny and posterity, but will act as loyally toward me and the land in which you stay as I have acted toward you." **24**To this Abraham replied, "I so swear."

25Abraham, however, reproached Abimelech about a well that Abimelech's men had seized by force. **26**"I have no idea who did that," Abimelech replied. "In fact, you never told me about it, nor did I ever hear of it until now."

27Then Abraham took sheep and cattle and gave them to Abimelech and the two made a pact. **28**Abraham also set apart seven ewe lambs of the flock, **29**and Abimelech asked him, "What is the purpose of these seven ewe lambs that you have set apart?" **30**Abraham answered, "The seven ewe lambs you shall accept from me that thus I may have your acknowledgment that the well was dug by me." **31**†This is why the place is called Beer-sheba; the two took an oath there. **32**When they had thus made the pact in Beer-sheba, Abimelech, along with Phicol, the commander of his army, left and returned to the land of the Philistines.

33†Abraham planted a tamarisk at Beer-sheba, and there he invoked by name the Lord, God the Eternal.

34Abraham resided in the land of the Philistines for many years.

The Testing of Abraham

22 **1***†SOME time after these events, God put Abraham to the test. He called to him, "Abraham!" "Ready!" he replied. **2***†Then God said: "Take your son Isaac, your only one, whom you love, and go to the land of Moriah. There you shall offer him up as a holocaust on a height that I will point out to you." **3**Early the next morning Abraham saddled his donkey, took with him his son Isaac, and two of his servants as well, and with the wood that he had cut for the holocaust, set out for the place of which God had told him.

4On the third day Abraham got sight of the place from afar. **5**Then he said to his servants: "Both of you stay here with the donkey, while the boy and I go on over yonder. We will worship and then come back to you." **6**Thereupon Abraham took the wood for the holocaust and laid it on his son Isaac's shoulders, while he himself carried the fire and the knife. As the two walked on together, **7**Isaac spoke to his father Abraham. "Father!" he said. "Yes, son," he replied. Isaac continued, "Here are the fire and the wood, but where is the sheep for the holocaust?" **8**"Son," Abraham answered, "God himself will provide the sheep for the holocaust." Then the two continued going forward.

9*When they came to the place of which God had told him, Abraham built an altar there and arranged the wood on it. Next he tied up his son Isaac, and put him on top of the wood on the altar. **10***Then he reached out and took the knife to slaughter his son. **11**But the Lord's messenger called to him from heaven, "Abraham, Abraham!" "Yes, Lord," he answered.

---

† 21, 14: *Placing the child on her back:* the phrase is translated from an emended form of the Hebrew text. In the current faulty Hebrew text, Abraham put the bread and the waterskin on Hagar's back, while her son apparently walked beside her. This reading seems to be a scribal attempt at harmonizing the present passage with the data of the Priestly source, in which Ishmael would have been at least fourteen years old when Isaac was born; compare 16, 16 with 21, 5; cf 17, 25. But in the present Elohist story Ishmael is obviously a litle boy, not much older than Isaac; cf vv 15.18.

21, 22: Here and in v 32 the Greek text has ". . . Abimelech, accompanied by Ahuzzath, his councilor, and Phicol . . . "; but this is probably a secondary harmonization with 26, 26. Abimelech took Phicol with him in order to intimidate Abraham by a show of strength.

21, 23: *This place:* Beer-sheba (v 31). Abimelech had come from Gerar (20, 2), about thirty miles west of Beer-sheba.

21, 31: *Beer-sheba:* the Hebrew name really means, "the well of the seven," i. e., the place where there are seven wells, alluded to in the episode of the *seven ewe lambs,* vv 28ff; but it can also be interpreted to mean "the well of the oath."

21, 33: *God the Eternal:* in Hebrew, *el olam,* perhaps the name of the deity of the pre-Israelite sanctuary at Beer-sheba, but used by Abraham merely as a title of Yahweh; cf Is 40, 28.

22, 1: *God put Abraham to the test:* to prove the firmness of Abraham's faith in God's promise that through Isaac all the nations of the earth would find blessing; cf 18, 10.18; 21, 12.

22, 2: *Only one:* uniquely precious, especially loved; therefore the same term is rendered in vv 12.17 as "beloved."

❋
    12: Rom 9, 7; Heb 11, 18.   2: 2 Chr 3, 1; 1
    17: 16, 7.   Mc 2, 52; Heb 11, 17.
    22/1: Sir 44, 20.   9: Jas 2, 21.
                                        10: Wis 10, 5.

12*"Do not lay your hand on the boy," said the messenger. "Do not do the least thing to him. I know now how devoted you are to God, since you did not withhold from me your own beloved son." **13**As Abraham looked about, he spied a ram caught by its horns in the thicket. So he went and took the ram and offered it up as a holocaust in place of his son. **14**†Abraham named the site Yahweh-yireh; hence people now say, "On the mountain the LORD will see."

15Again the LORD's messenger called to Abraham from heaven **16***and said: "I swear by myself, declares the LORD, that because you acted as you did in not withholding from me your beloved son, **17***I will bless you abundantly and make your descendants as countless as the stars of the sky and the sands of the seashore; your descendants shall take possession of the gates of their enemies, **18***and in your descendants all the nations of the earth shall find blessing—all this because you obeyed my command."

19Abraham then returned to his servants, and they set out together for Beer-sheba, where Abraham made his home.

Nahor's Descendants

20†Some time afterward, the news came to Abraham: "Milcah too has borne sons, to your brother Nahor: **21**Uz, his first-born, his brother Buz, Kemuel (the father of Aram), **22**Chesed, Hazo, Pildash, Jidlaph, and Bethuel." **23**Bethuel became the father of Rebekah. These eight Milcah bore to Abraham's brother Nahor. **24**His concubine, whose name was Reumah, also bore children: Tebah, Gaham, Tahash, and Maacah.

Purchase of a Burial Place

23 1THE span of Sarah's life was one hundred and twenty-seven years. **2**She died in Kiriath-arba (that is, Hebron) in the land of Canaan, and Abraham performed the customary mourning rites for her. **3**†Then he left the side of his dead one and addressed the Hittites: **4***†"Although I am a resident alien among you, sell me from your holdings a piece of property for a burial ground, that I may bury my dead wife." **5**The Hittites answered Abraham: "Please, sir, **6**listen to us! You are an elect of God among us. Bury your dead in the choicest of our burial sites. None of us would deny you his burial ground for the burial of your dead." **7**Abraham, however, began to bow low before the local citizens, the Hittites, **8**while he appealed to them: "If you will allow me room for burial of my dead, listen to me! Intercede for me with Ephron, son of Zohar, asking him **9**to sell me the cave of Machpelah that he owns; it is at the edge of his field. Let him sell it to me in your presence, at its full price, for a burial place."

10†Now Ephron was present with the Hittites. So Ephron the Hittite replied to Abraham in the hearing of the Hittites who sat on his town council: **11**"Please, sir, listen to me! I give you both the field and the cave in it; in the presence of my kinsmen I make this gift. Bury your dead!" **12**But Abraham, after bowing low before the local citizens, addressed Ephron in the hearing of these men: **13**"Ah, if only you would please listen to me! I will pay you the price of the field. Accept it from me, that I may bury my dead there." **14**Ephron replied to Abraham, "Please, **15**†sir, listen to me! A piece of land worth four hundred shekels of silver—what is that between you and me, as long as you can bury your dead?" **16***†Abraham accepted Ephron's terms; he weighed out to him the silver that Ephron had stipulated in the hearing of the Hittites, four hundred shekels of silver at the current market value.

17*Thus Ephron's field in Machpelah, facing Mamre, together with its cave and all the trees anywhere within its limits, was conveyed **18**to Abraham by purchase in the presence of all the Hittites who sat on Ephron's town council. After this transaction, **19**Abraham buried his wife Sarah in the cave of the field of Machpelah, facing Mamre (that is, Hebron) in the land of Canaan. **20**Thus the field with its cave was transferred from the Hittites to Abraham as a burial place.

Isaac and Rebekah

24 1ABRAHAM had now reached a ripe old age, and the LORD had blessed him in every way. **2***†Abraham said to the senior servant of his

---

† 22, 14: *Yahweh-yireh:* a Hebrew expression meaning "the Lord will see"; the reference is to the words in v 8, "God himself will see to it."

22, 20-24: A list of Aramean tribes who lived to the east and northeast of Israel, twelve in number, like the twelve tribes of Israel (35, 23) and the twelve tribes of Ishmael (25, 12-16).

23, 3: *The Hittites:* a non-Semitic people in Canaan; their relationship to the well-known Hittites of Asia Minor is uncertain.

23, 4: *A resident alien:* literally "a sojourner and a settler," i. e., a long-term resident alien. Such a one would normally not have the right to own property. The importance of Abraham's purchase of the field in Machpelah, which is worded in technical legal terms, lies in the fact that it gave his descendants their first, though small, land rights in the country that God had promised the patriarch they would one day inherit as their own. Abraham therefore insists on purchasing the field and not receiving it as a gift.

23, 10: *Who sat on his town council:* probable meaning of the literal translation, "who came in at the gate of his city"; so also in v 18.

23, 15: *Four hundred shekels:* probably an exorbitant sum; Jeremiah (32, 9) paid only seventeen shekels for his field in Anathoth, though the Babylonian invasion no doubt helped to reduce the price.

23, 16: *The current market value:* the standard weight called a shekel varied according to time and place.

24, 2: *Put your hand under my thigh:* the symbolism of this act was apparently connected with the Hebrew concept of children issuing from their father's "thigh" (46, 26; Ex 1, 5). Perhaps the man who took such an oath was thought to bring the curse of sterility on himself if he did not fulfill his sworn prom-

---

* 12: Rom 8, 32; 1 Jn 4, 9.
16f: 15, 5; Ex 32, 13; Lk 1, 73; Rom 4, 13; Heb 6, 13f; 11, 12.
17: 24, 60.
18: 12, 3; 18, 18; 26, 4; Sir 44, 21; Acts 3, 25; Gal 3, 16.
23/4: 33, 19; Acts 7, 16; Heb 11, 9.
16: Acts 7, 16.
17f: 49, 29f.
24/2f: 47, 29.

household, who had charge of all his possessions: "Put your hand under my thigh, **3*** and I will make you swear by the LORD, the God of heaven and the God of earth, that you will not procure a wife for my son from the daughters of the Canaanites among whom I live, **4** but that you will go to my own land and to my kindred to get a wife for my son Isaac." **5** The servant asked him: "What if the woman is unwilling to follow me to this land? Should I then take your son back to the land from which you migrated?" **6** "Never take my son back there for any reason," Abraham told him. **7*** "The LORD, the God of heaven, who took me from my father's house and the land of my kin, and who confirmed by oath the promise he then made to me, 'I will give this land to your descendants'—he will send his messenger before you, and you will obtain a wife for my son there. **8** If the woman is unwilling to follow you, you will be released from this oath. But never take my son back there!" **9** So the servant put his hand under the thigh of his master Abraham and swore to him in this undertaking.

10† The servant then took ten of his master's camels, and bearing all kinds of gifts from his master, he made his way to the city of Nahor in Aram Naharaim. **11** Near evening, at the time when women go out to draw water, he made the camels kneel by the well outside the city. **12†** Then he prayed: "LORD, God of my master Abraham, let it turn out favorably for me today and thus deal graciously with my master Abraham. **13** While I stand here at the spring and the daughters of the townsmen are coming out to draw water, **14** if I say to a girl, 'Please lower your jug, that I may drink,' and she answers, 'Take a drink, and let me give water to your camels, too,' let her be the one whom you have decided upon for your servant Isaac. In this way I shall know that you have dealt graciously with my master."

15* He had scarcely finished these words when Rebekah (who was born to Bethuel, son of Milcah, the wife of Abraham's brother Nahor) came out with a jug on her shoulder. **16** The girl was very beautiful, a virgin, untouched by man. She went down to the spring and filled her jug. As she came up, **17** the servant ran toward her and said, "Please give me a sip of water from your jug." **18** "Take a drink, sir," she replied, and quickly lowering the jug onto her hand, she gave him a drink. **19** When she had let him drink his fill, she said, "I will draw water for your camels, too, until they have drunk their fill." **20** With that, she quickly emptied her jug into the drinking trough and ran back to the well to draw more water, until she had drawn enough for all the camels. **21** The man watched her the whole time, silently waiting to learn whether or not the LORD had made his errand successful. **22** When the camels had finished drinking, the man took out a gold ring weighing half a shekel, which he fastened on her nose, and

two gold bracelets weighing ten shekels, which he put on her wrists. **23** Then he asked her: "Whose daughter are you? Tell me, please. And is there room in your father's house for us to spend the night?" **24** She answered: "I am the daughter of Bethuel the son of Milcah, whom she bore to Nahor. **25** There is plenty of straw and fodder at our place," she added, "and room to spend the night." **26** The man then bowed down in worship to the LORD, **27** saying: "Blessed be the LORD, the God of my master Abraham, who has not let his constant kindness toward my master fail. As for myself also, the LORD has led me straight to the house of my master's brother."

28 Then the girl ran off and told her mother's household about it. **29*** Now Rebekah had a brother named Laban. **30** As soon as he saw the ring and the bracelets on his sister Rebekah and heard her words about what the man had said to her, Laban rushed outside to the man at the spring. When he reached him, he was still standing by the camels at the spring. **31** So he said to him: "Come, blessed of the LORD! Why are you staying outside when I have made the house ready for you, as well as a place for the camels?" **32** The man then went inside; and while the camels were being unloaded and provided with straw and fodder, water was brought to bathe his feet and the feet of the men who were with him. **33** But when the table was set for him, he said, "I will not eat until I have told my tale." "Do so," they replied.

34 "I am Abraham's servant," he began. **35** "The LORD has blessed my master so abundantly that he has become a wealthy man; he has given him flocks and herds, silver and gold, male and female slaves, and camels and asses. **36** My master's wife Sarah bore a son to my master in her old age, and he has given him everything he owns. **37** My master put me under oath, saying: 'You shall not procure a wife for my son among the daughters of the Canaanites in whose land I live; **38** instead, you shall go to my father's house, to my own relatives, to get a wife for my son.' **39** When I asked my master, 'What if the woman will not follow me?,' **40*** he replied: 'The LORD, in whose presence I have always walked, will send his messenger with you and make your errand successful, and so you will get a wife for my son from my own kindred of my father's house. **41** Then you shall be released from my ban. If you visit my kindred and they refuse you, then, too, you shall be released from my ban.'

42 "When I came to the spring today, I prayed: 'LORD, God of my master Abraham, may it be your will to

---

† ise. Jacob made Joseph swear in the same way (Gn 47, 29). In both these instances, the oath was taken to carry out the last request of a man upon his death.

24, 10: *Nahor:* it is uncertain whether this is to be understood as the name of Abraham's brother (11, 27), Rebekah's grandfather (24, 15), or the city of the same name (as known from the Mari documents): *Aram Naharaim,* situated near Haran (11, 31) in northern Mesopotamia.

24, 12: *Let it turn out favorably for me:* let me have a favorable omen; cf end of v 14.

✿
3: 24, 37; 28, 1f;
   Jgs 14, 3; Tb 4, 12.
7: 12, 7; Ex 6, 8;
   Tb 5, 17; Gal 3, 16.
15: 22, 23.
29: 27, 43.
40: Tb 5, 17; 10, 13.

make successful the errand I am engaged on! **43**While I stand here at the spring, if I say to a young woman who comes out to draw water, Please give me a little water from your jug, **44**and she answers, Not only may you have a drink, but I will give water to your camels, too— let her be the woman whom the Lord has decided upon for my master's son.'

45"I had scarcely finished saying this prayer to myself when Rebekah came out with a jug on her shoulder. After she went down to the spring and drew water, I said to her, 'Please let me have a drink.' **46**She quickly lowered the jug she was carrying and said, 'Take a drink, and let me bring water for your camels, too.' So I drank, and she watered the camels also. **47**When I asked her, 'Whose daughter are you?' she answered, 'The daughter of Bethuel, son of Nahor, borne to Nahor by Milcah.' So I put the ring on her nose and the bracelets on her wrists. **48**Then I bowed down in worship to the Lord, blessing the Lord, the God of my master Abraham, who had led me on the right road to obtain the daughter of my master's kinsman for his son. **49**If, therefore, you have in mind to show true loyalty to my master, let me know; but if not, let me know that, too. I can then proceed accordingly."

50*Laban and his household said in reply: "This thing comes from the Lord; we can say nothing to you either for or against it. **51**Here is Rebekah, ready for you; take her with you, that she may become the wife of your master's son, as the Lord has said." **52**When Abraham's servant heard their answer, he bowed to the ground before the Lord. **53**Then he brought out objects of silver and gold and articles of clothing and presented them to Rebekah; he also gave costly presents to her brother and mother. **54***After he and the men with him had eaten and drunk, they spent the night there.

When they were up the next morning, he said, "Give me leave to return to my master." **55**Her brother and mother replied, "Let the girl stay with us a short while, say ten days; after that she may go." **56**But he said to them, "Do not detain me, now that the Lord has made my errand successful, let me go back to my master." **57**They answered, "Let us call the girl and see what she herself has to say about it."

58So they called Rebekah and asked her, "Do you wish to go with this man?" She answered, "I do." **59**At this they allowed their sister Rebekah and her nurse to take leave, along with Abraham's servant and his men. **60***Invoking a blessing on Rebekah, they said:

> "Sister, may you grow
>   into thousands of myriads;
> And may your descendants gain possession
>   of the gates of their enemies!"

61Then Rebekah and her maids started out; they mounted their camels and followed the man. So the servant took Rebekah and went on his way.

62*Meanwhile Isaac had gone from Beer-lahai-roi and was living in the region of the Negeb. **63†**One day toward evening he went out . . . in the field, and as he looked around, he noticed that camels were approaching. **64**Rebekah, too, was looking about, and when she saw him, she alighted from her camel **65**and asked the servant, "Who is the man out there, walking through the fields toward us?" "That is my master," replied the servant. Then she covered herself with her veil.

66The servant recounted to Isaac all the things he had done. **67**Then Isaac took Rebekah into his tent; he married her, and thus she became his wife. In his love for her Isaac found solace after the death of his mother Sarah.

Abraham's Sons by Keturah

25 **1*†**ABRAHAM married another wife, whose name was Keturah. **2**She bore him Zimran, Jokshan, Medan, Midian, Ishbak, and Shuah. **3***Jokshan became the father of Sheba and Dedan. The descendants of Dedan were the Asshurim, the Letushim, and the Leummim. **4**The descendants of Midian were Ephah, Epher, Hanoch, Abida, and Eldaah. All of these were descendants of Keturah.

5Abraham deeded everything that he owned to his son Isaac. **6†**To his sons by concubinage, however, he made grants while he was still living, as he sent them away eastward, to the land of Kedem, away from his son Isaac.

Death of Abraham

7The whole span of Abraham's life was one hundred and seventy-five years. **8**Then he breathed his last, dying at a ripe old age, grown old after a full life; and he was taken to his kinsmen. **9***His sons Isaac and Ishmael buried him in the cave of Machpelah, in the field of Ephron, son of Zohar the Hittite, which faces Mamre, **10**the field that Abraham had bought from the Hittites; there he was buried next to his wife Sarah. **11**After the death of Abraham, God blessed his son Isaac, who made his home near Beer-lahai-roi.

Descendants of Ishmael

12These are the descendants of Abraham's son Ishmael, whom Hagar the Egyptian, Sarah's slave, bore to Abraham. **13***These are the names of Ishmael's sons, listed in the order of their birth: Nebaioth (Ishmael's

---

50f: Tb 7, 12.
54: Tb 7, 14; 8, 20.
60: 22, 17.
62: 16, 13f; 25, 11.
25/1-4: 1 Chr 1, 32f.

3: Is 21, 13.
9f: 23, 3-20.
13-16: 1 Chr 1, 29ff.
13: Is 60, 7.

†
24, 63: *He went out:* the meaning of the Hebrew term that follows this is obscure.

25, 1-11: Though mentioned here, Abraham's marriage to a concubine, or wife of secondary rank, and his death are not to be understood as happening chronologically after the events narrated in the preceding chapter.

25, 6: *The land of Kedem:* or "the country of the East," the region inhabited by the Kedemites or Easterners (29, 1; Jgs 6, 3.33; Jb 1, 3; Is 11, 14). The names mentioned in vv 2ff, as far as they can be identified, are those of tribes in the Arabian desert.

first-born), Kedar, Adbeel, Mibsam, ¹⁴Mishma, Dumah, Massa, ¹⁵Hadad, Tema, Jetur, Naphish, and Kedemah. ¹⁶°These are the sons of Ishmael, their names by their villages and encampments; twelve chieftains of as many tribal groups.

¹⁷The span of Ishmael's life was one hundred and thirty-seven years. After he had breathed his last and died, he was taken to his kinsmen. ¹⁸†The Ishmaelites ranged from Havilah-by-Shur, which is on the border of Egypt, all the way to Asshur; and each of them pitched camp in opposition to his various kinsmen.

III: THE PATRIARCHS ISAAC AND JACOB

Birth of Esau and Jacob

¹⁹THIS IS THE FAMILY HISTORY of Isaac, son of Abraham; Abraham had begotten Isaac. ²⁰°Isaac was forty years old when he married Rebekah, the daughter of Bethuel the Aramean of Paddan-aram and the sister of Laban the Aramean. ²¹Isaac entreated the LORD on behalf of his wife, since she was sterile. The LORD heard his entreaty, and Rebekah became pregnant. ²²But the children in her womb jostled each other so much that she exclaimed, "If this is to be so, what good will it do me!" She went to consult the LORD, ²³°and he answered her:

"Two nations are in your womb,
    two peoples are quarreling while still within you;
But one shall surpass the other,
    and the older shall serve the younger."

²⁴°When the time of her delivery came, there were twins in her womb. ²⁵†The first to emerge was reddish, and his whole body was like a hairy mantle; so they named him Esau. ²⁶°†His brother came out next, gripping Esau's heel; so they named him Jacob. Isaac was sixty years old when they were born.

²⁷°As the boys grew up, Esau became a skillful hunter, a man who lived in the open; whereas Jacob was a simple man, who kept to his tents. ²⁸Isaac preferred Esau, because he was fond of game; but Rebekah preferred Jacob. ²⁹Once, when Jacob was cooking a stew, Esau came in from the open, famished. ³⁰†He said to Jacob, "Let me gulp down some of that red stuff; I'm starving." (That is why he was called Edom.) ³¹°†But Jacob replied, "First give me your birthright in exchange for it." ³²"Look," said Esau, "I'm on the point of dying. What good will any birthright do me?" ³³°But Jacob insisted, "Swear to me first!" So he sold Jacob his birthright under oath. ³⁴Jacob then

gave him some bread and the lentil stew; and Esau ate, drank, got up, and went his way. Esau cared little for his birthright.

Isaac and Abimelech

26 ¹°THERE was a famine in the land (distinct from the earlier one that had occurred in the days of Abraham), and Isaac went down to Abimelech, king of the Philistines in Gerar. ²The LORD appeared to him and said: "Do not go down to Egypt, but continue to camp wherever in this land I tell you. ³°Stay in this land, and I will be with you and bless you; for to you and your descendants I will give all these lands, in fulfillment of the oath that I swore to your father Abraham. ⁴°I will make your descendants as numerous as the stars in the sky and give them all these lands, and in your descendants all the nations of the earth shall find blessing—⁵this because Abraham obeyed me, keeping my mandate (my commandments, my ordinances, and my instructions)."

⁶So Isaac settled in Gerar. ⁷When the men of the place asked questions about his wife, he answered, "She is my sister." He was afraid, if he called her his wife, the men of the place would kill him on account of Rebekah, since she was very beautiful. ⁸But when he had been there for a long time, Abimelech, king of the Philistines, happened to look out of a window and was surprised to see Isaac fondling his wife Rebekah. ⁹He called for Isaac and said: "She must certainly be your wife! How could you have said, 'She is my sister'?" Isaac replied, "I thought I might lose my life on her account." ¹⁰"How could you do this to us!" exclaimed Abimelech. "It would have taken very little for one of the men to lie with your wife, and you would have thus brought guilt upon us!" ¹¹Abimelech therefore gave this warning to all his men: "Anyone who molests this man or his wife shall forthwith be put to death."

---

† 25, 18: *Pitched camp:* literally "fell"; the same Hebrew verb is used in Jgs 7, 12 in regard to the hostile encampment of Bedouin tribes. The present passage shows the fulfillment of the prediction contained in Gn 16, 12.

25, 25: *Reddish:* in Hebrew, *admoni*, a reference to Edom, another name for Esau (v 30; 36, 1). Edom, however, was really the name of the country south of Moab where the descendants of Esau lived. It was called the "red" country because of its reddish sandstone. *Hairy:* in Hebrew, *sear*, a reference to Seir, another name for Edom (36, 8). One might expect the text to say, "So they named him Seir"; but Esau (*esaw*) also means "hairy."

25, 26: *Esau's heel:* the Hebrew is *baaqeb esaw*, a reference to the name Jacob; cf 27, 36. Probably, however, the name Jacob has no true etymological connection with the Hebrew word for "heel" (*aqeb*) but is instead a shortened form of some such name as *yaaqob-el* ("may God protect").

25, 30: *Red stuff:* in Hebrew, *adom;* another play on the word "Edom," the "red" land.

25, 31: *Birthright:* the privilege that entitled the first-born son to a position of honor in the family and to a double share in the possessions inherited from the father.

26, 6-11: The Yahwist's version of the wife-sister episode at Gerar; the Elohist's version (20, 1-18) is connected with Abraham and Sarah.

✿
16: 17, 20.
18: 16, 12.
20: 24, 66.
23: 27, 29; Nm 24, 18; Mal 1, 2-5; Rom 9, 11f.
24: Hos 12, 3.
26: Mt 1, 2.
27: 27, 6f.
31: Dt 21, 17.

33: Heb 12, 16.
26/1-14: 12, 10-20.
1: 12, 1.
3: 12, 7; 15, 18; Ex 32, 13; Ps 105, 9; Sir 44, 22; Heb 11, 9.
4: 12, 3; 22, 17f; 28, 14; Ex 32, 13.

¹²†Isaac sowed a crop in that region and reaped a hundredfold the same year. Since the Lᴏʀᴅ blessed him, ¹³*he became richer and richer all the time, until he was very wealthy indeed. ¹⁴He acquired such flocks and herds, and so many work animals, that the Philistines became envious of him. ¹⁵*(The Philistines had stopped up and filled with dirt all the wells that his father's servants had dug back in the days of his father Abraham.) ¹⁶So Abimelech said to Isaac, "Go away from us; you have become far too numerous for us." ¹⁷Isaac left there and made the Wadi Gerar his regular campsite. ¹⁸(Isaac reopened the wells which his father's servants had dug back in the days of his father Abraham and which the Philistines had stopped up after Abraham's death; he gave them the same names that his father had given them.) ¹⁹But when Isaac's servants dug in the wadi and reached spring water in their well, ²⁰†the shepherds of Gerar quarreled with Isaac's servants, saying, "The water belongs to us!" So the well was called Esek, because they had challenged him there. ²¹†Then they dug another well, and they quarreled over that one too; so it was called Sitnah. ²²When he had moved on from there, he dug still another well; but over this one they did not quarrel. It was called Rehoboth, because he said, "The Lᴏʀᴅ has now given us ample room, and we shall flourish in the land."

²³From there Isaac went up to Beer-sheba. ²⁴*The same night the Lᴏʀᴅ appeared to him and said: "I am the God of your father Abraham. You have no need to fear, since I am with you. I will bless you and multiply your descendants for the sake of my servant Abraham." ²⁵So he built an altar there and invoked the Lᴏʀᴅ by name. After he had pitched his tent there, his servants began to dig a well nearby.

²⁶*Abimelech had meanwhile come to him from Gerar, accompanied by Ahuzzath, his councilor, and Phicol, the general of his army. ²⁷Isaac asked them, "Why have you come to me, seeing that you hate me and have driven me away from you?" ²⁸They answered: "We are convinced that the Lᴏʀᴅ is with you, so we propose that there be a sworn agreement between our two sides—between you and us. Let us make a pact with you: ²⁹you shall not act unkindly toward us, just as we have not molested you, but have always acted kindly toward you and have let you depart in peace. Henceforth, "The Lᴏʀᴅ's blessing be upon you!'" ³⁰Isaac then made a feast for them, and they ate and drank. ³¹Early the next morning they exchanged oaths. Then Isaac bade them farewell, and they departed from him in peace.

³²That same day Isaac's servants came and brought him news about the well they had been digging; they told him, "We have reached water!" ³³†He called it Shibah; hence the name of the city, Beer-sheba, to this day.

³⁴*†When Esau was forty years old, he married Judith, daughter of Beeri the Hittite, and Basemath, daughter of Elon the Hivite. ³⁵But they became a cause of embitterment to Isaac and Rebekah.

Jacob's Deception

27 ¹†WHEN Isaac was so old that his eyesight had failed him, he called his older son Esau and said to him, "Son!" "Yes, father!" he replied. ²Isaac then said, "As you can see, I am so old that I may now die at any time. ³Take your gear, therefore—your quiver and bow—and go out into the country to hunt some game for me. ⁴†With your catch prepare an appetizing dish for me, such as I like, and bring it to me to eat, so that I may give you my special blessing before I die."

⁵*Rebekah had been listening while Isaac was speaking to his son Esau. So when Esau went out into the country to hunt some game for his father, ⁶Rebekah said to her son Jacob, "Listen! I overheard your father tell your brother Esau, ⁷'Bring me some game and with it prepare an appetizing dish for me to eat, that I may give you my blessing with the Lᴏʀᴅ's approval before I die.' ⁸Now, son, listen carefully to what I tell you. ⁹Go to the flock and get me two choice kids. With these I will prepare an appetizing dish for your father, such as he likes. ¹⁰Then bring it to your father to eat, that he may bless you before he dies." ¹¹*"But my brother Esau is a hairy man," said Jacob to his mother Rebekah, "and I am smooth-skinned! ¹²Suppose my father feels me? He will think I am making sport of him, and I shall bring on myself a curse in-

13f: Jb 1, 3.
15-24: 21, 25-31.
24: 46, 3.
26-33: 21, 22-31; Prv 16, 7.
34f: 27, 46.
27/5: 25, 28.
11: 25, 25.

† 26, 12-33: The Yahwist's version of the story about the wells at Beer-sheba; again, the Elohist's version (21, 22f) is connected with Abraham. A redactor joined the two accounts by means of the parenthetical verses 15 and 18.
26, 20: Esek: "challenge."
26, 21: Sitnah: "opposition"; one might expect the text to be continued by some such words as "because they were in opposition there."
26, 33: Shibah: "seven," for the sake of a closer assonance with Beer-sheba; but the present version of the story says nothing about there being seven wells there as implied in 21, 28-31. The Greek version understood the Hebrew text more logically as shebua, "oath," in keeping with the present story.
26, 34f: These verses from the Priestly source, which have no logical connection with the preceding stories, serve as an introduction to the following section on Esau's loss of his birthright by suggesting a motivation for this in Isaac's and Rebekah's dislike for Esau's Canaanite wives.
27, 1-45: What Jacob did in deceiving his father and thereby cheating Esau out of Isaac's deathbed blessing is condemned as blameworthy, not only by Hosea (12, 4) and Jeremiah (9, 3), but also, indirectly, by the Yahwist narrator of the present story, who makes the reader sympathize with Esau as the innocent victim of a cruel plot, and shows that Jacob and his mother, the instigator of the plot, paid for it by a lifelong separation from each other. The story was told because it was part of the mystery of God's ways in salvation history—his use of weak, sinful men to achieve his own ultimate purpose.
27, 4: My special blessing: "the blessing of my soul." The same expression is used also in vv 19.25.31. In the context it must mean something like a solemn deathbed blessing, believed to be especially efficacious.

stead of a blessing." **13**His mother, however, replied: "Let any curse against you, son, fall on me! Just do as I say. Go and get me the kids."

14So Jacob went and got them and brought them to his mother; and with them she prepared an appetizing dish, such as his father liked. **15**Rebekah then took the best clothes of her older son Esau that she had in the house, and gave them to her younger son Jacob to wear; **16**and with the skins of the kids she covered up his hands and the hairless parts of his neck. **17**Then she handed her son Jacob the appetizing dish and the bread she had prepared.

18Bringing them to his father, Jacob said, "Father!" "Yes?" replied Isaac. "Which of my sons are you?" **19**Jacob answered his father: "I am Esau, your first-born. I did as you told me. Please sit up and eat some of my game, so that you may give me your special blessing." **20**But Isaac asked, "How did you succeed so quickly, son?" He answered, "The LORD, your God, let things turn out well with me." **21**Isaac then said to Jacob, "Come closer, son, that I may feel you, to learn whether you really are my son Esau or not." **22**So Jacob moved up closer to his father. When Isaac felt him, he said, "Although the voice is Jacob's, the hands are Esau's." **23**(He failed to identify him because his hands were hairy, like those of his brother Esau; so in the end he gave him his blessing.) **24**Again he asked him, "Are you really my son Esau?" "Certainly," he replied. **25**Then Isaac said, "Serve me your game, son, that I may eat of it and then give you my blessing." Jacob served it to him, and Isaac ate; he brought him wine, and he drank. **26**Finally his father Isaac said to him, "Come closer, son, and kiss me." **27***As Jacob went up and kissed him, Isaac smelled the fragrance of his clothes. With that, he blessed him, saying,

> "Ah, the fragrance of my son
>   is like the fragrance of a field
>   that the LORD has blessed!
>
> **28**"May God give to you
>   of the dew of the heavens
> And of the fertility of the earth
>   abundance of grain and wine.
>
> **29***"Let peoples serve you,
>   and nations pay you homage;
> Be master of your brothers,
>   and may your mother's sons bow down to you.
> Cursed be those who curse you,
>   and blessed be those who bless you."

30Jacob had scarcely left his father, just after Isaac had finished blessing him, when his brother Esau came back from his hunt. **31**Then he too prepared an appetizing dish with his game, and bringing it to his father, he said, "Please, father, eat some of your son's

game, that you may then give me your special blessing." **32**"Who are you?" his father Isaac asked him. "I am Esau," he replied, "your first-born son." **33**With that, Isaac was seized with a fit of uncontrollable trembling. "Who was it, then," he asked, "that hunted game and brought it to me? I finished eating it just before you came, and I blessed him. Now he must remain blessed!" **34**On hearing his father's words, Esau burst into loud, bitter sobbing. "Father, bless me too!" he begged. **35**When Isaac explained, "Your brother came here by a ruse and carried off your blessing," **36***†Esau exclaimed, "He has been well named Jacob! He has now supplanted me twice! First he took away my birthright, and now he has taken away my blessing." Then he pleaded, "Haven't you saved a blessing for me?" **37**Isaac replied: "I have already appointed him your master, and I have assigned to him all his kinsmen as his slaves; besides, I have enriched him with grain and wine. What then can I do for you, son?" **38***But Esau urged his father, "Have you only that one blessing, father? Bless me too!" Isaac, however, made no reply; and Esau wept aloud. **39***Finally Isaac spoke again and said to him:

> "Ah, far from the fertile earth
>   shall be your dwelling;
>   far from the dew of the heavens above!
> **40***"By your sword you shall live,
>   and your brother you shall serve;
> But when you become restive,
>   you shall throw off his yoke from your neck."

41*Esau bore Jacob a grudge because of the blessing his father had given him. He said to himself, "When the time of mourning for my father comes, I will kill my brother Jacob." **42**When Rebekah got news of what her older son Esau had in mind, she called her younger son Jacob and said to him: "Listen! Your brother Esau intends to settle accounts with you by killing you. **43**Therefore, son, do what I tell you: flee at once to my brother Laban in Haran, **44**and stay with him a while until your brother's fury subsides **45**[until your brother's anger against you subsides] and he forgets what you did to him. Then I will send for you and bring you back. Must I lose both of you in a single day?"

46*†Rebekah said to Isaac: "I am disgusted with life because of the Hittite women. If Jacob also should marry a Hittite woman, a native of the land, like these women, what good would life be to me?"

---

*   27: 22, 17f; Heb 11, 20.   40: 2 Kgs 8, 20.22;
      29: 25, 23; 49, 8; Nm 24, 9.   2 Chr 21, 8.
      36: 25, 26.29-34; Hos 12, 4.   41: Wis 10, 10; Ob 1, 10.
      38: Heb 12, 17.   46: 26, 34f.
      39: Heb 11, 20.

†   27, 36: *He has now supplanted me:* in Hebrew, *wayyaqebeni,* a wordplay on the name Jacob, *yaaqob;* see Jer 9, 3 and note, as well as Gn 25, 26. There is also a play between the Hebrew words *bekora* ("birthright") and *beraka* ("blessing").

27, 46-28, 9: This section, which is from the Priestly source and a direct sequel of 26, 34f, presents a different, though not contradictory, reason for Jacob's going to Paddan-aram: namely, to preserve racial purity among the chosen people. The account of Esau's marriages is given for the purpose of explaining the racial mixture of the Edomites, who were descended in part from tribes related to Israel, in part from older peoples in Edom called Hittites, Horites or Hivites, and in part from the Ishmaelite (Arabian) tribes who later invaded the region.

Jacob Sent to Laban

28 [1]*ISAAC therefore called Jacob, greeted him with a blessing, and charged him: "You shall not marry a Canaanite woman! [2]*Go now to Paddan-aram, to the home of your mother's father Bethuel, and there choose a wife for yourself from among the daughters of your uncle Laban. [3]May God Almighty bless you and make you fertile, multiply you that you may become an assembly of peoples. [4]*May he extend to you and your descendants the blessing he gave to Abraham, so that you may gain possession of the land where you are staying, which he assigned to Abraham." [5]*Then Isaac sent Jacob on his way; he went to Paddan-aram, to Laban, son of Bethuel the Aramean, and brother of Rebekah, the mother of Jacob and Esau.

[6]Esau noted that Isaac had blessed Jacob when he sent him to Paddan-aram to get himself a wife there, charging him, as he gave him his blessing, not to marry a Canaanite woman, [7]and that Jacob had obeyed his father and mother and gone to Paddan-aram. [8]Esau realized how displeasing the Canaanite women were to his father Isaac, [9]*so he went to Ishmael, and in addition to the wives he had, married Mahalath, the daughter of Abraham's son Ishmael and sister of Nebaioth.

Jacob's Dream at Bethel

[10]Jacob departed from Beer-sheba and proceeded toward Haran. [11]†When he came upon a certain shrine, as the sun had already set, he stopped there for the night. Taking one of the stones at the shrine, he put it under his head and lay down to sleep at that spot. [12]*†Then he had a dream: a stairway rested on the ground, with its top reaching to the heavens; and God's messengers were going up and down on it. [13]*And there was the LORD standing beside him and saying:

"I, the LORD, am the God of your forefather Abraham and the God of Isaac; the land on which you are lying I will give to you and your descendants. [14]*These shall be as plentiful as the dust of the earth, and through them you shall spread out east and west, north and south. In you and your descendants all the nations of the earth shall find blessing. [15]*Know that I am with you; I will protect you wherever you go, and bring you back to this land. I will never leave you until I have done what I promised you."

[16]When Jacob awoke from his sleep, he exclaimed, "Truly, the LORD is in this spot, although I did not know it!" [17]†In solemn wonder he cried out: "How awesome is this shrine! This is nothing else but an abode of God, and that is the gateway to heaven!" [18]*†Early the next morning Jacob took the stone that he had put under his head, set it up as a memorial stone, and poured oil on top of it. [19]*†He called that site Bethel, whereas the former name of the town had been Luz.

[20]Jacob then made this vow: "If God remains with me, to protect me on this journey I am making and to give me enough bread to eat and clothing to wear, [21]and I come back safe to my father's house, the LORD shall be my God. [22]This stone that I have set up as a memorial stone shall be God's abode. Of everything you give me, I will faithfully return a tenth part to you."

Arrival in Haran

29 [1]*†AFTER Jacob resumed his journey, he came to the land of the Easterners. [2]*Looking about, he saw a well in the open country, with three droves of sheep huddled near it, for droves were watered from that well. A large stone covered the mouth of the well. [3]Only when all the shepherds were assembled there could they roll the stone away from the mouth of the well and water the flocks. Then they would put the stone back again over the mouth of the well.

[4]Jacob said to them, "Friends, where are you from?" "We are from Haran," they replied. [5]*Then he asked them, "Do you know Laban, son of Nahor?" "We do," they answered. [6]He inquired further, "Is he well?" "He is," they answered; "and here comes his daughter Rachel with his flock." [7]Then he said: "There is still much daylight left; it is hardly the time to bring the animals home. Why don't you water the flocks now, and then continue pasturing them?" [8]"We cannot," they replied, "until all the shepherds are here to roll the stone away from the mouth of the well; only then can we water the flocks."

[9]While he was still talking with them, Rachel ar-

---

† 28, 11: *Shrine:* literally "place," often used specifically of a sacred site. Here the place was Bethel (v 19), a sacred site as early as the time of Abraham (12, 8).

28, 12: *Stairway:* in Hebrew, *sullam,* traditionally but inaccurately translated as "ladder." The corresponding verb, *salal,* means "to heap up" something, such as dirt for a highway or ramp. The imagery in Jacob's dream is derived from the Babylonian ziggurat or temple tower, "with its top in the sky" (11, 4), and with brick steps leading up to a small temple at the top.

28, 17: *This:* the stone Jacob used as a headrest; cf v 22. *That:* the stairway Jacob saw in his dream.

28, 18: *Memorial stone:* in Hebrew, *masseba,* a stone which might vary in shape and size, set upright and usually intended for some religious purpose. Since the custom of erecting such "sacred pillars" in Palestine went back to its pre-Israelite period, their pagan associations were often retained: therefore, later Israelite religion forbade their erection (Lv 26, 1; Dt 16, 22) and ordered the destruction of those that were associated with paganism (Ex 34, 31; Dt 12, 3).

28, 19: *Bethel:* i. e., "house of God"; the reference is to the abode of God in v 17.

29, 1: *Easterners:* see note on 25, 6.

* 28/1: 24, 3f; 26, 35.
　　2: 22, 22; 17, 1f.4f.
　　4: Ex 32, 13.
　　5: Jdt 8, 26.
　　9: 36, 2f.
　12: Jn 1, 51.
　13: Dt 1, 8; Mi 7, 28.
　14: 12, 3; 13, 14f; 15, 5f;
　　18, 18; 22, 17f; 26, 4;
　　Dt 19, 8; Sir 44, 21.

　15: 31, 3.
　18: 31, 13; 35, 14f.
　19: 35, 6; 48, 3; Jos 18, 13;
　　Jgs 1, 23; Hos 12, 4.
29/1: Wis 10, 10.
　　2: 24, 11f.
　　5: Tb 7, 4.

rived with her father's sheep; she was the one who tended them. ¹⁰As soon as Jacob saw Rachel, the daughter of his uncle Laban, with the sheep of his uncle Laban, he went up, rolled the stone away from the mouth of the well, and watered his uncle's sheep. ¹¹†Then Jacob kissed Rachel and burst into tears. ¹²He told her that he was her father's relative, Rebekah's son, and she ran to tell her father. ¹³When Laban heard the news about his sister's son Jacob, he hurried out to meet him. After embracing and kissing him, he brought him to his house. Jacob then recounted to Laban all that had happened, ¹⁴†and Laban said to him, "You are indeed my flesh and blood."

Marriage to Leah and Rachel

After Jacob had stayed with him a full month, ¹⁵Laban said to him: "Should you serve me for nothing just because you are a relative of mine? Tell me what your wages should be." ¹⁶Now Laban had two daughters; the older was called Leah, the younger Rachel. ¹⁷†Leah had lovely eyes, but Rachel was well formed and beautiful. ¹⁸†Since Jacob had fallen in love with Rachel, he answered Laban, "I will serve you seven years for your younger daughter Rachel." ¹⁹Laban replied, "I prefer to give her to you rather than to an outsider. Stay with me." ²⁰*So Jacob served seven years for Rachel, yet they seemed to him but a few days because of his love for her.

²¹Then Jacob said to Laban, "Give me my wife, that I may consummate my marriage with her, for my term is now completed." ²²So Laban invited all the local inhabitants and gave a feast. ²³At nightfall he took his daughter Leah and brought her to Jacob, and Jacob consummated the marriage with her. ²⁴(Laban assigned his slave girl Zilpah to his daughter Leah as her maidservant.) ²⁵†In the morning Jacob was amazed: it was Leah! So he cried out to Laban: "How could you do this to me! Was it not for Rachel that I served you? Why did you dupe me?" ²⁶"It is not the custom in our country," Laban replied, "to marry off a younger daughter before an older one. ²⁷*†Finish the bridal week for this one, and then I will give you the other too, in return for another seven years of service with me."

²⁸Jacob agreed. He finished the bridal week for Leah, and then Laban gave him his daughter Rachel in marriage. ²⁹(Laban assigned his slave girl Bilhah to his daughter Rachel as her maidservant.) ³⁰*Jacob then consummated his marriage with Rachel also, and he loved her more than Leah. Thus he remained in Laban's service another seven years.

Jacob's Children

³¹When the LORD saw that Leah was unloved, he made her fruitful, while Rachel remained barren.

³²*†Leah conceived and bore a son, and she named him Reuben; for she said, "It means, 'The LORD saw my misery; now my husband will love me.'" ³³†She conceived again and bore a son, and said, "It means, 'The LORD heard that I was unloved,' and therefore he has given me this one also"; so she named him Simeon. ³⁴†Again she conceived and bore a son, and she said, "Now at last my husband will become attached to me, since I have now borne him three sons"; that is why she named him Levi. ³⁵*†Once more she conceived and bore a son, and she said, "This time I will give grateful praise to the LORD"; therefore she named him Judah. Then she stopped bearing children.

30 ¹*WHEN Rachel saw that she failed to bear children to Jacob, she became envious of her sister. She said to Jacob, "Give me children or I shall die!" ²*In anger Jacob retorted, "Can I take the place of God, who has denied you the fruit of the womb?" ³*†She replied, "Here is my maidservant Bilhah. Have intercourse with her, and let her give birth on my knees, so that I too may have offspring, at least through her." ⁴†So she gave him her maidservant Bilhah as a consort, and Jacob had intercourse with her. When Bilhah conceived and bore a son, ⁶†Rachel said, "God has vindicated me; indeed he has heeded my plea and given me a son." Therefore she named him Dan. ⁷Rachel's maidservant Bilhah conceived

---

† 29, 11: *Burst into tears:* literally "raised his voice and wept," i. e., for joy.

29, 14: *Flesh and blood:* literally "bone and flesh," i. e., a close relative; on the Hebrew idiom, see 2, 23.

29, 17: *Lovely eyes:* the adjective modifying *eyes* is often translated as "weak," but "lovely" is the more probable word.

29, 18: Jacob offers to render service (Jos 15, 16f; 1 Sm 17, 25; 18, 17) in lieu of the customary bridal price (Ex 22, 16f; Dt 22, 29).

29, 25: *Jacob was amazed:* he had not recognized Leah because a bride was veiled when she was brought to her bridegroom; cf 24, 65.

29, 27: *The bridal week:* an ancient wedding lasted for seven days of festivities; cf Jgs 14, 12.

29, 32: *Reuben:* the literal meaning of the Hebrew name is "look, a son!" But in this case, as also with the names of all the other sons of Jacob, a symbolic rather than an etymological interpretation of the name is given, because the name and the persons were regarded as closely interrelated. The symbolic interpretation of Reuben's name, according to the Yahwist source, is based on the similar-sounding *raa beonyi,* "he saw my misery." In the Elohist source, the name is explained by the similar-sounding *yeehabani,* "he will love me."

29, 33: *Simeon:* in popular etymology, related to *shama,* "he heard."

29, 34: *Levi:* related to *yillaweh,* "he will become attached."

29, 35: *Judah:* related to *odeh,* "I will give grateful praise."

30, 3: *On my knees:* in the ancient Near East, a father would take a newborn child in his lap to signify that he acknowledged it as his own; Rachel uses this ceremony in order to adopt the child and establish her legal rights to it.

30, 4: *Consort:* The Hebrew word normally means "wife," but here it refers to a wife of secondary rank, who did not have the full legal rights of an ordinary wife.

30, 6: *Dan:* explained by the term *dannanni,* "he has vindicated me."

---

* 20: Hos 12, 13.   35: Mt 1, 2; Lk 3, 33.
27: Hos 12, 13.   30/1: Prv 30, 16.
30: Dt 21, 15ff.   2: 2 Kgs 5, 7.
32: 49, 3.   3: 16, 2ff.

again and bore a second son, ⁸†and Rachel said, "I engaged in a fateful struggle with my sister, and I prevailed." So she named him Naphtali.

⁹When Leah saw that she had ceased to bear children, she gave her maidservant Zilpah to Jacob as a consort. ¹⁰So Jacob had intercourse with Zilpah, and she conceived and bore a son. ¹¹Leah then said, "What good luck!" So she named him Gad. ¹²Then Leah's maidservant Zilpah bore a second son to Jacob; ¹³†and Leah said, "What good fortune!"—meaning, "Women call me fortunate." So she named him Asher.

¹⁴†One day, during the wheat harvest, when Reuben was out in the field, he came upon some mandrakes which he brought home to his mother Leah. Rachel asked Leah, "Please let me have some of your son's mandrakes." ¹⁵Leah replied, "Was it not enough for you to take away my husband, that you must now take my son's mandrakes too?" "Very well, then!" Rachel answered. "In exchange for your son's mandrakes, Jacob may lie with you tonight." ¹⁶That evening, when Jacob came home from the fields, Leah went out to meet him. "You are now to come in with me," she told him, "because I have paid for you with my son's mandrakes." So that night he slept with her, ¹⁷and God heard her prayer; she conceived and bore a fifth son to Jacob. ¹⁸†Leah then said, "God has given me my reward for having let my husband have my maidservant"; so she named him Issachar. ¹⁹Leah conceived again and bore a sixth son to Jacob; ²⁰†and she said, "God has brought me a precious gift. This time my husband will offer me presents, now that I have borne him six sons"; so she named him Zebulun. ²¹Finally, she gave birth to a daughter, and she named her Dinah.

²²Then God remembered Rachel; he heard her prayer and made her fruitful. ²³*She conceived and bore a son, and she said, "God has removed my disgrace." ²⁴†So she named him Joseph, meaning, "May the Lord add another son to this one for me!"

Jacob Outwits Laban

²⁵After Rachel gave birth to Joseph, Jacob said to Laban: "Give me leave to go to my homeland. ²⁶Let me have my wives, for whom I served you, and my children, too, that I may depart. You know very well the service that I have rendered you." ²⁷Laban answered him: "If you will please. . . .

"I have learned through divination that it is because of you that God has blessed me. ²⁸So," he continued, "state what wages you want from me, and I will pay them." ²⁹Jacob replied: "You know what work I did for you and how well your livestock fared under my care; ³⁰the little you had before I came has grown into very much, since the Lord's blessings came upon you in my company. Therefore I should now do something for my own household as well." ³¹"What should I pay you?" Laban asked. Jacob answered: "You do not have to pay me anything outright. I will again

pasture and tend your flock, if you do this one thing for me: ³²†go through your whole flock today and remove from it every dark animal among the sheep and every spotted or speckled one among the goats. Only such animals shall be my wages. ³³In the future, whenever you check on these wages of mine, let my honesty testify against me: any animal in my possession that is not a speckled or spotted goat, or a dark sheep, got there by theft!" ³⁴"Very well," agreed Laban. "Let it be as you say."

³⁵†That same day Laban removed the streaked and spotted he-goats and all the speckled and spotted she-goats, all those with some white on them, as well as the fully dark-colored sheep; these he left . . . in charge of his sons. ³⁶Then he put a three days' journey between himself and Jacob, while Jacob continued to pasture the rest of Laban's flock.

³⁷Jacob, however, got some fresh shoots of poplar, almond and plane trees, and he made white stripes in them by peeling off the bark down to the white core of the shoots. ³⁸The rods that he had thus peeled he then set upright in the watering troughs, so that they would be in front of the animals that drank from the troughs. When the animals were in heat as they came to drink, ³⁹†the goats mated by the rods, and so they brought forth streaked, speckled and spotted kids. ⁴⁰The sheep, on the other hand, Jacob kept apart, and he set these

---

† 30, 8: *Naphtali:* explained by the phrase *"naptule elohim niptalti,"* literally, "in a divine wrestling match I have wrestled," perhaps implying the concept of an ordeal; hence the above rendering, *I engaged in a fateful struggle.*

30, 11: *Gad:* explained by the Hebrew term *begad,* literally "in luck," i. e., *what good luck!*

30, 13: *Asher:* explained by the term *beoshri,* literally "in my good fortune." i. e., *what good fortune,* and by the term *ishsheruni* "they call me fortunate."

30, 14: *Mandrakes:* an herb whose root was anciently thought to promote conception. The Hebrew word for mandrakes, *dudaim,* has erotic connotations, since it sounds like the words *daddayim* ("breasts") and *dodim* ("sexual pleasure").

30, 18: *Issachar:* explained by the term *sekari,* "my reward," and in v 16, *sakor sekartika,* literally "I have hired you," i. e., *I have paid for you.*

30, 20: *Zebulun:* related to the Akkadian word *zubullum,* "bridegroom's gift," is explained by the terms *zebadani . . . zebed tob,* "he has brought me a precious gift," and *yizbeleni,* "he will offer me presents."

30, 24: *Joseph:* explained by the words *yosep,* "may he add," and in v 23, *asap,* "he has removed."

30, 32: *Dark . . . sheep . . . spotted or speckled goats:* In the Near East the normal color of sheep is light gray, whereas that of goats is uniform dark brown or black. Ordinarily, therefore, Jacob would have received but few animals.

30, 35: By giving the abnormally colored animals to his sons, Laban not only deprived Jacob of his first small wages, but he also designed to prevent in this way the future breeding of such animals in the part of his flock entrusted to Jacob.

30, 39-42: Jacob's stratagem was based on the widespread notion among simple people that visual stimuli can have prenatal effects on the offspring of breeding animals. Thus, the rods on which Jacob had whittled stripes or bands or chevron marks were thought to cause the female goats that looked at them to bear kids with lighter-colored marks on their dark hair, while the gray ewes were thought to bear lambs with dark marks on them simply by visual crossbreeding with the dark goats.

* 23: Lk 1, 25.

animals to face the streaked or fully dark-colored animals of Laban. Thus he produced special flocks of his own, which he did not put with Laban's flock. ⁴¹Moreover, whenever the hardier animals were in heat, Jacob would set the rods in the troughs in full view of these animals, so that they mated by the rods; ⁴²but with the weaker animals he would not put the rods there. So the feeble animals would go to Laban, but the sturdy ones to Jacob. ⁴³Thus the man grew increasingly prosperous, and he came to own, not only large flocks, but also male and female servants and camels and asses.

Flight from Laban

31 ¹JACOB learned that Laban's sons were saying, "Jacob has taken everything that belonged to our father, and he has accumulated all this wealth of his by using our father's property." ²Jacob perceived, too, that Laban's attitude toward him was not what it had previously been. ^{3*}Then the LORD said to Jacob, "Return to the land of your fathers, where you were born, and I will be with you."

⁴So Jacob sent for Rachel and Leah to meet him where he was in the field with his flock. ⁵There he said to them: "I have noticed that your father's attitude toward me is not as it was in the past; but the God of my father has been with me. ⁶You well know what effort I put into serving your father; ^{7*}yet your father cheated me and changed my wages time after time. God, however, did not let him do me any harm. ^{8†}Whenever your father said, 'The speckled animals shall be your wages,' the entire flock would bear speckled young; whenever he said, 'The streaked animals shall be your wages,' the entire flock would bear streaked young. ⁹Thus God reclaimed your father's livestock and gave it to me. ¹⁰Once, in the breeding season, I had a dream in which I saw mating he-goats that were streaked, speckled and mottled. ¹¹In the dream God's messenger called to me, 'Jacob!' 'Here!' I replied. ¹²Then he said: 'Note well. All the he-goats in the flock, as they mate, are streaked, speckled and mottled, for I have seen all the things that Laban has been doing to you. ^{13*}I am the God who appeared to you in Bethel, where you anointed a memorial stone and made a vow to me. Up, then! Leave this land and return to the land of your birth.'"

¹⁴Rachel and Leah answered him: "Have we still an heir's portion in our father's house? ^{15†}Are we not regarded by him as outsiders? He not only sold us; he has even used up the money that he got for us! ^{16*}All the wealth that God reclaimed from our father really belongs to us and our children. Therefore, do just as God has told you." ¹⁷Jacob proceeded to put his children and wives on camels, ¹⁸and he drove off with all his livestock and all the property he had acquired in Paddan-aram, to go to his father Isaac in the land of Canaan.

^{19*†}Now Laban had gone away to shear his sheep, and Rachel had meanwhile appropriated her father's household idols. ^{20†}Jacob had hoodwinked Laban the Aramean by not telling him of his intended flight. ²¹Thus he made his escape with all that he had. Once he was across the Euphrates, he headed for the highlands of Gilead.

²²On the third day, word came to Laban that Jacob had fled. ^{23†}Taking his kinsmen with him, he pursued him for seven days until he caught up with him in the hill country of Gilead. ^{24*}But that night God appeared to Laban the Aramean in a dream and warned him, "Take care not to threaten Jacob with any harm!"

Jacob and Laban in Gilead

²⁵When Laban overtook Jacob, Jacob's tents were pitched in the highlands; Laban also pitched his tents there, on Mount Gilead. ^{26*}"What do you mean," Laban demanded of Jacob, "by hoodwinking me and carrying off my daughters like war captives? ²⁷Why did you dupe me by stealing away secretly? You should have told me, and I would have sent you off with merry singing to the sound of tambourines and harps. ²⁸You did not even allow me a parting kiss to my daughters and grandchildren! What you have now done is a senseless thing. ²⁹I have it in my power to harm all of you; but last night the God of your father said to me, 'Take care not to threaten Jacob with any harm!' ³⁰Granted that you had to leave because you were desperately homesick for your father's house, why did you steal my gods?" ³¹"I was frightened," Jacob replied to Laban, "at the thought that you might take your daughters away from me by force. ³²But as for your gods, the one you find them with shall not remain alive! If, with my kinsmen looking on, you identify anything here as belonging to you, take it." Jacob, of course, had no idea that Rachel had stolen the idols.

³³Laban then went in and searched Jacob's tent and Leah's tent, as well as the tents of the two maidservants; but he did not find the idols. Leaving Leah's

† 31, 8-12: This Elohist account of the miraculous increase in Jacob's flock differs somewhat from the Yahwist account given in 30, 32-42.

31, 15: *Outsiders:* literally "foreign women"; they lacked the favored legal status of native women. *Used up:* literally "eaten, consumed"; the bridal price that a man received for giving his daughter in marriage was legally reserved as her inalienable dowry.

31, 19: *Household idols:* in Hebrew, *terapim,* figurines used in divination (Ez 21, 26; Zec 10, 2). Laban calls them his "gods" (v 30).

31, 20: *Hoodwinked:* literally "stolen the heart of," i. e., lulled the mind of. *Aramean:* The earliest extra-biblical references to the Arameans date from several centuries after the time of Jacob; to call Laban an *Aramean* and to have him speak Aramaic (v 47) would seem to be an anachronism.

31, 23: *For seven days:* literally "a way of seven days," a general term to designate a long distance; it would have taken a camel caravan many more days to travel from Haran to Gilead, the region east of the northern half of the Jordan.

31, 26: *War captives:* literally "women captured by the sword"; the women of a conquered people were treated as part of the victor's booty; cf 1 Sm 30, 2; 2 Kgs 5, 2.

* 31/3: 26, 3; 28, 15; 32, 10.   16: Wis 10, 10f.
7: Jdt 8, 26.   19: 19, 34; 1 Sm 19, 13.
13: 28, 18.   24: Wis 10, 12.

tent, he went into Rachel's. **34***Now Rachel had taken the idols, put them inside a camel cushion, and seated herself upon them. When Laban had rummaged through the rest of her tent without finding them, **35**Rachel said to her father, "Let not my lord feel offended that I cannot rise in your presence; a woman's period is upon me." So, despite his search, he did not find his idols.

36Jacob, now enraged, upbraided Laban. "What crime or offense have I committed," he demanded, "that you should hound me so fiercely? **37**Now that you have ransacked all my things, have you found a single object taken from your belongings? If so, produce it here before your kinsmen and mine, and let them decide between us two.

38"In the twenty years that I was under you, no ewe or she-goat of yours ever miscarried, and I have never feasted on a ram of your flock. **39*†**I never brought you an animal torn by wild beasts; I made good the loss myself. You held me responsible for anything stolen by day or night. **40**How often the scorching heat ravaged me by day, and the frost by night, while sleep fled from my eyes! **41**Of the twenty years that I have now spent in your household, I slaved fourteen years for your two daughters and six years for your flock, while you changed my wages time after time. **42***If my ancestral God, the God of Abraham and the Awesome One of Isaac, had not been on my side, you would now have sent me away empty-handed. But God saw my plight and the fruits of my toil, and last night he gave judgment."

43†Laban replied to Jacob: "The women are mine, their children are mine, and the flocks are mine; everything you see belongs to me. But since these women are my daughters, I will now do something for them and for the children they have borne. **44**Come, then, we will make a pact, you and I; the LORD shall be a witness between us."

45*Then Jacob took a stone and set it up as a memorial stone. **46**Jacob said to his kinsmen, "Gather some stones." So they got some stones and made a mound; and they had a meal there at the mound. **47†**Laban called it Jegar-sahadutha, but Jacob named it Galeed. **48**"This mound," said Laban, "shall be a witness from now on between you and me." That is why it was named Galeed—**49†**and also Mizpah, for he said: "May the LORD keep watch between you and me when we are out of each other's sight. **50**If you mistreat my daughters, or take other wives besides my daughters, remember that even though no one else is about, God will be witness between you and me."

51Laban said further to Jacob: "Here is this mound, and here is the memorial stone that I have set up between you and me. **52**This mound shall be witness, and this memorial stone shall be witness, that, with hostile intent, neither may I pass beyond this mound into your territory, nor may you pass beyond it into mine. **53**May the God of Abraham and the god of Nahor [their ancestral deities] maintain justice between us!" Jacob took the oath by the Awesome One of Isaac. **54**He then offered a sacrifice on the mountain and invited his kinsmen to share in the meal. When they had eaten, they passed the night on the mountain.

32 **1**EARLY the next morning, Laban kissed his grandchildren and his daughters goodbye; then he set out on his journey back home, **2**while Jacob continued on his own way. Then God's messengers encountered Jacob. **3†**When he saw them he said, "This is God's encampment." So he named that place Mahanaim.

Embassy to Esau

4*Jacob sent messengers ahead to his brother Esau in the land of Seir, the country of Edom, **5**with this message: "Thus shall you say to my lord Esau: 'Your servant Jacob speaks as follows: I have been staying with Laban and have been detained there until now. **6**I own cattle, asses and sheep, as well as male and female servants. I am sending my lord this information in the hope of gaining your favor.'" **7**When the messengers returned to Jacob, they said, "We reached your brother Esau. He is now coming to meet you, accompanied by four hundred men."

8Jacob was very much frightened. In his anxiety, he divided the people who were with him, as well as his flocks, herds and camels, into two camps. **9**"If Esau should attack and overwhelm one camp," he reasoned, "the remaining camp may still survive." **10***Then he prayed: "O God of my father Abraham and God of my father Isaac! You told me, O LORD, 'Go back to the land of your birth, and I will be good to you.' **11**I am unworthy of all the acts of kindness that you have loyally performed for your servant: although I crossed the Jordan here with nothing but my staff, I have now grown into two companies. **12***Save me, I pray, from the hand of my brother Esau! Otherwise I fear that when he comes he will strike me down and slay the

---

†

31, 39: Laban's actions were contrary to the customs of the ancient Near East, as recorded in the Code of Hammurabi: "If in a sheepfold an act of god has occurred, or a lion has made a kill, the shepherd shall clear himself before the deity, and the owner of the fold must accept the loss" (par. 266); cf Ex 22, 12.

31, 43-54: In this account of the treaty between Laban and Jacob, the Yahwist and Elohist sources are closely interwoven. The *mound* or cairn of stones comes from the Yahwist source, the *memorial stone* or stele from the Elohist.

31, 47: *Jegar-sahadutha:* an Aramaic term meaning "mound of witness." *Galeed:* in Hebrew, *galed*, with the same meaning; also offers an explanation of the regional name Gilead.

31, 49: *Mizpah:* a town in Gilead; cf Jgs 10, 17; 11, 11.34; Hos 5, 1. The Hebrew name *mispa* ("lookout") is allied to *yisep yhwh* ("may the Lord keep watch"), and also echoes the word *massēba* ("memorial pillar").

32, 3: *Mahanaim:* a town in Gilead (Jos 13, 26.30; 21, 38; 2 Sm 2, 8; etc.). The Hebrew name means "two camps." There are other allusions to the name in vv 8.11.

✿
34: 31, 19.   32/4: 36, 6.
39: Ex 22, 12.   10: 31, 3.
42: 19, 24.29.   12: 28, 14; 48, 16; Ex 32,
45: 28, 18; 35, 14.   13; Heb 11, 12.

mothers and children. ¹³You yourself said, 'I will be very good to you, and I will make your descendants like the sands of the sea, which are too numerous to count.'"

¹⁴After passing the night there, Jacob selected from what he had with him the following presents for his brother Esau: ¹⁵two hundred she-goats and twenty he-goats; two hundred ewes and twenty rams; ¹⁶thirty milch camels and their young; forty cows and ten bulls; twenty she-asses and ten he-asses. ¹⁷He put these animals in charge of his servants, in separate droves, and he told the servants, "Go on ahead of me, but keep a space between one drove and the next." ¹⁸To the servant in the lead he gave this instruction: "When my brother Esau meets you, he may ask you, 'Whose man are you? Where are you going? To whom do these animals ahead of you belong?' ¹⁹Then you shall answer, 'They belong to your brother Jacob, but they have been sent as a gift to my lord Esau; and Jacob himself is right behind us.'" ²⁰He gave similar instructions to the second servant and the third and to all the others who followed behind the droves, namely: "Thus and thus shall you say to Esau, when you reach him; ²¹and be sure to add, 'Your servant Jacob is right behind us.'" For Jacob reasoned, "If I first appease him with gifts that precede me, then later, when I face him, perhaps he will forgive me." ²²So the gifts went on ahead of him, while he stayed that night in the camp.

Struggle with the Angel

²³In the course of that night, however, Jacob arose, took his two wives, with the two maidservants and his eleven children, and crossed the ford of the Jabbok. ²⁴After he had taken them across the stream and had brought over all his possessions, ²⁵†Jacob was left there alone. Then some man wrestled with him until the break of dawn. ²⁶*When the man saw that he could not prevail over him, he struck Jacob's hip at its socket, so that the hip socket was wrenched as they wrestled. ²⁷The man then said, "Let me go, for it is daybreak." But Jacob said, "I will not let you go until you bless me." ²⁸*"What is your name?" the man asked. He answered, "Jacob." ²⁹†Then the man said, "You shall no longer be spoken of as Jacob, but as Israel, because you have contended with divine and human beings and have prevailed." ³⁰Jacob then asked him, "Do tell me your name, please." He answered, "Why should you want to know my name?" With that, he bade him farewell. ³¹*†Jacob named the place Peniel, "Because I have seen God face to face," he said, "yet my life has been spared."

³²At sunrise, as he left Penuel, Jacob limped along because of his hip. ³³That is why, to this day, the Israelites do not eat the sciatic muscle that is on the hip socket, inasmuch as Jacob's hip socket was struck at the sciatic muscle.

Jacob and Esau Meet

33 ¹JACOB looked up and saw Esau coming, accompanied by four hundred men. So he divided his children among Leah, Rachel and the two maidservants, ²putting the maids and their children first, Leah and her children next, and Rachel and Joseph last. ³He himself went on ahead of them, bowing to the ground seven times, until he reached his brother. ⁴Esau ran to meet him, embraced him, and flinging himself on his neck, kissed him as he wept.

⁵When Esau looked about, he saw the women and children. "Who are these with you?" he asked. Jacob answered, "They are the children whom God has graciously bestowed on your servant." ⁶Then the maidservants and their children came forward and bowed low; ⁷next, Leah and her children came forward and bowed low; lastly, Rachel and her children came forward and bowed low. ⁸Then Esau asked, "What did you intend with all those droves that I encountered?" Jacob answered, "It was to gain my lord's favor." ⁹"I have plenty," replied Esau; "you should keep what is yours, brother." ¹⁰"No, I beg you!" said Jacob. "If you will do me the favor, please accept this gift from me, since to come into your presence is for me like coming into the presence of God, now that you have received me so kindly. ¹¹Do accept the present I have brought you; God has been generous toward me, and I have an abundance." Since he so urged him, Esau accepted.

¹²Then Esau said, "Let us break camp and be on our way; I will travel alongside you." ¹³But Jacob replied: "As my lord can see, the children are frail. Besides, I am encumbered with the flocks and herds, which now have sucklings; if overdriven for a single day, the whole flock will die. ¹⁴Let my lord, then, go on ahead of me, while I proceed more slowly at the pace of the livestock before me and at the pace of my children, until I join my lord in Seir." ¹⁵Esau replied, "Let me at least put at your disposal some of the men who are with me." But Jacob said, "For what reason? Please indulge me in this, my lord." ¹⁶So on the same day that Esau began his journey back to Seir, ¹⁷†Jacob journeyed to Succoth. There he built a home for himself

---

† 32, 25: *Some man:* a messenger of the Lord in human form, as is clear from vv 29ff.

32, 29: *Israel:* the first part of the Hebrew name *Yisrael* is given a popular explanation in the word *sarita,* "you contended"; the second part is the first syllable of *elohim,* "divine beings." The present incident, with a similar allusion to the name Israel, is referred to in Hos 12, 5, where the mysterious wrestler is explicitly called an angel.

32, 31: *Peniel:* a variant of the word Penuel (v 32), the name of a town on the north bank of the Jabbok in Gilead (Jgs 8, 8f.17; 1 Kgs 12,25). The name is explained as meaning "the face of God," *peni-el.* Yet my life has been spared: see note on 16, 13.

33, 17: *Succoth:* an important town near the confluence of the Jabbok and the Jordan (Jos 13, 27; Jgs 8, 5-16; 1 Kgs 7, 46). *Booths:* in Hebrew, *sukkot,* of the same sound as the name of the town.

---

* 26: Hos 12, 4.   31: Jgs 13, 22.
28: 35, 10; 1 Kgs 18, 31;
    2 Kgs 17, 34.

and made booths for his livestock. That is why the place was called Succoth.

[18]*Having thus come from Paddan-aram, Jacob arrived safely at the city of Shechem, which is in the land of Canaan, and he encamped in sight of the city. [19]*†The plot of ground on which he had pitched his tent he bought for a hundred pieces of bullion from the descendants of Hamor, the founder of Shechem. [20]*He set up a memorial stone there and invoked "El, the God of Israel."

The Rape of Dinah

34 [1]†DINAH, the daughter whom Leah had borne to Jacob, went out to visit some of the women of the land. [2]†When Shechem, son of Hamor the Hivite, who was chief of the region, saw her, he seized her and lay with her by force. [3]Since he was strongly attracted to Dinah, daughter of Jacob, indeed was really in love with the girl, he endeavored to win her affection. [4]Shechem also asked his father Hamor, "Get me this girl for a wife."

[5]Meanwhile, Jacob heard that Shechem had defiled his daughter Dinah; but since his sons were out in the fields with his livestock, he held his peace until they came home. [6]Now Hamor, the father of Shechem, went out to discuss the matter with Jacob, [7]*just as Jacob's sons were coming in from the fields. When they heard the news, the men were shocked and seethed with indignation. What Shechem had done was an outrage in Israel; such a thing could not be tolerated.

[8]Hamor appealed to them, saying: "My son Shechem has his heart set on your daughter. Please give her to him in marriage. [9]Intermarry with us; give your daughters to us, and take our daughters for yourselves. [10]Thus you can live among us. The land is open before you; you can settle and move about freely in it, and acquire landed property here." [11]Then Shechem, too, appealed to Dinah's father and brothers: "Do me this favor, and I will pay whatever you demand of me. [12]No matter how high you set the bridal price, I will pay you whatever you ask; only give me the maiden in marriage."

Revenge of Jacob's Sons

[13]Jacob's sons replied to Shechem and his father Hamor with guile, speaking as they did because their sister Dinah had been defiled. [14]"We could not do such a thing," they said, "as to give our sister to an uncircumcised man; that would be a disgrace for us. [15]We will agree with you only on this condition, that you become like us by having every male among you circumcised. [16]Then we will give you our daughters and take yours in marriage; we will settle among you and become one kindred people with you. [17]But if you do not comply with our terms regarding circumcision, we will take our daughter and go away."

[18]Their proposal seemed fair to Hamor and his son Shechem. [19]The young man lost no time in acting in the matter, since he was deeply in love with Jacob's daughter. Moreover he was more highly respected than anyone else in his clan. [20]So Hamor and his son Shechem went to their town council and thus presented the matter to their fellow townsmen: [21]"These men are friendly toward us. Let them settle in the land and move about in it freely; there is ample room in the country for them. We can marry their daughters and give our daughters to them in marriage. [22]But the men will agree to live with us and form one kindred people with us only on this condition, that every male among us be circumcised as they themselves are. [23]Would not the livestock they have acquired—all their animals—then be ours? Let us, therefore, give in to them, so that they may settle among us."

[24]†All the able-bodied men of the town agreed with Hamor and his son Shechem, and all the males, including every able-bodied man in the community, were circumcised. [25]*On the third day, while they were still in pain, Dinah's full brothers Simeon and Levi, two of Jacob's sons, took their swords, advanced against the city without any trouble, and massacred all the males. [26]*After they had put Hamor and his son Shechem to the sword, they took Dinah from Shechem's house and left. [27]Then the other sons of Jacob followed up the slaughter and sacked the city in reprisal for their sister Dinah's defilement. [28]They seized their flocks, herds and asses, whatever was in the city and in the country around. [29]*They carried off all their wealth, their women, and their children, and took for loot whatever was in the houses.

[30]Jacob said to Simeon and Levi: "You have brought trouble upon me by making me loathsome to the inhabitants of the land, the Canaanites and the Perizzites. I have so few men that, if these people unite against me and attack me, I and my family will be wiped out." [31]But they retorted, "Should our sister have been treated like a harlot?"

† 33, 19: *Pieces of bullion:* in Hebrew, *kesita,* a monetary unit of which the value is now unknown. *Descendants of Hamor:* Hamorites, "the men of Hamor"; cf Jgs 9, 28. Hamor was regarded as the eponymous ancestor of the pre-Israelite inhabitants of Shechem.

34, 1-31: Behind the story of the rape of Dinah and the revenge of Jacob's sons on the men of the city of Shechem there probably lies a dimly recollected historical event connected with an armed conflict between the earliest Israelite tribes invading central Canaan and the Hurrian inhabitants of the Shechem region.

34, 2: *Hivite:* The Greek text has "Horite"; the terms were apparently used indiscriminately to designate the Hurrian or other non-Semitic elements in Palestine.

34, 24: *Every able-bodied man in the community:* literally "all those who go out at the gate of the city," apparently meaning the men who go out to war. By temporarily crippling them through circumcision, Jacob's sons deprived the city of its defenders.

33/18: 12, 6; Jn 4, 6.
19: Jos 24, 32; Jn 4, 5; Acts 7, 16.
20: Jgs 6, 24.
34/7: 2 Sm 13, 12.
25: 49, 6.
26: Jdt 9, 2.
29: Jdt 9, 3f.

Bethel Revisited

35 [1]*GOD said to Jacob: "Go up now to Bethel. Settle there and build an altar there to the God who appeared to you while you were fleeing from your brother Esau." [2]†So Jacob told his family and all the others who were with him: "Get rid of the foreign gods that you have among you; then purify yourselves and put on fresh clothes. [3]We are now to go up to Bethel, and I will build an altar there to the God who answered me in my hour of distress and who has been with me wherever I have gone." [4]†They therefore handed over to Jacob all the foreign gods in their possession and also the rings they had in their ears. [5]Then, as they set out, a terror from God fell upon the towns round about, so that no one pursued the sons of Jacob.

[6]*Thus Jacob and all the people who were with him arrived in Luz [that is, Bethel] in the land of Canaan. [7]*There he built an altar and named the place Bethel, for it was there that God had revealed himself to him when he was fleeing from his brother. [8]†Death came to Rebekah's nurse Deborah; she was buried under the oak below Bethel, and so it was called Allon-bacuth.

[9]On Jacob's arrival from Paddan-aram, God appeared to him again and blessed him. [10]*God said to him:

"You whose name is Jacob
shall no longer be called Jacob,
but Israel shall be your name."

Thus he was named Israel. [11]God also said to him:

"I am God Almighty;
be fruitful and multiply.
A nation, indeed an assembly of nations,
shall stem from you,
and kings shall issue from your loins.
[12]*The land I once gave
to Abraham and Isaac
I now give to you;
And to your descendants after you
will I give this land."

[13]Then God departed from him. [14]*On the site where God had spoken with him, Jacob set up a memorial stone, and upon it he made a libation and poured out oil. [15]Jacob named the site Bethel, because God had spoken with him there.

Jacob's Family

[16]Then they departed from Bethel; but while they still had some distance to go on the way to Ephrath, Rachel began to be in labor and to suffer great distress.

[17]When her pangs were most severe, her midwife said to her, "Have no fear! This time, too, you have a son." [18]†With her last breath—for she was at the point of death—she called him Ben-oni; his father, however, named him Benjamin. [19]*†Thus Rachel died; and she was buried on the road to Ephrath [that is, Bethlehem]. [20]Jacob set up a memorial stone on her grave, and the same monument marks Rachel's grave to this day.

[21]Israel moved on and pitched his tent beyond Migdaleder. [22]*While Israel was encamped in that region, Reuben went and lay with Bilhah, his father's concubine. When Israel heard of it, he was greatly offended.

The sons of Jacob were now twelve. [23]The sons of Leah: Reuben, Jacob's first-born, Simeon, Levi, Judah, Issachar, and Zebulun; [24]†the sons of Rachel: Joseph and Benjamin; [25]the sons of Rachel's maid Bilhah: Dan and Naphtali; [26]the sons of Leah's maid Zilpah: Gad and Asher. These are the sons of Jacob who were born to him in Paddan-aram.

[27]Jacob went home to his father Isaac at Mamre, in Kiriath-arba [that is, Hebron], where Abraham and Isaac had stayed. [28]The lifetime of Isaac was one hundred and eighty years; then he breathed his last. [29]After a full life, he died as an old man and was taken to his kinsmen. His sons Esau and Jacob buried him.

Edomite Lists

36 [1]THESE are the descendants of Esau [that is, Edom]. [2]*†Esau took his wives from among the Canaanite women: Adah, daughter of Elon the Hittite; Oholibamah, granddaughter through Anah of Zibeon the Hivite; [3]and Basemath, daughter

---

† 35, 2: *Foreign gods:* pagan images, including household idols (see note on 31, 19), that Jacob's people brought with them from Paddan-aram.

35, 4: *Rings:* Earrings were often worn as amulets connected with pagan magic.

35, 8: This verse may have stood originally in some other context. Rebekah's nurse is spoken of without a name in 24, 59. *Allon-bacuth:* the Hebrew name means "oak of weeping."

35, 18: *Ben-oni:* either "son of my vigor" or, more likely in the context, "son of affliction." *Benjamin:* "son of the right hand." This may be interpreted to signify a son who is his father's help and support, but more likely its original meaning was "southerner." In the Hebrew idiom, the south lies to one's right hand, and Benjamin was the southernmost of the Rachel tribes.

35, 19: *Bethlehem:* the gloss comes from a later tradition that identified the site with Bethlehem, also called Ephrath or Ephratha (Jos 15, 59; Ru 4, 11; Mi 5, 1). But Rachel's grave was actually near Ramah (Jer 31, 15), a few miles north of Jerusalem, in the territory of Benjamin (1 Sm 10, 2).

35, 24ff: Benjamin is here said to have been born in *Paddan-aram,* either because all twelve sons of Jacob are considered as a unit, or because the Priestly source, from which vv 23-29 are taken, follows a tradition different from that of the Elohistic source found in vv 16-20.

36, 2-14: The names of Esau's wives and of their fathers given here differ considerably from their names cited from other old sources in 26, 34 and 28, 9. *Zibeon the Hivite:* in v 20 he is called a *Horite;* see note on 34, 2.

✸
35/1: 28, 12f.
    6: 28, 19; Jos 18, 13;
        Jgs 1, 22f.
    7: 28, 12f.
  10: 1 Kgs 18, 31;
      2 Kgs 17, 34.

  12: Ex 32, 13; Heb 11, 9.
  14: 28, 18; 31, 45.
  19: 48, 7; 1 Sm 10, 2;
      Mi 5, 2.
  22: 49, 4; 1 Chr 5, 1.
36/2: 26, 34.

of Ishmael and sister of Nebaioth. **⁴***Adah bore Eliphaz to Esau; Basemath bore Reuel; **⁵***and Oholibamah bore Jeush, Jalam and Korah. These are the sons of Esau who were born to him in the land of Canaan.

⁶*Esau took his wives, his sons, his daughters, and all the members of his household, as well as his livestock comprising various animals and all the property he had acquired in the land of Canaan, and went to the land of Seir, out of the way of his brother Jacob. **⁷**Their possessions had become too great for them to dwell together, and the land in which they were staying could not support them because of their livestock. **⁸***So Esau settled in the highlands of Seir. [Esau is Edom.] **⁹**These are the descendants of Esau, ancestor of the Edomites, in the highlands of Seir.

¹⁰These are the names of Esau's sons: Eliphaz, son of Esau's wife Adah; and Reuel, son of Esau's wife Basemath. **¹¹***The sons of Eliphaz were Teman, Omar, Zepho, Gatam, and Kenaz. **¹²**(Esau's son Eliphaz had a concubine Timna, and she bore Amalek to Eliphaz.) These are the descendants of Esau's wife Adah. **¹³***The sons of Reuel were Nahath, Zerah, Shammah, and Mizzah. These are the descendants of Esau's wife Basemath. **¹⁴***The descendants of Esau's wife Oholibamah—granddaughter through Anah of Zibeon—whom she bore to Esau were Jeush, Jalam, and Korah.

¹⁵The following are the clans of Esau's descendants. The descendants of Eliphaz, Esau's first-born: the clans of Teman, Omar, Zepho, Kenaz, **¹⁶**Korah, Gatam, and Amalek. These are the clans of Eliphaz in the land of Edom; they are descended from Adah. **¹⁷**The descendants of Esau's son Reuel: the clans of Nahath, Zerah, Shammah, and Mizzah. These are the clans of Reuel in the land of Edom; they are descended from Esau's wife Basemath. **¹⁸**The descendants of Esau's wife Oholibamah: the clans of Jeush, Jalam, and Korah. These are the clans of Esau's wife Oholibamah, daughter of Anah. **¹⁹**Such are the descendants of Esau [that is, Edom] according to their clans.

²⁰*†The following are the descendants of Seir the Horite, the original settlers in the land: Lotan, Shobal, Zibeon, Anah, **²¹**Dishon, Ezer, and Dishan; they are the Horite clans descended from Seir, in the land of Edom. **²²***Lotan's descendants were Hori and Hemam, and Lotan's sister was Timna. **²³**Shobal's descendants were Alvan, Mahanath, Ebal, Shepho, and Onam. **²⁴**Zibeon's descendants were Aiah and Anah. (He is the Anah who found water in the desert while he was pasturing the asses of his father Zibeon.) **²⁵**The descendants of Anah were Dishon and Oholibamah, daughter of Anah. **²⁶**The descendants of Dishon were Hemdan, Eshban, Ithran, and Cheran. **²⁷**The descendants of Ezer were Bilhan, Zaavan, and Akan. **²⁸**The descend-

ants of Dishan were Uz and Aran. **²⁹**These are the Horite clans: the clans of Lotan, Shobal, Zibeon, Anah, **³⁰**Dishon, Ezer, and Dishan; they were the clans of the Horites, clan by clan, in the land of Seir.

³¹*†The following are the kings who reigned in the land of Edom before any king reigned over the Israelites. **³²**Bela, son of Beor, became king in Edom; the name of his city was Dinhabah. **³³**When Bela died, Jobab, son of Zerah, from Bozrah, succeeded him as king. **³⁴**When Jobab died, Husham, from the land of the Temanites, succeeded him as king. He defeated the Midianites in the country of Moab; the name of his city was Avith. **³⁵**When Husham died, **³⁶**Hadad, son of Bedad, succeeded him as king. When Hadad died, Samlah, from Masrekah, succeeded him as king. **³⁷**When Samlah died, Shaul, from Rehoboth-on-the-River, succeeded him as king. **³⁸**When Shaul died, Baal-hanan, son of Achbor, succeeded him as king. **³⁹**When Baal-hanan died, Hadar succeeded him as king; the name of his city was Pau. (His wife's name was Mehetabel; she was the daughter of Matred, son of Mezahab.)

⁴⁰The following are the names of the clans of Esau individually according to their subdivisions and localities: the clans of Timna, Alvah, Jetheth, **⁴¹**Oholibamah, Elah, Pinon, **⁴²**Kenaz, Teman, Mibzar, **⁴³**Magdiel, and Iram. These are the clans of the Edomites, according to their settlements in their territorial holdings. [Esau was the father of the Edomites.]

IV: JOSEPH AND HIS BROTHERS

Joseph Sold into Egypt

37 **¹**JACOB SETTLED IN THE LAND where his father had stayed, the land of Canaan. **²**This is his family history. When Joseph was seventeen years old, he was tending the flocks with his brothers; he was an assistant to the sons of his father's wives Bilhah and Zilpah, and he brought his father bad reports about them.

³Israel loved Joseph best of all his sons, for he was the child of his old age; and he had made him a long tunic. **⁴**When his brothers saw that their father loved him best of all his sons, they hated him so much that they would not even greet him.

⁵*Once Joseph had a dream, which he told to his brothers: **⁶**"Listen to this dream I had. **⁷**There we were, binding sheaves in the field, when suddenly my sheaf rose to an upright position, and your sheaves formed a ring around my sheaf and bowed down to it." **⁸***"Are you really going to make yourself king over

❀

4: 1 Chr 1, 35.
5: 1 Chr 1, 35.
6: 32, 4.
8: Dt 2, 4f; Jos 24, 4.
11f: 1 Chr 1, 36.
13: 1 Chr 1, 37.

14: 1 Chr 1, 35.
20f: 1 Chr 1, 38.
22-28: 1 Chr 1, 39-42.
31-43: 1 Chr 1, 43-54.
37/5: 42, 9.
8: 50, 17.

---

† 36, 20: *Seir the Horite:* according to Dt 2,12, the highlands of Seir were inhabited by Horites before they were occupied by the Edomites.

36, 31: *Before any king reigned over the Israelites:* obviously this statement was written after the time of Saul, Israel's first king.

us?" his brothers asked him. "Or impose your rule on us?" So they hated him all the more because of his talk about his dreams.

⁹Then he had another dream, and this one, too, he told to his brothers. "I had another dream," he said; "this time, the sun and the moon and eleven stars were bowing down to me." ¹⁰When he also told it to his father, his father reproved him. "What is the meaning of this dream of yours?" he asked. "Can it be that I and your mother and your brothers are to come and bow to the ground before you?" ¹¹So his brothers were wrought up against him but his father pondered the matter.

¹²One day, when his brothers had gone to pasture their father's flocks at Shechem, ¹³Israel said to Joseph, "Your brothers, you know, are tending our flocks at Shechem. Get ready; I will send you to them." "I am ready," Joseph answered. ¹⁴"Go then," he replied; "see if all is well with your brothers and the flocks, and bring back word." So he sent him off from the valley of Hebron. When Joseph reached Shechem, ¹⁵a man met him as he was wandering about in the fields. "What are you looking for?" the man asked him. ¹⁶"I am looking for my brothers," he answered. "Could you please tell me where they are tending the flocks?" ¹⁷The man told him, "They have moved on from here; in fact, I heard them say, 'Let us go on to Dothan.'" So Joseph went after his brothers and caught up with them in Dothan. ¹⁸They noticed him from a distance, and before he came up to them, they plotted to kill him. ¹⁹They said to one another: "Here comes that master dreamer! ²⁰*Come on, let us kill him and throw him into one of the cisterns here; we could say that a wild beast devoured him. We shall then see what comes of his dreams."

²¹†When Reuben heard this, he tried to save him from their hands, saying: "We must not take his life. ²²*Instead of shedding blood," he continued, "just throw him into that cistern there in the desert; but don't kill him outright." His purpose was to rescue him from their hands and restore him to his father. ²³So when Joseph came up to them, they stripped him of the long tunic he had on; ²⁴then they took him and threw him into the cistern, which was empty and dry.

²⁵*They then sat down to their meal. Looking up, they saw a caravan of Ishmaelites coming from Gilead, their camels laden with gum, balm, and resin to be taken down to Egypt. ²⁶*Judah said to his brothers: "What is to be gained by killing our brother and concealing his blood? ²⁷Rather, let us sell him to these Ishmaelites, instead of doing away with him ourselves. After all, he is our brother, our own flesh." His brothers agreed. ²⁸*†They sold Joseph to the Ishmaelites for twenty pieces of silver.

Some Midianite traders passed by, and they pulled Joseph up out of the cistern and took him to Egypt. ²⁹When Reuben went back to the cistern and saw that Joseph was not in it, he tore his clothes, ³⁰and returning to his brothers, he exclaimed: "The boy is gone! And I—where can I turn?" ³¹They took Joseph's tunic, and after slaughtering a goat, dipped the tunic in its blood. ³²Then they sent someone to bring the long tunic to their father, with the message: "We found this. See whether it is your son's tunic or not." ³³*He recognized it and exclaimed: "My son's tunic! A wild beast has devoured him! Joseph has been torn to pieces!" ³⁴Then Jacob rent his clothes, put sackcloth on his loins, and mourned his son many days. ³⁵*Though his sons and daughters tried to console him, he refused all consolation, saying, "No, I will go down mourning to my son in the nether world." Thus did his father lament him.

³⁶*The Midianites, meanwhile, sold Joseph in Egypt to Potiphar, a courtier of Pharaoh and his chief steward.

Judah and Tamar

38 ¹†ABOUT that time Judah parted from his brothers and pitched his tent near a certain Adullamite named Hirah. ²*There he met the daughter of a Canaanite named Shua, married her, and had relations with her. ³She conceived and bore a son, whom she named Er. ⁴Again she conceived and bore a son, whom she named Onan. ⁵*†Then she bore still another son, whom she named Shelah. They were in Chezib when he was born.

⁶Judah got a wife named Tamar for his first-born, Er. ⁷*But Er, Judah's first-born, greatly offended the LORD; so the LORD took his life. ⁸*†Then Judah said to

---

† 37, 21-36: The chapter thus far is from the Yahwist source, as are also vv 25-28a. But vv 21-24 and 28b-36 are from the Elohist source. In the latter, Reuben tries to rescue Joseph, who is taken in Reuben's absence by certain Midianites; in the Yahwist source, it is Judah who saves Joseph's life by having him sold to certain Ishmaelites. Although the two variant forms in which the story was handed down in early oral tradition differ in these minor points, they agree on the essential fact that Joseph was brought as a slave into Egypt because of the jealousy of his brothers.

37, 28: *They sold Joseph . . . silver:* in the Hebrew text, these words occur between *out of the cistern* and *and (they) took him to Egypt* at the end of the verse.

38, 1-30: This chapter, from the Yahwist source, has nothing to do with the Joseph story in which Judah is still living with his father and brothers. The sacred author inserted this independent account from the life of Judah at this place to mark the long lapse of time during which Joseph's family knew nothing of his life in Egypt. This is apparently a personalized history of the early days of the tribe of Judah, which inter-bred with several Canaanite clans, though some of these soon became extinct.

38, 5: *Chezib:* a variant form of Achzib (Jos 15, 44; Mi 1, 14), a town in the Judean Shephelah.

38, 8: *Preserve your brother's line:* literally "raise up seed for your brother." The ancient Israelites regarded as very important their law of levirate, or "brother-in-law" marriage; see notes on Dt 25, 5; Ru 2, 20. In the present story, it is primarily Onan's violation of this law, rather than the means he used to circumvent it, that brought on him God's displeasure (vv 9f).

✿
20: 44, 28.	35: 42, 38.
22: 42, 22.	36: Ps 105, 17.
25: 43, 11.	38/2: 1 Chr 2, 3.
26: Jb 16, 18.	5: 1 Chr 4, 21.
28: Ps 105, 17; Wis 10, 13;	7: 1 Chr 2, 3.
Acts 7, 9.	8: Dt 25, 5; Mt 22, 24;
33: 44, 28.	Mk 12, 19; Lk 20, 28.

Onan, "Unite with your brother's widow, in fulfillment of your duty as brother-in-law, and thus preserve your brother's line." ⁹Onan, however, knew that the descendants would not be counted as his; so whenever he had relations with his brother's widow, he wasted his seed on the ground, to avoid contributing offspring for his brother. ¹⁰What he did greatly offended the Lord, and the Lord took his life too. ¹¹Thereupon Judah said to his daughter-in-law Tamar, "Stay as a widow in your father's house until my son Shelah grows up"—for he feared that Shelah also might die like his brothers. So Tamar went to live in her father's house.

¹²Years passed, and Judah's wife, the daughter of Shua, died. After Judah completed the period of mourning, he went up to Timnah for the shearing of his sheep, in company with his friend Hirah the Adullamite. ¹³When Tamar was told that her father-in-law was on his way up to Timnah to shear his sheep, ¹⁴*she took off her widow's garb, veiled her face by covering herself with a shawl, and sat down at the entrance to Enaim, which is on the way to Timnah; for she was aware that, although Shelah was now grown up, she had not been given to him in marriage. ¹⁵When Judah saw her, he mistook her for a harlot, since she had covered her face. ¹⁶So he went over to her at the roadside, and not realizing that she was his daughter-in-law, he said, "Come, let me have intercourse with you." She replied, "What will you pay me for letting you have intercourse with me?" ¹⁷He answered, "I will send you a kid from the flock." "Very well," she said, "provided you leave a pledge until you send it." ¹⁸†Judah asked, "What pledge am I to give to you?" She answered, "Your seal and cord, and the staff you carry." So he gave them to her and had intercourse with her, and she conceived by him. ¹⁹When she went away, she took off her shawl and put on her widow's garb again.

²⁰Judah sent the kid by his friend the Adullamite to recover the pledge from the woman; but he could not find her. ²¹†So he asked the men of the place, "Where is the temple prostitute, the one by the roadside in Enaim?" But they answered, "There has never been a temple prostitute here." ²²He went back to Judah and told him, "I could not find her; and besides, the men of the place said there was no temple prostitute there." ²³"Let her keep the things," Judah replied; "otherwise we shall become a laughingstock. After all, I did send her the kid, even though you were unable to find her."

²⁴About three months later, Judah was told that his daughter-in-law Tamar had played the harlot and was then with child from her harlotry. "Bring her out," cried Judah; "she shall be burned." ²⁵But as they were bringing her out, she sent word to her father-in-law, "It is by the man to whom these things belong that I am with child. Please verify," she added, "whose seal and cord and whose staff these are." ²⁶Judah recognized them and said, "She is more in the right than I am, since I did not give her to my son Shelah." But he had no further relations with her.

²⁷*When the time of her delivery came, she was found to have twins in her womb. ²⁸While she was giving birth, one infant put out his hand; and the midwife, taking a crimson thread, tied it on his hand, to note that this one came out first. ²⁹*†But as he withdrew his hand, his brother came out; and she said, "What a breach you have made for yourself!" So he was called Perez. ³⁰*†Afterward his brother came out; he was called Zerah.

Joseph's Temptation

39 ¹†WHEN Joseph was taken down to Egypt, a certain Egyptian (Potiphar, a courtier of Pharaoh and his chief steward) bought him from the Ishmaelites who had brought him there. ²*But since the Lord was with him, Joseph got on very well and was assigned to the household of his Egyptian master. ³When his master saw that the Lord was with him and brought him success in whatever he did, ⁴*he took a liking to Joseph and made him his personal attendant; he put him in charge of his household and entrusted to him all his possessions. ⁵From the moment that he put him in charge of his household and all his possessions, the Lord blessed the Egyptian's house for Joseph's sake; in fact, the Lord's blessing was on everything he owned, both inside the house and out. ⁶Having left everything he owned in Joseph's charge, he gave no thought, with Joseph there, to anything but the food he ate.

Now Joseph was strikingly handsome in countenance and body. ⁷After a time, his master's wife began to look fondly at him and said, "Lie with me." ⁸But he refused. "As long as I am here," he told her, "my master does not concern himself with anything in the house, but has entrusted to me all he owns. ⁹He wields

---

† 38, 18: *Seal and cord:* the cylinder seal, through which a hole was bored lengthwise so that it could be worn from the neck by a cord, was a distinctive means of identification. Apparently a man's staff was also marked with his name (Nm 17, 16f) or other sign of identification.

38, 21: *Temple prostitute:* the Hebrew term *qedesha*, literally "consecrated woman," designates a woman who had ritual intercourse with men in pagan fertility rites; cf Dt 23, 18; Hos 4, 14, where the same Hebrew word is used. Hirah the Adullamite uses a word that refers to a higher social class than that designated by the term *zona*, common "harlot," used in vv 15.24.

38, 29: *He was called Perez:* the Hebrew word means "breach."

38, 30: *He was called Zerah:* a name connected here by popular etymology with a Hebrew verb for the red light of dawn, alluding apparently to the crimson thread.

39, 1: *(Potiphar . . . chief steward):* These words in the text serve to harmonize ch 39 from the Yahwist source with 37, 36 and 40, 1-23 from the Elohist. In the former, the Ishmaelites who bought Joseph from his brothers (37, 28) sold him to the unnamed "Egyptian master" of ch 39. In the latter, the Midianites who kidnaped Joseph (37, 28; 40, 15) sold him to Potiphar, Pharaoh's chief steward (37, 36), whose house was used as a royal prison (40, 2f).

---

* 14: Prv 7, 10.
27: 1 Chr 2, 4.
29: Rv 4, 12; Mt 1, 3; Lk 3, 33.
30: Nm 26, 20; 1 Chr 2, 4; Mt 1, 3.

39/2: 1 Sm 3, 19; 10, 7; 18, 14; 2 Sm 5, 10; 2 Kgs 18, 7; Acts 7, 9.
4: Dn 1, 9.

no more authority in this house than I do, and he has withheld from me nothing but yourself, since you are his wife. How, then, could I commit so great a wrong and thus stand condemned before God?" **10***Although she tried to entice him day after day, he would not agree to lie beside her, or even stay near her.

11One such day, when Joseph came into the house to do his work, and none of the household servants were then in the house, **12**she laid hold of him by his cloak, saying, "Lie with me!" But leaving the cloak in her hand, he got away from her and ran outside. **13**When she saw that he had left his cloak in her hand as he fled outside, **14**she screamed for her household servants and told them, "Look! my husband has brought in a Hebrew slave to make sport of us! He came in here to lie with me, but I cried out as loud as I could. **15**When he heard me scream for help, he left his cloak beside me and ran away outside."

16She kept the cloak with her until his master came home. **17**Then she told him the same story: "The Hebrew slave whom you brought here broke in on me, to make sport of me. **18**But when I screamed for help, he left his cloak beside me and fled outside." **19**As soon as the master heard his wife's story about how his slave had treated her, he became enraged. **20***He seized Joseph and threw him into the jail where the royal prisoners were confined.

But even while he was in prison, **21***the LORD remained with Joseph; he showed him kindness by making the chief jailer well-disposed toward him. **22**The chief jailer put Joseph in charge of all the prisoners in the jail, and everything that had to be done there was done under his management. **23**The chief jailer did not concern himself with anything at all that was in Joseph's charge, since the LORD was with him and brought success to all he did.

The Dreams Interpreted

40 **1**SOME time afterward, the royal cupbearer and baker gave offense to their lord, the king of Egypt. **2**Pharaoh was angry with his two courtiers, the chief cupbearer and the chief baker, **3**and he put them in custody in the house of the chief steward (the same jail where Joseph was confined). **4**The chief steward assigned Joseph to them, and he became their attendant.

After they had been in custody for some time, **5**the cupbearer and the baker of the king of Egypt who were confined in the jail both had dreams on the same night, each dream with its own meaning. **6**When Joseph came to them in the morning, he noticed that they looked disturbed. **7**So he asked Pharaoh's courtiers who were with him in custody in his master's house, "Why do you look so sad today?" **8***They answered him, "We have had dreams, but there is no one to interpret them for us." Joseph said to them,

"Surely, interpretations come from God. Please tell the dreams to me."

9Then the chief cupbearer told Joseph his dream. "In my dream," he said, "I saw a vine in front of me, **10**and on the vine were three branches. It had barely budded when its blossoms came out, and its clusters ripened into grapes. **11**Pharaoh's cup was in my hand; so I took the grapes, pressed them out into his cup, and put it in Pharaoh's hand." **12**Joseph said to him: "This is what it means. The three branches are three days; **13†**within three days Pharaoh will lift up your head and restore you to your post. You will be handing Pharaoh his cup as you formerly used to do when you were his cupbearer. **14**So if you will still remember, when all is well with you, that I was here with you, please do me the favor of mentioning me to Pharaoh, to get me out of this place. **15**The truth is that I was kidnaped from the land of the Hebrews, and here I have not done anything for which I should have been put into a dungeon."

16When the chief baker saw that Joseph had given this favorable interpretation, he said to him: "I too had a dream. In it I had three wicker baskets on my head; **17**in the top one were all kinds of bakery products for Pharaoh, but the birds were pecking at them out of the basket on my head." **18**Joseph said to him in reply: "This is what it means. The three baskets are three days; **19**within three days Pharaoh will lift up your head and have you impaled on a stake, and the birds will be pecking the flesh from your body."

20And in fact, on the third day, which was Pharaoh's birthday, when he gave a banquet to all his staff, with his courtiers around him, he lifted up the heads of the chief cupbearer and chief baker. **21**He restored the chief cupbearer to his office, so that he again handed the cup to Pharaoh; **22**but the chief baker he impaled —just as Joseph had told them in his interpretation. **23**Yet the chief cupbearer gave no thought to Joseph; he had forgotten him.

Pharaoh's Dream

41 **1**AFTER a lapse of two years, Pharaoh had a dream. He saw himself standing by the Nile, **2**when up out of the Nile came seven cows, handsome and fat; they grazed in the reed grass. **3**Behind them seven other cows, ugly and gaunt, came up out of the Nile; and standing on the bank of the Nile beside the others, **4**the ugly, gaunt cows ate up the seven handsome, fat cows. Then Pharaoh woke up.

5He fell asleep again and had another dream. He saw seven ears of grain, fat and healthy, growing on a single stalk. **6**Behind them sprouted seven ears of grain, thin and blasted by the east wind; **7**and the seven thin ears swallowed up the seven fat, healthy

---

† 40, 13: *Lift up your head:* signifying "pardon you." In v 19 "to lift up the head" means "to behead"; and finally, in v 20, the same expression means "to review the case (of someone)." Joseph couches his interpretation of the dreams in equivocal terms.

10: 1 Mc 2, 53.
20: Ps 105, 18.
21: Acts 7, 9f.
40/8: 41, 16.

ears. Then Pharaoh woke up, to find it was only a dream.

⁸Next morning his spirit was agitated. So he summoned all the magicians and sages of Egypt and recounted his dreams to them; but no one could interpret his dreams for him. ⁹Then the chief cupbearer spoke up and said to Pharaoh: "On this occasion I am reminded of my negligence. ¹⁰Once, when Pharaoh was angry, he put me and the chief baker in custody in the house of the chief steward. ¹¹Later, we both had dreams on the same night, and each of our dreams had its own meaning. ¹²*There with us was a Hebrew youth, a slave of the chief steward; and when we told him our dreams, he interpreted them for us and explained for each of us the meaning of his dream. ¹³And it turned out just as he had told us: I was restored to my post, but the other man was impaled."

¹⁴*Pharaoh therefore had Joseph summoned, and they hurriedly brought him from the dungeon. After he shaved and changed his clothes, he came into Pharaoh's presence. ¹⁵Pharaoh then said to him: "I had certain dreams that no one can interpret. But I hear it said of you that the moment you are told a dream you can interpret it." ¹⁶*"It is not I," Joseph replied to Pharaoh, "but God who will give Pharaoh the right answer."

¹⁷Then Pharaoh said to Joseph: "In my dream, I was standing on the bank of the Nile, ¹⁸when up from the Nile came seven cows, fat and well-formed; they grazed in the reed grass. ¹⁹Behind them came seven other cows, scrawny, most ill-formed and gaunt. Never have I seen such ugly specimens as these in all the land of Egypt! ²⁰The gaunt, ugly cows ate up the first seven fat cows. ²¹But when they had consumed them, no one could tell that they had done so, because they looked as ugly as before. Then I woke up. ²²In another dream I saw seven ears of grain, fat and healthy, growing on a single stalk. ²³Behind them sprouted seven ears of grain, shriveled and thin and blasted by the east wind; ²⁴and the seven thin ears swallowed up the seven healthy ears. I have spoken to the magicians, but none of them can give me an explanation."

²⁵Joseph said to Pharaoh: "Both of Pharaoh's dreams have the same meaning. God has thus foretold to Pharaoh what he is about to do. ²⁶The seven healthy cows are seven years, and the seven healthy ears are seven years—the same in each dream. ²⁷So also, the seven thin, ugly cows that came up after them are seven years, as are the seven thin, wind-blasted ears; they are seven years of famine. ²⁸It is just as I told Pharaoh: God has revealed to Pharaoh what he is about to do. ²⁹Seven years of great abundance are now coming throughout the land of Egypt; ³⁰but these will be followed by seven years of famine, when all the abundance in the land of Egypt will be forgotten. When the famine has ravaged the land, ³¹no trace of the abundance will be found in the land because of the famine that follows it—so utterly severe will that famine be. ³²That Pharaoh had the same dream twice means that the matter has been reaffirmed by God and that God will soon bring it about.

³³"Therefore, let Pharaoh seek out a wise and discerning man and put him in charge of the land of Egypt. ³⁴Pharaoh should also take action to appoint overseers, so as to regiment the land during the seven years of abundance. ³⁵They should husband all the food of the coming good years, collecting the grain under Pharaoh's authority, to be stored in the towns for food. ³⁶This food will serve as a reserve for the country against the seven years of famine that are to follow in the land of Egypt, so that the land may not perish in the famine."

³⁷*This advice pleased Pharaoh and all his officials. ³⁸"Could we find another like him," Pharaoh asked his officials, "a man so endowed with the spirit of God?" ³⁹So Pharaoh said to Joseph: "Since God has made all this known to you, no one can be as wise and discerning as you are. ⁴⁰*You shall be in charge of my palace, and all my people shall dart at your command. Only in respect to the throne shall I outrank you. ⁴¹Herewith," Pharaoh told Joseph, "I place you in charge of the whole land of Egypt." ⁴²†With that, Pharaoh took off his signet ring and put it on Joseph's finger. He had him dressed in robes of fine linen and put a gold chain about his neck. ⁴³†He then had him ride in the chariot of his vizier, and they shouted "Abrek!" before him.

Thus was Joseph installed over the whole land of Egypt. ⁴⁴"I, Pharaoh, proclaim," he told Joseph, "that without your approval no one shall move hand or foot in all the land of Egypt." ⁴⁵†Pharaoh also bestowed the name of Zaphenath-paneah on Joseph, and he gave him in marriage Asenath, the daughter of Potiphera, priest of Heliopolis. ⁴⁶Joseph was thirty years old when he entered the service of Pharaoh, king of Egypt.

After Joseph left Pharaoh's presence, he traveled throughout the land of Egypt. ⁴⁷During the seven years of plenty, when the land produced abundant crops, ⁴⁸he husbanded all the food of these years of plenty that the land of Egypt was enjoying and stored it in the towns, placing in each town the crops of the

---

† 41, 42: *Signet ring:* a finger ring in which was set a stamp seal, different from the cylinder seal such as Judah wore; see note on 38, 18. This is an authentic detail. By receiving Pharaoh's signet ring, Joseph was made vizier of Egypt (v 43); the vizier was known as "seal-bearer of the king of Lower Egypt." Another authentic detail is the *gold chain,* a symbol of high office in ancient Egypt.

41, 43: *Abrek:* apparently a cry of homage, though the word's derivation and actual meaning are uncertain.

41, 45: *Zaphenath-paneah:* a Hebrew transcription of an Egyptian name meaning "the god speaks and he (the new-born child) lives." *Asenath:* means "belonging to (the Egyptian goddess) Neith." *Potiphera:* means "he whom Ra (the Egyptian god) gave"; a shorter form of the same name was borne by Joseph's master (37, 36). *Heliopolis:* in Hebrew, *On,* a city seven miles northeast of modern Cairo, site of the chief temple of the sun god; it is mentioned also in v 50; 46, 20; Ez 30, 17.

* 41/12: Dn 1, 17.
     14: Ps 105, 20.
     16: 40, 8.
            37: Acts 7, 10.
            40: Ps 105, 21; Wis 10, 14;
                  1 Mc 2, 53; Acts 7, 10.

fields around it. ⁴⁹Joseph garnered grain in quantities like the sands of the sea, so vast that at last he stopped measuring it, for it was beyond measure.

⁵⁰*Before the famine years set in, Joseph became the father of two sons, borne to him by Asenath, daughter of Potiphera, priest of Heliopolis. ⁵¹†He named his first-born Manasseh, meaning, "God has made me forget entirely the sufferings I endured at the hands of my family"; ⁵²†and the second he named Ephraim, meaning, "God has made me fruitful in the land of my affliction."

⁵³When the seven years of abundance enjoyed by the land of Egypt came to an end, ⁵⁴*the seven years of famine set in, just as Joseph had predicted. Although there was famine in all the other countries, food was available throughout the land of Egypt. ⁵⁵When hunger came to be felt throughout the land of Egypt and the people cried to Pharaoh for bread, Pharaoh directed all the Egyptians to go to Joseph and do whatever he told them. ⁵⁶When the famine had spread throughout the land, Joseph opened all the cities that had grain and rationed it to the Egyptians, since the famine had gripped the land of Egypt. ⁵⁷In fact, all the world came to Joseph to obtain rations of grain, for famine had gripped the whole world.

The Brothers' First Journey to Egypt

42 ¹WHEN Jacob learned that grain rations were available in Egypt, he said to his sons: "Why do you keep gaping at one another? ²*I hear," he went on, "that rations of grain are available in Egypt. Go down there and buy some for us, that we may stay alive rather than die of hunger." ³So ten of Joseph's brothers went down to buy an emergency supply of grain from Egypt. ⁴It was only Joseph's full brother Benjamin that Jacob did not send with the rest, for he thought some disaster might befall him. ⁵*Thus, since there was famine in the land of Canaan also, the sons of Israel were among those who came to procure rations.

⁶*It was Joseph, as governor of the country, who dispensed the rations to all the people. When Joseph's brothers came and knelt down before him with their faces to the ground, ⁷he recognized them as soon as he saw them. But he concealed his own identity from them and spoke sternly to them. "Where do you come from?" he asked them. They answered, "From the land of Canaan, to procure food."

⁸When Joseph recognized his brothers, although they did not recognize him, ⁹*†he was reminded of the dreams he had about them. He said to them: "You are spies. You have come to see the nakedness of the land." ¹⁰"No, my lord," they replied. "On the contrary, your servants have come to procure food. ¹¹All of us are sons of the same man. We are honest men; your servants have never been spies." ¹²But he answered

them: "Not so! You have come to see the nakedness of the land." ¹³*"We your servants," they said, "were twelve brothers, sons of a certain man in Canaan; but the youngest one is at present with our father, and the other one is gone." ¹⁴"It is just as I said," Joseph persisted; "you are spies. ¹⁵This is how you shall be tested: unless your youngest brother comes here, I swear by the life of Pharaoh that you shall not leave here. ¹⁶So send one of your number to get your brother, while the rest of you stay here under arrest. Thus shall your words be tested for their truth; if they are untrue, as Pharaoh lives, you are spies!" ¹⁷With that, he locked them up in the guardhouse for three days.

¹⁸On the third day Joseph said to them: "Do this, and you shall live; for I am a God-fearing man. ¹⁹If you have been honest, only one of your brothers need be confined in this prison, while the rest of you may go and take home provisions for your starving families. ²⁰*But you must come back to me with your youngest brother. Your words will thus be verified, and you will not die." To this they agreed. ²¹*To one another, however, they said: "Alas, we are being punished because of our brother. We saw the anguish of his heart when he pleaded with us, yet we paid no heed; that is why this anguish has now come upon us." ²²*"Didn't I tell you," broke in Reuben, "not to do wrong to the boy? But you wouldn't listen! Now comes the reckoning for his blood." ²³They did not know, of course, that Joseph understood what they said, since he spoke with them through an interpreter. ²⁴But turning away from them, he wept. When he was able to speak to them again, he had Simeon taken from them and bound before their eyes. ²⁵Then Joseph gave orders to have their containers filled with grain, their money replaced in each one's sack, and provisions given them for their journey. After this had been done for them, ²⁶they loaded their donkeys with the rations and departed.

²⁷†At the night encampment, when one of them opened his bag to give his donkey some fodder, he was surprised to see his money in the mouth of his bag. ²⁸"My money has been returned!" he cried out to his brothers. "Here it is in my bag!" At that their hearts sank. Trembling, they asked one another, "What is this that God has done to us?"

²⁹When they got back to their father Jacob in the land of Canaan, they told him all that had happened to them. ³⁰"The man who is lord of the country," they said, "spoke to us sternly and put us in custody as if

---

† 41, 51: *Manasseh:* allusion to this name is in the Hebrew expression, *nishshani,* "he made me forget."

41, 52: *Ephraim:* related to the Hebrew expression *hiphrani,* "(God) has made me fruitful."

42, 9.12: *The nakedness of the land:* the military weakness of the land, like human nakedness, should not be seen by strangers.

42, 27-28: These two verses are from the Yahwist source, whereas the rest of the chapter is from the Elohist source, in which the men find the money in their sacks (not "bags"—a different Hebrew word) only when they arrive home (v 35); cf 43, 21.

❋
    50: 46, 20; 48, 5.   9: 37, 5.
    54: Ps 105, 16; Acts 7, 11.   13: 44, 20.
42/2: Acts 7, 12.   20: 43, 5.
    5: Jdt 5, 10; Acts 7, 11.   21: 37, 18-27.
    6: Ps 105, 21.   22: 37, 22.

we were spying on the land. ³¹But we said to him: 'We are honest men: we have never been spies. ³²There were twelve of us brothers, sons of the same father; but one is gone, and the youngest one is at present with our father in the land of Canaan.' ³³Then the man who is lord of the country said to us: 'This is how I shall know if you are honest men: leave one of your brothers with me, while the rest of you go home with rations for your starving families. ³⁴When you come back to me with your youngest brother, and I know that you are honest men and not spies, I will restore your brother to you, and you may move about freely in the land.'"

³⁵When they were emptying their sacks, there in each one's sack was his moneybag! At the sight of their moneybags, they and their father were dismayed. ³⁶Their father Jacob said to them: "Must you make me childless? Joseph is gone, and Simeon is gone, and now you would take away Benjamin! Why must such things always happen to me?" ³⁷Then Reuben told his father: "Put him in my care, and I will bring him back to you. You may kill my own two sons if I do not return him to you." ³⁸*But Jacob replied: "My son shall not go down with you. Now that his full brother is dead, he is the only one left. If some disaster should befall him on the journey you must make, you would send my white head down to the nether world in grief."

The Second Journey to Egypt

43 ¹†Now the famine in the land grew more severe. ²So when they had used up all the rations they had brought from Egypt, their father said to them, "Go back and procure us a little more food." ³*But Judah replied: "The man strictly warned us, 'You shall not appear in my presence unless your brother is with you.' ⁴If you are willing to let our brother go with us, we will go down to procure food for you. ⁵*But if you are not willing, we will not go down, because the man told us, 'You shall not appear in my presence unless your brother is with you.'" ⁶Israel demanded, "Why did you bring this trouble on me by telling the man that you had another brother?" ⁷They answered: "The man kept asking about ourselves and our family: 'Is your father still living? Do you have another brother?' We had to answer his questions. How could we know that he would say, 'Bring your brother down here'?"

⁸*Then Judah urged his father Israel: "Let the boy go with me, that we may be off and on our way if you and we and our children are to keep from starving to death. ⁹*I myself will stand surety for him. You can hold me responsible for him. If I fail to bring him back, to set him in your presence, you can hold it against me forever. ¹⁰Had we not dillydallied, we could have been there and back twice by now!"

¹¹*Their father Israel then told them: "If it must be so, then do this: Put some of the land's best products in your baggage and take them down to the man as gifts: some balm and honey, gum and resin, and pistachios and almonds. ¹²Also take extra money along, for you must return the amount that was put back in the mouths of your bags; it may have been a mistake. ¹³Take your brother, too, and be off on your way back to the man. ¹⁴May God Almighty dispose the man to be merciful toward you, so that he may let your other brother go, as well as Benjamin. As for me, if I am to suffer bereavement, I shall suffer it."

¹⁵So the men got the gifts, took double the amount of money with them, and, accompanied by Benjamin, were off on their way down to Egypt to present themselves to Joseph. ¹⁶When Joseph saw Benjamin with them, he told his head steward, "Take these men into the house, and have an animal slaughtered and prepared, for they are to dine with me at noon." ¹⁷Doing as Joseph had ordered, the steward conducted the men to Joseph's house. ¹⁸But on being led to his house, they became apprehensive. "It must be," they thought, "on account of the money put back in our bags the first time, that we are taken inside; they want to use it as a pretext to attack us and take our donkeys and seize us as slaves." ¹⁹So they went up to Joseph's head steward and talked to him at the entrance of the house. ²⁰*"If you please, sir," they said, "we came down here once before to procure food. ²¹*But when we arrived at a night's encampment and opened our bags, there was each man's money in the mouth of his bag—our money in the full amount! We have now brought it back. ²²We have brought other money to procure food with. We do not know who put the first money in our bags." ²³"Be at ease," he replied; "you have no need to fear. Your God and the God of your father must have put treasures in your bags for you. As for your money, I received it." With that, he led Simeon out to them.

²⁴The steward then brought the men inside Joseph's house. He gave them water to bathe their feet, and got fodder for their donkeys. ²⁵Then they set out their gifts to await Joseph's arrival at noon, for they had heard that they were to dine there. ²⁶When Joseph came home, they presented him with the gifts they had brought inside, while they bowed down before him to the ground. ²⁷*After inquiring how they were, he asked them, "And how is your aged father, of whom you spoke? Is he still in good health?" ²⁸"Your servant our father is thriving and still in good health," they said, as they bowed respectfully. ²⁹*When Joseph's eye fell on his full brother Benjamin, he asked, "Is this your youngest brother, of whom you told me?" Then he said to him, "May God be gracious to you, my boy!" ³⁰With that, Joseph had to hurry out, for he was so overcome with affection for his brother that he was

---

❊ 38: 37, 35.
43/3: 44, 23.
5: 42, 20.
8: 42, 37.
9: 44, 32.
11: 45, 23.
20: 42, 3.
21: 42, 27f.
27: Tb 7, 4.
29: 42, 13.

† 43, 1-34: This chapter and the following one are from the Yahwist source, in which Judah, not Reuben as in the Elohist source, volunteers to go surety for Benjamin.

on the verge of tears. He went into a private room and wept there. ³¹After washing his face, he reappeared and, now in control of himself, gave the order, "Serve the meal." ³²†It was served separately to him, to the brothers, and to the Egyptians who partook of his board. (Egyptians may not eat with Hebrews; that is abhorrent to them.) ³³When they were seated by his directions according to their age, from the oldest to the youngest, they looked at one another in amazement; ³⁴†and as portions were brought to them from Joseph's table, Benjamin's portion was five times as large as anyone else's. So they drank freely and made merry with him.

Final Test

44 ¹†THEN Joseph gave his head steward these instructions: "Fill the men's bags with as much food as they can carry, and put each man's money in the mouth of his bag. ²In the mouth of the youngest one's bag put also my silver goblet, together with the money for his rations." The steward carried out Joseph's instructions. ³At daybreak the men and their donkeys were sent off. ⁴They had not gone far out of the city when Joseph said to his head steward: "Go at once after the men! When you overtake them, say to them, 'Why did you repay good with evil? Why did you steal the silver goblet from me? ⁵†It is the very one from which my master drinks and which he uses for divination. What you have done is wrong.'"

⁶When the steward overtook them and repeated these words to them, ⁷they remonstrated with him: "How can my lord say such things? Far be it from your servants to do such a thing! ⁸We even brought back to you from the land of Canaan the money that we found in the mouths of our bags. Why, then, would we steal silver or gold from your master's house? ⁹If any of your servants is found to have the goblet, he shall die, and as for the rest of us, we shall become my lord's slaves." ¹⁰But he replied, "Even though it ought to be as you propose, only the one who is found to have it shall become my slave, and the rest of you shall be exonerated." ¹¹Then each of them eagerly lowered his bag to the ground and opened it; ¹²and when a search was made, starting with the oldest and ending with the youngest, the goblet turned up in Benjamin's bag. ¹³At this, they tore their clothes. Then, when each man had reloaded his donkey, they returned to the city.

¹⁴As Judah and his brothers reentered Joseph's house, he was still there; so they flung themselves on the ground before him. ¹⁵"How could you do such a thing?" Joseph asked them. "You should have known that such a man as I could discover by divination what happened." ¹⁶†Judah replied: "What can we say to my lord? How can we plead or how try to prove our innocence? God has uncovered your servants' guilt. Here we are, then, the slaves of my lord—the rest of us no less than the one in whose possession the goblet was found." ¹⁷"Far be it from me to act thus!" said Joseph. "Only the one in whose possession the goblet was found shall become my slave; the rest of you may go back safe and sound to your father."

¹⁸Judah then stepped up to him and said: "I beg you, my lord, let your servant speak earnestly to my lord, and do not become angry with your servant, for you are the equal of Pharaoh. ¹⁹†My lord asked your servants, 'Have you a father, or another brother?' ²⁰*So we said to my lord, 'We have an aged father, and a young brother, the child of his old age. This one's full brother is dead, and since he is the only one by that mother who is left, his father dotes on him.' ²¹Then you told your servants, 'Bring him down to me that my eyes may look on him.' ²²We replied to my lord, 'The boy cannot leave his father; his father would die if he were to leave him.' ²³*But you told your servants, 'Unless your youngest brother comes back with you, you shall not come into my presence again.' ²⁴When we returned to your servant our father, we reported to him the words of my lord.

²⁵"Later, our father told us to come back and buy some food for the family. ²⁶So we reminded him, 'We cannot go down there; only if our youngest brother is with us can we go, for we may not see the man if our youngest brother is not with us.' ²⁷Then your servant our father said to us, 'As you know, my wife bore me two sons. ²⁸*One of them, however, disappeared, and I had to conclude that he must have been torn to pieces by wild beasts; I have not seen him since. ²⁹If you now take this one away from me too, and some disaster befalls him, you will send my white head down to the nether world in grief.'

³⁰"If then the boy is not with us when I go back to your servant my father, whose very life is bound up with his, ³¹he will die as soon as he sees that the boy is missing; and your servants will thus send the white head of our father down to the nether world in grief. ³²*Besides, I, your servant, got the boy from his father by going surety for him, saying, 'If I fail to bring him

---

† 43, 32: *Separately to him:* that Joseph did not eat with the other Egyptians was apparently a matter of rank.

43, 34: *Five times as large as:* probably an idiomatic expression for "much larger than."

44, 1f: Replacement of the money in the men's bags is probably a redactional addition here, taken from the Yahwist account of the first visit. It is only the goblet in Benjamin's bag, not any replaced money, that plays a part in the rest of the chapter.

44, 5: *Divination:* seeking omens through liquids poured into a cup or bowl was a common practice in the ancient Near East; cf v 15. Even though divination was frowned on in later Israel (Lv 19, 31), it is in this place an authentic touch which the sacred author does not hesitate to ascribe to Joseph, the wisest man in Egypt.

44, 16: *Guilt:* in trying to do away with Joseph when he was young.

44, 19: *My lord . . . your servants:* such frequently repeated expressions in Judah's speech show the formal court style used by a subject in speaking to a high official.

✧
44/20: 42, 13.   28: 37, 20.33.
     23: 43, 3.   32: 43, 9.

back to you, father, you can hold it against me forever.' ³³Let me, your servant, therefore, remain in place of the boy as the slave of my lord, and let the boy go back with his brothers. ³⁴How could I go back to my father if the boy were not with me? I could not bear to see the anguish that would overcome my father."

The Truth Revealed

45 ¹JOSEPH could no longer control himself in the presence of all his attendants, so he cried out, "Have everyone withdraw from me!" Thus no one else was about when he made himself known to his brothers. ²But his sobs were so loud that the Egyptians heard him, and so the news reached Pharaoh's palace. ³*"I am Joseph," he said to his brothers. "Is my father still in good health?" But his brothers could give him no answer, so dumbfounded were they at him.

⁴"Come closer to me," he told his brothers. When they had done so, he said: "I am your brother Joseph, whom you once sold into Egypt. ⁵*But now do not be distressed, and do not reproach yourselves for having sold me here. It was really for the sake of saving lives that God sent me here ahead of you. ⁶For two years now the famine has been in the land, and for five more years tillage will yield no harvest. ⁷God, therefore, sent me on ahead of you to ensure for you a remnant on earth and to save your lives in an extraordinary deliverance. ⁸†So it was not really you but God who had me come here; and he has made of me a father to Pharaoh, lord of all his household, and ruler over the whole land of Egypt.

⁹*†"Hurry back, then, to my father and tell him: 'Thus says your son Joseph: God has made me lord of all Egypt; come to me without delay. ¹⁰†You will settle in the region of Goshen, where you will be near me—you and your children and grandchildren, your flocks and herds, and everything that you own. ¹¹Since five years of famine still lie ahead, I will provide for you there, so that you and your family and all that are yours may not suffer want.' ¹²Surely, you can see for yourselves, and Benjamin can see for himself, that it is I, Joseph, who am speaking to you. ¹³Tell my father all about my high position in Egypt and what you have seen. But hurry and bring my father down here." ¹⁴Thereupon he flung himself on the neck of his brother Benjamin and wept, and Benjamin wept in his arms. ¹⁵Joseph then kissed all his brothers, crying over each of them; and only then were his brothers able to talk with him.

¹⁶When the news reached Pharaoh's palace that Joseph's brothers had come, Pharaoh and his courtiers were pleased. ¹⁷So Pharaoh told Joseph: "Say to your brothers: 'This is what you shall do: Load up your animals and go without delay to the land of Canaan. ¹⁸*There get your father and your families, and then

come back here to me; I will assign you the best land in Egypt, where you will live off the fat of the land.' ¹⁹Instruct them further: 'Do this. Take wagons from the land of Egypt for your children and your wives and to transport your father on your way back here. ²⁰Do not be concerned about your belongings, for the best in the whole land of Egypt shall be yours.'"

²¹The sons of Israel acted accordingly. Joseph gave them the wagons, as Pharaoh had ordered, and he supplied them with provisions for the journey. ²²He also gave to each of them fresh clothing, but to Benjamin he gave three hundred shekels of silver and five sets of garments. ²³Moreover, what he sent to his father was ten jackasses loaded with the finest products of Egypt and ten jennies loaded with grain and bread and other provisions for his journey. ²⁴As he sent his brothers on their way, he told them, "Let there be no recriminations on the way."

²⁵So they left Egypt and made their way to their father Jacob in the land of Canaan. ²⁶When they told him, "Joseph is still alive—in fact, it is he who is ruler of all the land of Egypt," he was dumbfounded; he could not believe them. ²⁷But when they recounted to him all that Joseph had told them, and when he saw the wagons that Joseph had sent for his transport, the spirit of their father Jacob revived. ²⁸"It is enough," said Israel. "My son Joseph is still alive! I must go and see him before I die."

Migration to Egypt

46 ¹ISRAEL set out with all that was his. When he arrived at Beer-sheba, he offered sacrifices to the God of his father Isaac. ²There God, speaking to Israel in a vision by night, called, "Jacob! Jacob!" "Here I am," he answered. ³†Then he said: "I am God, the God of your father. Do not be afraid to go down to Egypt, for there I will make you a great nation. ⁴Not only will I go down to Egypt with you; I will also bring you back here, after Joseph has closed your eyes."

⁵So Jacob departed from Beer-sheba, and the sons of Israel put their father and their wives and children on the wagons that Pharaoh had sent for his transport. ⁶*They took with them their livestock and the possessions they had acquired in the land of Canaan. Thus Jacob and all his descendants migrated to Egypt. ⁷His sons and his grandsons, his daughters and his

---

* 45/3f: Acts 7, 13.
    5: 50, 20; Sir 49, 15.
    9: Acts 7, 14.

18: Acts 7, 14.
46/6: Ex 1, 1; Jos 24, 4;
    Jdt 5, 10; Acts 7, 15.

---

† 45, 8: *Father to Pharaoh:* a term applied to a vizier in ancient Egypt.

45, 9-15: In these verses, as in 46, 31—47, 5a, all from the Yahwist source, Joseph in his own name invites his father and brothers to come to Egypt. Only after their arrival is Pharaoh informed of the fact. On the other hand, in 45, 16-20, from the Elohist source, it is Pharaoh himself who invites Joseph's kinsmen to migrate to his domain.

45, 10: *The region of Goshen:* modern Wadi Tumilat in the eastern part of the Nile delta.

46, 3: *I am God:* more precisely according to the Hebrew text, "I am El." "El" is here a divine name, not the common noun "god."

granddaughters—all his descendants—he took with him to Egypt.

⁸*These are the names of the Israelites, Jacob and his descendants, who migrated to Egypt.

Reuben, Jacob's first-born, ⁹*†and the sons of Reuben: Hanoch, Pallu, Hezron, and Carmi. ¹⁰*The sons of Simeon: Nemuel, Jamin, Ohad, Jachin, Zohar, and Shaul, son of a Canaanite woman. ¹¹*The sons of Levi: Gershon, Kohath, and Merari. ¹²*The sons of Judah: Er, Onan, Shelah, Perez, and Zerah—but Er and Onan had died in the land of Canaan; and the sons of Perez were Hezron and Hamul. ¹³*The sons of Issachar: Tola, Puah, Jashub, and Shimron. ¹⁴*The sons of Zebulun: Sered, Elon, and Jahleel. ¹⁵These were the sons whom Leah bore to Jacob in Paddan-aram, along with his daughter Dinah—thirty-three persons in all, male and female.

¹⁶*The sons of Gad: Zephon, Haggi, Shuni, Ezbon, Eri, Arod, and Areli. ¹⁷*The sons of Asher: Imnah, Ishvah, Ishvi, and Beriah, with their sister Serah; and the sons of Beriah: Heber and Malchiel. ¹⁸These were the descendants of Zilpah, whom Laban had given to his daughter Leah; these she bore to Jacob—sixteen persons in all.

¹⁹The sons of Jacob's wife Rachel: Joseph and Benjamin. ²⁰*In the land of Egypt Joseph became the father of Manasseh and Ephraim, whom Asenath, daughter of Potiphera, priest of Heliopolis, bore to him. ²¹*The sons of Benjamin: Bela, Becher, Ashbel, Gera, Naaman, Ahiram, Shupham, Hupham, and Ard. ²²These were the sons whom Rachel bore to Jacob—fourteen persons in all.

²³*The sons of Dan: Hushim. ²⁴*The sons of Naphtali: Jahzeel, Guni, Jezer, and Shillem. ²⁵These were the sons of Bilhah, whom Laban had given to his daughter Rachel; these she bore to Jacob—seven persons in all.

²⁶*Jacob's people who migrated to Egypt—his direct descendants, not counting the wives of Jacob's sons—numbered sixty-six persons in all. ²⁷*†Together with Joseph's sons who were born to him in Egypt—two persons—all the people comprising Jacob's family who had come to Egypt amounted to seventy persons in all.

²⁸Israel had sent Judah ahead to Joseph, so that he might meet him in Goshen. On his arrival in the region of Goshen, ²⁹Joseph hitched the horses to his chariot and rode to meet his father Israel in Goshen. As soon as he saw him, he flung himself on his neck and wept a long time in his arms. ³⁰And Israel said to Joseph, "At last I can die, now that I have seen for myself that Joseph is still alive."

³¹Joseph then said to his brothers and his father's household: "I will go and inform Pharaoh, telling him: 'My brothers and my father's household, whose home is in the land of Canaan, have come to me. ³²The men are shepherds, having long been keepers of livestock; and they have brought with them their flocks and herds, as well as everything else they own.' ³³So when Pharaoh summons you and asks what your occupation is, you must answer, ³⁴'We your servants, like our ancestors, have been keepers of livestock from the beginning until now,' in order that you may stay in the region of Goshen, since all shepherds are abhorrent to the Egyptians."

Settlement in Goshen

47 ¹JOSEPH went and told Pharaoh, "My father and my brothers have come from the land of Canaan, with their flocks and herds and everything else they own; and they are now in the region of Goshen." ²He then presented to Pharaoh five of his brothers whom he had selected from their full number. ³When Pharaoh asked them what their occupation was, they answered, "We your servants, like our ancestors, are shepherds. ⁴*We have come," they continued, "in order to stay in this country, for there is no pasture for your servants' flocks in the land of Canaan, so severe has the famine been there. Please, therefore, let your servants settle in the region of Goshen." ⁵Pharaoh said to Joseph, "They may settle in the region of Goshen; and if you know any of them to be qualified, you may put them in charge of my own livestock."

Thus, when Jacob and his sons came to Joseph in Egypt, and Pharaoh, king of Egypt, heard about it, Pharaoh said to Joseph, "Now that your father and brothers have come to you, ⁶the land of Egypt is at your disposal; settle your father and brothers in the pick of the land." ⁷Then Joseph brought his father Jacob and presented him to Pharaoh. After Jacob had paid his respects to Pharaoh, ⁸Pharaoh asked him, "How many years have you lived?" ⁹†Jacob replied: "The years I have lived as a wayfarer amount to a hundred and thirty. Few and hard have been these years of my life, and they do not compare with the years my ancestors lived as wayfarers." ¹⁰Then Jacob bade Pharaoh farewell and withdrew from his presence.

✿

8: Ex 1, 2.
9: Ex 6, 14; Nm 26, 5; 1 Chr 5, 3.
10: Ex 6, 15; Nm 26, 12; 1 Chr 4, 24.
11: Ex 6, 16; Nm 3, 17; 26, 57; 1 Chr 6, 1.
12: 38, 3-10, 29f; Nm 26, 19; Rv 4, 18-22; 1 Chr 2, 5.
13: Nm 26, 23f; 1 Chr 7, 1.
14: Nm 26, 26.
16: Nm 26, 15f.
17: Nm 26, 44; 1 Chr 7, 30f.
20: 41, 50; Nm 26, 28.35.
21: Nm 26, 38; 1 Chr 7, 6; 8, 1-4.
23: Nm 26, 42.
24: Nm 26, 48f; 1 Chr 7, 13.
26: Ex 1, 5.
27: Ex 1, 5; Dt 10, 22; Acts 7, 14.
47/4: Ex 23, 9; Dt 23, 8.

---

†

46, 9-27: This genealogical list has here been inserted by a redactor who bases it on the clan lists (Nm 26, 5-50) at the time of Moses. Therefore it includes some of Jacob's grandchildren, who would hardly have been born when Joseph was still a relatively young man. The number *fourteen* (v 22) is based on a garbled version of the genealogical list.

46, 27: *Seventy persons:* either to be understood as a round number, or arrived at by including Jacob and Joseph with the preceding persons, who add up to sixty-eight.

47, 9: *Wayfarer . . . wayfarers:* man is merely a sojourner on earth; cf Ps 39, 13.

[11]†As Pharaoh had ordered, Joseph settled his father and brothers and gave them holdings in Egypt on the pick of the land, in the region of Rameses. [12]And Joseph sustained his father and brothers and his father's whole household, down to the youngest, with food.

Joseph's Land Policy

[13]Since there was no food in any country because of the extreme severity of the famine, and the lands of Egypt and Canaan were languishing from hunger, [14]Joseph gathered in, as payment for the rations that were being dispensed, all the money that was to be found in Egypt and Canaan, and he put it in Pharaoh's palace. [15]When all the money in Egypt and Canaan was spent, all the Egyptians came to Joseph, pleading, "Give us food or we shall perish under your eyes; for our money is gone." [16]"Since your money is gone," replied Joseph, "give me your livestock, and I will sell you bread in return for your livestock." [17]So they brought their livestock to Joseph, and he sold them food in return for their horses, their flocks of sheep and herds of cattle, and their donkeys. Thus he got them through that year with bread in exchange for all their livestock. [18]When that year ended, they came to him in the following one and said: "We cannot hide from my lord that, with our money spent and our livestock made over to my lord, there is nothing left to put at my lord's disposal except our bodies and our farm land. [19]Why should we and our land perish before your very eyes? Take us and our land in exchange for food, and we will become Pharaoh's slaves and our land his property; only give us seed, that we may survive and not perish, and that our land may not turn into a waste."

[20]Thus Joseph acquired all the farm land of Egypt for Pharaoh, since with the famine too much for them to bear, every Egyptian sold his field; so the land passed over to Pharaoh, [21]and the people were reduced to slavery, from one end of Egypt's territory to the other. [22]Only the priests' lands Joseph did not take over. Since the priests had a fixed allowance from Pharaoh and lived off the allowance Pharaoh had granted them, they did not have to sell their land.

[23]Joseph told the people: "Now that I have acquired you and your land for Pharaoh, here is your seed for sowing the land. [24]But when the harvest is in, you must give a fifth of it to Pharaoh, while you keep four-fifths as seed for your fields and as food for yourselves and your families [and as food for your children]." [25]"You have saved our lives!" they answered. "We are grateful to my lord that we can be Pharaoh's slaves." [26]Thus Joseph made it a law for the land in Egypt, which is still in force, that a fifth of its produce should go to Pharaoh. Only the land of the priests did not pass over to Pharaoh.

Jacob Blesses Ephraim and Manasseh

[27]*Thus Israel settled in the land of Egypt, in the region of Goshen. There they acquired property, were fertile, and increased greatly. [28]Jacob lived in the land of Egypt for seventeen years; the span of his life came to a hundred and forty-seven years. [29]When the time approached for Israel to die, he called his son Joseph and said to him: "If you really wish to please me, put your hand under my thigh as a sign of your constant loyalty to me; do not let me be buried in Egypt. [30]*When I lie down with my ancestors, have me taken out of Egypt and buried in their burial place." [31]†"I will do as you say," he replied. But his father demanded, "Swear it to me!" So Joseph swore to him. Then Israel bowed at the head of the bed.

48 [1]SOME time afterward, Joseph was informed, "Your father is failing." So he took along with him his two sons, Manasseh and Ephraim. [2]When Jacob was told, "Your son Joseph has come to you," he rallied his strength and sat up in bed.

[3]*†Jacob then said to Joseph: "God Almighty appeared to me at Luz in the land of Canaan, and blessing me, [4]he said, 'I will make you fertile and numerous and raise you into an assembly of tribes, and I will give this land to your descendants after you as a permanent possession.' [5]Your two sons, therefore, who were born to you in the land of Egypt before I joined you here, shall be mine; Ephraim and Manasseh shall be mine as much as Reuben and Simeon are mine. [6]Progeny born to you after them shall remain yours; but their heritage shall be recorded in the names of their two brothers. [7]*†I do this because, when I was returning from Paddan, your mother Rachel died, to my sorrow, during the journey in Canaan, while we were still a short distance from Ephrath; and I buried her there on the way to Ephrath [that is, Bethlehem]."

[8]When Israel saw Joseph's sons, he asked, "Who are these?" [9]"They are my sons," Joseph answered his father, "whom God has given me here." "Bring them to me," said his father, "that I may bless them." [10](Now Israel's eyes were dim from age, and he could not see well.) When Joseph brought his sons close to him, he kissed and embraced them. [11]Then Israel said to Jo-

---

† 47, 11: *The region of Rameses:* same as the region of Goshen; see note on 45, 10. The name Rameses, however, is an anachronism, since this royal name did not come into use before the end of the fourteenth century B. C., long after the time of Joseph.

47, 31: *Israel bowed at the head of the bed:* meaning perhaps that he gave a nod of assent and appreciation as he lay on his bed. By reading with different vowels the Hebrew word for "bed," the Greek version translated it as "staff," and understood the phrase to mean that he bowed in worship, leaning on the top of his staff; it is thus quoted in Heb 11, 21.

48, 3: *Luz:* an older name of Bethel (28, 19).

48, 7: Since her early death prevented Rachel from bearing more than two sons, Jacob feels justified in treating her two grandsons as if they were her own offspring.

✸
27: Ex 1, 7.   48/3f: 28, 12-15; 35, 6.
30: 50, 5.   7: 35, 19.

seph, "I never expected to see your face again, and now God has allowed me to see your descendants as well!"

[12]Joseph removed them from his father's knees and bowed down before him with his face to the ground. [13]Then Joseph took the two, Ephraim with his right hand, to Israel's left, and Manasseh with his left hand, to Israel's right, and led them to him. [14]But Israel, crossing his hands, put out his right hand and laid it on the head of Ephraim, although he was the younger, and his left hand on the head of Manasseh, although he was the first-born. [15]*Then he blessed them with these words:

"May the God in whose ways
    my fathers Abraham and Isaac walked,
The God who has been my shepherd
    from my birth to this day,
[16]The Angel who has delivered me from all harm,
    bless these boys
That in them my name be recalled,
    and the names of my fathers Abraham and Isaac,
And they may become teeming multitudes
    upon the earth!"

[17]When Joseph saw that his father had laid his right hand on Ephraim's head, this seemed wrong to him; so he took hold of his father's hand, to remove it from Ephraim's head to Manasseh's, [18]saying, "That is not right, father; the other one is the first-born; lay your right hand on his head!" [19]But his father resisted. "I know it, son," he said, "I know. That one too shall become a tribe, and he too shall be great. Nevertheless, his younger brother shall surpass him, and his descendants shall become a multitude of nations." [20]*So when he blessed them that day and said, "By you shall the people of Israel pronounce blessings; may they say, 'God make you like Ephraim and Manasseh,'" he placed Ephraim before Manasseh.

[21]Then Israel said to Joseph: "I am about to die. But God will be with you and will restore you to the land of your fathers. [22]*†As for me, I give to you, as to the one above his brothers, Shechem, which I captured from the Amorites with my sword and bow."

Jacob's Testament

49 [1]JACOB called his sons and said: "Gather around, that I may tell you what is to happen to you in days to come.

[2]"Assemble and listen, sons of Jacob,
    listen to Israel, your father.

[3]"You, Reuben, my first-born,
    my strength and the first fruit of my manhood,
    excelling in rank and excelling in power!
[4]*Unruly as water, you shall no longer excel,
    for you climbed into your father's bed
    and defiled my couch to my sorrow.

[5]†"Simeon and Levi, brothers indeed,
    weapons of violence are their knives.
[6]*Let not my soul enter their council,
    or my spirit be joined with their company;
For in their fury they slew men,
    in their willfulness they maimed oxen.

[7]Cursed be their fury so fierce,
    and their rage so cruel!
I will scatter them in Jacob,
    disperse them throughout Israel.

[8]"You, Judah, shall your brothers praise
    —your hand on the neck of your enemies;
    the sons of your father shall bow down to you.
[9]*Judah, like a lion's whelp,
    you have grown up on prey, my son.
He crouches like a lion recumbent,
    the king of beasts—who would dare rouse him?
[10]†The scepter shall never depart from Judah,
    or the mace from between his legs,
While tribute is brought to him,
    and he receives the peoples' homage.
[11]†He tethers his donkey to the vine,
    his purebred ass to the choicest stem.
In wine he washes his garments,
    his robe in the blood of grapes.
[12]His eyes are darker than wine,
    and his teeth are whiter than milk.

[13]"Zebulun shall dwell by the seashore
    [This means a shore for ships],
    and his flank shall be based on Sidon.

[14]"Issachar is a rawboned ass,
    crouching between the saddlebags.
[15]When he saw how good a settled life was,
    and how pleasant the country,
He bent his shoulder to the burden
    and became a toiling serf.

---

† 48, 22: Both the meaning of the Hebrew and the historical reference in this verse are obscure. By taking the Hebrew word for Shechem as a common noun meaning shoulder or mountain slope, some translators render the verse, "I give you one portion more than your brothers, which I captured. . . ." The reference may be to the capture of Shechem by the sons of Jacob (34, 24-29). Shechem lay near the border separating the tribal territory of Manasseh from that of Ephraim (Jos 16, 4-9; 17, 1f.7).

49, 5: *Knives:* if this is the meaning of the obscure Hebrew word here, the reference may be to the knives used in circumcising the men of Shechem (34, 24; cf Jos 5, 2).

49, 10: *While tribute is brought to him:* this translation is based on a slight change in the Hebrew text, which, as it stands, would seem to mean, "until he comes to Shiloh." A somewhat different reading of the Hebrew text would be, "until he comes to whom it belongs." This last has been traditionally understood in a Messianic sense. In any case, the passage foretells the supremacy of the tribe of Judah, which found its fulfillment in the Davidic dynasty and ultimately in the Messianic Son of David, Jesus Christ.

49, 11: *In wine . . . the blood of grapes:* Judah's clothes are poetically pictured as soaked with grape juice from trampling in the wine press, the rich vintage of his land; cf Is 63, 2.

✿
15: Heb 11, 21.
20: Heb 11, 21.
22: Jos 17, 14.17f; Jn 4, 5.

49/4: 35, 22; 1 Chr 5, 1f.
6: 34, 25.
9: 1 Chr 5, 2.

¹⁶†"Dan shall achieve justice for his kindred
    like any other tribe of Israel.
¹⁷Let Dan be a serpent by the roadside,
    a horned viper by the path,
    That bites the horse's heel,
      so that the rider tumbles backward.

¹⁸"[I long for your deliverance, O Lord!]

¹⁹†"Gad shall be raided by raiders,
    but he shall raid at their heels.

²⁰"Asher's produce is rich,
    and he shall furnish dainties for kings.

²¹"Naphtali is a hind let loose
    which brings forth lovely fawns.

²²"Joseph is a wild colt,
    a wild colt by a spring,
    a wild ass on a hillside.
²³Harrying and attacking,
    the archers opposed him;
²⁴But each one's bow remained stiff,
    as their arms were unsteady,
By the power of the Mighty One of Jacob,
    because of the Shepherd, the Rock of Israel,
²⁵†The God of your father, who helps you,
    God Almighty, who blesses you,
With the blessings of the heavens above,
    the blessings of the abyss that crouches below,
The blessings of breasts and womb,
   ²⁶the blessings of fresh grain and blossoms,
The blessings of the everlasting mountains,
    the delights of the eternal hills.
May they rest on the head of Joseph,
    on the brow of the prince among his brothers.

²⁷"Benjamin is a ravenous wolf;
    mornings he devours the prey,
    and evenings he distributes the spoils."

Farewell and Death

²⁸All these are the twelve tribes of Israel, and this is what their father said about them, as he bade them farewell and gave to each of them an appropriate message. ²⁹Then he gave them this charge: "Since I am about to be taken to my kindred, bury me with my fathers in the cave that lies in the field of Ephron the Hittite, ³⁰*the cave in the field of Machpelah, facing on Mamre, in the land of Canaan, the field that Abraham bought from Ephron the Hittite for a burial ground. ³¹There Abraham and his wife Sarah are buried, and so are Isaac and his wife Rebekah, and there, too, I buried Leah—³²the field and the cave in it that had been purchased from the Hittites."

³³When Jacob had finished giving these instructions to his sons, he drew his feet into the bed, breathed his last, and was taken to his kindred.

✿
  30: 23, 17.   13: 23, 16; Acts 7, 16.
  50/5: 47, 30.

Jacob's Funeral

50 ¹Joseph threw himself on his father's face and wept over him as he kissed him. ²Then he ordered the physicians in his service to embalm his father. When they embalmed Israel, ³they spent forty days at it, for that is the full period of embalming; and the Egyptians mourned him for seventy days. ⁴When that period of mourning was over, Joseph spoke to Pharaoh's courtiers. "Please do me this favor," he said, "and convey to Pharaoh this request of mine. ⁵*Since my father, at the point of death, made me promise on oath to bury him in the tomb that he had prepared for himself in the land of Canaan, may I go up there to bury my father and then come back?" ⁶Pharaoh replied, "Go and bury your father, as he made you promise on oath."

⁷So Joseph left to bury his father; and with him went all of Pharaoh's officials who were senior members of his court and all the other dignitaries of Egypt, ⁸as well as Joseph's whole household, his brothers, and his father's household; only their children and their flocks and herds were left in the region of Goshen. ⁹Chariots, too, and charioteers went up with him; it was a very large retinue.

¹⁰†When they arrived at Goren-ha-atad, which is beyond the Jordan, they held there a very great and solemn memorial service; and Joseph observed seven days of mourning for his father. ¹¹When the Canaanites who inhabited the land saw the mourning at Goren-ha-atad, they said, "This is a solemn funeral the Egyptians are having." That is why the place was named Abel-mizraim. It is beyond the Jordan.

¹²Thus Jacob's sons did for him as he had instructed them. ¹³*They carried him to the land of Canaan and buried him in the cave in the field of Machpelah, facing on Mamre, the field that Abraham had bought for a burial ground from Ephron the Hittite.

¹⁴After Joseph had buried his father he returned to Egypt, together with his brothers and all who had gone up with him for the burial of his father.

Plea for Forgiveness

¹⁵Now that their father was dead, Joseph's brothers became fearful and thought, "Suppose Joseph has been nursing a grudge against us and now plans to pay

†   49, 16: In Hebrew the verb for *achieve justice* is from the same root as the name *Dan*.

49, 19: In Hebrew there is a certain assonance between the name *Gad* and the words for "raided," "raiders" and "raid."

49, 25f: A very similar description of the agricultural riches of the tribal land of Joseph is given in Dt 33, 13-16.

50, 10f: *Goren-ha-atad*: "Threshing Floor of the Brambles." *Abel-mizraim*: although the name really means "watercourse of the Egyptians," it is understood here, by a play on the first part of the term, to mean "mourning of the Egyptians." The site has not been identified through either reading of the name. But it is difficult to see why the mourning rites should have been held in the land *beyond the Jordan* when the burial was at Hebron. Perhaps an earlier form of the story placed the mourning rites beyond the Wadi of Egypt, the traditional boundary between Canaan and Egypt (Nm 34, 5; Jos 15, 4.47).

us back in full for all the wrong we did him!" [16]So they approached Joseph and said: "Before your father died, he gave us these instructions: [17]'You shall say to Joseph, Jacob begs you to forgive the criminal wrongdoing of your brothers, who treated you so cruelly.' Please, therefore, forgive the crime that we, the servants of your father's God, committed." When they spoke these words to him, Joseph broke into tears. [18]Then his brothers proceeded to fling themselves down before him and said, "Let us be your slaves!" [19]But Joseph replied to them: "Have no fear. Can I take the place of God? [20]*Even though you meant harm to me, God meant it for good, to achieve his present end, the survival of many people. [21]*Therefore have no fear. I will provide for you and for your children." By thus speaking kindly to them, he reassured them.

[22]Joseph remained in Egypt, together with his father's family. He lived a hundred and ten years. [23]*He saw Ephraim's children to the third generation, and the children of Manasseh's son Machir were also born on Joseph's knees.

Death of Joseph

[24]*Joseph said to his brothers: "I am about to die. God will surely take care of you and lead you out of this land to the land that he promised on oath to Abraham, Isaac and Jacob." [25]*Then, putting the sons of Israel under oath, he continued, "When God thus takes care of you, you must bring my bones up with you from this place." [26]*Joseph died at the age of a hundred and ten. He was embalmed and laid to rest in a coffin in Egypt.

✿

20: 45, 5; Sir 49, 15.
21: 47, 12.
23: Nm 32, 39; Jos 17, 1.

24: Ex 3, 8; Jos 24, 32; Heb 11, 22.
25: Ex 13, 19; Heb 11, 22.
26: Sir 49, 15.

The Book of Exodus

Introduction

The second book of the Pentateuch is called Exodus from the Greek word for "departure," because the central event narrated in it is the departure of the Israelites from Egypt. It continues the history of the chosen people from the point where the Book of Genesis leaves off. It recounts the oppression by the Egyptians of the ever-increasing descendants of Jacob and their miraculous deliverance by God through Moses, who led them across the Red Sea to Mount Sinai where they entered into a special covenant with the Lord.

These events were of prime importance to the chosen people, for they became thereby an independent nation and enjoyed a unique relationship with God. Through Moses God gave to the Israelites at Mount Sinai the "law": the moral, civil and ritual legislation by which they were to become a holy people, in whom the promise of a Savior for all mankind would be fulfilled.

The principal divisions of Exodus are:
- I: The Israelites in Egypt (1, 1—12, 36)
- II: The Exodus from Egypt and the Journey to Sinai (12, 37—18, 27)
- III: The Covenant at Mount Sinai (19, 1—24, 18)
- IV: The Dwelling and Its Furnishings (25, 1—40, 38)

I: THE ISRAELITES IN EGYPT

Jacob's Descendants in Egypt

1 [1†]THESE ARE THE NAMES of the sons of Israel who, accompanied by their households, migrated with Jacob into Egypt: [2†]Reuben, Simeon, Levi and Judah; [3]Issachar, Zebulun and Benjamin; [4]Dan and Naphtali; Gad and Asher. [5*†]The total number of the direct descendants of Jacob was seventy. Joseph was already in Egypt.

[6*]Now Joseph and all his brothers and that whole generation died. [7]But the Israelites were fruitful and prolific. They became so numerous and strong that the land was filled with them.

The Oppression

[8*†]Then a new king, who knew nothing of Joseph, came to power in Egypt. [9]He said to his subjects, "Look how numerous and powerful the Israelite people are growing, more so than we ourselves! [10]Come, let us deal shrewdly with them to stop their increase; otherwise, in time of war they too may join our enemies to fight against us, and so leave our country."

[11*†]Accordingly, taskmasters were set over the Israelites to oppress them with forced labor. Thus they had to build for Pharaoh the supply cities of Pithom and Raamses. [12]Yet the more they were oppressed, the more they multiplied and spread. The Egyptians, then, dreaded the Israelites [13]and reduced them to cruel slavery, [14†]making life bitter for them with hard work in mortar and brick and all kinds of field work —the whole cruel fate of slaves.

Command to the Midwives

[15]The king of Egypt told the Hebrew midwives, one of whom was called Shiphrah and the other Puah, [16†]"When you act as midwives for the Hebrew women and see them giving birth, if it is a boy, kill him; but if it is a girl, she may live." [17]The midwives, however, feared God; they did not do as the king of Egypt had ordered them, but let the boys live. [18]So the king summoned the midwives and asked them, "Why have you acted thus, allowing the boys to live?" [19]The midwives answered Pharaoh, "The Hebrew women are not like the Egyptian women. They are robust and give birth before the midwife arrives." [20]Therefore God dealt well with the midwives. The people, too, increased and grew strong. [21]And because the midwives feared

---

†

1, 1: *Sons of Israel:* here literally the first-generation sons of Jacob. Cf v 5. However, beginning with 1, 7 the same Hebrew phrase refers to the more remote descendants of Jacob; hence, from there on, it is ordinarily rendered as "the Israelites." *Households:* the family in its fullest sense, including wives, children and servants.

1, 2: The sons of Jacob are listed here according to the respective mothers. Cf Gn 29, 31; 30, 20; 35, 16-26.

1, 5: *Direct descendants:* literally, persons coming from the loins of Jacob; hence, wives and servants are here excluded. Cf Gn 46, 26.

1, 8: *Who knew nothing of Joseph:* this king ignored the services that Joseph had rendered to Egypt.

1, 11: *Pharaoh:* not a personal name, but a title common to all the kings of Egypt.

1, 14: *Mortar:* either the wet clay with which the bricks were made, as in Na 3, 14, or the cement used between the bricks in building, as in Gn 11, 3.

1, 16: *And see them giving birth:* the Hebrew text is uncertain.

✿
1/5: Gn 46, 27; Dt 10, 22; Acts 7, 14.
6: Gn 50, 26.
8ff: Acts 7, 18.
11: Dt 26, 6.

God, he built up families for them. **22***†Pharaoh then commanded all his subjects, "Throw into the river every boy that is born to the Hebrews, but you may let all the girls live."

Birth and Adoption of Moses

2 **1***Now a certain man of the house of Levi married a Levite woman, **2***who conceived and bore a son. Seeing that he was a goodly child, she hid him for three months. **3**†When she could hide him no longer, she took a papyrus basket, daubed it with bitumen and pitch, and putting the child in it, placed it among the reeds on the river bank. **4**His sister stationed herself at a distance to find out what would happen to him.

5Pharaoh's daughter came down to the river to bathe, while her maids walked along the river bank. Noticing the basket among the reeds, she sent her handmaid to fetch it. **6**On opening it, she looked, and lo, there was a baby boy, crying! She was moved with pity for him and said, "It is one of the Hebrews' children." **7**Then his sister asked Pharaoh's daughter, "Shall I go and call one of the Hebrew women to nurse the child for you?" **8**"Yes, do so," she answered. So the maiden went and called the child's own mother. **9**Pharaoh's daughter said to her, "Take this child and nurse it for me, and I will repay you." The woman therefore took the child and nursed it. **10***†When the child grew, she brought him to Pharaoh's daughter, who adopted him as her son and called him Moses; for she said, "I drew him out of the water."

Moses' Flight to Midian

11*†On one occasion, after Moses had grown up, when he visited his kinsmen and witnessed their forced labor, he saw an Egyptian striking a Hebrew, one of his own kinsmen. **12**Looking about and seeing no one, he slew the Egyptian and hid him in the sand. **13**The next day he went out again, and now two Hebrews were fighting! So he asked the culprit, "Why are you striking your fellow Hebrew?" **14**But he replied, "Who has appointed you ruler and judge over us? Are you thinking of killing me as you killed the Egyptian?" Then Moses became afraid and thought, "The affair must certainly be known."

15*Pharaoh, too, heard of the affair and sought to put him to death. But Moses fled from him and stayed in the land of Midian. As he was seated there by a well, **16**seven daughters of a priest of Midian came to draw water and fill the troughs to water their father's flock. **17**But some shepherds came and drove them away. Then Moses got up and defended them and watered their flock. **18**†When they returned to their father Reuel, he said to them, "How is it you have returned so soon today?" **19**†They answered, "An Egyptian saved us from the interference of the shepherds. He even drew water for us and watered the flock!" **20**"Where is the man?" he asked his daughters. "Why did you leave him there? Invite him to have something to eat." **21**Moses agreed to live with him, and the man gave him his daughter Zipporah in marriage. **22***†She bore him a son, whom he named Gershom; for he said, "I am a stranger in a foreign land."

The Burning Bush

23*A long time passed, during which the king of Egypt died. Still the Israelites groaned and cried out because of their slavery. As their cry for release went up to God, **24***he heard their groaning and was mindful of his covenant with Abraham, Isaac and Jacob. **25**He saw the Israelites and knew. . . .

3 **1**†Meanwhile Moses was tending the flock of his father-in-law Jethro, the priest of Midian. Leading the flock across the desert, he came to Horeb, the mountain of God. **2***†There an angel of the Lord appeared to him in fire flaming out of a bush. As he looked on, he was surprised to see that the bush, though on fire, was not consumed. **3**So Moses decided, "I must go over to look at this remarkable sight, and see why the bush is not burned."

The Call of Moses

4When the Lord saw him coming over to look at it more closely, God called out to him from the bush, "Moses! Moses!" He answered, "Here I am." **5***God said, "Come no nearer! Remove the sandals from your feet, for the place where you stand is holy ground.

---

† 1, 22: *The river:* the Nile, which was "the" river for the Egyptians.

2, 3: *Basket:* literally, "chest" or "ark"; the same Hebrew word is used in Gn 6, 14 for Noah's ark. Here, however, the chest was made of papyrus stalks.

2, 10: *When the child grew:* probably when he was weaned or a little later. *Moses:* in Hebrew, *Mosheh;* the Hebrew word for "draw out" is *mashah.* This explanation of the name is not intended as a scientific etymology but as a play on words. The name is probably derived from an Egyptian word for "has been born," referring the birth to a god thought to be its sponsor.

2, 11: *After Moses had grown up:* Acts 7, 23 indicates that this was after an interval of nearly forty years. Cf Ex 7, 7. *Striking:* probably in the sense of "flogging"; according to some, "slaying."

2, 18: *Reuel:* he was also called Jethro. Cf 3, 1; 4, 18; 18, 1.

2, 19: *An Egyptian:* Moses was probably wearing Egyptian dress, or spoke Egyptian to Reuel's daughters.

2, 22: *Gershom:* the name is explained as if it came from the Hebrew word *ger,* "stranger," joined to the Hebrew word *sham,* "there." Some Greek and Latin manuscripts add here a passage taken from 18, 4.

3, 1: *The mountain of God:* probably given this designation because of the divine apparitions which took place there, such as on this occasion and when the Israelites were there after the departure from Egypt.

3, 2: *An angel of the Lord:* the visual form under which God appeared and spoke to men is referred to indifferently in some Old Testament texts either as God's angel or as God Himself. Cf Gn 16, 7.13; Ex 14, 19.24f; Nm 22, 22-35; Jgs 6, 11-18.

✧ 22: Acts 7, 19.
2/1: 6, 20; Nm 26, 59.
2: Acts 7, 20; Heb 11, 23.
10: Acts 7, 21; Heb 11, 24.
11-14: Acts 7, 23-28.
15: Acts 7, 29; Heb 11, 27.
22: 18, 3.
23: 3, 7.9; Dt 26, 7.
24: 6, 5; Pss 105, 8f; 106, 44f.
3/2-10: Acts 7, 30-35.
5: Jos 5, 15.

⁶*†"I am the God of your father," he continued, "the God of Abraham, the God of Isaac, the God of Jacob." Moses hid his face, for he was afraid to look at God. ⁷But the Lord said, "I have witnessed the affliction of my people in Egypt and have heard their cry of complaint against their slave drivers, so I know well what they are suffering. ⁸*†Therefore I have come down to rescue them from the hands of the Egyptians and lead them out of that land into a good and spacious land, a land flowing with milk and honey, the country of the Canaanites, Hittites, Amorites, Perizzites, Hivites and Jebusites. ⁹So indeed the cry of the Israelites has reached me, and I have truly noted that the Egyptians are oppressing them. ¹⁰Come, now! I will send you to Pharaoh to lead my people, the Israelites, out of Egypt."

¹¹†But Moses said to God, "Who am I that I should go to Pharaoh and lead the Israelites out of Egypt?" ¹²He answered, "I will be with you; and this shall be your proof that it is I who have sent you: when you bring my people out of Egypt, you will worship God on this very mountain." ¹³"But," said Moses to God, "when I go to the Israelites and say to them, 'The God of your fathers has sent me to you,' if they ask me, 'What is his name?' what am I to tell them?" ¹⁴†God replied, "I am who am." Then he added, "This is what you shall tell the Israelites: I Am sent me to you."

¹⁵*God spoke further to Moses, "Thus shall you say to the Israelites: The Lord, the God of your fathers, the God of Abraham, the God of Isaac, the God of Jacob, has sent me to you.

"This is my name forever;
   this is my title for all generations.

¹⁶†"Go and assemble the elders of the Israelites, and tell them: The Lord, the God of your fathers, the God of Abraham, Isaac and Jacob, has appeared to me and said: I am concerned about you and about the way you are being treated in Egypt; ¹⁷so I have decided to lead you up out of the misery of Egypt into the land of the Canaanites, Hittites, Amorites, Perizzites, Hivites and Jebusites, a land flowing with milk and honey.

¹⁸*"Thus they will heed your message. Then you and the elders of Israel shall go to the king of Egypt and say to him: The Lord, the God of the Hebrews, has sent us word. Permit us, then, to go a three days' journey in the desert, that we may offer sacrifice to the Lord, our God.

¹⁹"Yet I know that the king of Egypt will not allow you to go unless he is forced. ²⁰I will stretch out my hand, therefore, and smite Egypt by doing all kinds of wondrous deeds there. After that he will send you away. ²¹*I will even make the Egyptians so well-disposed toward this people that, when you leave, you will not go empty-handed. ²²†Every woman shall ask her neighbor and her house guest for silver and gold articles and for clothing to put on your sons and daughters. Thus you will despoil the Egyptians."

Confirmation of Moses' Mission

4 ¹"but," objected Moses, "suppose they will not believe me, nor listen to my plea? For they may say, 'The Lord did not appear to you.'" ²The Lord therefore asked him, "What is that in your hand?" "A staff," he answered. ³*The Lord then said, "Throw it on the ground." When he threw it on the ground it was changed into a serpent, and Moses shied away from it. ⁴"Now, put out your hand," the Lord said to him, "and take hold of its tail." So he put out his hand and laid hold of it, and it became a staff in his hand. ⁵"This will take place so that they may believe," he continued, "that the Lord, the God of their fathers, the God of Abraham, the God of Isaac, the God of Jacob, did appear to you."

⁶Again the Lord said to him, "Put your hand in your bosom." He put it in his bosom, and when he withdrew it, to his surprise his hand was leprous, like snow. ⁷The Lord then said, "Now, put your hand back in your bosom." Moses put his hand back in his bosom, and when he withdrew it, to his surprise it was again like the rest of his body. ⁸"If they will not believe you, nor heed the message of the first sign, they should believe the message of the second. ⁹*And if they will not believe even these two signs, nor heed your plea, take some water from the river and pour it on the dry land. The water you take from the river will become blood on the dry land."

---

† 3, 6: The appearance of God caused fear of death, since it was believed that no one could see God and live; cf Gn 32, 30. *The God of Abraham . . . Jacob:* cited by Christ in proof of the resurrection since the patriarchs, long dead, live on in God who is the God of the living. Cf Mt 22, 32; Mk 12, 26; Lk 20, 37.

3, 8: *I have come down:* a figure of speech signifying an extraordinary divine intervention in human affairs. Cf Gn 11, 5.7. *Flowing with milk and honey:* an expression denoting agricultural prosperity, which seems to have been proverbial in its application to Palestine. Cf 13, 5; Nm 13, 27; Jos 5, 6; Jer 11, 5; 32, 22; Ez 20, 6.15.

3, 11: *Who am I:* besides naturally shrinking from such a tremendous undertaking, Moses realized that, as a fugitive from Pharaoh, he could hardly hope to carry out a mission to him. Perhaps he also recalled that on one occasion even his own kinsmen questioned his authority. Cf 2, 14.

3, 14: *I am who am:* apparently this utterance is the source of the word *Yahweh*, the proper personal name of the God of Israel. It is commonly explained in reference to God as the absolute and necessary Being. It may be understood of God as the Source of all created beings. Out of reverence for this name, the term *Adonai*, "my Lord," was later used as a substitute. The word Lord in the present version represents this traditional usage. The word "Jehovah" arose from a false reading of this name as it is written in the current Hebrew text.

3, 16: *Elders:* the Israelite leaders, who were usually older men. They were representatives of the people.

3, 22: *Articles:* probably jewelry. *Despoil:* this was permissible, that the Israelites might compensate themselves for their many years of servitude; besides, the Egyptians would give these things willingly. Cf 12, 33-36.

---

* 6: 4, 5; Mt 22, 32; Mk 12, 36; Lk 20, 37.
8f: Gn 15, 19ff.
15: Ps 135, 13.
18: 5, 3.
21f: 11, 2f; 12, 35f.
4/3: 7, 10.
9: 7, 17.19f

Aaron's Office as Assistant

¹⁰*Moses, however, said to the LORD, "If you please, Lord, I have never been eloquent, neither in the past, nor recently, nor now that you have spoken to your servant; but I am slow of speech and tongue." ¹¹The LORD said to him, "Who gives one man speech and makes another deaf and dumb? Or who gives sight to one and makes another blind? Is it not I, the LORD? ¹²Go, then! It is I who will assist you in speaking and will teach you what you are to say." ¹³†Yet he insisted, "If you please, Lord, send someone else!" ¹⁴Then the LORD became angry with Moses and said, "Have you not your brother, Aaron the Levite? I know that he is an eloquent speaker. Besides, he is now on his way to meet you. ¹⁵*When he sees you, his heart will be glad. You are to speak to him, then, and put the words in his mouth. I will assist both you and him in speaking and will teach the two of you what you are to do. ¹⁶†He shall speak to the people for you: he shall be your spokesman, and you shall be as God to him. ¹⁷†Take this staff in your hand; with it you are to perform the signs."

Moses' Return to Egypt

¹⁸†After this Moses returned to his father-in-law Jethro and said to him, "Let me go back, please, to my kinsmen in Egypt, to see whether they are still living." Jethro replied, "Go in peace." ¹⁹*In Midian the LORD said to Moses, "Go back to Egypt, for all the men who sought your life are dead." ²⁰So Moses took his wife and his sons, and started back to the land of Egypt, with them riding the ass. The staff of God he carried with him. ²¹†The LORD said to him, "On your return to Egypt, see that you perform before Pharaoh all the wonders I have put in your power. I will make him obstinate, however, so that he will not let the people go. ²²*So you shall say to Pharaoh: Thus says the LORD: Israel is my son, my first-born. ²³*Hence I tell you: Let my son go, that he may serve me. If you refuse to let him go, I warn you, I will kill your son, your first-born."

²⁴†On the journey, at a place where they spent the night, the LORD came upon Moses and would have killed him. ²⁵*But Zipporah took a piece of flint and cut off her son's foreskin and, touching his person, she said, "You are a spouse of blood to me." ²⁶Then God let Moses go. At that time she said, "A spouse of blood," in regard to the circumcision.

²⁷The LORD said to Aaron, "Go into the desert to meet Moses." So he went, and when they met at the mountain of God, Aaron kissed him. ²⁸Moses informed him of all the LORD had said in sending him, and of the various signs he had enjoined upon him. ²⁹Then Moses and Aaron went and assembled all the elders of the Israelites. ³⁰Aaron told them everything the LORD had said to Moses, and he performed the signs before the people. ³¹The people believed, and when they heard that the LORD was concerned about them and had seen their affliction, they bowed down in worship.

Pharaoh's Obduracy

5 ¹AFTER that, Moses and Aaron went to Pharaoh and said, "Thus says the LORD, the God of Israel: Let my people go, that they may celebrate a feast to me in the desert." ²Pharaoh answered, "Who is the LORD, that I should heed his plea to let Israel go? I do not know the LORD; even if I did, I would not let Israel go." ³*They replied, "The God of the Hebrews has sent us word. Let us go a three days' journey in the desert, that we may offer sacrifice to the LORD, our God; otherwise he will punish us with pestilence or the sword."

⁴The king of Egypt answered them, "What do you mean, Moses and Aaron, by taking the people away from their work? Off to your labor! ⁵Look how numerous the people of the land are already," continued Pharaoh, "and yet you would give them rest from their labor!"

⁶†That very day Pharaoh gave the taskmasters and foremen of the people this order: ⁷†"You shall no longer supply the people with straw for their brickmaking as you have previously done. Let them go and gather straw themselves! ⁸Yet you shall levy upon them the same quota of bricks as they have previously made. Do not reduce it. They are lazy; that is why they are crying, 'Let us go to offer sacrifice to our God.' ⁹Increase the work for the men, so that they keep their mind on it and pay no attention to lying words."

¹⁰So the taskmasters and foremen of the people went out and told them, "Thus says Pharaoh: I will not provide you with straw. ¹¹Go and gather the straw yourselves, wherever you can find it. Yet there must not be the slightest reduction in your work." ¹²The

---

†

4, 13: *Send someone else:* literally, "Send by means of him whom you will send," that is, "Send whom you will."

4, 16: *Spokesman:* literally, "mouth"; Aaron was to serve as a mouthpiece for Moses, as a prophet does for God; hence the relation between Moses and Aaron is compared to that between God and his prophet. Cf 7, 1.

4, 17: *This staff:* probably the same as that of vv 2ff; but some understand it here of a new staff now given by God to Moses.

4, 18: Moses did not tell his father-in-law his main reason for returning to Egypt, but this secondary motive which he offered was also true.

4, 21: *Make him obstinate:* literally, "harden his heart." God permitted Pharaoh to be stubborn in his opposition to the departure of the Israelites. Cf Rom 9, 17f.

4, 24ff: Apparently God was angry with Moses for having failed to keep the divine command given to Abraham in Gn 17, 10ff. Moses' life is spared when his wife circumcises their son.

5, 6: *The taskmasters and foremen:* the former were higher officials and probably Egyptians; the latter were lower officials, chosen from the Israelites themselves. Cf v 14.

5, 7: Straw was mixed with the clay to give the sun-dried bricks greater consistency.

---

*

10: 6, 12.   23: 11, 5; 12, 29.
15f: 7, 1.   25: Is 6, 2; 7, 20.
19: 2, 15.23.   5/3: 3, 18.
22: Sir 36, 11.

people, then, scattered throughout the land of Egypt to gather stubble for straw, **13**while the taskmasters kept driving them on, saying, "Finish your work, the same daily amount as when your straw was supplied."

Complaint of the Foremen

14The foremen of the Israelites, whom the taskmasters of Pharaoh had placed over them, were beaten, and were asked, "Why have you not completed your prescribed amount of bricks yesterday and today, as before?"

15Then the Israelite foremen came and made this appeal to Pharaoh: "Why do you treat your servants in this manner? **16**No straw is supplied to your servants, and still we are told to make bricks. Look how your servants are beaten! It is you who are at fault." **17**Pharaoh answered, "It is just because you are lazy that you keep saying, 'Let us go and offer sacrifice to the Lord.' **18**Off to work, then! Straw shall not be provided for you, but you must still deliver your quota of bricks."

19The Israelite foremen knew they were in a sorry plight, having been told not to reduce the daily amount of bricks. **20**When, therefore, they left Pharaoh and came upon Moses and Aaron, who were waiting to meet them, **21**they said to them, "The Lord look upon you and judge! You have brought us into bad odor with Pharaoh and his servants and have put a sword in their hands to slay us."

Renewal of God's Promise

22Moses again had recourse to the Lord and said, "Lord, why do you treat this people so badly? And why did you send me on such a mission? **23**Ever since I went to Pharaoh to speak in your name, he has maltreated this people of yours, and you have done nothing to rescue them."

6 **1**THEN the Lord answered Moses, "Now you shall see what I will do to Pharaoh. Forced by my mighty hand, he will send them away; compelled by my outstretched arm, he will drive them from his land."

2God also said to Moses, "I am the Lord. **3***As God the Almighty I appeared to Abraham, Isaac and Jacob, but my name, Lord, I did not make known to them. **4***I also established my covenant with them, to give them the land of Canaan, the land in which they were living as aliens. **5***And now that I have heard the groaning of the Israelites, whom the Egyptians are treating as slaves, I am mindful of my covenant. **6**Therefore, say to the Israelites: I am the Lord. I will

free you from the forced labor of the Egyptians and will deliver you from their slavery. I will rescue you by my outstretched arm and with mighty acts of judgment. **7***I will take you as my own people, and you shall have me as your God. You will know that I, the Lord, am your God when I free you from the labor of the Egyptians **8**and bring you into the land which I swore to give to Abraham, Isaac and Jacob. I will give it to you as your own possession—I, the Lord!" **9**But when Moses told this to the Israelites, they would not listen to him because of their dejection and hard slavery.

10Then the Lord said to Moses, **11**"Go and tell Pharaoh, king of Egypt, to let the Israelites leave his land." **12***But Moses protested to the Lord, "If the Israelites would not listen to me, how can it be that Pharaoh will listen to me, poor speaker that I am!" **13**Still, the Lord, to bring the Israelites out of Egypt, spoke to Moses and Aaron and gave them his orders regarding both the Israelites and Pharaoh, king of Egypt.

Genealogy of Moses and Aaron

14*†These are the heads of the ancestral houses. The sons of Reuben, the first-born of Israel, were Hanoch, Pallu, Hezron and Carmi; these are the clans of Reuben. **15***The sons of Simeon were Jemuel, Jamin, Ohad, Jachin, Zohar and Shaul, who was the son of a Canaanite woman; these are the clans of Simeon. **16***The names of the sons of Levi, in their genealogical order, are Gershon, Kohath and Merari. Levi lived one hundred and thirty-seven years.

17*The sons of Gershon, as heads of clans, were Libni and Shimei. **18***The sons of Kohath were Amram, Izhar, Hebron and Uzziel. Kohath lived one hundred and thirty-three years. **19***The sons of Merari were Mahli and Mushi. These are the clans of Levi in their genealogical order.

20*†Amram married his aunt Jochebed, who bore him Aaron, Moses and Miriam. Amram lived one hundred and thirty-seven years. **21**The sons of Izhar were Korah, Nepheg and Zichri. **22**The sons of Uzziel were Mishael, Elzaphan and Sithri. **23***Aaron married Amminadab's daughter, Elisheba, the sister of Nahshon; she bore him Nadab, Abihu, Eleazar and Ithamar. **24**The sons of Korah were Assir, Elkanah and Abiasaph. These are the clans of the Korahites. **25**Aaron's son, Eleazar, married one of Putiel's daughters, who bore him Phinehas. These are the heads of the ancestral clans of the Levites. **26**This is the Aaron and this the Moses to whom the Lord said, "Lead the Israelites from the land of Egypt, company by company." **27**These are the ones who spoke to Pharaoh, king of

6/3: Gn 17, 1; 35, 11.
4: Gn 15, 18; 17, 4-8.
5: 2, 24.
7: Lv 26, 12.
12: 6, 30.
14: Nm 26, 5f; 1 Chr 5, 3.
15: Nm 26, 12; 1 Chr 4, 24.
16: Nm 3, 17; 1 Chr 6, 1.16; 23, 6.
17: Nm 3, 21; 1 Chr 6, 17; 23, 7.
18: Nm 3, 27; 1 Chr 6, 2.18.
19: Nm 3, 20; 1 Chr 6, 19; 23, 21.
20: Nm 26, 59.
23: Ru 4, 19f; 1 Chr 2, 10.

† 6, 14: The purpose of the genealogy here is to give the line from which Moses and Aaron sprang. Reuben and Simeon are first mentioned because, as older brothers of Levi, their names occur before his in the genealogy.

6, 20: *His aunt:* more exactly, "his father's sister." Later on such a marriage was forbidden. Cf Lv 18, 12. Hence, the Greek and Latin versions render here, "his cousin."

Egypt, to bring the Israelites out of Egypt—the same Moses and Aaron.

Moses and Aaron before Pharaoh

²⁸On the day the LORD spoke to Moses in Egypt ²⁹he said, "I am the LORD. Repeat to Pharaoh, king of Egypt, all that I tell you." ³⁰*But Moses protested to the LORD, "Since I am a poor speaker, how can it be that Pharaoh will listen to me?"

7 ¹*†THE LORD answered him, "See! I have made you as God to Pharaoh, and Aaron your brother shall act as your prophet. ²You shall tell him all that I command you. In turn, your brother Aaron shall tell Pharaoh to let the Israelites leave his land. ³Yet I will make Pharaoh so obstinate that, despite the many signs and wonders that I will work in the land of Egypt, ⁴he will not listen to you. Therefore I will lay my hand on Egypt and by great acts of judgment I will bring the hosts of my people, the Israelites, out of the land of Egypt, ⁵so that the Egyptians may learn that I am the LORD, as I stretch out my hand against Egypt and lead the Israelites out of their midst."

⁶Moses and Aaron did as the LORD had commanded them. ⁷Moses was eighty years old and Aaron eighty-three when they spoke to Pharaoh.

The Staff Turned into a Snake

⁸The LORD told Moses and Aaron, ⁹*"If Pharaoh demands that you work a sign or wonder, you shall say to Aaron: Take your staff and throw it down before Pharaoh, and it will be changed into a snake." ¹⁰Then Moses and Aaron went to Pharaoh and did as the LORD had commanded. Aaron threw his staff down before Pharaoh and his servants, and it was changed into a snake. ¹¹*Pharaoh, in turn, summoned wise men and sorcerers, and they also, the magicians of Egypt, did likewise by their magic arts. ¹²Each one threw down his staff, and it was changed into a snake. But Aaron's staff swallowed their staffs. ¹³Pharaoh, however, was obstinate and would not listen to them, just as the LORD had foretold.

First Plague: Water Turned into Blood

¹⁴†Then the LORD said to Moses, "Pharaoh is obdurate in refusing to let the people go. ¹⁵Tomorrow morning, when he sets out for the water, go and present yourself by the river bank, holding in your hand the staff that turned into a serpent. ¹⁶Say to him: The LORD, the God of the Hebrews, sent me to you with the message: Let my people go to worship me in the desert. But as yet you have not listened. ¹⁷*The LORD now says: This is how you shall know that I am the LORD. I will strike the water of the river with the staff I hold, and it shall be changed into blood. ¹⁸The fish

in the river shall die, and the river itself shall become so polluted that the Egyptians will be unable to drink its water."

¹⁹The LORD then said to Moses, "Say to Aaron: Take your staff and stretch out your hand over the waters of Egypt—their streams and canals and pools, all their supplies of water—that they may become blood. Throughout the land of Egypt there shall be blood, even in the wooden pails and stone jars."

²⁰Moses and Aaron did as the LORD had commanded. Aaron raised his staff and struck the waters of the river in full view of Pharaoh and his servants, and all the water of the river was changed into blood. ²¹The fish in the river died, and the river itself became so polluted that the Egyptians could not drink its water. There was blood throughout the land of Egypt. ²²But the Egyptian magicians did the same by their magic arts. So Pharaoh remained obstinate and would not listen to Moses and Aaron, just as the LORD had foretold. ²³He turned away and went into his house, with no concern even for this. ²⁴All the Egyptians had to dig in the neighborhood of the river for drinking water, since they could not drink the river water.

Second Plague: the Frogs

²⁵Seven days passed after the LORD had struck the river. ²⁶*†Then the LORD said to Moses, "Go to Pharaoh and tell him: Thus says the LORD: Let my people go to worship me. ²⁷If you refuse to let them go, I warn you, I will send a plague of frogs over all your territory. ²⁸The river will teem with frogs. They will come up into your palace and into your bedroom and onto your bed, into the houses of your servants, too, and your subjects, even into your ovens and your kneading bowls. ²⁹The frogs will swarm all over you and your subjects and your servants."

8 ¹THE LORD then told Moses, "Say to Aaron: Stretch out your hand and your staff over the streams and canals and pools, to make frogs overrun the land of Egypt." ²Aaron stretched out his hand over the waters of Egypt, and the frogs came up and covered the land of Egypt. ³But the magicians did the same by their magic arts. They, too, made frogs overrun the land of Egypt.

⁴Then Pharaoh summoned Moses and Aaron and said, "Pray the LORD to remove the frogs from me and my subjects, and I will let the people go to offer sacrifice to the LORD." ⁵Moses answered Pharaoh, "Do me the favor of appointing the time when I am to pray for you and your servants and your subjects, that the frogs

30: 6, 12.
7/1: 4, 15f.
9: 4, 3.
11: 2 Tm 3, 8.
17-21: 4, 9; Pss 78, 44;
105, 29; Wis 11, 5-7.
26-29: Pss 78, 45; 105, 30.

† 7, 1: Just as God had his prophets to speak to men in his name, so Moses had Aaron as his "prophet" to speak to Pharaoh. Cf 4, 16.

7, 14: Most of the ten plagues of Egypt seem to be similar to certain natural phenomena of that country; but they are represented as supernatural at least in their greater intensity and in their occurring exactly according to Moses' commands.

7, 26—8, 28: This is 8, 1-32 in the verse enumeration of the Vulgate.

may be taken away from you and your houses and be left only in the river." ⁶"Tomorrow," said Pharaoh. Then Moses replied, "It shall be as you have said, so that you may learn that there is none like the Lord, our God. ⁷The frogs shall leave you and your houses, your servants and your subjects; only in the river shall they be left."

⁸After Moses and Aaron left Pharaoh's presence, Moses implored the Lord to fulfill the promise he had made to Pharaoh about the frogs; ⁹†and the Lord did as Moses had asked. The frogs in the houses and courtyards and fields died off. ¹⁰Heaps and heaps of them were gathered up, and there was a stench in the land. ¹¹But when Pharaoh saw that there was a respite, he became obdurate and would not listen to them, just as the Lord had foretold.

Third Plague: the Gnats

¹²*†Thereupon the Lord said to Moses, "Tell Aaron to stretch out his staff and strike the dust of the earth, that it may be turned into gnats throughout the land of Egypt." ¹³They did so. Aaron stretched out his hand, and with his staff he struck the dust of the earth, and gnats came upon man and beast. The dust of the earth was turned into gnats throughout the land of Egypt. ¹⁴*Though the magicians tried to bring forth gnats by their magic arts, they could not do so. As the gnats infested man and beast, ¹⁵†the magicians said to Pharaoh, "This is the finger of God." Yet Pharaoh remained obstinate and would not listen to them, just as the Lord had foretold.

Fourth Plague: the Flies

¹⁶Again the Lord told Moses, "Early tomorrow morning present yourself to Pharaoh when he goes forth to the water, and say to him: Thus says the Lord: Let my people go to worship me. ¹⁷If you will not let my people go, I warn you, I will loose swarms of flies upon you and your servants and your subjects and your houses. The houses of the Egyptians and the very ground on which they stand shall be filled with swarms of flies. ¹⁸But on that day I will make an exception of the land of Goshen: there shall be no flies where my people dwell, that you may know that I am the Lord in the midst of the earth. ¹⁹I will make this distinction between my people and your people. This sign shall take place tomorrow." ²⁰*This the Lord did. Thick swarms of flies entered the house of Pharaoh and the houses of his servants; throughout Egypt the land was infested with flies.

²¹Then Pharaoh summoned Moses and Aaron and said to them, "Go and offer sacrifice to your God in this land." ²²†But Moses replied, "It is not right to do so, for the sacrifices we offer to the Lord, our God, are an abomination to the Egyptians. If before their very eyes we offer sacrifices which are an abomination to them,

will not the Egyptians stone us? ²³We must go a three days' journey in the desert to offer sacrifice to the Lord, our God, as he commands us." ²⁴"Well, then," said Pharaoh, "I will let you go to offer sacrifice to the Lord, your God, in the desert, provided that you do not go too far away and that you pray for me." ²⁵Moses answered, "As soon as I leave your presence I will pray to the Lord that the flies may depart tomorrow from Pharaoh and his servants and his subjects. Pharaoh, however, must not play false again by refusing to let the people go to offer sacrifice to the Lord." ²⁶When Moses left Pharaoh's presence, he prayed to the Lord; ²⁷and the Lord did as Moses had asked. He removed the flies from Pharaoh and his servants and subjects. Not one remained. ²⁸But once more Pharaoh became obdurate and would not let the people go.

Fifth Plague: the Pestilence

9 ¹Then the Lord said to Moses, "Go to Pharaoh and tell him: Thus says the Lord, the God of the Hebrews: Let my people go to worship me. ²If you refuse to let them go and persist in holding them, ³I warn you, the Lord will afflict all your livestock in the field—your horses, asses, camels, herds and flocks—with a very severe pestilence. ⁴But the Lord will distinguish between the livestock of Israel and that of Egypt, so that none belonging to the Israelites will die." ⁵And setting a definite time, the Lord added, "Tomorrow the Lord shall do this in the land." ⁶*And on the next day the Lord did so. All the livestock of the Egyptians died, but not one beast belonging to the Israelites. ⁷But though Pharaoh's messengers informed him that not even one beast belonging to the Israelites had died, he still remained obdurate and would not let the people go.

Sixth Plague: the Boils

⁸Then the Lord said to Moses and Aaron, "Take a double handful of soot from a furnace, and in the presence of Pharaoh let Moses scatter it toward the sky. ⁹It will then turn into fine dust over the whole land of Egypt and cause festering boils on man and beast throughout the land."

¹⁰So they took soot from a furnace and stood in the presence of Pharaoh. Moses scattered it toward the sky, and it caused festering boils on man and beast. ¹¹The magicians could not stand in Moses' presence, for there were boils on the magicians no less than on the rest of the Egyptians. ¹²But the Lord made Pharaoh obstinate, and he would not listen to them, just as the Lord had foretold to Moses.

---

† 8, 9: *Courtyards:* some render "farmhouses."

8, 12.17: *Gnats, flies:* it is uncertain what species of troublesome insects are here meant.

8, 15: *The finger of God:* understood by the magicians as the *staff* mentioned in 8, 13. Cf Lk 11, 20.

8, 22: The Egyptians would fiercely resent the sacrifice of any animal they considered sacred. Certain animals were worshiped in Egypt, at least as the symbols of various deities.

---

* 8/12f: Ps 105, 31.   20: Pss 78, 45; 105, 31;
     14: Wis 17, 7.   Wis 16, 9.
                           9/6: Ps 78, 48.

Seventh Plague: the Hail

13Then the LORD told Moses, "Early tomorrow morning present yourself to Pharaoh and say to him: Thus says the LORD, the God of the Hebrews: Let my people go to worship me, **14**or this time I will hurl all my blows upon you and your servants and your subjects, that you may know that there is none like me anywhere on earth. **15**For by now I would have stretched out my hand and struck you and your subjects with such pestilence as would wipe you from the earth. **16***†But this is why I have spared you: to show you my power and to make my name resound throughout the earth! **17**Will you still block the way for my people by refusing to let them go? **18**I warn you, then, tomorrow at this hour I will rain down such fierce hail as there has never been in Egypt from the day the nation was founded up to the present. **19**Therefore, order all your livestock and whatever else you have in the open fields to be brought to a place of safety. Whatever man or beast remains in the fields and is not brought to shelter shall die when the hail comes upon them." **20**Some of Pharaoh's servants feared the warning of the LORD and hurried their servants and livestock off to shelter. **21**Others, however, did not take the warning of the LORD to heart and left their servants and livestock in the fields.

22The LORD then said to Moses, "Stretch out your hand toward the sky, that hail may fall upon the entire land of Egypt, on man and beast and every growing thing in the land of Egypt." **23***When Moses stretched out his staff toward the sky, the LORD sent forth hail and peals of thunder. Lightning flashed toward the earth, and the LORD rained down hail upon the land of Egypt; **24**and lightning constantly flashed through the hail, such fierce hail as had never been seen in the land since Egypt became a nation. **25**It struck down every man and beast that was in the open throughout the land of Egypt; it beat down every growing thing and splintered every tree in the fields. **26**Only in the land of Goshen, where the Israelites dwelt, was there no hail.

27Then Pharaoh summoned Moses and Aaron and said to them, "I have sinned again! The LORD is just; it is I and my subjects who are at fault. **28**Pray to the LORD, for we have had enough of God's thunder and hail. Then I will let you go; you need stay no longer." **29**Moses replied, "As soon as I leave the city I will extend my hands to the LORD; the thunder will cease, and there will be no more hail. Thus you shall learn that the earth is the LORD's. **30**But you and your servants, I know, do not yet fear the LORD God."

31Now the flax and the barley were ruined, because the barley was in ear and the flax in bud. **32**But the wheat and the spelt were not ruined, for they grow later.

33When Moses had left Pharaoh's presence and had gone out of the city, he extended his hands to the LORD. Then the thunder and the hail ceased, and the rain no longer poured down upon the earth. **34**But Pharaoh, seeing that the rain and hail and thunder had ceased, sinned again: he with his servants became obdurate, **35**and in his obstinacy he would not let the Israelites go, as the LORD had foretold through Moses.

Eighth Plague: the Locusts

10 **1**THEN the LORD said to Moses, "Go to Pharaoh, for I have made him and his servants obdurate in order that I may perform these signs of mine among them **2***and that you may recount to your son and grandson how ruthlessly I dealt with the Egyptians and what signs I wrought among them, so that you may know that I am the LORD."

3So Moses and Aaron went to Pharaoh and told him, "Thus says the LORD, the God of the Hebrews: How long will you refuse to submit to me? Let my people go to worship me. **4**If you refuse to let my people go, I warn you, tomorrow I will bring locusts into your country. **5**They shall cover the ground, so that the ground itself will not be visible. They shall eat up the remnant you saved unhurt from the hail, as well as all the foliage that has since sprouted in your fields. **6**They shall fill your houses and the houses of your servants and of all the Egyptians; such a sight your fathers or grandfathers have not seen from the day they first settled on this soil up to the present day." With that he turned and left Pharaoh.

7But Pharaoh's servants said to him, "How long must he be a menace to us? Let the men go to worship the LORD, their God. Do you not yet realize that Egypt is being destroyed?" **8**So Moses and Aaron were brought back to Pharaoh, who said to them, "You may go and worship the LORD, your God. But how many of you will go?" **9**"Young and old must go with us," Moses answered, "our sons and daughters as well as our flocks and herds must accompany us. That is what a feast of the LORD means to us." **10**†"The LORD help you," Pharaoh replied, "if I ever let your little ones go with you! Clearly, you have some evil in mind. **11**†No, no! Just you men can go and worship the LORD. After all, that is what you want." With that they were driven from Pharaoh's presence.

12*The LORD then said to Moses, "Stretch out your hand over the land of Egypt, that locusts may swarm over it and eat up all the vegetation and whatever the hail has left." **13**†So Moses stretched out his staff

---

†

9, 16: *To show you:* some ancient versions read, "to show through you." Cf Rom 9, 17.

10, 10: *The Lord help you . . . :* literally, "May the LORD be with you in the same way as I let you . . . "; a sarcastic blessing intended as a curse.

10, 11: Pharaoh realized that if the men alone went they would have to return to their families. He suspected that the Hebrews had no intention of returning.

10, 13: *East wind:* coming across the desert from Arabia, the strong east wind brings Egypt the burning sirocco and, at times, locusts. Cf 14, 21.

---

*

16: Rom 9, 17.   10/2: Dt 6, 20ff.
23f: Pss 78, 47; 105, 32f.   12ff: Pss 78, 46; 105, 34f.

over the land of Egypt, and the Lord set an east wind blowing over the land all that day and all that night. At dawn the east wind brought the locusts. **14**They swarmed over the whole land of Egypt and settled down on every part of it. Never before had there been such a fierce swarm of locusts, nor will there ever be. **15**They covered the surface of the whole land, till it was black with them. They ate up all the vegetation in the land and the fruit of whatever trees the hail had spared. Nothing green was left on any tree or plant throughout the land of Egypt.

16Hastily Pharaoh summoned Moses and Aaron and said, "I have sinned against the Lord, your God, and against you. **17**But now, do forgive me my sin once more, and pray the Lord, your God, to take at least this deadly pest from me." **18**When Moses left the presence of Pharaoh, he prayed to the Lord, **19**†and the Lord changed the wind to a very strong west wind, which took up the locusts and hurled them into the Red Sea. But though not a single locust remained within the confines of Egypt, **20**the Lord made Pharaoh obstinate, and he would not let the Israelites go.

Ninth Plague: the Darkness

21†Then the Lord said to Moses, "Stretch out your hand toward the sky, that over the land of Egypt there may be such intense darkness that one can feel it." **22***So Moses stretched out his hand toward the sky, and there was dense darkness throughout the land of Egypt for three days. **23**Men could not see one another, nor could they move from where they were, for three days. But all the Israelites had light where they dwelt.

24Pharaoh then summoned Moses and Aaron and said, "Go and worship the Lord. Your little ones, too, may go with you. But your flocks and herds must remain." **25**Moses replied, "You must also grant us sacrifices and holocausts to offer up to the Lord, our God. **26**Hence, our livestock also must go with us. Not an animal must be left behind. Some of them we must sacrifice to the Lord, our God, but we ourselves shall not know which ones we must sacrifice to him until we arrive at the place itself." **27**But the Lord made Pharaoh obstinate, and he would not let them go. **28**"Leave my presence," Pharaoh said to him, "and see to it that you do not appear before me again! The day you appear before me you shall die!" **29**Moses replied, "Well said! I will never appear before you again."

Tenth Plague: the Death of the First-born

11 **1**THEN the Lord told Moses, "One more plague will I bring upon Pharaoh and upon Egypt. After that he will let you depart. In fact, he will not merely let you go; he will drive you away. **2***Instruct your people that every man is to ask his neighbor, and every woman her neighbor, for silver

and gold articles and for clothing." **3**The Lord indeed made the Egyptians well-disposed toward the people; Moses himself was very highly regarded by Pharaoh's servants and the people in the land of Egypt.

4*Moses then said, "Thus says the Lord: At midnight I will go forth through Egypt. **5***Every first-born in this land shall die, from the first-born of Pharaoh on the throne to the first-born of the slave-girl at the handmill, as well as all the first-born of the animals. **6**Then there shall be loud wailing throughout the land of Egypt, such as has never been, nor will ever be again. **7**But among the Israelites and their animals not even a dog shall growl, so that you may know how the Lord distinguishes between the Egyptians and the Israelites. **8***All these servants of yours shall then come down to me, and prostrate before me, they shall beg me, 'Leave us, you and all your followers!' Only then will I depart." With that he left Pharaoh's presence in hot anger.

9The Lord said to Moses, "Pharaoh refuses to listen to you that my wonders may be multiplied in the land of Egypt." **10**Thus, although Moses and Aaron performed these various wonders in Pharaoh's presence, the Lord made Pharaoh obstinate, and he would not let the Israelites leave his land.

The Passover Ritual Prescribed

12 **1**THE Lord said to Moses and Aaron in the land of Egypt, **2***†"This month shall stand at the head of your calendar; you shall reckon it the first month of the year. **3**Tell the whole community of Israel: On the tenth of this month every one of your families must procure for itself a lamb, one apiece for each household. **4**†If a family is too small for a whole lamb, it shall join the nearest household in procuring one and shall share in the lamb in proportion to the number of persons who partake of it. **5**The lamb must be a year-old male and without blemish. You may take it from either the sheep or the goats. **6**You shall keep it until the fourteenth day of this month, and then, with the whole assembly of Israel present, it shall be slaughtered during the evening twilight. **7**They shall take some of its blood and apply it to the two doorposts and the lintel of every house in which they partake of the lamb. **8**That same night they shall eat its roasted flesh with unleavened bread

† 10, 19: *The Red Sea:* according to the traditional translation, but the Hebrew is literally, "the Reed Sea"; hence the Red Sea of Exodus was probably a body of shallow water somewhat to the north of the present deep Red Sea.

10, 21: *Darkness:* at times a storm from the south, called the *khamsin*, blackens the sky of Egypt with sand from the Sahara; the dust in the air is then so thick that the darkness can, in a sense, "be felt."

12, 2: *This month:* Abib, the month of "ripe grain." Cf 13, 4; 23, 15; 34, 18; Dt 16, 1. It occurred near the vernal equinox, March-April. Later it was known by the Babylonian name of Nisan. Cf Neh 2, 1; Est 3, 7.

12, 4: *Share in the lamb:* probably, in the expenses of its purchase. Some explain, "reckon for the lamb the number of persons required to eat it." Cf 12, 10.

22: Ps 105, 28.
11/2f: 3, 21f; 12, 35f.
4: 12, 12.
5f: 12, 29f.
8: 12, 31ff.
12/2-20: Lv 23, 5-8;
Nm 9, 2-5; 28, 16ff;
Dt 16, 1-8.

and bitter herbs. [9]It shall not be eaten raw or boiled, but roasted whole, with its head and shanks and inner organs. [10]None of it must be kept beyond the next morning; whatever is left over in the morning shall be burned up.

[11]†"This is how you are to eat it: with your loins girt, sandals on your feet and your staff in hand, you shall eat like those who are in flight. It is the Passover of the LORD. [12]For on this same night I will go through Egypt, striking down every first-born of the land, both man and beast, and executing judgment on all the gods of Egypt—I, the LORD! [13]*But the blood will mark the houses where you are. Seeing the blood, I will pass over you; thus, when I strike the land of Egypt, no destructive blow will come upon you.

[14]"This day shall be a memorial feast for you, which all your generations shall celebrate with pilgrimage to the LORD, as a perpetual institution. [15]For seven days you must eat unleavened bread. From the very first day you shall have your houses clear of all leaven. Whoever eats leavened bread from the first day to the seventh shall be cut off from Israel. [16]On the first day you shall hold a sacred assembly, and likewise on the seventh. On these days you shall not do any sort of work, except to prepare the food that everyone needs.

[17]*"Keep, then, this custom of the unleavened bread. Since it was on this very day that I brought your ranks out of the land of Egypt, you must celebrate this day throughout your generations as a perpetual institution. [18]From the evening of the fourteenth day of the first month until the evening of the twenty-first day of this month you shall eat unleavened bread. [19]For seven days no leaven may be found in your houses. Anyone, be he a resident alien or a native, who eats leavened food shall be cut off from the community of Israel. [20]Nothing leavened may you eat; wherever you dwell you may eat only unleavened bread."

Promulgation of the Passover

[21]Moses called all the elders of Israel and said to them, "Go and procure lambs for your families, and slaughter them as Passover victims. [22]*†Then take a bunch of hyssop, and dipping it in the blood that is in the basin, sprinkle the lintel and the two doorposts with this blood. But none of you shall go outdoors until morning. [23]For the LORD will go by, striking down the Egyptians. Seeing the blood on the lintel and the two doorposts, the LORD will pass over that door and not let the destroyer come into your houses to strike you down.

[24]"You shall observe this as a perpetual ordinance for yourselves and your descendants. [25]Thus, you must also observe this rite when you have entered the land which the LORD will give you as he promised.

[26]*When your children ask you, 'What does this rite of yours mean?' [27]you shall reply, 'This is the Passover sacrifice of the LORD, who passed over the houses of the Israelites in Egypt; when he struck down the Egyptians, he spared our houses.'"

Then the people bowed down in worship, [28]and the Israelites went and did as the LORD had commanded Moses and Aaron.

Death of the First-born

[29]*At midnight the LORD slew every first-born in the land of Egypt, from the first-born of Pharaoh on the throne to the first-born of the prisoner in the dungeon, as well as all the first-born of the animals. [30]Pharaoh arose in the night, he and all his servants and all the Egyptians; and there was loud wailing throughout Egypt, for there was not a house without its dead.

Permission To Depart

[31]During the night Pharaoh summoned Moses and Aaron and said, "Leave my people at once, you and the Israelites with you! Go and worship the LORD as you said. [32]Take your flocks, too, and your herds, as you demanded, and begone; and you will be doing me a favor."

[33]The Egyptians likewise urged the people on, to hasten their departure from the land; they thought that otherwise they would all die. [34]The people, therefore, took their dough before it was leavened, in their kneading bowls wrapped in their cloaks on their shoulders. [35]*The Israelites did as Moses had commanded: they asked the Egyptians for articles of silver and gold and for clothing. [36]The LORD indeed had made the Egyptians so well-disposed toward the people that they let them have whatever they asked for. Thus did they despoil the Egyptians.

II: THE EXODUS FROM EGYPT AND THE JOURNEY TO SINAI

Departure from Egypt

[37]*THE ISRAELITES SET OUT from Rameses for Succoth, about six hundred thousand men on foot, not counting the children. [38]†A crowd of mixed ancestry also went up with them, besides their livestock, very numerous flocks and herds. [39]Since the dough they had brought out of Egypt was not leavened, they baked it into unleavened loaves. They had been rushed out of Egypt

---

† 12, 11: *Passover:* in Hebrew, *pesach,* in Aramaic, *pascha.* In the following verses the same root is used in the verb "to pass over." The word may be originally Egyptian, *pesach,* "the blow," i. e., the final plague which destroyed the Egyptian first-born.

12, 22: *Hyssop:* a plant with many woody branchlets that made a convenient sprinkler.

12, 38: *Mixed ancestry:* half-Hebrew and half-Egyptian. Cf Nm 11, 4; Lv 24, 10f.

13: Heb 11, 28.
17: 13, 3.
22f: 12, 7.13.
26f: 13, 8.14;
     Dt 6, 20f.

29f: 11, 4ff; Pss 78, 51; 105, 36; 136, 10;
     Wis 18, 10-16.
35f: 3, 21f; 11, 2f;
     Ps 105, 37f.
37: Nm 33, 3ff.

and had no opportunity even to prepare food for the journey.

40*†The time the Israelites had stayed in Egypt was four hundred and thirty years. **41**At the end of four hundred and thirty years, all the hosts of the LORD left the land of Egypt on this very date. **42**This was a night of vigil for the LORD, as he led them out of the land of Egypt; so on this same night all the Israelites must keep a vigil for the LORD throughout their generations.

Passover Regulations

43The LORD said to Moses and Aaron, "These are the regulations for the Passover. No foreigner may partake of it. **44**However, any slave who has been bought for money may partake of it, provided you have first circumcised him. **45**But no transient alien or hired servant may partake of it. **46***†It must be eaten in one and the same house; you may not take any of its flesh outside the house. You shall not break any of its bones. **47***The whole community of Israel must keep this feast. **48**If any aliens living among you wish to celebrate the Passover of the LORD, all the males among them must first be circumcised, and then they may join in its observance just like the natives. But no man who is uncircumcised may partake of it. **49**The law shall be the same for the resident alien as for the native."

50All the Israelites did just as the LORD had commanded Moses and Aaron. **51**On that same day the LORD brought the Israelites out of Egypt company by company.

Consecration of First-born

13 **1**THE LORD spoke to Moses and said, **2***"Consecrate to me every first-born that opens the womb among the Israelites, both of man and beast, for it belongs to me."

3*Moses said to the people, "Remember this day on which you came out of Egypt, that place of slavery. It was with a strong hand that the LORD brought you away. Nothing made with leaven must be eaten. **4**This day of your departure is in the month of Abib. **5**Therefore, it is in this month that you must celebrate this rite, after the LORD, your God, has brought you into the land of the Canaanites, Hittites, Amorites, Hivites and Jebusites, which he swore to your fathers he would give you, a land flowing with milk and honey. **6**For seven days you shall eat unleavened bread, and the seventh day shall also be a festival to the LORD. **7**Only unleavened bread may be eaten during the seven days; no leaven and nothing leavened may be

found in all your territory. **8**On this day you shall explain to your son, 'This is because of what the LORD did for me when I came out of Egypt.' **9***It shall be as a sign on your hand and as a reminder on your forehead; thus the law of the LORD will ever be on your lips, because with a strong hand the LORD brought you out of Egypt. **10**Therefore, you shall keep this prescribed rite at its appointed time from year to year.

11"When the LORD, your God, has brought you into the land of the Canaanites, which he swore to you and your fathers he would give you, **12***you shall dedicate to the LORD every son that opens the womb; and all the male firstlings of your animals shall belong to the LORD. **13**Every first-born of an ass you shall redeem with a sheep. If you do not redeem it, you shall break its neck. Every first-born son you must redeem. **14**If your son should ask you later on, 'What does this mean?' you shall tell him, 'With a strong hand the LORD brought us out of Egypt, that place of slavery. **15**When Pharaoh stubbornly refused to let us go, the LORD killed every first-born in the land of Egypt, every first-born of man and of beast. That is why I sacrifice to the LORD everything of the male sex that opens the womb, and why I redeem every first-born of my sons.' **16***Let this, then, be as a sign on your hand and as a pendant on your forehead: with a strong hand the LORD brought us out of Egypt."

Toward the Red Sea

17†Now, when Pharaoh let the people go, God did not lead them by way of the Philistines' land, though this was the nearest; for he thought, should the people see that they would have to fight, they might change their minds and return to Egypt. **18**Instead, he rerouted them toward the Red Sea by way of the desert road. In battle array the Israelites marched out of Egypt. **19***Moses also took Joseph's bones along, for Joseph had made the Israelites swear solemnly that, when God should come to them, they would carry his bones away with them.

20*Setting out from Succoth, they camped at Etham near the edge of the desert.

21*†The LORD preceded them, in the daytime by means of a column of cloud to show them the way, and at night by means of a column of fire to give them light. Thus they could travel both day and night. **22**Neither the column of cloud by day nor the column of fire by night ever left its place in front of the people.

40: Gn 15, 13; Acts 7, 6; Gal 3, 17.
46: Nm 9, 12; Jn 19, 36.
47f: Nm 9, 14.
13/2: 13, 12-15.
3-10: 12, 2-20.
9: 13, 16; Dt 6, 8; 11, 18.
12-15: 13, 2; 22, 29f; 34, 19f; Nm 3, 12f; 8, 16; 18, 15; Dt 15, 19.
16: 13, 9.
19: Gn 50, 25; Jos 24, 32.
20: Nm 33, 6.
21f: 40, 38; Nm 9, 15-22; Dt 1, 33; Neh 9, 19; Pss 78, 14; 105, 39; Wis 10, 17.

† 12, 40: *In Egypt:* according to some ancient sources, "in Canaan and Egypt," thus reckoning from the time of Abraham. Cf Gal 3, 17.

12, 46: *You shall not break any of its bones:* the application of these words to our Lord on the cross shows that the Paschal lamb was a prophetic type of Christ, immolated to free men from the bondage of sin. Cf also 1 Cor 5, 7; 1 Pt 1, 19.

13, 17: *By way of the Philistines' land:* the most direct route from Egypt to Palestine, along the shore of the Mediterranean.

13, 21: *A column of cloud . . . a column of fire:* probably one and the same preternatural phenomenon, a central nucleus of fire surrounded by smoke; only at night was its luminous nature visible. Cf 40, 38.

14

¹THEN the LORD said to Moses, ²*†"Tell the Israelites to turn about and camp before Pi-hahiroth, between Migdol and the sea. You shall camp in front of Baal-zephon, just opposite, by the sea. ³Pharaoh will then say, 'The Israelites are wandering about aimlessly in the land. The desert has closed in on them.' ⁴Thus will I make Pharaoh so obstinate that he will pursue them. Then I will receive glory through Pharaoh and all his army, and the Egyptians will know that I am the LORD."

This the Israelites did. ⁵*When it was reported to the king of Egypt that the people had fled, Pharaoh and his servants changed their minds about them. "What have we done!" they exclaimed. "Why, we have released Israel from our service!" ⁶So Pharaoh made his chariots ready and mustered his soldiers—⁷six hundred first-class chariots and all the other chariots of Egypt, with warriors on them all. ⁸So obstinate had the LORD made Pharaoh that he pursued the Israelites even while they were marching away in triumph. ⁹The Egyptians, then, pursued them; Pharaoh's whole army, his horses, chariots and charioteers, caught up with them as they lay encamped by the sea, at Pi-hahiroth, in front of Baal-zephon.

Crossing of the Red Sea

¹⁰Pharaoh was already near when the Israelites looked up and saw that the Egyptians were on the march in pursuit of them. In great fright they cried out to the LORD. ¹¹And they complained to Moses, "Were there no burial places in Egypt that you had to bring us out here to die in the desert? Why did you do this to us? Why did you bring us out of Egypt? ¹²Did we not tell you this in Egypt, when we said, 'Leave us alone. Let us serve the Egyptians'? Far better for us to be the slaves of the Egyptians than to die in the desert." ¹³But Moses answered the people, "Fear not! Stand your ground, and you will see the victory the LORD will win for you today. These Egyptians whom you see today you will never see again. ¹⁴The LORD himself will fight for you; you have only to keep still."

¹⁵Then the LORD said to Moses, "Why are you crying out to me? Tell the Israelites to go forward. ¹⁶And you, lift up your staff and, with hand outstretched over the sea, split the sea in two, that the Israelites may pass through it on dry land. ¹⁷But I will make the Egyptians so obstinate that they will go in after them. Then I will receive glory through Pharaoh and all his army, his chariots and charioteers. ¹⁸The Egyptians shall know that I am the LORD, when I receive glory through Pharaoh and his chariots and charioteers."

¹⁹The angel of God, who had been leading Israel's camp, now moved and went around behind them. The column of cloud also, leaving the front, took up its place behind them, ²⁰†so that it came between the camp of the Egyptians and that of Israel. But the cloud now became dark, and thus the night passed without the rival camps coming any closer together all night long. ²¹*Then Moses stretched out his hand over the sea, and the LORD swept the sea with a strong east wind throughout the night and so turned it into dry land. When the water was thus divided, ²²the Israelites marched into the midst of the sea on dry land, with the water like a wall to their right and to their left.

Destruction of the Egyptians

²³The Egyptians followed in pursuit; all Pharaoh's horses and chariots and charioteers went after them right into the midst of the sea. ²⁴In the night watch just before dawn the LORD cast through the column of the fiery cloud upon the Egyptian force a glance that threw it into a panic; ²⁵and he so clogged their chariot wheels that they could hardly drive. With that the Egyptians sounded the retreat before Israel, because the LORD was fighting for them against the Egyptians.

²⁶Then the LORD told Moses, "Stretch out your hand over the sea, that the water may flow back upon the Egyptians, upon their chariots and their charioteers." ²⁷So Moses stretched out his hand over the sea, and at dawn the sea flowed back to its normal depth. The Egyptians were fleeing head on toward the sea, when the LORD hurled them into its midst. ²⁸*As the water flowed back, it covered the chariots and the charioteers of Pharaoh's whole army which had followed the Israelites into the sea. Not a single one of them escaped. ²⁹But the Israelites had marched on dry land through the midst of the sea, with the water like a wall to their right and to their left. ³⁰Thus the LORD saved Israel on that day from the power of the Egyptians. When Israel saw the Egyptians lying dead on the seashore ³¹*and beheld the great power that the LORD had shown against the Egyptians, they feared the LORD and believed in him and in his servant Moses.

15

¹*†THEN Moses and the Israelites sang this song to the LORD:

I will sing to the LORD, for he is gloriously
　　triumphant;
　　horse and chariot he has cast into the sea.

---

† 14, 2: These places have not been definitively identified. Even the relative position of *Pi-hahiroth* and *Baal-zephon* is not clear; perhaps the former was on the west shore of the sea, where the Israelites were, and the latter on the opposite shore.

14, 20: *The cloud now became dark:* the light which it ordinarily cast at night would now have been a help to the Egyptians; its present obscurity serves as a shield for the Israelites. However, the reading of the original text here is not quite certain.

15, 1-21: This canticle (used in Christian liturgy) celebrates God's saving power, miraculously delivering his people from their enemies, and leading them to the victorious conquest of the Promised Land.

❀ 14/2: Nm 33, 7f.　　　　　　28f: Dt 11, 4; Ps 106, 11.
5-8: Wis 19, 3; 1 Mc 4, 9.　　31f: Ps 106, 12; Wis 10, 20:
21f: 15, 19; Pss 66, 6;　　　　15/1: 15, 21.
　　　78, 13; 136, 13f;
　　　Wis 10, 18; 19, 7f;
　　　Is 63, 12f; Heb 11, 29.

2*My strength and my courage is the LORD,
    and he has been my savior.
He is my God, I praise him;
    the God of my father, I extol him.
3The LORD is a warrior,
    LORD is his name!
4Pharaoh's chariots and army he hurled into the sea;
    the elite of his officers were submerged in the
    Red Sea.
5*The flood waters covered them,
    they sank into the depths like a stone.

6Your right hand, O LORD, magnificent in power,
    your right hand, O LORD, has shattered the
    enemy.
7In your great majesty you overthrew your
    adversaries;
    you loosed your wrath to consume them like
    stubble.
8At a breath of your anger the waters piled up,
    the flowing waters stood like a mound,
    the flood waters congealed in the midst of the sea.

9The enemy boasted, "I will pursue and overtake
    them;
    I will divide the spoils and have my fill of them;
    I will draw my sword; my hand shall despoil
    them!"
10When your wind blew, the sea covered them;
    like lead they sank in the mighty waters.

11Who is like to you among the gods, O LORD?
    Who is like to you, magnificent in holiness?
O terrible in renown, worker of wonders,
    12when you stretched out your right hand, the
    earth swallowed them!

13In your mercy you led the people you redeemed;
    in your strength you guided them to your holy
    dwelling.
14The nations heard and quaked;
    anguish gripped the dwellers in Philistia.
15Then were the princes of Edom dismayed;
    trembling seized the chieftains of Moab;
All the dwellers in Canaan melted away;
    16*terror and dread fell upon them.
By the might of your arm they were frozen like
    stone,
    while your people, O LORD, passed over,
    while the people you had made your own passed
    over.

17And you brought them in and planted them on the
    mountain of your inheritance—
    the place where you made your seat, O LORD,
    the sanctuary, O Lord, which your hands
    established.
18The LORD shall reign forever and ever.

19*They sang thus because Pharaoh's horses and chariots and charioteers had gone into the sea, and the LORD made the waters of the sea flow back upon them, though the Israelites had marched on dry land through the midst of the sea. **20**The prophetess Miriam, Aaron's sister, took a tambourine in her hand, while all the women went out after her with tambourines, dancing; **21***†and she led them in the refrain:

Sing to the LORD, for he is gloriously triumphant;
    horse and chariot he has cast into the sea.

At Marah and Elim

22*Then Moses led Israel forward from the Red Sea, and they marched out to the desert of Shur. After traveling for three days through the desert without finding water, **23**they arrived at Marah, where they could not drink the water, because it was too bitter. Hence this place was called Marah. **24**As the people grumbled against Moses, saying, "What are we to drink?" **25***he appealed to the LORD, who pointed out to him a certain piece of wood. When he threw this into the water, the water became fresh.

It was here that the LORD, in making rules and regulations for them, put them to the test. **26***"If you really listen to the voice of the LORD, your God," he told them, "and do what is right in his eyes: if you heed his commandments and keep all his precepts, I will not afflict you with any of the diseases with which I afflicted the Egyptians; for I, the LORD, am your healer."
27*Then they came to Elim, where there were twelve springs of water and seventy palm trees, and they camped there near the water.

The Desert of Sin

16 **1**†HAVING set out from Elim, the whole Israelite community came into the desert of Sin, which is between Elim and Sinai, on the fifteenth day of the second month after their departure from the land of Egypt. **2**Here in the desert the whole Israelite community grumbled against Moses and Aaron. **3**The Israelites said to them, "Would that we had died at the LORD's hand in the land of Egypt, as we sat by our fleshpots and ate our fill of bread! But you had to lead us into this desert to make the whole community die of famine!"

The Quail and Manna

4*†Then the LORD said to Moses, "I will now rain down bread from heaven for you. Each day the people

---

† 15, 21: *She led them:* Miriam's refrain re-echoes the first verse of this song and was probably sung as an antiphon after each verse.

16, 1: *On the fifteenth day of the second month:* just one full month after their departure from Egypt. Cf 12, 2.51; Nm 33, 3f. They encamped in the desert of Sin on a Friday; the murmuring (vv 2f) occurred on the sabbath, the arrival of the quail (v 13) the evening before Sunday, followed by six mornings (vv 14-27) of collecting manna before the next sabbath.

16, 4: *Bread from heaven:* as a gift from God, the manna is said to come down from the sky. Cf Ps 78, 25; Wis 16, 20. Per-

2: Ps 118, 14; Is 12, 2.
5: Neh 9, 11.
16f: Ps 78, 53ff.
19: 14, 21-29.
21: 15, 1.
22f: Nm 33, 8.
25: Sir 38, 5.
26: Dt 7, 15.
27: Nm 33, 9.
16/4: Pss 78, 24f; 105, 40;
    Jn 6, 31f; 1 Cor 10, 3.

are to go out and gather their daily portion; thus will I test them, to see whether they follow my instructions or not. **5**On the sixth day, however, when they prepare what they bring in, let it be twice as much as they gather on the other days." **6***So Moses and Aaron told all the Israelites, "At evening you will know that it was the LORD who brought you out of the land of Egypt; **7**and in the morning you will see the glory of the LORD, as he heeds your grumbling against him. But what are we that you should grumble against us? **8**When the LORD gives you flesh to eat in the evening," continued Moses, "and in the morning your fill of bread, as he heeds the grumbling you utter against him, what then are we? Your grumbling is not against us, but against the LORD."

9Then Moses said to Aaron, "Tell the whole Israelite community: Present yourselves before the LORD, for he has heard your grumbling." **10**When Aaron announced this to the whole Israelite community, they turned toward the desert, and lo, the glory of the LORD appeared in the cloud! **11**The LORD spoke to Moses and said, **12**"I have heard the grumbling of the Israelites. Tell them: In the evening twilight you shall eat flesh, and in the morning you shall have your fill of bread, so that you may know that I, the LORD, am your God."

13*In the evening quail came up and covered the camp. In the morning a dew lay all about the camp, **14**and when the dew evaporated, there on the surface of the desert were fine flakes like hoarfrost on the ground. **15*†**On seeing it, the Israelites asked one another, "What is this?" for they did not know what it was. But Moses told them, "This is the bread which the LORD has given you to eat.

Regulations Regarding the Manna

16"Now, this is what the LORD has commanded. So gather it that everyone has enough to eat, an omer for each person, as many of you as there are, each man providing for those of his own tent." **17**The Israelites did so. Some gathered a large and some a small amount. **18*†**But when they measured it out by the omer, he who had gathered a large amount did not have too much, and he who had gathered a small amount did not have too little. They so gathered that everyone had enough to eat. **19**Moses also told them, "Let no one keep any of it over until tomorrow morning." **20**But they would not listen to him. When some kept a part of it over until the following morning, it became wormy and rotten. Therefore Moses was displeased with them.

21Morning after morning they gathered it, till each had enough to eat; but when the sun grew hot, the manna melted away. **22**On the sixth day they gathered twice as much food, two omers for each person. When all the leaders of the community came and reported

this to Moses, **23**he told them, "That is what the LORD prescribed. Tomorrow is a day of complete rest, the sabbath, sacred to the LORD. You may either bake or boil the manna, as you please; but whatever is left put away and keep for the morrow." **24**When they put it away for the morrow, as Moses commanded, it did not become rotten or wormy. **25**Moses then said, "Eat it today, for today is the sabbath of the LORD. On this day you will not find any of it on the ground. **26**On the other six days you can gather it, but on the seventh day, the sabbath, none of it will be there." **27**Still, on the seventh day some of the people went out to gather it, although they did not find any. **28**Then the LORD said to Moses, "How long will you refuse to keep my commandments and laws? **29**Take note! The LORD has given you the sabbath. That is why on the sixth day he gives you food for two days. On the seventh day everyone is to stay home and no one is to go out." **30**After that the people rested on the seventh day.

31*†The Israelites called this food manna. It was like coriander seed, but white, and it tasted like wafers made with honey.

32Moses said, "This is what the LORD has commanded. Keep an omerful of manna for your descendants, that they may see what food I gave you to eat in the desert when I brought you out of the land of Egypt." **33*†**Moses then told Aaron, "Take an urn and put an omer of manna in it. Then place it before the LORD in safekeeping for your descendants." **34†**So Aaron placed it in front of the commandments for safekeeping, as the LORD had commanded Moses.

35*The Israelites ate this manna for forty years, until they came to settled land; they ate manna until they reached the borders of Canaan. **36**[An omer is one tenth of an ephah.]

Water from the Rock

17 **1***FROM the desert of Sin the whole Israelite community journeyed by stages, as the LORD directed, and encamped at Rephidim.

Here there was no water for the people to drink. **2***They quarreled, therefore, with Moses and said, "Give us water to drink." Moses replied, "Why do you quarrel with me? Why do you put the LORD to a test?"

---

†
haps it was similar to a natural substance that is still found in small quantities on the Sinai peninsula, but here it is, at least in part, clearly miraculous. Our Lord referred to the manna as a type of the Blessed Eucharist. Cf Jn 6, 32.49-52.

16, 15: *What is this:* the original *man hu* is thus rendered by the ancient versions, which understood the phrase as a popular etymology of the Hebrew word *man,* "manna"; some render, "This is manna."

16, 18: St. Paul cites this passage as an example of equitable sharing. Cf 2 Cor 8, 15.

16, 31: *Coriander seed:* small, round, aromatic seeds of bright brown color; the comparison, therefore, refers merely to the size and shape, not to the taste or color of the manna.

16, 33: *Urn:* according to the Greek translation, which is followed in Heb 9, 4, this was a golden vessel.

16, 34: *The commandments:* the two tablets of the ten commandments, which were kept in the ark. Cf 25, 16.21f.

✱
6f: 16, 12.
13: Nm 11, 31; Ps 78, 27f.
15: Dt 8, 3.
18: 2 Cor 8, 15.
31: Nm 11, 7.
33: Heb 9, 4.
35: Jos 5, 12.
17/1: Nm 33, 12ff.
2-7: Nm 20, 2-13.

³Here, then, in their thirst for water, the people grumbled against Moses, saying, "Why did you ever make us leave Egypt? Was it just to have us die here of thirst with our children and our livestock?" ⁴So Moses cried out to the LORD, "What shall I do with this people? A little more and they will stone me!" ⁵*The LORD answered Moses, "Go over there in front of the people, along with some of the elders of Israel, holding in your hand, as you go, the staff with which you struck the river. ⁶I will be standing there in front of you on the rock in Horeb. Strike the rock, and the water will flow from it for the people to drink." This Moses did, in the presence of the elders of Israel. ⁷*†The place was called Massah and Meribah, because the Israelites quarreled there and tested the LORD, saying, "Is the LORD in our midst or not?"

Battle with Amalek

⁸*†At Rephidim, Amalek came and waged war against Israel. ⁹Moses, therefore, said to Joshua, "Pick out certain men, and tomorrow go out and engage Amalek in battle. I will be standing on top of the hill with the staff of God in my hand." ¹⁰So Joshua did as Moses told him: he engaged Amalek in battle after Moses had climbed to the top of the hill with Aaron and Hur. ¹¹As long as Moses kept his hands raised up, Israel had the better of the fight, but when he let his hands rest, Amalek had the better of the fight. ¹²Moses' hands, however, grew tired; so they put a rock in place for him to sit on. Meanwhile Aaron and Hur supported his hands, one on one side and one on the other, so that his hands remained steady till sunset. ¹³And Joshua mowed down Amalek and his people with the edge of the sword.

¹⁴*Then the LORD said to Moses, "Write this down in a document as something to be remembered, and recite it in the ears of Joshua: I will completely blot out the memory of Amalek from under the heavens." ¹⁵†Moses also built an altar there, which he called Yahweh-nissi; ¹⁶for he said, "The LORD takes in hand his banner; the LORD will war against Amalek through the centuries."

Meeting with Jethro

18 ¹NOW Moses' father-in-law Jethro, the priest of Midian, heard of all that God had done for Moses and for his people Israel: how the LORD had brought Israel out of Egypt. ²So his father-in-law Jethro took along Zipporah, Moses' wife, whom Moses had sent back to him, ³*and her two sons. One of these was called Gershom; for he said, "I am a stranger in a foreign land." ⁴The other was called Eliezer; for he said, "My father's God is my helper; he has rescued me from Pharaoh's sword." ⁵Together with Moses' wife and sons, then, his father-in-law Jethro came to him in the desert where he was en-

camped near the mountain of God, ⁶and he sent word to Moses, "I, Jethro, your father-in-law, am coming to you, along with your wife and her two sons."

⁷Moses went out to meet his father-in-law, bowed down before him, and kissed him. Having greeted each other, they went into the tent. ⁸Moses then told his father-in-law of all that the LORD had done to Pharaoh and the Egyptians for the sake of Israel, and of all the hardships they had had to endure on their journey, and how the LORD had come to their rescue. ⁹Jethro rejoiced over all the goodness that the LORD had shown Israel in rescuing them from the hands of the Egyptians. ¹⁰"Blessed be the LORD," he said, "who has rescued his people from the hands of Pharaoh and the Egyptians. ¹¹Now I know that the LORD is a deity great beyond any other; for he took occasion of their being dealt with insolently to deliver the people from the power of the Egyptians." ¹²Then Jethro, the father-in-law of Moses, brought a holocaust and other sacrifices to God, and Aaron came with all the elders of Israel to participate with Moses' father-in-law in the meal before God.

Appointment of Minor Judges

¹³The next day Moses sat in judgment for the people, who waited about him from morning until evening. ¹⁴When his father-in-law saw all that he was doing for the people, he inquired, "What sort of thing is this that you are doing for the people? Why do you sit alone while all the people have to stand about you from morning till evening?" ¹⁵Moses answered his father-in-law, "The people come to me to consult God. ¹⁶Whenever they have a disagreement, they come to me to have me settle the matter between them and make known to them God's decisions and regulations."

¹⁷"You are not acting wisely," his father-in-law replied. ¹⁸*"You will surely wear yourself out, and not only yourself but also these people with you. The task is too heavy for you; you cannot do it alone. ¹⁹Now, listen to me, and I will give you some advice, that God may be with you. Act as the people's representative before God, bringing to him whatever they have to say. ²⁰Enlighten them in regard to the decisions and regulations, showing them how they are to live and what they are to do. ²¹*But you should also look among all the people for able and God-fearing men, trustworthy men who hate dishonest gain, and set them as officers over groups of thousands, of hundreds, of fifties, and of tens. ²²Let these men render decisions for the people in all ordinary cases. More important cases they should refer to you, but all the lesser cases they can settle themselves. Thus, your burden will be lightened, since they will bear it with you. ²³If you do this, when God gives you orders you will

---

5f: Dt 8, 15; Pss 78, 15f;
105, 41; Wis 11, 4;
Is 43, 20; 48, 21.
7: Ps 95, 8f.
8: Dt 25, 17; 1 Sm 15, 2.

14: Nm 24, 20;
1 Sm 15, 3.20.
18/3: 2, 22.
18: Nm 11, 14.
21.25: Dt 1, 15; 16, 18.

† 17, 7: *Massah . . . Meribah:* Hebrew words meaning respectively, "the (place of the) test," and, "the (place of the) quarreling."

17, 8: *Amalek:* the Amalekites were an aboriginal people of southern Palestine and the Sinai peninsula. Cf Nm 24, 20.

17, 15: *Yahweh-nissi:* meaning, "the LORD is my banner."

be able to stand the strain, and all these people will go home satisfied."

²⁴Moses followed the advice of his father-in-law and did all that he had suggested. ²⁵He picked out able men from all Israel and put them in charge of the people as officers over groups of thousands, of hundreds, of fifties, and of tens. ²⁶They rendered decisions for the people in all ordinary cases. The more difficult cases they referred to Moses, but all the lesser cases they settled themselves. ²⁷Then Moses bade farewell to his father-in-law, who went off to his own country.

III: THE COVENANT AT MOUNT SINAI

Arrival at Sinai

19 ¹*IN THE THIRD MONTH after their departure from the land of Egypt, on its first day, the Israelites came to the desert of Sinai. ²After the journey from Rephidim to the desert of Sinai, they pitched camp.

While Israel was encamped here in front of the mountain, ³Moses went up the mountain to God. Then the LORD called to him and said, "Thus shall you say to the house of Jacob; tell the Israelites: ⁴*You have seen for yourselves how I treated the Egyptians and how I bore you up on eagle wings and brought you here to myself. ⁵*Therefore, if you hearken to my voice and keep my covenant, you shall be my special possession, dearer to me than all other people, though all the earth is mine. ⁶*†You shall be to me a kingdom of priests, a holy nation. That is what you must tell the Israelites." ⁷So Moses went and summoned the elders of the people. When he set before them all that the LORD had ordered him to tell them, ⁸the people all answered together, "Everything the LORD has said, we will do." Then Moses brought back to the LORD the response of the people.

⁹*The LORD also told him, "I am coming to you in a dense cloud, so that when the people hear me speaking with you, they may always have faith in you also." When Moses, then, had reported to the LORD the response of the people, ¹⁰the LORD added, "Go to the people and have them sanctify themselves today and tomorrow. Make them wash their garments ¹¹and be ready for the third day; for on the third day the LORD will come down on Mount Sinai before the eyes of all the people. ¹²*Set limits for the people all around the mountain, and tell them: Take care not to go up the mountain, or even to touch its base. If anyone touches the mountain he must be put to death. ¹³No hand shall touch him; he must be stoned to death or killed with arrows. Such a one, man or beast, must not be allowed to live. Only when the ram's horn resounds may they go up to the mountain." ¹⁴Then Moses came down from the mountain to the people and had them sanctify themselves and wash their garments. ¹⁵He warned them, "Be ready for the third day. Have no intercourse with any woman."

The Great Theophany

¹⁶*On the morning of the third day there were peals of thunder and lightning, and a heavy cloud over the mountain, and a very loud trumpet blast, so that all the people in the camp trembled. ¹⁷But Moses led the people out of the camp to meet God, and they stationed themselves at the foot of the mountain. ¹⁸Mount Sinai was all wrapped in smoke, for the LORD came down upon it in fire. The smoke rose from it as though from a furnace, and the whole mountain trembled violently. ¹⁹The trumpet blast grew louder and louder, while Moses was speaking and God answering him with thunder.

²⁰When the LORD came down to the top of Mount Sinai, he summoned Moses to the top of the mountain, and Moses went up to him. ²¹Then the LORD told Moses, "Go down and warn the people not to break through toward the LORD in order to see him; otherwise many of them will be struck down. ²²The priests, too, who approach the LORD must sanctify themselves; else he will vent his anger upon them." ²³Moses said to the LORD, "The people cannot go up to Mount Sinai, for you yourself warned us to set limits around the mountain to make it sacred." ²⁴The LORD repeated, "Go down now! Then come up again along with Aaron. But the priests and the people must not break through to come up to the LORD; else he will vent his anger upon them." ²⁵So Moses went down to the people and told them this.

The Ten Commandments

20 ¹†THEN God delivered all these commandments:
²*"I, the LORD, am your God, who brought you out of the land of Egypt, that place of slavery. ³You shall not have other gods besides me. ⁴*You shall not carve idols for yourselves in the shape of anything in the sky above or on the earth below or in the waters

---

19/1f: Nm 33, 15.
    4: Dt 32, 11.
    5: Dt 7, 6; 14, 2; 26, 18f;
       32, 8f.
    6: 1 Pet 2, 9.
    9: 20, 21; 24, 15-18.
  12f: 34, 3; Heb 12, 18f.

16ff: Dt 4, 10ff.
20/2-17: Dt 5, 6-21.
    2: Lv 26, 13; Ps 81,
      10; Hos 13, 4.
    4: 34, 17; Lv 26, 1; Dt 4,
      15-19; 27, 15.

---

† 19, 6: *Kingdom of priests:* inasmuch as the whole Israelite nation was consecrated to God in a special way, it formed a race of royal priests who participated in the liturgical sacrifices, even though the actual offering of the sacrifices was the exclusive prerogative of the Aaronic priesthood. The same condition exists in the New Dispensation as regards the whole Christian people and the Christian priesthood in the strict sense. Cf Is 61, 6; 1 Pt 2, 5.9.

20, 1-17: The precise division of these precepts into "ten commandments" is somewhat uncertain. Traditionally among Catholics vv 1-6 are considered as only one commandment, and v 17 as two. Cf Dt 5, 6-21.

beneath the earth; **5***†you shall not bow down before them or worship them. For I, the Lord, your God, am a jealous God, inflicting punishment for their fathers' wickedness on the children of those who hate me, down to the third and fourth generation; **6**but bestowing mercy down to the thousandth generation, on the children of those who love me and keep my commandments.

7*"You shall not take the name of the Lord, your God, in vain. For the Lord will not leave unpunished him who takes his name in vain.

8*"Remember to keep holy the sabbath day. **9**Six days you may labor and do all your work, **10**but the seventh day is the sabbath of the Lord, your God. No work may be done then either by you, or your son or daughter, or your male or female slave, or your beast, or by the alien who lives with you. **11***In six days the Lord made the heavens and the earth, the sea and all that is in them; but on the seventh day he rested. That is why the Lord has blessed the sabbath day and made it holy.

12*"Honor your father and your mother, that you may have a long life in the land which the Lord, your God, is giving you.

13*"You shall not kill.

14*"You shall not commit adultery.

15*"You shall not steal.

16*"You shall not bear false witness against your neighbor.

17*"You shall not covet your neighbor's house. You shall not covet your neighbor's wife, nor his male or female slave, nor his ox or ass, nor anything else that belongs to him."

The Fear of God

18*When the people witnessed the thunder and lightning, the trumpet blast and the mountain smoking, they all feared and trembled. So they took up a position much farther away **19**and said to Moses, "You speak to us, and we will listen; but let not God speak to us, or we shall die." **20**Moses answered the people, "Do not be afraid, for God has come to you only to test you and put his fear upon you, lest you should sin." **21**Still the people remained at a distance, while Moses approached the cloud where God was.

22The Lord told Moses, "Thus shall you speak to the Israelites: You have seen for yourselves that I have spoken to you from heaven. **23***Do not make anything to rank with me; neither gods of silver nor gods of gold shall you make for yourselves.

24*†"An altar of earth you shall make for me, and upon it you shall sacrifice your holocausts and peace offerings, your sheep and your oxen. In whatever place I choose for the remembrance of my name I will come to you and bless you. **25***If you make an altar of stone for me, do not build it of cut stone, for by putting a tool to it you desecrate it. **26**You shall not go up by steps to my altar, on which you must not be indecently uncovered.

Laws Regarding Slaves

21 **1**†"THESE are the rules you shall lay before them. **2***When you purchase a Hebrew slave, he is to serve you for six years, but in the seventh year he shall be given his freedom without cost. **3**If he comes into service alone, he shall leave alone; if he comes with a wife, his wife shall leave with him. **4**But if his master gives him a wife and she bears him sons or daughters, the woman and her children shall remain the master's property and the man shall leave alone. **5**If, however, the slave declares, 'I am devoted to my master and my wife and children; I will not go free,' **6**†his master shall bring him to God and there, at the door or doorpost, he shall pierce his ear with an awl, thus keeping him as his slave forever.

7When a man sells his daughter as a slave, she shall not go free as male slaves do. **8**†But if her master, who had destined her for himself, dislikes her, he shall let her be redeemed. He has no right to sell her to a foreigner, since he has broken faith with her. **9**If he destines her for his son, he shall treat her like a daughter. **10**If he takes another wife, he shall not withhold her food, her clothing, or her conjugal rights. **11**If he does not grant her these three things, she shall be given her freedom absolutely, without cost to her.

Personal Injury

12*"Whoever strikes a man a mortal blow must be put to death. **13**He, however, who did not hunt a man down, but caused his death by an act of God, may flee to a place which I will set apart for this purpose. **14**But when a man kills another after maliciously scheming to do so, you must take him even from my altar and put him to death. **15**Whoever strikes his father or mother shall be put to death.

✿
5: 34, 7.14; Nm 14, 18; Dt 4, 24; 6, 15.	16: 23, 1; Dt 19, 16ff; Prv 19, 5.9; 24, 28.
7: Lv 19, 12; 24, 16.	17: Rom 7, 7.
8ff: 23, 12; 31, 13-16; 34, 21; 35, 2; Lv 23, 3.	18-21: Dt 4, 11; 5, 22-27; 18, 16; Heb 12, 18f.
11: 31, 17; Gn 2, 2f.	23: 20, 3f.
12-16: Mt 19, 18f; Mk 10, 19; Lk 18, 20; Rom 13, 9.	24: Dt 12, 5.11; 14, 23; 16, 6.
12: Mt 15, 4; Mk 7, 10; Eph 6, 2f.	25: Dt 27, 5; Jos 8, 31.
13: Mt 5, 21.	21/2-6: Lv 25, 39ff; Dt 15, 12-18; Jer 34, 14.
14: Lv 18, 20; 20, 10; Dt 22, 22; Mt 5, 27.	12ff: Lv 24, 17; Nm 35, 15-29; Dt 4, 41f; 19, 2-5.
15: Lv 19, 11.	

20, 5: *Jealous:* demanding exclusive allegiance, such as a wife must have for her husband.

20, 24: *I choose for the remembrance of my name:* literally, "where I make my name to be remembered": at the sacred site where God wishes to be worshiped and his name revered.

21, 1: *Rules:* judicial precedents to be used in settling questions of law and custom. This introductory phrase serves as the title of the following collection of civil and religious laws (chapters 21-23) which is called in 24, 7, *the book of the covenant.*

21, 6: *To God:* to the sanctuary; or perhaps the phrase is to be rendered, "to the gods," in the sense of "to the judges." Cf Ps 82, 1. Since the expression "to have an open ear" meant "to obey," a pierced ear lobe was an ancient symbol of obedience. Cf Ps 40, 7.

21, 8: *Destined her:* intended her as a wife of second rank.

16°"A kidnaper, whether he sells his victim or still has him when caught, shall be put to death. **17**°"Whoever curses his father or mother shall be put to death.

18"When men quarrel and one strikes the other with a stone or with his fist, not mortally, but enough to put him in bed, **19**the one who struck the blow shall be acquitted, provided the other can get up and walk around with the help of his staff. Still, he must compensate him for his enforced idleness and provide for his complete cure.

20"When a man strikes his male or female slave with a rod so hard that the slave dies under his hand, he shall be punished. **21**If, however, the slave survives for a day or two, he is not to be punished, since the slave is his own property.

22°"When men have a fight and hurt a pregnant woman, so that she suffers a miscarriage, but no further injury, the guilty one shall be fined as much as the woman's husband demands of him, and he shall pay in the presence of the judges. **23**†But if injury ensues, you shall give life for life, **24**eye for eye, tooth for tooth, hand for hand, foot for foot, **25**burn for burn, wound for wound, stripe for stripe.

26"When a man strikes his male or female slave in the eye and destroys the use of the eye, he shall let the slave go free in compensation for the eye. **27**If he knocks out a tooth of his male or female slave, he shall let the slave go free in compensation for the tooth.

28"When an ox gores a man or a woman to death, the ox must be stoned; its flesh may not be eaten. The owner of the ox, however, shall go unpunished. **29**But if an ox was previously in the habit of goring people and its owner, though warned, would not keep it in; should it then kill a man or a woman, not only must the ox be stoned, but its owner also must be put to death. **30**If, however, a fine is imposed on him, he must pay in ransom for his life whatever amount is imposed on him. **31**This law applies if it is a boy or a girl that the ox gores. **32**But if it is a male or a female slave that it gores, he must pay the owner of the slave thirty shekels of silver, and the ox must be stoned.

Property Damage

33"When a man uncovers or digs a cistern and does not cover it over again, should an ox or an ass fall into it, **34**the owner of the cistern must make good by restoring the value of the animal to its owner; the dead animal, however, he may keep.

35"When one man's ox hurts another's ox so badly that it dies, they shall sell the live ox and divide this money as well as the dead animal equally between them. **36**But if it was known that the ox was previously in the habit of goring and its owner would not keep it in, he must make full restitution, an ox for an ox; but the dead animal he may keep.

37°†"When a man steals an ox or a sheep and slaughters or sells it, he shall restore five oxen for the one ox, and four sheep for the one sheep.

22 **1**†[IF a thief is caught in the act of housebreaking and beaten to death, there is no bloodguilt involved. **2**But if after sunrise he is thus beaten, there is bloodguilt.] He must make full restitution. If he has nothing, he shall be sold to pay for his theft. **3**If what he stole is found alive in his possession, be it an ox, an ass or a sheep, he shall restore two animals for each one stolen.

4†"When a man is burning over a field or a vineyard, if he lets the fire spread so that it burns in another's field, he must make restitution with the best produce of his own field or vineyard. **5**If the fire spreads further, and catches on to thorn bushes, so that shocked grain or standing grain or the field itself is burned up, the one who started the fire must make full restitution.

Trusts and Loans

6"When a man gives money or any article to another for safekeeping and it is stolen from the latter's house, the thief, if caught, must make twofold restitution. **7**†If the thief is not caught, the owner of the house shall be brought to God, to swear that he himself did not lay hands on his neighbor's property. **8**In every question of dishonest appropriation, whether it be about an ox, or an ass, or a sheep, or a garment, or anything else that has disappeared, where another claims that the thing is his, both parties shall present their case before God; the one whom God convicts must make twofold restitution to the other.

9"When a man gives an ass, or an ox, or a sheep, or any other animal to another for safekeeping, if it dies, or is maimed or snatched away, without anyone witnessing the fact, **10**the custodian shall swear by the Lord that he did not lay hands on his neighbor's property; the owner must accept the oath, and no restitution is to be made. **11**But if the custodian is really guilty of theft, he must make restitution to the owner. **12**°If it has been killed by a wild beast, let him bring it as evidence, and he need not make restitution for the mangled animal.

---

† 21, 23ff: This section is known as the *lex talionis*, the law of tit for tat. The purpose of this law was not merely the enforcement of rigorous justice, but also the prevention of greater penalties than would be just. Christ refers to this passage when he exhorts Christians to cede their lawful rights for the sake of charity. Cf Mt 5, 38ff.

21, 37—22, 30: In the Vulgate, 22, 1-31.

22, 1f: *If a thief is caught:* this seems to be a fragment of what was once a longer law on housebreaking, which has been inserted here into the middle of a law on stealing animals. At night the householder would be justified in killing a burglar outright, but not so in the daytime, when the burglar could more easily be caught alive. *He must make full restitution:* this stood originally immediately after 21, 37.

22, 4: The Greek and Latin versions understood this verse as a prohibition against allowing one's cattle to graze in the field of another.

22, 7: *Brought to God:* see note on 21, 6. Cf also 22, 10.

° 16: Dt 24, 7. 17: Lv 20, 9; Prv 20, 20; Mt 15, 4; Mk 7, 10.   22-25: Lv 24, 18-21; Dt 19, 21; Mt 5, 38. 37: 2 Sm 12, 6.

¹³"When a man borrows an animal from his neighbor, if it is maimed or dies while the owner is not present, the man must make restitution. ¹⁴But if the owner is present, he need not make restitution. If it was hired, this was covered by the price of its hire.

Social Laws

¹⁵*"When a man seduces a virgin who is not betrothed, and lies with her, he shall pay her marriage price and marry her. ¹⁶†If her father refuses to give her to him, he must still pay him the customary marriage price for virgins.

¹⁷*"You shall not let a sorceress live.

¹⁸*"Anyone who lies with an animal shall be put to death.

¹⁹*"Whoever sacrifices to any god, except to the LORD alone, shall be doomed.

²⁰*"You shall not molest or oppress an alien, for you were once aliens yourselves in the land of Egypt. ²¹You shall not wrong any widow or orphan. ²²If ever you wrong them and they cry out to me, I will surely hear their cry. ²³My wrath will flare up, and I will kill you with the sword; then your own wives will be widows, and your children orphans.

²⁴*"If you lend money to one of your poor neighbors among my people, you shall not act like an extortioner toward him by demanding interest from him. ²⁵If you take your neighbor's cloak as a pledge, you shall return it to him before sunset; ²⁶for this cloak of his is the only covering he has for his body. What else has he to sleep in? If he cries out to me, I will hear him; for I am compassionate.

²⁷*†"You shall not revile God, nor curse a prince of your people.

²⁸"You shall not delay the offering of your harvest and your press. You shall give me the first-born of your sons. ²⁹*You must do the same with your oxen and your sheep; for seven days the firstling may stay with its mother, but on the eighth day you must give it to me.

³⁰*"You shall be men sacred to me. Flesh torn to pieces in the field you shall not eat; throw it to the dogs.

23 ¹*"YOU shall not repeat a false report. Do not join the wicked in putting your hand, as an unjust witness, upon anyone. ²Neither shall you allege the example of the many as an excuse for doing wrong, nor shall you, when testifying in a lawsuit, side with the many in perverting justice. ³*You shall not favor a poor man in his lawsuit.

⁴*"When you come upon your enemy's ox or ass going astray, see to it that it is returned to him. ⁵When you notice the ass of one who hates you lying prostrate under its burden, by no means desert him; help him, rather, to raise it up.

⁶"You shall not deny one of your needy fellow men his rights in his lawsuit. ⁷You shall keep away from anything dishonest. The innocent and the just you shall not put to death, nor shall you acquit the guilty. ⁸*Never take a bribe, for a bribe blinds even the most clear-sighted and twists the words even of the just. ⁹*You shall not oppress an alien; you well know how it feels to be an alien, since you were once aliens yourselves in the land of Egypt.

Religious Laws

¹⁰*"For six years you may sow your land and gather in its produce. ¹¹But the seventh year you shall let the land lie untilled and unharvested, that the poor among you may eat of it and the beasts of the field may eat what the poor leave. So also shall you do in regard to your vineyard and your olive grove.

¹²*"For six days you may do your work, but on the seventh day you must rest, that your ox and your ass may also have rest, and that the son of your maidservant and the alien may be refreshed. ¹³Give heed to all that I have told you.

"Never mention the name of any other god; it shall not be heard from your lips.

¹⁴*†"Three times a year you shall celebrate a pilgrim feast to me. ¹⁵†You shall keep the feast of Unleavened Bread. As I have commanded you, you must eat unleavened bread for seven days at the prescribed time in the month of Abib, for it was then that you came out of Egypt. No one shall appear before me empty-handed. ¹⁶You shall also keep the feast of the grain harvest with the first of the crop that you have sown in the field; and finally, the feast at the fruit harvest at the end of the year, when you gather in the produce from the fields. ¹⁷Thrice a year shall all your men appear before the Lord GOD.

¹⁸*"You shall not offer the blood of my sacrifice with leavened bread; nor shall the fat of my feast be kept overnight till the next day. ¹⁹†The choicest first fruits

---

✱ 15f: Dt 22, 28f.
  17: Lv 19, 26.31; 20, 6.27; Dt 18, 10f.
  18: Lv 18, 23; Dt 27, 21.
  19: Dt 13; 17, 2-7.
  20-23: 23, 9; Lv 19, 33f; Dt 10, 18f; 24, 17f; 27, 19; Zec 7, 10.
  24-26: Lv 25, 35-38; Dt 23, 19f; 24, 10-13; Ez 18, 7f.17f.
  27: Acts 23, 5.
  29: 13, 2; 34, 19; Lv 22, 27; Dt 15, 19.
  30: Lv 7, 24; 17, 15; 22, 8.
  23/1f: Dt 19, 16ff.
  3: Lv 19, 15.
  4: Dt 22, 1ff.
  8: Dt 16, 19; 27, 25; Sir 20, 28.
  9: 22, 21.
  10f: Lv 25, 3-7.
  12: 20, 8.
  14-17: 34, 18.22ff; Lv 23; Dt 16, 1-17.
  18f: 34, 25f.

† 22, 16: *The customary marriage price for virgins:* fifty shekels according to Dt 22, 29.

22, 27: *God:* or perhaps "the gods," in the sense of "the judges," as the parallel with *a prince of your people* suggests.

23, 14: These three feasts are elsewhere called the Passover, Pentecost and Booths. Cf 34, 18-26; Lv 23; Dt 16.

23, 15: *Appear before me:* the original expression was "see my face"; so also in several other places, as 23, 17; 34, 23f; Dt 16, 16; 31, 11.

23, 19: *Boil a kid in its mother's milk:* this was part of a Canaanite ritual; hence it is forbidden here as a pagan ceremony.

of your soil you shall bring to the house of the Lord, your God.

"You shall not boil a kid in its mother's milk.

Reward of Fidelity

20 "See, I am sending an angel before you, to guard you on the way and bring you to the place I have prepared. **21** Be attentive to him and heed his voice. Do not rebel against him, for he will not forgive your sin. My authority resides in him. **22** If you heed his voice and carry out all I tell you, I will be an enemy to your enemies and a foe to your foes.

23 "My angel will go before you and bring you to the Amorites, Hittites, Perizzites, Canaanites, Hivites and Jebusites; and I will wipe them out. **24** Therefore, you shall not bow down in worship before their gods, nor shall you make anything like them; rather, you must demolish them and smash their sacred pillars. **25** The Lord, your God, you shall worship; then I will bless your food and drink, and I will remove all sickness from your midst; **26** no woman in your land will be barren or miscarry; and I will give you a full span of life.

27 "I will have the fear of me precede you, so that I will throw into panic every nation you reach. I will make all your enemies turn from you in flight, **28** and ahead of you I will send hornets to drive the Hivites, Canaanites and Hittites out of your way. **29** But not in one year will I drive them all out before you; else the land will become so desolate that the wild beasts will multiply against you. **30** Instead, I will drive them out little by little before you, until you have grown numerous enough to take possession of the land. **31** I will set your boundaries from the Red Sea to the sea of the Philistines, and from the desert to the River; all who dwell in this land I will hand over to you to be driven out of your way. **32** You shall not make a covenant with them or their gods. **33** They must not abide in your land, lest they make you sin against me by ensnaring you into worshiping their gods."

Ratification of the Covenant

24 ¹MOSES himself was told, "Come up to the Lord, you and Aaron, with Nadab, Abihu, and seventy of the elders of Israel. You shall all worship at some distance, **2** but Moses alone is to come close to the Lord; the others shall not come too near, and the people shall not come up at all with Moses."

3 When Moses came to the people and related all the words and ordinances of the Lord, they all answered with one voice, "We will do everything that the Lord has told us." **4** Moses then wrote down all the words of the Lord and, rising early the next day, he erected at the foot of the mountain an altar and twelve pillars for the twelve tribes of Israel. **5** Then, having sent certain young men of the Israelites to offer holocausts and sacrifice young bulls as peace offerings to the Lord, **6** Moses took half of the blood and put it in large bowls; the other half he splashed on the altar. **7** Taking the book of the covenant, he read it aloud to the people, who answered, "All that the Lord has said, we will heed and do." **8** Then he took the blood and sprinkled it on the people, saying, "This is the blood of the covenant which the Lord has made with you in accordance with all these words of his."

9 Moses then went up with Aaron, Nadab, Abihu, and seventy elders of Israel, **10** and they beheld the God of Israel. Under his feet there appeared to be sapphire tilework, as clear as the sky itself. **11** Yet he did not smite these chosen Israelites. After gazing on God, they could still eat and drink.

Moses on the Mountain

12 The Lord said to Moses, "Come up to me on the mountain and, while you are there, I will give you the stone tablets on which I have written the commandments intended for their instruction." **13** So Moses set out with Joshua, his aide, and went up to the mountain of God. **14** The elders, however, had been told by him, "Wait here for us until we return to you. Aaron and Hur are staying with you. If anyone has a complaint, let him refer the matter to them." **15** After Moses had gone up, a cloud covered the mountain. **16** The glory of the Lord settled upon Mount Sinai. The cloud covered it for six days, and on the seventh day he called to Moses from the midst of the cloud. **17** To the Israelites the glory of the Lord was seen as a consuming fire on the mountaintop. **18** But Moses passed into the midst of the cloud as he went up on the mountain; and there he stayed for forty days and forty nights.

---

† 23, 21: *My authority resides in him:* literally, "My name is within him."

23, 24: *Make anything like them:* some render, "act according to their conduct." *Sacred pillars:* objects of religious veneration at Canaanite sanctuaries.

23, 28: *Hornets:* some understand this figuratively of various troublesome afflictions; others translate the Hebrew word as "leprosy." Cf Dt 7, 20; Jos 24, 12; Wis 12, 8.

23, 31: *The sea of the Philistines:* the Mediterranean. *The River:* the Euphrates. Only in the time of David and Solomon did the territory of Israel come near to reaching such distant borders.

24, 4: *Pillars:* stone shafts or slabs, erected as symbols of the fact that each of the twelve tribes had entered into this covenant with God; not idolatrous as in 23, 24, although the same Hebrew word is used in both passages. See note on Gn 28, 18.

24, 11: *After gazing on God:* the ancients thought that the sight of God would bring instantaneous death. Cf 33, 20; Gn 16, 13; 32, 31; Jgs 6, 22f; 13, 22. *Eat and drink:* partake of the sacrificial meal.

20: 14, 19; 32, 34; 33, 2.
23f: 34, 10-16; Nm 33, 51f; Dt 7, 24ff.
27ff: Dt 2, 25; 7, 20ff.
31: Gn 15, 18; Dt 11, 24; Jos 1, 4.
32f: 34, 12-16; Dt 7, 2ff.
24/3: 19, 8.
5-8: Heb 9, 18ff.
12: 31, 18; 32, 15; Dt 5, 22.
16: Sir 45, 4.
17: 19, 18; Heb 12, 18.
18: 34, 28; Dt 9, 9.

IV: THE DWELLING AND ITS FURNISHINGS

Collection of Materials

25 ¹*THIS IS WHAT THE LORD THEN SAID to Moses: ²"Tell the Israelites to take up a collection for me. From every man you shall accept the contribution that his heart prompts him to give me. ³*These are the contributions you shall accept from them: gold, silver and bronze; ⁴violet, purple and scarlet yarn; fine linen and goat hair; ⁵†rams' skins dyed red, and tahash skins; acacia wood; ⁶oil for the light; spices for the anointing oil and for the fragrant incense; ⁷onyx stones and other gems for mounting on the ephod and the breastpiece.

⁸*"They shall make a sanctuary for me, that I may dwell in their midst. ⁹*This Dwelling and all its furnishings you shall make exactly according to the pattern that I will now show you.

Plan of the Ark

¹⁰*"You shall make an ark of acacia wood, two and a half cubits long, one and a half cubits wide, and one and a half cubits high. ¹¹Plate it inside and outside with pure gold, and put a molding of gold around the top of it. ¹²Cast four gold rings and fasten them on the four supports of the ark, two rings on one side and two on the opposite side. ¹³Then make poles of acacia wood and plate them with gold. ¹⁴These poles you are to put through the rings on the sides of the ark, for carrying it; ¹⁵they must remain in the rings of the ark and never be withdrawn. ¹⁶In the ark you are to put the commandments which I will give you.

¹⁷†"You shall then make a propitiatory of pure gold, two cubits and a half long, and one and a half cubits wide. ¹⁸†Make two cherubim of beaten gold for the two ends of the propitiatory, ¹⁹fastening them so that one cherub springs direct from each end. ²⁰The cherubim shall have their wings spread out above, covering the propitiatory with them; they shall be turned toward each other, but with their faces looking toward the propitiatory. ²¹This propitiatory you shall then place on top of the ark. In the ark itself you are to put the commandments which I will give you. ²²There I will meet you and there, from above the propitiatory, between the two cherubim on the ark of the commandments, I will tell you all the commands that I wish you to give the Israelites.

The Table

²³*"You shall also make a table of acacia wood, two cubits long, a cubit wide, and a cubit and a half high. ²⁴Plate it with pure gold and make a molding of gold around it. ²⁵†Surround it with a frame, a handbreadth high, with a molding of gold around the frame. ²⁶You shall also make four rings of gold for it and fasten them at the four corners, one at each leg, ²⁷on two opposite sides of the frame as holders for the poles to carry the table. ²⁸These poles for carrying the table you shall make of acacia wood and plate with gold. ²⁹†Of pure gold you shall make its plates and cups, as well as its pitchers and bowls for pouring libations. ³⁰*On the table you shall always keep showbread set before me.

The Lampstand

³¹*"You shall make a lampstand of pure beaten gold—its shaft and branches—with its cups and knobs and petals springing directly from it. ³²Six branches are to extend from the sides of the lampstand, three branches on one side, and three on the other. ³³†On one branch there are to be three cups, shaped like almond blossoms, each with its knob and petals; on the opposite branch there are to be three cups, shaped like almond blossoms, each with its knob and petals; and so for the six branches that extend from the lampstand. ³⁴†On the shaft there are to be four cups, shaped like almond blossoms, with their knobs and petals, ³⁵including a knob below each of the three pairs of branches that extend from the lampstand. ³⁶Their knobs and branches shall so spring from it that the whole will form but a single piece of pure beaten gold. ³⁷*†You shall then make seven lamps for it and so set up the lamps that they shed their light on the space in front of the lampstand. ³⁸†These, as well as the trimming

---

† 25, 5: *Tahash:* perhaps the name of a marine animal, such as the dugong or the porpoise. The Greek and Latin versions took it for the color hyacinth.

25, 17: *Propitiatory:* this traditional rendering of the Hebrew term, which may mean merely "cover," is derived from its connection with the ceremony of the Day of Atonement whereby God was rendered "propitious." Cf Lv 16, 14ff.

25, 18ff: *Cherubim:* probably in the form of human-headed winged lions. The cherubim over the ark formed the throne for the invisible LORD. Cf Ps 80, 2. For a more detailed description of the somewhat different cherubim in the temple of Solomon, see 1 Kgs 6, 23-28; 2 Chr 3, 10-13.

25, 25: *A frame:* probably placed near the bottom of the legs to keep them steady. The golden table of Herod's temple is pictured thus on the Arch of Titus.

25, 29f: The *plates* held the showbread, that is, the holy bread which was placed upon the table every sabbath as an offering to God, and was later eaten by the priests. The *cups* held the incense which was strewn upon the bread. Cf Lv 24, 5-9. The libation wine was poured from the *pitchers* into the *bowls.* All these vessels were kept on the golden table.

25, 33: In keeping with the arrangement of the ornaments on the shaft, the three sets of ornaments on each branch were probably so placed that one was at the top and the other two equally spaced along the length of the branch. *Knob:* the cup-shaped seed capsule at the base of a flower.

25, 34f: Of the four ornaments on the shaft, one was at the top and one was below each of the three sets of side branches.

25, 37: The lamps were probably shaped like small boats, with the wick at one end; the end with the wick was turned toward the front of the lampstand.

25, 38: *Trays:* small receptacles for the burnt-out wicks.

25/1-7: 35, 4-9.20-29.   23-30: 37, 10-16.
3: 35, 4-9.   30: Lv 24, 5ff.
8f: 26, 1-30; 36, 8-38.   31-40: 37, 17-24.
9: Acts 7, 44.   37: Lv 24, 2ff; Nm 8, 2.
10-22: 37, 1-9; Heb 9, 1-5.

shears and trays, must be of pure gold. ³⁹Use a talent of pure gold for the lampstand and all its appurtenances. ⁴⁰*See that you make them according to the pattern shown you on the mountain.

The Tent Cloth

26 ¹*†THE Dwelling itself you shall make out of sheets woven of fine linen twined and of violet, purple and scarlet yarn, with cherubim embroidered on them. ²The length of each shall be twenty-eight cubits, and the width four cubits; all the sheets shall be of the same size. ³Five of the sheets are to be sewed together, edge to edge; and the same for the other five. ⁴Make loops of violet yarn along the edge of the end sheet in one set, and the same along the edge of the end sheet in the other set. ⁵There are to be fifty loops along the edge of the end sheet in the first set, and fifty loops along the edge of the corresponding sheet in the second set, and so placed that the loops are directly opposite each other. ⁶Then make fifty clasps of gold, with which to join the two sets of sheets, so that the Dwelling forms one whole.

⁷†"Also make sheets woven of goat hair, to be used as a tent covering over the Dwelling. ⁸Eleven such sheets are to be made; the length of each shall be thirty cubits, and the width four cubits: all eleven sheets shall be of the same size. ⁹†Sew five of the sheets, edge to edge, into one set, and the other six sheets into another set. Use the sixth sheet double at the front of the tent. ¹⁰Make fifty loops along the edge of the end sheet in one set, and fifty loops along the edge of the end sheet in the second set. ¹¹Also make fifty bronze clasps and put them into the loops, to join the tent into one whole. ¹²There will be an extra half sheet of tent covering, which shall be allowed to hang down over the rear of the Dwelling. ¹³Likewise, the sheets of the tent will have an extra cubit's length to be left hanging down on either side of the Dwelling to protect it. ¹⁴Over the tent itself you shall make a covering of rams' skins dyed red, and above that, a covering of tahash skins.

The Wooden Walls

¹⁵*"You shall make boards of acacia wood as walls for the Dwelling. ¹⁶The length of each board is to be ten cubits, and its width one and a half cubits. ¹⁷†Each board shall have two arms that shall serve to fasten the boards in line. In this way all the boards of the Dwelling are to be made. ¹⁸Set up the boards of the Dwelling as follows: twenty boards on the south side, ¹⁹with forty silver pedestals under the twenty boards, so that there are two pedestals under each board, at its two arms; ²⁰twenty boards on the other side of the Dwelling, the north side, ²¹with their forty silver pedestals, two under each board; ²²six boards for the rear of the Dwelling, to the west; ²³and two boards for the corners at the rear of the Dwelling. ²⁴These two shall be double at the bottom, and likewise double at the top, to the first ring. That is how both boards in the corners are to be made. ²⁵Thus, there shall be in the rear eight boards, with their sixteen silver pedestals, two pedestals under each board. ²⁶Also make bars of acacia wood: five for the boards on one side of the Dwelling, ²⁷five for those on the other side, and five for those at the rear, toward the west. ²⁸The center bar, at the middle of the boards, shall reach across from end to end. ²⁹Plate the boards with gold, and make gold rings on them as holders for the bars, which are also to be plated with gold. ³⁰You shall erect the Dwelling according to the pattern shown you on the mountain.

The Veils

³¹*"You shall have a veil woven of violet, purple and scarlet yarn, and of fine linen twined, with cherubim embroidered on it. ³²†It is to be hung on four gold-plated columns of acacia wood, which shall have hooks of gold and shall rest on four silver pedestals. ³³Hang the veil from clasps. The ark of the commandments you shall bring inside, behind this veil which divides the holy place from the holy of holies. ³⁴Set the propitiatory on the ark of the commandments in the holy of holies.

³⁵"Outside the veil you shall place the table and the lampstand, the latter on the south side of the Dwelling, opposite the table, which is to be put on the north side. ³⁶†For the entrance of the tent make a variegated curtain of violet, purple and scarlet yarn and of fine linen twined. ³⁷Make five columns of acacia wood for this curtain; have them plated with gold, with their hooks of gold; and cast five bronze pedestals for them.

The Altar of Holocausts

27 ¹*"YOU shall make an altar of acacia wood, on a square, five cubits long and five cubits wide; it shall be three cubits high. ²At the four corners there are to be horns, so made that they spring directly from the altar. You shall then plate it with bronze. ³Make pots for removing the ashes, as well as shovels, basins, forks and fire pans, all of which

---

† 26, 1: *Sheets:* strips of tapestry, woven of white linen, the colored threads being used for the cherubim which were embroidered on them. These sheets were stretched across the top of the Dwelling to form a roof, their free ends hanging down inside the boards which formed walls.

26, 7: *Tent covering:* the cloth made of sheets of goat hair to cover the Dwelling.

26, 9: Half the width of the end strip was folded back at the front of the Dwelling, thus leaving another half-strip to hang down at the rear. Cf v 12.

26, 17: *Arms:* literally, "hands." According to some, they served as "tongue and groove" to mortise the boards together; according to others, they were pegs at the bottom of the boards and fitted into sockets in the pedestals.

26, 32: *Hooks:* probably placed near the tops of the columns, to hold the rope from which the veils and curtains hung.

26, 36: *Variegated:* without definite designs such as the cherubim on the inner veil.

---

*
40: Heb 8, 5.   31: 2 Chr 3, 14.
26/1-14: 36, 8-19.   31-37: 36, 35-38.
15-30: 36, 20-34.   27/1-8: 38, 1-7.

shall be of bronze. **4**†Make a grating of bronze network for it; this to have four bronze rings, one at each of its four corners. **5**Put it down around the altar, on the ground. This network is to be half as high as the altar. **6**You shall also make poles of acacia wood for the altar, and plate them with bronze. **7**These poles are to be put through the rings, so that they are on either side of the altar when it is carried. **8**†Make the altar itself in the form of a hollow box, just as it was shown you on the mountain.

Court of the Dwelling

9*"You shall also make a court for the Dwelling. On the south side the court shall have hangings a hundred cubits long, woven of fine linen twined, **10**with twenty columns and twenty pedestals of bronze; the hooks and bands on the columns shall be of silver. **11**On the north side there shall be similar hangings, a hundred cubits long, with twenty columns and twenty pedestals of bronze; the hooks and bands on the columns shall be of silver. **12**On the west side, across the width of the court, there shall be hangings, fifty cubits long, with ten columns and ten pedestals. **13**The width of the court on the east side shall be fifty cubits. **14**On one side there shall be hangings to the extent of fifteen cubits, with three columns and three pedestals; **15**on the other side there shall be hangings to the extent of fifteen cubits, with three columns and three pedestals.

16"At the entrance of the court there shall be a variegated curtain, twenty cubits long, woven of violet, purple and scarlet yarn and of fine linen twined. It shall have four columns and four pedestals.

17"All the columns around the court shall have bands and hooks of silver, and pedestals of bronze. **18**The enclosure of the court is to be one hundred cubits long, fifty cubits wide, and five cubits high. Fine lined twined must be used, and the pedestals must be of bronze. **19**All the fittings of the Dwelling, whatever be their use, as well as all its tent pegs and all the tent pegs of the court, must be of bronze.

Oil for the Lamps

20*"You shall order the Israelites to bring you clear oil of crushed olives, to be used for the light, so that you may keep lamps burning regularly. **21**From evening to morning Aaron and his sons shall maintain them before the LORD in the meeting tent, outside the veil which hangs in front of the commandments. This shall be a perpetual ordinance for the Israelites throughout their generations.

The Priestly Vestments

28 **1***"FROM among the Israelites have your brother Aaron, together with his sons Nadab, Abihu, Eleazar and Ithamar, brought to you, that they may be my priests. **2**For the glorious adornment of your brother Aaron you shall have

sacred vestments made. **3**Therefore, to the various expert workmen whom I have endowed with skill, you shall give instructions to make such vestments for Aaron as will set him apart for his sacred service as my priest. **4**These are the vestments they shall make: a breastpiece, an ephod, a robe, a brocaded tunic, a miter and a sash. In making these sacred vestments which your brother Aaron and his sons are to wear in serving as my priests, **5**they shall use gold, violet, purple and scarlet yarn and fine linen.

The Ephod and Breastpiece

6*†"The ephod they shall make of gold thread and of violet, purple and scarlet yarn, embroidered on cloth of fine linen twined. **7**It shall have a pair of shoulder straps joined to its two upper ends. **8**The embroidered belt on the ephod shall extend out from it and, like it, be made of gold thread, of violet, purple and scarlet yarn, and of fine linen twined.

9"Get two onyx stones and engrave on them the names of the sons of Israel: **10**six of their names on one stone, and the other six on the other stone, in the order of their birth. **11**As a gem-cutter engraves a seal, so shall you have the two stones engraved with the names of the sons of Israel and then mounted in gold filigree work. **12**Set these two stones on the shoulder straps of the ephod as memorial stones of the sons of Israel. Thus Aaron shall bear their names on his shoulders as a reminder before the LORD. **13***Make filigree rosettes of gold, **14**as well as two chains of pure gold, twisted like cords, and fasten the cordlike chains to the filigree rosettes.

15*†"The breastpiece of decision you shall also have made, embroidered like the ephod with gold thread and violet, purple and scarlet yarn on cloth of fine linen twined. **16**It is to be square when folded double, a span high and a span wide. **17**†On it you shall mount four rows of precious stones: in the first row, a carnelian, a topaz and an emerald; **18**in the second row, a garnet, a sapphire and a beryl; **19**in the third row, a jacinth, an agate and an amethyst; **20**in the fourth row, a chrysolite, an onyx and a jasper. These stones are to

---

† 27, 4: *Grating:* it is not clear whether this was flush with the altar or at some small distance from it; in the latter case the space between the altar and the grating would be filled with stones and serve as a platform around the altar, which would otherwise be too high for the priest to reach conveniently.

27, 8: *Hollow:* probably filled with earth or stones when in use. Cf 20, 24f.

28, 6: *Ephod:* this Hebrew word is retained in the translation because it is the technical term for a peculiar piece of the priestly vestments, the exact nature of which is uncertain. It seems to have been a sort of apron that hung from the shoulders of the priest by *shoulder straps* (v 7) and was tied around his waist by the loose ends of the attached belt (v 8).

28, 15-30: *Breastpiece:* in shape like a modern altar burse, it was a pocketlike receptacle for holding the *Urim* and *Thummim* (v 30), and formed an integral part of the ephod, to which it was attached by an elaborate system of rings and chains. Both the ephod and its breastpiece were made of brocaded linen.

28, 17-20: The translation of the Hebrew names of some of these gems is quite conjectural.

---

*
9-19: 38, 9-20. 6-12: 39, 2-7; Sir 45, 8-14.
20f: Lv 24, 1-4. 13f: 28, 22.25; 39, 15.18.
28/1-5: 39, 1; Sir 45, 7. 15-21: 39, 15-21.

be mounted in gold filigree work, ²¹twelve of them to match the names of the sons of Israel, each stone engraved like a seal with the name of one of the twelve tribes.

²²"When the chains of pure gold, twisted like cords, have been made for the breastpiece, ²³you shall then make two rings of gold for it and fasten them to the two upper ends of the breastpiece. ²⁴The gold cords are then to be fastened to the two rings at the upper ends of the breastpiece, ²⁵the other two ends of the cords being fastened in front to the two filigree rosettes which are attached to the shoulder straps of the ephod. ²⁶Make two other rings of gold and put them on the two lower ends of the breastpiece, on its edge that faces the ephod. ²⁷Then make two more rings of gold and fasten them to the bottom of the shoulder straps next to where they join the ephod in front, just above its embroidered belt. ²⁸Violet ribbons shall bind the rings of the breastpiece to the rings of the ephod, so that the breastpiece will stay right above the embroidered belt of the ephod and not swing loose from it.

²⁹"Whenever Aaron enters the sanctuary, he will thus bear the names of the sons of Israel on the breastpiece of decision over his heart as a constant reminder before the Lord. ³⁰*†In this breastpiece of decision you shall put the Urim and Thummim, that they may be over Aaron's heart whenever he enters the presence of the Lord. Thus he shall always bear the decisions for the Israelites over his heart in the Lord's presence.

Other Vestments

³¹*"The robe of the ephod you shall make entirely of violet material. ³²It shall have an opening for the head in the center, and around this opening there shall be a selvage, woven as at the opening of a shirt, to keep it from being torn. ³³All around the hem at the bottom you shall make pomegranates, woven of violet, purple and scarlet yarn and fine linen twined, with gold bells between them; ³⁴first a gold bell, then a pomegranate, and thus alternating all around the hem of the robe. ³⁵Aaron shall wear it when ministering, that its tinkling may be heard as he enters and leaves the Lord's presence in the sanctuary; else he will die.

³⁶"You shall also make a plate of pure gold and engrave on it, as on a seal engraving, "Sacred to the Lord." ³⁷*This plate is to be tied over the miter with a violet ribbon in such a way that it rests on the front of the miter, ³⁸over Aaron's forehead. Since Aaron bears whatever guilt the Israelites may incur in consecrating any of their sacred gifts, this plate must always be over his forehead, so that they may find favor with the Lord.

³⁹*"The tunic of fine linen shall be brocaded. The miter shall be made of fine linen. The sash shall be of variegated work.

⁴⁰"Likewise, for the glorious adornment of Aaron's sons you shall have tunics and sashes and turbans made. ⁴¹†With these you shall clothe your brother Aaron and his sons. Anoint and ordain them, consecrating them as my priests. ⁴²*You must also make linen drawers for them, to cover their naked flesh from their loins to their thighs. ⁴³Aaron and his sons shall wear them whenever they go into the meeting tent or approach the altar to minister in the sanctuary, lest they incur guilt and die. This shall be a perpetual ordinance for him and for his descendants.

Consecration of the Priests

29 ¹*"This is the rite you shall perform in consecrating them as my priests. Procure a young bull and two unblemished rams. ²With fine wheat flour make unleavened cakes mixed with oil, and unleavened wafers spread with oil, ³and put them in a basket. Take the basket of them along with the bullock and the two rams. ⁴Aaron and his sons you shall also bring to the entrance of the meeting tent, and there wash them with water. ⁵Take the vestments and clothe Aaron with the tunic, the robe of the ephod, the ephod itself, and the breastpiece, fastening the embroidered belt of the ephod around him. ⁶Put the miter on his head, the sacred diadem on the miter. ⁷Then take the anointing oil and anoint him with it, pouring it on his head. ⁸Bring forward his sons also and clothe them with the tunics, ⁹*gird them with the sashes, and tie the turbans on them. Thus shall the priesthood be theirs by perpetual law, and thus shall you ordain Aaron and his sons.

Ordination Sacrifices

¹⁰*"Now bring forward the bullock in front of the meeting tent. There Aaron and his sons shall lay their hands on its head. ¹¹Then slaughter the bullock before the Lord, at the entrance of the meeting tent. ¹²Take some of its blood and with your finger put it on the horns of the altar. All the rest of the blood you shall pour out at the base of the altar. ¹³All the fat that covers its inner organs, as well as the lobe of its liver and its two kidneys, together with the fat that is on them, you shall take and burn on the altar. ¹⁴*But the flesh and hide and offal of the bullock you must burn up outside the camp, since this is a sin offering.

¹⁵"Then take one of the rams, and after Aaron and his sons have laid their hands on its head, ¹⁶slaughter it. The blood you shall take and splash on all the sides

---

† 28, 30: *Urim and Thummim:* both the meaning of these Hebrew words and the exact nature of the objects so designated are uncertain. They were apparently lots of some kind which were drawn or cast by the priest to ascertain God's decision in doubtful matters. Hence, the burse in which they were kept was called "the breastpiece of decision."

28, 41: *Ordain them:* literally, "fill their hands," a technical expression used solely for the installation of priests. The phrase probably originated in the custom of placing in the priests' hands the instruments or other symbols of the sacerdotal office.

❖
30: Lv 8, 8; Sir 45, 11.   42: Ez 44, 18.
31-35: 39, 20ff; Lv 8, 9.   29/1-8: Lv 8, 1-9.
    Sir 45, 10.   9: Lv 8, 13.
37: 39, 31; Lv 8, 9.   10-26: Lv 8, 14-30.
39-43: 39, 27ff.   14: Heb 13, 11.

of the altar. **17**Cut the ram into pieces; its inner organs and shanks you shall first wash, and then put them with the pieces and with the head. **18**The entire ram shall then be burned on the altar, since it is a holocaust, a sweet-smelling oblation to the Lord.

19"After this take the other ram, and when Aaron and his sons have laid their hands on its head, **20**slaughter it. Some of its blood you shall take and put on the tip of Aaron's right ear and on the tips of his sons' right ears and on the thumbs of their right hands and the great toes of their right feet. Splash the rest of the blood on all the sides of the altar. **21**Then take some of the blood that is on the altar, together with some of the anointing oil, and sprinkle this on Aaron and his vestments, as well as on his sons and their vestments, that his sons and their vestments may be sacred.

22†"Now, from this ram you shall take its fat: its fatty tail, the fat that covers its inner organs, the lobe of its liver, its two kidneys with the fat that is on them, and its right thigh, since this is the ordination ram; **23**then, out of the basket of unleavened food that you have set before the Lord, you shall take one of the loaves of bread, one of the cakes made with oil, and one of the wafers. **24**†All these things you shall put into the hands of Aaron and his sons, so that they may wave them as a wave offering before the Lord. **25**After you have received them back from their hands, you shall burn them on top of the holocaust on the altar as a sweet-smelling oblation to the Lord. **26**Finally, take the breast of Aaron's ordination ram and wave it as a wave offering before the Lord; this is to be your own portion.

27✽†"Thus shall you set aside the breast of whatever wave offering is waved, as well as the thigh of whatever raised offering is raised up, whether this be the ordination ram or anything else belonging to Aaron or to his sons. **28**Such things are due to Aaron and his sons from the Israelites by a perpetual ordinance as a contribution. From their peace offerings, too, the Israelites shall make a contribution, their contribution to the Lord.

29✽"The sacred vestments of Aaron shall be passed down to his descendants, that in them they may be anointed and ordained. **30**The descendant who succeeds him as priest and who is to enter the meeting tent to minister in the sanctuary shall be clothed with them for seven days.

31✽"You shall take the flesh of the ordination ram and boil it in a holy place. **32**At the entrance of the meeting tent Aaron and his sons shall eat the flesh of the ram and the bread that is in the basket. **33**They themselves are to eat of these things by which atonement was made at their ordination and consecration; but no layman may eat of them, since they are sacred. **34**If some of the flesh of the ordination sacrifice or

some of the bread remains over on the next day, this remnant must be burned up; it is not to be eaten, since it is sacred. **35**✽Carry out all these orders in regard to Aaron and his sons just as I have given them to you.

"Seven days you shall spend in ordaining them, **36**✽†sacrificing a bullock each day as a sin offering, to make atonement. Thus also shall you purge the altar in making atonement for it; you shall anoint it in order to consecrate it. **37**Seven days you shall spend in making atonement for the altar and in consecrating it. Then the altar will be most sacred, and whatever touches it will become sacred.

38✽†"Now, this is what you shall offer on the altar: two yearling lambs as the sacrifice established for each day; **39**one lamb in the morning and the other lamb at the evening twilight. **40**With the first lamb there shall be a tenth of an ephah of fine flour mixed with a fourth of a hin of oil of crushed olives and, as its libation, a fourth of a hin of wine. **41**The other lamb you shall offer at the evening twilight, with the same cereal offering and libation as in the morning. You shall offer this as a sweet-smelling oblation to the Lord. **42**Throughout your generations this established holocaust shall be offered before the Lord at the entrance of the meeting tent, where I will meet you and speak to you.

43✽"There, at the altar, I will meet the Israelites; hence, it will be made sacred by my glory. **44**Thus I will consecrate the meeting tent and the altar, just as I also consecrate Aaron and his sons to be my priests. **45**I will dwell in the midst of the Israelites and will be their God. **46**They shall know that I, the Lord, am their God who brought them out of the land of Egypt, so that I, the Lord, their God, might dwell among them.

Altar of Incense

30 **1**✽"For burning incense you shall make an altar of acacia wood, with a square surface, **2**a cubit long, a cubit wide, and two cubits high, with horns that spring directly from it. **3**Its grate on top, its walls on all four sides, and its horns you shall plate with pure gold. Put a gold molding around it. **4**Underneath the molding you shall put gold rings, two on one side and two on the opposite side, as holders for the poles used in carrying it. **5**Make the poles, too, of acacia wood and plate them with gold. **6**✽This altar you are to place in front of the veil that hangs

---

✽
27f: Lv 7, 31-34; 10, 14f;   Nm 18, 18f; Dt 18, 3.   29: Nm 20, 26.28.   31-34: Lv 8, 31f.   35: Lv 8, 36.

36f: Lv 8, 33ff.   38-42: Nm 28, 3-8.   43: 25, 22.   30/1-5: 37, 25-28.   6: 40, 26.

† 29, 22: *Fatty tail:* the thick layer of fat surrounding the tails of sheep and rams bred in Palestine even today. It is regarded as a choice food. Cf Lv 3, 9.

29, 24-26: *Wave offering:* the portions of a peace offering, breast and right thigh, which the officiating priest moved to and fro (waved) in the presence of the Lord. They were reserved for Aaron and his sons.

29, 27-30: These verses are a parenthetical interruption of the ordination ritual; v 31 belongs logically immediately after v 26.

29, 36f: *Purge the altar:* the construction of an altar by profane hands rendered it impure. The anointing and consecration of the altar purified it and made it sacred.

29, 38-42: A parenthesis inserted into the rubrics for consecrating the altar; v 43 belongs directly after v 37.

before the ark of the commandments where I will meet you.

7"On it Aaron shall burn fragrant incense. Morning after morning, when he prepares the lamps, **8**and again in the evening twilight, when he lights the lamps, he shall burn incense. Throughout your generations this shall be the established incense offering before the Lord. **9**On this altar you shall not offer up any profane incense, or any holocaust or cereal offering; nor shall you pour out a libation upon it. **10***Once a year Aaron shall perform the atonement rite on its horns. Throughout your generations this atonement is to be made once a year with the blood of the atoning sin offering. This altar is most sacred to the Lord."

Census Tax

11The Lord also said to Moses, **12***"When you take a census of the Israelites who are to be registered, each one, as he is enrolled, shall give the Lord a forfeit for his life, so that no plague may come upon them for being registered. **13***Everyone who enters the registered group must pay a half-shekel, according to the standard of the sanctuary shekel, twenty gerahs to the shekel. This payment of a half-shekel is a contribution to the Lord. **14**Everyone of twenty years or more who enters the registered group must give this contribution to the Lord. **15**The rich need not give more, nor shall the poor give less, than a half-shekel in this contribution to the Lord to pay the forfeit for their lives. **16***When you receive this forfeit money from the Israelites, you shall donate it to the service of the meeting tent, that there it may be the Israelites' reminder before the Lord, of the forfeit paid for their lives."

The Laver

17The Lord said to Moses, **18***"For ablutions you shall make a bronze laver with a bronze base. Place it between the meeting tent and the altar, and put water in it. **19***Aaron and his sons shall use it in washing their hands and feet. **20**When they are about to enter the meeting tent, they must wash with water, lest they die. Likewise when they approach the altar in their ministry, to offer an oblation to the Lord, **21**they must wash their hands and feet, lest they die. This shall be a perpetual ordinance for him and his descendants throughout their generations."

The Anointing Oil

22The Lord said to Moses, **23**"Take the finest spices: five hundred shekels of free-flowing myrrh; half that amount, that is, two hundred and fifty shekels, of fragrant cinnamon; two hundred and fifty shekels of fragrant cane; **24**five hundred shekels of cassia—all

according to the standard of the sanctuary shekel; together with a hin of olive oil; **25***and blend them into sacred anointing oil, perfumed ointment expertly prepared. **26***With this sacred anointing oil you shall anoint the meeting tent and the ark of the commandments, **27**the table and all its appurtenances, the lampstand and its appurtenances, the altar of incense **28**and the altar of holocausts with all its appurtenances, and the laver with its base. **29**When you have consecrated them, they shall be most sacred; whatever touches them shall be sacred. **30***Aaron and his sons you shall also anoint and consecrate as my priests. **31**To the Israelites you shall say: As sacred anointing oil this shall belong to me throughout your generations. **32**It may not be used in any ordinary anointing of the body, nor may you make any other oil of a like mixture. It is sacred, and shall be treated as sacred by you. **33**Whoever prepares a perfume like this, or whoever puts any of this on a layman, shall be cut off from his kinsmen."

The Incense

34*The Lord told Moses, "Take these aromatic substances: storax and onycha and galbanum, these and pure frankincense in equal parts; **35**and blend them into incense. This fragrant powder, expertly prepared, is to be salted and so kept pure and sacred. **36**Grind some of it into fine dust and put this before the commandments in the meeting tent where I will meet you. This incense shall be treated as most sacred by you. **37**You may not make incense of a like mixture for yourselves; you must treat it as sacred to the Lord. **38**Whoever makes an incense like this for his own enjoyment of its fragrance, shall be cut off from his kinsmen."

Choice of Artisans

31 **1***THE Lord said to Moses, **2**"See, I have chosen Bezalel, son of Uri, son of Hur, of the tribe of Judah, **3**and I have filled him with a divine spirit of skill and understanding and knowledge in every craft: **4**in the production of embroidery, in making things of gold, silver or bronze, **5**in cutting and mounting precious stones, in carving wood, and in every other craft. **6**As his assistant I have appointed Oholiab, son of Ahisamach, of the tribe of Dan. I have also endowed all the experts with the necessary skill to make all the things I have ordered you to make: **7***the meeting tent, the ark of the commandments with the propitiatory on top of it, all the furnishings of the tent, **8**the table with its appurtenances, the pure gold lampstand with all its appurtenances, the altar of incense, **9**the altar of holocausts with all its appurtenances, the laver with its base, **10**†the service cloths, the sacred vestments for Aaron the priest, the vestments for his sons in their ministry, **11**the anointing oil, and the fragrant incense for the sanctuary. All these things they shall make just as I have commanded you."

❋

10: Lv 16, 18.   26-29: 40, 9ff; Lv 8, 10;
12: Nm 1, 2f; 26, 2.   Nm 7, 1.
13: Mt. 17, 24-27.   30: 29, 7; Lv 8, 12.
16: 38, 25.   34ff: 25, 6; 37, 29.
18: 38, 8; 40, 7.30.   31/1-6: 35, 30-35.
19ff: 40, 31f.   7-11: 35, 10-19.
25: 37, 29.

---

† 31, 10: *The service cloths:* so the Greek. They were perhaps the colored cloths mentioned in Nm 4, 4-15.

Sabbath Laws

12*The Lord said to Moses, **13**"You must also tell the Israelites: Take care to keep my sabbaths, for that is to be the token between you and me throughout the generations, to show that it is I, the Lord, who make you holy. **14**Therefore, you must keep the sabbath as something sacred. Whoever desecrates it shall be put to death. If anyone does work on that day, he must be rooted out of his people. **15**Six days there are for doing work, but the seventh day is the sabbath of complete rest, sacred to the Lord. Anyone who does work on the sabbath day shall be put to death. **16**So shall the Israelites observe the sabbath, keeping it throughout their generations as a perpetual covenant. **17**Between me and the Israelites it is to be an everlasting token; for in six days the Lord made the heavens and the earth, but on the seventh day he rested at his ease."

18*When the Lord had finished speaking to Moses on Mount Sinai, he gave him the two tablets of the commandments, the stone tablets inscribed by God's own finger.

The Golden Calf

32 **1***When the people became aware of Moses' delay in coming down from the mountain, they gathered around Aaron and said to him, "Come, make us a god who will be our leader; as for the man Moses who brought us out of the land of Egypt, we do not know what has happened to him." **2**Aaron replied, "Have your wives and sons and daughters take off the golden earrings they are wearing, and bring them to me." **3**So all the people took off their earrings and brought them to Aaron, **4***who accepted their offering, and fashioning this gold with a graving tool, made a molten calf. Then they cried out, "This is your God, O Israel, who brought you out of the land of Egypt." **5**†On seeing this, Aaron built an altar before the calf and proclaimed, "Tomorrow is a feast of the Lord." **6***Early the next day the people offered holocausts and brought peace offerings. Then they sat down to eat and drink, and rose up to revel.

7*With that, the Lord said to Moses, "Go down at once to your people, whom you brought out of the land of Egypt, for they have become depraved. **8**They have soon turned aside from the way I pointed out to them, making for themselves a molten calf and worshiping it, sacrificing to it and crying out, 'This is your God, O Israel, who brought you out of the land of Egypt!' **9***I see how stiffnecked this people is," continued the Lord to Moses. **10**"Let me alone, then, that my wrath may blaze up against them to consume them. Then I will make of you a great nation."

11*But Moses implored the Lord, his God, saying, "Why, O Lord, should your wrath blaze up against your own people, whom you brought out of the land of Egypt with such great power and with so strong a hand? **12**Why should the Egyptians say, 'With evil intent he brought them out, that he might kill them in the mountains and exterminate them from the face of the earth'? Let your blazing wrath die down; relent in punishing your people. **13***Remember your servants Abraham, Isaac and Israel, and how you swore to them by your own self, saying, 'I will make your descendants as numerous as the stars in the sky; and all this land that I promised, I will give your descendants as their perpetual heritage.'" **14**So the Lord relented in the punishment he had threatened to inflict on his people.

15*Moses then turned and came down the mountain with the two tablets of the commandments in his hands, tablets that were written on both sides, front and back; **16***tablets that were made by God, having inscriptions on them that were engraved by God himself. **17**Now, when Joshua heard the noise of the people shouting, he said to Moses, "That sounds like a battle in the camp." **18**But Moses answered, "It does not sound like cries of victory, nor does it sound like cries of defeat; the sounds that I hear are cries of revelry." **19***As he drew near the camp, he saw the calf and the dancing. With that, Moses' wrath flared up, so that he threw the tablets down and broke them on the base of the mountain. **20***†Taking the calf they had made, he fused it in the fire and then ground it down to powder, which he scattered on the water and made the Israelites drink.

21Moses asked Aaron, "What did this people ever do to you that you should lead them into so grave a sin?" **22**Aaron replied, "Let not my lord be angry. You know well enough how prone the people are to evil. **23**They said to me, 'Make us a god to be our leader; as for the man Moses who brought us out of the land of Egypt, we do not know what has happened to him.' **24**So I told them, 'Let anyone who has gold jewelry take it off.' They gave it to me, and I threw it into the fire, and this calf came out."

25When Moses realized that, to the scornful joy of their foes, Aaron had let the people run wild, **26***he stood at the gate of the camp and cried, "Whoever is for the Lord, let him come to me!" All the Levites then rallied to him, **27**†and he told them, "Thus says the Lord, the God of Israel: Put your sword on your hip, every one of you! Now go up and down the camp,

---

❋ 12-17: 20, 8-11; 35, 1-3.
18: 24, 12; 32, 15f; Dt 5, 22.
32/1: 32, 23; Acts 7, 40.
4: 32, 8; 1 Kgs 12, 28.
6: 1 Cor 10, 7.
7f: Dt 9, 12.16.
9f: Dt 9, 13; Ps 106, 23.
11f: Nm 14, 13ff; Dt 9, 28.
13: Gn 22, 16f.
15: Dt 9, 15.
16: 31, 18.
19: Dt 9, 16f.
20: Dt 9, 21.
26-29: Dt 33, 8f.

† 32, 5: *The calf . . . a feast of the Lord:* from this it is clear that the golden calf was intended as an image, not of a false god, but of the Lord himself, his strength being symbolized by the strength of a young bull. The Israelites, however, had been forbidden to represent the Lord under any visible form. Cf 20, 4.

32, 20: *The water:* the stream that flowed down Mount Sinai. Cf Dt 9, 21.

32, 27: *Slay your own kinsmen . . . :* those who were especially guilty of the idolatry.

from gate to gate, and slay your own kinsmen, your friends and neighbors!" [28]The Levites carried out the command of Moses, and that day there fell about three thousand of the people. [29]†Then Moses said, "Today you have been dedicated to the LORD, for you were against your own sons and kinsmen, to bring a blessing upon yourselves this day."

The Atonement

[30]*On the next day Moses said to the people, "You have committed a grave sin. I will go up to the LORD, then; perhaps I may be able to make atonement for your sin." [31]So Moses went back to the LORD and said, "Ah, this people has indeed committed a grave sin in making a god of gold for themselves! [32]†If you would only forgive their sin! If you will not, then strike me out of the book that you have written." [33]The LORD answered, "Him only who has sinned against me will I strike out of my book. [34]Now, go and lead the people whither I have told you. My angel will go before you. When it is time for me to punish, I will punish them for their sin."

[35]Thus the LORD smote the people for having had Aaron make the calf for them.

33 [1]*THE LORD told Moses, "You and the people whom you have brought up from the land of Egypt, are to go up from here to the land which I swore to Abraham, Isaac and Jacob I would give to their descendants. [2]*Driving out the Canaanites, Amorites, Hittites, Perizzites, Hivites and Jebusites, I will send an angel before you [3]to the land flowing with milk and honey. But I myself will not go up in your company, because you are a stiff-necked people; otherwise I might exterminate you on the way." [4]When the people heard this bad news, they went into mourning, and no one wore his ornaments.

[5]The LORD said to Moses, "Tell the Israelites: You are a stiff-necked people. Were I to go up in your company even for a moment, I would exterminate you. Take off your ornaments, therefore; I will then see what I am to do with you." [6]So, from Mount Horeb onward, the Israelites laid aside their ornaments.

Moses' Intimacy with God

[7]*†The tent, which was called the meeting tent, Moses used to pitch at some distance away, outside the camp. Anyone who wished to consult the LORD would go to this meeting tent outside the camp. [8]Whenever Moses went out to the tent, the people would all rise and stand at the entrance of their own tents, watching Moses until he entered the tent. [9]As Moses entered the tent, the column of cloud would come down and stand at its entrance while the LORD spoke with Moses. [10]On seeing the column of cloud

stand at the entrance of the tent, all the people would rise and worship at the entrance of their own tents. [11]*The LORD used to speak to Moses face to face, as one man speaks to another. Moses would then return to the camp, but his young assistant, Joshua, son of Nun, would not move out of the tent.

[12]*Moses said to the LORD, "You, indeed, are telling me to lead this people on; but you have not let me know whom you will send with me. Yet you have said, 'You are my intimate friend,' and also, 'You have found favor with me.' [13]Now, if I have found favor with you, do let me know your ways so that, in knowing you, I may continue to find favor with you. Then, too, this nation is, after all, your own people." [14]†"I myself," the LORD answered, "will go along, to give you rest." [15]Moses replied, "If you are not going yourself, do not make us go up from here. [16]For how can it be known that we, your people and I, have found favor with you, except by your going with us? Then we, your people and I, will be singled out from every other people on the earth." [17]The LORD said to Moses, "This request, too, which you have just made, I will carry out, because you have found favor with me and you are my intimate friend."

[18]Then Moses said, "Do let me see your glory!" [19]*He answered, "I will make all my beauty pass before you, and in your presence I will pronounce my name, 'LORD'; I who show favors to whom I will, I who grant mercy to whom I will. [20]*But my face you cannot see, for no man sees me and still lives. [21]Here," continued the LORD, "is a place near me where you shall station yourself on the rock. [22]When my glory passes I will set you in the hollow of the rock and will cover you with my hand until I have passed by. [23]†Then I will remove my hand, so that you may see my back; but my face is not to be seen."

Renewal of the Tablets

34 [1]*THE LORD said to Moses, "Cut two stone tablets like the former, that I may write on them the commandments which were on the former tablets that you broke. [2]Get ready for tomorrow morning, when you are to go up Mount Sinai and there present yourself to me on the top of the mountain. [3]*No one shall come up with you, and no one is

---

† 32, 29: *Dedicated to the Lord:* because of their zeal for the true worship of the Lord, the Levites were chosen to be special ministers of the ritual service. However, the meaning of the Hebrew here is somewhat disputed.

32, 32: *The book that you have written:* the list of God's intimate friends. In a similar sense St. Paul wished to be anathema from Christ for the sake of his brethren. Cf Rom 9, 3.

33, 7-11: *The meeting tent* is mentioned here by anticipation; its actual construction is described in the following chapters.

33, 14: *I myself:* literally, "my face," that is, "my presence." *To give you rest:* in the Promised Land; some understand, "to put your mind at rest"; others, by a slight emendation in the text, render, "to lead you."

33, 23: *You may see my back:* man can see God's glory as reflected in creation, but his "face," that is, God as he is in himself, mortal man cannot behold. Cf 1 Cor 13, 12.

✿
30-34: Dt 9, 18ff.
33/1: Gn 12, 7.
    2: 23, 23.
    7: 29, 42f.
   11: Nm 12, 8; Dt 34, 10;
       Sir 45, 4-6.

12: 32, 34.
19: Rom 9, 15.
20: Jn 1, 18; 1 Tm 6, 16
34/1: Dt 10, 1f.
    3: 19, 12f.21.

even to be seen on any part of the mountain; even the flocks and the herds are not to go grazing toward this mountain." ⁴Moses then cut two stone tablets like the former, and early the next morning he went up Mount Sinai as the Lord had commanded him, taking along the two stone tablets.

⁵Having come down in a cloud, the Lord stood with him there and proclaimed his name, "Lord." ⁶*Thus the Lord passed before him and cried out, "The Lord, the Lord, a merciful and gracious God, slow to anger and rich in kindness and fidelity, ⁷continuing his kindness for a thousand generations, and forgiving wickedness and crime and sin; yet not declaring the guilty guiltless, but punishing children and grandchildren to the third and fourth generation for their fathers' wickedness!" ⁸Moses at once bowed down to the ground in worship. ⁹Then he said, "If I find favor with you, O Lord, do come along in our company. This is indeed a stiff-necked people; yet pardon our wickedness and sins, and receive us as your own."

Religious Laws

¹⁰"Here, then," said the Lord, "is the covenant I will make. Before the eyes of all your people I will work such marvels as have never been wrought in any nation anywhere on earth, so that this people among whom you live may see how awe-inspiring are the deeds which I, the Lord, will do at your side. ¹¹*But you, on your part, must keep the commandments I am giving you today.

"I will drive out before you the Amorites, Canaanites, Hittites, Perizzites, Hivites and Jebusites. ¹²*Take care, therefore, not to make a covenant with these inhabitants of the land that you are to enter; else they will become a snare among you. ¹³†Tear down their altars; smash their sacred pillars, and cut down their sacred poles. ¹⁴†You shall not worship any other god, for the Lord is 'the Jealous One'; a jealous God is he. ¹⁵Do not make a covenant with the inhabitants of that land; else, when they render their wanton worship to their gods and sacrifice to them, one of them may invite you and you may partake of his sacrifice. ¹⁶Neither shall you take their daughters as wives for your sons; otherwise, when their daughters render their wanton worship to their gods, they will make your sons do the same.

¹⁷*"You shall not make for yourselves molten gods.

¹⁸*"You shall keep the feast of Unleavened Bread. For seven days at the prescribed time in the month of Abib you are to eat unleavened bread, as I commanded you; for in the month of Abib you came out of Egypt.

¹⁹*"To me belongs every first-born male that opens the womb among all your livestock, whether in the herd or in the flock. ²⁰The firstling of an ass you shall redeem with one of the flock; if you do not redeem it, you must break its neck. The first-born among your sons you shall redeem.

"No one shall appear before me empty-handed.

²¹*"For six days you may work, but on the seventh day you shall rest; on that day you must rest even during the seasons of plowing and harvesting.

²²*†"You shall keep the feast of Weeks with the first of the wheat harvest; likewise, the feast at the fruit harvest at the close of the year. ²³Three times a year all your men shall appear before the Lord, the Lord God of Israel. ²⁴Since I will drive out the nations before you to give you a large territory, there will be no one to covet your land when you go up three times a year to appear before the Lord, your God.

²⁵*"You shall not offer me the blood of sacrifice with leavened bread, nor shall the sacrifice of the Passover feast be kept overnight for the next day.

²⁶"The choicest first fruits of your soil you shall bring to the house of the Lord, your God.

"You shall not boil a kid in its mother's milk."

Radiance of Moses' Face

²⁷Then the Lord said to Moses, "Write down these words, for in accordance with them I have made a covenant with you and with Israel." ²⁸*So Moses stayed there with the Lord for forty days and forty nights, without eating any food or drinking any water, and he wrote on the tablets the words of the covenant, the ten commandments.

²⁹As Moses came down from Mount Sinai with the two tablets of the commandments in his hands, he did not know that the skin of his face had become radiant while he conversed with the Lord. ³⁰When Aaron, then, and the other Israelites saw Moses and noticed how radiant the skin of his face had become, they were afraid to come near him. ³¹Only after Moses called to them did Aaron and all the rulers of the community come back to him. Moses then spoke to them. ³²Later on, all the Israelites came up to him, and he enjoined on them all that the Lord had told him on Mount Sinai. ³³*†When he finished speaking with them, he put a veil over his face. ³⁴Whenever Moses entered the

---

† 34, 13: *Sacred poles:* "Ashera" was the name of a Canaanite goddess. In her honor wooden poles (*asherot*) were erected, just as stone pillars (*massebot*) were erected in honor of the god Baal. Both were placed near the altar in a Canaanite shrine.

34, 14: *The Lord is "the Jealous One":* see note on 20, 5. Some, by a slight emendation, render, "The Lord is jealous for his name." Cf Ez 39, 25.

34, 22: *Feast of Weeks:* the festival of thanksgiving for the harvest, celebrated seven weeks or fifty days after the beginning of the harvest. It was also called Pentecost (fiftieth) and coincided with the giving of the law on Mount Sinai, fifty days after the offering of the first fruits (Lv 23, 10f; Dt 16, 9).

34, 33: *He put a veil over his face:* St. Paul sees in this a symbol of the failure of the Jews to recognize Jesus as the promised Messiah: the true spiritual meaning of the writings of Moses and the prophets is still veiled from the unbelieving Jews. Cf 2 Cor 3, 7-18.

---

*   6f: 20, 5f; Nm 14, 18; Dt 5, 9ff; Jer 32, 18.
11: 13, 5; 33, 2.
12-16: 23, 32f; Dt 7, 1-5; 12, 2f.
17: Lv 19, 4; 5, 8f.
18: 12, 15ff; 13, 3f.
19f: 13, 2.12f; 23, 15.

21: 20, 9f.
22f: 23, 16f; Dt 16, 10.13.16.
25f: 23, 18f.
28: 24, 18; Dt 9, 9.18; 10, 2.4.
33f: 2 Cor 3, 13.16.

presence of the LORD to converse with him, he removed the veil until he came out again. On coming out, he would tell the Israelites all that had been commanded. [35]Then the Israelites would see that the skin of Moses' face was radiant; so he would again put the veil over his face until he went in to converse with the LORD.

Sabbath Regulations

35 [1]*MOSES assembled the whole Israelite community and said to them, "This is what the LORD has commanded to be done. [2]On six days work may be done, but the seventh day shall be sacred to you as the sabbath of complete rest to the LORD. Anyone who does work on that day shall be put to death. [3]You shall not even light a fire in any of your dwellings on the sabbath day."

Collection of Materials

[4]Moses told the whole Israelite community, "This is what the LORD has commanded: [5]*Take up among you a collection for the LORD. Everyone, as his heart prompts him, shall bring, as a contribution to the LORD, gold, silver and bronze; [6]violet, purple and scarlet yarn; fine linen and goat hair; [7]rams' skins dyed red, and tahash skins; acacia wood; [8]oil for the light; spices for the anointing oil and for the fragrant incense; [9]onyx stones and other gems for mounting on the ephod and on the breastpiece.

Call for Artisans

[10]*"Let every expert among you come and make all that the LORD has commanded: the Dwelling, [11]with its tent, its covering, its clasps, its boards, its bars, its columns and its pedestals; [12]the ark, with its poles, the propitiatory, and the curtain veil; [13]the table, with its poles and all its appurtenances, and the showbread; [14]the lampstand, with its appurtenances, the lamps, and the oil for the light; [15]the altar of incense, with its poles; the anointing oil, and the fragrant incense; the entrance curtain for the entrance of the Dwelling; [16]the altar of holocausts, with its bronze grating, its poles, and all its appurtenances; the laver, with its base; [17]the hangings of the court, with their columns and pedestals; the curtain for the entrance of the court; [18]the tent pegs for the Dwelling and for the court, with their ropes; [19]the service cloths for use in the sanctuary; the sacred vestments for Aaron, the priest, and the vestments worn by his sons in their ministry."

The Contribution

[20]When the whole Israelite community left Moses' presence, [21]everyone, as his heart suggested and his spirit prompted, brought a contribution to the LORD for the construction of the meeting tent, for all its serv-

ices, and for the sacred vestments. [22]*Both the men and the women, all as their heart prompted them, brought brooches, earrings, rings, necklaces and various other gold articles. Everyone who could presented an offering of gold to the LORD. [23]Everyone who happened to have violet, purple or scarlet yarn, fine linen or goat hair, rams' skins dyed red or tahash skins, brought them. [24]Whoever could make a contribution of silver or bronze offered it to the LORD; and everyone who happened to have acacia wood for any part of the work, brought it. [25]All the women who were expert spinners brought hand-spun violet, purple and scarlet yarn and fine linen thread. [26]All the women who possessed the skill, spun goat hair. [27]The princes brought onyx stones and other gems for mounting on the ephod and on the breastpiece; [28]as well as spices, and oil for the light, anointing oil, and fragrant incense. [29]Every Israelite man and woman brought to the LORD such voluntary offerings as they thought best, for the various kinds of work which the LORD had commanded Moses to have done.

The Artisans

[30]*Moses said to the Israelites, "See, the LORD has chosen Bezalel, son of Uri, son of Hur, of the tribe of Judah, [31]and has filled him with a divine spirit of skill and understanding and knowledge in every craft: [32]in the production of embroidery, in making things of gold, silver or bronze, [33]in cutting and mounting precious stones, in carving wood, and in every other craft. [34]He has also given both him and Oholiab, son of Ahisamach, of the tribe of Dan, the ability to teach others. [35]He has endowed them with skill to execute all types of work: engraving, embroidering, the making of variegated cloth of violet, purple and scarlet yarn and fine linen thread, weaving, and all other arts and crafts.

36 [1]*"BEZALEL, therefore, will set to work with Oholiab and with all the experts whom the LORD has endowed with skill and understanding in knowing how to execute all the work for the service of the sanctuary, just as the LORD has commanded."

[2]Moses then called Bezalel and Oholiab and all the other experts whom the LORD had endowed with skill, men whose hearts moved them to come and take part in the work. [3]They received from Moses all the contributions which the Israelites had brought for establishing the service of the sanctuary. Still, morning after morning the people continued to bring their voluntary offerings to Moses. [4]Thereupon the experts who were executing the various kinds of work for the sanctuary, all left the work they were doing, [5]and told Moses, "The people are bringing much more than is needed to carry out the work which the LORD has commanded us to do." [6]Moses, therefore, ordered a proclamation to be made throughout the camp: "Let neither man nor woman make any more contributions for the sanctuary." So the people stopped bringing their of-

*

35/1-3: 31, 13-17.	22-28: 25, 3-7.
5-9: 25, 2-7.	30-35: 31, 1-6.
10-19: 31, 6-11.	36/1f: 31, 1.6.

ferings; **7**there was already enough at hand, in fact, more than enough, to complete the work to be done.

The Tent Cloth and Coverings

8*The various experts who were executing the work, made the Dwelling with its ten sheets woven of fine linen twined, having cherubim embroidered on them with violet, purple and scarlet yarn. **9**The length of each sheet was twenty-eight cubits, and the width four cubits; all the sheets were of the same size. **10**Five of the sheets were sewed together, edge to edge; and the same for the other five. **11**Loops of violet yarn were made along the edge of the end sheet in the first set, and the same along the edge of the end sheet in the second set. **12**Fifty loops were thus put on one inner sheet, and fifty loops on the inner sheet in the other set, with the loops directly opposite each other. **13**Then fifty clasps of gold were made, with which the sheets were joined so that the Dwelling formed one whole.

14Sheets of goat hair were also woven as a tent over the Dwelling. Eleven such sheets were made. **15**The length of each sheet was thirty cubits and the width four cubits; all eleven sheets were of the same size. **16**Five of these sheets were sewed edge to edge into one set; and the other six sheets into another set. **17**Fifty loops were made along the edge of the end sheet in one set, and fifty loops along the edge of the corresponding sheet in the other set. **18**Fifty bronze clasps were made with which the tent was joined so that it formed one whole. **19**A covering for the tent was made of rams' skins dyed red, and above that, a covering of tahash skins.

The Boards

20*Boards of acacia wood were made as walls for the Dwelling. **21**The length of each board was ten cubits, and the width one and a half cubits. **22**Each board had two arms, fastening them in line. In this way all the boards of the Dwelling were made. **23**They were set up as follows: twenty boards on the south side, **24**with forty silver pedestals under the twenty boards, so that there were two pedestals under each board, at its two arms; **25**twenty boards on the other side of the Dwelling, the north side, **26**with their forty silver pedestals, two under each board; **27**six boards at the rear of the Dwelling, to the west; **28**and two boards at the corners in the rear of the Dwelling. **29**These were double at the bottom, and likewise double at the top, to the first ring. That is how both boards in the corners were made. **30**Thus, there were in the rear eight boards, with their sixteen silver pedestals, two pedestals under each board. **31**Bars of acacia wood were also made, five for the boards on one side of the Dwelling, **32**five for those on the other side, and five for those at the rear, to the west. **33**The center bar, at the middle of the boards, was made to reach across from end to end. **34**The boards were plated with gold,

and gold rings were made on them as holders for the bars, which were also plated with gold.

The Veil

35*The veil was woven of violet, purple and scarlet yarn, and of fine linen twined, with cherubim embroidered on it. **36**Four gold-plated columns of acacia wood, with gold hooks, were made for it, and four silver pedestals were cast for them.

37The curtain for the entrance of the tent was made of violet, purple and scarlet yarn, and of fine linen twined, woven in a variegated manner. **38**Its five columns, with their hooks as well as their capitals and bands, were plated with gold; their five pedestals were of bronze.

The Ark

37 **1***BEZALEL made the ark of acacia wood, two and a half cubits long, one and a half cubits wide, and one and a half cubits high. **2**The inside and outside were plated with gold, and a molding of gold was put around it. **3**Four gold rings were cast and put on its four supports, two rings for one side and two for the opposite side. **4**Poles of acacia wood were made and plated with gold; **5**these were put through the rings on the sides of the ark, for carrying it.

6The propitiatory was made of pure gold, two and a half cubits long and one and a half cubits wide. **7**Two cherubim of beaten gold were made for the two ends of the propitiatory, **8**one cherub fastened at one end, the other at the other end, springing directly from the propitiatory at its two ends. **9**The cherubim had their wings spread out above, covering the propitiatory with them. They were turned toward each other, but with their faces looking toward the propitiatory.

The Table

10*The table was made of acacia wood, two cubits long, one cubit wide, and one and a half cubits high. **11**It was plated with pure gold, and a molding of gold was put around it. **12**A frame a handbreadth high was also put around it, with a molding of gold around the frame. **13**Four rings of gold were cast for it and fastened, one at each of the four corners. **14**The rings were alongside the frame as holders for the poles to carry the table. **15**These poles were made of acacia wood and plated with gold. **16**The vessels that were set on the table, its plates and cups, as well as its pitchers and bowls for pouring libations, were of pure gold.

The Lampstand

17*The lampstand was made of pure beaten gold— its shaft and branches as well as its cups and knobs and petals springing directly from it. **18**Six branches extended from its sides, three branches on one side and three on the other. **19**On one branch there were three cups, shaped like almond blossoms, each with its knob and petals; on the opposite branch there were

---

three cups, shaped like almond blossoms, each with its knob and petals; and so for the six branches that extended from the lampstand. [20]On the shaft there were four cups, shaped like almond blossoms, with their knobs and petals, [21]including a knob below each of the three pairs of branches that extended from the lampstand. [22]The knobs and branches sprang so directly from it that the whole formed but a single piece of pure beaten gold. [23]Its seven lamps, as well as its trimming shears and trays, were made of pure gold. [24]A talent of pure gold was used for the lampstand and its various appurtenances.

The Altar of Incense

[25]*The altar of incense was made of acacia wood, on a square, a cubit long, a cubit wide, and two cubits high, having horns that sprang directly from it. [26]Its grate on top, its walls on all four sides, and its horns were plated with pure gold; and a molding of gold was put around it. [27]Underneath the molding gold rings were placed, two on one side and two on the opposite side, as holders for the poles to carry it. [28]The poles, too, were made of acacia wood and plated with gold.

[29]*The sacred anointing oil and the fragrant incense were prepared in their pure form by a perfumer.

The Altar of Holocausts

38 [1]*THE altar of holocausts was made of acacia wood, on a square, five cubits long and five cubits wide; its height was three cubits. [2]At the four corners horns were made that sprang directly from the altar. The whole was plated with bronze. [3]All the utensils of the altar, the pots, shovels, basins, forks and fire pans, were likewise made of bronze. [4]A grating of bronze network was made for the altar and placed round it, on the ground, half as high as the altar itself. [5]Four rings were cast for the four corners of the bronze grating, as holders for the poles, [6]which were made of acacia wood and plated with bronze. [7]The poles were put through the rings on the sides of the altar for carrying it. The altar was made in the form of a hollow box.

[8]*†The bronze laver, with its bronze base, was made from the mirrors of the women who served at the entrance of the meeting tent.

The Court

[9]*The court was made as follows. On the south side of the court there were hangings, woven of fine linen twined, a hundred cubits long, [10]with twenty columns and twenty pedestals of bronze, the hooks and bands of the columns being of silver. [11]On the north side there were similar hangings, one hundred cubits long, with twenty columns and twenty pedestals of bronze,

the hooks and bands of the columns being of silver. [12]On the west side there were hangings, fifty cubits long, with ten columns and ten pedestals, the hooks and bands of the columns being of silver. [13]On the east side the court was fifty cubits long. [14]Toward one side there were hangings to the extent of fifteen cubits, with three columns and three pedestals; toward the other side, [15]beyond the entrance of the court, there were likewise hangings to the extent of fifteen cubits, with three columns and three pedestals. [16]The hangings on all sides of the court were woven of fine linen twined. [17]The pedestals of the columns were of bronze, while the hooks and bands of the columns were of silver; the capitals were silver-plated, and all the columns of the court were banded with silver.

[18]At the entrance of the court there was a variegated curtain, woven of violet, purple and scarlet yarn and of fine linen twined, twenty cubits long and five cubits wide, in keeping with the hangings of the court. [19]There were four columns and four pedestals of bronze for it, while their hooks were of silver. [20]All the tent pegs for the Dwelling and for the court around it were of bronze.

Amount of Metal Used

[21]The following is an account of the various amounts used on the Dwelling, the Dwelling of the commandments, drawn up at the command of Moses by the Levites under the direction of Ithamar, son of Aaron the priest. [22]*However, it was Bezalel, son of Uri, son of Hur, of the tribe of Judah, who made all that the LORD commanded Moses, [23]and he was assisted by Oholiab, son of Ahisamach, of the tribe of Dan, who was an engraver, an embroiderer, and a weaver of variegated cloth of violet, purple and scarlet yarn and of fine linen.

[24]All the gold used in the entire construction of the sanctuary, having previously been given as an offering, amounted to twenty-nine talents and seven hundred and thirty shekels, according to the standard of the sanctuary shekel. [25]The amount of the silver received from the community was one hundred talents and one thousand seven hundred and seventy-five shekels, according to the standard of the sanctuary shekel; [26]*one bekah apiece, that is, a half-shekel apiece, according to the standard of the sanctuary shekel, was received from every man of twenty years or more who entered the registered group; the number of these was six hundred and three thousand five hundred and fifty men. [27]One hundred talents of silver were used for casting the pedestals of the sanctuary and the pedestals of the veil, one talent for each pedestal, or one hundred talents for the one hundred pedestals. [28]The remaining one thousand seven hundred and seventy-five shekels were used for making the hooks on the columns, for plating the capitals, and

* 25-28: 30, 1-5.	9-20: 27, 9-19.
29: 30, 23ff.34ff.	22f: 31, 2.6; 35, 30.34;
38/1-7: 27, 1-8; 2 Chr 1, 5.	36, 1.
8: 30, 18-21.	26: Nm 1, 46.

† 38, 8: The reflecting surface of ancient mirrors was usually of polished bronze. *The women who served:* cf 1 Sm 2, 22.

for banding them with silver. **29**The bronze, given as an offering, amounted to seventy talents and two thousand four hundred shekels. **30**With this were made the pedestals at the entrance of the meeting tent, the bronze altar with its bronze gratings and all the appurtenances of the altar, **31**the pedestals around the court, the pedestals at the entrance of the court, and all the tent pegs for the Dwelling and for the court around it.

The Vestments

39 **1***WITH violet, purple and scarlet yarn were woven the service cloths for use in the sanctuary, as well as the sacred vestments for Aaron, as the LORD had commanded Moses.

2*The ephod was woven of gold thread and of violet, purple and scarlet yarn and of fine linen twined. **3**Gold was first hammered into gold leaf and then cut up into threads, which were woven with the violet, purple and scarlet yarn into an embroidered pattern on the fine linen. **4**Shoulder straps were made for it and joined to its two upper ends. **5**The embroidered belt on the ephod extended out from it, and like it, was made of gold thread, of violet, purple and scarlet yarn, and of fine linen twined, as the LORD had commanded Moses. **6**The onyx stones were prepared and mounted in gold filigree work; they were engraved like seal engravings with the names of the sons of Israel. **7**These stones were set on the shoulder straps of the ephod as memorial stones of the sons of Israel, just as the LORD had commanded Moses.

8*The breastpiece was embroidered like the ephod, with gold thread and violet, purple and scarlet yarn on cloth of fine linen twined. **9**It was square and folded double, a span high and a span wide in its folded form. **10**Four rows of precious stones were mounted on it: in the first row a carnelian, a topaz and an emerald; **11**in the second row, a garnet, a sapphire and a beryl; **12**in the third row a jacinth, an agate and an amethyst; **13**in the fourth row a chrysolite, an onyx and a jasper. They were mounted in gold filigree work. **14**These stones were twelve, to match the names of the sons of Israel, and each stone was engraved like a seal with the name of one of the twelve tribes.

15*Chains of pure gold, twisted like cords, were made for the breastpiece, **16**together with two gold filigree rosettes and two gold rings. The two rings were fastened to the two upper ends of the breastpiece. **17**The two gold chains were then fastened to the two rings at the ends of the breastpiece. **18**The other two ends of the two chains were fastened in front to the two filigree rosettes, which were attached to the shoulder straps of the ephod. **19**Two other gold rings were made and put on the two lower ends of the breastpiece, on the edge facing the ephod. **20**Two more gold rings were made and fastened to the bottom of the two shoulder straps next to where they joined the ephod in front, just above its embroidered belt. **21**Violet ribbons bound the rings of the breastpiece to the rings of the ephod, so that the breastpiece stayed right above the embroidered belt of the ephod and did not swing loose from it. All this was just as the LORD had commanded Moses.

The Other Vestments

22The robe of the ephod was woven entirely of violet yarn, **23**with an opening in its center like the opening of a shirt, with selvage around the opening to keep it from being torn. **24**At the hem of the robe pomegranates were made of violet, purple and scarlet yarn and of fine linen twined; **25**bells of pure gold were also made and put between the pomegranates all around the hem of the robe: **26**first a bell, then a pomegranate, and thus alternating all around the hem of the robe which was to be worn in performing the ministry—all this, just as the LORD had commanded Moses.

27*For Aaron and his sons there were also woven tunics of fine linen; **28**the miter of fine linen; the ornate turbans of fine linen; drawers of linen [of fine linen twined]; **29**and sashes of variegated work made of fine linen twined and of violet, purple and scarlet yarn, as the LORD had commanded Moses. **30***The plate of the sacred diadem was made of pure gold and inscribed, as on a seal engraving: "Sacred to the LORD." **31**It was tied over the miter with a violet ribbon, as the LORD had commanded Moses.

Presentation of the Work to Moses

32Thus the entire work of the Dwelling of the meeting tent was completed. The Israelites did the work just as the LORD had commanded Moses. **33**They then brought to Moses the Dwelling, the tent with all its appurtenances, the clasps, the boards, the bars, the columns, the pedestals, **34**the covering of rams' skins dyed red, the covering of tahash skins, the curtain veil; **35**the ark of the commandments with its poles, the propitiatory, **36**the table with all its appurtenances and the showbread, **37**the pure gold lampstand with its lamps set up on it and with all its appurtenances, the oil for the light, **38**the golden altar, the anointing oil, the fragrant incense; the curtain for the entrance of the tent, **39**the altar of bronze with its bronze grating, its poles and all its appurtenances, the laver with its base, **40**the hangings of the court with their columns and pedestals, the curtain for the entrance of the court with its ropes and tent pegs, all the equipment for the service of the Dwelling of the meeting tent; **41**the service cloths for use in the sanctuary, the sacred vestments for Aaron the priest, and the vestments to be worn by his sons in their ministry. **42**The Israelites had carried out all the work just as the LORD had commanded Moses. **43**So when Moses saw that all the work was done just as the LORD had commanded, he blessed them.

✶
39/1: 31, 10.
2-10: 28, 6-12.
8-14: 28, 15-21.
15-21: 28, 31-35.
27ff: 28, 39-42.
30f: 28, 36f.

Erection of the Dwelling

40 ¹THEN the Lord said to Moses, ²*†"On the first day of the first month you shall erect the Dwelling of the meeting tent. ³*Put the ark of the commandments in it, and screen off the ark with the veil. ⁴Bring in the table and set it. Then bring in the lampstand and set up the lamps on it. ⁵Put the golden altar of incense in front of the ark of the commandments, and hang the curtain at the entrance of the Dwelling. ⁶Put the altar of holocausts in front of the entrance of the Dwelling of the meeting tent. ⁷Place the laver between the meeting tent and the altar, and put water in it. ⁸Set up the court round about, and put the curtain at the entrance of the court.

⁹*"Take the anointing oil and anoint the Dwelling and everything in it, consecrating it and all its furnishings, so that it will be sacred. ¹⁰Anoint the altar of holocausts and all its appurtenances, consecrating it, so that it will be most sacred. ¹¹Likewise, anoint the laver with its base, and thus consecrate it.

¹²*"Then bring Aaron and his sons to the entrance of the meeting tent, and there wash them with water. ¹³Clothe Aaron with the sacred vestments and anoint him, thus consecrating him as my priest. ¹⁴Bring forward his sons also, and clothe them with the tunics. ¹⁵As you have anointed their father, anoint them also as my priests. Thus, by being anointed, shall they receive a perpetual priesthood throughout all future generations."

¹⁶Moses did exactly as the Lord had commanded him. ¹⁷On the first day of the first month of the second year the Dwelling was erected. ¹⁸It was Moses who erected the Dwelling. He placed its pedestals, set up its boards, put in its bars, and set up its columns. ¹⁹He spread the tent over the Dwelling and put the covering on top of the tent, as the Lord had commanded him. ²⁰*He took the commandments and put them in the ark; he placed poles alongside the ark and set the propitiatory upon it. ²¹He brought the ark into the Dwelling and hung the curtain veil, thus screening off the ark of the commandments, as the Lord had commanded him. ²²He put the table in the meeting tent, on the north side of the Dwelling, outside the veil, ²³*and arranged the bread on it before the Lord, as the Lord had commanded him. ²⁴He placed the lampstand in the meeting tent, opposite the table, on the south side of the Dwelling, ²⁵and he set up the lamps before the Lord, as the Lord had commanded him. ²⁶He placed the golden altar in the meeting tent, in front of the veil, ²⁷and on it he burned fragrant incense, as the Lord had commanded him. ²⁸He hung the curtain at the entrance of the Dwelling. ²⁹He put the altar of holocausts in front of the entrance of the Dwelling of the meeting tent, and offered holocausts and cereal offerings on it, as the Lord had commanded him. ³⁰*He placed the laver between the meeting tent and the altar, and put water in it for washing. ³¹Moses and Aaron and his sons used to wash their hands and feet there, ³²for they washed themselves whenever they went into the meeting tent or approached the altar, as the Lord had commanded Moses. ³³Finally, he set up the court around the Dwelling and the altar and hung the curtain at the entrance of the court. Thus Moses finished all the work.

God's Presence in the Dwelling

³⁴*Then the cloud covered the meeting tent, and the glory of the Lord filled the Dwelling. ³⁵Moses could not enter the meeting tent, because the cloud settled down upon it and the glory of the Lord filled the Dwelling. ³⁶Whenever the cloud rose from the Dwelling, the Israelites would set out on their journey. ³⁷But if the cloud did not lift, they would not go forward; only when it lifted did they go forward. ³⁸In the daytime the cloud of the Lord was seen over the Dwelling; whereas at night, fire was seen in the cloud by the whole house of Israel in all the stages of their journey.

---

*
40/2-8: 40, 16-33.   20ff: 25, 16.21; 26, 33ff.
    2: 26, 30.   23: 25, 30.
    3ff: 26, 33ff.   30ff: 30, 18ff.
    9ff: 30, 26-29.   34-38: Nm 9, 15-22.
    12-15: 28, 41; 29, 4-9;
        Lv 8, 1-13.

---

† 40, 2: *On the first day of the first month:* almost a year after the departure of the Israelites from Egypt. Cf v 17.

The Book of Leviticus

Introduction

The name "Leviticus" was bestowed on the third book of the Pentateuch by the ancient Greek translators because a good part of this book consists of sacrificial and other ritual laws prescribed for the priests of the tribe of Levi.

Continuing the legislation given by God to Moses at Mount Sinai, Leviticus is almost entirely legislative in character; the rare narrative portions are subordinate to the main legislative theme. Generally speaking, the laws contained in this book serve to teach the Israelites that they should always keep themselves in a state of legal purity, or external sanctity, as a sign of their intimate union with the LORD. Accordingly, the central idea of Leviticus is contained in its oft-repeated injunction: "You shall be holy, because I, the LORD, am holy."

The main divisions of Leviticus are:

I: Ritual of Sacrifices (1-7)
II: Ceremony of Ordination (8-10)
III: Laws regarding Legal Purity (11-16)
IV: Code of Legal Holiness (17-26)
V: Redemption of Offerings (27)

I: RITUAL OF SACRIFICES

Holocausts

1 [1]THE LORD CALLED MOSES, and from the meeting tent gave him this message: [2]*†"Speak to the Israelites and tell them: When any one of you wishes to bring an animal offering to the LORD, such an offering must be from the herd or from the flock.

[3]*†"If his holocaust offering is from the herd, it must be a male without blemish. To find favor with the LORD, he shall bring it to the entrance of the meeting tent [4]*and there lay his hand on the head of the holocaust, so that it may be acceptable to make atonement for him. [5]*He shall then slaughter the bull before the LORD, but Aaron's sons, the priests, shall offer up its blood by splashing it on the sides of the altar which is at the entrance of the meeting tent. [6]Then he shall skin the holocaust and cut it up into pieces. [7]After Aaron's

sons, the priests, have put some burning embers on the altar and laid some wood on them, [8]they shall lay the pieces of meat, together with the head and the suet, on top of the wood and embers on the altar. [9]*The inner organs and the shanks, however, the offerer shall first wash with water. The priest shall then burn the whole offering on the altar as a holocaust, a sweet-smelling oblation to the LORD.

[10]"If his holocaust offering is from the flock, that is, a sheep or a goat, he must bring a male without blemish. [11]This he shall slaughter before the LORD at the north side of the altar. Then Aaron's sons, the priests, shall splash its blood on the sides of the altar. [12]When the offerer has cut it up into pieces, the priest shall lay these, together with the head and suet, on top of the wood and the fire on the altar. [13]The inner organs and the shanks, however, the offerer shall first wash with water. The priest shall offer them up and then burn the whole offering on the altar as a holocaust, a sweet-smelling oblation to the LORD.

[14]*"If he offers a bird as a holocaust to the LORD, he shall choose a turtledove or a pigeon as his offering. [15]*Having brought it to the altar where it is to be burned, the priest shall snap its head loose and squeeze out its blood against the side of the altar. [16]Its crop and feathers shall be removed and thrown on the ash heap at the east side of the altar. [17]Then, having split the bird down the middle without separating the halves, the priest shall burn it on the altar, over the wood on the fire, as a holocaust, a sweet-smelling oblation to the LORD.

Cereal Offerings

2 [1]*"WHEN anyone wishes to bring a cereal offering to the LORD, his offering must consist of fine flour. He shall pour oil on it and put frankincense over it. [2]*†When he has brought it to Aaron's sons, the

---

*
   1/2: 22, 18.19.
   3: Ex 12, 5.
   4: 3, 2.8.13; 4, 15;
     8, 14.22; 16, 21;
     Ex 29, 10.15.
   5: 3, 8.

   9: 3, 5.16; Ex 29, 18.
   14: 5, 7; 12, 8; Lk 2, 24.
   15: 5, 8.
   2/1: Nm 15, 4.
   2: 6, 15.

† 1, 2: *From the herd or from the flock:* the only animals which could be used as sacrificial victims were either of the bovine class (bulls, cows and calves) or the ovine class (sheep and lambs, goats and kids). Excluded, therefore, were not only all wild animals, but also such "unclean" domestic animals as the camel and the ass. See note on 11, 1ff.

1, 3: *Holocaust:* from the Greek word meaning "wholly burned," this is the technical term for the special type of sacrifice in which an entire animal except its hide was consumed in the fire on the altar. The primary purpose of this complete gift was to render glory and praise to God.

2, 2: *Token offering:* literally, "reminder." Instead of burning the whole cereal offering, they burned only this part of it priests, one of them shall take a handful of this fine flour and oil, together with all the frankincense, and this he shall burn on the altar as a token offering, a sweet-smelling oblation to the LORD. **3***The rest of the cereal offering belongs to Aaron and his sons. It is a most sacred oblation to the LORD.

4"When the cereal offering you present is baked in an oven, it must be in the form of unleavened cakes made of fine flour mixed with oil, or of unleavened wafers spread with oil. **5***If you present a cereal offering that is fried on a griddle, it must be of fine flour mixed with oil and unleavened. **6**Such a cereal offering must be broken into pieces, and oil must be poured over it. **7**If you present a cereal offering that is prepared in a pot, it must be of fine flour, deep-fried in oil. **8**A cereal offering that is made in any of these ways you shall bring to the LORD, offering it to the priest, who shall take it to the altar. **9**Its token offering the priest shall then lift from the cereal offering and burn on the altar as a sweet-smelling oblation to the LORD. **10**The rest of the cereal offering belongs to Aaron and his sons. It is a most sacred oblation to the LORD.

11*"Every cereal offering that you present to the LORD shall be unleavened, for you shall not burn any leaven or honey as an oblation to the LORD. **12**Such you may indeed present to the LORD in the offering of first fruits, but they are not to be placed on the altar for a pleasing odor. **13***†However, every cereal offering that you present to the LORD shall be seasoned with salt. Do not let the salt of the covenant of your God be lacking from your cereal offering. On every offering you shall offer salt.

14"If you present a cereal offering of first fruits to the LORD, you shall offer it in the form of fresh grits of new ears of grain, roasted by fire. **15**On this cereal offering you shall put oil and frankincense. **16**For its token offering the priest shall then burn some of the grits and oil, together with all the frankincense, as an oblation to the LORD.

Peace Offerings

3 **1***†"IF someone in presenting a peace offering makes his offering from the herd, he may offer before the LORD either a male or a female animal, but it must be without blemish. **2***He shall lay his hand on the head of his offering, and then slaughter it at the entrance of the meeting tent; but Aaron's sons, the priests, shall splash its blood on the sides of the altar. **3***From the peace offering he shall offer as an oblation to the LORD the fatty membrane over the inner organs, and all the fat that adheres to them, **4**†as well as the two kidneys, with the fat on them near the loins, and the lobe of the liver, which he shall sever above the

kidneys. **5***All this Aaron's sons shall then burn on the altar with the holocaust, on the wood over the fire, as a sweet-smelling oblation to the LORD.

6"If the peace offering he presents to the LORD is from the flock, he may offer either a male or a female animal, but it must be without blemish. **7**If he presents a lamb as his offering, he shall bring it before the LORD, **8**and after laying his hand on the head of his offering, he shall slaughter it before the meeting tent; but Aaron's sons shall splash its blood on the sides of the altar. **9***†As an oblation to the LORD he shall present the fat of the peace offering: the whole fatty tail, which he must sever close to the spine, the fatty membrane over the inner organs, and all the fat that adheres to them, **10**as well as the two kidneys, with the fat on them near the loins, and the lobe of the liver, which he must sever above the kidneys. **11**All this the priest shall burn on the altar as the food of the LORD's oblation.

12"If he presents a goat, he shall bring it before the LORD, **13**and after laying his hand on its head, he shall slaughter it before the meeting tent; but Aaron's sons shall splash its blood on the sides of the altar. **14**From it he shall offer as an oblation to the LORD the fatty membrane over the inner organs, and all the fat that adheres to them, **15**as well as the two kidneys, with the fat on them near the loins, and the lobe of the liver, which he must sever above the kidneys. **16**All this the priest shall burn on the altar as the food of the sweet-smelling oblation. All the fat belongs to the LORD. **17***†This shall be a perpetual ordinance for your descendants wherever they may dwell. You shall not partake of any fat or any blood."

Sin Offerings: For Priests

4 **1**THE LORD said to Moses, **2***†"Tell the Israelites: When a person inadvertently commits a sin against some command of the LORD by doing one of the forbidden things, **3***†if it is the anointed

---

† on the altar; it thus corresponded to the fat of the peace offering. See note on 3, 1.

2, 13: *The salt of the covenant of your God:* the partaking in common of salt by those seated together at table was an ancient symbol of friendship and alliance. Cf Mk 9, 49 and Col 4, 6; and see note on Nm 18, 19.

3, 1: *Peace offering:* thus the ancient versions have rendered the Hebrew word, which perhaps means more exactly, "fulfillment sacrifice," offered up in fulfillment of a vow. Cf Prv 7, 14. Its characteristic feature was the sacred banquet at which the offerer and his guests partook of the meat of the sacrificed animal. Cf 7, 11-21.

3, 4: *The lobe of the liver:* some render, "the fatty covering of the liver."

3, 9: *The whole fatty tail:* see note on Ex 29, 22.

3, 17: *Any fat:* only the fat mentioned in vv 9f.14f is meant; other fat could be eaten by the Israelites.

4, 2: *A sin:* not necessarily a moral fault; included are all the cases of ritual uncleanness which people necessarily incurred in certain unavoidable circumstances.

4, 3: *The anointed priest:* his violation of the ceremonial law brought a sort of collective guilt on all the people whom he represented before God. *Sin offering:* more exactly, "sacrifice for remitting sin"; sin is here understood as explained above.

---

*

3: 7, 9f; Sir 7, 31; 1 Cor 9, 13.
5: 1 Chr 23, 29.
11: 6, 16f; Mt 16, 12; Mk 8, 15; Lk 12, 1; 1 Cor 5, 7; Gal 5, 9.
13: Ez 43, 24.
3/1: 22, 21.

2: 1, 4.
3: Ex 29, 13.22.
5: 6, 12.
9: 9, 19.
17: 17, 10-14; Gn 9, 4; Dt 12, 16.23; 15, 23.
4/2: 5, 15.17; Nm 15, 22-29.
3: Heb 7, 27.

priest who thus sins and thereby makes the people also become guilty, he shall present to the LORD a young, unblemished bull as a sin offering for the sin he committed. **4***Bringing the bullock to the entrance of the meeting tent, before the LORD, he shall lay his hand on its head and slaughter it before the LORD. **5**The anointed priest shall then take some of the bullock's blood and bring it into the meeting tent, **6***where, dipping his finger in the blood, he shall sprinkle it seven times before the LORD, toward the veil of the sanctuary. **7***The priest shall also put some of the blood on the horns of the altar of fragrant incense which is before the LORD in the meeting tent. The rest of the bullock's blood he shall pour out at the base of the altar of holocausts which is at the entrance of the meeting tent. **8**From the sin-offering bullock he shall remove all the fat: the fatty membrane over the inner organs, and all the fat that adheres to them, **9**as well as the two kidneys, with the fat on them near the loins, and the lobe of the liver, which he must sever above the kidneys. **10**This is the same as is removed from the ox of the peace offering; and the priest shall burn it on the altar of holocausts. **11***The hide of the bullock and all its flesh, with its head, legs, inner organs and offal, **12**in short, the whole bullock, shall be brought outside the camp to a clean place where the ashes are deposited and there be burned up in a wood fire. At the place of the ash heap, there it must be burned.

For the Community

13*"If the whole community of Israel inadvertently and without even being aware of it does something that the LORD has forbidden and thus makes itself guilty, **14**should it later on become known that the sin was committed, the community shall present a young bull as a sin offering. They shall bring it before the meeting tent, **15***and here, before the LORD, the elders of the community shall lay their hands on the bullock's head. When the bullock has been slaughtered before the LORD, **16**the anointed priest shall bring some of its blood into the meeting tent, **17**and dipping his finger in the blood, he shall sprinkle it seven times before the LORD, toward the veil. **18**He shall also put some of the blood on the horns of the altar of fragrant incense which is before the LORD in the meeting tent. The rest of the blood he shall pour out at the base of the altar of holocausts which is at the entrance of the meeting tent. **19**All of its fat he shall take from it and burn on the altar, **20**doing with this bullock just as he did with the other sin-offering bullock. Thus the priest shall make atonement for them, and they will be forgiven.

21This bullock must also be brought outside the camp and burned, just as has been prescribed for the other one. This is the sin offering for the community.

For the Princes

22"Should a prince commit a sin inadvertently by doing one of the things which are forbidden by some commandment of the LORD, his God, and thus become guilty, **23**if later on he learns of the sin he committed, he shall bring as his offering an unblemished male goat. **24**Having laid his hands on its head, he shall slaughter the goat as a sin offering before the LORD, in the place where the holocausts are slaughtered. **25**The priest shall then take some of the blood of the sin offering on his finger and put it on the horns of the altar of holocausts. The rest of the blood he shall pour out at the base of this altar. **26***All of the fat he shall burn on the altar like the fat of the peace offering. Thus the priest shall make atonement for the prince's sin, and it will be forgiven.

For Private Persons

27*"If a private person commits a sin inadvertently by doing one of the things which are forbidden by the commandments of the LORD, and thus becomes guilty, **28**should he later on learn of the sin he committed, he shall bring an unblemished she-goat as the offering for his sin. **29***Having laid his hand on the head of the sin offering, he shall slaughter it at the place of the holocausts. **30**The priest shall then take some of its blood on his finger and put it on the horns of the altar of holocausts. The rest of the blood he shall pour out at the base of the altar. **31***All the fat shall be removed, just as the fat is removed from the peace offering, and the priest shall burn it on the altar for an odor pleasing to the LORD. Thus the priest shall make atonement for him, and he will be forgiven.

32"If, however, for his sin offering he presents a lamb, he shall bring an unblemished female. **33**Having laid his hand on its head, he shall slaughter this sin offering in the place where the holocausts are slaughtered. **34**The priest shall then take some of the blood of the sin offering on his finger and put it on the horns of the altar of holocausts. The rest of the blood he shall pour out at the base of the altar. **35***All the fat shall be removed, just as the fat is removed from the peace-offering lamb, and the priest shall burn it on the altar with the other oblations of the LORD. Thus the priest shall make atonement for the man's sin, and it will be forgiven.

For Special Cases

5 **1***"IF any person refuses to give the information which, as a witness of something he has seen or learned, he has been adjured to give, and thus commits a sin and has guilt to bear; **2***or if someone, without being aware of it, touches any unclean thing, as the carcass of an unclean wild animal, or that of an unclean domestic animal, or that of an unclean swarming creature, and thus becomes unclean and guilty; **3**or

---

*

4: 1, 3f.	**26:** 3, 3-5.
6: 8, 11.	**27:** Nm 15, 27.
7: 8, 15; 9, 9; 16, 18;	**29:** 1, 4.
Ex 29, 12.	**31:** 1, 9; 3, 3-5.
11: 8, 17; 9, 11; Ex 29, 14;	**35:** 3, 3.9.
Nm 19, 5.	**5/1:** Prv 29, 24.
13: 5, 2-4; Nm 15, 24-26.	**2:** 11, 24.31.39; 12; 13;
15: 1, 4.	15.

if someone, without being aware of it, touches some human uncleanness, whatever kind of uncleanness this may be, and then recognizes his guilt; [4]*or if someone, without being aware of it, rashly utters an oath to do good or evil, such as men are accustomed to utter rashly, and then recognizes that he is guilty of such an oath; [5]*then whoever is guilty in any of these cases shall confess the sin he has incurred, [6]and as his sin offering for the sin he has committed he shall bring to the Lord a female animal from the flock, a ewe lamb or a she-goat. The priest shall then make atonement for his sin.

[7]*"If, however, he cannot afford an animal of the flock, he shall bring to the Lord as the sin offering for his sin two turtledoves or two pigeons, one for a sin offering and the other for a holocaust. [8]*He shall bring them to the priest, who shall offer the one for the sin offering first. Snapping its head loose at the neck, yet without breaking it off completely, [9]*he shall sprinkle some of the blood of the sin offering against the side of the altar. The rest of the blood shall be squeezed out against the base of the altar. Such is the offering for sin. [10]The other bird shall be offered as a holocaust in the usual way. Thus the priest shall make atonement for the sin the man committed, and it will be forgiven.

[11]"If he is unable to afford even two turtledoves or two pigeons, he shall present as a sin offering for his sin one tenth of an ephah of fine flour. He shall not put oil or frankincense on it, because it is a sin offering. [12]When he has brought it to the priest, the latter shall take a handful of this flour as a token offering, and this he shall burn as a sin offering on the altar with the other oblations of the Lord. [13]*Thus the priest shall make atonement for the sin that the man committed in any of the above cases, and it will be forgiven. The rest of the flour, like the cereal offerings, shall belong to the priest."

Guilt Offerings

[14]The Lord said to Moses, [15]†"If someone commits a sin by inadvertently cheating in the Lord's sacred dues, he shall bring to the Lord as his guilt offering an unblemished ram from the flock, valued at two silver shekels according to the standard of the sanctuary shekel. [16]*He shall also restore what he has sinfully withheld from the sanctuary, adding to it a fifth of its value. This is to be given to the priest, who shall then make atonement for him with the guilt-offering ram, and he will be forgiven.

[17]*†"If someone, without being aware of it, commits such a sin by doing one of the things which are forbidden by some commandment of the Lord, that he incurs guilt for which he must answer, [18]he shall bring as a guilt offering to the priest an unblemished ram of the flock of the established value. The priest shall then make atonement for the fault which was unwittingly committed, and it will be forgiven. [19]Such is the offering for guilt; the penalty of the guilt must be paid to the Lord."

[20]The Lord said to Moses, [21]"If someone commits a sin of dishonesty against the Lord by denying his neighbor a deposit or a pledge or a stolen article, or by otherwise retaining his neighbor's goods unjustly, [22]or if, having found a lost article, he denies the fact and swears falsely about it with any of the sinful oaths that men make in such cases, [23]he shall therefore, since he has incurred guilt by his sin, restore the thing that was stolen or unjustly retained by him or the deposit left with him or the lost article he found [24]or whatever else he swore falsely about; on the day of his guilt offering he shall make full restitution of the thing itself, and in addition, give the owner one fifth of its value. [25]As his guilt offering he shall bring to the Lord an unblemished ram of the flock of the established value. When he has presented this as his guilt offering to the priest, [26]the latter shall make atonement for him before the Lord, and he will be forgiven whatever guilt he may have incurred."

The Daily Holocaust

6 [1]THE Lord said to Moses, [2]†"Give Aaron and his sons the following command: This is the ritual for holocausts. The holocaust is to remain on the hearth of the altar all night until the next morning, and the fire is to be kept burning on the altar. [3]The priest, clothed in his linen robe and wearing linen drawers on his body, shall take away the ashes to which the fire has reduced the holocaust on the altar, and lay them at the side of the altar. [4]Then, having taken off these garments and put on other garments, he shall carry the ashes to a clean place outside the camp. [5]The fire on the altar is to be kept burning; it must not go out. Every morning the priest shall put firewood on it. On this he shall lay out the holocaust and burn the fat of the peace offerings. [6]The fire is to be kept burning continuously on the altar; it must not go out.

Daily Cereal Offering

[7]"This is the ritual of the cereal offering. One of Aaron's sons shall first present it before the Lord, in

---

† 5, 15: Cheating: not offering the full amount in tithes, first fruits, etc. Guilt offering: its characteristic was a certain additional penalty imposed as reparation for the injustice involved in the fault which was atoned for by this sacrifice. However, in certain passages, e. g., 14, 12f; Nm 6, 12; Ezr 10, 19, the term "guilt offering" is used for more important cases of "sin offerings" where no apparent injustice is involved.

5, 17: Without being aware of it: the case naturally presupposes that later on the offender learns of his mistake. Cf 4, 13f.

6, 2: Ritual: literally, "law, instruction." Here, and in the following paragraphs, are given additional prescriptions for various kinds of sacrifices which were, in part, treated of in the preceding chapters.

* 4: Jgs 11, 30f; 1 Sm 14, 24; Mk 6, 23; Acts 23, 12.
5: 26, 40; Nm 5, 7.
7: 12, 8; Lk 2, 24.
8: 1, 15.17.
9: 1, 15.
13: 4, 26.35.
16: 22, 14.
17: 4, 2.

front of the altar. [8]Then he shall take from it a handful of its fine flour and oil, together with all the frankincense that is on it, and this he shall burn on the altar as its token offering, a sweet-smelling oblation to the Lord. [9]The rest of it Aaron and his sons may eat; but it must be eaten in the form of unleavened cakes and in a sacred place: in the court of the meeting tent they shall eat it. [10]It shall not be baked with leaven. I have given it to them as their portion from the oblations of the Lord; it is most sacred, like the sin offering and the guilt offering. [11]All the male descendants of Aaron may partake of it as their rightful share in the oblations of the Lord perpetually throughout your generations. Whatever touches the oblations becomes sacred."

[12][†]The Lord said to Moses, [13]"This is the offering that Aaron and his sons shall present to the Lord [on the day he is anointed]: one tenth of an ephah of fine flour for the established cereal offering, half in the morning and half in the evening. [14]It shall be well kneaded and fried in oil on a griddle when you bring it in. Having broken the offering into pieces, you shall present it as a sweet-smelling oblation to the Lord. [15]Aaron's descendant who succeeds him as the anointed priest shall do likewise. This is a perpetual ordinance: for the Lord the whole offering shall be burned. [16]Every cereal offering of a priest shall be a whole burnt offering; it may not be eaten."

Sin Offerings

[17]The Lord said to Moses, [18][*]"Tell Aaron and his sons: This is the ritual for sin offerings. At the place where holocausts are slaughtered, there also, before the Lord, shall the sin offering be slaughtered. It is most sacred. [19][*]The priest who presents the sin offering may partake of it; but it must be eaten in a sacred place, in the court of the meeting tent. [20]Whatever touches its flesh shall become sacred. If any of its blood is spilled on a garment, the stained part must be washed in a sacred place. [21][*]A clay vessel in which it has been cooked shall thereafter be broken; if it is cooked in a bronze vessel, this shall be scoured afterward and rinsed with water. [22][*]All the males of the priestly line may partake of the sin offering, since it is most sacred. [23][*]But no one may partake of any sin offering of which some blood has been brought into the meeting tent to make atonement in the sanctuary; such an offering must be burned up in the fire.

Guilt Offerings

7 [1]"This is the ritual for guilt offerings, which are most sacred. [2][*]At the place where the holocausts are slaughtered, there also shall the guilt offering be slaughtered. Its blood shall be splashed on the sides of the altar. [3][*]All of its fat shall be taken from it and offered up: the fatty tail, the fatty membrane over the inner organs, [4]as well as the two kidneys with the fat on them near the loins, and the lobe of the liver, which must be severed above the kidneys. [5]All this the priest shall burn on the altar as an oblation to the Lord. This is the guilt offering. [6][*]All the males of the priestly line may partake of it; but it must be eaten in a sacred place, since it is most sacred.

[7]"Because the sin offering and the guilt offering are alike, both having the same ritual, the guilt offering likewise belongs to the priest who makes atonement with it. [8]Similarly, the priest who offers a holocaust for someone may keep for himself the hide of the holocaust that he has offered. [9][*]Also, every cereal offering that is baked in an oven or deep-fried in a pot or fried on a griddle shall belong to the priest who offers it, [10][*]whereas all cereal offerings that are offered up dry or mixed with oil shall belong to all of Aaron's sons without distinction.

Peace Offerings

[11]"This is the ritual for the peace offerings that are presented to the Lord. [12]When anyone makes a peace offering in thanksgiving, together with his thanksgiving sacrifice he shall offer unleavened cakes mixed with oil, unleavened wafers spread with oil, and cakes made of fine flour mixed with oil and well kneaded. [13][†]His offering shall also include loaves of leavened bread along with the victim of his peace offering for thanksgiving. [14]From each of his offerings he shall present one portion as a contribution to the Lord; this shall belong to the priest who splashes the blood of the peace offering.

[15]"The flesh of the thanksgiving sacrifice shall be eaten on the day it is offered; none of it may be kept till the next day. [16]However, if the sacrifice is a votive or a free-will offering, it should indeed be eaten on the day the sacrifice is offered, but what is left over may be eaten on the next day. [17]Should any flesh from the sacrifice be left over on the third day, it must be burned up in the fire. [18]If, therefore, any of the flesh of the peace offering is eaten on the third day, it shall not win favor for him nor shall it be reckoned to his credit; rather, it shall be considered as refuse, and anyone who eats of it shall have his guilt to bear. [19]Should the flesh touch anything unclean, it may not be eaten, but shall be burned up in the fire.

"All who are clean may partake of this flesh. [20]If, however, someone while in a state of uncleanness eats

[*]
6/18: 7, 2.
19: 10, 17.
21: 11, 33; 15, 12.
22: 7, 6; Nm 18, 10.
23: 4, 5; Heb 13, 11.
7/2: 6, 18.

3-5: 3, 4.9f.14-16; 4, 8f.
6: 6, 22.
9: 2, 3-10; Nm 18, 9; Ez 44, 29.
10: 2, 14f.
15-18: 19, 6f.

[†] 6, 12-16: This is another law about the daily or "established" cereal offering. It differs in some respects from the preceding law (vv 7-11) and also from the law in Ex 29, 38-42. Hence, the words *on the day he is anointed* were probably added by some later scribe in order to avoid the difficulty of harmonizing this law with the other two laws on the same matter.

7, 13: *Leavened bread:* these loaves were not burned on the altar (cf 2, 11), but were eaten at the "communion" meal which followed the sacrifice. See note on 3, 1.

any of the flesh of a peace offering belonging to the LORD, that person shall be cut off from his people. [21]Likewise, if someone touches anything unclean, whether the uncleanness be of human or of animal origin or from some loathsome crawling creature, and then eats of a peace offering belonging to the LORD, that person, too, shall be cut off from his people."

Prohibition against Blood and Fat

[22]The LORD said to Moses, [23]*†"Tell the Israelites: You shall not eat the fat of any ox or sheep or goat. [24]*Although the fat of an animal that has died a natural death or has been killed by wild beasts may be put to any other use, you may not eat it. [25]If anyone eats the fat of an animal from which an oblation is made to the LORD, such a one shall be cut off from his people. [26]Wherever you dwell, you shall not partake of any blood, be it of bird or of animal. [27]*Every person who partakes of any blood shall be cut off from his people."

The Portions for Priests

[28]The LORD said to Moses, [29]"Tell the Israelites: He who presents a peace offering to the LORD shall bring a part of it as his special offering to him, [30]†carrying in with his own hands the oblations to the LORD. The fat is to be brought in, together with the breast, which is to be waved as a wave offering before the LORD. [31]*The priest shall burn the fat on the altar, but the breast belongs to Aaron and his sons. [32]Moreover, from your peace offering you shall give to the priest the right leg as a raised offering. [33]The descendant of Aaron who offers up the blood and fat of the peace offering shall have the right leg as his portion, [34]*for from the peace offerings of the Israelites I have taken the breast that is waved and the leg that is raised up, and I have given them to Aaron, the priest, and to his sons by a perpetual ordinance as a contribution from the Israelites."

[35]†This is the priestly share from the oblations of the LORD, allotted to Aaron and his sons on the day he called them to be the priests of the LORD; [36]on the day he anointed them the LORD ordered the Israelites to give them this share by a perpetual ordinance throughout their generations.

[37]This is the ritual for holocausts, cereal offerings, sin offerings, guilt offerings, [ordination offerings] and peace offerings, [38]which the LORD enjoined on Moses at Mount Sinai at the time when he commanded the Israelites in the wilderness of Sinai to bring their offerings to the LORD.

II: CEREMONY OF ORDINATION

Ordination of Aaron and His Sons

8 [1]*†THE LORD SAID to Moses, [2]†"Take Aaron and his sons, together with the vestments, the anointing oil, the bullock for a sin offering, the two rams, and the basket of unleavened food. [3]Then assemble the whole community at the entrance of the meeting tent." [4]And Moses did as the LORD had commanded. When the community had assembled at the entrance of the meeting tent, [5]Moses told them what the LORD had ordered to be done. [6]*Bringing forward Aaron and his sons, he first washed them with water. [7]*Then he put the tunic on Aaron, girded him with the sash, clothed him with the robe, placed the ephod on him, and girded him with the embroidered belt of the ephod, fastening it around him. [8]*†He then set the breastpiece on him, with the Urim and Thummim in it, [9]*and put the miter on his head, attaching the gold plate, the sacred diadem, over the front of the miter, at his forehead, as the LORD had commanded him to do.

[10]*Taking the anointing oil, Moses anointed and consecrated the Dwelling, with all that was in it. [11]Then he sprinkled some of this oil seven times on the altar, and anointed the altar, with all its appurtenances, and the laver, with its base, thus consecrating them. [12]*He also poured some of the anointing oil on Aaron's head, thus consecrating him. [13]Moses likewise brought forward Aaron's sons, clothed them with tunics, girded them with sashes, and put turbans on them, as the LORD had commanded him to do.

Ordination Sacrifices

[14]When he had brought forward the bullock for a sin offering, Aaron and his sons laid their hands on its head. [15]*Then Moses slaughtered it, and taking some of its blood, with his finger he put it on the horns around the altar, thus purifying the altar. He also made atonement for the altar by pouring out the blood at its base when he consecrated it. [16]*Taking all the fat that was over the inner organs, as well as the lobe of the liver and the two kidneys with their fat, Moses burned them on the altar. [17]The bullock, however, with its hide and flesh and offal he burned in the fire

---

† 7, 23: *The fat:* only the particular portions specified in 3, 9f.14f are meant. *Ox or sheep or goat:* such animals as could be sacrificed; the fat of other clean animals could be eaten.

7, 30-34: *A wave offering . . . a raised offering:* these ceremonies are described in Ex 29, 24-28. The Hebrew word for "raised offering" is also rendered, in certain contexts, as "contribution."

7, 35: *The priestly share:* literally, "the anointed part."

8, 1—9, 21: Though presented in the form of a narrative, this description of Aaron's ordination was intended to serve as a guide for all future ordinations.

8, 2: *The vestments, etc.:* already described in Ex 28-29.

8, 8: *The Urim and Thummim:* see note on Ex 28, 30.

*
23: 3, 17.	7ff: Sir 45, 8-13.
24: 22, 8.	8: Ex 28, 30.
27: 17, 10.	9: Ex 28, 36.
31: 3, 11.16.	10: Ex 30, 26.
34: Ex 29, 27f.	12: Sir 45, 15.
8/1-36: cf Ex 29.	15: 4, 7; Heb 9, 22.
6f: Ex 40, 12f.	16f: 3, 4; 4, 8-11.

outside the camp, as the Lord had commanded him to do.

¹⁸He next brought forward the holocaust ram, and Aaron and his sons laid their hands on its head. ¹⁹When he had slaughtered it, Moses splashed its blood on all sides of the altar. ²⁰After cutting up the ram into pieces, he burned the head, the cut-up pieces and the suet; ²¹then, having washed the inner organs and the shanks with water, he also burned these remaining parts of the ram on the altar as a holocaust, a sweet-smelling oblation to the Lord, as the Lord had commanded him to do.

²²Then he brought forward the second ram, the ordination ram, and Aaron and his sons laid their hands on its head. ²³*When he had slaughtered it, Moses took some of its blood and put it on the tip of Aaron's right ear, on the thumb of his right hand, and on the big toe of his right foot. ²⁴Moses had the sons of Aaron also come forward, and he put some of the blood on the tips of their right ears, on the thumbs of their right hands, and on the big toes of their right feet. The rest of the blood he splashed on the sides of the altar. ²⁵He then took the fat: the fatty tail and all the fat over the inner organs, the lobe of the liver and the two kidneys with their fat, and likewise the right leg; ²⁶from the basket of unleavened food that was set before the Lord he took one unleavened cake, one loaf of bread made with oil, and one wafer; these he placed on top of the portions of fat and the right leg. ²⁷He then put all these things into the hands of Aaron and his sons, whom he had wave them as a wave offering before the Lord. ²⁸When he had received them back, Moses burned them with the holocaust on the altar as the ordination offering, a sweet-smelling oblation to the Lord. ²⁹He then took the breast and waved it as a wave offering before the Lord; this was Moses' own portion of the ordination ram. All this was in keeping with the Lord's command to Moses. ³⁰Taking some of the anointing oil and some of the blood that was on the altar, Moses sprinkled with it Aaron and his vestments, as well as his sons and their vestments, thus consecrating both Aaron and his vestments and his sons and their vestments.

³¹Finally, Moses said to Aaron and his sons, "Boil the flesh at the entrance of the meeting tent, and there eat it with the bread that is in the basket of the ordination offering, in keeping with the command I have received: 'Aaron and his sons shall eat of it.' ³²What is left over of the flesh and the bread you shall burn up in the fire. ³³Moreover, you are not to depart from the entrance of the meeting tent for seven days, until the days of your ordination are completed; for your ordination is to last for seven days. ³⁴†The Lord has commanded that what has been done today be done to make atonement for you. ³⁵Hence you must remain at the entrance of the meeting tent day and night for seven days, carrying out the prescriptions of the Lord; otherwise you shall die; for this is the com-

mand I have received." ³⁶So Aaron and his sons did all that the Lord had commanded through Moses.

Octave of the Ordination

9 ¹On the eighth day Moses summoned Aaron and his sons, together with the elders of Israel, ²and said to Aaron, "Take a calf for a sin offering and a ram for a holocaust, both without blemish, and offer them before the Lord. ³Tell the elders of Israel, too: Take a he-goat for a sin offering, a calf and a lamb, both unblemished yearlings, for a holocaust, ⁴and an ox and a ram for a peace offering, to sacrifice them before the Lord, along with a cereal offering mixed with oil; for today the Lord will reveal himself to you." ⁵So they brought what Moses had ordered. When the whole community had come forward and stood before the Lord, ⁶Moses said, "This is what the Lord orders you to do, that the glory of the Lord may be revealed to you. ⁷Come up to the altar," Moses then told Aaron, "and offer your sin offering and your holocaust in atonement for yourself and for your family; then present the offering of the people in atonement for them, as the Lord has commanded."

⁸Going up to the altar, Aaron first slaughtered the calf that was his own sin offering. ⁹When his sons presented the blood to him, he dipped his finger in the blood and put it on the horns of the altar. The rest of the blood he poured out at the base of the altar. ¹⁰He then burned on the altar the fat, the kidneys and the lobe of the liver that were taken from the sin offering, as the Lord had commanded Moses; ¹¹but the flesh and the hide he burned up in the fire outside the camp. ¹²Then Aaron slaughtered his holocaust. When his sons brought him the blood, he splashed it on all sides of the altar. ¹³They then brought him the pieces and the head of the holocaust, and he burned them on the altar. ¹⁴Having washed the inner organs and the shanks, he burned these also with the holocaust on the altar.

¹⁵Thereupon he had the people's offering brought up. Taking the goat that was for the people's sin offering, he slaughtered it and offered it up for sin as before. ¹⁶Then he brought forward the holocaust, other than the morning holocaust, and offered it in the usual manner. ¹⁷He then presented the cereal offering; taking a handful of it, he burned it on the altar. ¹⁸Finally he slaughtered the ox and the ram, the peace offering of the people. When his sons brought him the blood, Aaron splashed it on all sides of the altar. ¹⁹*The portions of fat from the ox and from the ram, the fatty tail, the fatty membrane over the inner organs, the two kidneys, with the fat that is on them, and the lobe of the liver, ²⁰he placed on top of the breasts and burned them on the altar, ²¹*having first waved the breasts

---

† 8, 34: The sense is not quite clear. Either the verse gives merely the reason why God ordered this ceremony, or it contains God's command that the same ceremony be used in all future ordinations, or it decrees a repetition of the entire ceremony on each of the seven days. At least a sin offering for atonement was made on each of these days. Cf Ex 29, 29-36.

and the right legs as a wave offering before the Lord, in keeping with the Lord's command to Moses.

Revelation of the Lord's Glory

²²Aaron then raised his hands over the people and blessed them. When he came down from offering the sin offering and holocaust and peace offering, ²³*Moses and Aaron went into the meeting tent. On coming out they again blessed the people. Then the glory of the Lord was revealed to all the people. ²⁴*Fire came forth from the Lord's presence and consumed the holocaust and the remnants of the fat on the altar. Seeing this, all the people cried out and fell prostrate.

Nadab and Abihu

10 ¹*†DURING this time Aaron's sons Nadab and Abihu took their censers and, strewing incense on the fire they had put in them, they offered up before the Lord profane fire, such as he had not authorized. ²*†Fire therefore came forth from the Lord's presence and consumed them, so that they died in his presence. ³*†Moses then said to Aaron, "This is as the Lord said:

Through those who approach me I will manifest my sacredness;
In the sight of all the people I will reveal my glory."

But Aaron said nothing. ⁴Then Moses summoned Mishael and Elzaphan, the sons of Aaron's uncle Uzziel, with the order, "Come, remove your kinsmen from the sanctuary and carry them to a place outside the camp." ⁵†So they went in and took them, in their tunics, outside the camp, as Moses had commanded.

Conduct of the Priests

⁶*†Moses said to Aaron and his sons Eleazar and Ithamar, "Do not bare your heads or tear your garments, lest you bring not only death on yourselves but God's wrath also on the whole community. Your kinsmen, the rest of the house of Israel, shall mourn for those whom the Lord's fire has smitten; ⁷but do not you go beyond the entry of the meeting tent, else you shall die; for the anointing oil of the Lord is upon you." So they did as Moses told them.

⁸The Lord said to Aaron, ⁹*"When you are to go to the meeting tent, you and your sons are forbidden under pain of death, by a perpetual ordinance throughout your generations, to drink any wine or strong drink. ¹⁰*You must be able to distinguish between what is sacred and what is profane, between what is

clean and what is unclean; ¹¹*you must teach the Israelites all the laws that the Lord has given them through Moses."

The Eating of the Priestly Portions

¹²*Moses said to Aaron and his surviving sons, Eleazar and Ithamar, "Take the cereal offering left over from the oblations of the Lord, and eat it beside the altar in the form of unleavened cakes. Since it is most sacred, ¹³you must eat it in a sacred place. This is your due from the oblations of the Lord, and that of your sons; such is the command I have received. ¹⁴*With your sons and daughters you shall also eat the breast of the wave offering and the leg of the raised offering, in a clean place; for these have been assigned to you and your children as your due from the peace offerings of the Israelites. ¹⁵The leg of the raised offering and the breast of the wave offering shall first be brought in with the oblations, the fatty portions, that are to be waved as a wave offering before the Lord. Then they shall belong to you and your children by a perpetual ordinance, as the Lord has commanded."

¹⁶†When Moses inquired about the goat of the sin offering, he discovered that it had all been burned. So he was angry with the surviving sons of Aaron, Eleazar and Ithamar, and said, ¹⁷*"Why did you not eat the sin offering in the sacred place, since it is most sacred? It has been given to you that you might bear the guilt of the community and make atonement for them before the Lord. ¹⁸If its blood was not brought into the inmost part of the sanctuary, you should certainly have eaten the offering in the sanctuary, in keeping with the command I had received." ¹⁹Aaron answered Moses, "Even though they presented their sin offering and holocaust before the Lord today, yet this misfortune has befallen me. Had I then eaten of the sin offering today, would it have been pleasing to the Lord?" ²⁰On hearing this, Moses was satisfied.

† 10, 1: *Nadab and Abihu:* the older sons of Aaron. Cf Ex 6, 23f.

10, 2: *Fire:* perhaps after the manner of lightning.

10, 3: *I will manifest my sacredness:* the presence of God is so sacred that it strikes dead those who approach him without the proper holiness. Cf Nm 20, 13; Ez 28, 22.

10, 5: *In their tunics:* they were buried just as they were, with no shroud or funeral solemnities.

10, 6: *Bare your heads:* go without the customary head covering, as a sign of mourning. Some interpreters, however, understand it as the cutting off of one's hair, which ordinarily all the Israelites, men as well as women, let grow long. Cf Is 15, 2; Jer 7, 29. Still others understand the verb to mean "to let one's hair hang loose and wild." Cf 13, 45; 21, 10, where the same phrase is used.

10, 16-19: *Eleazar and Ithamar* burned the entire goat of the sin offering (9, 15) instead of eating it in a sacred place (6, 19) to bear the guilt of the community. Aaron defends this action of his sons against Moses' displeasure by implying that they did not have sufficient sanctity to eat the flesh of the victim and thus perform the expiation of the people. They themselves still labored under the blow of the divine anger which struck their brothers Nadab and Abihu.

* 23: Nm 6, 23-26.
24: 1 Kgs 18, 38; 2 Chr 7, 1.
10/1: 16, 1; Nm 3, 4; 26, 61; 1 Chr 24, 2.
2: Nm 16, 35.
3: 21, 17.21.
6: 21, 10.
9: Ez 44, 21.
10: 11, 47; 20, 25; Ez 22, 26; 44, 23.
11: Sir 45, 16.
12: 6, 16.
14f: 7, 34.
17: 6, 18f.

III: LAWS REGARDING LEGAL PURITY

Clean and Unclean Food

11 ¹†THE LORD SAID to Moses and Aaron, ²"Speak to the Israelites and tell them: Of all land animals these are the ones you may eat: ³any animal that has hoofs you may eat, provided it is cloven-footed and chews the cud. ⁴But you shall not eat any of the following that only chew the cud or only have hoofs: the camel, which indeed chews the cud, but does not have hoofs and is therefore unclean for you; ⁵†the rock badger, which indeed chews the cud, but does not have hoofs and is therefore unclean for you; ⁶the hare, which indeed chews the cud, but does not have hoofs and is therefore unclean for you; ⁷and the pig, which does indeed have hoofs and is cloven-footed, but does not chew the cud and is therefore unclean for you. ⁸Their flesh you shall not eat, and their dead bodies you shall not touch; they are unclean for you.

⁹"Of the various creatures that live in the water, you may eat the following: whatever in the seas or in river waters has both fins and scales you may eat. ¹⁰But of the various creatures that crawl or swim in the water, whether in the sea or in the rivers, all those that lack either fins or scales are loathsome for you, ¹¹and you shall treat them as loathsome. Their flesh you shall not eat, and their dead bodies you shall loathe. ¹²Every water creature that lacks fins or scales is loathsome for you.

¹³†"Of the birds, these you shall loathe and, as loathsome, they shall not be eaten: the eagle, the vulture, the osprey, ¹⁴the kite, the various species of falcons, ¹⁵the various species of crows, ¹⁶the ostrich, the nightjar, the gull, the various species of hawks, ¹⁷the owl, the cormorant, the screech owl, ¹⁸the barn owl, the desert owl, the buzzard, ¹⁹†the stork, the various species of herons, the hoopoe, and the bat.

²⁰"The various winged insects that walk on all fours are loathsome for you. ²¹But of the various winged insects that walk on all fours you may eat those that have jointed legs for leaping on the ground; ²²†hence of these you may eat the following: the various kinds of locusts, the various kinds of grasshoppers, the various kinds of katydids, and the various kinds of crickets. ²³All other winged insects that have four legs are loathsome for you.

²⁴†"Such is the uncleanness that you contract, that everyone who touches their dead bodies shall be unclean until evening, ²⁵and everyone who picks up any part of their dead bodies shall wash his garments and be unclean until evening. ²⁶†All hoofed animals that are not cloven-footed or do not chew the cud are unclean for you; everyone who touches them becomes unclean. ²⁷†Of the various quadrupeds, all those that walk on paws are unclean for you; everyone who touches their dead bodies shall be unclean until evening, ²⁸and everyone who picks up their dead bodies shall wash his garments and be unclean until evening. Such is their uncleanness for you.

²⁹"Of the creatures that swarm on the ground, the following are unclean for you: the rat, the mouse, the various kinds of lizards, ³⁰the gecko, the chameleon, the agama, the skink, and the mole. ³¹Among the various swarming creatures, these are unclean for you. Everyone who touches them when they are dead shall be unclean until evening. ³²Everything on which one of them falls when dead becomes unclean. Any such article that men use, whether it be an article of wood, cloth, leather or goat hair, must be put in water and remain unclean until evening, when it again becomes clean. ³³Should any of these creatures fall into a clay vessel, everything in it becomes unclean, and the vessel itself you must break. ³⁴Any solid food that was in contact with water, and any liquid that men drink, in any such vessel become unclean. ³⁵Any object on which one of their dead bodies falls, becomes unclean; if it is an oven or a jar-stand, this must be broken to pieces; they are unclean and shall be treated as unclean by you. ³⁶†However, a spring or a cistern for collecting water remains clean; but whoever touches the dead body becomes unclean. ³⁷Any sort of cultivated grain remains clean even though one of their dead bodies falls on it; ³⁸but if the grain has become moistened, it becomes unclean when one of these falls on it.

³⁹"When one of the animals that you could otherwise eat, dies of itself, anyone who touches its dead body shall be unclean until evening; ⁴⁰*and anyone who eats of its dead body shall wash his garments and be unclean until evening; so also, anyone who removes its dead body shall wash his garments and be unclean until evening.

---

† 11, 1ff: These distinctions between edible and inedible meats were probably based on traditional ideas of hygiene, but they are here given a moral, religious basis: the inedible varieties are classified as "unclean" to remind the Israelites that they are to be a pure and holy people, dedicated to the LORD.

11, 5f: According to modern zoology, *the rock badger* (hyrax Syriacus) is classified as an ungulate, and *the hare* as a rodent; neither is a ruminant. They appear to chew their food as the true ruminants do, and it is upon this appearance that the classification in the text is based.

11, 13-19.30: The identification of the various Hebrew names for these birds and reptiles is in many cases uncertain.

11, 19: *The bat:* actually a mammal, but listed here with the birds because of its wings.

11, 22: The Hebrew distinguishes four classes of edible locust-like insects, but the difference between them is quite uncertain. Cf Mt 3, 4.

11, 24-28: This paragraph sharpens the prohibition against unclean animals: not only is their meat unfit for food, but contact with their dead bodies makes a person ritually unclean.

11, 26: *All hoofed animals that are not cloven-footed:* such as the horse and the ass.

11, 27: *All those that walk on paws:* such as dogs and cats.

11, 36: *Whoever touches the dead body:* to remove the dead insect from the water supply.

41"All the creatures that swarm on the ground are loathsome and shall not be eaten. 42Whether it crawls on its belly, goes on all fours, or has many legs, you shall eat no swarming creature: they are loathsome. 43*Do not make yourselves loathsome or unclean with any swarming creature through being contaminated by them. 44*For I, the LORD, am your God; and you shall make and keep yourselves holy, because I am holy. You shall not make yourselves unclean, then, by any swarming creature that crawls on the ground. 45Since I, the LORD, brought you up from the land of Egypt that I might be your God, you shall be holy, because I am holy.

46"This is the law for animals and birds and for all the creatures that move about in the water or swarm on the ground, 47*that you may distinguish between the clean and the unclean, between creatures that may be eaten and those that may not be eaten."

Uncleanness of Childbirth

12 1THE LORD said to Moses, 2*†"Tell the Israelites: When a woman has conceived and gives birth to a boy, she shall be unclean for seven days, with the same uncleanness as at her menstrual period. 3*On the eighth day, the flesh of the boy's foreskin shall be circumcised, 4and then she shall spend thirty-three days more in becoming purified of her blood; she shall not touch anything sacred nor enter the sanctuary till the days of her purification are fulfilled. 5If she gives birth to a girl, for fourteen days she shall be as unclean as at her menstruation, after which she shall spend sixty-six days in becoming purified of her blood.

6*"When the days of her purification for a son or for a daughter are fulfilled, she shall bring to the priest at the entrance of the meeting tent a yearling lamb for a holocaust and a pigeon or a turtledove for a sin offering. 7The priest shall offer them up before the LORD to make atonement for her, and thus she will be clean again after her flow of blood. Such is the law for the woman who gives birth to a boy or a girl child. 8*†If, however, she cannot afford a lamb, she may take two turtledoves or two pigeons, the one for a holocaust and the other for a sin offering. The priest shall make atonement for her, and thus she will again be clean."

Leprosy

13 1THE LORD said to Moses and Aaron, 2*†"If someone has on his skin a scab or pustule or blotch which appears to be the sore of leprosy, he shall be brought to Aaron, the priest, or to one of the priests among his descendants, 3who shall examine the sore on his skin. If the hair on the sore has turned white and the sore itself shows that it has

penetrated below the skin, it is indeed the sore of leprosy; the priest, on seeing this, shall declare the man unclean. 4If, however, the blotch on the skin is white, but does not seem to have penetrated below the skin, nor has the hair turned white, the priest shall quarantine the stricken man for seven days. 5On the seventh day the priest shall again examine him. If he judges that the sore has remained unchanged and has not spread on the skin, the priest shall quarantine him for another seven days, 6and once more examine him on the seventh day. If the sore is now dying out and has not spread on the skin, the priest shall declare the man clean; it was merely eczema. The man shall wash his garments and so become clean. 7But if, after he has shown himself to the priest to be declared clean, the eczema spreads at all on his skin, he shall once more show himself to the priest. 8Should the priest, on examining it, find that the eczema has indeed spread on the skin, he shall declare the man unclean; it is leprosy.

9"When someone is stricken with leprosy, he shall be brought to the priest. 10Should the priest, on examining him, find that there is a white scab on the skin which has turned the hair white and that there is raw flesh in it, 11it is skin leprosy that has long developed. The priest shall declare the man unclean without first quarantining him, since he is certainly unclean. 12†If leprosy breaks out on the skin and, as far as the priest can see, covers all the skin of the stricken man from head to foot, 13should the priest then, on examining him, find that the leprosy does cover his whole body, he shall declare the stricken man clean; since it has all turned white, the man is clean. 14But as soon as raw flesh appears on him, he is unclean; 15on observing the raw flesh, the priest shall declare him unclean, because raw flesh is unclean; it is leprosy. 16If, however, the raw flesh again turns white, he shall return to the priest; 17should the latter, on examining him, find that the sore has indeed turned white, he shall declare the stricken man clean, and thus he will be clean.

18"If a man who had a boil on his skin which later healed, 19should now in the place of the boil have a white scab or a pink blotch, he shall show himself to the priest. 20If the latter, on examination, sees that it

---

† 12, 2f: The uncleanness of the woman was more serious during the first period, the seven days after the birth of a boy or the fourteen days after the birth of a girl; only during this period would the rules given in 15, 19-24 apply.

12, 8: Forty days after the birth of Jesus, his Virgin Mother made this offering of the poor (Lk 2, 22.24); since the holocaust was offered in thanksgiving for the birth of the child, this was most fittingly offered by Mary. However, because of her miraculous delivery, she was not really obliged to make the sin offering of purification.

13, 2ff: Various kinds of skin blemishes are treated here which were not contagious but simply disqualified their subjects from association with others, especially in public worship, until they were declared ritually clean. The Hebrew term used does not refer to Hansen's disease, currently called leprosy.

13, 12ff: *If leprosy breaks out on the skin:* the symptoms described here point to a form of skin disease which is merely on the surface and therefore easily cured.

---

* 43f: 20, 25f.   3: Gn 17, 12; Jn 7, 22.
  44: 19, 2; 20, 7.26; Mt 5,   6: Lk 2, 22.
  48; 1 Pt 1, 16.   8: 1, 14; Lk 2, 24.
  47: 10, 10.   13/2: Dt 24, 8.
12/2: 15, 19.

is deeper than the skin and that the hair has turned white, he shall declare the man unclean; it is the sore of leprosy that has broken out in the boil. **21**But if the priest, on examining him, finds that there is no white hair in it and that it is not deeper than the skin and is already dying out, the priest shall quarantine him for seven days. **22**If it has then spread on the skin, the priest shall declare him unclean; the man is stricken. **23**But if the blotch remains in its place without spreading, it is merely the scar of the boil; the priest shall therefore declare him clean.

24"If a man had a burn on his skin, and the proud flesh of the burn now becomes a pink or a white blotch, **25**the priest shall examine it. If the hair has turned white on the blotch and this seems to have penetrated below the skin, it is leprosy that has broken out in the burn; the priest shall therefore declare him unclean and stricken with leprosy. **26**But if the priest, on examining it, finds that there is no white hair on the blotch and that this is not deeper than the skin and is already dying out, the priest shall quarantine him for seven days. **27**Should the priest, when examining it on the seventh day, find that it has spread at all on the skin, he shall declare the man unclean and stricken with leprosy. **28**But if the blotch remains in its place without spreading on the skin and is already dying out, it is merely the scab of the burn; the priest shall therefore declare the man clean, since it is only the scar of the burn.

29"When a man or a woman has a sore on the head or cheek, **30†**should the priest, on examining it, find that the sore has penetrated below the skin and that there is fine yellow hair on it, the priest shall declare the person unclean, for this is scall, a leprous disease of the head or cheek. **31**But if the priest, on examining the scall sore, finds that it has not penetrated below the skin, though the hair on it may not be black, the priest shall quarantine the person with scall sore for seven days, **32**and on the seventh day again examine the sore. If the scall has not spread and has no yellow hair on it and does not seem to have penetrated below the skin, **33**the man shall shave himself, but not on the diseased spot. Then the priest shall quarantine him for another seven days. **34**If the priest, when examining the scall on the seventh day, finds that it has not spread on the skin and that it has not penetrated below the skin, he shall declare the man clean; the latter shall wash his garments, and thus he will be clean. **35**But if the scall spreads at all on his skin after he has been declared clean, **36**the priest shall again examine it. If the scall has indeed spread on the skin, he need not look for yellow hair; the man is surely unclean. **37**If, however, he judges that the scall has remained in its place and that black hair has grown on it, the disease has been healed; the man is clean, and the priest shall declare him clean.

38"When the skin of a man or a woman is spotted with white blotches, **39†**the priest shall make an exam-ination. If the blotches on the skin are white and already dying out, it is only tetter that has broken out on the skin, and the person therefore is clean.

40"When a man loses the hair of his head, he is not unclean merely because of his bald crown. **41**So too, if he loses the hair on the front of his head, he is not unclean merely because of his bald forehead. **42**But when there is a pink sore on his bald crown or bald forehead, it is leprosy that is breaking out there. **43**The priest shall examine him; and if the scab on the sore of the bald spot has the same pink appearance as that of skin leprosy of the fleshy part of the body, **44**the man is leprous and unclean, and the priest shall declare him unclean by reason of the sore on his head.

45"The one who bears the sore of leprosy shall keep his garments rent and his head bare, and shall muffle his beard; he shall cry out, 'Unclean, unclean!' **46***As long as the sore is on him he shall declare himself unclean, since he is in fact unclean. He shall dwell apart, making his abode outside the camp.

Leprosy of Clothes

47†"When a leprous infection is on a garment of wool or of linen, **48**or on woven or knitted material of linen or wool, or on a hide or anything made of leather, **49**if the infection on the garment or hide, or on the woven or knitted material, or on any leather article is greenish or reddish, the thing is indeed infected with leprosy and must be shown to the priest. **50**Having examined the infection, the priest shall quarantine the infected article for seven days.

51"On the seventh day the priest shall again examine the infection. If it has spread on the garment, or on the woven or knitted material, or on the leather, what-ever be its use, the infection is malignant leprosy, and the article is unclean. **52**He shall therefore burn up the garment, or the woven or knitted material of wool or linen, or the leather article, whatever it may be, which is infected; since it has malignant leprosy, it must be destroyed by fire. **53**But if the priest, on examining the infection, finds that it has not spread on the garment, or on the woven or knitted material, or on the leather article, **54**he shall give orders to have the infected article washed and then quarantined for another seven days.

55"Then the priest shall again examine the infected article after it has been washed. If the infection has not changed its appearance, even though it may not have spread, the article is unclean and shall be destroyed by fire. **56**But if the priest, on examining the infection, finds that it is dying out after the washing, he shall tear the infected part out of the garment, or the leather, or the woven or knitted material. **57**If, however, the infection again appears on the garment, or on the woven or knitted material, or on the leather

---

† 13, 30: *Scall:* a scabby or scaly eruption of the scalp. According to some, "ringworm."

13, 39: *Tetter:* vitiligo, a harmless form of skin disease.

13, 47: *A leprous infection:* some mold or fungus growth resembling human leprosy.

article, it is still virulent and the thing infected shall be destroyed by fire. [58]But if, after the washing, the infection has left the garment, or the woven or knitted material, or the leather article, the thing shall be washed a second time, and thus it will be clean. [59]*This is the law for leprous infection on a garment of wool or linen, or on woven or knitted material, or on any leather article, to determine whether it is clean or unclean."

Purification after Leprosy

14 [1]THE LORD said to Moses, [2]*"This is the law for the victim of leprosy at the time of his purification. He shall be brought to the priest, [3]who is to go outside the camp to examine him. If the priest finds that the sore of leprosy has healed in the leper, [4]†he shall order the man who is to be purified, to get two live, clean birds, as well as some cedar wood, scarlet yarn, and hyssop. [5]†The priest shall then order him to slay one of the birds over an earthen vessel with spring water in it. [6]Taking the living bird with the cedar wood, the scarlet yarn and the hyssop, the priest shall dip them all in the blood of the bird that was slain over the spring water, [7]and then sprinkle seven times the man to be purified from his leprosy. When he has thus purified him, he shall let the living bird fly away over the countryside. [8]The man being purified shall then wash his garments and shave off all his hair and bathe in water; only when he is thus made clean may he come inside the camp; but he shall still remain outside his tent for seven days. [9]On the seventh day he shall again shave off all the hair of his head, his beard, his eyebrows, and any other hair he may have, and also wash his garments and bathe his body in water; and so he will be clean.

Purification Sacrifices

[10]"On the eighth day he shall take two unblemished male lambs, one unblemished yearling ewe lamb, three tenths of an ephah of fine flour mixed with oil for a cereal offering, and one log of oil. [11]The priest who performs the purification ceremony shall place the man who is being purified, as well as all these offerings, before the LORD at the entrance of the meeting tent. [12]Taking one of the male lambs, the priest shall present it as a guilt offering, along with the log of oil, waving them as a wave offering before the LORD. [13](This lamb he shall slaughter in the sacred place where the sin offering and the holocaust are slaughtered; because, like the sin offering, the guilt offering belongs to the priest and is most sacred.) [14]*Then the priest shall take some of the blood of the guilt offering and put it on the tip of the man's right ear, the thumb of his right hand, and the big toe of his right foot. [15]The priest shall also take the log of oil and

pour some of it into the palm of his own left hand; [16]then, dipping his right forefinger in it, he shall sprinkle it seven times before the LORD. [17]Of the oil left in his hand the priest shall put some on the tip of the man's right ear, the thumb of his right hand, and the big toe of his right foot, over the blood of the guilt offering. [18]The rest of the oil in his hand the priest shall put on the head of the man being purified. Thus shall the priest make atonement for him before the LORD. [19]Only after he has offered the sin offering in atonement for the man's uncleanness shall the priest slaughter the holocaust [20]and offer it, together with the cereal offering, on the altar before the LORD. When the priest has thus made atonement for him, the man will be clean.

Poor Leper's Sacrifice

[21]"If a man is poor and cannot afford so much, he shall take one male lamb for a guilt offering, to be used as a wave offering in atonement for himself, one tenth of an ephah of fine flour mixed with oil for a cereal offering, a log of oil, [22]†and two turtledoves or pigeons, which he can more easily afford, the one as a sin offering and the other as a holocaust. [23]On the eighth day of his purification he shall bring them to the priest, at the entrance of the meeting tent before the LORD. [24]Taking the guilt-offering lamb, along with the log of oil, the priest shall wave them as a wave offering before the LORD. [25]When he has slaughtered the guilt-offering lamb, he shall take some of its blood, and put it on the tip of the right ear of the man being purified, on the thumb of his right hand, and on the big toe of his right foot. [26]The priest shall then pour some of the oil into the palm of his own left hand [27]and with his right forefinger sprinkle it seven times before the LORD. [28]Some of the oil in his hand the priest shall also put on the tip of the man's right ear, the thumb of his right hand, and the big toe of his right foot, over the blood of the guilt offering. [29]The rest of the oil in his hand the priest shall put on the man's head. Thus shall he make atonement for him before the LORD. [30]Then, of the turtledoves or pigeons, such as the man can afford, [31]the priest shall offer up one as a sin offering and the other as a holocaust, along with the cereal offering. Thus shall the priest make atonement before the LORD for the man who is to be purified. [32]This is the law for one afflicted with leprosy who has insufficient means for his purification."

Leprosy of Houses

[33]The LORD said to Moses and Aaron, [34]"When you come into the land of Canaan, which I am giving you

---

*59: 14, 54.   14: 8, 23f.
14/2: Mt 8, 4; Mk 1, 44;
    Lk 5, 14.

†
  14, 4: *Scarlet yarn:* probably used for tying the hyssop sprig to the cedar branchlet.
  14, 5: *Spring water:* literally, "living water," taken from some source of running water, not from a cistern.
  14, 22: *Two turtledoves:* substitutes for the two additional lambs, similar to the offering of a poor woman after childbirth. Cf 12, 8.

to possess, if I put a leprous infection on any house of the land you occupy, **35**the owner of the house shall come and report to the priest, It looks to me as if my house were infected.' **36**The priest shall then order the house to be cleared out before he goes in to examine the infection, lest everything in the house become unclean. Only after this is he to go in to examine the house. **37**If the priest, on examining it, finds that the infection on the walls of the house consists of greenish or reddish depressions which seem to go deeper than the surface of the wall, **38**he shall close the door of the house behind him and quarantine the house for seven days. **39**On the seventh day the priest shall return to examine the house again. If he finds that the infection has spread on the walls, **40**he shall order the infected stones to be pulled out and cast in an unclean place outside the city. **41**The whole inside of the house shall then be scraped, and the mortar that has been scraped off shall be dumped in an unclean place outside the city. **42**Then new stones shall be brought and put in the place of the old stones, and new mortar shall be made and plastered on the house.

43"If the infection breaks out once more after the stones have been pulled out and the house has been scraped and replastered, **44**the priest shall come again; and if he finds that the infection has spread in the house, it is corrosive leprosy, and the house is unclean. **45**It shall be pulled down, and all its stones, beams and mortar shall be hauled away to an unclean place outside the city. **46**Whoever enters a house while it is quarantined shall be unclean until evening. **47**Whoever sleeps or eats in such a house shall also wash his garments. **48**If the priest finds, when he comes to examine the house, that the infection has in fact not spread after the plastering, he shall declare the house clean, since the infection has been healed. **49**To purify the house, he shall take two birds, as well as cedar wood, scarlet yarn, and hyssop. **50**One of the birds he shall slay over an earthen vessel with spring water in it. **51**Then, taking the cedar wood, the hyssop and the scarlet yarn, together with the living bird, he shall dip them all in the blood of the slain bird and the spring water, and sprinkle the house seven times. **52**Thus shall he purify the house with the bird's blood and the spring water, along with the living bird, the cedar wood, the hyssop, and the scarlet yarn. **53**He shall then let the living bird fly away over the countryside outside the city. When he has thus made atonement for it, the house will be clean.

54"This is the law for every kind of human leprosy and scall, **55***for leprosy of garments and houses, **56**as well as for scabs, pustules and blotches, **57**so that it may be manifest when there is a state of uncleanness and when a state of cleanness. This is the law for leprosy."

Personal Uncleanness

15 **1**THE LORD said to Moses and Aaron, **2***"Speak to the Israelites and tell them: Every man who is afflicted with a chronic flow from his private parts is thereby unclean. **3**Such is his uncleanness from this flow that it makes no difference whether the flow drains off or is blocked up; his uncleanness remains. **4**Any bed on which the man afflicted with the flow lies, is unclean, and any piece of furniture on which he sits, is unclean. **5**Anyone who touches his bed shall wash his garments, bathe in water, and be unclean until evening. **6**Whoever sits on a piece of furniture on which the afflicted man was sitting, shall wash his garments, bathe in water, and be unclean until evening. **7**Whoever touches the body of the afflicted man shall wash his garments, bathe in water, and be unclean until evening. **8**If the afflicted man spits on a clean man, the latter shall wash his garments, bathe in water, and be unclean until evening. **9**Any saddle on which the afflicted man rides, is unclean. **10**Whoever touches anything that was under him shall be unclean until evening; whoever lifts up any such thing shall wash his garments, bathe in water, and be unclean until evening. **11**Anyone whom the afflicted man touches with unrinsed hands shall wash his garments, bathe in water, and be unclean until evening. **12**Earthenware touched by the afflicted man shall be broken; and every wooden article shall be rinsed with water.

13"When a man who has been afflicted with a flow becomes free of his affliction, he shall wait seven days for his purification. Then he shall wash his garments and bathe his body in fresh water, and so he will be clean. **14**On the eighth day he shall take two turtledoves or two pigeons, and going before the LORD, to the entrance of the meeting tent, he shall give them to the priest, **15**who shall offer them up, the one as a sin offering and the other as a holocaust. Thus shall the priest make atonement before the LORD for the man's flow.

16"When a man has an emission of seed, he shall bathe his whole body in water and be unclean until evening. **17**Any piece of cloth or leather with seed on it shall be washed with water and be unclean until evening.

18"If a man lies carnally with a woman, they shall both bathe in water and be unclean until evening.

19*"When a woman has her menstrual flow, she shall be in a state of impurity for seven days. Anyone who touches her shall be unclean until evening. **20**Anything on which she lies or sits during her impurity shall be unclean. **21**Anyone who touches her bed shall wash his garments, bathe in water, and be unclean until evening. **22**Whoever touches any article of furniture on which she was sitting, shall wash his garments, bathe in water, and be unclean until evening. **23†**But

---

*

  55: 13, 47-58.   19: 12, 2.5.
  15/2: Nm 5, 2.

†
15, 23: What is added to the legislation by this verse is uncertain in both the Hebrew and the Greek.

if she is on the bed or on the seat when he touches it, he shall be unclean until evening. **24**If a man dares to lie with her, he contracts her impurity and shall be unclean for seven days; every bed on which he then lies also becomes unclean.

25"When a woman is afflicted with a flow of blood for several days outside her menstrual period, or when her flow continues beyond the ordinary period, as long as she suffers this unclean flow she shall be unclean, just as during her menstrual period. **26**Any bed on which she lies during such a flow becomes unclean, as it would during her menstruation, and any article of furniture on which she sits becomes unclean just as during her menstruation. **27**Anyone who touches them becomes unclean; he shall wash his garments, bathe in water, and be unclean until evening.

28"If she becomes freed from her affliction, she shall wait seven days, and only then is she to be purified. **29**On the eighth day she shall take two turtledoves or two pigeons and bring them to the priest at the entrance of the meeting tent. **30**The priest shall offer up one of them as a sin offering and the other as a holocaust. Thus shall the priest make atonement before the Lord for her unclean flow.

31"You shall warn the Israelites of their uncleanness, lest by defiling my Dwelling, which is in their midst, their uncleanness be the cause of their death.

32"This is the law for the man who is afflicted with a chronic flow, or who has an emission of seed, and thereby becomes unclean; **33**as well as for the woman who has her menstrual period, or who is afflicted with a chronic flow; the law for male and female; and also for the man who lies with an unclean woman."

The Day of Atonement

16 **1**AFTER the death of Aaron's two sons, who died when they approached the Lord's presence, the Lord spoke to Moses **2**and said to him, "Tell your brother Aaron that he is not to come whenever he pleases into the sanctuary, inside the veil, in front of the propitiatory on the ark; otherwise, when I reveal myself in a cloud above the propitiatory, he will die. **3**Only in this way may Aaron enter the sanctuary. He shall bring a young bullock for a sin offering and a ram for a holocaust. **4**He shall wear the sacred linen tunic, with the linen drawers next his flesh, gird himself with the linen sash and put on the linen miter. But since these vestments are sacred, he shall not put them on until he has first bathed his body in water. **5**From the Israelite community he shall receive two male goats for a sin offering and one ram for a holocaust.

6"Aaron shall bring in the bullock, his sin offering to atone for himself and for his household. **7**Taking the two male goats and setting them before the Lord at the entrance of the meeting tent, **8**he shall cast lots to determine which one is for the Lord and which for Azazel. **9**The goat that is determined by lot for the Lord, Aaron shall bring in and offer up as a sin offering. **10**But the goat determined by lot for Azazel he shall set alive before the Lord, so that with it he may make atonement by sending it off to Azazel in the desert.

11"Thus shall Aaron offer up the bullock, his sin offering, to atone for himself and for his family. When he has slaughtered it, **12**he shall take a censer full of glowing embers from the altar before the Lord, as well as a double handful of finely ground fragrant incense, and bringing them inside the veil, **13**there before the Lord he shall put incense on the fire, so that a cloud of incense may cover the propitiatory over the commandments; else he will die. **14**Taking some of the bullock's blood, he shall sprinkle it with his finger on the fore part of the propitiatory and likewise sprinkle some of the blood with his finger seven times in front of the propitiatory.

15"Then he shall slaughter the people's sin-offering goat, and bringing its blood inside the veil, he shall do with it as he did with the bullock's blood, sprinkling it on the propitiatory and before it. **16**Thus he shall make atonement for the sanctuary because of all the sinful defilements and faults of the Israelites. He shall do the same for the meeting tent, which is set up among them in the midst of their uncleanness. **17**No one else may be in the meeting tent from the time he enters the sanctuary to make atonement until he departs. When he has made atonement for himself and his household, as well as for the whole Israelite community, **18**he shall come out to the altar before the Lord and make atonement for it also. Taking some of the bullock's and the goat's blood, he shall put it on the horns around the altar, **19**and with his finger sprinkle some of the blood on it seven times. Thus he shall render it clean and holy, purged of the defilements of the Israelites.

The Scapegoat

20"When he has completed the atonement rite for the sanctuary, the meeting tent and the altar, Aaron shall bring forward the live goat. **21**Laying both hands on its head, he shall confess over it all the sinful faults and transgressions of the Israelites, and so put them on the goat's head. He shall then have it led into

---

16, 2: *The sanctuary, inside the veil:* the innermost part of the sanctuary, known also as "the holy of holies." Cf Ex 26, 33f. Here the high priest was allowed to enter only once a year, on *Yom Kippur,* the Day of Atonement. In Heb 9, 3-12 this ceremony is applied to Christ's single act of Redemption, whereby he won for us an everlasting atonement. *Propitiatory:* see note on Ex 25, 17.

16, 8: *Azazel:* perhaps a name for Satan, used only in this chapter. The ancient versions translated this word as "the escaping goat," whence the English word "scapegoat."

16, 13: *Else he will die:* the smoke is to conceal the resplendent majesty of God, the sight of which would strike any man dead.

24: 18, 19.
25: Mt 9, 20; Mk 5, 25; Lk 8, 43.
16/2: Heb 9, 6-12.
5: Nm 29, 11.
14: Heb 9, 13.25.
15: Heb 5, 1; 6, 19.
18: Ex 30, 12.
21: Is 53, 6; 2 Cor 5, 21.

the desert by an attendant. **22***Since the goat is to carry off their iniquities to an isolated region, it must be sent away into the desert.

23†"After Aaron has again gone into the meeting tent, he shall strip off and leave in the sanctuary the linen vestments he had put on when he entered there. **24**After bathing his body with water in a sacred place, he shall put on his vestments, and then come out and offer his own and the people's holocaust, in atonement for himself and for the people, **25**and also burn the fat of the sin offering on the altar.

26"The man who has led away the goat for Azazel shall wash his garments and bathe his body in water; only then may he enter the camp. **27***The sin-offering bullock and goat whose blood was brought into the sanctuary to make atonement, shall be taken outside the camp, where their hides and flesh and offal shall be burned up in the fire. **28**The one who burns them shall wash his garments and bathe his body in water; only then may he enter the camp.

The Fast

29*†"This shall be an everlasting ordinance for you: on the tenth day of the seventh month every one of you, whether a native or a resident alien, shall mortify himself and shall do no work. **30**Since on this day atonement is made for you to make you clean, so that you may be cleansed of all your sins before the LORD, **31**by everlasting ordinance it shall be a most solemn sabbath for you, on which you must mortify yourselves.

32"This atonement is to be made by the priest who has been anointed and ordained to the priesthood in succession to his father. He shall wear the linen garments, the sacred vestments, **33**and make atonement for the sacred sanctuary, the meeting tent and the altar, as well as for the priests and all the people of the community. **34***This, then, shall be an everlasting ordinance for you: once a year atonement shall be made for all the sins of the Israelites."

Thus was it done, as the LORD had commanded Moses.

IV: CODE OF LEGAL HOLINESS

Sacredness of Blood

17 **1**THE LORD SAID TO MOSES, **2**"Speak to Aaron and his sons, as well as to all the Israelites, and tell them: This is what the LORD has commanded. **3**†Any Israelite who slaughters an ox or a sheep or a goat, whether in the camp or outside of it, **4**without first bringing it to the entrance of the meeting tent to present it as an offering to the LORD in front of his Dwelling, shall be judged guilty of bloodshed; and for this, such a man shall be cut off from among his people. **5**Therefore, such sacrifices as they used to offer up in the open field the Israelites shall henceforth offer to the LORD, bringing them to the priest at the entrance of the meeting tent and sacrificing them there as peace offerings to the LORD. **6**The priest shall splash the blood on the altar of the LORD at the entrance of the meeting tent and there burn the fat for an odor pleasing to the LORD. **7***No longer shall they offer their sacrifices to the satyrs to whom they used to render their wanton worship. This shall be an everlasting ordinance for them and their descendants.

8"Tell them, therefore: Anyone, whether of the house of Israel or of the aliens residing among them, who offers a holocaust or sacrifice **9**without bringing it to the entrance of the meeting tent to offer it to the LORD, shall be cut off from his kinsmen. **10***And if anyone, whether of the house of Israel or of the aliens residing among them, partakes of any blood, I will set myself against that one who partakes of blood and will cut him off from among his people. **11***†Since the life of a living body is in its blood, I have made you put it on the altar, so that atonement may thereby be made for your own lives, because it is the blood, as the seat of life, that makes atonement. **12**That is why I have told the Israelites: No one among you, not even a resident alien, may partake of blood.

13"Anyone hunting, whether of the Israelites or of the aliens residing among them, who catches an animal or a bird that may be eaten, shall pour out its blood and cover it with earth. **14***Since the life of every living body is its blood, I have told the Israelites: You shall not partake of the blood of any meat. Since the life of every living body is its blood, anyone who partakes of it shall be cut off.

15*"Everyone, whether a native or an alien, who eats of an animal that died of itself or was killed by a wild beast, shall wash his garments, bathe in water, and be

---

† 16, 23: This verse is best read after v 25. According to later Jewish practice the high priest again went into the holy of holies to remove the censer.

16, 29: *Mortify himself:* literally, "afflict his soul"; traditionally understood by the Jews as signifying abstinence from all food. This is the only fast day prescribed in the Mosaic law.

17, 3ff: The ancients considered blood the seat and sign of life, and therefore something sacred, even in animals. Cf Gn 9, 4f. Hence, even the ordinary butchering of an animal for meat was looked upon as having a sacrificial character, so that it should be performed at the sanctuary. This law, however, could not be carried out without great difficulty when the Israelites were scattered throughout Palestine, and so was modified in Dt 12, 20ff.

17, 11: *That atonement may thereby be made for your own lives:* hence, the sacrifice of an animal was a symbolic act which substituted the victim's life for the life of the offerer, who thus acknowledged that he deserved God's punishments for his sins. This idea of sacrifice is applied in Heb 9-10 to the death of Christ, inasmuch as "without the shedding of blood there is no forgiveness" (Heb 9, 22).

---

*

22: Is 53, 11.12; Jn 1, 29; 1 Pt 2, 24.
27: Heb 13, 11.
29: 23, 27.32; Nm 29, 7.
34: Heb 9, 7.25.

17/7: Ex 34, 15; Dt 32, 17; 2 Chr 11, 15; 1 Cor 10, 20.
10: 3, 17.
11: Gn 9, 4.
14: 7, 26f.
15: 11, 39f; 22, 8.

unclean until evening, and then he will be clean. [16]If he does not wash or does not bathe his body, he shall have the guilt to bear."

The Sanctity of Sex

18 [1]THE LORD said to Moses, [2]"Speak to the Israelites and tell them: I, the LORD, am your God. [3]You shall not do as they do in the land of Egypt, where you once lived, nor shall you do as they do in the land of Canaan, where I am bringing you; do not conform to their customs. [4]My decrees you shall carry out, and my statutes you shall take care to follow. I, the LORD, am your God. [5]*Keep, then, my statutes and decrees, for the man who carries them out will find life through them. I am the LORD.

[6]†"None of you shall approach a close relative to have sexual intercourse with her. I am the LORD. [7]*You shall not disgrace your father by having intercourse with your mother. Besides, since she is your own mother, you shall not have intercourse with her. [8]*You shall not have intercourse with your father's wife, for that would be a disgrace to your father. [9]You shall not have intercourse with your sister, your father's daughter or your mother's daughter, whether she was born in your own household or born elsewhere. [10]You shall not have intercourse with your son's daughter or with your daughter's daughter, for that would be a disgrace to your own family. [11]You shall not have intercourse with the daughter whom your father's wife bore to him, since she, too, is your sister. [12]*You shall not have intercourse with your father's sister, since she is your father's relative. [13]You shall not have intercourse with your mother's sister, since she is your mother's relative. [14]*You shall not disgrace your father's brother by being intimate with his wife, since she, too, is your aunt. [15]You shall not have intercourse with your daughter-in-law; she is your son's wife, and therefore you shall not disgrace her. [16]*†You shall not have intercourse with your brother's wife, for that would be a disgrace to your brother. [17]You shall not have intercourse with a woman and also with her daughter, nor shall you marry and have intercourse with her son's daughter or her daughter's daughter; this would be shameful, because they are related to her. [18]While your wife is still living you shall not marry her sister as her rival; for thus you would disgrace your first wife.

[19]"You shall not approach a woman to have intercourse with her while she is unclean from menstruation. [20]You shall not have carnal relations with your neighbor's wife, defiling yourself with her. [21]*†You shall not offer any of your offspring to be immolated to Molech, thus profaning the name of your God. I am the LORD. [22]*You shall not lie with a male as with a woman; such a thing is an abomination. [23]*You shall not have carnal relations with an animal, defiling yourself with it; nor shall a woman set herself in front of an animal to mate with it; such things are abhorrent.

[24]"Do not defile yourselves by any of these things by which the nations whom I am driving out of your way have defiled themselves. [25]Because their land has become defiled, I am punishing it for its wickedness, by making it vomit out its inhabitants. [26]You, however, whether natives or resident aliens, must keep my statutes and decrees forbidding all such abominations [27]by which the previous inhabitants defiled the land; [28]otherwise the land will vomit you out also for having defiled it, just as it vomited out the nations before you. [29]Everyone who does any of these abominations shall be cut off from among his people. [30]*Heed my charge, then, not to defile yourselves by observing the abominable customs that have been observed before you. I, the LORD, am your God."

Various Rules of Conduct

19 [1]THE LORD said to Moses, [2]*"Speak to the whole Israelite community and tell them: Be holy, for I, the LORD, your God, am holy. [3]*Revere your mother and father, and keep my sabbaths. I, the LORD, am your God.

[4]*"Do not turn aside to idols, nor make molten gods for yourselves. I, the LORD, am your God.

[5]"When you sacrifice your peace offering to the LORD, if you wish it to be acceptable, [6]it must be eaten on the very day of your sacrifice or on the following day. Whatever is left over until the third day shall be burned up in the fire. [7]*If any of it is eaten on the third day, the sacrifice will be unacceptable as refuse; [8]whoever eats of it then shall pay the penalty for having profaned what is sacred to the LORD. Such a one shall be cut off from his people.

[9]"When you reap the harvest of your land, you shall not be so thorough that you reap the field to its very edge, nor shall you glean the stray ears of grain. [10]Likewise, you shall not pick your vineyard bare, nor gather up the grapes that have fallen. These things you shall leave for the poor and the alien. I, the LORD, am your God.

[11]*"You shall not steal. You shall not lie or speak

---

* 18/5: Gal 3, 12.
   7-16: 20, 11-21.
      8: Dt 23, 1; 27, 20; 1 Cor
         5, 1.
   12f: 20, 19.
    14: 20, 20.
    16: 20, 21; Mt 14, 3f;
         Mk 6, 18.
    21: 20, 2-5; Dt 18, 10;
         2 Kgs 16, 3; 21, 6.
    22: 20, 13; Rom 1, 27;
         1 Cor 6, 9f.
   23: 20, 15f; Ex 22, 18.
   30: 20, 23; Dt 18, 9.
19/2: 11, 44; Mt 5, 48;
         1 Pt 1, 16.
      3: Ex 20, 12.
      4: 26, 1; Ex 20, 3-5; 34,
         17; Dt 27, 15.
      7: 7, 18.
      9: 23, 22; Dt 24, 19ff.
    11: Ex 20, 15f.

---

† 18, 6-18: These laws are formulated as directed to the male Israelites only, but naturally the same norms of consanguinity and affinity would apply to the women as well. Marriage, as well as casual intercourse, is here forbidden between men and women of the specified degrees of relationship.

18, 16: *With your brother's wife:* it was the violation of this law which aroused the wrath of John the Baptist against Herod Antipas. Cf Mk 6, 18. An exception to this law is made in Dt 25, 5.

18, 21: *Immolated to Molech:* the reference is to the Canaanite custom of sacrificing children to the god Molech. The little victims were first slain and then cremated. Cf Ez 16, 20ff; 20, 26.31; 23, 37.

falsely to one another. **¹²***"You shall not swear falsely by my name, thus profaning the name of your God. I am the LORD.

¹³*"You shall not defraud or rob your neighbor. You shall not withhold overnight the wages of your day laborer. **¹⁴**You shall not curse the deaf, or put a stumbling block in front of the blind, but you shall fear your God. I am the LORD.

¹⁵*"You shall not act dishonestly in rendering judgment. Show neither partiality to the weak nor deference to the mighty, but judge your fellow men justly. **¹⁶**You shall not go about spreading slander among your kinsmen; nor shall you stand by idly when your neighbor's life is at stake. I am the LORD.

¹⁷*"You shall not bear hatred for your brother in your heart. Though you may have to reprove your fellow man, do not incur sin because of him. **¹⁸***†Take no revenge and cherish no grudge against your fellow countrymen. You shall love your neighbor as yourself. I am the LORD.

¹⁹"Keep my statutes: do not breed any of your domestic animals with others of a different species; do not sow a field of yours with two different kinds of seed; and do not put on a garment woven with two different kinds of thread.

²⁰†"If a man has carnal relations with a female slave who has already been living with another man but has not yet been redeemed or given her freedom, they shall be punished but not put to death, because she is not free. **²¹**The man, moreover, shall bring to the entrance of the meeting tent a ram as his guilt offering to the LORD. **²²**With this ram the priest shall make atonement before the LORD for the sin he has committed, and it will be forgiven him.

²³†"When you come into the land and plant any fruit tree there, first look upon its fruit as if it were uncircumcised. For three years, while its fruit remains uncircumcised, it may not be eaten. **²⁴**In the fourth year, however, all of its fruit shall be sacred to the LORD as a thanksgiving feast to him. **²⁵**Not until the fifth year may you eat its fruit. Thus it will continue its yield for you. I, the LORD, am your God.

²⁶*"Do not eat meat with the blood still in it. Do not practice divination or soothsaying. **²⁷***†Do not clip your hair at the temples, nor trim the edges of your beard. **²⁸**Do not lacerate your bodies for the dead, and do not tattoo yourselves. I am the LORD.

²⁹"You shall not degrade your daughter by making a prostitute of her; else the land will become corrupt and full of lewdness. **³⁰***Keep my sabbaths, and reverence my sanctuary. I am the LORD.

³¹*"Do not go to mediums or consult fortune tellers, for you will be defiled by them. I, the LORD, am your God.

³²"Stand up in the presence of the aged, and show respect for the old; thus shall you fear your God. I am the LORD.

³³*"When an alien resides with you in your land, do not molest him. **³⁴***You shall treat the alien who resides with you no differently than the natives born among you; have the same love for him as for yourself; for you too were once aliens in the land of Egypt. I, the LORD, am your God.

³⁵"Do not act dishonestly in using measures of length or weight or capacity. **³⁶***You shall have a true scale and true weights, an honest ephah and an honest hin. I, the LORD, am your God, who brought you out of the land of Egypt. **³⁷**Be careful, then, to observe all my statutes and decrees. I am the LORD."

Penalties for Various Sins

20 **¹**THE LORD said to Moses, **²***"Tell the Israelites: Anyone, whether an Israelite or an alien residing in Israel, who gives any of his offspring to Molech shall be put to death. Let his fellow citizens stone him. **³***I myself will turn against such a man and cut him off from the body of his people; for in giving his offspring to Molech, he has defiled my sanctuary and profaned my holy name. **⁴**Even if his fellow citizens connive at such a man's crime of giving his offspring to Molech, and fail to put him to death, **⁵**I myself will set my face against that man and his family and will cut off from their people both him and all who join him in his wanton worship of Molech. **⁶***Should anyone turn to mediums and fortunetellers and follow their wanton ways, I will turn against such a one and cut him off from his people. **⁷***Sanctify yourselves, then, and be holy; for I, the LORD, your God, am holy. **⁸**Be careful, therefore, to observe what I, the LORD, who make you holy, have prescribed.

⁹"Anyone who curses his father or mother shall be put to death; since he has cursed his father or mother, he has forfeited his life. **¹⁰***If a man commits adultery with his neighbor's wife, both the adulterer and the adulteress shall be put to death. **¹¹***If a man disgraces

✣
12: Ex 20, 7; Mt 5, 33.
13: Dt 24, 14f.
15: Ex 23, 2f; Dt 1, 17; 16, 19; Ps 82, 2; Prv 24, 23.
17: Mt 18, 15; Lk 17, 3; Gal 6, 1; 1 Jn 3, 14.
18: Mt 5, 43; 19, 19; 22, 39; Mk 12, 31; Rom 13, 9; Gal 5, 14; Jas 2, 8.
26: 3, 17; Dt 18, 10; 2 Kgs 17, 17; 21, 6; 2 Chr 33, 6.
27: 21, 5.
30: 26, 2; Ex 20, 8.
31: 20, 6.27; Dt 18, 11; Is 8, 19.
33: Ex 22, 20; 23, 9; Jer 22, 3; Mal 3, 5.
34: Dt 10, 19.
36: Dt 25, 13.15; Prv 11, 1; 16, 11; 20, 10; Ez 45, 10.
20/2: 18, 21.
3: Ez 23, 39.
6: 19, 31.
7: 11, 44; 19, 2; 1 Pt 1, 16.
9: Ex 21, 17; Prv 20, 20; Mt 15, 4; Mk 7, 10.
10: 18, 20; Dt 22, 22; Jn 8, 5.
11: 18, 7f.

† 19, 18: *You shall love your neighbor as yourself:* cited by our Lord as the second of the two most important commandments of God. Cf Mt 22, 39; Mk 12, 31. Although in the present context the word "neighbor" is restricted to "fellow countrymen," in Lk 10, 29-37 Christ extends its meaning to embrace all men, even enemies. Cf also Mt 5, 43ff.

19, 20ff: This law seems out of its proper context here; perhaps it stood originally after 20, 12. *Female slave . . . given her freedom:* reference is to the case treated of in Ex 21, 7-11.

19, 23ff: *Uncircumcised:* by analogy with a newborn boy, the newly planted tree was considered impure until "circumcised" by offering to the LORD all the fruit it bore in the fourth year.

19, 27: See note on 21, 5.

his father by lying with his father's wife, both the man and his stepmother shall be put to death; they have forfeited their lives. **12***If a man lies with his daughter-in-law, both of them shall be put to death; since they have committed an abhorrent deed, they have forfeited their lives. **13***If a man lies with a male as with a woman, both of them shall be put to death for their abominable deed; they have forfeited their lives. **14***If a man marries a woman and her mother also, the man and the two women as well shall be burned to death for their shameful conduct, so that such shamefulness may not be found among you. **15***If a man has carnal relations with an animal, the man shall be put to death, and the animal shall be slain. **16***If a woman goes up to any animal to mate with it, the woman and the animal shall be slain; let them both be put to death; their lives are forfeit. **17***If a man consummates marriage with his sister or his half-sister, they shall be publicly cut off from their people for this shameful deed; the man shall pay the penalty of having had intercourse with his own sister. **18***If a man lies in sexual intercourse with a woman during her menstrual period, both of them shall be cut off from their people, because they have laid bare the flowing fountain of her blood. **19***You shall not have intercourse with your mother's sister or your father's sister; whoever does so shall pay the penalty of incest. **20**If a man disgraces his uncle by having intercourse with his uncle's wife, the man and his aunt shall pay the penalty by dying childless. **21**If a man marries his brother's wife and thus disgraces his brother, they shall be childless because of this incest.

22"Be careful to observe all my statutes and all my decrees; otherwise the land where I am bringing you to dwell will vomit you out. **23***Do not conform, therefore, to the customs of the nations whom I am driving out of your way, because all these things that they have done have filled me with disgust for them. **24***But to you I have said: Their land shall be your possession, a land flowing with milk and honey. I am giving it to you as your own, I, the Lord, your God, who have set you apart from the other nations. **25***You, too, must set apart, then, the clean animals from the unclean, and the clean birds from the unclean, so that you may not be contaminated with the uncleanness of any beast or bird or of any swarming creature in the land that I have set apart for you. **26***To me, therefore, you shall be sacred; for I, the Lord, am sacred, I, who have set you apart from the other nations to be my own.

27*†"A man or a woman who acts as a medium or fortuneteller shall be put to death by stoning; they have no one but themselves to blame for their death."

Sanctity of the Priesthood

21 **1***†THE Lord said to Moses, "Speak to Aaron's sons, the priests, and tell them: None of you shall make himself unclean for any dead person among his people, **2**except for his nearest relatives, his mother or father, his son or daughter, his brother **3**or his maiden sister, who is of his own family while she remains unmarried; for these he may make himself unclean. **4**But for a sister who has married out of his family he shall not make himself unclean; this would be a profanation.

5†"The priests shall not make bare the crown of the head, nor shave the edges of the beard, nor lacerate the body. **6**†To their God they shall be sacred, and not profane his name; since they offer up the oblations of the Lord, the food of their God, they must be holy.

7"A priest shall not marry a woman who has been a prostitute or has lost her honor, nor a woman who has been divorced by her husband; for the priest is sacred to his God. **8**Honor him as sacred who offers up the food of your God; treat him as sacred, because I, the Lord, who have consecrated him, am sacred.

9"A priest's daughter who loses her honor by committing fornication and thereby dishonors her father also, shall be burned to death.

10†"The most exalted of the priests, upon whose head the anointing oil has been poured and who has been ordained to wear the special vestments, shall not bare his head or rend his garments, **11**nor shall he go near any dead person. Not even for his father or mother may he thus become unclean **12***or leave the sanctuary; otherwise he will profane the sanctuary of his God, for with the anointing oil upon him, he is dedicated to his God, to me, the Lord.

13"The priest shall marry a virgin. **14***Not a widow or a woman who has been divorced or a woman who has lost her honor as a prostitute, but a virgin, taken from his own people, shall he marry; **15**otherwise he will have base offspring among his people. I, the Lord, have made him sacred."

Irregularities

16The Lord said to Moses, **17**"Speak to Aaron and tell him: None of your descendants, of whatever generation, who has any defect shall come forward to offer up the food of his God. **18**Therefore, he who has any of the following defects may not come forward: he who is blind, or lame, or who has any disfigurement

---

12: 18, 15.
13: 18, 22.
14: 18, 17; Dt 27, 23.
15: Ex 22, 18; Dt 27, 21.
16: 18, 23.
17: 18, 9; Dt 27, 22.
18: 18, 19.
19: 18, 12f.
23: 18, 30.
24: Ex 3, 8.17; 6, 8.
25: 11, 2-47; Dt 14, 4-20.
26: 11, 44; Ex 19, 6; 1 Pt 1, 16.
27: 19, 31; Ex 22, 17; Dt 18, 11.
21/1: Ez 44, 25.
5: Ez 44, 20.
7: Ez 44, 22.
12: 10, 7.
14: Ez 44, 22.

† 20, 27: This verse is best read immediately after v 6.
21, 1: *Unclean for any dead person:* by preparing the corpse for burial. Cf Nm 6, 6; 19, 11-19.
21, 5: Such mourning customs of the Canaanites were forbidden to all the Israelites, but especially to the priests. Cf 19, 27f.
21, 6: *Sacred:* the same Hebrew word has both the active meaning of "holy," that is, keeping oneself free from profane impurities, and the passive meaning of "sacred," that is, set apart from what is profane and therefore treated with religious reverence.
21, 10: *Bare his head:* see note on 10, 6.

or malformation, ¹⁹or a crippled foot or hand, ²⁰or who is humpbacked or weakly or walleyed, or who is afflicted with eczema, ringworm or hernia. ²¹No descendant of Aaron the priest who has any such defect may draw near to offer up the oblations of the Lord; on account of his defect he may not draw near to offer up the food of his God. ²²He may, however, partake of the food of his God: of what is most sacred as well as of what is sacred. ²³Only, he may not approach the veil nor go up to the altar on account of his defect; he shall not profane these things that are sacred to me, for it is I, the Lord, who make them sacred."

²⁴Moses, therefore, told this to Aaron and his sons and to all the Israelites.

Sacrificial Banquets

22 ¹The Lord said to Moses, ²"Tell Aaron and his sons to respect the sacred offerings which the Israelites consecrate to me; else they will profane my holy name. I am the Lord.

³"Tell them: If any one of you, or of your descendants in any future generation, dares, while he is in a state of uncleanness, to draw near the sacred offerings which the Israelites consecrate to the Lord, such a one shall be cut off from my presence. I am the Lord.

⁴*"No descendant of Aaron who is stricken with leprosy, or who suffers from a flow, may eat of these sacred offerings, unless he again becomes clean. Moreover, if anyone touches a person who has become unclean by contact with a corpse, or if anyone has had an emission of seed, ⁵*or if anyone touches any swarming creature or any man whose uncleanness, of whatever kind it may be, is contagious, ⁶*the one who touches such as these shall be unclean until evening and may not eat of the sacred portions until he has first bathed his body in water; ⁷then, when the sun sets, he again becomes clean. Only then may he eat of the sacred offerings, which are his food. ⁸*He shall not make himself unclean by eating of any animal that has died of itself or has been killed by wild beasts. I am the Lord.

⁹"They shall keep my charge and not do wrong in this matter; else they will die for their profanation. I am the Lord who have consecrated them.

¹⁰*"Neither a lay person nor a priest's tenant or hired servant may eat of any sacred offering. ¹¹But a slave whom a priest acquires by purchase or who is born in his house may eat of his food. ¹²A priest's daughter who is married to a layman may not eat of the sacred contributions. ¹³But if a priest's daughter is widowed or divorced and, having no children, returns to her father's house, she may then eat of her father's food as in her youth. No layman, however,

may eat of it. ¹⁴*If such a one eats of a sacred offering through inadvertence, he shall make restitution to the priest for the sacred offering, with an increment of one fifth of the amount. ¹⁵*The sacred offerings which the Israelites contribute to the Lord the priests shall not allow to be profaned ¹⁶nor in the eating of the sacred offering shall they bring down guilt that must be punished; it is I, the Lord, who make them sacred."

Unacceptable Victims

¹⁷The Lord said to Moses, ¹⁸"Speak to Aaron and his sons and to all the Israelites, and tell them: When anyone of the house of Israel, or any alien residing in Israel, who wishes to offer a sacrifice, brings a holocaust as a votive offering or as a freewill offering to the Lord, ¹⁹*if it is to be acceptable, the ox or sheep or goat that he offers must be an unblemished male. ²⁰*You shall not offer one that has any defect, for such a one would not be acceptable for you. ²¹*When anyone presents a peace offering to the Lord from the herd or the flock in fulfillment of a vow, or as a freewill offering, if it is to find acceptance, it must be unblemished; it shall not have any defect. ²²One that is blind or crippled or maimed, or one that has a running sore or mange or ringworm, you shall not offer to the Lord; do not put such an animal on the altar as an oblation to the Lord. ²³An ox or a sheep that is in any way ill-proportioned or stunted you may indeed present as a freewill offering, but it will not be acceptable as a votive offering. ²⁴One that has its testicles bruised or crushed or torn out or cut off you shall not offer to the Lord. You shall neither do this in your own land ²⁵*nor receive from a foreigner any such animals to offer up as the food of your God; since they are deformed or defective, they will not be acceptable for you."

²⁶The Lord said to Moses, ²⁷*"When an ox or a lamb or a goat is born, it shall remain with its mother for seven days; only from the eighth day onward will it be acceptable, to be offered as an oblation to the Lord. ²⁸You shall not slaughter an ox or a sheep on one and the same day with its young. ²⁹Whenever you offer a thanksgiving sacrifice to the Lord, so offer it that it may be acceptable for you; ³⁰*it must, therefore, be eaten on the same day; none of it shall be left over until the next day. I am the Lord.

³¹"Be careful to observe the commandments which I, the Lord, give you, ³²and do not profane my holy name; in the midst of the Israelites I, the Lord, must be held as sacred. It is I who made you sacred ³³and led you out of the land of Egypt, that I, the Lord, might be your God."

Holy Days

23 ¹The Lord said to Moses, ²"Speak to the Israelites and tell them: The following are the festivals of the Lord, my feast days, which you shall celebrate with a sacred assembly.

³*"For six days work may be done; but the seventh day is the sabbath rest, a day for sacred assembly, on

22/4: 7, 20; 15, 16.
5: 11, 24.43.
6: Heb 10, 22.
8: 17, 15; Dt 14, 21; Ez 44, 31.
10: 1 Sm 21, 6; Mt 12, 4.
14: 5, 16; 27, 13.15.19.
15: 19, 8; Nm 18, 32.
19: 1, 3.10.
20: Dt 15, 21; 17, 1; Mal 1, 8.14.
21: 3, 1.6.
25: Mal 1, 14.
27: Ex 22, 29.
30: 7, 15.
23/3: Ex 20, 8-11; 23, 12; 31, 14f; 34, 21; Dt 5, 12-15; Lk 13, 14.

which you shall do no work. The sabbath shall belong to the LORD wherever you dwell.

Passover

4***"These, then, are the festivals of the LORD which you shall celebrate at their proper time with a sacred assembly. **5***The Passover of the LORD falls on the fourteenth day of the first month, at the evening twilight. **6***The fifteenth day of this month is the LORD's feast of Unleavened Bread. For seven days you shall eat unleavened bread. **7***On the first of these days you shall hold a sacred assembly and do no sort of work. **8**On each of the seven days you shall offer an oblation to the LORD. Then on the seventh day you shall again hold a sacred assembly and do no sort of work."

9The LORD said to Moses, **10**"Speak to the Israelites and tell them: When you come into the land which I am giving you, and reap your harvest, you shall bring a sheaf of the first fruits of your harvest to the priest, **11**†who shall wave the sheaf before the LORD that it may be acceptable for you. On the day after the sabbath the priest shall do this. **12**On this day, when your sheaf is waved, you shall offer to the LORD for a holocaust an unblemished yearling lamb. **13**Its cereal offering shall be two tenths of an ephah of fine flour mixed with oil, as a sweet-smelling oblation to the LORD; and its libation shall be a fourth of a hin of wine. **14**†Until this day, when you bring your God this offering, you shall not eat any bread or roasted grain or fresh kernels. This shall be a perpetual statute for you and your descendants wherever you dwell.

Pentecost

15*"Beginning with the day after the sabbath, the day on which you bring the wave-offering sheaf, you shall count seven full weeks, **16***†and then on the day after the seventh week, the fiftieth day, you shall present the new cereal offering to the LORD. **17**For the wave offering of your first fruits to the LORD, you shall bring with you from wherever you live two loaves of bread made of two tenths of an ephah of fine flour and baked with leaven. **18**Besides the bread, you shall offer to the LORD a holocaust of seven unblemished yearling lambs, one young bull, and two rams, along with their cereal offering and libations, as a sweet-smelling oblation to the LORD. **19***One male goat shall be sacrificed as a sin offering, and two yearling lambs as a peace offering. **20**The priest shall wave the bread of the first fruits and the two lambs as a wave offering before the LORD; these shall be sacred to the LORD and belong to the priest. **21**On this same day you shall by proclamation have a sacred assembly, and no sort of work may be done. This shall be a perpetual statute for you and your descendants wherever you dwell.

22"When you reap the harvest of your land, you shall not be so thorough that you reap the field to its very edge, nor shall you glean the stray ears of your grain. These things you shall leave for the poor and the alien. I, the LORD, am your God."

New Year's Day

23The LORD said to Moses, **24**"Tell the Israelites: On the first day of the seventh month you shall keep a sabbath rest, with a sacred assembly and with the trumpet blasts as a reminder; **25**you shall then do no sort of work, and you shall offer an oblation to the LORD."

The Day of Atonement

26*The LORD said to Moses, **27***"The tenth of this seventh month is the Day of Atonement, when you shall hold a sacred assembly and mortify yourselves and offer an oblation to the LORD. **28**On this day you shall not do any work, because it is the Day of Atonement, when atonement is made for you before the LORD, your God. **29**Anyone who does not mortify himself on this day shall be cut off from his people; **30**and if anyone does any work on this day, I will remove him from the midst of his people. **31**This is a perpetual statute for you and your descendants wherever you dwell: you shall do no work, **32**but shall keep a sabbath of complete rest and mortify yourselves. Beginning on the evening of the ninth of the month, you shall keep this sabbath of yours from evening to evening."

The Feast of Booths

33The LORD said to Moses, **34***†"Tell the Israelites: The fifteenth day of this seventh month is the LORD's feast of Booths, which shall continue for seven days. **35**On the first day there shall be a sacred assembly, and you shall do no sort of work. **36**For seven days you shall offer an oblation to the LORD, and on the eighth day you shall again hold a sacred assembly and offer an oblation to the LORD. On that solemn closing you shall do no sort of work.

37"These, therefore, are the festivals of the LORD on which you shall proclaim a sacred assembly, and offer

---

† 23, 11: *The sabbath:* according to the Jewish tradition this was the feast day itself, the fifteenth of Nisan, which was a special day of rest. Cf v 7. However, some understand here the Saturday of the Passover week, cf Jn 19, 31, or even the Saturday following it.

23, 14: *Any bread:* made from the new grain. The harvest had first to be sanctified for man's use by this offering to God.

23, 16: *The fiftieth:* from the Greek word for this we have the name "Pentecost." Cf 2 Mc 12, 31; Acts 2, 1. It was also called "the feast of the Seven Weeks," or simply "the feast of Weeks" (Nm 28, 26; Dt 16, 10; Tb 2, 1). *The new cereal offering:* of flour made from the new grain. Pentecost was the thanksgiving feast at the end of the grain harvest, which began after Passover. Later tradition made it a commemoration of the giving of the law at Sinai.

23, 34: *Feast of Booths:* the joyful observance of the vintage and fruit harvest. Cf Dt 16, 13. During the seven days of the feast the Israelites camped in booths of branches erected on the roofs of their houses or in the streets in commemoration of their wanderings in the desert, where they dwelt in booths.

---

*

4: Ex 23, 14-19.
5: Nm 9, 2f; 28, 16.
6: Ex 12, 18; 13.3.10; 23, 15; 34, 18.
7: Ex 12, 15; Nm 28, 18.25.
15: Ex 34, 22; Nm 28, 26; Dt 16, 9.

16: Acts 2, 1.
19: Nm 28, 30.
26: 25, 9.
27: 16, 29f; Nm 29, 7.
34: Nm 29, 12; Dt 16, 13; 2 Mc 1, 9.18; Jn 7, 2.

as an oblation to the Lord holocausts and cereal offerings, sacrifices and libations, as prescribed for each day, [38]in addition to those of the Lord's sabbaths, your donations, your various votive offerings and the freewill offerings that you present to the Lord.

[39]*"On the fifteenth day, then, of the seventh month, when you have gathered in the produce of the land, you shall celebrate a pilgrim feast of the Lord for a whole week. The first and the eighth day shall be days of complete rest. [40]†On the first day you shall gather foliage from majestic trees, branches of palms and boughs of myrtles and of valley poplars, and then for a week you shall make merry before the Lord, your God. [41]*By perpetual statute for you and your descendants you shall keep this pilgrim feast of the Lord for one whole week in the seventh month of the year. [42]During this week every native Israelite among you shall dwell in booths, [43]*that your descendants may realize that, when I led the Israelites out of the land of Egypt, I made them dwell in booths. I, the Lord, am your God."

[44]Thus did Moses announce to the Israelites the festivals of the Lord.

The Sanctuary Light

24 [1]THE Lord said to Moses, [2]*"Order the Israelites to bring you clear oil of crushed olives for the light, so that you may keep lamps burning regularly. [3]In the meeting tent, outside the veil that hangs in front of the commandments, Aaron shall set up the lamps to burn before the Lord regularly, from evening till morning. Thus, by a perpetual statute for you and your descendants, [4]*the lamps shall be set up on the pure gold lampstand, to burn regularly before the Lord.

The Showbread

[5]*"You shall take fine flour and bake it into twelve cakes, using two tenths of an ephah of flour for each cake [6]These you shall place in two piles, six in each pile, on the pure gold table before the Lord. [7]On each pile put some pure frankincense, which shall serve as an oblation to the Lord, a token offering for the bread. [8]*Regularly on each sabbath day this bread shall be set out afresh before the Lord, offered on the part of the Israelites by an everlasting agreement. [9]It shall belong to Aaron and his sons, who must eat it in a sacred place, since, as something most sacred among the various oblations to the Lord, it is his by perpetual right."

Punishment of Blasphemy

[10]Among the Israelites there was a man born of an Israelite mother (Shelomith, daughter of Dibri, of the tribe of Dan) and an Egyptian father. [11]This man quarreled publicly with another Israelite and cursed and blasphemed the Lord's name. So the people brought him to Moses, [12]who kept him in custody till a decision from the Lord should settle the case for them. [13]The Lord then said to Moses, [14]"Take the blasphemer outside the camp, and when all who heard him have laid their hands on his head, let the whole community stone him. [15]Tell the Israelites: Anyone who curses his God shall bear the penalty of his sin; [16]*whoever blasphemes the name of the Lord shall be put to death. The whole community shall stone him; alien and native alike must be put to death for blaspheming the Lord's name.

[17]*"Whoever takes the life of any human being shall be put to death; [18]*whoever takes the life of an animal shall make restitution of another animal. A life for a life! [19]Anyone who inflicts an injury on his neighbor shall receive the same in return. [20]*Limb for limb, eye for eye, tooth for tooth! The same injury that a man gives another shall be inflicted on him in return. [21]Whoever slays an animal shall make restitution, but whoever slays a man shall be put to death. [22]*You shall have but one rule, for alien and native alike. I, the Lord, am your God."

[23]*When Moses told this to the Israelites, they took the blasphemer outside the camp and stoned him; they carried out the command that the Lord had given Moses.

The Sabbatical Year

25 [1]THE Lord said to Moses on Mount Sinai, [2]"Speak to the Israelites and tell them: When you enter the land that I am giving you, let the land, too, keep a sabbath for the Lord. [3]*For six years you may sow your field, and for six years prune your vineyard, gathering in their produce. [4]*But during the seventh year the land shall have a complete rest, a sabbath for the Lord, when you may neither sow your field nor prune your vineyard. [5]†The aftergrowth of your harvest you shall not reap, nor shall you pick the grapes of your untrimmed vines in this year of sabbath rest for the land. [6]While the land has its sabbath, all its produce will be food equally for you yourself and for your male and female slaves, for your hired help and the tenants who live with you,

---

*
39: Ex 23, 16; Dt 16, 13.
41: Nm 29, 12-38.
43: Dt 31, 10-13.
24/2: Ex 27, 20f.
4: Ex 25, 31.
5: Ex 25, 30; 1 Kgs 7, 48;
   2 Chr 4, 19; 13, 11;
   Heb 9, 2.
8: 1 Chr 9, 32.
16: 1 Kgs 21, 10.13; Mt 26,
   65f; Jn 10, 33.

17: Gn 9, 5f; Ex 21, 12;
   Nm 35, 31; Dt 19, 11f.
18: Ex 21, 33f.
20: Dt 19, 21; Mt 5, 38.
22: 19, 34; Ex 12, 49;
   Nm 15, 16.
23: Acts 7, 57f.
25/3: Ex 23, 10f.
4: 1 Mc 6, 49.53.

† 23, 40: *Foliage:* literally, "fruit," but here probably used in the general sense of "produce, growth." These branches were used for constructing the "booths" or huts in which the people lived during the feast. Cf Neh 8, 15. However, from about the time of Christ on, the Jews have understood this of "fruit" in the strict sense; hence, branches of lemons and oranges were carried with the other branches in joyous procession.

25, 5ff: As long as the produce of the sabbatical year remains on the field, it remains available to everyone; cf v 12. In Ex 23, 10f the poor and the wild beasts that have no other source of nourishment are alone mentioned.

[7]and likewise for your livestock and for the wild animals on your land.

The Jubilee Year

[8]"Seven weeks of years shall you count—seven times seven years—so that the seven cycles amount to forty-nine years. [9]Then, on the tenth day of the seventh month let the trumpet resound; on this, the Day of Atonement, the trumpet blast shall re-echo throughout your land. [10]*†This fiftieth year you shall make sacred by proclaiming liberty in the land for all its inhabitants. It shall be a jubilee for you, when every one of you shall return to his own property, every one to his own family estate. [11]In this fiftieth year, your year of jubilee, you shall not sow, nor shall you reap the aftergrowth or pick the grapes from the untrimmed vines. [12]Since this is the jubilee, which shall be sacred for you, you may not eat of its produce, except as taken directly from the field.

[13]"In this year of jubilee, then, every one of you shall return to his own property. [14]Therefore, when you sell any land to your neighbor or buy any from him, do not deal unfairly. [15]*On the basis of the number of years since the last jubliee shall you purchase the land from him; and so also, on the basis of the number of years for crops, shall he sell it to you. [16]When the years are many, the price shall be so much the more; when the years are few, the price shall be so much the less. For it is really the number of crops that he sells you. [17]Do not deal unfairly, then; but stand in fear of your God. I, the LORD, am your God.

[18]"Observe my precepts and be careful to keep my regulations, for then you will dwell securely in the land. [19]*The land will yield its fruit and you will have food in abundance, so that you may live there without worry. [20]*Therefore, do not say, 'What shall we eat in the seventh year, if we do not then sow or reap our crop?' [21]I will bestow such blessings on you in the sixth year that there will then be crop enough for three years. [22]*When you sow in the eighth year, you will continue to eat from the old crop; and even into the ninth year, when the crop comes in, you will still have the old to eat from.

Redemption of Property

[23]*"The land shall not be sold in perpetuity; for the land is mine, and you are but aliens who have become my tenants. [24]Therefore, in every part of the country that you occupy, you must permit the land to be redeemed. [25]*When one of your countrymen is reduced to poverty and has to sell some of his property, his closest relative, who has the right to redeem it, may go and buy back what his kinsman has sold. [26]If, however, the man has no relative to redeem his land, but later on acquires sufficient means to buy it back in his own name, [27]he shall make a deduction from the price in proportion to the number of years since the sale, and then pay back the balance to the one to whom he sold it, so that he may thus regain his own property. [28]*But if he does not acquire sufficient means to buy back his land, what he has sold shall remain in the possession of the purchaser until the jubilee, when it must be released and returned to its original owner.

[29]"When someone sells a dwelling in a walled town, he has the right to buy it back during the time of one full year from its sale. [30]But if such a house in a walled town has not been redeemed at the end of a full year, it shall belong in perpetuity to the purchaser and his descendants; nor shall it be released in the jubilee. [31]However, houses in villages that are not encircled by walls shall be considered as belonging to the surrounding farm land; they may be redeemed at any time, and in the jubilee they must be released.

[32]"In levitical cities the Levites shall always have the right to redeem the town houses that are their property. [33]Any town house of the Levites in their cities that had been sold and not redeemed, shall be released in the jubilee; for the town houses of the Levites are their hereditary property in the midst of the Israelites. [34]*Moreover, the pasture land belonging to their cities shall not be sold at all; it must always remain their hereditary property.

[35]*"When one of your fellow countrymen is reduced to poverty and is unable to hold out beside you, extend to him the privileges of an alien or a tenant, so that he may continue to live with you. [36]Do not exact interest from your countryman either in money or in kind, but out of fear of God let him live with you. [37]*You are to lend him neither money at interest nor food at a profit. [38]I, the LORD, am your God, who brought you out of the land of Egypt to give you the land of Canaan and to be your God.

[39]*"When, then, your countryman becomes so impoverished beside you that he sells you his services, do not make him work as a slave. [40]Rather, let him be like a hired servant or like your tenant, working with you until the jubilee year, [41]when he, together with his children, shall be released from your service and return to his kindred and to the property of his ancestors. [42]Since those whom I brought out of the land of Egypt are servants of mine, they shall not be sold as slaves to any man. [43]Do not lord it over them harshly, but stand in fear of your God.

[44]"Slaves, male and female, you may indeed possess, provided you buy them from among the neighboring

---

*

10: Nm 36, 4; Is 61, 2; Ez 46, 17; Lk 4, 19.	25: Ru 2, 20; 4, 4.6; Jer 32, 7f.
15: 27, 18.23.	28: 27, 24.
19: 26, 5.	34: Nm 35, 3.
20: Mt 6, 25.31; Lk 12, 22.29.	35: Dt 15, 7.8.
22: 26, 10.	37: Dt 23, 19.
23: 1 Pt 2, 11.	39: 1 Kgs 9, 22.

---

†

25, 10: *Fiftieth year:* to arrive at this number, the preceding year of jubilee is included in the count, and therefore this is more exactly the forty-ninth year, the seventh sabbatical year. *Liberty:* Israelite slaves were set free (v 50) and landed property was returned to its original owner (v 13): two important laws for preserving the social and economic equilibrium. *Jubilee:* derived from the Hebrew word *yobel,* "ram's horn," which was blown on this occasion.

nations. **45**You may also buy them from among the aliens who reside with you and from their children who are born and reared in your land. Such slaves you may own as chattels, **46***and leave to your sons as their hereditary property, making them perpetual slaves. But you shall not lord it harshly over any of the Israelites, your kinsmen.

47"When one of your countrymen is reduced to such poverty that he sells himself to a wealthy alien who has a permanent or a temporary residence among you, or to one of the descendants of an immigrant family, **48**even after he has thus sold his services he still has the right of redemption; he may be redeemed by one of his own brothers, **49**or by his uncle or cousin, or by some other relative or fellow clansman; or, if he acquires the means, he may redeem himself. **50**With his purchaser he shall compute the years from the sale to the jubilee, distributing the sale price over these years as though he had been hired as a day laborer. **51**The more such years there are, the more of the sale price he shall pay back as ransom; **52**the fewer years there are left before the jubilee year, the more he has to his credit; in proportion to his years of service shall he pay his ransom. **53**The alien shall treat him as a servant hired on an annual basis, and he shall not lord it over him harshly under your very eyes. **54***If he is not thus redeemed, he shall nevertheless be released, together with his children, in the jubilee year. **55**For to me the Israelites belong as servants; they are servants of mine, because I brought them out of the land of Egypt, I, the LORD, your God.

The Reward of Obedience

26 **1***"DO not make false gods for yourselves. You shall not erect an idol or a sacred pillar for yourselves, nor shall you set up a stone figure for worship in your land; for I, the LORD, am your God. **2***Keep my sabbaths, and reverence my sanctuary. I am the LORD.

3†"If you live in accordance with my precepts and are careful to observe my commandments, **4***I will give you rain in due season, so that the land will bear its crops, and the trees their fruit; **5**your threshing will last till vintage time, and your vintage till the time for sowing, and you will have food to eat in abundance, so that you may dwell securely in your land. **6**I will establish peace in the land, that you may lie down to rest without anxiety. I will rid the country of ravenous beasts, and keep the sword of war from sweeping across your land. **7**You will rout your enemies and lay them low with your sword. **8**Five of you will put a hundred of your foes to flight, and a hundred of you

will chase ten thousand of them, till they are cut down by your sword. **9**I will look with favor upon you, and make you fruitful and numerous, as I carry out my covenant with you. **10***So much of the old crops will you have stored up for food that you will have to discard them to make room for the new. **11***I will set my Dwelling among you, and will not disdain you. **12**Ever present in your midst, I will be your God, and you will be my people; **13**for it is I, the LORD, your God, who brought you out of the land of the Egyptians and freed you from their slavery, breaking the yoke they had laid upon you and letting you walk erect.

Punishment of Disobedience

14"But if you do not heed me and do not keep all these commandments, **15**if you reject my precepts and spurn my decrees, refusing to obey all my commandments and breaking my covenant, **16**then I, in turn, will give you your deserts. I will punish you with terrible woes—with wasting and fever to dim the eyes and sap the life. You will sow your seed in vain, for your enemies will consume the crop. **17***I will turn against you, till you are beaten down before your enemies and lorded over by your foes. You will take to flight though no one pursues you.

18"If even after this you do not obey me, I will increase the chastisement for your sins sevenfold, **19**to break your haughty confidence. I will make the sky above you as hard as iron, and your soil as hard as bronze, **20**so that your strength will be spent in vain; your land will bear no crops, and its trees no fruit.

21"If then you become defiant in your unwillingness to obey me, I will multiply my blows another sevenfold, as your sins deserve. **22**I will unleash the wild beasts against you, to rob you of your children and wipe out your livestock, till your population dwindles away and your roads become deserted.

23"If, with all this, you still refuse to be chastened by me and continue to defy me, **24***I, too, will defy you and will smite you for your sins seven times harder than before. **25**I will make the sword, the avenger of my covenant, sweep over you. Though you then huddle together in your walled cities, I will send in pestilence among you, till you are forced to surrender to the enemy. **26***And as I cut off your supply of bread, ten women will need but one oven for baking all the bread they dole out to you in rations—not enough food to still your hunger.

27"If, despite all this, you still persist in disobeying and defying me, **28**I, also, will meet you with fiery defiance and will chastise you with sevenfold fiercer punishment for your sins, **29*†**till you begin to eat the

---

† 26, 3-45: Since God's covenant was with the Israelite nation as a whole, these promises and threats are made primarily to the entire community. The rewards and punishments are of a temporal nature because the community as such exists only here on earth, not in the hereafter.

26, 29: *Eat the flesh of your own sons and daughters:* extreme famine in cities under siege often forced their inhabitants to such dire means of subsistence. Cf Dt 28, 53; Jer 19, 9; Ez 5, 10; 2 Kgs 6, 28f.

*
46: Is 14, 1f.
54: Ex 21, 2f.
26/1: 19, 4; Ex 20, 4; Nm 33, 52; Dt 5, 8.
2: Ex 20, 8.
4: Ps 85, 13.
10: 25, 22.

11f: Ex 29, 45; Ez 37, 26ff; 2 Cor 6, 16.
17: Dt 28, 25.
24f: Jer 2, 30; Ez 5, 17; 14, 17.
26: Is 9, 19; Ez 4, 16; 5, 16; 14, 13; Mi 6, 14.
29: Is 9, 18.

flesh of your own sons and daughters. **30***I will demolish your high places, overthrow your incense stands, and cast your corpses on those of your idols. In my abhorrence of you, **31**I will lay waste your cities and devastate your sanctuaries, refusing to accept your sweet-smelling offerings. **32***So devastated will I leave the land that your very enemies who come to live there will stand aghast at the sight of it. **33***You yourselves I will scatter among the nations at the point of my drawn sword, leaving your countryside desolate and your cities deserted. **34***Then shall the land retrieve its lost sabbaths during all the time it lies waste, while you are in the land of your enemies; then shall the land have rest and make up for its sabbaths **35**during all the time that it lies desolate, enjoying the rest that you would not let it have on the sabbaths when you lived there.

36"Those of you who survive in the lands of their enemies I will make so fainthearted that, if leaves rustle behind them, they will flee headlong, as if from the sword, though no one pursues them; **37**stumbling over one another as if to escape a weapon, while no one is after them—so helpless will you be to take a stand against your foes! **38**You will be lost among the Gentiles, swallowed up in your enemies' country. **39***Those of you who survive in the lands of their enemies will waste away for their own and their fathers' guilt.

40"Thus they will have to confess that they and their fathers were guilty of having rebelled against me and of having defied me, **41**so that I, too, had to defy them and bring them into their enemies' land. Then, when their uncircumcised hearts are humbled and they make amends for their guilt, **42***I will remember my covenant with Jacob, my covenant with Isaac, and my covenant with Abraham; and of the land, too, I will be mindful. **43**But the land must first be rid of them, that in its desolation it may make up its lost sabbaths, and that they, too, may make good the debt of their guilt for having spurned my precepts and abhorred my statutes. **44**Yet even so, even while they are in their enemies' land, I will not reject or spurn them, lest, by wiping them out, I make void my covenant with them; for I, the LORD, am their God. **45***I will remember them because of the covenant I made with their forefathers, whom I brought out of the land of Egypt under the very eyes of the Gentiles, that I, the LORD, might be their God."

46†These are the precepts, decrees and laws which the LORD had Moses promulgate on Mount Sinai in the pact between himself and the Israelites.

V: REDEMPTION OF OFFERINGS

Redemption of Votive Offerings

27 **1**THE LORD SAID TO MOSES, **2**"Speak to the Israelites and tell them: When anyone fulfills a vow of offering one or more persons to the LORD, who are to be ransomed at a fixed sum of money, **3**for persons between the ages of twenty and sixty, the fixed sum, in sanctuary shekels, shall be fifty silver shekels for a man, **4**and thirty shekels for a woman; **5**for persons between the ages of five and twenty, the fixed sum shall be twenty shekels for a youth, and ten for a maiden; **6**for persons between the ages of one month and five years, the fixed sum shall be five silver shekels for a boy, and three for a girl; **7**for persons of sixty or more, the fixed sum shall be fifteen shekels for a man, and ten for a woman. **8**However, if the one who took the vow is too poor to meet the fixed sum, the person must be set before the priest, who shall determine the sum for his ransom in keeping with the means of the one who made the vow.

9"If the offering vowed to the LORD is an animal that may be sacrificed, every such animal, when vowed to the LORD, becomes sacred. **10**The offerer shall not present a substitute for it by exchanging either a better for a worse one or a worse for a better one. If he attempts to offer one animal in place of another, both the original and its substitute shall be treated as sacred. **11**If the animal vowed to the LORD is unclean and therefore unfit for sacrifice, it must be set before the priest, **12**†who shall determine its value in keeping with its good or bad qualities, and the value set by the priest shall stand. **13***If the offerer wishes to redeem the animal, he shall pay one fifth more than this valuation.

14"When someone dedicates his house as sacred to the LORD, the priest shall determine its value in keeping with its good or bad points, and the value set by the priest shall stand. **15**If the one who dedicated his house wishes to redeem it, he shall pay one fifth more than the price thus established, and then it will again be his.

16"If the object which someone dedicates to the LORD is a piece of his hereditary land, its valuation shall be made according to the amount of seed required to sow it, the acreage sown with a homer of barley seed being valued at fifty silver shekels. **17**If the dedication of a field is made at the beginning of a jubilee period, the full valuation shall hold; **18***but if

---

† 26, 46: The Book of Leviticus seems originally to have ended here; the following chapter is an appendix.

27, 12: *Determine its value:* fix the price at which the animal may be sold to someone else. Only the original owner must pay the twenty percent tax, as a penalty for buying back what he had vowed to God. So also for houses and fields that are vowed to the LORD, as treated of in the following verses. The money from the sale or from the redemption of such vowed property naturally goes to the sanctuary.

✳
  30: 2 Chr 14, 5; 34, 3.4.7;   39: Ez 4, 17; 24, 23; 33,
      Ez 6, 3-6.   10.
  32: 1 Kgs 9, 8; Jer 9, 11;   42: Ex 6, 5; 2 Kgs 13, 23;
      18, 16; 19, 8; 25, 18;   Ps 106, 45; Ez 16, 20.
      Ez 5, 15.   45: Ex 12, 51.
  33: Jer 9, 16; Zec 7, 14.   27/13: 22, 14.
  34: 25, 2; 2 Chr 36, 21.   18: 25, 15f.

it is some time after this, the priest shall estimate its money value according to the number of years left until the next jubilee year, with a corresponding rebate on the valuation. [19]If the one who dedicated his field wishes to redeem it, he shall pay one fifth more than the price thus established, and so reclaim it. [20]If, instead of redeeming such a field, he sells it to someone else, it may no longer be redeemed; [21]but at the jubilee it shall be released as sacred to the Lord; like a field that is doomed, it shall become priestly property.

[22]"If the field that some man dedicates to the Lord is one he had purchased and not a part of his hereditary property, [23]the priest shall compute its value in proportion to the number of years until the next jubilee, and on the same day the price thus established shall be given as sacred to the Lord; [24]at the jubilee, however, the field shall revert to the hereditary owner of this land from whom it had been purchased.

[25]"Every valuation shall be made according to the standard of the sanctuary shekel. There are twenty gerahs to the shekel.

Offerings Not To Be Redeemed

[26]"Note that a first-born animal, which as such already belongs to the Lord, may not be dedicated by vow to him. If it is an ox or a sheep, it shall be ceded to the Lord; [27]but if it is an unclean animal, it may be redeemed by paying one fifth more than its fixed value. If it is not redeemed, it shall be sold at its fixed value.

[28]"Note, also, that any one of his possessions which a man vows as doomed to the Lord, whether it is a human being or an animal or a hereditary field, shall be neither sold nor ransomed; everything that is thus doomed becomes most sacred to the Lord. [29]All human beings that are doomed lose the right to be redeemed; they must be put to death.

[30]"All tithes of the land, whether in grain from the fields or in fruit from the trees, belong to the Lord, as sacred to him. [31]If someone wishes to buy back any of his tithes, he shall pay one fifth more than their value. [32]The tithes of the herd and the flock shall be determined by ceding to the Lord as sacred every tenth animal as they are counted by the herdsman's rod. [33]It shall not matter whether good ones or bad ones are thus chosen, and no exchange may be made. If any exchange is attempted, both the original animal and its substitute shall be treated as sacred, without the right of being bought back."

[34]These are the commandments which the Lord gave Moses on Mount Sinai for the Israelites.

24: 25, 10.28.41.
26: Ex 13, 2.
28: 1 Sm 15, 21.
30: Nm 18, 21.24; 2 Chr 31, 5f.12; Mal 3, 8.10.

† 27, 27: *An unclean animal:* such as the first-born of an ass, which was unfit for sacrifice. According to Ex 13, 13; 34, 20, a first-born ass was to be redeemed by offering a sheep in its stead, or was to have its neck broken. The present law is probably a later modification of the earlier one.

27, 29: *All human beings that are doomed:* according to some interpreters, this signifies the idolatrous Canaanites, who were doomed to destruction by divine authority; according to others, this drastic law was enacted for the purpose of discouraging private persons from rashly vowing their slaves or other dependents as offerings to God. Cf Ex 22, 19; Dt 13, 13-19.

The Book of Numbers

Introduction

The Book of Numbers derives its name from the account of the two censuses of the Hebrew people taken, one near the beginning and the other toward the end of the journey in the desert (chapters 1 and 26). It continues the story of that journey, begun in Exodus, and describes briefly the experiences of the Israelites for a period of thirty-eight years, from the end of their encampment at Sinai to their arrival at the border of the Promised Land. Numerous legal ordinances are interspersed in the account, making the book a combination of law and history.

The various events described clearly indicate the action of God, who punishes the murmuring of the people by prolonging their stay in the desert, at the same time preparing them by this discipline to be his witnesses among the nations.

In the New Testament Christ and the Apostles derive useful lessons from such events in the Book of Numbers as the brazen serpent (Jn 3, 14f), the sedition of Korah and its consequences (1 Cor 10, 10), the prophecies of Balaam (2 Pt 2, 15f), and the water gushing from the rock (1 Cor 10, 4).

The chief divisions of the Book of Numbers are as follows:

  I: Preparation for the Departure from Sinai (1, 1—10, 10)
  II: From Sinai to the Plains of Moab (10, 11—22, 1)
  III: On the Plains of Moab (22, 2—36, 13)

I: PREPARATION FOR THE DEPARTURE FROM SINAI

The Census

1 ¹IN THE YEAR FOLLOWING THAT of the Israelites' departure from the land of Egypt, on the first day of the second month, the Lord said to Moses in the meeting tent in the desert of Sinai: ²*†"Take a census of the whole community of the Israelites, by clans and ancestral houses, registering each male individually. ³You and Aaron shall enroll in companies all the men in Israel of twenty years or more who are fit for military service.

Moses' Assistants

⁴"To assist you there shall be a man from each tribe, the head of his ancestral house. ⁵*These are the names of those who are to assist you:

from Reuben: Elizur, son of Shedeur;
⁶from Simeon: Shelumiel, son of Zurishaddai;
⁷from Judah: Nahshon, son of Amminadab;
⁸from Issachar: Nethanel, son of Zuar;
⁹from Zebulun: Eliab, son of Helon;
¹⁰from Ephraim: Elishama, son of Ammihud, and from Manasseh: Gamaliel, son of Pedahzur, for the descendants of Joseph;
¹¹from Benjamin: Abidan, son of Gideoni;
¹²from Dan: Ahiezer, son of Ammishaddai;
¹³from Asher: Pagiel, son of Ochran;
¹⁴from Gad: Eliasaph, son of Reuel;
¹⁵from Naphtali: Ahira, son of Enan."

¹⁶*†These were councilors of the community, princes of their ancestral tribes, chiefs of the troops of Israel. ¹⁷So Moses and Aaron took these men who had been designated, ¹⁸and assembled the whole community on the first day of the second month. Every man of twenty years or more then declared his name and lineage according to clan and ancestral house, ¹⁹as the Lord had commanded Moses.

Count of the Twelve Tribes

This is their census as taken in the desert of Sinai. ²⁰Of the descendants of Reuben, the first-born of Israel, registered by lineage in clans and ancestral houses: when all the males of twenty years or more who were fit for military service were polled, ²¹forty-six thousand five hundred were enrolled in the tribe of Reuben.

²²Of the descendants of Simeon, registered by lineage in clans and ancestral houses: when all the males of twenty years or more who were fit for military service were polled, ²³fifty-nine thousand three hundred were enrolled in the tribe of Simeon.

²⁴Of the descendants of Gad, registered by lineage in clans and ancestral houses: when all the males of twenty years or more who were fit for military service

---

1/2f: 14, 29; 26, 2-51.   16: Ex 18, 21.25.
5-15: 10, 14-27.

† 1, 2: All Israel was divided into tribes, each tribe into clans, and each clan into ancestral houses.
1, 16: *Troops:* literally "thousands"; this division of the Israelites, with its subdivisions of "hundreds, fifties and tens," was primarily for military and judicial purposes. Cf Ex 18, 21; 2 Sm 18, 1.

were polled, **25**forty-five thousand six hundred and fifty were enrolled in the tribe of Gad.

26Of the descendants of Judah, registered by lineage in clans and ancestral houses: when all the males of twenty years or more who were fit for military service were polled, **27**seventy-four thousand six hundred were enrolled in the tribe of Judah.

28Of the descendants of Issachar, registered by lineage in clans and ancestral houses: when all the males of twenty years or more who were fit for military service were polled, **29**fifty-four thousand four hundred were enrolled in the tribe of Issachar.

30Of the descendants of Zebulun, registered by lineage in clans and ancestral houses: when all the males of twenty years or more who were fit for military service were polled, **31**fifty-seven thousand four hundred were enrolled in the tribe of Zebulun.

32Of the descendants of Joseph—

Of the descendants of Ephraim, registered by lineage in clans and ancestral houses: when all the males of twenty years or more who were fit for military service were polled, **33**forty thousand five hundred were enrolled in the tribe of Ephraim.

34Of the descendants of Manasseh, registered by lineage in clans and ancestral houses: when all the males of twenty years or more who were fit for military service were polled, **35**thirty-two thousand two hundred were enrolled in the tribe of Manasseh.

36Of the descendants of Benjamin, registered by lineage in clans and ancestral houses: when all the males of twenty years or more who were fit for military service were polled, **37**thirty-five thousand four hundred were enrolled in the tribe of Benjamin.

38Of the descendants of Dan, registered by lineage in clans and ancestral houses: when all the males of twenty years or more who were fit for military service were polled, **39**sixty-two thousand seven hundred were enrolled in the tribe of Dan.

40Of the descendants of Asher, registered by lineage in clans and ancestral houses: when all the males of twenty years or more who were fit for military service were polled, **41**forty-one thousand five hundred were enrolled in the tribe of Asher.

42Of the descendants of Naphtali, registered by lineage in clans and ancestral houses: when all the males of twenty years or more who were fit for military service were polled, **43**fifty-three thousand four hundred were enrolled in the tribe of Naphtali.

44It was these who were registered, each according to his ancestral house, in the census taken by Moses and Aaron and the twelve princes of Israel. **45**The total number of the Israelites of twenty years or more who were fit for military service, registered by ancestral houses, **46**was six hundred and three thousand, five hundred and fifty.

Levites Omitted in the Census

47*†The Levites, however, were not registered by ancestral tribe with the others. **48**For the LORD had told Moses, **49**"The tribe of Levi alone you shall not enroll nor include in the census along with the other Israelites. **50***You are to give the Levites charge of the Dwelling of the commandments with all its equipment and all that belongs to it. It is they who shall carry the Dwelling with all its equipment and who shall be its ministers. They shall therefore camp around the Dwelling. **51***When the Dwelling is to move on, the Levites shall take it down; when the Dwelling is to be pitched, it is the Levites who shall set it up. Any layman who comes near it shall be put to death. **52***While the other Israelites shall camp by companies, each in his own division of the camp, **53***the Levites shall camp around the Dwelling of the commandments. Otherwise God's wrath will strike the Israelite community. The Levites, then, shall have charge of the Dwelling of the commandments." **54**All this the Israelites fulfilled as the LORD had commanded Moses.

Arrangement of the Tribes

2 **1**THE LORD said to Moses and Aaron: **2***"The Israelites shall camp, each in his own division, under the ensigns of their ancestral houses. They shall camp around the meeting tent, but at some distance from it.

3†"Encamped on the east side, toward the sunrise, shall be the divisional camp of Judah, arranged in companies. [The prince of the Judahites was Nahshon, son of Amminadab, **4**and his soldiers amounted in the census to seventy-four thousand six hundred.] **5**With Judah shall camp the tribe of Issachar [Their prince was Nethanel, son of Zuar, **6**and his soldiers amounted in the census to fifty-four thousand four hundred.] **7**and the tribe of Zebulun. [Their prince was Eliab, son of Helon, **8**and his soldiers amounted in the census to fifty-seven thousand four hundred. **9**The total number of those registered by companies in the camp of Judah was one hundred and eighty-six thousand four hundred.] These shall be first on the march.

10"On the south side shall be the divisional camp of Reuben, arranged in companies. [Their prince was Elizur, son of Shedeur, **11**and his soldiers amounted in the census to forty-six thousand five hundred.] **12**Beside them shall camp the tribe of Simeon [Their prince was Shelumiel, son of Zurishaddai, **13**and his soldiers amounted in the census to fifty-nine thousand three hundred.] **14**and next the tribe of Gad. [Their prince was Eliasaph, son of Reuel, **15**and his soldiers amounted in the census to forty-five thousand six hundred and fifty. **16**The total number of those registered

---

✸
47: 2, 33; 3, 14-39; 26, 57-62.
50: 3, 7f; 4, 2-49; 1 Chr 6, 48.
51: 3, 10.38; 18, 7; 2 Sm 6, 6f; 1 Chr 13, 10.
52: 2, 2.34.
53: 3, 7f.38; 8, 19; 18, 4f.
2/2: 1, 52.

†
1, 47: The Levites were not enrolled in this census, which was principally for military purposes, but a separate census was made of them. Cf 3, 15f.39.
2, 3-31: A similar arrangement of the tribes around the central sanctuary in the ideal Israelite state is given in Ez 48.

by companies in the camp of Reuben was one hundred and fifty-one thousand four hundred and fifty.] These shall be second on the march.

¹⁷"Then the meeting tent and the camp of the Levites shall set out in the middle of the line. As in camp, so also on the march, every man shall be in his proper place, with his own division.

¹⁸"On the west side shall be the divisional camp of Ephraim, arranged in companies. [Their prince was Elishama, son of Ammihud, ¹⁹and his soldiers amounted in the census to forty thousand five hundred.] ²⁰Beside them shall camp the tribe of Manasseh [Their prince was Gamaliel, son of Pedahzur, ²¹and his soldiers amounted in the census to thirty-two thousand two hundred.] ²²and the tribe of Benjamin. [Their prince was Abidan, son of Gideoni, ²³and his soldiers amounted in the census to thirty-five thousand four hundred. ²⁴The total number of those registered by companies in the camp of Ephraim was one hundred and eight thousand one hundred.] These shall be third on the march.

²⁵"On the north side shall be the divisional camp of Dan, arranged in companies. [Their prince was Ahiezer, son of Ammishaddai, ²⁶and his soldiers amounted in the census to sixty-two thousand seven hundred.] ²⁷Beside them shall camp the tribe of Asher [Their prince was Pagiel, son of Ochran, ²⁸and his soldiers amounted in the census to forty-one thousand five hundred.] ²⁹and next the tribe of Naphtali. [Their prince was Ahira, son of Enan, ³⁰and his soldiers amounted in the census to fifty-three thousand four hundred. ³¹The total number of those registered by companies in the camp of Dan was one hundred and fifty-seven thousand six hundred.] These shall be the last of the divisions on the march."

³²"This was the census of the Israelites taken by ancestral houses. The total number of those registered by companies in the camps was six hundred and three thousand five hundred and fifty. ³³The Levites, however, were not registered with the other Israelites, for so the LORD had commanded Moses. ³⁴The Israelites did just as the LORD had commanded Moses; both in camp and on the march they were in their own divisions, every man according to his clan and his ancestral house.

The Sons of Aaron

3 ¹THE following were the descendants of Aaron and Moses at the time that the LORD spoke to Moses on Mount Sinai. ²*The sons of Aaron were Nadab his first-born, Abihu, Eleazar, and Ithamar. ³These are the names of the sons of Aaron, the anointed priests who were ordained to exercise the priesthood. ⁴*But when Nadab and Abihu offered pro-

fane fire before the LORD in the desert of Sinai, they met death in the presence of the LORD, and left no sons. Thereafter only Eleazar and Ithamar performed the priestly functions under the direction of their father Aaron.

Levites in Place of the First-born

⁵Now the LORD said to Moses: ⁶*"Summon the tribe of Levi and present them to Aaron the priest, as his assistants. ⁷*They shall discharge his obligations and those of the whole community before the meeting tent by serving at the Dwelling. ⁸They shall have custody of all the furnishings of the meeting tent and discharge the duties of the Israelites in the service of the Dwelling. ⁹*You shall give the Levites to Aaron and his sons; they have been set aside from among the Israelites as dedicated to me. ¹⁰*But only Aaron and his descendants shall you appoint to have charge of the priestly functions. Any layman who comes near shall be put to death."

¹¹The LORD said to Moses, ¹²*"It is I who have chosen the Levites from the Israelites in place of every first-born that opens the womb among the Israelites. The Levites, therefore, are mine, ¹³because every first-born is mine. When I slew all the first-born in the land of Egypt, I made all the first-born in Israel sacred to me, both of man and of beast. They belong to me; I am the LORD."

Census of the Levites

¹⁴The LORD said to Moses in the desert of Sinai, ¹⁵*"Take a census of the Levites by ancestral houses and clans, registering every male of a month or more." ¹⁶Moses, therefore, took their census in accordance with the command the LORD had given him.

¹⁷*The sons of Levi were named Gershon, Kohath and Merari. ¹⁸The descendants of Gershon, by clans, were named Libni and Shimei. ¹⁹The descendants of Kohath, by clans, were Amram, Izhar, Hebron and Uzziel. ²⁰The descendants of Merari, by clans, were Mahli and Mushi. These were the clans of the Levites by ancestral houses.

Duties of the Levitical Clans

²¹To Gershon belonged the clan of the Libnites and the clan of the Shimeites; these were the clans of the Gershonites. ²²When all their males of a month or more were registered, they numbered seven thousand five hundred. ²³The clans of the Gershonites camped behind the Dwelling, to the west. ²⁴The prince of their ancestral house of Eliasaph, son of Lael. ²⁵*†At the meeting tent they had charge of whatever pertained to the Dwelling, the tent and its covering, the curtain at the entrance of the meeting tent, ²⁶the hangings of

---

32-33: 1, 46-49.
  3/2: Ex 6, 23.
    4: 26, 61; Lv 10, 1f;
       1 Chr 24, 2.
  6: 18, 2.
    7: 8, 24.
    9: 8, 19.
   10: 1, 51; 18, 7.

12f: 3, 41; 8, 16f; Ex 13, 2.
     12.15.
 15: 3, 39; 26, 62.
17-20: 26, 57; Gn 46, 11;
       Ex 6, 16-19;
       1 Chr 6, 1f.16-19.
25-26: Ex 26, 7.14.36; 36, 14.

† 3, 25f: The Gershonites had two wagons for transporting these things; cf 7, 7. For a description of *the Dwelling*, see Ex 26, 1-6; *the tent*, Ex 26, 7-13; *its covering*, Ex 26, 14; *the curtain at the entrance*, Ex 26, 36; *the hangings of the court*, Ex 27, 9-15; *the curtain at the entrance of the court*, Ex 27, 16; *the ropes* of the Dwelling, Ex 35, 18.

the court, the curtain at the entrance of the court enclosing both the Dwelling and the altar, and the ropes.

27To Kohath belonged the clans of the Amramites, the Izharites, the Hebronites, and the Uzzielites; these were the clans of the Kohathites. **28**When all their males of a month or more were registered, they numbered eight thousand three hundred. They had charge of the sanctuary. **29**The clans of the Kohathites camped at the south side of the Dwelling. **30**The prince of their ancestral house was Elizaphan, son of Uzziel. **31**†They had charge of whatever pertained to the ark, the table, the lampstand, the altars, the utensils with which the ministry of the sanctuary was exercised, and the veil. **32**The chief prince of the Levites, however, was Eleazar, son of Aaron the priest; he was supervisor over those who had charge of the sanctuary.

33To Merari belonged the clans of the Mahlites and the Mushites; these were the clans of Merari. **34**When all their males of a month or more were registered, they numbered six thousand two hundred. **35**The prince of the ancestral house of the clans of Merari was Zuriel, son of Abihail. They camped at the north side of the Dwelling. **36**†The Merarites were charged with the care of whatever pertained to the boards of the Dwelling, its bars, columns, pedestals, and all its fittings, **37**as well as the columns of the surrounding court with their pedestals, pegs and ropes.

38East of the Dwelling, that is, in front of the meeting tent, toward the sunrise, were camped Moses and Aaron and the latter's sons. They discharged the obligations of the sanctuary for the Israelites. Any layman who came near was to be put to death.

39The total number of male Levites a month old or more whom Moses had registered by clans in keeping with the Lord's command, was twenty-two thousand.

Census and Ransom of First-born

40The Lord then said to Moses, "Take a census of all the first-born males of the Israelites a month old or more, and compute their total number. **41**Then assign the Levites to me, the Lord, in place of all the first-born of the Israelites, as well as their cattle in place of all the first-born among the cattle of the Israelites." **42**So Moses took a census of all the first-born of the Israelites, as the Lord had commanded him. **43**When all the first-born males of a month or more were registered, they numbered twenty-two thousand two hundred and seventy-three.

44The Lord said to Moses: **45**"Take the Levites in place of all the first-born of the Israelites, and the Levites' cattle in place of their cattle, that the Levites may belong to me. I am the Lord. **46**As ransom for the two hundred and seventy-three first-born of the Israelites who outnumber the Levites, **47***you shall take five shekels for each individual, according to the standard of the sanctuary shekel, twenty gerahs to the shekel.

48Give this silver to Aaron and his sons as ransom for the extra number." **49**So Moses took the silver as ransom from those who were left when the rest had been redeemed by the Levites. **50**From the first-born of the Israelites he received in silver one thousand three hundred and sixty-five shekels according to the sanctuary standard. **51**He then gave this ransom silver to Aaron and his sons, as the Lord had commanded him.

Duties Further Defined

4 ¹THE Lord said to Moses and Aaron: **2**"Among the Levites take a total of the Kohathites, by clans and ancestral houses, all the men of the Kohathites **3***†between thirty and fifty years of age; these are to undertake obligatory tasks in the meeting tent.

4"The service of the Kohathites in the meeting tent concerns the most sacred objects. **5**†In breaking camp, Aaron and his sons shall go in and take down the screening curtain and cover the ark of the commandments with it. **6**Over these they shall put a cover of tahash skin, and on top of this spread an all-violet cloth. They shall then put the poles in place. **7**On the table of the Presence they shall spread a violet cloth and put on it the plates and cups, as well as the bowls and pitchers for libations; the established bread offering shall remain on the table. **8**Over these they shall spread a scarlet cloth and cover all this with tahash skin. They shall then put the poles in place. **9**They shall use a violet cloth to cover the lampstand with its lamps, trimming shears, and trays, as well as the various containers of oil from which it is supplied. **10**The lampstand with all its utensils they shall then enclose in a covering of tahash skin, and place on a litter. **11**†Over the golden altar they shall spread a violet cloth, and cover this also with a covering of tahash skin. They shall then put the poles in place. **12**Taking the utensils of the sanctuary service, they shall wrap them all in violet cloth and cover them with tahash skin. They shall then place them on a litter. **13**†After cleansing the altar of its ashes, they shall spread a purple cloth over it. **14**†On this they shall put

---

† 3, 31: The Kohathites had to carry these sacred objects on their shoulders; cf 7, 9. For a description of *the ark,* see Ex 25, 10-22; *the table,* Ex 25, 23-30; *the lampstand,* Ex 25, 31-40; *the altars,* Ex 27, 1-8; 30, 1-10.

3, 36f: The Merarites had four wagons for transporting this heavy material; cf 7, 8. For a description of *the boards, bars, etc., of the Dwelling,* see Ex 26, 15-30; *the columns, pedestals, etc., of the court,* Ex 27, 9-19.

4, 3: *Thirty:* at a later period the Levites began to serve when they were twenty-five (8, 24) or even only twenty years old (1 Chr 23, 24.27; 2 Chr 31, 17; Ezr 3, 8; but cf 1 Chr 23, 3).

4, 5: *The screening curtain:* the veil between the inner and the outer rooms of the sanctuary. Cf Ex 26, 31-33.

4, 11: *The golden altar:* the altar of incense. Cf Ex 30, 1-6.

4, 13: *The altar:* the bronze altar of holocausts. Cf Ex 27, 1-8.

4, 14: *Forks:* used in turning over the sacrificed animal on the fire of the altar. *Basins:* to receive the sacrificial blood; cf Zec 9, 15.

✷ 47: 18, 16; Ex 30, 13; Lv 27, 25; Ez 45, 12.   4/3: 8, 24; 1 Chr 23, 24-27.

all the utensils with which it is served: the fire pans, forks, shovels, basins, and all the utensils of the altar. They shall then spread a covering of tahash skin over this, and put the poles in place.

¹⁵*"Only after Aaron and his sons have finished covering the sacred objects and all their utensils on breaking camp, shall the Kohathites enter to carry them. But they shall not touch the sacred objects; if they do they will die. These, then, are the objects in the meeting tent that the Kohathites shall carry.

¹⁶"Eleazar, son of Aaron the priest, shall be in charge of the oil for the light, the fragrant incense, the established cereal offering, and the anointing oil. He shall be in charge of the whole Dwelling with all the sacred objects and utensils that are in it."

¹⁷The Lord said to Moses and Aaron: ¹⁸"Do not let the group of Kohathite clans perish from the body of the Levites. ¹⁹That they may live and not die when they approach the most sacred objects, this is what you shall do for them: Aaron and his sons shall go in and assign to each of them his task and what he must carry; ²⁰*but the Kohathites shall not go in to look upon the sacred objects, even for an instant; if they do, they will die."

²¹The Lord said to Moses, ²²"Take a total among the Gershonites also, by ancestral houses and clans, ²³of all the men between thirty and fifty years of age; these are to undertake obligatory tasks in the meeting tent. ²⁴This is the task of the clans of the Gershonites, what they must do and what they must carry: ²⁵they shall carry the sheets of the Dwelling, the meeting tent with its covering and the outer wrapping of tahash skin, the curtain at the entrance of the meeting tent, ²⁶the hangings of the court, the curtain at the entrance of the court that encloses both the Dwelling and the altar, together with their ropes and all other objects necessary in their use. Whatever is to be done with these things shall be their task. ²⁷The service of the Gershonites shall be entirely under the direction of Aaron and his sons, with regard to what they must do and what they must carry; you shall make each man of them responsible for what he is to carry; ²⁸This, then, is the task of the Gershonites in the meeting tent; and they shall be under the supervision of Ithamar, son of Aaron the priest.

²⁹"Among the Merarites, too, you shall enroll by clans and ancestral houses ³⁰all their men between thirty and fifty years of age; these are to undertake obligatory tasks in the meeting tent. ³¹*This is what they shall be responsible for carrying, all the years of their service in the meeting tent: the boards of the Dwelling with its bars, columns and pedestals, ³²and the columns of the surrounding court with their pedestals, pegs and ropes. You shall designate for each man of them all the objects connected with his service,

which he shall be responsible for carrying. ³³This, then, is the task of the clans of the Merarites during all their service in the meeting tent under the supervision of Ithamar, son of Aaron the priest."

Number of Adult Levites

³⁴So Moses and Aaron and the princes of the community made a registration among the Kohathites, by clans and ancestral houses, ³⁵of all the men between thirty and fifty years of age. These were to undertake obligatory tasks in the meeting tent; ³⁶as registered by clans, they numbered two thousand seven hundred and fifty. ³⁷Such was the census of all the men of the Kohathite clans who were to serve in the meeting tent, which Moses took, together with Aaron, as the Lord bade him.

³⁸The registration was then made among the Gershonites, by clans and ancestral houses, ³⁹of all the men between thirty and fifty years of age. These were to undertake obligatory tasks in the meeting tent; ⁴⁰as registered by clans and ancestral houses, they numbered two thousand six hundred and thirty. ⁴¹Such was the census of all the men of the Gershonite clans who were to serve in the meeting tent, which Moses took, together with Aaron, at the Lord's bidding.

⁴²Then the registration was made among the Merarites, by clans and ancestral houses, ⁴³of all the men from thirty up to fifty years of age. These were to undertake obligatory tasks in the meeting tent; ⁴⁴as registered by clans, they numbered three thousand two hundred. ⁴⁵Such was the census of the men of the Merarite clans which Moses took, together with Aaron, as the Lord bade him.

⁴⁶Therefore, when Moses and Aaron and the Israelite princes had completed the registration among the Levites, by clans and ancestral houses, ⁴⁷of all the men between thirty and fifty years of age who were to undertake tasks of service or transport of the meeting tent, ⁴⁸the total number registered was eight thousand five hundred and eighty. ⁴⁹According to the Lord's bidding to Moses, they gave them their individual assignments for service and for transport; so the Lord had commanded Moses.

The Unclean Expelled

5 ¹The Lord said to Moses: ²*†"Order the Israelites to expel from camp every leper, and everyone suffering from a discharge, and everyone who has become unclean by contact with a corpse. ³*Male and female alike, you shall compel them to go out of the camp; they are not to defile the camp in which I dwell." ⁴The Israelites obeyed the command that the Lord had given Moses; they expelled them from the camp.

15: 2 Sm 6, 6f; 1 Chr 13, 9f.
20: 1 Sm 6, 19.
31: 3, 36f.

5/2: 19, 11.13; Lv 13, 46; 21, 1; 22, 4.
3: 35, 34.

† 5, 2: For the laws regarding victims of leprosy, see Lv 13-14; those *suffering from a discharge,* Lv 15; the *unclean by contact with a corpse,* 19, 11-22; Lv 21, 1-4.

Unjust Possession

5†The Lord said to Moses, **6***"Tell the Israelites: If a man (or woman) commits a fault against his fellow man and wrongs him, thus breaking faith with the Lord, **7**he shall confess the wrong he has done, restore his ill-gotten goods in full, and in addition give one fifth of their value to the one he has wronged. **8**†However, if the latter has no next of kin to whom restoration of the ill-gotten goods can be made, the goods to be restored shall be the Lord's and shall fall to the priest; this is apart from the atonement ram with which the priest makes amends for the guilty man. **9***Likewise, every sacred contribution that the Israelites are bound to make shall fall to the priest. **10***Each Israelite man may dispose of his own sacred contributions; they become the property of the priest to whom he gives them."

Ordeal for a Suspected Adulteress

11The Lord said to Moses, **12**"Speak to the Israelites and tell them: If a man's wife goes astray and becomes unfaithful to him **13***by having intercourse with another man, though her husband has not sufficient evidence of the fact, so that her impurity remains unproved for lack of a witness who might have caught her in the act; **14**or if a man is overcome by a feeling of jealousy that makes him suspect his wife, whether she was actually impure or not: **15**he shall bring his wife to the priest and shall take along as an offering for her a tenth of an ephah of barley meal. However, he shall not pour oil on it nor put frankincense over it, since it is a cereal offering of jealousy, a cereal offering for an appeal in a question of guilt.

16"The priest shall first have the woman come forward and stand before the Lord. **17***†In an earthen vessel he shall meanwhile put some holy water, as well as some dust that he has taken from the floor of the Dwelling. **18**†Then, as the woman stands before the Lord, the priest shall uncover her head and place in her hands the cereal offering of her appeal, that is, the cereal offering of jealousy, while he himself shall hold the bitter water that brings a curse. **19**Then he shall adjure the woman, saying to her, 'If no other man has had intercourse with you, and you have not gone astray by impurity while under the authority of your husband, be immune to the curse brought by this bitter water. **20**But if you have gone astray while under the authority of your husband and have acted impurely by letting a man other than your husband have intercourse with you'—**21**†so shall the priest adjure the woman with this oath of imprecation—'may the Lord make you an example of malediction and imprecation among your people by causing your thighs to waste away and your belly to swell! **22***†May this water, then, that brings a curse, enter your body to make your belly swell and your thighs waste away!' And the woman shall say, 'Amen, amen!' **23**The priest shall put these imprecations in writing and shall then wash them off into the bitter water, **24**which he is to have the woman drink, so that it may go into her with all its bitter curse. **25**But first he shall take the cereal offering of jealousy from the woman's hand, and having waved this offering before the Lord, shall put it near the altar, **26***where he shall take a handful of the cereal offering as its token offering and burn it on the altar. Only then shall he have the woman drink the water. **27**Once she has done so, if she has been impure and unfaithful to her husband, this bitter water that brings a curse will go into her, and her belly will swell and her thighs will waste away, so that she will become an example of imprecation among her people. **28**If, however, the woman has not defiled herself, but is still pure, she will be immune and will still be able to bear children.

29"This, then, is the law for jealousy: When a woman goes astray while under the authority of her husband and acts impurely, **30**or when such a feeling of jealousy comes over a man that he becomes suspicious of his wife, he shall have her stand before the Lord, and the priest shall apply this law in full to her. **31**†The man shall be free from guilt, but the woman shall bear such guilt as she may have."

Laws Concerning Nazirites

6 **1**†THE Lord said to Moses: **2**"Speak to the Israelites and tell them: When a man (or a woman) solemnly takes the nazirite vow to dedicate himself to the Lord, **3***he shall abstain from wine and strong drink; he may neither drink wine vinegar, other vinegar, or any kind of grape juice, nor eat either fresh

---

† 5, 5-10: The basic law on unjust possession is given in Lv 5, 14-26. The new item here concerns the case where the injured party has died and left no heirs, in which case the restitution must be made to the priest.

5, 8: *Next of kin:* literally "redeemer," a technical term denoting the nearest relative, upon whom devolved the obligation of "redeeming" the family property, in order to keep it within the family. Cf Lv 25, 25; Ru 4, 1-6.

5, 17: *Holy water:* water from the laver that stood in the court of the Dwelling.

5, 18: *Appeal:* by which she invokes the Lord and refers her case to his decision.

5, 21: *An example of malediction and imprecation:* the woman's name would be used in curses and oaths to invoke a similar misfortune on another person or on oneself. Cf Is 65, 15; Jer 29, 22.

5, 22: *Amen:* a Hebrew word meaning, "certainly, truly," used to give assent to a statement, a curse, a blessing, a prayer, or the like; in this sense of "so be it," the Christian liturgy also uses it after prayers and blessings.

5, 31: *Free from guilt:* by fulfilling his obligation of obtaining a decision in the matter.

6, 1ff: *Nazirite:* from the Hebrew word *nazir,* meaning "set apart as sacred, dedicated, vowed." The nazirite vow could be either for a limited period or for life. Those bound by this vow had to abstain from all the products of the grapevine, from cutting or shaving their hair, and from contact with a corpse. They were regarded as men of God like the prophets; cf Am 2, 11f. Examples of lifelong nazirites were Samson (Jgs 13, 4f.7;

---

*   6ff: Lv 5, 21-25.   17: 19, 17.
     9: Dt 18, 3f; Ez 44, 29f.   22: Ps 109, 18.
   10: Lv 10, 12-15.   26: Lv 5, 12.
   13: Lv 18, 20; Jn 8, 4.   6/3f: Jgs 13, 7.14.

or dried grapes. **4**As long as he is a nazirite he shall not eat anything of the produce of the vine; not even unripe grapes or grapeskins. **5***While he is under the nazirite vow, no razor shall touch his hair. Until the period of his dedication to the LORD is over, he shall be sacred, and shall let the hair of his head grow freely. **6***As long as he is dedicated to the LORD, he shall not enter where a dead person is. **7**Not even for his father or mother, his sister or brother, should they die, may he become unclean, since his head bears his dedication to God. **8**As long as he is a nazirite he is sacred to the LORD.

9"If someone dies very suddenly in his presence, so that his dedicated head becomes unclean, he shall shave his head on the day of his purification, that is, on the seventh day. **10**On the eighth day he shall bring two turtledoves or two pigeons to the priest at the entrance of the meeting tent. **11**The priest shall offer up the one as a sin offering and the other as a holocaust, thus making atonement for him for the sin he has committed by reason of the dead person. On the same day he shall reconsecrate his head **12**and begin anew the period of his dedication to the LORD as a nazirite, bringing a yearling lamb as a guilt offering. The previous period is not valid, because his dedicated head became unclean.

13*"This is the ritual for the nazirite: On the day he completes the period of his dedication he shall go to the entrance of the meeting tent, **14**bringing as his offering to the LORD one unblemished yearling lamb for a holocaust, one unblemished yearling ewe lamb for a sin offering, one unblemished ram as a peace offering, along with their cereal offerings and libations, **15**and a basket of unleavened cakes of fine flour mixed with oil and of unleavened wafers spread with oil. **16**The priest shall present them before the LORD, and shall offer up the sin offering and the holocaust for him. **17**He shall then offer up the ram as a peace offering to the LORD, with its cereal offering and libation, and the basket of unleavened cakes. **18***Then at the entrance of the meeting tent the nazirite shall shave his dedicated head, collect the hair, and put it in the fire that is under the peace offering. **19**After the nazirite has shaved off his dedicated hair, the priest shall take a boiled shoulder of the ram, as well as one unleavened cake and one unleavened wafer from the basket, and shall place them in the hands of the nazirite. **20**The priest shall then wave them as a wave offering before the LORD. They become sacred and shall belong to the priest, along with the breast of the wave offering and the leg of the raised offering. Only after this may the nazirite drink wine.

21"This, then, is the law for the nazirite; this is the offering to the LORD which is included in his vow of dedication apart from anything else which his means may allow. Thus shall he carry out the law of his dedication in keeping with the vow he has taken."

The Priestly Blessing

22The LORD said to Moses: **23**"Speak to Aaron and his sons and tell them: This is how you shall bless the Israelites. Say to them:

24The LORD bless you and keep you!
25†The LORD let his face shine upon you, and be gracious to you!
26†The LORD look upon you kindly and give you peace!

27So shall they invoke my name upon the Israelites, and I will bless them."

Offerings of Princes

7 **1***NOW, when Moses had completed the erection of the Dwelling and had anointed and consecrated it with all its equipment (as well as the altar with all its equipment), **2**an offering was made by the princes of Israel, who were heads of ancestral houses; the same princes of the tribes who supervised the census. **3**The offering they brought before the LORD consisted of six baggage wagons and twelve oxen, that is, a wagon for every two princes, and an ox for every prince. These they presented as their offering before the Dwelling.

4The LORD then said to Moses, **5**"Accept their offering, that these things may be put to use in the service of the meeting tent. Assign them to the Levites, to each group in proportion to its duties." **6**So Moses accepted the wagons and oxen, and assigned them to the Levites. **7***He gave two wagons and four oxen to the Gershonites in proportion to their duties, **8**and four wagons and eight oxen to the Merarites in proportion to their duties, under the supervision of Ithamar, son of Aaron the priest. **9***He gave none to the Kohathites, because they had to carry on their shoulders the sacred objects which were their charge.

10*For the dedication of the altar also, the princes brought offerings before the altar on the day it was anointed. **11**But the LORD said to Moses, "Let one prince a day present his offering for the dedication of the altar."

12†The one who presented his offering on the first day was Nahshon, son of Amminadab, prince of the tribe of Judah. **13**His offering consisted of one silver plate weighing a hundred and thirty shekels according to the sanctuary standard and one silver basin weigh-

---

†
16, 17), Samuel (1 Sm 1, 11), and John the Baptizer (Lk 1, 15). At the time of Christ the practice of taking the nazirite vow for a limited period seems to have been quite common, even among the early Christians; cf Acts 18, 18; 21, 23f.26.

6, 25: *Let his face shine:* a Hebrew idiom for "smile."

6, 26: *Peace:* the Hebrew word includes the idea of "prosperity, happiness."

7, 12-88: The repetitious account of the same offerings brought by each of the twelve tribal princes and the summary of them are characteristic of an official registration.

✿
    5: Jgs 13, 5; 16, 17;   7/1: Ex 40, 17.
       1 Sm 1, 11.   7f: 4, 24-33.
    6: 19, 11.16; Lv 21, 11.   9: 3, 31; 4, 4-15.
  13: Acts 21, 24.26.   10: 7, 84.
  18: Acts 18, 18; 21, 24.

ing seventy shekels, both filled with fine flour mixed with oil for a cereal offering; ¹⁴one gold cup of ten shekels' weight filled with incense; ¹⁵one young bull, one ram, and one yearling lamb for a holocaust; ¹⁶one goat for a sin offering; ¹⁷and two oxen, five rams, five goats, and five yearling lambs for a peace offering. This was the offering of Nahshon, son of Amminadab.

¹⁸On the second day Nethanel, son of Zuar, prince of Issachar, made his offering. ¹⁹He presented as his offering one silver plate weighing a hundred and thirty shekels according to the sanctuary standard and one silver basin weighing seventy shekels, both filled with fine flour mixed with oil for a cereal offering; ²⁰one gold cup of ten shekels' weight filled with incense; ²¹one young bull, one ram, and one yearling lamb for a holocaust; ²²one goat for a sin offering; ²³and two oxen, five rams, five goats, and five yearling lambs for a peace offering. This was the offering of Nethanel, son of Zuar.

²⁴On the third day it was the turn of Eliab, son of Helon, prince of the Zebulunites. ²⁵His offering consisted of one silver plate weighing a hundred and thirty shekels according to the sanctuary standard and one silver basin weighing seventy shekels, both filled with fine flour mixed with oil for a cereal offering; ²⁶one gold cup of ten shekels' weight filled with incense; ²⁷one young bull, one ram, and one yearling lamb for a holocaust; ²⁸one goat for a sin offering; ²⁹and two oxen, five rams, five goats, and five yearling lambs for a peace offering. This was the offering of Eliab, son of Helon.

³⁰On the fourth day it was the turn of Elizur, son of Shedeur, prince of the Reubenites. ³¹His offering consisted of one silver plate weighing a hundred and thirty shekels according to the sanctuary standard and one silver basin weighing seventy shekels, both filled with fine flour mixed with oil for a cereal offering; ³²one gold cup of ten shekels' weight filled with incense; ³³one young bull, one ram, and one yearling lamb for a holocaust; ³⁴one goat for a sin offering; ³⁵and two oxen, five rams, five goats, and five yearling lambs for a peace offering. This was the offering of Elizur, son of Shedeur.

³⁶On the fifth day it was the turn of Shelumiel, son of Zurishaddai, prince of the Simeonites. ³⁷His offering consisted of one silver plate weighing a hundred and thirty shekels according to the sanctuary standard and one silver basin weighing seventy shekels, both filled with fine flour mixed with oil for a cereal offering; ³⁸one gold cup of ten shekels' weight filled with incense; ³⁹one young bull, one ram, and one yearling lamb for a holocaust; ⁴⁰one goat for a sin offering; ⁴¹and two oxen, five rams, five goats, and five yearling lambs for a peace offering. This was the offering of Shelumiel, son of Zurishaddai.

⁴²On the sixth day it was the turn of Eliasaph, son of Reuel, prince of the Gadites. ⁴³His offering consisted of one silver plate weighing a hundred and thirty shekels according to the sanctuary standard and one silver basin weighing seventy shekels, both

filled with fine flour mixed with oil for a cereal offering; ⁴⁴one gold cup of ten shekels' weight filled with incense; ⁴⁵one young bull, one ram, and one yearling lamb for a holocaust; ⁴⁶one goat for a sin offering; ⁴⁷and two oxen, five rams, five goats, and five yearling lambs for a peace offering. This was the offering of Eliasaph, son of Reuel.

⁴⁸On the seventh day it was the turn of Elishama, son of Ammihud, prince of the Ephraimites. ⁴⁹His offering consisted of one silver plate weighing a hundred and thirty shekels according to the sanctuary standard and one silver basin weighing seventy shekels, both filled with fine flour mixed with oil for a cereal offering; ⁵⁰one gold cup of ten shekels' weight filled with incense; ⁵¹one young bull, one ram, and one yearling lamb for a holocaust; ⁵²one goat for a sin offering; ⁵³and two oxen, five rams, five goats, and five yearling lambs for a peace offering. This was the offering of Elishama, son of Ammihud.

⁵⁴On the eighth day it was the turn of Gamaliel, son of Pedahzur, prince of the Manassehites. ⁵⁵His offering consisted of one silver plate weighing a hundred and thirty shekels according to the sanctuary standard, and one silver basin weighing seventy shekels, both filled with fine flour mixed with oil for a cereal offering; ⁵⁶one gold cup of ten shekels' weight filled with incense; ⁵⁷one young bull, one ram, and one yearling lamb for a holocaust; ⁵⁸one goat for a sin offering; ⁵⁹and two oxen, five rams, five goats, and five yearling lambs for a peace offering. This was the offering of Gamaliel, son of Pedahzur.

⁶⁰On the ninth day it was the turn of Abidan, son of Gideoni, prince of the Benjaminites. ⁶¹His offering consisted of one silver plate weighing a hundred and thirty shekels according to the sanctuary standard and one silver basin weighing seventy shekels, both filled with fine flour mixed with oil for a cereal offering; ⁶²one gold cup of ten shekels' weight filled with incense; ⁶³one young bull, one ram, and one yearling lamb for a holocaust; ⁶⁴one goat for a sin offering; ⁶⁵and two oxen, five rams, five goats, and five yearling lambs for a peace offering. This was the offering of Abidan, son of Gideoni.

⁶⁶On the tenth day it was the turn of Ahiezer, son of Ammishaddai, prince of the Danites. ⁶⁷His offering consisted of one silver plate weighing a hundred and thirty shekels according to the sanctuary standard and one silver basin weighing seventy shekels, both filled with fine flour mixed with oil for a cereal offering; ⁶⁸one gold cup of ten shekels' weight filled with incense; ⁶⁹one young bull, one ram, and one yearling lamb for a holocaust; ⁷⁰one goat for a sin offering; ⁷¹and two oxen, five rams, five goats, and five yearling lambs for a peace offering. This was the offering of Ahiezer, son of Ammishaddai.

⁷²On the eleventh day it was the turn of Pagiel, son of Ochran, prince of the Asherites. ⁷³His offering consisted of one silver plate weighing one hundred and thirty shekels according to the sanctuary standard and one silver basin weighing seventy shekels, both filled

with fine flour mixed with oil for a cereal offering; [74]one gold cup of ten shekels' weight filled with incense; [75]one young bull, one ram, and one yearling lamb for a holocaust; [76]one goat for a sin offering; [77]and two oxen, five rams, five goats, and five yearling lambs for a peace offering. This was the offering of Pagiel, son of Ochran.

[78]On the twelfth day it was the turn of Ahira, son of Enan, prince of the Naphtalites. [79]His offering consisted of one silver plate weighing a hundred and thirty shekels according to the sanctuary standard and one silver basin weighing seventy shekels, both filled with fine flour mixed with oil for a cereal offering; [80]one gold cup of ten shekels' weight filled with incense; [81]one young bull, one ram, and one yearling lamb for a holocaust; [82]one goat for a sin offering; [83]and two oxen, five rams, five goats, and five yearling lambs for a peace offering. This was the offering of Ahira, son of Enan.

[84]These were the offerings for the dedication of the altar, given by the princes of Israel on the occasion of its anointing: twelve silver plates, twelve silver basins, and twelve gold cups. [85]Each silver plate weighed a hundred and thirty shekels, and each silver basin seventy, so that all the silver of these vessels amounted to two thousand four hundred shekels, according to the sanctuary standard. [86]The twelve gold cups that were filled with incense weighed ten shekels apiece, according to the sanctuary standard, so that all the gold of the cups amounted to one hundred and twenty shekels. [87]The animals for the holocausts were, in all, twelve young bulls, twelve rams, and twelve yearling lambs, with their cereal offerings; those for the sin offerings were twelve goats. [88]The animals for the peace offerings were, in all, twenty-four oxen, sixty rams, sixty goats, and sixty yearling lambs. These, then, were the offerings for the dedication of the altar after it was anointed.

The Voice

[89]*When Moses entered the meeting tent to speak with him, he heard the voice addressing him from above the propitiatory on the ark of the commandments, from between the two cherubim; and it spoke to him. . . .

The Lamps Set Up

8 [1]THE LORD spoke to Moses, and said, [2]*"Give Aaron this command: When you set up the seven lamps, have them throw their light toward the front of the lampstand." [3]Aaron did so, setting up the lamps to face toward the front of the lampstand, just as the LORD had commanded Moses. [4]*The lampstand was made of beaten gold in both its shaft and its branches, according to the pattern which the LORD had shown Moses.

Purification of the Levites

[5]The LORD said to Moses: [6]†"Take the Levites from among the Israelites and purify them. [7]†This is what you shall do to them to purify them. Sprinkle them with the water of remission; then have them shave their whole bodies and wash their clothes, and so purify themselves. [8]They shall take a young bull, along with its cereal offering of fine flour mixed with oil; you shall take another young bull for a sin offering. [9]Then have the Levites come forward in front of the meeting tent, where you shall assemble also the whole community of the Israelites. [10]While the Levites are present before the LORD, the Israelites shall lay their hands upon them. [11]Let Aaron then offer the Levites before the LORD as a wave offering from the Israelites, thus devoting them to the service of the LORD. [12]The Levites in turn shall lay their hands on the heads of the bullocks, which shall then be immolated, the one as a sin offering and the other as a holocaust to the LORD, in atonement for the Levites. [13]Thus, then, shall you have the Levites stand before Aaron and his sons, to be offered as a wave offering to the LORD; [14]*and thus shall you set aside the Levites from the rest of the Israelites, that they may be mine.

[15]"Only then shall the Levites enter upon their service in the meeting tent. You shall purify them and offer them as a wave offering; [16]*because they, among the Israelites, are strictly dedicated to me; I have taken them for myself in place of every first-born that opens the womb among the Israelites. [17]*Indeed, all the first-born among the Israelites, both of man and of beast, belong to me; I consecrated them to myself on the day I slew all the first-born in the land of Egypt. [18]But in place of all the first-born Israelites I have taken the Levites; [19]*and I have given these dedicated Israelites to Aaron and his sons to discharge the duties of the Israelites in the meeting tent and to make atonement for them, so that no plague may strike among the Israelites should they come near the sanctuary."

[20]Thus, then, did Moses and Aaron and the whole community of the Israelites deal with the Levites, carrying out exactly the command which the LORD had given Moses concerning them. [21]†When the Levites had cleansed themselves of sin and washed their clothes, Aaron offered them as a wave offering before the LORD, and made atonement for them to purify them. [22]Only then did they enter upon their service in the meeting tent under the supervision of Aaron and his sons. The command which the LORD had given Moses concerning the Levites was carried out.

---

† 8, 6: *Purify them:* in the language of the Pentateuch only the priests were "consecrated," that is, made sacred or set aside for the Lord, in an elaborate ceremony described in Ex 29; Lv 8. The Levites were merely "purified," that is, made ritually clean for their special work.

8, 7: *Water of remission:* literally, "water of sin," that is, for the remission of sin.

8, 21: *Cleansed themselves of sin:* by having the "water of remission" sprinkled on them as prescribed in v 7.

---

*	89: Ex 25, 22.	16: 3, 12.45.
	8/2: Ex 25, 37.	17: 3, 13; 13, 2; Lk 2, 23.
	4: Ex 25, 31.40.	19: 3, 9f.
	14: 3, 45.	

Age Limits for Levitical Service

[23]THE LORD said to Moses: [24]*"This is the rule for the Levites. Each from his twenty-fifth year onward shall perform the required service in the meeting tent. [25]When he is fifty years old, he shall retire from the required service and work no longer. [26]His service with his fellow Levites shall consist in sharing their responsibilities in the meeting tent, but he shall not do the work. This, then, is how you are to regulate the duties of the Levites."

Second Passover

9 [1]IN the first month of the year following their departure from the land of Egypt, the LORD said to Moses in the desert of Sinai, [2]"Tell the Israelites to celebrate the Passover at the prescribed time. [3]The evening twilight of the fourteenth day of this month is the prescribed time when you shall celebrate it, observing all its rules and regulations." [4]Moses, therefore, told the Israelites to celebrate the Passover. [5]And they did so, celebrating the Passover in the desert of Sinai during the evening twilight of the fourteenth day of the first month, just as the LORD had commanded Moses.

[6]There were some, however, who were unclean because of a human corpse and so could not keep the Passover that day. These men came up to Moses and Aaron that same day [7]and said, "Although we are unclean because of a corpse, why should we be deprived of presenting the LORD's offering at its proper time along with the other Israelites?" [8]Moses answered them, "Wait until I learn what the LORD will command in your regard."

[9]*The LORD then said to Moses: [10]"Speak to the Israelites and say: If any one of you or of your descendants is unclean because of a corpse, or if he is absent on a journey, he may still keep the LORD's Passover. [11]*But he shall keep it in the second month, during the evening twilight of the fourteenth day of that month, eating it with unleavened bread and bitter herbs, [12]*and not leaving any of it over till morning, nor breaking any of its bones, but observing all the rules of the Passover. [13]However, anyone who is clean and not away on a journey, who yet fails to keep the Passover, shall be cut off from his people, because he did not present the LORD's offering at the prescribed time. That man shall bear the consequences of his sin.

[14]*†"If an alien who lives among you wishes to keep the LORD's Passover, he too shall observe the rules and regulations for the Passover. You shall have the same law for the resident alien as for the native of the land."

The Fiery Cloud

[15]*†On the day when the Dwelling was erected, the cloud covered the Dwelling, the tent of the command-

ments; but from evening until morning it took on the appearance of fire over the Dwelling. [16]It was always so: during the day the Dwelling was covered by the cloud, which at night had the appearance of fire. [17]*Whenever the cloud rose from the tent, the Israelites would break camp; wherever the cloud came to rest, they would pitch camp. [18]*At the bidding of the LORD the Israelites moved on, and at his bidding they encamped. As long as the cloud stayed over the Dwelling, they remained in camp. [19]Even when the cloud tarried many days over the Dwelling, the Israelites obeyed the LORD and would not move on; [20]yet sometimes the cloud was over the Dwelling only for a few days. It was at the bidding of the LORD that they stayed in camp, and it was at his bidding that they departed. [21]Sometimes the cloud remained there only from evening until morning; and when it rose in the morning, they would depart. Or if the cloud lifted during the day, or even at night, they would then set out. [22]Whether the cloud tarried over the Dwelling for two days or for a month or longer, the Israelites remained in camp and did not depart; but when it lifted, they moved on. [23]Thus, it was always at the bidding of the LORD that they encamped, and at his bidding that they set out; ever heeding the charge of the LORD, as he had bidden them through Moses.

The Silver Trumpets

10 [1]THE LORD said to Moses: [2]"Make two trumpets of beaten silver, which you shall use in assembling the community and in breaking camp. [3]When both are blown, the whole community shall gather round you at the entrance of the meeting tent; [4]but when one of them is blown, only the princes, the chiefs of the troops of Israel, shall gather round you. [5]When you sound the first alarm, those encamped on the east side shall set out; [6]when you sound the second alarm, those encamped on the south side shall set out; when you sound the third alarm, those encamped on the west side shall set out; when you sound the fourth alarm, those encamped on the north side shall set out. Thus shall the alarm be sounded for them to depart. [7]But in calling forth an assembly you are to blow an ordinary blast, without sounding the alarm.

[8]"It is the sons of Aaron, the priests, who shall blow the trumpets; and the use of them is prescribed by perpetual statute for you and your descendants. [9]*When in your own land you go to war against an enemy that is attacking you, you shall sound the alarm on the trumpets, and the LORD, your God, will remember you and save you from your foes. [10]*†On your days of celebration, your festivals, and your new moon feasts, you

---

† 9, 14: *An alien:* this passage presupposes that he is already circumcised as prescribed in Ex 12, 48.

9, 15: *The cloud:* already mentioned in the departure from Egypt; cf Ex 13, 21f.

10, 10: *Days of celebration:* special holidays, such as the occasion of a victory. *Festivals:* the great annual feasts of the Passover, Pentecost and Booths described in Lv 23; Nm 28-29.

❋
  24: 4, 3.23.
  9/3: Ex 12, 6; Lv 23, 5.
  11: 2 Chr 30, 2-15.
  12: Ex 12, 46; Jn 19, 36.
  14: Ex 12, 48f.

  15: Ex 13, 21.
  17: Wis 18, 3.
  18: 1 Cor 10, 1.
  10/9: 2 Chr 13, 14.
  10: 29, 1; 2 Chr 29, 26ff.

shall blow the trumpets over your holocausts and your peace offerings; this will serve as a reminder of you before your God. I, the Lord, am your God."

II: FROM SINAI TO THE PLAINS OF MOAB

Departure from Sinai

¹¹IN THE SECOND YEAR, on the twentieth day of the second month, the cloud rose from the Dwelling of the commandments. ¹²The Israelites moved on from the desert of Sinai by stages, until the cloud came to rest in the desert of Paran.

¹³The first time that they broke camp at the bidding of the Lord through Moses, ¹⁴*the camp of the Judahites, under its own standard and arranged in companies, was the first to set out. Nahshon, son of Amminadab, was over their host, ¹⁵and Nethanel, son of Zuar, over the host of the tribe of Issachar, ¹⁶and Eliab, son of Helon, over the host of the tribe of Zebulun. ¹⁷Then, after the Dwelling was dismantled, the clans of Gershon and Merari set out, carrying the Dwelling. ¹⁸The camp of the Reubenites, under its own standard and arranged in companies, was the next to set out, with Elizur, son of Shedeur, over their host, ¹⁹and Shelumiel, son of Zurishaddai, over the host of the tribe of Simeon, ²⁰and Eliasaph, son of Reuel, over the host of the tribe of Gad. ²¹The clan of Kohath then set out, carrying the sacred objects for the Dwelling, which was to be erected before their arrival. ²²The camp of the Ephraimites next set out, under its own standard and arranged in companies, with Elishama, son of Ammihud, over their host, ²³and Gamaliel, son of Pedahzur, over the host of the tribe of Manasseh, ²⁴and Abidan, son of Gideoni, over the host of the tribe of Benjamin. ²⁵Finally, as rear guard for all the camps, the camp of the Danites set out, under its own standard and arranged in companies, with Ahiezer, son of Ammishaddai, over their host, ²⁶and Pagiel, son of Ochran, over the host of the tribe of Asher, ²⁷and Ahira, son of Enan, over the host of the tribe of Naphtali. ²⁸This was the order of departure for the Israelites, company by company.

Hobab as Guide

As they were setting out, ²⁹Moses said to the brother-in-law Hobab, son of Reuel the Midianite, "We are setting out for the place which the Lord has promised to give us. Come with us, and we will be generous toward you, for the Lord has promised prosperity to Israel." ³⁰†But he answered, "No, I will not come. I am going instead to my own country and to my own kindred." ³¹Moses said, "Please, do not leave us; you know where we can camp in the desert, and you will serve as eyes for us. ³²If you come with us, we will share with you the prosperity the Lord will bestow on us."

Into the Desert

³³*†They moved on from the mountain of the Lord, a three days' journey, and the ark of the covenant of the Lord which was to seek out their resting place went the three days' journey with them. ³⁴And when they set out from camp, the cloud of the Lord was over them by day.

³⁵Whenever the ark set out, Moses would say,

"Arise, O Lord, that your enemies may be scattered,
     and those who hate you may flee before you."

³⁶And when it came to rest, he would say,

"Return, O Lord, you who ride upon the clouds,
     to the troops of Israel."

Discontent of the People

11 ¹*NOW the people complained in the hearing of the Lord; and when he heard it his wrath flared up so that the fire of the Lord burned among them and consumed the outskirts of the camp. ²But when the people cried out to Moses, he prayed to the Lord and the fire died out. ³†Hence that place was called Taberah, because there the fire of the Lord burned among them.

⁴*The foreign elements among them were so greedy for meat that even the Israelites lamented again, "Would that we had meat for food! ⁵*We remember the fish we used to eat without cost in Egypt, and the cucumbers, the melons, the leeks, the onions, and the garlic. ⁶But now we are famished; we see nothing before us but this manna."

⁷*†Manna was like coriander seed and had the appearance of bdellium. ⁸When they had gone about and gathered it up, the people would grind it between millstones or pound it in a mortar, then cook it in a pot and make it into loaves, which tasted like cakes made with oil. ⁹*At night, when the dew fell upon the camp, the manna also fell.

¹⁰When Moses heard the people, family after family, crying at the entrance of their tents, so that the Lord became very angry, he was grieved. ¹¹"Why do you treat your servant so badly?" Moses asked the Lord. "Why are you so displeased with me that you burden me with all this people? ¹²Was it I who conceived all this people? or was it I who gave them birth, that you tell me to carry them at my bosom, like a foster father

---

10, 30ff: Hobab wished to be coaxed before granting the favor. From Jgs 1, 16 it seems probable that he did accede to Moses' request.

10, 33: *The mountain of the Lord:* Sinai (Horeb), elsewhere always called "the mountain of God."

11, 3: *Taberah* means "the burning."

11, 7: *Coriander seed:* see note on Ex 16, 31. *Bdellium:* a transparent, amber-colored gum resin, which is also mentioned in Gn 2, 12.

14ff: 2, 3.5.7.
  33: Dt 1, 33.
11/1: Dt 9, 22.
  4: Ps 78, 18.
  5f: 21, 5; Ex 16, 3;
      Acts 7, 39.
7f: Ex 16, 14f.31;
    Ps 78, 24; Wis 16, 20;
    Jn 6, 31.
9: Ex 16, 14f.

carrying an infant, to the land you have promised under oath to their fathers? **13**Where can I get meat to give to all this people? For they are crying to me, 'Give us meat for our food.' **14**I cannot carry all this people by myself, for they are too heavy for me. **15**If this is the way you will deal with me, then please do me the favor of killing me at once, so that I need no longer face this distress."

The Seventy Elders

16Then the Lord said to Moses, "Assemble for me seventy of the elders of Israel, men you know for true elders and authorities among the people, and bring them to the meeting tent. When they are in place beside you, **17**I will come down and speak with you there. I will also take some of the spirit that is on you and will bestow it on them, that they may share the burden of the people with you. You will then not have to bear it by yourself.

18"To the people, however, you shall say: Sanctify yourselves for tomorrow, when you shall have meat to eat. For in the hearing of the Lord you have cried, 'Would that we had meat for food! Oh, how well off we were in Egypt!' Therefore the Lord will give you meat for food, **19**and you will eat it, not for one day, or two days, or five, or ten, or twenty days, **20**but for a whole month—until it comes out of your very nostrils and becomes loathsome to you. For you have spurned the Lord who is in your midst, and in his presence you have wailed, 'Why did we ever leave Egypt?'"

21But Moses said, "The people around me include six hundred thousand soldiers; yet you say, 'I will give them meat to eat for a whole month. **22**Can enough sheep and cattle be slaughtered for them? If all the fish of the sea were caught for them, would they have enough?" **23**The Lord answered Moses, "Is this beyond the Lord's reach? You shall see now whether or not what I have promised you takes place."

The Spirit on the Elders

24So Moses went out and told the people what the Lord had said. Gathering seventy elders of the people, he had them stand around the tent. **25**The Lord then came down in the cloud and spoke to him. Taking some of the spirit that was on Moses, he bestowed it on the seventy elders; and as the spirit came to rest on them, they prophesied.

26Now two men, one named Eldad and the other Medad, were not in the gathering but had been left in the camp. They too had been on the list, but had not gone out to the tent; yet the spirit came to rest on them also, and they prophesied in the camp. **27**So, when a young man quickly told Moses, "Eldad and Medad are prophesying in the camp," **28**Joshua, son of Nun, who from his youth had been Moses' aide, said,

"Moses, my lord, stop them." **29**But Moses answered him, "Are you jealous for my sake? Would that all the people of the Lord were prophets! Would that the Lord might bestow his spirit on them all!" **30**Then Moses retired to the camp, along with the elders of Israel.

The Quail

31*†There arose a wind sent by the Lord, that drove in quail from the sea and brought them down over the camp site at a height of two cubits from the ground for the distance of a day's journey all around the camp. **32***†All that day, all night, and all the next day the people gathered in the quail. Even the one who got the least gathered ten homers of them. Then they spread them out all around the camp. **33**But while the meat was still between their teeth, before it could be consumed, the Lord's wrath flared up against the people, and he struck them with a very great plague. **34**†So that place was named Kibroth-hattaavah, because it was there that the greedy people were buried.

35From Kibroth-hattaavah the people set out for Hazeroth.

Jealousy of Aaron and Miriam

12 WHILE they were in Hazeroth, **1**†Miriam and Aaron spoke against Moses on the pretext of the marriage he had contracted with a Cushite woman. **2**†They complained, "Is it through Moses alone that the Lord speaks? Does he not speak through us also?" And the Lord heard this. **3***Now, Moses himself was by far the meekest man on the face of the earth. **4**So at once the Lord said to Moses and Aaron and Miriam, "Come out, you three, to the meeting tent." And the three of them went. **5**Then the Lord came down in the column of cloud, and standing at the entrance of the tent, called Aaron and Miriam. When both came forward, **6**he said, "Now listen to the words of the Lord:

---

†   11, 25: *They prophesied:* in the sense, not of foretelling the future, but of speaking in enraptured enthusiasm. Such manifestations of mystic exaltation occurred in the early days of Hebrew prophecy (1 Sm 10, 10ff; 19, 20ff) and in the first years of the Church (Acts 2, 6-11.17; 19, 6; 1 Cor 12-14).

11, 31: *At a height of two cubits from the ground:* exhausted by the storm, the quail could take but short, low flights, so that they were easily captured. To give food to the hungry people, God may have used the natural phenomenon of the annual migration of quail across the Sinai Peninsula. In the spring large flocks of these birds cross the Gulf of Aqabah flying toward the west; in the fall they fly back eastward from the Mediterranean. *The sea* mentioned here probably refers to the former body of water.

11, 32: *They spread them out:* to cure by drying.

11, 34: *Kibroth-hattaavah* means "graves of greed."

12, 1: *Cushite woman:* apparently Zipporah, the Midianitess, is meant; cf Ex 2, 21. Perhaps the term is used here merely in the sense of "despised foreigner."

12, 2: The real reason for Miriam's quarrel with her brother Moses was her jealousy of his superior position; his *Cushite* wife served only as an occasion for the dispute. Aaron merely followed his sister in her rebellion; hence she alone was punished.

❖
  31: Ps 78, 26ff.   12/3: Sir 45, 1f.
32f: Ps 78, 26-31;
       1 Cor 10, 6-7.

Should there be a prophet among you,
   in visions will I reveal myself to him,
   in dreams will I speak to him;
7*Not so with my servant Moses!
   Throughout my house he bears my trust:
8*face to face I speak to him,
   plainly and not in riddles.
   The presence of the LORD he beholds.

Why, then, did you not fear to speak against my servant Moses?"

Miriam's Leprosy

9So angry was the LORD against them that when he departed, **10***†and the cloud withdrew from the tent, there was Miriam, a snow-white leper! When Aaron turned and saw her a leper, **11**"Ah, my lord!" he said to Moses, "please do not charge us with the sin that we have foolishly committed! **12**Let her not thus be like the stillborn babe that comes forth from its mother's womb with its flesh half consumed." **13**Then Moses cried to the LORD, "Please, not this! Pray, heal her!" **14**But the LORD answered Moses, "Suppose her father had spit in her face, would she not hide in shame for seven days? Let her be confined outside the camp for seven days; only then may she be brought back." **15**So Miriam was confined outside the camp for seven days, and the people did not start out again until she was brought back.

16After that the people set out from Hazeroth and encamped in the desert of Paran.

The Twelve Scouts

13 ¹THE LORD said to Moses, ²"Send men to reconnoiter the land of Canaan, which I am giving the Israelites. You shall send one man from each ancestral tribe, all of them princes." **3***So Moses dispatched them from the desert of Paran, as the LORD had ordered. All of them were leaders among the Israelites; **4**by name they were:

   Shammua, son of Zaccur, of the tribe of Reuben;
5Shaphat, son of Hori, of the tribe of Simeon;
6Caleb, son of Jephunneh, of the tribe of Judah;
7Igal [son of Joseph], of the tribe of Issachar;
10Gaddiel, son of Sodi, of the tribe of Zebulun;
11Gaddi, son of Susi, of the tribe of Manasseh, for the Josephites, with
8Hoshea, son of Nun, of the tribe of Ephraim;
9Palti, son of Raphu, of the tribe of Benjamin;
12Ammiel, son of Gemalli, of the tribe of Dan;
13Sethur, son of Michael, of the tribe of Asher;
14Nahbi, son of Vophsi, of the tribe of Naphtali;
15Geuel, son of Machi, of the tribe of Gad.

16†These are the names of the men whom Moses sent out to reconnoiter the land. But Hoshea, son of Nun, Moses called Joshua.

17In sending them to reconnoiter the land of Canaan, Moses said to them, "Go up here in the Negeb, up into the highlands, **18**and see what kind of land it is. Are the people living there strong or weak, few or many? **19**Is the country in which they live good or bad? Are the towns in which they dwell open or fortified? **20**Is the soil fertile or barren, wooded or clear? And do your best to get some of the fruit of the land." It was then the season for early grapes.

21†So they went up and reconnoitered the land from the desert of Zin as far as where Rehob adjoins Labo of Hamath. **22***†Going up by way of the Negeb, they reached Hebron, where Ahiman, Sheshai and Talmai, descendants of the Anakim, were living. [Hebron had been built seven years before Zoan in Egypt.] **23**†They also reached the Wadi Eshcol, where they cut down a branch with a single cluster of grapes on it, which two of them carried on a pole, as well as some pomegranates and figs. **24***It was because of the cluster the Israelites cut there that they called the place Wadi Eshcol.

Their Return

25After reconnoitering the land for forty days they returned, **26***met Moses and Aaron and the whole community of the Israelites in the desert of Paran at Kadesh, made a report to them all, and showed them the fruit of the country. **27**They told Moses: "We went into the land to which you sent us. It does indeed flow with milk and honey, and here is its fruit. **28***However, the people who are living in the land are fierce, and the towns are fortified and very strong. Besides, we saw descendants of the Anakim there. **29**Amalekites live in the region of the Negeb; Hittites, Jebusites and Amorites dwell in the highlands, and Canaanites along the seacoast and the banks of the Jordan."

30Caleb, however, to quiet the people toward Moses, said, "We ought to go up and seize the land, for we can certainly do so." **31**But the men who had gone up with him said, "We cannot attack these people; they

---

† 12, 10: *A snow-white leper:* afflicted with "white leprosy," a skin disease that generally is not serious or of long duration. Cf Lv 13, 3-6.

13, 16: *Joshua:* in Hebrew, "Jehoshua," which was later modified to "Jeshua," the Hebrew pronunciation of the name "Jesus." Hoshea and Joshua are variants of one original name meaning "the LORD saves." Cf Mt 1, 21.

13, 21: *The desert of Zin:* north of Paran and southwest of the Dead Sea. It is quite distinct from "the desert of Sin" near the border of Egypt (Ex 16, 1; 17, 1; Nm 33, 11). *Labo of Hamath:* a town near Riblah (Jer 39, 5f) at the southern border of *Hamath,* an independent kingdom in southern Syria. David's conquests extended as far as Hamath (2 Sm 8, 9ff), and Labo thus formed the northern border of the ideal extent of Israel's possessions (34, 7ff; Ez 47, 15; 48, 1). Some commentators think that this verse is a later addition to the text; cf Dt 1, 24.

13, 22.28: *Anakim:* an aboriginal race in southern Palestine, largely absorbed by the Canaanites before the Israelite invasion. Either because of their tall stature or because of the massive stone structures left by them the Israelites regarded them as giants.

13, 23: *Eshcol* means "cluster."

7: Sir 45, 3; Heb 3, 2.5.
8: Ex 33, 11; Dt 34, 10.
10: Dt 24, 9.
13/3-33: Dt 1, 22-28.
22: Jos 11, 21f.
24: 32, 9; Dt 1, 24f.
26f: Ex 3, 8.17.
28f: Dt 9, 1f.

are too strong for us." **32***So they spread discouraging reports among the Israelites about the land they had scouted, saying, "The land that we explored is a country that consumes its inhabitants. And all the people we saw there are huge men, **33*†**veritable giants [the Anakim were a race of giants]; we felt like mere grasshoppers, and so we must have seemed to them."

Threats of Revolt

14 **1**AT this, the whole community broke out with loud cries, and even in the night the people wailed. **2***All the Israelites grumbled against Moses and Aaron, the whole community saying to them, "Would that we had died in the land of Egypt, or that here in the desert we were dead! **3**Why is the LORD bringing us into this land only to have us fall by the sword? Our wives and little ones will be taken as booty. Would it not be better for us to return to Egypt?" **4**So they said to one another, "Let us appoint a leader and go back to Egypt."

5But Moses and Aaron fell prostrate before the whole assembled community of the Israelites; **6**while Joshua, son of Nun, and Caleb, son of Jephunneh, who had been in the party that scouted the land, tore their garments, **7***and said to the whole community of the Israelites, "The country which we went through and explored is a fine, rich land. **8**If the LORD is pleased with us, he will bring us in and give us that land, a land flowing with milk and honey. **9*†**But do not rebel against the LORD! You need not be afraid of the people of that land; they are but food for us! Their defense has left them, but the LORD is with us. Therefore, do not be afraid of them." **10**In answer, the whole community threatened to stone them.

The Lord's Sentence

But then the glory of the LORD appeared at the meeting tent to all the Israelites. **11***And the LORD said to Moses, "How long will this people spurn me? How long will they refuse to believe in me, despite all the signs I have performed among them? **12***I will strike them with pestilence and wipe them out. Then I will make of you a nation greater and mightier than they."

13*But Moses said to the LORD: "Are the Egyptians to hear of this? For by your power you brought out this people from among them. **14***And are they to tell of it to the inhabitants of this land? It has been heard that you, O LORD, are in the midst of this people; you, LORD, who plainly reveal yourself! Your cloud stands over them, and you go before them by day in a column of cloud and by night in a column of fire. **15**If now you

slay this whole people, the nations who have heard such reports of you will say, **16***'The LORD was not able to bring this people into the land he swore to give them; that is why he slaughtered them in the desert.' **17**Now then, let the power of my Lord be displayed in its greatness, even as you have said, **18***'The LORD is slow to anger and rich in kindness, forgiving wickedness and crime; yet not declaring the guilty guiltless, but punishing children to the third and fourth generation for their fathers' wickedness.' **19***Pardon, then, the wickedness of this people in keeping with your great kindness, even as you have forgiven them from Egypt until now."

20The LORD answered: "I pardon them as you have asked. **21**Yet, by my life and the LORD's glory that fills the whole earth, **22***of all the men who have seen my glory and the signs I worked in Egypt, and in the desert, and who nevertheless have put me to the test ten times already and have failed to heed my voice, **23**not one shall see the land which I promised on oath to their fathers. None of these who have spurned me shall see it. **24***But because my servant Caleb has a different spirit and follows me unreservedly, I will bring him into the land where he has just been, and his descendants shall possess it. **25†**But now, since the Amalekites and Canaanites are living the valleys, turn away tomorrow and set out in the desert on the Red Sea road."

26The LORD also said to Moses and Aaron: **27***"How long will this wicked community grumble against me? I have heard the grumblings of the Israelites against me. **28†**Tell them: By my life, says the LORD, I will do to you just what I have heard you say. **29***Here in the desert shall your dead bodies fall. Of all your men of twenty years or more registered in the census, who grumbled against me, **30**not one shall enter the land where I solemnly swore to settle you, except Caleb, son of Jephunneh, and Joshua, son of Nun. **31***Your little ones, however, who you said would be taken as booty, I will bring in, and they shall appreciate the land you spurned. **32**But as for you, your bodies shall fall here in the desert, **33***here where your children must wander for forty years, suffering for your faithlessness, till the last of you lies dead in the desert. **34**Forty days you spent in scouting the land; forty years shall you suffer for your crimes: one year for each day. Thus you will realize what it means to oppose me. **35**I, the LORD, have sworn to do this to all this wicked community that conspired against me: here in the desert they shall die to the last man."

32: 32, 9; Jos 14, 8.
33: Dt 2, 10.
14/2: Ex 16, 3; Ps 106, 25.
7f: Dt 1, 25.
9: Dt 7, 18.
11: Ps 78, 22.32.
12: Ex 32, 10.
13-16: Ex 32, 12; Dt 9, 26ff;
Ps 106, 23.
14: Ex 13, 21; Jos 2, 9f.
16: Ex 32, 12; Dt 9, 28.

18: Ex 20, 5; 34, 6f;
Pss 103, 8; 145, 8.
19: Ps 78, 38.
22f: Dt 1, 35.
24: Jos 14, 8f.
27: Ex 16, 7.12.
29: Dt 1, 35; Heb 3, 17.
31: Dt 1, 39.
33f: 13, 26; 32, 13;
Ps 95, 10; Ez 4, 6.

† 13, 33: *Giants:* in Hebrew, "nephilim." Cf Gn 6, 4.

14, 9: *They are but food for us:* that is, "we can easily consume and destroy them." This is the answer to the pessimistic report that this land "consumes its inhabitants" (13, 32).

14, 25: *The valleys:* the low-lying plains in the Negeb and along the seacoast and in the Jordan depression, as well as the higher valleys in the mountains farther north: cf 14, 45.

14, 28f: God punished the malcontents by giving them their wish; cf v 2. Their lack of faith and of confidence in God is cited in 1 Cor 10, 10, and Heb 3, 12-18, as a warning for Christians.

36*And so it happened to the men whom Moses had sent to reconnoiter the land and who on returning had set the whole community grumbling against him by spreading discouraging reports about the land; **37**these men who had given out the bad report about the land were struck down by the LORD and died. **38***Of all the men who had gone to reconnoiter the land, only Joshua, son of Nun, and Caleb, son of Jephunneh, survived.

Unsuccessful Invasion

39When Moses repeated these words to all the Israelites, the people felt great remorse. **40***Early the next morning they started up into the foothills, saying, "Here we are, ready to go up to the place that the LORD spoke of: for we were indeed doing wrong." **41**But Moses said, "Why are you again disobeying the LORD's orders? This cannot succeed. **42***Do not go up, because the LORD is not in your midst; if you go, you will be beaten down before your enemies. **43**For there the Amalekites and Canaanites face you, and you will fall by the sword. You have turned back from following the LORD; therefore the LORD will not be with you." **44***Yet they dared to go up into the foothills, even though neither the ark of the covenant of the LORD nor Moses left the camp. **45**†And the Amalekites and Canaanites who dwelt in that hill country came down and defeated them, beating them back as far as Hormah.

Secondary Offerings

15 **1**THE LORD said to Moses, **2**†"Give the Israelites these instructions: When you have entered the land that I will give you for your homesteads, **3**if you make to the LORD a sweet-smelling oblation from the herd or from the flock, in holocaust, in fulfillment of a vow, or as a freewill offering, or for one of your festivals, **4**whoever does so shall also present to the LORD a cereal offering consisting of a tenth of an ephah of fine flour mixed with a fourth of a hin of oil, **5**as well as a libation of a fourth of a hin of wine, with each lamb sacrificed in holocaust or otherwise. **6**With each sacrifice of a ram you shall present a cereal offering of two tenths of an ephah of fine flour mixed with a third of a hin of oil, **7**and a libation of a third of a hin of wine, thus making a sweet-smelling offering to the LORD. **8**When you sacrifice an ox as a holocaust, or in fulfillment of a vow, or as a peace offering to the LORD, **9**with it you shall present a cereal offering of three tenths of an ephah of fine flour mixed with half a hin of oil, **10**and a libation of half a hin of wine, as a sweet-smelling oblation to the LORD. **11**The same is to be done for each ox, ram, lamb or goat. **12**Whatever the number you offer, do the same for each of them.

13"All the native-born shall make these offerings in the same way, whenever they present a sweet-smelling oblation to the LORD. **14**Likewise, in any future generation, any alien residing with you permanently or for a time, who presents a sweet-smelling oblation to the LORD, shall do as you do. **15**There is but one rule for you and for the resident alien, a perpetual rule for all your descendants. Before the LORD you and the alien are alike, **16**with the same law and the same application of it for the alien residing among you as for yourselves."

17The LORD said to Moses, **18**"Speak to the Israelites and tell them: When you enter the land into which I will bring you **19***and begin to eat of the food of that land, you shall offer the LORD a contribution **20**†consisting of a cake of your first batch of dough. You shall offer it just as you offer a contribution from the threshing floor. **21**Throughout your generations you shall give a contribution to the LORD from your first batch of dough.

Sin Offerings

22*†"When through inadvertence you fail to carry out any of these commandments which the LORD gives to Moses, **23**and through Moses to you, from the time the LORD first issues the commandment down through your generations: **24**if the community itself unwittingly becomes guilty of the fault of inadvertence, the whole community shall offer the holocaust of one young bull as a sweet-smelling oblation pleasing to the LORD, along with its prescribed cereal offering and libation, as well as one he-goat as a sin offering. **25***Then the priest shall make atonement for the whole Israelite community; thus they will be forgiven the inadvertence for which they have brought their holocaust as an oblation to the LORD. **26**Not only the whole Israelite community, but also the aliens residing among you, shall be forgiven, since the fault of inadvertence affects all the people.

27*"However, if it is an individual who sins inadvertently, he shall bring a yearling she-goat as a sin offering, **28**and the priest shall make atonement before the LORD for him who sinned inadvertently; when atonement has been made for him, he will be forgiven. **29**You shall have but one law for him who sins inadvertently, whether he be a native Israelite or an alien residing with you.

---

† 14, 45: *Hormah:* one of the Canaanite royal cities in southern Judea (Jos 12, 14), known at this time as "Zephath"; the origin of the later name is told in 21, 3; Jgs 1, 17.

15, 2-16: These laws on sacrifice are complementary to those of Lv 1-3. Since the food of the Israelites consisted not only of meat but also of bread, oil and wine, so, besides the animal oblations, they offered flour, wine and oil in sacrifice to the Lord.

15, 20: *Dough:* some render, "barley grits." This word is used elsewhere only in Ez 44, 30 and Neh 10, 33; a related Hebrew word is used in Lv 2, 14.

15, 22ff: Although no moral guilt is incurred by an inadvertent violation of God's commandments, the sanctity of the law can require some reparation even for such violations.

⁑
    36f: 13, 17.32f;   44: Dt 1, 43.
        1 Cor 10, 10.   15/19-20: Ez 44, 30.
    38: 26, 65.   22f: Lv 4, 13f.
    40: 13, 18; Dt 1, 41.   25: Lv 4, 20.
    42: Dt 1, 42.   27f: Lv 4, 27f.

³⁰*"But anyone who sins defiantly, whether he be a native or an alien, insults the LORD, and shall be cut off from among his people. ³¹*Since he has despised the word of the LORD and has broken his commandment, he must be cut off. He has only himself to blame."

The Sabbath-breaker

³²While the Israelites were in the desert, a man was discovered gathering wood on the sabbath day. ³³Those who caught him at it brought him to Moses and Aaron and the whole assembly. ³⁴*†But they kept him in custody, for there was no clear decision as to what should be done with him. ³⁵Then the LORD said to Moses, "This man shall be put to death; let the whole community stone him outside the camp." ³⁶So the whole community led him outside the camp and stoned him to death, as the LORD had commanded Moses.

Tassels on the Cloak

³⁷The LORD said to Moses, ³⁸*†"Speak to the Israelites and tell them that they and their descendants must put tassels on the corners of their garments, fastening each corner tassel with a violet cord. ³⁹When you use these tassels, let the sight of them remind you to keep all the commandments of the LORD, without going wantonly astray after the desires of your hearts and eyes. ⁴⁰Thus you will remember to keep all my commandments and be holy to your God. ⁴¹*I, the LORD, am your God who, as God, brought you out of Egypt that I, the LORD, may be your God."

Rebellion of Korah

16 ¹†KORAH, son of Izhar, son of Kohath, son of Levi, [and Dathan and Abiram, sons of Eliab, son of Pallu, son of Reuben] took ²two hundred and fifty Israelites who were leaders in the community, members of the council and men of note. They stood before Moses, ³*and held an assembly against Moses and Aaron, to whom they said, "Enough from you! The whole community, all of them, are holy; the LORD is in their midst. Why then should you set yourselves over the LORD's congregation?"

⁴When Moses heard this, he fell prostrate. ⁵Then he said to Korah and to all his band, "May the LORD make known tomorrow morning who belongs to him and who is the holy one and whom he will have draw near to him! Whom he chooses, he will have draw near him. ⁶Do this: take your censers [Korah and all his band] ⁷and put fire in them and place incense in them before the LORD tomorrow. He whom the LORD then chooses is the holy one. Enough from you Levites!"

⁸Moses also said to Korah, "Listen to me, you Levites! ⁹*Is it too little for you that the God of Israel has singled you out from the community of Israel, to have you draw near him for the service of the LORD's Dwelling and to stand before the community to minister for them? ¹⁰He has allowed you and your kinsmen, the descendants of Levi, to approach him, and yet you now seek the priesthood too. ¹¹It is therefore against the LORD that you and all your band are conspiring. For what has Aaron done that you should grumble against him?"

Rebellion of Dathan and Abiram

¹²†Moses summoned Dathan and Abiram, sons of Eliab, but they answered, "We will not go. ¹³Are you not satisfied with having led us here away from a land flowing with milk and honey, to make us perish in the desert, that you must now lord it over us? ¹⁴†Far from bringing us to a land flowing with milk and honey, or giving us fields and vineyards for our inheritance, will you also gouge out our eyes? No, we will not go."

¹⁵*Then Moses became very angry and said to the LORD, "Pay no heed to their offering. I have never taken a single ass from them, nor have I wronged any one of them."

Korah

¹⁶Moses said to Korah, "You and all your band shall appear before the LORD tomorrow—you and they and Aaron too. ¹⁷Then each of your two hundred and fifty followers shall take his own censer, put incense in it, and offer it to the LORD; and you and Aaron, each with his own censer, shall do the same." ¹⁸So they all took their censers, and laying incense on the fire they had put in them, they took their stand by the entrance of the meeting tent along with Moses and Aaron. ¹⁹Then, when Korah had assembled all his band against them at the entrance of the meeting tent, the glory of the LORD appeared to the entire community, ²⁰and the

---

† 15, 34: *No clear decision:* they already knew that a willful violation of the sabbath was a capital offense, but they did not yet know how the death penalty was to be inflicted.

15, 38: *Tassels:* at the time of Christ these tassels were worn by all pious Jews, including our Lord (Mt 9, 20f; Mk 6, 56); the Pharisees wore very large ones in ostentation of their zeal for the law (Mt 23, 5).

16, 1ff: The evidence seems to show that there were two distinct rebellions: one of Korah and his band (27, 3) and the other of Dathan and Abiram (Dt 11, 6); cf Ps 106. The present account combines both events into one narrative; but even here it is rather easy to separate the two, once certain proper names (vv 1.6.24.32.35) have been identified as glosses. The rebellion of the Reubenites, Dathan and Abiram, was of a political nature, against Moses alone as the civil leader; these rebels were punished by being swallowed alive in an earthquake. The rebellion of Korah was of a religious nature, against the religious leadership of both Moses and Aaron; about two hundred and fifty malcontents joined Korah s *band;* they were punished by fire. The parts of the present section which refer to the rebellion of Dathan and Abiram are vv 12-15 and vv 25-34 of chapter 16; the rest of chapter 16 and all of chapter 17 concern the rebellion of Korah.

16, 12: *We will not go:* to appear before Moses' tribunal.

16, 14: *Gouge out our eyes:* blind us to the real state of affairs.

❋   30: Dt 17, 12.   16/3: Ps 106, 16ff;
      31: Prv 13, 13.   Sir 45, 19; 1 Cor 10, 10.
      34: Lv 24, 12.   9: Dt 10, 8.
      38: Dt 22, 12.   15: 1 Sm 12, 3.
      41: Lv 22, 32f.

LORD said to Moses and Aaron, ²¹"Stand apart from this band, that I may consume them at once." ²²But they fell prostrate and cried out, "O God, God of the spirits of all mankind, will one man's sin make you angry with the whole community?" ²³The LORD answered Moses, ²⁴"Speak to the community and tell them: Withdraw from the space around the Dwelling" [of Korah, Dathan and Abiram].

Punishment of Dathan and Abiram

²⁵†Moses, followed by the elders of Israel, arose and went to Dathan and Abiram. ²⁶Then he warned the community, "Keep away from the tents of these wicked men and do not touch anything that is theirs: otherwise you too will be swept away because of all their sins." ²⁷When Dathan and Abiram had come out and were standing at the entrances of their tents with their wives and sons and little ones, ²⁸Moses said, "This is how you shall know that it was the LORD who sent me to do all I have done, and that it was not I who planned it: ²⁹if these men die an ordinary death, merely suffering the fate common to all mankind, then it was not the LORD who sent me. ³⁰But if the LORD does something entirely new, and the ground opens its mouth and swallows them alive down into the nether world, with all belonging to them, then you will know that these men have defied the LORD." ³¹*No sooner had he finished saying all this than the ground beneath them split open, ³²and the earth opened its mouth and swallowed them and their families [and all of Korah's men] and all their possessions. ³³They went down alive to the nether world with all belonging to them; the earth closed over them, and they perished from the community. ³⁴But all the Israelites near them fled at their shrieks, saying, "The earth might swallow us too!"

Punishment of Korah

³⁵†So they withdrew from the space around the Dwelling [of Korah, Dathan and Abiram]. And fire from the LORD came forth which consumed the two hundred and fifty men who were offering the incense.

17 ¹THE LORD said to Moses, ²"Tell Eleazar, son of Aaron the priest, to remove the censers from the embers; and scatter the fire some distance away, ³†for these sinners have consecrated the censers at the cost of their lives. Have them hammered into plates to cover the altar, because in being presented before the LORD they have become sacred. In this way they shall serve as a sign to the Israelites." ⁴So Eleazar the priest had the bronze censers of those burned during the offering hammered into a covering for the altar, ⁵in keeping with the orders which the LORD had given him through Moses. This cover was to be a reminder to the Israelites that no layman, no one who was not a descendant of Aaron, should approach the altar to offer incense before the LORD, lest he meet the fate of Korah and his band.

⁶The next day the whole Israelite community grumbled against Moses and Aaron, saying, "It is you who have slain the LORD's people." ⁷But while the community was deliberating against them, Moses and Aaron turned toward the meeting tent, and the cloud now covered it and the glory of the LORD appeared. ⁸Then Moses and Aaron came to the front of the meeting tent, ⁹and the LORD said to Moses and Aaron, ¹⁰"Depart from this community, that I may consume them at once." But they fell prostrate.

¹¹*Then Moses said to Aaron, "Take your censer, put fire from the altar in it, lay incense on it, and bring it quickly to the community to make atonement for them; for wrath has come forth from the LORD and the blow is falling." ¹²Obeying the orders of Moses, Aaron took his censer and ran in among the community, where the blow was already falling on the people. Then, as he offered the incense and made atonement for the people, ¹³standing there between the living and the dead, the scourge was checked. ¹⁴Yet fourteen thousand seven hundred died from the scourge, in addition to those who died because of Korah. ¹⁵When the scourge had been checked, Aaron returned to Moses at the entrance of the meeting tent.

Aaron's Staff

¹⁶The LORD now said to Moses, ¹⁷†"Speak to the Israelites and get one staff from them for each ancestral house, twelve staffs in all, one from each of their tribal princes. Mark each man's name on his staff; ¹⁸†and mark Aaron's name on Levi's staff, for the head of Levi's ancestral house shall also have a staff. ¹⁹Then lay them down in the meeting tent, in front of the commandments, where I meet you. ²⁰There the staff of the man of my choice shall sprout. Thus will I suppress from my presence the Israelites' grumbling against you."

²¹So Moses spoke to the Israelites, and their princes gave him staffs, twelve in all, one from each tribal prince; and Aaron's staff was with them. ²²Then Moses

---

† 16, 25: Since Dathan and Abiram had refused to go to Moses (vv 12ff), he, with the elders as witnesses, was obliged to go to their tent.

16, 35: This verse continues v 24; the first sentence is transposed from v 27.

17, 3: Whatever was brought into intimate contact with something sacred shared in its sacredness. See note on 19, 20.

17, 17: The staff was not merely an article of practical use, but also a symbol of authority; cf Gn 49, 10; Nm 24, 17; Jer 48, 17. Hence, the staff of a leader of a tribe was considered the emblem of his tribe; in fact, certain Hebrew words for "staff" also mean "tribe." Perhaps for this reason, to avoid confusion, the author here uses the term "ancestral house" instead of the ordinary word for "tribe."

17, 18: *Levi's staff:* it is not clear whether this is considered as one of the twelve mentioned in the preceding verse, or as a thirteenth staff. Sometimes Levi is reckoned as one of the twelve tribes (e. g., Dt 27, 12f), but more often the number twelve is arrived at by counting the two sub-tribes of Joseph, i. e., Ephraim and Manasseh, as distinct tribes. In this passage also it seems probable that the tribe of Levi is considered apart from the other twelve.

* 31ff: 26, 10; Lv 10, 2;   17/11: Wis 18, 20f.
Dt 11, 6; Ps 106, 17f.

laid the staffs down before the LORD in the tent of the commandments. **23**The next day, when Moses entered the tent, Aaron's staff, representing the house of Levi, had sprouted and put forth not only shoots, but blossoms as well, and even bore ripe almonds! **24**Moses thereupon brought out all the staffs from the LORD's presence to the Israelites. After each prince identified his own staff and took it, **25**the LORD said to Moses, "Put back Aaron's staff in front of the commandments, to be kept there as a warning to the rebellious, so that their grumbling may cease before me; if it does not, they will die." **26**And Moses did as the LORD had commanded him.

Charge of the Sacred Things

27†Then the Israelites cried out to Moses, "We are perishing; we are lost, we are all lost! **28**Every time anyone approaches the Dwelling of the LORD, he dies! Are we to perish to the last man?"

18 **1**†THE LORD said to Aaron, "You and your sons as well as the other members of your ancestral house shall be responsible for the sanctuary; but the responsibility of the priesthood shall rest on you and your sons alone. **2**†Bring with you also your other kinsmen of the tribe of Levi, your ancestral tribe, as your associates and assistants, while you and your sons are in front of the tent of the commandments. **3**They shall look after your persons and the whole tent; however, they shall not come near the sacred vessels or the altar, lest both they and you die. **4**†As your associates they shall have charge of all the work connected with the meeting tent. But no layman shall come near you. **5**You shall have charge of the sanctuary and of the altar, that wrath may not fall again upon the Israelites.

6⁕"Remember, it is I who have taken your kinsmen, the Levites, from the body of the Israelites; they are a gift to you, dedicated to the LORD for the service of the meeting tent. **7**⁕†But only you and your sons are to have charge of performing the priestly functions in whatever concerns the altar and the room within the veil. I give you the priesthood as a gift. Any layman who draws near shall be put to death."

The Priests' Share of the Sacrifices

8⁕†The LORD said to Aaron, "I myself have given you charge of the contributions made to me in the various sacred offerings of the Israelites; by perpetual ordinance I have assigned them to you and to your sons as your priestly share. **9**You shall have the right to share in the oblations that are most sacred, in whatever they offer me as cereal offerings or sin offerings or guilt offerings; these shares shall accrue to you and to your sons. **10**In eating them you shall treat them as most sacred; every male among you may partake of them. As sacred, they belong to you.

11⁕†"You shall also have what is removed from the gift in every wave offering of the Israelites; by perpetual ordinance I have assigned it to you and to your sons and daughters. All in your family who are clean may partake of it. **12**⁕I have also assigned to you all the best of the new oil and of the new wine and grain that they give to the LORD as their first fruits; **13**and likewise, of whatever grows on their land, the first products that they bring in to the LORD shall be yours; all of your family who are clean may partake of them. **14**†Whatever is doomed in Israel shall be yours. **15**⁕Every living thing that opens the womb, whether of man or of beast, such as are to be offered to the LORD, shall be yours; but you must let the first-born of man, as well as of unclean animals, be redeemed. **16**The ransom for a boy is to be paid when he is a month old; it is fixed at five silver shekels according to the sanctuary standard, twenty gerahs to the shekel. **17**But the first-born of cattle, sheep or goats shall not be redeemed; they are sacred. Their blood you must splash on the altar and their fat you must burn as a sweet-smelling oblation to the LORD. **18**⁕Their meat, however, shall be yours, just as the breast and the right leg of the wave offering belong to you. **19**†By perpetual ordinance I have assigned to you and to your sons and daughters all the contributions from the sacred gifts which the Israelites make to the LORD; this is an inviolable covenant to last forever before the LORD, for you and for your descendants." **20**⁕†Then the LORD said to Aaron, "You shall not have any heritage in the land of the Israelites nor hold any portion

---

† 17, 27f: Logically these two verses belong immediately after 16, 35.

18, 1ff: This law, which kept unqualified persons from contact with sacred things, is the answer to the Israelites' cry in 17, 28. It is followed by other laws concerning priests and Levites.

18, 2: *Associates:* in Hebrew this word alludes to the popular etymology of the name "Levi." Cf Gn 29, 34.

18, 4: *Layman:* here, "one who is not a Levite"; in v 7, "one who is not a priest."

18, 7: *Veil:* the outer veil, or "curtain," is probably meant.

18, 8ff: Two classes of offerings are here distinguished: the *most sacred* offering, which only the male members of the priestly families could eat (vv 8ff), and the other offerings, which even the women of the priestly families could eat (vv 11-19).

18, 11: *Wave offering:* this included the breast and right leg (v 18), the shoulder of the peace offering (Lv 7, 30-34), and portions of the nazirite sacrifice (Nm 6, 19f).

18, 14: *Doomed:* in Hebrew, *herem,* which means here "set aside from profane use and made sacred to the Lord." Cf Lv 27, 21.28.

18, 19: *An inviolable covenant:* literally, "a covenant of salt." Cf 2 Chr 13, 5. The reference may perhaps be to the preservative power of salt (cf Mt 5, 13); but more likely the phrase refers to the custom of partaking of the same salt in common to render a contract unbreakable. See note on Lv 2, 13.

18, 20: The priests and Levites were forbidden to own hereditary land such as the other Israelites possessed; therefore in the allotment of the land they were not to receive any portion of it. Certain cities, however, were assigned to them for their residence; cf 35, 1-8.

⁕
18/6: 3, 9; 8, 19.
   7: 3, 10.
   8: 5, 9.
  11: Ex 29, 27f; Lv 7, 34; 10, 14.

12f: Dt 18, 4; 26, 2.
15: Ex 13, 2.
18: Lv 7, 31-34.
20: Dt 10, 9; 18, 1f; Jos 13, 33; Ez 44, 28.

among them; I will be your portion and your heritage among them.

Tithes Due the Levites

21* "To the Levites, however, I hereby assign all tithes in Israel as their heritage in recompense for the service they perform in the meeting tent. **22**The Israelites may no longer approach the meeting tent; else they will incur guilt deserving death. **23**Only the Levites are to perform the service of the meeting tent, and they alone shall be held responsible; this is a perpetual ordinance for all your generations. The Levites, therefore, shall not have any heritage among the Israelites, **24**for I have assigned to them as their heritage the tithes which the Israelites give as a contribution to the Lord. That is why I have ordered that they are not to have any heritage among the Israelites."

Tithes Paid by the Levites

25The Lord said to Moses, **26**"Give the Levites these instructions: When you receive from the Israelites the tithes I have assigned you from them as your heritage, you are to make a contribution from them to the Lord, a tithe of the tithes; **27**and your contribution will be credited to you as if it were grain from the threshing floor or new wine from the press. **28**Thus you too shall make a contribution from all the tithes you receive from the Israelites, handing over to Aaron the priest the part to be contributed to the Lord. **29**From all the gifts that you receive, and from the best parts, you are to consecrate to the Lord your own full contribution.

30"Tell them also: Once you have made your contribution from the best part, the rest of the tithes will be credited to you Levites as if it were produce of the threshing floor or of the wine press. **31**Your families, as well as you, may eat them anywhere, since they are your recompense for service at the meeting tent. **32**You will incur no guilt so long as you make a contribution of the best part. Do not profane the sacred gifts of the Israelites and so bring death on yourselves."

Ashes of the Red Heifer

19 **1**The Lord said to Moses and Aaron: **2**"This is the regulation which the law of the Lord prescribes. Tell the Israelites to procure for you a red heifer that is free from every blemish and defect and on which no yoke has ever been laid. **3†**This is to be given to Eleazar the priest, to be led outside the camp and slaughtered in his presence. **4†**Eleazar the priest shall take some of its blood on his finger and sprinkle it seven times toward the front of the meeting tent. **5**Then the heifer shall be burned in his sight, with its hide and flesh, its blood and offal; **6**and the priest shall take some cedar wood, hyssop and scarlet yarn and throw them into the fire in which the heifer is being burned. **7**The priest shall then wash his garments and bathe his body in water. He remains unclean until the evening, and only afterward may he

return to the camp. **8**Likewise, he who burned the heifer shall wash his garments, bathe his body in water, and be unclean until evening. **9**Finally, a man who is clean shall gather up the ashes of the heifer and deposit them in a clean place outside the camp. There they are to be kept for preparing lustral water for the Israelite community. The heifer is a sin offering. **10**He who has gathered up the ashes of the heifer shall also wash his garments and be unclean until evening. This is a perpetual ordinance, both for the Israelites and for the aliens residing among them.

Use of the Ashes

11"Whoever touches the dead body of any human being shall be unclean for seven days; **12**he shall purify himself with the water on the third and on the seventh day, and then he will be clean again. But if he fails to purify himself on the third and on the seventh day, he will not become clean. **13***Everyone who fails to purify himself after touching the body of any deceased person, defiles the Dwelling of the Lord and shall be cut off from Israel. Since the lustral water has not been splashed over him, he remains unclean: his uncleanness still clings to him.

14"This is the law: When a man dies in a tent, everyone who enters the tent, as well as everyone already in it, shall be unclean for seven days; **15**likewise, every vessel that is open, or with its lid unfastened, shall be unclean. **16**Moreover, everyone who in the open country touches a dead person, whether he was slain by the sword or died naturally, or who touches a human bone or a grave, shall be unclean for seven days. **17†**For anyone who is thus unclean, ashes from the sin offering shall be put in a vessel, and spring water shall be poured on them. **18**Then a man who is clean shall take some hyssop, dip it in this water, and sprinkle it on the tent and on all the vessels and persons that were in it, or on him who touched a bone, a slain person or other dead body, or a grave. **19**The clean man shall sprinkle the unclean on the third and on the seventh day; thus purified on the seventh day, he shall wash his garments and bathe his body in water, and in the evening he will be clean again. **20†**Any unclean man who fails to have himself purified shall be cut off from the community, because he defiles the sanctuary of the Lord. As long as the lustral water has not been

† 19, 3: *Outside the camp:* several Fathers of the Church saw in this a prefiguring of the sacrificial death of Christ outside the walls of Jerusalem; cf Jn 19, 20; Heb 13, 12; in the purifying water, into which the ashes of the red heifer were put, they saw a type of the water of Baptism.
19, 4: *Toward the front of the meeting tent:* since the tabernacle faced the east (Ex 26, 15-30), the killing of the heifer took place east of the camp; in later times it was done on the Mount of Olives, east of the Temple.
19, 17ff: "If . . . the sprinkled ashes of a heifer sanctify the unclean unto the cleansing of the flesh, how much more will the blood of Christ . . . cleanse your conscience from dead works?" (Heb 9, 13f).
19, 20: Ritual uncleanness is, as it were, contagious, so also sacredness; see note on 17, 3.

* 21: Heb 7, 5.　　　19/13: Lv 15, 31.

splashed over him, he remains unclean. **21**This shall be a perpetual ordinance for you.

"One who sprinkles the lustral water shall wash his garments, and anyone who comes in contact with this water shall be unclean until evening. **22**Moreover, whatever the unclean person touches becomes unclean itself, and anyone who touches it becomes unclean until evening." `

Death of Miriam

20 **1**†THE whole Israelite community arrived in the desert of Zin in the first month, and the people settled at Kadesh. It was here that Miriam died, and here that she was buried.

Water Famine at Kadesh

2As the community had no water, they held a council against Moses and Aaron. **3**The people contended with Moses, exclaiming, "Would that we too had perished with our kinsmen in the LORD's presence! **4**Why have you brought the LORD's community into this desert where we and our livestock are dying? **5**Why did you lead us out of Egypt, only to bring us to this wretched place which has neither grain nor figs nor vines nor pomegranates? Here there is not even water to drink!" **6**But Moses and Aaron went away from the assembly to the entrance of the meeting tent, where they fell prostrate.

Sin of Moses and Aaron

Then the glory of the LORD appeared to them, **7**and the LORD said to Moses, **8**"Take the staff and assemble the community, you and your brother Aaron, and in their presence order the rock to yield its waters. From the rock you shall bring forth water for the community and their livestock to drink." **9**So Moses took the staff from its place before the LORD, as he was ordered. **10***He and Aaron assembled the community in front of the rock, where he said to them, "Listen to me, you rebels! Are we to bring water for you out of this rock?" **11***†Then, raising his hand, Moses struck the rock twice with his staff, and water gushed out in abundance for the community and their livestock to drink. **12**†But the LORD said to Moses and Aaron, "Because you were not faithful to me in showing forth my sanctity before the Israelites, you shall not lead this community into the land I will give them."

13*These are the waters of Meribah, where the Israelites contended against the LORD, and where he revealed his sanctity among them.

Edom's Refusal

14†From Kadesh Moses sent men to the king of Edom with the message: "Your brother Israel has this to say: You know of all the hardships that have befallen us, **15**how our fathers went down to Egypt, where we stayed a long time, how the Egyptians maltreated us and our fathers, **16***and how, when we cried to the LORD, he heard our cry and sent an angel who led us out of Egypt. Now here we are at the town of Kadesh at the edge of your territory. **17**†Kindly let us pass through your country. We will not cross any fields or vineyards, nor drink any well water, but we will go straight along the royal road without turning to the right or to the left, until we have passed through your territory."

18But Edom answered him, "You shall not pass through here; if you do, I will advance against you with the sword." **19**The Israelites insisted, "We want only to go up along the highway. If we or our livestock drink any of your water, we will pay for it. Surely there is no harm in merely letting us march through." **20***But Edom still said, "No, you shall not pass through," and advanced against them with a large and heavily armed force. **21***Therefore, since Edom refused to let them pass through their territory, Israel detoured around them.

Death of Aaron

22†Setting out from Kadesh, the whole Israelite community came to Mount Hor. **23**There at Mount Hor, on the border of the land of Edom, the LORD said to Moses and Aaron, **24**"Aaron is about to be taken to his people; he shall not enter the land I am giving to the Israelites, because you both rebelled against my commandment at the waters of Meribah. **25***Take Aaron and his son Eleazar and bring them up on Mount Hor. **26**Then strip Aaron of his garments and put them on his son Eleazar; for there Aaron shall be taken in death."

27Moses did as the LORD commanded. When they had climbed Mount Hor in view of the whole com-

---

† 20, 1: *The first month:* we would expect the mention also of the day and of the year (after the exodus) when this took place; cf similar dates in 1, 1; 10, 11; 33, 38; Dt 1, 3. Here the full date seems to have been lost. Probably the Israelites arrived in Kadesh in the third year after the exodus. Cf Dt 1, 46. *The desert of Zin:* a barren region with a few good oases, southwest of the Dead Sea. See note on 13, 21.

20, 11: *Twice:* perhaps because he had not sufficient faith to work the miracle with the first blow. Cf v 12.

20, 12f: The sin of Moses and Aaron consisted in doubting God's mercy toward the ever-rebellious people. *In showing forth my sanctity:* God's sacred power and glory: an allusion to the name of the place, *Kadesh,* which means "sanctified, sacred." *Meribah* means "contention." Cf Ex 17, 7.

20, 14: *Your brother Israel:* the Edomites were descended from Esau, the brother of Jacob. Their country, to the southeast of the Dead Sea, was also known as Seir; cf Gn 25, 24ff; 36, 1.8f.

20, 17: *The royal road:* an important highway, running north and south along the plateau east of the Dead Sea. In ancient times it was much used by caravans and armies; later it was improved by the Romans, and large stretches of it are still clearly recognizable.

20, 22: *Mount Hor:* not definitively identified, but probably to be sought in the vicinity of Kadesh. According to Dt 10, 6, Aaron died at Moserah (cf "Moseroth" in Nm 33, 30f), which is apparently the name of the region in which Mount Hor is situated.

* 20/10: Ex 17, 5f.
    11: Ps 78, 15f.;
       Wis 11, 4; 1 Cor 10, 4.
    13: 27, 14; Ex 17, 7.

16: Ex 2, 23.
20: Jgs 11, 17.
21f: 33, 37.
25f: Dt 32, 50.

munity, **28***Moses stripped Aaron of his garments and put them on his son Eleazar. Then Aaron died there on top of the mountain. When Moses and Eleazar came down from the mountain, **29**all the community understood that Aaron had passed away; and for thirty days the whole house of Israel mourned him.

Victory over Arad

21 **1*†**WHEN the Canaanite king of Arad, who lived in the Negeb, heard that the Israelites were coming along the way of Atharim, he engaged them in battle and took some of them captive. **2***Israel then made this vow to the LORD: "If you deliver this people into my hand, I will doom their cities." **3*†**Later, when the LORD heeded Israel's prayer and delivered up the Canaanites, they doomed them and their cities. Hence that place was named Hormah.

The Bronze Serpent

4From Mount Hor they set out on the Red Sea road, to by-pass the land of Edom. But with their patience worn out by the journey, **5*†**the people complained against God and Moses, "Why have you brought us up from Egypt to die in this desert, where there is no food or water? We are disgusted with this wretched food!" **6*†**In punishment the LORD sent among the people saraph serpents, which bit the people so that many of them died. **7**Then the people came to Moses and said, "We have sinned in complaining against the LORD and you. Pray the LORD to take the serpents from us." So Moses prayed for the people, **8†**and the LORD said to Moses, "Make a saraph and mount it on a pole, and if anyone who has been bitten looks at it, he will recover." **9*†**Moses accordingly made a bronze serpent and mounted it on a pole, and whenever anyone who had been bitten by a serpent looked at the bronze serpent, he recovered.

Journey around Moab

10*The Israelites moved on and encamped in Oboth. **11†**Setting out from Oboth, they encamped in Iye-abarim in the desert fronting Moab on the east. **12**Setting out from there, they encamped in the Wadi Zered. **13**Setting out from there, they encamped on the other side of the Arnon, in the desert that extends from the territory of the Amorites; for the Arnon forms Moab's boundary with the Amorites. **14†**Hence it is said in the "Book of the Wars of the LORD":

"Waheb in Suphah and the wadies,
  15Arnon and the wadi gorges
That reach back toward the site of Ar
  and slant to the border of Moab."

16†From there they went to Beer, where there was the well of which the LORD said to Moses, "Bring the

people together, and I will give them water." **17**Then it was that Israel sang this song:

"Spring up, O well!—so sing to it—
  18The well that the princes sank,
    that the nobles of the people dug,
    with their scepters and their staffs."

From Beer they went to Mattanah, **19**from Mattanah to Nahaliel, from Nahaliel to Bamoth, **20†**from Bamoth to the cleft in the plateau of Moab at the headland of Pisgah that overlooks Jeshimon.

Victory over Sihon

21Now Israel sent men to Sihon, king of the Amorites, with the message, **22**"Let us pass through your country. We will not turn aside into any field or vineyard, nor will we drink any well water, but we will go straight along the royal road until we have passed through your territory." **23***Sihon, however, would not let Israel pass through his territory, but mustered all his forces and advanced into the desert against Israel. When he reached Jahaz, he engaged Israel in battle. **24**But Israel defeated him at the point of the sword, and took possession of his land from the Arnon to the Jabbok and as far as the country of the Ammonites, whose boundary was at Jazer. **25***Israel seized all the towns here and settled in these towns of the Amorites, in Heshbon and all its dependencies. **26**Now Heshbon was the capital of Sihon, king of the Amorites, who had fought against the former king of Moab and had seized all his land from Jazer to the Arnon. **27**That is why the poets say:

---

†

21, 1-3: The account of this episode seems to be a later insertion here, for 21, 4, belongs logically immediately after 20, 29. Perhaps this is the same event as that mentioned in Jgs 1, 16f.

21, 3: *Hormah:* related to the Hebrew word *herem,* meaning "doomed." See notes on 14, 45; 18, 14.

21, 5: *This wretched food:* apparently the manna is meant.

21, 6: *Saraph:* the Hebrew name for a certain species of venomous snakes; the word probably signifies "the fiery one," these snakes being so called from the burning effect of their poisonous bite.

21, 8: *If anyone who has been bitten looks at it, he will recover:* "and as Moses lifted up the serpent in the desert, even so must the Son of Man be lifted up, that those who believe in him may not perish, but may have life everlasting" (Jn 3, 14f).

21, 9: King Hezekiah, in his efforts to abolish idolatry, "smashed the bronze serpent which Moses had made" (2 Kgs 18, 4).

21, 11: *Iyeabarim* probably means "the ruins in the Abarim (Mountains)." See note on 27, 12.

21, 14: *The "Book of the Wars of the Lord":* an ancient collection of Israelite songs, now lost. *Waheb in Suphah:* since neither place is mentioned elsewhere, it is quite uncertain whether these dubious Hebrew words are even to be considered as place names; some Hebrew words apparently lost must have preceded this phrase.

21, 16: *Beer* means a well.

21, 20: *Jeshimon:* "the wasteland"; in 1 Sm 23, 19.24, and 26, 1.3, this is the desert of Judah, on the western side of the Dead Sea, but here and in Nm 23, 28, it seems to refer to the southern end of the Jordan valley where Beth-jeshimoth was situated.

✢
    28: 33, 38.   6: Dt 8, 15; Wis 16, 5;
  21/1: 33, 40.   1 Cor 10, 9.
    2: Jos 6, 17; Jgs 1, 17.   9: Wis 16, 6f.10; Jn 3, 14f.
    3: 14, 45.   10: 33, 43f.
    5: 11, 6; Ex 16, 3.   23: Dt 2, 32; Jgs 11, 20.
                          25f: Jos 21, 39; Jgs 11, 26.

"Come to Heshbon, let it be rebuilt,
    let Sihon's capital be firmly constructed.
28For fire went forth from Heshbon
    and a blaze from the city of Sihon;
It consumed the cities of Moab
    and swallowed up the high places of the Arnon.
29†Woe to you, O Moab!
    You are ruined, O people of Chemosh!
He let his sons become fugitives
    and his daughters be taken captive
    by the Amorite king Sihon.
30Their plowland is ruined from Heshbon to Dibon;
    Ar is laid waste; fires blaze as far as Medeba."

31When Israel had settled in the land of the Amorites, 32Moses sent spies to Jazer; Israel then captured it with its dependencies and dispossessed the Amorites who were there.

Victory over Og

33*Then they turned and went up along the road to Bashan. But Og, king of Bashan, advanced against them with all his people to give battle at Edrei. 34*The Lord, however, said to Moses, "Do not be afraid of him; for into your hand I will deliver him with all his people and his land. Do to him as you did to Sihon, king of the Amorites, who lived in Heshbon." 35So they struck him down with his sons and all his people, until not a survivor was left to him, and they took possession of his land.

22 1†THEN the Israelites moved on and encamped in the plains of Moab on the other side of the Jericho stretch of the Jordan.

III: ON THE PLAINS OF MOAB

Balaam Summoned

2NOW BALAK, SON OF ZIPPOR, saw all that Israel did to the Amorites. 3Indeed, Moab feared the Israelites greatly because of their numbers, and detested them. 4So Moab said to the elders of Midian, "Soon this horde will devour all the country around us as an ox devours the grass of the field." And Balak, Zippor's son, who was king of Moab at that time, 5sent messengers to Balaam, son of Beor, at Pethor on the Euphrates, in the land of the Amawites, summoning him with these words, "A people has come here from Egypt who now cover the face of the earth and are settling down opposite us! 6†Please come and curse this people for us; they are stronger than we are. We may then be able to defeat them and drive them out of the country. For I know that whoever you bless is blessed and whoever you curse is cursed." 7Then the elders of Moab and of Midian left with the divination

fee in hand and went to Balaam. When they had given him Balak's message, 8he said to them in reply, "Stay here overnight, and I will give you whatever answer the Lord gives me." So the princes of Moab lodged with Balaam.

9Then God came to Balaam and said, "Who are these men visiting you?" 10Balaam answered God, "Balak, son of Zippor, king of Moab, sent me the message: 11'This people that came here from Egypt now cover the face of the earth. Please come and lay a curse on them for us; we may then be able to give them battle and drive them out.'" 12But God said to Balaam, "Do not go with them and do not curse this people, for they are blessed." 13The next morning Balaam arose and told the princes of Balak, "Go back to your own country, for the Lord has refused to let me go with you." 14So the princes of Moab went back to Balak with the report, "Balaam refused to come with us."

Second Appeal to Balaam

15Balak again sent princes, who were more numerous and more distinguished than the others. 16On coming to Balaam they told him, "This is what Balak, son of Zippor, has to say: Please do not refuse to come to me. 17I will reward you very handsomely and will do anything you ask of me. Please come and lay a curse on this people for me." 18*But Balaam replied to Balak's officials, "Even if Balak gave me his house full of silver and gold, I could not do anything, small or great, contrary to the command of the Lord, my God. 19But, you too shall stay here overnight, till I learn what else the Lord may tell me."

20That night God came to Balaam and said to him, "If these men have come to summon you, you may go with them; yet only on the condition that you do exactly as I tell you." 21So the next morning when Balaam arose, he saddled his ass, and went off with the princes of Moab.

The Talking Ass

22†But now the anger of God flared up at him for going, and the angel of the Lord stationed himself on

---

† 21, 29: *Chemosh:* the chief god of the Moabites, and mentioned as such in the famous inscription of Mesha, king of Moab, who was the contemporary of the dynasty of Omri in Israel. Cf 1 Kgs 11, 7.33; 2 Kgs 23, 13; Jer 48, 7.13.
22, 1: *The plains of Moab:* the lowlands to the northeast of the Dead Sea, between the Jordan and the foothills below Mount Nebo. Here the Israelites remained until they crossed the Jordan, as told in Jos 1-4. *Jericho* lay to the west of the Jordan.
22, 6: *Curse this people for us:* Balak believed that if Balaam forecast an evil omen for Israel, this evil would come to pass, as if by magic. Balaam was a soothsayer or foreteller; cf Jos 13, 22.
22, 22: *The anger of God flared up:* not merely because Balaam was going to Balak, for he had God's permission for the journey (v 20), but perhaps because he was tempted by avarice to curse Israel against God's command. "They have followed the way of Balaam, son of Bosor, who loved the wages of wrongdoing" (2 Pt 2, 15); "and have rushed on thoughtlessly into the error of Balaam for the sake of gain" (Jude 11). Cf v 32 and compare Ex 4, 18-26.

* 33: Dt 3, 1ff.   22/18: 24, 13.
34: Ps 136, 17ff.

the road to hinder him as he was riding along on his ass, accompanied by two of his servants. **23**When the ass saw the angel of the Lord standing on the road with sword drawn, she turned off the road and went into the field, and Balaam had to beat her to bring her back on the road. **24**Then the angel of the Lord took his stand in a narrow lane between vineyards with a stone wall on each side. **25**When the ass saw the angel of the Lord there, she shrank against the wall; and since she squeezed Balaam's leg against it, he beat her again. **26**The angel of the Lord then went ahead, and stopped next in a passage so narrow that there was no room to move either to the right or to the left. **27**When the ass saw the angel of the Lord there, she cowered under Balaam. So, in anger, he again beat the ass with his stick.

28＊But now the Lord opened the mouth of the ass, and she asked Balaam, "What have I done to you that you should beat me these three times?" **29**"You have acted so willfully against me," said Balaam to the ass, "that if I but had a sword at hand, I would kill you here and now." **30**But the ass said to Balaam, "Am I not your own beast, and have you not always ridden upon me until now? Have I been in the habit of treating you this way before?" "No," replied Balaam.

31Then the Lord removed the veil from Balaam's eyes, so that he too saw the angel of the Lord standing on the road with sword drawn; and he fell on his knees and bowed to the ground. **32**But the angel of the Lord said to him, "Why have you beaten your ass these three times? It is I who have come armed to hinder you because this rash journey of yours is directly opposed to me. **33**When the ass saw me, she turned away from me these three times. If she had not turned away from me, I would have killed you; her I would have spared." **34**Then Balaam said to the angel of the Lord, "I have sinned. Yet I did not know that you stood against me to oppose my journey. Since it has displeased you, I will go back home." **35**But the angel of the Lord said to Balaam, "Go with the men; but you may say only what I tell you." So Balaam went on with the princes of Balak.

36When Balak heard that Balaam was coming, he went out to meet him at the boundary city Ir-Moab on the Arnon at the end of the Moabite territory. **37**And he said to Balaam, "I sent an urgent summons to you! Why did you not come to me? Did you think I could not reward you?" **38**Balaam answered him, "Well, I have come to you after all. But what power have I to say anything? I can speak only what God puts in my mouth." **39**Then Balaam went with Balak, and they came to Kiriath-huzoth. **40**Here Balak slaughtered oxen and sheep, and sent portions to Balaam and to the princes who were with him.

The First Oracle

41The next morning Balak took Balaam up on Bamoth-baal, and from there he saw some of the clans.

23

1THEN Balaam said to Balak, "Build me seven altars, and prepare seven bullocks and seven rams for me here." **2**So he did as Balaam had ordered, offering a bullock and a ram on each altar. And Balak said to him, "I have erected the seven altars, and have offered a bullock and a ram on each." **3**Balaam then said to him, "Stand here by your holocaust while I go over there. Perhaps the Lord will meet me, and then I will tell you whatever he lets me see." He went out on the barren height, **4**and God met him. **5**When he had put an utterance in Balaam's mouth, the Lord said to him, "Go back to Balak, and speak accordingly." **6**So he went back to Balak, who was still standing by his holocaust together with all the princes of Moab. **7**＊†Then Balaam gave voice to his oracle:

> From Aram has Balak brought me here,
>> Moab's king, from the Eastern Mountains:
> "Come and lay a curse for me on Jacob,
>> come and denounce Israel."
> **8**How can I curse whom God has not cursed?
>> How denounce whom the Lord has not
>>> denounced?
> **9**†For from the top of the crags I see him,
>> from the heights I behold him.
> Here is a people that lives apart
>> and does not reckon itself among the nations.
> **10**†Who has ever counted the dust of Jacob,
>> or numbered Israel's wind-borne particles?
> May I die the death of the just,
>> may my descendants be as many as theirs!

11"What have you done to me?" cried Balak to Balaam. "It was to curse my foes that I brought you here; instead, you have even blessed them." **12**Balaam replied, "Is it not what the Lord puts in my mouth that I must repeat with care?"

The Second Oracle

13†Then Balak said to him, "Please come with me to another place from which you can see only some and not all of them, and from there curse them for me." **14**So he brought him to the lookout field on the top of Pisgah, where he built seven altars and offered a bullock and a ram on each of them. **15**Balaam then said to

---

† 23, 7: *Aram:* the ancient name of the region later known as Syria. *The Eastern Mountains:* the low ranges in the Syrian desert near the Euphrates and Balaam's town of Pethor; cf 22, 5.

23, 9: *A people that lives apart:* Israel, as the chosen people of God, occupied a unique place among the nations, from which they kept themselves aloof.

23, 10: *The dust of Jacob . . . Israel's wind-borne particles:* the Israelites will be as numerous as dust in a desert sandstorm. *May I . . . as many as theirs:* a formula by which Balaam swears he is speaking the truth; he sees the reward of virtue in having numerous descendants.

23, 13: *To another place:* Balak thought that if Balaam would view Israel from a different site, he could forecast a different kind of omen.

Balak, "Stand here by your holocaust, while I seek a meeting over there." **16**Then the LORD met Balaam, and having put an utterance in his mouth, he said to him, "Go back to Balak, and speak accordingly." **17**So he went back to Balak, who was still standing by his holocaust together with the princes of Moab. When Balak asked him, "What did the LORD say?" **18**Balaam gave voice to his oracle:

> Be aroused, O Balak, and hearken;
>> give ear to my testimony, O son of Zippor!
> **19**God is not man that he should speak falsely,
>> nor human, that he should change his mind.
> Is he one to speak and not act,
>> to decree and not fulfill?
> **20**It is a blessing I have been given to pronounce;
>> a blessing which I cannot restrain.
> **21**†Misfortune is not observed in Jacob,
>> nor misery seen in Israel.
> The LORD, his God, is with him;
>> with him is the triumph of his King.
> **22***†It is God who brought him out of Egypt,
>> a wild bull of towering might.
> **23**No, there is no sorcery against Jacob,
>> nor omen against Israel.
> It shall yet be said of Jacob,
>> and of Israel, "Behold what God has wrought!"
> **24***Here is a people that springs up like a lioness,
>> and stalks forth like a lion;
> It rests not till it has devoured its prey
>> and has drunk the blood of the slain.

25"Even though you cannot curse them," said Balak to Balaam, "at least do not bless them." **26**But Balaam answered Balak, "Did I not warn you that I must do all that the LORD tells me?"

The Third Oracle

27Then Balak said to Balaam, "Come, let me bring you to another place; perhaps God will approve of your cursing them for me from there." **28**So he took Balaam to the top of Peor, that overlooks Jeshimon. **29**Balaam then said to him, "Here build me seven altars; and here prepare for me seven bullocks and seven rams." **30**And Balak did as Balaam had ordered, offering a bullock and a ram on each altar.

24 **1**BALAAM, however, perceiving that the LORD was pleased to bless Israel, did not go aside as before to seek omens, but turned his gaze toward the desert. **2**When he raised his eyes and saw Israel encamped, tribe by tribe, the spirit of God came upon him, **3**and he gave voice to his oracle:

> The utterance of Balaam, son of Beor,
>> the utterance of the man whose eye is true,

4The utterance of one who hears what God says,
>> and knows what the Most High knows,
> Of one who sees what the Almighty sees,
>> enraptured, and with eyes unveiled:
> **5**How goodly are your tents, O Jacob;
>> your encampments, O Israel!
> **6**They are like gardens beside a stream,
>> like the cedars planted by the LORD.
> **7**His wells shall yield free-flowing waters,
>> he shall have the sea within reach;
> His king shall rise higher than . . . .
>> and his royalty shall be exalted.
> **8***It is God who brought him out of Egypt,
>> a wild bull of towering might.
> He shall devour the nations like grass,
>> their bones he shall strip bare.
> **9***He lies crouching like a lion,
>> or like a lioness; who shall arouse him?
> Blessed is he who blesses you,
>> and cursed is he who curses you!

10*†Balak beat his palms together in a blaze of anger at Balaam and said to him, "It was to curse my foes that I summoned you here; yet three times now you have even blessed them instead! **11**Be off at once, then, to your home. I promised to reward you richly, but the LORD has withheld the reward from you!" **12**Balaam replied to Balak, "Did I not warn the very messengers whom you sent to me, **13***'Even if Balak gave me his house full of silver and gold, I could not of my own accord do anything, good or evil, contrary to the command of the LORD'? Whatever the LORD says I must repeat.

The Fourth Oracle

14"But now that I am about to go to my own people, let me first warn you what this people will do to your people in the days to come." **15**Then Balaam gave voice to his oracle:

> The utterance of Balaam, son of Beor,
>> the utterance of the man whose eye is true,
> **16**The utterance of one who hears what God says,
>> and knows what the Most High knows,
> Of one who sees what the Almighty sees,
>> enraptured and with eyes unveiled.
> **17***†I see him, though not now;
>> I behold him, though not near:

---

†   23, 21: *Misfortune . . . misery:* Balaam admits that he is unable to predict any evils for Israel.

23, 22: *A wild bull of towering might:* the reference is to Israel, rather than to God.

24, 10: *Balak beat his palms:* a sign of disclaiming any responsibility for paying the promised reward.

24, 17: *A star . . . a staff:* many of the Fathers have understood this as a Messianic prophecy, although it is not referred to anywhere in the New Testament; in this sense the *star* is Christ himself, just as he is the *staff from Israel;* cf Is 11, 1. But it is doubtful whether this passage is to be connected with the "star of the Magi" in Mt 2, 1-12. *The Shuthites:* mentioned in other documents of this period as nomads on the borders of Palestine.

✤
  22: 24, 8.   10: 23, 11.
  24: 24, 9; Gn 49, 9.   13: 22, 18.
24/8: 23, 22.   17: 2 Sm 8, 2.
  9: 23, 24; Gn 12, 3;
    27, 29; 49, 9.

A star shall advance from Jacob,
and a staff shall rise from Israel,
That shall smite the brows of Moab,
and the skulls of all the Shuthites,
18Till Edom is dispossessed,
and no fugitive is left in Seir.
Israel shall do valiantly,
19and Jacob shall overcome his foes.

20*†Upon seeing Amalek, Balaam gave voice to his oracle:

First of the peoples was Amalek,
but his end is to perish forever.

21†Upon seeing the Kenites, he gave voice to his oracle:

Your abode is enduring, O smith,
and your nest is set on a cliff;
22Yet destined for burning—
even as I watch—are your inhabitants.

23†Upon seeing . . . . he gave voice to his oracle:

Alas, who shall survive of Ishmael,
24to deliver his people from the hands of the Kittim?
When they have conquered Asshur and conquered Eber,
He too shall perish forever.

25Then Balaam set out on his journey home; and Balak also went his way.

Worship of Baal of Peor

25 **1*†**WHILE Israel was living at Shittim, the people degraded themselves by having illicit relations with the Moabite women. **2***These then invited the people to the sacrifices of their god, and the people ate of the sacrifices and worshiped their god. **3***When Israel thus submitted to the rites of Baal of Peor, the LORD's anger flared up against Israel, **4*†**and he said to Moses, "Gather all the leaders of the people, and hold a public execution of the guilty ones before the LORD, that his blazing wrath may be turned away from Israel." **5**So Moses told the Israelite judges, "Each of you shall kill those of his men who have submitted to the rites of Baal of Peor."

Zeal of Phinehas

6†Yet a certain Israelite came and brought in a Midianite woman to his clansmen in the view of Moses and of the whole Israelite community, while they were weeping at the entrance of the meeting tent. **7***When Phinehas, son of Eleazar, son of Aaron the priest, saw this, he left the assembly, and taking a lance in hand,

8followed the Israelite into his retreat where he pierced the pair of them, the Israelite and the woman. Thus the slaughter of Israelites was checked; **9**but only after twenty-four thousand had died.

10Then the LORD said to Moses, **11**"Phinehas, son of Eleazar, son of Aaron the priest, has turned my anger from the Israelites by his zeal for my honor among them; that is why I did not put an end to the Israelites for the offense to my honor. **12***Announce, therefore, that I hereby give him my pledge of friendship, **13**which shall be for him and for his descendants after him the pledge of an everlasting priesthood, because he was zealous on behalf of his God and thus made amends for the Israelites."

14†The Israelite slain with the Midianite woman was Zimri, son of Salu, prince of an ancestral house of the Simeonites. **15**The slain Midianite woman was Cozbi, daughter of Zur, who was head of a clan, an ancestral house, in Midian.

Vengeance on the Midianites

16†The LORD then said to Moses, **17***"Treat the Midianites as enemies and crush them, **18**for they have been your enemies by their wily dealings with you as regards Peor and as regards their kinswoman Cozbi, the daughter of a Midianite prince, who was killed at the time of the slaughter because of Peor."

---

† 24, 20: *First:* literally "the beginning." Amalek was an aboriginal people in Palestine and therefore considered as of great antiquity. There is a deliberate contrast here between the words *first* and *end.*

24, 21: *The Kenites* lived in high strongholds in the mountains of southern Palestine and the Sinai Peninsula, and were skilled in working the various metals found in their territory. Their name is connected, at least by popular etymology, with the Hebrew word for "smith"; of similar sound is the Hebrew word for "nest"—hence the play on words in the present passage.

24, 23f: The translation of this short oracle is based on a reconstructed text and is rather uncertain. *Ishmael:* the survival of Ishmael is indicated in Gn 17, 20; 21, 13.18.

25, 1: *Shittim:* the full name was Abel-shittim, a locality at the foot of the mountains in the northeastern corner of *the plains of Moab* (33, 49). *Illicit relations:* perhaps as part of the licentious worship of Baal of Peor.

25, 4: *Hold a public execution:* the same phrase occurs in 2 Sm 21, 6-14, where the context shows that at least a part of the penalty consisted in being denied honorable burial. In both passages, dismemberment as a punishment for the breaking of covenant pledges is a current understanding of the phrase.

25, 6: *Midianite woman:* at this time the Midianites were leagued with the Moabites in opposing Israel; cf 22, 4.7. Balaam had induced both the Midianites (31, 16) and the Moabites (Ap 2, 14) to lure the Israelites to the obscene rites of Baal of Peor. *They were weeping:* on account of the plague that had struck them; cf v 8.

25, 11: *For my honor:* by taking vengeance on those who had made Baal of Peor a rival of the Lord.

25, 14f: The nobility of the slain couple is mentioned in order to stress the courage of Phinehas in punishing them. The zeal of Phinehas became proverbial; cf Ps 106, 30; Sir 45, 23; 1 Mc 2, 26.54.

25, 16ff: The account of the execution of this command is given in Nm 31, 1-18.

20: Ex 17, 14; 1 Sm 15, 3.
25/1: 31, 16.
2: Ex 34, 15f.
3: Ps 106, 28; Hos 9, 10.
4: Dt 4, 3.
7: Ps 106, 30.
12f: Sir 45, 23f; Ps 106, 31; 1 Mc 2, 26.54.
17f: 31, 2-12.

The Second Census

26 AFTER the slaughter [1]the LORD said to Moses and Eleazar, son of Aaron the priest, [2*]"Take a census, by ancestral houses, throughout the community of the Israelites of all those of twenty years or more who are fit for military service in Israel." [3]So on the plains of Moab along the Jericho stretch of the Jordan, Moses and the priest Eleazar registered [4]those of twenty years or more, as the LORD had commanded Moses.

The Israelites who came out of the land of Egypt were as follows:

[5*]Of Reuben, the first-born of Israel, the Reubenites by clans were: through Hanoch the clan of the Hanochites, through Pallu the clan of the Palluites, [6]through Hezron the clan of the Hezronites, through Carmi the clan of the Carmites. [7]These were the clans of the Reubenites, of whom forty-three thousand seven hundred and thirty men were registered.

[8]From Pallu descended Eliab, [9*]and the descendants of Eliab were Dathan and Abiram—the same Dathan and Abiram, councilors of the community, who revolted against Moses and Aaron [like Korah's band when it rebelled against the LORD]. [10]The earth opened its mouth and swallowed them as a warning [Korah too and the band that died when the fire consumed two hundred and fifty men. [11]The descendants of Korah, however, did not die out].

[12†]The Simeonites by clans were: through Nemuel the clan of the Nemuelites, through Jamin the clan of the Jaminites, through Jachin the clan of the Jachinites, [13]through Sohar the clan of the Soharites, through Shaul the clan of the Shaulites. [14]These were the clans of the Simeonites, of whom twenty-two thousand two hundred men were registered.

[15]The Gadites by clans were: through Zephon the clan of the Zephonites, through Haggi the clan of the Haggites, through Shuni the clan of the Shunites, [16]through Ozni the clan of the Oznites, through Eri the clan of the Erites, [17]through Arod the clan of the Arodites, through Areli the clan of the Arelites. [18]These were the clans of the Gadites, of whom forty thousand five hundred men were registered.

[19*]The sons of Judah who died in the land of Canaan were Er and Onan. [20]The Judahites by clans were: through Shelah the clan of the Shelahites, through Perez the clan of the Perezites, through Zerah the clan of the Zerahites. [21]The Perezites were: through Hezron the clan of the Hezronites, through Hamul the clan of the Hamulites. [22]These were the clans of Judah, of whom seventy-six thousand five hundred men were registered.

[23]The Issacharites by clans were: through Tola the clan of the Tolaites, through Puvah the clan of the Puvahites, [24]through Jashub the clan of the Jashubites, through Shimron the clan of the Shimronites. [25]These were the clans of Issachar, of whom sixty-four thousand three hundred men were registered.

[26]The Zebulunites by clans were: through Sered the clan of the Seredites, through Elon the clan of the Elonites, through Jahleel the clan of the Jahleelites. [27]These were the clans of the Zebulunites, of whom sixty thousand five hundred men were registered.

[28]The sons of Joseph were Manasseh and Ephraim. [29]The Manassehites by clans were: through Machir the clan of the Machirites, through Gilead, a descendant of Machir, the clan of the Gileadites. [30]The Gileadites were: through Abiezer the clan of the Abiezrites, through Helek the clan of the Helekites, [31]through Asriel the clan of the Asrielites, through Shechem the clan of the Shechemites, [32]through Shemida the clan of the Shemidaites, through Hepher the clan of the Hepherites. [33*]Zelophehad, son of Hepher, had no sons, but only daughters, whose names were Mahlah, Noah, Hoglah, Milcah and Tirzah. [34]These were the clans of Manasseh, of whom fifty-two thousand seven hundred men were registered.

[35]The Ephraimites by clans were: through Shuthelah the clan of the Shuthelahites, through Becher the clan of the Bechrites, through Tahan the clan of the Tahanites. [36]The Shuthelahites were: through Eran the clan of the Eranites. [37]These were the clans of the Ephraimites, of whom thirty-two thousand five hundred men were registered.

These were the descendants of Joseph by clans.

[38]The Benjaminites by clans were: through Bela the clan of the Belaites, through Ashbel the clan of the Ashbelites, through Ahiram the clan of the Ahiramites, [39]through Shupham the clan of the Shuphamites, through Hupham the clan of the Huphamites. [40]The descendants of Bela were Arad and Naaman: through Arad the clan of the Aradites, through Naaman the clan of the Naamanites. [41]These were the Benjaminites by clans, of whom forty-five thousand six hundred men were registered.

[42]The Danites by clans were: through Shuham the clan of the Shuhamites. These were the clans of Dan, [43]of whom sixty-four thousand four hundred men were registered.

[44]The Asherites by clans were: through Imnah the clan of the Imnites, through Ishvi the clan of the Ishvites, through Beriah the clan of the Beriites, [45]through Heber the clan of the Heberites, through Malchiel the clan of the Malchielites. [46]The name of Asher's daughter was Serah. [47]These were the clans of Asher, of whom fifty-three thousand four hundred men were registered.

[48]The Naphtalites by clans were: through Jahzeel the clan of the Jahzeelites, through Guni the clan of the Gunites, [49]through Jezer the clan of the Jezerites, through Shillem the clan of the Shillemites. [50]These

---

✿
26/2: 1, 2f.   19: Gn 38, 7.10; 46, 12;
5f: 1 Chr 5, 3.   1 Chr 2, 3.
9f: 16, 1.32.   33: 27, 1; 36, 11; Jos 17, 3.

---

†
26, 12: *Nemuel:* so also in Gn 46, 10; 1 Chr 4, 24. In Ex 6, 15, the same man is called "Jemuel"; it is uncertain which form is correct.

were the clans of Naphtali, of whom forty-five thousand four hundred men were registered.

⁵¹These six hundred and one thousand seven hundred and thirty were the Israelites who were registered.

Allotment of the Land

⁵²†The Lord said to Moses, ⁵³*"Among these groups the land shall be divided as their heritage in keeping with the number of individuals in each group. ⁵⁴*To a large group you shall assign a large heritage, to a small group a small heritage, each group receiving its heritage in proportion to the number of men registered in it. ⁵⁵But the land shall be divided by lot, as the heritage of the various ancestral tribes. ⁵⁶As the lot falls shall each group, large or small, be assigned its heritage."

Census of the Levites

⁵⁷The Levites registered by clans were: through Gershon the clan of the Gershonites, through Kohath the clan of the Kohathites, through Merari the clan of the Merarites. ⁵⁸These also were clans of Levi: the clan of the Libnites, the clan of the Hebronites, the clan of the Mahlites, the clan of the Mushites, the clan of the Korahites.

Among the descendants of Kohath was Amram, ⁵⁹whose wife was named Jochebed. She also was of the tribe of Levi, born to the tribe in Egypt. To Amram she bore Aaron and Moses and their sister Miriam. ⁶⁰To Aaron were born Nadab and Abihu, Eleazar and Ithamar. ⁶¹But Nadab and Abihu died when they offered profane fire before the Lord.

⁶²*The total number of male Levites one month or more of age, who were registered, was twenty-three thousand. They were not registered with the other Israelites, however, for no heritage was given them among the Israelites.

⁶³These, then, were the men registered by Moses and the priest Eleazar in the census of the Israelites taken on the plains of Moab along the Jericho stretch of the Jordan. ⁶⁴Among them there was not a man of those who had been registered by Moses and the priest Aaron in the census of the Israelites taken in the desert of Sinai. ⁶⁵*For the Lord had told them that they would surely die in the desert, and not one of them was left except Caleb, son of Jephunneh, and Joshua, son of Nun.

Zelophehad's Daughters

27 ¹*ZELOPHEHAD, son of Hepher, son of Gilead, son of Machir, son of Manasseh, son of Joseph, had daughters named Mahlah, Noah, Hoglah, Milcah and Tirzah. They came forward, ²and standing in the presence of Moses, the priest Eleazar, the princes, and the whole community at the entrance of the meeting tent, said: ³†"Our father died in the desert. Although he did not join those who banded together against the Lord [in Korah's band], he died for his own sin without leaving any sons. ⁴But why should our father's name be withdrawn from his clan merely because he had no son? Let us, therefore, have property among our father's kinsmen."

Laws Concerning Heiresses

⁵†When Moses laid their case before the Lord, ⁶the Lord said to him, ⁷"The plea of Zelophehad's daughters is just; you shall give them hereditary property among their father's kinsmen, letting their father's heritage pass on to them. ⁸Therefore, tell the Israelites: If a man dies without leaving a son, you shall let his heritage pass on to his daughter; ⁹if he has no daughter, you shall give his heritage to his brothers; ¹⁰if he has no brothers, you shall give his heritage to his father's brothers; ¹¹*if his father had no brothers, you shall give his heritage to his nearest relative in his clan, who shall then take possession of it." This is the legal norm for the Israelites, as the Lord commanded Moses.

Joshua to Succeed Moses

¹²*†The Lord said to Moses, "Go up here into the Abarim Mountains and view the land that I am giving to the Israelites. ¹³*When you have viewed it, you too shall be taken to your people, as was your brother Aaron, ¹⁴*because in the rebellion of the community in the desert of Zin you both rebelled against my order to manifest my sanctity to them by means of the water." [This is the water of Meribah of Kadesh in the desert of Zin.]

¹⁵Then Moses said to the Lord, ¹⁶†"May the Lord, the God of the spirits of all mankind, set over the community a man ¹⁷who shall act as their leader in all things, to guide them in all their actions; that the

---

† 26, 52-56: The division of Canaan among the various tribes and clans and families was determined partly by the size of each group and partly by lot. Perhaps the lots determined the respective locality of each tribal land and the section reserved for each clan, while the relative size of the allotted locality and section depended on the numerical strength of each group. The Hebrews considered the outcome of the drawing of lots as an expression of God's will; cf Acts 1, 23-26.

27, 3: *He did not join . . . against the Lord:* had he done so, he and his heirs could have rightly been deprived of the privilege of receiving a portion in the Promised Land.

27, 5-11: The purpose of this law, as also that of the related laws in Nm 36, 2-10 (heiresses to marry within the same tribe), Dt 25, 5-10 (levirate marriage), and Lv 25, 10 (return of property in the jubilee year), was to keep the landed property within the proper domain of each tribe.

27, 12: *The Abarim Mountains:* the range on the eastern side of the Dead Sea.

27, 16: *The God of the spirits of all mankind:* the sense is either that God knows the character and abilities of all men and therefore knows best whom to appoint (cf Acts 1, 24), or, more probably, that God is Master of life and death and therefore can call Moses from this world whenever he wishes; cf the same phrase in Nm 16, 22, where "spirit" evidently means "the life principle."

53: Jos 11, 23.
54: 33, 54; 35, 8.
62: 3, 39.
65: 14, 22ff.29.
27/1: 26, 33; Jos 17, 3.
11: Jer 32, 6-9.
12: Dt 3, 27; 32, 49; 34, 1.
13f: 20, 12.24.
14: Dt 32, 51.

LORD's community may not be like sheep without a shepherd." **18*****†**And the LORD replied to Moses, "Take Joshua, son of Nun, a man of spirit, and lay your hand upon him. **19**Have him stand in the presence of the priest Eleazar and of the whole community, and commission him before their eyes. **20**Invest him with some of your own dignity, that the whole Israelite community may obey him. **21†**He shall present himself to the priest Eleazar, to have him seek out for him the decisions of the Urim in the LORD's presence; and as he directs, Joshua, all the Israelites with him, and the community as a whole shall perform all their actions."

22Moses did as the LORD had commanded him. Taking Joshua and having him stand in the presence of the priest Eleazar and of the whole community, **23**he laid his hands on him and gave him his commission, as the LORD had directed through Moses.

General Sacrifices

28 **1**THE LORD said to Moses, **2**"Give the Israelites this commandment: At the times I have appointed, you shall be careful to present to me the food offerings that are offered to me as sweet-smelling oblations.

Each Morning and Evening

3***†**"You shall tell them therefore: This is the oblation which you shall offer to the LORD: two unblemished yearling lambs each day as the established holocaust, **4**offering one lamb in the morning and the other during the evening twilight, **5†**each with a cereal offering of one tenth of an ephah of fine flour mixed with a fourth of a hin of oil of crushed olives. **6**This is the established holocaust that was offered at Mount Sinai as a sweet-smelling oblation to the LORD. **7†**And as the libation for the first lamb, you shall pour out to the LORD in the sanctuary a fourth of a hin of wine. **8**The other lamb, to be offered during the evening twilight, you shall offer with the same cereal offering and the same libation as in the morning, as a sweet-smelling oblation to the LORD.

On the Sabbath

9"On the sabbath day you shall offer two unblemished yearling lambs, with their cereal offering, two tenths of an ephah of fine flour mixed with oil, and with their libations. **10**Each sabbath there shall be the sabbath holocaust in addition to the established holocaust and its libation.

At the New Moon Feast

11†"On the first of each month you shall offer as a holocaust to the LORD two bullocks, one ram, and seven unblemished yearling lambs, **12**with three tenths of an ephah of fine flour mixed with oil as the cereal offering for each bullock, two tenths of an ephah of

fine flour mixed with oil as the cereal offering for the ram, **13**and one tenth of an ephah of fine flour mixed with oil as the cereal offering for each lamb, that the holocaust may be a sweet-smelling oblation to the LORD. **14**Their libations shall be half a hin of wine for each bullock, a third of a hin for the ram, and a fourth of a hin for each lamb. This is the new moon holocaust for every new moon of the year. **15**Moreover, one goat shall be sacrificed as a sin offering to the LORD. These are to be offered in addition to the established holocaust and its libation.

At the Passover

16***†**"On the fourteenth day of the first month falls the Passover of the LORD, **17**and the fifteenth day of this month is the pilgrimage feast. For seven days unleavened bread is to be eaten. **18***On the first of these days you shall hold a sacred assembly, and do no sort of work. **19**As an oblation you shall offer a holocaust to the LORD, which shall consist of two bullocks, one ram, and seven yearling lambs that you are sure are unblemished, **20**with their cereal offerings of fine flour mixed with oil; offering three tenths of an ephah for each bullock, two tenths for the ram, **21**and one tenth for each of the seven lambs; **22**and offer one goat as a sin offering in atonement for yourselves. **23**These offerings you shall make in addition to the established morning holocaust: **24**you shall make exactly the same offerings each day for seven days as food offerings, in addition to the established holocaust with its libation, for a sweet-smelling oblation to the LORD. **25***On the seventh day you shall hold a sacred assembly, and do no sort of work.

At Pentecost

26***†**"On the day of first fruits, on your feast of Weeks, when you present to the LORD the new cereal

---

†

27, 18: *A man of spirit:* literally, "a man in whom there is spirit": one who has the qualities of a good leader—courage, prudence, and strength of will. Cf Gn 41, 38; Dt 34, 9.

27, 21: *The Urim:* certain sacred objects which the Hebrew priests employed to ascertain the divine will, probably by obtaining a positive or negative answer to a given question. The full expression was "the Urim and Thummim"; cf Ex 28, 30; Lv 8, 8; Dt 33, 8; Ezr 2, 63; Neh 7, 65. Joshua was ordinarily not to receive direct revelations from God as Moses had received them.

28, 3: *The established holocaust:* "the tamid holocaust," the technical term for the daily sacrifice.

28, 5: *Oil of crushed olives:* this oil, made in a mortar, was purer and more expensive than oil extracted in the olive press.

28, 7: *In the sanctuary:* according to Sir 50, 15, it was at the base of the altar.

28, 11: *On the first of each month:* literally, "at the new moons"; beginning on the evening when the crescent of the new moon first appeared.

28, 16: *On the fourteenth day:* toward evening at the end of this day; cf Ex 12, 6.18.

28, 26: *The day of first fruits:* a unique term for this feast, which is usually called "the feast of Weeks"; it was celebrated as a thanksgiving for the wheat harvest seven weeks after the barley harvest (Passover). In the time of Christ it was commonly known by the Greek word "Pentecost," that is, "fiftieth" (day after the Passover); see note on Lv 23, 16.

18: Dt 34, 9.
28/3-8: Ex 29, 38-42.
16: Ex 12, 18; Lv 23, 5; Dt 16, 1.
18: Ex 12, 16; Lv 23, 7.
25: Ex 12, 16; 13, 6; Lv 23, 8.
26: Ex 34, 22.

offering, you shall hold a sacred assembly, and do no sort of work. [27]You shall offer as a sweet-smelling holocaust to the LORD two bullocks, one ram, and seven yearling lambs that you are sure are unblemished, [28]with their cereal offerings of fine flour mixed with oil; offering three tenths of an ephah for each bullock, two tenths for the ram, [29]and one tenth for each of the seven lambs. [30]Moreover, one goat shall be offered as a sin offering in atonement for yourselves. [31]You shall make these offerings, together with their libations, in addition to the established holocaust with its cereal offering.

On New Year's Day

29 [1]*†"ON the first day of the seventh month you shall hold a sacred assembly, and do no sort of work; it shall be a day on which you sound the trumpet. [2]You shall offer as a sweet-smelling holocaust to the LORD one bullock, one ram, and seven unblemished yearling lambs, [3]with their cereal offerings of fine flour mixed with oil; offering three tenths of an ephah for the bullock, two tenths for the ram, [4]and one tenth for each of the seven lambs. [5]Moreover, one goat shall be offered as a sin offering in atonement for yourselves. [6]These are to be offered in addition to the ordinary new moon holocaust with its cereal offering, and in addition to the established holocaust with its cereal offering, together with the libations prescribed for them, as a sweet-smelling oblation to the LORD.

On the Day of Atonement

[7]*†"On the tenth day of this seventh month you shall hold a sacred assembly, and mortify yourselves, and do no sort of work. [8]You shall offer as a sweet-smelling holocaust to the LORD one bullock, one ram, and seven yearling lambs that you are sure are unblemished, [9]with their cereal offerings of fine flour mixed with oil; offering three tenths of an ephah for the bullock, two tenths for the ram, [10]and one tenth for each of the seven lambs. [11]†Moreover, one goat shall be sacrificed as a sin offering. These are to be offered in addition to the atonement sin offering, the established holocaust with its cereal offering, and their libations.

On the Feast of Booths

[12]*†"On the fifteenth day of the seventh month you shall hold a sacred assembly, and do no sort of work; then, for seven days following, you shall celebrate a pilgrimage feast to the LORD. [13]†You shall offer as a sweet-smelling holocaust to the LORD thirteen bullocks, two rams, and fourteen yearling lambs that are unblemished, [14]with their cereal offerings of fine flour mixed with oil; offering three tenths of an ephah for each of the thirteen bullocks, two tenths for each of the two rams, [15]and one tenth for each of the fourteen lambs. [16]Moreover, one goat shall be sacrificed as a sin offering. These are to be offered in addition to the estab-

lished holocaust with its cereal offering and libation.

[17]"On the second day you shall offer twelve bullocks, two rams, and fourteen unblemished yearling lambs, [18]with their cereal offerings and libations as prescribed for the bullocks, rams and lambs in proportion to their number, [19]as well as one goat for a sin offering, besides the established holocaust with its cereal offering and libation.

[20]"On the third day you shall offer eleven bullocks, two rams, and fourteen unblemished yearling lambs, [21]with their cereal offerings and libations as prescribed for the bullocks, rams and lambs in proportion to their number, [22]as well as one goat for a sin offering, besides the established holocaust with its cereal offering and libation.

[23]"On the fourth day you shall offer ten bullocks, two rams, and fourteen unblemished yearling lambs, [24]with their cereal offerings and libations as prescribed for the bullocks, rams and lambs in proportion to their number, [25]as well as one goat for a sin offering, besides the established holocaust with its cereal offering and libation.

[26]"On the fifth day you shall offer nine bullocks, two rams, and fourteen unblemished yearling lambs, [27]*with their cereal offerings and libations as prescribed for the bullocks, rams and lambs in proportion to their number, [28]as well as one goat for a sin offering, besides the established holocaust with its cereal offering and libation.

[29]"On the sixth day you shall offer eight bullocks, two rams, and fourteen unblemished yearling lambs, [30]with their cereal offerings and libations as prescribed for the bullocks, rams and lambs in proportion to their number, [31]as well as one goat for a sin offering, besides the established holocaust with its cereal offering and libation.

[32]"On the seventh day you shall offer seven bullocks, two rams, and fourteen unblemished yearling lambs, [33]with their cereal offerings and libations as prescribed for the bullocks, rams and lambs in proportion to their number, [34]as well as one goat for a sin offering, besides the established holocaust with its cereal offering and libation.

[35]*†"On the eighth day you shall hold a solemn

---

† 29, 1: *The first day of the seventh month* (about September-October) is now the Jewish New Year's Day. In the older calendar the year began with the first of Nisan (March-April); cf Ex 12, 2.

29, 7: *The tenth day of this seventh month:* the Day of Atonement. *Mortify yourselves:* literally, "afflict your souls," that is, with fasting.

29, 11: *The atonement sin offering:* the bullock prescribed in Lv 16, 11f.

29, 12: This feast of Booths celebrating the vintage harvest was the most popular of all and therefore had the most elaborate ritual. See note on Lv 23, 34.

29, 13: *Thirteen bullocks:* the number of bullocks sacrificed before the octave day was seventy, arranged on a descending scale so that the number on the seventh day was the sacred number seven.

29, 35: *A solemn meeting:* the Hebrew word is the technical term for the closing celebration of the three major feasts of the

---

29/1: 10, 10; Lv 23, 24.　　　　27: 29, 30.37.
　　7: Lv 16, 29; 23, 27f.32.　　35: Lv 23, 36; Jn 7, 37.
　　12: Lv 23, 34f.

meeting, and do no sort of work. ³⁶You shall offer up in holocaust as a sweet-smelling oblation to the LORD one bullock, one ram, and seven unblemished yearling lambs, ³⁷with their cereal offerings and libations as prescribed for the bullocks, rams and lambs in proportion to their number, ³⁸as well as one goat for a sin offering, besides the established holocaust with its cereal offering and libation.

³⁹"These are the offerings you shall make to the LORD on your festivals, besides whatever holocausts, cereal offerings, libations, and peace offerings you present as your votive or freewill offerings."

30

¹MOSES then gave the Israelites these instructions, just as the LORD had ordered him.

Validity and Annulment of Vows

²Moses said to the heads of the Israelite tribes, "This is what the LORD has commanded: ³*†When a man makes a vow to the LORD or binds himself under oath to a pledge of abstinence, he shall not violate his word, but must fulfill exactly the promise he has uttered.

⁴"When a woman, while still a maiden in her father's house, makes a vow to the LORD, or binds herself to a pledge, ⁵if her father learns of her vow or the pledge to which she bound herself and says nothing to her about it, then any vow or any pledge she has made remains valid. ⁶But if on the day he learns of it her father expresses to her his disapproval, then any vow or any pledge she has made becomes null and void; and the LORD releases her from it, since her father has expressed to her his disapproval.

⁷"If she marries while under a vow or under a rash pledge to which she bound herself, ⁸and her husband learns of it, yet says nothing to her that day about it, then the vow or pledge she had made remains valid. ⁹But if on the day he learns of it her husband expresses to her his disapproval, he thereby annuls the vow she had made or the rash pledge to which she had bound herself, and the LORD releases her from it. ¹⁰The vow of a widow or of a divorced woman, or any pledge to which such a woman binds herself, is valid.

¹¹†"If it is in her husband's house that she makes a vow or binds herself under oath to a pledge, ¹²and her husband learns of it yet says nothing to express to her his disapproval, then any vow or any pledge she has made remains valid. ¹³But if on the day he learns of them her husband annuls them, then whatever she has expressly promised in her vow or in her pledge becomes null and void; since her husband has annulled them, the LORD releases her from them.

¹⁴"Any vow or pledge that she makes under oath to mortify herself, her husband can either allow to remain valid or render null and void. ¹⁵But if her husband, day after day, says nothing at all to her about them, he thereby allows as valid any vow or any pledge she has made; he has allowed them to remain

valid, because on the day he learned of them he said nothing to her about them. ¹⁶†If, however, he countermands them some time after he first learned of them, he is responsible for her guilt."

¹⁷These are the statutes which the LORD prescribed through Moses concerning the relationship between a husband and his wife, as well as between a father and his daughter while she is still a maiden in her father's house.

Extermination of the Midianites

31

¹†THE LORD said to Moses, ²"Avenge the Israelites on the Midianites, and then you shall be taken to your people." ³So Moses told the people, "Select men from your midst and arm them for war, to attack the Midianites and execute the LORD's vengeance on them. ⁴From each of the tribes of Israel you shall send a band of one thousand men to war." ⁵From the clans of Israel, therefore, a thousand men of each tribe were levied, so that there were twelve thousand men armed for war. ⁶Moses sent them out on the campaign, a thousand from each tribe, with Phinehas, son of Eleazar, the priest for the campaign, who had with him the sacred vessels and the trumpets for sounding the alarm. ⁷They waged war against the Midianites, as the LORD had commanded Moses, and killed every male among them. ⁸†Besides those slain in battle, they killed the five Midianite kings: Evi, Rekem, Zur, Hur and Reba; and they also executed Balaam, son of Beor, with the sword. ⁹But the Israelites kept the women of the Midianites with their little ones as captives, and all their herds and flocks and wealth as spoil, ¹⁰while they set on fire all the towns where they had settled and all their encampments. ¹¹Then they took all the booty, with the people and beasts they had captured, and brought the captives, together with the spoils and booty, ¹²to Moses and the priest Eleazar and to the Israelite community at their camp on the plains of Moab, along the Jericho stretch of the Jordan.

Treatment of the Captives

¹³When Moses and the priest Eleazar, with all the princes of the community, went outside the camp to meet them, ¹⁴Moses became angry with the officers of the army, the clan and company commanders, who

---

† Passover, Pentecost and Booths, or of other special feasts that lasted for a week. Cf Lv 23, 36; Dt 16, 8; 2 Chr 7, 9; Neh 8, 18.

30, 3: *A vow . . . a pledge:* here the former signifies the doing of some positive good deed, in particular the offering of some sacrifice; the latter signifies the abstaining from some otherwise licit action or pleasure; cf v 14.

30, 11: *In her husband's house:* after her marriage. This contrasts with the case given in vv 7ff.

30, 16: *He countermands them:* he prevents their fulfillment. Since he has first allowed the vows to remain valid, he can no longer annul them.

31, 1ff: The narrative of Israel's relations with Midian, which was interrupted after 25, 18, is now resumed.

31, 8: *The five Midianite kings:* they are called "Midianite princes, Sihon's vassals" in Jos 13, 21.

30/3: Dt 23, 22; Eccl 5, 3f.

were returning from combat. ¹⁵"So you have spared all the women!" he exclaimed. ¹⁶*"Why, they are the very ones who on Balaam's advice prompted the unfaithfulness of the Israelites toward the LORD in the Peor affair, which began the slaughter of the LORD's community. ¹⁷†Slay, therefore, every male child and every woman who has had intercourse with a man. ¹⁸But you may spare and keep for yourselves all girls who had no intercourse with a man.

Purification after Combat

¹⁹"Moreover, you shall stay outside the camp for seven days, and those of you who have slain anyone or touched anyone slain in battle shall purify yourselves on the third and on the seventh day. This applies both to you and to your captives. ²⁰You shall also purify every article of cloth, leather, goats' hair, or wood."

²¹Eleazar the priest told the soldiers who had returned from combat: "This is what the law, as prescribed by the LORD to Moses, ordains: ²²Whatever can stand fire, such as gold, silver, bronze, iron, tin and lead, ²³†you shall put into the fire, that it may become clean; however, it must also be purified with lustral water. But whatever cannot stand fire you shall put into the water. ²⁴On the seventh day you shall wash your clothes, and then you will again be clean. After that you may enter the camp."

Division of the Booty

²⁵The LORD said to Moses: ²⁶"With the help of the priest Eleazar and of the heads of the ancestral houses, count up all the human captives and the beasts that have been taken; ²⁷†then divide them evenly, giving half to those who took active part in the war by going out to combat, and half to the rest of the community. ²⁸You shall levy a tax for the LORD on the warriors who went out to combat: one out of every five hundred persons, oxen, asses and sheep ²⁹in their half of the spoil you shall turn over to the priest Eleazar as a contribution to the LORD. ³⁰From the Israelites' half you shall take one out of every fifty persons, and the same from the different beasts, oxen, asses and sheep, and give them to the Levites, who have charge of the LORD's Dwelling." ³¹So Moses and the priest Eleazar did this, as the LORD had commanded Moses.

Amount of Booty

³²This booty, what was left of the loot which the soldiers had taken, amounted to six hundred and seventy-five thousand sheep, ³³seventy-two thousand oxen, ³⁴sixty-one thousand asses, ³⁵and thirty-two thousand girls who were still virgins.

³⁶The half that fell to those who had gone out to combat was: three hundred and thirty-seven thousand five hundred sheep, ³⁷of which six hundred and seventy-five fell as tax to the LORD; ³⁸thirty-six thousand oxen, of which seventy-two fell as tax to the LORD; ³⁹thirty thousand five hundred asses, of which

sixty-one fell as tax to the LORD; ⁴⁰and sixteen thousand persons, of whom thirty-two fell as tax to the LORD. ⁴¹The taxes contributed to the LORD, Moses gave to the priest Eleazar, as the LORD had commanded him.

⁴²The half for the other Israelites, which fell to the community when Moses had taken it from the soldiers, was: ⁴³three hundred and thirty-seven thousand five hundred sheep, ⁴⁴thirty-six thousand oxen, ⁴⁵thirty thousand five hundred asses, ⁴⁶and sixteen thousand persons. ⁴⁷From this, the Israelites' share, Moses, as the LORD had ordered, took one out of every fifty, both of persons and of beasts, and gave them to the Levites, who had charge of the LORD's Dwelling.

Gifts of the Officers

⁴⁸Then the officers who had been clan and company commanders of the army came up to Moses ⁴⁹and said to him, "Your servants have counted up the soldiers under our command, and not one is missing. ⁵⁰†So, to make atonement for ourselves before the LORD, each of us will bring as an offering to the LORD some gold article he has picked up, such as an anklet, a bracelet, a ring, an earring, or a necklace." ⁵¹Moses and the priest Eleazar accepted this gold from them, all of it in well-wrought articles. ⁵²The gold that they gave as a contribution to the LORD amounted in all to sixteen thousand seven hundred and fifty shekels. This was from the clan and company commanders; ⁵³what the common soldiers had looted each one kept for himself. ⁵⁴Moses, then, and the priest Eleazar accepted the gold from the clan and company commanders, and put it in the meeting tent as a memorial for the Israelites before the LORD.

Request of Gad and Reuben

32 ¹†Now the Reubenites and Gadites had a very large number of livestock. Noticing that the land of Jazer and of Gilead was grazing country, ²they came to Moses and the priest Eleazar and to the princes of the community and said, ³†"The region of Ataroth, Dibon, Jazer, Nimrah, Heshbon,

---

† 31, 17: There are later references to Midian in Jgs 6-8; 1 Kgs 11, 18; Is 60, 6. The present raid was only against those Midianites who were dwelling at this time near the encampment of the Israelites.

31, 23: *Lustral water:* water mixed with the ashes of the red heifer as prescribed in Nm 19, 9.

31, 27: *Divide them evenly:* for a similar division of the booty into two equal parts, between those who engaged in the fray and those who stayed with the baggage, cf 1 Sm 30, 24. But note that here the tax on the booty of the noncombatants is ten times as much as that on the soldier's booty.

31, 50: The precise nature and use of some of these articles of gold is not certain.

32, 1: *Gilead:* the name of the western part of the plateau east of the Jordan, sometimes signifying the whole region from the Yarmuk to the Jordan, sometimes only the northern part of this region, and sometimes, as here, only its southern part. *Jazer* lay to the east of southern Gilead.

32, 3: The places named in this verse, as well as the additional ones given in vv 34-38, were all in the former kingdom of Sihon, that is, in the region between the Jabbok and the Arnon. Cf 21, 23f; Jos 13, 19-21.24-27.

---

* 31/16: 2 Pt 2, 15; Rv 2, 14.

Elealeh, Sebam, Nebo and Baal-meon, **4**which the LORD has laid low before the community of Israel, is grazing country. Now, since your servants have livestock," **5**they continued, "if we find favor with you, let this land be given to your servants as their property. Do not make us cross the Jordan."

Moses' Rebuke

6But Moses answered the Gadites and Reubenites: "Are your kinsmen, then, to engage in war, while you remain here? **7**Why do you wish to discourage the Israelites from crossing to the land the LORD has given them? **8***That is just what your fathers did when I sent them from Kadesh-barnea to reconnoiter the land. **9**They went up to the Wadi Eshcol and reconnoitered the land, then so discouraged the Israelites that they would not enter the land the LORD had given them. **10***At that time the wrath of the LORD flared up, and he swore, **11**'Because they have not followed me unreservedly, none of these men of twenty years or more who have come up from Egypt shall ever see this country I promised under oath to Abraham and Isaac and Jacob, **12*†**except the Kenizzite Caleb, son of Jephunneh, and Joshua, son of Nun, who have followed the LORD unreservedly.' **13**So in his anger with the Israelites the LORD made them wander in the desert forty years, until the whole generation that had done evil in the sight of the LORD had died out. **14**And now here you are, a brood of sinners, rising up in your fathers' place to add still more to the LORD's blazing wrath against the Israelites. **15**If you turn away from following him, he will make them stay still longer in the desert, and so you will bring about the ruin of this whole nation."

Counter Proposal

16But they were insistent with him: "We wish only to build sheepfolds here for our flocks, and towns for our families; **17***but we ourselves will march as troops in the van of the Israelites, until we have led them to their destination. Meanwhile our families can remain here in the fortified towns, safe from attack by the natives. **18**We will not return to our homes until every one of the Israelites has taken possession of his heritage, **19***and will not claim any heritage with them once we cross the Jordan, so long as we receive a heritage for ourselves on this eastern side of the Jordan."

Agreement Reached

20†Moses said to them in reply: "If you keep your word to march as troops in the LORD's vanguard **21**and to cross the Jordan in full force before the LORD until he has driven his enemies out of his way **22***and the land is subdued before him, then you may return here, quit of every obligation to the LORD and to Israel, and

this region shall be your possession before the LORD. **23**But if you do not do this, you will sin against the LORD, and you can be sure that you will not escape the consequences of your sin. **24**Build the towns, then, for your families, and the folds for your flocks, but also fulfill your express promise."

25The Gadites and Reubenites answered Moses, "Your servants will do as you command, my lord. **26***While our wives and children, our herds and other livestock remain in the towns of Gilead, **27**all your servants will go across as armed troops to battle before the LORD, just as your lordship says."

28Moses, therefore, gave this order in their regard to the priest Eleazar, to Joshua, son of Nun, and to the heads of the ancestral tribes of the Israelites: **29**"If all the Gadites and Reubenites cross the Jordan with you as combat troops before the LORD, you shall give them Gilead as their property when the land has been subdued before you. **30**But if they will not go across with you as combat troops before the LORD, you shall bring their wives and children and livestock across before you into Canaan, and they shall have their property with you in the land of Canaan."

31To this the Gadites and Reubenites replied, "We will do what the LORD has commanded us, your servants. **32**We ourselves will go across into the land of Canaan as troops before the LORD, but we will retain our hereditary property on this side of the Jordan." **33*†**So Moses gave them [the Gadites and Reubenites, as well as half the tribe of Manasseh, son of Joseph, the kingdom of Sihon, king of the Amorites, and the kingdom of Og, king of Bashan,] the land with its towns and the districts that surrounded them.

34The Gadites rebuilt the fortified towns of Dibon, Ataroth, Aroer, **35**Atroth-shophan, Jazer, Jogbehah, **36**Beth-nimrah and Beth-haran, and they built sheepfolds. **37**The Reubenites rebuilt Heshbon, Elealeh, Kiriathaim, **38†**Nebo, Baal-meon [names to be changed!], and Sibmah. These towns, which they rebuilt, they called by their old names.

Other Conquests

39The descendants of Machir, son of Manasseh, invaded Gilead and captured it, driving out the Amo-

---

†   32, 12: *Kenizzite:* a member of the clan of Kenaz, which, according to Gn 36, 11.15.42, was Edomitic; hence, although Caleb belonged to the tribe of Judah (Nm 13, 6; 34, 19), he must have had Edomite blood in his veins; cf also Jos 14, 6.14.

32, 20ff: Since the ark of the Lord was borne into battle with the Israelite army, the vanguard was said to march *before the Lord.*

32, 33: The preceding is concerned solely with the two tribes of Gad and Reuben and with the land of the former kingdom of Sihon; hence it seems probable that the sudden reference here to the half-tribe of Manasseh and to their territory in Bashan, the former kingdom of Og, is a later addition to the text.

32, 38: The phrase in brackets is a gloss, warning the reader either to change the order of the preceding names, or, more probably, to read some other word, such as *bosheth,* "shame," for *Baal. They called by their old names:* literally, "they called by their names" (see Textual Notes); however, some understand the current Hebrew text to mean, "they called by new names."

✼
32/8f: 13, 31ff; Dt 1, 22.
10f: Dt 1, 34f.
12: 14, 24; Dt 1, 36.
17: Jos 4, 12f.
19: Jos 13, 8.

22: Jos 1, 15.
26: Jos 1, 14.
33: Dt 3, 12; 29, 7;
    Jos 12, 6; 13, 8.

rites who were there. **40***[Moses gave Gilead to Machir, son of Manasseh, and he settled there.] **41***Jair, a Manassehite clan, campaigned against the tent villages, captured them and called them Havvoth-jair. **42**Nobah also campaigned against Kenath, captured it with its dependencies and called it Nobah after his own name.

Stages on the Journey

33 **1†**THE following are the stages by which the Israelites journeyed up by companies from the land of Egypt under the guidance of Moses and Aaron. **2**By the LORD's command Moses recorded the starting places of the various stages. The starting places of the successive stages were:

3†They set out from Rameses in the first month,
  on the fifteenth day of the first month.
On the Passover morrow the Israelites went forth
  in triumph, in view of all Egypt,
4*While the Egyptians buried their first-born
  all of whom the LORD had struck down;
  on their gods, too, the LORD executed judgments.

From Egypt to Sinai

5Setting out from Rameses, the Israelites camped at Succoth. **6**Setting out from Succoth, they camped at Etham near the edge of the desert. **7***Setting out from Etham, they turned back to Pi-hahiroth, which is opposite Baal-zephon, and they camped opposite Migdol. **8***Setting out from Pi-hahiroth, they crossed over through the sea into the desert, and after a three days' journey in the desert of Etham, they camped at Marah. **9***Setting out from Marah, they came to Elim, where there were twelve springs of water and seventy palm trees, and they camped there. **10**Setting out from Elim, they camped beside the Red Sea. **11**Setting out from the Red Sea, they camped in the desert of Sin. **12**Setting out from the desert of Sin, they camped at Dophkah. **13**Setting out from Dophkah, they camped at Alush. **14***Setting out from Alush, they camped at Rephidim, where there was no water for the people to drink. **15***Setting out from Rephidim, they camped in the desert of Sinai.

From Sinai to Kadesh

16Setting out from the desert of Sinai, they camped at Kibroth-hattaavah. **17***Setting out from Kibroth-hattaavah, they camped at Hazeroth. **18**Setting out from Hazeroth, they camped at Rithmah. **19**Setting out from Rithmah, they camped at Rimmon-perez. **20**Setting out from Rimmon-perez, they camped at Libnah. **21**Setting out from Libnah, they camped at Rissah. **22**Setting out from Rissah, they camped at Kehelathah. **23**Setting out from Kehelathah, they camped at Mount Shepher. **24**Setting out from Mount Shepher, they camped at Haradah. **25**Setting out from Haradah, they camped at Makheloth. **26**Setting out from Makheloth, they camped at Tahath. **27**Setting out from Tahath, they camped at Terah. **28**Setting out from Terah, they camped at Mithkah. **29**Setting out from Mithkah, they camped at Hashmonah. **30†**Setting out from Hashmonah,—

From Mount Hor to Ezion-geber

They camped at Moseroth. **31**Setting out from Moseroth, they camped at Bene-jaakan. **32**Setting out from Bene-jaakan, they camped at Mount Gidgad. **33**Setting out from Mount Gidgad, they camped at Jotbathah. **34**Setting out from Jotbathah, they camped at Abronah. **35**Setting out from Abronah, they camped at Ezion-geber. **36***Setting out from Ezion-geber,—

From Kadesh to Mount Hor

They camped in the desert of Zin, at Kadesh. **37**Setting out from Kadesh, they camped at Mount Hor on the border of the land of Edom. **38***[Aaron the priest ascended Mount Hor at the LORD's command, and there he died in the fortieth year from the departure of the Israelites from the land of Egypt, on the first day of the fifth month. **39**Aaron was a hundred and twenty-three years old when he died on Mount Hor. **40†**Now, when the Canaanite king of Arad, who lived in the Negeb in the land of Canaan, heard that the Israelites were coming. . . .] **41†**Setting out from Mount Hor,—

From Ezion-geber to the Plains of Moab

They camped at Zalmonah. **42**Setting out from Zalmonah, they camped at Punon. **43**Setting out from Punon, they camped at Oboth. **44**Setting out from Oboth, they camped at Iye-abarim on the border of Moab. **45**Setting out from Iye-abarim, they camped at Dibon-gad. **46**Setting out from Dibon-gad, they camped at Almon-diblathaim. **47**Setting out from Al-

---

† 33, 1ff: This list of camping sites was drawn up by Moses, as v 2 expressly states. However, in its present form it probably includes some glosses. Moreover, a comparison with the more detailed accounts of the journey as given elsewhere shows that this list is not complete. It records just forty camping sites, not counting the starting place, Rameses, and the terminus, the plains of Moab. This number, which corresponds exactly to the forty years of wandering in the desert, is probably a schematic device. Besides, it seems that in its present form the order of some of these names has been disturbed. Several names listed here are not recorded elsewhere.

33, 3f: These two verses were probably borrowed from some ancient song celebrating the exodus from Egypt.

33, 30-36: Moseroth is mentioned in Dt 10, 6 (in the form of "Moserah"), as the place where Aaron died. It must therefore have been close to Mount Hor; cf Nm 20, 22ff. It seems very probable that the section vv 36b-41a stood originally immediately after v 30a.

33, 40: The verse begins the same account of the victory over Arad as is given in 21, 1ff, where it also follows the account of Aaron's death.

33, 41b-49: It seems that this section stood originally immediately after v 36a.

40: Dt 3, 15.
41: Dt 3, 14.
33/4f: Ex 12, 12.29.37.
7: Ex 14, 2.
8: Ex 15, 22.
9: Ex 15, 27.
14: Ex 17, 1.
15: Ex 19, 2.
17f: Nm 11, 34f.
36f: 20, 1.22.
38: 20, 25; Dt 32, 50.

mon-diblathaim, they camped in the Abarim Mountains opposite Nebo. [48]Setting out from the Abarim Mountains, they camped on the plains of Moab along the Jericho stretch of the Jordan. [49]Their camp along the Jordan on the plains of Moab extended from Beth-jeshimoth to Abel-shittim.

Conquest and Division of Canaan

[50]The LORD spoke to Moses on the plains of Moab beside the Jericho stretch of the Jordan and said to him: [51]"Tell the Israelites: When you go across the Jordan into the land of Canaan, [52]*drive out all the inhabitants of the land before you; destroy all their stone figures and molten images, and demolish all their high places.

[53]"You shall take possession of the land and settle in it, for I have given you the land as your property. [54]*You shall apportion the land among yourselves by lot, clan by clan, assigning a large heritage to a large group and a small heritage to a small group. Wherever anyone's lot falls, there shall his property be within the heritage of his ancestral tribe.

[55]*"But if you do not drive out the inhabitants of the land before you, those whom you allow to remain will become as barbs in your eyes and thorns in your sides, and they will harass you in the country where you live, [56]and I will treat you as I had intended to treat them."

The Boundaries

34 [1]THE LORD said to Moses, [2]"Give the Israelites this order: When you enter the land of Canaan, this is the territory that shall fall to you as your heritage—the land of Canaan with its boundaries:

[3]*"Your southern boundary shall be at the desert of Zin along the border of Edom; on the east it shall begin at the end of the Salt Sea, [4]*and turning south of the Akrabbim Pass, it shall cross Zin, and extend south of Kadesh-barnea to Hazar-addar; thence it shall cross to Azmon, [5]*and turning from Azmon to the Wadi of Egypt, shall terminate at the Sea.

[6]†"For your western boundary you shall have the Great Sea with its coast; this shall be your western boundary.

[7]†"The following shall be your boundary on the north: from the Great Sea you shall draw a line to Mount Hor, [8]and shall continue it from Mount Hor to Labo in the land of Hamath, with the boundary extending through Zedad. [9]Thence the boundary shall reach to Ziphron and terminate at Hazar-enan. This shall be your northern boundary.

[10]"For your eastern boundary you shall draw a line from Hazar-enan to Shepham. [11]From Shepham the boundary shall go down to Ar-Baal, east of Ain, and descending further, shall strike the ridge on the east

side of the Sea of Chinnereth; [12]thence the boundary shall continue along the Jordan and terminate with the Salt Sea.

"This is the land that shall be yours, with the boundaries that surround it."

[13]Moses also gave this order to the Israelites: "This is the land, to be apportioned among you by lot, which the LORD has commanded to be given to the nine and one half tribes. [14]For all the ancestral houses of the tribe of Reuben, and the ancestral houses of the tribe of Gad, as well as half of the tribe of Manasseh, have already received their heritage; [15]these two and one half tribes have received their heritage on the eastern side of the Jericho stretch of the Jordan, toward the sunrise."

Supervisors of the Allotment

[16]The LORD said to Moses, [17]"These are the names of the men who shall apportion the land among you: Eleazar the priest, and Joshua, son of Nun, [18]*and one prince from each of the tribes whom you shall designate for this task. [19]These shall be as follows:

from the tribe of Judah: Caleb, son of Jephunneh,
[20]from the tribe of Simeon: Samuel, son of Ammihud;
[21]from the tribe of Benjamin: Elidad, son of Chislon;
[22]from the tribe of Dan: Bukki, son of Jogli;
[23]from the tribe of Manasseh: Hanniel, son of Ephod; and
[24]from the tribe of Ephraim: Kemuel, son of Shiphtan, for the descendants of Joseph;
[25]from the tribe of Zebulun: Elizaphan, son of Parnach;
[26]from the tribe of Issachar: Paltiel, son of Azzan;
[27]from the tribe of Asher: Ahihud, son of Shelomi;
[28]from the tribe of Naphtali: Pedahel, son of Ammihud."

[29]These are they whom the LORD commanded to assign the Israelites their heritage in the land of Canaan.

Cities for the Levites

35 [1]THE LORD gave these instructions to Moses on the plains of Moab beside the Jericho stretch of the Jordan: [2]*"Tell the Israelites that out of their hereditary property they shall give the Levites cities for homes, as well as pasture lands around the cities. [3]The cities shall serve them to dwell in, and the pasture lands shall serve their herds and flocks and other animals. [4]The pasture lands of the cities to be assigned the Levites shall extend a thousand cubits from the city walls in each direction. [5]Thus you shall measure out two thousand cubits outside the city along each side—east, south, west and north—with the city lying in the center. This shall serve them as the pasture lands of their cities.

✿
52: Ex 23, 31; 34, 13;
    Dt 7, 5; 12, 3.
54: 26, 53ff.
55: Jos 23, 13; Jgs 2, 3.
34/3: Jos 15, 1f.

4: Jos 15, 3.
5: Jos 15, 4.
18: 1, 4.
35/2: Jos 14, 3f; 21, 2.

---

† 34, 6: *The Great Sea:* the Mediterranean.
34, 7f: *Mount Hor:* different from the one where Aaron died; cf Nm 20, 22; 33, 37f.

⁶*"Now these are the cities you shall give to the Levites: the six cities of asylum which you must establish as places where a homicide can take refuge, and in addition forty-two other cities—⁷a total of forty-eight cities with their pasture lands to be assigned the Levites. ⁸†In assigning the cities from the property of the Israelites, take more from a larger group and fewer from a smaller one, so that each group will cede cities to the Levites in proportion to its own heritage."

Cities of Asylum

⁹The LORD said to Moses, ¹⁰*"Tell the Israelites: When you go across the Jordan into the land of Canaan, ¹¹select for yourselves cities to serve as cities of asylum, where a homicide who has killed someone unintentionally may take refuge. ¹²†These cities shall serve you as places of asylum from the avenger of blood, so that a homicide shall not be put to death unless he is first tried before the community. ¹³Six cities of asylum shall you assign: ¹⁴three beyond the Jordan, and three in the land of Canaan. ¹⁵These six cities of asylum shall serve not only the Israelites but all the resident or transient aliens among them, so that anyone who has killed another unintentionally may take refuge there.

Murder and Manslaughter

¹⁶*†"If a man strikes another with an iron instrument and causes his death, he is a murderer and shall be put to death. ¹⁷If a man strikes another with a death-dealing stone in his hand and causes his death, he is a murderer and shall be put to death. ¹⁸If a man strikes another with a death-dealing club in his hand and causes his death, he is a murderer and shall be put to death. ¹⁹The avenger of blood may execute the murderer, putting him to death on sight.

²⁰*"If a man pushes another out of hatred, or after lying in wait for him throws something at him, and causes his death, ²¹or if he strikes another out of enmity and causes his death, he shall be put to death as a murderer. The avenger of blood may execute the murderer on sight.

²²*"However, if a man pushes another accidentally and not out of enmity, or if without lying in wait for him he throws some object at him, ²³or without seeing him throws a death-dealing stone which strikes him and causes his death, although he was not his enemy nor seeking to harm him: ²⁴then the community, deciding the case between the slayer and the avenger of blood in accordance with these norms, ²⁵*shall free the homicide from the avenger of blood and shall remand him to the city of asylum where he took refuge; and he shall stay there until the death of the high priest who has been anointed with sacred oil. ²⁶If the homicide of his own accord leaves the bounds of the city of asylum where he has taken refuge, ²⁷and the avenger of blood finds him beyond these bounds and kills him, the avenger incurs no bloodguilt; ²⁸the homicide was bound to stay in his city of asylum until the death of the high priest. Only after the death of the high priest may the homicide return to his own district.

²⁹"These shall be norms for you and all your descendants, wherever you live, for rendering judgment.

Witnesses

³⁰*"Whenever someone kills another, the evidence of witnesses is required for the execution of the murderer. The evidence of a single witness is not sufficient for putting a person to death.

No Indemnity

³¹"You shall not accept indemnity in place of the life of a murderer who deserves the death penalty; he must be put to death. ³²Nor shall you accept indemnity to allow a refugee to leave his city of asylum and again dwell elsewhere in the land before the death of the high priest. ³³You shall not desecrate the land where you live. Since bloodshed desecrates the land, the land can have no atonement for the blood shed on it except through the blood of him who shed it. ³⁴*Do not defile the land in which you live and in the midst of which I dwell; for I am the LORD who dwells in the midst of the Israelites."

Property of Heiresses

36 ¹THE heads of the ancestral houses in the clan of descendants of Gilead, son of Machir, son of Manasseh—one of the Josephite clans—came up and laid this plea before Moses and the priest Eleazar and before the princes who were the heads of the ancestral houses of the other Israelites. ²*They said: "The LORD commanded you, my lord, to apportion the land by lot among the Israelites; and you, my lord, were also commanded by the LORD to give the heritage of our kinsman Zelophehad to his daughters. ³But if they marry into one of the other Israelite tribes, their heritage will be withdrawn from our ancestral heritage and will be added to that of the tribe into which they marry; thus the heritage that fell to us by lot will be diminished. ⁴†When the Israelites celebrate the jubilee year, the heritage of these women will be permanently added to that of the tribe into which they marry and will be withdrawn from that of our ancestral tribe."

---

† 35, 8: This provision was hardly observed in the actual assignment of the levitical cities as narrated in Jos 21.

35, 12: *The avenger of blood:* one of the close relatives of the slain (2 Sm 14, 7) who, as executor of public justice, had the right and duty to take the life of the murderer; cf Dt 19, 6.12; Jos 20, 3.5.9.

35, 16-25: Here, as also in Dt 19, 1-13, there is a casuistic development of the original law as stated in Ex 21, 12ff.

36, 4: Before the jubilee year various circumstances, such as divorce, could make such property revert to its original tribal owners; but in the jubilee year it became irrevocably attached to its new owners.

6: Dt 4, 41f; Jos 20, 2.
10ff: Dt 19, 2; Jos 20, 2ff.
16: Ex 21, 12; Lv 24, 17.
20: Ex 21, 14; Dt 19, 11.
22: Jos 20, 3.
25: Jos 20, 6.
30: Dt 17, 6; 19, 15; Jn 8, 17; 2 Cor 13, 1; 1 Tm 5, 19.
34: Ex 29, 45.
36/2: 26, 55; 27, 6; Jos 17, 3f.

[5]†So Moses gave this regulation to the Israelites according to the instructions of the LORD: "The tribe of the Josephites are right in what they say. [6]This is what the LORD commands with regard to the daughters of Zelophehad: They may marry anyone they please, provided they marry into a clan of their ancestral tribe, [7]so that no heritage of the Israelites will pass from one tribe to another, but all the Israelites will retain their own ancestral heritage. [8]Therefore, every daughter who inherits property in any of the Israelite tribes shall marry someone belonging to a clan of her own ancestral tribe, in order that all the Israelites may remain in possession of their own ancestral heritage. [9]Thus, no heritage can pass from one tribe to another, but all the Israelite tribes will retain their own ancestral heritage."

[10]The daughters of Zelophehad obeyed the command which the LORD had given to Moses. [11]Mahlah, Tirzah, Hoglah, Milcah and Noah, Zelophehad's daughters, married relatives on their father's side [12]within the clans of the descendants of Manasseh, son of Joseph; hence their heritage remained in the tribe of their father's clan.

Conclusion

[13]These are the commandments and decisions which the LORD prescribed for the Israelites through Moses, on the plains of Moab beside the Jericho stretch of the Jordan.

---

†   36, 5-9: This is a supplement to the law given in 27, 5-11.

The Book of Deuteronomy

Introduction

The fifth and last book of the Pentateuch is called Deuteronomy, meaning "second law." In reality, what it contains is not a new law but a partial repetition, completion and explanation of the law proclaimed on Mount Sinai. The historical portions of the book are also a résumé of what is related elsewhere in the Pentateuch.

The chief characteristic of this book is its vigorous oratorical style. In a series of eloquent discourses Moses presents the theme of covenant renewal in a vital liturgical framework. He exhorts, corrects and threatens his people, appealing to their past glory, their historic mission, and the promise of future triumph. His aim is to enforce among the Israelites the Lord's claim to their obedience, loyalty and love.

The events contained in the Book of Deuteronomy took place in the plains of Moab (1, 5) between the end of the wanderings in the desert (1, 3) and the crossing of the Jordan River (Jos 4, 19), a period of no more than forty days.

The Book of Deuteronomy, written after the Israelites had for centuries been resident in the Land of Promise, takes the form of a testament of Moses, the great leader and legislator, to his people on the eve of his death. At the time of our Lord's coming, it shared with the Psalms a preeminent religious influence among the Old Testament books.

The Savior quoted passages of Deuteronomy in overcoming the threefold temptation of Satan in the desert (Mt 4; Dt 6, 13.16; 8, 3; 10, 20), and in explaining to the lawyer the first and greatest commandment (Mt 22, 35-39; Dt 6, 4).

The book is divided as follows:
I: Historical Review and Exhortation (1, 1—4, 43)
II: God and His Covenant (4, 44—11, 32)
III: Exposition of the Law (12, 1—26, 19)
IV: Final Words of Moses (27, 1—34, 12)

I: HISTORICAL REVIEW AND EXHORTATION

Introduction

1 ¹†THESE ARE THE WORDS which Moses spoke to all Israel beyond the Jordan [in the desert, in the Arabah, opposite Suph, between Paran and Tophel, Laban, Hazeroth and Dizahab; ²it is a journey of eleven days from Horeb to Kadesh-barnea by way of the highlands of Seir].

³In the fortieth year, on the first day of the eleventh month, Moses spoke to the Israelites all the commands that the LORD had given him in their regard. ⁴*After he had defeated Sihon, king of the Amorites, who lived in Heshbon, and Og, king of Bashan, who lived in Ashtaroth and in Edrei, ⁵Moses began to explain the law in the land of Moab beyond the Jordan, as follows:

Departure from Horeb

⁶"The LORD, our God, said to us at Horeb, 'You have stayed long enough at this mountain. ⁷*†Leave here and go to the hill country of the Amorites and to all the surrounding regions, the land of the Canaanites in the Arabah, the mountains, the foothills, the Negeb and the seacoast; to Lebanon, and as far as the Great River [the Euphrates]. ⁸*I have given that land over to you. Go now and occupy the land I swore to your fathers, Abraham, Isaac and Jacob, I would give to them and to their descendants.'

Appointment of Elders

⁹†"At that time I said to you, 'Alone, I am unable to carry you. ¹⁰*The LORD, your God, has so multiplied you that you are now as numerous as the stars in the sky. ¹¹May the LORD, the God of your fathers, increase you a thousand times over, and bless you as he promised! ¹²But how can I alone bear the crushing burden that you are, along with your bickering? ¹³*Choose wise, intelligent and experienced men from each of your tribes, that I may appoint them as your leaders.' ¹⁴You answered me, 'We agree to do as you have proposed.' ¹⁵So I took outstanding men of your tribes, wise and experienced, and made them your leaders as officials over thousands, over hundreds, over fifties and over tens, and other tribal officers. ¹⁶*I charged your judges at that time, 'Listen to complaints among your kinsmen, and administer true justice to both parties even if one of them is an alien. ¹⁷In rendering judgment, do not consider who a person is; give ear to the lowly and to the great alike, fearing no man, for judgment is God's. Refer to me any case that is too

---

† 1, 1: The local setting of all these discourses is *in the land of Moab beyond the Jordan* (cf v 5), also known as *the plains of Moab* (Nm 36, 13).

1, 7: The Amorites and the Canaanites formed the principal part of the pre-Israelite population of Palestine. *The foothills*: the hills on the western slope of the Judean mountain range. *The Arabah*: the valley of the Jordan and the depression south of the Dead Sea. *The Negeb*: the arid land in southern Palestine.

1, 9: *Carry you*: cf v 31.

1/4: 3, 2; Nm 21, 21-35.
   7: Nm 13, 29.
   8: Gn 12, 7; 15, 18; 17, 7f; 28, 13f.
   10: 10, 22; Gn 15, 5.
13ff: Ex 18, 21-25.
16f: Ex 18, 26; 2 Chr 19, 6f; Prv 24, 23; Jn 7, 24; Jas 2, 9.

hard for you and I will hear it.' ¹⁸Thereupon I gave you all the commands you were to fulfill.

The Twelve Scouts

¹⁹*"Then, in obedience to the command of the LORD, our God, we set out from Horeb and journeyed through the whole desert, vast and fearful as you have seen, in the direction of the hill country of the Amorites. We had reached Kadesh-barnea ²⁰when I said to you, 'You have come to the hill country of the Amorites, which the LORD, our God, is giving us. ²¹The LORD, your God, has given this land over to you. Go up and occupy it, as the LORD, the God of your fathers, commands you. Do not fear or lose heart.' ²²*Then all of you came up to me and said, 'Let us send men ahead to reconnoiter the land for us and report to us on the road we must follow and the cities we must take.' ²³Agreeing with the proposal, I chose twelve men from your number, one from each tribe. ²⁴They set out into the hill country as far as the Wadi Eshcol, and explored it. ²⁵Then, taking along some of the fruit of the land, they brought it down to us and reported, 'The land which the LORD, our God, gives us is good.'

Threats of Revolt

²⁶*"But you refused to go up, and after defying the command of the LORD, your God, ²⁷*†you set to murmuring in your tents, 'Out of hatred for us the LORD has brought us up out of the land of Egypt, to deliver us into the hands of the Amorites and destroy us. ²⁸*What shall we meet with up there? Our kinsmen have made us fainthearted by reporting that the people are stronger and taller than we, and their cities are large and fortified to the sky; besides, they saw the Anakim there.'

²⁹"But I said to you, 'Have no dread or fear of them. ³⁰The LORD, your God, who goes before you, will himself fight for you, just as he took your part before your very eyes in Egypt, ³¹as well as in the desert, where you saw how the LORD, your God, carried you, as a man carries his child, all along your journey until you arrived at this place.' ³²Despite this, you would not trust the LORD, your God, ³³*who journeys before you to find you a resting place—by day in the cloud, and by night in the fire, to show the way you must go. ³⁴*When the LORD heard your words, he was angry; ³⁵and he swore, 'Not one man of this evil generation shall look upon the good land I swore to give to your fathers, ³⁶†except Caleb, son of Jephunneh; he shall see it. For to him and to his sons I will give the land he trod upon, because he has followed the LORD unreservedly.'

³⁷*"The LORD was angered against me also on your account, and said, 'Not even you shall enter there, ³⁸*but your aide Joshua, son of Nun, shall enter. Encourage him, for he is to give Israel its heritage. ³⁹*Your little ones, who you said would become booty, and your children, who as yet do not know good from bad—they shall enter; to them I will give it, and they shall occupy it. ⁴⁰But as for yourselves: turn about and proceed into the desert on the Red Sea road.'

Unsuccessful Invasion

⁴¹*"In reply you said to me, 'We have sinned against the LORD. We will go up ourselves and fight, just as the LORD, our God, commanded us.' And each of you girded on his weapons, making light of going up into the hill country. ⁴²But the LORD said to me, 'Warn them: Do not go up and fight, lest you be beaten down before your enemies, for I will not be in your midst.' ⁴³I gave you this warning but you would not listen. In defiance of the LORD's command you arrogantly marched off into the hill country. ⁴⁴Then the Amorites living there came out against you and, like bees, chased you, cutting you down in Seir as far as Hormah. ⁴⁵On your return you wept before the LORD, but he did not listen to your cry or give ear to you. ⁴⁶That is why you had to stay as long as you did at Kadesh.

Northward along Edom

2 ¹*"WHEN we did turn and proceed into the desert on the Red Sea road, as the LORD had commanded me, we circled around the highlands of Seir for a long time. ²Finally the LORD said to me, ³'You have wandered round these highlands long enough; turn and go north. ⁴Give this order to the people: You are now about to pass through the territory of your kinsmen, the descendants of Esau, who live in Seir. Though they are afraid of you, be very careful ⁵not to come in conflict with them, for I will not give you so much as a foot of their land, since I have already given Esau possession of the highlands of Seir. ⁶You shall purchase from them with silver the food you eat and the well water you drink. ⁷*The LORD, your God, has blessed you in all your undertakings; he has been concerned about your journey through this vast desert. It is now forty years that he has been with you, and you have never been in want.'

Along Moab

⁸*"Then we left behind us the Arabah route, Elath, Ezion-geber, and Seir, where our kinsmen, the descendants of Esau, live; and we went on toward the desert of Moab. ⁹*And the LORD said to me, 'Do not show hostility to the Moabites or engage them in battle, for I will not give you possession of any of their land, since I have given Ar to the descendants of Lot

19: 8, 15; 32, 10.
22-28: Nm 13, 2-34.
26: 9, 23.
27: 9, 28; Nm 14, 1-4; Ps 106, 25.
28: 9, 1f.
33: Ex 13, 21; Nm 10, 33f; 14, 14.
34ff: Nm 14, 22f.28-38; Jos 14, 9.
37: 4, 21; 34, 4; Nm 20, 12.
38: 31, 3.7; Nm 27, 18ff; 34, 17.
39f: Nm 14, 31.
41-45: Nm 14, 40.42-45.
2/1: 1, 40; Nm 14, 25; 21, 4.
7: 8, 2ff.
8: Jgs 11, 18.
9: Gn 19, 36f.

1, 27: *In your tents:* among yourselves.

1, 36: *Except Caleb:* Joshua also was allowed to enter, but he is not referred to here because special mention is made of him in v 38 as the successor of Moses.

as their own. **10***[Formerly the Emim lived there, a people strong and numerous and tall like the Anakim; **11**like them they were considered Rephaim. It was the Moabites who called them Emim. **12***In Seir, however, the former inhabitants were the Horites; the descendants of Esau dispossessed them, clearing them out of the way and taking their place, just as the Israelites have done in the land of their heritage which the Lord has given them.] **13***Get ready, then, to cross the Wadi Zered.' So we crossed it. **14***Thirty-eight years had elpased between our departure from Kadesh-barnea and that crossing; in the meantime the whole generation of soldiers had perished from the camp, as the Lord had sworn they should. **15**For it was the Lord's hand that was against them, till he wiped them out of the camp completely.

Along Ammon

16"When at length death had put an end to all the soldiers among the people, **17**the Lord said to me, **18**'You are now about to leave Ar and the territory of Moab behind. **19***As you come opposite the Ammonites, do not show hostility or come in conflict with them, for I will not give you possession of any land of the Ammonites, since I have given it to the descendants of Lot as their own. **20**[This also was considered a country of the Rephaim from its former inhabitants, whom the Ammonites called Zamzummim, **21**a people strong and numerous and tall like the Anakim. But these, too, the Lord cleared out of the way for the Ammonites, who ousted them and took their place. **22**He had done the same for the descendants of Esau, who dwell in Seir, by clearing the Horites out of their way, so that the descendants of Esau have taken their place down to the present. **23**†So also the Caphtorim, migrating from Caphtor, cleared away the Avvim, who once dwelt in villages as far as Gaza, and took their place.]

Defeat of Sihon

24*"'Advance now across the Wadi Arnon. I now deliver into your hands Sihon, the Amorite king of Heshbon, and his land. Begin the occupation; engage him in battle. **25**This day I will begin to put a fear and dread of you into every nation under the heavens, so that at the mention of your name they will quake and tremble before you.'

26"So I sent messengers from the desert of Kedemoth to Sihon, king of Heshbon, with this offer of peace: **27**'Let me pass through your country by the highway; I will go along it without turning aside to the right or to the left. **28**For the food I eat which you will supply, and for the water you give me to drink, you shall be paid in silver. Only let me march through, **29***as the descendants of Esau who dwell in Seir and the Moabites who dwell in Ar have done, until I cross the Jordan into the land which the Lord, our God, is about to give us.' **30**But Sihon, king of Heshbon, refused to let us pass through his land, because the Lord, your God, made him stubborn in mind and obstinate in heart that he might deliver him up to you, as indeed he has now done.

31"Then the Lord said to me, 'Now that I have already begun to hand over to you Sihon and his land, begin the actual occupation.' **32**So Sihon and all his people advanced against us to join battle at Jahaz; **33***but since the Lord, our God, had delivered him to us, we defeated him and his sons and all his people. **34***†At that time we seized all his cities and doomed them all, with their men, women and children; we left no survivor. **35**Our only booty was the livestock and the loot of the captured cities. **36***From Aroer on the edge of the Wadi Arnon and from the city in the wadi itself, as far as Gilead, no city was too well fortified for us to whom the Lord had delivered them up. **37***However, in obedience to the command of the Lord, our God, you did not encroach upon any of the Ammonite land, neither the region bordering on the Wadi Jabbok, nor the cities of the highlands.

Defeat of Og

3 **1***"THEN we turned and proceeded toward Bashan. But Og, king of Bashan, advanced against us with all his people to give battle at Edrei. **2***The Lord, however, said to me, 'Do not be afraid of him, for I have delivered him into your hand with all his people and his land. Do to him as you did to Sihon, king of the Amorites, who lived in Heshbon.' **3**And thus the Lord, our God, delivered into our hands Og, king of Bashan, with all his people. We defeated him so completely that we left him no survivor. **4**At that time we captured all his cities, none of them eluding our grasp, the whole region of Argob, the kingdom of Og in Bashan: sixty cities in all, **5**to say nothing of the great number of unwalled towns. All the cities were fortified with high walls and gates and bars. **6***As we had done to Sihon, king of Heshbon, so also here we doomed all the cities, with their men, women and children; **7**but all the livestock and the loot of each city we took as booty for ourselves.

8"And so at that time we took from the two kings of the Amorites beyond the Jordan the territory from the Wadi Arnon to Mount Hermon **9**[which is called Sirion by the Sidonians and Senir by the Amorites], **10**comprising all the cities of the plateau and all Gilead and all the cities of the kingdom of Og in Bashan including Salecah and Edrei. **11**†[Og, king of Bashan, was the last

---

*

10: 1, 28.
12: Gn 36, 20f.
13: Nm 21, 12.
14: Nm 14, 29.33.35.
19: Gn 19, 38.
24: Nm 21, 13;
    Jgs 11, 19-22.
29: 2, 5.8f; Jgs 11, 17.

33: 29, 7; Nm 21, 23-32.
34: 3, 6; 29, 7f.
36: 3, 12; Jos 13, 9.16;
    Jgs 11, 26.
37: Nm 21, 24; Jos 12, 2.
3/1: 29, 6; Nm 21, 33.
2f: Nm 21, 34f.
6: Ps 135, 10ff.

†

2, 23: *The Caphtorim:* members of one of the groups of sea peoples who invaded the coast of Egypt and the southern part of Palestine about 1200 B. C. *Caphtor:* the ancient name of the island of Crete. Cf Am 9, 7.

2, 34: *Doomed:* see notes on Nm 18, 14; 21, 3.

3, 11: *Bed of iron:* some translate, "a sarcophagus of basalt."

remaining survivor of the Rephaim. He had a bed of iron, nine regular cubits long and four wide, which is still preserved in Rabbah of the Ammonites.]

Allotment of the Conquered Lands

¹²*"When we occupied the land at that time, I gave Reuben and Gad the territory from Aroer, on the edge of the Wadi Arnon, halfway up into the highlands of Gilead, with the cities therein. ¹³The rest of Gilead and all of Bashan, the kingdom of Og, the whole Argob region, I gave to the half-tribe of Manasseh. [All this region of Bashan was once called a land of the Rephaim. ¹⁴*Jair, a Manassehite clan, took all the region of Argob as far as the border of the Geshurites and Maccathites, and called it after his own name Bashan Havvoth-jair, the name it bears today.] ¹⁵To Machir I gave Gilead, ¹⁶and to Reuben and Gad the territory from Gilead to the Wadi Arnon—including the wadi bed and its banks—and to the Wadi Jabbok, which is the border of the Ammonites, ¹⁷*as well as the Arabah with the Jordan and its eastern banks from Chinnereth to the Salt Sea of the Arabah, under the slopes of Pisgah.

¹⁸*†"At that time I charged them as follows: 'The Lord, your God, has given you this land as your own. But all you troops equipped for battle must cross over in the vanguard of your brother Israelites. ¹⁹*Only your wives and children, as well as your livestock, of which I know you have a large number, shall remain behind in the towns I have given you, ²⁰*until the Lord has settled your kinsmen as well, and they too possess the land which the Lord, your God, will give them on the other side of the Jordan. Then you may all return to the possessions I have given you.'

²¹"It was then that I instructed Joshua, 'Your eyes have seen all that the Lord, your God, has done to both these kings; so, too, will the Lord do to all the kingdoms which you will encounter over there. ²²Fear them not, for the Lord, your God, will fight for you.'

Refusal to Moses

²³"And it was then that I besought the Lord, ²⁴'O Lord God, you have begun to show to your servant your greatness and might. For what god in heaven or on earth can perform deeds as mighty as yours? ²⁵Ah, let me cross over and see this good land beyond the Jordan, this fine hill country, and the Lebanon!' ²⁶*But the Lord was angry with me on your account and would not hear me. 'Enough!' the Lord said to me. 'Speak to me no more of this. ²⁷*Go up to the top of Pisgah and look out to the west, and to the north, and

to the south, and to the east. Look well, for you shall not cross this Jordan. ²⁸*Commission Joshua, and encourage and strengthen him, for he shall cross at the head of this people and shall put them in possession of the land you are to see.' ²⁹This was while we were in the ravine opposite Beth-peor.

Advantages of Fidelity

4 ¹"Now, Israel, hear the statutes and decrees which I am teaching you to observe, that you may live, and may enter in and take possession of the land which the Lord, the God of your fathers, is giving you. ²*In your observance of the commandments of the Lord, your God, which I enjoin upon you, you shall not add to what I command you nor subtract from it. ³*You have seen with your own eyes what the Lord did at Baal-peor: the Lord, your God, destroyed from your midst everyone that followed the Baal of Peor; ⁴but you, who clung to the Lord, your God, are all alive today. ⁵Therefore, I teach you the statutes and decrees as the Lord, my God, has commanded me, that you may observe them in the land you are entering to occupy. ⁶Observe them carefully, for thus will you give evidence of your wisdom and intelligence to the nations, who will hear of all these statutes and say, 'This great nation is truly a wise and intelligent people.' ⁷*For what great nation is there that has gods so close to it as the Lord, our God, is to us whenever we call upon him? ⁸Or what great nation has statutes and decrees that are as just as this whole law which I am setting before you today?

Revelation at Horeb

⁹*"However, take care and be earnestly on your guard not to forget the things which your own eyes have seen, nor let them slip from your memory as long as you live, but teach them to your children and to your children's children: ¹⁰*†There was the day on which you stood before the Lord, your God, at Horeb, and he said to me, 'Assemble the people for me; I will have them hear my words, that they may learn to fear me as long as they live in the land and may so teach their children.' ¹¹*You came near and stood at the foot of the mountain, which blazed to the very sky with fire and was enveloped in a dense black cloud. ¹²*Then the Lord spoke to you from the midst of the fire. You heard the sound of the words, but saw no form; there was only a voice. ¹³*He proclaimed to you his covenant, which he commanded you to keep: the ten commandments, which he wrote on two tablets of stone. ¹⁴The Lord charged me at that time to teach you the statutes and decrees which you are to observe over in the land you will occupy.

✷

12f: Nm 32, 29.32f;
    Jos 13, 8.29.
14: Nm 32, 41;
    Jos 13, 11.13.
17: 4, 49; Jos 12, 3.
18: Jos 1, 14; 4, 12.
19: Nm 32, 1.4; Jos 1, 14.
20: Jos 22, 4.
26: 4, 21.
27: 34, 4; Nm 27, 12f.

28: 1, 38; 31, 7;
    Nm 27, 22f.
4/2: 13, 1.
3: Nm 25, 3-9.
7: 2 Sm 7, 23.
9: 11, 19; Ps 78, 3-6.
10: Heb 12, 18f.
11: Ex 19, 17f.
12: 4, 33.36; 5, 4.
13: Ex 24, 12; 31, 18;
    34, 28.

---

† 3, 18: *I charged them:* the words which follow were spoken to the men of Reuben and Gad (cf Nm 32).

4, 10: Beginning here and continuing on for several verses (at least to the end of v 14) is the "reminiscence," the account of the things that the Israelites should recall and teach their children.

Danger of Idolatry

15"You saw no form at all on the day the LORD spoke to you at Horeb from the midst of the fire. Be strictly on your guard, therefore, **16***not to degrade yourselves by fashioning an idol to represent any figure, whether it be the form of a man or of a woman, **17**of any animal on the earth or of any bird that flies in the sky, **18**of anything that crawls on the ground or of any fish in the waters under the earth. **19***And when you look up to the heavens and behold the sun or the moon or any star among the heavenly hosts, do not be led astray into adoring them and serving them. These the LORD, your God, has let fall to the lot of all other nations under the heavens; **20***†but you he has taken and led out of that iron foundry, Egypt, that you might be his very own people, as you are today. **21***Since the LORD was angered against me on your account and swore that I should not cross the Jordan nor enter the good land which he is giving you as a heritage, **22***I myself shall die in this country without crossing the Jordan; but you will cross over and take possession of that good land. **23***Take heed, therefore, lest, forgetting the covenant which the LORD, your God, has made with you, you fashion for yourselves against his command an idol in any form whatsoever. **24**For the LORD, your God, is a consuming fire, a jealous God.

God's Fidelity

25†"When you have children and grandchildren, and have grown old in the land, should you then degrade yourselves by fashioning an idol in any form and by this evil done in his sight provoke the LORD, your God, **26**I call heaven and earth this day to witness against you, that you shall all quickly perish from the land which you will occupy when you cross the Jordan. You shall not live in it for any length of time but shall be promptly wiped out. **27***The LORD will scatter you among the nations, and there shall remain but a handful of you among the nations to which the LORD will lead you. **28***There you shall serve gods fashioned by the hands of man out of wood and stone, gods which can neither see nor hear, neither eat nor smell. **29***Yet there too you shall seek the LORD, your God; and you shall indeed find him when you search after him with your whole heart and your whole soul. **30**In your distress, when all these things shall have come upon you, you shall finally return to the LORD, your God, and heed his voice. **31***Since the LORD, your God, is a merciful God, he will not abandon and destroy you, nor forget the covenant which under oath he made with your fathers.

Proofs of God's Love

32"Ask now of the days of old, before your time, ever since God created man upon the earth; ask from one end of the sky to the other: Did anything so great ever happen before? Was it ever heard of? **33***Did a people ever hear the voice of God speaking from the midst of fire, as you did, and live? **34***†Or did any god venture to go and take a nation for himself from the midst of another nation, by testings, by signs and wonders, by war, with his strong hand and outstretched arm, and by great terrors, all of which the LORD, your God, did for you in Egypt before your very eyes? **35**All this you were allowed to see that you might know the LORD is God and there is no other. **36**Out of the heavens he let you hear his voice to discipline you; on earth he let you see his great fire, and you heard him speaking out of the fire. **37**For love of your fathers he chose their descendants and personally led you out of Egypt by his great power, **38**driving out of your way nations greater and mightier than you, so as to bring you in and to make their land your heritage, as it is today. **39***This is why you must now know, and fix in your heart, that the LORD is God in the heavens above and on earth below, and that there is no other. **40***You must keep his statutes and commandments which I enjoin on you today, that you and your children after you may prosper, and that you may have long life on the land which the LORD, your God, is giving you forever."

Cities of Refuge

41*Then Moses set apart three cities in the region east of the Jordan, **42**that a homicide might take refuge there if he unwittingly killed his neighbor to whom he had previously borne no malice, and that he might save his life by fleeing to one of these cities: **43**Bezer in the desert, in the region of the plateau, for the Reubenites; Ramoth in Gilead for the Gadites; and Golan in Bashan for the Manassehites.

II: GOD AND HIS COVENANT

Introduction

44THIS IS THE LAW which Moses set before the Israelites. **45**These are the ordinances, statutes and decrees which he proclaimed to them when they had come out of Egypt **46**and were beyond the Jordan in the ravine opposite Beth-peor, in the land of Sihon, king of the

✿
16: 5, 8; Ex 20, 4.
19: 17, 3; Jb 31, 26ff.
20: 1 Kgs 8, 51; Jer 11, 4.
21: 1, 37; 3, 26.
22: 3, 27.
23: 4, 16.
27f: 28, 36.62.64.
28: Ps 135, 15ff; Is 44, 9.
29: Jer 29, 13.
31: 31, 8.

33: 4, 36; 5, 24.26; Ex 20, 19.
34: 7, 19; 26, 8; 29, 2; Ex 7, 3; 15, 3-10; Jer 32, 21.
39: 4, 35.
40: 6, 2f; 12, 28.
41ff: 19, 2-13; Nm 35, 6-29; Jos 20, 8; 21, 27.36f; 1 Chr 6, 71.80.

---

†

4, 20: Egypt is called an *iron foundry*, or furnace for smelting iron, because God allowed the Israelites to be afflicted there for the sake of their spiritual purification; the same expression for Egypt occurs also in 1 Kgs 8, 51; Jer 11, 4; compare the expression, "the furnace of affliction," in Is 48, 10.

4, 25: *Grown old:* Israel will lose the freshness of its youthful fervor.

4, 34: *Testings:* the demonstrations of God's power as in the ten great plagues of Egypt; cf 7, 19; 29, 2.

Amorites, who dwelt in Heshbon and whom Moses and the Israelites defeated after coming out of Egypt. **47**They occupied his land and the land of Og, king of Bashan, as well—the land of these two kings of the Amorites in the region east of the Jordan: **48**†from Aroer on the edge of the Wadi Arnon to Mount Sion (that is Hermon) **49***and all the Arabah east of the Jordan, as far as the Arabah Sea under the slopes of Pisgah.

The Covenant at Horeb

5 **1**MOSES summoned all Israel and said to them, "Hear, O Israel, the statutes and decrees which I proclaim in your hearing this day, that you may learn them and take care to observe them. **2***The LORD, our God, made a covenant with us at Horeb; **3**not with our fathers did he make this covenant, but with us, all of us who are alive here this day. **4**The LORD spoke with you face to face on the mountain from the midst of the fire. **5***Since you were afraid of the fire and would not go up the mountain, I stood between the LORD and you at that time, to announce to you these words of the LORD:

The Decalogue

6*'I, the LORD, am your God, who brought you out of the land of Egypt, that place of slavery. **7***You shall not have other gods besides me. **8***You shall not carve idols for yourselves in the shape of anything in the sky above or on the earth below or in the waters beneath the earth; **9***†you shall not bow down before them or worship them. For I, the LORD, your God, am a jealous God, inflicting punishments for their fathers' wickedness on the children of those who hate me, down to the third and fourth generation **10***but bestowing mercy, down to the thousandth generation, on the children of those who love me and keep my commandments.

11*'You shall not take the name of the LORD, your God, in vain. For the LORD will not leave unpunished him who takes his name in vain.

12'Take care to keep holy the sabbath day as the LORD, your God, commanded you. **13**Six days you may labor and do all your work; **14***but the seventh day is the sabbath of the LORD, your God. No work may be done then, whether by you, or your son or daughter, or your male or female slave, or your ox or ass or any of your beasts, or the alien who lives with you. Your male and female slave should rest as you do. **15***For remember that you too were once slaves in Egypt, and the LORD, your God, brought you from there with his strong hand and outstretched arm. This is why the LORD, your God, has commanded you to observe the sabbath day.

16*'Honor your father and your mother, as the LORD, your God, has commanded you, that you may have a long life and prosperity in the land which the LORD, your God, is giving you.

17*'You shall not kill.

18'You shall not commit adultery.

19'You shall not steal.

20'You shall not bear dishonest witness against your neighbor.

21'You shall not covet your neighbor's wife.

'You shall not desire your neighbor's house or field, nor his male or female slave, nor his ox or ass, nor anything that belongs to him.'

Moses as Mediator

22"These words, and nothing more, the LORD spoke with a loud voice to your entire assembly on the mountain from the midst of the fire and the dense cloud. He wrote them upon two tablets of stone and gave them to me. **23**But when you heard the voice from the midst of the darkness, while the mountain was ablaze with fire, you came to me in the person of all your tribal heads and elders, **24***and said, 'The LORD, our God, has indeed let us see his glory and his majesty! We have heard his voice from the midst of the fire and have found out today that a man can still live after God has spoken with him. **25***But why should we die now? Surely this great fire will consume us. If we hear the voice of the LORD, our God, any more, we shall die. **26**For what mortal has heard, as we have, the voice of the living God speaking from the midst of fire, and survived? **27***Go closer, you, and hear all that the LORD, our God, will say, and then tell us what the LORD, our God, tells you; we will listen and obey.'

28*"The LORD heard your words as you were speaking to me and said to me, 'I have heard the words these people have spoken to you, which are all well said. **29**Would that they might always be of such a mind, to fear me and to keep all my commandments! Then they and their descendants would prosper forever. **30**Go, tell them to return to their tents. **31**Then you wait here near me and I will give you all the commandments, the statutes and decrees you must teach them, that they may observe them in the land which I am giving them to possess.'

32"Be careful, therefore, to do as the LORD, your God, has commanded you, not turning aside to the right or to the left, **33***but following exactly the way prescribed for you by the LORD, your God, that you

❋
49: 3, 17.
5/2: 28, 69.
5: Ex 24, 2.
6-21: Ex 20, 2-17.
6: Ps 81, 11.
7: Ps 81, 10.
8: 27, 15; Lv 26,1;
　Ps 97, 7.
9: Ex 34, 14.
10: 7, 9; Ex 20, 6.
11: Mt 5, 33.
14: Gn 2, 2; Ex 20, 8; 23,
　12; Heb 4, 4.
15: 15, 15; 16, 12;
　24, 18.22.
16: Sir 3, 2-16; Mt 15, 4;
　Mk 7, 10; Lk 18, 20;
　Eph 6, 2.
17-20: Mt 5, 21.27; Lk 18, 20;
　Jas 2, 11.
24: 4, 33.
25: 18, 16.
27: Ex 20, 19.
28: 18, 17.
33: 4, 40.

†
4, 48: *Sion:* another name for Mount Hermon, besides those mentioned in 3, 9.

5, 9f: God does not punish us for another's sins, but because of the solidarity of human society, the good or evil deeds of one generation may make their effects felt even in later generations. Yet note how God's mercy allows the good effects of virtue to last much longer than the bad effects of vice: a thousand generations compared to three or four.

may live and prosper, and may have long life in the land which you are to occupy.

6 [1]*"THESE then are the commandments, the statutes and decrees which the LORD, your God, has ordered that you be taught to observe in the land into which you are crossing for conquest, [2]*so that you and your son and your grandson may fear the LORD, your God, and keep, throughout the days of your lives, all his statutes and commandments which I enjoin on you, and thus have long life. [3]Here then, Israel, and be careful to observe them, that you may grow and prosper the more, in keeping with the promise of the LORD, the God of your fathers, to give you a land flowing with milk and honey.

The Great Commandment

[4]*†"Hear, O Israel! The LORD is our God, the LORD alone! [5]*Therefore, you shall love the LORD, your God, with all your heart, and with all your soul, and with all your strength. [6]*Take to heart these words which I enjoin on you today. [7]Drill them into your children. Speak of them at home and abroad, whether you are busy or at rest. [8]*†Bind them at your wrist as a sign and let them be as a pendant on your forehead. [9]*Write them on the doorposts of your houses and on your gates.

Fidelity in Prosperity

[10]*"When the LORD, your God, brings you into the land which he swore to your fathers, Abraham, Isaac and Jacob, that he would give you, a land with fine, large cities that you did not build, [11]with houses full of goods of all sorts that you did not garner, with cisterns that you did not dig, with vineyards and olive groves that you did not plant; and when, therefore, you eat your fill, [12]*take care not to forget the LORD, who brought you out of the land of Egypt, that place of slavery. [13]*†The LORD, your God, shall you fear; him shall you serve, and by his name shall you swear. [14]*You shall not follow other gods, such as those of the surrounding nations, [15]lest the wrath of the LORD, your God, flare up against you and he destroy you from the face of the land; for the LORD, your God, who is in your midst, is a jealous God.

[16]*"You shall not put the LORD, your God, to the test, as you did at Massah. [17]But keep the commandments of the LORD, your God, and the ordinances and statutes he has enjoined on you. [18]Do what is right and good in the sight of the LORD, that you may, according to his word, prosper, and may enter in and possess the good

land which the LORD promised on oath to your fathers, [19]*thrusting all your enemies out of your way.

Instruction to Children

[20]*"Later on, when your son asks you what these ordinances, statutes and decrees mean which the LORD, our God, has enjoined on you, [21]*you shall say to your son, 'We were once slaves of Pharaoh in Egypt, but the LORD brought us out of Egypt with his strong hand [22]and wrought before our eyes signs and wonders, great and dire, against Egypt and against Pharaoh and his whole house. [23]He brought us from there to lead us into the land he promised on oath to our fathers, and to give it to us. [24]Therefore, the LORD commanded us to observe all these statutes in fear of the LORD, our God, that we may always have as prosperous and happy a life as we have today; [25]and our justice before the LORD, our God, is to consist in carefully observing all these commandments he has enjoined on us.'

Destruction of Pagans

7 [1]*"WHEN the LORD, your God, brings you into the land which you are to enter and occupy, and dislodges great nations before you—the Hittites, Girgashites, Amorites, Canaanites, Perizzites, Hivites and Jebusites: seven nations more numerous and powerful than you—[2]*and when the LORD, your God, delivers them up to you and you defeat them, you shall doom them. Make no covenant with them and show them no mercy. [3]*You shall not intermarry with them, neither giving your daughters to their sons nor taking their daughters for your sons. [4]For they would turn your sons from following me to serving other gods, and then the wrath of the LORD would flare up against you and quickly destroy you.

[5]*†"But this is how you must deal with them: Tear down their altars, smash their sacred pillars, chop down their sacred poles, and destroy their idols by fire. [6]*For you are a people sacred to the LORD, your God; he has chosen you from all the nations on the face of the earth to be a people peculiarly his own. [7]It was not because you are the largest of all nations that the LORD set his heart on you and chose you, for you are really the smallest of all nations. [8]It was because the LORD loved you and because of his fidelity to the oath he had

---

*   6/1: 4, 1; 5, 31; 12, 1.
2: 4, 40; 5, 29; 10, 12f.
4: Mk 12, 29.
5: 10, 12; 11, 13; Mt 22, 37; Mk 12, 30; Lk 10, 27.
6f: 4, 9; 11, 18; 32, 46.
8: 11, 18; Ex 13, 9.16; Mt 23, 5.
9: 11, 20.
10f: Jos 24, 13.
12: 5, 6.

13: 10, 20; Mt 4, 10; Lk 4, 8.
14f: 8, 19; 11, 16.28.
16: Nm 20, 1-13.
19: Ex 23, 27; 34, 11.
20: Ex 12, 26; 13, 14.
21: Ex 20, 2.
7/1: Ex 23, 23; 33, 2.
2: Ex 34, 12.
3f: Ex 34, 16; 1 Kgs 11, 1f.
5: 12, 3; Ex 34, 13.
6: 14, 2; 26, 18; Ex 19, 6.

†   6, 4f: This passage contains the basic principle of the whole Mosaic law, the keynote of the Book of Deuteronomy: since the Lord alone is God, we must love him with an undivided heart. Christ cited these words as "the greatest and the first commandment," embracing in itself the whole law of God (Mt 22, 37f and parallels).

6, 8: *Bind them . . . as a sign:* these injunctions were probably meant merely in a figurative sense; cf Ex 13, 9.16. However, the later Jews understood them literally, and tied on their wrists and foreheads "phylacteries," boxes containing strips of parchment on which these words were inscribed; cf Mt 23, 5.

6, 13: *Him shall you serve:* here, to "serve" God means especially to "worship" him; in this sense it is quoted by our Lord (Mt 4, 10) as an argument against worshiping the devil.

7, 5: *Sacred pillars . . . poles:* see note on Ex 34, 13.

sworn to your fathers, that he brought you out with his strong hand from the place of slavery, and ransomed you from the hand of Pharaoh, king of Egypt. [9]*Understand, then, that the LORD, your God, is God indeed, the faithful God who keeps his merciful covenant down to the thousandth generation toward those who love him and keep his commandments, [10]but who repays with destruction the person who hates him; he does not dally with such a one, but makes him personally pay for it. [11]You shall therefore carefully observe the commandments, the statutes and the decrees which I enjoin on you today.

Blessings of Obedience

[12]*"As your reward for heeding these decrees and observing them carefully, the LORD, your God, will keep with you the merciful covenant which he promised on oath to your fathers. [13]*He will love and bless and multiply you; he will bless the fruit of your womb and the produce of your soil, your grain and wine and oil, the issue of your herds and the young of your flocks, in the land which he swore to your fathers he would give you. [14]You will be blessed above all peoples; no man or woman among you shall be childless nor shall your livestock be barren. [15]The LORD will remove all sickness from you; he will not afflict you with any of the malignant diseases that you know from Egypt, but will leave them with all your enemies.

[16]"You shall consume all the nations which the LORD, your God, will deliver up to you. You are not to look on them with pity, lest you be ensnared into serving their gods. [17]*Perhaps you will say to yourselves, 'These nations are greater than we. How can we dispossess them?' [18]But do not be afraid of them. Rather, call to mind what the LORD, your God, did to Pharaoh and to all Egypt: [19]*the great testings which your own eyes have seen, the signs and wonders, his strong hand and outstretched arm with which the LORD, your God, brought you out. The same also will he do to all the nations of whom you are now afraid. [20]*Moreover, the LORD, your God, will send hornets among them, until the survivors who have hidden from you are destroyed. [21]Therefore, do not be terrified by them, for the LORD, your God, who is in your midst, is a great and awesome God. [22]*He will dislodge these nations before you little by little. You cannot exterminate them all at once, lest the wild beasts become too numerous for you. [23]*The LORD, your God, will deliver them up to you and will rout them utterly until they are annihilated. [24]*He will deliver their kings into your hand, that you may make their names perish from under the heavens. No man will be able to stand up against you,

till you have put an end to them. [25]The images of their gods you shall destroy by fire. Do not covet the silver or gold on them, nor take it for yourselves, lest you be ensnared by it; for it is an abomination to the LORD, your God. [26]You shall not bring any abominable thing into your house, lest you be doomed with it; loathe and abhor it utterly as a thing that is doomed.

God's Care

8 [1]*"BE careful to observe all the commandments I enjoin on you today, that you may live and increase, and may enter in and possess the land which the LORD promised on oath to your fathers. [2]*Remember how for forty years now the LORD, your God, has directed all your journeying in the desert, so as to test you by affliction and find out whether or not it was your intention to keep his commandments. [3]*†He therefore let you be afflicted with hunger, and then fed you with manna, a food unknown to you and your fathers, in order to show you that not by bread alone does man live, but by every word that comes forth from the mouth of the LORD. [4]*The clothing did not fall from you in tatters, nor did your feet swell these forty years. [5]So you must realize that the LORD, your God, disciplines you even as a man disciplines his son.

Danger of Prosperity

[6]"Therefore, keep the commandments of the LORD, your God, by walking in his ways and fearing him. [7]*For the LORD, your God, is bringing you into a good country, a land with streams of water, with springs and fountains welling up in the hills and valleys, [8]a land of wheat and barley, of vines and fig trees and pomegranates, of olive trees and of honey, [9]a land where you can eat bread without stint and where you will lack nothing, a land whose stones contain iron and in whose hills you can mine copper. [10]But when you have eaten your fill, you must bless the LORD, your God, for the good country he has given you. [11]Be careful not to forget the LORD, your God, by neglecting his commandments and decrees and statutes which I enjoin on you today: [12]lest, when you have eaten your fill, and have built fine houses and lived in them, [13]and have increased your herds and flocks, your silver and gold, and all your property, [14]you then become haughty of heart and unmindful of the LORD, your God, who brought you out of the land of Egypt, that place of slavery; [15]*who guided you through the vast and terrible desert with its saraph serpents and scorpions, its parched and waterless ground; who brought forth water for you from the flinty rock [16]and fed you in the desert with manna, a food unknown to your fathers, that he might afflict you and test you, but also make you prosperous in the end. [17]*Otherwise, you might say to yourselves, 'It is my own power and the

---

✿

9f: 5, 9f.
12-16: 28, 1-14; Ex 23, 22-26; Lv 26, 3-13.
13: 30, 9.
17f: 1, 28ff.
19: 4, 34.
20: Ex 23, 28ff.
22: Ex 23, 29f.
23: 7, 2.
24: 11, 25.

8/1: 4, 1; 6, 1.
2: 2, 7; 29, 4; Am 2, 10.
3: Ex 16, 12-15.35; Nm 11, 6-9; Mt 4, 4; Lk 4, 4.
4: 29, 4; Neh 9, 21.
7: 11, 10ff.
15: Wis 11, 4.
17: 9, 4.

---

† 8, 3: *Not by bread alone, etc:* quoted by our Lord in Mt 4, 4. The sense is: God takes care of those who love him even when natural means seem to fail them.

strength of my own hand that has obtained for me this wealth.' [18]Remember then, it is the LORD, your God, who gives you the power to acquire wealth, by fulfilling, as he has now done, the covenant which he swore to your fathers. [19]*But if you forget the LORD, your God, and follow other gods, serving and worshiping them, I forewarn you this day that you will perish utterly. [20]Like the nations which the LORD destroys before you, so shall you too perish for not heeding the voice of the LORD, your God.

Unmerited Success

9 [1]*"HEAR, O Israel! You are now about to cross the Jordan to enter in and dispossess nations greater and stronger than yourselves, having large cities fortified to the sky, [2]*the Anakim, a people great and tall. You know of them and have heard it said of them, 'Who can stand up against the Anakim?' [3]*Understand, then, today that it is the LORD, your God, who will cross over before you as a consuming fire; he it is who will reduce them to nothing and subdue them before you, so that you can drive them out and destroy them quickly, as the LORD promised you. [4]*After the LORD, your God, has thrust them out of your way, do not say to yourselves, 'It is because of my merits that the LORD has brought me in to possess this land'; for it is really because of the wickedness of these nations that the LORD is driving them out before you. [5]No, it is not because of your merits or the integrity of your heart that you are going in to take possession of their land; but the LORD, your God, is driving these nations out before you on account of their wickedness and in order to keep the promise which he made on oath to your fathers, Abraham, Isaac and Jacob. [6]Understand this, therefore: it is not because of your merits that the LORD, your God, is giving you this good land to possess, for you are a stiff-necked people.

The Golden Calf

[7]*"Bear in mind and do not forget how you angered the LORD, your God, in the desert. From the day you left the land of Egypt until you arrived in this place, you have been rebellious toward the LORD. [8]*At Horeb you so provoked the LORD that he was angry enough to destroy you, [9]*when I had gone up the mountain to receive the stone tablets of the covenant which the LORD made with you. Meanwhile I stayed on the mountain forty days and forty nights without eating or drinking, [10]*till the LORD gave me the two tablets of stone inscribed, by God's own finger, with a copy of all the words that the LORD spoke to you on the mountain from the midst of the fire on the day of

the assembly. [11]Then, at the end of the forty days and forty nights, when the LORD had given me the two stone tablets of the covenant, [12]*he said to me, 'Go down from here now, quickly, for your people whom you have brought out of Egypt have become depraved; they have already turned aside from the way I pointed out to them and have made for themselves a molten idol. [13]I have seen now how stiff-necked this people is,' the LORD said to me. [14]'Let me be, that I may destroy them and blot out their name from under the heavens. I will then make of you a nation mightier and greater than they.'

[15]*"When I had come down again from the blazing, fiery mountain, with the two tablets of the covenant in both my hands, [16]*I saw how you had sinned against the LORD, your God: you had already turned aside from the way which the LORD had pointed out to you by making for yourselves a molten calf! [17]Raising the two tablets with both hands I threw them from me and broke them before your eyes. [18]*Then, as before, I lay prostrate before the LORD for forty days and forty nights without eating or drinking, because of all the sin you had committed in the sight of the LORD and the evil you had done to provoke him. [19]*For I dreaded the fierce anger of the LORD against you: his wrath would destroy you. Yet once again the LORD listened to me. [20]With Aaron, too, the LORD was deeply angry, and would have killed him had I not prayed for him also at that time. [21]*Then, taking the calf, the sinful object you had made, and fusing it with fire, I ground it down to powder as fine as dust, which I threw into the wadi that went down the mountainside.

[22]*"At Taberah, at Massah, and at Kibroth-hattaavah likewise, you provoked the LORD to anger. [23]*And when he sent you up from Kadesh-barnea to take possession of the land he was giving you, you rebelled against this command of the LORD, your God, and would not trust or obey him. [24]Ever since I have known you, you have been rebels against the LORD.

[25]"Those forty days, then, and forty nights, I lay prostrate before the LORD, because he had threatened to destroy you. [26]This was my prayer to him: O Lord GOD, destroy not your people, the heritage which your majesty has ransomed and brought out of Egypt with your strong hand. [27]Remember your servants, Abraham, Isaac and Jacob. Look not upon the stubbornness of this people nor upon their wickedness and sin, [28]*lest the people from whose land you have brought us say, 'The LORD was not able to bring them into the land he promised them'; or 'Out of hatred for them, he brought them out to slay them in the desert.' [29]*They are, after all, your people and your heritage, whom you have brought out by your great power and with your outstretched arm.

10 [1]*"AT that time the LORD said to me, 'Cut two tablets of stone like the former; then come up the mountain to me. Also make an ark of wood. [2]I will write upon the tablets the commandments that were on the former tablets that you broke, and

* 19: 4, 25f; 30, 18.
9/1: 1, 28; 4, 38.
2: Nm 13, 33.
3: 31, 3; Ex 23, 27.
4: 8, 17.
7: 31, 27; Ex 14, 11; Nm 14, 11.
8: Ex 32, 4; Ps 106, 19.
9: Ex 24, 12.18; 34, 28.
10: Ex 31, 18.
12ff: Ex 32, 7-10.
15: Ex 32, 15.
16f: Ex 32, 19.
18: Ex 32, 31; 34, 28.
19: 10, 10; Ex 32, 10.
21: Ex 32, 20.
22: Ex 17, 7; Nm 11, 1ff.34.
23: Nm 14, 1-4; Ps 106, 24f.
28: Nm 14, 14ff.
29: 4, 20; Ex 6, 6f.
10/1: Ex 34, 1.

you shall place them in the ark.' **3***So I made an ark of acacia wood, and cut two tablets of stone like the former, and went up the mountain carrying the two tablets. **4***The Lord then wrote on them, as he had written before, the ten commandments which he spoke to you on the mountain from the midst of the fire on the day of the assembly. After the Lord had given them to me, **5***I turned and came down the mountain, and placed the tablets in the ark I had made. There they have remained, in keeping with the command the Lord gave me.

6*[The Israelites set out from Beeroth Bene-jaakan for Moserah, where Aaron died and was buried, his son Eleazar succeeding him in the priestly office. **7***From there they set out for Gudgodah, and from Gudgodah for Jotbathah, a region where there is water in the wadies.]

8*"At that time the Lord set apart the tribe of Levi to carry the ark of the covenant of the Lord, to be in attendance before the Lord and minister to him, and to give blessings in his name, as they have done to this day. **9***For this reason, Levi has no share in the heritage with his brothers; the Lord himself is his heritage, as the Lord, your God, has told him.

10"After I had spent these other forty days and forty nights on the mountain, and the Lord had once again heard me and decided not to destroy you, **11***he said to me, 'Go now and set out at the head of your people, that they may enter in and occupy the land which I swore to their fathers I would give them.'

The Lord's Majesty

12*"And now, Israel, what does the Lord, your God, ask of you but to fear the Lord, your God, and follow his ways exactly, to love and serve the Lord, your God, with all your heart and all your soul, **13**to keep the commandments and statutes of the Lord which I enjoin on you today for your own good? **14***†Think! The heavens, even the highest heavens, belong to the Lord, your God, as well as the earth and everything on it. **15***Yet in his love for your fathers the Lord was so attached to them as to choose you, their descendants, in preference to all other peoples, as indeed he has now done. **16**†Circumcise your hearts, therefore, and be no longer stiff-necked. **17***For the Lord, your God, is the God of gods, the Lord of lords, the great God, mighty and awesome, who has no favorites, accepts no bribes; **18**who executes justice for the orphan and the widow, and befriends the alien, feeding and clothing him. **19***So you too must befriend the alien, for you were once aliens yourselves in the land of Egypt. **20***The Lord, your God, shall you fear, and him shall you serve; hold fast to him and swear by his name. **21**He is your glory, he, your God, who has done for you those great and terrible things which your own eyes have seen. **22***Your ancestors went down to Egypt seventy strong, and now the Lord, your God, has made you as numerous as the stars of the sky.

The Wonders of the Lord

11 **1**"LOVE the Lord, your God, therefore, and always heed his charge: his statutes, decrees and commandments. **2**It is not your children, who have not known it from experience, but you yourselves who must now understand the discipline of the Lord, your God; his majesty, his strong hand and outstretched arm; **3***the signs and deeds he wrought among the Egyptians, on Pharaoh, king of Egypt, and on all his land; **4***what he did to the Egyptian army and to their horses and chariots, engulfing them in the water of the Red Sea as they pursued you, and bringing ruin upon them even to this day; **5**what he did for you in the desert until you arrived in this place; **6***and what he did to the Reubenites Dathan and Abiram, sons of Eliab, when the ground opened its mouth and swallowed them up out of the midst of Israel, with their families and tents and every living thing that belonged to them. **7**With your own eyes you have seen all these great deeds that the Lord has done. **8**Keep all the commandments, then, which I enjoin on you today, that you may be strong enough to enter in and take possession of the land into which you are crossing, **9**and that you may have long life on the land which the Lord swore to your fathers he would give to them and their descendants, a land flowing with milk and honey.

The Gift of Rain

10"For the land which you are to enter and occupy is not like the land of Egypt from which you have come, where you would sow your seed and then water it by hand, as in a vegetable garden. **11***No, the land into which you are crossing for conquest is a land of hills and valleys that drinks in rain from the heavens, **12**a land which the Lord, your God, looks after; his eyes are upon it continually from the beginning of the year to the end. **13***†If, then, you truly heed my commandments which I enjoin on you today, loving and serving the Lord, your God, with all your heart and all your soul, **14**†I will give the seasonal rain to your land,

---

3: Ex 34, 4.
4: Ex 20, 1-17; 34, 28.
5: Ex 40, 20; 1 Kgs 8, 9.
6: Nm 33, 31.
7: Nm 33, 32f.
8: Nm 3, 6; 6, 23-27; 16, 9.
9: Nm 18, 20.
11: Ex 32, 34; 33, 1.
12: 6, 2.5.
14: Neh 9, 6.
15: 7, 6ff.
17: 2 Chr 19, 7; Jb 34, 19;

Wis 6, 7, Acts 10,34; Rom 2, 11; Gal 2, 6.
19: Ex 22, 21; 23, 9; Lv 19, 33f.
20: 6, 13; Mt 4, 10; Lk 4, 8.
22: Gn 46, 27; Ex 1, 5; Acts 7, 14.
11/3: 6, 22; Ps 78, 42-51.
4: Ex 14, 26ff; 15, 9; Pss 78, 53; 106, 11.
6: Nm 16, 31ff.
11f: 8, 7.
13f: 10, 12; Lv 26, 4.

† 10, 14: *Even the highest heavens:* literally, "and the heavens of the heavens"; compare the phrase, "the third heaven," in 2 Cor 12, 2.

10, 16: *Circumcise your hearts:* cf 30, 6; Jer 4, 4; Rom 2, 29. The "uncircumcised heart" (Lv 26, 41; Jer 9, 25; Ez 44, 7.9) is closed and unreceptive to divine grace and guidance, just as "uncircumcised ears" (Jer 6, 10) are closed to sound, and "uncircumcised lips" (Ex 6, 12.30) do not open well in speech.

11, 13ff: As often in the Prophets, the discourse passes into the words of God himself. Cf 7, 4; 17, 3; 28, 20; 29, 4f.

11, 14: *The early rain:* the rains which begin in October or November and continue intermittently throughout the winter.

the early rain and the late rain, that you may have your grain, wine and oil to gather in; ¹⁵*and I will bring forth grass in your fields for your animals. Thus you may eat your fill. ¹⁶*But be careful lest your heart be so lured away that you serve other gods and worship them. ¹⁷For then the wrath of the Lord will flare up against you and he will close up the heavens, so that no rain will fall, and the soil will not yield its crops, and you will soon perish from the good land he is giving you.

Reward of Fidelity

¹⁸*"Therefore, take these words of mine into your heart and soul. Bind them at your wrist as a sign, and let them be a pendant on your forehead. ¹⁹Teach them to your children, speaking of them at home and abroad, whether you are busy or at rest. ²⁰And write them on the doorposts of your houses and on your gates, ²¹so that, as long as the heavens are above the earth, you and your children may live on in the land which the Lord swore to your fathers he would give them.

²²"For if you are careful to observe all these commandments I enjoin on you, loving the Lord, your God, and following his ways exactly, and holding fast to him, ²³*the Lord will drive all these nations out of your way, and you will dispossess nations greater and mightier than yourselves. ²⁴*†Every place where you set foot shall be yours: from the desert and from Lebanon, from the Euphrates River to the Western Sea, shall be your territory. ²⁵*None shall stand up against you; the Lord, your God, will spread the fear and dread of you through any land where you set foot, as he promised you.

A Blessing and a Curse

²⁶*"I set before you here, this day, a blessing and a curse: ²⁷a blessing for obeying the commandments of the Lord, your God, which I enjoin on you today; ²⁸a curse if you do not obey the commandments of the Lord, your God, but turn aside from the way I ordain for you today, to follow other gods, whom you have not known. ²⁹*†When the Lord, your God, brings you into the land which you are to enter and occupy, then you shall pronounce the blessing on Mount Gerizim, the curse on Mount Ebal. ³⁰[Are they not beyond the Jordan, on the other side of the western road in the country of the Canaanites who live in the Arabah, opposite the Gilgal beside the terebinth of Moreh?] ³¹For you are about to cross the Jordan to enter and occupy the land which the Lord, your God, is giving you. When, therefore, you take possession of it and settle there, ³²be careful to observe all the statutes and decrees that I set before you today.

III: EXPOSITION OF THE LAW

One Sanctuary

12 ¹"these are the statutes and decrees which you must be careful to observe in the land which the Lord, the God of your fathers, has given you to occupy, as long as you live on its soil. ²*Destroy without fail every place on the high mountains, on the hills, and under every leafy tree where the nations you are to dispossess worship their gods. ³Tear down their altars, smash their sacred pillars, destroy by fire their sacred poles, and shatter the idols of their gods, that you may stamp out the remembrance of them in any such place.

⁴"That is not how you are to worship the Lord, your God. ⁵*Instead, you shall resort to the place which the Lord, your God, chooses out of all your tribes and designates as his dwelling ⁶and there you shall bring your holocausts and sacrifices, your tithes and personal contributions, your votive and freewill offerings, and the firstlings of your herds and flocks. ⁷There, too, before the Lord, your God, you and your families shall eat and make merry over all your undertakings, because the Lord, your God, has blessed you. ⁸You shall not do as we are now doing; here, everyone does what seems right to himself, ⁹since you have not yet reached your resting place, the heritage which the Lord, your God, will give you. ¹⁰But after you have crossed the Jordan and dwell in the land which the Lord, your God, is giving you as a heritage, when he has given you rest from all your enemies round about and you live there in security, ¹¹then to the place which the Lord, your God, chooses as the dwelling place for his name you shall bring all the offerings I command you: your holocausts and sacrifices, your tithes and personal contributions, and every special offering you have vowed to the Lord. ¹²You shall make merry before the Lord, your God, with your sons and daughters, your male and female slaves, as well as with the Levite who belongs to your community but has no share of his own in your heritage. ¹³Take care not to offer up your holocausts in any place you fancy, ¹⁴but offer them up in the place which the Lord chooses from among your tribes; there you shall make whatever offerings I enjoin upon you.

Profane and Sacred Meals

¹⁵*"However, in any of your communities you may slaughter and eat to your heart's desire as much meat

---

The late rain: the heavy showers of March and April. In Palestine the crops are sown in the autumn and reaped in the spring.

11, 24: *The Western Sea:* the Mediterranean.

11, 29: *You shall pronounce the blessing . . . the curse:* for the full ceremony, see chapters 27 and 28. *Gerizim . . . Ebal:* adjacent mountains in Samaria with a deep ravine between them. Their summits command an excellent view of the entire country.

---

*

15: Ps 104, 14.
16f: 4, 25f; 6, 14.
18-21: 6, 6-9.
23: 7, 1; 9, 1.
24: Ex 23, 31.
25: 2, 25; 7, 24; Ex 23, 27.

26ff: 28, 2-45; 30, 1.15.19.
29: 27, 12f.
12/2f: 7, 5; Ex 23, 24; 34, 13.
5-7.11f: 14; 22-26; 15, 19f;
16, 2.10f.14f; 26, 2.

as the LORD, your God, has blessed you with; and the unclean as well as the clean may eat it, as they do the gazelle or the deer. [16]*Only, you shall not partake of the blood, but must pour it out on the ground like water. [17]Moreover, you shall not, in your own communities, partake of your tithe of grain or wine or oil, of the first-born of your herd or flock, of any offering you have vowed, of your freewill offerings, or of your personal contributions. [18]These you must eat before the LORD, your God, in the place he chooses, along with your son and daughter, your male and female slave, and the Levite who belongs to your community; and there, before the LORD, you shall make merry over all your undertakings. [19]*Take care, also, that you do not neglect the Levite as long as you live in the land.

[20]*†"After the LORD, your God, has enlarged your territory, as he promised you, when you wish meat for food, you may eat it at will, to your heart's desire; [21]and if the place which the LORD, your God, chooses for the abode of his name is too far, you may slaughter in the manner I have told you any of your herd or flock that the LORD has given you, and eat it to your heart's desire in your own community. [22]You may eat it as you would the gazelle or the deer: the unclean and the clean eating it alike. [23]But make sure that you do not partake of the blood; for blood is life, and you shall not consume this seat of life with the flesh. [24]Do not partake of the blood, therefore, but pour it out on the ground like water. [25]Abstain from it, that you and your children after you may prosper for doing what is right in the sight of the LORD. [26]However, any sacred gifts or votive offerings that you may have, you shall bring with you to the place which the LORD chooses, [27]*and there you must offer both the flesh and the blood of your holocausts on the altar of the LORD, your God; of your other sacrifices the blood indeed must be poured out against the altar of the LORD, your God, but their flesh may be eaten. [28]Be careful to heed all these commandments I enjoin on you, that you and your descendants may always prosper for doing what is good and right in the sight of the LORD, your God.

Pagan Rites

[29]"When the LORD, your God, removes the nations from your way as you advance to dispossess them, be on your guard! Otherwise, once they have been wiped out before you and you have replaced them and are settled in their land, [30]you will be lured into following them. Do not inquire regarding their gods, 'How did these nations worship their gods? I, too, would do the same.' [31]You shall not thus worship the LORD, your God, because they offered to their gods every abomination that the LORD detests, even burning their sons and daughters to their gods.

Penalties for Idolatry

13 [1]"EVERY command that I enjoin on you, you shall be careful to observe, neither adding to it nor subtracting from it.

[2]†"If there arises among you a prophet or a dreamer who promises you a sign or wonder, [3]urging you to follow other gods, whom you have not known, and to serve them: even though the sign or wonder he has foretold you comes to pass, [4]pay no attention to the words of that prophet or that dreamer; for the LORD, your God, is testing you to learn whether you really love him with all your heart and with all your soul. [5]The LORD, your God, shall you follow, and him shall you fear; his commandment shall you observe, and his voice shall you heed, serving him and holding fast to him alone. [6]*But that prophet or that dreamer shall be put to death, because, in order to lead you astray from the way which the LORD, your God, has directed you to take, he has preached apostasy from the LORD, your God, who brought you out of the land of Egypt and ransomed you from that place of slavery. Thus shall you purge the evil from your midst.

[7]"If your own full brother, or your son or daughter, or your beloved wife, or your intimate friend, entices you secretly to serve other gods, whom you and your fathers have not known, [8]gods of any other nation, near at hand or far away, from one end of the earth to the other: [9]do not yield to him or listen to him, nor look with pity upon him, to spare or shield him, [10]but kill him. Your hand shall be the first raised to slay him; the rest of the people shall join in with you. [11]You shall stone him to death, because he sought to lead you astray from the LORD, your God, who brought you out of the land of Egypt, that place of slavery. [12]And all Israel, hearing of it, shall fear and never again do such evil as this in your midst.

[13]"If, in any of the cities which the LORD, your God, gives you to dwell in, you hear it said [14]that certain scoundrels have sprung up among you and have led astray the inhabitants of their city to serve other gods whom you have not known, [15]you must inquire carefully into the matter and investigate it thoroughly. If you find that it is true and an established fact that this abomination has been committed in your midst, [16]*you shall put the inhabitants of that city to the sword, dooming the city and all life that is in it, even its cattle, to the sword. [17]Having heaped up all its spoils in the middle of its square, you shall burn the city with all its spoils as a whole burnt offering to the LORD, your God. Let it be a heap of ruins forever, never to be rebuilt. [18]You shall not retain anything that is doomed, that the blazing wrath of the LORD may die down and

---

† 12, 20: *Meat for food:* as on special feasts. Meat was not eaten every day in Israel, even by the wealthy.

13, 2.4.6: *Dreamer:* a false prophet who pretended to have received revelations from God in his dreams; cf Jer 23, 25-32; Zec 10, 2. But dreams could also be a channel of true prophecy (Nm 12, 6; Jl 3, 1) and of genuine revelations (Gn 20, 3.6; 31, 10.24; 37, 5.9; Mt 1, 20; 2.12f.19; etc.).

✿

16: 15, 23; Gn 9, 4;   27: Lv 17, 11.
    Lv 3, 17.   31: Lv 18, 21; Jer 7, 31.
19: 14, 27.   13/6-10.14: 6, 14; 17, 2-7.
20: 19, 8; Gn 28, 14;   16f: Jos 6, 18.24; 7, 26;
    Ex 34, 24.   8, 28.

he may show you mercy and in his mercy for you may multiply you as he promised your fathers on oath; [19]because you have heeded the voice of the Lord, your God, keeping all his commandments which I enjoin on you today, doing what is right in his sight.

Pagan Mourning Rites

14 [1]*"YOU are children of the Lord, your God. You shall not gash yourselves nor shave the hair above your foreheads for the dead. [2]*For you are a people sacred to the Lord, your God, who has chosen you from all the nations on the face of the earth to be a people peculiarly his own.

Clean and Unclean Animals

[3]*"You shall not eat any abominable thing. [4]*These are the animals you may eat: the ox, the sheep, the goat, [5]†the red deer, the gazelle, the roe deer, the ibex, the addax, the oryx, and the mountain sheep. [6]Any animal that has hoofs you may eat, provided it is cloven-footed and chews the cud. [7]But you shall not eat any of the following that only chew the cud or only have cloven hoofs: the camel, the hare and the rock badger, which indeed chew the cud, but do not have hoofs, and are therefore unclean for you; [8]*and the pig, which indeed has hoofs and is cloven-footed, but does not chew the cud and is therefore unclean for you. Their flesh you shall not eat, and their dead bodies you shall not touch.

[9]"Of the various creatures that live in the water, whatever has both fins and scales you may eat, [10]but all those that lack either fins or scales you shall not eat; they are unclean for you.

[11]"You may eat all clean birds. [12]But you shall not eat any of the following: the eagle, the vulture, the osprey, [13]the various kites and falcons, [14]all the various species of crows, [15]the ostrich, the nightjar, the gull, the various species of hawks, [16]the owl, the screech owl, the ibis, [17]the desert owl, the buzzard, the cormorant, [18]the stork, the various species of herons, the hoopoe, and the bat. [19]†All winged insects, too, are unclean for you and shall not be eaten. [20]But you may eat any clean winged creatures.

[21]*†"You must not eat any animal that has died of itself, for you are a people sacred to the Lord, your God. But you may give it to an alien who belongs to your community, and he may eat it, or you may sell it to a foreigner.

"You shall not boil a kid in its mother's milk.

Tithes

[22]*"Each year you shall tithe all the produce that grows in the field you have sown; [23]*then in the place which the Lord, your God, chooses as the dwelling place of his name you shall eat in his presence your tithe of the grain, wine and oil, as well as the firstlings of your herd and flock, that you may learn always to fear the Lord, your God. [24]†If, however, the journey is too much for you and you are not able to bring your tithe, because the place which the Lord, your God, chooses for the abode of his name is too far for you, considering how the Lord has blessed you, [25]you may exchange the tithe for money and, with the purse of money in hand, go to the place which the Lord, your God, chooses. [26]You may then exchange the money for whatever you desire, oxen or sheep, wine or strong drink, or anything else you would enjoy, and there before the Lord, your God, you shall partake of it and make merry with your family. [27]*But do not neglect the Levite who belongs to your community, for he has no share in the heritage with you.

[28]*"At the end of every third year you shall bring out all the tithes of your produce for that year and deposit them in community stores, [29]that the Levite who has no share in the heritage with you, and also the alien, the orphan and the widow who belongs to your community, may come and eat their fill; so that the Lord, your God, may bless you in all that you undertake.

Debts and the Poor

15 [1]*†"AT the end of every seven-year period you shall have a relaxation of debts, [2]which shall be observed as follows. Every creditor shall relax his claim on what he has loaned his neighbor; he must not press his neighbor, his kinsman, because a relaxation in honor of the Lord has been proclaimed. [3]*You may press a foreigner, but you shall relax the claim on your kinsman for what is yours. [4]Nay, more! since the Lord, your God, will bless you abundantly in the land he will give you to occupy as your heritage, there should be no one of you in need. [5]If you but heed the voice of the Lord, your God, and carefully observe all these commandments which I enjoin on you today, [6]*you will lend to many nations, and borrow from none; you will rule over many nations, and none will rule over you, since the Lord, your God, will bless you as he promised. [7]If one of your kinsmen in any com-

---

† 14, 5: *The gazelle, the addax, the oryx:* species of antelopes. *The ibex:* a species of wild goat.

14, 19f: The apparent contradiction is to be resolved in the light of Lv 11, 20-23: the *unclean winged insects* are those that walk on the ground; the *clean winged creatures* are those that leap on the ground, such as certain species of locusts.

14, 21: *Boil a kid in its mother's milk:* see note on Ex 23, 19.

14, 24: *Considering how the Lord has blessed you:* should the Israelite farmer be blessed with an abundant harvest, a tenth of this would be too much to transport for a great distance.

15, 1: *At the end of every seven-year period:* in every seventh, or sabbatical, year. Cf v 9; 31, 10; and compare Jer 34, 14 with Dt 15, 12. *A relaxation of debts:* it is uncertain whether a full cancellation of debts is meant, or merely a suspension of payment on them or on their interest among the Israelites. Cf Ex 23, 11 where the same Hebrew root is used of a field that is "let lie fallow" in the sabbatical year.

14/1: Lv 19, 28.
2: 7, 6.
3: Ez 4, 14; Acts 10, 14.
4-20: Lv 11, 2-23.
8: Lv 11, 26.
21: Ex 22, 30; 23, 19; 34, 26.
22: Lv 27, 30.
23f: 12, 5ff.
27: 12, 12.19.
28f: 26, 12.
15/1: Neh 10, 31.
3: 23, 20.
6: 28, 12f.

munity is in need in the land which the LORD, your God, is giving you, you shall not harden your heart nor close your hand to him in his need. **8***Instead, you shall open your hand to him and freely lend him enough to meet his need. **9**Be on your guard lest, entertaining the mean thought that the seventh year, the year of relaxation, is near, you grudge help to your needy kinsman and give him nothing; else he will cry to the LORD against you and you will be held guilty. **10**When you give to him, give freely and not with ill will; for the LORD, your God, will bless you for this in all your works and undertakings. **11***†The needy will never be lacking in the land; that is why I command you to open your hand to your poor and needy kinsman in your country.

Hebrew Slaves

12*"If your kinsman, a Hebrew man or woman, sells himself to you, he is to serve you for six years, but in the seventh year you shall dismiss him from your service, a free man. **13**When you do so, you shall not send him away empty-handed, **14**but shall weight him down with gifts from your flock and threshing floor and wine press, in proportion to the blessing the LORD, your God, has bestowed on you. **15***For remember that you too were once slaves in the land of Egypt, and the LORD, your God, ransomed you. That is why I am giving you this command today. **16***If, however, he tells you that he does not wish to leave you, because he is devoted to you and your household, since he fares well with you, **17**†you shall take an awl and thrust it through his ear into the door, and he shall then be your slave forever. Your female slave, also, you shall treat in the same way. **18**You must not be reluctant to let your slave go free, since the service he has given you for six years was worth twice a hired man's salary; then also the LORD, your God, will bless you in everything you do.

Firstlings

19*"You shall consecrate to the LORD, your God, all the male firstlings of your herd and of your flock. You shall not work the firstlings of your cattle, nor shear the firstlings of your flock. **20***Year after year you and your family shall eat them before the LORD, your God, in the place he chooses. **21***If, however, a firstling is lame or blind or has any other serious defect, you shall not sacrifice it to the LORD, your God, **22**but in your own communities you may eat it, the unclean and the clean eating it alike, as you would a gazelle or a deer. **23**Only, you shall not partake of its blood, which must be poured out on the ground like water.

Feast of the Passover

16 **1***†"OBSERVE the month of Abib by keeping the Passover of the LORD, your God, since it was in the month of Abib that he brought you by night out of Egypt. **2**You shall offer the Passover sacrifice from your flock or your herd to the LORD, your God, in the place which he chooses as the dwelling place of his name. **3***You shall not eat leavened bread with it. For seven days you shall eat with it only unleavened bread, the bread of affliction, that you may remember as long as you live the day of your departure from the land of Egypt; for in frightened haste you left the land of Egypt. **4**Nothing leavened may be found in all your territory for seven days, and none of the meat which you sacrificed on the evening of the first day shall be kept overnight for the next day.

5"You may not sacrifice the Passover in any of the communities which the LORD, your God, gives you; **6**only at the place which he chooses as the dwelling place of his name, and in the evening at sunset, on the anniversary of your departure from Egypt, shall you sacrifice the Passover. **7**You shall cook and eat it at the place the LORD, your God, chooses; then in the morning you may return to your tents. **8**For six days you shall eat unleavened bread, and on the seventh there shall be a solemn meeting in honor of the LORD, your God; on that day you shall not do any sort of work.

Feast of Weeks

9*"You shall count off seven weeks, computing them from the day when the sickle is first put to the standing grain. **10**†You shall then keep the feast of Weeks in honor of the LORD, your God, and the measure of your own freewill offering shall be in proportion to the blessing the LORD, your God, has bestowed on you. **11***In the place which the LORD, your God, chooses as the dwelling place of his name, you shall make merry in his presence together with your son and daughter, your male and female slave, and the Levite who belongs to your community, as well as the alien, the orphan and the widow among you. **12**Remember that you too were once slaves in Egypt, and carry out these statutes carefully.

Feast of Booths

13*†"You shall celebrate the feast of Booths for seven days, when you have gathered in the produce from your threshing floor and wine press. **14***You shall make merry at your feast, together with your son and daugh-

8: Lv 25, 35; Sir 29, 1f;
    Mt 5, 42.
11: 15, 8; Sir 29, 12.
12: Ex 21, 2; Jer 34, 14.
15: 5, 15.
16f: Ex 21, 5f.
19: Ex 13, 11.
20: 14, 23.
21ff: 12, 15f; Lv 22, 20.

16/1-8: Ex 12, 2-20; 23, 15;
        Nm 28, 16ff.24f.
3f: Ex 13, 6f; 34, 18.
9-12: Lv 23, 15-21.
11: 12, 5.7.12.18.
13-15: Ex 23, 16;
       Lv 23, 34-43;
       Nm 29, 12-38.
14: 16, 11.

---

† 15, 11: *The needy will never be lacking:* compare the words of Christ, "The poor you have always with you" (Mt 26, 11).

15, 17: *His ear:* cf Ex 21, 6 and the note there.

16, 1: *Abib:* "ear of grain, ripe grain," the name of the month in which the barley harvest fell, corresponding to our March and April; at a later period this month received the Babylonian name of "Nisan."

16, 10: *Feast of Weeks:* later known more commonly as "Pentecost."

16, 13: See note on Lv 23, 34.

ter, your male and female slave, and also the Levite, the alien, the orphan and the widow who belong to your community. [15]For seven days you shall celebrate this pilgrim feast in honor of the LORD, your God, in the place which he chooses; since the LORD, your God, has blessed you in all your crops and in all your undertakings, you shall do nought but make merry.

[16]*"Three times a year, then, every male among you shall appear before the LORD, your God, in the place which he chooses: at the feast of Unleavened Bread, at the feast of Weeks, and at the feast of Booths. No one shall appear before the LORD empty-handed, [17]but each of you with as much as he can give, in proportion to the blessings which the LORD, your God, has bestowed on you.

Judges

[18]"You shall appoint judges and officials throughout your tribes to administer true justice for the people in all the communities which the LORD, your God, is giving you. [19]*You shall not distort justice; you must be impartial. You shall not take a bribe; for a bribe blinds the eyes even of the wise and twists the words even of the just. [20]Justice and justice alone shall be your aim, that you may have life and may possess the land which the LORD, your God, is giving you.

Pagan Worship

[21]*†"You shall not plant a sacred pole of any kind of wood beside the altar of the LORD, your God, which you will build; [22]nor shall you erect a sacred pillar, such as the LORD, your God, detests.

17 [1]*"YOU shall not sacrifice to the LORD, your God, from the herd or from the flock an animal with any serious defect; that would be an abomination to the LORD, your God.

[2]*"If there is found among you, in any one of the communities which the LORD, your God, gives you, a man or a woman who does evil in the sight of the LORD, your God, and transgresses his covenant, [3]*by serving other gods, or by worshiping the sun or the moon or any of the host of the sky, against my command; [4]and if, on being informed of it, you find by careful investigation that it is true and an established fact that this abomination has been committed in Israel: [5]†you shall bring the man (or woman) who has done the evil deed out to your city gates and stone him to death. [6]*The testimony of two or three witnesses is required for putting a person to death; no one shall be put to death on the testimony of only one witness. [7]*At the execution, the witnesses are to be the first to raise their hands

against him; afterward all the people are to join in. Thus shall you purge the evil from your midst.

Judges

[8]"If in your own community there is a case at issue which proves too complicated for you to decide, in a matter of bloodshed or of civil rights or of personal injury, you shall then go up to the place which the LORD, your God, chooses, [9]*to the levitical priests or to the judge who is in office at that time. They shall study the case and then hand down to you their decision. [10]According to this decision that they give you in the place which the LORD chooses, you shall act, being careful to do exactly as they direct. [11]You shall carry out the directions they give you and the verdict they pronounce for you, without turning aside to the right or to the left from the decision they hand down to you. [12]†Any man who has the insolence to refuse to listen to the priest who officiates there in the ministry of the LORD, your God, or to the judge, shall die. Thus shall you purge the evil from your midst. [13]And all the people, on hearing of it, shall fear, and never again be so insolent.

The King

[14]*"When you have come into the land which the LORD, your God, is giving you, and have occupied it and settled in it, should you then decide to have a king over you like all the surrounding nations, [15]*you shall set that man over you as your king whom the LORD, your God, chooses. He whom you set over you as king must be your kinsman; a foreigner, who is no kin of yours, you may not set over you. [16]*†But he shall not have a great number of horses; nor shall he make his people go back again to Egypt to acquire them, against the LORD's warning that you must never go back that way again. [17]*Neither shall he have a great number of wives, lest his heart be estranged, nor shall he accumulate a vast amount of silver and gold. [18]*When he is enthroned in his kingdom, he shall have a copy of this law made from the scroll that is in the custody of the levitical priests. [19]He shall keep it with him and read it all the days of his life that he may learn to fear the LORD, his God, and to heed and fulfill all the words of this law and these statutes. [20]Let him not

---

† 16, 21—17, 7: This section seems to be out of its proper place, since it interrupts the natural sequence of the laws for the judges (16, 18-20 and 17, 8-13). It probably belongs to the similar section, 12-29—14, 2.

16, 21f: *Sacred pole . . . sacred pillar:* see note on Ex 34, 13.

17, 5: *Out to your city gates:* outside the gates in an unclean place; cf Lv 24, 14; Nm 15, 36; Acts 7, 58; Heb 13, 12.

17, 12: *The priest:* the high priest; *the judge:* a layman. The former presided over the court in cases which directly concerned religion, the latter in cases of a more secular nature; cf 2 Chr 19, 8-11.

17, 16: *Horses:* chariotry for war. *The Lord's warning:* the same warning is also referred to in 28, 68, although it is not mentioned explicitly elsewhere in the Pentateuch. We know from other sources that Egypt used to export war horses to Palestine. The danger envisioned here is that some king might make Israel a vassal of Egypt for the sake of such military aid.

❋
16: Ex 23, 14f.17; 34, 23;   7: 13, 10.
    2 Chr 8,13.   9: 21, 5; 2 Chr 19, 8.
19: 1, 17; Ex 23, 8.   14: 1 Sm 8, 5.19f.
21: 1 Kgs 14, 15;   15: 1 Sm 9, 16; 10, 24;
    2 Chr 33, 3.   16, 12.
17/1: Lv 22, 20.   16: 28, 68; 1 Kgs 4, 26;
2-7: 13, 6-15.   10, 26.
3: 4, 19.   17: 1 Kgs 11, 3f;
6: 19, 15; Nm 35, 30;   Neh 13, 26.
    Mt 18, 16; Jn 8, 17;   18: 31, 9.26.
    2 Cor 13, 1.

become estranged from his countrymen through pride, nor turn aside to the right or to the left from these commandments. Then he and his descendants will enjoy a long reign in Israel.

Priests

18 ¹*"THE whole priestly tribe of Levi shall have no share in the heritage with Israel; they shall live on the oblations of the LORD and the portions due to him. ²Levi shall have no heritage among his brothers; the LORD himself is his heritage, as he has told him. ³The priests shall have a right to the following things from the people: from those who are offering a sacrifice, whether the victim is from the herd or from the flock, the priest shall receive the shoulder, the jowls and the stomach. ⁴*You shall also give him the first fruits of your grain and wine and oil, as well as the first fruits of the shearing of your flock; ⁵for the LORD, your God, has chosen him and his sons out of all your tribes to be always in attendance to minister in the name of the LORD.

⁶"When a Levite goes from one of your communities anywhere in Israel in which he ordinarily resides, to visit, as his heart may desire, the place which the LORD chooses, ⁷he may minister there in the name of the LORD, his God, like all his fellow Levites who are in attendance there before the LORD. ⁸He shall then receive the same portions to eat as the rest, along with his monetary offerings and heirlooms.

Prophets

⁹*"When you come into the land which the LORD, your God, is giving you, you shall not learn to imitate the abominations of the peoples there. ¹⁰*†Let there not be found among you anyone who immolates his son or daughter in the fire, nor a fortuneteller, soothsayer, charmer, diviner, ¹¹or caster of spells, nor one who consults ghosts and spirits or seeks oracles from the dead. ¹²*Anyone who does such things is an abomination to the LORD, and because of such abominations the LORD, your God, is driving these nations out of your way. ¹³You, however, must be altogether sincere toward the LORD, your God. ¹⁴Though these nations whom you are to dispossess listen to their soothsayers and fortunetellers, the LORD, your God, will not permit you to do so.

¹⁵*†"A prophet like me will the LORD, your God, raise up for you from among your own kinsmen; to him you shall listen. ¹⁶*This is exactly what you requested of the LORD, your God, at Horeb on the day of the assembly, when you said, 'Let us not again hear the voice of the LORD, our God, nor see this great fire any more, lest we die.' ¹⁷And the LORD said to me, 'This was well said. ¹⁸I will raise up for them a prophet like you from among their kinsmen, and will put my words into his mouth; he shall tell them all that I command him. ¹⁹*If any man will not listen to my words which he speaks in my name, I myself will make him answer for it. ²⁰*But if a prophet presumes to speak in my name an oracle that I have not commanded him to speak, or speaks in the name of other gods, he shall die.'

²¹"If you say to yourselves, 'How can we recognize an oracle which the LORD has spoken?', ²²know that, even though a prophet speaks in the name of the LORD, if his oracle is not fulfilled or verified, it is an oracle which the LORD did not speak. The prophet has spoken it presumptuously, and you shall have no fear of him.

Cities of Refuge

19 ¹"WHEN the LORD, your God, removes the nations whose land he is giving you, and you have taken their place and are settled in their cities and houses, ²*†you shall set apart three cities in the land which the LORD, your God, is giving you to occupy. ³You shall thereby divide into three regions the land which the LORD, your God, will give you as a heritage, and so arrange the routes that every homicide will be able to find a refuge.

⁴*"It is in the following case that a homicide may take refuge in such a place to save his life: when someone unwittingly kills his neighbor to whom he had previously borne no malice. ⁵For example, if he goes with his neighbor to a forest to cut wood, and as he swings his ax to fell a tree, its head flies off the handle and hits his neighbor a mortal blow, he may take refuge in one of these cities to save his life. ⁶†Should the distance be too great, the avenger of blood may in the heat of his anger pursue the homicide and overtake him and strike him dead, even though he does not merit death since he had previously borne the slain man no malice. ⁷That is why I order you to set apart three cities.

---
† 18, 10f: *Immolates his son or daughter in the fire:* to Molech. See note on Lv 18, 21. Such human sacrifices are classed here with other pagan superstitions because they were believed to possess magical powers for averting a calamity; cf 2 Kgs 3, 27. Three other forms of superstition are listed here: augury (by a *fortuneteller,* a *soothsayer* or a *diviner*); black magic (by a *charmer . . . or caster of spells*); and necromancy (by *one who consults ghosts and spirits or seeks oracles from the dead*).

18, 15: *A prophet like me:* from the context (opposition to the pagan soothsayers) it seems that Moses is referring in general to all the true prophets who were to succeed him. But since Christ is the Great Prophet in whom the prophetic office finds its fulfillment and completion, this passage was understood in a special Messianic sense both by the Jews (Jn 6, 14; 7, 40) and by the Apostles (Acts 3, 22; 7, 37).

19, 2: *Set apart three cities:* the Israelites were to have at least six cities of refuge, three in the land east of the Jordan and three in the land of Canaan west of the Jordan (Nm 35, 9-34); but since the three cities east of the Jordan had now been appointed (Dt 4, 41-43, reference is made here only to the three west of the Jordan. The execution of this command is narrated in Jos 20.

19, 6: *The avenger of blood:* see note on Nm 35, 12.

18/1: Nm 18, 8f.20-24; 1 Cor 9, 13.
4: Nm 18, 12; 2 Chr 31, 5.
9: 12, 29ff; Lv 18, 26-30.
10f: Lv 18, 21; 19, 31; 20, 27; 1 Sm 28, 7; 2 Kgs 17, 17; 21, 6.
12: 9, 4.
15: Jn 1, 45; 6, 14;
Acts 3, 22; 7, 37.
16: Ex 20, 19.
19: Acts 3, 23.
20.22: 13, 2ff.
19/2: 4, 41ff; Ex 21, 13; Nm 35, 10-15; Jos 20, 2.8.
4: 4, 42; Nm 35, 15; Jos 20, 3.5.

8*"But if the Lord, your God, enlarges your territory, as he swore to your fathers, and gives you all the land he promised your fathers he would give **9**in the event that you carefully observe all these commandments which I enjoin on you today, loving the Lord, your God, and ever walking in his ways: then add three cities to these three. **10**Thus, in the land which the Lord, your God, is giving you as a heritage, innocent blood will not be shed and you will not become guilty of bloodshed.

11*"However, if someone lies in wait for his neighbor out of hatred for him, and rising up against him, strikes him mortally, and then takes refuge in one of these cities, **12**the elders of his own city shall send for him and have him taken from there, and shall hand him over to be slain by the avenger of blood. **13**Do not look on him with pity, but purge from Israel the stain of shedding innocent blood, that you may prosper.

Removal of Landmarks

14*"You shall not move your neighbor's landmarks erected by your forefathers in the heritage you receive in the land which the Lord, your God, is giving you to occupy.

False Witnesses

15*"One witness alone shall not take the stand against a man in regard to any crime or any offense of which he may be guilty; a judicial fact shall be established only on the testimony of two or three witnesses.

16"If an unjust witness takes the stand against a man to accuse him of a defection from the law, **17***the two parties in the dispute shall appear before the Lord in the presence of the priests or judges in office at that time; **18***and if after a thorough investigation the judges find that the witness is a false witness and has accused his kinsman falsely, **19**you shall do to him as he planned to do to his kinsman. Thus shall you purge the evil from your midst. **20**The rest, on hearing of it, shall fear, and never again do a thing so evil among you. **21***Do not look on such a man with pity. Life for life, eye for eye, tooth for tooth, hand for hand, and foot for foot!

Courage in War

20 **1**"WHEN you go out to war against your enemies and you see horses and chariots and an army greater than your own, do not be afraid of them, for the Lord, your God, who brought you up from the land of Egypt, will be with you.

2"When you are about to go into battle, the priest shall come forward and say to the soldiers: **3**'Hear, O Israel! Today you are going into battle against your enemies. Be not weakhearted or afraid; be neither alarmed nor frightened by them. **4***For it is the Lord, your God, who goes with you to fight for you against your enemies and give you victory.

5*"Then the officials shall say to the soldiers, 'Is there anyone who has built a new house and not yet had the housewarming? Let him return home, lest he die in battle and another dedicate it. **6**Is there anyone who has planted a vineyard and never yet enjoyed its fruits? Let him return home, lest he die in battle and another enjoy its fruits in his stead. **7***Is there anyone who has betrothed a woman and not yet taken her as his wife? Let him return home, lest he die in battle and another take her to wife.' **8***In fine, the officials shall say to the soldiers, 'Is there anyone who is afraid and weakhearted? Let him return home, lest he make his fellows as fainthearted as himself.'

9"When the officials have finished speaking to the soldiers, military officers shall be appointed over the army.

Cities of the Enemy

10"When you march up to attack a city, first offer it terms of peace. **11**If it agrees to your terms of peace and opens its gates to you, all the people to be found in it shall serve you in forced labor. **12**But if it refuses to make peace with you and instead offers you battle, lay siege to it, **13***and when the Lord, your God, delivers it into your hand, put every male in it to the sword; **14**but the women and children and livestock and all else in it that is worth plundering you may take as your booty, and you may use this plunder of your enemies which the Lord, your God, has given you.

15"That is how you shall deal with any city at a considerable distance from you, which does not belong to the peoples of this land. **16***But in the cities of those nations which the Lord, your God, is giving you as your heritage, you shall not leave a single soul alive. **17**You must doom them all—the Hittites, Amorites, Canaanites, Perizzites, Hivites and Jebusites—as the Lord, your God, has commanded you, **18**lest they teach you to make any such abominable offerings as they make to their gods, and you thus sin against the Lord, your God.

Trees of a Besieged City

19"When you are at war with a city and have to lay siege to it for a long time before you capture it, you shall not destroy its trees by putting an ax to them. You may eat their fruit, but you must not cut down the trees. After all, are the trees of the field men, that they should be included in your siege? **20**However, those trees which you know are not fruit trees you may destroy, cutting them down to build siegeworks with which to reduce the city that is resisting you.

❋

8: Gn 15, 18-21; 28, 14; Ex 23, 31; 34, 24.
11ff: Ex 21, 12.14; Nm 35, 20f.
14: 27, 17; Prv 23, 10; Hos 5, 10.
15: 17, 6; Nm 35, 30; Mt 18, 16; Jn 8, 17; 2 Cor 13, 1.
17: 17, 8f.

18f: Dn 13, 61f.
21: Ex 21, 23f; Lv 24, 20; Mt 5.38.
20/4: 1, 30; 3, 22; Jos 23, 10.
5ff: 1 Mc 3, 56.
7: 24, 5.
8: Jgs 7, 3.
13f: Nm 31, 7.9.11; Jos 22, 8.
16f: 7, 1f; Jos 10, 40; 11, 14.

Expiation of Untraced Murder

21 ¹†"IF the corpse of a slain man is found lying in the open on the land which the LORD, your God, is giving you to occupy, and it is not known who killed him, ²your elders and judges shall go out and measure the distances to the cities that are in the neighborhood of the corpse. ³When it is established which city is nearest the corpse, the elders of that city shall take a heifer that has never been put to work as a draft animal under a yoke, ⁴†and bringing it down to a wadi with an everflowing stream at a place that has not been plowed or sown, they shall cut the heifer's throat there in the wadi. ⁵*The priests, the descendants of Levi, shall also be present, for the LORD, your God, has chosen them to minister to him and to give blessings in his name, and every case of dispute or violence must be settled by their decision. ⁶†Then all the elders of that city nearest the corpse shall wash their hands over the heifer whose throat was cut in the wadi, ⁷†and shall declare, 'Our hands did not shed this blood, and our eyes did not see the deed. ⁸Absolve, O LORD, your people Israel, whom you have ransomed, and let not the guilt of shedding innocent blood remain in the midst of your people Israel.' Thus they shall be absolved from the guilt of bloodshed, ⁹and you shall purge from your midst the guilt of innocent blood, that you may prosper for doing what is right in the sight of the LORD.

Marriage with a Female Captive

¹⁰"When you go out to war against your enemies and the LORD, your God, delivers them into your hand, so that you take captives, ¹¹if you see a comely woman among the captives and become so enamored of her that you wish to have her as wife, ¹²†you may take her home to your house. But before she may live there, she must shave her head and pare her nails ¹³and lay aside her captive's garb. After she has mourned her father and mother for a full month, you may have relations with her, and you shall be her husband and she shall be your wife. ¹⁴However, if later on you lose your liking for her, you shall give her her freedom, if she wishes it; but you shall not sell her or enslave her, since she was married to you under compulsion.

Rights of the First-born

¹⁵"If a man with two wives loves one and dislikes the other; and if both bear him sons, but the first-born is of her whom he dislikes: ¹⁶when he comes to bequeath his property to his sons he may not consider as his first-born the son of the wife he loves, in preference to his true first-born, the son of the wife whom he dislikes. ¹⁷On the contrary, he shall recognize as his first-born the son of her whom he dislikes, giving him a double share of whatever he happens to own, since he is the first fruits of his manhood, and to him belong the rights of the first-born.

The Incorrigible Son

¹⁸"If a man has a stubborn and unruly son who will not listen to his father or mother, and will not obey them even though they chastise him, ¹⁹†his father and mother shall have him apprehended and brought out to the elders at the gate of his home city, ²⁰where they shall say to those city elders, 'This son of ours is a stubborn and unruly fellow who will not listen to us; he is a glutton and a drunkard.' ²¹Then all his fellow citizens shall stone him to death. Thus shall you purge the evil from your midst, and all Israel, on hearing of it, shall fear.

Corpse of a Criminal

²²†"If a man guilty of a capital offense is put to death and his corpse hung on a tree, ²³*†it shall not remain on the tree overnight. You shall bury it the same day; otherwise, since God's curse rests on him who hangs on a tree, you will defile the land which the LORD, your God, is giving you as an inheritance.

Care for Lost Animals

22 ¹*"YOU shall not see your kinsman's ox or sheep driven astray without showing concern about it; see to it that it is returned to your kinsman. ²If this kinsman does not live near you, or you do not know who he may be, take it to your own place and keep it with you until he claims it; then give it back to him. ³You shall do the same with his ass, or

---

† 21, 1-9: This paragraph is best read immediately after 19, 21. The *slain man* may not necessarily have been murdered; he may have been killed by a wild beast. But the blood of the slain cries out to God from the soil where it was shed; cf Gn 4, 10. Therefore a religious ceremony of propitiation is here prescribed in order to avert God's anger on the community.

21, 4: *They shall cut the heifer's throat there in the wadi:* its blood is to be carried away by the stream, signifying thereby the removal of the human blood from the soil. This is not a sacrifice but a symbolic action; the priests are present merely as official witnesses.

21, 6: *Wash their hands:* a symbolic gesture in protestation of one's own innocence when human blood is unjustly shed; cf Mt 27, 24.

21, 7: *This blood:* the blood of the slain man as symbolized by the heifer's blood.

21, 12f: *Shave her head . . . :* these symbolic actions are meant to signify the purification of the woman from her pagan defilement or perhaps the end of her period of mourning for her previous husband.

21, 19: *The gate:* in the city walls. This open space served as the forum for the administration of justice. Cf 22, 15; 25, 7; Ru 4, 1f.11; Is 29, 21; Am 5, 10.12.15.

21, 22: *Hung on a tree:* some understand, "impaled on a stake." In any case the hanging or impaling was not the means used to execute the criminal; he was first put to death by the ordinary means, stoning, and his corpse was then exposed on high as a salutary warning for others. Cf Jos 8, 29; 10, 26; 1 Sm 31, 10; 2 Sm 21, 9.

21, 23: *God's curse rests on him who hangs on a tree:* St. Paul quotes these words in Gal 3, 13, where he applies them to the crucified Savior, who "redeemed us from the curse of the law, becoming a curse for us."

---

* 21/5: 19, 17.   22/1-4: Ex 23, 4f.
23: Gal 3, 13.

his garment, or anything else which your kinsman loses and you happen to find; you may not be unconcerned about them. ⁴You shall not see your kinsman's ass or ox foundering on the road without showing concern about it; see to it that you help him lift it up.

Various Precepts

⁵"A woman shall not wear an article proper to a man, nor shall a man put on a woman's dress; for anyone who does such things is an abomination to the Lord, your God.

⁶"If, while walking along, you chance upon a bird's nest with young birds or eggs in it, in any tree or on the ground, and the mother bird is sitting on them, you shall not take away the mother bird along with her brood; ⁷you shall let her go, although you may take her brood away. It is thus that you shall have prosperity and a long life.

⁸"When you build a new house, put a parapet around the roof; otherwise, if someone falls off, you will bring bloodguilt upon your house.

⁹*†"You shall not sow your vineyard with two different kinds of seed; if you do, its produce shall become forfeit, both the crop you have sown and the yield of the vineyard. ¹⁰You shall not plow with an ox and an ass harnessed together. ¹¹You shall not wear cloth of two different kinds of thread, wool and linen, woven together.

¹²*†"You shall put twisted cords on the four corners of the cloak that you wrap around you."

Crimes against Marriage

¹³"If a man, after marrying a woman and having relations with her, comes to dislike her, ¹⁴and makes monstrous charges against her and defames her by saying, 'I married this woman, but when I first had relations with her I did not find her a virgin,' ¹⁵†the father and mother of the girl shall take the evidence of her virginity and bring it to the elders at the city gate. ¹⁶There the father of the girl shall say to the elders, 'I gave my daughter to this man in marriage, but he has come to dislike her, ¹⁷and now brings monstrous charges against her, saying: I did not find your daughter a virgin. But here is the evidence of my daughter's virginity!' And they shall spread out the cloth before the elders of the city. ¹⁸†Then these city elders shall take the man and chastise him, ¹⁹besides fining him one hundred silver shekels, which they shall give to the girl's father, because the man defamed a virgin in Israel. Moreover, she shall remain his wife, and he may not divorce her as long as he lives.

²⁰"But if this charge is true, and evidence of the girl's virginity is not found, ²¹they shall bring the girl to the entrance of her father's house and there her townsmen shall stone her to death, because she committed a crime against Israel by her unchasteness in her father's house. Thus shall you purge the evil from your midst.

²²*"If a man is discovered having relations with a woman who is married to another, both the man and the woman with whom he has had relations shall die. Thus shall you purge the evil from your midst.

²³†"If within the city a man comes upon a maiden who is betrothed, and has relations with her, ²⁴you shall bring them both out to the gate of the city and there stone them to death: the girl because she did not cry out for help though she was in the city, and the man because he violated his neighbor's wife. Thus shall you purge the evil from your midst.

²⁵"If, however, it is in the open fields that a man comes upon such a betrothed maiden, seizes her and has relations with her, the man alone shall die. ²⁶You shall do nothing to the maiden, since she is not guilty of a capital offense. This case is like that of a man who rises up against his neighbor and murders him: ²⁷it was in the open fields that he came upon her, and though the betrothed maiden may have cried out for help, there was no one to come to her aid.

²⁸*"If a man comes upon a maiden that is not betrothed, takes her and has relations with her, and their deed is discovered, ²⁹the man who had relations with her shall pay the girl's father fifty silver shekels and take her as his wife, because he has deflowered her. Moreover, he may not divorce her as long as he lives.

23 ¹†"A man shall not marry his father's wife, nor shall he dishonor his father's bed.

Membership in the Community

²"No one whose testicles have been crushed or whose penis has been cut off may be admitted into the community of the Lord. ³No child of an incestuous union may be admitted into the community of the Lord, nor any descendant of his even to the tenth generation. ⁴*No Ammonite or Moabite may ever be admitted into the community of the Lord, nor any descendants of theirs even to the tenth generation, ⁵*because they would not succor you with food and water on your journey after you left Egypt, and because Moab hired Balaam, son of Beor, from Pethor in Aram Naharaim, to curse you; ⁶though the Lord, your God, would not listen to Balaam and turned his curse into a blessing for you, because he loves you. ⁷Never promote their peace and prosperity as long as you live.

---

† 22, 9: *Become forfeit:* to the sanctuary; cf Lv 19, 19; Jos 6, 19.

22, 12: *Twisted cords:* referred to as "tassels" on "violet cords" in Nm 15, 38. See note there.

22, 15: *The evidence of her virginity:* the bridal garment or sheet stained with a little blood from the first nuptial relations.

22, 18: *Chastise him:* flog him, as prescribed in 25, 1-3.

22, 23: *A maiden who is betrothed:* a girl who is married but not yet brought to her husband's home and whose marriage is therefore still unconsummated.

23, 1: *Father's wife:* stepmother. *Dishonor:* cf 27, 20.

---

* 9.11: Lv 19, 19.
12: Nm 15, 38; Mt 23, 5.
22: Lv 20, 10; Jn 8, 4f.
28f: Ex 22, 16.
23/4: Neh 13, 1f.
5: Nm 24, 10.

⁸*But do not abhor the Edomite, since he is your brother, nor the Egyptian, since you were an alien in his country. ⁹Children born to them may in the third generation be admitted into the community of the LORD.

Cleanliness in Camp

¹⁰"When you are in camp during an expedition against your enemies, you shall keep yourselves from everything offensive. ¹¹If one of you becomes unclean because of a nocturnal emission, he shall go outside the camp, and not return until, ¹²toward evening, he has bathed in water; then, when the sun has set, he may come back into the camp. ¹³Outside the camp you shall have a place set aside to be used as a latrine. ¹⁴You shall also keep a trowel in your equipment and with it, when you go outside to ease nature, you shall first dig a hole and afterward cover up your excrement. ¹⁵Since the LORD, your God, journeys along within your camp to defend you and to put your enemies at your mercy, your camp must be holy; otherwise, if he sees anything indecent in your midst, he will leave your company.

Various Precepts

¹⁶"You shall not hand over to his master a slave who has taken refuge from him with you. ¹⁷†Let him live with you wherever he chooses, in any one of your communities that pleases him. Do not molest him. ¹⁸*†"There shall be no temple harlot among the Israelite women, nor a temple prostitute among the Israelite men. ¹⁹You shall not offer a harlot's fee or a dog's price as any kind of votive offering in the house of the LORD, your God; both these things are an abomination to the LORD, your God. ²⁰*"You shall not demand interest from your countrymen on a loan of money or of food or of anything else on which interest is usually demanded. ²¹You may demand interest from a foreigner, but not from your countryman, so that the LORD, your God, may bless you in all your undertakings on the land you are to enter and occupy. ²²"When you make a vow to the LORD, your God, you shall not delay in fulfilling it; otherwise you will be held guilty, for the LORD, your God, is strict in requiring it of you. ²³Should you refrain from making a vow, you will not be held guilty. ²⁴But you must keep your solemn word and fulfill the votive offering you have freely promised to the LORD.

²⁵"When you go through your neighbor's vineyard, you may eat as many of his grapes as you wish, but do not put them in your basket. ²⁶When you go through your neighbor's grainfield, you may pluck some of the ears with your hand, but do not put a sickle to your neighbor's grain.

Marriage Laws

24 ¹†"WHEN a man, after marrying a woman and having relations with her, is later displeased with her because he finds in her something indecent, and therefore he writes out a bill of divorce and hands it to her, thus dismissing her from his house: ²if on leaving his house she goes and becomes the wife of another man, ³and the second husband, too, comes to dislike her and dismisses her from his house by handing her a written bill of divorce; or if this second man who has married her, dies; ⁴then her former husband, who dismissed her, may not again take her as his wife after she has become defiled. That would be an abomination before the LORD, and you shall not bring such guilt upon the land which the LORD, your God, is giving you as a heritage.

⁵"When a man is newly wed, he need not go out on a military expedition, nor shall any public duty be imposed on him. He shall be exempt for one year for the sake of his family, to bring joy to the wife he has married.

Justice, Equity and Charity

⁶†"No one shall take a hand mill or even its upper stone as a pledge for debt, for he would be taking the debtor's sustenance as a pledge.

⁷*"If any man is caught kidnaping a fellow Israelite in order to enslave him and sell him, the kidnaper shall be put to death. Thus shall you purge the evil from your midst.

⁸*"In an attack of leprosy you shall be careful to observe exactly and to carry out all the directions of the levitical priests. Take care to act in accordance with the instructions I have given them. ⁹*Remember what

---

† 23, 17: *In any one of your communities:* from this it would seem that the slave in question is a fugitive from a foreign country.

23, 18f: The pagans believed that they could enter into special relationship with their gods and goddesses by having sexual relations with the pagan priests and priestesses who prostituted themselves for this purpose. The money paid for this was considered a sort of votive offering made to the pagan sanctuary. Such abominations were naturally forbidden in Israel. *A dog's price:* the money paid to the pagan priest for his indecent service.

24, 1-4: This law is directly concerned only with forbidding divorced couples to remarry each other, and indirectly with checking hasty divorces, by demanding sufficient cause and certain legal formalities. Divorce itself is taken for granted and tolerated as an existing custom whose evils this law seeks to lessen. Cf 22, 19.29; Mal 2, 14ff. Christ gave the authentic interpretation of this law: "Moses, by reason of the hardness of your heart, permitted you to put away your wives; but it was not so from the beginning" (Mt 19, 8f).

24, 1: *Something indecent:* a rather indefinite phrase, meaning perhaps "immodest conduct." At the time of Christ the rabbis differed in opinion concerning the sufficient grounds for divorce; cf Mt 19, 3.

24, 6: Since the Israelites ground their grain into flour only in sufficient quantity for their current need, to deprive a debtor of his hand mill was virtually equivalent to condemning him to starve to death.

---

*
 8: Gn 25, 24ff.
 18: 1 Kgs 14, 24; 22, 46;
  2 Kgs 23, 7.
 20: Ex 22, 25; Lv 25, 37;
  Lk 6, 34f.

 24/5: 20, 7.
 7: Ex 21, 16.
 8: Lv 14, 1-14.
 9: Nm 12, 10-15.

the LORD, your God, did to Miriam on the journey after you left Egypt.

10†"When you make a loan of any kind to your neighbor, you shall not enter his house to receive a pledge from him, 11but shall wait outside until the man to whom you are making the loan brings his pledge outside to you. 12If he is a poor man, you shall not sleep in the mantle he gives as a pledge, 13*but shall return it to him at sunset that he himself may sleep in it. Then he will bless you, and it will be a good deed of yours before the LORD, your God.

14*"You shall not defraud a poor and needy hired servant, whether he be one of your own countrymen or one of the aliens who live in your communities. 15You shall pay him each day's wages before sundown on the day itself, since he is poor and looks forward to them. Otherwise he will cry to the LORD against you, and you will be held guilty.

16*"Fathers shall not be put to death for their children, nor children for their fathers; only for his own guilt shall a man be put to death.

17*"You shall not violate the rights of the alien or of the orphan, nor take the clothing of a widow as a pledge. 18For, remember, you were once slaves in Egypt, and the LORD, your God, ransomed you from there; that is why I command you to observe this rule.

19*"When you reap the harvest in your field and overlook a sheaf there, you shall not go back to get it; let it be for the alien, the orphan or the widow, that the LORD, your God, may bless you in all your undertakings. 20When you knock down the fruit of your olive trees, you shall not go over the branches a second time; let what remains be for the alien, the orphan and the widow. 21When you pick your grapes, you shall not go over the vineyard a second time; let what remains be for the alien, the orphan, and the widow. 22For remember that you were once slaves in Egypt; that is why I command you to observe this rule.

25 1"WHEN men have a dispute and bring it to court, and a decision is handed down to them acquitting the innocent party and condemning the guilty party, 2if the latter deserves stripes, the judge shall have him lie down and in his presence receive the number of stripes his guilt deserves. 3*†Forty stripes may be given him, but no more; lest, if he were beaten with more stripes than these, your kinsman should be looked upon as disgraced because of the severity of the beating.

4*†"You shall not muzzle an ox when it is treading out grain.

Levirate Marriage

5*†"When brothers live together and one of them dies without a son, the widow of the deceased shall not marry anyone outside the family; but her husband's brother shall go to her and perform the duty of a brother-in-law by marrying her. 6*The first-born son she bears shall continue the line of the deceased brother, that his name may not be blotted out from Israel. 7If, however, a man does not care to marry his brother's wife, she shall go up to the elders at the gate and declare, 'My brother-in-law does not intend to perform his duty toward me and refuses to perpetuate his brother's name in Israel.' 8Thereupon the elders of his city shall summon him and admonish him. If he persists in saying, 'I am not willing to marry her,' 9†this sister-in-law, in the presence of the elders, shall go up to him and strip his sandal from his foot and spit in his face, saying publicly, 'This is how one should be treated who will not build up his brother's family!' 10And his lineage shall be spoken of in Israel as 'the family of the man stripped of his sandal.'

Various Precepts

11"When two men are fighting and the wife of one intervenes to save her husband from the blows of his opponent, if she stretches out her hand and seizes the latter by his private parts, 12you shall chop off her hand without pity.

13*"You shall not keep two differing weights in your bag, one large and the other small; 14nor shall you keep two different measures in your house, one large and the other small. 15But use a true and just weight, and a true and just measure, that you may have a long life on the land which the LORD, your God, is giving you. 16Everyone who is dishonest in any of these matters is an abomination to the LORD, your God.

17*†"Bear in mind what Amalek did to you on the

---

† 24, 10f: The debtor had the right to select the pledge that the creditor demanded as a guarantee for his loan.

25, 3: *Forty stripes:* a relatively mild punishment in ancient times. Later Jewish practice limited the number to thirty-nine; cf 2 Cor 11, 24.

25, 4: St. Paul argues from this verse that a laborer has the right to live on the fruits of his labor; cf 1 Cor 9, 9; 1 Tm 5, 18.

25, 5: *When brothers live together:* when relatives of the same clan, though married, hold their property in common. It was only in this case that the present law was to be observed, since one of its purposes was to keep the property of the deceased within the same clan. Such a marriage of a widow with her brother-in-law is known as a "levirate" marriage from the Latin word *levir,* meaning "a husband's brother."

25, 9f: The penalty decreed for a man who refuses to comply with this law of family loyalty is public disgrace (the widow is to *spit in his face*) and the curse of poverty; sandals were proverbially a man's cheapest possession (cf Am 2, 6; 8, 6), and therefore "a man without sandals" was the poorest of the poor. Some commentators, however, connect this symbolic act with the ceremony mentioned in Ru 4, 7f.

25, 17-19: This attack on Israel by Amalek is not mentioned elsewhere in the Old Testament, although it probably was connected with the battle mentioned in Ex 17, 8. A campaign against Amalek was carried out by Saul; cf 1 Sm 15.

✿
13: Ex 22, 26.
14f: Lv 19, 13; Tb 4, 15; Sir 34, 25f; Jer 22, 13.
16: 2 Kgs 14, 6; 2 Chr 25, 4; Ez 18, 20.
17: Ex 22, 22; 23, 9.
19ff: Lv 19, 9f; 23, 22.
25/3: 2 Cor 11, 24.

4: 1 Cor 9, 9; 1 Tm 5, 18.
5: Mt 22, 24; Mk 12, 19; Lk 20, 28.
6-9: Ru 4, 5-10.
13ff: Lv 19, 35f; Prv 16, 11; Ez 45, 10; Mi 6, 11.
17: Ex 17, 8.

journey after you left Egypt, [18]how without fear of any god he harassed you along the way, weak and weary as you were, and cut off at the rear all those who lagged behind. [19]*Therefore, when the LORD, your God, gives you rest from all your enemies round about in the land which he is giving you to occupy as your heritage, you shall blot out the memory of Amalek from under the heavens. Do not forget!

Thanksgiving for the Harvest

26 [1]"WHEN you have come into the land which the LORD, your God, is giving you as a heritage, and have occupied it and settled in it, [2]*you shall take some first fruits of the various products of the soil which you harvest from the land which the LORD, your God, gives you, and putting them in a basket, you shall go to the place which the LORD, your God, chooses for the dwelling place of his name. [3]There you shall go to the priest in office at that time and say to him, 'Today I acknowledge to the LORD, my God, that I have indeed come into the land which he swore to our fathers he would give us.' [4]The priest shall then receive the basket from you and shall set it in front of the altar of the LORD, your God. [5]*†Then you shall declare before the LORD, your God, 'My father was a wandering Aramean who went down to Egypt with a small household and lived there as an alien. But there he became a nation great, strong and numerous. [6]*When the Egyptians maltreated and oppressed us, imposing hard labor upon us, [7]we cried to the LORD, the God of our fathers, and he heard our cry and saw our affliction, our toil and our oppression. [8]*He brought us out of Egypt with his strong hand and outstretched arm, with terrifying power, with signs and wonders; [9]*and bringing us into this country, he gave us this land flowing with milk and honey. [10]Therefore, I have now brought you the first fruits of the products of the soil which you, O LORD, have given me.' And having set them before the LORD, your God, you shall bow down in his presence. [11]*Then you and your family, together with the Levite and the aliens who live among you, shall make merry over all these good things which the LORD, your God, has given you.

Prayer with the Tithes

[12]*†"When you have finished setting aside all the tithes of your produce in the third year, the year of the tithes, and you have given them to the Levite, the alien, the orphan and the widow, that they may eat their fill in your own community, [13]you shall declare before the LORD, your God, 'I have purged my house of the sacred portion and I have given it to the Levite, the alien, the orphan and the widow, just as you have commanded me. In this I have not broken or forgotten

any of your commandments: [14]†I have not eaten any of the tithe as a mourner; I have not brought any of it out as one unclean; I have not offered any of it to the dead. I have thus hearkened to the voice of the LORD, my God, doing just as you have commanded me. [15]Look down, then, from heaven, your holy abode, and bless your people Israel and the soil you have given us in the land flowing with milk and honey which you promised on oath to our fathers.'

The Covenant

[16]"This day the LORD, your God, commands you to observe these statutes and decrees. Be careful, then, to observe them with all your heart and with all your soul. [17]*Today you are making this agreement with the LORD: he is to be your God and you are to walk in his ways and observe his statutes, commandments and decrees, and to hearken to his voice. [18]*And today the LORD is making this agreement with you: you are to be a people peculiarly his own, as he promised you; and provided you keep all his commandments, [19]he will then raise you high in praise and renown and glory above all other nations he has made, and you will be a people sacred to the LORD, your God, as he promised."

IV: FINAL WORDS OF MOSES

Ceremonies

27 [1]THEN MOSES, WITH THE ELDERS of Israel, gave the people this order: "Keep all these commandments which I enjoin on you today. [2]On the day you cross the Jordan into the land which the LORD, your God, is giving you, set up some large stones and coat them with plaster. [3]*Also write on them, at the time you cross, all the words of this law, that you may thus enter into the land flowing with milk and honey, which the LORD, your God, and the God of your fathers, is giving you as he promised you. [4]When, moreover, you have crossed the Jordan, besides setting up on Mount Ebal these stones concerning which I command you today, and coating them with plaster, [5]*you shall also build to the LORD, your God, an altar made of stones that no iron tool has touched. [6]You shall make this altar of the LORD, your God, with undressed stones, and shall offer on its holocausts to the LORD, your God. [7]You shall also sacrifice peace offerings and eat them there, making merry before the LORD, your God. [8]On the stones you shall inscribe all the words of this law very clearly."

19: Ex 17, 14; 1 Sm 15, 2f.
26/2: Ex 23, 19; 34, 26.
5: Gn 46, 6f; Acts 7, 14f.
6f: Ex 1, 8-22; 2, 23ff; 3, 9; Nm 20, 15f.
8: Ex 12, 51.
9: Ex 3, 8.
11: 12, 7.12.
12: 14, 28f.
17: Ex 24, 7.
18f: 7, 6, 14, 2; 28, 1; Ex 19, 5.
27/3: Jos 8, 32.
5: Ex 20, 25; Jos 8, 31.

---

† 26, 5: *Aramean:* either in reference to the origin of the patriarchs from Aram Naharaim (cf Gn 24, 10; 25, 20; 28, 5; 31, 20.24), or merely in the sense of "nomad," in the same way as "Arab" was later used; cf Jer 3, 2.

26, 12: *And you have given them to the Levite, . . .* : as prescribed in 14, 28f.

26, 14: These are allusions to pagan religious practices.

27, 8: *On the stones:* cf vv 3f; not the stones of the altar.

9*Moses, with the levitical priests, then said to all Israel: "Be silent, O Israel, and listen! This day you have become the people of the Lord, your God. 10You shall therefore hearken to the voice of the Lord, your God, and keep his commandments and statutes which I enjoin on you today."

11That same day Moses gave the people this order: 12*"When you cross the Jordan, Simeon, Levi, Judah, Issachar, Joseph and Benjamin shall stand on Mount Gerizim to pronounce blessings over the people, 13while Reuben, Gad, Asher, Zebulun, Dan and Naphtali shall stand on Mount Ebal to pronounce curses.

The Twelve Curses

14"The Levites shall proclaim aloud to all the men of Israel: 15*†'Cursed be the man who makes a carved or molten idol—an abomination to the Lord, the product of a craftsman's hands—and sets it up in secret!' And all the people shall answer, 'Amen!'

16*'Cursed be he who dishonors his father or his mother!' And all the people shall answer, 'Amen!'

17*'Cursed be he who moves his neighbor's landmarks!' And all the people shall answer, 'Amen!'

18*'Cursed be he who misleads a blind man on his way!' And all the people shall answer, 'Amen!'

19*'Cursed be he who violates the rights of the alien, the orphan or the widow!' And all the people shall answer, 'Amen!'

20*'Cursed be he who has relations with his father's wife, for he dishonors his father's bed!' And all the people shall answer, 'Amen!'

21*'Cursed be he who has relations with any animal!' And all the people shall answer, 'Amen!'

22*'Cursed be he who has relations with his sister or his half-sister!' And all the people shall answer, 'Amen!'

23*'Cursed be he who has relations with his mother-in-law!' And all the people shall answer, 'Amen!'

24*'Cursed be he who slays his neighbor in secret!' And all the people shall answer, 'Amen!'

25'Cursed be he who accepts payment for slaying an innocent man!' And all the people shall answer, 'Amen!'

26*'Cursed be he who fails to fulfill any of the provisions of this law!' And all the people shall answer, 'Amen!'

Blessings for Obedience

28 1*†"THUS, then, shall it be: if you continue to heed the voice of the Lord, your God, and are careful to observe all his commandments which I enjoin on you today, the Lord, your God, will raise you high above all the nations of the earth. 2When you hearken to the voice of the Lord, your God, all these blessings will come upon you and overwhelm you:

3"May you be blessed in the city,
    and blessed in the country!

4*"Blessed be the fruit of your womb,
    the produce of your soil and the offspring of
        your livestock,
    the issue of your herds and the young of your
        flocks!

5"Blessed be your grain bin and your kneading
    bowl!

6†"May you be blessed in your coming in,
    and blessed in your going out!

Victory and Prosperity

7†"The Lord will beat down before you the enemies that rise up against you; though they come out against you from but one direction, they will flee before you in seven. 8The Lord will affirm his blessing upon you, on your barns and on all your undertakings, blessing you in the land that the Lord, your God, gives you. 9*Provided that you keep the commandments of the Lord, your God, and walk in his ways, he will establish you as a people sacred to himself, as he swore to you; 10*†so that, when all the nations of the earth see you bearing the name of the Lord, they will stand in awe of you. 11The Lord will increase in more than goodly measure the fruit of your womb, the offspring of your livestock, and the produce of your soil, in the land which he swore to your fathers he would give you. 12*The Lord will open up for you his rich treasure house of the heavens, to give your land rain in due season, blessing all your undertakings, so that you will lend to many nations and borrow from none. 13†The Lord will make you the head, not the tail, and you will always mount higher and not decline, as long as you obey the commandments of the Lord, your God, which I order you today to observe carefully; 14not turning

---

† 27, 15-26: *Amen:* see note on Nm 5, 22.

28, 1-69: This chapter would read better immediately after chapter 26.

28, 6: *In your coming in . . . in your going out:* at the beginning and end of every action, or in all actions in general.

28, 7.25: *From but one direction . . . in seven:* in one compact mass, contrasted with many scattered groups.

28, 10: *You bearing the name of the Lord:* literally, "The Lord's name is called over you," an expression signifying ownership and protection. Cf 2 Sm 12, 28; 1 Kgs 8, 43; Is 4, 1; 63, 19; Jer 7, 10f; 14, 9; 15, 16; 25, 29; Am 9, 12.

28, 13: *The head, not the tail:* in the honorable position as leader. Cf Is 9, 14; 19, 15.

9: 26, 17ff.
12f: 11, 29; Jos 8, 33f.
15: Ex 20, 4.23; Lv 19, 4; Wis 14, 8.
16: 21, 18-21; Ex 21, 17; Lv 20, 9.
17: 19, 14.
18: Lv 19, 14.
19: 24, 17; Ex 22, 21f.
20: 22, 23, 1; Lv 18, 8; 20, 11.
21: Ex 22, 18; Lv 18, 23; 20, 15.
22: Lv 18, 9; 20, 17.
23: Lv 18, 17; 20, 14.
24: Ex 20, 13; 21, 12; Nm 35, 20f.
26: Gal 3, 10.
28/1-68: Lv 26, 1-45.
1-14: 7, 12-16.
1: 26, 19.
4: 7, 13; 30, 9.
9: 26, 18; Ex 19, 5f.
10: 2, 25; 11, 25.
12: 15, 6.

aside to the right or to the left from any of the commandments which I now give you, in order to follow other gods and serve them.

Curses for Disobedience

15*"But if you do not hearken to the voice of the Lord, your God, and are not careful to observe all his commandments which I enjoin on you today, all these curses shall come upon you and overwhelm you:

16"May you be cursed in the city,
and cursed in the country!

17"Cursed be your grain bin and your kneading bowl!
18"Cursed be the fruit of your womb,
the produce of your soil and the offspring of your livestock,
the issue of your herds and the young of your flocks!

19"May you be cursed in your coming in,
and cursed in your going out!

Sickness and Defeat

20"The Lord will put a curse on you, defeat and frustration in every enterprise you undertake, until you are speedily destroyed and perish for the evil you have done in forsaking me. **21**The Lord will bring a pestilence upon you that will persist until he has exterminated you from the land you are entering to occupy. **22***The Lord will strike you with wasting and fever, with scorching, fiery drought, with blight and searing wind, that will plague you until you perish. **23**The sky over your heads will be like bronze and the earth under your feet like iron. **24**For rain the Lord will give your land powdery dust, which will come down upon you from the sky until you are destroyed. **25***The Lord will let you be beaten down before your enemies; though you advance against them from one direction, you will flee before them in seven, so that you will become a terrifying example to all the kingdoms of the earth. **26**Your carcasses will become food for all the birds of the air and for the beasts of the field, with no one to frighten them off. **27***The Lord will strike you with Egyptian boils and with tumors, eczema and the itch, until you cannot be cured. **28**And the Lord will strike you with madness, blindness and panic, **29**so that even at midday you will grope like a blind man in the dark, unable to find your way.

Despoilment

"You will be oppressed and robbed continually, with no one to come to your aid. **30**Though you betroth a wife, another man will have her. Though you build a house, you will not live in it. Though you plant a vineyard, you will not enjoy its fruits. **31**Your ox will be slaughtered before your eyes, and you will not eat of its flesh. Your ass will be stolen in your presence, but you will not recover it. Your flocks will be given to your enemies, with no one to come to your aid. **32**Your sons and daughters will be given to a foreign nation while you look on and grieve for them in constant helplessness. **33**A people whom you do not know will consume the fruit of your soil and of all your labor, and you will be oppressed and crushed at all times without surcease, **34**until you are driven mad by what your eyes must look upon. **35**†The Lord will strike you with malignant boils of which you cannot be cured, on your knees and legs, and from the soles of your feet to the crown of your head.

Exile

36*"The Lord will bring you, and your king whom you have set over you, to a nation which you and your fathers have not known, and there you will serve strange gods of wood and stone, **37**and will call forth amazement, reproach and barbed scorn from all the nations to which the Lord will lead you.

Fruitless Labors

38*"Though you spend much seed on your field, you will harvest but little, for the locusts will devour the crop. **39***Though you plant and cultivate vineyards, you will not drink or store up the wine, for the grubs will eat the vines clean. **40***Though you have olive trees throughout your country, you will have no oil for ointment, for your olives will drop off unripe. **41***Though you beget sons and daughters, they will not remain with you, but will go into captivity. **42**Buzzing insects will infest all your trees and the crops of your soil. **43**The alien residing among you will rise higher and higher above you, while you sink lower and lower. **44**He will lend to you, not you to him. He will become the head, you the tail.

45"All these curses will come upon you, pursuing you and overwhelming you, until you are destroyed, because you would not hearken to the voice of the Lord, your God, nor keep the commandments and statutes he gave you. **46**†They will light on you and your descendants as a sign and a wonder for all time. **47**Since you would not serve the Lord, your God, with joy and gratitude for abundance of every kind, **48**therefore in hunger and thirst, in nakedness and utter poverty, you will serve the enemies whom the Lord will send against you. He will put an iron yoke on your neck, until he destroys you.

Invasion and Siege

49*"The Lord will raise up against you a nation from afar, from the end of the earth, that swoops down like

15: Bar 1, 20; Dn 9, 11; Mal 2, 2.
22f: Lv 26, 19.
25: Lv 26, 17.37.
27: Ex 9, 9ff.
36f: 1 Kgs 9, 7ff; 2 Chr 7, 20ff; 33, 11; 36, 6.20.
38: Mi 6, 15; Hg 1, 6.
39: Zep 1, 13.
40: Mi 6, 15.
41: Lam 1, 5.
49-52: Jer 5, 15ff; Bar 4, 15f.

† 28, 35: This verse is best read with v 27.
28, 46: *A sign and a wonder:* an ominous example, attracting attention; cf 29, 21-28.

an eagle, a nation whose tongue you do not understand, ⁵⁰a nation of stern visage, that shows neither respect for the aged nor pity for the young. ⁵¹They will consume the offspring of your livestock and the produce of your soil, until you are destroyed; they will leave you no grain or wine or oil, no issue of your herds or young of your flocks, until they have brought about your ruin. ⁵²They will besiege you in each of your communities, until the great, unscalable walls you trust in come tumbling down all over your land. They will so besiege you in every community throughout the land which the Lord, your God, has given you, ⁵³*that in the distress of the siege to which your enemy subjects you, you will eat the fruit of your womb, the flesh of your own sons and daughters whom the Lord, your God, has given you. ⁵⁴The most refined and fastidious man among you will begrudge his brother and his beloved wife and his surviving children ⁵⁵any share in the flesh of his children that he himself is using for food when nothing else is left him in the straits of the siege to which your enemy will subject you in all your communities. ⁵⁶The most refined and delicate woman among you, so delicate and refined that she would not venture to set the sole of her foot on the ground, will begrudge her beloved husband and her son and daughter ⁵⁷the afterbirth that issues from her womb and the infant she brings forth when she secretly uses them for food for want of anything else, in the straits of the siege to which your enemy will subject you in your communities.

Plagues

⁵⁸"If you are not careful to observe every word of the law which is written in this book, and to revere the glorious and awesome name of the Lord, your God, ⁵⁹he will smite you and your descendants with severe and constant blows, malignant and lasting maladies. ⁶⁰*†He will again afflict you with all the diseases of Egypt which you dread, and they will persist among you. ⁶¹Should there be any kind of sickness or calamity not mentioned in this book of the law, that too the Lord will bring upon you until you are destroyed. ⁶²*Of you who were numerous as the stars in the sky, only a few will be left, because you would not hearken to the voice of the Lord, your God.

Exile

⁶³*"Just as the Lord once took delight in making you grow and prosper, so will he now take delight in ruining and destroying you, and you will be plucked out of the land you are now entering to occupy. ⁶⁴*The Lord will scatter you among all the nations from one end of the earth to the other, and there you will serve strange gods of wood and stone, such as you and your fathers

have not known. ⁶⁵†Among these nations you will find no repose, not a foot of ground to stand upon, for there the Lord will give you an anguished heart and wasted eyes and a dismayed spirit. ⁶⁶You will live in constant suspense and stand in dread both day and night, never sure of your existence. ⁶⁷In the morning you will say, 'Would that it were evening!' and in the evening you will say, 'Would that it were morning!' for the dread that your heart must feel and the sight that your eyes must see. ⁶⁸*†The Lord will send you back in galleys to Egypt, to the region I told you that you were never to see again; and there you will offer yourselves for sale to your enemies as male and female slaves, but there will be no buyer."

⁶⁹These are the words of the covenant which the Lord ordered Moses to make with the Israelites in the land of Moab, in addition to the covenant which he made with them at Horeb.

Past Favors Recalled

29 ¹Moses summoned all Israel and said to them, "You have seen all that the Lord did in the land of Egypt before your very eyes to Pharaoh and all his servants and to all his land; ²*the great testings your own eyes have seen, and those great signs and wonders. ³†But not even at the present day has the Lord yet given you a mind to understand, or eyes to see, or ears to hear. ⁴*'I led you for forty years in the desert. Your clothes did not fall from you in tatters nor your sandals from your feet; ⁵bread was not your food, nor wine or beer your drink. Thus you should know that I, the Lord, am your God.' ⁶*When we came to this place, Sihon, king of Heshbon, and Og, king of Bashan, came out to engage us in battle, but we defeated them ⁷*and took over their land, which we then gave as a heritage to the Reubenites, Gadites, and half the tribe of Manasseh. ⁸Keep the terms of this covenant, therefore, and fulfill them, that you may succeed in whatever you do.

All Israel Bound to the Covenant

⁹"You are all now standing before the Lord, your God—your chiefs and judges, your elders and officials, and all of the men of Israel, ¹⁰together with your wives and children and the aliens who live in your camp, down to those who hew wood and draw water for you —¹¹†that you may enter into the covenant of the Lord, your God, which he concluded with you today under this sanction of a curse; ¹²so that he may now estab-

---

† 28, 60: *He will again afflict you with all the diseases of Egypt:* such as the Lord had promised to remove from his people; cf 7, 15.

28, 65: *Wasted eyes:* worn out and disappointed in their longing gaze.

28, 68: *In galleys:* in the ships of the Phoenician slave traders (Ez 27, 13; Jl 4, 6; Am 1, 9), who also dealt with Egypt (Is 23, 3).

29, 3: *Eyes to see . . . ears to hear:* with inner, spiritual discernment. Cf Mt 13, 43.

29, 11: *Sanction of a curse:* the present pact binds under penalty of the curses mentioned in this book. Cf v 20.

53: Lv 26, 29; 2 Kgs 6, 28f;
    Jer 19, 9; Lam 4, 10;
    Bar 2, 3.
60: 28, 27.
62: 1, 10; Jer 42, 2.
63: 30, 9.
64: Lv 26, 33.

68: Hos 8, 13; 9, 3.
29/2: 4, 34; Ex 19, 4.
4: 8, 2.4.
6: 2, 24.32; 3, 1; Nm 21, 33ff.
7: 3, 16; Nm 32, 33.

lish you as his people and he may be your God, as he promised you and as he swore to your fathers Abraham, Isaac and Jacob. **13**But it is not with you alone that I am making this covenant, under this sanction of a curse; **14†**it is just as much with those who are not here among us today as it is with those of us who are now here present before the LORD, our God.

Warning against Idolatry

15"You know in what surroundings we lived in the land of Egypt and what we passed by in the nations we traversed, **16**and you saw the loathsome idols of wood and stone, of gold and silver, that they possess. **17**Let there be, then, no man or woman, no clan or tribe among you, who would now turn away their hearts from the LORD, our God, to go and serve these pagan gods! Let there be no root that would bear such poison and wormwood among you! **18†**If any such person, upon hearing the words of this curse, should beguile himself into thinking that he can safely persist in his stubbornness of heart, as though to sweep away both the watered soil and the parched ground, **19**the LORD will never consent to pardon him. Instead, the LORD's wrath and jealousy will flare up against that man, and every curse mentioned in this book will alight on him. The LORD will blot out his name from under the heavens **20**and will single him out from all the tribes of Israel for doom, in keeping with all the curses of the covenant inscribed in this book of the law.

Punishment for Infidelity

21"Future generations, your own descendants who will rise up after you, as well as the foreigners who will come here from far-off lands, when they see the calamities of this land and the ills with which the LORD has smitten it—**22***all its soil being nothing but sulphur and salt, a burnt-out waste, unsown and unfruitful, without a blade of grass, destroyed like Sodom and Gomorrah, Admah and Zeboiim, which the LORD overthrew in his furious wrath—**23***they and all the nations will ask, 'Why has the LORD dealt thus with this land? Why this fierce outburst of wrath?' **24**And the answer will be, 'Because they forsook the covenant which the LORD, the God of their fathers, had made with them when he brought them out of the land of Egypt, **25**and they went and served other gods and adored them, gods whom they did not know and whom he had not let fall to their lot: **26**that is why the LORD was angry with this land and brought on it all the imprecations listed in this book; **27***in his furious wrath and tremendous anger the LORD uprooted them from their soil and cast them out into a strange land, where they are today.' **28†**[Both what is still hidden and what has already been revealed concern us and our descendants

forever, that we may carry out all the words of this law.]

Mercy for the Repentant

30 **1***"WHEN all these things which I have set before you, the blessings and the curses, are fulfilled in you, and from among whatever nations the LORD, your God, may have dispersed you, you ponder them in your heart: **2***then, provided that you and your children return to the LORD, your God, and heed his voice with all your heart and all your soul, just as I now command you, **3**the LORD, your God, will change your lot; and taking pity on you, he will again gather you from all the nations wherein he has scattered you. **4**Though you may have been driven to the farthest corner of the world, even from there will the LORD, your God, gather you; even from there will he bring you back. **5**The LORD, your God, will then bring you into the land which your fathers once occupied, that you too may occupy it, and he will make you more prosperous and numerous than your fathers. **6*†**The LORD, your God, will circumcise your hearts and the hearts of your descendants, that you may love the LORD, your God, with all your heart and all your soul, and so may live. **7**But all those curses the LORD, your God, will assign to your enemies and the foes who persecuted you. **8**You, however, must again heed the LORD's voice and carry out all his commandments which I now enjoin on you. **9***Then the LORD, your God, will increase in more than goodly measure the returns from all your labors, the fruit of your womb, the offspring of your livestock, and the produce of your soil; for the LORD, your God, will again take delight in your prosperity, even as he took delight in your fathers', **10**if only you heed the voice of the LORD, your God, and keep his commandments and statutes that are written in this book of the law, when you return to the LORD, your God, with all your heart and all your soul.

God's Command Clear

11†"For this command which I enjoin on you today is not too mysterious and remote for you. **12**It is not up in the sky, that you should say, 'Who will go up in the sky to get it for us and tell us of it, that we may carry it out?' **13**Nor is it across the sea, that you should say,

---

† 29, 14: *Not here among us:* this includes their descendants.

29, 18: *To sweep away both the watered soil and the parched ground:* apparently a proverb signifying that such an unfaithful Israelite will cause God to punish the good with the wicked, to root out the good plants growing in irrigated soil, together with the worthless plants growing in the dry ground.

29, 28: *What is still hidden:* the events of the future. *What has already been revealed:* God's law and the punishments in store for those who break it. Leave the future to God; our business is to keep his law.

30, 6: *Circumcise your hearts:* see note on 10, 16.

30, 11-14: God has revealed his will so clearly that ignorance of his law can be no excuse. St. Paul in Rom 10, 6-10, applies these words to the ease with which we can come to faith and salvation in Christ.

✿ 22: Gn 14, 10f; 19, 24f. 30/1: 11, 26ff.
23f: 1 Kgs 9, 8f; Jer 22, 8f. 2f: Neh 1, 9.
27: Dn 9, 11-14. 6: 6, 5.
9: 28, 11.

'Who will cross the sea to get it for us and tell us of it, that we may carry it out?' [14]†No, it is something very near to you, already in your mouths and in your hearts; you have only to carry it out.

The Choice before Israel

[15]"Here, then, I have today set before you life and prosperity, death and doom. [16]If you obey the commandments of the LORD, your God, which I enjoin on you today, loving him, and walking in his ways, and keeping his commandments, statutes and decrees, you will live and grow numerous, and the LORD, your God, will bless you in the land you are entering to occupy. [17]If, however, you turn away your hearts and will not listen, but are led astray and adore and serve other gods, [18]I tell you now that you will certainly perish; you will not have a long life on the land which you are crossing the Jordan to enter and occupy. [19]*I call heaven and earth today to witness against you: I have set before you life and death, the blessing and the curse. Choose life, then, that you and your descendants may live, [20]by loving the LORD, your God, heeding his voice, and holding fast to him. For that will mean life for you, a long life for you to live on the land which the LORD swore he would give to your fathers Abraham, Isaac and Jacob."

The Lord's Leadership

31 [1]WHEN Moses had finished speaking these words to all Israel, [2]*he said to them, "I am now one hundred and twenty years old and am no longer able to move about freely; besides, the LORD has told me that I shall not cross this Jordan. [3]*It is the LORD, your God, who will cross before you; he will destroy these nations before you, that you may supplant them. [It is Joshua who will cross before you, as the LORD promised.] [4]*The LORD will deal with them just as he dealt with Sihon and Og, the kings of the Amorites whom he destroyed, and with their country. [5]*When, therefore, the LORD delivers them up to you, you must deal with them exactly as I have ordered you. [6]*Be brave and steadfast; have no fear or dread of them, for it is the LORD, your God, who marches with you; he will never fail you or forsake you."

Call of Joshua

[7]*Then Moses summoned Joshua and in the presence of all Israel said to him, "Be brave and steadfast, for you must bring this people into the land which the LORD swore to their fathers he would give them; you must put them in possession of their heritage. [8]It is the LORD who marches before you; he will be with you and will never fail you or forsake you. So do not fear or be dismayed."

The Reading of the Law

[9]When Moses had written down this law, he entrusted it to the levitical priests who carry the ark of the covenant of the LORD, and to all the elders of Israel, [10]*†giving them this order: "On the feast of Booths, at the prescribed time in the year of relaxation which comes at the end of every seven-year period, [11]†when all Israel goes to appear before the LORD, your God, in the place which he chooses, you shall read this law aloud in the presence of all Israel. [12]Assemble the people—men, women and children, as well as the aliens who live in your communities—that they may hear it and learn it, and so fear the LORD, your God, and carefully observe all the words of this law. [13]Their children also, who do not know it yet, must hear it and learn it, that they too may fear the LORD, your God, as long as you live on the land which you will cross the Jordan to occupy."

Commission of Joshua

[14]†The LORD said to Moses, "The time is now approaching for you to die. Summon Joshua, and present yourselves at the meeting tent that I may give him his commission." So Moses and Joshua went and presented themselves at the meeting tent. [15]And the LORD appeared at the tent in a column of cloud, which stood still at the entrance of the tent.

A Command to Moses

[16]*The LORD said to Moses, "Soon you will be at rest with your fathers, and then this people will take to rendering wanton worship to the strange gods among whom they will live in the land they are about to enter. They will forsake me and break the covenant which I have made with them. [17]At that time my anger will flare up against them; I will forsake them and hide my face from them, so that they will become a prey to be devoured, and many evils and troubles will befall them. At that time they will indeed say, 'Is it not because our God is not among us that these evils have befallen us?' [18]Yet I will be hiding my face from them at that time only because of all the evil they have done in turning to other gods. [19]*Write out this song, then, for yourselves. Teach it to the Israelites and have them recite it, so that this song may be a witness for me against the Israelites. [20]For when I have brought them into the land flowing with milk and honey which I promised on oath to their fathers, and they have eaten their fill and grown fat, if they turn to other gods and serve them, despising me and breaking my covenant; [21]then, when many evils and troubles befall them, this

---

30, 14: *In your mouths:* that you may readily talk about it; cf 6, 7; 11, 19. *And in your hearts:* that you may easily remember it; cf 6, 6; 11, 18.

31, 10: *The year of relaxation:* cf 15, 1ff and the note there.

31, 11ff: Reading the law not only instructed the people but also consoled them by the assurance of the divine goodness.

31, 14f.23: V 23 is best read immediately after v 15; perhaps the original order was vv 7-8.14-15.23.

19: 4, 26.
19: 11, 26ff; 28, 2.15.
31/2: 34, 7; Nm 20, 12.
3: 9, 3.
4: Nm 21, 21-35.
5: 7, 2.
6: 20, 3f.
7f: Jos 1, 6f.9.
10f: 16, 13ff.
16: Jgs 2, 12.17.
19: 31, 21; 32, 1-43.

song, which their descendants will not have forgotten to recite, will bear witness against them. For I know what they are inclined to do even at the present time, before I have brought them into the land which I promised on oath to their fathers." **22**So Moses wrote this song that same day, and he taught it to the Israelites.

Commission of Joshua

23*Then the LORD commissioned Joshua, son of Nun, and said to him, "Be brave and steadfast, for it is you who must bring the Israelites into the land which I promised them on oath. I myself will be with you."

The Law Placed in the Ark

24*When Moses had finished writing out on a scroll the words of the law in their entirety, **25**he gave the Levites who carry the ark of the covenant of the LORD this order: **26**"Take this scroll of the law and put it beside the ark of the covenant of the LORD, your God, that there it may be a witness against you. **27**For I already know how rebellious and stiff-necked you will be. Why, even now, while I am alive among you, you have been rebels against the LORD! How much more, then, after I am dead! **28***Therefore, assemble all your tribal elders and your officials before me, that I may speak these words for them to hear, and so may call heaven and earth to witness against them. **29***For I know that after my death you are sure to become corrupt and to turn aside from the way along which I directed you, so that evil will befall you in some future age because you have done evil in the LORD's sight, and provoked him by your deeds."

The Song of Moses

30Then Moses recited the words of this song from beginning to end, for the whole assembly of Israel to hear:

32   A

1†GIVE ear, O heavens, while I speak;
let the earth hearken to the words of my mouth!
2May my instruction soak in like the rain,
and my discourse permeate like the dew,
Like a downpour upon the grass,
like a shower upon the crops.

3For I will sing the LORD's renown.
Oh, proclaim the greatness of our God.
4*The Rock—how faultless are his deeds,
how right all his ways!
A faithful God, without deceit,
how just and upright he is!

5*Yet basely has he been treated by his degenerate children,
a perverse and crooked race!
6*Is the LORD to be thus repaid by you,
O stupid and foolish people?
Is he not your father who created you?
Has he not made you and established you?

7*Think back on the days of old,
reflect on the years of age upon age.
Ask your father and he will inform you,
ask your elders and they will tell you:

8*†When the Most High assigned the nations their heritage,
when he parceled out the descendants of Adam,
He set up the boundaries of the peoples
after the number of the sons of God;
9*While the LORD's own portion was Jacob,
His hereditary share was Israel.

10*He found them in a wilderness,
a wasteland of howling desert.
He shielded them and cared for them,
guarding them as the apple of his eye.

11*As an eagle incites its nestlings forth
by hovering over its brood,
So he spread his wings to receive them
and bore them up on his pinions.

12The LORD alone was their leader,
no strange god was with him.
13†He had them ride triumphant over the summits of the land
and live off the products of its fields,
Giving them honey to suck from its rocks
and olive oil from its hard, stony ground;

14†Butter from its cows and milk from its sheep,
with the fat of its lambs and rams;
Its Bashan bulls and its goats,
with the cream of its finest wheat;
and the foaming blood of its grapes you drank.

B

15*†[So Jacob ate his fill,]
the darling grew fat and frisky;
you became fat and gross and gorged.

23: 31, 7f; Jos 1, 5ff.
24f: 31, 9.
28: 32, 1-43.
29: Jgs 2, 19.
32/4: Ps 92, 15; Rv 15, 3.
5: 31, 29; Ps 78, 8; Lk 9, 41.
6: Ex 4, 22; Is 63, 16; 64, 8; Jer 31, 9.
7: 4, 32; Ps 44, 2.
8: Gn 10, 1-32; Acts 17, 26.
9: Ex 19, 5; Ps 33, 12.
10: 8, 15; Jer 2, 6; Zec 2, 8.
11: Ex 19, 4.
15: 31, 20.

---

† 32, 1-43: In the style of the great prophets, the speaker is often God himself. The whole song is a poetic sermon, having for its theme God's benefits to Israel (vv 1-14) and Israel's ingratitude and idolatry in turning to the gods of the pagans, which sins will be punished by the pagans themselves (vv 15-29); in turn, the foolish pride of the pagans will be punished, and the Lord's honor will be vindicated (vv 30-43).

32, 8: *The sons of God:* the angels; cf Jb 1, 6; 2, 1; 38, 7; Ps 89, 7f. Here the various nations are portrayed as having their respective guardian angels. Cf Dn 10, 20f; 12, 1.

32, 13: *The land:* Canaan.

32, 14: *Bashan:* a fertile grazing land east of the Jordan, famous for its strong cattle. Cf Ps 22, 13; Ez 39, 18; Am 4, 1.

32, 15: *The darling:* a probable meaning of the Hebrew word *yeshurun,* a term of endearment for "Israel." Cf 33, 5.26; Is 44, 2.

They spurned the God who made them
and scorned their saving Rock.
16*They provoked him with strange gods
and angered him with abominable idols.

17They offered sacrifice to demons, to "no-gods,"
to gods whom they had not known before,
To newcomers just arrived,
of whom their fathers had never stood in awe.
18*You were unmindful of the Rock that begot you,
You forgot the God who gave you birth.

19When the LORD saw this, he was filled with
loathing
and anger toward his sons and daughters.
20*"I will hide my face from them," he said,
"and see what will then become of them.
What a fickle race they are,
sons with no loyalty in them!

21*"Since they have provoked me with their 'no-god'
and angered me with their vain idols,
I will provoke them with a 'no-people';
with a foolish nation I will anger them.

22*"For by my wrath a fire is enkindled
that shall rage to the depths of the nether world,
Consuming the earth with its yield,
and licking with flames the roots of the
mountains.
23I will spend on them woe upon woe
and exhaust all my arrows against them:

24"Emaciating hunger and consuming fever
and bitter pestilence,
And the teeth of wild beasts I will send among
them,
with the venom of reptiles gliding in the dust.

25*"Snatched away by the sword in the street
and by sheer terror at home
Shall be the youth and the maiden alike,
the nursing babe as well as the hoary old man.

26"I would have said, 'I will make an end of them
and blot out their name from men's memories,'
27Had I not feared the insolence of their enemies,
feared that these foes would mistakenly boast,
'Our own hand won the victory;
the LORD had nothing to do with it.'"

28†For they are a people devoid of reason,
having no understanding.
29If they had insight they would realize what
happened,
they would understand their future and say,

C

30"How could one man rout a thousand,
or two men put ten thousand to flight,
Unless it was because their Rock sold them
and the LORD delivered them up?"
31Indeed, their "rock" is not like our Rock,
and our foes are under condemnation.

32They are a branch of Sodom's vinestock,
from the vineyards of Gomorrah.
Poisonous are their grapes
and bitter their clusters.
33Their wine is the venom of dragons
and the cruel poison of cobras.

34"Is not this preserved in my treasury,
sealed up in my storehouse,
35Against the day of vengeance and requital,
against the time they lose their footing?"
Close at hand is the day of their disaster,
and their doom is rushing upon them!

36*†Surely, the LORD shall do justice for his people;
on his servants he shall have pity.
When he sees their strength failing,
and their protected and unprotected alike
disappearing,

37*He will say, "Where are their gods
whom they relied on as their 'rock'?
38Let those who ate the fat of your sacrifices
and drank the wine of your libations
Rise up now and help you!
Let them be your protection!

39*"Learn then that I, I alone, am God,
and there is no god besides me.
It is I who bring both death and life,
I who inflict wounds and heal them,
and from my hand there is no rescue.

40"To the heavens I raise my hand and swear:
As surely as I live forever,
41I will sharpen my flashing sword,
and my hand shall lay hold of my quiver.

"With vengeance I will repay my foes
and requite those who hate me.
42I will make my arrows drunk with blood,
and my sword shall gorge itself with flesh—
With the blood of the slain and the captured,
Flesh from the heads of the enemy leaders."

43Exult with him, you heavens,
glorify him, all you angels of God;
For he avenges the blood of his servants
and purges his people's land.

---

*   16: Nm 25, 2f; Ps 78, 58.   25: Lv 26, 25.
18: Jer 2, 32.   36: 2 Mc 7, 6.
20: 31, 17.   37f: Jgs 10, 14; Jer 2, 28.
21: Rom 10, 19.   39: 4, 35; Tb 13, 2;
22: Lam 4, 11.   Wis 16, 13.

† 32, 28-35: The reference is to the pagan nations, not to
Israel.

32, 36: *Their protected and unprotected:* the meaning of the
Hebrew is uncertain; according to some, the idea is "slaves and
freemen."

[44]So Moses, together with Joshua, son of Nun, went and recited all the words of this song for the people to hear.

Final Appeal

[45]When Moses had finished speaking all these words to all Israel, [46]*he said, "Take to heart all the warning which I have now given you and which you must impress on your children, that you may carry out carefully every word of this law. [47]For this is no trivial matter for you; rather, it means your very life, since it is by this means that you are to enjoy a long life on the land which you will cross the Jordan to occupy."

Moses To View Canaan

[48]On that very day the LORD said to Moses, [49]*"Go up on Mount Nebo, here in the Abarim Mountains [it is in the land of Moab facing Jericho], and view the land of Canaan, which I am giving to the Israelites as their possession. [50]*Then you shall die on the mountain you have climbed, and shall be taken to your people, just as your brother Aaron died on Mount Hor and there was taken to his people; [51]*because both of you broke faith with me among the Israelites at the waters of Meribath-kadesh in the desert of Zin by failing to manifest my sanctity among the Israelites. [52]*You may indeed view the land at a distance, but you shall not enter that land which I am giving to the Israelites."

Blessing upon the Tribes

33 [1]THIS is the blessing which Moses, the man of God, pronounced upon the Israelites before he died. [2]*†He said:

"The LORD came from Sinai
　　and dawned on his people from Seir;
He shone forth from Mount Paran
　　and advanced from Meribath-kadesh,
While at his right hand a fire blazed forth
　　and his wrath devastated the nations.
[3]†But all his holy ones were in his hand;
　　they followed at his feet
　　and he bore them up on his pinions.
[4]*A law he gave to us;
　　he made the community of Jacob his domain,
[5]†and he became king of his darling,
　When the chiefs of the people assembled
　　and the tribes of Israel came together.

[6]*†"May Reuben live and not die out,
　　but let his men be few."

[7]*†The following is for Judah. He said:
"The LORD hears the cry of Judah;

　　you will bring him to his people.
His own hands defend his cause
　　and you will be his help against his foes."

[8]*†Of Levi he said:
"To Levi belong your Thummim,
　　to the man of your favor your Urim;
For you put him to the test at Massah
　　and you contended with him at the waters of Meribah.
[9]†He said of his father, 'I regard him not';
　　his brothers he would not acknowledge,
　　and his own children he refused to recognize.
Thus the Levites keep your words,
　　and your covenant they uphold.
[10]*They promulgate your decisions to Jacob
　　and your law to Israel.
They bring the smoke of sacrifice to your nostrils,
　　and burnt offerings to your altar.
[11]Bless, O LORD, his possessions
　　and accept the ministry of his hands.
Break the backs of his adversaries
　　and of his foes, that they may not rise."

[12]*Of Benjamin he said:
"Benjamin is the beloved of the LORD,
　　who shelters him all the day,
　　while he abides securely at his breast."

[13]*Of Joseph he said:
"Blessed by the LORD is his land
　　with the best of the skies above
　　and of the abyss crouching beneath;
[14]With the best of the produce of the year,
　　and the choicest sheaves of the months;
[15]With the finest gifts of the age-old mountains
　　and the best from the timeless hills;
[16]†With the best of the earth and its fullness,
　　and the favor of him who dwells in the bush.

---

† 33, 2-5.26-29: These verses seem to form an independent hymn describing, in the form of a theophany, the conquest of Canaan. The first section of this hymn (vv 2-5) serves here as an introduction to the various "blessings"; the second section (vv 26-29), as their conclusion.

33, 3: *His holy ones were in his hand:* the Israelites were protected by the Lord.

33, 5.26: *The darling:* see note on 32, 15.

33, 6: In keeping with the other blessings, probably this verse was once introduced by the phrase, "Of Reuben he said." It is to be noted that there is no blessing here for Simeon.

33, 7: *Bring him to his people:* this probably refers to the isolated position of the tribe of Judah during the conquest of the Promised Land (cf Jgs 1, 17-19); according to some commentators the reference is to the divided kingdom.

33, 8: *Thummim . . . Urim:* see note on Ex 28, 30.

33, 9: The reference is probably to the Levites' slaughter of their brethren after the affair of the golden calf in the desert; cf Ex 32, 27-29.

33, 16: *Him who dwells in the bush:* a title given to the Lord because of his appearance to Moses in the burning bush; cf Ex 3.

46: 4, 9.	6: Gn 49, 3f.
49: Nm 27, 12; 33, 47f.	7: Gn 49, 8-12.
50: Nm 20, 24ff.28; 27, 13; 33, 38.	8: Gn 49, 5; Ex 17, 7; 28, 30; Nm 20, 13.
51: Nm 20, 12; 27, 14.	10: Ex 30, 7f.
52: 3, 27; 34, 4.	12: Gn 49, 27.
33/2: Ex 19, 18.20; Jgs 5, 4f.	13-17: Gn 49, 22-26.
4: Jn 1, 17; 7, 19.	

These shall come upon the head of Joseph
    and upon the brow of the prince among his
        brothers,
¹⁷The majestic bull, his father's first-born,
    whose horns are those of the wild ox
With which to gore the nations,
    even those at the ends of the earth."
[These are the myriads of Ephraim,
    and these the thousands of Manasseh.]

¹⁸*Of Zebulun he said:
"Rejoice, O Zebulun, in your pursuits,
    and you, Issachar, in your tents!
    ¹⁹†You who invite the tribes to the mountains
    where feasts are duly held,
Because you suck up the abundance of the seas
    and the hidden treasures of the sand."

²⁰*Of Gad he said:
"Blessed be he who has made Gad so vast!
    He lies there like a lion
    that has seized the arm and head of the prey.
    ²¹*†He saw that the best should be his
    when the princely portion was assigned,
    while the heads of the people were gathered.
He carried out the justice of the LORD
    and his decrees respecting Israel."
²²*†Of Dan he said:
"Dan is a lion's whelp,
    that springs forth from Bashan!"

²³*†Of Naphtali he said:
"Naphtali is enriched with favors
    and filled with the blessings of the LORD;
The lake and south of it are his possession!"

²⁴*†Of Asher he said:
"More blessed than the other sons be Asher!
    May he be the favorite among his brothers,
    as the oil of his olive trees runs over his feet!
    ²⁵May your bolts be of iron and bronze;
    may your strength endure through all your
        days!"

²⁶"There is no god like the God of the darling,
    who rides the heavens in his power,
    and rides the skies in his majesty;
²⁷He spread out the primeval tent;
    he extended the ancient canopy.
He drove the enemy out of your way
    and the Amorite he destroyed.

²⁸*Israel has dwelt securely,
    and the fountain of Jacob has been
        undisturbed
In a land of grain and wine,
    where the heavens drip with dew.

²⁹*How fortunate you are, O Israel!
    Where else is a nation victorious in the LORD?
The LORD is your saving shield,
    and his sword is your glory.
Your enemies fawn upon you,
    as you stride upon their heights."

Death and Burial of Moses

34 ¹*THEN Moses went up from the plains of Moab to Mount Nebo, the headland of Pisgah which faces Jericho, and the LORD showed him all the land—Gilead, and as far as Dan, ²all Naphtali, the land of Ephraim and Manasseh, all the land of Judah as far as the Western Sea, ³the Negeb, the circuit of the Jordan with the lowlands at Jericho, city of palms, and as far as Zoar. ⁴*The LORD then said to him, "This is the land which I swore to Abraham, Isaac and Jacob that I would give to their descendants. I have let you feast your eyes upon it, but you shall not cross over." ⁵*So there, in the land of Moab, Moses, the servant of the LORD, died as the LORD had said; ⁶and he was buried in the ravine opposite Beth-peor in the land of Moab, but to this day no one knows the place of his burial. ⁷*Moses was one hundred and twenty years old when he died, yet his eyes were undimmed and his vigor unabated. ⁸For thirty days the Israelites wept for Moses in the plains of Moab, till they had completed the period of grief and mourning for Moses.

⁹*Now Joshua, son of Nun, was filled with the spirit of wisdom, since Moses had laid his hands upon him; and so the Israelites gave him their obedience, thus carrying out the LORD's command to Moses.

¹⁰*Since then no prophet has arisen in Israel like Moses, whom the LORD knew face to face. ¹¹*He had no equal in all the signs and wonders the LORD sent him to perform in the land of Egypt against Pharaoh and all his servants and against all his land, ¹²and for the might and the terrifying power that Moses exhibited in the sight of all Israel.

---

† 33, 19: *The abundance of the seas:* perhaps the wealth that comes from sea-borne trade or from fishing. *The hidden treasures of the sand:* possibly an allusion to the valuable purple dye extracted from certain marine shells found on the coast of northern Palestine.

33, 21: *The princely portion:* Moses gave the tribe of Gad their land on the east of the Jordan only on condition that they would help the other tribes conquer the land west of the river; cf Nm 32; Jos 22.

33, 22: The sense is, "May he leap up like a lion of Bashan"; the heavily wooded hills of Bashan were notorious for their lions, but the tribe of Dan was not settled in this region.

33, 23: *The lake:* The Lake of Gennesaret on which the land of this tribe bordered.

33, 24: The land of the tribe of Asher was covered with olive groves.

*

18f: Gn 49, 13ff.   29: 4, 7f.
20f: Gn 49, 19.   34/1: 3, 27.
21: Nm 32, 1.5.16-19.31f;   4: 3, 27; 32, 52; Gn 12, 7;
     Jos 1, 12-15; 1 Chr 5,   15, 18.
     18-22.   5: 32, 50.
22: Gn 49, 16f.   7: 31, 2.
23: Gn 49, 21; Jos 19, 32-   9: Nm 27, 18.23; Jos 1,
     39.   17.
24f: Gn 49, 20.   10: Ex 33, 11.
28: Gn 27, 28.   11: 4, 34.

The Book of Joshua

Introduction

The Book of Joshua derives its name from the successor of Moses, with whose deeds it is principally concerned. The purpose of the book is to demonstrate God's fidelity in giving to the Israelites the land he had promised them for an inheritance (Gn 15, 18ff; Jos 1, 2ff; 21, 41ff; 23, 14ff).

Their occupation of the country is begun with the crossing of the Jordan and the conquest of Jericho (ch 1—6), in both of which the Lord intervenes on their behalf. This is followed by a first foothold on the Palestinian mountain range, at Ai, Bethel, and Gibeon (ch 7—9), and two sweeping campaigns against the city states in the south of the country (ch 10) and in the north (ch 11), with a summary in ch 12. The broad claim to total sovereignty thus established is spelled out by a combined list of tribal boundaries and of the towns contained within each area or administrative district (ch 13—19), including cities of asylum and cities for the Levites (ch 20, 21). The book closes with a narrative about the tribes east of the Jordan (ch 22), a warning speech by Joshua (ch 23), and a renewal at Shechem (ch 24) of the covenant with the Lord, already affirmed there near the beginning of the conquest (8, 30-35).

Like the books which precede it, the Book of Joshua was built up by a long and complex process of editing traditional materials. Both Jewish and Christian believers have always regarded it as inspired.

The entire history of the conquest of the Promised Land is a prophecy of the spiritual conquest of the world through the church under the leadership of Jesus the Messiah.

The Book of Joshua may be divided as follows:

    I: Conquest of Canaan (1, 1—12, 24)
    II: Division of the Land (13, 1—21, 45)
    III: Return of the Transjordan Tribes and Joshua's Farewell (22, 1—24, 33)

I: CONQUEST OF CANAAN

Divine Promise of Assistance

1 [1]AFTER MOSES, the servant of the LORD, had died, the LORD said to Moses' aide Joshua, son of Nun: [2]"My servant Moses is dead. So prepare to cross the Jordan here, with all the people into the land I will give the Israelites. [3]*As I promised Moses, I will deliver to you every place where you set foot. [4]†Your domain is to be all the land of the Hittites, from the desert and from Lebanon east to the great river Euphrates and west to the Great Sea. [5]*No one can withstand you while you live. I will be with you as I was with Moses: I will not leave you nor forsake you. [6]Be firm and steadfast, so that you may give this people possession of the land which I swore to their fathers I would give them. [7]*Above all, be firm and steadfast, taking care to observe the entire law which my servant Moses enjoined on you. Do not swerve from it either to the right or to the left, that you may succeed wherever you go. [8]Keep this book of the law on your lips. Recite it by day and by night, that you may observe carefully all that is written in it; then you will successfully attain your goal. [9]I command you: be firm and steadfast! Do not fear nor be dismayed, for the LORD, your God, is with you wherever you go."

[10]So Joshua commanded the officers of the people: [11]*"Go through the camp and instruct the people, 'Prepare your provisions, for three days from now you shall cross the Jordan here, to march in and take possession of the land which the LORD, your God, is giving you.'"

The Transjordan Tribes

[12]Joshua reminded the Reubenites, the Gadites, and the half-tribe of Manasseh: [13]"Remember what Moses, the servant of the LORD, commanded you when he said, 'The LORD, your God, will permit you to settle in this land.' [14]*Your wives, your children, and your livestock shall remain in the land Moses gave you here beyond the Jordan. But all the warriors among you must cross over armed ahead of your kinsmen and you must help them [15]*until the LORD has settled your kinsmen, and they like you possess the land which the LORD, your God, is giving them. Afterward you may return and occupy your own land, which Moses, the servant of the LORD, has given you east of the Jordan." [16]"We will do all you have commanded us," they answered Joshua, "and we will go wherever you send us. We will obey you as completely as we obeyed Moses. [17]But may the LORD, your God, be with you as he was with Moses. [18]If anyone rebels against your orders and

---

*
1/3f: 14, 9; Gn 15, 18;
    Dt 11, 24.
5: Dt 31, 8; Heb 13, 5.
7.9: Dt 31, 7f.

11: Dt 11, 31.
14: Nm 32, 26.
15: 22, 4; Dt 3, 20.

---

† 1, 4: The ideal frontiers are given: in the south *the desert* of Sinai, in the north the *Lebanon* range, in the east the *Euphrates*, and in the west *the Great Sea*, the Mediterranean.

does not obey every command you give him, he shall be put to death. But be firm and steadfast."

Spies Saved by Rahab

2 **1*****†**THEN Joshua, son of Nun, secretly sent out two spies from Shittim, saying, "Go, reconnoiter the land and Jericho." When the two reached Jericho, they went into the house of a harlot named Rahab, where they lodged. **2**But a report was brought to the king of Jericho that some Israelites had come there that night to spy out the land. **3**So the king of Jericho sent Rahab the order, "Put out the visitors who have entered your house, for they have come to spy out the entire land." **4***The woman had taken the two men and hidden them, so she said, "True, the men you speak of came to me, but I did not know where they came from. **5**At dark, when it was time for the gate to be shut, they left, and I do not know where they went. You will have to pursue them immediately to overtake them." **6**†Now, she had led them to the roof, and hidden them among her stalks of flax spread out there. **7**But the pursuers set out along the way to the fords of the Jordan, and once they had left, the gate was shut.

8†Before the spies fell asleep, Rahab came to them on the roof **9***and said: "I know that the LORD has given you the land, that a dread of you has come upon us, and that all the inhabitants of the land are overcome with fear of you. **10***For we have heard how the LORD dried up the waters of the Red Sea before you when you came out of Egypt, and how you dealt with Sihon and Og, the two kings of the Amorites beyond the Jordan, whom you doomed to destruction. **11***At these reports, we are disheartened; everyone is discouraged because of you, since the LORD, your God, is God in heaven above and on earth below. **12***Now then, swear to me by the LORD that, since I am showing kindness to you, you in turn will show kindness to my family; and give me an unmistakable token **13**that you are to spare my father and mother, brothers and sisters, and all their kin, and save us from death." **14**"We pledge our lives for yours," the men answered her. "If you do not betray this errand of ours, we will be faithful in showing kindness to you when the LORD gives us the land."

15†Then she let them down through the window with a rope; for she lived in a house built into the city wall. **16**"Go up into the hill country," she suggested to them, "that your pursuers may not find you. Hide there for three days, until they return; then you may proceed on your way." **17**The men answered her, "This is how we will fulfill the oath you made us take: **18**When we come into the land, tie this scarlet cord in the window through which you are letting us down; and gather your father and mother, your brothers and all your family into your house. **19**Should any of them

pass outside the doors of your house, he will be responsible for his own death, and we shall be guiltless. But we shall be responsible if anyone in the house with you is harmed. **20**If, however, you betray this errand of ours, we shall be quit of the oath you have made us take." **21**"Let it be as you say," she replied, and bade them farewell. When they were gone, she tied the scarlet cord in the window.

22They went up into the hills, where they stayed three days until their pursuers, who had sought them all along the road without finding them, returned. **23**Then the two came back down from the hills, crossed the Jordan to Joshua, son of Nun, and reported all that had befallen them. **24**They assured Joshua, "The LORD has delivered all this land into our power; indeed, all the inhabitants of the land are overcome with fear of us."

Preparations for Crossing the Jordan

3 **1***EARLY the next morning, Joshua moved with all the Israelites from Shittim to the Jordan, where they lodged before crossing over. **2**Three days later the officers went through the camp **3**and issued these instructions to the people: "When you see the ark of the covenant of the LORD, your God, which the levitical priests will carry, you must also break camp and follow it, **4**that you may know the way to take, for you have not gone over this road before. But let there be a space of two thousand cubits between you and the ark. Do not come nearer to it." **5**Joshua also said to the people, "Sanctify yourselves, for tomorrow the LORD will perform wonders among you." **6**And he directed the priests to take up the ark of the covenant and go on ahead of the people; and they did so.

7*Then the LORD said to Joshua, "Today I will begin to exalt you in the sight of all Israel, that they may know I am with you, as I was with Moses. **8**Now command the priests carrying the ark of the covenant to come to a halt in the Jordan when they reach the edge of the waters."

9So Joshua said to the Israelites, "Come here and listen to the words of the LORD, your God." **10***He continued: "This is how you will know that there is a living God in your midst, who at your approach will

† 2, 1: *Harlot:* this is the regular equivalent of the Hebrew word, but perhaps it is used here of Rahab in the broader sense of a woman who kept a public house. Joshua's spies hoped to remain undetected at such an inn.

2, 6: *Stalks of flax spread out:* to dry in the sun, after they had been soaked in water, according to the ancient process of preparing flax for linen-making. In the Near East the flax harvest occurs near the time of the feast of the Passover (4, 19; 5, 10); cf Ex 9, 31.

2, 8-11: Rahab's faith and good works are praised in the New Testament; cf Heb 11, 31; Jas 2, 25.

2, 15: *A house built into the city wall:* such houses, which used the city wall for their own inner walls, have been found at ancient sites. The upper story of Rahab's house was evidently higher than the city wall. It was through the window of such a house that St. Paul escaped from Damascus; cf Acts 9, 25; 2 Cor 11, 33.

❋
2/1: Mt 1, 5; Jas 2, 25.
4: 6, 17.
9: Ex 15, 15f; 23, 27.
10: 4, 23; Ex 14, 21; Nm 21, 23-26.33ff.
11: Dt 4, 39.
12: 2, 18; 6, 23.25.
3/1: 2, 1.
7: 1, 5; 4, 14.
10: Ex 33, 2; Dt 7, 1.

dispossess the Canaanites, Hittites, Hivites, Perizzites, Girgashites, Amorites and Jebusites. **11**The ark of the covenant of the Lord of the whole earth will precede you into the Jordan. **12***[Now choose twelve men, one from each of the tribes of Israel.] **13**When the soles of the feet of the priests carrying the ark of the LORD, the Lord of the whole earth, touch the water of the Jordan, it will cease to flow; for the water flowing down from upstream will halt in a solid bank."

The Crossing Begun

14The people struck their tents to cross the Jordan, with the priests carrying the ark of the covenant ahead of them. **15**†No sooner had these priestly bearers of the ark waded into the waters at the edge of the Jordan, which overflows all its banks during the entire season of the harvest, **16***†than the waters flowing from upstream halted, backing up in a solid mass for a very great distance indeed, from Adam, a city in the direction of Zarethan; while those flowing downstream toward the Salt Sea of the Arabah disappeared entirely. Thus the people crossed over opposite Jericho. **17***While all Israel crossed over on dry ground, the priests carrying the ark of the covenant of the LORD remained motionless on dry ground in the bed of the Jordan until the whole nation had completed the passage.

Memorial Stones

4 **1**AFTER the entire nation had crossed the Jordan, the LORD said to Joshua, **2***"Choose twelve men from the people, one from each tribe, **3***and instruct them to take up twelve stones from this spot in the bed of the Jordan where the priests have been standing motionless. Carry them over with you, and place them where you are to stay tonight."

4Summoning the twelve men whom he had selected from among the Israelites, one from each tribe, **5**Joshua said to them: "Go to the bed of the Jordan in front of the ark of the LORD, your God; lift to your shoulders one stone apiece, so that they will equal in number the tribes of the Israelites. **6**In the future, these are to be a sign among you. When your children ask you what these stones mean to you, **7***you shall answer them, 'The waters of the Jordan ceased to flow before the ark of the covenant of the LORD when it crossed the Jordan.' Thus these stones are to serve as a perpetual memorial to the Israelites." **8**The twelve Israelites did as Joshua had commanded: they took up as many stones from the bed of the Jordan as there were tribes of the Israelites, and carried them along to the camp site, where they placed them, according to the LORD's direction. **9**Joshua also had twelve stones set up in the bed of the Jordan on the spot where the priests stood who were carrying the ark of the covenant. They are there to this day.

10†The priests carrying the ark remained in the bed of the Jordan until everything had been done that the LORD had commanded Joshua to tell the people. The people crossed over quickly, **11**and when all had reached the other side, the ark of the LORD, borne by the priests, also crossed to its place in front of them. **12***The Reubenites, Gadites, and half-tribe of Manasseh, armed, marched in the vanguard of the Israelites, as Moses had ordered. **13**About forty thousand troops equipped for battle passed over before the LORD to the plains of Jericho.

14*That day the LORD exalted Joshua in the sight of all Israel, and thenceforth during his whole life they respected him as they had respected Moses.

15Then the LORD said to Joshua, **16***"Command the priests carrying the ark of the commandments to come up from the Jordan." **17**Joshua did so, **18**and when the priests carrying the ark of the covenant of the LORD had come up from the bed of the Jordan, as the soles of their feet regained the dry ground, the waters of the Jordan resumed their course and as before overflowed all its banks.

19The people came up from the Jordan on the tenth day of the first month, and camped in Gilgal on the eastern limits of Jericho. **20**At Gilgal Joshua set up the twelve stones which had been taken from the Jordan, **21**saying to the Israelites, "In the future, when the children among you ask their fathers what these stones mean, **22**you shall inform them, 'Israel crossed the Jordan here on dry ground.' **23***For the LORD, your God, dried up the waters of the Jordan in front of you until you crossed over, just as the LORD, your God, had done at the Red Sea, which he dried up in front of us until we crossed over; **24**in order that all the peoples of the earth may learn that the hand of the LORD is mighty, and that you may fear the LORD, your God, forever."

Rites at Gilgal

5 **1**WHEN all the kings of the Amorites to the west of the Jordan and all the kings of the Canaanites by the sea heard that the LORD had dried up the waters of the Jordan before the Israelites until they crossed over, they were disheartened and lost courage at their approach.

2On this occasion the LORD said to Joshua, "Make

---

† 3, 15: *Season of the harvest:* toward the end of March and the beginning of April, when the grain and other crops that grew during the rainy season of winter were reaped. The crossing took place "on the tenth day of the first month" of the Hebrew year, which began with the first new moon after the spring equinox; cf 4, 19. At this time of the year the Jordan would be swollen as a result of the winter rains and the melting snow of Mount Hermon.

3, 16: The sudden damming of the river could have been caused by a landslide, as has happened on other occasions. The miraculous character of this event would not thereby be removed because God, who foretold it (3, 13), also caused it to take place at precisely the right moment (3, 15), whether or not he used natural forces to accomplish his will.

4, 10-18: After the digression about the two sets of memorial stones, the author resumes the narrative by briefly repeating the story of the crossing, which he had already told in 3, 14-17.

✿
12: 4, 2.4.   7: 3, 13.16.
16: Ps 114, 3.   12: Dt 3, 18.
17: 4, 7.22.   14: 3, 7.
4/2: 3, 12.   16: 3, 6.
3: 3, 13; 4, 8f; Dt 27, 2.   23: Ex 14, 21.

flint knives and circumcise the Israelite nation for the second time." [3]†So Joshua made flint knives and circumcised the Israelites at Gibeath-haaraloth, [4]*under these circumstances: Of all the people who came out of Egypt, every man of military age had died in the desert during the journey after they left Egypt. [5]Though all the men who came out were circumcised, none of those born in the desert during the journey after the departure from Egypt were circumcised. [6]*Now the Israelites had wandered forty years in the desert, until all the warriors among the people that came forth from Egypt died off because they had not obeyed the command of the LORD. For the LORD swore that he would not let them see the land flowing with milk and honey which he had promised their fathers he would give us. [7]*It was the children whom he raised up in their stead whom Joshua circumcised, for these were yet with foreskins, not having been circumcised on the journey. [8]When the rite had been performed, the whole nation remained in camp where they were, until they recovered. [9]*†Then the LORD said to Joshua, "Today I have removed the reproach of Egypt from you." Therefore the place is called Gilgal to the present day.

[10]*†While the Israelites were encamped at Gilgal on the plains of Jericho, they celebrated the Passover on the evening of the fourteenth of the month. [11]On the day after the Passover they ate of the produce of the land in the form of unleavened cakes and parched grain. On that same day [12]*after the Passover on which they ate of the produce of the land, the manna ceased. No longer was there manna for the Israelites, who that year ate of the yield of the land of Canaan.

Siege at Jericho

[13]*†While Joshua was near Jericho, he raised his eyes and saw one who stood facing him, drawn sword in hand. Joshua went up to him and asked, "Are you one of us or of our enemies?" [14]He replied, "Neither. I am the captain of the host of the LORD and I have just arrived." Then Joshua fell prostrate to the ground in worship, and said to him, "What has my lord to say to his servant?" [15]*The captain of the host of the LORD replied to Joshua, "Remove your sandals from your feet, for the place on which you are standing is holy." And Joshua obeyed.

6 [1]NOW Jericho was in a state of siege because of the presence of the Israelites, so that no one left or entered. [2]And to Joshua the LORD said, "I have delivered Jericho and its king into your power. [3]Have all the soldiers circle the city, marching once around it. Do this for six days, [4]*with seven priests carrying ram's horns ahead of the ark. On the seventh day march around the city seven times, and have the priests blow the horns. [5]When they give a long blast on the ram's horns and you hear that signal, all the people shall shout aloud. The wall of the city will collapse, and they will be able to make a frontal attack."

[6]Summoning the priests, Joshua, son of Nun, then ordered them to take up the ark of the covenant with seven of the priests carrying ram's horns in front of the ark of the LORD. [7]And he ordered the people to proceed in a circle around the city, with the picked troops marching ahead of the ark of the LORD. [8]At this order they proceeded, with the seven priests who carried the ram's horns before the LORD blowing their horns, and the ark of the covenant of the LORD following them. [9]In front of the priests with the horns marched the picked troops; the rear guard followed the ark, and the blowing of horns was kept up continually as they marched. [10]But the people had been commanded by Joshua not to shout or make any noise or outcry until he gave the word: only then were they to shout. [11]So he had the ark of the LORD circle the city, going once around it, after which they returned to camp for the night.

[12]Early the next morning, Joshua had the priests take up the ark of the LORD. [13]The seven priests bearing the ram's horns marched in front of the ark of the LORD, blowing their horns. Ahead of these marched the picked troops, while the rear guard followed the ark of the LORD, and the blowing of horns was kept up continually. [14]On this second day they again marched around the city once before returning to camp; and for six days in all they did the same.

[15]On the seventh day, beginning at daybreak, they marched around the city seven times in the same manner; on that day only did they march around the city seven times. [16]The seventh time around, the priests blew the horns and Joshua said to the people, "Now shout, for the LORD has given you the city [17]*and everything in it. It is under the LORD's ban. Only the harlot Rahab and all who are in the house with her are to be spared, because she hid the messengers we sent. [18]*†But be careful not to take, in your greed, anything that is under the ban; else you will bring upon

---

5, 3: *Gibeath-haaraloth:* "Hill of the Foreskins."

5, 9: *The place is called Gilgal:* by popular etymology, because of the similarity of sound with the Hebrew word *gallôthi,* "I have removed." Gilgal probably means "(the place of) the circle of standing stones." Cf 4, 4-8.

5, 10: *The month:* the first month of the year, later called Nisan; see note on 3, 15. The crossing of the Jordan occurred, therefore, about the same time of the year as did the equally miraculous crossing of the Red Sea; cf Ex 12-14.

5, 13—6, 26: The account of the siege of Jericho embraces: (1) The command of the Lord, through his angel, to Joshua (5, 13—6, 5); (2) Joshua's instructions to the Israelites, with a brief summary of how these orders were carried out (6, 6-11); (3) a description of the action on each of the first six days (6, 12-14); (4) the events on the seventh day (6, 15-26).

6, 18: *That is under the ban:* that is doomed to destruction; see notes on Lv 27, 29; Nm 18, 14; 21, 3.

     ❋

    5/4: Nm 14, 29; 26, 64f;   12: Ex 16, 35.
        Dt 2, 16; Ps 106, 26;   13: Ex 23, 20.
        1 Cor 10, 5.   15: Ex 3, 5; Acts 7, 33.
    6: Nm 14, 29;   6/4: Nm 10, 8f.
        Heb 3, 11.17.   17: 2, 4; Dt 20, 17;
    7: Dt 1, 39.   Heb 11, 31.
    9: 4, 19.   18: 7, 12.25; Dt 13, 18.
   10: Ex 12, 6; Lv 23, 5;
        Nm 9, 3-5.

the camp of Israel this ban and the misery of it. ¹⁹All silver and gold, and the articles of bronze or iron, are sacred to the Lord. They shall be put in the treasury of the Lord."

The Fall of Jericho

²⁰*†As the horns blew, the people began to shout. When they heard the signal horn, they raised a tremendous shout. The wall collapsed, and the people stormed the city in a frontal attack and took it. ²¹*They observed the ban by putting to the sword all living creatures in the city: men and women, young and old, as well as oxen, sheep and asses.

²²*Joshua directed the two men who had spied out the land, "Go into the harlot's house and bring out the woman with all her kin, as you swore to her you would do." ²³*The spies entered and brought out Rahab, with her father, mother, brothers, and all her kin. Her entire family they led forth and placed them outside the camp of Israel. ²⁴*The city itself they burned with all that was in it, except the silver, gold, and articles of bronze and iron, which were placed in the treasury of the house of the Lord. ²⁵†Because Rahab the harlot had hidden the messengers whom Joshua had sent to reconnoiter Jericho, Joshua spared her with her family and all her kin, who continue in the midst of Israel to this day.

²⁶*†On that occasion Joshua imposed the oath: Cursed before the Lord be the man who attempts to rebuild this city, Jericho. He shall lose his first-born when he lays its foundation, and he shall lose his youngest son when he sets up its gates. ²⁷*Thus the Lord was with Joshua so that his fame spread throughout the land.

Defeat at Ai

7 ¹*BUT the Israelites violated the ban; Achan, son of Carmi, son of Zerah, son of Zara of the tribe of Judah, took goods that were under the ban, and the anger of the Lord flared up against the Israelites.

²Joshua next sent men from Jericho to Ai, which is near Bethel on its eastern side, with instructions to go up and reconnoiter the land. When they had explored Ai, ³they returned to Joshua and advised, "Do not send all the people up; if only about two or three thousand go up, they can overcome Ai. The enemy there are few; you need not call for an effort from all the people." ⁴About three thousand of the people made the attack, but they were defeated by those at Ai, ⁵who killed some thirty-six of them. They pressed them back across the clearing in front of the city gate till they broke ranks, and defeated them finally on the descent, so that the confidence of the people melted away like water.

⁶Joshua, together with the elders of Israel, rent his garments and lay prostrate before the ark of the Lord until evening; and they threw dust on their heads. ⁷"Alas, O Lord God," Joshua prayed, "why did you ever allow this people to pass over the Jordan, delivering us into the power of the Amorites, that they might destroy us? Would that we had been content to dwell on the other side of the Jordan. ⁸Pray, Lord, what can I say, now that Israel has turned its back to its enemies? ⁹When the Canaanites and the other inhabitants of the land hear of it, they will close in around us and efface our name from the earth. What will you do for your great name?"

¹⁰The Lord replied to Joshua: "Stand up. Why are you lying prostrate? ¹¹*Israel has sinned: they have violated the covenant which I enjoined on them. They have stealthily taken goods subject to the ban, and have deceitfully put them in their baggage. ¹²*If the Israelites cannot stand up to their enemies, but must turn their back to them, it is because they are under the ban. I will not remain with you unless you remove from among you whoever has incurred the ban. ¹³*Rise, sanctify the people. Tell them to sanctify themselves before tomorrow, for the Lord, the God of Israel, says: You are under the ban, O Israel. You cannot stand up to your enemies until you remove from among you whoever has incurred the ban. ¹⁴In the morning you must present yourselves by tribes. The tribe which the Lord designates shall come forward by clans; the clan which the Lord designates shall come forward by families; the family which the Lord designates shall come forward one by one. ¹⁵He who is designated as having incurred the ban shall be destroyed by fire, with all that is his, because he has violated the covenant of the Lord and has committed a shameful crime in Israel."

Achan's Guilt and Punishment

¹⁶†Early the next morning Joshua had Israel come forward by tribes, and the tribe of Judah was designated. ¹⁷*Then he had the clans of Judah come forward, and the clan of Zerah was designated. He had the clan of Zerah come forward by families, and Zabdi was designated. ¹⁸Finally he had that family come forward one by one, and Achan, son of Carmi, son of Zabdi, son of Zerah of the tribe of Judah, was desig-

---

† 6, 20: *The wall collapsed:* by the miraculous intervention of God. The blowing of the horns and the shouting of the people were a customary feature of ancient warfare, here intended by God as a test of the people's obedience and of their faith in his promise; cf Heb 11, 30.

6, 25: From Mt 1, 5, we learn that Rahab married Salmon of the tribe of Judah and thus became the great-great-grandmother of David, Christ's ancestor; cf Ru 4, 18-22.

6, 26: *He shall lose his first-born . . . its gates:* this curse was fulfilled when Hiel rebuilt Jericho as a fortified city during the reign of Ahab, king of Israel; cf 1 Kgs 16, 34. Till then Jericho was merely an unwalled village; cf Jos 18, 12.21; Jgs 3, 13; 2 Sm 10, 5.

7, 16ff: *Was designated:* probably by means of the Urim and Thummim; cf 1 Sm 14, 38-42. See note on Ex 28, 30.

20: 2 Mc 12, 15; Heb 11, 30.
21: Dt 7, 2.
22: 2, 14.
23: 2, 13; Heb 11, 31.
24: 8, 2.
26: 1 Kgs 16, 34.
27: 1, 5.
7/1: 6, 18; 22, 20; 1 Chr 2, 7.
11: 6, 17-19.
12: 6, 18.
13: 3, 5; Lv 20, 7; 1 Sm 16, 5.
17: Nm 26, 20.

nated. ¹⁹Joshua said to Achan, "My son, give to the LORD, the God of Israel, glory and honor by telling me what you have done; do not hide it from me." ²⁰Achan answered Joshua, "I have indeed sinned against the LORD, the God of Israel. This is what I have done: ²¹Among the spoils, I saw a beautiful Babylonian mantle, two hundred shekels of silver, and a bar of gold fifty shekels in weight; in my greed I took them. They are now hidden in the ground inside my tent, with the silver underneath." ²²The messengers whom Joshua sent hastened to the tent and found them hidden there, with the silver underneath. ²³They took them from the tent, brought them to Joshua and all the Israelites, and spread them out before the LORD.

²⁴Then Joshua and all Israel took Achan, son of Zerah, with the silver, the mantle, and the bar of gold, and with his sons and daughters, his ox, his ass and his sheep, his tent, and all his possessions, and led them off to the Valley of Achor. ²⁵*Joshua said, "The LORD bring upon you today the misery with which you have afflicted us!" And all Israel stoned him to death ²⁶*†and piled a great heap of stones over him, which remains to the present day. Then the anger of the LORD relented. That is why the place is called the Valley of Achor to this day.

Capture of Ai

8 ¹*THE LORD then said to Joshua, "Do not be afraid or dismayed. Take all the army with you and prepare to attack Ai. I have delivered the king of Ai into your power, with his people, city, and land. ²*Do to Ai and its king what you did to Jericho and its king; except that you may take its spoil and livestock as booty. Set an ambush behind the city." ³†So Joshua and all the soldiers prepared to attack Ai. Picking out thirty thousand warriors, Joshua sent them off by night ⁴with these orders: "See that you ambush the city from the rear, at no great distance; then all of you be on the watch. ⁵The rest of the people and I will come up to the city, and when they make a sortie against us as they did the last time, we will flee from them. ⁶They will keep coming out after us until we have drawn them away from the city, for they will think we are fleeing from them as we did the last time. When this occurs, ⁷rise from ambush and take possession of the city, which the LORD, your God, will deliver into your power. ⁸When you have taken the city, set it afire in obedience to the LORD's command. These are my orders to you." ⁹Then Joshua sent them away. They went to the place of ambush, taking up their position to the west of Ai, toward Bethel. Joshua, however, spent that night in the plain.

¹⁰Early the next morning Joshua mustered the army and went up to Ai at its head, with the elders of Israel. ¹¹When all the troops he led were drawn up in position

before the city, they pitched camp north of Ai, on the other side of the ravine. ¹²[He took about five thousand men and set them in ambush between Bethel and Ai, west of the city.] ¹³Thus the people took up their stations, with the main body north of the city and the ambush west of it, and Joshua waited overnight among his troops. ¹⁴The king of Ai saw this, and he and all his army came out very early in the morning to engage Israel in battle at the descent toward the Arabah, not knowing that there was an ambush behind the city. ¹⁵Joshua and the main body of the Israelites fled in seeming defeat toward the desert, ¹⁶till the last of the soldiers in the city had been called out to pursue them. ¹⁷Since they were drawn away from the city, with every man engaged in this pursuit of Joshua and the Israelites, not a soldier remained in Ai [or Bethel], and the city was open and unprotected.

¹⁸Then the LORD directed Joshua, "Stretch out the javelin in your hand toward Ai, for I will deliver it into your power." Joshua stretched out the javelin in his hand toward the city, ¹⁹and as soon as he did so, the men in ambush rose from their post, rushed in, captured the city, and immediately set it on fire. ²⁰By the time the men of Ai looked back, the smoke from the city was already sky-high. Escape in any direction was impossible, because the Israelites retreating toward the desert now turned on their pursuers; ²¹for when Joshua and the main body of Israelites saw that the city had been taken from ambush and was going up in smoke, they struck back at the men of Ai. ²²*Since those in the city came out to intercept them, the men of Ai were hemmed in by Israelites on either side, who cut them down without any fugitives or survivors ²³except the king, whom they took alive and brought to Joshua.

²⁴All the inhabitants of Ai who had pursued the Israelites into the desert were slain by the sword there in the open, down to the last man. Then all Israel returned and put to the sword those inside the city. ²⁵There fell that day a total of twelve thousand men and women, the entire population of Ai. ²⁶*Joshua kept the javelin in his hand stretched out until he had fulfilled the doom on all the inhabitants of Ai. ²⁷However, the Israelites took for themselves as booty the livestock and the spoil of that city, according to the command of the LORD issued to Joshua. ²⁸*Then Joshua destroyed the place by fire, reducing it to an everlasting mound of ruins, as it remains today. ²⁹*He had the king of Ai hanged on a tree until evening; then at sunset Joshua ordered the body removed from the tree and cast at the entrance of the city gate, where a

---

† 7, 26: *Achor:* "misery, affliction." The reference is to the saying of Joshua in v 25, with an allusion also to the similar-sounding name of Achan.

8, 3: *Thirty thousand warriors:* this figure of the Hebrew text, which seems extremely high, may be due to a copyist's error; some manuscripts of the Septuagint have "three thousand," which is the number of the whole army in the first, unsuccessful attack (7, 4); the variant reading in v 12 mentions "five thousand."

❋

25: 6, 18; 22, 20;   22: Dt 7, 2.
    1 Chr 2, 7.   26: Ex 17, 11ff.
26: 8, 29.   28: Dt 13, 16.
8/1: 2, 24.   29: 10, 26f; Dt 21, 22f;
2: 6, 21.24; Dt 20, 14.   Jn 19, 31.

great heap of stones was piled up over it, which remains to the present day.

Altar on Mount Ebal

30†Later Joshua built an altar to the LORD, the God of Israel, on Mount Ebal, **31***of unhewn stones on which no iron tool had been used, in keeping with the command to the Israelites of Moses, the servant of the LORD, as recorded in the book of the law. On this altar they offered holocausts and peace offerings to the LORD. **32***There, in the presence of the Israelites, Joshua inscribed upon the stones a copy of the law written by Moses. **33***And all Israel, stranger and native alike, with their elders, officers and judges, stood on either side of the ark facing the levitical priests who were carrying the ark of the covenant of the LORD. Half of them were facing Mount Gerizim and half Mount Ebal, thus carrying out the instructions of Moses, the servant of the LORD, for the blessing of the people of Israel on this first occasion. **34***Then were read aloud all the words of the law, the blessings and the curses, exactly as written in the book of the law. **35***Every single word that Moses had commanded, Joshua read aloud to the entire community, including the women and children, and the strangers who had accompanied Israel.

Confederacy against Israel

9 **1***WHEN the news reached the kings west of the Jordan, in the mountain regions and in the foothills, and all along the coast of the Great Sea as far as Lebanon: Hittites, Amorites, Canaanites, Perizzites, Hivites and Jebusites, **2**they all formed an alliance to launch a common attack against Joshua and Israel.

The Gibeonite Deception

3*On learning what Joshua had done to Jericho and Ai, the inhabitants of Gibeon **4**put into effect a device of their own. They chose provisions for a journey, making use of old sacks for their asses, and old wineskins, torn and mended. **5**They wore old, patched sandals and shabby garments; and all the bread they took was dry and crumbly. **6***Thus they journeyed to Joshua in the camp at Gilgal, where they said to him and to the men of Israel, "We have come from a distant land to propose that you make an alliance with us." **7**†But the men of Israel replied to the Hivites, "You may be living in land that is ours. How, then, can we make an alliance with you?" **8**But they answered Joshua, "We are your servants." Then Joshua asked them, "Who are you? Where do you come from?" **9***They answered him, "Your servants have come from

a far-off land, because of the fame of the LORD, your God. For we have heard reports of all that he did in Egypt **10***and all that he did to the two kings of the Amorites beyond the Jordan, Sihon, king of Heshbon, and Og, king of Bashan, who lived in Ashtaroth. **11**So our elders and all the inhabitants of our country said to us, 'Take along provisions for the journey and go to meet them. Say to them: We are your servants; we propose that you make an alliance with us.' **12**This bread of ours was still warm when we brought it from home as provisions the day we left to come to you, but now it is dry and crumbled. **13**Here are our wineskins, which were new when we filled them, but now they are torn. Look at our garments and sandals, which are worn out from the very long journey." **14***Then the Israelite princes partook of their provisions, without seeking the advice of the LORD. **15***So Joshua made an alliance with them and entered into an agreement to spare them, which the princes of the community sealed with an oath.

Gibeonites Made Vassals

16Three days after the agreement was entered into, the Israelites learned that these people were from nearby, and would be living in Israel. **17**The third day on the road, the Israelites came to their cities of Gibeon, Chephirah, Beeroth and Kiriath-jearim, **18**but did not attack them, because the princes of the community had sworn to them by the LORD, the God of Israel. When the entire community grumbled against the princes, **19**these all remonstrated with the people, "We have sworn to them by the LORD, the God of Israel, and so we cannot harm them. **20**Let us therefore spare their lives and so deal with them that we shall not be punished for the oath we have sworn to them." **21**†Thus the princes recommended that they be let live, as hewers of wood and drawers of water for the entire community; and the community did as the princes advised them.

22Joshua summoned the Gibeonites and said to them, "Why did you lie to us and say that you lived at a great distance from us, when you will be living in our very midst? **23**For this are you accursed: every one of you shall always be a slave [hewers of wood and drawers of water] for the house of my God." **24***They answered Joshua, "Your servants were fully informed of how the LORD, your God, commanded his servant Moses that you be given the entire land and that all its inhabitants be destroyed before you. Since, therefore, at your advance, we were in great fear for our lives, we acted as we did. **25**And now that we are in your

---

❀

31: Ex 20, 24f; Dt 27, 5f.
32: Dt 27, 2.8.
33: 3, 3; Dt 11, 27; 27, 12; 31, 9.12.
34: Dt 28, 2-68; 30, 19; 31, 11; Neh 8, 2f.
35: Dt 31, 12.
9/1: 3, 10; Ex 3, 8.17; 23, 23; Dt 1, 7.

3: 6, 21.24; 11, 19.
6: Ex 23, 32; Dt 7, 2.
9: 2, 10.
10: Nm 21, 25.33.
14: Nm 27, 21.
15: 11, 19; 2 Sm 21, 2.
24: Ex 23, 27f; Dt 7, 1f.

†
8, 30-35: These ceremonies were prescribed in Dt 11, 29 and 27, 2-26. See notes on those passages.

9, 7: *The Hivites:* apparently the Gibeonites belonged to this larger ethnic group (cf also 11, 19), although in 2 Sm 21, 2 they are classed as Amorites; both groups are listed among the *seven nations* in Canaan whom the Israelites were to exterminate; cf Dt 7, 1f.

9, 21: *Hewers of wood and drawers of water:* proverbial terms for the lowest social class in the Israelite community; cf Dt 29, 10f.

power, do with us what you think fit and right." [26]†Joshua did what he had decided: while he saved them from being killed by the Israelites, [27]*at the same time he made them, as they still are, hewers of wood and drawers of water for the community and for the altar of the LORD, in the place of the LORD's choice.

The Siege of Gibeon

10 [1]*NOW Adonizedek, king of Jerusalem, heard that, in the capture and destruction of Ai, Joshua had done to that city and its king as he had done to Jericho and its king. He heard also that the inhabitants of Gibeon had made their peace with Israel, remaining among them, [2]and that there was great fear abroad, because Gibeon was large enough for a royal city, larger even than the city of Ai, and all its men were brave. [3]So Adonizedek, king of Jerusalem, sent for Hoham, king of Hebron, Piram, king of Jarmuth, Japhia, king of Lachish, and Debir, king of Eglon, [4]*to come to his aid for an attack on Gibeon, since it had concluded peace with Joshua and the Israelites. [5]†The five Amorite kings, of Jerusalem, Hebron, Jarmuth, Lachish and Eglon, united all their forces and marched against Gibeon, where they took up siege positions. [6]*Thereupon, the men of Gibeon sent an appeal to Joshua in his camp at Gilgal: "Do not abandon your servants. Come up here quickly and save us. Help us, because all the Amorite kings of the mountain country have joined forces against us."

Joshua's Victory

[7]So Joshua marched up from Gilgal with his picked troops and the rest of his soldiers. [8]Meanwhile the LORD said to Joshua, "Do not fear them, for I have delivered them into your power. Not one of them will be able to withstand you." [9]And when Joshua made his surprise attack upon them after an all-night march from Gilgal, [10]the LORD threw them into disorder before him. The Israelites inflicted a great slaughter on them at Gibeon and pursued them down the Beth-horon slope, harassing them as far as Azekah and Makkedah.

[11]*†While they fled before Israel along the descent from Beth-horon, the LORD hurled great stones from the sky above them all the way to Azekah, killing many. More died from these hailstones than the Israelites slew with the sword. [12]On this day, when the LORD delivered up the Amorites to the Israelites,

Joshua prayed to the LORD,
and said in the presence of Israel:
Stand still, O sun, at Gibeon,
O moon, in the valley of Aijalon!

[13]*†And the sun stood still,
and the moon stayed,
while the nation took vengeance on its foes.

Is this not recorded in the Book of Jashar? The sun halted in the middle of the sky; not for a whole day did it resume its swift course. [14]Never before or since was there a day like this, when the LORD obeyed the voice of a man; for the LORD fought for Israel. [15][Then Joshua and all Israel returned to the camp at Gilgal.]

Execution of Amorite Kings

[16]Meanwhile the five kings who had fled, hid in a cave at Makkedah. [17]When Joshua was told that the five kings had been discovered hiding in a cave at Makkedah, [18]he said, "Roll large stones to the mouth of the cave and post men over it to guard them. [19]But do not remain there yourselves. Pursue your enemies, and harry them in the rear. Do not allow them to escape to their cities, for the LORD, your God, has delivered them into your power." [20]Once Joshua and the Israelites had finally inflicted the last blows in this very great slaughter, and the survivors had escaped from them into the fortified cities, [21]all the army returned safely to Joshua and the camp at Makkedah, no man uttering a sound against the Israelites. [22]Then Joshua said, "Open the mouth of the cave and bring out those five kings to me." [23]Obediently, they brought out to him from the cave the five kings, of Jerusalem, Hebron, Jarmuth, Lachish and Eglon. [24]When they had done so, Joshua summoned all the men of Israel and said to the commanders of the soldiers who had marched with him, "Come forward and put your feet on the necks of these kings." They came forward and put their feet upon their necks. [25]Then Joshua said to them, "Do not be afraid or dismayed, be firm and steadfast. This is what the LORD will do to all the enemies against whom you fight." [26]*Thereupon Joshua struck and killed them, and hanged them on five trees, where they remained hanging until evening. [27]At sunset they were removed from the trees at the command of Joshua and cast into the cave where they had hidden; over the mouth of the cave large stones were placed, which remain until this very day.

---

† 9, 26f: Later on, Saul violated the immunity of the Gibeonites, but David vindicated it; cf 2 Sm 21, 1-9.

10, 5: *Hebron . . . Eglon:* these four cities were to the south and southwest of Jerusalem.

10, 11: *Great stones from the sky:* the hailstones mentioned in the next sentence.

10, 13: *Is this not recorded:* the reference is to the preceding, poetic passage. Evidently the *Book of Jashar,* like the *Book of the Wars of the Lord* (Nm 21, 14), recounted in epic style the exploits of Israel's early heroes. *The sun halted:* though it is widely supposed that this passage describes in popular language and according to external appearances a miraculous lengthening of the day, it is equally probable that Joshua's prayer was rather for an abrupt obscuration of the sun, which would impede his enemies in their flight homeward and also prevent them from rallying their forces; this request would have been answered by the hailstorm (cf Sir 46, 5) and by a darkness relieved only twenty-four hours later, well into the next day.

✿
27: Dt 12, 5.   11: Job 38, 22.
10/1: 9, 15; 6, 21.24;   13: Sir 46, 4; Is 28, 21;
      8, 26-29.   Heb 3, 11.
   4: 9, 15.   26f: 8, 29; Dt 21, 22f.
   6: 9, 6.

Conquest of Southern Canaan

28*Makkedah, too, Joshua captured and put to the sword at that time. He fulfilled the doom on the city, on its king, and on every person in it, leaving no survivors. Thus he did to the king of Makkedah what he had done to the king of Jericho. **29**Joshua then passed on with all Israel from Makkedah to Libnah, which he attacked. **30**Libnah also, with its king, the Lord delivered into the power of Israel. He put it to the sword with every person there, leaving no survivors. Thus he did to its king what he had done to the king of Jericho. **31**Joshua next passed on with all Israel from Libnah to Lachish, where they set up a camp during the attack. **32**The Lord delivered Lachish into the power of Israel, so that on the second day Joshua captured it and put it to the sword with every person in it, just as he had done to Libnah. **33**At that time Horam, king of Gezer, came up to help Lachish, but Joshua defeated him and his people, leaving him no survivors. **34**From Lachish, Joshua passed on with all Israel to Eglon; encamping near it, they attacked it **35**and captured it the same day, putting it to the sword. He fulfilled the doom that day on every person in it, just as he had done at Lachish. **36**From Eglon, Joshua went up with all Israel to Hebron, which they attacked **37**and captured. They put it to the sword with its king, all its towns, and every person there, leaving no survivors, just as Joshua had done to Eglon. He fulfilled the doom on it and on every person there. **38**Then Joshua and all Israel turned back to Debir and attacked it, **39**capturing it with its king and all its towns. They put them to the sword and fulfilled the doom on every person there, leaving no survivors. Thus was done to Debir and its king what had been done to Hebron, as well as to Libnah and its king.

40*Joshua conquered the entire country; the mountain regions, the Negeb, the foothills, and the mountain slopes, with all their kings. He left no survivors, but fulfilled the doom on all who lived there, just as the Lord, the God of Israel, had commanded. **41**†Joshua conquered from Kadesh-barnea to Gaza, and all the land of Goshen to Gibeon. **42**All these kings and their lands Joshua captured in a single campaign, for the Lord, the God of Israel, fought for Israel. **43**Thereupon Joshua with all Israel returned to the camp at Gilgal.

Northern Confederacy

11 **1**†when Jabin, king of Hazor, learned of this, he sent a message to Jobab, king of Madon, to the king of Shimron, to the king of Achshaph, **2***and to the northern kings in the mountain regions and in the Arabah near Chinneroth, in the foothills, and in Naphath-dor to the west. **3**These were Canaanites to the east and west, Amorites, Hittites, Perizzites and Jebusites in the mountain regions, and Hivites at the foot of Hermon in the land of Mizpah. **4**They came out with all their troops, an army numerous as the sands on the seashore, and with a multitude of horses and chariots. **5**†All these kings joined forces and marched to the waters of Merom, where they encamped together to fight against Israel.

6The Lord said to Joshua, "Do not fear them, for by this time tomorrow I will stretch them slain before Israel. You must hamstring their horses and burn their chariots." **7**Joshua with his whole army came upon them at the waters of Merom in a surprise attack. **8***The Lord delivered them into the power of the Israelites, who defeated them and pursued them to Greater Sidon, to Misrephoth-maim, and eastward to the valley of Mizpeh. They struck them all down, leaving no survivors. **9**Joshua did to them as the Lord had commanded: he hamstrung their horses and burned their chariots.

Conquest of Northern Canaan

10At that time Joshua, turning back, captured Hazor and slew its king with the sword; for Hazor formerly was the chief of all those kingdoms. **11**He also fulfilled the doom by putting every person there to the sword, till none was left alive. Hazor itself he burned. **12***Joshua thus captured all those kings with their cities and put them to the sword, fulfilling the doom on them, as Moses, the servant of the Lord, had commanded. **13**However, Israel did not destroy by fire any of the cities built on raised sites, except Hazor, which Joshua burned. **14**The Israelites took all the spoil and livestock of these cities as their booty; but the people they put to the sword, until they had exterminated the last of them, leaving none alive. **15***As the Lord had commanded his servant Moses, so Moses commanded Joshua, and Joshua acted accordingly. He left nothing undone that the Lord had commanded Moses should be done.

Survey of the Conquest

16*So Joshua captured all this land: the mountain regions, the entire Negeb, all the land of Goshen, the foothills, the Arabah, as well as the mountain regions and foothills of Israel, **17***from Mount Halak that rises toward Seir as far as Baal-gad in the Lebanon valley at the foot of Mount Hermon. All their kings he captured and put to death. **18**Joshua waged war against

---

† 10, 41: *Goshen:* a town and its surrounding district at the southern end of the Judean mountains (cf 11, 16; 15, 51); not to be confused with the *land of Goshen* in northeastern Egypt (Gn 45, 10), although in the current Hebrew Bible both names are spelled the same.

11, 1ff: *Hazor, Madon, Shimron,* and *Chinneroth:* cities and their surrounding districts in eastern Galilee. *Achshaph* and *Naphath-dor:* southwest of Galilee. *The mountain regions:* in central and northern Galilee.

11, 5: *The waters of Merom:* a stream in central Galilee that flows southeast to water the fertile Arabah, or plain of Chinneroth on the western shore of the Lake of Gennesaret.

---

*

28: 6, 21.
40: Dt 20, 16f.
11/2: 12, 3; Jgs 1, 27.
  8: 13, 6.

12: Dt 7, 2; 20, 16f.
15: Dt 7, 2.
16: 10, 41; 12, 8.
17: 12, 7; Dt 7, 24.

all these kings for a long time. **19***With the exception of the Hivites who lived in Gibeon, no city made peace with the Israelites; all were taken in battle. **20***For it was the design of the LORD to encourage them to wage war against Israel, that they might be doomed to destruction and thus receive no mercy, but be exterminated, as the LORD had commanded Moses.

21*†At that time Joshua penetrated the mountain regions and exterminated the Anakim in Hebron, Debir, Anab, the entire mountain region of Judah, and the entire mountain region of Israel. Joshua fulfilled the doom on them and on their cities, **22**so that no Anakim were left in the land of the Israelites. However, some survived in Gaza, in Gath, and in Ashdod. **23*†**Thus Joshua captured the whole country, just as the LORD had foretold to Moses. Joshua gave it to Israel as their heritage, apportioning it among the tribes. And the land enjoyed peace.

Lists of Conquered Kings

12 **1†**THE kings of the land east of the Jordan, from the River Arnon to Mount Hermon, including all the eastern section of the Arabah, whom the Israelites conquered and whose lands they occupied, were: **2***First, Sihon, king of the Amorites, who lived in Heshbon. His domain extended from Aroer, which is on the bank of the Wadi Arnon, to include the wadi itself, and the land northward through half of Gilead to the Wadi Jabbok, **3***as well as the Arabah from the eastern side of the Sea of Chinnereth, as far south as the eastern side of the Salt Sea of the Arabah in the direction of Beth-jeshimoth, to a point under the slopes of Pisgah. **4***Secondly, Og, king of Bashan, a survivor of the Rephaim, who lived at Ashtaroth and Edrei. **5**He ruled over Mount Hermon, Salecah, and all Bashan as far as the boundary of the Geshurites and Maacathites, and over half of Gilead as far as the territory of Sihon, king of Heshbon. **6***After Moses, the servant of the LORD, and the Israelites conquered them, he assigned their land to the Reubenites, the Gadites, and the half-tribe of Manasseh, as their property.

7This is a list of the kings whom Joshua and the Israelites conquered west of the Jordan and whose land, from Baal-gad in the Lebanon valley to Mount Halak which rises toward Seir, Joshua apportioned to the tribes of Israel. **8**It included the mountain regions and foothills, the Arabah, the slopes, the desert, and the Negeb, belonging to the Hittites, Amorites, Canaanites, Perizzites, Hivites and Jebusites. **9***They were the kings of Jericho, Ai (which is near Bethel), **10***Jerusalem, Hebron, **11**Jarmuth, Lachish, **12***Eglon, Gezer, **13***Debir, Geder, **14**Hormah, Arad, **15***Libnah, Adullam, **16***Makkedah, Bethel, **17***Tappuah, Hepher, **18***Aphek, Lasharon, **19***Madon, Hazor, **20***Shimron, Achshaph, **21***Taanach, Megiddo, **22***Kedesh, Jokneam (at Carmel), **23***and Dor (in Naphath-dor), the foreign king at Gilgal, **24**and the king of Tirzah: thirty-one kings in all.

II: DIVISION OF THE LAND

Division of Land Commanded

13 **1***WHEN JOSHUA WAS OLD and advanced in years, the LORD said to him: "Though now you are old and advanced in years, a very large part of the land still remains to be conquered. **2†**This additional land includes all Geshur and all the districts of the Philistines **3***(from the stream adjoining Egypt to the boundary of Ekron in the north is reckoned Canaanite territory, though held by the five lords of the Philistines in Gaza, Ashdod, Ashkelon, Gath and Ekron); also where the Avvim are in the south; **4**all the land of the Canaanites from Mearah of the Sidonians to Aphek, and the boundaries of the Amorites; **5**and the Gebalite territory; and all the Lebanon on the east, from Baal-gad at the foot of Mount Hermon to Labo in the land of Hamath. **6***At the advance of the Israelites I will drive out all the Sidonian inhabitants of the mountain regions between Lebanon and Misrephoth-maim; at least include these areas in the division of the Israelite heritage, just as I have commanded you. **7**Now, therefore, apportion among the nine tribes and the half-tribe of Manasseh the land which is to be their heritage."

The Eastern Tribes

8*Now the other half of the tribe of Manasseh as well as the Reubenites and Gadites, had received their heritage which Moses, the servant of the LORD, had given them east of the Jordan: **9**from Aroer on the

---

† 11, 21ff: Most of the land assigned to the tribe of Judah was not conquered by it till the early period of the Judges. See note on Jgs 1, 1-36.

11, 23: *The land enjoyed peace:* of a limited and temporary nature. Many of the individual tribes had still to fight against the remaining Canaanites; cf 15, 13-17; 17, 12f. This verse forms the conclusion to the first part of the book. Cf note on 12, 1-24.

12, 1-24: This chapter, inserted between the two principal parts of the book (chapters 1-11 and 13-21), resembles the lists of conquered cities which are inscribed on monuments of the Egyptian and Assyrian monarchs. Perhaps it was copied here from some such public Israelite record.

13, 2: *Geshur:* not to be confused with the large Aramaean district of the same name in Bashan (vv 11-13; Dt 3, 14); here it is a region to the south of the Philistine country, since vv 2-5 list the unconquered lands along the coast from south to north; cf also 1 Sm 27, 8.

❀	
19: 9, 3.7.15.	15: 10, 29f; 15, 35.
20: Dt 2, 30; 20, 16f.	16: 8, 17; 10, 28.
21: Jos 15, 13f; Nm 13, 22;	17: 15, 34.
Dt 1, 28.	18: 15, 53.
23: 14, 1-19, 51; Nm 34,	19: 11, 1.10.
2-12.	20: 11, 1.
12/2-5: Nm 21, 21-26.33ff.	21: 17, 11.
3: 13, 20.	22: 19, 37.
4: 13, 11f.	23: 11, 2.
6: Nm 32, 33; Dt 3, 12f.	13/1: 23, 1.
9: 6, 2; 8, 23.	3: Jgs 3, 3.
10f: 10, 23.	6: 11, 8.
12: 10, 23.33.	8: 12, 6; Nm 32, 33.
13: 10, 38f; 15, 36.	

bank of the Wadi Arnon and the city in the wadi itself, through the tableland of Medeba and Dibon, [10]with the rest of the cities of Sihon, king of the Amorites, who reigned in Heshbon, to the boundary of the Ammonites; [11]also Gilead and the territory of the Geshurites and Maacathites, all Mount Hermon, and all Bashan as far as Salecah, [12]the entire kingdom in Bashan of Og, a survivor of the Rephaim, who reigned at Ashtaroth and Edrei. Though Moses conquered and occupied these territories, [13]the Israelites did not dislodge the Geshurites and Maacathites, so that Geshur and Maacath survive in the midst of Israel to this day. [14]*However, to the tribe of Levi Moses assigned no heritage since, as the LORD had promised them, the LORD, the God of Israel, is their heritage.

Reuben

[15]*What Moses gave to the Reubenite clans: [16]Their territory reached from Aroer, on the bank of the Wadi Arnon, and the city in the wadi itself, through the tableland about Medeba, [17]to include Heshbon and all its towns which are on the tableland, Dibon, Bamoth-baal, Beth-baal-meon, [18]Jahaz, Kedemoth, Mephaath, [19]Kiriathaim, Sibmah, Zereth-shahar on the knoll within the valley, [20]Beth-peor, the slopes of Pisgah, Beth-jeshimoth, [21]*and the other cities of the tableland and, generally, of the kingdom of Sihon. This Amorite king, who reigned in Heshbon, Moses had killed, with his vassals, the princes of Midian, who were settled in the land: Evi, Rekem, Zur, Hur and Reba; [22]*and among their slain followers the Israelites put to the sword also the soothsayer Balaam, son of Beor. [23]The boundary of the Reubenites was the bank of the Jordan. These cities and their villages were the heritage of the clans of the Reubenites.

Gad

[24]*What Moses gave to the Gadite clans: [25]Their territory included Jazer, all the cities of Gilead, and half the land of the Ammonites as far as Aroer, toward Rabbah [26](that is, from Heshbon to Ramath-mizpeh and Betonim, and from Mahanaim to the boundary of Lodebar); [27]and in the Jordan valley: Beth-haram, Beth-nimrah, Succoth, Zaphon, the other part of the kingdom of Sihon, king of Heshbon, with the bank of the Jordan to the southeastern tip of the Sea of Chinnereth. [28]These cities and their villages were the heritage of the clans of the Gadites.

Manasseh

[29]*What Moses gave to the clans of the half-tribe of Manasseh: [30]*Their territory included Mahanaim, all of Bashan, the entire kingdom of Og, king of Bashan, and all the villages of Jair, which are sixty cities in Bashan. [31]Half of Gilead, with Ashtaroth and Edrei, once the royal cities of Og in Bashan, fell to the descendants of Machir, son of Manasseh, for half the clans descended from Machir.

[32]These are the portions which Moses gave when he was in the plains of Moab, beyond the Jordan east of Jericho. [33]*However, Moses gave no heritage to the tribe of Levi, since the LORD himself, the God of Israel, is their heritage, as he promised.

The Western Tribes

14 [1]*HERE follow the portions which the Israelites received in the land of Canaan. Eleazar the priest, Joshua, son of Nun, and the heads of families in the tribes of the Israelites determined [2]*their heritage by lot, in accordance with the instructions the LORD had given through Moses concerning the remaining nine and a half tribes. [3]*For to two and a half tribes Moses had already given a heritage beyond the Jordan; and though the Levites were given no heritage among the tribes, [4]*the descendants of Joseph formed two tribes, Manasseh and Ephraim. The Levites themselves received no share of the land except cities to live in, with their pasture lands for the cattle and flocks.

[5]Thus, in apportioning the land, did the Israelites carry out the instructions of the LORD to Moses.

Caleb's Portion

[6]*When the Judahites came up to Joshua in Gilgal, the Kenizzite Caleb, son of Jephunneh, said to him: "You know what the LORD said to the man of God, Moses, about you and me in Kadesh-barnea. [7]*I was forty years old when the servant of the LORD, Moses, sent me from Kadesh-barnea to reconnoiter the land; and I brought back to him a conscientious report. [8]*My fellow scouts who went up with me discouraged the people, but I was completely loyal to the LORD, my God. [9]On that occasion Moses swore this oath, 'The land where you have set foot shall become your heritage and that of your descendants forever, because you have been completely loyal to the LORD, my God.' [10]*Now, as he promised, the LORD has preserved me while Israel was journeying through the desert, for the forty-five years since the LORD spoke thus to Moses; and although I am now eighty-five years old, [11]*I am still as strong today as I was the day Moses sent me forth, with no less vigor whether for war or for ordinary tasks. [12]*Give me, therefore, this mountain region which the LORD promised me that day, as you yourself heard. True, the Anakim are there, with large fortified cities, but if the LORD is with me I shall be able to drive them out, as the LORD promised." [13]*Joshua blessed Caleb, son of Jephunneh, and

---

✱   14: 14, 3f; Nm 18, 20-24.
15-31: Dt 3, 12-17.
15-23: Nm 21, 25-31; 32, 37f.
    21: Nm 21, 24; 31, 8; Dt 3, 10.
    22: Nm 31, 8.
24-28: Nm 32, 34ff.
29-31: Nm 32, 39ff.
    30: Nm 32, 41.
    33: 18, 7; Nm 18, 20.
14/1: 17, 4; 21, 1; Nm 34, 17f.
    2: Nm 26, 55; 33, 54; 34, 13.

    3: 13, 8.14.33.
    4: 21, 3-40; Gn 48, 5.
    6: Nm 14, 24.30; 32, 12; Dt 1, 36.38.
    7: Nm 14, 6-9.
    8: Nm 13, 31ff; 14, 24; 32, 12; Dt 1, 36.
  10: Nm 14, 30.
  11: Sir 46, 1ff.
  12: 11, 21.
  13: 10, 36f; 15, 13-19; 21, 11f.

gave him Hebron as his heritage. [14]Therefore Hebron remains the heritage of the Kenizzite Caleb, son of Jephunneh, to the present day, because he was completely loyal to the LORD, the God of Israel. [15]*Hebron was formerly called Kiriath-arba, for Arba, the greatest among the Anakim. And the land enjoyed peace.

Boundaries of Judah

15 [1]*THE lot for the clans of the Judahite tribe fell in the extreme south toward the boundary of Edom, the desert of Zin in the Negeb. [2]*The boundary there ran from the bay that forms the southern end of the Salt Sea, [3]southward below the pass of Akrabbim, across through Zin, up to a point south of Kadesh-barnea, across to Hezron, and up to Addar; from there, looping around Karka, [4]it crossed to Azmon and then joined the Wadi of Egypt before coming out at the sea. [This is your southern boundary.] [5]The eastern boundary was the Salt Sea as far as the mouth of the Jordan.

[6]*The northern boundary climbed from the bay where the Jordan meets the sea, up to Beth-hoglah, and ran north of Beth-arabah, up to Eben-Bohan-ben-Reuben. [7]*Thence it climbed to Debir, north of the vale of Achor, in the direction of the Gilgal that faces the pass of Adummim, on the south side of the wadi; from there it crossed to the waters of En-shemesh and emerged at En-rogel. [8]*†Climbing again to the Valley of Ben-hinnom on the southern flank of the Jebusites [that is, Jerusalem], the boundary rose to the top of the mountain at the northern end of the Valley of Rephaim, which bounds the Valley of Hinnom on the west. [9]*From the top of the mountain it ran to the fountain of waters of Nephtoah, extended to the cities of Mount Ephron, and continued to Baalah, or Kiriath-jearim. [10]From Baalah the boundary curved westward to Mount Seir and passed north of the ridge of Mount Jearim (that is, Chesalon); thence it descended to Beth-shemesh, and ran across to Timnah. [11]It then extended along the northern flank of Ekron, continued through Shikkeron, and across to Mount Baalah, thence to include Jabneel, before it came out at the sea. [12]The western boundary was the Great Sea and its coast. This was the complete boundary of the clans of the Judahites.

Conquest by Caleb

[13]*As the LORD had commanded, Joshua gave Caleb, son of Jephunneh, a portion among the Judahites, namely, Kiriath-arba (Arba was the father of Anak), that is, Hebron. [14]*And Caleb drove out from there the three Anakim, the descendants of Anak: Sheshai, Ahiman and Talmai. [15]*From there he marched up against the inhabitants of Debir, which was formerly called Kiriath-sepher. [16]Caleb said, "I will give my daughter Achsah in marriage to the one who attacks Kiriath-sepher and captures it." [17]†Othniel, son of Caleb's brother Kenaz, captured it, and so Caleb gave him his daughter Achsah in marriage. [18]On the day of her marriage to Othniel, she induced him to ask her father for some land. Then, as she alighted from the ass, Caleb asked her, "What is troubling you?" [19]She answered, "Give me an additional gift! Since you have assigned to me land in the Negeb, give me also pools of water." So he gave her the upper and the lower pools.

Cities of Judah

[20]†This is the heritage of the clans of the tribe of Judahites: [21]The cities of the tribe of the Judahites in the extreme southern district toward Edom were: Kabzeel, Eder, Jagur, [22]Kinah, Dimonah, Adadah, [23]Kedesh, Hazor and Ithnan; [24]Ziph, Telem, Bealoth, [25]Hazor-hadattah, and Kerioth-hezron (that is, Hazor); [26]Amam, Shema, Moladah, [27]Hazar-gaddah, Heshmon, Beth-pelet, [28]Hazar-shual, Beer-sheba and Biziothiah; [29]Baalah, Iim, Ezem, [30]Eltolad, Chesil, Hormah, [31]*Ziklag, Madmannah, Sansannah, [32]Lebaoth, Shilhim and En-rimmon; a total of twenty-nine cities with their villages.

[33]†In the foothills: Eshtaol, Zorah, Ashnah, [34]Zanoah, Engannim, Tappuah, Enam, [35]Jarmuth, Adullam, Socoh, Azekah, [36]Shaaraim, Adithaim, Gederah, and Gederothaim; fourteen cities and their villages. [37]Zenan, Hadashah, Migdalgad, [38]Dilean, Mizpeh, Joktheel, [39]Lachish, Bozkath, Eglon, [40]Cabbon, Lahmam, Chitlish, [41]Gederoth, Beth-dagon, Naamah and Makkedah; sixteen cities and their villages. [42]Libnah, Ether, Ashan, [43]Iphtah, Ashnah, Nezib, [44]Keilah, Achzib and Mareshah; nine cities and their villages. [45]Ekron and its towns and villages; [46]from Ekron to the sea, all the towns that lie alongside Ashdod, and their villages; [47]Ashdod and its towns and villages; Gaza and its towns and villages, as far as the Wadi of Egypt and the coast of the Great Sea.

[48]In the mountain regions: Shamir, Jattir, Socoh, [49]Dannah, Kiriath-sannah (that is, Debir), [50]Anab, Eshtemoh, Anim, [51]Goshen, Holon and Giloh; eleven

---

† 15, 8: *The Valley of Ben-hinnom:* the southern limit of Jerusalem. *Ben-hinnom* means "son of Hinnom." The place was also called *Valley of Hinnom,* in Hebrew *gē-hinnom,* whence the word "Gehenna" is derived.

15, 17-19: The story of Othniel is told again in Jgs 1, 13-15; cf also Jgs 3, 9-11.

15, 20-62: This elaborate list of the cities of Judah was probably taken from a document made originally for administrative purposes; the cities are divided into four provincial districts, some of which have further subdivisions. For similar lists of the cities of Judah, cf 19, 2-7; 1 Chr 4, 28-32; Neh 11, 25-30. This list has suffered in transmission, so that the totals given in vv 32 and 36 are not exact, and some of the names are probably misspelled; many of the cities cannot be identified.

15, 33: *In the foothills:* see note on Dt 1, 7.

❀
 15: Jgs 1, 10.   9: 18, 15.
15/1: Nm 34, 3.   13-19: Jgs 1, 10-15.
2-4: Nm 34, 3ff.   13: 14, 13ff.
 6: 18, 18f.22.   14: Nm 13, 22; Jgs 1, 20.
 7: 7, 26; 18, 16ff; 15: 10, 38.
  2 Sm 17, 17.   31: 1 Sm 27, 6.
 8: 18, 16.

cities and their villages. ⁵²Arab, Dumah, Eshan, ⁵³Janim, Beth-tappuah, Aphekah, ⁵⁴Humtah, Kiriath-arba (that is, Hebron), and Zior; nine cities and their villages. ⁵⁵Maon, Carmel, Ziph, Juttah, ⁵⁶Jezreel, Jokdeam, Zanoah, ⁵⁷Kain, Gibbeah, and Timnah; ten cities and their villages. ⁵⁸Halhul, Beth-zur, Gedor, ⁵⁹Maarath, Beth-anoth and Eltekon; six cities and their villages. Tekoa, Ephrathah (that is, Bethlehem), Peor, Etam, Kulom, Tatam, Zores, Karim, Gallim, Bether and Manoko; eleven cities and their villages. ⁶⁰*Kiriath-baal (that is, Kiriath-jearim) and Rabbah; two cities and their villages.

⁶¹†In the desert: Beth-arabah, Middin, Secacah, ⁶²Nibshan, Ir-hamelah and En-gedi; six cities and their villages. ⁶³*[But the Jebusites who lived in Jerusalem the Judahites could not drive out; so the Jebusites dwell in Jerusalem beside the Judahites to the present day.]

The Joseph Tribes

16 ¹†THE lot that fell to the Josephites extended from the Jordan at Jericho to the waters of Jericho east of the desert; then the boundary went up from Jericho to the heights at Bethel. ²Leaving Bethel for Luz, it crossed the ridge to the border of the Archites at Ataroth, ³*and descended westward to the border of the Japhletites, to that of the Lower Beth-horon, and to Gezer, ending thence at the sea.

Ephraim

⁴Within the heritage of Manasseh and Ephraim, sons of Joseph, ⁵*†the dividing line for the heritage of the clans of the Ephraimites ran from east of Ataroth-addar to Upper Beth-horon ⁶*and thence to the sea. From Michmethath on the north, their boundary curved eastward around Taanath-shiloh, and continued east of it to Janoah; ⁷from there it descended to Ataroth and Naarah, and skirting Jericho, it ended at the Jordan. ⁸*From Tappuah the boundary ran westward to the Wadi Kanah and ended at the sea. This was the heritage of the clans of the Ephraimites, ⁹*including the villages that belonged to each city set aside for the Ephraimites within the territory of the Manassehites. ¹⁰*But they did not drive out the Canaanites living in Gezer, who live on within Ephraim to the present day, though they have been impressed as laborers.

Manasseh

17 ¹*NOW as for the lot that fell to the tribe of Manasseh as the first-born of Joseph: since his eldest son, Machir, the father of Gilead, was a warrior, who had already obtained Gilead and Bashan, ²*the allotment was now made to the other descendants of Manasseh, the clans of Abiezer, Helek, Asriel, Shechem, Hepher and Shemida, the other male children of Manasseh, son of Joseph.

³*Furthermore, Zelophehad, son of Hepher, son of Gilead, son of Machir, son of Manasseh, had had no sons, but only daughters, whose names were Mahlah, Noah, Hoglah, Milcah, and Tirzah. ⁴*These presented themselves to Eleazar the priest, to Joshua, son of Nun, and to the princes, saying, "The LORD commanded Moses to give us a heritage among our kinsmen." So in obedience to the command of the LORD a heritage was given to each of them among their father's kinsmen. ⁵*Thus ten shares fell to Manasseh apart from the land of Gilead and Bashan beyond the Jordan, ⁶since these female descendants of Manasseh received each a portion among his sons. The land of Gilead fell to the rest of the Manassehites.

⁷†Manasseh bordered on Asher. From Michmethath near Shechem, another boundary ran southward to include the natives of En-Tappuah, ⁸because the district of Tappuah belonged to Manasseh, although Tappuah itself was an Ephraimite city on the border of Manasseh. ⁹*This same boundary continued down to the Wadi Kanah. The cities that belonged to Ephraim from among the cities in Manasseh were those to the south of that wadi; thus the territory of Manasseh ran north of the wadi and ended at the sea. ¹⁰The land on the south belonged to Ephraim and that on the north to Manasseh; with the sea as their common boundary, they reached Asher on the north and Issachar on the east.

¹¹*Moreover, in Issachar and in Asher Manasseh was awarded Beth-shean and its towns, Ibleam and its towns, Dor and its towns and the natives there, Endor and its towns and natives, Taanach and its towns and natives, and Megiddo and its towns and natives [the third is Naphathdor]. ¹²Since the Manassehites could not conquer these cities, the Canaanites persisted in

---

† 15, 61: *In the desert:* in the Jordan rift near the Dead Sea.

16, 1—17, 18: The boundaries and cities of Judah, the most important tribe, having been given, the land of the next most important group, the two Josephite tribes of Ephraim and Manasseh, is now described, though it was separated from Judah by the territories of Benjamin (18, 11-20) and Dan (19, 40-48).

16, 1-3: This line formed the southern boundary of Ephraim and the northern boundaries of Benjamin and of Dan.

16, 5: *The dividing line:* separating Ephraim from Manasseh. Ephraim's northern border (v 5) is given in an east-to-west direction; its eastern border (v 6f) in a north-to-south direction.

17, 7: *Manasseh bordered on Asher:* only at the extreme northwestern section of Manasseh's territory. The boundary given in the following sentences (vv 7-10) is a more detailed description of the one already mentioned in 16, 5ff, as separating Manasseh from Ephraim.

✿   60: 18, 14.
       63: Jgs 1, 21; 2 Sm 5, 6.
   16/3: 10, 10.33.
       5: 18, 13.
       6: 17, 7.
       8: 17, 7.
       9: 17, 9.
     10: Jgs 1, 29.
   17/1: Gn 41, 51; 46, 20; 48, 18; 50, 23; Nm 26, 29; Dt 3, 13.15.

       2: Nm 26, 29-32.
       3: Nm 26, 33; 27, 1; 36, 2.
       4: Nm 27, 6f; 36, 2.
       5: 13, 30f.
       9: 16, 8f.
     11: 1 Chr 7, 29.
   11ff: Jgs 1, 27f.

this region. [13]When the Israelites grew stronger they impressed the Canaanites as laborers, but they did not drive them out.

Protest of Joseph Tribes

[14]*The descendants of Joseph said to Joshua, "Why have you given us only one lot and one share as our heritage? Our people are too many, because of the extent to which the LORD has blessed us." [15]Joshua answered them, "If you are too many, go up to the forest and clear out a place for yourselves there in the land of the Perizzites and Rephaim, since the mountain regions of Ephraim are so narrow." [16]*For the Josephites said, "Our mountain regions are not enough for us; on the other hand, the Canaanites living in the valley region all have iron chariots, in particular those in Beth-shean and its towns, [17]and those in the valley of Jezreel." Joshua therefore said to Ephraim and Manasseh, the house of Joseph, "You are a numerous people and very strong. You shall have not merely one share, [18]for the mountain region which is now forest shall be yours when you clear it. Its adjacent land shall also be yours if, despite their strength and iron chariots, you drive out the Canaanites."

18 [1]*AFTER they had subdued the land, the whole community of the Israelites assembled at Shiloh, where they set up the meeting tent.

The Seven Remaining Portions

[2]Seven tribes among the Israelites had not yet received their heritage. [3]Joshua therefore said to the Israelites, "How much longer will you put off taking steps to possess the land which the LORD, the God of your fathers, has given you? [4]Choose three men from each of your tribes; I will commission them to begin a survey of the land, which they shall describe for purposes of inheritance. When they return to me [5]*you shall divide it into seven parts. Judah is to retain its territory in the south, and the house of Joseph its territory in the north. [6]You shall bring here to me the description of the land in seven sections. I will then cast lots for you here before the LORD, our God. [7]*For the Levites have no share among you, because the priesthood of the LORD is their heritage; while Gad, Reuben, and the half-tribe of Manasseh have already received the heritage east of the Jordan which Moses, the servant of the LORD, gave them."

[8]When those who were to map out the land were ready for the journey, Joshua instructed them to survey the land, prepare a description of it, and return to him; then he would cast lots for them there before the LORD in Shiloh. [9]So they went through the land, listed its cities in writing in seven sections, and returned to Joshua in the camp at Shiloh. [10]Joshua then divided up the land for the Israelites into their separate shares, casting lots for them before the LORD in Shiloh.

Benjamin

[11]One lot fell to the clans of the tribe of Benjaminites. The territory allotted them lay between the descendants of Judah and those of Joseph. [12]*†Their northern boundary began at the Jordan and went over the northern flank of Jericho, up westward into the mountains, till it reached the desert of Beth-aven. [13]*From there it crossed over to the southern flank of Luz (that is, Bethel). Then it ran down to Ataroth-addar, on the mountaintop south of Lower Beth-horon. [14]For the western border, the boundary line swung south from the mountaintop opposite Beth-horon till it reached Kiriath-baal (that is, Kiriath-jearim), which city belonged to the Judahites. This was the western boundary. [15]The southern boundary began at the limits of Kiriath-jearim and projected to the spring at Nephtoah. [16]*It went down to the edge of the mountain on the north of the Valley of Rephaim, where it faces the Valley of Ben-hinnom; and continuing down the Valley of Hinnom along the southern flank of the Jebusites, reached En-rogel. [17]Inclining to the north, it extended to En-shemesh, and thence to Geliloth, opposite the pass of Adummim. Then it dropped to Eben-Bohan-ben-Reuben, [18]*across the northern flank of the Arabah overlook, down into the Arabah. [19]From there the boundary continued across the northern flank of Beth-hoglah and extended to the northern tip of the Salt Sea, at the southern end of the Jordan. This was the southern boundary. [20]The Jordan bounded it on the east. This was how the heritage of the clans of the Benjaminites was bounded on all sides.

[21]Now the cities belonging to the clans of the tribe of the Benjaminites were: Jericho, Beth-hoglah, Emek-keziz, [22]Beth-arabah, Zemaraim, Bethel, [23]Avvim, Parah, Ophrah, [24]Chephar-ammoni, Ophni and Geba; twelve cities and their villages. [25]Also Gibeon, Ramah, Beeroth, [26]Mizpeh, Chephirah, Mozah, [27]Rekem, Irpeel, Taralah, [28]Zela, Haeleph, the Jebusite city (that is, Jerusalem), Gibeah and Kiriath; fourteen cities and their villages. This was the heritage of the clans of Benjaminites.

Simeon

19 [1]THE second lot fell to Simeon. The heritage of the clans of the tribe of Simeonites lay within that of the Judahites. [2]*For their heritage they received Beer-sheba, Shema, Moladah, [3]Hazar-shual, Balah, Ezem, [4]Eltolad, Bethul, Hormah, [5]Ziklag, Bethmar-caboth, Hazar-susah, [6]Beth-lebaoth and Sharuhen; thirteen cities and their villages. [7]Also En-rimmon, Ether and Ashan; four cities and their

---

✣
14: 16, 4; Gn 48, 19f.22.   12: 16, 1.
16: Jgs 6, 33.   13: 16, 2f.5; Gn 28, 19.
18/1: 19, 51.   16: 15, 7f.
5: 15, 1-17, 18.   18: 15, 6.
7: 13, 8.33.   19/2-8: 1 Chr 4, 28-33.

---

† 18, 12-20: Benjamin's *northern boundary* (vv 12f) corresponded to part of the southern boundary of Ephraim (16, 1f). Their *western border* (v 14) was the eastern border of Dan (cf 19, 40-47). Their *southern boundary* (vv 15-19) corresponded to part of the northern boundary of Judah (15, 6-9).

villages, [8]besides all the villages around these cities as far as Baalath-beer (that is, Ramoth-negeb). This was the heritage of the clans of the tribe of the Simeonites. [9]This heritage of the Simeonites was within the confines of the Judahites; for since the portion of the latter was too large for them, the Simeonites obtained their heritage within it.

Zebulun

[10][†]The third lot fell to the clans of the Zebulunites. The limit of their heritage was at Sarid. [11]Their boundary went up west . . . and through Mareal, reaching Dabbesheth and the wadi that is near Jokneam. [12]From Sarid eastward it ran to the district of Chisloth-tabor, on to Daberath, and up to Japhia. [13]From there it continued eastward to Gath-hepher and to Eth-kazin, extended to Rimmon, and turned to Neah. [14]Skirting north of Hannathon, the boundary ended at the valley of Iphtahel. [15]Thus, with Kattath, Nahalal, Shimron, Idalah and Bethlehem, there were twelve cities and their villages [16]to comprise the heritage of the clans of the Zebulunites.

Issachar

[17][†]The fourth lot fell to Issachar. The territory of the clans of the Issacharites [18]included Jezreel, Chesulloth, Shunem, [19]Hapharaim, Shion, Anaharath, [20]Rabbith, Kishion, Ebez, [21]Remeth, En-gannim, En-haddah and Beth-pazzez. [22]The boundary reached Tabor, Shahazumah and Beth-shemesh, ending at the Jordan. These sixteen cities and their villages [23]were the heritage of the clans of the Issacharites.

Asher

[24][†]The fifth lot fell to the clans of the tribe of the Asherites. [25]Their territory included Helkath, Hali, Beten, Achshaph, [26]Allammelech, Amad and Mishal, and reached Carmel on the west, and Shihor-libnath. [27]In the other direction, it ran eastward of Beth-dagon, reached Zebulun and the valley of Iphtahel; then north of Beth-emek and Neiel, it extended to Cabul, [28][*]Mishal, Abdon, Rehob, Hammon and Kanah, near Greater Sidon. [29]Then the boundary turned back to Ramah and to the fortress city of Tyre; thence it cut back to Hosah and ended at the sea. Thus, with Mahalab, Achzib, [30]Ummah, Acco, Aphek and Rehob, there were twenty-two cities and their villages [31]to comprise the heritage of the clans of the tribe of the Asherites.

Naphtali

[32][†]The sixth lot fell to the Naphtalites. The boundary of the clans of the Naphtalites [33]extended from Heleph, from the oak at Zaanannim to Lakkum, including Adami-nekeb and Jabneel, and ended at the Jordan. [34]In the opposite direction, westerly, it ran through Aznoth-tabor and from there extended to Hukkok; it touched Zebulun on the south, Asher on the west, and the Jordan on the east. [35]The fortified cities were Ziddim, Zer, Hammath, Rakkath, Chinnereth, [36]Adamah, Ramah, Hazor, [37]Kedesh, Edrei, En-hazor, [38][*]Yiron, Migdal-el, Horem, Beth-anath and Beth-shemesh; nineteen cities and their villages, [39]to comprise the heritage of the clans of the tribe of the Naphtalites.

Dan

[40][†]The seventh lot fell to the clans of the tribe of Danites. [41]Their heritage was the territory of Zorah, Eshtaol, Ir-shemesh, [42][*]Sha-alabbin, Aijalon, Ithlah, [43]Elon, Timnah, Ekron, [44]Eltekoh, Gibbethon, Baalath, [45]Jehud, Bene-berak, Gath-rimmon, [46]Mejarkon and Rakkon, with the coast at Joppa. [47][*][†]But the territory of the Danites was too small for them; so the Danites marched up and attacked Leshem, which they captured and put to the sword. Once they had taken possession of Leshem, they renamed the settlement after their ancestor Dan. [48]These cities and their villages were the heritage of the clans of the tribe of the Danites.

Joshua's City

[49]When the last of them had received the portions of the land they were to inherit, the Israelites assigned a heritage in their midst to Joshua, son of Nun. [50][*]In obedience to the command of the Lord, they gave him the city which he requested, Timnah-serah in the mountain region of Ephraim. He rebuilt the city and made it his home.

[51]These are the final portions into which Eleazar the priest, Joshua, son of Nun, and the heads of families in the tribes of the Israelites divided the land by lot in

---

28f: Jgs 1, 31.   47: Jgs 18, 27-29.
38: Jgs 1, 33.   50: 24, 30; Jgs 2, 9.
42: Jgs 1, 35.

[†] 19, 10-16: Zebulun's territory was in the central section of the Plain of Esdraelon and of southern Galilee; it was bounded on the south by Manasseh, on the southeast by Issachar, on the northeast and north by Naphtali, and on the west by Asher. The site of the later city of Nazareth was within its borders. *Bethlehem* of Zebulun was, of course, distinct from the city of the same name in Judah. *Twelve cities:* apparently seven of the names are missing from v 15, unless some of the places mentioned in vv 12-14 are to be included in the number.

19, 17-23: Issachar's land was on the eastern watershed of the Plain of Esdraelon, but also included the southeastern end of the Galilean mountains. It was surrounded by Manasseh on the south and east, by Naphtali on the north, and by Zebulun on the west. *Jezreel* (v 18) dominated the plain to which it gave its name, the later form of which was Esdraelon.

19, 24-31: Asher inherited the western slope of the Galilean hills as far as the sea, with Manasseh to the south, Zebulun and Naphtali to the east, and Phoenicia to the north.

19, 32-39: Naphtali received eastern Galilee; Asher was to the west and Zebulun and Issachar were to the south, while the upper Jordan and Mount Hermon formed the eastern border. Part of the tribe of Dan later on occupied the northern extremity of Naphtali's lands, at the sources of the Jordan (v 47).

19, 40-46: The original territory of Dan was a small enclave between Judah, Benjamin, Ephraim and the Philistines.

19, 47: *Leshem:* called *Laish* in Jgs 18, where the story of the migration of the Danites is told at greater length.

the presence of the LORD, at the door of the meeting tent in Shiloh.

Cities of Asylum

20 [1]†THE LORD said to Joshua: [2]*"Tell the Israelites to designate the cities of which I spoke to them through Moses, [3]to which one guilty of accidental and unintended homicide may flee for asylum from the avenger of blood. [4]To one of these cities the killer shall flee, and standing at the entrance of the city gate, he shall plead his case before the elders, who must receive him and assign him a place in which to live among them. [5]Though the avenger of blood pursues him, they are not to deliver up the homicide who slew his fellow man unintentionally and not out of previous hatred. [6]*Once he has stood judgment before the community, he shall live on in that city till the death of the high priest who is in office at the time. Then the killer may go back home to his own city from which he fled."

List of Cities

[7]*So they set apart Kedesh in Galilee in the mountain region of Naphtali, Shechem in the mountain region of Ephraim, and Kiriath-arba (that is, Hebron) in the mountain region of Judah. [8]*And beyond the Jordan east of Jericho they designated Bezer on the open tableland in the tribe of Reuben, Ramoth in Gilead in the tribe of Gad, and Golan in Bashan in the tribe of Manasseh. [9]*These were the designated cities to which any Israelite or stranger living among them who had killed a person accidentally might flee to escape death at the hand of the avenger of blood, until he could appear before the community.

Levitical Cities

21 [1]*†THE heads of the Levite families came up to Eleazar the priest, to Joshua, son of Nun, and to the heads of families of the other tribes of the Israelites [2]*at Shiloh in the land of Canaan, and said to them, "The LORD commanded, through Moses, that cities be given us to dwell in, with pasture lands for our livestock." [3]Out of their own heritage, in obedience to this command of the LORD, the Israelites gave the Levites the following cities with their pasture lands.

[4]When the first lot among the Levites fell to the clans of the Kohathites, the descendants of Aaron the priest obtained thirteen cities by lot from the tribes of Judah, Simeon and Benjamin. [5]The rest of the Kohathites obtained ten cities by lot from the clans of the tribe of Ephraim, from the tribe of Dan, and from the half-tribe of Manasseh. [6]The Gershonites obtained thirteen cities by lot from the clans of the tribe of Issachar, from the tribe of Asher, from the tribe of Naphtali, and from the half-tribe of Manasseh. [7]The clans of the Merarites obtained twelve cities from the tribes of Reuben, Gad and Zebulun. [8]*These cities with their pasture lands the Israelites allotted to the Levites in obedience to the LORD's command through Moses.

Cities of the Priests

[9]*From the tribes of the Judahites and Simeonites they designated the following cities, [10]and assigned them to the descendants of Aaron in the Kohathite clan of the Levites, since the first lot fell to them: [11]first, Kiriath-arba (Arba was the father of Anak), that is, Hebron, in the mountain region of Judah, with the adjacent pasture lands, [12]*although the open country and villages belonging to the city had been given to Caleb, son of Jephunneh, as his property. [13]Thus to the descendants of Aaron the priest were given the city of asylum for homicides at Hebron, with its pasture lands; also, Libnah with its pasture lands, [14]Jattir with its pasture lands, Eshtemoa with its pasture lands, [15]Holon with its pasture lands, Debir with its pasture lands, [16]Ashan with its pasture lands, Juttah with its pasture lands, and Beth-shemesh with its pasture lands: nine cities from the two tribes mentioned. [17]From the tribe of Benjamin they obtained the four cities of Gibeon with its pasture lands, Geba with its pasture lands, [18]*Anathoth with its pasture lands, and Almon with its pasture lands. [19]These cities which with their pasture lands belonged to the priestly descendants of Aaron, were thirteen in all.

Cities of the Other Kohathites

[20]*The rest of the Kohathite clans among the Levites obtained by lot, from the tribe of Ephraim, four cities. [21]They were assigned, with its pasture lands, the city of asylum for homicides at Shechem in the mountain region of Ephraim; also Gezer with its pasture lands, [22]Kibzaim with its pasture lands, and Beth-horon with its pasture lands. [23]From the tribe of Dan they obtained the four cities of Elteke with its pasture lands, Gibbethon with its pasture lands. [24]Aijalon with its pasture lands, and Gath-rimmon with its pasture lands; [25]and from the half-tribe of Manasseh the two cities of Taanach with its pasture lands and Ibleam with its pasture lands. [26]These cities which with their pasture lands belonged to the rest of the Kohathite clans were ten in all.

---

† 20, 1-9: The laws concerning the cities of refuge are given in Nm 35, 9-28; Dt 19, 1-13; see notes on Nm 35, 16-25; Dt 19, 2.

21, 1: The order to establish special cities for the Levites is given in Nm 35, 1-8. The forty-eight cities listed here were hardly the exclusive possession of the Levites; at least the more important of them, such as Hebron, Shechem and Ramoth in Gilead, were certainly peopled for the most part by the tribe in whose territory they were situated. But in all these cities the Levites had special property rights which they did not possess in other cities; cf Lv 25, 32ff.

20/2: Ex 21, 13; Nm 35, 10-14; Dt 4, 41-43; 19, 2-9.
6: Nm 35, 12.24f.
7: 15, 13; 19, 37; 21, 21.
8: 21, 27.36f.
9: Nm 35, 15.
21/1: Ex 6, 16-19; Nm 3, 17-20.
2: Nm 35, 2.
8: Nm 35, 2.
9-19: 1 Chr 6, 54-60.
12: 14, 14; 15, 13.
18: Jer 1, 1.
20-26: 1 Chr 6, 66-70.

Cities of the Gershonites

27* The Gershonite clan of the Levites received from the half-tribe of Manasseh two cities: the city of asylum for homicides at Golan, with its pasture lands; and also Beth-ashtaroth with its pasture lands. **28**From the tribe of Issachar they obtained the four cities of Kishion with its pasture lands, Daberath with its pasture lands, **29**Jarmuth with its pasture lands, and En-gannim with its pasture lands; **30**from the tribe of Asher, the four cities of Mishal with its pasture lands, Abdon with its pasture lands, **31**Helkath with its pasture lands, and Rehob with its pasture lands; **32**and from the tribe of Naphtali, three cities: the city of asylum for homicides at Kedesh in Galilee, with its pasture lands; also Hammath with its pasture lands, and Rakkath with its pasture lands. **33**These cities which with their pasture lands belonged to the Gershonite clans were thirteen in all.

Cities of the Merarites

34* The Merarite clans, the last of the Levites, received from the tribe of Zebulun the four cities of Jokneam with its pasture lands, Kartah with its pasture lands, **35**Rimmon with its pasture lands, and Nahalal with its pasture lands; **36**also, across the Jordan, from the tribe of Reuben, four cities: the city of asylum for homicides at Bezer with its pasture lands, Jahaz with its pasture lands, **37**Kedemoth with its pasture lands, and Mephaath with its pasture lands; **38**and from the tribe of Gad a total of four cities: the city of asylum for homicides at Ramoth in Gilead with its pasture lands, also Mahanaim with its pasture lands, **39**Heshbon with its pasture lands, and Jazer with its pasture lands. **40**The cities which were allotted to the Merarite clans, the last of the Levites, were therefore twelve in all.

41* Thus the total number of cities within the territory of the Israelites which, with their pasture lands, belonged to the Levites, was forty-eight. **42**With each and every one of these cities went the pasture lands round about it.

43* And so the LORD gave Israel all the land he had sworn to their fathers he would give them. Once they had conquered and occupied it, **44**the LORD gave them peace on every side, just as he had promised their fathers. Not one of their enemies could withstand them; the LORD brought all their enemies under their power. **45***Not a single promise that the LORD made to the house of Israel was broken; every one was fulfilled.

III: RETURN OF THE TRANSJORDAN TRIBES AND JOSHUA'S FAREWELL

The Eastern Tribes Dismissed

22 **1**AT THAT TIME Joshua summoned the Reubenites, the Gadites, and the half-tribe of Manasseh **2***and said to them: "You have done all that Moses, the servant of the LORD, commanded you, and have obeyed every command I gave you. **3**For many years now you have not once abandoned your kinsmen, but have faithfully carried out the commands of the LORD, your God. **4***Since, therefore, the LORD, your God, has settled your kinsmen as he promised them, you may now return to your tents beyond the Jordan; to your own land, which Moses, the servant of the LORD, gave you. **5***But be very careful to observe the precept and law which Moses, the servant of the LORD, enjoined upon you: love the LORD, your God; follow him faithfully; keep his commandments; remain loyal to him; and serve him with your whole heart and soul." **6**Joshua then blessed them and sent them away to their own tents.

7* (For, to half the tribe of Manasseh Moses had assigned land in Bashan; and to the other half Joshua had given a portion along with their kinsmen west of the Jordan.) What Joshua said to them when he sent them off to their tents with his blessing was, **8***"Now that you are returning to your own tents with great wealth, with very numerous livestock, with silver, gold, bronze and iron, and with a very large supply of clothing, divide these spoils of your enemies with your kinsmen there." **9***So the Reubenites, the Gadites, and the half-tribe of Manasseh left the other Israelites at Shiloh in the land of Canaan and returned to the land of Gilead, their own property, which they had received according to the LORD's command through Moses.

The Altar beside the Jordan

10When the Reubenites, the Gadites, and the half-tribe of Manasseh came to the region of the Jordan in the land of Canaan, they built there at the Jordan a conspicuously large altar. **11***†The other Israelites heard the report that the Reubenites, the Gadites, and the half-tribe of Manasseh had built an altar in the region of the Jordan facing the land of Canaan, across from them, **12†**and therefore they assembled their whole community at Shiloh to declare war on them.

27-33: 1 Chr 6, 71-76.
34-38: 1 Chr 6, 77-81.
41: Nm 35, 7.
43: Gn 12, 7; 13, 15; 15, 18; 26, 3; 28, 4.13.
45: 23, 14f.
22/2: 1, 16f; Nm 32, 20ff; Dt 3, 18ff.
4: 1, 13; 13, 8; Nm 32, 33.
5: Dt 6, 5f.17; 10, 12; 11, 1.13.22.
7: 17, 5.
8: Nm 31, 27.
9: 18, 1; Nm 32, 1.26.29.
11: Dt 13, 13ff.

† 22, 11: *In the region of the Jordan facing the land of Canaan:* on the eastern side of the Jordan valley. The river itself formed the boundary between these eastern tribes and the rest of the tribes who lived in what was formerly Canaan—though the term *Canaan* could also be used of both sides of the Jordan valley (cf v 10). The Transjordan tribes naturally built their altar in their own territory.

22, 12: *To declare war on them:* the western Israelites considered this altar, which seemed to violate the customary unity of the sanctuary (cf Lv 17, 1-9; Dt 12, 4-14), as a sign of seces-

Accusation of the Western Tribes

13* First, however, they sent to the Reubenites, the Gadites, and the half-tribe of Manasseh in the land of Gilead an embassy consisting of Phinehas, son of Eleazar the priest, **14** and ten princes, one from every tribe of Israel, each one being both prince and military leader of his ancestral house. **15** When these came to the Reubenites, the Gadites, and the half-tribe of Manasseh in the land of Gilead, they said to them: **16*** "The whole community of the LORD sends this message: What act of treachery is this you have committed against the God of Israel? You have seceded from the LORD this day, and rebelled against him by building an altar of your own! **17*** For the sin of Peor, a plague came upon the community of the LORD. **18** We are still not free of that; must you now add to it? You are rebelling against the LORD today and by tomorrow he will be angry with the whole community of Israel! **19*†** If you consider the land you now possess unclean, cross over to the land the LORD possesses, where the Dwelling of the LORD stands, and share that with us. But do not rebel against the LORD, nor involve us in rebellion, by building an altar of your own in addition to the altar of the LORD, our God. **20*†** When Achan, son of Zerah, violated the ban, did not wrath fall upon the entire community of Israel? Though he was but a single man, he did not perish alone for his guilt!"

Reply of the Eastern Tribes

21 The Reubenites, the Gadites, and the half-tribe of Manasseh replied to the military leaders of the Israelites: "The LORD is the God of gods. **22†** The LORD, the God of gods, knows and Israel shall know. If now we have acted out of rebellion or treachery against the LORD, our God, **23** and if we have built an altar of our own to secede from the LORD, or to offer holocausts, grain offerings or peace offerings upon it, the LORD himself will exact the penalty. **24** We did it rather out of our anxious concern lest in the future your children should say to our children: 'What have you to do with the LORD, the God of Israel? **25** For the LORD has placed the Jordan as a boundary between you and us. You descendants of Reuben and Gad have no share in the LORD.' Thus your children would prevent ours from revering the LORD. **26** So we decided to guard our interests by building this altar of our own: not for holocausts or for sacrifices, **27*** but as evidence for you on behalf of ourselves and our descendants, that we have the right to worship the LORD in his presence with our holocausts, sacrifices, and peace offerings. Now in the future your children cannot say to our children, 'You have no share in the LORD.' **28†** Our thought was, that if in the future they should speak thus to us or to our descendants, we could answer: 'Look at the model of the altar of the LORD which our fathers made, not for holocausts or for sacrifices, but to witness between you and us.' **29** Far be it from us to rebel against the LORD or to secede now from the LORD by building an altar for holocaust, grain offering, or sacrifice in addition to the altar of the LORD, our God, which stands before his Dwelling."

30 When Phinehas the priest and the princes of the community, the military leaders of the Israelites, heard what the Reubenites, the Gadites and the Manassehites had to say, they were satisfied. **31** Phinehas, son of Eleazar the priest, said to the Reubenites, the Gadites and the Manassehites, "Now we know that the LORD is with us. Since you have not committed this act of treachery against the LORD, you have kept the Israelites free from punishment by the LORD."

32 Phinehas, son of Eleazar the priest, and the princes returned from the Reubenites and the Gadites in the land of Gilead to the Israelites in the land of Canaan, and reported the matter to them. **33** The report satisfied the Israelites, who blessed God and decided against declaring war on the Reubenites and Gadites or ravaging the land they occupied.

34† The Reubenites and the Gadites gave the altar its name as a witness among them that the LORD is God.

Joshua's Final Plea

23 **1*** MANY years later, after the LORD had given the Israelites rest from all their enemies round about them, and when Joshua was old and advanced in years, **2** he summoned all Israel (including their elders, leaders, judges and officers) and said to them: "I am old and advanced in years. **3** You have seen all that the LORD, your God, has done for you against all these nations; for it has been the LORD, your God, himself who fought for you. **4*** Bear in mind that I have apportioned among your tribes as their heritage the nations that survive [as well as those I destroyed] between the Jordan and the Great Sea in the west. **5** The LORD, your God, will drive them out and dislodge them at your approach, so that you will take possession of their land as the LORD, your

---

† sion and dangerous to national unity. The motives for the war were political as well as religious.

22, 19: *Unclean:* not sanctified by the Dwelling of the Lord.

22, 20: *Achan . . . did not perish alone:* his guilt caused the failure of the first attack on Ai (7, 4-23); this fact is adduced as an argument for the solidarity and mutual responsibility of all the Israelites.

22, 22: *The Lord, the God of gods:* the Hebrew, which cannot be adequately rendered in English here, adds to the divine name Yahweh ("the LORD") two synonymous words for "God," *el* and *elohim.* The repetition of these three sacred words adds force to the protestations of fidelity and innocence.

22, 28: *To witness:* far from being destined to form a rival sanctuary, the *model of the altar* was intended by the eastern tribes solely as a means of teaching their children to be faithful to the one true sanctuary beyond the Jordan.

22, 34: The name of this altar was the Hebrew word for "witness," *ᵉed.*

13: Ex 6, 25; Sir 45, 28.
16: Lv 17, 8f.
17: Nm 25, 3f; Dt 4, 3.
19: 18, 1.
20: 7, 1.5.
27: Dt 12, 5f.17f.
23/1: 13, 1.
4: 13, 2-7; 14, 2; 18, 10; Ps 78, 55.

God, promised you. **6***Therefore strive hard to observe and carry out all that is written in the book of the law of Moses, not straying from it in any way, **7***or mingling with these nations while they survive among you. You must not invoke their gods, or swear by them, or serve them, or worship them, **8**but you must remain loyal to the LORD, your God, as you have been to this day. **9**At your approach the LORD has driven out large and strong nations, and to this day no one has withstood you. **10***One of you puts to flight a thousand, because it is the LORD, your God, himself who fights for you, as he promised you. **11**Take great care, however, to love the LORD, your God. **12***For if you ever abandon him and ally yourselves with the remnant of these nations while they survive among you, by intermarrying and intermingling with them, **13**know for certain that the LORD, your God, will no longer drive these nations out of your way. Instead they will be a snare and a trap for you, a scourge for your sides and thorns for your eyes, until you perish from this good land which the LORD, your God, has given you.

14†"Today, as you see, I am going the way of all men. So now acknowledge with your whole heart and soul that not one of all the promises the LORD, your God, made to you has remained unfulfilled. Every promise has been fulfilled for you, with not one single exception. **15*†**But just as every promise the LORD, your God, made to you has been fulfilled for you, so will he fulfill every threat, even so far as to exterminate you from this good land which the LORD, your God, has given you. **16**If you transgress the covenant of the LORD, your God, which he enjoined on you, serve other gods and worship them, the anger of the LORD will flare up against you and you will quickly perish from the good land which he has given you."

Reminder of the Divine Goodness

24 **1**JOSHUA gathered together all the tribes of Israel at Shechem, summoning their elders, their leaders, their judges and their officers. When they stood in ranks before God, **2*†**Joshua addressed all the people: "Thus says the LORD, the God of Israel: In times past your fathers, down to Terah, father of Abraham and Nahor, dwelt beyond the River and served other gods. **3***But I brought your father Abraham from the region beyond the River and led him through the entire land of Canaan. I made his descendants numerous, and gave him Isaac. **4***To Isaac I gave Jacob and Esau. To Esau I assigned the mountain region of Seir in which to settle, while Jacob and his children went down to Egypt.

5*"Then I sent Moses and Aaron, and smote Egypt with the prodigies which I wrought in her midst. **6***Afterward I led you out of Egypt, and when you reached the sea, the Egyptians pursued your fathers to the Red Sea with chariots and horsemen. **7***Because they cried out to the LORD, he put darkness between your people and the Egyptians, upon whom he brought the sea so that it engulfed them. After you witnessed what I did to Egypt, and dwelt a long time in the desert, **8***I brought you into the land of the Amorites who lived east of the Jordan. They fought against you, but I delivered them into your power. You took possession of their land, and I destroyed them [the two kings of the Amorites] before you. **9***Then Balak, son of Zippor, king of Moab, prepared to war against Israel. He summoned Balaam, son of Beor, to curse you; **10***but I would not listen to Balaam. On the contrary, he had to bless you, and I saved you from him. **11***Once you crossed the Jordan and came to Jericho, the men of Jericho fought against you, but I delivered them also into your power. **12*†**And I sent the hornets ahead of you which drove them [the Amorites, Perizzites, Canaanites, Hittites, Girgashites, Hivites and Jebusites] out of your way; it was not your sword or your bow.

13*"I gave you a land which you had not tilled and cities which you had not built, to dwell in; you have eaten of vineyards and olive groves which you did not plant.

14*"Now, therefore, fear the LORD and serve him completely and sincerely. Cast out the gods your fathers served beyond the River and in Egypt, and serve the LORD. **15*†**If it does not please you to serve the LORD, decide today whom you will serve, the gods your fathers served beyond the River or the gods of the Amorites in whose country you are dwelling. As for me and my household, we will serve the LORD."

Renewal of the Covenant

16But the people answered, "Far be it from us to forsake the LORD for the service of other gods. **17**For it was the LORD, our God, who brought us and our fathers up out of the land of Egypt, out of a state of slavery. He performed those great miracles before our very eyes and protected us along our entire journey and among all the peoples through whom we passed. **18**At our approach the LORD drove out [all the peoples, including] the Amorites who dwelt in the land. Therefore we also will serve the LORD, for he is our God."

✦
   6: 1, 7.
   7: Dt 7, 2ff.
  10: Ex 14, 14; Lv 26, 8;
     Dt 3, 22.
  12: Ex 34, 16; Dt 7, 3.
  15: Lv 26, 14-39; Dt 28,
     15-68.
24/2: Gn 11, 26.31; 31, 53.
   3: Gn 12, 1; Acts 7, 2-4.
   4: Gn 25, 24ff; 36, 8; 46,
     1.6; Acts 7, 15.
   5: Ex 3, 10; 7, 14—12, 30.

   6: Ex 12, 37.51; 14, 9.
   7: Ex 14, 10.20.27f.
   8: Nm 21, 21-35.
   9: Nm 22, 2-5.
  10: Nm 23, 1—24, 25.
  11: 3, 14; 6, 1.
  12: 11, 20; Ex 23, 28;
     Dt 7, 20.
  13: Dt 6, 10f.
  14: Dt 10, 12; 1 Sm 7, 3;
     12, 24; Tb 14, 9.
  15: Dt 30, 15-19.

---

† 23, 14: *Going the way of all men:* drawing near to death, the inevitable goal of all; cf 1 Kgs 2, 1f.

23, 15: *Every threat:* mentioned especially in Dt 28, 15-68.

24, 2: *Beyond the River:* east of the Euphrates; cf Gn 11, 28-31.

24, 12: *The hornets:* see note on Ex 23, 28.

24, 15: *The gods your fathers served:* Abraham's ancestors were polytheists.

¹⁹*†Joshua in turn said to the people, "You may not be able to serve the Lord, for he is a holy God; he is a jealous God who will not forgive your transgressions or your sins. ²⁰If, after the good he has done for you, you forsake the Lord and serve strange gods, he will do evil to you and destroy you."

²¹But the people answered Joshua, "We will still serve the Lord." ²²Joshua therefore said to the people, "You are your own witnesses that you have chosen to serve the Lord." They replied, "We are, indeed!" ²³"Now, therefore, put away the strange gods that are among you and turn your hearts to the Lord, the God of Israel." ²⁴Then the people promised Joshua, "We will serve the Lord, our God, and obey his voice."

²⁵So Joshua made a covenant with the people that day and made statutes and ordinances for them at Shechem, ²⁶*which he recorded in the book of the law of God. Then he took a large stone and set it up there under the oak that was in the sanctuary of the Lord. ²⁷*And Joshua said to all the people, "This stone shall be our witness, for it has heard all the words which the Lord spoke to us. It shall be a witness against you, should you wish to deny your God." ²⁸*Then Joshua dismissed the people, each to his own heritage.

Death of Joshua

²⁹*After these events, Joshua, son of Nun, servant of the Lord, died at the age of a hundred and ten. ³⁰*He was buried within the limits of his heritage at Timnath-serah in the mountain region of Ephraim north of Mount Gaash. ³¹Israel served the Lord during the entire lifetime of Joshua and that of the elders who outlived Joshua and knew all that the Lord had done for Israel. ³²*†The bones of Joseph, which the Israelites had brought up from Egypt, were buried in Shechem in the plot of ground Jacob had bought from the sons of Hamor, father of Shechem, for a hundred pieces of money. This was a heritage of the descendants of Joseph. ³³*When Eleazar, son of Aaron, also died, he was buried on the hill which had been given to his son Phinehas in the mountain region of Ephraim.

---

† 24, 19: *You may not be able:* fidelity to God's service is not easy, and therefore those who take such solemn obligations on themselves must be ever vigilant against human weakness.

24, 32: *The bones of Joseph:* the mummified body of Joseph (Gn 50, 25f), which the Israelites took with them as they left Egypt (Ex 13, 19), was fittingly buried at the ancient city of Shechem, near the border between the two Josephite tribes of Ephraim and Manasseh.

19: Ex 20, 5; 23, 21; 34, 14; Lv 19, 2.
26: Gn 28, 18; 31, 45; Jgs 9, 6.
27: Gn 31, 48.52; Dt 31, 19.21.26.
28: Jgs 2, 6.
29ff: Jgs 2, 7ff.
30: 19, 50; Jgs 2, 9.
32: Gn 33, 19; 50, 24; Ex 13, 19.
33: 22, 13.

The Book of Judges

Introduction

The Book of Judges derives its title from the twelve heroes of Israel whose deeds it records. They were not magistrates, but military leaders sent by God to aid and to relieve his people in time of external danger. They exercised their activities in the interval of time between the death of Joshua and the institution of the monarchy in Israel. Six of them—Othniel, Ehud, Barak, Gideon, Jephthah and Samson—are treated in some detail and have accordingly been styled the Major Judges. The other six, of whose activities this book preserves but a summary record, are called the Minor Judges. There were two other judges, whose judgeships are described in 1 Samuel—Eli and Samuel, who seem to have ruled the entire nation of Israel just before the institution of the monarchy. The twelve judges of the present book, however, very probably exercised their authority, sometimes simultaneously, over one or another tribe of Israel, never over the entire nation.

The purpose of the book is to show that the fortunes of Israel depended upon the obedience or disobedience of the people to God's law. Whenever they rebelled against him, they were oppressed by pagan nations; when they repented, he raised up judges to deliver them (cf 2, 10-23).

The accounts of various events, whether written shortly after their occurrence or orally transmitted, were later skillfully unified according to the moral purpose of the redactor some time during the Israelite monarchy.

The book is divided as follows:
  I: Palestine after the Death of Joshua (1, 1—3, 6)
  II: Stories of the Judges (3, 7—16, 31)
  III: The Tribes of Dan and Benjamin in the Days of the Judges (17, 1—21, 25)

I: PALESTINE AFTER THE DEATH OF JOSHUA

Pagan Survivors in Palestine

1 [1]*†AFTER THE DEATH OF JOSHUA the Israelites consulted the LORD, asking, "Who shall be first among us to attack the Canaanites and to do battle with them?" [2]The LORD answered, "Judah shall attack: I have delivered the land into his power." [3]Judah then said to his brother Simeon, "Come up with me into the territory allotted to me, and let us engage the Canaanites in battle. I will likewise accompany you into the territory allotted to you." So Simeon went with him.

[4]When the forces of Judah attacked, the LORD delivered the Canaanites and Perizzites into their power, and they slew ten thousand of them in Bezek. [5]It was in Bezek that they came upon Adonibezek and fought against him. When they defeated the Canaanites and Perizzites, [6]Adonibezek fled. They set out in pursuit, and when they caught him, cut off his thumbs and his big toes. [7]At this Adonibezek said, "Seventy kings, with their thumbs and big toes cut off, used to pick up scraps under my table. As I have done, so has God repaid me." He was brought to Jerusalem, and there he died. [8][The Judahites fought against Jerusalem and captured it, putting it to the sword; then they destroyed the city by fire.]

[9]*Afterward the Judahites went down to fight against the Canaanites who lived in the mountain region, in the Negeb, and in the foothills. [10]*Judah also marched against the Canaanites who dwelt in Hebron, which was formerly called Kiriath-arba, and defeated Sheshai, Ahiman and Talmai. [11]From there they marched against the inhabitants of Debir, which was formerly called Kiriath-sepher. [12]And Caleb said, "I will give my daughter Achsah in marriage to the one who attacks Kiriath-sepher and captures it." [13]*Othniel, son of Caleb's younger brother Kenaz, captured it; so Caleb gave him his daughter Achsah in marriage. [14]On the day of her marriage to Othniel she induced him to ask her father for some land. Then, as she alighted from the ass, Caleb asked her, "What is troubling you?" [15]"Give me an additional gift," she answered. "Since you have assigned land in the Negeb to me, give me also pools of water." So Caleb gave her the upper and the lower pool. [16]*†The descendants of the Kenite, Moses' father-in-law, came up with the Judahites from the city of palms to the desert at Arad [which is in the Negeb]. But they later left and settled among the Amalekites.

✷

1/1: 20, 18; Nm 27, 21.
9: Jos 10, 40; 11, 16;
12, 8.
10-15: Jos 15, 13-19.

10: Nm 13, 22; Jos 14, 15.
13: 3, 9.
16: 4, 11; Nm 10, 29-32.

† 1, 1-36: This chapter summarizes events most of which occurred shortly after the death of Joshua. Perhaps because they were planned and inaugurated by him, they are also attributed to him in the last half of the preceding book (Jos 14—22).

1, 16: *Moses' father-in-law:* Reuel; cf Nm 10, 29-32 and note. *City of palms:* Jericho (cf Dt 34, 3) or a town in the Negeb.

17* Judah then went with his brother Simeon, and they defeated the Canaanites who dwelt in Zephath. After having doomed the city to destruction, they renamed it Hormah. **18*** Judah, however, did not occupy Gaza with its territory, Ashkelon with its territory, or Ekron with its territory. **19*** Since the Lord was with Judah, he gained possession of the mountain region. Yet he could not dislodge those who lived on the plain, because they had iron chariots. **20*** As Moses had commanded, Hebron was given to Caleb, who then drove from it the three sons of Anak.

21*† The Benjaminites did not dislodge the Jebusites who dwelt in Jerusalem, with the result that the Jebusites live in Jerusalem beside the Benjaminites to the present day.

22 The house of Joseph, too, marched up against Bethel, and the Lord was with them. **23*** The house of Joseph had a reconnaissance made of Bethel, which formerly was called Luz. **24** The scouts saw a man coming out of the city and said to him, "Show us a way into the city, and we will spare you." **25** He showed them a way into the city, which they then put to the sword; but they let the man and his whole clan go free. **26** He then went to the land of Hittites, where he built a city and called it Luz, as it is still called.

27* Manasseh did not take possession of Beth-shean with its towns or of Taanach with its towns. Neither did he dislodge the inhabitants of Dor and its towns, those of Ibleam and its towns, or those of Megiddo and its towns. The Canaanites kept their hold in this district. **28** When the Israelites grew stronger, they impressed the Canaanites as laborers, but did not drive them out. **29*** Similarly, the Ephraimites did not drive out the Canaanites living in Gezer, and so the Canaanites live in Gezer in their midst.

30 Zebulun did not dislodge the inhabitants of Kitron or those of Nahalol; the Canaanites live among them, but have become forced laborers.

31* Nor did Asher drive out the inhabitants of Acco or those of Sidon, or take possession of Mahaleb, Achzib, Helbah, Aphik or Rehob. **32** The Asherites live among the Canaanite natives of the land, whom they have not dislodged.

33* Naphtali did not drive out the inhabitants of Beth-shemesh or those of Beth-anath, and so they live among the Canaanite natives of the land. However, the inhabitants of Beth-shemesh and Beth-anath have become forced laborers for them.

34* The Amorites hemmed in the Danites in the mountain region, not permitting them to go down into the plain, **35** The Amorites had a firm hold in Har-heres, Aijalon and Shaalbim, but as the house of Joseph gained the upper hand, they were impressed as laborers.

36 The territory of the Amorites extended from the Akrabbim pass to Sela and beyond.

Infidelities of the Israelites

2 **1*** An angel of the Lord went up from Gilgal to Bochim and said, "It was I who brought you up from Egypt and led you into the land which I promised on oath to your fathers. I said that I would never break my covenant with you, **2*** but that you were not to make a pact with the inhabitants of this land, and you were to pull down their altars. Yet you have not obeyed me. What did you mean by this? **3*** For now I tell you, I will not clear them out of your way; they shall oppose you and their gods shall become a snare for you."

4 When the angel of the Lord had made these threats to all the Israelites, the people wept aloud; **5†** and so that place came to be called Bochim. They offered sacrifice there to the Lord.

6* When Joshua dismissed the people, each Israelite went to take possession of his own hereditary land. **7** The people served the Lord during the entire lifetime of Joshua, and of those elders who outlived Joshua and who had seen all the great work which the Lord had done for Israel. **8** Joshua, son of Nun, the servant of the Lord, was a hundred and ten years old when he died; **9*** and they buried him within the borders of his heritage at Timnath-heres in the mountain region of Ephraim north of Mount Gaash.

10 But once the rest of that generation were gathered to their fathers, and a later generation arose that did not know the Lord, or what he had done for Israel, **11*†** the Israelites offended the Lord by serving the Baals. **12** Abandoning the Lord, the God of their fathers, who had led them out of the land of Egypt, they followed the other gods of the various nations around them, and by their worship of these gods provoked the Lord.

13† Because they had thus abandoned him and served Baal and the Ashtaroth, **14** the anger of the Lord flared up against Israel, and he delivered them over to plunderers who despoiled them. He allowed them to fall into the power of their enemies round about whom they were no longer able to withstand. **15*** Whatever they undertook, the Lord turned into disaster for them, as in his warning he had sworn he would do, till

17: Nm 21, 3.
18: Jos 11, 22.
19: Jos 17, 16ff.
20: Jos 14, 9.13; 15, 14.
21: Jos 15, 63.
23: Gn 28, 19; 35, 6; 48, 3; Jos 18, 13.
27f: Jos 17, 11ff.
29: Jos 16, 10.
31f: Jos 19, 24-31.
33: Jos 19, 32-39.
34: Jos 19, 47f.
2/1ff: 6, 8ff.
2: Ex 34, 12f.15; Dt 7, 2.5; 12, 2f.
3: Nm 33, 55; Jos 23,13.
6-9: Jos 24, 28-31.
9: Jos 19, 50.
11.14: 3, 7f; 4, 1f; 6, 1; 10, 6f; 13, 1.
15: Dt 28, 15-68.

† 1, 21: According to Jos 18, 16, Jerusalem was assigned to the tribe of Benjamin. But it was not actually taken from the Jebusites until David captured it (2 Sm 5, 6-9) and made it his capital, outside the tribal organization.

2, 5: *Bochim:* the Hebrew word for "weepers."

2, 11: *Baals:* the chief god of the Canaanites and the Phoenicians was called "Baal," a word meaning "lord." He was honored by various titles, hence the plural form here, equivalent to "the pagan gods."

2, 13: *Ashtaroth:* the Canaanite Phoenician goddess of love and fertility was Astarte. The plural form used here refers to her various titles and images and is equivalent to "goddesses."

they were in great distress. **16**Even when the Lord raised up judges to deliver them from the power of their despoilers, **17**they did not listen to their judges, but abandoned themselves to the worship of other gods. They were quick to stray from the way their fathers had taken, and did not follow their example of obedience to the commandments of the Lord. **18**Whenever the Lord raised up judges for them, he would be with the judge and save them from the power of their enemies as long as the judge lived; it was thus the Lord took pity on their distressful cries of affliction under their oppressors. **19***But when the judge died, they would relapse and do worse than their fathers, following other gods in service and worship, relinquishing none of their evil practices or stubborn conduct.

20*In his anger toward Israel the Lord said, "Inasmuch as this nation has violated my covenant which I enjoined on their fathers, and has disobeyed me, **21**I for my part will not clear away for them any more of the nations which Joshua left when he died." **22**Through these nations the Israelites were to be made to prove whether or not they would keep to the way of the Lord and continue in it as their fathers had done; **23**therefore the Lord allowed them to remain instead of expelling them immediately, or delivering them into the power of Israel.

3 **1**THE following are the nations which the Lord allowed to remain, so that through them he might try all those Israelites who had no experience of the battles with Canaan [just to instruct, by training them in battle, **2**those generations only of the Israelites who would not have had that previous experience]: **3*†**the five lords of the Philistines; and all the Canaanites, the Sidonians, and the Hivites who dwell in the mountain region of Lebanon between Baal-hermon and the entrance to Hamath. **4**These served to put Israel to the test, to determine whether they would obey the commandments the Lord had enjoined on their fathers through Moses. **5**Besides, the Israelites were living among the Canaanites, Hittites, Amorites, Perizzites, Hivites and Jebusites. **6**In fact, they took their daughters in marriage, and gave their own daughters to their sons in marriage, and served their gods.

II: STORIES OF THE JUDGES

Othniel

7*†BECAUSE THE ISRAELITES had offended the Lord by forgetting the Lord, their God, and serving the Baals and the Asherahs, **8**the anger of the Lord flared up against them, and he allowed them to fall into the power of Cushan-rishathaim, king of Aram Naharaim, whom they served for eight years. **9**But when the Israelites cried out to the Lord, he raised up for them a savior, Othniel, son of Caleb's younger brother Kenaz, who rescued them. **10***The spirit of the Lord came upon him, and he judged Israel. When he went out to war, the Lord delivered Cushan-rishathaim, king of Aram, into his power, so that he made him subject. **11***The land then was at rest for forty years, until Othniel, son of Kenaz, died.

Ehud

12Again the Israelites offended the Lord, who because of this offense strengthened Eglon, king of Moab, against Israel. **13**In alliance with the Ammonites and Amalekites, he attacked and defeated Israel, taking possession of the city of palms. **14**The Israelites then served Eglon, king of Moab, for eighteen years.

15But when the Israelites cried out to the Lord, he raised up for them a savior, the Benjaminite Ehud, son of Gera, who was left-handed. It was by him that the Israelites sent their tribute to Eglon, king of Moab. **16**Ehud made himself a two-edged dagger a foot long, and wore it under his clothes over his right thigh. **17**He presented the tribute to Eglon, king of Moab, who was very fat, **18**and after the presentation went off with the tribute bearers. **19**He returned, however, from where the idols are, near Gilgal, and said, "I have a private message for you, O king." And the king said, "Silence!" Then when all his attendants had left his presence, **20**and Ehud went in to him where he sat alone in his cool upper room, Ehud said, "I have a message from God for you." So the king rose from his chair, **21**and then Ehud with his left hand drew the dagger from his right thigh, and thrust it into Eglon's belly. **22**The hilt also went in after the blade, and the fat closed over the blade because he did not withdraw the dagger from his body.

23Then Ehud went out into the hall, shutting the doors of the upper room on him and locking them. **24**When Ehud had left and the servants came, they saw that the doors of the upper room were locked, and thought, "He must be easing himself in the cool chamber." **25**They waited until they finally grew suspicious. Since he did not open the doors of the upper room, they took the key and opened them. There on the floor, dead, lay their lord!

26During their delay Ehud made good his escape and, passing the idols, took refuge in Seirah. **27**On his arrival he sounded the horn in the mountain region of Ephraim, and the Israelites went down from the mountains with him as their leader. **28***"Follow me," he said to them, "for the Lord has delivered your ene-

---

†   3, 3: *The Philistines:* non-Semitic invaders who gave their name to all Palestine, although they occupied only its southwestern plains. Their confederation embraced the five leading cities of Gaza, Ashkelon, Ashdod, Gath and Ekron.

    3, 7: *Asherahs:* elsewhere rendered "sacred poles." See note on Ex 34, 13; and on Dt 7, 5. Here the word seems to mean "goddesses."

❋
19: 3, 12; 4, 1; 6, 1; 8, 33.   10: 6, 34; 11, 29; 13, 25;
20f: Jos 23, 16.   14, 6.19; 15, 14.
3/3: Jos 13, 2-6.   11: 5, 31; 8, 28.
    7: 2, 11ff.   28: 4, 7.14; 7, 9.15.

mies the Moabites into your power." So they followed him down and seized the fords of the Jordan leading to Moab, permitting no one to cross. 29On that occasion they slew about ten thousand Moabites, all of them strong and valiant men. Not a man escaped. 30Thus was Moab brought under the power of Israel at that time; and the land had rest for eighty years.

Shamgar

31After him there was Shamgar, son of Anath, who slew six hundred Philistines with an oxgoad. He, too, rescued Israel.

Deborah and Barak

4 1AFTER Ehud's death, however, the Israelites again offended the LORD. 2*So the LORD allowed them to fall into the power of the Canaanite king, Jabin, who reigned in Hazor. The general of his army was Sisera, who dwelt in Harosheth-ha-goiim. 3But the Israelites cried out to the LORD; for with his nine hundred iron chariots he sorely oppressed the Israelites for twenty years.

4At this time the prophetess Deborah, wife of Lappidoth, was judging Israel. 5She used to sit under Deborah's palm tree, situated between Ramah and Bethel in the mountain region of Ephraim, and there the Israelites came up to her for judgment. 6*She sent and summoned Barak, son of Abinoam, from Kedesh of Naphtali. "This is what the LORD, the God of Israel, commands," she said to him; "go, march on Mount Tabor, and take with you ten thousand Naphtalites and Zebulunites. 7*I will lead Sisera, the general of Jabin's army, out to you at the Wadi Kishon, together with his chariots and troops, and will deliver them into your power." 8But Barak answered her, "If you come with me, I will go; if you do not come with me, I will not go." 9"I will certainly go with you," she replied, "But you shall not gain the glory in the expedition on which you are setting out, for the LORD will have Sisera fall into the power of a woman." So Deborah joined Barak and journeyed with him to Kedesh.

10*Barak summoned Zebulun and Naphtali to Kedesh, and ten thousand men followed him. Deborah also went up with him. 11*†Now the Kenite Heber had detached himself from his own people, the descendants of Hobab, Moses' brother-in-law, and had pitched his tent by the terebinth of Zaanannim, which was near Kedesh.

12It was reported to Sisera that Barak, son of Abinoam, had gone up to Mount Tabor. 13So Sisera assembled from Harosheth-ha-goiim at the Wadi Kishon all nine hundred of his iron chariots and all his forces. 14Deborah then said to Barak, "Be off, for this is the day on which the LORD has delivered Sisera into your power. The LORD marches before you." So Barak went down Mount Tabor, followed by his ten thousand men. 15*And the LORD put Sisera and all his chariots and all his forces to rout before Barak. Sisera himself dismounted from his chariot and fled on foot. 16Barak, however, pursued the chariots and the army as far as Harosheth-ha-goiim. The entire army of Sisera fell beneath the sword, not even one man surviving.

17†Sisera, in the meantime, had fled on foot to the tent of Jael, wife of the Kenite Heber, since Jabin, king of Hazor, and the family of the Kenite Heber were at peace with one another. 18Jael went out to meet Sisera and said to him, "Come in, my lord, come in with me; do not be afraid." So he went into her tent, and she covered him with a rug. 19*He said to her, "Please give me a little water to drink. I am thirsty." But she opened a jug of milk for him to drink, and then covered him over. 20"Stand at the entrance of the tent," he said to her. "If anyone comes and asks, 'Is there someone here?' say, 'No!'" 21*Instead Jael, wife of Heber, got a tent peg and took a mallet in her hand. While Sisera was sound asleep, she stealthily approached him and drove the peg through his temple down into the ground, so that he perished in death. 22Then when Barak came in pursuit of Sisera, Jael went out to meet him and said to him, "Come, I will show you the man you seek." So he went in with her, and there lay Sisera dead, with the tent peg through his temple.

23Thus on that day God humbled the Canaanite king, Jabin, before the Israelites; 24their power weighed ever heavier upon him, till at length they destroyed the Canaanite king, Jabin.

Canticle of Deborah

5 1ON that day Deborah [and Barak, son of Abinoam,] sang this song:

2†Of chiefs who took the lead in Israel,
    of noble deeds by the people who bless the LORD,

3Hear, O kings! Give ear, O princes!
    I to the LORD will sing my song,
    my hymn to the LORD, the God of Israel.

4O LORD, when you went out from Seir,
    when you marched from the land of Edom,
The earth quaked and the heavens were shaken,
    while the clouds sent down showers.

5*Mountains trembled
    in the presence of the LORD, the One of Sinai,
    in the presence of the LORD, the God of Israel.

4/2: Jos 11, 1.10; Ps 83, 10; 1 Sm 12, 9.
6: Heb 11, 32.
7: 5, 21; Ps 83, 10.
10: 5, 18.
11: Nm 10, 29.
15: Ps 83, 10.
19: 5, 25.
21: 5, 26.
5/5: Dt 33, 2; 2 Sm 22, 8; Pss 18, 8; 68, 9. Ex 19, 16; Dt 4, 11; Ps 97, 5.

† 4, 11: Most of the Kenites occupied a district in the southern part of Judah (1, 16). A group of them, however, had detached themselves and settled in lower Galilee.

4, 17-22: It is to be noted that the sacred author merely records the fact of the murder of Sisera. We must not construe this as approval of Jael's action.

5, 2-31: This canticle is an excellent example of early Hebrew poetry, even though some of its verses are now obscure.

⁶*In the days of Shamgar, son of Anath,
    in the days of slavery caravans ceased:
Those. who traveled the roads
    went by roundabout paths.
⁷Gone was freedom beyond the walls,
    gone indeed from Israel.

When I, Deborah, rose,
    when I rose, a mother in Israel,
⁸†New gods were their choice;
    then the war was at their gates.
Not a shield could be seen, nor a lance,
    among forty thousand in Israel!

⁹My heart is with the leaders of Israel,
    nobles of the people who bless the Lord;
¹⁰They who ride on white asses,
    seated on saddlecloths as they go their way;
¹¹Sing of them to the strains of the harpers at the
    wells,
where men recount the just deeds of the Lord,
    his just deeds that brought freedom to Israel.

¹²Awake, awake, Deborah!
    awake, awake, strike up a song.
Strength! arise, Barak,
    make despoilers your spoil, son of Abinoam.
¹³Then down came the fugitives with the mighty,
    the people of the Lord came down for me as
    warriors.
¹⁴†From Ephraim, princes were in the valley;
    behind you was Benjamin, among your troops.
From Machir came down commanders,
    from Zebulun wielders of the marshal's staff.
¹⁵*With Deborah were the princes of Issachar;
    Barak, too, was in the valley, his course
    unchecked.

Among the clans of Reuben
    great were the searchings of heart.
¹⁶Why do you stay beside your hearths
    listening to the lowing of the herds?
Among the clans of Reuben
    great were the searchings of heart!

¹⁷Gilead, beyond the Jordan, rests;
    why does Dan spend his time in ships?
Asher, who dwells along the shore,
    is resting in his coves.
¹⁸*Zebulun is the people defying death;
    Naphtali, too, on the open heights!

¹⁹*The kings came and fought;
    then they fought, those kings of Canaan,
At Taanach by the waters of Megiddo;
    no silver booty did they take.
²⁰*†From the heavens the stars, too, fought;
    from their courses they fought against Sisera.

²¹*The Wadi Kishon swept them away;
    a wadi . . . , the Kishon.
²²Then the hoofs of the horses pounded,
    with the dashing, dashing of his steeds.

²³†"Curse Meroz," says the Lord,
    "hurl a curse at its inhabitants!
For they came not to my help,
    as warriors to the help of the Lord."

²⁴*Blessed among women be Jael,
    blessed among tent-dwelling women.
²⁵*He asked for water, she gave him milk;
    in a princely bowl she offered curds.
²⁶With her left hand she reached for the peg,
    with her right, for the workman's mallet.

She hammered Sisera, crushed his head;
    she smashed, stove in his temple.
²⁷At her feet he sank down, fell, lay still;
    down at her feet he sank and fell;
    where he sank down, there he fell, slain.

²⁸From the window peered down and wailed
    the mother of Sisera, from the lattice:
"Why is his chariot so long in coming?
    why are the hoofbeats of his chariots delayed?"
²⁹The wisest of her princesses answers her,
    and she, too, keeps answering herself:

³⁰"They must be dividing the spoil they took:
    there must be a damsel or two for each man,
Spoils of dyed cloth as Sisera's spoil,
    an ornate shawl or two for me in the spoil."

³¹*May all your enemies perish thus, O Lord!
    but your friends be as the sun rising in its might!

And the land was at rest for forty years.

The Call of Gideon

6 ¹THE Israelites offended the Lord, who therefore delivered them into the power of Midian for seven years, ²so that Midian held Israel subject. For fear of Midian the Israelites established the fire signals on the mountains, the caves for refuge, and the strongholds. ³*And it used to be that when the Israelites had completed their sowing, Midian, Amalek

---

† 5, 8: *New gods:* pagan deities; cf Dt 32, 16-18. God punished the idolatry of the Israelites by leaving them relatively unarmed before the attacks of their enemies, who had better weapons, made of iron; cf 1 Sm 13, 19-22.

5, 14-22: Praise for the tribes which formed the Israelite league against Sisera: Ephraim, Benjamin, Manasseh (represented by Machir), Zebulun, Issachar, and Naphtali (led by Barak). The tribes of Reuben, Gad (Gilead), Dan, and Asher are chided for their lack of co-operation. The more distant tribes of Judah and Simeon are not mentioned.

5, 20f: It would seem that nature aided the Hebrews in some way. Perhaps the torrential rains swelled the waters of Kishon, which then overwhelmed the Canaanites.

5, 23: *Meroz:* an unknown locality in which Hebrews probably resided, since its inhabitants are cursed for their failure to proffer aid.

* 6: 3, 31.
15: 4, 14.
18: 4, 10.
19: 1, 27; Jos 17, 11.
20: 4, 15; Jos 10, 14.
21: 4, 7.13.
24: 4, 17; Jdt 13, 17; Lk 1, 28.42.
25f: 4, 19.21.
31: Ps 83, 10-19.
6/3f: 7, 12; Dt 28, 30ff.

and the Kedemites would come up, ⁴encamp opposite them, and destroy the produce of the land as far as the outskirts of Gaza, leaving no sustenance in Israel, nor sheep, oxen or asses. ⁵For they would come up with their livestock, and their tents would become as numerous as locusts; and neither they nor their camels could be numbered, when they came into the land to lay it waste. ⁶Thus was Israel reduced to misery by Midian, and so the Israelites cried out to the LORD.

⁷When Israel cried out to the LORD because of Midian, ⁸*he sent a prophet to the Israelites who said to them, "The LORD, the God of Israel, says: I led you up from Egypt; I brought you out of the place of slavery. ⁹I rescued you from the power of Egypt and of all your other oppressors. I drove them out before you and gave you their land. ¹⁰And I said to you: I, the LORD, am your God; you shall not venerate the gods of the Amorites in whose land you are dwelling. But you did not obey me."

¹¹Then the angel of the LORD came and sat under the terebinth in Ophrah that belonged to Joash the Abiezrite. While his son Gideon was beating out wheat in the wine press to save it from the Midianites, ¹²the angel of the LORD appeared to him and said, "The LORD is with you, O champion!" ¹³"My lord," Gideon said to him, "if the LORD is with us, why has all this happened to us? Where are his wondrous deeds of which our fathers told us when they said, 'Did not the LORD bring us up from Egypt?' For now the LORD has abandoned us and has delivered us into the power of Midian." ¹⁴The LORD turned to him and said, "Go with the strength you have and save Israel from the power of Midian. It is I who send you." ¹⁵But he answered him, "Please, my lord, how can I save Israel? My family is the meanest in Manasseh, and I am the most insignificant in my father's house." ¹⁶"I shall be with you," the LORD said to him, "and you will cut down Midian to the last man." ¹⁷He answered him, "If I find favor with you, give me a sign that you are speaking with me. ¹⁸Do not depart from here, I pray you, until I come back to you and bring out my offering and set it before you." He answered, "I will await your return."

¹⁹So Gideon went off and prepared a kid and an ephah of flour in the form of unleavened cakes. Putting the meat in a basket and the broth in a pot, he brought them out to him under the terebinth and presented them. ²⁰*The angel of God said to him, "Take the meat and unleavened cakes and lay them on this rock; then pour out the broth." When he had done so, ²¹the angel of the LORD stretched out the tip of the staff he held, and touched the meat and unleavened cakes. Thereupon a fire came up from the rock which consumed the meat and unleavened cakes, and the angel of the LORD disappeared from sight. ²²*Gideon, now aware that it had been the angel of the LORD, said, "Alas, Lord GOD, that I have seen the angel of the LORD

face to face!" ²³The LORD answered him, "Be calm, do not fear. You shall not die." ²⁴†So Gideon built there an altar to the LORD and called it Yahweh-shalom. To this day it is still in Ophrah of the Abiezrites.

²⁵†That same night the LORD said to him, "Take the seven-year-old spare bullock and destroy your father's altar to Baal and cut down the sacred pole that is by it. ²⁶You shall build, instead, the proper kind of altar to the LORD, your God, on top of this stronghold. Then take the spare bullock and offer it as a holocaust on the wood from the sacred pole you have cut down." ²⁷So Gideon took ten of his servants and did as the LORD had commanded him. But through fear of his family and of the townspeople, he would not do it by day, but did it at night. ²⁸Early the next morning the townspeople found that the altar of Baal had been destroyed, the sacred pole near it cut down, and the spare bullock offered on the altar that was built. ²⁹They asked one another, "Who did this?" Their inquiry led them to the conclusion that Gideon, son of Joash, had done it. ³⁰So the townspeople said to Joash, "Bring out your son that he may die, for he has destroyed the altar of Baal and has cut down the sacred pole that was near it." ³¹But Joash replied to all who were standing around him, "Do you intend to act in Baal's stead, or be his champion? If anyone acts for him, he shall be put to death by morning. If he whose altar has been destroyed is a god, let him act for himself!" ³²*†So on that day Gideon was called Jerubbaal, because of the words, "Let Baal take action against him, since he destroyed his altar."

³³Then all Midian and Amalek and the Kedemites mustered and crossed over into the valley of Jezreel, where they encamped. ³⁴The spirit of the LORD enveloped Gideon; he blew the horn that summoned Abiezer to follow him. ³⁵He sent messengers, too, throughout Manasseh, which also obeyed his summons; through Asher, Zebulun and Naphtali, likewise, he sent messengers and these tribes advanced to meet the others. ³⁶Gideon said to God, "If indeed you are going to save Israel through me, as you promised, ³⁷I am putting this woolen fleece on the threshing floor. If dew comes on the fleece alone, while all the ground is dry, I shall know that you will save Israel through me, as you promised." ³⁸That is what took place. Early the next morning he wrung the dew from the fleece, squeezing out of it a bowlful of water. ³⁹Gideon then said to God, "Do not be angry with me if I speak once more. Let me make just one more test with the fleece. Let the fleece alone be dry, but let there be dew on all the ground." ⁴⁰That night God did so; the fleece alone was dry, but there was dew on all the ground.

✣   8ff: 2, 1f; 10, 11-14.   22f: Gn 32, 31; Dt 5, 24ff.
      20: 13, 19.   32: 1 Sm 12, 11.

†   6, 24: *Yahweh-shalom:* Hebrew for "the LORD is peace," a reference to the LORD's words, "Be calm," literally, "Peace be to you!"

     6, 25: *The sacred pole:* see note on Ex 34, 13.

     6, 32: *Jerubbaal:* similar in sound to the Hebrew words meaning, "Let Baal take action."

Defeat of Midian

7 [1]*EARLY the next morning Jerubbaal (that is, Gideon) encamped by En-harod with all his soldiers. The camp of Midian was in the valley north of Gibeath-hammoreh. [2]The LORD said to Gideon, "You have too many soldiers with you for me to deliver Midian into their power, lest Israel vaunt itself against me and say, 'My own power brought me the victory.' [3]*Now proclaim to all the soldiers, 'If anyone is afraid or fearful, let him leave.'" When Gideon put them to this test on the mountain, twenty-two thousand of the soldiers left, but ten thousand remained. [4]The LORD said to Gideon, "There are still too many soldiers. Lead them down to the water and I will test them for you there. If I tell you that a certain man is to go with you, he must go with you. But no one is to go if I tell you he must not." [5]†When Gideon led the soldiers down to the water, the LORD said to him, "You shall set to one side everyone who laps up the water as a dog does with its tongue; to the other, everyone who kneels down to drink." [6]Those who lapped up the water raised to their mouths by hand numbered three hundred, but all the rest of the soldiers knelt down to drink the water. [7]The LORD said to Gideon, "By means of the three hundred who lapped up the water I will save you and will deliver Midian into your power. So let all the other soldiers go home." [8]Their horns, and such supplies as the soldiers had with them, were taken up, and Gideon ordered the rest of the Israelites to their tents, but kept the three hundred men. Now the camp of Midian was beneath him in the valley.

[9]That night the LORD said to Gideon, "Go, descend on the camp, for I have delivered it up to you. [10]If you are afraid to attack, go down to the camp with your aide Purah. [11]When you hear what they are saying, you will have the courage to descend on the camp." So he went down with his aide Purah to the outposts of the camp. [12]The Midianites, Amalekites, and all the Kedemites lay in the valley, as numerous as locusts. Nor could their camels be counted, for these were as many as the sands on the seashore. [13]†When Gideon arrived, one man was telling another about a dream. "I had a dream," he said, "that a round loaf of barley bread was rolling into the camp of Midian. It came to our tent and struck it, and as it fell it turned the tent upside down." [14]"This can only be the sword of the Israelite Gideon, son of Joash," the other replied. "God has delivered Midian and all the camp into his power." [15]When Gideon heard the description and explanation of the dream, he prostrated himself. Then returning to the camp of Israel, he said, "Arise, for the LORD has delivered the camp of Midian into your power."

[16]He divided the three hundred men into three companies, and provided them all with horns and with empty jars and torches inside the jars. [17]"Watch me and follow my lead," he told them. "I shall go to the edge of the camp, and as I do, you must do also. [18]When I and those with me blow horns all around the camp and cry out, 'For the LORD and for Gideon!'" [19]†So Gideon and the hundred men who were with him came to the edge of the camp at the beginning of the middle watch, just after the posting of the guards. They blew the horns and broke the jars they were holding. [20]All three companies blew horns and broke their jars. They held the torches in their left hands, and in their right the horns they were blowing, and cried out, "A sword for the LORD and Gideon!" [21]They all remained standing in place around the camp, while the whole camp fell to running and shouting and fleeing. [22]*But the three hundred men kept blowing the horns, and throughout the camp the LORD set the sword of one against another. The army fled as far as Beth-shittah in the direction of Zarethan, near the border of Abel-meholah at Tabbath.

[23]The Israelites were called to arms from Naphtali, from Asher, and from all Manasseh, and they pursued Midian. [24]Gideon also sent messengers throughout the mountain region of Ephraim to say, "Go down to confront Midian, and seize the water courses against them as far as Beth-barah, as well as the Jordan." So all the Ephraimites were called to arms, and they seized the water courses as far as Beth-barah, and the Jordan as well. [25]*They captured the two princes of Midian, Oreb and Zeeb, killing Oreb at the rock of Oreb and Zeeb at the wine press of Zeeb. Then they pursued Midian and carried the heads of Oreb and Zeeb to Gideon beyond the Jordan.

8 [1]BUT the Ephraimites said to him, "What have you done to us, not calling us when you went to fight against Midian?" And they quarreled bitterly with him. [2]*"What have I accomplished now in comparison with you?" he answered them. "Is not the gleaning of Ephraim better than the vintage of Abiezer? [3]Into your power God delivered the princes of Midian, Oreb and Zeeb. What have I been able to do in comparison with you?" When he said this, their anger against him subsided.

[4]When Gideon reached the Jordan and crossed it with his three hundred men, they were exhausted and famished. [5]So he said to the men of Succoth, "Will you give my followers some loaves of bread? They are exhausted, and I am pursuing Zebah and Zalmunna,

---

† 7, 5: The LORD desired not numerous but reliable soldiers. Those who drank from their hands were alert, standing ready to resist attack, whereas the others were careless and undependable. the cowardly soldiers had already been dismissed (v 3); cf Dt 20, 8.

7, 13: The barley loaf represents the agricultural Hebrews while the tent refers to the nomadic Midianites. The overthrow of the tent indicates the victory of the Hebrews over their Midianite oppressors.

7, 19: *At the beginning of the middle watch:* about two hours before midnight. The ancient Hebrews divided the night into three watches of about four hours each. At the beginning of a watch the sentinels were changed.

❋
7/1: 6, 32.
3: Dt 20, 8.
22f: Ps 83, 10; Is 9, 4.

25: 8, 3; Ps 83, 12;
Is 10, 26.
8/2: 6, 34.

kings of Midian." [6†]But the princes of Succoth replied, "Are the hands of Zebah and Zalmunna already in your possession, that we should give food to your army?" [7]Gideon said, "Very well; when the LORD has delivered Zebah and Zalmunna into my power, I will grind your flesh in with the thorns and briers of the desert." [8]He went up from there to Penuel and made the same request of them, but the men of Penuel answered him as had the men of Succoth. [9]So to the men of Penuel, too, he said, "When I return in triumph, I will demolish this tower."

[10]Now Zebah and Zalmunna were in Karkor with their force of about fifteen thousand men; these were all who were left of the whole Kedemite army, a hundred and twenty thousand swordsmen having fallen. [11]Gideon went up by the route of the nomads east of Nobah and Jogbehah, and attacked the camp when it felt secure. [12]Zebah and Zalmunna fled. He pursued them and took the two kings of Midian, Zebah and Zalmunna, captive, throwing the entire army into panic.

[13]Then Gideon, son of Joash, returned from battle by the pass of Heres. [14]He captured a young man of Succoth, who upon being questioned listed for him the seventy-seven princes and elders of Succoth. [15]So he went to the men of Succoth and said, "Here are Zebah and Zalmunna, with whom you taunted me, 'Are the hands of Zebah and Zalmunna already in your possession, that we should give food to your weary followers?'" [16]He took the elders of the city, and thorns and briers of the desert, and ground these men of Succoth into them. [17]He also demolished the tower of Penuel and slew the men of the city.

[18]Then he said to Zebah and Zalmunna, "Where now are the men you killed at Tabor?" "They all resembled you," they replied. "They appeared to be princes." [19]"They were my brothers, my mother's sons," he said. "As the LORD lives, if you had spared their lives, I should not kill you." [20]Then he said to his first-born, Jether, "Go, kill them." Since Jether was still a boy, he was afraid and did not draw his sword. [21]Zebah and Zalmunna said, "Come, kill us yourself, for a man's strength is like the man." So Gideon stepped forward and killed Zebah and Zalmunna. He also took the crescents that were on the necks of their camels.

[22]The Israelites then said to Gideon, "Rule over us—you, your son, and your son's son—for you rescued us from the power of Midian." [23]But Gideon answered them, "I will not rule over you, nor shall my son rule over you. The LORD must rule over you."

[24†]Gideon went on to say, "I should like to make a request of you. Will each of you give me a ring from his booty?" (For being Ishmaelites, the enemy had gold rings.) [25]"We will gladly give them," they replied, and spread out a cloak into which everyone threw a ring from his booty. [26]The gold rings that he requested weighed seventeen hundred gold shekels, in addition to the crescents and pendants, the purple garments worn by the kings of Midian, and the trappings that were on the necks of their camels. [27]Gideon made an ephod out of the gold and placed it in his city Ophrah. However, all Israel paid idolatrous homage to it there, and caused the ruin of Gideon and his family.

[28]Thus was Midian brought into subjection by the Israelites; no longer did they hold their heads high. And the land had rest for forty years, during the lifetime of Gideon.

Gideon's Son Abimelech

[29]Then Jerubbaal, son of Joash, went back home to stay. [30*]Now Gideon had seventy sons, his direct descendants, for he had many wives. [31†]His concubine who lived in Shechem also bore him a son, whom he named Abimelech. [32]At a good old age Gideon, son of Joash, died and was buried in the tomb of his father Joash in Ophrah of the Abiezrites. [33†]But after Gideon was dead, the Israelites again abandoned themselves to the Baals, making Baal of Berith their god [34]and forgetting the LORD, their God, who had delivered them from the power of their enemies all around them. [35]Nor were they grateful to the family of Jerubbaal [Gideon] for all the good he had done for Israel.

9 [1*]ABIMELECH, son of Jerubbaal, went to his mother's kinsmen in Shechem, and said to them and to the whole clan to which his mother's family belonged, [2]"Put this question to all the citizens of Shechem: 'Which is better for you: that seventy men, or all Jerubbaal's sons, rule over you, or that one man rule over you?' You must remember that I am your own flesh and bone." [3]When his mother's kin repeated these words to them on his behalf, all the citizens of Shechem sympathized with Abimelech, thinking, "He is our kinsman." [4]They also gave him seventy silver shekels from the temple of Baal of Berith, with which Abimelech hired shiftless men and ruffians as his followers. [5]He then went to his ancestral house in Ophrah, and slew his brothers, the seventy sons of Jerubbaal, on one stone. Only the youngest son of Jerubbaal, Jotham, escaped, for he was hidden. [6]Then all the citizens of Shechem and all Beth-millo came together and proceeded to make Abimelech king by the terebinth at the memorial pillar in Shechem.

[7]When this was reported to him, Jotham went to the top of Mount Gerizim, and standing there, cried out to them in a loud voice: "Hear me, citizens of Shechem, that God may then hear you! [8*]Once the trees

---

[†] 8, 6: *Are the hands . . . in your possession . . . ?*: i. e., can you already boast of victory? The hands as well as the heads of slain enemies were cut off and counted as trophies; cf 2 Sm 4, 8; 2 Kgs 10, 7f; and the Ugaritic Anath Epic, V AB, II 10ff.

8, 24: *Ishmaelites*: here as in Gn 37, 25-28, the designation is not ethnic; it refers rather to their status as nomads.

8, 31: *Concubine*: a wife of secondary rank.

8, 33: *Baal of Berith*: one of the titles of Baal as worshiped by the Canaanites of Shechem, meaning "the lord of the covenant."

---

went to anoint a king over themselves. So they said to the olive tree, 'Reign over us.' **9**†But the olive tree answered them, 'Must I give up my rich oil, whereby men and gods are honored, and go to wave over the trees?' **10**Then the trees said to the fig tree, 'Come; you reign over us!' **11**But the fig tree answered them, 'Must I give up my sweetness and my good fruit, and go to wave over the trees?' **12**Then the trees said to the vine, 'Come you, and reign over us.' **13**†But the vine answered them, 'Must I give up my wine that cheers gods and men, and go to wave over the trees?' **14**Then all the trees said to the buckthorn, 'Come; you reign over us!' **15**But the buckthorn replied to the trees, 'If you wish to anoint me king over you in good faith, come and take refuge in my shadow. Otherwise, let fire come from the buckthorn and devour the cedars of Lebanon.'

16†"Now then, if you have acted in good faith and honorably in appointing Abimelech your king, if you have dealt well with Jerubbaal and with his family, and if you have treated him as he deserved—**17**for my father fought for you at the risk of his life when he saved you from the power of Midian; **18***but you have risen against his family this day and have killed his seventy sons upon one stone, and have made Abimelech, the son of his handmaid, king over the citizens of Shechem, because he is your kinsman—**19**if, then, you have acted in good faith and with honor toward Jerubbaal and his family this day, rejoice in Abimelech and may he in turn rejoice in you. **20**But if not, let fire come forth from Abimelech to devour the citizens of Shechem and Beth-millo, and let fire come forth from the citizens and from Beth-millo to devour Abimelech." **21**Then Jotham went in flight to Beer, where he remained for fear of his brother Abimelech.

22When Abimelech had ruled Israel for three years, **23**God put bad feelings between Abimelech and the citizens of Shechem, who rebelled against Abimelech. **24**This was to repay the violence done to the seventy sons of Jerubbaal and to avenge their blood upon their brother Abimelech, who killed them, and upon the citizens of Shechem, who encouraged him to kill his brothers. **25**The citizens of Shechem then set men in ambush for him on the mountaintops, and these robbed all who passed them on the road. But it was reported to Abimelech.

26Now Gaal, son of Ebed, came over to Shechem with his kinsmen. The citizens of Shechem put their trust in him, **27**and went out into the fields, harvested their grapes and trod them out. Then they held a festival and went to the temple of their god, where they ate and drank and cursed Abimelech. **28***Gaal, son of Ebed, said, "Who is Abimelech? And why should we of Shechem serve him? Were not the son of Jerubbaal and his lieutenant Zebul once subject to the men of Hamor, father of Shechem? Why should we serve him? **29**Would that this people were entrusted to my command! I would depose Abimelech. I would say to Abimelech, 'Get a larger army and come out!' "

30At the news of what Gaal, son of Ebed, had said, Zebul, the ruler of the city, was angry **31**and sent messengers to Abimelech in Arumah with the information: "Gaal, son of Ebed, and his kinsmen have come to Shechem and are stirring up the city against you. **32**Now rouse yourself; set an ambush tonight in the fields, you and the men who are with you. **33**Promptly at sunrise tomorrow morning, make a raid on the city. When he and his followers come out against you, deal with him as best you can."

34During the night Abimelech advanced with all his soldiers and set up an ambush for Shechem in four companies. **35**Gaal, son of Ebed, went out and stood at the entrance of the city gate. When Abimelech and his soldiers rose from their place of ambush, **36**Gaal saw them and said to Zebul, "There are men coming down from the hilltops!" But Zebul answered him, "You see the shadow of the hills as men." **37**But Gaal went on to say, "Men are coming down from the region of Tabbur-Haares, and one company is coming by way of Elon-Meonenim." **38**Zebul said to him, "Where now is the boast you uttered, 'Who is Abimelech that we should serve him?' Are these not the men for whom you expressed contempt? Go out now and fight with them." **39**So Gaal went out at the head of the citizens of Shechem and fought against Abimelech. **40**But Abimelech routed him, and he fled before him; and many fell slain right up to the entrance of the gate. **41**Abimelech returned to Arumah, but Zebul drove Gaal and his kinsmen from Shechem, which they had occupied.

42The next day, when the people were taking the field, it was reported to Abimelech, **43**who divided the men he had into three companies, and set up an ambush in the fields. He watched till he saw the people leave the city, and then rose against them for the attack. **44**Abimelech and the company with him dashed in and stood by the entrance of the city gate, while the other two companies rushed upon all who were in the field and attacked them. **45**†That entire day Abimelech fought against the city, and captured it. He then killed its inhabitants and demolished the city, sowing the site with salt.

46When they heard of this, all the citizens of Migdalshechem went into the crypt of the temple of

---

† 9, 9: *Whereby men and gods are honored:* oil was used in the worship both of the true God and of false gods; it was prescribed in the worship of Yahweh (Lv 2, 1.6.15; 24, 2). It was also used to consecrate prophets, priests and kings (Ex 30, 25.30; 1 Sm 10, 1; 16, 13).

9, 13: *Cheers gods:* wine was used in the libations both of the Temple of Jerusalem and of pagan temples.

9, 16: Just as the noble trees refused the honor of royalty and were made subject to a mean plant, so did Abimelech of less noble birth than the seventy sons of Gideon now tyrannize over the people.

9, 45: *Sowing the site with salt:* a severe measure, which was a symbol of desolation, and even more, since it actually rendered the ground barren and useless.

✣   18: 8, 31.   28: Gn 34, 2.6.

El-berith. **⁴⁷**It was reported to Abimelech that all the citizens of Migdal-shechem were gathered together. **⁴⁸**So he went up Mount Zalmon with all his soldiers, took his axe in his hand, and cut down some brushwood. This he lifted to his shoulder, then said to the men with him, "Hurry! Do just as you have seen me do." **⁴⁹**So all the men likewise cut down brushwood, and following Abimelech, placed it against the crypt. Then they set the crypt on fire over their heads, so that every one of the citizens of Migdal-shechem, about a thousand men and women, perished.

⁵⁰Abimelech proceeded to Thebez, which he invested and captured. **⁵¹**Now there was a strong tower in the middle of the city, and all the men and women, in a word all the citizens of the city, fled there, shutting themselves in and going up to the roof of the tower. **⁵²**Abimelech came up to the tower and fought against it, advancing to the very entrance of the tower to set it on fire. **⁵³***But a certain woman cast the upper part of a millstone down on Abimelech's head, and it fractured his skull. **⁵⁴***He immediately called his armor-bearer and said to him, "Draw your sword and dispatch me, lest they say of me that a woman killed me." So his attendant ran him through and he died. **⁵⁵**When the Israelites saw that Abimelech was dead, they all left for their homes.

⁵⁶Thus did God requite the evil Abimelech had done to his father in killing his seventy brothers. **⁵⁷**God also brought all their wickedness home to the Shechemites, for the curse of Jotham, son of Jerubbaal, overtook them.

Tola

10 **¹**AFTER Abimelech there rose to save Israel the Issacharite Tola, son of Puah, son of Dodo, a resident of Shamir in the mountain region of Ephraim. **²**When he had judged Israel twenty-three years, he died and was buried in Shamir.

Jair

³Jair the Gileadite came after him and judged Israel twenty-two years. **⁴***†He had thirty sons who rode on thirty saddle-asses and possessed thirty cities in the land of Gilead; these are called Havvoth-jair to the present day. **⁵**Jair died and was buried in Kamon.

Oppression by the Ammonites

⁶The Israelites again offended the LORD, serving the Baals and Ashtaroth, the gods of Aram, the gods of Sidon, the gods of Moab, the gods of the Ammonites, and the gods of the Philistines. Since they had abandoned the LORD and would not serve him, **⁷**the LORD became angry with Israel and allowed them to fall into the power of [the Philistines and] the Ammonites. **⁸**For eighteen years they afflicted and oppressed the Israelites in Bashan, and all the Israelites in the Amorite land beyond the Jordan in Gilead. **⁹**The Ammonites also crossed the Jordan to fight against Judah, Benjamin, and the house of Ephraim, so that Israel was in great distress.

¹⁰Then the Israelites cried out to the LORD, "We have sinned against you; we have forsaken our God and have served the Baals." **¹¹***The LORD answered the Israelites: "Did not the Egyptians, the Amorites, the Ammonites, the Philistines, **¹²***the Sidonians, the Amalekites, and the Midianites oppress you? Yet when you cried out to me, and I saved you from their grasp, **¹³**you still forsook me and worshiped other gods. Therefore I will save you no more. **¹⁴**Go and cry out to the gods you have chosen; let them save you now that you are in distress." **¹⁵**But the Israelites said to the LORD, "We have sinned. Do to us whatever you please. Only save us this day." **¹⁶**And they cast out the foreign gods from their midst and served the LORD, so that he grieved over the misery of Israel.

¹⁷*The Ammonites had gathered for war and encamped in Gilead, while the Israelites assembled and encamped in Mizpah. **¹⁸***And among the people the princes of Gilead said to one another, "The one who begins the war against the Ammonites shall be leader of all the inhabitants of Gilead."

Jephthah

11 **¹**THERE was a chieftain, the Gileadite Jephthah, born to Gilead of a harlot. **²**Gilead's wife had also borne him sons, and on growing up the sons of the wife had driven Jephthah away, saying to him, "You shall inherit nothing in our family, for you are the son of another woman." **³**So Jephthah had fled from his brothers and had taken up residence in the land of Tob. A rabble had joined company with him, and went out with him on raids.

⁴Some time later, the Ammonites warred on Israel. **⁵**When this occurred the elders of Gilead went to bring Jephthah from the land of Tob. **⁶**"Come," they said to Jephthah, "be our commander that we may be able to fight the Ammonites." **⁷**"Are you not the ones who hated me and drove me from my father's house?" Jephthah replied to the elders of Gilead. "Why do you come to me now, when you are in distress?" **⁸**The elders of Gilead said to Jephthah, "In any case, we have now come back to you, if you go with us to fight against the Ammonites, you shall be the leader of all of us who dwell in Gilead." **⁹**Jephthah answered the elders of Gilead, "If you bring me back to fight against the Ammonites and the LORD delivers them up to me, I shall be your leader." **¹⁰**The elders of Gilead said to Jephthah, "The LORD is witness between us that we will do as you say."

¹¹*So Jephthah went with the elders of Gilead, and the people made him their leader and commander. In Mizpah, Jephthah settled all his affairs before the LORD. **¹²**Then he sent messengers to the king of the

---

❋
　　53: 2 Sm 11, 21.
　　54: 1 Sm 31, 4; 1 Chr 10, 4.
　10/4: Dt 3, 14.
　11-14: 2, 1ff; 6, 8ff.
　　11: Nm 21, 21-32.

　　12: 6, 3.
　　17: 11, 29.
　　18: 11, 5-11.
　11/11: 10, 18.

---

†
　10, 4: *Saddle-asses:* a sign of rank and wealth; cf 5, 10; 12, 14.

Ammonites to say, "What have you against me that you come to fight with me in my land?" **13***He answered the messengers of Jephthah, "Israel took away my land from the Arnon to the Jabbok and the Jordan when they came up from Egypt. Now restore the same peaceably."

14Again Jephthah sent messengers to the king of the Ammonites, **15***saying to him, "This is what Jephthah says: Israel did not take the land of Moab or the land of the Ammonites. **16**For when they came up from Egypt, Israel went through the desert to the Red Sea and came to Kadesh. **17***Israel then sent messengers to the king of Edom saying, 'Let me pass through your land.' But the king of Edom did not give consent. They also sent to the king of Moab, but he too was unwilling. So Israel remained in Kadesh. **18***Then they went through the desert, and by-passing the land of Edom and the land of Moab, went east of the land of Moab and encamped across the Arnon. Thus they did not go through the territory of Moab, for the Arnon is the boundary of Moab. **19***Then Israel sent messengers to Sihon, king of the Amorites, king of Heshbon. Israel said to him, 'Let me pass through your land to my own place.' **20**But Sihon refused to let Israel pass through his territory. On the contrary, he gathered all his soldiers, who encamped at Jahaz and fought Israel. **21**But the Lord, the God of Israel, delivered Sihon and all his men into the power of Israel, who defeated them and occupied all the land of the Amorites dwelling in that region, **22**the whole territory from the Arnon to the Jabbok, from the desert to the Jordan. **23**If now the Lord, the God of Israel, has cleared the Amorites out of the way of his people, are you to dislodge Israel? **24***†Should you not possess that which your god Chemosh gave you to possess, and should we not possess all that the Lord, our God, has cleared out for us? **25***Again, are you any better than Balak, son of Zippor, king of Moab? Did he ever quarrel with Israel, or did he war against them **26***when Israel occupied Heshbon and its villages, Aroer and its villages, and all the cities on the banks of the Arnon? Three hundred years have passed; why did you not recover them during that time? **27**I have not sinned against you, but you wrong me by warring against me. Let the Lord, who is judge, decide this day between the Israelites and the Ammonites!" **28**But the king of the Ammonites paid no heed to the message Jephthah sent him.

Jephthah's Vow

29The spirit of the Lord came upon Jephthah. He passed through Gilead and Manasseh, and through Mizpah-Gilead as well, and from there he went on

to the Ammonites. **30**†Jephthah made a vow to the Lord. "If you deliver the Ammonites into my power," he said, **31**"whoever comes out of the doors of my house to meet me when I return in triumph from the Ammonites shall belong to the Lord. I shall offer him up as a holocaust."

32Jephthah then went on to the Ammonites to fight against them, and the Lord delivered them into his power, **33**so that he inflicted a severe defeat on them, from Aroer to the approach of Minnith (twenty cities in all) and as far as Abel-keramin. Thus were the Ammonites brought into subjection by the Israelites. **34**When Jephthah returned to his house in Mizpah, it was his daughter who came forth, playing the tambourines and dancing. She was an only child: he had neither son nor daughter besides her. **35***When he saw her, he rent his garments and said, "Alas, daughter, you have struck me down and brought calamity upon me. For I have made a vow to the Lord and I cannot retract." **36**"Father," she replied, "you have made a vow to the Lord. Do with me as you have vowed, because the Lord has wrought vengeance for you on your enemies the Ammonites." **37**†Then she said to her father, "Let me have this favor. Spare me for two months, that I may go off down the mountains to mourn my virginity with my companions." **38**"Go," he replied, and sent her away for two months. So she departed with her companions and mourned her virginity on the mountains. **39**At the end of the two months she returned to her father, who did to her as he had vowed. She had not been intimate with man. It then became a custom in Israel **40**for Israelite women to go yearly to mourn the daughter of Jephthah the Gileadite for four days of the year.

The Shibboleth Incident

12 **1***THE men of Ephraim gathered together and crossed over to Zaphon. They said to Jephthah, "Why do you go on to fight with the Ammonites without calling us to go with you? We will burn your house over you." **2**Jephthah answered them, "My soldiers and I were engaged in a critical contest with the Ammonites. I summoned you, but you did not rescue me from their power. **3**When I saw that you would not effect a rescue, I took my life in my own

---

† 11, 24: *Chemosh:* the chief god of the Moabites—not of the Ammonites, whose leading deity was called Molech or Milcom; cf Nm 21, 29; 1 Kgs 11, 7; 2 Kgs 23, 13. The error is probably due to an ancient copyist. Jephthah argues from the viewpoint of his adversaries, the Ammonites, that they were entitled to all the land they had conquered with the aid of their god. It does not necessarily follow that Jephthah himself believed in the actual existence of this pagan god.

11, 30-40: The text clearly implies that Jephthah vowed a human sacrifice, according to the custom of his pagan neighbors; cf 2 Kgs 3, 27. The inspired author merely records the fact; he does not approve of the action.

11, 37: *Mourn my virginity:* to bear children was woman's greatest pride; to be childless was regarded as a great misfortune. Hence Jephthah's daughter asks permission to mourn the fact that she will be put to death before she can bear children.

13: Nm 21, 13.24ff.
15: Dt 2, 9.19.
17: Nm 20, 1.14.18-21;
    Dt 1, 46.
18: Nm 21, 4.11.13;
    22, 36; Dt 2, 8.
19-22: Nm 21, 21-26;
    Dt 2, 26-36.

24: Nm 21, 29; 1 Kgs 11, 7.
25: Nm 22, 2; Jos 24, 9;
    Mi 6, 5.
26: Nm 21, 25; Dt 2, 36.
35: Nm 30, 3.
12/1: 8, 1.

hand and went on to the Ammonites, and the LORD delivered them into my power. Why, then, do you come up against me this day to fight with me?"

⁴Then Jephthah called together all the men of Gilead and fought against Ephraim, whom they defeated; for the Ephraimites had said, "You of Gilead are Ephraimite fugitives in territory belonging to Ephraim and Manasseh." ⁵The Gileadites took the fords of the Jordan toward Ephraim. When any of the fleeing Ephraimites said, "Let me pass," the men of Gilead would say to him, "Are you an Ephraimite?" If he answered, "No!" ⁶†they would ask him to say "Shibboleth." If he said "Sibboleth," not being able to give the proper pronunciation, they would seize him and kill him at the fords of the Jordan. Thus forty-two thousand Ephraimites fell at that time.

⁷After having judged Israel for six years, Jephthah the Gileadite died and was buried in his city in Gilead.

Ibzan

⁸After him Ibzan of Bethlehem judged Israel. ⁹He had thirty sons. He also had thirty daughters married outside the family, and he brought in as wives for his sons thirty young women from outside the family. After having judged Israel for seven years, ¹⁰Ibzan died and was buried in Bethlehem.

Elon

¹¹After him the Zebulunite Elon judged Israel. When he had judged Israel for ten years, ¹²the Zebulunite Elon died and was buried in Elon in the land of Zebulun.

Abdon

¹³After him the Pirathonite Abdon, son of Hillel, judged Israel. ¹⁴He had forty sons and thirty grandsons who rode on seventy saddle-asses. After having judged Israel for eight years, ¹⁵the Pirathonite Abdon, son of Hillel, died and was buried in Pirathon in the land of Ephraim on the mountain of the Amalekites.

The Birth of Samson

13 ¹*THE Israelites again offended the LORD, who therefore delivered them into the power of the Philistines for forty years.

²There was a certain man from Zorah, of the clan of the Danites, whose name was Manoah. His wife was barren and had borne no children. ³*An angel of the LORD appeared to the woman and said to her, "Though you are barren and have had no children, yet you will conceive and bear a son. ⁴Now, then, be careful to take no wine or strong drink and to eat nothing unclean. ⁵*†As for the son you will conceive and bear, no razor shall touch his head, for this boy is to be consecrated to God from the womb. It is he who will begin the deliverance of Israel from the power of the Philistines."

⁶The woman went and told her husband, "A man of God came to me; he had the appearance of an angel of God, terrible indeed. I did not ask him where he came from, nor did he tell me his name. ⁷But he said to me, 'You will be with child and will bear a son. So take neither wine nor strong drink, and eat nothing unclean. For the boy shall be consecrated to God from the womb, until the day of his death.'" ⁸Manoah then prayed to the LORD. "O LORD, I beseech you," he said, "may the man of God whom you sent, return to us to teach us what to do for the boy who will be born."

⁹God heard the prayer of Manoah, and the angel of God came again to the woman as she was sitting in the field. Since her husband Manoah was not with her, ¹⁰the woman ran in haste and told her husband. "The man who came to me the other day has appeared to me," she said to him; ¹¹so Manoah got up and followed his wife. When he reached the man, he said to him, "Are you the one who spoke to my wife?" "Yes," he answered. ¹²Then Manoah asked, "Now, when that which you say comes true, what are we expected to do for the boy?" ¹³The angel of the LORD answered Manoah, "Your wife is to abstain from all the things of which I spoke to her. ¹⁴She must not eat anything that comes from the vine, nor take wine or strong drink, nor eat anything unclean. Let her observe all that I have commanded her." ¹⁵Then Manoah said to the angel of the LORD, "Can we persuade you to stay, while we prepare a kid for you?" ¹⁶But the angel of the LORD answered Manoah, "Although you press me, I will not partake of your food. But if you will, you may offer a holocaust to the LORD." Not knowing that it was the angel of the LORD, ¹⁷Manoah said to him, "What is your name, that we may honor you when your words come true?" ¹⁸*†The angel of the LORD answered him, "Why do you ask my name, which is mysterious?" ¹⁹*Then Manoah took the kid with a cereal offering and offered it on the rock to the LORD, whose works are mysteries. While Manoah and his wife were looking on, ²⁰as the flame rose to the sky from the altar, the angel of the LORD ascended in the flame of the altar. When Manoah and his wife saw this, they fell prostrate to the ground; ²¹*but the angel of the LORD was seen no more by Manoah and his wife. Then Manoah, realizing that it was the angel of the LORD, ²²said to his wife, "We will certainly die, for we have seen God." ²³But his wife pointed out to him, "If the LORD had meant to kill us, he would not have

---

† 12, 6: *Shibboleth:* "an ear of grain." But this Hebrew word can also mean "flood water" as in Ps 69, 3.16. Apparently the Gileadites engaged the Ephraimites in conversation about the "flood water" of the Jordan. Differences in enunciating the initial siblant of the Hebrew word betrayed different tribal affinities.

13, 5: *Consecrated:* in Hebrew, *nazir.* Samson therefore was for life to be under the nazirite vow, which obliged him to abstain from drinking wine or having his hair cut; cf Nm 6, 2-8.

13, 18: *Mysterious:* incomprehensible, above human understanding. Hence, the angel speaks in the name of the LORD himself, to whom Manoah at once offers a sacrifice.

13/1: 10, 6.
3f: 1 Sm 1, 20; Lk 1, 31.
5: Nm 6, 5.
18: Gn 32, 29.
19f: 6, 19ff.
21f: 6, 22f.

accepted a holocaust and cereal offering from our hands! Nor would he have let us see all this just now, or hear what we have heard."

24*The woman bore a son and named him Samson. The boy grew up and the LORD blessed him; **25**the spirit of the LORD first stirred him in Mahaneh-dan, which is between Zorah and Eshtaol.

Marriage of Samson

14 **1†**SAMSON went down to Timnah and saw there one of the Philistine women. **2**On his return he told his father and mother, "There is a Philistine woman I saw in Timnah whom I wish you to get as a wife for me." **3**His father and mother said to him, "Can you find no wife among your kinsfolk or among all our people, that you must go and take a wife from the uncircumcised Philistines?" But Samson answered his father, "Get her for me, for she pleases me." **4***Now his father and mother did not know that this had been brought about by the LORD, who was providing an opportunity against the Philistines; for at that time they had dominion over Israel.

5†So Samson went down to Timnah with his father and mother. When they had come to the vineyards of Timnah, a young lion came roaring to meet him. **6**But the spirit of the LORD came upon Samson, and although he had no weapons, he tore the lion in pieces as one tears a kid. **7**However, on the journey to speak for the woman, he did not mention to his father or mother what he had done. **8**Later, when he returned to marry the woman who pleased him, he stepped aside to look at the remains of the lion and found a swarm of bees and honey in the lion's carcass. **9**So he scooped the honey out into his palms and ate it as he went along. When he came to his father and mother, he gave them some to eat, without telling them that he had scooped the honey from the lion's carcass.

10His father also went down to the woman, and Samson gave a banquet there, since it was customary for the young men to do this. **11†**When they met him, they brought thirty men to be his companions. **12**Samson said to them, "Let me propose a riddle to you. If within the seven days of the feast you solve it for me successfully, I will give you thirty linen tunics and thirty sets of garments. **13**But if you cannot answer it for me, you must give me thirty tunics and thirty sets of garments." "Propose your riddle," they responded; "we will listen to it." **14**So he said to them,

"Out of the eater came forth food,
   and out of the strong came forth sweetness."

After three days' failure to answer the riddle, **15**they said on the fourth day to Samson's wife, "Coax your husband to answer the riddle for us, or we will burn you and your family. Did you invite us here to reduce us to poverty?" **16**At Samson's side, his wife wept and said, "You must hate me; you do not love me, for you

have proposed a riddle to my countrymen, but have not told me the answer." He said to her, "If I have not told it even to my father or my mother, must I tell it to you?" **17**But she wept beside him during the seven days the feast lasted. On the seventh day, since she importuned him, he told her the answer, and she explained the riddle to her countrymen. **18**On the seventh day, before the sun set, the men of the city said to him,

"What is sweeter than honey,
   and what is stronger than a lion?"

He replied to them,

"If you had not plowed with my heifer,
   you would not have solved my riddle."

19The spirit of the LORD came upon him, and he went down to Ashkelon, where he killed thirty of their men and despoiled them; he gave their garments to those who had answered the riddle. Then he went off to his own family in anger, **20***and Samson's wife was married to the one who had been best man at his wedding.

Samson Defeats the Philistines

15 **1**AFTER some time, in the season of the wheat harvest, Samson visited his wife, bringing a kid. But when he said, "Let me be with my wife in private," her father would not let him enter, **2**saying, "I thought it certain you wished to repudiate her; so I gave her to your best man. Her younger sister is more beautiful than she; you may have her instead." **3**Samson said to them, "This time the Philistines cannot blame me if I harm them." **4**So Samson left and caught three hundred foxes. Turning them tail to tail, he tied between each pair of tails one of the torches he had at hand. **5**He then kindled the torches and set the foxes loose in the standing grain of the Philistines, thus burning both the shocks and the standing grain, and the vineyards and olive orchards as well.

6*When the Philistines asked who had done this, they were told, "Samson, the son-in-law of the Timnite, because his wife was taken and given to his best man." So the Philistines went up and destroyed her and her family by fire. **7**Samson said to them, "If this is how you act, I will not stop until I have taken revenge on you." **8**And with repeated blows, he inflicted

---

† 14, 1-3: Marriages were arranged by the parents of the bridegroom as well as of the bride; cf Gn 24, 2-8; 34, 3-6. The Mosaic law specified only seven pagan nations, not including the Philistines, in the prohibition against mixed marriages; cf Dt 7, 1-4. But national and religious sentiment was against any marriage with a non-Israelite; cf Gn 28, 1f; 1 Kgs 11, 1-10.

14, 5ff: Although Samson was accompanied by his parents on the journey to Timnah, v 7 implies that he was not near them when *he tore the lion in pieces.*

14, 11: *Companions:* known at a later period as "the friends of the bridegroom" (1 Mc 9, 39; Mk 2, 19), the best man and his fellows. Here they are Philistines (v 16), appointed by the family of the bride, who would also have several bridesmaids; cf Mt 25, 1-13.

*
24: Heb 11, 32.   20: 15, 2.6.
14/4: 15, 11.   15/6: 14, 20.

a great slaughter on them. Then he went down and remained in a cavern of the cliff of Etam.

⁹The Philistines went up and, from a camp in Judah, deployed against Lehi. ¹⁰When the men of Judah asked, "Why have you come up against us?" they answered, "To take Samson prisoner; to do to him as he has done to us." ¹¹Three thousand men of Judah went down to the cavern in the cliff of Etam and said to Samson, "Do you not know that the Philistines are our rulers? Why, then, have you done this to us?" He answered them, "As they have done to me, so have I done to them." ¹²They said to him, "We have come to take you prisoner, to deliver you over to the Philistines." Samson said to them, "Swear to me that you will not kill me yourselves." ¹³*"No," they replied, "we will certainly not kill you but will only bind you and deliver you over to them." So they bound him with two new ropes and brought him up from the cliff. ¹⁴When he reached Lehi, and the Philistines came shouting to meet him, the spirit of the LORD came upon him: the ropes around his arms became as flax that is consumed by fire and his bonds melted away from his hands. ¹⁵Near him was the fresh jawbone of an ass; he reached out, grasped it, and with it killed a thousand men. ¹⁶Then Samson said,

"With the jawbone of an ass
    I have piled them in a heap;
With the jawbone of an ass
    I have slain a thousand men."

¹⁷†As he finished speaking he threw the jawbone from him; and so that place was named Ramath-lehi. ¹⁸Being very thirsty, he cried to the LORD and said, "You have granted this great victory by the hand of your servant. Must I now die of thirst or fall into the hands of the uncircumcised?" ¹⁹†Then God split the cavity in Lehi, and water issued from it, which Samson drank till his spirit returned and he revived. Hence that spring in Lehi is called En-hakkore to this day.

²⁰*Samson judged Israel for twenty years in the days of the Philistines.

16 ¹ONCE Samson went to Gaza, where he saw a harlot and visited her. ²Informed that Samson had come there, the men of Gaza surrounded him with an ambush at the city gate all night long. And all the night they waited, saying, "Tomorrow morning we will kill him." ³Samson rested there until midnight. Then he rose, seized the doors of the city gate and the two gateposts, and tore them loose, bar and all. He hoisted them on his shoulders and carried them to the top of the ridge opposite Hebron.

Samson and Delilah

⁴After that he fell in love with a woman in the Wadi Sorek whose name was Delilah. ⁵The lords of the Philistines came to her and said, "Beguile him and find

out the secret of his great strength, and how we may overcome and bind him so as to keep him helpless. We will each give you eleven hundred shekels of silver."

⁶So Delilah said to Samson, "Tell me the secret of your great strength and how you may be bound so as to be kept helpless." ⁷"If they bind me with seven fresh bowstrings which have not dried," Samson answered her, "I shall be as weak as any other man." ⁸So the lords of the Philistines brought her seven fresh bowstrings which had not dried, and she bound him with them. ⁹*She had men lying in wait in the chamber and so she said to him, "The Philistines are upon you, Samson!" But he snapped the strings as a thread of tow is severed by a whiff of flame; and the secret of his strength remained unknown.

¹⁰Delilah said to Samson, "You have mocked me and told me lies. Now tell me how you may be bound." ¹¹*"If they bind me tight with new ropes, with which no work has been done," he answered her, "I shall be as weak as any other man." ¹²So Delilah took new ropes and bound him with them. Then she said to him, "The Philistines are upon you, Samson!" For there were men lying in wait in the chamber. But he snapped them off his arms like thread.

¹³Delilah said to Samson again, "Up to now you have mocked me and told me lies. Tell me how you may be bound." He said to her, "If you weave my seven locks of hair into the web and fasten them with the pin, I shall be as weak as any other man." ¹⁴So while he slept, Delilah wove his seven locks of hair into the web, and fastened them in with the pin. Then she said, "The Philistines are upon you, Samson!" Awakening from his sleep, he pulled out both the weaver's pin and the web.

¹⁵Then she said to him, "How can you say that you love me when you do not confide in me? Three times already you have mocked me, and not told me the secret of your great strength!" ¹⁶She importuned him continually and vexed him with her complaints till he was deathly weary of them. ¹⁷*So he took her completely into his confidence and told her, "No razor has touched my head, for I have been consecrated to God from my mother's womb. If I am shaved, my strength will leave me, and I shall be as weak as any other man." ¹⁸When Delilah saw that he had taken her completely into his confidence, she summoned the lords of the Philistines, saying, "Come up this time, for he has opened his heart to me." So the lords of the Philistines came and brought up the money with them. ¹⁹She had him sleep on her lap, and called for a man who shaved off his seven locks of hair. Then she began to mistreat him, for his strength had left him. ²⁰When she said, "The Philistines are upon you, Samson!", and he woke from his sleep, he thought he could make good his escape as he had done time and again, for he did not realize that the LORD had left him. ²¹But the

13: 16, 11f.
20: 16, 31.
16/9: 15, 14.

11: 15, 13.
17: 13, 5.

† 15, 17: *Ramath-lehi:* "heights of the jawbone."
15, 19: *En-hakkore:* "the spring of him who cries out," an allusion to Samson's cry in v 18.

Philistines seized him and gouged out his eyes. Then they brought him down to Gaza and bound him with bronze fetters, and he was put to grinding in the prison. **22**But the hair of his head began to grow as soon as it was shaved off.

The Death of Samson

23*†The lords of the Philistines assembled to offer a great sacrifice to their god Dagon and to make merry. They said,

> "Our god has delivered into our power
> Samson our enemy."

25When their spirits were high, they said, "Call Samson that he may amuse us." So they called Samson from the prison, and he played the buffoon before them. **24**When the people saw him, they praised their god. For they said,

> "Our god has delivered into our power
> our enemy, the ravager of our land,
> the one who has multiplied our slain."

Then they stationed him between the columns. **26**Samson said to the attendant who was holding his hand, "Put me where I may touch the columns that support the temple and may rest against them." **27**The temple was full of men and women: all the lords of the Philistines were there, and from the roof about three thousand men and women looked on as Samson provided amusement. **28**Samson cried out to the LORD and said, "O Lord GOD, remember me! Strengthen me, O God, this last time that for my two eyes I may avenge myself once and for all on the Philistines." **29**Samson grasped the two middle columns on which the temple rested and braced himself against them, one at his right hand, the other at his left. **30**And Samson said, "Let me die with the Philistines!" He pushed hard, and the temple fell upon the lords and all the people who were in it. Those he killed at his death were more than those he had killed during his lifetime.

31*All his family and kinsmen went down and bore him up for burial in the grave of his father Manoah between Zorah and Eshtaol. He had judged Israel for twenty years.

III: THE TRIBES OF DAN AND BENJAMIN IN THE DAYS OF THE JUDGES

Micah and the Levite

17 **1**THERE WAS A MAN in the mountain region of Ephraim whose name was Micah. **2**He said to his mother, "The eleven hundred shekels of silver over which you pronounced a curse in my hearing when they were taken from you, are in my possession. It was I who took them; so now I will restore them to you." **3*†**When he restored the eleven hundred shekels of silver to his mother, she took two hundred of them and gave them to the silversmith, who made of them a carved idol overlaid with silver. **4**Then his mother said, "May the LORD bless my son! I have consecrated the silver to the LORD as my gift in favor of my son, by making a carved idol overlaid with silver." It remained in the house of Micah. **5***Thus the layman Micah had a sanctuary. He also made an ephod and household idols, and consecrated one of his sons, who became his priest. **6***In those days there was no king in Israel; everyone did what he thought best.

7There was a young Levite who had resided within the tribe of Judah at Bethlehem of Judah. **8**From that city he set out to find another place of residence. On his journey he came to the house of Micah in the mountain region of Ephraim. **9**Micah said to him, "Where do you come from?" He answered him, "I am a Levite from Bethlehem in Judah, and am on my way to find some other place of residence." **10***"Stay with me," Micah said to him. "Be father and priest to me, and I will give you ten silver shekels a year, a set of garments, and your food." **11**So the young Levite decided to stay with the man, to whom he became as one of his own sons. **12†**Micah consecrated the young Levite, who became his priest, remaining in his house. **13**Therefore Micah said, "Now I know that the LORD will prosper me, since the Levite has become my priest."

Migration of the Danites

18 **1*†**AT that time there was no king in Israel. Moreover the tribe of Danites were in search of a district to dwell in, for up to that time they had received no heritage among the tribes of Israel.

2So the Danites sent from their clan a detail of five valiant men of Zorah and Eshtaol, to reconnoiter the land and scout it. With their instructions to go and scout the land, they traveled as far as the house of Micah in the mountain region of Ephraim, where they passed the night. **3*†**Near the house of Micah, they recognized the voice of the young Levite and turned in that direction. "Who brought you here and what are you doing here?" they asked him. "What is your

---

✿
23: 1 Sm 5, 2-5.
31: 15, 20.
17/3: Ex 20, 4; Lv 19, 4.
5: 18, 14.17.
6: 18, 1; 21, 25.
10: 18, 19.
18/1: Jos 19, 40-48.
3: 17, 7.

---

† 16, 23: Dagon was originally a Mesopotamian deity, whom the Philistines came to worship as their own god of grain.

17, 3: *Idol:* an image, not of a pagan god, but of the LORD. The Mosaic law forbade the making of an image even of the true God.

17, 12f: According to Nm 18, 1-7 only those Levites who were descended from Aaron could be consecrated as priests.

18, 1: The tribe of Dan had been assigned a territory with definite limits in central Palestine. However they were unable to gain possession of the better portion of their land (1, 34). So they now seek territory elsewhere in Palestine.

18, 3: *Recognized the voice:* perhaps they noticed the peculiar pronunciation of his south Hebrew dialect.

interest here?" **4***"This is how Micah treats me," he replied to them. "He pays me a salary and I am his priest." **5**They said to him, "Consult God, that we may know whether the undertaking we are engaged in will succeed." **6**The priest said to them, "Go and prosper: the LORD is favorable to the undertaking you are engaged in."

7So the five men went on and came to Laish. They saw that the people dwelling there lived securely after the manner of the Sidonians, quiet and trusting, with no lack of any natural resources. They were distant from the Sidonians and had no contact with other people. **8**When the five returned to their kinsmen in Zorah and Eshtaol and were asked for a report, **9**they replied, "Come, let us attack them, for we have seen the land and it is very good. Are you going to hesitate? Do not be slothful about beginning your expedition to possess the land. **10**Those against whom you go are a trusting people, and the land is ample. God has indeed given it into your power: a place where no natural resource is lacking."

11So six hundred men of the clan of the Danites, fully armed with weapons of war, set out from where they were in Zorah and Eshtaol, **12***and camped in Judah, up near Kiriath-jearim; hence to this day the place, which lies west of Kiriath-jearim, is called Mahaneh-dan.

13From there they went on to the mountain region of Ephraim and came to the house of Micah. **14***The five men who had gone to reconnoiter the land of Laish said to their kinsmen, "Do you know that in these houses there are an ephod, household idols, and a carved idol overlaid with silver? Now decide what you must do!" **15**So turning in that direction, they went to the house of the young Levite at the home of Micah and greeted him. **16**The six hundred men girt with weapons of war, who were Danites, stood by the entrance of the gate, and the priest stood there also. **17**Meanwhile the five men who had gone to reconnoiter the land went up and entered the house of Micah. **18**When they had gone in and taken the ephod, the household idols, and the carved idol overlaid with silver, the priest said to them, "What are you doing?" **19***They said to him, "Be still: put your hand over your mouth. Come with us and be our father and priest. Is it better for you to be priest for the family of one man or to be priest for a tribe and a clan in Israel?" **20**The priest, agreeing, took the ephod, household idols, and carved idol and went off in the midst of the band. **21**As they turned to depart, they placed their little ones, their livestock, and their goods at the head of the column.

22The Danites had already gone some distance, when those in the houses near that of Micah took up arms and overtook them. **23**They called to the Danites, who turned about and said to Micah, "What do you want, that you have taken up arms?" **24**"You have

taken my god, which I made, and have gone off with my priest as well," he answered. "What is left for me? How, then, can you ask me what I want?" **25**The Danites said to him, "Let us hear no further sound from you, lest fierce men fall upon you and you and your family lose your lives." **26**The Danites then went on their way, and Micah, seeing that they were stronger than he, returned home.

27Having taken what Micah had made, and the priest he had had, they attacked Laish, a quiet and trusting people; they put them to the sword and destroyed their city by fire. **28**No one came to their aid, since the city was far from Sidon and they had no contact with other people. The Danites then rebuilt the city, which was in the valley that belongs to Beth-rehob, and lived there. **29**They named it Dan after their ancestor Dan, son of Israel. However, the name of the city was formerly Laish. **30**†The Danites set up the carved idol for themselves, and Jonathan, son of Gershom, son of Moses, and his descendants were priests for the tribe of the Danites until the time of the captivity of the land. **31**They maintained the carved idol Micah had made as long as the house of God was in Shiloh.

The Levite from Ephraim

19 **1***AT that time, when there was no king in Israel, there was a Levite residing in remote parts of the mountain region of Ephraim who had taken for himself a concubine from Bethlehem of Judah. **2**His concubine was unfaithful to him and left him for her father's house in Bethlehem of Judah, where she stayed for some four months. **3**Her husband then set out with his servant and a pair of asses, and went after her to forgive her and take her back. She brought him into her father's house, and on seeing him, the girl's father joyfully made him welcome. **4**He was detained by the girl's father, and so he spent three days with this father-in-law of his, eating and drinking and passing the night there. **5**†On the fourth day they rose early in the morning and he prepared to go. But the girl's father said to his son-in-law, "Fortify yourself with a little food; you can go later on." **6**So they stayed and the two men ate and drank together. Then the girl's father said to the husband, "Why not decide to spend the night here and enjoy yourself?" **7**The man still made a move to go, but when his father-in-law pressed him he went back and spent the night there.

8On the fifth morning he rose early to depart, but the girl's father said, "Fortify yourself and tarry until the afternoon." When he and his father-in-law had eaten, **9**and the husband was ready to go with his concubine and servant, the girl's father said to him, "It is already growing dusk. Stay for the night. See, the day

---

---

† 18, 30: *Until . . . land:* about the year 734 B. C., when the Assyrian emperor Tiglath-pileser III subjected northern Palestine.

19, 5-9: Such importuning of guests to prolong their stay at the home of their host is characteristic of Oriental hospitality.

is coming to an end. Spend the night here and enjoy yourself. Early tomorrow you can start your journey home." **10**The man, however, refused to stay another night; he and his concubine set out with a pair of saddled asses, and traveled till they came opposite Jebus, which is Jerusalem. **11**Since they were near Jebus with the day far gone, the servant said to his master, "Come, let us turn off to this city of the Jebusites and spend the night in it." **12***But his master said to him, "We will not turn off to a city of foreigners, who are not Israelites, but will go on to Gibeah. **13***Come," he said to his servant, "let us make for some other place, either Gibeah or Ramah, to spend the night." **14**So they continued on their way till the sun set on them when they were abreast of Gibeah of Benjamin.

15*†There they turned off to enter Gibeah for the night. The man waited in the public square of the city he had entered, but no one offered them the shelter of his home for the night. **16**In the evening, however, an old man came from his work in the field; he was from the mountain region of Ephraim, though he lived among the Benjaminite townspeople of Gibeah. **17**When he noticed the traveler in the public square of the city, the old man asked where he was going, and whence he had come. **18**He said to him, "We are traveling from Bethlehem of Judah far up into the mountain region of Ephraim, where I belong. I have been to Bethlehem of Judah and am now going back home; but no one has offered us the shelter of his house. **19**We have straw and fodder for our asses, and bread and wine for the woman and myself and for our servant; there is nothing else we need." **20**"You are welcome," the old man said to him, "but let me provide for all your needs, and do not spend the night in the public square." **21***So he led them to his house and provided fodder for the asses. Then they washed their feet, and ate and drank.

The Outrage at Gibeah

22*†While they were enjoying themselves, the men of the city, who were corrupt, surrounded the house and beat on the door. They said to the old man whose house it was, "Bring out your guest, that we may abuse him." **23**The owner of the house went out to them and said, "No, my brothers; do not be so wicked. Since this man is my guest, do not commit this crime. **24**Rather let me bring out my maiden daughter or his concubine. Ravish them, or do whatever you want with them; but against the man you must not commit this wanton crime." **25**When the men would not listen to his host, the husband seized his concubine and thrust her outside to them. They had relations with her and abused her all night until the following dawn, when they let her go. **26**Then at daybreak the woman came

and collapsed at the entrance of the house in which her husband was a guest, where she lay until the morning. **27**When her husband rose that day and opened the door of the house to start out again on his journey, there lay the woman, his concubine, at the entrance of the house with her hands on the threshold. **28**He said to her, "Come, let us go"; but there was no answer. So the man placed her on an ass and started out again for home.

29†On reaching home, he took a knife to the body of his concubine, cut her into twelve pieces, and sent them throughout the territory of Israel. **30***Everyone who saw this said, "Nothing like this has been done or seen from the day the Israelites came up from the land of Egypt to this day. Take note of it, and state what you propose to do."

Assembly of Israelites

20 **1†**so all the Israelites came out as one man: from Dan to Beer-sheba, and from the land of Gilead, the community was gathered to the Lord at Mizpah. **2**The leaders of all the people and all the tribesmen of Israel, four hundred thousand foot soldiers who were swordsmen, presented themselves in the assembly of the people of God. **3**Meanwhile, the Benjaminites heard that the Israelites had gone up to Mizpah. The Israelites asked to be told how the crime had taken place, **4***and the Levite, the husband of the murdered woman, testified: "My concubine and I went into Gibeah of Benjamin for the night. **5***But the citizens of Gibeah rose up against me by night and surrounded the house in which I was. Me they attempted to kill, and my concubine they abused so that she died. **6***So I took my concubine and cut her up and sent her through every part of the territory of Israel, because of the monstrous crime they had committed in Israel. **7*†**Now that you are all here, O Israelites, state what you propose to do." **8**All the people rose as one man to say, "None of us is to leave for his tent or return to his home. **9**Now as for Gibeah, this is what we will do: We will proceed against it by lot, **10**taking from all the tribes of Israel ten men for every hundred, a hundred for every thousand, a thousand for every ten thousand, and procuring supplies for the soldiers who will go to deal fully and suitably with Gibeah of Benjamin for the crime it committed in Israel."

11When, therefore, all the men of Israel without ex-

---

† 19, 15: Private hospitality was the customary means of providing comfort for travelers where public facilities were so rare.

19, 22: *Who were corrupt:* literally "sons of Belial," indicating extreme perversion; cf Gn 19, 4-8. This crime and its punishment made the name *Gibeah* proverbial as a place of shameful wickedness; cf Hos 9, 9; 10, 9.

19, 29: A drastic means for arousing the tribes to avenge the unheard of crime of the Benjaminites.

20, 1: *From Dan to Beer-sheba:* from north to south. *The land of Gilead:* all the territory east of the Jordan.

20, 7: The Israelites were asked to decide at once what action to take concerning this crime; cf 2 Sm 16, 20. The Levite undoubtedly addressed the tribal heads who would speak in behalf of the multitude.

✱
12: 1, 21.	30: Hos 9, 9; 10, 9.
13: Jos 18, 25.	20/4: 19, 14f.
15: 20, 4.	5: 19, 22-27.
21: Gn 18, 4; 24, 32; 43, 24.	6: 19, 29.
	7: 19, 30.
22-25: Gn 19, 4-9.	

ception were leagued together against the city, **12**†the tribes of Israel sent men throughout the tribe of Benjamin to say, "What is this evil which has occurred among you? **13**Now give up these corrupt men of Gibeah, that we may put them to death and thus purge the evil from Israel." But the Benjaminites refused to accede to the demand of their brothers, the Israelites. **14**Instead, the Benjaminites assembled from their other cities to Gibeah, to do battle with the Israelites. **15**The number of the Benjaminite swordsmen from the other cities on that occasion was twenty-six thousand, in addition to the inhabitants of Gibeah. **16**Included in this total were seven hundred picked men who were left-handed, every one of them able to sling a stone at a hair without missing. **17**Meanwhile the other Israelites who, without Benjamin, mustered four hundred thousand swordsmen ready for battle, **18***†moved on to Bethel and consulted God. When the Israelites asked who should go first in the attack on the Benjaminites, the LORD said, "Judah shall go first." **19**The next day the Israelites advanced on Gibeah with their forces.

War with Benjamin

20On the day the Israelites drew up in battle array at Gibeah for the combat with Benjamin, **21**the Benjaminites came out of the city and felled twenty-two thousand men of Israel. **23**Then the Israelites went up and wept before the LORD until evening. "Shall I again engage my brother Benjamin in battle?" they asked the LORD; and the LORD answered that they should. **22**But though the Israelite soldiers took courage and again drew up for combat in the same place as on the previous day, **24**when they met the Benjaminites for the second time, **25**once again the Benjaminites who came out of Gibeah against them felled eighteen thousand Israelites, all of them swordsmen. **26**So the entire Israelite army went up to Bethel, where they wept and remained fasting for the LORD until evening of that day, besides offering holocausts and peace offerings before the LORD. **27***When the Israelites consulted the LORD (for the ark of the covenant of God was there in those days, **28**and Phinehas, son of Eleazar, son of Aaron, was ministering to him in those days), and asked, "Shall I go out again to battle with Benjamin, my brother, or shall I desist?" the LORD said, "Attack! for tomorrow I will deliver him into your power." **29***†So Israel set men in ambush around Gibeah.

30The Israelites went up against the Benjaminites for the third time and formed their line of battle at Gibeah as on other occasions. **31**The Benjaminites went out to meet them, and in the beginning they killed off about thirty of the Israelite soldiers in the open field, just as on the other occasions. **32**Therefore the Benjaminites thought, "We are defeating them as before"; not realizing that disaster was about to overtake them. The Israelites, however, had planned the flight so as to draw them away from the city onto the highways. They were drawn away from the city onto the highways, of which the one led to Bethel, the other to Gibeon. **33**And then all the men of Israel rose from their places. They re-formed their ranks at Baal-tamar, and the Israelites in ambush rushed from their place west of Gibeah, **34**ten thousand picked men from all Israel, and advanced against the city itself. In a fierce battle, **35**the LORD defeated Benjamin before Israel; and on that day the Israelites killed twenty-five thousand one hundred men of Benjamin, all of them swordsmen.

36To the Benjaminites it had looked as though the enemy were defeated, for the men of Israel gave ground to Benjamin, trusting in the ambush they had set at Gibeah. **37**But then the men in ambush made a sudden dash into Gibeah, overran it, and put the whole city to the sword. **38**Now, the other Israelites had agreed with the men in ambush on a smoke signal they were to send up from the city. **39**And though the men of Benjamin had begun by killing off some thirty of the men of Israel, under the impression that they were defeating them as surely as in the earlier fighting, the Israelites wheeled about to resist **40**as the smoke of the signal column began to rise up from the city. It was when Benjamin looked back and saw the whole city in flames against the sky **41**that the men of Israel wheeled about. Therefore the men of Benjamin were thrown into confusion, for they realized the disaster that had overtaken them. **42**They retreated before the men of Israel in the direction of the desert, with the fight being pressed against them. In their very midst, meanwhile, those who had been in the city were spreading destruction. **43**The men of Benjamin had been surrounded, and were now pursued to a point east of Gibeah, **44**while eighteen thousand of them fell, warriors to a man. **45***The rest turned and fled through the desert to the rock Rimmon. But on the highways the Israelites picked off five thousand men among them, and chasing them up to Gidom, killed another two thousand of them there. **46**Those of Benjamin who fell on that day were in all twenty-five thousand swordsmen, warriors to a man. **47**But six hundred others who turned and fled through the desert reached the rock Rimmon, where they remained for four months.

---

† 20, 12: Before the crime at Gibeah was punished, the Benjaminites were invited to join their brethren, the Irsaelites, in punishing the crime. Since they failed to respond, special messengers were sent asking them to deliver up the guilty ones. They replied by gathering their forces for combat.

20, 18: *Judah shall go first:* the same response as in 1, 1f, but without the assurance of immediate success. Only after the Israelites were punished at the hands of the Benjaminites for their own grossness, and had performed penance, did they succeed in punishing the latter for their part in the crime of rape and murder, by gaining the victory over them.

20, 29-46: This stratagem proved more useful to the Israelites than force, as in the siege of Ai (Jos 8, 3-21). In the parallel accounts the first (vv 29-35) is a summary of the second (vv 36-46).

---

*   18: 1, 1f.   29-46: Jos 8, 4-24.
     27: 1 Sm 4, 3f.   45: 21, 13.

48The men of Israel withdrew through the territory of the Benjaminites, putting to the sword the inhabitants of the cities, the livestock, and all they chanced upon. Moreover they destroyed by fire all the cities they came upon.

Wives for the Survivors

21 **1†**NOW the men of Israel had sworn at Mizpah that none of them would give his daughter in marriage to anyone from Benjamin. **2***So the people went to Bethel and remained there before God until evening, raising their voices in bitter lament. **3**They said, "LORD, God of Israel, why has it come to pass in Israel that today one tribe of Israel should be lacking?" **4**Early the next day the people built an altar there and offered holocausts and peace offerings. **5***Then the Israelites asked, "Are there any among all the tribes of Israel who did not come up to the LORD for the assembly?" For they had taken a solemn oath that anyone who did not go up to the LORD at Mizpah should be put to death without fail.

6†The Israelites were disconsolate over their brother Benjamin and said, "Today one of the tribes of Israel has been cut off. **7**What can we do about wives for the survivors, since we have sworn by the LORD not to give them any of our daughters in marriage?" **8**And when they asked whether anyone among the tribes of Israel had not come up to the LORD in Mizpah, they found that none of the men of Jabesh-gilead had come to the encampment for the assembly. **9**A roll call of the army established that none of the inhabitants of that city were present. **10**The community, therefore, sent twelve thousand warriors with orders to go to Jabesh-gilead and put those who lived there to the sword, including the women and children. **11*†**They were told to include under the ban all males and every woman who was not still a virgin. **12**Finding among the inhabitants of Jabesh-gilead four hundred young virgins, who had had no relations with men, they brought them to the camp at Shiloh in the land of Canaan. **13***Then the whole community sent a message to the Benjaminites at the rock Rimmon, offering them peace. **14**When Benjamin returned at that time, they gave them as wives the women of Jabesh-gilead whom they had spared; but these proved to be not enough for them.

15†The people were still disconsolate over Benjamin because the LORD had made a breach among the tribes of Israel. **16**And the elders of the community said, "What shall we do for wives for the survivors? For every woman in Benjamin has been put to death." **17**They said, "Those of Benjamin who survive must have heirs, else one of the Israelite tribes will be wiped out. **18†**Yet we cannot give them any of our daughters in marriage, because the Israelites have sworn, 'Cursed be he who gives a woman to Benjamin!'" **19**Then they thought of the yearly feast of the LORD at Shiloh, north of Bethel, east of the highway that goes up from Bethel to Shechem, and south of Lebonah. **20**And they instructed the Benjaminites, "Go and lie in wait in the vineyards. **21**When you see the girls of Shiloh come out to do their dancing, leave the vineyards and each of you seize one of the girls of Shiloh for a wife, and go to the land of Benjamin. **22**When their fathers or their brothers come to complain to us, we shall say to them, 'Release them to us as a kindness, since we did not take a woman apiece in the war. Had you yourselves given them these wives, you would now be guilty.'"

23The Benjaminites did this; they carried off a wife for each of them from their raid on the dancers, and went back to their own territory, where they rebuilt and occupied the cities. **24**Also at that time the Israelites dispersed; each of them left for his own heritage in his own clan and tribe.

25*†In those days there was no king in Israel; everyone did what he thought best.

---

† 21, 1-3: The anger of the Israelites led them to destroy their brethren, the Benjaminites. Having realized their goal, however, they were soon filled with dismay, and sought to restore the tribe they had all but exterminated.

21, 6-9: This account is summarized in the parallel passage in vv 2-5.

21, 11: *Under the ban:* see note on Nm 21, 3.

21, 15: *Had made a breach:* what is here attributed to God was in reality the free and deliberate act of the Israelites and happened only by the permissive will of God. The ancients attributed to the first primary cause what is more directly due to secondary causes.

21, 18: Regardless of the serious consequences of their vow, the Israelites considered themselves obliged to fulfill it; cf 11, 31.35f.39.

21, 25: Cf 17, 6; 18, 1; 19, 1. The verse gives the reason why the lawlessness of the period of judges, and the events described herein, were possible.

✻ 21/2: 20, 26.
5: 20, 8ff.
11: Nm 31, 17.
13: 20, 47.
25: 17, 6; 18, 1; 19, 1.

The Book of Ruth

Introduction

The Book of Ruth is named after the Moabite woman who was joined to the Israelite people by her marriage with the influential Boaz of Bethlehem.

The book contains a beautiful example of filial piety, pleasing to the Hebrews especially because of its connection with King David, and useful both to Hebrews and to Gentiles. Its aim is to demonstrate the divine reward for such piety even when practiced by a stranger. Ruth's piety (2, 11), her spirit of self-sacrifice, and her moral integrity were favored by God with the gift of faith and an illustrious marriage whereby she became the ancestress of David and of Christ. In this, the universality of the messianic salvation is foreshadowed.

In the Greek and Latin canons the Book of Ruth is placed just after Judges, to which it is closely related because of the time of its action, and just before Samuel, for which it is an excellent introduction, since it traces the ancestry of the Davidic dynasty. One might characterize the literary form of this book as dramatic, since about two-thirds of it is in dialogue. Yet there is every indication that, as tradition has always held, it contains true history.

There is no certainty about the author of the book. It was written long after the events had passed (4, 7), which took place "in the time of the judges" (1, 1).

Naomi in Moab

1 [1†]ONCE in the time of the judges there was a famine in the land; so a man from Bethlehem of Judah departed with his wife and two sons to reside on the plateau of Moab. [2]The man was named Elimelech, his wife Naomi, and his sons Mahlon and Chilion; they were Ephrathites from Bethlehem of Judah. Some time after their arrival on the Moabite plateau, [3]Elimelech, the husband of Naomi, died, and she was left with her two sons, [4]who married Moabite women, one named Orpah, the other Ruth. When they had lived there about ten years, [5]both Mahlon and Chilion died also, and the woman was left with neither her two sons nor her husband. [6]She then made ready to go back from the plateau of Moab because word reached her there that the LORD had visited his people and given them food.

[7]She and her two daughters-in-law left the place where they had been living. Then as they were on the road back to the land of Judah, [8†]Naomi said to her two daughters-in-law, "Go back, each of you, to your mother's house! May the LORD be kind to you as you

were to the departed and to me! [9]May the LORD grant each of you a husband and a home in which you will find rest." She kissed them good-by, but they wept with loud sobs, [10]and told her they would return with her to her people. [11†]"Go back, my daughters!" said Naomi. "Why should you come with me? Have I other sons in my womb who may become your husbands? [12]Go back, my daughters! Go, for I am too old to marry again. And even if I could offer any hopes, or if tonight I had a husband or had borne sons, [13]would you then wait and deprive yourselves of husbands until those sons grew up? No, my daughters! my lot is too bitter for you, because the LORD has extended his hand against me." [14]Again they sobbed aloud and wept; and Orpah kissed her mother-in-law good-by, but Ruth stayed with her.

[15]"See now!" she said, "your sister-in-law has gone back to her people and her god. Go back after your sister-in-law!" [16†]But Ruth said, "Do not ask me to abandon or forsake you! for wherever you go I will go, wherever you lodge I will lodge, your people shall be my people, and your God my God. [17]Wherever you die I will die, and there be buried. May the LORD do so and so to me, and more besides, if aught but death separates me from you!" [18]Naomi then ceased to urge her, for she saw she was determined to go with her.

The Return to Bethlehem

[19]So they went on together till they reached Bethlehem. On their arrival there, the whole city was astir over them, and the women asked, "Can this be

---

† 1, 1f: *In the time of the judges:* three generations before the end of the period of judges; cf 4, 21f. *Bethlehem of Judah:* to distinguish it from the town of the same name in the tribe of Zebulun (Jos 19, 15). *Ephrathites from Bethlehem:* belonging to a Judean clan which settled in Bethlehem; cf 1 Sm 17, 12; 1 Chr 2, 50f; 4, 4.

1, 8: *Mother's house:* the women's part of the dwelling; cf Jgs 4, 17; Sg 3, 4.

1, 11: *Have I other sons . . . husbands?* Naomi insisted that her daughters-in-law remain in their own country only for the sake of posterity. If she had had other sons, the levirate law would have obliged them to marry the widows of her deceased sons to perpetuate the names of the deceased; cf Gn 38, 8; Dt 25, 5f.

1, 16f: An example of heroic fidelity and piety. Ruth's decision, confirmed with an oath, to adhere to her mother-in-law impelled her to abandon her country and its pagan worship.

Naomi?" **20*†**But she said to them, "Do not call me Naomi. Call me Mara, for the Almighty has made it very bitter for me. **21**I went away with an abundance, but the LORD has brought me back destitute. Why should you call me Naomi, since the LORD has pronounced against me and the Almighty has brought evil upon me?" **22†**Thus it was that Naomi returned with the Moabite daughter-in-law, Ruth, who accompanied her back from the plateau of Moab. They arrived in Bethlehem at the beginning of the barley harvest.

The Meeting

2 **1***NAOMI had a prominent kinsman named Boaz, of the clan of her husband Elimelech. Ruth the Moabite said to Naomi, **2*†**"Let me go and glean ears of grain in the field of anyone who will allow me that favor." Naomi said to her, "Go, my daughter," **3**and she went. The field she entered to glean after the harvesters happened to be the section belonging to Boaz of the clan of Elimelech. **4†**Boaz himself came from Bethlehem and said to the harvesters, "The LORD be with you!" and they replied, "The LORD bless you!" **5**Boaz asked the overseer of his harvesters, "Whose girl is this?" **6***The overseer of the harvesters answered, "She is the Moabite girl who returned from the plateau of Moab with Naomi. **7**She asked leave to gather the gleanings into sheaves after the harvesters; and ever since she came this morning she has remained here until now, with scarcely a moment's rest."

8Boaz said to Ruth, "Listen, my daughter! Do not go to glean in anyone else's field; you are not to leave here. Stay here with my women servants. **9**Watch to see which field is to be harvested, and follow them; I have commanded the young men to do you no harm. When you are thirsty, you may go and drink from the vessels the young men have filled." **10**Casting herself prostrate upon the ground, she said to him, "Why should I, a foreigner, be favored with your notice?" **11***Boaz answered her: "I have had a complete account of what you have done for your mother-in-law after your husband's death; you have left your father and your mother and the land of your birth, and have come to a people whom you did not know previously. **12**May the LORD reward what you have done! May you receive a full reward from the LORD, the God of Israel, under whose wings you have come for refuge." **13**She said, "May I prove worthy of your kindness, my lord: you have comforted me, your servant, with your consoling words; would indeed that I were a servant of yours!" **14**At mealtime Boaz said to her, "Come here and have some food; dip your bread in the sauce." Then as she sat near the reapers, he handed her some roasted grain and she ate her fill and had some left over. **15**She rose to glean, and Boaz instructed his servants to let her glean among the sheaves themselves without scolding her, **16**and even to let drop some handfuls and leave them for her to glean without being rebuked.

17She gleaned in the field until evening, and when she beat out what she had gleaned it came to about an ephah of barley, **18**which she took into the city and showed to her mother-in-law. Next she brought out and gave her what she had left over from lunch. **19**So her mother-in-law said to her, "Where did you glean today? Where did you go to work? May he who took notice of you be blessed!" Then she told her mother-in-law with whom she had worked. "The man at whose place I worked today is named Boaz," she said. **20*†**"May he be blessed by the LORD, who is ever merciful to the living and to the dead," Naomi exclaimed to her daughter-in-law; and she continued, "He is a relative of ours, one of our next of kin." **21**"He even told me," added Ruth the Moabite, "that I should stay with his servants until they complete his entire harvest." **22**"You would do well, my dear," Naomi rejoined, "to go out with his servants; for in someone else's field you might be insulted." **23**So she stayed gleaning with the servants of Boaz until the end of the barley and wheat harvests.

Ruth Again Presents Herself

3 WHEN she was back with her mother-in-law, **1**Naomi said to her, "My daughter, I must seek a home for you that will please you. **2***Now is not Boaz, with whose servant you were, a relative of ours? This evening he will be winnowing barley at the threshing floor. **3**So bathe and anoint yourself; then put on your best attire and go down to the threshing floor. Do not make yourself known to the man before he has finished eating and drinking. **4†**But when he lies down, take note of the place where he does so. Then go, uncover a place at his feet, and lie down. He will tell you what to do." **5**"I will do whatever you advise," Ruth replied. **6**So she went down to the threshing floor

---

† 1, 20f: *Naomi:* "amiable" or "pleasant," suggesting God's favor toward her. *The Almighty has brought evil upon me:* the ancients regarded adversity as a punishment from God for personal sin, as if good and evil were always repaid in a temporal and material manner.

1, 22: *Barley harvest:* early April. This circumstance favored the events of the narrative that follow.

2, 2: *Let me go and glean . . . grain:* even the poor, the widow, the stranger, and the orphan had a right to glean at harvest time; cf Lv 19, 9f; 23, 22; Dt 24, 19-22.

2, 4: *The Lord be with you:* courtesy and religious feeling characterize the salutations of the Hebrews. This greeting is used in the Christian liturgy.

2, 20: *One of our next of kin:* literally "our redeemer," a near relative of the same clan who had the right and duty to restore the land which an impoverished kinsman had alienated (Lv 25, 25-28), and to marry the widow of a relative who had died without male offspring so as to raise up posterity to his name (Dt 25, 5-10).

3, 4: *Uncover a place at his feet, . . . :* confident of the virtue of Ruth and Boaz, Naomi advises this unusual expedient to her daughter-in-law for the purpose of introducing her claim.

❋
1/20: Ex 15, 23.   11: 1, 14-17.
2/1: 3, 2.12; 4, 21; Mt 1, 5.   20: 3, 9.
2: Dt 24, 19.   3/2: 1.
6: 1, 22.

and did just as her mother-in-law had instructed her.

⁷Boaz ate and drank to his heart's content. Then when he went and lay down at the edge of the sheaves, she stole up, uncovered a place at his feet, and lay down. ⁸In the middle of the night, however, the man gave a start and turned around to find a woman lying at his feet. ⁹†He asked, "Who are you?" And she replied, "I am your servant Ruth. Spread the corner of your cloak over me, for you are my next of kin." ¹⁰*He said, "May the Lord bless you, my daughter! You have been even more loyal now than before in not going after the young men, whether poor or rich. ¹¹So be assured, daughter, I will do for you whatever you say; all my townspeople know you for a worthy woman. ¹²*†Now, though indeed I am closely related to you, you have another relative still closer. ¹³*Stay as you are for tonight, and tomorrow, if he wishes to claim you, good! let him do so. But if he does not wish to claim you, as the Lord lives, I will claim you myself. Lie there until morning." ¹⁴So she lay at his feet until morning, but rose before men could recognize one another. Boaz said, "Let it not be known that this woman came to the threshing floor." ¹⁵*Then he said to her, "Take off your cloak and hold it out." When she did so, he poured out six measures of barley, helped her lift the bundle, and left for the city.

¹⁶Ruth went home to her mother-in-law, who asked, "How have you fared, my daughter?" So she told her all the man had done for her, ¹⁷and concluded, "He gave me these six measures of barley because he did not wish me to come back to my mother-in-law empty-handed!" ¹⁸Naomi then said, "Wait here, my daughter, until you learn what happens, for the man will not rest, but will settle the matter today."

Boaz Marries Ruth

4 ¹*†Boaz went and took a seat at the gate; and when he saw the closer relative of whom he had spoken come along, he called to him by name, "Come and sit beside me!" And he did so. ²†Then Boaz picked out ten of the elders of the city and asked them to sit nearby. When they had done this, ³he said to the near relative: "Naomi, who has come back from the Moabite plateau, is putting up for sale the piece of land that belonged to our kinsman Elimelech. ⁴*†So I thought I would inform you, bidding you before those here present, including the elders of my people, to put in your claim for it if you wish to acquire it as next of kin. But if you do not wish to claim it, tell me so, that I may be guided accordingly, for no one has a prior claim to yours, and mine is next." He answered, "I will put in my claim."

⁵*†Boaz continued, "Once you acquire the field from Naomi, you must take also Ruth the Moabite, the widow of the late heir, and raise up a family for the

departed on his estate." ⁶The near relative replied, "I cannot exercise my claim lest I depreciate my own estate. Put in a claim yourself in my stead, for I cannot exercise my claim." ⁷†Now it used to be the custom in Israel that, to make binding a contract of redemption or exchange, one party would take off his sandal and give it to the other. This was the form of attestation in Israel. ⁸So the near relative, in saying to Boaz, "Acquire it for yourself," drew off his sandal. ⁹Boaz then said to the elders and to all the people, "You are witnesses today that I have acquired from Naomi all the holdings of Elimelech, Chilion and Mahlon. ¹⁰I also take Ruth the Moabite, the widow of Mahlon, as my wife, in order to raise up a family for her late husband on his estate, so that the name of the departed may not perish among his kinsmen and fellow citizens. Do you witness this today?" ¹¹*All those at the gate, including the elders, said, "We do so. May the Lord make this wife come into your house like Rachel and Leah, who between them built up the house of Israel. May you do well in Ephrathah and win fame in Bethlehem. ¹²*†With the offspring the Lord will give you from this girl, may your house become like the house of Perez, whom Tamar bore to Judah."

¹³Boaz took Ruth. When they came together as man and wife, the Lord enabled her to conceive and she bore a son. ¹⁴Then the women said to Naomi, "Blessed is the Lord who has not failed to provide you today with an heir! May he become famous in Israel! ¹⁵He will be your comfort and the support of your old age, for his mother is the daughter-in-law who loves you. She is worth more to you than seven sons!" ¹⁶†Naomi took the child, placed him on her lap, and became his

---

† 3, 9: *Spread the corner of your cloak over me:* be my protector by marrying me according to the duty of a near kinsman; cf Dt 25, 5; Ez 16, 8.

3, 12: *Relative still closer:* who had a prior right and duty to marry Ruth.

4, 1: *Took a seat at the gate:* i. e., of the city, where business affairs were settled.

4, 2: *Ten of the elders:* to serve as judges in legal matters as well as witnesses of the settlement of business affairs; cf Dt 25, 7-9.

4, 4: Poverty had obliged Naomi to sell the land of her deceased husband. The law permitted the nearest kinsman to redeem the land and thus preserve the family patrimony; cf Lv 25, 25.

4, 5f: The heir of Elimelech's field had died without children (1, 5). The nearest of kin could now redeem the land but he must also take Ruth, *the widow of the late heir,* to wife to perpetuate the family of the deceased; cf Dt 25, 5f. The first male child of such a marriage would be the legal son of Mahlon and grandson of Elimelech.

4, 7: *Take off his sandal . . . .:* by this act the near relative renounced his legal right, both to the field of Elimelech and to the marriage with Ruth. The custom mentioned in Dt 25, 6 is somewhat different.

4, 12: *Perez, whom Tamar bore to Judah:* the right which Judah unwittingly satisfied for his daughter-in-law Tamar (Gn 38), Boaz willingly rendered to Ruth.

4, 16: *Placed him on her lap:* took him as her own; cf Gn 30, 3; 48, 12; Nm 11, 12.

✦
10: Dt 25, 5.   4: Lv 25, 25.
12: 4, 1.   5: 3, 13; Dt 25, 5.
13: 3, 4, 5; Dt 25, 5.   11: Gn 29, 31–30, 24;
15: 2, 17.   35, 19.
4/1: 3, 12.   12: Gn 38, 29.

nurse. [17]*†And the neighbor women gave him his name, at the news that a grandson had been born to Naomi. They called him Obed. He was the father of Jesse, the father of David.

[18]*These are the descendants of Perez: Perez was the father of Hezron, [19]Hezron was the father of Ram, Ram was the father of Amminadab, [20]*Amminadab was the father of Nahshon, Nahshon was the father of Salmon, [21]Salmon was the father of Boaz, Boaz was the father of Obed, [22]*Obed was the father of Jesse, and Jesse became the father of David.

17: Lk 1, 58.
18-22: 1 Chr 2, 4-15; Mt 1, 3-6.
18: Gn 46, 12; 1 Chr 4, 1.
20: Ex 6, 23; Nm 1, 7.
22: 1 Sm 16, 10-13.

†

4, 17: *The father of Jesse, the father of David:* indicating the place of Obed, Jesse and David in the line of Judah and the ancestry of Christ, the Messiah; cf Mt 1, 5f.

The Historical Books

THE HISTORICAL BOOKS include 1 and 2 Samuel, 1 and 2 Kings, 1 and 2 Chronicles, Ezra, Nehemiah, 1 and 2 Maccabees. To these are added the special literary group of Tobit, Judith and Esther.

The books of Tobit, Judith, and 1 and 2 Maccabees, as well as parts of Esther, are called deuterocanonical: they are not contained in the Hebrew canon but have been accepted by the Catholic Church as canonical and inspired.

By means of a series of episodes involving the persons of Samuel, Saul, and David, a century of history unfolds in 1 and 2 Samuel from the close of the period of Judges to the rise and establishment of the monarchy in Israel. Most important is God's promise to David of a lasting dynasty (2 Sm 7), from which royal messianism in the Bible developed.

In 1 and 2 Kings the religious history of Israel extends another four centuries, from the last days of David to the Babylonian captivity and the destruction of Jerusalem (587 B.C.). The various sources for these books are woven into a uniform pattern based on the principle of fidelity to Yahweh for rulers and people alike. The sequence of regnal chronicles in both books is interrupted by a cycle of traditions surrounding the prophets Elijah (1 Kgs) and Elisha (2 Kgs).

Chronicles, Ezra and Nehemiah form a historical work, uniform in style and basic ideas. Chronicles records the long period from the reign of Saul to the return from exile, not so much with exactitude of detail as with concern for the meaning of the facts which demonstrate God's intervention in history. The Ezra-Nehemiah chronicle constitutes the most important source for the formation of the Jewish religious community after the Babylonian exile; the two persons most responsible for the reorganization of Jewish life were Ezra and Nehemiah.

1 and 2 Maccabees contain independent accounts of partially identical events which accompanied the attempted suppression of Judaism in Palestine in the second century B.C. Vigorous reaction to this attempt established for a time the religious and political independence of the Jews. 1 Maccabees portrays God as the eternal benefactor of the Jews and their unfailing source of help. The people are required to be devoted to his exclusive worship and to observe exactly the law he has given them. 2 Maccabees, besides supplementing the former volume, gives a theological interpretation of the history of the period and contains teaching on the resurrection from the dead, intercession of the saints, and suffrages for the dead.

Tobit, Judith, and Esther are examples of free composition—the religious novel used for purposes of edification and instruction. Interest in whatever historical data these books may contain is merely intensified by the addition of vivid details. Judith is a lesson in Providence: a pious reflection on the annual Passover observance to convey the reassurance that God is still the master of history who saves Israel from her enemies. Esther's purpose is the glorification of the Jewish people and the explanation of the origin, significance, and date of the feast of Purim. It is a literary development of the principle of reversal of fortune through punishment of the prosperous rich and reward for the virtuous who are oppressed.

Samuel to Maccabees demonstrates that before as well as during the millennium of history with which it is concerned, Israel was a covenanted people, bound to Yahweh, Lord of the universe, by the ties of faith and obedience. This required observance of the law and worship in his temple, the consequent rewards of which were divine favor and protection. In this way these books anticipate and prepare for the coming of him who would bring type and prophecy to fulfillment, history to term, and holiness to perfection: Christ, the Son of David and the promised Messiah.

The First Book of Samuel

Introduction

Originally but one book, the scroll of Samuel was early divided into two. The Greek translators called these the first and second Books of Kingdoms, a title St. Jerome later modified to "Kings." The Hebrew title, "Samuel," alludes to the leading figure in the first book, who was responsible for the enthronement of David. It is David's history that the second book recounts.

This sacred work thus comprises the history of about a century, describing the close of the age of the Judges and the beginnings of monarchy in Israel under Saul and David. It is not a complete and continuous history, nor a systematic account of the period, but rather a series of episodes centered around the persons of Samuel, Saul and David, the principal figures leading up to the establishment of the royal dynasty of David.

The final editor is unknown, nor are we certain of the time at which the various strands of the narrative were put together, though one may think of the period, perhaps late in the seventh century B. C., when the other volumes of the "Former Prophets," from Joshua through Kings, were built into a more or less continuous historical corpus. The Samuel-Saul-David narratives clearly depend on several written sources: a Samuel cycle, two sets of stories about Saul and David, and a family history of David. This last (2 Sm 9-20; 1 Kgs 1-2), one of the most vivid historical narratives surviving from ancient times, probably originated early in the reign of Solomon.

One of the most significant theological contributions of the Old Testament is found in 2 Samuel 7, the oracle of Nathan. David is here promised an eternal dynasty, and this becomes the basis for the development of royal messianism throughout the Bible. With this promise to David one should compare 2 Chr 17; Pss 89, 20-38 and 132, 11ff; Acts 2, 30; and Heb 1, 5.

The contents of this work may be divided as follows:
- I: History of the Last Judges, Eli and Samuel (1 Sm 1, 1—7, 17)
- II: Establishment of the Monarchy in Israel (1 Sm 8, 1—12, 25)
- III: Saul and David (1 Sm 13, 1—2 Sm 2, 7)
- IV: Reign of David (2 Sm 2, 8—20, 26)
- V: Appendixes (2 Sm 21, 1—24, 25)

I: HISTORY OF THE LAST JUDGES, ELI AND SAMUEL

Elkanah and His Family at Shiloh

1 1*THERE WAS A CERTAIN MAN from Ramathaim, Elkanah by name, a Zuphite from the hill country of Ephraim. He was the son of Jeroham, son of Elihu, son of Tohu, son of Zuph, an Ephraimite. ²He had two wives, one named Hannah, the other Peninnah; Peninnah had children, but Hannah was childless. ³*This man regularly went on pilgrimage from his city to worship the LORD of hosts and to sacrifice to him at Shiloh, where the two sons of Eli, Hophni and Phinehas, were ministering as priests of the LORD. ⁴When the day came for Elkanah to offer sacrifice, he used to give a portion each to his wife Peninnah and to all her sons and daughters, ⁵*but a double portion to Hannah because he loved her, though the LORD had made her barren. ⁶*Her rival, to upset her, turned it into a constant reproach to her that the LORD had left her barren. ⁷This went on year after year; each time they made their pilgrimage to the sanctuary of the LORD, Peninnah would approach her, and Hannah would weep and refuse to eat. ⁸*Her husband Elkanah used to ask her: "Hannah, why do you weep, and why do you refuse to eat? Why do you grieve? Am I not more to you than ten sons?"

Hannah's Prayer

⁹Hannah rose after one such meal at Shiloh, and presented herself before the LORD; at the time, Eli the priest was sitting on a chair near the doorpost of the LORD's temple. ¹⁰In her bitterness she prayed to the LORD, weeping copiously, ¹¹*†and she made a vow, promising: "O LORD of hosts, if you look with pity on the misery of your handmaid, if you remember me and do not forget me, if you give your handmaid a male child, I will give him to the LORD for as long as he lives; neither wine nor liquor shall he drink, and no razor shall ever touch his head." ¹²As she remained long at prayer before the LORD, Eli watched her mouth, ¹³for Hannah was praying silently; though her lips were moving, her voice could not be heard. Eli, thinking her drunk, ¹⁴said to her, "How long will you make a drunken show of yourself? Sober up from your

---

1/1: 1 Chr 6, 19f.
3: Ex 23, 14-17; 34, 23; Dt 16, 16; Jgs 21, 19.
5: Dt 21, 15ff.
6: Gn 16, 4f.
8: Ru 4, 15.
11: Nm 6, 1-5; Jgs 13, 2-5; 16, 17; Lk 1, 15.

† 1, 11: *Give him to the Lord:* some ancient texts call Samuel a *nazir* in this context; see note on Nm 6, 1ff.

wine!" ¹⁵"It isn't that, my lord," Hannah answered. "I am an unhappy woman. I have had neither wine nor liquor; I was only pouring out my troubles to the Lord. ¹⁶Do not think your handmaid a ne'er-do-well; my prayer has been prompted by my deep sorrow and misery." ¹⁷Eli said, "Go in peace, and may the God of Israel grant you what you have asked of him." ¹⁸She replied, "Think kindly of your maidservant," and left. She went to her quarters, ate and drank with her husband, and no longer appeared downcast. ¹⁹Early the next morning they worshiped before the Lord, and then returned to their home in Ramah.

Hannah Bears a Son

When Elkanah had relations with his wife Hannah, the Lord remembered her. ²⁰She conceived, and at the end of her term bore a son whom she called Samuel, since she had asked the Lord for him. ²¹The next time her husband Elkanah was going up with the rest of his household to offer the customary sacrifice to the Lord and to fulfill his vows, ²²Hannah did not go, explaining to her husband, "Once the child is weaned, I will take him to appear before the Lord and to remain there forever; I will offer him as a perpetual nazirite." ²³Her husband Elkanah answered her: "Do what you think best; wait until you have weaned him. Only, may the Lord bring your resolve to fulfillment!" And so she remained at home and nursed her son until she had weaned him.

Samuel Is Offered to God

²⁴Once he was weaned, she brought him up with her, along with a three-year-old bull, an ephah of flour, and a skin of wine, and presented him at the temple of the Lord in Shiloh. ²⁵After the boy's father had sacrificed the young bull, Hannah, his mother, approached Eli ²⁶and said: "Pardon, my lord! As you live, my lord, I am the woman who stood near you here, praying to the Lord. ²⁷I prayed for this child, and the Lord granted my request. ²⁸Now I, in turn, give him to the Lord; as long as he lives, he shall be dedicated to the Lord." She left him there;

2 ¹and as she worshiped the Lord, she said:

"My heart exults in the Lord,
my horn is exalted in my God.
I have swallowed up my enemies;
I rejoice in my victory.
²There is no Holy One like the Lord;
there is no Rock like our God.

³"Speak boastfully no longer,
nor let arrogance issue from your mouths.
For an all-knowing God is the Lord,
a God who judges deeds.
⁴The bows of the mighty are broken,
while the tottering gird on strength.
⁵The well-fed hire themselves out for bread,
while the hungry batten on spoil.
The barren wife bears seven sons,
while the mother of many languishes.

⁶"The Lord puts to death and gives life;
he casts down to the nether world;
he raises up again.
⁷The Lord makes poor and makes rich,
he humbles, he also exalts.
⁸He raises the needy from the dust;
from the ash heap he lifts up the poor,
To seat them with nobles
and make a glorious throne their heritage.
He gives to the vower his vow,
and blesses the sleep of the just.

"For the pillars of the earth are the Lord's,
and he has set the world upon them.
⁹He will guard the footsteps of his faithful ones,
but the wicked shall perish in the darkness.
For not by strength does man prevail;
¹⁰the Lord's foes shall be shattered.
The Most High in heaven thunders;
the Lord judges the ends of the earth,
Now may he give strength to his king,
and exalt the horn of his anointed!"

¹¹When Elkanah returned home to Ramah, the child remained in the service of the Lord under the priest Eli.

Wickedness of Eli's Sons

¹²Now the sons of Eli were wicked; they had respect neither for the Lord ¹³nor for the priests' duties toward the people. When someone offered a sacrifice, the priest's servant would come with a three-pronged fork, while the meat was still boiling, ¹⁴and would thrust it into the basin, kettle, caldron, or pot. Whatever the fork brought up, the priest would keep. That is how all the Israelites were treated who came to the

---

† 1, 20: *Since she had asked:* this explanation would be more directly appropriate for the name Saul, which means "asked"; Samuel means "name of God."

1, 24: *An ephah:* a little more than a bushel.

2, 1-10: A hymn attributed to Hannah, the mother of Samuel, as her thanksgiving to God because she has borne a son despite her previous sterility. She praises God as the helper of the weak (1f), who casts down the mighty and raises up the lowly (3ff), and who alone is the source of true strength (8ff); the hymn ends with a prayer for the king (v 10). This canticle has several points of resemblance with our Lady's *Magnificat.*

2, 1: *Horn:* the symbol of strength; cf Pss 18, 3; 75, 5; 89, 18; 112, 9.

2, 3: *Speak ... mouths:* addressed to the *enemies* mentioned in v 1.

2/1: Dt 33, 17; 2 Sm 22, 3; Ps 18, 2; Is 61, 10; Lk 1, 47.69.
2: 2 Sm 22, 3; Ps 18, 2.
3: Ps 75, 4.
4: Is 40, 29.
6: Dt 32, 39; Tb 4, 19; Jb 5, 11; Ps 30, 4; Wis 16, 13; Lk 1, 52.
8: Jb 9, 6; 38, 6; Ps 104, 5; 121, 3.
10: Ps 98, 9.
13-15: Ex 29, 27f; Lv 7, 29-36; Dt 18, 3.

sanctuary at Shiloh. **15**In fact, even before the fat was burned, the priest's servant would come and say to the man offering the sacrifice, "Give me some meat to roast for the priest. He will not accept boiled meat from you, only raw meat." **16***And if the man protested to him, "Let the fat be burned first as is the custom, then take whatever you wish," he would reply, "No, give it to me now, or else I will take it by force." **17**Thus the young men sinned grievously in the presence of the LORD; they treated the offerings to the LORD with disdain.

The Lord Rewards Hannah

18†Meanwhile the boy Samuel, girt with a linen apron, was serving in the presence of the LORD. **19**His mother used to make a little garment for him, which she would bring him each time she went up with her husband to offer the customary sacrifice. **20**And Eli would bless Elkanah and his wife, as they were leaving for home. He would say, "May the LORD repay you with children from this woman for the gift she has made to the LORD!" **21***The LORD favored Hannah so that she conceived and gave birth to three more sons and two daughters, while young Samuel grew up in the service of the LORD.

Eli's Futile Rebuke

22†When Eli was very old, he heard repeatedly how his sons were treating all Israel [and that they were having relations with the women serving at the entry of the meeting tent]. **23**So he said to them: "Why are you doing such things? **24**No, my sons, you must not do these things! It is not a good report that I hear the people of the LORD spreading about you. **25**If a man sins against another man, one can intercede for him with the LORD; but if a man sins against the LORD, who can intercede for him?" But they disregarded their father's warning, since the LORD had decided on their death. **26***Meanwhile, young Samuel was growing in stature and in worth in the estimation of the LORD and of men.

Doom of Eli's House

27†A man of God came to Eli and said to him: "This is what the LORD says: 'I went so far as to reveal myself to your father's family when they were in Egypt as slaves to the house of Pharaoh. **28*†**I chose them out of all the tribes of Israel to be my priests, to go up to my altar, to burn incense, and to wear the ephod before me; and I assigned all the oblations of the Israelites to your father's family. **29**Why do you keep a greedy eye on my sacrifices and on the offerings which I have prescribed? And why do you honor your sons in preference to me, fattening yourselves with

the choicest part of every offering of my people Israel?' **30***This, therefore, is the oracle of the LORD, the God of Israel: 'I said in the past that your family and your father's family should minister in my presence forever. But now,' the LORD declares, 'away with this! for I will honor those who honor me, but those who spurn me shall be accursed. **31**Yes, the time is coming when I will break your strength and the strength of your father's family, so that no man in your family shall reach old age. **32**You shall witness as a disappointed rival all the benefits enjoyed by Israel, but there shall never be an old man in your family. **33**I will permit some of your family to remain at my altar, to wear out their eyes in consuming greed; but the rest of the men of your family shall die by the sword. **34***You shall have a sign in what will happen to your two sons, Hophni and Phinehas: both shall die on the same day. **35**I will choose a faithful priest who shall do what I have in heart and mind. I will establish a lasting house for him which shall function in the presence of my anointed forever. **36***Then whoever is left of your family will come to grovel before him for a piece of silver or a loaf of bread, and will say: Appoint me, I beg you, to a priestly function, that I may have a morsel of bread to eat.'"

Revelation to Samuel

3 **1†**DURING the time young Samuel was minister to the Lord under Eli, a revelation of the LORD was uncommon and vision infrequent. **2**One day Eli was asleep in his usual place. His eyes had lately grown so weak that he could not see. **3***The lamp of God was not yet extinguished, and Samuel was sleeping in the temple of the LORD where the ark of God was. **4**The LORD called to Samuel, who answered, "Here I am." **5**He ran to Eli and said, "Here I am. You called me." "I did not call you," Eli said. "Go back to sleep." So he went back to sleep. **6**Again the LORD called Samuel, who rose and went to Eli. "Here I am," he said. "You called me." But he answered, "I did not

---

†

2, 18: *Linen apron:* called in Hebrew "ephod," but not the same as the high priest's ephod (Ex 28, 6-14) or the ephod used in divination (v 28). Samuel wore a simple apron such as was worn by the priests (22, 18), and on one occasion also by David (2 Sm 6, 14).

2, 22: The bracketed words, which recall Ex 38, 8, are a gloss in the received text; they are lacking in the oldest Greek translation, and in a Hebrew manuscript from Qumran.

2, 27-36: These verses propose the punishment of Eli from a point of view contemporary with the reform of Josiah (2 Kgs 23, 9; cf v 36); they hint at the events recorded in 22, 18-23 and 1 Kgs 2, 27. The older story of this divine warning is that in 3, 11-14.

2, 28: *Ephod:* a portable container, presumably of cloth, for the lots used in ritual consultation of God during the days of the Judges (Jgs 17, 5; 18, 14-15) and down into the time of David (14, 3ff; 23, 6ff; 30, 7f). The ephod of the high priest described in Ex 28, 6ff becomes a garment upon which a *breast-piece of decision* symbolizes, but no longer serves for, such consultation. The Exodus text codifies a later form of the tradition.

3, 1: *Uncommon:* prophetic communications from God were almost unknown.

16: Lv 3, 3ff.
21: 3, 19.
26: Lk 2, 52.
28: 23, 9; 30, 7f; Jgs 17, 5.
30f: 2 Sm 22, 26; 1 Kgs 2, 27; Ps 18, 25.
34: 4, 11.
36: 2 Kgs 23, 9.
3/3: Ex 25, 22; 27, 20f; Lv 24, 2.4; 2 Chr 13, 11.

call you, my son. Go back to sleep." **7**At that time Samuel was not familiar with the LORD, because the LORD had not revealed anything to him as yet. **8**The LORD called Samuel again, for the third time. Getting up and going to Eli, he said, "Here I am. You called me." Then Eli understood that the LORD was calling the youth. **9**So he said to Samuel, "Go to sleep, and if you are called, reply, 'Speak, LORD, for your servant is listening.'" When Samuel went to sleep in his place, **10**the LORD came and revealed his presence, calling out as before, "Samuel, Samuel!" Samuel answered, "Speak, for your servant is listening." **11**The LORD said to Samuel: "I am about to do something in Israel that will cause the ears of everyone who hears it to ring. **12**On that day I will carry out in full against Eli everything I threatened against his family. **13***I announce to him that I am condemning his family once and for all, because of this crime: though he knew his sons were blaspheming God, he did not reprove them. **14**Therefore, I swear to the family of Eli that no sacrifice or offering will ever expiate its crime." **15**Samuel then slept until morning, when he got up early and opened the doors of the temple of the LORD. He feared to tell Eli the vision, **16**but Eli called to him, "Samuel, my son!" He replied, "Here I am." **17**†Then Eli asked, "What did he say to you? Hide nothing from me! May God do thus and so to you if you hide a single thing he told you." **18**So Samuel told him everything, and held nothing back. Eli answered, "He is the LORD. He will do what he judges best."

Samuel Acknowledged as Prophet

19*Samuel grew up, and the LORD was with him, not permitting any word of his to be without effect. **20***Thus all Israel from Dan to Beer-sheba came to know that Samuel was an accredited prophet of the LORD. **21**The LORD continued to appear at Shiloh; he manifested himself to Samuel at Shiloh through his word,

Defeat of the Israelites

4 **1**and Samuel spoke to all Israel. At that time, the Philistines gathered for an attack on Israel. Israel went out to engage them in battle and camped at Ebenezer, while the Philistines camped at Aphek. **2**The Philistines then drew up in battle formation against Israel. After a fierce struggle Israel was defeated by the Philistines, who slew about four thousand men on the battlefield. **3**When the troops retired to the camp, the elders of Israel said, "Why has the LORD permitted us to be defeated today by the Philistines? Let us fetch the ark of the LORD from Shiloh that it may go into battle among us and save us from the grasp of our enemies."

Loss of the Ark

4*†So the people sent to Shiloh and brought from there the ark of the LORD of hosts, who is enthroned upon the cherubim. The two sons of Eli, Hophni and Phinehas, were with the ark of God. **5**When the ark of the LORD arrived in the camp, all Israel shouted so loudly that the earth resounded. **6**The Philistines, hearing the noise of shouting, asked, "What can this loud shouting in the camp of the Hebrews mean?" On learning that the ark of the LORD had come into the camp, **7**the Philistines were frightened. They said, "Gods have come to their camp." They said also, "Woe to us! This has never happened before. **8**†Woe to us! Who can deliver us from the power of these mighty gods? These are the gods that struck the Egyptians with various plagues and with pestilence. **9**Take courage and be manly, Philistines; otherwise you will become slaves to the Hebrews, as they were your slaves. So fight manfully!" **10***The Philistines fought and Israel was defeated; every man fled to his own tent. It was a disastrous defeat, in which Israel lost thirty thousand foot soldiers. **11***The ark of God was captured, and Eli's two sons, Hophni and Phinehas, were among the dead.

Death of Eli

12*A Benjaminite fled from the battlefield and reached Shiloh that same day, with his clothes torn and his head covered with dirt. **13**When he arrived, Eli was sitting in his chair beside the gate, watching the road, for he was troubled at heart about the ark of God. The man, however, went into the city to divulge his news, which put the whole city in an uproar. **14**Hearing the outcry of the men standing near him, Eli inquired, "What does this commotion mean?" **15**(Eli was ninety-eight years old, and his eyes would not focus, so that he could not see.) **16**The man quickly came up to Eli and said, "It is I who have come from the battlefield; I fled from there today." He asked, "What happened, my son?" **17**And the messenger answered: "Israel fled from the Philistines; in fact, the troops suffered heavy losses. Your two sons, Hophni and Phinehas, are among the dead, and the ark of God has been captured." **18**At this mention of the ark of God, Eli fell backward from his chair into the gateway; since he was an old man and heavy, he died of a broken neck. He had judged Israel for forty years.

19His daughter-in-law, the wife of Phinehas, was

---

† 3, 17: *May God do thus and so to you:* the Biblical writers avoid repeating for us the specific terms of a curse as the speaker would have uttered it.

4, 4: *Enthroned upon the cherubim:* this title of the Lord seems to have originated in the sanctuary at Shiloh; it represents the divine Majesty as seated upon a throne on which he can be borne through the heaven by winged creatures somewhat as in the visions of Ez 1 and 10.

4, 8: *These mighty gods:* the Philistines, who were polytheists, are represented as supposing the Israelites honored several gods.

❋

13: 2, 27-36.   10: Ps 78, 61.
19: 2, 21.   11: 2, 34.
20: Jgs 20, 1.   12: Jos 7, 6; 2 Sm 1, 2;
4/4: Ex 25, 22.   Jer 7, 12.

with child and at the point of giving birth. When she heard the news concerning the capture of the ark and the deaths of her father-in-law and her husband, she was seized with the pangs of labor, and gave birth. **20***She was about to die when the women standing around her said to her, "Never fear! You have given birth to a son." Yet she neither answered nor paid any attention. **21**[She named the child Ichabod, saying, "Gone is the glory from Israel," with reference to the capture of the ark of God and to her father-in-law and her husband.] **22***She said, "Gone is the glory from Israel," because the ark of God had been captured.

The Ark in the Temple of Dagon

5 **1***THE Philistines, having captured the ark of God, transferred it from Ebenezer to Ashdod. **2**They then took the ark of God and brought it into the temple of Dagon, placing it beside Dagon. **3**When the people of Ashdod rose early the next morning, Dagon was lying prone on the ground before the ark of the LORD. So they picked Dagon up and replaced him. **4**But the next morning early, when they arose, Dagon lay prone on the ground before the ark of the LORD, his head and hands broken off and lying on the threshold, his trunk alone intact. **5**For this reason, neither the priests of Dagon nor any others who enter the temple of Dagon tread on the threshold of Dagon in Ashdod to this very day; they always step over it.

The Ark Is Carried About

6*†Now the LORD dealt severely with the people of Ashdod. He ravaged and afflicted the city and its vicinity with hemorrhoids; he brought upon the city a great and deadly plague of mice that swarmed in their ships and overran their fields. **7**On seeing how matters stood, the men of Ashdod decided, "The ark of the God of Israel must not remain with us, for he is handling us and our god Dagon severely." **8**So they summoned all the Philistine lords and inquired of them, "What shall we do with the ark of the God of Israel?" The men of Gath replied, "Let them move the ark of the God of Israel on to us." **9**So they moved the ark of the God of Israel to Gath! But after it had been brought there, the LORD threw the city into utter turmoil: he afflicted its inhabitants, young and old, and hemorrhoids broke out on them. **10**The ark of God was next sent to Ekron; but as it entered that city, the people there cried out, "Why have they brought the ark of the God of Israel here to kill us and our kindred?" **11**Then they, too, sent a summons to all the Philistine lords and pleaded: "Send away the ark of the God of Israel. Let it return to its own place, that it may not kill us and our kindred." A deadly panic had seized the whole city, since the hand of God had been very heavy upon it. **12**Those who escaped death were afflicted with hemorrhoids, and the outcry from the city went up to the heavens.

The Ark To Be Returned

6 **1**THE ark of the LORD had been in the land of the Philistines seven months **2**when they summoned priests and fortune-tellers to ask, "What shall we do with the ark of the LORD? Tell us what we should send back with it." **3**†They replied: "If you intend to send away the ark of the God of Israel, you must not send it alone, but must, by all means, make amends to him through a guilt offering. Then you will be healed, and will learn why he continues to afflict you." **4**When asked further, "What guilt offering should be our amends to him?", they replied:

"Five golden hemorrhoids and five golden mice to correspond to the number of Philistine lords, since the same plague has struck all of you and your lords. **5**Therefore, make images of the hemorrhoids and of the mice that are infesting your land and give them as a tribute to the God of Israel. Perhaps then he will cease to afflict you, your gods, and your land. **6***Why should you become stubborn, as the Egyptians and Pharaoh were stubborn? Was it not after he had dealt ruthlessly with them that the Israelites were released and departed? **7***So now set to work and make a new cart. Then take two milch cows that have not borne the yoke; hitch them to the cart, but drive their calves indoors away from them. **8**You shall next take the ark of the LORD and place it on the cart, putting in a box beside it the golden articles that you are offering, as amends for your guilt. Start it on its way, and let it go. **9**Then watch! If it goes up to Beth-shemesh along the route to his own territory, he has brought this great calamity upon us; if not, we will know it was not he who struck us, but that an accident happened to us."

The Ark in Beth-shemesh

10They acted upon this advice. Taking two milch cows, they hitched them to the cart but shut up their calves indoors. **11**Then they placed the ark of the LORD on the cart, along with the box containing the golden mice and the images of the hemorrhoids. **12**The cows went straight for the route to Beth-shemesh and continued along this road, mooing as they went, without turning right or left. The Philistine lords followed them as far as the border of Beth-shemesh. **13**The people of Beth-shemesh were harvesting the wheat in the valley. When they looked up and spied the ark, they greeted it with rejoicing. **14***The cart came to the field of Joshua the Beth-shemite and stopped there. At a large stone in the field, the wood of the cart was split

✿
    20: 14, 3; Gn 35, 16ff.
      22: Ps 78, 61.
  5/1-5: Jgs 16, 23-30; Is 45,
      5f.20f.
    6: Ps 78, 66.

  6/6: Ex 7, 14; 8, 15; 9, 34.
    7: Nm 19, 2; Dt 21, 3;
      2 Sm 6, 3.
   14: 2 Sm 24, 21ff.

†
    5, 6: *Hemorrhoids . . . mice:* a double calamity fell upon them —a plague of mice or rats, and a severe epidemic of pestilential tumors, probably the bubonic plague.

    6, 3: *A guilt offering:* a propitiatory offering customary after unwitting transgression of the ordinances of God regarding holy things or property rights; cf Lv 6, 1ff.

up and the cows were offered as a holocaust to the Lord. [15]The Levites, meanwhile, had taken down the ark of God and the box beside it, in which the golden articles were, and had placed them on the great stone. The men of Beth-shemesh also offered other holocausts and sacrifices of the Lord that day. [16]After witnessing this, the five Philistine lords returned to Ekron the same day.

Guilt Offering

[17]The golden hemorrhoids the Philistines sent back as a guilt offering to the Lord were as follows: one for Ashdod, one for Gaza, one for Ashkelon, one for Gath, and one for Ekron. [18]The golden mice, however, corresponded to the number of all the cities of the Philistines belonging to the five lords, including fortified cities and open villages. The large stone on which the ark of the Lord was placed is still in the field of Joshua the Beth-shemite at the present time.

Penalty for Irreverence

[19]The descendants of Jeconiah did not join in the celebration with the inhabitants of Beth-shemesh when they greeted the ark of the Lord, and seventy of them were struck down. The people went into mourning at this great calamity with which the Lord had afflicted them. [20]The men of Beth-shemesh asked, "Who can stand in the presence of this Holy One? To whom shall he go from us?" [21]They then sent messengers to the inhabitants of Kiriath-jearim, saying, "The Philistines have returned the ark of the Lord; come down and get it."

7 [1]so the inhabitants of Kiriath-jearim came for the ark of the Lord and brought it into the house of Abinadab on the hill, appointing his son Eleazar as guardian of the ark of the Lord.

Religious Reform

[2]From the day the ark came to rest in Kiriath-jearim a long time—twenty years—elapsed, and the whole Israelite population turned to the Lord. [3]*Samuel said to them: "If you wish with your whole heart to return to the Lord, put away your foreign gods and your Ashtaroth, devote yourselves to the Lord, and worship him alone. Then he will deliver you from the power of the Philistines." [4]So the Israelites put away their Baals and Ashtaroth, and worshiped the Lord alone. [5]*Samuel then gave orders, "Gather all Israel to Mizpah, that I may pray to the Lord for you." [6]*†When they were gathered at Mizpah, they drew water and poured it out on the ground before the Lord, and they fasted that day, confessing, "We have sinned against the

Lord." It was at Mizpah that Samuel began to judge the Israelites.

Rout of the Philistines

[7]When the Philistines heard that the Israelites had gathered at Mizpah, their lords went up against Israel. Hearing this, the Israelites became afraid of the Philistines [8]*and said to Samuel, "Implore the Lord our God unceasingly for us, to save us from the clutches of the Philistines." [9]*Samuel therefore took an unweaned lamb and offered it entire as a holocaust to the Lord. He implored the Lord for Israel, and the Lord heard him. [10]While Samuel was offering the holocaust, the Philistines advanced to join battle with Israel. That day, however, the Lord thundered loudly against the Philistines, and threw them into such confusion that they were defeated by Israel. [11]Thereupon the Israelites sallied forth from Mizpah and pursued the Philistines, harrying them down beyond Beth-car. [12]†Samuel then took a stone and placed it between Mizpah and Jeshanah; he named it Ebenezer, explaining, "To this point the Lord helped us." [13]*Thus were the Philistines subdued, never again to enter the territory of Israel, for the Lord was severe with them as long as Samuel lived. [14]The cities from Ekron to Gath which the Philistines had taken from Israel were restored to them. Israel also freed the territory of these cities from the dominion of the Philistines. Moreover there was peace between Israel and the Amorites.

[15]Samuel judged Israel as long as he lived. [16]He made a yearly journey, passing through Bethel, Gilgal and Mizpah and judging Israel at each of these sanctuaries. [17]*Then he used to return to Ramah, for that was his home. There, too, he judged Israel and built an altar to the Lord.

II: ESTABLISHMENT OF THE MONARCHY IN ISRAEL

Request for a King

8 [1]†IN HIS OLD AGE Samuel appointed his sons judges over Israel. [2]His first-born was named Joel, his second son, Abijah; they judged at Beersheba. [3]*His sons did not follow his example but sought illicit gain and accepted bribes, perverting jus-

---

7/3: 12, 10.20.24; Jos 24, 23; Jgs 6, 6-10; 10, 10-16.
5: 10, 17; Jgs 20, 1.
6: 10, 20.26; Ps 22, 14; Lam 2, 19.
8: Ex 17, 9-13.

9f: 2 Sm 22, 14f; Sir 46, 16ff.
13: Jgs 3, 30; 8, 28; 11, 33.
17: 9, 12; 14, 35.
8/3: Ex 23, 8; Dt 16, 19; Prv 17, 23.

†

7, 6: *Poured it out on the ground:* for the symbolism, cf 2 Sm 14, 14.

7, 12: *Ebenezer:* or *eben ha-ezer,* means "stone of help."

8, 1: From this chapter on, the First Book of Samuel gives us two and sometimes three viewpoints on most of the events with which it is concerned, such as the appointment of Saul as king, the reasons for his downfall, his relationship with David, even the circumstances of Saul's death (1 Sm 31; 2 Sm 1). The choice of Saul as king is seen, in ch 8, followed by 10, 17-24 and ch 12, as motivated by the people's defection from the proper service of God; this later editorial approach incorporates not only narratives with which it is consistent, but also early traditions (9, 1-10.16; ch 11) which portray the events and their motivation quite differently.

tice. **4**Therefore all the elders of Israel came in a body to Samuel at Ramah **5***and said to him, "Now that you are old, and your sons do not follow your example, appoint a king over us, as other nations have, to judge us."

God Grants the Request

6Samuel was displeased when they asked for a king to judge them. He prayed to the Lord, however, **7***who said in answer: "Grant the people's every request. It is not you they reject, they are rejecting me as their king. **8**As they have treated me constantly from the day I brought them up from Egypt to this day, deserting me and worshiping strange gods, so do they treat you too. **9**Now grant their request; but at the same time, warn them solemnly and inform them of the rights of the king who will rule them."

The Rights of a King

10Samuel delivered the message of the Lord in full to those who were asking him for a king. **11***He told them: "The rights of the king who will rule you will be as follows: He will take your sons and assign them to his chariots and horses, and they will run before his chariot. **12***He will also appoint from among them his commanders of groups of a thousand and of a hundred soldiers. He will set them to do his plowing and his harvesting, and to make his implements of war and the equipment of his chariots. **13**He will use your daughters as ointment-makers, as cooks, and as bakers. **14***He will take the best of your fields, vineyards, and olive groves, and give them to his officials. **15**He will tithe your crops and your vineyards, and give the revenue to his eunuchs and his slaves. **16**He will take your male and female servants, as well as your best oxen and your asses, and use them to do his work. **17***He will tithe your flocks and you yourselves will become his slaves. **18**When this takes place, you will complain against the king whom you have chosen, but on that day the Lord will not answer you."

Persistent Demand

19*The people, however, refused to listen to Samuel's warning and said, "Not so! There must be a king over us. **20**We too must be like other nations, with a king to rule us and to lead us in warfare and fight our battles." **21**When Samuel had listened to all the people had to say, he repeated it to the Lord, **22**who then said to him, "Grant their request and appoint a king to rule them." Samuel thereupon said to the men of Israel, "Each of you go to his own city."

9 **1***There was a stalwart man from Benjamin named Kish, who was the son of Abiel, son of Zeror, son of Becorath, son of Aphiah, a Benjaminite. **2***He had a son named Saul, who was a handsome young man. There was no other Israelite handsomer than Saul; he stood head and shoulders above the people.

The Lost Asses

3Now the asses of Saul's father, Kish, had wandered off. Kish said to his son Saul, "Take one of the servants with you and go out and hunt for the asses." **4**Accordingly they went through the hill country of Ephraim, and through the land of Shalishah. Not finding them there, they continued through the land of Shaalim without success. They also went through the land of Benjamin, but they failed to find the animals. **5**When they came to the land of Zuph, Saul said to the servant who was with him, "Come, let us turn back, lest my father forget about the asses and become anxious about us." **6**The servant replied, "Listen! There is a man of God in this city, a man held in high esteem; all that he says is sure to come true. Let us go there now! Perhaps he can tell us how to accomplish our errand." **7***But Saul said to his servant, "If we go, what can we offer the man? There is no bread in our bags, and we have no present to give the man of God. What have we?" **8**†Again the servant answered Saul, "I have a quarter of a silver shekel. If I give that to the man of God, he will tell us our way." **10**Saul then said to his servant, "Well said! Come on, let us go!" And they went to the city where the man of God lived.

Quest for Samuel's Aid

11*As they were going up the ascent to the city, they met some girls coming out to draw water and inquired of them, "Is the seer in town?" **9***†(In former times in Israel, anyone who went to consult God used to say, "Come, let us go to the seer." For he who is now called prophet was formerly called seer.) **12***†The girls answered, "Yes, there—straight ahead. Hurry now; just today he came to the city, because the people have a sacrifice today on the high place. **13**When you enter the city, you may reach him before he goes up to the high place to eat. The people will not eat until he arrives; only after he blesses the sacrifice will the invited guests eat. Go up immediately, for you should find him right now."

Samuel's Revelation about Saul

14So they went up to the city. As they entered it, Samuel was coming toward them on his way to the

5f: Dt 17, 14f; Hos 13, 10; Acts 13, 21.
7f: 12, 1.12f; Jgs 8, 22f; 10, 13; 1 Kgs 9, 9.
11: 10, 25; Dt 17, 14-20; 1 Kgs 12.
12: 2 Sm 15, 1; 1 Kgs 1, 5.
14: 22, 7; 1 Kgs 21, 1-24; Ez 46, 18.
17: 1 Kgs 12, 4.
19: 10, 19.
9/1: 14, 51; 1 Chr 8, 33.
2: 10, 23.
7f: Nm 22, 7; 1 Kgs 14, 3; 2 Kgs 4, 42; 5, 15; 8, 8f.
9: Sir 46, 15.
11: Gn 24, 11ff; Ex 2, 16.
12: 7, 17; 16, 2.5; 20, 6.29; Dt 12, 13; 1 Kgs 3, 2.4.

† 9, 8: *A quarter of a silver shekel:* about a tenth of an ounce of silver.
9, 9: This verse is a later explanation of the term *seer*, first used in the text in 9, 11.
9, 12: *On the high place:* the local sanctuary on the top of a hill, where the sacrifice was offered and the sacrificial meal eaten.

high place. **¹⁵***The day before Saul's arrival, the LORD had given Samuel the revelation: **¹⁶***"At this time tomorrow I will send you a man from the land of Benjamin whom you are to anoint as commander of my people Israel. He shall save my people from the clutches of the Philistines, for I have witnessed their misery and accepted their cry for help." **¹⁷**When Samuel caught sight of Saul, the LORD assured him, "This is the man of whom I told you; he is to govern my people."

¹⁸Saul met Samuel in the gateway and said, "Please tell me where the seer lives." **¹⁹**Samuel answered Saul: "I am the seer. Go up ahead of me to the high place and eat with me today. In the morning, before dismissing you, I will tell you whatever you wish. **²⁰**As for the asses you lost three days ago, do not worry about them, for they have been found. Whom does Israel desire ardently if not you and your father's family?" **²¹***Saul replied: "Am I not a Benjaminite, of one of the smallest tribes of Israel, and is not my clan the least among the clans of the tribe of Benjamin? Why say such things to me?"

²²Samuel then took Saul and his servant and brought them to the room, where he placed them at the head of the guests, of whom there were about thirty. **²³**He said to the cook, "Bring the portion I gave you and told you to put aside." **²⁴†**So the cook took up the leg and what went with it, and placed it before Saul. Samuel said: "This is a reserved portion that has been set before you. Eat, for it was kept for you until your arrival; I explained that I was inviting some guests." Thus Saul dined with Samuel that day. **²⁵**When they came down from the high place into the city, a mattress was spread for Saul on the roof, **²⁶**and he slept there.

Saul's Anointing

At daybreak Samuel called to Saul on the roof, "Get up, and I will start you on your journey." Saul rose, and he and Samuel went outside the city together. **²⁷**As they were approaching the edge of the town, Samuel said to Saul, "Tell the servant to go on ahead of us, but stay here yourself for the moment, that I may give you a message from God."

10 **¹***THEN, from a flask he had with him, Samuel poured oil on Saul's head; he also kissed him, saying: "The LORD anoints you commander over his heritage. You are to govern the LORD's people Israel, and to save them from the grasp of their enemies round about.

"This will be the sign for you that the LORD has anointed you commander over his heritage: **²*†**When you leave me today, you will meet two men near Rachel's tomb at Zelzah in the territory of Benjamin, who will say to you, 'The asses you went to look for have been found. Your father is no longer worried about the asses, but is anxious about you and says, What shall I do about my son?' **³**Farther on, when you arrive at the terebinth of Tabor, you will be met by three men going up to God at Bethel; one will be bringing three kids, another three loaves of bread, and the third a skin of wine. **⁴**They will greet you and offer you two wave offerings of bread, which you will take from them. **⁵*†**After that you will come to Gibeath-elohim, where there is a garrison of the Philistines. As you enter that city, you will meet a band of prophets, in a prophetic state, coming down from the high place preceded by lyres, tambourines, flutes and harps. **⁶***The spirit of the LORD will rush upon you, and you will join them in their prophetic state and will be changed into another man. **⁷**When you see these signs fulfilled, do whatever you judge feasible, because God is with you. **⁸*†**Now go down ahead of me to Gilgal, for I shall come down to you, to offer holocausts and to sacrifice peace offerings. Wait seven days until I come to you; I shall then tell you what you must do."

Fulfillment of the Signs

⁹As Saul turned to leave Samuel, God gave him another heart. That very day all these signs came to pass. . . . **¹⁰*†**When they were going from there to Gibeah, a band of prophets met him, and the spirit of God rushed upon him, so that he joined them in their prophetic state. **¹¹***When all who had known him previously saw him in a prophetic state among the prophets, they said to one another, "What has happened to the son of Kish? Is Saul also among the prophets?" **¹²**And someone from that district added, "And who is their father?" Thus the proverb arose, "Is Saul also among the prophets?" **¹³**When he came out of the prophetic state, he went home.

---

† 9, 24: *And what went with it:* a slight change would give "and the fatty tail" as perhaps the original reading. Sheep in the Near East are exceptionally fat-tailed, and such a portion would be thought a special delicacy by the Hebrews. However, the ritual legislation as we know it (Lv 3, 9) would require that the fat tail be burned on the altar. If this general rule was later than the time of Samuel, the present text may have been retouched so as not to seem to contravene it. A Qumran text has "the festive (leg)" here.

10, 2: Here, as in Jer 31, 15, Rachel's tomb is placed north of Jerusalem. Later tradition understood Gn 35, 19f in the sense given by Mt 2, 16ff, and placed the tomb at Bethlehem, farther south.

10, 5: *A garrison of the Philistines:* the Hebrew word for "garrison" has been explained alternatively to mean a pillar erected to mark the Philistine occupation, or an inspector or officer for the collection of taxes. *In a prophetic state:* in an ecstatic condition due to strong feelings of religious enthusiasm induced by a communal observance, possibly accompanied by music and dancing.

10, 8: By inserting this verse, with its *seven days*, an editor has prepared for one narrative of the rejection of Saul (13, 8-15) in the very context of Saul's anointing.

10, 10: The story has here been abridged by omitting the fulfillment of the first two signs given by Samuel (10, 2ff).

❋
15: Acts 13, 21.
16: 10, 1.
21: 15, 17.
10/1: 9, 16f; 24, 7; Jgs 9, 9; 1 Kgs 1, 39; Acts 13, 21.
2: Jer 31, 15; Mk 14, 13.
5f: 13, 3; 16, 13; 19, 20f.

6: 11, 6; 16, 13; Jgs 14, 6.19; 15, 14; 2 Kgs 3, 15.
8: 13, 8; Lv 3, 1.
10: 19, 20-24; Nm 11, 25.
11: 19, 24.

Silence about the Kingship

14Saul's uncle inquired of him and his servant, "Where have you been?" Saul replied, "To look for the asses. When we could not find them, we went to Samuel." **15**Then Saul's uncle said, "Tell me, then, what Samuel said to you." **16**Saul said to his uncle, "He assured us that the asses had been found." But he mentioned nothing to him of what Samuel had said about the kingship.

Saul Chosen King by Lot

17* Samuel called the people together to the LORD at Mizpah **18*** and addressed the Israelites: "Thus says the LORD, the God of Israel, 'It was I who brought Israel up from Egypt and delivered you from the power of the Egyptians and from the power of all the kingdoms that oppressed you.' **19*** But today you have rejected your God, who delivers you from all your evils and calamities, by saying to him, 'Not so, but you must appoint a king over us.' Now, therefore, take your stand before the LORD according to tribes and families." **20**So Samuel had all the tribes of Israel come forward, and the tribe of Benjamin was chosen. **21**Next he had the tribe of Benjamin come forward in clans, and the clan of Matri was chosen, and finally Saul, son of Kish, was chosen. But they looked for him in vain. **22*** Again they consulted the LORD, "Has he come here?" The LORD answered, "He is hiding among the baggage." **23*** They ran to bring him from there; and when he stood among the people, he was head and shoulders above all the crowd. **24*** Samuel said to all the people, "Do you see the man whom the LORD has chosen? There is none like him among all the people!" Then all the people shouted, "Long live the king!"

25*†Samuel next explained to the people the law of royalty and wrote it in a book, which he placed in the presence of the LORD. This done, Samuel dismissed the people, each to his own place. **26**Saul also went home to Gibeah, accompanied by warriors whose hearts the LORD had touched. **27*** But certain worthless men said, "How can this fellow save us?" They despised him and brought him no present.

Defeat of the Ammonites

11 **1*†**ABOUT a month later, Nahash the Ammonite went up and laid siege to Jabesh-gilead. All the men of Jabesh begged Nahash, "Make a treaty with us, and we will be your subjects." **2**But Nahash the Ammonite replied, "This is my condition for a treaty with you: I must gouge out every man's right eye, that I may thus bring ignominy on all Israel." **3**The elders of Jabesh said to him: "Give us seven days to send messengers throughout the territory of Israel. If no one rescues us, we will surrender to you." **4**When the messengers arrived at Gibeah of Saul, they related the news to the people, all of whom wept aloud.

5Just then Saul came in from the field, behind his oxen. "Why are the people weeping?" he asked. The message of the inhabitants of Jabesh was repeated to him. **6*** As he listened to this report, the spirit of God rushed upon him and he became very angry. **7*** Taking a yoke of oxen, he cut them into pieces, which he sent throughout the territory of Israel by couriers with the message, "If anyone does not come out to follow Saul [and Samuel], the same as this will be done to his oxen!" In dread of the LORD, the people turned out to a man. **8**When he reviewed them in Bezek, there were three hundred thousand Israelites and seventy thousand Judahites.

9To the messengers who had come he said, "Tell the inhabitants of Jabesh-gilead that tomorrow, while the sun is hot, they will be rescued." The messengers came and reported this to the inhabitants of Jabesh, who were jubilant, **10**and said to Nahash, "Tomorrow we will surrender to you, and you may do whatever you please with us." **11**On the appointed day, Saul arranged his troops in three companies and invaded the camp during the dawn watch. They slaughtered Ammonites until the heat of the day; by then the survivors were so scattered that no two were left together.

Saul Accepted as King

12*†The people then said to Samuel: "Who questioned whether Saul should rule over us? Hand over the men and we will put them to death." **13*** But Saul broke in to say, "No man is to be put to death this day, for today the LORD has saved Israel." **14**Samuel said to the people, "Come, let us go to Gilgal to inaugurate the kingdom there." **15**So all the people went to Gilgal, where, in the presence of the LORD, they made Saul king. They also sacrificed peace offerings there before the LORD, and Saul and all the Israelites celebrated the occasion with great joy.

Samuel's Integrity

12 **1***SAMUEL addressed all Israel: "I have granted your request in every respect," he said. "I have set a king over you **2**and now the king is your leader. As for me, I am old and gray, and have sons among you. I have lived with you from my

---

† 10, 25: *The law of royalty:* the charter defining the rights of the king.

11, 1: *About a month later:* there is ancient evidence for a longer introduction to this campaign. The time indication here may refer to its earlier stages rather than to the events of ch 10.

11, 12-14: With these verses, an editor has harmonized the account of the acknowledgment of Saul as king at Mizpah (10, 17-24) with the public acclamation at Gilgal (11, 15) after the defeat of the Ammonites (11, 1-11). The Greek text of 11, 15 reads "and Samuel anointed Saul as king," instead of *they made Saul king.*

* 17: 7, 5.
18: Ex 20, 2; Lv 11, 45; 25, 38; Nm 15, 41; Dt 5, 6; Jgs 6, 8f.
19: 8, 19.
22: 30, 24.
23: 9, 2; 16, 7.
24: 2 Sm 16, 16; 1 Kgs 1, 25; 2 Kgs 11, 12.
25: 8, 11; Dt 17, 14-20.
27: 11, 12.
11/1: 12, 12; 31, 11.
6: 16, 13; Jgs 14, 6.19.
7: 1 Kgs 11, 30; 2 Kgs 13, 18.
12: 10, 27.
13: 2 Sm 19, 23.
12/1: 8, 7.9.22.

youth to the present day. **3***Here I stand! Answer me in the presence of the LORD and of his anointed. Whose ox have I taken? Whose ass have I taken? Whom have I cheated? Whom have I oppressed? From whom have I accepted a bribe and overlooked his guilt? I will make restitution to you." **4**They replied, "You have neither cheated us, nor oppressed us, nor accepted anything from anyone." **5**So he said to them, "The LORD is witness against you this day, and his anointed as well, that you have found nothing in my possession." "He is witness," they agreed.

Samuel Upbraids the People

6*Continuing, Samuel said to the people: "The LORD is witness, who appointed Moses and Aaron, and who brought your fathers up from the land of Egypt. **7**Now, therefore, take your stand, and I shall arraign you before the LORD, and shall recount for you all the acts of mercy the LORD has done for you and your fathers. **8***When Jacob and his sons went to Egypt and the Egyptians oppressed them, your fathers appealed to the LORD, who sent Moses and Aaron to bring them out of Egypt, and he gave them this place to live in. **9***But they forgot the LORD their God; and he allowed them to fall into the clutches of Sisera, the captain of the army of Jabin, king of Hazor, into the grasp of the Philistines, and into the grip of the king of Moab, who made war against them. **10***Each time they appealed to the LORD and said, 'We have sinned in forsaking the LORD and worshiping Baals and Ashtaroth; but deliver us now from the power of our enemies, and we will worship you.' **11***Accordingly, the LORD sent Jerubbaal, Barak, Jephthah, and Samson; he delivered you from the power of your enemies on every side, so that you were able to live in security. **12***Yet, when you saw Nahash, king of the Ammonites, advancing against you, you said to me, 'Not so, but a king must rule us,' even though the LORD your God is your king.

Warnings for People and King

13*"Now you have the king you want, a king the LORD has given you. **14**If you fear the LORD and worship him, if you are obedient to him and do not rebel against the LORD's command, if both you and the king who rules you follow the LORD your God—well and good. **15**But if you do not obey the LORD and if you rebel against his command, the LORD will deal severely with you and your king, and destroy you. **16**Now then, stand ready to witness the great marvel the LORD is about to accomplish before your eyes. **17***Are we not in the harvest time for wheat? Yet I shall call to the LORD, and he will send thunder and rain. Thus you will see and understand how greatly the LORD is displeased that you have asked for a king." **18**Samuel then called to the LORD, and the LORD sent thunder and rain that day.

Assistance Promised

As a result, all the people dreaded the LORD and Samuel. **19**They said to Samuel, "Pray to the LORD your God for us, your servants, that we may not die for having added to all our other sins the evil of asking for a king." **20**"Do not fear," Samuel answered them. "It is true you have committed all this evil; still, you must not turn from the LORD, but must worship him with your whole heart. **21***Do not turn to meaningless idols which can neither profit nor save; they are nothing. **22***For the sake of his own great name the LORD will not abandon his people, since the LORD himself chose to make you his people. **23***As for me, far be it from me to sin against the LORD by ceasing to pray for you and to teach you the good and right way. **24**But you must fear the LORD and worship him faithfully with your whole heart; keep in mind the great things he has done among you. **25**If instead you continue to do evil, both you and your king shall perish."

III: SAUL AND DAVID

13 **1*†**[SAUL was . . . years old when he became king and he reigned . . . (two) years over Israel.]

Saul Offers Sacrifice

2SAUL CHOSE THREE THOUSAND MEN of Israel, of whom two thousand remained with him in Michmash and in the hill country of Bethel, and one thousand were with Jonathan in Gibeah of Benjamin. He sent the rest of the people back to their tents. **3*†**Now Jonathan overcame the Philistine garrison which was in Gibeah, and the Philistines got word of it. Then Saul sounded the horn throughout the land, with a proclamation, "Let the Hebrews hear!" **4**Thus all Israel learned that Saul had overcome the garrison of the Philistines and that Israel had brought disgrace upon the Philistines; and the soldiers were called up to Saul in Gilgal. **5**The Philistines also assembled for battle, with three thousand chariots, six thousand horsemen,

---

✿

3: Ex 20, 17; 23, 8;
Nm 16, 15; Dt 16, 19;
Sir 46, 19.
6: Mi 6, 4.
8: Gn 46, 5; Ex 1, 11;
2, 23ff.
9: Jgs 3, 12ff; 4, 2f; 10, 7;
13, 1.
10: 7, 3f.
11: Jgs 6, 14.32; 11, 1.

12: 8, 6f.19; 11, 1f;
Jgs 8, 23.
13: 8, 7.
17: Ex 9, 23.28ff;
1 Kgs 18, 1.
21: Dt 32, 37ff.
22: Jer 14, 21; Ez 20, 9;
Dn 3, 34.
23: Ex 32, 11.
13/3: 14, 1-15; Jgs 3, 27;
6, 34; 2 Sm 20, 1f.

† 13, 1: A formula like that of 2 Sm 5, 4 was introduced here at some time; but the age of Saul when he became king remains a blank, and the *two years* assigned for his reign in the received text cannot be correct. Tradition (Acts 13, 21) offers the round number, "forty years."

13, 3-4: *The Philistine garrison:* see note on 10, 5. *Let the Hebrews hear:* a different reading of these verses, based on the Greek, would yield: "And the Philistines heard that the Hebrews (*or:* the slaves) had revolted. Saul in the meantime sounded the trumpet throughout all the land (v 4), and all Israel heard that Saul. . . ."

and foot soldiers as numerous as the sands of the sea-shore. Moving up against Israel, they encamped in Michmash, east of Beth-aven. [6]*Some Israelites, aware of the danger and of the difficult situation, hid them-selves in caves, in thickets, among rocks, in caverns, and in cisterns, [7]†and other Hebrews passed over the Jordan into the land of Gad and Gilead. Saul, however, held out at Gilgal, although all his followers were seized with fear. [8]*He waited seven days—the time Samuel had determined. When Samuel did not arrive at Gilgal, the men began to slip away from Saul. [9]He then said, "Bring me the holocaust and peace offer-ings," and he offered up the holocaust.

King Saul Reproved

[10]He had just finished this offering when Samuel arrived. Saul went out to greet him, [11]and Samuel asked him, "What have you done?" Saul replied: "When I saw that the men were slipping away from me, since you had not come by the specified time, and with the Philistines assembled at Michmash, [12]I said to myself, 'Now the Philistines will come down against me at Gilgal, and I have not yet sought the LORD's blessing.' So in my anxiety I offered up the holocaust." [13]Samuel's response was: "You have been foolish! Had you kept the command the LORD your God gave you, the LORD would now establish your kingship in Israel as lasting; [14]*but as things are, your kingdom shall not endure. The LORD has sought out a man after his own heart and has appointed him commander of his peo-ple, because you broke the LORD's command."

Philistine Invasion

[15]*Then Samuel set out from Gilgal and went his own way; but the rest of the people went up after Saul to meet the soldiers, going from Gilgal to Gibeah of Benjamin. Saul then numbered the soldiers he had with him, who were about six hundred. [16]Saul, his son Jonathan, and the soldiers they had with them were now occupying Geba of Benjamin, and the Philistines were encamped at Michmash. [17]*Meanwhile, raiders left the camp of the Philistines in three bands. One band took the Ophrah road toward the district of Shual; [18]another turned in the direction of Beth-horon; and the third took the road for Geba that overlooks the Valley of the Hyenas toward the desert.

Disarmament of Israel

[19]*Not a single smith was to be found in the whole land of Israel, for the Philistines had said, "Otherwise the Hebrews will make swords or spears." [20]All Israel, therefore, had to go down to the Philistines to sharpen their plowshares, mattocks, axes, and sickles. [21]The price for the plowshares and mattocks was two-thirds of a shekel, and a third of a shekel for sharpening the axes and for setting the ox-goads. [22]And so on the day of battle neither sword nor spear could be found in the possession of any of the soldiers with Saul or Jonathan. Only Saul and his son Jonathan had them.

Jonathan's Exploit

[23]*An outpost of the Philistines had pushed forward to the pass of Michmash.

14 [1]*ONE day Jonathan, son of Saul, said to his armor-bearer, "Come, let us go over to the Philistine outpost on the other side." But he did not inform his father. [2](Saul's command post was under the pomegranate tree near the threshing floor on the outskirts of Geba; those with him numbered about six hundred men. [3]*Ahijah, son of Ahitub, brother of Ichabod, who was the son of Phinehas, son of Eli, the priest of the LORD at Shiloh, was wearing the ephod.) Nor did the soldiers know that Jonathan had gone. [4]Flanking the ravine through which Jonathan intended to get over to the Philistine outpost there was a rocky crag on each side, one called Bozez, the other Seneh. [5]One crag was to the north, toward Mich-mash, the other to the south, toward Geba. [6]*Jonathan said to his armor-bearer: "Come, let us go over to that outpost of the uncircumcised. Perhaps the LORD will help us, because it is no more difficult for the LORD to grant victory through a few than through many." [7]His armor-bearer replied, "Do whatever you are inclined to do; I will match your resolve." [8]Jonathan continued: "We shall go over to those men and show ourselves to them. [9]If they say to us, 'Stay there until we can come to you,' we shall stop where we are; we shall not go up to them. [10]But if they say, 'Come up to us,' we shall go up, because the LORD has delivered them into our grasp. That will be our sign." [11]Accordingly, the two of them appeared before the outpost of the Philistines, who said, "Look, some Hebrews are coming out of the holes where they have been hiding." [12]The men of the outpost called to Jonathan and his armor-bearer. "Come up here," they said, "and we will teach you a lesson." So Jonathan said to his armor-bearer, "Climb up after me, for the LORD has delivered them into the grasp of Israel." [13]Jonathan clambered up with his armor-bearer behind him; as the Philistines turned to flee him, he cut them down, and his armor-bearer fol-lowed him and finished them off. [14]In this first exploit Jonathan and his armor-bearer slew about twenty men within half a furlong. [15]Then panic spread to the army and to the countryside, and all the soldiers, including the outpost and the raiding parties, were terror-stricken. The earth also shook, so that the panic was beyond human endurance.

6: 14, 22.
8: 10, 8.
14: 25, 30; 2 Sm 7, 15f;
      Ps 78, 70; Acts 13, 22.
15: 14, 2.
17: 14, 15.
19: Jgs 5, 8.

23: 14, 15.
14/1: 13, 3.
3: 2, 28; 4, 21; 14, 18;
      23, 9; 30, 7.
6: 17, 26.36.47; Sir 39, 18;
      1 Mc 3, 19.

---

† 13, 7-15: These verses, like 10, 8, anticipate the rejection of Saul; a different occasion and motivation for this are given in ch 15, resumed in 28, 17f.

Rout of the Philistines

16The lookouts of Saul in Geba of Benjamin saw that the enemy camp had scattered and were running about in all directions. **17**Saul said to those around him, "Count the troops and find out if any of us are missing." When they had investigated, they found Jonathan and his armor-bearer missing. **18**†Saul then said to Ahijah, "Bring the ephod here." (Ahijah was wearing the ephod in front of the Israelites at that time.) **19**While Saul was speaking to the priest, the tumult in the Philistine camp kept increasing. So he said to the priest, "Withdraw your hand." **20***And Saul and all his men shouted and rushed into the fight, where the Philistines, wholly confused, were thrusting swords at one another. **21***In addition, the Hebrews who had previously sided with the Philistines and had gone up with them to the camp, turned to join the Israelites under Saul and Jonathan. **22***Likewise, all the Israelites who were hiding in the hill country of Ephraim, on hearing that the Philistines were fleeing, pursued them in the rout. **23**†Thus the LORD saved Israel that day.

Saul's Oath

24The battle continued past Beth-horon; the whole people, about ten thousand combatants, were with Saul, and there was scattered fighting in every town in the hill country of Ephraim. And Saul swore a very rash oath that day, putting the people under this ban: "Cursed be the man who takes food before evening, before I am able to avenge myself on my enemies." So none of the people tasted food. **25**Indeed, there was a honeycomb lying on the ground, **26**and when the soldiers came to the comb the swarm had left it; yet no one would raise a hand to his mouth from it, because the people feared the oath.

Violation of the Oath

27Jonathan, who had not heard that his father had put the people under oath, thrust out the end of the staff he was holding and dipped it into the honey. Then he raised it to his mouth and his eyes lit up. **28**At this one of the soldiers spoke up: "Your father put the people under a strict oath, saying, 'Cursed be the man who takes food this day!' As a result the people are weak." **29**Jonathan replied: "My father brings trouble to the land. Look how bright my eyes are from this small taste of honey I have had. **30**What is more, if the people had eaten freely today of their enemy's booty when they came across it, would not the slaughter of the Philistines by now have been the greater for it?"

Use of Flesh with Blood Forbidden

31After the Philistines were routed that day from Michmash to Aijalon, the people were completely exhausted. **32***So they pounced upon the spoil and took sheep, oxen and calves, slaughtering them on the ground and eating the flesh with blood. **33**Informed that the people were sinning against the LORD by eating the flesh with blood, Saul said: "You have broken faith. Roll a large stone here for me." **34**He continued: "Mingle with the people and tell each of them to bring his ox or his sheep to me. Slaughter it here and then eat, but you must not sin against the LORD by eating the flesh with blood." So everyone brought to the LORD whatever ox he had seized, and they slaughtered them there; **35***and Saul built an altar to the LORD—this was the first time he built an altar to the LORD.

Jonathan in Danger of Death

36Then Saul said, "Let us go down in pursuit of the Philistines by night, to plunder among them until daybreak and to kill them all off." They replied, "Do what you think best." But the priest said, "Let us consult God." **37***So Saul inquired of God: "Shall I go down in pursuit of the Philistines? Will you deliver them into the power of Israel?" But he received no answer on this occasion. **38**Saul then said, "Come here, all officers of the army. We must investigate and find out how this sin was committed today. **39**As the LORD lives who has given victory to Israel, even if my son Jonathan has committed it, he shall surely die!" But none of the people answered him. **40***So he said to all Israel, "Stand on one side, and I and my son Jonathan will stand on the other." The people responded, "Do what you think best." **41***†And Saul said to the LORD, the God of Israel: "Why did you not answer your servant this time? If the blame for this resides in me or my son Jonathan, LORD, God of Israel, respond with Urim; but if this guilt is in your people Israel, respond with Thummim." Jonathan and Saul were designated, and the people went free. **42**Saul then said, "Cast lots between me and my son Jonathan." And Jonathan was designated. **43**Saul said to Jonathan, "Tell me what you have done." Jonathan replied, "I only tasted a little honey from the end of the staff I was holding. Am I to die for this?" **44***Saul said, "May God do thus and so to me if you do not indeed die, Jonathan!"

---

†   14, 18: *Ephod:* to be used in consulting God; see note on v 41, and that on 2, 28 above.

14, 23: *Past Beth-horon:* this is a textual correction influenced by 13, 18; the received Hebrew text refers to Bethel (Beth-aven), but the effect of the victory would seem to have been that the main ridge of mountains in the territories of Benjamin and Ephraim was cleared of Philistines.

14, 41: The *Urim* and *Thummim,* or sacred lots, were a device for ascertaining the will of God; they ceased to be used after the time of David. The material and the shape of these objects, and the manner in which they were used, are unknown. They gave a "yes" or "no" answer to specific questions.

*
20: Jgs 7, 22.
21: 29, 4.
22: 13, 6.
32: 15, 19.21; Lv 3, 17; 7, 26f; 17, 10-14; Acts 15, 20.29.
35: 7, 17; Jgs 6, 24.
37: 28, 6.15.
40: Jos 7, 13ff.
41: 28, 6; Ex 28, 30; Dt 33, 8.
44: 3, 17; Ru 1, 17.

Rescue of Jonathan

⁴⁵*†But the army said to Saul: "Is Jonathan to die, though it was he who brought Israel this great victory? This must not be! As the LORD lives, not a single hair of his head shall fall to the ground, for God was with him in what he did today!" Thus the soldiers were able to rescue Jonathan from death. ⁴⁶After that Saul gave up the pursuit of the Philistines, who returned to their own territory.

Wars and Victories

⁴⁷*After taking over the kingship of Israel, Saul waged war on all their surrounding enemies—Moab, the Ammonites, Aram, Beth-rehob, the king of Zobah, and the Philistines. Wherever he turned, he was successful ⁴⁸and fought bravely. He defeated Amalek and delivered Israel from the hands of those who were plundering them.

Saul's Family

⁴⁹*†The sons of Saul were Jonathan, Ishvi, and Malchishua; his two daughters were named, the elder, Merob, and the younger, Michal. ⁵⁰Saul's wife, who was named Ahinoam, was the daughter of Ahimaaz. The name of his general was Abner, son of Saul's uncle, Ner; ⁵¹*Kish, Saul's father, and Ner, Abner's father, were sons of Abiel.

⁵²An unremitting war was waged against the Philistines during Saul's lifetime. When Saul saw any strong or brave man, he took him into his service.

15 ¹SAMUEL said to Saul: "It was I the LORD sent to anoint you king over his people Israel. Now, therefore, listen to the message of the LORD. ²*This is what the LORD of hosts has to say: 'I will punish what Amalek did to Israel when he barred his way as he was coming up from Egypt. ³*†Go, now, attack Amalek, and deal with him and all that he has under the ban. Do not spare him, but kill men and women, children and infants, oxen and sheep, camels and asses.'"

Disobedience of Saul

⁴†Saul alerted the soldiers, and at Telaim reviewed two hundred thousand foot soldiers and ten thousand men of Judah. ⁵Saul went to the city of Amalek, and after setting an ambush in the wadi, ⁶*warned the Kenites: "Come! Leave Amalek and withdraw, that I may not have to destroy you with them, for you were kind to the Israelites when they came up from Egypt."

After the Kenites left, ⁷*Saul routed Amalek from Havilah to the approaches of Shur, on the frontier of Egypt. ⁸He took Agag, king of Amalek, alive, but on the rest of the people he put into effect the ban of destruction by the sword. ⁹He and his troops spared Agag and the best of the fat sheep and oxen, and the lambs. They refused to carry out the doom on anything that was worthwhile, dooming only what was worthless and of no account.

Saul Is Reproved

¹⁰Then the LORD spoke to Samuel: ¹¹†"I regret having made Saul king, for he has turned from me and has not kept my command." At this Samuel grew angry and cried out to the LORD all night. ¹²Early in the morning he went to meet Saul, but was informed that Saul had gone to Carmel, where he erected a trophy in his own honor, and that on his return he had passed on and gone down to Gilgal. ¹³When Samuel came to him, Saul greeted him: "The LORD bless you! I have kept the command of the LORD." ¹⁴But Samuel asked, "What, then, is the meaning of this bleating of sheep that comes to my ears, and the lowing of oxen that I hear?" ¹⁵Saul replied: "They were brought from Amalek. The men spared the best sheep and oxen to sacrifice to the LORD, your God; but we have carried out the ban on the rest." ¹⁶Samuel said to Saul: "Stop! Let me tell you what the LORD said to me last night." "Speak!" he replied. ¹⁷*Samuel then said: "Though little in your own esteem, are you not leader of the tribes of Israel? The LORD anointed you king of Israel ¹⁸*and sent you on a mission, saying, 'Go and put the sinful Amalekites under a ban of destruction. Fight against them until you have exterminated them.' ¹⁹*Why then have you disobeyed the LORD? You have pounced on the spoil, thus displeasing the LORD." ²⁰Saul answered Samuel: "I did indeed obey the LORD and fulfill the mission on which the LORD sent me. I have brought back Agag, and I have destroyed Amalek under the ban. ²¹*But from the spoil the men took sheep and oxen, the best of what had been banned, to sacrifice to the LORD their God in Gilgal."

---

† 14, 45: *Rescue:* the Hebrew word used is that for the "redemption" of the first-born (Ex 13, 13ff).

14, 49: *Ishvi:* known also as Ishbaal, in 2 Sm 2, 8 and elsewhere. The name may once have read "Ishyo" here.

15, 3: *Under the ban:* in such wars of extermination, all things (men, cities, beasts, etc.) were to be blotted out; nothing could be reserved for private use. The interpretation of God's will here attributed to Samuel is in keeping with the abhorrent practices of blood revenge prevalent among pastoral, seminomadic peoples such as the Hebrews had recently been. The slaughter of the innocent has never been in conformity with the will of God.

15, 4: The numbers here are not realistic; compare 14, 24 above.

15, 11: *I regret:* God manifests "regret" when, offended by men, he takes away his benefits, graces and favors. It is not God, but men, who change, to their own detriment.

45: 2 Sm 14, 11; 1 Kgs 1, 52.
47: 2 Sm 1, 22; 8, 2-5.
49: 18, 20.25; 31, 2; 1 Chr 8, 33; 9, 39; 10, 2.
51: 9, 1.
15/2: Ex 17, 8-10.16; Dt 25, 17ff.
3: 27, 8; 30, 17; Ex 17, 16; Nm 24, 20.
6: Nm 24, 21.
7: 27, 8.
17: 9, 21.
18: 28, 18.
19: 14, 32.
21: Lv 27, 28.

22*†But Samuel said:

"Does the Lord so delight in holocausts and sacrifices
    as in obedience to the command of the Lord?
Obedience is better than sacrifice,
    and submission than the fat of rams.
23For a sin like divination is rebellion,
    and presumption is the crime of idolatry.
Because you have rejected the command of the Lord,
    he, too, has rejected you as ruler."

Saul Asks Forgiveness

24*Saul replied to Samuel: "I have sinned, for I have disobeyed the command of the Lord and your instructions. In my fear of the people, I did what they said. **25**Now forgive my sin, and return with me, that I may worship the Lord." **26***But Samuel said to Saul, "I will not return with you, because you rejected the command of the Lord and the Lord rejects you as king of Israel." **27***As Samuel turned to go, Saul seized a loose end of his mantle, and it tore off. **28***So Samuel said to him: "The Lord has torn the kingdom of Israel from you this day, and has given it to a neighbor of yours, who is better than you. **29***The Glory of Israel neither retracts nor repents, for he is not man that he should repent." **30**But he answered: "I have sinned, yet honor me now before the elders of my people and before Israel. Return with me that I may worship the Lord your God." **31**And so Samuel returned with him, and Saul worshiped the Lord.

Agag Is Cut Down

32Afterward Samuel commanded, "Bring Agag, king of Amalek, to me." Agag came to him struggling and saying, "So it is bitter death!" **33***And Samuel said,

"As your sword has made women childless,
    so shall your mother be childless among women."

Then he cut Agag down before the Lord in Gilgal.
34Samuel departed for Ramah, while Saul went up to his home in Gibeah of Saul. **35***Never again, as long as he lived, did Samuel see Saul. Yet he grieved over Saul, because the Lord regretted having made him king of Israel.

Samuel Sent to Bethlehem

16 **1*†**THE LORD said to Samuel: "How long will you grieve for Saul, whom I have rejected as king of Israel? Fill your horn with oil, and be on your way. I am sending you to Jesse of Bethlehem, for I have chosen my king from among his sons." **2**But Samuel replied: "How can I go? Saul will hear of it and kill me." To this the Lord answered: "Take a heifer along and say, 'I have come to sacrifice to the Lord.' **3**Invite Jesse to the sacrifice, and I myself will tell you what to do; you are to anoint for me the one I point out to you."

4Samuel did as the Lord had commanded him. When he entered Bethlehem, the elders of the city came trembling to meet him and inquired, "Is your visit peaceful, O seer?" **5***He replied: "Yes! I have come to sacrifice to the Lord. So cleanse yourselves and join me today for the banquet." He also had Jesse and his sons cleanse themselves and invited them to the sacrifice. **6**As they came, he looked at Eliab and thought, "Surely the Lord's anointed is here before him." **7***But the Lord said to Samuel: "Do not judge from his appearance or from his lofty stature, because I have rejected him. Not as man sees does God see, because man sees the appearance but the Lord looks into the heart." **8***Then Jesse called Abinadab and presented him before Samuel, who said, "The Lord has not chosen him." **9**Next Jesse presented Shammah, but Samuel said, "The Lord has not chosen this one either." **10**In the same way Jesse presented seven sons before Samuel, but Samuel said to Jesse, "The Lord has not chosen any one of these." **11***Then Samuel asked Jesse, "Are these all the sons you have?" Jesse replied, "There is still the youngest, who is tending the sheep." Samuel said to Jesse, "Send for him; we will not begin the sacrificial banquet until he arrives here." **12***Jesse sent and had the young man brought to them. He was ruddy, a youth handsome to behold and making a splendid appearance. The Lord said, "There—anoint him, for this is he!" **13***Then Samuel, with the horn of oil in hand, anointed him in the midst of his brothers; and from that day on, the spirit of the Lord rushed upon David. When Samuel took his leave, he went to Ramah.

Saul's Spirit of Melancholy

14*†The spirit of the Lord had departed from Saul, and he was tormented by an evil spirit sent by the Lord. **15**So the servants of Saul said to him: "Please! An evil spirit from God is tormenting you. **16**If your lordship will order it, we, your servants here in attendance on you, will look for a man skilled in playing the harp. When the evil spirit from God comes over you, he will play and you will feel better." **17**Saul then told his servants, "Find me a skillful harpist and bring

---

22: Prv 21, 3; Hos 6, 6;
    Am 5, 21-25; Zec 10, 2;
    Mt 9, 13; 12, 7;
    Heb 10, 9.
24: 26, 21.
26: 1 Kgs 11, 11.30f.
27: 24, 6.
28: 28, 17; 2 Sm 7, 15f.
29: Nm 23, 19.
33: Ex 21, 23.
35: Gn 6, 6.
16/1: 1 Kgs 1, 39; Ru 4, 17-
    22; 1 Chr 11, 3; Is 11,
    1; Lk 2, 4.

5: 9, 12f; 20, 26; Ex 19,
    10; Jb 1, 5.
7: 10, 23f; 1 Chr 28, 9;
    Prv 15, 11; Jer 17, 10;
    20, 12; Lk 16, 15;
    Acts 1, 24.
8ff: 17, 12f; 1 Chr 2, 13ff.
11: 17, 15.28.34; 2 Sm 7, 8.
12: 9, 2.
13: 10, 6; 11, 6; Jgs 3, 10;
    9, 9; Sir 46, 13.
14: 18, 10f.

---

† 15, 22: Samuel is disapproving, not of sacrifices in general, but of merely external sacrifices offered in defiance of God's commandment and without heartfelt obedience.

16, 1: The anointing here prepared for is unknown to David's brother Eliab in the next chapter (17, 28), and David is twice anointed after Saul's death (2 Sm 2, 4; 5, 3).

16, 14: *An evil spirit sent by the Lord:* the Lord permitted Saul to be tormented with violent fits of rage.

him to me." **18***†A servant spoke up to say: "I have observed that one of the sons of Jesse of Bethlehem is a skillful harpist. He is also a stalwart soldier, besides being an able speaker, and handsome. Moreover, the LORD is with him."

David Made Armor-bearer

19Accordingly, Saul dispatched messengers to ask Jesse to send him his son David, who was with the flock. **20***Then Jesse took five loaves of bread, a skin of wine, and a kid, and sent them to Saul by his son David. **21***Thus David came to Saul and entered his service. Saul became very fond of him, made him his armor-bearer, **22**and sent Jesse the message, "Allow David to remain in my service, for he meets with my approval." **23**Whenever the spirit from God seized Saul, David would take the harp and play, and Saul would be relieved and feel better, for the evil spirit would leave him.

The Challenge of Goliath

17 **1**THE Philistines rallied their forces for battle at Socoh in Judah and camped between Socoh and Azekah at Ephes-dammim. **2**Saul and the Israelites also gathered and camped in the Vale of the Terebinth, drawing up their battle line to meet the Philistines. **3**The Philistines were stationed on one hill and the Israelites on an opposite hill, with a valley between them.

4A champion named Goliath of Gath came out from the Philistine camp; he was six and a half feet tall. **5**He had a bronze helmet on his head and wore a bronze corselet of scale armor weighing five thousand shekels, **6**†and bronze greaves, and had a bronze scimitar slung from a baldric. **7***†The shaft of his javelin was like a weaver's heddle-bar, and its iron head weighed six hundred shekels. His shield-bearer went before him. **8**He stood and shouted to the ranks of Israel: "Why come out in battle formation? I am a Philistine, and you are Saul's servants. Choose one of your men, and have him come down to me. **9**If he beats me in combat and kills me, we will be your vassals; but if I beat him and kill him, you shall be our vassals and serve us." **10**The Philistine continued: "I defy the ranks of Israel today. Give me a man and let us fight together." **11**Saul and all the men of Israel, when they heard this challenge of the Philistine, were dismayed and terror-stricken.

David Comes to the Camp

12*†[David was the son of an Ephrathite named Jesse, who was from Bethlehem in Judah. He had eight sons, and in the days of Saul was old and well on in years. **13**The three oldest sons of Jesse had followed

Saul to war; these three sons who had gone off to war were named, the first-born Eliab, the second son Abinadab, and the third Shammah. **14**David was the youngest. While the three oldest had joined Saul, **15***David would go and come from Saul to tend his father's sheep at Bethlehem.

16[Meanwhile the Philistine came forward and took his stand morning and evening for forty days.

17[Now Jesse said to his son David: "Take this ephah of roasted grain and these ten loaves for your brothers, and bring them quickly to your brothers in the camp. **18**Also take these ten cheeses for the field officer. Greet your brothers and bring home some token from them. **19**Saul, and they, and all Israel are fighting against the Philistines in the Vale of the Terebinth." **20***Early the next morning, having left the flock with a shepherd, David set out on his errand, as Jesse had commanded him. He reached the barricade of the camp just as the army, on their way to the battleground, were shouting their battle cry. **21**The Israelites and the Philistines drew up opposite each other in battle array. **22***David entrusted what he had brought to the keeper of the baggage and hastened to the battle line, where he greeted his brothers. **23**While he was talking with them, the Philistine champion, by name Goliath of Gath, came up from the ranks of the Philistines and spoke as before, and David listened. **24**When the Israelites saw the man, they all retreated before him, very much afraid. **25***The Israelites had been saying: "Do you see this man coming up? He comes up to insult Israel. If anyone should kill him, the king would give him great wealth, and his daughter as well, and would grant exemption to his father's family in Israel." **26***David now said to the men standing by: "What will be done for the man who kills this Philistine and frees Israel of the disgrace? Who is this uncircumcised Philistine in any case, that he should insult the armies of the living God?" **27**They repeated the same words to him and said, "That is how the man who kills him will be rewarded." **28**When Eliab, his oldest brother, heard him speaking with the men, he grew angry with David and said: "Why did you come down? With whom have you left those sheep in the desert meanwhile? I know your arrogance and your evil intent. You came down to enjoy the battle!"

---

† 16, 18: Of the two traditions which describe the coming of David into Saul's service, the oldest Greek translation retains only the one comprised in 16, 14-23; 17, 1-11.32-54. This effort at consistency is not in accord with the character of the rest of the book; see note on 8, 1. Though square brackets are used in this edition to indicate the passages lacking in the oldest translation, this is meant only to help the reader follow one account at a time. Both are equally a part of the inspired text, as are also the various amplifications and retouchings of the narrative given within brackets in chs 18 and 19.

17, 6: *Scimitar:* the Hebrew word for this is rather rare, and the nature of the weapon was in doubt until recent years. It is not the same as the *sword* of v 45.

17, 7: *Six hundred shekels:* over 15 pounds.

17, 12-31: An alternative account of how David came to undertake the combat with the Philistine is here inserted; it is continued in 17, 55—18, 6. See note on 16, 18.

18: 2 Sm 17, 8.
20: 9, 7f; 10, 4.27; 16, 1; 17, 27ff.
21: 18, 2.
17/7: 2 Sm 21, 19; 1 Chr 11, 23; 20, 5.
12: 16, 1.10; Ru 1, 2.

15: 18, 2; 2 Sm 7, 8.
20: 26, 5.
22: 25, 13.
25: 18, 17; Jos 15, 16.
26: 18, 25; Jgs 15, 18; 2 Kgs 19, 4; Is 37, 4.

²⁹David replied, "What have I done now?—I was only talking." **³⁰**Yet he turned from him to another and asked the same question; and everyone gave him the same answer as before. **³¹**The words that David had spoken were overheard and reported to Saul, who sent for him.]

David Fights Goliath

³²Then David spoke to Saul: "Let your majesty not lose courage. I am at your service to go and fight this Philistine." **³³**But Saul answered David, "You cannot go up against this Philistine and fight with him, for you are only a youth, while he has been a warrior from his youth." **³⁴***Then David told Saul: "Your servant used to tend his father's sheep, and whenever a lion or bear came to carry off a sheep from the flock, **³⁵**I would go after it and attack it and rescue the prey from its mouth. If it attacked me, I would seize it by the jaw, strike it, and kill it. **³⁶**Your servant has killed both a lion and a bear, and this uncircumcised Philistine will be as one of them, because he has insulted the armies of the living God." **³⁷***David continued: "The Lord, who delivered me from the claws of the lion and the bear, will also keep me safe from the clutches of this Philistine." Saul answered David, "Go! the Lord will be with you."

Preparation for the Encounter

³⁸Then Saul clothed David in his own tunic, putting a bronze helmet on his head and arming him with a coat of mail. **³⁹**David also girded himself with Saul's sword over the tunic. He walked with difficulty, however, since he had never tried armor before. He said to Saul, "I cannot go in these, because I have never tried them before." So he took them off. **⁴⁰**Then, staff in hand, David selected five smooth stones from the wadi and put them in the pocket of his shepherd's bag. With his sling also ready to hand, he approached the Philistine.

David's Victory

⁴¹With his shield-bearer marching before him, the Philistine also advanced closer and closer to David. **⁴²**When he had sized David up, and seen that he was youthful, and ruddy, and handsome in appearance, he held him in contempt. **⁴³**The Philistine said to David, "Am I a dog that you come against me with a staff?" Then the Philistine cursed David by his gods **⁴⁴***and said to him, "Come here to me, and I will leave your flesh for the birds of the air and the beasts of the field." **⁴⁵**David answered him:

"You come against me with sword and spear and scimitar, but I come against you in the name of the Lord of hosts, the God of the armies of Israel that you have insulted. **⁴⁶**Today the Lord shall deliver you into my hand; I will strike you down and cut off your head. This very day I will leave your corpse and the corpses of the Philistine army for the birds of the air and the beasts of the field; thus the whole land shall learn that Israel has a God. **⁴⁷***All this multitude, too, shall learn that it is not by sword or spear that the Lord saves. For the battle is the Lord's, and he shall deliver you into our hands."

⁴⁸The Philistine then moved to meet David at close quarters, while David ran quickly toward the battle line in the direction of the Philistine. **⁴⁹**David put his hand into the bag and took out a stone, hurled it with the sling, and struck the Philistine on the forehead. The stone embedded itself in his brow, and he fell prostrate on the ground. **⁵⁰***[Thus David overcame the Philistine with sling and stone; he struck the Philistine mortally, and did it without a sword.] **⁵¹***Then David ran and stood over him; with the Philistine's own sword [which he drew from its sheath] he dispatched him and cut off his head.

Flight of the Philistines

When they saw that their hero was dead, the Philistines took to flight. **⁵²**Then the men of Israel and Judah, with loud shouts, went in pursuit of the Philistines to the approaches of Gath and to the gates of Ekron, and Philistines fell wounded along the road from Shaaraim as far as Gath and Ekron. **⁵³**On their return from the pursuit of the Philistines, the Israelites looted their camp. **⁵⁴***†David took the head of the Philistine and brought it to Jerusalem; but he kept Goliath's armor in his own tent.

David Presented to Saul

⁵⁵[When Saul saw David go out to meet the Philistine, he asked his general Abner, "Abner, whose son is that youth?" Abner replied, "As truly as your majesty is alive, I have no idea." **⁵⁶**And the king said, "Find out whose son the lad is." **⁵⁷**So when David returned from slaying the Philistine, Abner took him and presented him to Saul. David was still holding the Philistine's head. **⁵⁸**Saul then asked him, "Whose son are you, young man?" David replied, "I am the son of your servant Jesse of Bethlehem."

David and Jonathan

18 **¹***[By the time David finished speaking with Saul, Jonathan had become as fond of David as if his life depended on him; he loved him as he loved himself. **²***Saul laid claim to David that day and did not allow him to return to his father's house. **³**And Jonathan entered into a bond with David, because he loved him as himself. **⁴***Jonathan divested himself of the mantle he was wearing and gave it to David, along with his military dress, and his sword, his bow and his belt. **⁵**David then carried out successfully

---

34f: Jgs 14, 6; Sir 47, 3.
37: Prv 28, 1.
44: Dt 28, 26; Is 18, 6; Jer 15, 3.
47: 14, 6; Ps 33, 16.
50: Sir 47, 4; 1 Mc 4, 30.
51: 21, 10.
54: 31, 9.
18/1: 19, 1-7; 20, 17; 23, 16; 2 Sm 1, 26; 9, 1.
2: 16, 21; 17, 15.
4: 2 Sm 1, 22.

---

† 17, 54: At the time supposed by this narrative, Jerusalem was still Jebusite, and David had no military tent of his own; the verse is a later gloss.

every mission on which Saul sent him. So Saul put him in charge of his soldiers, and this was agreeable to the whole army, even to Saul's own officers.]

Saul's Jealousy

6*At the approach of Saul and David (on David's return after slaying the Philistine), women came out from each of the cities of Israel to meet King Saul, singing and dancing, with tambourines, joyful songs, and sistrums. **7***The women played and sang:

> "Saul has slain his thousands,
> and David his ten thousands."

8Saul was very angry and resentful of the song, for he thought: "They give David ten thousands, but only thousands to me. All that remains for him is the kingship." **9**[And from that day on, Saul was jealous of David.]

10*[The next day an evil spirit from God came over Saul, and he raged in his house. David was in attendance, playing the harp as at other times, while Saul was holding his spear. **11**Saul poised the spear, thinking to nail David to the wall, but twice David escaped him.] **12**Saul then began to fear David, [because the LORD was with him, but had departed from Saul himself.] **13**Accordingly, Saul removed him from his presence by appointing him a field officer. So David led the people on their military expeditions, **14**and prospered in all his enterprises, for the LORD was with him. **15**Seeing how successful he was, Saul conceived a fear of David; **16***on the other hand, all Israel and Judah loved him, since he led them on their expeditions.

17*[Saul said to David, "There is my older daughter, Merob, whom I will give you in marriage if you become my champion and fight the battles of the LORD." Saul had in mind, "I shall not touch him; let the Philistines strike him." **18**But David answered Saul: "Who am I? And who are my kin or my father's clan in Israel that I should become the king's son-in-law?" **19***However, when it was time for Saul's daughter Merob to be given to David, she was given in marriage to Adriel the Meholathite instead.]

20*Now Saul's daughter Michal loved David, and it was reported to Saul, who was pleased at this, **21**for he thought, "I will offer her to him to become a snare for him, so that the Philistines may strike him." [Thus for the second time Saul said to David, "You shall become my son-in-law today."] **22**Saul then ordered his servants to speak to David privately and to say: "The king is fond of you, and all his officers love you. You should become the king's son-in-law." **23**But when Saul's servants mentioned this to David, he said: "Do you think it easy to become the king's son-in-law? I am poor and insignificant." **24**When his servants reported to him the

nature of David's answer, **25***Saul commanded them to say this to David: "The king desires no other price for the bride than the foreskins of one hundred Philistines, that he may thus take vengeance on his enemies." Saul intended in this way to bring about David's death through the Philistines. **26**When the servants reported this offer to David, he was pleased with the prospect of becoming the king's son-in-law. [Before the year was up,] **27**David made preparations and sallied forth with his men and slew two hundred Philistines. He brought back their foreskins and counted them out before the king, that he might thus become the king's son-in-law. So Saul gave him his daughter Michal in marriage. **28**Saul thus came to recognize that the LORD was with David; besides, his own daughter Michal loved David. **29**Therefore Saul feared David all the more [and was his enemy ever after].

30[The Philistine chiefs continued to make forays, but each time they took the field, David was more successful against them than any other of Saul's officers, and as a result acquired great fame.]

Persecution of David

19 **1***SAUL discussed his intention of killing David with his son Jonathan and with all his servants. But Saul's son Jonathan, who was very fond of David, **2**told him: "My father Saul is trying to kill you. Therefore, please be on your guard tomorrow morning; get out of sight and remain in hiding. **3**I, however, will go out and stand beside my father in the countryside where you are, and will speak to him about you. If I learn anything, I will let you know."

4Jonathan then spoke well of David to his father Saul, saying to him: "Let not your majesty sin against his servant David, for he has committed no offense against you, but has helped you very much by his deeds. **5***When he took his life in his hands and slew the Philistine, and the LORD brought about a great victory for all Israel through him, you were glad to see it. Why, then, should you become guilty of shedding innocent blood by killing David without cause?" **6**Saul heeded Jonathan's plea and swore, "As the LORD lives, he shall not be killed." **7**So Jonathan summoned David and repeated the whole conversation to him. Jonathan then brought David to Saul, and David served him as before.

8When war broke out again, David went out to fight against the Philistines and inflicted a great defeat upon them, putting them to flight. **9***Then an evil spirit from the LORD came upon Saul as he was sitting in his house with spear in hand and David was playing the harp nearby. **10**Saul tried to nail David to the wall with the spear, but David eluded Saul, so that the spear struck only the wall, and David got away safe.

11†The same night, Saul sent messengers to David's house to guard it, that he might kill him in the morn-

---

✿

    6: Ex 15, 20f; Jgs 11, 34;
      Jdt 15, 12.
    7: 21, 12; 29, 5; Sir 47, 6f.
    10f: 16, 14; 19, 9f; 20, 33;
       22, 6; 26, 8.
    16: 2 Sm 5, 2.
    17: 14, 49; 17, 25.

    19: 21, 8; 24, 16.
    20: 14, 49; 25, 44; 26, 23;
      2 Sm 3, 13.
    25: 17, 26; Gn 34, 12.
    19/1: 18, 1; 20, 1ff.
    5: Dt 19, 10; Ps 119, 109.
    9f: 16, 14; 18, 10f.

---

† 19, 11: This story in all probability originally followed 18, 29, placing the episode of David's escape on the night of his marriage with Michal.

ing. David's wife Michal informed him, "Unless you save yourself tonight, tomorrow you will be killed." [12]*Then Michal let David down through a window, and he made his escape in safety. [13]*Michal took the household idol and laid it in the bed, putting a net of goat's hair at its head and covering it with a spread. [14]When Saul sent messengers to arrest David, she said, "He is sick." [15]Saul, however, sent the messengers back to see David and commanded them, "Bring him up to me in the bed, that I may kill him." [16]But when the messengers entered, they found the household idol in the bed, with the net of goat's hair at its head. [17]Saul therefore asked Michal: "Why did you play this trick on me? You have helped my enemy to get away!" Michal answered Saul: "He threatened me, 'Let me go or I will kill you.'"

David and Samuel in Ramah

[18]Thus David got safely away; he went to Samuel in Ramah, informing him of all that Saul had done to him. Then he and Samuel went to stay in the sheds. [19]When Saul was told that David was in the sheds near Ramah, [20]*he sent messengers to arrest David. But when they saw the band of prophets, presided over by Samuel, in a prophetic frenzy, they too fell into the prophetic state. [21]Informed of this, Saul sent other messengers, who also fell into the prophetic state. For the third time Saul sent messengers, but they too fell into the prophetic state.

Saul among the Prophets

[22]Saul then went to Ramah himself. Arriving at the cistern of the threshing floor on the bare hilltop, he inquired, "Where are Samuel and David?", and was told, "At the sheds near Ramah." [23]As he set out from the hilltop toward the sheds, the spirit of God came upon him also, and he continued on in a prophetic condition until he reached the spot. At the sheds near Ramah [24]*he, too, stripped himself of his garments and he, too, remained in the prophetic state in the presence of Samuel; all that day and night he lay naked. That is why they say, "Is Saul also among the prophets?"

David Consults with Jonathan

20 [1]*DAVID fled from the sheds near Ramah, and went to Jonathan. "What have I done?" he asked him. "What crime or what offense does your father hold against me that he seeks my life?" [2]Jonathan answered him: "Heaven forbid that you should die! My father does nothing, great or small, without disclosing it to me. Why, then, should my father conceal this from me? This cannot be so!" [3]But David replied: "Your father is well aware that I am

favored with your friendship, so he has decided, 'Jonathan must not know of this lest he be grieved.' Nevertheless, as the LORD lives and as you live, there is but a step between me and death." [4]Jonathan then said to David, "I will do whatever you wish." [5]*David answered: "Tomorrow is the new moon, when I should in fact dine with the king. Let me go and hide in the open country until evening. [6]If it turns out that your father misses me, say, 'David urged me to let him go on short notice to his city Bethlehem, because his whole clan is holding its seasonal sacrifice there.' [7]If he says, 'Very well,' your servant is safe. But if he becomes quite angry, you can be sure he has planned some harm. [8]*Do this kindness for your servant because of the LORD's bond between us, into which you brought me: if I am guilty, kill me yourself! Why should you give me up to your father?" [9]But Jonathan answered: "Not I! If ever I find out that my father is determined to inflict injury upon you, I will certainly let you know." [10]David then asked Jonathan, "Who will tell me if your father gives you a harsh answer?"

Mutual Agreement

[11][Jonathan replied to David, "Come, let us go out into the field." When they were out in the open country together, [12]Jonathan said to David: "As the LORD, the God of Israel, lives, I will sound out my father about this time tomorrow. Whether he is well disposed toward David or not, I will send you the information. [13]*Should it please my father to bring any injury upon you, may the LORD do thus and so to Jonathan if I do not apprise you of it and send you on your way in peace. May the LORD be with you even as he was with my father. [14]Only this: if I am still alive, may you show me the kindness of the LORD. But if I die, [15]never withdraw your kindness from my house. And when the LORD exterminates all the enemies of David from the surface of the earth, [16]the name of Jonathan must never be allowed by the family of David to die out from among you, or the LORD will make you answer for it." [17]And in his love for David, Jonathan renewed his oath to him, because he loved him as his very self.]

[18]Jonathan then said to him: "Tomorrow is the new moon; and you will be missed, since your place will be vacant. [19]*On the following day you will be missed all the more. Go to the spot where you hid on the other occasion and wait near the mound there. [20]On the third day of the month I will shoot arrows, as though aiming at a target. [21]I will then send my attendant to go and recover the arrows. If in fact I say to him, 'Look, the arrow is this side of you; pick it up,' come, for you are safe. As the LORD lives, there will be nothing to fear. [22]But if I say to the boy, 'Look, the arrow is beyond you,' go, for the LORD sends you away. [23]However, in the matter which you and I have discussed, the LORD shall be between you and me forever." [24]So David hid in the open country.

On the day of the new moon, when the king sat at table to dine, [25]taking his usual place against the wall, Jonathan sat facing him, while Abner sat at the king's

✷

12: Jos 2, 15; Acts 9, 25;   20/1: 19, 1-7.11-17.
    2 Cor 11, 33.   5: Nm 10, 10; 28, 11-15.
13: Gn 31, 19; Jgs 17, 5;   8f: 23, 17f.
    18, 14.18.20.   13-16: 24, 22f; 2 Sm 9, 1-13;
20: 10, 5f.10; Nm 11, 25.   21, 7.
24: 10, 10ff.   19: 19, 1-7.

side, and David's place was vacant. **²⁶*†**Saul, however, said nothing that day, for he thought, "He must have become unclean by accident, and not yet have been cleansed." **²⁷**On the next day, the second day of the month, David's place was vacant. Saul inquired of his son Jonathan, "Why has the son of Jesse not come to table yesterday or today?" **²⁸**Jonathan answered Saul: "David urgently asked me to let him go to his city, Bethlehem. **²⁹**'Please let me go,' he begged, 'for we are to have a clan sacrifice in our city, and my brothers insist on my presence. Now, therefore, if you think well of me, give me leave to visit my brothers.' That is why he has not come to the king's table." **³⁰**But Saul was extremely angry with Jonathan and said to him: "Son of a rebellious woman, do I not know that, to your own shame and to the disclosure of your mother's shame, you are the companion of Jesse's son? **³¹***Why, as long as the son of Jesse lives upon the earth, you cannot make good your claim to the kingship! So send for him, and bring him to me, for he is doomed." **³²**But Jonathan asked his father Saul: "Why should he die? What has he done?" **³³***At this Saul brandished his spear to strike him, and thus Jonathan learned that his father was resolved to kill David. **³⁴**Jonathan sprang up from the table in great anger and took no food that second day of the month, for he was grieved on David's account, since his father had railed against him.

Jonathan's Farewell

³⁵The next morning Jonathan went out into the field with a little boy for his appointment with David. **³⁶**There he said to the boy, "Run and fetch the arrow." And as the boy ran, he shot an arrow beyond him in the direction of the city. **³⁷**When the boy made for the spot where Jonathan had shot the arrow, Jonathan called after him, "The arrow is farther on!" **³⁸**Again he called to his lad, "Hurry, be quick, don't delay!" Jonathan's boy picked up the arrow and brought it to his master. **³⁹**The boy knew nothing; only Jonathan and David knew what was meant. **⁴⁰**Then Jonathan gave his weapons to this boy of his and said to him, "Go, take them to the city." **⁴¹**When the boy had left, David rose from beside the mound and prostrated himself on the ground three times before Jonathan in homage. They kissed each other and wept aloud together. **⁴²***At length Jonathan said to David, "Go in peace, in keeping with what we two have sworn by the name of the Lord: 'The Lord shall be between you and me, and between your posterity and mine forever.'"

21 **¹**THEN David departed on his way, while Jonathan went back into the city.

The Holy Bread

²*David went to Ahimelech, the priest of Nob, who came trembling to meet him and asked, "Why are you alone? Is there no one with you?" **³**David answered the priest: "The king gave me a commission and told me to let no one know anything about the business on which he sent me or the commission he gave me. For that reason I have arranged a meeting place with my men. **⁴***Now what have you on hand? Give me five loaves, or whatever you can find." **⁵†**But the priest replied to David, "I have no ordinary bread on hand, only holy bread; if the men have abstained from women, you may eat some of that." **⁶**David answered the priest: "We have indeed been segregated from women as on previous occasions. Whenever I go on a journey, all the young men are consecrated—even for a secular journey. All the more so today, when they are consecrated at arms!" **⁷***So the priest gave him holy bread, for no other bread was on hand except the showbread which had been removed from the Lord's presence and replaced by fresh bread when it was taken away. **⁸**One of Saul's servants was there that day, detained before the Lord; his name was Doeg the Edomite, and he was Saul's chief henchman.

The Sword of Goliath

⁹David then asked Ahimelech: "Do you have a spear or a sword on hand? I brought along neither my sword nor my weapons, because the king's business was urgent." **¹⁰***The priest replied: "The sword of Goliath the Philistine, whom you killed in the Vale of the Terebinth, is here [wrapped in a mantle] behind an ephod. If you wish to take that, take it; there is no sword here except that one." David said: "There is none to match it. Give it to me!"

David a Fugitive

¹¹*That same day David took to flight from Saul, going to Achish, king of Gath. **¹²***But the servants of Achish said, "Is this not David, the king of the land? During their dances do they not sing,

'Saul has slain his thousands,
    but David his ten thousands'?"

¹³David took note of these remarks and became very much afraid of Achish, king of Gath. **¹⁴**So, as they watched, he feigned insanity and acted like a madman in their hands, drumming on the doors of the gate and drooling onto his beard. **¹⁵**Finally Achish said to his servants: "You see the man is mad. Why did you

---

†

20, 26: The meal on the first day of the month would have religious overtones, and a ritual impurity (Lv 15, 16; Dt 23, 10ff) would bar David from sharing in it.

21, 5f: *From women:* the high priest, willing to distribute the holy bread to David and his men, requires that they be free from ritual uncleanness, associated in Old Testament times (Lv 15, 18) with the marriage act. David's answer supposes the discipline of a military campaign under the conditions of "holy war" (Dt 23, 10).

26: 16, 5; Lv 7, 20f; 15, 1ff.
31: 2 Sm 12, 5.
33: 18, 11.
42: 2 Sm 9, 1; 21, 7.
21/2: Is 10, 32; Mk 2, 26.
4: Lv 24, 5.9.

7: 22, 9; Lv 24, 5-9;
    Mt 12, 3f; Mk 2, 26;
    Lk 6, 3ff.
10: 17, 51.54.
11: 27, 2; 29, 5.
12: 18, 7; 29, 5.

bring him to me? [16]Do I not have enough madmen, that you bring in this one to carry on in my presence? Should this fellow come into my house?"

22

[1]*DAVID left Gath and escaped to the cave of Adullam. When his brothers and the rest of his family heard about it, they came down to him there. [2]He was joined by all those who were in difficulties or in debt, or who were embittered, and he became their leader. About four hundred men were with him.

[3]From there David went to Mizpeh of Moab and said to the king of Moab, "Let my father and mother stay with you, until I learn what God will do for me." [4]†He left them with the king of Moab, and they stayed with him as long as David remained in the refuge.

[5]But the prophet Gad said to David: "Do not remain in the refuge. Leave, and go to the land of Judah." And so David left and went to the forest of Hereth.

Doeg Betrays Ahimelech

[6]*Now Saul heard that David and his men had been located. At the time he was sitting in Gibeah under a tamarisk tree on the high place, holding his spear, while all his servants were standing by. [7]*So he said to them: "Listen, men of Benjamin! Will the son of Jesse give all of you fields and vineyards? Will he make each of you an officer over a thousand or a hundred men, [8]that you have all conspired against me and no one tells me that my son has made an agreement with the son of Jesse? None of you shows sympathy for me or discloses to me that my son has stirred up my servant to be an enemy against me, as is the case today." [9]*Then Doeg the Edomite, who was standing with the officers of Saul, spoke up: "I saw the son of Jesse come to Ahimelech, son of Ahitub, in Nob. [10]He consulted the LORD for him and gave him supplies, and the sword of Goliath the Philistine as well."

Slaughter of the Priests

[11]At this the king sent a summons to Ahimelech the priest, son of Ahitub, and to all his family who were priests in Nob; and they all came to the king. [12]Then Saul said, "Listen, son of Ahitub!" He replied, "Yes, my lord." [13]Saul asked him, "Why did you conspire against me with the son of Jesse by giving him food and a sword and by consulting God for him, that he might rebel against me and become my enemy, as is the case today?" [14]Ahimelech answered the king: "And who among all your servants is as loyal as David, the king's son-in-law, captain of your bodyguard, and honored in your own house? [15]Is this the first time I have consulted God for him? No indeed! Let not the king accuse his servant or anyone in my family of such a thing. Your servant knows nothing at all, great

or small, about the whole matter." [16]But the king said, "You shall die, Ahimelech, with all your family." [17]*The king then commanded his henchmen standing by: "Make the rounds and kill the priests of the LORD, for they assisted David. They knew he was a fugitive and yet failed to inform me." But the king's servants refused to lift a hand to strike the priests of the LORD.

[18]The king therefore commanded Doeg, "You make the rounds and kill the priests!" So Doeg the Edomite went from one to the next and killed the priests himself, slaying on that day eighty-five who wore the linen ephod. [19]Saul also put the priestly city of Nob to the sword, including men and women, children and infants, and oxen, asses and sheep.

Abiathar Escapes

[20]*One son of Ahimelech, son of Ahitub, named Abiathar, escaped and fled to David. [21]When Abiathar told David that Saul had slain the priests of the LORD, [22]David said to him: "I knew that day, when Doeg the Edomite was there, that he would surely tell Saul. I am responsible for the death of all your family. [23]Stay with me. Fear nothing; he that seeks your life must seek my life also. You are under my protection."

Keilah Liberated

23

[1]*DAVID received information that the Philistines were attacking Keilah and plundering the threshing floors. [2]*So he consulted the LORD, inquiring, "Shall I go and defeat these Philistines?" The LORD answered, "Go, for you will defeat the Philistines and rescue Keilah." [3]But David's men said to him: "We are afraid here in Judah. How much more so if we go to Keilah against the forces of the Philistines!" [4]Again David consulted the LORD, who answered, "Go down to Keilah, for I will deliver the Philistines into your power." [5]David then went with his men to Keilah and fought with the Philistines. He drove off their cattle and inflicted a severe defeat on them, and thus rescued the inhabitants of Keilah.

[6]*Abiathar, son of Ahimelech, who had fled to David, went down with David to Keilah, taking the ephod with him.

Flight from Keilah

[7]When Saul was told that David had entered Keilah, he said: "God has put him in my grip. Now he has shut himself in, for he has entered a city with gates and bars." [8]Saul then called all the people to war, in order to go down to Keilah and besiege David and his men. [9]*When David found out that Saul was planning to harm him, he said to the priest Abiathar, "Bring forward the ephod." [10]David then said: "O LORD God of Israel, your servant has heard a report that Saul plans to come to Keilah, to destroy the city on my account. [11]Will they hand me over? And now: will Saul come down as your servant has heard? O LORD God of Israel, tell your servant." The LORD an-

---

22/1: 2 Sm 23, 13; Ps 63;   20: 23, 6; 30, 7;
     Mi 1, 15.   1 Kgs 2, 26f.
    6: Ps 52.   23/1: Jos 15, 44.
    7: 8, 14.   2: 28, 6.
   9f: 21, 2-10.   6: 22, 20; 30, 7.
   17: 2, 31.33; 21, 7.   9: 2, 28.

22, 4-5: *Refuge:* seemingly connected with the cave complex spoken of in v 1.

swered, "He will come down." [12]David then asked, "Will the citizens of Keilah deliver me and my men into the grasp of Saul?" And the LORD answered, "Yes." [13]So David and his men, about six hundred in number, left Keilah and wandered from place to place. When Saul was informed that David had escaped from Keilah, he abandoned the expedition.

David and Jonathan in Horesh

[14]David now lived in the refuges in the desert, or in the barren hill country near Ziph. Though Saul sought him continually, the LORD did not deliver David into his grasp. [15]David was apprehensive because Saul had come out to seek his life; but while he was at Horesh in the barrens near Ziph, [16]*Saul's son, Jonathan, came down there to David and strengthened his resolve in the LORD. [17]He said to him: "Have no fear, my father Saul shall not lay a hand to you. You shall be king of Israel and I shall be second to you. Even my father Saul knows this." [18]*They made a joint agreement before the LORD in Horesh, where David remained, while Jonathan returned to his home.

Treachery of the Ziphites

[19]*Some of the Ziphites went up to Saul in Gibeah and said, "David is hiding among us, now in the refuges, and again at Horesh, or on the hill of Hachilah, south of the wasteland. [20]Therefore, whenever the king wishes to come down, let him do so. It will be our task to deliver him into the king's grasp." [21]*Saul replied: "The LORD bless you for your sympathy toward me. [22]Go now and make sure once more! Take note of the place where he sets foot" (for he thought, perhaps they are playing some trick on me). [23]"Look around and learn in which of all the various hiding places he is holding out. Then come back to me with sure information, and I will go with you. If he is in the region, I will search him out among all the families of Judah." [24]*So they went off to Ziph ahead of Saul. At this time David and his men were in the desert below Maon, in the Arabah south of the wasteland.

Escape from Saul

[25]When Saul and his men came looking for him, David got word of it and went down to the gorge in the desert below Maon. Saul heard of this and pursued David into the desert below Maon. [26]As Saul moved along one rim of the gorge, David and his men took to the other. David was in anxious flight to escape Saul, and Saul and his men were attempting to outflank David and his men in order to capture them, [27]when a messenger came to Saul, saying, "Come quickly, because the Philistines have invaded the land." [28]Saul interrupted his pursuit of David and went

to meet the Philistines. This is how that place came to be called the Gorge of Divisions.

David Spares Saul

24 [1]DAVID then went up from there and stayed in the refuges behind Engedi. [2]And when Saul returned from the pursuit of the Philistines, he was told that David was in the desert near Engedi. [3]So Saul took three thousand picked men from all Israel and went in search of David and his men in the direction of the wild goat crags. [4]*When he came to the sheepfolds along the way, he found a cave, which he entered to ease nature. David and his men were occupying the inmost recesses of the cave.

[5]David's servants said to him, "This is the day of which the LORD said to you, 'I will deliver your enemy into your grasp; do with him as you see fit.'" So David moved up and stealthily cut off an end of Saul's mantle. [6]*Afterward, however, David regretted that he had cut off an end of Saul's mantle. [7]*He said to his men, "The LORD forbid that I should do such a thing to my master, the LORD's anointed, as to lay a hand on him, for he is the LORD's anointed." [8]With these words David restrained his men and would not permit them to attack Saul. Saul then left the cave and went on his way. [9]David also stepped out of the cave, calling to Saul, "My lord the king!" When Saul looked back, David bowed to the ground in homage [10]and asked Saul:

"Why do you listen to those who say, 'David is trying to harm you'? [11]You see for yourself today that the LORD just now delivered you into my grasp in the cave. I had some thought of killing you, but I took pity on you instead. I decided, 'I will not raise a hand against my lord, for he is the LORD's anointed and a father to me.' [12]*Look here at this end of your mantle which I hold. Since I cut off an end of your mantle and did not kill you, see and be convinced that I plan no harm and no rebellion. I have done you no wrong, though you are hunting me down to take my life. [13]The LORD will judge between me and you, and the LORD will exact justice from you in my case. I shall not touch you. [14]The old proverb says, 'From the wicked comes forth wickedness.' So I will take no action against you. [15]Against whom are you on campaign, O king of Israel? Whom are you pursuing? A dead dog, or a single flea! [16]*The LORD will be the judge; he will decide between me and you. May he see this, and take my part, and grant me justice beyond your reach!"

Saul's Remorse

[17]When David finished saying these things to Saul, Saul answered, "Is that your voice, my son David?" And he wept aloud. [18]Saul then said to David: "You are in the right rather than I; you have treated me generously, while I have done you harm. [19]Great is the generosity you showed me today, when the LORD delivered me into your grasp and you did not kill me. [20]For if a man meets his enemy, does he send him away unharmed? May the LORD reward you gen-

---

✿

16: 18, 1.
18: 18, 3; 20, 8.
19: 26, 1-3; Ps 54.
21: 2 Sm 2, 5.
24: 25, 2.
24/4: Ps 57.
6: 15, 27.

7: 10, 1; 31, 4;
   2 Sm 1, 14.
12: Rom 12, 19.
16: 18, 19.31; 26, 19;
   Pss 35, 1ff; 43, 1.

erously for what you have done this day. **21***And now, since I know that you shall surely be king and that sovereignty over Israel shall come into your possession, **22***swear to me by the LORD that you will not destroy my descendants and that you will not blot out my name and family." **23**David gave Saul his oath and Saul returned home, while David and his men went up to the refuge.

Death of Samuel

25 **1***SAMUEL died, and all Israel gathered to mourn him; they buried him at his home in Ramah.

Nabal and Abigail

Then David went down to the desert of Maon. **2***There was a man of Maon who had property in Carmel; he was very wealthy, owning three thousand sheep and a thousand goats. At this time he was present for the shearing of his flock in Carmel. **3***The man was named Nabal, his wife, Abigail. The woman was intelligent and attractive, but Nabal himself, a Calebite, was harsh and ungenerous in his behavior. **4**When David heard in the desert that Nabal was shearing his flock, **5**he sent ten young men, instructing them: "Go up to Carmel. Pay Nabal a visit and greet him in my name. **6**Say to him, 'Peace be with you, my brother, and with your family, and with all who belong to you. **7**I have just heard that shearers are with you. Now, when your shepherds were with us, we did them no injury, neither did they miss anything all the while they were in Carmel. **8**Ask your servants and they will tell you so. Look kindly on these young men, since we come at a festival time. Please give your servants and your son David whatever you can manage.'"

9When David's young men arrived, they delivered this message fully to Nabal in David's name, and then waited. **10**But Nabal answered the servants of David: "Who is David? Who is the son of Jesse? Nowadays there are many servants who run away from their masters. **11**Must I take my bread, my wine, my meat that I have slaughtered for my own shearers, and give them to men who come from I know not where?" **12**So David's young men retraced their steps and on their return reported to him all that had been said. **13**Thereupon David said to his men, "Let everyone gird on his sword." And so everyone, David included, girded on his sword. About four hundred men went up after David, while two hundred remained with the baggage.

14But Nabal's wife Abigail was informed of this by one of the servants, who said: "David sent messengers from the desert to greet our master, but he flew at them screaming. **15**Yet these men were very good to us. We were done no injury, neither did we miss any-

thing all the while we were living among them during our stay in the open country. **16**For us they were like a rampart night and day the whole time we were pasturing the sheep near them. **17**Now, see what you can do, for you must realize that otherwise evil is in store for our master and for his whole family. He is so mean that no one can talk to him." **18**Abigail quickly got together two hundred loaves, two skins of wine, five dressed sheep, five seahs of roasted grain, a hundred cakes of pressed raisins, and two hundred cakes of pressed figs, and loaded them on asses. **19**She then said to her servants, "Go on ahead; I will follow you." But she did not tell her husband Nabal.

20As she came down through a mountain defile riding on an ass, David and his men were also coming down from the opposite direction. When she met them, **21**David had just been saying: "Indeed, it was in vain that I guarded all this man's possessions in the desert, so that he missed nothing. He has repaid good with evil. **22***May God do thus and so to David, if by morning I leave a single male alive among all those who belong to him." **23**As soon as Abigail saw David, she dismounted quickly from the ass and, falling prostrate on the ground before David, did him homage. **24**As she fell at his feet she said:

"My lord, let the blame be mine. Please let your handmaid speak to you, and listen to the words of your handmaid. **25**†Let not my lord pay attention to that worthless man Nabal, for he is just like his name. Fool is his name, and he acts the fool. I, your handmaid, did not see the young men whom my lord sent. **26**†Now, therefore, my lord, as the LORD lives, and as you live, it is the LORD who has kept you from shedding blood and from avenging yourself personally. May your enemies and those who seek to harm my lord become as Nabal! **27**Accept this present, then, which your maidservant has brought for my lord, and let it be given to the young men who follow my lord. **28**Please forgive the transgression of your handmaid, for the LORD shall certainly establish a lasting dynasty for my lord, because your lordship is fighting the battles of the LORD, and there is no evil to be found in you your whole life long. **29***†If anyone rises to pursue you and to seek your life, may the life of my lord be bound in the bundle of the living in the care of the LORD your God; but may he hurl out the lives of your enemies as from the hollow of a sling. **30***And when the LORD carries out for my lord the promise of success he has made concerning you, and appoints you as commander over Israel, **31**you shall not have this as a qualm or burden on your conscience, my lord, for

---

† 25, 25: *Fool is his name:* Nabal in Hebrew means "a fool."

25, 26: Abigail anticipates that some misfortune will shortly overtake Nabal, as in fact it does (vv 37-38).

25, 29: *The bundle of the living:* the figure is perhaps taken from the practice of tying up valuables in a kerchief or bag for safekeeping. Abigail desires that David enjoy permanent peace and security, but that his enemies be subject to constant agitation and humiliation like a stone whirled about, cast out of the sling, and thereafter disregarded.

❋
21: 26, 25.
22: 2 Sm 9, 1ff.
25/1: 28, 3; Sir 46, 13-20.
2: 23, 24; Jos 15, 55.
3: 27, 3; Jos 14, 6;
    1 Chr 2, 42.45.

22: 1 Kgs 16, 11; 21, 21;
    2 Kgs 9, 8.
29: Ps 69, 28.
30: 13, 14; 2 Sm 3, 10.

having shed innocent blood or for having avenged yourself personally. When the LORD confers this benefit on your lordship, remember your handmaid."

³²David said to Abigail: "Blessed be the LORD, the God of Israel, who sent you to meet me today. ³³Blessed be your good judgment and blessed be you yourself, who this day have prevented me from shedding blood and from avenging myself personally. ³⁴Otherwise, as the LORD, the God of Israel, lives, who has restrained me from harming you, if you had not come so promptly to meet me, by dawn Nabal would not have had a single man or boy left alive." ³⁵David then took from her what she had brought him and said to her: "Go up to your home in peace! See, I have granted your request as a personal favor."

Nabal's Death

³⁶When Abigail came to Nabal, there was a drinking party in his house like that of a king, and Nabal was merry because he was very drunk. So she told him nothing at all before daybreak the next morning. ³⁷But then, when Nabal had become sober, his wife told him what had happened. At this his courage died within him, and he became like a stone. ³⁸About ten days later the LORD struck him and he died. ³⁹On hearing that Nabal was dead, David said: "Blessed be the LORD, who has requited the insult I received at the hand of Nabal, and who restrained his servant from doing evil, but has punished Nabal for his own evil deeds."

David Marries Abigail and Ahinoam

David then sent a proposal of marriage to Abigail. ⁴⁰When David's servants came to Abigail in Carmel, they said to her, "David has sent us to you that he may take you as his wife." ⁴¹Rising and bowing to the ground, she answered, "Your handmaid would become a slave to wash the feet of my lord's servants." ⁴²*She got up immediately, mounted an ass, and followed David's messengers, with her five maids following in attendance upon her. She became his wife, ⁴³*and David also married Ahinoam of Jezreel. Thus both of them were his wives; but Saul gave David's wife Michal, Saul's own daughter, to Palti, son of Laish, who was from Gallim.

Saul's Life Again Spared

26 ¹*MEN from Ziph came to Saul in Gibeah, reporting that David was hiding on the hill of Hachilah at the edge of the wasteland. ²So Saul went off down to the desert of Ziph with three thousand picked men of Israel, to search for David in the desert of Ziph. ³Saul camped beside the road on the hill of Hachilah, at the edge of the waste-

land. David, who was living in the desert, saw that Saul had come into the desert after him ⁴and sent out scouts, who confirmed Saul's arrival. ⁵*David himself then went to the place where Saul was encamped and examined the spot where Saul and Abner, son of Ner, the general, had their sleeping quarters. Saul's were within the barricade, and all his soldiers were camped around him. ⁶*David asked Ahimelech the Hittite, and Abishai, son of Zeruiah and brother of Joab, "Who will go down into the camp with me to Saul?" Abishai replied, "I will." ⁷So David and Abishai went among Saul's soldiers by night and found Saul lying asleep within the barricade, with his spear thrust into the ground at his head and Abner and his men sleeping around him.

⁸*Abishai whispered to David: "God has delivered your enemy into your grasp this day. Let me nail him to the ground with one thrust of the spear; I will not need a second thrust!" ⁹But David said to Abishai, "Do not harm him, for who can lay hands on the LORD's anointed and remain unpunished? ¹⁰As the LORD lives," David continued, "it must be the LORD himself who will strike him, whether the time comes for him to die, or he goes out and perishes in battle. ¹¹But the LORD forbid that I touch his anointed! Now take the spear which is at his head and the water jug, and let us be on our way." ¹²So David took the spear and the water jug from their place at Saul's head, and they got away without anyone's seeing or knowing or awakening. All remained asleep, because the LORD had put them into a deep slumber.

David Taunts Abner

¹³Going across to an opposite slope, David stood on a remote hilltop at a great distance from Abner, son of Ner, and the troops. ¹⁴He then shouted, "Will you not answer, Abner?" And Abner answered, "Who is it that calls me?" ¹⁵David said to Abner: "Are you not a man whose like does not exist in Israel? Why, then, have you not guarded your lord the king when one of his subjects went to kill the king, your lord? ¹⁶This is no creditable service you have performed. As the LORD lives, you people deserve death because you have not guarded your lord, the LORD's anointed. Go, look: where are the king's spear and the water jug that was at his head?"

Saul Admits His Guilt

¹⁷Saul recognized David's voice and asked, "Is that your voice, my son David?" David answered, "Yes, my lord the king." ¹⁸He continued: "Why does my lord pursue his servant? What have I done? What evil do I plan? ¹⁹*†Please, now, let my lord the king listen to the words of his servant. If the LORD has incited you against me, let an offering appease him; but if men, may they be cursed before the LORD, because they

---

✲
  42: 27, 3.   5: 17, 20.
  43: 18, 20; 27, 3; 30, 5;   6: 1 Chr 2, 16.
      2 Sm 3, 2.13ff;   8: 18, 11; 19, 10.
      1 Chr 3, 1.   19: 24, 16.
  26/1f: 23, 19f; Ps 54.

---

† 26, 19: *The Lord's inheritance:* the land of Israel (Dt 32, 8f), under the Lord's special protection, where he could be freely worshiped.

have exiled me so that this day I have no share in the LORD's inheritance, but am told: 'Go, serve other gods!' ²⁰Do not let my blood flow to the ground far from the presence of the LORD. For the king of Israel has come out to seek a single flea as if he were hunting partridge in the mountains." ²¹Then Saul said: "I have done wrong. Come back, my son David, I will not harm you again, because you have held my life precious today. Indeed, I have been a fool and have made a serious mistake." ²²But David answered: "Here is the king's spear. Let an attendant come over to get it. ²³*The LORD will reward each man for his justice and faithfulness. Today, though the LORD delivered you into my grasp, I would not harm the LORD's anointed. ²⁴As I valued your life highly today, so may the LORD value my life highly and deliver me from all difficulties." ²⁵*Then Saul said to David: "Blessed are you, my son David! You shall certainly succeed in whatever you undertake." David went his way, and Saul returned to his home.

Refuge among Philistines

27 ¹BUT David said to himself: "I shall perish some day at the hand of Saul. I have no choice but to escape to the land of the Philistines; then Saul will give up his continual search for me throughout the land of Israel, and I shall be out of his reach." ²*Accordingly, David departed with his six hundred men and went over to Achish, son of Maoch, king of Gath. ³*David and his men lived in Gath with Achish; each one had his family, and David had his two wives, Ahinoam from Jezreel and Abigail, the widow of Nabal from Carmel. ⁴When Saul was told that David had fled to Gath, he no longer searched for him.

In Ziklag

⁵David said to Achish: "If I meet with your approval, let me have a place to live in one of the country towns. Why should your servant live with you in the royal city?" ⁶*†That same day Achish gave him Ziklag, which has, therefore, belonged to the kings of Judah up to the present time. ⁷*In all, David lived a year and four months in the country of the Philistines.

Raids on Israel's Foes

⁸*David and his men went up and made raids on the Geshurites, Girzites, and Amalekites—peoples living in the land between Telam, on the approach to Shur, and the land of Egypt. ⁹In attacking the land David would not leave a man or woman alive, but would carry off sheep, oxen, asses, camels, and clothes. On his return he brought these to Achish, ¹⁰*who

asked, "Whom did you raid this time?" And David answered, "The Negeb of Judah," or "The Negeb of Jerahmeel," or "The Negeb of the Kenites." ¹¹But David would not leave a man or woman alive to be brought to Gath, fearing that they would betray him by saying, "This is what David did." This was his custom as long as he lived in the country of the Philistines. ¹²And Achish trusted David, thinking, "He must certainly be detested by his people Israel. I shall have him as my vassal forever."

28 ¹IN those days the Philistines mustered their military forces to fight against Israel. So Achish said to David, "You realize, of course, that you and your men must go out on campaign with me to Jezreel." ²David answered Achish, "Good! Now you shall learn what your servant can do." Then Achish said to David, "I shall appoint you my permanent bodyguard."

³*Now Samuel had died and, after being mourned by all Israel, was buried in his city, Ramah. Meanwhile Saul had driven mediums and fortune-tellers out of the land.

Saul in Dismay

⁴The Philistine levies advanced to Shunem and encamped. Saul, too, mustered all Israel; they camped on Gilboa. ⁵When Saul saw the camp of the Philistines, he was dismayed and lost heart completely. ⁶*He therefore consulted the LORD; but the LORD gave no answer, whether in dreams or by the Urim or through prophets. ⁷*Then Saul said to his servants, "Find me a woman who is a medium, to whom I can go to seek counsel through her." His servants answered him, "There is a woman in Endor who is a medium."

The Witch of Endor

⁸*So he disguised himself, putting on other clothes, and set out with two companions. They came to the woman by night, and Saul said to her, "Tell my fortune through a ghost; conjure up for me the one I ask you to." ⁹But the woman answered him, "You are surely aware of what Saul has done, in driving the mediums and fortune-tellers out of the land. Why, then, are you laying snares for my life, to have me killed?" ¹⁰But Saul swore to her by the LORD, "As the LORD lives, you shall incur no blame for this." ¹¹Then the woman asked him, "Whom do you want me to conjure up?" and he answered, "Samuel."

Samuel Appears

¹²†When the woman saw Samuel, she shrieked at the top of her voice and said to Saul, "Why have you

---

✻

23: 18, 20.
25: 24, 21.
27/2: 21, 11-16.
   3: 25, 3.44; 30, 3ff;
     2 Sm 2, 3.
   6: 30, 1.
   7: 29, 3.
   8: 15, 3.7.

10: 30, 14.29;
    1 Chr 2, 9.25.42.
28/3: 25, 1; Sir 46, 20.
   6: 14, 37.41; Ex 28, 30;
     Lv 8, 8.
   7: Lv 19, 31; 20, 27;
     Dt 18, 10ff; 1 Chr 10,
     13f; Acts 16, 16.
   8: 1 Kgs 14, 2.

---

† 27, 6: *Has . . . belonged to the kings of Judah:* as a personal holding, outside the system of tribal lands; Jerusalem, when taken by David, had a similar status (2 Sm 5, 7-9).

28, 12: Human beings cannot communicate at will with the souls of the dead. God may, however, permit a departed soul to appear to the living and even to disclose things unknown to them. Saul's own prohibition of necromancy and divination deceived me? You are Saul!" ¹³But the king said to her, "Have no fear. What do you see?" The woman answered Saul, "I see a preternatural being rising from the earth." ¹⁴"What does he look like?" asked Saul. And she replied, "It is an old man who is rising, clothed in a mantle." Saul knew that it was Samuel, and so he bowed face to the ground in homage.

Saul's Doom

¹⁵*Samuel then said to Saul, "Why do you disturb me by conjuring me up?" Saul replied: "I am in great straits; for the Philistines are waging war against me and God has abandoned me. Since he no longer answers me through prophets or in dreams, I have called you to tell me what I should do." ¹⁶*To this Samuel said: "But why do you ask me, if the Lord has abandoned you and is with your neighbor? ¹⁷The Lord has done to you what he foretold through me: he has torn the kingdom from your grasp and has given it to your neighbor David.

¹⁸*"Because you disobeyed the Lord's directive and would not carry out his fierce anger against Amalek, the Lord has done this to you today. ¹⁹*Moreover, the Lord will deliver Israel, and you as well, into the clutches of the Philistines. By tomorrow you and your sons will be with me, and the Lord will have delivered the army of Israel into the hands of the Philistines."

Saul's Despair

²⁰Immediately Saul fell full length on the ground, for he was badly shaken by Samuel's message. Moreover, he had no bodily strength left, since he had eaten nothing all that day and night. ²¹Then the woman came to Saul, and seeing that he was quite terror-stricken, said to him: "Remember, your maidservant obeyed you: I took my life in my hands and fulfilled the request you made of me. ²²Now you, in turn, please listen to your maidservant. Let me set something before you to eat, so that you may have strength when you go on your way." ²³But he refused, saying, "I will not eat." However, when his servants joined the woman in urging him, he listened to their entreaties, got up from the ground, and sat on a couch. ²⁴The woman had a stall-fed calf in the house, which she now quickly slaughtered. Then taking flour, she kneaded it and baked unleavened bread. ²⁵She set the meal before Saul and his servants, and they ate. Then they stood up and left the same night.

David's Aid Rejected

29 ¹*Now the Philistines had mustered all their forces in Aphek, and the Israelites were encamped at the spring of Harod near Jezreel. ²As the Philistine lords were marching their groups of a hundred and a thousand, David and his men were

marching in the rear guard with Achish. ³*The Philistine chiefs asked, "What are those Hebrews doing here?" And Achish answered them: "Why, that is David, the officer of Saul, king of Israel. He has been with me now for a year or two, and I have no fault to find with him from the day he came over to me until the present." ⁴*But the Philistine chiefs were angered at this and said to him: "Send that man back! Let him return to the place you picked out for him. He must not go down into battle with us, lest during the battle he become our enemy. For how else can he win back his master's favor, if not with the heads of these men of ours? ⁵*Is this not the David of whom they sing during their dances,

> 'Saul has slain his thousands,
> but David his ten thousands'?"

⁶So Achish summoned David and said to him: "As the Lord lives, you are honest, and I should be pleased to have you active with me in the camp, for I have found nothing wrong with you from the day of your arrival to this day. But you are not welcome to the lords. ⁷Withdraw peaceably, now, and do nothing that might displease the Philistine lords." ⁸But David said to Achish: "What have I done? Or what have you against your servant from the first day I have been with you to this day, that I cannot go to fight against the enemies of my lord the king?" ⁹"You know," Achish answered David, "that you are acceptable to me. But the Philistine chiefs have determined you are not to go up with us to battle. ¹⁰So the first thing tomorrow, you and your lord's servants who came with you, go to the place I picked out for you. Do not decide to take umbrage at this; you are as acceptable to me as an angel of God. But make an early morning start, as soon as it grows light, and be on your way." ¹¹So David and his men left early in the morning to return to the land of the Philistines. The Philistines, however, went on up to Jezreel.

Ziklag in Ruins

30 ¹*Before David and his men reached Ziklag on the third day, the Amalekites had raided the Negeb and Ziklag, had stormed the city, and had set it on fire. ²They had taken captive the women and all who were in the city, young and old, killing no one; they had carried them off when they left. ³David and his men arrived at the city to find it burned to the ground and their wives, sons and daughters taken captive. ⁴Then David and those who were with him wept aloud until they could weep no more. ⁵*David's two wives, Ahinoam of Jezreel and Abigail, the widow of Nabal from Carmel, had also been carried off with the rest. ⁶Now David found himself in great difficulty, for the men spoke of stoning him, so

---

15: Sir 46, 20.
16: 15, 27f.
18: 15, 18f.26.
19: 31, 2-6; Sir 46, 20.
29/1: 4, 1.

3: 27, 7.
4: 1 Chr 12, 19f.
5: 18, 6f; 21, 11.
30/1: 27, 6.10; 1 Chr 12, 21.
5: 25, 42; 27, 3; 30, 5.

† (v 3) was in keeping with the consistent teaching of the Old Testament. If we are to credit the reality of the apparition to Saul, it was due, not to the summons of the witch, but to God's will; the woman merely furnished the occasion.

bitter were they over the fate of their sons and daughters. But with renewed trust in the LORD his God, [7]*David said to Abiathar, the priest, son of Ahimelech, "Bring me the ephod!" When Abiathar brought him the ephod, [8]David inquired of the LORD, "Shall I pursue these raiders? Can I overtake them?" The LORD answered him, "Go in pursuit, for you shall surely overtake them and effect a rescue."

Raid of the Amalekites

[9]So David went off with his six hundred men and came as far as the Wadi Besor, where those who were to remain behind halted. [10]David continued the pursuit with four hundred men, but two hundred were too exhausted to cross the Wadi Besor and remained behind. [11]An Egyptian was found in the open country and brought to David. He was provided with food, which he ate, and given water to drink; [12]a cake of pressed figs and two cakes of pressed raisins were also offered to him. When he had eaten, he revived; he had not taken food nor drunk water for three days and three nights. [13]Then David asked him, "To whom do you belong, and where do you come from?" He replied: "I am an Egyptian, the slave of an Amalekite. My master abandoned me because I fell sick three days ago today. [14]*We raided the Negeb of the Cherethites, the territory of Judah, and the Negeb of Caleb; and we set Ziklag on fire." [15]David then asked him, "Will you lead me down to this raiding party?" He answered, "Swear to me by God that you will not kill me or deliver me to my master, and I will lead you to the raiding party." [16]He did lead them, and there were the Amalekites scattered all over the ground, eating, drinking, and in a festive mood because of all the rich booty they had taken from the land of the Philistines and from the land of Judah.

The Booty Recovered

[17]*From dawn to sundown David attacked them, putting them under the ban so that none escaped except four hundred young men, who mounted their camels and fled. [18]David recovered everything the Amalekites had taken, and rescued his two wives. [19]Nothing was missing, small or great, booty or sons or daughters, of all that the Amalekites had taken. David brought back everything. [20]Moreover, David took all the sheep and oxen, and as they drove these before him, they shouted, "This is David's spoil!"

Division of the Spoils

[21]When David came to the two hundred men who had been too exhausted to follow him, and whom he had left behind at the Wadi Besor, they came out to meet David and the men with him. On nearing them David greeted them. [22]But all the stingy and worthless men among those who had accompanied David spoke up to say, "Since they did not accompany us, we will not give them anything from the booty, except to each man his wife and children. Let them take those along and be on their way." [23]But David said: "You must not do this, my brothers, after what the LORD has given us. He has protected us and delivered into our grip the band that came against us. [24]*Who could agree with this proposal of yours? Rather, the share of the one who goes down to battle and that of the one who remains with the baggage shall be the same; they shall share alike." [25]*And from that day forward he made it a law and a custom in Israel, as it still is today.

David's Gifts to Judah

[26]When David came to Ziklag, he sent part of the spoil to the elders of Judah, city by city, saying, "This is a gift to you from the spoil of the enemies of the LORD": [27]to those in Bethel, to those in Ramoth-negeb, to those in Jattir, [28]to those in Aroer, to those in Siphmoth, to those in Eshtemoa, [29]*to those in Racal, to those in the Jerahmeelite cities, to those in the Kenite cities, [30]to those in Hormah, to those in Borashan, to those in Athach, [31]to those in Hebron, and to all the places frequented by David and his men.

Death of Saul and His Sons

31 [1]*As they pressed their attack on Israel, with the Israelites fleeing before them and falling mortally wounded on Mount Gilboa, [2]*the Philistines pursued Saul and his sons closely, and slew Jonathan, Abinadab, and Malchishua, sons of Saul. [3]The battle raged around Saul, and the archers hit him; he was pierced through the abdomen. [4]*Then Saul said to his armor-bearer, "Draw your sword and run me through, lest these uncircumcised come and make sport of me." But his armor-bearer, badly frightened, refused to do it. So Saul took his own sword and fell upon it. [5]*†When the armor-bearer saw that Saul was dead, he too fell upon his sword and died with him. [6]Thus Saul, his three sons, and his armor-bearer died together on that same day.

[7]When the Israelites on the slope of the valley and those along the Jordan saw that the men of Israel had fled and that Saul and his sons were dead, they too abandoned their cities and fled. Then the Philistines came and lived in those cities.

[8]The day after the battle the Philistines came to strip the slain, and found Saul and his three sons lying on Mount Gilboa. [9]*They cut off Saul's head and stripped him of his armor, and then sent the good news throughout the land of the Philistines to their idols and to the people. [10]They put his armor in the temple of Astarte, but impaled his body on the wall of Bethshan.

✿

7f: 2, 28; 23, 6; Ex 28, 30.
14: 27, 10; Ez 25, 16.
17: 15, 3; Jos 6, 17;
    Jgs 7, 12.
24: 17, 22; 25, 13.
25: Nm 31, 27.
29: 27, 10.
31/1-13: 1 Chr 10, 1-12; 2 Sm 1,
    1-16; 4, 4.

2: 14, 49; 28, 19;
   1 Chr 10, 2f.
4: 24, 7; Jgs 9, 54;
   1 Chr 10, 4.
5: 10, 1; 26, 9;
   2 Mc 14, 42.
9: 17, 54; 2 Sm 1, 20;
   2 Mc 15, 35.

† 31, 5: This report of the suicidal act of Saul is presented as a part of his downfall, to be judged accordingly.

Burial of Saul

11*When the inhabitants of Jabesh-gilead heard what the Philistines had done to Saul, 12†all their warriors set out, and after marching throughout the night, removed the bodies of Saul and his sons from the wall

of Beth-shan, and brought them to Jabesh, where they cremated them. 13Then they took their bones and buried them under the tamarisk tree in Jabesh, and fasted for seven days.

---

* 11ff: 11, 1-11; 2 Sm 2, 4-7.

† 31, 12: *Cremated them:* cremation was not normally practiced in Israel, though it was known in the country from pre-Israelite times.

The Second Book of Samuel

Report of Saul's Death

1 [1]*AFTER THE DEATH OF SAUL, David returned from his defeat of the Amalekites and spent two days in Ziklag. [2]On the third day a man came from Saul's camp, with his clothes torn and dirt on his head. Going to David, he fell to the ground in homage. [3]David asked him, "Where do you come from?" He replied, "I have escaped from the Israelite camp." [4]"Tell me what happened," David bade him. He answered that the soldiers had fled the battle and that many of them had fallen and were dead, among them Saul and his son Jonathan. [5]Then David said to the youth who was reporting to him, "How do you know that Saul and his son Jonathan are dead?" [6]*The youthful informant replied: "It was by chance that I found myself on Mount Gilboa and saw Saul leaning on his spear, with chariots and horsemen closing in on him. [7]He turned around and, seeing me, called me to him. When I said, 'Here I am,' [8]he asked me, 'Who are you?' and I replied, 'An Amalekite.' [9]Then he said to me, 'Stand up to me, please, and finish me off, for I am in great suffering, yet fully alive.' [10]So I stood up to him and dispatched him, for I knew that he could not survive his wound. I removed the crown from his head and the armlet from his arm and brought them here to my lord."

[11]*David seized his garments and rent them, and all the men who were with him did likewise. [12]*They mourned and wept and fasted until evening for Saul and his son Jonathan, and for the soldiers of the LORD of the clans of Israel, because they had fallen by the sword. [13]Then David said to the young man who had brought him the information, "Where are you from?" He replied, "I am the son of an Amalekite immigrant." [14]*David said to him, "How is it that you were not afraid to put forth your hand to desecrate the LORD's anointed?" [15]David then called one of the attendants and said to him, "Come, strike him down"; and the youth struck him a mortal blow. [16]Meanwhile David said to him, "You are responsible for your own death, for you testified against yourself when you said, 'I dispatched the LORD's anointed.'"

Elegy for Saul and Jonathan

[17]Then David chanted this elegy for Saul and his son Jonathan, [18]*which is recorded in the Book of Jashar to be taught to the Judahites. He sang:

[19]"Alas! the glory of Israel, Saul,
    slain upon your heights;
    how can the warriors have fallen!

[20]*"Tell it not in Gath,
    herald it not in the streets of Ashkelon,
Lest the Philistine maidens rejoice,
    lest the daughters of the strangers exult!
[21]*†Mountains of Gilboa,
    may there be neither dew nor rain upon you,
    nor upsurgings of the deeps!
Upon you lie begrimed the warriors' shields,
    the shield of Saul, no longer anointed with oil.

[22]*"From the blood of the slain,
    from the bodies of the valiant,
The bow of Jonathan did not turn back,
    or the sword of Saul return unstained.
[23]Saul and Jonathan, beloved and cherished,
    separated neither in life nor in death,
    swifter than eagles, stronger than lions!
[24]Women of Israel, weep over Saul,
    who clothed you in scarlet and in finery,
    who decked your attire with ornaments of gold.

[25]"How can the warriors have fallen—
    in the thick of the battle,
    slain upon your heights!

[26]*"I grieve for you, Jonathan my brother!
    most dear have you been to me;
More precious have I held love for you
    than love for women.

[27]"How can the warriors have fallen,
    the weapons of war have perished!"

David Anointed King

2 [1]AFTER this David inquired of the LORD, "Shall I go up into one of the cities of Judah?" The LORD replied to him, "Yes." Then David asked, "Where shall I go?" He replied, "To Hebron." [2]*So David went up there accompanied by his two wives, Ahinoam of

1/1: 1 Sm 30, 17-20; 31,
    1-13.
6-10: 4, 10; 1 Sm 31, 1-4;
    1 Chr 10, 1-4.
11: 13, 31.
12: 1 Sm 31, 13.
14: 1 Sm 10, 1; 24, 7;
    Ps 105, 15.
18: Jos 10, 13.
20: Jgs 16, 23; 1 Sm 31, 9;
    Mi 1, 10.
21: Gn 27, 28.
22: 1 Sm 14, 47.
26: 1 Sm 18, 1; 1 Mc 9, 21.
2/2: 1 Sm 25, 42f.

† 1, 21: *Upsurgings of the deeps:* this reading attempts to recover from an unintelligible Hebrew phrase the poetic parallel to dew and rain. The sense would be a wish that the mountain

Jezreel and Abigail, the widow of Nabal of Carmel. 3David also brought up his men with their families, and they dwelt in the cities near Hebron. 4*Then the men of Judah came there and anointed David king of the Judahites.

A report reached David that the men of Jabesh-gilead had buried Saul. 5So David sent messengers to the men of Jabesh-gilead and said to them: "May you be blessed by the LORD for having done this kindness to your lord Saul in burying him. 6And now may the LORD be kind and faithful to you. I, too, will be generous to you for having done this. 7Take courage, therefore, and prove yourselves valiant men, for though your lord Saul is dead, the Judahites have anointed me their king."

IV: THE REIGN OF DAVID

Ishbaal King of Israel

8*ABNER, SON OF NER, Saul's general, took Ishbaal, son of Saul, and brought him over to Mahanaim, 9where he made him king over Gilead, the Ashurites, Jezreel, Ephraim, Benjamin, and the rest of Israel. 10Ishbaal, son of Saul, was forty years old when he became king over Israel, and he reigned for two years. The Judahites alone followed David. 11*In all, David spent seven years and six months in Hebron as king of the Judahites.

Combat near Gibeon

12Now Abner, son of Ner, and the servants of Ishbaal, Saul's son, left Mahanaim for Gibeon. 13Joab, son of Zeruiah, and David's servants also set out and met them at the pool of Gibeon. And they sat down, one group on one side of the pool and the other on the opposite side. 14Then Abner said to Joab, "Let the young men rise and perform for us." Joab replied, "All right!" 15So they rose and were counted off: twelve of the Benjaminites of Ishbaal, son of Saul, and twelve of David's servants. 16†Then each one grasped his opponent's head and thrust his sword into his opponent's side, and all fell down together. And so that place, which is in Gibeon, was named the Field of the Sides.

Death of Asahel

17After a very fierce battle that day, Abner and the men of Israel were defeated by David's servants. 18*The three sons of Zeruiah were there—Joab, Abishai, and Asahel. Asahel, who was as fleet of foot as a gazelle in the open field, 19*set out after Abner, turning neither right nor left in his pursuit. 20Abner turned around and said, "Is that you, Asahel?" He replied, "Yes." 21Abner said to him, "Turn right or left;

seize one of the young men and take what you can strip from him." But Asahel would not desist from his pursuit. 22*Once more Abner said to Asahel: "Stop pursuing me! Why must I strike you to the ground? How could I face your brother Joab?" 23Still he refused to stop. So Abner struck him in the abdomen with the heel of his javelin, and the weapon protruded from his back. He fell there and died on the spot. And all who came to the place where Asahel had fallen and died, came to a halt. 24Joab and Abishai, however, continued the pursuit of Abner. The sun had gone down when they came to the hill of Ammah which lies east of the valley toward the desert near Geba.

Truce between Joab and Abner

25Here the Benjaminites rallied around Abner, forming a single group, and made a stand on the hilltop. 26Then Abner called to Joab and said: "Must the sword destroy to the utmost? Do you not know that afterward there will be bitterness? How much longer will you refrain from ordering the people to stop the pursuit of their brothers?" 27Joab replied, "As God lives, if you had not spoken, the soldiers would not have been withdrawn from the pursuit of their brothers until morning." 28Joab then sounded the horn, and all the soldiers came to a halt, pursuing Israel no farther and fighting no more.

29Abner and his men marched all night long through the Arabah, crossed the Jordan, marched all through the morning, and came to Mahanaim. 30Joab, after interrupting the pursuit of Abner, assembled all the men. Besides Asahel, nineteen other servants of David were missing. 31But David's servants had fatally wounded three hundred and sixty men of Benjamin, followers of Abner. 32They took up Asahel and buried him in his father's tomb in Bethlehem. Joab and his men made an all-night march, and dawn found them in Hebron.

3 1THERE followed a long war between the house of Saul and that of David, in which David grew stronger, but the house of Saul weaker.

Sons Born in Hebron

2*Sons were born to David in Hebron: his firstborn, Amnon, of Ahinoam from Jezreel; 3*the second, Chileab, of Abigail the widow of Nabal of Carmel; the third, Absalom, son of Maacah the daughter of Talmai, king of Geshur; 4*the fourth, Adonijah, son of Haggith; the fifth, Shephatiah, son of Abital; 5and the sixth, Ithream, of David's wife Eglah. These were born to David in Hebron.

Ishbaal and Abner Quarrel

6During the war between the house of Saul and that of David, Abner was gaining power in the house of

---

*

4: 1 Sm 31, 11ff.
8: 1 Sm 14, 50.
11: 5, 5; 1 Kgs 2, 11.
18: 23, 24; 1 Chr 2, 16.
19: 1 Chr 27, 7.

22: 3, 27f.30.
3/2-5: 1 Chr 3, 14.
3: 13, 37; 15, 8.
4: 1 Kgs 1, 5.

†
should have neither moisture from above nor water from springs or wells.

2, 16: The nature of this gruesome game is not clear, and the place name is variously given in the older texts.

Saul. **7***Now Saul had had a concubine, Rizpah, the daughter of Aiah. And Ishbaal, son of Saul, said to Abner, "Why have you been intimate with my father's concubine?" **8**Enraged at the words of Ishbaal, Abner said, "Am I a dog's head in Judah? At present I am doing a kindness to the house of your father Saul, to his brothers and his friends, by keeping you out of David's clutches; yet this day you charge me with a crime involving a woman! **9***May God do thus and so to Abner if I do not carry out for David what the LORD swore to him—**10***that is, take away the kingdom from the house of Saul and establish the throne of David over Israel and over Judah from Dan to Beer-sheba." **11**In his fear of Abner, Ishbaal was no longer able to say a word to him.

Abner and David Reconciled

12Then Abner sent messengers to David in Telam, where he was at the moment, to say, "Make an agreement with me, and I will aid you by bringing all Israel over to you." **13***He replied, "Very well, I will make an agreement with you. But one thing I require of you. You must not appear before me unless you bring back Michal, Saul's daughter, when you come to present yourself to me." **14**At the same time David sent messengers to Ishbaal, son of Saul, to say, "Give me my wife Michal, whom I espoused by paying a hundred Philistine foreskins." **15***Ishbaal sent for her and took her away from her husband Paltiel, son of Laish, **16**who followed her weeping as far as Bahurim. But Abner said to him, "Go back!" And he turned back.

17Abner then said in discussion with the elders of Israel: "For a long time you have been seeking David as your king. **18**Now take action, for the LORD has said of David, 'By my servant David I will save my people Israel from the grasp of the Philistines and from the grasp of all their enemies.'" **19**Abner also spoke personally to Benjamin, and then went to make his own report to David in Hebron concerning all that would be agreeable to Israel and to the whole house of Benjamin. **20**When Abner, accompanied by twenty men, came to David in Hebron, David prepared a feast for Abner and for the men who were with him. **21**Then Abner said to David, "I will now go to assemble all Israel for my lord the king, that they may make an agreement with you; you will then be king over all whom you wish to rule." So David bade Abner farewell, and he went away in peace.

Death of Abner

22Just then David's servants and Joab were coming in from an expedition, bringing much plunder with them. Abner, having been dismissed by David, was no longer with him in Hebron but had gone his way in peace. **23**When Joab and the whole force he had with

him arrived, he was informed, "Abner, son of Ner, came to David; he has been sent on his way in peace." **24**So Joab went to the king and said: "What have you done? Abner came to you. Why did you let him go peacefully on his way? **25**Are you not aware that Abner came to deceive you and to learn the ins and outs of all that you are doing?" **26**Joab then left David, and without David's knowledge sent messengers after Abner, who brought him back from the cistern of Sirah. **27***When Abner returned to Hebron, Joab took him aside within the city gate as though to speak with him privately. There he stabbed him in the abdomen, and he died in revenge for the killing of Joab's brother Asahel. **28***Later David heard of it and said: "Before the LORD, I and my kingdom are forever innocent. **29**May the full responsibility for the death of Abner, son of Ner, be laid to Joab and to all his family. May the men of Joab's family never be without one suffering from a discharge, or a leper, or one unmanly, one falling by the sword, or one in need of bread!" **30**[Joab and his brother Abishai had lain in wait for Abner because he killed their brother Asahel in battle at Gibeon.]

David Mourns Abner

31*Then David said to Joab and to all the people who were with him, "Rend your garments, gird yourselves with sackcloth, and mourn over Abner." King David himself followed the bier. **32**When they had buried Abner in Hebron, the king wept aloud at the grave of Abner, and the people also wept. **33**And the king sang this elegy over Abner:

> "Would Abner have died like a fool?
> **34**Your hands were not bound with chains,
> nor your feet placed in fetters;
> as men fall before the wicked, you fell."

And all the people continued to weep for him. **35***Then they went to console David with food while it was still day. But David swore, "My God do thus and so to me if I eat bread or anything else before sunset." **36**All the people noted this with approval, just as they were pleased with everything that the king did. **37**So on that day all the people and all Israel came to know that the king had no part in the killing of Abner, son of Ner. **38**The king then said to his servants: "You must recognize that a great general has fallen today in Israel. **39***Although I am the anointed king, I am weak this day, and these men, the sons of Zeruiah, are too ruthless for me. May the LORD requite the evildoer in accordance with his evil deed."

Death of Ishbaal

4 **1**WHEN Ishbaal, son of Saul, heard that Abner had died in Hebron, he ceased to resist and all Israel was alarmed. **2***Ishbaal, son of Saul, had two company leaders named Baanah and Rechab, sons of Rimmon the Beerothite, of the tribe of Benjamin. [Beeroth, too, was ascribed to Benjamin: **3***the Beerothites fled to Gittaim, where they have been resi-

❋

7: 21, 8ff.
9: Ru 1, 17.
10: 5, 2; 1 Sm 25, 30.
13: 1 Sm 18, 20-27.
15: 1 Sm 25, 44.
27: 1 Kgs 2, 5.32.

28.30: 2, 22f.
31: 21, 10.
35: Ru 1, 17.
39: Ps 28, 4; Is 3, 11.
4/2: 9, 3; Jos 9, 17f.
3: Jos 18, 25.

dent aliens to this day. **⁴*†**Jonathan, son of Saul, had a son named Meribbaal with crippled feet. He was five years old when the news about Saul and Jonathan came from Jezreel, and his nurse took him up and fled. But in their hasty flight, he fell and became lame.] **⁵**The sons of Rimmon the Beerothite, Rechab and Baanah, came into the house of Ishbaal during the heat of the day, while he was taking his siesta. **⁶**The portress of the house had dozed off while sifting wheat, and was asleep. So Rechab and his brother Baanah slipped past **⁷**and entered the house while Ishbaal was lying asleep in his bedroom. They struck and killed him, and cut off his head. Then, taking the head, they traveled on the Arabah road all night long.

The Murder Avenged

⁸They brought the head of Ishbaal to David in Hebron and said to the king: "This is the head of Ishbaal, son of your enemy Saul, who sought your life. Thus has the LORD this day avenged my lord the king on Saul and his posterity." **⁹**But David replied to Rechab and his brother Baanah, sons of Rimmon the Beerothite: "As the LORD lives, who rescued me from all difficulty, **¹⁰***in Ziklag I seized and put to death the man who informed me of Saul's death, thinking himself the bearer of good news for which I ought to give him a reward. **¹¹**How much more now, when wicked men have slain an innocent man in bed at home, must I hold you responsible for his death and destroy you from the earth!" **¹²***So at a command from David, the young men killed them and cut off their hands and feet, hanging them up near the pool in Hebron. But he took the head of Ishbaal and buried it in Abner's grave in Hebron.

David King of Israel

5 **¹***ALL the tribes of Israel came to David in Hebron and said: "Here we are, your bone and your flesh. **²***In days past, when Saul was our king, it was you who led the Israelites out and brought them back. And the LORD said to you, 'You shall shepherd my people Israel and shall be commander of Israel.'" **³**When all the elders of Israel came to David in Hebron, King David made an agreement with them there before the LORD, and they anointed him king of Israel. **⁴**David was thirty years old when he became king, and he reigned for forty years: **⁵***seven years and six months in Hebron over Judah, and thirty-three years in Jerusalem over all Israel and Judah.

Capture of Zion

⁶*†Then the king and his men set out for Jerusalem against the Jebusites who inhabited the region. David was told, "You cannot enter here: the blind and the lame will drive you away!" which was their way of saying, "David cannot enter here." **⁷**But David did take the stronghold of Zion, which is the City of David. **⁸***On that day David said: "All who wish to attack the Jebusites must strike at them through the water shaft. The lame and the blind shall be the personal enemies of David." That is why it is said, "The blind and the lame shall not enter the palace."

⁹*David then dwelt in the stronghold, which was called the City of David; he built up the area from Millo to the palace. **¹⁰***David grew steadily more powerful, for the LORD of hosts was with him. **¹¹***Hiram, king of Tyre, sent ambassadors to David; he furnished cedar wood, as well as carpenters and masons, who built a palace for David. **¹²**And David knew that the LORD had established him as king of Israel and had exalted his rule for the sake of his people Israel.

David's Family in Jerusalem

¹³*David took more concubines and wives in Jerusalem after he had come from Hebron, and more sons and daughters were born to him in Jerusalem. **¹⁴**These are the names of those who were born to him in Jerusalem: Shammua, Shobab, Nathan, Solomon, **¹⁵**Ibhar, Elishua, Nepheg, Japhia, **¹⁶**Elishama, Baaliada, and Eliphelet.

Rout of the Philistines

¹⁷†When the Philistines heard that David had been anointed king of Israel, they all took the field in search of him. On hearing this, David went down to the refuge. **¹⁸†**The Philistines came and overran the valley of Rephaim. **¹⁹**David inquired of the LORD, "Shall I attack the Philistines—will you deliver them into my grip?" The LORD replied to David, "Attack, for I will surely deliver the Philistines into your grip." **²⁰†**David then went to Baal-perazim, where he defeated them. He said, "The LORD has scattered my enemies before me like waters that have broken free." That is why the place is called Baal-perazim. **²¹**They abandoned their gods there, and David and his men carried them away. **²²**But the Philistines came up again and overran the valley of Rephaim. **²³**So David inquired of the LORD,

---

† 4, 4: Saul's grandson Meribbaal is the subject of chapter 9 below. The text of this verse may owe its present place to the fact that pre-Christian copies of the Books of Samuel tended to confuse his name with that of his uncle Ishbaal, Saul's son and successor, a principal figure in chapters 2-4.

5, 6-12: David's most important military exploit, the taking of Jerusalem, is here presented before his battles with the Philistines, vv 17-25, which were earlier in time. The sense of vv 6 and 8 is in doubt.

5, 17: *Refuge:* probably near Adullam (1 Sm 22, 1-5).

5, 18-25: The successive defeats of the Philistines in the *valley of Rephaim* southwest of Jerusalem had the effect of blocking their access to the mountain ridge near *Gibeon,* and confining them to their holdings on the coast and in the foothills beyond Gezer to the west and south.

5, 20: *Baal-perazim:* means approximately "the lord of scatterings."

---

*
    4: 9, 3; 19, 25.   6: Jos 15, 63; Jgs 1, 19.21;
    10: 1, 6-10.14.16.   Is 29, 3.
    12: Dt 21, 22f; 1 Sm 31, 10.   8: Lv 21, 18; Mt 21, 14f.
    5/1ff: 1 Chr 11, 1ff.   9: 1 Kgs 3, 1; 11, 27.
      2: 3, 10; Dt 17, 15;   10: Pss 78, 70ff.89; 132, 13.
         1 Sm 18, 16.   11-25: 1 Chr 14, 1-16.
      5: 2, 11; 1 Kgs 2, 11;   11f: 1 Kgs 5, 15;
         1 Chr 3, 4.   1 Chr 14, 1f.
    6-10: 1 Chr 11, 4-9.   13-16: 1 Chr 3, 5-8; 14, 3-7.

who replied: "You must not attack frontally, but circle their rear and meet them before the mastic trees. ²⁴†When you hear a sound of marching in the tops of the mastic trees, act decisively, for the LORD will have gone forth before you to attack the camp of the Philistines." ²⁵David obeyed the LORD's command and routed the Philistines from Gibeon as far as Gezer.

The Ark Brought to Jerusalem

6 ¹*DAVID again assembled all the picked men of Israel, thirty thousand in number. ²*Then David and all the people who were with him set out for Baala of Judah to bring up from there the ark of God, which bears the name of the LORD of hosts enthroned above the cherubim. ³*The ark of God was placed on a new cart and taken away from the house of Abinadab on the hill. Uzzah and Ahio, sons of Abinadab, guided the cart, ⁴with Ahio walking before it, ⁵*while David and all the Israelites made merry before the LORD with all their strength, with singing and with citharas, harps, tambourines, sistrums and cymbals.

⁶When they came to the threshing floor of Nodan, Uzzah reached out his hand to the ark of God and steadied it, for the oxen were making it tip. ⁷But the LORD was angry with Uzzah; God struck him on that spot, and he died there before God. ⁸*David was disturbed because the LORD had vented his anger on Uzzah. (The place has been called Perez-uzzah down to the present day.) ⁹David feared the LORD that day and said, "How can the ark of the LORD come to me?" ¹⁰So David would not have the ark of the LORD brought to him in the City of David, but diverted it to the house of Obed-edom the Gittite.

¹¹*The ark of the LORD remained in the house of Obed-edom the Gittite for three months, and the LORD blessed Obed-edom and his whole house. ¹²*When it was reported to King David that the LORD had blessed the family of Obed-edom and all that belonged to him, David went to bring up the ark of God from the house of Obed-edom into the City of David amid festivities. ¹³As soon as the bearers of the ark of the LORD had advanced six steps, he sacrificed an ox and a fatling. ¹⁴*Then David, girt with a linen apron, came dancing before the LORD with abandon, ¹⁵as he and all the Israelites were bringing up the ark of the LORD with shouts of joy and to the sound of the horn. ¹⁶As the ark of the LORD was entering the City of David, Saul's daughter Michal looked down through the window and saw King David leaping and dancing before the LORD, and she despised him in her heart. ¹⁷*The

ark of the LORD was brought in and set in its place within the tent David had pitched for it. Then David offered holocausts and peace offerings before the LORD. ¹⁸When he finished making these offerings, he blessed the people in the name of the LORD of hosts. ¹⁹He then distributed among all the people, to each man and each woman in the entire multitude of Israel, a loaf of bread, a cut of roast meat, and a raisin cake. With this, all the people left for their homes.

²⁰*When David returned to bless his own family, Saul's daughter Michal came out to meet him and said, "How the king of Israel has honored himself today, exposing himself to the view of the slave girls of his followers, as a commoner might do!" ²¹*But David replied to Michal: "I was dancing before the LORD. As the LORD lives, who preferred me to your father and his whole family when he appointed me commander of the LORD's people, Israel, not only will I make merry before the LORD, ²²but I will demean myself even more. I will be lowly in your esteem, but in the esteem of the slave girls you spoke of I will be honored." ²³And so Saul's daughter Michal was childless to the day of her death.

David's Concern for the Ark

7 ¹*WHEN King David was settled in his palace, and the LORD had given him rest from his enemies on every side, ²*he said to Nathan the prophet, "Here I am living in a house of cedar, while the ark of God dwells in a tent!" ³*Nathan answered the king, "Go, do whatever you have in mind, for the LORD is with you." ⁴But that night the LORD spoke to Nathan and said: ⁵*"Go, tell my servant David, 'Thus says the LORD: Should you build me a house to dwell in? ⁶I have not dwelt in a house from the day on which I led the Israelites out of Egypt to the present, but I have been going about in a tent under cloth. ⁷In all my wanderings everywhere among the Israelites, did I ever utter a word to any one of the judges whom I charged to tend my people Israel, to ask: Why have you not built me a house of cedar?'

The Lord's Promises

⁸*†"Now then, speak thus to my servant David, 'The LORD of hosts has this to say: It was I who took you from the pasture and from the care of the flock to be commander of my people Israel. ⁹*I have been with you wherever you went, and I have destroyed all your enemies before you. And I will make you famous like

---

6/1-11: 1 Chr 13, 1-14.
    2: Ex 25, 10; Jos 15, 9;
      Ps 132, 8f; 1 Chr 1, 4.
    3: 1 Sm 4, 3f; 6, 7f; 7, 1;
      Dn 3, 55.
    5: Pss 68, 25f; 150, 3.5.
    8: 1 Kgs 8, 1.
  11: 1 Chr 26, 4.
 12-23: 1 Chr 15, 1-29;
      Ps 24, 7-10.
  14: 1 Sm 2, 18.
 17ff: Lv 1, 1-17; 3, 1-17;
      1 Chr 16, 1ff.

20: 1 Chr 16, 43.
21: 1 Sm 13, 14; 15, 28.
7/1-29: 1 Chr 17, 1-27.
  1: 1 Kgs 5, 4.
  2: Dt 12, 10; 25, 19.
  3: Ps 132, 1-5.
  5: 1 Kgs 5, 17; 8, 16.27;
      1 Chr 22, 8; 28, 3;
      Is 66, 1; Acts 7, 48.
  8: 1 Sm 16, 13; 17, 15-20;
      Ps 78, 70f; Am 7, 14.
  9: Ps 89, 27.

---

† 5, 24: *Sound of marching:* the wind in the treetops suggestive of the Lord's footsteps.

7, 8-16: The prophecy to David contained in these verses is cited again, in poetic form, in Ps 89, 20-38, and alluded to in Ps 132. The promise regarding the people of Israel, vv 10-11, is a part of the promise to David at least as old as the composition of this chapter of Samuel, where it is anticipated in vv 6-7, and alluded to in David's thanksgiving, vv 23-24; it applies to the people an expression used of David in Ps 89, 23.

The prophecy to David is the basis for Jewish expectation of a messiah, son of David, which Jesus Christ fulfilled in a transcendent way; cf Acts 2, 30; Heb 1, 5.

the great ones of the earth. [10]I will fix a place for my people Israel; I will plant them so that they may dwell in their place without further disturbance. Neither shall the wicked continue to afflict them as they did of old, [11]*since the time I first appointed judges over my people Israel. I will give you rest from all your enemies. The Lord also reveals to you that he will establish a house for you. [12]*And when your time comes and you rest with your ancestors, I will raise up your heir after you, sprung from your loins, and I will make his kingdom firm. [13]It is he who shall build a house for my name. And I will make his royal throne firm forever. [14]I will be a father to him, and he shall be a son to me. And if he does wrong, I will correct him with the rod of men and with human chastisements; [15]*but I will not withdraw my favor from him as I withdrew it from your predecessor Saul, whom I removed from my presence. [16]*Your house and your kingdom shall endure forever before me; your throne shall stand firm forever.'"

[17]Nathan reported all these words and this entire vision to David.

King David's Prayer

[18]Then King David went in and sat before the Lord and said, "Who am I, Lord God, and who are the members of my house, that you have brought me to this point? [19]†Yet even this you see as too little, Lord God; you have also spoken of the house of your servant for a long time to come: this too you have shown to man, Lord God! [20]What more can David say to you? You know your servant, Lord God! [21]For your servant's sake and as you have had at heart, you have brought about this entire magnificent disclosure to your servant. [22]*And so—

"Great are you, Lord God! There is none like you and there is no God but you, just as we have heard it told. [23]*What other nation on earth is there like your people Israel, which God has led, redeeming it as his people; so that you have made yourself renowned by doing this magnificent deed, and by doing awe-inspiring things as you cleared nations and their gods out of the way of your people, which you redeemed for yourself from Egypt? [24]*You have established for yourself your people Israel as yours forever, and you, Lord, have become their God. [25]And now, Lord God, confirm for all time the prophecy you have made concerning your servant and his house, and do as you have promised. [26]Your name will be forever great, when men say, 'The Lord of hosts is God of Israel,' and the house of your servant David stands firm before you.

[27]It is you, Lord of hosts, God of Israel, who said in a revelation to your servant, 'I will build a house for you.' Therefore your servant now finds the courage to make this prayer to you. [28]*And now, Lord God, you are God and your words are truth; you have made this generous promise to your servant. [29]Do, then, bless the house of your servant that it may be before you forever; for you, Lord God, have promised, and by your blessing the house of your servant shall be blessed forever."

Summary of David's Wars

8 [1]*†AFTER this David attacked the Philistines and conquered them, wresting . . . from the Philistines. [2]†He also defeated Moab and then measured them with a line, making them lie down on the ground. He told off two lengths of line for execution, and a full length to be spared. Thus the Moabites became tributary to David. [3]*Next David defeated Hadadezer, son of Rehob, king of Zobah, when he went to reestablish his dominion at the Euphrates River. [4]*David captured from him one thousand seven hundred horsemen and twenty thousand foot soldiers. And he hamstrung all the chariot horses, preserving only enough for a hundred chariots. [5]When the Arameans of Damascus came to the aid of Hadadezer, king of Zobah, David slew twenty-two thousand of them. [6]David then placed garrisons in Aram of Damascus, and the Arameans became subjects, tributary to David. The Lord brought David victory in all his undertakings. [7]David also took away the golden shields used by Hadadezer's servants and brought them to Jerusalem. [These Shishak, king of Egypt, took away when he came to Jerusalem in the days of Rehoboam, son of Solomon.] [8]From Tebah and Berothai, towns of Hadadezer, King David removed a very large quantity of bronze. [9]When Toi, king of Hamath, heard that David had defeated all the forces of Hadadezer, [10]he sent his son Hadoram to King David to greet him and to congratulate him for his victory over Hadadezer in battle, because Toi had been in many battles with Hadadezer. Hadoram also brought with him articles of silver, gold, and bronze. [11]These, too, King David consecrated to the Lord, together with the silver and gold he had taken from every nation he had conquered: [12]from Edom and Moab, from

---

† 7, 19: *This too you have shown to man:* the text as transmitted has, rather, "and this is instruction for (*or:* the law of) mankind." The author of Chronicles (1 Chr 17, 17) saw approximately the same phrase, which he endeavored to fit into the context in a quite different sense. The above is conjectural; cf Dt 5, 24.

8, 1: *Wresting . . . :* the Hebrew text here gives "the bridle of the cubit"; 1 Chr 18, 1 understood "Gath and its dependent villages"; others implausibly read "dominion of the capital city."

8, 2: *Two lengths . . . a full length:* usually taken to mean that two-thirds of them were executed; but it could mean that two-thirds were spared, if the line was used full length in their case but doubled on itself to make "two lines" for those to be put to death.

---

*
11: 23, 5; 1 Kgs 2, 4-24.
12ff: 1 Kgs 5, 19; 8, 19; 1 Chr 22, 10; 2 Chr 7, 18; Ps 89, 5.27f.30.37f; Lk 1, 32; Heb 1, 5.
15: 23, 5; 1 Sm 13, 14; 15, 26.28; 2 Kgs 19, 34; 1 Chr 17, 11-14; Ps 89, 34.
16: 23, 5; Dn 2, 45; 1 Mc 2, 57; Mk 11, 10; Lk 1,

32f; Heb 1, 8.
18: 1 Chr 17, 16.
22: Ex 15, 11; Is 45, 5.
23: Dt 4, 7.34.
24f: Ex 6, 7; Dt 7, 6; 26, 17; 29, 12.
28: Nm 23, 19; Jn 17, 17.
8/1-18: 1 Chr 18, 1-17.
3-8: 10, 15-19.
3: 10, 6; 1 Kgs 11, 23.
4: Jos 11, 6.9.

the Ammonites, from the Philistines, from the Amalekites, and from the plunder of Hadadezer, son of Rehob, king of Zobah.

13***†**On his return, David became famous for having slain eighteen thousand Edomites in the Salt Valley; **14**after which he placed garrisons in Edom. Thus all the Edomites became David's subjects, and the LORD brought David victory in all his undertakings.

David's Officials

15*David reigned over all Israel, judging and administering justice to all his people. **16**Joab, son of Zeruiah, was in command of the army. Jehoshaphat, son of Ahilud, was chancellor. **17**Zadok, son of Ahitub, and Ahimelech, son of Abiathar, were priests. Shawsha was scribe. **18***Benaiah, son of Jehoiada, was in command of the Cherethites and Pelethites. And David's sons were priests.

David and Meribbaal

9 **1***DAVID asked, "Is there any survivor of Saul's house to whom I may show kindness for the sake of Jonathan?" **2***Now there was a servant of the family of Saul named Ziba. He was summoned to David, and the king asked him, "Are you Ziba?" He replied, "Your servant." **3***Then the king inquired, "Is there any survivor of Saul's house to whom I may show God's kindness?" Ziba answered the king, "There is still Jonathan's son, whose feet are crippled." **4***The king said to him, "Where is he?" and Ziba answered, "He is in the house of Machir, son of Ammiel, in Lodebar." **5**So King David sent for him and had him brought from the house of Machir, son of Ammiel, in Lodebar. **6**When Meribbaal, son of Jonathan, son of Saul, came to David, he fell prostrate in homage. David said, "Merribbaal," and he answered, "Your servant." **7**"Fear not," David said to him, "I will surely be kind to you for the sake of your father Jonathan. I will restore to you all the lands of your grandfather Saul, and you shall always eat at my table." **8***Bowing low, he answered, "What is your servant that you should pay attention to a dead dog like me?" **9**The king then called Ziba, Saul's attendant, and said to him: "I am giving your lord's son all that belonged to Saul and to all his family. **10**You and your sons and servants must till the land for him. You shall bring in the produce, which shall be food for your lord's family to eat. But Meribbaal, your lord's son, shall always eat at my table." Ziba, who had fifteen sons and twenty servants, **11***said to the king, "Your servant shall do just as my lord the king has commanded him." And so Meribbaal ate at David's table like one of the king's sons.

12*Meribbaal had a young son whose name was Mica; and all the tenants of Ziba's family worked for Meribbaal. **13***But Meribbaal lived in Jerusalem, because he always ate at the king's table. He was lame in both feet.

Insults of the Ammonites

10 **1***†SOME time later the king of the Ammonites died, and his son Hanun succeeded him as king. **2**David thought, "I will be kind to Hanun, son of Nahash, as his father was kind to me." So David sent his servants with condolences to Hanun for the loss of his father. But when David's servants entered the country of the Ammonites, **3**the Ammonite princes said to their lord Hanun: "Do you think that David is honoring your father by sending men with condolences? Is it not rather to explore the city, to spy on it, and to overthrow it, that David has sent his messengers to you?" **4***Hanun, therefore, seized David's servants and, after shaving off half their beards and cutting away the lower halves of their garments at the buttocks, sent them away. **5**When he was told of it, King David sent out word to them, since the men were quite ashamed. "Stay in Jericho until your beards grow," he said, "and then come back."

Ammonites Defeated

6*†In view of the offense they had given to David, the Ammonites sent for and hired twenty thousand Aramean foot soldiers from Beth-rehob and Zobah, as well as the king of Maacah with one thousand men, and twelve thousand men from Tob. **7***On learning this, David sent out Joab with the entire levy of trained soldiers. **8**The Ammonites came out and drew up in battle formation at the entrance of their city gate, while the Arameans of Zobah and Rehob and the men of Tob and Maacah remained apart in the open country. **9**When Joab saw the battle lines drawn up against him, both front and rear, he made a selection from all the picked troops of Israel and arrayed them against the Arameans. **10**He placed the rest of the soldiers under the command of his brother Abishai, who arrayed them against the Ammonites. **11**Joab said, "If the Arameans are stronger than I, you shall help me. But if the Ammonites are stronger than you, I will come to help you. **12**Be brave; let us prove our valor for the sake of our people and the cities of our God; the LORD will do what he judges best." **13**When Joab and

---

† 8, 13: *On his return:* possibly to Jerusalem, after the revolt of Absalom, a circumstance which this catalogue of victories would avoid mentioning. 1 Chr 18, 13 attributes the defeat of the Edomites to Abishai.

10, 1: *Some time later:* early in the reign of David, since Hanun's father had been ruling in Ammon at the beginning of Saul's reign (1 Sm 11) and Solomon was as yet unborn (2 Sm 11, 1; 12, 24).

10, 6-9: A Hebrew text from Qumran (4Q Samᵃ) comes closer in these verses to what is given in 1 Chr 19, 6-9. The scene of the conflict is more likely Rabbath-Ammon, with Josephus (Ant., vii, 123), than Madeba, as in 1 Chr; compare ch 11.

✿
     13: 2 Kgs 14, 7.   8: 1 Sm 24, 15.
  15-18: 20, 23-26; 1 Kgs 4, 1-6;   11: 19, 29.
         1 Chr 18, 14-17.   12: 1 Chr 8, 34.
     18: 15, 18; 20, 7.23; 23, 20.   13: 21, 7.
       20, 8ff.15f.18.   10/1-19: 1 Chr 19, 1-19.
  9/1: 21, 7; 1 Sm 18, 1-4;   4: Is 20, 4.
      2: 16, 1-4; 19, 27.   6: 8, 3; 1 Sm 14, 47.
      3: 4, 4.   7: 11, 1.
      4: 17, 27.

the soldiers who were with him approached the Arameans for battle, they fled before him. ¹⁴The Ammonites, seeing that the Arameans had fled, also fled from Abishai and withdrew into the city. Joab then ceased his attack on the Ammonites and returned to Jerusalem.

Arameans Defeated

¹⁵*Then the Arameans responded to their defeat by Israel with a full mustering of troops; ¹⁶Hadadezer sent for and enlisted Arameans from beyond the Euphrates. They came to Helam, with Shobach, general of Hadadezer's army, at their head. ¹⁷On receiving this news, David assembled all Israel, crossed the Jordan, and went to Helam. The Arameans drew up in formation against David and fought with him. ¹⁸But the Arameans gave way before Israel, and David's men killed seven hundred charioteers and forty thousand of the Aramean foot soldiers. Shobach, general of the army, was struck down and died on the field. ¹⁹All of Hadadezer's vassal kings, in view of their defeat by Israel, then made peace with the Israelites and became their subjects. And the Arameans were afraid to give further aid to the Ammonites.

David's Sin

11 ¹*†AT the turn of the year, when kings go out on campaign, David sent out Joab along with his officers and the army of Israel, and they ravaged the Ammonites and besieged Rabbah. David, however, remained in Jerusalem. ²One evening David rose from his siesta and strolled about on the roof of the palace. From the roof he saw a woman bathing, who was very beautiful. ³*David had inquiries made about the woman and was told, "She is Bathsheba, daughter of Eliam, and wife of [Joab's armor-bearer] Uriah the Hittite." ⁴*Then David sent messengers and took her. When she came to him, he had relations with her, at a time when she was just purified after her monthly period. She then returned to her house. ⁵But the woman had conceived, and sent the information to David, "I am with child."

⁶David therefore sent a message to Joab, "Send me Uriah the Hittite." So Joab sent Uriah to David. ⁷When he came, David questioned him about Joab, the soldiers, and how the war was going, and Uriah answered that all was well. ⁸David then said to Uriah, "Go down to your house and bathe your feet." Uriah left the palace, and a portion was sent out after him from the king's table. ⁹But Uriah slept at the entrance of the royal palace with the other officers of his lord, and did not go down to his own house. ¹⁰David was told that Uriah had not gone home. So he said to Uriah, "Have you not come from a journey? Why,

then, did you not go down to your house?" ¹¹*Uriah answered David, "The ark and Israel and Judah are lodged in tents, and my lord Joab and your majesty's servants are encamped in the open field. Can I go home to eat and to drink and to sleep with my wife? As the LORD lives and as you live, I will do no such thing." ¹²Then David said to Uriah, "Stay here today also; tomorrow I shall dismiss you." So Uriah remained in Jerusalem that day. On the day following, ¹³David summoned him, and he ate and drank with David, who made him drunk. But in the evening he went out to sleep on his bed among his lord's servants, and did not go down to his home. ¹⁴The next morning David wrote a letter to Joab which he sent by Uriah. ¹⁵In it he directed: "Place Uriah up front, where the fighting is fierce. Then pull back and leave him to be struck down dead." ¹⁶So while Joab was besieging the city, he assigned Uriah to a place where he knew the defenders were strong. ¹⁷When the men of the city made a sortie against Joab, some officers of David's army fell, and among them Uriah the Hittite died.

¹⁸Then Joab sent David a report of all the details of the battle, ¹⁹instructing the messenger, "When you have finished giving the king all the details of the battle, ²⁰the king may become angry and say to you: 'Why did you go near the city to fight? Did you not know that they would shoot from the wall above? ²¹*Who killed Abimelech, son of Jerubbaal? Was it not a woman who threw a millstone down on him from the wall above, so that he died in Thebez? Why did you go near the wall?' Then you in turn shall say, 'Your servant Uriah the Hittite is also dead.'" ²²†The messenger set out, and on his arrival he relayed to David all the details as Joab had instructed him. ²³He told David: "The men had us at a disadvantage and came out into the open against us, but we pushed them back to the entrance of the city gate. ²⁴Then the archers shot at your servants from the wall above, and some of the king's servants died, among them your servant Uriah." ²⁵David said to the messenger: "This is what you shall convey to Joab: 'Do not be chagrined at this, for the sword devours now here and now there. Strengthen your attack on the city and destroy it.' Encourage him."

²⁶When the wife of Uriah heard that her husband had died, she mourned her lord. ²⁷But once the mourning was over, David sent for her and brought her into his house. She became his wife and bore him a son. But the LORD was displeased with what David had done.

15-19: 8, 3-8; 1 Chr 9, 16-19.　　4: Lv 15, 19.
11/1: 10, 7; 1 Chr 20, 1.　　11: 1 Sm 4, 3f.
3: 23, 39.　　21: Jgs 9, 50-54.

Nathan's Parable

12 **¹***†THE LORD sent Nathan to David, and when he came to him, he said: "Judge this case for me! In a certain town there were two men, one rich, the other poor. **²**The rich man had flocks and herds in great numbers. **³**But the poor man had nothing at all except one little ewe lamb that he had bought. He nourished her, and she grew up with him and his children. She shared the little food he had and drank from his cup and slept in his bosom. She was like a daughter to him. **⁴**Now, the rich man received a visitor, but he would not take from his own flocks and herds to prepare a meal for the wayfarer who had come to him. Instead he took the poor man's ewe lamb and made a meal of it for his visitor." **⁵**David grew very angry with that man and said to Nathan: "As the LORD lives, the man who has done this merits death! **⁶***He shall restore the ewe lamb fourfold because he has done this and has had no pity."

David's Punishment

⁷*Then Nathan said to David: "You are the man! Thus says the LORD God of Israel: 'I anointed you king of Israel. I rescued you from the hand of Saul. **⁸**I gave you your lord's house and your lord's wives for your own. I gave you the house of Israel and of Judah. And if this were not enough, I could count up for you still more. **⁹**Why have you spurned the LORD and done evil in his sight? You have cut down Uriah the Hittite with the sword; you took his wife as your own, and him you killed with the sword of the Ammonites. **¹⁰***Now, therefore, the sword shall never depart from your house, because you have despised me and have taken the wife of Uriah to be your wife.' **¹¹***Thus says the LORD: 'I will bring evil upon you out of your own house. I will take your wives while you live to see it, and will give them to your neighbor. He shall lie with your wives in broad daylight. **¹²**You have done this deed in secret, but I will bring it about in the presence of all Israel, and with the sun looking down.'"

David's Repentance

¹³*Then David said to Nathan, "I have sinned against the LORD." Nathan answered David: "The LORD on his part has forgiven your sin: you shall not die. **¹⁴**But since you have utterly spurned the LORD by this deed, the child born to you must surely die." **¹⁵**Then Nathan returned to his house.

The LORD struck the child that the wife of Uriah had borne to David, and it became desperately ill. **¹⁶**David besought God for the child. He kept a fast, retiring for the night to lie on the ground clothed in sackcloth. **¹⁷**The elders of his house stood beside him urging him to rise from the ground; but he would not, nor would he take food with them. **¹⁸**On the seventh day, the child died. David's servants, however, were afraid to tell him that the child was dead, for they said: "When the child was alive, we spoke to him, but he would not listen to what we said. How can we tell him the child is dead? He may do some harm!" **¹⁹**But David noticed his servants whispering among themselves and realized that the child was dead. He asked his servants, "Is the child dead?" They replied, "Yes, he is." **²⁰**Rising from the ground, David washed and anointed himself, and changed his clothes. Then he went to the house of the LORD and worshiped. He returned to his own house, where at his request food was set before him, and he ate. **²¹**His servants said to him: "What is this you are doing? While the child was living, you fasted and wept and kept vigil; now that the child is dead, you rise and take food." **²²**He replied: "While the child was living, I fasted and wept, thinking, 'Perhaps the LORD will grant me the child's life.' **²³***But now he is dead. Why should I fast? Can I bring him back again? I shall go to him, but he will not return to me."

²⁴Then David comforted his wife Bathsheba. He went and slept with her; and she conceived and bore him a son, who was named Solomon. The LORD loved him **²⁵**and sent the prophet Nathan to name him Jedidiah, on behalf of the LORD.

Ammonite War Ends

²⁶*Joab fought against Rabbah of the Ammonites and captured this royal city. **²⁷**He sent messengers to David with the word: "I have fought against Rabbah and have taken the water-city. **²⁸**Therefore, assemble the rest of the soldiers, join the siege against the city and capture it, lest it be I that capture the city and it be credited to me." **²⁹**So David assembled the rest of the soldiers and went to Rabbah. When he had fought against it and captured it, **³⁰**†he took the crown from Milcom's head. It weighed a talent, of gold and precious stones; it was placed on David's head. He brought out immense booty from the city, **³¹**and also led away the inhabitants, whom he assigned to work with saws, iron picks, and iron axes, or put to work at the brickmold. This is what he did to all the Ammonite cities. David and all the soldiers then returned to Jerusalem.

The Crime of Amnon

13 **¹***SOME time later the following incident occurred. David's son Absalom had a beautiful sister named Tamar, and David's son Amnon loved her. **²**He was in such straits over his sister Tamar that he became sick; since she was a virgin, Amnon

---

† 12, 1-4: This utterance of Nathan is in regular lines in Hebrew, resembling English blank verse.

12, 30: *Weighed a talent:* since this would be more than 75 pounds, some commentators picture the idol's crown as displaying a single precious stone of large size, which David took to wear; but the text does not say this.

12/1: Sir 47, 1.
6: Ex 21, 37; Lk 19, 8.
7: 1 Sm 16, 13.
10: 13, 28f; 18, 14.
11: 16, 11.22.
13: 1 Kgs 21, 29; Pss 32, 5; 50, 6; Sir 47, 11.
23: Job 7, 9.
26-31: 1 Chr 20, 1-3.
13/1: 3, 2f; 1 Chr 3, 9.

thought it impossible to carry out his designs toward her. **3***Now Amnon had a friend named Jonadab, son of David's brother Shimeah, who was very clever. **4**He asked him, "Prince, why are you so dejected morning after morning? Why not tell me?" So Amnon said to him, "I am in love with Tamar, my brother Absalom's sister." **5**Then Jonadab replied, "Lie down on your bed and pretend to be sick. When your father comes to visit you, say to him, 'Please let my sister Tamar come and encourage me to take food. If she prepares something appetizing in my presence, for me to see, I will eat it from her hand.'" **6**So Amnon lay down and pretended to be sick. When the king came to visit him, Amnon said to the king, "Please let my sister Tamar come and prepare some fried cakes before my eyes, that I may take nourishment from her hand."

7David then sent home a message to Tamar, "Please go to the house of your brother Amnon and prepare some nourishment for him." **8**Tamar went to the house of her brother Amnon, who was in bed. Taking dough and kneading it, she twisted it into cakes before his eyes and fried the cakes. **9**Then she took the pan and set out the cakes before him. But Amnon would not eat; he said, "Have everyone leave me." When they had all left him, **10**Amnon said to Tamar, "Bring the nourishment into the bedroom, that I may have it from your hand." So Tamar picked up the cakes she had prepared and brought them to her brother Amnon in the bedroom. **11**But when she brought them to him to eat, he seized her and said to her, "Come! Lie with me, my sister!" **12***But she answered him, "No, my brother! Do not shame me! That is an intolerable crime in Israel. Do not commit this insensate deed. **13***Where would I take my shame? And you would be a discredited man in Israel. So please, speak to the king; he will not keep me from you."

14Not heeding her plea, he overpowered her; he shamed her and had relations with her. **15**Then Amnon conceived an intense hatred for her, which far surpassed the love he had had for her. "Get up and leave," he said to her. **16**She replied, "No, brother, because to drive me out would be far worse than the first injury you have done me." He would not listen to her, **17**but called the youth who was his attendant and said, "Put her outside, away from me, and bar the door after her." **18**Now she had on a long tunic, for that is how maiden princesses dressed in olden days. When his attendant put her out and barred the door after her, **19**Tamar put ashes on her head and tore the long tunic in which she was clothed. Then, putting her hands to her head, she went away crying loudly. **20**Her brother Absalom said to her: "Has your brother Amnon been with you? Be still now, my sister; he is your brother. Do not take this affair to heart." But Tamar remained grief-stricken

and forlorn in the house of her brother Absalom. **21**King David, who got word of the whole affair, became very angry. He did not, however, spark the resentment of his son Amnon, whom he favored because he was his first-born. **22**Absalom, moreover, said nothing at all to Amnon, although he hated him for having shamed his sister Tamar.

Absalom's Plot

23After a period of two years, Absalom had shearers in Baal-hazor near Ephraim, and he invited all the princes. **24**Absalom went to the king and said: "Your servant is having shearers. Please, your majesty, come with all your retainers to your servant." **25**But the king said to Absalom, "No, my son, all of us should not go lest we be a burden to you." And though Absalom urged him, he refused to go and began to bid him goodbye. **26**Absalom then said, "If you will not come yourself, please let my brother Amnon come to us." The king asked him, "Why should he go to you?" **27**At Absalom's urging, however, he sent Amnon and all the other princes with him. Absalom prepared a banquet fit for royalty. **28***But he had instructed his servants: "Now watch! When Amnon is merry with wine and I say to you, 'Kill Amnon,' put him to death. Do not be afraid, for it is I who order you to do it. Be resolute and act manfully."

Death of Amnon

29When the servants did to Amnon as Absalom had commanded, all the other princes rose, mounted their mules, and fled. **30**While they were still on the road, a report reached David that Absalom had killed all the princes and that not one of them had survived. **31***The king stood up, rent his garments, and then lay on the ground. All his servants standing by him also rent their garments. **32**But Jonadab, son of David's brother Shimeah, spoke up: "Let not my lord think that all the young princes have been killed! Amnon alone is dead, for Absalom was determined on this ever since Amnon shamed his sister Tamar. **33**So let not my lord the king put faith in the report that all the princes are dead. Amnon alone is dead." **34**Meanwhile, Absalom had taken flight. Then the servant on watch looked about and saw a large group coming down the slope from the direction of Bahurim. He came in and reported this, telling the king that he had seen some men coming down the mountainside from the direction of Bahurim. **35**So Jonadab said to the king: "There! The princes have come. It is as your servant said." **36**No sooner had he finished speaking than the princes came in, weeping aloud. The king, too, and all his servants wept very bitterly. **37***But Absalom, who had taken flight, went to Talmai, son of Ammihud, king of Geshur, **38**and stayed in Geshur for three years.

Efforts for Absalom's Return

39The king continued during all that time to mourn over his son; but his longing reached out for Absalom as he became reconciled to the death of Amnon.

3: 21, 21.
12: Lv 18, 9; 20, 17;
    Dt 27, 22.
13: Gn 34, 7.
28f: 12, 10.
31: 1, 11.
37: 3, 3; 15, 8.

14

1WHEN Joab, son of Zeruiah, observed how the king felt toward Absalom, **2**he sent to Tekoa and brought from there a gifted woman, to whom he said: "Pretend to be in mourning. Put on mourning apparel and do not anoint yourself with oil, that you may appear to be a woman who has been long in mourning for a departed one. **3**Then go to the king and speak to him in this manner." And Joab instructed her what to say.

4So the woman of Tekoa went to the king and fell prostrate to the ground in homage, saying, "Help, your majesty!" **5***The king said to her, "What do you want?" She replied: "Alas, I am a widow; my husband is dead. **6**Your servant had two sons, who quarreled in the field. There being no one to part them, one of them struck his brother and killed him. **7*†**Then the whole clan confronted your servant and demanded: 'Give up the one who killed his brother. We must put him to death for the life of his brother whom he has slain; we must extinguish the heir also.' Thus they will quench my remaining hope and leave my husband neither name nor posterity upon the earth." **8**The king then said to the woman: "Go home. I will issue a command on your behalf." **9**The woman of Tekoa answered him, "Let me and my family be to blame, my lord king; you and your throne are innocent." **10**Then the king said, "If anyone says a word to you, have him brought to me, and he shall not touch you again." **11**But she went on to say, "Please, your majesty, keep in mind the LORD your God, that the avenger of blood may not go too far in destruction and that my son may not be done away with." He replied, "As the LORD lives, not a hair of your son shall fall to the ground."

12The woman continued, "Please let your servant say still another word to my lord the king." He replied, "Speak." **13**So the woman said: "Why, then, do you think of this same kind of thing against the people of God? In pronouncing as he has, the king shows himself guilty, for not bringing back his own banished son. **14*†**We must indeed die; we are then like water that is poured out on the ground and cannot be gathered up. Yet, though God does not bring back life, he does take thought how not to banish anyone from him. **15**And now, if I have presumed to speak of this matter to your majesty, it is because the people have given me cause to fear. And so your servant thought: 'Let me speak to the king. Perhaps he will grant the petition of his maidservant. **16**For the king must surely consent to free his servant from the grasp of one who would seek to destroy me and my son as well from God's inheritance.'" **17*†**And the woman concluded: "Let the word of my lord the king provide a resting place; indeed, my lord the king is like an angel of God, evaluating good and bad. The LORD your God be with you."

18The king answered the woman, "Now do not conceal from me anything I may ask you!" The woman said, "Let my lord the king speak." **19**So the king asked, "Is Joab involved with you in all this?" And the woman answered: "As you live, my lord the king, it is just as your majesty has said, and not otherwise. It was your servant Joab who instructed me and told your servant all these things she was to say. **20**Your servant Joab did this to come at the issue in a roundabout way. But my lord is as wise as an angel of God, so that he knows all things on earth."

Absalom's Return

21Then the king said to Joab: "I hereby grant this request. Go, therefore, and bring back young Absalom." **22**Falling prostrate to the ground in homage and blessing the king, Joab said, "This day I know that I am in good favor with you, my lord the king, since the king has granted the request of his servant." **23**Joab then went off to Geshur and brought Absalom to Jerusalem. **24**But the king said, "Let him go to his own house; he shall not appear before me." So Absalom went off to his house and did not appear before the king.

25In all Israel there was not a man who could so be praised for his beauty as Absalom, who was without blemish from the sole of his foot to the crown of his head. **26**When he shaved his head—which he used to do at the end of every year, because his hair became too heavy for him—the hair weighed two hundred shekels according to the royal standard. **27***Absalom had three sons born to him, besides a daughter named Tamar, who was a beautiful woman.

Absalom Is Pardoned

28Absalom lived in Jerusalem for two years without appearing before the king. **29**Then he summoned Joab to send him to the king, but Joab would not come to him. Although he summoned him a second time, Joab refused to come. **30***He therefore instructed his servants: "You see Joab's field that borders mine, on which he has barley. Go, set it on fire." And so Absalom's servants set the field on fire. Joab's farmhands came to him with torn garments and reported to him what had been done. **31**At this, Joab went to Absalom in his house and asked him, "Why have your servants set my field on fire?" **32**Absalom answered Joab: "I was summoning you to come here, that I may send you to the king to say: 'Why did I come back from Geshur? I would be better off if I were still there!' Now, let me appear before the king. If I am guilty, let him put me to death.'" **33**Joab went to the king and reported this. The king then called Absalom, who came to him and

---

† 14, 7: *Hope:* literally, "glowing coal." The image is similar to that of the lighted lamp, e. g., Ps 89, 17, to keep alive the ancestral name.

14, 14: *How not to banish:* a possible allusion to the religious institution of cities of refuge for involuntary murderers; see Nm 35, 9-15.

14, 17: *A resting place:* cf Ps 95, 11; Heb 3, 7–4, 11. The reference here is to return home for Absalom to Israel.

❀

14/5f: 2 Kgs 6, 26f.   17-20: 1 Sm 29, 9.
   7: Nm 35, 19.   27: 18, 18.
  14: Jb 7, 9; 14, 7-12;   30: Jgs 15, 4f.
      Ps 88, 5.11ff.

in homage fell on his face to the ground before the king. Then the king kissed him.

Absalom's Plot

15 ¹*AFTER this Absalom provided himself with chariots, horses, and fifty henchmen. ²Moreover, Absalom used to rise early and stand alongside the road leading to the gate. If someone had a lawsuit to be decided by the king, Absalom would call to him and say, "From what city are you?" And when he replied, "Your servant is of such and such a tribe of Israel," ³Absalom would say to him, "Your suit is good and just, but there is no one to hear you in the king's name." ⁴And he would continue: "If only I could be appointed judge in the land! Then everyone who has a lawsuit to be decided might come to me and I would render him justice." ⁵Whenever a man approached him to show homage, he would extend his hand, hold him, and kiss him. ⁶By behaving in this way toward all the Israelites who came to the king for judgment, Absalom was stealing away the loyalties of the men of Israel.

Conspiracy in Hebron

⁷After a period of four years, Absalom said to the king: "Allow me to go to Hebron and fulfill a vow I made to the LORD. ⁸*For while living in Geshur in Aram, your servant made this vow: 'If the LORD ever brings me back to Jerusalem, I will worship him in Hebron.'" ⁹The king wished him a safe journey, and he went off to Hebron. ¹⁰Then Absalom sent spies throughout the tribes of Israel to say, "When you hear the sound of the horn, declare Absalom king in Hebron." ¹¹Two hundred men had accompanied Absalom from Jerusalem. They had been invited and went in good faith, knowing nothing of the plan. ¹²*Absalom also sent to Ahithophel the Gilonite, David's counselor, an invitation to come from his town, Giloh, for the sacrifices he was about to offer. So the conspiracy gained strength, and the people with Absalom increased in numbers.

David Flees Jerusalem

¹³*An informant came to David with the report, "The Israelites have transferred their loyalty to Absalom." ¹⁴At this, David said to all his servants who were with him in Jerusalem: "Up! Let us take flight, or none of us will escape from Absalom. Leave quickly, lest he hurry and overtake us, then visit disaster upon us and put the city to the sword." ¹⁵The king's officers answered him, "Your servants are ready, whatever our lord the king chooses to do." ¹⁶*Then the king set out, accompanied by his entire household, except for ten concubines whom he left behind to take care of the palace. ¹⁷As the king left the city, with all his officers accompanying him, they halted opposite the ascent of the Mount of Olives, at a distance, ¹⁸*while the whole army marched past him.

David and Ittai

As all the Cherethites and Pelethites, and the six hundred men of Gath who had accompanied him from that city, were passing in review before the king, ¹⁹he said to Ittai the Gittite: "Why should you also go with us? Go back and stay with the king, for you are a foreigner and you, too, are an exile from your own country. ²⁰You came only yesterday, and shall I have you wander about with us today, wherever I have to go? Return and take your brothers with you, and may the LORD be kind and faithful to you." ²¹*But Ittai answered the king, "As the LORD lives, and as my lord the king lives, your servant shall be wherever my lord the king may be, whether for death or for life." ²²So the king said to Ittai, "Go, then, march on." And Ittai the Gittite, with all his men and all the dependents that were with him, marched on. ²³Everyone in the countryside wept aloud as the last of the soldiers went by, and the king crossed the Kidron Valley with all the soliders moving on ahead of him by way of the Mount of Olives, toward the desert.

David and the Priests

²⁴Zadok, too [with all the Levite bearers of the ark of the covenant of God], and Abiathar brought the ark of God to a halt until the soldiers had marched out of the city. ²⁵Then the king said to Zadok: "Take the ark of God back to the city. If I find favor with the LORD, he will bring me back and permit me to see it and its lodging. ²⁶*But if he should say, 'I am not pleased with you,' I am ready; let him do to me as he sees fit." ²⁷The king also said to the priest Zadok: "See to it that you and Abiathar return to the city in peace, and both your sons with you, your own son Ahimaaz, and Abiathar's son Jonathan. ²⁸Remember, I shall be waiting at the fords near the desert until I receive information from you." ²⁹So Zadok and Abiathar took the ark of God back to Jerusalem and remained there.

³⁰*As David went up the Mount of Olives, he wept without ceasing. His head was covered, and he was walking barefoot. All those who were with him also had their heads covered and were weeping as they went. ³¹*When David was informed that Ahithophel was among the conspirators with Absalom, he said, "O LORD, turn the counsel of Ahithophel to folly!"

David and Hushai

³²*When David reached the top, where men used to worship God, Hushai the Archite was there to meet him, with rent garments and dirt upon his head. ³³David said to him: "If you come with me, you will be a burden to me. ³⁴*But if you return to the city and say to Absalom, 'Let me be your servant, O king; I was formerly your father's servant, but now I will be yours,' you will undo for me the counsel of Ahithophel. ³⁵You

15/1: 1 Sm 8, 11; 1 Kgs 1, 5.
8: 3, 3; 13, 37.
12: 16, 23.
13: Ps 3.
16: 16, 21f; 20, 3.
18: 8, 18.
21: Ru 1, 16.
26: 16, 10.
30: 19, 5; Mi 1, 8.
31: 16, 23; 17, 14.23.
32: 16, 16.
34: 16, 19.

will have the priests Zadok and Abiathar there with you. If you hear anything from the royal palace, you shall report it to the priests Zadok and Abiathar, **36**who have there with them both Zadok's son Ahimaaz and Abiathar's son Jonathan. Through them you shall send on to me whatever you hear." **37**So David's friend Hushai went into the city of Jerusalem as Absalom was about to enter it.

David and Ziba

16 **1***DAVID had gone a little beyond the top when Ziba, the servant of Meribbaal, met him with saddled asses laden with two hundred loaves of bread, an ephah of cakes of pressed raisins, an ephah of summer fruits, and a skin of wine. **2**The king said to Ziba, "What do you plan to do with these?" Ziba replied: "The asses are for the king's household to ride on. The bread and summer fruits are for your servants to eat, and the wine for those to drink who are weary in the desert." **3***Then the king said, "And where is your lord's son?" Ziba answered the king, "He is staying in Jerusalem, for he said, 'Now the Israelites will restore to me my father's kingdom.'" **4***The king therefore said to Ziba, "So! Everything Meribbaal had is yours." Then Ziba said: "I pay you homage, my lord the king. May I find favor with you!"

David and Shimei

5*As David was approaching Bahurim, a man named Shimei, the son of Gera of the same clan as Saul's family, was coming out of the place, cursing as he came. **6**He threw stones at David and at all the king's officers, even though all the soldiers, including the royal guard, were on David's right and on his left. **7**Shimei was saying as he cursed: "Away, away, you murderous and wicked man! **8†**The LORD has requited you for all the bloodshed in the family of Saul, in whose stead you became king, and the LORD has given over the kingdom to your son Absalom. And now you suffer ruin because you are a murderer." **9***Abishai, son of Zeruiah, said to the king: "Why should this dead dog curse my lord the king? Let me go over, please, and lop off his head." **10***But the king replied: "What business is it of mine or of yours, sons of Zeruiah, that he curses? Suppose the LORD has told him to curse David; who then will dare to say, 'Why are you doing this?'" **11***Then the king said to Abishai and to all his servants: "If my own son, who came forth from my loins, is seeking my life, how much more might this Benjaminite do so! Let him alone and let him curse, for the LORD has told him to. **12**Perhaps the LORD will look upon my affliction and make it up to me with benefits for the curses he is uttering this day."

13*David and his men continued on the road, while Shimei kept abreast of them on the hillside, all the while cursing and throwing stones and dirt as he went. **14**The king and all the soldiers with him arrived at the Jordan tired out, and stopped there for a rest.

Absalom's Counselors

15In the meantime Absalom, accompanied by Ahithophel, entered Jerusalem with all the Israelites. **16***When David's friend Hushai the Archite came to Absalom, he said to him: "Long live the king! Long live the king!" **17**But Absalom asked Hushai: "Is this your devotion to your friend? Why did you not go with your friend?" **18**Hushai replied to Absalom: "On the contrary, I am his whom the LORD and all this people and all Israel have chosen, and with him I will stay. **19***Furthermore, as I was in attendance upon your father, so will I be before you. Whom should I serve, if not his son?" **20**Then Absalom said to Ahithophel, "Offer your counsel on what we should do." **21***Ahithophel replied to Absalom: "Have relations with your father's concubines, whom he left behind to take care of the palace. When all Israel hears how odious you have made yourself to your father, all your partisans will take courage." **22***So a tent was pitched on the roof for Absalom, and he visited his father's concubines in view of all Israel. **23***Now the counsel given by Ahithophel at that time was as though one had sought divine revelation. Such was all his counsel both to David and to Absalom.

Counsel of Ahithophel

17 **1**AHITHOPHEL went on to say to Absalom: "Please let me choose twelve thousand men, and be off in pursuit of David tonight. **2**If I come upon him when he is weary and discouraged, I shall cause him panic. When all the people with him flee, I shall strike down the king alone. **3**Then I can bring back the rest of the people to you, as a bride returns to her husband. It is the death of only one man you are seeking; then all the people will be at peace." **4**This plan was agreeable to Absalom and to all the elders of Israel.

Counsel of Hushai

5Then Absalom said, "Now call Hushai the Archite also; let us hear what he too has to say." **6**When Hushai came to Absalom, Absalom said to him: "This is what Ahithophel proposed. Shall we follow his proposal? If not, speak up." **7**Hushai replied to Absalom, "This time Ahithophel has not given good counsel." **8***And he went on to say: "You know that your father and his men are warriors, and that they are as fierce as a bear in the wild robbed of her cubs. Moreover, since your father is skilled in warfare, he will not spend the night with the people. **9**Even now he lies hidden in one of the caves or in some other place. And if some of our

---

16/1: 4, 4; 9, 1-13; 19, 18.25.   11: 12, 11.
     3: 19, 26f.   13: 19, 19-24.
     4: 19, 30.   16: 15, 32-37.
     5: 3, 16; 19, 17.22f;   19: 15, 34.
        1 Kgs 2, 8.   21: 15, 16; 20, 3.
     9: 19, 23.29; 1 Sm 24, 15;   22: 12, 11f.
        26, 6.   23: 15, 12.31; 17, 23.
    10: 15, 25f; 19, 23.   17/8: Hos 13, 8.

---

† 16, 8: *Bloodshed . . . Saul:* refers to the episode recounted in 21, 1-14.

soliders should fall at the first attack, whoever hears of it will say, 'Absalom's followers have been slaughtered.' [10]Then even the brave man with the heart of a lion will lose courage. For all Israel knows that your father is a warrior and that those who are with him are brave.

[11]"This is what I counsel: Let all Israel from Dan to Beer-sheba, who are as numerous as the sands by the sea, be called up for combat; and go with them yourself. [12]We can then attack him wherever we find him, settling down upon him as dew alights on the ground. None shall survive—neither he nor any of his followers. [13]And if he retires into a city, all Israel shall bring ropes to that city and we can drag it into the gorge, so that not even a pebble of it can be found." [14]*Then Absalom and all the Israelites pronounced the counsel of Hushai the Archite better than that of Ahithophel. For the LORD had decided to undo Ahithophel's good counsel, in order thus to bring Absalom to ruin.

David Told of the Plan

[15]Then Hushai said to the priests Zadok and Abiathar: "This is the counsel Ahithophel gave Absalom and the elders of Israel, and this is what I counseled. [16]So send a warning to David immediately, not to spend the night at the fords near the desert, but to cross over without fail. Otherwise the king and all the people with him will be destroyed." [17]Now Jonathan and Ahimaaz were staying at En-rogel, since they could not risk being seen entering the city. A maid-servant was to come with information for them, and they in turn were to go and report to King David. [18]But an attendant saw them and informed Absalom. They sped on their way and reached the house of a man in Bahurim who had a cistern in his courtyard. They let themselves down into this, [19]and the housewife took the cover and spread it over the cistern, strewing ground grain on the cover so that nothing could be noticed. [20]When Absalom's servants came to the woman at the house, they asked, "Where are Ahimaaz and Jonathan?" The woman replied, "They went by a short while ago toward the water." They searched, but found no one, and so returned to Jerusalem. [21]As soon as they left, Ahimaaz and Jonathan came up out of the cistern and went on to inform King David. They said to him: "Leave! Cross the water at once, for Ahithophel has given the following counsel in regard to you." [22]So David and all his people moved on and crossed the Jordan. By daybreak, there was no one left who had not crossed.

[23]*When Ahithophel saw that his counsel was not acted upon, he saddled his ass and departed, going to his home in his own city. Then, having left orders concerning his family, he hanged himself. And so he died and was buried in his father's tomb.

[24]Now David had gone to Mahanaim when Absalom crossed the Jordan accompanied by all the Israelites. [25]*Absalom had put Amasa in command of the army in Joab's place. Amasa was the son of an Ishmaelite named Ithra, who had married Abigail, daughter of Jesse and sister of Joab's mother Zeruiah. [26]Israel and Absalom encamped in the territory of Gilead.

[27]*When David came to Mahanaim, Shobi, son of Nahash from Rabbah of the Ammonites, Machir, son of Ammiel from Lodebar, and Barzillai, the Gileadite from Rogelim, [28]*brought couches, coverlets, basins and earthenware, as well as wheat, barley, flour, roasted grain, beans, lentils, [29]honey, butter and cheese from the flocks and herds, for David and those who were with him to eat; for they said, "The people have been hungry and tired and thirsty in the desert."

Preparation for Battle

18 [1]AFTER mustering the troops he had with him, David placed officers in command of groups of a thousand and groups of a hundred. [2]David then put a third part of the soldiers under Joab's command, a third under command of Abishai, son of Zeruiah and brother of Joab, and a third under command of Ittai the Gittite. The king then said to the soliders, "I intend to go out with you myself." [3]But they replied: "You must not come out with us. For if we should flee, we shall not count; even if half of us should die, we shall not count. You are equal to ten thousand of us. Therefore it is better that we have you to help us from the city." [4]So the king said to them, "I will do what you think best"; and he stood by the gate as all the soldiers marched out in units of a hundred and of a thousand. [5]But the king gave this command to Joab, Abishai and Ittai: "Be gentle with young Absalom for my sake." All the soldiers heard the king instruct the various leaders with regard to Absalom.

Defeat of Absalom

[6]David's army then took the field against Israel, and a battle was fought in the forest near Mahanaim. [7]The forces of Israel were defeated by David's servants, and the casualties there that day were heavy—twenty thousand men. [8]The battle spread out over that entire region, and the thickets consumed more combatants that day than did the sword.

Death of Absalom

[9]Absalom unexpectedly came up against David's servants. He was mounted on a mule, and, as the mule passed under the branches of a large terebinth, his hair caught fast in the tree. He hung between heaven and earth while the mule he had been riding ran off. [10]Someone saw this and reported to Joab that he had seen Absalom hanging from a terebinth. [11]Joab said to his informant: "If you saw him, why did you not strike him to the ground on the spot? Then it would have been my duty to give you fifty pieces of silver and a belt." [12]But the man replied to Joab: "Even if I already held a thousand pieces of silver in my two hands, I

14: 15, 31.
23: 15, 31; 16, 23.
25: 19, 14; 20, 4-13.

27: 9, 4; 19, 32; 1 Kgs 2, 7.
28: 19, 32; Ezr 2, 61.

would not harm the king's son, for the king charged you and Abishai and Ittai in our hearing to protect the youth Absalom for his sake. [13]Had I been disloyal and killed him, the whole matter would have come to the attention of the king, and you would stand aloof." [14]*Joab replied, "I will not waste time with you in this way." And taking three pikes in hand, he thrust for the heart of Absalom, still hanging from the tree alive. [15]Next, ten of Joab's young armor-bearers closed in on Absalom, and killed him with further blows. [16]*Joab then sounded the horn, and the soldiers turned back from the pursuit of the Israelites, because Joab called on them to halt. [17]*Absalom was taken up and cast into a deep pit in the forest, and a very large mound of stones was erected over him. And all the Israelites fled to their own tents.

[18]*During his lifetime Absalom had taken a pillar and erected it for himself in the King's Valley, for he said, "I have no son to perpetuate my name." The pillar which he named for himself is called Yad-abshalom to the present day.

David Told of Absalom's Death

[19]Then Ahimaaz, son of Zadok, said, "Let me run to take the good news to the king that the LORD has set him free from the grasp of his enemies." [20]But Joab said to him: "You are not the man to bring the news today. On some other day you may take the good news, but today you would not be bringing good news, for in fact the king's son is dead." [21]Then Joab said to a Cushite, "Go, tell the king what you have seen." The Cushite bowed to Joab and sped away. [22]But Ahimaaz, son of Zadok, said to Joab again, "Come what may, permit me also to run after the Cushite." Joab replied: "Why do you want to run, my son? You will receive no reward." [23]But he insisted, "Come what may, I want to run." Joab said to him, "Very well." Ahimaaz sped off by way of the Jordan plain and outran the Cushite.

[24]Now David was sitting between the two gates, and a lookout mounted to the roof of the gate above the city wall, where he looked about and saw a man running all alone. [25]The lookout shouted to inform the king, who said, "If he is alone, he has good news to report." As he kept coming nearer, [26]the lookout spied another runner. From his place atop the gate he cried out, "There is another man running by himself." And the king responded, "He, too, is bringing good news." [27]*Then the lookout said, "I notice that the first one runs like Ahimaaz, son of Zadok." The king replied, "He is a good man; he comes with good news." [28]Then Ahimaaz called out and greeted the king. With face to the ground he paid homage to the king and said, "Blessed be the LORD your God, who has delivered up the men who rebelled against my lord the king." [29]But the king asked, "Is the youth Absalom safe?" And Ahimaaz replied, "I saw a great disturbance when the king's servant Joab sent your servant on, but I do not know what it was." [30]The king said, "Step aside and remain in attendance here." So he stepped aside and remained there. [31]When the Cushite came in, he said, "Let my lord the king receive the good news that this day the LORD has taken your part, freeing you from the grasp of all who rebelled against you." [32]But the king asked the Cushite, "Is young Absalom safe?" The Cushite replied, "May the enemies of my lord the king and all who rebel against you with evil intent be as that young man!"

19 [1]THE king was shaken, and went up to the room over the city gate to weep. He said as he wept, "My son Absalom! My son, my son Absalom! If only I had died instead of you, Absalom, my son, my son!"

Joab Reproves David

[2]Joab was told that the king was weeping and mourning for Absalom; [3]and that day's victory was turned into mourning for the whole army when they heard that the king was grieving for his son. [4]The soldiers stole into the city that day like men shamed by flight in battle. [5]*Meanwhile the king covered his face and cried out in a loud voice, "My son Absalom! Absalom! My son, my son!" [6]Then Joab went to his residence and said: "Though they saved your life and your sons' and daughters' lives, also the lives of your wives and those of your concubines, you have put all your servants to shame today [7]by loving those who hate you and hating those who love you. For you have shown today that officers and servants mean nothing to you. Indeed I am now certain that if Absalom were alive today and all of us dead, you would think that more suitable. [8]Now then, get up! Go out and speak kindly to your servants. I swear by the LORD that if you do not go out, not a single man will remain with you overnight, and this will be a far greater disaster for you than any that has afflicted you from your youth until now." [9]So the king stepped out and sat at the gate. When all the people were informed that the king was sitting at the gate, they came into his presence.

The Reconciliation

Now the Israelites had fled to their separate tents, [10]but throughout the tribes of Israel all the people were arguing among themselves, saying to one another: "The king delivered us from the clutches of our enemies, and it was he who rescued us from the grip of the Philistines. But now he has fled from the country before Absalom, [11]and Absalom, whom we anointed over us, died in battle. Why, then, should you remain silent about restoring the king to his palace?" When the talk of all Israel reached the king, [12]David sent word to the priests Zadok and Abiathar: "Say to the elders of Judah: 'Why should you be last to restore the king to his palace? [13]You are my brothers, you are my bone and flesh. Why should you be last to restore the king?' [14]*Also say to Amasa: 'Are you not my bone

---

18/14: 12, 10; 13, 28f.　　　　　27: 2 Kgs 9, 20.
　　16: 20, 23-26.　　　　　　　19/5: 15, 30.
　　17: Jos 7, 26; 8, 29; 10, 27.　　14: 17, 25; 20, 4.
　　18: 14, 27.

and flesh? May God do thus and so to me, if you do not become my general permanently in place of Joab.'" **15**He won over all the Judahites as one man, and so they summoned the king to return, with all his servants.

David and Shimei

16When the king, on his return, reached the Jordan, Judah had come to Gilgal to meet him and to escort him across the Jordan. **17***Shimei, son of Gera, the Benjaminite from Bahurim, hurried down with the Judahites to meet King David, **18***accompanied by a thousand men from Benjamin. Ziba, too, the servant of the house of Saul, accompanied by his fifteen sons and twenty servants, hastened to the Jordan before the king. **19***They crossed over the ford to bring the king's household over and to do whatever he wished. When Shimei, son of Gera, crossed the Jordan, he fell down before the king **20**and said to him: "May my lord not hold me guilty, and may he not remember and take to heart the wrong that your servant did the day my lord the king left Jerusalem. **21**For your servant knows that he has done wrong. Yet realize that I have been the first of the whole house of Joseph to come down today to meet my lord the king." **22**But Abishai, son of Zeruiah, countered: "Shimei must be put to death for this. He cursed the LORD's anointed." **23***David replied: "What has come between you and me, sons of Zeruiah, that you would create enmity for me this day? Should anyone die today in Israel? Am I not aware that today I am king of Israel?" **24**Then the king said to Shimei, "You shall not die." And the king gave him his oath.

David and Meribbaal

25Meribbaal, son of Saul, also went down to meet the king. He had not washed his feet nor trimmed his mustache nor washed his clothes from the day the king left until he returned safely. **26***When he came from Jerusalem to meet the king, the king asked him, "Why did you not go with me, Meribbaal?" **27***He replied: "My lord the king, my servant betrayed me. For your servant, who is lame, said to him, 'Saddle the ass for me, that I may ride on it and go with the king.' **28**But he slandered your servant before my lord the king. But my lord the king is like an angel of God. Do what you judge best. **29***For though my father's entire house deserved only death from my lord the king, yet you placed your servant among the guests at your table. What right do I still have to make further appeal to the king?" **30***But the king said to him: "Why do you go on talking? I say, 'You and Ziba shall divide the property.'" **31**Meribbaal answered the king, "Indeed let

him have it all, now that my lord the king has returned safely to his palace."

David and Barzillai

32*Barzillai the Gileadite also came down from Rogelim and escorted the king to the Jordan for his crossing, taking leave of him there. **33**It was Barzillai, a very old man of eighty and very wealthy besides, who had provisioned the king during his stay in Mahanaim. **34**The king said to Barzillai, "Cross over with me, and I will provide for your old age as my guest in Jerusalem." **35**But Barzillai answered the king: "How much longer have I to live, that I should go up to Jerusalem with the king? **36**I am now eighty years old. Can I distinguish between good and bad? Can your servant taste what he eats and drinks, or still appreciate the voices of singers and songstresses? Why should your servant be any further burden to my lord the king? **37**In escorting the king across the Jordan, your servant is doing little enough! Why should the king give me this reward? **38**Please let your servant go back to die in his own city by the tomb of his father and mother. Here is your servant Chimham. Let him cross over with my lord the king. Do for him whatever you will." **39**Then the king said to him, "Chimham shall come over with me, and I will do for him as you would wish. And anything else you would like me to do for you, I will do." **40**Then all the people crossed over the Jordan, but the king remained; he kissed Barzillai and bade him Godspeed as he returned to his own district. **41**Finally the king crossed over to Gilgal, accompanied by Chimham.

Israel and Judah Quarrel

All the people of Judah and half of the people of Israel had escorted the king across. **42**But all these Israelites began coming to the king and saying, "Why did our brothers the Judahites steal you away and escort the king and his household across the Jordan, along with all David's men?" **43**All the Judahites replied to the men of Israel: "Because the king is our relative. Why are you angry over this affair? Have we had anything to eat at the king's expense? Or have portions from his table been given to us?" **44***The Israelites answered the Judahites: "We have ten shares in the king. Also, we are the first-born rather than you. Why do you slight us? Were we not first to speak of restoring the king?" Then the Judahites in turn spoke even more fiercely than the Israelites.

Sheba's Rebellion

20 **1***NOW a rebellious individual from Benjamin named Sheba, the son of Bichri, happened to be there. He sounded the horn and cried out,

> "We have no portion in David,
> nor any share in the son of Jesse.
> Every man to his tent, O Israel!"

2So all the Israelites left David for Sheba, son of Bichri.

❋

17: 16, 5-13.
18: 16, 1-4; 19, 25-31.
19ff: 16, 13; Ex 22, 27;
    1 Kgs 2, 8.
23: 16, 9f; 1 Sm 11, 13;
    1 Kgs 2, 8.38.46.
26: 16, 3.

27: 9, 2-13; Dt 21, 12f.
29: 9, 9ff.
30: 16, 4.
32: 17, 27ff; 1 Kgs 2, 7;
    Ezr 2, 61.
44: 1 Kgs 11, 31.
20/1: 1 Kgs 12, 16.

But from the Jordan to Jerusalem the Judahites remained loyal to their king. ³*When King David came to his palace in Jerusalem, he took the ten concubines whom he had left behind to take care of the palace and placed them in confinement. He provided for them, but had no further relations with them. And so they remained in confinement to the day of their death, lifelong widows.

Amasa's Death

⁴*Then the king said to Amasa: "Summon the Judahites for me within three days. Then present yourself here." ⁵Accordingly Amasa set out to summon Judah, but delayed beyond the time set for him by David. ⁶Then David said to Abishai: "Sheba, son of Bichri, may now do us more harm than Absalom did. Take your lord's servants and pursue him, lest he find fortified cities and take shelter while we look on." ⁷*So Joab and the Cherethites and Pelethites and all the warriors marched out behind Abishai from Jerusalem to campaign in pursuit of Sheba, son of Bichri. ⁸*†They were at the great stone in Gibeon when Amasa met them. Now Joab had a belt over this tunic, from which was slung, in its sheath near his thigh, a sword that could be drawn with a downward movement. ⁹And Joab asked Amasa, "How are you, my brother?" With his right hand Joab held Amasa's beard as if to kiss him. ¹⁰*And since Amasa was not on his guard against the sword in Joab's other hand, Joab stabbed him in the abdomen with it, so that his entrails burst forth to the ground, and he died without receiving a second thrust. Then Joab and his brother Abishai pursued Sheba, son of Bichri. ¹¹One of Joab's attendants stood by Amasa and said, "Let him who favors Joab and is for David follow Joab." ¹²Amasa lay covered with blood in the middle of the highroad, and the man noticed that all the soldiers were stopping. So he removed Amasa from the road to the field and placed a garment over him, because all who came up to him were stopping. ¹³When he had been removed from the road, everyone went on after Joab in pursuit of Sheba, son of Bichri.

Joab Pursues Sheba

¹⁴Sheba passed through all the tribes of Israel to Abel Beth-maacah. Then all the Bichrites assembled and they too entered the city after him. ¹⁵So David's servants came and besieged him in Abel Beth-maacah. They threw up a mound against the city, and all the soldiers who were with Joab began battering the wall to throw it down. ¹⁶Then a wise woman from the city stood on the outworks and called out, "Listen, listen! Tell Joab to come here, that I may speak with him." ¹⁷When Joab had come near her, the woman said, "Are you Joab?" And he replied, "Yes." She said to him, "Listen to what your maidservant has to say." He replied, "I am listening." ¹⁸*†Then she went on to say: "There is an ancient saying, 'Let them ask if they will in Abel ¹⁹or in Dan whether loyalty is finished or ended in Israel.' You are seeking to beat down a city that is a mother in Israel. Why do you wish to destroy the inheritance of the Lord?" ²⁰Joab answered, "Not at all, not at all! I do not wish to destroy or to ruin anything. ²¹That is not the case at all. A man named Sheba, son of Bichri, from the hill country of Ephraim has rebelled against King David. Surrender him alone, and I will withdraw from the city." Then the woman said to Joab, "His head shall be thrown to you across the wall." ²²She went to all the people with her advice, and they cut off the head of Sheba, son of Bichri, and threw it out to Joab. He then sounded the horn, and they scattered from the city to their own tents, while Joab returned to Jerusalem to the king.

David's Officials

²³*Joab was in command of the whole army of Israel. Benaiah, son of Jehoiada, was in command of the Cherethites and Pelethites. ²⁴Adoram was in charge of the forced labor. Jehoshaphat, son of Ahilud, was the chancellor. ²⁵*Shawsha was the scribe. Zadok and Abiathar were priests. ²⁶Ira the Jairite was also David's priest.

V: APPENDIXES

Gibeonite Vengeance

21 ¹*DURING DAVID'S REIGN there was a famine for three successive years. David had recourse to the Lord, who said, "There is bloodguilt on Saul and his family because he put the Gibeonites to death." ²*So the king called the Gibeonites and spoke to them. (Now the Gibeonites were not Israelites, but survivors of the Amorites; and although the Israelites had given them their oath, Saul had attempted to kill them off in his zeal for the men of Israel and Judah.) ³David said to the Gibeonites, "What must I do for you and how must I make atonement, that you may bless the inheritance of the Lord?" ⁴The Gibeonites answered him, "We have no claim against Saul and his house for silver or gold, nor is it our place to put any man to death in Israel." Then he said, "I will do for you whatever you propose." ⁵They said to the king, "As for the man who was exterminating us and who intended to destroy us that we might have no place in all the territory of Israel, ⁶let seven men from among his descendants be given to us, that we may dismember them before the Lord in Gibeon, on the Lord's mountain." The king replied, "I will give them up." ⁷*The king, however, spared Meribbaal, son of Jona-

---

3: 15, 16; 16, 20ff.   23: 8, 16ff; 23, 20.
4: 17, 25; 19, 14.   25: 8, 17f.
7: 8, 18.   21/1: 24, 13.
8: 2, 13.   2: Jos 9, 3-27.
10: 1 Kgs 2, 5.   7: 9, 13; 1 Sm 18, 3;
18: Gn 49, 16.   20, 8ff.15f.42.

20, 8: The text of this verse is quite uncertain.

20, 18f: The proverbial expression here has been poorly transmitted, and its sense is doubtful.

than, son of Saul, because of the LORD's oath that formed a bond between David and Saul's son Jonathan. **8°**But the king took Armoni and Meribbaal, the two sons that Aiah's daughter Rizpah had borne to Saul, and the five sons of Saul's daughter Merob that she had borne to Adriel, son of Barzillai the Meholathite, **9**and surrendered them to the Gibeonites. They then dismembered them on the mountain before the LORD. The seven fell at the one time; they were put to death during the first days of the harvest—that is, at the beginning of the barley harvest.

10°Then Rizpah, Aiah's daughter, took sackcloth and spread it out for herself on the rock from the beginning of the harvest until rain came down on them from the sky, fending off the birds of the sky from settling on them by day, and the wild animals by night. **11**When David was informed of what Rizpah, Aiah's daughter, the concubine of Saul, had done, **12°**he went and obtained the bones of Saul and of his son Jonathan from the citizens of Jabesh-gilead, who had carried them off secretly from the public square of Beth-shan, where the Philistines had hanged them at the time they killed Saul on Gilboa. **13**When he had brought up from there the bones of Saul and of his son Jonathan, the bones of those who had been dismembered were also gathered up. **14°**Then the bones of Saul and of his son Jonathan were buried in the tomb of his father Kish at Zela in the territory of Benjamin. After all that the king commanded had been carried out, God granted relief to the land.

Exploits in Philistine Wars

15There was another battle between the Philistines and Israel. David went down with his servants and fought the Philistines, but David grew tired. **16**Dadu, one of the Rephaim, whose bronze spear weighed three hundred shekels, was about to take him captive. Dadu was girt with a new sword and planned to kill David, **17°**but Abishai, son of Zeruiah, came to his assistance and struck and killed the Philistine. Then David's men swore to him, "You must not go out to battle with us again, lest you quench the lamp of Israel."

18°After this there was another battle with the Philistines in Gob. On that occasion Sibbecai, from Husha, killed Saph, one of the Rephaim. **19°**There was another battle with the Philistines in Gob, in which Elhanan, son of Jair from Bethlehem, killed Goliath of Gath, who had a spear with a shaft like a weaver's heddle-bar. **20**There was another battle at Gath in which there was a man of large stature with six fingers on each hand and six toes on each foot—twenty-four in all. He too was one of the Rephaim. **21°**And when he

insulted Israel, Jonathan, son of David's brother Shimei, killed him. **22**These four were Rephaim in Gath, and they fell at the hands of David and his servants.

Song of Thanksgiving

22 **1°†**DAVID sang the words of this song to the LORD when the LORD had rescued him from the grasp of all his enemies and from the hand of Saul. **2°**This is what he sang:

A

I

"O LORD, my rock, my fortress, my deliverer,
　3°†my God, my rock of refuge!
My shield, the horn of my salvation,
　my stronghold, my refuge,
　my savior, from violence you keep me safe.
4Praised be the LORD,' I exclaim,
　and I am safe from my enemies.

II

5°"The breakers of death surged round about me,
　the floods of perdition overwhelmed me;
6The cords of the nether world enmeshed me,
　the snares of death overtook me.
7†In my distress I called upon the LORD
　and cried out to my God;
From his temple he heard my voice,
　and my cry reached his ears.

III

8†"The earth swayed and quaked;
　the foundations of the heavens trembled
　and shook when his wrath flared up.
9Smoke rose from his nostrils,
　and a devouring fire from his mouth;
　he kindled coals into flame.
10°He inclined the heavens and came down,
　with dark clouds under his feet.
11°†He mounted a cherub and flew,
　borne on the wings of the wind.

---

† 22, 1-51: This song of thanksgiving is also given, with a few small variants, in Ps 18. In both places it is attributed to David. Two main sections can be distinguished. In the first part, after an introductory stanza of praise to God (2-4), David describes the peril he was in (5-7), and then poetically depicts, under the form of a theophany, God's intervention in his behalf (8-20), concluding with an acknowledgment of God's justice (21-31). In the second part, God is praised for having prepared the psalmist for war (32-35), given him victory over his enemies (36-39), whom he put to flight (40-43), and bestowed on him dominion over many peoples (44-46). The entire song ends with a paean of grateful praise (47-51).

22, 3: *The horn of my salvation:* my strong savior. The horn, the dreadful weapon of an enraged bull, was a symbol of strength; cf Lk 1, 69.

22, 5f: These verses are to be understood figuratively.

22, 7f: *His temple:* his heavenly abode.

22, 8ff: God's intervention is graphically portrayed under the figures of an earthquake (vv 8.16) and a thunderstorm (vv 9-15); cf Jgs 5, 4f; Pss 29; 97, 2-6; Hb 3.

22, 11: *He mounted a cherub:* since God makes the winds his messengers, or "angels" (Ps 104, 4), he is spoken of poet-

°
　8: 3, 7.
　10: 3, 31; 12, 16.
　12: 1 Sm 31, 10-13.
　14: 24, 25.
　17: 1 Kgs 11, 36; 15, 4;
　　2 Kgs 8, 19.
18-22: 1 Chr 20, 4-8.
　18: 23, 27.

19f: 1 Sm 17, 4.7.
　21: 13, 3.
22/1: Ps 18, 1.
2-51: Ps 18, 3-51.
　3: 1 Sm 2, 1f.
　10: Ps 144, 5.
　11: Ex 25, 18.

¹²He made darkness the shelter about him,
    with spattering rain and thickening clouds.
¹³From the brightness of his presence
    coals were kindled to flame.

¹⁴"The Lord thundered from heaven;
    the Most High gave forth his voice.
¹⁵He sent forth arrows to put them to flight;
    he flashed lightning and routed them.
¹⁶Then the wellsprings of the sea appeared,
    the foundations of the earth were laid bare,
At the rebuke of the Lord,
    at the blast of the wind of his wrath.

¹⁷"He reached out from on high and grasped me;
    he drew me out of the deep waters.
¹⁸He rescued me from my mighty enemy,
    from my foes, who were too powerful for me.
¹⁹They attacked me on my day of calamity,
    but the Lord came to my support.
²⁰He set me free in the open,
    and rescued me, because he loves me.

IV
²¹"The Lord rewarded me according to my justice;
    according to the cleanness of my hands he
        requited me.
²²For I kept the ways of the Lord
    and was not disloyal to my God.
²³For his ordinances were all present to me,
    and his statutes I put not from me;
²⁴But I was wholehearted toward him,
    and I was on my guard against guilt.
²⁵And the Lord requited me according to my
        justice,
    according to my innocence in his sight.

²⁶†"Toward the faithful you are faithful;
    toward the wholehearted you are whole-
        hearted;
²⁷Toward the sincere you are sincere;
    but toward the crooked you are astute.
²⁸You save lowly people,
    though on the lofty your eyes look down.
²⁹†You are my lamp, O Lord!
    O my God, you brighten the darkness about me.
³⁰For with your aid I run against an armed band,
    and by the help of my God I leap over a wall.
³¹God's way is unerring;
    the promise of the Lord is fire-tried;
    he is a shield to all who take refuge in him."

B
I
³²"For who is God except the Lord?
    Who is a rock save our God?
³³The God who girded me with strength
    and kept my way unerring;

³⁴†Who made my feet swift as those of hinds
    and set me on the heights;
³⁵Who trained my hands for war
    till my arms could bend a bow of brass.

II
³⁶"You have given me your saving shield,
    and your help has made me great.
³⁷You made room for my steps;
    unwavering was my stride.
³⁸I pursued my enemies and destroyed them,
    nor did I turn again till I made an end of them.
³⁹I smote them and they did not rise;
    they fell beneath my feet.

III
⁴⁰"You girded me with strength for war;
    you subdued my adversaries beneath me.
⁴¹My enemies you put to flight before me
    and those who hated me I destroyed.
⁴²They cried for help—but no one saved them;
    to the Lord—but he answered them not.
⁴³I ground them fine as the dust of the earth;
    like the mud in the streets I trampled them
        down.

IV
⁴⁴"You rescued me from the strife of my people;
    you made me head over nations.
A people I had not known became my slaves;
    ⁴⁵as soon as they heard me, they obeyed.
⁴⁶The foreigners fawned and cringed before me;
    they staggered forth from their fortresses."

C
⁴⁷"The Lord live! And blessed be my Rock!
    Extolled be my God, rock of my salvation.
⁴⁸O God, who granted me vengeance,
    who made peoples subject to me
    ⁴⁹and helped me escape from my enemies,
Above my adversaries you exalt me
    and from the violent man you rescue me.
⁵⁰Therefore will I proclaim you, O Lord, among the
        nations,
    and I will sing praise to your name,
⁵¹You who gave great victories to your king
    and showed kindness to your anointed,
    to David and his posterity forever."

15: Ps 144, 6.
17: Ps 144, 7.
26f: 1 Sm 2, 30.
31: Prv 30, 5.
50: Ps 22, 23; Rom 15, 9.

† ically as riding on the clouds, or on the angelic creatures called "cherubim." His earthly throne above the ark of the covenant was likewise associated with two winged cherubim; cf Ex 37, 7ff. In both senses the Lord is enthroned upon the cherubim; cf Pss 79, 2; 99, 1.

22, 26f: Men are treated by God in the same way they treat him and their fellow men.

22, 29: *My lamp:* a figure of life and happiness; cf 1 Kgs 11, 36.

22, 34: *The heights:* a natural stronghold safe from attack; cf Ps 62, 3; Hb 3, 19.

The Last Words of David

23

¹*†THESE are the last words of David:

"The utterance of David, son of Jesse;
    the utterance of the man God raised up,
Anointed of the God of Jacob,
    favorite of the Mighty One of Israel.
²*The spirit of the LORD spoke through me;
    his word was on my tongue.
³*The God of Israel spoke;
    of me the Rock of Israel said,
'He that rules over men in justice,
    that rules in the fear of God,
⁴*Is like the morning light at sunrise
    on a cloudless morning,
    making the greensward sparkle after rain.'
⁵*Is not my house firm before God?
    He has made an eternal covenant with me,
    set forth in detail and secured.
Will he not bring to fruition
    all my salvation and my every desire?
⁶*But the wicked are all like thorns to be cast away;
    they cannot be taken up by hand.
⁷He who wishes to touch them
    must arm himself with iron and the shaft of a
        spear,
    and they must be consumed by fire."

David's Warriors

⁸*†These are the names of David's warriors. Ishbaal, son of Hachamoni, was the first of the Three. It was he who brandished his battle-ax over eight hundred slain in a single encounter. ⁹*Next to him, among the Three warriors, was Eleazar, son of Dodo the Ahohite. He was with David at Ephes-dammim when the Philistines assembled there for battle. The Israelites had retreated, ¹⁰but he stood his ground and fought the Philistines until his hand grew tired and became cramped, holding fast to the sword. The LORD brought about a great victory on that day; the soldiers turned back after Eleazar, but only to strip the slain. ¹¹*Next to him was Shammah, son of Agee the Hararite. The Philistines had assembled at Lehi, where there was a plot of land full of lentils. When the soldiers fled from the Philistines, ¹²he took his stand in the middle of the plot and defended it. He slew the Philistines, and the LORD brought about a great victory. Such were the deeds of the Three warriors.

¹³*During the harvest three of the Thirty went down to David in the cave of Adullam, while a Philistine clan was encamped in the Vale of Rephaim. ¹⁴At that time David was in the refuge, and there was a garrison of Philistines in Bethlehem. ¹⁵Now David had a strong craving and said, "Oh, that someone would give me a drink of water from the cistern that is by the gate of Bethlehem!" ¹⁶So the Three warriors broke through the Philistine camp and drew water from the cistern that is by the gate of Bethlehem. But when they brought it to David he refused to drink it, and instead poured it out to the LORD, ¹⁷saying: "The LORD forbid that I do this! Can I drink the blood of these men who went at the risk of their lives?" So he refused to drink it.

¹⁸Abishai, brother of Joab, son of Zeruiah, was at the head of the Thirty. It was he who brandished his spear over three hundred slain. He was listed among the Thirty ¹⁹and commanded greater respect than the Thirty, becoming their leader. However, he did not attain to the Three.

²⁰*Benaiah, son of Jehoiada, a stalwart from Kabzeel, was a man of great achievements. It was he who slew the two lions in Moab. He also went down and killed the lion in the cistern at the time of the snow. ²¹It was he, too, who slew an Egyptian of large stature. Although the Egyptian was armed with a spear, he went against him with a club and wrested the spear from the Egyptian's hand, then killed him with his own spear. ²²Such were the deeds performed by Benaiah, son of Jehoiada. He was listed among the Thirty warriors ²³*and commanded greater respect than the Thirty. However, he did not attain to the Three. David put him in command of his bodyguard. ²⁴*†Asahel, brother of Joab. . . .

Among the Thirty were: Elhanan, son of Dodo, from Bethlehem; ²⁵Shammah from En-harod; Elika from En-harod; ²⁶Helez from Beth-pelet; Ira, son of Ikkesh, from Tekoa; ²⁷*Abiezer from Anathoth; Sibbecai from Hushah; ²⁸Zalmon from Ahoh; Maharai from Netophah; ²⁹Heled, son of Baanah, from Netophah; Ittai, son of Ribai, from Gibeah of the Benjaminites; ³⁰Benaiah from Pirathon; Hiddai from Nahale-gaash; ³¹Abibaal from Beth-arabah; Azmaveth from Bahurim; ³²Eliahba from Shaalbon; Jashen the Gunite; Jonathan, ³³son of Shammah the Hararite; Ahiam, son of Sharar the Hararite; ³⁴Eliphelet, son of Ahasbai, from Beth-maacah; Eliam, son of Ahithophel, from Gilo; ³⁵Hezrai from Carmel; Paarai the Arbite; ³⁶Igal, son of

---

† 23, 1-7: The text of this short composition in the spirit of the wisdom writers (Prv 30, 1-6) is difficult in places; it views David's career in retrospect.

23, 8ff: There are thirty-seven warriors in all mentioned in this list. First there are the Three warriors most noted for single-handed exploits (vv 8-12). Then comes the story of a daring adventure by three unnamed members of the larger group (vv 13-17). Next come the commanders of the king's bodyguard, Abishai (vv 18-19) and Benaiah (vv 20-23), with whom must be counted Asahel (v 24) and Joab (vv 18.24.37), and finally the group of the Thirty (vv 24-39).

23, 24: A more complete notice about Asahel, who died early in his career (2 Sm 2, 16-23), is to be presumed lost at this point. Elhanan is the first of the Thirty.

❋ 23/1: 1 Kgs 2, 3-9; Sir 47, 8.
    2: Is 59, 21; Jer 1, 9.
    3: Ps 72, 1-4.
    4: Jgs 5, 31; Ps 72, 6.
    5: 7, 11.15f; Ps 89, 30;
       Is 55, 3.
    6: Dt 13, 14.
  8-39: 1 Chr 11-41; 27, 1-15.

    9: 1 Sm 17, 1.
   11: Jgs 15, 9.
   13: 1 Sm 22, 1; Mi 1, 15.
   20: 8, 18; 20, 23; Jgs 14, 6;
       1 Kgs 2, 29f.
   23: 1 Sm 22, 14.
   24: 2, 18-23.
   27: 21, 18.

Nathan, from Zobah; Bani the Gadite; **37**Zelek the Ammonite; Naharai from Beeroth; armor-bearer of Joab, son of Zeruiah; **38**Ira from Jattir; Gareb from Jattir; **39***Uriah the Hittite—thirty-seven in all.

Census of the People

24 **1***†THE LORD's anger against Israel flared again, and he incited David against the Israelites by prompting him to number Israel and Judah. **2**Accordingly the king said to Joab and the leaders of the army who were with him, "Tour all the tribes in Israel from Dan to Beer-sheba and register the people, that I may know their number." **3**But Joab said to the king: "May the LORD your God increase the number of people a hundredfold for your royal majesty to see it with his own eyes. But why does it please my lord the king to order a thing of this kind?" **4**The king, however, overruled Joab and the leaders of the army, so they left the king's presence in order to register the people of Israel. **5**Crossing the Jordan, they began near Aroer, south of the city in the wadi, and went in the direction of Gad, toward Jazer. **6**They continued on to Gilead and to the district below Mount Hermon. Then they proceeded to Dan; from there they turned toward Sidon, **7**going to the fortress of Tyre and to all the cities of the Hivites and Canaanites, and ending up at Beer-sheba in the Negeb of Judah. **8**Thus they toured the whole country, reaching Jerusalem again after nine months and twenty days. **9**Joab then reported to the king the number of people registered: in Israel, eight hundred thousand men fit for military service; in Judah, five hundred thousand.

The Pestilence

10*†Afterward, however, David regretted having numbered the people, and said to the LORD: "I have sinned grievously in what I have done. But now, LORD, forgive the guilt of your servant, for I have been very foolish." **11**When David rose in the morning, the LORD had spoken to the prophet Gad, David's seer, saying: **12**"Go and say to David, 'This is what the LORD says: I offer you three alternatives; choose one of them, and I will inflict it on you.'" **13***Gad then went to David to inform him. He asked: "Do you want a three years' famine to come upon your land, or to flee from your enemy three months while he pursues you, or to have a three days' pestilence in your land? Now consider and decide what I must reply to him who sent me."

14David answered Gad: "I am in very serious difficulty. Let us fall by the hand of God, for he is most merciful; but let me not fall by the hand of man." **15**Thus David chose the pestilence. Now it was the time of the wheat harvest when the plague broke out among the people. [The LORD then sent a pestilence over Israel from morning until the time appointed, and seventy thousand of the people from Dan to Beer-sheba died.] **16***But when the angel stretched forth his hand toward Jerusalem to destroy it, the LORD regretted the calamity and said to the angel causing the destruction among the people, "Enough now! Stay your hand." The angel of the LORD was then standing at the threshing floor of Araunah the Jebusite. **17**†When David saw the angel who was striking the people, he said to the LORD: "It is I who have sinned; it is I, the shepherd, who have done wrong. But these are sheep; what have they done? Punish me and my kindred."

Sacrifice of Atonement

18On the same day Gad went to David and said to him, "Go up and build an altar to the LORD on the threshing floor of Araunah the Jebusite." **19**Following Gad's bidding, David went up as the LORD had commanded. **20**Now Araunah looked down and noticed the king and his servants coming toward him while he was threshing wheat. So he went out and paid homage to the king, with face to the ground. **21**Then Araunah asked, "Why does my lord the king come to his servant?" David replied, "To buy the threshing floor from you, to build an altar to the LORD, that the plague may be checked among the people." **22***But Araunah said to David: "Let my lord the king take and offer up whatever he may wish. Here are oxen for holocausts, and threshing sledges and the yokes of the oxen for wood. **23**All this does Araunah give to the king." Araunah then said to the king, "May the LORD your God accept your offering." **24**The king, however, replied to Araunah, "No, I must pay you for it, for I cannot offer to the LORD my God holocausts that cost nothing." So David bought the threshing floor and the oxen for fifty silver shekels. **25**Then David built an altar there to the LORD, and offered holocausts and peace offerings. The LORD granted relief to the country, and the plague was checked in Israel.

---

†

39: 11, 3f.
24/1-25: 1 Chr 21, 1-27.
10: 1 Sm 24, 6; 1 Chr 21, 7.
13: 21, 1.
16: Ex 12, 23; 2 Kgs 19, 35.
22f: 1 Sm 6, 14; 1 Kgs 19, 21.

24, 1ff: This story was probably joined at one time to 21, 1-14.

24, 10: The narrative supposes that since the people belonged to the Lord rather than to the king, only the Lord should know their exact number.

24, 17: Before this verse a Qumran manuscript (4Q Samᵃ) gives the fuller text of 1 Chr 21, 16, an alternative to the words *When David saw the angel who was striking the people.*

The First Book of Kings

Introduction

The two Books of Kings were originally, like 1 and 2 Samuel, a single historical work. In conjunction with the Books of Samuel, they extend the consecutive history of Israel from the birth of Samuel to the destruction of Jerusalem in 587 B. C. This combined work is designed as a religious history; hence in Kings the temple, which is the chosen site for the worship of Yahweh, occupies the center of attention.

The Books of Kings show clearly the theological bent of a Deuteronomic editor. In them, as already in Judges, material from various sources, such as the "book of the acts of Solomon" (1 Kgs 11, 41) and the "book of the chronicles of the kings of Israel" (1 Kgs 14, 19), is forged into structural unity by an editor whose principal interest is in the fidelity to Yahweh of rulers and people. The reigns of individual kings are adapted to an editorial framework consisting of a presentation and an obituary notice for each, in stereotyped formulas. In between, the achievements of the king are reported—above all, his fidelity or lack of fidelity to Yahweh. The faithful prosper; the unfaithful pay for their defections. Since this is basically a narrative of sin and retribution, it would not be inappropriate to entitle the Books of Kings "The Rise and Fall of the Israelite Monarchy."

Without minimizing the complexity of the process by which this material was transmitted for many centuries, one may speak of two editions of the Books: the first at some time between 621 B. C. and 597 B. C., and the second, final edition during the Exile; probably shortly after Jehoiachin was released from his Babylonian prison (561 B. C.).

1 Kings carries the history of Israel from the last days and death of David to the accession in Samaria of Ahaziah, son of Ahab, near the end of the reign of Jehoshaphat, king of Judah. Judgment is passed on Ahaziah's reign but the details are given only later, in 2 Kings. We should note the two large cycles of traditions which grew up around the great prophetic figures of Elijah and Elisha, the former in 1 Kings and the latter chiefly in 2 Kings. These cycles, which interrupt the sequence of regnal chronicles, were very probably preserved and transmitted by the prophetic communities to which there are references in the same traditions. The Elijah cycle is the more important since it dramatically underscores Israel's critical struggle with the religion of Canaan.

The principal divisions of the Books of Kings are:

I: THE REIGN OF SOLOMON

1 **¹WHEN KING DAVID WAS OLD** and advanced in years, though they spread covers over him he could not keep warm. ²His servants therefore said to him, "Let a young virgin be sought to attend you, lord king, and to nurse you. If she sleeps with your royal majesty, you will be kept warm." ³So they sought for a beautiful girl throughout the territory of Israel, and found Abishag the Shunamite, whom they brought to the king. ⁴The maiden, who was very beautiful, nursed the king and cared for him, but the king did not have relations with her.

Ambition of Adonijah

⁵Adonijah, son of Haggith, began to display his ambition to be king. He acquired chariots, drivers, and fifty henchmen. ⁶Yet his father never rebuked him or asked why he was doing this. Adonijah was also very handsome, and next in age to Absalom by the same mother. ⁷He conferred with Joab, son of Zeruiah, and with Abiathar the priest, and they supported him. ⁸However, Zadok the priest, Benaiah, son of Jehoiada, Nathan the prophet, and Shimei and his companions, the pick of David's army, did not side with Adonijah. ⁹†When he slaughtered sheep, oxen, and fatlings at the stone Zoheleth, near En-rogel, Adonijah invited all his brothers, the king's sons, and all the royal officials of Judah. ¹⁰But he did not invite the prophet Nathan, or Benaiah, or the pick of the army, or his brother Solomon.

Solomon Proclaimed King

¹¹Then Nathan said to Bathsheba, Solomon's mother: "Have you not heard that Adonijah, son of Haggith, has become king without the knowledge of our lord David? ¹²Come now, let me advise you so that you may save your life and that of your son Solomon.

---

† 1, 9: *En-rogel:* the modern Job's Well southeast of Jerusalem. It marked the ancient boundary between the tribes of Benjamin and Judah (Jos 15, 7; 18, 16). Here David's men sought information about Absalom's revolt (2 Sm 17, 17).

¹³Go, visit King David, and say to him, 'Did you not, lord king, swear to your handmaid: Your son Solomon shall be king after me and shall sit upon my throne? Why, then, has Adonijah become king?' ¹⁴And while you are still there speaking to the king, I will come in after you and confirm what you have said."

¹⁵So Bathsheba visited the king in his room, while Abishag the Shunamite was attending him because of his advanced age. ¹⁶Bathsheba bowed in homage to the king, who said to her, "What do you wish?" ¹⁷She answered him: "My lord, you swore to me your handmaid by the LORD, your God, that my son Solomon should reign after you and sit upon your throne. ¹⁸But now Adonijah has become king, and you, my lord king, do not know it. ¹⁹He has slaughtered oxen, fatlings, and sheep in great numbers; he has invited all the king's sons, Abiathar the priest, and Joab, the general of the army, but not your servant Solomon. ²⁰†Now, my lord king, all Israel is waiting for you to make known to them who is to sit on the throne after your royal majesty. ²¹If this is not done, when my lord the king sleeps with his fathers, I and my son Solomon will be considered criminals."

²²While she was still speaking to the king, the prophet Nathan came in. ²³When he had been announced, the prophet entered the king's presence and, bowing to the floor, did him homage. ²⁴Then Nathan said: "Have you decided, my lord king, that Adonijah is to reign after you and sit on your throne? ²⁵He went down today and slaughtered oxen, fatlings, and sheep in great numbers; he invited all the king's sons, the commanders of the army, and Abiathar the priest, and they are eating and drinking in his company and saying, 'Long live King Adonijah!' ²⁶But me, your servant, he did not invite; nor Zadok the priest, nor Benaiah, son of Jehoiada, nor your servant Solomon. ²⁷Was this done by my royal master's order without my being told who was to succeed to your majesty's kingly throne?"

²⁸King David answered, "Call Bathsheba here." When she re-entered the king's presence and stood before him, ²⁹the king swore, "As the LORD lives, who has delivered me from all distress, ³⁰this very day I will fulfill the oath I swore to you by the LORD, the God of Israel, that your son Solomon should reign after me and should sit upon my throne in my place." ³¹Bowing to the floor in homage to the king, Bathsheba said, "May my lord, King David, live forever!" ³²Then King David summoned Zadok the priest, Nathan the prophet, and Benaiah, son of Jehoiada. When they had entered the king's presence, ³³he said to them: "Take with you the royal attendants. Mount my son Solomon upon my own mule and escort him down to Gihon. ³⁴There Zadok the priest and Nathan the prophet are to anoint him king of Israel, and you shall blow the horn and cry, 'Long live King Solomon!' ³⁵When you come back in his train, he is to go in and sit upon my throne and reign in my place. I designate him ruler of Israel and of Judah." ³⁶In answer to the king, Benaiah, son of Jehoiada, said: "So be it! May the LORD, the God of my lord the king, so decree! ³⁷As the

LORD has been with your royal majesty, so may he be with Solomon, and exalt his throne even more than that of my lord, King David!"

³⁸†So Zadok the priest, Nathan the prophet, Benaiah, son of Jehoiada, and the Cherethites and Pelethites went down, and mounting Solomon on King David's mule, escorted him to Gihon. ³⁹Then Zadok the priest took the horn of oil from the tent and anointed Solomon. They blew the horn and all the people shouted, "Long live King Solomon!" ⁴⁰Then all the people went up after him, playing flutes and rejoicing so much as to split open the earth with their shouting.

⁴¹Adonijah and all the guests who were with him heard it, just as they ended their banquet. When Joab heard the sound of the horn, he asked, "What does this uproar in the city mean?" ⁴²As he was speaking, Jonathan, son of Abiathar the priest, arrived. "Come," said Adonijah, "you are a man of worth and must bring good news." ⁴³"On the contrary!" Jonathan answered him. "Our lord, King David, has made Solomon king. ⁴⁴The king sent with him Zadok the priest, Nathan the prophet, Benaiah, son of Jehoiada, and the Cherethites and Pelethites, and they mounted him upon the king's own mule. ⁴⁵Zadok the priest and Nathan the prophet anointed him king at Gihon, and they went up from there rejoicing, so that the city is in an uproar. That is the noise you heard. ⁴⁶Besides, Solomon took his seat on the royal throne, ⁴⁷and the king's servants went in and paid their respects to our lord, King David, saying, 'May God make Solomon more famous than you and exalt his throne more than your own!' And the king in his bed worshiped God, ⁴⁸and this is what he said: 'Blessed be the LORD, the God of Israel, who has this day seated one of my sons upon my throne, so that I see it with my own eyes.'"

⁴⁹All the guests of Adonijah left in terror, each going his own way. ⁵⁰†Adonijah, in fear of Solomon, also left; he went and seized the horns of the altar. ⁵¹It was reported to Solomon that Adonijah, in his fear of King Solomon, had seized the horns of the altar and said, "Let King Solomon first swear that he will not kill me, his servant, with the sword." ⁵²Solomon answered, "If he proves himself worthy, not a hair shall fall from his head. But if he is found guilty of crime, he shall die." ⁵³King Solomon sent to have him brought down from the altar, and he came and paid homage to the king. Solomon then said to him, "Go to your home."

---

† 1, 20: At this time, neither law nor the right of primogeniture, but the will of the ruling monarch, determined succession to the throne.

1, 38: *Cherethites and Pelethites:* mercenaries in David's bodyguard. They became part of his retinue after he defeated the Philistines and established himself in Jerusalem; cf 2 Sm 8, 18; 15, 18; 20, 23.

1, 50: *Horns of the altar:* the protuberances on each of the four corners of the altar were surrounded with a special degree of holiness (Ex 27, 2; 29, 12), and constituted a place of asylum for transgressors of the law (Ex 21, 13f; 1 Kgs 2, 28).

David's Last Instructions and Death

2 ¹†WHEN the time of David's death drew near, he gave these instructions to his son Solomon: ²"I am going the way of all mankind. Take courage and be a man. ³*Keep the mandate of the LORD, your God, following his ways and observing his statutes, commands, ordinances, and decrees as they are written in the law of Moses, that you may succeed in whatever you do, wherever you turn, ⁴*and the LORD may fulfill the promise he made on my behalf when he said, 'If your sons so conduct themselves that they remain faithful to me with their whole heart and with their whole soul, you shall always have someone of your line on the throne of Israel.' ⁵*You yourself know what Joab, son of Zeruiah, did to me when he slew the two generals of Israel's armies, Abner, son of Ner, and Amasa, son of Jether. He took revenge for the blood of war in a time of peace, and put blood shed without provocation on the belt about my waist and the sandal on my foot. ⁶Act with the wisdom you possess; you must not allow him to go down to the grave in peaceful old age.

⁷*"But be kind to the sons of Barzillai the Gileadite, and have them eat at your table. For they received me kindly when I was fleeing your brother Absalom.

⁸*"You also have with you Shimei, son of Gera, the Benjaminite of Bahurim, who cursed me balefully when I was going to Mahanaim. Because he came down to meet me at the Jordan, I swore to him by the LORD that I would not put him to the sword. ⁹But you must not let him go unpunished. You are a prudent man and will know how to deal with him to send down his hoary head in blood to the grave."

¹⁰*David rested with his ancestors and was buried in the City of David. ¹¹*The length of David's reign over Israel was forty years: he reigned seven years in Hebron and thirty-three years in Jerusalem.

The Kingdom Made Secure

¹²When Solomon was seated on the throne of his father David, with his sovereignty firmly established, ¹³Adonijah, son of Haggith, went to Bathsheba, the mother of Solomon. "Do you come as a friend?" she asked. "Yes," he answered, ¹⁴and added, "I have something to say to you." She replied, "Say it." ¹⁵So he said: "You know that the kingdom was mine, and all Israel expected me to be king. But the kingdom escaped me and became my brother's, for the LORD gave it to him. ¹⁶But now there is one favor I would ask of you. Do not refuse me." And she said, "Speak on." ¹⁷†He said, "Please ask King Solomon, who will not refuse you, to give me Abishag the Shunamite for my wife." ¹⁸"Very well," replied Bathsheba, "I will speak to the king for you."

¹⁹So Bathsheba went to King Solomon to speak to him for Adonijah, and the king stood up to meet her and paid her homage. Then he sat down upon his throne, and a throne was provided for the king's mother, who sat at his right. ²⁰"There is one small favor I would ask of you," she said. "Do not refuse me." "Ask it, my mother," the king said to her, ²¹"for I will not refuse you." So she said, "Let Abishag the Shunamite be given to your brother Adonijah for his wife." ²²"And why do you ask Abishag the Shunamite for Adonijah?" King Solomon answered his mother. "Ask the kingdom for him as well, for he is my elder brother and has with him Abiathar the priest and Joab, son of Zeruiah." ²³And King Solomon swore by the LORD: "May God do thus and so to me, and more besides, if Adonijah has not proposed this at the cost of his life. ²⁴And now, as the LORD lives, who has seated me firmly on the throne of my father David and made of me a dynasty as he promised, this day shall Adonijah be put to death." ²⁵Then King Solomon sent Benaiah, son of Jehoiada, who struck him dead.

²⁶The king said to Abiathar the priest: "Go to your land in Anathoth. Though you deserve to die, I will not put you to death this time, because you carried the ark of the Lord GOD before my father David and shared in all the hardships my father endured." ²⁷*So Solomon deposed Abiathar from his office of priest of the LORD, thus fulfilling the prophecy which the LORD had made in Shiloh about the house of Eli.

²⁸When the news came to Joab, who had sided with Adonijah, though not with Absalom, he fled to the tent of the LORD and seized the horns of the altar. ²⁹King Solomon was told that Joab had fled to the tent of the LORD and was at the altar. He sent Benaiah, son of Jehoiada, with the order, "Go, strike him down." ³⁰Benaiah went to the tent of the LORD and said to him, "The king says, 'Come out.'" But he answered, "No! I will die here." Benaiah reported to the king, "This is what Joab said to me in reply." ³¹The king answered him: "Do as he has said. Strike him down and bury him, and you will remove from me and from my family the blood which Joab shed without provocation. ³²*The LORD will hold him responsible for his own blood, because he struck down two men better and more just than himself, and slew them with the sword without my father David's knowledge: Abner, son of Ner, general of Israel's army, and Amasa, son of Jether, general of Judah's army. ³³Joab and his descendants

---

† 2, 1-6.8-9: Solomon is expected to remove from his father's family the imputation of blood guilt brought upon it by Joab in the unwarranted killings of Abner (2 Sm 3, 27-29) and Amasa (2 Sm 19, 9-10); and likewise to punish Shimei for his curse, the effects of which David had pledged himself not to avenge in person (2 Sm 19, 21-23). The standards of morality presumed in these verses are far from the Christian ones.

2, 17.22-25: *Abishag* had been the concubine of King David (1, 4). His successor, Solomon, inherited his father's harem. When Adonijah requested Abishag as his wife, he was subtly undermining the security of Solomon's throne and exposing himself to the suspicion of insurrection that would cost him his life; cf 2 Sm 3, 6-11; 16, 22.

2/3: Dt 17, 19.
4: 2 Sm 7, 11-16; Ps 132, 11f.
5: 2 Sm 3, 27; 20, 10.
7: 2 Sm 19, 33ff.
8: 2 Sm 16, 5; 19, 19.
10: Acts 2, 29.
11: 1 Chr 29, 27.
27: 1 Sm 2, 31.
32: 2 Sm 3, 27; 20, 10.

shall be responsible forever for their blood. But there shall be the peace of the Lord forever for David, and his descendants, and his house, and his throne." ³⁴Benaiah, son of Jehoiada, went back, struck him down and killed him; he was buried in his house in the desert. ³⁵The king appointed Benaiah, son of Jehoiada, over the army in his place, and put Zadok the priest in place of Abiathar.

³⁶Then the king summoned Shimei and said to him: "Build yourself a house in Jerusalem and live there. Do not go anywhere else. ³⁷For if you leave, and cross the Kidron Valley, be certain you shall die without fail. You shall be responsible for your own blood." ³⁸Shimei answered the king: "I accept. Your servant will do just as the king's majesty has said." So Shimei stayed in Jerusalem for a long time. ³⁹But three years later, two of Shimei's servants ran away to Achish, son of Maacah, king of Gath, and Shimei was informed that his servants were in Gath. ⁴⁰So Shimei rose, saddled his ass, and went to Achish in Gath in search of his servants, whom he brought back. ⁴¹When Solomon was informed that Shimei had gone from Jerusalem to Gath, and had returned, ⁴²the king summoned Shimei and said to him: "Did I not have you swear by the Lord to your clear understanding of my warning that, if you left and went anywhere else, you should die without fail? And you answered, 'I accept and obey.' ⁴³Why, then, have you not kept the oath of the Lord and the command that I gave you?" ⁴⁴And the king said to Shimei: "You know in your heart the evil that you did to my father David. Now the Lord requites you for your own wickedness. ⁴⁵But King Solomon shall be blessed, and David's throne shall endure before the Lord forever." ⁴⁶The king then gave the order to Benaiah, son of Jehoiada, who struck him dead as he left.

Wisdom of Solomon

3 ¹*WITH the royal power firmly in his grasp, Solomon allied himself by marriage with Pharaoh, king of Egypt. The daughter of Pharaoh, whom he married, he brought to the City of David, until he should finish building his palace, and the temple of the Lord, and the wall around Jerusalem.

²However, the people were sacrificing on the high places, for up to that time no temple had been built to the name of the Lord. ³Solomon loved the Lord, and obeyed the statutes of his father David; yet he offered sacrifice and burned incense on the high places.

⁴The king went to Gibeon to sacrifice there, because that was the most renowned high place. Upon its altar Solomon offered a thousand holocausts. ⁵In Gibeon the Lord appeared to Solomon in a dream at night. God said, "Ask something of me and I will give it to you." ⁶Solomon answered: "You have shown great favor to your servant, my father David, because he behaved faithfully toward you, with justice and an

upright heart; and you have continued this great favor toward him, even today, seating a son of his on his throne. ⁷O Lord, my God, you have made me, your servant, king to succeed my father David; but I am a mere youth, not knowing at all how to act. ⁸I serve you in the midst of the people whom you have chosen, a people so vast that it cannot be numbered or counted. ⁹*Give your servant, therefore, an understanding heart to judge your people and to distinguish right from wrong. For who is able to govern this vast people of yours?"

¹⁰The Lord was pleased that Solomon made this request. ¹¹So God said to him: "Because you have asked for this—not for a long life for yourself, nor for riches, nor for the life of your enemies, but for understanding so that you may know what is right—¹²I do as you requested. I give you a heart so wise and understanding that there has never been anyone like you up to now, and after you there will come no one to equal you. ¹³*In addition, I give you what you have not asked for, such riches and glory that among kings there is not your like. ¹⁴And if you follow me by keeping my statutes and commandments, as your father David did, I will give you a long life."

¹⁵When Solomon awoke from his dream, he went to Jerusalem, stood before the ark of the covenant of the Lord, offered holocausts and peace offerings, and gave a banquet for all his servants.

Solomon's Judgment

¹⁶Later, two harlots came to the king and stood before him. ¹⁷One woman said: "By your leave, my lord, this woman and I live in the same house, and I gave birth in the house while she was present. ¹⁸On the third day after I gave birth, this woman also gave birth. We were alone in the house; there was no one there but us two. ¹⁹This woman's son died during the night; she smothered him by lying on him. ²⁰Later that night she got up and took my son from my side, as I, your handmaid, was sleeping. Then she laid him in her bosom, after she had laid her dead child in my bosom. ²¹I rose in the morning to nurse my child, and I found him dead. But when I examined him in the morning light, I saw it was not the son whom I had borne."

²²The other woman answered, "It is not so! The living one is my son, the dead one is yours." But the first kept saying, "No, the dead one is your child, the living one is mine!" Thus they argued before the king. ²³Then the king said: "One woman claims, 'This, the living one, is my child, and the dead one is yours.' The other answers, 'No! The dead one is your child; the living one is mine.'" ²⁴The king continued, "Get me a sword." When they brought the sword before him, ²⁵he said, "Cut the living child in two, and give half to one woman and half to the other." ²⁶The woman whose son it was, in the anguish she felt for it, said to the king, "Please, my lord, give her the living child—please do not kill it!" The other, however, said, "It shall be neither mine nor yours. Divide it!" ²⁷The

king then answered, "Give the first one the living child! By no means kill it, for she is the mother."

²⁸When all Israel heard the judgment the king had given, they were in awe of him, because they saw that the king had in him the wisdom of God for giving judgment.

Chief Officers of the Kingdom

4 ¹SOLOMON was king over all Israel, ²and these were the officials he had in his service:

Azariah, son of Zadok, priest;

³Elihoreph and Ahijah, sons of Shisha, scribes; Jehoshaphat, son of Ahilud, chancellor;

⁴[Benaiah, son of Jehoiada, commander of the army; Zadok and Abiathar, priests;]

⁵Azariah, son of Nathan, chief of the commissaries; Zabud, son of Nathan, companion to the king;

⁶Ahishar, major-domo of the palace; and Adoniram, son of Abda, superintendent of the forced labor.

Solomon's Royal State

⁷†Solomon had twelve commissaries for all Israel who supplied food for the king and his household, each having to provide for one month in the year. ⁸Their names were:

the son of Hur in the hill country of Ephraim;

⁹the son of Deker in Makaz, Shaalbim, Beth-shemesh, Elon and Beth-hanan;

¹⁰the son of Hesed in Arubboth, as well as in Socoh and the whole region of Hepher;

¹¹the son of Abinadab, who was married to Solomon's daughter Taphath, in all the Naphath-dor;

¹²Baana, son of Ahilud, in Taanach and Megiddo, and beyond Jokmeam, and in all Beth-shean, and in the country around Zarethan below Jezreel from Beth-shean to Abel-meholah;

¹³the son of Geber in Ramoth-gilead, having charge of the villages of Jair, son of Manasseh, in Gilead; and of the district of Argob in Bashan —sixty large walled cities with gates barred with bronze;

¹⁴Ahinadab, son of Iddo, in Mahanaim;

¹⁵Ahimaaz, who was married to Basemath, another daughter of Solomon, in Naphtali;

¹⁶Baana, son of Hushai, in Asher and along the rocky coast;

¹⁷Jehoshaphat, son of Paruah, in Issachar;

¹⁸Shimei, son of Ela, in Benjamin;

¹⁹†Geber, son of Uri, in the land of Gilead, the land of Sihon, king of the Amorites, and of Og, king of Bashan.

There was one prefect besides, in the king's own land.

5/⁷These commissaries, one for each month, provided food for King Solomon and for all the guests at the royal table. They left nothing unprovided. 5/⁸For the chariot horses and draft animals also, each brought his quota of barley and straw to the required place.

²⁰Judah and Israel were as numerous as the sands by the sea; they ate and drank and made merry.

5 ¹*SOLOMON ruled over all the kingdoms from the River to the land of the Philistines, down to the border of Egypt; they paid Solomon tribute and were his vassals as long as he lived.

²Solomon's supplies for each day were thirty kors of fine flour, sixty kors of meal, ³ten fatted oxen, twenty pasture-fed oxen, and a hundred sheep, not counting harts, gazelles, roebucks, and fatted fowl.

⁴He ruled over all the land west of the Euphrates, from Tiphsah to Gaza, and over all its kings, and he had peace on all his borders round about. ⁵Thus Judah and Israel lived in security, every man under his vine or under his fig tree from Dan to Beer-sheba, as long as Solomon lived.

⁶*Solomon had four thousand stalls for his twelve thousand chariot horses.

⁹*Moreover, God gave Solomon wisdom and exceptional understanding and knowledge, as vast as the sand on the seashore. ¹⁰Solomon surpassed all the Cedemites and all the Egyptians in wisdom. ¹¹He was wiser than all other men—than Ethan the Ezrahite, or Heman, Chalcol, and Darda, the musicians—and his fame spread throughout the neighboring nations. ¹²*Solomon also uttered three thousand proverbs, and his songs numbered a thousand and five. ¹³He discussed plants, from the cedar on Lebanon to the hyssop growing out of the wall, and he spoke about beasts, birds, reptiles, and fishes. ¹⁴Men came to hear Solomon's wisdom from all nations, sent by all the kings of the earth who had heard of his wisdom.

Preparations for the Temple

¹⁵When Hiram, king of Tyre, heard that Solomon had been anointed king in place of his father, he sent an embassy to him; for Hiram had always been David's friend. ¹⁶Solomon sent back this message to Hiram: ¹⁷"You know that my father David, because of the enemies surrounding him on all sides, could not build a temple in honor of the LORD, his God, until such a time as the LORD should put these enemies under the soles of his feet. ¹⁸But now the LORD, my God, has given me peace on all sides. There is no enemy or threat of danger. ¹⁹*So I propose to build a temple in honor of the LORD, my God, as the LORD predicted to

---

† 4, 7-19: The administration of the kingdom thus initiated by Solomon continued in its main features for the duration of the monarchy in Israel and Judah.

4, 19: *One prefect . . . in the king's own land:* the royal territory of Judah had its own peculiar administration different from that of the twelve districts which had to supply the king and his household with a month's provisions of food each year (v 7).

5/1: Sir 47, 15f; 2 Chr 9, 26.   12: 3, 12.
6: 2 Chr 9, 25f.   19: 2 Sm 7, 13; 1 Chr
9-14: Sir 47, 16f.   22, 10.

my father David when he said: 'It is your son whom I will put upon your throne in your place who shall build the temple in my honor.' [20]Give orders, then, to have cedars from the Lebanon cut down for me. My servants shall accompany yours, since you know that there is no one among us who is skilled in cutting timber like the Sidonians, and I will pay you whatever you say for your servants' salary."

[21]When he had heard the words of Solomon, Hiram was pleased and said, "Blessed be the Lord this day, who has given David a wise son to rule this numerous people. [22]Hiram then sent word to Solomon, "I agree to the proposal you sent me, and I will provide all the cedars and fir trees you wish. [23]My servants shall bring them down from the Lebanon to the sea, and I will arrange them into rafts in the sea and bring them wherever you say. There I will break up the rafts, and you shall take the lumber. You, for your part, shall furnish the provisions I desire for my household."

[24]So Hiram continued to provide Solomon with all the cedars and fir trees he wished; [25]while Solomon every year gave Hiram twenty thousand kors of wheat to provide for his household, and twenty thousand measures of pure oil. [26]The Lord, moreover, gave Solomon wisdom as he promised him, and there was peace between Hiram and Solomon, since they were parties to a treaty.

[27]King Solomon conscripted thirty thousand workmen from all Israel. [28]He sent them to the Lebanon each month in relays of ten thousand, so that they spent one month in the Lebanon and two months at home. Adoniram was in charge of the draft. [29]Solomon had seventy thousand carriers and eighty thousand stonecutters in the mountain, [30]in addition to three thousand three hundred overseers, answerable to Solomon's prefects for the work, directing the people engaged in the work. [31]By order of the king, fine, large blocks were quarried to give the temple a foundation of hewn stone. [32]Solomon's and Hiram's builders, along with the Gebalites, hewed them out, and prepared the wood and stones for building the temple.

Building of the Temple

6 [1]*[IN the four hundred and eightieth year from the departure of the Israelites from the land of Egypt, in the fourth year of Solomon's reign over Israel, in the month of Ziv, which is the second month, the construction of the temple of the Lord was begun.

[2]The temple which King Solomon built for the Lord was sixty cubits long, twenty wide, and twenty-five high. [3]The porch in front of the temple was twenty cubits from side to side, along the width of the nave, and ten cubits deep in front of the temple. [4]Splayed windows with trellises were made for the temple, [5]and adjoining the wall of the temple, which enclosed the nave and the sanctuary, an annex of several stories was built. [6]Its lowest story was five cubits wide, the middle one six cubits wide, the third seven cubits

wide, because there were offsets along the outside of the temple so that the beams would not be fastened into the walls of the temple. [7](The temple was built of stone dressed at the quarry, so that no hammer, axe, or iron tool was to be heard in the temple during its construction.) [8]The entrance to the lowest floor of the annex was at the right side of the temple, and stairs with intermediate landings led up to the middle story and from the middle story to the third. [9]When the temple was built to its full height, it was roofed in with rafters and boards of cedar. [10]The annex, with its lowest story five cubits high, was built all along the outside of the temple, to which it was joined by cedar beams.

[11][This word of the Lord came to Solomon: [12]*"As to this temple you are building—if you observe my statutes, carry out my ordinances, keep and obey all my commands, I will fulfill toward you the promise I made to your father David. [13]*I will dwell in the midst of the Israelites and will not forsake my people Israel."

[14]When Solomon finished building the temple, [15]its walls were lined from floor to ceiling beams with cedar paneling, and its floor was laid with fir planking. [16]At the rear of the temple a space of twenty cubits was set off by cedar partitions from the floor to the rafters, enclosing the sanctuary, the holy of holies. [17]The nave, or part of the temple in front of the sanctuary, was forty cubits long. [18]The cedar in the interior of the temple was carved in the form of gourds and open flowers; all was of cedar, and no stone was to be seen.

[19][In the innermost part of the temple was located the sanctuary to house the ark of the Lord's covenant, [20][twenty cubits long, twenty wide, and twenty high. [21]Solomon overlaid the interior of the temple with pure gold. He made in front of the sanctuary a cedar altar, overlaid it with gold, and looped it with golden chains. [22]The entire temple was overlaid with gold so that it was completely covered with it; the whole altar before the sanctuary was also overlaid with gold. [23]In the sanctuary were two cherubim, each ten

---

† 6, 1: *Construction of the temple of the Lord* is here paralleled in importance with the founding of the nation after the departure from Egypt. In both, God is the central figure who chose Israel as his people, and now chooses the place where his temple should be built (Dt 12, 4-18.26). The year is given in a round number, 480, which corresponds to twelve generations. The *fourth year of Solomon's reign:* c. 968 B. C.

6, 11ff: *The word of the Lord . . . my people Israel:* the oracle, which came as a climax at the completion of the work, was an expression of God's acceptance and approval. Nevertheless the fulfillment of God's promises to David and his royal descendants will depend on their observance of his ordinances and commands.

6, 19: *The innermost part of the temple:* the sanctuary or holy of holies reserved exclusively for the Lord. Here through his presence he dwelt as on a throne between the cherubim above the ark of the covenant (23-28; 2 Chr 3, 10-13). See note on Ex 25, 18ff.

6, 20: *Twenty (cubits) high:* it is usually supposed that the holy of holies was of this height because it had a raised floor, five cubits above the floor level of the nave, rather than a dropped ceiling. The building was twenty-five cubits high (v 2) according to the reading here followed.

6/1: 2 Chr 3, 1.　　　13: 1 Chr 22, 9f.
12: 2 Sm 7, 13.

cubits high, made of olive wood. **24**Each wing of a cherub measured five cubits so that the space from wing tip to wing tip of each was ten cubits. **25**The cherubim were identical in size and shape, **26**and each was exactly ten cubits high. **27**The cherubim were placed in the inmost part of the temple, with their wings spread wide, so that one wing of each cherub touched a side wall while the other wing, pointing toward the middle of the room, touched the corresponding wing of the second cherub. **28**The cherubim, too, were overlaid with gold.

29The walls on all sides of both the inner and the outer rooms had carved figures of cherubim, palm trees, and open flowers. **30**The floor of both the inner and the outer rooms was overlaid with gold. **31**At the entrance of the sanctuary, doors of olive wood were made; the doorframes had beveled posts. **32**The two doors were of olive wood, with carved figures of cherubim, palm trees, and open flowers. The doors were overlaid with gold, which was also molded to the cherubim and the palm trees. **33**The same was done at the entrance to the nave, where the doorposts of olive wood were rectangular. **34**The two doors were of fir wood; each door was banded by a metal strap, front and back, **35**and had carved cherubim, palm trees, and open flowers, over which gold was evenly applied.

36The inner court was walled off by means of three courses of hewn stones and one course of cedar beams.

37The foundations of the LORD's temple were laid in the month of Ziv **38**in the fourth year, and it was completed in all particulars, exactly according to plan, in the month of Bul, the eighth month, in the eleventh year. Thus it took Solomon seven years to build it.

Building of the Palace

7 **1***HIS own palace Solomon completed after thirteen years of construction. **2**He built the hall called the Forest of Lebanon one hundred cubits long, fifty wide, and thirty high; it was supported by four rows of cedar columns, with cedar capitals upon the columns. **3**Moreover, it had a ceiling of cedar above the beams resting on the columns; these beams numbered forty-five, fifteen to a row. **4**There were three window frames at either end, with windows in strict alignment. **5**The posts of all the doorways were rectangular, and the doorways faced each other, three at either end. **6**The porch of the columned hall he made fifty cubits long and thirty wide. The porch extended the width of the columned hall, and there was a canopy in front. **7**He also built the vestibule of the throne where he gave judgment—that is, the tribunal; it was paneled with cedar from floor to ceiling beams. **8***His living quarters were in another court, set in deeper than the tribunal and of the same construction. A palace like this tribunal was built for Pharaoh's daughter, whom Solomon had married.

9All these buildings were of fine stones, hewn to size and trimmed front and back with a saw, from the foundation to the bonding course. **10**(The foundation was made of fine, large blocks, some ten cubits and some eight cubits. **11**Above were fine stones hewn to size, and cedar wood.) **12**The great court was enclosed by three courses of hewn stones and a bonding course of cedar beams. So also were the inner court of the temple of the LORD and the temple porch.

Furnishing of the Temple

13King Solomon had Hiram brought from Tyre. **14**He was a bronze worker, the son of a widow from the tribe of Naphtali; his father had been from Tyre. He was endowed with skill, understanding, and knowledge of how to produce any work in bronze. He came to King Solomon and did all his metal work.

15*†Two hollow bronze columns were cast, each eighteen cubits high and twelve cubits in circumference; their metal was of four fingers' thickness. **16**There were also two capitals cast in bronze, to place on top of the columns, each of them five cubits high. **17**Two pieces of network with a chainlike mesh were made to cover the (nodes of the) capitals on top of the columns, one for each capital. **18**Four hundred pomegranates were also cast; two hundred of them in a double row encircled the piece of network on each of the two capitals. **19**The capitals on top of the columns were finished wholly in a lotus pattern **20**above the level of the nodes and their enveloping network. **21**The columns were then erected adjacent to the porch of the temple, one to the right, called Jachin, and the other to the left, called Boaz. **22**Thus the work on the columns was completed.

23*†The sea was then cast; it was made with a circular rim, and measured ten cubits across, five in height, and thirty in circumference. **24**Under the brim, gourds encircled it, ten to the cubit all the way around; the gourds were in two rows and were cast in one mold with the sea. **25**This rested on twelve oxen, three facing north, three facing west, three facing south, and three facing east, with their haunches all toward the center, where the sea was set upon them. **26**It was a handbreadth thick, and its brim resembled that of a cup, being lily-shaped. Its capacity was two thousand measures.

27Ten stands were also made of bronze, each four cubits long, four wide, and three high. **28**When these stands were constructed, panels were set within the framework. **29**On the panels between the frames there were lions, oxen, and cherubim; and on the frames likewise, above and below the lions and oxen, there were wreaths in relief.

30Each stand had four bronze wheels and bronze axles. **32**The four wheels were below the paneling, and

7/1: 1 Kgs 9, 10.
8: 3, 1.
15: Jer 52, 21.
23: 2 Chr 4, 2.

† 7, 15-21: The *two hollow bronze columns*, Jachin and Boaz (2 Chr 3, 17), stood free to the right and left of the temple porch. The names are related to God's power (*Boaz*) founding (*Jachin*) the temple and his people.

7, 23-26: *The sea . . . rested on twelve oxen:* this was a large circular tank containing about twelve thousand gallons of water.

the axle-trees of the wheels and the stand were of one piece. Each wheel was a cubit and a half high. **33**The wheels were constructed like chariot wheels; their axles, fellies, spokes, and hubs were all cast.

The four legs of each stand had cast braces, which were under the basin; they had wreaths on each side. **34**These four braces, extending to the corners of each stand, were of one piece with the stand. **35**On top of the stand there was a raised collar half a cubit high, with supports and panels which were of one piece with the top of the stand. 7/**31**This was surmounted by a crown one cubit high within which was a rounded opening to provide a receptacle a cubit and a half in depth. There was carved work at the opening, on panels that were angular, not curved. **36**On the surfaces of the supports and on the panels, wherever there was a clear space, cherubim, lions, and palm trees were carved, as well as wreaths all around. **37**This was how the ten stands were made, all of the same casting, the same size, the same shape. **38**Ten bronze basins were then made, each four cubits in diameter with a capacity of forty measures, one basin for the top of each of the ten stands. **39**The stands were placed, five on the south side of the temple and five on the north. The sea was placed off to the southeast from the south side of the temple.

40When Hiram made the pots, shovels, and bowls, he therewith completed all his work for King Solomon in the temple of the LORD: **41**two columns, two nodes for the capitals on top of the columns, two pieces of network covering the nodes for the capitals on top of the columns, **42**four hundred pomegranates in double rows on both pieces of network that covered the two nodes of the capitals where they met the columns, **43**ten stands, ten basins on the stands, **44**one sea, twelve oxen supporting the sea, **45**pots, shovels, and bowls. All these articles which Hiram made for King Solomon in the temple of the LORD were of burnished bronze. **46**The king had them cast in the neighborhood of the Jordan, in the clayey ground between Succoth and Zarethan. **47**Solomon did not weigh all the articles because they were so numerous; the weight of the bronze, therefore, was not determined.

48Solomon had all the articles made for the interior of the temple of the LORD: the golden altar; the golden table on which the showbread lay; **49**the lampstands of pure gold, five to the right and five to the left before the sanctuary, with their flowers, lamps, and tongs of gold; **50**basins, snuffers, bowls, cups, and fire pans of pure gold; and hinges of gold for the doors of the inner room, or holy of holies, and for the doors of the outer room, the nave.

51When all the work undertaken by King Solomon in the temple of the LORD was completed, he brought in the dedicated offerings of his father David, putting the silver, gold, and other articles in the treasuries of the temple of the LORD.

Dedication of the Temple

8 **1**AT the order of Solomon, the elders of Israel and all the leaders of the tribes, the princes in the ancestral houses of the Israelites, came to King Solomon in Jerusalem, to bring up the ark of the LORD's covenant from the City of David [which is Zion]. **2**All the men of Israel assembled before King Solomon during the festival in the month of Ethanim (the seventh month). **3**When all the elders of Israel had arrived, the priests took up the ark; **4**they carried the ark of the LORD and the meeting tent with all the sacred vessels that were in the tent. (The priests and Levites carried them.)

5King Solomon and the entire community of Israel present for the occasion sacrificed before the ark sheep and oxen too many to number or count. **6**†The priests brought the ark of the covenant of the LORD to its place beneath the wings of the cherubim in the sanctuary, the holy of holies of the temple. **7**The cherubim had their wings spread out over the place of the ark, sheltering the ark and its poles from above. **8**The poles were so long that their ends could be seen from that part of the holy place adjoining the sanctuary; however, they could not be seen beyond. (They have remained there to this day.) **9**There was nothing in the ark but the two stone tablets which Moses had put there at Horeb, when the LORD made a covenant with the Israelites at their departure from the land of Egypt.

10When the priests left the holy place, the cloud filled the temple of the LORD **11**so that the priests could no longer minister because of the cloud, since the LORD's glory had filled the temple of the LORD. **12**Then Solomon said, "The LORD intends to dwell in the dark cloud; **13**I have truly built you a princely house, a dwelling where you may abide forever."

14The king turned and greeted the whole community of Israel as they stood. **15**He said to them: "Blessed be the LORD, the God of Israel, who with his own mouth made a promise to my father David and by his hand has brought it to fulfillment. It was he who said, **16**'Since the day I brought my people Israel out of Egypt, I have not chosen a city out of any tribe of Israel for the building of a temple to my honor; but I choose David to rule my people Israel.' **17**When my father David wished to build a temple to the honor of the LORD, the God of Israel, **18**the LORD said to him, 'In wishing to build a temple to my honor, you do well. **19**It will not be you, however, who will build the temple; but the son who will spring from you, he shall build the temple to my honor.' **20**And now the LORD has fulfilled the promise that he made: I have suc-

---

† 8, 6-9: The transfer of the ark of the covenant into the newly constructed temple building, and the oracle of God's acceptance (9, 3-9), and his act of possession (8, 10-13), constituted the temple's solemn dedication, and made of it the abiding dwelling of God among his people for which David had hoped (2 Sm 6, 12-15; 7, 1-3). The concurrence of the feast of Booths marks an appropriate transition of God's dwelling among nomadic tribes to his permanent abode among a settled people.

✱
51: 2 Chr 5, 1. 12: 2 Chr 6, 1.
8/1: 2 Chr 5, 2. 17: 2 Sm 7, 5.
9: Ex 34, 27; Heb 9, 4.

ceeded my father David and sit on the throne of Israel, as the Lord foretold, and I have built this temple to honor the Lord, the God of Israel. **21**I have provided in it a place for the ark in which is the covenant of the Lord, which he made with our fathers when he brought them out of the land of Egypt."

Solomon's Prayer

22Solomon stood before the altar of the Lord in the presence of the whole community of Israel, and stretching forth his hands toward heaven, **23**he said, "Lord, God of Israel, there is no God like you in heaven above or on earth below; you keep your covenant of kindness with your servants who are faithful to you with their whole heart. **24**You have kept the promise you made to my father David, your servant. You who spoke that promise, have this day, by your own power, brought it to fulfillment. **25***Now, therefore, Lord, God of Israel, keep the further promise you made to my father David, your servant, saying, 'You shall always have someone from your line to sit before me on the throne of Israel, provided only that your descendants look to their conduct so that they live in my presence, as you have lived in my presence.' **26**Now, Lord, God of Israel, may this promise which you made to my father David, your servant, be confirmed.

27"Can it indeed be that God dwells among men on earth? If the heavens and the highest heavens cannot contain you, how much less this temple which I have built! **28**Look kindly on the prayer and petition of your servant, O Lord, my God, and listen to the cry of supplication which I, your servant, utter before you this day. **29**May your eyes watch night and day over this temple, the place where you have decreed you shall be honored; may you heed the prayer which I, your servant, offer in this place. **30**Listen to the petitions of your servant and of your people Israel which they offer in this place. Listen from your heavenly dwelling and grant pardon.

31"If a man sins against his neighbor and is required to take an oath sanctioned by a curse, when he comes and takes the oath before your altar in this temple, **32**listen in heaven; take action and pass judgment on your servants. Condemn the wicked and punish him for his conduct, but acquit the just and establish his innocence.

33†"If your people Israel sin against you and are defeated by an enemy, and if then they return to you, praise your name, pray to you, and entreat you in this temple, **34**listen in heaven and forgive the sin of your people Israel, and bring them back to the land you gave their fathers.

35"If the sky is closed, so that there is no rain, because they have sinned against you and you afflict them, and if then they repent of their sin, and pray, and praise your name in this place, **36**listen in heaven

and forgive the sin of your servant and of your people Israel, teaching them the right way to live and sending rain upon this land of yours which you have given to your people as their heritage.

37"If there is famine in the land or pestilence; or if blight comes, or mildew, or a locust swarm, or devouring insects; if an enemy of your people besieges them in one of their cities; whatever plague or sickness there may be, **38**if then any one [of your entire people Israel] has remorse of conscience and offers some prayer or petition, stretching out his hands toward this temple, **39**listen from your heavenly dwelling place and forgive. You who alone know the hearts of all men, render to each one of them according to his conduct; knowing their hearts, so treat them **40**that they may fear you as long as they live on the land you gave our fathers.

41"To the foreigner, likewise, who is not of your people Israel, but comes from a distant land to honor you **42**(since men will learn of your great name and your mighty hand and your outstretched arm), when he comes and prays toward this temple, **43**listen from your heavenly dwelling. Do all that the foreigner asks of you, that all the peoples of the earth may know your name, may fear you as do your people Israel, and may acknowledge that this temple which I have built is dedicated to your honor.

44"Whatever the direction in which you may send your people forth to war against their enemies, if they pray to you, O Lord, toward the city you have chosen and the temple I have built in your honor, **45**listen in heaven to their prayer and petition, and defend their cause.

46*"When they sin against you (for there is no man who does not sin), and in your anger against them you deliver them to the enemy, so that their captors deport them to a hostile land, far or near, **47**may they repent in the land of their captivity and be converted. If then they entreat you in the land of their captors and say, 'We have sinned and done wrong; we have been wicked'; **48**if with their whole heart and soul they turn back to you in the land of the enemies who took them captive, pray to you toward the land you gave their fathers, the city you have chosen, and the temple I have built in your honor, **49**listen from your heavenly dwelling. **50**Forgive your people their sins and all the offenses they have committed against you, and grant them mercy before their captors, so that these will be merciful to them. **51**For they are your people and your inheritance, whom you brought out of Egypt, from the midst of an iron furnace.

52"Thus may your eyes be open to the petition of your servant and to the petition of your people Israel. Hear them whenever they call upon you, **53**because you have set them apart among all the peoples of the earth for your inheritance, as you declared through

---

* 25: 2 Sm 7, 12.   46: 2 Chr 6, 36; Eccl 7, 20; 1 Jn 1, 8.

† 8, 33-34.46-53: These references to deportation of Israelites to *a hostile land* are an expansion of Solomon's prayer dating from the Babylonian exile four centuries later.

your servant Moses when you brought our fathers out of Egypt, O Lord God."

⁵⁴When Solomon finished offering this entire prayer of petition to the LORD, he rose from before the altar of the LORD, where he had been kneeling with his hands outstretched toward heaven. ⁵⁵He stood and blessed the whole community of Israel, saying in a loud voice: ⁵⁶"Blessed be the LORD who has given rest to his people Israel, just as he promised. Not a single word has gone unfulfilled of the entire generous promise he made through his servant Moses. ⁵⁷May the LORD, our God, be with us as he was with our fathers and may he not forsake us nor cast us off. ⁵⁸May he draw our hearts to himself, that we may follow him in everything and keep the commands, statutes, and ordinances which he enjoined on our fathers. ⁵⁹May this prayer I have offered to the LORD, our God, be present to him day and night, that he may uphold the cause of his servant and of his people Israel as each day requires, ⁶⁰that all the peoples of the earth may know the LORD is God and there is no other. ⁶¹You must be wholly devoted to the LORD, our God, observing his statutes and keeping his commandments, as on this day."

⁶²The king and all Israel with him offered sacrifices before the LORD. ⁶³Solomon offered as peace offerings to the LORD twenty-two thousand oxen and one hundred twenty thousand sheep. Thus the king and all the Israelites dedicated the temple of the LORD. ⁶⁴On that day the king consecrated the middle of the court facing the temple of the LORD; he offered there the holocausts, the cereal offerings, and the fat of the peace offerings, because the bronze altar before the LORD was too small to hold these offerings.

⁶⁵On this occasion Solomon and all the Israelites, who had assembled in large numbers from Labo of Hamath to the Wadi of Egypt, celebrated the festival before the LORD, our God, for seven days. ⁶⁶On the eighth day he dismissed the people, who bade the king farewell and went to their homes, rejoicing and happy over all the blessings the LORD had given to his servant David and to his people Israel.

Promise and Warning to Solomon

9 ¹AFTER Solomon finished building the temple of the LORD, the royal palace, and everything else that he had planned, ²*the LORD appeared to him a second time, as he had appeared to him in Gibeon. ³The LORD said to him: "I have heard the prayer of petition which you offered in my presence. I have consecrated this temple which you have built; I confer my name upon it forever, and my eyes and my heart shall be there always. ⁴As for you, if you live in my presence as your father David lived, sincerely and uprightly, doing just as I have commanded you, keeping my statutes and decrees, ⁵*I will establish your throne

of sovereignty over Israel forever, as I promised your father David when I said, 'You shall always have someone from your line on the throne of Israel.' ⁶But if you and your descendants ever withdraw from me, fail to keep the commandments and statutes which I set before you, and proceed to venerate and worship strange gods, ⁷I will cut off Israel from the land I gave them and repudiate the temple I have consecrated to my honor. Israel shall become a proverb and a byword among all nations, ⁸*and this temple shall become a heap of ruins. Every passerby shall catch his breath in amazement, and ask, 'Why has the LORD done this to the land and to this temple?' ⁹Men will answer: 'They forsook the LORD, their God, who brought their fathers out of the land of Egypt; they adopted strange gods which they worshiped and served. That is why the LORD has brought down upon them all this evil.'"

Other Acts of the King

¹⁰After the twenty years during which Solomon built the two houses, the temple of the LORD and the palace of the king ¹¹—Hiram, king of Tyre, supplying Solomon with all the cedar wood, fir wood, and gold he wished—King Solomon gave Hiram twenty cities in the land of Galilee. ¹²Hiram left Tyre to see the cities Solomon had given him, but was not satisfied with them. ¹³So he said, "What are these cities you have given me, my brother?" And he called them the land of Cabul, as they are called to this day. ¹⁴†Hiram, however, had sent King Solomon one hundred and twenty talents of gold.

¹⁵†This is an account of the forced labor which King Solomon levied in order to build the temple of the LORD, his palace, Millo, the wall of Jerusalem, Hazor, Megiddo, Gezer ¹⁶(Pharaoh, king of Egypt, had come up and taken Gezer and, after destroying it by fire and slaying all the Canaanites living in the city, had given it as dowry to his daughter, Solomon's wife; ¹⁷Solomon then rebuilt Gezer), Lower Beth-horon, ¹⁸Baalath, Tamar in the desert of Judah, ¹⁹all his cities for supplies, cities for chariots and for horses, and whatever else Solomon decided should be built in Jerusalem, in Lebanon, and in the entire land under his dominion. ²⁰All the non-Israelite people who remained in the land, descendants of the Amorites, Hittites, Perizzites, Hivites, and Jebusites ²¹whose doom the Israelites had been unable to accomplish, Solomon conscripted as forced laborers, as they are to this day. ²²But Solomon enslaved none of the Israelites, for they were his fighting force, his ministers, commanders, adjutants, chariot officers, and charioteers. ²³The supervisors of Solomon's works who policed the people engaged in the work numbered five hundred and fifty.

²⁴As soon as Pharaoh's daughter went up from the

9, 14: *One hundred and twenty talents of gold:* approximately three million six hundred thousand dollars.

9, 15: *Millo:* probably means a filling, and may refer to an artificial earthwork or platform of stamped ground south of the temple area. It was begun by David (2 Sm 5, 9); cf 9, 24; 11, 27.

9/2: 3, 5; 11, 9; 2 Chr 7, 12.   8: Dt 29, 23; Jer 22, 8.
5: 2 Sm 7, 12-16.

City of David to her palace, which he had built for her, Solomon built Millo.

²⁵Three times a year Solomon used to offer holocausts and peace offerings on the altar which he had built to the Lord, and to burn incense before the Lord; and he kept the temple in repair.

²⁶†King Solomon also built a fleet at Ezion-geber, which is near Elath on the shore of the Red Sea in the land of Edom. ²⁷In this fleet Hiram placed his own expert seamen with the servants of Solomon. ²⁸They went to Ophir, and brought back four hundred and twenty talents of gold to King Solomon.

Visit of the Queen of Sheba

10 ¹*†THE queen of Sheba, having heard of Solomon's fame, came to test him with subtle questions. ²She arrived in Jerusalem with a very numerous retinue, and with camels bearing spices, a large amount of gold, and precious stones. She came to Solomon and questioned him on every subject in which she was interested. ³King Solomon explained everything she asked about, and there remained nothing hidden from him that he could not explain to her.

⁴When the queen of Sheba witnessed Solomon's great wisdom, the palace he had built, ⁵the food at his table, the seating of his ministers, the attendance and garb of his waiters, his banquet service, and the holocausts he offered in the temple of the Lord, she was breathless. ⁶"The report I heard in my country about your deeds and your wisdom is true," she told the king. ⁷"Though I did not believe the report until I came and saw with my own eyes, I have discovered that they were not telling me the half. Your wisdom and prosperity surpass the report I heard. ⁸Happy are your men, happy these servants of yours, who stand before you always and listen to your wisdom. ⁹Blessed be the Lord, your God, whom it has pleased to place you on the throne of Israel. In his enduring love for Israel, the Lord has made you king to carry out judgment and justice." ¹⁰Then she gave the king one hundred and twenty gold talents, a very large quantity of spices, and precious stones. Never again did anyone bring such an abundance of spices as the queen of Sheba gave to King Solomon.

¹¹†Hiram's fleet, which used to bring gold from Ophir, also brought from there a large quantity of cabinet wood and precious stones. ¹²With the wood the king made supports for the temple of the Lord and for the palace of the king, and harps and lyres for the chanters. No more such wood was brought or seen to the present day.

¹³King Solomon gave the queen of Sheba everything she desired and asked for, besides such presents as were given her from Solomon's royal bounty. Then she returned with her servants to her own country.

Solomon's Wealth

¹⁴The gold that Solomon received every year weighed six hundred and sixty-six gold talents, ¹⁵in addition to what came from the Tarshish fleet, from the traffic of merchants, and from all the kings of Arabia and the governors of the country. ¹⁶*Moreover, King Solomon made two hundred shields of beaten gold (six hundred gold shekels went into each shield) ¹⁷and three hundred bucklers of beaten gold (three minas of gold went into each buckler); and he put them in the hall of the Forest of Lebanon. ¹⁸The king also had a large ivory throne made, and overlaid it with refined gold. ¹⁹The throne had six steps, a back with a round top, and an arm on each side of the seat. Next to each arm stood a lion; ²⁰and twelve other lions stood on the steps, two to a step, one on either side of each step. Nothing like this was produced in any other kingdom. ²¹In addition, all King Solomon's drinking vessels were of gold, and all the utensils in the hall of the Forest of Lebanon were of pure gold. There was no silver, for in Solomon's time it was considered worthless. ²²†The king had a fleet of Tarshish ships at sea with Hiram's fleet. Once every three years the fleet of Tarshish ships would come with a cargo of gold, silver, ivory, apes, and monkeys. ²³Thus King Solomon surpassed in riches and wisdom all the kings of the earth. ²⁴And the whole world sought audience with Solomon, to hear from him the wisdom which God had put in his heart. ²⁵Each one brought his yearly tribute: silver or gold articles, garments, weapons, spices, horses and mules.

²⁶*Solomon collected chariots and drivers; he had one thousand four hundred chariots and twelve thousand drivers; these he allocated among the chariot cities and to the king's service in Jerusalem. ²⁷The king made silver as common in Jerusalem as stones, and cedars as numerous as the sycamores of the foothills. ²⁸Solomon's horses were imported from Cilicia, where the king's agents purchased them. ²⁹A chariot imported from Egypt cost six hundred shekels, a horse one hundred and fifty shekels; they were exported at these rates to all the Hittite and Aramean kings.

---

† 9, 26: *Ezion-geber . . . Edom:* the first mention of maritime commerce in the Israelite kingdom (to which the land of Edom was subject after its conquest by King David; cf 2 Sm 8, 14).

10, 1: *Queen of Sheba:* women rulers among the Arabs are recorded in eighth-century-B. C. Assyrian inscriptions. Sheba was for centuries the leading principality in what is now the Yemen.

10, 11f: *Cabinet:* an unknown wood, probably fragrant.

10, 22: *Tarshish ships:* large, strong vessels for long voyages. *Tarshish* was the ancient Tartessus, a Phoenician colony in southern Spain, the name of which denotes a center for smelting metallic ore.

---

* 10/1: 2 Chr 9, 1; Mt 12, 42;   16: 14, 26.
  Lk 11, 31.   26: 2 Chr 1, 14.

The Sins of Solomon

11 [1]*†KING Solomon loved many foreign women besides the daughter of Pharaoh (Moabites, Ammonites, Edomites, Sidonians, and Hittites), [2]*from nations with which the LORD had forbidden the Israelites to intermarry, "because," he said, "they will turn your hearts to their gods." But Solomon fell in love with them. [3]He had seven hundred wives of princely rank and three hundred concubines, and his wives turned his heart.

[4]When Solomon was old his wives had turned his heart to strange gods, and his heart was not entirely with the LORD, his God, as the heart of his father David had been. [5]By adoring Astarte, the goddess of the Sidonians, and Milcom, the idol of the Ammonites, [6]Solomon did evil in the sight of the LORD; he did not follow him unreservedly as his father David had done. [7]Solomon then built a high place to Chemosh, the idol of Moab, and to Molech, the idol of the Ammonites, on the hill opposite Jerusalem. [8]He did the same for all his foreign wives who burned incense and sacrificed to their gods. [9]*The LORD, therefore, became angry with Solomon, because his heart was turned away from the LORD, the God of Israel, who had appeared to him twice [10](for though the LORD had forbidden him this very act of following strange gods, Solomon had not obeyed him).

[11]So the LORD said to Solomon: "Since this is what you want, and you have not kept my covenant and my statutes which I enjoined on you, I will deprive you of the kingdom and give it to your servant. [12]*I will not do this during your lifetime, however, for the sake of your father David; it is your son whom I will deprive. [13]Nor will I take away the whole kingdom. I will leave your son one tribe for the sake of my servant David and of Jerusalem, which I have chosen."

[14]The LORD then raised up an adversary to Solomon: Hadad the Edomite, who was of the royal line in Edom. [15]*Earlier, when David had conquered Edom, Joab, the general of the army, while going to bury the slain, put to death every male in Edom. [16]Joab and all Israel remained there six months until they had killed off every male in Edom. [17]Meanwhile, Hadad, who was only a boy, fled toward Egypt with some Edomite servants of his father. [18]They left Midian and passing through Paran, where they picked up additional men, they went into Egypt to Pharaoh, king of Egypt, who gave Hadad a house, appointed him rations, and assigned him land.

[19]Hadad won great favor with Pharaoh, so that he gave him in marriage the sister of Queen Tahpenes, his own wife. [20]Tahpenes' sister bore Hadad a son, Genubath. After his weaning, the queen kept him in Pharaoh's palace, where he then lived with Pharaoh's own sons. [21]When Hadad in Egypt heard that David rested with his ancestors and that Joab, the general of the army, was dead, he said to Pharaoh, "Give me leave to return to my own country." [22]Pharaoh said to him, "What do you lack with me, that you are seeking to return to your own country?" "Nothing," he said, "but please let me go!"

[23]God raised up against Solomon another adversary, in Rezon, the son of Eliada, who had fled from his lord, Hadadezer, king of Zobah, [24]when David defeated them with slaughter. Rezon gathered men about him and became leader of a band, went to Damascus, settled there, and became king in Damascus. [25]He was an enemy of Israel as long as Solomon lived; this added to the harm done by Hadad, who made a rift in Israel by becoming king over Edom.

[26]*Solomon's servant Jeroboam, son of Nebat, an Ephraimite from Zeredah with a widowed mother, Zeruah, also rebelled against the king. [27]This is why he rebelled. King Solomon was building Millo, closing up the breach of his father's City of David. [28]Jeroboam was a man of means, and when Solomon saw that he was also an industrious young man, he put him in charge of the entire labor force of the house of Joseph. [29]*At that time Jeroboam left Jerusalem, and the prophet Ahijah the Shilonite met him on the road. The two were alone in the area, and the prophet was wearing a new cloak. [30]Ahijah took off his new cloak, tore it into twelve pieces, [31]*and said to Jeroboam:

"Take ten pieces for yourself; the LORD, the God of Israel, says: 'I will tear away the kingdom from Solomon's grasp and will give you ten of the tribes. [32]One tribe shall remain to him for the sake of David my servant, and of Jerusalem, the city I have chosen out of all the tribes of Israel. [33]The ten I will give you because he has forsaken me and has worshiped Astarte, goddess of the Sidonians, Chemosh, god of Moab, and Milcom, god of the Ammonites; he has not followed my ways or done what is pleasing to me according to my statutes and my decrees, as his father David did. [34]Yet I will not take any of the kingdom from Solomon himself, but will keep him a prince as long as he lives for the sake of my servant David, whom I chose, who kept my commandments and statutes. [35]But I will take the kingdom from his son and will give it to you—that is, the ten tribes. [36]I will give his son one tribe, that my servant David may always have a lamp before me in

---

† 11, 1-3.7: The glorious rise of Solomon, his piety and wisdom, administrative skill and wealth, the extension of his kingdom, his prestige among neighboring rulers, his reign of peace, above all his friendship with God—these are now eclipsed by his sins of intermarriage with great numbers of pagan wives and the consequent forbidden worship of their gods (Ex 34, 11-16; Dt 7, 1-5). His construction of temples in their honor merited the punishment of loss of a united kingdom to his posterity, and the opposition of adversaries to himself (vv 14.23-37). Hadad the Edomite rebelled against Solomon at the beginning of his reign (v 25). Rezon of Syria established a new kingdom in Damascus; Jeroboam of Israel constituted the greatest threat because of his revolt from within. This threefold threat culminated in the breakup of Solomon's kingdom.

✳

11/1: Dt 17, 17; Sir 47, 19f.   15: 2 Sm 8, 14.
  2: Ex 34, 16.   26: 2 Chr 13, 6.
  9: 9, 2.   29: 14, 2; 2 Chr 10, 15.
  12: 12, 15.   31: 12, 15.

Jerusalem, the city in which I choose to be honored. **37**I will take you; you shall reign over all that you desire and shall become king of Israel. **38**If, then, you heed all that I command you, follow my ways, and please me by keeping my statutes and my commandments like my servant David, I will be with you. I will establish for you, as I did for David, a lasting dynasty; I will give Israel to you. **39**I will punish David's line for this, but not forever.'"

40When Solomon tried to have Jeroboam killed for his rebellion, he escaped to King Shishak, in Egypt, where he remained until Solomon's death.

41The rest of the acts of Solomon, with all his deeds and his wisdom, are recorded in the book of the chronicles of Solomon. **42**The time that Solomon reigned in Jerusalem over all Israel was forty years. **43**Solomon rested with his ancestors; he was buried in his father's City of David, and his son Rehoboam succeeded him as king.

II: JUDAH AND ISRAEL TO THE TIME OF AHAB

Secession of Israel

12 **1**†REHOBOAM WENT TO SHECHEM, where all Israel had come to proclaim him king. **3**They said to Rehoboam: **4**"Your father put on us a heavy yoke. If you now lighten the harsh service and the heavy yoke your father imposed on us, we will serve you." **5**"Come back to me in three days," he answered them. When the people had departed, **6**King Rehoboam consulted the elders who had been in his father's service while he was alive, and asked, "What answer do you advise me to give this people?" **7**They replied, "If today you will be the servant of this people and submit to them, giving them a favorable answer, they will be your servants forever." **8**But he ignored the advice the elders had given him, and consulted the young men who had grown up with him and were in his service. **9**He said to them, "What answer do you advise me to give this people, who have asked me to lighten the yoke my father imposed on them?" **10**The young men who had grown up with him replied, "This is what you must say to this people who have asked you to lighten the yoke your father put on them: 'My little finger is thicker than my father's body. **11**Whereas my father put a heavy yoke on you, I will make it heavier. My father beat you with whips, but I will beat you with scorpions.'"

12On the third day all Israel came back to King Rehoboam, as he had instructed them to do. **13**Ignoring the advice the elders had given him, the king gave the people a harsh answer. **14**He said to them, as the young men had advised: "My father put on you a heavy yoke, but I will make it heavier. My father beat

you with whips, but I will beat you with scorpions." **15***The king did not listen to the people, for the LORD brought this about to fulfill the prophecy he had uttered to Jeroboam, son of Nebat, through Ahijah the Shilonite.

16†When all Israel saw that the king did not listen to them, the people answered the king:

"What share have we in David?
We have no heritage in the son of Jesse.
To your tents, O Israel!
Now look to your own house, David."

So Israel went off to their tents, **17**but Rehoboam reigned over the Israelites who lived in the cities of Judah. **18**King Rehoboam then sent out Adoram, superintendent of the forced labor, but all Israel stoned him to death. Rehoboam managed to mount his chariot to flee to Jerusalem, **19**and Israel went into rebellion against David's house to this day. **2**Jeroboam, son of Nebat, who was still in Egypt, where he had fled from King Solomon, returned from Egypt as soon as he learned this. **20**When all Israel heard that Jeroboam had returned, they summoned him to an assembly and made him king over all Israel. None remained loyal to David's house except the tribe of Judah alone.

21On his arrival in Jerusalem, Rehoboam gathered together all the house of Judah and the tribe of Benjamin—one hundred eighty thousand seasoned warriors—to fight against the house of Israel, to restore the kingdom to Rehoboam, son of Solomon. **22***However, the LORD spoke to Shemaiah, a man of God: **23**"Say to Rehoboam, son of Solomon, king of Judah, and to the house of Judah and to Benjamin, and to the rest of the people: **24**"Thus says the LORD: You must not march out to fight against your brother Israelites. Let every man return home, for I have brought this about.'" They accepted this message of the LORD and gave up the expedition accordingly.

25Jeroboam built up Shechem in the hill country of Ephraim and lived there. Then he left it and built up Penuel.

Religious Rebellion

26†Jeroboam thought to himself: "The kingdom will return to David's house. **27**If now this people go up to offer sacrifices in the temple of the LORD in Jerusalem,

---

† 12, 1: *Shechem:* chief city of the northern tribes, where a covenant of fidelity had previously been made between the Lord and his people and a stone of witness had been erected in memory of the event (Jos 24, 25ff).

12, 16: *What share have we in David:* even in David's time the northern tribes seemed ready to withdraw from Judah (2 Sm 20, 1). The unreasonable attitude of Rehoboam toward them intensified the discontent caused by the oppression of Solomon (v 4) and thus precipitated the establishment of a rival monarchy (v 20).

12, 26-32: *Jeroboam* feared reunification of the divided kingdom through worship in the single temple in Jerusalem. To prevent this he encouraged shrines on the high places, and appointed false priests to supplement those of levitical descent. The golden bullocks he installed in two of his sanctuaries, the hearts of this people will return to their master, Rehoboam, king of Judah, and they will kill me." **28***After taking counsel, the king made two calves of gold and said to the people: "You have been going up to Jerusalem long enough. Here is your God, O Israel, who brought you up from the land of Egypt." **29†**And he put one in Bethel, the other in Dan. **30**This led to sin, because the people frequented these calves in Bethel and in Dan. **31***He also built temples on the high places and made priests from among the people who were not Levites. **32**Jeroboam established a feast in the eighth month on the fifteenth day of the month to duplicate in Bethel the pilgrimage feast of Judah, with sacrifices to the calves he had made; and he stationed in Bethel priests of the high places he had built.

Message of the Prophet from Judah

33Jeroboam ascended the altar he built in Bethel on the fifteenth day of the eighth month, the month in which he arbitrarily chose to establish a feast for the Israelites; he was going to offer sacrifice.

13 **1**A MAN of God came from Judah to Bethel by the word of the LORD, while Jeroboam was standing at the altar to offer sacrifice. **2***He cried out against the altar the word of the LORD: "O altar, altar, the LORD says, 'A child shall be born to the house of David, Josiah by name, who shall slaughter upon you the priests of the high places who offer sacrifice upon you, and he shall burn human bones upon you.'" **3**He gave a sign that same day and said: "This is the sign that the LORD has spoken: The altar shall break up and the ashes on it shall be strewn about."

4When King Jeroboam heard what the man of God was crying out against the altar, he stretched forth his hand from the altar and said, "Seize him!" But the hand he stretched forth against him withered, so that he could not draw it back. **5**Moreover, the altar broke up and the ashes from it were strewn about—the sign the man of God had given as the word of the LORD. **6**Then the king appealed to the man of God. "Entreat the LORD, your God," he said, "and intercede for me that I may be able to withdraw my hand." So the man of God entreated the LORD, and the king recovered the normal use of his hand. **7**"Come home with me for some refreshment," the king invited the man of God, "and I will give you a present." **8**"If you gave me half your kingdom," the man of God said to the king, "I would not go with you, nor eat bread or drink water in this place. **9**For I was instructed by the word of the LORD not to eat bread or drink water and not to return by the way I came." **10**So he departed by another road and did not go back the way he had come to Bethel.

11There was an old prophet living in the city, whose sons came and told him all that the man of God had done that day in Bethel. When they repeated to their father the words he had spoken to the king, **12**the fa-ther asked them, "Which way did he go?" And his sons pointed out to him the road taken by the man of God who had come from Judah. **13**Then he said to his sons, "Saddle the ass for me." When they had saddled it, he mounted **14**and followed the man of God, whom he found seated under a terebinth. When he asked him, "Are you the man of God who came from Judah?" he answered, "Yes." **15**Then he said, "Come home with me and have some bread." **16**"I cannot go back with you, and I cannot eat bread or drink water with you in this place," he answered, **17**"for I was told by the word of the LORD neither to eat bread nor drink water here, and not to go back the way I came." **18**But he said to him, "I, too, am a prophet like you, and an angel told me in the word of the LORD to bring you back with me to my house and to have you eat bread and drink water." He was lying to him, however.

19So he went back with him, and ate bread and drank water in his house. **20**But while they were sitting at table, the LORD spoke to the prophet who had brought him back, **21**and he cried out to the man of God who had come from Judah: "The LORD says, 'Because you rebelled against the command of the LORD and did not keep the command which the LORD, your God, gave you, **22**but returned and ate bread and drank water in the place where he told you to do neither, your corpse shall not be brought to the grave of your ancestors.'"

23After he had eaten bread and drunk water, the ass was saddled for him, and he again **24**set out. But a lion met him on the road, and killed him. His corpse lay sprawled on the road, and the ass remained standing by it, and so did the lion. **25**Some passers-by saw the body lying in the road, with the lion standing beside it, and carried the news to the city where the old prophet lived. **26**On hearing it, the prophet who had brought him back from his journey said: "It is the man of God who rebelled against the command of the LORD. He has delivered him to a lion, which mangled and killed him, as the LORD predicted to him." **27**Then he said to his sons, "Saddle the ass for me." When they had saddled it, **28**he went off and found the body lying in the road with the ass and the lion standing beside it. The lion had not eaten the body nor had it harmed the ass. **29**The prophet lifted up the body of the man of God and put it on the ass, and brought it back to the city to mourn over it and to bury it. **30**He laid the man's body in his own grave, and they mourned over it: "Alas, my brother!" **31**After he had buried him, he said to his sons, "When I die, bury me in the grave where the man of God is buried. Lay my remains beside his. **32**For the word of the LORD which he proclaimed

---

† though probably intended as bearers of the invisible Divine Majesty, quickly became occasions for idolatry. Thus Jeroboam caused Israel to sin, and sealed his doom and that of his royal house (13, 34; 14, 7-14).

12, 29: *Bethel* and *Dan:* at the southern and northern boundaries of the separate kingdom of Israel, where sanctuaries had existed in the past (Gn 12, 8; 13, 3; 18, 10-22; 25, 1-16; Jgs 18, 1-31).

---

* 28: Tb 1, 5; Ex 32, 8.   13/2: 2 Kgs 23, 16.
31: 2 Chr 11, 15.

against the altar in Bethel and against all the shrines on the high places in the cities of Samaria shall certainly come to pass."

33Jeroboam did not give up his evil ways after this event, but again made priests for the high places from among the common people. Whoever desired it was consecrated and became a priest of the high places. 34This was a sin on the part of the house of Jeroboam for which it was to be cut off and destroyed from the earth.

Death of Abijah

14 1AT that time Abijah, son of Jeroboam, took sick. 2*So Jeroboam said to his wife, "Get ready and disguise yourself so that none will recognize you as Jeroboam's wife. Then go to Shiloh, where you will find the prophet Ahijah. It was he who predicted my reign over this people. 3Take along ten loaves, some cakes, and a jar of preserves, and go to him. He will tell you what will happen to the child." 4The wife of Jeroboam obeyed. She made the journey to Shiloh and entered the house of Ahijah who could not see because age had dimmed his sight.

5The LORD had said to Ahijah: "Jeroboam's wife is coming to consult you about her son, for he is sick. This is what you must tell her. When she comes, she will be in disguise." 6So Ahijah, hearing the sound of her footsteps as she entered the door, said, "Come in, wife of Jeroboam. Why are you in disguise? I have been commissioned to give you bitter news. 7Go, tell Jeroboam, 'This is what the LORD, the God of Israel, says: I exalted you from among the people and made you ruler of my people Israel. 8I deprived the house of David of the kingdom and gave it to you. Yet you have not been like my servant David, who kept my commandments and followed me with his whole heart, doing only what pleased me. 9You have done worse than all who preceded you: you have gone and made for yourself strange gods and molten images to provoke me; but me you have cast behind your back. 10*Therefore, I am bringing evil upon the house of Jeroboam: I will cut off every male in Jeroboam's line, whether slave or freeman in Israel, and will burn up the house of Jeroboam completely, as though dung were being burned. 11*When one of Jeroboam's line dies in the city, dogs will devour him; when one of them dies in the field, he will be devoured by the birds of the sky. For the LORD has spoken!' 12So leave; go home! As you step inside the city, the child will die, 13and all Israel will mourn him and bury him, for he alone of Jeroboam's line will be laid in the grave, since in him alone of Jeroboam's house has something pleasing to the LORD, the God of Israel, been found. 14Today, at this very moment, the LORD will raise up for himself a king of Israel who will destroy the house of Jeroboam. 15The LORD will strike Israel like a reed tossed about in the water and will pluck out Israel from this good land which he gave their fathers, scattering them beyond the River, because they made sacred poles for themselves and thus provoked the LORD. 16He will give up Israel because of the sins Jeroboam has committed and caused Israel to commit."

17So Jeroboam's wife started back; when she reached Tirzah and crossed the threshold of her house, the child died. 18He was buried with all Israel mourning him, as the LORD had prophesied through his servant the prophet Ahijah.

19The rest of the acts of Jeroboam, with his warfare and his reign, are recorded in the book of the chronicles of the kings of Israel. 20The length of Jeroboam's reign was twenty-two years. He rested with his ancestors, and his son Nadab succeeded him as king.

Reign of Rehoboam

21*Rehoboam, son of Solomon, reigned in Judah. He was forty-one years old when he became king, and he reigned seventeen years in Jerusalem, the city in which, out of all the tribes of Israel, the LORD chose to be honored. His mother was the Ammonite named Naamah.

22Judah did evil in the sight of the LORD, and by their sins angered him even more than their fathers had done. 23They, too, built for themselves high places, pillars, and sacred poles, upon every high hill and under every green tree. 24There were also cult prostitutes in the land. Judah imitated all the abominable practices of the nations whom the LORD had cleared out of the Israelites' way.

25†In the fifth year of King Rehoboam, Shishak, king of Egypt, attacked Jerusalem. 26*He took everything, including the treasures of the temple of the LORD and those of the royal palace, as well as all the gold shields made under Solomon. 27To replace them, King Rehoboam had bronze shields made, which he entrusted to the officers of the guard on duty at the entrance of the royal palace. 28Whenever the king visited the temple of the LORD, those on duty would carry the shields, and then return them to the guardroom.

29The rest of the acts of Rehoboam, with all that he did, are recorded in the book of the chronicles of the kings of Judah. 30There was constant warfare between Rehoboam and Jeroboam. 31Rehoboam rested with his ancestors; he was buried with them in the City of David. His mother was the Ammonite named Naamah. His son Abijam succeeded him as king.

---

† 14, 25: *In the fifth year . . . Shishak, king of Egypt, attacked Jerusalem:* c. 926 B. C. According to 2 Chr 12, 1-12, the repentance of King Rehoboam and of the princes of Israel after the warning of the prophet Shemaiah diverted the actual attack on Jerusalem. Shishak, however, *carried off the treasures of the temple of the Lord and of the king's palace* (2 Chr 12, 9). A bas-relief of this Pharaoh in the temple of Amon at Karnak commemorates his conquest of some hundred and fifty Palestinian and Transjordanian cities and towns.

14/2: 11, 29.
10: 15, 29.
11: 16, 4.

21: 2 Chr 12, 13.
26: 10, 16.

Reign of Abijam

15 ¹*IN the eighteenth year of King Jeroboam, son of Nebat, Abijam became king of Judah; ²he reigned three years in Jerusalem. His mother's name was Maacah, daughter of Abishalom. ³He imitated all the sins his father had committed before him, and his heart was not entirely with the Lord, his God, like the heart of his grandfather David. ⁴Yet for David's sake the Lord, his God, gave him a lamp in Jerusalem, raising up his son after him and permitting Jerusalem to endure; ⁵*because David had pleased the Lord and did not disobey any of his commands as long as he lived, except in the case of Uriah the Hittite.

⁷*The rest of Abijam's acts, with all that he did, are written in the book of the chronicles of the kings of Judah. ⁶There was war between Abijam and Jeroboam. ⁸Abijam rested with his ancestors; he was buried in the City of David, and his son Asa succeeded him as king.

Reign of Asa

⁹In the twentieth year of Jeroboam, king of Israel, Asa, king of Judah, began to reign; ¹⁰he reigned forty-one years in Jerusalem. His grandmother's name was Maacah, daughter of Abishalom. ¹¹Asa pleased the Lord like his forefather David, ¹²banishing the temple prostitutes from the land and removing all the idols his father had made. ¹³He also deposed his grandmother Maacah from her position as queen mother, because she had made an outrageous object for Asherah. Asa cut down this object and burned it in the Kidron Valley. ¹⁴The high places did not disappear; yet Asa's heart was entirely with the Lord as long as he lived. ¹⁵He brought into the temple of the Lord his father's and his own votive offerings of silver, gold, and various utensils.

¹⁶There was war between Asa and Baasha, king of Israel, as long as they both reigned. ¹⁷*Baasha, king of Israel, attacked Judah and fortified Ramah to prevent communication with Asa, king of Judah. ¹⁸†Asa then took all the silver and gold remaining in the treasuries of the temple of the Lord and of the royal palace. Entrusting them to his ministers, King Asa sent them to Ben-hadad, son of Tabrimmon, son of Hezion, king of Aram, resident in Damascus. He said: ¹⁹"There is a treaty between you and me, as there was between your father and my father. I am sending you a present of silver and gold. Go, break your treaty with Baasha, king of Israel, that he may withdraw from me." ²⁰Ben-hadad agreed with King Asa and sent the leaders of his troops against the cities of Israel. They attacked Ijon, Dan, Abel-beth-maacah, and all Chinnereth, besides all the land of Naphtali. ²¹When Baasha heard of

it, he left off fortifying Ramah, and stayed in Tirzah. ²²Then King Asa summoned all Judah without exception, and they carried away the stones and beams with which Baasha was fortifying Ramah. With them King Asa built Geba of Benjamin and Mizpeh.

²³The rest of the acts of Asa, with all his valor and accomplishments, and the cities he built, are written in the book of the chronicles of the kings of Judah. In his old age, Asa had an infirmity in his feet. ²⁴*He rested with his ancestors; he was buried in his forefather's City of David, and his son Jehoshaphat succeeded him as king.

Reign of Nadab

²⁵In the second year of Asa, king of Judah, Nadab, son of Jeroboam, became king of Israel; he reigned over Israel two years. ²⁶He did evil in the Lord's sight, imitating his father's conduct and the sin which he had caused Israel to commit. ²⁷Baasha, son of Ahijah, of the house of Issachar, plotted against him and struck him down at Gibbethon of the Philistines, which Nadab and all Israel were besieging. ²⁸Baasha killed him in the third year of Asa, king of Judah, and reigned in his stead. ²⁹*Once he was king, he killed off the entire house of Jeroboam, not leaving a single soul to Jeroboam but destroying him utterly, according to the warning which the Lord had pronounced through his servant, Ahijah the Shilonite, ³⁰because of the sins Jeroboam committed and caused Israel to commit, by which he provoked the Lord, the God of Israel, to anger.

³¹The rest of the acts of Nadab, with all that he did, are written in the book of the chronicles of the kings of Israel. ³²[There was war between Asa and Baasha, king of Israel, as long as they lived.]

Reign of Baasha

³³In the third year of Asa, king of Judah, Baasha, son of Ahijah, began his twenty-four-year reign over Israel in Tirzah. ³⁴He did evil in the Lord's sight, imitating the conduct of Jeroboam and the sin he had caused Israel to commit.

16 ¹THE LORD spoke against Baasha to Jehu, son of Hanani, and said: ²"Inasmuch as I lifted you up from the dust and made you ruler of my people Israel, but you have imitated the conduct of Jeroboam and have caused my people Israel to sin, provoking me to anger by their sins, ³*I will destroy you, Baasha, and your house; ⁴*I will make your house like that of Jeroboam, son of Nebat. If anyone of Baasha's line dies in the city, dogs shall devour him; if he dies in the field, he shall be devoured by the birds of the sky."

⁵*The rest of the acts of Baasha, with all his valor and accomplishments, are written in the book of the

---

✱

15/1: 2 Chr 13, 1f.   29: 14, 10; 21, 22.
    5: 2 Sm 11, 4.   16/3: 21, 22.
    7: 2 Chr 13, 2.   4: 14, 11.
  17: 2 Chr 16, 1.   5: 2 Chr 16, 1.
  24: 2 Chr 17, 1.

---

† 15, 18: *Ben-hadad . . . king of Aram:* Ben-hadad I, third successor of Rezon, who had thrown off the yoke of the Israelites during the reign of Solomon and become king of Aram (11, 23f).

chronicles of the kings of Israel. ⁶Baasha rested with his ancestors; he was buried in Tirzah, and his son Elah succeeded him as king. ⁷[Through the prophet Jehu, son of Hanani, the LORD had threatened Baasha and his house, because of all the evil Baasha did in the sight of the LORD, provoking him to anger by his evil deeds, so that he became like the house of Jeroboam; and because he killed Nadab.]

Reign of Elah

⁸In the twenty-sixth year of Asa, king of Judah, Elah, son of Baasha, began his two-year reign over Israel in Tirzah. ⁹His servant Zimri, commander of half his chariots, plotted against him. As he was in Tirzah, drinking to excess in the house of Arza, superintendent of his palace in Tirzah, ¹⁰*Zimri entered; he struck and killed him in the twenty-seventh year of Asa, king of Judah, and reigned in his place. ¹¹Once he was seated on the royal throne, he killed off the whole house of Baasha, not sparing a single male relative or friend of his. ¹²Zimri destroyed the entire house of Baasha, as the LORD had prophesied to Baasha through the prophet Jehu, ¹³because of all the sins which Baasha and his son Elah committed and caused Israel to commit, provoking the LORD, the God of Israel, to anger by their idols.

¹⁴The rest of the acts of Elah, with all that he did, are written in the book of the chronicles of the kings of Israel.

Reign of Zimri

¹⁵In the twenty-seventh year of Asa, king of Judah, Zimri reigned seven days in Tirzah. The army was besieging Gibbethon of the Philistines ¹⁶when they heard that Zimri had formed a conspiracy and had killed the king. So that day in the camp all Israel proclaimed Omri, general of the army, king of Israel. ¹⁷Omri marched up from Gibbethon, accompanied by all Israel, and laid siege to Tirzah. ¹⁸When Zimri saw the city was captured, he entered the citadel of the royal palace and burned down the palace over him. He died ¹⁹because of the sins he had committed, doing evil in the sight of the LORD by imitating the sinful conduct of Jeroboam, thus causing Israel to sin.

²⁰The rest of the acts of Zimri, with the conspiracy he carried out, are written in the book of the chronicles of the kings of Israel.

²¹At that time the people of Israel were divided, half following Tibni, son of Ginath, to make him king, and half for Omri. ²²The partisans of Omri prevailed over those of Tibni, son of Ginath. Tibni died and Omri became king.

Reign of Omri

²³In the thirty-first year of Asa, king of Judah, Omri became king; he reigned over Israel twelve years, the first six of them in Tirzah. ²⁴He then bought the hill of Samaria from Shemer for two silver talents and built upon the hill, naming the city he built Samaria after Shemer, the former owner. ²⁵But Omri did evil in the LORD's sight beyond any of his predecessors. ²⁶He closely imitated the sinful conduct of Jeroboam, son of Nebat, causing Israel to sin and to provoke the LORD, the God of Israel, to anger by their idols.

²⁷The rest of the acts of Omri, with all his valor and accomplishments, are written in the book of the chronicles of the kings of Israel. ²⁸Omri rested with his ancestors; he was buried in Samaria, and his son Ahab succeeded him as king.

Reign of Ahab

²⁹In the thirty-eighth year of Asa, king of Judah, Ahab, son of Omri, became king of Israel; he reigned over Israel in Samaria for twenty-two years. ³⁰Ahab, son of Omri, did evil in the sight of the LORD more than any of his predecessors. ³¹It was not enough for him to imitate the sins of Jeroboam, son of Nebat. He even married Jezebel, daughter of Ethbaal, king of the Sidonians, and went over to the veneration and worship of Baal. ³²Ahab erected an altar to Baal in the temple of Baal which he built in Samaria, ³³and also made a sacred pole. He did more to anger the LORD, the God of Israel, than any of the kings of Israel before him.

³⁴*During his reign, Hiel from Bethel rebuilt Jericho. He lost his first-born son, Abiram, when he laid the foundation, and his youngest son, Segub, when he set up the gates, as the LORD had foretold through Joshua, son of Nun.

III: STORIES OF THE PROPHETS

Drought Predicted by Elijah

17 ¹*†ELIJAH THE TISHBITE, from Tishbe in Gilead, said to Ahab: "As the LORD, the God of Israel, lives, whom I serve, during these years there shall be no dew or rain except at my word." ²The LORD then said to Elijah: ³"Leave here, go east and hide in the Wadi Cherith, east of the Jordan. ⁴You shall drink of the stream, and I have commanded ravens to feed you there." ⁵So he left and did as the LORD had commanded. He went and remained by the Wadi Cherith, east of the Jordan. ⁶Ravens brought him bread and meat in the morning, and bread and meat in the evening, and he drank from the stream.

---

† 17, 1: *Elijah the Tishbite:* one of the most important figures in Old Testament history. As his name indicates ("Yahweh is my God"), Elijah was the successful leader in the struggle to preserve the knowledge and worship of Yahweh against the encroaching worship of Baal introduced into Israel by Jezebel, the Tyrian wife of Ahab. The Elijah cycle of narratives includes, besides the above struggle, miracle stories, denunciations of kings, and a preparation for the prophet's role as eschatological forerunner of the "great day of the Lord"; cf Mal 3, 23-24; Mt 17; 10-13; Lk 1, 17.

❖ 10: 2 Kgs 9, 31.　　　　17/1: Sir 48, 3; Jas 5, 17.
34: Jos 6, 26.

Elijah and the Widow

7After some time, however, the brook ran dry, because no rain had fallen in the land. **8**So the LORD said to him: **9**"Move on to Zarephath of Sidon and stay there. I have designated a widow there to provide for you." **10***He left and went to Zarephath. As he arrived at the entrance of the city, a widow was gathering sticks there; he called out to her, "Please bring me a small cupful of water to drink." **11**She left to get it, and he called out after her, "Please bring along a bit of bread." **12**"As the LORD, your God, lives," she answered, "I have nothing baked; there is only a handful of flour in my jar and a little oil in my jug. Just now I was collecting a couple of sticks, to go in and prepare something for myself and my son; when we have eaten it, we shall die." **13**"Do not be afraid," Elijah said to her. "Go and do as you propose. But first make me a little cake and bring it to me. Then you can prepare something for yourself and your son. **14**For the LORD, the God of Israel, says, 'The jar of flour shall not go empty, nor the jug of oil run dry, until the day when the LORD sends rain upon the earth.'" **15**She left and did as Elijah had said. She was able to eat for a year, and he and her son as well; **16**the jar of flour did not go empty, nor the jug of oil run dry, as the LORD had foretold through Elijah.

17Some time later the son of the mistress of the house fell sick, and his sickness grew more severe until he stopped breathing. **18**So she said to Elijah, "Why have you done this to me, O man of God? Have you come to me to call attention to my guilt and to kill my son?" **19**"Give me your son," Elijah said to her. Taking him from her lap, he carried him to the upper room where he was staying, and laid him on his own bed. **20**He called out to the LORD: "O LORD, my God, will you afflict even the widow with whom I am staying by killing her son?" **21**Then he stretched himself out upon the child three times and called out to the LORD: "O LORD, my God, let the life breath return to the body of this child." **22**The LORD heard the prayer of Elijah; the life breath returned to the child's body and he revived. **23**Taking the child, Elijah brought him down into the house from the upper room and gave him to his mother. "See!" Elijah said to her, "your son is alive." **24**"Now indeed I know that you are a man of God," the woman replied to Elijah. "The word of the LORD comes truly from your mouth."

Elijah and the Prophets of Baal

18 **1**LONG afterward, in the third year, the LORD spoke to Elijah. "Go, present yourself to Ahab," he said, "that I may send rain upon the earth." **2**So Elijah went to present himself to Ahab.

3Now the famine in Samaria was bitter, **4**and Ahab had summoned Obadiah, his vizier, who was a zealous follower of the LORD. When Jezebel was murdering the prophets of the LORD, Obadiah took a hundred prophets, hid them away fifty each in two caves, and supplied them with food and drink. **5**Ahab said to Obadiah, "Come, let us go through the land to all sources of water and to all the streams. We may find grass and save the horses and mules, so that we shall not have to slaughter any of the beasts." **6**Dividing the land to explore between them, Ahab went one way by himself, Obadiah another way by himself.

7As Obadiah was on his way, Elijah met him. Recognizing him, Obadiah fell prostrate and asked, "Is it you, my lord Elijah?" **8**"Yes," he answered. "Go tell your master, 'Elijah is here!'" **9**But Obadiah said, "What sin have I committed, that you are handing me over to Ahab to have me killed? **10**As the LORD, your God, lives, there is no nation or kingdom where my master has not sent in search of you. When they replied, 'He is not here,' he made each kingdom and nation swear they could not find you. **11**And now you say, 'Go tell your master: Elijah is here!' **12**After I leave you, the spirit of the LORD will carry you to some place I do not know, and when I go to inform Ahab and he does not find you, he will kill me. Your servant has revered the LORD from his youth. **13**Have you not been told, my lord, what I did when Jezebel was murdering the prophets of the LORD—that I hid a hundred of the prophets of the LORD, fifty each in two caves, and supplied them with food and drink? **14**And now you say, 'Go tell your master: Elijah is here!' He will kill me!" **15**Elijah answered, "As the LORD of hosts lives, whom I serve, I will present myself to him today."

16So Obadiah went to meet Ahab and informed him. Ahab came to meet Elijah, **17**and when he saw Elijah, said to him, "Is it you, you disturber of Israel?" **18**"It is not I who disturb Israel," he answered, "but you and your family, by forsaking the commands of the LORD and following the Baals. **19**Now summon all Israel to me on Mount Carmel, as well as the four hundred and fifty prophets of Baal and the four hundred prophets of Asherah who eat at Jezebel's table." **20**So Ahab sent to all the Israelites and had the prophets assemble on Mount Carmel.

21Elijah appealed to all the people and said, "How long will you straddle the issue? If the LORD is God, follow him; if Baal, follow him." The people, however, did not answer him. **22**So Elijah said to the people, "I am the only surviving prophet of the LORD, and there are four hundred and fifty prophets of Baal. **23**Give us two young bulls. Let them choose one, cut it into pieces, and place it on the wood, but start no fire. I shall prepare the other and place it on the wood, but shall start no fire. **24**You shall call on your gods, and I will call on the LORD. The God who answers with fire is God." All the people answered, "Agreed!"

25Elijah then said to the prophets of Baal, "Choose one young bull and prepare it first, for there are more of you. Call upon your gods, but do not start the fire." **26**Taking the young bull that was turned over to them, they prepared it and called on Baal from morning to noon, saying, "Answer us, Baal!" But there was no sound, and no one answering. And they hopped around the altar they had prepared. ²⁷When it was noon, Elijah taunted them: "Call louder, for he is a god and may be meditating, or may have retired, or may be on a journey. Perhaps he is asleep and must be awakened." ²⁸They called out louder and slashed themselves with swords and spears, as was their custom, until blood gushed over them. ²⁹Noon passed and they remained in a prophetic state until the time for offering sacrifice. But there was not a sound; no one answered, and no one was listening.

³⁰Then Elijah said to all the people, "Come here to me." When they had done so, he repaired the altar of the LORD which had been destroyed. ³¹He took twelve stones, for the number of tribes of the sons of Jacob, to whom the LORD had said, "Your name shall be Israel." ³²He built an altar in honor of the LORD with the stones, and made a trench around the altar large enough for two seahs of grain. ³³When he had arranged the wood, he cut up the young bull and laid it on the wood. ³⁴"Fill four jars with water," he said, "and pour it over the holocaust and over the wood." "Do it again," he said, and they did it again. "Do it a third time," he said, and they did it a third time. ³⁵The water flowed around the altar, and the trench was filled with the water.

³⁶At the time for offering sacrifice, the prophet Elijah came forward and said, "LORD, God of Abraham, Isaac, and Israel, let it be known this day that you are God in Israel and that I am your servant and have done all these things by your command. ³⁷Answer me, LORD! Answer me, that this people may know that you, LORD, are God and that you have brought them back to their senses." ³⁸The LORD's fire came down and consumed the holocaust, wood, stones, and dust, and it lapped up the water in the trench. ³⁹Seeing this, all the people fell prostrate and said, "The LORD is God! The LORD is God!" ⁴⁰Then Elijah said to them, "Seize the prophets of Baal. Let none of them escape!" They were seized, and Elijah had them brought down to the brook Kishon and there he slit their throats.

⁴¹Elijah then said to Ahab, "Go up, eat and drink, for there is the sound of a heavy rain." ⁴²So Ahab went up to eat and drink, while Elijah climbed to the top of Carmel, crouched down to the earth, and put his head between his knees. ⁴³"Climb up and look out to sea," he directed his servant, who went up and looked, but reported, "There is nothing." Seven times he said, "Go, look again!" ⁴⁴And the seventh time the youth reported, "There is a cloud as small as a man's hand rising from the sea." Elijah said, "Go and say to Ahab, 'Harness up and leave the mountain before the rain stops you.'" ⁴⁵In a trice, the sky grew dark with clouds and wind, and a heavy rain fell. Ahab mounted his chariot and made for Jezreel. ⁴⁶But the hand of the LORD was on Elijah, who girded up his clothing and ran before Ahab as far as the approaches to Jezreel.

Flight to Horeb

19 ¹AHAB told Jezebel all that Elijah had done— that he had put all the prophets to the sword. ²Jezebel then sent a messenger to Elijah and said, "May the gods do thus and so to me if by this time tomorrow I have not done with your life what was done to each of them." ³Elijah was afraid and fled for his life, going to Beer-sheba of Judah. He left his servant there ⁴and went a day's journey into the desert, until he came to a broom tree and sat beneath it. He prayed for death: "This is enough, O LORD! Take my life, for I am no better than my fathers." ⁵He lay down and fell asleep under the broom tree, but then an angel touched him and ordered him to get up and eat. ⁶He looked and there at his head was a hearth cake and a jug of water. After he ate and drank, he lay down again, ⁷but the angel of the LORD came back a second time, touched him, and ordered, "Get up and eat, else the journey will be too long for you!" ⁸He got up, ate and drank; then strengthened by that food, he walked forty days and forty nights to the mountain of God, Horeb.

⁹There he came to a cave, where he took shelter. But the word of the LORD came to him, "Why are you here, Elijah?" ¹⁰He answered: "I have been most zealous for the LORD, the God of hosts, but the Israelites have forsaken your covenant, torn down your altars, and put your prophets to the sword. I alone am left, and they seek to take my life." ¹¹†Then the LORD said, "Go outside and stand on the mountain before the LORD; the LORD will be passing by." A strong and heavy wind was rending the mountains and crushing rocks before the LORD—but the LORD was not in the wind. After the wind there was an earthquake—but the LORD was not in the earthquake. ¹²After the earthquake there was fire—but the LORD was not in the fire. After the fire there was a tiny whispering sound. ¹³When he heard this, Elijah hid his face in his cloak and went and stood at the entrance of the cave. A voice said to him, "Elijah, why are you here?" ¹⁴*He replied, "I have been most zealous for the LORD, the God of hosts. But the Israelites have forsaken your covenant, torn down your altars, and put your prophets to the sword. I alone am left, and they seek to take my life." ¹⁵†"Go, take

---

† 19, 11ff: Compare these divine manifestations to Elijah with those to Moses (Ex 19, 1-23; 33, 21ff; 34, 5) on the same Mount Horeb (Sinai) (Dt 4, 10-15). Though various phenomena, such as wind, storms, earthquakes, fire (Ex 19, 18f), herald the divine presence, they do not constitute the presence itself which, like the *tiny whispering sound*, is imperceptible and bespeaks the spirituality of God. It was fitting that Elijah, whose mission it was to re-establish the covenant and restore the pure faith, should have returned to Horeb where the covenant was revealed to Moses and through him to the Israelite people (Ex 3, 1-4.17; 33, 18-34, 9). Moses and Elijah appeared with Christ at the time of his transfiguration (Mt 17, 1-9; Mk 9, 1-7; Lk 9, 28-36).

19, 15-17: Elijah himself carried out only the third of the commissions entrusted to him (vv 19-21); Elisha was deputed to perform the first in person (2 Kgs 8, 7-19), and the second through one of his followers (2 Kgs 9, 1-10).

---

the road back to the desert near Damascus," the LORD said to him. "When you arrive, you shall anoint Hazael as king of Aram. **16***Then you shall anoint Jehu, son of Nimshi, as king of Israel, and Elisha, son of Shaphat of Abel-meholah, as prophet to succeed you. **17**If anyone escapes the sword of Hazael, Jehu will kill him. If he escapes the sword of Jehu, Elisha will kill him. **18***Yet I will leave seven thousand men in Israel—all those who have not knelt to Baal or kissed him."

Call of Elisha

19†Elijah set out, and came upon Elisha, son of Shaphat, as he was plowing with twelve yoke of oxen; he was following the twelfth. Elijah went over to him and threw his cloak over him. **20**Elisha left the oxen, ran after Elijah, and said, "Please, let me kiss my father and mother goodbye, and I will follow you." "Go back!" Elijah answered. "Have I done anything to you?" **21**Elisha left him and, taking the yoke of oxen, slaughtered them; he used the plowing equipment for fuel to boil their flesh, and gave it to his people to eat. Then he left and followed Elijah as his attendant.

Ahab's Victories over Ben-hadad

20 **1**BEN-HADAD, king of Aram, gathered all his forces, and accompanied by thirty-two kings with horses and chariotry, proceeded to invest and attack Samaria. **2**He sent couriers to Ahab, king of Israel, within the city, **3**and said to him, "This is Ben-hadad's message: 'Your silver and gold are mine, and your wives and your promising sons are mine.'" **4**The king of Israel answered, "As you say, my lord king, I and all I have are yours." **5**But the couriers came again and said, "This is Ben-hadad's message: 'I sent you word to give me your silver and gold, your wives and your sons. **6**Now, however, at this time tomorrow I will send my servants to you, and they shall ransack your house and the houses of your servants. They shall seize and take away whatever they consider valuable.'"

7The king of Israel then summoned all the elders of the land and said: "Understand clearly that this man wants to ruin us. When he sent to me for my wives and sons, my silver and my gold, I did not refuse him." **8**All the elders and all the people said to him, "Do not listen. Do not give in." **9**Accordingly he directed the couriers of Ben-hadad, "Say to my lord the king, 'I will do all that you demanded of your servant the first time. But this I cannot do.'" The couriers left and reported this. **10**Ben-hadad then sent him the message, "May the gods do thus and so to me if there is enough dust in Samaria to make handfuls for all my followers." **11**The king of Israel replied, "Tell him, 'It is not for the man who is buckling his armor to boast as though he were taking it off.'" **12**Ben-hadad was drinking in the pavilions with the kings when he heard

this reply. "Prepare the assault," he commanded his servants; and they made ready to storm the city.

13Then a prophet came up to Ahab, king of Israel, and said: "The LORD says, 'Do you see all this huge army? When I deliver it up to you today, you will know that I am the LORD.'" **14**But Ahab asked, "Through whom will it be delivered up?" He answered, "The LORD says, 'Through the retainers of the governors of the provinces.'" Then Ahab asked, "Who is to attack?" He replied, "You are." **15**So Ahab called up the retainers of the governors of the provinces, two hundred thirty-two of them. Behind them he mustered all the Israelite soldiery, who numbered seven thousand. **16**They marched out at noon, while Ben-hadad was drinking heavily in the pavilions with the thirty-two kings who were his allies. **17**When the retainers of the governors of the provinces marched out first, Ben-hadad received word that some men had marched out of Samaria. **18**He answered, "Whether they have come out for peace or for war, in any case take them alive." **19**But when these had come out of the city—the soldiers of the governors of the provinces with the army following them **20**—each of them struck down his man. The Arameans fled with Israel pursuing them, while Ben-hadad, king of Aram, escaped on a chariot steed. **21**The king of Israel went out, took the horses and chariots, and inflicted a severe defeat on Aram.

22†Then the prophet went up to the king of Israel and said to him: "Go, regroup your forces. Mark well what you do, for at the beginning of the year the king of Aram will attack you." **23**On the other hand, the servants of the king of Aram said to him: "Their gods are gods of mountains. That is why they defeated us. But if we fight them on level ground, we shall be sure to defeat them. **24**This is what you must do: Take the kings from their posts and put prefects in their places. **25**Mobilize an army as large as the army that has deserted you, horse for horse, chariot for chariot. Let us fight them on level ground, and we shall surely defeat them." He took their advice and did this.

26At the beginning of the year, Ben-hadad mobilized Aram and went up to Aphek to fight against Israel. **27**The Israelites, too, were called to arms and supplied with provisions; then they went out to engage the foe. The Israelites, encamped opposite them, seemed like a couple of small flocks of goats, while Aram covered the countryside. **28**A man of God came up and said to the king of Israel: "The LORD says, 'Because Aram has said the LORD is a god of mountains, not a god of plains, I will deliver up to you all this large army, that you may know I am the LORD.'" **29**They were encamped opposite each other for seven days. On the

---

† 19, 19-21: Elijah's act of throwing his mantle over the shoulders of Elisha expressed the divine call to share the prophetic mission. Elisha's prompt response through destruction of his plow and oxen is an example of total obedience and detachment from his former manner of living in order to promote the glory of God.

20, 22: *At the beginning of the year:* in the spring.

❧   16: 2 Kgs 9, 2.   18: Rom 11, 4.

seventh day battle was joined, and the Israelites struck down one hundred thousand foot soldiers of Aram in one day. **30**The survivors, twenty-seven thousand of them, fled into the city of Aphek, and there the wall collapsed. Ben-hadad, too, fled, and took refuge within the city, in an inside room.

31His servants said to him: "We have heard that the kings of the land of Israel are merciful kings. Allow us, therefore, to garb ourselves in sackcloth, with cords around our heads, and go out to the king of Israel. Perhaps he will spare your life." **32**So they dressed in sackcloth girded at the waist, and wearing cords around their heads, they went to the king of Israel. "Your servant Ben-hadad pleads for his life," they said. "Is he still alive?" the king asked. "He is my brother." **33**Hearing this as a good omen, the men quickly took him at his word and said, "Ben-hadad is your brother." He answered, "Go and get him." When Ben-hadad came out to him, the king had him mount his chariot. **34**Ben-hadad said to him, "I will restore the cities which my father took from your father, and you may make yourself bazaars in Damascus, as my father did in Samaria." "On these terms," Ahab replied, "I will set you free." So he made an agreement with him and then set him free.

35One of the guild prophets was prompted by the LORD to say to his companion, "Strike me." But he refused to strike him. **36**Then he said to him, "Since you did not obey the voice of the LORD, a lion will kill you when you leave me." When they parted company, a lion came upon him and killed him. **37**The prophet met another man and said, "Strike me." The man struck him a blow and wounded him. **38**The prophet went on and waited for the king on the road, having disguised himself with a bandage over his eyes. **39**As the king was passing, he called out to the king and said: "Your servant went into the thick of the battle, and suddenly someone turned and brought me a man and said, 'Guard this man. If he is missing, you shall have to pay for his life with your life or pay out a talent of silver.' **40**But while your servant was looking here and there, the man disappeared." The king of Israel said to him, "That is your sentence. You have decided it yourself." **41**He immediately removed the bandage from his eyes, and the king of Israel recognized him as one of the prophets. **42***He said to him: "The LORD says, 'Because you have set free the man I doomed to destruction, your life shall pay for his life, your people for his people.'" **43**Disturbed and angry, the king of Israel went off homeward and entered Samaria.

Seizure of Naboth's Vineyard

21 **1**SOME time after this, as Naboth the Jezreelite had a vineyard in Jezreel next to the palace of Ahab, king of Samaria, **2**Ahab said to Naboth, "Give me your vineyard to be my vegetable garden, since it is close by, next to my house. I will give you a better vineyard in exchange, or, if you prefer, I will give you its value in money." **3**"The LORD forbid," Naboth answered him, "that I should give you my ancestral heritage." **4**Ahab went home disturbed and angry at the answer Naboth the Jezreelite had made to him: "I will not give you my ancestral heritage." Lying down on his bed, he turned away from food and would not eat.

5His wife Jezebel came to him and said to him, 'Why are you so angry that you will not eat?" **6**He answered her, "Because I spoke to Naboth the Jezreelite and said to him, 'Sell me your vineyard, or, if you prefer, I will give you a vineyard in exchange.' But he refused to let me have his vineyard." **7**"A fine ruler over Israel you are indeed!" his wife Jezebel said to him. "Get up. Eat and be cheerful. I will obtain the vineyard of Naboth the Jezreelite for you."

8So she wrote letters in Ahab's name and, having sealed them with his seal, sent them to the elders and to the nobles who lived in the same city with Naboth. **9**This is what she wrote in the letters: "Proclaim a fast and set Naboth at the head of the people. **10**Next, get two scoundrels to face him and accuse him of having cursed God and king. Then take him out and stone him to death." **11**His fellow citizens—the elders and the nobles who dwelt in his city—did as Jezebel had ordered them in writing, through the letters she had sent them. **12**They proclaimed a fast and placed Naboth at the head of the people. **13**Two scoundrels came in and confronted him with the accusation, "Naboth has cursed God and king." And they led him out of the city and stoned him to death. **14**Then they sent the information to Jezebel that Naboth had been stoned to death.

15When Jezebel learned that Naboth had been stoned to death, she said to Ahab, "Go on, take possession of the vineyard of Naboth the Jezreelite which he refused to sell you, because Naboth is not alive, but dead." **16**On hearing that Naboth was dead, Ahab started off on his way down to the vineyard of Naboth the Jezreelite, to take possession of it.

17But the LORD said to Elijah the Tishbite: **18**"Start down to meet Ahab, king of Israel, who rules in Samaria. He will be in the vineyard of Naboth, of which he has come to take possession. **19***†This is what you shall tell him, 'The LORD says: After murdering, do you also take possession? For this, the LORD says: In the place where the dogs licked up the blood of Naboth, the dogs shall lick up your blood, too.'" **20**†"Have you

---

† 21, 19: The response of Ahab to this divine judgment is described in v 27, and the consequences are given in vv 28-29, and in 2 Kgs 9, 21-26.

21, 20-26: In these verses the Judean editor of the Books of Kings substitutes, for the message of Elijah prepared for in v 19, a sweeping and definitive judgment against the whole family of Ahab in the same terms as were used against the families of Jeroboam I (14, 9-11) and Baasha (16, 2-4). This judgment is the fruit of later theological reflection; it is not occasioned directly by the crime against Naboth, but by the idolatry of Ahab and Jezebel. The judgment on Jezebel herself (v 23) may have been uttered by Elijah during the Naboth episode; it finds its

---

found me out, my enemy?" Ahab said to Elijah. "Yes," he answered. "Because you have given yourself up to doing evil in the LORD's sight, **21***I am bringing evil upon you: I will destroy you and will cut off every male in Ahab's line, whether slave or freeman, in Israel. **22***I will make your house like that of Jeroboam, son of Nebat, and like that of Baasha, son of Ahijah, because of how you have provoked me by leading Israel into sin." **23***(Against Jezebel, too, the LORD declared, "The dogs shall devour Jezebel in the district of Jezreel.") **24**"When one of Ahab's line dies in the city, dogs will devour him; when one of them dies in the field, the birds of the sky will devour him." **25**Indeed, no one gave himself up to the doing of evil in the sight of the LORD as did Ahab, urged on by his wife Jezebel. **26**He became completely abominable by following idols, just as the Amorites had done, whom the LORD drove out before the Israelites.

27When Ahab heard these words, he tore his garments and put on sackcloth over his bare flesh. He fasted, slept in the sackcloth, and went about subdued. **28**Then the LORD said to Elijah the Tishbite, **29***"Have you seen that Ahab has humbled himself before me? Since he has humbled himself before me, I will not bring the evil in his time. I will bring the evil upon his house during the reign of his son."

Campaign against Ramoth-gilead

22 **1***THREE years passed without war between Aram and Israel. **2**In the third year, however, King Jehoshaphat of Judah came down to the king of Israel, **3**who said to his servants, "Do you not know that Ramoth-gilead is ours and we are doing nothing to take it from the king of Aram?" **4**He asked Jehoshaphat, "Will you come with me to fight against Ramoth-gilead?" Jehoshaphat answered the king of Israel, "You and I are as one, and your people and my people, your horses and my horses as well." **5**Jehoshaphat also said to the king of Israel, "Seek the word of the LORD at once."

6The king of Israel gathered together the prophets, about four hundred of them, and asked, "Shall I go to attack Ramoth-gilead or shall I refrain?" "Go up," they answered. "The LORD will deliver it over to the king." **7**But Jehoshaphat said, "Is there no other prophet of the LORD here whom we may consult?" **8**The king of Israel answered, "There is one other through whom we might consult the LORD, Micaiah, son of Imlah; but I hate him because he prophesies not good but evil about me." Jehoshaphat said, "Let not your majesty speak of evil against you."

9So the king of Israel called an official and said to him, "Get Micaiah, son of Imlah, at once." **10**The king of Israel and King Jehoshaphat of Judah were seated, each on his throne, clothed in their robes of state on a threshing floor at the entrance of the gate of Samaria, and all the prophets were prophesying before them.

11Zedekiah, son of Chenaanah, made himself horns of iron and said, "The LORD says, 'With these you shall gore Aram until you have destroyed them.'" **12**The other prophets prophesied in a similar vein, saying: "Go up to Ramoth-gilead; you shall succeed. The LORD will deliver it over to the king."

13The messenger who had gone to call Micaiah said to him, "Look now, the prophets are unanimously predicting good for the king. Let your word be the same as any of theirs; predict good." **14**"As the LORD lives," Micaiah answered, "I shall say whatever the LORD tells me."

15When he came to the king, the king said to him, "Micaiah, shall we go to fight against Ramoth-gilead, or shall we refrain?" "Go up," he answered, "you shall succeed! The LORD will deliver it over to the king." **16**But the king answered him, "How many times must I adjure you to tell me nothing but the truth in the name of the LORD?" **17**So Micaiah said:

"I see all Israel
    scattered on the mountains,
    like sheep without a shepherd,
    and the LORD saying, 'These have no master!
Let each of them go back home in peace.'"

18The king of Israel said to Jehoshaphat, "Did I not tell you he prophesies not good but evil about me?" **19**†Micaiah continued: "Therefore hear the word of the LORD: I saw the LORD seated on his throne, with the whole host of heaven standing by to his right and to his left. **20**The LORD asked, 'Who will deceive Ahab, so that he will go up and fall at Ramoth-gilead?' And one said this, another that, **21**until one of the spirits came forth and presented himself to the LORD, saying, 'I will deceive him.' The LORD asked, 'How?' **22**He answered, 'I will go forth and become a lying spirit in the mouths of all his prophets.' The LORD replied, 'You shall succeed in deceiving him. Go forth and do this.' **23**So now, the LORD has put a lying spirit in the mouths of all these prophets of yours, but the LORD himself has decreed evil against you."

24Thereupon Zedekiah, son of Chenaanah, came up and slapped Micaiah on the cheek, saying, "Has the spirit of the LORD, then, left me to speak with you?" **25**"You shall find out," Micaiah replied, "on that day when you retreat into an inside room to hide." **26**The king of Israel then said, "Seize Micaiah and take him back to Amon, prefect of the city, and to Joash, the king's son, **27**and say, 'This is the king's order: Put this man in prison and feed him scanty rations of bread

---

† fulfillment in 2 Kgs 9, 36-37. Still another theological explanation for the death of Ahab is given by the North Israelite writer of 20, 35-42 above.

22, 19-23: The prophet Micaiah uses as a last resort to deter Ahab from his foolhardy design of fighting against Ramoth-gilead the literary device of describing false prophets as messengers of a lying spirit which God, after holding counsel with his angels, permits to deceive them.

and water until I return in safety.'" **28**†But Micaiah said, "If ever you return in safety, the Lord has not spoken through me."

29The king of Israel and King Jehosphaphat of Judah went up to Ramoth-gilead, **30**and the king of Israel said to Jehoshaphat, "I will disguise myself and go into battle, but you put on your own clothes." So the king of Israel disguised himself and entered the fray. **31**In the meantime the king of Aram had given his thirty-two chariot commanders the order, "Do not fight with anyone at all except the king of Israel." **32**When the chariot commanders saw Jehoshaphat, they cried out, "That must be the king of Israel!" and shifted to fight him. But Jehoshaphat shouted his battle cry, **33**and the chariot commanders, aware that he was not the king of Israel, gave up pursuit of him. **34**Someone, however, drew his bow at random, and hit the king of Israel between the joints of his breastplate. He ordered his charioteer, "Rein about and take me out of the ranks, for I am disabled." **35**❋The battle grew fierce during the day, and the king, who was propped up in his chariot facing the Arameans, died in the evening. The blood from his wound flowed to the bottom of the chariot. **36**At sunset a cry went through the army, "Every man to his city, every man to his land, **37**for the king is dead!" So they went to Samaria, where they buried the king. **38**❋When the chariot was washed at the pool of Samaria, the dogs licked up his blood and harlots bathed there, as the Lord had prophesied.

39The rest of the acts of Ahab, with all that he did, including the ivory palace and all the cities he built, are recorded in the book of the chronicles of the kings of Israel. **40**Ahab rested with his ancestors, and his son Ahaziah succeeded him as king.

Reign of Jehoshaphat

41Jehoshaphat, son of Asa, began to reign over Judah in the fourth year of Ahab, king of Israel. **42**Je-

hoshaphat was thirty-five years old when he began to reign, and he reigned twenty-five years in Jerusalem. His mother's name was Azubah, daughter of Shilhi. **43**He followed all the ways of his father Asa unswervingly, doing what was right in the Lord's sight. **44**Nevertheless, the high places did not disappear, and the people continued to sacrifice and to burn incense on the high places. **45**Jehoshaphat also made peace with the king of Israel. **46**The rest of the acts of Jehoshaphat, with his prowess, what he did and how he fought, are recorded in the book of the chronicles of the kings of Judah.

47He removed from the land the rest of the cult prostitutes who had remained in the reign of his father Asa. **48**There was no king in Edom, but an appointed regent. **49**Jehosphaphat made Tarshish ships to go to Ophir for gold; but in fact the ships did not go, because they were wrecked at Ezion-geber. **50**Then Ahaziah, son of Ahab, said to Jehoshaphat, "Let my servants accompany your servants in the ships." But Jehoshaphat would not agree. **51**Jehoshaphat rested with his ancestors; he was buried in his forefathers' City of David. His son Jehoram succeeded him as king.

Reign of Ahaziah

52†Ahaziah, son of Ahab, began to reign over Israel in Samaria in the seventeenth year of Jehoshaphat, king of Judah; he reigned two years over Israel. **53**He did evil in the sight of the Lord, behaving like his father, his mother, and Jeroboam, son of Nebat, who caused Israel to sin. **54**He served and worshiped Baal, thus provoking the Lord, the God of Israel, just as his father had done.

❋   35: 20, 42.   38: 21, 19.

---

†   22, 28: A note in the Hebrew text after this verse attributes to Micaiah ben Imlah the first words of the book of a different Micaiah, the minor prophet of Moreshet.

22, 52: *Seventeenth year:* so the present Hebrew text. More consistent with 2 Kgs 1, 17 would be a date in the twenty-fourth year of Jehoshaphat for Ahab's death; see note on 2 Kgs 3, 1.

The Second Book of Kings

I: THE KINGDOMS OF ISRAEL AND JUDAH

Ahaziah Consults Baalzebub

1 ¹*AFTER AHAB'S DEATH, Moab rebelled against Israel. ²†Ahaziah had fallen through the lattice of his roof terrace at Samaria and had been injured. So he sent out messengers with the instructions: "Go and inquire of Baalzebub, the god of Ekron, whether I shall recover from this injury."

³Meanwhile, the angel of the LORD said to Elijah the Tishbite: "Go, intercept the messengers of Samaria's king, and ask them, 'Is it because there is no God in Israel that you are going to inquire of Baalzebub, the god of Ekron?' ⁴For this, the LORD says: 'You shall not leave the bed upon which you lie; instead, you shall die.'" And with that, Elijah departed. ⁵The messengers then returned to Ahaziah, who asked them, "Why have you returned?" ⁶"A man came up to us," they answered, "who said to us, 'Go back to the king who sent you and tell him: The LORD says, Is it because there is no God in Israel that you are sending to inquire of Baalzebub, the god of Ekron? For this you shall not leave the bed upon which you lie; instead, you shall die.'" ⁷The king asked them, "What was the man like who came up to you and said these things to you?" ⁸*†"Wearing a hairy garment," they replied, "with a leather girdle about his loins." "It is Elijah the Tishbite!" he exclaimed.

Death of Two Captains

⁹Then the king sent a captain with his company of fifty men after Elijah. The prophet was seated on a hilltop when he found him. "Man of God," he ordered, "the king commands you to come down." ¹⁰*"If I am a man of God," Elijah answered the captain, "may fire come down from heaven and consume you and your fifty men." And fire came down from heaven and consumed him and his fifty men. ¹¹Ahaziah sent another captain with his company of fifty men after Elijah. "Man of God," he called out to Elijah, "the king commands you to come down immediately." ¹²†"If I am a man of God," Elijah answered him, "may fire come down from heaven and consume you and your fifty men." And divine fire came down from heaven, consuming him and his fifty men.

Death of the King

¹³Again, for the third time, Ahaziah sent a captain with his company of fifty men. When the third captain arrived, he fell to his knees before Elijah, pleading with him. "Man of God," he implored him, "let my life and the lives of these fifty men, your servants, count for something in your sight! ¹⁴Already fire has come down from heaven, consuming two captains with their companies of fifty men. But now, let my life mean something to you!" ¹⁵Then the angel of the LORD said to Elijah, "Go down with him; you need not be afraid of him."

¹⁶*So Elijah left and went down with him and stated to the king: "Thus says the LORD: 'Because you sent messengers to inquire of Baalzebub, the god of Ekron, you shall not leave the bed upon which you lie; instead, you shall die.'"

¹⁷†Ahaziah died in fulfillment of the prophecy of the LORD spoken by Elijah. Since he had no son, his brother Joram succeeded him as king, in the second year of Jehoram, son of Jehoshaphat, king of Judah. ¹⁸The rest of the acts of Ahaziah are recorded in the book of chronicles of the kings of Israel.

---

† 1, 2: *Baalzebub:* in this form, "Baal of flies." The name in the Hebrew text is a derisive alteration of Baalzebul, "Prince Baal." The best New Testament evidence supports the latter form in Mt 10, 25; Lk 11, 15. Later associations with Aramaic *beeldebaba,* "enemy," gave the ancient name its connotation of "devil."

1, 8: *Hairy garment:* a sign of ascetical and prophetic calling, imitated by John the Baptizer; see Mt 3, 4; Mk 1, 6.

1, 12: *Divine fire:* literally, "fire of God," which in Hebrew sounds quite like *man of God.* The play on words is the basis for Elijah's alleged retort. This story was told among the people to enhance the dignity of the prophet and to reflect the power of God whom he served. The mercy which God extends even to the wicked is described in Wis 11, 17—12, 22, and the prophet Elijah was well aware of it (1 Kgs 21, 28f).

1, 17: *Joram:* in the Second Book of Kings the name Joram (*yoram*), alternately Jehoram (*yehoram*), appears in numerous passages to designate both the king of Judah, son and successor of Jehoshaphat (848-841 B. C.), and the contemporary king of Israel, son of Ahab (852-841 B. C.). For the convenience of the reader in distinguishing these two kings, the longer form, Jehoram, is used to designate the king of Judah and the shorter form, Joram, to designate the king of Israel. See note on 3, 1.

✿
1/1: 3, 4-27.   10: Lv 10, 2; Sir 48, 3f;
8: Zec 13, 4.   Lk 9, 54f.
16: Sir 48, 6.

Elijah and Elisha

2 ¹†WHEN the LORD was about to take Elijah up to heaven in a whirlwind, he and Elisha were on their way from Gilgal. ²"Stay here, please," Elijah said to Elisha. "The LORD has sent me on to Bethel." "As the LORD lives, and as you yourself live," Elisha replied, "I will not leave you." So they went down to Bethel, ³where the guild prophets went out to Elisha and asked him, "Do you know that the LORD will take your master from over you today?" "Yes, I know it," he replied. "Keep still."

⁴Then Elijah said to him, "Stay here, please, Elisha, for the LORD has sent me on to Jericho." "As the LORD lives, and as you yourself live," Elisha replied, "I will not leave you." ⁵They went on to Jericho, where the guild prophets approached Elisha and asked him, "Do you know that the LORD will take your master from over you today?" "Yes, I know it," he replied. "Keep still."

⁶Elijah said to Elisha, "Please stay here; the LORD has sent me on to the Jordan." "As the LORD lives, and as you yourself live," Elisha replied, "I will not leave you." And so the two went on together. ⁷Fifty of the guild prophets followed, and when the two stopped at the Jordan, stood facing them at a distance. ⁸*Elijah took his mantle, rolled it up and struck the water, which divided, and both crossed over on dry ground.

Elisha Succeeds Elijah

⁹†When they had crossed over, Elijah said to Elisha, "Ask for whatever I may do for you, before I am taken from you." Elisha answered, "May I receive a double portion of your spirit." ¹⁰*"You have asked something that is not easy," he replied. "Still, if you see me taken up from you, your wish will be granted; otherwise not." ¹¹*As they walked on conversing, a flaming chariot and flaming horses came between them, and Elijah went up to heaven in a whirlwind. ¹²*†When Elisha saw it happen he cried out, "My father! my father! Israel's chariots and drivers!" But when he could no longer see him, Elisha gripped his own garment and tore it in two.

¹³*Then he picked up Elijah's mantle which had fallen from him, and went back and stood at the bank of the Jordan. ¹⁴Wielding the mantle which had fallen from Elijah, he struck the water in his turn and said, "Where is the LORD, the God of Elijah?" When Elisha struck the water it divided and he crossed over.

¹⁵The guild prophets in Jericho, who were on the other side, saw him and said, "The spirit of Elijah rests on Elisha." They went to meet him, bowing to the ground before him. ¹⁶*"Among your servants are fifty brave men," they said. "Let them go in search of your master. Perhaps the spirit of the LORD has carried him away to some mountain or some valley." "Do not send them," he answered. ¹⁷However, they kept urging him, until he was embarrassed and said, "Send them." So they sent the fifty men, who searched for three days without finding him. ¹⁸When they returned to Elisha in Jericho, where he was staying, he said to them, "Did I not tell you not to go?"

Healing of the Water

¹⁹Once the inhabitants of the city complained to Elisha, "The site of the city is fine indeed, as my lord can see, but the water is bad and the land unfruitful." ²⁰"Bring me a new bowl," Elisha said, "and put salt into it." When they had brought it to him, ²¹he went out to the spring and threw salt into it, saying, "Thus says the LORD, 'I have purified this water. Never again shall death or miscarriage spring from it.'" ²²And the water has stayed pure even to this day, just as Elisha prophesied.

The Prophet's Curse

²³†From there Elisha went up to Bethel. While he was on the way, some small boys came out of the city and jeered at him. "Go up, baldhead," they shouted, "go up, baldhead!" ²⁴The prophet turned and saw them, and he cursed them in the name of the LORD. Then two she-bears came out of the woods and tore forty-two of the children to pieces.

²⁵From there he went to Mount Carmel, and thence he returned to Samaria.

Campaign of Joram against Moab

3 ¹†JORAM, son of Ahab, became king of Israel in Samaria [in the eighteenth year of Jehoshaphat, king of Judah, and he reigned for twelve years]. ²He did evil in the LORD's sight, though not as much as his father and mother. He did away with the pillar of Baal, which his father had made, ³but he still clung

---

2, 1: *Gilgal:* commonly identified with Jiljulieh, about seven miles north of Bethel, and different from the Gilgal in Dt 11, 30 near Shechem, and that in Jos 4 and 5, passim, near Jericho.

2, 9: *Double portion of your spirit:* as the first-born son inherited a double portion of his father's property (Dt 21, 17), so Elisha asks to inherit from Elijah his spirit of prophecy in the degree befitting his principal disciple. In Nm 11, 17.25, God bestows some of the spirit of Moses on others.

2, 12: *My father:* a religious title accorded prophetic leaders; cf 6, 21; 8, 9. *Israel's chariots and drivers:* Elijah was worth more than a whole army in defending Israel and the true religion. King Joash of Israel uses the same phrase of Elisha himself (13, 14).

2, 23f: This story, like the one about Elijah and the captains (ch. 1), is preserved for us in Scripture to convey a popular understanding of the dignity of the prophet. Told in popular vein, it becomes a caricature, in which neither Elisha nor the bears behave in character. See note on 1, 12 and the contrasting narrative in ch. 4.

3, 1: The sequence of the reigns between Ahab and Jehu of Israel may be reconstructed as follows: Jehoshaphat of Judah outlived Ahab by a short time, so that Ahaziah of Israel was his contemporary. Jehoram of Judah succeeded his father Jehoshaphat while Ahaziah of Israel was still alive. Jehoram (Joram) of Israel became king, following his brother Ahaziah, in the second

2/8: Ex 14, 16.22.
10: Nm 11, 17.25.
11: Gn 5, 24; 1 Mc 2, 58; Acts 1, 9.
12: 13, 14; Sir 48, 9.12.
13: 1 Kgs 19, 19.
16: 1 Kgs 18, 12.

to the sin to which Jeroboam, son of Nebat, had lured Israel; this he did not give up.

⁴Now Mesha, king of Moab, who raised sheep, used to pay the king of Israel as tribute a hundred thousand lambs and the wool of a hundred thousand rams. ⁵But when Ahab died, the king of Moab had rebelled against the king of Israel. ⁶Joram as king mustered all Israel, and when he set out on a campaign from Samaria, ⁷*he sent the king of Judah the message: "The king of Moab is in rebellion against me. Will you join me in battle against Moab?" "I will," he replied. "You and I shall be as one, your people and mine, and your horses and mine as well." ⁸They discussed the route for their attack, and settled upon the route through the desert of Edom.

⁹So the king of Israel set out, accompanied by the king of Judah and the king of Edom. After their roundabout journey of seven days the water gave out for the army and for the animals with them. ¹⁰"Alas!" exclaimed the king of Israel. "The LORD has called together these three kings to put them in the grasp of Moab." ¹¹*But the king of Judah asked, "Is there no prophet of the LORD here through whom we may inquire of the LORD?" One of the officers of the king of Israel replied, "Elisha, son of Shaphat, who poured water on the hands of Elijah, is here." ¹²"He has the word of the LORD," the king of Judah agreed. So the kings of Israel, Judah, and Edom went down to Elisha. ¹³"What do you want with me?" Elisha asked the king of Israel. "Go to the prophets of your father and to the prophets of your mother." "No," the king of Israel replied. "The LORD has called these three kings together to put them in the grasp of Moab." ¹⁴*Then Elisha said, "As the LORD of hosts lives, whom I serve, were it not that I respect the king of Judah, I should neither look at you nor notice you at all. ¹⁵Now get me a minstrel."

When the minstrel played, the power of the LORD came upon Elisha ¹⁶and he announced: "Thus says the LORD, 'Provide many catch basins in this wadi.' ¹⁷For the LORD says, 'Though you will see neither wind nor rain, yet this wadi will be filled with water for you, your livestock, and your pack animals to drink.' ¹⁸And since the LORD does not consider this enough, he will also deliver Moab into your grasp. ¹⁹*You shall destroy every fortified city, fell every fruit tree, stop up all the springs, and ruin every fertile field with stones."

²⁰*In the morning, at the time of the sacrifice, water came from the direction of Edom and filled the land. ²¹Meanwhile, all Moab heard that the kings had come to give them battle; every man capable of bearing arms was called up and stationed at the border. ²²†Early that morning, when the sun shone on the water, the Moabites saw the water at a distance as red as blood. ²³"This is blood!" they exclaimed. "The kings have fought among themselves and killed one another.

Quick! To the spoils, Moabites!" ²⁴But when they reached the camp of Israel, the Israelites rose up and attacked the Moabites, who fled from them. They ranged through the countryside striking down the Moabites, and ²⁵*†destroying the cities; each of them cast stones onto every fertile field till they had loaded it down; all the springs they stopped up and every useful tree they felled. Finally only Kir-hareseth was left behind its stone walls, and the slingers had surrounded it and were attacking it. ²⁶When he saw that he was losing the battle, the king of Moab took seven hundred swordsmen to break through to the king of Aram, but he failed. ²⁷*†So he took his firstborn, his heir apparent, and offered him as a holocaust upon the wall. The wrath against Israel was so great that they gave up the siege and returned to their own land.

The Widow's Oil

4 ¹*†A certain woman, the widow of one of the guild prophets, complained to Elisha: "My husband, your servant, is dead. You know that he was a God-fearing man, yet now his creditor has come to take my two children as his slaves." ²"How can I help you?" Elisha answered her. "Tell me what you have in the house." "This servant of yours has nothing in the house but a jug of oil," she replied. ³"Go out," he said, "borrow vessels from all your neighbors—as many empty vessels as you can. ⁴Then come back and close the door on yourself and your children; pour the oil into all the vessels, and as each is filled, set it aside." ⁵She went and did so, closing the door on herself and her children. As they handed her the vessels, she would pour in oil. ⁶When all the vessels were filled, she said to her son, "Bring me another vessel." "There is none left," he answered her. And then the oil

---

† year of Jehoram of Judah (2 Kgs 1, 17); this is one datum on which the earliest Greek evidence and the standard Hebrew text are in agreement.

The two Jehorams were contemporary for much of their reigns; Jehoram of Judah was succeeded by Ahaziah something more than a year before Jehu did away with the rulers of both kingdoms (2 Kgs 9, 1-29).

The Moabite campaign of 2 Kgs 3, 4-27 is thus best placed under the two Kings Jehoram, before the Edomite rebellion mentioned in 2 Kgs 8, 20. In the received Hebrew text, Jehoshaphat has been made the Judahite protagonist in the campaign against Moab as a tribute to his piety; this assimilates the story of 2 Kgs 3 to that of 1 Kgs 22, but creates difficulties in the chronology which the extant data leave partly unresolved. An older practice for stories of the Israelite kings was to leave them and their fellow kings without identification by name; cf 2 Kgs 6, 8-7, 20. The name of Jehoshaphat has been omitted from a number of places in 2 Kgs 3-8, in this translation; cf 1 Kgs 22, 51.

3, 22: *Red as blood:* possibly caused by the red sandstone of the Wadi Zered (Dt 2, 13), south of Moab.

3, 25: *Kir-hareseth:* modern Kerak, east of the Dead Sea; cf Is 16, 7. 11; Jer 48, 31. 36.

3, 27: *The wrath against Israel:* probably the wrath of Chemosh, the Moabite god to whom the child was offered. He was feared by the Israelites who lost heart on foreign soil.

4, 1: *His creditor . . . slaves:* Hebrew law permitted the selling of wife and children as chattels for debt; cf Ex 21, 7; Am 2, 6; 8, 6; Is 50.

✿
3/7: 1 Kgs 22, 4.   20: 1 Kgs 18, 29.
11: 1 Kgs 22, 7.   25: Jb 5, 23.
14: 1 Kgs 18, 15.   27: Jgs 11, 30f.
19: Dt 20, 19.   4/1: 1 Kgs 17, 8-16.

stopped. **7**She went and told the man of God, who said, "Go and sell the oil to pay off your creditor; with what remains, you and your children can live."

Elisha and the Shunammite

8One day Elisha came to Shunem, where there was a woman of influence, who urged him to dine with her. Afterward, whenever he passed by, he used to stop there to dine. **9**So she said to her husband, "I know that he is a holy man of God. Since he visits us often, **10**let us arrange a little room on the roof and furnish it for him with a bed, table, chair, and lamp, so that when he comes to us he can stay there." **11**Sometime later Elisha arrived and stayed in the room overnight. **12**Then he said to his servant Gehazi, "Call this Shunammite woman." He did so, and when she stood before Elisha, **13**he told Gehazi, "Say to her, 'You have lavished all this care on us; what can we do for you? Can we say a good word for you to the king or to the commander of the army?'" She replied, "I am living among my own people." **14**Later Elisha asked, "Can something be done for her?" Yes!" Gehazi answered. "She has no son, and her husband is getting on in years." **15**"Call her," said Elisha. When she had been called, and stood at the door, **16***Elisha promised, "This time next year you will be fondling a baby son." "Please, my lord," she protested, "you are a man of God; do not deceive your servant." **17**Yet the woman conceived, and by the same time the following year she had given birth to a son, as Elisha promised.

18*The day came when the child was old enough to go out to his father among the reapers. **19**"My head hurts!" he complained to his father. "Carry him to his mother," the father said to a servant. **20**The servant picked him up and carried him to his mother; he stayed with her until noon, when he died in her lap. **21**The mother took him upstairs and laid him on the bed of the man of God. Closing the door on him, she went out **22**and called to her husband, "Let me have a servant and a donkey. I must go quickly to the man of God, and I will be back." **23**"Why are you going to him today?" he asked. "It is neither the new moon nor the sabbath." But she bade him good-bye, **24**and when the donkey was saddled, said to her servant: "Lead on! Do not stop my donkey unless I tell you to." **25**She kept going till she reached the man of God on Mount Carmel. When he spied her at a distance, the man of God said to his servant Gehazi: "There is the Shunammite! **26**†Hurry to meet her, and ask if all is well with her, with her husband, and with the boy." "Greetings," she replied. **27**But when she reached the man of God on the mountain, she clasped his feet. Gehazi came near to push her away, but the man of God said: "Let her alone, she is in bitter anguish; the Lord hid it from me and did not let me know." **28**"Did I ask my lord for a son?" she cried out. "Did I not beg you not to deceive

me?" **29**†"Gird your loins," Elisha said to Gehazi, "take my staff with you and be off; if you meet anyone, do not greet him, and if anyone greets you, do not answer. Lay my staff upon the boy." **30**But the boy's mother cried out: "As the Lord lives and as you yourself live, I will not release you." So he started to go back with her.

31*Meanwhile, Gehazi had gone on ahead and had laid the staff upon the boy, but there was no sound or sign of life. He returned to meet Elisha and informed him that the boy had not awakened. **32**When Elisha reached the house, he found the boy lying dead. **33***He went in, closed the door on them both, and prayed to the Lord. Then he lay upon the child on the bed, placing his mouth upon the child's mouth, his eyes upon the eyes, and his hands upon the hands. As Elisha stretched himself over the child, the body became warm. **35***He arose, paced up and down the room, and then once more lay down upon the boy, who now sneezed seven times and opened his eyes. **36**Elisha summoned Gehazi and said, "Call the Shunammite." She came at his call, and Elisha said to her, "Take your son." **37**She came in and fell at his feet in gratitude; then she took her son and left the room.

The Poisoned Stew

38When Elisha returned to Gilgal, there was a famine in the land. Once, when the guild prophets were seated before him, he said to his servant, "Put the large pot on, and make some vegetable stew for the guild prophets." **39**Someone went out into the field to gather herbs and found a wild vine, from which he picked a clothful of wild gourds. On his return he cut them up into the pot of vegetable stew without anybody's knowing it. **40**The stew was poured out for the men to eat, but when they began to eat it, they exclaimed, "Man of God, there is poison in the pot!" And they could not eat it. **41**"Bring some meal," Elisha said. He threw it into the pot and said, "Serve it to the people to eat." And there was no longer anything harmful in the pot.

Multiplication of Loaves

42A man came from Baal-shalishah bringing the man of God twenty barley loaves made from the first fruits, and fresh grain in the ear. "Give it to the people to eat," Elisha said. **43**But his servant objected, "How can I set this before a hundred men?" "Give it to the people to eat," Elisha insisted. "For thus says the Lord, 'They shall eat and there shall be some left over.'" **44**And when they had eaten, there was some left over, as the Lord had said.

16: Gn 18, 10.　　　33: 1 Kgs 17, 21-23.
18: 1 Kgs 17, 17-24.　　35: Heb 11, 35.
31-36: Acts 20, 10ff.

---

† 4, 26: *Greetings:* the conventional answer to Gehazi's question, which tells him nothing.

4, 29: *Do not greet him:* the profuse exchange of compliments among Orientals meeting and greeting one another consumed time. Urgency necessitated their omission, as our Lord counseled his disciples (Lk 10, 4).

Cure of Naaman

5 **¹**NAAMAN, the army commander of the king of Aram, was highly esteemed and respected by his master, for through him the LORD had brought victory to Aram. But valiant as he was, the man was a leper. **²**Now the Arameans had captured from the land of Israel in a raid a little girl, who became the servant of Naaman's wife. **³**"If only my master would present himself to the prophet in Samaria," she said to her mistress, "he would cure him of his leprosy." **⁴**Naaman went and told his lord just what the slave girl from the land of Israel had said. **⁵**"Go," said the king of Aram. "I will send along a letter to the king of Israel." So Naaman set out, taking along ten silver talents, six thousand gold pieces, and ten festal garments. **⁶**To the king of Israel he brought the letter, which read: "With this letter I am sending my servant Naaman to you, that you may cure him of his leprosy."

⁷*When he read the letter, the king of Israel tore his garments and exclaimed: "Am I a god with power over life and death, that this man should send someone to me to be cured of leprosy? Take note! You can see he is only looking for a quarrel with me!" **⁸**When Elisha, the man of God, heard that the king of Israel had torn his garments, he sent word to the king: "Why have you torn your garments? Let him come to me and find out that there is a prophet in Israel."

⁹Naaman came with his horses and chariots and stopped at the door of Elisha's house. **¹⁰***The prophet sent him the message: "Go and wash seven times in the Jordan, and your flesh will heal, and you will be clean." **¹¹**But Naaman went away angry, saying, "I thought that he would surely come out and stand there to invoke the LORD his God, and would move his hand over the spot, and thus cure the leprosy. **¹²**†Are not the rivers of Damascus, the Abana and the Pharpar, better than all the waters of Israel? Could I not wash in them and be cleansed?" With this, he turned about in anger and left.

¹³But his servants came up and reasoned with him. "My father," they said, "if the prophet had told you to do something extraordinary, would you not have done it? All the more now, since he said to you, 'Wash and be clean,' should you do as he said." **¹⁴***So Naaman went down and plunged into the Jordan seven times at the word of the man of God. His flesh became again like the flesh of a little child, and he was clean.

¹⁵He returned with his whole retinue to the man of God. On his arrival he stood before him and said, "Now I know that there is no God in all the earth, except in Israel. Please accept a gift from your servant."
¹⁶"As the LORD lives whom I serve, I will not take it," Elisha replied; and despite Naaman's urging, he still refused. **¹⁷**†Naaman said: "If you will not accept, please let me, your servant, have two mule-loads of earth, for I will no longer offer holocaust or sacrifice to any other god except to the LORD. **¹⁸**But I trust the LORD will forgive your servant this: when my master enters the temple of Rimmon to worship there, then I, too, as his adjutant, must bow down in the temple of Rimmon. May the LORD forgive your servant this." **¹⁹**†"Go in peace," Elisha said to him.

Naaman had gone some distance **²⁰**when Gehazi, the servant of Elisha, the man of God, thought to himself: "My master was too easy with this Aramean Naaman, not accepting what he brought. As the LORD lives, I will run after him and get something out of him." **²¹**So Gehazi hurried after Naaman. Aware that someone was running after him, Naaman alighted from his chariot to wait for him. "Is everything all right?" he asked. **²²**"Yes," Gehazi replied, "but my master sent me to say, 'Two young men have just come to me, guild prophets from the hill country of Ephraim. Please give them a talent of silver and two festal garments.'" **²³**"Please take two talents," Naaman said, and pressed them upon him. He tied up these silver talents in bags and gave them, with the two festal garments, to two of his servants, who carried them before Gehazi. **²⁴**When they reached the hill, Gehazi took what they had, carried it into the house, and sent the men on their way.

²⁵He went in and stood before Elisha his master, who asked him, "Where have you been, Gehazi?" He answered, "Your servant has not gone anywhere." **²⁶**But Elisha said to him: "Was I not present in spirit when the man alighted from his chariot to wait for you? Is this a time to take money or to take garments, olive orchards or vineyards, sheep or cattle, male or female servants? **²⁷***The leprosy of Naaman shall cling to you and your descendants forever." And Gehazi left Elisha, a leper white as snow.

Recovery of the Lost Ax

6 **¹**THE guild prophets once said to Elisha: "There is not enough room for us to continue to live here with you. **²**Let us go to the Jordan, where by getting one beam apiece we can build ourselves a place to live." "Go," Elisha said. **³**"Please agree to accompany your servants," one of them requested. "Yes, I will come," he replied.

⁴So he went with them, and when they arrived at the Jordan they began to fell trees. **⁵**While one of them was felling a tree trunk, the iron axhead slipped into the water. "O master," he cried out, "it was borrowed!" **⁶**"Where did it fall?" asked the man of God.

---

† 5, 12: *Wash in them and be cleansed:* typical of the ambiguity in ritual healing or cleanliness. The muddy waters of the Jordan are no match hygienically for the mountain spring waters of Damascus; ritually, it is the other way around.

5, 17: *Two mule-loads of earth:* Israelite earth on which to erect in Aram an altar to the God of Israel.

5, 19: *Go in peace:* Elisha understands and approves the situation of Naaman who, though a proselyte as regards belief in and worship of the God of Israel, is required by his office to assist his master, the king, worshiping in the pagan temple of Rimmon.

❉
5/7: Gn 30, 2; 1 Sm 2, 6;　　14: Lk 4, 27.
　　Jn 5, 21.　　　　　　　　　27: Ex 4, 6; Nm 12, 10.
10: Jn 9, 7.

When he pointed out the spot, Elisha cut off a stick, threw it into the water, and brought the iron to the surface. **7**"Pick it up," he said. And the man reached down and grasped it.

Aramean Ambush

8When the king of Aram was waging war on Israel, he would make plans with his servants to attack a particular place. **9**But the man of God would send word to the king of Israel, "Be careful! Do not pass by this place, for Aram will attack there." **10**So the king of Israel would send word to the place which the man of God had indicated, and alert it; then they would be on guard. This happened several times.

11Greatly disturbed over this, the king of Aram called together his officers. "Will you not tell me," he asked them, "who among us is for the king of Israel?" **12**"No one, my lord king," answered one of the officers. "The Israelite prophet Elisha can tell the king of Israel the very words you speak in your bedroom." **13**"Go, find out where he is," he said, "so that I may take him captive."

Blinded Aramean Soldiers

Informed that Elisha was in Dothan, **14**he sent there a strong force with horses and chariots. They arrived by night and surrounded the city. **15**Early the next morning, when the attendant of the man of God arose and went out, he saw the force with its horses and chariots surrounding the city. "Alas!" he said to Elisha. "What shall we do, my lord?" **16**"Do not be afraid," Elisha answered. "Our side outnumbers theirs." **17***Then he prayed, "O LORD, open his eyes, that he may see." And the LORD opened the eyes of the servant, so that he saw the mountainside filled with horses and fiery chariots around Elisha.

18When the Arameans came down to get him, Elisha prayed to the LORD, "Strike this people blind, I pray you." And in answer to the prophet's prayer the LORD struck them blind. **19**Then Elisha said to them: "This is the wrong road, and this is the wrong city. Follow me! I will take you to the man you want." And he led them to Samaria. **20**When they entered Samaria, Elisha prayed, "O LORD, open their eyes that they may see." The LORD opened their eyes, and they saw that they were inside Samaria. **21**When the king of Israel saw them, he asked, "Shall I kill them, my father?" **22**†"You must not kill them," replied Elisha. "Do you slay those whom you have taken captive with your sword or bow? Serve them bread and water. Let them eat and drink, and then go back to their master." **23**The king spread a great feast for them. When they had eaten and drunk he sent them away, and they went back to their master. No more Aramean raiders came into the land of Israel.

Siege of Samaria

24After this, Ben-hadad, king of Aram, mustered his whole army and laid siege to Samaria. **25**Because of the siege the famine in Samaria was so severe that an ass's head sold for eighty pieces of silver, and a fourth of a kab of wild onion for five pieces of silver.

26One day, as the king of Israel was walking on the city wall, a woman cried out to him, "Help, my lord king!" **27**"No," he replied, "the LORD help you! Where could I find help for you: from the threshing floor or the winepress?" **28***Then the king asked her, "What is your trouble?" She replied: "This woman said to me, 'Give up your son that we may eat him today; then tomorrow we will eat my son.' **29**So we boiled my son and ate him. The next day I said to her, 'Now give up your son that we may eat him.' But she hid her son." **30***When the king heard the woman's words, he tore his garments. And as he was walking on the wall, the people saw that he was wearing sackcloth underneath, next to his skin.

31"May God do thus and so to me," the king exclaimed, "if the head of Elisha, son of Shaphat, stays on him today!" **32**Meanwhile, Elisha was sitting in his house in conference with the elders. The king had sent a man ahead before he himself should come to him. Elisha had said to the elders: "Do you know that this son of a murderer is sending someone to cut off my head? When the messenger comes, see that you close the door and hold it fast against him. His master's footsteps are echoing behind him." **33**While Elisha was still speaking, the king came down to him and said, "This evil is from the LORD. Why should I trust in the LORD any longer?"

7 **1**†ELISHA said: "Hear the word of the LORD! Thus says the LORD, 'At this time tomorrow a seah of fine flour will sell for a shekel, and two seahs of barley for a shekel, in the market of Samaria.'" **2***But the adjutant on whose arm the king leaned, answered the man of God, "Even if the LORD were to make windows in heaven, how could this happen?" "You shall see it with your own eyes," Elisha said, "but you shall not eat of it."

The Lepers at the Gate

3*At the city gate were four lepers who were deliberating, "Why should we sit here until we die? **4**If we decide to go into the city, we shall die there, for there is famine in the city. If we remain here ,we shall die too. Come, let us desert to the camp of the Arameans. If they spare us, we live; if they kill us, we die." **5**At twilight they left for the Arameans; but when they

---

* 6/17: 7, 6; Ps 67, 18.   7/2: 7, 17; Ps 78, 23; 28: Dt 28, 53-57.   Is 24, 18. 30: 1 Kgs 20, 31; 21, 27.   3: Lv 13, 46.

† 6, 22: *With your sword or bow:* since the king would not slay prisoners who had surrendered to his power, much less should he slay prisoners captured by God's power. By oriental custom they became guests within Samaria's walls.

7, 1: *Market:* literally "gate," the principal place of trading in ancient walled cities in time of peace.

reached the edge of the camp, no one was there. ⁶*†The Lord had caused the army of the Arameans to hear the sound of chariots and horses, the din of a large army, and they had reasoned among themselves, "The king of Israel has hired the kings of the Hittites and the kings of the borderlands to fight us." ⁷Then in the twilight they fled, abandoning their tents, their horses, and their asses, the whole camp just as it was, and fleeing for their lives.

⁸After the lepers reached the edge of the camp, they went first into one tent, ate and drank, and took silver, gold, and clothing from it, and went out and hid them. Back they came into another tent, took things from it, and again went out and hid them. ⁹Then they said to one another: "We are not doing right. This is a day of good news, and we are keeping silent. If we wait until morning breaks, we shall be blamed. Come, let us go and inform the palace."

¹⁰They came and summoned the city gatekeepers. "We went to the camp of the Arameans," they said, "but no one was there—not a human voice, only the horses and asses tethered, and the tents just as they were left." ¹¹The gatekeepers announced this and it was reported within the palace. ¹²Though it was night, the king got up; he said to his servants: "Let me tell you what the Arameans have done to us. Knowing that we are in famine, they have left their camp to hide in the field, hoping to take us alive and enter our city when we leave it." ¹³One of his servants, however, suggested: "Since those who are left in the city are no better off than all the throng that has perished, let some of us take five of the abandoned horses and send scouts to investigate."

End of the Siege

¹⁴They took two chariots, and horses, and the king sent them to reconnoiter the Aramean army. "Go and find out," he ordered. ¹⁵They followed the Arameans as far as the Jordan, and the whole route was strewn with garments and other objects that the Arameans had thrown away in their haste. The messengers returned and told the king.

¹⁶The people went out and plundered the camp of the Arameans; and then a seah of fine flour sold for a shekel and two seahs of barley for a shekel, as the LORD had said.

¹⁷The king put in charge of the gate the officer who was his adjutant; but the people trampled him to death at the gate, just as the man of God had predicted when the king visited him. ¹⁸Thus was fulfilled the prophecy of the man of God to the king, "Two seahs of barley will sell for a shekel, and one seah of fine flour for a shekel at this time tomorrow at the gate of Samaria." ¹⁹The adjutant had answered the man of God, "Even if the LORD were to make windows in heaven, how could this happen?" And Elisha had re-

plied, "You shall see it with your own eyes, but you shall not eat of it." ²⁰And that is what happened to him, for the people trampled him to death at the gate.

Prediction of Famine

8 ¹*ELISHA once said to the woman whose son he had restored to life: "Get ready! Leave with your family and settle wherever you can, because the LORD has decreed a seven-year famine which is coming upon the land." ²The woman got ready and did as the man of God said, setting out with her family and settling in the land of the Philistines for seven years. ³At the end of the seven years, the woman returned from the land of the Philistines and went out to the king to claim her house and her field. ⁴The king was talking with Gehazi, the servant of the man of God. "Tell me," he said, "all the great things that Elisha has done." ⁵Just as he was relating to the king how his master had restored a dead person to life, the very woman whose son Elisha had restored to life came to the king to claim her house and field. "My lord king," Gehazi said, "this is the woman, and this is that son of hers whom Elisha restored to life." ⁶†The king questioned the woman, and she told him her story. With that the king placed an official at her disposal, saying, "Restore all her property to her, with all that the field produced from the day she left the land until now."

Death of Ben-hadad Foretold

⁷Elisha came to Damascus at a time when Ben-hadad, king of Aram, lay sick. When he was told that the man of God had come there, ⁸the king said to Hazael, "Take a gift with you and go call on the man of God. Have him consult the LORD as to whether I shall recover from this sickness." ⁹Hazael went to visit him, carrying a present, and with forty camel loads of the best goods of Damascus. On his arrival, he stood before the prophet and said, "Your son Ben-hadad, king of Aram, has sent me to ask you whether he will recover from his sickness." ¹⁰"Go and tell him," Elisha answered, "that he will surely recover. However, the LORD has showed me that he will in fact die." ¹¹Then he stared him down until Hazael became ill at ease. The man of God wept, ¹²*and Hazael asked, "Why are you weeping, my lord?" Elisha replied, "Because I know the evil that you will inflict upon the Israelites. You will burn their fortresses, you will slay their youth with the sword, you will dash their little children to pieces, you will rip open their pregnant women." ¹³*†Hazael exclaimed, "How can a dog like me, your

---

† 7, 6: *Kings of the borderlands:* from Musur in Anatolia rather than Egypt.

8, 6: *An official:* literally "eunuch," and perhaps actually so in this instance.

8, 13: *A dog . . . your servant:* Hazael feigns humility (1 Sm 24, 14; 2 Sm 9, 8), without attending to the crimes he would commit after usurping the royal power as the prophet predicts. *Anything so important:* literally "a great deed" for a patriotic Syrian.

---

*
6f: 6, 17; 19, 35f; 2 Sm 5, 24.
8/1: 4, 36.
12: 13, 7.
13: 15, 16; 1 Kgs 19, 15.

servant, do anything so important?" "The LORD has showed you to me as king over Aram," replied Elisha.

¹⁴Hazael left Elisha and returned to his master. "What did Elisha tell you?" asked Ben-hadad. "He told me that you would surely recover," replied Hazael. ¹⁵The next day, however, Hazael took a cloth, dipped it in water, and spread it over the king's face, so that he died. And Hazael reigned in his stead.

Reign of Jehoram of Judah

¹⁶†In the fifth year of Joram, son of Ahab, king of Israel, Jehoram, son of Jehoshaphat, king of Judah, became king. ¹⁷*He was thirty-two years old when he began to reign, and he reigned eight years in Jerusalem. ¹⁸He conducted himself like the kings of Israel of the line of Ahab, since the sister of Ahab was his wife; and he did evil in the LORD's sight. ¹⁹*Even so, the LORD was unwilling to destroy Judah, because of his servant David. For he had promised David that he would leave him a lamp in the LORD's presence for all time. ²⁰During Jehoram's reign, Edom revolted against the sovereignty of Judah and chose a king of its own. ²¹Thereupon Jehoram with all his chariots crossed over to Zair. He arose by night and broke through the Edomites when they had surrounded him and the commanders of his chariots. Then his army fled homeward. ²²*To this day Edom has been in revolt against the rule of Judah. Libnah also revolted at that time. ²³The rest of the acts of Jehoram, with all that he did, are recorded in the book of the chronicles of the kings of Judah. ²⁴Jehoram rested with his ancestors and was buried with them in the City of David. His son Ahaziah succeeded him as king.

Accession of Ahaziah

²⁵†Ahaziah, son of Jehoram, king of Judah, became king in the twelfth year of Joram, son of Ahab, king of Israel. ²⁶He was twenty-two years old when he began his reign, and he reigned one year in Jerusalem. His mother's name was Athaliah; she was the daughter of Omri, king of Israel. ²⁷He conducted himself like the house of Ahab, doing evil in the LORD's sight as they did, since he was related to them by marriage. ²⁸*He joined Joram, son of Ahab, in battle against Hazael, king of Aram, at Ramoth-gilead, where the Arameans wounded Joram. ²⁹King Joram returned to Jezreel to be healed of the wounds which the Arameans had inflicted on him at Ramah in his battle against Hazael, king of Aram. Then Ahaziah, son of Jehoram, king of Judah, went down to Jezreel to visit him there in his illness.

Anointing of Jehu

9 ¹*THE prophet Elisha called one of the guild prophets and said to him: "Gird your loins, take this flask of oil with you, and go to Ramoth-gilead. ²*When you get there, look for Jehu, son of Jehoshaphat, son of Nimshi. Enter and take him away from his companions into an inner chamber. ³*From the flask you have, pour oil on his head, and say, 'Thus says the LORD: I anoint you king over Israel.' Then open the door and flee without delay." ⁴The young man (the guild prophet) went to Ramoth-gilead. ⁵When he arrived, the commanders of the army were in session. "I have a message for you, commander," he said. "For which one of us?" asked Jehu. "For you, commander," he answered. ⁶Jehu got up and went into the house. Then the young man poured the oil on his head and said, "Thus says the LORD, the God of Israel: 'I anoint you king over the people of the LORD, over Israel. ⁷†You shall destroy the house of Ahab your master; thus will I avenge the blood of my servants the prophets, and the blood of all the other servants of the LORD shed by Jezebel, ⁸*and by all the rest of the family of Ahab. I will cut off every male in Ahab's line, whether slave or freeman in Israel. ⁹I will deal with the house of Ahab as I dealt with the house of Jeroboam, son of Nebat, and with the house of Baasha, son of Ahijah. ¹⁰Dogs shall devour Jezebel at the confines of Jezreel, so that no one can bury her.'" Then he opened the door and fled.

¹¹When Jehu rejoined his master's servants, they asked him, "Is all well? Why did that madman come to you?" "You know that kind of man and his talk," he replied. ¹²But they said, "Not at all! Come, tell us." So he told them what the young man had said to him, and finally, "Thus says the LORD: 'I anoint you king over Israel.'" ¹³*At once each took his garment, spread it under Jehu on the bare steps, blew the trumpet, and cried out, "Jehu is king!"

¹⁴*Thus Jehu, son of Jehoshaphat, son of Nimshi, formed a conspiracy against Joram. Joram, with all Israel, had been besieging Ramoth-gilead against Hazael, king of Aram, ¹⁵but had returned to Jezreel to be healed of the wounds the Arameans had inflicted on him in the battle against Hazael, king of Aram.

Murder of Joram

"If you are truly with me," Jehu said, "see that no one escapes from the city to report in Jezreel." ¹⁶Then Jehu mounted his chariot and drove to Jezreel, where

---

† 8, 16: *Jehoram* of Judah succeeded his father Jehoshaphat during the reign of Ahaziah of Israel. See note on 3, 1.

8, 25: *Twelfth year of Joram:* i. e., of Israel, who probably reigned only eight years.

9, 7-10: The editors of the Books of Kings have here added to the prophet's message the same type of indictment and sanctions against *the family of Ahab* as were invoked against the dynasties of *Jeroboam* (1 Kgs 14, 10f), *Baasha* (1 Kgs 16, 3f), and *Ahab* on a previous occasion (1 Kgs 21, 21-24).

---

*
17ff: 2 Chr 21, 5ff.	9/1: 1 Kgs 21, 29; Hos 1, 4.
19: 2 Sm 7, 11-16; 21, 17;	2: 1 Kgs 19, 16.
1 Kgs 11, 36; 15, 4;	3: 1 Kgs 19, 16.
2 Chr 21, 7.	8ff: 1 Kgs 14, 10f; 16, 3f;
22: Gn 27, 40; 2 Chr 21,	21, 21-24.
8ff.	13: Mt 21, 8.
28: 9, 14f.	14f: 8, 28f; 1 Kgs 22, 3f.

Joram lay ill and Ahaziah, king of Judah, had come to visit him.

¹⁷The watchman standing on the tower in Jezreel saw the troop of Jehu coming and reported, "I see chariots." "Get a driver," Joram said, "and send him to meet them and to ask whether all is well." ¹⁸So a driver went out to meet him and said, "The king asks whether all is well." "What does it matter to you how things are?" Jehu said. "Get behind me." The watchman reported to the king, "The messenger has reached them, but is not returning."

¹⁹Joram sent a second driver, who went to them and said, "The king asks whether all is well." "What does it matter to you how things are?" Jehu replied. "Get behind me."

²⁰The watchman reported, "The messenger has reached them, but is not returning. The driving is like that of Jehu, son of Nimshi, in its fury." ²¹"Prepare my chariot," said Joram. When they had done so, Joram, king of Israel, and Ahaziah, king of Judah, set out, each in his own chariot, to meet Jehu. They reached him near the field of Naboth the Jezreelite. ²²†When Joram recognized Jehu, he asked, "Is all well, Jehu?" "How can all be well," Jehu replied, "as long as the many fornications and witchcrafts of your mother Jezebel continue?" ²³Joram reigned about and fled, crying to Ahaziah, "Treason, Ahaziah!" ²⁴But Jehu drew his bow and shot Joram between the shoulders, so that the arrow went through his heart and he collapsed in his chariot. ²⁵*Then Jehu said to his adjutant Bidkar, "Take him and throw him into the field of Naboth the Jezreelite. For I remember that when we were driving teams behind his father Ahab, the LORD delivered this oracle against him: ²⁶'As surely as I saw yesterday the blood of Naboth and the blood of his sons,' says the LORD, 'I will repay you for it in that very plot of ground, says the LORD.' So now take him into this plot of ground, in keeping with the word of the LORD."

Death of Ahaziah

²⁷*Seeing what was happening, Ahaziah, king of Judah, fled toward Beth-haggan. Jehu pursued him, shouting, "Kill him too!" And they pierced him as he rode through the pass of Gur near Ibleam. He continued his flight as far as Megiddo and died there. ²⁸His servants brought him in a chariot to Jerusalem and buried him in the tomb of his ancestors in the City of David. ²⁹Ahaziah had become king of Judah in the eleventh year of Joram, son of Ahab.

Death of Jezebel

³⁰When Jezebel learned that Jehu had arrived in Jezreel, she shadowed her eyes, adorned her hair, and looked down from her window. ³¹*As Jehu came through the gate, she cried out, "Is all well, Zimri, murderer of your master?" ³²Jehu looked up to the window and shouted, "Who is on my side? Anyone?" At this, two or three eunuchs looked down toward him. ³³"Throw her down," he ordered. They threw her down, and some of her blood spurted against the wall and against the horses. Jehu rode in over her body ³⁴and, after eating and drinking, he said: "Attend to that accursed woman and bury her; after all, she was a king's daughter." ³⁵But when they went to bury her, they found nothing of her but the skull, the feet, and the hands. ³⁶*They returned to Jehu, and when they told him, he said, "This is the sentence which the LORD pronounced through his servant Elijah the Tishbite: 'In the confines of Jezreel dogs shall eat the flesh of Jezebel. ³⁷The corpse of Jezebel shall be like dung in the field in the confines of Jezreel, so that no one can say: This was Jezebel.'"

Killing of Ahab's Descendants

10 ¹*AHAB had seventy descendants in Samaria. Jehu prepared letters and sent them to the city rulers, to the elders, and to the guardians of Ahab's descendants in Samaria. ²"Since your master's sons are with you," he wrote, "and you have the chariots, the horses, a fortified city, and the weapons, when this letter reaches you ³decide which is the best and the fittest of your master's offspring, place him on his father's throne, and fight for your master's house." ⁴They were overcome with fright and said, "If two kings could not withstand him, how can we?" ⁵So the vizier and the ruler of the city, along with the elders and the guardians, sent this message to Jehu: "We are your servants, and we will do everything you tell us. We will proclaim no one king; do whatever you think best." ⁶So Jehu wrote them a second letter: "If you are on my side and will obey me, count the heads of your master's sons and come to me in Jezreel at this time tomorrow." [The seventy princes were in the care of prominent men of the city, who were rearing them.]

⁷When the letter arrived, they took the princes and slew all seventy of them, put their heads in baskets, and sent them to Jehu in Jezreel. ⁸"They have brought the heads of the princes," a messenger came in and told him. "Pile them in two heaps at the entrance of the city until morning," he ordered. ⁹Going out in the morning, he stopped and said to all the people: "You are not responsible, and although I conspired against my lord and slew him, yet who killed all these? ¹⁰*Know that not a single word which the LORD has spoken against the house of Ahab shall go unfulfilled. The LORD has accomplished all that he foretold through his servant Elijah." ¹¹*Thereupon Jehu slew all who were left of the family of Ahab in Jezreel, as well as all his powerful supporters, intimates, and priests, leaving him no survivor.

---

*
25f: 1 Kgs 21, 9-16.
27ff: 2 Chr 22, 7ff.
31: 1 Kgs 16, 9ff.
36: 1 Kgs 21, 23.
10/1: Jgs 9, 5; 1 Kgs 15, 29;
    16, 11.
10: 1 Kgs 21, 17-24.29.
11: Hos 1, 4.

---

† 9, 22: *Fornications and witchcrafts*: the worship of foreign gods.

Ahaziah's Kinsmen

12*Then he set out for Samaria, and at Beth-eked-haroim on the way, **13**he came across kinsmen of Ahaziah, king of Judah. "Who are you?" he asked. "We are kinsmen of Ahaziah," they replied. "We are going down to visit the princes and the family of the queen mother." **14**"Take them alive," Jehu ordered. They were taken alive, forty-two in number, then slain at the pit of Beth-eked. Not one of them was spared.

Jehu in Samaria

15*When he left there, Jehu met Jehonadab, son of Rechab, on the road. He greeted him and asked, "Are you sincerely disposed toward me, as I am toward you?" "Yes," replied Jehonadab. "If you are," continued Jehu, "give me your hand." Jehonadab gave him his hand, and Jehu drew him up into his chariot. **16**"Come with me," he said, "and see my zeal for the Lord." And he took him along in his own chariot.

17When he arrived in Samaria, Jehu slew all who remained there of Ahab's line, doing away with them completely and thus fulfilling the prophecy which the Lord had spoken to Elijah.

Baal's Temple Destroyed

18*Jehu gathered all the people together and said to them: "Ahab served Baal to some extent, but Jehu will serve him yet more. **19**Now summon for me all Baal's prophets, all his worshipers, and all his priests. See that no one is absent, for I have a great sacrifice for Baal. Whoever is absent shall not live." This Jehu did as a ruse, so that he might destroy the worshipers of Baal. **20**Jehu said further, "Proclaim a solemn assembly in honor of Baal." They did so, **21**and Jehu sent word of it throughout the land of Israel. All the worshipers of Baal without exception came into the temple of Baal, which was filled to capacity. **22***Then Jehu said to the custodian of the wardrobe, "Bring out the garments for all the worshipers of Baal." When he had brought out the garments for them, **23**Jehu, with Jehonadab, son of Rechab, entered the temple of Baal and said to the worshipers of Baal, "Search and be sure that there is no worshiper of the Lord here with you, but only worshipers of Baal." **24**Then they proceeded to offer sacrifices and holocausts. Now Jehu had stationed eighty men outside with this warning, "If one of you lets anyone escape of those whom I shall deliver into your hands, he shall pay life for life." **25**As soon as he finished offering the holocaust, Jehu said to the guards and officers, "Go in and slay them. Let no one escape." So the guards and officers put them to the sword and cast them out. Afterward they went into the inner shrine of the temple of Baal, **26**took out the stele of Baal, and burned the shrine. **27**Then they smashed the stele of Baal, tore down the building, and turned it into a latrine, as it remains today.

28Thus Jehu rooted out the worship of Baal from Israel. **29***However, he did not desist from the sins which Jeroboam, son of Nebat, had caused Israel to commit, as regards the golden calves at Bethel and at Dan. **30***The Lord said to Jehu, "Because you have done well what I deem right, and have treated the house of Ahab as I desire, your sons to the fourth generation shall sit upon the throne of Israel." **31**But Jehu was not careful to observe wholeheartedly the law of the Lord, the God of Israel, since he did not desist from the sins which Jeroboam caused Israel to commit.

32*At that time the Lord began to dismember Israel. Hazael defeated the Israelites throughout their territory **33**east of the Jordan (all the land of Gilead, of the Gadites, Reubenites and Manassehites), from Aroer on the river Arnon up through Gilead and Bashan.

34The rest of the acts of Jehu, his valor and all his accomplishments, are written in the book of chronicles of the kings of Israel. **35**Jehu rested with his ancestors and was buried in Samaria. His son Jehoahaz succeeded him as king. **36**The length of Jehu's reign over Israel in Samaria was twenty-eight years.

Rule of Athaliah

11 **1***when Athaliah, the mother of Ahaziah, saw that her son was dead, she began to kill off the whole royal family. **2**†But Jehosheba, daughter of King Jehoram and sister of Ahaziah, took Joash, his son, and spirited him away, along with his nurse, from the bedroom where the princes were about to be slain. She concealed him from Athaliah, and so he did not die **3**For six years he remained hidden in the temple of the Lord, while Athaliah ruled the land.

4*But in the seventh year, Jehoiada summoned the captains of the Carians and of the guards. He had them come to him in the temple of the Lord, exacted from them a sworn commitment, and then showed them the king's son. **5**He gave them these orders: "This is what you must do: the third of you who come on duty on the sabbath shall guard the king's palace; **6**another third shall be at the gate Sur; and the last third shall be at the gate behind the guards. **7**The two of your divisions who are going off duty that week shall keep guard over the temple of the Lord for the king. **8**You shall surround the king, each with drawn weapons, and if anyone tries to approach the cordon, kill him; stay with the king, whatever he may do."

9*The captains did just as Jehoiada the priest commanded. Each one with his men, both those going on duty for the sabbath and those going off duty that week, came to Jehoiada the priest. **10***He gave the captains King David's spears and shields, which were in the temple of the Lord. **11**And the guards, with drawn weapons, lined up from the southern to the

---

❋

12ff: 2 Chr 22, 8f.

15: 1 Chr 2, 55; Jer 35, 1-11.

18: 1 Kgs 16, 30ff.

22: 1 Kgs 16, 32.

29: 1 Kgs 12, 28f.

30: 15, 12ff.

32: Am 1, 3.

11/1: Jgs 9, 5.

4-8: 2 Chr 23, 1-7.

9-12: 2 Chr 23, 8-11.

10ff: 2 Sm 8, 7; 1 Kgs 1, 33f.

---

†

11, 2: *Jehosheba* was the wife of Jehoida, the high priest; cf 2 Chr 22, 11.

northern limit of the enclosure, surrounding the altar and the temple on the king's behalf. [12]*Then Jehoiada led out the king's son and put the crown and the insignia upon him. They proclaimed him king and anointed him, clapping their hands and shouting, "Long live the king!"

[13]*Athaliah heard the noise made by the people, and appeared before them in the temple of the LORD. [14]†When she saw the king standing by the pillar, as was the custom, and the captains and trumpeters near him, with all the people of the land rejoicing and blowing trumpets, she tore her garments and cried out, "Treason, treason!" [15]Then Jehoiada the priest instructed the captains in command of the force: "Bring her outside through the ranks. If anyone follows her," he added, "let him die by the sword." He had given orders that she should not be slain in the temple of the LORD. [16]She was led out forcibly to the horse gate of the royal palace, where she was put to death.

[17]*Then Jehoiada made a covenant between the LORD as one party and the king and the people as the other, by which they would be the LORD's people; and another covenant, between the king and the people. [18]Thereupon all the people of the land went to the temple of Baal and demolished it. They shattered its altars and images completely, and slew Mattan, the priest of Baal, before the altars. After appointing a detachment for the temple of the LORD, Jehoiada [19]with the captains, the Carians, the guards, and all the people of the land, led the king down from the temple of the LORD through the guards' gate to the palace, where Joash took his seat on the royal throne. [20]All the people of the land rejoiced and the city was quiet, now that Athaliah had been slain with the sword at the royal palace.

Reign of Joash

12 [1]*JOASH was seven years old when he became king. [2]Joash began to reign in the seventh year of Jehu, and he reigned forty years in Jerusalem. His mother, who was named Zibiah, was from Beer-sheba. [3]Joash did what was pleasing to the LORD as long as he lived, because the priest Jehoiada guided him. [4]Still, the high places did not disappear; the people continued to sacrifice and to burn incense there.

[5]*For the priests Joash made this rule: "All the funds for sacred purposes that are brought to the temple of the LORD—the census tax, personal redemption money, and whatever funds are freely brought to the temple of the LORD—[6]the priests may take for themselves, each from his own clients. However, they must make whatever repairs on the temple may prove necessary." [7]Nevertheless, as late as the twenty-third year of the reign of King Joash, the priests had not made needed repairs on the temple. [8]Accordingly, King Joash summoned the priest Jehoiada and the other priests. "Why do you not repair the temple?" he asked them. "You must no longer take funds from your clients, but you shall turn them over for the repairs." [9]*So the priests agreed that they would neither take funds from the people nor make the repairs on the temple.

[10]The priest Jehoiada then took a chest, bored a hole in its lid, and set it beside the stele, on the right as one entered the temple of the LORD. The priests who guarded the entry would put into it all the funds that were brought to the temple of the LORD. [11]When they noticed that there was a large amount of silver in the chest, the royal scribe [and the priest] would come up, and they would melt down all the funds that were in the temple of the LORD, and weigh them. [12]The amount thus realized they turned over to the master workmen in the temple of the LORD. They in turn would give it to the carpenters and builders working in the temple of the LORD, [13]and to the lumbermen and stone cutters, and for the purchase of the wood and hewn stone used in repairing the breaches, and for any other expenses that were necessary to repair the temple. [14]None of the funds brought to the temple of the LORD were used there to make silver cups, snuffers, basins, trumpets, or any gold or silver article. [15]Instead, they were given to the workmen, and with them they repaired the temple of the LORD. [16]Moreover, no reckoning was asked of the men who were provided with the funds to give to the workmen, because they held positions of trust. [17]The funds from guilt-offerings and from sin-offerings, however, were not brought to the temple of the LORD; they belonged to the priests.

[18]*Then King Hazael of Aram mounted a siege against Gath. When he had taken it, Hazael decided to go on to attack Jerusalem. [19]But King Jehoash of Judah took all the dedicated offerings presented by his forebears, Jehoshaphat, Jehoram, and Ahaziah, kings of Judah, as well as his own, and all the gold there was in the treasuries of the temple and the palace, and sent them to King Hazael of Aram, who then led his forces away from Jerusalem. [20]The rest of the acts of Joash, with all that he did, are recorded in the book of the chronicles of the kings of Judah. [21]Certain of his officials entered into a plot against him and killed him at Beth-millo. [22]Jozacar, son of Shimeath, and Jehozabad, son of Shomer, were the officials who killed him. He was buried in his forefathers' City of David, and his son Amaziah succeeded him as king.

Reign of Jehoahaz of Israel

13 [1]IN the twenty-third year of Joash, son of Ahaziah, king of Judah, Jehoahaz, son of Jehu, began his seventeen-year reign over Israel in Samaria. [2]He did evil in the LORD's sight, conducting himself like Jeroboam, son of Nebat, and not renouncing the sin he had caused Israel to commit.

❋
12: 2 Sm 1, 10.　　　　　　5-8: 2 Chr 24, 5-10.
13-16: 2 Chr 23, 12-15.　　9-16: 2 Chr 24, 11-14.
17-20: 2 Chr 23, 16-21.　　18: 8, 12.
12/1f: 2 Chr 24, 1f.　　　　18-22: 2 Chr 24, 23-27.

† 11, 14: *By the pillar:* see note on 2 Chr 23, 13.

³The LORD was angry with Israel and for a long time left them in the power of Hazael, king of Aram, and of Ben-hadad, son of Hazael. ⁴*Then Jehoahaz entreated the LORD, who heard him, since he saw the oppression to which the king of Aram had subjected Israel. ⁵†So the LORD gave Israel a savior, and the Israelites, freed from the power of Aram, dwelt in their own homes as formerly. ⁶*†Nevertheless, they did not desist from the sins which the house of Jeroboam had caused Israel to commit, but persisted in them. The sacred pole also remained standing in Samaria. ⁷No soldiers were left to Jehoahaz, except fifty horsemen with ten chariots and ten thousand foot soldiers, since the king of Aram had destroyed them and trampled them like dust. ⁸The rest of the acts of Jehoahaz, with all his valor and accomplishments, are recorded in the book of the chronicles of the kings of Israel. ⁹Jehoahaz rested with his ancestors and was buried in Samaria. His son Joash succeeded him as king.

Reign of Joash of Israel

¹⁰In the thirty-seventh year of Joash, king of Judah, Jehoash, son of Jehoahaz, began his sixteen-year reign over Israel in Samaria. ¹¹He did evil in the sight of the LORD; he did not desist from any of the sins which Jeroboam, son of Nebat, had caused Israel to commit, but persisted in them. ¹²*†[The rest of the acts of Joash, the valor with which he fought against Amaziah, king of Judah, and all his accomplishments, are recorded in the book of the chronicles of the kings of Israel. ¹³Joash rested with his ancestors, and Jeroboam occupied the throne. Joash was buried with the kings of Israel in Samaria.]

¹⁴*†When Elisha was suffering from the sickness of which he was to die, King Joash of Israel went down to visit him. "My father, my father!" he exclaimed, weeping over him. "Israel's chariots and horsemen!" ¹⁵"Take a bow and some arrows," Elisha said to him. When he had done so, ¹⁶†Elisha said to the king of Israel, "Put your hand on the bow." As the king held the bow, Elisha placed his hands over the king's hands ¹⁷and said, "Open the window toward the east." He opened it. Elisha said, "Shoot," and he shot. The prophet exclaimed, "The LORD's arrow of victory! The arrow of victory over Aram! You will completely conquer Aram at Aphec."

¹⁸Then he said to the king of Israel, "Take the arrows," which he did. Elisha said to him, "Strike the ground!" He struck the ground three times and stopped. ¹⁹Angry with him, the man of God said: "You should have struck five or six times; you would have defeated Aram completely. Now, you will defeat Aram only three times."

²⁰Elisha died and was buried. At the time, bands of Moabites used to raid the land each year. ²¹*Once some people were burying a man, when suddenly they spied such a raiding band. So they cast the dead man into the grave of Elisha, and everyone went off. But when the man came in contact with the bones of Elisha, he came back to life and rose to his feet.

²²King Hazael of Aram oppressed Israel during the entire reign of Jehoahaz. ²³*But the LORD was merciful with Israel and looked on them with compassion because of his covenant with Abraham, Isaac, and Jacob. He was unwilling to destroy them or to cast them out from his presence. ²⁴So when King Hazael of Aram died and his son Ben-hadad succeeded him as king, ²⁵Joash, son of Jehoahaz, took back from Ben-hadad, son of Hazael, the cities which Hazael had taken in battle from his father Jehoahaz. Joash defeated Ben-hadad three times, and thus recovered the cities of Israel.

Amaziah of Judah

14 ¹†IN the second year of Joash, son of Jehoahaz, king of Israel, Amaziah, son of Joash, king of Judah, began to reign. ²*He was twenty-five years old when he became king, and he reigned twenty-nine years in Jerusalem. His mother, whose name was Jehoaddin, was from Jerusalem. ³He pleased the LORD, yet not like his forefather David, since he did just as his father Joash had done. ⁴Thus the high places did not disappear, but the people continued to sacrifice and to burn incense on them. ⁵*When Amaziah had the kingdom firmly in hand, he slew the officials who had murdered the king, his father. ⁶*But the children of the murderers he did not put to death, obeying the LORD's command written in the book of the law of Moses, "Fathers shall not be put to death for their children, nor shall children be put to death for their fathers; each one shall die for his own sin."

⁷*Amaziah slew ten thousand Edomites in the Salt Valley, and took Sela in battle. He renamed it Joktheel, the name it has to this day.

⁸*Then Amaziah sent messengers to Jehoash, son of Jehoahaz, son of Jehu, king of Israel, with this chal-

---

† 13, 5: *A savior:* by this language, typical of the Book of Judges (3, 9. 15), Jeroboam II of Israel is meant; cf 14, 27.

13, 6: *Sacred pole:* see note on Ex 34, 13.

13, 12f: The conclusion to the reign of Joash is given again in 14, 15f, where it is more appropriate.

13, 14: *My father, my father:* the king expresses here the same sentiments as those with which Elisha addressed Elijah.

13, 16-19: Symbolic acts similar to these are seen in Ex 17, 8ff; Jos 8, 18ff; Ez 4, 1ff.

14, 1f: *In the second year . . . twenty-nine years in Jerusalem:* the reigns of the kings of Judah between Athaliah and Ahaz are assigned too many years in all to correspond to the reigns in Israel from Jehu to the fall of Samaria. It seems probable that Amaziah was murdered as soon as his son Azariah was old enough to rule, and that Amaziah's reign was nearer nineteen than twenty-nine years. The correlation, in 15, 1, of the beginning of Azariah's reign with the 27th year of Jeroboam II can hardly be correct; and the sixteen-year reign of Joatham of Judah (15, 33) consisted for the most part of a regency during the illness of his father (15, 5).

---

* 13/4: 14, 26f.
　6: Ex 34, 13.
　12: 14, 8-16.
　14: 2, 12.
　21: Sir 48, 14.
　23: Dt 9, 27.

14/2f: 2 Chr 25, 1f.
　5f: 2 Chr 25, 3f.
　6: Dt 24, 16; Ez 18, 20.
　7: 2 Sm 8, 13f; 2 Chr 25, 11.
　8: 13, 12; Jgs 9, 8-15.

lenge, "Come, let us meet face to face." ⁹King Jehoash of Israel sent this reply to the king of Judah: "The thistle of Lebanon sent word to the cedar of Lebanon, 'Give your daughter to my son in marriage,' but an animal of Lebanon passed by and trampled the thistle underfoot. ¹⁰You have indeed conquered Edom, and you have become ambitious. Enjoy your glory, but stay at home! Why involve yourself and Judah with you in misfortune and failure?"

¹¹But Amaziah would not listen. King Jehoash of Israel then advanced, and he and King Amaziah of Judah met in battle at Beth-shemesh of Judah. ¹²Judah was defeated by Israel, and all the Judean soldiery fled homeward. ¹³King Jehoash of Israel captured Amaziah, son of Jehoash, son of Ahaziah, king of Judah, at Beth-shemesh. He went on to Jerusalem where he tore down four hundred cubits of the city wall, from the Gate of Ephraim to the Corner Gate. ¹⁴He took all the gold and silver and all the utensils there were in the temple of the LORD and in the treasuries of the palace, and hostages as well. Then he returned to Samaria. ¹⁵*The rest of the acts of Jehoash, his valor, and how he fought Amaziah, king of Judah, are recorded in the book of the chronicles of the kings of Israel. ¹⁶Jehoash rested with his ancestors; he was buried in Samaria with the kings of Israel. His son Jeroboam succeeded him as king.

¹⁷†Amaziah, son of Joash, king of Judah, survived Jehoash, son of Jehoahaz, king of Israel, by fifteen years. ¹⁸The rest of the acts of Amaziah are written in the book of the chronicles of the kings of Judah. ¹⁹When a conspiracy was formed against him in Jerusalem, he fled to Lachish. But he was pursued to Lachish and killed there. ²⁰He was brought back on horses and buried with his ancestors in the City of David in Jerusalem. ²¹*†Thereupon all the people of Judah took the sixteen-year-old Azariah and proclaimed him king to succeed his father Amaziah. ²²It was Azariah who rebuilt Elath and restored it to Judah, after King Amaziah rested with his ancestors.

Jeroboam II of Israel

²³In the fifteenth year of Amaziah, son of Joash, king of Judah, Jeroboam, son of Joash, king of Israel, began his forty-one-year reign in Samaria. ²⁴He did evil in the sight of the LORD; he did not desist from any of the sins which Jeroboam, son of Nebat, had caused Israel to commit. ²⁵†He restored the boundaries of Israel from Labo-of-Hamath to the sea of the Arabah, just as the LORD, the God of Israel, had prophesied through his servant, the prophet Jonah, son of Amittai, from Gathhepher. ²⁶*For the LORD saw the very bitter affliction of Israel, where there was neither slave nor freeman, no one at all to help Israel. ²⁷Since the LORD had not determined to blot out the name of Israel from under the heavens, he saved them through Jeroboam, son of Joash. ²⁸The rest of the acts of Jeroboam, his valor and all his accomplishments, how he fought with Damascus and turned back Hamath from Israel, are recorded in the book of the chronicles of the kings of Israel. ²⁹Jeroboam rested with his ancestors, the kings of Israel, and his son Zechariah succeeded him as king.

Azariah of Judah

15 ¹*†AZARIAH, son of Amaziah, king of Judah, became king in the twenty-seventh year of Jeroboam, king of Israel. ²He was sixteen years old when he began to reign, and he reigned fifty-two years in Jerusalem. His mother, whose name was Jecholiah, was from Jerusalem. ³He pleased the LORD just as his father Amaziah had done. ⁴Yet the high places did not disappear; the people continued to sacrifice and to burn incense on them. ⁵*The LORD afflicted the king, and he was a leper to the day of his death. He lived in a house apart, while Jotham, the king's son, was vizier and regent for the people of the land. ⁶The rest of the acts of Azariah, and all his accomplishments, are recorded in the book of the chronicles of the kings of Judah. ⁷Azariah rested with his ancestors, and was buried with them in the City of David. His son Jotham succeeded him as king.

Zechariah of Israel

⁸In the thirty-eighth year of Azariah, king of Judah, Zechariah, son of Jeroboam, was king of Israel in Samaria for six months. ⁹He did evil in the sight of the LORD as his fathers had done, and did not desist from the sins which Jeroboam, son of Nebat, had caused Israel to commit. ¹⁰Shallum, son of Jabesh, conspired against Zechariah, attacked and killed him at Ibleam, and reigned in his place. ¹¹The rest of the acts of Zechariah are recorded in the book of the chronicles of the kings of Israel. ¹²*Thus the LORD's promise to Jehu, "Your descendants to the fourth generation shall sit upon the throne of Israel," was fulfilled.

Shallum of Israel

¹³Shallum, son of Jabesh, became king in the thirty-ninth year of Uzziah, king of Judah; he reigned one month in Samaria. ¹⁴Menahem, son of Gadi, came up from Tirzah to Samaria, where he attacked and killed Shallum, son of Jabesh, and reigned in his place. ¹⁵The rest of the acts of Shallum, and the fact of his conspiracy, are recorded in the book of the chronicles of the kings of Israel. ¹⁶At that time, Menahem punished Tappuah, all the inhabitants of the town and of its whole district, because on his way from Tirzah they did not let him in. He punished them even to ripping open all the pregnant women.

❋
15: 13, 12f.   15/1ff: 2 Chr 26, 3f.
21: 2 Chr 26, 1f.   5ff: 2 Chr 26, 21ff.
26: 13, 4f; 1 Kgs 14, 10.   12: 10, 30.

---

†
14, 17: See note on 14, 1f.
14, 21: *Azariah:* also called Uzziah in many texts.
14, 25: *Sea of the Arabah:* the Dead Sea. *Jonah:* see note on Jon 1, 1.
15, 1: *Twenty-seventh year:* see note on 14, 1f.

Menahem of Israel

[17]In the thirty-ninth year of Azariah, king of Judah, Menahem, son of Gadi, began his ten-year reign over Samaria. [18]He did evil in the sight of the LORD, not desisting from the sins which Jeroboam, son of Nebat, had caused Israel to commit. During his reign, [19]†Pul, king of Assyria, invaded the land, and Menahem gave him a thousand talents of silver to have his assistance in strengthening his hold on the kingdom. [20]Menahem secured the money to give to the king of Assyria by exacting it from all the men of substance in the country, fifty silver shekels from each. The king of Assyria did not remain in the country but withdrew. [21]The rest of the acts of Menahem, and all his accomplishments, are recorded in the book of the chronicles of the kings of Israel. [22]Menahem rested with his ancestors, and his son Pekahiah succeeded him as king.

Pekahiah of Israel

[23]In the fiftieth year of Azariah, king of Judah, Pekahiah, son of Menahem, began his two-year reign over Israel in Samaria. [24]He did evil in the sight of the LORD, not desisting from the sins which Jeroboam, son of Nebat, had caused Israel to commit. [25]His adjutant Pekah, son of Remaliah, who had with him fifty men from Gilead, conspired against him, killed him within the palace stronghold in Samaria, and reigned in his place. [26]The rest of the acts of Pekahiah, and all his accomplishments, are recorded in the book of the chronicles of the kings of Israel.

Pekah of Israel

[27]†In the fifty-second year of Azariah, king of Judah, Pekah, son of Remaliah, began his twenty-year reign over Israel in Samaria. [28]He did evil in the sight of the LORD, not desisting from the sins which Jeroboam, son of Nebat, had caused Israel to commit. [29]During the reign of Pekah, king of Israel, Tiglath-pileser, king of Assyria, came and took Ijon, Abel-beth-maacah, Janoah, Kedesh, Hazor, all the territory of Naphtali, Gilead, and Galilee, deporting the inhabitants to Assyria. [30]Hoshea, son of Elah, conspired against Pekah, son of Remaliah; he attacked and killed him, and reigned in his place [in the twentieth year of Jotham, son of Uzziah]. [31]The rest of the acts of Pekah, and all his accomplishments, are recorded in the book of the chronicles of the kings of Israel.

Jotham of Judah

[32]*In the second year of Pekah, son of Remaliah, king of Israel, Jotham, son of Uzziah, king of Judah, began to reign. [33]He was twenty-five years old when he became king, and he reigned sixteen years in Jerusalem. His mother's name was Jerusha, daughter of Zadok. [34]He pleased the LORD, just as his father Uzziah had done. [35]†Nevertheless the high places did not disappear and the people continued to sacrifice and to burn incense on them. It was he who built the Upper Gate of the temple of the LORD. [36]The rest of the acts of Jotham, and all his accomplishments, are recorded in the book of the chronicles of the kings of Judah. [37]It was at that time that the LORD first loosed Rezin, king of Aram, and Pekah, son of Remaliah, against Judah. [38]Jotham rested with his ancestors and was buried with them in his forefather's City of David. His son Ahaz succeeded him as king.

Ahaz of Judah

16 [1]*IN the seventeenth year of Pekah, son of Remaliah, Ahaz, son of Jotham, king of Judah, began to reign. [2]Ahaz was twenty years old when he became king, and he reigned sixteen years in Jerusalem. He did not please the LORD, his God, like his forefather David, [3]*but conducted himself like the kings of Israel, and even immolated his son by fire, in accordance with the abominable practice of the nations whom the LORD had cleared out of the way of the Israelites. [4]*Further, he sacrificed and burned incense on the high places, on hills, and under every leafy tree.

[5]*Then Rezin, king of Aram, and Pekah, son of Remaliah, king of Israel, came up to Jerusalem to attack it. Although they besieged Ahaz, they were unable to conquer him. [6]*At the same time the king of Edom recovered Elath for Edom, driving the Judeans out of it. The Edomites then entered Elath, which they have occupied until the present.

[7]*Meanwhile, Ahaz sent messengers to Tiglath-pileser, king of Assyria, with the plea: "I am your servant and your son. Come up and rescue me from the clutches of the king of Aram and the king of Israel, who are attacking me." [8]*Ahaz took the silver and gold that were in the temple of the LORD and in the palace treasuries and sent them as a present to the king of Assyria, [9]†who listened to him and moved against

---

† 15, 19: *Pul:* The Babylonian throne name of the Assyrian Tiglath-pileser III; cf 15, 29.

15, 27: The twenty years here ascribed to *Pekah* are an impossibility; the calculation which made his reign, of five years at most, appear so long may have been based on the attempt to give Jotham of Judah a full sixteen-year reign independently of his regency. See 16, 1 and the note on 14, 1f.

15, 35: *The Upper Gate:* also the Gate of Benjamin; cf Jer 20, 2; Ez 9, 2.

16, 9: Firmly dated events bearing on chapters 16 through 20 are: the fall of Damascus (16, 9) in 732 B. C., the fall of Samaria (18, 9-11) in 721 B. C., and Sennacherib's invasion of Judah (18, 3) in 701 B. C., which is equated both in Kgs and in Is 36, 1 with the 14th year of Hezekiah. These data make it necessary to credit Ahaz with at least a twenty-year reign, between 735 and c. 715 B. C., and to exclude the correlations between Hoshea of Israel and Hezekiah in chapter 18.

If the 14th-year correspondence for 701 B. C. is given up, other arrangements are possible. The alleged ages of Jotham (15, 33), Ahaz (16, 2), and Hezekiah (18, 2) at their successive accessions to the throne do not argue for an early date for Hezekiah; but one or more of these may be artificial. Azariah (15, 1-7; Is 6, 1) was still on the throne of Judah in 743 B. C.

❀
32-38: 2 Chr 27, 1-4.7-9.   5: 2 Chr 28, 5f.
16/1-4: 2 Chr 28, 1-4.   6: 2 Chr 28, 17.
  3: Lv 18, 21.   7: 2 Chr 28, 16.
  4: Dt 12, 2.   8: 2 Chr 28, 21.

Damascus, which he captured. He deported its inhabitants to Kir and put Rezin to death.

¹⁰King Ahaz went to Damascus to meet Tiglath-pileser, king of Assyria. When he saw the altar in Damascus, King Ahaz sent to Uriah the priest a model of the altar and a detailed design of its construction. ¹¹Uriah the priest built an altar according to the plans which King Ahaz sent him from Damascus, and had it completed by the time the king returned home. ¹²On his arrival from Damascus, the king inspected this altar, then went up to it and offered sacrifice on it, ¹³*burning his holocaust and cereal-offering, pouring out his libation, and sprinkling the blood of his peace-offerings on the altar. ¹⁴The bronze altar that stood before the Lord he brought from the front of the temple—that is, from the space between the new altar and the temple of the Lord—and set it on the north side of his altar. ¹⁵*†"Upon the large altar," King Ahaz commanded Uriah the priest, "burn the morning holocaust and the evening cereal-offering, the royal holocaust and cereal-offering, as well as the holocausts, cereal-offerings, and libations of the people. You must also sprinkle on it all the blood of holocausts and sacrifices. But the old bronze altar shall be mine for consultation." ¹⁶Uriah the priest did just as King Ahaz had commanded. ¹⁷*King Ahaz detached the frames from the bases and removed the lavers from them; he also took down the bronze sea from the bronze oxen that supported it, and set it on a stone pavement. ¹⁸†In deference to the king of Assyria he removed from the temple of the Lord the emplacement which had been built in the temple for a throne, and the outer entrance for the king. ¹⁹*The rest of the acts of Ahaz are recorded in the book of the chronicles of the kings of Judah. ²⁰Ahaz rested with his ancestors and was buried with them in the City of David. His son Hezekiah succeeded him as king.

Hoshea of Israel

17 ¹In the twelfth year of Ahaz, king of Judah, Hoshea, son of Elah, began his nine-year reign over Israel in Samaria. ²He did evil in the sight of the Lord, yet not to the extent of the kings of Israel before him. ³*†Shalmaneser, king of Assyria, advanced against him, and Hoshea became his vassal and paid him tribute. ⁴But the king of Assyria found Hoshea guilty of conspiracy for sending envoys to the king of Egypt at Sais, and for failure to pay the annual tribute to his Assyrian overlord. ⁵For this, the king of Assyria arrested and imprisoned Hoshea; he then occupied the whole land and attacked Samaria, which he besieged for three years. ⁶*†In the ninth year of Hoshea, the king of Assyria took Samaria, and de-

ported the Israelites to Assyria, settling them in Halah, at the Habor, a river of Gozan, and in the cities of the Medes.

⁷This came about because the Israelites sinned against the Lord, their God, who had brought them up from the land of Egypt, from under the domination of Pharaoh, king of Egypt, and because they venerated other gods. ⁸They followed the rites of the nations whom the Lord had cleared out of the way of the Israelites [and the kings of Israel whom they set up]. ⁹They adopted unlawful practices toward the Lord, their God. They built high places in all their settlements, the watchtowers as well as the walled cities. ¹⁰*They set up pillars and sacred poles for themselves on every high hill and under every leafy tree. ¹¹There, on all the high places, they burned incense like the nations whom the Lord had sent into exile at their coming. They did evil things that provoked the Lord, ¹²and served idols, although the Lord had told them, "You must not do this."

¹³*And though the Lord warned Israel and Judah by every prophet and seer, "Give up your evil ways and keep my commandments and statutes, in accordance with the entire law which I enjoined on your fathers and which I sent you by my servants the prophets," ¹⁴they did not listen, but were as stiff-necked as their fathers, who had not believed in the Lord, their God. ¹⁵*They rejected his statutes, the covenant which he had made with their fathers, and the warnings which he had given them. The vanity they pursued, they themselves became: they followed the surrounding nations whom the Lord had commanded them not to imitate. ¹⁶*They disregarded all the commandments of the Lord, their God, and made for themselves two molten calves; they also made a sacred pole and worshiped all the host of heaven, and served Baal. ¹⁷*They immolated their sons and daughters by fire, practiced fortune-telling and divination, and sold themselves into evildoing in the Lord's sight, provoking him ¹⁸till, in his great anger against Israel, the Lord put them away out of his sight. Only the tribe of Judah was left.

¹⁹Even the people of Judah, however, did not keep the commandments of the Lord, their God, but followed the rites practiced by Israel. ²⁰So the Lord rejected the whole race of Israel. He afflicted them and delivered them over to plunderers, finally casting them out from before him. ²¹*When he tore Israel away from the house of David, they made Jeroboam, son of Nebat, king; he drove the Israelites away from the Lord, causing them to commit a great sin. ²²The Israelites imitated Jeroboam in all the sins he committed, nor would they desist from them. ²³*Finally, the Lord put Israel away out of his sight as he had

---

* 13: 2 Chr 28, 23.
15: Ex 29, 38f; Nm 28, 3f.
17: 2 Chr 28, 24.
19: 2 Chr 28, 26f.
17/3: 18, 9; Tb 1, 2.
6: 18, 10f.
10: Ex 23, 24; 34, 13; Dt 12, 2.
13: Jer 25, 5, Dt 9, 13.
15: Jer 2, 5.
16: 1 Kgs 12, 28; Ex 34, 13; Dt 4, 19; 17, 2f.
17: Lv 18, 21; Dt 18, 10.
21: 1 Kgs 12, 19f; 12, 26-33.
23: Jer 25, 9.

† 16, 15: *For consultation:* perhaps the introduction into Judah of the Babylonian practice of omen sacrifices; cf Ez 21, 16.

16, 18: *Emplacement . . . for a throne, and the outer entrance for the king:* signs of sovereignty for the Hebrew kings.

17, 3: *Shalmaneser:* son and successor of Tiglath-pileser.

17, 6: *The king of Assyria:* Shalmaneser's successor and usurper, Sargon II.

foretold through all his servants, the prophets; and Israel went into exile from their native soil to Assyria, an exile lasting to the present.

24The king of Assyria brought people from Babylon, Cuthah, Avva, Hamath, and Sepharvaim, and settled them in the cities of Samaria in place of the Israelites. They took possession of Samaria and dwelt in its cities. 25When they first settled there, they did not venerate the Lord, so he sent lions among them that killed some of their number. 26A report reached the king of Assyria: "The nations whom you deported and settled in the cities of Samaria do not know how to worship the God of the land, and he has sent lions among them that are killing them, since they do not know how to worship the God of the land." 27The king of Assyria gave the order, "Send back one of the priests whom I deported, to go there and settle, to teach them how to worship the God of the land." 28So one of the priests who had been deported from Samaria returned and settled in Bethel, and taught them how to venerate the Lord.

29*But these peoples began to make their own gods in the various cities in which they were living; in the shrines on the high places which the Samarians had made, each people set up gods. 30Thus the Babylonians made Marduk and his consort; the men of Cuth made Nergal; the men of Hamath made Ashima; 31the men of Avva made Nibhaz and Tartak; and the men of Sepharvaim immolated their children by fire to their city gods, King Hadad and his consort Anath. 32*They also venerated the Lord, choosing from their number priests for the high places, who officiated for them in the shrines on the high places. 33But, while venerating the Lord, they served their own gods, following the worship of the nations from among whom they had been deported.

34*†To this day they worship according to their ancient rites. [They did not venerate the Lord nor observe the statutes and regulations, the law and commandments, which the Lord enjoined on the descendants of Jacob, whom he had named Israel. 35*When he made a covenant with them, he commanded them: "You must not venerate other gods, nor worship them, nor serve them, nor offer sacrifice to them. 36The Lord, who brought you up from the land of Egypt with great power and outstretched arm: him shall you venerate, him shall you worship, and to him shall you sacrifice. 37You must be careful to observe forever the statutes and regulations, the law and commandment, which he wrote for you, and you must not venerate other gods. 38The covenant which I made with you, you must not forget; you must not venerate other gods. 39But the Lord, your God, you must venerate; it is he who will

deliver you from the power of all your enemies." 40They did not listen, however, but continued in their earlier manner.] 41Thus these nations venerated the Lord, but also served their idols. And their sons and grandsons, to this day, are doing as their fathers did.

II: THE KINGDOM OF JUDAH AFTER 721 B. C.

Hezekiah

18 1*IN THE THIRD YEAR of Hoshea, son of Elah, king of Israel, Hezekiah, son of Ahaz, king of Judah, began to reign. 2He was twenty-five years old when he became king, and he reigned twenty-nine years in Jerusalem. His mother's name was Abi, daughter of Zechariah. 3He pleased the Lord, just as his forefather David had done. 4*It was he who removed the high places, shattered the pillars, and cut down the sacred poles. He smashed the bronze serpent called Nehushtan which Moses had made, because up to that time the Israelites were burning incense to it. 5He put his trust in the Lord, the God of Israel; and neither before him nor after him was there anyone like him among all the kings of Judah. 6Loyal to the Lord, Hezekiah never turned away from him, but observed the commandments which the Lord had given Moses. 7The Lord was with him, and he prospered in all that he set out to do. He rebelled against the king of Assyria and did not serve him. 8He also subjugated the watchtowers and walled cities of the Philistines, all the way to Gaza and its territory.

9In the fourth year of King Hezekiah, which was the seventh year of Hoshea, son of Elah, king of Israel, Shalmaneser, king of Assyria, attacked Samaria, laid siege to it, 10*and after three years captured it. In the sixth year of Hezekiah, the ninth year of Hoshea, king of Israel, Samaria was taken. 11The king of Assyria then deported the Israelites to Assyria and settled them in Halah, at the Habor, a river of Gozan, and in the cities of the Medes. 12*This came about because they had not heeded the warning of the Lord, their God, but violated his covenant, not heeding and not fulfilling the commandments of Moses, the servant of the Lord.

Invasion of Sennacherib

13*†In the fourteenth year of King Hezekiah, Sennacherib, king of Assyria, went on an expedition against all the fortified cities of Judah and captured

✿
29: Jn 4, 9.
32: 1 Kgs 12, 31.
34: Gn 32, 29.
35: Ex 20, 3ff.
18/1ff: 2 Chr 28, 27; 29, 1f.
4: Ex 23, 24; 34, 13;
Nm 21, 9; Dt 12, 2;
2 Chr 31, 1; Wis 16, 6;
Jn 3, 14.

10f: 17, 6; Tb 1, 2.
12: 17, 7-18.
13: 2 Chr 32, 1ff;
Sir 48, 18; Is 36, 1.

† 17, 34-40: *They did not . . . earlier manner:* this passage is an adaptation of language denouncing the Israelites to make it applicable to the later Samaritan sect of postexilic times. The original bearing of the discourse [13-15] can be seen by reading it between 22 and 23. Cf also 18, 12.

18, 9: See note on 16, 9.

18, 13: *Sennacherib* succeeded Sargon II as king of Assyria. His Judean campaign was waged in 701 B. C. See note on 16, 9.

18, 13—20, 11: Duplication of Is 36, 1—38, 8.21.22.

them. ¹⁴Hezekiah, king of Judah, sent this message to the king of Assyria at Lachish: "I have done wrong. Leave me, and I will pay whatever tribute you impose on me." The king of Assyria exacted three hundred talents of silver and thirty talents of gold from Hezekiah, king of Judah. ¹⁵Hezekiah paid him all the funds there were in the temple of the Lord and in the palace treasuries. ¹⁶*He broke up the door panels and the uprights of the temple of the Lord which he himself had ordered to be overlaid with gold, and gave the gold to the king of Assyria.

¹⁷*†The king of Assyria sent the general, the lord chamberlain, and the commander from Lachish with a great army to King Hezekiah at Jerusalem. They went up, and on their arrival in Jerusalem, stopped at the conduit of the upper pool on the highway of the fuller's field. ¹⁸*They called for the king, who sent out to them Eliakim, son of Hilkiah, the master of the palace; Shebnah the scribe; and the herald Joah, son of Asaph. ¹⁹The commander said to them, "Tell Hezekiah, 'Thus says the great king, the king of Assyria: On what do you base this confidence of yours? ²⁰Do you think mere words substitute for strategy and might in war? On whom, then, do you rely, that you rebel against me? ²¹*This Egypt, the staff on which you rely, is in fact a broken reed which pierces the hand of anyone who leans on it. That is what Pharaoh, king of Egypt, is to all who rely on him. ²²But if you say to me, We rely on the Lord, our God, is not he the one whose high places and altars Hezekiah has removed, commanding Judah and Jerusalem to worship before this altar in Jerusalem?'

²³"Now, make a wager with my lord, the king of Assyria: I will give you two thousand horses if you can put riders on them. ²⁴How then can you repulse even one of the least servants of my lord, relying as you do on Egypt for chariots and horsemen? ²⁵Was it without the Lord's will that I have come up to destroy this place? The Lord said to me, 'Go up and destroy that land!'"

²⁶Then Eliakim, son of Hilkiah, and Shebnah and Joah said to the commander: "Please speak to your servants in Aramaic; we understand it. Do not speak to us in Judean within earshot of the people who are on the wall." ²⁷But the commander replied: "Was it to your master and to you that my lord sent me to speak these words? Was it not rather to the men sitting on the wall, who, with you, will have to eat their own excrement and drink their urine?" ²⁸Then the commander stepped forward and cried out in a loud voice in Judean, "Listen to the words of the great king, the king of Assyria. ²⁹Thus says the king: 'Do not let Hezekiah deceive you, since he cannot deliver you out of my hand. ³⁰Let not Hezekiah induce you to rely on the

Lord, saying, The Lord will surely save us; this city will not be handed over to the king of Assyria. ³¹Do not listen to Hezekiah, for the king of Assyria says: Make peace with me and surrender! Then each of you will eat of his own vine and of his own fig-tree, and drink the water of his own cistern, ³²until I come to take you to a land like your own, a land of grain and wine, of bread and orchards, of olives, oil and fruit syrup. Choose life, not death. Do not listen to Hezekiah when he would seduce you by saying, The Lord will rescue us. ³³Has any of the gods of the nations ever rescued his land from the hand of the king of Assyria? ³⁴*Where are the gods of Hamath and Arpad? Where are the gods of Sepharvaim, Hena, and Avva? Where are the gods of the land of Samaria? ³⁵Which of the gods for all these lands ever rescued his land from my hand? Will the Lord then rescue Jerusalem from my hand?'" ³⁶But the people remained silent and did not answer him one word, for the king had ordered them not to answer him.

³⁷Then the master of the palace, Eliakim, son of Hilkiah, Shebnah the scribe, and the herald Joah, son of Asaph, came to Hezekiah with their garments torn, and reported to him what the commander had said.

Hezekiah and Isaiah

19 ¹*WHEN King Hezekiah heard this, he tore his garments, wrapped himself in sackcloth, and went into the temple of the Lord. ²He sent Eliakim, the master of the palace, Shebnah the scribe, and the elders of the priests, wrapped in sackcloth, to tell the prophet Isaiah, son of Amoz, ³†"Thus says Hezekiah: 'This is a day of distress, of rebuke, and of disgrace. Children are at the point of birth, but there is no strength to bring them forth. ⁴Perhaps the Lord, your God, will hear all the words of the commander, whom his master, the king of Assyria, sent to taunt the living God, and will rebuke him for the words which the Lord, your God, has heard. So send up a prayer for the remnant that is here.'" ⁵When the servants of King Hezekiah had come to Isaiah, ⁶*he said to them, "Tell this to your master: 'Thus says the Lord: Do not be frightened by the words you have heard, with which the servants of the king of Assyria have blasphemed me. ⁷I am about to put in him such a spirit that, when he hears a certain report, he will return to his own land, and there I will cause him to fall by the sword.'"

⁸When the commander, on his return, heard that the king of Assyria had withdrawn from Lachish, he found him besieging Libnah. ⁹The king of Assyria heard a report that Tirhakah, king of Ethiopia, had come out to fight against him. Again he sent envoys to Hezekiah with this message: ¹⁰"Thus shall you say to

16: 1 Kgs 6, 20-22.
17: 2 Chr 32, 9; Is 36, 1ff.
18: Is 22, 13-25.
21: Is 30, 1-7; 31, 1-3; Ez 29, 6-7.
34: 17, 24.
19/1-7: Is 37, 1-7.
6: Is 10, 5-19.

† 18, 17: *General, the lord chamberlain . . . commander:* the text lists three major functionaries by their Assyrian titles, of which only the first, more nearly "lord lieutenant," is military in origin; the *commander* was technically the king's chief butler.
19, 3: See note on Is 37, 3.

Hezekiah, king of Judah: 'Do not let your God on whom you rely deceive you by saying that Jerusalem will not be handed over to the king of Assyria. ¹¹You have heard what the kings of Assyria have done to all other countries: they doomed them! Will you, then, be saved? ¹²*Did the gods of the nations whom my fathers destroyed save them? Gozan, Haran, Rezeph, or the Edenites in Telassar? ¹³*Where are the king of Hamath, the king of Arpad, or the kings of the cities Sepharvaim, Hena and Avva?'"

¹⁴*Hezekiah took the letter from the hand of the messengers and read it; then he went up to the temple of the LORD, and spreading it out before him, ¹⁵*he prayed in the LORD's presence: "O LORD, God of Israel, enthroned upon the cherubim! You alone are God over all the kingdoms of the earth. You have made the heavens and the earth. ¹⁶Incline your ear, O LORD, and listen! Open your eyes, O LORD, and see! Hear the words of Sennacherib which he sent to taunt the living God. ¹⁷Truly, O LORD, the kings of Assyria have laid waste the nations and their lands, ¹⁸*and cast their gods into the fire; they destroyed them because they were not gods, but the work of human hands, wood and stone. ¹⁹*Therefore, O LORD, our God, save us from the power of this man, that all the kingdoms of the earth may know that you alone, O LORD, are God."

Punishment of Sennacherib

²⁰Then Isaiah, son of Amoz, sent this message to Hezekiah: "Thus says the LORD, the God of Israel, in answer to your prayer for help against Sennacherib, king of Assyria: I have listened! ²¹†This is the word the LORD has spoken concerning him:

"'She despises you, laughs you to scorn,
    the virgin daughter Zion!
Behind you she wags her head,
    daughter Jerusalem.
²²Whom have you insulted and blasphemed,
    against whom have you raised your voice
And lifted up your eyes on high?
    Against the Holy One of Israel!
²³Through your servants you have insulted the Lord.
    You said: With my many chariots
I climbed the mountain heights,
    the recesses of Lebanon;
I cut down its lofty cedars,
    its choice cypresses;
I reached the remotest heights,
    its forest park.
²⁴I dug wells and drank water in foreign lands;
    I dried up with the soles of my feet
    all the rivers of Egypt.

²⁵"'Have you not heard?
    Long ago I prepared it,
From days of old I planned it.
    Now I have brought it to pass:
That you should reduce fortified cities
    into heaps of ruins,
²⁶While their inhabitants, shorn of power,
    are dismayed and ashamed,
Becoming like the plants of the field,
    like the green growth,
    like the scorched grass on the housetops.
²⁷*I am aware whether you stand or sit;
    I know whether you come or go,
    ²⁸and also your rage against me.
Because of your rage against me
    and your fury which has reached my ears,
I will put my hook in your nose
    and my bit in your mouth,
    and make you return the way you came.

²⁹"'This shall be a sign for you:
    this year you shall eat the aftergrowth,
    next year, what grows of itself;
But in the third year, sow and reap,
    plant vineyards and eat their fruit!
³⁰The remaining survivors of the house of Judah
    shall again strike root below
    and bear fruit above.
³¹For out of Jerusalem shall come a remnant,
    and from Mount Zion, survivors.
The zeal of the LORD of hosts shall do this.'

³²"Therefore, thus says the LORD concerning the king of Assyria: 'He shall not reach this city, nor shoot an arrow at it, nor come before it with a shield, nor cast up siege-works against it. ³³He shall return by the same way he came, without entering the city, says the LORD. ³⁴*I will shield and save this city for my own sake, and for the sake of my servant David.'"

³⁵*That night the angel of the LORD went forth and struck down one hundred and eighty-five thousand men in the Assyrian camp. Early the next morning, there they were, all the corpses of the dead. ³⁶So Sennacherib, the king of Assyria, broke camp, and went back home to Nineveh.

³⁷When he was worshiping in the temple of his god Nisroch, his sons Adrammelech and Sharezer slew him with the sword and fled into the land of Ararat. His son Esarhaddon reigned in his stead.

Hezekiah's Illness

20 ¹*IN those days, when Hezekiah was mortally ill, the prophet Isaiah, son of Amoz, came and said to him: "Thus says the LORD: 'Put your house in order, for you are about to die; you shall not recover.'" ²He turned his face to the wall and prayed to the LORD: ³"O LORD, remember how faithfully and wholeheartedly I conducted myself in

12: 17, 6.
13: 18, 34.
14-19: 2 Chr 32, 20;
    Is 37, 14-20.
15: Ex 25, 18.
18: Jer 10, 3.
19: 1 Kgs 18, 24.

27: Ps 139, 2f.
34: 2 Sm 7, 12; Hos 1, 7.
35: Sir 48, 21; 2 Chr 32,
    21f; Is 37, 36-38;
    1 Mc 7, 41; 2 Mc 8, 19.
20/1-9: 2 Chr 32, 24; Is 38, 1-8.

† 19, 21-31: vv 21-28 are addressed to Sennacherib, vv 29-31 to Judah.

your presence, doing what was pleasing to you!" And Hezekiah wept bitterly.

⁴Before Isaiah had left the central courtyard, the word of the Lord came to him: ⁵"Go back and tell Hezekiah, the leader of my people: 'Thus says the Lord, the God of your forefather David: I have heard your prayer and seen your tears. I will heal you. In three days you shall go up to the Lord's temple; ⁶I will add fifteen years to your life. I will rescue you and this city from the hand of the king of Assyria; I will be a shield to this city for my own sake, and for the sake of my servant David.'"

⁷Isaiah then ordered a poultice of figs to be brought and applied to the boil, that he might recover. ⁸Then Hezekiah asked Isaiah, "What is the sign that the Lord will heal me and that I shall go up to the temple of the Lord on the third day?" ⁹Isaiah replied, "This will be the sign for you from the Lord that he will do what he has promised: Shall the shadow go forward or back ten steps?"

¹⁰"It is easy for the shadow to advance ten steps," Hezekiah answered. "Rather, let it go back ten steps." ¹¹So the prophet Isaiah invoked the Lord, who made the shadow retreat the ten steps it had descended on the staircase to the terrace of Ahaz.

¹²*†At that time, when Merodach-baladan, son of Baladan, king of Babylon, heard that Hezekiah had been ill, he sent letters and gifts to him. ¹³Hezekiah was pleased at this, and therefore showed the messengers his whole treasury, his silver, gold, spices and fine oil, his armory, and all that was in his storerooms; there was nothing in his house or in all his realm that Hezekiah did not show them.

¹⁴Then Isaiah the prophet came to King Hezekiah and asked him: "What did these men say to you? Where did they come from?" "They came from a distant land, from Babylon," replied Hezekiah. ¹⁵"What did they see in your house?" the prophet asked. "They saw everything in my house," answered Hezekiah. "There is nothing in my storerooms that I did not show them."

¹⁶Then Isaiah said to Hezekiah: "Hear the word of the Lord: ¹⁷The time is coming when all that is in your house, and everything that your fathers have stored up until this day, shall be carried off to Babylon; nothing shall be left, says the Lord. ¹⁸Some of your own bodily descendants shall be taken and made servants in the palace of the king of Babylon."

¹⁹Hezekiah replied to Isaiah, "The word of the Lord which you have spoken is favorable." For he thought, "There will be peace and security in my lifetime."

²⁰*†The rest of the acts of Hezekiah, all his valor, and his construction of the pool and conduit by which water was brought into the city, are written in the book of the chronicles of the kings of Judah. ²¹Heze-

kiah rested with his ancestors and his son Manasseh succeeded him as king.

Reign of Manasseh

21 ¹*Manasseh was twelve years old when he began to reign, and he reigned fifty-five years in Jerusalem. ²His mother's name was Hephzibah. He did evil in the sight of the Lord, following the abominable practices of the nations whom the Lord had cleared out of the way of the Israelites. ³*He rebuilt the high places which his father Hezekiah had destroyed. He erected altars to Baal, and also set up a sacred pole, as Ahab, king of Israel, had done. He worshiped and served the whole host of heaven. ⁴He built altars in the temple of the Lord, about which the Lord had said, "I will establish my name in Jerusalem"— ⁵*altars for the whole host of heaven, in the two courts of the temple.

⁶He immolated his son by fire. He practiced soothsaying and divination, and reintroduced the consulting of ghosts and spirits. He did much evil in the Lord's sight and provoked him to anger.

⁷*The Asherah idol he had made, he set up in the temple, of which the Lord had said to David and to his son Solomon: "In this temple and in Jerusalem, which I have chosen out of all the tribes of Israel, I shall place my name forever. ⁸I will not in future allow Israel to be driven off the land I gave their fathers, provided that they are careful to observe all I have commanded them, the entire law which my servant Moses enjoined upon them." ⁹But they did not listen, and Manasseh misled them into doing even greater evil than the nations whom the Lord had destroyed at the coming of the Israelites.

¹⁰Then the Lord spoke through his servants the prophets: ¹¹*"Because Manasseh, king of Judah, has practiced these abominations and has done greater evil than all that was done by the Amorites before him, and has led Judah into sin by his idols, ¹²therefore thus says the Lord, the God of Israel: 'I will bring such evil on Jerusalem and Judah that, whenever anyone hears of it, his ears shall ring. ¹³*I will measure Jerusalem with the same cord as I did Samaria, and with the plummet I used for the house of Ahab. I will wipe Jerusalem clean as one wipes a dish, wiping it inside and out. ¹⁴I will cast off the survivors of my inheritance and deliver them into enemy hands, to become a prey and a booty for all their enemies, ¹⁵because they have done evil in my sight and provoked me from the day their fathers came forth from Egypt until today.'"

¹⁶In addition to the sin which he caused Judah to commit, Manasseh did evil in the sight of the Lord, shedding so much innocent blood as to fill the length and breadth of Jerusalem. ¹⁷*The rest of the acts of Manasseh, the sin he committed and all that he did, are written in the book of the chronicles of the kings

---

＊
12f: Is 39, 1f; 2 Chr 32, 27ff.	7: 2 Sm 7, 13; 1 Kgs 8, 16; 9, 3.

12f: Is 39, 1f; 2 Chr 32, 27ff.
20: 2 Chr 32, 30; Sir 48, 17.
21/1-10: 2 Chr 33, 1-10.
3: 17, 16; 1 Kgs 18, 4; 16, 32f.
5: Lv 18, 21.

7: 2 Sm 7, 13; 1 Kgs 8, 16; 9, 3.
11: 1 Kgs 21, 26; Jer 15, 4.
13: Is 34, 11; Am 7, 7-9; Lam 2, 8.
17: 2 Chr 33, 18ff.

†
20, 12-19: Duplication of Is 39, 1-8.
20, 20: *Pool and conduit:* Hezekiah's tunnel; cf 2 Chr 32, 30.

of Judah. ¹⁸Manasseh rested with his ancestors and was buried in his palace garden, the garden of Uzza. His son Amon succeeded him as king.

Reign of Amon

¹⁹*Amon was twenty-two years old when he began to reign, and he reigned two years in Jerusalem. His mother's name was Meshullemeth, daughter of Haruz of Jotbah. ²⁰He did evil in the sight of the LORD, as his father Manasseh had done. ²¹He followed exactly the path his father had trod, serving and worshiping the idols his father had served. ²²He abandoned the LORD, the God of his fathers, and did not follow the path of the LORD. ²³Subjects of Amon conspired against him and slew the king in his palace, ²⁴but the people of the land then slew all who had conspired against King Amon, and proclaimed his son Josiah king in his stead. ²⁵The rest of the acts that Amon did are written in the book of the chronicles of the kings of Judah. ²⁶He was buried in his own grave in the garden of Uzza, and his son Josiah succeeded him as king.

Reign of Josiah

22 ¹*JOSIAH was eight years old when he began to reign, and he reigned thirty-one years in Jerusalem. His mother's name was Jedidah, daughter of Adaiah of Bozkath. ²He pleased the LORD and conducted himself unswervingly just as his ancestor David had done.

³*†In his eighteenth year, King Josiah sent the scribe Shaphan, son of Azaliah, son of Meshullam, to the temple of the LORD with orders to ⁴*go to the high priest Hilkiah and have him smelt down the precious metals that had been donated to the temple of the LORD, which the doorkeepers had collected from the people. ⁵They were to be consigned to the master workmen in the temple of the LORD, who should then pay them out to the carpenters, builders, and lumbermen making repairs on the temple, ⁶and for the purchase of wood and hewn stone for the temple repairs. ⁷No reckoning was asked of them regarding the funds consigned to them, because they held positions of trust.

The Book of the Law

⁸The high priest Hilkiah informed the scribe Shaphan, "I have found the book of the law in the temple of the LORD." Hilkiah gave the book to Shaphan, who read it. ⁹Then the scribe Shaphan went to the king and reported, "Your servants have smelted down the metals available in the temple and have consigned them to the master workmen in the temple of the LORD." ¹⁰The scribe Shaphan also informed the king that the priest Hilkiah had given him a book, and then read it aloud to the king. ¹¹*When the king had heard the contents of the book of the law, he tore his garments ¹²and issued this command to Hilkiah the priest,

Ahikam, son of Shaphan, Achbor, son of Micaiah, the scribe Shaphan, and the king's servant Asaiah: ¹³"Go, consult the LORD for me, for the people, for all Judah, about the stipulations of this book that has been found, for the anger of the LORD has been set furiously ablaze against us, because our fathers did not obey the stipulations of this book, nor fulfill our written obligations."

¹⁴So Hilkiah the priest, Ahikam, Achbor, Shaphan, and Asaiah betook themselves to the Second Quarter in Jerusalem, where the prophetess Huldah resided. She was the wife of Shallum, son of Tikvah, son of Harhas, keeper of the wardrobe. When they had spoken to her, ¹⁵she said to them, "Thus says the LORD, the God of Israel: 'Say to the man who sent you to me, ¹⁶Thus says the LORD: I will bring upon this place and upon its inhabitants all the evil that is threatened in the book which the king of Judah has read. ¹⁷Because they have forsaken me and have burned incense to other gods, provoking me by everything to which they turn their hands, my anger is ablaze against this place and it cannot be extinguished.'

¹⁸"But to the king of Judah who sent you to consult the LORD, give this response: 'Thus says the LORD, the God of Israel: As for the threats you have heard, ¹⁹because you were heartsick and have humbled yourself before the LORD when you heard my threats that this place and its inhabitants would become a desolation and a curse; because you tore your garments and wept before me; I in turn have listened, says the LORD. ²⁰I will therefore gather you to your ancestors; you shall go to your grave in peace, and your eyes shall not see all the evil I will bring upon this place.'" This they reported to the king.

23 ¹*THE king then had all the elders of Judah and of Jerusalem summoned together before him. ²The king went up to the temple of the LORD with all the men of Judah and all the inhabitants of Jerusalem: priests, prophets, and all the people, small and great. He had the entire contents of the book of the covenant that had been found in the temple of the LORD, read out to them. ³Standing by the column, the king made a covenant before the LORD that they would follow him and observe his ordinances, statutes and decrees with their whole hearts and souls, thus reviving the terms of the covenant which were written in this book. And all the people stood as participants in the covenant.

⁴*Then the king commanded the high priest Hilkiah, his vicar, and the doorkeepers to remove from the temple of the LORD all the objects that had been made for Baal, Asherah, and the whole host of heaven. He had these burned outside Jerusalem on the slopes of the Kidron and their ashes carried to Bethel. ⁵*He

---

19-26: 2 Chr 33, 21-25.　　11-20: 2 Chr 34, 19-28.
22/1f: 2 Chr 34, 1f.　　23/1-5: 2 Chr 34, 29-33.
3-13: 2 Chr 34, 8-21.　　4: 2 Chr 34, 3-5; Sir 49, 3.
4-7: 12, 11-16.　　5: Dt 17, 3ff.

† 22, 3: *Shaphan:* head of a prominent family in the reign of Josiah, secretary to the king, bearer and reader of the newfound book of the law (3-13; 2 Chr 34, 8f.15-20). He and his sons favored the reform of King Josiah and supported the prophet Jeremiah; cf Jer 26, 24.

also put an end to the pseudo-priests whom the kings of Judah had appointed to burn incense on the high places in the cities of Judah and in the vicinity of Jerusalem, as well as those who burned incense to Baal, to the sun, moon, and signs of the Zodiac, and to the whole host of heaven. **6***From the temple of the LORD he also removed the sacred pole, to the Kidron Valley, outside Jerusalem; there he had it burned and beaten to dust, which was then scattered over the common graveyard. **7***†He tore down the apartments of the cult prostitutes which were in the temple of the LORD, and in which the women wove garments for the Asherah.

8*He brought in all the priests from the cities of Judah, and then defiled, from Geba to Beer-sheba, the high places where they had offered incense. He also tore down the high place of the satyrs, which was at the entrance of the Gate of Joshua, governor of the city, to the left as one enters the city gate. **9**The priests of the high places could not function at the altar of the LORD in Jerusalem; but they, along with their relatives, ate the unleavened bread.

10*†The king also defiled Topheth in the Valley of Ben-hinnom, so that there would no longer be any immolation of sons or daughters by fire in honor of Molech. **11**†He did away with the horses which the kings of Judah had dedicated to the sun; these were at the entrance of the temple of the LORD, near the chamber of Nathan-melech the eunuch, which was in the large building. The chariots of the sun he destroyed by fire. **12***He also demolished the altars made by the kings of Judah on the roof (the roof terrace of Ahaz), and the altars made by Manasseh in the two courts of the temple of the LORD. He pulverized them and threw the dust into the Kidron Valley. **13***†The king defiled the high places east of Jerusalem, south of the Mount of Misconduct, which Solomon, king of Israel, had built in honor of Astarte, the Sidonian horror, of Chemosh, the Moabite horror, and of Milcom, the idol of the Ammonites. **14***He broke to pieces the pillars, cut down the sacred poles, and filled the places where they had been with human bones. **15***Likewise the altar which was at Bethel, the high place built by Jeroboam, son of Nebat, who caused Israel to sin— this same altar and high place he tore down, breaking up the stones and grinding them to powder, and burning the Asherah.

16When Josiah turned and saw the graves there on the mountainside, he ordered the bones taken from the graves and burned on the altar, and thus defiled it in fulfillment of the word of the LORD which the man of God had proclaimed as Jeroboam was standing by the altar on the feast day. When the king looked up and saw the grave of the man of God who had proclaimed these words, **17**he asked, "What is that tombstone I see?" The men of the city replied, "It is the grave of the man of God who came from Judah and predicted the very things you have done to the altar of Bethel." **18***†"Let him be," he said, "let no one move his bones." So they left his bones undisturbed together with the bones of the prophet who had come from Samaria.

19*Josiah also removed all the shrines on the high places near the cities of Samaria which the kings of Israel had erected, thereby provoking the LORD; he did the very same to them as he had done in Bethel. **20**He slaughtered upon the altars all the priests of the high places that were at the shrines, and burned human bones upon them. Then he returned to Jerusalem.

21*The king issued a command to all the people to observe the Passover of the LORD, their God, as it was prescribed in that book of the covenant. **22**No Passover such as this had been observed during the period when the Judges ruled Israel, or during the entire period of the kings of Israel and the kings of Judah, **23**until the eighteenth year of King Josiah, when this Passover of the LORD was kept in Jerusalem.

24*†Further, Josiah did away with the consultation of ghosts and spirits, with the household gods, idols, and all the other horrors to be seen in the land of Judah and in Jerusalem, so that he might carry out the stipulations of the law written in the book that the priest Helkiah had found in the temple of the LORD.

25*Before him there had been no king who turned to the LORD as he did, with his whole heart, his whole soul, and his whole strength, in accord with the entire law of Moses; nor could any after him compare with him.

26Yet, because of all the provocations that Manasseh had given, the LORD did not desist from his fiercely burning anger against Judah. **27***The LORD said: "Even Judah will I put out of my sight as I did Israel. I will reject this city, Jerusalem, which I chose, and the temple of which I said, 'There shall my name be.'"

28*The rest of the acts of Josiah, with all that he did, are written in the book of the chronicles of the kings of Judah. **29***In his time Pharaoh Neco, king of Egypt, went up toward the river Euphrates to the king of As-

---

† 23, 7: *Cult prostitutes:* of both sexes; cf 1 Kgs 14, 24.

23, 10: *Topheth . . . by fire:* condemned by Deuteronomic law and denounced by Jeremiah (Dt 12, 31; Jer 7, 29ff; Jer 19).

23, 11: *Large building:* to the west of the temple area (1 Chr 26, 18), named in the Hebrew by an Egyptian name for a similar construction.

23, 13: *Mount of Misconduct:* a paranomasia on "Mount of Olives" (in Hebrew *Maschit/mishcheh*) as suggested by the Targum. Cf Vulgate, "Mount of Offense." *Horror . . . idol:* in all three phrases here the Hebrew uses a pejorative designation meaning "abomination."

23, 18: *From Samaria:* more narrowly, from Bethel; cf 1 Kgs 13, 31f.

23, 24: *Household gods, idols:* teraphim. See note on Gn 31, 19.

*
6: Dt 16, 21; 1 Kgs 14, 23.
7: 1 Kgs 14, 24; Dt 23, 18f.
8: Dt 12, 2f.
10: Lv 18, 21.
12: 21, 5.
13: 1 Kgs 11, 7.
14: Dt 16, 21f; 1 Kgs 14, 23.
15: 1 Kgs 12, 31f; 13, 32.
18: 1 Kgs 13, 31.
19: 2 Chr 34, 6f.
21: Dt 16, 1-8; 2 Chr 35, 1ff.18f.
24: 21, 6; Gn 31, 19; Dt 18, 11; Jgs 18, 14.
25: Dt 6, 5.
27: 24, 2.
28: 2 Chr 35, 26f.
29: 2 Chr 35, 20-24.

syria. King Josiah set out to confront him, but was slain at Megiddo at the first encounter. ³⁰†His servants brought his body on a chariot from Megiddo to Jerusalem, where they buried him in his own grave. Then the people of the land took Jehoahaz, son of Josiah, anointed him, and proclaimed him king to succeed his father.

Reign of Jehoahaz

³¹*Jehoahaz was twenty-three years old when he began to reign, and he reigned three months in Jerusalem. His mother, whose name was Hamutal, daughter of Jeremiah, was from Libnah. ³²He did evil in the sight of the LORD, just as his forebears had done. ³³†Pharaoh Neco took him prisoner at Riblah in the land of Hamath, thus ending his reign in Jerusalem. He imposed a fine upon the land of a hundred talents of silver and a talent of gold. ³⁴Pharaoh Neco then appointed Eliakim, son of Josiah, king in place of his father Josiah; he changed his name to Jehoiakim. Jehoahaz he took away with him to Egypt, where he died. ³⁵Jehoiakim gave the silver and gold to Pharaoh, but taxed the land to raise the amount Pharaoh demanded. He exacted the silver and gold from the people of the land, from each proportionately, to pay Pharaoh Neco.

Reign of Jehoiakim

³⁶*Jehoiakim was twenty-five years old when he began to reign, and he reigned eleven years in Jerusalem. His mother's name was Zebidah, daughter of Pedaiah, from Rumah. ³⁷He did evil in the sight of the LORD, just as his forebears had done.

24 ¹*DURING his reign Nebuchadnezzar, king of Babylon, moved against him, and Jehoiakim became his vassal for three years. Then Jehoiakim turned and rebelled against him. ²*The LORD loosed against him bands of Chaldeans, Arameans, Moabites, and Ammonites; he loosed them against Judah to destroy it, as the LORD had threatened through his servants the prophets. ³This befell Judah because the LORD had stated that he would inexorably put them out of his sight for the sins Manasseh had committed in all that he did; ⁴*and especially because of the innocent blood he shed, with which he filled Jerusalem, the LORD would not forgive.

⁵*The rest of the acts of Jehoiakim, with all that he did, are written in the book of the chronicles of the kings of Judah. ⁶Jehoiakim rested with his ancestors, and his son Jehoiachin succeeded him as king. ⁷The king of Egypt did not again leave his own land, for the king of Babylon had taken all that belonged to the king of Egypt from the Wadi of Egypt to the Euphrates River.

Reign of Jehoiachin

⁸†Jehoiachin was eighteen years old when he began to reign, and he reigned three months in Jerusalem. His mother's name was Nehushta, daughter of Elnathan of Jerusalem. ⁹He did evil in the sight of the LORD, just as his forebears had done.

¹⁰*At that time the officials of Nebuchadnezzar, king of Babylon, attacked Jerusalem, and the city came under siege. ¹¹Nebuchadnezzar, king of Babylon, himself arrived at the city while his servants were besieging it. ¹²Then Jehoiachin, king of Judah, together with his mother, his ministers, officers, and functionaries, surrendered to the king of Babylon, who, in the eighth year of his reign, took him captive. ¹³*He carried off all the treasures of the temple of the LORD and those of the palace, and broke up all the gold utensils that Solomon, king of Israel, had provided in the temple of the LORD, as the LORD had foretold. ¹⁴He deported all Jerusalem: all the officers and men of the army, ten thousand in number, and all the craftsmen and smiths. None were left among the people of the land except the poor. ¹⁵*He deported Jehoiachin to Babylon, and also led captive from Jerusalem to Babylon the king's mother and wives, his functionaries, and the chief men of the land. ¹⁶The king of Babylon also led captive to Babylon all seven thousand men of the army, and a thousand craftsmen and smiths, all of them trained soldiers. ¹⁷In place of Jehoiachin, the king of Babylon appointed his uncle Mattaniah king, and changed his name to Zedekiah.

Reign of Zedekiah

¹⁸*Zedekiah was twenty-one years old when he became king, and he reigned eleven years in Jerusalem. His mother's name was Hamutal, daughter of Jeremiah of Libnah. ¹⁹He also did evil in the sight of the LORD, just as Jehoiakim had done. ²⁰*The LORD's anger befell Jerusalem and Judah till he cast them out from his presence. Thus Zedekiah rebelled against the king of Babylon.

25 ¹*†IN the tenth month of the ninth year of Zedekiah's reign, on the tenth day of the month, Nebuchadnezzar, king of Babylon, and his whole army advanced against Jerusalem, encamped around it, and built siege walls on every side. ²The siege of the city continued until the eleventh year of Zedekiah. ³On the ninth day of the fourth month, when famine had gripped the city, and the people had

---

*
31: 2 Chr 36, 2f.	13: 20, 17; Is 39, 6.
36f: 2 Chr 36, 4f.	15: Est A, 3; 2, 6.
24/1-5: 2 Chr 36, 6ff.	18: 2 Chr 36, 9;
2: 23, 27.	Jer 37, 1f; 52, 1ff.
4: 21, 16.	20: 22, 17; 23, 27.
5: 2 Chr 36, 8.	25/1-21: Jer 39, 1-10; 52, 4-28.
10: 2 Chr 36, 10; Dn 1, 1f.	

†
23, 30.35: *People of the land:* in this period, the phrase referred to "landed gentry"; in later times it meant "the poor." Cf 24, 14.

23, 33: *A talent of gold:* some manuscripts of the Greek and Syriac texts have "ten talents."

24, 8: *He reigned three months:* in the year 597 B. C.

25, 1-30: This chapter parallels Jer 39 and 52; see notes to those parts of Jeremiah.

no more bread, ⁴the city walls were breached. Then the king and all the soldiers left the city by night through the gate between the two walls which was near the king's garden. Since the Chaldeans had the city surrounded, they went in the direction of the Arabah. ⁵But the Chaldean army pursued the king and overtook him in the desert near Jericho, abandoned by his whole army.

⁶The king was therefore arrested and brought to Riblah to the king of Babylon, who pronounced sentence on him. ⁷He had Zedekiah's sons slain before his eyes. Then he blinded Zedekiah, bound him with fetters, and had him brought to Babylon.

⁸On the seventh day of the fifth month (this was in the nineteenth year of Nebuchadnezzar, king of Babylon), Nebuzaradan, captain of the bodyguard, came to Jerusalem as the representative of the king of Babylon. ⁹*He burned the house of the LORD, the palace of the king, and all the houses of Jerusalem; every large building was destroyed by fire. ¹⁰Then the Chaldean troops who were with the captain of the guard tore down the walls that surrounded Jerusalem.

¹¹†Then Nebuzaradan, captain of the guard, led into exile the last of the people remaining in the city, and those who had deserted to the king of Babylon, and the last of the artisans. ¹²But some of the country's poor, Nebuzaradan, captain of the guard, left behind as vinedressers and farmers.

¹³*The bronze pillars that belonged to the house of the LORD, and the wheeled carts and the bronze sea in the house of the LORD, the Chaldeans broke into pieces; they carried away the bronze to Babylon. ¹⁴*They took also the pots, the shovels, the snuffers, the bowls, the pans and all the bronze vessels used for service. ¹⁵The fire-holders and the bowls which were of gold or silver the captain of the guard also carried off. ¹⁶The weight in bronze of the two pillars, the bronze sea, and the wheeled carts, all of them furnishings which Solomon had made for the house of the LORD, was never calculated. ¹⁷*Each of the pillars was eighteen cubits high; a bronze capital five cubits high surmounted each pillar, and a network with pomegranates encircled the capital, all of bronze; and so for the other pillar, as regards the network.

¹⁸The captain of the guard also took Seraiah the high priest, Zephaniah the second priest, and the three keepers of the entry. ¹⁹And from the city he took one courtier, a commander of soldiers, five men in the personal service of the king who were still in the city, the scribe of the army commander, who mustered the people of the land, and sixty of the common people still remaining in the city. ²⁰The captain of the guard, Nebuzaradan, arrested these and brought them to the king of Babylon at Riblah; ²¹the king had them struck down and put to death in Riblah, in the land of Hamath. Thus was Judah exiled from her land.

Governorship of Gedaliah

²²*As for the people whom he had allowed to remain in the land of Judah, Nebuchadnezzar, king of Babylon, appointed as their governor Gedaliah, son of Ahikam, son of Shaphan. ²³Hearing that the king of Babylon had appointed Gedaliah governor, all the army commanders with their men came to him at Mizpah: Ishmael, son of Nethaniah, Johanan, son of Kareah, Seraiah, son of Tanhumeth the Netophathite, and Jaazaniah, from Beth-maacah. ²⁴Gedaliah gave the commanders and their men his oath. "Do not be afraid of the Chaldean officials," he said to them. "Remain in the country and serve the king of Babylon, and all will be well with you."

²⁵But in the seventh month Ishmael, son of Nethaniah, son of Elishama, of royal descent, came with ten men, attacked Gedaliah and killed him, along with the Jews and Chaldeans who were in Mizpah with him. ²⁶Then all the people, great and small, left with the army commanders and went to Egypt for fear of the Chaldeans.

Release of Jehoiachin

²⁷*In the thirty-seventh year of the exile of Jehoiachin, king of Judah, on the twenty-seventh day of the twelfth month, Evil-merodach, king of Babylon, in the inaugural year of his own reign, raised up Jehoiachin, king of Judah, from prison. ²⁸He spoke kindly to him and gave him a throne higher than that of the other kings who were with him in Babylon. ²⁹Jehoiachin took off his prison garb and ate at the king's table as long as he lived. ³⁰The allowance granted him by the king was a perpetual allowance, in fixed daily amounts, for as long as he lived.

❋

9: 2 Chr 36, 19; Ps 74, 7.
13: 16, 17; 1 Kgs 7, 15-39;
    2 Chr 3, 15; 36, 18;
    Jer 27, 19.
14: 1 Kgs 7, 48ff.

17: 1 Kgs 7, 15;
     Jer 52, 21ff.
22-26: Jer 40, 5.7-41, 1-3.
27-30: Jer 52, 31-34.

†
25, 11: *Those who had deserted:* perhaps on the advice of Jeremiah; cf Jer 38, 2f.

The First Book of Chronicles

Introduction

Originally the two books of Chronicles formed, with the Books of Ezra and Nehemiah, a single historical work, uniform in style and basic ideas. The Greek title, *paraleipomena,* means "things omitted, or passed over (in Samuel and Kings)." The Books of Chronicles, however, are more than a supplement to Samuel and Kings; a comparison of the two histories discloses striking differences in scope and purpose. The Books of Chronicles record in some detail the lengthy span from the reign of Saul to the return from the Exile. Unlike the exact science of history today, wherein factual accuracy and impartiality of judgment are the standards for estimating what is of permanent worth, ancient biblical history, with rare exceptions, was less concerned with reporting in precise detail all the facts of a situation than with explaining the meaning of those facts. Such history was primarily interpretative and, in the Old Testament, its purpose was to disclose the action of the living God in the affairs of men. For this reason we speak of it as "sacred history"; its writer's first concern was to bring out the divine or supernatural dimension in history.

This is apparent when we examine the primary objective of the Chronicler in compiling his work. In view of the situation which confronted the Jewish people at this time (the end of the fifth century B. C.), the Chronicler realized that Israel's political greatness was a thing of the past. It would be a people under God, or nothing. Yet Israel's past held the key to her future. The Chronicler proposed to establish and defend the legitimate claims of the Davidic monarchy in Israel's history, and to underscore the place of Jerusalem and its divinely established temple worship as the center of religious life for the Jewish community of his day. If Judaism was to survive and prosper, it would have to heed the lessons of the past and devoutly serve Yahweh in the place where he had chosen to dwell, the temple of Jerusalem. From the Chronicler's point of view, David's reign was the ideal to which all subsequent rule in Judah must aspire.

The Chronicler was much more interested in David's religious and cultic influence than in his political power. There is little of royal messianism in his book. He apparently regarded as something of the distant past the prophet Zechariah's abortive attempt to have the Davidic kingdom reestablished in the time of Zerubbabel at the end of the sixth century B. C. (Zec 6, 9-15). He saw David's primary importance as deriving from the establishment of Jerusalem and its temple as the center of the true worship of the Lord. Furthermore, he presented David as the one who had authorized the elaborate ritual (which, in point of fact, only gradually evolved in the temple built by Zerubbabel) and who had also appointed Levites to supervise the liturgical services there.

There are good reasons for believing that originally the Books of Ezra and Nehemiah formed the last part of a single literary work that began with 1 and 2 Chronicles. Some authors even regard Ezra himself as having been the anonymous Chronicler. In any case, the Chronicler's Hebrew as well as his religious and political outlook points to c. 400 B. C. as the time of composition of this work.

The Chronicler used sources in writing his history. Besides the canonical Books of Genesis, Exodus, Numbers, Joshua and Ruth, and especially the Books of Samuel and Kings, he cites the titles of many other works no longer extant. "The books of the kings of Israel," or "the books of the kings of Israel and Judah," "the history of Samuel the seer," "the history of Nathan the prophet," "the history of Gad the seer," "the commentary of the Books of Kings," are some of the documents mentioned as historical sources.

In addition, the Chronicler's work contains early preexilic material not found in the Books of Kings. At one time scholars discounted the value of this material, but modern research has shown that, even though the Chronicler may have at times treated the material rather freely, he derived it from authentic and reliable sources.

The principal divisions of 1 Chronicles are as follows:
I: Genealogical Tables (1, 1—9, 34)
II: The History of David (9, 35—29, 30)

I: GENEALOGICAL TABLES

From Adam to Abraham

1 [1]* †ADAM, SETH, ENOSH, [2]*Kenan, Mahalalel, Jared, [3]*Enoch, Methuselah, Lamech, [4]*Noah, Shem, Ham, and Japheth. [5]*The descendants of Japheth were Gomer, Magog, Madai, Javan, Tubal, Meshech, and Tiras. [6]The descendants of Gomer were Ashkenaz,

---

1/1: 4, 25f; Gn 5, 3.6.9.   4: Gn 5, 32; 6, 10; 9, 18.
2ff: Gn 5, 9-32; 10, 2ff.   5ff: Gn 10, 2ff.
3: Gn 4, 25.

† 1, 1—9, 34: The Chronicler set as his task the retelling, from his particular viewpoint, of the story of God's people from the beginning to his own day. Since his primary interest was the history of David and the Davidic dynasty of Judah, he presents through mere genealogical lists a summary of what preceded

Riphath, and Togarmah. ⁷The descendants of Javan were Elishah, Tarshish, the Kittim, and the Rodanim.

⁸*The descendants of Ham were Cush, Mesraim, Put, and Canaan. ⁹The descendants of Cush were Seba, Havilah, Sabta, Raama, and Sabteca. The descendants of Raama were Sheba and Dedan. ¹⁰Cush became the father of Nimrod, who was the first to be a conqueror on the earth. ¹¹*Mesraim became the father of the Ludim, Anamim, Lehabim, Naphtuhim, ¹²Pathrusim, Casluhim, and Caphtorim, from whom the Philistines sprang. ¹³Canaan became the father of Sidon, his first-born, and Heth, ¹⁴and the Jebusite, the Amorite, the Girgashite, ¹⁵the Hivite, the Arkite, the Sinite, ¹⁶the Arvadite, the Zemarite, and the Hamathite.

¹⁷*The descendants of Shem were Elam, Asshur, Arpachshad, Lud, and Aram. The descendants of Aram were Uz, Hul, Gether, and Mash. ¹⁸Arpachshad became the father of Shelah, and Shelah became the father of Eber. ¹⁹Two sons were born to Eber; the first was named Peleg (for in his time the world was divided), and his brother was Joktan. ²⁰Joktan became the father of Almodad, Sheleph, Hazarmaveth, Jerah, ²¹Hadoram, Uzal, Diklah, ²²Ebal, Abimael, Sheba, ²³Ophir, Havilah, and Jobab; all these were the sons of Joktan.

²⁴*Shem, Arpachshad, Shelah, ²⁵Eber, Peleg, Reu, ²⁶Serug, Nahor, Terah, ²⁷*Abram, who was Abraham.

From Abraham to Jacob

²⁸*The sons of Abraham were Isaac and Ishmael. ²⁹*These were their descendants:

Nebaioth, the first-born of Ishmael, then Kedar, Adbeel, Mibsam, ³⁰Mishma, Dumah, Massa, Hadad, Tema, ³¹Jetur, Naphish, and Kedemah. These were the descendants of Ishmael.

³²*The descendants of Keturah, Abraham's concubine: she bore Zimran, Jokshan, Medan, Midian, Ishbak, and Shuah. The sons of Jokshan were Sheba and Dedan. ³³The descendants of Midian were Ephah, Epher, Hanoch, Abida, and Eldaah. All these were the descendants of Keturah.

³⁴*Abraham became the father of Isaac. The sons of Isaac were Esau and Israel.

³⁵*The sons of Esau were Eliphaz, Reuel, Jeush, Jalam, and Korah. ³⁶The sons of Eliphaz were Teman, Omar, Zephi, Gatam, Kenaz, [Timna,] and Amalek.

³⁷The sons of Reuel were Nahath, Zerah, Shammah, and Mizzah.

³⁸*†The descendants of Seir were Lotan, Shobal, Zibeon, Anah, Dishon, Ezer, and Dishan. ³⁹The sons of Lotan were Hori and Homam; Timna was the sister of Lotan. ⁴⁰The sons of Shobal were Alian, Manahath, Ebal, Shephi, and Onam. The sons of Zibeon were Aiah and Anah. ⁴¹The sons of Anah: Dishon. The sons of Dishon were Hemdan, Eshban, Ithran, and Cheran. ⁴²The sons of Ezer were Bilhan, Zaavan, and Jaakan. The sons of Dishan were Uz and Aran.

⁴³*The kings who reigned in the land of Edom before they had Israelite kings were the following: Bela, son of Beor, the name of whose city was Dinhabah. ⁴⁴*When Bela died, Jobab, son of Zerah, from Bozrah, succeeded him. ⁴⁵*When Jobab died, Husham, from the land of the Temanites, succeeded him. ⁴⁶Husham died and Hadad, son of Bedad, succeeded him. He overthrew the Midianites on the Moabite plateau, and the name of his city was Avith. ⁴⁷Hadad died and Samlah of Masrekah succeeded him. ⁴⁸Samlah died and Shaul from Rehoboth-han-nahar succeeded him. ⁴⁹When Shaul died, Baalhanan, son of Achbor, succeeded him. ⁵⁰Baalhanan died and Hadad succeeded him. The name of his city was Pai, and his wife's name was Mehetabel. She was the daughter of Matred, who was the daughter of Mezahab. ⁵¹*After Hadad died. . . .

These were the chiefs of Edom: the chiefs of Timna, Aliah, Jetheth, ⁵²Oholibamah, Elah, Pinon, ⁵³Kenaz, Teman, Mibzar, ⁵⁴Magdiel, and Iram were the chiefs of Edom.

2 ¹*THESE were the sons of Israel: Reuben, Simeon, Levi, Judah, Issachar, Zebulun, ²*Dan, Joseph, Benjamin, Naphtali, Gad, and Asher.

Judah

³*†The sons of Judah were: Er, Onan, and Shelah; these three were born to him of Bathshua, a Canaanite woman. But Judah's first-born, Er, was wicked in the sight of the LORD, so he killed him. ⁴*Judah's daughter-in-law Tamar bore him Perez and Zerah, so that he had five sons in all.

⁵*The sons of Perez were Hezron and Hamul. ⁶*The sons of Zerah were Zimri, Ethan, Heman, Calcol, and Darda—five in all. ⁷*The sons of Zimri: Carmi. The sons of Carmi: Achar, who brought trouble upon Israel by violating the ban. ⁸The sons of Ethan: Azariah.

❋
8f: Gn 10, 8.	44: Is 34, 6; 63, 1;
11-16: Gn 10, 13-18.	Jer 49, 13.22.
17-23: Gn 10, 22-29;	45: Gn 36, 11; Jb 2, 11;
11, 10-18.	Jer 49, 7.20.
24-27: Gn 11, 10-26;	51-54: Gn 36, 40-43.
Lk 3, 34ff.	2/1: Gn 29, 32-35;
27: Gn 17, 5; Neh 9, 7.	30, 18.20; 35, 23.
28: Gn 16, 11.15; 21, 2f;	2: Gn 30, 6.8.11.13.24;
Gal 4, 22f; Heb 11, 11.	35, 18.24ff.
29ff: Gn 25, 13-16.	3: 4, 21; Gn 38, 1-5;
32f: Gn 25, 1-4.	46, 12.
34: Gn 21, 2f; 25, 19.25f;	4: Gn 38, 7.13-30; 46, 12;
32, 28f; Mt 1, 2;	Rv 4, 12.18; Mt 1, 3.
Lk 3, 34.	5: Gn 46, 12.
35ff: Gn 36, 4f.10-13.15ff.	6: 1 Kgs 5, 11.
38-42: Gn 36, 20-28.	7: Jos 7, 1.18ff.24f; 22, 20.
43-54: Gn 36, 31-43.	

† the reign of Saul, David's predecessor in the kingdom. The sources for these genealogies are mostly the canonical Hebrew Scriptures that were already in their present form in his time. The cross references in this book indicate in each case the scriptural sources used.

1, 38: Seir: another name for Esau (v 35) or Edom (v 43).

2, 3—4, 23: For two reasons, the Chronicler places the genealogy of the tribe of Judah before that of the other tribes, giving it also at greater length than the others: because of his interest in David and because in the Chronicler's time the people of God were almost exclusively Jews. Both David and the Jews were of the tribe of Judah.

9***†**The sons born to Hezron were Jerahmeel, Ram, and Chelubai.

10***†**Ram became the father of Amminadab, and Amminadab became the father of Nahshon, a prince of the Judahites. **11***Nahshon became the father of Salma. Salma became the father of Boaz. **12**Boaz became the father of Obed. Obed became the father of Jesse. **13***Jesse became the father of Eliab, his first-born, of Abinadab, the second son, Shimea, the third, **14**Nethanel, the fourth, Raddai, the fifth, **15**Ozem, the sixth, and David, the seventh. **16***Their sisters were Zeruiah and Abigail. Zeruiah had three sons: Abishai, Joab, and Asahel. **17***Abigail bore Amasa, whose father was Jether the Ishmaelite.

18***†**By his wife Azubah, Caleb, son of Hezron, became the father of a daughter, Jerioth. Her sons were Jesher, Shobab, and Ardon. **19***When Azubah died, Caleb married Ephrath, who bore him Hur. **20***Hur became the father of Uri, and Uri became the father of Bezalel. **21***Then Hezron had relations with the daughter of Machir, the father of Gilead, having married her when he was sixty years old. She bore him Segub. **22***Segub became the father of Jair, who possessed twenty-three cities in the land of Gilead. **23***Geshur and Aram took from them the villages of Jair, that is, Kenath and its towns, sixty cities in all, which had belonged to the sons of Machir, the father of Gilead. **24***After the death of Hezron, Caleb had relations with Ephrathah, the widow of his father Hezron, and she bore him Ashhur, the father of Tekoa.

25***†**The sons of Jerahmeel, the first-born of Hezron, were Ram, the first-born, then Bunah, Oren, and Ozem, his brothers. **26**Jerahmeel also had another wife, Atarah by name, who was the mother of Onam. **27**The sons of Ram, the first-born of Jerahmeel, were Maaz, Jamin, and Eker. **28**The sons of Onam were Shammai and Jada. The sons of Shammai were Nadab and Abishur. **29**Abishur's wife, who was named Abihail, bore him Ahban and Molid. **30**The sons of Nadab were Seled and Appaim. Seled died without sons. **31***The sons of Appaim: Ishi. The sons of Ishi: Sheshan. The sons of Sheshan: Ahlai. **32**The sons of Jada, the brother of Shammai, were Jether and Jonathan. Jether died without sons. **33**The sons of Jonathan were Peleth and Zaza. These were the descendants of Jerahmeel. **34**Sheshan, who had no sons, only daughters, had an Egyptian slave named Jarha. **35**Sheshan gave his daughter in marriage to his slave Jarha, and she bore him Attai. **36**Attai became the father of Nathan.

Nathan became the father of Zabad. **37**Zabad became the father of Ephlal. Ephlal became the father of Obed. **38**Obed became the father of Jehu. Jehu became the father of Azariah. **39**Azariah became the father of Helez. Helez became the father of Eleasah. **40**Eleasah became the father of Sismai. Sismai became the father of Shallum. **41**Shallum became the father of Jekamiah. Jekamiah became the father of Elishama.

42†The descendants of Caleb, the brother of Jerahmeel: [Mesha] his first-born, who was the father of Ziph. Then the sons of Mareshah, who was the father of Hebron. **43**The sons of Hebron were Korah, Tappuah, Rekem, and Shema. **44**Shema became the father of Raham, who was the father of Jorkeam. Rekem became the father of Shammai. **45**The son of Shammai: Maon, who was the father of Beth-zur. **46**Ephah, Caleb's concubine, bore Haran, Moza, and Gazez. Haran became the father of Gazez. **47**The sons of Jahdai were Regem, Jotham, Geshan, Pelet, Ephah, and Shaaph. **48**Maacah, Caleb's concubine, bore Sheber and Tirhanah. **49***She also bore Shaaph, the father of Madmannah, Sheva, the father of Machbenah, and the father of Gibea. Achsah was Caleb's daughter.

50†These were descendants of Caleb, sons of Hur, the first-born of Ephrathah: Shobal, the father of Kiriath-jearim, **51**Salma, the father of Bethlehem, and Hareph, the father of Bethgader. **52**The sons of Shobal, the father of Kiriath-jearim, were Reaiah, half the Manahathites, **53***and the clans of Kiriath-jearim: the Ithrites, the Puthites, the Shumathites, and the Mishraites. From these the people of Zorah and the Eshtaolites derived. **54**The descendants of Salma were Bethlehem, the Netophathites, Atroth-beth-Joab, half the Manahathites, and the Zorites. **55***The clans of the Sopherim dwelling in Jabez were the Tirathites, the Shimeathites, and the Sucathites. They were the Kenites, who came from Hammath of the ancestor of the Rechabites.

3 **1*****†**THE following were the sons of David who were born to him in Hebron: the first-born, Amnon, by Ahinoam of Jezreel; the second, Daniel, by Abigail of Carmel; **2**the third, Absalom, son of Maacah, who was the daughter of Talmai, king of Geshur;

---

*

9: Rv 4, 19; Mt 1, 3.
10: Rv 4, 19; Mt 1, 4.
11f: Nm 1, 7; Rv 4, 20f;
    Mt 1, 4f.
13: 2 Chr 11, 18.
13ff: 1 Sm 16, 6-13; 17, 13f.
16: 2 Sm 2, 18.
17: 2 Sm 17, 25; 19, 14;
    20, 4-13.
18: 2, 24.
19: 2, 24.
20: Ex 24, 14; 31, 2;
    35, 30; 2 Chr 1, 5.
21: Nm 26, 29; 27, 1;
    32, 39; Jos 13, 31;
    Jgs 5, 14.

22: Nm 32, 41; 1 Kgs 4, 13.
23: Dt 3, 14; Jos 13, 30;
    Jgs 10, 4.
24: 2, 19; 2 Sm 14, 2;
    2 Chr 11, 6.
25: 1 Sm 27, 10; 30, 29;
    Jb 32, 2.
31: 4, 20.
49: Jos 15, 16; Jgs 1, 12.
53: Jgs 18, 2.
55: Nm 24, 21; Jgs 1, 16;
    4, 11; 1 Sm 15, 6.
3/1-4: 2 Sm 3, 2-5.

†

2, 9: *Chelubai:* a variant form of the name *Caleb* (vv 18.42), distinct from *Chelub* of 4, 11.

2, 10-17: Immediate ancestors of David. A similar list is given in Ru 4, 19-22; each list, independent of the other, derives from a common source.

2, 18-24: Descendants of Caleb. In 4, 15, as is often the case in the Pentateuch (Nm 13, 6; 14, 6.30; 26, 65; etc.), Caleb is called *son of Jephunneh.* Here he is called *son of Hezron*, perhaps because the Calebites were reckoned as part of the clan of the Hezronites.

2, 25-41: The Jerahmeelites were a clan in the Negeb of Judah.

2, 42-49: Another list, dating from preexilic times, of the Calebites, a clan that inhabited the south of Judah.

2, 50-55: The Hurites, a clan dwelling to the south and west of Jerusalem and related to the Calebites.

3, 1-9: David's sons.

3, 1: *Daniel:* called *Chileab* in 2 Sm 3, 3.

the fourth, Adonijah, son of Haggith; ³the fifth, Shephatiah, by Abital; the sixth, Ithream, by his wife Eglah. ⁴*Six in all were born to him in Hebron, where he reigned seven years and six months. Then he reigned thirty-three years in Jerusalem, ⁵*†where the following were born to him: Shimea, Shobab, Nathan, Solomon—four by Bathsheba, the daughter of Ammiel; ⁶Ibhar, Elishua, Eliphelet, ⁷Nogah, Nepheg, Japhia, ⁸Elishama, Eliada, and Eliphelet—nine. ⁹*All these were sons of David, in addition to other sons by concubines; and Tamar was their sister.

¹⁰*†The son of Solomon was Rehoboam, whose son was Abijah, whose son was Asa, whose son was Jehoshaphat, ¹¹*whose son was Joram, whose son was Ahaziah, whose son was Joash, ¹²*whose son was Amaziah, whose son was Azariah, whose son was Jotham, ¹³*whose son was Ahaz, whose son was Hezekiah, whose son was Manasseh, ¹⁴*whose son was Amon, whose son was Josiah. ¹⁵*†The sons of Josiah were: the first-born, Johanan; the second, Jehoiakim; the third, Zedekiah; the fourth, Shallum. ¹⁶*The sons of Jehoiakim were: Jeconiah, his son; Zedekiah, his son.

¹⁷*†The sons of Jeconiah the captive were: Shealtiel, ¹⁸†Malchiram, Pedaiah, Shenazzar, Jekamiah, Shama, and Nedabiah. ¹⁹†The sons of Pedaiah were Zerubbabel and Shimei. The sons of Zerubbabel were Meshullam and Hananiah; Shelomith was their sister. ²⁰The sons of Meshullam were Hashubah, Ohel, Berechiah, Hasadiah, Jushab-hesed—five. ²¹The sons of Hananiah were Pelatiah, Jeshaiah, Rephaiah, Arnan, Obadiah, and Shecaniah. ²²*The sons of Shecaniah were Shemiah, Hattush, Igal, Bariah, Neariah, Shaphat—six. ²³The sons of Neariah were Elioenai, Hizkiah, and Azrikam—three. ²⁴The sons of Elioenai were Hodaviah, Eliashib, Pelaiah, Akkub, Johanan, Delaiah, and Anani—seven.

4 ¹*†THE descendants of Judah were: Perez, Hezron, Carmi, Hur, and Shobal. ²Reaiah, the son of Shobal, became the father of Jahath, and Jahath became the father of Ahumai and Lahad. These were the clans of the Zorathites.

³These were the descendants of Hareph, the father of Etam: Jezreel, Ishma, and Idbash; their sister was named Hazzelelponi. ⁴Penuel was the father of Gedor, and Ezer the father of Hushah. These were the descendants of Hur, the first-born of Ephrathah, the father of Bethlehem.

⁵*Ashhur, the father of Tekoa, had two wives, Helah and Naarah. ⁶Naarah bore him Ahuzzam, Hepher, the Temenites and the Ahashtarites. These were the descendants of Naarah. ⁷The sons of Helah were Zereth, Izhar, Ethnan, and Koz. ⁸Koz became the father of Anub and Zobebah, as well as of the clans of Aharhel, son of Harum. ⁹Jabez was the most distinguished of the brothers. His mother had named him Jabez, saying, "I bore him with pain." ¹⁰Jabez prayed to the God of Israel: "Oh, that you may truly bless me and extend my boundaries! Help me and make me free of misfortune, without pain!" And God granted his prayer.

¹¹Chelub, the brother of Shuhah, became the father of Mehir, who was the father of Eshton. ¹²Eshton became the father of Bethrapha, Paseah, and Tehinnah, the father of the city of Nahash. These were the men of Recah.

¹³*The sons of Kenaz were Othniel and Seraiah. The sons of Othniel were Hathath and Meonothai; ¹⁴Meonothai became the father of Ophrah. Seraiah became the father of Joab, the father of Geharashim, so called because they were craftsmen. ¹⁵*The sons of Caleb, son of Jephunneh, were Ir, Elah, and Naam. The sons of Elah were . . . and Kenaz.

¹⁶The sons of Jehallelel were Ziph, Ziphah, Tiria, and Asarel. ¹⁷*The sons of Ezrah were Jether, Mered, Epher, and Jalon. Jether became the father of Miriam, Shammai, and Ishbah, the father of Eshtemoa. ¹⁸[. . .] His (Mered's) Egyptian wife bore Jered, the father of Gedor, Heber, the father of Soco, and Jekuthiel, the father of Zanoah. These were the sons of Bithiah, the daughter of Pharaoh, whom Mered married. ¹⁹The sons of his Jewish wife, the sister of Naham, the father of Keilah, were Shimon the Garmite and Ishi the Maacathite. ²⁰The sons of Shimon were Amnon, Rinnah, Benhanan, and Tilon. The son of Ishi was Zoheth and the son of Zoheth. . . .

²¹*The descendants of Shelah, son of Judah, were:

✱

4: 2 Sm 2, 11; 5, 5.	15: 2 Kgs 23, 34; 24, 17;
5-8: 2 Sm 5, 14ff.	2 Chr 36, 4.10.
5: 2 Sm 5, 5.	16: 2 Kgs 24, 6.17;
9: 2 Sm 13, 1f.	2 Chr 36, 8.10.
10-17: Mt 1, 7-12.	17.19: Ezr 2, 2; 3, 2.8; 5, 2;
10: 1 Kgs 11, 43; 14, 31;	Sir 49, 11;
15, 1.8.24; 2 Chr 9, 31;	Hg 1, 1.12.14;
12, 16; 13, 23; 17, 1.	Mt 1, 12f; Lk 3, 27.
11: 1 Kgs 22, 51; 2 Chr 21,	22: Neh 3, 29.
1; 22, 1; 24, 1.27.	4/1: 2, 4f.7.9.50; Gn 38, 29;
12: 2 Kgs 12, 21; 14, 21;	46, 12; Mt 1, 3.
15, 7; 2 Chr 25, 1;	5: 2, 24.
26, 1.23; 27, 1.	13: Jos 15, 17; Jgs 1, 13;
13: 2 Kgs 15, 38; 16, 20;	3, 9.11.
20, 21; 2 Chr 28, 1.27;	15: Nm 13, 6; 14, 6;
32, 33.	32, 12; Jos 14, 6.14.
14: 2 Kgs 21, 18.26;	17: 1 Sm 30, 28.
2 Chr 33, 20.25.	21: 2, 3; Gn 38, 5; 46, 12;
	Nm 26, 20.

†

3, 5: *Shimea:* called *Shammua* in 2 Sm 5, 14. *Ammiel:* called *Eliam* in 2 Sm 11, 3.

3, 10-16: The kings of Judah from Solomon to the destruction of Jerusalem by the Babylonians.

3, 15: *Shallum:* the same as Jehoahaz, Josiah's successor; cf Jer 22, 11.

3, 17-24: The descendants of King *Jechoniah* up to the time of the Chronicler. If twenty-five years are allowed to each generation, the ten generations between *Jechoniah* and *Anani* (the last name on the list) would bring the birth of the latter to about 405 B. C.—an important item in establishing the approximate date of the Chronicler.

3, 18: *Shenazzar:* presumably the same as *Sheshbazzar* of Ezr 1, 8.11; 5, 14ff, the prince of Judah who was the first Jewish governor of Judah after the exile. Both forms of the name probably go back to the Babylonian name Sin-ab-ussar signifying, "O [god] Sin, protect [our] father!"

3, 19: *Zerubbabel:* here called the son of *Pedaiah,* though elsewhere (Hg 1, 12.14; 2, 2.23; Ezr 3, 2.8; 5, 2; Neh 12, 1) called *son of Shealtiel.* The latter term may merely mean that Zerubbabel succeeded Shealtiel as head of the house of David.

4, 1-43: The southern tribes.

Er, the father of Lecah; Laadah, the father of Mareshah; the clans of the linen weavers' guild in Bethashbea; **22**Jokim; the men of Cozeba; and Joash and Saraph, who held property in Moab, but returned to Bethlehem. [These are events of old.] **23**They were potters and inhabitants of Netaim and Gederah, where they lived in the king's service.

Simeon

24*The sons of Simeon were Nemuel, Jamin, Jachin, Zerah, and Shaul, **25**whose son was Shallum, whose son was Mibsam, whose son was Mishma. **26**The descendants of Mishma were his son Hammuel, whose son was Zaccur, whose son was Shimei. **27**Shimei had sixteen sons and six daughters. His brothers, however, did not have many sons, and as a result all their clans did not equal the number of the Judahites. **28***They dwelt in Beer-sheba, Moladah, Hazar-shual, **29**Bilhah, Ezem, Tolad, **30**Bethuel, Hormah, Ziklag, **31**Beth-marcaboth, Hazar-susim, Bethbiri, and Shaaraim. Until David came to reign, these were their cities **32**and their villages. Etam, also, and Ain, Rimmon, Tochen, and Ashan—five cities, **33**together with all their outlying villages as far as Baal. Here is where they dwelt, and so it was inscribed of them in their family records.

34Meshobab, Jamlech, Joshah, son of Amaziah, **35**Joel, Jehu, son of Joshibiah, son of Seraiah, son of Asiel, **36**Elioenai, Jaakobath, Jeshohaiah, Asaiah, Adiel, Jesimiel, Benaiah, **37**Ziza, son of Shiphi, son of Allon, son of Jedaiah, son of Shimri, son of Shemaiah— **38***these just named were princes in their clans, and their ancestral houses spread out to such an extent **39†**that they went to the approaches of Gedor, east of the valley, seeking pasture for their flocks. **40**They found abundant and good pastures, and the land was spacious, quiet, and peaceful. **41***They who have just been listed by name set out during the reign of Hezekiah, king of Judah, and attacked the tents of Ham (for Hamites dwelt there formerly) and also the Meunites who were there. They pronounced against them the ban that is still in force and dwelt in their place because they found pasture there for their flocks.

42Five hundred of them (the Simeonites) went to Mount Seir under the leadership of Pelatiah, Neariah, Rephaiah, and Uzziel, sons of Ishi. **43***They attacked the surviving Amalekites who had escaped, and have resided there to the present day.

Reuben

5 **1*†**THE sons of Reuben, the first-born of Israel. (He was indeed the first-born, but because he disgraced the couch of his father his birthright was given to the sons of Joseph, son of Israel, so that he is not listed in the family records according to birthright. **2***Judah, in fact, became powerful among his brothers, so that the ruler came from him, though the birthright had been Joseph's.) **3***The sons of Reuben, the first-born of Israel, were Hanoch, Pallu, Hezron, and Carmi. **4**His son was Joel, whose son was Shemaiah, whose son was Gog, whose son was Shimei, **5**whose son was Micah, whose son was Reaiah, whose son was Baal, **6***whose son was Beerah, whom Tiglath-pileser, the king of Assyria, took into exile; he was a prince of the Reubenites. **7**His brothers who belonged to his clans, when they were listed in the family records according to their descendants, were: Jeiel, the chief, and Zechariah, **8***and Bela, son of Azaz, son of Shema, son of Joel. The Reubenites lived in Aroer and as far as Nebo and Baal-meon; **9***toward the east they dwelt as far as the desert which extends from the Euphrates River, for they had much livestock in the land of Gilead. **10***During the reign of Saul they waged war with the Hagrites, and when they had defeated them they occupied their tents throughout the region east of Gilead.

Gad

11*The Gadites lived alongside them in the land of Bashan as far as Salecah. **12***Joel was chief, Shapham was second in command, and Janai was judge in Bashan. **13**Their brothers, corresponding to their ancestral houses, were: Michael, Meshullam, Sheba, Jorai, Jacan, Zia, and Eber—seven. **14**These were the sons of Abihail, son of Huri, son of Jaroah, son of Gilead, son of Michael, son of Jeshishai, son of Jahdo, son of Buz. **15**Ahi, son of Abdiel, son of Guni, was the head of their ancestral houses. **16**They dwelt in Gilead, in Bashan and its towns, and in all the pasture lands of Sirion to the borders. **17**All were listed in the family records in the time of Jotham, king of Judah, and of Jeroboam, king of Israel.

18The Reubenites, Gadites, and half-tribe of Manasseh were warriors, men who bore shield and sword and who drew the bow, trained in warfare—forty-four thousand seven hundred and sixty men fit for military service. **19***When they waged war against the Hagrites and against Jetur, Naphish, and Nodab, **20***they received help so that they mastered the Hagrites and all who were with them. For during the battle they called on God, and he heard them because they had put their trust in him. **21**Along with one hundred thousand men they also captured their livestock: fifty thousand camels, two hundred fifty thousand sheep, and two

24: Gn 46, 10; Ex 6, 15; Nm 26, 12f.
28-32: Jos 19, 2-8.
38: Nm 1, 2.
41: 2 Kgs 18, 1f; 2 Chr 29, 1.
43: Ex 17, 8.14; Dt 25, 17ff; 1 Sm 14, 48; 15, 3.7f; 2 Sm 8, 12.
5/1: Gn 35, 22; 48, 5.15-22; 49, 3f; Dt 33, 6.
2: 28, 4; Gn 49, 8ff.
3: Gn 46, 9; Ex 6, 14; Nm 26, 5f.
6: 2 Kgs 15, 29.
8: Jos 13, 9.16f; Nm 32, 3.38.
9: Jos 22, 9.
10: Ps 83, 6.
11: Jos 13, 11.24-28.
12: Gn 46, 16.
19: 1, 31; 5, 10; Gn 25, 15; Ps 83, 6.
20: Dt 33, 20f.

4, 39: *Gedor:* in the Greek, Gerar, no doubt correct.
5, 1-26: The Transjordan tribes.

thousand asses. **22***Many had fallen in battle, for victory is from God; and they took over their dwelling place until the time of the exile.

East Manasseh

23The numerous members of the half-tribe of Manasseh lived in the land of Bashan as far as Baal-hermon, Senir, and Mount Hermon. **24**The following were the heads of their ancestral houses: Epher, Ishi, Eliel, Azriel, Jeremiah, Hodaviah, and Jahdiel—men who were warriors, famous men, and heads over their ancestral houses.

25*However, they offended the God of their fathers by lusting after the gods of the natives of the land, whom God had cleared out of their way. **26***†Therefore the God of Israel incited against them the anger of Pul, king of Assyria, and of Tiglath-pileser, king of Assyria, who deported the Reubenites, the Gadites, and the half-tribe of Manasseh and brought them to Halah, Habor, and Hara, and to the river Gozan, where they have remained to this day.

Levi

27*†The sons of Levi were Gershon, Kohath, and Merari. **28***The sons of Kohath were Amram, Izhar, Hebron, and Uzziel. **29***The children of Amram were Aaron, Moses, and Miriam. The sons of Aaron were Nadab, Abihu, Eleazar, and Ithamar. **30**†Eleazar became the father of Phinehas. Phinehas became the father of Abishua. **31**Abishua became the father of Bukki. Bukki became the father of Uzzi. **32**Uzzi became the father of Zerahiah. Zerahiah became the father of Meraioth. **33**Meraioth became the father of Amariah. Amariah became the father of Ahitub. **34**Ahitub became the father of Zadok. Zadok became the father of Ahimaaz. **35**Ahimaaz became the father of Azariah. Azariah became the father of Johanan. **36**Johanan became the father of Azariah, who served as priest in the temple Solomon built in Jerusalem. **37**Azariah became the father of Amariah. Amariah became the father of Ahitub. **38**Ahitub became the father of Zadok. Zadok became the father of Shallum. **39**Shallum became the father of Hilkiah. Hilkiah became the father of Azariah. **40**Azariah became the father of Seraiah. Seraiah became the father of Jehozadak. **41**Jehozadak was one of those who went into the exile which the LORD inflicted on Judah and Jerusalem through Nebuchadnezzar.

6 **1***THE sons of Levi were Gershon, Kohath, and Merari. **2***The sons of Gershon were named Libni and Shimei. **3***The sons of Kohath were Amram, Izhar, Hebron, and Uzziel. **4***The sons of Merari were Mahli and Mushi.

The following were the clans of Levi, distributed according to their ancestors: **5**of Gershon: his son Libni, whose son was Jahath, whose son was Zimmah, **6**whose son was Joah, whose son was Iddo, whose son was Zerah, whose son was Jetherai.

7The descendants of Kohath were: his son Amminadab, whose son was Korah, whose son was Assir, **8**whose son was Elkanah, whose son was Ebiasaph, whose son was Assir, **9**whose son was Tahath, whose son was Uriel, whose son was Uzziah, whose son was Shaul. **10**The sons of Elkanah were Amasai and Ahimoth, **11**whose son was Elkanah, whose son was Zophai, whose son was Nahath, **12**whose son was Eliab, whose son was Jeroham, whose son was Elkanah, whose son was Samuel. **13**The sons of Samuel were Joel, the first-born, and Abijah, the second.

14*The descendants of Merari were Mahli, whose son was Libni, whose son was Shimei, whose son was Uzzah, **15**whose son was Shimea, whose son was Haggiah, whose son was Asaiah.

16†The following were entrusted by David with the choir services in the LORD's house from the time when the ark had obtained a permanent resting place. **17**They served as singers before the Dwelling of the meeting tent until Solomon built the temple of the LORD in Jerusalem, and they performed their services in an order prescribed for them. **18**Those who so performed are the following, together with their descendants.

Among the Kohathites: Heman, the chanter, son of Joel, son of Samuel, **19**son of Elkanah, son of Jeroham, son of Eliel, son of Toah, **20**son of Zuth, son of Elkanah, son of Mahath, son of Amasi, **21**son of Elkanah, son of Joel, son of Azariah, son of Zaphaniah, **22***son of Tahath, son of Assir, son of Ebiasaph, son of Korah, **23**son of Izhar, son of Kohath, son of Levi, son of Israel.

24His brother Asaph stood at his right hand. Asaph was the son of Berechiah, son of Shimea, **25**son of Michael, son of Baaseiah, son of Malchijah, **26**son of Ethni, son of Zerah, son of Adaiah, **27***son of Ethan,

---

† 5, 26: *Pul:* the name which the Assyrian king *Tiglath-pileser* III (745-727 B. C.) took as king of Babylon.

5, 27—6, 66: The tribe of Levi. The list gives special prominence to Levi's son *Kohath*, from whom were descended both the Aaronite priests (5, 28-41) and the leading group of temple singers (6, 18-23).

5, 30-41: The line of preexilic priests. The list seems to be confused in vv 36ff, which repeat the names, mostly in inverse order, that occur in vv 34f. A similar but shorter list is given, with variations, in Ezr 7, 1-5.

6, 16-32: The origin of the *choir services* performed by the levitical families in the postexilic temple at the time of the Chronicler is here attributed to David, somewhat as all the laws in the Pentateuch are attributed to Moses.

✿
22: Nm 32, 39; Dt 3, 8ff; Jgs 3, 3.
25: Ex 34, 14ff; 2 Kgs 17, 7.
26: 2 Kgs 15, 9.29; 17, 6.
27: 6, 1; 23, 6; Gn 46, 11; Ex 6, 16; Nm 26, 57.
28: 6, 3; Ex 6, 18.
29: Ex 6, 20; Nm 26, 59f.
6/1: 5, 27; 23, 6; Gn 46, 11; Ex 6, 16; Nm 26, 57.

2: Ex 6, 17.
3: Ex 6, 18; Nm 3, 19; 26, 59.
4: 6, 14; Ex 6, 19; Nm 3, 20; 26, 58.
14: 6, 4; Ex 6, 19; Nm 3, 20; 26, 58.
22: Ex 6, 24.
27: 6, 2.5.

son of Zimmah, son of Shimei, **28**son of Jahath, son of Gershon, son of Levi.

29Their brothers, the Merarites, stood at the left: Ethan, son of Kishi, son of Abdi, son of Malluch, **30**son of Hashabiah, son of Amaziah, son of Hilkiah, **31**son of Amzi, son of Bani, son of Shemer, **32***son of Mahli, son of Mushi, son of Merari, son of Levi.

33*Their brother Levites were appointed to all the other services of the Dwelling of the house of God. **34***However, it was Aaron and his descendants who burnt the offerings on the altar of holocausts and on the altar of incense; they alone had charge of the holy of holies and of making atonement for Israel, as Moses, the servant of God, had ordained.

35These were the descendants of Aaron: his son Eleazar, whose son was Phinehas, whose son was Abishua, **36**whose son was Bukki, whose son was Uzzi, whose son was Zerahiah, **37**whose son was Meraioth, whose son was Amariah, whose son was Ahitub, **38**whose son was Zadok, whose son was Ahimaaz.

39†The following were their dwelling places to which their encampment was limited. To the descendants of Aaron who belonged to the clan of the Kohathites, since the first lot fell to them, **40**was assigned Hebron with its adjacent pasture lands in the land of Judah, **41**although the open country and the villages belonging to the city had been given to Caleb, the son of Jephunneh. **42**There were assigned to the descendants of Aaron: Hebron, a city of asylum, Libnah with its pasture lands, Jattir with its pasture lands, Eshtemoa with its pasture lands, **43**Holon with its pasture lands, Debir with its pasture lands, **44**Ashan with its pasture lands, Jetta with its pasture lands, and Bethshemesh with its pasture lands. **45**Also from the tribe of Benjamin: Gibeon with its pasture lands, Geba with its pasture lands, Almon with its pasture lands, Anathoth with its pasture lands. In all, they had thirteen cities with their pasture lands. **49**The Israelites assigned these cities with their pasture lands to the Levites, **50**designating them by name and assigning them by lot from the tribes of the Judahites, Simeonites, and Benjaminites.

46The other Kohathites obtained ten cities by lot for their clans from the tribe of Ephraim, from the tribe of Dan, and from the half-tribe of Manasseh. **47**The clans of the Gershonites obtained thirteen cities from the tribes of Issachar, Asher, and Naphtali, and from the half-tribe of Manasseh in Bashan. **48**The clans of the Merarites obtained twelve cities by lot from the tribes of Reuben, Gad, and Zebulun.

51The clans of the Kohathites obtained cities by lot from the tribe of Ephraim. **52**They were assigned: Shechem in the mountain region of Ephraim, a city of asylum, with its pasture lands, Gezer with its pasture lands, **53**Kibzaim with its pasture lands, and Bethhoron with its pasture lands. **54**From the tribe of Dan:

Elteke with its pasture lands, Gibbethon with its pasture lands, Aijalon with its pasture lands, and Gathrimmon with its pasture lands. **55**From the half-tribe of Manasseh: Taanach with its pasture lands and Ibleam with its pasture lands. These belonged to the rest of the Kohathite clan.

56The clans of the Gershonites received from the half-tribe of Manasseh: Golan in Bashan with its pasture lands and Ashtaroth with its pasture lands. **57**From the tribe of Issachar: Kedesh with its pasture lands, Daberath with its pasture lands, **58**Ramoth with its pasture lands, and En-gannim with its pasture lands. **59**From the tribe of Asher: Mashal with its pasture lands, Abdon with its pasture lands, **60**Hilkath with its pasture lands, and Rehob with its pasture lands. **61**From the tribe of Naphtali: Kedesh in Galilee with its pasture lands, Hammon with its pasture lands, and Kiriathaim with its pasture lands.

62The rest of the Merarites received from the tribe of Zebulun: Jokneam with its pasture lands, Kartah with its pasture lands, Rimmon with its pasture lands, and Tabor with its pasture lands. **63**Across the Jordan at Jericho [that is, east of the Jordan] they received from the tribe of Reuben: Bezer in the desert with its pasture lands, Jahzah with its pasture lands, **64**Kedemoth with its pasture lands, and Mephaath with its pasture lands. **65**From the tribe of Gad: Ramoth in Gilead with its pasture lands, Mahanaim with its pasture lands, **66**Heshbon with its pasture lands, and Jazer with its pasture lands.

Issachar

7 **1***†THE sons of Issachar were Tola, Puah, Jashub, and Shimron: four. **2***The sons of Tola were Uzzi, Rephaiah, Jeriel, Jahmai, Ibsam, and Shemuel, warrior heads of the ancestral houses of Tola. Their kindred numbered twenty-two thousand six hundred in the time of David. **3**The sons of Uzzi: Izarahiah. The sons of Izarahiah were Michael, Obadiah, Joel, and Isshiah. All five of these were chiefs. **4**Their kindred, by ancestral houses, numbered thirty-six thousand men in organized military troops, since they had more wives and sons **5**than their fellow tribesmen. In all the clans of Issachar there was a total of eighty-seven thousand warriors in their family records.

Benjamin

6*The sons of Benjamin were Bela, Becher, and Jediael—three. **7**The sons of Bela were Ezbon, Uzzi, Uzziel, Jerimoth, and Iri—five. They were heads of their ancestral houses and warriors. Their family records listed twenty-two thousand and thirty-four. **8***The sons of Becher were Zemirah, Joash, Eliezer, Elioenai, Omri, Jeremoth, Abijah, Anathoth, and Alemeth—all these were sons of Becher. **9**Their family records listed twenty thousand two hundred of their kindred who

---

---

†

    6, 39-66: Regarding the nature of the rights of Levites in the cities assigned to them, see note on Jos 21, 1.

    7, 1-40: The northern tribes.

were heads of their ancestral houses and warriors. ¹⁰The sons of Jediael: Bilhan. The sons of Bilhan were Jeush, Benjamin, Ehud, Chenaanah, Zethan, Tarshish, and Ahishahar. ¹¹*All these were descendants of Jediael, heads of ancestral houses and warriors. They numbered seventeen thousand two hundred men fit for military service . . . Shupham and Hupham.

Dan, Naphtali and Manasseh

¹²*The sons of Dan: Hushim. ¹³The sons of Naphtali were Jahziel, Guni, Jezer, and Shallum. These were descendants of Bilhah. ¹⁴*The sons of Manasseh, whom his Aramean concubine bore: she bore Machir, the father of Gilead. ¹⁵*Machir took a wife whose name was Maacah; his sister's name was Molecheth. Manasseh's second son was named Zelophehad, but to Zelophehad only daughters were born. ¹⁶Maacah, Machir's wife, bore a son whom she named Peresh. He had a brother named Sheresh, whose sons were Ulam and Rakem. ¹⁷The sons of Ulam: Bedan. These were the descendants of Gilead, the son of Machir, the son of Manasseh. ¹⁸His sister Molecheth bore Ishhod, Abiezer, and Mahlah. ¹⁹The sons of Shemida were Ahian, Shechem, Likhi, and Aniam.

Ephraim

²⁰*The sons of Ephraim: Shuthelah, whose son was Bered, whose son was Tahath, whose son was Eleadah, whose son was Tahath, ²¹whose son was Zabad. Ephraim's son Shuthelah, and Ezer and Elead, who were born in the land, were slain by the inhabitants of Gath because they had gone down to take away their livestock. ²²Their father Ephraim mourned a long time, but after his kinsmen had come and comforted him, ²³*he visited his wife, who conceived and bore a son whom he named Beriah, since evil had befallen his house. ²⁴He had a daughter, Sheerah, who built lower and upper Beth-horon and Uzzen-sheerah. ²⁵Zabad's son was Rephah, whose son was Resheph, whose son was Telah, whose son was Tahan, ²⁶*whose son was Ladan, whose son was Ammihud, whose son was Elishama, ²⁷whose son was Nun, whose son was Joshua.

²⁸*Their property and their dwellings were in Bethel and its towns, Naaran to the east, Gezer and its towns to the west, and also Shechem and its towns as far as Ayyah and its towns. ²⁹*Manasseh, however, had possession of Beth-shean and its towns, Taanach and its towns, Megiddo and its towns, and Dor and its towns. In these dwelt the descendants of Joseph, the son of Israel.

Asher

³⁰*The sons of Asher were Imnah, Iishvah, Ishvi, and Beriah; their sister was Serah. ³¹Beriah's sons were Heber and Malchiel, who was the father of Birzaith. ³²Heber became the father of Japhlet, Shomer, Hotham, and their sister Shua. ³³The sons of Japhlet were Pasach, Bimhal, and Ashvath; these were the sons of Japhlet. ³⁴The sons of Shomer were Ahi, Rohgah, Jehubbah, and Aram. ³⁵The sons of his brother Hotham were Zophah, Imna, Shelesh, and Amal. ³⁶The sons of Zophah were Suah, Harnepher, Shual, Beri, Imrah, ³⁷Bezer, Hod, Shamma, Shilshah, Ithran, and Beera. ³⁸The sons of Jether were Jephunneh, Pispa, and Ara. ³⁹The sons of Ulla were Arah, Hanniel, and Rizia. ⁴⁰All these were descendants of Asher, heads of ancestral houses, distinguished men, warriors, and chiefs among the princes. Their family records numbered twenty-six thousand men fit for military service.

Benjamin

8 ¹*†BENJAMIN became the father of Bela, his first-born, Ashbel, the second son, Aharah, the third, ²Nohah, the fourth, and Rapha, the fifth. ³The sons of Bela were Addar and Gera, the father of Ehud. ⁴*The sons of Ehud were Abishua, Naaman, Ahoah, ⁵Gera, Shephuphan, and Huram. ⁶These were the sons of Ehud, family heads over those who dwelt in Geba and were deported to Manahath. ⁷Also Naaman, Ahijah, and Gera. The last, who led them into exile, became the father of Uzza and Ahihud. ⁸Shaharaim became a father on the Moabite plateau after he had put away his wives Hushim and Baara. ⁹By his wife Hodesh he became the father of Jobab, Zibia, Mesha, Malcam, ¹⁰Jeuz, Sachia, and Mirmah. These were his sons, family heads. ¹¹By Hushim he became the father of Abitub and Elpaal. ¹²*The sons of Elpaal were Eber, Misham, Shemed, who built Ono and Lod with its nearby towns, ¹³Beriah, and Shema. They were family heads of those who dwelt in Aijalon, and they put the inhabitants of Gath to flight. ¹⁴Their brethren were Elpaal, Shashak, and Jeremoth. ¹⁵Zebadiah, Arad, Eder, ¹⁶Michael, Ishpah, and Joha were the sons of Beriah. ¹⁷Zebadiah, Meshullam, Hizki, Heber, ¹⁸Ishmerai, Izliah, and Jobab were the sons of Elpaal. ¹⁹Jakim, Zichri, Zabdi, ²⁰Elienai, Zillethai, Eliel, ²¹Adaiah, Beraiah, and Shimrath were the sons of Shimei. ²²Ishpan, Eber, Eliel, ²³Abdon, Zichri, Hanan, ²⁴Hananiah, Elam,, Anthothijah, ²⁵Iphdeiah, and Penuel were the sons of Shashak. ²⁶Shamsherai, Shehariah, Athaliah, ²⁷Jaareshiah, Elijah, and Zichri were the sons of Jeroham. ²⁸These were family heads over their kindred, chiefs who dwelt in Jerusalem.

²⁹*In Gibeon dwelt Jeiel, the founder of Gibeon, whose wife's name was Maacah; ³⁰also his first-born son, Abdon, and Zur, Kish, Baal, Ner, Nadab, ³¹Gedor, Ahio, Zecher, and Mikloth. ³²Mikloth became the fa-

---

❊
  11: Nm 26, 39.
  12f: Gn 46, 24; Nm 26, 48f.
  14-19: Nm 26, 29-32.
  14: Nm 26, 29; Jos 17, 1.
  15: Nm 26, 33; Jos 17, 3.
  20: Nm 26, 35.
  23: 8, 13.
  26: Nm 1, 10; 2, 18; 7, 48;
      10, 22.

  28: Gn 12, 8; 1 Kgs 9, 16.
  29: Jos 17, 11.
  30: Gn 46, 17; Nm 26, 44ff.
  8/1: 7, 6; Gn 46, 21;
       Nm 26, 38ff.
  4: Jgs 3, 15.
  12: Neh 11, 35.
  29-32: 9, 35-38.

---

† 8, 1-40: A second, variant list of the Benjaminites, with special prominence given to Saul's family (vv 33-40).

ther of Shimeah. These, too, dwelt with their relatives in Jerusalem, opposite their fellow tribesmen. **33***Ner became the father of Kish, and Kish became the father of Saul. Saul became the father of Jonathan, Malchishua, Abinadab, and Eshbaal. **34***The son of Jonathan was Meribbaal, and Meribbaal became the father of Micah. **35**The sons of Micah were Pithon, Melech, Tarea, and Ahaz. **36***Ahaz became the father of Jehoaddah, and Jehoaddah became the father of Alemeth, Azmaveth, and Zimri. Zimri became the father of Moza. **37***Moza became the father of Binea, whose son was Raphah, whose son was Eleasah, whose son was Azel. **38**Azel had six sons, whose names were Azrikam, his first-born, Ishmael, Sheariah, Azariah, Obadiah, and Hanan; all these were the sons of Azel. **39**The sons of Eshek, his brother, were Ulam, his first-born, Jeush, the second son, and Eliphelet, the third. **40**The sons of Ulam were combat archers, and many were their sons and grandsons: one hundred and fifty. All these were the descendants of Benjamin.

9 **1***THUS all Israel was inscribed in its family records which are recorded in the book of the kings of Israel.

Now Judah had been carried in captivity to Babylon because of its rebellion. **2***†The first to settle again in their cities and dwell there were certain lay Israelites, the priests, the Levites, and the temple slaves.

Jerusalemites

3In Jerusalem lived Judahites and Benjaminites; also Ephraimites and Manassehites. **4**Among the Judahites was Uthai, son of Ammihud, son of Omri, son of Imri, son of Bani, one of the descendants of Perez, son of Judah. **5**Among the Shelanites were Asaiah, the first-born, and his sons. **6**Among the Zerahites were Jeuel and six hundred and ninety of their brethren. **7**Among the Benjaminites were Sallu, son of Meshullam, son of Hodaviah, son of Hassenuah; **8**Ibneiah, son of Jeroham; Elah, son of Uzzi, son of Michri; Meshullam, son of Shephatiah, son of Reuel, son of Ibnijah. **9**Their kindred of various families were nine hundred and fifty-six. All those named were heads of their ancestral houses.

10Among the priests were Jedaiah; Jehoiarib; Jachin; **11**Azariah, son of Hilkiah, son of Meshullam, son of Zadok, son of Meraioth, son of Ahitub, the ruler of the house of God; **12**Adaiah, son of Jeroham, son of Pashhur, son of Malchijah; Maasai, son of Adiel, son of Jahzerah, son of Meshullam, son of Meshillemith,

son of Immer. **13**Their brethren, heads of their ancestral houses, were one thousand seven hundred and sixty, valiant for the work of the service of the house of God.

14Among the Levites were Shemaiah, son of Hasshub, son of Azrikam, son of Hashabiah, one of the descendants of Merari; **15**Bakbakkar; Heresh; Galal; Mattaniah, son of Mica, son of Zichri, a descendant of Asaph; **16**Obadiah, son of Shemaiah, son of Galal, a descendant of Jeduthun; and Berechiah, son of Asa, son of Elkanah, whose family lived in the villages of the Netophathites.

17The gatekeepers were Shallum, Akkub, Talmon, Ahiman, and their brethren; Shallum was the chief. **18**Previously they had stood guard at the king's gate on the east side; now they became gatekeepers for the encampments of the Levites. **19**Shallum, son of Kore, son of Ebiasaph, a descendant of Korah, and his brethren of the same ancestral house of the Korahites had as their assigned task the guarding of the threshold of the tent, just as their fathers had guarded the entrance to the encampment of the LORD. **20***Phinehas, son of Eleazar, had been their chief in times past—the LORD be with him! **21***Zechariah, son of Meshelemiah, guarded the gate of the meeting tent. **22**In all, those who were chosen for gatekeepers at the threshold were two hundred and twelve. They were inscribed in the family records of their villages. David and Samuel the seer had established them in their position of trust. **23**Thus they and their sons kept guard over the gates of the house of the LORD, the house which was then a tent. **24***The gatekeepers were stationed at the four sides, to the east, the west, the north, and the south. **25***Their kinsmen who lived in their own villages took turns in assisting them for seven-day periods, **26**while the four chief gatekeepers were on constant duty. These were the Levites who also had charge of the chambers and treasures of the house of God. **27**At night they lodged about the house of God, for it was in their charge and they had the duty of opening it each morning.

28Some of them had charge of the liturgical equipment, tallying it as it was brought in and taken out. **29**Others were appointed to take care of the utensils and all the sacred vessels, as well as the fine flour, the wine, the oil, the frankincense, and the spices. **30***It was the sons of priests, however, who mixed the spiced ointments. **31***Mattithiah, one of the Levites, the first-born of Shallum the Koreite, was entrusted with preparing the cakes. **32***Benaiah the Kohathite, one of their brethren, was in charge of setting out the showbread each sabbath.

33These were the chanters and the gatekeepers, family heads over the Levites. They stayed in the chambers when free of duty, for day and night they had to

---

33-38: 9, 39-44.
33: 10, 2; 1 Sm 9, 1; 14, 49.51; 31, 2.
34: 2 Sm 4, 4; 9, 6.10.12.
36: 9, 42.
37: 9, 43.
9/1: 2 Chr 16, 11; 20, 34; 25, 26; 27, 7; 33, 18; 36, 8.
2-22: Neh 11, 3-19.

2: Ezr 2, 70; 7, 7; Neh 11, 3.
20: Ex 6, 25; Nm 25, 7.11; Jgs 20, 28.
21: 26, 2.14.
24: 26, 13.
25: 2 Chr 23, 4f.
30: Ex 30, 22-33.
31f: 23, 29; Lv 2, 1ff; 6, 13ff; 7, 11.
32: Ex 25, 30; Lv 24, 5-8.

---

† 9, 2-34: The inhabitants of Jerusalem after the exile. A similar list, with many variants in the names, is given in Neh 11, 3-24.

be ready for service. ³⁴These were the levitical family heads over their kindred, chiefs who dwelt in Jerusalem.

II: THE HISTORY OF DAVID

Genealogy of Saul

³⁵*IN GIBEON DWELT JEIEL, the founder of Gibeon, whose wife's name was Maacah. ³⁶His first-born son was Abdon; then came Zur, Kish, Baal, Ner, Nadab, ³⁷Gedor, Ahio, Zechariah, and Mikloth. ³⁸Mikloth became the father of Shimeam. These, too, with their brethren, dwelt opposite their brethren in Jerusalem. ³⁹Ner became the father of Kish, and Kish became the father of Saul. Saul became the father of Jonathan, Malchishua, Abinadab, and Eshbaal. ⁴⁰The son of Jonathan was Meribbaal, and Meribbaal became the father of Micah. ⁴¹The sons of Micah were Pithon, Melech, Tahrea, and Ahaz. ⁴²Ahaz became the father of Jehoaddah, and Jehoaddah became the father of Alemeth, Azmaveth, and Zimri. Zimri became the father of Moza. ⁴³Moza became the father of Binea, whose son was Rephaiah, whose son was Eleasah, whose son was Azel. ⁴⁴Azel had six sons, whose names were Azrikam, his first-born, Ishmael, Sheariah, Azariah, Obadiah, and Hanan; these were the sons of Azel.

His Death and Burial

10 ¹*NOW the Philistines were at war with Israel; the Israelites fled before the Philistines, and a number of them fell, slain on Mount Gilboa. ²The Philistines pressed hard after Saul and his sons. When the Philistines had killed Jonathan, Abinadab, and Malchishua, sons of Saul, ³the whole fury of the battle descended upon Saul. Then the archers found him, and wounded him with their arrows.

⁴Saul said to his armor-bearer, "Draw your sword and thrust me through with it, that these uncircumcised may not come and maltreat me." But the armor-bearer, in great fear, refused. So Saul took his own sword and fell on it; ⁵and seeing him dead, the armor-bearer also fell on his sword and died. ⁶Thus, with Saul and his three sons, his whole house died at one time. ⁷When all the Israelites who were in the valley saw that Saul and his sons had died in the rout, they left their cities and fled; thereupon the Philistines came and occupied them.

⁸On the following day, when the Philistines came to strip the slain, they found Saul and his sons where they had fallen on Mount Gilboa. ⁹They stripped him, cut off his head, and took his armor; these they sent throughout the land of the Philistines to convey the good news to their idols and their people. ¹⁰His armor they put in the house of their gods, but his skull they impaled on the temple of Dagon.

¹¹When all the inhabitants of Jabesh-gilead had heard what the Philistines had done to Saul, ¹²*its warriors rose to a man, recovered the bodies of Saul and his sons, and brought them to Jabesh. They buried their bones under the oak of Jabesh, and fasted seven days.

¹³*†Thus Saul died because of his rebellion against the LORD in disobeying his command, and also because he had sought counsel of a necromancer, ¹⁴*and had not rather inquired of the LORD. Therefore the LORD slew him, and transferred his kingdom to David, the son of Jesse.

David Is Made King

11 ¹*THEN all Israel gathered about David in Hebron, and they said: "Surely, we are of the same bone and flesh as you. ²*Even formerly, when Saul was still the king, it was you who led Israel in all its battles. And now the LORD, your God, has said to you, 'You shall shepherd my people Israel and be ruler over them.'" ³*Then all the elders of Israel came to the king at Hebron, and there David made a covenant with them in the presence of the LORD; and they anointed him king over Israel, in accordance with the word of the LORD as revealed through Samuel.

Jerusalem Captured

⁴*Then David and all Israel went to Jerusalem, that is, Jebus, where the natives of the land were called Jebusites. ⁵The inhabitants of Jebus said to David, "You shall not enter here." David nevertheless captured the fortress of Zion, which is the City of David. ⁶*David said, "Whoever strikes the Jebusites first shall be made the chief commander." Joab, the son of Zeruiah, was the first to go up; and so he became chief. ⁷David took up his residence in the fortress, which thenceforth was called the City of David. ⁸*He rebuilt the city on all sides, from the Millo all the way around, while Joab restored the rest of the city. ⁹David became more and more powerful, for the LORD of hosts was with him.

David's Warriors

¹⁰*These were David's chief warriors who, together with all Israel, supported him in his reign in order to make him true king, even as the LORD had commanded

35-44: 8, 29-38.
10/1-12: 1 Sm 31, 1-13.
12: 2 Sm 2, 5.
13: Dt 18, 10ff;
1 Sm 13, 13f;
15, 3.11.26.
14: 1 Sm 15, 28;
2 Sm 3, 9f.
11/1-9: 2 Sm 5, 1-10.
2: 1 Sm 18, 5.13-16.30;
19, 8.
3: 1 Sm 16, 1.13;
2 Sm 2, 4.
4: Jos 15, 8; Jgs 1, 21;
19, 10f.
6: 2 Sm 2, 13ff; 8, 16.
8: 1 Kgs 9, 15.24; 11, 27;
2 Chr 32, 5.
10-41: 2 Sm 23, 8-39.

† 10, 13f: The Chronicler's comment on why Saul met his tragic end: he had disobeyed the Lord's command given through the prophet Samuel (1 Sm 15, 3-9), and *had sought counsel of a necromancer* (1 Sm 28, 6-19), contrary to the Mosaic law against necromancy (Dt 18, 10f).

concerning Israel. **11**†Here is the list of David's warriors:

Ishbaal, the son of Hachamoni, chief of the Three. He brandished his spear against three hundred, whom he slew in a single encounter.

12*Next to him Eleazar, the son of Dodo the Ahohite, one of the Three warriors. **13***He was with David at Pas-dammim, where the Philistines had massed for battle. The plowland was fully planted with barley, but its defenders were retreating before the Philistines. **14**He made a stand on the sown ground, kept it safe, and cut down the Philistines. Thus the Lord brought about a great victory.

15*Three of the Thirty chiefs went down to the rock, to David, who was in the cave of Adullam while the Philistines were encamped in the valley of Rephaim. **16**David was then in the stronghold, and a Philistine garrison was at Bethlehem. **17**David expressed a desire: "Oh, that someone would give me a drink from the cistern that is by the gate at Bethlehem!" **18**Thereupon the Three broke through the encampment of the Philistines, drew water from the cistern by the gate at Bethlehem, and carried it back to David. But David refused to drink it. Instead, he poured it out as a libation to the Lord, **19**saying, "God forbid that I should do such a thing! Could I drink the blood of these men who risked their lives?" For at the risk of their lives they brought it; and so he refused to drink it. Such deeds as these the Three warriors performed.

20*†Abishai, the brother of Joab. He was the chief of the Thirty; he brandished his spear against three hundred, and slew them. Thus he had a reputation like that of the Three. **21**He was twice as famous as any of the Thirty and became their commander, but he did not attain to the Three.

22Benaiah, son of Jehoiada, a valiant man of mighty deeds, from Kabzeel. He killed the two sons of Ariel of Moab, and also, on a snowy day, he went down and killed the lion in the cistern. **23**He likewise slew the Egyptian, a huge man five cubits tall. The Egyptian carried a spear that was like a weaver's heddle-bar, but he came against him with a staff, wrested the spear from the Egyptian's hand, and killed him with his own spear. **24**Such deeds as these of Benaiah, the son of Jehoiada, gave him a reputation like that of the Three. **25***He was more famous than any of the Thirty, but he did not attain to the Three. David put him in charge of his bodyguard.

26*Also these warriors: Asahel, the brother of Joab; Elhanan, son of Dodo, from Bethlehem; **27**Shammoth, from En-harod; Helez, from Palti; **28**Ira, son of Ikkesh, from Tekoa; Abiezer, from Anathoth; **29***Sibbecai, from Husha; Ilai, from Ahoh; **30***Maharai, from Netophah; Heled, son of Baanah, from Netophah; **31***Ithai,

son of Ribai, from Gibeah of Benjamin; Benaiah, from Pirathon; **32**Hurai, from the valley of Gaash; Abiel, from Betharabah; **33**Azmaveth, from Bahurim; Eliahba, from Shaalbon; **34**Jashen the Gunite; Jonathan, son of Shagee, from En-harod; **35**Ahiam, son of Sachar, from En-harod; **36**Elipheleth, son of Ahasabi, from Beth-maacah; Ahijah, from Gilo; **37**Hezro, from Carmel; Naarai, the son of Ezbai; **38**Joel, brother of Nathan, from Rehob, the Gadite; **39**Zelek the Ammonite; Naharai, from Beeroth, the armor-bearer of Joab, son of Zeruiah; **40**Ira, from Jattir; Gareb, from Jattir; **41**Uriah the Hittite; Zabad, son of Ahlai, **42**and, in addition to the Thirty, Adina, son of Shiza, the Reubenite, chief of the tribe of Reuben; **43**Hanan, from Beth-maacah; Joshaphat the Mithnite; **44**Uzzia, from Ashterath; Shama and Jeiel, sons of Hotham, from Aroer; **45**Jediael, son of Shimri, and Joha, his brother, the Tizite; **46**Eliel the Mahavite; Jeribai and Joshaviah, sons of Elnaam; Ithmah, from Moab; **47**Eliel, Obed, and Jaasiel the Mezobian.

David's Early Followers

12 **1***The following men came to David in Ziklag while he was still under banishment from Saul, son of Kish; they, too, were among the warriors who helped him in his battles. **2**They were archers who could use either the right or the left hand, both in slinging stones and in shooting arrows with the bow. They were some of Saul's kinsmen, from Benjamin. **3***Ahiezer was their chief, along with Joash, both sons of Shemaah of Gibeah; also Jeziel and Pelet, sons of Azmaveth; Beracah; Jehu, from Anathoth; **4**Ishmaiah the Gibeonite, a warrior on the level of the Thirty, and in addition to their number; **5**Jeremiah; Jahaziel; Johanan; Jozabad from Gederah; **6**Eluzai; Jerimoth; Bealiah; Shemariah; Shephatiah the Haruphite; **7**Elkanah, Isshiah, Azarel, Joezer, and Ishbaal, who were Korahites; **8**Joelah, finally, and Zebadiah, sons of Jeroham, from Gedor.

9*Some of the Gadites also went over to David when he was at the stronghold in the wilderness. They were valiant warriors, experienced soldiers equipped with shield and spear, who bore themselves like lions, and were as swift as the gazelles on the mountains. **10**Ezer was their chief, Obadiah was second, Eliab third, **11**Mishmannah fourth, Jeremiah fifth, **12**Attai sixth, Eliel seventh, **13**Johanan eighth, Elzabad ninth, **14**Jeremiah tenth, and Machbannai eleventh. **15**These Gadites were army commanders, the lesser placed over hundreds and the greater over thousands. **16**It was they who crossed over the Jordan when it was overflowing both its banks in the first month, and dispersed all who were in the valleys to the east and to the west.

17Some Benjaminites and Judahites also came to

❋
12: 27, 4.
13: 1 Sm 17, 1.
15: 14, 9; 2 Sm 5, 18.22.
20f: 2 Sm 23, 18f.
20: 18, 12; 1 Sm 26, 6ff;
   2 Sm 16, 9; 18, 2;
21, 17.
25: 2 Sm 8, 18; 20, 23.

26: 2, 16; 27, 7.
29: 27, 11.
30: 27, 13.
31: 27, 14.
12/1: 1 Sm 27, 1-7.
3: 27, 12.
9: Dt 33, 20.

---

†
11, 11f: *The Three:* the Chronicler names only two of them: *Ishbaal* and *Eleazar.* According to 2 Sm 23, 8-12, the Three were *Ishbaal, Eleazar,* and *Shammah.*

11, 20: *The Thirty:* listed by name in vv 26-47. The list given in 2 Sm 23, 8-39 often differs in names and spellings; for the numbers, see the note there.

David at the stronghold. [18]David went out to meet them and addressed them in these words: "If you come peacefully, to help me, I am of a mind to have you join me. But if you have come to betray me to my enemies though my hands have done no wrong, may the God of our fathers see and punish you."

[19]Then spirit enveloped Amasai, the chief of the Thirty, who spoke:

> "We are yours, O David,
>   we are with you, O son of Jesse.
> Peace, peace to you,
>   and peace to him who helps you;
>   your God it is who helps you."

So David received them and placed them among the leaders of his troops.

[20]Men from Manasseh also deserted to David when he came with the Philistines to battle against Saul. However, he did not help the Philistines, for their lords took counsel and sent him home, saying, "At the cost of our heads he will desert to his master Saul." [21]As he was returning to Ziklag, therefore, these deserted to him from Manasseh: Adnah, Jozabad, Jediael, Michael, Jozabad, Elihu, and Zillethai, chiefs of thousands of Manasseh. [22]They helped David by taking charge of his troops, for they were all warriors and became commanders of his army. [23]And from day to day men kept coming to David's help until there was a vast encampment, like an encampment of angels.

The Assembly at Hebron

[24]This is the muster of the detachments of armed troops that came to David at Hebron to transfer to him Saul's kingdom, as the LORD had ordained. [25]†Judahites bearing shields and spears: six thousand eight hundred armed troops. [26]Of the Simeonites, warriors fit for battle: seven thousand one hundred. [27]Of the Levites: four thousand six hundred, [28]along with Jehoiada, leader of the line of Aaron, with another three thousand seven hundred, [29]and Zadok, a young warrior, with twenty-two princes of his father's house. [30]Of the Benjaminites, the brethren of Saul: three thousand—until this time, most of them had held their allegiance to the house of Saul. [31]Of the Ephraimites: twenty thousand eight hundred warriors, men renowned in their ancestral houses. [32]Of the half-tribe of Manasseh: eighteen thousand, designated by name to come and make David king. [33]Of the Issacharites, their chiefs who were endowed with an understanding of the times and who knew what Israel had to do: two hundred chiefs, together with all their brethren under their command. [34]From Zebulun, men fit for military service, set in battle array with every kind of weapon for war: fifty thousand men rallying with a single purpose. [35]From Naphtali: one thousand captains, and with them, armed with shield and lance,

thirty-seven thousand men. [36]Of the Danites, set in battle array: twenty-eight thousand six hundred. [37]From Asher, fit for military service and set in battle array: forty thousand. [38]From the other side of the Jordan, of the Reubenites, Gadites, and the half-tribe of Manasseh, men equipped with every kind of weapon of war: one hundred and twenty thousand.

[39]All these soldiers, drawn up in battle order, came to Hebron with the resolute intention of making David king over all Israel. The rest of Israel was likewise of one mind to make David king. [40]They remained with David for three days, feasting and drinking, for their brethren had prepared for them. [41]Moreover, their neighbors from as far as Issachar, Zebulun, and Naphtali came bringing food on asses, camels, mules, and oxen—provisions in great quantity of meal, pressed figs, raisins, wine, oil, oxen, and sheep. For there was rejoicing in Israel.

Transfer of the Ark

13 [1]*AFTER David had taken counsel with his commanders of thousands and of hundreds, that is to say, with every one of his leaders, [2]*he said to the whole assembly of Israel: "If it seems good to you, and is so decreed by the LORD our God, let us summon the rest of our brethren from all the districts of Israel, and also the priests and the Levites from their cities with pasture lands, that they may join us; [3]and let us bring the ark of our God here among us, for in the days of Saul we did not visit it." [4]And the whole assembly agreed to do this, for the idea was pleasing to all the people.

[5]*†Then David assembled all Israel, from Shihor of Egypt to Labo of Hamath, to bring the ark of God from Kiriath-jearim. [6]*David and all Israel went up to Baalah, that is, to Kiriath-jearim, of Judah, to bring back the ark of God, which was known by the name "LORD enthroned upon the cherubim." [7]They transported the ark of God on a new cart from the house of Abinadab; Uzzah and Ahio were guiding the cart, [8]while David and all Israel danced before God with great enthusiasm, amid songs and music on lyres, harps, tambourines, cymbals, and trumpets.

[9]†As they reached the threshing floor of Chidon, Uzzah stretched out his hand to steady the ark, for the oxen were upsetting it. [10]Then the LORD became angry with Uzzah and struck him; he died there in God's presence, because he had laid his hand on the ark. [11]†David was disturbed because the LORD's anger had

---

† 12, 25-38: The Chronicler fills out the pageantry of joyous occasions in keeping with his much later appreciation of the significance of the event in the history of God's people: the numbers in attendance at David's crowning in Hebron (cf 2 Sm 5, 1ff) are recounted in the same spirit of enthusiasm which in v 23 compares David's band of desert freebooters to a numerous encampment of angels.

13, 5: *Shihor of Egypt:* the eastern branch of the Nile delta. *Labo of Hamath:* in southern Syria.

13, 9: *Chidon:* in 2 Sm 6, 6, *Nodan.*

13, 11: *Perez-uzza:* a Hebrew term meaning "the breaking out against Uzza."

✱
13/1-14: 2 Sm 6, 1-11.
    2: Nm 35, 1ff; Jos 14, 4;
      21, 2ff.
    5: 15, 3; Jos 13, 3.5;

1 Sm 6, 21; 7, 1f;
2 Sm 6, 1-11.
6: Jos 15, 9; 18, 14;
1 Sm 4, 4; 7, 1.

broken out against Uzzah. Therefore that place has been called Perez-uzza even to this day.

[12]David was now afraid of God, and he said, "How can I bring the ark of God with me?" [13]Therefore he did not take the ark back with him to the City of David, but he took it instead to the house of Obed-edom the Gittite. [14]*The ark of God remained in the house of Obed-edom with his family for three months, and the Lord blessed Obed-edom's household and all that he possessed.

David in Jerusalem

14 [1]*HIRAM, king of Tyre, sent envoys to David along with masons and carpenters, and cedar wood to build him a house. [2]David now understood that the Lord had truly confirmed him as king over Israel, for his kingdom was greatly exalted for the sake of his people Israel. [3]*David took other wives in Jerusalem and became the father of more sons and daughters. [4]These are the names of those who were born to him in Jerusalem: Shammua, Shobab, Nathan, Solomon, [5]Ibhar, Elishua, Elpelet, [6]Nogah, Nepheg, Japhia, [7]Elishama, Beeliada, and Eliphelet.

The Philistine Wars

[8]When the Philistines had heard that David was anointed king over all Israel, they went up in unison to seek him out. But when David heard of this, he marched out against them. [9]*Meanwhile the Philistines had come and raided the valley of Rephaim. [10]David inquired of God, "Shall I advance against the Philistines, and will you deliver them into my power?" The Lord answered him, "Advance, for I will deliver them into your power." [11]They advanced, therefore, to Baal-perazim, and David defeated them there. Then David said, "God has used me to break through my enemies just as water breaks through a dam." Therefore that place was called Baal-perazim. [12]*The Philistines had left their gods there, and David ordered them to be burnt.

[13]Once again the Philistines raided the valley, [14]and again David inquired of God. But God answered him: "Do not try to pursue them, but go around them and come upon them from the direction of the mastic trees. [15]When you hear the sound of marching in the tops of the mastic trees, then go forth to battle, for God has already gone before you to strike the army of the Philistines." [16]David did as God commanded him, and they routed the Philistine army from Gibeon to Gezer.

[17]Thus David's fame was spread abroad through every land, and the Lord made all the nations fear him.

The Ark Brought to Jerusalem

15 [1]DAVID built houses for himself in the City of David and prepared a place for the ark of God, pitching a tent for it there. [2]*At that time he said, "No one may carry the ark of God except the Levites, for the Lord chose them to carry the ark of the Lord and to minister to him forever." [3]*Then David assembled all Israel in Jerusalem to bring the ark of the Lord to the place which he had prepared for it. [4]David also called together the sons of Aaron and the Levites: [5]of the sons of Kohath, Uriel, their chief, and one hundred and twenty of his brethren; [6]of the sons of Merari, Asaiah, their chief, and two hundred and twenty of his brethren; [7]of the sons of Gershon, Joel, their chief, and one hundred and thirty of his brethren; [8]of the sons of Elizaphan, Shemaiah, their chief, and two hundred of his brethren; [9]of the sons of Hebron, Eliel, their chief, and eighty of his brethren; [10]of the sons of Uzziel, Amminadab, their chief, and one hundred and twelve of his brethren.

[11]*David summoned the priests Zadok and Abiathar, and the Levites Uriel, Asaiah, Joel, Shemaiah, Eliel, and Amminadab, [12]*and said to them: "You, the heads of the levitical families, must sanctify yourselves along with your brethren and bring the ark of the Lord, the God of Israel, to the place which I have prepared for it. [13]*Because you were not with us the first time, the wrath of the Lord our God burst upon us, for we did not seek him aright." [14]Accordingly, the priests and the Levites sanctified themselves to bring up the ark of the Lord, the God of Israel. [15]*The Levites bore the ark of God on their shoulders with poles, as Moses had ordained according to the word of the Lord.

[16]*David commanded the chiefs of the Levites to appoint their brethren as chanters, to play on musical instruments, harps, lyres, and cymbals, to make a loud sound of rejoicing. [17]*Therefore the Levites appointed Heman, son of Joel, and, among his brethren, Asaph, son of Berechiah; and among the sons of Merari, their brethren, Ethan, son of Kushaiah; [18]and, together with these, their brethren of the second rank: the gatekeepers Zechariah, Uzziel, Shemiramoth, Jehiel, Unni, Eliab, Benaiah, Maaseiah, Mattithiah, Eliphelehu, Mikneiah, Obed-edom, and Jeiel. [19]The chanters, Heman, Asaph, and Ethan, sounded brass cymbals. [20]†Zechariah, Uzziel, Shemiramoth, Jehiel, Unni, Eliab, Maaseiah, and Benaiah played on harps set to "Alamoth." [21]But Mattithiah, Eliphelehu, Mikneiah, Obed-edom, and Jeiel led the chant on lyres set to "the eighth." [22]*Chenaniah was the chief of the Levites in the chanting; he directed the chanting, for he

---

❋

14:	26, 4f.	12:	2 Chr 29, 5.15.34;
14/1-16:	2 Sm 5, 11-25.		30, 3.15.24.
1:	1 Kgs 5, 1; 2 Chr 2, 3.	13:	13, 3.
3-7:	3, 5-8; 2 Sm 5, 13-16.	15:	Ex 25, 13ff; Nm 1, 50;
9:	11, 15.		7, 9; 2 Chr 35, 3.
12:	Dt 7, 5.25.	16:	13, 8; 16, 5;
15/2:	Nm 1, 50; 7, 9;		2 Chr 5, 12; 29, 25;
	Dt 10, 8; 31, 25;		Neh 12, 27.
	1 Sm 6, 15; Jos 3, 8.	17:	6, 31-47; 25, 1-8.
3:	13, 5; 2 Sm 6, 15.17.	22:	26, 29.
11:	16, 39; 2 Sm 8, 17;		
	15, 29.35.		

---

† 15, 20: *Alamoth:* a musical term (literally, "young women") of uncertain meaning, occurring also in Ps 46, 1, where it is rendered as *virgins.* Perhaps it may mean something like "soprano," whereas the term "eighth" (Hebrew *sheminith,* v 21) may then mean "bass"; cf Pss 6, 1; 12, 1.

was skillful. ²³Berechiah and Elkanah were gatekeepers before the ark. ²⁴*The priests, Shebaniah, Joshaphat, Nethanel, Amasai, Zechariah, Benaiah, and Eliezer, sounded the trumpets before the ark of God. Obed-edom and Jeiel were also gatekeepers before the ark.

²⁵*Thus David, the elders of Israel, and the commanders of thousands went to bring up the ark of the covenant of the Lord with joy from the house of Obededom. ²⁶*While the Levites, with God's help, were bearing the ark of the covenant of the Lord, seven bulls and seven rams were sacrificed. ²⁷*David was clothed in a robe of fine linen, as were all the Levites who carried the ark, the singers, and Chenaniah, the leader of the chant; David was also wearing a linen ephod. ²⁸Thus all Israel brought back the ark of the covenant of the Lord with joyful shouting, to the sound of horns, trumpets, and cymbals, and the music of harps and lyres. ²⁹*But as the ark of the covenant of the Lord was entering the City of David, Michal, daughter of Saul, looked down from her window, and when she saw King David leaping and dancing, she despised him in her heart.

16 ¹*THEY brought in the ark of God and set it within the tent which David had pitched for it. Then they offered up holocausts and peace offerings to God. ²When David had finished offering up the holocausts and peace offerings, he blessed the people in the name of the Lord, ³and distributed to every Israelite, to every man and every woman, a loaf of bread, a piece of meat, and a raisin cake.

The Ministering Levites

⁴*He now appointed certain Levites to minister before the ark of the Lord, to celebrate, thank, and praise the Lord, the God of Israel. ⁵Asaph was their chief, and second to him were Zechariah, Uzziel, Shemiramoth, Jehiel, Mattithiah, Eliab, Benaiah, Obededom, and Jeiel. These were to play on harps and lyres, while Asaph was to sound the cymbals, ⁶and the priests Benaiah and Jahaziel were to be the regular trumpeters before the ark of the covenant of God.

⁷Then, on that same day, David appointed Asaph and his brethren to sing for the first time these praises of the Lord:

⁸*†Give thanks to the Lord, invoke his name;
    make known among the nations his deeds.
⁹Sing to him, sing his praise,
    proclaim all his wondrous deeds.
¹⁰Glory in his holy name;
    rejoice, O hearts that seek the Lord!
¹¹Look to the Lord in his strength;
    seek to serve him constantly.

¹²Recall the wondrous deeds that he has wrought,
    his portents, and the judgments he has uttered,
¹³You descendants of Israel, his servants,
    sons of Jacob, his chosen ones!

¹⁴He, the Lord, is our God;
    throughout the earth his judgments prevail.
¹⁵He remembers forever his covenant
    which he made binding for a thousand generations—
¹⁶Which he entered into with Abraham
    and by his oath to Isaac;
¹⁷Which he established for Jacob by statute,
    for Israel as an everlasting covenant,
¹⁸Saying, "To you will I give the land of Canaan
    as your allotted inheritance."

¹⁹When they were few in number,
    a handful, and strangers there,
²⁰Wandering from nation to nation,
    from one kingdom to another people,
²¹He let no one oppress them,
    and for their sake he rebuked kings:
²²"Touch not my anointed,
    and to my prophets do no harm."

²³*Sing to the Lord, all the earth,
    announce his salvation, day after day
²⁴Tell his glory among the nations;
    among all peoples, his wondrous deeds.
²⁵For great is the Lord and highly to be praised;
    and awesome is he, beyond all gods.
²⁶For all the gods of the nations are things of nought,
    but the Lord made the heavens.
²⁷Splendor and majesty go before him;
    praise and joy are in his holy place.

²⁸Give to the Lord, you families of nations,
    give to the Lord glory and praise;
  ²⁹give to the Lord the glory due his name!
Bring gifts, and enter his presence;
    worship the Lord in holy attire.
³⁰Tremble before him, all the earth;
    he has made the world firm, not to be moved.

³¹Let the heavens be glad and the earth rejoice;
    let them say among the nations: The Lord is king.
³²Let the sea and what fills it resound;
    let the plains rejoice and all that is in them!
³³Then shall all the trees of the forest exult
    before the Lord, for he comes:
    he comes to rule the earth.

³⁴*Give thanks to the Lord, for he is good,
    for his kindness endures forever;
³⁵And say, "Save us, O God, our savior,
    gather us and deliver us from the nations,
That we may give thanks to your holy name
    and glory in praising you."

✿
    24: Nm 10, 8; Jos 6, 4ff.   16/1-3: 2 Sm 6, 17ff.
  25-29: 2 Sm 6, 12-16.   1: 15, 1.
    26: 2 Sm 6, 17;   4: Sir 47, 9.
       2 Chr 29, 21.   8-22: Ps 105, 1-15.
    27: 1 Sm 2, 18; 2 Sm 6, 14.   23-33: Ps 96, 1-13.
    29: 2 Sm 6, 20ff.   34ff: Ps 106, 1.47f.

---

†   16, 8-36: A hymn composed of parts, with textual variants, from several Psalms: vv 8-22=Ps 105, 1-15; vv 23-33=Ps 96, 1-13; vv 34-36=Ps 106, 1.47f.

36Blessed be the Lord, the God of Israel, through all eternity!

Let all the people say, Amen! Alleluia.

37Then David left Asaph and his brethren there before the ark of the covenant of the Lord to minister before the ark regularly according to the daily ritual; **38***he also left there Obed-edom and sixty-eight of his brethren, including Obed-edom, son of Jeduthun, and Hosah, to be gatekeepers. **39***But the priest Zadok and his priestly brethren he left before the Dwelling of the Lord on the high place at Gibeon, **40***to offer holocausts to the Lord on the altar of holocausts regularly, morning and evening, and to do all that is written in the law of the Lord which he has decreed for Israel. **41***With them were Heman and Jeduthun and the others who were chosen and designated by name to give thanks to the Lord, "because his kindness endures forever," **42***with trumpets and cymbals for accompaniment, and instruments for the sacred chant. The sons of Jeduthun kept the gate.

43*Then all the people departed, each to his own home, and David returned to bless his household.

The Oracle of Nathan

17 **1***After David had taken up residence in his house, he said to Nathan the prophet, "See, I am living in a house of cedar, but the ark of the covenant of the Lord dwells under tentcloth." **2**Nathan replied to David, "Do, therefore, whatever you desire, for God is with you."

3But that same night the word of God came to Nathan: **4***"Go and tell my servant David, Thus says the Lord: It is not you who are to build a house for me to dwell in. **5**For I have never dwelt in a house, from the time when I led Israel onward, even to this day, but I have been lodging in tent or pavilion **6**as long as I have wandered about with all of Israel. Did I ever say a word to any of the judges of Israel whom I commanded to guide my people, such as, 'Why have you not built me a house of cedar?' **7***Therefore, tell my servant David, Thus says the Lord of hosts: I took you from the pasture, from following the sheep, that you might become ruler over my people Israel. **8**I was with you wherever you went, and I cut down all your enemies before you. I will make your name great like that of the greatest on the earth. **9**I will assign a place for my people Israel and I will plant them in it to dwell there henceforth undisturbed; nor shall wicked men ever again oppress them, as they did at first, **10**and during all the time when I appointed judges over my people Israel. And I will subdue all your enemies. Moreover, I declare to you that I, the Lord, will build you a house; **11***so that when your days have been completed and you must join your fathers, I will raise up your offspring after you who will be one of your own sons, and I will establish his kingdom. **12***He it is who shall build me a house, and I will establish his throne forever. **13***I will be a father to him, and he shall be a son to me, and I will not withdraw my favor from him as I withdrew it from him who preceded you; **14**but I will maintain him in my house and in my kingdom forever, and his throne shall be firmly established forever."

15All these words and this whole vision Nathan related exactly to David.

David's Thanksgiving

16Then David came in and sat in the Lord's presence, saying: "Who am I, O Lord God, and what is my family, that you should have brought me as far as I have come? **17***And yet, even this you now consider too little, O God! For you have made a promise regarding your servant's family reaching into the distant future, and you have looked on me as henceforth the most notable of men, O Lord God. **18**What more can David say to you? You know your servant. **19**O Lord, for your servant's sake and in keeping with your purpose, you have done this great thing. **20***O Lord, there is no one like you and there is no God but you, just as we have always understood.

21*"Is there, like your people Israel, whom you redeemed from Egypt, another nation on earth whom a god went to redeem as his people? You won for yourself a name for great and awesome deeds by driving out the nations before your people. **22**You made your people Israel your own forever, and you, O Lord, became their God. **23**Therefore, O Lord, may the promise that you have uttered concerning your servant and his house remain firm forever. Bring about what you have promised, **24**that your renown as Lord of hosts, God of Israel, may be great and abide forever, while the house of David, your servant, is established in your presence.

25*"Because you, O my God, have revealed to your servant that you will build him a house, your servant has made bold to pray before you. **26**Since you, O Lord, are truly God and have promised this good thing to your servant, **27***and since you have deigned to bless the house of your servant, so that it will remain forever—since it is you, O Lord, who blessed it, it is blessed forever."

David's Victories

18 **1***After this, David defeated the Philistines and subdued them; and he took Gath and its towns away from the control of the Philistines. **2**He also defeated Moab, and the Moabites became his subjects, paying tribute.

3David then defeated Hadadezer, king of Zobah toward Hamath, when the latter was on his way to

---

❋

38: 15, 24.
39: 1 Kgs 3, 4.
40: Ex 29, 38-42; Lv 6, 9; Nm 28, 3.6; 2 Chr 13, 11.
41: 2 Chr 5, 12; 7, 3.6; 20, 21; Ezr 3, 11.
42: 2 Chr 29, 27.
43: 2 Sm 6, 19f.
17/1-27: 2 Sm 7, 1-29.
   1: 15, 1; 2 Sm 5, 11.

4: 28, 3; 1 Kgs 8, 19.
7: 1 Sm 16, 11.
11: 2 Sm 7, 12f.
12: 22, 10; 28, 6.10.
13: 2 Sm 7, 14.
17: 2 Sm 7, 19.
20: Sir 36, 4.
21: Dt 4, 7; 2 Sm 7, 23.
25: 2 Sm 7, 27.
27: Nm 22, 6.
18/1-13: 2 Sm 8, 1-14.

set up his victory stele at the river Euphrates. ⁴*David took from him twenty thousand foot soldiers, one thousand chariots, and seven thousand horsemen. Of the chariot horses, David hamstrung all but one hundred. ⁵The Arameans of Damascus came to the aid of Hadadezer, king of Zobah, but David also slew twenty-two thousand of their men. ⁶Then David set up garrisons in the Damascus region of Aram, and the Arameans became his subjects, paying tribute. Thus the LORD made David victorious in all his campaigns.

⁷David took the golden shields that were carried by Hadadezer's attendants and brought them to Jerusalem. ⁸*He likewise took away from Tibhath and Cun, cities of Hadadezer, large quantities of bronze, which Solomon later used to make the bronze sea and the pillars and the vessels of bronze.

⁹When Tou, king of Hamath, heard that David had defeated the entire army of Hadadezer, king of Zobah, ¹⁰*he sent his son Hadoram to wish King David well and to congratulate him on having waged a victorious war against Hadadezer; for Hadadezer had been at war with Tou. He also sent David gold, silver and bronze utensils of every sort. ¹¹These also King David consecrated to the LORD along with all the silver and gold that he had taken from the nations: from Edom, Moab, the Ammonites, the Philistines, and Amalek.

¹²*Abishai, the son of Zeruiah, also slew eighteen thousand Edomites in the Valley of Salt. ¹³He set up garrisons in Edom, and all the Edomites became David's subjects. Thus the LORD made David victorious in all his campaigns.

David's Officials

¹⁴*David reigned over all Israel and dispensed justice and right to all his people. ¹⁵*Joab, son of Zeruiah, was in command of the army; Jehoshaphat, son of Ahilud, was herald; ¹⁶*†Zadok, son of Ahitub, and Ahimelech, son of Abiathar, were priests; Shavsha was scribe; ¹⁷*†Benaiah, son of Jehoiada, was in command of the Cherethites and the Pelethites; and David's sons were the chief assistants to the king.

Campaigns against Ammon

19 ¹*AFTERWARD Nahash, king of the Ammonites, died and his son succeeded him as king. ²David said, "I will show kindness to Hanun, the son of Nahash, for his father treated me with kindness." Therefore he sent envoys to him to comfort him over the death of his father. But when David's servants had entered the land of the Ammonites to comfort Hanun, ³the Ammonite princes said to Hanun, "Do you think David is doing this—sending you these consolers—to honor your father? Have not his servants

rather come to you to explore the land, spying it out for its overthrow?" ⁴Thereupon Hanun seized David's servants and had them shaved and their garments cut off half-way at the hips. Then he sent them away. ⁵When David was informed of what had happened to his men, he sent messengers to meet them, for the men had been greatly disgraced. "Remain at Jericho," the king told them, "until your beards have grown again; and then you may come back here."

⁶When the Ammonites realized that they had put themselves in bad odor with David, Hanun and the Ammonites sent a thousand talents of silver to hire chariots and horsemen from Aram Naharaim, from Aram-maacah, and from Zobah. ⁷They hired thirty-two thousand chariots along with the king of Maacah and his army, who came and encamped before Medeba. The Ammonites also assembled from their cities and came out for war.

⁸When David heard of this, he sent Joab and his whole army of warriors against them. ⁹The Ammonites marched out and lined up for battle at the gate of the city, while the kings who had come to their help remained apart in the open field. ¹⁰*When Joab saw that there was a battle line both in front of and behind him, he chose some of the best fighters among the Israelites and set them in array against the Arameans; ¹¹*the rest of the army, which he placed under the command of his brother Abishai, then lined up to oppose the Ammonites. ¹²And he said: "If the Arameans prove too strong for me, you must come to my help; and if the Ammonites prove too strong for you, I will save you. ¹³Hold steadfast and let us show ourselves courageous for the sake of our people and the cities of our God; then may the LORD do what seems best to him." ¹⁴Joab therefore advanced with his men to engage the Arameans in battle; but they fled before him. ¹⁵And when the Ammonites saw that the Arameans had fled, they also took to flight before his brother Abishai, and reentered the city. Joab then returned to Jerusalem.

¹⁶Seeing themselves vanquished by Israel, the Arameans sent messengers to bring out the Arameans from the other side of the River, with Shophach, the general of Hadadezer's army, at their head. ¹⁷When this was reported to David, he gathered all Israel together,

---

† 18, 16: *Zadok . . . and Ahimelech, son of Abiathar, were priests:* as in the Chronicler's source, 2 Sm 8, 17. But according to 2 Sm 15, 24.29.35; 17, 15; 19, 11; 20, 25, and even 1 Chr 15, 11, it was Abiathar who shared the priestly office with Zadok, and he remained in this office even during the early years of Solomon's reign (1 Kgs 2, 26; 4, 4). Moreover, according to 1 Sm 22, 20; 23, 6; 30, 7, Ahimelech was the father, not the son, of Abiathar. If the text *Ahimelech, son of Abiathar,* is not due to a scribal change, one must assume that Abiathar had a son who was named after his grandfather and who shared the priestly office with his father during the last years of David's reign.

18, 17: *David's sons were the chief assistants to the king:* in the parallel passage, 2 Sm 8, 18, which was the Chronicler's source, *David's sons were priests.* The change is characteristic of the Chronicler, for whom only Aaron's descendants could be priests.

✱
    4: 2 Sm 8, 14;
        Jos 11, 6.9.
    8: 2 Sm 8, 8;
        1 Kgs 7, 15.23.27.
  10: 2 Sm 8, 10.
  12: 2 Sm 8, 13;
       2 Kgs 14, 7.
14-17: 2 Sm 8, 15-18.

  15: 11, 6; 2 Sm 8, 16;
      1 Kgs 4, 3.
  16: 24, 3.6.31; 2 Sm 8, 17.
  17: 11, 22; 2 Sm 8, 18;
      1 Kgs 1, 38.44.
19/1-19: 2 Sm 10, 1-19.
  10: 20, 23; 1 Kgs 2, 28.34.
  11: 23, 18f.

crossed the Jordan, and met them. With the army of David drawn up to fight the Arameans, they gave battle. **18**But the Arameans fled before Israel, and David slew seven thousand of their chariot fighters and forty thousand of their foot soldiers; he also killed Shophach, the general of the army. **19**When the vassals of Hadadezer saw themselves vanquished by Israel, they made peace with David and became his subjects. After this, the Arameans refused to come to the aid of the Ammonites.

20 **1**AT the beginning of the following year, the time when kings go to war, Joab led the army out in force, laid waste the land of the Ammonites, and went on to besiege Rabbah, while David himself remained in Jerusalem. When Joab had attacked Rabbah and destroyed it, **2***David took the crown of Milcom from the idol's head. It was found to weigh a talent of gold; and it contained precious stones, which David wore on his own head. He also brought out a great amount of booty from the city. **3**He deported the people of the city and set them to work with saws, iron picks, and axes. Thus David dealt with all the cities of the Ammonites. Then he and his whole army returned to Jerusalem.

Victories over the Philistines

4*Afterward there was another battle with the Philistines, at Gezer. At that time, Sibbecai the Hushathite slew Sippai, one of the descendants of the Raphaim, and the Philistines were subdued. **5***†Once again there was war with the Philistines, and Elhanan, the son of Jair, slew Lahmi, the brother of Goliath of Gath, whose spear shaft was like a weaver's heddlebar.

6In still another battle, at Gath, they encountered a giant, also a descendant of the Raphaim, who had six fingers to each hand and six toes to each foot; twenty-four in all. **7**He defied Israel, and Jonathan, the son of Shimea, David's brother, slew him. **8**These were the descendants of the Raphaim of Gath who died at the hands of David and his servants.

David's Census; the Plague

21 **1***†A SATAN rose up against Israel, and he enticed David into taking a census of Israel. **2**David therefore said to Joab and to the other generals of the army, "Go, find out the number of the Israelites from Beer-sheba to Dan, and report back to me that I may know their number." **3**But Joab replied: "May the LORD increase his people a hundredfold! My lord king, are not all of them my lord's subjects? Why does my lord seek to do this thing? Why will he bring guilt upon Israel?" **4**However, the king's command prevailed over Joab, who departed and traversed all of Israel, and then returned to Jerusalem. **5**Joab reported the result of the census to David: of men capable of wielding a sword, there were in all Israel one million one hundred thousand, and in Judah four hundred and seventy thousand. **6***Levi and Benjamin, however, he did not include in the census, for the king's command was repugnant to Joab. **7**This command displeased God, who began to punish Israel. **8**Then David said to God, "I have sinned greatly in doing this thing. Take away your servant's guilt, for I have acted very foolishly."

9*Then the LORD spoke to Gad, David's seer, in these words: **10**"Go, tell David: Thus says the LORD: I offer you three alternatives; choose one of them, and I will inflict it on you." **11**Accordingly, Gad went to David and said to him; "Thus says the LORD: Decide now—**12**will it be three years of famine; or three months of fleeing your enemies, with the sword of your foes ever at your back; or three days of the LORD's own sword, a pestilence in the land, with the LORD's destroying angel in every part of Israel? Therefore choose: What answer am I to give him who sent me?" **13**Then David said to Gad: "I am in dire straits. But I prefer to fall into the hand of the LORD, whose mercy is very great, than into the hands of men."

14Therefore the LORD sent pestilence upon Israel, and seventy thousand men of Israel died. **15***God also sent an angel to destroy Jerusalem; but as he was on the point of destroying it, the LORD saw and decided against the calamity, and said to the destroying angel, "Enough now! Stay your hand!"

Ornan's Threshing Floor

The angel of the LORD was then standing by the threshing floor of Ornan the Jebusite. **16**When David raised his eyes, he saw the angel of the LORD standing between earth and heaven, with a naked sword in his hand stretched out against Jerusalem. David and the elders, clothed in sackcloth, prostrated themselves face to the ground, **17**and David prayed to God: "Was it not I who ordered the census of the people? I am the one who sinned, I did this wicked thing. But these sheep, what have they done? O LORD, my God, strike me and my father's family, but do not afflict your people with this plague!"

18*Then the angel of the LORD commanded Gad to

20, 5: *Elhanan . . . slew Lahmi, the brother of Goliath:* the Chronicler thus solves the difficulty of the apparent contradiction between 1 Sm 17, 49ff (David killed Goliath) and 2 Sm 21, 19 (*Elhanan killed Goliath*).

21, 1: *A satan:* in the parallel passage of 2 Sm 24, 1, *the Lord's anger.* The change in the term reflects the changed theological outlook of postexilic Israel, when evil could no longer be attributed directly to God. At an earlier period the Hebrew word *satan* ("adversary," or, especially in a court of law, "accuser"), when not used of men, designated an angel who accused men before God (Jb 1, 6-12; 2, 1-7; Zec 3, 1f). Here, as in later Judaism (Wis 2, 24) and in the New Testament, *satan,* or the "devil" (from the Greek translation of the word), designates an evil spirit who tempts men to wrongdoing.

20/2f: 2 Sm 12, 30f.
    4-8: 2 Sm 21, 18-22.
    4: 11, 29; 27, 11.
    5: 11, 26; 1 Sm 17, 4.23.
21/1-7: 2 Sm 24, 1-25.
    1: Zec 3, 1f.
    6: 27, 24; Nm 1, 49.

9: 29, 29; 1 Sm 9, 9; 2 Chr 29, 25.
15: Gn 6, 6; Ex 32, 14; 2 Sm 24, 16; Jon 3, 10.
18: 2 Chr 3, 1.

tell David to go up and erect an altar to the Lord on the threshing floor of Ornan the Jebusite. [19]David went up at Gad's command, given in the name of the Lord. [20]While Ornan was threshing wheat, he turned around and saw the king, and his four sons who were with him, without recognizing them. [21]But as David came on toward him, he looked up and saw that it was David. Then he left the threshing floor and bowed down before David, his face to the ground. [22]David said to Ornan: "Sell me the ground of this threshing floor, that I may build on it an altar to the Lord. Sell it to me at its full price, that the plague may be stayed from the people." [23]But Ornan said to David: "Take it as your own, and let my lord the king do what seems best to him. See, I also give you the oxen for the holocausts, the threshing sledges for the wood, and the wheat for the cereal offering. I give it all to you." [24]But King David replied to Ornan: "No! I will buy it from you properly, at its full price. I will not take what is yours for the Lord, nor offer up holocausts that cost me nothing." [25]†So David paid Ornan six hundred shekels of gold for the place.

Altar of Holocausts

[26]*David then built an altar there to the Lord, and offered up holocausts and peace offerings. When he called upon the Lord, he answered him by sending down fire from heaven upon the altar of holocausts. [27]Then the Lord gave orders to the angel to return his sword to its sheath. [28]Once David saw that the Lord had heard him on the threshing floor of Ornan the Jebusite, he continued to offer sacrifices there. [29]*The Dwelling of the Lord, which Moses had built in the desert, and the altar of holocausts were at that time on the high place at Gibeon. [30]But David could not go there to worship God, for he was fearful of the sword of the angel of the Lord.

22 [1]*THEREFORE David said, "This is the house of the Lord God, and this is the altar of holocausts for Israel."

Material for the Temple

[2]*†David then ordered that all the aliens who lived in the land of Israel be brought together, and he appointed them stonecutters to hew out stone blocks for building the house of God. [3]*He also laid up large stores of iron to make nails for the doors of the gates, and clamps, together with so much bronze that it could not be weighed, [4]*and cedar trees without number. The Sidonians and Tyrians brought great stores

of cedar logs to David, [5]*who said: "My son Solomon is young and immature; but the house that is to be built for the Lord must be made so magnificent that it will be renowned and glorious in all countries. Therefore I will make preparations for it." Thus before his death David laid up materials in abundance.

Charge to Solomon

[6]Then he called for his son Solomon and commanded him to build a house for the Lord, the God of Israel. [7]*David said to Solomon: "My son, it was my purpose to build a house myself for the honor of the Lord, my God. [8]But this word of the Lord came to me: 'You have shed much blood, and you have waged great wars. You may not build a house in my honor, because you have shed too much blood upon the earth in my sight. [9]*†However, a son is to be born to you. He will be a peaceful man, and I will give him rest from all his enemies on every side. For Solomon shall be his name, and in his time I will bestow peace and tranquillity on Israel. [10]*It is he who shall build a house in my honor; he shall be a son to me, and I will be a father to him, and I will establish the throne of his kingship over Israel forever.' [11]Now, my son, the Lord be with you, and may you succeed in building the house of the Lord your God, as he has said you shall. [12]May the Lord give you prudence and discernment when he brings you to rule over Israel, so that you keep the law of the Lord, your God. [13]*Only then shall you succeed, if you are careful to observe the precepts and decrees which the Lord gave Moses for Israel. Be brave and steadfast; do not fear or lose heart. [14]*†See, with great effort I have laid up for the house of the Lord a hundred thousand talents of gold, a million talents of silver, and bronze and iron in such great quantities that they cannot be weighed. I have also stored up wood and stones, to which you must add. [15]Moreover, you have available an unlimited supply of workmen, stonecutters, masons, carpenters, and every kind of craftsman [16]skilled in gold, silver, bronze, and

---

† 21, 25: *Six hundred shekels of gold:* about 10,000 dollars. According to 2 Sm 24, 24, David paid 50 shekels of silver, about 20 dollars, for Ornan's threshing floor; but for the Chronicler the site of the temple was much more precious than that.

22, 2ff: According to 1 Kgs 5, 15-32, it was Solomon who made the material preparations for building the temple, even though David had wished to do so (1 Kgs 5, 17ff). The Chronicler, however, sought to have David, who was Israel's ideal king, more closely connected with Israel's most sacred sanctuary, the temple of Jerusalem.

22, 9: The Hebrew word for peace, *shalom,* is reflected in the name Solomon, in Hebrew, *Shelomo.* A contrast is drawn here between Solomon, the *peaceful man,* and David, who *waged great wars* (v 8). David was prevented from building the temple, not only because all his time was taken up in waging war (1 Kgs 5, 17), but also, because he *shed much blood* (v 8), and in the eyes of the Chronicler this made him ritually unfit for the task.

22, 14: *A hundred thousand talents of gold:* about 3,775 tons of gold. *A million talents of silver:* about 37,750 tons of silver. The fantastically exaggerated figures are intended merely to stress the inestimable value of the temple as the center of Israelite worship. More modest figures are given in 1 Kgs 9, 14.28; 10, 10.14.

✻
    26: Lv 9, 24; Jgs 6, 21;   4: 10, 27; Ezr 3, 7.
           1 Kgs 18, 38;   5: 29, 1.
           2 Chr 7, 1; 2 Mc 2, 10ff.   7-10: 17, 1-14; 28, 2-7;
    29: 16, 39; 1 Kgs 3, 4;   2 Sm 7, 1-16;
           2 Chr 1, 3.   1 Kgs 5, 3ff; 8, 17-21.
   22/1: 21, 18.26.28;   9: 2 Sm 12, 24.
           2 Chr 3, 1.   10: Heb 1, 5.
      2: 1 Kgs 5, 31f; 9, 20f;   13: 28, 7.20; Dt 31, 6.23;
           2 Chr 2, 16f.   Jos 1, 6f.9; 1 Kgs 2, 2f.
      3: 18, 8; 1 Kgs 7, 47.   14: 29, 2ff.

iron. Set to work, therefore, and the Lord be with you!"

Charge to the Leaders

17David also commanded all of Israel's leaders to help his son Solomon: **18***"Is not the Lord your God with you? Has he not given you rest on every side? Indeed, he has delivered the occupants of the land into my power, and the land is subdued before the Lord and his people. **19***Therefore, devote your hearts and souls to seeking the Lord your God. Proceed to build the sanctuary of the Lord God, that the ark of the covenant of the Lord and God's sacred vessels may be brought into the house built in honor of the Lord."

The Levitical Classes

23 **1***WHEN David had grown old and was near the end of his days, he made his son Solomon king over Israel. **2**He then gathered together all the leaders of Israel, together with the priests and the Levites.

3*The Levites thirty years old and above were counted, and their total number was found to be thirty-eight thousand men. **4**Of these, twenty-four thousand were to direct the service of the house of the Lord, six thousand were to be officials and judges, **5***four thousand were to be gatekeepers, and four thousand were to praise the Lord with the instruments which David had devised for praise. **6***David divided them into classes according to the sons of Levi: Gershon, Kohath, and Merari.

7To the Gershonites belonged Ladan and Shimei. **8***The sons of Ladan: Jehiel the chief, then Zetham and Joel; three in all. **9**The sons of Shimei were Shelomoth, Haziel, and Haran; three. These were the heads of the families of Ladan. **10**The sons of Shimei were Jahath, Zizah, Jeush, and Beriah; these were the sons of Shimei, four in all. **11**Jahath was the chief and Zizah was second to him; but Jeush and Beriah had not many sons, and therefore they were classed as a single family, fulfilling a single office.

12*The sons of Kohath: Amram, Izhar, Hebron, and Uzziel; four in all. **13***The sons of Amram were Aaron and Moses. Aaron was set apart to be consecrated as most holy, he and his sons forever, to offer sacrifice before the Lord, to minister to him, and to bless his name forever. **14**As for Moses, however, the man of God, his sons were counted as part of the tribe of Levi. **15***The sons of Moses were Gershom and Eliezer. **16***The sons of Gershom: Shubael the chief. **17**The sons of Eliezer were Rehabiah the chief—Eliezer had no other sons, but the sons of Rehabiah were very numerous. **18**The sons of Izhar: Shelomith the chief. **19***The sons of Hebron: Jeriah, the chief, Amariah, the second, Jahaziel, the third, and Jekameam, the fourth. **20***The sons of Uzziel: Micah, the chief, and Isshiah, the second.

21*The sons of Merari: Mahli and Mushi. The sons of Mahli: Eleazar and Kish. **22***Eleazar died leaving no sons, only daughters; the sons of Kish, their kinsmen, married them. **23***The sons of Mushi: Mahli, Eder, and Jeremoth; three in all.

24*These were the sons of Levi according to their ancestral houses, the family heads as they were enrolled one by one according to their names. They performed the work of the service of the house of the Lord from twenty years of age upward, **27**for David's final orders were to enlist the Levites from the time they were twenty years old.

25*David said: "The Lord, the God of Israel, has given rest to his people, and has taken up his dwelling in Jerusalem. **26***Henceforth the Levites need not carry the Dwelling or any of its furnishings or equipment. **28**Rather, their duty shall be to assist the sons of Aaron in the service of the house of the Lord, having charge of the courts, the chambers, and the preservation of everything holy: they shall take part in the service of the house of God. **29***They shall also have charge of the showbread, of the fine flour for the cereal offering, of the wafers of unleavened bread, and of the baking and mixing, and of all measures of quantity and size. **30***They must be present every morning to offer thanks and to praise the Lord, and likewise in the evening; **31***and at every offering of holocausts to the Lord on sabbaths, new moons, and feast days, in such numbers as are prescribed, they must always be present before the Lord. **32***They shall observe what is prescribed for them concerning the meeting tent, the sanctuary, and the sons of Aaron, their brethren, in the service of the house of the Lord."

The Priestly Classes

24 **1***THE descendants of Aaron also were divided into classes. The sons of Aaron were Nadab, Abihu, Eleazar, and Ithamar. **2***Nadab and Abihu died before their father, leaving no sons; therefore only Eleazar and Ithamar served as priests. **3***David, with Zadok, a descendant of Eleazar, and Ahimelech, a descendant of Ithamar, assigned the functions for the priestly service. **4**But since the descendants of Eleazar were found to be more numerous than those of Ithamar, the former were divided into sixteen groups, and the latter into eight groups, each under its family head. **5**Their functions were as-

*

18: 23, 25; Jos 21, 44;
     23, 1; 2 Sm 7, 1.
19: 1 Kgs 8, 6.21;
     2 Chr 5, 7; 6, 11.
23/1: 28, 5; 1 Kgs 1, 30.
   3: Nm 4, 3.23.30.35.39.
     43.47; 8, 23-26;
     2 Chr 31, 17.
   5: 9, 22.
   6: 6, 1.16-30; 26, 1-19;
     Ex 6, 16; Nm 3, 17;
     26, 57.
   8: 26, 21f; 29, 8.
  12: 26, 23; Ex 6, 18;
     Nm 3, 19; 26, 23ff.
  13: 6, 49; Ex 6, 20; 28, 1;
     Nm 6, 23.
  15: Ex 2, 22; 18, 3f.
  16: 26, 24.
  19: 24, 23.

20: 24, 24f.
21: 6, 29; 24, 26.28f;
     Ex 6, 19; Nm 3, 20, 33.
22: 24, 28f.
23: 6, 47; 24, 30.
24: 2 Chr 31, 17; Ezr 3, 8.
25: 22, 18; Ps 132, 13.
26: 15, 15; 2 Chr 35, 3.
29: 9, 29.31f; Lv 2, 1.4f;
     24, 5-8.
30: Nm 28, 3-8.
31: Nm 28, 2-29, 39.
32: Nm 3, 6-9; 18, 2-5.
24/1: Ex 6, 23; Nm 3, 2ff;
     26, 60.
   2: Lv 10, 1-7.12;
     Nm 3, 2.4.
   3: 18, 16; 2 Sm 8, 17;
     2 Chr 8, 14.

signed impartially by lot, for there were officers of the holy place, and officers of the divine presence, descended both from Eleazar and from Ithamar. **6***†The scribe Shemaiah, son of Nethanel, a Levite, made a record of it in the presence of the king, and of the leaders, of Zadok the priest, and of Ahimelech, son of Abiathar, and of the heads of the ancestral houses of the priests and of the Levites, listing two successive family groups from Eleazar before each one from Ithamar.

7*The first lot fell to Jehoiarib, the second to Jedaiah, **8**the third to Harim, the fourth to Seorim, **9**the fifth to Malchijah, the sixth to Mijamin, **10***the seventh to Hakkoz, the eighth to Abijah, **11**the ninth to Jeshua, the tenth to Shecaniah, **12**the eleventh to Eliashib, the twelfth to Jakim, **13**the thirteenth to Huppah, the fourteenth to Ishbaal, **14**the fifteenth to Bilgah, the sixteenth to Immer, **15**the seventeenth to Hezir, the eighteenth to Happizzez, **16**the nineteenth to Pethahiah, the twentieth to Jehezkel, **17**the twenty-first to Jachin, the twenty-second to Gamul, **18**the twenty-third to Delaiah, the twenty-fourth to Maaziah. **19***This was the appointed order of their service when they functioned in the house of the LORD in keeping with the precepts given them by Aaron, their father, as the LORD, the God of Israel, had commanded him.

Other Levites

20*Of the remaining Levites, there were Shubael, of the descendants of Amram, and Jehdeiah, of the descendants of Shubael; **21**Isshiah, the chief, of the descendants of Rehabiah; **22**Shelomith of the Izharites, and Jahath of the descendants of Shelomith. **23**The descendants of Hebron were Jeriah, the chief, Amariah, the second, Jahaziel, the third, Jekameam, the fourth. **24**The descendants of Uzziel were Micah; Shamir, of the descendants of Micah; **25**Isshiah, the brother of Micah; and Zechariah, a descendant of Isshiah. **26**The descendants of Merari were Mahli, Mushi, and the descendants of his son Uzziah. **27**The descendants of Merari through his son Uzziah: Shoham, Zaccur, and Ibri. **28**Descendants of Mahli were Eleazar, who had no sons, **29**and Jerahmeel, of the descendants of Kish. **30**The descendants of Mushi were Mahli, Eder, and Jerimoth.

These were the descendants of the Levites according to their ancestral houses. **31***They too, in the same manner as their relatives, the descendants of Aaron, cast lots in the presence of King David, Zadok, Ahimelech, and the heads of the priestly and levitical families; the more important family did so in the same way as the less important one.

The Singers

25 **1***DAVID and the leaders of the liturgical cult set apart for service the descendants of Asaph, Heman, and Jeduthun, as singers of inspired songs to the accompaniment of lyres and harps and cymbals.

This is the list of those who performed this service: **2**†Of the sons of Asaph: Zaccur, Joseph, Nethaniah, and Asharelah, sons of Asaph, under the direction of Asaph, who sang inspired songs under the guidance of the king. **3**Of Jeduthun, these sons of Jeduthun: Gedaliah, Zeri, Jeshaiah, Shimei, Hashabiah, and Mattithiah; six, under the direction of their father Jeduthun, who sang inspired songs to the accompaniment of a lyre, to give thanks and praise to the LORD. **4**Of Heman, these sons of Heman: Bukkiah, Mattaniah, Uzziel, Shubael, and Jerimoth; Hananiah, Hanani, Eliathah, Giddalti, Romamti-ezer, Joshbekashah, Mallothi, Hothir, and Mahazioth. **5***All these were the sons of Heman, the king's seer in divine matters; to enhance his prestige, God gave Heman fourteen sons and three daughters. **6***All these, whether of Asaph, Jeduthun, or Heman, were under their fathers' direction in the singing in the house of the LORD to the accompaniment of cymbals, harps and lyres, serving in the house of God, under the guidance of the king. **7**Their number, together with that of their brethren who were trained in singing to the LORD, all of them skilled men, was two hundred and eighty-eight. **8***They cast lots for their functions equally, young and old, master and pupil alike.

9The first lot fell to Asaph, the family of Joseph; he and his sons and his brethren were twelve. Gedaliah was the second; he and his brethren and his sons were twelve. **10**The third was Zaccur, his sons, and his brethren: twelve. **11**The fourth fell to Izri, his sons, and his brethren: twelve. **12**The fifth was Nethaniah, his sons, and his brethren: twelve. **13**The sixth was Bukkiah, his sons, and his brethren: twelve. **14**The seventh was Jesarelah, his sons, and his brethren: twelve. **15**The eighth was Jeshaiah, his sons, and his brethren: twelve. **16**The ninth was Mattaniah, his sons, and his brethren: twelve. **17**The tenth was Shimei, his sons, and his brethren: twelve. **18**The eleventh was Uzziel, his sons, and his brethren: twelve. **19**The twelfth fell to Hashabiah, his sons, and his brethren: twelve. **20**The thirteenth was Shubael, his sons, and his brethren: twelve. **21**The fourteenth was Mattithiah, his sons, and his brethren: twelve. **22**The fifteenth fell to Jeremoth,

---

✻   6: 18, 16; 2 Sm 8, 17.
7-10: 9, 10ff; Ezr 2, 36ff;
     Neh 7, 39ff; 11, 10ff.
10: Lk 1, 5.
19: 2 Chr 23, 8.
20-31: 23, 7-23.
31: 25, 8; 26, 13.

25/1: 6, 31ff; 15, 16f.19;
     16, 37; 2 Chr 5, 12;
     35, 15; Neh 12, 27.45.
5: 2 Chr 35, 15.
6: 15, 16.
8: 24, 31.

---

†   24, 6: *Ahimelech, son of Abiathar:* see note on 18, 16.

25, 2-31: This list of twenty-four classes of temple singers balances the list of the twenty-four classes of priests (24, 4-19). The last nine names in 25, 4, which seem to form a special group, appear to have been originally fragments or *incipits* of hymns. With some slight changes in the vocalization, the names would mean: "Have mercy on me, O LORD," "Have mercy on me," "You are my God," "I magnify," "I extol the help of . . . ," "Sitting in adversity," "I have fulfilled," "He made abundant," and "Visions."

his sons, and his brethren: twelve. ²³The sixteenth fell to Hananiah, his sons, and his brethren: twelve. ²⁴The seventeenth fell to Joshbekashah, his sons, and his brethren: twelve. ²⁵The eighteenth fell to Hanani, his sons, and his brethren: twelve. ²⁶The nineteenth fell to Mallothi, his sons, and his brethren: twelve. ²⁷The twentieth fell to Eliathah, his sons, and his brethren: twelve. ²⁸The twenty-first fell to Hothir, his sons, and his brethren: twelve. ²⁹The twenty-second fell to Giddalti, his sons, and his brethren: twelve. ³⁰The twenty-third fell to Mahazioth, his sons, and his brethren: twelve. ³¹The twenty-fourth fell to Romamti-ezer, his sons, and his brethren: twelve.

Classes of Gatekeepers

26 ¹*As for the classes of gatekeepers. Of the Korahites was Meshelemiah, the son of Kore, one of the sons of Abiasaph. ²Meshelemiah's sons: Zechariah, the first-born, Jediael, the second son, Zebadiah, the third, Jathniel, the fourth, ³Elam, the fifth, Jehohanan, the sixth, Eliehoenai, the seventh. ⁴Obed-edom's sons: Shemaiah, the first-born, Jehozabad, a second son, Joah, the third, Sachar, the fourth, Nethanel, the fifth, ⁵Ammiel, the sixth, Issachar, the seventh, Peullethai, the eighth, for God blessed him. ⁶To his son Shemaiah were born sons who ruled over their family, for they were warriors. ⁷The sons of Shemaiah were Othni, Rephael, Obed, and Elzabad; also his brethren who were men of might, Elihu and Semachiah. ⁸All these were of the sons of Obed-edom, who, together with their sons and their brethren, were mighty men, fit for the service. Of Obed-edom, sixty-two. ⁹Of Meshelemiah, eighteen sons and brethren, mighty men.

¹⁰*Hosah, a descendant of Merari, had these sons: Shimri, the chief (for though he was not the first-born, his father made him chief), ¹¹Hilkiah, the second son, Tebaliah, the third, Zechariah, the fourth. All the sons and brethren of Hosah were thirteen.

¹²To these classes of gatekeepers, under their chief men, were assigned watches in the service of the house of the Lord, for each group in the same way. ¹³They cast lots for each gate, the small and the large families alike. ¹⁴*When the lot was cast for the east side, it fell to Meshelemiah. Then they cast lots for his son Zechariah, a prudent counselor, and the north side fell to his lot. ¹⁵To Obed-edom fell the south side, and to his sons the storehouse. ¹⁶To Hosah fell the west side with the Shallecheth gate at the ascending highway. For each family, watches were established. ¹⁷On the east, six watched each day, on the north, four each day, on the south, four each day, and at the storehouse they were two and two; ¹⁸†as for the large building on the west, there were four at the highway and two at the large building. ¹⁹These were the classes of the gatekeepers, descendants of Kore and Merari.

Treasurers

²⁰*Their brother Levites superintended the stores for the house of God and the stores of votive offerings. ²¹*Among the descendants of Ladan the Gershonite, the family heads were descendants of Jehiel: the descendants of Jehiel, ²²*Zetham and his brother Joel, who superintended the treasures of the house of the Lord. ²³From the Amramites, Izharites, Hebronites, and Uzzielites, ²⁴Shubael, son of Gershon, son of Moses, was chief superintendent over the treasures. ²⁵*His associate pertained to Eliezer, whose son was Rehabiah, whose son was Jeshaiah, whose son was Joram, whose son was Zichri, whose son was Shelomith. ²⁶*This Shelomith and his brethren superintended all the stores of the votive offerings dedicated by King David, the heads of the families, the commanders of thousands and of hundreds, and the commanders of the army, ²⁷from the booty they had taken in the wars, for the enhancement of the house of the Lord. ²⁸Also, whatever Samuel the seer, Saul, son of Kish, Abner, son of Ner, Joab, son of Zeruiah, and all others had consecrated, was under the charge of Shelomith and his brethren.

Magistrates

²⁹*Among the Izharites, Chenaniah and his sons were in charge of Israel's civil affairs as officials and judges. ³⁰*Among the Hebronites, Hashabiah and his brethren, one thousand seven hundred police officers, had the administration of Israel on the western side of the Jordan in all the work of the Lord and in the service of the king. ³¹*Among the Hebronites, Jerijah was their chief according to their family records. In the fortieth year of David's reign search was made, and there were found among them outstanding officers at Jazer of Gilead. ³²His brethren were also police officers, two thousand seven hundred heads of families. King David appointed them to the administration of the Reubenites, the Gadites, and the half-tribe of Manasseh in everything pertaining to God and to the king.

Army Commanders

27 ¹†THIS is the list of the Israelite family heads, commanders of thousands and of hundreds, and other officers who served the king in all that pertained to the divisions, of twenty-four thousand men each, that came and went month by month throughout the year.

* 26/1: 9, 19; 2 Chr 8, 14; 23, 19; 35, 15; Neh 12, 45. 10: 16, 38. 14: 9, 24. 20: 28, 12; 1 Kgs 7, 51. 21: 23, 7f; 29, 8. 22ff: 23, 8.12.16. 25: 23, 17f; 24, 21. 26: 2 Sm 8, 11. 29: 23, 4. 30: 27, 17; Neh 11, 15f. 31: 23, 19; 29, 27; Jos 13, 25.

† 26, 18: The large building (in the Hebrew text Parbar): see note on 2 Kgs 23, 11.

27, 1-15: This list of army commanders is similar to, but distinct from, the list of David's warriors as given in 11, 10-47. The schematic enumeration of the soldiers as presented here is, no doubt, artificial and grossly exaggerated (12x24,000=288,000 men!), unless the Hebrew word (eleph) for thousand is under-

²Over the first division for the first month was Ishbaal, son of Zabdiel, and in his division were twenty-four thousand men; ³a descendant of Perez, he was chief over all the commanders of the army for the first month. ⁴*Over the division of the second month was Eleazar, son of Dodo, from Ahoh, and in his division were twenty-four thousand men. ⁵*The third army commander, chief for the third month, was Benaiah, son of Jehoiada the priest, and in his division were twenty-four thousand men. ⁶This Benaiah was a warrior among the Thirty and over the Thirty. His son Ammizabad was over his division. ⁷*Fourth, for the fourth month, was Asahel, brother of Joab, and after him his son Zebadiah, and in his division were twenty-four thousand men. ⁸Fifth, for the fifth month, was the commander Shamhuth, a descendant of Zerah, and in his division were twenty-four thousand men. ⁹Sixth, for the sixth month, was Ira, son of Ikkesh, from Tekoa, and in his division were twenty-four thousand men. ¹⁰Seventh, for the seventh month, was Hellez, from Beth-phelet, of the sons of Ephraim, and in his division were twenty-four thousand men. ¹¹*Eighth, for the eighth month, was Sibbecai the Hushathite, a descendant of Zerah, and in his division were twenty-four thousand men. ¹²Ninth, for the ninth month, was Abiezer from Anathoth, of Benjamin, and in his division were twenty-four thousand men. ¹³Tenth, for the tenth month, was Maharai from Netophah, a descendant of Zerah, and in his division were twenty-four thousand men. ¹⁴Eleventh, for the eleventh month, was Benaiah the Pirathonite, of Ephraim, and in his division were twenty-four thousand men. ¹⁵Twelfth, for the twelfth month, was Heldai the Netophathite, of the family of Othniel, and in his division were twenty-four thousand men.

Tribal Heads

¹⁶Over the tribes of Israel, for the Reubenites the leader was Eliezer, son of Zichri; for the Simeonites, Shephatiah, son of Maacah; ¹⁷for Levi, Hashabiah, son of Kemuel; for Aaron, Zadok; ¹⁸*for Judah, Eliab, one of David's brothers; for Issachar, Omri, son of Michael; ¹⁹for Zebulun, Ishmaiah, son of Obadiah; for Naphtali, Jeremoth, son of Azriel; ²⁰for the sons of Ephraim, Hoshea, son of Azaziah; for the half-tribe of Manasseh, Joel, son of Pedaiah; ²¹for the half-tribe of Manasseh in Gilead, Iddo, son of Zechariah; for Benjamin, Jaasiel, son of Abner; ²²for Dan, Azarel, son of Jeroham. These were the commanders of the tribes of Israel.

²³*David did not count those who were twenty years of age or younger, for the LORD had promised to multiply Israel like the stars of the heavens. ²⁴*Joab, son of Zeruiah, began to take the census, but he did not complete it, for because of it wrath fell upon Israel. Therefore the number did not enter into the book of chronicles of King David.

Overseers

²⁵*Over the treasures of the king was Azmaveth, the son of Adiel. Over the stores in the country, the cities, the villages, and the towers was Jonathan, son of Uzziah. ²⁶Over the farm workers who tilled the soil was Ezri, son of Chelub. ²⁷Over the vineyards was Shimei from Ramah, and over their produce for the wine cellars was Zabdi the Shiphmite. ²⁸Over the olive trees and sycamores of the foothills was Baalhanan the Gederite, and over the stores of oil was Joash. ²⁹Over the cattle that grazed in Sharon was Shitrai the Sharonite, and over the cattle in the valleys was Shaphat, the son of Adlai; ³⁰over the camels was Obil the Ishmaelite; over the she-asses was Jehdeiah the Meronothite; ³¹and over the flocks was Jaziz the Hagrite. All these were the overseers of King David's possessions.

David's Court

³²Jonathan, David's uncle and a man of intelligence, was counselor and scribe; he and Jehiel, the son of Hachmoni, were tutors of the king's sons. ³³*Ahithophel was also the king's counselor, and Hushai the Archite was the king's confidant. ³⁴†After Ahithophel came Jehoiada, the son of Benaiah, and Abiathar. The commander of the king's army was Joab.

The Assembly at Jerusalem

28 ¹*DAVID assembled at Jerusalem all the leaders of Israel, the heads of the tribes, the commanders of the divisions who were in the service of the king, the commanders of thousands and of hundreds, the overseers of all the king's estates and possessions, and his sons, together with the courtiers, the warriors, and every important man. ²*†King David rose to his feet and said: "Hear me, my brethren and my people. It was my purpose to build a house of repose myself for the ark of the covenant of the LORD, the footstool for the feet of our God; and I was preparing to build it. ³But God said to me, 'You may not build a house in my honor, for you are a man who fought wars and shed blood.' ⁴*However, the LORD, the God

---

† stood as designating a military unit of much smaller size; see note on 12, 25-38.

27, 34: *After Ahithophel:* after his suicide (2 Sm 17, 23). Jehoiada then succeeded him as the king's counselor. *Abiathar:* the priest. The Chronicler does not mention his office because he regards only the Zadokites as legitimate high priests.

28, 2: *The ark . . . , the footstool . . . of our God:* the Lord, who was invisibly enthroned upon the cherubim that were associated with the ark of the covenant at Shiloh and later in the Jerusalem temple, had the ark as his footstool; cf Pss 99, 5; 132, 7. The *propitiatory* (28, 11) and the *chariot throne* (28, 18) reflect the different circumstances of the postexilic community, for whom only the place of the ark was a focal point of worship, though the ark itself was no longer present.

---

* 27/4: 9, 37; 11, 12;   33: 2 Sm 15, 12.32-37;
     2 Sm 23, 9.   16, 16-19.23;
   5f: 11, 22ff; 18, 17;   17, 5-16.23.
      2 Sm 23, 20ff.   28/1: 27, 2-22.25-31; 11,
   7: 2 Sm 2, 18; 23, 24.   10ff.
  11: 11, 29; 20, 4;   2f: 17, 4; 22, 7ff;
      2 Sm 21, 18.   2 Sm 7, 5; 1 Kgs 5, 3;
  18: 2, 13.   Ps 132, 3-7.
  23: 22, 17.   4: 17, 23; Gn 49, 8ff;
  24: 2 Sm 24, 10.   1 Sm 16, 6-13.
  25: 2 Sm 23, 31.

of Israel, chose me from all my father's family to be king over Israel forever. For he chose Judah as leader, then one family of Judah, that of my father; and finally, among all the sons of my father, it pleased him to make me king over all Israel. **5***And of all my sons—for the LORD has given me many sons—he has chosen my son Solomon to sit on the LORD's royal throne over Israel. **6***For he said to me: 'It is your son Solomon who shall build my house and my courts, for I have chosen him for my son, and I will be a father to him. **7**I will establish his kingdom forever, if he perseveres in keeping my commandments and decrees as he keeps them now.' **8***Therefore, in the presence of all Israel, the assembly of the LORD, and in the hearing of our God, I exhort you to keep and to carry out all the commandments of the LORD, your God, that you may continue to possess this good land and afterward leave it as an inheritance to your children forever.

9*"As for you, Solomon, my son, know the God of your father and serve him with a perfect heart and a willing soul, for the LORD searches all hearts and understands all the mind's thoughts. If you seek him, he will let himself be found by you; but if you abandon him, he will cast you off forever. **10**See, then! The LORD has chosen you to build a house as his sanctuary. Take courage and set to work."

Temple Plans Given to Solomon

11*Then David gave to his son Solomon the pattern of the portico and of the building itself, with its storerooms, its upper rooms and inner chambers, and the room with the propitiatory. **12**He provided also the pattern for all else that he had in mind by way of courts for the house of the LORD, with the surrounding compartments for the stores for the house of God and the stores of the votive offerings, **13**as well as for the divisions of the priests and Levites, for all the work of the service of the house of the LORD, and for all the liturgical vessels of the house of the LORD. **14**He specified the weight of gold to be used in the golden vessels for the various services and the weight of silver to be used in the silver vessels for the various services; **15***likewise for the golden lampstands and their lamps he specified the weight of gold for each lampstand and its lamps, and for the silver lampstands he specified the weight of silver for each lampstand and its lamps, depending on the use to which each lampstand was to be put. **16**He specified the weight of gold for each table to hold the showbread, and the silver for the silver tables; the pure gold to be used for the forks and

pitchers; **17**the amount of gold for each golden bowl and the silver for each silver bowl; **18***†the refined gold, and its weight, to be used for the altar of incense; and, finally, gold for what would suggest a chariot throne: the cherubim that spread their wings and covered the ark of the covenant of the LORD. **19**He had successfully committed to writing the exact specifications of the pattern, because the hand of the LORD was upon him.

20*Then David said to his son Solomon: "Be firm and steadfast; go to work without fear or discouragement, for the LORD God, my God, is with you. He will not fail you or abandon you before you have completed all the work for the service of the house of the LORD. **21***The classes of the priests and Levites are ready for all the service of the house of God; they will help you in all your work with all those who are eager to show their skill in every kind of craftsmanship. Also the leaders and all the people will do everything that you command."

Offerings for the Temple

29 **1***KING David then said to the whole assembly: "My son Solomon, whom alone God has chosen, is still young and immature; the work, however, is great, for this castle is not intended for man, but for the LORD God. **2***For this reason I have stored up for the house of my God, as far as I was able, gold for what will be made of gold, silver for what will be made of silver, bronze for what will be made of bronze, iron for what will be made of iron, wood for what will be made of wood, onyx stones and settings for them, carnelian and mosaic stones, every other kind of precious stone, and great quantities of marble. **3**But now, because of the delight I take in the house of my God, in addition to all that I stored up for the holy house, I give to the house of my God my personal fortune in gold and silver: **4***three thousand talents of Ophir gold, and seven thousand talents of refined silver, for overlaying the walls of the rooms, **5***for the various utensils to be made of gold and silver, and for every work that is to be done by artisans. Now, who else is willing to contribute generously this day to the LORD?"

6*Then the heads of the families, the leaders of the tribes of Israel, the commanders of thousands and of hundreds, and the overseers of the king's affairs came forward willingly **7***and contributed for the service of the house of God five thousand talents and ten thousand darics of gold, ten thousand talents of silver, eighteen thousand talents of bronze, and one hundred thousand talents of iron. **8***Those who had precious stones gave them into the keeping of Jehiel the Gershonite for the treasury of the house of the LORD. **9***The people rejoiced over these free-will offerings, which had been contributed to the LORD wholeheartedly. King David also rejoiced greatly.

✿

5: 3, 1-9; 14, 3-7; 22, 9;
   23, 1; Wis 9, 7.
6: 17, 11ff; 22, 9f;
   2 Sm 7, 12f.
8: Dt 4, 5.
9: 29, 17; 2 Chr 15, 2;
   1 Kgs 8, 61.
11: Ex 25, 9.40; 26, 30.
15: Ex 25, 31-37.
18: Ex 25, 18-22; 30, 1-10;
   1 Kgs 6, 23-28.
20: 22, 13.16; Jos 1, 5.

21: Ex 36, 1-5.
29/1: 22, 5; 28, 5.
2: 22, 14.
4: 2 Chr 9, 10; 1 Kgs 9,
   28; 10, 11.
5: Ex 25, 2; 35, 5f.
6: 27, 1.25-31; 28, 1.
7: Ezr 2, 69; 8, 27;
   Neh 7, 70ff.
8: 23, 8; 26, 21.
9: 2 Kgs 12, 4.

---

† 28, 18: *Chariot throne:* probably suggested by Ez 1, 4-24; 10, 1-22.

David's Prayer

¹⁰Then David blessed the Lord in the presence of the whole assembly, praying in these words:

"Blessed may you be, O Lord,
God of Israel our father,
from eternity to eternity.

¹¹"Yours, O Lord, are grandeur and power,
majesty, splendor, and glory.
For all in heaven and on earth is yours;
yours, O Lord, is the sovereignty;
you are exalted as head over all.

¹²*"Riches and honor are from you,
and you have dominion over all.
In your hand are power and might;
it is yours to give grandeur and strength to all.
¹³Therefore, our God, we give you thanks
and we praise the majesty of your name."

¹⁴"But who am I, and who are my people, that we should have the means to contribute so freely? For everything is from you, and we only give you what we have received from you. ¹⁵*For we stand before you as aliens: we are only your guests, like all our fathers. Our life on earth is like a shadow that does not abide. ¹⁶O Lord our God, all this wealth that we have brought together to build you a house in honor of your holy name comes from you and is entirely yours. ¹⁷I know, O my God, that you put hearts to the test and that you take pleasure in uprightness. With a sincere heart I have willingly given all these things, and now with joy I have seen your people here present also giving to you generously. ¹⁸*O Lord, God of our fathers Abraham, Isaac, and Israel, keep such thoughts in the hearts and minds of your people forever, and direct their hearts toward you. ¹⁹Give to my son Solomon a wholehearted desire to keep your commandments, precepts, and statutes, that he may carry out all these plans and build the castle for which I have made preparation."

²⁰Then David besought the whole assembly, "Now bless the Lord your God!" And the whole assembly blessed the Lord, the God of their fathers, bowing down and prostrating themselves before the Lord and before the king. ²¹On the following day they offered sacrifices and holocausts to the Lord, a thousand bulls, a thousand rams, and a thousand lambs, together with their libations and many other sacrifices for all Israel; ²²†and on that day they ate and drank in the Lord's presence with great rejoicing.

Solomon Anointed

Then for a second time they proclaimed David's son Solomon king, and they anointed him as the Lord's prince, and Zadok as priest. ²³*Thereafter Solomon sat on the throne of the Lord as king in place of his father David; he prospered, and all Israel obeyed him. ²⁴All the leaders and warriors, and also all the other sons of King David, swore allegiance to King Solomon. ²⁵*And the Lord exalted Solomon greatly in the eyes of all Israel, giving him a glorious reign such as had not been enjoyed by any king over Israel before him.

Death of David

²⁶Thus David, the son of Jesse, had reigned over all Israel. ²⁷*The time that he reigned over Israel was forty years: in Hebron he reigned seven years, and in Jerusalem thirty-three. ²⁸*He died at a ripe old age, rich in years and wealth and glory, and his son Solomon succeeded him as king.

²⁹*Now the deeds of King David, first and last, can be found written in the history of Samuel the seer, the history of Nathan the prophet, and the history of Gad the seer, ³⁰together with the particulars of his reign and valor, and of the events that affected him and all Israel and all the kingdoms of the surrounding lands.

12: 2 Chr 20, 6; Wis 6, 3.
15: Lv 25, 23; Wis 2, 5; 5, 9.
18: Ex 3, 6.15f; 4, 5; 1 Kgs 18, 36.
23: 28, 5; 2 Chr 9, 8; 1 Kgs 2, 10ff.
25: 2 Chr 1, 12; 1 Kgs 3, 13.
27: 2 Sm 5, 5; 1 Kgs 2, 11.
28: 23, 1.
29: 21, 9; 1 Sm 22, 5.

29, 22: *For a second time:* the first time is referred to in 23, 1. Here there is a solemn public ratification of David's earlier appointment of Solomon as his successor.

Second Book of Chronicles

Introduction

The Second Book of Chronicles takes up the history of the monarchy where the First Book breaks off. It begins with the account of the reign of Solomon from the special viewpoint of the Chronicler. The portrait of Solomon is an idealized one; he appears as second only to David. The great achievement of the building of the temple and the magnificence of Solomon's court are described in detail while the serious defects of his reign are passed over without comment. All this is in keeping with the Chronicler's purpose of stressing the supreme importance of the temple and its worship. He wishes to impress on his readers the splendor of God's dwelling and the magnificence of the liturgy of sacrifice, prayer and praise offered there. Judah's kings are judged by their attitude toward the temple and its cult. To this ideal of one people, united in the worship of the one true God at the temple of Jerusalem founded by David and Solomon, the restored community would have to conform.

In treating the period of divided monarchy, the Chronicler gives practically all his attention to the kingdom of Judah. His omission of the northern Israelite kings is significant. In his view, the northern tribes of Israel were in religious schism as long as they worshiped Yahweh in a place other than the temple of Jerusalem. The Chronicler makes no mention of the important sanctuaries of Yahweh at Dan and Bethel—as though they had never existed. Nevertheless he retains the ancient ideal of "all Israel" (a phrase occurring forty-one times in Chronicles) as the people of God. The condition he places for a united people is that "the whole congregation of Israel" worship the Lord only in his temple at Jerusalem. This explains his praise of Kings Hezekiah and Josiah for striving, after the fall of Samaria, to unite the remnants of the northern tribes of Israel into the kingdom of Judah.

At the end of the fifth century B. C., during the Chronicler's own time, "the people of the land" were the descendants of the people of all the tribes (including Judah) who had not gone into exile. These had become intermingled with aliens and had evolved a religion of Yahweh very different from the Judaism that developed during the Babylonian exile. Thus, religious and political cooperation between the returned exiles and these "people of the land" was out of the question for the Chronicler. This he clearly shows in the last part of his work, the Books of Ezra and Nehemiah.

The Second Book of Chronicles is divided as follows:

I: THE REIGN OF SOLOMON

Solomon at Gibeon

1 [1]SOLOMON, SON OF DAVID, strengthened his hold on the kingdom, for the Lord, his God, was with him, constantly making him more renowned. [2]He sent a summons to all Israel, to the commanders of thousands and of hundreds, the judges, the princes of all Israel, and the family heads; [3*]and, accompanied by the whole assembly, he went to the high place at Gibeon, because the meeting tent of God, made in the desert by Moses, the Lord's servant, was there. [4](The ark of God, however, David had brought up from Kiriath-jearim to Jerusalem, where he had provided a place and pitched a tent for it.) [5*†]The bronze altar made by Bezalel, son of Uri, son of Hur, he put in front of the Lord's Dwelling on the high place. There Solomon and the assembly consulted the Lord, [6]and Solomon offered sacrifice in the Lord's presence on the bronze altar at the meeting tent; he offered a thousand holocausts upon it.

[7]That night God appeared to Solomon and said to him, "Make a request of me, and I will grant it to you." [8]Solomon answered God: "You have shown great favor to my father David, and you have allowed me to succeed him as king. [9]Now, Lord God, may your promise to my father David be fulfilled, for you have made me king over a people as numerous as the dust of the earth. [10]Give me, therefore, wisdom and knowledge to lead this people, for otherwise who could rule this great people of yours?" [11]God then replied to Solomon: "Since this has been your wish and you have not asked for riches, treasures and glory, nor for the life of those

---

† 1, 5: *The bronze altar . . . the* Lord's *Dwelling:* the Chronicler justifies Solomon's worship at the high place of Gibeon. He pictures *the* Lord's *Dwelling,* i. e., the Mosaic meeting tent, and *the bronze altar* made at Moses' command (Ex 31, 1-9) as still at Gibeon after David had removed the ark of the covenant from there to a new tent in Jerusalem (1 Chr 15, 1.25; 16, 1). The altar made by Bezalel is described as being of acacia wood plated with bronze (Ex 27, 1f). Solomon later made an all-bronze altar for the temple in Jerusalem (2 Chr 4, 1).

who hate you, nor even for a long life for yourself, but have asked for wisdom and knowledge in order to rule my people over whom I have made you king, [12]wisdom and knowledge are given you; but I will also give you riches, treasures and glory, such as kings before you never had, nor will those have them who come after you."

Solomon's Wealth

[13]Solomon returned to Jerusalem from the high place at Gibeon, from the meeting tent, and became king over Israel. [14*]He gathered together chariots and drivers, so that he had one thousand four hundred chariots and twelve thousand drivers he could station in the chariot cities and with the king in Jerusalem. [15*]The king made silver and gold as common in Jerusalem as stones, while cedars became as numerous as the sycamores of the foothills. [16*†]Solomon also imported horses from Egypt and Cilicia. The king's agents would acquire them by purchase from Cilicia, [17*]and would then bring up chariots from Egypt and export them at six hundred silver shekels, with the horses going for a hundred and fifty shekels. At these rates they served as middlemen for all the Hittite and Aramean kings.

Preparations for the Temple

[18]Solomon gave orders for the building of a house to honor the Lord and also of a house for his own royal estate.

2 [1*]HE conscripted seventy thousand men to carry stone and eighty thousand to cut the stone in the mountains, and over these he placed three thousand six hundred overseers. [2*]Moreover, Solomon sent this message to Huram, king of Tyre: "As you dealt with my father David, sending him cedars to build a house for his dwelling, so deal with me. [3*]I intend to build a house for the honor of the Lord, my God, and to consecrate it to him, for the burning of fragrant incense in his presence, for the perpetual display of the showbread, for holocausts morning and evening, and for the sabbaths, new moons, and festivals of the Lord, our God: such is Israel's perpetual obligation. [4]And the house I intend to build must be large, for our God is greater than all other gods. [5*]Yet who is really able to build him a house, since the heavens and even the highest heavens cannot contain him? And who am I that I should build him a house, unless it be to offer incense in his presence? [6]Now, send me men skilled at work in gold, silver, bronze and iron, in purple, crimson, and violet fabrics, and who know how to do

engraved work, to join the craftsmen who are with me in Judah and Jerusalem, whom my father David appointed. [7]Also send me boards of cedar, cypress and cabinet wood from Lebanon, for I realize that your servants know how to cut the wood of the Lebanon. My servants will labor with yours [8]in order to prepare for me a great quantity of wood, since the house I intend to build must be lofty and wonderful. [9*]I will furnish as food for your servants, the hewers who cut the wood, twenty thousand kors of wheat, twenty thousand kors of barley, twenty thousand measures of wine, and twenty thousand measures of oil."

[10]Huram, king of Tyre, wrote an answer which he sent to Solomon: "Because the Lord loves his people, he has placed you over them as king." [11*]He added: "Blessed be the Lord, the God of Israel, who made heaven and earth, for having given King David a wise son of intelligence and understanding, who will build a house for the Lord and also a house for his royal estate. [12*]I am now sending you a craftsman of great skill, Huram-abi, [13†]son of a Danite woman and of a father from Tyre; he knows how to work with gold, silver, bronze and iron, with stone and wood, with purple, violet, fine linen and crimson, and also how to do all kinds of engraved work and to devise every type of artistic work that may be given him and your craftsmen and the craftsmen of my lord David your father. [14*]And now, let my lord send to his servants the wheat, barley, oil and wine which he has promised. [15*]For our part, we will cut trees on Lebanon, as many as you need, and float them down to you at the port of Joppa, whence you may take them up to Jerusalem."

[16*]Thereupon Solomon took a census of all the alien men who were in the land of Israel (following the census David his father had taken of them), who were found to number one hundred fifty-three thousand six hundred. [17*]Of these he made seventy thousand carriers and eighty thousand cutters in the mountains, and three thousand six hundred overseers to keep the people working.

Building of the Temple

3 [1*†]THEN Solomon began to build the house of the Lord in Jerusalem on Mount Moriah, which had been pointed out to his father David, on the spot which David had selected, the threshing-floor of Ornan the Jebusite. [2]He began to build in the second

---

† 1, 16f: *Egypt . . . Cilicia:* it seems likely that the horses came from Cilicia and the chariots from Egypt. Some read the source of these data in 1 Kgs 10, 28f as containing the name (Musur) of a mountain district north of Cilicia, rather than of Egypt; but the author of Chronicles surely understood *Egypt;* cf 9, 28.

2, 13: *A Danite woman:* a widow of the tribe of Naphtali (1 Kgs 7, 14). The Danites had settled in the northern section of Naphtali's territory (Jgs 18, 27ff). Bezalel's fellow craftsman was of the tribe of Dan (Ex 31, 6).

3, 1: *Mount Moriah:* the *height* in *the land of Moriah* (Gn 22, 2). This is the only place in the Bible where the temple mount is identified with the site where Abraham was to sacrifice Isaac.

✻

14: 9, 25; 10, 26-29.
15: 1 Kgs 10, 27.
16: 1 Kgs 10, 28.
17: 1 Kgs 10, 29.
2/1: 2, 17; 5, 29f.
2-9: 1 Kgs 5, 15-20;
　　　1 Chr 14, 1.
3: Lv 24, 5-8; Nm 28—29.
5: 6, 18.
9: 1 Kgs 5, 25; Ezr 3, 7.

11: 1 Kgs 5, 21.
12f: 1 Kgs 7, 13f;
　　　Ex 31, 1-5.
14f: 1 Kgs 5, 22-26.
15: Ezr 3, 7.
16f: 1 Chr 22, 2.
17: 2, 1.
3/1f: Gn 22, 2; 1 Kgs 6, 1;
　　　1 Chr 21, 22-26.

month of the fourth year of his reign. **³*** These were the specifications laid down by Solomon for building the house of God: the length was sixty cubits according to the old measure, and the width was twenty cubits; **⁴*†** the porch which lay before the nave along the width of the house was also twenty cubits, and it was twenty cubits high. He overlaid its interior with pure gold. **⁵*** The nave he overlaid with cypress wood which he covered with fine gold, embossing on it palms and chains. **⁶** He also decorated the building with precious stones. **⁷** The house, its beams and thresholds, as well as its walls and its doors, he overlaid with gold, and he engraved cherubim upon the walls. (The gold was from Parvaim.) **⁸*** He also made the room of the holy of holies. Its length corresponded to the width of the house, twenty cubits, and its width was also twenty cubits. He overlaid it with fine gold to the amount of six hundred talents. **⁹** The weight of the nails was fifty gold shekels. The upper chambers he likewise covered with gold.

¹⁰* For the room of the holy of holies he made two cherubim of carved workmanship, which were then overlaid with gold. **¹¹** The wings of the cherubim spanned twenty cubits: **¹²** one wing of each cherub, five cubits in length, extended to a wall of the building, while the other wing, also five cubits in length, touched the corresponding wing of the second cherub. **¹³** The combined wingspread of the two cherubim was thus twenty cubits. They stood upon their own feet, facing toward the nave. **¹⁴*†** He made the veil of violet, purple, crimson and fine linen, and had cherubim embroidered upon it.

¹⁵* In front of the building he set two columns thirty-five cubits high; the capital topping each was of five cubits. **¹⁶** He worked out chains in the form of a collar with which he encircled the capitals of the columns, and he made a hundred pomegranates which he set on the chains. **¹⁷** He set up the columns to correspond with the nave, one for the right side and the other for the left, and he called the one to the right Jachin and the one to the left Boaz.

4 **¹*** THEN he made a bronze altar twenty cubits long, twenty cubits wide and ten cubits high. **²*** He also made the molten sea. It was perfectly round, ten cubits in diameter, five in depth, and thirty in circumference; **³†** below the rim a ring of figures of oxen encircled the sea, ten to the cubit, all the way around; there were two rows of these cast in the same mold with the sea. **⁴** It rested on twelve oxen, three facing north, three west, three south, and three east, with their haunches all toward the center; the sea

rested on their backs. **⁵†** It was a handbreadth thick, and its brim was made like that of a cup, being lily-shaped. It had a capacity of three thousand measures.

⁶* Then he made ten basins for washing, placing five of them to the right and five to the left. Here were cleansed the victims for the holocausts; but the sea was for the priests to wash in.

⁷* He made the lampstands of gold, ten of them as was prescribed, and placed them in the nave, five to the right and five to the left. **⁸*** He made ten tables and had them set in the nave, five to the right and five to the left; and he made a hundred golden bowls. **⁹*** He made the court of the priests and the great courtyard and the gates of the courtyard; the gates he overlaid with bronze. **¹⁰*** The sea was placed off to the southeast from the right side of the temple.

¹¹* Huram also made the pots, the shovels and the bowls. Huram thus completed the work he had to do for King Solomon in the house of God: **¹²** two columns, two nodes for the capitals topping these two columns, and two networks covering the nodes of the capitals topping the columns; **¹³** also four hundred pomegranates for the two networks, with two rows of pomegranates to each network, to cover the two nodes of the capitals topping the columns. **¹⁴** He made the stands, and the basins on the stands; **¹⁵** one sea, and the twelve oxen under it; **¹⁶** likewise the pots, the shovels and the forks. Huram-abi made all these articles for King Solomon from polished bronze for the house of the LORD. **¹⁷** The king had them cast in the Jordan region, in the clayey ground between Succoth and Zeredah. **¹⁸** Solomon made all these vessels, so many in number that the weight of the bronze was not ascertained.

¹⁹ Solomon had all these articles made for the house of God: the golden altar, the tables on which the showbread lay, **²⁰** the lampstands and their lamps of pure gold which were to burn according to prescription before the sanctuary, **²¹** flowers, lamps and gold tongs [this was the purest gold], **²²** snuffers, bowls, cups and firepans of pure gold. As for the entry to the house, its inner doors to the holy of holies, as well as the doors to the nave, were of gold.

---

† 3, 4: *The porch . . . twenty cubits high:* this measurement, not given in the Books of Kings, is here based on a variant Greek text that may be a later revision. The received Hebrew text says, "one hundred and twenty cubits high." The height of the two free-standing columns adjacent to the porch (1 Kgs 7, 15-16) is nearly doubled by the Chronicler (3, 15).

3, 14: *The veil:* at the entrance of the holy of holies, as also in the Mosaic meeting tent (Ex 26, 31f). Solomon's temple had doors at this place (1 Kgs 6, 31). Apparently there was a veil here in the temple of the Chronicler's time as there was also in Herod's temple (Mt 27, 51; Mk 15, 38; Lk 23, 45).

4, 3: *Oxen:* in 1 Kgs 7, 24 this double row of ornaments is described as being gourds. The text of Kings available to the Chronicler may have been faulty on this point as the words are similar in sound. In 4, 16 the *forks* correspond in a similar way to *bowls* in the text of 1 Kings (7, 40).

4, 5: *Three thousand measures:* according to 1 Kgs 7, 26, *two thousand measures.*

✿
3:	1 Kgs 6, 2; Ez 40, 5.	2-5:	1 Kgs 7, 23-26;
4:	1 Kgs 6, 3; Ez 40, 48.		Ez 43, 13.
5:	1 Kgs 6, 15; Ez 41, 1.	6:	1 Kgs 7, 38f; Ez 40, 38.
8:	1 Kgs 6, 16f.20;	7:	1 Kgs 7, 49.
	Ez 41, 3.	8:	1 Kgs 7, 50;
10-13:	1 Kgs 6, 23-27.		1 Chr 28, 16.
14:	Mt 27, 51.	9:	1 Kgs 7, 12.
15ff:	1 Kgs 7, 15-22;	10:	1 Kgs 7, 39.
	Ez 40, 49.	11-22:	1 Kgs 7, 40-51.
4/1:	Ez 43, 13-17.		

Dedication of the Temple

5 ¹*WHEN all the work undertaken by Solomon for the temple of the LORD had been completed, he brought in the dedicated offerings of his father David, putting the silver, the gold and all the other articles in the treasuries of the house of God. ²At Solomon's order the elders of Israel and all the leaders of the tribes, the princes of the Israelite ancestral houses, came to Jerusalem to bring up the ark of the LORD's covenant from the City of David (which is Zion). ³All the men of Israel assembled before the king during the festival of the seventh month. ⁴*†When all the elders of Israel had arrived, the Levites took up the ark, ⁵and they carried the ark and the meeting tent with all the sacred vessels that were in the tent; it was the levitical priests who carried them.

⁶King Solomon and the entire community of Israel gathered about him before the ark were sacrificing sheep and oxen so numerous that they could not be counted or numbered. ⁷The priests brought the ark of the covenant of the LORD to its place beneath the wings of the cherubim in the sanctuary, the holy of holies of the temple. ⁸The cherubim had their wings spread out over the place of the ark, sheltering the ark and its poles from above. ⁹†The poles were long enough so that their ends could be seen from that part of the holy place nearest the sanctuary; however, they could not be seen beyond. The ark has remained there to this day. ¹⁰There was nothing in it but the two tablets which Moses put there on Horeb, the tablets of the covenant which the LORD made with the Israelites at their departure from Egypt.

¹¹When the priests came out of the holy place (all the priests who were present had purified themselves without reference to the rotation of their various classes), ¹²the Levites who were singers, all who belonged to Asaph, Heman, Jeduthun, and their sons and brothers, clothed in fine linen, with cymbals, harps and lyres, stood east of the altar, and with them a hundred and twenty priests blowing trumpets.

¹³When the trumpeters and singers were heard as a single voice praising and giving thanks to the LORD, and when they raised the sound of the trumpets, cymbals and other musical instruments to "give thanks to the LORD, for he is good, for his mercy endures forever," the building of the LORD's temple was filled with a cloud. ¹⁴*The priests could not continue to minister because of the cloud, since the LORD's glory filled the house of God.

6 ¹*THEN Solomon said: "The LORD intends to dwell in the dark cloud. ²I have truly built you a princely house and dwelling, where you may abide forever." ³*Turning about, the king greeted the whole community of Israel as they stood. ⁴He said:

"Blessed be the LORD, the God of Israel, who with his own mouth made a promise to my father David and by his own hands brought it to fulfillment. He said: ⁵'Since the day I brought my people out of the land of Egypt, I have not chosen any city from among all the tribes of Israel for the building of a temple to my honor, nor have I chosen any man to be commander of my people Israel; ⁶but now I choose Jerusalem, where I shall be honored, and I choose David to rule my people Israel.' ⁷My father David wished to build a temple to the honor of the LORD, the God of Israel, ⁸but the LORD said to him: 'In wishing to build a temple to my honor, you do well. ⁹However, you shall not build the temple; rather, your son whom you will beget shall build the temple to my honor.'

¹⁰"Now the LORD has fulfilled the promise that he made. I have succeeded my father David and have taken my seat on the throne of Israel, as the LORD foretold, and I have built the temple to the honor of the LORD, the God of Israel. ¹¹And I have placed there the ark, in which abides the covenant of the LORD which he made with the Israelites."

Solomon's Prayer

¹²*Solomon then took his place before the altar of the LORD in the presence of the whole community of Israel and stretched forth his hands. ¹³†He had made a bronze platform five cubits long, five cubits wide, and three cubits high, which he had placed in the middle of the courtyard. Having ascended it, Solomon knelt in the presence of the whole of Israel and stretched forth his hands toward heaven. ¹⁴Thus he prayed: "LORD, God of Israel, there is no god like you in heaven or on earth; you keep your covenant and show kindness to your servants who are wholeheartedly faithful to you. ¹⁵You have kept the promise you made to my father David, your servant. With your own mouth you spoke it, and by your own hand you have brought it to fulfillment this day. ¹⁶Now, therefore, LORD, God of Israel, keep the further promise you made to my father David, your servant, when you said, 'You shall always have someone from your line to sit before me on the throne of Israel, provided only that your descendants look to their conduct so as always to live according to my law, even as you have lived in my presence.' ¹⁷Now, LORD, God of Israel, may this promise which you made to your servant David be confirmed.

¹⁸"Can it indeed be that God dwells with mankind on earth? If the heavens and the highest heavens can-

---

† 5, 4: *The Levites:* The parallel passage in 1 Kgs 8, 3 has *the priests;* but see 2 Chr 5, 5, where the Deuteronomic term *levitical priests* is used, as also in 23, 18; 30, 27.

5, 9: *The ark has remained there to this day:* the Chronicler must have copied this from his source (1 Kgs 8, 8) without reflecting that the ark was lost in the Babylonian destruction of Jerusalem; cf 2 Mc 2, 4-8.

6, 13: This verse is not found in the Chronicler's source; cf 1 Kgs 8, 22f. He has Solomon praying on *a bronze platform . . . in the middle of the courtyard* because at the time of the Chronicler only the priests prayed before the altar.

---

* 5/1-14: 1 Kgs 7, 51—8, 13.   6/1f: 1 Kgs 8, 12f.
  4f: 35, 3.   3-11: 1 Kgs 8, 14-21.
  14: 7, 2; 1 Kgs 8, 10f.   12-41: 1 Kgs 8, 22-53.

not contain you, how much less this temple which I have built! **¹⁹**Look kindly on the prayer and petition of your servant, O Lᴏʀᴅ, my God, and listen to the cry of supplication your servant makes before you. **²⁰**May your eyes watch day and night over this temple, the place where you have decreed you shall be honored; may you heed the prayer which I your servant offer toward this place. **²¹**Listen to the petitions of your servant and of your people Israel which they direct toward this place. Listen from your heavenly dwelling, and when you have heard, pardon.

²²"When any man sins against his neighbor and is required to take an oath of execration against himself, and when he comes for the oath before your altar in this temple, **²³**listen from heaven: take action and pass judgment on your servants, requiting the wicked man and holding him responsible for his conduct, but absolving the innocent and rewarding him according to his virtue. **²⁴**When your people Israel have sinned against you and are defeated by the enemy, but afterward they return and praise your name, and they pray to you and entreat you in this temple, **²⁵**listen from heaven and forgive the sin of your people Israel, and bring them back to the land which you gave them and their fathers. **²⁶**When the sky is closed so that there is no rain, because they have sinned against you, but then they pray toward this place and praise your name, and they withdraw from sin because you afflict them, **²⁷**listen in heaven and forgive the sin of your servants and of your people Israel. But teach them the right way to live, and send rain upon your land which you gave your people as their heritage. **²⁸**When there is famine in the land, when there is pestilence, or blight, or mildew, or locusts, or caterpillars; when their enemies besiege them at any of their gates; whenever there is a plague or sickness of any kind; **²⁹**when any Israelite of all your people offers a prayer or petition of any kind, and in awareness of his affliction and pain, stretches out his hands toward this temple, **³⁰**listen from your heavenly dwelling place, and forgive. Knowing his heart, render to everyone according to his conduct, for you alone know the hearts of men. **³¹**So may they fear you and walk in your ways as long as they live on the land you gave our fathers.

³²"For the foreigner, too, who is not of your people Israel, when he comes from a distant land to honor your great name, your mighty power, and your outstretched arm, when they come in prayer to this temple, **³³**listen from your heavenly dwelling place, and do whatever the foreigner entreats you, that all the peoples of the earth may know your name, fearing you as do your people Israel, and knowing that this house which I have built is dedicated to your honor.

³⁴"When your people go forth to war against their enemies, wherever you send them, and pray to you in the direction of this city and of the house I have built to your honor, **³⁵**listen from heaven to their prayer and petition, and defend their cause. **³⁶**When they sin against you (for there is no man who does not sin), and in your anger against them you deliver them to the enemy, so that their captors deport them to another land, far or near, **³⁷**when they repent in the land where they are captive and are converted, when they entreat you in the land of their captivity and say, 'We have sinned and done wrong; we have been wicked,' **³⁸**and with their whole heart and with their whole soul they turn back to you in the land of those who hold them captive, when they pray in the direction of their land which you gave their fathers, and of the city you have chosen, and of the house which I have built to your honor, **³⁹**listen from your heavenly dwelling place, hear their prayer and petitions, and uphold their cause. Forgive your people who have sinned against you. **⁴⁰**My God, may your eyes be open and your ears attentive to the prayer of this place. **⁴¹**And now,

"Advance, Lᴏʀᴅ God, to your resting place,
    you and the ark of your majesty.
May your priests, Lᴏʀᴅ God, be clothed with
    salvation,
    may your faithful ones rejoice in good things.
⁴²Lᴏʀᴅ God, reject not the plea of your anointed,
    remember the devotion of David, your servant."

7 **¹***ᴡʜᴇɴ Solomon had ended his prayer, fire came down from heaven and consumed the holocaust and the sacrifices, and the glory of the Lᴏʀᴅ filled the house. **²***But the priests could not enter the house of the Lᴏʀᴅ, for the glory of the Lᴏʀᴅ had filled the house of the Lᴏʀᴅ. **³**All the Israelites looked on while the fire came down and the glory of the Lᴏʀᴅ was upon the house, and they fell down upon the pavement with their faces to the earth and adored, praising the Lᴏʀᴅ, "for he is good, for his mercy endures forever." **⁴***The king and all the people were offering sacrifices before the Lᴏʀᴅ. **⁵***King Solomon offered as sacrifice twenty-two thousand oxen, and one hundred twenty thousand sheep.

End of the Dedication

⁶*Thus the king and all the people dedicated the house of God. The priests were standing at their stations, as were the Levites, with the musical instruments of the Lᴏʀᴅ which King David had made for "praising the Lᴏʀᴅ, for his mercy endures forever," when David used them to accompany the hymns. Across from them the priests blew the trumpets and all Israel stood.

⁷*Then Solomon consecrated the middle part of the court which lay before the house of the Lᴏʀᴅ; there he offered the holocausts and the fat of the peace offerings, since the bronze altar which Solomon had made could not hold the holocausts, the cereal offerings and the fat.

⁸*On this occasion Solomon and with him all Israel,

7/1-10: 1 Kgs 8, 54-66; Jgs 6,
    21; 1 Chr 21, 26;
    2 Mc 2, 10.
2: 5, 14; Ex 24, 16;
    1 Kgs 8, 10f.
4: 5, 13; 1 Kgs 8, 62;
    Ps 136, 1.
5: 1 Kgs 8, 62f.
6: Nm 10, 8.10; Ps 136, 1.
7: 1 Kgs 8, 64.
8: 1 Kgs 8, 65.

who had assembled in very large numbers from Labo of Hamath to the Wadi of Egypt, celebrated the festival for seven days. **9*****†**On the eighth day they held a special meeting, for they had celebrated the dedication of the altar for seven days and the feast for seven days. **10**On the twenty-third day of the seventh month he sent the people back to their tents, rejoicing and glad at heart at the good things the Lord had done for David, for Solomon, and for his people Israel. **11***Solomon completed the house of the Lord and the royal palace; he successfully accomplished everything he had planned to do in regard to the house of the Lord and his own house.

God's Promise to Solomon

12The Lord appeared to Solomon during the night and said to him: "I have heard your prayer, and I have chosen this place for my house of sacrifice. **13**If I close heaven so that there is no rain, if I command the locust to devour the land, if I send pestilence among my people, **14**and if my people, upon whom my name has been pronounced, humble themselves and pray, and seek my presence and turn from their evil ways, I will hear them from heaven and pardon their sins and revive their land. **15**Now my eyes shall be open and my ears attentive to the prayer of this place. **16**And now I have chosen and consecrated this house that my name may be there forever; my eyes and my heart also shall be there always.

17"As for you, if you live in my presence as your father David did, doing all that I have commanded you and keeping my statutes and ordinances, **18**I will establish your royal throne as I covenanted with your father David when I said, 'There shall never be lacking someone of yours as ruler in Israel.' **19**But if you turn away and forsake my statutes and commands which I placed before you, if you proceed to venerate and worship strange gods, **20**then I will uproot the people from the land I gave them; I will cast from my sight this house which I have consecrated to my honor, and I will make it a proverb and a byword among all peoples. **21**This temple which is so exalted—everyone passing by it will be amazed and ask: 'Why has the Lord done this to this land and to this house?' **22**And men will answer: 'They forsook the Lord, the God of their fathers, who brought them out of the land of Egypt, and they adopted strange gods and worshiped them and served them. That is why he has brought down upon them all this evil.'"

Public Works

8 **1***After the twenty years during which Solomon built the house of the Lord and his own house, **2**†he built up the cities which Huram had given him, and settled Israelites there. **3**Then Solomon went to Hamath of Zoba and conquered it. **4**†He built Tad-

mor in the desert region and all the supply cities, which he built in Hamath. **5***He built Upper Beth-horon and Lower Beth-horon, fortified cities with walls, gates and bars; **6**also Baalath, all the supply cities belonging to Solomon, and all the cities for the chariots, the cities for the horsemen, and whatever else Solomon decided should be built in Jerusalem, in the Lebanon, and in the entire land under his dominion. **7**All the people that remained of the Hittites, Amorites, Perizzites, Hivites, and Jebusites, who were not of Israel—**8**that is, their descendants remaining in the land, whom the Israelites had not destroyed—Solomon subjected to forced labor, as they continue to this day. **9**But Solomon did not enslave the Israelites for his works. They became soldiers, commanders of his warriors, and commanders of his chariots and his horsemen. **10**They were also King Solomon's two hundred and fifty overseers who had charge of the people.

Solomon's Piety

11Solomon brought the daughter of Pharaoh up from the City of David to the palace which he had built for her, for he said, "No wife of mine shall dwell in the house of David, king of Israel, for the places where the ark of the Lord has come are holy."

12In those times Solomon offered holocausts to the Lord upon the altar of the Lord which he had built in front of the porch, **13***as was required day by day according to the command of Moses, and in particular on the sabbaths, at the new moons, and on the fixed festivals three times a year: on the feast of the Unleavened Bread, the feast of Weeks and the feast of Booths.

14*And according to the ordinance of his father David he appointed the various classes of the priests for their service, and the Levites according to their functions of praise and ministry alongside the priests, as the daily duty required. The gatekeepers of the various classes stood guard at each gate, since such was the command of David, the man of God. **15**There was no deviation from the king's command in any respect relating to the priests and Levites or the treasuries. **16**All of Solomon's work was carried out successfully from the day the foundation of the house of the

---

7, 9f: *The feast:* of Booths, celebrated on the fifteenth day of the seventh month and followed by a solemn octave lasting through the twenty-second day (Lv 23, 33-36; Nm 29, 12-35); the people are therefore sent home on the twenty-third day (v 10). The festival (v 8) for *the dedication of the altar* and of the temple lasted for seven days before the feast of Booths, from the seventh to the fourteenth day. According to 1 Kgs 8, 65f, the people are dismissed at the end of these seven days.

8, 2: *The cities which Huram had given him:* according to 1 Kgs 9, 10-14, Solomon had ceded the cities as payment for the timber and gold received from Tyre. But since Huram was dissatisfied, he may have returned the cities to Solomon.

8, 4: *Tadmor:* later known as Palmyra, an important caravan city in the Syrian desert. The parallel passage in 1 Kgs 9, 18 has *Tamar,* in southern Judah; cf Ez 47, 19; 48, 28. But Solomon may well have fortified Tadmor against the Arameans.

9f: 1 Kgs 8, 66.
11-22: 1 Kgs 9, 1-9.
8/1f: 1 Kgs 9, 10f.
5-12: 1 Kgs 9, 18-25.
13: 1 Kgs 9, 25; Ex 23, 14; Nm 28—29.
14: 1 Chr 23—26; Neh 12, 46.

LORD was laid until the house of the LORD had been completed in every detail.

Glories of the Court

[17]In those times Solomon went to Ezion-geber and to Elath on the seashore of the land of Edom. [18]Huram, through his servants, sent him ships and crewmen acquainted with the sea, who accompanied Solomon's servants to Ophir and brought back from there four hundred and fifty talents of gold to King Solomon.

9 [1]WHEN the queen of Sheba heard of Solomon's fame, she came to Jerusalem to test him with subtle questions, accompanied by a very numerous retinue and by camels bearing spices, much gold, and precious stones. She came to Solomon and questioned him on every subject in which she was interested. [2]Solomon explained to her everything she asked about, and there remained nothing hidden from Solomon that he could not explain to her.

[3]When the queen of Sheba witnessed Solomon's wisdom, the palace he had built, [4]the food at his table, the seating of his ministers, the attendance of his servants and their dress, his cupbearers and their dress, and the holocausts he offered in the house of the LORD, it took her breath away. [5]"The account I heard in my country about your deeds and your wisdom is true," she told the king. [6]"Yet I did not believe the report until I came and saw with my own eyes. I have discovered that they did not tell me the half of your great wisdom; you have surpassed the stories I heard. [7]Happy are your men, happy these servants of yours, who stand before you always and listen to your wisdom. [8]Blessed be the LORD, your God, who has been so pleased with you as to place you on his throne as king for the LORD, your God. Because your God has so loved Israel as to will to make it last forever, he has appointed you over them as king to administer right and justice." [9]Then she gave the king one hundred and twenty gold talents and a very large quantity of spices, as well as precious stones. There was no other spice like that which the queen of Sheba gave to King Solomon.

[10]The servants of Huram and of Solomon who brought gold from Ophir also brought cabinet wood and precious stones. [11]With the cabinet wood the king made stairs for the temple of the LORD and the palace of the king; also lyres and harps for the chanters. The like of these had not been seen before in the land of Judah.

[12]King Solomon gave the queen of Sheba everything she desired and asked him for, more than she had brought to the king. Then she returned to her own country with her servants.

[13]The gold that Solomon received each year weighed six hundred and sixty-six gold talents, [14]in addition to what was collected from travelers and what the merchants brought. All the kings of Arabia also, and the governors of the country, brought gold and silver to Solomon.

[15]Moreover, King Solomon made two hundred large shields of beaten gold, six hundred shekels of beaten gold going into each shield, [16]and three hundred bucklers of beaten gold, three hundred shekels of gold going into each buckler; these the king put in the hall of the Forest of Lebanon.

[17]King Solomon also made a large ivory throne which he overlaid with fine gold. [18]The throne had six steps; a footstool of gold was fastened to it, and there was an arm on each side of the seat, with two lions standing beside the arms. [19]Twelve other lions also stood there, one on either side of each step. Nothing like this had ever been produced in any other kingdom. [20]Furthermore, all of King Solomon's drinking vessels were of gold, and all the utensils in the hall of the Forest of Lebanon were of pure gold; silver was not considered of value in Solomon's time. [21]For the king had ships that went to Tarshish with the servants of Huram. Once every three years the fleet of Tarshish would return with a cargo of gold and silver, ivory, apes and monkeys. [22]Thus King Solomon surpassed all the other kings of the earth in riches as well as in wisdom.

[23]All the kings of the earth sought audience with Solomon, to hear from him the wisdom which God had put in his heart. [24]Year in and year out, each one would bring his tribute—silver and gold articles, garments, weapons, spices, horses and mules. [25]Solomon also had four thousand stalls of horses, chariots, and twelve thousand horsemen, which he assigned to the chariot cities and to the king in Jerusalem. [26]He was ruler over all the kings from the River to the land of the Philistines and down to the border of Egypt. [27]The king made silver as common in Jerusalem as stones, while cedars became as numerous as the sycamores of the foothills. [28]†Horses were imported for Solomon from Egypt and from all the lands.

The Death of Solomon

[29]The rest of the acts of Solomon, first and last, are written, as is well known, in the acts of Nathan the prophet, in the prophecy of Ahijah the Shilonite, and in the visions of Iddo the seer which concern Jeroboam, son of Nebat. [30]Solomon reigned in Jerusalem over all Israel for forty years. [31]He rested with his ancestors; he was buried in his father's City of David, and his son Rehoboam succeeded him as king.

17: 1 Kgs 9, 26; Mt 12, 42;
Lk 11, 31.
18: 1 Kgs 9, 27f.

9/1: 1 Kgs 10, 1f; Mt 12,
42; Lk 11, 31.
13-28: 1 Kgs 10, 14-28.
29ff: 1 Kgs 11, 41ff.

†
9, 28: See note on 1, 16f.

II: THE MONARCHY BEFORE HEZEKIAH

Division of the Kingdom

10 [1]*†REHOBOAM WENT TO SHECHEM, for all Israel had come to Shechem to proclaim him king. [2]When Jeroboam, son of Nebat, heard of this in Egypt where he had fled from King Solomon, he returned from Egypt. [3]Jeroboam was summoned to the assembly, and he and all Israel said to Rehoboam: [4]"Your father laid a heavy yoke upon us. If you now lighten the harsh service and the heavy yoke that your father imposed on us, we will serve you." [5]"In three days," he answered them, "come back to me."

When the people had departed, [6]King Rehoboam consulted the elders who had been in the service of his father during Solomon's lifetime, asking, "What answer do you advise me to give this people?" [7]They replied, "If you will deal kindly with this people and give in to them, acceding to their request, they will be your servants forever." [8]But he ignored the advice the elders had given him and consulted the young men who had grown up with him and were in his service. [9]He said to them, "What answer do you advise me to give this people, who have asked me to lighten the yoke my father imposed on them?" [10]The young men who had grown up with him replied: "This is the answer you should give to this people who have said to you, 'Your father laid a heavy yoke upon us, but do you lighten our yoke'; this you should say to them: 'My little finger is thicker than my father's body. [11]Whereas my father put a heavy yoke on you, I will make it heavier! My father beat you with whips, but I will beat you with scorpions!'"

[12]On the third day, Jeroboam and all the people came back to King Rehoboam as he had instructed them to do. [13]Ignoring the advice the elders had given him, the king gave them a harsh answer, [14]speaking to them according to the advice of the young men: "My father laid a heavy yoke on you, but I will make it heavier. My father beat you with whips, but I will beat you with scorpions." [15]*The king would not listen to the people, for this turn of events was divinely ordained to fulfill the prophecy the LORD had uttered to Jeroboam, the son of Nebat, through Ahijah the Shilonite.

[16]*When all Israel saw that the king would not listen to them, the people answered the king,

"What share have we in David?
We have no heritage in the son of Jesse.
Everyone to your tents, O Israel!
Now look to your own house, David!"

So all Israel went off to their tents. [17]Rehoboam, therefore, reigned over only those Israelites who lived in the cities of Judah. [18]King Rehoboam then sent out Hadoram, who was superintendent of the forced labor, but the Israelites stoned him to death. Rehoboam himself managed to mount his chariot and flee to Jerusalem. [19]Thus Israel has been in rebellion against David's house to this day.

11 [1]*ON his arrival in Jerusalem Rehoboam gathered together the house of Judah and Benjamin, a hundred and eighty thousand seasoned warriors, to have them fight against Israel and restore the kingdom to him. [2]However, the word of the LORD came to Shemaiah, a man of God: [3]"Say to Rehoboam, son of Solomon, king of Judah, and to all the Israelites in Judah and Benjamin: [4]'Thus says the LORD: You must not march out to fight against your brothers. Let every man return home, for what has occurred I have brought about.'" They obeyed this message of the LORD and gave up the expedition against Jeroboam.

Rehoboam's Works

[5]†Rehoboam took up residence in Jerusalem and built fortified cities in Judah. [6]He built up Bethlehem, Etam, Tekoa, [7]Beth-zur, Soco, Adullam, [8]Gath, Mareshah, Ziph, [9]Adoraim, Lachish, Azekah, [10]Zorah, Aijalon, and Hebron; these were fortified cities in Judah and Benjamin. [11]Then he strengthened the fortifications and put commanders in them, with supplies of food, oil and wine. [12]In every city were shields and spears, and he made them very strong. Thus Judah and Benjamin remained his.

Refugees from the North

[13]Now the priests and Levites throughout Israel presented themselves to him from all parts of their land, [14]*for the Levites left their assigned pasture lands and their holdings and came to Judah and Jerusalem, because Jeroboam and his sons repudiated them as priests of the LORD. [15]*In their place, he himself appointed priests for the high places and satyrs and calves he had made. [16]After them, all those of the Israelite tribes who firmly desired to seek the LORD, the God of Israel, came to Jerusalem to sacrifice to the LORD, the God of their fathers. [17]Thus they strengthened the kingdom of Judah and made Rehoboam, son of Solomon, prevail for three years; for they walked in the way of David and Solomon three years.

Rehoboam's Family

[18]Rehoboam took to himself as wife Mahalath, daughter of Jerimoth, son of David and of Abihail,

10/1-14: 1 Kgs 12, 1-14.
　15: 1 Kgs 11, 29-39; 12, 15.
16-19: 1 Kgs 12, 16-19.
11/1-4: 1 Kgs 12, 21-24.
　14: 1 Kgs 12, 32.
　15: 1 Kgs 12, 32; Lv 17, 7.

† 10, 1: *All Israel:* as in the original source (1 Kgs 12, 1), the northern tribes, distinct from Judah and Benjamin. Contrast the Chronicler's own terms, *those Israelites who lived in the cities of Judah* (v 17), and *all the Israelites* [literally, all Israel] *in Judah and Benjamin* (11, 3).

11, 5-12: These verses, though not found in 1 Kgs, are apparently based on a reliable, ancient source.

daughter of Eliab, son of Jesse. **19**She bore him sons: Jehush, Shemariah and Zaham. **20***After her, he married Maacah, daughter of Absalom, who bore him Abijah, Attai, Ziza and Shelomith. **21**Rehoboam loved Maacah, daughter of Absalom, more than all his other wives and concubines; he had taken eighteen wives and sixty concubines, and he fathered twenty-eight sons and sixty daughters. **22**Rehoboam constituted Abijah, son of Maacah, commander among his brothers, for he intended to make him king. **23**He acted prudently, distributing various of his sons throughout all the districts of Judah and Benjamin, in all the fortified cities; and he furnished them with copious provisions and sought an abundance of wives for them.

His Apostasy

12 **1***AFTER Rehoboam had consolidated his rule and had become powerful, he abandoned the law of the LORD, he and all Israel with him. **2***Thus it happened that in the fifth year of King Rehoboam, Shishak, king of Egypt, attacked Jerusalem, for they had been unfaithful to the LORD. **3†**He came up with twelve hundred chariots and sixty thousand horsemen, and there was no counting the army that came with him from Egypt—Libyans, Sukkites and Ethiopians. **4**They captured the fortified cities of Judah and came as far as Jerusalem. **5***Then Shemaiah the prophet came to Rehoboam and the commanders of Judah who had gathered at Jerusalem because of Shishak, and said to them: "Thus says the LORD: 'You have abandoned me, and therefore I have abandoned you to the power of Shishak.'"

6However, the commanders of Israel and the king humbled themselves, saying, "The LORD is just." **7**When the LORD saw that they had humbled themselves, the word of the LORD came to Shemaiah: "Because they have humbled themselves, I will not destroy them; I will give them some deliverance, and my wrath shall not be poured out upon Jerusalem through Shishak. **8**But they shall be his servants, that they may know what it is to serve me and what it is to serve earthly kingdoms." **9***Therefore Shishak, king of Egypt, attacked Jerusalem and carried off the treasures of the temple of the LORD and of the king's palace. He took everything, including the gold bucklers that Solomon had made. **10**(To replace them, King Rehoboam made bronze bucklers, which he entrusted to the officers of the guard on duty at the entrance of the royal palace. **11**Whenever the king visited the temple of the LORD, the troops would come bearing them, and then they would return them to the guardroom.) **12**Because he had humbled himself, the anger of the LORD turned from him so that it did not destroy him completely; and in Judah, moreover, good deeds were found.

13*King Rehoboam consolidated his power in Jerusalem and continued to rule; he was forty-one years old when he became king, and he reigned seventeen years in Jerusalem, the city in which, out of all the tribes of Israel, the LORD chose to be honored. Rehoboam's mother was named Naamah, an Ammonite. **14**He did evil, for he had not truly resolved to seek the LORD. **15***The acts of Rehoboam, first and last, are written, as is well known, in the history of Shemaiah the prophet and of Iddo the seer [his family record]. There was war continually between Rehoboam and Jeroboam. **16**Rehoboam rested with his ancestors; he was buried in the City of David. His son Abijah succeeded him as king.

War between Abijah and Jeroboam

13 **1***IN the eighteenth year of King Jeroboam, Abijah became king of Judah; **2**he reigned three years in Jerusalem. His mother was named Michaiah, daughter of Uriel of Gibeah. There was war between Abijah and Jeroboam.

3Abijah joined battle with a force of four hundred thousand picked warriors, while Jeroboam lined up against him in battle with eight hundred thousand picked and valiant warriors. **4†**Abijah stood on Mount Zemaraim, which is in the highlands of Ephraim, and said: "Listen to me, Jeroboam and all Israel! **5**Do you not know that the LORD, the God of Israel, has given the kingdom of Israel to David forever, to him and to his sons, by a covenant made in salt? **6***Yet Jeroboam, son of Nebat, the servant of Solomon, son of David, has stood up and rebelled against his lord! **7**Worthless men, scoundrels, joined him and overcame Rehoboam, son of Solomon, when Rehoboam was young and unthinking, and no match for them. **8**But now, do you think you are a match for the kingdom of the LORD commanded by the sons of David, simply because you are a huge multitude and have with you the golden calves which Jeroboam made you for gods?

9"Have you not expelled the priests of the LORD, the sons of Aaron, and the Levites, and made for yourselves priests like the peoples of foreign lands? Everyone who comes to consecrate himself with a young bull and seven rams becomes a priest of no-gods. **10**But as for us, the LORD is our God, and we have not forsaken him. The priests ministering to the LORD are sons of Aaron, and the Levites also have their offices. **11**They burn holocausts to the LORD and fragrant incense morning after morning and evening after evening; they display the showbread on the pure table, and the lamps of the golden lampstand burn evening after evening; for we observe our duties to the LORD, our God, but you have abandoned him. **12**See, God is with us, at our head, and his priests are here with trumpets to sound the attack against you. Do not

---

✿
 20: 1 Kgs 15, 2.
12/1: 1 Kgs 11, 4; 14, 22.
 2: 1 Kgs 14, 25.
 5: 11, 2.
 9ff: 1 Kgs 14, 25-28.
    13: 1 Kgs 14, 21.
    15f: 1 Kgs 14, 29ff.
    13/1f: 1 Kgs 15, 1f.
    6: 1 Kgs 11, 26.

---

†
 12, 3: *Sukkites:* foreign mercenaries in the Egyptian army.
 13, 4-12: This is a free composition of the Chronicler to show that this was a religious, rather than a political, war.

battle against the LORD, the God of your fathers, O Israelites, for you will not succeed!" ¹³But Jeroboam had an ambush go around them to come at them from the rear; so that while his army faced Judah, his ambush lay behind them. ¹⁴When Judah turned and saw that they had to battle on both fronts, they cried out to the LORD and the priests sounded the trumpets. ¹⁵Then the men of Judah shouted; and when they did so, God defeated Jeroboam and all Israel before Abijah and Judah. ¹⁶The Israelites fled before Judah, and God delivered them into their hands. ¹⁷Abijah and his people inflicted a severe defeat upon them; five hundred thousand picked men of Israel fell slain. ¹⁸The Israelites were subdued on that occasion and the Judahites were victorious because they relied on the LORD, the God of their fathers. ¹⁹Abijah pursued Jeroboam and took cities from him: Bethel and its dependencies, Jeshanah and its dependencies, and Ephron and its dependencies. ²⁰Jeroboam did not regain power during the time of Abijah; the LORD struck him down and he died, ²¹while Abijah continued to grow stronger. He took to himself fourteen wives and fathered twenty-two sons and sixteen daughters.

Death of Abijah

²²*The rest of Abijah's acts, his deeds and his words, are written in the midrash of the prophet Iddo. ²³Abijah rested with his ancestors; they buried him in the City of David. His son Asa succeeded him as king. During his time, ten years of peace began in the land.

Asa the Reformer

14 ¹*ASA did what was good and pleasing to the LORD, his God, ²removing the heathen altars and the high places, breaking to pieces the sacred pillars, and cutting down the sacred poles. ³He commanded Judah to seek the LORD, the God of their fathers, and to observe the law and its commands. ⁴He removed the high places and incense stands from all the cities of Judah, and under him the kingdom had peace. ⁵He built fortified cities in Judah, for the land had peace and no war was waged against him during these years, because the LORD had given him peace. ⁶He said to Judah: "Let us build these cities and surround them with walls, towers, gates and bars. The land is still ours, for we have sought the LORD, our God; we sought him, and he has given us rest on every side." So they built and prospered.

The Ethiopian Invasion

⁷†Asa had an army of three hundred thousand shield- and lance-bearers from Judah, and two hundred and eighty thousand from Benjamin who carried bucklers and were archers, all of them valiant war-

riors. ⁸*Zerah the Ethiopian moved against them with a force of one million men and three hundred chariots, and he came as far as Mareshah. ⁹Asa went out to meet him and set himself in battle array in the valley of Zephathah, near Mareshah. ¹⁰*Asa called upon the LORD, his God, praying: "O LORD, there is none like you to help the powerless against the strong. Help us, O LORD, our God, for we rely on you, and in your name we have come against this multitude. You are the LORD, our God; let no man prevail against you." ¹¹*And so the LORD defeated the Ethiopians before Asa and Judah, and they fled. ¹²Asa and those with him pursued them as far as Gerar, and the Ethiopians fell until there were no survivors, for they were crushed before the LORD and his army, which carried away enormous spoils. ¹³Then the Judahites conquered all the cities around Gerar, for the fear of the LORD was upon them; they despoiled all the cities, for there was much booty in them. ¹⁴They attacked also the tents of the cattle-herders and carried off a great number of sheep and camels. Then they returned to Jerusalem.

Cult Reform

15 ¹UPON Azariah, son of Oded, came the spirit of God. ²*He went forth to meet Asa and said to him: "Hear me, Asa and all Judah and Benjamin! The LORD is with you when you are with him, and if you seek him he will be present to you; but if you abandon him, he will abandon you. ³For a long time Israel had no true God, no priest-teacher and no law, ⁴*but when in their distress they turned to the LORD, the God of Israel, and sought him, he was present to them. ⁵In that former time there was no peace for anyone to go or come, but there were many terrors upon the inhabitants of the lands. ⁶*Nation crushed nation and city crushed city, for God destroyed them by every kind of adversity. ⁷*But as for you, be strong and do not relax, for your work shall be rewarded."

⁸When Asa heard these words and the prophecy [Oded the prophet], he was encouraged to remove the detestable idols from the whole land of Judah and Benjamin and from the cities he had taken in the highlands of Ephraim, and to restore the altar of the LORD which was before the vestibule of the LORD. ⁹Then he convened all Judah and Benjamin, together with those of Ephraim, Manasseh and Simeon who sojourned with them; for many had fled to him from Israel when they saw that the LORD, his God, was with him. ¹⁰†They gathered at Jerusalem in the third month of

---

*
   22f: 12, 15; 1 Kgs 15, 7ff.   11: Pss 20, 7f; 60, 11f.
   14/1f: 33, 15; Ex 23, 24; 34,   15/2: Jer 29, 13f; Hos 3, 4f.
       13; 1 Kgs 15, 11f.   4: Dt 4, 29f.
    8: 16, 8.   6: Is 19, 2.
   10: 32, 8.   7: Is 7, 4; Jer 31, 16.

---

† 14, 7-14: An Ethiopian invasion of Judah is mentioned only in 1 Chronicles. This account may be a legend contrived to show how the pious King Asa was rewarded through divine assistance. There may, however, have been an incursion of nomads from the Negeb at this time; cf vv 13f.

15, 10ff: With this description of a covenant ceremony in the *third month* of a year beginning in the spring, the Chronicler lays a foundation for celebrating the ancient feast of Pentecost (Weeks) as the time for a solemn renewal of the people's covenant with God on Mount Sinai; see Ex 19, 1ff; Lv 23, 16 and the fifteenth year of Asa's reign, **¹¹**and sacrificed to the LORD at that time seven hundred oxen and seven thousand sheep of the booty they had brought. **¹²**They entered into a covenant to seek the LORD, the God of their fathers, with all their heart and soul; **¹³***and everyone who would not seek the LORD, the God of Israel, was to be put to death, whether small or great, whether man or woman. **¹⁴**They swore to the LORD with a loud voice, with shouting and with trumpets and horns. **¹⁵***All Judah rejoiced over the oath, for they had sworn with their whole heart and sought him with complete desire, so that he was present to them. And the LORD gave them rest on every side.

¹⁶*Maacah, the mother of King Asa, he deposed as queen mother because she had made an outrageous object for Asherah; Asa cut this down, smashed it, and burnt it in the Kidron Valley. **¹⁷**Although the high places did not disappear from Israel, yet Asa's heart was undivided as long as he lived. **¹⁸**He brought into the house of God his father's votive offerings and his own: silver, gold, and various utensils. **¹⁹**There was no war until the thirty-fifth year of Asa's reign.

Asa's Infidelity

16 **¹***IN the thirty-sixth year of Asa's reign, Baasha, king of Israel, attacked Judah and fortified Ramah to prevent any communication with Asa, king of Judah. **²**Asa then brought out silver and gold from the treasuries of the temple of the LORD and of the royal palace and sent them to Ben-hadad, king of Aram, who lived in Damascus, with this message: **³**"There is a treaty between you and me, as there was between your father and my father. See, I am sending you silver and gold. Go, break your treaty with Baasha, king of Israel, that he may withdraw from me." **⁴**Ben-hadad agreed to King Asa's request and sent the leaders of his troops against the cities of Israel. They attacked Ijon, Dan, Abelmaim, and all the store cities of Naphtali. **⁵**When Baasha heard of it, he left off fortifying Ramah; he stopped his work. **⁶**Then King Asa commandeered all of Judah to carry away the stone and wood with which Baasha had been fortifying Ramah, and with them he fortified Geba and Mizpah.

⁷†At that time Hanani the seer came to Asa, king of Judah, and said to him: "Because you relied on the king of Aram and did not rely on the LORD, your God, the army of the king of Aram has escaped your hand. **⁸***Were not the Ethiopians and Libyans a vast army, with great numbers of chariots and drivers? And yet, because you relied on the LORD, he delivered them into your power. **⁹***The eyes of the LORD roam over the whole earth, to encourage those who are devoted to him wholeheartedly. You have acted foolishly in this

matter, for from now on you will have wars." **¹⁰**But Asa became angry with the seer and imprisoned him in the stocks, so greatly was he enraged at him over this. Asa also oppressed some of his people at this time.

¹¹*Now the acts of Asa, first and last, can be found recorded in the book of the kings of Judah and Israel. **¹²**In the thirty-ninth year of his reign, Asa contracted a serious disease in his feet. But even in his sickness he did not seek the LORD, but only the physicians. **¹³**Asa rested with his ancestors; he died in the forty-first year of his reign. **¹⁴**They buried him in the tomb he had hewn for himself in the City of David, having laid him upon a couch which was filled with spices and various kinds of aromatics compounded into an ointment. They also burned a very great funeral pyre for him.

Zeal of Jehoshaphat for the Law

17 **¹***HIS son Jehoshaphat succeeded him as king and strengthened his hold against Israel. **²**He placed armed forces in all the fortified cities of Judah, and put garrisons in the land of Judah and in the cities of Ephraim which his father Asa had taken. **³†**The LORD was with Jehoshaphat, for he walked in the ways his father had pursued in the beginning, and he did not consult the Baals. **⁴**Rather, he sought the God of his father and observed his commands, and not the practices of Israel. **⁵**As a result, the LORD made his kingdom secure, and all Judah gave Jehoshaphat gifts, so that he enjoyed great wealth and glory. **⁶***Thus he was encouraged to follow the LORD's ways, and again he removed the high places and the sacred poles from Judah.

⁷In the third year of his reign he sent his leading men, Ben-hail, Obadiah, Zechariah, Nethanel and Micaiah, to teach in the cities of Judah. **⁸***With them he sent the Levites Shemaiah, Nethaniah, Zebadiah, Asahel, Shemiramoth, Jehonathan, Adonijah and Tobijah, together with the priests Elishama and Jehoram. **⁹***They taught in Judah, having with them the book containing the law of the LORD; they traveled through all the cities of Judah and taught among the people.

His Power

¹⁰Now the fear of the LORD was upon all the kingdoms of the countries surrounding Judah, so that they did not war against Jehoshaphat. **¹¹**Some of the Philistines brought Jehoshaphat gifts and a tribute of silver; and the Arabs also brought him a flock of seven thousand seven hundred rams and seven thousand seven hundred he-goats.

---

the note there. This is also the background for Pentecost as the "birthday of the Church."

16, 7: *The king of Aram . . . escaped:* according to the Lucianic recension, "the king of Israel escaped": this may well be the original reading; Asa was friendly with Aram.

17, 3: *The Lord was with Jehoshaphat:* along with Hezekiah and Josiah, Jehoshaphat was one of the Chronicler's favorite kings.

✷
13: Neh 10, 30.
15: Dt 4, 29.
16ff: 1 Kgs 15, 13ff.
16/1-6: 1 Kgs 15, 16-21.
8: 14, 8-14.
9: Ps 33, 13ff.

11-14: 1 Kgs 15, 23f.
17/1: 1 Kgs 15, 24.
6: 20, 33; Ex 34, 13.
8: 19, 8.
9: Ezr 7, 25.

¹²Jehoshaphat grew steadily greater. He built strongholds and store cities in Judah. ¹³He carried out many works in the cities of Judah, and he had soldiers, valiant warriors, in Jerusalem. ¹⁴This was their mustering according to their ancestral houses. Of Judah, the commanders of thousands: Adnah the commander, and with him three hundred thousand valiant warriors. ¹⁵Next to him, Jehohanan the commander, and with him two hundred eighty thousand. ¹⁶Next to him, Amasiah, son of Zichri, who offered himself to the LORD, and with him two hundred thousand valiant warriors. ¹⁷From Benjamin: Eliada, a valiant warrior, and with him two hundred thousand armed with bow and buckler. ¹⁸Next to him, Jozabad, and with him one hundred and eighty thousand equipped for war. ¹⁹These were at the service of the king; in addition were those whom the king had placed in the fortified cities throughout all Judah.

Alliance with Israel

18 ¹*JEHOSHAPHAT therefore had wealth and glory in abundance; but he became related to Ahab by marriage. ²After some years he went down to Ahab at Samaria; Ahab offered numerous sheep and oxen for him and the people with him, and persuaded him to go up against Ramoth-gilead. ³Ahab, king of Israel, asked Jehoshaphat, king of Judah, "Will you come with me to Ramoth-gilead?" "You and I are as one," was his answer; "your people and my people as well. We will be with you in the battle." ⁴But Jehoshaphat also said to the king of Israel, "Seek the word of the LORD at once."

The Prophets

⁵The king of Israel gathered his prophets, four hundred in number, and asked them, "Shall we go to attack Ramoth-gilead, or shall I refrain?" "Go up," they answered. "God will deliver it over to the king." ⁶But Jehoshaphat said, "Is there no other prophet of the LORD here whom we may consult?" ⁷The king of Israel answered Jehoshaphat, "There is still another through whom we may consult the LORD, but I hate him, for he prophesies not good but always evil about me. That is Micaiah, son of Imlah." Jehoshaphat said, "Let not your Majesty speak of evil against you." ⁸So the king of Israel called an official, to whom he said, "Get Micaiah, son of Imlah, at once." ⁹The king of Israel and King Jehoshaphat of Judah were seated each on his throne, clothed in their robes of state on a threshing floor at the entrance of the gate of Samaria, and all the prophets were prophesying before them.

¹⁰Zedekiah, son of Chenaanah, made iron horns for himself and said: "The LORD says, 'With these you shall gore Aram until you have destroyed them.'" ¹¹The other prophets prophesied in the same vein, saying: "Go up to Ramoth-gilead. You shall succeed; the LORD will deliver it over to the king." ¹²†The messenger who had gone to call Micaiah said to him: "Look now, the prophets unanimously predict good for the king. Let your word, like each of theirs, predict good." ¹³"As the LORD lives," Micaiah answered, "I will say what my God tells me."

¹⁴When he came to the king, the king said to him, "Micaiah, shall we go to fight against Ramoth-gilead, or shall I refrain?" "Go up," he answered, "and succeed; they will be delivered into your power." ¹⁵But the king said to him, "How many times must I adjure you to tell me nothing but the truth in the name of the LORD?" ¹⁶Then Micaiah answered:

"I see all Israel
    scattered on the mountains,
    like sheep without a shepherd,
    and the LORD saying, 'These have no master!
    Let each of them go back home in peace.'"

¹⁷The king of Israel said to Jehoshaphat, "Did I not tell you that he prophesies no good about me, but only evil?" ¹⁸But Micaiah continued:

"Therefore hear the word of the LORD: I saw the LORD seated on his throne, with the whole host of heaven standing by to his right and to his left. ¹⁹The LORD asked, 'Who will deceive Ahab, king of Israel, so that he will go up and fall at Ramoth-gilead?' And one said this, another that, ²⁰until a spirit came forward and presented himself to the LORD saying, 'I will deceive him.' The LORD asked, 'How?' ²¹He answered, 'I will go forth and become a lying spirit in the mouths of all his prophets.' The LORD agreed: 'You shall succeed in deceiving him. Go forth and do this.' ²²So now the LORD has put a lying spirit in the mouths of these your prophets, but the LORD himself has decreed evil against you."

²³Thereupon Zedekiah, son of Chenaanah, came up and slapped Micaiah on the cheek, saying, "Which way did the spirit of the LORD go when he left me to speak to you?" ²⁴"You shall find out," Micaiah replied, "on that day when you enter an innermost chamber to hide." ²⁵The king of Israel then said: "Seize Micaiah and take him back to Amon, prefect of the city, and to Joash the king's son, ²⁶and say, 'This is the king's order: Put this man in prison and feed him scanty rations of bread and water until I return in safety!'" ²⁷†But Micaiah said, "If ever you return in safety, the LORD has not spoken through me." And he said, "Hear, O peoples, all of you!"

Ahab's Death

²⁸The king of Israel and King Jehoshaphat of Judah went up to Ramoth-gilead ²⁹and the king of Israel said to Jehoshaphat, "I will go into battle disguised, but you put on your own clothes." So the king of Israel dis-

---

† 18, 12-22: See note on 1 Kgs 22, 19-23.
  18, 27: "Hear, O peoples, all of you!": this quotation, which appears in some texts of 1 Kgs 22, 28, ascribes to the prophet Micaiah ben Imlah the opening words of the prophetic utterance of Micah of Moresheth (Mi 1, 2), a century later.

guised himself and they entered the fray. ³⁰Meanwhile, the king of Aram had given his chariot commanders the order, "Fight with no one, small or great, except the king of Israel." ³¹When the commanders saw Jehoshaphat, they exclaimed, "That must be the king of Israel!" and shifted to fight him. But Jehoshaphat cried out and the LORD helped him; God induced them to leave him. ³²The chariot commanders became aware that he was not the king of Israel and gave up their pursuit of him. ³³*Someone, however, drew his bow at random and hit the king of Israel between the joints of his breastplate. He ordered his charioteer, "Rein about and take me out of the ranks, for I am disabled." ³⁴The battle grew fierce during the day, and the king of Israel braced himself up on his chariot facing the Arameans until evening. He died as the sun was setting.

Jehoshaphat Rebuked

19 ¹KING Jehoshaphat of Judah returned in safety to his house in Jerusalem. ²†Jehu the seer, son of Hanani, met King Jehoshaphat and said to him: "Should you help the wicked and love those who hate the LORD? For this reason, wrath is upon you from the LORD. ³Yet some good things are to be found in you, since you have removed the sacred poles from the land and have been determined to seek God."

Judges Appointed

⁴Jehoshaphat dwelt in Jerusalem; but he went out again among the people from Beer-sheba to the highlands of Ephraim and brought them back to the LORD, the God of their fathers. ⁵He appointed judges in the land, in all the fortified cities of Judah, city by city, ⁶*and he said to them: "Take care what you do, for you are judging, not on behalf of man, but on behalf of the LORD; he judges with you. ⁷*And now, let the fear of the LORD be upon you. Act carefully, for with the LORD, our God, there is no injustice, no partiality, no bribe-taking." ⁸*In Jerusalem also, Jehoshaphat appointed some Levites and priests and some of the family heads of Israel to judge in the name of the LORD and to settle quarrels among the inhabitants of Jerusalem. ⁹He gave them this command: "You shall act faithfully and wholeheartedly in the fear of the LORD. ¹⁰*And in every dispute that your brethren living in their cities bring to you, whether it concerns bloodguilt or questions of law, command, statutes, or judgments, warn them lest they become guilty before the LORD and his wrath come upon you and your brethren. Do that and you shall be guiltless. ¹¹See now, Amariah is high priest over you in everything that pertains to the LORD, and Zebadiah, son of Ishmael, is leader of the house of Judah in all that pertains to the

king; and the Levites will be your officials. Act firmly, and the LORD will be with the good."

Invasion from Edom

20 ¹†AFTER this the Moabites, the Ammonites, and with them some Meunites came to fight against Jehoshaphat. ²The message was brought to Jehoshaphat: "A great multitude is coming against you from across the sea, from Edom; they are already in Hazazon-tamar" (which is En-gedi). ³Jehoshaphat was frightened, and he hastened to consult the LORD. He proclaimed a fast for all Judah. ⁴*Then Judah gathered to seek help from the LORD; from every one of the cities of Judah they came to seek the LORD.

Prayer of Jehoshaphat

⁵Jehoshaphat stood up in the assembly of Judah and Jerusalem in the house of the LORD before the new court, ⁶*and he said: "LORD, God of our fathers, are you not the God in heaven, and do you not rule over all the kingdoms of the nations? In your hand is power and might, and no one can withstand you. ⁷*Was it not you, our God, who drove out the inhabitants of this land before your people Israel and gave it forever to the descendants of Abraham, your friend? ⁸They have dwelt in it and they built in it a sanctuary to your honor, saying, ⁹'When evil comes upon us, the sword of judgment, or pestilence, or famine, we will stand before this house and before you, for your name is in this house, and we will cry out to you in our affliction, and you will hear and save!' ¹⁰*And now, see the Ammonites, Moabites, and those of Mount Seir whom you did not allow Israel to invade when they came from the land of Egypt, but instead they passed them by and did not destroy them. ¹¹See how they are now repaying us by coming to drive us out of the possession you have given us. ¹²O our God, will you not pass judgment on them? We are powerless before this vast multitude that comes against us. We are at a loss what to do, hence our eyes are turned toward you."

Victory Prophesied

¹³All Judah was standing before the LORD, with their little ones, their wives, and their young sons. ¹⁴And the spirit of the LORD came upon Jahaziel, son of Zechariah, son of Benaiah, son of Jeiel, son of Mattaniah, a Levite of the clan of Asaph, in the midst of the assembly, ¹⁵and he said: "Listen, all of Judah, inhabitants of Jerusalem, and King Jehoshaphat! The LORD says to you: 'Do not fear or lose heart at the sight of this vast

---

†

19, 2: *Jehu the seer, son of Hanani:* hardly the same seer as Jehu, son of Hanani, who prophesied against Baasha almost fifty years earlier (1 Kgs 16, 1).

20, 1-30: Although the account here seems to be a free composition of the Chronicler, there is probably a basis in fact for it; there could well have been a raid of nomads against Judah in the reign of Jehoshaphat, similar to Zerah's attack on Asa (14, 8-14). The story may also, in some way, be connected with the campaign of Israel and Judah against Moab through the territory of Edom (2 Kgs 3, 4-27).

---

*

    33: 35, 23; 1 Kgs 22, 34.   10: Nm 35, 19.
19/6: Dt 1, 16ff; 16, 19f.   20/4: Jer 36, 6; Jb 1, 14.
    7: Dt 10, 17.   6: 32, 7; Dt 4, 39.
    8: 17, 8f; Dt 17, 8-13;   7: Dn 3, 35.
       Ps 122, 3ff.   10: Dt 2, 4f.9f.18f.

multitude, for the battle is not yours but God's. ¹⁶Go down against them tomorrow. You will see them coming up by the ascent of Ziz, and you will come upon them at the end of the wadi which opens on the wilderness of Jeruel. ¹⁷*You will not have to fight in this encounter. Take your places, stand firm, and see how the LORD will be with you to deliver you, Judah and Jerusalem. Do not fear or lose heart. Tomorrow go out to meet them, and the LORD will be with you.' " ¹⁸Then Jehoshaphat knelt down with his face to the ground, and all Judah and the inhabitants of Jerusalem fell down before the LORD in worship. ¹⁹Levites from among the Kohathites and Korahites rose to sing the praises of the LORD, the God of Israel, in a resounding chorus.

The Invaders Destroyed

²⁰*In the early morning they hastened out to the wilderness of Tekoa. As they were going out, Jehoshaphat halted and said: "Listen to me, Judah and inhabitants of Jerusalem! Trust in the LORD, your God, and you will be found firm. Trust in his prophets and you will succeed." ²¹*†After consulting with the people, he appointed some to sing to the LORD and some to praise the holy Appearance as it went forth at the head of the army. They sang: "Give thanks to the LORD, for his mercy endures forever." ²²At the moment they began their jubilant hymn, the LORD laid an ambush against the Ammonites, Moabites, and those of Mount Seir who were coming against Judah, so that they were vanquished. ²³*For the Ammonites and Moabites set upon the inhabitants of Mount Seir and completely exterminated them. And when they had finished with the inhabitants of Seir, they began to destroy each other.

²⁴When Judah came to the watchtower of the desert and looked toward the throng, they saw only corpses fallen on the ground, with no survivors. ²⁵Jehoshaphat and his people came to take plunder, and they found an abundance of cattle and personal property, garments and precious vessels. They took so much that they were unable to carry it all; they were three days taking the spoil, so great was it. ²⁶†On the fourth day they held an assembly in the Valley of Beracah—for there they blessed the LORD; therefore that place has ever since been called the Valley of Beracah. ²⁷Then all the men of Judah and Jerusalem, with Jehoshaphat at their head, turned back toward Jerusalem celebrating the joyful victory the LORD had given them over their enemies. ²⁸They came to Jerusalem, to the house of the LORD, with harps, lyres and trumpets. ²⁹And the fear of God came upon all the kingdoms of the surrounding lands when they heard how the LORD had fought against the enemies of Israel. ³⁰Thereafter Je-

hoshaphat's kingdom enjoyed peace, for his God gave him rest on every side.

Jehoshaphat's Other Deeds

³¹*Thus Jehoshaphat reigned over Judah. He was thirty-five years old when he became king, and he reigned twenty-five years in Jerusalem. His mother was named Azubah, daughter of Shilhi. ³²He followed the path of his father Asa unswervingly, doing what was right in the LORD's sight. ³³But the high places were not removed, nor as yet had the people fixed their hearts on the God of their fathers.

³⁴The rest of the acts of Jehoshaphat, first and last, can be found written in the chronicle of Jehu, son of Hanani, which is inserted in the book of the kings of Israel. ³⁵After this, King Jehoshaphat of Judah allied himself with King Ahaziah of Israel, who did evil. ³⁶*He joined with him in building ships to sail to Tarshish; the fleet was built at Ezion-geber. ³⁷But Eliezer, son of Dodavahu from Mareshah, prophesied against Jehoshaphat, saying, "Because you have joined with Ahaziah, the LORD will shatter your work." And the ships were wrecked and were unable to sail to Tarshish.

21 ¹*JEHOSHAPHAT rested with his ancestors; he was buried with them in the City of David. Jehoram, his son, succeeded him as king. ²His brothers, sons of Jehoshaphat, were Azariah, Jehiel, Zechariah, Azariah, Michael and Shephatiah; all these were sons of King Jehoshaphat of Judah. ³Their father gave them numerous gifts of silver, gold and precious objects, together with fortified cities in Judah, but the kingship he gave to Jehoram because he was the first-born.

Evil Deeds of Jehoram

⁴When Jehoram had come into his father's kingdom and had consolidated his power, he put to the sword all his brothers and also some of the princes of Israel. ⁵*Jehoram was thirty-two years old when he became king, and he reigned eight years in Jerusalem. ⁶†He conducted himself like the kings of Israel of the line of Ahab, because one of Ahab's daughters was his wife. He did evil in the sight of the LORD, ⁷*but the LORD would not destroy the house of David because of the covenant he had made with David and because of his promise to give him and his sons a lamp for all time.

⁸*During his time Edom revolted against the sovereignty of Judah; they chose a king of their own. ⁹Thereupon Jehoram crossed over with his officers and all the chariots he had. He arose by night and

---

17: Is 8, 10.
20: Is 7, 9.
21: Ps 136, 1.
23: Jos 6, 17; Ez 38, 21.
31-34: 1 Kgs 22, 41-45.
36f: 1 Kgs 22, 48f.

21/1: 1 Kgs 22, 51.
5ff: 2 Kgs 8, 17ff.
7: 1 Kgs 11, 36; 2 Kgs 8, 19.
8ff: Gn 27, 40; 2 Kgs 8, 20ff.

† 20, 21: *Holy Appearance:* the Lord, who is with the Israelite army (v 17), manifests himself (the same language is in Ps 29, 2) in bring Israel the victory (Ex 14, 14.24).
20, 26: *Beracah:* the Hebrew word for "blessing."
21, 6: *One of Ahab's daughters:* Athaliah. In 22, 2 (and its source, 2 Kgs 8, 26) she is called Omri's daughter; but this should probably be understood in the sense of granddaughter.

broke through the Edomites when they had surrounded him and the commanders of his chariots. [10]However, Edom has continued in revolt against the sovereignty of Judah down to the present time. Libhah also revolted at that time against Jehoram's sovereignty because he had forsaken the LORD, the God of his fathers. [11]He also set up high places in the mountains of Judah; he led the inhabitants of Jerusalem into idolatry and seduced Judah.

Retribution

[12†]He received a letter from the prophet Elijah with this message: "Thus says the LORD, the God of your ancestor David: 'Because you have not followed the path of your father Jehoshaphat, nor of Asa, king of Judah, [13]but instead have walked in the way of the kings of Israel and have led Judah and the inhabitants of Jerusalem into idolatry, as did the house of Ahab, and also because you have murdered your brothers of your father's house who were better than you, [14]the LORD will strike your people, your children, your wives, and all that is yours with a great plague; [15]and you shall have severe pains from a disease in your bowels, while your bowels issue forth because of the disease, day after day.'"

[16]Then the LORD stirred up against Jehoram the animosity of the Philistines and of the Arabs who bordered on the Ethiopians. [17]They came up against Judah, invaded it, and carried away all the wealth found in the king's palace, along with his sons and his wives; there was left to him only one son, Jehoahaz, his youngest. [18]After these events, the LORD afflicted him with an incurable disease of the bowels. [19]As time went on until a period of two years had elapsed, his bowels issued forth because of the disease and he died in great pain. His people did not make a pyre for him like that of his fathers. [20*]He was thirty-two years old when he became king, and he reigned eight years in Jerusalem. He departed unloved and was buried in the City of David, but not in the tombs of the kings.

Ahaziah

22 [1*]THEN the inhabitants of Jerusalem made Ahaziah, his youngest son, king in his stead, since all the older sons had been slain by the band that had come into the fort with the Arabs. Thus Ahaziah, son of Jehoram, reigned as king of Judah. [2]He was twenty-two years old when he became king, and he reigned one year in Jerusalem. His mother was named Athaliah, daughter of Omri. [3]He, too, followed the ways of the house of Ahab, because his mother counseled him to act sinfully. [4]To his own destruction, he did evil in the sight of the LORD, as did the house of Ahab, since they were his counselors after the death of his father.

[5]He was also following their counsel when he accompanied Jehoram, son of Ahab, king of Israel, to battle against Hazael, king of Aram, at Ramoth-gilead. There Jehoram was wounded by the Arameans. [6]He returned to Jezreel to be healed of the wounds he had received at Rama in his battle against Hazael, king of Aram. Because of this illness, Ahaziah, son of Jehoram, king of Judah, went down to visit Jehoram, son of Ahab, in Jezreel. [7*]Now it was willed by God for Ahaziah's downfall that he should join Jehoram, for after his arrival he rode out with Jehoram to Jehu, son of Nimshi, whom the LORD had anointed to cut down the house of Ahab. [8*]While Jehu was executing judgment on the house of Ahab, he also encountered the princes of Judah and the nephews of Ahaziah who were his attendants, and he slew them. [9*†]Then he looked for Ahaziah himself. They caught him where he was hiding in Samaria and brought him to Jehu, who put him to death. They buried him, for they said, "He was the grandson of Jehoshaphat, who sought the LORD with his whole heart." There remained in Ahaziah's house no one powerful enough to wield the kingship.

Usurpation of Athaliah

[10*]When Athaliah, mother of Ahaziah, learned that her son was dead, she proceeded to kill off all the royal offspring of the house of Judah. [11]But Jehosheba, a royal princess, secretly took Ahaziah's son Joash from among the king's sons who were about to be slain, and put him and his nurse in a bedroom. In this way Jehosheba, who was the daughter of King Jehoram, a sister of Ahaziah, and wife of Jehoiada the priest, hid the child from Athaliah's sight, so that she did not put him to death. [12]For six years he remained hidden with them in the house of God, while Athaliah ruled over the land.

Athaliah Overthrown

23 [1*]IN the seventh year, Jehoiada took courage and entered a conspiracy with certain captains: Azariah, son of Jeroham; Ishmael, son of Jehohanan; Azariah, son of Obed; Masseiah, son of Adaiah; and Elishaphat, son of Zichri. [2]They journeyed about Judah, gathering the Levites from all the cities of Judah and also the heads of the Israelite families. When they had come to Jerusalem, [3]the whole assembly made a covenant with the king in the house of God. Jehoiada said to them: "Here is the king's son who must reign, as the LORD promised concerning the sons of David. [4]This is what you must do: a third of your number, both priests and Levites, who come in on the sabbath must guard the thresholds, [5]another third must be at the king's palace, and the

20: 2 Kgs 8, 24.
22/1-6: 2 Kgs 8, 24-29.
7: 2 Kgs 9, 21; 10, 12ff.
8: 2 Kgs 10, 12ff.
9: 2 Kgs 9, 27f.
10ff: 2 Kgs 11, 1f.
23/1-17.19ff: 2 Kgs 11, 4-20.

† 21, 12: *Elijah:* the only mention by the Chronicler of this prophet of the northern kingdom of Israel. It is doubtful that Elijah was still living in the reign of Jehoram of Judah; in any case, the attribution of the letter to him is most likely an imaginative filling out of the narration.

22, 9: This account of the death of Ahaziah of Judah is not derived from 2 Kgs 9, 27f, with which it is at variance.

final third at the Foundation Gate, when all the people will be in the courts of the LORD's temple. ⁶Let no one enter the LORD's house except the priests and those Levites who are ministering. They may enter because they are holy; but all the other people must observe the prescriptions of the LORD. ⁷The Levites shall surround the king on all sides, each with his weapon drawn. Whoever tries to enter the house must be slain. Stay with the king wherever he goes."

⁸*The Levites and all Judah did just as Jehoiada the priest commanded. Each brought his men, those who were to come in on the sabbath as well as those who were to depart on the sabbath, since Jehoiada the priest had not dismissed any of the divisions. ⁹Jehoiada the priest gave the captains the spears, shields and bucklers of King David which were in the house of God. ¹⁰He stationed all the people, each with his spear in hand, from the southern to the northern extremity of the enclosure, around the altar and the temple on the king's behalf. ¹¹Then they brought out the king's son, set the crown and the insignia upon him, and made him king. Jehoiada and his sons anointed him, and they cried, "Long live the king!"

¹²When Athaliah heard the din of the people running and acclaiming the king, she went to the people in the temple of the LORD. ¹³†She looked, and there was the king standing beside his pillar at the entrance, the officers and the trumpeters around him, and all the people of the land rejoicing and blowing trumpets, while the singers with their musical instruments were leading the acclaim. Athaliah tore her garments and cried out, "Treason! treason!" ¹⁴Then Jehoiada the priest sent out the captains who were in command of the army; he said to them: "Take her outside through the ranks, and if anyone tries to follow her, let him die by the sword. For," the priest continued, "you must not put her to death in the LORD's temple." ¹⁵So they seized her, and when she arrived at the entrance to the Horse Gate of the palace, they put her to death there.

¹⁶Then Jehoiada made a covenant between himself and all the people and the king, that they should be the LORD's people. ¹⁷And all the people went to the temple of Baal and tore it down. They smashed its altars and images, and they slew Mattan, the priest of Baal, before the altars. ¹⁸*Then Jehoiada gave the charge of the LORD's temple into the hands of the levitical priests, to whom David had assigned turns in the temple for offering the holocausts of the LORD, as is written in the law of Moses, with rejoicing and song, as David had provided. ¹⁹Moreover, he stationed guards at the gates of the LORD's temple, so that no one unclean in any respect might enter. ²⁰Then he took the captains, the nobles, the rulers among the people, and all the people of the land, and led the king out of the LORD's house. When they had come within the upper gate of the king's house, they seated the king upon the royal throne. ²¹All the people of the land rejoiced and the city was quiet, now that Athaliah had been put to death by the sword.

The Temple Restored

24 ¹*JOASH was seven years old when he became king, and he reigned forty years in Jerusalem. His mother, named Zibiah, was from Beer-sheba. ²Joash did what was pleasing to the LORD as long as Jehoiada the priest lived. ³Jehoiada provided him with two wives, and he became the father of sons and daughters.

⁴After some time, Joash decided to restore the LORD's temple. ⁵†He called together the priests and Levites and said to them: "Go out to all the cities of Judah and collect money from all Israel that you may repair the house of your God over the years. You must hasten this affair." But the Levites did not hasten. ⁶*Then the king summoned Jehoiada, who was in charge, and said to him: "Why have you not required the Levites to bring in from Judah and Jerusalem the tax levied by Moses, the servant of the LORD, and by the assembly of Israel, for the tent of the testimony?" ⁷For the wicked Athaliah and her sons had damaged the house of God and had even turned over to the Baals the dedicated resources of the LORD's temple.

⁸*At the king's command, therefore, they made a chest, which they put outside the gate of the LORD's temple. ⁹*They had it proclaimed throughout Judah and Jerusalem that the tax which Moses, the servant of God, had imposed on Israel in the desert should be brought to the LORD. ¹⁰All the princes and the people rejoiced; they brought what was asked and cast it into the chest until it was filled. ¹¹Whenever the chest was brought to the royal officials by the Levites and they saw that it contained much money, the royal scribe and an overseer for the high priest came, emptied the chest, then took it back and returned it to its place. This they did day after day until they had collected a large sum of money. ¹²Then the king and Jehoiada gave it to the workmen in charge of the labor on the LORD's temple, who hired masons and carpenters to restore the temple, and also iron- and bronze-smiths to repair it. ¹³The workmen labored, and the task of restoration progressed under their hands. They restored the house of God according to its original

---

† 23, 13: *Beside his pillar:* the king had a special place in the eastern gateway of the temple court that contained the altar of holocausts. He occupied this place on feasts and sabbaths at the time of the statutory offerings, or when he made freewill offerings of his own; cf 2 Kgs 11, 4 and also Ez 46, 1-8 for a later reflection of this.

24, 5: *Collect money:* according to 2 Kgs 12, 5, the people themselves brought the money to the temple; it consisted, at least in part, of voluntary contributions. At the time of the Chronicler (see Neh 10, 32) there was a fixed head tax for the upkeep of the temple (2 Chr 34, 9), based on Ex 30, 12-16. This was still in force in New Testament times (Mt 17, 24f).

---

*   8: 2 Kgs 11, 9;   6: Ex 25, 1-9; Neh 10, 33.
        1 Chr 24, 19.   8: 34, 9.
     18: 1 Chr 23, 13.   9: Ex 30, 13.
  24/1-14: 2 Kgs 12, 1-13.

form, and reinforced it. ¹⁴After they had finished, they brought the rest of the money to the king and to Jehoiada, who had it made into utensils for the LORD's temple, utensils for the service and the holocausts, and basins and other gold and silver utensils. They offered holocausts in the LORD's temple continually throughout the lifetime of Jehoiada. ¹⁵Jehoiada lived to a ripe old age; he was a hundred and thirty years old when he died. ¹⁶He was buried in the City of David with the kings, because he had done good in Israel, in particular with respect to God and his temple.

Apostasy of King Joash

¹⁷After the death of Jehoiada, the princes of Judah came and paid homage to the king, and the king then listened to them. ¹⁸*They forsook the temple of the LORD, the God of their fathers, and began to serve the sacred poles and the idols; and because of this crime of theirs, wrath came upon Judah and Jerusalem. ¹⁹Although prophets were sent to them to convert them to the LORD, the people would not listen to their warnings. ²⁰Then the spirit of God possessed Zechariah, son of Jehoiada the priest. He took his stand above the people and said to them: "God says, 'Why are you transgressing the LORD's commands, so that you cannot prosper? Because you have abandoned the LORD, he has abandoned you.'" ²¹But they conspired against him, and at the king's order they stoned him to death in the court of the LORD's temple. ²²Thus King Joash was unmindful of the devotion shown him by Jehoiada, Zechariah's father, and slew his son. And as he was dying, he said, "May the LORD see and avenge."

Retribution

²³*At the turn of the year a force of Arameans came up against Joash. They invaded Judah and Jerusalem, did away with all the princes of the people, and sent all their spoil to the king of Damascus. ²⁴*Though the Aramean force came with few men, the LORD surrendered a very large force into their power, because Judah had abandoned the LORD, the God of their fathers. So punishment was meted out to Joash. ²⁵*After the Arameans had departed from him, leaving him in grievous suffering, his servants conspired against him because of the murder of the son of Jehoiada the priest. They killed him on his sickbed. He was buried in the City of David, but not in the tombs of the kings.

²⁶These conspired against him: Zabad, son of Shimeath from Ammon, and Jehozabad, son of Shimrith from Moab. ²⁷*Of his sons, and the great tribute imposed on him, and of his rebuilding of the house of God, there is a written account in the midrash of the book of the kings. His son Amaziah succeeded him as king.

Campaign in Edom

25 ¹*AMAZIAH was twenty-four years old when he became king, and he reigned twenty-nine years in Jerusalem. His mother, named Jehoaddan, was from Jerusalem. ²He did what was pleasing in the sight of the LORD, though not wholeheartedly. ³After he had strengthened his hold on the kingdom, he slew those of his servants who had killed the king, his father; ⁴*but he did not put their children to death, for he acted according to what is written in the law, in the Book of Moses, as the LORD commanded: "Fathers shall not be put to death for their children, nor children for their fathers; but only for his own guilt shall a man be put to death."

⁵Amaziah mustered Judah and placed them, out of all Judah and Benjamin according to their ancestral houses, under leaders of thousands and of hundreds. When he had counted those of twenty years and over, he found them to be three hundred thousand picked men fit for war, capable of handling lance and shield. ⁶He also hired a hundred thousand valiant warriors from Israel for a hundred talents of silver. ⁷But a man of God came to him and said: 'O king, let not the army of Israel go with you, for the LORD is not with Israel, with any Ephraimite. ⁸Instead, go on your own, strongly prepared for the conflict; otherwise the LORD will defeat you in the face of the enemy. It is God who has the power to reinforce or to defeat." ⁹Amaziah answered the man of God, "But what is to be done about the hundred talents that I paid for the troops of Israel?" The man of God replied, "The LORD can give you much more than that." ¹⁰Amaziah then disbanded the troops that had come to him from Ephraim, and sent them home. They, however, became furiously angry with Judah, and returned home blazing with resentment.

¹¹*Amaziah now assumed command of his army. They proceeded to the Valley of Salt, and there they killed ten thousand men of Seir. ¹²The Judahites also brought back another ten thousand alive, whom they led to the summit of the Rock and then cast down, so that they were all crushed. ¹³Meanwhile, the mercenaries whom Amaziah had dismissed from battle service with him raided the cities of Judah from Samaria to Beth-horon. They killed three thousand of the inhabitants and took away much booty.

Infidelity of Amaziah

¹⁴When Amaziah returned from his conquest of the Edomites he brought back with him the gods of the people of Seir, which he set up as his own gods; he bowed down before them and offered sacrifice to them. ¹⁵Then the anger of the LORD blazed out against Amaziah, and he sent a prophet to him who said: "Why have you had recourse to this people's gods that could not save their own people from your hand?" ¹⁶While he was still speaking, however, the king said to him: "Have you been made the king's counselor? Be silent! Why should it be necessary to kill you?" There-

---

✿

18: Ex 34, 13.
23: 2 Kgs 12, 17f.
24: Dt 32, 30.
25f: 2 Kgs 12, 21f.
27: 2 Kgs 12, 19.22.

25/1-4: 2 Kgs 14, 1-6.
4: Dt 24, 16; 2 Kgs 14, 5f;
Ez 18, 20.
11: 2 Kgs 14, 7.

fore the prophet desisted. "I know, however," he said, "that God has let you take counsel to your own destruction, because you have done this thing and have refused to hear my counsel."

Retribution

17*Having taken counsel, King Amaziah of Judah sent messengers to Joash, son of Jehoahaz, son of Jehu, the king of Israel, saying, "Come, let us meet each other face to face." **18***King Joash of Israel sent this reply to King Amaziah of Judah: "The thistle of the Lebanon sent a message to the cedar of the Lebanon, saying, 'Give your daughter to my son for his wife.' But the wild beasts of the Lebanon passed by and trampled the thistle down. **19**You are thinking, 'See, I have beaten Edom!', and thus ambition makes you proud. Remain at home. Why involve yourself, and Judah with you, in misfortune and failure?" **20**But Amaziah would not listen, for God had determined to hand them over because they had had recourse to the gods of Edom.

21Therefore King Joash of Israel advanced and he and King Amaziah met in battle at Beth-shemesh of Judah. **22**There Judah was defeated by Israel, and all the Judean soldiers fled homeward. **23**King Joash of Israel captured Amaziah, king of Judah, son of Joash, son of Jehoahaz, at Beth-shemesh and brought him to Jerusalem. Then he tore down the wall of Jerusalem from the Ephraim Gate to the Corner Gate, a distance of four hundred cubits. **24**†He took away all the gold and silver and all the vessels he found in the house of God with Obed-edom, together with the treasures of the palace, and hostages as well. Then he returned to Samaria.

25*Amaziah, son of Joash, king of Judah, survived Joash, son of Jehoahaz, king of Israel, by fifteen years. **26**The rest of the acts of Amaziah, first and last, can be found written, as is well known, in the book of the kings of Judah and Israel. **27**Now from the time that Amaziah ceased to follow the Lord, a conspiracy was formed against him in Jerusalem; hence he fled to Lachish. But they pursued him to Lachish and put him to death there. **28**†They brought him back on horses and buried him with his ancestors in the City of Judah.

The Works of Uzziah

26 **1***ALL the people of Judah chose Uzziah, though he was but sixteen years of age, and proclaimed him king to succeed his father Amaziah. **2**He rebuilt Elath and restored it to Judah; this was after King Amaziah had gone to rest with his ancestors. **3**Uzziah was sixteen years old when he became king, and he reigned fifty-two years in Jerusalem. His mother, named Jecoliah, was from Jerusalem. **4**He pleased the Lord, just as his father Amaziah had done.

5*†He was prepared to seek God as long as Zechariah lived, who taught him to fear God; and as long as he sought the Lord, God made him prosper. **6***He went out and fought the Philistines and razed the walls of Gath, Jabneh and Ashdod [and built cities in the district of Ashdod and in Philistia]. **7**God helped him against the Philistines, against the Arabs who dwelt in Gurbaal, and against the Meunites. **8**The Ammonites paid tribute to Uzziah and his fame spread as far as Egypt, for he grew stronger and stronger. **9**Moreover, Uzziah built towers in Jerusalem at the Corner Gate, at the Valley Gate, and at the Angle, and he fortified them. **10**He built towers in the desert and dug numerous cisterns, for he had many cattle. He had plowmen in the foothills and the plains, and vinedressers in the highlands and the garden land. He was a lover of the soil.

11Uzziah also had a standing army of fit soldiers divided into bands according to the number in which they were mustered by Jeiel the scribe and Maaseiah the recorder, under the command of Hananiah, one of the king's officials. **12**The entire number of family heads over these valiant warriors was two thousand six hundred, **13**and at their disposal was a mighty army of three hundred seven thousand five hundred fighting men of great valor to help the king against his enemies. **14**Uzziah provided for them—for the entire army—bucklers, lances, helmets, breastplates, bows and slingstones. **15**He also built machines in Jerusalem, devices contrived to stand on the towers and at the angles of the walls to shoot arrows and cast large stones. His fame spread far and wide, and his power was ascribed to the marvelous help he had received.

Pride and Fall

16But after he had become strong, he became proud to his own destruction and broke faith with the Lord, his God. He entered the temple of the Lord to make an offering on the altar of incense. **17**But Azariah the priest, and with him eighty other priests of the Lord, courageous men, followed him. **18***They opposed King Uzziah, saying to him: "It is not for you, Uzziah, to burn incense to the Lord, but for the priests, the sons of Aaron, who have been consecrated for this purpose. Leave the sanctuary, for you have broken faith and no longer have a part in the glory that comes from the Lord God." **19***Uzziah, who was holding a censer for burning the incense, became angry, but at the moment he showed his anger to the priests, while they were looking at him in the house of the Lord beside the altar

---

† 25, 24: *With Obed-edom:* possibly a reference to the priest of an Edomite false worship (cf v 14), if not to a levitical family of gatekeepers; cf 1 Chr 15, 18; 26, 12-15.

25, 28: *The City of Judah:* in the parallel passage of 2 Kgs 14, 20, *the City of David.* The Chronicler is referring, by this term, to the capital of Judah, Jerusalem.

26, 5: *Zechariah:* this person, not otherwise identified, is referred to in language suggesting a pious layman rather than a priest or prophet; cf 29, 1.

---

* 17-24: 2 Kgs 14, 8-14.
  18: Jgs 9, 7-15; 2 Kgs 14, 9.
  25-28: 2 Kgs 14, 17-20.
  26/1-4: 2 Kgs 14, 21f; 15, 1ff.

5: 24, 2.
6: Am 1, 8.
18: Ex 30, 7.
19: Nm 12, 10.

of incense, leprosy broke out on his forehead. **20***Azariah the chief priest and all the other priests examined him, and when they saw that his forehead was leprous, they expelled him from the temple. He himself fled willingly, for the LORD had afflicted him. **21***King Uzziah remained a leper to the day of his death. As a leper he dwelt in a segregated house, for he was excluded from the house of the LORD. Therefore his son Jotham was regent of the palace and ruled the people of the land.

22The prophet Isaiah, son of Amos, wrote the rest of the acts of Uzziah, first and last. **23**Uzziah rested with his ancestors; he was buried with them in the field adjoining the royal cemetery, for they said, "He was a leper." His son Jotham succeeded him as king.

Jotham

27 **1***JOTHAM was twenty-five years old when he became king, and he reigned sixteen years in Jerusalem. His mother was named Jerusa, daughter of Zadok. **2**He pleased the LORD just as his father Uzziah had done, though he did not enter the temple of the LORD; the people, however, continued to act sinfully.

3He built the upper gate of the LORD's house and had much construction done on the wall of Ophel. **4**Moreover, he built cities in the hill country of Judah, and in the forest land he set up fortresses and towers. **5**He fought with the king of the Ammonites and conquered them. That year the Ammonites paid him one hundred talents of silver, together with ten thousand kors of wheat and ten thousand of barley. They brought the same to him also in the second and in the third year. **6**Thus Jotham continued to grow strong because he lived resolutely in the presence of the LORD, his God. **7***The rest of the acts of Jotham, his wars and his activities, can be found written in the book of the kings of Israel and Judah. **8**He was twenty-five years old when he became king, and he reigned sixteen years in Jerusalem. **9**Jotham rested with his ancestors and was buried in the City of David, and his son Ahaz succeeded him as king.

III: REFORMS OF HEZEKIAH AND JOSIAH

Impiety of Ahaz

28 **1***AHAZ WAS TWENTY YEARS OLD when he became king, and he reigned sixteen years in Jerusalem. He did not please the LORD as his forefather David had done, **2**but conducted himself like the kings of Israel and even made molten idols of the Baals. **3***Moreover, he offered sacrifice in the

Valley of Ben-hinnom, and immolated his sons by fire according to the abominable practice of the nations which the LORD had cleared out before the Israelites. **4**He offered sacrifice and incense on the high places, on hills, and under every leafy tree.

Retribution

5*Therefore the LORD, his God, delivered him into the power of the king of Aram. The Arameans defeated him and carried away captive a large number of his people, whom they brought to Damascus. He was also delivered into the power of the king of Israel, who defeated him with great slaughter. **6**For Pekah, son of Remaliah, slew one hundred and twenty thousand of Judah in a single day, all of them valiant men, because they had abandoned the LORD, the God of their fathers. **7**Zichri, an Ephraimite warrior, killed Maaseiah, the king's son, and Azrikam, the master of the palace, and also Elkanah, who was second to the king. **8**The Israelites took away as captives two hundred thousand of their brethren's wives, sons and daughters; they also took from them much plunder, which they brought to Samaria.

The Prophecy of Oded

9In Samaria there was a prophet of the LORD by the name of Oded. He went out to meet the army returning to Samaria and said to them: "It was because the LORD, the God of your fathers, was angry with Judah that he delivered them into your hands. You, however, have slaughtered them with a fury that has reached up to heaven. **10**And now you are planning to make the children of Judah and Jerusalem your slaves and bondwomen. Are not you yourselves, therefore, guilty of a crime against the LORD, your God? **11**Now listen to me: send back the captives you have carried off from among your brethren, for the burning anger of the LORD is upon you."

12At this, some of the Ephraimite leaders, Azariah, son of Johanan, Berechiah, son of Meshillemoth, Jehizkiah, son of Shallum, and Amasa, son of Hadlai, themselves stood up in opposition to those who had returned from the war. **13**They said to them: "Do not bring the captives here, for what you propose will make us guilty before the LORD and increase our sins and our guilt. Our guilt is already great, and there is a burning anger upon Israel." **14**Therefore the soldiers left their captives and the plunder before the princes and the whole assembly. **15***Then the men just named proceeded to help the captives. All of them who were naked they clothed from the booty; they clothed them, put sandals on their feet, gave them food and drink, anointed them, and all who were weak they set on asses. They brought them to Jericho, the city of palms, to their brethren. Then they returned to Samaria.

Further Sins of Ahaz

16*At that time King Ahaz sent an appeal for help to the kings of Assyria. **17***The Edomites had returned, attacked Judah, and carried off captives. **18**The Philis-

---

❋

21ff: 2 Kgs 15, 5ff; Lv 13, 46; Nm 19, 20.
27/1-3: 2 Kgs 15, 32-35.
7-9: 2 Kgs 15, 36ff.
28/1-4: 2 Kgs 16, 1-4.

3: 2 Kgs 16, 3; Lv 18, 21.
5: 2 Kgs 16, 5; Is 7, 1-9.
15: Lk 10, 25-37.
16: 2 Kgs 16, 7.
17: 2 Kgs 16, 6.

tines too had raided the cities of the foothills and the Negeb of Judah; they captured Beth-shemesh, Aijalon, Gederoth, Soco and its dependencies, Timnah and its dependencies, and Gimzo and its dependencies, and occupid them. ¹⁹†For the LORD had brought Judah low because of Ahaz, king of Israel, who let Judah go its own way and proved utterly faithless to the LORD. ²⁰*Tilgath-pilneser, king of Assyria, did indeed come to him, but to oppress him rather than to help him. ²¹*Though Ahaz plundered the LORD's house and the houses of the king and the princes to make payment to the king of Assyria, it availed him nothing.

²²While he was already in distress, the same King Ahaz became even more unfaithful to the LORD. ²³*He sacrificed to the gods of Damascus who had defeated him, saying, "Since it was the gods of the kings of Aram who helped them, I will sacrifice to them that they may help me also." However, they only caused further disaster to him and to all Israel. ²⁴*Ahaz gathered up the utensils of God's house and broke them in pieces. He closed the doors of the LORD's house and had altars made for himself in every corner of Jerusalem. ²⁵In every city throughout Judah he set up high places to offer sacrifice to other gods. Thus he angered the LORD, the God of his fathers.

²⁶*The rest of his deeds and his activities, first and last, can be found written in the book of the kings of Judah and Israel. ²⁷Ahaz rested with his ancestors and was buried in Jerusalem—in the city, for they did not bring him to the tombs of the kings of Israel. His son Hezekiah succeeded him as king.

Reforms of Hezekiah

29 ¹*HEZEKIAH was twenty-five years old when he became king, and he reigned twenty-nine years in Jerusalem. His mother was named Abia, daughter of Zechariah. ²He pleased the LORD just as his forefather David had done. ³*It was he who, in the first month of the first year of his reign, opened the doors of the LORD's house and repaired them. ⁴He summoned the priests and Levites, gathered them in the open space to the east, ⁵and said to them: "Listen to me, you Levites! Sanctify yourselves now and sanctify the house of the LORD, the God of your fathers, and clean out the filth from the sanctuary. ⁶Our fathers acted faithlessly and did evil in the eyes of the LORD, our God. They abandoned him, turned away their faces from the LORD's dwelling, and turned their backs on him. ⁷*They also closed the doors of the vestibule, extinguished the lamps, and refused to burn incense and offer holocausts in the sanctuary to the honor of the God of Israel. ⁸*Therefore the anger of the LORD has come upon Judah and Jerusalem; he has made them an object of terror, astonishment and mockery, as you see with your own eyes. ⁹For our fa-

thers, as you know, fell by the sword, and our sons, our daughters and our wives have been taken captive because of this. ¹⁰Now, I intend to make a covenant with the LORD, the God of Israel, that his burning anger may withdraw from us. ¹¹My sons, be not negligent any longer, for it is you whom the LORD has chosen to stand before him, to minister to him, to be his ministers and to offer incense."

¹²Then the Levites arose: Mahath, son of Amasai, and Joel, son of Azariah, descendants of the Kohathites; of the sons of Merari: Kish, son of Abdi, and Azariah, son of Jehallel; of the Gershonites: Joah, son of Zimmah, and Eden, son of Joah; ¹³of the sons of Elizaphan: Shimri and Jeuel; of the sons of Asaph: Zechariah and Mattaniah; ¹⁴of the sons of Heman: Jehuel and Shimei; of the sons of Jeduthun: Shemiah and Uzziel. ¹⁵They gathered their brethren together and sanctified themselves; then they came as the king had ordered, to cleanse the LORD's house in keeping with his words.

¹⁶The priests entered the interior of the LORD's house to cleanse it; and whatever they found in the LORD's temple that was unclean they brought out to the court of the LORD's house, where the Levites took it from them and carried it out to the Kidron Valley. ¹⁷They began the work of consecration on the first day of the first month, and on the eighth day of the month they arrived at the vestibule of the LORD; they consecrated the LORD's house during eight days, and on the sixteenth day of the first month, they had finished.

¹⁸Then they went inside to King Hezekiah and said: "We have cleansed the entire house of the LORD, the altar of holocausts with all its utensils, and the table for the showbread with all its utensils. ¹⁹All the articles which King Ahaz during his reign had thrown away because of his apostasy, we have restored and consecrated, and they are now before the LORD's altar."

The Rite of Expiation

²⁰Then King Hezekiah hastened to convoke the princes of the city and went up to the LORD's house. ²¹Seven bulls, seven rams, seven lambs and seven he-goats were brought for a sin offering for the kingdom, for the sanctuary, and for Judah, and he ordered the sons of Aaron, the priests, to offer them on the altar of the LORD. ²²They slaughtered the bulls, and the priests collected the blood and cast it on the altar. Then they slaughtered the rams and cast the blood on the altar; then they slaughtered the lambs and cast the blood on the altar. ²³Then the he-goats for the sin offering were led before the king and the assembly, who laid their hands upon them. ²⁴The priests then slaughtered them and offered their blood on the altar to atone for the sin of all Israel; for "The holocaust and the sin offering," the king had said, "is for all Israel."

²⁵He stationed the Levites in the LORD's house with

20: 2 Kgs 16, 10;   **26f:** 2 Kgs 16, 19f.
Is 7, 17-20; 8, 5-8.   **29/1ff:** 2 Kgs 18, 1ff.
21: 2 Kgs 16, 8.   **3:** 28, 24.
23: 2 Kgs 16, 12f; Is 10, 20.   **7:** 2 Kgs 16, 15.
24: 29, 3; 30, 14;   **8f:** Lv 26, 32f; Dt 28, 25;
2 Kgs 16, 17.   Jer 25, 18.

---

† 28, 19: *Ahaz, king of Israel:* in the period of the divided kingdom the term *king of Israel* would elsewhere mean "king of the northern kingdom of Israel."

cymbals, harps and lyres according to the prescriptions of David, of Gad the king's seer, and of Nathan the prophet; for the prescriptions were from the LORD through his prophets. [26]The Levites were stationed with the instruments of David, and the priests with the trumpets. [27]Then Hezekiah ordered the holocaust to be sacrificed on the altar, and in the same instant that the holocaust began, they also began the song of the LORD, to the accompaniment of the trumpets and the instruments of David, king of Israel. [28]The entire assembly prostrated itself, and they continued to sing the song and to sound the trumpets until the holocaust had been completed. [29]As the holocaust was completed, the king and all who were with him knelt and prostrated themselves. [30]King Hezekiah and the princes then commanded the Levites to sing the praises of the LORD in the words of David and of Asaph the seer. They sang praises till their joy was full, then fell down and prostrated themselves.

[31]Hezekiah now spoke out this command: "You have undertaken a work for the LORD. Approach, and bring forward the sacrifices and thank offerings for the house of the LORD." Then the assembly brought forward the sacrifices and thank offerings and all the holocausts which were free-will offerings. [32]The number of holocausts that the assembly brought forward was seventy oxen, one hundred rams, and two hundred lambs: all of these as a holocaust to the LORD. [33]As consecrated gifts there were six hundred oxen and three thousand sheep. [34]*Since the priests were too few in number to be able to skin all the victims for the holocausts, their brethren the Levites assisted them until the task was completed and the priests had sanctified themselves; the Levites, in fact, were more willing than the priests to sanctify themselves. [35]Also, the holocausts were many, along with the fat of the peace offerings and the libations for the holocausts. Thus the service of the house of the LORD was reestablished. [36]Hezekiah and all the people rejoiced over what God had reestablished for the people, and at how suddenly this had been done.

Invitation to the Passover

30 [1]*HEZEKIAH sent a message to all Israel and Judah, and even wrote letters to Ephraim and Manasseh saying that they should come to the house of the LORD in Jerusalem to celebrate the Passover in honor of the LORD, the God of Israel. [2]*The king, his princes, and the entire assembly in Jerusalem had agreed to celebrate the Passover during the second month, [3]for they could not celebrate it at the time of the restoration: the priests had not sanctified themselves in sufficient numbers, and the people were not gathered at Jerusalem. [4]When this proposal had been approved by the king and the entire assembly, [5]they issued a decree to be proclaimed throughout all Israel from Beer-sheba to Dan, that everyone should come to Jerusalem to celebrate the Passover in honor of the LORD, the God of Israel; for not many had kept it in the manner prescribed. [6]Accordingly the couriers, with the letters written by the king and his princes, traversed all Israel and Judah, and at the king's command they said: "Israelites, return to the LORD, the God of Abraham, Isaac and Israel, that he may return to you, the remnant left from the hands of the Assyrian kings. [7]*Be not like your fathers and your brethren who proved faithless to the LORD, the God of their fathers, so that he delivered them over to desolation, as you yourselves now see. [8]Be not obstinate, as your fathers were; extend your hands to the LORD and come to his sanctuary that he has consecrated forever, and serve the LORD, your God, that he may turn away his burning anger from you. [9]*For when you return to the LORD, your brethren and your children will find mercy with their captors and return to this land; for merciful and compassionate is the LORD, your God, and he will not turn away his face from you if you return to him."

[10]So the couriers passed from city to city in the land of Ephraim and Manasseh and as far as Zebulun, but they were derided and scoffed at. [11]Nevertheless, some from Asher, Manasseh and Zebulun humbled themselves and came to Jerusalem. [12]In Judah, however, the power of God brought it about that the people were of one mind to carry out the command of the king and the princes in accordance with the word of the LORD. [13]Thus many people gathered in Jerusalem to celebrate the feast of Unleavened Bread in the second month; it was a very great assembly.

The Passover Celebrated

[14]*They proceeded to take down the altars that were in Jerusalem; also they removed all the altars of incense and cast them into the Kidron Valley. [15]They slaughtered the Passover on the fourteenth day of the second month. The priests and Levites, touched with shame, sanctified themselves and brought holocausts into the house of the LORD. [16]They stood in the places prescribed for them according to the law of Moses, the man of God. The priests sprinkled the blood given them by the Levites; [17]*for many in the assembly had not sanctified themselves, and the Levites were in charge of slaughtering the Passover victims for all who were unclean and therefore could not consecrate them to the LORD. [18]The greater part of the people, in fact, chiefly from Ephraim, Manasseh, Issachar and Zebulun, had not cleansed themselves. Nevertheless they ate the Passover, contrary to the prescription; for Hezekiah prayed for them, saying, "May the LORD, who is good, grant pardon to [19]everyone who has resolved to seek God, the LORD, the God of his fathers, though he be not clean as holiness requires." [20]The LORD heard Hezekiah and spared the people.

[21]Thus the Israelites who were in Jerusalem celebrated the feast of Unleavened Bread with great rejoicing for seven days, and the Levites and the priests

---

❋
    34: 1 Chr 15, 12.   9: 1 Kgs 8, 50.
30/1: Ex 12, 1-28.   14: 28, 24f.
    2ff: Nm 9, 6-13.   17: 35, 6.
    7: Acts 7, 51.

sang the praises of the Lord day after day with all their strength. ²²Hezekiah spoke encouragingly to all the Levites who had shown themselves well skilled in the service of the Lord. And when they had completed the seven days of festival, slaying peace offerings and singing praises to the Lord, the God of their fathers, ²³the whole assembly agreed to celebrate another seven days. With joy, therefore, they continued the festivity seven days longer. ²⁴King Hezekiah of Judah had contributed a thousand bulls and seven thousand sheep to the assembly, and the princes had contributed to the assembly a thousand bulls and ten thousand sheep. The priests sanctified themselves in great numbers, ²⁵and the whole assembly of Judah rejoiced, together with the priests and Levites and the rest of the assembly that had come from Israel, as well as the sojourners from the land of Israel and those that lived in Judah. ²⁶There was great rejoicing in Jerusalem, for since the days of Solomon, son of David, king of Israel, there had not been the like in the city. ²⁷Then the levitical priests rose and blessed the people; their voice was heard and their prayer reached heaven, God's holy dwelling.

Liturgical Reform

31 ¹*AFTER all this was over, those Israelites who had been present went forth to the cities of Judah and smashed the sacred pillars, cut down the sacred poles, and tore down the high places and altars throughout Judah, Benjamin, Ephraim and Manasseh, until all were destroyed. Then the Israelites returned to their various cities, each to his own possession.

²Hezekiah reestablished the classes of the priests and the Levites according to their former classification, assigning to each priest and Levite his proper service, whether in regard to holocausts or peace offerings, thanksgiving or praise, or ministering in the gates of the encampment of the Lord. ³*From his own wealth the king allotted a portion for holocausts, those of morning and evening and those on sabbaths, new moons and festivals, as prescribed in the law of the Lord. ⁴He also commanded the people living in Jerusalem to provide the support of the priests and Levites, that they might devote themselves entirely to the law of the Lord.

⁵*As soon as the order was promulgated, the Israelites brought, in great quantities, the best of their grain, wine, oil and honey, and all the produce of the fields; they gave a generous tithe of everything. ⁶*Israelites and Judahites living in other cities of Judah also brought in tithes of oxen, sheep, and things that had been consecrated to the Lord, their God; these they

brought in and set out in heaps. ⁷†It was in the third month that they began to establish these heaps, and they completed them in the seventh month. ⁸When Hezekiah and the princes had come and seen the heaps, they blessed the Lord and his people Israel. ⁹Then Hezekiah questioned the priests and the Levites concerning the heaps, ¹⁰*and the priest Azariah, head of the house of Zadoc, answered him, "Since they began to bring the offerings to the house of the Lord, we have eaten to the full and have had much left over, for the Lord has blessed his people. This great supply is what was left over."

¹¹Hezekiah then gave orders that chambers be constructed in the house of the Lord. When this had been done, ¹²the offerings, tithes and consecrated things were deposited there in safekeeping. The overseer of these things was Conaniah the Levite, and his brother Shimei was second in charge. ¹³Jehiel, Azaziah, Nahath, Asahel, Jerimoth, Jozabad, Eliel, Ismachiah, Mahath and Benaiah were supervisors subject to Conaniah and his brother Shimei by appointment of King Hezekiah and of Azariah, the prefect of the house of God. ¹⁴Kore, the son of Imnah, a Levite and the keeper of the eastern gate, was in charge of the free-will gifts made to God; he distributed the offerings made to the Lord and the most holy of the consecrated things. ¹⁵Under him in the priestly cities were Eden, Miniamin, Jeshua, Shemaiah, Amariah and Shecaniah, who faithfully made the distribution to their brethren, great and small alike, according to their classes.

¹⁶*There was also a register by ancestral houses of males thirty years of age and over, for all priests who were eligible to enter the house of the Lord according to the daily rule to fulfill their service in the order of their classes. ¹⁷*The priests were inscribed in their family records according to their ancestral houses, and the Levites of twenty years and over according to their various offices and classes. ¹⁸A distribution was also made to all who were inscribed in the family records, for their little ones, wives, sons and daughters—thus for the entire assembly, since they were to sanctify themselves by sharing faithfully in the consecrated things. ¹⁹The sons of Aaron, the priests who lived on the lands attached to their cities, had in every city men designated by name to distribute portions to every male among the priests and to every Levite listed in the family records.

²⁰This Hezekiah did in all Judah. He did what was good, upright and faithful before the Lord, his God. ²¹*Everything that he undertook, for the service of the house of God or for the law and the commandments, was to do the will of his God. He did this wholeheartedly, and he prospered.

❋
31/1: 34, 3f; 2 Kgs 18, 4.
　　3: 1 Chr 29, 3; Ez 45, 17;
　　　　Nm 28-29.
　　5: Nm 18, 8-24;
　　　　Dt 14, 22f.
　　6: Nm 12, 44-47; 13, 10-
　　　　13.
　10: Lv 25, 19-22.
　16: 1 Chr 23, 3f.
　17: 1 Chr 23, 6-24.
　21: Ps 119, 2f.

† 31, 7: *Third month . . . seventh month:* between the feast of Pentecost and that of Booths, an interval without rain in Palestine, at the end of which the problem of storage (v 11) would become more urgent.

Invasion of Sennacherib

32 **¹***BUT after he had proved his fidelity by such deeds, Sennacherib, king of Assyria, came. He invaded Judah, besieged the fortified cities, and proposed to take them by storm. **²**When Hezekiah saw that Sennacherib was coming with the intention of attacking Jerusalem, **³**he decided in counsel with his princes and warriors to stop the waters of the springs outside the city. When they had pledged him their support, **⁴***a large crowd was gathered which stopped all the springs and also the running stream in the valley nearby. For they said, "Why should the kings of Assyria come and find an abundance of water?" **⁵***He then looked to his defenses: he rebuilt the wall where it was broken down, raised towers upon it, and built another wall outside. He strengthened the Millo of the City of David and had a great number of spears and shields prepared. **⁶**Then he appointed army commanders over the people. He gathered them together in his presence in the open space at the gate of the city and encouragd them with these words: **⁷***"Be brave and steadfast; do not be afraid or dismayed because of the king of Assyria and all the throng that is coming with him, for there is more with us than with him. **⁸***For he has only an arm of flesh, but we have the LORD, our God, to help us and to fight our battles." And the people took confidence from the words of King Hezekiah of Judah.

Threat of Sennacherib

⁹*After this, while Sennacherib, king of Assyria, himself remained at Lachish with all his forces, he sent his officials to Jerusalem with this message for King Hezekiah of Judah, and all the Judahites who were in Jerusalem: **¹⁰**"King Sennacherib of Assyria has this to say: On what are you relying, while you remain under siege in Jerusalem? **¹¹**Has not Hezekiah deceived you, delivering you over to a death of famine and thirst, by his claim that 'the LORD, our God, will save us from the grasp of the king of Assyria'? **¹²**Has not this same Hezekiah removed his high places and altars and commanded Judah and Jerusalem, 'You shall prostrate yourselves before one altar only, and on it alone you shall offer incense'? **¹³**Do you not know what my fathers and I have done to all the peoples of other lands? Were the gods of the nations in those lands able to save their lands from my hand? **¹⁴**Who among all the gods of those nations which my fathers put under the ban was able to save his people from my hand? Will your god, then, be able to save you from my hand?

¹⁵Let not Hezekiah mislead you further and deceive you in any such way. Do not believe him! Since no other god of any other nation or kingdom has been able to save his people from my hand or the hands of my fathers, how much the less shall your god save you from my hand!"

¹⁶His officials said still more against the LORD God and against his servant Hezekiah, **¹⁷***for he had written letters to deride the LORD, the God of Israel, speaking of him in these terms: "As the gods of the nations in other lands have not saved their people from my hand, neither shall Hezekiah's god save his people from my hand." **¹⁸**In a loud voice they shouted in the Judean language to the people of Jerusalem who were on the wall, to frighten and terrify them so that they might capture their city. **¹⁹**They spoke of the God of Israel as though he were one of the gods of the other peoples of the earth, a work of human hands. **²⁰***But because of this, King Hezekiah and the prophet Isaiah, son of Amos, prayed and called out to heaven.

Defeat of Sennacherib

²¹*Then the LORD sent an angel, who destroyed every valiant warrior, leader and commander in the camp of the Assyrian king, so that he had to return shamefaced to his own country. And when he entered the temple of his god, some of his own offspring struck him down there with the sword. **²²**Thus the LORD saved Hezekiah and the inhabitants of Jerusalem from the hand of Sennacherib, king of Assyria, as from every other power; he gave them rest on every side. **²³***Many brought gifts for the LORD to Jerusalem and costly objects for King Hezekiah of Judah, who thereafter was exalted in the eyes of all the nations.

Hezekiah's Other Deeds

²⁴*In those days Hezekiah became mortally ill. He prayed to the LORD, who answered him by giving him a sign. **²⁵**Hezekiah, however, did not then discharge his debt of gratitude, for he had become proud. Therefore anger descended upon him and upon Judah and Jerusalem. **²⁶***But then Hezekiah humbled himself for his pride—both he and the inhabitants of Jerusalem; and therefore the LORD did not vent his anger on them during the time of Hezekiah.

²⁷*Hezekiah possessed very great wealth and glory. He had treasuries made for his silver, gold, precious stones, spices, jewels, and other precious things of all kinds; **²⁸**also storehouses for the harvest of grain, for wine and oil, and barns for the various kinds of cattle and for the flocks. **²⁹**He built cities for himself, and he acquired sheep and oxen in great numbers, for God gave him very great riches. **³⁰***This same Hezekiah stopped the upper outflow of water from Gihon and led it underground westward to the City of David. Hezekiah prospered in all his undertakings. **³¹**Nevertheless, in respect to the ambassadors [princes] sent to him from Babylon to investigate the sign that had occurred in the land, God forsook him to test him, that he might know all that was in his heart.

✿
32/1: 2 Kgs 18, 13.
    4: Is 22, 9.11.
    5: Neh 2, 17f.
    7: 14, 10; 20, 6-12.
    8: Is 31, 3.
    9-20: 2 Kgs 18, 17-37;
        Is 36, 1-22.
    17: 2 Kgs 19, 9-13;
        Is 37, 9-13.
    20: 2 Kgs 19, 14-19;
        Is 37, 14-20.

21: 2 Kgs 19, 35ff;
    Is 37, 36ff.
23: 14, 6.
24: 2 Kgs 20, 1-11;
    Is 38, 1-8.
26.31: 2 Kgs 20, 12-19;
        Is 39, 1-8.
27f: 2 Kgs 20, 13; Is 39, 2.
30: 2 Kgs 20, 20f.

[32]The rest of Hezekiah's acts, including his pious works, can be found written in the Vision of the Prophet Isaiah, son of Amos, and in the book of the kings of Judah and Israel. [33]†Hezekiah rested with his ancestors; he was buried at the approach to the tombs of the descendants of David. All Judah and the inhabitants of Jerusalem paid him honor at his death. His son Manasseh succeeded him as king.

Impiety of Manasseh

33 [1]*MANASSEH was twelve years old when he became king, and he reigned fifty-five years in Jerusalem. [2]He did evil in the sight of the LORD, following the abominable practices of the nations whom the LORD had cleared out of the way of the Israelites. [3]He rebuilt the high places which his father Hezekiah had torn down, erected altars for the Baals, made sacred poles, and prostrated himself before the whole host of heaven and worshiped them. [4]He even built altars in the temple of the LORD, of which the LORD had said, "In Jerusalem shall my name be forever": [5]he built altars to the whole host of heaven in the two courts of the LORD's house. [6]It was he, too, who immolated his sons by fire in the Valley of Ben-hinnom. He practiced augury, divination and magic, and appointed necromancers and diviners of spirits, so that he provoked the LORD with the great evil that he did in his sight. [7]He placed an idol that he had carved in the house of God, of which God had said to David and his son Solomon: "In this house and in Jerusalem which I have chosen from all the tribes of Israel I shall place my name forever. [8]I will not again allow Israel's feet to leave the land which I assigned to your fathers, provided they are careful to observe all that I commanded them, keeping the whole law and the statutes and the ordinances given by Moses." [9]Manasseh misled Judah and the inhabitants of Jerusalem into doing even greater evil than the nations which the LORD had destroyed at the coming of the Israelites. [10]The LORD spoke to Manasseh and his people, but they paid no attention.

His Conversion

[11]*†Therefore the LORD brought against them the army commanders of the Assyrian king; they took Manasseh with hooks, shackled him with chains, and transported him to Babylon. [12]In this distress, he began to appease the LORD, his God. He humbled himself abjectly before the God of his fathers [13]†and prayed to him. The LORD let himself be won over: he heard his prayer and restored him to his kingdom in Jerusalem. Then Manasseh understood that the LORD is indeed God.

[14]Afterward he built an outer wall for the City of David to the west of Gihon in the valley, extending to the Fish Gate and encircling Ophel; he built it very high. He stationed army officers in all the fortified cities of Judah. [15]*He removed the foreign gods and the idol from the LORD's house and all the altars he had built on the mount of the LORD's house and in Jerusalem, and he cast them outside the city. [16]He restored the altar of the LORD, and sacrificed on it peace offerings and thank offerings, and commanded Judah to serve the LORD, the God of Israel. [17]Though the people continued to sacrifice on the high places, they now did so to the LORD, their God.

[18]*The rest of the acts of Manasseh, his prayer to his God, and the words of the seers who spoke to him in the name of the LORD, the God of Israel, can be found written in the chronicles of the kings of Israel. [19]His prayer and how his supplication was heard, all his sins and his infidelity, the sites where he built high places and erected sacred poles and carved images before he humbled himself, all can be found written down in the history of his seers. [20]Manasseh rested with his ancestors and was buried in his own palace. His son Amon succeeded him as king.

Amon

[21]*Amon was twenty-two years old when he became king, and he reigned two years in Jerusalem. [22]He did evil in the sight of the LORD, just as his father Manasseh had done. Amon offered sacrifice to all the idols which his father Manasseh had made, and worshiped them. [23]Moreover, he did not humble himself before the LORD as his father Manasseh had done; on the contrary, Amon only increased his guilt. [24]His servants conspired against him and put him to death in his own house. [25]But the people of the land slew all those who had conspired against King Amon, and then they, the people of the land, made his son Josiah king in his stead.

Reforms of Josiah

34 [1]*JOSIAH was eight years old when he became king, and he reigned thirty-one years in Jerusalem. [2]He pleased the LORD, following the path of his ancestor David. [3]*†In the eighth year of his reign, while he was still a youth, he began to seek after the God of his forefather David, and in

---

† 32, 33: *The approach to the tombs:* literally, "the ascent of the tombs," which may mean "the upper section of the tombs," their most prominent and honored place.

33, 11: There is no evidence elsewhere for an imprisonment of King Manasseh in Babylon. However, according to the Assyrian inscriptions, he paid tribute to the Assyrian kings Esarhaddon (680-669 B. C.) and Asshurbanipal (668-627 B. C.). He may well have been obliged to go to Nineveh to take the oath of allegiance as vassal to the king of Assyria.

33, 13: *And prayed to him:* these words led an unknown writer to compose the apocryphal "Prayer of Manasseh," which is added as an appendix to many editions of the Vulgate Bible and is used in the public prayers of the church.

34, 3: *In his twelfth year:* c 628 B. C., the year after Asshurbanipal's death, when Judah could free itself from Assyrian domination. From 2 Kgs 22, 1—23, 25 alone, one might think

---

* 33/1-10: 2 Kgs 21, 1-9.   21-25: 2 Kgs 21, 19-26.
    11: Jb 36, 7f; Ez 19, 9.   34/1f: 2 Kgs 22, 1f.
    15: 14, 2.   3-7: 14, 1-4; 31, 1;
    18.20: 2 Kgs 21, 17f.   2 Kgs 23, 4-20.

his twelfth year he began to purge Judah and Jerusalem of the high places, the sacred poles and the carved and molten images. [4]In his presence, the altars of the Baals were destroyed; the incense stands erected above them were torn down; the sacred poles and the carved and molten images were shattered and beaten into dust, which was strewn over the tombs of those who had sacrificed to them; [5]and the bones of the priests he burned upon their altars. Thus he purged Judah and Jerusalem. [6]He did likewise in the cities of Manasseh, Ephraim, Simeon, and in the ruined villages of the surrounding country as far as Naphtali; [7]he destroyed the altars, broke up the sacred poles and carved images and beat them into dust, and tore down the incense stands throughout the land of Israel. Then he returned to Jerusalem.

The Temple Restored

[8]*In the eighteenth year of his reign, in order to cleanse the temple as well as the land, he sent Shaphan, son of Azaliah, Maaseiah, the ruler of the city, and Joah, son of Joahaz, the chamberlain, to restore the house of the Lord, his God. [9]*They came to Hilkiah the high priest and turned over the money brought to the house of God which the Levites, the guardians of the threshold, had collected from Manasseh, Ephraim, and all the remnant of Israel, as well as from all of Judah, Benjamin, and the inhabitants of Jerusalem. [10]They turned it over to the master workmen in the house of the Lord, and these in turn used it to pay the workmen in the Lord's house who were restoring and repairing the temple. [11]They also gave it to the carpenters and the masons to buy hewn stone and timber for the tie beams and rafters of the buildings which the kings of Judah had allowed to fall into ruin. [12]The men worked faithfully at their task; their overseers were Jahath and Obadiah, Levites of the line of Merari, and Zechariah and Meshullam, of the Kohathites, who directed them. All those Levites who were skillful with musical instruments [13]were in charge of the men who carried the burdens, and they directed all the workers in every kind of labor. Some of the other Levites were scribes, officials and gatekeepers.

The Finding of the Law

[14]*When they brought out the money that had been deposited in the house of the Lord, Hilkiah the priest found the book of the law of the Lord given through Moses. [15]He reported this to Shaphan the scribe, saying, "I have found the book of the law in the house of the Lord." [16]Hilkiah gave the book to Shaphan, who brought it to the king at the same time that he was making his report to him. He said, "Your servants are doing everything that has been entrusted to them; [17]they have turned into bullion the metals deposited in the Lord's house and have handed it over to the overseers and the workmen." [18]Then Shaphan the scribe announced to the king, "Hilkiah the priest has given me a book." And Shaphan read from it before the king.

[19]When the king heard the words of the law, he tore his garments [20]and issued this command to Hilkiah, to Ahikam, son of Shaphan, to Abdon, son of Michah, to Shaphan the scribe, and to Asaiah, the king's servant: [21]"On behalf of myself and those who are left in Israel and Judah, go, consult the Lord concerning the words of the book that has been found. For the anger of the Lord has been set furiously ablaze against us, since our fathers have not kept the word of the Lord and have not done all that is written in this book." [22]Then Hilkiah and the other men from the king went to the prophetess Huldah, the wife of Shallum, son of Tokhath, son of Hasrah, the guardian of the wardrobe; she dwelt in Jerusalem, in the new quarter. They spoke to her as they had been instructed, [23]and she said to them: "Thus says the Lord, the God of Israel: 'Tell the one who sent you to me, [24]The Lord says: I am prepared to bring evil upon this place and upon its inhabitants, all the curses written in the book that has been read before the king of Judah. [25]Because they have abandoned me and have offered incense to other gods, provoking me by every deed that they have performed, my anger is ablaze against this place and cannot be extinguished.'

[26]"But to the king of Judah who sent you to consult the Lord, give this response: 'Thus says the Lord, the God of Israel, concerning the threats you have heard: [27]Because you were heartsick and have humbled yourself before God on hearing his words spoken against this place and its inhabitants; because you have humbled yourself before me, have torn your garments, and have wept before me, I in turn have listened—so declares the Lord. [28]I will gather you to your ancestors and you shall be taken to your grave in peace. Your eyes shall not see all the evil I will bring upon this place and upon its inhabitants.'"

They brought back this message to the king.

Renewal of the Covenant

[29]*The king now convened all the elders of Judah and Jerusalem. [30]He went up to the house of the Lord with all the men of Judah and the inhabitants of Jerusalem, the priests, the Levites, and all the people, great and small; and he had read aloud to them the entire text of the book of the covenant that had been found in the house of the Lord. [31]†Standing at his post, the king made a covenant before the Lord to follow the Lord and to keep his commandments, decrees, and statutes with his whole heart and soul, thus observing

---

† that Josiah's reform began only after the discovery of the book of the law in the temple, in the eighteenth year of his reign. But the Chronicler is no doubt right in placing the beginning of the reform at an earlier period. The very repair of the temple, which led to the finding of the book of the law, must have been occasioned by a cultic reform.

34, 31: *Standing at his post:* see note on 23, 13.

*
8-13: 2 Kgs 22, 3-7.   14-28: 2 Kgs 22, 8-20.
9: 24, 8f.   29-32: 2 Kgs 23, 1ff.

the terms of the covenant written in this book. [32]He thereby committed all who were of Jerusalem and Benjamin, and the inhabitants of Jerusalem conformed themselves to the covenant of God, the God of their fathers. [33]*Josiah removed every abominable thing from all the territory belonging to the Israelites, and he obliged all who were in Israel to serve the LORD, their God. During his lifetime they did not desert the LORD, the God of their fathers.

The Passover

35 [1]*JOSIAH celebrated in Jerusalem a Passover to honor the LORD; the Passover sacrifice was slaughtered on the fourteenth day of the first month. [2]He reappointed the priests to their duties and encouraged them in the service of the LORD's house. [3]*He said to the Levites who were to instruct all Israel, and who were consecrated to the LORD: "Put the holy ark in the house built by Solomon, son of David, king of Israel. It shall no longer be a burden on your shoulders. Serve now the LORD, your God, and his people Israel. [4]Prepare yourselves in your ancestral houses and your classes according to the prescriptions of King David of Israel and his son Solomon. [5]*Stand in the sanctuary according to the divisions of the ancestral houses of your brethren, the common people, so that the distribution of the Levites and the families may be the same. [6]*Slay the Passover sacrifice, sanctify yourselves, and be at the disposition of your brethren, that all may be carried out according to the word of the LORD given through Moses."

[7]*Josiah contributed to the common people a flock of lambs and kids, thirty thousand in number, each to serve as a Passover victim for any who were present, and also three thousand oxen; these were from the king's property. [8]*His princes also gave a free-will gift to the people, the priests and the Levites. Hilkiah, Zechariah and Jehiel, prefects of the house of God, gave to the priests two thousand six hundred Passover victims together with three hundred oxen. [9]Conaniah and his brothers Shemaiah, Nethanel, Hashabiah, Jehiel and Jozabad, the rulers of the Levites, contributed to the Levites five thousand Passover victims, together with five hundred oxen.

[10]When the service had been arranged, the priests took their places, as did the Levites in their classes according to the king's command. [11]The Passover sacrifice was slaughtered, whereupon the priests sprinkled some of the blood and the Levites proceeded to the skinning. [12]They separated what was destined for the holocaust and gave it to various groups of the ancestral houses of the common people to offer to the LORD, as is prescribed in the book of Moses. They did the same with the oxen. [13]*They cooked the Passover on the fire as prescribed, and also cooked the sacred meals in pots, caldrons and pans, then brought them quickly to all the common people. [14]Afterward they prepared the Passover for themselves and for the priests. Indeed the priests, the sons of Aaron, were busy offering holocausts and the fatty portions until night; therefore the Levites prepared for themselves and for the priests, the sons of Aaron. [15]The singers, the sons of Asaph, were at their posts as prescribed by David: Asaph, Heman and Jeduthun, the king's seer. The gatekeepers were at every gate; there was no need for them to leave their stations, for their brethren, the Levites, prepared for them. [16]Thus the entire service of the LORD was arranged that day so that the Passover could be celebrated and the holocausts offered on the altar of the LORD, as King Josiah had commanded. [17]The Israelites who were present on that occasion kept the Passover and the feast of the Unleavened Bread for seven days. [18]*No such Passover had been observed in Israel since the time of the prophet Samuel, nor had any king of Israel kept a Passover like that of Josiah, the priests and Levites, all of Judah and Israel that were present, and the inhabitants of Jerusalem. [19]It was in the eighteenth year of Josiah's reign that this Passover was observed.

Josiah's Reign Ends

[20]After Josiah had done all this to restore the temple, Neco, king of Egypt, came up to fight at Carchemish on the Euphrates, and Josiah went out to intercept him. [21]Neco sent messengers to him, saying: "What quarrel is between us, king of Judah? I have not come against you this day, for my war is with another kingdom, and God has told me to hasten. Do not interfere with God who is with me, as otherwise he will destroy you." [22]But Josiah would not withdraw from him, for he had sought a pretext for fighting with him. Therefore he would not listen to the words of Neco that came from the mouth of God, but went out to fight in the plain of Magiddo. [23]*Then the archers shot King Josiah, who said to his servants, "Take me away, for I am seriously wounded." [24]His servants removed him from his own chariot, placed him in another he had in reserve, and brought him to Jerusalem, where he died. He was buried in the tombs of his ancestors, and all Judah and Jerusalem mourned him. [25]†Jeremiah also composed a lamentation over Josiah, which is recited to this day by all the male and female singers in their lamentations over Josiah. These have been made obligatory for Israel, and can be found written in the Lamentations.

[26]*The rest of the chronicle of Josiah, his pious deeds in regard to what is written in the law of the LORD, and his acts, first and last, can be found written in the book of the kings of Israel and Judah.

✼
    33: 2 Kgs 23, 4-20.   7: Ex 12, 5.
35/1-19: 2 Kgs 23, 21ff.   8: Nm 7, 1-83.
     1: Ex 12, 1-28;   13: Nm 12, 8f.
         2 Kgs 23, 21.   18f: 2 Kgs 23, 22f.
     3: 5, 4; 1 Chr 15, 12.15.   23: 18, 33f.
     5: 1 Chr 24—26.   26: 2 Kgs 23, 28.
     6: 30, 17.

†   35, 25: The reference to a *lamentation over Josiah* composed by Jeremiah is not found either in 2 Kgs or Jer; but see note on Zec 12, 11. *Their lamentations:* probably a reference to the canonical Book of Lamentations.

36

1*THE people of the land took Jehoahaz, son of Josiah, and made him king in Jerusalem in his father's stead.

IV: END OF THE KINGDOM

Jehoahaz

2JEHOAHAZ WAS TWENTY-THREE YEARS OLD when he became king, and he reigned three months in Jerusalem. 3The king of Egypt deposed him in Jerusalem and fined the land one hundred talents of silver and a talent of gold. 4Then the king of Egypt made his brother Eliakim king over Judah and Jerusalem, and changed his name to Jehoiakim. Neco took his brother Jehoahaz away and brought him to Egypt.

Jehoiakim

5*Jehoiakim was twenty-five years old when he became king, and he reigned eleven years in Jerusalem. He did evil in the sight of the LORD, his God. 6*†Nebuchadnezzar, king of Babylon, came up against him and bound him with chains to take him to Babylon. 7Nebuchadnezzar also carried away to Babylon some of the vessels of the house of the LORD and put them in his palace in Babylon. 8*The rest of the acts of Jehoiakim, the abominable things that he did, and what therefore happened to him, can be found written in the book of the kings of Israel and Judah. His son Jehoiachin succeeded him as king.

Jehoiachin

9*Jehoiachin was eighteen years old when he became king, and he reigned three months [and ten days] in Jerusalem. He did evil in the sight of the LORD. 10*†At the turn of the year, King Nebuchadnezzar sent for him and had him brought to Babylon, along with precious vessels from the temple of the LORD. He made his brother Zedekiah king over Judah and Jerusalem.

Zedekiah

11*Zedekiah was twenty-one years old when he became king, and he reigned eleven years in Jerusalem. 12*He did evil in the sight of the LORD, his God, and he did not humble himself before the prophet Jeremiah, who spoke the word of the LORD. 13*He also rebelled against King Nebuchadnezzar, who had made him swear by God. He became stiff-necked and hardened his heart rather than return to the LORD, the God of

Israel. 14Likewise all the princes of Judah, the priests and the people added infidelity to infidelity, practicing all the abominations of the nations and polluting the LORD's temple which he had consecrated in Jerusalem.

Dissolution of Judah

15*Early and often did the LORD, the God of their fathers, send his messengers to them, for he had compassion on his people and his dwelling place. 16*But they mocked the messengers of God, despised his warnings, and scoffed at his prophets, until the anger of the LORD against his people was so inflamed that there was no remedy. 17*Then he brought up against them the king of the Chaldeans, who slew their young men in their own sanctuary building, sparing neither young man nor maiden, neither the aged nor the decrepit; he delivered all of them over into his grip. 18*All the utensils of the house of God, the large and the small, and the treasures of the LORD's house and of the king and his princes, all these he brought to Babylon. 19*They burnt the house of God, tore down the walls of Jerusalem, set all its palaces afire, and destroyed all its precious objects. 20Those who escaped the sword he carried captive to Babylon, where they became his and his sons' servants until the kingdom of the Persians came to power. 21All this was to fulfill the word of the LORD spoken by Jeremiah: "Until the land has retrieved its lost sabbaths, during all the time it lies waste it shall have rest while seventy years are fulfilled."

Decree of Cyrus

22*†In the first year of Cyrus, king of Persia, in order to fulfill the word of the LORD spoken by Jeremiah, the LORD inspired King Cyrus of Persia to issue this proclamation throughout his kingdom, both by word of mouth and in writing: 23"Thus says Cyrus, king of Persia: 'All the kingdoms of the earth the LORD, the God of heaven, has given to me, and he has also charged me to build him a house in Jerusalem, which is in Judah. Whoever, therefore, among you belongs to any part of his people, let him go up, and may his God be with him!'"

---

†

36, 6: *Nebuchadnezzar . . . bound him with chains to take him to Babylon:* the Chronicler does not say that Jehoiakim was actually taken to Babylon. According to 2 Kgs 24, 1-6, Jehoiakim revolted after being Nebuchadnezzar's vassal for three years; he died in Jerusalem before the Babylonian king could reach the city. However, Dn 1, 1f, apparently based on 2 Chr 36, 6f, speaks of Jehoiakim's deportation to Babylon.

36, 10: *His brother Zedekiah:* Zedekiah was actually the brother of Jehoiakim and the uncle of *Jehoiachin* (2 Kgs 24, 17; Jer 37, 1), though scarcely older than his nephew (2 Kgs 24, 8.18; 2 Chr 36, 9.11).

36, 22f: The words of these verses are identical with those of Ezr 1, 1-3a. Originally Ezra-Nehemiah formed the last part of the single work of the Chronicler, of which 1 and 2 Chronicles formed the first part. But when Ezra-Nehemiah was regarded as a natural sequence to the Books of Samuel and of Kings, it was separated from 1 and 2 Chronicles and placed before them. Thus, 1 and 2 Chronicles became the last part of the Hebrew Bible. To prevent this work from ending on a note of doom, Ezr 1, 1-3a was repeated as 2 Chr 36, 22f.

---

* 36/1-4: 2 Kgs 23, 30-34;
     1 Chr 3, 15f.
  5: 2 Kgs 23, 36f;
    Jer 22, 18f.
  6: 2 Kgs 24, 1f.
  8: 2 Kgs 24, 5.
  9: 2 Kgs 24, 8f.
  10: 2 Kgs 24, 10-16.
  11: 2 Kgs 24, 18ff;
    Jer 52, 1ff.

12: Jer 37, 1ff.
13: 2 Kgs 25, 1; Jer 52, 4;
    Ez 17, 13-16.
15: Jer 7, 25; Heb 1, 1.
16: Mt 23, 34ff.
17: Lam 1, 15; 5, 11-14.
18: 2 Kgs 25, 14f.
19: 2 Kgs 25, 9f; Lam 2, 8.
22: Ezr 1, 1ff.

The Book of Ezra

Introduction

The last four books of the Hebrew canon are Ezra, Nehemiah, 1 and 2 Chronicles, in that order. Originally, however, Ezra and Nehemiah followed the Books of Chronicles, and formed with them a unified historical work so homogeneous in spirit that one usually speaks of a single author for the four books. He is called "the Chronicler." The treatment of Ezra-Nehemiah as a single book by the earliest chroniclers was undoubtedly due to the fact that in ancient times the two books were put under the one name—Ezra. The combined work Ezra-Nehemiah is our most important literary source for the formation of the Jewish religious community after the Babylonian exile. This is known as the period of the Restoration, and the two men most responsible for the reorganization of Jewish life at this time were Ezra and Nehemiah.

In the present state of the Ezra-Nehemiah text, there are several dislocations of large sections so that the chronological or logical sequence is disrupted. The major instances are pointed out in the footnotes. Although Ezra appears before Nehemiah in this work, it seems probable that Nehemiah's activity preceded his.

What is known of Ezra and his work is due almost exclusively to Ezra 7–10 (the "Ezra Memoirs") and to Neh 8–9. Strictly speaking, the term "Ezra Memoirs" should be used only of that section in which Ezra speaks in the first person, i. e., 7, 27–9, 15. Compare the "Nehemiah Memoirs" in Neh 1, 1–7, 72a; 11, 1f; 12, 27-43; 13, 4-31. The Chronicler combined this material with other sources at his disposal. The personality of Ezra is less known than that of Nehemiah. Ben Sirach, in his praise of the fathers, makes no mention of Ezra. The genealogy of Ezra (7, 1-5) traces his priesthood back to Aaron, brother of Moses. This was the accepted way of establishing the legality of one's priestly office. He is also called *a scribe, well-versed in the law of Moses* (7, 6), indicating Ezra's dedication to the study of the Torah, which he sought to make the basic rule of life in the restored community. It was in religious and cultic reform rather than in political affairs that Ezra made his mark as a postexilic leader. Jewish tradition holds him in great honor; the Talmud even regards him as a second Moses, claiming that the Torah would have been given to Israel through Ezra had not Moses preceded him.

Ezra is sometimes accused of having been a mere legalist who gave excessive attention to the letter of the law. His work, however, should be seen and judged within a specific historical context. He gave to his people a cohesion and spiritual unity which prevented the disintegration of the small Jewish community. Had it not been for the intransigence of Ezra and of those who adopted his ideal, it is doubtful that Judaism would have so effectively resisted Hellenism, then or in later centuries. Ezra set the tone of the postexilic community, and it was characterized by fidelity to the Torah, Judaism's authentic way of life. It is in this light that we can judge most fairly the work of Ezra during the Restoration.

The Book of Ezra is divided as follows:
    I: The Return from Exile (1, 1–6, 22)
    II: The Deeds of Ezra (7, 1–10, 44)

The following list of the kings of Persia, with the dates of their reigns, will be useful for dating the events mentioned in Ezra-Nehemiah:

Cyrus	538-529 B.C.
Cambyses	529-521 B.C.
Darius I	521-485 B.C.
Xerxes	485-464 B.C.
Artaxerxes I	464-423 B.C.
Darius II	423-404 B.C.
Artaxerxes II	404-358 B.C.
Artaxerxes III	358-337 B.C.
End of the Persian Empire (Defeat of Darius III)	331 B.C.

I: THE RETURN FROM EXILE

The Decree of Cyrus

1 ¹*†IN THE FIRST YEAR OF CYRUS, king of Persia, in order to fulfill the word of the LORD spoken by Jeremiah, the LORD inspired King Cyrus of Persia to issue this proclamation throughout his kingdom, both by word of mouth and in writing: ²"Thus says Cyrus, king of Persia: 'All the kingdoms of the earth the LORD, the God of heaven, has given to me, and he has also charged me to build him a house in Jerusalem, which is in Judah. ³Whoever, therefore, among you belongs to any part of his people, let him go up, and may his God be with him! ⁴Let everyone who has survived, in whatever place he may have dwelt, be assisted by the people of that place with silver, gold, goods, and cattle, together with free-will offerings for the house of God in Jerusalem.'"

⁵Then the family heads of Judah and Benjamin and the priests and Levites—everyone, that is, whom God had inspired to do so—prepared to go up to build the house of the LORD in Jerusalem. ⁶*All their neighbors

---

† 1, 1: *In the first year of Cyrus*: as sovereign over the world empire which began with his conquest of Babylon; that is, 538 B.C.

❉ 1/1ff: 36, 22f; Jer 25, 11f; 29, 10; Zec 1, 12.   6: Ex 3, 22; 11, 2; 12, 35.

gave them help in every way, with silver, gold, goods, and cattle, and with many precious gifts besides all their free-will offerings. ⁷King Cyrus, too, had the utensils of the house of the LORD brought forth which Nebuchadnezzar had taken away from Jerusalem and placed in the house of his god. ⁸†Cyrus, king of Persia, had them brought forth by the treasurer Mithredath, and counted out to Sheshbazzar, the prince of Judah. ⁹This was the inventory: sacks of goldware, thirty; sacks of silverware, one thousand and twenty-nine; ¹⁰golden bowls, thirty; silver bowls, four hundred and ten; other ware, one thousand pieces. ¹¹†Total of the gold- and silver-ware: five thousand four hundred pieces. All these Sheshbazzar took with him when the exiles were brought back from Babylon to Jerusalem.

Census of the Province

2 ¹*†THESE are the inhabitants of the province who returned from the captivity of the exiles, whom Nebuchadnezzar, king of Babylon, had carried away to Babylon, and who came back to Jerusalem and Judah, each man in his own city ²(those who returned with Zerubbabel, Jeshua, Nehemiah, Seraiah, Reelaiah, Mordecai, Bilshan, Mispereth, Bigvai, Rehum, and Baanah):

The census of the men of Israel: ³sons of Parosh, two thousand one hundred and seventy-two; ⁴sons of Shephatiah, three hundred and seventy-two; ⁵sons of Arah, seven hundred and seventy-five; ⁶sons of Pahath-moab, who were sons of Jeshua and Joab, two thousand eight hundred and twelve; ⁷sons of Elam, one thousand two hundred and fifty-four; ⁸sons of Zattu, nine hundred and forty-five; ⁹sons of Zaccai, seven hundred and sixty; ¹⁰sons of Bani, six hundred and forty-two; ¹¹sons of Bebai, six hundred and twenty-three; ¹²sons of Azgad, one thousand two hundred and twenty-two; ¹³sons of Adonikam, six hundred and sixty-six; ¹⁴sons of Bigvai, two thousand and fifty-six; ¹⁵sons of Adin, four hundred and fifty-four; ¹⁶sons of Ater, who were sons of Hezekiah, ninety-eight; ¹⁷sons of Bezai, three hundred and twenty-three; ¹⁸sons of Jorah, one hundred and twelve; ¹⁹sons of Hashum, two hundred and twenty-three; ²⁰sons of Gibeon, ninety-five; ²¹sons of Bethlehem, one hundred and twenty-three; ²²men of Netophah, fifty-six; ²³men of Anathoth, one hundred and twenty-eight; ²⁴men of Beth-azmaveth, forty-two; ²⁵men of Kiriath-jearim, Chephirah, and Beeroth, seven hundred and forty-three; ²⁶men of Ramah and Geba, six hundred and twenty-one; ²⁷men of Michmas, one hundred and twenty-two; ²⁸men of Bethel and Ai, two hundred and twenty-three; ²⁹sons of Nebo, fifty-two; ³⁰sons of Magbish, one hundred and fifty-six; ³¹sons of the other Elam, one thousand two hundred and fifty-four; ³²sons of Harim, three hundred and twenty; ³³sons of Lod, Hadid, and Ono, seven hundred and twenty-five;

³⁴sons of Jericho, three hundred and forty-five; ³⁵sons of Senaah, three thousand six hundred and thirty.

³⁶The priests: sons of Jedaiah, who were of the house of Jeshua, nine hundred and seventy-three; ³⁷sons of Immer, one thousand and fifty-two; ³⁸sons of Pashhur, one thousand two hundred and forty-seven; ³⁹sons of Harim, one thousand and seventeen.

⁴⁰*The Levites: sons of Jeshua, Kadmiel, Binnui, and Hodaviah, seventy-four.

⁴¹The singers: sons of Asaph, one hundred and twenty-eight.

⁴²The gatekeepers: sons of Shallum, sons of Ater, sons of Talmon, sons of Akkub, sons of Hatita, sons of Shobai, one hundred and thirty-nine in all.

⁴³The temple slaves: sons of Ziha, sons of Hasupha, sons of Tabbaoth, ⁴⁴sons of Keros, sons of Siaha, sons of Padon, ⁴⁵sons of Lebanah, sons of Hagabah, sons of Akkub, ⁴⁶sons of Hagab, sons of Shamlai, sons of Hanan, ⁴⁷sons of Giddel, sons of Gahar, sons of Reaiah, ⁴⁸sons of Rezin, sons of Nekoda, sons of Gazzam, ⁴⁹sons of Uzza, sons of Paseah, sons of Besai, ⁵⁰sons of Asnah, sons of the Meunites, sons of the Nephusites, ⁵¹sons of Bakbuk, sons of Hakupha, sons of Harhur, ⁵²sons of Bazluth, sons of Mehida, sons of Harsha, ⁵³sons of Barkos, sons of Sisera, sons of Temah, ⁵⁴sons of Neziah, sons of Hatipha.

⁵⁵Descendants of the slaves of Solomon: sons of Sotai, sons of Hassophereth, sons of Peruda, ⁵⁶sons of Jaalah, sons of Darkon, sons of Giddel, ⁵⁷sons of Shephatiah, sons of Hattil, sons of Pochereth-hazzebaim, sons of Ami. ⁵⁸The total of the temple slaves and the descendants of the slaves of Solomon was three hundred and ninety-two.

⁵⁹The following who returned from Tel-melah, Tel-harsha, Cherub, Addan, and Immer were unable to prove that their ancestral houses and their descent were Israelite: ⁶⁰sons of Delaiah, sons of Tobiah, sons of Nekoda, six hundred and fifty-two. ⁶¹*Also, of the priests: sons of Habaiah, sons of Hakkoz, sons of Barzillai (he had married one of the daughters of Barzillai the Gileadite and became known by his name). ⁶²These men searched their family records, but their names could not be found written there; hence they were degraded from the priesthood, ⁶³†and His Excellency ordered them not to partake of the most holy foods until there should be a priest bearing the Urim and Thummim.

---

† 1, 8: *Sheshbazzar:* very probably the fourth son of Jehoiachin, king of Judah, taken captive to Babylon in 598 B. C., listed in 1 Chr 3, 18 as Senneser; if so, he was the uncle of Zerubbabel (3, 2ff); see note on 1 Chr 3, 18.

1, 11: *Total . . . five thousand four hundred pieces:* either this figure or the figures given for one or more of the items listed (vv 9f) have been corrupted in the transmission of the text.

2, 1-67: As it now stands, this list is an expanded form of the lists of returned captives from the sixth century B. C.; see Neh 7, 6-72, where it reappears.

2, 63: *His Excellency:* the deputy of the Persian government; from the context, he was one of the Jewish exile leaders. Nehemiah as governor receives the same title (Neh 8, 9; 10, 2). *Urim and Thummim:* see note on Ex 28, 30.

⁶⁴The entire assembly taken together came to forty-two thousand three hundred and sixty, ⁶⁵not counting their male and female slaves, who were seven thousand three hundred and thirty-seven. They also had two hundred male and female singers. ⁶⁶Their horses were seven hundred and thirty-six, their mules two hundred and forty-five, ⁶⁷their camels four hundred and thirty-five, their asses six thousand seven hundred and twenty.

⁶⁸When they arrived at the house of the Lord in Jerusalem, some of the family heads made free-will offerings for the house of God, to rebuild it in its place. ⁶⁹According to their means they contributed to the treasury for the temple service: sixty-one thousand drachmas of gold, five thousand minas of silver, and one hundred garments for the priests. ⁷⁰The priests, the Levites, and some of the common people took up residence in Jerusalem; but the singers, the gatekeepers, and the temple slaves dwelt in their cities. Thus all the Israelites dwelt in their cities.

Restoration of the Altar

3 ¹*†Now when the seventh month came, after the Israelites had settled in their cities, the people gathered at Jerusalem as one man. ²Then Jeshua, son of Jozadak, together with his brethren the priests, and Zerubbabel, son of Shealtiel, together with his brethren, set about rebuilding the altar of the God of Israel in order to offer on it the holocausts prescribed in the law of Moses, the man of God. ³*Despite their fear of the peoples of the land, they replaced the altar on its foundations and offered holocausts to the Lord on it, both morning and evening. ⁴*They also kept the feast of Booths in the manner prescribed, and they offered the daily holocausts in the proper number required for each day. ⁵Thereafter they offered the established holocaust, the sacrifices prescribed for the new moons and all the festivals sacred to the Lord, and those which anyone might offer as a free-will gift to the Lord. ⁶From the first day of the seventh month they began to offer holocausts to the Lord, though the foundation of the temple of the Lord had not yet been laid.

Founding of the Temple

⁷*Then they hired stonecutters and carpenters, and sent food and drink and oil to the Sidonians and Tyrians that they might ship cedar trees from the Lebanon to the port of Joppa, as Cyrus, king of Persia, had authorized. ⁸In the year after their coming to the house of God in Jerusalem, in the second month, Zerubbabel, son of Shealtiel, and Jeshua, son of Jozadak, together with the rest of their brethren, the priests and Levites and all who had come from the captivity to Jerusalem, began by appointing the Levites twenty years of age and over to supervise the work on the house of the Lord. ⁹Jeshua and his sons and brethren, with Kadmiel and Binnui, son of Henadad, and their sons and their brethren, the Levites, stood as one man to supervise those who were engaged in the work on the house of God. ¹⁰*When the builders had laid the foundation of the Lord's temple, the vested priests with the trumpets and the Levites, sons of Asaph, were stationed there with the cymbals to praise the Lord in the manner laid down by David, king of Israel. ¹¹*They alternated in songs of praise and thanksgiving to the Lord, "for he is good, for his kindness to Israel endures forever"; and all the people raised a great shout of joy, praising the Lord because the foundation of the Lord's house had been laid. ¹²*Many of the priests, Levites, and family heads, the old men who had seen the former house, cried out in sorrow as they watched the foundation of the present house being laid. Many others, however, lifted up their voices in shouts of joy, ¹³*and no one could distinguish the sound of the joyful shouting from the sound of those who were weeping; for the people raised a mighty clamor which was heard afar off.

Samaritan Interference

4 ¹When the enemies of Judah and Benjamin heard that the exiles were building a temple for the Lord, the God of Israel, ²they approached Zerubbabel and the family heads and said to them, "Let us build with you, for we seek your God just as you do, and we have sacrificed to him since the days of Esarhaddon, king of Assyria, who had us brought here." ³But Zerubbabel, Jeshua, and the rest of the family heads of Israel answered them, "It is not your responsibility to build with us a house for our God, but we alone must build it for the Lord, the God of Israel, as King Cyrus of Persia has commanded us." ⁴Thereupon the people of the land set out to intimidate and dishearten the people of Judah so as to keep them from building. ⁵†They also suborned counselors to work against them and thwart their plans during the remaining years of Cyrus, king of Persia, and until the reign of Darius, king of Persia.

† 3, 1f: *The seventh month:* Tishri (September-October), apparently of 538 B. C.; cf 1, 1; 4, 5. In this case, it was Sheshbazzar who erected the first altar, since he began the work on the foundations of the temple in Jerusalem; cf 5, 16. It was in the second year of Darius I, i. e., in 520 B. C., that *Jeshua* and *Zerubbabel* resumed the work on the temple that had been temporarily interrupted (4, 24—5, 1; Hg 1, 1; 2, 1). The Chronicler or a later editor of the text here attributes to them the beginning of the work which, in reality, they merely completed. *Shealtiel:* the eldest son of King Jehoiachin of Judah and the brother of Sheshbazzar (1 Chr 3, 18f); Zerubbabel was therefore the grandson of Jehoiachin; see note on 1, 8.

4, 5: *Darius:* Darius I (521-485 B. C.). The temple-building narrative continues in 4, 24. In between (4, 6-23) is a series of notes about the opposition to the returned exiles voiced at the Persian court in the early fifth century B. C., after the temple had been reestablished.

* 3/1: Neh 7, 73—8, 1.
3: 1 Kgs 8, 64; Dn 9, 25.
4: Ex 23, 16; Nm 28, 3-8.
7: 1 Chr 22, 4; 2 Chr 2, 9.
10: 2, 41.
11: Pss 100, 5; 136; Jer 33, 11.
12: Hg 2, 3.
13: Tb 14, 5.

Later Hostility

6Also at the beginning of the reign of Ahashuerus they prepared a written accusation against the inhabitants of Judah and Jerusalem.

7†Again, in the time of Artaxerxes, Mithredath wrote in concert with Tabeel and the rest of his fellow officials to Artaxerxes, king of Persia. The document was written in Aramaic and was accompanied by a translation. [Aramaic:]

8†Then Rehum, the governor, and Shimshai, the scribe, wrote the following letter against Jerusalem to King Artaxerxes: **9**"Rehum, the governor, Shimshai, the scribe, and their fellow judges, officials, and agents from among the Persian, Urukian, Babylonian, Susian (that is Elamite), **10**and the other peoples whom the great and illustrious Assurbanipal transported and settled in the city of Samaria and elsewhere in the province West-of-Euphrates, as follows. . . ." **11**This is a copy of the letter that they sent to him:

"To King Artaxerxes, your servants, the men of West-of-Euphrates, as follows: **12**Let it be known to the king that the Jews who came up from you to us have arrived at Jerusalem and are now rebuilding this rebellious and evil city. They are raising up its walls, and the foundations have already been laid. **13**Now let it be known to the king that if this city is rebuilt and its walls are raised up again, they will no longer pay taxes, tributes, or tolls; thus it can only result in harm to the throne. **14**Now, since we partake of the salt of the palace, we ought not simply to look on while the king is being dishonored. Therefore we have sent this message to inform you, O king, **15**so that inquiry may be made in the historical records of your fathers. In the historical records you can discover and verify that this city is a rebellious city which has proved fatal to kings and provinces, and that sedition has been fostered there since ancient times. For that reason this city was destroyed. **16**We inform you, O king, that if this city is rebuilt and its walls are raised up again, by that very fact you will no longer own any part of West-of-Euphrates."

17The king sent this answer: "To Rehum, the governor, Shimshai, the scribe, and their fellow officials living in Samaria and elsewhere in the province West-of-Euphrates, greetings and the following: **18**The communication which you sent us has been read plainly in my presence. **19**When at my command inquiry was made, it was verified that from ancient times this city has risen up against kings and that rebellion and sedition have been fostered there. **20**Powerful kings were once in Jerusalem who ruled over all West-of-Euphrates, and taxes, tributes, and tolls were paid to them. **21**Give orders, therefore, that will stop the work of these men. This city may not be rebuilt until a further

decree has been issued by me. **22**Take care that you do not neglect this matter, lest the evil grow to the detriment of the throne."

23✶As soon as a copy of King Artaxerxes' letter had been read before Rehum, the governor, Shimshai, the scribe, and their fellow officials, they went in all haste to the Jews in Jerusalem and stopped their work by force of arms.

Rebuilding of the Temple

24†Thus it was that the work on the house of God in Jerusalem was halted. This inaction lasted until the second year of the reign of Darius, king of Persia.

5 **1**✶†THEN the prophets Haggai and Zechariah, son of Iddo, began to prophesy to the Jews in Judah and Jerusalem in the name of the God of Israel. **2**Thereupon Zerubbabel, son of Shealtiel, and Jeshua, son of Jozadak, began again to build the house of God in Jerusalem, with the prophets of God giving them support. **3**At that time there came to them Tattenai, governor of West-of-Euphrates, and Shethar-bozenai, and their fellow officials, who asked of them: "Who issued the decree for you to build this house and raise this edifice? **4**What are the names of the men who are building this structure?" **5**But their God watched over the elders of the Jews so that they were not hindered, until a report could go to Darius and then a written order be sent back concerning this matter.

6A copy of the letter sent to King Darius by Tattenai, governor of West-of-Euphrates, and Shethar-bozenai, and their fellow officials from West-of-Euphrates; **7**they sent him a report in which was written the following:

"To King Darius, all good wishes! **8**Let it be known to the king that we have visited the province of Judah and the house of the great God: it is being rebuilt of cut stone and the walls are being reinforced with timber; the work is being carried on diligently and is making good progress under their hands. **9**We then questioned the elders, addressing to them the following words: 'Who issued the decree for you to build this house and raise this edifice?' **10**We also asked them

---

† 4, 7: *Aramaic:* this word in the original text seems to be a note indicating a change of language from Hebrew to Aramaic, which in fact takes place here. The Aramaic section ends with 6, 18, but again in 7, 12-26 a royal letter is cited in Aramaic.

4, 8-23: The central question here is the rebuilding of the fortification walls of Jerusalem, not the building of the temple. The interruption of work on the city wall some time before 445 B. C. was the occasion for the coming of Nehemiah to Palestine (Neh 1, 1-4; 2, 1-5). *Artaxerxes:* Artaxerxes I (464-423 B. C.).

4, 24: *The second year . . . of Darius:* that is, 520 B. C.; it marks the beginning of the successful restoration of the temple, which was accomplished within the five years following (5, 1—16, 8).

5, 1: *The prophets Haggai and Zechariah:* two of the Minor Prophets, whose books record their role in the encouragement of this work.

✶ 4/23: Neh 1, 3.   5/1: Hg 1, 14—2, 9; Zec 4, 9.

their names, to report them to you in a list of the men who are their leaders. [11]This was their answer to us: 'We are the servants of the God of heaven and earth, and we are rebuilding the house built here long years ago, which a great king of Israel built and finished. [12]But because our fathers provoked the wrath of the God of heaven, he delivered them into the power of the Chaldean, Nebuchadnezzar, king of Babylon, who destroyed this house and led the people captive to Babylon. [13]However, in the first year of Cyrus, king of Babylon, King Cyrus issued a decree for the rebuilding of this house of God. [14]Moreover, the gold and silver utensils of the house of God which Nebuchadnezzar had taken from the temple in Jerusalem and carried off to the temple in Babylon, King Cyrus ordered to be removed from the temple in Babylon and consigned to a certain Sheshbazzar, whom he named governor. [15]And he commanded him: Take these utensils and deposit them in the temple of Jerusalem, and let the house of God be rebuilt on its former site. [16]Then this same Sheshbazzar came and laid the foundations of the house of God in Jerusalem. Since that time the building has been going on, and it is not yet completed.' [17]Now, if it please the king, let a search be made in the royal archives of Babylon to discover whether a decree really was issued by King Cyrus for the rebuilding of this house of God in Jerusalem. And may the king's pleasure in this matter be communicated to us."

The Decree of Darius

6 [1]THEREUPON King Darius issued an order to search the archives in which the Babylonian records were stored away; [2*]and in Ecbatana, the stronghold in the province of Media, a scroll was found containing the following text: "Memorandum. [3]In the first year of King Cyrus, King Cyrus issued a decree: The house of God in Jerusalem. The house is to be rebuilt as a place for offering sacrifices and bringing burnt offerings. Its height is to be sixty cubits and its width sixty cubits. [4]It shall have three courses of cut stone for each one of timber. The costs are to be borne by the royal palace. [5]Also, the gold and silver utensils of the house of God which Nebuchadnezzar took from the temple of Jerusalem and brought to Babylon are to be sent back: to be returned to their place in the temple of Jerusalem and deposited in the house of God.

[6]"Now, therefore, Tattenai, governor of West-of-Euphrates, and Shethar-bozenai, and you, their fellow officials in West-of-Euphrates, do not interfere in that place. [7]Let the governor and the elders of the Jews continue the work on that house of God; they are to rebuild it on its former site. [8]I also issue this decree concerning your dealing with these elders of the Jews

in the rebuilding of that house of God: From the royal revenue, the taxes of West-of-Euphrates, let these men be repaid for their expenses, in full and without delay. [9]Whatever else is required—young bulls, rams, and lambs for holocausts to the God of heaven, wheat, salt, wine, and oil, according to the requirements of the priests who are in Jerusalem—is to be delivered to them day by day without fail, [10]that they may continue to offer sacrifices of pleasing odor to the God of heaven and pray for the life of the king and his sons. [11]I also issue this decree: If any man violates this edict, a beam is to be taken from his house, and he is to be lifted up and impaled on it; and his house is to be reduced to rubble for this offense. [12]And may the God who causes his name to dwell there overthrow every king or people who may undertake to alter this or to destroy this house of God in Jerusalem. I, Darius, have issued this decree; let it be carefully executed."

[13]Then Tattenai, the governor of West-of-Euphrates, and Shethar-bozenai, and their fellow officials carried out fully the instructions King Darius had sent them. [14]The elders of the Jews continued to make progress in the building, supported by the message of the prophets, Haggai and Zechariah, son of Iddo. They finished the building according to the command of the God of Israel and the decrees of Cyrus and Darius [and of Artaxerxes, king of Persia]. [15]They completed this house on the third day of the month Adar, in the sixth year of the reign of King Darius. [16]The Israelites —priests, Levites, and the other returned exiles—celebrated the dedication of this house of God with joy. [17]For the dedication of this house of God, they offered one hundred bulls, two hundred rams, and four hundred lambs, together with twelve he-goats as a sin-offering for all Israel, in keeping with the number of the tribes of Israel. [18]Finally, they set up the priests in their classes and the Levites in their divisions for the service of God in Jerusalem, as is prescribed in the book of Moses.

The Passover

[19*]The exiles kept the Passover on the fourteenth day of the first month. [20]The Levites, every one of whom had purified himself for the occasion, sacrificed the Passover for the rest of the exiles, for their brethren the priests, and for themselves. [21*]The Israelites who had returned from the exile partook of it together with all those who had separated themselves from the uncleanness of the peoples of the land to join them in seeking the LORD, the God of Israel. [22†]They joyfully kept the feast of Unleavened Bread for seven days, for the LORD had filled them with joy by making the king of Assyria favorable to them, so that he gave them help in their work on the house of God, the God of Israel.

---

*   6/2-12: 1, 4-11.   21: Ps 47, 9.
      19-22: Ex 12, 1-20.

†   6, 22: *Assyria:* used here in a broad sense for the Persian Empire.

II: THE DEEDS OF EZRA

Ezra the Scribe

7 ¹†AFTER THESE EVENTS, during the reign of Artaxerxes, king of Persia, Ezra, son of Seraiah, son of Azariah, son of Hilkiah, ²son of Shallum, son of Zadok, son of Ahitub, ³son of Amariah, son of Azariah, son of Meraioth, ⁴son of Zerahiah, son of Uzzi, son of Bukki, ⁵son of Abishua, son of Phinehas, son of Eleazar, son of the high priest Aaron—⁶*this Ezra came up from Babylon. He was a scribe, well-versed in the law of Moses which was given by the LORD, the God of Israel. Because the hand of the LORD, his God, was upon him, the king granted him all that he requested.

⁷Some of the Israelites and some priests, Levites, singers, gatekeepers, and temple slaves also came up to Jerusalem in the seventh year of King Artaxerxes. ⁸Ezra came to Jerusalem in the fifth month of that seventh year of the king. ⁹On the first day of the first month he resolved on the journey up from Babylon, and on the first day of the fifth month he arrived at Jerusalem, for the favoring hand of his God was upon him. ¹⁰*Ezra had set his heart on the study and practice of the law of the LORD and on teaching statutes and ordinances in Israel.

The Decree of Artaxerxes

¹¹This is a copy of the rescript which King Artaxerxes gave to Ezra the priest-scribe, the scribe of the text of the LORD's commandments and statutes for Israel:

¹²*"Artaxerxes, king of kings, to Ezra the priest, scribe of the law of the God of heaven (then, after greetings): ¹³I have issued this decree, that anyone in my kingdom belonging to the people of Israel, its priests or Levites, who is minded to go up to Jerusalem with you, may do so. ¹⁴You are the envoy from the king and his seven counselors to supervise Judah and Jerusalem in respect of the law of your God which is in your possession, ¹⁵and to bring with you the silver and gold which the king and his counselors have freely contributed to the God of Israel, whose dwelling is in Jerusalem, ¹⁶as well as all the silver and gold which you may receive throughout the province of Babylon, together with the free-will offerings which the people and priests freely contribute for the house of their God in Jerusalem. ¹⁷You must take care, therefore, to use this money to buy bulls, rams, lambs, and the cereal offerings and libations proper to these, and to offer them on the altar of the house of your God in Jerusalem. ¹⁸You and your brethren may do whatever seems best to you with the remainder of the silver and gold, conformably to the will of your God. ¹⁹The utensils consigned to you for the service of the house of your God you are to deposit before the God of Jerusalem. ²⁰Whatever else you may be required to supply for the needs of the house of your God, you may draw from the royal treasury. ²¹I, Artaxerxes the king, issue this decree to all the treasurers of West-of-Euphrates: Whatever Ezra the priest, scribe of the law of the God of heaven, requests of you, dispense to him accurately, ²²within these limits: silver, one hundred talents; wheat, one hundred kors; wine, one hundred baths; oil, one hundred baths; salt, without limit. ²³Let everything that is ordered by the God of heaven be carried out exactly for the house of the God of heaven, that wrath may not come upon the realm of the king and his sons. ²⁴We also inform you that it is not permitted to impose taxes, tributes, or tolls on any priest, Levite, singer, gatekeeper, temple slave, or any other servant of that house of God.

²⁵*†"As for you, Ezra, in accordance with the wisdom of your God which is in your possession, appoint magistrates and judges to administer justice to all the people in West-of-Euphrates, to all, that is, who know the laws of your God. Instruct those who do not know these laws. ²⁶Whoever does not obey the law of your God and the law of the king, let strict judgment be executed upon him, whether death, or corporal punishment, or a fine on his goods, or imprisonment."

Ezra and His Companions

²⁷Blessed be the LORD, the God of our fathers, who thus disposed the mind of the king to glorify the house of the LORD in Jerusalem, ²⁸*and who let me find favor with the king, with his counselors, and with all the most influential royal officials. I therefore took courage and, with the hand of the LORD, my God, upon me, I gathered together Israelite family heads to make the return journey with me.

8 ¹THIS is the list of the family heads who returned with me from Babylon during the reign of King Artaxerxes:

²Of the sons of Phinehas, Gershon; of the sons of Ithamar, Daniel; of the sons of David, Hattush, ³son of Shecaniah; of the sons of Parosh, Zechariah, and with him one hundred and fifty males were enrolled; ⁴of the sons of Pahath-moab, Eliehoenai, son of Zerahiah, and with him two hundred males; ⁵of the sons of Zattu, Shecaniah, son of Jahaziel, and with him three hundred males; ⁶of the sons of Adin, Ebed, son of Jonathan, and with him fifty males; ⁷of the sons of

---

† 7, 1-8: The date of Ezra's journey to Palestine is not known with certainty. The *seventh year* of King Artaxerxes I would be 458 B. C., and the present order of the text suggests that date. The narratives of Ezra and Nehemiah make it seem to many, however, that the arrival of Nehemiah in 445 B. C. should precede that of Ezra. If so, Ezra may be thought to have come in 398 B. C., the seventh year of King Artaxerxes II. Others argue for the thirty-seventh year of Artaxerxes I, that is, 428 B. C.; this would suppose that the date given in the text has suffered in transmission.

7, 25: *The wisdom of your God:* the Mosaic law; cf vv 6, 14.

✤
7/6: 7, 28; 8, 18;   12-17: 1, 2ff.
   Neh 2, 8.18.   25: 2 Chr 17, 9.
10: Ps 119, 45.   28: 7, 6.

Elam, Jeshaiah, son of Athaliah, and with him seventy males; [8]of the sons of Shephatiah, Zebadiah, son of Michael, and with him eighty males; [9]of the sons of Joab, Obadiah, son of Jehiel, and with him two hundred and eighteen males; [10]of the sons of Bani, Shelomith, son of Josiphiah, and with him one hundred and sixty males; [11]of the sons of Bebai, Zechariah, son of Bebai, and with him twenty-eight males; [12]of the sons of Azgad, Johanan, son of Hakkatan, and with him one hundred and ten males; [13]of the sons of Adonikam, younger sons, whose names were Eliphelet, Jeiel, and Shemaiah, and with them sixty males; [14]of the sons of Bigvai, Uthai, son of Zakkur, and with him seventy males.

The Journey to Jerusalem

[15†]I had them assemble by the river that flows toward Ahava, where we made camp for three days. There I perceived that both laymen and priests were present, but I could not discover a single Levite. [16]Therefore I sent Eliezer, Ariel, Shemaiah, Jarib, Elnathan, Nathan, Zechariah, and Meshullam, wise leaders, [17]with a command for Iddo, the leader in the place Casiphia, instructing them what to say to Iddo and his brethren, and to the temple slaves in Casiphia, in order to procure for us ministers for the house of our God. [18*]They sent to us—for the favoring hand of our God was upon us—a well-instructed man, one of the sons of Mahli, son of Levi, son of Israel, namely Sherebiah, with his sons and brethren, eighteen men. [19]They also sent us Hashabiah, and with him Jeshaiah, sons of Merari, and their brethren and their sons, twenty men. [20*]Of the temple slaves (those whom David and the princes appointed to serve the Levites) there were two hundred and twenty. All these men were enrolled by name.

[21]Then I proclaimed a fast, there by the river of Ahava, that we might humble ourselves before our God to petition from him a safe journey for ourselves, our children, and all our possessions. [22*]For I would have been ashamed to ask the king for troops and horsemen to protect us against enemies along the way, since we had said to the king, "The favoring hand of our God is upon all who seek him, but his mighty wrath is against all who forsake him." [23]So we fasted, and prayed to our God for this, and our petition was granted. [24]Next I selected twelve of the priestly leaders along with Sherebiah, Hashabiah, and ten of their brethren, [25]and I weighed out before them the silver and the gold and the utensils offered for the house of our God by the king, his counselors, his officials, and all the Israelites of that region. [26]I consigned it to them in these amounts: silver, six hundred and fifty talents; silver utensils, one hundred; gold, one hundred talents; [27]twenty golden bowls valued at a thousand darics; two vases of excellent polished bronze, as precious as gold. [28]I addressed them in these words: "You are consecrated to the LORD, and the utensils are also consecrated; the silver and the gold are a free-will offering to the LORD, the God of your fathers. [29]Keep good watch over them till you weigh them out in Jerusalem in the presence of the chief priests and Levites and the family leaders of Israel, in the chambers of the house of the LORD." [30]The priests and the Levites then took over the silver, the gold, and the utensils that had been weighed out, to bring them to Jerusalem, to the house of our God.

[31]We set out for Jerusalem from the river of Ahava on the twelfth day of the first month. The hand of our God remained upon us, and he protected us from enemies and bandits along the way. [32]Thus we arrived in Jerusalem, where we first rested for three days. [33]On the fourth day, the silver, the gold, and the utensils were weighed out in the house of our God and consigned to the priest Meremoth, son of Uriah, who was assisted by Eleazar, son of Phinehas; they were assisted by the Levites Jozabad, son of Jeshua, and Noadiah, son of Binnui. [34]Everything was in order as to number and weight, and the total weight was registered. At that same time, [35]those who had returned from the captivity, the exiles, offered as holocausts to the God of Israel twelve bulls for all Israel, ninety-six rams, seventy-seven lambs, and twelve goats as sin-offerings: all these as a holocaust to the LORD. [36†]Finally, the orders of the king were presented to the king's satraps and to the governors in West-of-Euphrates, who gave their support to the people and to the house of God.

Denunciation of Mixed Marriages

9 [1*]WHEN these matters had been concluded, the leaders approached me with this report: "Neither the Israelite laymen nor the priests nor the Levites have kept themselves aloof from the peoples of the land and their abominations [Canaanites, Hittites, Perizzites, Jebusites, Ammonites, Moabites, Egyptians, and Amorites]; [2]for they have taken some of their daughters as wives for themselves and their sons, and thus they have desecrated the holy race with the peoples of the land. Furthermore, the leaders and rulers have taken a leading part in this apostasy!"

Ezra's Exhortation

[3*]When I had heard this thing, I tore my cloak and my mantle, plucked hair from my head and beard, and sat there stupefied. [4*]Around me gathered all who were in dread of the sentence of the God of Israel on this apostasy of the exiles, while I remained motionless until the evening sacrifice. [5]Then, at the time of

8/18: 7, 6.
20: 2, 43.
22: Neh 2, 9.

9/1f: Dt 7, 1; Neh 9, 2.
3: Ps 119, 136.
4: Is 66, 2.

† 8, 15: Ahava: a town at an unidentified site in Babylonia. The river that flowed toward it was probably a branch or canal of the Euphrates.

8, 36: The story of Ezra's mission is seemingly continued from this point by Neh 7, 72b—8, 18, which may be read before Ezr 9, 1.

the evening sacrifice, I rose in my wretchedness, and with cloak and mantle torn I fell on my knees, stretching out my hands to the LORD my God.

6*I said: "My God, I am too ashamed and confounded to raise my face to you, O my God, for our wicked deeds are heaped up above our heads and our guilt reaches up to heaven. 7†From the time of our fathers even to this day great has been our guilt, and for our wicked deeds we have been delivered over, we and our kings and our priests, to the will of the kings of foreign lands, to the sword, to captivity, to pillage, and to disgrace, as is the case today.

8*"And now, but a short time ago, mercy came to us from the LORD our God, who left us a remnant and gave us a stake in his holy place; thus our God has brightened our eyes and given us relief in our servitude. 9*For slaves we are, but in our servitude our God has not abandoned us; rather, he has turned the good will of the kings of Persia toward us. Thus he has given us new life to raise again the house of our God and restore its ruins, and has granted us a fence in Judah and Jerusalem. 10But now, O our God, what can we say after all this? For we have abandoned your commandments, 11*which you gave through your servants the prophets: the land which you are entering to take as your possession is a land unclean with the filth of the peoples of the land, with the abominations with which they have filled it from one end to the other in their uncleanness. 12*Do not, then, give your daughters to their sons in marriage, and do not take their daughters for your sons. Never promote their peace and prosperity; thus you will grow strong, enjoy the produce of the land, and leave it as an inheritance to your children forever.

13"After all that has come upon us for our evil deeds and our great guilt—though you, our God, have made less of our sinfulness than it deserved and have allowed us to survive as we do—14shall we again violate your commandments by intermarrying with these abominable peoples? Would you not become so angered with us as to destroy us without remnant or survivor? 15O LORD, God of Israel, you are just; yet we have been spared, the remnant we are today. Here we are before you in our sins. Because of all this, we can no longer stand in your presence."

The People's Response

10 1WHILE Ezra prayed and acknowledged their guilt, weeping and prostrate before the house of God, a very large assembly of Israelites gathered about him, men, women, and children; and the people wept profusely. 2Then Shecaniah, the son of Jehiel, one of the sons of Elam, made this appeal to Ezra: "We have indeed betrayed our God by taking as wives foreign women of the peoples of the land. Yet even now there remains a hope for Israel. 3Let us

therefore enter into a covenant before our God to dismiss all our foreign wives and the children born of them, in keeping with what you, my lord, advise, and those who fear the commandments of our God. Let the law be observed! 4Rise, then, for this is your duty! We will stand by you, so have courage and take action!"

5Ezra rose to his feet and demanded an oath from the chiefs of the priests, from the Levites and from all Israel that they would do as had been proposed; and they swore it. 6†Then Ezra retired from his place before the house of God and entered the chamber of Johanan, son of Eliashib, where he spent the night neither eating food nor drinking water, for he was in mourning over the betrayal by the exiles. 7A proclamation was made throughout Judah and Jerusalem that all the exiles should gather together in Jerusalem, 8and that whoever failed to appear within three days would, according to the judgment of the leaders and elders, suffer the confiscation of all his possessions, and himself be excluded from the assembly of the exiles.

9†All the men of Judah and Benjamin gathered together in Jerusalem within the three-day period: it was in the ninth month, on the twentieth day of the month. All the people, standing in the open place before the house of God, were trembling both over the matter at hand and because it was raining. 10Then Ezra, the priest, stood up and said to them: "Your unfaithfulness in taking foreign women as wives has added to Israel's guilt. 11*But now, give praise to the LORD, the God of your fathers, and do his will: separate yourselves from the peoples of the land and from these foreign women." 12In answer, the whole assembly cried out with a loud voice: "Yes, it is our duty to do as you say! 13But the people are numerous and it is the rainy season, so that we cannot remain out-of-doors; besides, this is not a task that can be performed in a single day or even two, for those of us who have sinned in this regard are many. 14Let our leaders represent the whole assembly; then let all those in our cities who have taken foreign women for wives appear at appointed times, accompanied by the elders and magistrates of each city in question, till we have turned away from us our God's burning anger over this affair." 15Only Jonathan, son of Asahel, and Jahzeiah, son of Tikvah, were against this proposal, with Meshullam and Shabbethai the Levite supporting them.

---

† 9, 7: After this verse, the next part of the prayer attributed to Ezra is perhaps to be found in Neh 9, 6-37, which may be read as leading up to Ezr 9, 8-15.

10, 6: *Johanan, son of Eliashib:* actually, the grandson of Eliashib; the father of Johanan was Eliashib's son Joiada (Neh 12, 10f.22). Since Eliashib was high priest at the time of Nehemiah (Neh 3, 1.20f; 13, 4.7) and Johanan, if not yet high priest, was at least old enough to have his own separate quarters (*chamber*) in the temple at the time of Ezra, it is practically certain that Nehemiah's activity in Jerusalem must have preceded that of Ezra.

10, 9: *Ninth month:* Chislev (November-December), during the "early rains" in Palestine. Since the assembly took place *in the open . . . all the people . . . were trembling . . . because it was raining.*

---

* 6: Ps 38, 4.   11: Lv 18, 24f; Ez 36, 17.
8: Is 4, 3.   12: Dt 7, 3.
9: Ps 106, 46.   10/11: Neh 9, 2.

The Guilty

16†The exiles did as agreed. Ezra appointed as his assistants men who were family heads, one for each family, all of them designated by name. They held sessions to examine the matter, beginning with the first day of the tenth month. **17**By the first day of the first month they had passed judgment on all the men who had taken foreign women for wives.

18Among the priests, the following were found to have taken foreign women for wives: Of the sons of Jeshua, son of Jozadak, and his brethren: Maaseiah, Eliezer, Jarib, and Gedaliah. **19**They pledged themselves to dismiss their wives, and as a guilt-offering for their guilt they gave a ram from the flock. **20**Of the sons of Immer: Hanani and Zebadiah; **21**of the sons of Harim: Maaseiah, Elijah, Shemaiah, Jehiel, and Uzziah; **22**of the sons of Pashhur: Elioenai, Maaseiah, Ishmael, Nethanel, Jozabad, and Elasah.

23*Of the Levites: Jozabad, Shimei, Kelaiah (also called Kelita), Pethahiah, Judah, and Eliezer.

24Of the singers: Eliashib and Zakkur; of the gatekeepers: Shallum, Telem, and Uri.

25Among the other Israelites: Of the sons of Parosh: Ramiah, Izziah, Malchijah, Mijamin, Eleazar, Malchijah, and Benaiah; **26**of the sons of Elam: Mattaniah, Zechariah, Jehiel, Abdi, Jeremoth, and Elijah; **27**of the sons of Zattu: Elioenai, Eliashib, Mattaniah, Jeremoth, Zabad, and Aziza; **28**of the sons of Bebai: Jehohanan, Hananiah, Zabbai, and Athlai; **29**of the sons of Bani: Meshullam, Malluch, Adaiah, Jashub, Sheal, and Jeremoth; **30**of the sons of Pahath-moab: Adna, Chelal, Benaiah, Maaseiah, Mattaniah, Bezalel, Binnui, and Manasseh; **31**of the sons of Harim: Eliezer, Isshijah, Malchijah, Shemaiah, Shimeon, **32**Benjamin, Malluch, Shemariah; **33**of the sons of Hashum: Mattenai, Mattattah, Zabad, Eliphelet, Jeremai, Manasseh, Shimei; **34**of the sons of Begui: Maadai, Amram, Uel, **35**Benaiah, Bedeiah, Cheluhi, **36**Vaniah, Meremoth, Eliashib, **37**Mattaniah, Mattenai, and Jaasu; **38**of the sons of Binnui: Shimei, **39**Shelemiah, Nathan, and Adaiah; **40**of the sons of Zachai: Shashai, Sharai, **41**Azarel, Shelemiah, Shemariah, **42**Shallum, Amariah, Joseph; **43**of the sons of Nebo: Jeiel, Mattithiah, Zabad, Zebina, Jaddai, Joel, Benaiah.

44†All these had taken foreign wives; but they sent them away, both the women and their children.

---

*   23: Neh 8, 7; 10, 11.

---

†   10, 16f: The work of the committee lasted three months, from *the first day of the tenth month*, Tebet (December-January), to *the first day of the first month*, Nisan (March-April), of the following Jewish year.

10, 44: The account of the problem of mixed marriages at the time of Ezra is continued in Neh 9, 1-5; this may be read immediately after Ezr 10, 44, though the date given in Neh 9, 1 fits more precisely after Ezr 10, 15; cf Hg 2, 10-14.

The Book of Nehemiah

Introduction

Problems common to the combined Books Ezra-Nehemiah have been pointed out in the Introduction to the Book of Ezra. The achievements of the two men were complementary; each helped to make it possible for Judaism to maintain its identity during the difficult days of the Restoration. Nehemiah was the man of action who rebuilt the walls of Jerusalem and introduced necessary administrative reforms. Ezra in turn was the great religious reformer who succeeded in establishing the Torah as the constitution of the returned community.

The biblical sources for Nehemiah's life and work are the autobiographical portions scattered through the book. They are called the "Memoirs of Nehemiah," and have been used more extensively and effectively by "the Chronicler" than the "Memoirs of Ezra." No competent scholar questions the authenticity of Nehemiah's memoirs. From these and other sources, the picture emerges of a man dedicated to the single purpose of the welfare of his people. Despite temperamental shortcomings, Nehemiah was a man of good practical sense combined with deep faith in God. In view of his selfless service to a community capable of severely testing any leader, we can be indulgent toward his numerous appeals to God to credit him with the work he had done. Nehemiah was a layman, and his generous dedication of talents to the service of God and of God's people remains an example of undiminished force for laymen today.

The Book of Nehemiah is divided as follows:
I: The Deeds of Nehemiah (1, 1—7, 72)
II: Promulgation of the Law (8, 1—13, 31)

I: THE DEEDS OF NEHEMIAH

Nehemiah's Vocation

1 ¹†THE WORDS OF NEHEMIAH, the son of Hacaliah.
In the month Chislev of the twentieth year, I was in the citadel of Susa ²when Hanani, one of my brothers, came with other men from Judah. I asked them about the Jews, the remnant preserved after the captivity, and about Jerusalem, ³and they answered me: "The survivors of the captivity there in the province are in great distress and under reproach. Also, the wall of Jerusalem lies breached, and its gates have been gutted with fire." ⁴When I heard this report, I began to weep and continued mourning for several days; I fasted and prayed before the God of heaven.

⁵*I prayed: "O LORD, God of heaven, great and awesome God, you who preserve your covenant of mercy toward those who love you and keep your commandments, ⁶*may your ear be attentive, and your eyes open, to heed the prayer which I, your servant, now offer in your presence day and night for your servants the Israelites, confessing the sins which we of Israel have committed against you, I and my father's house included. ⁷*Grievously have we offended you, not keeping the commandments, the statutes, and the ordinances which you committed to your servant Moses. ⁸*But remember, I pray, the promise which you gave through Moses, your servant, when you said: 'Should you prove faithless, I will scatter you among the nations; ⁹but should you return to me and carefully keep my commandments, even though your outcasts have been driven to the farthest corner of the world, I will gather them from there, and bring them back to the place which I have chosen as the dwelling place for my name.' ¹⁰*They are your servants, your people, whom you freed by your great might and your strong hand. ¹¹*†O Lord, may your ear be attentive to my prayer and that of all your willing servants who revere your name. Grant success to your servant this day, and let him find favor with this man"—for I was cupbearer to the king.

Appointment by the King

2 ¹IN the month Nisan of the twentieth year of King Artaxerxes, when the wine was in my charge, I took some and offered it to the king. As I had never before been sad in his presence, ²the king asked me, "Why do you look sad? If you are not sick, you must be sad at heart." Though I was seized with great fear, ³I answered the king: "May the king live forever! How could I not look sad when the city where my ancestors are buried lies in ruins, and its gates have been eaten out by fire?" ⁴The king asked me, "What

---

†

1, 1: The first mission of Nehemiah, from the *twentieth year* of Artaxerxes I, lasted from the spring (2, 1) of 445 B. C. until 433 B. C. (5, 14). It is recounted in Neh 1, 1—6, 15; 12, 27-43; 6, 16—7, 5; 11, 1-21, which may be read in that order.

1, 11: *Cupbearer to the king:* an important official in the royal household. Because Nehemiah could appear in the queen's presence (2, 6), it is commonly presumed that he was a eunuch; but this is not necessarily so.

❋
1/5: Dt 7, 9.12; Dn 9, 4.
6: 2 Chr 6, 40.
7: Dn 3, 29f.

8f: Dt 30, 1-5.
10: Dt 9, 29.
11: Ps 118, 25.

is it, then, that you wish?" I prayed to the God of heaven [5]and then answered the king: "If it please the king, and if your servant is deserving of your favor, send me to Judah, to the city of my ancestors' graves, to rebuild it." [6]Then the king, and the queen seated beside him, asked me how long my journey would take and when I would return. I set a date that was acceptable to him, and the king agreed that I might go.

[7]I asked the king further: "If it please the king, let letters be given to me for the governors of West-of-Euphrates, that they may afford me safe-conduct till I arrive in Judah; [8]*also a letter for Asaph, the keeper of the royal park, that he may give me wood for timbering the gates of the temple-citadel and for the city wall and the house that I shall occupy." The king granted my requests, for the favoring hand of my God was upon me. [9]*Thus I proceeded to the governors of West-of-Euphrates and presented the king's letters to them. The king also sent with me army officers and cavalry.

[10]†When Sanballat the Horonite and Tobiah the Ammonite slave had heard of this, they were very much displeased that someone had come to seek the welfare of the Israelites.

Circuit of the City

[11]When I had arrived in Jerusalem, I first rested there for three days. [12]Then I set out by night with only a few other men (for I had not told anyone what my God had inspired me to do for Jerusalem) and with no other animals but my own mount. [13]†I rode out at night by the Valley Gate, passed by the Dragon Spring, and came to the Dung Gate, observing how the walls of Jerusalem lay in ruins and its gates had been eaten out by fire. [14]Then I passed over to the Spring Gate and to the King's Pool. Since there was no room here for my mount to pass with me astride, [15]I continued on foot up the wadi by night, inspecting the wall all the while till I once more reached the Valley Gate, by which I went back in. [16]The magistrates knew nothing of where I had gone or what I was doing, for as yet I had disclosed nothing to the Jews, neither to the priests, nor to the nobles, nor to the magistrates, nor to the others who would be concerned about the matter.

Rebuilding Jerusalem's Walls

[17]Afterward I said to them: "You see the evil plight in which we stand: how Jerusalem lies in ruins and its gates have been gutted by fire. Come, let us rebuild the wall of Jerusalem, so that we may no longer be an object of derision!" [18]*Then I explained to them how the favoring hand of my God had rested upon me, and what the king had said to me. They replied, "Let us be up and building!" And they undertook the good work with vigor.

[19]On hearing of this, Sanballat the Horonite, Tobiah the Ammonite slave, and Geshem the Arab mocked us and ridiculed us. "What is this that you are about?" they asked. "Are you rebelling against the king?" [20]†My answer to them was this: "It is the God of heaven who will grant us success. We, his servants, shall set about the rebuilding; but for you there is to be neither share nor claim nor memorial in Jerusalem."

List of Workers

3 [1]*†ELIASHIB the high priest and his priestly brethren took up the task of rebuilding the Sheep Gate. They timbered it and set up its doors, its bolts, and its bars, then continued the rebuilding to the Tower of Hananel. [2]At their side the men of Jericho were rebuilding, and next to them was Zaccur, son of Imri. [3]*The Fish Gate was rebuilt by the sons of Hassenaah; they timbered it and set up its doors, its bolts, and its bars. [4]At their side Meremoth, son of Uriah, son of Hakkoz, carried out the work of repair; next to him was Meshullam, son of Berechiah, son of Meshezabel; and next to him was Zadok, son of Baana. [5]Next to him the Tekoites carried out the work of repair; however, some of their outstanding men would not submit to the labor asked by their lords. [6]The New City Gate was repaired by Joiada, son of Paseah; and Meshullam, son of Besodeiah; they timbered it and set up its doors, its bolts, and its bars. [7]At their side were Melatiah the

---

† 2, 10: *Sanballat the Horonite:* the governor of the province of Samaria (3, 33f), apparently a native of one of the Bethhorons. A letter from the Jews living at Elephantine in southern Egypt, dated 408-407 B. C., mentions "Delayah and Shelemyah, the sons of Sanballat, the governor of Samaria." Although his own name was Babylonian—*Sin-uballit,* i. e., "Sin (the moon god) has given life"—his two sons had names referring to Yahweh. *Tobiah, the Ammonite slave:* the governor of the province of Ammon in Transjordan. His honorary title, "servant" (in Hebrew, *ebed*), i. e., of the king, could also be understood as *slave,* and Nehemiah no doubt meant it in this derogatory sense. The Tobiads remained a powerful family even in Maccabean times (2 Mc 3, 11). Sanballat and Tobiah, together with Geshem the Arab (2, 19; 6, 1f), who was probably in charge of Edom and the regions to the south and southeast of Judah, opposed the rebuilding of Jerusalem's walls on political grounds; the city was the capital of a rival province.

2, 13ff: Nehemiah left Jerusalem by *the Valley Gate* near the northwestern end of the old City of David and went south down the Tyropoean Valley toward *the Dragon Spring* (or the Enrogel of Jos 15, 7; 18, 16; 2 Sm 17, 17; 1 Kgs 1, 9, now known as Job's Well) at the juncture of the Valley of Hinnom and the Kidron Valley; he then turned north at *the Dung Gate* (or *the Potsherd Gate* of Jer 19, 2) at the southern end of the city and proceeded up *the wadi,* that is, the Kidron Valley, passing *the Spring Gate* (at the Spring of Gihon) and *the King's Pool* (unidentified); finally he turned west and then south to his starting point.

2, 20: *Neither share nor claim nor memorial:* although Sanballat and Tobiah were Yahwist, Nehemiah would not let them participate in any of the rights of the religious community in Jerusalem.

3, 1-32: The construction work on the gates and walls of the city is described in counterclockwise direction, beginning and ending at *the Sheep Gate* (to the north of the temple). The exact sites of many of the topographical points mentioned are uncertain.

---

* 2/8: Ezr 7, 6.   3/1: Jer 31, 38.
9: Ezr 8, 22.   3: Ezr 2, 35; Zep 1, 10.
18: Ezr 7, 6.

Gibeonite, Jadon the Meronothite, and the men of Gibeon and of Mizpah, who were under the jurisdiction of the governor of West-of-Euphrates. 8†Next to them the work of repair was carried out by Uzziel, son of Harhaiah, a member of the goldsmiths' guild, and at his side was Hananiah, one of the perfumers' guild. They restored Jerusalem as far as the wall of the public square. 9Next to them the work of repair was carried out by Rephaiah, son of Hur, leader of half the district of Jerusalem, 10and at his side was Jedaiah, son of Harumaph, who repaired opposite his own house. Next to him Hattush, son of Hashabneiah, carried out the work of repair. 11The adjoining sector, as far as the Oven Tower, was repaired by Malchijah, son of Harim, and Hasshub, of Pahath-moab. 12At their side the work of repair was carried out by Shallum, son of Hallohesh, leader of half the district of Jerusalem, by himself and his daughters. 13The Valley Gate was repaired by Hanun and the inhabitants of Zanoah; they rebuilt it and set up its doors, its bolts, and its bars. They also repaired a thousand cubits of the wall up to the Dung Gate. 14The Dung Gate was repaired by Malchijah, son of Rechab, leader of the district of Beth-haccherem; he rebuilt it and set up its doors, its bolts, and its bars. 15The Spring Gate was repaired by Shallum, son of Colhozeh, leader of the district of Mizpah; he rebuilt it, roofed it over, and set up its doors, its bolts, and its bars. He also repaired the wall of the Aqueduct Pool near the king's garden as far as the steps that lead down from the City of David. 16After him, the work of repair was carried out by Nehemiah, son of Azbuk, leader of half the district of Beth-zur, to a place opposite the tombs of David, as far as the artificial pool and the barracks.

17After him, the Levites carried out the work of repair: Rehum, son of Bani. Next to him, for his own district, was Hashabiah, leader of half the district of Keilah. 18After him, their brethren carried out the work of repair: Binnui, son of Henadad, leader of half the district of Keilah; 19next to him Ezer, son of Jeshua, leader of Mizpah, who repaired the adjoining sector, the Corner, opposite the ascent to the arsenal. 20After him, Baruch, son of Zabbai, repaired the adjoining sector from the Corner to the entrance of the house of Eliashib, the high priest. 21After him, Meremoth, son of Uriah, son of Hakkoz, repaired the adjoining sector from the entrance of Eliashib's house to the end of the house.

22After him, the work of repair was carried out by the priests, men of the surrounding country. 23After them, Benjamin and Hasshub carried out the repair in front of their houses; after them, Azariah, son of Maaseiah, son of Ananiah, made the repairs alongside his house. 24After him, Binnui, son of Henadad, repaired the adjoining sector from the house of Azariah to the Corner [that is, to the Angle]. 25After him, Palal, son of Uzai, carried out the work of repair opposite the

Corner and the tower projecting from the Upper Palace at the quarters of the guard. After him, Pedaiah, son of Parosh, carried out the work of repair 26to a point opposite the Water Gate on the east, and the projecting tower. 27After him, the Tekoites repaired the adjoining sector opposite the great projecting tower, to the wall of Ophel [the temple slaves were dwelling on Ophel].

28Above the Horse Gate the priests carried out the work of repair, each before his own house. 29*After them Zadok, son of Immer, carried out the repair before his house, and after him the repair was carried out by Shemaiah, son of Shecaniah, keeper of the East Gate. 30After him, Hananiah, son of Shelemiah, and Hanun, the sixth son of Zalaph, repaired the adjoining sector; after them, Meshullam, son of Berechiah, repaired the place opposite his own lodging. 31After him, Malchijah, a member of the goldsmiths' guild, carried out the work of repair as far as the quarters of the temple slaves and the merchants, before the Gate of Inspection and as far as the upper chamber of the Angle. 32Between the upper chamber of the Angle and the Sheep Gate, the goldsmiths and the merchants carried out the work of repair.

Opposition from Judah's Foes

33When Sanballat heard that we were rebuilding the wall, it roused his anger and he became very much incensed. He ridiculed the Jews, 34saying in the presence of his brethren and the troops of Samaria: "What are these miserable Jews trying to do? Will they complete their restoration in a single day? Will they recover these stones, burnt as they are, from the heaps of dust?" 35Tobiah the Ammonite was beside him, and he said: "It is a rubble heap they are building. Any fox that attacked it would breach their wall of stones!" 36Take note, O our God, how we were mocked! Turn back their derision upon their own heads and let them be carried away to a land of captivity! 37*Hide not their crime and let not their sin be blotted out in your sight, for they insulted the builders to their face! 38We, however, continued to build the wall, which was soon filled in and completed up to half its height. The people worked with a will.

4 1WHEN Sanballat, Tobiah, the Arabs, the Ammonites, and the Ashdodites heard that the restoration of the walls of Jerusalem was progressing—for the gaps were beginning to be closed up—they became extremely angry. 2Thereupon they all plotted together to come and fight against Jerusalem and thus to throw us into confusion. 3We prayed to our God and posted a watch against them day and night for fear of what they might do. 4Meanwhile the Judahites were saying:

29: Ezr 40, 6.   37: Jer 18, 23.

† 3, 8: *Wall of the public square:* that is, the section of wall bounding the place of assembly outside the Gate of Ephraim, or New City Gate; cf 3, 6; 8, 16.

"Slackened is the bearers' strength,
there is no end to the rubbish;
Never shall we be able
the wall to rebuild."

5Our enemies thought, "Before they are aware of it or see us, we shall come into their midst, kill them, and put an end to the work." **6**When the Jews who lived near them had come to us from one place after another, and had told us ten times over that they were about to attack us, **7**I stationed guards down below, behind the wall, near the exposed points, assigning them by family groups with their swords, their spears, and their bows. **8**I made an inspection, then addressed these words to the nobles, the magistrates, and the rest of the people: "Have no fear of them! Keep in mind the Lord, who is great and to be feared, and fight for your brethren, your sons and daughters, your wives and your homes." **9**When our enemies became aware that we had been warned and that God had upset their plan, we all went back each to his own task at the wall.

10From that time on, however, only half my able men took a hand in the work, while the other half, armed with spears, bucklers, bows, and breastplates, stood guard behind the whole house of Judah **11**as they rebuilt the wall. The load carriers, too, were armed; each did his work with one hand and held a weapon with the other. **12**Every builder, while he worked, had his sword girt at his side. Also, a trumpeter stood beside me, **13**for I had said to the nobles, the magistrates, and the rest of the people: "Our work is scattered and extensive, and we are widely separated from one another along the wall; **14**wherever you hear the trumpet sound, join us there; our God will fight with us." **15**Thus we went on with the work, half of the men with spears at the ready, from daybreak till the stars came out.

16At the same time I told the people to spend the nights inside Jerusalem, each man with his own attendant, so that they might serve as a guard by night and a working force by day. **17**Neither I, nor my kinsmen, nor any of my attendants, nor any of the bodyguard that accompanied me took off his clothes; everyone kept his weapon at his right hand.

Antisocial Conduct

5 **1**THEN there rose a great outcry of the common people and their wives against certain of their fellow Jews. **2**Some said: "We are forced to pawn our sons and daughters in order to get grain to eat that we may live." **3**Others said: "We are forced to pawn our fields, our vineyards, and our houses, that we may have grain during the famine." **4**Still others said: "To pay the king's tax we have borrowed money on our fields and our vineyards. **5**And though these are our own kinsmen and our children are as good as theirs, we have had to reduce our sons and daughters to slavery, and violence has been done to some of our daughters! Yet we can do nothing about it, for our fields and our vineyards belong to others."

Nehemiah's Action

6I was extremely angry when I heard the reasons they had for complaint. **7**After some deliberation, I called the nobles and magistrates to account, saying to them, "You are exacting interest from your own kinsmen!" I then rebuked them severely, **8**saying to them: "As far as we were able, we bought back our fellow Jews who had been sold to Gentiles; you, however, are selling your own brothers, to have them bought back by us." They remained silent, for they could find no answer. **9**I continued: "What you are doing is not good. Should you not walk in the fear of our God, and put an end to the derision of our Gentile enemies? **10**I myself, my kinsmen, and my attendants have lent the people money and grain without charge. Let us put an end to this usury! **11**I ask that you return to them this very day their fields, their vineyards, their olive groves, and their houses, together with the interest on the money, the grain, the wine, and the oil that you have lent them." **12**They answered: "We will return everything and exact nothing further from them. We will do just what you ask." Then I called for the priests and had them administer an oath to these men that they would do as they had promised. **13**I also shook out the folds of my garment, saying, "Thus may God shake from his home and his fortune every man who fails to keep this promise, and may he thus be shaken out and emptied!" And the whole assembly answered, "Amen," and praised the LORD. Then the people did as they had promised.

Nehemiah's Lack of Self-interest

14Moreover, from the time that King Artaxerxes appointed me governor in the land of Judah, from his twentieth to his thirty-second year—during these twelve years neither I nor my brethren lived from the governor's allowance. **15**The earlier governors, my predecessors, had laid a heavy burden on the people, taking from them each day forty silver shekels for their food; then too, their men oppressed the people. But I, because I feared God, did not act thus. **16**Moreover, though I had acquired no land of my own, I did my part in this work on the wall, and all my men were gathered there for the work. **17**Though I set my table for a hundred and fifty persons, Jews and magistrates, as well as those who came to us from the nations round about, **18**and though the daily preparations were made at my expense—one beef, six choice muttons, poultry—besides all kinds of wine in abundance every ten days, despite this I did not claim the governor's allowance, for the labor lay heavy upon this people. **19**Keep in mind, O my God, in my favor all that I did for this people.

4/10: Ps 149, 6.
5/1f: Jer 34, 8-22.

5: Ex 21, 7; Lv 25, 39.
8: Lv 25, 48.

5, 7: *You are exacting interest from your own kinsmen!:* contrary to the Mosaic law (Dt 23, 20).

Plots against Nehemiah

6 ¹WHEN it had been reported to Sanballat, Tobiah, Geshem the Arab, and our other enemies that I had rebuilt the wall and that there was no breach left in it (though up to that time I had not yet set up the doors in the gates), ²Sanballat and Geshem sent me this message: "Come, let us hold council together at Caphirim in the plain of Ono." They were planning to do me harm. ³However, I sent messengers to them with this reply: "I am engaged in a great enterprise and am unable to come down; why should the work stop, while I leave it to come down to you?" ⁴Four times they sent me this same proposal, and each time I gave the same reply. ⁵Then, the fifth time, Sanballat sent me the same message by one of his servants, who bore an unsealed letter ⁶containing this text: "Among the nations it has been reported—Geshem is witness to this—that you and the Jews are planning a rebellion; that for this reason you are rebuilding the wall; and that you are to be their king"—and so on. ⁷"Also, that you have set up prophets in Jerusalem to proclaim you king of Judah. Now, since matters like these must reach the ear of the king, come, let us hold council together." ⁸I sent him this answer: "Nothing of what you report has taken place; rather, it is the invention of your own mind." ⁹They were all trying to frighten us, thinking, "Their hands will slacken in the work, and it will never be completed." But instead, I now redoubled my efforts.

¹⁰I went to the house of Shemaiah, son of Delaiah, son of Mehetabel, who was unable to go about, and he said:

"Let us meet in the house of God,
    inside the temple building;
    let us lock the doors of the temple.
For men are coming to kill you;
    by night they are coming to kill you."

¹¹My answer was: "A man like me take flight? Can a man like me enter the temple to save his life? I will not go!" ¹²For on consideration it was plain to me that God had not sent him; rather, because Tobiah and Sanballat had bribed him, he voiced this prophecy concerning me ¹³that I might act on it out of fear and commit this sin. Then they would have had a shameful story with which to discredit me. ¹⁴*Keep in mind Tobiah and Sanballat, O my God, because of these things they did; keep in mind as well Noadiah the prophetess and the other prophets who were trying to frighten me.

Conclusion of the Work

¹⁵†The wall was finished on the twenty-fifth day of Elul; it had taken fifty-two days. ¹⁶*When all our enemies had heard of this, and all the nations round about had taken note of it, our enemies lost much face in the eyes of the nations, for they knew that it was with our God's help that this work had been completed. ¹⁷†At that same time, however, many letters were going to Tobiah from the nobles of Judah, and Tobiah's letters were reaching them, ¹⁸for many in Judah were in league with him, since he was the son-in-law of Shecaniah, son of Arah, and his son Jehohanan had married the daughter of Meshullam, son of Berechiah. ¹⁹Thus they would praise his good deeds in my presence and relate to him whatever I said; and Tobiah sent letters trying to frighten me.

7 ¹WHEN the wall had been rebuilt, I had the doors set up, and the gatekeepers [and the singers and the Levites] were put in charge of them. ²Over Jerusalem I placed Hanani, my brother, and Hananiah, the commander of the citadel, who was a more trustworthy and God-fearing man than most. ³I said to them: "The gates of Jerusalem are not to be opened until the sun is hot, and while the sun is still shining they shall shut and bar the doors. Appoint as watchmen the inhabitants of Jerusalem, some at their watch posts, and others before their own houses."

Census of the Province

⁴Now the city was quite wide and spacious, but its population was small, and none of the houses had been rebuilt. ⁵When my God had put it into my mind to gather together the nobles, the magistrates, and the common people, and to examine their family records, I came upon the family list of those who had returned in the earliest period. There I found the following written:

⁶*†These are the inhabitants of the province who returned from the captivity of the exiles whom Nebuchadnezzar, king of Babylon, had carried away, and who came back to Jerusalem and Judah, each man to his own city ⁷(those who returned with Zerubbabel, Jeshua, Nehemiah, Azariah, Raamiah, Nahamani, Mordecai, Bilshan, Mispereth, Bigvai, Nehum, and Baanah).

The census of the men of Israel: ⁸sons of Parosh, two thousand one hundred and seventy-two; ⁹sons of Shephatiah, three hundred and seventy-two; ¹⁰sons of Arah, six hundred and fifty-two; ¹¹sons of Pahath-moab who were sons of Jeshua and Joab, two thousand eight hundred and eighteen; ¹²sons of Elam, one thousand two hundred and fifty-four; ¹³sons of Zattu, eight hundred and forty-five; ¹⁴sons of Zaccai, seven hundred and sixty; ¹⁵sons of Binnui, six hundred and forty-eight; ¹⁶sons of Bebai, six hundred and twenty-eight; ¹⁷sons of Azgad, two thousand three hundred and twenty-two; ¹⁸sons of Adonikam, six hundred and sixty-seven; ¹⁹sons of Bigvai, two thousand and sixty-

6/14: Jer 23, 9-40; Zec 13, 3.   7/6-72: Ezr 2, 1-70.
16: Ps 118, 22f; 127, 1.

† 6, 15: *Elul:* the sixth month (August-September). *Fifty-two days:* according to Josephus (*Antiquities* XI, v 8), the rebuilding of the walls of Jerusalem by Nehemiah took two years and four months, which seems more probable.
6, 17ff: These verses should be read immediately after v 14.
7, 6-72a: See note on Ezr 2, 1-67.

seven; [20]sons of Adin, six hundred and fifty-five; [21]sons of Ater who were sons of Hezekiah, ninety-eight; [22]sons of Hashum, three hundred and twenty-eight; [23]sons of Bezai, three hundred and twenty-four; [24]sons of Hariph, one hundred and twelve; [25]sons of Gibeon, ninety-five; [26]men of Bethlehem and Netophah, one hundred and eighty-eight; [27]men of Anathoth, one hundred and twenty-eight; [28]men of Beth-azmaveth, forty-two; [29]men of Kiriath-jearim, Chephirah, and Beeroth, seven hundred and forty-three; [30]men of Ramah and Geba, six hundred and twenty-one; [31]men of Michmas, one hundred and twenty-two; [32]men of Bethel and Ai, one hundred and twenty-three; [33]men of Nebo, fifty-two; [34]sons of another Elam, one thousand two hundred and fifty-four; [35]sons of Harim, three hundred and twenty; [36]sons of Jericho, three hundred and forty-five; [37]sons of Lod, Hadid, and Ono, seven hundred and twenty-one; [38]sons of Senaah, three thousand nine hundred and thirty.

[39]The priests: sons of Jedaiah who were of the house of Jeshua, nine hundred and seventy-three; [40]sons of Immer, one thousand and fifty-two; [41]sons of Pashhur, one thousand two hundred and forty-seven; [42]sons of Harim, one thousand and seventeen.

[43]The Levites: sons of Jeshua, Kadmiel, Binnui, Hodeviah, seventy-four.

[44]The singers: sons of Asaph, one hundred and forty-eight.

[45]The gatekeepers: sons of Shallum, sons of Ater, sons of Talmon, sons of Akkub, sons of Hatita, sons of Shobai, one hundred and thirty-eight.

[46]The temple slaves: sons of Ziha, sons of Hasupha, sons of Tabbaoth, [47]sons of Keros, sons of Sia, sons of Padon, [48]sons of Lebana, sons of Hagaba, sons of Shalmai, [49]sons of Hanan, sons of Giddel, sons of Gahar, [50]sons of Reaiah, sons of Rezin, sons of Nekoda, [51]sons of Gazzam, sons of Uzza, sons of Paseah, [52]sons of Besai, sons of the Meunites, sons of the Nephusites, [53]sons of Bakbuk, sons of Hakupha, sons of Harhur, [54]sons of Bazlith, sons of Mehida, sons of Harsha, [55]sons of Barkos, sons of Sisera, sons of Temah, [56]sons of Neziah, sons of Hatipha.

[57]Descendants of the slaves of Solomon: sons of Sotai, sons of Sophereth, sons of Perida, [58]sons of Jaala, sons of Darkon, sons of Giddel, [59]sons of Shephatiah, sons of Hattil, sons of Pochereth-hazzebaim, sons of Amon. [60]The total of the temple slaves and the descendants of the slaves of Solomon was three hundred and ninety-two.

[61]The following who returned from Tel-melah, Tel-harsha, Cherub, Addon, and Immer were unable to prove that their ancestral houses and their descent were Israelite: [62]sons of Delaiah, sons of Tobiah, sons of Nekoda, six hundred and forty-two. [63]Also, of the priests: sons of Hobaiah, sons of Hakkoz, sons of Barzillai (he had married one of the daughters of Barzillai the Gileadite and became known by his name). [64]These men searched their family records, but their names

could not be found written there; hence they were degraded from the priesthood, [65][†]and His Excellency ordered them not to partake of the most holy foods until there should be a priest bearing the Urim and Thummim.

[66]The entire assembly taken together came to forty-two thousand three hundred and sixty, [67]not counting their male and female slaves, who were seven thousand three hundred and thirty-seven. They also had two hundred male and female singers. Their horses were seven hundred and thirty-six, their mules two hundred and forty-five, [68]their camels four hundred and thirty-five, their asses six thousand seven hundred and twenty.

[69]Certain of the family heads contributed to the service. His Excellency put into the treasury one thousand drachmas of gold, fifty basins, thirty garments for priests, and five hundred minas of silver. [70]Some of the family heads contributed to the treasury for the temple service: twenty thousand drachmas of gold and two thousand two hundred minas of silver. [71]The contributions of the rest of the people amounted to twenty thousand drachmas of gold, two thousand minas of silver, and sixty-seven garments for priests.

[72][†]The priests, the Levites, the gatekeepers, the singers, the temple slaves, and all Israel took up residence in their cities.

II: PROMULGATION OF THE LAW

Ezra Reads the Law

8 NOW WHEN THE SEVENTH MONTH CAME, [1][*]the whole people gathered as one man in the open space before the Water Gate, and they called upon Ezra the scribe to bring forth the book of the law of Moses which the LORD prescribed for Israel. [2]On the first day of the seventh month, therefore, Ezra the priest brought the law before the assembly, which consisted of men, women, and those children old enough to understand. [3]Standing at one end of the open place that was before the Water Gate, he read out of the book from daybreak till midday, in the presence of the men, the women, and those children old enough to understand; and all the people listened attentively to the book of the law. [4]Ezra the scribe stood on a wooden platform that had been made for the occasion; at his right side stood Mattithiah, Shema, Anaiah, Uriah, Hilkiah, and Maaseiah, and on his left Pedaiah, Mishael, Malchijah, Hashum, Hashbaddanah, Zechariah, Meshullam. [5]Ezra opened the scroll

---

8/1: Ezr 3, 1.

[†]
7, 65.69: *His Excellency:* see note on Ezr 2, 63.

7, 72b-8, 18: to be read after Ezr 8, 36. The gloss mentioning *Nehemiah* in v 9 was inserted in this Ezra section after the dislocation of several parts of Ezra-Nehemiah had occurred. There is no clear evidence of a simultaneous presence of Nehemiah and Ezra in Jerusalem; Neh 12, 26 and 12, 36 are also scribal glosses.

so that all the people might see it (for he was standing higher up than any of the people); and, as he opened it, all the people rose. ⁶Ezra blessed the LORD, the great God, and all the people, their hands raised high, answered, "Amen, amen!" Then they bowed down and prostrated themselves before the LORD, their faces to the ground. ⁷*[The Levites Jeshua, Bani, Sherebiah, Jamin, Akkub, Shabbethai, Hodiah, Maaseiah, Kelita, Azariah, Jozabad, Hanan, and Pelaiah explained the law to the people, who remained in their places.] ⁸*Ezra read plainly from the book of the law of God, interpreting it so that all could understand what was read. ⁹Then [Nehemiah, that is, His Excellency, and] Ezra the priest-scribe [and the Levites who were instructing the people] said to all the people: "Today is holy to the LORD your God. Do not be sad, and do not weep"—for all the people were weeping as they heard the words of the law. ¹⁰*He said further: "Go, eat rich foods and drink sweet drinks, and allot portions to those who had nothing prepared; for today is holy to our Lord. Do not be saddened this day, for rejoicing in the LORD must be your strength!" ¹¹[And the Levites quieted all the people, saying, "Hush, for today is holy, and you must not be saddened."] ¹²Then all the people went to eat and drink, to distribute portions, and to celebrate with great joy, for they understood the words that had been expounded to them.

The Feast of Booths

¹³On the second day, the family heads of the whole people and also the priests and the Levites gathered around Ezra the scribe and examined the words of the law more closely. ¹⁴*They found it written in the law prescribed by the LORD through Moses that the Israelites must dwell in booths during the feast of the seventh month; ¹⁵*and that they should have this proclamation made throughout their cities and in Jerusalem: "Go out into the hill country and bring in branches of olive trees, oleasters, myrtle, palm, and other leafy trees, to make booths, as the law prescribes." ¹⁶The people went out and brought in branches with which they made booths for themselves, on the roofs of their houses, in their courtyards, in the courts of the house of God, and in the open spaces of the Water Gate and the Gate of Ephraim. ¹⁷Thus the entire assembly of the returned exiles made booths and dwelt in them. Now the Israelites had done nothing of this sort from the days of Jeshua, son of Nun, until this occasion; therefore there was very great joy. ¹⁸Ezra read from the book of the law of God day after day, from the first day to the last. They kept the feast for seven days, and the solemn assembly on the eighth day, as was required.

Confession of the People

9 ¹*[†]ON the twenty-fourth day of this month, the Israelites gathered together fasting and in sackcloth, their heads covered with dust. ²*Those of Israelite descent separated themselves from all who were of foreign extraction, then stood forward and confessed their sins and the guilty deeds of their fathers. ³When they had taken their places, they read from the book of the law of the LORD their God, for a fourth part of the day, and during another fourth part they made their confession and prostrated themselves before the LORD their God. ⁴Standing on the platform of the Levites were Jeshua, Binnui, Kadmiel, Shebaniah, Bunni, Sherebiah, Bani, and Chenani, who cried out to the LORD their God, with a loud voice. ⁵*The Levites Jeshua, Kadmiel, Bani, Hashabneiah, Sherebiah, Hodiah, Shebaniah, and Pethahiah said,

> "Arise, bless the LORD, your God,
> from eternity to eternity!"

The Israelites answered with the blessing,

> "Blessed is your glorious name,
> and exalted above all blessing and praise."

⁶[†]Then Ezra said: "It is you, O LORD, you are the only one; you made the heavens, the highest heavens and all their host, the earth and all that is upon it, the seas and all that is in them. To all of them you give life, and the heavenly hosts bow down before you.

⁷"You, O LORD, are the God who chose Abram, who brought him out from Ur of the Chaldees, and named him Abraham. ⁸*When you had found his heart faithful in your sight, you made the covenant with him to give to him and his posterity the land of the Canaanites, Hittites, Amorites, Perizzites, Jebusites, and Girgashites. These promises of yours you fulfilled, for you are just.

> ⁹*"You saw the affliction of our fathers in Egypt,
> you heard their cry by the Red Sea;
> ¹⁰*You worked signs and wonders against Pharaoh,
> against all his servants and the people of his land,
> Because you knew of their insolence toward them;
> thus you made for yourself a name even to this day.
> ¹¹*The sea you divided before them,
> on dry ground they passed through the midst of the sea;
> Their pursuers you hurled into the depths,
> like a stone into the mighty waters.

❊
  7: 10, 11.   2: Ezr 9, 1f; 10, 11.
  8: Ezr 7, 6.   5: Dn 2, 20; 3, 52.
  10: Est 9, 19.   7: Gn 12, 1; 17, 5.
  14: Ex 23, 14;   8: Gn 15, 18f.
      Lv 23, 33-36.   9: Ex 2, 23f.
  15: Ps 118, 27.   10: Ex 7—11; 14.
  9/1: Dn 9, 3.   11: Ex 15, 5.10.

---

† 9, 1-5: This is a continuation of the account concerning the problem of mixed marriages at the time of Ezra; it should be read immediately after Ezr 10, 44.

9, 6-37: The prayer of Ezra which began in Ezr 9, 6f is here continued; see note on Ezr 9, 7.

¹²*With a column of cloud you led them by day,
    and by night with a column of fire,
To light the way of their journey,
    the way in which they must travel.
¹³*On Mount Sinai you came down,
    you spoke with them from heaven;
You gave them just ordinances, firm laws,
    good statutes, and commandments;
¹⁴*Your holy sabbath you made known to them,
    commandments, statutes, and law you pre-
    scribed for them,
    by the hand of Moses your servant.
¹⁵*Food from heaven you gave them in their hunger,
    water from a rock you sent them in their thirst.
You bade them enter and occupy the land
    which you had sworn with upraised hand to give
    them.

¹⁶"But they, our fathers, proved to be insolent; they held their necks stiff and would not obey your commandments. ¹⁷*They refused to obey and no longer remembered the miracles you had worked for them. They stiffened their necks and turned their heads to return to their slavery in Egypt. But you are a God of pardons, gracious and compassionate, slow to anger and rich in mercy; you did not forsake them. ¹⁸*Though they made for themselves a molten calf, and proclaimed, 'Here is your God who brought you up out of Egypt,' and were guilty of great effronteries, ¹⁹yet in your great mercy you did not forsake them in the desert. The column of cloud did not cease to lead them by day on their journey, nor did the column of fire by night cease to light for them the way by which they were to travel.

²⁰*"Your good spirit you bestowed on them, to give them understanding; your manna you did not withhold from their mouths, and you gave them water in their thirst. ²¹*Forty years in the desert you sustained them: they did not want; their garments did not become worn, and their feet did not become swollen. ²²*You gave them kingdoms and peoples, which you divided up among them as border lands. They possessed the land of Sihon, king of Heshbon, and the land of Og, king of Bashan.

²³*"You made their children as numerous as the stars of the heavens, and you brought them into the land which you had commanded their fathers to enter and possess. ²⁴The sons went in to take possession of the land, and you humbled before them the Canaanite inhabitants of the land and delivered them over into their power, their kings as well as the peoples of the land, to do with them as they would. ²⁵*They captured fortified cities and fertile land; they took possession of houses filled with all good things, cisterns already dug, vineyards, olive groves, and fruit trees in abundance. They could eat and have their fill, fatten and feast themselves on your immense good gifts.

²⁶*"But they were contemptuous and rebellious: they cast your law behind their backs, they slew your prophets who bore witness against them in order to bring them back to you, and they were guilty of great effronteries. ²⁷*Therefore you delivered them into the power of their enemies, who oppressed them. But in the time of their oppression they would cry out to you, and you would hear them from heaven, and according to your great mercy give them saviors to deliver them from the power of their enemies.

²⁸"As soon as they had relief, they would go back to doing evil in your sight. Then again you abandoned them to the power of their enemies, who crushed them. Then they cried out to you, and you heard them from heaven and delivered them according to your mercy, many times over. ²⁹*You bore witness against them, in order to bring them back to your law. But they were insolent and would not obey your commandments; they sinned against your ordinances, from which men draw life when they practice them. They turned stubborn backs, stiffened their necks, and would not obey. ³⁰You were patient with them for many years, bearing witness against them through your spirit, by means of your prophets; still they would not listen. Thus you delivered them over into the power of the peoples of the lands. ³¹Yet in your great mercy you did not completely destroy them and you did not forsake them, for you are a kind and merciful God.

³²*"Now, therefore, O our God, great, mighty, and awesome God, you who in your mercy preserve the covenant, take into account all the disasters that have befallen us, our kings, our princes, our priests, our prophets, our fathers, and your entire people, from the time of the kings of Assyria until this day! ³³*In all that has come upon us you have been just, for you kept faith while we have done evil. ³⁴Yes, our kings, our princes, our priests, and our fathers have not kept your law; they paid no attention to your commandments and the obligations of which you reminded them. ³⁵While they were yet in their kingdom, in the midst of the many good things that you had given them and in the wide and fertile land that you had spread out before them, they did not serve you nor did they turn away from their evil deeds. ³⁶But, see, we today are slaves; and as for the land which you gave our fathers that they might eat its fruits and good things—see, we have become slaves upon it! ³⁷Its rich produce goes to the kings whom you set over us because of our sins, who rule over our bodies and our cattle as they please. We are in great distress!"

✿
  12: Ex 13, 21f.   23: Dt 1, 10.
  13: Ex 19—20.   25: Dt 3, 5; 6, 10f; 11, 11;
  14: Ex 20, 8.   32, 15.
  15: Ex 16, 4; 17, 1f.   26: Wis 2, 10-20.
  17: Nm 14, 1-4; Ex 34, 6;   27: Dn 9, 19.
       Dn 9, 9.   29: Lv 18, 5; 30, 16;
  18: Ex 32, 4.   32, 47.
  20: Dt 2, 7.   32: Lam 5.
  21: Dt 8, 4.   33: Dn 3, 27; 9, 14.
  22: Nm 21, 21-35; Dt 1, 4;
       2, 26-3, 11.

Agreement of the People

10 ¹*†IN view of all this, we are entering into a firm pact, which we are putting into writing. On the sealed document appear the names of our princes, our Levites, and our priests.

²On the sealed document: His Excellency Nehemiah, son of Hacaliah, and Zedekiah.

³Seraiah, Azariah, Jeremiah, ⁴Pashhur, Amariah, Malchijah, ⁵Hattush, Shebaniah, Malluch, ⁶Harim, Meremoth, Obadiah, ⁷Daniel, Ginnethon, Baruch, ⁸Meshullam, Abijah, Mijamin, ⁹Maaziah, Bilgai, Shemaiah: these are the priests.

¹⁰The Levites: Jeshua, son of Azaniah; Binnui, of the sons of Henadad; Kadmiel; ¹¹*and their brethren Shebaniah, Hodiah, Kelita, Pelaiah, Hanan, ¹²Mica, Rehob, Hashabiah, ¹³Zaccur, Sherebiah, Shebaniah, ¹⁴Hodiah, Bani, Beninu.

¹⁵The leaders of the people: Parosh, Pahath-moab, Elam, Zattu, Bani, ¹⁶Bunni, Azgad, Bebai, ¹⁷Adonijah, Bigvai, Adin, ¹⁸Ater, Hezekiah, Azzur, ¹⁹Hodiah, Hashum, Bezai, ²⁰Hariph, Anathoth, Nebai, ²¹Magpiash, Meshullam, Hezir, ²²Meshezabel, Zadok, Jaddua, ²³Pelatiah, Hanan, Anaiah, ²⁴Hoshea, Hananiah, Hasshub, ²⁵Hallohesh, Pilha, Shobek, ²⁶Rehum, Hashabnah, Maaseiah, ²⁷Ahiah, Hanan, Anan, ²⁸Malluch, Harim, Baanah.

Provisions of the Pact

²⁹The rest of the people, priests, Levites, gatekeepers, singers, temple slaves, and all others who have separated themselves from the peoples of the lands in favor of the law of God, with their wives, their sons, their daughters, all who are of the age of discretion, ³⁰*join with their brethren who are their princes, and with the sanction of a curse take this oath to follow the law of God which was given through Moses, the servant of God, and to observe carefully all the commandments of the LORD, our Lord, his ordinances and his statutes.

³¹*Agreed, that we will not marry our daughters to the peoples of the land, and that we will not take their daughters for our sons.

³²*When the peoples of the land bring in merchandise or any kind of grain for sale on the sabbath day, we will not buy from them on the sabbath or on any other holyday. We will forgo the seventh year, as well as every kind of debt.

³³*We impose these commandments on ourselves: to give a third of a shekel each year for the service of the house of our God, ³⁴for the showbread, for the daily cereal offering, for the daily holocaust, for the sabbaths, new moons, and festivals, for the holy offerings, for sin offerings to make atonement for Israel, and for every service of the house of our God. ³⁵*We, priests, Levites, and people, have determined by lot concerning the procurement of wood: it is to be brought to the house of our God by each of our family houses at stated times each year, to be burnt on the altar of the LORD, our God, as the law prescribes. ³⁶*We have agreed to bring each year to the house of the LORD the first fruits of our fields and of our fruit trees, of whatever kind; ³⁷also, as is prescribed in the law, to bring to the house of our God, to the priests who serve in the house of our God, the first-born of our children and our animals, including the first-born of our flocks and herds. ³⁸*The first batch of our dough, and our offerings of the fruit of every tree, of wine and of oil, we will bring to the priests, to the chambers of the house of our God. The tithe of our fields we will bring to the Levites; they, the Levites, shall take the tithe in all the cities of our service. ³⁹An Aaronite priest shall be with the Levites when they take the tithe, and the Levites shall bring the tithe of the tithes to the house of our God, to the chambers of the treasury. ⁴⁰For to these chambers the Israelites and Levites bring the offerings of grain, wine, and oil; there also are housed the utensils of the sanctuary, and the ministering priests, the gatekeepers, and the singers. We will not neglect the house of our God.

Repeopling of Jerusalem

11 ¹*†THE leaders of the people took up residence in Jerusalem, and the rest of the people cast lots to bring one man in ten to reside in Jerusalem, the holy city, while the other nine would remain in the other cities. ²The people applauded all those men who willingly agreed to take up residence in Jerusalem.

The Residents of Jerusalem

³*These are the heads of the province who took up residence in Jerusalem. (In the cities of Judah dwelt lay Israelites, priests, Levites, temple slaves, and the descendants of the slaves of Solomon, each man on the property he owned in his own city.)

⁴In Jerusalem dwelt both Judahites and Benjaminites. Of the Judahites: Athaiah, son of Uzziah, son of Zechariah, son of Amariah, son of Shephatiah, son of Mehallalel, of the sons of Perez; ⁵Maaseiah, son of Baruch, son of Col-hozeh, son of Hazaiah, son of Adaiah, son of Joiarib, son of Zechariah, a son of the Shelanites. ⁶The total of the sons of Perez who dwelt in Jerusalem was four hundred and sixty-eight valiant men.

*
10/1: 12, 12-26.
11: Ezr 10, 23.
30: 13, 23-27.
31: 13, 15-22.
32: 5, 1-13; Ex 20, 8;
    Lv 25, 2-7.
33: 2 Chr 24, 6.9f;
    Lv 24, 5-9.
35: 13, 31.
36f: Ex 13, 1.11ff; Dt 26, 1.
38: 13, 10-14;
    Nm 18, 21.24ff.
11/1: 7, 4.
3-19: 1 Chr 9, 2-34.

†
10, 1-40: This section belongs to the Nehemiah narrative rather than to that of Ezra. It is best read after Neh 13, 31. *In view of all this:* considering the situation described in Neh 13, 4-31.

11, 1-19: This list of the family heads who lived in Jerusalem at the time of Nehemiah is best read after 7, 72a. It is basically the same as that given in 1 Chr 9, 2-17, but there are many differences between the two lists.

⁷These were the Benjaminites: Sallu, son of Meshullam, son of Joed, son of Pedaiah, son of Kolaiah, son of Maaseiah, son of Ithiel, son of Jeshaiah, ⁸and his brethren, warriors, nine hundred and twenty-eight in number. ⁹Joel, son of Zichri, was their commander, and Judah, son of Hassenuah, was second in charge of the city.

¹⁰Among the priests were: Jedaiah; Joiarib; Jachin; ¹¹Seraiah, son of Hilkiah, son of Meshullam, son of Zadok, son of Meraioth, son of Ahitub, the ruler of the house of God, ¹²and their brethren who carried out the temple service, eight hundred and twenty-two; Adaiah, son of Jeroham, son of Pelaliah, son of Amzi, son of Zechariah, son of Pashhur, son of Malchijah, ¹³and his brethren, family heads, two hundred and forty-two; and Amasai, son of Azarel, son of Ahzai, son of Meshillemoth, son of Immer, ¹⁴and his brethren, warriors, one hundred and twenty-eight. Their commander was Zabdiel, son of Haggadol.

¹⁵Among the Levites were Shemaiah, son of Hasshub, son of Azrikam, son of Hashabiah, son of Bunni; ¹⁶Shabbethai and Jozabad, levitical chiefs who were placed over the external affairs of the house of God; ¹⁷Mattaniah, son of Micah, son of Zabdi, son of Asaph, director of the psalms, who led the thanksgiving at prayer; Bakbukiah, second in rank among his brethren; and Abda, son of Shammua, son of Galal, son of Jeduthun. ¹⁸The total of the Levites in the holy city was two hundred and eighty-four.

¹⁹The gatekeepers were Akkub, Talmon, and their brethren, who kept watch over the gates; one hundred and seventy-two in number.

²⁰The rest of Israel, including priests and Levites, were in all the other cities of Judah, each man in his inheritance.

²¹The temple slaves lived on Ophel. Ziha and Gishpa were in charge of the temple slaves.

²²*The prefect of the Levites in Jerusalem was Uzzi, son of Bani, son of Hashabiah, son of Mattaniah, son of Micah; he was one of the sons of Asaph, the singers appointed to the service of the house of God—²³for they had been appointed by royal decree, and there was a fixed schedule for the singers assigning them their daily duties.

²⁴Pethahiah, son of Meshezabel, a descendant of Zerah, son of Judah, was royal deputy in all affairs that concerned the people.

The Other Cities

²⁵As concerns their villages in the country: Judahites lived in Kiriath-arba and its dependencies, in Dibon and its dependencies, in Jekabzeel and its villages, ²⁶in Jeshua, Moladah, Beth-pelet, ²⁷in Hazar-shual, in Beer-sheba and its dependencies, ²⁸in Ziklag, in Meconah and its dependencies, ²⁹in En-rimmon, Zorah, Jarmuth, ³⁰Zanoah, Adullam, and their villages, La-

chish and its countryside, Azekah and its dependencies. They were settled from Beer-sheba to Ge-hinnom.

³¹Benjaminites were in Geba, Michmash, Aija, Bethel and its dependencies, ³²Anathoth, Nob, Ananiah, ³³Hazor, Ramah, Gittaim, ³⁴Hadid, Zeboim, Neballat, ³⁵Lod, Ono, and the Valley of the Artisans. ³⁶Some sections of the Levites from Judah settled in Benjamin.

Priests and Levites under Zerubbabel

12 ¹*THE following are the priests and Levites who returned with Zerubbabel, son of Shealtiel, and Jeshua: Seraiah, Jeremiah, Ezra, ²Amariah, Malluch, Hattush, ³Shecaniah, Rehum, Meremoth, ⁴Iddo, Ginnethon, Abijah, ⁵Mijamin, Maadiah, Bilgah, ⁶Shemaiah, and Joiarib, Jedaiah, ⁷Sallu, Amok, Hilkiah, Jedaiah. These were the priestly heads and their brethren in the days of Jeshua.

⁸The Levites were Jeshua, Binnui, Kadmiel, Sherebiah, Judah, Mattaniah; the last-mentioned, together with his brethren, was in charge of the hymns, ⁹while Bakbukiah and Unno and their brethren ministered opposite them by turns.

High Priests

¹⁰†Jeshua became the father of Joiakim, Joiakim became the father of Eliashib, and Eliashib became the father of Joiada. ¹¹Joiada became the father of Johanan, and Johanan became the father of Jaddua.

Priests and Levites under Joiakim

¹²*In the days of Joiakim these were the priestly family heads: for Seraiah, Meraiah; for Jeremiah, Hananiah; ¹³for Ezra, Meshullam; for Amariah, Jehohanan; ¹⁴for Malluch, Jonathan; for Shebaniah, Joseph; ¹⁵for Harim, Adna; for Meremoth, Helkai; ¹⁶for Iddo, Zechariah; for Ginnethon, Meshullam; ¹⁷for Abijah, Zichri; for Miamin, . . . ; for Maadiah, Piltai; ¹⁸for Bilgah, Shammua; for Shemaiah, Jehonathan; ¹⁹and for Joiarib, Mattenai; for Jedaiah, Uzzi; ²⁰for Sallu, Kallai; for Amok, Eber; ²¹for Hilkiah, Hashabiah; for Jedaiah, Nethanel.

²²In the time of Eliashib, Joiada, Johanan, and Jaddua, the family heads of the priests were written down in the Book of Chronicles, up until the reign of Darius the Persian. ²³The sons of Levi: the family heads were

---

† 12, 10f: *Jeshua*, the high priest when Zerubbabel was governor, i. e., the last decades of the sixth century B. C. (Hg 1, 1.12.14; 2, 2.4). He was the grandfather of *Eliashib*, the high priest at least in the early period of Nehemiah's governorship, i. e., 445-433 B. C. (Ezr 10, 6; Neh 3, 1.20f; 13, 4.7). Eliashib, in turn, was the grandfather of *Johanan*, a grown man, if not yet a high priest, at the time of Ezra, i. e., c. 400 B. C. (Ezr 10, 6; and note). According to Josephus (*Antiquities* XI, v), whose testimony here is doubtful, *Jaddua*, son of Johanan, died as an old man about the time that Alexander the Great died, i. e., 323 B. C. If this list of the postexilic high priests, at least as far as Johanan, comes, as seems probable (cf v 23), from the Chronicler himself and not from a later scribe, it is of prime importance for dating the Chronicler's work in the first decades of the fourth century B. C.

written down in the Book of Chronicles, up until the time of Johanan, the son of Eliashib.

24*The heads of the Levites were Hashabiah, Sherebiah, Jeshua, Binnui, Kadmiel. Their brethren who stood opposite them to sing praises and thanksgiving in fulfillment of the command of David, the man of God, one section opposite the other, **25***were Mattaniah, Bakbukiah, Obadiah.

Meshullam, Talmon, and Akkub were gatekeepers. They kept watch over the storerooms at the gates.

26All these lived in the time of Joiakim, son of Jeshua, son of Jozadak [and in the time of Nehemiah the governor and of Ezra the priest-scribe].

Dedication of the City Wall

27†At the dedication of the wall of Jerusalem, the Levites were sought out wherever they lived and were brought to Jerusalem to celebrate a joyful dedication with thanksgiving hymns and the music of cymbals, harps, and lyres. **28**The levitical singers gathered together from the region about Jerusalem, from the villages of the Netophathites, **29**from Beth-gilgal, and from the plains of Geba and Azmaveth (for the singers had built themselves settlements about Jerusalem). **30**The priests and Levites first purified themselves, then they purified the people, the gates, and the wall.

31I had the princes of Judah mount the wall, and I arranged two great choirs. The first of these proceeded to the right, along the top of the wall, in the direction of the Dung Gate, **32**followed by Hoshaiah and half the princes of Judah, **33**along with Azariah, Ezra, Meshullam, **34**Judah, Benjamin, Shemaiah, and Jeremiah, **35**priests with the trumpets, and also Zechariah, son of Jonathan, son of Shemaiah, son of Mattaniah, son of Micaiah, son of Zaccur, son of Asaph, **36**and his brethren Shemaiah, Azarel, Milalai, Gilalai, Maai, Nethanel, Judah, and Hanani, with the musical instruments of David, the man of God. [Ezra the scribe was at their head.] **37**At the Spring Gate they went straight up by the steps of the City of David and continued along the top of the wall above the house of David until they came to the Water Gate on the east.

38The second choir proceeded to the left, followed by myself and the other half of the princes of the people, along the top of the wall past the Oven Tower as far as the Broad Wall, **39**then past the Ephraim Gate [the New City Gate], the Fish Gate, the Tower of Hananel, and the Hundred Tower, as far as the Sheep Gate [and they came to a halt at the Prison Gate].

40The two choirs took up a position in the house of God; I, too, who had with me half the magistrates, **41**the priests Eliakim, Maaseiah, Minjamin, Micaiah, Elioenai, Zechariah, Hananiah, with the trumpets, **42**and Maaseiah, Shemaiah, Eleazar, Uzzi, Jehohanan,

Malchijah, Elam, and Ezer. The singers were heard under the leadership of Jezrahiah. **43**Great sacrifices were offered on that day, and there was rejoicing over the great feast of the Lord in which they shared. The women and the children joined in, and the rejoicing at Jerusalem could be heard from afar off.

Offerings for Priests and Levites

44*†At that time men were appointed over the chambers set aside for stores, offerings, first fruits, and tithes; in them they were to collect from the fields of the various cities the portions legally assigned to the priests and Levites. For Judah rejoiced in its appointed priests and Levites **45**who carried out the ministry of their God and the ministry of purification (as did the singers and the gatekeepers) in accordance with the prescriptions of David and of Solomon, his son. **46***For the heads of the families of the singers and the hymns of praise and thanksgiving to God came down from the days of David and Asaph in times of old. **47***Thus all Israel, in the days of Zerubbabel [and in the days of Nehemiah], gave the singers and the gatekeepers their portions, according to their daily needs. They made their consecrated offering to the Levites, and the Levites made theirs to the sons of Aaron.

Separation from Aliens

13 **1***†AT that time, when there was reading from the book of Moses in the hearing of the people, it was found written there that "no Ammonite or Moabite may ever be admitted into the assembly of God; **2***for they would not succor the Israelites with food and water, but they hired Balaam to curse them, though our God turned the curse into a blessing." **3***When they had heard the law, they separated from Israel every foreign element.

Reform in the Temple

4†Before this, the priest Eliashib, who had been placed in charge of the chambers of the house of our God and who was an associate of Tobiah, **5***had set aside for the latter's use a large chamber in which had previously been stored the cereal offerings, incense and utensils, the tithes in grain, wine, and oil allotted to the Levites, singers, and gatekeepers, and the offer-

---

† 12, 27-43: *The dedication of the wall of Jerusalem* took place, no doubt, soon after the restoration of the wall and its gates had been completed. Therefore, this section is best read after 6, 15.

12, 44-47: This account of the provisions made for the temple services is apparently a composition of the Chronicler. *At that time:* a mere connective; no particular time is meant, but the account fits best after that of the restoration of the temple (Ezr 6, 13-18) in the days of Zerubbabel (v 47). The gloss mentioning Nehemiah is not in the ancient Greek version.

13, 1ff: These verses were composed by the Chronicler to serve as an introduction to the reforms that Nehemiah instituted during his second mission in Jerusalem (vv 4-31). The part of *the book of Moses* read to the people is freely quoted here from Dt 23, 3-6.

13, 4-31: This part of the "Memoirs of Nehemiah"; it is continued in 10, 1-40.

---

*
24: Ezr 2, 40.
25: 11, 17.
44f: 1 Chr 23—26;
   2 Chr 8, 14.
46: 2 Chr 29, 30; 35, 15.

47: 13, 10f; 10, 39;
   Nm 18, 26.
13/1ff: Dt 23, 3-6.
2: Nm 22—24.
3: 23-28.
5: 12, 44.

ings due the priests. **6**†During all this time I had not been in Jerusalem, for in the thirty-second year of Artaxerxes, king of Babylon, I had gone back to the king. After due time, however, I asked leave of the king **7**and returned to Jerusalem, where I discovered the evil thing that Eliashib had done for Tobiah, in setting aside for him a chamber in the courts of the house of God. **8**This displeased me very much, and I had all of Tobiah's household goods thrown outside the chamber. **9**Then I gave orders to purify the chambers, and I had them replace there the utensils of the house of God, the cereal offerings, and the incense.

10I learned, too, that the portions due the Levites were no longer being given, so that the Levites and the singers who should have been carrying out the services had deserted, each man to his own field. **11**I took the magistrates to task, demanding, "Why is the house of God abandoned?" Then I brought the Levites together and had them resume their stations. **12***All Judah once more brought in the tithes of grain, wine, and oil to the storerooms; **13**and in charge of the storerooms I appointed the priest Shelemiah, Zadok the scribe, and Pedaiah, one of the Levites, together with Hanan, son of Zaccur, son of Mattaniah, as their assistant; for these men were held to be trustworthy. It was their duty to make the distribution to their brethren. **14**Remember this to my credit, O my God! Let not the devotion which I showed for the house of my God and its services be forgotten!

Sabbath Observance

15*In those days I perceived that men in Judah were treading the winepresses on the sabbath; that they were bringing in sheaves of grain, loading them on their asses, together with wine, grapes, figs, and every other kind of burden, and bringing them to Jerusalem on the sabbath day. I warned them to sell none of these victuals. **16**In Jerusalem itself the Tyrians who were resident there were importing fish and every other kind of merchandise and selling it to the Judahites on the sabbath. **17**I took the nobles of Judah to task, demanding of them: "What is this evil thing that you are doing, profaning the sabbath day? **18**Did not your fathers act in this same way, with the result that our God has brought all this evil upon us and upon this city? Would you add to the wrath against Israel by once more profaning the sabbath?"

19When the shadows were falling on the gates of Jerusalem before the sabbath, I ordered the doors to be closed and forbade them to be reopened till after the sabbath. I posted some of my own men at the gates so that no burden might enter on the sabbath day. **20**The merchants and sellers of various kinds of merchandise spent the night once or twice outside Jerusalem, **21**but then I warned them, saying to them: "Why do you spend the night alongside the wall? If you keep this up, I will lay hands on you!" From that time on, they did not return on the sabbath. **22**Then I ordered the Levites to purify themselves and to go and watch the gates, so that the sabbath day might be kept holy. This, too, remember in my favor, O my God, and have mercy on me in accordance with your great mercy!

Mixed Marriages

23*Also in those days I saw Jews who had married Ashdodite, Ammonite, or Moabite wives. **24**†Of their children, half spoke Ashdodite, and none of them knew how to speak Jewish; and so it was in regard to the languages of the various other peoples. **25**I took them to task and cursed them; I had some of them beaten and their hair pulled out; and I adjured them by God: "You shall not marry your daughters to their sons nor take any of their daughters for your sons or for yourselves! **26***Did not Solomon, the king of Israel, sin because of them? Though among the many nations there was no king like him, and though he was beloved of his God and God had made him king over all Israel, yet even he was made to sin by foreign women. **27**Must it also be heard of you that you have done this same very great evil, betraying our God by marrying foreign women?"

28*One of the sons of Joiada, son of Eliashib the high priest, was the son-in-law of Sanballat the Horonite! I drove him from my presence. **29**Remember against them, O my God, how they defiled the priesthood and the covenant of the priesthood and the Levites!

30Thus I cleansed them of all foreign contamination. I established the various functions for the priests and Levites, so that each had his appointed task. **31***I also provided for the procurement of wood at stated times and for the first fruits. Remember this in my favor, O my God!

---

*
12: 10, 38f; 12, 44f.47; 2 Chr 31, 6.
15: 10, 32; Ex 20, 8.
23: 10, 31; 13, 1ff; Dt 23, 3.
26: 1 Kgs 11, 1-13.
28: 2, 10; 13, 4f.7ff.
31: 10, 35f.

† 13, 6: *After due time:* It is not known when Nehemiah returned to Jerusalem or how long his second period of activity there lasted, but it probably ended before Ezra came to Palestine; see note on Ezr 7, 1-8.

13, 24: *Ashdodite:* the language spoken at Ashdod, more likely an Aramaic rather than a Philistine dialect. *Jewish:* Hebrew as spoken in postexilic Judah.

The Book of Tobit

Introduction

The Book of Tobit, named after its principal hero, combines specifically Jewish piety and morality with oriental folklore in a fascinating story that has enjoyed wide popularity in both Jewish and Christian circles. Prayers, psalms, and words of wisdom, as well as the skillfully constructed story itself, provide valuable insights into the faith and the religious milieu of its unknown author. The book was probably written early in the second century B. C.; it is not known where.

Tobit, a devout and wealthy Israelite living among the captives deported to Nineveh from the northern kingdom of Israel in 721 B. C., suffers severe reverses and is finally blinded. Because of his misfortunes he begs the Lord to let him die. But recalling the large sum he had formerly deposited in far-off Media, he sends his son Tobiah there to bring back the money. In Media, at this same time, a young woman, Sarah, also prays for death, because she has lost seven husbands, each killed in turn on her wedding night by the demon Asmodeus. God hears the prayers of Tobit and Sarah, and sends the angel Raphael in disguise to aid them both.

Raphael makes the trip to Media with Tobiah. When Tobiah is attacked by a large fish as he bathes, Raphael orders him to seize it and to remove its gall, heart, and liver because they make "useful medicines." Later, at Raphael's urging, Tobiah marries Sarah, and uses the fish's heart and liver to drive Asmodeus from the bridal chamber. Returning to Nineveh with his wife and his father's money, Tobiah rubs the fish's gall into his father's eyes and cures them. Finally, Raphael reveals his true identity and returns to heaven. Tobit then utters his beautiful hymn of praise. Before dying, Tobit tells his son to leave Nineveh because God will destroy that wicked city. After Tobiah buries his father and mother, he and his family depart for Media, where he later learns that the destruction of Nineveh has taken place.

The inspired author of the book used the literary form of religious novel (as in Jonah and Judith) for the purpose of instruction and edification. There may have been a historical nucleus around which the story was composed, but this possibility has nothing to do with the teaching of the book. The seemingly historical data—names of kings, cities, etc.—are used merely as vivid details to create interest and charm.

Although the Book of Tobit is usually listed with the historical books, it more correctly stands midway between them and the wisdom literature. It contains numerous maxims like those found in the wisdom books (cf 4, 3-19.21; 12, 6-10; 14, 7.9) as well as the customary sapiential themes: fidelity to the law, the intercessory function of angels, piety toward parents, the purity of marriage, reverence for the dead, and the value of almsgiving, prayer, and fasting. The book makes Tobit a relative of *Ahiqar,* a hero of ancient Near Eastern folklore.

Written in Aramaic, the original of the book was lost for centuries. The Greek translation, existing in three different recensions, in our primary source. In 1955, fragments of the book in Aramaic and in Hebrew were recovered from Cave IV at Qumran. These texts are in substantial agreement with the Greek recension that has served as the basis for the present translation.

The divisions of the Book of Tobit are:
  I: Tobit's Ordeals (1, 3–3, 6)
  II: Sarah's Plight (3, 7-17)
  III: Tobiah's Journey and Marriage to Sarah (4, 1–9, 6)
  IV: Tobiah's Return; Cure of Tobit's Blindness (10, 1—11, 18)
  V: Raphael Reveals His Identity (12, 1-22)
  VI: Tobit's Song of Praise (13, 1-18)
  VII: Epilogue (14, 1-15)

Tobit

1 ¹†THIS BOOK TELLS THE STORY OF TOBIT, son of Tobiel, son of Hananiel, son of Aduel, son of Gabael of the family of Asiel, of the tribe of Naphtali, ²*who during the reign of Shalmaneser, king of Assyria, was taken captive from Thisbe, which is south of Kedesh Naphtali in upper Galilee, above and to the west of Asser, north of Phogor.

I: TOBIT'S ORDEALS

His Virtue

³I, TOBIT, HAVE WALKED all the days of my life on the paths of truth and righteousness. I performed many

---

† 1, 1: *Tobit:* in the fragments of the book found at Qumran, is given as *Tôbî,* an abbreviated form of *Tôbiyāh* (v 9; Ezr 2, 60) or of *Tôbiyāhû* (2 Chr 17, 8), a name which means "Yahweh is good." *Tobiel,* "God is good"; *Hananiel,* "God is merciful." The book abounds in theophoric names.
  1, 2: *Shalmaneser* (V) (727-722 B. C.): began the siege of Samaria; the inhabitants of the northern kingdom were taken into captivity by his successor, Sargon II (722-705). *Thisbe* and *Phogor:* towns of Galilee that have not been identified; Thisbe in Gilead was perhaps the birthplace of Elijah. *Kedesh:* cf Jos 20, 7. *Asser:* Hazor (Jos 11, 1).

charitable works for my kinsmen and my people who had been deported with me to Nineveh, in Assyria. [4]When I lived as a young man in my own country, Israel, the entire tribe of my forefather Naphtali had broken away from the house of David and from Jerusalem. This city had been singled out of all Israel's tribes, so that they all might offer sacrifice in the place where the temple, God's dwelling, had been built and consecrated for all generations to come. [5]*†All my kinsmen, like the rest of the tribe of my forefather Naphtali, used to offer sacrifice on all the mountains of Galilee as well as to the young bull which Jeroboam, king of Israel, had made in Dan.

[6]*†I, for my part, would often make the pilgrimage alone to Jerusalem for the festivals, as is prescribed for all Israel by perpetual decree. Bringing with me the first fruits of the field and the firstlings of the flock, together with a tenth of my income and the first shearings of the sheep, I would hasten to Jerusalem [7]*and present them to the priests, Aaron's sons, at the altar. To the Levites who were doing service in Jerusalem I would give the tithe of grain, wine, olive oil, pomegranates, figs, and other fruits. And except for sabbatical years, I used to give a second tithe in money, which each year I would go and disburse in Jerusalem. [8]The third tithe I gave to orphans and widows, and to converts who were living with the Israelites. Every third year I would bring them this offering, and we ate it in keeping with the decree of the Mosaic law and the commands of Deborah, the mother of my father Tobiel; for when my father died, he left me an orphan.

[9]When I reached manhood, I married Anna, a woman of our own lineage. By her I had a son whom I named Tobiah. [10]*Now, after I had been deported to Nineveh, all my brothers and relatives ate the food of heathens, [11]but I refrained from eating that kind of food. [12]Because of this wholehearted service of God, [13]the Most High granted me favor and status with Shalmaneser, so that I became purchasing agent for all his needs. [14]†Every now and then until his death I would go to Media to buy goods for him. I also deposited several pouches containing a great sum of money with my kinsman Gabael, son of Gabri, who lived at Rages, in Media. [15]†But when Shalmaneser died and his son Sennacherib succeeded him as king, the roads to Media became unsafe, so I could no longer go there.

Courage in Burying the Dead

[16]During Shalmaneser's reign I performed many charitable works for my kinsmen and my people. [17]*†I

would give my bread to the hungry and my clothing to the naked. If I saw one of my people who had died and been thrown outside the walls of Nineveh, I would bury him. [18]*I also buried anyone whom Sennacherib slew when he returned as a fugitive from Judea during the days of judgment decreed against him by the heavenly King because of the blasphemies he had uttered. In his rage he killed many Israelites, but I used to take their bodies by stealth and bury them; so when Sennacherib looked for them, he could not find them. [19]But a certain citizen of Nineveh informed the king that it was I who buried the dead. When I found out that the king knew all about me and wanted to put me to death, I went into hiding; then in my fear I took to flight. [20]Afterward, all my property was confiscated; I was left with nothing. All that I had was taken to the king's palace, except for my wife Anna and my son Tobiah.

[21]*†But less than forty days later the king was assassinated by two of his sons, who then escaped into the mountains of Ararat. His son Esarhaddon, who succeeded him as king, placed Ahiqar, my brother Anael's son, in charge of all the accounts of his kingdom, so that he took control over the entire administration. [22]Then Ahiqar interceded on my behalf, and I was able to return to Nineveh. For under Sennacherib, king of Assyria, Ahiqar had been chief cupbearer, keeper of the seal, administrator, and treasurer; and Esarhaddon reappointed him. He was a close relative—in fact, my nephew.

---

† 1, 5: Jeroboam established sanctuaries in Dan and Bethel so that the people would no longer go to Jerusalem for the festivals. The gold statues of bulls which he placed in the sanctuaries were considered the throne of Yahweh; but the people soon came to worship the images themselves. Jeroboam also encouraged the high places or hilltop shrines (1 Kgs 12, 26-33).

1, 6ff: *Perpetual decree:* Dt 12, 11.13-14. Refusing to worship at Jeroboam's shrines, the faithful Tobit continued to bring his offerings to Jerusalem; see 2 Chr 11, 16. For the various tithes, cf Nm 18, 20-32; 2 Chr 31, 4-6; Dt 14, 22-29; 26, 12f.

1, 14: *A great sum of money:* literally, "ten silver talents," about ten thousand dollars. *Rages:* modern Rai, about five miles southeast of Teheran. *Media:* the northwestern part of modern Iran.

1, 15: *Sennacherib* (705-681 B. C.): the son of Sargon (722-705 B. C.); neither was descended from Shalmaneser. Inconsistencies such as this point to the fact that the Book of Tobit is a religious novel (see Introduction; also notes on 5, 6 and 14, 15).

1, 17-18: Tobit risked his own life to bury the dead. Deprivation of burial was viewed with horror by the Jews. Cf 4, 3-4; 6, 15; 14, 12-13.

1, 21: *Esarhaddon:* 681-669 B. C. *Ahiqar:* a hero of ancient folklore, known for his outstanding wisdom. The *Story* (or *Wisdom*) *of Ahiqar* was very popular in antiquity and is extant in many different forms: Aramaic, Syriac, Armenian, Arabic (*Arabian Nights*), Greek (*Aesop's Fables*), Slavonic, Ethiopic, and Romanian. The sacred author makes Tobit the uncle of the famous Ahiqar in order to enhance Tobit's own prestige. See note on 14, 10.

※
    5: 1 Kgs 12, 26-32.
    6: Ex 23, 14f.17; 34, 23; Dt 16, 16.
    7f: Nm 18, 12f.24; Dt 14, 22-29; 18, 4f.
    10: Lv 11; Dt 14, 3-21; Acts 15, 29; 1 Cor 8, 7ff.

    17: Jb 31, 16-20.
    18: 22.25.30-35; 19. 4-7.35ff.
    21: 2 Kgs 19, 37; 2 Chr 32, 21; Sir 48, 21; Is 37, 38; 2 Mc 8, 19.

2 ¹*†THUS under King Esarhaddon I returned to my home, and my wife Anna and my son Tobiah were restored to me. Then on our festival of Pentecost, the feast of Weeks, a fine dinner was prepared for me, and I reclined to eat. ²†The table was set for me, and when many different dishes were placed before me, I said to my son Tobiah: "My son, go out and try to find a poor man from among our kinsmen exiled here in Nineveh. If he is a sincere worshiper of God, bring him back with you, so that he can share this meal with me. Indeed, son, I shall wait for you to come back."

³Tobiah went out to look for some poor kinsman of ours. When he returned he exclaimed, "Father!" I said to him, "What is it, son?" He answered, "Father, one of our people has been murdered! His body lies in the market place where he was just strangled!" ⁴I sprang to my feet, leaving the dinner untouched; and I carried the dead man from the street and put him in one of the rooms, so that I might bury him after sunset. ⁵*†Returning to my own quarters, I washed myself and ate my food in sorrow. ⁶*I was reminded of the oracle pronounced by the prophet Amos against Bethel:

> "Your festivals shall be turned into mourning,
> And all your songs into lamentation."

⁷And I wept. Then at sunset I went out, dug a grave, and buried him.

⁸The neighbors mocked me, saying to one another: "Will this man never learn! Once before he was hunted down for execution because of this very thing; yet now that he has escaped, here he is again burying the dead!"

Tobit's Blindness

⁹That same night I bathed, and went to sleep next to the wall of my courtyard. Because of the heat I left my face uncovered. ¹⁰†I did not know there were birds perched on the wall above me, till their warm droppings settled in my eyes, causing cataracts. I went to see some doctors for a cure, but the more they anointed my eyes with various salves, the worse the cataracts became, until I could see no more. For four years I was deprived of eyesight, and all my kinsmen were grieved at my condition. Ahiqar, however, took care of me for two years, until he left for Elymais.

¹¹At that time my wife Anna worked for hire at weaving cloth, the kind of work women do. ¹²†When she sent back the goods to their owners, they would pay her. Late in winter she finished the cloth and sent it back to the owners. They paid her the full salary, and also gave her a young goat for the table. ¹³On

entering my house the goat began to bleat. I called to my wife and said: "Where did this goat come from? Perhaps it was stolen! Give it back to its owners; we have no right to eat stolen food!" ¹⁴*†But she said to me, "It was given to me as a bonus over and above my wages." Yet I would not believe her, and told her to give it back to its owners. I became very angry with her over this. So she retorted: "Where are your charitable deeds now? Where are your virtuous acts? See! Your true character is finally showing itself!"

3 ¹GRIEF-STRICKEN in spirit, I groaned and wept aloud. Then with sobs I began to pray:

Tobit's Prayer for Death

²*"You are righteous, O Lord,
and all your deeds are just;
All your ways are mercy and truth;
you are the judge of the world.

³*And now, O Lord, may you be mindful of me,
and look with favor upon me.
Punish me not for my sins,
nor for my inadvertent offenses,
nor for those of my fathers.

"They sinned against you,
⁴*and disobeyed your commandments.
So you handed us over to plundering, exile, and death,
till we were an object lesson, a byword, a reproach
in all the nations among whom you scattered us.

⁵"Yes, your judgments are many and true
in dealing with me as my sins
and those of my fathers deserve.
For we have not kept your commandments,
nor have we trodden the paths of truth before you.

⁶*†"So now, deal with me as you please,
and command my life breath to be taken from me,
that I may go from the face of the earth into dust.

⁂
2/1: Lv 23, 15-21; Nm 28, 26-31; Dt 16, 9-12.
5: Nm 19, 11-22.
6: Am 8, 10; 1 Mc 1, 39.
14: Jb 2, 9.
3/2: Pss 25, 10; 119, 137; Dn 3, 27.
3: Ex 34, 7.
4: Dt 28, 15; Bar 1, 16-22; 2, 4f; 3, 8; Dn 9, 5f.
6: Nm 11, 15; 1 Kgs 19, 4; Jb 7, 15; Jon 4, 3.8.

---

† 2, 1: *The feast of Weeks:* also called by its Greek name *Pentecost,* was celebrated fifty days after the Passover. Cf Lv 23, 15-21; Dt 16, 9-12.

2, 2: Almsgiving and charity to the poor are important virtues taught by the book (4, 7-11.16f; 12, 8f; 14, 10f).

2, 5: *I washed myself:* because of ritual defilement from touching a corpse (Nm 19, 11-13).

2, 10: *Cataracts:* literally, "white scales, or films." *Elymais:* the Greek name of ancient Elam, a district northeast of the head of the Persian Gulf.

2, 12: *Late in winter:* literally, "seventh of Dystros," the Macedonian month which corresponds to the Jewish month of Shebat (January-February). *For the table:* literally, "for the hearth"; the gift had probably been made in view of some springtime festival like the Jewish Purim.

2, 14: Anna's sharp rebuke calls to mind the words of Job's wife (Jb 2, 9).

3, 6: *It is better for me to die than to live:* in his distress Tobit

It is better for me to die than to live,
    because I have heard insulting calumnies,
    and I am overwhelmed with grief.

"Lord, command me to be delivered from such
        anguish;
    let me go to the everlasting abode;
    Lord, refuse me not.
For it is better for me to die
    than to endure so much misery in life,
    and to hear these insults!"

II: SARAH'S PLIGHT

Sarah Falsely Accused

7†ON THE SAME DAY, at Ecbatana in Media, it so happened that Raguel's daughter Sarah also had to listen to abuse, from one of her father's maids. **8**†For she had been married to seven husbands, but the wicked demon Asmodeus killed them off before they could have intercourse with her, as it is prescribed for wives. So the maid said to her: "You are the one who strangles your husbands! Look at you! You have already been married seven times, but you have had no joy with any one of your husbands. **9**Why do you beat us? Because your husbands are dead? Then why not join them! May we never see a son or daughter of yours!"
10✻That day she was deeply grieved in spirit. She went in tears to an upstairs room in her father's house with the intention of hanging herself. But she reconsidered, saying to herself: "No! People would level this insult against my father: 'You had only one beloved daughter, but she hanged herself because of ill fortune!' And thus would I cause my father in his old age to go down to the nether world laden with sorrow. It is far better for me not to hang myself, but to beg the Lord to have me die, so that I need no longer live to hear such insults."
11✻†At that time, then, she spread out her hands, and facing the window, poured out this prayer:

Sarah's Prayer for Death

"Blessed are you, O Lord, merciful God!
    Forever blessed and honored is your holy name;
    may all your works forever bless you.
12And now, O Lord, to you I turn my face
    and raise my eyes.
13Bid me to depart from the earth,
    never again to hear such insults.

14"You know, O Master, that I am innocent
    of any impure act with a man,
15And that I have never defiled my own name
    or my father's name in the land of my exile.

"I am my father's only daughter,
    and he has no other child to make his heir,
Nor does he have a close kinsman or other relative
    whom I might bide my time to marry.
I have already lost seven husbands;
    why then should I live any longer?
But if it please you, Lord, not to slay me,
    look favorably upon me and have pity on me;
    never again let me hear these insults!"

An Answer to Prayer

16At that very time, the prayer of these two suppliants was heard in the glorious presence of Almighty God. **17**✻†So Raphael was sent to heal them both: to remove the cataracts from Tobit's eyes, so that he might again see God's sunlight; and to marry Raguel's daughter Sarah to Tobit's son Tobiah, and then drive the wicked demon Asmodeus from her. For Tobiah had the right to claim her before any other who might wish to marry her.

In the very moment that Tobit returned from the courtyard to his house, Raguel's daughter Sarah came downstairs from her room.

III: TOBIAH'S JOURNEY AND MARRIAGE TO SARAH

A Father's Instruction

4 **1**THAT SAME DAY Tobit remembered the money he had deposited with Gabael at Rages in Media, and he thought, **2**"Now that I have asked for death, why should I not call my son Tobiah and let him know about this money before I die?" **3**✻†So he

---

† uses the words of the petulant Jonah (Jon 4, 3.8), who wished to die because God did not destroy the hated Ninevites. In similar circumstances, Moses (Nm 11, 15), Elijah (1 Kgs 19, 4), and Job (Jb 7, 15) also prayed for death. *Everlasting abode:* a reference to Sheol, the dismal abode of the dead from which no one returns (Jb 7, 9-10; 14, 12; Is 26, 14). The revelation of a blessed immortality had not yet been made. See note on 4, 6.

3, 7: From here on, the story is told in the third person. V 7 relates one of the several marvelous coincidences which the storyteller uses to heighten interest; see also vv 16.17; 4, 1; 5, 4. *Ecbatana: Hamadan* in modern Iran; this was the capital of ancient Media. *Raguel:* "friend of God."

3, 8: *Asmodeus:* in Persian *aeshma daeva,* "demon of wrath," adopted into Aramaic with the sense of "the Destroyer." He will be subdued (8, 3) by Raphael (v 17), "God heals."

3, 11: *Facing the window:* that is, looking toward Jerusalem; cf Dn 6, 11.
Blessed are you and "Blessed be God" are traditional openings of Jewish prayers (8, 5.15; 11, 14; 13, 1).

3, 17: *Tobiah had the right:* according to the patriarchal custom of marriage within the family group. Tobiah was Sarah's closest eligible relative (6, 12). Cf 4, 12-13; Gn 24.

4, 3-19: A collection of maxims which parallel those in the wisdom literature, especially Prv and Sir (see Introduction): duties toward parents (3-4); cf also 14, 13; perseverance in virtue and avoidance of evil (5-6.14b); necessity and value of almsgiving and charity (7-11.16-17); marriage to a kinsman (12-13a); industry (13b); prompt payment of wages (14a); the golden rule (15a); temperance (15b); docility (18); prayer (19).

✻ 10: 6, 15; Gn 37, 35; 42, 38; 44, 29.31.
11: 1 Kgs 8, 44.48; Pss 28, 2; 134, 2; Dn 6, 11.

17: 4, 12f; 6, 12f; Gn 24, 3f.
4/3: Ex 20, 12; Prv 23, 22; Sir 7, 27.

called his son Tobiah; and when he came, he said to him: "My son, when I die, give me a decent burial. Honor your mother, and do not abandon her as long as she lives. Do whatever pleases her, and do not grieve her spirit in any way. **⁴**Remember, my son, that she went through many trials for your sake while you were in her womb. And when she dies, bury her in the same grave with me.

⁵"Through all your days, my son, keep the Lord in mind, and suppress every desire to sin or to break his commandments. Perform good works all the days of your life, and do not tread the paths of wrongdoing. **⁶*†**For if you are steadfast in your service, your good works will bring success, not only to you, but also to all those who live uprightly.

⁷*"Give alms from your possessions. Do not turn your face away from any of the poor, and God's face will not be turned away from you. **⁸**Son, give alms in proportion to what you own. If you have great wealth, give alms out of your abundance; if you have but little, distribute even some of that. But do not hesitate to give alms; **⁹***you will be storing up a goodly treasure for yourself against the day of adversity. **¹⁰**Almsgiving frees one from death, and keeps one from going into the dark abode. **¹¹***Alms are a worthy offering in the sight of the Most High for all who give them.

¹²*"Be on your guard, son, against every form of immorality, and above all, marry a woman of the lineage of your forefathers, Do not marry a stranger who is not of your father's tribe, because we are sons of the prophets. My boy, keep in mind Noah, Abraham, Isaac, and Jacob, our fathers from of old: all of them took wives from among their own kinsmen and were blessed in their children. Remember that their posterity shall inherit the land. **¹³**Therefore, my son, love your kinsmen. Do not be so proudhearted toward your kinsmen, the sons and daughters of your people, as to refuse to take a wife for yourself from among them. For in such arrogance there is ruin and great disorder. Likewise, in worthlessness there is decay and dire poverty, for worthlessness is the mother of famine.

¹⁴*"Do not keep with you overnight the wages of any man who works for you, but pay him immediately. If you thus behave as God's servant, you will receive your reward. Keep a close watch on yourself, my son, in everything you do, and discipline yourself in all your conduct. **¹⁵***Do to no one what you yourself dislike. Do not drink wine till you become drunk, nor let drunkenness accompany you on your way.

¹⁶*"Give to the hungry some of your bread, and to the naked some of your clothing. Whatever you have left over, give away as alms; and do not begrudge the alms you give. **¹⁷*†**Be lavish with your bread and wine at the burial of the virtuous, but do not share them with sinners.

¹⁸"Seek counsel from every wise man, and do not think lightly of any advice that can be useful. **¹⁹*†**At all times bless the Lord God, and ask him to make all your paths straight and to grant success to all your endeavors and plans. For no pagan nation possesses good counsel, but the Lord himself gives all good things. If the Lord chooses, he raises a man up; but if he should decide otherwise, he casts him down to the deepest recesses of the nether world. So now, my son, keep in mind my commandments, and never let them be erased from your heart.

²⁰"And now, son, I wish to inform you that I have deposited a great sum of money with Gabri's son Gabael at Rages in Media. **²¹***Do not be discouraged, my child, because of our poverty. You will be a rich man if you fear God, avoid all sin, and do what is right before the Lord your God."

The Angel Raphael

5 **¹**THEN Tobiah replied to his father Tobit: "Everything that you have commanded me, father, I will do. **²**But how shall I be able to obtain the money from him, since he does not know me nor do I know him? What can I show him to make him recognize me and trust me, so that he will give me the money? I do not even know which roads to take for the journey into Media!" **³†**Tobit answered his son Tobiah: "We exchanged signatures on a document written in duplicate; I divided it into two parts, and each of us kept one; his copy I put with the money. Think of it, twenty years have already passed since I deposited that money! So now, my son, find yourself a trustworthy man who will make the journey with you. We will, of course, give him a salary when you return; but get back that money from Gabael."

⁴*†Tobiah went to look for someone acquainted with the roads who would travel with him to Media. As soon as he went out, he found the angel Raphael

---

† 4, 6: Before the revelation of retribution for all men in the afterlife—a doctrine taught in the Book of Wisdom—Old Testament man believed that virtue guaranteed earthly prosperity, and sin earthly disaster (cf Dt 28).

4, 17: Tobit counsels his son either to give alms in honor of the dead, or, more probably, to give the "bread of consolation" to the family of the deceased. Cf Jer 16, 7; Ez 24, 17.

4, 19: Prayer is the foundation of a moral life.

5, 3: *Document:* in Greek *cheirographon.* In the Middle Ages, notably in England, a deed and its duplicate were written on one piece of parchment, with the Latin word *chirographum* inscribed across the top of the sheet or between the two copies of the text. The document was then cut in two in either a straight or a wavy line, the parts being given to the persons concerned. Perhaps this procedure derived from the present verse of Tobit. Duplicate documents, usually one open and the other sealed, are well known from the ancient Near East.

5, 4: *He did not know:* the theme of an angel in disguise occurs frequently in folklore as well as in the Old Testament (Gn 18; cf Heb 13, 2).

*

6: 13, 6; Jn 3, 21; Eph 4, 15.
7f: 12, 8ff; Dt 15, 7f.11; Prv 19, 17; Sir 4, 1-6; 14, 13; Lk 14, 13; 1 Jn 3, 17.
9: Mt 6, 20f.
11: Sir 3, 30; 29, 12.
12: 3, 15.17; 6, 12; Gn 11, 29.31; 25, 20; 28, 1-4; 29, 15-30; Ex 34, 16; Dt 7, 3; Jgs 14, 3.
14: Lv 19, 13; Dt 24, 15.
15: Mt 7, 12; Lk 6, 31.
16: Dt 15, 10; Is 58, 7; Mt 25, 35f; 2 Cor 9, 7.
17: Jer 16, 7; Lk 14, 13.
19: Dt 4, 6; Ps 119, 10.
21: 1 Tm 6, 6ff.
5/4: Heb 13, 2.

standing before him, though he did not know that this was an angel of God. **5**Tobiah said to him, "Who are you, young man?" He replied, "I am an Israelite, one of your kinsmen. I have come to work." Tobiah said, "Do you know the way to Media?" **6†**The other replied: "Yes, I have been there many times. I know the place well and I know all the routes. I have often traveled to Media; I used to stay with our kinsman Gabael, who lives at Rages in Media. It is a good two days' travel from Ecbatana to Rages, for Rages is situated at the mountains, Ecbatana out on the plateau." **7***Tobiah said to him, "Wait for me, young man, till I go back and tell my father; for I need you to make the journey with me. I will, of course, pay you." **8**Raphael replied, "Very well, I will wait for you; but do not be long."

9Tobiah went back to tell his father Tobit what had happened. He said to him, "I have just found a man who is one of our own Israelite kinsmen!" Tobit said, "Call the man, so that I may find out what family and tribe he comes from, and whether he is trustworthy enough to travel with you, son." Tobiah went out to summon the man, saying, "Young man, my father would like to see you."

10†When Raphael entered the house, Tobit greeted him first. Raphael said, "Hearty greetings to you!" Tobit replied: "What joy is left for me any more? Here I am, a blind man who cannot see God's sunlight, but must remain in darkness, like the dead who no longer see the light! Though alive, I am among the dead. I can hear a man's voice, but I cannot see him." Raphael said, "Take courage! God has healing in store for you; so take courage!" Tobit then said: "My son Tobiah wants to go to Media. Can you go with him to show him the way? I will of course pay you, brother." Raphael answered: "Yes, I can go with him, for I know all the routes. I have often traveled to Media and crossed all its plains and mountains; so I know every road well." **11**Tobit asked, "Brother, tell me, please, what family and tribe are you from?" **12***Raphael said: "Why? Do you need a tribe and a family? Or are you looking for a hired man to travel with your son?" Tobit replied, "I wish to know truthfully whose son you are, brother, and what your name is."

13†Raphael answered, "I am Azariah, son of Hananiah the elder, one of your own kinsmen." **14**Tobit exclaimed: "Welcome! God save you, brother! Do not be provoked with me, brother, for wanting to learn the truth about your family. So it turns out that you are a kinsman, and from a noble and good line! I knew Hananiah and Nathaniah, the two sons of Shemaiah the elder; with me they used to make the pilgrimage to Jerusalem, where we would worship together. No, they did not stray from the right path; your kinsmen are good men. You are certainly of good lineage, and welcome!"

15†Then he added: "For each day you are away I will give you the normal wages, plus expenses for you and for my son. If you go with my son, **16**I will even add a bonus to your wages!" Raphael replied: "I will go with him; have no fear. In good health we shall leave you, and in good health we shall return to you, for the way is safe." **17**Tobit said, "God bless you, brother." Then he called his son and said to him: "My son, prepare whatever you need for the journey, and set out with your kinsman. May God in heaven protect you on the way and bring you back to me safe and sound; and may his angel accompany you for safety, my son."

Before setting out on his journey, Tobiah kissed his father and mother. Tobit said to him, "Have a safe journey." **18**But his mother began to weep. She said to Tobit: "Why have you decided to send my child away? Is he not the staff to which we cling, ever there with us in all that we do? **19**I hope more money is not your chief concern! Rather let it be a ransom for our son! **20**What the Lord has given us to live on is certainly enough for us." **21**Tobit reassured her: "Have no such thought. Our son will leave in good health and come back to us in good health. Your own eyes will see the day when he returns to you safe and sound. **22†**So, no such thought; do not worry about them, my love. For a good angel will go with him, his journey will be successful, and he will return unharmed."

6

1THEN she stopped weeping.

Journey to Rages

2When the boy left home, accompanied by the angel, the dog followed Tobiah out of the house and went with them. The travelers walked till nightfall, and made camp beside the Tigris River. **3**Now when the boy went down to wash his feet in the river, a large fish suddenly leaped out of the water and tried to swallow his foot. He shouted in alarm. **4**But the angel said to him, "Take hold of the fish and don't let it get away!" They boy seized the fish and hauled it up on the shore. **5†**The angel then told him: "Cut the fish

---

† 5, 6: *It is a good two days' travel from Ecbatana to Rages:* Alexander's army took eleven days in forced marches to cover this distance, about 180 miles. The author is merely using popular impressions about faraway places; he is not teaching geography. (See notes on 1, 15; 3, 7 and Introduction.)

5, 10: *Hearty greetings* and *what joy* form a wordplay on the Greek verb *chairein,* "to greet" and "to be joyful."

5, 13-14: *Azariah,* "Yahweh helps"; *Hananiah,* "Yahweh is merciful"; *Nathaniah,* "Yahweh gives"; *Shemaiah,* "Yahweh hears."

5, 15: *The normal wages:* literally, "a drachma," about seventeen cents, a day's wages for a workingman.

5, 22: *My love:* literally, "sister," a term of endearment applied to one's wife; cf 7, 11.15; 8, 4.21; 10, 6.13; Sg 4, 9.10.12; 5, 1f.

A good angel: a reference to the guardian angel, though Tobit does not know, of course, that Raphael himself, disguised as Azariah, is the good angel in this case.

6, 5: *Its gall . . . medicines:* belief in the healing power of these organs was common among even the physicians of antiquity.

---

open and take out its gall, heart, and liver, and keep them with you; but throw away the entrails. Its gall, heart, and liver make useful medicines." **6**After the lad had cut the fish open, he put aside the gall, heart, and liver. Then he broiled and ate part of the fish; the rest he salted and kept for the journey.

Raphael's Instructions

7Afterward they traveled on together till they were near Media. The boy asked the angel this question: "Brother Azariah, what medicinal value is there in the fish's heart, liver, and gall?" **8**He answered: "As regards the fish's heart and liver, if you burn them so that the smoke surrounds a man or a woman who is afflicted by a demon or evil spirit, the affliction will leave him completely, and no demons will ever return to him again. **9**And as for the gall, if you rub it on the eyes of a man who has cataracts, blowing into his eyes right on the cataracts, his sight will be restored."

10When they had entered Media and were getting close to Ecbatana, **11**Raphael said to the boy, "Brother Tobiah!" He answered, "Yes, what is it?" Raphael continued: "Tonight we must stay with Raguel, who is a relative of yours. He has a daughter named Sarah, **12***but no other child. Since you are Sarah's closest relative, you before all other men have the right to marry her. Also, her father's estate is rightfully yours to inherit. Now the girl is sensible, courageous, and very beautiful; and her father loves her dearly." **13**†He continued: "Since you have the right to marry her, listen to me, brother. Tonight I will ask the girl's father to let us have her as your bride. When we return from Rages, we will hold the wedding feast for her. I know that Raguel cannot keep her from you or let her become engaged to another man; that would be a capital crime according to the decree in the Book of Moses, and he knows that it is your right, before all other men, to marry his daughter. So heed my words, brother; tonight we must speak for the girl, so that we may have her engaged to you. And when we return from Rages, we will take her and bring her back with us to your house."

14Tobiah objected, however: "Brother Azariah, I have heard that this woman has already been married seven times, and that her husbands died in their bridal chambers. On the very night they approached her, they dropped dead. And I have heard it said that it was a demon who killed them. **15***So now I too am afraid of this demon. Because he loves her, he does not harm her; but he does slay any man who wishes to come close to her. I am my father's only child. If I should die, I would bring my father and mother down to their grave in sorrow over me. And they have no other son to bury them!"

16Raphael said to him: "Do you not remember your father's orders? He commanded you to marry a woman from your own family. So now listen to me, brother; do not give another thought to this demon, but marry

Sarah. I know that tonight you shall have her for your wife! **17**When you go into the bridal chamber, take the fish's liver and heart, and place them on the embers for the incense. **18**†As soon as the demon smells the odor they give off, he will flee and never again show himself near her. Then when you are about to have intercourse with her, both of you first rise up to pray. Beg the Lord of heaven to show you mercy and grant you deliverance. But do not be afraid, for she was set apart for you before the world existed. You will save her, and she will go with you. And I suppose that you will have children by her, who will take the place of brothers for you. So do not worry."

When Tobiah heard Raphael say that she was his kinswoman, of his own family's lineage, he fell deeply in love with her, and his heart became set on her.

At the House of Raguel

7 **1**WHEN they entered Ecbatana, Tobiah said, "Brother Azariah, lead me straight to our kinsman Raguel." So he brought him to the house of Raguel, whom they found seated by his courtyard gate. They greeted him first. He said to them, "Greetings to you too, brothers! Good health to you, and welcome!" When he brought them into his home, **2**he said to his wife Edna, "This young man looks just like my kinsman Tobit!" **3**So Edna asked them, "Who are you, brothers?" They answered, "We are of the exiles from Naphtali at Nineveh." **4**She said, "Do you know our kinsman Tobit?" They answered, "Indeed we do!" She asked, "Is he well?" **5**They answered, "Yes, he is alive and well." Then Tobiah exclaimed, "He is my father!" **6**Raguel sprang up and kissed him, shedding tears of joy. **7**But when he heard that Tobit had lost his eyesight, he was grieved and wept aloud. He said to Tobiah: "My child, God bless you! You are the son of a noble and good father. But what a terrible misfortune that such a righteous and charitable man should be afflicted with blindness!" He continued to weep in the arms of his kinsman Tobiah. **8**His wife Edna also wept for Tobit; and even their daughter Sarah began to weep.

Marriage of Tobiah and Sarah

9Afterward, Raguel slaughtered a ram from the flock and gave them a cordial reception. When they had bathed and reclined to eat, Tobiah said to Raphael, "Brother Azariah, ask Raguel to let me marry my kinswoman Sarah." **10**Raguel overheard the words; so he said to the boy: "Eat and drink and be merry tonight, for no man is more entitled to marry my daughter Sarah than you, brother. Besides, not even I have the right to give her to anyone but you, because you are my closest relative. But I will explain the situation

---

† 6, 13: *Raguel . . . Book of Moses:* Nm 36, 6-8 prescribed marriage within the ancestral tribe, but no death penalty is mentioned.

6, 18: *Rise up to pray:* prayer is needed to drive out the demon.

to you very frankly. ¹¹I have given her in marriage to seven men, all of whom were kinsmen of ours, and all died on the very night they approached her. But now, son, eat and drink. I am sure the Lord will look after you both." Tobiah answered, "I will eat or drink nothing until you set aside what belongs to me."

Raguel said to him: "I will do it. She is yours according to the decree of the Book of Moses. Your marriage to her has been decided in heaven! Take your kinswoman; from now on you are her love, and she is your beloved. She is yours today and ever after. And tonight, son, may the lord of heaven prosper you both. May he grant you mercy and peace." ¹²*Then Raguel called his daughter Sarah, and she came to him. He took her by the hand and gave her to Tobiah with the words: "Take her according to the law. According to the decree written in the Book of Moses she is your wife. Take her and bring her back safely to your father. And may the God of heaven grant both of you peace and prosperity." ¹³*He then called her mother and told her to bring a scroll, so that he might draw up a marriage contract stating that he gave Sarah to Tobiah as his wife according to the decree of the Mosaic law. Her mother brought the scroll, and he drew up the contract, to which they affixed their seals.

¹⁴Afterward they began to eat and drink. ¹⁵Later Raguel called his wife Edna and said, "My love, prepare the other bedroom and bring the girl there." ¹⁶She went and made the bed in the room, as she was told, and brought the girl there. After she had cried over her, she wiped away the tears and said: ¹⁷"Be brave, my daughter. May the Lord of heaven grant you joy in place of your grief. Courage, my daughter." Then she left.

Expulsion of the Demon

8 ¹WHEN they had finished eating and drinking, the girl's parents wanted to retire. They brought the young man out of the dining room and led him into the bedroom. ²†At this point Tobiah, mindful of Raphael's instructions, took the fish's liver and heart from the bag which he had with him, and placed them on the embers for the incense. ³†The demon, repelled by the odor of the fish, fled into Upper Egypt; Raphael pursued him there and bound him hand and foot. Then Raphael returned immediately.

⁴When the girl's parents left the bedroom and closed the door behind them, Tobiah arose from bed and said to his wife, "My love, get up. Let us pray and beg our Lord to have mercy on us and to grant us deliverance." ⁵*She got up, and they started to pray and beg that deliverance might be theirs. He began with these words:

"Blessed are you, O God of our fathers;
praised be your name forever and ever.
Let the heavens and all your creation
praise you forever.

⁶*You made Adam and you gave him his wife Eve
to be his help and support;
and from these two the human race descended.
You said, 'It is not good for the man to be alone;
let us make him a partner like . . . . himself,'
⁷Now, Lord, you know that I take this wife of mine
not because of lust,
but for a noble purpose.
Call down your mercy on me and on her,
and allow us to live together to a happy old age."

⁸They said together, "Amen, amen," ⁹and went to bed for the night.

But Raguel got up and summoned his servants. With him they went out to dig a grave, ¹⁰for he said, "I must do this, because if Tobiah should die, we would be subjected to ridicule and insult." ¹¹When they had finished digging the grave, Raguel went back into the house and called his wife, ¹²saying, "Send one of the maids in to see whether Tobiah is alive or dead, so that if necessary we may bury him without anyone's knowing about it." ¹³She sent the maid, who lit a lamp, opened the bedroom door, went in, and found them sound asleep together. ¹⁴The maid went out and told the girl's parents that Tobiah was alive, and that there was nothing wrong. ¹⁵Then Raguel praised the God of heaven in these words:

"Blessed are you, O God, with every holy and pure blessing!
Let all your chosen ones praise you;
let them bless you forever!
¹⁶Blessed are you, who have made me glad;
what I feared did not happen.
Rather you have dealt with us
according to your great mercy.
¹⁷Blessed are you, for you were merciful
toward two only children.
Grant them, Master, mercy and deliverance,
and bring their lives to fulfillment
with happiness and mercy."

¹⁸Then he told his servants to fill in the grave before dawn.

Wedding Feast

¹⁹He asked his wife to bake many loaves of bread; he himself went out to the herd and picked out two steers and four rams which he ordered to be slaughtered. So the servants began to prepare the feast. ²⁰†He

---

† 8, 2f: The manner of coping with demonic influences among the ancients seems quaint to us. However, the fish here is part of the story, and not a recipe for exorcism. It is clear that the author places primary emphasis on the value of prayer to God (6, 18; 8, 4-8), on the role of the angel as God's agent, and on the pious dispositions of Tobiah.

8, 3: *Into Upper Egypt:* to the desert there. The desert was considered the dwelling place of demons. Cf Is 13, 21; 34, 14; Mt 4, 1; 12, 43.

8, 20: *For fourteen days:* because of the happy, and unexpected, turn of events, Raguel doubles the time of the wedding feast. When Tobiah returns home, the usual seven-day feast is held (11, 18). Cf Jgs 14, 12.

7/12: Gn 24, 50f.
13: 6, 12.
8/5: Dn 3, 26.
6: Gn 2, 18-23.

summoned Tobiah and made an oath in his presence, saying: "For fourteen days you shall not stir from here, but shall remain here eating and drinking with me; and you shall bring joy to my daughter's sorrowing spirit. ²¹Take, to begin with, half of whatever I own when you go back in good health to your father; the other half will be yours when I and my wife die. Be of good cheer, my son! I am your father, and Edna is your mother; and we belong to you and to your beloved now and forever. So be happy, son!"

The Money Recovered

9 ¹THEN Tobiah called Raphael and said to him: ²"Brother Azariah, take along with you four servants and two camels and travel to Rages. Go to Gabael's house and give him this bond. Get the money and then bring him along with you to the wedding celebration. ⁴For you know that my father is counting the days. If I should delay my return by a single day, I would cause him intense grief. ³You witnessed the oath that Raguel has sworn; I cannot violate his oath." ⁵So Raphael, together with the four servants and two camels, traveled to Rages in Media, where they stayed at Gabael's house. Raphael gave Gabael his bond and told him about Tobit's son Tobiah, and that he had married and was inviting him to the wedding celebration. Gabael promptly checked over the sealed moneybags, and they placed them on the camels.

⁶The following morning they got an early start and traveled to the wedding celebration. When they entered Raguel's house, they found Tobiah reclining at table. He sprang up and greeted Gabael, who wept and blessed him, exclaiming: "O noble and good child, son of a noble and good, upright and charitable man, may the Lord grant heavenly blessing to you and to your wife, and to your wife's father and mother. Blessed be God, because I have seen the very image of my cousin Tobit!"

IV: TOBIAH'S RETURN; CURE OF TOBIT'S BLINDNESS

Anxiety of the Parents

10 ¹MEANWHILE, DAY BY DAY, Tobit was keeping track of the time Tobiah would need to go and to return. When the number of days was reached and his son did not appear, ²he said, "I wonder what has happened. Perhaps he has been detained there; or perhaps Gabael is dead, and there is no one to give him the money." ³And he began to worry. ⁴His wife Anna said, "My son has perished and is no longer among the living!" And she began to weep aloud and to wail over her son: ⁵"Alas, my child, light of my eyes, that I let you make this journey!" ⁶But Tobit kept telling her: "Hush, do not think about it, my love; he is

safe! Probably they have to take care of some unexpected business there. The man who is traveling with him is trustworthy, and is one of our own kinsmen. So do not worry over him, my love. He will be here soon." ⁷*But she retorted, "Stop it, and do not lie to me! My child has perished!" She would go out and keep watch all day at the road her son had taken, and she ate nothing. At sunset she would go back home to wail and cry the whole night through, getting no sleep at all.

Departure from Ecbatana

Now at the end of the fourteen-day wedding celebration which Raguel had sworn to hold for his daughter, Tobiah went to him and said: "Please let me go, for I know that my father and mother do not believe they will ever see me again. So I beg you, father, let me go back to my father. I have already told you how I left him." ⁸Raguel said to Tobiah: "Stay, my child, stay with me. I am sending messengers to your father Tobit, and they will give him news of you." ⁹But Tobiah insisted, "No, I beg you to let me go back to my father."

¹⁰Raguel then promptly handed over to Tobiah Sarah his wife, together with half of all his property: male and female slaves, oxen and sheep, asses and camels, clothing, money, and household goods. ¹¹Bidding them farewell, he let them go. He embraced Tobiah and said to him: "Good-bye, my son. Have a safe journey. May the Lord of heaven grant prosperity to you and to your wife Sarah. And may I see children of yours before I die!" ¹²Then he kissed his daughter Sarah and said to her: "My daughter, honor your father-in-law and your mother-in-law, because from now on they are as much your parents as the ones who brought you into the world. Go in peace, my daughter; let me hear good reports about you as long as I live." Finally he said good-bye to them and sent them away.

Then Edna said to Tobiah: ¹³"My child and beloved kinsman, may the Lord bring you back safely, and may I live long enough to see children of you and of my daughter Sarah before I die. Before the Lord, I entrust my daughter to your care. Never cause her grief at any time in your life. Go in peace, my child. From now on I am your mother, and Sarah is your beloved. May all of us be prosperous all the days of our lives." She kissed them both and sent them away in peace.

¹⁴When Tobiah left Raguel, he was full of happiness and joy, and he blessed the Lord of heaven and earth, the King of all, for making his journey so successful. Finally he said good-bye to Raguel and his wife Edna, and added, "May I honor you all the days of my life!"

Homeward Journey

11 ¹THEN they left and began their return journey. When they were near Kaserin, just before Nineveh, ²Raphael said: "You know how we left your father. ³Let us hurry on ahead of your wife to prepare the house while the rest of the party are still on the way." ⁴So they both went on ahead and

---

10/7: Gn 45, 26.

Raphael said to Tobiah, "Have the gall in your hand!" And the dog ran along behind them.

⁵Meanwhile, Anna sat watching the road by which her son was to come. ⁶When she saw him coming, she exclaimed to his father, "Tobit, your son is coming, and the man who traveled with him!"

⁷Raphael said to Tobiah before he reached his father: "I am certain that his eyes will be opened. ⁸Smear the fish gall on them. This medicine will make the cataracts shrink and peel off from his eyes; then your father will again be able to see the light of day."

Sight Restored

⁹*Then Anna ran up to her son, threw her arms around him, and said to him, "Now that I have seen you again, son, I am ready to die!" And she sobbed aloud. ¹⁰Tobit got up and stumbled out through the courtyard gate. Tobiah went up to him ¹¹with the fish gall in his hand, and holding him firmly, blew into his eyes. "Courage, father," he said. ¹²Next he smeared the medicine on his eyes, ¹³and it made them smart. Then, beginning at the corners of Tobit's eyes, Tobiah used both hands to peel off the cataracts. When Tobit saw his son, he threw his arms around him ¹⁴and wept. He exclaimed, "I can see you, son, the light of my eyes!" Then he said:

> "Blessed be God,
>   and praised be his great name,
>   and blessed be all his holy angels.
> May his holy name be praised
>   throughout all the ages,
> ¹⁵*Because it was he who scourged me,
>   and it is he who has had mercy on me.
> Behold, I now see my son Tobiah!"

Then Tobit went back in, rejoicing and praising God with full voice. Tobiah told his father that his journey had been a success; that he had brought back the money; and that he had married Raguel's daughter Sarah, who would arrive shortly, for she was approaching the gate of Nineveh.

¹⁶Rejoicing and praising God, Tobit went out to the gate of Nineveh to meet his daughter-in-law. When the people of Nineveh saw him walking along briskly, with no one leading him by the hand, they were amazed. ¹⁷Before them all Tobit proclaimed how God had mercifully restored sight to his eyes. When Tobit reached Sarah, the wife of his son Tobiah, he greeted her: "Welcome, my daughter! Blessed be your God for bringing you to us, daughter! Blessed are your father and your mother. Blessed is my son Tobiah, and blessed are you, daughter! Welcome to your home with blessing and joy. Come in, daughter!" That day there was joy for all the Jews who lived in Nineveh. ¹⁸Ahiqar and his nephew Nadab also came to rejoice

with Tobit. They celebrated Tobiah's wedding feast for seven happy days, and he received many gifts.

V: RAPHAEL REVEALS HIS IDENTITY

Raphael's Wages

12 ¹†WHEN THE WEDDING CELEBRATION came to an end, Tobit called his son Tobiah and said to him, "Son, see to it that you give what is due to the man who made the journey with you; give him a bonus too." ²*Tobiah said: "Father, how much shall I pay him? It would not hurt me at all to give him half of all the wealth he brought back with me. ³He led me back safe and sound; he cured my wife; he brought the money back with me; and he cured you. How much of a bonus should I give him?" ⁴Tobit answered, "It is only fair, son, that he should receive half of all that he brought back." ⁵So Tobiah called Raphael and said, "Take as your wages half of all that you have brought back, and go in peace."

Exhortation

⁶†Raphael called the two men aside privately and said to them: "Thank God! Give him the praise and the glory. Before all the living, acknowledge the many good things he has done for you, by blessing and extolling his name in song. Before all men, honor and proclaim God's deeds, and do not be slack in praising him. ⁷A king's secret it is prudent to keep, but the works of God are to be declared and made known. Praise them with due honor. Do good, and evil will not find its way to you. ⁸*†Prayer and fasting are good, but better than either is almsgiving accompanied by righteousness. A little with righteousness is better than abundance with wickedness. It is better to give alms than to store up gold; ⁹*for almsgiving saves one from death and expiates every sin. Those who regularly give alms shall enjoy a full life; ¹⁰but those habitually guilty of sin are their own worst enemies.

Raphael's Identity

¹¹"I will now tell you the whole truth; I will conceal nothing at all from you. I have already said to you, 'A king's secret it is prudent to keep, but the works of God are to be made known with due honor.' ¹²*†I can

---

† 12, 1-5: Tobit and his son generously agree to give Azariah far more than the wages agreed upon in 5, 15-16.

12, 6-10: In the fashion of a wisdom teacher, Raphael gives the two men a short exhortation similar to the one Tobit gave his son in 4, 3-19.

12, 6f: The Jews considered the duty of praising God their most esteemed privilege. Without praise of God, life was meaningless. Cf Is 38, 16-20.

12, 8: Prayer . . . fasting . . . almsgiving . . . righteousness: these, together with the proper attitude toward wealth, are treated in great detail by Christ our Lord in the Sermon on the Mount (Mt 6).

12, 12.15: Raphael is one of the seven specially designated intercessors who present man's prayers to God. Angelology was

    11/9: Gn 33, 4; 45, 14; 46,
        29f; Lk 15, 20.
    15: 13, 2; Dt 32, 39; 1 Sm
        2, 6; Tb 13, 2.
    12/2: 5, 3.7.15f.

    8: 4, 7-11; Sir 29, 8-13.
    9: Dn 4, 24.
    12: Jb 33, 23f; Acts 10, 4;
        Rv 8, 3f.

now tell you that when you, Tobit, and Sarah prayed, it was I who presented and read the record of your prayer before the Glory of the Lord; and I did the same thing when you used to bury the dead. **¹³**When you did not hesitate to get up and leave your dinner in order to go and bury the dead, **¹⁴†**I was sent to put you to the test. At the same time, however, God commissioned me to heal you and your daughter-in-law Sarah. **¹⁵***I am Raphael, one of the seven angels who enter and serve before the Glory of the Lord."

¹⁶Stricken with fear, the two men fell to the ground. **¹⁷**But Raphael said to them: "No need to fear; you are safe. Thank God now and forever. **¹⁸**As for me, when I came to you it was not out of any favor on my part, but because it was God's will. So continue to thank him every day; praise him with song. **¹⁹**Even though you watched me eat and drink, I did not really do so; what you were seeing was a vision. **²⁰***So now get up from the ground and praise God. Behold, I am about to ascend to him who sent me; write down all these things that have happened to you." **²¹**When Raphael ascended, they rose to their feet and could no longer see him. **²²**They kept thanking God and singing his praises; and they continued to acknowledge these marvelous deeds which he had done when the angel of God appeared to them.

VI: TOBIT'S SONG OF PRAISE

13

¹*†THEN TOBIT COMPOSED this joyful prayer:

Blessed be God who lives forever,
   because his kingdom lasts for all ages.
²*For he scourges and then has mercy;
   he casts down to the depths of the nether world,
   and he brings up from the great abyss.
No one can escape his hand.

³Praise him, you Israelites, before the Gentiles,
   for though he has scattered you among them,
⁴he has shown you his greatness even there.
Exalt him before every living being,
   because he is the Lord our God,
   our Father and God forever.

⁵*He scourged you for your iniquities,
   but will again have mercy on you all.
He will gather you from all the Gentiles
   among whom you have been scattered.

⁶*When you turn back to him with all your heart,
   to do what is right before him,
Then he will turn back to you,
   and no longer hide his face from you.

So now consider what he has done for you,
   and praise him with full voice.
Bless the Lord of righteousness,
   and exalt the King of the ages.

In the land of my exile I praise him,
   and show his power and majesty to a sinful
     nation.
"Turn back, you sinners! do the right before him:
   perhaps he may look with favor upon you
   and show you mercy.

⁷"As for me, I exalt my God,
   and my spirit rejoices in the King of heaven.
⁸Let all men speak of his majesty,
   and sing his praises in Jerusalem."

⁹*†O Jerusalem, holy city,
   he scourged you for the works of your hands,
   but will again pity the children of the righteous.
¹⁰*Praise the Lord for his goodness,
   and bless the King of the ages,
   so that his tent may be rebuilt in you with joy.
May he gladden within you all who were captives;
   all who were ravaged may he cherish within you
   for all generations to come.

¹¹*A bright light will shine to all parts of the earth;
   many nations shall come to you from afar,
And the inhabitants of all the limits of the earth,
   drawn to you by the name of the Lord God,
Bearing in their hands their gifts
   for the King of heaven.
Every generation shall give joyful praise in you,
   and shall call you the chosen one,
   through all ages forever.

¹²*Accursed are all who speak a harsh word against
     you;
   accursed are all who destroy you
   and pull down your walls,
And all who overthrow your towers
   and set fire to your homes;
   but forever blessed are all those who build you
   up.

---

† developing in this period. The names of two other angels are given in the Bible: Gabriel (Dn 8, 16; 9, 21; Lk 1, 19.26) and Michael (Dn 10, 13.21; 12, 1; Jude 9; Rv 12, 7).

12, 14: *I was sent . . . test:* God often sends trials to purify his faithful servants further. Cf Jb 1—2.

13, 1-18: Tobit's hymn of praise (cf Ex 15, 1-18; Jdt 16, 1-17) is divided into two parts. The first part (vv 1-8) is a song of praise that echoes themes from the hymns and psalms of the kingdom; the second (vv 9-18) is addressed to Jerusalem in the style of the prophets who spoke of a new and ideal Jerusalem (Is 60); cf Rv 21.

13, 9: *Works of your hands:* idols.

✿
   15: Lk 1, 19; Rv 8, 2.
   20: Jgs 13, 20.
  13/1: 3, 11; 8, 5.15;
     1 Chr 29, 10; Dn 3, 26.
   2: 11, 15; 13, 9;
     Dt 32, 39; 1 Sm 2, 6;
     Wis 16, 13.
   5: Dt 30, 3; Neh 1, 9.

   6: Dt 30, 2.
   9: 11, 15; Mi 7, 19; Rv 21.
  10: Is 44, 26.28; Am 9, 11;
     Zec 1, 16.
  11: Is 2, 3f; 9, 1; 49, 6;
     60, 1; Mi 4, 2;
     Zec 8, 22.
  12: Bar 4, 31f.

13Go, then, rejoice over the children of the righteous,
who shall all be gathered together
and shall bless the Lord of the ages.
14*Happy are those who love you,
and happy those who rejoice in your prosperity.

Happy are all the men who shall grieve over you,
over all your chastisements,
For they shall rejoice in you
as they behold all your joy forever.

15My spirit blesses the Lord, the great King;
16*Jerusalem shall be rebuilt as his home forever.
Happy for me if a remnant of my offspring survive
to see your glory and to praise the King of
heaven!

The gates of Jerusalem shall be built with sapphire
and emerald,
and all your walls with precious stones.
The towers of Jerusalem shall be built with gold,
and their battlements with pure gold.
17The streets of Jerusalem shall be paved
with rubies and stones of Ophir;
18The gates of Jerusalem shall sing hymns of
gladness,
and all her houses shall cry out, "Alleluia!

"Blessed be God who has raised you up!
may he be blessed for all ages!"
For in you they shall praise his holy name forever.

The end of Tobit's hymn of praise.

VII: EPILOGUE

Parting Advice

14 **1**TOBIT DIED PEACEFULLY at the age of a hundred and twelve, and received an honorable burial in Nineveh. **2**He was sixty-two years old when he lost his eyesight, and after he recovered it he lived in prosperity, giving alms and continually blessing God and praising the divine Majesty.

3*Just before he died, he called his son Tobiah and Tobiah's seven sons, and gave him this command: "Son, take your children **4***†and flee into Media, for I believe God's word which was spoken by Nahum against Nineveh. It shall all happen, and shall overtake Assyria and Nineveh; indeed, whatever was said by Israel's prophets, whom God commissioned, shall occur. Not one of all the oracles shall remain unfulfilled, but everything shall take place in the time appointed for it. So it will be safer in Media than in Assyria or Babylon. For I know and believe that whatever God has spoken will be accomplished. It shall happen, and not a single word of the prophecies shall prove false.

"As for our kinsmen who dwell in Israel, they shall all be scattered and led away into exile from the Good Land. The entire country of Israel shall become desolate; even Samaria and Jerusalem shall become desolate! God's temple there shall be burnt to the ground and shall be desolate for a while. **5***†But God will again have mercy on them and bring them back to the land of Israel. They shall rebuild the temple, but it will not be like the first one, until the era when the appointed times shall be completed. Afterward all of them shall return from their exile, and they shall rebuild Jerusalem with splendor. In her the temple of God shall also be rebuilt; yes, it will be rebuilt for all generations to come, just as the prophets of Israel said of her. **6***†All the nations of the world shall be converted and shall offer God true worship; all shall abandon their idols which have deceitfully led them into error, **7***and shall bless the God of the ages in righteousness. Because all the Israelites who are to be saved in those days will truly be mindful of God, they shall be gathered together and go to Jerusalem; in security shall they dwell forever in the land of Abraham, which will be given over to them. Those who sincerely love God shall rejoice, but those who become guilty of sin shall completely disappear from the land.

9"Now, children, I give you this command: serve God faithfully and do what is right before him; you must tell your children to do what is upright and to give alms, to be mindful of God and at all times to bless his name sincerely and with all their strength.

8"Now, as for you, my son, depart from Nineveh; do not remain here. **10***†The day you bury your mother next to me, do not even stay overnight within the confines of the city. For I see that people here shamelessly commit all sorts of wickedness and treachery. Think, my son, of all that Nadab did to Ahiqar, the very one who brought him up: Ahiqar went down alive into

---

† 14, 4f: *Nahum:* one of the minor prophets, whose book contains oracles of doom against Nineveh. Here, in keeping with the period to which he assigns his story, the sacred author makes Tobit speak as if the punishment of Nineveh, the destruction of Jerusalem (587 B. C.), the exile from Judah and the return, would all take place in the future. The technique of using the facts of past history as seemingly future predictions, is a frequent device of apocalyptic writers. *The Good Land:* a favorite name for the promised land. Cf Dt 1, 35; 3, 25; 4, 21.22.

14, 5: *Until the era . . . completed:* a reference to the advent of messianic times, in which a new, more perfect temple was to be expected. Cf Heb 9, 1-14.

14, 6: Conversion of the Gentiles is also to come in the messianic era.

14, 10: *Nadab:* In the *Story of Ahiqar,* the hero Ahiqar, chancellor under the Assyrian kings Sennacherib and Esarhaddon, adopts his nephew Nadab and prepares him to become his successor. But Nadab treacherously plots to have his uncle put to death. Ahiqar hides in a friend's house, and is finally vindicated (*came out again into the light*) when Nadab's scheme is discovered. Thereupon Nadab is thrown into a dungeon where he dies (*went into everlasting darkness*). It was Ahiqar's almsgiving that delivered him from death; see note on 2, 2.

✷
    14: Ps 122, 6; Is 66, 10.
    16: 14, 5; Is 54, 11-13;
        62, 2; Rv 21, 10-21.
  14/3: Gn 47, 29f.
    4: Na 2, 2–3, 19.
    5: Neh 12, 27; Jer 31, 38.

    6: 45, 14; Is 60, 1-4.
    7: Is 60, 21; Jer 32, 37;
        Ez 34, 28; 37, 25;
        39, 26.
  10: 1, 21f.

the earth! Yet God made Nadab's disgraceful crime rebound against him. Ahiqar came out again into the light, but Nadab went into the everlasting darkness, for he had tried to kill Ahiqar. Because Ahiqar had given alms to me, he escaped from the deadly trap Nadab had set for him. But Nadab himself fell into the deadly trap, and it destroyed him. [11]So, my children, note well what almsgiving does, and also what wickedness does—it kills! But now my spirit is about to leave me."

Death of Tobit and Tobiah

They placed him on his bed and he died; and he received an honorable burial. [12]*When Tobiah's mother died, he buried her next to his father. He then

---

　　　*　　12: 4, 4.

departed with his wife and children for Media, where he settled in Ecbatana with his father-in-law Raguel. [13]He took respectful care of his aging father-in-law and mother-in-law; and he buried them at Ecbatana in Media. Then he inherited Raguel's estate as well as that of his father Tobit. [14]He died at the venerable age of a hundred and seventeen. [15]†But before he died, he heard of the destruction of Nineveh and saw its effects. He witnessed the exile of the city's inhabitants when Cyaxares, king of Media, led them captive into Media. Tobiah praised God for all that he had done against the citizens of Nineveh and Assyria. Before dying he rejoiced over Nineveh's destruction, and he blessed the Lord God forever and ever. Amen.

---

† 14, 15: *Cyaxares:* Nabopolassar, king of Babylon, and Cyaxares conquered and destroyed Nineveh in 612 B. C.; see note on 1, 15.

The Book of Judith

Introduction

The Book of Judith is a vivid story relating how, in a grave crisis, God delivered the Jewish people through the instrumentality of a woman. The unknown author composed this edifying narrative of divine providence at the end of the second or the beginning of the first century B. C. The original was almost certainly written in Hebrew, but the Greek text shows so much freedom in adapting from the Septuagint the language of older biblical books that it must be regarded as having a literary character of its own. It is this Greek form of the book, accepted as canonical by the Catholic Church, which is translated here. St. Jerome, who prepared (with some reluctance) a Latin text of Judith, based his work on a secondary Aramaic text available to him in Palestine, combined with an older Latin rendering from the Greek. The long hymn of chapter 16 he took in its entirety from that earlier Latin text.

Since it is no longer possible to determine with any precision the underlying events which may have given rise to this narrative, it is enough to note that the author sought to strengthen the faith of his people in God's abiding presence among them. The Book of Judith is a tract for difficult times; the reader, it was hoped, would take to heart the lesson that God was still the Master of history, who could save Israel from her enemies. Note the parallel with the time of the Exodus: as God had delivered his people by the hand of Moses, so he could deliver them by the hand of the pious widow Judith (see note on 2, 12).

The story can be divided into two parts. In the first (cc 1—7), Holofernes, commander-in-chief of the armies of Nebuchadnezzar, leads an overwhelming Assyrian force in a punitive campaign against the vassals who refused to help in the Assyrian war against the Medes. The Jewish people stubbornly resist the enemy at Bethulia, guarding the route of access to Jerusalem. Despite the warning of Achior that the Jews cannot be conquered unless they sin against God, the proud general lays siege to the town and cuts off its water supply. After a siege of thirty-four days, the exhausted defenders are desperate and ready to surrender.

At this point, the climax of the story, Judith (the name means "Jewess") appears and promises to defeat the Assyrians. The rest of the story is too well known to repeat in detail. Having fasted and prayed, Judith dresses in her finest garments and proceeds to the Assyrian camp, where she succeeds in killing Holofernes while he lies in a drunken stupor. The Assyrians panic when they discover this, and the Jews are able to rout and slaughter them. The beautiful hymn of the people honoring Judith (15, 9-10) is often applied to Mary in the liturgy.

Any attempt to read the book directly against the backdrop of Jewish history in relation to the empires of the ancient world is bound to fail. The story was written as a pious reflection on the meaning of the yearly Passover observance. It draws its inspiration from the Exodus narrative (especially Ex 14, 31) and from the texts of Isaiah and the Psalms portraying the special intervention of God for the preservation of Jerusalem. The theme of God's hand as the agent of this providential activity, reflected of old in the hand of Moses and now in the hand of Judith, is again exemplified at a later time in Jewish synagogue art. God's hand reaching down from heaven appears as part of the scene at Dura-Europos (before A. D. 256) in paintings of the Exodus, of the sacrifice of Isaac (Gn 22), and of Ezekiel's valley of dry bones (Ez 37).

The Book of Judith is divided as follows:
> I: Peril of the Jews (1, 1—7, 32)
> II: Deliverance of the Jews (8, 1—14, 10)
> III: Victory (14, 11—16, 25)

I: PERIL OF THE JEWS

War against the Medes

1 [1]IT WAS THE TWELFTH YEAR of the reign of Nebuchadnezzar, king of the Assyrians in the great city of Nineveh. At that time Arphaxad ruled over the Medes in Ecbatana. [2]Around this city he built a wall of blocks of stone, each three cubits in height and six in length. He made the wall seventy cubits high and fifty thick. [3]At the gates he raised towers of a hundred cubits, with a thickness of sixty cubits at the base. [4]The gateway he built to a height of seventy cubits, with an opening forty cubits wide for the passage of his chariot forces and the marshaling of his infantry. [5]Then King Nebuchadnezzar waged war against King Arphaxad in the vast plain, in the district of Ragae. [6][†]To him there rallied all the inhabitants of the mountain region, all who dwelt along the Euphrates, the Tigris, and the Hydaspes, and King Arioch of the Elamites, in the plain. Thus many nations came together to resist the people of Cheleoud.

Ultimatum to the West

[7]Now Nebuchadnezzar, king of the Assyrians, sent messengers to all the inhabitants of Persia, and to all those who dwelt in the West: to the inhabitants of

---

[†] 1, 6: *Cheleoud:* probably the Chaldeans are meant.

Cilicia and Damascus, Lebanon and Anti-Lebanon, to all who dwelt along the seacoast, **8**to the peoples of Carmel, Gilead, Upper Galilee, and the vast plain of Esdraelon, **9**to all those in Samaria and its cities, and west of the Jordan as far as Jerusalem, Bethany, Chelous, Kadesh, and the River of Egypt; to Tahpanhes, Raamses, all the land of Goshen, **10**Tanis, Memphis and beyond, and to all the inhabitants of Egypt as far as the borders of Ethiopia.

11But the inhabitants of all that land disregarded the summons of Nebuchadnezzar, king of the Assyrians, and would not go with him to the war. They were not afraid of him but regarded him as a lone individual opposed to them, and turned away his envoys empty-handed, in disgrace. **12†**Then Nebuchadnezzar fell into a violent rage against all that land, and swore by his throne and his kingdom that he would avenge himself on all the territories of Cilicia and Damascus and Syria, and also destroy with his sword all the inhabitants of Moab, Ammon, the whole of Judea, and those living anywhere in Egypt as far as the borders of the two seas.

Defeat of Arphaxad

13In the seventeenth year he proceeded with his army against King Arphaxad, and was victorious in his campaign. He routed the whole force of Arphaxad, his entire cavalry and all his chariots, **14**and took possession of his cities. He pressed on to Ecbatana and took its towers, sacked its market places, and turned its glory into shame. **15**Arphaxad himself he overtook in the mountains of Ragae, ran him through with spears, and utterly destroyed him. **16**°Then he returned home with all his numerous, motley horde of warriors; and there he and his army relaxed and feasted for a hundred and twenty days.

Council of War against the West

2 **1**IN the eighteenth year, on the twenty-second day of the first month, there was a discussion in the palace of Nebuchadnezzar, king of the Assyrians, about taking revenge on the whole world, as he had threatened. **2**He summoned all his ministers and nobles, laid before them his secret plan, and urged the total destruction of those countries. **3**They decided to do away with all those who had refused to comply with the order he had issued.

4When he had completed his plan, Nebuchadnezzar, king of the Assyrians, summoned Holofernes, general in chief of his forces, second to himself in command, and said to him:

5°"Thus says the great king, the lord of all the earth: Go forth from my presence, take with you men of proven valor, a hundred and twenty thousand infantry and twelve thousand cavalry, **6**and proceed against all the land of the West, because they did not comply with the order I issued. **7†**Tell them to have earth and water

ready, for I will come against them in my wrath; I will cover all the land with the feet of my soldiers, to whom I will deliver them as spoils. **8**Their slain shall fill their ravines and wadies, the swelling torrent shall be choked with their dead; **9**and I will deport them as exiles to the very ends of the earth.

10"You go before me and take possession of all their territories for me. If they surrender to you, guard them for me till the day of their punishment. **11**As for those who resist, show them no quarter, but deliver them up to slaughter and plunder in each country you occupy. **12†**For as I live, and by the strength of my kingdom, what I have spoken I will accomplish by my power. **13**Do not disobey a single one of the orders of your lord; fulfill them exactly as I have commanded you, and do it without delay."

Campaign of Holofernes

14So Holofernes left the presence of his lord, and summoned all the princes, and the generals and officers of the Assyrian army. **15**He mustered a hundred and twenty thousand picked troops, as his lord had commanded, and twelve thousand mounted archers, **16**and grouped them into a complete combat force. **17**He took along a very large number of camels, asses, and mules for their baggage; innumerable sheep, cattle, and goats for their food supply; **18**abundant provisions for each man, and much gold and silver from the royal palace.

19Then he and his whole army proceeded on their expedition in advance of King Nebuchadnezzar, to cover all the western region with their chariots and cavalry and regular infantry. **20**°A huge, irregular force, too many to count, like locusts or the dust of the earth, went along with them.

21After a three-day march from Nineveh, they reached the plain of Bectileth, and from Bectileth they next encamped near the mountains to the north of Upper Cilicia. **22**From there Holofernes took his whole force, the infantry, cavalry, and chariots, and marched into the mountain region. **23†**He devastated Put and Lud, and plundered all the Rassisites and the Ishmaelites on the border of the desert toward the south of Chaldea.

---

† 1, 12: *The two seas:* the ancient rulers in Mesopotamia often designated the limits of their realm as extending from the Upper Sea (the Mediterranean) to the Lower Sea (the Persian Gulf).

2, 7: *Earth and water:* in the Persian period, the offering of these to a conqueror was a symbolic gesture of unconditional surrender.

2, 12: *As I live:* in the Old Testament, an oath proper to divinity; cf Dt 32, 40. Nebuchadnezzar is making himself equal to God; see 6, 2. *By my power:* literally "by my hand." The hand of Nebuchadnezzar raised in opposition to God and to his people is the occasion for Judith's intervention *by a woman's hand;* cf 9, 9f; Is 10, 5-14.

2, 23: *Put and Lud:* the same as the "Put and Lud" mentioned in Ez 30, 5 as allies of Egypt, and in Ez 27, 10 as supplying mercenary soldiers to Tyre. Here they seem inserted to embellish the narrative with assonance and prophetic associations rather than to indicate definite localities.

° 1/16: Est 1, 3f.   20: Jgs 7, 12.
2/5f: Est 3, 8f.

24Then, following the Euphrates, he went through Mesopotamia, and battered down every fortified city along the Wadi Abron, until he reached the sea. **25**He seized the territory of Cilicia, and cut down everyone who resisted him. Then he proceeded to the southern borders of Japheth, toward Arabia. **26**He surrounded all the Midianites, burned their tents, and plundered their sheepfolds. **27**Descending to the plain of Damascus at the time of the wheat harvest, he set fire to all their fields, destroyed their flocks and herds, despoiled their cities, devastated their plains, and put all their youths to the sword.

28The fear and dread of him fell upon all the inhabitants of the coastland, upon those in Sidon and Tyre, and those who dwelt in Sur and Ocina, and the inhabitants of Jamnia. Those in Azotus and Ascalon also feared him greatly.

Submission of the West

3 **1**THEY therefore sent messengers to him to sue for peace in these words: **2**"We, the servants of Nebuchadnezzar the great king, lie prostrate before you; do with us as you will. **3**Our dwellings and all our wheat fields, our flocks and herds, and all our encampments are at your disposal; make use of them as you please. **4**Our cities and their inhabitants are also at your service; come and deal with them as you see fit."

5After the spokesmen had reached Holofernes and given him this message, **6**he went down with his army to the seacoast, and stationed garrisons in the fortified cities; from them he impressed picked troops as auxiliaries. **7**The people of these cities and all the inhabitants of the countryside received him with garlands and dancing to the sound of timbrels. **8***Nevertheless, he devastated their whole territory and cut down their sacred groves, for he had been commissioned to destroy all the gods of the earth, so that every nation might worship Nebuchadnezzar alone, and every people and tribe invoke him as a god. **9**At length Holofernes reached Esdraelon in the neighborhood of Dothan, the approach to the main ridge of the Judean mountains; **10**†he set up his camp between Geba and Scythopolis, and stayed there a whole month to refurbish all the equipment of his army.

Israelite Defense

4 **1**WHEN the Israelites who dwelt in Judea heard of all that Holofernes, commander in chief of Nebuchadnezzar, king of the Assyrians, had done to the nations, and how he had despoiled all their temples and destroyed them, **2**they were in extreme dread of him, and greatly alarmed for Jerusalem and the temple of the Lord, their God. **3**†Now, they had lately returned from exile, and only recently had all the people of Judea been gathered together, and the vessels, the altar, and the temple been purified

from profanation. **4**So they sent word to the whole region of Samaria, to Kona, Beth-horon, Belmain, and Jericho, to Choba and Aesora, and to the valley of Salem. **5**The people there posted guards on all the summits of the high mountains, fortified their villages, and since their fields had recently been harvested, stored up provisions in preparation for war.

6†Joakim, who was high priest in Jerusalem in those days, wrote to the inhabitants of Bethulia [and Betomesthaim], which is on the way to Esdraelon, facing the plain near Dothan, **7**and instructed them to keep firm hold of the mountain passes, since these offered access to Judea. It would be easy to ward off the attacking forces, as the defile was only wide enough for two abreast. **8**†The Israelites carried out the orders given them by Joakim, the high priest, and the senate of the whole people of Israel, which met in Jerusalem.

Prayer and Penance

9All the men of Israel cried to God with great fervor and did penance—**10***†they, along with their wives, and children, and domestic animals. All their resident aliens, hired laborers, and slaves also girded themselves with sackcloth. **11**†And all the Israelite men, women, and children who lived in Jerusalem prostrated themselves in front of the temple building, with ashes strewn on their heads, displaying their sackcloth covering before the Lord. **12***The altar, too, they draped in sackcloth; and with one accord they cried out fervently to the God of Israel not to allow their children to be seized, their wives to be taken captive, the cities of their inheritance to be ruined, or the sanctuary to be profaned and mocked for the nations to gloat over.

13*The Lord heard their cry and had regard for their distress. For the people observed a fast of many days' duration throughout Judea, and before the sanctuary of the Lord Almighty in Jerusalem. **14**The high priest Joakim, and all the priests in attendance on the Lord who served his altar, were also girded with sackcloth as they offered the daily holocaust, the votive offerings, and the free-will offerings of the people. **15**With ashes upon their turbans, they cried to the Lord with

---

† 3, 10: *Geba:* perhaps originally "Gelboe," the mountain range near the eastern end of which lay *Scythopolis,* the Greek name for ancient Beth-shean (Jos 17, 11).

4, 3: *Returned from exile . . . profanation:* these allusions are variously attributed—to the Persian period (538-323 B. C.), or even to a condition in the days of Antiochus Epiphanes (175-164 B. C.).

4, 6: *Joakim, who was high priest:* see Bar 1, 7 and the footnote on Bar 1, 8f; this name for a high priest cannot be used in dating the events in Jdt.

4, 8: The organization of the Jewish nation as subject to a *high priest* and a *senate,* or council of elders, was proper to the Greek period (after 323 B. C.), and is reflected in the coinage of John Hyrcanus (135-104 B. C.).

4, 10: *Domestic animals:* see note on Jon 3, 8.

4, 11: *Prostrated themselves in front of the temple building:* for a parallel to this ceremony of entreaty, see Jl 1, 13f; 2, 15ff, and the note on Jl 2, 17.

---

*   3/8: Ex 34, 13.   12: Est 4, 1f.
     4/10f: Jon 3, 7f.   13: Est 4, 16.

all their strength to look with favor on the whole house of Israel.

Council against the Israelites

5 ¹IT was reported to Holofernes, commander in chief of the Assyrian army, that the Israelites were ready for battle, and had blocked the mountain passes, fortified the summits of all the higher peaks, and placed roadblocks in the plains. ²In great anger he summoned all the rulers of the Moabites, the generals of the Ammonites, and all the satraps of the seacoast ³and said to them: "Now tell me, you Canaanites, what sort of people is this that dwells in the mountains? Which cities do they inhabit? How large is their army? In what does their power and strength consist? Who has set himself up as their king and the leader of their army? ⁴Why have they refused to come out to meet me along with all the other inhabitants of the West?"

Achior's Speech

⁵*Then Achior, the leader of all the Ammonites, said to him: "My lord, hear this account from your servant; I will tell you the truth about this people that lives near you [that inhabits this mountain region]; no lie shall escape your servant's lips.

⁶†"These people are descendants of the Chaldeans. ⁷*They formerly dwelt in Mesopotamia, for they did not wish to follow the gods of their forefathers who were born in the land of the Chaldeans. ⁸Since they abandoned the way of their ancestors, and acknowledged with divine worship the God of heaven, their forefathers expelled them from the presence of their gods. So they fled to Mesopotamia and dwelt there a long time. ⁹*Their God bade them leave their abode and proceed to the land of Canaan. Here they settled, and grew very rich in gold, silver, and a great abundance of livestock. ¹⁰*Later, when famine had gripped the whole land of Canaan, they went down into Egypt. They stayed there as long as they found sustenance, and grew into such a great multitude that the number of their race could not be counted. ¹¹*The king of Egypt, however, rose up against them, shrewdly forced them to labor at brickmaking, oppressed and enslaved them. ¹²But they cried to their God, and he struck the land of Egypt with plagues for which there was no remedy. When the Egyptians expelled them, ¹³*God dried up the Red Sea before them, ¹⁴and led them along the route to Sinai and Kadesh-barnea. First they drove out all the inhabitants of the desert; ¹⁵*then they settled in the land of the Amorites, destroyed all the Heshbonites by

main force, crossed the Jordan, and took possession of the whole mountain region. ¹⁶*They expelled the Canaanites, the Perizzites, the Jebusites, the Shechemites, and all the Gergesites; and they lived in these mountains a long time.

¹⁷*"As long as the Israelites did not sin in the sight of their God, they prospered, for their God, who hates wickedness, was with them. ¹⁸*But when they deviated from the way he prescribed for them, they were ground down steadily, more and more, by frequent wars, and finally taken as captives into foreign lands. The temple of their God was razed to the ground, and their cities were occupied by their enemies. ¹⁹But now that they have returned to their God, they have come back from the Dispersion wherein they were scattered, and have repossessed Jerusalem, where their sanctuary is, and have settled again in the mountain region which was unoccupied.

²⁰*"So now, my lord and master, if these people are at fault, and are sinning against their God, and if we verify this offense of theirs, then we shall be able to go up and conquer them. ²¹But if they are not a guilty nation, then your lordship should keep his distance; otherwise their Lord and God will shield them, and we shall become the laughingstock of the whole world."

²²Now when Achior had concluded his recommendation, all the people standing round about the tent murmured; and the officers of Holofernes and all the inhabitants of the seacoast and of Moab alike said he should be cut to pieces. ²³"We are not afraid of the Israelites," they said, "for they are a powerless people, incapable of a strong defense. ²⁴*Let us therefore attack them; your great army, Lord Holofernes, will swallow them up."

Holofernes' Answer

6 ¹WHEN the noise of the crowd surrounding the council had subsided, Holofernes, commander in chief of the Assyrian army, said to Achior, in the presence of the whole throng of coastland peoples, of the Moabites, and of the Ammonite mercenaries: ²*"Who are you, Achior, to prophesy among us as you have done today, and to tell us not to fight against the Israelites because their God protects them? What god is there beside Nebuchadnezzar? He will send his force and destroy them from the face of the earth. Their God will not save them; ³*but we, the servants of Nebuchadnezzar, will strike them down as one man, for they will be unable to withstand the force of our cavalry. ⁴*We will overwhelm them with it, and the mountains shall be drunk with their blood, and their plains filled with their corpses. Not a trace of

---

* 5/5: 11, 9-19.
    7: Gn 11, 31.
    9: Gn 11, 31—12, 5.
    10: Gn 42, 1-5; 46, 1-7;
       Ex 1, 7.
    11f: Ex 5, 4-21; 7, 1-9.
    13f: Ex 14, 21f.29.
    15: Nm 21, 21-32;
      Jos 2, 10.

    16: Dt 7.1.
    17f: Dt 28—30;
      Ps 106, 40-46; Is 59, 2.
    18: 2 Kgs 25.
    20f: 8, 18ff; 11, 10.
    24: 6, 2; 9, 7; 16, 2.
    6/2: 3, 8; 9, 7.
     3: Is 36, 18ff.
     4: 6, 17.

† 5, 6-9: Achior outlines the early history of the Hebrews, whose forefather, Abraham, first lived in Ur of the *Chaldeans* (Gn 11, 28) and then migrated to Haran (Gn 11, 31) in Aram Naharaim (Gn 24, 10), which was called *Mesopotamia* by the Greeks. *The gods of their forefathers* were the pagan deities worshiped by Abraham's relatives (Jos 24, 2).

them shall survive our attack: they shall utterly perish, says King Nebuchadnezzar, lord of all the earth; for he has spoken, and his words shall not remain unfulfilled. ⁵As for you, Achior, you Ammonite mercenary, for saying these things in a moment of perversity you shall not see my face after today, until I have taken revenge on this race of people from Egypt. ⁶*Then at my return, the sword of my army or the spear of my servants will pierce your sides, and you shall fall among their slain. ⁷My servants will now conduct you to the mountain region, and leave you at one of the towns along the ascent. ⁸You shall not die till you are destroyed together with them. ⁹If you still cherish the hope that they will not be taken, then there is no need for you to be downcast. I have spoken, and my words shall not prove false in any respect."

Achior in Bethulia

¹⁰Then Holofernes ordered the servants who were standing by in his tent to seize Achior, conduct him to Bethulia, and hand him over to the Israelites. ¹¹So the servants took him in custody and brought him out of the camp into the plain. From there they led him into the mountain region till they reached the springs below Bethulia. ¹²When the men of the city saw them, they seized their weapons and ran out of the city to the crest of the ridge; and all the slingers blocked the ascent of Holofernes' servants by hurling stones upon them. ¹³So they took cover below the mountain, where they bound Achior and left him lying at the foot of the mountain; then they returned to their lord.

¹⁴The Israelites came down to him from their city, loosed him, and brought him into Bethulia. They haled him before the rulers of the city, ¹⁵who in those days were Uzziah, son of Micah of the tribe of Simeon, Chabris, son of Gothoniel, and Charmis, son of Melchiel. ¹⁶They then convened all the elders of the city; and all their young men, as well as the women, gathered in haste at the place of assembly. They placed Achior in the center of the throng, and Uzziah questioned him about what had happened. ¹⁷He replied by giving them an account of what was said in the council of Holofernes, and of all his own words among the Assyrian officers, and of all the boasting threats of Holofernes against the house of Israel.

¹⁸At this the people fell prostrate and worshiped God; and they cried out: ¹⁹†"Lord, God of heaven, behold their arrogance! Have pity on the lowliness of our people, and look with favor this day on those who are consecrated to you." ²⁰Then they reassured Achior and praised him highly. ²¹Uzziah brought him from the assembly to his home, where he gave a banquet for the elders. That whole night they called upon the God of Israel for help.

Siege of Bethulia

7 ¹THE following day Holofernes ordered his whole army, and all the allied troops that had come to his support, to move against Bethulia, seize the mountain passes, and engage the Israelites in battle. ²That same day all their fighting men went into action. Their forces numbered a hundred and seventy thousand infantry and twelve thousand horsemen, not counting the baggage train or the men who accompanied it on foot—a very great army. ³They encamped at the spring in the valley near Bethulia, and spread out in breadth toward Dothan as far as Balbaim, and in length from Bethulia to Cyamon, which faces Esdraelon.

⁴When the Israelites saw how many there were, they said to one another in great dismay: "Soon they will devour the whole country. Neither the high mountains nor the valleys and hills can support the mass of them." ⁵†Yet they all seized their weapons, lighted fires on their bastions, and kept watch throughout the night.

⁶On the second day Holofernes led out all his cavalry in the sight of the Israelites who were in Bethulia. ⁷He reconnoitered the approaches to their city and located their sources of water; these he seized, stationing armed detachments around them, while he himself returned to his troops.

⁸All the commanders of the Edomites and all the leaders of the Ammonites, together with the generals of the seacoast, came to Holofernes and said: ⁹"Sir, listen to what we have to say, that there may be no losses among your troops. ¹⁰*These Israelites do not rely on their spears, but on the height of the mountains where they dwell; it is not easy to reach the summit of their mountains. ¹¹Therefore, sir, do not attack them in regular formation; thus not a single one of your troops will fall. ¹²Stay in your camp, and spare all your soldiers. Have some of your servants keep control of the source of water that flows out at the base of the mountain, ¹³*for that is where the inhabitants of Bethulia get their water. Then thirst will begin to carry them off, and they will surrender their city. Meanwhile, we and our men will go up to the summits of the nearby mountains, and encamp there to guard against anyone's leaving the city. ¹⁴They and their wives and children will languish with hunger, and even before the sword strikes them they will be laid low in the streets of their city. ¹⁵Thus you will render them dire punishment for their rebellion and their refusal to meet you peacefully."

---

† 6, 19: The Latin Vulgate (6, 15) has a longer form of this prayer: "Lord, God of heaven and earth, behold their arrogance; regard our lowliness and look with favor on your holy ones; show that you do not abandon those who trust in you, but that you humble those who trust in themselves and glory in their own strength."

7, 5: *Lighted fires on their bastions:* to serve as signals for alerting the neighboring towns. Reference to fire signals in time of siege is made in the Lachish ostraca at the beginning of the sixth century B. C. *Kept watch throughout the night:* to prevent a surprise attack.

6: 5, 22.
7/10: 1 Kgs 20, 23.28.

13: Ex 5, 21.

¹⁶Their words pleased Holofernes and all his ministers, and he ordered their proposal to be carried out. ¹⁷Thereupon the Moabites moved camp, together with five thousand Assyrians. They encamped in the valley, and held the water supply and the springs of the Israelites. ¹⁸The Edomites and the Ammonites went up and encamped in the mountain region opposite Dothan; and they sent some of their men to the south and to the east opposite Egrebel, near Chusi, which is on Wadi Mochmur. The rest of the Assyrian army was encamped in the plain, covering the whole countryside. Their enormous store of tents and equipment was spread out in profusion everywhere.

¹⁹*The Israelites cried to the Lord, their God, for they were disheartened, since all their enemies had them surrounded, and there was no way of slipping through their lines. ²⁰The whole Assyrian camp, infantry, chariots, and cavalry, kept them thus surrounded for thirty-four days. All the reservoirs of water failed the inhabitants of Bethulia, ²¹and the cisterns ran dry, so that on no day did they have enough to drink, but their drinking water was rationed. ²²Their children fainted away, and the women and youths were consumed with thirst and were collapsing in the streets and gateways of the city, with no strength left in them.

²³All the people, therefore, including youths, women, and children, went in a crowd to Uzziah and the rulers of the city. They set up a great clamor and said before the elders: ²⁴"God judge between you and us! You have done us grave injustice in not making peace with the Assyrians. ²⁵There is no help for us now! Instead, God has sold us into their power by laying us prostrate before them in thirst and utter exhaustion. ²⁶Therefore, summon them and deliver the whole city as booty to the troops of Holofernes and to all his forces; ²⁷we would be better off to become their prey. We should indeed be made slaves, but at least we should live, and not have to behold our little ones dying before our eyes and our wives and children breathing out their souls. ²⁸We adjure you by heaven and earth, and by our God, the Lord of our forefathers, who is punishing us for our sins and those of our forefathers, to do as we have proposed, this very day."

²⁹All in the assembly with one accord broke into shrill wailing and loud cries to the Lord their God. ³⁰But Uzziah said to them, "Courage, my brothers! Let us wait five days more for the Lord our God, to show his mercy toward us; he will not utterly forsake us. ³¹But if those days pass without help coming to us, I will do as you say." ³²Then he dispersed the men to their posts, and they returned to the walls and towers of the city; the women and children he sent to their homes. Throughout the city they were in great misery.

II: DELIVERANCE OF THE JEWS

Judith

8 ¹†NOW IN THOSE DAYS Judith, daughter of Merari, son of Joseph, son of Oziel, son of Elkiah, son of Ananias, son of Gideon, son of Raphain, son of Ahitob, son of Elijah, son of Hilkiah, son of Eliab, son of Nathanael, son of Salamiel, son of Sarasadai, son of Simeon, son of Israel, heard of this. ²Her husband, Manasseh, of her own tribe and clan, had died at the time of the barley harvest. ³While he was in the field supervising those who bound the sheaves, he suffered sunstroke; and he died of this illness in Bethulia, his native city. He was buried with his forefathers in the field between Dothan and Balamon. ⁴The widowed Judith remained three years and four months at home, ⁵†where she set up a tent for herself on the roof of her house. She put sackcloth about her loins and wore widow's weeds. ⁶*She fasted all the days of her widowhood, except sabbath eves and sabbaths, new moon eves and new moons, feastdays and holidays of the house of Israel. ⁷She was beautifully formed and lovely to behold. Her husband, Manasseh, had left her gold and silver, servants and maids, livestock and fields, which she was maintaining. ⁸No one had a bad word to say about her, for she was a very God-fearing woman.

Her Words to the Elders

⁹When Judith, therefore, heard of the harsh words which the people, discouraged by their lack of water, had spoken against their ruler, and of all that Uzziah had said to them in reply, swearing that he would hand over the city to the Assyrians at the end of five days, ¹⁰she sent the maid who was in charge of all her things to ask Uzziah, Chabris, and Charmis, the elders of the city, to visit her. ¹¹When they came, she said to them: "Listen to me, you rulers of the people of Bethulia. What you said to the people today is not proper. When you promised to hand over the city to our enemies at the end of five days unless within that time the Lord comes to our aid, you interposed between God and yourselves this oath which you took. ¹²*Who are you, then, that you should have put God to the test this day, setting yourselves in the place of God in human affairs? ¹³It is the Lord Almighty for whom you are laying down conditions; will you never understand anything? ¹⁴*You cannot plumb the depths of the human heart or grasp the workings of the human mind; how then can you fathom God, who has made all these things, discern his mind, and understand his plan?

"No, my brothers, do not anger the Lord our God.

19: Ps 106, 6.
8/6: Lk 2, 37.
12: Jb 38, 2; 40, 2.7f; 42, 3.

14: Jb 41, 3; Prv 14, 10; Wis 9, 13; Is 40, 13; Rom 11, 33f; 1 Cor 2, 11.

† 8, 1: *Salamiel, son of Sarasadai:* head of the tribe of *Simeon* during the wanderings of the Israelites in the desert (Nm 1, 6).

8, 5: *A tent:* erected by Judith on the roof of her house (v 5); it was here that the elders came to confer with her (v 11).

¹⁵For if he does not wish to come to our aid within the five days, he has it equally within his power to protect us at such time as he pleases, or to destroy us in the face of our enemies. ¹⁶It is not for you to make the Lord our God give surety for his plans.

"God is not man that he should be moved by threats,
    nor human, that he may be given an ultimatum.

¹⁷"So while we wait for the salvation that comes from him, let us call upon him to help us, and he will hear our cry if it is his good pleasure. ¹⁸*For there has not risen among us in recent generations, nor does there exist today, any tribe, or clan, or town, or city of ours that worships gods made by hands, as happened in former days. ¹⁹*It was for such conduct that our forefathers were handed over to the sword and to pillage, and fell with great destruction before our enemies. ²⁰But since we acknowledge no other god but the Lord, we hope that he will not disdain us or any of our people. ²¹If we are taken, all Judea will fall, our sanctuary will be plundered, and God will make us pay for its profanation with our life's blood. ²²For the slaughter of our kinsmen, for the taking of exiles from the land, and for the devastation of our inheritance, he will lay the guilt on our heads. Wherever we shall be enslaved among the nations, we shall be a mockery and a reproach in the eyes of our masters. ²³Our enslavement will not be turned to our benefit, but the Lord our God will maintain it to our disgrace.

²⁴"Therefore, my brothers, let us set an example for our kinsmen. Their lives depend on us, and the defense of the sanctuary, the temple, and the altar rests with us. ²⁵*Besides all this, we should be grateful to the Lord our God, for putting us to the test, as he did our forefathers. ²⁶Recall how he dealt with Abraham, and how he tried Isaac, and all that happened to Jacob in Syrian Mesopotamia while he was tending the flocks of Laban, his mother's brother. ²⁷*Not for vengeance did the Lord put them in the crucible to try their hearts, nor has he done so with us. It is by way of admonition that he chastises those who are close to him."

Uzziah's Response

²⁸Then Uzziah said to her: "All that you have said was spoken with good sense, and no one can gainsay your words. ²⁹Not today only is your wisdom made evident, but from your earliest years all the people have recognized your prudence, which corresponds to the worthy dispositions of your heart. ³⁰The people, however, were so tortured with thirst that they forced us to speak to them as we did, and to bind ourselves by an oath that we cannot break. ³¹But now, God-fearing woman that you are, pray for us that the Lord may

send rain to fill up our cisterns, lest we be weakened still further."

³²Then Judith said to them: "Listen to me! I will do something that will go down from generation to generation among the descendants of our race. ³³Stand at the gate tonight to let me pass through with my maid; and within the days you have specified before you will surrender the city to our enemies, the Lord will rescue Israel by my hand. ³⁴You must not inquire into what I am doing, for I will not tell you until my plan has been accomplished." ³⁵Uzziah and the rulers said to her, "Go in peace, and may the Lord God go before you to take vengeance upon our enemies!" ³⁶Then they withdrew from the tent and returned to their posts.

The Prayer of Judith

9 ¹*JUDITH threw herself down prostrate, with ashes strewn upon her head, and wearing nothing over her sackcloth. While the incense was being offered in the temple of God in Jerusalem that evening, Judith prayed to the Lord with a loud voice: ²*†"Lord, God of my forefather Simeon! You put a sword into his hand to take revenge upon the foreigners who had immodestly loosened the maiden's girdle, shamefully exposed her thighs, and disgracefully violated her body. This they did, though you forbade it. ³†Therefore you had their rulers slaughtered; and you covered with their blood the bed in which they lay deceived, the same bed that had felt the shame of their own deceiving. You smote the slaves together with their princes, and the princes together with their servants. ⁴Their wives you handed over to plunder, and their daughters to captivity; and all the spoils you divided among your favored sons, who burned with zeal for you, and in their abhorrence of the defilement of their kinswoman, called on you for help.

⁵*"O God, my God, hear me also, a widow. It is you who were the author of those events and of what preceded and followed them. The present, also, and the future you have planned. Whatever you devise comes into being; ⁶*the things you decide on come forward and say, 'Here we are!' All your ways are in readiness, and your judgment is made with foreknowledge.

⁷*"Here are the Assyrians, a vast force, priding themselves on horse and rider, boasting of the power of their infantry, trusting in shield and spear, bow and sling. They do not know that

⁸"'You, the Lord, crush warfare; Lord is your name.'

"Shatter their strength in your might, and crush their force in your wrath; for they have resolved to

---

† 9, 2: *The maiden:* Dinah, Jacob's daughter, who was violated by Shechem, the Hivite (Gn 34, 2).

9, 3: Because Shechem had deceived and violated Dinah, her brothers, Simeon and Levi, tricked Shechem and the men of his city into being circumcised, and then slew them while they were confined to bed from the circumcision; cf Gn 34, 13-29.

❋
18: 5, 20f; 11, 10.
19: Pss 78, 56f; 106, 13f;
    Jer 7, 16-20; 14, 7.
25f: Gn 22, 1-12; 29, 22-30.
27: Dt 4, 7.
9/1: Ex 30, 7f; Ps 141, 2.

2: Gn 34.
5: Is 44, 7.
6: Jb 38, 35; Is 46, 9-13;
    Bar 3, 35.
7f: 5, 23; 6, 2; 16, 2.

profane your sanctuary, to defile the tent where your glorious name resides, and to overthrow with iron the horns of your altar. ⁹*See their pride, and send forth your wrath upon their heads. Give me, a widow, the strong hand to execute my plan. ¹⁰With the guile of my lips, smite the slave together with the ruler, the ruler together with his servant; crush their pride by the hand of a woman.

¹¹"Your strength is not in numbers, nor does your power depend upon stalwart men; but you are the God of the lowly, the helper of the oppressed, the supporter of the weak, the protector of the forsaken, the savior of those without hope.

¹²"Please, please, God of my forefather, God of the heritage of Israel, Lord of heaven and earth, Creator of the waters, King of all you have created, hear my prayer! ¹³*Let my guileful speech bring wound and wale on those who have planned dire things against your covenant, your holy temple, Mount Zion, and the homes your children have inherited. ¹⁴Let your whole nation and all the tribes know clearly that you are the God of all power and might, and that there is no other who protects the people of Israel but you alone."

Judith's Departure

10 ¹As soon as Judith had thus concluded, and ceased her invocation to the God of Israel, ²she rose from the ground. She called her maid and they went down into the house, which she used only on sabbaths and feast days. ³*She took off the sackcloth she had on, laid aside the garments of her widowhood, washed her body with water, and anointed it with rich ointment. She arranged her hair and bound it with a fillet, and put on the festive attire she had worn while her husband, Manasseh, was living. ⁴*She chose sandals for her feet, and put on her anklets, bracelets, rings, earrings, and all her other jewelry. Thus she made herself very beautiful, to captivate the eyes of all the men who should see her.

⁵*She gave her maid a leather flask of wine and a cruse of oil. She filled a bag with roasted grain, fig cakes, bread and cheese; all these provisions she wrapped up and gave to the maid to carry.

⁶Then they went out to the gate of the city of Bethulia and found Uzziah and the elders of the city, Chabri and Charmis, standing there. ⁷When these men saw Judith transformed in looks and differently dressed, they were very much astounded at her beauty and said to her, ⁸"May the God of our fathers bring you to favor, and make your undertaking a success, for the glory of the Israelites and the exaltation of Jerusalem."

Judith bowed down to God. Then she said to them, ⁹"Order the gate of the city opened for me, that I may go to carry out the business we discussed." So they ordered the youths to open the gate for her as she requested. ¹⁰When they did so, Judith and her maid went out. The men of the city kept her in view as she went down the mountain and crossed the valley; then they lost sight of her.

Judith Captured

¹¹As Judith and her maid walked directly across the valley, they encountered the Assyrian outpost. ¹²†The men took her in custody and asked her, "To what people do you belong? Where do you come from, and where are you going?" She replied: "I am a daughter of the Hebrews, and I am fleeing from them, because they are about to be delivered up to you as prey. ¹³*I have come to see Holofernes, the general in chief of your forces, to give him a trustworthy report; I will show him the route by which he can ascend and take possession of the whole mountain district without a single one of his men suffering injury or loss of life."

¹⁴When the men heard her words and gazed upon her face, which appeared wondrously beautiful to them, they said to her, ¹⁵"By coming down thus promptly to see our master, you have saved your life. Now go to his tent; some of our men will accompany you to present you to him. ¹⁶When you stand before him, have no fear in your heart; give him the report you speak of, and he will treat you well." ¹⁷So they detailed a hundred of their men as an escort for her and her maid, and these conducted them to the tent of Holofernes.

¹⁸When the news of her arrival spread among the tents, a crowd gathered in the camp. They came and stood around her as she waited outside the tent of Holofernes, while he was being informed about her. ¹⁹They marveled at her beauty, regarding the Israelites with wonder because of her, and they said to one another, "Who can despise this people that has such women among them? It is not wise to leave one man of them alive, for if any were to be spared they could beguile the whole world."

Judith Meets Holofernes

²⁰The guard of Holofernes and all his servants came out and ushered her into the tent. ²¹Now Holofernes was reclining on his bed under a canopy with a netting of crimson and gold, emeralds and other precious stones. ²²When they announced her to him, he came out to the antechamber, preceded by silver lamps; ²³and when Holofernes and his servants beheld Judith, they all marveled at the beauty of her face. She threw herself down prostrate before him, but his servants raised her up.

✤   9: Ps 33, 16.   4: 9, 13.
            13: 10, 4; 11, 20.23; 16,   5: 12, 2.
              6.9.   13: 11, 5f.
          10/3: 8, 6ff.

†   10, 12f: The deceitful means used by Judith against Holofernes, here and in 11, 5-19, are to be judged in the light of the moral concepts of Old Testament times; cf Gn 27, 1-25; 34, 13-29; 37, 32ff; Jos 2, 1-7; Jgs 4, 17-22.

11

¹THEN Holofernes said to her: "Take courage, lady; have no fear in your heart! Never have I harmed anyone who chose to serve Nebuchadnezzar, king of all the earth. ²Nor would I have raised my spear against your people who dwell in the mountain region, had they not despised me and brought this upon themselves. ³But now tell me why you fled from them and came to us. In any case, you have come to safety. Take courage! Your life is spared tonight and for the future. ⁴No one at all will harm you. Rather, you will be well treated, as are all the servants of my lord, King Nebuchadnezzar."

⁵*Judith answered him: "Listen to the words of your servant, and let your handmaid speak in your presence! I will tell no lie to my lord this night, ⁶and if you follow out the words of your handmaid, God will give you complete success, and my lord will not fail in any of his undertakings. ⁷*By the life of Nebuchadnezzar, king of all the earth, and by the power of him who has sent you to set all creatures aright! not only do men serve him through you; but even the wild beasts and the cattle and the birds of the air, because of your strength, will live for Nebuchadnezzar and his whole house. ⁸Indeed, we have heard of your wisdom and sagacity, and all the world is aware that throughout the kingdom you alone are competent, rich in experience, and distinguished in military strategy.

⁹*"As for Achior's speech in your council, we have heard of it. When the men of Bethulia spared him, he told them all he had said to you. ¹⁰*So then, my lord and master, do not disregard his word, but bear it in mind, for it is true. For our people are not punished, nor does the sword prevail against them, except when they sin against their God. ¹¹But now their guilt has caught up with them, by which they bring the wrath of their God upon them whenever they do wrong; so that my lord will not be repulsed and fail, but death will overtake them. ¹²Since their food gave out and all their water ran low, they decided to kill their animals, and determined to consume all the things which God in his laws forbade them to eat. ¹³They decreed that they would use up the first fruits of grain and the tithes of wine and oil which they had sanctified and reserved for the priests who minister in the presence of our God in Jerusalem: things which no layman should even touch with his hands. ¹⁴They have sent messengers to Jerusalem to bring back to them authorization from the council of the elders; for the inhabitants there have also done these things. ¹⁵On the very day when the response reaches them and they act upon it, they will be handed over to you for destruction.

¹⁶"As soon as I, your handmaid, learned all this, I fled from them. God has sent me to perform with you such deeds that people throughout the world will be astonished on hearing of them. ¹⁷Your handmaid is, indeed, a God-fearing woman, serving the God of heaven night and day. Now I will remain with you, my lord; but each night your handmaid will go out to the ravine and pray to God. He will tell me when the Israelites have committed their crimes. ¹⁸Then I will come and let you know, so that you may go out with your whole force, and not one of them will be able to withstand you. ¹⁹I will lead you through Judea, till you come to Jerusalem, and there I will set up your judgment seat. You will drive them like sheep that have no shepherd, and not even a dog will growl at you. This was told me, and announced to me in advance, and I in turn have been sent to tell you."

²⁰*Her words pleased Holofernes and all his servants; they marveled at her wisdom and exclaimed, ²¹"No other woman from one end of the world to the other looks so beautiful and speaks so wisely!" ²²Then Holofernes said to her: "God has done well in sending you ahead of your people, to bring victory to our arms, and destruction to those who have despised my lord. ²³*You are fair to behold, and your words are well spoken. If you do as you have said, your God will be my God; you shall dwell in the palace of King Nebuchadnezzar, and shall be renowned throughout the earth."

Judith's Conduct

12

¹THEN he ordered them to lead her into the room where his silverware was kept, and bade them set a table for her with his own delicacies to eat and his own wine to drink. ²*But Judith said, "I will not partake of them, lest it be an occasion of sin; but I shall be amply supplied from the things I brought with me." ³Holofernes asked her: "But if your provisions give out, where shall we get more of the same to provide for you? None of your people are with us." ⁴Judith answered him, "As surely as you, my lord, live, your handmaid will not use up her supplies till the Lord accomplishes by my hand what he has determined."

⁵Then the servants of Holofernes led her into the tent, where she slept till midnight. In the night watch just before dawn, she rose ⁶and sent this message to Holofernes, "Give orders, my lord, to let your handmaid go out for prayer." ⁷So Holofernes ordered his bodyguard not to hinder her. Thus she stayed in the camp three days. Each night she went out to the ravine of Bethulia, where she washed herself at the spring of the camp. ⁸After bathing, she besought the Lord, the God of Israel, to direct her way for the triumph of his people. ⁹Then she returned purified to the tent, and remained there until her food was brought to her toward evening.

Holofernes' Banquet

¹⁰†On the fourth day Holofernes gave a banquet for his servants alone, to which he did not invite any of

---

✳

11/5f: 10, 13.
　7: Jer 27, 6; Bar 3, 16f;
　　　Dn 2, 38.
　9f: 5, 5.

10: 5, 21; 8, 18.
20: 9, 13.
23: 9, 13.
12/2: 10, 5; Dn 1, 8.

†

12, 10: *Banquet for his servants alone . . . officers:* Holofernes invited the officials of his household, but not the officers of his army, who were needed for military duty.

the officers. **11**And he said to Bagoas, the eunuch in charge of his household: "Go and persuade this Hebrew woman in your care to come and to eat and drink with us. **12**It would be a disgrace for us to have such a woman with us without enjoying her company. If we do not entice her, she will laugh us to scorn."

13So Bagoas left the presence of Holofernes, and came to Judith and said, "So fair a maiden should not be reluctant to come to my lord to be honored by him, to enjoy drinking wine with us, and to be like one of the Assyrian women who live in the palace of Nebuchadnezzar." **14**She replied, "Who am I to refuse my lord? Whatever is pleasing to him I will promptly do. This will be a joy for me till the day of my death."

15Thereupon she proceeded to put on her festive garments and all her feminine adornments. Meanwhile her maid went ahead and spread out on the ground for her in front of Holofernes the fleece Bagoas had furnished for her daily use in reclining at her dinner. **16**Then Judith came in and reclined on it. The heart of Holofernes was in rapture over her, and his spirit was shaken. He was burning with the desire to possess her, for he had been biding his time to seduce her from the day he saw her. **17**Holofernes said to her, "Drink and be merry with us!" **18**Judith replied, "I will gladly drink, my lord, for at no time since I was born have I ever enjoyed life as much as I do today." **19**She then took the things her maid had prepared, and ate and drank in his presence. **20**Holofernes, charmed by her, drank a great quantity of wine, more than he had ever drunk on one single day in his life.

13 **1**WHEN it grew late, his servants quickly withdrew. Bagoas closed the tent from the outside and excluded the attendants from their master's presence. They went off to their beds, for they were all tired from the prolonged banquet. **2**Judith was left alone in the tent with Holofernes, who lay prostrate on his bed, for he was sodden with wine. **3**She had ordered her maid to stand outside the bedroom and wait, as on the other days, for her to come out; she said she would be going out for her prayer. To Bagoas she had said this also.

Beheading of Holofernes

4When all had departed, and no one, small or great, was left in the bedroom, Judith stood by Holofernes' bed and said within herself: "O Lord, God of all might, in this hour look graciously on my undertaking for the exaltation of Jerusalem; **5**now is the time for aiding your heritage and for carrying out my design to shatter the enemies who have risen against us." **6**She went to the bedpost near the head of Holofernes, and taking his sword from it, **7**drew close to the bed, grasped the hair of his head, and said, "Strengthen me this day, O God of Israel!" **8***Then with all her might she struck him twice in the neck and cut off his head. **9**She rolled his body off the bed and took the canopy from its supports. Soon afterward, she came out and handed over the head of Holofernes to her maid, **10**who put it into her food pouch; and the two went off together as they were accustomed to do for prayer.

The Return to Bethulia

They passed through the camp, and skirting the ravine, reached Bethulia on the mountain. As they approached its gates, **11**Judith shouted to the guards from a distance: "Open! Open the gate! God, our God, is with us. Once more he has made manifest his strength in Israel and his power against our enemies; he has done it this very day." **12**When the citizens heard her voice, they quickly descended to their city gate and summoned the city elders. **13**All the people, from the least to the greatest, hurriedly assembled, for her return seemed unbelievable. They opened the gate and welcomed the two women. They made a fire for light; and when they gathered around the two, **14**Judith urged them with a loud voice: "Praise God, praise him! Praise God, who has not withdrawn his mercy from the house of Israel, but has shattered our enemies by my hand this very night." **15***Then she took the head out of the pouch, showed it to them, and said: "Here is the head of Holofernes, general in charge of the Assyrian army, and here is the canopy under which he lay in his drunkenness. The Lord struck him down by the hand of a woman. **16**As the Lord lives, who has protected me in the path I have followed, I swear that it was my face that seduced Holofernes to his ruin, and that he did not sin with me to my defilement or disgrace."

17All the people were greatly astonished. They bowed down and worshiped God, saying with one accord, "Blessed are you, our God, who today have brought to nought the enemies of your people." **18***Then Uzziah said to her: "Blessed are you, daughter, by the Most High God, above all the women on earth; and blessed be the Lord God, the creator of heaven and earth, who guided your blow at the head of the chief of our enemies. **19**Your deed of hope will never be forgotten by those who tell of the might of God. **20**May God make this redound to your everlasting honor, rewarding you with blessings, because you risked your life when your people were being oppressed, and you averted our disaster, walking uprightly before our God." And all the people answered, "Amen! Amen!"

Judith's Counsel

14 **1**THEN Judith said to them: "Listen to me, my brothers. Take this head and hang it on the parapet of your wall. **2**At daybreak, when the sun rises on the earth, let each of you seize his weapons, and let all the able-bodied men rush out of the city under command of a captain, as if about to go down into the plain against the advance guard of the Assyrians, but without going down. **3**They will seize their armor and hurry to their camp to awaken the

---

13/8: Jgs 4, 21.   18: Jgs 5, 24; Lk 1, 28.42.
    15: 14, 18.

generals of the Assyrian army. When they run to the tent of Holofernes and do not find him, panic will seize them, and they will flee before you. ⁴Then you and all the other inhabitants of the whole territory of Israel will pursue them and strike them down in their tracks. ⁵But before doing this, summon for me Achior the Ammonite, that he may see and recognize the one who despised the house of Israel and sent him here to meet his death."

Achior Summoned

⁶†So they called Achior from the house of Uzziah. When he came and saw the head of Holofernes in the hand of one of the men in the assembly of the people, he fell forward in a faint. ⁷Then, after they lifted him up, he threw himself at the feet of Judith in homage, saying: "Blessed are you in every tent of Judah; and in every foreign nation, all who hear of you will be struck with terror. ⁸But now, tell me all that you did during these days." So Judith told him, in the presence of the people, all that she had been doing from the day she left till the time she began speaking to them. ⁹When she finished her account, the people cheered loudly, and their city resounded with shouts of joy. ¹⁰Now Achior, seeing all that the God of Israel had done, believed firmly in him. He had the flesh of his foreskin circumcised, and he has been united with the house of Israel to the present day.

III: VICTORY

Consternation in the Camp

¹¹AT DAYBREAK THEY HUNG the head of Holofernes on the wall. Then all the Israelite men took up their arms and went to the slopes of the mountain. ¹²When the Assyrians saw them, they notified their captains; these, in turn, went to the generals and division leaders and all their other commanders. ¹³They came to the tent of Holofernes and said to the one in charge of all his things, "Waken our master, for the slaves have dared come down to give us battle, to their utter destruction."

¹⁴Bagoas went in, and knocked at the entry of the tent, presuming that he was sleeping with Judith. ¹⁵As no one answered, he parted the curtains, entered the bedroom, and found him lying on the floor, a headless corpse. ¹⁶He broke into a loud clamor of weeping, groaning, and howling, and rent his garments. ¹⁷Then he entered the tent where Judith had her quarters; and, not finding her, he rushed out to the troops and cried: ¹⁸*"The slaves have duped us! A single Hebrew woman has brought disgrace on the house of King Nebuchadnezzar. Here is Holofernes headless on the ground!"

¹⁹When the commanders of the Assyrian army heard these words, they rent their tunics and were seized with consternation. Loud screaming and howling arose in the camp.

15 ¹ON hearing what had happened, those still in their tents were amazed, ²and overcome with fear and trembling. No one kept ranks any longer; they scattered in all directions, and fled along every road, both through the valley and in the mountains. ³Those also who were stationed in the mountain district around Bethulia took to flight. Then all the Israelite warriors overwhelmed them.

Pursuit

⁴Uzziah sent messengers to Betomasthaim, to Choba and Kona, and to the whole country of Israel to report what had happened, that all might fall upon the enemy and destroy them. ⁵On hearing this, all the Israelites, with one accord, attacked them and cut them down as far as Choba. Even those from Jerusalem and the rest of the mountain region took part in this, for they too had been notified of the happenings in the camp of their enemies. The Gileadites and the Galileans struck the enemy's flanks with great slaughter, even beyond Damascus and its territory. ⁶The remaining inhabitants of Bethulia swept down on the camp of the Assyrians, plundered it, and acquired great riches. ⁷*The Israelites who returned from the slaughter took possession of what was left, till the towns and villages in the mountains and on the plain were crammed with the enormous quantity of booty they had seized.

⁸*The high priest Joakim and the elders of the Israelites, who dwelt in Jerusalem, came to see for themselves the good things that the Lord had done for Israel, and to meet and congratulate Judith. ⁹†When they had visited her, all with one accord blessed her, saying:

"You are the glory of Jerusalem,
    the surpassing joy of Israel;
    You are the splendid boast of our people.
¹⁰With your own hand you have done all this;
    You have done good to Israel,
    and God is pleased with what you have wrought.
May you be blessed by the Lord Almighty
    forever and ever!"

And all the people answered, "Amen!"

---

† 14, 6-10: In recognizing the head of Holofernes, whom he had known personally, Achior was so overcome with the evidence of the Lord's power exerted through a woman that he believed in the God of Israel.

15, 9: *You are the glory of Jerusalem, the surpassing joy of Israel; you are the splendid boast of our people:* these words are used in the liturgy of the church in regard to the Blessed Virgin Mary.

---

* 14/18: 13, 15; 16, 5-9; Jgs 9,
    54.   15/7: Est 9, 5.16.
                    8: Est 9, 10.

11For thirty days the whole populace plundered the camp, giving Judith the tent of Holofernes, with all his silver, his couches, his dishes, and all his furniture, which she accepted. She harnessed her mules, hitched her wagons to them, and loaded these things on them. **12***All the women of Israel gathered to see her; and they blessed her and performed a dance in her honor. She took branches in her hands and distributed them to the women around her, **13**and she and the other women crowned themselves with garlands of olive leaves. At the head of all the people, she led the women in the dance, while the men of Israel followed in their armor, wearing garlands and singing hymns.

Hymn of Praise

14Judith led all Israel in this song of thanksgiving, and the people swelled this hymn of praise:

16 **1***"STRIKE up the instruments,
    a song to my God with timbrels,
      chant to the Lord with cymbals;
Sing to him a new song,
    exalt and acclaim his name.
2*For the Lord is God; he crushes warfare,
    and sets his encampment among his people;
    he snatched me from the hands of my
      persecutors.

3"The Assyrian came from the mountains of the
      north,
    with the myriads of his forces he came;
Their numbers blocked the torrents,
    their horses covered the hills.
4He threatened to burn my land,
    put my youths to the sword,
Dash my babes to the ground,
    make my children a prey,
    and seize my virgins as spoil.

5*"But the Lord Almighty thwarted them,
    by a woman's hand he confounded them.
6*Not by youths was their mighty one struck down,
    nor did titans bring him low,
    nor huge giants attack him;
But Judith, the daughter of Merari,
    by the beauty of her countenance disabled him.
7She took off her widow's garb
    to raise up the afflicted in Israel.
She anointed her face with fragrant oil;
    8with a fillet she fastened her tresses,
    and put on a linen robe to beguile him.

9*Her sandals caught his eyes,
    and her beauty captivated his mind.
    The sword cut through his neck.

10"The Persians were dismayed at her daring,
    the Medes appalled at her boldness.
11When my lowly ones shouted, they were terrified;
    when my weaklings cried out, they trembled;
    at the sound of their war cry, they took to flight.
12Sons of slave girls pierced them through;
    the supposed sons of rebel mothers cut them
      down;
    they perished before the ranks of my Lord.

13*"A new hymn I will sing to my God.
    O Lord, great are you and glorious,
    wonderful in power and unsurpassable.
14*Let your every creature serve you;
    for you spoke, and they were made,
You sent forth your spirit, and they were created;
    no one can resist your word.
15*The mountains to their bases, and the seas, are
      shaken;
    the rocks, like wax, melt before your glance.

"But to those who fear you,
    you are very merciful.
16*Though the sweet odor of every sacrifice is a trifle,
    and the fat of all holocausts but little in your
      sight,
    one who fears the Lord is forever great.

17*†"Woe to the nations that rise against my people!
    the Lord Almighty will requite them;
    in the day of judgment he will punish them:
He will send fire and worms into their flesh,
    and they shall burn and suffer forever."

Thanksgiving

18The people then went to Jerusalem to worship God; when they were purified, they offered their holocausts, free-will offerings, and gifts. **19***Judith dedicated, as a votive offering to God, all the things of Holofernes that the people had given her, as well as the canopy that she herself had taken from his bedroom. **20**For three months the people continued their celebration in Jerusalem before the sanctuary, and Judith remained with them.

Judith's Renown

21When those days were over, each one returned to his inheritance. Judith went back to Bethulia and remained on her estate. For the rest of her life she was renowned throughout the land. **22**Many wished to marry her, but she gave herself to no man all the days of her life from the time of the death and burial of her husband, Manasseh. **23***She lived to be very old in the house of her husband, reaching the advanced age of a

---

12: Ex 15, 20f; Jgs 11, 34; 1 Sm 18, 6; Jer 31, 4.13.
16/1: Pss 81, 2f; 135, 1ff; 149, 1ff.
  2: 5, 23; 6, 2; 9, 7f; Ex 15, 3; Ps 46, 10.
  5: 14, 8.
  6: 9, 13.
  9: 9, 13.
13: Ps 144, 9.
14: Pss 33, 9; 104, 30; 148, 5.
15: Jgs 5, 5; Ps 97, 5.
16: Ps 86, 11; Sir 34, 13-17.
17: Is 66, 24.
19: Nm 31, 48-54; Dt 13, 13-18; Jos 6, 18f.
23: Gn 23, 19; 49, 29-32.

---

† 16, 17: *Fire and worms into their flesh:* see footnote on Is 66, 24.

hundred and five. She died in Bethulia, where they buried her in the tomb of her husband, Manasseh; [24]and the house of Israel mourned her for seven days. Before she died, she distributed her goods to the relatives of her husband, Manasseh, and to her own relatives; and to the maid she gave her freedom.

✽

    25: Jgs 3, 11.30; 5, 31; 8, 28.

[25]✽†During the life of Judith and for a long time after her death, no one again disturbed the Israelites.

---

† 16, 25: The Vulgate adds: "The feast day of this victory was adopted by the Hebrews into the calendar of their holy days, and has been celebrated by the Jews from that time to the present." However, there is no other evidence of such a festivity; and it is the ancient feast of Passover to which the narrative is especially suited.

The Book of Esther

Introduction

The Book of Esther is named after its Jewish heroine. It tells the story of the plot of Haman the Agagite, jealous and powerful vizier of King Xerxes (Ahasuerus) of Persia (485-464 B. C.), to destroy in a single day all the Jews living in the Persian Empire. He is moved to this out of hatred for the Jewish servant Mordecai, who for religious motives refuses to render him homage. The day of the proposed massacre is determined by lot. Meanwhile Esther, niece and adopted daughter of Mordecai, is chosen queen by King Xerxes in place of Vashti. She averts the pogrom planned against her people and has the royal decree of extermination reversed against Haman and the enemies of the Jews. Mordecai replaces Haman, and together with Esther, works for the welfare of their people. The event is celebrated with feasting and great joy, and the memory of it is to be perpetuated by the annual observance of the feast of Purim (lots), when the lot of destruction for the Jews was reversed for one of deliverance and triumph by Queen Esther and her uncle Mordecai.

The purpose of the book is didactic: the glorification of the Jewish people and the explanation of the origin, significance and date of the feast of Purim on the fourteenth and fifteenth of Adar (February-March). The book was intended as a consolation for Israel, a reminder that God's providence continually watches over them, never abandoning them when they serve him faithfully or turn to him in sincere repentance. There is no justification for interpreting the story in mythological or cultic terms, as though Mordecai and Esther represented Marduk and Ishtar in their mythological triumph over two Elamite deities.

The Hebrew text of Esther is found in the Hebrew Bible, where it is the last of the five *megilloth* (scrolls) read on special feasts of the Jewish liturgical year.

The book is a free composition—not a historical document, despite the Achaemenian coloring of the narrative. Its time of composition may well have been at the end of the Persian Empire, toward the close of the fourth century B. C. The author shows skill in developing his story and in using the art of contrast for instruction and edification. The solution to the difficulties of the book is to be found in its literary presentation rather than in a forced attempt to square detailed data of the narrative with facts. The evident literary motif of the reversal of fortune of the prosperous wicked and the oppressed virtuous through eventual punishment of the former and triumph of the latter, finds parallels in the story of Joseph (Gn 37; 39—45) and of Judith (8—16). The book is vindictive, but it should be remembered that the precept of love of enemies had not yet been taught by the word and example of Christ.

The text of Esther, written originally in Hebrew, was transmitted in two forms: a short Hebrew form and a longer Greek version. The latter contains 107 additional verses, inserted at appropriate places within the Hebrew form of the text. A few of these seem to have a Hebrew origin while the rest are Greek in original composition. It is possible that the Hebrew form of the text is original throughout. If it systematically omits reference to God and his Providence over Israel, this is perhaps due to fear of irreverent response (see note on 4, 14). The Greek text with the above-mentioned additions is probably a later literary paraphrase in which the author seeks to have the reader share his sentiments. This standard Greek text is pre-Christian in origin. The church has accepted the additions as equally inspired with the rest of the book.

In the present translation, the portions preceded by the letters A through F indicate the underlying Greek additions referred to above. The regular chapter numbers apply to the Hebrew text.

The book may be divided as follows:

  I: Prologue (A, 1-17)
  II: Elevation of Esther (1, 1—2, 23)
  III: Haman's Plot against the Jews (3, 1-13; B, 1-7; 3, 4, 48; B, 8; 4, 9-16; C, 1—D, 16; 5, 1-14)
  IV: Vindication of the Jews (6, 1—8, 12; E, 1-24; 8, 13—10, 3)
  V: Epilogue (F, 1-11)

The order of the Vulgate text in relation to the order of the Greek text is as follows:

  Vulg. 11, 2—12, 6 = A, 1—17 at the beginning of the book.
      13, 1-7 = B, 1—7 after 3, 13.
      13, 8—15, 3-19 = C, 1—D, 16 after 4, 16.
      15, 1-2 = B, 8.9 after 4, 8.
      16, 1—24 = E, 1-24 after 8, 12.
      10, 4—10, 13 = F, 1-10 after 10, 3.

I: PROLOGUE

Dream of Mordecai

A 1*†IN THE SECOND YEAR of the reign of the great King Ahasuerus, on the first day of Nisan, Mordecai, son of Jair, son of Shimei, son of Kish, of the tribe of Benjamin, had a dream. ²He was a Jew residing in the city of Susa, a prominent man who

---

† A, 1: *King Ahasuerus:* Xerxes I (486-465 B. C.).
Mordecai: a Babylonian name, after the god Marduk. The genealogy of Mordecai is designed to reflect opposition to

served at the king's court, **3***and one of the captives whom Nebuchadnezzar, king of Babylon, had taken from Jerusalem with Jeconiah, king of Judah.

4*†This was his dream. There was noise and tumult, thunder and earthquake—confusion upon the earth. **5**Two great dragons came on, both poised for combat. They uttered a mighty cry, **6**and at their cry every nation prepared for war, to fight against the race of the just. **7**It was a dark and gloomy day. Tribulation and distress, evil and great confusion, lay upon the earth. **8**The whole race of the just were dismayed with fear of the evils to come upon them, and were at the point of destruction. **9***Then they cried out to God, and as they cried, there appeared to come forth a great river, a flood of water from a little spring. **10**The light of the sun broke forth; the lowly were exalted and they devoured the nobles.

11Having seen this dream and what God intended to do, Mordecai awoke. He kept it in mind, and tried in every way, until night, to understand its meaning.

The Plot Discovered

12*Mordecai lodged at the court with Bagathan and Thares, two eunuchs of the king who were court guards. **13**He overheard them plotting, investigated their plans, and discovered that they were preparing to lay hands on King Ahasuerus. So he informed the king about them, **14**and the king had the two eunuchs questioned and, upon their confession, put to death. **15**Then the king had these things recorded; Mordecai, too, put them into writing. **16*†**The king also appointed Mordecai to serve at the court, and rewarded him for his actions.

17*†Haman, however, son of Hammedatha the Agagite, who was in high honor with the king, sought to harm Mordecai and his people because of the two eunuchs of the king.

II: ELEVATION OF ESTHER

The Banquet of Ahasuerus

1 **1†**DURING THE REIGN OF AHASUERUS—this was the Ahasuerus who ruled over a hundred and twenty-seven provinces from India to Ethiopia **2†**—while he was occupying the royal throne in the stronghold of Susa, **3***in the third year of his reign, he presided over a feast for all his officers and ministers: the Persian and Median aristocracy, the nobles, and the governors of the provinces. **4**For as many as a hundred and eighty days, he displayed the glorious riches of his kingdom and the resplendent wealth of his royal estate.

5At the end of this time the king gave a feast of seven days in the garden court of the royal palace for all the people, great and small, who were in the stronghold of Susa. **6**There were white cotton draperies and violet hangings, held by cords of crimson byssus from silver rings on marble pillars. Gold and silver couches were on the pavement, which was of porphyry, marble, mother-of-pearl, and colored stones. **7**Liquor was served in a variety of golden cups, and the royal wine flowed freely, as befitted the king's munificence. **8**By ordinance of the king the drinking was unstinted, for he had instructed all the stewards of his household to comply with the good pleasure of everyone.

9†Queen Vashti also gave a feast for the women inside the royal palace of King Ahasuerus.

Deposal of Vashti

10*On the seventh day, when the king was merry with wine, he instructed Mehuman, Biztha, Harbona, Bigtha, Abagtha, Zethar, and Carkas, the seven eunuchs who attended King Ahasuerus, **11**to bring Queen Vashti into his presence wearing the royal crown, that he might display her beauty to the populace and the officials, for she was lovely to behold. **12**But Queen Vashti refused to come at the royal order issued through the eunuchs. At this the king's wrath flared up, and he burned with fury. **13**He conferred with the wise men versed in the law, because the king's business was conducted in general consultation with lawyers and jurists. **14***He summoned Carshena, Shethar, Admatha, Tarshish, Meres, Marsena and Memucan, the seven Persian and Median officials who were in the king's personal service and held first rank in the realm, **15**and asked them, "What is to be done by law with Queen Vashti for disobeying the order of King Ahasuerus issued through the eunuchs?"

16In the presence of the king and of the officials, Memucan answered: "Queen Vashti has not wronged

---

†
Israel's enemy, as narrated in 1 Sm 15, 7ff, where Saul (whose father's name was *Kish, of the Tribe of Benjamin*) conquered Agag the Amalekite; in A, 17 Haman is said to be the son of an Agagite. Further emphasis on the Benjaminite-Agagite opposition can be seen in *Shimei*, the Benjaminite who reviled David (2 Sm 16, 5ff). Jair appears to be the minor Judge, a Transjordanian Manassehite (Jgs 10, 3). The chronology of the book would make Mordecai well over one hundred years old, since he was deported with Jehoiachin about 598 B. C.; cf 2, 5f.

A, 4: The interpretation of this dream is given in F, 1-6.

A, 16: *Rewarded him:* this reward comes only later; see the sequence of events from the Hebrew text of Esther at 2, 22f, and 6, 3 below.

A, 17: *Haman . . . the Agagite:* opposed Mordecai the Benjaminite, by whom, however, he was overcome (7, 9f), just as King Agag, the Amalekite, was conquered by King Saul, ancestor of Mordecai (1 Sm 15, 7ff).

1, 1: *From India to Ethiopia:* from western India to Upper Egypt, the greatest extent of the Persian Empire achieved under Darius the Great, father of Ahasuerus.

1, 2: *Susa:* ancient capital of Elam (Gn 14, 1); under the Achamenid kings, one of the two capitals of the Persian Empire. The other was Persepolis, the summer palace of the kings.

1, 9: *Queen Vashti:* Herodotus (*Histories* 7, 61) relates that the wife of Ahasuerus was Amestris.

✿
    3: 2, 6; 2 Kgs 24, 15;   16: 6, 3.
         2 Chr 36, 9f; Jer 22,   17: 3, 1-15; B, 1-7; E, 13.
         24ff; 24, 1; 29, 1f.   1/3: Jdt 1, 16.
    4ff: F, 2, 4ff.   10: Dn 5, 1.
    9f: F, 3.   14: Ezr 7, 14.
    12-15: 2, 21ff; 6, 1ff.

the king alone, but all the officials and the populace throughout the provinces of King Ahasuerus. [17]For the queen's conduct will become known to all the women, and they will look with disdain upon their husbands when it is reported, 'King Ahasuerus commanded that Queen Vashti be ushered into his presence, but she would not come.' [18]This very day the Persian and Median ladies who hear of the queen's conduct will rebel against all the royal officials, with corresponding disdain and rancor. [19]*†If it pleases the king, let an irrevocable royal decree be issued by him and inscribed among the laws of the Persians and Medes, forbidding Vashti to come into the presence of King Ahasuerus and authorizing the king to give her royal dignity to one more worthy than she. [20]Thus, when the decree which the king will issue is published throughout his realm, vast as it is, all wives will honor their husbands, from the greatest to the least."

[21]This proposal found acceptance with the king and the officials, and the king acted on the advice of Memucan. [22]†He sent letters to all the royal provinces, to each province in its own script and to each people in its own language, to the effect that every man should be lord in his own home.

Esther Made Queen

2 [1]AFTER this, when King Ahasuerus' wrath had cooled, he thought over what Vashti had done and what had been decreed against her. [2]Then the king's personal attendants suggested: "Let beautiful young virgins be sought for the king. [3]Let the king appoint commissaries in all the provinces of his realm to bring together all beautiful young virgins to the harem in the stronghold of Susa. Under the care of the royal eunuch Hegai, custodian of the women, let cosmetics be given them. [4]Then the girl who pleases the king shall reign in place of Vashti." This suggestion pleased the king, and he acted accordingly.

[5]There was in the stronghold of Susa a certain Jew named Mordecai, son of Jair, son of Shimei, son of Kish, a Benjaminite, [6]*who had been exiled from Jerusalem with the captives taken with Jeconiah, king of Judah, whom Nebuchadnezzar, king of Babylon, had deported. [7]*†He was foster father to Hadassah, that is, Esther, his cousin; for she had lost both father and mother. The girl was beautifully formed and lovely to behold. On the death of her father and mother, Mordecai had taken her as his own daughter.

[8]When the king's order and decree had been obeyed and many maidens brought together to the stronghold of Susa under the care of Hegai, Esther also was brought in to the royal palace under the care of Hegai, custodian of the women. [9]The girl pleased him and won his favor. So he promptly furnished her with cosmetics and provisions. Then picking out seven maids for her from the royal palace, he transferred

both her and her maids to the best place in the harem. [10]Esther did not reveal her nationality or family, for Mordecai had commanded her not to do so.

[11]Day by day Mordecai would walk about in front of the court of the harem, to learn how Esther was faring and what was to become of her.

[12]Each girl went in turn to visit King Ahasuerus after the twelve months' preparation decreed for the women. Of this period of beautifying treatment, six months were spent with oil of myrrh, and the other six months with perfumes and cosmetics. [13]Then, when the girl was to visit the king, she was allowed to take with her from the harem to the royal palace whatever she chose. [14]*She would go in the evening and return in the morning to a second harem under the care of the royal eunuch Shaashgaz, custodian of the concubines. She could not return to the king unless he was pleased with her and had her summoned by name.

[15]As for Esther, daughter of Abihail and adopted daughter of his nephew Mordecai, when her turn came to visit the king, she did not ask for anything but what the royal eunuch Hegai, custodian of the women, suggested. Yet she won the admiration of all who saw her. [16]Esther was led to King Ahasuerus in his palace in the tenth month, Tebeth, in the seventh year of his reign. [17]The king loved Esther more than all other women, and of all the virgins she won his favor and benevolence. So he placed the royal diadem on her head and made her queen in place of Vashti. [18]†Then the king gave a great feast in honor of Esther to all his officials and ministers, granting a holiday to the provinces and bestowing gifts with royal bounty.

The Plot Discovered

[19]*†[To resume: From the time the virgins had been brought together, and while Mordecai was passing his time at the king's gate, [20]Esther had not revealed her family or nationality, because Mordecai had told her not to; and Esther continued to follow Mordecai's instructions, just as she had when she was being brought up by him. [21]*†And during the time that Mordecai spent at the king's gate, Bagathan and Thares, two of the royal eunuchs who guarded the entrance, had

---

†

1, 19: *Irrevocable royal decree:* the historian Siculus indicates that such a concept of *irrevocable* laws existed in the time of Darius III (335-331 B. C.), the last of the Persian kings; cf 8, 8.

1, 22: *To each province . . . script and to each people . . . language:* many languages were spoken in the Persian Empire, the principal ones being Persian, Elamite, Babylonian, Aramaic, Phoenician, Egyptian, and Greek. Each of them had its own script.

2, 7: *Hadassah* (the feminine form of *hadas,* myrtle), was the name by which this woman would be known among her Jewish compatriots. *Esther* is a variant of the name of the Babylonian goddess Ishtar.

2, 18: *A holiday:* or perhaps, "a remission of taxes."

2, 19-23: This is a resumption, in a slightly different form, of the story already told in A, 12-15.

2, 21: *Mordecai . . . at the king's gate:* to exercise watchful care for Esther. Some understand this to mean that Mordecai was stationed at the gate to render royal service; cf A, 2.

✿

19: 8, 5.8; Dn 6, 8f.
2/6: A, 3; 2 Kgs 24, 15;
    2 Chr 36, 9f; Jer 22,
    24ff; 24, 1; 29, 1f.

7: 2, 15.
14: 2, 19f; 4, 11.16.
19f: 2, 14.
21ff: A, 12-15; 6, 1ff.

plotted in anger to lay hands on King Ahasuerus. [22]When the plot became known to Mordecai, he told Queen Esther, who in turn informed the king for Mordecai. [23]†The matter was investigated and verified, and both of them were hanged on a gibbet. This was written in the annals for the king's use.]

III: HAMAN'S PLOT AGAINST THE JEWS

Mordecai Refuses to Honor Haman

3 [1]*AFTER THESE EVENTS King Ahasuerus raised Haman, son of Hammedatha the Agagite, to high rank, seating him above all his fellow officials. [2]*†All the king's servants who were at the royal gate would kneel and bow down to Haman, for that is what the king had ordered in his regard. Mordecai, however, would not kneel and bow down. [3]*The king's servants who were at the royal gate said to Mordecai, "Why do you disobey the king's order?" [4]When they had reminded him day after day and he would not listen to them, they informed Haman, to see whether Mordecai's explanation was acceptable, since he had told them that he was a Jew.

Haman's Reprisal

[5]When Haman observed that Mordecai would not kneel and bow down to him, he was filled with anger. [6]Moreover, he thought it was not enough to lay hands on Mordecai alone. Since they had told Haman of Mordecai's nationality, he sought to destroy all the Jews, Mordecai's people, throughout the realm of King Ahasuerus. [7]*†In the first month, Nisan, in the twelfth year of King Ahasuerus, the *pur,* or lot, was cast in Haman's presence to determine the day and the month for the destruction of Mordecai's people on a single day, and the lot fell on the thirteenth day of the twelfth month, Adar.

Decree against the Jews

[8]*Then Haman said to King Ahasuerus: "Dispersed among the nations throughout the provinces of your kingdom, there is a certain people living apart, with laws different from those of every other people. They do not obey the laws of the king, and so it is not proper for the king to tolerate them. [9]*If it please the king, let a decree be issued to destroy them; and I will deliver to the procurators ten thousand silver talents for deposit in the royal treasury." [10]*†The king took the signet ring from his hand and gave it to Haman, son of Hammedatha the Agagite, the enemy of the Jews. [11]"The silver you may keep," the king said to Haman,

"but as for this people, do with them whatever you please."

[12]So the royal scribes were summoned; and on the thirteenth day of the first month they wrote, at the dictation of Haman, an order to the royal satraps, the governors of every province, and the officials of every people, to each province in its own script and to each people in its own language. It was written in the name of King Ahasuerus and sealed with the royal signet ring. [13]*Letters were sent by couriers to all the royal provinces, that all the Jews, young and old, including women and children, should be killed, destroyed, wiped out in one day, the thirteenth day of the twelfth month, Adar, and that their goods should be seized as spoil.

B [1]THIS is a copy of the letter:
"The great King Ahasuerus writes to the satraps of the hundred and twenty-seven provinces from India to Ethiopia, and the governors subordinate to them, as follows: [2]*When I came to rule many peoples and to hold sway over the whole world, I determined not to be carried away with the sense of power, but always to deal fairly and with clemency; to provide for my subjects a life of complete tranquillity; and by making my government humane and effective as far as the borders, to restore the peace desired by all men. [3]*When I consulted my counselors as to how this might be accomplished, Haman, who excels among us in wisdom, who is outstanding for constant devotion and steadfast loyalty, and who has gained the second rank in the kingdom, [4]*brought it to our attention that, mixed in with all the races throughout the world, there is one people of bad will, which by its laws is opposed to every other people and continually disregards the decrees of kings, so that the unity of empire blamelessly designed by us cannot be established.

[5]"Having noted, therefore, that this most singular people is continually at variance with all men, lives by divergent and alien laws, is inimical to our interests, and commits the worst crimes, so that stability of government cannot be obtained, [6]*†we hereby decree

---

† 2, 23: *Hanged on a gibbet:* impaled, perhaps, after the Babylonian manner.

3, 2: *Mordecai . . . would not kneel and bow down:* in order not to render to man the homage which he regarded as belonging to God alone; cf C, 5ff.

3, 7: *Pur:* a Babylonian word which the Hebrew translates as *goral,* "lot." This word is preserved in the text because its plural, *purim,* became the name of the feast of Purim commemorating the deliverance of the Jews; cf 9, 24.26.

3, 10: *Signet ring:* a ring containing a seal which was impressed on documents to authenticate them. By giving this ring to Haman, the king bestowed on him the power to authenticate royal decrees.

B, 6: *Fourteenth day:* the Hebrew text, as in 2, 13 above, and the Greek text here translated do not agree on the day of the month specified by the king; in fact, a two-day celebration is decreed in chapter 9, and the 13th, 14th and 15th of Adar are all mentioned; see 9, 15.18.

✸
3/1: B, 3; 5, 11; E, 11.　　　　　10: Gn 41, 42.
2: C, 5; 5, 9.13; 6, 10.12.　　　13: B, 6; 7, 4.
3: 4, 16.　　　　　　　　　　　B/2: E, 8f.
7: 9, 24ff; F, 10.　　　　　　　3: 3, 1; 5, 11; E, 11.
8: 3, 13; B, 4; E, 24;　　　　　4: 3, 8; E, 24.
　　Dn 3, 8-12; Wis 2, 14f.　　6: 3, 13; 7, 4; E, 11ff.
9: 7, 4.

that all those who are indicated to you in the letters of Haman, who is in charge of the administration and is a second father to us, shall, together with their wives and children, be utterly destroyed by the swords of their enemies, without any pity or mercy, on the fourteenth day of the twelfth month, Adar, of the current year; **7**so that when these people, whose present ill will is of long standing, have gone down into the nether world by a violent death on a single day, they may at least leave our affairs stable and undisturbed for the future."

3/**14**A copy of the decree to be promulgated as law in every province was published to all the peoples, that they might be prepared for that day. 3/**15**The couriers set out in haste at the king's command; meanwhile, the decree was promulgated in the stronghold of Susa. The king and Haman then sat down to feast, but the city of Susa was thrown into confusion.

Esther's Aid Sought by Mordecai

4 **1***WHEN Mordecai learned all that was happening, he tore his garments, put on sackcloth and ashes, and walked through the city crying out loudly and bitterly, **2**till he came before the royal gate, which no one clothed in sackcloth might enter. **3**(Likewise in each of the provinces, wherever the king's legal enactment reached, the Jews went into deep mourning, with fasting, weeping, and lament; they all slept on sackcloth and ashes.)

4Queen Esther's maids and eunuchs came and told her. Overwhelmed with anguish, she sent garments for Mordecai to put on, so that he might take off his sackcloth; but he refused. **5**Esther then summoned Hathach, one of the king's eunuchs whom he had placed at her service, and commanded him to find out what this action of Mordecai meant and the reason for it. **6**So Hathach went out to Mordecai in the public square in front of the royal gate, **7**and Mordecai told him all that had happened, as well as the exact amount of silver Haman had promised to pay to the royal treasury for the slaughter of the Jews. **8**He also gave him a copy of the written decree for their destruction which had been promulgated in Susa, to show and explain to Esther. He was to instruct her to go to the king; she was to plead and intercede with him in behalf of her people. B/**8**"Remember the days of your lowly estate," Mordecai had him say, "when you were brought up in my charge; for Haman, who is second to the king, has asked for our death. B/**9**Invoke the Lord and speak to the king for us; save us from death."

9Hathach returned to Esther and told her what Mordecai had said. **10**Then Esther replied to Hathach and gave him this message for Mordecai: **11***"All the servants of the king and the people of his provinces know that any man or woman who goes to the king in the inner court without being summoned, suffers the automatic penalty of death, unless the king extends to him the golden scepter, thus sparing his life. Now as for me, I have not been summoned to the king for thirty days."

12When Esther's words were reported to Mordecai, **13**he had this reply brought to her: "Do not imagine that because you are in the king's palace, you alone of all the Jews will escape. **14†**Even if you now remain silent, relief and deliverance will come to the Jews from another source; but you and your father's house will perish. Who knows but that it was for a time like this that you obtained the royal dignity?"

15Esther sent back to Mordecai the response: **16***Go and assemble all the Jews who are in Susa; fast on my behalf, all of you, not eating or drinking, night or day, for three days. I and my maids will also fast in the same way. Thus prepared, I will go to the king, contrary to the law. If I perish, I perish!"

Prayer of Mordecai

C MORDECAI went away and did exactly as Esther had commanded. **1**Recalling all that the Lord had done, he prayed to him **2**and said: "O Lord God, almighty King, all things are in your power, and there is no one to oppose you in your will to save Israel. **3**You made heaven and earth and every wonderful thing under the heavens. **4**You are Lord of all, there is no one who can resist you, Lord. **5***You know all things. You know, O Lord, that it was not out of insolence or pride or desire for fame that I acted thus in not bowing down to the proud Haman. **6**Gladly would I have kissed the soles of his feet for the salvation of Israel. **7**But I acted as I did so as not to place the honor of man above that of God. I will not bow down to anyone but you, my Lord. It is not out of pride that I am acting thus. **8**And now, Lord God, King, God of Abraham, spare your people, for our enemies plan our ruin and are bent upon destroying the inheritance that was yours from the beginning. **9**Do not spurn your portion, which you redeemed for yourself out of Egypt. **10**Hear my prayer; have pity on your inheritance and turn our sorrow into joy: thus we shall live to sing praise to your name, O Lord. Do not silence those who praise you."

11All Israel, too, cried out with all their strength, for death was staring them in the face.

Prayer of Esther

12*Queen Esther, seized with mortal anguish, likewise had recourse to the Lord. **13**Taking off her splendid garments, she put on garments of distress and mourning. In place of her precious ointments she covered her head with dirt and ashes. She afflicted her body severely; all her festive adornments were put aside, and her hair was wholly disheveled.

14Then she prayed to the Lord, the God of Israel, saying: "My Lord, our King, you alone are God. Help

❋
4/1: Jdt 4, 12.
11: 2, 14; 4, 12; D, 12.
16: C, 12f.

C/5ff: 3, 2; 5, 9.
12f: 4, 16.

†
4, 14: *From another source:* very probably Mordecai refers to divine aid; the Greek additions (C) are explicit about this.

me, who am alone and have no help but you, [15]*for I am taking my life in my hand. [16]*As a child I was wont to hear from the people of the land of my forefathers that you, O Lord, chose Israel from among all peoples, and our fathers from among all their ancestors, as a lasting heritage, and that you fulfilled all your promises to them. [17]But now we have sinned in your sight, and you have delivered us into the hands of our enemies, [18]because we worshiped their gods. You are just, O Lord. [19]But now they are not satisfied with our bitter servitude, but have undertaken [20]to do away with the decree you have pronounced, and to destroy your heritage; to close the mouths of those who praise you, and to extinguish the glory of your temple and your altar; [21]to open the mouths of the heathen to acclaim their false gods, and to extol an earthly king forever.

[22]"O Lord, do not relinquish your scepter to those that are nought. Let them not gloat over our ruin, but turn their own counsel against them and make an example of our chief enemy. [23]Be mindful of us, O Lord. Manifest yourself in the time of our distress and give me courage, King of gods and Ruler of every power. [24]Put in my mouth persuasive words in the presence of the lion, and turn his heart to hatred for our enemy, so that he and those who are in league with him may perish. [25]Save us by your power, and help me, who am alone and have no one but you, O Lord.

"You know all things. [26]You know that I hate the glory of the pagans, and abhor the bed of the uncircumcised or of any foreigner. [27]You know that I am under constraint, that I abhor the sign of grandeur which rests on my head when I appear in public; abhor it like a polluted rag, and do not wear it in private. [28]†I, your handmaid, have never eaten at the table of Haman, nor have I graced the banquet of the king or drunk the wine of libations. [29]From the day I was brought here till now, your handmaid has had no joy except in you, O Lord, God of Abraham. [30]O God, more powerful than all, hear the voice of those in despair. Save us from the power of the wicked, and deliver me from my fear."

Esther Is Received by the King

D[1]ON the third day, putting an end to her prayers, she took off her penitential garments and arrayed herself in royal attire. [2]In making her state appearance, after invoking the all-seeing God and savior, she took with her two maids; [3]on the one she leaned gently for support, [4]while the other followed her, bearing her train. [5]She glowed with the perfection of her beauty and her countenance was as joyous as it was lovely, though her heart was shrunk with fear. [6]She passed through all the portals till she stood face to face with the king, who was seated on his royal throne, clothed in full robes of state, and covered with gold and precious stones, so that he inspired great awe. [7]As he looked up, his features ablaze with the height of majestic anger, the queen staggered, changed color, and leaned weakly against the head of the maid in front of her. [8]But God changed the king's anger to gentleness. In great anxiety he sprang from his throne, held her in his arms until she recovered, and comforted her with reassuring words. [9]"What is it, Esther?" he said to her. "I am your brother. Take courage! [10]You shall not die because of this general decree of ours. [11]Come near!" [12]*Raising the golden scepter, he touched her neck with it, embraced her, and said, "Speak to me."

[13]She replied: "I saw you, my lord, as an angel of God, and my heart was troubled with fear of your majesty. [14]For you are awesome, my lord, though your glance is full of kindness." [15]As she said this, she fainted. [16]The king became troubled and all his attendants tried to revive her.

5 [1]†[NOW on the third day, Esther put on her royal garments and stood in the inner courtyard, looking toward the royal palace, while the king was seated on his royal throne in the audience chamber, facing the palace doorway. [2]He saw Queen Esther standing in the courtyard, and made her welcome by extending toward her the golden staff which he held. She came up to him, and touched the top of the staff.]

[3]*Then the king said to her, "What is it, Queen Esther? What is your request? Even if it is half of my kingdom, it shall be granted you." [4]"If it please your majesty," Esther replied, "come today with Haman to a banquet I have prepared." [5]And the king ordered, "Have Haman make haste to fulfill the wish of Esther."

First Banquet of Esther

So the king went with Haman to the banquet Esther had prepared. [6]*During the drinking of the wine, the king said to Esther, "Whatever you ask for shall be granted, and whatever request you make shall be honored, even if it is for half my kingdom." [7]Esther replied: "This is my petition and request: [8]if I have found favor with the king and if it pleases your majesty to grant my petition and honor my request, come with Haman tomorrow to a banquet which I shall prepare for you; and then I will do as you ask."

Haman's Plot against Mordecai

[9]*That day Haman left happy and in good spirits. But when he saw that Mordecai at the royal gate did not rise, and showed no fear of him, he was filled with anger toward him. [10]Haman restrained himself, however, and went home, where he summoned his friends and his wife Zeresh. [11]*He recounted the greatness of

---

✻
  15: 4, 16.
  16: Dt 4, 20; 7, 6; 9, 29;
      14, 2; 26, 18; 32, 9.
D/12: 4, 11.
  5/3: 5, 6; 7, 2; 9, 12.

  6: 5, 3.
  9: 3, 2f; C, 5ff; 6, 10.12.
  11: 3, 1; B, 3; E, 11;
      9, 6-10.

†
  C, 28: *Wine of libations:* offered in sacrifice to the gods.
  5, 1f: The Hebrew text here translated is a short form of the
account already given in Greek.

his riches, the large number of his sons, and just how the king had promoted him and placed him above the officials and royal servants. **12**"Moreover," Haman added, "Queen Esther invited no one but me to the banquet with the king; again tomorrow I am to be her guest, with the king. **13***Yet none of this satisfies me as long as I continue to see the Jew Mordecai sitting at the royal gate." **14***His wife Zeresh and all his friends said to him, "Have a gibbet set up, fifty cubits in height, and in the morning ask the king to have Mordecai hanged on it. Then go to the banquet with the king in good cheer." This suggestion pleased Haman, and he had the gibbet erected.

IV: VINDICATION OF THE JEWS

Mordecai's Reward from the King

6 **1**THAT NIGHT THE KING, unable to sleep, asked that the chronicle of notable events be brought in. While this was being read to him, **2***the passage occurred in which Mordecai reported Bagathan and Teresh, two of the royal eunuchs who guarded the entrance, for seeking to lay hands on King Ahasuerus. **3***The king asked, "What was done to reward and honor Mordecai for this?" The king's attendants replied, "Nothing was done for him."

4*"Who is in the court?" the king asked. Now Haman had entered the outer court of the king's palace to suggest to the king that Mordecai should be hanged on the gibbet he had raised for him. **5**The king's servants answered him, "Haman is waiting in the court." "Let him come in," the king said. **6**When Haman entered, the king said to him, "What should be done for the man whom the king wishes to reward?" Now Haman thought to himself, "Whom would the king more probably wish to reward than me?" **7**So he replied to the king: "For the man whom the king wishes to reward **8**there should be brought the royal robe which the king wore and the horse on which the king rode when the royal crown was placed on his head. **9***The robe and the horse should be consigned to one of the noblest of the king's officials, who must clothe the man the king wishes to reward, have him ride on the horse in the public square of the city, and cry out before him, 'This is what is done for the man whom the king wishes to reward!'" **10***Then the king said to Haman: "Hurry! Take the robe and horse as you have proposed, and do this for the Jew Mordecai, who is sitting at the royal gate. Do not omit anything you proposed." **11**So Haman took the robe and horse, clothed

Mordecai, had him ride in the public square of the city, and cried out before him, "This is what is done for the man whom the king wishes to reward!"

12*Mordecai then returned to the royal gate, while Haman hurried home, his head covered in grief. **13**When he told his wife Zeresh and all his friends everything that had happened to him, his advisers and his wife Zeresh said to him, "If Mordecai, before whom you are beginning to decline, is of the Jewish race, you will not prevail against him, but will surely be defeated by him."

Esther's Second Banquet

14While they were speaking with him, the king's eunuchs arrived and hurried Haman off to the banquet Esther had prepared.

7 **1**so the king and Haman went to the banquet with Queen Esther. **2***Again, on this second day, during the drinking of the wine, the king said to Esther, "Whatever you ask, Queen Esther, shall be granted you. Whatever request you make shall be honored, even for half the kingdom." **3**Queen Esther replied: "If I have found favor with you, O king, and if it pleases your majesty, I ask that my life be spared, and I beg that you spare the lives of my people. **4***For my people and I have been delivered to destruction, slaughter, and extinction. If we were to be sold into slavery I would remain silent, but as it is, the enemy will be unable to compensate for the harm done to the king." **5***"Who and where," said King Ahasuerus to Queen Esther, "is the man who has dared to do this?" **6**Esther replied, "The enemy oppressing us is this wicked Haman." At this, Haman was seized with dread of the king and queen.

7The king left the banquet in anger and went into the garden of the palace, but Haman stayed to beg Queen Esther for his life, since he saw that the king had decided on his doom. **8**When the king returned from the garden of the palace to the banquet hall, Haman had thrown himself on the couch on which Esther was reclining; and the king exclaimed, "Will he also violate the queen while she is with me in my own house!" Scarcely had the king spoken when the face of Haman was covered over.

Punishment of Haman

9*Harbona, one of the eunuchs who attended the king, said, "At the house of Haman stands a gibbet fifty cubits high. Haman prepared it for Mordecai, who gave the report that benefited the king." The king answered, "Hang him on it." **10**So they hanged Haman on the gibbet which he had made ready for Mordecai, and the anger of the king abated.

8 **1***THAT day King Ahasuerus gave the house of Haman, enemy of the Jews, to Queen Esther; and Mordecai was admitted to the king's presence, for Esther had revealed his relationship to her. **2***The king removed his signet ring from Haman, and

---

❊

13: 3, 2f; 6, 10.12.
14: 6, 4; 7, 9f.
6/2: A, 12ff; 2, 21ff.
  3: A, 16.
  4: 5, 14; 7, 9f.
  9: Gn 41, 42f;
    1 Kgs 1, 33; Dn 5, 29.
 10: 2, 21; 3, 2f; 5, 9.13.

12: 2, 21; 3, 2f; 5, 9.13.
7/2: 5, 3.
  4: 3, 13; B, 6.
  5: 3, 8f.
 9f: 5, 14; 6, 4.
8/1: 9, 1; Prv 11, 8; 26, 27;
    Mt 7, 2.
  2: Prv 13, 22; Dn 2, 48f.

transferred it into the keeping of Mordecai; and Esther put Mordecai in charge of the house of Haman.

The Second Royal Decree

3In another audience with the king, Esther fell at his feet and tearfully implored him to revoke the harm done by Haman the Agagite, and the plan he had devised against the Jews. **4**The king stretched forth the golden scepter to Esther. So she rose and, standing in his presence, **5***said: "If it pleases your majesty and seems proper to you, and if I have found favor with you and you love me, let a document be issued to revoke the letters which that schemer Haman, son of Hammedatha the Agagite, wrote for the destruction of the Jews in all the royal provinces. **6**For how can I witness the evil that is to befall my people, and how can I behold the destruction of my race?"

7King Ahasuerus then said to Queen Esther and to the Jew Mordecai: "Now that I have given Esther the house of Haman, and they have hanged him on the gibbet because he attacked the Jews, **8***†you in turn may write in the king's name what you see fit concerning the Jews and seal the letter with the royal signet ring." For whatever is written in the name of the king and sealed with the royal signet ring cannot be revoked.

9At that time, on the twenty-third day of the third month, Sivan, the royal scribes were summoned. Exactly as Mordecai dictated, they wrote to the Jews and to the satraps, governors, and officials of the hundred and twenty-seven provinces from India to Ethiopia: to each province in its own script and to each people in its own language, and to the Jews in their own script and language. **10**These letters, which he wrote in the name of King Ahasuerus and sealed with the royal signet ring, he sent by mounted couriers riding thoroughbred royal steeds. **11***In these letters the king authorized the Jews in each and every city to group together and defend their lives, and to kill, destroy, wipe out, along with their wives and children, every armed group of any nation or province which should attack them, and to seize their goods as spoil **12**throughout the provinces of King Ahasuerus, on a single day, the thirteenth of the twelfth month, Adar.

E **1**THE following is a copy of the letter: "King Ahasuerus the Great to the governors of the provinces in the hundred and twenty-seven satrapies from India to Ethiopia, and to those responsible for our interests: Greetings! **2**"Many have become the more ambitious the more they were showered with honors through the bountiful generosity of their patrons. **3**Not only do they seek to do harm to our subjects; incapable of bearing such greatness, they even begin plotting against their own benefactors. **4**Not only do they drive out gratitude

from among men; with the arrogant boastfulness of those to whom goodness has no meaning, they suppose they will escape the vindictive judgment of the all-seeing God.

5"Often, too, the fair speech of friends entrusted with the administration of affairs has induced many placed in authority to become accomplices in the shedding of innocent blood, and has involved them in irreparable calamities **6**by deceiving with malicious slander the sincere good will of rulers. **7**This can be verified in the ancient stories that have been handed down to us, but more fully when one considers the wicked deeds perpetrated in your midst by the pestilential influence of those undeserving of authority. **8***We must provide for the future, so as to render the kingdom undisturbed and peaceful for all men, **9**taking advantage of changing conditions and deciding always with equitable treatment matters coming to our attention.

10†"For instance, Haman, son of Hammedatha, a Macedonian, certainly not of Persian blood, and very different from us in generosity, was hospitably received by us. **11***He so far enjoyed the good will which we have toward all peoples that he was proclaimed 'father of the king,' before whom everyone was to bow down; he attained the rank second to the royal throne. **12**But, unequal to this dignity, he strove to deprive us of kingdom and of life; **13***and by weaving intricate webs of deceit, he demanded the destruction of Mordecai, our savior and constant benefactor, and of Esther, our blameless royal consort, together with their whole race. **14**For by such measures he hoped to catch us defenseless and to transfer the rule of the Persians to the Macedonians. **15**But we find that the Jews, who were doomed to extinction by this arch-criminal, are not evildoers, but rather are governed by very just laws **16**and are the children of the Most High, the living God of majesty, who has maintained the kingdom in a flourishing condition for us and for our forebears.

17"You will do well, then, to ignore the letter sent by Haman, son of Hammedatha, **18***for he who composed it has been hanged, together with his entire household, before the gates of Susa. Thus swiftly has God, who governs all, brought just punishment upon him.

19"You shall exhibit a copy of this letter publicly in every place, to certify that the Jews may follow their own laws, **20**and that you may help them on the day

---

† 8, 8: *Whatever is written . . . cannot be revoked:* the king cannot directly grant Esther's request (v 5) to revoke the previous decree against the Jews because of the irrevocable character of the laws of the Medes and Persians (1, 19; Dn 6, 9); but he empowers Esther to issue a new decree in his name which renders the earlier decree without effect; cf 3, 12f.

E, 10: *Macedonian:* a redactor of the book in the Hellenistic period used the designation *Macedonian,* here and in v 14, to express, after Macedonia's conquest of Persia, the most odious kind of man that a Persian ruler could be supposed to think of; the Hebrew text, for a similar reason, called Haman an Agagite. See note on A, 17.

---

*
    5: 1, 19.   11: B, 3.6.
    8: 1, 19.   13: A, 17.
    11f: 9, 1-4.   18: 7, 10; 9, 14.
    E/8f: B, 2.

set for their ruin, the thirteenth day of the twelfth month, Adar, to defend themselves against those who attack them. **21**For God, the ruler of all, has turned that day for them from one of destruction of the chosen race into one of joy. **22**Therefore, you too must celebrate this memorable day among your designated feasts with all rejoicing, **23**so that both now and in the future it may be, for us and for loyal Persians, a celebration of victory, and for those who plot against us a reminder of destruction.

24⁎"Every city and province, without exception, that does not observe this decree shall be ruthlessly destroyed with fire and sword, so that it will be left not merely untrodden by men, but even shunned by wild beasts and birds forever."

8/13†A copy of the letter to be promulgated as law in each and every province was published among all the peoples, so that the Jews might be prepared on that day to avenge themselves on their enemies. **8/14**Couriers mounted on royal steeds sped forth in haste at the king's order, and the decree was promulgated in the stronghold of Susa.

8/15⁎Mordecai left the king's presence clothed in a royal robe of violet and of white cotton, with a large crown of gold and a cloak of crimson byssus. The city of Susa shouted with joy, **8/16**and there was splendor and merriment for the Jews, exultation and triumph. **8/17**⁎In each and every province and in each and every city, wherever the king's order arrived, there was merriment and exultation, banqueting and feasting for the Jews. And many of the peoples of the land embraced Judaism, for they were seized with a fear of the Jews.

Victory of the Jews

9 **1**⁎WHEN the day arrived on which the order decreed by the king was to be carried out, the thirteenth day of the twelfth month, Adar, on which the enemies of the Jews had expected to become masters of them, the situation was reversed: the Jews became masters of their enemies. **2**The Jews mustered in their cities throughout the provinces of King Ahasuerus to attack those who sought to do them harm, and no one could withstand them, but all peoples were seized with a fear of them. **3**Moreover, all the officials of the provinces, the satraps, governors, and royal procurators supported the Jews from fear of Mordecai; **4**for Mordecai was powerful in the royal palace, and the report was spreading through all the provinces that he was continually growing in power.

5⁎The Jews struck down all their enemies with the sword, killing and destroying them; they did to their enemies as they pleased. **6**⁎In the stronghold of Susa, the Jews killed and destroyed five hundred men. **7**They

also killed Parshandatha, Dalphon, Aspatha, **8**Porathai, Adalia, Aridatha, **9**Parmashta, Arisai, Aridai, and Vaizatha, **10**⁎†the ten sons of Haman, son of Hammedatha, the foe of the Jews. However, they did not engage in plundering.

11On the same day, when the number of those killed in the stronghold of Susa was reported to the king, **12**he said to Queen Esther: "In the stronghold of Susa the Jews have killed and destroyed five hundred men, as well as the ten sons of Haman. What must they have done in the other royal provinces! You shall again be granted whatever you ask, and whatever you request shall be honored." **13**So Esther said, "If it pleases your majesty, let the Jews in Susa be permitted again tomorrow to act according to today's decree, and let the ten sons of Haman be hanged on gibbets." **14**⁎The king then gave an order to this effect, and the decree was published in Susa. So the ten sons of Haman were hanged, **15**⁎†and the Jews in Susa mustered again on the fourteenth of the month of Adar and killed three hundred men in Susa. However, they did not engage in plundering.

16⁎†The other Jews, who dwelt in the royal provinces, also mustered and defended themselves, and obtained rest from their enemies. They killed seventy-five thousand of their foes, without engaging in plunder, **17**on the thirteenth day of the month of Adar. On the fourteenth of the month they rested, and made it a day of feasting and rejoicing.

18(The Jews in Susa, however, mustered on the thirteenth and fourteenth of the month. But on the fifteenth they rested, and made it a day of feasting and rejoicing.) **19**That is why the rural Jews, who dwell in villages, celebrate the fourteenth of the month of Adar as a day of rejoicing and feasting, a holiday on which they send gifts of food to one another.

The Feast of Purim

20Mordecai recorded these events and sent letters to all the Jews, both near and far, in all the provinces of King Ahasuerus. **21**He ordered them to celebrate every year both the fourteenth and the fifteenth of the month of Adar **22**as the days on which the Jews obtained rest from their enemies and as the month which was turned for them from sorrow into joy, from mourning into festivity. They were to observe these days with feasting and gladness, sending food to one another and gifts to the poor. **23**⁎The Jews took upon themselves for the future this observance which they instituted at the written direction of Mordecai.

⁎

24: 3, 8f; B, 4.
8/15: Dn 5, 7.
    17: 9, 27.
9/1f: 8, 11f.
    5: Jdt 15, 6.
    6-10: 5, 11; B, 3; E, 11.

10: 9, 15; Jdt 15, 7.11.
14: 7, 10; E, 18.
15: 9, 10.
16: Jdt 15, 6.
23: 9, 29.

---

†

8, 13: *Avenge themselves on their enemies:* partly in self-defense (E, 20), and partly to express the fact that the extreme cruelty designed against the Jews by their enemies now recoiled upon the latter as a punishment. Cf 9, 1f.

9, 10: *They did not engage in plundering:* in contrast to the Israelites who fought Agag (1 Sm 15, 9); cf also vv 15f.

9, 15: This second slaughter explains the two dates (13th and 14th) of the Purim celebration by Jews in Susa (v 18).

9, 16: *Seventy-five thousand:* according to the Greek text this number was fifteen thousand.

24[*]Haman, son of Hammedatha the Agagite, the foe of all the Jews, had planned to destroy them and had cast the *pur,* or lot, for the time of their defeat and destruction. **25**[*]Yet, when Esther entered the royal presence, the king ordered in writing that the wicked plan Haman had devised against the Jews should instead be turned against Haman and that he and his sons should be hanged on gibbets. **26**And so these days have been named Purim after the word *pur.*

Thus, because of all that was contained in this letter, and because of what they had witnessed and experienced in this affair, **27**[*]the Jews established and took upon themselves, their descendants, and all who should join them, the inviolable obligation of celebrating these two days every year in the manner prescribed by this letter, and at the time appointed. **28**These days were to be commemorated and kept in every generation, by every clan, in every province, and in every city. These days of Purim were never to fall into disuse among the Jews, nor into oblivion among their descendants.

29[†]Queen Esther, daughter of Abihail and of Mordecai the Jew, wrote to confirm with full authority this second letter about Purim, **30**[*]when Mordecai sent documents concerning peace and security to all the Jews in the hundred and twenty-seven provinces of Ahasuerus' kingdom. **31**[†]Thus were established, for their appointed time, these days of Purim which Mordecai the Jew and Queen Esther had designated for the Jews, just as they had previously enjoined upon themselves and upon their race the duty of fasting and supplication. **32**The command of Esther confirmed these prescriptions for Purim and was recorded in the book.

10 **1**KING Ahasuerus laid tribute on the land and on the islands of the sea. **2**All the acts of his power and valor, as well as a detailed account of the greatness of Mordecai, whom the king promoted, are recorded in the chronicles of the kings of Media and Persia. **3**[*]The Jew Mordecai was next in rank to King Ahasuerus, in high standing among the Jews, and was regarded with favor by his many brethren, as the promoter of his people's welfare and the herald of peace for his whole race.

V: EPILOGUE

Mordecai's Dream Fulfilled

F¹[*]THEN MORDECAI SAID: "This is the work of God. **2**I recall the dream I had about these very things, and not a single detail has been left unfulfilled**3**—the tiny spring that grew into a river, the light of the sun, the many waters. The river is Esther, whom the king married and made queen. **4**The two dragons are myself and Haman. **5**The nations are those who assembled to destroy the name of the Jews, **6**but my people is Israel, who cried to God and was saved.

"The LORD saved his people and delivered us from all these evils. God worked signs and great wonders, such as have not occurred among the nations. **7**[†]For this purpose he arranged two lots: one for the people of God, the second for all the other nations. **8**These two lots were fulfilled in the hour, the time, and the day of judgment before God and among all the nations. **9**God remembered his people and rendered justice to his inheritance.

10[*]"Gathering together with joy and happiness before God, they shall celebrate these days on the fourteenth and fifteenth of the month Adar throughout all future generations of his people Israel."

[†] 9, 29: *Queen Esther, daughter of Abihail and of Mordecai:* the natural offspring of Abihail and adopted daughter of Mordecai; cf 2, 15. *This second letter:* for the burden of this letter see 9, 20ff. It was endorsed by Queen Esther. The first letter, written in the king's name, is referred to in 8, 9.

9, 31: *Fasting and supplication:* as the Jews had previously undertaken the duty of fasting and supplication to prevent the impending disaster, they now observe days of festival to commemorate their deliverance—in both cases (cf 4, 3.15f) at the request of Mordecai and Esther.

F, 7: *Two lots:* in this passage of the Greek text, which gives a more religious interpretation of the feast, the *two lots* are drawn by God to determine, respectively, the destiny of Israel and that of the nations. In 3, 7 above, translated from the Hebrew text, the feast is called *Purim* because of the lots which Aman cast to determine the day for the extinction of the Jews.

NOTE ON THE GREEK TEXT OF ESTHER

The Greek text of Esther contains a postscript as follows:

In the fourth year of the reign of Ptolemy and Cleopatra, Dositheus, who said he was a priest and Levite, and his son Ptolemy brought the present letter of Purim, saying that it was genuine and that Lysimachus, son of Ptolemy, of the community of Jerusalem, had translated it.

The date referred to in this postscript is most probably 78-77 B.C., in the reign of Ptolemy XII and Cleopatra V.

---

* 24ff: 3, 7; F, 10.   10/3: 2 Mc 15, 14.
25: 6, 5-13.   F/1-6: A, 4-10.
27: 8, 12.17.   10: 3, 7; 9, 17f.21.24-28.
30: 9, 23-26.

The First Book of Maccabees

Introduction

The name Maccabee, probably meaning "hammer," is actually applied in the Books of Maccabees to only one man, Judas, third son of the priest Mattathias and first leader of the revolt against the Seleucid kings who persecuted the Jews (1 Mc 2, 4.66; 2 Mc 8, 5.16; 10, 1.16). Traditionally the name has come to be applied to the brothers of Judas, his supporters, and even to other Jewish heroes of the period, such as the seven brothers (2 Mc 7).

The two Books of Maccabees, placed last in the Douai Version of the Old Testament, contain independent accounts of events in part identical which accompanied the attempted suppression of Judaism in Palestine in the second century B. C. The vigorous reaction to this attempt established for a time the religious and political independence of the Jews.

1 Maccabees was written about 100 B. C., in Hebrew, but the original has not come down to us. Instead, we have an early, pre-Christian, Greek translation full of Hebrew idioms. The author, probably a Palestinian Jew, is unknown. He was familiar with the traditions and sacred books of his people and had access to much reliable information on their recent history (from 175 to 134 B. C.). He may well have played some part in it himself in his youth. His purpose in writing is to record the salvation of Israel which God worked through the family of Mattathias (5, 62)—especially through his three sons, Judas, Jonathan, and Simon, and his grandson, John Hyrcanus. Implicitly the writer compares their virtues and their exploits with those of the ancient heroes, the Judges, Samuel, and David.

There are seven poetic sections in the book which imitate the style of classical Hebrew poetry: four laments (1, 25-28.36-40; 2, 8-13; 3, 45), and three hymns of praise of "our fathers" (2, 51-64), of Judas (3, 3-9), and of Simon (14, 4-15).

The doctrine expressed in the book is the customary belief of Israel, without the new developments which appear in 2 Maccabees and Daniel. The people of Israel have been specially chosen by the one true God as his covenant-partner, and they alone are privileged to know him and worship him. He is their eternal benefactor and their unfailing source of help. The people, in turn, must be loyal to his exclusive worship and must observe exactly the precepts of the law he has given them.

There is no doctrine of individual immortality except in the survival of one's name and fame, nor does the book express any messianic expectation, though messianic images are applied historically to "the days

of Simon" (14, 4-17). In true deuteronomic tradition, the author insists on fidelity to the law as the expression of Israel's love for God. The contest which he describes is a struggle, not simply between Jew and Gentile, but between those who would uphold the law and those, Jews or Gentiles, who would destroy it. His severest condemnation goes, not to the Seleucid politicians, but to the lawless apostates among his own people, adversaries of Judas and his brothers, who are models of faith and loyalty.

1 Maccabees has importance also for the New Testament. Salvation is paralleled with Jewish national aspirations (1 Mc 4, 46—14, 41), in contrast to the universal reign of God taught by Christ in the Gospel (Mt 13, 47-50; 22, 1-14). Also, destruction of the wall of the temple separating Jew from Gentile is an act of desecration in 1 Mc 9, 54, but in Eph 2, 14, an act of redemption and unification of both through Christ. On the other hand, association, in 1 Mc 2, 52, of Abraham's offering up of Isaac (Gn 22) with his justification by God (Gn 15, 6) is reflected in Jn 2, 21f, just as the Scriptures are regarded as a source of consolation in 1 Mc 12, 9 and in Rom 15, 4.

The Books of Maccabees, though regarded by Jews and Protestants as apocryphal, i. e., not inspired Scripture, because not contained in the Palestinian Canon or list of books drawn up at the end of the first century A. D., have nevertheless always been accepted by the Catholic Church as inspired, on the basis of apostolic tradition.

1 Maccabees is divided as follows:

I: INTRODUCTION: HELLENISM IN ASIA MINOR

Conquests and Death of Alexander

1 ¹*†AFTER ALEXANDER THE MACEDONIAN, Philip's son, who came from the land of Kittim, had defeated Darius, king of the Persians and Medes, he became king in his place, having first ruled in

---

1/1-10: Dn 8, 20ff; 11, 3f.21.

---

† 1, 1: *Land of Kittim:* Greece. The name referred originally to inhabitants of Kiti, capital of the isle of Cyprus, then to any Cypriots (Is 23, 1; Jer 2, 10), later to Greeks in general, and finally even to Romans. See note on Dn 11, 30. *Darius:* Darius III, Codoman (336-331 B. C.).

Greece. ²He fought many campaigns, captured fortresses, and put kings to death. ³He advanced to the ends of the earth, gathering plunder from many nations; the earth fell silent before him, and his heart became proud and arrogant. ⁴He collected a very strong army and conquered provinces, nations, and rulers, and they became his tributaries. ⁵But after all this he took to his bed, realizing that he was going to die. ⁶He therefore summoned his officers, the nobles, who had been brought up with him from his youth, to divide his kingdom among them while he was still alive. ⁷†Alexander had reigned twelve years when he died.

⁸So his officers took over his kingdom, each in his own territory, ⁹and after his death they all put on royal crowns, and so did their sons after them for many years, causing much distress over the earth.

II: THE MACCABEAN REVOLT

Pact between Jews and Gentiles

¹⁰*†THERE SPRANG FROM THESE a sinful off-shoot, Antiochus Epiphanes, son of King Antiochus, once a hostage at Rome. He became king in the year one hundred and thirty-seven of the kingdom of the Greeks.

¹¹*In those days there appeared in Israel men who were breakers of the law, and they seduced many people, saying: "Let us go and make an alliance with the Gentiles all around us; since we separated from them, many evils have come upon us." ¹²The proposal was agreeable; ¹³*some from among the people promptly went to the king, and he authorized them to introduce the way of living of the Gentiles. ¹⁴†Thereupon they built a gymnasium in Jerusalem according to the Gentile custom. ¹⁵*They covered over the mark of their circumcision and abandoned the holy covenant; they allied themselves with the Gentiles and sold themselves to wrongdoing.

Egyptian Campaign of Antiochus

¹⁶When his kingdom seemed secure, Antiochus proposed to become king of Egypt, so as to rule over both kingdoms. ¹⁷*†He invaded Egypt with a strong force, with chariots and elephants, and with a large fleet, ¹⁸to make war on Ptolemy, king of Egypt. Ptolemy was frightened at his presence and fled, leaving many casualties. ¹⁹The fortified cities in the land of Egypt were captured, and Antiochus plundered the land of Egypt.

Persecution of the Jews

²⁰*†After Antiochus had defeated Egypt in the year one hundred and forty-three, he returned and went up to Israel and to Jerusalem with a strong force. ²¹He insolently invaded the sanctuary and took away the golden altar, the lampstand for the light with all its fixtures, ²²the offering table, the cups and the bowls, the golden censers, the curtain, the crowns, and the golden ornament on the façade of the temple. He stripped off everything, ²³and took away the gold and silver and the precious vessels; he also took all the hidden treasures he could find. ²⁴Taking all this, he went back to his own country, after he had spoken with great arrogance and shed much blood.

²⁵And there was great mourning for Israel, in every
    place where they dwelt,
²⁶and the rulers and the elders groaned.
Virgins and young men languished,
    and the beauty of the women was disfigured.
²⁷Every bridegroom took up lamentation,
    she who sat in the bridal chamber mourned,
²⁸And the land was shaken on account of its inhabitants,
    and all the house of Jacob was covered with shame.

²⁹*Two years later, the king sent the Mysian commander to the cities of Judah, and he came to Jerusalem with a strong force. ³⁰He spoke to them deceitfully in peaceful terms, and won their trust. Then he attacked the city suddenly, in a great onslaught, and destroyed many of the people in Israel. ³¹He plundered the city and set fire to it, demolished its houses and its surrounding walls, ³²took captive the women and children, and seized the cattle. ³³*†Then they

† 1, 7: *Twelve years:* 336-323 B.C.

1, 10: *The year one hundred and thirty-seven:* Antiochus IV seized the throne in September, 175 B.C. Dates are given in this book according to the Seleucid era, which however was reckoned in two different ways. Antiochians considered this date to be October, 312 B.C. (Syrian calendar), while Babylonians and Jewish priests accepted April, 311 B.C. as the commencement of the era (temple calendar). The author of 1 Mc dates political events by the Syrian calendar but religious events by the temple calendar. Accordingly, the civil New Year occurred variously in September or October, the religious New Year in March or April.

1, 14: *Gymnasium:* symbol and center of athletic and intellectual life, it was the chief instrument of Hellenistic propaganda. Jewish youth were attracted by sports and encouraged to join youth clubs. They received training in military skills and in the duties of citizens. Through participation in the intellectual life, many were gradually won over to paganism.

1, 17: *Elephants:* an important part of Seleucid armament. About 300 B.C. Seleucus I, founder of the dynasty, procured five hundred of them from India; cf 6, 34-37.

1, 20: *Defeated Egypt in the year one hundred and forty-three:* 169 B.C. No mention is made in 1 Mc of the second expedition to Egypt a year later, described in 2 Mc 5, 1.11. Dn 11, 25.29 records both.

1, 33: *City of David:* not Mount Zion on the eastern hill of Jerusalem, which David captured from the Jebusites (2 Sm 5, 7), but a new fortress built on the western hill and overlooking the temple and its courts on Mount Zion. It was occupied for twenty-six years by the Syro-Macedonian garrison, together with apostate Jews, and was a continual threat to the temple and the Jewish people (v 36); cf 13, 49ff.

* 10: 2 Mc 4, 7.
11: 2 Mc 4, 9-17.
13ff: 2 Mc 4, 7-17.
15: 1 Cor 7, 18.
17: 2 Mc 5, 1; Dn 11, 25-28.
20-24: 2 Mc 5, 11-21.
29-32: 2 Mc 5, 24ff.
33: 6, 18.

built up the City of David with a high, massive wall and strong towers, and it became their citadel. **34**There they installed a sinful race, perverse men, who fortified themselves inside it, **35**storing up weapons and provisions, and depositing there the plunder they had collected from Jerusalem. And they became a great threat.

36The citadel became an ambush against the sanctuary,
and a wicked adversary to Israel at all times.
37And they shed innocent blood around the sanctuary;
they defiled the sanctuary.
38Because of them the inhabitants of Jerusalem fled away,
and she became the abode of strangers.
She became a stranger to her own offspring,
and her children forsook her.
39*Her sanctuary was as desolate as a wilderness;
her feasts were turned into mourning,
Her sabbaths to shame,
her honor to contempt.
40Her dishonor was as great as her glory had been,
and her exaltation was turned into mourning.

Prohibitions against Religion

41Then the king wrote to his whole kingdom that all should be one people, **42**each abandoning his particular customs. All the Gentiles conformed to the command of the king, **43**and many Israelites were in favor of his religion; they sacrificed to idols and profaned the sabbath.

44*The king sent messengers with letters to Jerusalem and to the cities of Judah, ordering them to follow customs foreign to their land: **45**to prohibit holocausts, sacrifices, and libations in the sanctuary, to profane the sabbaths and feast days, **46***to desecrate the sanctuary and the sacred ministers, to build pagan altars and temples and shrines, **47**to sacrifice swine and unclean animals, **48**to leave their sons uncircumcised, and to let themselves be defiled with every kind of impurity and abomination, **49**so that they might forget the law and change all their observances. **50***Whoever refused to act according to the command of the king should be put to death.

51Such were the orders he published throughout his kingdom. He appointed inspectors over all the people, and he ordered the cities of Judah to offer sacrifices, each city in turn. **52**Many of the people, those who abandoned the law, joined them and committed evil in the land. **53**Israel was driven into hiding, wherever places of refuge could be found.

54*†On the fifteenth day of the month Chislev, in the year one hundred and forty-five, the king erected the horrible abomination upon the altar of holocausts, and in the surrounding cities of Judah they built pagan altars. **55**They also burnt incense at the doors of houses and in the streets. **56**†Any scrolls of the law which they found they tore up and burnt. **57***Whoever was found with a scroll of the covenant, and whoever observed the law, was condemned to death by royal decree. **58**So they used their power against Israel, against those who were caught, each month, in the cities. **59**On the twenty-fifth day of each month they sacrificed on the altar erected over the altar of holocausts. **60***Women who had had their children circumcised were put to death, in keeping with the decree, **61**with the babies hung from their necks; their families also and those who had circumcised them were killed. **62**But many in Israel were determined and resolved in their hearts not to eat anything unclean; **63***they preferred to die rather than to be defiled with unclean food or to profane the holy covenant; and they did die. Terrible affliction was upon Israel.

Mattathias and His Sons

2 **1**†IN those days Mattathias, son of John, son of Simeon, a priest of the family of Joarib, left Jerusalem and settled in Modein. **2***He had five sons: John, who was called Gaddi; **3**Simon, who was called Thassi; **4**Judas, who was called Maccabeus; **5**Eleazar, who was called Avaran; and Jonathan, who was called Apphus. **6**When he saw the sacrileges that were being committed in Judah and in Jerusalem, **7**he said: "Woe is me! Why was I born to see the ruin of my people and the ruin of the holy city, and to sit idle while it is given into the hands of enemies, and the sanctuary into the hands of strangers?

8"Her temple has become like a man disgraced,
9*her glorious ornaments have been carried off as spoils,
Her infants have been murdered in her streets,
her young men by the sword of the enemy.
10What nation has not taken its share of her realm,
and laid its hand on her possessions?
11All her adornment has been taken away.
From being free, she has become a slave.
12We see our sanctuary and our beauty
and our glory laid waste,
And the Gentiles have defiled them!
13Why are we still alive?"

14Then Mattathias and his sons tore their garments, put on sackcloth, and mourned bitterly.

1, 54: *Fifteenth day of the month Chislev, in the year one hundred and forty-five:* December 6, 167 B. C. *Horrible abomination:* in the original Hebrew, a contemptuous pun on the title "Lord of heaven" given to the god Zeus Olympios, to whom an image or perhaps an altar was erected *upon the altar of holocausts* in the temple of Jerusalem; cf Dn 9, 27; 11, 31.

1, 56f: *Scrolls of the law:* one or more of the first five books of the Old Testament.

2, 1: *Modein:* a village twenty miles northwest of Jerusalem.

*
39f: Tb 2, 6; Am 8, 10.   57: 2 Mc 2, 14.
44-63: 2 Mc 6, 1-11.   60f: 2 Mc 6, 10.
46: 2 Mc 6, 2; Dn 9, 27.   63: 2 Mc 6, 10.
50: 2 Mc 6, 18—7, 41.   2/2: 1 Chr 24, 7.
54: 6, 7; Dn 9, 27; 11, 31.   9: Lam 2, 11.21.

Pagan Worship Refused

¹⁵The officers of the king in charge of enforcing the apostasy came to the city of Modein to organize the sacrifices. ¹⁶Many of Israel joined them, but Mattathias and his sons gathered in a group apart. ¹⁷Then the officers of the king addressed Mattathias: "You are a leader, an honorable and great man in this city, supported by sons and kinsmen. ¹⁸†Come now, be the first to obey the king's command, as all the Gentiles and the men of Judah and those who are left in Jerusalem have done. Then you and your sons shall be numbered among the King's Friends, and shall be enriched with silver and gold and many gifts." ¹⁹But Mattathias answered in a loud voice: "Although all the Gentiles in the king's realm obey him, so that each forsakes the religion of his fathers and consents to the king's orders, ²⁰yet I and my sons and my kinsmen will keep to the covenant of our fathers. ²¹God forbid that we should forsake the law and the commandments. ²²We will not obey the words of the king nor depart from our religion in the slightest degree."

²³As he finished saying these words, a certain Jew came forward in the sight of all to offer sacrifice on the altar in Modein according to the king's order. ²⁴When Mattathias saw him, he was filled with zeal; his heart was moved and his just fury was aroused; he sprang forward and killed him upon the altar. ²⁵At the same time, he also killed the messenger of the king who was forcing them to sacrifice, and he tore down the altar. ²⁶*Thus he showed his zeal for the law, just as Phinehas did with Zimri, son of Salu.

²⁷Then Mattathias went through the city shouting, "Let everyone who is zealous for the law and who stands by the covenant follow after me!" ²⁸*Thereupon he fled to the mountains with his sons, leaving behind in the city all their possessions. ²⁹†Many who sought to live according to righteousness and religious custom went out into the desert to settle there, ³⁰they and their sons, their wives and their cattle, because misfortunes pressed so hard on them.

³¹It was reported to the officers and soldiers of the king who were in the City of David, in Jerusalem, that certain men who had flouted the king's order had gone out to the hiding places in the desert. ³²*Many hurried out after them, and having caught up with them, camped opposite and prepared to attack them on the sabbath. ³³"Enough of this!" the pursuers said to them. "Come out and obey the king's command, and your lives will be spared." ³⁴But they replied, "We will not come out, nor will we obey the king's command to profane the sabbath." ³⁵Then the enemy attacked them at once; ³⁶but they did not retaliate; they neither threw stones, nor blocked up their own hiding places. ³⁷They said, "Let us all die without reproach; heaven and earth are our witnesses that you destroy us unjustly." ³⁸So the officers and soldiers attacked them on the sabbath, and they died with their wives, their children and their cattle, to the number of a thousand persons.

³⁹When Mattathias and his friends heard of it, they mourned deeply for them. ⁴⁰"If we all do as our kinsmen have done," they said to one another, "and do not fight against the Gentiles for our lives and our traditions, they will soon destroy us from the earth." ⁴¹On that day they came to this decision: "Let us fight against anyone who attacks us on the sabbath, so that we may not all die as our kinsmen died in the hiding places."

⁴²†Then they were joined by a group of Hasideans, valiant Israelites, all of them devout followers of the law. ⁴³And all those who were fleeing from the disaster joined them and supported them. ⁴⁴*They gathered an army and struck down sinners in their anger and lawbreakers in their wrath, and the survivors fled to the Gentiles for safety. ⁴⁵Mattathias and his friends went about and tore down the pagan altars; ⁴⁶they also enforced circumcision for any uncircumcised boys whom they found in the territory of Israel. ⁴⁷They put to flight the arrogant, and the work prospered in their hands. ⁴⁸They saved the law from the hands of the Gentiles and of the kings and did not let the sinner triumph.

Death of Mattathias

⁴⁹When the time came for Mattathias to die, he said to his sons: "Arrogance and scorn have now grown strong; it is a time of disaster and violent anger. ⁵⁰Therefore, my sons, be zealous for the law and give your lives for the covenant of our fathers.

⁵¹"Remember the deeds that our fathers did in their times, and you shall win great glory and an everlasting name.
⁵²*Was not Abraham found faithful in trial, and it was reputed to him as uprightness?
⁵³*Joseph, when in distress, kept the commandment, and he became master of Egypt.
⁵⁴*Phinehas our father, for his burning zeal, received the covenant of an everlasting priesthood.
⁵⁵*Joshua, for executing his commission, became a judge in Israel.

† 2, 18: *The King's Friends:* a regular order of nobility at Hellenistic courts. The various grades are frequently mentioned in this book: Friends, Chief Friends, Kinsmen.

2, 29: *The desert:* the sparsely inhabited mountain country southward from Jerusalem and west of the Dead Sea. It was an arid region with some perennial springs and a fair amount of rain in winter.

2, 42: *Hasideans:* in Hebrew *hasidim*, "pious ones," a religious group devoted to the strict observance of the law. They were the forerunners of both the Pharisees and the Essenes. They first supported the Maccabean movement, but subsequently opposed it, regarding it as too political.

* 26: 2, 54; Nm 25, 6-14.
28: 2 Mc 5, 27.
32-38: 2 Mc 6, 11.
44: Is 63, 3.
52: Gn 15, 6; 22, 1ff.
53: Gn 39, 7-10; 41, 39-43.
54: Nm 25, 10-13; Sir 45, 28ff.
55: Jos 1, 2.5.

56*Caleb, for bearing witness before the assembly,
  received an inheritance in the land.
57*David, for his piety,
  received as a heritage a throne of everlasting
    royalty.
58*Elijah, for his burning zeal for the law,
  was taken up to heaven.
59*Hananiah, Azariah and Mishael, for their faith,
  were saved from the fire.
60*Daniel, for his innocence,
  was delivered from the jaws of lions.
61And so, consider this from generation to genera-
    tion,
  that none who hope in him shall fail in strength.
62Do not fear the words of a sinful man,
  for his glory ends in corruption and worms.
63Today he is exalted, and tomorrow he is not to be
    found,
  because he has returned to his dust,
  and his schemes have perished.
64Children! be courageous and strong in keeping
    the law,
  for by it you shall be glorified.

65"Here is your brother Simeon who I know is a wise man; listen to him always, and he will be a father to you. **66**And Judas Maccabeus, a warrior from his youth, shall be the leader of your army and direct the war against the nations. **67**You shall also gather about you all who observe the law, and you shall avenge the wrongs of your people. **68**Pay back the Gentiles what they deserve, and observe the precepts of the law."

69Then he blessed them, and he was united with his fathers. **70†**He died in the year one hundred and forty-six, and was buried in the tombs of his fathers in Modein, and all Israel mourned him greatly.

III: LEADERSHIP OF JUDAS MACCABEUS

Defeat of Apollonius and Seron

3 **1**THEN HIS SON JUDAS, who was called Maccabeus, took his place. **2**All his brothers and all who had joined his father supported him, and they carried on Israel's war joyfully.

3*He spread abroad the glory of his people,
  and put on his breastplate like a giant.
He armed himself with weapons of war;
  he planned battles and protected the camp with
    his sword.
4In his actions he was like a lion,
  like a young lion roaring for prey.
5He pursued the wicked, hunting them out,

and those who troubled his people he destroyed
    by fire.
6The lawbreakers were cowed by fear of him,
  and all evildoers were dismayed.
By his hand redemption was happily achieved,
  7and he afflicted many kings;
He made Jacob glad by his deeds,
  and his memory is blessed forever.
8He went about the cities of Judah
  destroying the impious there.
He turned away wrath from Israel
  9and was renowned to the ends of the earth;
  he gathered together those who were perishing.

10†Then Apollonius gathered the Gentiles, together with a large army from Samaria, to fight against Israel. **11**When Judas learned of it, he went out to meet him and defeated and killed him. Many fell wounded, and the rest fled. **12**Their possessions were seized and the sword of Apollonius was taken by Judas, who fought with it the rest of his life.

13But Seron, commander of the Syrian army, heard that Judas had gathered many about him, an assembly of faithful men ready for war. **14**So he said, "I will make a name for myself and win glory in the kingdom by defeating Judas and his followers, who have despised the king's command." **15**And again a large company of renegades advanced with him to help him take revenge on the Israelites. **16†**When he reached the ascent of Beth-horon, Judas went out to meet him with a few men. **17**But when they saw the army coming against them, they said to Judas: "How can we, few as we are, fight such a mighty host as this? Besides, we are weak today from fasting." **18**But Judas said: "It is easy for many to be overcome by a few; in the sight of Heaven there is no difference between deliverance by many or by few; **19***for victory in war does not depend upon the size of the army, but on strength that comes from Heaven. **20**With great presumption and lawlessness they come against us to destroy us and our wives and children and to despoil us; **21**but we are fighting for our lives and our laws. **22†**He himself will crush them before us; so do not be afraid of them." **23**When he finished speaking, he rushed suddenly upon Seron and his army, who were crushed before him. **24*†**He pursued Seron down the descent of Beth-horon into

---

† 2, 70: *In the year one hundred and forty-six:* 166 B. C.

3, 10: *Apollonius:* the Mysian commander mentioned in 1, 29 and in 2 Mc 5, 24.

3, 16: *Beth-horon:* the famous pass leading up from the coastal plain to the Judean hill country. Here Joshua won an important battle (Jos 10, 10f), and in 66 A. D. a Roman force under Cestius was trapped and massacred.

3, 22: *He himself:* out of reverence for God, the author of 1 Mc prefers to use this and other expressions, such as "Heaven," instead of the divine name. Cf 1 Mc 3, 50.

3, 24: *About eight hundred:* the figures given in this book for strength of armies and number of casualties are not to be taken literally. In accordance with biblical usage, they indicate rather the importance of the battle described or the greatness of the victory.

56: Nm 13, 30; 14, 6-9.24;   59: Dn 3, 50.
  Jos 14, 14.   60: Dn 6, 23; 14, 31-42.
57: 2 Sm 2, 4; 7, 16.   3/3: 2 Mc 8, 5.
58: 1 Kgs 19, 10.14;   19: 1 Sm 14, 6.
  2 Kgs 2, 11.   24: Jos 10, 10.

the plain. About eight hundred of their men fell, and the rest fled to the country of the Philistines. **25**Then Judas and his brothers began to be feared, and dread fell upon the Gentiles about them. **26**His fame reached the king, and all the Gentiles talked about the battles of Judas.

Regency of Lysias

27When Antiochus heard about these events, he was angry; so he ordered a muster of all the forces of his kingdom, a very strong army. **28**He opened his treasure chests, gave his soldiers a year's pay, and commanded them to be prepared for anything. **29**He then found that this exhausted the money in his treasury; moreover the income from the province was small, because of the dissension and distress he had brought upon the land by abolishing the laws which had been in effect from of old. **30**He feared that, as had happened more than once, he would not have enough for his expenses and for the gifts that he had previously given with a more liberal hand than the preceding kings. **31**Greatly perplexed, he decided to go to Persia and levy tribute on those provinces, and so raise a large sum of money. **32**He left Lysias, a nobleman of royal blood, in charge of the king's affairs from the Euphrates River to the frontier of Egypt, **33**and commissioned him to take care of his son Antiochus until his own return. **34**He entrusted to him half of the army, and the elephants, and gave him instructions concerning everything he wanted done. As for the inhabitants of Judea and Jerusalem, **35**Lysias was to send an army against them to crush and destroy the power of Israel and the remnant of Jerusalem and efface their memory from the land. **36**He was to settle foreigners in all their territory and distribute their land by lot.

37†The king took the remaining half of the army and set out from Antioch, his capital, in the year one hundred and forty-seven; he crossed the Euphrates River and advanced inland.

The Victories of Judas

38*†Lysias chose Ptolemy, son of Dorymenes, and Nicanor and Gorgias, capable men among the King's Friends, **39**and with them he sent forty thousand men and seven thousand cavalry to invade the land of Judah and ravage it according to the king's orders. **40**†Setting out with all their forces, they came and pitched their camp near Emmaus in the plain. **41**When the merchants of the country heard of their fame, they came to the camp, bringing fetters and a large sum of silver and gold, to buy the Israelites as slaves. A force from Idumea and from Philistia joined with them.

42Judas and his brothers saw that the situation had become critical now that armies were encamped within their territory; they knew of the orders which the king had given to destroy and utterly wipe out the people. **43**So they said to one another, "Let us restore our people from their ruined estate, and fight for our people and our sanctuary!"

44The assembly gathered together to prepare for battle and to pray and implore mercy and compassion.

45Jerusalem was uninhabited, like a desert;
    not one of her children entered or came out.
The sanctuary was trampled on,
    and foreigners were in the citadel;
    it was a habitation of Gentiles.
Joy had disappeared from Jacob,
    and the flute and the harp were silent.

46*†Thus they assembled and went to Mizpah near Jerusalem, because there was formerly at Mizpah a place of prayer for Israel. **47**That day they fasted and wore sackcloth; they sprinkled ashes on their heads and tore their clothes. **48**†They unrolled the scroll of the law, to learn about the things for which the Gentiles consulted the images of their idols. **49***†They brought with them the priestly vestments, the first fruits, and the tithes; and they brought forward the nazirites who had completed the time of their vows. **50**And they cried aloud to Heaven: "What shall we do with these men, and where shall we take them? **51**For your sanctuary has been trampled on and profaned, and your priests are in mourning and humiliation. **52**Now the Gentiles are gathered together against us to destroy us. You know what they plot against us. **53**How shall we be able to resist them unless you help us?" **54**Then they blew the trumpets and cried out loudly.

55After this Judas appointed officers among the people, over thousands, over hundreds, over fifties, and over tens. **56***He proclaimed that those who were building houses, or were just married, or were planting vineyards, and those who were afraid, could each return to his home, according to the law. **57**Then the army moved off, and they camped to the south of Emmaus. **58**Judas said: "Arm yourselves and be brave; in the morning be ready to fight these Gentiles who have assembled against us to destroy us and our sanctuary. **59***It is better for us to die in battle than to witness the ruin of our nation and our sanctuary. Whatever Heaven wills, he will do."

---

† 3, 37: This expedition, in the spring of 165 B. C., resulted in failure; cf ch 6.

3, 38: *Nicanor:* the leader of another attack against the Jews four years later. He was finally killed by Judas; cf 7, 26-46.

3, 40: *Emmaus:* probably not the village mentioned in Lk 24, 13, but a settlement about twenty miles west of Jerusalem at the edge of the hill country.

3, 46: . . . *Mizpah a place of prayer for Israel:* a holy place established of old eight miles north and slightly west of Jerusalem. It was here that Samuel began to judge the Israelites (1 Sm 7, 5-11; 10, 17).

3, 48: *To learn . . . idols:* favorable omens for the coming battle. A contrast is intended between the idol worship of the pagans and the consultation of the word of God by the Jews; cf 2 Mc 8, 23.

3, 49: *Nazirites:* see note on Nm 6, 1ff.

---

*
38-44: 2 Mc 8, 8-15.
    38f: 7, 26; 2 Mc 4, 45; 8,   16-23.
        8f; 10, 14.   49: Nm 6, 2-5.
    46ff: 1 Sm 7, 5f; 2 Mc 8,   56: Dt 20, 5-8; Jgs 7, 3.
                           59: 2, 21f.

4 ¹NOW Gorgias took five thousand infantry and a thousand picked cavalry, and this detachment set out at night ²in order to attack the camp of the Jews and take them by surprise. Some men from the citadel were their guides. ³Judas heard of it, and himself set out with his soldiers to attack the king's army at Emmaus, ⁴while the latter's forces were still scattered away from the camp. ⁵During the night Gorgias came into the camp of Judas, and found no one there; so he began to hunt for them in the mountains, saying, "They are fleeing from us."

⁶But at daybreak Judas appeared in the plain with three thousand men, who lacked such armor and swords as they would have wished. ⁷They saw the army of the Gentiles, strong and breastplated, flanked with cavalry, and made up of expert soldiers. ⁸Judas said to the men with him: "Do not be afraid of their numbers or dread their attack. ⁹*Remember how our fathers were saved in the Red Sea, when Pharaoh pursued them with an army. ¹⁰*So now let us cry to Heaven in the hope that he will favor us, remember his covenant with our fathers, and destroy this army before us today. ¹¹All the Gentiles shall know that there is One who redeems and delivers Israel."

¹²When the foreigners looked up and saw them marching toward them, ¹³they came out of their camp for battle, and the men with Judas blew the trumpet. ¹⁴The battle was joined and the Gentiles were defeated and fled toward the plain. ¹⁵†Their whole rearguard fell by the sword, and they were pursued as far as Gazara and the plains of Judea, to Azotus and Jamnia. About three thousand of their men fell.

¹⁶When Judas and the army returned from the pursuit, ¹⁷he said to the people: "Do not be greedy for the plunder, for there is a fight ahead of us, ¹⁸and Gorgias and his army are near us on the mountain. But now stand firm against our enemies and overthrow them. Afterward you can freely take the plunder."

¹⁹As Judas was finishing this speech, a detachment appeared, looking down from the mountain. ²⁰They saw that their army had been put to flight and their camp was being burned. The smoke that could be seen indicated what had happened. ²¹When they realized this, they were terrified; and when they also saw the army of Judas in the plain ready to attack, ²²†they all fled to Philistine territory.

²³Then Judas went back to plunder the camp, and his men collected much gold and silver, violet and crimson cloth, and great treasure. ²⁴*As they returned, they were singing hymns and glorifying Heaven, "for he is good, for his mercy endures forever." ²⁵Thus Israel had a great deliverance that day.

Victory over Lysias

²⁶*But those of the foreigners who had escaped went and told Lysias all that had occurred. ²⁷When he heard it he was disturbed and discouraged, because things in Israel had not turned out as he intended and as the king had ordered.

²⁸So the following year he gathered together sixty thousand picked men and five thousand cavalry, to subdue them. ²⁹†They came into Idumea and camped at Beth-zur, and Judas met them with ten thousand men. ³⁰*Seeing that the army was strong, he prayed thus:

"Blessed are you, O Savior of Israel, who broke the rush of the mighty one by the hand of your servant David and delivered the camp of the Philistines into the hand of Jonathan, the son of Saul, and his armor-bearer. ³¹Give this army into the hands of your people Israel; make them ashamed of their troops and their cavalry. ³²Strike them with fear, weaken the boldness of their strength, and let them tremble at their own destruction. ³³Strike them down by the sword of those who love you, that all who know your name may hymn your praise."

³⁴Then they engaged in battle, and about five thousand of Lysias' men fell in hand-to-hand fighting. ³⁵†When Lysias saw his ranks beginning to give way, and the increased boldness of Judas, whose men were ready either to live or to die bravely, he withdrew to Antioch and began to recruit mercenaries so as to return to Judea with greater numbers.

Purification of the Temple

³⁶*†Then Judas and his brothers said, "Now that our enemies have been crushed, let us go up to purify the sanctuary and rededicate it." ³⁷So the whole army assembled, and went up to Mount Zion. ³⁸*They found the sanctuary desolate, the altar desecrated, the gates burnt, weeds growing in the courts as in a forest or on some mountain, and the priests' chambers demolished. ³⁹Then they tore their clothes and made great lamentation; they sprinkled their heads with ashes ⁴⁰and fell with their faces to the ground. And when the signal was given with trumpets, they cried out to Heaven.

⁴¹Judas appointed men to attack those in the citadel,

---

† 4, 15: *Gazara: Gezer* of the Hebrew Bible, five miles northwest of Emmaus; *Azotus*, Hebrew *Ashdod*, lay to the southwest; and *Jamnia*, Hebrew *Jabneel* (Jos 15, 11) or *Jabneh* (2 Chr 26, 6), to the west of Gazara.

4, 22: *Philistine territory:* the coastal cities of southern Palestine, traditionally hostile to Jerusalem. Jamnia in particular was an important base for the Seleucid power.

4, 29: *Beth-zur:* an important frontier city in the mountain area, fifteen miles south of Jerusalem. Its inhabitants were sympathetic to the Maccabees and refused to receive Lysias.

4, 35: According to 2 Mc 11, 13-15, peace negotiations followed between Lysias and Judas.

4, 36: *The sanctuary:* the whole temple area with its walls, courts and outbuildings, to be distinguished from the temple proper, the oblong edifice with porch, main room and inner shrine.

* 4/9: Ex 14, 21ff.
10: 2, 21.
24: Ps 118, 1ff.29.
26-35: 2 Mc 11, 1-12.
30: 1 Sm 17, 48ff.
36-59: 2 Mc 10, 1-8.
38: Ps 74, 2-7.

while he purified the sanctuary. **⁴²**He chose blameless priests, devoted to the law; **⁴³**these purified the sanctuary and carried away the stones of the Abomination to an unclean place. **⁴⁴***They deliberated what ought to be done with the altar of holocausts that had been desecrated. **⁴⁵***The happy thought came to them to tear it down, lest it be a lasting shame to them that the Gentiles had defiled it; so they tore down the altar. **⁴⁶**They stored the stones in a suitable place on the temple hill, until a prophet should come and decide what to do with them. **⁴⁷***Then they took uncut stones, according to the law, and built a new altar like the former one. **⁴⁸**They also repaired the sanctuary and the interior of the temple and purified the courts. **⁴⁹***They made new sacred vessels and brought the lampstand, the altar of incense, and the table into the temple. **⁵⁰***Then they burned incense on the altar and lighted the lamps on the lampstand, and these illuminated the temple. **⁵¹**They also put loaves on the table and hung up the curtains. Thus they finished all the work they had undertaken.

⁵²†Early in the morning on the twenty-fifth day of the ninth month, that is, the month of Chislev, in the year one hundred and forty-eight, **⁵³***they arose and offered sacrifice according to the law on the new altar of holocausts that they had made. **⁵⁴**On the anniversary of the day on which the Gentiles had defiled it, on that very day it was reconsecrated with songs, harps, flutes, and cymbals. **⁵⁵**All the people prostrated themselves and adored and praised Heaven, who had given them success.

⁵⁶For eight days they celebrated the dedication of the altar and joyfully offered holocausts and sacrifices of deliverance and praise. **⁵⁷**They ornamented the facade of the temple with gold crowns and shields; they repaired the gates and the priests' chambers and furnished them with doors. **⁵⁸**There was great joy among the people now that the disgrace of the Gentiles was removed. **⁵⁹*†**Then Judas and his brothers and the entire congregation of Israel decreed that the days of the dedication of the altar should be observed with joy and gladness on the anniversary every year for eight days, from the twenty-fifth day of the month Chislev.

⁶⁰At that time they built high walls and strong towers around Mount Zion, to prevent the Gentiles from coming and trampling over it as they had done before. **⁶¹**Judas also placed a garrison there to protect it, and likewise fortified Beth-zur, that the people might have a stronghold facing Idumea.

Punishment of Hostile Acts

5 **¹*†**WHEN the Gentiles round about heard that the altar had been rebuilt and the sanctuary consecrated as before, they were very angry. **²**So

they decided to destroy the descendants of Jacob who were among them, and they began to massacre and persecute the people. **³*†**Then Judas attacked the sons of Esau at Akrabattene in Idumea, because they were blockading Israel; he defeated them heavily, overcame and despoiled them. **⁴†**He also remembered the malice of the sons of Baean, who had become a snare and a stumblingblock to the people by ambushing them along the roads. **⁵**He forced them to take refuge in towers, which he besieged; he vowed their annihilation and burned down the towers along with all the persons in them. **⁶†**Then he crossed over to the Ammonites, where he found a strong army and a large body of people with Timothy as their leader. **⁷**He fought many battles with them, routed them, and struck them down. **⁸**After seizing Jazer and its villages, he returned to Judea.

Liberation of Galilean Jews

⁹The Gentiles in Gilead assembled to attack and destroy the Israelites who were in their territory; these then fled to the stronghold of Dathema. **¹⁰**They sent a letter to Judas and his brothers saying: "The Gentiles around us have combined against us to destroy us, **¹¹**and they are preparing to come and seize this stronghold to which we have fled. Timothy is the leader of their army. **¹²**Come at once and rescue us from them, for many of us have fallen. **¹³***All our kinsmen who were among the Tobiads have been killed; the Gentiles have carried away their wives and children and their goods, and they have slain there about a thousand men."

¹⁴While they were reading this letter, suddenly other messengers, in torn clothes, arrived from Galilee to deliver a similar message: **¹⁵†**that the inhabitants of Ptolemais, Tyre, and Sidon, and the whole of Gentile Galilee had joined forces to destroy them. **¹⁶**When Judas and the people heard this, a great assembly convened to consider what they should do for their unfortunate kinsmen who were being attacked by enemies.

¹⁷Judas said to his brother Simon: "Choose men for yourself, and go, rescue your kinsmen in Galilee; I and my brother Jonathan will go to Gilead."

¹⁸In Judea he left Joseph, son of Zechariah, and

---

†

4, 52: *Twenty-fifth day of the ninth month . . . in the year one hundred and forty-eight:* December 14, 164 B. C.

4, 59: *Days of the dedication . . . Chislev:* institution of the feast of Hannukah, also called the feast of Dedication (Jn 10, 22). Josephus Flavius calls it the feast of Lights.

5, 1: The events of this chapter occurred within the year 163 B. C.

5, 3: *Akrabattene:* a district southwest of the Dead Sea.

5, 4: *Sons of Baean:* 2 Mc 10, 15-23 calls them simply Idumeans.

5, 6ff: This summary anticipates the order of events and would fit better between vv 36 and 37. It corresponds to 2 Mc 12, 17-23. The action was probably a reprisal for the massacre referred to in v 13. Timothy was the Seleucid governor of Transjordan. *Jazer:* a town on the road from the Jordan to Amman.

5, 15: *Ptolemais:* Hebrew *Acco* (Jgs 1, 31), modern Acre, on the coast north of Haifa.

---

*

44: 1 Kgs 8, 64.
45: 6, 7.
47: Ex 20, 25.
49: Ex 25, 23-39; 30, 1-6.
50: Ex 30, 7ff.

53.56: Ex 30, 10; Ez 43, 18-27.
59: Jn 10, 22.
5/1f: 13, 6.
3ff: 2 Mc 10, 15-23.
13: 2 Mc 12, 17.

Azariah, leader of the people, with the rest of the army to guard it. [19]"Take charge of these people," he commanded them, "but do not fight against the Gentiles until we return." [20]Three thousand men were allotted to Simon, to go into Galilee, and eight thousand men to Judas, for Gilead.

[21]Simon went into Galilee and fought many battles with the Gentiles. They were crushed before him, [22]and he pursued them to the very gate of Ptolemais. About three thousand men of the Gentiles fell, and he gathered their spoils. [23]He took with him the Jews who were in Galilee and in Arbatta, with their wives and children and all that they had, and brought them to Judea with great rejoicing.

Rescue in Gilead

[24]*Judas Maccabeus and his brother Jonathan crossed the Jordan and marched for three days through the desert. [25]†There they met some Nabateans, who received them peacefully and told them all that had happened to the Jews in Gilead: [26]"Many of them have been imprisoned in Bozrah, in Bosor near Alema, in Chaspho, Maked, and Carnaim"—all of these are large, fortified cities—[27]"and some have been imprisoned in other cities of Gilead. Tomorrow their enemies plan to attack the strongholds and to seize and destroy all these people in one day."

[28]Thereupon Judas suddenly changed direction with his army, marched across the desert to Bozrah, and captured the city. He slaughtered all the male population, took all their possessions, and set fire to the city. [29]He led his army from that place by night, and they marched toward the stronghold of Dathema. [30]When morning came, they looked ahead and saw a countless multitude of people, with ladders and devices for capturing the stronghold, and beginning to attack the people within. [31]When Judas perceived that the struggle had begun and that the noise of the battle was resounding to heaven with trumpet blasts and loud shouting, [32]he said to the men of his army, "Fight for our kinsmen today."

[33]He came up behind them with three columns blowing their trumpets and shouting in prayer. [34]When the army of Timothy realized that it was Maccabeus, they fell back before him, and he inflicted on them a crushing defeat. About eight thousand of their men fell that day. [35]Then he turned toward Alema and attacked and captured it; he killed all the male population, plundered the place, and burned it down. [36]From there he moved on and took Chaspho, Maked, Bosor, and the other cities of Gilead.

[37]*After these events Timothy assembled another army and camped opposite Raphon, on the other side of the stream. [38]Judas sent men to spy on the camp, and they reported to him: "All the Gentiles around us have rallied to him, making a very large force; [39]they

have also hired Arabs to help them, and have camped beyond the stream, ready to attack you." So Judas went forward to attack them.

[40]*As Judas and his army were approaching the running stream, Timothy said to the officers of his army: "If he crosses over to us first, we shall not be able to resist him; he will certainly defeat us. [41]But if he is afraid and camps on the other side of the river, we will cross over to him and defeat him."

[42]But when Judas reached the running stream, he stationed the officers of the people beside the stream and gave them this order: "Do not allow any man to pitch a tent; all must go into battle." [43]He was the first to cross to the attack, with all the people behind him, and the Gentiles were crushed before them; they threw away their arms and fled to the temple enclosure at Carnaim. [44]*The Jews captured that city and burnt the enclosure with all who were in it. So Carnaim was subdued, and Judas met with no more resistance.

[45]Then he assembled all the Israelites, great and small, who were in Gilead, with their wives and children and their goods, a great crowd of people, to go into the land of Judah. [46]*†When they reached Ephron, a large and strongly fortified city along the way, they found it impossible to encircle it on either the right or the left; they would have to march right through it. [47]*But the men in the city shut them out and blocked up the gates with stones. [48]Then Judas sent them this peaceful message: "We wish to cross your territory in order to reach our own; no one will harm you; we will only march through." But they would not open to him.

[49]So Judas ordered a proclamation to be made in the camp that everyone make an attack from the place where he was. [50]When the men of the army took up their positions, he assaulted the city all that day and night, and it was delivered to him. [51]He slaughtered every male, razed and plundered the city, and passed through it over the slain.

[52]Then they crossed the Jordan to the great plain in front of Beth-shan; [53]and Judas kept rounding up the stragglers and encouraging the people the whole way, until he reached the land of Judah. [54]They ascended Mount Zion in joy and gladness and offered holocausts, because not one of them had fallen; they had returned in safety.

Joseph and Azariah Defeated

[55]During the time that Judas and Jonathan were in the land of Gilead, and Simon his brother was in Galilee opposite Ptolemais, [56]Joseph, son of Zechariah, and

---

*
24-36: 2 Mc 12, 10ff.
37-44: 2 Mc 12, 20-26.
  40: 1 Sm 14, 9f.
  44: 2 Mc 12, 21.

46-54: 2 Mc 12, 27-31.
  47: Nm 20, 17-21;
     21, 21-25.

---

†
5, 25: *Nabateans:* an Arab people who acquired wealth and power as caravan merchants in the final two centuries B. C. They settled down, established Petra as their capital, and for a time controlled all of Transjordan, even as far as Damascus. It was from a Nabatean governor that St. Paul escaped about 38 A. D. (2 Cor 11, 32f).

5, 46: *Ephron:* a city in Transjordan opposite Beth-shan, about five miles east of the Jordan River. Situated on a height, it dominated the valleys of the two tributaries of the Jordan.

Azariah, the leaders of the army, heard about the brave deeds and the fighting that they were doing. **57**They said, "Let us also make a name for ourselves by going out and fighting against the Gentiles around us."

58They gave orders to the men of their army who were with them, and marched toward Jamnia. **59**But Gorgias and his men came out of the city to meet them in battle. **60**Joseph and Azariah were beaten, and were pursued to the frontiers of Judea, and about two thousand Israelites fell that day. **61**It was a bad defeat for the people, because they had not obeyed Judas and his brothers, thinking that they would do brave deeds. **62**But they did not belong to the family of those men to whom it was granted to achieve Israel's salvation. **63**The valiant Judas and his brothers were greatly renowned in all Israel and among all the Gentiles, wherever their name was heard; **64**and men gathered about them and praised them.

65†Then Judas and his brothers went out and attacked the sons of Esau in the country toward the south; he took Hebron and its villages, and he destroyed its strongholds and burned the towers around it. **66**He then set out for the land of the Philistines and passed through Marisa. **67**At that time some priests fell in battle who had gone out rashly to fight in their desire to distinguish themselves. **68**Judas then turned toward Azotus in the land of the Philistines. He destroyed their altars and burned the statues of their gods; and after plundering their cities he returned to the land of Judah.

Defeat and Death of Antiochus IV

6 **1***†As King Antiochus was traversing the inland provinces, he heard that in Persia there was a city called Elymais, famous for its wealth in silver and gold, **2**and that its temple was very rich, containing gold helmets, breastplates, and weapons left there by Alexander, son of Philip, king of Macedon, the first king of the Greeks. **3**He went therefore and tried to capture and pillage the city. But he could not do so, because his plan became known to the people of the city **4**who rose up in battle against him. So he retreated and in great dismay withdrew from there to return to Babylon.

5While he was in Persia, a messenger brought him news that the armies sent into the land of Judah had been put to flight; **6**that Lysias had gone at first with a strong army and been driven back by the Israelites; that they had grown strong by reason of the arms, men, and abundant possessions taken from the armies they had destroyed; **7***that they had pulled down the Abomination which he had built upon the altar in Jerusalem; and that they had surrounded with high walls both the sanctuary, as it had been before, and his city of Beth-zur.

8When the king heard this news, he was struck with fear and very much shaken. Sick with grief because his designs had failed, he took to his bed. **9**There he remained many days, overwhelmed with sorrow, for he knew he was going to die.

10So he called in all his Friends and said to them: "Sleep has departed from my eyes, for my heart is sinking with anxiety. **11**I said to myself: 'Into what tribulation have I come, and in what floods of sorrow am I now! **12**Yet I was kindly and beloved in my rule.' But I now recall the evils I did in Jerusalem, when I carried away all the vessels of gold and silver that were in it, and for no cause gave orders that the inhabitants of Judah be destroyed. **13**I know that this is why these evils have overtaken me; and now I am dying, in bitter grief, in a foreign land."

14Then he summoned Philip, one of his Friends, and put him in charge of his whole kingdom. **15**He gave him his crown, his robe, and his signet ring, so that he might guide the king's son Antiochus and bring him up to be king. **16**†King Antiochus died in Persia in the year one hundred and forty-nine.

The Citadel Besieged

17*†When Lysias learned that the king was dead, he set up the king's son Antiochus, whom he had reared as a child, to be king in his place; and he gave him the title Eupator.

18*The men in the citadel were hemming in Israel around the sanctuary, continually trying to harm them and to strengthen the Gentiles. **19**But Judas planned to destroy them, and called all the people together to besiege them. **20**†So in the year one hundred and fifty they assembled and stormed the citadel, for which purpose he constructed catapults and other devices. **21**Some of the besieged escaped, joined by impious Israelites; **22**they went to the king and said:

"How long will you fail to do justice and avenge our kinsmen? **23**We agreed to serve your father and to follow his orders and obey his edicts. **24**And for this the sons of our people have become our enemies; they have put to death as many of us as they could find and have plundered our estates. **25**They have acted aggressively not only against us, but throughout their whole territory. **26**Look! They have now besieged the citadel

---

---

†

5, 65: *Sons of Esau:* Idumeans.

6, 1: *Elymais:* the mountainous region of Elam, north of the Persian Gulf. This section continues the story from 3, 37 and pertains to events preceding those in 4, 37ff.

6, 16: *The year one hundred and forty-nine:* September 22, 164, to October 9, 163 B. C. A Babylonian list of the Seleucid kings indicates that Antiochus died in November or early December of 164.

6, 17: *The king's son Antiochus:* Antiochus V Eupator, then about nine years old. He was in Antioch, still in the charge of Lysias, who proceeded to govern and wage wars in his name. Both were put to death two years later, when Demetrius, brother of Antiochus IV, arrived to claim the kingship; cf 7, 1ff.

6, 20: *The year one hundred and fifty:* October, 163, to September, 162 B. C.

in Jerusalem in order to capture it, and they have fortified the sanctuary and Beth-zur. [27]Unless you quickly forestall them, they will do even worse things than these, and you will not be able to stop them."

Campaign against Judas

[28]*When the king heard this he was angry, and he called together all his Friends, the officers of his army, and the commanders of the cavalry. [29]Mercenary forces also came to him from other kingdoms and from the islands of the seas. [30]His army numbered a hundred thousand foot-soldiers, twenty thousand cavalry, and thirty-two elephants trained for war. [31]They passed through Idumea and camped before Beth-zur. For many days they attacked it; they constructed siege-devices, but the besieged made a sortie and burned these, and they fought bravely.

[32]Then Judas marched away from the citadel and moved his camp to Beth-zechariah, on the way to the king's camp. [33]The king, rising before dawn, moved his force hastily along the road to Beth-zechariah; and the armies prepared for battle, while the trumpets sounded. [34]They made the elephants drunk on grape and mulberry wine to provoke them to fight. [35]The beasts were distributed along the phalanxes, each elephant having assigned to it a thousand men in coats of mail, with bronze helmets, and five hundred picked cavalry. [36]These anticipated the beast wherever it was; and wherever it moved, they moved too and never left it. [37]A strong wooden tower covering each elephant, and fastened to it by a harness, held, besides the Indian mahout, three soldiers who fought from it. [38]The remaining cavalry were stationed on one or the other of the two flanks of the army, to harass the enemy and to be protected from the phalanxes. [39]When the sun shone on the gold and bronze shields, the mountains gleamed with their brightness and blazed like flaming torches. [40]Part of the king's army extended over the heights, while some were on low ground, but they marched forward steadily and in good order. [41]All who heard the noise of their numbers, the tramp of their marching, and the clashing of the arms, trembled; for the army was very great and strong.

[42]Judas with his army advanced to fight, and six hundred men of the king's army fell. [43]*Eleazar, called Avaran, saw one of the beasts bigger than any of the others and covered with royal armor, and he thought the king must be on it. [44]So he gave up his life to save his people and win an everlasting name for himself. [45]He dashed up to it in the middle of the phalanx, killing men right and left, so that they fell back from him on both sides. [46]He ran right under the elephant and stabbed it in the belly, killing it. The beast fell to the ground on top of him, and he died there.

[47]When the Jews saw the strength of the royal army and the ardor of its forces, they retreated from them. [48]*A part of the king's army went up to Jerusalem to attack them, and the king established camps in Judea and at Mount Zion. [49]*†He made peace with the men of Beth-zur, and they evacuated the city, because they had no food there to enable them to stand a siege, for that was a sabbath year in the land. [50]The king took Beth-zur and stationed a garrison there to hold it. [51]For many days he besieged the sanctuary, setting up artillery and machines, fire-throwers, catapults and mechanical bows for shooting arrows and slingstones. [52]The Jews countered by setting up machines of their own, and kept up the fight a long time. [53]But there were no provisions in the storerooms, because it was the seventh year, and the tide-over provisions had been eaten up by those who had been rescued from the Gentiles and brought to Judea. [54]Few men remained in the sanctuary; the rest scattered, each to his own home, for the famine was too much for them.

Peace Treaty

[55]*Lysias heard that Philip, whom King Antiochus, before his death, had appointed to train his son Antiochus to be king, [56]had returned from Persia and Media with the army that accompanied the king, and that he was seeking to take over the government. [57]*So he hastily resolved to withdraw. He said to the king, the leaders of the army, and the soldiers: "We are growing weaker every day, our provisions are scanty, the place we are besieging is strong, and it is our duty to take care of the affairs of the kingdom. [58]Therefore let us now come to terms with these men, and make peace with them and all their nation. [59]Let us grant them freedom to live according to their own laws as formerly; it was on account of their laws, which we abolished, that they became angry and did all these things."

[60]The proposal found favor with the king and the leaders; he sent peace terms to the Jews, and they accepted. [61]So the king and the leaders swore an oath to them, and on these terms they evacuated the fortification. [62]But when the king entered Mount Zion and saw how the place was fortified, he broke the oath he had sworn and gave orders for the encircling wall to be destroyed. [63]Then he departed in haste and returned to Antioch, where he found Philip in possession of the city. He fought against him and took the city by force.

✴   28-54: 2 Mc 13, 1-23.   49: Lv 25, 2.
     28ff: 2 Mc 13, 1f.   55-63: 2 Mc 13, 23-26.
     43: 2 Mc 13, 15.   57: 2 Mc 11, 13ff.
     48f: 2 Mc 13, 22-23.

---

† 6, 49: *A sabbath year in the land:* when sowing and reaping were prohibited (Ex 23, 10f; Lv 25, 2-7). The year without a harvest (autumn of 164 to autumn of 163) was followed by a food shortage.

Expedition of Bacchides and Alcimus

7 ¹*†IN the year one hundred and fifty-one, Demetrius, son of Seleucus, set out from Rome, arrived with a few men in a city on the seacoast, and began to rule there. ²As he was preparing to enter the royal palace of his ancestors, the soldiers seized Antiochus and Lysias to bring them to him. ³When he was informed of this, he said, "Do not show me their faces." ⁴So the soldiers killed them, and Demetrius sat on the royal throne.

⁵†Then all the lawless and impious men of Israel came to him. They were led by Alcimus, who desired to be high priest. ⁶They made this accusation to the king against the people: "Judas and his brothers have destroyed all your friends and have driven us out of our country. ⁷So now, send a man whom you trust to go and see all the havoc Judas has done to us and to the king's land, and let him punish them and all their supporters."

⁸Then the king chose Bacchides, one of the King's Friends, governor of West-of-Euphrates, a great man in the kingdom, and faithful to the king. ⁹*He sent him and the impious Alcimus, to whom he granted the high priesthood, with orders to take revenge on the Israelites. ¹⁰They set out and, on arriving in the land of Judah with a great army, sent messengers who spoke deceitfully to Judas and his brothers in peaceful terms. ¹¹But these paid no attention to their words, seeing that they had come with a great army. ¹²A group of scribes, however, gathered about Alcimus and Bacchides to ask for a just agreement. ¹³*The Hasideans were the first among the Israelites to seek peace with them, ¹⁴for they said, "A priest of the line of Aaron has come with the army, and he will not do us any wrong." ¹⁵He spoke with them peacefully and swore to them, "We will not try to injure you or your friends." ¹⁶So they trusted him. But he arrested sixty of them and killed them in one day, according to the text of Scripture:

¹⁷*"The flesh of your saints they have strewn,
     and their blood they have shed round about
         Jerusalem,
     and there was no one to bury them."

¹⁸Then fear and dread of them came upon all the people, who said: "There is no truth or justice among them; they violated the agreement and the oath that they swore."

¹⁹†Bacchides withdrew from Jerusalem and pitched his camp in Beth-zaith. He had many of the men arrested who deserted to him, throwing them into the great pit. ²⁰He handed the province over to Alcimus, leaving troops to help him, while he himself returned to the king.

²¹Alcimus spared no pains to maintain his high priesthood, ²²and all those who were disturbing their people gathered about him. They took possession of the land of Judah and caused great distress in Israel. ²³When Judas saw all the evils that Alcimus and his men were bringing upon the Israelites, more than even the Gentiles had done, ²⁴he went about all the borders of Judea and took revenge on the men who had deserted, preventing them from going out into the country. ²⁵But when Alcimus saw that Judas and his followers were gaining strength and realized that he could not oppose them, he returned to the king and accused them of grave crimes.

Defeat of Nicanor

²⁶*Then the king sent Nicanor, one of his famous officers, who was a bitter enemy of Israel, with orders to destroy the people. ²⁷†Nicanor came to Jerusalem with a large force and deceitfully sent to Judas and his brothers this peaceable message: ²⁸"Let there be no fight between me and you. I will come with a few men to meet you peaceably."

²⁹So he came to Judas, and they greeted one another peaceably. But Judas' enemies were prepared to seize him. ³⁰*When he became aware that Nicanor had come to him with treachery in mind, Judas was afraid and would not meet him again. ³¹†When Nicanor saw that his plan had been discovered, he went out to fight Judas near Caphar-salama.³²About five hundred men of Nicanor's army fell; the rest fled to the City of David.

³³*After this, Nicanor went up to Mount Zion. Some of the priests from the sanctuary and some of the elders of the people came out to greet him peaceably and to show him the holocaust that was being offered for the king. ³⁴†But he mocked and ridiculed them, defiled them, and spoke disdainfully. ³⁵In a rage he swore: "If Judas and his army are not delivered to me at once, when I return victorious I will burn this tem-

---

* 7/1-7: 2 Mc 14, 1-11.
9ff: 2 Mc 14, 46.
13f: 2, 42.
17: Ps 79, 1ff.

26f: 3, 38; 2 Mc 8, 9;
14, 12f.
30: 2 Mc 14, 30.
33-38: 2 Mc 14, 31-36.

† 7, 1ff: *The year one hundred and fifty-one:* the spring of 161 B. C. *Demetrius,* son of Seleucus, was the lawful heir to the kingdom; but when only nine years old, he was taken as a hostage at Rome in place of his uncle, who ruled as Antiochus IV Epiphanes. At the age of twenty-five Demetrius fled secretly from Rome and, with the support of the Syrians, overcame his rival Antiochus V and put him to death. *The royal palace:* at Antioch.

7, 5f: *Alcimus:* a renegade Jew hostile to the Maccabees, who became high priest after the death of Menelaus (2 Mc 14, 3). He received confirmation in his office from the new King Demetrius (v 9), and brought malicious charges against *Judas and his brothers* and the people (v 6). He wrought more evils on the Israelites than the Gentiles had done (v 23).

7, 19: *Beth-zaith:* about three miles north of Beth-zur and twelve miles south of Jerusalem.

7, 27: *Nicanor . . . deceitfully sent to Judas:* a more favorable picture of Nicanor, as an honest man who became a personal friend of Judas, is given in 2 Mc 14, 17-25. Their friendship was broken by the intrigues of Alcimus (2 Mc 14, 26-30).

7, 31: *Caphar-salama:* a village seven miles north-northwest of Jerusalem, on the road leading to Beth-horon.

7, 34: *Defiled them:* spitting on the priests caused them to become legally defiled.

ple down." He went away in great anger. **³⁶***The priests, however, went in and stood before the altar and the sanctuary. They wept and said: **³⁷**"You have chosen this house to bear your name, to be a house of prayer and petition for your people. **³⁸**Take revenge on this man and his army, and let them fall by the sword. Remember their blasphemies, and do not let them continue."

³⁹Nicanor left Jerusalem and pitched his camp at Beth-horon, where the Syrian army joined him. **⁴⁰**†But Judas camped in Adasa with three thousand men. Here Judas uttered this prayer: **⁴¹***"When they who were sent by the king blasphemed, your angel went out and killed a hundred and eighty-five thousand of them. **⁴²***In the same way, crush this army before us today, and let the rest know that Nicanor spoke wickedly against your sanctuary; judge him according to his wickedness."

⁴³*The armies met in battle on the thirteenth day of the month Adar. Nicanor's army was crushed, and he himself was the first to fall in the battle. **⁴⁴**When his army saw that Nicanor was dead, they threw down their arms and fled. **⁴⁵**The Jews pursued them a day's journey, from Adasa to near Gazara, blowing the trumpets behind them as signals. **⁴⁶**From all the surrounding villages of Judea people came out and closed in on them. They hemmed them in, and all the enemies fell by the sword; not a single one escaped.

⁴⁷Then the Jews collected the spoils and the booty; they cut off Nicanor's head and his right arm, which he had lifted up so arrogantly. These they brought to Jerusalem and displayed there. **⁴⁸**The people rejoiced greatly, and observed that day as a great festival. **⁴⁹**†They decreed that it should be observed every year on the thirteenth of Adar. **⁵⁰**†And for a short time the land of Judah was quiet.

Treaty with the Romans

8 **¹**†JUDAS had heard of the reputation of the Romans. They were valiant fighters and acted amiably to all who took their side. They established a friendly alliance with all who applied to them. **²**†He was also told of their battles and the brave deeds that they had performed against the Gauls, conquering them and forcing them to pay tribute. **³**They had gotten possession of the silver and gold mines in Spain, **⁴**and by planning and persistence had conquered the whole country, although it was very remote from their own. They had crushed the kings who had come against them from the far corners of the earth and had inflicted on them severe defeat, and the rest paid tribute to them every year. **⁵**†Philip and Perseus, king of the Macedonians, and the others who opposed them in battle had been overwhelmed and subjugated. **⁶**†Antiochus the Great, king of Asia, who had fought against them with a hundred and twenty elephants and with cavalry and chariots and a very great army,

had been defeated by them. **⁷**They had taken him alive and obliged him and the kings who succeeded him to pay a heavy tribute, to give hostages and a section of **⁸**†Lycia, Mysia, and Lydia from among their best provinces. The Romans took these from him and gave them to King Eumenes. **⁹**†When the men of Greece had planned to come and destroy them, **¹⁰**the Romans discovered it, and sent against the Greeks a single general who made war on them. Many were wounded and fell, and the Romans took their wives and children captive. They plundered them, took possession of their land, tore down their strongholds and reduced them to slavery even to this day. **¹¹**All the other kingdoms and islands that had ever opposed them they destroyed and enslaved; **¹²**with their friends, however, and those who relied on them, they maintained friendship. They had conquered kings both far and near, and all who heard of their fame were afraid of them. **¹³**In truth, those whom they desired to help to a king-

---

†

7, 40: *Adasa:* a village southeast of Caphar-salama.

7, 49: *The thirteenth of Adar:* March 27, 160 B. C. This day in the Jewish calendar was called the "Day of Nicanor" (2 Mc 15, 36), but it was not long celebrated by the Jews.

7, 50: *A short time:* about one month following the death of Nicanor. After that began the attack of Bacchides resulting in the death of Judas (9, 1-18).

8, 1: This chapter contains the account of the embassy which Judas sent to Rome, probably before the death of Nicanor, to conclude a treaty of alliance between Rome and the Jewish nation. Without precise chronology, the pertinent data are gathered into a unified theme.

The image of the Roman Republic greatly impressed the smaller Eastern peoples seeking support against their overlords (1-16), because of Roman success in war (2-11) and effective aid to their allies (12-13). Numerous interventions by Rome in the politics of the Near East bear witness to its power and prestige in the second century B. C. Cf 1 Mc 1, 10; 7, 2; 12, 3; 15, 15-24; 2 Mc 11, 34. With the Roman control of Palestine in 63 B. C., the Republic and later the Empire became heartily detested. The eulogy of Rome in this chapter is one of the reasons why 1 Maccabees was not preserved by the Palestinian Jews of the century that followed.

8, 2: *Gauls:* probably the Celts of northern Italy and southern France, subdued by the Romans in 222 B. C., and again in 200-191 B. C.; but perhaps also those in Asia Minor (the Galatians), whom the Romans defeated in 189 B. C.

8, 5: *Philip:* Philip V of Macedonia, defeated by a Graeco-Roman alliance at Cynoscephalae in 197 B. C. *Perseus,* his son, was defeated at Pydna in 168 B. C., and died a prisoner. With this, the kingdom of Macedonia came to an end.

8, 6: *Antiochus:* Antiochus III, greatest of the Seleucid kings. He was defeated at Magnesia in 190 B. C. By the Treaty of Apamea in 189, he was obliged to pay Rome a crushing indemnity of 15,000 talents. It was the weakening of Antiochene power and the growing military and economic influence of Rome that led Antiochus IV to adopt the policy of political, religious and cultural unification of Syria and Palestine.

8, 8: *Lycia, Mysia:* regions in western Asia Minor. These names are restored here by conjectural emendation; the Greek text has "India, Media," most likely through scribal error. *Eumenes:* Eumenes II (197-158), king of Pergamum, an ally of Rome who benefited greatly from Antiochus' losses.

8, 9f: The revolt of the Achaean League, inserted here, occurred in 146 B. C., after Judas' time. It was crushed by the Roman consul Lucius Mummius and marked the end of Greek independence. The author regards all Greeks as the enemies of God.

---

*
36: Jl 2, 17.   42: Is 37, 36ff.
41f: 2 Mc 8, 19; 15, 22ff.   43: 2 Mc 15, 25-35.

dom became kings, and those whom they wished to depose they deposed; and they were greatly exalted. [14]Yet with all this, none of them put on a crown or wore purple as a display of grandeur. [15]They had made for themselves a senate house, and every day three hundred and twenty men took counsel, deliberating on all that concerned the people and their well-being. [16]†They entrusted their government to one man every year, to rule over their entire country, and they all obeyed that one, and there was no envy or jealousy among them.

[17]*So Judas chose Eupolemus, son of John, son of Accos, and Jason, son of Eleazar, and sent them to Rome to establish an alliance of friendship with them. [18]He did this to get rid of the yoke, for it was obvious that the kingdom of the Greeks was subjecting Israel to slavery. [19]After making a very long journey to Rome, the envoys entered the senate and spoke as follows: [20]"Judas, called Maccabeus, and his brothers, with the Jewish people, have sent us to you to make a peaceful alliance with you, and to enroll ourselves among your allies and friends." [21]The proposal pleased the Romans, [22]*†and this is a copy of the reply they inscribed on bronze tablets and sent to Jerusalem, to remain there with the Jews as a record of peace and alliance:

[23]"May it be well with the Romans and the Jewish nation at sea and on land forever; may sword and enemy be far from them. [24]But if war is first made on Rome, or any of its allies in any of their dominions, [25]the Jewish nation will help them wholeheartedly, as the occasion shall demand; [26]and to those who wage war they shall not give nor provide grain, arms, money, or ships; this is Rome's decision. They shall fulfill their obligations without receiving any recompense. [27]In the same way, if war is made first on the Jewish nation, the Romans will help them willingly, as the occasion shall demand, [28]and to those who are attacking them there shall not be given grain, arms, money, or ships; this is Rome's decision. They shall fulfill their obligations without deception. [29]On these terms the Romans have made an agreement with the Jewish people. [30]But if both parties hereafter decide to add or take away anything, they shall do as they choose, and whatever they shall add or take away shall be valid.

[31]"Moreover, concerning the wrongs that King Demetrius has done to them, we have written to him thus: 'Why have you made your yoke heavy upon our friends and allies the Jews? [32]If they complain about you again, we will do them justice and make war on you by land and sea.'"

Invasion of Judah

9 [1]WHEN Demetrius heard that Nicanor and his army had fallen in battle, he again sent Bacchides and Alcimus into the land of Judah, along with the right wing of his army. [2]†They took the road to Galilee, and camping opposite the ascent at Arbela,

8/17: 12, 1f; 15, 15-22.   22: 14, 18.

they captured it and killed many people. [3]†In the first month of the year one hundred and fifty-two, they encamped against Jerusalem. [4]Then they set out for Berea with twenty thousand men and two thousand cavalry. [5]Judas, with three thousand picked men, had camped at Elasa. [6]When his men saw the great number of the troops, they were very much afraid, and many slipped away from the camp, until only eight hundred men remained.

[7]As Judas saw that his army was melting away just when the battle was imminent, he was panic-stricken, because he had no time to gather them together. [8]But in spite of his discouragement, he said to those who remained: "Let us go forward to meet our enemies; perhaps we can put up a good fight against them." [9]They tried to dissuade him, saying: "We certainly cannot. Let us save our lives now, and come back with our kinsmen, and then fight against them. Now we are too few." [10]But Judas said: "Far be it from me to do such a thing as to flee from them! If our time has come, let us die bravely for our kinsmen and not leave a stain upon our glory!"

Death of Judas

[11]Then the army of Bacchides moved out of camp and took its position for combat. The cavalry were divided into two squadrons, and the slingers and the archers came on ahead of the army, and all the valiant men were in the front line. [12]Bacchides was on the right wing. Flanked by the two squadrons, the phalanx attacked as they blew their trumpets. Those who were on Judas' side also blew their trumpets. [13]The earth shook with the noise of the armies, and the battle raged from morning until evening. [14]Seeing that Bacchides was on the right, with the main force of his army, Judas, with all the most stouthearted rallying to him, [15]†drove back the right wing and pursued

---

† 8, 16: *They entrusted their government to one man:* actually the Roman Republic always had two consuls as joint heads of the government. Presumably, a single one dealt with embassies and answered letters, hence the impression the Jews received; cf 15, 16.

8, 22: *The reply . . . on bronze tablets and sent to Jerusalem:* The decree of the Senate would be inscribed on bronze and kept in the Roman Capitol, with only a copy in letter form sent to Jerusalem. The translation of the decree into Hebrew and then into Greek, as found here in 1 Mc, may have occasioned this error.

9, 2: *They took the road . . . Arbela, they captured it:* This passage is restored, in part, by conjectural emendation. The present Greek text could be translated, "They took the road to Gilgal, and camping opposite Mesaloth at Arbela, they captured it." But Arbela (modern Khirbet Irbid) was in Galilee—on a high hill overlooking the western shore of the Sea of Galilee. Gilgal, on the contrary, was in the Jordan valley near Jericho. "Mesaloth" is probably a corrupt form of a Hebrew word meaning "steps, ascent."

9, 3: *The first month of the year one hundred and fifty-two:* April/May 160 B. C., by the temple calendar.

9, 15: *As far as the mountain slopes:* conjectural emendation. The Greek text has "as far as Mount Azotus"; this is most unlikely. Apparently the Greek translator mistook the Hebrew word *ashdôt,* "slopes," *for aśdôd,* "Azotus."

them as far as the mountain slopes. ¹⁶But when the men on the left wing saw that the right wing was driven back, they turned and followed Judas and his men, taking them in the rear. ¹⁷The battle was fought desperately, and many on both sides fell wounded. ¹⁸Then Judas fell, and the rest fled.

¹⁹Jonathan and Simon took their brother Judas and buried him in the tomb of their fathers at Modein. ²⁰All Israel bewailed him in great grief. They mourned for him many days, and they said, ²¹*"How the mighty one has fallen, the savior of Israel!" ²²The other acts of Judas, his battles, the brave deeds he performed, and his greatness have not been recorded; but they were very many.

IV: LEADERSHIP OF JONATHAN

Bacchides and Jonathan

²³ᴬꜰᴛᴇʀ ᴛʜᴇ ᴅᴇᴀᴛʜ ᴏꜰ ᴊᴜᴅᴀs, the transgressors of the law raised their heads in every part of Israel, and all kinds of evildoers appeared. ²⁴In those days there was a very great famine, and the country deserted to them. ²⁵Bacchides chose impious men and made them masters of the country. ²⁶These sought out and hunted down the friends of Judas and brought them to Bacchides, who punished and derided them. ²⁷There had not been such great distress in Israel since the time prophets ceased to appear among the people.

²⁸Then all the friends of Judas came together and said to Jonathan: ²⁹"Since your brother Judas died, there has been no one like him to oppose our enemies, Bacchides and those who are hostile to our nation. ³⁰Now therefore we have chosen you today to be our ruler and leader in his place, and to fight our battle." ³¹From that moment Jonathan accepted the leadership, and took the place of Judas his brother.

³²When Bacchides learned of it, he sought to kill him. ³³†But Jonathan and his brother Simon and all the men with him discovered this, and they fled to the desert of Tekoa and camped by the waters of the pool of Asphar.

³⁵*Jonathan sent his brother as leader of the convoy to ask permission of his friends, the Nabateans, to deposit with them their great quantity of baggage. ³⁶†But the sons of Jambri from Medaba made a raid and seized and carried off John and everything he had. ³⁷After this, word was brought to Jonathan and his brother Simon: "The sons of Jambri are celebrating a great wedding, and with a large escort they are bringing the bride, the daughter of one of the great princes of Canaan, from Nadabath." ³⁸Remembering the blood of John their brother, they went up and hid themselves under cover of the mountain. ³⁹They watched, and suddenly saw a noisy crowd with baggage; the bridegroom and his friends and kinsmen had come out to meet the bride's party with tambourines

and musicians and much equipment. ⁴⁰The Jews rose up against them from their ambush and killed them. Many fell wounded, and after the survivors fled toward the mountain, all their spoils were taken. ⁴¹Thus the wedding was turned into mourning, and the sound of music into lamentation. ⁴²Having taken their revenge for the blood of their brother, the Jews returned to the marshes of the Jordan.

⁴³When Bacchides heard of it, he came on the sabbath to the banks of the Jordan with a large force. ⁴⁴Then Jonathan said to his companions, "Let us get up now and fight for our lives, for today is not like yesterday and the day before. ⁴⁵†The battle is before us, and behind us are the waters of the Jordan on one side, marsh and thickets on the other, and there is no way of escape. ⁴⁶Cry out now to Heaven for deliverance from our enemies." ⁴⁷When they joined battle, Jonathan raised his arm to strike Bacchides, but Bacchides backed away from him. ⁴⁸Jonathan and his men jumped into the Jordan and swam across to the other side, but the enemy did not pursue them across the Jordan. ⁴⁹A thousand men on Bacchides' side fell that day.

⁵⁰†On returning to Jerusalem, Bacchides built strongholds in Judea: the Jericho fortress, as well as Emmaus, Beth-horon, Bethel, Timnath, Pharathon, and Tephon, with high walls and gates and bars. ⁵¹In each he put a garrison to oppose Israel. ⁵²He fortified the city of Beth-zur, Gazara and the citadel, and put soldiers in them and stores of provisions. ⁵³*He took as hostages the sons of the leaders of the country and put them in custody in the citadel at Jerusalem.

⁵⁴†In the year one hundred and fifty-three, in the second month, Alcimus ordered the wall of the inner court of the sanctuary to be torn down, thus destroying the work of the prophets. But he only began to tear it down. ⁵⁵Just at that time he had a stroke, and his work was interrupted; his mouth was closed and he was paralyzed, so that he could no longer utter a word to give orders concerning his house. ⁵⁶Finally he died in great agony. ⁵⁷Seeing that Alcimus was dead, Bacchides returned to the king, and the land of Judah was quiet for two years.

⁵⁸Then all the transgressors of the law held a council and said: "Jonathan and his companions are living in peace and security. Now then, let us have Bacchides return, and he will capture all of them in a single night." ⁵⁹So they went and took counsel with him. ⁶⁰When Bacchides was setting out with a large force,

---

† 9, 33: *Tekoa:* home of the prophet Amos in the wild country above the Dead Sea, southeast of Jerusalem.
9, 34: Omitted: it is a dittography of v 43.
9, 35: Jonathan sent his brother: this was John, who was called Gaddi (2, 2; cf 9, 36, 38).
9, 36: *Medaba:* northeast of the Dead Sea.
9, 45: Jonathan's force was apparently trapped in one of the many oxbows of the lower Jordan. Bacchides had crossed and caught them still on the east bank.
9, 50: These sites constitute a ring on the edges of the province of Judea.
9, 54: *In the year . . . second month:* May, 159 B.C.

* 9/21: 2 Sm 1, 27.　　53: 10, 9.
35: 5, 25.

he sent letters secretly to all his allies in Judea, telling them to seize Jonathan and his companions. They were not able to do this, however, because their plot became known. ⁶¹In fact, Jonathan's men seized about fifty of the men of the country who were ringleaders in the mischief and put them to death. ⁶²†Then Jonathan and Simon and their companions withdrew to Bethbasi in the desert; they rebuilt and strengthened its fortifications that had been demolished. ⁶³When Bacchides learned of this, he gathered together his whole force and sent word to those who were in Judea. ⁶⁴He came and pitched his camp before Bethbasi, and constructing siege-machines, he fought against it for many days.

⁶⁵Leaving his brother Simon in the city, Jonathan, accompanied by a small group of men, went out into the field. ⁶⁶He struck down Odomera and his kinsmen and the sons of Phasiron in their encampment; these men had set out to go up to the siege with their forces. ⁶⁷Simon and his men then sallied forth from the city and set fire to the machines. ⁶⁸They fought against Bacchides, and he was beaten. This caused him great distress. Because the enterprise he had planned came to nought, ⁶⁹he was angry with the lawless men who had advised him to invade the province. He killed many of them and resolved to return to his own country.

⁷⁰Jonathan learned of this and sent ambassadors to make peace with him and to obtain the release of the prisoners. ⁷¹He agreed to do as Jonathan had asked. He swore an oath to him that he would never try to injure him for the rest of his life; ⁷²and he released the prisoners he had previously taken from the land of Judah. He returned to his own country and never came into their territory again.

⁷³†Then the sword ceased in Israel. Jonathan settled in Michmash; he began to judge the people, and he destroyed the impious in Israel.

Revolt of Alexander

10 ¹†IN the year one hundred and sixty, Alexander, who was called Epiphanes, son of Antiochus, came up and took Ptolemais. He was accepted and began to reign there. ²When King Demetrius heard of it, he mustered a very large army and marched out to engage him in combat. ³Demetrius sent a letter to Jonathan written in peaceful terms, to pay him honor; ⁴for he said: "Let us be the first to make peace with him, before he makes peace with Alexander against us, ⁵since he will remember all the wrongs we have done to him, his brothers, and his nation."

⁶So Demetrius authorized Jonathan, as his ally, to gather an army and procure arms as his ally; and he ordered that the hostages in the citadel be released to him. ⁷Accordingly Jonathan went up to Jerusalem and read the letter to all the people. The men in the citadel ⁸were struck with fear when they heard that the king

had given him authority to gather an army. ⁹*They released the hostages to Jonathan, and he gave them back to their parents. ¹⁰Thereafter Jonathan dwelt in Jerusalem, and began to build and restore the city. ¹¹He ordered the workmen to build the walls and encircle Mount Zion with square stones for its fortification, which they did. ¹²The foreigners in the strongholds that Bacchides had built, took flight; ¹³each one of them left his place and returned to his own country. ¹⁴Only in Beth-zur did some remain of those who had abandoned the law and the commandments, for they used it as a place of refuge.

Jonathan Supports Alexander

¹⁵King Alexander heard of the promises that Demetrius had made to Jonathan; he was also told of the battles and valiant deeds of Jonathan and his brothers and the troubles that they had endured. ¹⁶He said, "Shall we ever find another man like him? Let us now make him our friend and ally." ¹⁷So he sent Jonathan a letter written in these terms: ¹⁸"King Alexander sends greetings to his brother Jonathan. ¹⁹We have heard of you, that you are a mighty warrior and worthy to be our friend. ²⁰*We have therefore appointed you today to be high priest of your nation; you are to be called the King's Friend, and you are to look after our interests and preserve amity with us." He also sent him a purple robe and a crown of gold.

²¹†Jonathan put on the sacred vestments in the seventh month of the year one hundred and sixty at the feast of Booths, and he gathered an army and procured many arms. ²²When Demetrius heard of these things, he was distressed and said: ²³"Why have we allowed Alexander to get ahead of us by gaining the friendship of the Jews and thus strengthening himself? ²⁴I too will write them conciliatory words and offer dignities and gifts, so that they may be an aid to me."

²⁵So he sent them this message: "King Demetrius sends greetings to the Jewish nation. ²⁶We have heard how you have kept the treaty with us and continued in our friendship and not gone over to our enemies, and we are glad. ²⁷Continue, therefore, to keep faith

---

† 9, 62: *Bethbasi:* two miles east of Bethlehem and six miles north of Tekoa.

9, 73: *Began to judge:* exercise the governing authority as in the book of Judges. With Jerusalem and the garrison towns (v 50) firmly in Seleucid hands, Jonathan's freedom of action was greatly restricted. *Michmash,* southeast of Bethel, famous for the exploit of the former Jonathan, son of Saul; cf 1 Sm 14.

10, 1: *The year one hundred and sixty:* 152 B.C. *Alexander . . . Antiochus:* Alexander Balas claimed to be a son of Antiochus IV. He had the backing of the Romans, who had never forgiven Demetrius for becoming king without their permission. The latter meanwhile had become unpopular with his own people as well as with the Jews.

10, 21: *Jonathan . . . feast of Booths:* Jonathan began to discharge the office of high priest October 23-30, 152 B.C. For seven years after the death of Alcimus there had been no high priest in Jerusalem. It was taken for granted that the king, though a Gentile, had the power to appoint one. The Maccabees, though a priestly family, were not of the line of Zadok, and some in Israel regarded Jonathan's tenure as a usurpation.

with us, and we will reward you with favors in return for what you do in our behalf. **²⁸**We will grant you many exemptions and will bestow gifts on you.

²⁹°"I now free you, as I also exempt all the Jews, from the tribute, the salt tax, and the crown levies. **³⁰**°†Instead of collecting the third of the grain and the half of the fruit of the trees that should be my share, I renounce the right from this day forward. Neither now nor in the future will I collect them from the land of Judah or from the three districts annexed from Samaria. **³¹**Let Jerusalem and her territory, her tithes and her tolls, be sacred and free from tax. **³²**I also yield my authority over the citadel in Jerusalem, and I transfer it to the high priest, that he may put in it such men as he shall choose to guard it. **³³**Every one of the Jews who has been carried into captivity from the land of Judah into any part of my kingdom I set at liberty without ransom; and let all their taxes, even those on their cattle, be canceled. **³⁴**Let all feast days, sabbaths, new moon festivals, appointed days, and the three days that precede each feast day, and the three days that follow, be days of immunity and exemption for every Jew in my kingdom. **³⁵**Let no man have authority to exact payment from them or to molest any of them in any matter.

³⁶"Let thirty thousand Jews be enrolled in the king's army and allowances be given them, as is due to all the king's soldiers. **³⁷**Let some of them be stationed in the king's principal strongholds, and of these let some be given positions of trust in the affairs of the kingdom. Let their superiors and their rulers be taken from among them, and let them follow their own laws, as the king has commanded in the land of Judah.

³⁸"Let the three districts that have been added to Judea from the province of Samaria be incorporated with Judea so that they may be under one man and obey no other authority than the high priest. **³⁹**Ptolemais and its confines I give as a present to the sanctuary in Jerusalem for the necessary expenses of the sanctuary. **⁴⁰**I make a yearly personal grant of fifteen thousand silver shekels out of the royal revenues, from appropriate places. **⁴¹**All the additional funds that the officials did not hand over as they had done in the first years, shall henceforth be handed over for the services of the temple. **⁴²**Moreover, the dues of five thousand silver shekels that used to be taken from the revenue of the sanctuary every year shall be canceled, since these funds belong to the priests who perform the services. **⁴³**Whoever takes refuge in the temple of Jerusalem or in any of its precincts, because of money he owes the king, or because of any other debt, shall be released, together with all the goods he possesses in my kingdom. **⁴⁴**The cost of rebuilding and restoring the structures of the sanctuary shall be covered out of the royal revenue. **⁴⁵**Likewise the cost of building the walls of Jerusalem and fortifying it all

around, and of building walls in Judea, shall be donated from the royal revenue."

⁴⁶When Jonathan and the people heard these words, they neither believed nor accepted them, for they remembered the great evil that Demetrius had done in Israel, and how sorely he had afflicted them. **⁴⁷**They therefore decided in favor of Alexander, for he had been the first to address them peaceably, and they remained his allies for the rest of his life.

⁴⁸King Alexander gathered together a large army and encamped opposite Demetrius. **⁴⁹**The two kings joined battle, and when the army of Demetrius fled, Alexander pursued him, and overpowered his soldiers. **⁵⁰**He pressed the battle hard until sunset, and Demetrius fell that day.

Treaty of Ptolemy and Alexander

⁵¹Alexander sent ambassadors to Ptolemy, king of Egypt, with this message: **⁵²**"Now that I have returned to my realm, taken my seat on the throne of my fathers, and established my role by crushing Demetrius and gaining control of my country—**⁵³**for I engaged him in battle, defeated him and his army, and recovered the royal throne—**⁵⁴**let us now establish friendship with each other. Give me your daughter for my wife; and as your son-in-law, I will give to you and to her gifts worthy of you."

⁵⁵King Ptolemy answered in these words: "Happy the day on which you returned to the land of your fathers and took your seat on their royal throne! **⁵⁶**I will do for you what you have written; but meet me in Ptolemais, so that we may see each other, and I will become your father-in-law as you have proposed."

⁵⁷†So Ptolemy with his daughter Cleopatra set out from Egypt and came to Ptolemais in the year one hundred and sixty-two. **⁵⁸**There King Alexander met him, and Ptolemy gave him his daughter Cleopatra in marriage. Their wedding was celebrated at Ptolemais with great splendor according to the custom of kings.

⁵⁹King Alexander also wrote to Jonathan to come and meet him. **⁶⁰**°So he went with pomp to Ptolemais, where he met the two kings and gave them and their friends silver and gold and many gifts and thus won their favor. **⁶¹**Some pestilent Israelites, transgressors of the law, united against him to accuse him, but the king paid no heed to them. **⁶²**He ordered Jonathan to be divested of his ordinary garments and to be clothed in royal purple; and so it was done. **⁶³**The king also had him seated at his side. He said to his magistrates: "Go with him to the center of the city and make a proclamation that no one is to bring charges against him on any grounds or be troublesome to him in any way."

⁶⁴°When his accusers saw the honor paid to him in

°

29: 11, 28f.35.   60: 2, 18.
30: 11, 28.34.   64f: 2, 18; 11, 27.

†
10, 30: *The three districts annexed from Samaria:* mentioned by name in 11, 34. The present Greek text, by a scribal error, has added "and Galilee" after "Samaria."

10, 57: *Cleopatra:* Cleopatra Thea, then about fifteen years old. She later married Demetrius II, and later still, his brother Antiochus VII. *The year one hundred and sixty-two:* 151/150 B. C.

the proclamation, and the purple with which he was clothed, they all fled. 65The king also honored him by numbering him among his Chief Friends and made him military commander and governor of the province. 66So Jonathan returned in peace and happiness to Jerusalem.

Victory over Apollonius

67†In the year one hundred and sixty-five, Demetrius, son of Demetrius, came from Crete to the land of his fathers. 68When King Alexander heard of it he was greatly troubled, and returned to Antioch. 69Demetrius appointed Apollonius governor of Coelesyria. Having gathered a large army, Apollonius pitched his camp at Jamnia. From there he sent this message to Jonathan the high priest:

70"You are the only one who resists us. I am laughed at and put to shame on your account. Why are you displaying power against us in the mountains? 71If you have confidence in your forces, come down now to us in the plain, and let us test each other's strength there; the city forces are on my side. 72Inquire and learn who I am and who the others are who are helping me. Men say that you cannot make a stand against us because your fathers were twice put to flight in their own land. 73Now you too will be unable to withstand our cavalry and such a force as this in the plain, where there is not a stone or a pebble or a place to flee."

74When Jonathan heard the message of Apollonius, he was roused. Choosing ten thousand men, he set out from Jerusalem, and Simon his brother joined him to help him. 75He pitched camp near Joppa, but the men in the city shut him out because Apollonius had a garrison there. When the Jews besieged it, 76†the men of the city became afraid and opened the gates, and so Jonathan took possession of Joppa.

77When Apollonius heard of it, he drew up three thousand horsemen and an innumerable infantry. He marched on Azotus as though he were going on through the country, but at the same time he advanced into the plain, because he had such a large number of horsemen to rely on. 78Jonathan followed him to Azotus, and they engaged in battle. 79Apollonius, however, had left a thousand cavalry in hiding behind them. 80When Jonathan discovered that there was an ambush behind him, his army was surrounded. From morning until evening they showered his men with arrows. 81But his men held their ground, as Jonathan had commanded, whereas the enemy's horses became tired out. 82When the horsemen were exhausted, Simon attacked the phalanx, overwhelmed it and put it to flight. 83The horsemen too were scattered over the plain. The enemy fled to Azotus and entered Bethdagon, the temple of their idol, to save themselves. 84*But Jonathan burned and plundered Azotus with its neighboring towns, and destroyed by fire both the

temple of Dagon and the men who had taken refuge in it. 85Those who fell by the sword, together with those who were burned alive, came to about eight thousand men. 86Then Jonathan left there and pitched his camp at Ashkalon, and the people of that city came out to meet him with great pomp. 87He and his men then returned to Jerusalem, laden with much booty. 88When King Alexander heard of these events, he accorded new honors to Jonathan. 89†He sent him a gold buckle, such as is usually given to King's Kinsmen; he also gave him Ekron and all its territory as a possession.

Alliance of Demetrius and Ptolemy

11 1THE king of Egypt gathered his forces, as numerous as the sands of the seashore, and many ships; and he sought by deceit to take Alexander's kingdom and add it to his own. 2He entered Syria with peaceful words, and the people in the cities opened their gates to welcome him, as King Alexander had ordered them to do, since Ptolemy was his father-in-law. 3But when Ptolemy entered the cities, he stationed garrison troops in each one. 4*When he reached Azotus, he was shown the temple of Dagon destroyed by fire, Azotus and its suburbs demolished, corpses lying about, and the charred bodies of those burned by Jonathan in the war and stacked up along his route. 5To prejudice the king against Jonathan, he was told what the latter had done; but the king said nothing. 6Jonathan met the king with pomp at Joppa, and they greeted each other and spent the night there. 7†Jonathan accompanied the king as far as the river called Eleutherus and then returned to Jerusalem.

8†Plotting evil against Alexander, King Ptolemy took possession of the cities along the seacoast as far as Seleucia-by-the-Sea. 9He sent ambassadors to King Demetrius, saying: "Come, let us make a pact with each other; I will give you my daughter whom Alexander has married, and you shall reign over your father's kingdom. 10†I regret that I gave him my daughter, for he has sought to kill me." 11His real reason for accusing Alexander, however, was that he coveted Alexander's kingdom. 12After taking his daughter away and giving her to Demetrius, Ptolemy broke with Alexander; their enmity became open. 13Then

---

†

10, 67: *The year one hundred and sixty-five:* 147 B.C. *Demetrius:* Demetrius II Nicator.

10, 76: *Joppa:* about forty miles northwest of Jerusalem. For the first time the Maccabees took possession of a seaport; nominally it was on behalf of King Alexander.

10, 89: *Kinsmen:* a class higher than Chief Friends.

11, 7: *Eleutherus:* modern Nahr el-Kebir, the northern border of modern Lebanon; in the second century B.C. the northern limit of Coelesyria.

11, 8: *Seleucia-by-the-Sea:* at the mouth of the Orontes, the port city of Antioch.

11, 10: *I regret . . . to kill me:* according to Josephus, Ammonius, a friend of Alexander, had tried to assassinate Ptolemy, and the latter claimed that Alexander was the instigator, thus calumniating him to gain his kingdom (v 11).

✸   84: 11, 4; 1 Sm 5, 2-5.   11/4: 10, 84.

Ptolemy entered Antioch and assumed the crown of Asia; he thus wore two crowns on his head, that of Egypt and that of Asia.

Deaths of Alexander and Ptolemy

14King Alexander was in Cilicia at that time, because the people of that region had revolted. **15**When Alexander heard the news, he came to challenge Ptolemy in battle. Ptolemy marched out and met him with a strong force and put him to flight. **16**Alexander fled to Arabia to seek protection. King Ptolemy's triumph was complete **17**when the Arab Zabdiel cut off Alexander's head and sent it to Ptolemy. **18**But three days later King Ptolemy himself died, and his men in the fortified cities were killed by the inhabitants of the strongholds. **19†**Thus Demetrius became king in the year one hundred and sixty-seven.

Pact with Demetrius

20At that time Jonathan gathered together the men of Judea to attack the citadel in Jerusalem, and they set up many machines against it. **21**Some transgressors of the law, enemies of their own nation, went to the king and informed him that Jonathan was besieging the citadel. **22**When Demetrius heard this, he was furious, and set out immediately for Ptolemais. He wrote to Jonathan to discontinue the siege and to meet him for a conference at Ptolemais as soon as possible.

23On hearing this, Jonathan ordered the siege to continue. He selected some elders and priests of Israel and exposed himself to danger **24**by going to the king at Ptolemais. He brought with him silver, gold apparel, and many other presents, and found favor with the king. **25**Although some impious men of his own nation brought charges against him, **26**the king treated him just as his predecessors had done and showed him great honor in the presence of all his Friends. **27**He confirmed him in the high priesthood and in all the honors he had previously held, and had him enrolled among his Chief Friends.

28*Jonathan asked the king to exempt Judea and the three districts of Samaria from tribute, promising him in return three hundred talents. **29**The king agreed and wrote the following letter to Jonathan about all these matters:

30*†"King Demetrius sends greetings to his brother Jonathan and to the Jewish nation. **31†**We are sending you, for your information, a copy of the letter that we wrote to Lasthenes our kinsman concerning you. **32**'King Demetrius sends greetings to his father Lasthenes. **33**Because of the good will they show us, we have decided to bestow benefits on the Jewish nation, who are our friends and who observe their obligations to us. **34*†**Therefore we confirm their possession, not only of the territory of Judea, but also of the three districts of Aphairema, Lydda, and Ramathaim. These districts, together with all their dependencies, were transferred from Samaria to Judea in favor of all those who offer sacrifices for us in Jerusalem instead of paying the royal taxes that formerly the king received from them each year from the produce of the soil and the fruit of the trees. **35**From this day on we grant them release from payment of all other things that would henceforth be due to us, that is, of tithes and tribute and of the tax on the salt pans and the crown tax. **36**Henceforth none of these provisions shall ever be revoked. **37**Be sure, therefore, to have a copy of these instructions made and given to Jonathan, that it may be displayed in a conspicuous place on the holy hill.'"

The Intrigue of Trypho

38When King Demetrius saw that the land was peaceful under his rule and that he had no opposition, he dismissed his entire army, every man to his home, except the foreign troops which he had hired from the islands of the nations. So all the soldiers who had served under his predecessors hated him. **39***When a certain Trypho, who had previously belonged to Alexander's party, saw that all the troops were grumbling at Demetrius, he went to Imalkue the Arab, who was bringing up Alexander's young son Antiochus. **40**Trypho kept urging Imalkue to hand over the boy to him, that he might make him king in his father's place. During his stay there of many days, he told him of all that Demetrius had done and of the hatred that his soldiers had for him.

Jonathan Aids Demetrius

41Meanwhile Jonathan sent the request to King Demetrius to withdraw his troops from the citadel of Jerusalem and from the other strongholds, for they were constantly hostile to Israel. **42**Demetrius, in turn, sent this word to Jonathan: "I will not only do this for you and your nation, but I will greatly honor you and your nation when I find the opportunity. **43**Do me the favor, therefore, of sending men to fight for me, because all my troops have revolted." **44**So Jonathan sent three thousand good fighting men to him at Antioch. When they came to the king, he was delighted over their arrival, **45**for the populace, one hundred and twenty thousand strong, had massed

† 11, 19: *The year one hundred and sixty-seven:* 146/145 B.C. The two deaths (vv 17-18) occurred in the summer of 145 B.C.
11, 30: *Brother:* this title and *father* in v 32 are honorific titles used of the Kinsmen.
11, 31: *Lasthenes:* leader of the mercenary troops who had come with Demetrius from Crete. He was now the young king's chief minister and was apparently responsible for the disastrous policy (v 38) of disbanding the national army.
11, 34: *Aphairema:* the Ophrah of Jos 18, 23; 1 Sm 23, 6; the Ephron of 2 Chr 13, 19; and the Ephraim of Jn 11, 54—modern et-Taiyibeh, five miles northeast of Bethel. *Lydda:* the Lod of the postexilic Jews (Ez 2, 33; Neh 11, 35) and the hometown of Aeneas, who was cured by Peter (Acts 9, 32ff). It is ten miles southeast of Joppa. *Ramathaim:* the Ramathaim-zophim of 1 Sm 1, 1, and the Arimathea of Mt 27, 57—modern Rentis, nine miles northeast of Lydda.

28: 10, 29; 11, 34.   34f: 10, 29; 11, 28.
30-37: 10, 26-45.   39: 12, 39.

in the center of the city in an attempt to kill him. ⁴⁶But he took refuge in the palace, while the populace gained control of the main streets and began to fight. ⁴⁷So the king called the Jews to his aid. They all rallied around him and spread out through the city. On that day they killed about a hundred thousand men in the city, ⁴⁸which, at the same time, they set on fire and plundered on a large scale. Thus they saved the king's life. ⁴⁹When the populace saw that the Jews held the city at their mercy, they lost courage and cried out to the king in supplication, ⁵⁰"Give us your terms and let the Jews stop attacking us and our city." So they threw down their arms and made peace. ⁵¹The Jews thus gained glory in the eyes of the king and all his subjects, and they became renowned throughout his kingdom. Finally they returned to Jerusalem with much spoil.

⁵²But when King Demetrius was sure of his royal throne, and the land was peaceful under his rule, ⁵³he broke all his promises and became estranged from Jonathan. Instead of rewarding Jonathan for all the favors he had received from him, he caused him much trouble.

Alliance with Trypho

⁵⁴*After this, Trypho returned and brought with him the young boy Antiochus, who became king and wore the royal crown. ⁵⁵All the soldiers whom Demetrius had discharged rallied around Antiochus and fought against Demetrius, who was routed and fled. ⁵⁶Trypho captured the elephants and occupied Antioch. ⁵⁷Then young Antiochus wrote to Jonathan: "I confirm you in the high priesthood and appoint you ruler over the four districts and wish you to be one of the King's Friends." ⁵⁸*He also sent him gold dishes and a dinner service, gave him the right to drink from gold cups, to dress in royal purple, and to wear a gold buckle. ⁵⁹†Likewise, he made Jonathan's brother Simon governor of the region from the Ladder of Tyre to the frontier of Egypt.

⁶⁰†Jonathan set out and traveled through West-of-Euphrates and its cities, and all the forces of Syria espoused his cause as allies. When he arrived at Ashkalon, the citizens welcomed him with pomp. ⁶¹But when he set out for Gaza, the people of Gaza locked their gates against him. So he besieged it and burned and plundered its suburbs. ⁶²Then the people of Gaza appealed to him for mercy, and he granted them peace. He took the sons of their chief men as hostages and sent them to Jerusalem. He then traveled on through the province as far as Damascus.

War with Demetrius

⁶³Jonathan heard that the generals of Demetrius had come with a strong force to Kadesh in Galilee, intending to remove him from office. ⁶⁴So he went to meet them, leaving his brother Simon in the province. ⁶⁵Simon besieged Beth-zur, attacked it for many days, and blockaded the inhabitants. ⁶⁶When they sued for peace, he granted it to them. He expelled them from the city, took possession of it, and put a garrison there. ⁶⁷†Meanwhile, Jonathan and his army pitched their camp near the waters of Gennesaret, and at daybreak they went to the plain of Hazor. ⁶⁸There, in front of him on the plain, was the army of the foreigners. This army attacked him in the open, having first detached an ambush against him in the mountains. ⁶⁹Then the men in ambush rose out of their places and joined in the battle. ⁷⁰All of Jonathan's men fled; no one stayed except the army commanders Mattathias, son of Absalom, and Judas, son of Chalphi. ⁷¹Jonathan tore his clothes, threw earth on his head, and prayed. ⁷²Then he went back to the combat and so overwhelmed the enemy that they took to flight. ⁷³Those of his men who were running away saw it and returned to him; and with him they pursued the enemy as far as their camp in Kadesh, where they pitched their own camp. ⁷⁴Three thousand of the foreign troops fell on that day. Then Jonathan returned to Jerusalem.

Alliances with Rome and Sparta

12 ¹*when Jonathan saw that the times favored him, he sent selected men to Rome to confirm and renew his friendship with the Romans. ²He also sent letters to Sparta and other places for the same purpose.

³After reaching Rome, the men entered the senate chamber and said, "The high priest Jonathan and the Jewish people have sent us to renew the earlier friendship and alliance between you and them." ⁴The Romans gave them letters addressed to the authorities in the various places, requesting them to provide the envoys with safe conduct to the land of Judah.

⁵This is a copy of the letter that Jonathan wrote to the Spartans: ⁶"Jonathan the high priest, the senate of the nation, the priests, and the rest of the Jewish people send greetings to their brothers the Spartans. ⁷*†Long ago a letter was sent to the high priest Onias from Arius, who then reigned over you, stating that you are our brothers, as the attached copy shows. ⁸Onias welcomed the envoy with honor and received the letter, which clearly referred to alliance and friendship. ⁹*†Though we have no need of these

---

† 11, 59: *Ladder of Tyre:* modern Rās en-Nāqūrah, on the border between Lebanon and Israel, where the mountains reach the sea, so that the coastal road must ascend in a series of steps.

11, 60: *West-of-Euphrates:* refers here to the territory of Palestine and Coelesyria, but not Upper Syria; cf 3, 32; 7, 8.

11, 67: *Plain of Hazor:* the site of the ancient Canaanite city (Jos 11, 10), ten miles north of the Lake of Gennesaret.

12, 7: *Onias:* Onias I, high priest from 323-300 or 290 B. C. *Arius:* Arius I, king from 309 to 265 B. C. The letter was sent *long ago,* i. e., a century and a half before.

12, 9: *The sacred books . . . in our possession:* a reference to "the law, the prophets and other books," as mentioned in the Prologue to Sirach (v 1), after 132 B. C.

* 54: 11, 39; 12, 39. 58: 2, 18. 12/1: 8, 17. 7: 12, 20-23. 9: Rom 15, 4.

things, since we have for our encouragement the sacred books that are in our possession, ¹⁰we have ventured to send word to you for the renewal of brotherhood and friendship, so as not to become strangers to you altogether; a long time has passed since your mission to us. ¹¹We, on our part, have never ceased to remember you in the sacrifices and prayers that we offer on our feasts and other appropriate days, as it is right and proper to remember brothers. ¹²We likewise rejoice in your renown. ¹³But many hardships and wars have beset us, and the kings around us have attacked us. ¹⁴We did not wish to be troublesome to you and to the rest of our allies and friends in these wars; ¹⁵with the help of Heaven for our support, we have been saved from our enemies, and they have been humbled. ¹⁶*So we have chosen Numenius, son of Antiochus, and Antipater, son of Jason, and we have sent them to the Romans to renew our former friendship and alliance with them. ¹⁷We have also ordered them to come to you and greet you, and to deliver to you our letter about the renewal of our brotherhood. ¹⁸Therefore kindly send us an answer on this matter."

¹⁹This is a copy of the letter that was sent to Onias: ²⁰*"Arius, king of the Spartans, sends greetings to Onias the high priest. ²¹A document has been found stating that the Spartans and the Jews are brothers; both nations descended from Abraham. ²²Now that we have learned this, kindly write to us about your welfare. ²³We, on our part, are informing you that your cattle and your possessions are ours, and ours are yours. We have, therefore, given orders that you should be told of this."

Demetrius Repelled

²⁴Jonathan heard that the generals of Demetrius had returned to attack him with a stronger army than before. ²⁵†He set out from Jerusalem and went into the country of Hamath to meet them, giving them no time to enter his province. ²⁶The spies he had sent into their camp came back and reported that the enemy had made ready to attack the Jews that very night. ²⁷Therefore, when the sun set, Jonathan ordered his men to be on guard and to remain armed, ready for combat, throughout the night. He also set outposts all around the camp. ²⁸When the enemy heard that Jonathan and his men were ready for battle, their hearts sank with fear and dread. They lighted fires and then withdrew. ²⁹But because Jonathan and his men were watching the lights burning, they did not know what had happened until morning. ³⁰Then Jonathan pursued them, but he could not overtake them, for they had crossed the river Eleutherus. ³¹So Jonathan turned aside against the Arabs who are called Zabadeans, overwhelming and plundering them. ³²Then he marched on to Damascus and traversed that whole region.

³³Simon also set out and went as far as Ashkalon and its neighboring strongholds. He then turned to Joppa and occupied it, ³⁴for he heard that its men had intended to hand over this stronghold to the supporters of Demetrius. He left a garrison there to guard it.

³⁵When Jonathan returned, he assembled the elders of the people, and with them he made plans for building strongholds in Judea, ³⁶for making the walls of Jerusalem still higher, and for erecting a high barrier between the citadel and the city, that would isolate the citadel and so prevent its garrison from commerce with the city. ³⁷The people therefore worked together on building up the city, for part of the east wall above the ravine had collapsed. The quarter called Chaphenatha was also repaired. ³⁸Simon likewise built up Adida in the Shephelah, and strengthened its fortifications by providing them with gates and bars.

Capture of Jonathan

³⁹*Trypho was determined to become king of Asia, assume the crown, and do away with King Antiochus. ⁴⁰But he was afraid that Jonathan would not permit him, but would fight against him. Looking for a way to seize and kill him, he set out and reached Beth-shan. ⁴¹Jonathan marched out against him with forty thousand picked fighting men and came to Beth-shan. ⁴²But when Trypho saw that Jonathan had arrived with a large army, he was afraid to offer him violence. ⁴³Instead, he received him with honor, introduced him to all his friends, and gave him presents. He also ordered his friends and soldiers to obey him as they would himself. ⁴⁴Then he said to Jonathan: "Why have you put all your soldiers to so much trouble when we are not at war? ⁴⁵Pick out a few men to stay with you, send the rest back home, and then come with me to Ptolemais. I will hand it over to you together with other strongholds and their garrisons, as well as the officials, then I will leave and go home. That is why I came here."

⁴⁶Jonathan believed him and did as he said. He dismissed his troops, and they returned to the land of Judah. ⁴⁷But he kept with him three thousand men, of whom he sent two thousand to Galilee while one thousand accompanied him. ⁴⁸Then as soon as Jonathan had entered Ptolemais, the men of the city closed the gates and seized him; all who had entered with him, they killed with the sword.

⁴⁹†Trypho sent soldiers and cavalry to Galilee and the Great Plain to destroy all Jonathan's men. ⁵⁰These, upon learning that Jonathan had been captured and his companions killed, encouraged one another and went out in compact body ready to fight. ⁵¹As their pursuers saw that they were ready to fight for their lives, they turned back. ⁵²Thus all these men of Jonathan came safely into the land of Judah. They mourned

---

† 12, 25: *Country of Hamath:* the Seleucid territory of Upper Syria northeast of Coelesyria and separated from it by the Eleutherus River. The latter territory was under the command of Jonathan (11, 59f).

12, 49: *The Great Plain:* of Beth-shan (v 41), where Jonathan's disbanded troops remained.

✿　16: 14, 22; 15, 15.　　　　39: 11, 39f.54f.
20-23: 12, 6f.

over Jonathan and his men, and were in great fear, and all Israel fell into deep mourning.

⁵³*All the nations round about sought to destroy them. They said, "Now that they have no leader to help them, let us make war on them and wipe out their memory from among men."

V: SIMON, HIGH PRIEST AND ETHNARCH

Simon, Leader of the Jews

13 ¹WHEN SIMON HEARD that Trypho was gathering a large army to invade and ravage the land of Judah, ²and saw that the people were in dread and terror, he went up to Jerusalem. There he assembled the people ³and exhorted them in these words: "You know what I, my brothers, and my father's house have done for the laws and the sanctuary; what battles and disasters we have been through. ⁴It was for the sake of these, for the sake of Israel, that all my brothers have perished, and I alone am left. ⁵Far be it from me, then, to save my own life in any time of distress, for I am not better than my brothers. ⁶*Rather will I avenge my nation and the sanctuary, as well as your wives and children, for all the nations out of hatred have united to destroy us."

⁷As the people heard these words, their spirit was rekindled. ⁸They shouted in reply: "You are our leader in place of your brothers Judas and Jonathan. ⁹Fight our battles, and we will do everything that you tell us." ¹⁰So Simon mustered all the men able to fight, and quickly completing the walls of Jerusalem, fortified it on every side. ¹¹He sent Jonathan, son of Absalom, to Joppa with a large force; Jonathan drove out the occupants and remained there.

Deceit and Treachery of Trypho

¹²Then Trypho moved from Ptolemais with a large army to invade the land of Judah, bringing Jonathan with him as a prisoner. ¹³But Simon pitched his camp at Adida, facing the plain. ¹⁴When Trypho learned that Simon had succeeded his brother Jonathan, and that he intended to fight him, he sent envoys to him with this message: ¹⁵"We have detained your brother Jonathan on account of the money that he owed the royal treasury in connection with the offices that he held. ¹⁶Therefore, if you send us a hundred talents of silver, and two of his sons as hostages to guarantee that when he is set free he will not revolt against us, we will release him."

¹⁷Although Simon knew that they were speaking deceitfully to him, he gave orders to get the money and the boys, for fear of provoking much hostility among the people, who might say ¹⁸that Jonathan perished because Simon would not send Trypho the money and the boys. ¹⁹So he sent the boys and the hundred talents; but Trypho broke his promise and would not let

Jonathan go. ²⁰†Next he began to invade and ravage the country. His troops went around by the road that leads to Adora, but Simon and his army moved along opposite him everywhere he went. ²¹The men in the citadel sent messengers to Trypho, urging him to come to them by way of the desert, and to send them provisions. ²²Although Trypho got all his cavalry ready to go, there was a heavy fall of snow that night, and he could not go. So he left for Gilead. ²³†When he was approaching Baskama, he had Jonathan killed and buried there. ²⁴Then Trypho returned to his own country.

Jonathan's Tomb

²⁵Simon sent for the remains of his brother Jonathan, and buried him in Modein, the city of his fathers. ²⁶All Israel bewailed him with solemn lamentation, mourning over him for many days. ²⁷Then Simon erected over the tomb of his father and his brothers a monument of stones, polished front and back, and raised high enough to be seen at a distance. ²⁸He set up seven pyramids facing one another for his father and his mother and his four brothers. ²⁹For the pyramids he devised a setting of big columns, on which he carved suits of armor as a perpetual memorial, and next to the armor he placed carved ships, which could be seen by all who sailed the sea. ³⁰This tomb which he built at Modein is there to the present day.

Pact between Simon and Demetrius

³¹Trypho dealt treacherously with the young King Antiochus. He killed him ³²and assumed the kingship in his place, putting on the crown of Asia. Thus he brought much evil on the land. ³³Simon, on his part, built up the strongholds of Judea, strengthening their fortifications with high towers, thick walls, and gates with bars, and he stored up provisions in the fortresses. ³⁴Simon also sent chosen men to King Demetrius with the request that he grant the land a release from taxation, for all that Trypho did was to plunder the land. ³⁵In reply, King Demetrius sent him the following letter:

³⁶"King Demetrius sends greetings to Simon the high priest, the friend of kings, and to the elders and the Jewish people. ³⁷We have received the gold crown and the palm branch that you sent. We are willing to be on most peaceful terms with you and to write to our official to grant you release from tribute. ³⁸Whatever we have guaranteed to you remains in force, and the strongholds that you have built shall remain yours. ³⁹We remit any oversights and defaults incurred up to now, as well as the crown tax that you owe. Any other tax that may have been collected in Jerusalem shall no longer be collected there. ⁴⁰If any of you are quali-

---

* 53: 5, 2; 13, 6.   13/6: 5, 2; 12, 53.

† 13, 20f: The invaders made a wide flanking movement to invade Judea from the south. *Adora* was a few miles southwest of Beth-zur. They would avoid Beth-zur itself and other strongholds of the Maccabees by following the *way of the desert.*

13, 23: *Baskama:* northeast of the Sea of Galilee.

fied for enrollment in our service, let them be enrolled. Let there be peace between us."

41†Thus in the year one hundred and seventy, the yoke of the Gentiles was removed from Israel, **42**and the people began to write in their records and contracts, "In the first year of Simon, high priest, governor, and leader of the Jews."

Capture of Gazara and the Citadel

43✱†In those days Simon besieged Gazara and surrounded it with troops. He made a siege machine, pushed it up against the city, and attacked and captured one of the towers. **44**The men who had been on the siege machine jumped down into the city and caused a great tumult there. **45**The men of the city, joined by their wives and children, went up on the wall, with their garments rent, and cried out in loud voices, begging Simon to grant them peace. **46**"Do not treat us according to our evil deeds," they said, "but according to your mercy."

47So Simon came to terms with them and did not destroy them. He made them leave the city, however, and he purified the houses in which there were idols. Then he entered the city with hymns and songs of praise. **48**After removing from it everything that was impure, he settled there men who observed the law. He improved its fortifications and built himself a residence.

49The men in the citadel in Jerusalem were prevented from going out into the country and back for the purchase of food; they suffered greatly from hunger, and many of them died of starvation. **50**They finally cried out to Simon for peace, and he gave them peace. He expelled them from the citadel and cleansed it of impurities. **51**✱†On the twenty-third day of the second month, in the year one hundred and seventy-one, the Jews entered the citadel with shouts of jubilation, waving of palm branches, the music of harps and cymbals and lyres, and the singing of hymns and canticles, because a great enemy of Israel had been destroyed. **52**Simon decreed that this day should be celebrated every year with rejoicing. He also strengthened the fortifications of the temple hill alongside the citadel, and he and his companions dwelt there. **53**†Seeing that his son John was now a grown man, Simon made him commander of all his soldiers, with his residence in Gazara.

Capture of Demetrius

14 **1**†IN the year one hundred and seventy-two, King Demetrius assembled his army and marched into Media to obtain help so that he could fight Trypho. **2**†When Arsaces, king of Persia and Media, heard that Demetrius had invaded his territory, he sent one of his generals to take him alive.

3The general went forth and defeated the army of Demetrius; he captured him and brought him to Arsaces, who put him in prison.

Glory of Simon

4✱The land was at rest all the days of Simon,
    who sought the good of his nation.
His people were delighted with his power
    and his magnificence throughout his reign.
  5As his crowning glory he captured the port of Joppa
    and made it a gateway to the isles of the sea.
  6✱He enlarged the borders of his nation
    and gained control of the country.
  7He took many enemies prisoners of war
    and made himself master of Gazara, Beth-zur,
      and the citadel.
He cleansed the citadel of its impurities;
    there was no one to withstand him.
  8✱The people cultivated their land in peace;
    the land yielded its produce
    and the trees of the field their fruit.
  9✱Old men sat in the squares,
    all talking about the good times,
    while the young men wore the glorious apparel
      of war.
10He supplied the cities with food
    and equipped them with means of defense,
    till his glorious name reached the ends of the
      earth.
11✱He brought peace to the land,
    and Israel was filled with happiness.
12✱Every man sat under his vine and his fig tree,
    with no one to disturb him.
13No one was left to attack them in their land;
    the kings in those days were crushed.
14He strengthened all the lowly among his people
    and was zealous for the law;
    he suppressed all the lawless and the wicked.
15He made the temple splendid
    and enriched its equipment.

Alliance with Rome and Sparta

16†When people heard in Rome and even in Sparta that Jonathan had died, they were deeply grieved.

---

† 13, 41: *The year one hundred and seventy:* March, 142, to April, 141 B. C., by the temple calendar.

13, 43: *Gazara:* a key position in the Shephelah, fortified by Bacchides in 160 B. C.; cf 9, 52.

13, 51: *The twenty-third day of the second month:* June 3, 141 B. C.

13, 53: *John:* John Hyrcanus, who was to succeed his father as ruler and high priest; cf 16, 23f.

14, 1: *The year one hundred and seventy-two:* 141-140 B. C. The expedition began most probably in the spring of 140.

14, 2: *Arsaces:* Arsaces VI, also called Mithridates I, the Parthian king (171-138 B. C.). Parthians had overrun Persia and now held Babylonia, both of which had hitherto belonged to the Seleucid empire. The Greeks and Macedonians in these countries had appealed to Demetrius for help.

14, 16: The embassy to Rome and Sparta was sent soon after Simon's accession to power, and the replies were received before Demetrius' expedition (vv 1-3)—probably in 142 B. C.

✱
    43: 2 Mc 10, 32-38.   8: Zec 8, 12.
    51: 1, 36.   9: Zec 8, 4f.
    14/4: 3, 3-9.   11: Lv 26, 6.
    6: Ex 34, 24.   12: Mi 4, 4; Zec 3, 10.

[17]But when the Romans heard that his brother Simon had been made high priest in his place and was master of the country and the cities, [18]*they sent him inscribed tablets of bronze to renew with him the friendship and alliance that they had established with his brothers Judas and Jonathan. [19]These were read before the assembly in Jerusalem.

[20]This is a copy of the letter that the Spartans sent: "The rulers and the citizens of Sparta send greetings to Simon the high priest, the elders, the priests, and the rest of the Jewish people, our brothers. [21]The envoys you sent to our people have informed us of your glory and fame, and we were happy that they came. [22]*In accordance with what they said we have recorded the following in the public decrees: Since Numenius, son of Antiochus, and Antipater, son of Jason, envoys of the Jews, have come to us to renew their friendship with us, [23]the people have voted to receive the men with honor, and to deposit a copy of their words in the public archives, so that the people of Sparta may have a record of them. A copy of this decree has been made for Simon the high priest."

[24]*After this, Simon sent Numenius to Rome with a great gold shield weighing a thousand minas, to confirm the alliance with the Romans.

Decree of Honor

[25]When the people heard of these things, they said, "How can we thank Simon and his sons? [26]He and his brothers and his father's house have stood firm and repulsed Israel's enemies. They have thus preserved its liberty." So they made an inscription on bronze tablets, which they affixed to pillars on Mount Zion. [27]†The following is a copy of the inscription:

"On the eighteenth day of Elul, in the year one hundred and seventy-two, that is, the third year under Simon the high priest in Asaramel, [28]in a great assembly of priests, people, rulers of the nation, and elders of the country, the following proclamation was made:

[29]"'Since there have often been wars in our country, Simon, son of the priest Mattathias, descendant of Joarib, and his brothers have put themselves in danger and resisted the enemies of their nation, so that their sanctuary and law might be maintained, and they have thus brought great glory to their nation. [30]After Jonathan had rallied his nation and become their high priest, he was gathered to his kinsmen. [31]When the enemies of the Jews sought to invade and devastate their country and to lay hands on their temple, [32]Simon rose up and fought for his nation, spending large sums of his own money to equip the men of his nation's armed forces and giving them their pay. [33]He fortified the cities of Judea, especially the frontier city of Bethzur, where he stationed a garrison of Jewish soldiers, and where previously the enemy's arms had been stored. [34]He also fortified Joppa by the sea and Gazara on the border of Azotus, a place previously occupied by the enemy; these cities he resettled with Jews, and furnished them with all that was necessary for their restoration. [35]When the Jewish people saw Simon's loyalty and the glory he planned to bring to his nation, they made him their leader and high priest because of all he had accomplished and the loyalty and justice he had shown his nation. In every way he sought to exalt his people.

[36]"'In his time and under his guidance they succeeded in driving the Gentiles out of their country, especially those in the City of David in Jerusalem, who had built for themselves a citadel from which they used to sally forth to defile the environs of the temple and inflict grave injury on its purity. [37]In this citadel he stationed Jewish soldiers, and he strengthened its fortifications for the defense of the land and the city, while he also raised the wall of Jerusalem to a greater height. [38]Consequently, King Demetrius confirmed him in the high priesthood, [39]*made him one of his Friends, and conferred the highest honors on him. [40]He had indeed heard that the Romans had addressed the Jews as friends, allies, and brothers and that they had received Simon's envoys with honor.

[41]"'The Jewish people and their priest have, therefore, made the following decisions. Simon shall be their permanent leader and high priest until a true prophet arises. [42]He shall act as governor general over them, and shall have charge of the temple, to make regulations concerning its functions and concerning the country, its weapons and strongholds; [43]he shall be obeyed by all. All contracts made in the country shall be dated by his name. He shall have the right to wear royal purple and gold ornaments. [44]It shall not be lawful for any of the people or priests to nullify any of these decisions, or to contradict the orders given by him, or to convene an assembly in the country without his consent, to be clothed in royal purple or wear an official gold brooch. [45]Whoever acts otherwise or violates any of these prescriptions shall be liable to punishment.

[46]"'All the people approved of granting Simon the right to act in accord with these decisions, [47]†and Simon accepted and agreed to act as high priest, governor general, and ethnarch of the Jewish people and priests and to exercise supreme authority over all.'"

[48]It was decreed that this inscription should be engraved on bronze tablets, to be set up in a conspicuous place in the precincts of the temple, [49]and that copies of it should be deposited in the treasury, where they would be available to Simon and his sons.

---

† 14, 27: *Eighteenth day of Elul:* September 13, 140 B. C. *Asaramel:* a Hebrew name meaning "court of the people of God."

14, 47: *Ethnarch:* a subaltern ruler over a racial group whose office needed confirmation by a higher authority within the empire.

* 18: 8, 22.　　　　　　24: 12, 16; 15, 15.
22: 12, 16; 15, 15.　　39f: 2, 18.

Letter of Antiochus

15 ¹†ANTIOCHUS, son of King Demetrius, sent a letter from the islands of the sea to Simon, the priest and ethnarch of the Jews, and to all the nation, ²which read as follows:

"King Antiochus sends greetings to Simon, the priest and ethnarch, and to the Jewish nation. ³Whereas certain villains have gained control of the kingdom of my ancestors, I intend to reclaim it, that I may restore it to its former state. I have recruited a large number of mercenary troops and equipped warships ⁴to make a landing in my country and take revenge on those who have ruined it and laid waste many cities in my realm.

⁵"Now, therefore, I confirm to you all the tax exemptions that the kings before me granted you and whatever other privileges they conferred on you. ⁶I authorize you to coin your own money, as legal tender in your country. ⁷Jerusalem and its temple shall be free. All the weapons you have prepared and all the strongholds you have built and now occupy shall remain in your possession. ⁸All debts, present or future, due to the royal treasury shall be canceled for you, now and for all time. ⁹When we recover our kingdom, we will greatly honor you and your nation and the temple, so that your glory will be manifest in all the earth."

¹⁰†In the year one hundred and seventy-four, Antiochus invaded the land of his ancestors, and all the troops rallied to him, so that few were left with Trypho. ¹¹†Pursued by Antiochus, Trypho fled to Dor, by the sea, ¹²realizing what a mass of troubles had come upon him now that his soldiers had deserted him. ¹³Antiochus encamped before Dor with a hundred and twenty thousand infantry and eight thousand horsemen. ¹⁴While he invested the city, his ships closed in along the coast, so that he blockaded it by land and sea and let no one go in or out.

Roman Alliance Renewed

¹⁵*Meanwhile, Numenius and his companions left Rome with letters such as this addressed to various kings and countries:

¹⁶†"Lucius, Consul of the Romans, sends greetings to King Ptolemy. ¹⁷Certain envoys of the Jews, our friends and allies, have come to us to renew their earlier alliance of friendship. They had been sent by Simon the high priest and the Jewish people, ¹⁸*and they brought with them a gold shield worth a thousand minas. ¹⁹Therefore we have decided to write to various kings and countries, that they are not to harm them, or wage war against them or their cities or their country, and are not to assist those who fight against them. ²⁰We have also decided to accept the shield from them. ²¹If, then, any troublemakers from their country take refuge with you, hand them over to Simon the high priest, so that he may punish them according to their law."

²²†The consul sent similar letters to Kings Demetrius, Attalus, Ariarthes and Arsaces; to all the countries—²³Sampsames, Sparta, Delos, Myndos, Sicyon, Caria, Samos, Pamphylia, Lycia, Halicarnassus, Rhodes, Phaselis, Cos, Side, Aradus, Gortyna, Cnidus, Cyprus, and Cyrene. ²⁴A copy of the letter was also sent to Simon the high priest.

Hostility of Antiochus

²⁵When King Antiochus was encamped before Dor, he assaulted it continuously both with troops and with the siege machines he had made. He blockaded Trypho by preventing anyone from going in or out. ²⁶Simon sent to Antiochus' support two thousand elite troops, together with gold and silver and much equipment. ²⁷But he refused to accept the aid; in fact, he broke all the agreements he had previously made with Simon and became hostile toward him.

²⁸He sent Athenobius, one of his Friends, to confer with Simon and say: "You are occupying Joppa and Gazara and the citadel of Jerusalem; these are cities of my kingdom. ²⁹You have laid waste their territories, done great harm to the land, and taken possession of many districts in my realm. ³⁰Therefore, give up the cities you have seized and the tribute money of the districts outside the territory of Judea of which you have taken possession; ³¹or instead, pay me five hundred talents of silver for the devastation you have caused and five hundred talents more for the tribute money of the cities. If you do not do this, we will come and make war on you."

³²So Athenobius, the king's Friend, came to Jerusalem, and on seeing the splendor of Simon's court, the gold and silver plate on the sideboard, and the rest of his rich display, he was amazed. When he gave him the king's message, ³³Simon said to him in reply:

"We have not seized any foreign land; what we took is not the property of others, but our ancestral heritage which for a time had been unjustly held by our enemies. ³⁴Now that we have the opportunity, we are holding on to the heritage of our ancestors. ³⁵As for

† 15, 1: *Antiochus:* Antiochus VII Sidetes, son of Demetrius I, and younger brother of Demetrius II, now a prisoner of the Parthians. At the age of twenty he set out from the island of Rhodes to take his brother's place and drive out the usurper Trypho.

15, 10: *The year one hundred and seventy-four:* 138 B. C.

15, 11: *Dor, by the sea:* a fortress on the Palestinian coast, fifteen miles south of Carmel.

15, 16: *Lucius:* perhaps Lucius Caecilius Metellus, consul in 142 B. C., or Lucius Calpurnicus Piso, consul in 140-139 B. C. This document pertains to Simon's first years as leader.

15, 22: *Attalus:* Attalus II of Pergamum, reigned 159-138 B. C. *Ariarthes:* Ariarthes V of Cappadocia, reigned 162-130 B. C. *Arsaces:* see note on 14, 2.

* 15/15: 8, 17; 12, 16; 14, 22.24.   18: 14, 24.

Joppa and Gazara, which you demand, the men of these cities were doing great harm to our people and laying waste our country; however, we are willing to pay you a hundred talents for these cities."

³⁶Athenobius made no reply, but returned to the king in anger. When he told him of Simon's words, of his splendor, and of all he had seen, the king fell into a violent rage.

Victory over Cendebeus

³⁷†Trypho had gotten aboard a ship and escaped to Orthosia. ³⁸Then the king appointed Cendebeus commander-in-chief of the seacoast, and gave him infantry and cavalry forces. ³⁹†He ordered him to move his troops against Judea and to fortify Kedron and strengthen its gates, so that he could launch attacks against the Jewish people. Meanwhile the king went in pursuit of Trypho. ⁴⁰When Cendebeus came to Jamnia, he began to harass the people and to make incursions into Judea, where he took people captive or massacred them. ⁴¹As the king ordered, he fortified Kedron and stationed horsemen and infantry there, so that they could go out and patrol the roads of Judea.

16 ¹JOHN then went up from Gazara and told his father Simon what Cendebeus was doing. ²Simon called his two oldest sons, Judas and John, and said to them: "I and my brothers and my father's house have fought the battles of Israel from our youth until today, and many times we succeeded in saving Israel. ³I have now grown old, but you, by the mercy of Heaven, have come to man's estate. Take my place and my brother's, and go out and fight for our nation; and may the help of Heaven be with you!"

⁴John then mustered in the land twenty thousand warriors and horsemen. Setting out against Cendebeus, they spent the night at Modein, ⁵rose early, and marched into the plain. There, facing them, was an immense army of foot soldiers and horsemen, and between the two armies was a stream. ⁶John and his men took their position against the enemy. Seeing that his men were afraid to cross the stream, John crossed first. When his men saw this, they crossed over after him. ⁷Then he divided his infantry into two corps and put his cavalry between them, for the enemy's horsemen were very numerous. ⁸They blew the trumpets, and Cendebeus and his army were put to flight; many of them fell wounded, and the rest fled toward the stronghold. ⁹It was then that John's brother Judas fell wounded; but John pursued them until Cendebeus reached Kedron, which he had fortified. ¹⁰Some took refuge in the towers on the plain of Azotus, but John

set fire to these, and about two thousand of the enemy perished. He then returned to Judea in peace.

Murder of Simon and His Sons

¹¹Ptolemy, son of Abubus, had been appointed governor of the plain of Jericho, and he had much silver and gold, ¹²being the son-in-law of the high priest. ¹³But he became ambitious and sought to get control of the country. So he made treacherous plans to do away with Simon and his sons. ¹⁴†As Simon was inspecting the cities of the country and providing for their needs, he and his sons Mattathias and Judas went down to Jericho in the year one hundred and seventy-seven, in the eleventh month (that is, the month Shebat). ¹⁵†The son of Abubus gave them a deceitful welcome in the little stronghold called Dok which he had built. While serving them a sumptuous banquet, he had his men hidden there. ¹⁶Then, when Simon and his sons had drunk freely, Ptolemy and his men sprang up, weapons in hand, rushed upon Simon in the banquet hall, and killed him, his two sons, and some of his servants. ¹⁷By this vicious act of treason he repaid good with evil.

¹⁸Then Ptolemy wrote an account of this and sent it to the king, asking that troops be sent to help him and that the country be turned over to him. ¹⁹He sent other men to Gazara to do away with John. To the army officers he sent letters inviting them to come to him so that he might present them with silver, gold, and gifts. ²⁰He also sent others to seize Jerusalem and the mount of the temple. ²¹But someone ran ahead and brought word to John at Gazara that his father and his brothers had perished, and that Ptolemy had sent men to kill him also. ²²On hearing this, John was utterly astounded. When the men came to kill him, he had them arrested and put to death, for he knew what they meant to do.

²³†Now the rest of the history of John, his wars and the brave deeds he performed, his rebuilding of the walls, and his other achievements—²⁴these things are recorded in the chronicle of his pontificate, from the time that he succeeded his father as high priest.

---

†

15, 37: *Orthosia:* a port between Tripoli and the Eleutherus River.

15, 39: *Kedron:* a few miles southeast of Jamnia and facing the fortress of Gazara held by John Hyrcanus.

16, 14: *In the year one hundred and seventy-seven, in the eleventh month:* January-February, 134 B. C., by the temple calendar.

16, 15: *Dok:* a fortress built on a cliff three miles northwest of Jericho, near modern Ain Duq.

16, 23f: John Hyrcanus was ruler and high priest from 134 B. C. till his death in 104 B. C. These verses suggest that the book was written, or at least completed, only after he died.

The Second Book of Maccabees

Introduction

Although this book, like the preceding one, receives its title from its protagonist, Judas Maccabee (or Maccabeus), it is not a sequel to 1 Maccabees. The two differ in many respects. Whereas the first covers the period from the beginning of the reign of Antiochus IV (175 B.C.) to the accession of John Hyrcanus I (134 B.C.), this present book treats of the events in Jewish history from the time of the high priest Onias III and King Seleucus IV (c. 180 B.C.) to the defeat of Nicanor's army (161 B.C.).

The author of 2 Maccabees states (2, 23) that his one-volume work is an abridgment of a certain five-volume work by Jason of Cyrene; but since this latter has not survived, it is difficult to determine its relationship to the present epitome. One does not know how freely the anonymous epitomizer may have rewritten his shorter composition, or how closely he may have followed the wording of the original in the excerpts he made. Some parts of the text here, clearly not derived from Jason's work, are the Preface (2, 19-32), the Epilogue (15, 37-39), and probably also certain moralizing reflections (e. g., 5, 17-20; 6, 12-17). It is certain, however, that both works were written in Greek, which explains why the Second Book of Maccabees was not included in the canon of the Hebrew Bible.

The book is not without genuine historical value in supplementing 1 Maccabees, and it contains some apparently authentic documents (11, 16-38). Its purpose, whether intended by Jason himself or read into it by the compiler, is to give a theological interpretation to the history of the period. There is less interest, therefore, in the actual exploits of Judas Maccabeus than in God's marvelous interventions. These direct the course of events, both to punish the sacrilegious and blasphemous pagans, and to purify God's holy temple and restore it to his faithful people. The author sometimes effects his purpose by transferring events from their proper chronological order, and giving exaggerated figures for the size of armies and the numbers killed in battle; he also places long, edifying discourses and prayers in the mouths of his heroes, and inclines to elaborate descriptions of celestial apparitions (3, 24-34; 5, 2ff; 10, 29f; 15, 11-16). He is the earliest known composer of stories that glorify God's holy martyrs (6, 18—7, 42; 14, 37-46).

Of theological importance are the author's teachings on the resurrection of the just on the last day (7, 9.11.14.23; 14, 46), the intercession of the saints in heaven for people living on earth (15, 11-16), and the power of the living to offer prayers and sacrifices for the dead (12, 39-46).

The beginning of 2 Maccabees consists of two letters sent by the Jews of Jerusalem to their coreligionists in Egypt. They deal with the observance of the feast commemorating the central event of the book, the purification of the temple. It is uncertain whether the author or a later scribe prefixed these letters to the narrative proper. If the author is responsible for their insertion, he must have written his book some time after 124 B.C., the date of the more recent of the two letters. In any case, Jason's five-volume work very likely continued the history of the Jews well into the Hasmonean period, so that 2 Maccabees would probably not have been produced much before the end of the second century B.C.

The main divisions of 2 Maccabees are:
   I: Letters to the Jews in Egypt (1, 1—2, 18)
  II: Author's Preface (2, 19-32)
 III: Heliodorus' Attempt To Profane the Temple (3, 1-40)
  IV: Profanation and Persecution (4, 1—7, 42)
   V: Victories of Judas and Purification of the Temple (8, 1—10, 8)
  VI: Renewed Persecution (10, 9—15, 36)
 VII: Epilogue (15, 37-39)

I: LETTERS TO THE JEWS IN EGYPT

First Letter 124 B.C.

1 [1]THE JEWS IN JERUSALEM and in the land of Judea send greetings to their brethren, the Jews in Egypt, and wish them true peace! [2]May God bless you and remember his covenant with his faithful servants, Abraham, Isaac and Jacob. [3]May he give to all of you a heart to worship him and to do his will readily and generously. [4]May he open your heart to his law and his commandments and grant you peace. [5]May he hear your prayers, and be reconciled to you, and never forsake you in time of adversity. [6]Even now we are praying for you here.

[7]*†In the reign of Demetrius, the year one hundred and sixty-nine, we Jews wrote to you during the

---

† 1, 7: *Demetrius:* Demetrius II, king of Syria (145-139, 129-125 B. C.). *The year one hundred and sixty-nine* of the Seleucid era, 143 B. C. Regarding the dates in 1 and 2 Mc, see note on 1 Mc 1, 10. On the troubles caused by *Jason* and his revolt against *the kingdom,* i. e., the rule of the legitimate high priest, see 4, 7-22.

trouble and violence that overtook us in those years after Jason and his followers had revolted against the holy land and the kingdom, [8]*†setting fire to the gatehouse and shedding innocent blood. But we prayed to the Lord, and our prayer was heard; we offered sacrifices and fine flour; we lighted the lamps and set out the loaves of bread. [9]†We are now reminding you to celebrate the feast of Booths in the month of Chislev. [10]†Dated in the year one hundred and eighty-eight.

Festival Letter 164 B.C.

The people of Jerusalem and Judea, the senate, and Judas send greetings and good wishes to Aristobulus, counselor of King Ptolemy and member of the family of the anointed priests, and to the Jews in Egypt. [11]†Since we have been saved by God from grave dangers, we give him great thanks for having fought on our side against the king; [12]*it was he who drove out those who fought against the holy city. [13]†When their leader arrived in Persia with his seemingly irresistible army, they were cut to pieces in the temple of the goddess Nanea through a deceitful stratagem employed by Nanea's priests. [14]†On the pretext of marrying the goddess, Antiochus with his Friends had come to the place to get its great treasures by way of dowry. [15]When the priests of the Nanaeon had displayed the treasures, Antiochus with a few attendants came to the temple precincts. As soon as he entered the temple, the priests locked the doors. [16]Then they opened a hidden trapdoor in the ceiling, hurled stones at the leader and his companions and struck them down. They dismembered the bodies, cut off their heads and tossed them to the people outside. [17]Forever blessed be our God, who has thus punished the wicked!

[18]†We shall be celebrating the purification of the temple on the twenty-fifth day of the month Chislev, so we thought it right to inform you that you too may celebrate the feast of Booths and of the fire that appeared when Nehemiah, the rebuilder of the temple and the altar, offered sacrifices. [19]†When our fathers were being exiled to Persia, devout priests of the time took some of the fire from the altar and hid it secretly in the hollow of a dry cistern, making sure that the place would be unknown to anyone. [20]Many years later, when it so pleased God, Nehemiah, commissioned by the king of Persia, sent the descendants of the priests who had hidden the fire to look for it. [21]When they informed us that they could not find any fire, but only muddy water, he ordered them to scoop some out and bring it. After the material for the sacrifices had been prepared, Nehemiah ordered the priests to sprinkle with the water the wood and what lay on it. [22]When this was done and in time the sun, which had been clouded over, began to shine, a great fire blazed up, so that everyone marveled. [23]While the sacrifice was being burned, the priests recited a prayer, and all present joined in with them, Jonathan leading and the rest responding with Nehemiah.

[24]The prayer was as follows: "Lord, Lord God, creator of all things, awesome and strong, just and merciful, the only king and benefactor, [25]who alone are gracious, just, almighty, and eternal, Israel's savior from all evil, who chose our forefathers and sanctified them: [26]accept this sacrifice on behalf of all your people Israel and guard and sanctify your heritage. [27]Gather together our scattered people, free those who are the slaves of the Gentiles, look kindly on those who are despised and detested, and let the Gentiles know that you are our God. [28]Punish those who tyrannize over us and arrogantly mistreat us. [29]*Plant your people in your holy place, as Moses promised."

[30]Then the priests began to sing hymns. [31]After the sacrifice was burned, Nehemiah ordered the rest of the liquid to be poured upon large stones. [32]As soon as this was done, a flame blazed up, but its light was lost in the brilliance cast from a light on the altar. [33]When the event became known and the king of the Persians was told that, in the very place where the exiled priests had hidden the fire, a liquid was found with which Nehemiah and his people had burned the sacrifices, [34]the king, after verifying the fact, fenced the place off and declared it sacred. [35]To those on whom the king wished to bestow favors he distributed the large revenues he received there. [36]†Nehemiah and his companions called the liquid nephthar, meaning purification, but most people name it naphtha.

---

† 1, 8: *Our prayer was heard:* in the ultimate victory of the Maccabees.

1, 9: *Feast of Booths in the month of Chislev:* really the feast of the Dedication of the temple (10, 1-8), celebrated on the twenty-fifth of Chislev (Nov.-Dec.). Its solemnity resembles that of the true feast of Booths (Lv 23, 33-43), celebrated on the fifteenth of Tishri (Sept.-Oct.); cf 1, 18.

1, 10: 124 B. C. The date pertains to the preceding, not the following letter.

1, 10: *King Ptolemy:* Ptolemy VI Philometor, ruler of Egypt from 180 to 145 B. C.; he is mentioned also in 1 Mc 1, 18; 10, 51-59.

1, 11f: *The king:* Antiochus IV of Syria, the bitter persecutor of the Jews, who, as *leader* of the Syrian army that invaded Persia, perished there in 164 B. C.

1, 13: *Nanea:* an oriental goddess comparable to Artemis of the Greeks.

1, 14-17: A different account of the death of Antiochus IV is given in 9, 1-29, and another variant account in 1 Mc 6, 1-16. The writer of this letter had probably heard a distorted rumor of the king's death. This fact and other indications show that the letter was written very soon after Antiochus IV died, hence in 164 B. C.

1, 18-36: This purely legendary account of Nehemiah's miraculous fire is incorporated in the letter because of its connection with the temple and its rededication.

1, 18: *Nehemiah, the rebuilder of the temple:* he rebuilt the walls of Jerusalem, but the temple had been rebuilt by Zerubbabel almost a century before.

1, 19: *Persia:* actually Babylonia, which later became part of the Persian Empire.

1, 36: By a play on words, the Greek term *naphtha* (petroleum) is assimilated to some Semitic word, perhaps *nephthar,* meaning "loosened."

---

* 8: 1 Mc 4, 38.
12-17: 9, 1-29; 1 Mc 6, 1-13.

29: 2, 18; Dt 30, 3ff.

2 ¹†YOU will find in the records, not only that Jeremiah the prophet ordered the deportees to take some of the aforementioned fire with them, ²*but also that the prophet, in giving them the law, admonished them not to forget the commandments of the Lord or be led astray in their thoughts, when seeing the gold and silver idols and their ornaments. ³With other similar words he urged them not to let the law depart from their hearts. ⁴*†The same document also tells how the prophet, following a divine revelation, ordered that the tent and the ark should accompany him and how he went off to the mountain which Moses climbed to see God's inheritance. ⁵When Jeremiah arrived there, he found a room in a cave in which he put the tent, the ark, and the altar of incense; then he blocked up the entrance. ⁶Some of those who followed him came up intending to mark the path, but they could not find it. ⁷When Jeremiah heard of this, he reproved them: "The place is to remain unknown until God gathers his people together again and shows them mercy. ⁸*†Then the Lord will disclose these things, and the glory of the Lord will be seen in the cloud, just as it appeared in the time of Moses and when Solomon prayed that the Place might be gloriously sanctified."

⁹It is also related how Solomon in his wisdom offered a sacrifice at the dedication and the completion of the temple. ¹⁰*Just as Moses prayed to the Lord and fire descended from the sky and consumed the sacrifices, so Solomon also prayed and fire came down and burned up the holocausts. ¹¹*†Moses had said, "Because it had not been eaten, the sin offering was burned up." ¹²Solomon also celebrated the feast in the same way for eight days.

¹³†Besides these things, it is also told in the records and in Nehemiah's Memoirs how he collected the books about the kings, the writings of the prophets and of David, and the royal letters about sacred offerings. ¹⁴*In like manner Judas also collected for us the books that had been scattered because of the war, and we now have them in our possession. ¹⁵If you need them, send messengers to get them for you.

¹⁶As we are about to celebrate the feast of the purification of the temple, we are writing to you requesting you also to please celebrate the feast. ¹⁷It is God who has saved all his people and has restored to all of them their heritage, the kingdom, the priesthood, and the sacred rites, ¹⁸*as he promised through the law. We trust in God, that he will soon have mercy on us and gather us together from everywhere under the heavens to his holy Place, for he has rescued us from great perils and has purified his Place.

II: AUTHOR'S PREFACE

¹⁹THIS IS THE STORY of Judas Maccabeus and his brothers, of the purification of the great temple, the dedication of the altar, ²⁰†the campaigns against Antiochus Epiphanes and his son Eupator, ²¹and of the heavenly manifestations accorded to the heroes who fought bravely for Judaism, so that, few as they were, they seized the whole land, put to flight the barbarian hordes, ²²regained possession of the world-famous temple, liberated the city, and reestablished the laws that were in danger of being abolished, while the Lord favored them with all his generous assistance. ²³All this, which Jason of Cyrene set forth in detail in five volumes, we will try to condense into a single book.

Purpose and Method

²⁴In view of the flood of statistics, and the difficulties encountered by those who wish to plunge into historical narratives where the material is abundant, ²⁵we have aimed to please those who prefer simple reading, as well as to make it easy for the studious who wish to commit things to memory, and to be helpful to all. ²⁶For us who have taken upon ourselves the labor of making this digest, the task, far from being easy, is one of sweat and of sleepless nights, ²⁷just as the preparation of a festive banquet is no light matter for one who thus seeks to give enjoyment to others. Similarly, to win the gratitude of many we will gladly endure these inconveniences, ²⁸while we leave the responsibility for exact details to the original author, and confine our efforts to giving only a summary outline. ²⁹As the architect of a new house must give his attention to the whole structure, while the man who undertakes the decoration and the frescoes has only to concern himself with what is needed for ornamentation, so I think it is with us. ³⁰To enter into questions and examine them thoroughly from all sides is the task of the professional historian; ³¹but the man who is making an adaptation should be allowed to aim at brevity of expression and to omit detailed treatment of the matter. ³²Here, then, we shall begin our account without further ado; it would be nonsense to write a long preface to a story and then abbreviate the story itself.

---

† 2, 1-8: This legendary account of how Jeremiah hid the sacred tent (which was not mentioned after the time of Solomon!), the ark, and the altar is given for the purpose of explaining why the postexilic temple was the legitimate place of worship even without these sacred objects.

2, 4: *The mountain:* Nebo; cf Dt 34, 1.

2, 8: *The Place:* the temple of Jerusalem.

2, 11: The statement attributed here to Moses seems to be based on Lv 10, 16-20.

2, 13: *Nehemiah's Memoirs:* a lost apocryphal work.

2, 20: For the account of *the campaigns against Antiochus IV Epiphanes,* see 4, 7—10, 9; and for the account of those against *his son* Antiochus V *Eupator,* see 10, 10—13, 26.

III: HELIODORUS' ATTEMPT TO PROFANE THE TEMPLE

Treachery of Simon

3 [1]*†WHILE THE HOLY CITY lived in perfect peace and the laws were strictly observed because of the piety of the high priest Onias and his hatred of evil, [2]the kings themselves honored the Place and glorified the temple with the most magnificent gifts. [3]†Thus Seleucus, king of Asia, defrayed from his own revenues all the expenses necessary for the sacrificial services. [4]*†But a certain Simon, of the priestly course of Bilgah, who had been appointed superintendent of the temple, had a quarrel with the high priest about the supervision of the city market. [5]Since he could not prevail against Onias, he went to Apollonius of Tarsus, who at that time was governor of Coelesyria and Phoenicia, [6]and reported to him that the treasury in Jerusalem was so full of untold riches that the total sum of money was incalculable and out of all proportion to the cost of the sacrifices, and that it would be possible to bring it all under the control of the king.

Mission of Heliodorus

[7]When Apollonius had an audience with the king, he informed him about the riches that had been reported to him. The king chose his minister Heliodorus and sent him with instructions to expropriate the aforesaid wealth. [8]So Heliodorus immediately set out on his journey, ostensibly to visit the cities of Coelesyria and Phoenicia, but in reality to carry out the king's purpose. [9]When he arrived in Jerusalem and had been graciously received by the high priest of the city, he told him about the information that had been given, and explained the reason for his presence, and he asked if these things were really true. [10]*The high priest explained that part of the money was a care fund for widows and orphans, [11]†and a part was the property of Hyrcanus, son of Tobias, a man who occupied a very high position. Contrary to the calumnies of the impious Simon, the total amounted to four hundred talents of silver and two hundred of gold. [12]He added that it was utterly unthinkable to defraud those who had placed their trust in the sanctity of the Place and in the sacred inviolability of a temple venerated all over the world. [13]But because of the orders he had from the king, Heliodorus said that in any case the money must be confiscated for the royal treasury. [14]So on the day he had set he went in to take an inventory of the funds.

Anguish of the Faithful

There was great distress throughout the city. [15]Priests prostrated themselves in their priestly robes before the altar, and loudly begged him in heaven who had given the law about deposits to keep the deposits safe for those who had made them. [16]Whoever saw the appearance of the high priest was pierced to the heart, for the changed color of his face manifested the anguish of his soul. [17]The terror and bodily trembling that had come over the man clearly showed those who saw him the pain that lodged in his heart. [18]People rushed out of their houses in crowds to make public supplication, because the Place was in danger of being profaned. [19]Women, girded with sackcloth below their breasts, filled the streets; maidens secluded indoors ran together, some to the gates, some to the walls, others peered through the windows, [20]all of them with hands raised toward heaven, making supplication. [21]It was pitiful to see the populace variously prostrated in prayer and the high priest full of dread and anguish.

Divine Intervention

[22]While they were imploring the almighty Lord to keep the deposits safe and secure for those who had placed them in trust, [23]Heliodorus went on with his plan. [24]But just as he was approaching the treasury with his bodyguards, the Lord of spirits who holds all power manifested himself in so striking a way that those who had been bold enough to follow Heliodorus were panic-stricken at God's power and fainted away in terror. [25]There appeared to them a richly caparisoned horse, mounted by a dreadful rider. Charging furiously, the horse attacked Heliodorus with its front hoofs. The rider was seen to be wearing golden armor. [26]Then two other young men, remarkably strong, strikingly beautiful, and splendidly attired, appeared before him. Standing on each side of him, they flogged him unceasingly until they had given him innumerable blows. [27]Suddenly he fell to the ground, enveloped in great darkness. Men picked him up and laid him on a stretcher. [28]The man who a moment before had entered that treasury with a great retinue and his whole bodyguard was carried away helpless, having clearly experienced the sovereign power of God. [29]While he lay speechless and deprived of all hope of aid, due to an act of God's power, [30]the Jews praised the Lord who had marvelously glorified his holy Place; and the temple, charged so shortly before with fear and commotion, was filled with joy and gladness, now that the almighty Lord had manifested himself.

---

† 3, 1-40: This legendary episode about Heliodorus is recounted here for the purpose of stressing the inviolability of the temple of Jerusalem; its later profanation was allowed by God because of the people's sins; cf 5, 17f.

3, 1: *The high priest Onias:* Onias III, who was high priest from 196 to 175 B. C., and died in 171 B. C. He was the son of Simon, whose praises are sung in Sir 50, 1-21.

3, 3: *Seleucus:* Seleucus IV Philopator, who reigned from 187 to 175 B. C.

3, 4: *Bilgah:* a priestly family mentioned in Neh 12, 5.18.

3, 11: *Son of Tobias:* a member of the Tobiad family of Transjordan (Neh 2, 10; 6, 17ff; 13, 4-8). Hyrcanus' father was Joseph, whose mother was the sister of the high priest Onias II.

---

* 3/1ff: 5, 19f; 15, 12.　　　10: Dt 14, 29.
　4: 4, 23.

³¹Soon some of the companions of Heliodorus begged Onias to invoke the Most High, praying that the life of the man who was about to expire might be spared. ³²Fearing that the king might think that Heliodorus had suffered some foul play at the hands of the Jews, the high priest offered a sacrifice for the man's recovery. ³³While the high priest was offering the sacrifice of atonement, the same young men in the same clothing again appeared and stood before Heliodorus. "Be very grateful to the high priest Onias," they told him. "It is for his sake that the Lord has spared your life. ³⁴Since you have been scourged by Heaven, proclaim to all men the majesty of God's power." When they had said this, they disappeared.

Testimony of Heliodorus

³⁵After Heliodorus had offered a sacrifice to the Lord and made most solemn vows to him who had spared his life, he bade Onias farewell, and returned with his soldiers to the king. ³⁶Before all men he gave witness to the deeds of the most high God that he had seen with his own eyes. ³⁷When the king asked Heliodorus who would be a suitable man to be sent to Jerusalem next, he answered: ³⁸"If you have an enemy or a plotter against the government, send him there, and you will receive him back well-flogged, if indeed he survives at all; for there is certainly some special divine power about the Place. ³⁹He who has his dwelling in heaven watches over that Place and protects it, and he strikes down and destroys those who come to harm it." ⁴⁰This was how the matter concerning Heliodorus and the preservation of the treasury turned out.

IV: PROFANATION AND PERSECUTION

Onias Appeals to the King

4 ¹THE SIMON MENTIONED ABOVE as the informer about the funds against his own country, made false accusation that it was Onias who threatened Heliodorus and instigated the whole miserable affair. ²He dared to brand as a plotter against the government the man who was a benefactor of the city, a protector of his compatriots, and a zealous defender of the laws. ³When Simon's hostility reached such a point that murders were being committed by one of his henchmen, ⁴Onias saw that the opposition was serious and that Apollonius, son of Menestheus, the governor of Coelesyria and Phoenicia, was abetting Simon's wickedness. ⁵So he had recourse to the king, not as an accuser of his countrymen, but as a man looking to the general and particular good of all the people. ⁶He saw that, unless the king intervened, it would be impossible to have a peaceful government, and that Simon would not desist from his folly.

Jews Led by Jason To Apostatize

⁷*†But Seleucus died, and when Antiochus surnamed Epiphanes succeeded him on the throne, Onias' brother Jason obtained the high priesthood by corrupt means: ⁸in an interview, he promised the king three hundred and sixty talents of silver, as well as eighty talents from another source of income. ⁹†Besides this he agreed to pay a hundred and fifty more, if he were given authority to establish a gymnasium and a youth club for it and to enroll men in Jerusalem as Antiochians.

¹⁰When Jason received the king's approval and came into office, he immediately initiated his countrymen into the Greek way of life. ¹¹*†He set aside the royal concessions granted to the Jews through the mediation of John, father of Eupolemus (that Eupolemus who would later go on an embassy to the Romans to establish a treaty of friendship with them); he abrogated the lawful institutions and introduced customs contrary to the law. ¹²*†He quickly established a gymnasium at the very foot of the acropolis, where he induced the noblest young men to wear the Greek hat. ¹³The craze for Hellenism and foreign customs reached such a pitch, through the outrageous wickedness of the ungodly pseudo-high-priest Jason, ¹⁴that the priests no longer cared about the service of the altar. Disdaining the temple and neglecting the sacrifices, they hastened, at the signal for the discus-throwing, to take part in the unlawful exercises on the athletic field. ¹⁵They despised what their ancestors had regarded as honors, while they highly prized what the Greeks esteemed as glory. ¹⁶Precisely because of this, they found themselves in serious trouble: the very people whose manner of life they emulated, and whom they desired to imitate in everything, became their enemies and oppressors. ¹⁷It is no light matter to flout the laws of God, as the following period will show.

¹⁸When the quinquennial games were held at Tyre in the presence of the king, ¹⁹the vile Jason sent envoys as representatives of the Antiochians of Jerusalem, to bring there three hundred silver drachmas for the sacrifice to Hercules. But the bearers themselves decided that the money should not be spent on

---

† 4, 7: *Seleucus died:* he was murdered by Heliodorus. *Antiochus Epiphanes* was his younger brother. Onias' brother showed his love for *the Greek way of life* (v 10) by changing his Hebrew name Joshua, or Jesus, to the Greek name *Jason.*

4, 9: *Youth club:* an educational institution in which young men were trained both in Greek intellectual culture and in physical fitness. *Antiochians:* honorary citizens of Antioch, a Hellenistic city of the Seleucid Kingdom that had a corporation of such Antiochians, who enjoyed certain political and commercial privileges.

4, 11: *Eupolemus:* one of the two envoys sent to Rome by Judas Maccabeus (1 Mc 8, 17).

4, 12: Since the *gymnasium,* where the youth exercised naked (Greek *gymnos*), lay in the Tyropoeon Valley to the east of the citadel, it was directly next to the temple on its eastern side. *The Greek hat:* a wide-brimmed hat, traditional headgear of Hermes, the patron god of athletic contests; it formed part of the distinctive costume of the members of the "youth club."

✻
4/7: 1, 7; 1 Mc 1, 10.   12: 1 Mc 1, 14.
11: 1 Mc 8, 17.

a sacrifice, as that was not right, but should be used for some other purpose. **20**†So the contribution destined by the sender for the sacrifice to Hercules was in fact applied, by those who brought it, to the construction of triremes.

21†When Apollonius, son of Menestheus, was sent to Egypt for the coronation of King Philometor, Antiochus learned that the king was opposed to his policies; so he took measures for his own security. **22**After going to Joppa, he proceeded to Jerusalem. There he was received with great pomp by Jason and the people of the city, who escorted him with torchlights and acclamations; following this, he led his army into Phoenicia.

Menelaus Supplants Jason

23†Three years later Jason sent Menelaus, brother of the aforementioned Simon, to deliver the money to the king, and to obtain decisions on some important matters. **24**When he had been introduced to the king, he flattered him with such an air of authority that he secured the high priesthood for himself, outbidding Jason by three hundred talents of silver. **25**He returned with the royal commission, but with nothing that made him worthy of the high priesthood; he had the temper of a cruel tyrant and the rage of a wild beast. **26**Then Jason, who had cheated his own brother and now saw himself cheated by another man, was driven out as a fugitive to the country of the Ammonites.

27Although Menelaus had obtained the office, he did not make any payments of the money he had promised to the king, **28**in spite of the demand of Sostratus, the commandant of the citadel, whose duty it was to collect the taxes. For this reason, both were summoned before the king. **29**Menelaus left his brother Lysimachus as his substitute in the high priesthood, while Sostratus left Crates, commander of the Cypriots, as his substitute.

Murder of Onias

30†While these things were taking place, the people of Tarsus and Mallus rose in revolt, because their cities had been given as a gift to Antiochis, the king's mistress. **31**The king, therefore, went off in haste to settle the affair, leaving Andronicus, one of his nobles, as his deputy. **32**Then Menelaus, thinking this a good opportunity, stole some gold vessels from the temple and presented them to Andronicus; he had already sold some other vessels in Tyre and in the neighboring cities. **33**When Onias had clear evidence of the facts, he made a public protest, after withdrawing to the inviolable sanctuary at Daphne, near Antioch. **34**Thereupon Menelaus approached Andronicus privately and asked him to lay hands on Onias. So Andronicus went to Onias, and by treacherously reassuring him through sworn pledges with right hands joined, persuaded him, in spite of his suspicions, to leave the sanctuary. Then, without any regard for justice, he immediately put him to death.

35As a result, not only the Jews, but many people of other nations as well, were indignant and angry over the unjust murder of the man. **36**†When the king returned from the region of Cilicia, the Jews of the city, together with the Greeks who detested the crime, went to see him about the murder of Onias. **37**Antiochus was deeply grieved and full of pity; he wept as he recalled the prudence and noble conduct of the deceased. **38**Inflamed with anger, he immediately stripped Andronicus of his purple robe, tore off his other garments, and had him led through the whole city to the very place where he had committed the outrage against Onias; and there he put the murderer to death. Thus the LORD rendered him the punishment he deserved.

Riot against Lysimachus

39†Many sacrilegious thefts had been committed by Lysimachus in the city with the connivance of Menelaus. When word was spread that a large number of gold vessels had been stolen, the people assembled in protest against Lysimachus. **40**As the crowds, now thoroughly enraged, began to riot, Lysimachus launched an unjustified attack against them with about three thousand armed men under the leadership of Auranus, a man as advanced in folly as he was in years. **41**Reacting against Lysimachus' attack, the people picked up stones or pieces of wood or handfuls of the ashes lying there and threw them in wild confusion at Lysimachus and his men. **42**As a result, they wounded many of them and even killed a few, while they put all the rest to flight. The sacrilegious thief himself they slew near the treasury.

43Charges about this affair were brought against Menelaus. **44**†When the king came to Tyre, three men sent by the senate presented to him the justice of their cause. **45***But Menelaus, seeing himself on the losing side, promised Ptolemy, son of Dorymenes, a substantial sum of money if he would win the king over. **46**So Ptolemy retired with the king under a colonnade, as if to get some fresh air, and persuaded him to change his mind. **47**Menelaus, who was the cause of all the trouble, the king acquitted of the charges, while he condemned to death those poor men who would have been declared innocent even if they had pleaded their case before Scythians. **48**Thus, those who had prose-

---

† 4, 20: *Triremes:* war vessels with three banks of oars.
4, 21: *Philometor:* Ptolemy VI, king of Egypt, c. 172 to c. 145 B. C.
4, 23: *Menelaus:* Jewish high priest from c. 172 to his execution in 162 B. C. (13, 3-8).
4, 30: *Mallus:* a city of Cilicia (v 36) in southeastern Asia Minor, about thirty miles east of *Tarsus.*
4, 36: *The city:* Antioch. But some understand the Greek to mean "each city."
4, 39: *The city:* Jerusalem. *Menelaus* was still in Syria.
4, 44: *The senate:* the council of Jewish elders at Jerusalem; cf 1 Mc 12, 6.

cuted the case for the city, for the people, and for the sacred vessels, quickly suffered unjust punishment. [49]For this reason, even some Tyrians were indignant over the crime and provided sumptuously for their burial. [50]But Menelaus, thanks to the covetousness of the men in power, remained in office, where he grew in wickedness and became the chief plotter against his fellow citizens.

Sedition and Death of Jason

5 [1]*†ABOUT this time Antiochus sent his second expedition into Egypt. [2]*It then happened that all over the city, for nearly forty days, there appeared horsemen charging in midair, clad in garments interwoven with gold—companies fully armed with lances [3]and drawn swords; squadrons of cavalry in battle array, charges and countercharges on this side and that, with brandished shields and bristling spears, flights of arrows and flashes of gold ornaments, together with armor of every sort. [4]Therefore all prayed that this vision might be a good omen.

[5]†But when a false rumor circulated that Antiochus was dead, Jason gathered fully a thousand men and suddenly attacked the city. As the defenders on the walls were forced back and the city was finally being taken, Menelaus took refuge in the citadel. [6]Jason then slaughtered his fellow citizens without mercy, not realizing that triumph over one's own kindred was the greatest failure, but imagining that he was winning a victory over his enemies, not his fellow countrymen. [7]Even so, he did not gain control of the government, but in the end received only disgrace for his treachery, and once again took refuge in the country of the Ammonites. [8]†At length he met a miserable end. Called to account before Aretas, king of the Arabs, he fled from city to city, hunted by all men, hated as a transgressor of the laws, abhorred as the butcher of his country and his countrymen. After being driven into Egypt, [9]he crossed the sea to the Spartans, among whom he hoped to find protection because of his relations with them. There he who had exiled so many from their country perished in exile; [10]and he who had cast out so many to lie unburied went unmourned himself with no funeral of any kind or any place in the tomb of his ancestors.

The City Ravaged

[11]*When these happenings were reported to the king, he thought that Judea was in revolt. Raging like a wild animal, he set out from Egypt and took Jerusalem by storm. [12]He ordered his soldiers to cut down without mercy those whom they met and to slay those who took refuge in their houses. [13]There was a massacre of young and old, a killing of women and children, a slaughter of virgins and infants. [14]In the space

of three days, eighty thousand were lost, forty thousand meeting a violent death, and the same number being sold into slavery. [15]Not satisfied with this, the king dared to enter the holiest temple in the world; Menelaus, that traitor both to the laws and to his country, served as guide. [16]He laid his impure hands on the sacred vessels and gathered up with profane hands the votive offerings made by other kings for the advancement, the glory, and the honor of the Place. [17]*Puffed up in spirit, Antiochus did not realize that it was because of the sins of the city's inhabitants that the Lord was angry for a little while and hence disregarded the holy Place. [18]If they had not become entangled in so many sins, this man, like Heliodorus, who was sent by King Seleucus to inspect the treasury, would have been flogged and turned back from his presumptuous action as soon as he approached. [19]*†The Lord, however, had not chosen the people for the sake of the Place, but the Place for the sake of the people. [20]Therefore, the Place itself, having shared in the people's misfortunes, afterward participated in their good fortune; and what the Almighty had forsaken in his anger was restored in all its glory, once the great Sovereign became reconciled.

[21]*Antiochus carried off eighteen hundred talents from the temple, and hurried back to Antioch. In his arrogance he planned to make the land navigable and the sea passable on foot, so carried away was he with pride. [22]†But he left governors to harass the nation: at Jerusalem, Philip, a Phrygian by birth, and in character more cruel than the man who appointed him; [23]†at Mount Gerizim, Andronicus; and besides these, Menelaus, who lorded it over his fellow citizens worse than the others did. Out of hatred for the Jewish citizens, [24]*†the king sent Apollonius, commander of the Mysians, at the head of an army of twenty-two thousand men, with orders to kill all the grown men and sell the women and young men into slavery. [25]When this man arrived in Jerusalem, he pretended to be peacefully disposed and waited until the holy day of the sabbath; then, finding the Jews refraining from

† 5, 1: *Second expedition:* the first invasion of Egypt by Antiochus in 169 B. C. (1 Mc 1, 16-20) is not mentioned in 2 Mc, unless the coming of the Syrian army to Palestine (2 Mc 4, 21f) is regarded as the first invasion. The author of 2 Mc apparently combines the first pillage of Jerusalem in 169 B. C. after Antiochus' first invasion of Egypt (1 Mc 1, 20-28; cf 2 Mc 5, 5ff) with the second pillage of the city two years later (167 B. C.), following the king's second invasion of Egypt in 168 B. C. (1 Mc 1, 29-35; cf 2 Mc 5, 24ff).
5, 5: *Jason:* brother of Onias III, was claimant of the high priesthood (4, 7-10). Later he was supplanted by Menelaus who drove him into Transjordan (4, 26).
5, 8: *Aretas:* King Aretas I of the Nabateans; cf 1 Mc 5, 25.
5, 19: Man is more important than even the most sacred institutions; cf Mk 2, 27.
5, 22: *Philip, a Phrygian by birth:* the Philip of 6, 11 and 8, 8, but probably not the same as Philip the regent of 9, 29 and 1 Mc 6, 14.
5, 23: *Mount Gerizim:* the sacred mountain of the Samaritans at Shechem; cf 6, 2.
5, 24: *Apollonius:* the *Mysian commander* of 1 Mc 1, 29; mentioned also in 2 Mc 3, 5; 4, 4.

5/1: 1 Mc 1, 17.
2f: 3, 24ff; 10, 29f; 11, 8.
11-21: 1 Mc 1, 20-24.
17: 6, 12-16; 7, 16-19.32-38.
19f: 3, 1ff; 1 Chr 17, 9; Mk 2, 27.
21: 1 Mc 1, 23f.
24ff: 1 Mc 1, 29f.

work, he ordered his men to parade fully armed. **26**All those who came out to watch, he massacred, and running through the city with armed men, he cut down a large number of people.

27*But Judas Maccabeus and about nine others withdrew to the wilderness, where he and his companions lived like wild animals in the hills, continuing to eat what grew wild to avoid sharing the defilement.

The Temple Desecrated

6 **1***NOT long after this the king sent an Athenian senator to force the Jews to abandon the customs of their ancestors and live no longer by the laws of God; **2***†also to profane the temple in Jerusalem and dedicate it to Olympian Zeus, and that on Mount Gerizim to Zeus the Hospitable, as the inhabitants of the place requested. **3**This intensified the evil in an intolerable and utterly disgusting way. **4**†The Gentiles filled the temple with debauchery and revelry; they amused themselves with prostitutes and had intercourse with women even in the sacred court. They also brought into the temple things that were forbidden, **5**so that the altar was covered with abominable offerings prohibited by the laws.

Abolition of the Law

6A man could not keep the sabbath or celebrate the traditional feasts, nor even admit that he was a Jew. **7**†Moreover, at the monthly celebration of the king's birthday the Jews had, from bitter necessity, to partake of the sacrifices, and when the festival of Dionysus was celebrated, they were compelled to march in his procession, wearing wreaths of ivy.

8At the suggestion of the citizens of Ptolemais, a decree was issued ordering the neighboring Greek cities to act in the same way against the Jews: oblige them to partake of the sacrifices, **9**and put to death those who would not consent to adopt the customs of the Greeks. It was obvious, therefore, that disaster impended. **10***Thus, two women who were arrested for having circumcised their children were publicly paraded about the city with their babies hanging at their breasts and then thrown down from the top of the city wall. **11***Others, who had assembled in nearby caves to observe the sabbath in secret, were betrayed to Philip and all burned to death. In their respect for the holiness of that day, they had scruples about defending themselves.

Purpose of Divine Judgment

12*Now I beg those who read this book not to be disheartened by these misfortunes, but to consider that these chastisements were meant not for the ruin but for the correction of our nation. **13**It is, in fact, a sign of great kindness to punish sinners promptly instead of letting them go for long. **14***Thus, in dealing with other nations, the Lord patiently waits until they reach the full measure of their sins before he punishes them; but with us he has decided to deal differently, **15**in order that he may not have to punish us more severely later, when our sins have reached their fullness. **16**He never withdraws his mercy from us. Although he disciplines us with misfortunes, he does not abandon his own people. **17**Let these words suffice for recalling this truth. Without further ado we must go on with our story.

Martyrdom of Eleazar

18*†Eleazar, one of the foremost scribes, a man of advanced age and noble appearance, was being forced to open his mouth to eat pork. **19**But preferring a glorious death to a life of defilement, he spat out the meat, and went forward of his own accord to the instrument of torture, **20**as men ought to do who have the courage to reject the food which it is unlawful to taste even for love of life. **21**Those in charge of that unlawful ritual meal took the man aside privately, because of their long acquaintance with him, and urged him to bring meat of his own providing, such as he could legitimately eat, and to pretend to be eating some of the meat of the sacrifice prescribed by the king; **22**in this way he would escape the death penalty, and be treated kindly because of their old friendship with him. **23**But he made up his mind in a noble manner, worthy of his years, the dignity of his advanced age, the merited distinction of his gray hair, and of the admirable life he had lived from childhood; and so he declared that above all he would be loyal to the holy laws given by God.

He told them to send him at once to the abode of the dead, explaining: **24**"At our age it would be unbecoming to make such a pretense; many young men would think the ninety-year-old Eleazar had gone over to an alien religion. **25**Should I thus dissimulate for the sake of a brief moment of life, they would be led astray by me, while I would bring shame and dishonor on my old age. **26**Even if, for the time being, I avoid the punishment of men, I shall never, whether alive or dead, escape the hands of the Almighty. **27**Therefore, by manfully giving up my life now, I will prove myself worthy of my old age, **28**and I will leave to the young a noble example of how to die willingly and generously for the revered and holy laws."

---

† 6, 2: *Olympian Zeus:* equated with the Syrian Baal Shamen ("the lord of the heavens"), a term which the Jews rendered as "Shiqqus shomem," *horrible abomination* (Dn 9, 27; 11, 31; 12, 11; 1 Mc 1, 54).

6, 4: *Amused themselves with prostitutes:* as in the fertility cults of the ancient Near East; see notes on Bar 6, 10.42f.

6, 7: *Dionysus:* called also Bacchus, the god of the grape harvest and of wine; *ivy* was one of his symbols.

6, 18—7, 42: The stories of Eleazar and of the mother and her seven sons, among the earliest models of "martyrology," were understandably popular among the Christians of the early centuries. Written originally to encourage God's people in times of persecution, they add gruesome details to the record of tortures, and place long speeches in the mouths of the martyrs.

---

*
27: 1 Mc 2, 28.
6/1-11: 1 Mc 1, 44-63.
   2: 1 Mc 1, 46; Dn 9, 27.
  10: 1 Mc 1, 60f.
11: 1 Mc 2, 32-38.
12-16: 5, 17; 7, 16-19.32-38.
14: Wis 11, 9f; 12, 2.22.
18: Lv 11, 7f; Heb 11, 35.

He spoke thus, and went immediately to the instrument of torture. ²⁹Those who shortly before had been kindly disposed, now became hostile toward him because what he had said seemed to them utter madness. ³⁰When he was about to die under the blows, he groaned and said: "The Lord in his holy knowledge knows full well that, although I could have escaped death, I am not only enduring terrible pain in my body from this scourging, but also suffering it with joy in my soul because of my devotion to him." ³¹This is how he died, leaving in his death a model of courage and an unforgettable example of virtue not only for the young but for the whole nation.

Martyrdom of a Mother and Her Sons

7 ¹*It also happened that seven brothers with their mother were arrested and tortured with whips and scourges by the king, to force them to eat pork in violation of God's law. ²One of the brothers, speaking for the others, said: "What do you expect to achieve by questioning us? We are ready to die rather than transgress the laws of our ancestors." ³At that the king, in a fury, gave orders to have pans and caldrons heated. ⁴While they were being quickly heated, he commanded his executioners to cut out the tongue of the one who had spoken for the others, to scalp him and cut off his hands and feet, while the rest of his brothers and his mother looked on. ⁵When he was completely maimed but still breathing, the king ordered them to carry him to the fire and fry him. As a cloud of smoke spread from the pan, the brothers and their mother encouraged one another to die bravely, saying such words as these: ⁶*"The Lord God is looking on, and he truly has compassion on us, as Moses declared in his canticle, when he protested openly with the words, 'And he will have pity on his servants.'"

⁷When the first brother had died in this manner, they brought the second to be made sport of. After tearing off the skin and hair of his head, they asked him, "Will you eat the pork rather than have your body tortured limb by limb?" ⁸Answering in the language of his forefathers, he said, "Never!" So he too in turn suffered the same tortures as the first. ⁹*†At the point of death he said: "You accursed fiend, you are depriving us of this present life, but the King of the world will raise us up to live again forever. It is for his laws that we are dying."

¹⁰After him the third suffered their cruel sport. He put out his tongue at once when told to do so, and bravely held out his hands, ¹¹*as he spoke these noble words: "It was from Heaven that I received these; for the sake of his laws I disdain them; from him I hope to receive them again." ¹²Even the king and his attendants marveled at the young man's courage, because he regarded his sufferings as nothing.

¹³After he had died, they tortured and maltreated the fourth brother in the same way. ¹⁴When he was near death, he said, "It is my choice to die at the hands of men with the God-given hope of being restored to life by him; but for you, there will be no resurrection to life."

¹⁵They next brought forward the fifth brother and maltreated him. ¹⁶*Looking at the king, he said: "Since you have power among men, mortal though you are, do what you please. But do not think that our nation is forsaken by God. ¹⁷Only wait, and you will see how his great power will torment you and your descendants."

¹⁸After him they brought the sixth brother. When he was about to die, he said: "Have no vain illusions. We suffer these things on our own account, because we have sinned against our God; that is why such astonishing things have happened to us. ¹⁹*Do not think, then, that you will go unpunished for having dared to fight against God."

²⁰Most admirable and worthy of everlasting remembrance was the mother, who saw her seven sons perish in a single day, yet bore it courageously because of her hope in the Lord. ²¹Filled with a noble spirit that stirred her womanly heart with manly courage, she exhorted each of them in the language of their forefathers with these words: ²²"I do not know how you came into existence in my womb; it was not I who gave you the breath of life, nor was it I who set in order the elements of which each of you is composed. ²³Therefore, since it is the Creator of the universe who shapes each man's beginning, as he brings about the origin of everything, he, in his mercy, will give you back both breath and life, because you now disregard yourselves for the sake of his law."

²⁴Antiochus, suspecting insult in her words, thought he was being ridiculed. As the youngest brother was still alive, the king appealed to him, not with mere words, but with promises on oath, to make him rich and happy if he would abandon his ancestral customs: he would make him his Friend and entrust him with high office. ²⁵When the youth paid no attention to him at all, the king appealed to the mother, urging her to advise her boy to save his life. ²⁶After he had urged her for a long time, she went through the motions of persuading her son. ²⁷In derision of the cruel tyrant, she leaned over close to her son and said in their native language: "Son, have pity on me, who carried you in my womb for nine months, nursed you for three years, brought you up, educated and supported you to your present age. ²⁸†I beg you, child, to look at the heavens and the earth and see all that is in them; then you will know that God did not make them out of existing

---

† 7, 9: *The King of the world will raise us up:* here, and in vv 11.14.23.29.36, belief in the future resurrection of the body, at least for the just, is clearly stated; cf also 12, 44; 14, 46; Dn 12, 2.

7, 28: *God did not make them out of existing things:* that is, God made all things solely by his omnipotent will and his creative word; cf Heb 11, 3.

✽
7/1: Jer 15, 9.　　　　　11: 12, 43ff.
6: Dt 32, 36.　　　　16-19: 5, 17; 6, 12-16.
9: 12, 44; 14, 46.　　　19: Acts 5, 39.

things; and in the same way the human race came into existence. ²⁹Do not be afraid of this executioner, but be worthy of your brothers and accept death, so that in the time of mercy I may receive you again with them."

³⁰She had scarcely finished speaking when the youth said: "What are you waiting for? I will not obey the king's command. I obey the command of the law given to our forefathers through Moses. ³¹But you, who have contrived every kind of affliction for the Hebrews, will not escape the hands of God. ³²We, indeed, are suffering because of our sins. ³³Though our living Lord treats us harshly for a little while to correct us with chastisements, he will again be reconciled with his servants. ³⁴But you, wretch, vilest of all men! do not, in your insolence, concern yourself with unfounded hopes, as you raise your hand against the children of Heaven. ³⁵You have not yet escaped the judgment of the almighty and all-seeing God. ³⁶My brothers, after enduring brief pain, have drunk of never-failing life, under God's covenant, but you, by the judgment of God, shall receive just punishments for your arrogance. ³⁷Like my brothers, I offer up my body and my life for our ancestral laws, imploring God to show mercy soon to our nation, and by afflictions and blows to make you confess that he alone is God. ³⁸Through me and my brothers, may there be an end to the wrath of the Almighty that has justly fallen on our whole nation." ³⁹At that, the king became enraged and treated him even worse than the others, since he bitterly resented the boy's contempt. ⁴⁰Thus he too died undefiled, putting all his trust in the Lord. ⁴¹The mother was last to die, after her sons.

⁴²Enough has been said about the sacrificial meals and the excessive cruelties.

V: VICTORIES OF JUDAS AND PURIFICATION OF THE TEMPLE

Judas Maccabeus

8 ¹JUDAS MACCABEUS AND HIS COMPANIONS entered the villages secretly, summoned their kinsmen, and by also enlisting others who remained faithful to Judaism, assembled about six thousand men. ²They implored the Lord to look kindly upon his people, who were being oppressed on all sides; to have pity on the temple, which was profaned by godless men; ³to have mercy on the city, which was being destroyed and about to be leveled to the ground; to hearken to the blood that cried out to him; ⁴to remember the criminal slaughter of innocent children and the blasphemies uttered against his name; and to manifest his hatred of evil. ⁵Once Maccabeus got his men or-

ganized, the Gentiles could not withstand him, for the Lord's wrath had now changed to mercy. ⁶Coming unexpectedly upon towns and villages, he would set them on fire. He captured strategic positions, and put to flight a large number of the enemy. ⁷He preferred the nights as being especially helpful to such attacks. Soon the fame of his valor spread everywhere.

First Victory over Nicanor

⁸When Philip saw that Judas was gaining ground little by little and that his successful advances were becoming more frequent, he wrote to Ptolemy, governor of Coelesyria and Phoenicia, to come to the aid of the king's government. ⁹Ptolemy promptly selected Nicanor, son of Patroclus, one of the Chief Friends, and sent him at the head of at least twenty thousand armed men of various nations to wipe out the entire Jewish race. With him he associated Gorgias, a professional military commander, well-versed in the art of war. ¹⁰Nicanor planned to raise the two thousand talents of tribute owed by the king to the Romans by selling captured Jews into slavery. ¹¹So he immediately sent word to the coastal cities, inviting them to buy Jewish slaves and promising to deliver ninety slaves for a talent—little did he dream of the punishment that was to fall upon him from the Almighty.

¹²When Judas learned of Nicanor's advance and informed his companions about the approach of the army, ¹³the cowardly and those who lacked faith in God's justice deserted and got away. ¹⁴But the others sold everything they had left, and at the same time besought the Lord to deliver those whom the ungodly Nicanor had sold before even meeting them. ¹⁵They begged the Lord to do this, if not for their sake, at least for the sake of the covenants made with their forefathers, and because they themselves bore his holy, glorious name. ¹⁶Maccabeus assembled his men, six thousand strong, and exhorted them not be panic-stricken before the enemy, nor to fear the large number of the Gentiles attacking them unjustly, but to fight courageously, ¹⁷keeping before their eyes the lawless outrage perpetrated by the Gentiles against the holy Place and the affliction of the humiliated city, as well as the subversion of their ancestral way of life. ¹⁸"They trust in weapons and acts of daring," he said, "but we trust in almighty God, who can by a mere nod destroy not only those who attack us, but the whole world." ¹⁹He went on to tell them of the times when help had been given their ancestors: both the time of Sennacherib, when a hundred and eighty-five thousand of his men were destroyed, ²⁰and the time of the battle in Babylonia against the Galatians, when only eight thousand Jews fought along with four thousand Macedonians; yet when the Macedonians were hard

32.38: 5, 17; 6, 12-16; 17, 16-19.
40f: Heb 11, 35.
8/1-7: 5, 27; 1 Mc 3, 10-26.
5ff: 1 Mc 3, 3-9.
8: 4, 45; 1 Mc 3, 38.
9: 1 Mc 7, 26.
19: 15, 22; 2 Kgs 19, 35; Is 37, 36.

† 8, 8-29.34ff: This account of the campaign of Nicanor and Gorgias against Judas is paralleled, with certain differences, in 1 Mc 3, 38—4, 24.

pressed, the eight thousand routed one hundred and twenty thousand and took a great quantity of booty, because of the help they received from Heaven. [21]With such words he encouraged them and made them ready to die for their laws and their country.

Then Judas divided his army into four, [22†]placing his brothers, Simon, Joseph, and Jonathan, each over a division, assigning to each fifteen hundred men. [23*](There was also Eleazar.) After reading to them from the holy book and giving them the watchword, "The Help of God," he himself took charge of the first division and joined in battle with Nicanor. [24]With the Almighty as their ally, they killed more than nine thousand of the enemy, wounded and disabled the greater part of Nicanor's army, and put all of them to flight. [25]They also seized the money of those who had come to buy them as slaves. When they had pursued the enemy for some time, [26]they were obliged to return by reason of the late hour. It was the day before the sabbath, and for that reason they could not continue the pursuit. [27]They collected the enemy's arms and stripped them of their spoils, and then observed the sabbath with fervent praise and thanks to the Lord who kept them safe for that day on which he let descend on them the first dew of his mercy. [28]After the sabbath, they gave a share of the booty to the persecuted and to widows and orphans; the rest they divided among themselves and their children. [29]When this was done, they made supplication in common, imploring the merciful Lord to be completely reconciled with his servants.

Timothy and Bacchides Defeated

[30]They also challenged the forces of Timothy and Bacchides, killed more than twenty thousand of them, and captured some very high fortresses. They divided the enormous plunder, allotting half to themselves and the rest to the persecuted, to orphans, widows, and the aged. [31]They collected the enemies' weapons and carefully stored them in suitable places; the rest of the spoils they carried to Jerusalem. [32]They also killed the commander of Timothy's forces, a most wicked man, who had done great harm to the Jews. [33]While celebrating the victory in their ancestral city, they burned both those who had set fire to the sacred gates and Callisthenes, who had taken refuge in a little house; so he received the reward his wicked deeds deserved.

Humiliation of Nicanor

[34*]The accursed Nicanor, who had brought the thousand slave dealers to buy the Jews, [35]after being humbled through the Lord's help by those whom he had thought of no account, laid aside his fine clothes and fled alone across country like a runaway slave, until he reached Antioch. He was eminently successful in destroying his own army. [36]So he who had promised to

provide tribute for the Romans by the capture of the people of Jerusalem testified that the Jews had a champion, and that they were invulnerable for the very reason that they followed the laws laid down by him.

Punishment and Death of Antiochus

9 [1*†]ABOUT that time Antiochus retreated in disgrace from the region of Persia. [2]He had entered the city called Persepolis and attempted to rob the temple and gain control of the city. Thereupon the people had swift recourse to arms, and Antiochus' men were routed, so that in the end Antiochus was put to flight by the natives and forced to beat a shameful retreat. [3]On his arrival in Ecbatana, he learned what had happened to Nicanor and to Timothy's forces. [4]Overcome with anger, he planned to make the Jews suffer for the injury done by those who had put him to flight. Therefore he ordered his charioteer to drive without stopping until he finished the journey.

Yet the condemnation of Heaven rode with him, since he said in his arrogance, "I will make Jerusalem the common graveyard of the Jews as soon as I arrive there." [5*]So the all-seeing Lord, the God of Israel, struck him down with an unseen but incurable blow; for scarcely had he uttered those words when he was seized with excruciating pains in his bowels and sharp internal torment, [6]a fit punishment for him who had tortured the bowels of others with many barbarous torments. [7]Far from giving up his insolence, he was all the more filled with arrogance. Breathing fire in his rage against the Jews, he gave orders to drive even faster. As a result he hurtled from the dashing chariot, and every part of his body was racked by the violent fall. [8*]Thus he who previously, in his superhuman presumption, thought he could command the waves of the sea, and imagined he could weigh the mountaintops in his scales, was now thrown to the ground and had to be carried on a litter, clearly manifesting to all the power of God. [9*]The body of this impious man swarmed with worms, and while he was still alive in hideous torments, his flesh rotted off, so that the entire army was sickened by the stench of his corruption. [10]Shortly before, he had thought that he could reach the stars of heaven, and now, no one could endure to transport the man because of this intolerable stench.

[11]At last, broken in spirit, he began to give up his excessive arrogance, and to gain some understanding,

---

† 8, 22: *Joseph*: called John in 1 Mc 2, 2; 9, 36.38; this paragraph interrupts the story of Nicanor's defeat, which is resumed in v 34. The purpose of the author apparently is to group together the defeats suffered by the Syrians on various occasions. Battles against Timothy are recounted in 1 Mc 5, 37-44 and 2 Mc 12, 10-25; against Bacchides, in 1 Mc 7, 8-20.

9, 1-28: In order to keep together the various accounts of God's punishment of the persecutors of his people, the author places here the stories of Antiochus' illness and death (in actuality the king died only after the purification of the temple; cf 1 Mc 4, 36-59; 6, 1-16; 2 Mc 10, 1-8); of Judas' campaigns in Idumea and Transjordan; cf 1 Mc 5, 1-51; 2 Mc 10, 14-38; and of the first expedition of Lysias (1 Mc 4, 26-35; 2 Mc 11, 1-15).

23: 1 Mc 3, 48.
34f: 8, 23f; 1 Mc 7, 26.
9/1-29: 1, 12-17; 1 Mc 6, 1-13.
5: Acts 12, 20-23.
8: Jb 38, 8-11; Ps 65, 6f; Is 40, 12.
9: Acts 12, 23.

under the scourge of God, for he was racked with pain unceasingly. [12]When he could no longer bear his own stench, he said, "It is right to be subject to God, and not to think one's mortal self divine." [13]Then this vile man vowed to the Lord, who would no longer have mercy on him, [14]that he would set free the holy city, toward which he had been hurrying with the intention of leveling it to the ground and making it a common graveyard; [15]he would put on perfect equality with the Athenians all the Jews, whom he had judged not even worthy of burial, but fit only to be thrown out with their children to be eaten by vultures and wild animals; [16]he would adorn with the finest offerings the holy temple which he had previously despoiled; he would restore all the sacred vessels many times over; and would provide from his own revenues the expenses required for the sacrifices. [17]Besides all this, he would become a Jew himself and visit every inhabited place to proclaim there the power of God. [18]But since God's punishment had justly come upon him, his sufferings were not lessened, so he lost hope for himself and wrote the following letter to the Jews in the form of a supplication. It reads thus:

[19]†"To my esteemed Jewish citizens, Antiochus, their king and general, sends hearty greetings and best wishes for their health and happiness. [20]If you and your children are well and your affairs are going as you wish, I thank God very much, for my hopes are in heaven. [21]Now that I am ill, I recall with affection the esteem and good will you bear me. On returning from the regions of Persia, I fell victim to a troublesome illness; so I thought it necessary to form plans for the general welfare of all. [22]Actually, I do not despair about my health, since I have great hopes of recovering from my illness. [23]Nevertheless, I know that my father, whenever he went on campaigns in the hinterland, would name his successor, [24]so that, if anything unexpected happened or any unwelcome news came, the people throughout the realm would know to whom the government had been entrusted, and so not be disturbed. [25]†I am also bearing in mind that the neighboring rulers, especially those on the borders of our kingdom, are on the watch for opportunities and waiting to see what will happen. I have therefore appointed as king my son Antiochus, whom I have often before entrusted and commended to most of you, when I made hurried visits to the outlying provinces. I have written to him the letter copied below. [26]Therefore I beg and entreat each of you to remember the general and individual benefits you have received, and to continue to show good will toward me and my son. [27]I am confident that, following my policy, he will treat you with mildness and kindness in his relations with you."

[28]So this murderer and blasphemer, after extreme sufferings, such as he had inflicted on others, died a miserable death in the mountains of a foreign land. [29]His foster brother Philip brought the body home;

but fearing Antiochus' son, he later withdrew into Egypt, to Ptolemy Philometor.

Purification of Temple and City

10 [1]*WHEN Maccabeus and his companions, under the Lord's leadership, had recovered the temple and the city, [2]they destroyed the altars erected by the Gentiles in the marketplace and the sacred enclosures. [3]†After purifying the temple, they made a new altar. Then, with fire struck from flint, they offered sacrifice for the first time in two years, burned incense, and lighted lamps. They also set out the showbread. [4]When they had done this, they prostrated themselves and begged the Lord that they might never again fall into such misfortunes, and that if they should sin at any time, he might chastise them with moderation and not hand them over to blasphemous and barbarous Gentiles. [5]On the anniversary of the day on which the temple had been profaned by the Gentiles, that is, the twenty-fifth of the same month Chislev, the purification of the temple took place. [6]The Jews celebrated joyfully for eight days as on the feast of Booths, remembering how, a little while before, they had spent the feast of Booths living like wild animals in caves on the mountains. [7]Carrying rods entwined with leaves, green branches and palms, they sang hymns of grateful praise to him who had brought about the purification of his own Place. [8]By public edict and decree they prescribed that the whole Jewish nation should celebrate these days every year.

VI: RENEWED PERSECUTION

Death of Ptolemy

[9]*SUCH WAS THE END OF ANTIOCHUS surnamed Epiphanes. [10]Now we shall relate what happened under Antiochus Eupator, the son of that godless man, and shall give a summary of the chief evils caused by the wars. [11]When Eupator succeeded to the kingdom, he put a certain Lysias in charge of the government as commander-in-chief of Coelesyria and Phoenicia. [12]†Ptolemy, surnamed Macron, had taken the lead in treating the Jews fairly because of the previous injustice that had been done them, and he endeavored to have peaceful relations with them. [13]As a result, he

---

† 9, 19-27: Despite the statement in v 18, this letter is not really a *supplication*. It is rather a notification to all the king's subjects of the appointment of his son as his successor and a request that they be loyal to the new king. Apparently the same letter, which has every appearance of being authentic, was sent to the various peoples throughout the kingdom, with only a few words of address changed for each group.

9, 25: *The letter copied below*: not included in the text of 2 Mc.

10, 3: *Two years*: three years according to 1 Mc 1, 54 and 4, 52.

10, 12: *Ptolemy Macron*: son of Dorymenes (4, 45), was formerly hostile to the Jews (6, 8).

was accused before Eupator by the King's Friends. In fact, on all sides he heard himself called a traitor for having abandoned Cyprus, which Philometor had entrusted to him, and for having gone over to Antiochus Epiphanes. Since he could not command the respect due to his high office, he ended his life by taking poison.

Victory over the Idumeans

¹⁴†When Gorgias became governor of the region, he employed foreign troops and used every opportunity to attack the Jews. ¹⁵*At the same time the Idumeans, who held some important strongholds, were harassing the Jews; they welcomed fugitives from Jerusalem and endeavored to continue the war. ¹⁶Maccabeus and his companions, after public prayers asking God to be their ally, moved quickly against the strongholds of the Idumeans. ¹⁷Attacking vigorously, they gained control of the places, drove back all who manned the walls, and cut down those who opposed them, killing as many as twenty thousand men. ¹⁸When at least nine thousand took refuge in two very strong towers, containing everything necessary to sustain a siege, ¹⁹Maccabeus left Simon and Joseph, along with Zacchaeus and his men, in sufficient numbers to besiege them, while he himself went off to places where he was more urgently needed. ²⁰But some of the men in Simon's force who were money lovers let themselves be bribed by some of the men in the towers; on receiving seventy thousand drachmas, they allowed a number of them to escape. ²¹When Maccabeus was told what had happened, he assembled the rulers of the people and accused those men of having sold their kinsmen for money by setting their enemies free to fight against them. ²²So he put them to death as traitors, and without delay captured the two towers. ²³As he was successful at arms in all his undertakings, he destroyed more than twenty thousand men in the two strongholds.

Victory over Timothy

²⁴†Timothy, who had previously been defeated by the Jews, gathered a tremendous force of foreign troops and collected a large number of cavalry from Asia; then he appeared in Judea, ready to conquer it by force. ²⁵At his approach, Maccabeus and his men made supplication to God, sprinkling earth upon their heads and girding their loins in sackcloth. ²⁶*Lying prostrate at the foot of the altar, they begged him to be gracious to them, and to be an enemy to their enemies, and a foe to their foes, as the law declares. ²⁷After the prayer, they took up their arms and advanced a considerable distance from the city, halting when they were close to the enemy. ²⁸†As soon as dawn broke, the armies joined battle, the one having as pledge of success and victory not only their valor

but also their reliance on the Lord, and the other taking fury as their leader in the fight.

²⁹*In the midst of the fierce battle, there appeared to the enemy from the heavens five majestic men riding on golden-bridled horses, who led the Jews on. ³⁰They surrounded Maccabeus, and shielding him with their own armor, kept him from being wounded. They shot arrows and hurled thunderbolts at the enemy, who were bewildered and blinded, thrown into confusion and routed. ³¹Twenty-five hundred of their foot soldiers and six hundred of their horsemen were slain. ³²*Timothy, however, fled to a well-fortified stronghold called Gazara, where Chaereas was in command. ³³For four days Maccabeus and his men eagerly besieged the fortress. ³⁴Those inside, relying on the strength of the place, kept repeating outrageous blasphemies and uttering abominable words. ³⁵When the fifth day dawned, twenty young men in the army of Maccabeus, angered over such blasphemies, bravely stormed the wall and with savage fury cut down everyone they encountered. ³⁶Others who climbed up the same way swung around on the defenders, taking the besieged in the rear; they put the towers to the torch, spread the fire and burned the blasphemers alive. Still others broke down the gates and let in the rest of the troops, who took possession of the city. ³⁷†Timothy had hidden in a cistern, but they killed him, along with his brother Chaereas, and Apollophanes. ³⁸On completing these exploits, they blessed, with hymns of grateful praise, the Lord who shows great kindness to Israel and grants them victory.

Defeat of Lysias

11 ¹*†VERY soon afterward, Lysias, guardian and Kinsman of the king and head of the government, being greatly displeased at what had happened, ²mustered about eighty thousand infantry and all his cavalry and marched against the Jews. His plan was to make Jerusalem a Greek settlement; ³to levy tribute on the temple, as he did on the sanctuaries of the other nations; and to put the high priesthood up for sale every year. ⁴He did not take God's power into account at all, but felt exultant confidence in his myriads of foot soldiers, his thousands of horsemen, and his eighty elephants. ⁵So he invaded Judea, and when he reached Beth-zur, a fortified place about twenty miles from Jerusalem, launched a strong attack against it. ⁶*When Maccabeus and his men learned that Lysias was besieging the strongholds, they and all the

---

† 10, 14-23: Probably the same campaign of Judas against the Idumeans that is mentioned in 1 Mc 5, 1-3.

10, 24: *Timothy, . . . previously . . . defeated by the Jews:* as recounted in 8, 30ff.

10, 28: *As soon as dawn broke:* the same battle at dawn as in 1 Mc 5, 30-34.

10, 37: *Timothy . . . they killed:* apparently, the same Timothy is still alive in 12, 2.18-25. The present passage is not in chronological order; Gazara, v 32 (Gezer) was not captured by the Jews until much later (cf 1 Mc 9, 50ff; 13, 53).

11, 1-12: The defeat of Lysias at Beth-zur probably occurred before the purification of the temple; cf 1 Mc 4, 26-35.

✻
15-23: 1 Mc 5, 3ff.
    26: Ex 23, 22.
29f: 3, 24ff; 5, 2f; 10, 29f;
    11, 8.

    32: 1 Mc 13, 43-48.
11/1-12: 1 Mc 4, 26-35.
    6: Ex 23, 20.

people begged the Lord with lamentations and tears to send a good angel to save Israel. [7]Maccabeus himself was the first to take up arms, and he exhorted the others to join him in risking their lives to help their kinsmen. Then they resolutely set out together. [8]*Suddenly, while they were still near Jerusalem, a horseman appeared at their head, clothed in white garments and brandishing gold weapons. [9]Then all of them together thanked God for his mercy, and their hearts were filled with such courage that they were ready to assault not only men, but the most savage beasts, yes, even walls of iron. [10]Now that the Lord had shown his mercy toward them, they advanced in battle order with the aid of their heavenly ally. [11]Hurling themselves upon the enemy like lions, they laid low eleven thousand foot soldiers and sixteen hundred horsemen, and put all the rest to flight. [12]Most of those who got away were wounded and stripped of their arms, while Lysias himself escaped only by shameful flight.

Peace with the Syrians

[13]*But Lysias was not a stupid man. He reflected on the defeat he had suffered, and came to realize that the Hebrews were invincible because the mighty God was their ally. He therefore sent a message [14]persuading them to settle everything on just terms, and promising to persuade the king also, and to induce him to become their friend. [15]Maccabeus, solicitous for the common good, agreed to all that Lysias proposed; and the king, on his part, granted in behalf of the Jews all the written requests of Maccabeus to Lysias.

Official Letters

[16]These are the terms of the letter which Lysias wrote to the Jews: "Lysias sends greetings to the Jewish people. [17]John and Absalom, your envoys, have presented your signed communication and asked about the matters contained in it. [18]Whatever had to be referred to the king I called to his attention, and the things that were acceptable he has granted. [19]If you maintain your loyalty to the government, I will endeavor to further your interests in the future. [20]On the details of these matters I have authorized my representatives, as well as your envoys, to confer with you. [21]†Farewell." The year one hundred and forty-eight, the twenty-fourth of Dioscorinthius.

[22]The king's letter read thus: "King Antiochus sends greetings to his brother Lysias. [23]Now that our father has taken his place among the gods, we wish the subjects of our kingdom to be undisturbed in conducting their own affairs. [24]We understand that the Jews do not agree with our father's policy concerning Greek customs but prefer their own way of life. They are petitioning us to let them retain their own customs. [25]Since we desire that this people too should be undisturbed, our decision is that their temple be restored to them and that they live in keeping with the customs of their ancestors. [26]Accordingly, please send them

messengers to give them our assurances of friendship, so that, when they learn of our decision, they may have nothing to worry about but may contentedly go about their own business."

[27]The king's letter to the people was as follows: "King Antiochus sends greetings to the Jewish senate and to the rest of the Jews. [28]If you are well, it is what we desire. We too are in good health. [29]Menelaus has told us of your wish to return home and attend to your own affairs. [30]Therefore, those who return by the thirtieth of Xanthicus will have our assurance of full permission [31]to observe their dietary laws and other laws, just as before, and none of the Jews shall be molested in any way for faults committed through ignorance. [32]I have also sent Menelaus to reassure you. [33]†Farewell." In the year one hundred and forty-eight, the fifteenth of Xanthicus.

[34]The Romans also sent them a letter as follows: "Quintus Memmius and Titus Manius, legates of the Romans, send greetings to the Jewish people. [35]Whatever Lysias, kinsman of the king, has granted you, we also approve. [36]But the matters on which he passed judgment should be submitted to the king. As soon as you have considered them, send someone to us with your decisions so that we may present them to your advantage, for we are on our way to Antioch. [37]Make haste, then, to send us those who can inform us of your intentions. [38]†Farewell." In the year one hundred and forty-eight, the fifteenth of Xanthicus.

Persecution Renewed

12 [1]AFTER these agreements were made, Lysias returned to the king, and the Jews went about their farming. [2]†But some of the local governors, Timothy and Apollonius, son of Gennaeus, as also Hieronymus and Demophon, to say nothing of Nicanor, the commander of the Cyprians, would not allow them to live in peace.

[3]Some people of Joppa also committed this outrage: they invited the Jews who lived among them, together with their wives and children, to embark on boats which they had provided. There was no hint of enmity toward them; [4]this was done by public vote of the city. When the Jews, not suspecting treachery and wishing to live on friendly terms, accepted the invitation, the people of Joppa took them out to sea and drowned at least two hundred of them.

---

† 11, 21: *The year one hundred and forty-eight:* 164 B. C. The reading of the name of the month and its position in the calendar are uncertain.

11, 33: The date, which is the same as the date of the Romans' letter (v 38), cannot be correct. The king's letter must be connected with the peace treaty of the year 149 of the Seleucid era, i. e., 163 B. C. Perhaps the mention of the month of Xanthicus in the body of the letter (v 30) caused the date of the Romans' letter to be transferred to this one.

11, 38: The date is March 12, 164 B. C.

12, 2: *Apollonius, son of Gennaeus:* not the Apollonius who was the son of Menestheus (4, 21). *Nicanor:* probably distinct from the Nicanor of 14, 2.

✿   8: 3, 24ff; 5, 2f; 10, 29f.   13-33: 1 Mc 6, 57-61.

Activity of Judas

[5]As soon as Judas heard of the barbarous deed perpetrated against his countrymen, he summoned his men; [6]and after calling upon God, the just judge, he marched against the murderers of his kinsmen. In a night attack he set the harbor on fire, burnt the boats, and put to the sword those who had taken refuge there. [7]When the gates of the town were shut, he withdrew, intending to come back later and wipe out the entire population of Joppa.

[8]On hearing that the men of Jamnia planned to give like treatment to the Jews who lived among them, [9]he attacked the Jamnian populace by night, setting fire to the harbor and the fleet, so that the glow of the flames was visible as far as Jerusalem, thirty miles away.

[10]*†When the Jews had gone about a mile from there in the campaign against Timothy, they were attacked by Arabs numbering at least five thousand foot soldiers, and five hundred horsemen. [11]After a hard fight, Judas and his companions, with God's help, were victorious. The defeated nomads begged Judas to make friends with them and promised to supply the Jews with cattle and to help them in every other way. [12]Realizing that they could indeed be useful in many respects, Judas agreed to make peace with them. After the pledge of friendship had been exchanged, the Arabs withdrew to their tents.

[13]He also attacked a certain city called Caspin, fortified with earthworks and ramparts and inhabited by a mixed population of Gentiles. [14]Relying on the strength of their walls and their supply of provisions, the besieged treated Judas and his men with contempt, insulting them and even uttering blasphemies and profanity. [15]*But Judas and his men invoked the aid of the great Sovereign of the world, who, in the day of Joshua, overthrew Jericho without battering-ram or siege machine; then they furiously stormed the ramparts. [16]Capturing the city by the will of God, they inflicted such indescribable slaughter on it that the adjacent pool, which was about a quarter of a mile wide, seemed to be filled with the blood that flowed into it.

[17]*†When they had gone on some ninety miles, they reached Charax, where there were certain Jews known as Toubiani. [18]But they did not find Timothy in that region, for he had already departed from there without having done anything except to leave behind in one place a very strong garrison. [19]But Dositheus and Sosipater, two of Maccabeus' captains, marched out and destroyed the force of more than ten thousand men that Timothy had left in the stronghold. [20]Meanwhile, Maccabeus divided his army into cohorts, with a commander over each cohort, and went in pursuit of Timothy, who had a force of a hundred and twenty thousand foot soldiers and twenty-five hundred horsemen. [21]When Timothy learned of the approach of Ju-

das, he sent on ahead of him the women and children, as well as the baggage, to a place called Karnion, which was hard to besiege and even hard to reach because of the difficult terrain of that region. [22]But when Judas' first cohort appeared, the enemy was overwhelmed with fear and terror at the manifestation of the All-seeing. Scattering in every direction, they rushed away in such headlong flight that in many cases they wounded one another, pierced by the swords of their own men. [23]Judas pressed the pursuit vigorously, putting the sinners to the sword and destroying as many as thirty thousand men.

[24]Timothy himself fell into the hands of the men under Dositheus and Sosipater; but with great cunning, he asked them to spare his life and let him go, because he had in his power the parents and relatives of many of them, and could make these suffer. [25]When he had fully confirmed his solemn pledge to restore them unharmed, they let him go for the sake of saving their brethren.

Further Successes

[26]†Judas then marched to Karnion and the shrine of Atargatis, where he killed twenty-five thousand people. [27]*After the defeat and destruction of these, he moved his army to Ephron, a fortified city inhabited by people of many nationalities. Robust young men took up their posts in defense of the walls, from which they fought valiantly; inside were large supplies of machines and missiles. [28]But the Jews, invoking the Sovereign who forcibly shatters the might of his enemies, got possession of the city and slaughtered twenty-five thousand of the people in it. [29]†Then they set out from there and hastened on to Scythopolis, seventy-five miles from Jerusalem. [30]But when the Jews who lived there testified to the good will shown by the Scythopolitans and to their kind treatment even in times of adversity, [31]Judas and his men thanked them and exhorted them to be well disposed to their race in the future also. Finally they arrived in Jerusalem, shortly before the feast of Weeks.

[32]After this feast called Pentecost, they lost no time in marching against Gorgias, governor of Idumea, [33]who opposed them with three thousand foot soldiers and four hundred horsemen. [34]In the ensuing battle, a few of the Jews were slain. [35]†A man called Dositheus, a powerful horseman and one of Bacenor's men, caught hold of Gorgias, grasped his military cloak and dragged him along by main strength, intending to

---

† 12, 10: *From there:* not from the aforesaid Jamnia (vv 8f) or Joppa (vv 3-7), but from a place in Transjordan; vv 10-26 parallel the account given in 1 Mc 5, 9-13.24-54 of Judas' campaign in northern Transjordan.

12, 17: *Certain Jews known as Toubiani:* because they lived "in the land of Tob" (1 Mc 5, 13).

12, 26: *Atargatis:* a Syrian goddess, represented by the body of a fish.

12, 29: *Scythopolis:* the Greek name of the city of Beth-shan; cf 1 Mc 5, 52.

12, 35: *One of Bacenor's men:* certain ancient witnesses to the text have "one of the Toubiani"; cf v 17.

---

*
12/10-16: 1 Mc 5, 24-36.   17: 1 Mc 5, 13.
  15: Jos 6, 1-21.   27-31: 5, 45-54.
  17-26: 1 Mc 5, 37-44.

capture the vile wretch alive, when a Thracian horse-man attacked Dositheus and cut off his arm at the shoulder. Then Gorgias fled to Marisa. [36]After Esdris and his men had been fighting for a long time and were weary, Judas called upon the Lord to show him-self their ally and leader in the battle. [37]Then, raising a battle cry in his ancestral language, and with songs, he charged Gorgias' men when they were not expect-ing it and put them to flight.

Expiation for the Dead

[38]Judas rallied his army and went to the city of Adullam. As the week was ending, they purified them-selves according to custom and kept the sabbath there. [39]On the following day, since the task had now be-come urgent, Judas and his men went to gather up the bodies of the slain and bury them with their kins-men in their ancestral tombs. [40]*But under the tunic of each of the dead they found amulets sacred to the idols of Jamnia, which the law forbids the Jews to wear. So it was clear to all that this was why these men had been slain. [41]They all therefore praised the ways of the Lord, the just judge who brings to light the things that are hidden. [42]†Turning to supplication, they prayed that the sinful deed might be fully blotted out. The noble Judas warned the soldiers to keep themselves free from sin, for they had seen with their own eyes what had happened because of the sin of those who had fallen. [43]He then took up a collection among all his soldiers, amounting to two thousand silver drachmas, which he sent to Jerusalem to provide for an expiatory sacrifice. In doing this he acted in a very excellent and noble way, inasmuch as he had the resurrection of the dead in view; [44]for if he were not expecting the fallen to rise again, it would have been useless and foolish to pray for them in death. [45]But if he did this with a view to the splendid reward that awaits those who had gone to rest in godliness, it was a holy and pious thought. [46]Thus he made atonement for the dead that they might be freed from this sin.

The Syrians Invade Judea

13 [1]†IN the year one hundred and forty-nine, Judas and his men learned that Antiochus Eupator was invading Judea with a large force, [2]*†and that with him was Lysias, his guardian, who was in charge of the government. They led a Greek army of one hundred and ten thousand foot soldiers, fifty-three hundred horsemen, twenty-two elephants, and three hundred chariots armed with scythes.

Death of Menelaus

[3]Menelaus also joined them, and with great duplic-ity kept urging Antiochus on, not for the welfare of his country, but in the hope of being established in office. [4]*†But the King of kings aroused the anger of Antiochus against the scoundrel. When the king was shown by Lysias that Menelaus was to blame for all the trouble, he ordered him to be taken to Beroea and executed there in the customary local method. [5]†There is at that place a tower seventy-five feet high, full of ashes, with a circular rim sloping down steeply on all sides toward the ashes. [6]A man guilty of sacrilege or notorious for certain other crimes is brought up there and then hurled down to destruction. [7]In such a man-ner was Menelaus, the transgressor of the law, fated to die; he was deprived even of decent burial. [8]It was altogether just that he who had committed so many sins against the altar with its pure fire and ashes should meet his death in ashes.

Skirmish near Modein

[9]The king was advancing, his mind full of savage plans for inflicting on the Jews worse things than those they suffered in his father's time. [10]When Judas learned of this, he urged the people to call upon the Lord night and day, to help them now, if ever, [11]when they were about to be deprived of their law, their country, and their holy temple; and not to allow this nation, which had just begun to revive, to be sub-jected again to blasphemous Gentiles. [12]When they had all joined in doing this, and had implored the merciful Lord continuously with weeping and fasting and prostrations for three days, Judas encouraged them and told them to stand ready. [13]After a private meeting with the elders, he decided that, before the king's army could invade Judea and take possession of the city, the Jews should march out and settle the matter with God's help. [14]Leaving the outcome to the Creator of the world, and exhorting his followers to fight nobly to death for the laws, the temple, the city, the country, and the government, he pitched his camp near Modein. [15]*†Giving his men the battle cry "God's Victory," he made a night attack on the king's pavilion with a picked force of the bravest young men and killed about two thousand in the camp. They also slew the lead elephant and its rider. [16]†Finally they with-

---

† 12, 42-46: This is the earliest statement of the doctrine that prayers (v 42) and sacrifices (v 43) for the dead are efficacious. The statement is made here, however, only for the purpose of proving that Judas believed in the resurrection of the just (7, 9.14.23.36). That is, he believed that expiation could be made for certain sins of otherwise good men—soldiers who had given their lives for God's cause. Thus, they could share in the resur-rection. His belief was similar to, but not quite the same as, the Catholic doctrine of purgatory.

13, 1: *In the year one hundred and forty-nine:* 163-162 B. C.

13, 2: *They led:* the Greek means literally "Each (of them) led," but it is unlikely that the author meant the already im-mense numbers to be doubled; the numbers are similar to those in 1 Mc 6, 30.

13, 4: *Beroea:* the Greek name of Aleppo.

13, 5: *Ashes:* probably smoldering ashes; the *tower* resembles the ancient Persian fire towers.

13, 15: *Slew:* literally "stabbed"; the deed was done by Eleazar (1 Mc 6, 43-46).

13, 16: *They withdrew in triumph:* according to 1 Mc 6, 47 they fled.

---

*
　　40: Dt 7, 25.　　　　　　　19, 16.
　13/2: 1 Mc 6, 30.　　　15: 1 Mc 6, 43-46.
　　　4: 1 Tm 6, 15; Rv 17, 14;

drew in triumph, having filled the camp with terror and confusion. [17]Day was just breaking when this was accomplished with the help and protection of the Lord.

Treaty with Antiochus V

[18]*The king, having had a taste of the Jews' daring, tried to take their positions by a stratagem. [19]So he marched against Beth-zur, a strong fortress of the Jews; but he was driven back, checked, and defeated. [20]Judas then sent supplies to the men inside, [21]†but Rhodocus, of the Jewish army, betrayed military secrets to the enemy. He was found out, arrested, and imprisoned. [22]The king made a second attempt by negotiating with the men of Beth-zur. After giving them his pledge and receiving theirs, he withdrew [23]and attacked Judas and his men. But he was defeated. Next he heard that Philip, who was left in charge of the government in Antioch, had rebelled. Dismayed, he parleyed with the Jews, submitted to their terms, and swore to observe their rights. Having come to this agreement, he offered a sacrifice, and honored the temple with a generous donation. [24]†He approved of Maccabeus and left him as military and civil governor of the territory from Ptolemais to the region of the Gerrenes. [25]When he came to Ptolemais, the people of that city were angered by the peace treaty; in fact they were so indignant that they wanted to annul its provisions. [26]But Lysias took the platform, defended the treaty as well as he could, and won them over by persuasion. After calming them and gaining their good will, he returned to Antioch.

That is how the king's attack and withdrawal went.

Antagonism of Alcimus

14 [1]*†THREE years later, Judas and his men learned that Demetrius, son of Seleucus, had sailed into the port of Tripolis with a powerful army and a fleet, [2]and that he had occupied the country, after doing away with Antiochus and his guardian Lysias.

[3]A certain Alcimus, a former high priest, who had willfully incurred defilement at the time of the revolt, realized that there was no way for him to salvage his position and regain access to the holy altar. [4]*So he went to King Demetrius in the year one hundred and fifty-one and presented him with a gold crown and a palm branch, as well as some of the customary olive branches from the temple. On that occasion he kept quiet. [5]But he found an opportunity to further his mad scheme when he was invited to the council by Demetrius and questioned about the dispositions and intentions of the Jews. He replied: [6]"Those Jews called Hasideans, led by Judas Maccabeus, are warmongers, who stir up sedition and keep the kingdom from enjoying peace and quiet. [7]For this reason, now that I am

deprived of my ancestral dignity, that is to say, the high priesthood, I have come here—[8]first, out of my genuine concern for the king's interests, and secondly, out of consideration for my own countrymen, since our entire nation is suffering great affliction from the unreasonable conduct of the people just mentioned. [9]When you have informed yourself in detail on these matters, O king, act in the interest of our country and its hard-pressed people with the same gracious consideration that you show toward all. [10]As long as Judas is around, it is impossible for the state to enjoy peace." [11]When he had said this, the other Friends who were hostile to Judas quickly added fuel to Demetrius' indignation.

Dealings with Nicanor

[12]*The king immediately chose Nicanor, who had been in command of the elephants, and appointed him governor of Judea. He sent him off [13]with orders to put Judas to death, to disperse his followers, and to set up Alcimus as high priest of the great temple. [14]†The Gentiles from Judea, who would have banished Judas, came flocking to Nicanor, thinking that the misfortunes and calamities of the Jews would mean prosperity for themselves. [15]*When the Jews heard of Nicanor's coming, and that the Gentiles were rallying to him, they sprinkled themselves with earth and prayed to him who established his people forever, and who always comes to the aid of his heritage. [16]At their leader's command, they set out at once and came upon the enemy at the village of Adasa. [17]Judas' brother Simon had engaged Nicanor, but because of the sudden appearance of the enemy suffered a slight repulse. [18]However, when Nicanor heard of the valor of Judas and his men, and the great courage with which they fought for their country, he shrank from deciding the issue by bloodshed. [19]So he sent Posidonius, Theodotus and Mattathias to arrange an agreement. [20]After a long discussion of the terms, each leader communicated them to his troops; and when general agreement was expressed, they assented to the treaty. [21]A day was set on which the leaders would meet by themselves. From each side a chariot came forward and thrones were set in place. [22]Judas had posted armed men in readiness at suitable points for fear that the enemy might suddenly carry out some treacherous plan. But the conference was held in the proper way. [23]Nicanor stayed on in Jerusalem, where he did nothing out of place. He got rid of the throngs of ordinary

---

† 13, 21: *Military secrets:* probably about the lack of provisions in the besieged city; cf 1 Mc 6, 49.

13, 24: The Greek text is uncertain and may be rendered: "He approved of Maccabeus, then left Hegemonides as governor of the territory. . . ." *Gerrenes:* probably the inhabitants of Gerar, southeast of Gaza.

14, 1: *Three years later:* actually, *Demetrius* (I Soter), *son of Seleucus* (IV), landed at *Tripolis* in the year 151 of the Seleucid era (v 4), i. e., 162-161 B. C.; cf 1 Mc 7, 1-7.

14, 14: *Who would have banished Judas:* the meaning of the Greek is uncertain; some render it: "who had fled before Judas."

---

* 18-23: 1 Mc 6, 48-53.   12f: 8, 9; 1 Mc 3, 38f.
14/1-11: 1 Mc 7, 1-7.   15-19: 1 Mc 7, 26-32.
     4: 1 Mc 7, 7.25.

people who gathered around him; 24but he always kept Judas in his company, for he had a cordial affection for the man. 25He urged him to marry and have children; so Judas married, settled down, and shared the common life.

Threats against Judas

26When Alcimus saw their friendship for each other, he took the treaty that had been made, went to Demetrius, and said that Nicanor was plotting against the state, and that he had appointed Judas, the conspirator against the kingdom, to be his successor. 27Stirred up by the villain's calumnies, the king became enraged. He wrote to Nicanor, stating that he was displeased with the treaty, and ordering him to send Maccabeus as a prisoner to Antioch without delay. 28When this message reached Nicanor he was dismayed, for he hated to break his agreement with a man who had done no wrong. 29However, there was no way of opposing the king, so he watched for an opportunity to carry out this order by a stratagem. 30But Maccabeus noticed that Nicanor was becoming cool in his dealings with him, and acting with unaccustomed rudeness when they met; he concluded that this coldness betokened no good. So he gathered together a large number of his men, and went into hiding from Nicanor. 31*When Nicanor realized that he had been disgracefully outwitted by the man, he went to the great and holy temple, at a time when the priests were offering the customary sacrifices, and ordered them to surrender Judas. 32As they declared under oath that they did not know where the wanted man was, 33he raised his right hand toward the temple and swore this oath: "If you do not hand Judas over to me as prisoner, I will level this shrine of God to the ground; I will tear down the altar, and erect here a splendid temple to Dionysus." 34With these words he went away. The priests stretched out their hands toward heaven, calling upon the unfailing defender of our nation in these words: 35*"Lord of all, though you are in need of nothing, you have approved of a temple for your dwelling place among us. 36Therefore, O holy One, Lord of all holiness, preserve forever undefiled this house, which has been so recently purified."

The Story of Razis

37†A certain Razis, one of the elders of Jerusalem, was denounced to Nicanor as a patriot. A man highly regarded, he was called a father of the Jews because of his love for them. 38In the early days of the revolt, he had been convicted of Judaism, and had risked body and life in his ardent zeal for it. 39Nicanor, to show his detestation of the Jews, sent more than five hundred soldiers to arrest him. 40He thought that by arresting such a man he would deal the Jews a hard blow. 41But when these troops, on the point of captur-

ing the tower, were forcing the outer gate and calling for fire to set the door ablaze, Razis, now caught on all sides, turned his sword against himself, 42preferring to die nobly rather than fall into the hands of vile men and suffer outrages unworthy of his noble birth. 43In the excitement of the struggle he failed to strike exactly. So while the troops rushed in through the doors, he gallantly ran up to the top of the wall and with manly courage threw himself down into the crowd. 44But as they quickly drew back and left an opening, he fell into the middle of the empty space. 45Still breathing, and inflamed with anger, he got up and ran through the crowd, with blood gushing from his frightful wounds. 46*Then, standing on a steep rock, as he lost the last of his blood, he tore out his entrails and flung them with both hands into the crowd, calling upon the Lord of life and of spirit to give these back to him again. Such was the manner of his death.

Nicanor's Blasphemy

15 1WHEN Nicanor learned that Judas and his companions were in the territory of Samaria, he decided to attack them in all safety on the day of rest. 2The Jews who were forced to follow him pleaded, "Do not massacre them in that way, like a savage barbarian, but show respect for the day which the All-seeing has exalted with holiness above all other days." 3*At this the thrice-sinful wretch asked if there was a ruler in heaven who prescribed the keeping of the sabbath day. 4When they replied that there was indeed such a ruler in heaven, the living Lord himself, who commanded the observance of the sabbath day, 5he said, "I, on my part, am ruler on earth, and my orders are that you take up arms and carry out the king's business." Nevertheless he did not succeed in carrying out his cruel plan.

Fresh Hope

6†In his utter boastfulness and arrogance Nicanor had determined to erect a public monument of victory over Judas and his men. 7But Maccabeus remained confident, fully convinced that he would receive help from the Lord. 8He urged his men not to fear the enemy, but mindful of the help they had received from Heaven in the past, to expect that now, too, victory would be given them by the Almighty. 9†By encouraging them with words from the law and the prophets, and by reminding them of the battles they had already won, he filled them with fresh enthusiasm. 10Having stirred up their courage, he gave his orders and pointed out at the same time the perfidy of the Gentiles and their violation of oaths. 11When he had armed each of them, not so much with the safety of

† 14, 37-46: The story of Razis belongs to the "martyrology" class of literature; it is similar to the stories in 6, 18—7, 42.

15, 6: Public monument of victory: a heap of stones covered with the arms and armor of the fallen enemy.

15, 9: The law and the prophets: the first of the three parts of the Hebrew Scriptures, called the sacred books (1 Mc 12, 9).

* 31-36: 1 Mc 7, 33-38.　　46: 7, 9ff.
　35: Acts 17, 25.　　15/3: 1 Mc 7, 34.

shield and spear as with the encouragement of noble words, he cheered them all by relating a dream, a kind of vision, worthy of belief.

12*†What he saw was this: Onias, the former high priest, a good and virtuous man, modest in appearance, gentle in manners, distinguished in speech, and trained from childhood in every virtuous practice, was praying with outstretched arms for the whole Jewish community. **13**Then in the same way another man appeared, distinguished by his white hair and dignity, and with an air about him of extraordinary, majestic authority. **14†**Onias then said of him, "This is God's prophet Jeremiah, who loves his brethren and fervently prays for his people and their holy city." Stretching out his right hand, **15**Jeremiah presented a gold sword to Judas. As he gave it to him he said, **16**"Accept this holy sword as a gift from God; with it you shall crush your adversaries."

Defeat and Death of Nicanor

17Encouraged by Judas' noble words, which had power to instill valor and stir young hearts to courage, the Jews determined not to delay, but to charge gallantly and decide the issue by hand-to-hand combat with the utmost courage, since their city and its temple with the sacred vessels were in danger. **18***They were not so much concerned about their wives and children or their brothers and kinsmen; their first and foremost fear was for the consecrated sanctuary. **19**Those who remained in the city suffered a like agony, anxious as they were about the battle in the open country.

20Everyone now awaited the decisive moment. The enemy were already drawing near with their troops drawn up in battle line, their elephants placed in strategic positions, and their cavalry stationed on the flanks. **21**Maccabeus, contemplating the hosts before him, their elaborate equipment, and the fierceness of their elephants, stretched out his hands toward heaven and called upon the Lord who works miracles; for he knew that it is not through arms but through the Lord's decision that victory is won by those who deserve it. **22***He prayed to him thus: "You, O Lord, sent your angel in the days of King Hezekiah of Judea, and he slew a hundred and eighty-five thousand men of Sennacherib's army. **23**Sovereign of the heavens, send a good angel now to spread fear and dread before us. **24**By the might of your arm may those be struck down who have blasphemously come against your holy people!" With this he ended his prayer.

25*Nicanor and his men advanced to the sound of trumpets and battle songs. **26**But Judas and his men met the army with supplication and prayers. **27**Fighting with their hands and praying to God with their hearts, they laid low at least thirty-five thousand, and rejoiced greatly over this manifestation of God's power. **28**When the battle was over and they were joyfully departing, they discovered Nicanor lying there in all his armor; **29**so they raised tumultuous shouts in their native tongue in praise of the divine Sovereign.

30Then Judas, who was ever in body and soul the chief defender of his fellow citizens, and had maintained from youth his affection for his countrymen, ordered Nicanor's head and whole right arm to be cut off and taken to Jerusalem. **31†**When he arrived there, he assembled his countrymen, stationed the priests before the altar, and sent for those in the citadel. **32**He showed them the vile Nicanor's head and the wretched blasphemer's arm that had been boastfully stretched out against the holy dwelling of the Almighty. **33**He cut out the tongue of the godless Nicanor, saying he would feed it piecemeal to the birds and would hang up the other wages of his folly opposite the temple. **34**At this, everyone looked toward heaven and praised the Lord who manifests his divine power, saying, "Blessed be he who has kept his own Place undefiled!"

35*Judas hung up Nicanor's head on the wall of the citadel, a clear and evident proof to all of the Lord's help. **36***†By public vote it was unanimously decreed never to let this day pass unobserved, but to celebrate it on the thirteenth day of the twelfth month, called Adar in Aramaic, the eve of Mordecai's Day.

VII: EPILOGUE

Author's Apology

37SINCE NICANOR'S DOINGS ended in this way, with the city remaining in possession of the Hebrews from that time on, I will bring my own story to an end here too. **38**If it is well written and to the point, that is what I wanted; if it is poorly done and mediocre, that is the best I could do. **39**Just as it is harmful to drink wine alone or water alone, whereas mixing wine with water makes a more pleasant drink that increases delight, so a skillfully composed story delights the ears of those who read the work. Let this, then, be the end.

---

† 15, 12: *Onias, the former high priest:* Onias III (3, 1-40). Evidently the author believed that the departed just were in some way alive even before the resurrection.

15, 14: *Jeremiah:* regarded by the postexilic Jews as one of the greatest figures in their history; cf 2, 1; Mt 16, 14. *Who . . . prays for his people:* a clear belief in the intercession of the saints.

15, 31: *Those in the citadel:* presumably Jewish soldiers; actually, the citadel was still in the possession of the Syrians.

15, 36: *Mordecai's Day:* the feast of Purim, celebrated on the fourteenth and fifteenth days of Adar (Est 9, 17-22).

* 12: 3, 1ff.
18: 1 Mc 4, 36.
22f: 8, 19; 2 Kgs 19, 35; Is 37, 36; I Mc 7, 40f.
25-36: 8, 39-50.
35: 1 Sm 31, 9f.
36: 1 Mc 7, 49.

THE HOLY
SACRIFICE

OF THE
MASS

*The events
of the Mass-drama
illustrated
with thirty photographs
in full color
and descriptive text*

The Mass

is, essentially, the renewal of Christ's infinite sacrifice of Redemption on Calvary. It is a true, but unbloody, sacrifice, in which the Body and Blood of Christ are offered to God under the appearance of bread and wine. On the Cross the sacrifice of Christ was physical and personal; in the Mass Christ is both priest and victim, and the sacrifice is made through the ministry of His priests. At the Last Supper Christ instituted the Sacrament of Holy Eucharist to continue the Sacrifice of the Cross in the Church so that the merits of Christ's death on the Cross, which was made for the redemption of mankind, could be made continually available to the faithful.

The Mass *is* the renewal of Christ's sacrifice; but it is more. It is a renewal and a making present of the entire redemptive life, death, resurrection and glorification of Jesus Christ. Our understanding of the mystery of redemption depends on human words and thought patterns. This means that we can understand the profound act of Christ in various ways. The sacraments are mysteries and their depths can never be encompassed by any human expressions. The basic "data" in any theological explanation of redemption remains the same: Jesus is one Person who is truly God and truly man. It is because of His coming-to-flesh (Incarnation) and His entire life of giving glory to God that we are saved. His total giving climaxed in His death on the cross which is inseparable from His bodily resurrection into glory. The mystery of Christ's "going to the Father" through His suffering, death, resurrection, and ascension is called the "Paschal Mystery" (or Easter mystery). It is this entire mystery which Christ makes dynamically present in each and every Mass. It is, therefore, true to say that the Mass is the renewal of the resurrection of Christ by which He raises us up and pledges eternal glory to us. It is true to say that the Mass is a fellowship by which the Christian community celebrates the real meaning of life in Christ which will culminate in glory. It is true to say that the Mass is a love-feast by which we are united with our savior in love of God and love of neighbor. All of these aspects of the Mass are true; none of them is exhaustive. However, because the Church has historically seen in the sacrificial death of Christ the primary emphasis in the redemptive activity of Christ, the primary emphasis in understanding the Mass must always be on sacrifice, as we said in the previous paragraph.

Pope Pius XII indicated the role the laity should play in the celebration of the Mass. Each, in his own way, must unite himself interiorly with Jesus by devoutly contemplating the sufferings and death He underwent for our salvation. Moreover, Pius indicated that the laity should participate more fully in the Mass outwardly also, by ceremonial gesture, prayers, singing, and by joining in the response prayers. The faithful are no longer to be mere spectators at the Mass, but are to participate in it, along with the priest.

The Second Vatican Council convened under Pope John XXIII and Pope Paul VI, further declared: "The Church, therefore, earnestly desires that Christ's faithful, when present at this Mystery of Faith, should not be there as strangers or silent spectators. On the contrary, through a proper appreciation of the rites and prayers they should participate knowingly, devoutly, and actively. They should be instructed by God's word and be refreshed at the table of the Lord's body . . . by offering the Immaculate Victim, not only through the hands of the priest, but also with him, they should learn to offer themselves too. Through Christ the Mediator, they should be drawn day by day into ever closer union with God and with each other . . . ."

The Mass consists of two principal divisions: the *Liturgy of the Word of God,* which proclaims and explains God's message to His people, and the *Liturgy of the Eucharist,* which focuses on the essential act of sacrifice in the Consecration and on the Eucharistic Banquet of Holy Communion. To make the Mass more immediately intelligible, informative, and meaningful, vernacular languages are used by priest and people for parts of the Mass that pertain to the people, while lay commentators and cantors lead the congregation in participation.

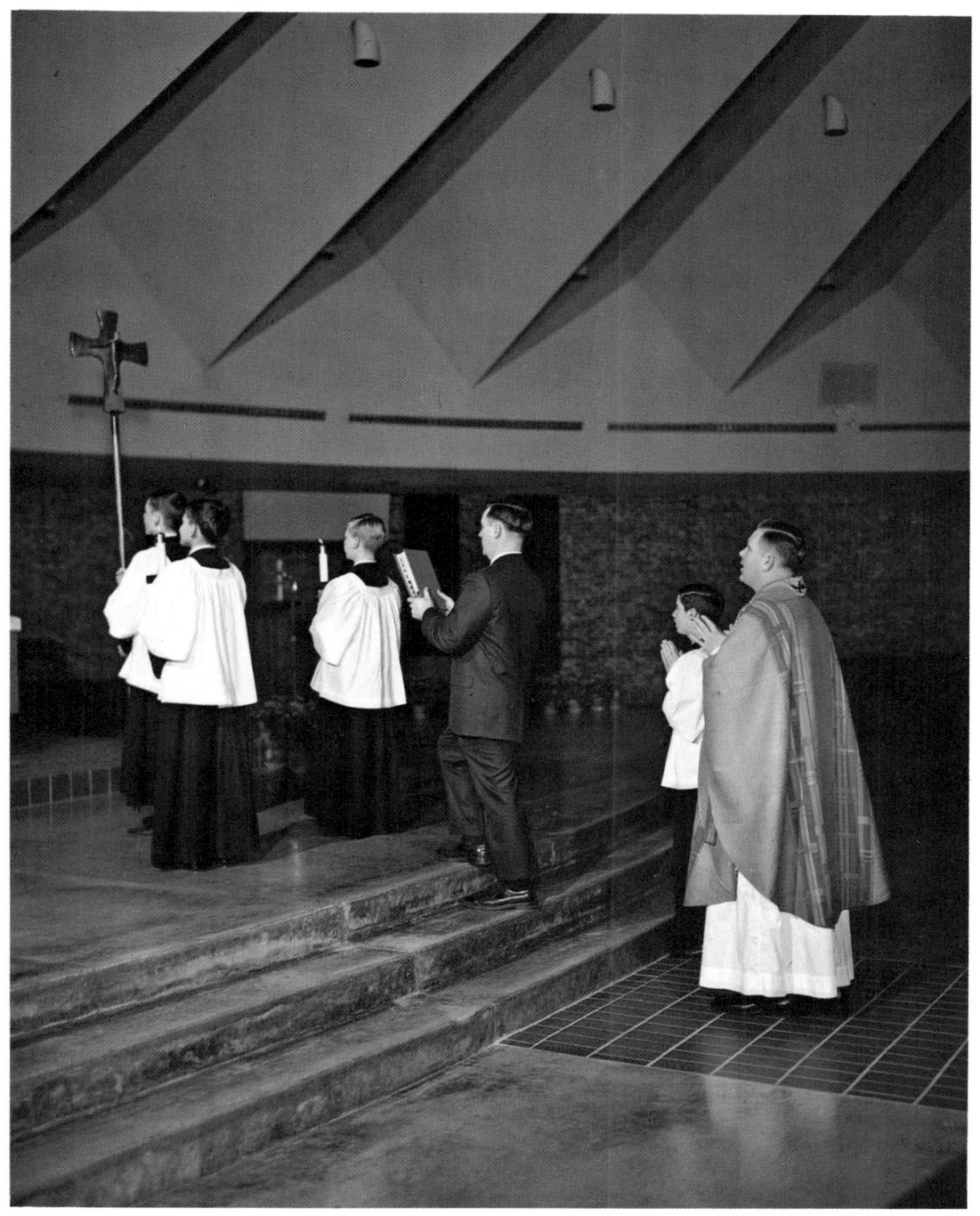

ENTRANCE RITE OR PROCESSION (*Liturgy of the Word of God*).   The Mass begins with a processional song, a psalm or hymn to greet Christ and to prepare for worship. The priest arrives at the altar and venerates his symbol of Christ. He then goes to his chair to greet the people.

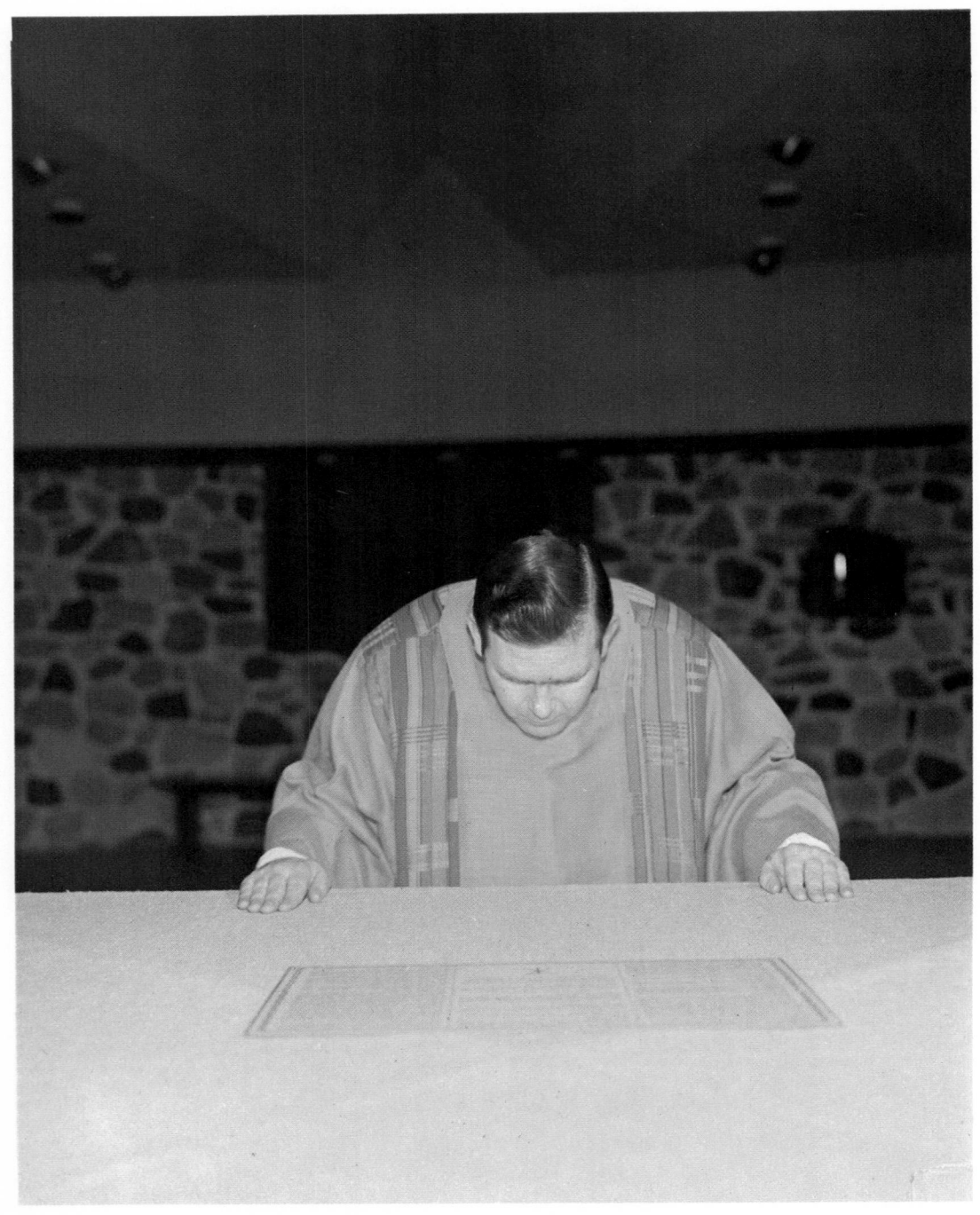

THE CELEBRANT GREETS THE ALTAR (*Liturgy of the Word of God*).   After the priest reverences the altar, he goes to his chair to preside over the Liturgy of the Word. He greets the people, and then priest and people prepare to enter into God's presence by a common confession of unworthiness.

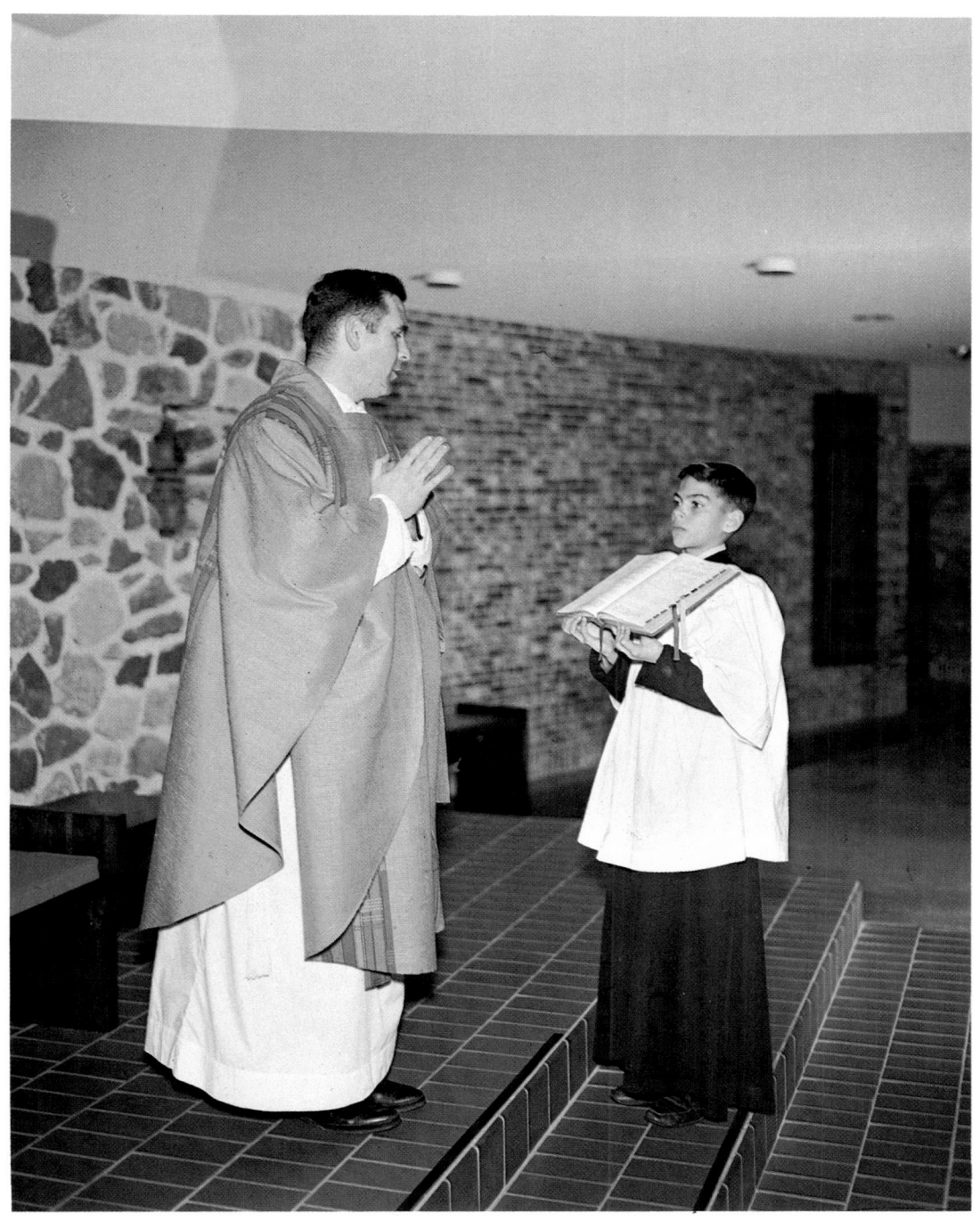

THE LORD HAVE MERCY AND GLORY TO GOD (*Liturgy of the Word of God*). The Lord Have Mercy (Kyrie Eleison) may be combined with the expression of unworthiness (penitential rite) described previously. On Sundays outside of Advent and Lent, priest and people sing or pray together the "Glory to God in the Highest." The first words of this ancient hymn were those sung by the angels on the first Christmas.

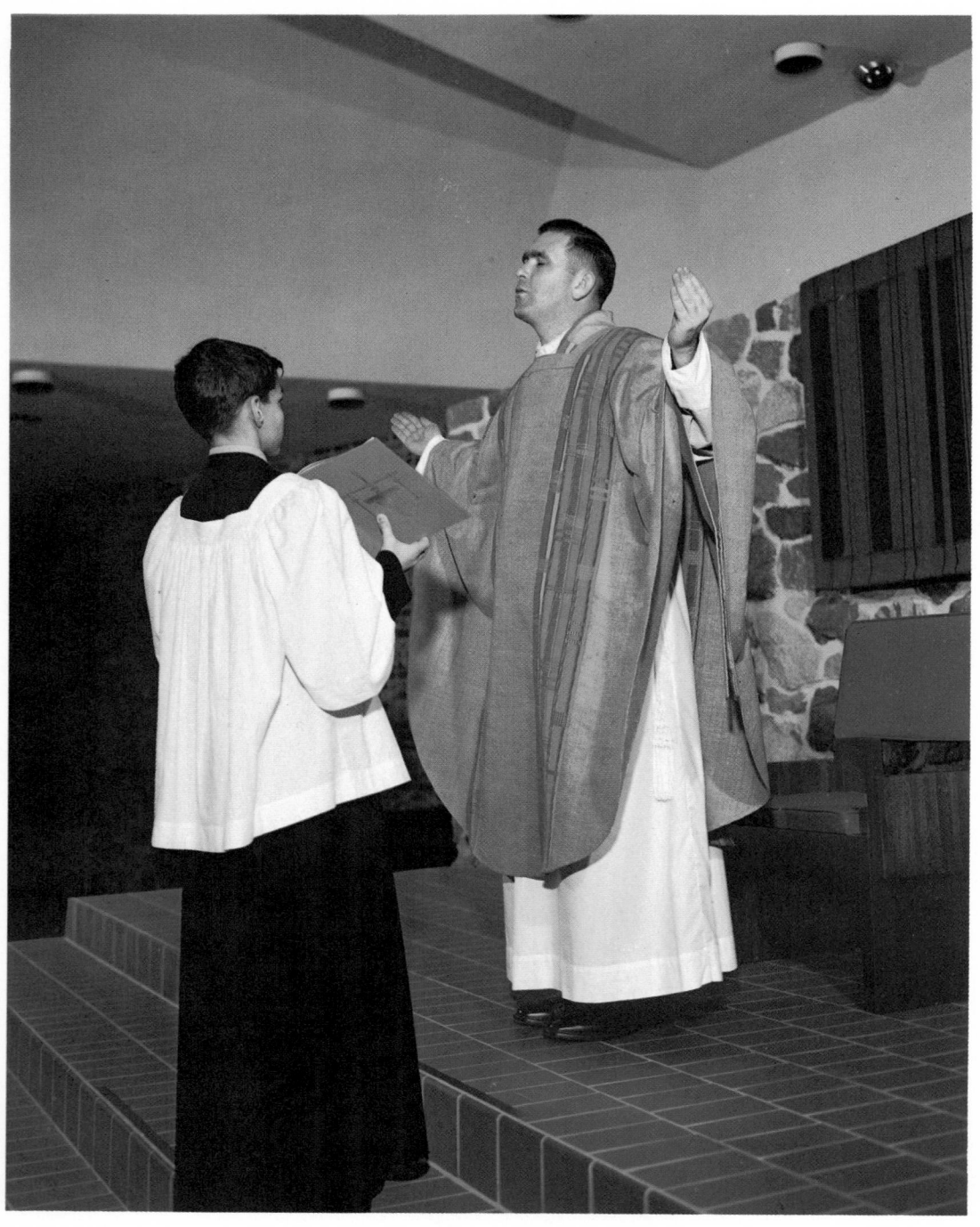

THE CELEBRANT COLLECTS THE PRAYERS OF THE ASSEMBLY (*Liturgy of the Word of God*).   Each of those present having privately formulated their own petitions according to their own needs and desires, the celebrant then "collects" these many requests and in behalf of the worshipping community petitions God to grant them in the name of His divine Son, Jesus Christ, our Mediator. He asks God for all the graces we need to save our souls, for His forgiveness, and for His help. The prayers are short, but pointed and forceful.

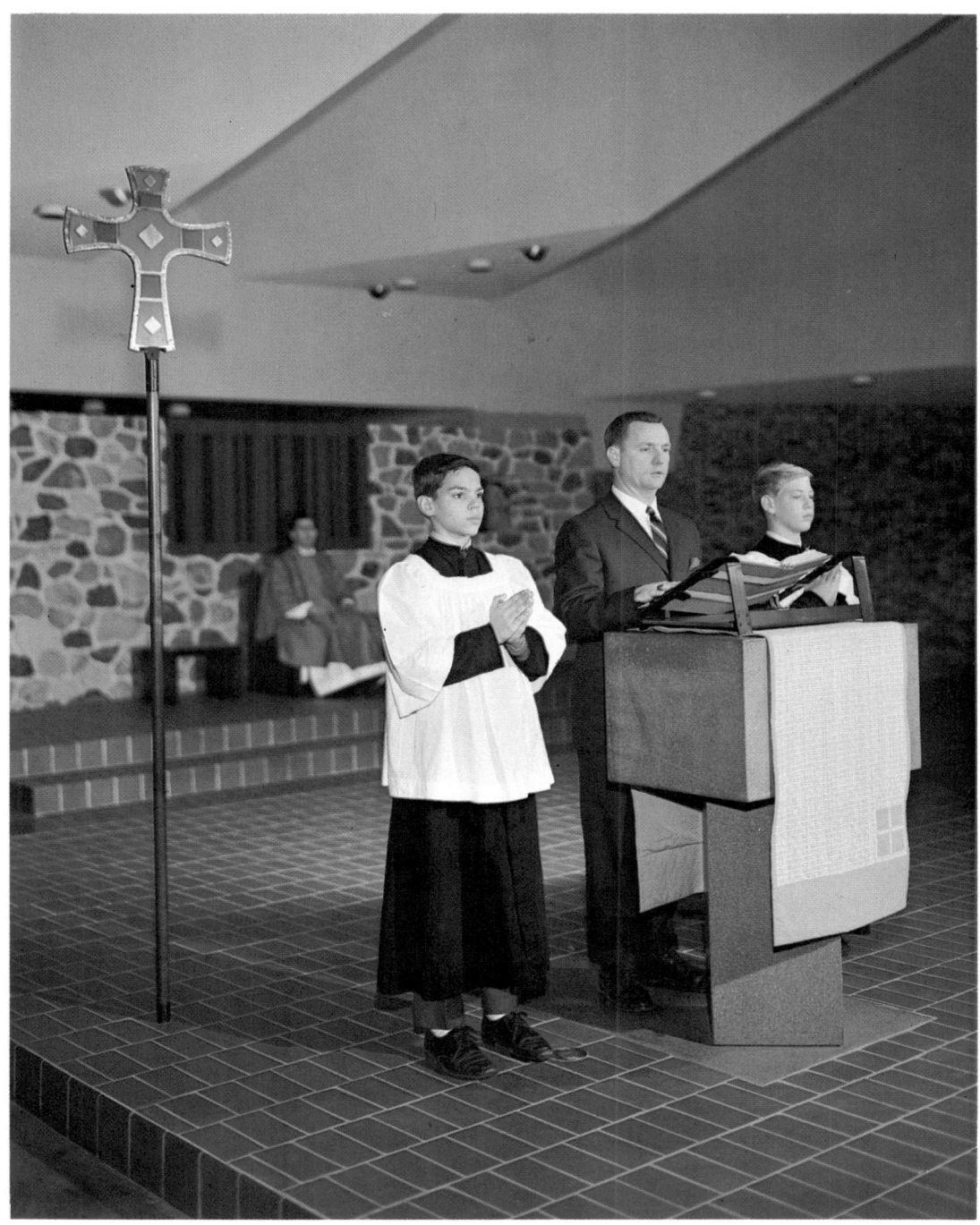

THE FIRST OR SCRIPTURAL READING (*Liturgy of the Word of God.*) The Liturgy of the Word usually contains three lessons from the Bible. The first of these is ordinarily taken from the Old Testament. The lay lector proclaims this lesson to the people. The lesson is followed by the Responsorial Psalm. This is an antiphonal arrangement of a psalm which is intended to be a meditation on the Word of God. Although this psalm should be sung, it may also be recited alternately by lector and congregation.

THE EPISTLE (*Liturgy of the Word of God*).   The second lesson is proclaimed by the lector. This lesson, always taken from the New Testament, is usually from one of the Epistles. Following the Epistle, all stand for the singing of the Alleluia and verse in preparation for the proclamation of the Gospel. During Lent, the Alleluia is not sung; in its place a Gospel acclamation is used.

THE CELEBRANT (OR DEACON OR ANOTHER PRIEST) PROCLAIMS THE GOSPEL (*Liturgy of the Word of God*). A selection from Matthew, Mark, Luke, or John is proclaimed at each Mass. The Gospel and the previous Scripture lessons are arranged on a three year cycle so that once every three years the entire Bible is proclaimed. The word Gospel means "good news." It is the proclamation that Jesus has come to save us through the mystery of His life, death, and resurrection.

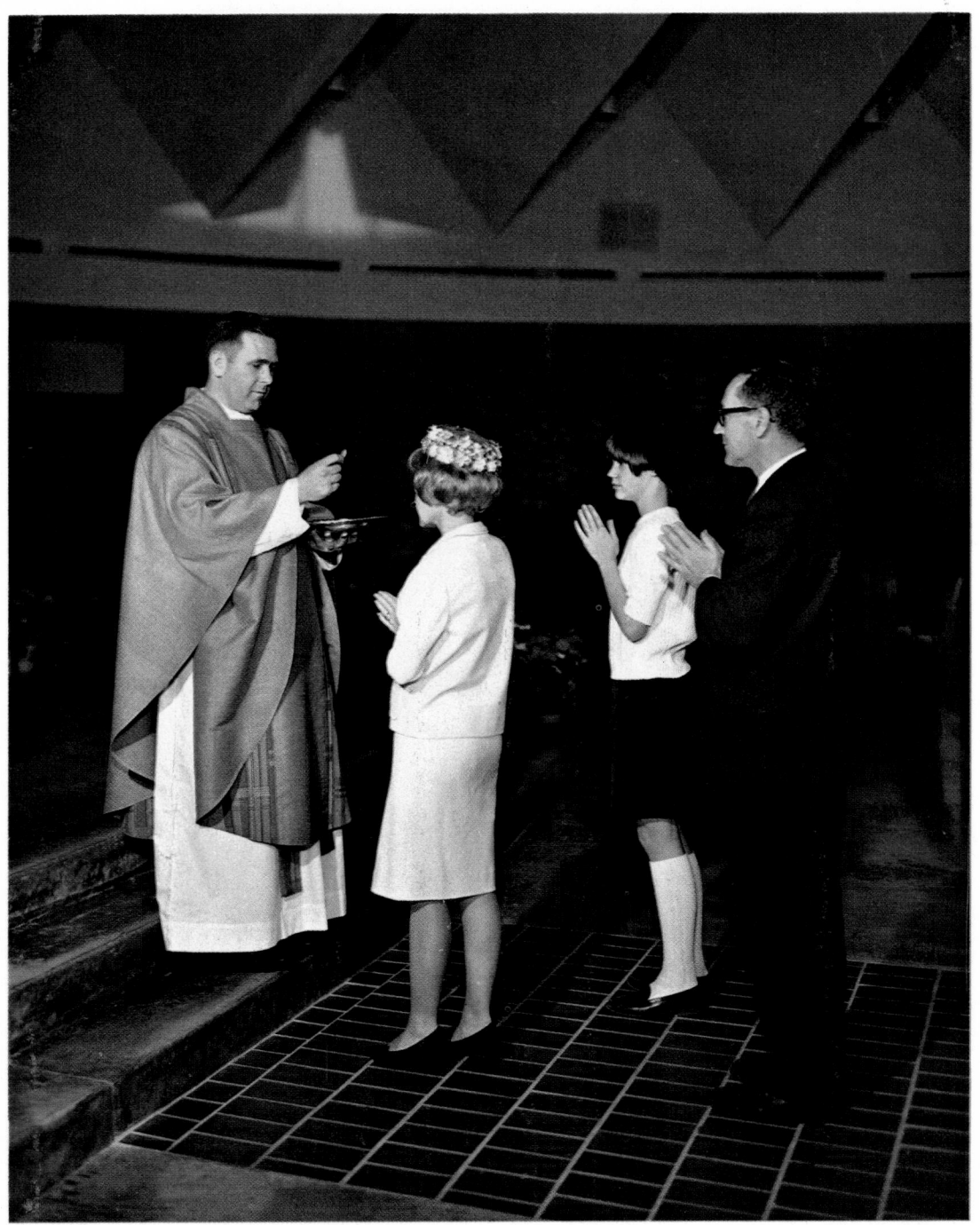

THE COMMUNION PROCESSION (*Liturgy of the Eucharist*).   Having humbly confessed their unworthiness, and asking for forgiveness, mercy, and peace, the communicants proceed to the foot of the altar to receive Holy Communion. The priest holds the Consecrated Host before each communicant saying: "The Body of Christ!" and each communicant replies: "Amen." During the distribution of Holy Communion the communion verse or a hymn may be sung by the congregation.

THE PRAYER AFTER COMMUNION (*Liturgy of the Eucharist*).   After Communion, the congregation and celebrant may observe a period of silent thanksgiving. Then, the celebrant prays the final prayer of Mass, the Prayer after Communion. It is a prayer of thanksgiving for the great gift of the Eucharist, and a petition that we shall bear fruit, having been refreshed by the Body and Blood of Christ. This Prayer, as well as the Prayer of the Assembly, and the Prayer over the Gifts, is different in each Mass.

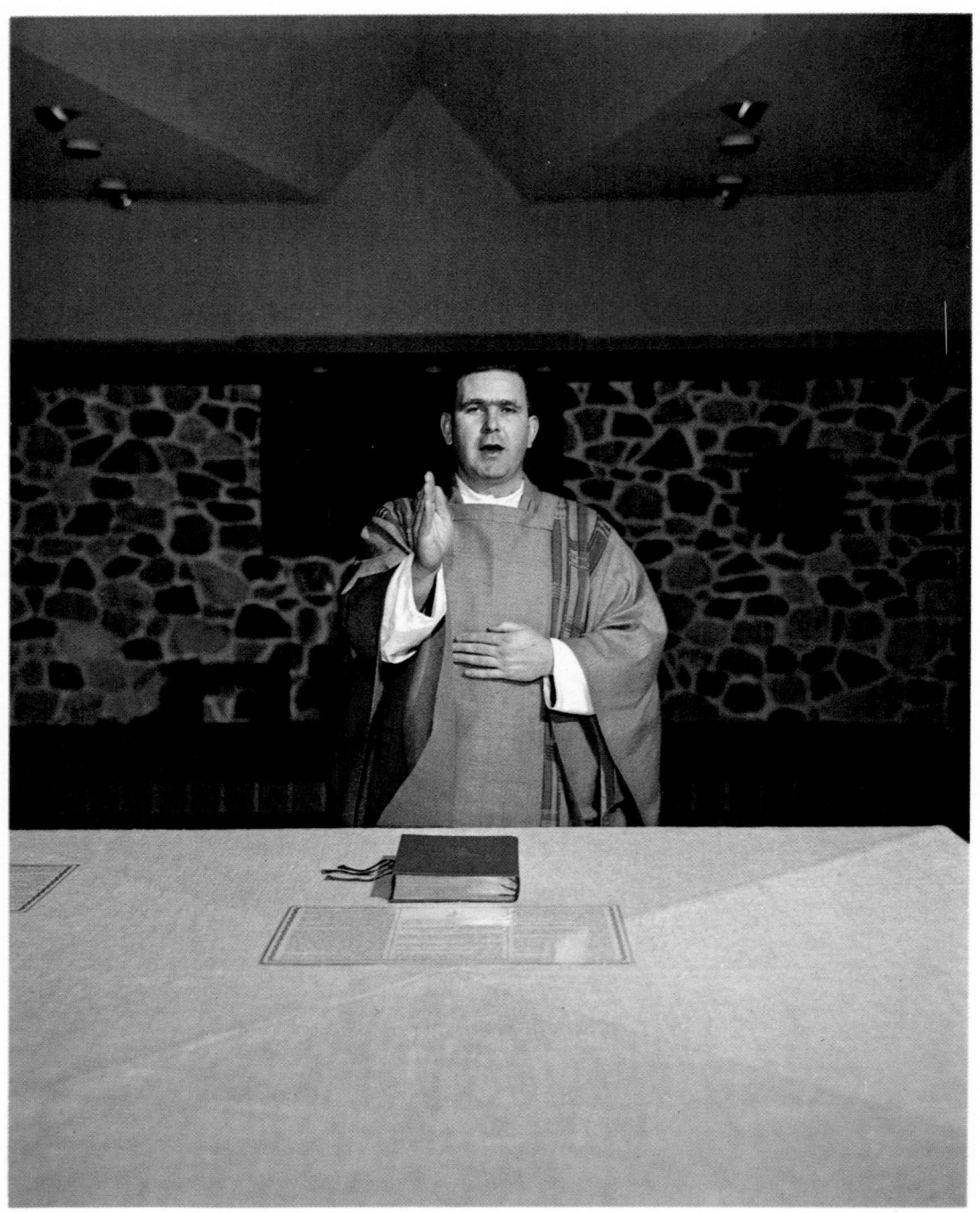

THE BLESSING OF THE FAITHFUL (*Liturgy of the Eucharist*). The celebrant blesses the congregation in the name of the Father, the Son, and the Holy Spirit. Then he sends us forth to live in the spirit of the Lord. One of the optional dismissals is: "Go in peace to love and serve the Lord." To this, all answer a hearty "Thanks be to God."

RECESSIONAL HYMN (*Liturgy of the Eucharist*). At Sunday Masses and other Masses with some solemnity, the recessional hymn is sung after the dismissal as the procession leaves the altar. This hymn is intended to send us on our way to live the Mass: As Jesus has offered Himself for us, forgiven us, restored us to the grace of the Father, so now we resolve that we shall be the light of the world and the salt of the earth: that we shall lead all men to Him by our lives of sacrificial love.

PRAYERS

PRAYER BEFORE A CRUCIFIX

Look upon me, meek and merciful Jesus. I kneel humbly before You and ardently pray that You will inspire me to fervent faith, hope and charity. Give me true sorrow for my sins and a genuine desire to correct whatever wrongdoing I have done. As I look upon the cross, I meditate with great love on Your complete sacrifice for me which is shown in the wounds of Your hands, Your feet and Your side. You have fulfilled the saying of David your prophet: "They have pierced my hands and my feet; I can count all my bones."

ANIMA CHRISTI

Spirit of Christ, give me life.
Body of Christ, be my salvation.
Blood of Christ, quench my thirst.
Water from Christ's side, cleanse me.
Suffering of Christ, enable me to suffer courageously.
   Merciful Jesus, hear me.
   Keep me always close to You.
   From Satan's wiles defend me.
   In death's hour, call me.
   Summon me to Your presence,
   That forever with Your saints I may praise You. Amen.

MORNING OFFERING

Almighty Father, You have so loved the world that You sent Your Son to save us. You have poured Your Spirit into our hearts that we may be witnesses united with Your Son. All good comes to us through the life, death and resurrection of Your Son; all praise comes to You through the same mystery of Christ Jesus. At the beginning of this day, I offer You every thought, desire, word and action. Through the merit and power of Your Son, I consecrate myself to do Your will today. Fill me with Your Holy Spirit so that I may keep this resolution, that I may avoid all sin, and that I may be what You have called me to be: the light of the world and the salt of the earth. Amen.

The Wisdom Books

THE BOOKS of Job, Psalms, Proverbs, Ecclesiastes, the Song of Songs, Wisdom, and Sirach are all versified by the skillful use of parallelism, that is, of the balanced and symmetrical phrases peculiar to Hebrew poetry. With the exception of the Psalms, the majority of which are devotional lyrics, and the Song of Songs, a nuptial hymn, these books belong to the general class of wisdom or didactic literature, strictly so called because their chief purpose is instruction.

The wisdom literature of the Bible is the fruit of a movement among ancient oriental people to gather, preserve and express, usually in aphoristic style, the results of human experience as an aid toward understanding and solving the problems of life. In Israel especially, the movement concerned itself with such basic and vital problems as man's origin and destiny, his quest for happiness, the problem of suffering, of good and evil in human conduct, of death, and the state beyond the grave. Originating with oral tradition, these formulations found their way into the historical books of the Old Testament in the shape of proverbs, odes, chants, epigrams, and also into those psalms intended for instruction.

The developed compositions of this literature form the sapiential books. The Book of Proverbs is a collection of sentences or practical norms for moral conduct. The Book of Job is an artistic dialogue skillfully handling the problem of suffering though only from the standpoint of temporal life. Ecclesiastes examines a wide range of human experience only to conclude that all things are vanity except the fear of the Lord and observance of his commandments, and that God requites man in his own good time. Sirach gathers and presents the fruits of past experience, thus preparing for the Book of Wisdom, which sees for the just man seeking happiness the full hope of immortality (Wis 3, 4).

Those who cultivated wisdom were called sages. Men of letters, scribes, skilled in the affairs of government, and counselors to rulers, they were instructors of the people, especially of youth (Sir 51, 13-30). In times of crisis they guided the people by revaluating tradition, thus helping to preserve unity, peace and good will. The most illustrious of the sages, and the originator of wisdom literature in Israel, was Solomon. Because of his fame, some of the wisdom books of which he was not the author bear his name.

Despite numerous resemblances, sometimes exaggerated, between the sapiential literature of pagan nations and the wisdom books of the Bible, the former are often replete with vagaries and abound in polytheistic conceptions; the latter remained profoundly human, universal, fundamentally moral, and essentially religious and monotheistic. Under the influence of the law and the prophets, wisdom became piety and virtue; impiety and vice were folly. The teachers of wisdom were regarded as men of God, and their books were placed beside the law and the prophets. The highest wisdom became identified with the spirit of God through which the world was created and preserved (Prv 8, 22-31), and mankind was enlightened.

The limitations of Old Testament wisdom served to crystallize the problems of human life and destiny, thus preparing for their solution through New Testament revelation. Ecclesiastes' vain search for success and happiness on earth ends when the Savior assures these things to his followers, not in this world but in the bliss of heaven. The anxiety in the Book of Job over reconciling God's justice and wisdom with the suffering of the innocent is relieved by the account of the crucified and risen Redeemer in the gospel. By fulfilling all that the Psalms foretold concerning him, Jesus makes the Psalter his prayer book and that of the church for all time. The love of God for the chosen people which underlies the Song of Songs is perfected in the union of Christ with his church. The personification of the wisdom of Proverbs, Wisdom and Sirach shines forth in resplendent reality in the Word who was with God, and who was God, and who became incarnate to dwell among us; cf Jn 1, 2.14.

The Book of Job

Introduction

The Book of Job, named after its protagonist, is an exquisite dramatic poem which treats of the problem of the suffering of the innocent, and of retribution. The contents of the book, together with its artistic structure and elegant style, place it among the literary masterpieces of all time.

Job, an oriental chieftain, pious and upright, richly endowed in his own person and in domestic prosperity, suffers a sudden and complete reversal of fortune. He loses his property and his children; a loathsome disease afflicts his body; and sorrow oppresses his soul. Nevertheless, Job does not complain against God. When some friends visit him to condole with him, Job protests his innocence and does not understand why he is afflicted. He curses the day of his birth and longs for death to bring an end to his sufferings. The debate which ensues consists of three cycles of speeches. Job's friends insist that his plight can only be a punishment for personal wrongdoing and an invitation from God to repentance. Job rejects their inadequate explanation and calls for a response from God himself. At this point, the speeches of a youth named Elihu (chs 32—37) interrupt the development.

In response to Job's plea that he be allowed to see God and hear from him the cause of his suffering, God answers, not by justifying his action before men, but by referring to his own omniscience and almighty power. Job is content with this. He recovers his attitude of humility and trust in God, which is deepened now and strengthened by his experience of suffering.

The author of the book is not known; it was composed some time between the seventh and fifth centuries B.C. Its literary form, with speeches, prologue and epilogue disposed according to a studied plan, indicates that the purpose of the writing is didactic. The lesson is that even the just may suffer here, and their sufferings are a test of their fidelity. They shall be rewarded in the end. Man's finite mind cannot probe the depths of the divine omniscience that governs the world. The problems we encounter can be solved by a broader and deeper awareness of God's power, presence (42, 5) and wisdom.

The divisions of the Book of Job are as follows:

I: PROLOGUE

Job's Wealth and Piety

1 ¹*†IN THE LAND OF UZ there was a blameless and upright man named Job, who feared God and avoided evil. ²†Seven sons and three daughters were born to him; ³†and he had seven thousand sheep, three thousand camels, five hundred yoke of oxen, five hundred she-asses, and a great number of work animals, so that he was greater than any of the men of the East. ⁴His sons used to take turns giving feasts, sending invitations to their three sisters to eat and drink with them. ⁵And when each feast had run its course, Job would send for them and sanctify them, rising early and offering holocausts for every one of them. For Job said, "It may be that my sons have sinned and blasphemed God in their hearts." This Job did habitually.

⁶*†One day, when the sons of God came to present themselves before the LORD, Satan also came among them. ⁷*And the LORD said to Satan, "Whence do you come?" Then Satan answered the LORD and said, "From roaming the earth and patrolling it." ⁸And the LORD said to Satan, "Have you noticed my servant Job, and that there is no one on earth like him, blameless and upright, fearing God and avoiding evil?" ⁹But Satan answered the LORD and said, "Is it for nothing that Job is God-fearing? ¹⁰Have you not surrounded him and his family and all that he has with your protection? You have blessed the work of his hands, and his livestock are spread over the land. ¹¹*But now put forth your hand and touch anything that he has, and surely he will blaspheme you to your face." ¹²And the LORD said to Satan, "Behold, all that he has is in your

---

1/1: 2, 3.
6ff: 2, 1ff.
6: Gn 6, 2.4; Zec 3, 1;

Lk 22, 31; Rv 12, 9.
7: 1 Pt 5, 8.
11: 2, 5.

† 1, 1: *Uz:* somewhere in Edom or Arabia. *Job:* a not uncommon name in ancient Semitic circles; its original meaning was "enemy."

1, 2f: The numbers mentioned here indicate Job's great wealth and happiness, external proof of God's friendship.

1, 3: *Men of the East:* that is, east of Palestine.

1, 6: *Sons of God:* angels. *Satan:* literally, "adversary."

power; only do not lay a hand upon his person." So Satan went forth from the presence of the LORD.

The First Trial

[13]And so one day, while his sons and his daughters were eating and drinking wine in the house of their eldest brother, [14]a messenger came to Job and said, "The oxen were plowing and the asses grazing beside them, [15]†and the Sabeans carried them off in a raid. They put the herdsmen to the sword, and I alone have escaped to tell you." [16]†While he was yet speaking, another came and said, "Lightning has fallen from heaven and struck the sheep and their shepherds and consumed them; and I alone have escaped to tell you." [17]While he was yet speaking, another came and said, "The Chaldeans formed three columns, seized the camels, carried them off, and put those tending them to the sword, and I alone have escaped to tell you." [18]While he was yet speaking, another came and said, "Your sons and daughters were eating and drinking wine in the house of their eldest brother, [19]when suddenly a great wind came across the desert and smote the four corners of the house. It fell upon the young people and they are dead; and I alone have escaped to tell you." [20]Then Job began to tear his cloak and cut off his hair. He cast himself prostrate upon the ground, [21]*†and said,

"Naked I came forth from my mother's womb,
     and naked shall I go back again.
The LORD gave and the LORD has taken away;
     blessed be the name of the LORD!"

[22]*In all this Job did not sin, nor did he say anything disrespectful of God.

The Second Trial

2 [1]*ONCE again the sons of God came to present themselves before the LORD, and Satan also came with them. [2]And the LORD said to Satan, "Whence do you come?" And Satan answered the LORD and said, "From roaming the earth and patrolling it." [3]*And the LORD said to Satan, "Have you noticed my servant Job, and that there is no one on earth like him, faultless and upright, fearing God and avoiding evil? He still holds fast to his innocence although you incited me against him to ruin him without cause." [4]†And Satan answered the LORD and said, "Skin for skin! All that a man has will he give for his life. [5]*But now put forth your hand and touch his bone and his flesh, and surely he will blaspheme you to your face." [6]And the LORD said to Satan, "He is in your power; only spare his life." [7]So Satan went forth from the presence of the LORD and smote Job with severe boils from the soles of his feet to the crown of his head. [8]And he took a potsherd to scrape himself, as he sat among the ashes. [9]*†Then his

wife said to him, "Are you still holding to your innocence? Curse God and die." [10]*But he said to her, "Are even you going to speak as senseless women do? We accept good things from God; and should we not accept evil?" Through all this, Job said nothing sinful.

Job's Three Friends

[11]†Now when three of Job's friends heard of all the misfortune that had come upon him, they set out each one from his own place: Eliphaz from Teman, Bildad from Shuh, and Zophar from Naamath. They met and journeyed together to give him sympathy and comfort. [12]But when, at a distance, they lifted up their eyes and did not recognize him, they began to weep aloud; they tore their cloaks and threw dust upon their heads. [13]Then they sat down upon the ground with him seven days and seven nights, but none of them spoke a word to him; for they saw how great was his suffering.

II: FIRST CYCLE OF SPEECHES

Job's Plaint

3 [1]AFTER THIS, JOB OPENED HIS MOUTH and cursed his day. [2]Job spoke out and said:

[3]*   Perish the day on which I was born,
     the night when they said, "The child is a boy!"

[4]   May that day be darkness:
     let not God above call for it,
     nor light shine upon it!

[5]   May darkness and gloom claim it,
     clouds settle upon it,
     the blackness of night affright it!

[6]   May obscurity seize that day;
     let it not occur among the days of the year,
     nor enter into the count of the months!

[7]   May that night be barren;
     let no joyful outcry greet it!

[8]†   Let them curse it who curse the sea,
     the appointed disturbers of Leviathan!

[9]   May the stars of its twilight be darkened;
     may it look for daylight, but have none,
     nor gaze on the eyes of the dawn,

---

† 1, 15: *Sabeans:* from southern Arabia.

1, 16: *Lightning:* literally, "God's fire."

1, 21: *Go back again:* to the earth; cf Gn 2, 7; Sir 40, 1.

2, 4: *Skin for skin:* an expression which, as applied to Job, means that he has borne his suffering patiently thus far only because he seeks to avoid greater suffering and to receive greater favors from God.

2, 9: *Curse God and die:* you have nothing to hope for from God and therefore nothing to live for.

2, 11: The names of Job's friends suggest Edomite origin. The Edomites (Ab 8f) and more specifically the Temanites (Jer 49, 7) enjoyed a reputation for wisdom.

3, 8: *Leviathan:* in 40, 25, the crocodile; here the reference is probably to a mythological sea monster symbolizing primeval chaos. Cf 9, 13; 26, 13; Pss 74, 13f; 104, 26; Is 27, 1.

✿   21: Eccl 5, 14; 1 Tm 6, 7.
     22: 2, 10; Jas 5, 11.
     2/1: 1, 6.
     3: 1, 1.
     5: 1, 11.

9: 19, 17.
10: 1, 22; Sir 2, 4; Jas 5, 11.
3/3: Jer 20, 14.

10 Because it kept not shut the doors of the
womb
to shield my eyes from trouble!

11⁕ Why did I not perish at birth,
come forth from the womb and expire?

16† Or why was I not buried away like an
untimely birth,
like babes that have never seen the
light?

12 Wherefore did the knees receive me?
or why did I suck at the breasts?

13 For then I should have lain down and been
tranquil;
had I slept, I should then have been at
rest

14 With kings and counselors of the earth
who built where now there are ruins

15 Or with princes who had gold
and filled their houses with silver.

17† There the wicked cease from troubling,
there the weary are at rest.

18 There the captives are at ease together,
and hear not the voice of the slave
driver.

19 Small and great are there the same,
and the servant is free from his master.

20 Why is light given to the toilers,
and life to the bitter in spirit?

21 They wait for death and it comes not;
they search for it rather than for hidden
treasures,

22 Rejoice in it exultingly,
and are glad when they reach the grave:

23 Men whose path is hidden from them,
and whom God has hemmed in!

24 For sighing comes more readily to me than
food,
and my groans well forth like water.

25 For what I fear overtakes me,
and what I shrink from comes upon me.

26 I have no peace nor ease;
I have no rest, for trouble comes!

Eliphaz's First Speech

4 ¹THEN spoke Eliphaz the Temanite, who said:

2 If someone attempts a word with you, will
you mind?
For how can anyone refrain from
speaking?

3 Behold, you have instructed many,
and have made firm their feeble hands.

4 Your words have upheld the stumbler;
you have strengthened his faltering
knees.

5 But now that it comes to you, you are
impatient;
when it touches yourself, you are
dismayed.

6 Is not your piety a source of confidence,
and your integrity of life your hope?

7⁕ Reflect now, what innocent person
perishes?
Since when are the upright destroyed?

8 As I see it, those who plow for mischief
and sow trouble, reap the same.

9⁕ By the breath of God they perish,
and by the blast of his wrath they are
consumed.

10† Though the lion roars, though the king of
beasts cries out,
yet the teeth of the young lions are
broken;

11 The old lion perishes for lack of prey,
and the cubs of the lioness are scattered.

12† For a word was stealthily brought to me,
and my ear caught a whisper of it.

13⁕ In my thoughts during visions of the night,
when deep sleep falls on men,

14 Fear came upon me, and shuddering,
that terrified me to the bones.

15 Then a spirit passed before me,
and the hair of my flesh stood up.

16 It paused, but its likeness I could not
discern;
a figure was before my eyes,
and I heard a still voice:

17⁕ "Can a man be righteous as against God?
Can a mortal be blameless against his
Maker?

18⁕ Lo, he puts no trust in his servants,
and with his angels he can find fault.

19 How much more with those that dwell in
houses of clay,
whose foundation is in the dust,
who are crushed more easily than the
moth!

---

† 3, 16: This verse has been placed between vv 11 and 12 where it probably stood originally. There is reason to believe that here, as well as in several other places in Job, the original order of the poetic lines was accidentally disturbed in the early transmission of the text; so in chapters 12-15; 19-21; 24-31; 34; 36; 38-42. The verse numbers given in such cases are always those of the current Hebrew text, though the arrangement may differ. The footnotes will advise the reader of the difficulties and provide him with further indications for following the progress of thought in the book.

3, 17: *There:* in death.

4, 10: *The lion:* used figuratively here for the violent, rapacious sinner who cannot prevail against God.

4, 12-21: A dramatic presentation of the idea of man's nothingness in contrast to God's greatness.

⁕
11: 10, 18f.
4/7: Ps 37, 25.
  9: Ps 18, 16; Is 11, 4;
    2 Thes 2, 8.
13: 33, 15.

17: 9, 2; 15, 14ff; 25, 4;
    Pss 130, 3; 143, 2.
18: 15, 15; 2 Pt 2, 4;
    Jude 6.

20 Morning or evening they may be
  shattered;
    with no heed paid to it, they perish
    forever.

21 The pegs of their tent are plucked up;
    they die without knowing wisdom."

5 ¹ Call now! Will anyone respond to you?
    To which of the holy ones will you
    appeal?

2 Nay, impatience kills the fool
    and indignation slays the simpleton.

3* I have seen a fool spreading his roots,
    but his household suddenly decayed.

4† His children shall be far from safety;
    they shall be crushed at the gate
    without a rescuer.

5 What they have reaped the hungry shall
  eat up;
    [or God shall take it away by blight;]
    and the thirsty shall swallow their
    substance.

6 For mischief comes not out of the earth,
    nor does trouble spring out of the
    ground;

7† But man himself begets mischief,
    as sparks fly upward.

8 In your place, I would appeal to God,
    and to God I would state my plea.

10 He gives rain upon the earth
    and sends water upon the fields;

11* He sets up on high the lowly,
    and those who mourn he exalts to safety.

12 He frustrates the plans of the cunning,
    so that their hands achieve no success;

13* He catches the wise in their own ruses,
    and the designs of the crafty are routed.

14 They meet with darkness in the daytime,
    and at noonday they grope as though it
    were night.

15 But the poor from the edge of the sword
    and from the hand of the mighty, he
    saves.

16 Thus the unfortunate have hope,
    and iniquity closes her mouth.

17 Happy is the man whom God reproves!
    The Almighty's chastening do not reject.

18* For he wounds, but he binds up;
    he smites, but his hands give healing.

19† Out of six troubles he will deliver you,
    and at the seventh no evil shall touch
    you.

20 In famine he will deliver you from death,
    and in war from the threat of the sword;

21 From the scourge of the tongue you shall
  be hidden,
    and shall not fear approaching ruin.

22 At destruction and want you shall laugh;
    the beasts of the earth you need not
    dread.

23 You shall be in league with the stones of
  the field,
    and the wild beasts shall be at peace
    with you.

24 And you shall know that your tent is
  secure;
    taking stock of your household,
    you shall miss nothing.

25 You shall know that your descendants are
  many,
    and your offspring as the grass of the
    earth.

26 You shall approach the grave in full vigor,
    as a shock of grain comes in at its season.

27 Lo, this we have searched out; so it is!
    This we have heard, and you should
    know.

Job's First Reply

6 ¹THEN Job answered and said:

2 Ah, could my anguish but be measured
    and my calamity laid with it in the
    scales,

3 They would now outweigh the sands of the
  sea!
    Because of this I speak without
    restraint.

4* For the arrows of the Almighty pierce me,
    and my spirit drinks in their poison;
    the terrors of God are arrayed against
    me.

5† Does the wild ass bray when he has grass?
    Does the ox low over his fodder?

6 Can a thing insipid be eaten without salt?
    Is there flavor in the white of an egg?

7 I refuse to touch them;
    they are loathsome food to me.

8 Oh, that I might have my request,
    and that God would grant what I long
    for:

---

† 5, 4: *At the gate:* of the city, where justice was administered.

5, 7: *Sparks:* in Hebrew, "sons of resheph," which the ancient versions took as the name of a bird.

5, 9: Omitted here; it is a duplicate of 9, 10.

5, 19: *Six . . . the seventh:* proverbial expression for any large number; cf Prv 24, 16; Lk 17, 4.

6, 5f: Job would not complain if his life were as pleasant to him as fodder to a hungry animal; but his life is as disagreeable as insipid food. *White of an egg:* thus the obscure Hebrew has been understood in Jewish tradition; some render it "mallow juice."

---

* 5/3: Ps 37, 35f.   13: 1 Cor 3, 19.
  11: 1 Sm 2, 7f; Ps 113, 7;   18: Hos 6, 1f.
    Lk 1, 52.   6/4: Ps 88, 17.

9 Even that God would decide to crush me,
that he would put forth his hand and
cut me off!

10 Then I should still have consolation
and could exult through unremitting
pain,
because I have not transgressed the
commands of the Holy One.

11 What strength have I that I should
endure,
and what is my limit that I should be
patient?

12 Have I the strength of stones,
or is my flesh of bronze?

13* Have I no helper,
and has advice deserted me?

14 A friend owes kindness to one in despair,
though he have forsaken the fear of the
Almighty.

15 My brethren are undependable as a brook,
as watercourses that run dry in the
wadies;

16 Though they may be black with ice,
and with snow heaped upon them,

17 Yet once they flow, they cease to be;
in the heat, they disappear from their
place.

18 Caravans turn aside from their routes;
they go into the desert and perish.

19† The caravans of Tema search,
the companies of Sheba have hopes;

20 They are disappointed, though they were
confident;
they come there and are frustrated.

21 It is thus that you have now become for
me;
you see a terrifying thing and are afraid.

22 Have I asked you to give me anything,
to offer a gift for me from your
possessions,

23 Or to deliver me from the enemy,
or to redeem me from oppressors?

24 Teach me, and I will be silent;
prove to me wherein I have erred.

25 How agreeable are honest words;
yet how unconvincing is your argument!

26 Do you consider your words as proof,
but the sayings of a desperate man as
wind?

27 You would even cast lots for the orphan,
and would barter away your friend!

28 Come, now, give me your attention;
surely I will not lie to your face.

29 Think it over; let there be no injustice.
Think it over; I still am right.

30 Is there insincerity on my tongue,
or cannot my taste discern falsehood?

7

1*† Is not man's life on earth a drudgery?
Are not his days those of a hireling?

2 He is a slave who longs for the shade,
a hireling who waits for his wages.

3 So I have been assigned months of misery,
and troubled nights have been told off
for me.

4 If in bed I say, "When shall I arise?"
then the night drags on;
I am filled with restlessness until the
dawn.

5* My flesh is clothed with worms and scabs;
my skin cracks and festers;

6 My days are swifter than a weaver's
shuttle;
they come to an end without hope.

7* Remember that my life is like the wind;
I shall not see happiness again.

8 The eye that now sees me shall no more
behold me;
as you look at me, I shall be gone.

9* As a cloud dissolves and vanishes,
so he who goes down to the nether
world shall come up no more.

10 He shall not again return to his house;
his place shall know him no more.

11 My own utterance I will not restrain;
I will speak in the anguish of my spirit;
I will complain in the bitterness of my
soul.

12† Am I the sea, or a monster of the deep,
that you place a watch over me?
Why have you set me up as an object of
attack;
or why should I be a target for you?

13 When I say, "My bed shall comfort me,
my couch shall ease my complaint,"

14 Then you affright me with dreams
and with visions terrify me,

15 So that I should prefer choking
and death rather than my pains.

16* I waste away: I cannot live forever;
let me alone, for my days are but a
breath.

17 What is man, that you make much of him,
or pay him any heed?

18* You observe him with each new day
and try him at every moment!

---

* 13: 19, 14f.
7/1: 14, 14.
  5: 2, 7f.
  7: Pss 8, 5; 144, 3.

9f: 10, 21; 14, 10ff; 2 Sm
    12, 23; 14, 14;
    Wis 2, 1.
16: 14, 1ff.5.
18: Ps 17, 3.

† 6, 19: *Tema:* in northwest Arabia. *Sheba:* see note on 1, 15.
7, 1: *Drudgery:* taken by some to refer to military service;
cf also 14, 14.

7, 12: An allusion in poetic imagery to primeval chaos as a
monstrous ocean vanquished by God at the world's creation.
7, 12-21: Job now speaks, not to his friends, but to God.

19 How long will it be before you look away
    from me,
    and let me alone long enough to swallow
    my spittle?
20 Though I have sinned, what can I do to
    you,
    O watcher of men?
21 Why do you not pardon my offense,
    or take away my guilt?
    For soon I shall lie down in the dust;
    and should you seek me I shall then be
    gone.

Bildad's First Speech

8 ¹BILDAD the Shuhite spoke out and said:

2 How long will you utter such things?
    The words from your mouth are like a
    mighty wind!
3* Does God pervert judgment,
    and does the Almighty distort justice?
4 If your children have sinned against him
    and he has left them in the grip of their
    guilt,
5 Still, if you yourself have recourse to God
    and make supplication to the Almighty,
6 Should you be blameless and upright,
    surely now he will awake for you
    and restore your rightful domain;
7 Your former state will be of little moment,
    for in time to come you will flourish
    indeed.
8* If you inquire of the former generations,
    and give heed to the experience of the
    fathers
9* (As we are but of yesterday and have no
    knowledge,
    because our days on earth are but a
    shadow),
10 Will they not teach you and tell you
    and utter their words of understanding?
11† Can the papyrus grow up without mire?
    Can the reed grass flourish without
    water?
12 While it is yet green and uncut,
    it withers quicker than any grass.
13 So is the end of everyone who forgets God,
    and so shall the hope of the godless man
    perish.
14 His confidence is but a gossamer thread
    and his trust is a spider's web.
15 He shall rely upon his family, but it shall
    not last;
    he shall cling to it, but it shall not
    endure.

16 He is full of sap before sunrise,
    and beyond his garden his shoots go
    forth;
17 About a heap of stones are his roots
    entwined;
    among the rocks he takes hold.
18 Yet if one tears him from his place,
    it will disown him: "I have never seen
    you!"
19 There he lies rotting beside the road,
    and out of the soil another sprouts.

20 Behold, God will not cast away the
    upright;
    neither will he take the hand of the
    wicked.
21 Once more will he fill your mouth with
    laughter,
    and your lips with rejoicing.
22 They that hate you shall be clothed with
    shame,
    and the tent of the wicked shall be no
    more.

Job's Second Reply

9 ¹THEN Job answered and said:

2 I know well that it is so;
    but how can a man be justified before
    God?
3 Should one wish to contend with him,
    he could not answer him once in a
    thousand times.
4 God is wise in heart and mighty in
    strength;
    who has withstood him and remained
    unscathed?
5 He removes the mountains before they
    know it;
    he overturns them in his anger.
6* He shakes the earth out of its place,
    and the pillars beneath it tremble.
7 He commands the sun, and it rises not;
    he seals up the stars.
8* He alone stretches out the heavens
    and treads upon the crests of the sea.
9 He made the Bear and Orion,
    the Pleiades and the constellations of
    the south;
10 He does great things past finding out,
    marvelous things beyond reckoning.

11 Should he come near me, I see him not;
    should he pass by, I am not aware of
    him;

---

†
    8, 11ff: As marsh plants need water, so man needs God. These
verses are taken by some as a quotation from the teaching of
the forefathers; cf v 10.

12 Should he seize me forcibly, who can say
    him nay?
    Who can say to him, "What are you
      doing?"

13† He is God and he does not relent;
    the helpers of Rahab bow beneath him.

14 How much less shall I give him any
    answer,
    or choose out arguments against him!

15✶ Even though I were right, I could not
    answer him,
    but should rather beg for what was due
    me.

16 If I appealed to him and he answered my
    call,
    I could not believe that he would
      hearken to my words;

17 With a tempest he might overwhelm me,
    and multiply my wounds without cause;

18 He need not suffer me to draw breath,
    but might fill me with bitter griefs.

19 If it be a question of strength, he is mighty;
    and if of judgment, who will call him to
      account?

20✶ Though I were right, my own mouth might
    condemn me;
    were I innocent, he might put me in the
      wrong.

21 Though I am innocent, I myself cannot
    know it;
    I despise my life.

22✶ It is all one! therefore I say:
    Both the innocent and the wicked he
      destroys.

23 When the scourge slays suddenly,
    he laughs at the despair of the innocent.

24 The earth is given into the hands of the
    wicked;
    he covers the faces of its judges.
    If it is not he, who then is it?

25✶ My days are swifter than a runner,
    they flee away; they see no happiness;

26 They shoot by like skiffs of reed,
    like an eagle swooping upon its prey.

27 If I say: I will forget my complaining,
    I will lay aside my sadness and be of
      good cheer,

28† Then I am in dread of all my pains;
    I know that you will not hold me
      innocent.

29 If I must be accounted guilty,
    why then should I strive in vain?

30 If I should wash myself with snow
    and cleanse my hands with lye,

31 Yet you would plunge me in the ditch,
    so that my garments would abhor me.

32 For he is not a man like myself, that I
    should answer him,
    that we should come together in
      judgment.

33 Would that there were an arbiter
    between us,
    who could lay his hand upon us both

34 and withdraw his rod from me.
    Would that his terrors did not frighten
      me;

35 that I might speak without being
    afraid of him.
    Since this is not the case with me,

10

1✶ I loathe my life.

I will give myself up to complaint;
    I will speak from the bitterness of my
      soul.

2 I will say to God: Do not put me in the
    wrong!
    Let me know why you oppose me.

3 Is it a pleasure for you to oppress,
    to spurn the work of your hands,
    and smile on the plan of the wicked?

4 Have you eyes of flesh?
    Do you see as man sees?

5✶ Are your days as the days of a mortal,
    and are your years as a man's lifetime,

6 That you seek for guilt in me
    and search after my sins,

7✶ Even though you know that I am not
    wicked,
    and that none can deliver me out of
      your hand?

8 Your hands have formed me and
    fashioned me;
    will you then turn and destroy me?

9✶ Oh, remember that you fashioned me
    from clay!
    Will you then bring me down to dust
      again?

10 Did you not pour me out as milk,
    and thicken me like cheese?

11 With skin and flesh you clothed me,
    with bones and sinews knit me
      together.

12 Grace and favor you granted me,
    and your providence has preserved
      my spirit.

✶
15: 10, 15.
20: 15, 6.
22: Eccl 9, 2.
25: 7, 6.
10/1: 9, 21.

5: 36, 26.
7: 2, 3.9; Dt 32, 39;
    Wis 16, 15.
9: 4, 19; 33, 6; Gn 2, 7;
    3, 19; Ps 146, 4.

†
9, 13: *Rahab:* cf 26, 12. See note on Ps 89, 11.
9, 28-31: *You:* refers to God.

13 Yet these things you have hidden in your
heart;
I know that they are your purpose:

14 If I should sin, you would keep a watch
against me,
and from my guilt you would not
absolve me.

15 If I should be wicked, alas for me!
if righteous, I dare not hold up my
head,
filled with ignominy and sodden with
affliction!

16 Should it lift up, you hunt me like a
lion:
repeatedly you show your wondrous
power against me,

17 You renew your attack upon me
and multiply your harassment of me;
in waves your troops come against me.

18* Why then did you bring me forth from
the womb?
I should have died and no eye have
seen me.

19 I should be as though I had never lived;
I should have been taken from the
womb to the grave.

20 Are not the days of my life few?
Let me alone, that I may recover a
little

21* Before I go whence I shall not return,
to the land of darkness and of gloom,

22 The black, disordered land
where darkness is the only light.

Zophar's First Speech

11 [1]AND Zophar the Naamathite spoke out and
said:

2 Should not the man of many words be
answered,
or must the garrulous man necessarily
be right?

3 Shall your babblings keep men silent,
and shall you deride and no one give
rebuke?

4 Shall you say: "My teaching is pure,
and I am clean in your sight"?

5 But oh, that God would speak,
and open his lips against you,

6 And tell you that the secrets of wisdom
are twice as effective:
So you might learn that God
will make you answer for your guilt.

7* Can you penetrate the designs of God?
Dare you vie with the perfection of
the Almighty?

8 It is higher than the heavens; what can
you do?
It is deeper than the nether world;
what can you know?

9 It is longer than the earth in measure,
and broader than the sea.

10 If he seize and imprison
or call to judgment, who then can say
him nay?

11 For he knows the worthlessness of men
and sees iniquity; will he then ignore
it?

12* Will empty man then gain
understanding,
and the wild jackass be made docile?

13 If you set your heart aright
and stretch out your hands toward
him,

14 If you remove all iniquity from your
conduct,
and let not injustice dwell in your
tent,

15 Surely then you may lift up your face in
innocence;
you may stand firm and unafraid.

16 For then you shall forget your misery,
or recall it like waters that have ebbed
away.

17 Then your life shall be brighter than the
noonday;
its gloom shall become as the
morning,

18* And you shall be secure, because there
is hope;
you shall look round you and lie down
in safety,

19 and you shall take your rest with none
to disturb.

Many shall entreat your favor,
20 but the wicked, looking on, shall be
consumed with envy.
Escape shall be cut off from them,
they shall wait to expire.

Job's Third Reply

12 [1]THEN Job replied and said:

2 No doubt you are the intelligent folk,
and with you wisdom shall die!

3* But I have intelligence as well as you;
for who does not know such things as
these?

4*† I have become the sport of my
neighbors:

---

*   18: 3, 3.11.   18: Lv 26, 6; Ps 4, 9.
21: 7, 9f; 16, 22.   12/3: 13, 2; 15, 9.
11/7: Rom 11, 33.   4: 21, 3; 30, 1.
12: 39, 5-8.

†   12, 4f: The Hebrew is somewhat obscure, but the general
sense is that the wicked mock at the pious when the latter appear to be abandoned by God; cf Ps 22, 7ff; Mt 27, 39-43.

"The one whom God answers when
he calls upon him,
the just, the perfect man," is a
laughingstock;

5 The undisturbed esteem my downfall a
disgrace
such as awaits unsteady feet;

6 Yet the tents of robbers are prosperous,
and those who provoke God are
secure.

7 But now ask the beasts to teach you,
and the birds of the air to tell you;

8 Or the reptiles on earth to instruct you,
and the fish of the sea to inform you.

9 Which of all these does not know
that the hand of God has done this?

10* In his hand is the soul of every living
thing,
and the life breath of all mankind.

11* Does not the ear judge words
as the mouth tastes food?

12* So with old age is wisdom,
and with length of days
understanding.

13 With him are wisdom and might;
his are counsel and understanding.

14* If he breaks a thing down, there is no
rebuilding;
if he imprisons a man, there is no
release.

15* He holds back the waters and there is
drought;
he sends them forth and they
overwhelm the land.

18† He loosens the bonds imposed by kings
and leaves but a waistcloth to bind
the king's own loins.

21 He breaks down the barriers of the
streams

19 and lets their never-failing waters
flow away.

16 With him are strength and prudence;
the misled and the misleaders are his.

17 He sends counselors away barefoot,
and of judges he makes fools.

20 He silences the trusted adviser,
and takes discretion from the aged.

22 The recesses of the darkness he
discloses,
and brings the gloom forth to the
light.

23 He makes nations great and he destroys
them;
he spreads peoples abroad and he
abandons them.

24 He takes understanding from the
leaders of the land,

25 till they grope in the darkness
without light;
he makes them stagger like drunken
men.

13

1 Lo, all this my eye has seen;
my ear has heard and perceived it.

2* What you know, I also know;
I fall not short of you.

3* But I would speak with the Almighty;
I wish to reason with God.

4 You are glossing over falsehoods
and offering vain remedies, every one
of you!

5 Oh, that you would be altogether silent!
This for you would be wisdom.

6 Hear now the rebuke I shall utter
and listen to the reproof from my lips.

7 Is it for God that you speak falsehood?
Is it for him that you utter deceit?

8 Is it for him that you show partiality?
Do you play advocate on behalf of
God?

9 Will it be well when he shall search you
out?
Would you impose on him as one does
on men?

10 He will openly rebuke you
if even in secret you show partiality.

11 Surely will his majesty affright you
and the dread of him fall upon you.

12 Your reminders are ashy maxims,
your fabrications are mounds of clay.

13 Be silent, let me alone! that I may speak
and give vent to my feelings.

14† I will carry my flesh between my teeth,
and take my life in my hand.

15* Slay me though he might, I will wait for
him;
I will defend my conduct before him.

16 And this shall be my salvation,
that no impious man can come into
his presence.

17 Pay careful heed to my speech,
and give my statement a hearing.

18* Behold, I have prepared my case,
I know that I am in the right.

19 If anyone can make a case against me,
then I shall be silent and die.

---

† 12, 18: *Waistcloth . . . loins:* he reduces kings to the condition of slaves, who wear only a cloth wrapped about the waist.

13, 14: The second half of the verse is a common biblical expression for risking one's life; cf Jgs 12, 3; 1 Sm 19, 5; 28, 21; Ps 119, 109; the first half of the verse must have a similar meaning. Job is so confident of his innocence that he is willing to risk his life by going to judgment with God.

✿ 10: Acts 17, 28.   13/2: 12, 3; 15, 9.
11: 34, 3.   3: 23, 4.
12: 32, 7.   15: 27, 5.
14: Rv 3, 7.   18: 33, 9.
15: Gn 7, 11-24.

20† These things only do not use against me,
　　　then from your presence I need not
　　　　hide:
21 Withdraw your hand far from me,
　　　and let not the terror of you frighten
　　　　me.
22 Then call me, and I will respond;
　　　or let me speak first, and answer me.

23 What are my faults and my sins?
　　　My misdeeds and my sins make
　　　　known to me!
24✻ Why do you hide your face
　　　and consider me your enemy?
25 Will you harass a wind-driven leaf,
　　　or pursue a withered straw?
26 For you draw up bitter indictments
　　　against me,
　　　and punish in me the faults of my
　　　　youth.
27 You put my feet in the stocks;
　　　you watch all my paths
　　　and trace out all my footsteps.

14 1✻ Man born of woman
　　　is short-lived and full of trouble,
2✻ Like a flower that springs up and fades,
　　　swift as a shadow that does not abide.
3 Upon such a one will you cast your eyes
　　　so as to bring him into judgment
　　　　before you,
13/28 Though he wears out like a leather
　　　bottle,
　　　like a garment that the moth has
　　　　consumed?
4✻ Can a man be found who is clean of
　　　defilement?
　　　There is none, 5however short his
　　　　days.
　　　You know the number of his months;
　　　you have fixed the limit which he
　　　　cannot pass.
6 Look away from him and let him be,
　　　while, like a hireling, he completes his
　　　　day.

7 For a tree there is hope,
　　　if it be cut down, that it will sprout
　　　　again
　　　and that its tender shoots will not
　　　　cease.
8 Even though its root grow old in the
　　　earth,
　　　and its stump die in the dust,

9 Yet at the first whiff of water it may
　　　flourish again
　　　and put forth branches like a young
　　　　plant.
10✻ But when a man dies, all vigor leaves
　　　him;
　　　when man expires, where then is he?
11 As when the waters of a lake fail,
　　　or a stream grows dry and parches,
12✻ So men lie down and rise not again.
　　　Till the heavens are no more, they
　　　　shall not awake,
　　　nor be roused out of their sleep.

13 Oh, that you would hide me in the
　　　nether world
　　　and keep me sheltered till your wrath
　　　　is past;
　　　would fix a time for me, and then
　　　　remember me!
14✻ When a man has died, were he to live
　　　again,
　　　all the days of my drudgery I would
　　　　wait,
　　　until my relief should come.
15 You would call, and I would answer
　　　you;
　　　you would esteem the work of your
　　　　hands.
16✻ Surely then you would count my steps,
　　　and not keep watch for sin in me.
17† My misdeeds would be sealed up in a
　　　pouch,
　　　and you would cover over my guilt.

18 But as a mountain falls at last
　　　and its rock is moved from its place,
19 As waters wear away the stones
　　　and floods wash away the soil of the
　　　　land,
　　　so you destroy the hope of man.
20 You prevail once for all against him and
　　　he passes on;
　　　with changed appearance you send
　　　　him away.
21 If his sons are honored, he is not aware
　　　of it;
　　　if they are in disgrace, he does not
　　　　know about them.
22 Only his own flesh pains him,
　　　and his soul grieves for him.

✻
24: 19, 11; 33, 10.　　　　4: Ps 51, 4.7.
14/1: 10, 20; 15, 14;　　　10: 20, 7.
Pss 39, 5f; 89, 46;　　　12: 7, 10.
Wis 2, 1.　　　　　　　14: 7, 1.
2: 8, 9; Pss 90, 6; 102, 12;　16: 31, 4; 34, 21.
103, 15; 109, 23; 144,
4; Is 40, 6f; Jas 1, 10.

† 13, 20: From here to the end of chapter 14, Job pleads his case, addressing God rather than his three friends.
14, 17: *Sealed up in a pouch:* hidden away and forgotten.

III: SECOND CYCLE OF SPEECHES

Second Speech of Eliphaz

15 ¹THEN ELIPHAZ THE TEMANITE spoke and said:

2   Should a wise man answer with airy
opinions,
      or puff himself up with wind?

3   Should he argue in speech which does
not avail,
      and in words which are to no profit?

4   You in fact do away with piety,
      and you lessen devotion toward God,

5   Because your wickedness instructs your
mouth,
      and you choose to speak like the
crafty.

6*   Your own mouth condemns you, not I;
      your own lips refute you.

7   Are you indeed the first-born of
mankind,
      or were you brought forth before the
hills?

8*   Are you privy to the counsels of God,
      and do you restrict wisdom to
yourself?

9*   What do you know that we do not
know?
      What intelligence have you which we
have not?

10   There are gray-haired old men among us
      more advanced in years than your
father.

11   Are the consolations of God not enough
for you,
      and speech that deals gently with
you?

12   Why do your notions carry you away,
      and why do your eyes blink,

13   So that you turn your anger against God
      and let such words escape your
mouth!

14*   What is a man that he should be
blameless,
      one born of woman that he should be
righteous?

15*   If in his holy ones God places no
confidence,
      and if the heavens are not clean in his
sight,

16   How much less so is the abominable,
the corrupt:
      man, who drinks in iniquity like
water!

17   I will show you, if you listen to me;
      what I have seen I will tell—

18   What wise men relate
      and have not contradicted since the
days of their fathers,

19   To whom alone the land was given,
      when no foreigner moved among
them.

20   The wicked man is in torment all his
days,
      and limited years are in store for the
tyrant;

21   The sound of terrors is in his ears;
      when all is prosperous, the spoiler
comes upon him.

22   He despairs of escaping the darkness,
      and looks ever for the sword;

23   A wanderer, food for the vultures,
      he knows that his destruction is
imminent.

24   By day the darkness fills him with dread;
      distress and anguish overpower him.

25   Because he has stretched out his hand
against God
      and bade defiance to the Almighty,

26   One shall rush sternly upon him
      with the stout bosses of his shield,
      like a king prepared for the charge.

27   Because he has blinded himself with his
crassness,
      padding his loins with fat,

28   He shall dwell in ruinous cities,
      in houses that are deserted,
      That are crumbling into clay

29   with no shadow to lengthen over the
ground.

      He shall not be rich, and his possessions
shall not endure;

31   for vain shall be his bartering.

30   A flame shall wither him up in his early
growth,
      and with the wind his blossoms shall
disappear.

32   His stalk shall wither before its time,
      and his branches shall be green no
more.

33   He shall be like a vine that sheds its
grapes unripened,
      and like an olive tree casting off its
bloom.

34*   For the breed of the impious shall be
sterile,
      and fire shall consume the tents of
extortioners.

✿
  15/6: 9, 20.
      8: 11, 7; Wis 9, 13;
        Jer 23, 18; Rom 11, 34;
        1 Cor 2, 11.16.
      9: 12, 3; 13, 2.
      14ff: 25, 4ff.
      14: 14, 4.
      15: 4, 18f.
      34: Wis 3, 11.18.

35*† They conceive malice and bring forth
        emptiness;
      they give birth to failure.

Job's Fourth Reply

16 ¹THEN Job answered and said:

2*   I have heard this sort of thing many
        times.
      Wearisome comforters are you all!

3   Is there no end to windy words?
      Or what sickness have you that you
        speak on?

4   I also could talk as you do,
      were you in my place.
    I could declaim over you,
      or wag my head at you;

5   I could strengthen you with talk,
      or shake my head with silent lips.

6   If I speak, this pain I have will not be
        checked;
      if I leave off, it will not depart from
        me.

7   But now that I am exhausted and
        stunned,
      all my company has closed in on me.

8   As a witness there rises up
      my traducer, speaking openly against
        me;

9   I am the prey his wrath assails,
      he gnashes his teeth against me.
    My enemies lord it over me;

10   their mouths are agape to bite me.
    They smite me on the cheek
        insultingly;
      they are all enlisted against me.

11   God has given me over to the impious;
      into the clutches of the wicked he has
        cast me.

12   I was in peace, but he dislodged me;
      he seized me by the neck and dashed
        me to pieces.

    He has set me up for a target;

13   his arrows strike me from all
        directions,
    He pierces my sides without mercy,
      he pours out my gall upon the ground.

14   He pierces me with thrust upon thrust;
      he attacks me like a warrior.

15   I have fastened sackcloth over my skin,
      and have laid my brow in the dust.

16   My face is inflamed with weeping
      and there is darkness over my eyes,

17   Although my hands are free from
        violence,
      and my prayer is sincere.

18†   O earth, cover not my blood,
      nor let my outcry come to rest!

19†   Even now, behold, my witness is in
        heaven,
      and my spokesman is on high.

20   My friends it is who wrong me;
      before God my eyes drop tears,

21   That he may do justice for a mortal in his
        presence
      and decide between a man and his
        neighbor.

22   For my years are numbered now,
      and I am on a journey from which I
        shall not return.

17 ¹ MY SPIRIT is broken, my lamp of life
        extinguished;
      my burial is at hand.

2   I am indeed mocked,
      and, as their provocation mounts, my
        eyes grow dim.

3†   Grant me one to offer you a pledge on
        my behalf:
      who is there that will give surety for
        me?

4   You darken their minds to knowledge;
      therefore they do not understand.

5   My lot is described as evil,

6*   and I am made a byword of the
        people;
      their object lesson I have become.

7   My eye has grown blind with anguish,
      and all my frame is shrunken to a
        shadow.

8   Upright men are astonished at this,
      and the innocent aroused against the
        wicked.

9   Yet the righteous shall hold to his way,
      and he who has clean hands increase
        in strength.

10   But turn now, and come on again;
      for I shall not find a wise man among
        you!

11   My days are passed away, my plans are
      at an end,
      the cherished purposes of my heart.

---

† 15, 35: *They give birth to failure:* their wicked plans yield nothing but futile results. Cf Ps 17, 15; Is 59, 4.

16, 18: As the blood of those who were unjustly slain cries to heaven for vengeance (Gn 4, 10; Ez 24, 6-9), so Job's sufferings demand redress.

16, 19: *Witness:* refers either to God or, more probably, to Job's prayer.

17, 3: Addressed to God; v 10 to Job's friends.

✿
35: Ps 7, 15; Is 59, 4.   17/6: 30, 9.
16/2: 12, 3.

12 Such men change the night into day;
where there is darkness they talk of
approaching light.

13 If I look for the nether world as my
dwelling,
if I spread my couch in the darkness,

14 If I must call corruption "my father,"
and the maggot "my mother" and
"my sister,"

15 Where then is my hope,
and my prosperity, who shall see?

16 Will they descend with me into the
nether world?
Shall we go down together into the
dust?

Bildad's Second Speech

18 ¹THEN Bildad the Shuhite replied and said:

2 When will you put an end to words?
Reflect, and then we can have
discussion.

3 Why are we accounted like the beasts,
their equals in your sight?

4† You who tear yourself in your anger,
shall the earth be neglected on your
account
[or the rock be moved out of its
place]?

5 Truly, the light of the wicked is
extinguished;
no flame brightens his hearth.

6✸ The light is darkened in his tent;
in spite of him, his lamp goes out.

7 His vigorous steps are hemmed in,
and his own counsel casts him down.

8 For he rushes headlong into a net,
and he wanders into a pitfall.

9 A trap seizes him by the heel,
and a snare lays hold of him.

10 A noose for him is hid on the ground,
and the toils for him on the way.

11✸ On every side terrors affright him;
they harry him at each step.

12 Disaster is ready at his side,

13† the first-born of death consumes his
limbs.

14† Fiery destruction lodges in his tent,
and marches him off to the king of
terrors.

He is plucked from the security of his
tent;

15 over his abode brimstone is scattered.

16 Below, his roots dry up,
and above, his branches wither.

17✸ His memory perishes from the land,
and he has no name on the earth.

18 He is driven from light into darkness,
and banished out of the world.

19 He has neither son nor grandson among
his people,
nor any survivor where once he dwelt.

20 They who come after shall be appalled
at his fate;
they who went before are struck with
horror.

21 So is it then with the dwelling of the
impious man,
and such is the place of him who
knows not God!

Job's Fifth Reply

19 ¹THEN Job answered and said:

2 How long will you vex my soul,
grind me down with words?

3 These ten times you have reviled me,
have assailed me without shame!

4 Be it indeed that I am at fault
and that my fault remains with me,

5 Even so, if you would vaunt yourselves
against me
and cast up to me my reproach,

6 Know then that God has dealt unfairly
with me,
and compassed me round with his net.

7✸ If I cry out "Injustice!" I am not heard.
I cry for help, but there is no redress.

8 He has barred my way and I cannot
pass;
he has veiled my path in darkness;

9 He has stripped me of my glory,
and taken the diadem from my brow.

10 He breaks me down on every side, and I
am gone;
my hope he has uprooted like a tree.

11✸ His wrath he has kindled against me;
he counts me among his enemies.

12 His troops advance as one man;
they build up their road to attack me,
and they encamp around my tent.

13✸ My brethren have withdrawn from me,
and my friends are wholly estranged.

✸ 18/6: 21, 17;
Prv 13, 9; 24, 20.
11: 15, 20-24; 27, 20.
17: Ps 34, 17;
Prv 2, 22; 10, 7.

19/7: 30, 20.
11: 13, 24; 33, 10.
13: 6, 13.

---

† 18, 4: Job himself is portrayed as having the heedless rage of
wild beasts, despite which God does not forsake the usual
course of Divine Providence.

18, 13: *First-born of death:* that is, disease, plague.

18, 14: *The king of terrors:* of the nether world, death; however, the Hebrew is obscure.

14 My kinsfolk and companions neglect
me,
and my guests have forgotten me.
15 Even my handmaids treat me as a
stranger;
I am an alien in their sight.
16 I call my servant, but he gives no
answer,
though in my speech I plead with
him.
17✤ My breath is abhorred by my wife;
I am loathsome to the men of my
family.
18 The young children, too, despise me;
when I appear, they speak against me.
19✤ All my intimate friends hold me in
horror;
those whom I loved have turned
against me!
20† My bones cleave to my skin,
and I have escaped with my flesh
between my teeth.
21 Pity me, pity me, O you my friends,
for the hand of God has struck me!
22† Why do you hound me as though you
were divine,
and insatiably prey upon me?
23✤† Oh, would that my words were written
down!
Would that they were inscribed in a
record:
24 That with an iron chisel and with lead
they were cut in the rock forever!
25✤† But as for me, I know that my Vindicator
lives,
and that he will at last stand forth
upon the dust;
27 Whom I myself shall see:
my own eyes, not another's, shall
behold him,
26 And from my flesh I shall see God;
my inmost being is consumed with
longing.
28 But you who say, "How shall we
persecute him,
seeing that the root of the matter is
found in him?"
29 Be afraid of the sword for yourselves,
for these crimes deserve the sword;
that you may know that there is a
judgment.

Zophar's Second Speech

20 **1**THEN Zophar the Naamathite spoke and
said:

3 A rebuke which puts me to shame I
hear,
2 and because of this I am disturbed.
So now my thoughts provide me with an
answer,
and from my understanding a spirit
gives me a reply.
4 Do you not know this from olden time,
since man was placed upon the earth,
5✤ That the triumph of the wicked is short
and the joy of the impious but for a
moment?
6 Though his pride mount up to the
heavens
and his head reach to the clouds,
7✤ Yet he perishes forever like the fuel of
his fire,
and the onlookers say, "Where is he?"
8 Like a dream he takes flight and is not
found again;
he fades away like a vision of the
night.
9 The eye which saw him does so no
more;
nor shall his dwelling again behold
him.
11 Though his frame is full of youthful
vigor,
this shall lie with him in the dust.
12 Though wickedness is sweet in his
mouth,
and he hides it under his tongue,
13 Though he retains it and will not let
it go
but keeps it still within his mouth,
14 Yet in his stomach the food shall turn;
it shall be venom of asps inside him.
15 The riches he swallowed he shall
disgorge;

---

† 19, 20: *With my flesh between my teeth:* meaning perhaps
that Job has been reduced to such an extremity that he scarcely
has thin lips over his teeth. But the current Hebrew text of this
line is probably corrupt.
19, 22: *Divine:* possessing God's attributes of judgment and
authority to punish.
19, 23f: Job regards what he is about to say as so important
that he wishes it recorded in a permanent manner.
19, 25.27: The meaning of this passage is obscure because the
original text has been poorly preserved and the ancient versions
do not agree among themselves. It is certain that Job expresses
his belief in a future vindication by God (called here in the Hebrew "Goel"), but the time and manner of this vindication are
undefined. In the Vulgate Job is made to indicate a belief in
physical resurrection after death, but the Hebrew and the
other ancient versions are less specific.

✤
17: 2, 9.   20/5: 21, 13; Ps 37, 35f.
19: Sir 6, 8.   7: 14, 10;
23: 31, 35.   Ps 37, 10.36.
25ff: Phil 3, 20; Ti 2, 13.

God shall compel his belly to disown
   them.

16 The poison of asps he shall drink in;
   the viper's fangs shall slay him.

17† He shall see no streams of oil,
   no torrents of honey or milk.

18 Restoring his gains, he shall not enjoy
   them;
   though his wealth increases, he shall
   not rejoice.

19 Because he has oppressed the poor,
   and stolen a patrimony he had not
   built up,

21 Therefore his prosperity shall not
   endure,

10✷ and his hands shall yield up his
   riches.

20✷ Though he has known no quiet in his
   greed,
   his treasures shall not save him.

22✷ When he abounds to overflowing, he
   shall be brought into straits,
   and nought shall be left of his goods.

23 God shall send against him the fury of
   his wrath
   and rain down his missiles of war
   upon him.

24 Should he escape the iron weapon,
   the bow of bronze shall pierce him
   through;

25 The dart shall come out of his back;
   terrors shall fall upon him.

26✷ Complete darkness is in store for him;
   the fire which shall consume him
   needs not to be fanned.

27 The heavens shall reveal his guilt,
   and the earth shall rise up against
   him.

28 The flood shall sweep away his house
   with the waters that run off in the day
   of God's anger.

29✷ This is the portion of a wicked man,
   and the heritage appointed him by
   God.

Job's Sixth Reply

21 ¹THEN Job said in reply:

2✷ At least listen to my words,
   and let that be the consolation you
   offer.

3 Bear with me while I speak;
   and after I have spoken, you can
   mock!

4 Is my complaint toward man?
   And why should I not be impatient?

5 Look at me and be astonished,
   put your hands over your mouths.

6 When I think of it, I am dismayed,
   and horror takes hold on my flesh.

7✷ Why do the wicked survive,
   grow old, become mighty in power?

8 Their progeny is secure in their sight;
   they see before them their kinsfolk
   and their offspring.

9 Their homes are safe and without fear,
   nor is the scourge of God upon them.

10 Their bulls gender without fail;
   their cows calve and do not miscarry.

11 These folk have infants numerous as
   lambs,
   and their children dance.

12 They sing to the timbrel and harp,
   and make merry to the sound of the
   flute.

13✷ They live out their days in prosperity,
   and tranquilly go down to the nether
   world.

14✷ Yet they say to God, "Depart from us,
   for we have no wish to learn your
   ways!

15✷ What is the Almighty that we should
   serve him?
   And what gain shall we have if we
   pray to him?"

16✷ If their happiness is not in their own
   hands
   and if the counsel of the wicked is
   repulsive to God,

17 How often is the lamp of the wicked
   put out?
   How often does destruction come
   upon them,
   the portion he allots in his anger?

18 Let them be like straw before the wind,
   and like chaff which the storm
   snatches away!

19 May God not store up the man's misery
   for his children;
   let him requite the man himself so
   that he feels it,

20 Let his own eyes see the calamity,
   and the wrath of the Almighty let
   him drink!

✷

10: 27, 14.
20: Eccl 5, 9; Lk 12, 20.
22: 15, 20-35.
26: Dt 32, 22.
29: 27, 13.
21/2: 13, 17.

7: 12, 6; Pss 37, 35;
   73, 3; Eccl 8, 14;
   Jer 12, 1f; Mal 3, 14f.
13: 34, 20.
14: 22, 17.
15: Mal 3, 14.
16: 22, 18.

---

† 20, 17: *Oil:* olive oil, one of the main agricultural products of Palestine, a land proverbially rich in *honey* and *milk.*

21   For what interest has he in his family
after him,
    when the number of his months is
finished?

23   One dies in his full vigor,
    wholly at ease and content;

24   His figure is full and nourished,
    and his bones are rich in marrow.

25.   Another dies in bitterness of soul,
    having never tasted happiness.

26   Alike they lie down in the dust,
    and worms cover them both.

27   Behold, I know your thoughts,
    and the arguments you rehearse
against me.

28   For you say, "Where is the house of
the magnate,
    and where the dwelling place of the
wicked?"

29   Have you not asked the wayfarers
    and do you not recognize their
monuments?

30   Nay, the evil man is spared calamity
when it comes;

32   and on the day he is carried to the
grave

31   Who will charge him with his conduct
to his face,
    and for what he has done who will
repay him?

33   Sweet to him are the clods of the valley,
    and over him the funeral mound
keeps watch,
    While all the line of mankind follows
him,
    and the countless others who have
gone before.

34   How then can you offer me vain
comfort,
    while in your answers perfidy
remains?

IV: THIRD CYCLE OF SPEECHES

Eliphaz's Third Speech

22   [1]THEN ELIPHAZ THE TEMANITE answered and said:

2✸   Can a man be profitable to God?
    Though to himself a wise man be
profitable!

21/22†   Can anyone teach God knowledge,
    seeing that he judges those on high?

3✸   Is it of advantage to the Almighty if
you are just?
    Or is it a gain to him if you make your
ways perfect?

4   Is it because of your piety that he
reproves you—
    that he enters with you into
judgment?

5   Is not your wickedness manifold?
    Are not your iniquities endless?

6✸†   You have unjustly kept your kinsmen's
goods in pawn,
    left them stripped naked of their
clothing.

7   To the thirsty you have given no water
to drink,
    and from the hungry you have
withheld bread;

8   As if the land belonged to the man of
might,
    and only the privileged were to dwell
in it.

9✸   You have sent widows away empty-
handed,
    and the resources of orphans you
have destroyed.

10✸   Therefore snares are round about you,
    and a sudden terror causes you
dismay,

11   Or darkness, in which you cannot see;
    a deluge of waters covers you.

12✸   Does not God, in the heights of the
heavens,
    behold the stars, high though they
are?

13✸   Yet you say, "What does God know?
    Can he judge through the thick
darkness?

14   Clouds hide him so that he cannot see;
    he walks upon the vault of the
heavens!"

15   Do you indeed keep to the ancient way
    trodden by worthless men,

16   Who were snatched away before their
time;
    whose foundations a flood swept
away?

17   These men said to God, "Depart from
us!"
    and, "What can the Almighty do
to us?"

✸
22/2: 9, 2.   10: 18, 8ff.
   3: 35, 7.   12: 11, 8.
   6: 24, 3; Dt 24, 6.17;   13f: Pss 10, 11; 73, 11;
     Ez 18, 12.16.   94, 7; Is 29, 15;
   9: Dt 24, 17; 27, 19.   Ez 8, 12; 9, 9.

† 21, 22: *Those on high:* the angels.

22, 6ff: This criticism of Job by Eliphaz is altogether untrue, but it is made to dramatize the latter's argument that God always acts justly when he causes someone to suffer. V 8 is misplaced.

18*† [Yet he had filled their houses with
          good things!
      But far be from me the mind of the
          impious!]

19* The just look on and are gladdened,
      and the innocent deride them:

20 "Truly these have been destroyed
          where they stood,
      and such as were left, fire has
          consumed!"

21 Come to terms with him to be at peace.
      In this shall good come to you:

22 Receive instruction from his mouth,
      and lay up his words in your heart.

23 If you return to the Almighty, you will
          be restored;
      if you put iniquity far from your tent,

24† And treat raw gold like dust,
      and the fine gold of Ophir as pebbles
          from the brook,

25 Then the Almighty himself shall be
          your gold
      and your sparkling silver.

26 For then you shall delight in the
          Almighty
      and you shall lift up your face toward
          God.

27* You shall entreat him and he will hear
          you,
      and your vows you shall fulfill.

28 When you make a decision, it shall
          succeed for you,
      and upon your ways the light shall
          shine.

29* For he brings down the pride of the
          haughty,
      but the man of humble mien he saves.

30* God delivers him who is innocent;
      you shall be delivered through
          cleanness of hands.

Job's Seventh Reply

23 ¹AGAIN Job answered and said:

2 Though I know my complaint is bitter,
      his hand is heavy upon me in my
          groanings.

3 Oh, that today I might find him,
      that I might come to his judgment
          seat!

4 I would set out my cause before him,
      and fill my mouth with arguments;

5 I would learn the words with which he
          would answer,
      and understand what he would
          reply to me.

6 Even should he contend against me
          with his great power,
      yet, would that he himself might
          heed me!

7 There the upright man might reason
          with him,
      and I should once and for all
          preserve my rights.

8 But if I go to the east, he is not there;
      or to the west, I cannot perceive him;

9 Where the north enfolds him, I behold
          him not;
      by the south he is veiled, and I see
          him not.

10* Yet he knows my way;
      if he proved me, I should come forth
          as gold.

11 My foot has always walked in his steps;
      his way I have kept and have not
          turned aside.

12 From the commands of his lips I have
          not departed;
      the words of his mouth I have
          treasured in my heart.

13* But he has decided, and who can say
          him nay?
      What he desires, that he does.

14 For he will carry out what is
          appointed for me;
      and many such things may yet be in
          his mind.

15 Therefore am I dismayed before him;
      when I take thought, I fear him.

16 Indeed God has made my courage fail;
      the Almighty has put me in dismay.

17 Yes, would that I had vanished in
          darkness,
      and that thick gloom were before me
          to conceal me.

24 1† WHY are not times set by the Almighty,
      and why do his friends not see his
          days?

2 The wicked remove landmarks;
      they steal away herds and pasture
          them.

3 The asses of orphans they drive away;
      they take the widow's ox for a pledge.

---

*
18: 21, 16.
19: Ps 107, 42.
27: 33, 26.
29: Ps 138, 6; Prv 29, 23;
  Mt 23, 12; Lk 1, 52;
  Jas 4, 10; 1 Pt 5, 5.

30: 17, 9; Ps 18, 21.25.
23/10: Ps 66, 10; Prv 17, 3;
  Mal 3, 3; 1 Pt 1, 7.
13: 42, 2; Pss 115, 3;
  135, 6.

†
22, 18: A gloss, taken partly from 21, 16.
22, 24: *Ophir:* cf note to Ps 45, 10.
24, 1: Why does not God favor his friends by the speedy
punishment of his enemies? (The text and order of verses in
this chapter are not certain; note the omission of v 9 which
duplicates words of vv 2-4.)

4 They force the needy off the road;
    all the poor of the land are driven
       into hiding.

5 Like wild asses in the desert, these go
    forth
    to their task of seeking food;
    The steppe provides food for the young
       among them;

6   they harvest at night in the untilled
       land.

7 They pass the night naked, without
       clothing,
    for they have no covering against the
       cold;

8 They are drenched with the rain of the
       mountains,
    and for want of shelter they cling to
       the rock.

11 Between the rows they press out the oil;
    they glean in the vineyard of the
       wicked.
    They tread the wine presses, yet suffer
       thirst,

10   and famished are those who carry the
       sheaves.

12 From the dust the dying groan,
    and the souls of the wounded cry out
    [yet God does not treat it as
       unseemly].

13❊ There are those who are rebels against
       the light;
    they know not its ways;
    they abide not in its paths.

14 When there is no light the murderer
       rises,
    to kill the poor and needy.

15❊ The eye of the adulterer watches for the
       twilight;
    he says, "No eye will see me."
    In the night the thief roams about,
    and he puts a mask over his face;

16   in the dark he breaks into houses.
    By day they shut themselves in;
    none of them know the light,

17†   for daylight they regard as darkness.

❊   ❊   ❊

18 Their portion in the land is accursed,
20   and wickedness is splintered like
       wood.

19.21 . . . .

22 To him who rises without assurance of
       his life

23   he gives safety and support.
    He sustains the mighty by his strength,
    and his eyes are on their ways.

24 They are exalted for a while, and then
       they are gone;
    they are laid low and, like all others,
       are gathered up;
    like ears of grain they shrivel.

❊   ❊   ❊

25 If this be not so, who will confute me,
    and reduce my argument to nought?

Bildad's Third Speech

25 ¹THEN Bildad the Shuhite answered and said:

2   Dominion and awesomeness are his
       who brings about harmony in his
       heavens.

3†   Is there any numbering of his troops?
       Yet to which of them does not his
       light extend?

4❊   How can a man be just in God's sight,
       or how can any woman's child be
       innocent?

5   Behold, even the moon is not bright
       and the stars are not clear in his sight.

6❊   How much less man, who is but a
       maggot,
       the son of man, who is only a worm?

Job's Reply

26 ¹†THEN Job spoke again and said:

2   What help you give to the powerless,
       what strength to the feeble arm!

3   How you counsel, as though he had no
       wisdom;
       how profuse is the advice you offer!

4❊   With whose help have you uttered
       those words,
       and whose is the breath that comes
       forth from you?

5❊†   The shades beneath writhe in terror,
       the waters, and the inhabitants.

---

† 24, 17: The asterisks which follow this verse mark off a passage (vv 18-24) which cannot be ascribed to Job with certainty. Vv 17-24 are in general poorly preserved; and much of vv 18-21 has not been translated because these verses are obscure. St. Jerome renders them as follows: (18) "He is light upon the face of the water, cursed be his portion on the earth; let him not walk by the way of vineyards. (19) Let him pass from the snow waters to excessive heat, and his sin even to hell. (20) Let mercy forget him; may worms be his sweetness; let him be remembered no more, but be broken in pieces as an unfruitful tree. (21) For he has fed the barren that bears not, and to the widow he has done no good."

25, 3: *His troops:* the heavenly hosts, the stars or the angels. *His light:* compare the wording in 24, 13: *those who are rebels against the light.*

26, 1-14: Probably to be read as Job's reply to Bildad's short speech. Some, however, would make it the reply to Zophar (27, 13-21); it would thus lead up to the poem of ch 28.

26, 5: *Shades:* the dead in Sheol, the nether world; cf Pss 6, 6; 88, 11.

❊
24/13: Jn 3, 19f.   6: 4, 19; 15, 16.
  15: Prv 7, 9f.   26/4: Gn 2, 7.
  25/4: 4, 17ff; 9, 2.   5: Prv 9, 18.

6*† Naked before him is the nether world,
and Abaddon has no covering.

7† He stretches out the North over empty
space,
and suspends the earth over nothing
at all;

8 He binds up the waters in his clouds,
yet the cloud is not rent by their
weight;

9 He holds back the appearance of the
full moon
by spreading his clouds before it.

10*† He has marked out a circle on the
surface of the deep
as the boundary of light and
darkness.

11* The pillars of the heavens tremble
and are stunned at his thunderous
rebuke;

12† By his power he stirs up the sea,
and by his might he crushes Rahab;

13* With his angry breath he scatters the
waters,

27/22† and he hurls the lightning against
them relentlessly;
His hand pierces the fugitive dragon
as from his hand it strives to flee.

14 Lo, these are but the outlines of his
ways,
and how faint is the word we hear!

Job's Reply

27   **11** I will teach you the manner of God's
dealings,
and the way of the Almighty I will
not conceal.

2*† As God lives, who withholds my deserts,
the Almighty, who has made bitter
my soul,

3 So long as I still have life in me
and the breath of God is in my
nostrils,

4 My lips shall not speak falsehood,
nor my tongue utter deceit!

5* Far be it from me to account you right;
till I die I will not renounce my
innocence.

6 My justice I maintain and I will not
relinquish it;
my heart does not reproach me for
any of my days.

7 Let my enemy be as the wicked
and my adversary as the unjust!

8 For what can the impious man expect
when he is cut off,
when God requires his life?

9 Will God then attend to his cry
when calamity comes upon him?

10 Will he then delight in the Almighty
and call upon him constantly?

12 Behold, you yourselves have all seen it;
why then do you spend yourselves in
idle words!

* * *

13*† This is the portion of a wicked man
from God,
the inheritance an oppressor receives
from the Almighty:

14 Though his children be many, the
sword is their destiny.
His offspring shall not be filled with
bread.

15 His survivors, when they die, shall have
no burial,
and their widows shall not be
mourned.

16 Though he heap up silver like dust
and store away mounds of clothing,

17 What he has stored the just man shall
wear,
and the innocent shall divide the
silver.

18 He builds his house as of cobwebs,
or like a booth put up by the
vine-keeper.

19* He lies down a rich man, one last time;
he opens his eyes and nothing
remains to him.

20 Terrors rush upon him by day;
at night the tempest carries him off.

21† The storm wind seizes him and he
disappears;
it sweeps him out of his place.

* * *

---

†   26, 6: *Nether world:* cf note to Ps 6, 6. *Abaddon:* Hebrew for "(place of) destruction," a synonym for *nether world;* cf 28, 22; Rv 9, 11.

26, 7: *The North:* used here as a synonym for the firmament, the heavens; cf Is 14, 13.

26, 10: *Circle:* the horizon of the ocean which serves as the boundary for the activity of light and darkness.

26, 12: *Rahab:* cf 9, 13; see note on Ps 89, 11.

27, 22: *The fugitive dragon:* the same term occurs in Is 27, 1 in apposition to Leviathan; see note on 3, 8.

27, 2-12: This is probably to be read as Job's reply to Zophar's speech of 27, 13-21. In the current Hebrew text the heading for this chapter (27, 1, here omitted) is identical with 29, 1; we should expect rather such a heading as in 21, 1; 23, 1; 26, 1.

27, 13-21: This is probably to be read as Zophar's third speech. The asterisks are present to indicate it is not likely that the sacred writer intended these words to be ascribed to Job.

27, 21: The Hebrew has two more verses: v 22 (read above with 26, 13); and v 23, a variant form of v 21.

*
6: Ps 139, 7-12.
10: 38, 8-11; Prv 8, 29.
11: 9, 6.
13: Is 27, 1.

27/2: 34, 5.
5: 2, 3.9; 13, 15; 33, 9.
13: 20, 4-29.
19: Pss 49, 18; 76, 6.

28 · The Inaccessibility of Wisdom

28

1† THERE is indeed a mine for silver,
   and a place for gold which men
   refine.

2 Iron is taken from the earth,
   and copper is melted out of stone.

4 . . . .

5 The earth, though out of it comes forth
   bread,
   is in fiery upheaval underneath.

6 Its stones are the source of sapphires,
   and there is gold in its dust.

12✶ But whence can wisdom be obtained,
   and where is the place of
   understanding?

13 Man knows nothing to equal it,
   nor is it to be had in the land of the
   living.

15✶ Solid gold cannot purchase it,
   nor can its price be paid with silver.

16† It cannot be bought with gold of Ophir,
   with the precious onyx or the
   sapphire.

17 Gold or crystal cannot equal it,
   nor can golden vessels reach its
   worth.

18 Neither coral nor jasper should be
   thought of;
   it surpasses pearls and [19]Arabian
   topaz.

20 Whence, then, comes wisdom,
   and where is the place of
   understanding?

21 It is hid from the eyes of any beast;
   from the birds of the air it is
   concealed.

7 The path to it no bird of prey knows,
   nor has the hawk's eye seen that path.

8 The proud beasts have not trodden it,
   nor has the lion gone that way.

14 The abyss declares, "It is not in me";
   and the sea says, "I have it not."

22† Abaddon and Death say,
   "Only by rumor have we heard of it."

23✶ God knows the way to it;
   it is he who is familiar with its place.

24 For he beholds the ends of the earth
   and sees all that is under the heavens.

3 He has set a boundary for the darkness;
   to the farthest confines he penetrates.

9 He sets his hand to the flinty rock,
   and overturns the mountains at their
   foundations.

10 He splits channels in the rocks;
   his eyes behold all that is precious.

11 He probes the wellsprings of the
   streams,
   and brings hidden things to light.

25 He has weighed out the wind,
   and fixed the scope of the waters;

26✶ When he made rules for the rain
   and a path for the thunderbolts,

27 Then he saw wisdom and appraised it,
   gave it its setting, knew it through
   and through.

28✶ And to man he said:
   Behold, the fear of the LORD is
   wisdom;
   and avoiding evil is understanding.

V: JOB'S FINAL SUMMARY OF HIS CAUSE

29

1 JOB TOOK UP HIS THEME anew and said:

2✶ Oh, that I were as in the months past!
   as in the days when God watched
   over me,

3 While he kept his lamp shining above
   my head,
   and by his light I walked through
   darkness;

4 As I was in my flourishing days,
   when God sheltered my tent;

5 When the Almighty was yet with me,
   and my children were round about
   me;

6† When my footsteps were bathed in
   milk,
   and the rock flowed with streams of
   oil;

7 When I went forth to the gate of the city
   and set up my seat in the square—

8 Then the young men saw me and
   withdrew,
   while the elders rose up and stood;

✶ 28/12: Eccl 7, 24f;
   Bar 3, 14f.29-33.
15: Prv 3, 14; 8, 10f.19;
   16, 16; Wis 7, 7-11.
23-27: Prv 8, 22-31.
23: Prv 2, 6; Sir 1, 1;

Jas 1, 5.
26: 38, 25; Prv 3, 20.
28: Ps 111, 10; Prv 1, 7;
   9, 10; Sir 1, 16.
29/2: 1, 10.

---

† 28, 1-28: Note the changed order of verses; v 4 is uncertain. This chapter contains a beautifully vivid description of that Wisdom which is beyond the attainment of creatures; known only to God, it is reflected in the order and majesty of his creation. Man, however, can, in a way, participate in this Wisdom by fearing the LORD and avoiding evil. Scholars are not agreed regarding the authorship of this poem, though it is altogether worthy of the author of the Book of Job. Used here as a counterpoise to ch 3 at the beginning of the dialogue, it may have been first conceived as an independent poem.

28, 16: *Ophir:* cf note to Ps 45, 10.

28, 22: *Abaddon:* cf note to 26, 6.

29, 6: Hyperbole to express abundance; see note on 20, 17.

9* The chief men refrained from speaking
  and covered their mouths with their
    hands;

10 The voice of the princes was silenced,
  and their tongues stuck to the roofs
    of their mouths.

21 For me they listened and waited;
  they were silent for my counsel.

22 Once I spoke, they said no more,
  but received my pronouncement
    drop by drop.

23 They waited for me as for the rain;
  they drank in my words like the
    spring rains.

24 When I smiled on them they were
    reassured;
  mourners took comfort from my
    cheerful glance.
  I chose out their way and presided;
  I took a king's place in the armed
    forces.

11 Whoever heard of me blessed me;
  those who saw me commended me.

12 For I rescued the poor who cried out for
    help,
  the orphans, and the unassisted;

13 The blessings of those in extremity
    came upon me,
  and the heart of the widow I made
    joyful.

14 I wore my honesty like a garment;
  justice was my robe and my turban.

15 I was eyes to the blind,
  and feet to the lame was I;

16 I was a father to the needy;
  the rights of the stranger I studied,

17 And I broke the jaws of the wicked
    man;
  from his teeth I forced the prey.

18† Then I said: "In my own nest I shall
    grow old;
  I shall multiply years like the
    phoenix.

19 My root is spread out to the waters;
  the dew rests by night on my
    branches.

20 My glory is fresh within me,
  and my bow is renewed in my hand!"

30 1* BUT now they hold me in derision
  who are younger in years than I;
  Whose fathers I should have disdained
    to rank with the dogs of my flock.

2 Such strength as they had, to me meant
    nought;
  they were utterly destitute.

3* In want and hunger was their lot,
  they who fled to the parched
    wastelands:

4† They plucked saltwort and shrubs;
  the roots of the broom plant were
    their food.

5 They were banished from among men,
  with an outcry like that against a
    thief—

6 To dwell on the slopes of the wadies,
  in caves of sand and stone;

7 Among the bushes they raised their
    raucous cry;
  under the nettles they huddled
    together.

8 Irresponsible, nameless men,
  they were driven out of the land.

9* Yet now they sing of me in mockery;
  I am become a byword among them.

10 They abhor me, they stand aloof from
    me,
  they do not hesitate to spit in my face!

11 Indeed, they have loosed their bonds;
    they lord it over me,
  and have thrown off restraint in my
    presence.

12 To subvert my paths they rise up;
  they build their approaches for my
    ruin.

13 To destroy me, they attack with none to
    stay them;

14 as through a wide breach they
    advance.
  Amid the uproar they come on in
    waves;

15 over me rolls the terror.

My dignity is borne off on the wind,
  and my welfare vanishes like a cloud.

18† One with great power lays hold of my
    clothing;
  by the collar of my tunic he seizes
    me:

19 He has cast me into the mire;
  I am leveled with the dust and ashes.

20* I cry to you, but you do not answer me;
  you stand off and look at me,

---

† 29, 18: *Phoenix:* a legendary bird which, after several centuries of life, consumed itself in fire, then rose from its ashes in youthful freshness. This meaning, originally intended in the Greek, later came to mean "palm tree." Some render the Hebrew as "sand."

30, 4: *Saltwort:* found in salt marshes and very sour to the taste; eaten by the extremely poor as a cooked vegetable. *Broom plant:* the juniper or brushwood; cf Ps 120, 4; a figure of bitterness and poverty, because of its bitter-tasting roots which are practically inedible.

30, 18-23: Job here refers to God's stern treatment of him.

※
  9: Wis 8, 10ff.   9: 17, 6.
30/1: 12, 4; 19, 18.   20: 19, 7.
  3-8: 24, 5f.

21 Then you turn upon me without mercy
and with your strong hand you buffet
me.

22 You raise me up and drive me before
the wind;
I am tossed about by the tempest.

23* Indeed I know you will turn me back in
death
to the destined place of everyone
alive.

24 Yet should not a hand be held out
to help a wretched man in his
calamity?

25* Or have I not wept for the hardships of
others;
was not my soul grieved for the
destitute?

26 Yet when I looked for good, then evil
came;
when I expected light, then came
darkness.

16 My soul ebbs away from me;
27 days of affliction have overtaken me.

17 My frame takes no rest by night;
my inward parts seethe and will not
be stilled.

28 I go about in gloom, without the sun;
I rise up in public to voice my grief.

29 I have become the brother of jackals,
companion to the ostrich.

30 My blackened skin falls away from me;
the heat scorches my very frame.

31 My harp is turned to mourning,
and my reed pipe to sounds of
weeping.

31 **2** BUT what is man's lot from God above,
his inheritance from the Almighty on
high?

3 Is it not calamity for the unrighteous,
and woe for evildoers?

4* Does he not see my ways,
and number all my steps?

6* Let God weigh me in the scales of
justice;
thus will he know my innocence!

5† If I have walked in falsehood
and my foot has hastened to deceit;

7 If my steps have turned out of the way,
and my heart has followed my eyes,
or any stain clings to my hands,

8 Then may I sow, but another eat of it,
or may my planting be rooted up!

38 If my land has cried out against me
till its very furrows complained;

39 If I have eaten its produce without
payment
and grieved the hearts of its tenants;

40 Then let the thistles grow instead of
wheat
and noxious weeds instead of barley!

1† If I have made an agreement with my
eyes
and entertained any thoughts against
a maiden;

9 If my heart has been enticed toward a
woman,
and I have lain in wait at my
neighbor's door;

10 Then may my wife grind for another,
and may others cohabit with her!

11* For that would be heinous,
a crime to be condemned;

12* A fire that should burn down to the
abyss
till it consumed all my possessions to
the roots.

13 Had I refused justice to my manservant
or to my maid, when they had a claim
against me,

14 What then should I do when God rose
up;
what could I answer when he
demand an account?

15 Did not he who made me in the womb
make him?
Did not the same One fashion us
before our birth?

16* If I have denied anything to the poor,
or allowed the eyes of the widow to
languish

17 While I ate my portion alone,
with no share in it for the fatherless,

18 Though like a father God has reared me
from my youth,
guiding me even from my mother's
womb—

19 If I have seen a wanderer without
clothing,
or a poor man without covering,

20 Whose limbs have not blessed me
when warmed with the fleece of my
sheep;

21† If I have raised my hand against the
innocent

---

*
23: Heb 9, 27.   6: 23, 10.
25: 29, 12-16.   11: Ex 20, 14; Lv 20, 10;
31/4: 14, 16; 34, 21;   Dt 22, 22.
Ps 139, 3;   12: Sir 9, 8f.
Prv 5, 21.   16-23: 29, 12-16.

†
31, 5-34: Job's final protestation of his innocence.
31, 1.9: Note the gradation: avoidance of sinful glances
and thoughts against a maiden; desire for another's wife.
31, 21: *Gate:* cf notes on Jb 5, 4; Ru 4, 1.

because I saw that I had supporters
at the gate—

22 Then may my arm fall from the
shoulder,
my forearm be broken at the elbow!

23 For the dread of God will be upon me,
and his majesty will overpower me.

24 Had I put my trust in gold
or called fine gold my security;

25 Or had I rejoiced that my wealth was
great,
or that my hand had acquired
abundance—

26*† Had I looked upon the sun as it shone,
or the moon in the splendor of its
progress,

27 And had my heart been secretly enticed
to waft them a kiss with my hand;

28* This too would be a crime for
condemnation,
for I should have denied God above.

29* Had I rejoiced at the destruction of my
enemy
or exulted when evil fell upon him,

30 Even though I had not suffered my
mouth to sin
by uttering a curse against his life—

31† Had not the men of my tent exclaimed,
"Who has not been fed with his
meat!"

32 Because no stranger lodged in the
street,
but I opened my door to wayfarers—

33† Had I, out of human weakness, hidden
my sins
and buried my guilt in my bosom

34 Because I feared the noisy multitude
and the scorn of the tribes terrified
me—
then I should have remained silent,
and not come out of doors!

35* Oh, that I had one to hear my case,
and that my accuser would write out
his indictment!

36† Surely, I should wear it on my shoulder
or put it on me like a diadem;

37† Of all my steps I should give him an
account;
like a prince I should present myself
before him.

This is my final plea; let the Almighty
answer me!

The words of Job are ended.

VI: ELIHU'S SPEECHES

32 ¹*THEN THE THREE MEN CEASED to answer Job,
because he was righteous in his own eyes.
²*†But the anger of Elihu, son of Barachel the Buzite,
of the family of Ram, was kindled. He was angry with
Job for considering himself rather than God to be in
the right. ³*He was angry also with the three friends
because they had not found a good answer and had not
condemned Job. ⁴But since these men were older than
he, Elihu bided his time before addressing Job. ⁵When,
however, Elihu saw that there was no reply in the
mouths of the three men, his wrath was inflamed. ⁶So
Elihu, son of Barachel the Buzite, spoke out and said:

I am young and you are very old;
therefore I held back and was afraid
to declare to you my knowledge.

7* Days should speak, I thought,
and many years teach wisdom!

8* But it is a spirit in man,
the breath of the Almighty, that gives
him understanding.

9 It is not those of many days who are
wise,
nor the aged who understand the
right.

10 Therefore I say, hearken to me;
let me too set forth my knowledge!

11 Behold, I have waited for your
discourses,
and have given ear to your
arguments.

---

† 31, 26ff: Job never sinned by worshiping the sun or the
moon; *waft them a kiss:* an act of idolatrous worship.

31, 31: The members of his household will testify to his
hospitality.

31, 33f: Job's present protest is made, not in spite of hidden
sins which he had been unwilling to disclose, but out of genuine
innocence.

31, 36: *On my shoulder:* i. e., boldly, proudly.

31, 37: *Like a prince:* not as a frightened criminal. *Final
plea:* literally, "tau," the last letter of the Hebrew alphabet;
in the current Hebrew text this line is in v 35, while the following one ends v 40.

32, 2: *Elihu* means "My God is he." This speaker was from
Buz, which, according to Jer 25, 23, was near Tema and Dedan.
A young man, he impetuously and impatiently upbraids Job for
his boldness toward God, and the three friends for not successfully answering Job. He undertakes to defend God's absolute
justice and to explain more clearly why there is suffering. While
fundamentally his position is the same as that of the three
friends, he does locate more definitely, though not perfectly, the
place of suffering in the divine plan.

✿
26f: Dt 4, 19.
28: Dt 17, 2-7.
29: Prv 24, 17.
35: 19, 23; 23, 3-7.
32/1: 33, 9.

2: 13, 18; 27, 6;
34, 5; 35, 2.
3: 22, 5.
7: 12, 12.
8: 33, 4.

12 Yes, I followed you attentively
as you searched out what to say;
And behold, there is none who has
convicted Job,
not one of you who could refute his
statements.

13† Yet do not say, "We have met wisdom.
God may vanquish him but not man!"

14 For had he addressed his words to me,
I should not then have answered him
as you have done.

15 They are dismayed, they make no more
reply;
words fail them.

16 Must I wait? Now that they speak no
more,
and have ceased to make reply,

17 I too will speak my part;
I also will show my knowledge!

18 For I am full of matters to utter;
the spirit within me compels me.

19 Like a new wineskin with wine under
pressure,
my bosom is ready to burst.

20 Let me speak and obtain relief;
let me open my lips, and make reply.

21 I would not be partial to anyone,
nor give flattering titles to any.

22 For I know nought of flattery;
if I did, my Maker would soon take
me away.

33

1 THEREFORE, O Job, hear my discourse,
and hearken to all my words.

2 Behold, now I open my mouth;
my tongue and my voice form words.

3 I will state directly what is in my mind,
my lips shall utter knowledge
sincerely;

4✲ For the spirit of God has made me,
the breath of the Almighty keeps me
alive.

5 If you are able, refute me;
draw up your arguments and stand
forth.

6✲ Behold I, like yourself, have been taken
from the same clay by God.

7 Therefore no fear of me should dismay
you,
nor should my presence weigh
heavily upon you.

8 But you have said in my hearing,
as I listened to the sound of your
words:

9✲ "I am clean and without transgression;
I am innocent; there is no guilt in me.

10✲ Yet he invents pretexts against me
and reckons me as his enemy.

11✲ He puts my feet in the stocks;
he watches all my ways!"

12 In this you are not just, let me tell you;
for God is greater than man.

13✲ Why, then, do you make complaint
against him
that he gives no account of his
doings?

14 For God does speak, perhaps once,
or even twice, though one perceive
it not.

15 In a dream, in a vision of the night,
[when deep sleep falls upon men]
as they slumber in their beds,

16 It is then he opens the ears of men
and as a warning to them, terrifies
them;

17 By turning man from evil
and keeping pride away from him,

18 He withholds his soul from the pit
and his life from passing to the grave.

19 Or a man is chastened on his bed by
pain
and unceasing suffering within his
frame,

20✲ So that to his appetite food becomes
repulsive,
and his senses reject the choicest
nourishment.

21 His flesh is wasted so that it cannot be
seen,
and his bones, once invisible, appear;

22 His soul draws near to the pit,
his life to the place of the dead.

23† If then there be for him an angel,
one out of a thousand, a mediator,
To show him what is right for him
and bring the man back to justice,

24 He will take pity on him and say,
"Deliver him from going down to the
pit;
I have found him a ransom."

25 Then his flesh shall become soft as a
boy's;
he shall be again as in the days of his
youth.

26✲ He shall pray and God will favor him;
he shall see God's face with rejoicing.

✲
33/4: 32, 8.
6: 31, 15.
9: 10, 7; 13, 18; 27, 5f;
29, 14; 32, 1; 34, 5.
10: 13, 24; 19, 11.
11: 13, 27; 31, 4.
13: 31, 35.
20: 6, 7.
26: 22, 26-29.

†
32, 13: *Met wisdom:* in Job's arguments.

33, 23: *Angel:* one of the thousands who stand between God
and man as intermediaries, reminding man of his duties and
giving God an account of their fulfillment.

27 He shall sing before men and say,
  "I sinned and did wrong,
    yet he has not punished me
      accordingly.
28 He delivered my soul from passing to
    the pit,
  and I behold the light of life."

29 Lo, all these things God does,
    twice, or thrice, for a man,
30 Bringing back his soul from the pit
    to the light, in the land of the living.
31 Be attentive, O Job; listen to me!
    Be silent and I will speak.
32 If you have aught to say, then answer
    me.
  Speak out! I should like to see you
    justified.
33 If not, then do you listen to me;
    be silent while I teach you wisdom.

34 ¹THEN Elihu continued and said:

2   Hear, O wise men, my discourse,
      and you that have knowledge, hear
        me!
3* For the ear tests words,
      as the taste does food.
4   Let us discern for ourselves what is
        right;
      let us learn between us what is good.
5* For Job has said, "I am innocent,
      but God has taken what is my due.
6* Notwithstanding my right I am set at
        nought;
      in my wound the arrow rankles,
        sinless though I am."

7   What man is like Job?
      He drinks in blasphemies like water,
8   Keeps company with evildoers
      and goes along with wicked men,
9* When he says, "It profits a man nought
        that he is pleasing to God."

10* Therefore, men of understanding,
      hearken to me:
    far be it from God to do wickedness;
      far from the Almighty to do wrong!
11* Rather, he requites men for their
        conduct,
      and brings home to a man his way of
        life.

12* Surely, God cannot act wickedly,
      the Almighty cannot violate justice.
13* Who gave him government over the
        earth,
      or who else set all the land in its
        place?
14 If he were to take back his spirit to
        himself,
      withdraw to himself his breath,
15* All flesh would perish together,
      and man would return to the dust.

16 Now, do you, O Job, hear this!
      Hearken to the words I speak!
17 Can an enemy of justice indeed be in
        control,
      or will you condemn the supreme
        Just One,
18 Who says to a king, "You are worthless!"
      and to nobles, "You are wicked!"
19* Who neither favors the person of
        princes,
      nor respects the rich more than the
        poor?
20* For they are all the work of his hands:
      in a moment they die, even at
        midnight.
    He brings on nobles, and takes them
        away,
      removing the powerful without
        lifting a hand;
21 For his eyes are upon the ways of man,
      and he beholds all his steps.
22 There is no darkness so dense
      that evildoers can hide in it.
25 Therefore he discerns their works;
      he turns at night and crushes them.
23 For he forewarns no man of his time
      to come before God in judgment.
24* Without a trial he breaks the mighty,
      and sets others in their stead,
27 Because they turned away from him
      and heeded none of his ways,
28 But caused the cries of the poor to reach
        him,
      so that he heard the plea of the
        afflicted.
29† If he remains tranquil, who then can
        condemn?
      If he hides his face, who then can
        behold him?
30 . . . .
31 When anyone says to God,
      "I was misguided; I will offend no
        more.

*
34/3: 12, 11.
  5: 33, 9f.
  6: 9, 20.
  9: 9, 22f.30f; 21, 15;
     35, 3.
  10: 36, 23.
  11: Ps 62, 13; Prv 24, 12;
      Mt 16, 27; Rom 2, 6;
      2 Cor 5, 10; Rv 22, 12.

  12: 8, 3.
  13: 38, 4-7.
  15: 10, 9.
  19: Dt 10, 17; 2 Chr 19, 7;
      Wis 6, 7; Acts 10, 34;
      Rom 2, 11; Eph 6, 9;
      Col 3, 25; 1 Pt 1, 17.
  20: 21, 3.
  24: Ps 2, 9.

† 34, 26.29f: The extant Hebrew text of these verses contains several added phrases which either represent duplication or are very obscure.

32 Teach me wherein I have sinned;
if I have done wrong, I will do so no
more,"
33 Would you then say that God must
punish,
since you reject what he is doing?
It is you who must choose, not I;
speak, therefore, what you know.

34 Men of understanding will say to me,
every wise man who hears my views:
35✻ "Job speaks without intelligence,
and his words are without sense."
36 Let Job be tried to the limit,
since his answers are those of the
impious;
37 For he is adding rebellion to his sin
by brushing off our arguments
and addressing many words to God.

35 ¹THEN Elihu proceeded and said:
2✻ Do you think it right to say,
"I am just rather than God"?
3✻ To say, "What does it profit me;
what advantage have I more than if I
had sinned?"
4† I have words for a reply to you
and your three companions as well.
5 Look up to the skies and behold;
regard the heavens high above you.
6 If you sin, what injury do you do to
God?
Even if your offenses are many, how
do you hurt him?
7✻ If you are righteous, what do you give
him,
or what does he receive from your
hand?
8 Your wickedness can affect only a man
like yourself;
and your justice only a fellow human
being.

9 In great oppression men cry out;
they call for help because of the
power of the mighty,
10 Saying, "Where is God, my Maker,
who has given visions in the night,
11 Taught us rather than the beasts of the
earth,
and made us wise rather than the
birds of the heavens?"
12 Though thus they cry out, he answers
not
against the pride of the wicked.

13 But it is idle to say God does not hear
or that the Almighty does not take
notice.
14† Even though you say that you see him
not,
the case is before him; with
trembling should you wait upon
him.
15 But now that you have done otherwise,
God's anger punishes,
nor does he show concern that a man
will die.
16✻ Yet Job to no purpose opens his mouth,
and without knowledge multiplies
words.

36 ¹ELIHU proceeded further and said:
2 Wait yet a little and I will instruct you,
for there are still words to be said on
God's behalf.
3 I will bring my knowledge from afar,
and to my Maker I will accord the
right.
4 For indeed, my theme cannot fail me:
the one perfect in knowledge I set
before you.
5† Behold, God rejects the obstinate in
heart;
he preserves not the life of the
wicked.
6✻ He withholds not the just man's rights,
but grants vindication to the
oppressed,
7✻ And with kings upon thrones
he sets them, exalted forever.
8 Or if they are bound with fetters
and held fast by bonds of affliction,
9 Then he makes known to them what
they have done
and their sins of boastful pride.
10 He opens their ears to correction
and exhorts them to turn back from
evil.
11 If they obey and serve him,
they spend their days in prosperity,
their years in happiness.
12† But if they obey not, they perish;
they die for lack of knowledge.

✻
35: 35, 16; 38, 2; 42, 3.   16: 34, 35; 38, 2; 42, 3.
35/2: 32, 2.   36/6: Ps 72, 4.12f.
3: 34, 9.   7: Ps 113, 7f.
7: 22, 3; 41, 2; Lk 17, 10;
Rom 11, 35.

† 35, 4: *A reply to you:* Elihu refers to Job's statement that the innocent suffer as much as the wicked, and especially to Eliphaz's words in 22, 2f.
35, 14f: The text here is uncertain. It seems to indicate that Job should have realized God's indifference is only apparent, and that, because he has not done so, God will punish him.
36, 5-21: Perhaps this section should be read between vv 6 and 7 of chapter 34.
36, 12: *Knowledge:* practical wisdom in serving God, which they lack because they refused it when warned (cf v 10).

13 The impious in heart lay up anger for
themselves;
they cry not for help when he
enchains them;

14† Therefore they expire in youth,
and perish among the reprobate.

15 But he saves the unfortunate through
their affliction,
and instructs them through distress.

16†-20 . . . .

21 Take heed, turn not to evil;
for you have preferred carousal to
affliction.

22 Behold, God is sublime in his power.
What teacher is there like him?

23❀ Who prescribes for him his conduct,
or who can say, "You have done
wrong"?

24 Remember, you should extol his work,
which men have praised in song.

25 All men contemplate it;
man beholds it from afar.

26 Lo, God is great beyond our
knowledge;
the number of his years is past
searching out.

27 He holds in check the waterdrops
that filter in rain through his mists,

28 Till the skies run with them
and the showers rain down on
mankind.

31† For by these he nourishes the nations,
and gives them food in abundance.

29†-30 Lo! he spreads the clouds in layers
as the carpeting of his tent.

32 In his hands he holds the lightning,
and he commands it to strike the
mark.

33 His thunder speaks for him
and incites the fury of the storm.

37

1 At this my heart trembles
and leaps out of its place,

2† To hear his angry voice
as it rumbles forth from his mouth!

3 Everywhere under the heavens he
sends it,
with his lightning, to the ends of the
earth.

4 Again his voice roars—
the majestic sound of his thunder.

5 He does great things beyond our
knowing;
wonders past our searching out.

6 For he says to the snow, "Fall to the
earth";
likewise to his heavy, drenching rain.

7 He shuts up all mankind indoors;

8 the wild beasts take to cover
and remain quietly in their dens.

9† Out of its chamber comes forth the
tempest;
from the north winds, the cold.

10❀ With his breath God brings the frost,
and the broad waters become
congealed.

11 With hail, also, the clouds are laden,
as they scatter their flashes of light.

12† He it is who changes their rounds,
according to his plans,
in their task upon the surface of the
earth,

13 whether for punishment or mercy,
as he commands.

14 Hearken to this, O Job!
Stand and consider the wondrous
works of God!

15 Do you know how God lays his
commands upon them,
and makes the light shine forth from
his clouds?

16 Do you know how the clouds are
banked,
the wondrous work of him who is
perfect in knowledge?

17 You, whom the streams of water fail
when a calm from the south comes
over the land,

18† Do you spread out with him the
firmament of the skies,
hard as a brazen mirror?

---

† 36, 14: *Reprobate:* cf Dt 23, 18f.

36, 16-20: The Hebrew text here is in disorder. The Vulgate has: "(16) Therefore he will give you most ample salvation from the narrow mouth which has no foundations beneath it; but the repose of your table will be filled with fatness. (17) Your case has been judged as that of the wicked; case and judgment you will receive. (18) Let no wrath, then, overcome you, that you oppress anyone; nor let numerous gifts mislead you. (19) Lay down your greatness without tribulation, and all who are mighty in strength. (20) Do not draw out the night, that people may go in place of them."

36, 31: *These:* refers to *the showers* of v 28, if the verse order indicated above is correct.

36, 29f: Because of the uncertainty of the text, no translation of these verses has received unanimous approval from exegetes.

37, 2: *Voice:* the thunder.

37, 9: *Chamber:* where it was popularly believed storms were kept enclosed.

37, 12: *Their rounds:* of *rain* (36, 27), of *clouds* (36, 29f), of *lightning* and *thunder* (36, 32f), of *snow* (37, 6), of *winds* (37, 9).

37, 18: *The firmament . . . mirror:* the ancients thought of the sky as a ceiling above which were the "upper waters" (cf Gn 1, 6f; 7, 11); when this ceiling became as hard as metal, the usual rain failed to fall on the earth (cf Lv 26, 19; Dt 28, 23).

❀ 23: 34, 10; Is 40, 13.　　　37/10: Ps 148, 17.

19 Teach us then what we shall say to him;
    we cannot, for the darkness, make our plea.

20† Will he be told about it when I speak,
    or when a man says he is being destroyed?

21† Nay, rather, it is as the light which men see not
    while it is obscured among the clouds,
    till the wind comes by and sweeps the clouds away.

22† From the North the splendor comes,
    surrounding God's awesome majesty!

23 The Almighty! we cannot discover him,
    pre-eminent in power and judgment;
    his great justice owes no one an accounting.

24 Therefore men revere him,
    though none can see him, however wise their hearts.

VII: THE LORD'S SPEECH

38 ¹†THEN THE LORD ADDRESSED JOB out of the storm and said:

2 Who is this that obscures divine plans with words of ignorance?

3†* Gird up your loins now, like a man;
    I will question you, and you tell me the answers!

4 Where were you when I founded the earth?
    Tell me, if you have understanding.

5 Who determined its size; do you know?
    Who stretched out the measuring line for it?

6 Into what were its pedestals sunk,
    and who laid the cornerstone,

7† While the morning stars sang in chorus
    and all the sons of God shouted for joy?

8* And who shut within doors the sea,
    when it burst forth from the womb;

9 When I made the clouds its garment
    and thick darkness its swaddling bands?

10 When I set limits for it
    and fastened the bar of its door,

11 And said: Thus far shall you come but no farther,
    and here shall your proud waves be stilled!

12 Have you ever in your lifetime commanded the morning
    and shown the dawn its place

13 For taking hold of the ends of the earth,
    till the wicked are shaken from its surface?

14 The earth is changed as is clay by the seal,
    and dyed as though it were a garment;

15 But from the wicked the light is withheld,
    and the arm of pride is shattered.

16 Have you entered into the sources of the sea,
    or walked about in the depths of the abyss?

17 Have the gates of death been shown to you,
    or have you seen the gates of darkness?

18 Have you comprehended the breadth of the earth?
    Tell me, if you know all:

19 Which is the way to the dwelling place of light,
    and where is the abode of darkness,

20 That you may take them to their boundaries
    and set them on their homeward paths?

21† You know, because you were born before them,
    and the number of your years is great!

22† Have you entered the storehouse of the snow,
    and seen the treasury of the hail

23 Which I have reserved for times of stress,

---

† 37, 20: Will an angel bring this to God's attention?

37, 21: Even though God seems not to know our circumstances, he does know them, just as surely as the sun shines, unseen by man, behind the clouds.

37, 22: Now the storms of doubt and ignorance disappear, and *from the North,* used here as a symbol for God's mysterious abode, comes *the splendor* of the manifestation of God's majestic ways.

38, 1: Now the LORD enters the debate and addresses two discourses (38—39 and 40—41) to Job, in which he speaks of his wisdom and power, which are altogether beyond the capacity of Job, who therefore should never dare to demand a reason for the divine actions. *Out of the storm:* frequently the background of the appearances of the LORD in the Old Testament; cf Pss 18; 50; Na 1, 3; Hb 3.

38, 3: *Gird up your loins:* prepare for combat—figuratively, be ready to defend yourself in debate.

38, 7: *Sons of God:* angels; cf 1, 6.

38, 21: Divine irony.

38, 22f: *Hail . . . of war:* thus God used a hailstorm to rout Joshua's foes in the battle of Gibeon; cf Jos 10, 11; Sir 46, 5.

for the days of war and of battle?

24 Which way to the parting of the winds,
whence the east wind spreads over
the earth?

25 Who has laid out a channel for the
downpour
and for the thunderstorm a path

26 To bring rain to no man's land,
the unpeopled wilderness;

27 To enrich the waste and desolate
ground
till the desert blooms with verdure?

28 Has the rain a father;
or who has begotten the drops of
dew?

29 Out of whose womb comes the ice,
and who gives the hoarfrost its birth
in the skies,

30 When the waters lie covered as though
with stone
that holds captive the surface of the
deep?

31† Have you fitted a curb to the Pleiades,
or loosened the bonds of Orion?

32 Can you bring forth the Mazzaroth in
their season,
or guide the Bear with its train?

33 Do you know the ordinances of the
heavens;
can you put into effect their plan on
the earth?

34† Can you raise your voice among the
clouds,
or veil yourself in the waters of the
storm?

35† Can you send forth the lightnings on
their way,
or will they say to you, "Here we
are"?

37 Who counts the clouds in his wisdom?
Or who tilts the water jars of heaven

38 So that the dust of earth is fused into a
mass
and its clods made solid?

39 Do you hunt the prey for the lioness
or appease the hunger of her cubs,

40 While they crouch in their dens,
or lie in wait in the thicket?

36† Who puts wisdom in the heart,
and gives the cock its understanding?

41✱ Who provides nourishment for the
ravens
when their young ones cry out to
God,
and they rove abroad without food?

39

1 Do you know about the birth of the
mountain goats,
watch for the birth pangs of the
hinds,

2 Number the months that they must
fulfill,
and fix the time of their bringing
forth?

3 They crouch down and bear their
young;
they deliver their progeny in the
desert.

4 When their offspring thrive and grow,
they leave and do not return.

5 Who has given the wild ass his freedom,
and who has loosed him from bonds?

6 I have made the wilderness his home
and the salt flats his dwelling.

7 He scoffs at the uproar of the city,
and hears no shouts of a driver.

8 He ranges the mountains for pasture,
and seeks out every patch of green.

9 Will the wild ox consent to serve you,
and to pass the nights by your
manger?

10 Will a rope bind him in the furrow,
and will he harrow the valleys after
you?

11 Will you trust him for his great strength
and leave to him the fruits of your
toil?

12 Can you rely on him to thresh out your
grain
and gather in the yield of your
threshing floor?

13† The wings of the ostrich beat idly;
her plumage is lacking in pinions.

14† When she leaves her eggs on the ground
and deposits them in the sand,

15 Unmindful that a foot may crush them,
that the wild beasts may trample
them,

16 She cruelly disowns her young
and ruthlessly makes nought of her
brood;

---

† 38, 31f: *Pleiades . . . Orion . . . Bear:* cf 9, 9. *Mazzaroth:* It is
uncertain what astronomical group is meant by this Hebrew
word; perhaps a southern constellation (cf 9, 9).

38, 34: *Veil yourself . . . storm:* wrap yourself in a cloud, as
God comes in a theophany; cf Ps 18, 12.

38, 35: *Here we are:* at your service.

38, 36: *Understanding:* the reflection of divine Wisdom discernible in the created animal instincts of the *cock.*

39, 13: *The wings of the ostrich* cannot raise her from the
ground, but they help her to run swiftly.

39, 14ff: It was popularly believed that, because the ostrich
laid her eggs on the sand, she was thereby cruelly abandoning
them; cf Lam 4, 3.

✱ 41: Ps 147, 9.

17 For God has withheld wisdom from her
   and has given her no share in
   understanding.
18 Yet in her swiftness of foot
   she makes sport of the horse and his
   rider.
19† Do you give the horse his strength,
   and endow his neck with splendor?
20 Do you make the steed to quiver
   while his thunderous snorting
   spreads terror?
21 He jubilantly paws the plain
   and rushes in his might against the
   weapons.
22 He laughs at fear and cannot be
   deterred;
   he turns not back from the sword.
23 Around him rattles the quiver,
   flashes the spear and the javelin.
24 Frenzied and trembling he devours the
   ground;
   he holds not back at the sound of the
   trumpet,
25   but at each blast he cries, "Aha!"
   Even from afar he scents the battle,
   the roar of the chiefs and the
   shouting.
26 Is it by your discernment that the hawk
   soars,
   that he spreads his wings toward the
   south?
27 Does the eagle fly up at your command
   to build his nest aloft?
28 On the cliff he dwells and spends the
   night,
   on a spur of the cliff or the fortress.
29 From thence he watches for his prey;
   his eyes behold it afar off.
30* His young ones greedily drink blood;
   where the slain are, there is he.

40 ¹THE LORD then said to Job:

2* Will we have arguing with the
   Almighty by the critic?
   Let him who would correct God give
   answer!

³Then Job answered the LORD and said:

4 Behold, I am of little account; what can
   I answer you?
   I put my hand over my mouth.
5 Though I have spoken once, I will not
   do so again;
   though twice, I will do so no more.

⁶Then the LORD addressed Job out of the
storm and said:

7 Gird up your loins now, like a man.
   I will question you, and you tell me
   the answers!
8 Would you refuse to acknowledge my
   right?
   Would you condemn me that you
   may be justified?
9 Have you an arm like that of God,
   or can you thunder with a voice like
   his?
10 Adorn yourself with grandeur and
   majesty,
   and array yourself with glory and
   splendor.
11 Let loose the fury of your wrath;
12   tear down the wicked and shatter
   them.
   Bring down the haughty with a glance;
13   bury them in the dust together;
   in the hidden world imprison them.
14 Then will I too acknowledge
   that your own right hand can save
   you.
15† See, besides you I made Behemoth,
   that feeds on grass like an ox.
16 Behold the strength in his loins,
   and his vigor in the sinews of his
   belly.
17 He carries his tail like a cedar;
   the sinews of his thighs are like
   cables.
18 His bones are like tubes of bronze;
   his frame is like iron rods.
19 He came at the beginning of God's
   ways,
   and was made the taskmaster of his
   fellows;
20 For the produce of the mountains is
   brought to him,
   and of all wild animals he makes
   sport.
21 Under the lotus trees he lies,
   in coverts of the reedy swamp.
22 The lotus trees cover him with their
   shade;
   all about him are the poplars on the
   bank.
23 If the river grows violent, he is not
   disturbed;
   he is tranquil though the torrent
   surges about his mouth.
24† Who can capture him by his eyes,
   or pierce his nose with a trap?

---

† 39, 19-25: The famous description of a war horse.
40, 15: *Behemoth:* the hippopotamus.
40, 24: *Eyes . . . nose:* the only exposed parts of the submerged beast.

---

* 39/30: Mt 24, 28; Lk 17, 37.   40/2: 38, 3.

25† Can you lead about Leviathan with a
      hook,
    or curb his tongue with a bit?
26 Can you put a rope into his nose,
      or pierce through his cheek with a
      gaff?
27 Will he then plead with you, time after
      time,
    or address you with tender words?
28 Will he make an agreement with you
      that you may have him as a slave
      forever?
29 Can you play with him, as with a bird?
      Can you put him in leash for your
      maidens?
30† Will the traders bargain for him?
      Will the merchants divide him up?

31 Can you fill his hide with barbs,
      or his head with fish spears?
32 Once you but lay a hand upon him,
      no need to recall any other conflict!

41

2† Is he not relentless when aroused;
      who then dares stand before him?
1   Whoever might vainly hope to do so
      need only see him to be overthrown.
3   Who has assailed him and come off
      safe—
    Who under all the heavens?

4   I need hardly mention his limbs,
      his strength, and the fitness of his
      armor.
5   Who can strip off his outer garment,
      or penetrate his double corselet?
6   Who can force open the doors of his
      mouth,
    close to his terrible teeth?
7   Rows of scales are on his back,
      tightly sealed together;
8   They are fitted each so close to the next
      that no space intervenes;
9   So joined one to another
      that they hold fast and cannot be
      parted.

10 When he sneezes, light flashes forth;
      his eyes are like those of the dawn.
11 Out of his mouth go forth firebrands;
      sparks of fire leap forth.
12 From his nostrils issues steam,
      as from a seething pot or bowl.
13 His breath sets coals afire;
      a flame pours from his mouth.
14 Strength abides in his neck,
      and terror leaps before him.

15.16 His heart is hard as stone;
      his flesh, as the lower millstone.
17† When he rises up, the mighty are
      afraid;
    the waves of the sea fall back.
18 Should the sword reach him, it will not
      avail;
    nor will the spear, nor the dart, nor
      the javelin.
19 He regards iron as straw,
      and bronze as rotten wood.
20 The arrow will not put him to flight;
      slingstones used against him are but
      straws.
21 Clubs he esteems as splinters;
      he laughs at the crash of the spear.

22 His belly is sharp as pottery fragments;
      he spreads like a threshing sledge
      upon the mire.
23 He makes the depths boil like a pot;
      the sea he churns like perfume in a
      kettle.
24 Behind him he leaves a shining path;
      you would think the deep had the
      hoary head of age.
25 Upon the earth there is not his like,
      intrepid he was made.
26 All, however lofty, fear him;
      he is king over all proud beasts.

42

1THEN Job answered the LORD and said:

2† I know that you can do all things,
      and that no purpose of yours can be
      hindered.
3* I have dealt with great things that I do
      not understand;
    things too wonderful for me, which I
      cannot know.
5   I had heard of you by word of mouth,
      but now my eye has seen you.
6   Therefore I disown what I have said,
      and repent in dust and ashes.

---

† 40, 25: *Leviathan* here is the crocodile. But cf 3, 8.

40, 30: *Merchants:* literally, "Canaanites," whose reputation for trading was so widespread that their name came to be used for merchants; cf Prv 31, 24. The meaning of this verse is that the crocodile is too powerful a creature to be sold like common fish.

41, 2: *Before him:* some read, "before me," i. e., God; also in v 3.

41, 17: The text here is uncertain.

42, 2-6: In the current Hebrew text, this final utterance of Job is interrupted by words ascribed to God (vv 3f) which are in large part a duplication of 38, 2f.

VIII: EPILOGUE

Job's Restoration

7†AND IT CAME TO PASS after the LORD had spoken these words to Job, that the LORD said to Eliphaz the Temanite, "I am angry with you and with your two friends; for you have not spoken rightly concerning me, as has my servant Job. 8†Now, therefore, take seven bullocks and seven rams, and go to my servant Job, and offer up a holocaust for yourselves; and let my servant Job pray for you; for his prayer I will accept, not to punish you severely. For you have not spoken rightly concerning me, as has my servant Job." 9Then Eliphaz the Temanite, and Bildad the Shuhite, and Zophar the Naamathite, went and did as the LORD had commanded them. And the LORD accepted the intercession of Job.

10Also, the LORD restored the prosperity of Job, after he had prayed for his friends; the LORD even gave to Job twice as much as he had before. 11†Then all his brethren and his sisters came to him, and all his former acquaintances, and they dined with him in his house. They condoled with him and comforted him for all the evil which the LORD had brought upon him; and each one gave him a piece of money and a gold ring.

12*Thus the LORD blessed the latter days of Job more than his earlier ones. For he had fourteen thousand sheep, six thousand camels, a thousand yoke of oxen, and a thousand she-asses. 13And he had seven sons and three daughters, 14†of whom he called the first Jemimah, the second Keziah, and the third Keren-happuch. 15In all the land no other women were as beautiful as the daughters of Job; and their father gave them an inheritance among their brethren. 16*†After this, Job lived a hundred and forty years; and he saw his children, his grandchildren, and even his great-grandchildren. 17Then Job died, old and full of years.

* 12: 1, 3.   16: 5, 25f.

† 42, 7: The three friends of Job (Elihu is ignored in the Epilogue) are criticized by the LORD because they had (even though in good faith) leveled false charges against him.

42, 8: Job becomes the intercessor for his friends, as were other great Old Testament characters, e. g., Abraham and Moses, and as our Lord would be, whom he prefigured. *Seven:* a symbolic number.

42, 11: *A piece of money:* the term is the same as that used in Gn 33, 19; Jos 24, 32. *Gold ring:* for the nose or ear.

42, 14: Job's daughters had names symbolic of their charms: *Jemimah,* dove; *Keziah,* precious perfume (cf Ps 45, 9); *Keren-happuch,* cosmetic jar—more precisely, a container for a black powder that was used like modern mascara.

42, 15: Ordinarily daughters did not inherit property unless there were no sons; cf Nm 27, 1-11.

42, 16: As his other rewards were *twice as much as he had before* (v 10), so Job's *hundred and forty years* were double the expected span of human life; cf Ps 90, 10.

The Book of Psalms

Introduction

The Book of Psalms, or Psalter, is a collection of religious songs, traditionally listed as 150. This number, however, is only approximately correct, for several psalms contain two or more originally independent songs, while others, which were originally a single unit, have been broken up into two or more psalms. Moreover, certain psalms and parts of psalms occur more than once in this collection.

The present collection is divided into five "books," perhaps in imitation of the five Books of the Pentateuch. But internal evidence shows that there existed at an earlier period more numerous, smaller collections which were gradually gathered together to form the present Psalter.

In form and subject matter the psalms are most varied. Some were composed for liturgical use in the temple, others, for recitation elsewhere. In some psalms the singer is an individual; in others, the community. One of the most common types is that of supplication to God for his help in various spiritual and temporal needs. But hymns of thanksgiving and of praise are also numerous. Less frequent are poems written primarily to discuss some problem or to teach some lesson.

Prefixed to most of the psalms are certain words and phrases which offer traditional information about the psalm, such as the tone in which it is to be sung, the musical instruments which are to accompany its singing, the historical circumstances connected in some way with its composition, the name of its author, and so forth. These "titles," as they are called, were added, at least in most cases, by later writers. It cannot be proved that they were divinely inspired. They have some value, however, as representing ancient tradition. They are printed here in smaller type.

About half of the psalms are attributed in these "titles" to David. The Davidic authorship of some of these is taken for granted in the New Testament. Some other psalms are attributed to certain groups of temple singers known as "the sons of Korah" and "the sons of Asaph." One psalm each is ascribed to Moses, Solomon, Heman and Ethan. About a third of the psalms have no author's name prefixed to them. Although some of the psalms appear to have been composed during the early postexilic period (the fifth and fourth centuries B.C.), it cannot be demonstrated that any psalms are as late as the Maccabean age.

I: THE FIRST BOOK—Psalms 1-41

True Happiness

I

1 † **1**† Happy the man who follows not
  the counsel of the wicked
Nor walks in the way of sinners,
  nor sits in the company of the insolent,
2✶ But delights in the law of the LORD
  and meditates on his law day and night.
3✶ He is like a tree
  planted near running water,
That yields its fruit in due season,
  and whose leaves never fade.
  [Whatever he does, prospers.]

II

4 Not so the wicked, not so;
  they are like chaff which the wind drives away.
5 Therefore in judgment the wicked shall not stand,
  nor shall sinners, in the assembly of the just.
6✶ For the LORD watches over the way of the just,
  but the way of the wicked vanishes.

The Universal Reign of the Messiah

I

2 † **1**✶ Why do the nations rage
  and the peoples utter folly?
2† The kings of the earth rise up,

---

† Ps 1: A preface to the whole Book of Psalms; it outlines the lot of the good and of the wicked.

1, 1: *The way:* a common biblical term for "manner of living" or moral conduct.

Ps 2: A messianic psalm, i. e., it refers to the Messiah, Christ. The psalmist depicts the revolt of the nations against God and his anointed Son (1-3), God's answer (4-6), the Messianic decree (7-9), and the warning given to the rebels (10-12).

2, 2: *Anointed:* in Hebrew, *Mashiah* (whence the word "Messiah"), which the Greek translated as *Christos*. Among the He-

✶
 1/2: Jos 1, 8.   6: Ps 37, 18.
 3: Jer 17, 8.   2/1f: Acts 4, 25ff.

and the princes conspire together
  against the Lord and against his
  anointed:
3 "Let us break their fetters
  and cast their bonds from us!"

II

4 He who is throned in heaven laughs;
  the Lord derides them.
5 Then in anger he speaks to them;
  he terrifies them in his wrath:
6 "I myself have set up my king
  on Zion, my holy mountain."

III

7* I will proclaim the decree of the Lord:
  The Lord said to me, "You are my
  son;
  this day I have begotten you.
8 Ask of me and I will give you
  the nations for an inheritance
  and the ends of the earth for your
  possession.
9* You shall rule them with an iron rod;
  you shall shatter them like an earthen
  dish."

IV

10 And now, O kings, give heed;
  take warning, you rulers of the earth.
11† Serve the Lord with fear, and rejoice
  before him;
  with trembling ¹²pay homage to him,
  Lest he be angry and you perish from
  the way,
  when his anger blazes suddenly.
  Happy are all who take refuge in
  him!

Trust in God in Time of Danger

3 ¹* A psalm of David, when he fled from his son
  Absalom.

I

2 O Lord, how many are my adversaries!
  Many rise up against me!
3 Many are saying of me,
  "There is no salvation for him in
  God."
4 But you, O Lord, are my shield;
  my glory, you lift up my head!

II

5 When I call out to the Lord,
  he answers me from his holy
  mountain.

6 When I lie down in sleep,
  I wake again, for the Lord sustains
  me.
7 I fear not the myriads of people
  arrayed against me on every side.

III

8 Rise up, O Lord!
  Save me, my God!
  For you strike all my enemies on the
  cheek;
  the teeth of the wicked you break.
9 Salvation is the Lord's!
  Upon your people be your blessing!

Joyful Confidence in God

4 † ¹† For the leader; with stringed instruments. A
  psalm of David.

I

2 When I call, answer me, O my just God,
  you who relieve me when I am in
  distress;
  Have pity on me, and hear my prayer!

II

3 Men of rank, how long will you be dull
  of heart?
  Why do you love what is vain and
  seek after falsehood?
4 Know that the Lord does wonders for
  his faithful one;
  the Lord will hear me when I call
  upon him.
5*† Tremble, and sin not;
  reflect, upon your beds, in silence.
6 Offer just sacrifices,
  and trust in the Lord.

---

† brews both the kings (Jgs 9, 8; 1 Sm 9, 16; 16, 12f) and the high priests (Lv 8, 12; Nm 3, 3) received the power of their office by being anointed with oil.

2, 11f: *And rejoice before him; with trembling pay homage to him:* a shorter reading, "pay homage to him with trembling," may have been the original. *Pay homage:* literally, "kiss his feet."

Ps 3: The psalmist, surrounded by enemies, implores God's help (2-4), arouses himself to trust in God (5-7), and prays for himself and the people (8f).

Ps 4: The psalmist begs God's aid (2), admonishes the incredulous worldings to put their trust in God (3-6), and reaffirms his own confidence in him (7-9).

4, 1: *For the leader:* very many of the psalms have this phrase prefixed to them. It probably signifies that they were copied from a collection which once belonged "to the choirmaster." Cf 1 Chr 15, 21.

4, 5: An admonition not to utter rash words against the Lord, even in distress or affliction; the right conduct, after silent acceptance of trials, is proposed in v 6. *Tremble:* the Hebrew verb means, "to be deeply moved" with any emotion; in the present context, "with fear or dismay." The Greek understood it as, "to be moved with anger," and thus it is quoted in Eph 4, 26.

7: Acts 13, 33; Heb 1, 5.   3/1: 2 Sm 15, 13ff.
9: Rv 2, 27; 12, 5; 19, 15.   4/5: Eph 4, 26.

III

7 Many say, "Oh, that we might see
    better times!"
    O Lord, let the light of your
    countenance shine upon us!

8 You put gladness into my heart,
    more than when grain and wine
    abound.

9 As soon as I lie down, I fall peacefully
    asleep,
    for you alone, O Lord,
    bring security to my dwelling.

Prayer for Divine Help

5 † 1 For the leader; with wind instruments.
    A psalm of David.

I

2 Hearken to my words, O Lord,
    attend to my sighing.

3 Heed my call for help,
    my king and my God!
    To you I pray, 4O Lord;
    at dawn you hear my voice;
    at dawn I bring my plea expectantly
    before you.

II

5 For you, O God, delight not in
    wickedness;
    no evil man remains with you;

6   the arrogant may not stand in your
    sight.
    You hate all evildoers;

7✻   you destroy all who speak falsehood;
    The bloodthirsty and the deceitful
    the Lord abhors.

III

8 But I, because of your abundant
    kindness,
    will enter your house;
    I will worship at your holy temple
    in fear of you, 9†O Lord;
    Because of my enemies, guide me in
    your justice;
    make straight your way before me.

IV

10† For in their mouth there is no sincerity;
    their heart teems with treacheries.
    Their throat is an open grave;
    they flatter with their tongue.

11✻ Punish them, O God;
    let them fall by their own devices;

For their many sins, cast them out
    because they have rebelled against
    you.

V

12 But let all who take refuge in you
    be glad and exult forever.
    Protect them, that you may be the joy
    of those who love your name.

13 For you, O Lord, bless the just man;
    you surround him with the shield of
    your good will.

Prayer in Time of Distress

6 † 1 For the leader; with stringed instruments,
    "upon the eighth." A psalm of David.

I

2✻ O Lord, reprove me not in your anger,
    nor chastise me in your wrath.

3 Have pity on me, O Lord, for I am
    languishing;
    heal me, O Lord, for my body is in
    terror;

4† My soul, too, is utterly terrified;
    but you, O Lord, how long . . .?

II

5 Return, O Lord, save my life;
    rescue me because of your kindness,

6✻† For among the dead no one remembers
    you;
    in the nether world who gives you
    thanks?

III

7 I am wearied with sighing;
    every night I flood my bed with
    weeping;
    I drench my couch with my tears.

8 My eyes are dimmed with sorrow;
    they have aged because of all my foes.

---

† Ps 5: At dawn the psalmist calls upon God (2-4), who hates sinners (5-7); trusting in divine guidance for himself (8f), he asks God to punish the wicked (10f) and protect the just (12f).

5, 9: The Greek reads, "Make straight my way before you."

5, 10: *An open grave:* while they feign words of friendship, their hidden thoughts, the words in *their throat,* i. e., in their heart, are murderous, ready to swallow up men to death. Cf Jer 5, 16.

Ps 6: The first of the Penitential Psalms. In his affliction the psalmist begs God for mercy (2-4); praying to be saved from death (5f), he describes his mercy (7f); then, certain of being heard, he rejects all fellowship with sinners (9-11).

6, 4: *How long:* an elliptical exclamation for, "How long will it be before you answer my prayer?" Cf Ps 13, 2ff.

6, 6: The ancient concept of the abode of the dead (*the nether world,* in Hebrew, *Sheol*) supposed no activity or lofty emotion among the deceased, who were pictured as surrounded by the darkness of oblivion. The Hebrews shared in this common idea almost to the time of Christ, when God revealed a clearer notion of the hereafter. Cf Wis 3.

✻ 5/7: Wis 14, 9.
    11: Rom 3, 13.
    6/2: Ps 38, 2.
                          6: Pss 30, 10; 88, 11f;
                            113, 17; Is 38, 18.

IV

9* Depart from me, all evildoers,
for the LORD has heard the sound of
my weeping;

10 The LORD has heard my plea;
the LORD has accepted my prayer.

11* All my enemies shall be put to shame in
utter terror;
they shall fall back in sudden shame.

An Appeal to the Divine Judge

7† 1 A plaintive song of David, which he sang to
the LORD because of Cush the Benjaminite.

I

2 O LORD, my God, in you I take refuge;
save me from all my pursuers and
rescue me,

3 Lest I become like the lion's prey,
to be torn to pieces, with no one to
rescue me,

II

4† O LORD, my God, if I am at fault in this,
if there is guilt on my hands,

5† If I have repaid my friend with evil,
I who spared those who without
cause were my foes—

6 Let the enemy pursue and overtake me;
let him trample my life to the ground,
and lay my glory in the dust.

III

7 Rise up, O LORD, in your anger;
rise against the fury of my foes;
wake to the judgment you have
decreed.

8 Let the assembly of the peoples
surround you;
above them on high be enthroned.

9* [The LORD judges the nations.]
Do me justice, O LORD, because I am
just,
and because of the innocence that is
mine.

10* Let the malice of the wicked come to an
end,
but sustain the just,
O searcher of heart and soul, O just
God.

IV

11 A shield before me is God,
who saves the upright of heart;

12 A just judge is God,
a God who punishes day by day.

13 Unless they be converted, God will
sharpen his sword;
he will bend and aim his bow,

14 Prepare his deadly weapons against
them,
and use fiery darts for arrows.

V

15* He who conceived iniquity and was
pregnant with mischief,
brings forth failure.

16* He has opened a hole, he has dug it
deep,
but he falls into the pit which he has
made.

17 His mischief shall recoil upon his own
head;
upon the crown of his head his
violence shall rebound.

18 I will give thanks to the LORD for his
justice,
and sing praise to the name of the
LORD Most High.

The Majesty of God
and the Dignity of Man

8† 1 For the leader; "upon the *gittith*." A psalm of
David.

I

2 O LORD, our Lord,
how glorious is your name over all
the earth!
You have exalted your majesty above
the heavens.

3* Out of the mouths of babes and
sucklings
you have fashioned praise because of
your foes,
to silence the hostile and the
vengeful.

4 When I behold your heavens, the work
of your fingers,
the moon and the stars which you set
in place—

---

* 9: Ps 119, 115; Mt 7, 23;
  Lk 13, 27.
11: Pss 35, 4; 40, 15.
7/9: Pss 26, 1; 35, 24;
  43, 1.

10: Jer 11, 20; 17, 10;
  20, 12.
15: Jb 15, 35; Is 59, 4.
16: Ps 57, 7; Prv 26, 27;
  Eccl 10, 8; Sir 27, 26.
8/3: Mt 21, 16.

---

† Ps. 7: Slandered by his enemies, the psalmist prays for help
against them (2f), as he swears that he is innocent (4-6) and calls
upon God, the just judge of the world, to defend him (7-10);
confident of God's justice (11-14), he foretells the punishment
of his calumniators (15-17), and promises a thanksgiving sacrifice (18).

7, 4: *At fault in this:* in these accusations made against the
psalmist.

7, 5: *I who spared:* cf David's generous treatment of Saul
(1 Sm 24, 11; 26, 9).

Ps 8: After contrasting man's finite nature with God's infinite
majesty (2-5), the psalmist extols the dignity and power to which
God has raised man (6-10).

5*   What is man that you should be
mindful of him,
or the son of man that you should
care for him?

II

6†   You have made him little less than the
angels,
and crowned him with glory and
honor.

7*   You have given him rule over the
works of your hands,
putting all things under his feet:

8   All sheep and oxen,
yes, and the beasts of the field,

9   The birds of the air, the fishes of the
sea,
and whatever swims the paths of
the seas.

10†   O Lord, our Lord,
how glorious is your name over all
the earth!

Thanksgiving for the Otherthrow of Hostile Nations

9 **†** **1**   For the leader; according to *Muth labben.*
A psalm of David.

I

2   I will give thanks to you, O Lord, with
all my heart;
I will declare all your wondrous
deeds.

3   I will be glad and exult in you;
I will sing praise to your name,
Most High,

4   Because my enemies are turned back,
overthrown and destroyed before
you.

II

5   For you upheld my right and my cause,
seated on your throne, judging justly.

6   You rebuked the nations and destroyed
the wicked;
their name you blotted out forever
and ever.

7   The enemies are ruined completely
forever;
the remembrance of the cities you
uprooted has perished.

III

8   But the Lord sits enthroned forever;
he has set up his throne for judgment.

9*   He judges the world with justice;
he governs the peoples with equity.

10   The Lord is a stronghold for the
oppressed,
a stronghold in times of distress.

11   They trust in you who cherish your
name,
for you forsake not those who seek
you, O Lord.

IV

12   Sing praise to the Lord enthroned in
Zion;
proclaim among the nations his
deeds;

13   For the avenger of blood has
remembered;
he has not forgotten the cry of the
afflicted.

V

14   Have pity on me, O Lord; see how I am
afflicted by my foes,
you who have raised me up from the
gates of death,

15†   That I may declare all your praises
and, in the gates of the daughter of
Zion, rejoice in your salvation.

VI

16   The nations are sunk in the pit they
have made;
in the snare they set, their foot is
caught;

17†   In passing sentence, the Lord is
manifest;
the wicked are trapped by the work
of their own hands.

---

†   8, 6: *The angels:* in Hebrew, *elohim,* which is the ordinary word for "God" or "the gods"; hence, some translate, "a little less than godlike." Cf Pss 45, 7; 58, 2; 82, 1; 97, 7. But the ancient versions generally understood the term as referring to the heavenly spirits. Cf Ps 138, 1. In Heb 2, 9 this passage is shown to be eminently fulfilled in the God-man Jesus Christ. Cf 1 Cor 15, 27 also, where St. Paul applies to Christ the words, *putting all things under his feet.*

8, 10: The verse with which this psalm begins is repeated as a refrain at the end.

Ps 9: The Vulgate consists of two parts (A and B), each of which forms a separate psalm (Pss 9 and 10) in the current Hebrew text. In favor of the original unity of this psalm is its acrostic character, now partially lost in the poorly preserved text: the first letter of each stanza (of two couplets apiece) originally followed the order of the Hebrew alphabet consecutively throughout both halves of the psalm. Those who consider the two halves as separate psalms point to their somewhat diverse subject matter, the prayer in the first being mainly against the enemies of Israel, that in the second mainly against the wicked within Israel. However, as in all the alphabetic psalms, there is not much logical sequence between the verses.

9, 15: *The daughter of Zion:* or, "daughter Zion"; Hebrew idiom for "the city of Zion."

9, 17: God's honor and glory are vindicated when he judges and punishes the wicked.

---

*   5: Ps 144, 3.   7ff: Gn 1, 26.28; Wis 9, 2.
5ff: Heb 2, 6ff.   9/9: Pss 96, 10; 98, 9.

VII

18 To the nether world the wicked shall turn back,
all the nations that forget God.

19 For the needy shall not always be forgotten,
nor shall the hope of the afflicted forever perish.

20 Rise, O Lord, let not man prevail;
let the nations be judged in your presence.

21 Strike them with terror, O Lord;
let the nations know that they are but men.

Prayer for Help against Oppressors

I

10

1 Why, O Lord, do you stand aloof?
Why hide in times of distress?

2 Proudly the wicked harass the afflicted,
who are caught in the devices the wicked have contrived.

II

3 For the wicked man glories in his greed,
and the covetous blasphemes, sets the Lord at nought.

4 The wicked man boasts, "He will not avenge it";
"There is no God," sums up his thoughts.

5† His ways are secure at all times;
your judgments are far from his mind;
all his foes he scorns.

6 He says in his heart, "I shall not be disturbed;
from age to age I shall be without misfortune."

7* His mouth is full of cursing, guile and deceit;
under his tongue are mischief and iniquity.

8 He lurks in ambush near the villages;
in hiding he murders the innocent;
his eyes spy upon the unfortunate.

9 He waits in secret like a lion in his lair;
he lies in wait to catch the afflicted;
he catches the afflicted and drags them off in his net.

10 He stoops and lies prone
till by his violence fall the unfortunate.

11* He says in his heart, "God has forgotten;
he hides his face, he never sees."

III

12 Rise, O Lord! O God, lift up your hand!
Forget not the afflicted!

13 Why should the wicked man despise God,
saying in his heart, "He will not avenge it"?

14 You do see, for you behold misery and sorrow,
taking them in your hands.
On you the unfortunate man depends;
of the fatherless you are the helper.

15 Break the strength of the wicked and of the evildoer;
punish their wickedness; let them not survive.

IV

16 The Lord is king forever and ever;
the nations have perished out of his land.

17 The desire of the afflicted you hear, O Lord;
strengthening their hearts, you pay heed

18 To the defense of the fatherless and and the oppressed,
that man, who is of earth, may terrify no more.

Unshaken Confidence in God

11†

1 For the leader. Of David.

I

In the Lord I take refuge; how can you say to me,
"Flee to the mountain like a bird!

2 For, see, the wicked bend the bow;
they place the arrow on the string
to shoot in the dark at the upright of heart.

---

† 10, 5: *Are far from his mind:* the current Hebrew text may be read, "are lofty beyond him."

Ps 11: While fainthearted friends advise flight in the present peril (1-3), the psalmist reaffirms his confidence in the all-knowing Lord who gives just retribution to both the good and the wicked (4-7).

10/7: Rom 3, 14.   11: Pss 73, 11; 94, 7.

3†   When the pillars are overthrown,
     what can the just man do?"

II

4   The LORD is in his holy temple;
     the LORD's throne is in heaven.
   His eyes behold,
     his searching glance is on
     mankind.
5   The LORD searches the just and the
     wicked;
     the lover of violence he hates.
6*†   He rains upon the wicked fiery coals
     and brimstone;
     a burning blast is their allotted
     cup.
7   For the LORD is just, he loves just
     deeds;
     the upright shall see his face.

Prayer against Evil Tongues

12† 1   For the leader; "upon the eighth." A psalm
of David.

I

2   Help, O LORD! for no one now is
     dutiful;
     faithfulness has vanished from
     among men.
3   Everyone speaks falsehood to his
     neighbor;
     with smooth lips they speak, and
     double heart.

II

4   May the LORD destroy all smooth
     lips,
     every boastful tongue,
5   Those who say, "We are heroes with
     our tongues;
     our lips are our own; who is lord
     over us?"

III

6†   "Because they rob the afflicted, and
     the needy sigh,
     now will I arise," says the LORD;
     "I will grant safety to him who
     longs for it."

IV

7   The promises of the LORD are sure,
     like tried silver, freed from dross,
     sevenfold refined.
8   You, O LORD, will keep us
     and preserve us always from this
     generation,

9   While about us the wicked strut
     and in high place are the basest of
     men.

Prayer of One in Sorrow

13† 1   For the leader. A psalm of David.

I

2   How long, O LORD? Will you utterly
     forget me?
   How long will you hide your face
     from me?
3   How long shall I harbor sorrow in
     my soul,
     grief in my heart day after day?
   How long will my enemy triumph
     over me?
4   Look, answer me, O LORD, my
     God!

II

   Give light to my eyes that I may not
     sleep in death
5   lest my enemy say, "I have
     overcome him";
   Lest my foes rejoice at my downfall
6   though I trusted in your kindness.
   Let my heart rejoice in your
     salvation;
     let me sing of the LORD, "He has
     been good to me."

A Lament over Widespread Corruption

14† 1*   For the leader. Of David.

I

   The fool says in his heart,
     "There is no God."
   Such are corrupt; they do
     abominable deeds;
     there is not one who does good.

---

†   11, 3: *The pillars:* usually understood as "the foundations of
public order." Cf Ps 82, 5.
   11, 6: *Allotted cup:* the cup which God gives men to drink is
a common biblical figure for the destiny he assigns them. Cf Pss
16, 5; 23, 5; 75, 9; Mt 20, 22; 26, 39; Rv 14, 10.
   Ps 12: The psalmist prays for help against the deceit (2f)
and pride (4f) of the wicked; God's promises (6) fill him with
confidence (7-9).
   12, 6-9: The Hebrew text is obscure in part, and the versions
differ; the above translation follows the revised Latin Psalter.
   Ps 13: Oppressed by foes, the psalmist laments his desolation
(2-4a) and prays for God's help (4b-6).
   Ps 14: Bewailing the widespread corruption of the godless
(1-3), the psalmist foretells their punishment (4-6), as he prays
for his people (7). This psalm is repeated in almost identical
form as Ps 53.

---

*   11/6: Gn 19, 24.   14/1-7: Ps 53, 2-7.

2 The LORD looks down from heaven
upon the children of men,
to see if there be one who is wise
and seeks God.

3† All alike have gone astray; they have
become perverse;
there is not one who does good,
not even one.

II

4 Will all these evildoers never learn,
they who eat up my people just as
they eat bread?
They have not called upon the LORD;

5 then they shall be in great fear,
for God is with the just generation.

6 You would confound the plans of the
afflicted,
but the LORD is his refuge.

III

7 Oh, that out of Zion would come the
salvation of Israel!
When the LORD restores the
well-being of his people,
then shall Jacob exult and Israel
be glad.

The Guest of God

15 **†** **1** A psalm of David.

I

O LORD, who shall sojourn in your
tent?
Who shall dwell on your holy
mountain?

II

2 He who walks blamelessly and does
justice;
who thinks the truth in his heart

3 and slanders not with his tongue;
Who harms not his fellow man,
nor takes up a reproach against his
neighbor;

4 By whom the reprobate is despised,
while he honors those who fear the
LORD;
Who, though it be to his loss,
changes not his pledged word;

5 who lends not his money at usury
and accepts no bribe against the
innocent.

III

He who does these things
shall never be disturbed.

God the Supreme Good

16 **†** **1** A *miktam* of David.

I

Keep me, O God, for in you I take
refuge;

2 I say to the LORD, "My Lord are
you.
Apart from you I have no good."

3 How wonderfully has he made me
cherish
the holy ones who are in his land!

4† They multiply their sorrows
who court other gods.
Blood libations to them I will not
pour out,
nor will I take their names upon
my lips.

5† O LORD, my allotted portion and my
cup,
you it is who hold fast my lot.

6 For me the measuring lines have
fallen on pleasant sites;
fair to me indeed is my
inheritance.

II

7 I bless the LORD who counsels me;
even in the night my heart exhorts
me.

8✻ I set the LORD ever before me;
with him at my right hand I shall
not be disturbed.

9 Therefore my heart is glad and my
soul rejoices,
my body, too, abides in
confidence;

10† Because you will not abandon my
soul to the nether world,
nor will you suffer your faithful
one to undergo corruption.

---

† 14, 3: Here many Greek and Latin texts insert the Old Testament quotations which were first combined in Rom 3, 13-18.

Ps 15: Lists the moral qualities which he should possess who would enter the Lord's sanctuary worthily; the social virtues of justice and charity are especially emphasized.

Ps 16: Pledging his loyalty to God, the psalmist proclaims his hostility toward the idolaters and his friendship toward the faithful in Israel (1-6); therefore he is aware of the constant presence of God, who will keep him in this blessed union by granting him bodily resurrection and everlasting life (7-11).

16, 4: *Take their names:* the pious Israelite not only refrained from praying to false gods and from swearing by them; he would not even mention their names. Cf Hos 2, 18.

16, 5: In the worship of the true God the psalmist finds his best inheritance.

16, 10: *To undergo corruption:* some commentators render this: "to see the grave," understanding this to mean that God will not let the psalmist die in the present circumstances. But the Hebrew word *shahath* means not only "the pit," "the grave," but also "corruption." In the latter sense the ancient Greek ver-

11   You will show me the path to life,
fullness of joys in your presence,
the delights at your right hand
forever.

Prayer against Persecutors

17†   **1**   A prayer of David.

I

Hear, O LORD, a just suit;
attend to my outcry;
hearken to my prayer from lips
without deceit.

2   From you let my judgment come;
your eyes behold what is right.

3   Though you test my heart, searching
it in the night,
though you try me with fire, you
shall find no malice in me.

4   My mouth has not transgressed
after the manner of man;
according to the words of your lips
I have kept the ways of the law.

5   My steps have been steadfast in your
paths,
my feet have not faltered.

II

6   I call upon you, for you will answer
me, O God;
incline your ear to me; hear my
word.

7   Show your wondrous kindness,
O savior of those who flee
from their foes to refuge at your
right hand.

8   Keep me as the apple of your eye;
hide me in the shadow of your
wings

9   from the wicked who use violence
against me.

III

My ravenous enemies beset me;

10   they shut up their cruel hearts,
their mouths speak proudly.

11   Their steps even now surround me;
crouching to the ground, they fix
their gaze,

12   Like lions hungry for prey,
like young lions lurking in hiding.

IV

13   Rise, O LORD, confront them and
cast them down;
rescue me by your sword from the
wicked,

14   by your hand, O LORD, from
mortal men:
From mortal men whose portion in
life is in this world,
where with your treasures you fill
their bellies.
Their sons are enriched
and bequeath their abundance to
their little ones.

15†   But I in justice shall behold your face;
on waking, I shall be content in
your presence.

Thanksgiving for Help and Victory

18†   **1**   For the leader. Of David, the servant of the
LORD, who sang to the LORD the words of
this song when the LORD had rescued him
from the grasp of all his enemies and from
the hand of Saul.

A

I

2✱   I love you, O LORD, my strength,

3†   O LORD, my rock, my fortress, my
deliverer.
My God, my rock of refuge,
my shield, the horn of my
salvation, my stronghold!

4   Praised be the LORD, I exclaim,
and I am safe from my enemies.

II

5✱†   The breakers of death surged round
about me,
the destroying floods overwhelmed me;

---

† sion rendered this passage, and it was thus quoted by St. Peter (Acts 2, 25-32) and St. Paul (Acts 13, 35-37), both of whom interpret this as referring to Christ's resurrection.

Ps 17: Certain of his innocence, the psalmist appeals to God's just judgment (1-5), imploring his help against the enemies (6-9) who persecute him (10-12); these worldlings shall be punished, whereas the psalmist shall enjoy God's presence hereafter (13-15).

17, 15: *On waking:* to a new life after death. Death is often compared to sleep. Cf Ps 76, 6; Dn 12, 2.

Ps 18: This psalm of thanksgiving is also given, with a few small variants, in 2 Sm 22. In both places it is attributed to David. Two main sections can be distinguished. In the first part, after an introductory stanza of praise to God (2-4), the royal psalmist describes the peril he was in (5-7), and then poetically depicts, under the form of a theophany, God's intervention in his behalf (8-20), concluding with an acknowledgment of God's justice (21-31). In the second part, God is praised for having prepared the psalmist for war (32-35), given him victory over his enemies (36-39), whom he put to flight (40-43), and bestowed on him dominion over many peoples (44-46). The whole psalm ends with a pæan of grateful praise (47-51).

18, 3: *The horn of my salvation;* my strong savior. The horn, the dreadful weapon of an enraged bull, was a symbol of strength. Cf Lk 1, 69.

18, 5f: These verses are to be understood figuratively.

✱ 18/2-51: 2 Sm 22, 2-51.   5: Ps 116, 3; Jon 2, 3.

6* The cords of the nether world
        enmeshed me,
    the snares of death overtook me.
7† In my distress I called upon the
        LORD
    and cried out to my God;
    From his temple he heard my voice,
        and my cry to him reached his
        ears.

III

8† The earth swayed and quaked;
    the foundations of the mountains
        trembled
    and shook when his wrath flared
        up.
9 Smoke rose from his nostrils,
    and a devouring fire from his
        mouth
    that kindled coals into flame.
10* And he inclined the heavens and
        came down,
    with dark clouds under his feet.
11† He mounted a cherub and flew,
    borne on the wings of the wind.
12* And he made darkness the cloak
        about him;
    dark, misty rain-clouds his wrap.
13 From the brightness of his presence
    coals were kindled to flame.
14 And the LORD thundered from
        heaven,
    the Most High gave forth his
        voice;
15 He sent forth his arrows to put them
        to flight,
    with frequent lightnings he routed
        them.
16 Then the bed of the sea appeared,
    and the foundations of the world
        were laid bare,
    At the rebuke of the LORD,
    at the blast of the wind of his
        wrath.
17 He reached out from on high and
        grasped me;
    he drew me out of the deep waters.
18 He rescued me from my mighty
        enemy
    and from my foes, who were too
        powerful for me.
19 They attacked me in the day of my
        calamity,
    but the LORD came to my support.
20 He set me free in the open,
    and rescued me, because he loves
        me.

IV

21 The LORD rewarded me according to
        my justice;
    according to the cleanness of my
        hands he requited me;
22 For I kept the ways of the LORD
    and was not disloyal to my God;
23 For his ordinances were all present
        to me,
    and his statutes I put not from me,
24 But I was wholehearted toward him,
    and I was on my guard against
        guilt.
25 And the LORD requited me
        according to my justice,
    according to the cleanness of my
        hands in his sight.
26† Toward the faithful you are faithful,
    toward the wholehearted you are
        wholehearted,
27 Toward the sincere you are sincere,
    but toward the crooked you are
        astute;
28 For lowly people you save
    but haughty eyes you bring low;
29† You indeed, O LORD, give light to my
        lamp;
    O my God, you brighten the
        darkness about me;
30 For with your aid I run against an
        armed band,
    and by the help of my God I leap
        over a wall.
31 God's way is unerring,
    the promise of the LORD is
        fire-tried;
    he is a shield to all who take refuge
        in him.

B

I

32 For who is God except the LORD?
    Who is a rock, save our God?

---

† 18, 7: *His temple:* his heavenly abode.

18, 8ff: God's intervention is graphically portrayed under the figures of an earthquake (8, 16), and a thunderstorm (9-15). Cf Jgs 5, 4f; Pss 29; 97, 2-6; Hb 3.

18, 11: *He mounted a cherub:* since God makes the winds his *messengers,* or "angels" (Ps 104, 4), he is also spoken of poetically as riding on the storm clouds, or on the angelic creatures called *cherubim.* His earthly throne on the ark of the covenant was likewise formed by two winged *cherubim.* Cf Ex 37, 7-9. In both senses the Lord is enthroned upon the cherubim. Cf Pss 80, 2; 99, 1.

18, 26f: Men are treated by God in the same way they treat him and their fellow men.

18, 29: *Light to my lamp:* a figure of life and happiness. Cf 1 Kgs 11, 36.

---

* 6: Jn 2, 3.   12: Ps 97, 2.
10: Ps 144, 5.

33 The God who girded me with
strength
and kept my way unerring;

34† Who made my feet swift as those of
hinds
and set me on the heights;

35✱ Who trained my hands for war
and my arms to bend a bow of
brass.

II

36 You have given me your saving
shield;
your right hand has upheld me,
and you have stooped to make me
great.

37 You made room for my steps;
unwavering was my stride.

38 I pursued my enemies and overtook
them,
nor did I turn again till I made an
end of them.

39 I smote them and they could not rise;
they fell beneath my feet.

III

40 And you girded me with strength for
war;
you subdued my adversaries
beneath me.

41 My enemies you put to flight before
me,
and those who hated me you
destroyed.

42 They cried for help—but no one
saved them;
to the Lord—but he answered
them not.

43 I ground them fine as the dust before
the wind;
like the mud in the streets I
trampled them down.

IV

44 You rescued me from the strife of the
people;
you made me head over nations;
A people I had not known became
my slaves;

45 as soon as they heard me they
obeyed.
The foreigners fawned and cringed
before me;

46 they staggered forth from their
fortresses.

C

47 The Lord live! And blessed be my
Rock!
Extolled be God my savior.

48 O God, who granted me vengeance,
who made peoples subject to me

49 and preserved me from my
enemies,
Truly above my adversaries you
exalt me
and from the violent man you have
rescued me.

50✱ Therefore will I proclaim you,
O Lord, among the nations,
and I will sing praise to your name,

51 You who gave great victories to your
king
and showed kindness to your
anointed,
to David and his posterity forever.

God's Glory in the Heavens
and in the Law

19† **1** For the leader. A psalm of David.

A

I

2 The heavens declare the glory of
God,
and the firmament proclaims his
handiwork.

3† Day pours out the word to day,
and night to night imparts
knowledge;

4† Not a word nor a discourse
whose voice is not heard;

5✱† Through all the earth their voice
resounds,
and to the ends of the world, their
message.

II

He has pitched a tent there for the
sun,

---

† 18, 34: *The heights:* a natural stronghold, safe from attack.
Cf Ps 61, 3; Hb 3, 19.

Ps 19 consists of two distinct parts, perhaps originally two
independent psalms. The first section presents the heavenly
firmament, especially the sun, as singing the glories of the
Creator (2-7). In the second section the psalmist praises God's
moral law (8-11) and prays for grace to keep it (12-15).

19, 3: *Day pours out the word:* as if under divine inspiration,
each day proclaims to the next the message of God's grandeur.

19, 4: *Not a word:* this message is so clear that the hearts and
minds of all men cannot help but hear it. However, some commentators interpret the passage to mean, "Although no physical
sound is heard, yet the heavens have a language of their own
that is understood throughout the world."

19, 5: *Through all the earth:* these two lines are applied in
Rom 10, 18 to the preachers of the Gospel. *There:* in the heavens, below the horizon.

✱   35: Ps 144, 1.   19/5: Rom 10, 18.
    50: Rom 15, 9.

6† which comes forth like the groom
from his bridal chamber
and, like a giant, joyfully runs its
course.

7 At one end of the heavens it comes
forth,
and its course is to their other end;
nothing escapes its heat.

B

I

8† The law of the Lord is perfect,
refreshing the soul;
The decree of the Lord is
trustworthy,
giving wisdom to the simple.

9 The precepts of the Lord are right,
rejoicing the heart;
The command of the Lord is clear,
enlightening the eye;

10 The fear of the Lord is pure,
enduring forever;
The ordinances of the Lord are true,
all of them just;

11 They are more precious than gold,
than a heap of purest gold;
Sweeter also than syrup
or honey from the comb.

II

12 Though your servant is careful of
them,
very diligent in keeping them,

13 Yet who can detect failings?
Cleanse me from my unknown
faults!

14 From wanton sin especially, restrain
your servant;
let it not rule over me.
Then shall I be blameless and
innocent
of serious sin.

15 Let the words of my mouth and the
thought of my heart
find favor before you,
O Lord, my rock and my
redeemer.

**Prayer for the King
in Time of War**

20 † 1 For the leader. A psalm of David.

I

2 The Lord answer you in time of
distress;
the name of the God of Jacob
defend you!

3 May he send you help from the
sanctuary,
from Zion may he sustain you.

4 May he remember all your offerings
and graciously accept your
holocaust.

5 May he grant you what is in your
heart
and fulfill your every plan.

6 May we shout for joy at your victory
and raise the standards in the
name of our God.
The Lord grant all your requests!

II

7 Now I know that the Lord has given
victory to his anointed,
that he has answered him from his
holy heaven
with the strength of his victorious
right hand.

8† Some are strong in chariots; some,
in horses;
but we are strong in the name of
the Lord, our God.

9 Though they bow down and fall,
yet we stand erect and firm.

10 O Lord, grant victory to the king,
and answer us when we call upon
you.

**Thanksgiving and Prayers
for the King**

21 † 1 For the leader. A psalm of David.

I

2 O Lord, in your strength the king is
glad;
in your victory how greatly he
rejoices!

3 You have granted him his heart's
desire;
you refused not the wish of his
lips.

4 For you welcomed him with goodly
blessings,
you placed on his head a crown of
pure gold.

5 He asked life of you: you gave him
length of days forever and ever.

---

† 19, 6: *A giant:* literally, "a powerful man"; used also in the sense of "a champion," "a hero," and here perhaps, "an athlete."
19, 8-10: Six synonyms are used for the same idea, divine law Cf Ps 119.
Pss 20 and 21 are complementary, having a similar structure. The former, sung before the battle, expresses good wishes for the king (2-6), with assurance of victory (7-9). The latter, sung after the battle, thanks God for the victory (2-8) and again invokes God's blessing on the king (9-13). Both psalms end with a refrain sung by the people.
20, 8: The pious place their trust, not in material means, but in the help of God whom they invoke. Cf 1 Sm 17, 45; Is 31, 1; 36, 9.

6 Great is his glory in your victory;
     majesty and splendor you
       conferred upon him.
7 For you made him a blessing
       forever;
     you gladdened him with the joy of
       your presence.
8 For the king trusts in the LORD,
     and through the kindness of the
       Most High he stands unshaken.

    II

9† May your hand reach all your
       enemies,
     may your right hand reach your
       foes!
10 Make them burn as though in a fiery
       furnace,
     when you appear.
   May the LORD consume them in his
       anger;
     let fire devour them.
11 Destroy their fruit from the earth
     and their posterity from among
       men.
12 Though they intend evil against you,
     devising plots, they cannot
       succeed,
13 For you shall put them to flight;
     you shall aim your shafts against
       them.
14 Be extolled, O LORD, in your
       strength!
   We will sing, chant the praise of
     your might.

Passion and Triumph
of the Messiah

22 † 1 For the leader; according to "The hind of
           the dawn." A psalm of David.

    A

    I

2*† My God, my God, why have you
       forsaken me,
     far from my prayer, from the
       words of my cry?
3† O my God, I cry out by day, and you
       answer not;
     by night, and there is no relief for
       me.
4 Yet you are enthroned in the holy
       place,
     O glory of Israel!
5 In you our fathers trusted;
     they trusted, and you delivered
       them.

6 To you they cried, and they escaped;
     in you they trusted, and they were
       not put to shame.
7 But I am a worm, not a man;
     the scorn of men, despised by the
       people.
8*† All who see me scoff at me;
     they mock me with parted lips,
       they wag their heads:
9*† "He relied on the LORD; let him
       deliver him,
     let him rescue him, if he loves
       him."
10† You have been my guide since I was
       first formed,
     my security at my mother's breast.
11† To you I was committed at birth,
     from my mother's womb you are
       my God.

12 Be not far from me, for I am in
       distress;
     be near, for I have no one to help
       me.   *(II)*
13† Many bullocks surround me;
     the strong bulls of Bashan encircle
       me.

---

† 21, 9ff: These words are addressed to the king.

Ps 22 is one of the most important of the messianic psalms. Our Lord himself on the cross repeated its first line, and several other verses are directly quoted, or at least alluded to, in the New Testament as pertaining to his Passion. Of no other person is this touching description of spiritual and physical suffering so eminently true as it is of Jesus Christ. Hence, the entire psalm has been traditionally interpreted in the Catholic Church as referring to him. The psalmist, therefore, speaks in Christ's name when in the first section (2-22) he describes the Messiah's dereliction (2-6), opprobrium (7-9) and physical sufferings (13-19), together with his unshaken confidence in the heavenly Father (10-12.20-22); and in the second part, the fruits of his redemption: the grateful praise of the redeemed (23-27), the conversion of the Gentiles (28-30d), and the glory of God and his beloved Son (30e-32).

22, 2: *Far from my prayer:* when he prays, God seems too distant to hear his cry.

22, 3: *There is no relief for me:* the Hebrew phrase here is obscure; the revised Latin Psalter renders it, "You heed me not."

22, 8: *Parted lips:* a sign of scorn. *They wag their heads:* another gesture of derision; it was indulged in by Christ's enemies on Calvary.

22, 9: These words were spoken, in unwitting fulfillment of the prophecy, by the Jews at our Lord's crucifixion. Cf Mt 27, 42. *If he loves him:* the natural sense seems to be, "If God loves the sufferer"; but some understand it as, "Since he (the sufferer) has loved him (the LORD)."

22, 10: *My guide:* so in the revised Latin Psalter, but the meaning of the Hebrew is uncertain.

22, 11: *To you I was committed:* literally, "upon you I was thrown." Some see in this a reference to the ancient custom of placing a newborn baby upon its father's lap, so that he might acknowledge its paternity. But more probably the meaning is simply, "I was given to your care."

22, 13: *Bashan:* a fertile grazing land east of the Jordan, famous for its strong cattle. Cf Dt 32, 14; Ez 39, 18; Am 4, 1. The various beasts mentioned here are, of course, to be understood figuratively, as signifying cruel persecutors.

✿ 22/2: Mt 27, 46; Mk 15, 34.   9: Mt 27, 43.
   8: Mt 27, 39; Mk 15, 29.

14 They open their mouths against me
like ravening and roaring lions.

15 I am like water poured out;
all my bones are racked.
My heart has become like wax
melting away within my bosom.

16 My throat is dried up like baked
clay,
my tongue cleaves to my jaws;
to the dust of death you have
brought me down.

17† Indeed, many dogs surround me,
a pack of evildoers closes in upon
me;
They have pierced my hands and
my feet;

18 I can count all my bones.
They look on and gloat over me;

19*† they divide my garments among
them,
and for my vesture they cast lots.

III

20 But you, O Lord, be not far from me;
O my help, hasten to aid me.

21† Rescue my soul from the sword,
my loneliness from the grip of the
dog.

22 Save me from the lion's mouth;
from the horns of the wild bulls,
my wretched life.

B

I

23*† I will proclaim your name to my
brethren;
in the midst of the assembly I will
praise you:

24 "You who fear the Lord, praise him;
all you descendants of Jacob, give
glory to him;
revere him, all you descendants of
Israel!

25 For he has not spurned nor
disdained
the wretched man in his misery,
Nor did he turn his face away from
him,
but when he cried out to him, he
heard him."

26 So by your gift will I utter praise in
the vast assembly;
I will fulfill my vows before those
who fear him.

27† The lowly shall eat their fill;
they who seek the Lord shall
praise him:
"May your hearts be ever merry!"

II

28 All the ends of the earth
shall remember and turn to the
Lord;
All the families of the nations
shall bow down before him.

29 For dominion is the Lord's,
and he rules the nations.

30† To him alone shall bow down
all who sleep in the earth;
Before him shall bend
all who go down into the dust.

(III)

And to him my soul shall live;
31 my descendants shall serve him.
Let the coming generation be told of
the Lord

32 that they may proclaim to a
people yet to be born
the justice he has shown.

The Lord, Shepherd and Host

23† 1† A psalm of David.

I

The Lord is my shepherd; I shall not
want.
2 In verdant pastures he gives me
repose;
Beside restful waters he leads me;
3 he refreshes my soul.
He guides me in right paths
for his name's sake.

---

† 22, 17: *They have pierced my hands:* so in the ancient versions. The current Hebrew text reads, "Like the lion my hands," which hardly makes good sense. This passage finds its complete fulfillment in the nailing of Christ's hands and feet to the cross.

22, 19: Explicitly cited in Jn 19, 24 as a prophecy fulfilled in the dividing of our Lord's garments by the soldiers on Calvary.

22, 21: *My loneliness:* his desolate soul. Cf Ps 35, 17.

22, 23: The transition from deepest sorrow to the great joy of the risen Savior. The language of vv 23-27 is based on the custom whereby a person who offered a thanksgiving sacrifice in the temple would recount to his fellow worshipers the favor received from God and then invite them to share in his sacrificial banquet.

22, 27: *May your hearts be ever merry:* addressed to *the lowly.* Cf Ps 69, 33.

22, 30f: The Hebrew text is poorly preserved here. The translation given above follows the revised Latin Psalter in restoring the text to accord with the ancient versions.

Ps 23: God's loving care for his devoted servant is here portrayed under the figures of a shepherd's solicitude for his sheep (1-4) and a host's generosity toward his guest (5f).

23, 1: The idea of God as the good shepherd of his flock is common in both the Old and the New Testament. Cf especially Jn 10, 11-18.

19: Jn 19, 24.   23: Heb 2, 12.

4† Even though I walk in the dark
valley
  I fear no evil; for you are at my
  side
With your rod and your staff
  that give me courage.

II

5† You spread the table before me
  in the sight of my foes;
You anoint my head with oil;
  my cup overflows.
6 Only goodness and kindness follow
me
  all the days of my life;
And I shall dwell in the house of the
LORD
  for years to come.

The Lord's Solemn Entry Into Zion

24 **†** **1*** A psalm of David.

I

The LORD's are the earth and its
fullness;
  the world and those who dwell
  in it.
2† For he founded it upon the seas
  and established it upon the rivers.

II

3*† Who can ascend the mountain of the
LORD?
  or who may stand in his holy
  place?
4 He whose hands are sinless, whose
heart is clean,
  who desires not what is vain,
  nor swears deceitfully to his
  neighbor.
5 He shall receive a blessing from the
LORD,
  a reward from God his savior.
6 Such is the race that seeks for him,
  that seeks the face of the God of
  Jacob.

III

7† Lift up, O gates, your lintels;
  reach up, you ancient portals,
  that the king of glory may come in!
8 Who is this king of glory?
  The LORD, strong and mighty,
  the LORD, mighty in battle.
9 Lift up, O gates, your lintels;
  reach up, you ancient portals,
  that the king of glory may come in!

10 Who is this king of glory?
  The LORD of hosts; he is the king
  of glory.

Prayer for Guidance and Help

25 **†** **1*** Of David.

I

To you I lift up my soul,
  O LORD, **2**my God.
In you I trust; let me not be put to
shame,
  let not my enemies exult over me.
3 No one who waits for you shall be
put to shame;
  those shall be put to shame who
  heedlessly break faith.

4* Your ways, O LORD, make known to
me;
  teach me your paths,
5† Guide me in your truth and teach
me,
  for you are God my savior,
  and for you I wait all the day.
6 Remember that your compassion,
O LORD,
  and your kindness are from of old.
7 The sins of my youth and my
frailties remember not;
  in your kindness remember me,
  because of your goodness, O LORD.

II

8 Good and upright is the LORD;
  thus he shows sinners the way.

---

†
23, 4: *Your rod and your staff:* to guide and defend the sheep.
23, 5: *Oil:* a perfumed ointment, used especially at banquets. Cf Mt 26, 7; Lk 7, 37.46; Jn 12, 3.
Ps 24: After a strophe in praise of God's universal dominion (1f), the psalm lays down the moral requirements for assisting at divine worship (3-6), and then gives the words which were sung when the ark, representing God's presence, was carried to Zion or into the temple (7-10). From the dialogue structure it seems probable that this psalm was composed for liturgical use, to be sung by alternating choirs. Cf 2 Sm 6, 12ff.
24, 2: According to the ancient notion of the world, the earth was regarded as a flat disk resting on a vast underground sea, "the deep." Cf Ps 33, 7.
24, 3-6: Ps 15 is similar in structure and content: a question, an answer giving the conditions, and a conclusion.
24, 7.9: *Your lintels:* literally, "your heads." The doorway is pictured as too low for the great God to enter. The *gates* and *portals* are either those of the temple or of the *ancient* citadel of the Jebusites.
Ps 25: An alphabetic psalm. Cf Ps 9. The thoughts are rather loosely connected, but the first part (1-7) is principally a prayer for guidance and pardon; the second (8-15), a meditation on God's goodness toward the just; the third (16-22), a prayer for protection and consolation.
25, 5: *And for you I wait all the day:* perhaps the third line of v 7 should be inserted immediately after these words. Elsewhere in this psalm there are two lines apiece for each letter of the Hebrew alphabet.

---

*
24/1: Ps 50, 12; 1 Cor 10, 26.   25/1: Pss 86, 4; 143, 8.
3-5: Ps 15, 1-5.   4f: Ps 86, 11.

9   He guides the humble to justice,
    he teaches the humble his way.
10   All the paths of the Lord are
    kindness and constancy
    toward those who keep his
    covenant and his decrees.
11   For your name's sake, O Lord,
    you will pardon my guilt, great as
    it is.

12   When a man fears the Lord,
    he shows him the way he should
    choose.
13   He abides in prosperity,
    and his descendants inherit the
    land.
14   The friendship of the Lord is with
    those who fear him,
    and his covenant, for their
    instruction.
15   My eyes are ever toward the Lord,
    for he will free my feet from the
    snare.

III

16   Look toward me, and have pity on
    me,
    for I am alone and afflicted.
17   Relieve the troubles of my heart,
    and bring me out of my distress.
18†   Put an end to my affliction and my
    suffering,
    and take away all my sins.
19   Behold, my enemies are many,
    and they hate me violently.
20   Preserve my life, and rescue me;
    let me not be put to shame, for I
    take refuge in you.
21   Let integrity and uprightness
    preserve me,
    because I wait for you, O Lord.
22†   Redeem Israel, O God,
    from all its distress!

Prayer of an Innocent Man

26 † 1   Of David.

I

Do me justice, O Lord! for I have
    walked in integrity,
    and in the Lord I trust without
    wavering.
2   Search me, O Lord, and try me;
    test my soul and my heart.

II

3   For your kindness is before my eyes,
    and I walk in your truth.

4   I stay not with worthless men,
    nor do I consort with hypocrites.
5   I hate the assembly of evildoers,
    and with the wicked I will not
    stay.
6*†   I wash my hands in innocence,
    and I go around your altar,
    O Lord,
7   Giving voice to my thanks,
    and recounting all your wondrous
    deeds.
8   O Lord, I love the house in which
    you dwell,
    the tenting-place of your glory.

III

9   Gather not my soul with those of
    sinners,
    nor with men of blood my life.
10   On their hands are crimes,
    and their right hands are full of
    bribes.
11   But I walk in integrity;
    redeem me, and have pity on me.
12†   My foot stands on level ground;
    in the assemblies I will bless the
    Lord.

Trust in God

27 † 1   Of David.

A

I

The Lord is my light and my
    salvation;
    whom should I fear?
The Lord is my life's refuge;
    of whom should I be afraid?

---

† 25, 18f: The wording and the order of these verses are not wholly free from doubt.

25, 22: This final verse is an addition to the original psalm.

Ps 26: Protesting his innocence (1f), the psalmist enumerates his virtues (3-8), that God may not condemn him with the wicked (9-12).

26, 6: *I wash my hands:* although the washing of hands was a liturgical act (Ex 30, 19.21; 40, 31), here it is probably to be understood figuratively, as in Is 1, 16. The words from here to the end of the psalm were long recited in the Roman rite Mass, at the washing . . . Cf Ps 73, 13.

26, 12: *On level ground:* in safety, where there is no danger of tripping and falling; here used figuratively. Some join the two lines of this verse to read, "When my feet stand on level ground, . . . I will bless the Lord." *In the assemblies:* in the temple, where the psalmist will offer a sacrifice of thanksgiving.

Ps 27: Asserting his boundless confidence that God will rescue him (1-3), the psalmist longs for the shelter of the temple where, united with the Lord, he will be safe from his enemies (4-6). The second half seems originally to have been an independent psalm. Here the psalmist prays that he may not be abandoned by God (7-10), asks for guidance and protection (11f), and ends on a note of confidence (13f).

2† When evildoers come at me
    to devour my flesh,
My foes and my enemies
    themselves stumble and fall.

3 Though an army encamp against me,
    my heart will not fear;
Though war be waged upon me,
    even then will I trust.

II

4*† One thing I ask of the LORD;
    this I seek:
To dwell in the house of the LORD
    all the days of my life,
That I may gaze on the loveliness of
    the LORD
    and contemplate his temple.

5 For he will hide me in his abode
    in the day of trouble;
He will conceal me in the shelter of
    his tent,
    he will set me high upon a rock.

6 Even now my head is held high
    above my enemies on every side.
And I will offer in his tent
    sacrifices with shouts of gladness;
I will sing and chant praise to the
    LORD.

B

I

7 Hear, O LORD, the sound of my call;
    have pity on me, and answer me.

8 Of you my heart speaks; you my
    glance seeks;
    your presence, O LORD, I seek.

9 Hide not your face from me;
    do not in anger repel your servant.
You are my helper: cast me not off;
    forsake me not, O God my savior.

10 Though my father and mother
    forsake me,
    yet will the LORD receive me.

II

11† Show me, O LORD, your way,
    and lead me on a level path,
    because of my adversaries.

12 Give me not up to the wishes of my
    foes;
    for false witnesses have risen up
    against me,
    and such as breathe out violence.

13† I believe that I shall see the bounty
    of the LORD
    in the land of the living.

14 Wait for the LORD with courage;
    be stouthearted, and wait for the
    LORD.

Petition and Thanksgiving

28 † **1*** Of David.

I

To you, O LORD, I call;
    O my Rock, be not deaf to me,
Lest, if you heed me not,
    I become one of those going down
    into the pit.

2† Hear the sound of my pleading,
    when I cry to you,
    lifting up my hands toward your
    holy shrine.

3 Drag me not away with the wicked,
    with those who do wrong,
Who speak civilly to their neighbors
    though evil is in their hearts.

4† Repay them for their deeds,
    for the evil of their doings.
For the work of their hands repay
    them;
    give them their deserts.

5 Because they consider not
    the deeds of the LORD nor the work
    of his hands,
    may he tear them down and not
    build them up.

II

6 Blessed be the LORD,
    for he has heard the sound of my
    pleading;

7 the LORD is my strength and my
    shield.
In him my heart trusts, and I find
    help;
    then my heart exults, and with my
    song I give him thanks.

---

† 27, 2: *To devour my flesh:* to destroy me completely. Cf Ps 14, 4; Mi 3, 3.

27, 4: *Contemplate his temple:* the meaning of the Hebrew is not quite certain. Some render it as, "visit his temple at dawn."

27, 11: *A level path:* see note on Ps 26, 12.

27, 13: *In the land of the living:* the meaning is, "While I am still living here on earth." But these words may also be used in an accommodated sense, as the church uses them in the Office of the Dead, to mean, "In heaven, where there is true life."

Ps 28 consists of a prayer asking that the psalmist may not be punished with the wicked (1-5), followed by anticipated thanksgiving to God for having heard him (6f), and ending with an intercession for the king and the nation (8f).

28, 2: *Your holy shrine:* the innermost part of the temple, the holy of holies, containing the ark of the Lord.

28, 4f: Since the wicked have no care for God, he will have no care for them.

✶   27/4: Pss 23, 6; 61, 5; 65, 5.   28/1: Pss 30, 4; 88, 5; 143, 7;   Prv 1, 12.

III

8 The Lord is the strength of his
     people,
   the saving refuge of his anointed.
9 Save your people, and bless your
     inheritance;
   feed them, and carry them forever!

God's Majesty in the Storm

29† ¹*†   A psalm of David.

I

Give to the Lord, you sons of God,
   give to the Lord glory and praise,
2 Give to the Lord the glory due his
     name;·
   adore the Lord in holy attire.

II

3† The voice of the Lord is over the
     waters,
   the God of glory thunders,
   the Lord, over vast waters.
4 The voice of the Lord is mighty;
   the voice of the Lord is majestic.
5 The voice of the Lord breaks the
     cedars,
   the Lord breaks the cedars of
     Lebanon.
6† He makes Lebanon leap like a calf
   and Sirion like a young bull.
7 The voice of the Lord strikes fiery
     flames;
8† the voice of the Lord shakes the
     desert,
   the Lord shakes the wilderness of
     Kadesh.
9 The voice of the Lord twists the
     oaks and strips the forests,
   and in his temple all say, "Glory!"

III

10 The Lord is enthroned above the
     flood;
   the Lord is enthroned as king
     forever.
11 May the Lord give strength to his
     people;
   may the Lord bless his people with
     peace!

Thanksgiving for Deliverance from Death

30† ¹†   A psalm. A song for the dedication of the
temple. Of David.

2   I will extol you, O Lord, for you
     drew me clear

and did not let my enemies rejoice
   over me.

A

3 O Lord, my God,
   I cried out to you and you healed
     me.
4* O Lord, you brought me up from the
     nether world;
   you preserved me from among
     those going down into the pit.
5 Sing praise to the Lord, you his
     faithful ones,
   and give thanks to his holy name.
6 For his anger lasts but a moment;
   a lifetime, his good will.
At nightfall, weeping enters in,
   but with the dawn, rejoicing.

B

I

7 Once, in my security, I said,
   "I shall never be disturbed."
8 O Lord, in your good will you had
     endowed me with majesty and
     strength;
   but when you hid your face I was
     terrified.

II

9 To you, O Lord, I cried out;
   with the Lord I pleaded:

---

† Ps 29: After an invocation to praise the Lord (1f), this strik-ing psalm describes a magnificent theophany, the revelation of God's majesty in a tremendous thunderstorm (3-10), and ends with a prayer for the people (11).

29, 1: *Sons of God:* although this phrase regularly refers to the angels, as in Jb 1, 6; 2, 1; 38, 7, here it may be understood of "godly, virtuous men"; in Ps 96, 7ff, a very similar invocation is addressed to the families of nations. Cf Ps 89, 7.

29, 3: *The voice of the Lord:* the thunder and the thunder-bolt, the sound of which is here attributed directly to God.

29, 6: *He makes Lebanon leap:* the mountains are pictured as trembling with fear; perhaps an earthquake is meant. Cf Ps 114, 4.6f. *Sirion:* the Phœnician name for Mount Hermon. Cf Dt 3, 9. Several expressions in this psalm are also found in the Canaanite texts written in the fifteenth century B. C. at Ugarit, in the north of Phœnicia.

29, 8: *The wilderness of Kadesh:* formerly identified with the oasis of Kadesh in the northern part of the Sinai peninsula. Cf Nm 20, 1. More probably, however, it was north of Palestine, for it is also mentioned in one of the Ugaritic texts, and in the pres-ent context seems to be in the neighborhood of Lebanon and Hermon.

Ps 30: The psalmist, after announcing his theme (2), thanks God for having restored him to health when sickness was about to bring him to the grave (3-6). He then gives the details of what had occurred: confident of robust health, he was suddenly stricken with some disease (7f), but he cried to the Lord for help (9-11), and his prayer was heard (12f).

30, 1: *For the dedication of the temple:* a later adaptation of this psalm.

10*† "What gain would there be from my
lifeblood,
from my going down into the
grave?
Would dust give you thanks
or proclaim your faithfulness?
11 Hear, O Lord, and have pity on me;
O Lord, be my helper."

III

12† You changed my mourning into
dancing;
you took off my sackcloth and
clothed me with gladness,
13 That my soul might sing praise to
you without ceasing;
O Lord, my God, forever will I
give you thanks.

Prayer in Distress and Thanksgiving for Escape

31† **1** For the leader. A psalm of David.

I

2* In you, O Lord, I take refuge;
let me never be put to shame.
In your justice rescue me,
3 incline your ear to me,
make haste to deliver me!
Be my rock of refuge,
a stronghold to give me safety.
4 You are my rock and my fortress;
for your name's sake you will lead
and guide me.
5 You will free me from the snare they
set for me,
for you are my refuge.
6*† Into your hands I commend my
spirit;
you will redeem me, O Lord,
O faithful God.
7 You hate those who worship vain
idols,
but my trust is in the Lord.
8 I will rejoice and be glad of your
kindness,
when you have seen my affliction
and watched over me in my
distress,
9 Not shutting me up in the grip of the
enemy
but enabling me to move about at
large.

II

10 Have pity on me, O Lord, for I am
in distress;
with sorrow my eye is consumed;
my soul also, and my body.

11 For my life is spent with grief
and my years with sighing;
My strength has failed through
affliction,
and my bones are consumed.
12 For all my foes I am an object of
reproach,
a laughingstock to my neighbors,
and a dread to my friends;
they who see me abroad flee from
me.
13† I am forgotten like the unremem-
bered dead;
I am like a dish that is broken.
14*† I hear the whispers of the crowd,
that frighten me from every
side,
as they consult together against
me, plotting to take my life.
15 But my trust is in you, O Lord;
I say, "You are my God."
16 In your hands is my destiny; rescue
me
from the clutches of my enemies
and my persecutors.
17 Let your face shine upon your
servant;
save me in your kindness.
18 O Lord, let me not be put to shame,
for I call upon you;
let the wicked be put to shame; let
them be reduced to silence in
the nether world.
19 Let dumbness strike their lying lips
that speak insolence against the
just in pride and scorn.

III

20 How great is the goodness, O Lord,
which you have in store for those
who fear you,

---

† 30, 10: See note on Ps 6, 6.

30, 12: *Sackcloth:* worn in times of mourning and penance. Cf 2 Sm 3, 31; 1 Kgs 21, 27; Pss 35, 13; 69, 12.

Ps 31: In the first two sections (2-19) the psalmist describes in pathetic words his extreme misery and affliction, while with unshaken confidence in God's goodness he prays for heavenly aid. The third section (20-25) is a typical hymn of thanksgiving. If it was originally joined to the preceding verses and not an independent psalm, it must be considered as an anticipated acknowledgment of favors the psalmist hopes to receive.

31, 6: *Into your hands I commend my spirit:* our Lord made these words his own as he died on the cross. Cf Lk 23, 46. Hence the whole psalm may be fittingly considered as an expression of Christ's feelings of anguish, joined with filial confidence in his heavenly Father, during his bitter Passion.

31, 13: *Like a dish that is broken:* a common comparison for something ruined and useless. Cf Is 30, 14; Jer 19, 11; 22, 28.

31, 14: *That frighten me from every side:* literally, "terror from round about." This phrase occurs several times also in Jeremiah. Cf Jer 6, 25; 20, 3.10; 46, 5; 49, 29. There are certain other marks of similarity between this psalm and the writings of that prophet.

---

* 10: Ps 6, 6.   6: Lk 23, 46.
31/2-4: Ps 71, 1-3.   14: Jer 20, 10.

And which, toward those who take
    refuge in you,
    you show in the sight of men.

21 You hide them in the shelter of your
    presence
    from the plottings of men;
You screen them within your abode
    from the strife of tongues.

22 Blessed be the LORD whose
    wondrous kindness
    he has shown me in a fortified city.

23 Once I said in my anguish,
    "I am cut off from your sight";
Yet you heard the sound of my
    pleading
    when I cried out to you.

24 Love the LORD, all you his faithful
    ones!
The LORD keeps those who are
    constant,
    but more than requites those who
    act proudly.

25 Take courage and be stouthearted,
    all you who hope in the LORD.

Remission of Sin

32 † **1*** Of David. A *maskil.*

I

Happy is he whose fault is taken
    away,
    whose sin is covered.

2† Happy the man to whom the LORD
    imputes not guilt,
    in whose spirit there is no guile.

II

3† As long as I would not speak, my
    bones wasted away
    with my groaning all the day,

4 For day and night your hand was
    heavy upon me;
    my strength was dried up as by the
    heat of summer.

5† Then I acknowledged my sin to you,
    my guilt I covered not.
I said, "I confess my faults to the
    LORD,"
    and you took away the guilt of my
    sin.

6 For this shall every faithful man
    pray to you
    in time of stress.
Though deep waters overflow,
    they shall not reach him.

7 You are my shelter; from distress you
    will preserve me;
    with glad cries of freedom you will
    ring me round.

III

8 I will instruct you and show you the
    way you should walk;
    I will counsel you, keeping my eye
    on you.

9† Be not senseless like horses or mules:
    with bit and bridle their temper
    must be curbed,
    else they will not come near you.

IV

10 Many are the sorrows of the wicked,
    but kindness surrounds him who
    trusts in the LORD.

11 Be glad in the LORD and rejoice, you
    just;
    exult, all you upright of heart.

Praise of the Lord's Power and Providence

I

33 † **1** Exult, you just, in the LORD;
    praise from the upright is fitting.

2 Give thanks to the LORD on the harp;
    with the ten-stringed lyre chant
    his praises.

3 Sing to him a new song;
    pluck the strings skillfully, with
    shouts of gladness.

4 For upright is the word of the LORD,
    and all his works are trustworthy.

5 He loves justice and right;
    of the kindness of the LORD the
    earth is full.

II

6† By the word of the LORD the heavens
    were made;

---

† Ps 32: The second of the Penitential Psalms, and a favorite of St. Augustine's. The psalmist describes the blessedness of having one's sins forgiven by God (1f), as well as his own spiritual consolation when he confessed his sins (3-7); he then exhorts others to be submissive to God's will (8f), and to confide with joy in his goodness (10f).

32, 2: *No guile:* no hypocrisy in acknowledging his sins.

32, 3: *I would not speak:* I refused at first to confess my sins.

32, 5: St. Augustine's comment is that, even before the sin is acknowledged by the penitent's lips, God hears the cry of his heart. Pardon at once follows sincere contrition. Cf 2 Sm 12, 13.

32, 9: The Hebrew text of this verse is obscure, and is variously interpreted.

Ps 33: A hymn of praise in which the just are invited to chant the glories of God (1-3), because he is ever faithful to his promises (4f), the all-powerful Creator (6f), and the wise and mighty Ruler of the world (8-12), who sees and knows all things (13-15) and who alone is the source of victory and salvation (16-19). The hymn concludes with an expression of confidence in God's goodness (20-22).

33, 6: *All their host:* by a common figure, the countless stars of the sky are viewed as a vast army. Cf Neh 9, 6; Is 40, 26; 45, 12; Jer 33, 22.

✤ 32/1f: Rom 4, 7f.

by the breath of his mouth all their
host.

7† He gathers the waters of the sea as
in a flask;
in cellars he confines the deep.

III

8 Let all the earth fear the LORD;
let all who dwell in the world
revere him.

9 For he spoke, and it was made;
he commanded, and it stood forth.

10 The LORD brings to nought the plans
of nations;
he foils the designs of peoples.

11 But the plan of the LORD stands
forever;
the design of his heart, through all
generations.

12* Happy the nation whose God is the
LORD,
the people he has chosen for his
own inheritance.

IV

13 From heaven the LORD looks down;
he sees all mankind.

14 From his fixed throne he beholds
all who dwell on the earth,

15 He who fashioned the heart of each,
he who knows all their works.

V

16 A king is not saved by a mighty
army,
nor is a warrior delivered by great
strength.

17 Useless is the horse for safety;
great though its strength, it cannot
provide escape.

18 But see, the eyes of the LORD are
upon those who fear him,
upon those who hope for his
kindness,

19 To deliver them from death
and preserve them in spite of
famine.

VI

20 Our soul waits for the LORD,
who is our help and our shield,

21 For in him our hearts rejoice;
in his holy name we trust.

22 May your kindness, O LORD, be
upon us
who have put our hope in you.

Praise of God, the Protector of the Just

34 † **1*†** Of David, when he feigned madness before
Abimelech, who forced him to depart.

I

2 I will bless the LORD at all times;
his praise shall be ever in my
mouth.

3 Let my soul glory in the LORD;
the lowly will hear me and be
glad.

4 Glorify the LORD with me,
let us together extol his name.

II

5 I sought the LORD, and he answered
me
and delivered me from all my
fears.

6 Look to him that you may be radiant
with joy,
and your faces may not blush with
shame.

7† When the afflicted man called out,
the LORD heard,
and from all his distress he saved
him.

8 The angel of the LORD encamps
around those who fear him, and
delivers them.

9† Taste and see how good the LORD is;
happy the man who takes refuge
in him.

10 Fear the LORD, you his holy ones,
for nought is lacking to those who
fear him.

11* The great grow poor and hungry;
but those who seek the LORD want
for no good thing.

---

†
33, 7: The ancients marveled at the power which kept the
mighty seas from overwhelming the dry land. According to
pagan mythology, this was achieved by a fierce battle in which
the heavenly gods triumphed over the gods of the deep. For the
Lord, however, this is as simple as putting water into a bottle;
he can store away the immense subterranean ocean as easily as
a man stores wine in his cellar.

Ps 34: An alphabetic psalm having no apparent connection
with the events mentioned in v 1. After an exhortation to glorify
the Lord (2-4), the psalmist sings his grateful praise to God
for having rescued him from danger (5-11), and concludes with
an admonition to fear the Lord and keep his commandments
(12-23).

34, 1: It was at the court of the Philistine King Achish that
David feigned insanity after he had departed from the priest
Abimelech. Some early scribe appears to have confused these
two names here.

34, 7: *When the afflicted man called out, the Lord heard:*
some render the passage, "Here is an afflicted man who called
out, and the LORD heard him." The psalmist himself would then
be this *afflicted man.*

34, 9: *Taste and see:* figurative language for, "know by experience."

---

*
33/12: Ps 144, 15.   11: Lk 1, 53.
34/1: 1 Sm 21, 1-22, 1.

III

12† Come, children, hear me;
  I will teach you the fear of the
  LORD.

13* Which of you desires life,
  and takes delight in prosperous
  days?

14 Keep your tongue from evil
  and your lips from speaking guile;

15 Turn from evil, and do good;
  seek peace, and follow after it.

16* The LORD has eyes for the just,
  and ears for their cry.

17 The LORD confronts the evildoers,
  to destroy remembrance of them
  from the earth.

18 When the just cry out, the LORD
  hears them,
  and from all their distress he
  rescues them.

19 The LORD is close to the
  brokenhearted;
  and those who are crushed in spirit
  he saves.

20 Many are the troubles of the just
  man,
  but out of them all the LORD
  delivers him;

21 He watches over all his bones;
  not one of them shall be broken.

22 Vice slays the wicked,
  and the enemies of the just pay for
  their guilt.

23 But the LORD redeems the lives of his
  servants;
  no one incurs guilt who takes
  refuge in him.

Prayer for Help against Unjust Enemies

35 † **1†** Of David.

I

Fight, O LORD, against those who
  fight me;
  war against those who make war
  upon me.

2 Take up the shield and buckler,
  and rise up in my defense.

3 Brandish the lance, and block the
  way
  in the face of my pursuers;
  Say to my soul,
  "I am your salvation."

4 Let those be put to shame and
  disgraced
  who seek my life;
  Let those be turned back and
  confounded
  who plot evil against me.

5 Let them be like chaff before the
  wind,
  with the angel of the LORD driving
  them on.

6 Let their way be dark and slippery,
  with the angel of the LORD
  pursuing them.

II

7 For without cause they set their
  snare for me,
  without cause they dug a pit
  against my life.

8 Let ruin come upon them unawares,
  and let the snare they have set
  catch them;
  into the pit they have dug let them
  fall.

9 But I will rejoice in the LORD,
  I will be joyful because of his
  salvation.

10* All my being shall say,
  "O LORD, who is like you,
  The rescuer of the afflicted man from
  those too strong for him,
  of the afflicted and the needy
  from their despoilers?"

11 Unjust witnesses have risen up;
  things I knew not of, they lay to
  my charge.

12 They have repaid me evil for good,
  bringing bereavement to my soul.

III

13† But I, when they were ill, put on
  sackcloth;
  I afflicted myself with fasting
  and poured forth prayers within
  my bosom.

---

† 34, 12: *Children:* in Hebrew wisdom literature a rabbi or teacher customarily addresses his disciples in this way.

Ps 35: Calling upon God to defend him (1-6), the psalmist describes the wickedness (7-12) and ingratitude (13-16) of his enemies, and then reiterates his plea for divine assistance (17-28).

35, 1-3: The martial language is purely figurative; the psalmist's enemies are not actually armed against him, but rather are those who have falsely accused him of serious crimes. Cf vv 11.21.

35, 13.15-17: In several places the Hebrew text of these verses is obscure and their translation somewhat uncertain.

35, 13: *And poured forth prayers within my bosom:* literally, "my prayers returned upon my bosom." Some take this to mean that he prayed with deeply bowed head so that his voice reverberated against his chest; but more probably it refers to the saying of silent prayers which remained within his heart.

13-17: 1 Pt 3, 10-12.   35/10: Ex 15, 11; Pss 71, 19;
  16: Sir 15, 19.   89, 7.9; 113, 5.

¹⁴ As though it were a friend of mine,
      or a brother, I went about;
    like one bewailing a mother, I was
      bowed down in mourning.
¹⁵ Yet when I stumbled they were glad
      and gathered together;
    they gathered together striking me
      unawares.
They tore at me without ceasing;
¹⁶   they put me to the test; they
      mocked me,
    gnashing their teeth at me.

IV

¹⁷ O Lord, how long will you look on?
    Save me from the roaring beasts;
      from the lions, my only life.
¹⁸ I will give you thanks in the vast
      assembly,
    in the mighty throng I will praise
      you.
^{19†} Let not my unprovoked enemies
      rejoice over me;
    let not my undeserved foes wink
      knowingly.
²⁰ For civil words they speak not,
    but against the peaceful in the
      land
    they fashion treacherous speech.
²¹ And they open wide their mouths
      against me,
    saying, "Aha, aha! We saw him
      with our own eyes!"
²² You, O Lord, have seen; be not
      silent;
    Lord, be not far from me!
²³ Awake, and be vigilant in my
      defense;
    in my cause, my God and my Lord.
²⁴ Do me justice, because you are just,
      O Lord;
    my God, let them not rejoice over
      me.
²⁵ Let them not say in their hearts,
      "Aha! This is what we wanted!"
    Let them not say, "We have
      swallowed him up!"

²⁶ Let all be put to shame and
      confounded
    who are glad at my misfortune.
    Let those be clothed with shame and
      disgrace
    who glory over me.
²⁷ But let those shout for joy and be
      glad
    who favor my just cause;

And may they ever say, "The Lord
      be glorified;
    he wills the prosperity of his
      servant!"
²⁸ Then my tongue shall recount your
      justice,
    your praise, all the day.

Human Wickedness and Divine Providence

36^{† 1} For the leader. Of David, the servant of the
    Lord.

I

^{2*†} Sin speaks to the wicked man in his
      heart;
    there is no dread of God before his
      eyes,
^{3†} For he beguiles himself with the
      thought
    that his guilt will not be found out
      or hated.
⁴ The words of his mouth are empty
      and false;
    he has ceased to understand how
      to do good.
⁵ He plans wickedness in his bed;
    he sets out on a way that is not
      good, with no repugnance for
      evil.

II

⁶ O Lord, your kindness reaches to
      heaven;
    your faithfulness, to the clouds.
^{7†} Your justice is like the mountains of
      God;
    your judgments, like the mighty
      deep;
    man and beast you save, O Lord.
⁸ How precious is your kindness,
      O God!
    The children of men take refuge
      in the shadow of your wings.
⁹ They have their fill of the prime gifts
      of your house;
    from your delightful stream you
      give them to drink.

---

† 35, 19: *Unprovoked . . . undeserved:* he has never given them a just reason for hating and persecuting him.

Ps 36: The thought of man's wickedness, which leads him to forget or ignore the just punishments due to his sins (2-5), is here contrasted with God's loving care for mankind (6-10). Hence, the psalmist prays to be delivered from wicked men (11-13).

36, 2: *Speaks:* the Hebrew word used here is used elsewhere only of the Lord speaking to his inspired prophets. Hence the sense here is, "It is the sinfulness in man's heart that inspires, or instigates, him to wickedness."

36, 3: *Hated:* punished by God.

36, 7: *Like the mountains of God:* as immense as the loftiest mountains.

36/2: Rom 3, 18.

10*† For with you is the fountain of life,
    and in your light we see light.

III

11 Keep up your kindness toward your
    friends,
    your just defense of the upright of
    heart.

12 Let not the foot of the proud
    overtake me
    nor the hand of the wicked
    disquiet me.

13 See how the evildoers have fallen;
    they are thrust down and cannot
    rise.

The Fate of Sinners and the Reward of the Just

37† 1 Of David.

    Be not vexed over evildoers,
    nor jealous of those who do wrong;

2 For like grass they quickly wither,
    and like green herbs they wilt.

3† Trust in the LORD and do good,
    that you may dwell in the land and
    enjoy security.

4 Take delight in the LORD,
    and he will grant you your heart's
    requests.

5 Commit to the LORD your way;
    trust in him, and he will act.

6 He will make justice dawn for you
    like the light;
    bright as the noonday shall be
    your vindication.

7 Leave it to the LORD,
    and wait for him;
    Be not vexed at the successful path
    of the man who does malicious
    deeds.

8 Give up your anger, and forsake
    wrath;
    be not vexed, it will only harm you.

9 For evildoers shall be cut off,
    but those who wait for the LORD
    shall possess the land.

10 Yet a little while, and the wicked
    man shall be no more;
    though you mark his place he will
    not be there.

11* But the meek shall possess the land,
    they shall delight in abounding
    peace.

12 The wicked man plots against the
    just
    and gnashes his teeth at them;

13 But the Lord laughs at him,
    for he sees that his day is coming.

14 A sword the wicked draw; they bend
    their bow
    to bring down the afflicted and the
    poor,
    to slaughter those whose path is
    right.

15 But their swords shall pierce their
    own hearts,
    and their bows shall be broken.

16 Better is the scanty store of the just
    than the great wealth of the
    wicked,

17 For the power of the wicked shall be
    broken,
    but the LORD supports the just.

18 The LORD watches over the lives of
    the wholehearted;
    their inheritance lasts forever.

19 They are not put to shame in an evil
    time;
    in days of famine they have plenty.

20 But the wicked perish,
    and the enemies of the LORD, like
    the beauty of the meadows,
    vanish; like smoke they vanish.

21 The wicked man borrows and does
    not repay;
    the just man is kindly and gives,

22 But those whom he blesses shall
    possess the land,
    while those he curses shall be cut
    off.

23 By the LORD are the steps of a man
    made firm,
    and he approves his way.

24 Though he fall, he does not lie
    prostrate,
    for the hand of the LORD sustains
    him.

---

† 36, 10: *In your light we see light:* light is the symbol of goodness and happiness; hence, "Through your goodness we enjoy true happiness."

Ps 37 treats of the problem of evil: why the wicked seem to prosper while the good suffer. The answer of the psalmist is that this seeming injustice is short-lived. God will reward the good and punish the wicked even here on earth. Since this is an alphabetic psalm, these thoughts are repeated without much logical sequence throughout the whole psalm.

37, 3.9.11.22.29.34: *The land:* the Promised Land, Palestine, which however is a type or figure of heaven. Cf Heb 11, 9f.13-16. Therefore, when our Lord in the Beatitudes (Mt 5, 4) quoted v 11 of this psalm, he meant it in the sense of, "The meek shall possess the kingdom of heaven."

25. Neither in my youth, nor now that I
      am old,
      have I seen a just man forsaken
      nor his descendants begging
      bread.

26. All the day he is kindly and lends,
      and his descendants shall be
      blessed.

27. Turn from evil and do good,
      that you may abide forever;

28. For the LORD loves what is right,
      and forsakes not his faithful ones.

Criminals are destroyed,
      and the posterity of the wicked is
      cut off.

29. The just shall possess the land
      and dwell in it forever.

30. The mouth of the just man tells of
      wisdom
      and his tongue utters what is right.

31* The law of his God is in his heart,
      and his steps do not falter.

32. The wicked man spies on the just,
      and seeks to slay him.

33. The LORD will not leave him in his
      power
      nor let him be condemned when
      he is on trial.

34. Wait for the LORD,
      and keep his way;
      He will promote you to ownership of
      the land;
      when the wicked are destroyed,
      you shall look on.

35. I saw a wicked man, fierce,
      and stalwart as a flourishing,
      age-old tree.

36. Yet as I passed by, lo! he was no
      more;
      I sought him, but he could not be
      found.

37† Watch the wholehearted man, and
      mark the upright;
      for there is a future for the man of
      peace.

38. Sinners shall all alike be destroyed;
      the future of the wicked shall be
      cut off.

39. The salvation of the just is from the
      LORD;
      he is their refuge in time of
      distress.

40. And the LORD helps them and
      delivers them;

he delivers them from the wicked
      and saves them,
      because they take refuge in him.

Prayer of an Afflicted Sinner

38† 1*† A psalm of David. For remembrance.

I

2* O LORD, in your anger punish me
      not,
      in your wrath chastise me not;

3. For your arrows have sunk deep in
      me,
      and your hand has come down
      upon me.

4. There is no health in my flesh
      because of your indignation;
      there is no wholeness in my bones
      because of my sin,

5. For my iniquities have overwhelmed
      me;
      they are like a heavy burden,
      beyond my strength.

II

6. Noisome and festering are my sores
      because of my folly,

7. I am stooped and bowed down
      profoundly;
      all the day I go in mourning,

8. For my loins are filled with burning
      pains;
      there is no health in my flesh.

9. I am numbed and severely crushed;
      I roar with anguish of heart.

10. O LORD, all my desire is before you;
      from you my groaning is not hid.

11. My heart throbs; my strength
      forsakes me;
      the very light of my eyes has
      failed me.

12. My friends and my companions
      stand back because of my
      affliction;
      my neighbors stand afar off.

13. Men lay snares for me seeking my
      life;
      they look to my misfortune, they
      speak of ruin,
      treachery they talk of all the day.

---

† 37, 37f: *A future for the man of peace . . . the future of the wicked:* in his own life and in his offspring.

Ps 38: The third of the Penitential Psalms. Acknowledging that his sickness is a punishment for his sins (2-5), the psalmist describes his misery (6-13), which he is patiently bearing with trust in God (14-17), whose pardon and help he implores (18-23).

38, 1: *For remembrance:* or, "For the memorial sacrifice." Cf Lv 2, 2.9.16; 5, 12; Is 66, 3.

III

14 But I am like a deaf man, hearing
  not,
  like a dumb man who opens not his
  mouth.
15 I am become like a man who neither
  hears
  nor has in his mouth a retort.
16 Because for you, O Lord, I wait;
  you, O Lord my God, will answer
17 When I say, "Let them not be glad
  on my account
  who, when my foot slips, glory
  over me."

IV

18 For I am very near to falling,
  and my grief is with me always.
19 Indeed, I acknowledge my guilt;
  I grieve over my sin.
20 But my undeserved enemies are
  strong;
  many are my foes without cause.
21† Those who repay evil for good
  harass me for pursuing good.
22 Forsake me not, O Lord;
  my God, be not far from me!
23 Make haste to help me,
  O Lord my salvation!

The Brevity and Vanity of Life

39 **†** **1*** For the leader, for Jeduthun. A psalm of
David.

I

2 I said, "I will watch my ways,
  so as not to sin with my tongue;
  I will set a curb on my mouth."
  While the wicked man was before
  me
3 I kept dumb and silent;
  I refrained from rash speech.
  But my grief was stirred up;
4 hot grew my heart within me;
  in my thoughts, a fire blazed forth.
  I spoke out with my tongue:

II

5 Let me know, O Lord, my end
  and what is the number of my
  days,
  that I may learn how frail I am.
6 A short span you have made my
  days,
  and my life is as nought before
  you;

only a breath is any human
  existence.
7 A phantom only, man goes his
  ways;
  like vapor only are his restless
  pursuits;
  he heaps up stores, and knows not
  who will use them.

III

8 And now, for what do I wait,
  O Lord?
  In you is my hope.
9 From all my sins deliver me;
  a fool's taunt let me not suffer.

IV

10 I was speechless and opened not my
  mouth,
  because it was your doing;
11 Take away your scourge from me;
  at the blow of your hand I wasted
  away.
12 With rebukes for guilt you chasten
  man;
  you dissolve like a cobweb all that
  is dear to him;
  only a breath is any man.
13 Hear my prayer, O Lord;
  to my cry give ear;
  to my weeping be not deaf!
  For I am but a wayfarer before you,
  a pilgrim like all my fathers.
14† Turn your gaze from me, that I may
  find respite
  ere I depart and be no more.

Gratitude and Prayer for Help

40 **†** **1** For the leader. A psalm of David.

A

I

2 I have waited, waited for the Lord,
  and he stooped toward me and
  heard my cry.

---

† 38, 21: *Harass:* the Hebrew expression, from which the word
"Satan" is derived, signifies either "to harass" or "to slander."
Cf Ps 109, 4.

Ps 39: Although he had resolved not to complain (2-4), the
psalmist, like Ecclesiastes, laments the brevity and vanity of life
(5-7); yet his hope is in the Lord (8f), to whom he prays for
pardon and health (10-14).

39, 14: *And be no more:* here on earth. The psalmist naturally
shared the common belief in a certain kind of life in the nether
world after death. Job also complained in a similar strain of the
brevity of life and the finality of death, while asserting at the
same time his faith in a future life. Cf Jb 3, 13-19.

Ps 40 consists of two distinct parts, probably once independent psalms. In the first section (2-11) the psalmist thanks
God for having rescued him from the danger of death (2-4),
and praises the Lord for his goodness toward all who trust in
him (5f); to do God's will is the best sacrifice, he says (7-9), as

3 He drew me out of the pit of
destruction,
    out of the mud of the swamp;
He set my feet upon a crag;
    he made firm my steps.

4† And he put a new song into my
mouth,
    a hymn to our God.
Many shall look on in awe
    and trust in the Lord.

II

5 Happy the man who makes the Lord
his trust;
    who turns not to idolatry
    or to those who stray after
falsehood.

6 How numerous have you made,
    O Lord, my God, your wondrous
deeds!
And in your plans for us
    there is none to equal you;
Should I wish to declare or to tell
them,
    they would be too many to
recount.

III

7† Sacrifice or oblation you wished not,
    but ears open to obedience you
gave me.
Holocausts or sin-offerings you
sought not;

8   then said I, "Behold I come;
    in the written scroll it is prescribed
for me.

9 To do your will, O my God, is my
delight,
    and your law is within my heart!"

10 I announced your justice in the vast
assembly;
    I did not restrain my lips, as you,
O Lord, know.

11 Your justice I kept not hid within my
heart;
    your faithfulness and your
salvation I have spoken of;
I have made no secret of your
kindness and your truth
    in the vast assembly.

B

I

12 Withhold not, O Lord, your
compassion from me;
    may your kindness and your truth
ever preserve me.

13 For all about me are evils beyond
reckoning;
    my sins so overcome me that I
cannot see;
They are more numerous than the
hairs of my head,
    and my heart fails me.

II

14 Deign, O Lord, to rescue me;
    O Lord, make haste to help me.

15 Let all be put to shame and
confusion
    who seek to snatch away my life.
Let them be turned back in disgrace
    who desire my ruin.

16 Let them be dismayed in their
shame
    who say to me, "Aha, aha!"

17 But may all who seek you
    exult and be glad in you,
And may those who love your
salvation
    say ever, "The Lord be glorified."

18 Though I am afflicted and poor,
    yet the Lord thinks of me.
You are my help and my deliverer;
    O my God, hold not back!

Thanksgiving after Sickness

41† **1** For the leader. A psalm of David.

I

2 Happy is he who has regard for the
lowly and the poor;
    in the day of misfortune the Lord
will deliver him.

3† The Lord will keep and preserve
him;
    he will make him happy on the
earth,

---

† he offers up this hymn of thanksgiving among the worshipers in the temple (10f). The second section (12-18), which is the same as Ps 70, is a typical supplication of one afflicted and persecuted.

40, 4: *A new song:* the hymn of thanksgiving in vv 5-11. Many hymns of praise and thanksgiving are thus described because they represent a complete change from the attitude of lamentation.

40, 7-9: Obedience is better than sacrifice. Cf 1 Sm 15, 22; Is 1, 10-20; Mi 6, 6-8. In Heb 10, 5-7 this passage, according to the somewhat different form of the ancient Greek version, is quoted and most fittingly applied to Christ, whose sacrifice of perfect obedience immeasurably surpasses the liturgical sacrifices of the old law.

Ps 41: After speaking in general terms about the merciful man obtaining God's mercy (2-4), the psalmist recounts how he had once prayed for that mercy when, in his sickness, he was reviled and persecuted even by his friends (5-11); therefore he now acknowledges with gratitude that God has heard his prayer (12-13).

41, 3: In the form of a prayer, "May the Lord keep," etc., this verse is employed in the liturgy of the church as an invocation for the pope.

40/7-9: Heb 10, 5-7.   14-18: Ps 70, 2-6.

and not give him over to the will of
   his enemies.

4 The Lord will help him on his
   sickbed,
   he will take away all his ailment
      when he is ill.

II

5 Once I said, "O Lord, have pity on
   me;
   heal me, though I have sinned
      against you.

6 My enemies say the worst of me:
   'When will he die and his name
      perish?'

7 When one comes to see me, he
   speaks without sincerity;
   his heart stores up malice;
   when he leaves he gives voice to it
      outside.

8 All my foes whisper together against
   me;
   against me they imagine the
      worst:

9 'A malignant disease fills his frame';
   and 'Now that he lies ill, he will
      not rise again.'

10 * † Even my friend who had my trust
   and partook of my bread, has
   raised his heel against me. (*III*)

11 But you, O Lord, have pity on me,
   and raise me up,
   that I may repay them."

12 That you love me I know by this,
   that my enemy does not triumph
      over me,

13 But because of my integrity you
   sustain me
   and let me stand before you
      forever.

❉   ❉   ❉

14 † Blessed be the Lord, the God of
   Israel,
   from all eternity and forever.
   Amen. Amen.

II: THE SECOND BOOK—Psalms 42-72

Desire for God and His Temple

42 † 1 For the leader. A *maskil* of the sons of
Korah.

I

2 † As the hind longs for the running
   waters,
   so my soul longs for you, O God.

3 † Athirst is my soul for God, the living
   God.
   When shall I go and behold the
      face of God?

4 † My tears are my food day and night,
   as they say to me day after day,
   "Where is your God?"

5 Those times I recall,
   now that I pour out my soul within
      me,
   When I went with the throng
   and led them in procession to the
      house of God,
   Amid loud cries of joy and
      thanksgiving,
   with the multitude keeping
      festival.

6 Why are you so downcast, O my
   soul?
   Why do you sigh within me?
   Hope in God! For I shall again
      be thanking him,
   in the presence of my savior
      and my God.

II

7 † Within me my soul is downcast;
   so will I remember you
   From the land of the Jordan and of
      Hermon,
   from Mount Mizar.

8 † Deep calls unto deep
   in the roar of your cataracts;
   All your breakers and your billows
      pass over me.

---

† 41, 10: These words were cited by our Lord at the Last
Supper in regard to Judas, the perfect fulfillment of this type of
treacherous friend. Cf Jn 13, 18.

41, 14: Doxology closing the First Book of the Psalter. It is
not part of the psalm to which it is appended.

Pss 42-43 represent respectively two thirds and one third of
what was originally a single psalm. Each of the three parts ends
in an identical refrain (42, 6.12; 43, 5). The psalmist is in exile
north of Palestine, far from Jerusalem. Homesick for the solemn
services of the temple, he keeps up his courage by an ardent
hope and an unshaken trust in God. The high lyrical style of this
psalm makes it one of the finest poems in the Bible.

42, 2: *O God:* in the Second Book of the Psalms the proper
name of God, *Yahweh,* "The Lord," was changed in almost all
places by some early scribe to read, *Elohim,* "God." Thus we
have the strange phrase, "O God, my God," instead of the original, "O Lord, my God," e. g., in Ps 43, 4.

42, 3: *Go and behold the face of God:* a Hebrew idiom meaning, "Visit the temple." Cf Ex 23, 17.

42, 4: *Where is your God?:* God gives no evidence of coming
to his aid.

42, 7: *The land of the Jordan:* the region at the sources of the
Jordan, at the foot of Mount Hermon. *Mount Mizar:* probably
means, "the small mountain," presumably one of Hermon's foothills.

42, 8: *Deep calls unto deep:* the 're-echoing roar of stormy
waters. The figure of affliction as a raging sea is common. Cf Pss
18, 5; 69, 2ff.15f; Jn 2, 3-6. Here, however, the thought may
also have been suggested by the cataracts of the upper Jordan.

❉ 41/10: Ps 55, 14f; Jn 13, 18.

9† By day the LORD bestows his grace,
and at night I have his song,
a prayer to my living God.

10 I sing to God, my rock:
"Why do you forget me?
Why must I go about in mourning,
with the enemy oppressing me?"

11 It crushes my bones that my foes
mock me,
as they say to me day after day,
"Where is your God?"

12 Why are you so downcast, O my
soul?
Why do you sigh within me?
Hope in God! For I shall again
be thanking him,
in the presence of my savior
and my God.

III

43 1 Do me justice, O God, and fight my
fight
against a faithless people;
from the deceitful and impious
man rescue me.

2 For you, O God, are my strength.
Why do you keep me so far away?
Why must I go about in mourning,
with the enemy oppressing me?

3 Send forth your light and your
fidelity;
they shall lead me on
And bring me to your holy mountain,
to your dwelling-place.

4† Then will I go in to the altar of God,
the God of my gladness and joy;
Then will I give you thanks upon the
harp,
O God, my God!

5 Why are you so downcast, O my
soul?
Why do you sigh within me?
Hope in God! For I shall again
be thanking him,
in the presence of my savior
and my God.

Israel's Past Glory and Present Need

44† 1 For the leader. A *maskil* of the sons of
Korah.

I

2✱ O God, our ears have heard,
our fathers have declared to us,
The deeds you did in their days,
in days of old:

3✱ How with your own hand you rooted
out the nations and planted
them;
you smashed the peoples, but for
them you made room.

4 For not with their own sword did
they conquer the land,
nor did their own arm make them
victorious,
But it was your arm and your right
hand
and the light of your countenance,
in your love for them.

5 You are my king and my God,
who bestowed victories on Jacob.

6 Our foes through you we struck
down;
through your name we trampled
down our adversaries.

7 For not in my bow did I trust,
nor did my sword save me;

8 But you saved us from our foes,
and those who hated us you put to
shame.

9 In God we gloried day by day;
your name we praised always.

II

10 Yet now you have cast us off and put
us in disgrace,
and you go not forth with our
armies.

11 You have let us be driven back by
our foes;
those who hated us plundered us
at will.

12✱ You marked us out as sheep to be
slaughtered;
among the nations you scattered
us.

---

† 42, 9: *My living God:* literally "the God of my life"; hence some understand it as, "the God who gives me life." Perhaps Ps 42, 3 also was originally, "the God of my life." Cf Ps 43, 4.

Ps 43: The church frequently uses as a responsorial psalm following the first scriptural reading at Mass.

Ps 44: A supplication of the community, reminding God of his past favors to Israel (2-9) in contrast to the present sad state of affairs, when the nation suffers from military defeat (10-17) and seems abandoned by him (18-23); therefore the people cry out to him to come to their aid (24-27). The historical circumstances of the psalm cannot be determined with certainty. The occasion may have been the invasion of the Assyrians under Sennacherib at the time of King Hezekiah (2 Kgs 18-19) or the calamities which followed on the defeat of King Josiah and the invasion of the Babylonians (2 Kgs 23, 29—25, 26), or the time of national degradation during the Persian period, the fifth to the fourth century B. C. But there are no compelling reasons to put this psalm as late as the Maccabean times.

✱ 44/2: Ps 78, 3.   12: Lv 26, 33; Dt 4, 27.
     3: Ps 80, 9.

13 You sold your people for no great
price;
  you made no profit from the sale
  of them.
14 You made us the reproach of our
neighbors,
  the mockery and the scorn of those
  around us.
15 You made us a byword among the
nations,
  a laughingstock among the
  peoples.
16 All the day my disgrace is before me,
  and shame covers my face
17 At the voice of him who mocks and
blasphemes,
  and in the presence of the enemy
  and the avenger.

III

18 All this has come upon us, though we
have not forgotten you,
  nor have we been disloyal to your
  covenant;
19 Our hearts have not shrunk back,
  nor our steps turned aside from
  your path,
20 Though you thrust us down into a
place of misery
  and covered us over with darkness.
21 If we had forgotten the name of our
God
  and stretched out our hands to a
  strange god,
22 Would not God have discovered
this?
  For he knows the secrets of the
  heart.
23 Yet for your sake we are being slain
all the day;
  we are looked upon as sheep to be
  slaughtered.

IV

24 Awake! Why are you asleep,
O LORD?
  Arise! Cast us not off forever!
25 Why do you hide your face,
  forgetting our woe and our
  oppression?
26 For our souls are bowed down to the
dust,
  our bodies are pressed to the earth.
27 Arise, help us!
  Redeem us for your kindness' sake.

*Nuptial Ode for the
Messianic King*

45 † **1** For the leader; according to "Lilies." A
maskil of the sons of Korah. A love song.

I

2 My heart overflows with a goodly
theme;
  as I sing my ode to the king,
  my tongue is nimble as the pen of
  a skillful scribe.

II

3† Fairer in beauty are you than the
sons of men;
  grace is poured out upon your lips;
  thus God has blessed you forever.
4 Gird your sword upon your thigh,
O mighty one!
  In your splendor and your majesty
  ride on triumphant
5 In the cause of truth and for the sake
of justice;
  and may your right hand show you
  wondrous deeds.
6 Your arrows are sharp; peoples are
subject to you;
  the king's enemies lose heart.
7† Your throne, O God, stands forever
and ever;
  a tempered rod is your royal
  scepter.
8 You love justice and hate
wickedness;
  therefore God, your God, has
  anointed you
  with the oil of gladness above your
  fellow kings.
9 With myrrh and aloes and cassia
your robes are fragrant;
  from ivory palaces string music
  brings you joy.

† Ps 45: After a dedicatory prologue (2), the psalmist sings the praises of the royal bridegroom (3-10) and his bride (11f); he then describes the wedding procession (13-16) and wishes the king illustrious offspring (17f). The occasion of this epithalamium may have been the marriage of some prince of the Davidic dynasty, perhaps Solomon, with a foreign princess who was apparently from Tyre. But Catholic tradition, in keeping with the inspired interpretation given in Heb 1, 8f, has always understood this psalm as referring, at least in a typical sense, to Christ and his bride, the church. Cf Eph 5, 25ff.
45, 3: *Fairer . . . than the sons of men:* i. e., than other men; or, "Fairest among the sons of men."
45, 7: *Your throne, O God:* the Hebrew king was called *Elohim,* "God," not in the polytheistic sense common among the ancient pagans, but as meaning "godlike," or, "taking the place of God." Cf Pss 58, 2; 82, 1.6. Of Christ alone can this passage be understood in its full literal sense. Some, however, amend the text to read, "Your throne is the throne of God." Cf 1 Chr 29, 23, where Solomon's throne is referred to as "the throne of the LORD."

14: Pss 79, 4; 80, 7.   45/7f: Heb 1, 8f.
23: Rom 8, 36.

10† The daughters of kings come to meet
     you;
     the queen takes her place at your
        right hand in gold of Ophir.

III

11 Hear, O daughter, and see; turn your
     ear,
     forget your people and your
        father's house.
12† So shall the king desire your beauty;
     for he is your lord, and you must
        worship him.
13† And the city of Tyre is here with
     gifts;
     the rich among the people seek
        your favor.
14 All glorious is the king's daughter as
     she enters;
     her raiment is threaded with spun
        gold.
15 In embroidered apparel she is borne
     in to the king;
     behind her the virgins of her train
        are brought to you.
16 They are borne in with gladness and
     joy;
     they enter the palace of the king.

IV

17 The place of your fathers your sons
     shall have;
     you shall make them princes
        through all the land.
18 I will make your name memorable
     through all generations;
     therefore shall nations praise you
        forever and ever.

God the Refuge of Israel

46† 1 For the leader. A song of the sons of Korah;
according to "Virgins."

I

2 God is our refuge and our strength,
     an ever-present help in distress.
3† Therefore we fear not, though the
     earth be shaken
     and mountains plunge into the
        depths of the sea;
4 Though its waters rage and foam
     and the mountains quake at its
        surging.
        The LORD of hosts is with us;
        our stronghold is the God of
          Jacob.

II

5† There is a stream whose runlets
     gladden the city of God,

the holy dwelling of the Most
     High.
6 God is in its midst; it shall not be
     disturbed;
     God will help it at the break of
        dawn.
7 Though nations are in turmoil,
     kingdoms totter,
     his voice resounds, the earth melts
        away,
8   The LORD of hosts is with us;
        our stronghold is the God of
          Jacob.

III

9 Come! behold the deeds of the LORD,
     the astounding things he has
        wrought on earth:
10 He has stopped wars to the end of
     the earth:
     the bow he breaks; he splinters the
        spears;
     he burns the shields with fire.
11 Desist! and confess that I am God,
     exalted among the nations, exalted
        upon the earth.
12   The LORD of hosts is with us;
        our stronghold is the God of
          Jacob.

The Lord the King of All Nations

47† 1 For the leader. A psalm of the sons of
Korah.

I

2 All you peoples, clap your hands,
     shout to God with cries of
        gladness,

---

† 45, 10: *Ophir:* a region on the coast of southern Arabia or eastern Africa, famous for its gold. Cf 1 Kgs 9, 28; 10, 11.22; Jb 22, 24.

45, 12: *Worship him:* pay him homage and be submissive to him.

45, 13: *Your favor:* in the current Hebrew text this is read as addressed to the bride, but it should probably be understood as referring to the king. The *you* in v 15 certainly signifies the king.

Ps 46: A hymn of victory whose dominant note is the refrain, *The Lord of hosts is with us.* The first strophe (2-4) sings of Israel's unshaken trust in the Lord; the second (5-8), of God's protection over Zion; the third (9-12), of his victory over war itself.

46, 3f: Figurative language for social and political upheavals.

46, 5: *There is a stream:* merely a symbol of divine favors. Jerusalem is not situated on a river, and its natural water supply is very meager.

Ps 47: A hymn calling on all the nations of the earth to acknowledge the God of Israel as the only true God (2-5); when the Lord manifests himself as King of all (6f), the whole earth will proclaim his dominion (8-10). This prophecy finds its fulfillment only in the universal kingship of Christ.

3 For the LORD, the Most High, the
    awesome,
      is the great king over all the earth.
4 He brings peoples under us;
      nations under our feet.
5 He chooses for us our inheritance,
      the glory of Jacob, whom he loves.

II

6 God mounts his throne amid shouts
    of joy;
      the LORD, amid trumpet blasts.
7 Sing praise to God, sing praise;
      sing praise to our king, sing praise.

III

8 For king of all the earth is God;
      sing hymns of praise.
9 God reigns over the nations,
      God sits upon his holy throne.
10† The princes of the peoples are
    gathered together
      with the people of the God of
      Abraham.
For God's are the guardians of the
    earth;
      he is supreme.

Thanksgiving for Jerusalem's Deliverance

48† **1** A psalm of the sons of Korah; a song.

I

2 Great is the LORD and wholly to be
    praised
      in the city of our God.
His holy mountain, **3†**fairest of heights,
      is the joy of all the earth;
Mount Zion, "the recesses of the
    North,"
      is the city of the great King.
4 God is with her castles;
      renowned is he as a stronghold.

II

5 For lo! the kings assemble,
      they come on together;
6 They also see, and at once are
    stunned,
      terrified, routed;
7 Quaking seizes them there;
      anguish, like a woman's in labor,
8† As though a wind from the east
      were shattering ships of Tarshish.

III

9† As we had heard, so have we seen
      in the city of the LORD of hosts,
In the city of our God;
      God makes it firm forever.

10 O God, we ponder your kindness
      within your temple.
11 As your name, O God, so also your
    praise
      reaches to the ends of the earth.
Of justice your right hand is full;
12   let Mount Zion be glad,
Let the cities of Judah rejoice,
      because of your judgments.

IV

13 Go about Zion, make the round;
      count her towers.
14 Consider her ramparts,
      examine her castles,
That you may tell a future
      generation
15†   that such is God,
Our God forever and ever;
      he will guide us.

The Vanity of Worldly Riches

49† **1** For the leader. A psalm of the sons of
Korah.

2 Hear this, all you peoples;
      hearken, all who dwell in the
      world,
3 Of lowly birth or high degree,
      rich and poor alike.

---

† 47, 10: *With the people of the God of Abraham:* perhaps, with the ancient versions, to be read simply, "With the God of Abraham." By *the princes of the peoples* and *the guardians of the earth* are probably meant the angelic spirits who watch over the various nations. Cf Dt 32, 8-9; Dn 10, 13.

Ps 48: A hymn of thanksgiving, sung in the temple after Jerusalem had successfully withstood an attack launched by a league of hostile kings. It is uncertain which of the many attacks on Jerusalem is referred to here. This magnificent pæan of triumph first praises God as Israel's true bulwark (2-4); then, briefly recounting how the enemies' attack was repulsed (5-8), the psalmist proclaims the Lord as the author of this great victory (9-12); finally, the people are invited to gaze with wonder on the strong fortifications of the city (13-15).

48, 3: *"The recesses of the North":* in Palestine and Syria, a traditional name for the earthly abode of God. Cf Is 14, 13.

48, 8: *Ships of Tarshish:* large ocean-going vessels, named after the distant land or port of Tarshish, probably ancient Tartessus in southern Spain, although other identifications have been proposed. Cf Is 2, 16; 60, 9; Jon 1, 3. Here the phrase is merely part of the figure and does not imply that the hostile kings came by boat.

48, 9: *As we had heard* of the wonders that God did in the days of our forefathers, *so have we seen* similar wonders now with our own eyes.

48, 15: *He will guide us:* "through the ages" should perhaps be added, with some ancient sources.

Ps 49: A sapiential psalm, treating of the problem as to why the wicked prosper. Here the answer is that wealth cannot save anyone from death, but for the good there is the hope of blessedness after death. Cf Pss 37; 73. After inviting all to listen to his wise words (2-5), the psalmist teaches that we should not envy the unjust rich, who must all die and leave their wealth behind (6-13.17-21); they shall be brought to nought, but God will save the just (14-16).

4   My mouth shall speak wisdom;
     prudence shall be the utterance of
       my heart.

5*†   My ear is intent upon a proverb;
     I will set forth my riddle to the
       music of the harp.

I

6   Why should I fear in evil days
     when my wicked ensnarers ring
       me round?

7   They trust in their wealth;
     the abundance of their riches is
       their boast.

8†   Yet in no way can a man redeem
       himself,
     or pay his own ransom to God;

9   Too high is the price to redeem one's
       life; he would never have
       enough

10   to remain alive always and not see
       destruction.

11*   For he can see that wise men die,
     and likewise the senseless and the
       stupid pass away,
     leaving to others their wealth.

12   Tombs are their homes forever,
     their dwellings through all
       generations,
     though they have called lands by
       their names.

13   Thus man, for all his splendor,
       does not abide;
     he resembles the beasts that
       perish.

II

14   This is the way of those whose trust
       is folly,
     the end of those contented with
       their lot:

15   Like sheep they are herded into the
       nether world;
     death is their shepherd, and the
       upright rule over them.
     Quickly their form is consumed;
     the nether world is their palace.

16*   But God will redeem me
     from the power of the nether
       world by receiving me.

III

17   Fear not when a man grows rich,
     when the wealth of his house
       becomes great,

18*   For when he dies, he shall take none
       of it;
     his wealth shall not follow him
       down.

19   Though in his lifetime he counted
       himself blessed,
     "They will praise you for doing
       well for yourself,"

20   He shall join the circle of his
       forebears
     who shall never more see light.

21   Man, for all his splendor, if he
       have not prudence,
     resembles the beasts that
       perish.

The Acceptable Sacrifice

50† 1†   A psalm of Asaph.

I

     God the LORD has spoken and
       summoned the earth,
     from the rising of the sun to its
       setting.

2   From Zion, perfect in beauty,
     God shines forth.

3*   May our God come and not be deaf
       to us!
     Before him is a devouring fire;
     around him is a raging storm.

4*   He summons the heavens from
       above,
     and the earth, to the trial of his
       people:

5   "Gather my faithful ones before me,
     those who have made a covenant
       with me by sacrifice."

6   And the heavens proclaim his
       justice;
     for God himself is the judge.

II

7*   "Hear, my people, and I will speak;
     Israel, I will testify against you;
     God, your God, am I.

---

†   49, 5: *My riddle:* this enigma, the problem of evil.

49, 8f: No man is rich enough to buy God off in order to save himself from death.

Ps 50: Like the prophets of old, the psalmist shows the worthlessness of external worship when it is divorced from true morality. God calls a solemn assembly (1-6), in which he tells his people he does not need their liturgical sacrifices but wants of them the true sacrifice of prayer (7-15); he then rebukes the hypocritical sinner (16-21), for without true worship, joined with true morality, there can be no salvation (22f).

50, 1: *God the Lord:* the Hebrew text has two synonyms for God (*El* and *Elohim*) before the word *Yahweh* (*the Lord*). A translation cannot adequately render this.

---

*   49/5: Ps 78, 2; Mt 13, 35.
     11: Eccl 2, 14.16.
     16: Pss 86, 13; 103, 4;
       116, 8.
     18: Eccl 5, 15f; Sir 11, 19f.
     50/3: Ex 19, 16-18; Dt 5, 22f.
     4: Dt 4, 26; 31, 28; 32, 1.
     7: Ex 20, 2.

8 Not for your sacrifices do I rebuke
    you,
    for your holocausts are before me
    always.

9 I take from your house no bullock,
    no goats out of your fold.

10 For mine are all the animals of the
    forests,
    beasts by the thousands on my
    mountains.

11 I know all the birds of the air,
    and whatever stirs in the plains,
    belongs to me.

12* If I were hungry, I should not tell
    you,
    for mine are the world and its
    fullness.

13 Do I eat the flesh of strong bulls,
    or is the blood of goats my drink?

14 Offer to God praise as your sacrifice
    and fulfill your vows to the Most
    High;

15 Then call upon me in time of
    distress;
    I will rescue you, and you shall
    glorify me."

III

16 But to the wicked man God says:
    "Why do you recite my statutes,
    and profess my covenant with
    your mouth,

17 Though you hate discipline
    and cast my words behind you?

18 When you see a thief, you keep pace
    with him,
    and with adulterers you throw in
    your lot.

19 To your mouth you give free rein for
    evil,
    you harness your tongue to deceit.

20 You sit speaking against your
    brother;
    against your mother's son you
    spread rumors.

21† When you do these things, shall I be
    deaf to it?
    Or do you think that I am like
    yourself?
    I will correct you by drawing them
    up before your eyes.

IV

22 "Consider this, you who forget God,
    lest I rend you and there be no one
    to rescue you.

23 He that offers praise as a sacrifice
    glorifies me;
    and to him that goes the right way
    I will show the salvation of
    God."

The Miserere:
Prayer of Repentance

51 **† 1*** For the leader. A psalm of David, **2**when
Nathan the prophet came to him after
his sin with Bathsheba.

A

3 Have mercy on me, O God, in your
    goodness;
    in the greatness of your
    compassion wipe out my
    offense.

4 Thoroughly wash me from my guilt
    and of my sin cleanse me.

B

I

5 For I acknowledge my offense,
    and my sin is before me always:

6*† "Against you only have I sinned,
    and done what is evil in your
    sight"—
    That you may be justified in your
    sentence,
    vindicated when you condemn.

7*† Indeed, in guilt was I born,
    and in sin my mother conceived
    me;

8 Behold, you are pleased with
    sincerity of heart,
    and in my inmost being you teach
    me wisdom.

---

† 50, 21: *That I am like yourself:* perhaps the original was, "that I, the LORD, am like yourself."

Ps 51: The fourth and most famous of the Penitential Psalms. The psalmist begs pardon for his sins (3f), which he sincerely confesses (5-8); he prays to be restored to grace and purity (9-14); in return, he will make God's mercy known to others and will offer him the sacrifice of a contrite heart (15-19). An added strophe asks for the restoration of Jerusalem (20f).

51, 6: *Against you only have I sinned:* although sin may also be an injustice against a fellow man, yet the very essence of sin consists in its being an offense against God. *That you may be justified:* this refers to v 5 and gives the reason why the psalmist confesses his sins: when men see God punishing him, they will know that he is receiving his deserts.

51, 7: The penitent offers the fact of his innate sinfulness partly as a mitigating circumstance and partly as a humble acknowledgment of his profound corruption. Catholic tradition sees in this passage a foreshadowing of the basic Christian doctrine of original sin, which was not clearly revealed before the time of Christ. Cf Rom 5, 12-19; Eph 2, 3.

12: Ps 24, 1.   6: Rom 3, 4.
51/1: 2 Sm 12, 1.   7: Jb 14, 4; 15, 14.

II

9† Cleanse me of sin with hyssop, that
 I may be purified;
 wash me, and I shall be whiter
 than snow.

10 Let me hear the sounds of joy and
 gladness;
 the bones you have crushed shall
 rejoice.

11 Turn away your face from my sins,
 and blot out all my guilt.

III

12 A clean heart create for me, O God,
 and a steadfast spirit renew within
 me.

13 Cast me not out from your presence,
 and your holy spirit take not from
 me.

14 Give me back the joy of your
 salvation,
 and a willing spirit sustain in me.

IV

15 I will teach transgressors your ways,
 and sinners shall return to you.

16† Free me from blood guilt, O God,
 my saving God;
 then my tongue shall revel in your
 justice.

17 O Lord, open my lips,
 and my mouth shall proclaim your
 praise.

18 *† For you are not pleased with
 sacrifices;
 should I offer a holocaust, you
 would not accept it.

19 My sacrifice, O God, is a contrite
 spirit;
 a heart contrite and humbled,
 O God, you will not spurn.

C

20† Be bountiful, O Lord, to Zion in your
 kindness
 by rebuilding the walls of
 Jerusalem;

21 Then shall you be pleased with due
 sacrifices,
 burnt offerings and holocausts;
 then shall they offer up bullocks on
 your altar.

The Deceitful Tongue

52 † 1 For the leader. A *maskil* of David, 2when
Doeg the Edomite went and told Saul,
"David went to the house of Ahimelech."

I

3 Why do you glory in evil,
 you champion of infamy?
 All the day 4you plot harm;
 your tongue is like a sharpened
 razor, you practiced deceiver!

5 You love evil rather than good,
 falsehood rather than honest
 speech.

6 You love all that means ruin,
 you of the deceitful tongue!

II

7 God himself shall demolish you;
 forever he shall break you;
 He shall pluck you from your tent,
 and uproot you from the land of
 the living.

III

8 The just shall look on with awe;
 then they shall laugh at him:

9 "This is the man who made not
 God the source of his strength,
 But put his trust in his great wealth,
 and his strength in harmful plots."

10† But I, like a green olive tree
 in the house of God,
 Trust in the kindness of God
 forever and ever.

11 I will thank you always for what you
 have done,
 and proclaim the goodness of your
 name
 before your faithful ones.

---

† 51, 9: *Hyssop:* a small bush whose many woody twigs made a natural sprinkler. It was prescribed in the Mosaic law as an instrument for scattering sacrificial blood or lustral water on persons to be ritually cleansed. Cf Ex 12, 22; Lv 14, 4; Nm 19, 18. These ceremonies were mere symbols of purification; here the psalmist prays that God may effectively "un-sin" him, as the Hebrew literally means.

51, 16: *Blood guilt:* the guilt of murder. This is in keeping with the traditional ascription of this psalm to David. Cf 2 Sm 11, 6f; 12, 9.

51, 18: *Not pleased with sacrifices:* the mere offering of ritual sacrifice apart from good dispositions is not acceptable to God. Cf Ps 50. Others explain that the Mosaic law prescribes no sacrifice to expiate sins of adultery and murder, such as David was guilty of.

51, 20f: These two verses were added to the psalm some time after the destruction of Jerusalem by the Babylonians.

Ps 52: The psalmist inveighs against his deceitful enemy (3-6), foretelling the divine punishment in store for him (7) when God avenges the just (8-11).

52, 10: The just will flourish as unshaken in the house of God as a green olive tree which is well rooted in the soil. The words do not imply that olive trees grew in the courts of the temple. Cf Pss 92, 14; 128, 3.

✻ 18: Pss 40, 7; 50, 8-13.

Lament over Widespread Corruption

53 † 1 For the leader; according to *Mahalath*. A *maskil* of David.

I

2* The fool says in his heart,
   "There is no God."
Such are corrupt; they do
   abominable deeds;
   there is not one who does good.

3 God looks down from heaven upon
   the children of men
   to see if there be one who is wise
   and seeks God.

4* All alike have gone astray; they have
   become perverse;
   there is not one who does good,
   not even one.

II

5 Will all these evildoers never learn,
   they who eat up my people just as
   they eat bread,
   who call not upon God?

6† There they were in great fear,
   where no fear was,
For God has scattered the bones of
   your besiegers;
   they are put to shame, because
   God has rejected them.

III

7 Oh, that out of Zion would come the
   salvation of Israel!
   When God restores the well-being
   of his people,
   then shall Jacob exult and Israel
   be glad.

Confident Prayer in Great Peril

54 † 1 For the leader; with stringed instruments. A *maskil* of David, 2*when the Ziphites went and said to Saul, "David is hiding among us."

I

3† O God, by your name save me,
   and by your might defend my
   cause.

4 O God, hear my prayer;
   hearken to the words of my
   mouth.

5 For haughty men have risen up
   against me,
   and fierce men seek my life;
   they set not God before their eyes.

II

6 Behold, God is my helper;
   the Lord sustains my life.

7 Turn back the evil upon my foes;
   in your faithfulness destroy them.

8 Freely will I offer you sacrifice;
   I will praise your name, O LORD,
   for its goodness,

9 Because from all distress you have
   rescued me,
   and my eyes look down upon my
   enemies.

Complaint against Enemies and a Disloyal Companion

55 † 1 For the leader; with stringed instruments. A *maskil* of David.

I

2 Hearken, O God, to my prayer;
   turn not away from my pleading;

3 give heed to me, and answer me.
I rock with grief, and am troubled

4 at the voice of the enemy and the
   clamor of the wicked.
For they bring down evil upon me,
   and with fury they persecute me.

5 My heart quakes within me;
   the terror of death has fallen upon
   me.

6 Fear and trembling come upon me.
   and horror overwhelms me,

7 And I say, "Had I but wings like a
   dove,
   I would fly away and be at rest.

8 Far away I would flee;
   I would lodge in the wilderness.

9 I would hasten to find shelter
   from the violent storm and the
   tempest."

II

10† Engulf them, O Lord; divide their
   counsels,

---

† Ps 53: With a few slight differences this is the same as Ps 14.
53, 6: *God has scattered the bones of your besiegers:* a reference, perhaps to the annihilation of Sennacherib's army before the walls of Jerusalem. Cf 2 Kgs 19, 35.
Ps 54: The psalmist implores God's assistance against foes that seek his life (3-5) and, confident of this aid, promises a sacrifice of thanksgiving (6-9).
54, 3: *By your name:* through the power of the Lord. God's name is his nature as revealed to man; hence this term is frequently used as practically synonymous with God himself, his majesty, power, etc.
Ps 55: Vividly describing his fear and his longing to flee (2-9), the psalmist bewails the disorders about him, especially the treachery of a former friend (10-15); full of confidence in God, he prays for the overthrow of the wicked and his own deliverance (16-24).
55, 10: *Divide their counsels:* some see here an allusion to the story of the tower of Babel. Cf Gn 11, 1-9.

53/2-6: Ps 14, 1-5.   54/2: 1 Sm 23, 19f; 26, 1.
4: Rom 3, 12.

for in the city I see violence and
strife;

11   day and night they prowl about
upon its walls.

Evil and mischief are in its midst;

12†   [treachery is in its midst;]
oppression and fraud never depart
from its streets.

13   If an enemy had reviled me,
I could have borne it;

If he who hates me had vaunted
himself against me,
I might have hidden from him.

14   But you, my other self,
my companion and my bosom
friend!

15   You, whose comradeship I enjoyed;
at whose side I walked in
procession in the house of God!

III

16†   Let death surprise them;
let them go down alive to the
nether world,
for evil is in their dwellings, in
their very midst.

17   But I will call upon God,
and the Lord will save me.

18   In the evening, and at dawn, and at
noon,
I will grieve and moan,
and he will hear my voice.

19   He will give me freedom and peace
from those who war against me,
for many there are who oppose
me.

20   God will hear me and will humble
them
from his eternal throne;
For improvement is not in them,
nor do they fear God.

21   Each one lays hands on his
associates,
and violates his pact.

22   Softer than butter is his speech,
but war is in his heart;

His words are smoother than oil,
but they are drawn swords.

23*   Cast your care upon the Lord,
and he will support you;
never will he permit the just man
to be disturbed.

24   And you, O God, will bring them
down
into the pit of destruction;
Men of blood and deceit shall not
live out half their days.
But I trust in you, O Lord.

Trust in God, the Helper in Need

56 **†** **1***   For the leader; according to *Jonath . . .
rehokim.* A *miktam* of David, when the
Philistines held him in Gath.

I

2   Have pity on me, O God, for men
trample upon me;
all the day they press their attack
against me.

3   My adversaries trample upon me all
the day;
yes, many fight against me.

O Most High, **4**when I begin to fear,
in you will I trust.

5   In God, in whose promise I
glory,
in God I trust without fear;
what can flesh do against me?

II

6   All the day they molest me in my
efforts;
their every thought is of evil
against me.

7   They gather together in hiding,
they watch my steps.

As they have waited for my life,

8   because of their wickedness keep
them in view:
in your wrath bring down the
peoples, O God.

9†   My wanderings you have counted;
my tears are stored in your flask;
are they not recorded in your
book?

10   Then do my enemies turn back,
when I call upon you;
now I know that God is with me.

11   In God, in whose promise I
glory,

12   in God I trust without fear;
what can flesh do against me?

III

13*   I am bound, O God, by vows to you;
your thank offerings I will fulfill.

---

† 55, 12: *Treachery is in its midst:* apparently this is merely a
variant reading of the preceding line.

55, 16: *Go down alive to the nether world:* die a sudden
death. Perhaps there is an allusion here to the death of Korah
and his fellow rebels. Cf Nm 16, 31ff.

Ps 56: The psalmist prays for help against his enemies (2-4)
and bewails their machinations (6-10); in a twice-repeated refrain (5.11) he expresses his confidence in God, to whom he
vows a thanksgiving sacrifice (13).

56, 9: *My tears are stored in your flask:* a quaint figure to express that God knows the psalmist's weeping and will requite it,
for he is carefully collecting all his tears in a bottle.

❋
55/23: 1 Pt 5, 7.   13: Ps 49, 16.
56/1: 1 Sm 21, 10.

14 For you have rescued me from
     death,
   my feet, too, from stumbling;
   that I may walk before God in the
     light of the living.

Confident Prayer for Deliverance

57 † **1***† For the leader. (Do not destroy!) A *miktam*
       of David, when he fled away from Saul
       into the cave.

I

2 Have pity on me, O God; have pity
     on me,
   for in you I take refuge.
   In the shadow of your wings I take
     refuge,
   till harm pass by.
3 I call to God the Most High,
   to God, my benefactor.
4 May he send from heaven and save
     me;
   may he make those a reproach
     who trample upon me;
   may God send his kindness and his
     faithfulness.
5 I lie prostrate in the midst of lions
   which devour men;
   Their teeth are spears and arrows,
     their tongue is a sharp sword.
6   Be exalted above the heavens,
       O God;
     above all the earth be your
       glory!

II

7 They have prepared a net for my
     feet;
   they have bowed me down;
   They have dug a pit before me,
     but they fall into it.
8† My heart is steadfast, O God;
     my heart is steadfast;
   I will sing and chant praise.
9† Awake, O my soul; awake, lyre and
     harp!
   I will wake the dawn.
10 I will give thanks to you among the
     peoples, O Lord.
   I will chant your praise among the
     nations,
11 For your kindness towers to the
     heavens,
   and your faithfulness to the skies.

12   Be exalted above the heavens,
        O God;
      above all the earth be your
        glory!

Against Unjust Judges

58 † **1** For the leader. (Do not destroy!) A *miktam*
       of David.

I

2† Do you indeed like gods pronounce
     justice
   and judge fairly, you men of rank?
3 Nay, you willingly commit crimes;
   on earth you look to the fruits of
     extortion.
4 From the womb the wicked are
     perverted;
   astray from birth have the liars
     gone.
5† Theirs is poison like a serpent's,
   like that of a stubborn snake that
     stops its ears,
6 That it may not hear the voice of
     enchanters
   casting cunning spells.

II

7 O God, smash their teeth in their
     mouths;
   the jaw-teeth of the lions, break,
     O LORD!
8 Let them vanish like water flowing
     off;
   when they draw the bow, let their
     arrows be headless shafts.
9† Let them dissolve like a melting
     snail,

---

† Ps 57: Each of the two equal strophes contains a prayer for
help, accompanied by joyful trust in God (2-5.7-11), and each
strophe ends with the same refrain to God's glory (6.12).

57, 1: *Do not destroy:* here and in the next two psalms, as
well as in Ps 75, this is probably a mere annotation by some
early scribe who wished to keep his copy from being discarded.

57, 8-12: With a few small variations these verses appear
again at the beginning of Ps 108.

57, 9: *I will wake the dawn:* by a bold figure of speech the
psalmist imagines that the sound he makes at night with his
singing and music will arouse a new day to life.

Ps 58: The psalmist rebukes certain unjust judges (2-6), and
invokes God's punishment upon them (7-12).

58, 2: *Like gods:* literally, "O gods!" Here, as also in Ps 82,
judges are called "gods" in the sense of "possessing godlike
power," or of "taking God's place in pronouncing judgment."
See note on Ps 45, 7.

58, 5f: Two figures derived from snake life are here skillfully
combined: the harm done by these wicked judges is as deadly as
a serpent's venom, and these men are as unresponsive to God's
teachings as certain stubborn snakes are to the music of the
snake charmer.

58, 9: *Like a melting snail:* the Hebrew is not entirely certain,
but if the text is correct, it would seem that the ancients thought
a snail "melted" or gradually wasted away to nothing—an idea

like an untimely birth that never
       sees the sun.
10† Unexpectedly, like a thorn-bush,
       or like thistles, let the whirlwind
       carry them away.
11† The just man shall be glad when he
       sees vengeance;
       he shall bathe his feet in the blood
       of the wicked.
12 And men shall say, "Truly there is a
       reward for the just;
       truly there is a God who is judge
       on earth!"

Against Bloodthirsty Enemies

59† 1* For the leader. (Do not destroy!) A *miktam*
of David when Saul sent men to watch his
house and put him to death.

I

2 Rescue me from my enemies, O my
       God;
       from my adversaries defend me.
3 Rescue me from evildoers;
       from bloodthirsty men save me.
4 For behold, they lie in wait for my
       life;
       mighty men come together against
       me.
Not for any offense or sin of mine,
       O LORD;
5   for no guilt of mine they hurry to
       take up arms.
Rouse yourself to see it, and aid me,
6   for you are the LORD of hosts, the
       God of Israel.
Arise; punish all the nations;
       have no pity on any worthless
       traitors.

7   Each evening they return, they
       snarl like dogs
       and prowl about the city.
8† Though they bay with their mouths,
       and blasphemies are on their lips—
       "Who is there to listen?"—
9 You, O LORD, laugh at them;
       you deride all the nations.
10   O my strength! for you I watch;
       for you, O God, are my
       stronghold,
11   my gracious God!

II

May God come to my aid;
       may he show me the fall of my
       foes.

12 O God, slay them, lest they beguile
       my people;
       shake them by your power, and
       bring them down,
       O Lord our shield!
13 By the sin of their mouths and the
       word of their lips
       let them be caught in their
       arrogance,
       for the lies they have told under
       oath.
14 Consume them in wrath; consume,
       till they are no more;
       that men may know that God is
       the ruler of Jacob,
       yes, to the ends of the earth.

15   Each evening they return, they
       snarl like dogs
       and prowl about the city;
16 They wander about as scavengers;
       if they are not filled, they howl.
17 But I will sing of your strength
       and revel at dawn in your
       kindness;
       You have been my stronghold,
       my refuge in the day of distress.
18   O my strength! your praise will
       I sing;
       for you, O God, are my
       stronghold,
       my gracious God!

Prayer after Defeat in Battle

60† 1 For the leader; according to "The Lily
of . . . ." A *miktam* of David (for teaching)
2* when he fought against Aram Naharaim
and Aram-zobah; and Joab, coming back,
killed twelve thousand Edomites in the
"valley of salt."

I

3 O God, you have rejected us and
       broken our defenses;
       you have been angry; rally us!

---

† derived, perhaps, from the sight of the trail of slime a snail
leaves behind as it moves along and from the fact that dead
snails are soon but empty shells.

58, 10: The Hebrew text of this verse is obscure and is variously reconstructed.

58, 11: *He shall bathe his feet in the blood:* by the figure of
hyperbole, victorious soldiers may be said to wade through the
blood of the vanquished. Cf Ps 68, 24; Is 63, 1-6.

Ps 59: In each of the two similar strophes (2-6.11b-14) the
psalmist beseeches God to defend him against his wicked enemies. In the two similar refrains (7-11a.15-18) he compares the
wicked to ravenous dogs.

59, 8: *Who is there to listen?:* this is their blasphemy, that
they say, "God does not even hear of our wickedness."

Ps 60: Bewailing a military disaster, the psalmist first thanks
God for having saved at least a part of the army (3-7); then,
recalling God's promise to subjugate the neighboring nations
(8-10), he puts his trust in the Lord's strong assistance (11-14).

✿   59/1: 1 Sm 19, 11.   60/2: 2 Sm 8, 3ff.8; 10, 6ff;
                                        1 Chr 18, 12f.

4 You have rocked the country and
    split it open;
    repair the cracks in it, for it is
      tottering.
5 You have made your people feel
    hardships;
    you have given us stupefying
      wine.
6 You have raised for those who fear
    you a banner
    to which they may flee out of
      bowshot
7*† That your loved ones may escape;
    help us by your right hand, and
      answer us!

II

8† God promised in his sanctuary:
    "Exultantly I will apportion
      Shechem,
    and measure off the valley of
      Succoth.
9† Mine is Gilead, and mine Manasseh;
    Ephraim is the helmet for my
      head; Judah, my scepter;
10† Moab shall serve as my washbowl;
    upon Edom I will set my shoe;
    I will triumph over Philistia."

III

11† Who will bring me into the fortified
    city?
    Who will lead me into Edom?
12 Have not you, O God, rejected us,
    so that you go not forth, O God,
      with our armies?
13 Give us aid against the foe,
    for worthless is the help of men.
14 Under God we shall do valiantly;
    it is he who will tread down our
      foes.

Prayer of the King in Exile

61† 1 For the leader; with stringed instruments.
Of David.

I

2 Hear, O God, my cry;
    listen to my prayer!
3 From the earth's end I call to you
    as my heart grows faint.
    You will set me high upon a rock;
    you will give me rest,
4 for you are my refuge,
    a tower of strength against the
      enemy.

5 Oh, that I might lodge in your tent
    forever,
    take refuge in the shelter of your
      wings!

II

6 You indeed, O God, have accepted
    my vows;
    you granted me the heritage of
      those who fear your name.
7 Add to the days of the king's life;
    let his years be many generations;
8 Let him sit enthroned before God
    forever;
    bid kindness and faithfulness
      preserve him.
9 So will I sing the praises of your
    name forever,
    fulfilling my vows day by day.

Trust in God Alone

62† 1 For the leader; *'al Jeduthun.* A psalm of
David.

I

2 Only in God is my soul at rest;
    from him comes my salvation.
3 He only is my rock and my
    salvation,
    my stronghold; I shall not be
      disturbed at all.
4 How long will you set upon a man
    and all together beat him down
    as though he were a sagging fence,
      a battered wall?

---

† 60, 7-14: These verses occur again as the second half of Ps 108.

60, 8: *I will apportion . . . and measure off:* God will claim these places as his own. *The valley of Succoth:* probably the lower stretch of the Jabbok valley. Cf Gn 32, 23; 33, 17.

60, 9: *Judah, my scepter:* an allusion to the Blessing of Jacob. Cf Gn 49, 10.

60, 10: *Moab shall serve as my washbowl:* the Moabites shall perform menial service for Israel; possibly there is also an allusion to the "basin" of the Dead Sea, which formed the western border of Moab. *Upon Edom I will set my shoe:* God will use Edom as his footstool; thus the ancient kings treated their conquered enemies. Cf Ps 110, 1. Some render, "Upon Edom I will throw my shoe," and understand this casting of a shoe on conquered territory as a sign of possession.

60, 11: *The fortified city:* perhaps Bozrah, the impregnable capital of Edom. Cf Is 34, 6; 63, 1; Am 1, 12.

Ps 61: Far away from Jerusalem, the psalmist longs for God's help and the shelter of his abode (2-5); confident of being heard, he prays for the king (6-9). This may be interpreted as a prayer of David when he had to flee from Jerusalem during the rebellion of Absalom. Cf 2 Sm 15-19.

Ps 62: The keynote of trust in God is struck in the twice-repeated refrain (2f.6f); though attacked by his enemies (4f), the psalmist asserts his unshaken confidence in the Lord (8f), for true strength comes not from earthly power but from God's grace (10-13).

---

* 7-14: Ps 108, 7-14.

5† Truly from my place on high they
      plan to dislodge me;
      they delight in lies;
They bless with their mouths,
      but inwardly they curse.

II

6   Only in God be at rest, my soul,
       for from him comes my hope.
7   He only is my rock and my
        salvation,
        my stronghold; I shall not be
        disturbed.
8   With God is my safety and my glory,
      he is the rock of my strength; my
      refuge is in God.
9   Trust in him at all times, O my
      people!
      Pour out your hearts before him;
      God is our refuge!

III

10   Only a breath are mortal men;
      an illusion are men of rank;
In a balance they prove lighter,
      all together, than a breath.
11   Trust not in extortion; in plunder
      take no empty pride;
      though wealth abound, set not
      your heart upon it.
12†   One thing God said; these two things
      which I heard:
      that power belongs to God,
13✱   and yours, O Lord, is kindness;
      and that you render to everyone
      according to his deeds.

Ardent Longing for God

63† 1✱   A psalm of David, when he was in the
wilderness of Judah.

I

2   O God, you are my God whom I
      seek;
      for you my flesh pines and my soul
      thirsts
      like the earth, parched, lifeless
      and without water.
3   Thus have I gazed toward you in the
      sanctuary
      to see your power and your glory,
4   For your kindness is a greater good
      than life;
      my lips shall glorify you.

II

5   Thus will I bless you while I live;
      lifting up my hands, I will call
      upon your name.
6   As with the riches of a banquet shall
      my soul be satisfied,
      and with exultant lips my mouth
      shall praise you.
7   I will remember you upon my couch,
      and through the night-watches I
      will meditate on you:
8   That you are my help,
      and in the shadow of your wings I
      shout for joy.
9   My soul clings fast to you;
      your right hand upholds me.

III

10   But they shall be destroyed who seek
      my life,
      they shall go into the depths of the
      earth;
11†   They shall be delivered over the
      sword,
      and shall be the prey of jackals.
12   The king, however, shall rejoice in
      God;
      everyone who swears by him shall
      glory,
      but the mouths of those who speak
      falsely shall be stopped.

Treacherous Conspirators Punished by God

64† 1   For the leader. A psalm of David.

I

2   Hear, O God, my voice in my
      lament;
      from the dread enemy preserve
      my life.
3   Shelter me against the council of
      malefactors,
      against the tumult of evildoers,

---

† 62, 5: *My place on high:* a place of safety such as a fortress set on a cliff.

62, 12: *One thing . . . two things:* such use of progressive numbers is a device of Hebrew poetry. Cf Am 1, 3; Prv 6, 16-19; 30, 15.18.21.

Ps 63: Homesick for God's sanctuary (2-4), the psalmist holds fast to the Lord in spirit (5-9), confident that his enemies will be destroyed while the king and his loyal followers will triumph (10-12).

63, 11: *The prey of jackals:* their dead bodies shall be devoured by wild animals. Lack of proper burial was dreaded by the ancients.

Ps 64: The psalmist prays for God's help against deceitful foes who secretly plot against him (2-7); God will repay them with exemplary punishment (8-11).

✱ 62/13: Mt 16, 27; Rom 2, 6.   63/1: 1 Sm 24.

4 Who sharpen their tongues like
swords,
who aim like arrows their bitter
words,

5 Shooting from ambush at the
innocent man,
suddenly shooting at him without
fear.

6 They resolve on their wicked plan;
they conspire to set snares,
saying, "Who will see us?"

7 They devise a wicked scheme,
and conceal the scheme they have
devised;
deep are the thoughts of each
heart.

II

8 But God shoots his arrows at them;
suddenly they are struck.

9† He brings them down by their own
tongues;
all who see them nod their
heads.

10 And all men fear and proclaim the
work of God,
and ponder what he has done.

11 The just man is glad in the LORD and
takes refuge in him;
in him glory all the upright of
heart.

Thanksgiving for God's Blessings

65† 1 For the leader. A psalm of David. A song.

I

2† To you we owe our hymn of praise,
O God, in Zion;
To you must vows be fulfilled,
you who hear prayers.

3† To you all flesh must come
4 because of wicked deeds.
We are overcome by our sins;
it is you who pardon them.

5 Happy the man you choose, and
bring
to dwell in your courts.
May we be filled with the good
things of your house,
the holy things of your temple!

II

6 With awe-inspiring deeds of justice
you answer us,
O God our savior,
The hope of all the ends of the earth
and of the distant seas.

7 You set the mountains in place by
your power,
you who are girt with might;

8 You still the roaring of the seas,
the roaring of their waves and the
tumult of the peoples.

9 And the dwellers at the earth's ends
are in fear at your marvels;
the farthest east and west you
make resound with joy.

III

10 You have visited the land and
watered it;
greatly have you enriched it.
God's watercourses are filled;
you have prepared the grain.

11 Thus have you prepared the land:
drenching its furrows,
breaking up its clods,
Softening it with showers,
blessing its yield.

12† You have crowned the year with
your bounty,
and your paths overflow with a
rich harvest;

13 The untilled meadows overflow
with it,
and rejoicing clothes the hills.

14 The fields are garmented with flocks
and the valleys blanketed with
grain.
They shout and sing for joy.

Praise of God, Israel's Deliverer

66† 1 For the leader. A psalm; a song.

Shout joyfully to God, all you on
earth,
2 sing praise to the glory of his
name;
proclaim his glorious praise.

---

† 64, 9: *Nod their heads:* a gesture of derision. Cf Pss 22, 8;
44, 15; 109, 25.

Ps 65: A hymn of thanksgiving, sung by the community for
a bountiful harvest. Humbly acknowledging that they are unworthy of God's favors (2-5), the people praise him for his power
over all the earth (6-9), and thank him for the rains which produced such abundant crops (10-14).

65, 2: *Vows:* the Israelites were accustomed to promise sacrifices in the temple if their prayers were heard.

65, 3: *To you all flesh must come:* all men must have recourse
to God's mercy.

65, 12: *Your paths overflow with a rich harvest:* literally,
"Your wagon-wheel tracks drip with oil."

Ps 66: There are two distinct parts here, which perhaps originally were two independent psalms. The first part (1-12) is a
hymn of the community praising God's omnipotence as revealed
throughout history, especially at the Exodus (5-7), and now in
the recent restoration of the nation from some calamity (8-12).
The second part (13-20) is the thanksgiving hymn of an individual fulfilling his vows in the temple (13-15) and recounting
how the Lord had heard his prayer (16-20).

3† Say to God, "How tremendous are
your deeds!
for your great strength your
enemies fawn upon you.
4 Let all on earth worship and sing
praise to you,
sing praise to your name!"

I

5 Come and see the works of God,
his tremendous deeds among men.
6✻ He has changed the sea into dry
land;
through the river they passed on
foot;
therefore let us rejoice in him.
7 He rules by his might forever;
his eyes watch the nations;
rebels may not exalt themselves.
8 Bless our God, you peoples,
loudly sound his praise;
9 He has given life to our souls,
and has not let our feet slip.
10 For you have tested us, O God!
You have tried us as silver is tried
by fire;
11 You have brought us into a snare;
you laid a heavy burden on our
backs.
12 You let men ride over our heads;
we went through fire and water,
but you have led us out to
refreshment.

II

13 I will bring holocausts to your house;
to you I will fulfill the vows
14 Which my lips uttered
and my words promised in my
distress.
15 Holocausts of fatlings I will offer
you,
with burnt offerings of rams;
I will sacrifice oxen and goats.
16 Hear now, all you who fear God,
while I declare
what he has done for me.
17† When I appealed to him in words,
praise was on the tip of my
tongue.
18 Were I to cherish wickedness in my
heart,
the Lord would not hear;
19 But God has heard;
he has hearkened to the sound of
my prayer.
20 Blessed be God who refused me not
my prayer or his kindness!

Harvest Prayer that All Men May Worship God

67 **† 1** For the leader; with stringed instruments.
A psalm; a song.

I

2✻† May God have pity on us and bless
us;
may he let his face shine upon us.
3 So may your way be known upon
earth;
among all nations, your salvation.
4† May the peoples praise you,
O God;
may all the peoples praise
you!

II

5 May the nations be glad and exult
because you rule the peoples in
equity;
the nations on the earth you guide.
6 May the peoples praise you,
O God;
may all the peoples praise
you!

III

7 The earth has yielded its fruits;
God, our God, has blessed us.
8 May God bless us,
and may all the ends of the earth
fear him!

God's Triumphal Procession

68 **† 1** For the leader. A psalm of David; a song.

I

2✻† God arises; his enemies are scattered,
and those who hate him flee
before him.

---

† 66, 3: *Fawn upon you:* pay an unwilling tribute of praise.
Cf Pss 18, 45; 81, 16.

66, 17: *Praise was on the tip of my tongue:* literally, "praise
was under my tongue." Even while the psalmist was praying
aloud for help, he was already thanking God silently for having
heard his prayer.

Ps 67: The refrain (4.6 and perhaps originally after 8) calls
on all the nations of the earth to praise the Lord, because he
blesses Israel (2f), governs all peoples wisely (5), and bestows
an abundant harvest (7). Israel's hope of seeing the Lord acknowledged as the only God by all the nations was based on,
and found its sole fulfillment in, the promise of the Messiah.
Cf Gn 12, 2f.

67, 2: These words are similar to the priestly blessing of Nm
6, 22-27.

67, 4.6: *Praise:* the Hebrew means more exactly, "give grateful praise"; hence, according to the context, it is often translated, "give thanks."

Ps 68: One of the most magnificent but, at the same time,
one of the most difficult hymns of the Psalter. In several places
the Hebrew text is poorly preserved. It was written to be sung

✻ 66/6: Ex 14, 21f.   68/2: Nm 10, 35.
67/2: Nm 6, 24f.

3 As smoke is driven away, so are they
　　driven;
　　　as wax melts before the fire,
　　　so the wicked perish before God.
4 But the just rejoice and exult before
　　God;
　　　they are glad and rejoice.

II

5*† Sing to God, chant praise to his
　　name,
　　　extol him who rides upon the
　　　clouds,
　　Whose name is the LORD;
　　　exult before him.
6 The father of orphans and the
　　defender of widows
　　　is God in his holy dwelling.
7 God gives a home to the forsaken;
　　he leads forth prisoners to
　　　prosperity;
　　　only rebels remain in the parched
　　　land.

III

8* O God, when you went forth at the
　　head of your people,
　　　when you marched through the
　　　wilderness,
9 The earth quaked; it rained from
　　heaven at the presence of God,
　　　at the presence of God, the God of
　　　Israel, the One of Sinai.
10 A bountiful rain you showered
　　down, O God, upon your
　　　inheritance;
　　　you restored the land when it
　　　languished;
11 Your flock settled in it;
　　in your goodness, O God, you
　　　provided it for the needy.

IV

12† The Lord give the word;
　　women bear the glad tidings, a
　　　vast army:
13 "Kings and their hosts are fleeing,
　　fleeing,
　　　and the household shall divide the
　　　spoils.
14† Though you rested among the
　　sheepfolds,
　　　the wings of the dove shone with
　　　silver,
　　　and her pinions with a golden hue.
15 While the Almighty dispersed the
　　kings there,
　　　snow fell on Zalmon."

V

16 High the mountains of Bashan;
　　rugged the mountains of Bashan.
17† Why look you jealously, you rugged
　　mountains,
　　　at the mountain God has chosen
　　　for his throne,
　　　where the LORD himself will dwell
　　　forever?
18 The chariots of God are myriad,
　　thousands on thousands;
　　　the Lord advances from Sinai to
　　　the sanctuary.
19*† You have ascended on high, taken
　　captives,
　　　received men as gifts—
　　　even rebels; the LORD God enters
　　　his dwelling.

VI

20 Blessed day by day be the Lord,
　　who bears our burdens; God, who
　　　is our salvation.
21 God is a saving God for us;
　　the LORD, my Lord, controls the
　　　passageways of death.

---

† as the ark of the covenant was carried in solemn procession into the temple. Beginning with the ancient war cry of Israel, which was used when the ark was carried into battle (2), the opening strophe proclaims the defeat of the wicked and the triumph of the just (3f). After general praise of God's goodness (5-7), the Lord's victorious march from Egypt to Sinai (8-11) and the conquest of the Promised Land (12-15) are briefly and poetically recounted; reference is then made to God's choice of Zion for his dwelling (16-19), as well as to all his victories (20-24); finally, with a description of the present procession serving as an interlude (25-28), God is implored to spread his mighty rule (29-32) until all the earth sings his glory (33-36).

68, 2: What is here stated as a fact is given in the form of a prayer in Nm 10, 35.

68, 5: *Extol him who rides upon the clouds:* the meaning of the Hebrew is not entirely certain. The revised Latin Psalter has, "Lay a road for him who rides through the desert." However, the expression "The Rider of the Clouds" as a divine epithet is very ancient, since it occurs in Canaanite literature even before the time of Moses, and it is not uncommon in the Old Testament. Cf Dt 33, 26; Pss 18, 10ff; 68, 34; Is 19, 1; Hb 3, 8.

68, 12: The Israelite women took an active part in celebrating a victory. Cf Ex 15, 20; 1 Sm 18, 6f.

68, 14f: The Hebrew text of these verses is very obscure. The translation given above follows the revised Latin Psalter. *The dove:* perhaps a figure of the victorious army of Israel. Cf Ps 74, 19. *Snow fell:* either literally, or figuratively of the fallen enemy lying as thick as snowflakes on the battlefield. *Zalmon:* probably a mountain in the Hauran or in Bashan. The historical event referred to is uncertain. Cf Nm 21, 33ff; Dt 3, 1-10.

68, 17: *The mountain God has chosen:* Mount Zion.

68, 19: *Ascended on high:* to the divine throne, either on Zion or in heaven. *Received men as gifts:* St. Paul quotes this somewhat freely according to the Greek version as, "He gave gifts to men," and then applies it to Christ bestowing his charismatic graces on the Church after his ascension into heaven. Cf Eph 4, 8.

✿ 5: Ex 15, 3.　　　　　　　19: Eph 4, 8.
　8f: Jgs 5, 4f.

22 Surely God crushes the heads of his
enemies,
the hairy crowns of those who
stalk about in their guilt.

23 The Lord said: "I will fetch them
back from Bashan;
I will fetch them back from the
depths of the sea,

24 So that you will bathe your feet in
blood;
the tongues of your dogs will have
their share of your enemies."

VII

25 They view your progress, O God,
the progress of my God, my King,
into the sanctuary;

26 The singers lead, the minstrels
follow,
in their midst the maidens play on
timbrels.

27 In your choirs bless God;
bless the Lord, you of Israel's
wellspring!

28 There is Benjamin, the youngest,
leading them;
the princes of Judah in a body,
the princes of Zebulun, the
princes of Naphtali.

VIII

29 Show forth, O God, your power,
the power, O God, with which you
took our part;

30 For your temple in Jerusalem
let the kings bring you gifts.

31† Rebuke the wild beast of the reeds,
the herd of strong bulls and the
bullocks, the nations.
Let them prostrate themselves with
bars of silver;
scatter the peoples who delight in
war.

32 Let nobles come from Egypt;
let Ethiopia extend its hands to
God.

IX

33 You kingdoms of the earth, sing to
God,
chant praise to the Lord

34† who rides on the heights of the
ancient heavens.
Behold, his voice resounds, the voice
of power:

35 "Confess the power of God!"
Over Israel is his majesty;
his power is in the skies.

36 Awesome in his sanctuary is God,
the God of Israel;
he gives power and strength to his
people.
Blessed be God!

A Cry of Anguish
in Great Distress

69† 1 For the leader; according to "Lilies." Of
David.

I

2† Save me, O God,
for the waters threaten my life;

3 I am sunk in the abysmal swamp
where there is no foothold;
I have reached the watery depths;
the flood overwhelms me.

4 I am wearied with calling,
my throat is parched;
My eyes have failed
with looking for my God.

5*† Those outnumber the hairs of my
head
who hate me without cause.
Too many for my strength
are they who wrongfully are my
enemies.
Must I restore what I did not
steal?

II

6† O God, you know my folly,
and my faults are not hid from
you.

7 Let not those who wait for you be
put to shame through me,
O Lord, GOD of hosts.

---

† 68, 31: *The wild beast of the reeds:* most probably Egypt. Cf
Ez 29, 2ff. *Bars of silver:* tribute from the foreign nations
brought to Zion.

68, 34: *Who rides:* see note on v 5.

Ps 69: A lamentation similar to Ps 22. The psalmist describes
his extreme misery (2-5) and unmerited disgrace (6-13), imploring God to vindicate him (14-22) and punish his enemies (23-
29); in return he will offer God a sacrifice of praise (30-35). As
in Ps 51, two verses were added at the end foretelling the restoration of Israel from exile in Babylon (36f). Since several passages are quoted in the New Testament in reference to Christ,
Catholic tradition has always considered this psalm as at least
indirectly messianic.

69, 2: *The waters:* a common metaphor for affliction. Cf Pss
18, 5; 42, 8; 88, 8.

69, 5: *Who hate me without cause:* according to our Lord's
own statement these words were fully verified in the hatred his
enemies bore him. Cf Jn 15, 25.

69, 6: *My folly, and my faults:* the psalmist is guilty, he admits, of certain sins, but not of the grave crimes his enemies
charge him with. This verse cannot be interpreted in a messianic sense except in so far as Christ took upon himself the sins
of the world.

---

* 69/5: Jn 15, 25.

Let not those who seek you blush for
me,
O God of Israel,

8 Since for your sake I bear insult,
and shame covers my face.

9 I have become an outcast to my
brothers,
a stranger to my mother's sons,

10*† Because zeal for your house
consumes me,
and the insults of those who
blaspheme you fall upon me.

11 I humbled myself with fasting,
and this was made a reproach to
me.

12 I made sackcloth my garment,
and I became a byword for them.

13 They who sit at the gate gossip
about me,
and drunkards make me the butt
of their songs.

III

14 But I pray to you, O LORD,
for the time of your favor, O God!
In your great kindness answer me
with your constant help.

15 Rescue me out of the mire; may I not
sink!
may I be rescued from my foes,
and from the watery depths.

16 Let not the flood-waters overwhelm
me,
nor the abyss swallow me up,
nor the pit close its mouth over
me.

17 Answer me, O LORD, for bounteous
is your kindness;
in your great mercy turn toward
me.

18 Hide not your face from your
servant;
in my distress, make haste to
answer me.

19 Come and ransom my life;
as an answer for my enemies,
redeem me.

20 You know my reproach, my shame
and my ignominy;
before you are all my foes.

21 Insult has broken my heart, and I am
weak,
I looked for sympathy, but there
was none;
for comforters, and I found none.

22*† Rather they put gall in my food,
and in my thirst they gave me
vinegar to drink.

IV

23*† Let their own table be a snare before
them,
and a net for their friends.

24 Let their eyes grow dim so that they
cannot see,
and keep their backs always
feeble.

25 Pour out your wrath upon them;
let the fury of your anger overtake
them.

26*† Let their encampment become
desolate;
in their tents let there be no one to
dwell.

27 For they kept after him whom you
smote,
and added to the pain of him you
wounded.

28 Heap guilt upon their guilt,
and let them not attain to your
reward.

29 May they be erased from the book of
of the living,
and not be recorded with the just!

V

30 But I am afflicted and in pain;
let your saving help, O God,
protect me.

31 I will praise the name of God in
song,
and I will glorify him with
thanksgiving;

32 This will please the LORD more than
oxen
or bullocks with horns and divided
hooves:

33 "See, you lowly ones, and be glad;
you who seek God, may your
hearts be merry!

34 For the LORD hears the poor,
and his own who are in bonds he
spurns not.

10: Jn 2, 17; Rom 15, 3.   23f: Rom 11, 9f.
22: Mt 27, 34.48;   26: Acts 1, 20.
Mk 15, 23.

† 69, 10: *Zeal for your house consumes me:* eminently fulfilled
in Christ's cleansing of the temple. Cf Jn 2, 17. *The insults of
those who blaspheme you fall upon me:* cited by St. Paul as an
example of our Lord's unselfishness. Cf Rom 15, 3.

69, 22: A prophecy fulfilled in the bitter drink given to Christ
on the cross. Cf Jn 19, 28. *Gall:* the Hebrew word probably signifies the juice of some bitter and poisonous plant.

69, 23: *Table:* a mere tablecloth spread on the ground, on
which one might trip.

69, 26: Applied to Judas in Acts 1, 20.

35   Let the heavens and the earth praise
      him,
        the seas and whatever moves in
        them!"

36   For God will save Zion
        and rebuild the cities of Judah.
      They shall dwell in the land and own
        it,

37   and the descendants of his
        servants shall inherit it,
        and those who love his name shall
        inhabit it.

Prayer for Divine Help

70 †   1   For the leader; of David. For remembrance.

2*   Deign, O God, to rescue me;
      O Lord, make haste to help me.

3   Let them be put to shame and
      confounded
      who seek my life.
     Let them be turned back in disgrace
      who desire my ruin.

4   Let them retire in their shame
      who say to me, "Aha, aha!"

5   But may all who seek you
      exult and be glad in you,
     And may those who love your
      salvation
      say ever, "God be glorified!"

6   But I am afflicted and poor;
      O God, hasten to me!
     You are my help and my deliverer;
      O Lord, hold not back!

Humble Prayer in Time of Old Age

I

71 †   1   In you, O Lord, I take refuge;
      let me never be put to shame.

2   In your justice rescue me, and
      deliver me;
      incline your ear to me, and save
      me.

3   Be my rock of refuge,
      a stronghold to give me safety,
      for you are my rock and my
      fortress.

4   O my God, rescue me from the hand
      of the wicked,
      from the grasp of the criminal and
      the violent.

5   For you are my hope, O Lord;
      my trust, O God, from my youth.

6†   On you I depend from birth;
      from my mother's womb you are
      my strength;
      constant has been my hope in you.

7†   A portent am I to many,
      but you are my strong refuge!

8   My mouth shall be filled with your
      praise,
      with your glory day by day.

II

9   Cast me not off in my old age;
      as my strength fails, forsake me
      not,

10   For my enemies speak against me,
      and they who keep watch against
      my life take counsel together.

11   They say, "God has forsaken him;
      pursue and seize him,
      for there is no one to rescue him."

12   O God, be not far from me;
      my God, make haste to help me.

13   Let them be put to shame and
      consumed who attack my life;
      let them be wrapped in ignominy
      and disgrace who seek to harm
      me.

14   But I will always hope
      and praise you ever more and
      more.

15†   My mouth shall declare your justice,
      day by day your salvation,
      though I know not their extent.

16   I will treat of the mighty works of
      the Lord;
      O God, I will tell of your singular
      justice.

III

17   O God, you have taught me from my
      youth,
      and till the present I proclaim
      your wondrous deeds;

---

† Ps 70: Almost identical with Ps 40, 14-18.

Ps 71: The aged psalmist, who has always put his trust in the Lord, implores his aid (1-7) now that he is afflicted and persecuted (9-13); each of these two sections ends with a promise of grateful praise (8.14-16); almost all of the third section (17-24) likewise describes the same confident expectation of being heard by God.

71, 6: *My strength:* the exact meaning of the Hebrew is uncertain. The revised Latin Psalter still retains "my protector" of the older Latin version.

71, 7: *A portent:* many marvel that the psalmist is so afflicted, looking on him as cursed by God. Cf Dt 28, 46. Some commentators, however, understand this as, "Many marvel at my invincible confidence in God and at the great graces he bestows on me."

71, 15: *Though I know not their extent:* the psalmist admits that God's acts of kindness toward him are more numerous than he himself realizes.

---

* 70/2-6: Ps 40, 14-18.

18 And now that I am old and gray,
O God, forsake me not
Till I proclaim your strength
to every generation that is to
come.

19 Your power and your justice,
O God, reach to heaven.
You have done great things;
O God, who is like you?

20 Though you have made me feel
many bitter afflictions,
you will again revive me;
from the depths of the earth you
will once more raise me.

21 Renew your benefits toward me,
and comfort me over and over.

22 So will I give you thanks with music
on the lyre,
for your faithfulness, O my God!
I will sing your praises with the harp,
O Holy One of Israel!

23 My lips shall shout for joy
as I sing your praises;
My soul also, which you have
redeemed,

24 and my tongue day by day shall
discourse on your justice.
How shamed and how disgraced
are those who sought to harm me!

The Kingdom of the Messiah

72 † 1†   Of Solomon.

I

O God, with your judgment endow
the king,
and with your justice, the king's
son;

2† He shall govern your people with
justice
and your afflicted ones with
judgment.

3 The mountains shall yield peace for
the people,
and the hills justice.

4 He shall defend the afflicted among
the people,
save the children of the poor,
and crush the oppressor.

II

5 May he endure as long as the sun,
and like the moon through all
generations.

6 He shall be like rain coming down on
the meadow,
like showers watering the earth.

7 Justice shall flower in his days,
and profound peace, till the moon
be no more.

III

8† May he rule from sea to sea,
and from the River to the ends of
the earth.

9 His foes shall bow before him,
and his enemies shall lick the dust.

10*† The kings of Tarshish and the Isles
shall offer gifts;
the kings of Arabia and Seba shall
bring tribute.

11 All kings shall pay him homage,
all nations shall serve him.

IV

12 For he shall rescue the poor man
when he cries out,
and the afflicted when he has no
one to help him.

13 He shall have pity for the lowly and
the poor;
the lives of the poor he shall save.

14 From fraud and violence he shall
redeem them,
and precious shall their blood be
in his sight.

V

15 May he live to be given the gold of
Arabia,
and to be prayed for continually;
day by day shall they bless him.

16 May there be an abundance of grain
upon the earth;

---

† Ps 72: a song of good wishes for the king, perhaps composed originally for the coronation ceremonies of one of David's successors. But some of the expressions cannot be understood of any earthly monarch except as pure hyperbole. They find their complete fulfillment only in Christ. Hence the traditional interpretation rightly treats the psalm as messianic, at least in a typical sense. The earthly king is here a type or figure of Christ the King. The Hebrew verbs seem to vary between the future and the jussive. Some commentators render them all in the future. The thoughts here expressed concern the king's just rule (1-4), his long and glorious reign (5-7), his universal dominion (8-11), his defense of the poor and oppressed (12-14), and the prosperity of his kingdom (15-17).

72, 1: *The king . . . the king's son:* the same individual is meant; his father was also a king.

72, 2: *With judgment:* he shall procure their rights for them.

72, 8: Indicates the boundaries of the civilized world at that time: from the Mediterranean Sea to the Persian Gulf (the "Eastern Sea"), and from the Euphrates (*the River*) to the islands and lands of southwestern Europe, then considered *the ends of the earth.*

72, 10: *Tarshish and the Isles:* the far west. Cf Ps 48, 8. *Arabia and Seba: the far south.* Cf 1 Kgs 10, 1.

on the tops of the mountains the
    crops shall rustle like Lebanon;
the city dwellers shall flourish like
    the verdure of the fields.

17† May his name be blessed forever;
    as long as the sun his name shall
       remain.
In him shall all the tribes of the earth
    be blessed;
    all the nations shall proclaim his
       happiness.

* * *

18*† Blessed be the LORD, the God of
    Israel,
    who alone does wondrous deeds.
19 And blessed forever be his glorious
    name;
    may the whole earth be filled with
       his glory.
    Amen. Amen.

20† The prayers of David the son of
    Jesse are ended.

III: THE THIRD BOOK—Psalms 73-89

The False Happiness
of the Wicked

73† 1 A psalm of Asaph.

How good God is to the upright;
    the LORD, to those who are clean
       of heart!
2 But, as for me, I almost lost my
    balance;
    my feet all but slipped,
3 Because I was envious of the
    arrogant
    when I saw them prosper though
       they were wicked.

I

4 For they are in no pain;
    their bodies are sound and sleek;
5 They are free from the burdens of
    mortals,
    and are not afflicted like the rest
       of men.
6 So pride adorns them as a necklace;
    as a robe violence enwraps them.
7 Out of their crassness comes
    iniquity;
    their fancies overflow their hearts.

8 They scoff and speak evil;
    outrage from on high they
       threaten.
9† They set their mouthings in place of
    heaven,
    and their pronouncements roam
       the earth:
10† "So he brings his people to such a
    pass
    that they have not even water!"
11 And they say, "How does God
    know?"
    And, "Is there any knowledge in
       the Most High?"
12 Such, then, are the wicked;
    always carefree, while they
       increase in wealth.

II

13† Is it but in vain I have kept my heart
    clean
    and washed my hands as an
       innocent man?
14 For I suffer affliction day after day
    and chastisement with each new
       dawn.
15 Had I thought, "I will speak as they
    do,"
    I had been false to the fellowship
       of your children.
16 Though I tried to understand this
    it seemed to me too difficult,
17† Till I entered the sanctuary of God
    and considered their final destiny.

---

† 72, 17: *In him . . . be blessed:* either, "Because of him all men shall receive God's blessings," or, "All men shall use his name in giving a blessing, saying, 'May you be as blessed as this king.'" Cf Gn 48, 20.

72, 18f: The doxology at the end of the Second Book of the Psalms; a later addition. Cf 41, 14.

72, 20: This note shows that Ps 72 once constituted the end of a certain collection of Davidic psalms. It does not exclude the possibility of some other Davidic psalms being incorporated in the following collections.

Ps 73: Like Pss 37 and 49, this sapiential psalm is concerned with the problem of why the wicked seem to prosper. After showing how dangerous the thought of such apparent injustice may be (1-3), the psalmist sets forth the difficulty in clear terms by describing the earthly happiness of the wicked who blaspheme God with seeming impunity (4-12), whereas the good apparently suffer in vain (13-16); the only solution, as he has learned from God himself, lies in the hereafter (17), where the fortunes of the prosperous sinner will suddenly be reversed (18-22) while the good will enjoy God's presence forever (23-28).

73, 9: *They set their mouthings in place of heaven:* literally, "They set their mouths in heaven," which seems to mean, "They speak as if they were God." The revised Latin Psalter renders it, "They attack heaven with their mouths."

73, 10: This verse is defective in the current Hebrew text. The translation given above understands it as one of the blasphemies uttered by the wicked, ridiculing God's justice. The revised Latin Psalter understands it as said by the psalmist himself, "So my people turn to them, and they suck up water in abundance."

73, 17: *I entered the sanctuary of God:* in spirit the psalmist penetrated God's heavenly sanctuary.

---

* 18f: Pss 41, 14; 89, 53;   73/13: Ps 26, 6.
    106, 48.

III

18 You set them, indeed, on a slippery
road;
you hurl them down to ruin.

19 How suddenly they are made
desolate!
They are completely wasted away
amid horrors.

20† As though they were the dream of
one who had awakened,
O Lord,
so will you, when you arise, set at
nought these phantoms.

21† Because my heart was embittered
and my soul was pierced,

22 I was stupid and understood not;
I was like a brute beast in your
presence.

IV

23 Yet with you I shall always be;
you have hold of my right hand;

24 With your counsel you guide me,
and in the end you will receive me
in glory.

25 Whom else have I in heaven?
And when I am with you, the
earth delights me not.

26 Though my flesh and my heart waste
away,
God is the rock of my heart and
my portion forever.

27 For indeed, they who withdraw
from you perish;
you destroy everyone who is
unfaithful to you.

28 But for me, to be near God is my
good;
to make the Lord GOD my refuge.
I shall declare all your works
in the gates of the daughter of
Zion.

Prayer in Time of National Calamity

74† 1† A *maskil* of Asaph.

I

Why, O God, have you cast us off
forever?
Why does your anger smolder
against the sheep of your
pasture?

2✠ Remember your flock which you
built up of old,

the tribe you redeemed as your
inheritance,
Mount Zion, where you took up
your abode.

3 Turn your steps toward the utter
ruins;
toward all the damage the enemy
has done in the sanctuary.

4 Your foes roar triumphantly in your
shrine;
they have set up their tokens of
victory.

5† They are like men coming up with
axes to a clump of trees;

6 and now with chisel and hammer
they hack at all its paneling.

7✠ They set your sanctuary on fire;
the place where your name abides
they have razed and profaned.

8 They said in their hearts, "Let us
destroy them;
burn all the shrines of God in the
land."

9✠† Deeds on our behalf we do not see;
there is no prophet now,
and no one of us knows how
long. . . .

10 How long, O God, shall the foe
blaspheme?
Shall the enemy revile your name
forever?

11 Why draw back your hand
and keep your right hand idle
beneath your cloak?

II

12 Yet, O God, my king from of old,
you doer of saving deeds on earth,

---

† 73, 20: *When you arise:* in judgment. The Lord seems to act as if he were asleep. Cf Ps 78, 65. The temporary injustice will prove to be but a bad dream.

73, 21f: The psalmist reverts to the time when he was scandalized by the prosperity of the wicked.

Ps 74: A lamentation over the destruction of the temple. The event referred to is probably the taking of Jerusalem by the Babylonians in 587 B. C. The psalmist graphically describes the frightful havoc and desolation in the temple as he implores God to be mindful of his people (1-11); then, recalling the glorious deeds the Lord has done of old (12-17), he humbly reminds God that his own honor is at stake in the fate of his chosen people (18-23).

74, 1: *Forever:* this word seems to imply that the disaster is already of long duration.

74, 5: The Hebrew text of this verse is rather obscure.

74, 9: *Deeds on our behalf:* literally, "our signs," which probably means, "signs done for us," wonderful exploits such as God performed for the Israelites during the Exodus. *There is no prophet now:* Jeremiah and Ezekiel may have been dead, or at least may not have been in Jerusalem. There is no need, because of these words, to fix the date of this psalm as late as Maccabean times. Cf Lam 2, 9.

74/2: Pss 68, 17; 132, 13.   9: Lam 2, 9.
7: 2 Kgs 25, 8f; Ps 79, 1.

13† You stirred up the sea by your might;
    you smashed the heads of the
    dragons in the waters.

14 You crushed the heads of Leviathan,
    and made food of him for the
    dolphins.

15 You released the springs and
    torrents;
    you brought dry land out of the
    primeval waters.

16* Yours is the day, and yours the night;
    you fashioned the moon and the
    sun.

17 You fixed all the limits of the land;
    summer and winter you made.

18 Remember how the enemy has
    blasphemed you, O Lord,
    and how a stupid people has
    reviled your name.

19† Give not to the vulture the life of
    your dove;
    be not forever unmindful of the
    lives of your afflicted ones.

20 Look to your covenant,
    for the hiding places in the land
    and the plains are full of
    violence.

21 May the humble not retire in
    confusion;
    may the afflicted and the poor
    praise your name.

22 Arise, O God; defend your cause;
    remember how the fool
    blasphemes you day after day.

23 Be not unmindful of the voice of
    your foes;
    the uproar of those who rebel
    against you is unceasing.

God the Just Judge
of the Wicked

75† 1 For the leader. (Do not destroy!) A psalm
of Asaph; a song.

I

2 We give you thanks, O God, we give
    thanks,
    and we invoke your name; we
    declare your wondrous deeds.

II

3 "When I seize the appointed time,
    I will judge with equity.

4 Though the earth and all who dwell
    in it quake,
    I have set firm its pillars.

5† I say to the boastful: Boast not;
    and to the wicked: Lift not up
    your horns."

6 Lift not up your horns against the
    Most High;
    speak not haughtily against the
    Rock.

7† For neither from the east nor from
    the west,
    neither from the desert nor from
    the mountains—

8 But God is the judge;
    one he brings low; another he lifts
    up.

9*† For a cup is in the Lord's hand,
    full of spiced and foaming wine,
    And he pours out from it; even to the
    dregs they shall drain it;
    all the wicked of the earth shall
    drink.

III

10 But as for me, I will exult forever;
    I will sing praise to the God of
    Jacob.

11 And I will break off the horns of all
    the wicked;
    the horns of the just shall be lifted
    up.

Thanksgiving for the Overthrow
of Israel's Foes

76† 1 For the leader; a psalm with stringed instruments. A song of Asaph.

I

2 God is renowned in Judah,
    in Israel great is his name.

---

† **74, 13-17:** These verses were probably borrowed from some much older hymn. The imagery used here to describe God's creative power at the beginning of the world may have been taken over in part from the ancient Canaanite literature. *The dragons . . . Leviathan:* mythological monsters. Cf Is 27, 1. Here they are the personification of the watery chaos at the beginning of creation. Cf Ps 89, 11.

74, 19: *The vulture:* the ferocious foes. *Your dove:* Israel. Cf Ps 68, 14.

Ps 75: After an introductory verse of praise sung by the community (2), the word of the Lord is heard, foretelling the condemnation of the proud (3-5); the psalmist then repeats and develops the same thought (6-9), praising God for this victory over the sinners (10f).

75, 5f.11: *Horns:* the symbol of power. See note on Ps 18, 3.

75, 7: The sentence is intentionally left incomplete; for the sense, add, "does justice come." *The desert:* the south. *The mountains:* the north.

75, 9: *A cup:* see note on Ps 11, 6. Here it is "the cup of God's wrath," the punishment he inflicts on sinners. Cf 51, 17; Jer 25, 15-29; 49, 12; Ez 23, 31ff. *Spiced:* literally, "a mixed drink"; spices or drugs were put into wine to make it more intoxicating. Cf Is 5, 22; Prv 9, 2.5.

Ps 76: A hymn of triumph in which Jerusalem's victory is

✱   16: Gn 1, 14-19.   75/9: Jer 25, 15-29.

³† In Salem is his abode;
  his dwelling is in Zion.
⁴ There he shattered the flashing
  shafts of the bow,
  shield and sword, and weapons of
  war.

II

⁵† Resplendent you came, O powerful
  One,
  from the everlasting mountains.
⁶† Despoiled are the stouthearted;
  they sleep their sleep;
  the hands of all the mighty ones
  have failed.
⁷ At your rebuke, O God of Jacob,
  chariots and steeds lay stilled.

III

⁸ You are terrible; and who can
  withstand you
  for the fury of your anger?
⁹ From heaven you made your
  intervention heard;
  the earth feared and was silent
¹⁰ When God arose for judgment,
  to save all the afflicted of the earth.

IV

¹¹† For wrathful Edom shall glorify you,
  and the survivors of Hamath shall
  keep your festivals.
¹² Make vows to the LORD, your God,
  and fulfill them;
  let all round about him bring gifts
  to the terrible Lord
¹³† Who checks the pride of princes,
  who is terrible to the kings of the
  earth.

Lament and Comfort in Time of Distress

77† ¹ For the leader; 'al Jeduthun. A psalm of
Asaph.

I

² Aloud to God I cry;
  aloud to God, to hear me;
³ on the day of my distress I seek
  the Lord.
  By night my hands are stretched out
  without flagging;
  my soul refuses comfort.
⁴ When I remember God, I moan;
  when I ponder, my spirit grows
  faint.
⁵ You keep my eyes watchful;
  I am troubled and cannot speak.

⁶* I consider the days of old;
  the years long past ⁷I remember.
  In the night I meditate in my heart;
  I ponder, and my spirit broods:
⁸ "Will the Lord reject forever
  and nevermore be favorable?
⁹ Will his kindness utterly cease,
  his promise fail for all
  generations?
¹⁰ Has God forgotten pity?
  Does he in anger withhold his
  compassion?"
¹¹† And I say, "This is my sorrow,
  that the right hand of the Most
  High is changed."
¹² I remember the deeds of the LORD;
  yes, I remember your wonders of
  old.
¹³ And I meditate on your works;
  your exploits I ponder.

II

¹⁴* O God, your way is holy;
  what great god is there like our
  God?
¹⁵ You are the God who works
  wonders;
  among the peoples you have made
  known your power.
¹⁶ With your strong arm you redeemed
  your people,
  the sons of Jacob and Joseph.
¹⁷ The waters saw you, O God;
  the waters saw you and
  shuddered;
  the very depths were troubled.

---

† attributed primarily to God (2-4). He has overwhelmed the enemy (5-7) and avenged the oppressed (8-10); to him, therefore, sacrifices of thanksgiving are due (11-13).

76, 3: *Salem:* Jerusalem. Perhaps on account of its allusion to the Hebrew word for peace, this ancient form of the city's name was chosen here. Cf Gn 14, 18; Heb 7, 1f.

76, 5: *From the everlasting mountains:* from the temple on Mount Zion, the "ancient," age-old fortress of the Jebusites. Cf Ps 24, 7.9.

76, 6: *Their sleep:* of death.

76, 11: *Edom . . . Hamath:* the words are not certain. The reference would be to Israel's pagan neighbors south and north. The current Hebrew text may perhaps be rendered, "For the wrath of man must be turned to your praise, and the survivors of fury shall keep your festivals."

76, 13: *Checks the pride:* or perhaps, "Cuts short the courage"; literally, "Shortens (or cuts off) the spirit." The Syriac version renders this as, "Humbles the pride"; the Greek version as, "Cuts off the life."

Ps 77: The first section (2-13) is a lamentation in which the psalmist bewails, probably not his own misfortune, but rather the seeming abandonment of his nation by God; the second section (14-21) is in the tones of a typical hymn of praise, which the psalmist perhaps borrowed from an older hymn, in order to contrast the present situation with God's glorious deeds in the past, particularly in the Exodus.

77, 11: *The right hand of the Most High:* God's strong guidance and protection. Cf Pss 17, 7; 18, 36; Is 41, 10.

77/6: Dt 32, 7; Ps 143, 5.　　　14f: Ex 15, 11; Ps 86, 10.

18 The clouds poured down water;
  the skies gave forth their voice;
  your arrows also sped abroad.
19 Your thunder resounded in the
    whirlwind;
  your lightning illumined the
    world;
  the earth quivered and quaked.
20 Through the sea was your way,
  and your path through the deep
    waters,
  though your footsteps were not
    seen.
21* You led your people like a flock
  under the care of Moses and
    Aaron.

God's Goodness despite Israel's Ingratitude

78† 1 A *maskil* of Asaph.

Hearken, my people, to my teaching;
  incline your ears to the words of
    my mouth.
2*† I will open my mouth in a parable,
  I will utter mysteries from of old.
3* What we have heard and know,
  and what our fathers have
    declared to us,
4 We will not hide from their sons;
  we will declare to the generation
    to come
The glorious deeds of the LORD and
    his strength
  and the wonders that he wrought.
5 He set it up as a decree in Jacob,
  and established it as a law in
    Israel,
That what he commanded our
    fathers
  they should make known to their
    sons;
6 So that the generation to come might
    know,
  their sons yet to be born,
That they too may rise and declare
    to their sons
7 that they should put their hope in
    God,
And not forget the deeds of God
  but keep his commands,
8 And not be like their fathers,
  a generation wayward and
    rebellious,

A generation that kept not its heart
    steadfast
  nor its spirit faithful toward God.

I

9† The sons of Ephraim, ordered ranks
    of bowmen,
  retreated in the day of battle.
10 They kept not the covenant with
    God;
  according to his law they would
    not walk;
11 And they forgot his deeds,
  the wonders he had shown them.
12† Before their fathers he did wondrous
    things,
  in the land of Egypt, in the plain
    of Zoan.
13* He cleft the sea and brought them
    through,
  and he made the waters stand as
    in a mound.
14* He led them with a cloud by day,
  and all night with a glow of fire.
15* He cleft the rocks in the desert
  and gave them water in copious
    floods.
16 He made streams flow from the crag
  and brought the waters forth in
    rivers.

II

17* But they sinned yet more against
    him,
  rebelling against the Most High in
    the wasteland,

---

† Ps 78: A didactic psalm, drawing salutary lessons from Israel's history. Cf Pss 106; 107. After an elaborate introduction on the importance of handing down the tradition of God's dealings with his people (1-8), the psalmist teaches that the Northern Kingdom of Israel became disloyal to God (9-11), just as did their forefathers for whom God had worked wonders in the Exodus (12-16) and in the journey through the wilderness (17-31); these ancestors were punished for giving mere lip service to God (32-39) although they had witnessed his power in the plagues of Egypt (40-51) and in the journey to the Promised Land (52-55); so also God rejected their descendants, the Israelites of the northern kingdom (56-64) and chose Judah and the house of David (65-72).

78, 2: This verse is applied by St. Matthew to our Lord's teaching in parables (Mt 13, 35). *A parable:* the Hebrew word *mashal* signifies properly, "a comparison," then any saying in which some deeper meaning lies, to be understood by means of the hidden comparison; here the entire psalm is a *mashal. Mysteries from of old:* the meanings which the psalmist sees hidden in the ancient history of his ancestors.

78, 9: *Ephraim:* the most important of the northern tribes of Israel; hence here, as often, the northern kingdom in general.

78, 12.43: *Zoan:* a city in the delta of the Nile, the capital of Egypt at the time of the Exodus.

✿
21: Ex 12, 51; Ps 78, 52f;
  Is 63, 11f; Hos 12, 13.
78/2: Ps 49, 4; Mt 13, 35.
  3: Ps 44, 2.
  13: Ex 14, 21f; 15, 8;
  Ps 136, 13.
14: Ex 13, 21; Wis 18, 3.
15f: Ex 17, 6; Nm 20, 11;
  Dt 8, 15; Pss 105, 41;
  114, 8; Wis 11, 4.
17: Dt 9, 7.

18* And they tempted God in their
     hearts
      by demanding the food they
      craved.

19 Yes, they spoke against God, saying,
     "Can God spread a table in the
     desert?

20 For when he struck the rock, waters
     gushed forth,
      and the streams overflowed;
     Can he also give bread
      and provide meat for his people?"

21* Then the LORD heard and was
     enraged;
      and fire blazed up against Jacob,
     and anger rose against Israel,

22 Because they believed not God
     nor trusted in his help.

23 Yet he commanded the skies above
     and the doors of heaven he
     opened;

24* He rained manna upon them for
     food
      and gave them heavenly bread.

25† The bread of the mighty was eaten
     by men;
      even a surfeit of provisions he sent
     them.

26* He stirred up the east wind in the
     heavens,
      and by his power brought on the
     south wind.

27 And he rained meat upon them like
     dust,
      and, like the sand of the sea,
     winged fowl,

28 Which fell in the midst of their camp
     round about their tents.

29 So they ate and were wholly
     surfeited;
      he had brought them what they
     craved.

30 They had not given over their
     craving,
      and their food was still in their
     mouths,

31 When the anger of God rose against
     them
      and slew their best men,
     and laid low the young men of
     Israel.

III

32 Yet for all this they sinned still more
     and believed not in his wonders.

33 Therefore he quickly ended their
     days
      and their years with sudden
     destruction.

34 While he slew them they sought
     him
      and inquired after God again,

35 Remembering that God was their
     rock
      and the Most High God, their
     redeemer.

36 But they flattered him with their
     mouths
      and lied to him with their tongues,

37 Though their hearts were not
     steadfast toward him,
      nor were they faithful to his
     covenant.

38 Yet he, being merciful, forgave their
     sin
      and destroyed them not;
     Often he turned back his anger
      and let none of his wrath be
     roused.

39 He remembered that they were
     flesh,
      a passing breath that returns not.

IV

40 How often they rebelled against him
     in the desert
      and grieved him in the wilderness!

41 Again and again they tempted God
     and provoked the Holy One of
     Israel.

42 They remembered not his hand
     nor the day he delivered them
     from the foe,

43* When he wrought his signs in Egypt
     and his marvels in the plain of
     Zoan,

44 And changed into blood their
     streams—
      their running water, so that they
     could not drink;

45 He sent among them flies that
     devoured them
      and frogs that destroyed them.

46 He gave their harvest to the
     caterpillar,
      the fruits of their toil to the locust.

47 He killed their vines with hail
     and their sycamores with frost.

48 He gave over to the hail their beasts
     and their flocks to the lightning.

49 He loosed against them his fierce
     anger,

---

* 18ff: Ex 16, 3; Nm 11, 5f;   24: Ex 16, 4.14f; Wis 16,
   Ps 106, 14.   20; Jn 6, 31.
   21: Nm 11, 1.   26-31: Nm 11, 31ff.
                    43-51: Ex 7-12; Ps 105, 27-36.

† 78, 25: *The mighty:* the angels, according to the Greek version and Wis 16, 20. Cf Ps 103, 20.

wrath and fury and strife,
a detachment of messengers of
doom.

50† When he measured the course of his
anger
he spared them not from death,
and delivered their beasts to the
plague.

51 He smote every first-born in Egypt,
the first fruits of manhood in the
tents of Ham;

52* But his people he led forth like sheep
and guided them like a herd in the
desert.

53 He led them on secure and unafraid,
while he covered their enemies
with the sea.

54* And he brought them to his holy
land,
to the mountains his right hand
had won.

55 And he drove out nations before
them;
he distributed their inheritance by
lot,
and settled the tribes of Israel in
their tents.

V

56 But they tempted and rebelled
against God the Most High,
and kept not his decrees.

57 They turned back and were faithless
like their fathers;
they recoiled like a treacherous
bow.

58* They angered him with their high
places
and with their idols roused his
jealousy.

59 God heard and was enraged
and utterly rejected Israel.

60* And he forsook the tabernacle in
Shiloh,
the tent where he dwelt among
men.

61 And he surrendered his strength
into captivity,
his glory into the hands of the foe.

62 He abandoned his people to the
sword
and was enraged against his
inheritance.

63 Fire consumed their young men,
and their maidens were not
betrothed.

64 Their priests fell by the sword,
and their widows sang no dirges.

VI

65 Then the Lord awoke, as wakes from
sleep
a champion overcome with wine;

66† And he put his foes to flight
and cast them into everlasting
disgrace.

67 And he rejected the tent of Joseph,
and the tribe of Ephraim he chose
not;

68 But he chose the tribe of Judah,
Mount Zion which he loved.

69 And he built his shrine like heaven,
like the earth which he founded
forever.

70* And he chose David, his servant,
and took him from the sheepfolds;

71 From following the ewes he brought
him
to shepherd Jacob, his people,
and Israel, his inheritance.

72 And he tended them with a sincere
heart,
and with skillful hands he guided
them.

The Destruction of Jerusalem and Its Temple

79† **1** A psalm of Asaph.

I

O God, the nations have come into
your inheritance;
they have defiled your holy
temple,
they have laid Jerusalem in ruins.

2*† They have given the corpses of your
servants

---

† 78, 50: *Measured*: with his eye, surveyed.

78, 66: *He put his foes to flight*: literally, "He struck his foes back," or, "in the back"; some commentators see in this an allusion to 1 Sm 5, 6.9.

Ps 79: A lamentation of the people over the havoc wrought by the enemy in Jerusalem. The situation may well have been the capture of the city by the Babylonians in 587 B. C. Cf Ps 74. Here the people bewail the destruction and slaughter in the city (1-4), and pray God to avenge them and pardon their sins (5-8) for the sake of his own honor and glory (9f); if he frees the captive Jews and punishes their enemies, they will offer him eternal thanks (11-13).

79, 2f: *The flesh . . . to bury them*: these four lines are quoted somewhat freely in 1 Mc 7, 17 as describing the treacherous slaughter of sixty pious Jews in Jerusalem during the Maccabean wars. But this does not prove that the psalm was written at such a late period.

---

*
52: Ps 77, 21.
54: Ex 15, 17.
58: Lv 26, 30.
60: 1 Sm 4, 3-11; Jer 7,
12-15; 26, 6-9.

70f: 1 Sm 16, 10-13; 2 Sm
7, 8; 2 Chr 6, 6.
79/2f: 1 Mc 7, 17.

as food to the birds of heaven,
the flesh of your faithful ones to
the beasts of the earth.

3 They have poured out their blood
like water
round about Jerusalem,
and there is no one to bury them.

4* We have become the reproach of our
neighbors,
the scorn and derision of those
around us.

II

5 O Lord, how long? Will you be
angry forever?
Will your jealousy burn like fire?

6* Pour out your wrath upon the
nations that acknowledge you
not,
upon the kingdoms that call not
upon your name;

7 For they have devoured Jacob
and laid waste his dwelling.

8 Remember not against us the
iniquities of the past;
may your compassion quickly
come to us,
for we are brought very low.

III

9 Help us, O God our savior,
because of the glory of your name;
Deliver us and pardon our sins
for your name's sake.

10 Why should the nations say,
"Where is their God?"
Let it be known among the nations
in our sight
that you avenge the shedding of
your servants' blood.

IV

11 Let the prisoners' sighing come
before you;
with your great power free those
doomed to death.

12† And repay our neighbors sevenfold
into their bosoms
the disgrace they have inflicted on
you, O Lord.

13 Then we, your people and the sheep
of your pasture,
will give thanks to you forever;
through all generations we will
declare your praise.

Prayer for the Restoration of the Lord's Vineyard

80 **† 1** For the leader; according to "Lilies."
Eduth. A psalm of Asaph.

I

2* O shepherd of Israel, hearken,
O guide of the flock of Joseph!
From your throne upon the
cherubim, shine forth

3 before Ephraim, Benjamin and
Manasseh.
Rouse your power,
and come to save us.

4† O Lord of hosts, restore us;
if your face shine upon us,
then we shall be safe.

II

5 O Lord of hosts, how long will you
burn with anger
while your people pray?

6 You have fed them with the bread of
tears
and given them tears to drink in
ample measure.

7* You have left us to be fought over by
our neighbors,
and our enemies mock us.

8 O Lord of hosts, restore us;
if your face shine upon us,
then we shall be safe.

III

9† A vine from Egypt you transplanted;
you drove away the nations and
planted it.

10 You cleared the ground for it,
and it took root and filled the land.

11† The mountains were hidden in its
shadow;
by its branches, the cedars of God.

---

†
79, 12: *Into their bosoms:* the ample folds at the front of full-length garments were used in accepting gifts or rewards of grain. Cf Lk 6, 38. The same figure is used here for full (sevenfold) punishment.

Ps 80: The Lord's help is besought for Israel, especially for the northern tribes (2f), for they are sorely oppressed by their enemies (5-7); they were once God's well-tended vine (9-12), but now this vineyard is devastated (13-16); therefore his saving help is implored (17-19). The refrain after the first, second and fifth stanzas (4.8.20) perhaps stood originally after the third and fourth stanzas also.

80, 4: *If your face shine upon us:* if God brighten their lives with his gracious smile.

80, 9: *A vine:* a frequent metaphor for Israel. Cf Is 5, 1-7; 27, 2f; Jer 2, 21; Hos 10, 1; Mt 21, 33.

80, 11: *The cedars of God:* the giant cedars of Lebanon, considered as especially planted by God. Cf Nm 24, 6.

4: Ps 44, 14.
6f: Jer 10, 25.
80/2: Ex 25, 22; 1 Sm 4, 4; 2 Sm 6, 2.
7: Ps 44, 14.

12† It put forth its foliage to the Sea,
    its shoots as far as the River.

IV

13 Why have you broken down its
    walls,
    so that every passer-by plucks its
    fruit,
14 The boar from the forest lays it
    waste,
    and the beasts of the field feed
    upon it?
15 Once again, O Lord of hosts,
    look down from heaven, and see;
Take care of this vine,
16†   and protect what your right hand
    has planted
    [the son of man whom you
    yourself made strong].

V

17† Let those who would burn it with
    fire or cut it down
    perish before you at your rebuke.
18 May your help be with the man of
    your right hand,
    with the son of man whom you
    yourself made strong.
19 Then we will no more withdraw
    from you;
    give us new life, and we will call
    upon your name.
20   O Lord of hosts, restore us;
      if your face shine upon us,
      then we shall be safe.

Festive Song with an Admonition to Fidelity

81† 1 For the leader; "upon the *gittith*." Of
Asaph.

A

2 Sing joyfully to God our strength;
    acclaim the God of Jacob.
3 Take up a melody, and sound the
    timbrel,
    the pleasant harp and the lyre.
4✷† Blow the trumpet at the new moon,
    at the full moon, on our solemn
    feast;
5 For it is a statute in Israel,
    an ordinance of the God of Jacob,
6† Who made it a decree for Joseph
    when he came forth from the land
    of Egypt.

B

I

    An unfamiliar speech I hear:
7†   "I relieved his shoulder of the
    burden;
    his hands were freed from the
    basket.
8✷ In distress you called, and I rescued
    you;
    Unseen, I answered you in
    thunder;
    I tested you at the waters of
    Meribah.
9 Hear, my people, and I will
    admonish you;
    O Israel, will you not hear me?
10✷ There shall be no strange god among
    you
    nor shall you worship any alien
    god.
11† I, the Lord, am your God
    who led you forth from the land of
    Egypt;
    open wide your mouth, and I will
    fill it.

II

12 "But my people heard not my voice,
    and Israel obeyed me not;
13 So I gave them up to the hardness of
    their hearts;
    they walked according to their
    own counsels.

---

† 80, 12: *The Sea:* the Mediterranean. *The River:* the Euphrates. Cf Ps 72, 8.

80, 16: *The son of man:* this line is presumably an accidental duplication of the similar line in v 18.

80, 17: *Let those who would burn it:* this line, as here translated, is a reconstruction; but the two halves of the Hebrew line do not properly belong together.

Ps 81: Two distinct sections. The first section (2-6a) is a short song sung on the feast of Booths. The second section (6b-17) is a divine oracle in which the Lord reminds the people that it was he who led them out of Egypt and commanded them at that time to worship no other God but him (7-11); he has punished them for their disobedience, but will now give them victory and prosperity if they obey him (12-17).

81, 4: *Blow the trumpet:* to assemble the people for the feast. This custom was observed on various feasts, but it was especially prescribed for the first day of each month, that is, for the feast of *the new moon,* and in particular for the first day of the seventh month, during which month the feast of Booths, a very *solemn feast,* was celebrated on the fifteenth day, *the full moon.* Cf Lv 23, 24.34-43; Nm 10, 10; 29, 1.12.

81, 6: *An unfamiliar speech I hear:* these words are uttered by a prophet, who then continues to speak in God's name.

81, 7: A reference to the liberation of Israel from slavery in Egypt. *The basket:* for carrying clay to make bricks. Cf Ex 1, 14.

81, 11: *Open wide your mouth, and I will fill it:* God tells the people that, no matter how great their desires, he will fulfill them.

✷ 81/4: Lv 23, 24.34ff;   8: Ex 2, 23f; 19, 16;
    Nm 29, 1.   Nm 20, 13.
                            10f: Ex 20, 2f; Dt 5, 6f.

14 If only my people would hear me,
and Israel walk in my ways,

15 Quickly would I humble their
enemies;
against their foes I would turn my
hand.

16 Those who hated the LORD would
seek to flatter me,
but their fate would endure
forever,

17*† While Israel I would feed with the
best of wheat,
and with honey from the rock I
would fill them."

Judgment against Wicked Judges

82 † 1† A psalm of Asaph.

God arises in the divine assembly;
he judges in the midst of the gods.

I

2 "How long will you judge unjustly
and favor the cause of the wicked?

3 Defend the lowly and the fatherless;
render justice to the afflicted and
the destitute.

4 Rescue the lowly and the poor;
from the hand of the wicked
deliver them.

II

5† "They know not, neither do they
understand;
they go about in darkness;
all the foundations of the earth are
shaken.

6*† I said: You are gods,
all of you sons of the Most High;

7† Yet like men you shall die,
and fall like any prince."

8† Rise, O God; judge the earth,
for yours are all the nations.

Prayer against a Hostile Alliance

83 † 1 A song; a psalm of Asaph.

I

2 O God, do not remain unmoved;
be not silent, O God, and be not
still!

3 For behold, your enemies raise a
tumult,
and they who hate you lift up their
heads.

4 Against your people they plot
craftily;
they conspire against those whom
you protect.

5 They say, "Come, let us destroy their
nation;
let the name of Israel be
remembered no more!"

6 Yes, they consult together with one
mind,
and against you they are allied:

7† The tents of Edom and the
Ishmaelites,
Moab and the people of Hagar,

8 Gebal and Ammon and Amalek,
Philistia with the inhabitants of
Tyre;

9 The Assyrians, too, are leagued with
them;
they are the forces of the sons of
Lot.

II

10† Deal with them as with Midian;
as with Sisera and Jabin at the
torrent Kishon,

11 Who perished at Endor;
they became dung on the ground.

12 Make their nobles like Oreb and
Zeeb;
all their chiefs like Zebah and
Zalmunna,

13 Who said, "Let us take for ourselves
the dwelling place of God."

---

† 81, 17: *Honey . . . rock:* extreme abundance. Cf Jl 4, 18.

Ps 82: The psalmist presents God himself (1) rebuking the unjust judges (2-4) and passing sentences on them (5-7). A short prayer for universal justice concludes the psalm (8). Cf Is 3, 13ff for a similar judgment scene.

82, 1: *The gods:* human judges, who are "godlike" in their prerogative of establishing justice on earth. Cf Ps 58, 2.

82, 5: *The foundations of the earth:* the very basis of law and order. Cf Ps 11, 3.

82, 6: *I said: You are gods:* our Lord's own comment on these words is, "He called them gods to whom the word of God was addressed." Cf Jn 10, 34.

82, 7: *Like men:* like the rest of men.

82, 8: This verse can be fittingly understood as addressed to Christ, to whom all judgment has been given. Cf Jn 5, 22.

Ps 83: The psalmist prays for divine aid against a powerful league of hostile nations (2-5), which he enumerates (6-9), asking God to overcome them as he did Israel's enemies of old (10-13), and to destroy them completely (14-19).

83, 7ff: Apart from *the Assyrians,* all the nations listed here were neighbors of Israel. *The people of Hagar:* a seminomadic tribe of the desert regions east of *Ammon* and *Moab;* cf 1 Chr 5, 10.19f. *Gebal* was a mountain region south of the Dead Sea. History knows of no occasion when all these peoples were leagued together against Israel. Perhaps their names are used here poetically as figures of the hostile Gentiles in general.

83, 10ff: For the historical events here referred to, see Jgs 4-8.

---

* 17: Dt 32, 13f.   82/6: Jn 10, 34.

14 O my God, make them like leaves in
    a whirlwind,
    like chaff before the wind.
15 As a fire raging in a forest,
    as a flame setting the mountains
      ablaze,
16 So pursue them with your tempest
    and rout them with your storm.
17 Darken their faces with disgrace,
    that men may seek your name,
      O LORD.
18 Let them be shamed and put to rout
    forever;
    let them be confounded and
      perish,
19 Knowing that you alone are the
    LORD,
    the Most High over all the earth.

Desire for the Sanctuary

84 † 1 For the leader; "upon the *gittith*." A psalm
of the sons of Korah.

I

2 How lovely is your dwelling place,
    O LORD of hosts!
3 My soul yearns and pines
    for the courts of the LORD.
    My heart and my flesh
      cry out for the living God.
4† Even the sparrow finds a home,
    and the swallow a nest
    in which she puts her young—
    Your altars, O LORD of hosts,
      my king and my God!

II

5 Happy they who dwell in your
    house!
    continually they praise you.
6† Happy the men whose strength you
    are!
    their hearts are set upon the
      pilgrimage:
7 When they pass through the valley
    of the mastic trees
    they make a spring of it;
    the early rain clothes it with
      generous growth.
8 They go from strength to strength;
    they shall see the God of gods in
      Zion.

III

9 O LORD of hosts, hear my prayer;
    hearken, O God of Jacob!
10† O God, behold our shield,
    and look upon the face of your
      anointed.

11 I had rather one day in your courts
    than a thousand elsewhere;
    I had rather lie at the threshold of
      the house of my God
    than dwell in the tents of the
      wicked.
12 For a sun and a shield is the LORD
    God;
    grace and glory he bestows;
    The LORD withholds no good thing
      from those who walk in sincerity.
13 O LORD of hosts,
    happy the men who trust in you!

Prayer for Complete Restoration

85 † 1 For the leader. A psalm of the sons of
Korah.

I

2 You have favored, O LORD, your
    land;
    you have restored the well-being
      of Jacob.
3 You have forgiven the guilt of your
    people;
    you have covered all their sins.
4* You have withdrawn all your wrath;
    you have revoked your burning
      anger.

II

5 Restore us, O God our savior,
    and abandon your displeasure
      against us.
6 Will you be ever angry with us,
    prolonging your anger to all
      generations?
7 Will you not instead give us life;
    and shall not your people rejoice
      in you?

---

† Ps 84: Although similar in style and general content to Pss 42-43, this seems to be one of the "Pilgrim Songs" sung on the journeys to the temple for the annual feasts. The psalmist expresses his ardent longing to visit the house of the Lord (2-4), describing the happiness of those who dwell there at all times or who at least have the privilege of going there as pilgrims (5-8); hence he prays that this privilege may be his (9-13).

84, 4: Since in God's providence even "the birds of the air have nests" (Mt 8, 20), all the more will the Lord welcome his pious pilgrims to the shelter of his sanctuary and the refuge of his altars.

84, 6ff: The Hebrew text of these two verses is obscure in several places.

84, 10: *Our shield:* the king. Cf Ps 89, 19.

Ps 85: After thanking God for the blessings so far received (2-4), the people beseech him to remove the hardships which they still suffer (5-8); then a prophet tells them of the coming happiness which the Lord has revealed to him (9-14). The situation suggests the conditions in Judea during the early postexilic period, fifth century B. C.; the thoughts are likewise similar to those expressed by the postexilic prophets. Cf Hg 1, 5-11; 2, 6-9; Mal 3, 13-21.

---

* 85/4: Ps 14, 7.

8 Show us, O LORD, your kindness,
  and grant us your salvation.

III

9† I will hear what God proclaims;
  the LORD—for he proclaims peace
To his people, and to his faithful
  ones,
  and to those who put in him their
  hope.
10† Near indeed is his salvation to those
  who fear him,
  glory dwelling in our land.
11† Kindness and truth shall meet;
  justice and peace shall kiss.
12 Truth shall spring out of the earth,
  and justice shall look down from
  heaven.
13 The LORD himself will give his
  benefits;
  our land shall yield its increase.
14 Justice shall walk before him,
  and salvation, along the way of
  his steps.

Prayer in Time of Distress

86 † 1 A prayer of David.

I

Incline your ear, O LORD; answer me,
  for I am afflicted and poor.
2 Keep my life, for I am devoted to
  you;
  save your servant who trusts in
  you.
3 You are my God; have pity on me,
  O Lord,
  for to you I call all the day.
4 Gladden the soul of your servant,
  for to you, O Lord, I lift up my
  soul;
5✣ For you, O Lord, are good and
  forgiving,
  abounding in kindness to all who
  call upon you.
6 Hearken, O LORD, to my prayer
  and attend to the sound of my
  pleading.
7 In the day of my distress I call upon
  you,
  for you will answer me.

II

8✣† There is none like you among the
  gods, O Lord,
  and there are no works like yours.
9✣ All the nations you have made shall
  come

and worship you, O Lord,
  and glorify your name.
10 For you are great, and you do
  wondrous deeds;
  you alone are God.

III

11 Teach me, O LORD, your way
  that I may walk in your truth;
  direct my heart that it may fear
  your name.
12 I will give thanks to you, O LORD my
  God,
  with all my heart,
  and I will glorify your name
  forever.
13✣ Great has been your kindness
  toward me;
  you have rescued me from the
  depths of the nether world.
14 O God, the haughty have risen up
  against me,
  and the company of fierce men
  seeks my life,
  nor do they set you before their
  eyes.
15 But you, O Lord, are a God merciful
  and gracious,
  slow to anger, abounding in
  kindness and fidelity.
16 Turn toward me, and have pity on
  me;
  give your strength to your servant,
  and save the son of your
  handmaid.
17 Grant me a proof of your favor,
  that my enemies may see, to their
  confusion,
  that you, O LORD, have helped and
  comforted me.

Zion the Home of All Nations

87 † 1 A psalm of the sons of Korah. A song.

His foundation upon the holy
  mountains

---

† 85, 9: The prophet listens for God's revelation. Cf Hb 2, 1.

85, 10: *Glory:* the glory of the Lord which departed from Jerusalem when the temple was destroyed. Cf Ez 11, 23. Now it returns to the Holy Land. Cf Hg 2, 9.

85, 11-14: The social virtues are here poetically personified as courtiers of the returning king.

Ps 86: A supplication for help (1-7.11-17), divided in the middle by a short hymn of praise (8-10). Several of the verses occur in similar form in various other psalms, and they are here joined together with no close logical sequence.

86, 8: *The gods:* those whom the pagans call "gods." In v 10 the psalmist clearly denies their reality. Cf Ex 15, 11; Dt 4, 7. Some translate the word *elohim* here not as "gods" but as "angels."

Ps 87: A song of Zion, extolling the holy city as the spiritual home of all the nations of the earth.

✣
86/5: Jl 2, 13.   9: Zec 14, 16.
  8: Ex 15, 11; Ps 89, 7.   13: Ps 30, 4.

2†   the LORD loves,
The gates of Zion,
    more than any dwelling of Jacob.

3   Glorious things are said of you,
    O city of God!

4†   I tell of Egypt and Babylon
    among those that know the LORD;
Of Philistia, Tyre, Ethiopia:
    "This man was born there."

5†   And of Zion they shall say:
    "One and all were born in her;
And he who has established her
    is the Most High LORD."

6   They shall note, when the peoples
    are enrolled:
    "This man was born there."

7   And all shall sing, in their festive
    dance:
    "My home is within you."

Lament and Prayer in Affliction

88† 1   A song; a psalm of the sons of Korah. For
the leader; according to *Mahalath*. For
singing; a *maskil* of Heman the Ezrahite.

I

2   O LORD, my God, by day I cry out;
    at night I clamor in your presence.

3   Let my prayer come before you;
    incline your ear to my call for help,

4   For my soul is surfeited with
    troubles
    and my life draws near to the
    nether world.

5*   I am numbered with those who go
    down into the pit;
    I am a man without strength.

6†   My couch is among the dead,
    like the slain who lie in the grave,
Whom you remember no longer
    and who are cut off from your
    care.

7   You have plunged me into the
    bottom of the pit,
    into the dark abyss.

8   Upon me your wrath lies heavy,
    and with all your billows you
    overwhelm me.

9   You have taken my friends away
    from me;
    you have made me an
    abomination to them;
    I am imprisoned, and I cannot
    escape.

II

10   My eyes have grown dim through
    affliction;

    daily I call upon you, O LORD;
    to you I stretch out my hands.

11*†   Will you work wonders for the dead?
    Will the shades arise to give you
    thanks?

12   Do they declare your kindness in the
    grave,
    your faithfulness among those
    who have perished?

13   Are your wonders made known in
    the darkness,
    or your justice in the land of
    oblivion?

III

14   But I, O LORD, cry out to you;
    with my morning prayer I wait
    upon you.

15   Why, O LORD, do you reject me;
    why hide from me your face?

16   I am afflicted and in agony from my
    youth;
    I am dazed with the burden of
    your dread.

17   Your furies have swept over me;
    your terrors have cut me off.

18   They encompass me like water all
    the day;
    on all sides they close in upon me.

19   Companion and neighbor you have
    taken away from me;
    my only friend is darkness.

Prayer for the Fulfillment of God's Promises to David

89† 1   A *maskil* of Ethan the Ezrahite.

I

2†   The favors of the LORD I will sing
    forever;
    through all generations my mouth
    shall proclaim your faithfulness.

---

†

87, 2: *The gates:* the city itself, a common Hebrew idiom.

87, 4: *Egypt:* literally, "Rahab," the name of an ocean monster; here used poetically for Egypt. Cf Ps 89, 11; Is 30, 7.

87, 5: *Of Zion they shall say:* most manuscripts of the Greek version read, "'Mother Zion,' they shall say." St. Paul is probably alluding to this reading when in Gal 4, 26 he speaks of "Jerusalem which is our mother."

Ps 88: The supplication of a desolate man in mortal illness. The psalmist complains that God seems to have abandoned him (2-9); he reminds the Lord that, if he dies, he can no longer praise him (10-13), and bitterly bewails his misery (14-19).

88, 6: *My couch:* the meaning of the Hebrew is uncertain. *Who lie in the grave:* Hebrew thought would lead us to expect, "who are deprived of any grave," and this may have been the original reading. Cf Ps 63, 11.

88, 11ff: See note on Ps 6, 6.

Ps 89: An exilic or post-exilic psalm, but composed in part from older sources. Having announced his theme—God's covenant with David—(2-5), the psalmist first sings the praise of the Lord in phrases reminiscent of much older hymns (6-19).

88/5: Ps 28, 1.   11-13: Ps 6, 6; Is 38, 18;
                             Bar 2, 17.

3   For you have said, "My kindness is
established forever";
in heaven you have confirmed
your faithfulness:

4   "I have made a covenant with my
chosen one,
I have sworn to David my servant:

5*   Forever will I confirm your posterity
and establish your throne for all
generations."

II

6†   The heavens proclaim your wonders,
O Lord,
and your faithfulness, in the
assembly of the holy ones.

7*   For who in the skies can rank with
the Lord?
Who is like the Lord among the
sons of God?

8   God is terrible in the council of the
holy ones;
he is great and awesome beyond
all round about him.

9   O Lord, God of hosts, who is like
you?
Mighty are you, O Lord, and your
faithfulness surrounds you.

10   You rule over the surging of the sea;
you still the swelling of its waves.

11†   You have crushed Rahab with a
mortal blow;
with your strong arm you have
scattered your enemies.

12   Yours are the heavens, and yours is
the earth;
the world and its fullness you have
founded;

13†   North and south you created;
Tabor and Hermon rejoice at your
name.

14   Yours is a mighty arm;
strong is your hand, exalted your
right hand.

15   Justice and judgment are the
foundation of your throne;
kindness and truth go before you.

16†   Happy the people who know the
joyful shout;
in the light of your countenance,
O Lord, they walk.

17   At your name they rejoice all the
day,
and through your justice they are
exalted.

18†   For you are the splendor of their
strength,
and by your favor our horn is
exalted.

19   For to the Lord belongs our shield,
and to the Holy One of Israel, our
king.

III

20*†   Once you spoke in a vision,
and to your faithful ones you said:
"On a champion I have placed a
crown;
over the people I have set a youth.

21*   I have found David, my servant;
with my holy oil I have anointed
him,

22   That my hand may be always with
him,
and that my arm may make him
strong.

23   "No enemy shall deceive him,
nor shall the wicked afflict him.

24   But I will crush his foes before him
and those who hate him I will
smite.

25   My faithfulness and my kindness
shall be with him,
and through my name shall his
horn be exalted.

---

† The divine promises to David, as narrated in 2 Sm 7, 8-16, are then retold here at considerable length (20-38), in order to contrast these with the present sad state of affairs (39-46), when God seems to have forgotten his promises (47-52).

89, 2: *The favors of the Lord:* the promise of an everlasting dynasty which God made to David through the prophet Nathan. Cf v 50.

89, 6, 8: *The holy ones:* the heavenly spirits, called the *sons of God* in v 7.

89, 11: *Rahab:* a mythological sea monster whose name is used in the Bible mainly as a poetical personification of the primeval chaos of Gn 1, 2.6f. Here it is a symbol of God's dominion over the sea and over all rebellious creatures. Cf Jb 9, 13; 26, 12; Ps 74, 13f; Is 51, 9.

89, 13: *North and south:* in Hebrew, *saphon* and *yamin,* which some retain here as proper nouns, the names of mountains sacred to the ancients, in order to have a better parallelism with the two mountains *Tabor and Hermon,* in the second half of the verse. "Saphon" is indeed mentioned elsewhere in a similar sense. Cf Ps 48, 3; Is 14, 13. However, no "Mount Yamin" is known; perhaps it may be taken here as a synonym for Sinai.

89, 16: *The joyful shout:* one of the characteristic features of Israelite public worship of God.

89, 18.25: *Horn:* a symbol of strength. See note on Ps 18, 3.

89, 20: *Your faithful ones:* Nathan and David.

* 89/5: 2 Sm 7, 16; Ps 132, 11.   20-38: 2 Sm 7, 4.8-16;
     7ff: Ex 15, 11; Ps 86, 8.   1 Chr 17, 3.7-14.
                                 21: Acts 13, 22.

26†   I will set his hand upon the sea,
     his right hand upon the rivers.

27   "He shall say of me, 'You are my
     father,
     my God, the rock, my savior.'

28   And I will make him the first-born,
     highest of the kings of the earth.

29   Forever I will maintain my kindness
     toward him,
     and my covenant with him stands
     firm.

30†   I will make his posterity endure
     forever
     and his throne as the days of
     heaven.

31*†   "If his sons forsake my law
     and walk not according to my
     ordinances,

32   If they violate my statutes
     and keep not my commands,

33   I will punish their crime with a rod
     and their guilt with stripes.

34   Yet my kindness I will not take from
     him,
     nor will I belie my faithfulness.

35   "I will not violate my covenant;
     the promise of my lips I will not
     alter.

36   Once, by my holiness, have I sworn;
     I will not be false to David.

37   His posterity shall continue forever,
     and his throne shall be like the sun
     before me;

38   Like the moon, which remains
     forever—
     a faithful witness in the sky."

IV

39*   Yet you have rejected and spurned
     and been enraged at your
     anointed.

40   You have renounced the covenant
     with your servant,
     and defiled his crown in the dust.

41   You have broken down all his walls;
     you have laid his strongholds in
     ruins.

42   All who pass by the way have
     plundered him;
     he is made the reproach of his
     neighbors.

43   You have exalted the right hands of
     his foes,
     you have gladdened all his
     enemies.

44   You have turned back his sharp
     sword
     and have not sustained him in
     battle.

45†   You have deprived him of his luster
     and hurled his throne to the
     ground.

46   You have shortened the days of his
     youth;
     you have covered him with shame.

V

47   How long, O Lord? Will you hide
     yourself forever?
     Will your wrath burn like fire?

48   Remember how short my life is;
     how frail you created all the
     children of men!

49   What man shall live, and not see
     death,
     but deliver himself from the
     power of the nether world?

50   Where are your ancient favors,
     O Lord,
     which you pledged to David by
     your faithfulness?

51   Remember, O Lord, the insults to
     your servants:
     I bear in my bosom all the
     accusations of the nations

52   With which your enemies have
     reviled, O Lord,
     with which they have reviled your
     anointed on his way!

*   *   *

53*†   Blessed be the Lord forever.
     Amen, and amen!

IV: THE FOURTH BOOK—Psalms 90-106

God's Eternity and Man's Frailty

90†   1   A prayer of Moses, the man of God.

I

O Lord, you have been our refuge
     through all generations.

---

† 89, 26: *The sea:* the Mediterranean to the west. *The rivers:* the Euphrates and its tributaries to the east.

89, 30: *As the days of heaven:* as steadfast as the sun in the sky. Cf Ps 72, 5.17 and vv 37f of this psalm.

89, 31-38: Note that God's promises are in part provisional and in part absolute. Inasmuch as David's descendants failed to carry out the conditions of the covenant, God did not fulfill his promises to them. But as absolute promises they find complete fulfillment in the Son of God who is also the Son of David.

89, 45: The Hebrew text of this verse is somewhat obscure.

89, 53: The doxology at the end of the Third Book of the Psalms; it is not a part of the preceding psalm.

Ps 90: A meditation on the brevity and misery of life. The

31-33: Lv 26, 14-33.   53: Pss 41, 14; 72, 18f;
39-46: Ps 44, 10-25.   106, 48.

2 Before the mountains were begotten
　　and the earth and the world were
　　　brought forth,
　　from everlasting to everlasting
　　　you are God.

3† You turn man back to dust,
　　saying, "Return, O children of
　　　men."

4† For a thousand years in your sight
　　are as yesterday, now that it is
　　　past,
　　or as a watch of the night.

5† You make an end of them in their
　　　sleep;
　　the next morning they are like the
　　　changing grass,

6† Which at dawn springs up anew,
　　but by evening wilts and fades.

II

7 Truly we are consumed by your
　　　anger,
　　and by your wrath we are put to
　　　rout.

8 You have kept our iniquities before
　　　you,
　　our hidden sins in the light of your
　　　scrutiny.

9 All our days have passed away in
　　　your indignation;
　　we have spent our years like a sigh.

10 Seventy is the sum of our years,
　　or eighty, if we are strong,
　　And most of them are fruitless toil,
　　　for they pass quickly and we drift
　　　away.

11 Who knows the fury of your anger
　　or your indignation toward those
　　　who should fear you?

III

12 Teach us to number our days aright,
　　that we may gain wisdom of heart.

13 Return, O Lord! How long?
　　Have pity on your servants!

14 Fill us at daybreak with your
　　　kindness;
　　that we may shout for joy and
　　　gladness all our days.

15† Make us glad, for the days when you
　　　afflicted us,
　　for the years when we saw evil.

16 Let your work be seen by your
　　　servants
　　and your glory by their children;

17† And may the gracious care of the
　　　Lord our God be ours;

prosper the work of our hands for
　　us!
[Prosper the work of our hands!]

Security under God's Protection

I

91 **1** You who dwell in the shelter of the
　　　Most High,
　　who abide in the shadow of the
　　　Almighty,

2 Say to the Lord, "My refuge and
　　　my fortress,
　　my God, in whom I trust."

3 For he will rescue you from the snare
　　of the fowler,
　　from the destroying pestilence.

4 With his pinions he will cover you,
　　and under his wings you shall take
　　　refuge;
　　his faithfulness is a buckler and a
　　　shield.

5 You shall not fear the terror of the
　　　night
　　nor the arrow that flies by day;

6 Not the pestilence that roams in
　　　darkness
　　nor the devastating plague at
　　　noon.

7 Though a thousand fall at your side,
　　ten thousand at your right side,
　　near you it shall not come.

8† Rather with your eyes shall you
　　　behold
　　and see the requital of the wicked,

9 Because you have the Lord for your
　　　refuge;
　　you have made the Most High
　　　your stronghold.

---

psalmist contrasts God's eternity with man's short span of life on earth (1-6), and sees in suffering and death the punishment for sin (7-11); he prays God to grant him some respite of happiness before death (12-17).

90, 3: *Saying, "Return . . .":* one word of God is enough to reduce man to the dust from which he was created. There is an allusion here to the sentence passed on Adam after the fall. Cf Gn 2, 7; 3, 19.

90, 4: *A watch of the night:* the Hebrews divided the night into three sentry periods or "watches." Cf Jgs 7, 19.

90, 5: The Hebrew text is obscure and variously translated. The revised Latin Psalter renders it, "You make an end of them; they become like sleep at dawn."

90, 6: The transitory nature of grass under the scorching sun of the Orient was proverbial. Cf Pss 103, 15f; 129, 6; Is 40, 6ff.

90, 15: *For the days when:* either, "as a recompense for the days when," or, "for as many days as."

90, 17: *Prosper the work of our hands:* the second occurrence of these words is probably an accidental repetition.

Ps 91: By means of various metaphors the psalmist indicates the benefits of trusting in God (1-13); in the epilogue God himself speaks, confirming the psalmist's words (14-16).

91, 8: *Rather with your eyes:* the pious man will be a spectator of these plagues and afflictions without being struck himself.

90/2: Ps 93, 2; Hb 1, 12.　　　　91/2: 2 Sm 22, 3; Ps 18, 3.
10: Sir 18, 8; Is 65, 20.

10 No evil shall befall you,
   nor shall affliction come near your
     tent,
11*† For to his angels he has given
   command about you,
     that they guard you in all your
     ways.
12 Upon their hands they shall bear you
   up,
     lest you dash your foot against a
     stone.
13 You shall tread upon the asp and the
   viper;
     you shall trample down the lion
     and the dragon.

II

14 Because he clings to me, I will
   deliver him;
     I will set him on high because he
     acknowledges my name.
15 He shall call upon me, and I will
   answer him;
     I will be with him in distress;
     I will deliver him and glorify him;
16   with length of days I will gratify
     him
     and will show him my salvation.

Praise of God's Just Government of Mankind

92 † 1 A psalm; a song for the sabbath day.

I

2 It is good to give thanks to the LORD,
   to sing praise to your name, Most
     High,
3 To proclaim your kindness at dawn
   and your faithfulness throughout
     the night,
4 With ten-stringed instrument and
   lyre,
     with melody upon the harp.
5 For you make me glad, O LORD, by
   your deeds;
     at the works of your hands I
     rejoice.

II

6* How great are your works, O LORD!
   How very deep are your thoughts!
7 A senseless man knows not,
   nor does a fool understand this.
8 Though the wicked flourish like
   grass
     and all evildoers thrive,

9 They are destined for eternal
   destruction;
     while you, O LORD, are the Most
     High forever.

III

10 For behold, your enemies, O LORD,
   for behold, your enemies shall
     perish;
     all evildoers shall be scattered.
11† You have exalted my horn like the
   wild bull's;
     you have anointed me with rich
     oil.
12 And my eye has looked down upon
   my foes,
     and my ears have heard of the fall
     of my wicked adversaries.

IV

13 The just man shall flourish like the
   palm tree,
     like a cedar of Lebanon shall he
     grow.
14† They that are planted in the house
   of the LORD
     shall flourish in the courts of our
     God.
15 They shall bear fruit even in old age;
   vigorous and sturdy shall they be,
16 Declaring how just is the LORD,
   my Rock, in whom there is no
     wrong.

The Glory of the Lord's Kingdom

93 † 1† The LORD is king, in splendor robed;
   robed is the LORD and girt about
     with strength;
    And he has made the world firm,
     not to be moved.

---

† 91, 11f: These words were quoted by Satan when he tempted Christ to presumption against God's providence. This promise would not be true if we should put ourselves unnecessarily into danger. *His angels:* the doctrine of guardian angels is common in the Old Testament. Cf Gn 24, 7; Ex 23,20; Ps 34, 8.

Ps 92: A hymn extolling God's just deeds (2-5); the wicked fail to understand them (6-9), but they will receive their due punishment (10-12), whereas the just will be rewarded with blessedness (13-16).

92, 11: *My horn like the wild bull's:* see note on Ps 18, 3. The horns of the wild bull, the *bos primigenius,* were especially formidable. Cf Ps 22, 22; Dt 33, 17.

92, 14: *Planted:* the pious are so steadfast in their attendance in the temple that they can figuratively be said to be rooted there. These words do not imply that cedars and palm trees actually grew in the temple. Cf Pss 52, 10; 128, 3.

Ps 93: A hymn in praise of the eternal kingship of the Lord (1f), who triumphs over the stormy forces of rebellion (3f); hence he is always to be obeyed and worshiped (5).

93, 1: *Is king:* literally, "has become a king." This is the cry

11: Mt 4, 6; Lk 4, 10f.   92/6: Ps 104, 24.

2 Your throne stands firm from of old;
from everlasting you are, O Lord.

3† The floods lift up, O Lord,
the floods lift up their voice;
the floods lift up their tumult.

4 More powerful than the roar of
many waters,
more powerful than the breakers
of the sea—
powerful on high is the Lord.

5 Your decrees are worthy of trust
indeed:
holiness befits your house,
O Lord, for length of days.

A Warning to Israel's Oppressors

A

I

94†
1 God of vengeance, Lord,
God of vengeance, show yourself.

2 Rise up, judge of the earth;
render their deserts to the proud.

3 How long, O Lord, shall the wicked,
how long shall the wicked glory,

4 Mouthing insolent speeches,
boasting, all the evildoers?

II

5 Your people, O Lord, they trample
down,
your inheritance they afflict.

6 Widow and stranger they slay,
the fatherless they murder,

7 And they say, "The Lord sees not;
the God of Jacob perceives not."

III

8 Understand, you senseless ones
among the people;
and, you fools, when will you be
wise?

9 Shall he who shaped the ear not
hear?
or he who formed the eye not see?

10 Shall he who instructs nations not
chastise,
he who teaches men knowledge?

11 The Lord knows the thoughts of
men,
and that they are vain.

B

I

12 Happy the man whom you instruct,
O Lord,
whom by your law you teach,

13 Giving him rest from evil days,
till the pit be dug for the wicked.

14 For the Lord will not cast off his
people,
nor abandon his inheritance;

15† But judgment shall again be with
justice,
and all the upright of heart shall
follow it.

II

16 Who will rise up for me against the
wicked?
Who will stand by me against the
evildoers?

17 Were not the Lord my help,
I would soon dwell in the silent
grave.

18 When I say, "My foot is slipping,"
your kindness, O Lord, sustains
me;

19 When cares abound within me,
your comfort gladdens my soul.

III

20 How could the tribunal of wickedness be leagued with you,
which creates burdens in the guise
of law?

21 Though they attack the life of the
just
and condemn innocent blood,

22 Yet the Lord is my stronghold,
and my God the rock of my refuge.

23 And he will requite them for their
evildoing,
and for their wickedness he will
destroy them;
the Lord, our God, will destroy
them.

---

† with which the people acclaimed a new king at his coronation. Therefore this psalm as well as Pss 96, 97 and 99 can be understood as enthronement psalms of the Messiah celebrating the inauguration of his reign.

93, 3: The raging storm is here a figure of chaos and rebellion.

Ps 94: A fervent prayer to God together with an indictment of wicked tyrants and unjust judges. Calling down divine vengeance upon these (1-4), as he sets forth their crimes and blasphemies (5-7), the psalmist directly rebukes them for their folly (8-11); then in a calmer tone he speaks of the blessedness of justice and fidelity to God's law (12-15). Confident of the Lord's assistance (16-19), he affirms his unwavering faith in the triumph of righteousness (20-23).

94, 15: The decisions of the judges will again be just.

A Call to Praise and Obedience

I

95 † **1** Come, let us sing joyfully to the
LORD;
let us acclaim the Rock of our
salvation.
2 Let us greet him with thanksgiving;
let us joyfully sing psalms to him.
3 For the LORD is a great God,
and a great king above all gods;
4 In his hands are the depths of the
earth,
and the tops of the mountains are
his.
5 His is the sea, for he has made it,
and the dry land, which his hands
have formed.

II

6 Come, let us bow down in worship;
let us kneel before the LORD who
made us.
7* For he is our God,
and we are the people he
shepherds, the flock he guides.

III

Oh, that today you would hear his
voice:
8† "Harden not your hearts as at
Meribah,
as in the day of Massah in the
desert,
9* Where your fathers tempted me;
they tested me though they had
seen my works.
10 Forty years I loathed that
generation,
and I said: They are a people of
erring heart,
and they know not my ways.
11† Therefore I swore in my anger:
They shall not enter into my rest."

The Glories of the Lord, the King of the Universe

I

96 † **1*** Sing to the LORD a new song;
sing to the LORD, all you lands.
2 Sing to the LORD; bless his name;
announce his salvation, day after
day.
3 Tell his glory among the nations;
among all peoples, his wondrous
deeds.

II

4 For great is the LORD and highly to
be praised;
awesome is he, beyond all gods.
5* For all the gods of the nations are
things of nought,
but the LORD made the heavens.
6 Splendor and majesty go before him;
praise and grandeur are in his
sanctuary.

III

7* Give to the LORD, you families of
nations,
give to the LORD glory and praise;
8 give to the LORD the glory due his
name!
Bring gifts, and enter his courts;
9 worship the LORD in holy attire.
Tremble before him, all the earth;
10 say among the nations: The LORD
is king.
He has made the world firm, not to
be moved;
he governs the peoples with
equity.

IV

11 Let the heavens be glad and the
earth rejoice;
let the sea and what fills it
resound;
12 let the plains be joyful and all that
is in them!
Then shall all the trees of the forest
exult
13 before the LORD, for he comes;
for he comes to rule the earth.
He shall rule the world with justice
and the peoples with his
constancy.

---

† Ps 95: The *Venite Exsultemus*, the psalm which daily opens the Divine Office of the church. Twice the psalmist invites the people to praise and worship the Lord (1f.6), for he is king of all his creatures (3-5) and shepherd of his flock (7a-b). In the last strophe the psalmist, speaking in God's name, warns the people to be more faithful to him than were their forefathers in the journey to the Promised Land (7c-11).

95, 8: *Meribah:* literally, "contention"; the place where the Israelites quarreled with the Lord. *Massah:* the place of "testing," where they put him to the trial. Cf Ex 17, 7; Nm 20, 13.

95, 11: *My rest:* in Heb 4 this is applied to the eternal rest of heaven; here it refers directly to the Promised Land.

Ps 96: A hymn inviting all mankind to praise the glories of the Lord (1-3), for he alone is God (4-6); to the just king of all men belongs adoration (7-10); even inanimate creation should praise him (11ff). This psalm somewhat altered occurs in 1 Chr 16, 23-33.

95/7c-11: Heb 3, 7-11.15;   96/1-13; 1 Chr 16, 23-33.
     4, 3.5.7.   5: 1 Cor 8, 4.
     9: Nm 14, 22.   7ff: Ps 29, 2.

The Divine King, the Just Judge of All

I

97 † 1   The LORD is king; let the earth rejoice;
    let the many isles be glad.
2*   Clouds and darkness are round about him,
    justice and judgment are the foundation of his throne.
3   Fire goes before him
    and consumes his foes round about.
4   His lightnings illumine the world;
    the earth sees and trembles.
5   The mountains melt like wax before the LORD,
    before the Lord of all the earth.
6   The heavens proclaim his justice,
    and all peoples see his glory.

II

7†   All who worship graven things are put to shame,
    who glory in the things of nought;
    all gods are prostrate before him.
8   Zion hears and is glad,
    and the cities of Judah rejoice
    because of your judgments,
    O LORD.
9   Because you, O LORD, are the Most High over all the earth,
    exalted far above all gods.
10   The LORD loves those that hate evil;
    he guards the lives of his faithful ones;
    from the hand of the wicked he delivers them.
11   Light dawns for the just;
    and gladness, for the upright of heart.
12   Be glad in the LORD, you just,
    and give thanks to his holy name.

The Lord, the Victorious King and Just Judge

98 † 1†   A psalm.

I

Sing to the LORD a new song,
    for he has done wondrous deeds;
His right hand has won victory for him,
    his holy arm.

2   The LORD has made his salvation known:
    in the sight of the nations he has revealed his justice.
3   He has remembered his kindness
    and his faithfulness
    toward the house of Israel.
All the ends of the earth have seen
    the salvation by our God.

II

4   Sing joyfully to the LORD, all you lands;
    break into song; sing praise.
5   Sing praise to the LORD with the harp,
    with the harp and melodious song.
6   With trumpets and the sound of the horn
    sing joyfully before the King, the LORD.

III

7   Let the sea and what fills it resound,
    the world and those who dwell in it;
8   Let the rivers clap their hands,
    the mountains shout with them for joy
9   Before the LORD, for he comes,
    for he comes to rule the earth;
He will rule the world with justice
    and the peoples with equity.

The Lord the Holy King

I

99 † 1†   The LORD is king; the peoples tremble;
    he is throned upon the cherubim;
    the earth quakes.

---

†

Ps 97: The first stanza of this hymn is a theophany portraying the coming of the Lord as judge (1-6); Israel rejoices to behold the overthrow of paganism (7-9) and the rewarding of the true worshipers of God (10-12).

97, 7: *All gods:* some render, with the Greek, "All the angels." Cf Heb 1, 6.

Ps 98: A hymn of praise, very similar to Ps 96, extolling the Lord for the victory he has given to Israel (1-3); all the nations of the earth and even inanimate creation should welcome the just Savior with joy (4-9).

98, 1: *His right hand . . . his holy arm:* concrete expressions for God's infinite power.

Ps 99: Another hymn in praise of the Lord as king, but here with special emphasis on his holiness. Each of the three strophes ends in a varying refrain (3b.5.9). The people extol the Lord's majesty (1-3a) and just rule (4), as well as his dealings with their great leaders of old (6-8).

99, 1: *The cherubim:* the figures of angels with outspread wings on the ark of the covenant. Cf Ex 25, 22; 1 Sm 4, 4; 2 Sm 6, 2; Ps 80, 2.

❖
97/2: Ex 19, 16; Dt 4, 11;
    5, 22; 1 Kgs 8, 12.

2 The Lord in Zion is great,
  he is high above all the peoples.

3 Let them praise your great and
    awesome name;
      holy is he!

II

4 The King in his might loves
    justice;
  you have established equity;
  justice and judgment in Jacob
    you have wrought.

5† Extol the Lord, our God,
    and worship at his
    footstool;
      holy is he!

III

6 Moses and Aaron were among his
    priests,
  and Samuel, among those who
    called upon his name;
  they called upon the Lord, and
    he answered them.

7✣ From the pillar of cloud he spoke
    to them;
  they heard his decrees and the
    law he gave them.

8 O Lord, our God, you answered
    them;
  a forgiving God you were to
    them,
  though requiting their mis-
    deeds.

9 Extol the Lord, our God,
    and worship at his holy
    mountain;
      for holy is the Lord, our
      God.

Processional Hymn

100† 1 A psalm of thanksgiving.

Sing joyfully to the Lord, all you
    lands;

2 serve the Lord with gladness;
  come before him with joyful
    song.

3† Know that the Lord is God;
  he made us, his we are;
  his people, the flock he tends.

4 Enter his gates with thanksgiving,
    his courts with praise;
  Give thanks to him; bless his
    name, **5**for he is good:
    the Lord, whose kindness
    endures forever,
  and his faithfulness, to all
    generations.

Norm of Life for Rulers

101† 1 A psalm of David.

Of kindness and judgment I will
    sing;
  to you, O Lord, I will sing
    praise.

2† I will persevere in the way of
    integrity;
  when will you come to me?

I will walk in the integrity of my
    heart,
  within my house;

3 I will not set before my eyes
  any base thing.
I hate him who does perversely;
  he shall not remain with me.

4 A crooked heart shall be far from
    me;
  evil I will not know.

5 Whoever slanders his neighbor in
    secret,
  him will I destroy.
The man of haughty eyes and
    puffed-up heart
  I will not endure.

6 My eyes are upon the faithful of
    the land,
  that they may dwell with me.
He who walks in the way of
    integrity
  shall be in my service.

7 He shall not dwell within my
    house
  who practices deceit.
He who speaks falsehood shall not
    stand
  before my eyes.

8† Each morning I will destroy
  all the wicked of the land,
And uproot from the city of the
    Lord
  all evildoers.

---

† 99, 5: *His footstool:* the ark itself. Cf 1 Chr 28, 2; Ps 132, 7.
Ps 100: A short hymn, sung at the solemn entry into the temple, probably in connection with the offering up of a thanksgiving sacrifice.

100, 3: Although the people call on all the nations of the earth to join them in their hymn, they are conscious of being the chosen people of the one true God.

Ps 101: After an introductory strophe setting forth his theme (1-2b), the psalmist pronounces several good resolutions concerning the exercise of his authority, both in his own conduct (2c-4) and in his suppression of evil in others (5-8).

101, 2: *When will you come to me?:* as a reward for his virtue, the psalmist desires union with God. With a slight emendation of the Hebrew text some render, "I will attend to the affairs of the wholehearted man whenever he comes to me."

101, 8: *Each morning:* the normal time for administering justice. Cf 2 Sm 15, 2; Jer 21, 12.

✣ 99/7: Ex 33, 9; Nm 12, 5.

Prayer in Time of Distress

102 † 1   The prayer of an afflicted one when he is faint and pours out his anguish before the Lord.

I

2   O Lord, hear my prayer,
and let my cry come to you.

3   Hide not your face from me
in the day of my distress.
Incline your ear to me;
in the day when I call, answer
me speedily.

4   For my days vanish like smoke,
and my bones burn like fire.

5   Withered and dried up like grass
is my heart;
I forget to eat my bread.

6   Because of my insistent sighing
I am reduced to skin and bone.

7†   I am like a desert owl;
I have become like an owl
among the ruins.

8   I am sleepless, and I moan;
I am like a sparrow alone on the
housetop.

9†   All the day my enemies revile me;
in their rage against me they
make a curse of me.

10   For I eat ashes like bread
and mingle my drink with tears,

11   Because of your fury and your
wrath;
for you lifted me up only to cast
me down.

12 ❋†   My days are like a lengthening
shadow,
and I wither like grass.

II

13   But you, O Lord, abide forever,
and your name through all
generations.

14   You will arise and have mercy on
Zion,
for it is time to pity her,
for the appointed time has
come.

15   For her stones are dear to your
servants,
and her dust moves them to
pity.

16 ❋   And the nations shall revere your
name, O Lord,
and all the kings of the earth
your glory,

17   When the Lord has rebuilt Zion
and appeared in his glory;

18   When he has regarded the prayer
of the destitute,
and not despised their prayer.

19   Let this be written for the
generation to come,
and let his future creatures
praise the Lord:

20   "The Lord looked down from his
holy height,
from heaven he beheld the
earth,

21   To hear the groaning of the
prisoners,
to release those doomed to
die"—

22   That the name of the Lord may be
declared in Zion;
and his praise, in Jerusalem,

23 ❋   When the peoples gather together,
and the kingdoms to serve the
Lord.

III

24   He has broken down my strength
in the way;
he has cut short my days.

25†   I say: O my God,
Take me not hence in the midst of
my days;
through all generations your
years endure.

26 ❋   Of old you established the earth,
and the heavens are the work of
your hands.

27   They shall perish, but you remain
though all of them grow old like
a garment.
Like clothing you change them,
and they are changed,

28   but you are the same, and your
years have no end.

---

† Ps 102: A composite psalm of three distinct parts. In the first section (2-12), the psalmist prays as a man who is very ill and abandoned by all; in the second, he prays for the restoration of Zion (13-18) and for her exiled children (19-23); the third section is a meditation on the brevity of human life compared to God's unchanging eternity (24-29). The psalm in its present form is perhaps a compilation made from parts of older psalms. This is the fifth of the Penitential Psalms.

102, 7: *A desert owl:* what exact species of birds the Hebrew words signify is uncertain, but evidently the solitary life of these birds as well as their desolate surroundings forms the point of comparison. Cf v 8b.

102, 9: *They make a curse of me:* the enemies of the psalmist use his name when they curse, saying to others, "May you be as miserable as this man."

102, 12: *A lengthening shadow:* life's day draws to a close.

102, 25: *In the midst of my days:* when the normal span of life is but half completed. Cf Is 38, 10; Jer 17, 11.

❋
102/12: Jb 8, 9; 14, 2;
Pss 109, 23; 144, 4;
Wis 2, 5.
16: Is 59, 19.
23: Zec 2, 15; 8, 22.
26ff: Heb 1, 10ff.

29 The children of your servants
    shall abide,
  and their posterity shall
    continue in your presence.

Praise of Divine Goodness

103 † 1 Of David.

I

Bless the LORD, O my soul;
  and all my being, bless his holy
    name.
2 Bless the LORD, O my soul,
  and forget not all his benefits;
3 He pardons all your iniquities,
  he heals all your ills.
4 He redeems your life from
    destruction,
  he crowns you with kindness
    and compassion,
5† He fills your lifetime with good;
  your youth is renewed like the
    eagle's.

II

6 The LORD secures justice
  and the rights of all the
    oppressed.
7 He has made known his ways to
    Moses,
  and his deeds to the children of
    Israel.
8❋ Merciful and gracious is the LORD,
  slow to anger and abounding in
    kindness.
9 He will not always chide,
  nor does he keep his wrath
    forever.
10 Not according to our sins does he
    deal with us,
  nor does he requite us according
    to our crimes.

III

11 For as the heavens are high above
    the earth,
  so surpassing is his kindness
    toward those who fear him.
12 As far as the east is from the west,
  so far has he put our
    transgressions from us.
13 As a father has compassion on his
    children,
  so the LORD has compassion on
    those who fear him,
14 For he knows how we are formed;
  he remembers that we are dust.

15 Man's days are like those of grass;
  like a flower of the field he
    blooms;
16 The wind sweeps over him and he
    is gone,
  and his place knows him no
    more.
17 But the kindness of the LORD is
    from eternity
  to eternity toward those who
    fear him,
  And his justice toward children's
    children
18   among those who keep his
      covenant
  and remember to fulfill his
    precepts.

IV

19 The LORD has established his
    throne in heaven,
  and his kingdom rules over all.
20❋ Bless the LORD, all you his angels,
  you mighty in strength, who do
    his bidding,
  obeying his spoken word.
21 Bless the LORD, all you his hosts,
  his ministers, who do his will.
22 Bless the LORD, all his works,
  everywhere in his domain.
  Bless the LORD, O my soul!

Praise of God the Creator

I

104 † 1 Bless the LORD, O my soul!
  O LORD, my God, you are great
    indeed!
  You are clothed with majesty and
    glory,

---

† Ps 103: A hymn of thanksgiving, remarkable for its tender piety, in praise of the Lord's generosity to the psalmist himself (1-5) as well as to his nation (6-10). God's mercy is so great because he knows man's frailty (11-18); therefore the psalmist calls upon the heavenly spirits and all creation to join him in his hymn of grateful praise (19-22).

103, 5: *Your youth is renewed like the eagle's:* because of its long life—sometimes covering the span of a hundred years—the eagle was a symbol of perennial youth and vigor. Cf Is 40, 31. It is doubtful whether there is any allusion here to the fabled phœnix.

Ps 104: A magnificent hymn praising God's creative wisdom and power. Filled with wonder at the glorious works of the Creator, the psalmist depicts in vivid colors the marvels of the atmosphere and sky (1-4); of the dry land and the ocean (5-9); of the streams and fields that give drink and food to man and beast and bird (10-18); of the sun and moon, with the activities of day and night (19-23); and of the manifold life in the mighty sea (24-26). Acknowledging that it is the Lord who governs and sustains all his creatures (27-30), the psalmist proclaims his omnipotence and sanctity (31-35).

103/8: Ex 34, 6; Nm 14, 18.   20f: Ps 148, 2.

2† robed in light as with a cloak.
You have spread out the heavens
like a tent-cloth;

3† you have constructed your
palace upon the waters.
You make the clouds your chariot;
you travel on the wings of the
wind.

4✻† You make the winds your
messengers,
and flaming fire your ministers.

II

5† You fixed the earth upon its
foundation,
not to be moved forever;

6† With the ocean, as with a garment,
you covered it;
above the mountains the waters
stood.

7 At your rebuke they fled,
at the sound of your thunder
they took to flight;

8 As the mountains rose, they went
down the valleys
to the place you had fixed for
them.

9 You set a limit they may not pass,
nor shall they cover the earth
again.

III

10 You send forth springs into the
watercourses
that wind among the mountains,

11 And give drink to every beast of
the field,
till the wild asses quench their
thirst.

12 Beside them the birds of heaven
dwell;
from among the branches they
send forth their song.

13† You water the mountains from
your palace;
the earth is replete with the fruit
of your works.

14 You raise grass for the cattle,
and vegetation for men's use,
Producing bread from the earth,

15 and wine to gladden men's
hearts,
So that their faces gleam with oil,
and bread fortifies the hearts of
men.

16 Well watered are the trees of the
LORD,
the cedars of Lebanon, which he
planted;

17 In them the birds build their nests;
fir trees are the home of the
stork.

18† The high mountains are for wild
goats;
the cliffs are a refuge for
rock-badgers.

IV

19✻ You made the moon to mark the
seasons;
the sun knows the hour of its
setting.

20 You bring darkness, and it is night;
then all the beasts of the forest
roam about;

21 Young lions roar for the prey
and seek their food from God.

22 When the sun rises, they withdraw
and couch in their dens.

23 Man goes forth to his work
and to his tillage till the
evening.

V

24✻ How manifold are your works,
O LORD!
In wisdom you have wrought
them all—
the earth is full of your
creatures;

25 The sea also, great and wide,
in which are schools without
number
of living things both small and
great,

---

†
104, 2: *Light:* created on the first day. In general the psalmist follows the order of creation as given in Gn 1.

104, 3: *Your palace upon the waters:* God's heavenly dwelling above the upper waters of the sky. Cf Gn 1, 6f; Ps 29, 9f.

104, 4: *Flaming fire:* lightning. In Heb 1, 7 this verse is cited as an argument for the superiority of Christ over the angels: if God uses mere wind and lightning as his messengers and ministers, then the ministering spirits in heaven whom God also uses as his messengers must be immeasurably lower than the eternal Son of God. In Greek the argument is more striking because the word *pneuma* means both "wind" and "spirit," while the word *angelos* means both "messenger" and "angel."

104, 5: The ancients compared the earth to a large building set upon firm foundations.

104, 6-9: According to Gn 1, 9f the whole earth was once covered with water; by elevating a part of the earth, God made the dry land appear.

104, 13: God is pictured as sending down the rain from the reservoir of the upper waters referred to in v 3. Cf Gn 7, 11; Jb 38, 22; Sir 43, 14.

104, 18: *Rock-badgers:* the *hyrax syriacus,* a small harelike, ungulate mammal. Cf Lv 11, 5; Dt 14, 7; Prv 30, 26.

✻
104/4: Heb 1, 7.   24: Ps 92, 6.
  19: Sir 43, 6ff.

26† And where ships move about
with Leviathan, which you
formed to make sport of it.

VI

27† They all look to you
to give them food in due time.
28 When you give it to them, they
gather it,
when you open your hand, they
are filled with good things.
29 If you hide your face, they are
dismayed;
if you take away their breath,
they perish
and return to their dust.
30† When you send forth your spirit,
they are created,
and you renew the face of the
earth.

VII

31† May the glory of the Lord endure
forever;
may the Lord be glad in his
works!
32 He who looks upon the earth, and
it trembles;
who touches the mountains,
and they smoke!
33✱ I will sing to the Lord all my life;
I will sing praise to my God
while I live.
34 Pleasing to him be my theme;
I will be glad to the Lord.
35 May sinners cease from the earth,
and may the wicked be no more.
Bless the Lord, O my soul!
Alleluia.

God's Fidelity to His Promise

I

105† 1✱ Give thanks to the Lord, invoke
his name;
make known among the nations
his deeds.
2 Sing to him, sing his praise,
proclaim all his wondrous
deeds.
3 Glory in his holy name;
rejoice, O hearts that seek the
Lord!
4 Look to the Lord in his strength;
seek to serve him constantly.

5 Recall the wondrous deeds that he
has wrought,
his portents, and the judgments
he has uttered,
6 You descendants of Abraham, his
servants,
sons of Jacob, his chosen ones!

7 He, the Lord, is our God;
throughout the earth his
(*II*) judgments prevail.
8 He remembers forever his
covenant
which he made binding for a
thousand generations—
9 Which he entered into with
Abraham
and by his oath to Isaac;
10 Which he established for Jacob by
statute,
for Israel as an everlasting
covenant,
11✱ Saying, "To you will I give the
land of Canaan
as your allotted inheritance."

III

12✱ When they were few in number,
a handful, and strangers there,
13 Wandering from nation to nation
and from one kingdom to
another people,
14† He let no man oppress them,
and for their sake he rebuked
kings:
15† "Touch not my anointed,
and to my prophets do no
harm."

---

†   104, 26: *Ships:* some emend the Hebrew text to read, "sea dragons," for the sake of the parallelism with *Leviathan.* The latter was the name of a mythological sea monster personifying primeval chaos. Cf Ps 74, 14; Is 27, 1. However, in Jb 40, 25 it stands for the crocodile, and here it may well signify the dolphin or some other large marine creature.

104, 27: *They all:* all the creatures, man included, mentioned in vv 10-26.

104, 30: *Your spirit:* the "breath" or spirit of God is the divine creative power, the source of all life in nature. Cf Gn 1, 2; 2, 7. So also the Holy Spirit of God is the source of all supernatural life. Hence, this verse is applied by the church to the Third Person of the Blessed Trinity.

104, 31: *Glad in his works:* Cf Gn 1, 31, "God saw that all he had made was very good."

Ps 105: A hymn in praise of God's goodness as shown in Israel's history. Cf Pss 78; 106; 136. After the introductory invocation (1-7), the psalmist recounts the Lord's promise to the patriarchs (8-11), their early wanderings in Canaan (12-15), the story of Joseph (16-22) and of the Israelites in Egypt (23-27), the Egyptian plagues (28-38), the journey through the desert (39-43), and the occupation of the Promised Land (44f).

105, 14: *Kings:* Pharaoh, and Abimelech of Gerar. Cf Gn 12, 17; 20, 6f.

105, 15: *My anointed . . . my prophets:* the patriarchs, Abra-

---

✱
     33: Ps 146, 2.   11: Gn 12, 7; 15, 18.
105/1-15: 1 Chr 16, 8-22.   12f: Dt 26, 5.

IV

16*† When he called down a famine on
          the land
          and ruined the crop that
          sustained them,

17* He sent a man before them,
          Joseph, sold as a slave;

18* They had weighed him down with
          fetters,
          and he was bound with chains,

19* Till his prediction came to pass
          and the word of the Lord
          proved him true.

20* The king sent and released him,
          the ruler of the peoples set him
          free.

21* He made him lord of his house
          and ruler of all his possessions,

22   That he might train his princes to
          be like him
          and teach his elders wisdom.

V

23*† Then Israel came to Egypt,
          and Jacob sojourned in the land
          of Ham.

24* He greatly increased his people
          and made them stronger than
    (VI) their foes,

25* Whose hearts he changed, so that
          they hated his people,
          and dealt deceitfully with his
          servants.

26   He sent Moses his servant;
          Aaron, whom he had chosen.

27* They wrought his signs among
          them,
          and wonders in the land of
          Ham.

VII

28† He sent the darkness; it grew dark,
          but they rebelled against his
          words.

29   He turned their waters into blood
          and killed their fish.

30   Their land swarmed with frogs,
          even in the chambers of their
          kings.

31   He spoke, and there came swarms
          of flies;
          gnats, throughout all their
          borders.

32   For rain he gave them hail,
          with flashing fires throughout
          their land.

33   He struck down their vines and
          their fig trees
          and shattered the trees
          throughout their borders.

34   He spoke, and there came locusts
          and grasshoppers without
          number;

35   And they devoured every plant
          throughout the land;
          they devoured the fruit of their
          soil.

36   Then he struck every first-born
          throughout their land,
          the first fruits of all their
          manhood.

37* And he led them forth laden with
          silver and gold,
          with not a weakling among their
          tribes.

38   Egypt rejoiced at their going,
          for the dread of them had fallen
          upon it.

VIII

39* He spread a cloud to cover them
          and fire to give them light by
          night.

40* They asked, and he brought them
          quail,
          and with bread from heaven he
          satisfied them.

41* He cleft the rock, and the water
          gushed forth;
          it flowed through the dry lands
          like a stream,

42   For he remembered his holy word
          to his servant Abraham.

43   And he led forth his people with
          joy;
          with shouts of joy, his chosen
          ones.

IX

44   And he gave them the lands of the
          nations,
          and they took what the peoples
          had toiled for,

45   That they might keep his statutes
          and observe his laws.   Alleluia.

†
ham, Isaac and Jacob, who were in a certain sense "anointed," that is, consecrated to God, and were the recipients of his revelations.

105, 16b: Literally, "And broke every staff of bread."

105, 23.27: *The land of Ham*: a synonym for Egypt. Cf Gn 10, 6, where Mizraim is the Hebrew name for Egypt.

105, 28-38: Here, as also in Ps 78, 43-51, the plagues of Egypt are retold with some poetic license, so that the order of the plagues is not quite the same as in Ex 7, 14—12, 30.

*
16: Gn 41, 57.	24: Ex 1, 7; Acts 7, 17.
17: Gn 37, 28.36.	25: Ex 1, 8-14.
18: Gn 39, 20.	27-36: Ex 7-12; Ps 78, 43-51.
19: Gn 40, 21f.	37f: Ex 12, 33-36.
20: Gn 41, 14.	39: Ex 13, 21; Ps 78, 14.
21: Gn 41, 41.44;	40: Ex 16, 13-15; Nm 11,
Acts 7, 10.	31; Ps 78, 24-27.
23: Gn 46, 6; Acts 7, 15.	41: Nm 20, 11.

Israel's Confession of Sin

106 † 1 Alleluia.

A

Give thanks to the LORD, for he is
    good,
    for his kindness endures forever.

2 Who can tell the mighty deeds of
    the LORD,
    or proclaim all his praises?

3 Happy are they who observe what
    is right,
    who do always what is just.

4 Remember me, O LORD, as you
    favor your people;
    visit me with your saving help,

5 That I may see the prosperity of
    your chosen ones,
    rejoice in the joy of your people,
    and glory with your inheritance.

B

I

6 We have sinned, we and our
    fathers;
    we have committed crimes; we
    have done wrong.

7✻ Our fathers in Egypt
    considered not your wonders;
    They remembered not your
    abundant kindness,
    but rebelled against the Most
    High at the Red Sea.

8 Yet he saved them for his name's
    sake,
    to make known his power.

9✻ He rebuked the Red Sea, and it
    was dried up,
    and he led them through the
    deep as through a desert.

10 He saved them from hostile hands
    and freed them from the hands
    of the enemy.

11 The waters covered their foes;
    not one of them was left.

12✻ Then they believed his words
    and sang his praises.

II

13✻ But soon they forgot his works;
    they waited not for his counsel.

14 They gave way to craving in the
    desert
    and tempted God in the
    wilderness.

15 He gave them what they asked
    but sent a wasting disease
    against them.

III

16✻ They envied Moses in the camp,
    and Aaron, the holy one of the
    LORD.

17 The earth opened and swallowed
    up Dathan,
    and covered the faction of
    Abiram.

18 Fire broke out against their
    faction;
    a flame consumed the wicked.

IV

19✻ They made a calf in Horeb
    and adored a molten image;

20 They exchanged their glory
    for the image of a grass-eating
    bullock.

21 They forgot the God who had
    saved them,
    who had done great deeds in
    Egypt,

22 Wondrous deeds in the land of
    Ham,
    terrible things at the Red Sea.

23 Then he spoke of exterminating
    them,
    but Moses, his chosen one,
    Withstood him in the breach
    to turn back his destructive
    wrath.

V

24✻ Yet they despised the desirable
    land;
    they believed not his word.

25 They murmured in their tents,
    and obeyed not the voice of the
    LORD.

26 Then with raised hand he swore
    against them
    to let them perish in the desert,

✻ 106/7: Ex 14, 11f.
9-11: Ex 14, 21-31.
12: Ex 15, 1ff.
13ff: Nm 11, 4ff.31ff;
    Ps 78, 26-31.
16ff: Nm 16.
19-23: Ex 32; Dt 9, 8-29;
    Acts 7, 41.
24-27: Nm 14.

---

†   Ps 106: Like the preceding psalm, this hymn reviews Israel's history, but here the salient thought is the rebellious spirit of the chosen people despite God's goodness to them. After an introductory prayer for God's mercy on himself and on his nation (1-5), the psalmist recounts the lack of faith shown by the Israelites at the Exodus (6-12), their craving for meat in the desert (13-15), the rebellions of Korah, Dathan and Abiram (16-18), the worship of the golden calf at Sinai (19-23), the cowardice and foolhardiness of the Israelites at their first contact with the Canaanites (24-27), their paganism at Peor (28-31), their causing Moses to sin at Meribah (32f), and their mingling with the Canaanites (34-39); confessing that it was their wickedness which made God punish them with repeated calamities and defeats (40-46), the psalmist prays for the return and restoration of scattered Israel (47).

27 To scatter their descendants
among the nations,
and to disperse them over the
lands.

VI

28* And they submitted to the rights of
Baal of Peor
and ate the sacrifices of dead
gods.

29 They provoked him by their
deeds,
and a plague attacked them.

30 Then Phinehas stood forth in
judgment
and the plague was checked;

31 And it was imputed to him for
merit
through all generations forever.

VII

32† They angered him at the waters of
Meribah,
and Moses fared ill on their
account,

33 For they embittered his spirit,
and the rash utterance passed
his lips.

VIII

34* They did not exterminate the
peoples,
as the LORD had commanded
them,

35* But mingled with the nations
and learned their works.

36* They served their idols,
which became a snare for them.

37* They sacrificed their sons
and their daughters to demons,

38 And they shed innocent blood,
the blood of their sons and their
daughters,
Whom they sacrificed to the idols
of Canaan,
desecrating the land with
bloodshed;

39 They became defiled by their
works,
and wanton in their crimes.

C

40 And the LORD grew angry with his
people,
and abhorred his inheritance;

41 He gave them over into the hands
of the nations,
and their foes ruled over them.

42 Their enemies oppressed them,
and they were humbled under
their power.

43 Many times did he rescue them,
but they embittered him with
their counsels
and were brought low by their
guilt.

44 Yet he had regard for their
affliction
when he heard their cry;

45 And for their sake he was mindful
of his covenant
and relented, in his abundant
kindness,

46 And he won for them compassion
from all who held them captive.

47* Save us, O LORD, our God,
and gather us from among the
nations,
That we may give thanks to your
holy name
and glory in praising you.

* * *

48† Blessed be the LORD, the God of
Israel, through all eternity!
Let all the people say, Amen!
Alleluia.

V: THE FIFTH BOOK—Psalms 107-150

God the Savior of Men in Distress

107† 1† "Give thanks to the LORD, for he is
good,
for his kindness endures
forever!"

---

† 106, 32: *Moses fared ill:* refers to the fact that he was not
allowed to enter the Promised Land. Cf Nm 20, 12.

106, 48: The doxology at the end of the Fourth Book of the
Psalms; a later addition.

Ps 107: Besides the prologue (1-3), in which the people thank
the Lord for their return from exile, this psalm consists of two
parts. In the first (4-32), where each of the four stanzas has
the same divided refrain, God is praised as the helper and rescuer of wanderers lost in the wilderness (4-9), of the imprisoned
(10-16), of the sick (17-22), and of storm-tossed seafarers (23-
32). The second part (33-43) describes how God's beneficent
providence changed deserts into fertile fields (33-35) where the
needy found prosperity (36-38); and how, when bad rulers
brought hard times upon them, God restored the fortunes of
the poor (39-41). All this, therefore, should be recognized as
coming from him (42f).

107, 1: A standard cry of praise in the liturgy of the temple,

* 28-31: Nm 25.   37: 2 Kgs 16, 3.
34: Jgs 1, 21.27-35.   47f: 1 Chr 16, 35f;
35: Jgs 3, 5f.   Ps 41, 14.
36: Jgs 2, 12f.17.19.

2 Thus let the redeemed of the Lord
say,
those whom he has redeemed
from the hand of the foe
3 And gathered from the lands,
from the east and the west, from
the north and the south.

A

I

4 They went astray in the desert
wilderness;
the way to an inhabited city
they did not find.
5 Hungry and thirsty,
their life was wasting away
within them.
6 They cried to the Lord in
their distress;
from their straits he
rescued them.
7 And he led them by a direct way
to reach an inhabited city.
8 Let them give thanks to the
Lord for his kindness
and his wondrous deeds
to the children of men,
9 Because he satisfied the longing
soul
and filled the hungry soul with
good things.

II

10* They dwelt in darkness and
gloom,
bondsmen in want and in
chains,
11 Because they had rebelled against
the words of God
and scorned the counsel of the
Most High.
12 And he humbled their hearts with
trouble;
when they stumbled, there was
no one to help them.
13 They cried to the Lord in
their distress;
from their straits he
rescued them.
14 And he led them forth from
darkness and gloom
and broke their bonds asunder.
15 Let them give thanks to the
Lord for his kindness
and his wondrous deeds
to the children of men,

16 Because he shattered the gates of
brass
and burst the bars of iron.

III

17 Stricken because of their wicked
ways
and afflicted because of their
sins,
18 They loathed all manner of food,
so that they were near the gates
of death.
19 They cried to the Lord in
their distress;
from their straits he
rescued them.
20 He sent forth his word to heal
them
and to snatch them from
destruction.
21 Let them give thanks to the
Lord for his kindness
and his wondrous deeds
to the children of men.
22 Let them make thank offerings
and declare his works with
shouts of joy.

IV

23 They who sailed the sea in ships,
trading on the deep waters,
24 These saw the works of the Lord
and his wonders in the abyss.
25 His command raised up a storm
wind
which tossed its waves on high.
26 They mounted up to heaven; they
sank to the depths;
their hearts melted away in
their plight.
27 They reeled and staggered like
drunken men,
and all their skill was swallowed
up.
28 They cried to the Lord in
their distress;
from their straits he
rescued them.
29 He hushed the storm to a gentle
breeze,
and the billows of the sea were
stilled;
30 They rejoiced that they were
calmed,
and he brought them to their
desired haven.

---

† and frequently cited in the Bible. Cf 1 Chr 16, 34; Pss 118, 1;
136, 1; Jer 33, 11; Dn 3, 89; 1 Mc 4, 24.

31 Let them give thanks to the
LORD for his kindness
and his wondrous deeds
to the children of men.

32 Let them extol him in the
assembly of the people
and praise him in the council of
the elders.

B

33◊ He changed rivers into desert,
water springs into thirsty
ground,

34 Fruitful land into salt marsh,
because of the wickedness of its
inhabitants.

35 He changed the desert into pools
of water,
waterless land into water
springs.

36† And there he settled the hungry,
and they built a city to dwell in.

37 They sowed fields and planted
vineyards,
and they obtained a fruitful
yield.

38 He blessed them, and they became
very many;
nor did he suffer their cattle to
decrease.

39 And they dwindled and were
brought low
through oppression, affliction
and sorrow.

40◊ But he who pours out contempt
upon princes,
and sends them astray through
a trackless waste,

41 Lifted up the needy out of misery
and made the families numerous
like flocks.

42 The upright see this and rejoice,
and all wickedness closes its
mouth.

43◊ Who is wise enough to observe
these things
and to understand the favors of
the LORD?

Prayer for Victory

108† **1** A song; a psalm of David.

I

2◊ My heart is steadfast, O God; my
heart is steadfast;
I will sing and chant praise.

3 Awake, O my soul; awake, lyre
and harp;
I will wake the dawn.

4 I will give thanks to you among
the peoples, O LORD;
I will chant your praise among
the nations,

5 For your kindness towers to the
heavens,
and your faithfulness to the
skies.

6 Be exalted above the heavens,
O God;
over all the earth be your glory!

7◊ That your loved ones may escape,
help us by your right hand, and
answer us.

II

8 God promised in his sanctuary:
"Exultantly I will apportion
Shechem,
and measure off the valley of
Succoth;

9 Mine is Gilead, and mine
Manasseh,
Ephraim is the helmet for my
head; Judah, my scepter;

10 Moab shall serve as my washbowl;
upon Edom I will set my shoe;
I will triumph over Philistia."

11 Who will bring me into the
fortified city?
Who will lead me into Edom?

12 Have not you, O God, rejected us,
so that you go not forth, O God,
with our armies?

13 Give us aid against the foe,
for worthless is the help of men.

14 Under God we shall do valiantly;
it is he who will tread down our
foes.

Prayer against a Slanderous Enemy

109† **1** For the leader. A psalm of David.

I

O God, whom I praise, be not
silent,

◊
33f: Is 35, 7; 41, 18; 42, 15.   108/2-6: Ps 57, 8-12.
40: Jb 12, 21.24.   7-14: Ps 60, 7-14.
43: Hos 14, 10.

---

† 107, 36-41: Although his words seem to refer to God's providence in general, the psalmist probably has in mind the settlement and development of the Promised Land (36ff), the hard
times caused by the Assyrian and Babylonian invasions (39), the
humiliation and exile of the last kings of Judah (40), and the
restoration of Zion after the exile (41).

Ps 108: A compilation of parts from two other psalms: 2-6
are the same as Ps 57, 8-12; 7-14 are the same as Ps 60, 7-14.

Ps 109: The first and the third sections are prayers of supplication from one who is cursed and calumniated by numerous
enemies (1-5.20-31). The middle section is a series of strong

2　for they have opened wicked
and treacherous mouths
against me.
They have spoken to me with
lying tongues,

3　and with words of hatred they
have encompassed me
and attacked me without cause.

4　In return for my love they
slandered me,
but I prayed.

5　They repaid me evil for good
and hatred for my love.

II

6†　Raise up a wicked man against
him,
and let the accuser stand at his
right hand.

7　When he is judged, let him go
forth condemned,
and may his plea be in vain.

8*　May his days be few;
may another take his office.

9　May his children be fatherless,
and his wife a widow.

10　May his children be roaming
vagrants and beggars;
may they be cast out of the ruins
of their homes.

11　May the usurer ensnare all his
belongings,
and strangers plunder the fruit
of his labors.

12　May there be no one to do him a
kindness,
nor anyone to pity his orphans.

13　May his posterity meet with
destruction;
in the next generation may their
name be blotted out.

14　May the guilt of his fathers be
remembered by the LORD;
let not his mother's sin be
blotted out;

15　May they be continually before
the LORD,
till he banish the memory of
these parents from the earth,

16　Because he remembered not to
show kindness,
but persecuted the wretched
and poor
and the brokenhearted, to do
them to death.

17　He loved cursing; may it come
upon him;
he took no delight in blessing;
may it be far from him.

18　And may he be clothed with
cursing as with a robe;
may it penetrate into his entrails
like water
and like oil into his bones;

19　May it be for him like a garment
which covers him,
like a girdle which is always
about him.

III

20†　May this be the recompense from
the LORD upon my accusers
and upon those who speak evil
against me.

21　But do you, O GOD, my Lord, deal
kindly with me for your
name's sake;
in your generous kindness
rescue me;

22　For I am wretched and poor,
and my heart is pierced within
me.

23†　Like a lengthening shadow I pass
away;
I am swept away like the locust.

24　My knees totter from my fasting,
and my flesh is wasted of its
substance.

25　And I am become a mockery to
them;
when they see me, they shake
their heads.

26　Help me, O LORD, my God;
save me, in your kindness,

---

†
curses against a certain individual (6-19). Whether the imprecations of this section were uttered by the psalmist himself against
one of his foes, or by these foes against him, is a disputed question; the answer depends principally on the interpretation of
v 20. See note on this verse.

109, 6: *The accuser:* the Hebrew word is *satan.* Cf Zec 3, 1,
where Satan stands at the right hand of the high priest to bring
accusations against him before the Lord. But here a human
accuser is meant, unless the phrase, *a wicked man,* is rendered,
"the wicked one," that is, the devil.

109, 20: *Recompense:* the Hebrew word means either "work
done" or "wages for work done." The above translation takes it
in the latter sense. Accordingly, the preceding dire curses may be
understood either as directly spoken by the psalmist against his
chief enemy, or as spoken first by his enemies against him and
then willed by him to recoil on them. The other possible translation would be, "This is the work of those who would bring
harm upon me from the LORD." In this case the only imprecations of the psalmist himself would be those in v 29, which are
comparatively mild.

109, 23: *Swept away:* a strong wind sometimes ends a plague
of locusts by blowing them out into the sea. Cf Ex 10, 19; Jl 2,
20. Some render, "Shaken off," and understand this of the custom of knocking locusts off the plants in order to kill them on
the ground.

109/8: Acts 1, 20.

27† And let them know that this is
your hand;
that you, O Lord, have done
this.

28† Let them curse, but do you bless;
may my adversaries be put to
shame,
but let your servant rejoice.

29 Let my accusers be clothed with
disgrace
and let them wear their shame
like a mantle.

30 I will speak my thanks earnestly to
the Lord,
and in the midst of the throng I
will praise him,

31 For he stood at the right hand of
the poor man,
to save him from those who
would condemn him.

The Messiah: King, Priest and Conqueror

110 † **1*†** A psalm of David.

I

The Lord said to my Lord: "Sit at
my right hand
till I make your enemies your
footstool."

2 The scepter of your power the
Lord will stretch forth from
Zion:
"Rule in the midst of your
enemies.

3† Yours is princely power in the day
of your birth, in holy
splendor;
before the daystar, like the dew,
I have begotten you."

II

4*† The Lord has sworn, and he will
not repent:
"You are a priest forever,
according to the order of
Melchizedek."

III

5 The Lord is at your right hand;
he will crush kings on the day of
his wrath.

6 He will do judgment on the
nations, heaping up corpses;
he will crush heads over the
wide earth.

7† From the brook by the wayside he
will drink;
therefore will he lift up his
head.

Praise of God for His Goodness

111 † **1*†** Alleluia.

I will give thanks to the Lord with
all my heart
in the company and assembly of
the just.

2 Great are the works of the Lord,
exquisite in all their delights.

3 Majesty and glory are his work,
and his justice endures forever.

4 He has won renown for his
wondrous deeds;
gracious and merciful is the
Lord.

---

† 109, 27: *This:* both the misery suffered and the deliverance expected from the Lord.

109, 28: *Let them curse:* this gives some probability to the view that the imprecations in vv 6-19 were uttered by the enemies of the psalmist.

Ps 110: One of the most important of the messianic psalms. Following the teaching of our Lord and the Apostles, Catholic tradition has constantly and unanimously interpreted this psalm as referring to Christ. However, in some verses the Hebrew text is obscure and the interpretation uncertain. Here is set forth the dignity of the Messiah as the king appointed by God (1-3), as the royal priest (4), and as victor over his foes (5-7).

110, 1: *The Lord said to my Lord:* literally, "The oracle of the Lord (Yahweh) for my Lord." *My Lord:* a Hebrew phrase of polite address, equivalent to "you," and used when a subject addresses his superior. Cf 1 Sm 25, 25ff; 2 Sm 1, 10. The force of our Lord's argument from this passage is as follows: David was universally recognized as the author of this psalm, which was acknowledged by all as referring to the Messiah; but the psalmist addresses the Messiah here as his superior; therefore the Messiah must be David's superior and not merely his "son" or descendant. Cf Mt 22, 41-45 and parallels. *At my right hand:* the place of honor next to the royal throne. Cf 1 Kgs 2, 19. *Your footstool:* in ancient times vanquished enemies had to suffer the victor's putting his feet on their prostrate bodies as a sign of their submission.

110, 3: The current Hebrew text is obscure and seems corrupt. The translation here follows the reading of the revised Latin Psalter, which is based on the ancient versions. *Before the daystar:* when the sun had not yet been created, that is, from all eternity. *Like the dew:* in a secret, mysterious manner.

110, 4: *According to the order of Melchizedek:* in the same way as Melchizedek was a priest. There are three main points of resemblance between Melchizedek, the prophetic type, and Christ who fulfilled this prophecy: both are kings as well as priests, both offer bread and wine to God, and both have their priesthood directly from God and not through Aaron, since neither belongs to the tribe of Levi. Cf Gn 14, 18; Heb 7.

110, 7: Figurative language of uncertain significance. The sense, according to some, is: The messianic King will bow down in humility to drink of the waters of divine assistance, and then go on to new victories. Cf Is 8, 6; Jer 2, 13.17f.

Ps 111: An alphabetic hymn in praise of God's law and of his merciful deeds for Israel. As is customary in such psalms, the thoughts here are rather loosely strung together.

111, 1: *In the company and assembly of the just:* in the temple. Cf Ps 149, 1.

110/1: Mt 22, 44; Acts 2, 34f;   4: Heb 5, 6; 7, 21.
1 Cor 15, 25;   111/1: Ps 138, 1.
Heb 1, 13; 10, 13.

5† He has given food to those who
fear him;
   he will forever be mindful of his
covenant.

6 He has made known to his people
the power of his works,
   giving them the inheritance of
the nations.

7 The works of his hands are faithful
and just;
   sure are all his precepts,

8 Reliable forever and ever,
   wrought in truth and equity.

9 He has sent deliverance to his
people;
   he has ratified his covenant
forever;
   holy and awesome is·his name.

10*† The fear of the LORD is the
beginning of wisdom;
   prudent are all who live by it.
   His praise endures forever.

The Blessings of the Just Man

112† **1** Alleluia.

Happy the man who fears the
LORD,
   who greatly delights in his
commands.

2 His posterity shall be mighty upon
the earth;
   the upright generation shall be
blessed.

3† Wealth and riches shall be in his
house;
   his generosity shall endure
forever.

4† He dawns through the darkness, a
light for the upright;
   he is gracious and merciful and
just.

5 Well for the man who is gracious
and lends,
   who conducts his affairs with
justice;

6 He shall never be moved;
   the just man shall be in
everlasting remembrance.

7 An evil report he shall not fear;
   his heart is firm, trusting in the
LORD.

8 His heart is steadfast; he shall not
fear
   till he looks down upon his foes.

9*† Lavishly he gives to the poor;
his generosity shall endure
forever;
   his horn shall be exalted in
glory.

10 The wicked man shall see it and be
vexed;
   he shall gnash his teeth and pine
away;
   the desire of the wicked shall
perish.

Praise of the Lord for His Care of the Lowly

113† **1†** Alleluia.

I

Praise, you servants of the LORD,
   praise the name of the LORD.

2 Blessed be the name of the LORD
   both now and forever.

3† From the rising to the setting of
the sun
   is the name of the LORD to be
praised.

II

4 High above all nations is the
LORD;
   above the heavens is his glory.

5 Who is like the LORD, our God,
   who is enthroned on high

6 and looks upon the heavens and
the earth below?

---

† 111, 5: *Food to those who fear him:* the manna in the desert. In the liturgy of the church these words are applied to the Blessed Eucharist, of which the manna was the type or figure. Cf Jn 6, 31ff.49ff.

111, 10: *The fear of the Lord:* reverence for God; the Hebrew term for "religion."

Ps 112: An alphabetic psalm of didactic character, lauding the virtues of the God-fearing man. In style and diction this is very similar to the preceding psalm; both may well have had the same author.

112, 3: *Generosity:* the original meaning of the Hebrew word is "justice," but in a later period of the language it also acquired the meaning of "liberality, almsgiving." Cf Sir 3, 30; 7, 10; also Mt 6, 1.

112, 4: Some interpret this verse as said of God. Cf Ps 111, 4b. But more probably the subject of this sentence is the same as the subject of all the preceding and following sentences, that is, the just man. He acts in the same way as God does.

112, 9: *His horn:* his power, dignity and authority. Cf note on Ps 18, 3.

Ps 113: A hymn praying that God may be glorified at all times and in all places (1-3), because he who is supreme over all (4-6) stoops down to raise up the lowly and the barren (7-9).

113, 1: *Servants of the Lord:* devout worshipers; in particular, the Levites. Cf Pss 134, 1; 135, 1; Dn 3, 85.

113, 3: *From the rising to the setting of the sun:* either temporally, "from morning to evening," or spatially," from the east to the west." Cf Mal 1, 11.

❀   10: Jb 28, 28; Prv 1, 7;   112/9: 2 Cor 9, 9.
        9, 10; Sir 1, 16.

III

7 He raises up the lowly from the
dust;
from the dunghill he lifts up the
poor

8 To seat them with princes,
with the princes of his own
people.

9† He establishes in her home the
barren wife
as the joyful mother of children.

The Lord's Wonders at the Exodus

114† **1** Alleluia.

When Israel came forth from
Egypt,
the house of Jacob from a
people of alien tongue,

2 Judah became his sanctuary,
Israel his domain.

3 The sea beheld and fled;
Jordan turned back.

4† The mountains skipped like rams,
the hills like the lambs of the
flock.

5 Why is it, O sea, that you flee?
O Jordan, that you turn back?

6 You mountains, that you skip like
rams?
You hills, like the lambs of the
flock?

7 Before the face of the Lord,
tremble, O earth,
before the face of the God of
Jacob,

8 Who turned the rock into pools of
water,
the flint into flowing springs.

The Greatness and Goodness of the True God

I

115† **1** Not to us, O LORD, not to us
but to your name give glory
because of your kindness,
because of your truth.

2† Why should the pagans say,
"Where is their God?"

3 Our God is in heaven;
whatever he wills, he does.

II

4 Their idols are silver and gold,
the handiwork of men.

5 They have mouths but speak not;
they have eyes but see not;

6 They have ears but hear not;
they have noses but smell not;

7 They have hands but feel not;
they have feet but walk not;
they utter no sound from their
throat.

8 Their makers shall be like them,
everyone that trusts in them.

III

9† The house of Israel trusts in the
LORD;
he is their help and their shield.

10 The house of Aaron trusts in the
LORD;
he is their help and their shield.

11 Those who fear the LORD trust in
the LORD;
he is their help and their shield.

12 The LORD remembers us and will
bless us:
he will bless the house of Israel;
he will bless the house of Aaron;

13 He will bless those who fear the
LORD,
both the small and the great.

14 May the LORD bless you more and
more,
both you and your children.

15 May you be blessed by the LORD,
who made heaven and earth.

---

† 113, 9: Because of the importance in Israel of large families, the barren wife was considered disgraced and cursed by God. Cf Gn 16, 4f; 1 Sm 1, 5f.11; 2, 5; Lk 1, 25.

Ps 114: A song commemorating Israel's deliverance from Egypt. When the Lord chose Israel as his own special people (1f), marvelous things took place in nature (3f) of which he was the cause (5-8). In the Greek and Latin versions, this song is joined to the following one to form a single psalm, but originally they were probably distinct.

114, 4: A poetic description of the earthquake that took place when God appeared on Mount Sinai. Cf Ex 19, 16ff.

Ps 115: A song in praise of the living God (1-3) and in derision of the lifeless idols of the pagans (4-8). To this are added a brief "liturgy," consisting of a litany in which the various classes of the people express their confidence in God (9-11); a blessing given by the priests (12-15); and a short hymn of praise (16-18). In Ps 135, 15-18 a very similar song in mockery of the pagan gods occurs, and there also it is followed by a similar litany and hymn (vv 19ff).

115, 2: *Where is their God?*: implying that God does not help them.

115, 9ff: *The house of Israel . . . the house of Aaron . . . those who fear the Lord:* the laity of Israelite birth, the priests, and the converts to Judaism. Cf Pss 118, 2ff; 135, 19ff. In the New Testament likewise, the phrase, "those who fear the Lord," is used for the proselytes or converts to Judaism. Cf Acts 10, 2.22.35; 13, 16.26.

113/7f: 1 Sm 2, 8.   8: Ex 17, 6; Nm 20, 11. 114/3: Ex 14, 21f; Jos 3, 14ff.   115/4-10: Ps 135, 15-19.

16 Heaven is the heaven of the Lord,
  but the earth he has given to the
  children of men.

17*† It is not the dead who praise the
  Lord,
  nor those who go down into
  silence;

18 But we bless the Lord,
  both now and forever.

Thanksgiving to God for Help in Need

A

116† 1 Alleluia.

I

I love the Lord because he has
  heard
  my voice in supplication,

2 Because he has inclined his ear to
  me
  the day I called.

3*† The cords of death encompassed
  me;
  the snares of the nether world
  seized upon me;
  I fell into distress and sorrow,

4 And I called upon the name of the
  Lord,
  "O Lord, save my life!"

II

5 Gracious is the Lord and just;
  yes, our God is merciful.

6 The Lord keeps the little ones;
  I was brought low, and he saved
  me.

7 Return, O my soul, to your
  tranquillity,
  for the Lord has been good to
  you.

8 For he has freed my soul from
  death,
  my eyes from tears, my feet
  from stumbling.

9 I shall walk before the Lord
  in the lands of the living.

B

10*† I believed, even when I said,
  "I am greatly afflicted";

11* I said in my alarm,
  "No man is dependable."

12 How shall I make a return to the
  Lord
  for all the good he has done for
  me?

13† The cup of salvation I will take up,
  and I will call upon the name of
  the Lord;

14 My vows to the Lord I will pay
  in the presence of all his people.

15† Precious in the eyes of the Lord
  is the death of his faithful ones.

16 O Lord, I am your servant;
  I am your servant, the son of
  your handmaid;
  you have loosed my bonds.

17 To you will I offer sacrifice of
  thanksgiving,
  and I will call upon the name of
  the Lord.

18 My vows to the Lord I will pay
  in the presence of all his people,

19 In the courts of the house of the
  Lord,
  in your midst, O Jerusalem.

Doxology of All the Nations

117† 1* Alleluia.

Praise the Lord, all you nations;
  glorify him, all you peoples!

2 For steadfast is his kindness
  toward us,
  and the fidelity of the Lord
  endures forever.

---

† 115, 17: See note on Ps 6, 6.

Pss 116: The Greek and Latin versions divide this psalm into two parts: Ps 144 (vv 1-9), Ps 115 (vv 10-19). This is a hymn of thanksgiving sung in the temple by an individual who, when mortally ill, had been cured by the Lord. Recalling how he prayed when he was at death's door (1-4), the psalmist now praises God for having heard his prayer (5-9). Referring again to his former period of need (10f), he offers up his sacrifice and hymn of grateful praise (12-19).

116, 3: Death is pictured as a trapper catching his prey. Cf Ps 18, 6.

116, 10: *I believed:* the psalmist did not doubt that God would be faithful to his promise of help.

116, 13: *The cup of salvation:* the libation of wine poured out in gratitude for having been saved. Cf Ex 25, 29; Nm 15, 1-10. This verse was very appropriately chosen as the prayer which the priest said before drinking the Precious Blood at Holy Mass.

116, 15: Humanly speaking, the Lord looks upon the death of his faithful servants and the consequent loss of their praise as too costly for him to allow. The sentiment of the psalmist is naturally connected with his ideas of the nether world. Cf Ps 6, 6. In the liturgy this verse was used, after the reading of the Martyrology at Prime, in an applied sense: in the eyes of God the death of his holy martyrs is as precious as gold which has been proved in a furnace. Cf Wis 3, 4-7.

Ps 117: The shortest of all the psalms; a brief hymn of praise calling on all mankind to glorify the Lord for his kindness and

---

✿ 17: Pss 6, 6; 88, 11ff;
  Sir 17, 27f(25f);
  Is 38; 18.
116/3: Ps 18, 5; Jon 2, 3.

10: 2 Cor 4, 13.
11: Rom 3, 4.
117/1: Rom 15, 11.

*Hymn of Thanksgiving
to the Savior of Israel*

118 †

1 Alleluia.

A

Give thanks to the LORD, for he is good,
   for his mercy endures forever.
2† Let the house of Israel say,
   "His mercy endures forever."
3 Let the house of Aaron say,
   "His mercy endures forever."
4 Let those who fear the LORD say,
   "His mercy endures forever."

B

I

5† In my straits I called upon the
   LORD;
   the LORD answered me and set
   me free.
6* The LORD is with me; I fear not;
   what can man do against me?
7 The LORD is with me to help me,
   and I shall look down upon my
   foes.
8* It is better to take refuge in the
   LORD
   than to trust in man.
9 It is better to take refuge in the
   LORD
   than to trust in princes.

II

10 All the nations encompassed me;
   in the name of the LORD I
   crushed them.
11 They encompassed me on every
   side;
   in the name of the LORD I
   crushed them.
12 They encompassed me like bees,
   they flared up like fire among
   thorns;
   in the name of the LORD I
   crushed them.
13 I was hard pressed and was
   falling,
   but the LORD helped me.
14* My strength and my courage is the
   LORD,
   and he has been my savior.

III

15 The joyful shout of victory
   in the tents of the just:
   "The right hand of the LORD has
   struck with power:

16 the right hand of the LORD is
   exalted;
   the right hand of the LORD has
   struck with power."
17 I shall not die, but live,
   and declare the works of the
   LORD.
18 Though the LORD has indeed
   chastised me,
   yet he has not delivered me to
   death.

C

I

19† Open to me the gates of justice;
   I will enter them and give
   thanks to the LORD.
20 This gate is the LORD's;
   the just shall enter it.
21 I will give thanks to you, for you
   have answered me
   and have been my savior.
22*† The stone which the builders
   rejected
   has become the cornerstone.
23 By the LORD has this been done;
   it is wonderful in our eyes.
24 This is the day the LORD has made;
   let us be glad and rejoice in it.
25† O LORD, grant salvation!
   O LORD, grant prosperity!

---

† fidelity to his promises. This invitation to all the nations finds its fulfillment in Christ's universal kingdom. Cf Rom 15, 11.

Ps 118: A dramatic "liturgy" of thanksgiving. After an invocation in the form of a litany (1-4), the psalmist, who very likely is speaking here in the name of the whole community, describes how the nation confidently implored the Lord's help (5-9) when hostile peoples threatened its life (10-14); in vivid words he recounts how God came to the rescue (15-18). Then follows a dialogue between the priests at the temple gates and the psalmist as he enters to offer the thanksgiving sacrifice (19-25); finally the priests impart their blessing (26f), and the psalmist sings his hymn of grateful praise (28f).

118, 2ff: See note on Ps 115, 9ff.

118, 5-18: Although many of the phrases in this section resemble those used in the supplications of individuals, other phrases make it probable that the psalmist is speaking here in the name of the whole nation. The occasion may have been such as described in Neh 12, 27-43.

118, 19-29: In this dramatic dialogue the words of the representative of the people seem to be limited to vv 19.21ff.28f. Probably vv 20.24-27 are spoken by the priests.

118, 22: *The stone which the builders rejected:* directly, Israel, which the empire-builders thought unworthy of a place in their worldly plans. But Israel is here a type of Christ, in whom this prophecy has been most eminently fulfilled; hence these words are often cited in the New Testament as referring to our Lord's rejection by the Jews.

118, 25: *Grant salvation:* the Hebrew for this cry, as far as English letters can represent it, is "Hosanna." This word and the words in the next line were used as a welcome to Christ when he entered the temple on Palm Sunday. Cf Mk 11, 10f.

* 118/6: Heb 13, 6.   22: Mt 21, 42; Lk 20, 17;
   8f: Ps 146, 3.   Acts 4, 11; Rom 9, 33;
   14: Ex 15, 2; Is 12, 2.   1 Pt 2, 7.

II

26*†   Blessed is he who comes in the
      name of the Lord;
      we bless you from the house of
      the Lord.

27†   The Lord is God, and he has
      given us light.
      Join in procession with leafy
      boughs
      up to the horns of the altar.

28   You are my God, and I give thanks
      to you;
      O my God, I extol you.

29   Give thanks to the Lord, for he is
      good;
      for his kindness endures
      forever.

Praise of God's Law

Aleph

119† 1   Happy are they whose way is
      blameless,
      who walk in the law of the
      Lord.

2   Happy are they who observe his
      decrees,
      who seek him with all their
      heart,

3   And do no wrong,
      but walk in his ways.

4   You have commanded that your
      precepts
      be diligently kept.

5   Oh, that I might be firm in the
      ways
      of keeping your statutes!

6   Then should I not be put to shame
      when I beheld all your
      commands.

7   I will give you thanks with an
      upright heart
      when I have learned your just
      ordinances.

8   I will keep your statutes;
      do not utterly forsake me.

Beth

9   How shall a young man be
      faultless in his way?
      By keeping to your words.

10   With all my heart I seek you;
      let me not stray from your
      commands.

11   Within my heart I treasure your
      promise,
      that I may not sin against you.

12   Blessed are you, O Lord;
      teach me your statutes.

13   With my lips I declare
      all the ordinances of your
      mouth.

14   In the way of your decrees I
      rejoice,
      as much as in all riches.

15   I will meditate on your precepts
      and consider your ways.

16   In your statutes I will delight;
      I will not forget your words.

Gimel

17   Be good to your servant, that I
      may live
      and keep your words.

18   Open my eyes, that I may consider
      the wonders of your law.

19†   I am a wayfarer of earth;
      hide not your commands from
      me.

20   My soul is consumed with longing
      for your ordinances at all times.

21   You rebuke the accursed proud,
      who turn away from your
      commands.

22   Take away from me reproach and
      contempt,
      for I observe your decrees.

23   Though princes meet and talk
      against me,
      your servant meditates on your
      statutes.

24   Yes, your decrees are my delight;
      they are my counselors.

Daleth

25   I lie prostrate in the dust;
      give me life according to your
      word.

---

† 118, 26: The sense is, "May he who now comes into the temple be blessed by having the Lord's name invoked upon him."

118, 27: *The horns of the altar:* the four corners of the altar of holocausts. Cf Ex 27, 2; 38, 2; Lv 4, 25.30.34.

Ps 119: An alphabetic psalm of didactic nature; in the form of prayer it inculcates the excellence of keeping the divinely revealed law. Some of the strophes show a certain logical development of thought, but on the whole there is merely a constant repetition of the main theme with numerous disconnected variations of it. The external form is based on an elaborately constructed scheme. The psalmist chose eight synonyms—law, statutes, commands, ordinances, decrees, precepts, words and promise—and in his strophes of eight verses apiece planned perhaps to use a different synonym in each verse. In the present form of the text, however, this plan is not perfectly carried out, nor is it certain whether these departures are due to mistakes of later copyists or to the original author himself. This psalm is the longest by far of any in the Psalter. Each of the eight verses of the first strophe begins with the first letter of the Hebrew alphabet, each verse of the second strophe with the second letter, and so on for all the twenty-two letters. Hence, the whole consists of 176 verses.

119, 19: *A wayfarer of earth:* the psalmist realizes that he has but a short life here below. Cf Ps 39, 13. Some render, "I am a stranger in the land"; the desire of the psalmist would then

---

✱   26: Mt 21, 9; 23, 39.

26 I declared my ways, and you
answered me;
teach me your statutes.

27 Make me understand the way of
your precepts,
and I will meditate on your
wondrous deeds.

28 My soul weeps for sorrow;
strengthen me according to your
words.

29 Remove from me the way of
falsehood,
and favor me with your law.

30 The way of truth I have chosen;
I have set your ordinances
before me.

31 I cling to your decrees;
O Lord, let me not be put to
shame.

32 I will run the way of your
commands
when you give me a docile
heart.

He

33 Instruct me, O Lord, in the way of
your statutes,
that I may exactly observe
them.

34 Give me discernment, that I may
observe your law
and keep it with all my heart.

35 Lead me in the path of your
commands,
for in it I delight.

36 Incline my heart to your decrees
and not to gain.

37 Turn away my eyes from seeing
what is vain;
by your way give me life.

38 Fulfill for your servant
your promise to those who fear
you.

39 Turn away from me the reproach
which I dread,
for your ordinances are good.

40 Behold, I long for your precepts;
in your justice give me life.

Waw

41 Let your kindness come to me,
O Lord,
your salvation according to your
promise.

42 So shall I have an answer for those
who reproach me,
for I trust in your words.

43 Take not the word of truth from
my mouth,
for in your ordinances is my
hope;

44 And I will keep your law
continually,
forever and ever.

45 And I will walk at liberty,
because I seek your precepts.

46 I will speak of your decrees before
kings
without being ashamed.

47 And I will delight in your
commands,
which I love.

48† And I will lift up my hands to your
commands
and meditate on your statutes.

Zayin

49 Remember your word to your
servant
since you have given me hope.

50 My comfort in my affliction is
that your promise gives me life.

51 Though the proud scoff bitterly at
me,
I turn not away from your law.

52 I remember your ordinances of
old, O Lord,
and I am comforted.

53 Indignation seizes me because of
the wicked
who forsake your law.

54 Your statutes are the theme of my
song
in the place of my exile.

55 By night I remember your name,
O Lord,
and I will keep your law.

56 This I have had,
that I have observed your
precepts.

Heth

57 I have said, O Lord, that my part
is to keep your words.

58 I entreat you with all my heart,
have pity on me according to
your promise.

59 I considered my ways
and turned my feet to your
decrees.

60 I was prompt and did not hesitate
in keeping your commands.

61 Though the snares of the wicked
are twined about me
your law I have not forgotten.

---

† be that he might learn all the laws and customs of the land that
God has chosen for his people.

119, 48: *I will lift up my hands:* an ancient and natural gesture of supplication. Some render, "I will put my hand to (the
task of keeping) your commands."

62 At midnight I rise to give you
        thanks
      because of your just ordinances.
63 I am the companion of all who
        fear you
      and keep your precepts.
64 Of your kindness, O Lord, the
        earth is full;
      teach me your statutes.

Teth

65 You have done good to your
        servant,
      O Lord, according to your
        word.
66 Teach me wisdom and knowledge,
      for in your commands I trust.
67 Before I was afflicted I went
        astray,
      but now I hold to your promise.
68 You are good and bountiful;
      teach me your statutes.
69 Though the proud forge lies
        against me,
      with all my heart I will observe
        your precepts.
70† Their heart has become gross and
        fat;
      as for me, your law is my
        delight.
71 It is good for me that I have been
        afflicted,
      that I may learn your statutes.
72 The law of your mouth is to me
        more precious
      than thousands of gold and
        silver pieces.

Yodh

73✶ Your hands have made me and
        fashioned me;
      give me discernment that I may
        learn your commands.
74 Those who fear you shall see me
        and be glad,
      because I hope in your word.
75 I know, O Lord, that your
        ordinances are just,
      and in your faithfulness you·
        have afflicted me.
76 Let your kindness comfort me
      according to your promise to
        your servants.
77 Let your compassion come to me
        that I may live,
      for your law is my delight.
78 Let the proud be put to shame for
        oppressing me unjustly;
      I will meditate on your
        precepts.

79 Let those turn to me who fear you
      and acknowledge your decrees.
80 Let my heart be perfect in your
        statutes,
      that I be not put to shame.

Kaph

81 My soul pines for your salvation;
      I hope in your word.
82 My eyes strain after your promise;
      when will you comfort me?
83† Though I am shriveled like a
        leathern flask in the smoke,
      I have not forgotten your
        statutes.
84 How many are the days of your
        servant?
      When will you do judgment on
        my persecutors?
85† The proud have dug pits for me;
      this is against your law.
86 All your commands are steadfast;
      they persecute me wrongfully;
        help me!
87 They have all but put an end to me
        on the earth,
      but I have not forsaken your
        precepts.
88 In your kindness give me life,
      that I may keep the decrees of
        your mouth.

Lamedh

89 Your word, O Lord, endures
        forever;
      it is firm as the heavens.
90 Through all generations your
        truth endures;
      you have established the earth,
        and it stands firm.
91 According to your ordinances
        they still stand firm:
      all things serve you.
92 Had not your law been my
        delight,
      I should have perished in my
        affliction.
93 Never will I forget your precepts,
      for through them you give me
        life.
94 I am yours; save me,
      for I have sought your precepts.
95 Sinners wait to destroy me,
      but I pay heed to your decrees.

---

† 119, 70: *Their heart has become gross and fat:* a Hebrew
idiom for, "Their mind has become dull and insensitive." But it
may also be understood to signify a "cruel heart." Cf Ps 17, 10.

119, 83: *A leathern flask:* tanned hides were used for holding
water or wine; such containers, if kept in the dry heat near the
fireplace, gradually became brittle and useless.

119, 85: *This is against your law:* or perhaps the sense may
be, "that is, to make me act against your law."

96 I see that all fulfillment has its
limits;
broad indeed is your command.

Mem

97 How I love your law, O LORD!
It is my meditation all the day.
98 Your command has made me
wiser than my enemies,
for it is ever with me.
99 I have more understanding than
all my teachers
when your decrees are my
meditation.
100 I have more discernment than the
elders,
because I observe your
precepts.
101 From every evil way I withhold
my feet,
that I may keep your words.
102 From your ordinances I turn not
away,
for you have instructed me.
103 How sweet to my palate are your
promises,
sweeter than honey to my
mouth!
104 Through your precepts I gain
discernment;
therefore I hate every false way.

Nun

105 A lamp to my feet is your word,
a light to my path.
106 I resolve and swear
to keep your just ordinances.
107 I am very much afflicted;
O LORD, give me life according
to your word.
108 Accept, O LORD, the free homage
of my mouth,
and teach me your decrees.
109† Though constantly I take my life
in my hands,
yet I forget not your law.
110 The wicked have laid a snare for
me,
but from your precepts I have
not strayed.
111 Your decrees are my inheritance
forever;
the joy of my heart they are.
112 I intend in my heart to fulfill your
statutes
always, to the letter.

Samekh

113† I hate men of divided heart,
but I love your law.

114 You are my refuge and my shield;
in your word I hope.
115 Depart from me, you wrongdoers,
and I will observe the
commands of my God.
116 Sustain me as you have promised,
that I may live;
disappoint me not in my hope.
117 Help me, that I may be safe
and ever delight in your
statutes.
118 You despise all who stray from
your statutes,
for their deceitfulness is in vain.
119 You account all the wicked of the
earth as dross;
therefore I love your decrees.
120 My flesh shudders with dread of
you,
and I fear your ordinances.

Ayin

121 I have fulfilled just ordinances;
leave me not to my oppressors.
122 Be surety for the welfare of your
servant;
let not the proud oppress me.
123 My eyes strain after your salvation
and your just promise.
124 Deal with your servant according
to your kindness,
and teach me your statutes.
125 I am your servant; give me
discernment
that I may know your decrees.
126 It is time for the LORD to act:
they have broken your law.
127 For I love your command
more than gold, however fine.
128 For in all your precepts I go
forward;
every false way I hate.

Peh

129 Wonderful are your decrees;
therefore I observe them.
130 The revelation of your words
sheds light,
giving understanding to the
simple.
131 I gasp with open mouth
in my yearning for your
commands.
132 Turn to me in pity
as you turn to those who love
your name.

---

† 119, 109f: The psalmist's life is always threatened by the
wicked who persecute him for keeping God's law.
119, 113: *Men of divided heart:* those who hesitate between
fidelity and infidelity to God. Cf 1 Kgs 18, 21.

133 Steady my footsteps according to
  your promise,
   and let no iniquity rule over
   me.

134 Redeem me from the oppression of
  men,
   that I may keep your precepts.

135† Let your countenance shine upon
  your servant,
   and teach me your statutes.

136 My eyes shed streams of tears
  because your law has not been
  kept.

Sadhe

137 You are just, O Lord,
  and your ordinance is right.

138 You have pronounced your
  decrees in justice
   and in perfect faithfulness.

139 My zeal consumes me,
  because my foes forget your
  words.

140† Your promise is very sure,
  and your servant loves it.

141 I am mean and contemptible,
  but your precepts I have not
  forgotten.

142 Your justice is everlasting justice,
  and your law is permanent.

143 Though distress and anguish have
  come upon me,
   your commands are my delight.

144 Your decrees are forever just;
  give me discernment that I may
  live.

Qoph

145 I call out with all my heart;
  answer me, O Lord;
   I will observe your statutes.

146 I call upon you; save me,
  and I will keep your decrees.

147 Before dawn I come and cry out;
  I hope in your words.

148† My eyes greet the night watches
  in meditation on your promise.

149 Hear my voice according to your
  kindness, O Lord;
   according to your ordinance
   give me life.

150 I am attacked by malicious
  persecutors
   who are far from your law.

151 You, O Lord, are near,
  and all your commands are
  permanent.

152 Of old I know from your decrees,
  that you have established them
  forever.

Resh

153 Behold my affliction, and rescue
  me,
   for I have not forgotten your
   law.

154 Plead my cause, and redeem me;
  for the sake of your promise
  give me life.

155 Far from sinners is salvation,
  because they seek not your
  statutes.

156 Your compassion is great, O Lord;
  according to your ordinances
  give me life.

157 Though my persecutors and my
  foes are many,
   I turn not away from your
   decrees.

158 I beheld the apostates with
  loathing,
   because they kept not to your
   promise.

159 See how I love your precepts,
  O Lord;
   in your kindness give me life.

160 Permanence is your word's chief
  trait;
   each of your just ordinances is
   everlasting.

Shin

161 Princes persecute me without
  cause
   but my heart stands in awe of
   your word.

162 I rejoice at your promise,
  as one who has found rich spoil.

163 Falsehood I hate and abhor;
  your law I love.

164† Seven times a day I praise you
  for your just ordinances.

165 Those who love your law have
  great peace,
   and for them there is no
   stumbling block.

166 I wait for your salvation, O Lord,
  and your commands I fulfill.

---

† 119, 135: *Let your countenance shine:* the psalmist asks God to smile on him with favor. Cf Nm 6, 25; Pss 67, 2; 80, 4.

119, 140: *Very sure:* literally, "fire-tried," said of purified metals that are genuine and reliable. Cf Ps 12, 7.

119, 148: *The night watches:* even at the time when people are usually asleep, the psalmist meditates on God's word. Cf v 62 and Ps 77, 3.5.

119, 164: *Seven times:* a Hebrew idiom for "many times." Cf Gn 4, 24; Ps 12, 7; Prv 24, 16; Mt 18, 21f; Lk 17, 4.

167 I keep your decrees
  and love them deeply.
168 I keep your precepts and your
    decrees,
  for all my ways are before you.

Taw

169 Let my cry come before you,
    O Lord;
  in keeping with your word, give
    me discernment.
170 Let my supplication reach you;
  rescue me according to your
    promise.
171 My lips pour forth your praise,
  because you teach me your
    statutes.
172 May my tongue sing of your
    promise,
  for all your commands are just.
173 Let your hand be ready to help
    me,
  for I have chosen your precepts.
174 I long for your salvation, O Lord,
  and your law is my delight.
175 Let my soul live to praise you,
  and may your ordinances help
    me.
176 I have gone astray [like a lost
    sheep]; seek your servant,
  because your commands I do
    not forget.

A Complaint against Treacherous Tongues

120 † 1† A song of ascents.

I

In my distress I called to the Lord,
  and he answered me.
2 O Lord, deliver me from lying lip,
  from treacherous tongue.

II

3† What will he inflict on you, with
    more besides,
  O treacherous tongue?
4† Sharp arrows of a warrior
  with fiery coals of brushwood.

III

5† Woe is me that I sojourn in
    Meshech,
  that I dwell amid the tents of
    Kedar!
6 All too long have I dwelt
  with those who hate peace.
7 When I speak of peace,
  they are ready for war.

The Lord Our Guardian

121 † 1† A song of ascents.

I

I lift up my eyes toward the
    mountains;
  whence shall help come to me?
2 My help is from the Lord,
  who made heaven and earth.

II

3 May he not suffer your foot to slip;
  may he slumber not who guards
    you:
4 Indeed he neither slumbers nor
    sleeps,
  the guardian of Israel.

III

5 The Lord is your guardian; the
    Lord is your shade;
  he is beside you at your right
    hand.
6† The sun shall not harm you by
    day,
  nor the moon by night.

---

† Ps 120: The psalmist implores God's help against his deceitful foe (1f); he asks the Lord to punish this enemy (3f) as he bewails his long exile among hostile strangers (5-7).

120, 1: *A song of ascents:* this title also occurs in each of the next fourteen psalms. The most probable explanation is that these fifteen psalms form a little collection of "Pilgrim Psalms," that is, songs which were sung by the pilgrims when they "went up" to Jerusalem for the great annual feasts. Cf Ex 23, 17; Dt 16, 16; 1 Kgs 12, 28; Mt 20, 17; Lk 2, 41f. Less probable explanations are that these psalms were sung by the returning exiles when they "went up" to Jerusalem from Babylon (Ezr 7, 9), or that they were sung by the Levites on the fifteen steps by which they ascended from the Court of the Women to the Court of the Israelites in the temple. Hence, these psalms are also known as the "Gradual Psalms," or "Psalms of the Steps."

120, 3: *With more besides:* the common formula of a curse in Hebrew was, "May the Lord do such and such evils to you (the evils being specified), and add still more to them." Cf 1 Sm 3, 17; 14, 44; 25, 22. Here the psalmist is at a loss for a suitable malediction.

120, 4: The punishment which the psalmist finally decides to wish on his enemy is that the latter may be shot in battle or overwhelmed with glowing charcoal. *Brushwood:* more exactly, the broom plant; charcoal made of this wood burns with an intense heat.

120, 5: *Meshech:* an ancient people dwelling in northeastern Asia Minor. Cf Gn 10, 2. *Kedar:* a tribe of the north Arabian desert. Cf Gn 25, 13. Probably these names are used here merely in a metaphorical sense for barbarians in general.

Ps 121: Since he himself is full of confidence in the Lord's help (1f), the psalmist also reassures his companion of God's protection (3-8).

121, 1: *The mountains:* the ridge on which Mount Zion with its temple was situated. Cf Pss 87, 1; 125, 2.

121, 6: The harm caused by sunstroke was known to the ancients. Cf 2 Kgs 4, 18ff. The Orientals even today think that the

IV

7 The LORD will guard you from all
   evil;
   he will guard your life.
8*† The LORD will guard your coming
   and your going,
   both now and forever.

The Pilgrim's Greetings to Jerusalem

122† 1 A song of ascents. Of David.

I

I rejoiced because they said to me,
   "We will go up to the house of
   the LORD."
2 And now we have set foot
   within your gates,
   O Jerusalem—
3 Jerusalem, built as a city
   with compact unity.

II

4 To it the tribes go up,
   the tribes of the LORD,
According to the decree for Israel,
   to give thanks to the name of the
   LORD.
5 In it are set up judgment seats,
   seats for the house of David.

III

6† Pray for the peace of Jerusalem!
   May those who love you
   prosper!
7 May peace be within your walls,
   prosperity in your buildings.
8 Because of my relatives and
   friends
   I will say, "Peace be within
   you!"
9 Because of the house of the LORD,
   our God,
   I will pray for your good.

Israel's Prayer in Persecution

123† 1 A song of ascents.

I

To you I lift up my eyes
   who are enthroned in heaven.
2 Behold, as the eyes of servants
   are on the hands of their
   masters,
As the eyes of a maid
   are on the hands of her mistress,

So are our eyes on the LORD, our
   God,
   till he have pity on us.

II

3 Have pity on us, O LORD, have
   pity on us,
   for we are more than sated with
   contempt;
4 Our souls are more than sated
   with the mockery of the
   arrogant,
   with the contempt of the proud.

The Lord the Rescuer of His People

124† 1† A song of ascents. Of David.

I

Had not the LORD been with us,
   let Israel say,
2   had not the LORD been with us—
When men rose up against us,
3   then would they have
   swallowed us alive.
When their fury was inflamed
   against us,
4†   then would the waters have
   overwhelmed us;
The torrent would have swept
   over us;
5   over us then would have swept
   the raging waters.

II

6 Blessed be the LORD, who did not
   leave us
   a prey to their teeth.

---

† moon also may have harmful effects. Some amend the Hebrew text to read, "Nor the cold by night." Cf Gn 31, 40.

121, 8: *Your coming and your going:* by a common idiom, the Hebrew uses the expression "to come in and to go out" to signify all ordinary human activity. Cf Dt 28, 6; 31, 2; Jos 14, 11; 2 Sm 3, 25.

Ps 122: A song of Zion. Full of joy at his arrival in the Holy City (1-3), the psalmist lauds Jerusalem as the goal of pilgrims and the seat of government (4f); he asks God's blessings upon it (6-9).

122, 6ff: *Peace:* shalom, the regular greeting in Hebrew; it is wider in meaning than the English word peace, and includes the idea of happiness, prosperity.

Ps 123: A supplication of the people. Protesting their loyal obedience to the Lord (1f), they beg him to have mercy on them in their humiliation (3f).

Ps 124: A hymn of thanksgiving in which the people acknowledge that without the Lord's help they would have been utterly destroyed (1-5); they praise him, therefore, for having rescued them from their enemies (6-8).

124, 1: *Of David:* missing in some ancient sources.

124, 4f: *The waters:* a figure of affliction. Cf Pss 18, 5.17; 69, 2f.

121/8: Dt 28, 6.

7 We were rescued like a bird
   from the fowlers' snare;
Broken was the snare,
   and we were freed.
8 Our help is in the name of the Lord,
   who made heaven and earth.

The Lord the Protector of Israel

125 † 1† A song of ascents.

I

They who trust in the Lord are
   like Mount Zion,
which is immovable; which
   forever stands.
2 Mountains are round about
   Jerusalem;
so the Lord is round about his
   people,
both now and forever.

II

3 For the scepter of the wicked shall
   not remain
upon the territory of the just,
Lest the just put forth
   to wickedness their hands.

III

4 Do good, O Lord, to the good
   and to the upright of heart.
5 But such as turn aside to crooked
   ways
may the Lord lead away with
   the evildoers!
Peace be upon Israel!

The People's Prayer for Full Restoration

126 † 1† A song of ascents.

I

When the Lord brought back the
   captives of Zion,
we were like men dreaming.
2 Then our mouth was filled with
   laughter,
and our tongue with rejoicing.
Then they said among the nations,
   "The Lord has done great
   things for them."
3 The Lord has done great things
   for us;
we are glad indeed.

II

4† Restore our fortunes, O Lord,
   like the torrents in the southern
   desert.

5 Those that sow in tears
   shall reap rejoicing.
6 Although they go forth weeping,
   carrying the seed to be sown,
They shall come back rejoicing,
   carrying their sheaves.

The Need of God's Blessing: His Gift of Sons

127 † 1 A song of ascents. Of Solomon.

I

Unless the Lord build the house,
   they labor in vain who build it.
Unless the Lord guard the city,
   in vain does the guard keep
   vigil.
2† It is vain for you to rise early,
   or put off your rest,
You that eat hard-earned bread,
   for he gives to his beloved in
   sleep.

II

3† Behold, sons are a gift from the
   Lord;
   the fruit of the womb is a
   reward.
4 Like arrows in the hand of a
   warrior
   are the sons of one's youth.
5† Happy the man whose quiver is
   filled with them;
   they shall not be put to shame
   when they contend
   with enemies at the gate.

---

† Ps 125: A supplication in which the people, affirming their confidence in the Lord's protection (1f), pray that the reign of wickedness may end (3) and that the good may enjoy God's blessings (4f).

125, 1ff: Although Jerusalem itself is situated on a high hill, a rampart of still higher mountains surrounds it.

Ps 126: Grateful for their happy return from exile (1-3), the people beseech the Lord that he will prosper their present struggle to rebuild their homeland (4-6). Cf Ps 85.

126, 1: *Like men dreaming:* the change from exile to their own country was almost too good to be believed. One can also understand, "like men restored to health."

126, 4: As the infrequent rains cause the sudden rush of waters through the dry and empty channels, so may the Lord quickly restore the fortunes of the exiles.

Ps 127: Two short songs; the first (1f) stresses the truth that without God's blessing all human endeavor is futile, the second (3-5) congratulates the man whom God has blessed with many children.

127, 2: Our Lord taught the same truth, that God's blessings come to those who do not worry but trust in his loving providence. Cf Mt 6, 25-34; Mk 4, 26-29; Lk 12, 22-31.

127, 3: *Sons:* the word might also be rendered, "children"; but boys were more welcome than girls in an Israelite family.

127, 5: *Enemies at the gate:* the sense is not "foes besieging the walls of the city," but "adversaries in the forum, in the court of justice." Local government functioned in the large open space

The Happy Home of the Just Man

128[†] **1**   A song of ascents.

I

   Happy are you who fear the LORD,
     who walk in his ways!
2 For you shall eat the fruit of your
     handiwork;
     happy shall you be, and
     favored.
3[†] Your wife shall be like a fruitful
     vine
     in the recesses of your home;
     Your children like olive plants
     around your table.
4 Behold, thus is the man blessed
     who fears the LORD.

II

5 The LORD bless you from Zion:
     may you see the prosperity of
     Jerusalem
     all the days of your life;
6 May you see your children's
     children.
     Peace be upon Israel!

Prayer for the Overthrow of Israel's Foes

129[†] **1**   A song of ascents.

I

   Much have they oppressed me
     from my youth,
     let Israel say,
2 Much have they oppressed me
     from my youth;
     yet they have not prevailed
     against me.
3[†] Upon my back the plowers
     plowed;
     long did they make their
     furrows.
4 But the just LORD has severed
     the cords of the wicked.

II

5 May all be put to shame and fall
     back
     that hate Zion.
6[†] May they be like grass on the
     housetops,
     which withers before it is
     plucked;
7 With which the reaper fills not
     his hand,
     nor the gatherer of sheaves his
     arms;

8[†] And those that pass by say not,
     "The blessing of the LORD be
     upon you!
     We bless you in the name of the
     LORD!"

Prayer for Pardon and Mercy

130[†] **1**[†]   A song of ascents.

I

   Out of the depths I cry to you,
     O LORD;
     Lord, hear my voice!
2 Let your ears be attentive
     to my voice in supplication:

II

3 If you, O LORD, mark iniquities,
     Lord, who can stand?
4[†] But with you is forgiveness,
     that you may be revered.

III

5 I trust in the LORD;
     my soul trusts in his word.
6 My soul waits for the LORD
     more than sentinels wait for the
     dawn.

IV

   More than sentinels wait for the
     dawn,

[†]

inside the city's gate. The larger a man's family, the greater his influence there. Cf Prv 31, 23.

Ps 128: Like Ps 127, 3ff, this is a song celebrating the blessings of family life. The psalmist congratulates the man to whom the Lord has given a fruitful wife and sturdy children (1-4), and wishes him prosperity and long life (5f).

128, 3: *Vine . . . olive plants:* merely for the purpose of comparison; not to be understood as if these plants grew inside a house. Cf Pss 52, 10; 92, 13ff.

Ps 129: Bewailing the affliction that has so often been Israel's lot (1-4), the people pray that their foes may be brought to nought (5-8).

129, 3: *Upon my back the plowers plowed:* Israel's towns were changed into plowland. Some understand the words to mean that Israel was scourged like a slave.

129, 6f: The flat roofs of the houses in Palestine were coated with a protective covering of clay; the grass that sprouted in this clay after a heavy rain was short-lived and worthless.

129, 8: Harvesters greeted one another with such blessings. Cf Ru 2, 4.

Ps 130: The sixth of the Penitential Psalms, the *De Profundis,* used in the liturgy of the church as a prayer for the faithful departed. In deep sorrow the psalmist cries to the Lord (1f), begging pardon for his sins (3f); as he himself trusts in God's mercy (5-6b), so also should Israel wait in hope for the Lord's redemption (6c-8).

130, 1: *The depths:* of spiritual, not physical misery.

130, 4: *That you may be revered:* the thought of God's merciful forgiveness should lead one to seek his pardon and to fear offending him in the future. Cf Rom 2, 4.

7† let Israel wait for the LORD,
For with the LORD is kindness
and with him is plenteous
redemption;

8 And he will redeem Israel
from all their iniquities.

Humble Trust in God

131 † 1 A song of ascents. Of David.

O LORD, my heart is not proud,
nor are my eyes haughty;
I busy not myself with great
things,
nor with things too sublime for
me.

2 Nay rather, I have stilled and
quieted
my soul like a weaned child.
Like a weaned child on its
mother's lap,
[so is my soul within me.]

3 O Israel, hope in the LORD,
both now and forever.

The Pact between David and the Lord

132 † 1† A song of ascents.

A

I

Remember, O LORD, for David
all his anxious care:

2† How he swore to the LORD,
vowed to the Mighty One of
Jacob:

3 "I will not enter the house I live in,
nor lie on the couch where I
sleep;

4 I will give my eyes no sleep
my eyelids no rest,

5 Till I find a place for the LORD,
a dwelling for the Mighty One
of Jacob."

II

6† Behold, we heard of it in
Ephrathah;
we found it in the fields of Jaar.

7† Let us enter into his dwelling,
let us worship at his footstool.

8✻ Advance, O LORD, to your resting
place
you and the ark of your majesty.

9 May your priests be clothed with
justice;
let your faithful ones shout
merrily for joy.

10† For the sake of David your
servant,
reject not the plea of your
anointed.

B

I

11✻ The LORD swore to David
a firm promise from which he
will not withdraw:
"Your own offspring
I will set upon your throne;

12 If your sons keep my covenant
and the decrees which I shall
teach them,
Their sons, too, forever
shall sit upon your throne."

13 For the LORD has chosen Zion;
he prefers her for his dwelling.

II

14 "Zion is my resting place forever;
in her will I dwell, for I prefer
her.

15 I will bless her with abundant
provision,
her poor I will fill with bread.

16 Her priests I will clothe with
salvation,
and her faithful ones shall shout
merrily for joy.

17† In her will I make a horn to sprout
forth for David;
I will place a lamp for my
anointed.

---

† 130, 7f: The redemption of Israel from all their iniquities
was achieved by Christ, the divine Redeemer. Cf Lk 2, 38.

Ps 131: A protestation of humility. The psalmist asserts that
he is free from all worldly ambition (1) and as simple as a child
(2); he hopes that Israel will likewise have childlike confidence
in the Lord (3).

Ps 132: A song reminding the people of the Lord's great
promise to David that his descendants would always rule in
Zion. It is similar to Ps 89 but differs from it in its lack of
lamentation over present miseries. The psalmist first recalls how
David vowed to build a new dwelling place for the Lord (1-5);
he then recounts how the ark was brought to Zion (6-10). There
follows the Lord's promise to David to bless his dynasty (11-13)
and Zion, his capital (14-18).

132, 1: *All his anxious care:* to build the temple. Cf 2 Sm
7, 1ff; 1 Kgs 8, 17.

132, 2.5: *The Mighty One of Jacob:* one of the titles of the
Lord. Cf Gn 49, 24; Is 49, 26; 60, 16.

132, 6: *Ephrathah:* Bethlehem, David's birthplace. Cf Ru 4,
11. *The fields of Jaar:* "Forestfield," the same as Kiriath-jearim,
"Foresttown," where the ark remained for several generations.
Cf 1 Sm 7, 1f; 2 Sm 6, 2; 1 Chr 13, 5f.

132, 7: *His footstool:* the ark. Cf Ps 99, 5.

132, 10: *Your anointed:* the royal descendant of David, con-
temporaneous with the psalmist. According to some, this proves
that the psalm is pre-exilic; according to others, the "anointed"
of the Lord is Zerubbabel, the post-exilic descendant of David.
Cf Ezr 3, 2; Hg 1, 1-2.23; Zec 4.

132, 17: *A horn to sprout forth for David:* a strong offspring
of David. This refers pre-eminently to Christ, who is called a

18 His enemies I will clothe with
   shame,
     but upon him my crown shall
     shine."

The Benefits of Brotherly Concord

133 † 1 A song of ascents. Of David.

Behold, how good it is, and how
   pleasant,
     where brethren dwell at one!
2 It is as when the precious ointment
   upon the head
     runs down over the beard, the
     beard of Aaron,
     till it runs down upon the collar
     of his robe.
3 It is a dew like that of Hermon,
   which comes down upon the
   mountains of Zion;
     For there the LORD has pro-
     nounced his blessing,
     life forever.

Exhortation to the Night Watch to Bless the Lord

134 † 1† A song of ascents.

Come, bless the LORD,
   all you servants of the LORD
Who stand in the house of the
   LORD
     during the hours of night.
2 Lift up your hands toward the
   sanctuary,
     and bless the LORD.

3 May the LORD bless you from Zion,
   the maker of heaven and earth.

Praise of God, the Lord and Benefactor of Israel

135 † 1† Alleluia.

A

Praise the name of the LORD;
   Praise, you servants of the LORD
2 Who stand in the house of the
   LORD,
     in the courts of the house of our
     God.
3 Praise the LORD, for the LORD is
   good;
     sing praise to his name, which
     we love;

4† For the LORD has chosen Jacob for
   himself,
     Israel for his own possession.

B

I

5 For I know that the LORD is great;
   our Lord is greater than all
   gods.
6* All that the LORD wills he does
   in heaven and on earth,
     in the seas and in all the deeps.
7* He raises storm clouds from the
   end of the earth;
     with the lightning he makes the
     rain;
     he brings forth the winds from
     his storehouse.

II

8* He smote the first-born in Egypt,
   both of man and of beast.
9 He sent signs and wonders
   into your midst, O Egypt,
     against Pharaoh and against all
     his servants.
10* He smote many nations
   and slew mighty kings:

---

† "sprout" of David by the prophets. Cf Jer 23, 5; 33, 15; Zec 3, 8; 6, 12. *I will place a lamp:* the ever-burning lamp in a house was a symbol of perpetual offspring; when a man died without descendants, his lamp was said to be put out. Cf 1 Kgs 11, 36; 15, 4; 2 Kgs 8, 19.

Ps 133: The psalmist rejoices in the compact settlement of the Israelite families as an evidence of God's blessing (1), just as the same divine blessing would be signified by the fragrant oil of anointing (2) used at the consecration of the high priest (Ex 30, 22-33), or by the rich dew (Gn 27, 27ff; Hos 14, 6; Jl 4, 17f) covering the mountain slopes round about Jerusalem (3). *Hermon* is the majestic snow-capped mountain at the north of the Holy Land. Its copious waters are the type of the divine blessing that fructifies the soil. Similarly, *Aaron* is the type for any high priest consecrated with the same precious oil. The *life forever* was understood in the first place of the preservation of earthly life; it is capable of a fuller application in the light of the gospel. The similes used seem to suppose that the psalmist saw the returned exiles living in and about the Holy City, crowning its mountaintop and spreading down over its slopes like a precious oil or a heaven-sent dew.

Ps 134: This short song seems to have been sung in the temple as an encouragement for the priests and Levites who were on duty there during the night (1f); they respond by blessing the people (3).

134, 1: *Servants of the Lord:* the priests and Levites. Cf Dt 10, 8; Pss 113, 1; 135, 1; Dn 3, 84f.

Ps 135: This hymn begins (1-4) and ends (19-21) with an exhortation to glorify God, who is the almighty Lord of creation (5-7) and the defender of his chosen people (8-14), whereas the pagan gods are lifeless idols (15-18). Many of the verses were borrowed from other psalms.

135, 1f: Very similar to Ps 134, 1.

135, 4: All nations belong to the Lord, but he has chosen Israel as his own in a special sense. Cf Ex 19, 5; Dt 7, 6; 14, 2; 26, 18; 32, 9.

---

* 135/6: Ps 115, 3.
  7: Jer 10, 13.
  8f: Pss 105, 27.36; 136, 10.

10ff: Nm 21, 21-35;
  Dt 3, 8-11;
  Ps 136, 17-22.

11 Sihon, king of the Amorites,
        and Og, king of Bashan,
        and all the kings of Canaan;
12 And he made their land a heritage,
        the heritage of Israel his people.
13* Your name, O LORD, endures
        forever;
        LORD is your title through all
            generations,
14* For the LORD defends his people,
        and is merciful to his servants.

III

15† The idols of the nations are silver
        and gold,
        the handiwork of men.
16 They have mouths but speak not;
        they have eyes but see not;
17 They have ears but hear not,
        nor is there breath in their
            mouths.
18 Their makers shall be like them,
        everyone that trusts in them.

C

19† House of Israel, bless the LORD,
        house of Aaron, bless the LORD,
20 House of Levi, bless the LORD;
        you who fear the LORD, bless
            the LORD.
21 Blessed from Zion be the LORD,
        who dwells in Jerusalem.

Hymn of Thanksgiving for the Everlasting Kindness of the Lord

136† 1 Alleluia.
        Give thanks to the LORD, for he is
            good,
            for his mercy endures forever;
2† Give thanks to the God of gods,
        for his mercy endures forever;
3 Give thanks to the Lord of lords,
        for his mercy endures forever;

I

4 Who alone does great wonders,
        for his mercy endures forever;
5* Who made the heavens in wisdom,
        for his mercy endures forever;
6 Who spread out the earth upon
            the waters,
        for his mercy endures forever;
7 Who made the great lights,
        for his mercy endures forever;

8 The sun to rule over the day,
        for his mercy endures forever;
9 The moon and the stars to rule
            over the night,
        for his mercy endures forever;

II

10* Who smote the Egyptians in their
            first-born,
        for his mercy endures forever;
11 And brought out Israel from their
            midst,
        for his mercy endures forever;
12 With a mighty hand and an
            outstretched arm,
        for his mercy endures forever;
13 Who split the Red Sea in twain,
        for his mercy endures forever;
14 And led Israel through its midst,
        for his mercy endures forever;
15 But swept Pharaoh and his army
            into the Red Sea,
        for his mercy endures forever;
16 Who led his people through the
            wilderness,
        for his mercy endures forever;
17† Who smote great kings,
        for his mercy endures forever;
18 And slew powerful kings,
        for his mercy endures forever;
19 Sihon, king of the Amorites,
        for his mercy endures forever;
20 And Og, king of Bashan,
        for his mercy endures forever;
21 And made their land a heritage,
        for his mercy endures forever;
22 The heritage of Israel his servant,
        for his mercy endures forever;

III

23† Who remembered us in our
            abjection,
        for his mercy endures forever;
24 And freed us from our foes,
        for his mercy endures forever;

---

† 135, 15-18: Almost identical with Ps 115, 4ff.8.

135, 19ff: Similar to Ps 118, 1-4.

Ps 136: This hymn has the form of a "litany," that is, each half-verse is followed by a refrain, the former probably sung by a soloist and the latter by the people. It seems fairly certain that at least the main section, vv 4-25, did not originally have this invariable refrain, which now interrupts the grammatical structure of the sentences. Besides the introductory and concluding invitations to give grateful praise (1-3.26), this hymn extols the Lord's greatness in creating the universe (4-9), as well as his goodness in bringing Israel to the Promised Land (10-22) and in having pity on the misery of the people (23-25).

136, 2: *The God of gods:* the supreme and only God.

136, 17-22: These verses occur in similar form but without the refrain in Ps 135, 10ff.

136, 23f: The reference seems to be to the Babylonian exile.

---

*
13: Ps 102, 13.   10-16: Ex 12, 29.51; 14,
14: Dt 32, 36.   22.28; 15, 22;
136/5-9: Gn 1, 8-18.   Ps 78, 51ff.

25 Who gives food to all flesh,
  for his mercy endures forever.
26 Give thanks to the God of heaven,
  for his mercy endures forever.

The Exile's Remembrance of Zion

I

137† 1† By the streams of Babylon
  we sat and wept
  when we remembered Zion.
2† On the aspens of that land
  we hung up our harps,
3 Though there our captors asked
    of us
  the lyrics of our songs,
And our despoilers urged us to be
    joyous:
  "Sing for us the songs of Zion!"

II

4 How could we sing a song of the
    LORD
  in a foreign land?
5 If I forget you, Jerusalem,
  may my right hand be forgotten!
6 May my tongue cleave to my
    palate
  if I remember you not,
If I place not Jerusalem
  ahead of my joy.

III

7† Remember, O LORD, against the
    children of Edom,
  the day of Jerusalem,
When they said, "Raze it, raze it
  down to its foundations!"
8† O daughter of Babylon, you
    destroyer,
  happy the man who shall repay
    you
  the evil you have done us!
9† Happy the man who shall seize
    and smash
  your little ones against the rock!

Hymn of a Grateful Heart

138† 1† Of David.

I

I will give thanks to you, O LORD,
    with all my heart,
  [for you have heard the words
    of my mouth;]
  in the presence of the angels I
    will sing your praise;
2 I will worship at your holy temple
  and give thanks to your name,

Because of your kindness and your
    truth;
  for you have made great above
    all things
  your name and your promise.
3 When I called, you answered me;
  you built up strength within me.

II

4 All the kings of the earth shall give
    thanks to you, O LORD,
  when they hear the words of
    your mouth;
5 And they shall sing of the ways of
    the LORD:
  "Great is the glory of the LORD."
6 The LORD is exalted, yet the lowly
    he sees,
  and the proud he knows from
    afar.

III

7 Though I walk amid distress,
  you preserve me;
  against the anger of my
    enemies you raise your hand;
  your right hand saves me.

---

†

Ps 137: The psalmist, now apparently returned from exile, recalls how the Jews refused to sing for their captors (1-3) because they thought joyful songs out of harmony with their mournful remembrance of Zion (4-6); condign punishment is wished upon cruel Edom and Babylon (7-9).

137, 1: *The streams of Babylon:* the Euphrates and Tigris, with the numerous irrigation-canals which branched off from them.

137, 2: *The aspens:* not, "the willows," as the older versions generally rendered it; the Hebrew word most probably signifies the *populus euphraticus,* the Mesopotamian aspen.

137, 7: *The day of Jerusalem:* the time when the Holy City was captured and destroyed by the Babylonians. In league with the latter were the Edomites, the southern neighbors and rivals of Judah. The prophets often threaten dire punishment to Edom for its hatred of Israel. Cf Is 34, 5-15; Jer 49, 7-22; Lam 4, 21f; Ez 25, 12ff; Am 1, 11f; Ob 1, 1-18.

137, 8: *Daughter of Babylon:* a Hebrew idiom for "city of Babylon."

137, 9: According to the ruthless custom of ancient warfare, children were indeed thus cruelly killed. Cf 2 Kgs 8, 12; Hos 9, 16. But it seems more probable that here the psalmist is personifying "the daughter of Babylon" as a mother whose *little ones* are the adult citizens, not the infants, of the city. Cf Lk 19, 44.

Ps 138: Thanking God for having heard his prayer (1-3), the psalmist wishes that all the great ones of the earth might join him in his hymn of gratitude (4-6), for he is confident of the Lord's continual help (7f).

138, 1: The words in brackets are in the Greek version but not in the current Hebrew text. They are probably a variant of v 4b accidentally inserted here. *The angels:* in Hebrew, *elohim,* which is the word for "God," "gods," and sometimes "godlike beings," such as the angels. Cf Pss 8, 6; 97, 7. Some render, "In the face of the gods," that is, despite the false gods of the pagans.

8 The Lord will complete what he
has done for me;
your kindness, O Lord, endures
forever;
forsake not the work of your
hands.

The All-knowing and Ever-present God

139 † **1** For the leader. A psalm of David.

I

O Lord, you have probed me and
you know me;
2† you know when I sit and when I
stand;
you understand my thoughts
from afar.
3 My journeys and my rest you
scrutinize,
with all my ways you are
familiar.
4 Even before a word is on my
tongue,
behold, O Lord, you know the
whole of it.
5 Behind me and before, you hem
me in
and rest your hand upon me.
6 Such knowledge is too wonderful
for me;
too lofty for me to attain.

II

7 Where can I go from your spirit?
from your presence where can I
flee?
8✦ If I go up to the heavens, you are
there;
if I sink to the nether world, you
are present there.
9† If I take the wings of the dawn,
if I settle at the farthest limits of
the sea,
10 Even there your hand shall guide
me,
and your right hand hold me
fast.
11 If I say, "Surely the darkness shall
hide me,
and night shall be my light"—
12† For you darkness itself is not dark,
and night shines as the day.
[Darkness and light are the
same.]

III

13 Truly you have formed my inmost
being;
you knit me in my mother's
womb.
14 I give you thanks that I am
fearfully, wonderfully made;
wonderful are your works.
My soul also you knew full well;
15† nor was my frame unknown to
you
When I was made in secret,
when I was fashioned in the
depths of the earth.
16† Your eyes have seen my actions;
in your book they are all
written;
my days were limited before
one of them existed.
17 How weighty are your designs,
O God;
how vast the sum of them!
18† Were I to recount them, they
would outnumber the sands;
did I reach the end of them,
I should still be with you.

IV

19 If only you would destroy the
wicked, O God,
and the men of blood were to
depart from me!
20 Wickedly they invoke your name;
your foes swear faithless oaths.
21 Do I not hate, O Lord, those who
hate you?
Those who rise up against you
do I not loathe?

---

† Ps 139: A hymn to God's omnipresence and omniscience, in the form of a meditation in which the psalmist ponders the truths that the Lord sees and knows him no matter where he may be (1-6); that there is no escape from the all-seeing eye of God (7-12); and that the divine Creator of man is also the Author of his destiny (13-18). He therefore resolves to abhor the wicked and to live sincerely in God's sight (19-24). The current Hebrew text is rather poorly preserved, and the interpretation of a few passages is somewhat doubtful.

139, 2: *When I sit and when I stand:* in all human activity.

139, 9: *Take the wings of the dawn:* go to the most distant extremities of the east. *The farthest limits of the sea:* the uttermost bounds of the west.

139, 12: *Darkness and light are the same:* as far as God is concerned; an explanatory gloss on the two preceding lines.

139, 15: *The depths of the earth:* figurative language for "the womb"; stressing not so much the darkness of the place as the hidden, mysterious nature of the operations which occur there.

139, 16ff: The text of these three verses is obscure in several places.

139, 18: *I should still be with you:* even though the psalmist might reach the end of his own capacity for understanding the divine attributes, the infinity of God's nature would still stand before him as if he had not even begun to comprehend it.

22 With a deadly hatred I hate them;
    they are my enemies.
23 Probe me, O God, and know my
    heart;
    try me, and know my thoughts;
24† See if my way is crooked,
    and lead me in the way of old.

Prayer for Deliverance from the Snares of the Wicked

140† 1 For the leader. A psalm of David.

I

2 Deliver me, O Lord, from evil
    men;
    preserve me from violent men;
3 From those who devise evil in
    their hearts,
    and stir up wars every day.
4✣† They make their tongues sharp as
    those of serpents;
    the venom of asps is under their
    lips.

II

5 Save me, O Lord, from the hands
    of the wicked;
    preserve me from violent men
    Who plan to trip up my feet—
6†   the proud who have hidden a
    trap for me;
    They have spread cords for a net;
    by the wayside they have laid
    snares for me.
7 I say to the Lord, you are my God;
    hearken, O Lord, to my voice in
    supplication.
8 O God, my Lord, my strength and
    my salvation;
    you are my helmet in the day of
    battle!

III

9 Grant not, O Lord, the desires of
    the wicked;
    further not their plans.
10 Those who surround me lift up
    their heads;
    may the mischief which they
    threaten overwhelm them.
11 May he rain burning coals upon
    them;
    may he cast them into the
    depths, never to rise.

IV

12 A man of wicked tongue shall not
    abide in the land;

    evil shall abruptly entrap the
    violent man.
13 I know that the Lord renders
    justice to the afflicted, judgment
    to the poor.
14 Surely the just shall give thanks to
    your name;
    the upright shall dwell in your
    presence.

Prayer of a Just Man to Be Saved from Wickedness

141† 1 A psalm of David.

I

O Lord, to you I call; hasten to
    me;
    hearken to my voice when I call
    upon you.
2† Let my prayer come like incense
    before you;
    the lifting up of my hands, like
    the evening sacrifice.

II

3 O Lord, set a watch before my
    mouth,
    a guard at the door of my lips.
4 Let not my heart incline to the
    evil
    of engaging in deeds of
    wickedness
    With men who are evildoers;
    and let me not partake of their
    dainties.
5 Let the just man strike me; that is
    kindness;
    let him reprove me; it is oil for
    the head,
    Which my head shall not refuse,
    but I will still pray under these
    afflictions.

---

† 139, 24: *The way of old:* the manner of living of the ancient patriarchs. Cf Jer 6, 16.

Ps 140: The psalmist beseeches God to rescue him from his violent, treacherous foes (2-4); they lay a trap for his life (5f), but he trusts in the Lord's protection (7f). Therefore he prays that their evil plans may recoil upon themselves (9-11), and that God will render due justice to both the wicked and the good (12-14).

140, 4: Similar metaphors for a wicked tongue are used in Pss 52, 4; 55, 22; 58, 5.

140, 6: The same figure, taken from the custom of a hunter laying a trap for his prey, occurs in Pss 9, 16; 31, 5; 35, 7; 57, 7; 64, 6. Cf Mt 22, 15; Lk 11, 54.

Ps 141: After calling for divine aid in general (1f), the psalmist prays that he may not be led astray by the seductions of the wicked, whose end is destruction (3-7), and that their evil may harm only themselves (8-10).

141, 2: *Incense:* literally, "smoke," that is, the fragrant fumes which rose from the altar at the burning of sacrificial animals or of aromatic spices, including frankincense; also used in Rv 5, 8

✣ 140/4: Rom 3, 13.

6† Their judges were cast down over
the crag,
    and they heard how pleasant
    were my words.

7 As when a plowman breaks
furrows in the field,
    so their bones are strewn by the
    edge of the nether world.

III

8 For toward you, O God, my Lord,
my eyes are turned;
    in you I take refuge; strip me
    not of life.

9 Keep me from the trap they have
set for me,
    and from the snares of evildoers.

10 Let all the wicked fall, each into
his own net,
    while I escape.

Prayer of a Prisoner
in Dire Straits

142 † **1†** A *maskil* of David. A prayer when he
was in the cave.

I

2 With a loud voice I cry out to the
Lord;
    with a loud voice I beseech the
    Lord.

3 My complaint I pour out before
him;
    before him I lay bare my
    distress.

4 When my spirit is faint within me,
you know my path.

II

In the way along which I walk
    they have hid a trap for me.

5 I look to the right to see,
    but there is no one who pays me
    heed.
I have lost all means of escape;
    there is no one who cares for my
    life.

III

6 I cry out to you, O Lord;
    I say, "You are my refuge,
    my portion in the land of the
    living."

7 Attend to my cry,
    for I am brought low indeed.
Rescue me from my persecutors,
    for they are too strong for me.

8† Lead me forth from prison,
    that I may give thanks to your
    name.
The just shall gather around me
    when you have been good to me.

Prayer of a Penitent
in Distress

143 † **1†** A psalm of David.

I

O Lord, hear my prayer;
    hearken to my pleading in your
    faithfulness;
    in your justice answer me.

2 And enter not into judgment with
your servant,
    for before you no living man is
    just.

II

3 For the enemy pursues me;
    he has crushed my life to the
    ground;
    he has left me dwelling in the
    dark, like those long dead.

4 And my spirit is faint within me,
    my heart within me is appalled.

5* I remember the days of old;
    I meditate on all your doings,
    the works of your hands I
    ponder.

6 I stretch out my hands to you;
    my soul thirsts for you like
    parched land.

III

7 Hasten to answer me, O Lord,
    for my spirit fails me.
Hide not your face from me
    lest I become like those who go
    down into the pit.

---

as a symbol of prayer. *The lifting up of my hands:* the gesture of supplication. Cf Pss 28, 2; 63, 5; 77, 3; 88, 10; 119, 48; 134, 2; 143, 6.

141, 6f: The text of these two verses is very obscure, and their interpretation quite uncertain.

Ps 142: Imploring the Lord to behold his sad plight (2-4b), the psalmist tells how his enemies have hemmed him in (4c-5), and beseeches God to rescue him (6-8).

142, 1: *In the cave:* cf 1 Sm 22, 1; 24, 1f; Ps 57, 1.

142, 8: *The just shall gather around me:* in the temple, when the psalmist offers up his thanksgiving sacrifice.

Ps 143: The seventh of the Penitential Psalms. Pleading for divine assistance despite his sinfulness (1f), the psalmist describes his external and internal afflictions (3f) as he longs for the help which God has always offered his faithful servants (5f). He begs to be rescued from his enemies (7-9), and prays for God's saving guidance and the destruction of his foes (10-12).

143, 1f: Confident that God, in justice to his own promise, will answer his prayer, the psalmist admits that in strict justice to himself he does not deserve to be heard because of his sins.

---

* 143/5: Ps 77, 6.12f.

8* At dawn let me hear of your
    kindness,
      for in you I trust.
Show me the way in which I
    should walk,
      for to you I lift up my soul.

9 Rescue me from my enemies,
    O LORD,
      for in you I hope.

IV

10† Teach me to do your will,
    for you are my God.
May your good spirit guide me
    on level ground.

11 For your name's sake, O LORD,
    preserve me;
      in your justice free me from
      distress,

12 And in your kindness destroy my
    enemies;
      bring to nought all my foes,
      for I am your servant.

**Prayer for Victory
and Prosperity**

144†   1†   Of David.

I

Blessed be the LORD, my rock,
    who trains my hands for battle,
      my fingers for war;
2 My refuge and my fortress,
    my stronghold, my deliverer,
My shield, in whom I trust,
    who subdues peoples under me.

II

3† LORD, what is man, that you notice
    him;
      the son of man, that you take
      thought of him?
4† Man is like a breath;
    his days, like a passing shadow.
5† Incline your heavens; O LORD,
    and come down;
      touch the mountains, and they
      shall smoke;
6 Flash forth lightning, and put
    them to flight,
      shoot your arrows, and rout
      them;
7 Reach out your hand from on
    high—
        Deliver me and rescue me
          from many waters,
          from the hands of aliens,

8 Whose mouths swear false
    promises
      while their right hands
      are raised in perjury.

III

9† O God, I will sing a new song to
    you;
      with a ten-stringed lyre I will
      chant your praise,
10 You who give victory to kings,
    and deliver David, your servant.
11   From the evil sword deliver
      me;
      and rescue me from the
      hands of aliens,
    Whose mouths swear false
      promises
      while their right hands
      are raised in perjury.

IV

12† May our sons be like plants
    well-nurtured in their youth,
Our daughters like wrought
    columns
      such as stand at the corners of
      the temple.
13 May our garners be full,
    affording every kind of store;
May our sheep be in the
    thousands,
      and increase to myriads in our
      meadows;
14   may our oxen be well laden.
May there be no breach in the
    walls, no exile,
      no outcry in our streets.
15 Happy the people for whom
    things are thus;
      happy the people whose God is
      the LORD.

---

†   143, 10: *On level ground:* some ancient sources read, "On a level path." Cf Pss 26, 12; 27, 11.

Ps 144: Except for its final section, this psalm is made up almost entirely of verses borrowed from various other psalms; hence it is somewhat lacking in logical unity. The first section (1f) is a prayer of thanks for victory in war; the second (3-7a), a humble acknowledgment of man's nothingness and a supplication that God show forth his saving might; the third (9f), a promise of future thanksgiving; the fourth (12-15), a wish for prosperity and peace. A slightly varying refrain, which contains a prayer for deliverance from treacherous foes, occurs after the second and third sections (7b-8, 11).

144, 1f: Composed of phrases from Ps 18, 3.35.47f.

144, 3: Very similar to Ps 8, 5.

144, 4: Composed of phrases from Pss 39, 6; 102, 12.

144, 5ff: Adapted in large part from Pss 18, 10.15.17; 104, 32.

144, 9f: Similar to Pss 18, 51; 33, 2f.

144, 12: *Like wrought columns . . . of the temple:* well-formed, shapely. But the Hebrew text of these two lines is obscure, and the allusion is uncertain.

✼   8: Pss 25, 1; 86, 4.

The Greatness and Goodness of God

145 † 1 Praise. Of David.

I will extol you, O my God and
King,
and I will bless your name
forever and ever.
2 Every day will I bless you,
and I will praise your name
forever and ever.
3* Great is the LORD and highly to be
praised;
his greatness is unsearchable.
4 Generation after generation
praises your works
and proclaims your might.

5 They speak of the splendor of your
glorious majesty
and tell of your wondrous
works.
6* They discourse of the power of
your terrible deeds
and declare your greatness.
7 They publish the fame of your
abundant goodness
and joyfully sing of your justice.
8* The LORD is gracious and merciful,
slow to anger and of great
kindness.
9 The LORD is good to all
and compassionate toward all
his works.

10 Let all your works give you
thanks, O LORD,
and let your faithful ones bless
you.
11 Let them discourse of the glory of
your kingdom
and speak of your might,
12 Making known to men your might
and the glorious splendor of
your kingdom.
13* Your kingdom is a kingdom for all
ages,
and your dominion endures
through all generations.

The LORD is faithful in all his
words
and holy in all his works.
14 The LORD lifts up all who are
falling
and raises up all who are bowed
down.

15 The eyes of all look hopefully to
you,
and you give them their food in
due season;
16* You open your hand
and satisfy the desire of every
living thing.

17 The LORD is just in all his ways
and holy in all his works.
18 The LORD is near to all who call
upon him,
to all who call upon him in
truth.
19 He fulfills the desire of those who
fear him,
he hears their cry and saves
them.
20 The LORD keeps all who love him,
but all the wicked he will
destroy.

21 May my mouth speak the praise of
the LORD,
and may all flesh bless his holy
name
forever and ever.

Trust in God Alone

146 † 1 Alleluia.

Praise the LORD, O my soul;
2* I will praise the LORD all my life;
I will sing praise to my God while
I live.

I

3* Put not your trust in princes,
in man, in whom there is no
salvation.
4 When his spirit departs he returns
to his earth;
on that day his plans perish.

II

5 Happy he whose help is the God
of Jacob,
whose hope is in the LORD, his
God,

---

† Ps 145: An alphabetic psalm of which many of the phrases
occur in similar form in other psalms or in other books of the
Bible. The main thoughts of this hymn are concerned with God's
sovereign majesty and loving providence.

Ps 146: A hymn in praise of the kindness and generosity of
God. After a short introductory strophe (1f), the psalmist exposes the folly of trusting in merely human aid (3f), and then
extols the goodness of God toward those who put their trust in
him alone (5-10).

❋ 145/3: Ps 48, 2.   16: Ps 104, 27.
     6: Ps 66, 3.   146/2: Ps 104, 33.
     8f: Ps 86, 5.15.   3: Ps 118, 8f.
    13: Dn 4, 31.

6* Who made heaven and earth,
　　the sea and all that is in them;
　　Who keeps faith forever,
7　　secures justice for the
　　　oppressed,
　　gives food to the hungry.
　　The Lord sets captives free;
8　　the Lord gives sight to the
　　　blind.
　　The Lord raises up those that were
　　　bowed down;
　　the Lord loves the just.
9　　The Lord protects strangers;
　　the fatherless and the widow he
　　　sustains,
　　but the way of the wicked he
　　　thwarts.
10　　The Lord shall reign forever;
　　your God, O Zion, through all
　　　generations.　Alleluia.

Zion's Grateful Praise to Her Bountiful Lord

I

147† 1　Praise the Lord, for he is good;
　　sing praise to our God, for he is
　　　gracious;
　　it is fitting to praise him.
2*　The Lord rebuilds Jerusalem;
　　the dispersed of Israel he
　　　gathers.
3*　He heals the brokenhearted
　　and binds up their wounds.
4*　He tells the number of the stars;
　　he calls each by name.
5　　Great is our Lord and mighty in
　　　power:
　　to his wisdom there is no limit.
6　　The Lord sustains the lowly;
　　the wicked he casts to the
　　　ground.

II

7　Sing to the Lord with
　　thanksgiving;
　　sing praise with the harp to our
　　　God,
8*† Who covers the heavens with
　　clouds,
　　who provides rain for the earth;
　　Who makes grass sprout on the
　　　mountains
　　and herbs for the service of
　　　men;

9* Who gives food to the cattle,
　　and to the young ravens when
　　　they cry to him.
10† In the strength of the steed he
　　delights not,
　　nor is he pleased with the
　　　fleetness of men.
11　The Lord is pleased with those
　　who fear him,
　　with those who hope for his
　　　kindness.

III

12　Glorify the Lord, O Jerusalem;
　　praise your God, O Zion.
13　For he has strengthened the bars
　　　of your gates;
　　he has blessed your children
　　　within you.
14* He has granted peace in your
　　　borders;
　　with the best of wheat he fills
　　　you.
15　He sends forth his command to
　　　the earth;
　　swiftly runs his word!
16　He spreads snow like wool;
　　frost he strews like ashes.
17* He scatters his hail like crumbs;
　　before his cold the waters
　　　freeze.
18　He sends his word and melts
　　　them;
　　he lets his breeze blow and the
　　　waters run.
19* He has proclaimed his word to
　　　Jacob,
　　his statutes and his ordinances
　　　to Israel.
20　He has not done thus for any other
　　　nation;
　　his ordinances he has not made
　　　known to them.　Alleluia.

---

† Ps 147: The Greek and Latin versions divide this psalm into two parts: Ps 146 (vv 1-11), Ps 147 (vv 12-20). The psalm sings the praises of God as the restorer of exiled Israel (1-6) who sustains the needy (7-11), and as the benefactor of Zion (12-20).

147, 8f: Just as the heavenly Father clothes the mountains with vegetation for the nourishment of man and beast, so does his loving providence feed the birds, especially the ravens, whose loud cawing is poetically taken as a cry to God for food. Cf Mt 6, 26-30.

147, 10f: Trust in his own natural strength makes a man proud and displeasing to God, who delights only in a humble confidence toward himself. Cf Pss 20, 8; 33, 16ff.

* 6: Acts 14, 14; Rv 14, 7.　　9: Jb 38, 41.
147/2: Is 11, 12.　　　　　　14: Ps 81, 17.
3: Is 61, 1.　　　　　　　　17: Jb 37, 9f.
4: Is 40, 26.　　　　　　　19f: Dt 4, 7f.
8: Ps 104, 13f.

Hymn of All Creation
to the Almighty Creator

148 † 1   Alleluia.

I

Praise the LORD from the heavens,
   praise him in the heights;
2✻ Praise him, all you his angels,
   praise him, all you his hosts.
3 Praise him, sun and moon;
   praise him, all you shining stars.
4† Praise him, you highest heavens,
   and you waters above the
   heavens.
5 Let them praise the name of the
   LORD,
   for he commanded and they
   were created;
6 He established them forever and
   ever;
   he gave them a duty which shall
   not pass away.

II

7 Praise the LORD from the earth,
   you sea monsters and all depths;
8 Fire and hail, snow and mist,
   storm winds that fulfill his
   word;
9 You mountains and all you hills,
   you fruit trees and all you
   cedars;
10 You wild beasts and all tame
   animals,
   you creeping things and you
   winged fowl.

III

11 Let the kings of the earth and all
   peoples,
   the princes and all the judges of
   the earth,
12 Young men too, and maidens,
   old men and boys,
13 Praise the name of the LORD,
   for his name alone is exalted;
   His majesty is above earth and
   heaven,
14† and he has lifted up the horn of
   his people.
   Be this his praise from all his
   faithful ones,
   from the children of Israel,
   the people close to him.
   Alleluia.

Invitation to Glorify the Lord
with Song and Sword

149 † 1   Alleluia.

I

Sing to the LORD a new song
   of praise in the assembly of the
   faithful.
2 Let Israel be glad in their maker,
   let the children of Zion rejoice in
   their king.
3✻† Let them praise his name in the
   festive dance,
   let them sing praise to him with
   timbrel and harp.
4 For the LORD loves his people,
   and he adorns the lowly with
   victory.
5 Let the faithful exult in glory;
   let them sing for joy upon their
   couches;
6 let the high praises of God be in
   their throats.

II

And let two-edged swords be in
   their hands:
7   to execute vengeance on the
   nations,
   punishments on the peoples;
8 To bind their kings with chains,
   their nobles with fetters of iron;
9 To execute on them the written
   sentence.
   This is the glory of all his
   faithful.   Alleluia.

---

† Ps 148: All creatures in the heavens (1-6) and on earth (7-10) are called upon to join in the hymn of praise that universal mankind, and especially Israel, should sing to the Lord of all (11-14).

148, 4: *Highest heavens:* literally, "the heavens of the heavens," that is, the space above the firmament, where the "upper waters" are stored. Cf Gn 1, 6ff; Dt 10, 14; 1 Kgs 8, 27; Ps 104, 3.13.

148, 14: *Lifted up the horn of his people:* restored their power. Cf note on Ps 18, 3.

Ps 149: While the people are invited to praise the Lord with sacred music in the temple (1-6a), they stand with sword in hand for the defense of Zion (6b-9). Cf Neh 4, 16-23 (10-17); 1 Mc 4, 37f.54; 2 Mc 15, 26f.

149, 3: *The festive dance:* Cf Ex 15, 20; 2 Sm 6, 5.14.16.

✻
148/2ff: Dn 3, 58-63.   149/3: Ps 150, 3f.

Final Doxology with Full Orchestra

150 † 1† Alleluia.

Praise the LORD in his sanctuary,
  praise him in the firmament of
  his strength.
2 Praise him for his mighty deeds,
  praise him for his sovereign
  majesty.
3 Praise him with the blast of the
  trumpet,
  praise him with lyre and harp,
4 Praise him with timbrel and
  dance,
  praise him with strings and
  pipe.

5 Praise him with sounding
  cymbals,
  praise him with clanging
  cymbals.
6 Let everything that has breath
  praise the LORD!   Alleluia.

---

† Ps 150: As a grand finale, the psalmist calls upon all the musical instruments of the temple service to join in the praise of the Lord; thus, the psalm serves as the closing doxology, not only to the Fifth Book of the Psalms, but to the whole Psalter.

150, 1: *Praise the Lord:* in Hebrew, *hallelu-yah,* which through the Greek and Latin versions has become our "Alleluia."

The Book of Proverbs

Introduction

The first word of this book, *Mishle,* has provided the title by which it is generally designated in Jewish and Christian circles. The name "Proverbs," while not an exact equivalent of *Mishle,* describes the main contents satisfactorily, even though it is hardly an adequate designation for such parts as 1, 1–9, 18 or 31, 10-31. Among some early Christian writers the book was also known by the name of "Wisdom," and in the Roman Missal it was for many centuries.

The Book of Proverbs is an anthology of didactic poetry forming part of the sapiential literature of the Old Testament. Its primary purpose, indicated in the first sentence (1, 2f), is to teach wisdom. It is thus directed particularly to the young and inexperienced (1, 4); but also to those who desire advanced training in wisdom (1, 5f). The wisdom which the book teaches, covers a wide field of human and divine activity, ranging from matters purely secular to most lofty moral and religious truths, such as God's omniscience (5, 21; 15, 3-11), power (19, 21; 21, 30), providence (20, 1-24), goodness (15, 29), and the joy and strength resulting from abandonment to him (3, 5; 16, 20; 18, 10). The teaching of the entire book is placed on a firm religious foundation by the principle that "the fear of the LORD is the beginning of knowledge" (1, 7; cf 9, 10).

To Solomon are explicitly ascribed parts II and V of the book; he is the patron of Hebrew wisdom. Of Agur (part VI) and Lemuel (part VIII), nothing further is known. Parts III and IV are attributed to "the wise." The remaining parts are anonymous.

The manner of compilation is conjectural. Parts II and V may have circulated first as independent collections, compiled before the fall of Jerusalem, as the references to Solomon (10, 1) and Hezekiah (25, 1) suggest. Parts III, IV and VII would seem to belong together as a third collection of a similar kind.

The author of the first nine chapters, a religious sage familiar with the earlier sacred books, was the editor of the whole as we have it, probably in the early part of the fifth century B. C.

Christ and the Apostles often expressly quoted the Proverbs (Jn 7, 38; Rom 12, 20; Jas 4, 6) or repeated their teaching; compare Lk 10, 14, and Prv 25, 7; 1 Pt 4, 8; Jas 5, 20 and Prv 10, 12. The book has an important place in the Latin and Greek liturgies.

On the basis of titles, subject matter, and poetic structure the Book of Proverbs may be divided as follows:

I: INTRODUCTION: THE VALUE OF WISDOM

Purpose of the Proverbs of Solomon

1 ¹*† THE PROVERBS OF SOLOMON, the son of David, king of Israel:

²† That men may appreciate wisdom and discipline,
may understand words of intelligence;

³ May receive training in wise conduct,
in what is right, just and honest;

⁴† That resourcefulness may be imparted to the simple,
to the young man knowledge and discretion.

⁵ A wise man by hearing them will advance in learning,
an intelligent man will gain sound guidance,

⁶ That he may comprehend proverb and parable,
the words of the wise and their riddles.

⁷*† The fear of the LORD is the beginning of knowledge;
wisdom and instruction fools despise.

---

† 1, 1-6: This prologue explains the purpose of the book: to educate the inexperienced in knowledge and right conduct, and to increase the learning of the wise man by proverbs, parables and riddles.

1, 2: *Discipline:* education or formation which dispels ignorance and corrects vice.

1, 4: *Simple:* immature and inexperienced, hence easily influenced for good or evil.

1, 7: *Fear of the Lord:* reverential fear and respect for God on account of his sovereignty, goodness and justice toward men. This is the foundation of religion.

The Path of the Wicked:
Greed and Violence

8† Hear, my son, your father's instruction,
    and reject not your mother's teaching;

9 A graceful diadem will they be for your
      head;
    a torque for your neck.

10 My son, should sinners entice you, 11and
      say,
    "Come along with us!
    Let us lie in wait for the honest man,
      let us, unprovoked, set a trap for the
      innocent;

12 Let us swallow them up, as the nether
      world does, alive,
    in the prime of life, like those who go
      down to the pit!

13 All kinds of precious wealth shall we gain,
    we shall fill our houses with booty;

14 Cast in your lot with us,
    we shall all have one purse!"—

15 My son, walk not in the way with them,
    hold back your foot from their path!

16✸ [For their feet run to evil,
    they hasten to shed blood.]

17† It is in vain that a net is spread
    before the eyes of any bird—

18 These men lie in wait for their own blood,
    they set a trap for their own lives.

19 This is the fate of everyone greedy of loot:
    unlawful gain takes away the life of him
      who acquires it.

Wisdom in Person Gives Warning

20✸† Wisdom cries aloud in the street,
    in the open squares she raises her voice;

21 Down the crowded ways she calls out,
    at the city gates she utters her words:

22 "How long, you simple ones, will you love
      inanity,

23   how long will you turn away at my
      reproof?
    Lo! I will pour out to you my spirit,
    I will acquaint you with my words.

24✸ "Because I called and you refused,
    I extended my hand and no one took
      notice;

25 Because you disdained all my counsel,
    and my reproof you ignored—

26 I, in my turn, will laugh at your doom;
    I will mock when terror overtakes you;

27 When terror comes upon you like a storm,
    and your doom approaches like a
      whirlwind;
    when distress and anguish befall you.

28† "Then they call me, but I answer not;
    they seek me, but find me not;

29 Because they hated knowledge,
    and chose not the fear of the Lᴏʀᴅ;

30 They ignored my counsel,
    they spurned all my reproof;
    And in their arrogance they preferred
      arrogance,
    and like fools they hated knowledge:

31† "Now they must eat the fruit of their own
      way,
    and with their own devices be glutted.

32 For the self-will of the simple kills them,
    the smugness of fools destroys them.

33✸ But he who obeys me dwells in security,
    in peace, without fear of harm."

The Blessings of Wisdom

2† 1† My son, if you receive my words
    and treasure my commands,

2† Turning your ear to wisdom,
    inclining your heart to understanding;

3 Yes, if you call to intelligence,
    and to understanding raise your voice;

4 If you seek her like silver,
    and like hidden treasures search her out:

5 Then will you understand the fear of the
      Lᴏʀᴅ;
    the knowledge of God you will find;

6✸ For the Lᴏʀᴅ gives wisdom,
    from his mouth come knowledge and
      understanding;

---

† 1, 8-19: A warning against association with the greedy and the violent who seek to destroy the honest man and to steal his possessions (11-14). The trap which the wicked set for the innocent (11), in the end (19) takes away the life of the wicked themselves.

1, 17: Instructed by the wise man, the youth (of v 4) will recognize the invitation of the wicked (11-14) as a *net* spread before him, and he will thus, like the *bird,* be protected against falling into it.

1, 20-33: Wisdom is here personified; with divine authority she sets forth and proclaims the moral order, instructing and threatening (24-33) the multitudes in the streets and places of assembly.

1, 28: Overtaken by doom, the foolish seek wisdom, but in vain because they do so too late. Cf Jn 7, 34; 8, 21.

1, 31: Sinners are punished by the bad fruits which their sins produce. Cf Wis 11, 16.

2—7: These chapters form an ordered discourse in seven "columns" of twenty-two verses each. Chapter 2 introduces the four topics about which the sage instructs his pupil: the service of God (3, 1-12.25-34), the search for wisdom (3, 13-24.35; 4, 1-9), the avoidance of evil companions among men (4, 10-27; 5, 21-23), and among women (5, 1-20; 6, 20—7, 27). The last topic is treated at a length equal to the first three because the discourse is meant especially for youths (cf 1, 4).

2, 1-22: The search for wisdom (1-4) leads to the protection of God (5-8) and of wisdom herself (9ff; cf 1, 20-33) and to deliverance from evil men (12-15) and evil women (16-19), and so to lasting happiness (20ff).

2, 2f: *Wisdom, understanding, intelligence:* various names or aspects of the same gift.

✸
16: Is 59, 7.
20: 8, 1-3; 9, 3.
24: Is 65, 2.12; 66, 4;
   Jer 7, 13.

33: 8, 33f.
2/6: Jb 32, 8; Wis 7, 25;
   Sir 1, 1; Jas 1, 5.

7 He has counsel in store for the upright,
    he is the shield of those who walk
      honestly,

8 Guarding the paths of justice,
    protecting the way of his pious ones.

9 Then you will understand rectitude and
    justice,
    honesty, every good path;

10 For wisdom will enter your heart,
    knowledge will please your soul,

11 Discretion will watch over you,
    understanding will guard you;

12 Saving you from the way of evil men,
    from men of perverse speech,

13 Who leave the straight paths
    to walk in ways of darkness,

14 Who delight in doing evil,
    rejoice in perversity;

15 Whose ways are crooked,
    and devious their paths;

16 Saving you from the wife of another,
    from the adulteress with her smooth
      words,

17 Who forsakes the companion of her youth
    and forgets the pact with her God;

18 For her path sinks down to death,
    and her footsteps lead to the shades;

19 None who enter thereon come back again,
    or gain the paths of life.

20 Thus you may walk in the way of good men,
    and keep to the paths of the just.

21 For the upright will dwell in the land,
    the honest will remain in it;

22 But the wicked will be cut off from the land,
    the faithless will be rooted out of it.

Attitude toward the Lord

3 **1** My son, forget not my teaching,
    keep in mind my commands;

2 For many days, and years of life,
    and peace, will they bring you.

3 Let not kindness and fidelity leave you;
    bind them around your neck;

4 Then will you win favor and good esteem
    before God and man.

5 Trust in the LORD with all your heart,
    on your own intelligence rely not;

6 In all your ways be mindful of him,
    and he will make straight your paths.

7 Be not wise in your own eyes,
    fear the LORD and turn away from evil;

8 This will mean health for your flesh
    and vigor for your bones.

9 Honor the LORD with your wealth,
    with first fruits of all your produce;

10 Then will your barns be filled with grain,
    with new wine your vats will overflow.

11 The discipline of the LORD, my son, disdain
    not;
    spurn not his reproof;

12 For whom the LORD loves he reproves,
    and he chastises the son he favors.

The Value of Wisdom

13 Happy the man who finds wisdom,
    the man who gains understanding!

14 For her profit is better than profit in silver,
    and better than gold is her revenue;

15 She is more precious than corals,
    and none of your choice possessions can
      compare with her.

16 Long life is in her right hand,
    in her left are riches and honor;

17 Her ways are pleasant ways,
    and all her paths are peace;

18 She is a tree of life to those who grasp her,
    and he is happy who holds her fast.

19 The LORD by wisdom founded the earth,
    established the heavens by understand-
      ing;

20 By his knowledge the depths break open,
    and the clouds drop down dew.

21 My son, let not these slip out of your sight:
    keep advice and counsel in view;

22 So will they be life to your soul,
    and an adornment for your neck.

23 Then you may securely go your way;
    your foot will never stumble;

24 When you lie down, you need not be afraid,
    when you rest, your sleep will be sweet.

35 Honor is the possession of wise men,
    but fools inherit shame.

---

† 3, 1-12: Many are the rewards for fidelity and trust in God, and for diffidence of self (1-8). Cf Dt 30, 20; Is 38, 19. The offering of material things for divine worship is blessed by an increase of such goods (9f). Even correction and chastisement are a mark of God's love and favor (11f).

3, 13-24: Wisdom, or understanding, is more valuable than silver and gold. Its fruit is long life, riches, honor and happiness (13-18). Even the creation of the universe and its adornment (Gn 1) were not done without wisdom (19f). It is the life of the soul and gives security in work and in repose (21-24).

3, 15: *Corals:* some precious stone may be intended.

3, 18: *A tree of life:* cf 11, 30; 13, 12; Gn 2, 9.

3, 20: For the Hebrews, *the depths* enclosed the great subterranean ocean; the rain and the dew descended from the celestial ocean above the firmament; cf Gn 1, 6-10; Jb 26, 8.12; Pss 18, 16; 24, 2.

16: 5, 3.20; 6, 24; 7, 5;
  22, 14.
18: 5, 5f; 7, 27.
21f: 10, 7.30; Jb 18, 17;
  Pss 21, 9-13; 37, 22.28.
3/2: 4, 10; 9, 11; 10, 27.
  7: Rom 11, 25; 12, 16.
  9: Ex 34, 26; Lv 27, 30;
  Dt 26, 2; Sir 7, 31;
  35, 7.
11: Heb 12, 5f.
12: Jdt 8, 27; Rv 3, 19.
13: 8, 34f.
15: 8, 11.19; Wis 7, 8-11.
18: 4, 13; 8, 35; 11, 30;
  Gn 2, 9; 3, 22.

Attitude toward Fellow Men

25† Be not afraid of sudden terror,
of the ruin of the wicked when it comes;

26 For the LORD will be your confidence,
and will keep your foot from the snare.

27 Refuse no one the good on which he has a claim
when it is in your power to do it for him.

28 Say not to your neighbor, "Go, and come again,
tomorrow I will give," when you can give at once.

29 Plot no evil against your neighbor,
against him who lives at peace with you.

30 Quarrel not with a man without cause,
with one who has done you no harm.

31* Envy not the lawless man
and choose none of his ways:

32 To the LORD the perverse man is an abomination,
but with the upright is his friendship.

33 The curse of the LORD is on the house of the wicked,
but the dwelling of the just he blesses;

34* When he is dealing with the arrogant, he is stern,
but to the humble he shows kindness.

Wisdom: the Supreme Guide of Men

4 1† Hear, O children, a father's instruction,
be attentive, that you may gain understanding!

2 Yes, excellent advice I give you;
my teaching do not forsake.

3 When I was my father's child,
frail, yet the darling of my mother,

4* He taught me, and said to me:
"Let your heart hold fast my words:
keep my commands, that you may live!

5 "Get wisdom, get understanding!
Do not forget or turn aside from the words I utter.

6 Forsake her not, and she will preserve you;
love her, and she will safeguard you;

7 The beginning of wisdom is: get wisdom;
at the cost of all you have, get understanding.

8 Extol her, and she will exalt you;
she will bring you honors if you embrace her;

9 She will put on your head a graceful diadem;
a glorious crown will she bestow on you."

The Good and the Evil Way

10*† Hear, my son, and receive my words,
and the years of your life shall be many.

11 On the way of wisdom I direct you,
I lead you on straightforward paths.

12 When you walk, your step will not be impeded,
and should you run, you will not stumble.

13 Hold fast to instruction, never let her go;
keep her, for she is your life.

14 The path of the wicked enter not,
walk not on the way of evil men;

15 Shun it, cross it not,
turn aside from it, and pass on.

16 For they cannot rest unless they have done evil;
to have made no one stumble steals away their sleep.

17 For they eat the bread of wickedness
and drink the wine of violence.

19 The way of the wicked is like darkness;
they know not on what they stumble.

18† But the path of the just is like shining light,
that grows in brilliance till perfect day.

20 My son, to my words be attentive,
to my sayings incline your ear;

21 Let them not slip out of your sight,
keep them within your heart;

22* For they are life to those who find them,
to man's whole being they are health.

23 With closest custody, guard your heart,
for in it are the sources of life.

24 Put away from you dishonest talk,
deceitful speech put far from you.

25 Let your eyes look straight ahead
and your glance be directly forward.

26 Survey the path for your feet,
and let all your ways be sure.

27 Turn neither to right nor to left,
keep your foot far from evil.

---

† 3, 25-34: Serving God with confidence in him (25f) requires serving one's neighbor through kindness (27f), peace with the good (29ff), no envy of the wicked (31), because the Lord's friendship and kindness are with the just; his curse is with the wicked.

3, 25: *The ruin of the wicked:* i. e., the ruin that comes upon the wicked.

4, 1-9: The sage speaks as a father admonishing his children to secure wisdom at any cost.

4, 10-27: The way of wisdom leads directly to life (10-13); it is a light that grows brighter (18). The wise man is bound to shun (14-17) the dark and violent path of the wicked (19). Singleness of purpose and right conduct proceed from the heart of a wise man as from the source of life (23-26); they save him from destruction on evil paths (4, 27; 5, 21ff).

4, 18: *Till perfect day:* literally, "till the day is established"; this may refer to full daylight or to noonday.

---

* 31: 23, 17; 24, 1.19;   4/4: 1 Kgs 2, 2ff.
      Ps 37, 1.   10: 3, 2.
     34: 1, 26.   22: 8, 35.

Warning against Adultery

5   1†   My son, to my wisdom be attentive,
to my knowledge incline your ear,

2   That discretion may watch over you,
and understanding may guard you.

3*   The lips of an adulteress drip with honey,
and her mouth is smoother than oil;

4   But in the end she is as bitter as wormwood,
as sharp as a two-edged sword.

5*   Her feet go down to death,
to the nether world her steps attain;

6   Lest you see before you the road to life,
her paths will ramble, you know not
where.

7   So now, O children, listen to me,
go not astray from the words of my
mouth.

8*   Keep your way far from her,
approach not the door of her house,

9*†   Lest you give your honor to others,
and your years to a merciless one;

10   Lest strangers have their fill of your wealth,
your hard-won earnings go to an alien's
house;

11   And you groan in the end,
when your flesh and your body are
consumed;

12   And you say, "Oh, why did I hate
instruction,
and my heart spurn reproof!

13   Why did I not listen to the voice of my
teachers,
nor to my instructors incline my ear!

14   I have all but come to utter ruin,
condemned by the public assembly!"

15   Drink water from your own cistern,
running water from your own well.

16   How may your water sources be dispersed
abroad,
streams of water in the streets?

17   Let your fountain be yours alone,
not one shared with strangers;

18   And have joy of the wife of your youth,

19†   your lovely hind, your graceful doe.
Her love will invigorate you always,
through her love you will flourish
continually,

6/22   When you lie down she will watch over you,
and when you wake, she will share your
concerns;
wherever you turn, she will guide you.

20   Why then, my son, should you go astray for
another's wife
and accept the embraces of an
adulteress?

21*†   For each man's ways are plain to the Lord's
sight;
all their paths he surveys;

22   By his own iniquities the wicked man will
be caught,
in the meshes of his own sin he will be
held fast;

23   He will die from lack of discipline,
through the greatness of his folly he will
be lost.

Miscellaneous Proverbs

6   1*†   My son, if you have become surety to your
neighbor,
given your hand in pledge to another,

2   You have been snared by the utterance of
your lips,
caught by the words of your mouth;

3   So do this, my son, to free yourself,
since you have fallen into your neighbor's power:
Go, hurry, stir up your neighbor!

4   Give no sleep to your eyes,
nor slumber to your eyelids;

5   Free yourself as a gazelle from the snare,
or as a bird from the hand of the fowler.

6*   Go to the ant, O sluggard,
study her ways and learn wisdom;

7   For though she has no chief,
no commander or ruler,

8   She procures her food in the summer,
stores up her provisions in the harvest.

9   How long, O sluggard, will you rest?
when will you rise from your sleep?

10†   A little sleep, a little slumber,
a little folding of the arms to rest—

---

† 5, 1-20: Understanding and discretion guard a man against the wiles of an adulteress, which lead astray and beget bitterness, bloodshed and death (1-6). They destroy honor, waste the years of life, despoil hard-earned wealth, consume the flesh, and bring remorse in the end (7-14). Conjugal fidelity and love for one wife only bring happiness and security (15-20). Cf 6, 20—7, 27.

5, 9: *Honor:* the words "life" and "wealth" have also been read in this place. *A merciless one:* the offended husband; cf 6, 34f.

5, 19: *Lovely hind . . . graceful doe:* oriental symbols of feminine beauty and charm; cf Sg 2, 7.9.17.

5, 21-23: These verses are best read after 4, 27.

6, 1-19: These verses interrupt the discourse of chapters 2-7, which should be read apart from them; they contain four shorter proverbs akin to those in chapter 30.

6, 1: *Given your hand in pledge:* literally, "struck your hands"; this was probably the legal method for closing a contract.

6, 10: This verse may be regarded as the sluggard's reply or as a continuation of the remonstrance.

✿   5/3: 7, 5.   21: Jb 14, 16; 31, 4; 34, 21.
5: 2, 18; 7, 27.   6/1f: 11, 15; 22, 26;
8: 7, 25.   Sir 8, 13; 29, 19.
9f: Sir 9, 6.   6: 30, 25.

11   Then will poverty come upon you like a
        highwayman,
        and want like an armed man.

12   A scoundrel, a villain, is he
        who deals in crooked talk.

13   He winks his eyes,
        shuffles his feet,
        makes signs with his fingers;

14   He has perversity in his heart,
        is always plotting evil,
        sows discord.

15   Therefore suddenly ruin comes upon him;
        in an instant he is crushed beyond cure.

16†   There are six things the LORD hates,
        yes, seven are an abomination to him;

17   Haughty eyes, a lying tongue,
        and hands that shed innocent blood;

18   A heart that plots wicked schemes,
        feet that run swiftly to evil,

19   The false witness who utters lies,
        and he who sows discord among
        brothers.

Warning against Adultery

20†   Observe, my son, your father's bidding,
        and reject not your mother's teaching;

21   Keep them fastened over your heart always,
        put them around your neck;

23   For the bidding is a lamp, and the teaching
        a light,
        and a way to life are the reproofs of
        discipline;

24✻   To keep you from your neighbor's wife,
        from the smooth tongue of the adulteress.

25✻   Lust not in your heart after her beauty,
        let her not captivate you with her glance!

26†   For the price of a loose woman
        may be scarcely a loaf of bread,
        But if she is married,
        she is a trap for your precious life.

27   Can a man take fire to his bosom,
        and his garments not be burned?

28   Or can a man walk on live coals,
        and his feet not be scorched?

29✻   So with him who goes in to his neighbor's
        wife—
        none who touches her shall go
        unpunished.

30   Men despise not the thief if he steals
        to satisfy his appetite when he is hungry;

31   Yet if he be caught he must pay back
        sevenfold;
        all the wealth of his house he may yield
        up.

32   But he who commits adultery is a fool;
        he who would destroy himself does it.

33   A degrading beating will he get,
        and his disgrace will not be wiped away;

34   For vindictive is the husband's wrath,
        he will have no pity on the day of
        vengeance;

35   He will not consider any restitution,
        nor be satisfied with the greatest gifts.

7   1   My son, keep my words,
        and treasure my commands.

2   Keep my commands and live,
        my teaching as the apple of your eye;

3✻   Bind them on your fingers,
        write them on the tablet of your heart.

4   Say to Wisdom, "You are my sister!"
        call Understanding, "Friend!"

5✻   That they may keep you from another's
        wife,
        from the adulteress with her smooth
        words.

6   For at the window of my house,
        through my lattice I looked out—

7   And I saw among the simple ones,
        I observed among the young men,
        a youth with no sense,

8   Going along the street near the corner,
        then walking in the direction of her
        house—

9   In the twilight, at dusk of day,
        at the time of the dark of night.

10   And lo! the woman comes to meet him,
        robed like a harlot, with secret designs—

11   She is fickle and unruly,
        in her home her feet cannot rest;

12   Now she is in the streets, now in the open
        squares,
        and at every corner she lurks in ambush—

13   When she seizes him, she kisses him,
        and with an impudent look says to him:

14†   "I owed peace offerings,
        and today I have fulfilled my vows;

---

†   6, 16-19: The seven vices symbolized for the most part by bodily organs are pride, lying, murder, intrigue, readiness to do evil, false witness, and the stirring up of discord.

6, 20—7, 27: Parental training and the love of wisdom are an invaluable and constant help for the young (6, 20-23; 7, 1-4). They are the best defense against adultery (6, 24; 7, 5.24f), which involves the guilty in many dangers and punishments (6, 26-35; 7, 6-27). Cf 5, 1-20.

6, 26: Some interpret the verse in a progressive sense, i. e., to satisfy the increasing demands of a courtesan a man is reduced to poverty; if the woman is married, even his very life is endangered.

7, 14: *"Peace offerings . . . vows"*: a portion of the sacrifice reverted to the donor and had to be eaten on the same day at a family festival (Lv 7, 11-15). In this figure, the adulteress offers to share with the foolish young man the deadly feast of her sensuality.

✻
24: 2, 16; 7, 5.   29: Sir 9, 9.
25: Ex 20, 17; Dt 5, 21;   7/3: Dt 6, 8.
     Sir 9, 8; 25, 20;   5: 2, 16; 6, 24.
     Mt 5, 28.

15 So I came out to meet you,
    to look for you, and I have found you!

16 With coverlets I have spread my couch,
    with brocaded cloths of Egyptian linen;

17 I have sprinkled my bed with myrrh,
    with aloes, and with cinnamon.

18 "Come, let us drink our fill of love,
    until morning, let us feast on love!

19 For my husband is not at home,
    he has gone on a long journey;

20 A bag of money he took with him,
    not till the full moon will he return
        home."

21* She wins him over by her repeated urging,
    with her smooth lips she leads him
        astray;

22 He follows her stupidly,
    like an ox that is led to slaughter;
    Like a stag that minces toward the net,

23 till an arrow pierces its liver;
    Like a bird that rushes into a snare,
        unaware that its life is at stake.

24 So now, O children, listen to me,
    be attentive to the words of my mouth!

25 Let not your heart turn to her ways,
    go not astray in her paths;

26 For many are those she has struck down
        dead,
    numerous, those she has slain.

27* Her house is made up of ways to the nether
        world,
    leading down into the chambers of death.

The Discourse of Wisdom

8 1*† Does not Wisdom call,
        and Understanding raise her voice?

2 On the top of the heights along the road,
    at the crossroads she takes her stand;

3 By the gates at the approaches of the city,
    in the entryways she cries aloud:

4 "To you, O men, I call;
    my appeal is to the children of men.

5† You simple ones, gain resource,
    you fools, gain sense.

6 "Give heed! for noble things I speak;
    honesty opens my lips.

7† Yes, the truth my mouth recounts,
    but wickedness my lips abhor.

8 Sincere are all the words of my mouth,
    no one of them is wily or crooked;

9 All of them are plain to the man of
        intelligence,
    and right to those who attain knowledge.

10 Receive my instruction in preference to
        silver,
    and knowledge rather than choice gold.

11* [For Wisdom is better than corals,
    and no choice possessions can compare
        with her.]

12 "I, Wisdom, dwell with experience,
    and judicious knowledge I attain.

13* [The fear of the LORD is to hate evil;]
    Pride, arrogance, the evil way,
        and the perverse mouth I hate.

14† Mine are counsel and advice;
    Mine is strength; I am understanding.

15 By me kings reign,
    and lawgivers establish justice;

16 By me princes govern,
    and nobles; all the rulers of earth.

17 "Those who love me I also love,
    and those who seek me find me.

18* With me are riches and honor,
    enduring wealth and prosperity.

19* My fruit is better than gold, yes, than pure
        gold,
    and my revenue than choice silver.

20 On the way of duty I walk,
    along the paths of justice,

21 Granting wealth to those who love me,
    and filling their treasuries.

22*† "The LORD begot me, the firstborn of his
        ways,
    the forerunner of his prodigies of long
        ago;

23*† From of old I was poured forth,
    at the first, before the earth.

21: 5, 3; 6, 24.   18: 3, 16.
27: 2, 18f; 5, 5.   19: 3, 14.
8/1: 1, 20f; 9, 3.   22: Wis 9, 9; Sir 1, 1; 24, 9.
11: 3, 15; Wis 7, 8.   23: Sir 1, 4.
13: 6, 16f; 16, 5.

† 8, 1-36: Wisdom is here personified as in 1, 20-33, to confirm the words of the teacher of wisdom. She exalts her grandeur and origin, and invites all (1-11) to be attentive to her salutary influence in human society (12-21), for she was privileged to be present at the creation of the world (22-31). Finally, she promises life and the favor of God to those who find her, death to those who despise her.

8, 5: *Simple ones . . . fools:* see note on 1, 4.

8, 7f: The truth and sincerity of wisdom are absolute because they are divine. They can neither deceive nor tolerate deception. An intelligent man understands and accepts them.

8, 14: What is here predicated of wisdom is elsewhere attributed to God (Jb 12, 13-16).

8, 22-31: Wisdom is of divine origin. It is here represented as a being which existed before all things (22-26) and concurred with God when he planned and executed the creation of the universe, adorned it with beauty and variety, and established its wonderful order (27-30). Here that plurality of divine Persons is foreshadowed which was afterward to be fully revealed when Wisdom in the Person of Jesus Christ became incarnate.

8, 23: *Poured forth:* the exact meaning of the Hebrew is uncertain; the expression must imply the equivalent of "born." The Hebrews liken the movement of air and of spirit to that of liquids.

24† When there were no depths I was brought
       forth,
   when there were no fountains or springs
       of water;

25 Before the mountains were settled into
       place,
   before the hills, I was brought forth;

26 While as yet the earth and the fields were
       not made,
   nor the first clods of the world.

27* "When he established the heavens I was
       there,
   when he marked out the vault over the
       face of the deep;

28 When he made firm the skies above,
   when he fixed fast the foundations of the
       earth;

29 When he set for the sea its limit,
   so that the waters should not transgress
       his command;

30*† Then was I beside him as his craftsman,
   and I was his delight day by day,
 Playing before him all the while,

31   playing on the surface of his earth;
   and I found delight in the sons of men.

32 "So now, O children, listen to me;
33   instruction and wisdom do not reject!
 Happy the man who obeys me,
   and happy those who keep my ways,

34 Happy the man watching daily at my gates,
   waiting at my doorposts;

35* For he who finds me finds life,
   and wins favor from the LORD;

36 But he who misses me harms himself;
   all who hate me love death."

The Two Banquets

9 1† Wisdom has built her house,
   she has set up her seven columns;

2 She has dressed her meat, mixed her wine,
   yes, she has spread her table.

3*† She has sent out her maidens; she calls
   from the heights out over the city:

4 "Let whoever is simple turn in here;
   to him who lacks understanding, I say,

5 Come, eat of my food,
   and drink of the wine I have mixed!

6 Forsake foolishness that you may live;
   advance in the way of understanding.

11* For by me your days will be multiplied
   and the years of your life increased."

7 He who corrects an arrogant man earns
       insult;
   and he who reproves a wicked man
       incurs opprobrium.

8* Reprove not an arrogant man, lest he hate
       you;
   reprove a wise man, and he will love you.

9 Instruct a wise man, and he becomes still
       wiser;
   teach a just man, and he advances in
       learning.

10* The beginning of wisdom is the fear of the
       LORD,
   and knowledge of the Holy One is
       understanding.

12 If you are wise, it is to your own advantage;
   and if you are arrogant, you alone shall
       bear it.

13* The woman Folly is fickle,
   she is inane, and knows nothing.

14 She sits at the door of her house
   upon a seat on the city heights,

15 Calling to passers-by
   as they go on their straight way:

16 "Let whoever is simple turn in here,
   or who lacks understanding; for to him I
       say,

17† Stolen water is sweet,
   and bread gotten secretly is pleasing!"

18† Little he knows that the shades are there,
   that in the depths of the nether world are
       her guests!

II: FIRST COLLECTION OF THE PROVERBS OF SOLOMON

10 1*† THE PROVERBS of Solomon:

   A wise son makes his father glad,
   but a foolish son is a grief to his
       mother.

2*   Ill-gotten treasures profit nothing,
   but virtue saves from death.

---

† 8, 24-26: The formless mass from which God created the heavens and the earth; cf Gn 1, 1f; 2, 4ff.

8, 30: *His craftsman:* furnishing God with the plan, as it were, for the creation of all things; cf. Jb 38, 1f; Wis 7, 22—8, 1. *I was his delight:* the ever-present object of God's complacency.

9, 1-6.13-18: Wisdom and folly are represented as matrons, each inviting people to her banquet. Wisdom offers the food and drink of divine doctrine and virtue which give life (1-6). Unstable and senseless folly furnishes the stolen bread and water of deceit and vice which bring death to her guests.

9, 3: *She calls:* i. e., indirectly, through her maidens; but the text could also mean that wisdom herself publicly proclaims her invitation.

9, 17: The secrecy implies wrongdoing.

9, 18: The banquet chamber of folly is a tomb from which no one who enters it is released.

10, 1—22, 16: The varied contents of this first collection of

* 27: 3, 19; Sir 24, 4f.   11: 3, 2.16; 4, 10; 10, 27.
30: Wis 9, 9.   13-18: 7, 7-27.
35: 3, 13-18; 4, 22.   10/1: 1, 1; 15, 20; 17, 25;
9/3: 8, 1f.   19, 13; 25, 1; 29, 15.
  8: Sir 10, 7.   2: 11, 4.6.
 10: 1, 7; Jb 28, 28;
    Ps 111, 10; Sir 1, 16.

3 The LORD permits not the just to hunger,
   but the craving of the wicked he
   thwarts.

4* The slack hand impoverishes,
   but the hand of the diligent enriches.

5 A son who fills the granaries in summer is
   a credit;
   a son who slumbers during harvest, a
   disgrace.

6 Blessings are for the head of the just,
   but a rod for the back of the fool.

7 The memory of the just will be blessed,
   but the name of the wicked will rot.

8 A wise man heeds commands,
   but a prating fool will be overthrown.

9 He who walks honestly walks securely,
   but he whose ways are crooked will
   fare badly.

10 He who winks at a fault causes trouble,
   but he who frankly reproves promotes
   peace.

11 A fountain of life is the mouth of the just,
   but the mouth of the wicked conceals
   violence.

12*† Hatred stirs up disputes,
   but love covers all offenses.

13 On the lips of the intelligent is found
   wisdom,
   [but the mouth of the wicked conceals
   violence].

14 Wise men store up knowledge,
   but the mouth of a fool is imminent
   ruin.

15† The rich man's wealth is his strong city;
   the ruination of the lowly is their
   poverty.

16* The just man's recompense leads to life,
   the gains of the wicked, to sin.

17* A path to life is his who heeds
   admonition,
   but he who disregards reproof goes
   astray.

18 It is the lips of the liar that conceal
   hostility;
   but he who spreads accusations is a
   fool.

19* Where words are many, sin is not
   wanting;
   but he who restrains his lips does well.

20 Like choice silver is the just man's
   tongue;
   the heart of the wicked is of little
   worth.

21 The just man's lips nourish many,
   but fools die for want of sense.

22*† It is the LORD's blessing that brings
   wealth,
   and no effort can substitute for it.

23 Crime is the entertainment of the fool;
   so is wisdom for the man of sense.

24 What the wicked man fears will befall
   him,
   but the desire of the just will be
   granted.

25 When the tempest passes, the wicked
   man is no more;
   but the just man is established forever.

26 As vinegar to the teeth, and smoke to the
   eyes,
   is the sluggard to those who use him as
   a messenger.

27* The fear of the LORD prolongs life,
   but the years of the wicked are brief.

28 The hope of the just brings them joy,
   but the expectation of the wicked
   comes to nought.

29 The LORD is a stronghold to him who
   walks honestly,
   but to evildoers, their downfall.

30 The just man will never be disturbed,
   but the wicked will not abide in the
   land.

31 The mouth of the just yields wisdom,
   but the perverse tongue will be cut off.

32 The lips of the just know how to please,
   but the mouth of the wicked, how to
   pervert.

---

† Solomon's proverbs apply mostly to individual life. Each of its three hundred and seventy-five proverbs is meant to be distinct from the others, developing one idea through contrasting parallelism in chapters 10-15, and a climactic treatment in 16-22.

10, 12: *Love covers all offenses:* a favorite maxim of the Apostles; cf 1 Cor 13, 7; Jas 5, 20; 1 Pt 4, 8; also Prv 17, 9.

10, 15: The inspired author reflects upon the reality of the power of money and the defeat of poverty, without approving these things.

10, 22: The blessing of God rather than our own industry crowns our efforts with success; cf Ps 127, 1f; Mt 6, 25-34.

❋
4: 6, 11, 12, 24; 13, 4;   19: 17, 27; Sir 20, 17;
   20, 13; 28, 19.   Jas 1, 19.
12: 1 Cor 13, 4-7; 1 Pt 4, 8.   22: Sir 11, 22.
16: 11, 18f.   27: 3, 2; 4, 10; 9, 11;
17: 15, 10.   14, 27.

11 1* False scales are an abomination to the
LORD,
but a full weight is his delight.

2 When pride comes, disgrace comes;
but with the humble is wisdom.

3 The honesty of the upright guides them;
the faithless are ruined by their
duplicity.

4*† Wealth is useless on the day of wrath,
but virtue saves from death.

5* The honest man's virtue makes his way
straight,
but by his wickedness the wicked man
falls.

6 The virtue of the upright saves them,
but the faithless are caught in their
own intrigue.

7* When a wicked man dies his hope
perishes,
and what is expected from strength
comes to nought.

8 The just man escapes trouble,
and the wicked man falls into it in his
stead.

9* With his mouth the impious man would
ruin his neighbor,
but through their knowledge the just
make their escape.

10* When the just prosper, the city rejoices;
and when the wicked perish, there is
jubilation.

11 Through the blessing of the righteous the
city is exalted,
but through the mouth of the wicked it
is overthrown.

12 He who reviles his neighbor has no sense,
but the intelligent man keeps silent.

13* A newsmonger reveals secrets,
but a trustworthy man keeps a
confidence.

14* For lack of guidance a people falls;
security lies in many counselors.

15* He is in a bad way who becomes surety
for another,
but he who hates giving pledges is
safe.

16 A gracious woman wins esteem,
but she who hates virtue is covered
with shame.

[The slothful become impoverished,
but the diligent gain wealth.]

17 A kindly man benefits himself,
but a merciless man harms himself.

18* The wicked man makes empty profits,
but he who sows virtue has a sure
reward.

19 Virtue directs toward life,
but he who pursues evil does so to his
death.

20 The depraved in heart are an abomination to the LORD,
but those who walk blamelessly are his
delight.

21 Truly the evil man shall not go
unpunished,
but those who are just shall escape.

22 Like a golden ring in a swine's snout
is a beautiful woman with a rebellious
disposition.

23 The desire of the just ends only in good;
the expectation of the wicked is wrath.

24 One man is lavish yet grows still richer;
another is too sparing, yet is the poorer.

25 He who confers benefits will be amply
enriched,
and he who refreshes others will
himself be refreshed.

26 Him who monopolizes grain, the people
curse—
but blessings upon the head of him
who distributes it!

27 He who seeks the good commands favor,
but he who pursues evil will have evil
befall him.

28* He who trusts in his riches will fall,
but like green leaves the just flourish.

29 He who upsets his household has empty
air for a heritage;
and the fool will become slave to the
wise man.

30 The fruit of virtue is a tree of life,
but violence takes lives away.

31* If the just man is punished on earth,
how much more the wicked and the
sinner!

---

* 11/1: 16, 11; 20, 10;
     Lv 19, 35f.
  4: 10, 2.
  5: 28, 18.
  7: 10, 28; Wis 3, 18.
  9: 29, 5.
  10: 28, 12; 29, 2.

13: 20, 19.
14: 15, 22; 20, 18; 24, 6.
15: 6, 1f.
18: 10, 16.
28: Ps 52, 9f.
31: 1 Pt 4, 18.

---

† 11, 4: *Wealth . . . death:* not what a man is worth but what
he is, counts before God.

12
1* He who loves correction loves knowledge,
   but he who hates reproof is stupid.

2 The good man wins favor from the Lord,
   but the schemer is condemned by him.

3 No man is built up by wickedness,
   but the root of the just will never be
   disturbed.

4* A worthy wife is the crown of her
   husband,
   but a disgraceful one is like rot in his
   bones.

5 The plans of the just are legitimate;
   the designs of the wicked are deceitful.

6 The words of the wicked are a deadly
   ambush,
   but the speech of the upright saves
   them.

7 The wicked are overthrown and are no
   more,
   but the house of the just stands firm.

8 According to his good sense a man is
   praised,
   but one with a warped mind is
   despised.

9* Better a lowly man who supports himself
   than one of assumed importance who
   lacks bread.

10 The just man takes care of his beast,
   but the heart of the wicked is merciless.

11* He who tills his own land has food in
   plenty,
   but he who follows idle pursuits is a
   fool.

12 The stronghold of evil men will be
   demolished,
   but the root of the just is enduring.

13 In the sin of his lips the evil man is
   ensnared,
   but the just comes free of trouble.

14*† From the fruit of his words a man has his
   fill of good things,
   and the work of his hands comes back
   to reward him.

15 The way of the fool seems right in his
   own eyes,
   but he who listens to advice is wise.

16 The fool immediately shows his anger,
   but the shrewd man passes over an
   insult.

17* He tells the truth who states what he is
   sure of,
   but a lying witness speaks deceitfully.

18 The prating of some men is like sword
   thrusts,
   but the tongue of the wise is healing.

19 Truthful lips endure forever,
   the lying tongue, for only a moment.

20 Deceit is in the hands of those who plot
   evil,
   but those who counsel peace have joy.

21 No harm befalls the just,
   but the wicked are overwhelmed with
   misfortune.

22* Lying lips are an abomination to the
   Lord,
   but those who are truthful are his
   delight.

23 A shrewd man conceals his knowledge,
   but the hearts of fools gush forth folly.

24* The diligent hand will govern,
   but the slothful will be enslaved.

25* Anxiety in a man's heart depresses it,
   but a kindly word makes it glad.

26 The just man surpasses his neighbor,
   but the way of the wicked leads them
   astray.

27 The slothful man catches not his prey,
   but the wealth of the diligent man is
   great.

28 In the path of justice there is life,
   but the abominable way leads to
   death.

13
1 A wise son loves correction,
   but the senseless one heeds no rebuke.

2* From the fruit of his words a man eats
   good things,
   but the treacherous one craves
   violence.

3* He who guards his mouth protects his
   life;
   to open wide one's lips brings
   downfall.

4 The soul of the sluggard craves in vain,
   but the diligent soul is amply satisfied.

---

* 12/1: 15, 5.10; 29, 1;
   Sir 19, 5; 21, 6.
   4: Sir 26, 1.16.
   9: Sir 10, 26.
   11: 28, 19; Sir 20, 27.
   14: 13, 2; 18, 20.
   17: 14, 5.
   22: 6, 17.
   24: 10, 4; 13, 4.
   25: 15, 13; 17, 22.
   13/2: 12, 14; 18, 20.
   3: 18, 7; 21, 23.

† 12, 14: Cf Mt 7, 17; Gal 6, 8.

5 Anything deceitful the just man hates,
but the wicked brings shame and
disgrace.

6* Virtue guards one who walks honestly,
but the downfall of the wicked is sin.

7 One man pretends to be rich, yet has
nothing;
another pretends to be poor, yet has
great wealth.

8 A man's riches serve as ransom for his
life,
but the poor man heeds no rebuke.

9*† The light of the just shines gaily,
but the lamp of the wicked goes out.

10 The stupid man sows discord by his
insolence,
but with those who take counsel is
wisdom.

11* Wealth quickly gotten dwindles away,
but amassed little by little, it grows.

12 Hope deferred makes the heart sick,
but a wish fulfilled is a tree of life.

13† He who despises the word must pay for it,
but he who reveres the commandment
will be rewarded.

14 The teaching of the wise is a fountain of
life,
that a man may avoid the snares of
death.

15 Good sense brings favor,
but the way of the faithless is their
ruin.

16 The shrewd man does everything with
prudence,
but the fool peddles folly.

17 A wicked messenger brings on disaster,
but a trustworthy envoy is a healing
remedy.

18 Poverty and shame befall the man who
disregards correction,
but he who heeds reproof is honored.

19 Lust indulged starves the soul,
but fools hate to turn from evil.

20* Walk with wise men and you will become
wise,
but the companion of fools will fare
badly.

21 Misfortune pursues sinners,
but the just shall be recompensed with
good.

22 The good man leaves an inheritance to
his children's children,
but the wealth of the sinner is stored
up for the just.

23 A lawsuit devours the tillage of the poor,
but some men perish for lack of a law
court.

24* He who spares his rod hates his son,
but he who loves him takes care to
chastise him.

25 When the just man eats, his hunger is
appeased;
but the belly of the wicked suffers
want.

14 1 Wisdom builds her house,
but Folly tears hers down with her
own hands.

2 He who walks uprightly fears the Lord,
but he who is devious in his ways
spurns him.

3 In the mouth of the fool is a rod for his
back,
but the lips of the wise preserve them.

4 Where there are no oxen, the crib
remains empty;
but large crops come through the
strength of the bull.

5* A truthful witness does not lie,
but a false witness utters lies.

6 The senseless man seeks in vain for
wisdom,
but knowledge is easy to the man of
intelligence.

7 To avoid the foolish man, take steps!
But knowing lips one meets with by
surprise.

8 The shrewd man's wisdom gives him
knowledge of his way,
but the folly of fools is their deception.

9 Guilt lodges in the tents of the arrogant,
but favor in the house of the just.

10 The heart knows its own bitterness,
and in its joy no one else shares.

11* The house of the wicked will be
destroyed,
but the tent of the upright will flourish.

6: 11, 3.5f. 9: 24, 20. 11: 28, 20.22. 20: Sir 6, 34; 8, 8.17.
24: 19, 18; 22, 15; 23, 13f; 29, 15; Sir 30, 1.8-13. 14/5: 12, 17. 11: 3, 33; 12, 7; 15, 25.

† 13, 9: *Light . . . lamp:* symbols of life and prosperity; cf 4, 18f.
13, 13: *Word:* advice, or God's law.

12* Sometimes a way seems right to a man,
    but the end of it leads to death!

13 Even in laughter the heart may be sad,
    and the end of joy may be sorrow.

14 The scoundrel suffers the consequences
    of his ways,
    and the good man reaps the fruit of his
    paths.

15 The simpleton believes everything,
    but the shrewd man measures his
    steps.

16 The wise man is cautious and shuns evil;
    the fool is reckless and sure of himself.

17 The quick-tempered man makes a fool of
    himself,
    but the prudent man is at peace.

18 The adornment of simpletons is folly,
    but shrewd men gain the crown of
    knowledge.

19 Evil men must bow down before the
    good,
    and the wicked, at the gates of the just.

20* Even by his neighbor the poor man is
    hated,
    but the friends of the rich are many.

21 He sins who despises the hungry;
    but happy is he who is kind to the
    poor!

22 Do not those who plot evil go astray?
    But those intent on good gain kindness
    and constancy.

23 In all labor there is profit,
    but mere talk tends only to penury.

24 The crown of the wise is resourcefulness;
    the diadem of fools is folly.

25 The truthful witness saves lives,
    but he who utters lies is a betrayer.

26 In the fear of the LORD is a strong
    defense;
    even for one's children he will be a
    refuge.

27 The fear of the LORD is a fountain of life,
    that a man may avoid the snares of
    death.

28 In many subjects lies the glory of the
    king;
    but if his people are few, it is the
    prince's ruin.

29* The patient man shows much good sense,
    but the quick-tempered man displays
    folly at its height.

30 A tranquil mind gives life to the body,
    but jealousy rots the bones.

31* He who oppresses the poor blasphemes
    his Maker,
    but he who is kind to the needy
    glorifies him.

32 The wicked man is overthrown by his
    wickedness,
    but the just man finds a refuge in his
    honesty.

33 In the heart of the intelligent wisdom
    abides,
    but in the bosom of fools it is unknown.

34 Virtue exalts a nation,
    but sin is a people's disgrace.

35 The king favors the intelligent servant,
    but the worthless one incurs his wrath.

15

1* A mild answer calms wrath,
    but a harsh word stirs up anger.

2 The tongue of the wise pours out
    knowledge,
    but the mouth of fools spurts forth
    folly.

3 The eyes of the LORD are in every place,
    keeping watch on the evil and the
    good.

4 A soothing tongue is a tree of life,
    but a perverse one crushes the spirit.

5* The fool spurns his father's admonition,
    but prudent is he who heeds reproof.

6 In the house of the just there are ample
    resources,
    but the earnings of the wicked are in
    turmoil.

7 The lips of the wise disseminate
    knowledge,
    but the heart of fools is perverted.

8* The sacrifice of the wicked is an
    abomination to the LORD,
    but the prayer of the upright is his
    delight.

9* The way of the wicked is an abomination
    to the LORD,
    but he loves the man who pursues
    virtue.

10 Severe punishment is in store for the man
    who goes astray;
    he who hates reproof will die.

12: 16, 25.
20: 19, 4.7; Sir 6, 8.12.
29: 16, 32; 19, 11;
    Jas 1, 19.
31: 17, 5.

15/1: 25, 15; Sir 6, 5.
    5: 12, 1; 13, 18.
    8: 21, 27; Eccl 4, 17;
        Sir 34, 18ff; Is 1, 11-15.
    9: 11, 20; 21, 21.

11† The nether world and the abyss lie open
   before the Lord;
   how much more the hearts of men!

12 The senseless man loves not to be
   reproved;
   to wise men he will not go.

13* A glad heart lights up the face,
   but by mental anguish the spirit is
   broken.

14 The mind of the intelligent man seeks
   knowledge,
   but the mouth of fools feeds on folly.

15 Every day is miserable for the depressed,
   but a lighthearted man has a continual
   feast.

16† Better a little with fear of the Lord
   than a great fortune with anxiety.

17 Better a dish of herbs where love is
   than a fatted ox and hatred with it.

18* An ill-tempered man stirs up strife,
   but a patient man allays discord.

19 The way of the sluggard is hemmed in as
   with thorns,
   but the path of the diligent is a
   highway.

20* A wise son makes his father glad,
   but a fool of a man despises his mother.

21 Folly is joy to the senseless man,
   but the man of understanding goes the
   straight way.

22* Plans fail when there is no counsel,
   but they succeed when counselors are
   many.

23* There is joy for a man in his utterance;
   a word in season, how good it is!

24 The path of life leads the prudent man
   upward,
   that he may avoid the nether world
   below.

25 The Lord overturns the house of the
   proud,
   but he preserves intact the widow's
   landmark.

26* The wicked man's schemes are an
   abomination to the Lord,
   but the pure speak what is pleasing to
   him.

27 He who is greedy of gain brings ruin on
   his own house,
   but he who hates bribes will live.

28 The just man weighs well his utterance,
   but the mouth of the wicked pours out
   evil.

29 The Lord is far from the wicked,
   but the prayer of the just he hears.

30 A cheerful glance brings joy to the heart;
   good news invigorates the bones.

31* He who listens to salutary reproof
   will abide among the wise.

32 He who rejects admonition despises his
   own soul,
   but he who heeds reproof gains
   understanding.

33* The fear of the Lord is training for
   wisdom,
   and humility goes before honors.

16   **1†** Man may make plans in his heart,
   but what the tongue utters is from the
   Lord.

2* All the ways of a man may be pure in his
   own eyes,
   but it is the Lord who proves the spirit.

3 Entrust your works to the Lord,
   and your plans will succeed.

4† The Lord has made everything for his
   own ends,
   even the wicked for the evil day.

5* Every proud man is an abomination to
   the Lord;
   I assure you that he will not go
   unpunished.

6 By kindness and piety guilt is expiated,
   and by the fear of the Lord man avoids
   evil.

7 When the Lord is pleased with a man's
   ways,
   he makes even his enemies be at peace
   with him.

8 Better a little with virtue,
   than a large income with injustice.

---

*
13: 12, 25; 17, 22;
   Sir 30, 22.
18: 26, 21; 29, 22;
   Sir 28, 11.
20: 10, 1; 29, 3.
22: 11, 14.

23: 25, 11; Sir 20, 6.
26: 6, 18.
31: 25, 12.
33: 1, 7; Sir 1, 24.
16/2: 21, 2.
5: 6, 16f; 8, 13.

---

† 15, 11: *Nether world . . . abyss:* the abode of the dead, signifying the profound obscurity which is open nevertheless to the
sight and power of God.

15, 16f: Not the amount of temporal goods but the virtue of
their possessor makes them a source of happiness.

16, 1: Words, like actions, often produce results different from
those which were planned.

16, 4: Even the wicked, in their punishment, cannot escape
glorifying God's justice.

9❋ In his mind a man plans his course,
   but the Lord directs his steps.

10† The king's lips are an oracle;
   no judgment he pronounces is false.

11❋ Balance and scales belong to the Lord;
   all the weights used with them are his
   concern.

12❋ Kings have a horror of wrongdoing,
   for by righteousness the throne
   endures.

13❋ The king takes delight in honest lips,
   and the man who speaks what is right
   he loves.

14❋ The king's wrath is like messengers of
   death,
   but a wise man can pacify it.

15 In the light of the king's countenance is
   life,
   and his favor is like a rain cloud in
   spring.

16❋ How much better to acquire wisdom
   than gold!
   To acquire understanding is more
   desirable than silver.

17 The path of the upright avoids misfortune;
   he who pays attention to his way
   safeguards his life.

18❋ Pride goes before disaster,
   and a haughty spirit before a fall.

19 It is better to be humble with the meek
   than to share plunder with the proud.

20 He who plans a thing will be successful;
   happy is he who trusts in the Lord!

21 The wise man is esteemed for his discernment,
   yet pleasing speech increases his
   persuasiveness.

22 Good sense is a fountain of life to its
   possessor,
   but folly brings chastisement on fools.

23 The mind of the wise man makes him
   eloquent,
   and augments the persuasiveness of his
   lips.

24 Pleasing words are a honeycomb,
   sweet to the taste and healthful to the
   body.

25❋ Sometimes a way seems right to a man,
   but the end of it leads to death!

26❋ The laborer's appetite labors for him,
   for his mouth urges him on.

27 A scoundrel is a furnace of evil,
   and on his lips there is a scorching fire.

28❋ An intriguer sows discord,
   and a talebearer separates bosom
   friends.

29 A lawless man allures his neighbor,
   and leads him into a way that is not
   good.

30 He who winks his eye is plotting trickery;
   he who compresses his lips has
   mischief ready.

31❋ Gray hair is a crown of glory;
   it is gained by virtuous living.

32❋ A patient man is better than a warrior,
   and he who rules his temper, than he
   who takes a city.

33† When the lot is cast into the lap,
   its decision depends entirely on the
   Lord.

17 1 Better a dry crust with peace
   than a house full of feasting with strife.

2† An intelligent servant will rule over a
   worthless son,
   and will share the inheritance with the
   brothers.

3 The crucible for silver, and the furnace
   for gold,
   but the tester of hearts is the Lord.

4† The evil man gives heed to wicked lips,
   and listens to falsehood from a mis-
   chievous tongue.

5❋ He who mocks the poor blasphemes his
   Maker;
   he who is glad at calamity will not go
   unpunished.

---

† 16, 10: Decisions of supreme judicial authority were presumed disinterested and correct.

16, 33: The favorable or unfavorable results of chance depends on God. Deciding strifes and doubts by lot was practiced
by the ancient Hebrews; cf Ex 28, 15-30; Lv 16, 8; Jos 7, 14;
1 Sm 10, 20f.

17, 2: Intelligence and ability are esteemed more highly than
nobility of blood.

17, 4: To justify his own evil ways, a wicked man judges evil
of others. Cf Mt 7, 1-5.

❋
9: 19, 21; 20, 24.   25: 14, 12.
11: 11, 1.   26: 10, 4.
12: 25, 5.   28: 6, 14.19; 17, 9; 26, 22;
13: 14, 35; 22, 11.   Sir 28, 15.
14: 19, 12; 20, 2.   31: 20, 29.
16: 8, 10f.19.   32: 14, 29.
18: 11, 2.   17/5: 14, 31.

6 Grandchildren are the crown of old men,
and the glory of children is their
parentage.

7 Fine words are out of place in a fool;
how much more, lying words in a
noble!

8 A man who has a bribe to offer rates it a
magic stone;
at every turn it brings him success.

9 He who covers up a misdeed fosters
friendship,
but he who gossips about it separates
friends.

10 A single reprimand does more for a man
of intelligence
than a hundred lashes for a fool.

11 On rebellion alone is the wicked man
bent,
but a merciless messenger will be sent
against him.

12 Face a bear robbed of her cubs,
but never a fool in his folly!

13* If a man returns evil for good,
from his house evil will not depart.

14 The start of strife is like the opening of a
dam;
therefore, check a quarrel before it
begins!

15* He who condones the wicked, he who
condemns the just,
are both an abomination to the LORD.

16 Of what use in the fool's hand are the
means
to buy wisdom, since he has no mind
for it?

17* He who is a friend is always a friend,
and a brother is born for the time of
stress.

18* Senseless is the man who gives his hand
in pledge,
who becomes surety for his neighbor.

19*† He who loves strife loves guilt;
he who builds his gate high courts
disaster.

20 He who is perverse in heart finds no good,
and a double-tongued man falls into
trouble.

21 To be a fool's parent is grief for a man;
the father of a numskull has no joy.

22* A joyful heart is the health of the body,
but a depressed spirit dries up the
bones.

23 The wicked man accepts a concealed
bribe
to pervert the course of justice.

24* The man of intelligence fixes his gaze on
wisdom,
but the eyes of a fool are on the ends of
the earth.

25* A foolish son is vexation to his father,
and bitter sorrow to her who bore him.

26 It is wrong to fine an innocent man,
but beyond reason to scourge princes.

27* He who spares his words is truly wise,
and he who is chary of speech is a man
of intelligence.

28 Even a fool, if he keeps silent,
is considered wise;
if he closes his lips, intelligent.

18 **1** In estrangement one seeks pretexts:
with all persistence he picks a quarrel.

2 The fool takes no delight in understanding,
but rather in displaying what he
thinks.

3 With wickedness comes contempt,
and with disgrace comes scorn.

4* The words from a man's mouth are deep
waters,
but the source of wisdom is a flowing
brook.

5* It is not good to be partial to the guilty,
and so to reject a rightful claim.

6 The fool's lips lead him into strife,
and his mouth provokes a beating.

7* The fool's mouth is his ruin;
his lips are a snare to his life.

8* The words of a talebearer are like dainty
morsels
that sink into one's inmost being.

9 The man who is slack in his work
is own brother to the man who is
destructive.

10† The name of the LORD is a strong tower;
the just man runs to it and is safe.

13: Mt 5, 39; Rom 12, 17;
    1 Thes 5, 15; 1 Pt 3, 9.
15: 24, 24; Is 5, 23.
17: 18, 24.
18: 6, 1f; 11, 15.
19: 15, 18.
22: 12, 25; 15, 13.
24: Eccl 8, 1.

25: 10, 1; 29, 15.
27: 10, 19; Sir 1, 21;
    Jas 1, 19.
18/4: 20, 5; Jn 7, 38.
  5: 24, 23; 28, 21.
  7: 10, 14; 12, 13; 13, 3;
    Eccl 10, 12.
  8: 26, 22.

† 17, 19: *Builds . . . high:* a symbol of arrogance.
18, 10f: Religion is a strong support and sure refuge in the

11* The rich man's wealth is his strong city;
he fancies it a high wall.

12*† Before his downfall a man's heart is haughty,
but humility goes before honors.

13*† He who answers before he hears—
his is the folly and the shame.

14 A man's spirit sustains him in infirmity—
but a broken spirit who can bear?

15 The mind of the intelligent gains knowledge,
and the ear of the wise seeks knowledge.

16* A man's gift clears the way for him,
and gains him access to great men.

17 The man who pleads his case first seems to be in the right;
then his opponent comes and puts him to the test.

18† The lot puts an end to disputes,
and is decisive in a controversy between the mighty.

19 A brother is a better defense than a strong city,
and a friend is like the bars of a castle.

20*† From the fruit of his mouth a man has his fill;
with the yield of his lips he sates himself.

21* Death and life are in the power of the tongue;
those who make it a friend shall eat its fruit.

22* He who finds a wife finds happiness;
it is a favor he receives from the LORD.

23 The poor man implores,
but the rich man answers harshly.

24* Some friends bring ruin on us,
but a true friend is more loyal than a brother.

19 **1*** Better a poor man who walks in his integrity
than he who is crooked in his ways and rich.

2 Without knowledge even zeal is not good;
and he who acts hastily, blunders.

3 A man's own folly upsets his way,
but his heart is resentful against the LORD.

4* Wealth adds many friends,
but the friend of the poor man deserts him.

5* The false witness will not go unpunished,
and he who utters lies will not escape.

6 Many curry favor with a noble;
all are friends of the man who has something to give.

7 All the poor man's brothers hate him;
how much more do his friends shun him!

8 He who gains intelligence is his own best friend;
he who keeps understanding will be successful.

9 The false witness will not go unpunished,
and he who utters lies will perish.

10 Luxury is not befitting a fool;
much less should a slave rule over princes.

11 It is good sense in a man to be slow to anger,
and it is his glory to overlook an offense.

12* The king's wrath is like the roaring of a lion,
but his favor, like dew on the grass.

13* The foolish son is ruin to his father,
and the nagging of a wife is a persistent leak.

14* Home and possessions are an inheritance from parents,
but a prudent wife is from the LORD.

15* Laziness plunges a man into deep sleep,
and the sluggard must go hungry.

16* He who keeps the precept keeps his life,
but the despiser of the word will die.

---

† struggle of life. The rich foolishly rely on their wealth for such support.

18, 12: Compare the Savior's words: "Whoever exalts himself shall be humbled, but whoever humbles himself shall be exalted" (Mt 23, 12).

18, 13: To speak without first listening is characteristic of a fool; cf 10, 14; Sir 11, 8.

18, 18: See note on 16, 33.

18, 20f: Everyone must accept the consequences, of benefit or harm to himself, which his words produce.

✿
11: 10, 15.
12: 11, 2; 16, 18; Sir 10, 15.
13: Sir 11, 8.
16: 21, 14.
20: 12, 14; 13, 2.
21: Sir 37, 18.
22: 12, 4; 19, 14; Sir 7, 26.
24: 17, 17.

19/1: 28, 6.
4: 14, 20; Sir 13, 20ff.
5: Dt 19, 16-20; Dn 13, 61.
12: 20, 2.
13: 10, 1; 17, 25.
14: 18, 22.
15: 6, 9ff.
16: 13, 13; 16, 17.

17 *† He who has compassion on the poor lends
  to the LORD,
    and he will repay him for his good
      deed.

18 * Chastise your son, for in this there is
  hope;
    but do not desire his death.

19 The man of violent temper pays the
  penalty;
    even if you rescue him, you will have
      it to do again.

20 Listen to counsel and receive instruction,
  that you may eventually become wise.

21 * Many are the plans in a man's heart,
  but it is the decision of the LORD that
    endures.

22 From a man's greed comes his shame;
  rather be a poor man than a liar.

23 The fear of the LORD is an aid to life;
  one eats and sleeps without being
    visited by misfortune.

24 * The sluggard loses his hand in the dish;
  he will not even lift it to his mouth.

25 * If you beat an arrogant man, the simple
  learn a lesson;
    if you rebuke an intelligent man,
      he gains knowledge.

26 * He who mistreats his father, or drives
  away his mother,
    is a worthless and disgraceful son.

27 If a son ceases to hear instruction,
  he wanders from words of knowledge.

28 An unprincipled witness perverts justice,
  and the mouth of the wicked pours out
    iniquity.

29 * Rods are prepared for the arrogant,
  and blows for the backs of fools.

20 **1*** Wine is arrogant, strong drink is
  riotous;
    none who goes astray for it is wise.

2* The dread of the king is as when a lion
  roars;
    he who incurs his anger forfeits his
      life.

3 It is honorable for a man to shun strife,
  while every fool starts a quarrel.

4 In seedtime the sluggard plows not;
  when he looks for the harvest, it is not
    there.

5* The intention in the human heart is like
  water far below the surface,
    but the man of intelligence draws it
      forth.

6 Many are declared to be men of virtue:
  but who can find one worthy of trust?

7 When a man walks in integrity and
  justice,
    happy are his children after him!

8 A king seated on the throne of judgment
  dispels all evil with his glance.

9*† Who can say, "I have made my heart
  clean,
    I am cleansed of my sin"?

10* Varying weights, varying measures,
  are both an abomination to the LORD.

11 Even by his manners the child betrays
  whether his conduct is innocent and
    right.

12 The ear that hears, and the eye that
  sees—
    the LORD has made them both.

13 Love not sleep, lest you be reduced to
  poverty;
    eyes wide open mean abundant food.

14† "Bad, bad!" says the buyer;
  but once he has gone his way,
    he boasts.

15 Like gold or a wealth of corals,
  wise lips are a precious ornament.

16*† Take his garment who becomes surety
  for another,
    and for strangers yield it up!

17 The bread of deceit is sweet to a man,
  but afterward his mouth will be filled
    with gravel.

18 Plans made after advice succeed;
  so with wise guidance wage your war.

19 A newsmonger reveals secrets;
  so have nothing to do with a babbler!

---

*
17: 14, 21; 22, 9; 28, 27.   2: 19, 12.
18: 13, 24; 23, 13f.   5: 18, 4.
21: 16, 9.   9: 1 Kgs 8, 46;
24: 26, 15.   2 Chr 6, 36;
25: 17, 10; 21, 11.   Eccl 7, 20; 1 Jn 1, 8.
26: Sir 3, 16.   10: 11, 1; 20, 23.
29: 26, 3.   16: 27, 13.
20/1: 23, 29-35.

†
  19, 17: Cf Mt 25, 34-40.
  20, 9: Man can be free of sin only by the power of God. Cf
1 Kgs 8, 46ff; Jb 4, 17; 14, 4; Pss 51, 2ff; 130, 3f; Rom 3, 23f;
1 Jn 1, 8.
  20, 14: What one wishes to buy is valued cheaply in order
that it may be obtained at a low price; once purchased, it is
deemed more valuable.
  20, 16: Caution is again advised in the matter of becoming
surety; cf 6, 1ff.

20*† If one curses his father or mother,
his lamp will go out at the coming of
darkness.

21 Possessions gained hastily at the outset
will in the end not be blessed.

22* Say not, "I will repay evil!"
Trust in the Lord and he will help you.

23* Varying weights are an abomination to
the Lord,
and false scales are not good.

24*† Man's steps are from the Lord;
how, then, can a man understand his
way?

25† Rashly to pledge a sacred gift is a trap
for a man,
or to regret a vow once made.

26 A wise king winnows the wicked,
and threshes them under the cart-
wheel.

27 A lamp from the Lord is the breath of
man;
it searches through all his inmost
being.

28* Kindness and piety safeguard the king,
and he upholds his throne by justice.

29* The glory of young men is their strength,
and the dignity of old men is gray hair.

30 Evil is cleansed away by bloody lashes,
and a scourging to the inmost being.

21 **1** Like a stream is the king's heart in the
hand of the Lord;
wherever it pleases him, he directs it.

2* All the ways of a man may be right in his
own eyes,
but it is the Lord who proves hearts.

3*† To do what is right and just
is more acceptable to the Lord than
sacrifice.

4 Haughty eyes and a proud heart—
the tillage of the wicked is sin.

5 The plans of the diligent are sure of
profit,
but all rash haste leads certainly to
poverty.

6 He who makes a fortune by a lying
tongue
is chasing a bubble over deadly snares.

7 The oppression of the wicked will sweep
them away,
because they refuse to do what is
right.

8 The way of the culprit is crooked,
but the conduct of the innocent is
right.

9* It is better to dwell in a corner of the
housetop
than in a roomy house with a quarrelsome woman.

10 The soul of the wicked man desires evil;
his neighbor finds no pity in his eyes.

11* When the arrogant man is punished, the
simple are the wiser;
when the wise man is instructed, he
gains knowledge.

12 The just man appraises the house of the
wicked:
there is one who brings down the
wicked to ruin.

13 He who shuts his ear to the cry of the
poor
will himself also call and not be heard.

14 A secret gift allays anger,
and a concealed present, violent
wrath.

15* To practice justice is a joy for the just,
but terror for evildoers.

16† The man who strays from the way of
good sense
will abide in the assembly of the
shades.

17 He who loves pleasure will suffer want;
he who loves wine and perfume will
not be rich.

18*† The wicked man serves as ransom for the
just,
and the faithless man for the
righteous.

---

† 20, 20: *His lamp will go out:* misfortune, even death, awaits
him; cf 13, 9; Ex 21, 17.
  20, 24: Man is dependent upon God and cannot fully foresee
his own course.
  20, 25: This verse cautions against making vows without
proper reflection; cf Dt 23, 22ff; Eccl 5, 4f.
  21, 3: External rites or sacrifices do not please God unless
accompanied by internal worship and right moral conduct; cf
15, 8; 21, 27; Is 1, 11-15; Am 5, 22; Mal 1, 12.
  21, 16: *Assembly of the shades:* cf note on Jb 26, 5.
  21, 18: *Wicked . . . ransom for the just:* exemplified in the
history of God's chosen people whom he ransomed from Egypt

✿
20: 30, 11.17; Ex 21, 17;   29: 16, 31.
    Lv 20, 9; Mt 15, 4.   21/2: 16, 2.
22: 24, 29; Sir 28, 1;   3: 1 Sm 15, 22; Hos 6, 6.
    Mt 5, 39; Rom 12,   9: 21, 19; 25, 24; 27, 15;
    17.19; 1 Thes 5, 15;   Sir 25, 23.
    1 Pt 3, 9.   11: 19, 25.
23: 11, 1; 20, 10.   15: 10, 29.
24: 16, 9.   18: 11, 8.
28: 16, 12.

19 It is better to dwell in a wilderness
than with a quarrelsome and
vexatious wife.

20 Precious treasure remains in the house
of the wise,
but the fool consumes it.

21 He who pursues justice and kindness
will find life and honor.

22 The wise man storms a city of the
mighty,
and overthrows the stronghold in
which it trusts.

23✱ He who guards his mouth and his tongue
keeps himself from trouble.

24 Arrogant is the name for the man of overbearing pride
who acts with scornful effrontery.

25 The sluggard's propensity slays him,
for his hands refuse to work.

26 Some are consumed with avarice all the
day,
but the just man gives unsparingly.

27✱ The sacrifice of the wicked is an
abomination,
the more so when they offer it with a
bad intention.

28✱ The false witness will perish,
but he who listens will finally have his
say.

29 The wicked man is brazenfaced,
but the upright man pays heed to his
ways.

30 There is no wisdom, no understanding,
no counsel, against the Lord.

31 The horse is equipped for the day of
battle,
but victory is the Lord's.

22 **1**✱ A good name is more desirable than
great riches,
and high esteem, than gold and silver.

2✱ Rich and poor have a common bond:
the Lord is the maker of them all.

3✱ The shrewd man perceives evil and
hides,
while simpletons continue on and
suffer the penalty.

4 The reward of humility and fear of the
Lord
is riches, honor and life.

5 Thorns and snares are on the path of the
crooked;
he who would safeguard his life will
shun them.

6 Train a boy in the way he should go;
even when he is old, he will not swerve
from it.

7 The rich rule over the poor,
and the borrower is the slave of the
lender.

8✱ He who sows iniquity reaps calamity,
and the rod destroys his labors.

9 The kindly man will be blessed,
for he gives of his sustenance to the
poor.

10 Expel the arrogant man and discord goes
out;
strife and insult cease.

11✱ The Lord loves the pure of heart;
the man of winning speech has the
king for his friend.

12 The eyes of the Lord safeguard knowledge,
but he defeats the projects of the
faithless.

13✱† The sluggard says, "A lion is outside;
in the streets I might be slain."

14✱ The mouth of the adulteress is a deep pit;
he with whom the Lord is angry will
fall into it.

15 Folly is close to the heart of a child,
but the rod of discipline will drive it
far from him.

16† He who oppresses the poor to enrich
himself
will yield up his gains to the rich as
sheer loss.

---

† at the cost of the life of Pharaoh and his army (Ex 14, 23-31),
and from Babylon by giving to Cyrus, the Persian conqueror,
Egypt, Ethiopia and Seba, the richest lands of the world (Is 43,
1ff).

22, 13: To avoid the effort required for doing good, *the sluggard* exaggerates the difficulties that must be overcome.

22, 16: Money gained by exploiting the poor is in turn lost to
those who are more wealthy.

✱
23: 13, 3.   8: Jb 4, 8; Sir 7, 3;
27: 15, 8; Sir 34, 18ff.   Hos 8, 7.
28: 19, 5.9.   11: Mt 5, 8.
22/1: Eccl 7, 1.   13: 26, 13.
2: 29, 13.   14: 23, 27.
3: 27, 12.

III: SAYINGS OF THE WISE

17 THE SAYINGS of the wise:

Incline your ear, and hear my words,
   and apply your heart to my doctrine;

18 For it will be well if you keep them in
   your bosom,
   if they all are ready on your lips.

19† That your trust may be in the LORD,
   I make known to you the words of
   Amen-em-Ope.

20 Have I not written for you the "Thirty,"
   with counsels and knowledge,

21 To teach you truly
   how to give a dependable report to
   one who sends you?

22 Injure not the poor because they are
   poor,
   nor crush the needy at the gate;

23 For the LORD will defend their cause,
   and will plunder the lives of those who
   plunder them.

24 Be not friendly with a hotheaded man,
   nor the companion of a wrathful man,

25 Lest you learn his ways,
   and get yourself into a snare.

26 Be not one of those who give their hand
   in pledge,
   of those who become surety for debts;

27 For if you have not the means to pay,
   your bed will be taken from under
   you.

28 Remove not the ancient landmark
   which your fathers set up.

29 You see a man skilled at his work?
   He will stand in the presence of kings;
   he will not stand in the presence of
   obscure men.

23 **1** When you sit down to dine with a ruler,
   keep in mind who is before you;

2† And put a knife to your throat
   if you have a ravenous appetite.

3 Do not desire his delicacies;
   they are deceitful food.

4 Toil not to gain wealth,
   cease to be concerned about it;

5 While your glance flits to it, it is gone!
   for assuredly it grows wings,
   like the eagle that flies toward heaven.

6 Do not take food with a grudging man,
   and do not desire his dainties;

7 For in his greed he is like a storm.
   "Eat and drink," he says to you,
   though his heart is not with you;

8 The little you have eaten you will vomit
   up,
   and you will have wasted your agreeable words.

9 Speak not for the fool's hearing;
   he will despise the wisdom of your
   words.

10 Remove not the ancient landmark,
   nor invade the fields of orphans;

11 For their redeemer is strong;
   he will defend their cause against you.

12 Apply your heart to instruction,
   and your ears to words of knowledge.

13 Withhold not chastisement from a boy;
   if you beat him with the rod, he will
   not die.

14 Beat him with the rod,
   and you will save him from the nether
   world.

15 My son, if your heart be wise,
   my own heart also will rejoice;

16 And my inmost being will exult,
   when your lips speak what is right.

17 Let not your heart emulate sinners,
   but be zealous for the fear of the LORD
   always;

---

† 22, 17–24, 22: This collection of proverbs, introduced as *sayings of the wise,* is given in the more intimate and personal form of an address to a pupil called the *son* and is arranged in strophes instead of couplets.

22, 17–23, 35: The maxims warn against: oppression of the poor and defenseless (22, 22f), anger (24f), giving surety for debts (26f), bad manners at a king's table (23, 1f), anxiety for riches (4f), a grudging host (6ff), intemperance in food and drink (19ff.29-35), and adultery (26ff). They exhort to: careful workmanship (22, 29), respect for the rights of orphans (23, 10f), correction of the young (13f), filial piety (15f.22-25), and fear of the LORD (17f).

22, 19f: *Amen-em-Ope:* an Egyptian scribe to whom is attributed a collection of maxims in *Thirty* chapters (v 20) composed for the instruction of his children and addressed to a young man who wishes to enter upon a career. The inspired editor of Proverbs does not translate these, but uses their materials in constructing a similar collection of proverbs.

23, 2: *Put a knife to your throat:* a metaphor for self-restraint.

✿ 17: 5, 1.
   23: 23, 11.
   26: 6, 1f; 11, 15; 17, 18.
   28: 23, 10; Dt 19, 14;
      27, 17.
   23/9: 9, 7.

   10: 22, 28.
   11: 22, 23.
   13: 13, 24; 19, 18;
      Sir 30, 1.
   14: 29, 15.17.
   17: 3, 31; 24, 1.19.

18 For you will surely have a future,
and your hope will not be cut off.

19 Hear, my son, and be wise,
and guide your heart in the right way.

20 Consort not with winebibbers,
nor with those who eat meat to excess;

21 For the drunkard and the glutton come
to poverty,
and torpor clothes a man in rags.

22 Listen to your father who begot you,
and despise not your mother when she
is old.

23 Get the truth, and sell it not—
wisdom, instruction and understanding.

24 The father of a just man will exult with
glee;
he who begets a wise son will have joy
in him.

25 Let your father and mother have joy;
let her who bore you exult.

26 My son, give me your heart,
and let your eyes keep to my ways.

27 For the harlot is a deep ditch,
and the adulteress a narrow pit;

28 Yes, she lies in wait like a robber,
and increases the faithless among men.

29 Who scream? Who shriek?
Who have strife? Who have anxiety?
Who have wounds for nothing?
Who have black eyes?

30 Those who linger long over wine,
those who engage in trials of blended
wine.

31 Look not on the wine when it is red,
when it sparkles in the glass.
It goes down smoothly;

32 But in the end it bites like a serpent,
or like a poisonous adder.

33 Your eyes behold strange sights,
and your heart utters disordered
thoughts;

34 You are like one now lying in the depths
of the sea,
now sprawled at the top of the mast.

35 "They struck me, but it pained me not;
they beat me, but I felt it not;
When shall I awake
to seek wine once again?"

24 **1** Be not emulous of evil men,
and desire not to be with them;

2 For their hearts plot violence,
and their lips speak of foul play.

3 By wisdom is a house built,
by understanding is it made firm;

4 And by knowledge are its rooms filled
with every precious and pleasing
possession.

5 A wise man is more powerful than a
strong man,
and a man of knowledge than a man
of might;

6 For it is by wise guidance that you wage
your war,
and the victory is due to a wealth of
counselors.

7 For a fool, to be silent is wisdom;
not to open his mouth at the gate.

8 He who plots evil doing—
men call him an intriguer.

9 Beyond intrigue and folly and sin,
it is arrogance that men find
abominable.

10 If you remain indifferent in time of
adversity,
your strength will depart from you.

11 Rescue those who are being dragged to
death,
and from those tottering to execution
withdraw not.

12 If you say, "I know not this man!"
does not he who tests hearts perceive
it?
He who guards your life knows it,
and he will repay each one according
to his deeds.

13 If you eat honey, my son, because it is
good,
if virgin honey is sweet to your taste;

† 23, 29-35: A vivid description of the evil effects, physical and psychological, of drunkenness.

23, 35: Wine makes the drunkard insensible to bodily and moral harm. His one desire is to indulge again.

24, 1-22: These verses continue an exhortation to wisdom (vv 3-7.13f), and against: violence (1f), pride and intrigue (8f), callousness (10-12), injustice (15f), joy in the failure of others (17f) or scandal at their success (19f), and rebellion against authority (21f).

24, 7: At the gate: of the city, where justice was administered and public affairs discussed; see note on Ru 4, 1. Cf also Pss 69, 13; 127, 5; Prv 22, 22; 31, 23.31.

24, 10: Indifferent: to those who suffer unjustly.

24, 11: Rescue . . . death: most probably refers to the legal rescue of those unjustly condemned to death.

✻
18: 24, 14.
24: 10, 1.
28: 7, 10-27.
30: 20, 1; Sir 19, 2;
     Hos 4, 11.
24/1: 3, 31; 23, 17.

5: 21, 22.
6: 20, 18.
7: Sir 6, 21.
12: Ps 62, 13; Sir 16, 12;
     Mt 16, 27; Rom 2, 6.

14* Such, you must know, is wisdom to your soul.
If you find it, you will have a future,
and your hope will not be cut off.

15 Lie not in wait against the home of the just man,
ravage not his dwelling place;

16† For the just man falls seven times and rises again,
but the wicked stumble to ruin.

17 Rejoice not when your enemy falls,
and when he stumbles, let not your heart exult,

18 Lest the Lord see it, be displeased with you,
and withdraw his wrath from your enemy.

19 Be not provoked with evildoers,
nor envious of the wicked;

20* For the evil man has no future,
the lamp of the wicked will be put out.

21† My son, fear the Lord and the king;
have nothing to do with those who rebel against them;

22 For suddenly arises the destruction they send,
and the ruin from either one, who can measure?

IV: OTHER SAYINGS OF THE WISE

23*† THESE ALSO ARE SAYINGS of the wise:

To show partiality in judgment is not good.

24 He who says to the wicked man, "You are just"—
men will curse him, people will denounce him;

25 But those who convict the evildoer will fare well,
and on them will come the blessing of prosperity.

26† He gives a kiss on the lips
who makes an honest reply.

27† Complete your outdoor tasks,
and arrange your work in the field;
afterward you can establish your house.

28* Be not a witness against your neighbor without just cause,
thus committing folly with your lips.

29*† Say not, "As he did to me, so will I do to him;
I will repay the man according to his deeds."

30 I passed by the field of the sluggard,
by the vineyard of the man without sense;

31 And behold! it was all overgrown with thistles;
its surface was covered with nettles,
and its stone wall broken down.

32 And as I gazed at it, I reflected;
I saw and learned the lesson:

33* A little sleep, a little slumber,
a little folding of the arms to rest—

34 Then will poverty come upon you like a highwayman,
and want like an armed man.

V: SECOND COLLECTION OF THE PROVERBS OF SOLOMON

25 1*† THESE ALSO ARE PROVERBS of Solomon. The men of Hezekiah, king of Judah, transmitted them.

2 God has glory in what he conceals,
kings have glory in what they fathom.

3 As the heavens in height, and the earth in depth,
the heart of kings is unfathomable.

---

† 24, 16: *The just man* overcomes every misfortune which oppresses him. *Seven times:* i. e., an indefinite number; cf Mt 18, 21f; Lk 17, 4.

24, 21f: One owes obedience to God and to supreme civil authority (Mt 22, 21; Rom 13, 1ff; 1 Pt 2, 13f). The punishments for failure in either duty transcend the limits of private justice.

24, 23-34: This collection of sayings continues in the same vein as the preceding: it instructs in fairness (23-26) and preparation for the future (27); and warns against vengeance (28f) and slothfulness (30-34).

24, 26: *He gives a kiss on the lips:* shows himself a true friend.

24, 27: This verse is commonly interpreted as advocating careful and practical preparation for marriage.

24, 29: This verse indicates great progress from the principle of the law of Talion (see note on Ex 21, 23ff) toward the teaching found in Rom 12, 17ff. Cf also Prv 25, 21ff.

25, 1: *The men of Hezekiah:* literary men at the royal court of Hezekiah who are represented as transcribing the proverbs from other collections. Hezekiah was a reformer of national religious life (2 Chr 29, 25-30).

✿
14: 23, 18.   28: 19, 5; 25, 18.
20: 13, 9.   29: 20, 22.
23: 18, 5; 28, 21; Lv 19,   33f: 6, 10f.
     15; Dt 1, 17; 16, 19.   25/1: 1, 1.

4 Remove the dross from silver,
and it comes forth perfectly purified;

5 Remove the wicked from the presence of
the king,
and his throne is made firm through
righteousness.

6† Claim no honor in the king's presence,
nor occupy the place of great men;

7* For it is better that you be told, "Come
up closer!"
than that you be humbled before the
prince.

8 What your eyes have seen
bring not forth hastily against an
opponent;
For what will you do later on
when your neighbor puts you to
shame?

9 Discuss your case with your neighbor,
but another man's secret do not
disclose;

10 Lest, hearing it, he reproach you,
and your ill repute cease not.

11 Like golden apples in silver settings
are words spoken at the proper time.

12 Like a golden earring, or a necklace of
fine gold,
is a wise reprover to an obedient ear.

13 Like the coolness of snow in the heat of
the harvest
is a faithful messenger for the one who
sends him.
[He refreshes the soul of his master.]

14 Like clouds and wind when no rain
follows
is the man who boastfully promises
what he never gives.

15* By patience is a ruler persuaded,
and a soft tongue will break a bone.

16 If you find honey, eat only what you
need,
lest you become glutted with it and
vomit it up.

17 Let your foot be seldom in your
neighbor's house,
lest he have more than enough of you,
and hate you.

18 Like a club, or a sword, or a sharp arrow,
is the man who bears false witness
against his neighbor.

19 Like an infected tooth or an unsteady
foot
is [dependence on] a faithless man in
time of trouble.

20* Like a moth in clothing, or a maggot in
wood,
sorrow gnaws at the human heart.

21*† If your enemy be hungry, give him food
to eat,
if he be thirsty, give him to drink;

22 For live coals you will heap on his head,
and the Lord will vindicate you.

23 The north wind brings rain,
and a backbiting tongue an angry
countenance.

24* It is better to dwell in a corner of the
housetop
than in a roomy house with a
quarrelsome woman.

25 Like cool water to one faint from thirst
is good news from a far country.

26 Like a troubled fountain or a polluted
spring
is a just man who gives way before the
wicked.

27† To eat too much honey is not good;
nor to seek honor after honor.

28 Like an open city with no defenses
is the man with no check on his
feelings.

26 1† Like snow in summer, or rain in harvest,
honor for a fool is out of place.

2 Like the sparrow in its flitting, like the
swallow in its flight,
a curse uncalled-for arrives nowhere.

3* The whip for the horse, the bridle for the
ass,
and the rod for the back of fools.

4† Answer not the fool according to his
folly,
lest you too become like him.

---

† 25, 6f: Compare the lesson on humility which was taught by
Christ (Lk 14, 7-11).

25, 21f: Charity is invaluable in resolving enmities and restoring peace. *Live coals:* i. e., either remorse and embarrass-
ment for the harm done, or increased punishment for refusing
reconciliation. Cf Mt 5, 44; Rom 12, 20.

25, 27: *Nor . . . honor after honor:* the text is uncertain.

26, 1-28: Concrete images describe the vices of fools (1-12),
of sluggards (13-16), of meddlers (17-19), of talebearers (20ff),
and of flatterers (23-28).

26, 4f: There is no contradiction between these two proverbs.
In any answer the wise man gives he must protect his own interest against the fool.

---

*   7: Lk 14, 8ff.   21: Rom 12, 20.
     15: 15, 1.4.   24: 21, 9.
     20: Sir 30, 24.   26/3: 19, 29; Sir 33, 25.

5 Answer the fool according to his folly,
   lest he become wise in his own eyes.

6 He cuts off his feet, he drinks down
   violence,
   who sends messages by a fool.

7† A proverb in the mouth of a fool
   hangs limp, like crippled legs.

8 Like one who entangles the stone in the
   sling
   is he who gives honor to a fool.

9 Like a thorn stick brandished by the
   hand of a drunkard
   is a proverb in the mouth of fools.

10 Like an archer wounding all who pass by
   is he who hires a drunken fool.

11* As the dog returns to his vomit,
   so the fool repeats his folly.

12 You see a man wise in his own eyes?
   There is more hope for a fool than for
   him.

13* The sluggard says, "There is a lion in the
   street,
   a lion in the middle of the square!"

14 The door turns on its hinges,
   the sluggard, on his bed!

15* The sluggard loses his hand in the dish;
   he is too weary to lift it to his mouth.

16 The sluggard imagines himself wiser
   than seven men who answer with good
   sense.

17 Like the man who seizes a passing dog
   by the ears
   is he who meddles in a quarrel not his
   own.

18 Like a crazed archer
   scattering firebrands and deadly
   arrows

19 Is the man who deceives his neighbor,
   and then says, "I was only joking."

20 For lack of wood, the fire dies out;
   and when there is no talebearer, strife
   subsides.

21* What a bellows is to live coals, what
   wood is to fire,
   such is a contentious man in
   enkindling strife.

22* The words of a talebearer are like dainty
   morsels
   that sink into one's inmost being.

23 Like a glazed finish on earthenware
   are smooth lips with a wicked heart.

24 With his lips an enemy pretends,
   but in his inmost being he maintains
   deceit;

25*† When he speaks graciously, trust him
   not,
   for seven abominations are in his
   heart.

26 A man may conceal hatred under
   dissimulation,
   but his malice will be revealed in the
   assembly.

27* He who digs a pit falls into it;
   and a stone comes back upon him who
   rolls it.

28 The lying tongue is its owner's enemy,
   and the flattering mouth works ruin.

27 1 Boast not of tomorrow,
   for you know not what any day may
   bring forth.

2 Let another praise you—not your own
   mouth;
   someone else—not your own lips.

3* Stone is heavy, and sand a burden,
   but a fool's provocation is heavier than
   both.

4 Anger is relentless, and wrath
   overwhelming—
   but before jealousy who can stand?

5 Better is an open rebuke
   than a love that remains hidden.

6 Wounds from a friend may be accepted
   as well meant,
   but the greetings of an enemy one
   prays against.

7 One who is full, tramples on virgin
   honey;
   but to the man who is hungry, any
   bitter thing is sweet.

8 Like a bird that is far from its nest
   is a man who is far from his home.

9 Perfume and incense gladden the heart,
   but by grief the soul is torn asunder.

❀

11: 2 Pt 2, 22.
13: 22, 13.
15: 19, 24.
21: 15, 18; 29, 22.

22: 18, 8.
25: Sir 12, 10; 27, 23.
27: Eccl 10, 8; Sir 27, 25f.
27/3: Sir 22, 14f.

---

† 26, 7ff: The fool abuses whatever knowledge he possesses.
26, 25: *Seven abominations:* many evil intentions.

10 Your own friend and your father's friend
    forsake not;
    but if ruin befalls you, enter not a
    kinsman's house.
    Better is a neighbor near at hand than a
    brother far away.

11 If you are wise, my son, you will gladden
    my heart,
    and I will be able to rebut him who
    taunts me.

12* The shrewd man perceives evil and
    hides;
    simpletons continue on and suffer the
    penalty.

13*† Take his garment who becomes surety
    for another,
    and for the sake of a stranger, yield it
    up!

14† When one greets his neighbor with a
    loud voice in the early morning,
    a curse can be laid to his charge.

15* For a persistent leak on a rainy day
    the match is a quarrelsome woman.

16 He who keeps her stores up a stormwind;
    he cannot tell north from south.

17 As iron sharpens iron,
    so man sharpens his fellow man.

18 He who tends a fig tree eats its fruit,
    and he who is attentive to his master
    will be enriched.

19 As one face differs from another,
    so does one human heart from
    another.

20* The nether world and the abyss are
    never satisfied;
    so too the eyes of men.

21 As the crucible tests silver and the
    furnace gold,
    so a man is tested by the praise he
    receives.

22 Though you should pound the fool to
    bits
    with the pestle, amid the grits in a
    mortar,
    his folly would not go out of him.

23† Take good care of your flocks,
    give careful attention to your herds;

24 For wealth lasts not forever,
    nor even a crown from age to age.

25 When the grass is taken away and the
    aftergrowth appears,
    and the mountain greens are gathered
    in,

26 The lambs will provide you with
    clothing,
    and the goats will bring the price of a
    field,

27 And there will be ample goat's milk to
    supply you,
    [to supply your household,]
    and maintenance for your maidens.

28

1 The wicked man flees although no one
    pursues him;
    but the just man, like a lion, feels sure
    of himself.

2† If a land is rebellious, its princes will be
    many;
    but with a prudent man it knows
    security.

3 A rich man who oppresses the poor
    is like a devastating rain that leaves no
    food.

4† Those who abandon the law praise the
    wicked man,
    but those who keep the law war
    against him.

5 Evil men understand nothing of justice,
    but those who seek the Lord
    understand all.

6* Better a poor man who walks in his
    integrity
    than he who is crooked in his ways and
    rich.

7 He who keeps the law is a wise son,
    but the gluttons' companion disgraces
    his father.

8† He who increases his wealth by interest
    and overcharge
    gathers it for him who is kind to the
    poor.

---

† 27, 13: See note on 20, 16.
27, 14: The *loud voice* suggests hypocrisy in the greeting.
27, 23-27: The land of Palestine was very suitable for flocks and herds, which formed the principal source of wealth for their owners.
28, 2: The meaning of this poorly preserved verse seems to be that frequent changes of rulers often result from moral corruption and political disorder.
28, 4: *The law*: religious and moral teaching.
28, 8: *Interest and overcharge* were strictly forbidden in the old law among Israelites because it was presumed that the borrower was in distress; cf Ex 22, 25; Lv 25, 35ff; Dt 23, 19; Ps 15, 5; Ez 18, 8. Civil and divine law will take the offender's wealth from him.

---

* 12: 22, 3.
13: 20, 16.
15: 21, 9; 25, 24.
20: 30, 16; Eccl 4, 8.
28/6: 19, 1.

9*† When one turns away his ear from
hearing the law,
even his prayer is an abomination.

10 He who seduces the upright into an evil
way
will himself fall into his own pit.
[And blameless men will gain
prosperity.]

11 The rich man is wise in his own eyes,
but a poor man who is intelligent sees
through him.

12 When the just are triumphant, there is
great jubilation;
but when the wicked gain
pre-eminence, people hide.

13 He who conceals his sins prospers not,
but he who confesses and forsakes
them obtains mercy.

14 Happy the man who is always on his
guard;
but he who hardens his heart will fall
into evil.

15 Like a roaring lion or a ravenous bear
is a wicked ruler over a poor people.

16 The less prudent the prince, the more his
deeds oppress.
He who hates ill-gotten gain prolongs his
days.

17 Though a man burdened with human
blood
were to flee to the grave, none should
support him.

18 He who walks uprightly is safe,
but he whose ways are crooked falls
into the pit.

19* He who cultivates his land will have
plenty of food,
but from idle pursuits a man has his
fill of poverty.

20* The trustworthy man will be richly
blessed;
he who is in haste to grow rich will not
go unpunished.

21* To show partiality is never good:
for even a morsel of bread a man may
do wrong.

22 The avaricious man is perturbed about
his wealth,
and he knows not when want will
come upon him.

23 He who rebukes a man gets more thanks
in the end
than one with a flattering tongue.

24* He who defrauds father or mother and
calls it no sin,
is a partner of the brigand.

25 The greedy man stirs up disputes,
but he who trusts in the LORD will
prosper.

26 He who trusts in himself is a fool,
but he who walks in wisdom is safe.

27* He who gives to the poor suffers no want,
but he who ignores them gets many a
curse.

28 When the wicked gain pre-eminence,
other men hide;
but at their fall the just flourish.

29

1 The man who remains stiff-necked and
hates rebuke
will be crushed suddenly beyond cure.

2* When the just prevail, the people rejoice;
but when the wicked rule, the people
groan.

3* He who loves wisdom makes his father
glad,
but he who consorts with harlots
squanders his wealth.

4 By justice a king gives stability to the
land;
but he who imposes heavy taxes ruins
it.

5 The man who flatters his neighbor
is spreading a net under his feet.

6* The wicked man steps into a snare,
but the just man runs on joyfully.

7 The just man has a care for the rights of
the poor;
the wicked man has no such concern.

8* Arrogant men set the city ablaze,
but wise men calm the fury.

9 If a wise man disputes with a fool,
he may rage or laugh but can have no
peace.

10 Bloodthirsty men hate the honest man,
but the upright show concern for his
life.

*   9: 21, 27.   27: 19, 17; Sir 4, 3-8.
19: 12, 11.   29/2: 11, 10.
20: 13, 11.   3: 5, 10; 10, 1.
21: 24, 23.   6: Dt 4, 2.
24: Mk 7, 11ff.   8: 11, 11.

† 28, 9: Prayers offered in bad faith are displeasing to God.

11* The fool gives vent to all his anger;
but by biding his time, the wise man calms it.

12 If a ruler listens to lying words,
his servants all become wicked.

13*† The poor and the oppressor have a common bond:
the LORD gives light to the eyes of both.

14 If a king is zealous for the rights of the poor,
his throne stands firm forever.

15* The rod of correction gives wisdom,
but a boy left to his whims disgraces his mother.

16 When the wicked prevail, crime increases;
but their downfall the just will behold.

17 Correct your son, and he will bring you comfort,
and give delight to your soul.

18 Without prophecy the people become demoralized;
but happy is he who keeps the law.

19* By words no servant can be trained;
for he understands what is said, but obeys not.

20* Do you see a man hasty in his words?
More can be hoped for from a fool!

21 If a man pampers his servant from childhood,
he will turn out to be stubborn.

22* An ill-tempered man stirs up disputes,
and a hotheaded man is the cause of many sins.

23* Man's pride causes his humiliation,
but he who is humble of spirit obtains honor.

24† The accomplice of a thief is his own enemy:
he hears himself put under a curse, yet discloses nothing.

25 The fear of man brings a snare,
but he who trusts in the LORD is safe.

26 Many curry favor with the ruler,
but the rights of each are from the LORD.

27 The evildoer is an abomination to the just,
and he who walks uprightly is an abomination to the wicked.

VI: THE WORDS OF AGUR

30 **1†** THE WORDS OF AGUR, son of Jakeh the Massaite:

The pronouncement of mortal man:
"I am not God;
I am not God, that I should prevail.

2 Why, I am the most stupid of men,
and have not even human intelligence;

3 Neither have I learned wisdom,
nor have I the knowledge of the Holy One.

4 Who has gone up to heaven and come down again—
who has cupped the wind in his hands?
Who has bound up the waters in a cloak—
who has marked out all the ends of the earth?
What is his name, what is his son's name, if you know it?"

5* Every word of God is tested;
he is a shield to those who take refuge in him.

6* Add nothing to his words,
lest he reprove you, and you be exposed as a deceiver.

VII: NUMERICAL PROVERBS

7 Two things I ask of you,
deny them not to me before I die:

8 Put falsehood and lying far from me,
give me neither poverty nor riches;
[provide me only with the food I need;]

9 Lest, being full, I deny you,
saying, "Who is the LORD?"
Or, being in want, I steal,
and profane the name of my God.

† 29, 13: God gives life to all classes of people; cf 22, 2.

29, 24: *Is his own enemy:* because he not only incurs guilt as an accomplice but, by his silence, brings down on himself the curse invoked on the unknown guilty partner.

30, 1: *Agur:* an unknown person. *Massaite:* from Massa in northern Arabia, elsewhere referred to as an encampment of the Ishmaelites (Gn 25, 14). But the word may not be intended as a place name; it might signify "an oracle," "a prophecy."

30, 1ff: Agur wishes to stress man's insignificance when he is compared to God; cf Jb 38—39.

* 11: 12, 16; 25, 28; Sir 21, 26.
13: 22, 2.
15: 13, 24; 22, 15; 23, 13f; Sir 22, 6; 30, 1.
19: Sir 33, 25f.
20: Eccl 5, 1.
22: 15, 18; 26, 21.
23: 11, 2; 16, 18; 18, 12; Jb 22, 29.
30/5: Ps 12, 7.

10 Slander not a servant to his master,
lest he curse you, and you have to pay the penalty.

11*† There is a group of people that curses its father,
and blesses not its mother.

12 There is a group that is pure in its own eyes,
yet is not purged of its filth.

13 There is a group—how haughty their eyes!
how overbearing their glance!

14 There is a group whose incisors are swords,
whose teeth are knives,
Devouring the needy from the earth,
and the poor from among men.

15† The two daughters of the leech are, "Give, Give."
Three things are never satisfied,
four never say, "Enough!"

16* The nether world, and the barren womb;
the earth, that is never saturated with water,
and fire, that never says, "Enough!"

17 The eye that mocks a father,
or scorns an aged mother,
Will be plucked out by the ravens in the valley;
the young eagles will devour it.

18† Three things are too wonderful for me,
yes, four I cannot understand:

19 The way of an eagle in the air,
the way of a serpent upon a rock,
The way of a ship on the high seas,
and the way of a man with a maiden.

20† Such is the way of an adulterous woman:
she eats, wipes her mouth,
and says, "I have done no wrong."

21 Under three things the earth trembles,
yes, under four it cannot bear up:

22* Under a slave when he becomes king,
and a fool when he is glutted with food;

23 Under an odious woman when she is wed,
and a maidservant when she displaces her mistress.

24 Four things are among the smallest on the earth,
and yet are exceedingly wise:

25 Ants—a species not strong,
yet they store up their food in the summer;

26† Rock-badgers—a species not mighty,
yet they make their home in the crags;

27 Locusts—they have no king,
yet they migrate all in array;

28 Lizards—you can catch them with your hands,
yet they find their way into kings' palaces.

29 Three things are stately in their stride,
yes, four are stately in their carriage:

30 The lion, mightiest of beasts,
who retreats before nothing;

31 The strutting cock, and the he-goat,
and the king at the head of his people.

32† If you have foolishly been proud
or presumptuous—put your hand on your mouth;

33 For the stirring of milk brings forth curds,
and the stirring of anger brings forth blood.

VIII: THE WORDS OF LEMUEL

31 **1** THE WORDS OF LEMUEL, king of Massa.
The advice which his mother gave him:

2 What, my son, my first-born!
what, O son of my womb;
what, O son of my vows!

3* Give not your vigor to women,
nor your strength to those who ruin kings.

4* It is not for kings, O Lemuel,
not for kings to drink wine;
strong drink is not for princes!

5 Lest in drinking they forget what the law decrees,
and violate the rights of all who are in need.

6 Give strong drink to one who is perishing,
and wine to the sorely depressed;

---

† 30, 11-14: Perverted people are here classified as unfilial (11), self-righteous (12), proud (13) and rapacious (14).

30, 15ff: *The two daughters . . . "Give, Give"*: the text is obscure but the sense seems to be that *the leech* is insatiable in its desire for blood, just as are *the nether world* for victims, *the barren womb* for offspring, the parched *earth* for *water,* and *fire* for fuel (16).

30, 18f: The soaring flight of the eagle, the mysterious movement upon a rock of the serpent which has no feet, the path of the ship through the trackless deep, and the marvelous procreation of human life, excite great wonderment.

30, 20: This verse portrays the indifference of an adulterous woman who thinks there is no trace of her wicked act.

30, 26: *Rock-badgers:* cf note to Ps 104, 18.

30, 32f: The anger aroused by overweening pride threatens an awesome punishment.

7   When they drink, they will forget their
       misery,
       and think no more of their burdens.

8   Open your mouth in behalf of the dumb,
       and for the rights of the destitute;

9   Open your mouth, decree what is just,
       defend the needy and the poor!

IX: THE IDEAL WIFE

10*   WHEN ONE FINDS a worthy wife,
       her value is far beyond pearls.

11   Her husband, entrusting his heart to her,
       has an unfailing prize.

12†   She brings him good, and not evil,
       all the days of her life.

13   She obtains wool and flax
       and makes cloth with skillful hands.

14†   Like merchant ships,
       she secures her provisions from afar.

15   She rises while it is still night,
       and distributes food to her household.

16   She picks out a field to purchase;
       out of her earnings she plants a
       vineyard.

17   She is girt about with strength,
       and sturdy are her arms.

18†   She enjoys the success of her dealings;
       at night her lamp is undimmed.

19   She puts her hands to the distaff,
       and her fingers ply the spindle.

20   She reaches out her hands to the poor,
       and extends her arms to the needy.

---

* 10-31: Sir 26, 1ff.13-18.

21   She fears not the snow for her household;
       all her charges are doubly clothed.

22   She makes her own coverlets;
       fine linen and purple are her clothing.

23   Her husband is prominent at the city
       gates
       as he sits with the elders of the land.

24   She makes garments and sells them,
       and stocks the merchants with belts.

25†   She is clothed with strength and dignity,
       and she laughs at the days to come.

26   She opens her mouth in wisdom,
       and on her tongue is kindly counsel.

27   She watches the conduct of her
       household,
       and eats not her food in idleness.

28   Her children rise up and praise her;
       her husband, too, extols her:

29   "Many are the women of proven worth,
       but you have excelled them all."

30†   Charm is deceptive and beauty fleeting;
       the woman who fears the LORD is to be
       praised.

31   Give her a reward of her labors,
       and let her works praise her at the city
       gates.

---

† 31, 12: *Good, and not evil:* i. e., prosperity, not adversity.

31, 14: *Merchant:* literally, "Canaanite" (cf v 24), probably because the merchant class had been composed chiefly of Canaanites.

31, 18: *Her lamp is undimmed:* indicates abundance of productive work and its accompanying prosperity; cf 20, 20; Jb 18, 6.

31, 25: *Laughs at the days to come:* anticipates the future with gladness free from anxiety.

31, 30: The true charm of the ideal wife is her religious spirit, for she *fears the Lord;* cf note on 1, 7.

The Book of Ecclesiastes

Introduction

The title *Ecclesiastes* given to this book is the Greek translation of the Hebrew name Qoheleth meaning, perhaps, "one who convokes an assembly." The book, however, does not consist of public addresses, but is a treatise, more or less logically developed, on the vanity of all things. Reflections in prose and aphorisms in verse are intermingled in Ecclesiastes, which contains, besides, an introduction and an epilogue.

The book is concerned with the purpose and value of human life. While admitting the existence of a divine plan, it considers such a plan to be hidden from man, who seeks happiness without ever finding it here below (3, 11; 8, 7.17). Ecclesiastes applies his "Vanity of vanities" to everything "under the sun," even to that wisdom which seeks to find at least a semblance of good in the things of the world. Merit does not yield happiness for it is often tried by suffering. Riches and pleasures do not avail. Existence is monotonous, enjoyment fleeting and vain; darkness quickly follows. Life, then, as an enigma beyond human ability to solve.

While Ecclesiastes concedes that there is an advantage for man in the enjoyment of certain legitimate pleasures lest he lapse into pessimism and despair, he nevertheless considers this indulgence also vanity unless man returns due thanks to the Creator who has given him all. Under this aspect, earthly wisdom would rise to the higher level of true spiritual wisdom. This true wisdom is not found "under the sun" but is perceived only by the light of faith, inasmuch as it rests with God, who is the final Judge of the good and the bad, and whose reign endures forever. The Epilogue gives the clue to this thought (12, 13f).

The moral teaching of the book is imperfect, like the Old Testament itself (Heb 7, 19), yet it marks an advance in the development of the doctrine of divine retribution. While rejecting the older solution of earthly rewards and punishments, Ecclesiastes looks forward to a more lasting one. The clear answer to the problem was to come with the light of Christ's teaching concerning future life.

The author of the book was a teacher of popular wisdom (12, 9). Qoheleth was obviously only his literary name. Because he is called "David's son, king in Jerusalem," it was commonly thought that he was King Solomon. Such personation, however, was but a literary device to lend greater dignity and authority to the book—

a circumstance which does not in any way impugn its inspired character. The Epilogue seems to have been written by an editor, probably a disciple of Qoheleth. The entire work differs considerably in language and style from earlier books of the Old Testament. It reflects a late period of Hebrew, and was probably written about three centuries before Christ.

1 [1*†] THE WORDS OF DAVID's SON, Qoheleth, king in Jerusalem:

Vanity of Toil without Profit

[2*†] Vanity of vanities, says Qoheleth,
    vanity of vanities! All things are vanity!
[3*†] What profit has man from all the labor
    which he toils at under the sun?
[4] One generation passes and another comes,
    but the world forever stays.
[5] The sun rises and the sun goes down;
    then it presses on to the place where it rises.
[6] Blowing now toward the south, then toward the north,
    the wind turns again and again, resuming its rounds.
[7] All rivers go to the sea,
    yet never does the sea become full.
To the place where they go,
    the rivers keep on going.
[8*†] All speech is labored;
    there is nothing man can say.
The eye is not satisfied with seeing
    nor is the ear filled with hearing.

[9*] What has been, that will be; what has been done, that will be done. Nothing is new under the sun. [10*] Even the thing of which we say, "See, this is new!" has already existed in the ages that preceded us. [11*†] There is no remembrance of the men of old; nor of those to come will there be any remembrance among those who come after them.

---

† 1, 1: *Qoheleth:* see Introduction.

1, 2: *Vanity of vanities:* a Hebrew superlative expressing the supreme degree of futility and emptiness.

1, 3: *Under the sun:* used throughout this book to signify "on the earth."

1, 8: *All speech . . . man can say:* or "All things are wearisome beyond man's power to tell."

1, 11: Men remember nothing long, God never forgets.

---

* 1/1: 7, 27; 12, 8f.
  2: 12, 8.
  3: 2, 11.22; 3, 9; 5, 15.
  8: 8, 17.
  9: 3, 15; 6, 10.
  10: 3, 15.
  11: 2, 16.

I: QOHELETH'S INVESTIGATION OF LIFE

Twofold Introduction

12 I, QOHELETH, WAS KING over Israel in Jerusalem, **13*** and I applied my mind to search and investigate in wisdom all things that are done under the sun.

> A thankless task God has appointed
> for men to be busied about.

14*† I have seen all things that are done under the sun, and behold, all is vanity and a chase after wind.

> **15** What is crooked cannot be made straight,
> and what is missing cannot be supplied.

16* Though I said to myself, "Behold, I have become great and stored up wisdom beyond all who were before me in Jerusalem, and my mind has broad experience of wisdom and knowledge"; **17*** yet when I applied my mind to know wisdom and knowledge, madness and folly, I learned that this also is a chase after wind.

18 For in much wisdom there is much sorrow,
> and he who stores up knowledge stores up grief.

Study of Pleasure-seeking

2 **1*†** I said to myself, "Come, now, let me try you with pleasure and the enjoyment of good things." But behold, this too was vanity. **2** Of laughter I said: "Mad!" and of mirth: "What good does this do?" **3†** I thought of beguiling my senses with wine, though my mind was concerned with wisdom, and of taking up folly, until I should understand what is best for men to do under the heavens during the limited days of their life. **4** I undertook great works; I built myself houses and planted vineyards; **5** I made gardens and parks, and set out in them fruit trees of all sorts. **6** And I constructed for myself reservoirs to water a flourishing woodland. **7** I acquired male and female slaves, and slaves were born in my house. I also had growing herds of cattle and flocks of sheep, more than all who had been before me in Jerusalem. **8** I amassed for myself silver and gold, and the wealth of kings and provinces. I got for myself male and female singers and all human luxuries. **9** I became great, and I stored up more than all others before me in Jerusalem; my wisdom, too, stayed with me. **10*** Nothing that my eyes desired did I deny them, nor did I deprive myself of any joy, but my heart rejoiced in the fruit of all my toil. This was my share for all my toil. **11*** But when I turned to all the works that my hands had wrought, and to the toil at which I had taken such pains, behold! all was vanity and a chase after wind, with nothing gained under the sun. **12** For what will the man do who is to come after the king? What men have already done!

Study of Wisdom and Folly

I went on to the consideration of wisdom, madness and folly. **13** And I saw that wisdom has the advantage over folly as much as light has the advantage over darkness.

> **14*** The wise man has eyes in his head,
> but the fool walks in darkness.

Yet I knew that one lot befalls both of them. **15** So I said to myself, if the fool's lot is to befall me also, why then should I be wise? Where is the profit for me? And I concluded in my heart that this too is vanity. **16*** Neither of the wise man nor of the fool will there be an abiding remembrance, for in days to come both will have been forgotten. How is it that the wise man dies as well as the fool! **17** Therefore I loathed life, since for me the work that is done under the sun is evil; for all is vanity and a chase after wind.

Study of the Fruits of Toil
To Others the Profits

18 And I detested all the fruits of my labor under the sun, because I must leave them to a man who is to come after me.

19 And who knows whether he will be a wise man or a fool? Yet he will have control over all the fruits of my wise labor under the sun. This also is vanity. **20** So my feelings turned to despair of all the fruits of my labor under the sun. **21** For here is a man who has labored with wisdom and knowledge and skill, and to another, who has not labored over it, he must leave his property. This also is vanity and a great misfortune. **22*** For what profit comes to a man from all the toil and anxiety of heart with which he has labored under the sun? **23** All his days sorrow and grief are his occupation; even at night his mind is not at rest. This also is vanity.

24*† There is nothing better for man than to eat and drink and provide himself with good things by his labors. Even this, I realized, is from the hand of God. **25** For who can eat or drink apart from him? **26*** For to whatever man he sees fit he gives wisdom and knowledge and joy; but to the sinner he gives the task of gathering possessions to be given to whatever man God sees fit. This also is vanity and a chase after wind.

---

† 1, 14: *Chase after wind:* futility, like an attempt to corral the winds. Cf Hos 12, 2. The ancient versions understand "affliction of spirit." These words are used to conclude sections of the discourse, as far as 6, 9.

2, 1-11: The author here assumes the role of Solomon.

2, 3: *Though my mind . . . wisdom:* while indulging in pleasure the author hopes to discover wherein man's true happiness consists.

2, 24: Unrestrained indulgence, is not advocated here, but legitimate pleasure and the cheerfulness it begets.

---

* 13: 8, 9.
14: 2, 11.17.
16: 2, 9.
17: 2, 3; 7, 25.
2/1: Wis 2, 6.
10: 3, 22; 5, 18.

11: 1, 17; Sir 44, 9.
14f: 6, 8; 9, 2f.
16: 1, 11; Wis 2, 4.
22: 1, 3.
24: 3, 12f.22; 5, 17f; 8, 15.
26: Prv 13, 22.

Man Cannot Hit on the Right Time to Act

3 ¹ There is an appointed time for everything,
and a time for every affair under the
heavens.

² A time to be born, and a time to die;
a time to plant, and a time to uproot the
plant.

³ A time to kill, and a time to heal;
a time to tear down, and a time to build.

⁴ A time to weep, and a time to laugh;
a time to mourn, and a time to dance.

⁵ A time to scatter stones, and a time to
gather them;
a time to embrace, and a time to be far
from embraces.

⁶ A time to seek, and a time to lose;
a time to keep, and a time to cast away.

⁷ A time to rend, and a time to sew;
a time to be silent, and a time to speak.

⁸ A time to love, and a time to hate;
a time of war, and a time of peace.

⁹*What advantage has the worker from his toil? ¹⁰I have considered the task which God has appointed for men to be busied about. ¹¹*He has made everything appropriate to its time, and has put the timeless into their hearts, without men's ever discovering, from beginning to end, the work which God has done. ¹²I recognized that there is nothing better than to be glad and to do well during life. ¹³*For every man, moreover, to eat and drink and enjoy the fruit of all his labor is a gift of God. ¹⁴I recognized that whatever God does will endure forever; there is no adding to it, or taking from it. Thus has God done that he may be revered. ¹⁵*†What now is has already been; what is to be, already is; and God restores what would otherwise be displaced.

The Problem of Retribution

¹⁶*And still under the sun in the judgment place I saw wickedness, and in the seat of justice, iniquity. ¹⁷*And I said to myself, both the just and the wicked God will judge, since there is a time for every affair and on every work a judgment. ¹⁸I said to myself: As for the children of men, it is God's way of testing them and of showing that they are in themselves like beasts. ¹⁹For the lot of man and of beast is one lot; the one dies as well as the other. Both have the same life-breath, and man has no advantage over the beast; but all is vanity. ²⁰*Both go to the same place; both were made from dust, and to the dust they both return. ²¹*Who knows if the life-breath of the children of men

goes upward and the life-breath of beasts goes earthward? ²²*And I saw that there is nothing better for a man than to rejoice in his work; for this is his lot. Who will let him see what is to come after him?

Vanity of Toil

4 ¹*AGAIN I considered all the oppressions that take place under the sun: the tears of the victims with none to comfort them! From the hand of their oppressors comes violence, and there is none to comfort them! ²*And those now dead, I declared more fortunate in death than are the living to be still alive. ³And better off than both is the yet unborn, who has not seen the wicked work that is done under the sun. ⁴Then I saw that all toil and skillful work is the rivalry of one man for another. This also is vanity and a chase after wind.

⁵†"The fool folds his arms
and consumes his own flesh"—
⁶Better is one handful with tranquility
than two with toil and a chase after wind!

Companions and Successors

⁷Again I found this vanity under the sun: ⁸a solitary man with no companion; with neither son nor brother. Yet there is no end to all his toil, and riches do not satisfy his greed. "For whom do I toil and deprive myself of good things?" This also is vanity and a worthless task. Two are better than one: ⁹they get a good wage for their labor. ¹⁰If the one falls, the other will lift up his companion. Woe to the solitary man! For if he should fall, he has no one to lift him up. ¹¹So also, if two sleep together, they keep each other warm. How can one alone keep warm? ¹²Where a lone man may be overcome, two together can resist. A three-ply cord is not easily broken.

¹³Better is a poor but wise youth than an old but foolish king who no longer knows caution; ¹⁴†for from a prison house one comes forth to rule, since even in his royalty he was poor at birth. ¹⁵†Then I saw all those who are to live and move about under the sun with the heir apparent who will succeed to his place. ¹⁶There is no end to all these people, to all over whom he takes precedence; yet the later generations will not applaud him. This also is vanity and a chase after wind.

Vanity of Many Words

¹⁷*†Guard your step when you go to the house of God. Let your approach be obedience, rather than the

---

† 3, 15: *God restores:* the meaning is probably that God allows no part of his creation to drop out of existence.

4, 5: *Consumes his own flesh:* refuses to work for the necessities of life and consequently suffers hunger and impairs his bodily health.

4, 14: *Prison house:* probably his mother's womb, from which the king issues without possessions. Cf 5, 14.

4, 15: The king is no sooner dead than the people transfer their allegiance to his successor.

4, 17: *The fools' . . . sacrifice:* unacceptable to God because of their disobedience; cf 1 Sm 15, 22; Hos 6, 6.

---

* 3/9: 1, 3.
11: 8, 17; 11, 5; Gn 1, 31.
13: 2, 24.
15: 1, 9.
16: 4, 1.
17: 12, 14.

20: 12, 7; Gn 2, 7; 3, 19;
Ps 103, 14; Wis 2, 3;
Sir 10, 9; 17, 1; 40, 11.
21: Wis 2, 2.
22: 8, 7; 10, 14.
4/1: 5, 7.
2: 7, 2.
17: 1 Sm 15, 22; Hos 6, 6.

fools' offering of sacrifice; for they know not how to keep from doing evil.

5 ¹BE not hasty in your utterance and let not your heart be quick to make a promise in God's presence. God is in heaven and you are on earth; therefore let your words be few.

²†For nightmares come with many cares,
and a fool's utterance with many words.

³*When you make a vow to God, delay not its fulfillment. For God has no pleasure in fools; fulfill what you have vowed. ⁴You had better not make a vow than make it and not fulfill it. ⁵Let not your utterances make you guilty, and say not before his representative, "It was a mistake," lest God be angered by such words and destroy the works of your hands. ⁶*Rather, fear God!"

Gain and Loss of Goods

⁷*If you see oppression of the poor, and violation of rights and justice in the realm, do not be shocked by the fact, for the high official has another higher than he watching him and above these are others higher still—. ⁸†Yet an advantage for a country in every respect is a king for the arable land.

⁹*The covetous man is never satisfied with money, and the lover of wealth reaps no fruit from it; so this too is vanity. ¹⁰Where there are great riches, there are also many to devour them. Of what use are they to the owner except to feast his eyes upon? ¹¹Sleep is sweet to the laboring man, whether he eats little or much, but the rich man's abundance allows him no sleep.

¹²*This is a grievous evil which I have seen under the sun: riches kept by their owner to his hurt. ¹³Should the riches be lost through some misfortune, he may have a son when he is without means. ¹⁴*As he came forth from his mother's womb, so again shall he depart, naked as he came, having nothing from his labor that he can carry in his hand. ¹⁵This too is a grievous evil, that he goes just as he came. What then does it profit him to toil for wind? ¹⁶All the days of his life are passed in gloom and sorrow, under great vexation, sickness and wrath.

¹⁷*Here is what I recognize as good: it is well for a man to eat and drink and enjoy all the fruits of his labor under the sun during the limited days of the life which God gives him; for this is his lot. ¹⁸Any man to whom God gives riches and property, and grants power to partake of them, so that he receives his lot and finds joy in the fruits of his toil, has a gift from God. ¹⁹†For he will hardly dwell on the shortness of his life, because God lets him busy himself with the joy of his heart.

Limited Worth of Enjoyment

6 ¹THERE is another evil which I have seen under the sun, and it weighs heavily upon man: ²*there is the man to whom God gives riches and property and honor, so that he lacks none of all the things he craves; yet God does not grant him power to partake of them, but a stranger devours them. This is vanity and a dire plague. ³†Should a man have a hundred children and live many years, no matter to what great age, still if he has not the full benefit of his goods, or if he is deprived of burial, of this man I proclaim that the child born dead is more fortunate than he. ⁴Though it came in vain and goes into darkness and its name is enveloped in darkness; ⁵though it has not seen or known the sun, yet the dead child is at rest rather than such a man. ⁶†Should he live twice a thousand years and not enjoy his goods, do not both go to the same place?

⁷†All man's toil is for his mouth, yet his desire is not fulfilled. ⁸For what advantage has the wise man over the fool, or what advantage has the poor man in knowing how to conduct himself in life? ⁹*"What the eyes see is better than what the desires wander after." This also is vanity and a chase after wind.

II: QOHELETH'S CONCLUSIONS

¹⁰†WHATEVER IS, WAS LONG AGO GIVEN ITS NAME, and the nature of man is known, and that he cannot contend in judgment with one who is stronger than he. ¹¹For though there are many sayings that multiply vanity, what profit is there for a man? ¹²*For who knows what is good for a man in life, the limited days of his vain life (which God has made like a shadow)? Because—who is there to tell a man what will come after him under the sun?

A

Man Cannot Find Out What Is Good for Him to Do

CRITIQUE OF SAGES ON THE DAY OF ADVERSITY

7 ¹*† A good name is better than good ointment, and the day of death than the day of birth.

---

†
5, 2: *Nightmares:* literally, "dreams."
5, 8: The wording of this verse has perhaps never been adequately explained.
5, 19: The meaning is that the joys of life, though temporary, keep a man from dwelling on the ills which afflict humanity.
6, 3: A large family, a long life, an honorable burial, all were highly esteemed by the Hebrews, and it was considered a great misfortune to be deprived of them.
6, 6: *Same place:* the grave.
6, 7: *Mouth:* appetite, and therefore, body.
6, 9: *Better . . . wander after:* the good that is present to us is better than that which is absent and, perhaps, unattainable.
6, 10: The one who is stronger than man is God.
7, 1: *Ointment:* applied to the child at birth; *a good name* remains even after death.

*
5/3: Nm 30, 3; Dt 23, 23; Ps 50, 14.
6: 12, 13; Dt 10, 12.
7: 3, 16; 4, 1.
9: Prv 28, 22.
12: Jb 20, 20.
14: Jb 1, 21; 1 Tm 6, 7.
17f: 2, 24.
6/2: 2, 18f.
12: Jb 8, 9; 14, 2; Ps 102, 12.
7/1: 4, 2; Prv 22, 1; Sir 41, 13.

2*   It is better to go to the house of mourning
         than to the house of feasting,
      For that is the end of every man,
         and the living should take it to heart.

3   Sorrow is better than laughter,
      because when the face is sad the heart
         grows wiser.

4   The heart of the wise is in the house of
         mourning,
      but the heart of fools is in the house of
         mirth.

5   It is better to hearken to the wise man's
         rebuke
      than to hearken to the song of fools;

6   For as the crackling of thorns under a pot,
      so is the fool's laughter.

        This also is vanity,

7   For oppression can make a fool of a wise
         man,
      and a bribe corrupts the heart.

8   Better is the end of speech than its
         beginning;
      better is the patient spirit than the lofty
         spirit.

9   Do not in spirit become quickly
         discontented,
      for discontent lodges in the bosom of a
         fool.

10Do not say: How is it that former times were better than these? For it is not in wisdom that you ask about this.

11Wisdom and an inheritance are good,
      and an advantage to those that see the sun.

12For the protection of wisdom is as the protection of money; and the advantage of knowledge is that wisdom preserves the life of its owner.

13Consider the work of God. Who can make straight what he has made crooked? 14On a good day enjoy good things, and on an evil day consider: Both the one and the other God has made, so that man cannot find fault with him in anything.

CRITIQUE OF SAGES ON JUSTICE AND WICKEDNESS

15I have seen all manner of things in my vain days: a just man perishing in his justice, and a wicked one surviving in his wickedness. 16*†"Be not just to excess, and be not overwise, lest you be ruined. 17†Be not wicked to excess, and be not foolish. Why should you die before your time?" 18†It is good to hold to this rule, and not to let that one go; but he who fears God will win through at all events.

19Wisdom is a better defense for the wise man than would be ten princes in the city, 20*†yet there is no man on earth so just as to do good and never sin. 21*Do not give heed to every word that is spoken lest you hear your servant speaking ill of you, 22for you know in your heart that you have many times spoken ill of others.

23All these things I probed in wisdom. I said, "I will acquire wisdom"; but it was beyond me. 24What exists is far-reaching; it is deep, very deep: who can find it out? 25*I turned my thoughts toward knowledge; I sought and pursued wisdom and reason, and I recognized that wickedness is foolish and folly is madness.

Critique of Sages on Women

26*More bitter than death I find the woman who is a hunter's trap, whose heart is a snare and whose hands are prison bonds. He who is pleasing to God will escape her, but the sinner will be entrapped by her. 27Behold, this have I found, says Qoheleth, adding one thing to another that I might discover the answer 28†which my soul still seeks and has not found: One man out of a thousand have I come upon, but a woman among them all I have not found. 29†Behold, only this have I found out: God made mankind straight, but men have had recourse to many calculations.

CRITIQUE OF SAGES ON THE WISE MAN AND THE KING

8   1   Who is like the wise man,
         and who knows the explanation of
           things?

       A man's wisdom illumines his face,
         but an impudent look is resented.

2Observe the precept of the king, and in view of your oath to God, 3be not hasty to withdraw from the king; do not join in with a base plot, for he does whatever he pleases, 4because his word is sovereign, and who can say to him, "What are you doing?"

5"He who keeps the commandment experiences no evil, and the wise man's heart knows times and judgments; 6for there is a time and a judgment for everything."—Yet it is a great affliction for man 7*that he is ignorant of what is to come; for who will make known to him how it will be? 8There is no man who is master of the breath of life so as to retain it, and none has mastery of the day of death. There is no exemption

---

†   7, 16: St. Jerome explains the warning against excessive justice in reference to the self-righteous man who is so stern that he is never willing to forgive sin in others; cf vv 20ff.

7, 17: Untimely death was traditionally recognized as a divine punishment of the wicked; cf 1 Sm 2, 31-34; Jer 17, 11; Ps 55, 24; Prv 10, 27. This warning against presumptuous wickedness is not an endorsement of any lesser degree of misconduct.

7, 18: *This rule . . . that one:* the sayings cited in vv 16f. Others refer *this* and *that* to riches and wisdom (cf 7, 12), justice and wisdom, or justice and wickedness. This last supposition makes the author's thought hard to follow.

7, 20: This is to be understood in the sense of Rom 5, 12. See note there.

7, 28: The author found sincerity rare among men, but among women still more rare.

7, 29: *Calculations:* the many vain attempts and schemes of men to attain happiness by their own efforts.

❋
    2: 4, 2.   21f: 1 Kgs 8, 46.
    16f: 8, 12ff.   25: 1, 17.
    20: Jb 25, 4; Prv 20, 9;   26: Prv 5, 4.
        1 Kgs 8, 46; Rom 3, 23;   8/7: 3, 22; 10, 14.
        Jas 3, 2; 1 Jn 1, 8.

from the struggle, nor are the wicked saved by their wickedness. **9***All these things I considered and I applied my mind to every work that is done under the sun, while one man tyrannizes over another to his hurt.

The Problem of Retribution

10†Meanwhile I saw wicked men approach and enter; and as they left the sacred place, they were praised in the city for what they had done. This also is vanity. **11**Because the sentence against evildoers is not promptly executed, therefore the hearts of men are filled with the desire to commit evil— **12**because the sinner does evil a hundred times and survives. Though indeed I know that it shall be well with those who fear God, for their reverence toward him; **13**†and that it shall not be well with the wicked man, and he shall not prolong his shadowy days, for his lack of reverence toward God.

14This is a vanity which occurs on earth: there are just men treated as though they had done evil and wicked men treated as though they had done justly. This, too, I say is vanity. **15***†Therefore I commend mirth, because there is nothing good for man under the sun except eating and drinking and mirth: for this is the accompaniment of his toil during the limited days of the life which God gives him under the sun.

16*When I applied my heart to know wisdom and to observe what is done on earth, **17***I recognized that man is unable to find out all God's work that is done under the sun, even though neither by day nor by night do his eyes find rest in sleep. However much man toils in searching, he does not find it out; and even if the wise man says that he knows, he is unable to find it out.

B
Man Does Not Know What Is to Come

9   **1**†ALL this I have kept in mind and recognized: the just, the wise, and their deeds are in the hand of God. Love from hatred man cannot tell; both appear equally vain, **2***in that there is the same lot for all, for the just and the wicked, for the good and the bad, for the clean and the unclean, for him who offers sacrifice and him who does not. As it is for the good man, so it is for the sinner; as it is for him who swears rashly, so it is for him who fears an oath. **3**Among all the things that happen under the sun, this is the worst, that things turn out the same for all. Hence the minds of men are filled with evil, and madness is in their hearts during life; and afterward they go to the dead.

4Indeed, for any among the living there is hope; a live dog is better off than a dead lion. **5***For the living know that they are to die, but the dead no longer know anything. There is no further recompense for them, because all memory of them is lost. **6**For them, love and hatred and rivalry have long since perished. They

will never again have part in anything that is done under the sun.

7*Go, eat your bread with joy and drink your wine with a merry heart, because it is now that God favors your works. **8**At all times let your garments be white, and spare not the perfume for your head. **9**Enjoy life with the wife whom you love, all the days of the fleeting life that is granted you under the sun. This is your lot in life, for the toil of your labors under the sun. **10**Anything you can turn your hand to, do with what power you have; for there will be no work, nor reason, nor knowledge, nor wisdom in the nether world where you are going.

The Evil Time Not Known

11Again I saw under the sun that the race is not won by the swift, nor the battle by the valiant, nor a livelihood by the wise, nor riches by the shrewd, nor favor by the experts; for a time of calamity comes to all alike. **12**†Man no more knows his own time than fish taken in the fatal net, or birds trapped in the snare; like these the children of men are caught when the evil time falls suddenly upon them.

THE UNCERTAIN FUTURE AND THE SAGES

13On the other hand I saw this wise deed under the sun, which I thought sublime. **14**Against a small city with few men in it advanced a mighty king, who surrounded it and threw up great siegeworks about it. **15**But in the city lived a man who, though poor, was wise, and he delivered it through his wisdom. Yet no one remembered this poor man. **16***Though I had said, "Wisdom is better than force," yet the wisdom of the poor man is despised and his words go unheeded.

17"The quiet words of the wise are better heeded
    than the shout of a ruler of fools"—!

18"A fly that dies can spoil the perfumer's ointment,
    and a single slip can ruin much that is good."

10   **1**   More weighty than wisdom or wealth is
      a little folly!
     2†   The wise man's understanding turns him
      to his right;
      the fool's understanding turns him to
      his left.

3When the fool walks through the street, in his lack of understanding he calls everything foolish.

---

†   8, 10: The text is obscure. The Latin has "wicked men buried, who, while still alive, were in the holy place and were praised in the city as if their works were just."

8, 13: *Shadowy:* perhaps an addition here; cf 6, 12.

8, 15: See notes on 2, 24; 5, 19.

9, 1-10: These statements are based on a very imperfect concept of life beyond the grave. With Christian revelation about the future life came the only satisfactory solution of the problem which so perplexed the author.

9, 1: *Love from hatred:* divine favor or disfavor.

9, 12: *His own time:* the time of death or sudden disaster.

10, 2: It is doubtful whether the author is endorsing either direction; cf Prv 4, 25ff.

❉
   9: 1, 13f.   9/2: 2, 14.
15: 2, 24; 9, 7.   5: 1, 11.
16: 1, 13; 3, 10.   7: 2, 1.24; 8, 15; 11, 9.
17: 3, 11.   16: Prv 24, 5.

⁴Should the anger of the ruler burst upon you, forsake not your place; for mildness abates great offenses.

⁵I have seen under the sun another evil, like a mistake that proceeds from the ruler: ⁶a fool put in lofty position while the rich sit in lowly places. ⁷I have seen slaves on horseback, while princes walked on the ground like slaves.

⁸*He who digs a pit may fall into it,
 and he who breaks through a wall may be bitten by a serpent.

⁹He who moves stones may be hurt by them,
 and he who chops wood is in danger from it.

¹⁰If the iron becomes dull, though at first he made easy progress, he must increase his efforts; but the craftsman has the advantage of his skill.

11 If the serpent bites because it has not been charmed,
 then there is no advantage for the charmer.

12* Words from the wise man's mouth win favor,
 but the fool's lips consume him.

13 The beginning of his words is folly,
 and the end of his talk is utter madness;

14* yet the fool multiplies words.
 Man knows not what is to come,
 for who can tell him what is to come after him?

15† When will the fool be weary of his labor,
 he who knows not the way to the city?

MAN DOES NOT KNOW WHAT EVIL WILL COME

16 Woe to you, O land, whose king was a servant,
 and whose princes dine in the morning!

17 Blessed are you, O land, whose king is of noble birth,
 and whose princes dine at the right time
 (for vigor and not in drinking bouts).

18 When hands are lazy, the rafters sag;
 when hands are slack, the house leaks.

19 Bread and oil call forth merriment
 and wine makes the living glad,
 but money answers for everything.

20 Even in your thoughts do not make light of the king,
 nor in the privacy of your bedroom revile the rich,
 Because the birds of the air may carry your voice,
 a winged creature may tell what you say.

11

1† Cast your bread upon the waters;
 after a long time you may find it again.

2† Make seven or eight portions;
 you know not what misfortune may come upon the earth.

MAN DOES NOT KNOW WHAT GOOD WILL COME

3 When the clouds are full,
 they pour out rain upon the earth.
 Whether a tree falls to the south or to the north,
 wherever it falls, there shall it lie.

4 One who pays heed to the wind will not sow,
 and one who watches the clouds will never reap.

5* Just as you know not how the breath of life
 fashions the human frame in the mother's womb,
 So you know not the work of God
 which he is accomplishing in the universe.

6 In the morning sow your seed,
 and at evening let not your hand be idle:
 For you know not which of the two will be successful,
 or whether both alike will turn out well.

Poem on Youth and Old Age

⁷Light is sweet! and it is pleasant for the eyes to see the sun. ⁸However many years a man may live, let him, as he enjoys them all, remember that the days of darkness will be many. All that is to come is vanity.

9 Rejoice, O young man, while you are young
 and let your heart be glad in the days of your youth.
 Follow the ways of your heart,
 the vision of your eyes;
 Yet understand that as regards all this
 God will bring you to judgment.

10† Ward off grief from your heart
 and put away trouble from your presence,
 though the dawn of youth is fleeting.

---

† 10, 15: *He who . . . city:* perhaps a proverbial expression for supreme stupidity.

11, 1: This may refer to a spirit of adventure in business or to generosity in almsgiving. *Waters:* of the ocean, which sometimes carry lost treasures to the shore.

11, 2: This verse refers either to almsgiving or to the wisdom of not putting all one's cargo into a single vessel.

11, 10: *Dawn . . . fleeting:* literally, "youth and the dawn [of life] are vanity."

10/8f: Prv 26, 27; Sir 27, 29.   14: 5, 2; 8, 7.
12: Sir 21, 19.   11/5: 8, 17.

12 ¹ Remember your Creator in the days of
　　　your youth,
　　　　before the evil days come
　　　And the years approach of which you
　　　　will say,
　　　　I have no pleasure in them;
^{2†} Before the sun is darkened,
　　　　and the light, and the moon, and the
　　　　stars,
　　　　while the clouds return after the rain;
^{3†} When the guardians of the house
　　　　tremble,
　　　　and the strong men are bent,
　　　And the grinders are idle because they
　　　　are few,
　　　　and they who look through the win-
　　　　dows grow blind;
^{4†} When the doors to the street are shut,
　　　　and the sound of the mill is low;
　　　When one waits for the chirp of a bird,
　　　　but all the daughters of song are sup-
　　　　pressed;
^{5†} And one fears heights,
　　　　and perils in the street;
　　　When the almond tree blooms,
　　　　and the locust grows sluggish
　　　　and the caper berry is without effect,
　　　Because man goes to his lasting home,
　　　　and mourners go about the streets;
^{6†} Before the silver cord is snapped
　　　　and the golden bowl is broken,
　　　And the pitcher is shattered at the spring,
　　　　and the broken pulley falls into the
　　　　well,

^{7*} And the dust returns to the earth as it
　　　　once was,
　　　　and the life breath returns to God who
　　　　gave it.
^{8*} Vanity of vanities, says Qoheleth,
　　　　all things are vanity!

Epilogue

⁹Besides being wise, Qoheleth taught the people knowledge, and weighed, scrutinized and arranged many proverbs. ¹⁰Qoheleth sought to find pleasing sayings, and to write down true sayings with precision. ^{11†}The sayings of the wise are like goads; like fixed spikes are the topics given by one collector. ^{12*}As to more than these, my son, beware. Of the making of many books there is no end, and in much study there is weariness for the flesh.

^{13*†}The last word, when all is heard: Fear God and keep his commandments, for this is man's all; ^{14*}because God will bring to judgment every work, with all its hidden qualities, whether good or bad.

---

†

12, 2: *The sun . . . return:* the cloudy and rainy Palestinian winter, a natural symbol of old age.

12, 3: *Guardians:* the arms; *strong men:* the legs; *grinders:* the teeth; *they who . . . windows:* the eyes.

12, 4: *Doors:* the tightly compressed lips; *sound of the mill:* perhaps the sound of mastication; *daughters of song:* the voice.

12, 5: *The almond tree blooms:* resembling the white hair of age. *The locust . . . sluggish:* an image of the stiffness in movement of the aged. *The caper berry:* a stimulant for appetite.

12, 6: *The golden bowl* suspended by *the silver cord* was a symbol of life; the snapping of the cord and the breaking of the bowl, a symbol of death. *The pitcher . . . the broken pulley:* another pair of metaphors for life and its ending.

12, 11: *Goads . . . one collector:* the *sayings* were stimulants to thought and also *spikes* or centers around which to group correlated pronouncements *of the wise.*

12, 13: *Man's all:* St. Jerome explains: "Unto this is every man born, that, knowing his Maker, he may revere him in fear, honor, and the observance of his commandments."

✿

12/7: 3, 20f; Jb 34, 15.   13: 5, 6.
   8: 1, 2.   14: 11, 9.
  12: 1, 18.

The Song of Songs

Introduction

The Song of Songs, meaning the greatest of songs (1, 1), contains in exquisite poetic form the sublime portrayal and praise of the mutual love of the Lord and his people. The Lord is the Lover and his people are the beloved. Describing this relationship in terms of human love, the author simply follows Israel's tradition. Isaiah (5, 1-7; 54, 4-8), Jeremiah (2, 2f.32), and Ezekiel (16; 23) all characterize the covenant between the Lord and Israel as a marriage. Hosea the prophet sees the idolatry of Israel in the adultery of Gomer (1-3). He also represents the Lord speaking to Israel's heart (2, 16) and changing her into a new spiritual people, purified by the Babylonian captivity and betrothed anew to her divine Lover "in justice and uprightness, in love and mercy" (2, 21).

The author of the Song, using the same literary figure, paints a beautiful picture of the ideal Israel, the chosen people of the Old and New Testaments, whom the Lord led by degrees to an exalted spiritual union with himself in the bond of perfect love. When the Song is thus interpreted there is no reason for surprise at the tone of the poem, which employs in its descriptions the courtship and marriage customs of the author's time. Moreover, the poem is not an allegory in which each remark, e. g., in the dialogue of the lovers, has a higher meaning. It is a parable in which the true meaning of mutual love comes from the poem as a whole.

While the Song is thus commonly understood by most Catholic scholars, it is also possible to see in it an inspired portrayal of ideal human love. Here we would have from God a description of the sacredness and the depth of married union.

Although the poem is attributed to Solomon in the traditional title (1, 1), the language and style of the work, among other considerations, point to a time after the end of the Babylonian Exile (538 B.C.) as that in which an unknown poet composed this masterpiece. The structure of the Song is difficult to analyze; here it is regarded as a lyric dialogue, with dramatic movement and interest.

The use of marriage as a symbol, characteristic of the Song, is found extensively also in the New Testament (Mt 9, 15; 25, 1-13; Jn 3, 29; 2 Cor 11, 2; Eph 5, 23-32; Rv 19, 7ff; 21, 9ff). In Christian tradition, the Song has been interpreted in terms of the union between Christ and the Church and, particularly by St. Bernard, of the union between Christ and the individual soul. Throughout the liturgy, especially in the Little Office, there is a consistent application of the Song of Songs to the Blessed Virgin Mary.

1 [1] THE SONG OF SONGS by Solomon.

Love's Desires

[2B*†] Let him kiss me with kisses of his mouth!

[3] More delightful is your love than wine!
    Your name spoken is a spreading perfume—
    that is why the maidens love you.

[4*] Draw me!—

[D]   We will follow you eagerly!

[B]   Bring me, O king, to your chambers.

[D] With you we rejoice and exult,
    we extol your love; it is beyond wine:
    how rightly you are loved!

Love's Boast

[5B†] I am as dark—but lovely,
    O daughters of Jerusalem—
    As the tents of Kedar,
    as the curtains of Salma.

[6†] Do not stare at me because I am swarthy,
    because the sun has burned me.
    My brothers have been angry with me;
    they charged me with the care of the vineyards:
    my own vineyard I have not cared for.

Love's Inquiry

[7B†] Tell me, you whom my heart loves,
    where you pasture your flock,
    where you give them rest at midday,
    Lest I be found wandering
    after the flocks of your companions.

---

† 1, 2ff: The marginal letters indicate the speaker of the verses: *B*—Bride; *D*—Daughters of Jerusalem; *G*—Bridegroom. In vv 2-7 the bride and the daughters address the bridegroom who appears here as a king, but more often in the poem as a shepherd. King and shepherd are familiar figures of the Lord in the Sacred Scriptures. Cf Ps 23, 1; Is 40, 11; Jn 10, 1-16.

1, 5: *Daughters of Jerusalem:* the chorus whom the bride addresses and who ask her questions (5, 9; 6, 1), thus developing action within the poem. *Kedar:* a Syrian desert region whose name suggests blackness; tents were often made of black goat hair. *Curtains:* tent coverings of *Salma,* a region close to Kedar.

1, 6: *Swarthy:* tanned by the sun from working in her brothers' vineyards. *My own vineyard:* the bride herself; cf Is 5, 1-7, where Israel is designated as the vineyard and the Lord is the Lover.

1, 7: Here and elsewhere in the Song (3, 1; 5, 8; 6, 1), the bride expresses her desire to be in the company of her lover.

---

* 1/2f: 4, 10.   4: 4, 10.

8G If you do not know,
    O most beautiful among women,
Follow the tracks of the flock
    and pasture the young ones
    near the shepherds' camps.

Love's Vision

9G† To the steeds of Pharaoh's chariots
    would I liken you, my beloved:
10 Your cheeks lovely in pendants,
    your neck in jewels.
11 We will make pendants of gold for you,
    and silver ornaments.

Love's Union

12B† For the king's banquet
    my nard gives forth its fragrance.
13† My lover is for me a sachet of myrrh
    to rest in my bosom.
14† My lover is for me a cluster of henna
    from the vineyards of Engedi.

15G✳† Ah, you are beautiful, my beloved,
    ah, you are beautiful; your eyes are
    doves!

16B† Ah, you are beautiful, my lover—
    yes, you are lovely.
Our couch, too, is verdant;
17   the beams of our house are cedars,
    our rafters, cypresses.

2 **1†** I am a flower of Sharon,
    a lily of the valley.

2G As a lily among thorns,
    so is my beloved among women.

3B As an apple tree among the trees of the
    woods,
    so is my lover among men.
I delight to rest in his shadow,
    and his fruit is sweet to my mouth.
4✳† He brings me into the banquet hall
    and his emblem over me is love.
5✳ Strengthen me with raisin cakes,
    refresh me with apples,
    for I am faint with love.
6✳ His left hand is under my head
    and his right arm embraces me.
7✳† I adjure you, daughters of Jerusalem,
    by the gazelles and hinds of the field,
Do not arouse, do not stir up love
    before its own time.

A Tryst in the Spring

8B† Hark! my lover—here he comes
    springing across the mountains,
    leaping across the hills.

9 My lover is like a gazelle
    or a young stag.
Here he stands behind our wall,
    gazing through the windows,
    peering through the lattices.
10 My lover speaks; he says to me,
    "Arise, my beloved, my beautiful one,
    and come!

11 "For see, the winter is past,
    the rains are over and gone.
12 The flowers appear on the earth,
    the time of pruning the vines has come,
    and the song of the dove is heard in our
    land.
13 The fig tree puts forth its figs,
    and the vines, in bloom, give forth
    fragrance.
Arise, my beloved, my beautiful one,
    and come!

14† "O my dove in the clefts of the rock,
    in the secret recesses of the cliff,
Let me see you,
    let me hear your voice,
For your voice is sweet,
    and you are lovely."

15B† Catch us the foxes, the little foxes
    that damage the vineyards; for our vine-
    yards are in bloom!

16✳ My lover belongs to me and I to him;
    he browses among the lilies.

---

† These verses point to a certain tension in the poem. Only at the end (8, 5ff) does mutual possession of the lovers become final.

1, 9ff: The bridegroom compares the girl's beauty to the rich adornment of the royal chariot of Pharaoh.

1, 12: *Nard:* a precious perfume, a figure of the bride; cf 4, 14.

1, 13: *Myrrh:* produced from aromatic resin of balsam or roses.

1, 14: *Henna:* a plant which bears white scented flowers.

1, 15: *Doves:* suggesting innocence and charm.

1, 16f: Though the meeting place of the lovers is but a shepherd's hut of green branches, it becomes a palace with beams of cedar and rafters of cypress when adorned with their love.

2, 1: *Flower of Sharon:* probably the narcissus, which grows in the fertile Plain of Sharon lying between Mount Carmel and Jaffa on the Mediterranean coast.

2, 4ff: *The banquet hall,* the sweet things of the table, the embrace of the bride and bridegroom, express the delicacy of their affection and the intimacy of their love.

2, 7: *By the gazelles and hinds:* the swiftness of these animals and the luster and soft expression of their eyes are suggestive of love; cf Prv 5, 19.

2, 8ff: In this sudden change of scene, the bride pictures her lover hastening toward her dwelling until his voice is heard bidding her come to him.

2, 14: The bride is addressed as though she were a dove in a mountain fastness out of sight and reach.

2, 15: A snatch of song in answer to the request of v 14; cf 8, 13f. *Foxes:* all who threaten to disturb the security of love symbolized by the vineyard; cf v 16.

✳ 15: 4, 1.7.   6: 8, 3.
2/4: 1, 4.   7: 3, 5; 8, 4.
   5: 5, 8.   16: 6, 3; 7, 10.

17*†
Until the day breathes cool and the
    shadows lengthen,
      roam, my lover,
Like a gazelle or a young stag
    upon the mountains of Bether.

Loss and Discovery

3 **1B*†**
On my bed at night I sought him
    whom my heart loves—
      I sought him but I did not find him.

2
I will rise then and go about the city;
    in the streets and crossings I will seek
Him whom my heart loves.
    I sought him but I did not find him.

3
The watchmen came upon me
    as they made their rounds of the city:
      Have you seen him whom my heart
      loves?

4*
I had hardly left them
    when I found him whom my heart loves.
I took hold of him and would not let him
    go
    till I should bring him to the home of
    my mother,
      to the room of my parent.

5*
I adjure you, daughters of Jerusalem,
    by the gazelles and hinds of the field,
Do not arouse, do not stir up love
    before its own time.

Regal State of the Bridegroom

6D*†
What is this coming up from the desert,
    like a column of smoke
Laden with myrrh, with frankincense,
    and with the perfume of every exotic
    dust?

7
Ah, it is the litter of Solomon;
    sixty valiant men surround it,
    of the valiant men of Israel:

8
All of them expert with the sword,
    skilled in battle,
Each with his sword at his side
    against danger in the watches of the
    night.

9
King Solomon made himself a carriage
    of wood from Lebanon.

10
He made its columns of silver,
    its roof of gold,
Its seat of purple cloth,
    its framework inlaid with ivory.

11
Daughters of Jerusalem, come forth
    and look upon King Solomon

In the crown with which his mother has
    crowned him
    on the day of his marriage,
    on the day of the joy of his heart.

The Charms of the Beloved

4 **1G***
Ah, you are beautiful, my beloved,
    ah, you are beautiful!
Your eyes are doves
    behind your veil.
Your hair is like a flock of goats
    streaming down the mountains of
    Gilead.

2†
Your teeth are like a flock of ewes to be
    shorn,
    which come up from the washing,
All of them big with twins,
    none of them thin and barren.

3†
Your lips are like a scarlet strand;
    your mouth is lovely.
Your cheek is like a half-pomegranate
    behind your veil.

4*†
Your neck is like David's tower
    girt with battlements;
A thousand bucklers hang upon it,
    all the shields of valiant men.

5*
Your breasts are like twin fawns,
    the young of a gazelle
    that browse among the lilies.

6*†
Until the day breathes cool and the
    shadows lengthen,
    I will go to the mountain of myrrh,
    to the hill of incense.

7†
You are all-beautiful, my beloved,
    and there is no blemish in you.

8†
Come from Lebanon, my bride,
    come from Lebanon, come!
Descend from the top of Amana,
    from the top of Senir and Hermon,
From the haunts of lions,
    from the leopards' mountains.

---

†
   2, 17: *Breathes cool:* in the evening when the sun is going down. Cf Gn 3, 8. *Bether:* a very obscure word; some interpret it in the sense of ruggedness; others, of spices; still others, of sacrifice (Gn 15, 10).

   3, 1ff: See the parallel in 5, 2-8.

   3, 6ff: The lover is portrayed as King Solomon, escorted by sixty armed men, coming in royal procession to meet his bride.

   4, 2: *Teeth:* praised for whiteness and regularity.

   4, 3: *Pomegranate:* a fruit somewhat like an orange, with a firm skin and deep red color. The girl's cheek is compared, in roundness and tint, to a half-pomegranate.

   4, 4: The ornaments about her neck are compared to the trophies on the city walls. Cf 1 Kgs 10, 10; 14, 26ff; Ez 27, 10.

   4, 6: *Mountain of myrrh . . . hill of incense:* spoken figuratively of the bride; cf 8, 14.

   4, 7: Cf St. Paul's description of the church in Eph 5, 27. This verse is also applied to Our Lady, especially in the liturgy of the feast of the Immaculate Conception.

   4, 8: *Amana . . . Senir and Hermon:* these rugged heights symbolize obstacles that would separate the lovers; cf 2, 14.

✱
17: 4, 6; 8, 14.   4/1: 1, 15.
3/1ff: 5, 2ff.   1ff: 6, 5ff.
4: 8, 2.   4: 7, 5.
5: 2, 7; 8, 4.   5: 7, 4.
6: 6, 10; 8, 5.   6: 2, 17.

9*† You have ravished my heart, my sister, my
bride;
> you have ravished my heart with one
> glance of your eyes,
> with one bead of your necklace.

10* How beautiful is your love, my sister, my
bride,
> how much more delightful is your love
> than wine,
> and the fragrance of your ointments
> than all spices!

11† Your lips drip honey, my bride,
> sweetmeats and milk are under your
> tongue;
> And the fragrance of your garments
> is the fragrance of Lebanon.

The Lover and His Garden

12G*† You are an enclosed garden, my sister, my
bride,
> an enclosed garden, a fountain sealed.

13 You are a park that puts forth
> pomegranates,
> with all choice fruits;

14† Nard and saffron, calamus and cinnamon,
> with all kinds of incense;
> Myrrh and aloes,
> with all the finest spices.

15 You are a garden fountain, a well of water
> flowing fresh from Lebanon.

16† Arise, north wind! Come, south wind!
> blow upon my garden
> that its perfumes may spread abroad.

B Let my lover come to his garden
> and eat its choice fruits.

5 **1G*†** I have come to my garden, my sister, my
bride;
> I gather my myrrh and my spices,
> I eat my honey and my sweetmeats,
> I drink my wine and my milk.

D Eat, friends; drink! Drink freely of love!

A Fruitless Search

2B*† I was sleeping, but my heart kept vigil;
> I heard my lover knocking:
> "Open to me, my sister, my beloved,
> my dove, my perfect one!
> For my head is wet with dew,
> my locks with the moisture of the
> night."

3† I have taken off my robe,
> am I then to put it on?
> I have bathed my feet,
> am I then to soil them?

4 My lover put his hand through the
> opening;
> my heart trembled within me,
> and I grew faint when he spoke.

5 I rose to open to my lover,
> with my hands dripping myrrh:
> With my fingers dripping choice myrrh
> upon the fittings of the lock.

6*† I opened to my lover—
> but my lover had departed, gone.
> I sought him but I did not find him;
> I called to him but he did not answer
> me.

7*† The watchmen came upon me
> as they made their rounds of the city;
> They struck me, and wounded me,
> and took my mantle from me,
> the guardians of the walls.

8* I adjure you, daughters of Jerusalem,
> if you find my lover—
> What shall you tell him?—
> that I am faint with love.

The Charms of the Lost Lover

9D How does your lover differ from any
> other,
> O most beautiful among women?
> How does your lover differ from any
> other,
> that you adjure us so?

10B† My lover is radiant and ruddy;
> he stands out among thousands.

11 His head is pure gold;
> his locks are palm fronds,
> black as the raven.

12 His eyes are like doves
> beside running waters,
> His teeth would seem bathed in milk,
> and are set like jewels.

---

† 4, 9: *Sister:* a term of endearment; it forms part of the conventional language of love used in this canticle.

4, 11: *Honey:* sweet words. Cf Prv 5, 3.

4, 12: *Enclosed garden . . . fountain sealed:* reserved for the bridegroom alone. The bride's fidelity is implied. Cf Prv 5, 15-19.

4, 14: These plants are all known for their sweet scent.

4, 16: The last two lines of the verse are spoken by the girl, inviting her lover to herself, the *garden*.

5, 1: *Eat, friends; drink!:* the lovers are encouraged to enjoy the delights of their love, symbol of Christ's union with the church.

5, 2-8: A trial similar to that in 3, 1ff.

5, 3f: The bride's hesitation is due, not to levity, but to strong emotion.

5, 6: The disappearance of the lover seems to be a deliberate trial and test inflicted on the girl.

5, 7: *The watchmen* do not know the reason for the girl's appearance in the city streets; cf 3, 2ff.

5, 10f: In answer to the question of v 9, the girl sings her lover's praises (vv 10-16). *Gold:* indicates how precious the lover is. *Palm fronds:* his thick, luxuriant growth of hair.

❋
9: 6, 5.	2ff: 3, 1f.
10: 1, 2f.	6: 3, 1.
12: 6, 2.11.	7: 3, 3.
5/1: 6, 2.	8: 2, 5.

13 His cheeks are like beds of spice
with ripening aromatic herbs.
His lips are red blossoms;
they drip choice myrrh.

14 His arms are rods of gold
adorned with chrysolites.
His body is a work of ivory
covered with sapphires.

15 His legs are columns of marble
resting on golden bases.
His stature is like the trees on Lebanon,
imposing as the cedars.

16 His mouth is sweetness itself;
he is all delight.
Such is my lover, and such my friend,
O daughters of Jerusalem.

Discovery

6 **1D†** Where has your lover gone,
O most beautiful among women?
Where has your lover gone
that we may seek him with you?

2B✿† My lover has come down to his garden,
to the beds of spice,
To browse in the garden
and to gather lilies.

3✿ My lover belongs to me and I to him;
he browses among the lilies.

The Charms of the Beloved

4G† You are as beautiful as Tirzah, my
beloved,
as lovely as Jerusalem,
as awe-inspiring as bannered troops.

5✿ Turn your eyes from me,
for they torment me.
Your hair is like a flock of goats
streaming down from Gilead.

6✿ Your teeth are like a flock of ewes
which come up from the washing,
All of them big with twins,
none of them thin and barren.

7 Your cheek is like a half-pomegranate
behind your veil.

8 There are sixty queens, eighty concubines,
and maidens without number—

9 One alone is my dove, my perfect one,
her mother's chosen,
the dear one of her parent.
The daughters saw her and declared her
fortunate,
the queens and concubines, and they
sang her praises;

10D✿ Who is this that comes forth like the dawn,
as beautiful as the moon, as resplendent
as the sun,
as awe-inspiring as bannered troops?

Love's Meeting

11B✿ I came down to the nut garden
to look at the fresh growth of the valley,
To see if the vines were in bloom,
if the pomegranates had blossomed.

12† Before I knew it, my heart had made me
the blessed one of my kinswomen.

The Beauty of the Bride

7 **1D†** Turn, turn, O Shulammite,
turn, turn, that we may look at you!

B Why would you look at the Shulammite
as at the dance of the two companies?

2D† How beautiful are your feet in sandals,
O prince's daughter!
Your rounded thighs are like jewels,
the handiwork of an artist.

3 Your navel is a round bowl
that should never lack for mixed wine.
Your body is a heap of wheat
encircled with lilies.

4✿ Your breasts are like twin fawns,
the young of a gazelle.

5✿† Your neck is like a tower of ivory.
Your eyes are like the pools in Heshbon
by the gate of Bath-rabbim.
Your nose is like the tower on Lebanon
that looks toward Damascus.

6, 1: The daughters of Jerusalem are won by this description of the lover and offer their aid in seeking him.

6, 2f: Determined to share her lover with no one, the girl refuses the aid offered by the daughters in seeking him. She implies that she had never really lost him, for he *has come down to his garden.*

6, 4-9: The lover again celebrates her beauty. *Tirzah:* probably meaning "pleasant"; it was the early capital of the northern kingdom of Israel (1 Kgs 16).

6, 12: The text is obscure in Hebrew and in the ancient versions. The Vulgate reads: "I did not know; my soul disturbed me because of the chariots of Aminadab."

7, 1: *Shulammite:* so called either because the girl is considered to be from Shulam in the plain of Esdraelon (cf 1 Kgs 1, 3) or because the name may mean "the peaceful one," and thus recall the name of Solomon. *As at the dance of the two companies:* the meaning is uncertain. The question in this verse could be construed as a refusal to dance; more probably, however, the girl accedes, as the following verses suggest.

7, 2-6: A flattering description of the girl's charms. *Rounded . . . jewels:* the meaning of these Hebrew words is not certain. *Wine* and *wheat* are symbolic of fertility; they are here associated with parts of the body which have a close relation to fruitfulness.

7, 5: The comparison emphasizes the stateliness and whiteness of the neck, and the limpidity of the eyes. *Bath-rabbim:* a proper name which occurs only here; there was a city of Rabbah northeast of *Heshbon* in Transjordan. Cf Jer 49, 3.

✿   6/2: 4, 12; 5, 1.   10: 3, 6; 8, 5.
      3: 2, 16; 7, 11.   11: 4, 12ff; 7, 13.
      5: 4, 9.   7/4: 4, 5.
      6f: 4, 1ff.   5: 4, 4.

6 Your head rises like Carmel;
  your hair is like draperies of purple;
  a king is held captive in its tresses.

Love's Desires

7G How beautiful you are, how pleasing,
  my love, my delight!
8† Your very figure is like a palm tree,
  your breasts are like clusters.
9 I said: I will climb the palm tree,
  I will take hold of its branches.
  Now let your breasts be like clusters of the
    vine
    and the fragrance of your breath like
      apples,
10† And your mouth like an excellent wine—

Love's Union

B that flows smoothly for my lover,
  spreading over the lips and the teeth.
11✤† I belong to my lover
  and for me he yearns.
12 Come, my lover, let us go forth to the
    fields
  and spend the night among the villages.
13✤ Let us go early to the vineyards, and see
  if the vines are in bloom,
  If the buds have opened,
  if the pomegranates have blossomed;
  There will I give you my love.
14† The mandrakes give forth fragrance,
  and at our doors are all choice fruits;
  Both fresh and mellowed fruits, my lover,
  I have kept in store for you.

8 **1** Oh, that you were my brother,
  nursed at my mother's breasts!
  If I met you out of doors, I would kiss you
  and none would taunt me.
2✤ I would lead you, bring you in
  to the home of my mother.
  There you would teach me to give you
  spiced wine to drink, and pomegranate
    juice.
3✤ His left hand is under my head
  and his right arm embraces me.
4✤ I adjure you, daughters of Jerusalem,
  by the gazelles and hinds of the field,
  Do not arouse, do not stir up love,
  before its own time.

Homecoming

5D✤† Who is this coming up from the desert,
  leaning upon her lover?

G Under the apple tree I awakened you;
  it was there that your mother conceived
    you,
  it was there that your parent conceived.

True Love

6B† Set me as a seal on your heart,
  as a seal on your arm;
  For stern as death is love,
  relentless as the nether world is
    devotion;
  its flames are a blazing fire.
7 Deep waters cannot quench love,
  nor floods sweep it away.
  Were one to offer all he owns to purchase
    love,
  he would be roundly mocked.

Chastity and Its Welcome

8† "Our sister is little
  and she has no breasts as yet.
  What shall we do for our sister
  when her courtship begins?
9 If she is a wall,
  we will build upon it a silver parapet;
  If she is a door,
  we will reinforce it with a cedar plank."
10 I am a wall,
  and my breasts are like towers.
  So now in his eyes I have become
  one to be welcomed.

---

† 7, 8f: *Palm tree:* a figure of stateliness. The bridegroom is eager to enjoy the possession of his bride.

7, 10: The bride delicately turns his compliment into an expression of the love and tenderness she feels for him.

7, 11-14: The girl's answer assures him of her affection and invites him to return with her to the rural delights which are associated with their love and which recall the meeting described in 6, 11f.

7, 14: *Mandrakes:* herbs believed to have power to arouse love and promote fertility; cf Gn 30, 14ff.

8, 5: The lovers are pictured walking homeward, enjoying the fulfillment of the desire which the girl expressed in vv 1f. The groom speaks of their first meeting.

8, 6f: *Seal:* this could be worn bound to the arm, as here, or suspended at the neck, or as a ring (Jer 22, 24). It was used for identification and signatures. *Stern . . . relentless:* in human experience, death and the nether world are inevitable, unrelenting; in the end they always triumph. Love, which is just as certain of its victory, matches its strength against the natural enemies of life; waters cannot extinguish it nor floods carry it away. It is more priceless than all riches.

8, 8ff: The bride affirms her chastity. In 8, 9 she quotes the course of action which her elder brothers had decided on. While she is yet immature, they will shelter her in view of eventual marriage. If she is virtuous, she will be honored; if she is unchaste, she will be kept under strict vigilance. In reply to this she proclaims her virtue and boasts of having found welcome from her lover.

✤ 11: 2, 16; 6, 3.   3: 2, 6.
  13: 6, 11.   4: 2, 7; 3, 5.
  8/2: 3, 4.   5: 3, 6; 6, 10.

The Bride and Her Dowry

11B† Solomon had a vineyard at Baal-hamon;
     he gave over the vineyard to caretakers.
     For its fruit one would have to pay
     a thousand silver pieces.

12 My vineyard is at my own disposal;
     the thousand pieces are for you, O
     Solomon,
     and two hundred for the caretakers of
     its fruit.

✿ 14: 2, 9.17; 4, 6.

Life Together

13G† O garden-dweller,
     my friends are listening for your voice,
     let me hear it!

14B✿ Be swift, my lover,
     like a gazelle or a young stag
     on the mountains of spices!

---

†   8, 11f: These enigmatic verses have been variously interpreted. In v 11 the girl alludes to a vineyard of great value which is compared to her own self in v 12. Her enormous dowry, *a thousand silver pieces*, is in keeping with her intrinsic worth. She has been the generous lover, giving herself and a dowry to her lover, referred to as *Solomon*, and also smaller gifts to her brothers, *the caretakers* (cf vv 8ff).

8, 13f: As in 2, 14f, her lover asks for a word or a song and she replies in words similar to those found in 2, 17.

The Book of Wisdom

Introduction

The Book of Wisdom was written about a hundred years before the coming of Christ. Its author, whose name is not known to us, was a member of the Jewish community at Alexandria, in Egypt. He wrote in Greek, in a style patterned on that of Hebrew verse. At times he speaks in the person of Solomon, placing his teachings on the lips of the wise king of Hebrew tradition in order to emphasize their value. His profound knowledge of the earlier Old Testament writings is reflected in almost every line of the book, and marks him, like Ben Sira, as an outstanding representative of religious devotion and learning among the sages of postexilic Judaism.

The primary purpose of the sacred author was the edification of his co-religionists in a time when they had experienced suffering and oppression, in part at least at the hands of apostate fellow Jews. To convey his message he made use of the most popular religious themes of his time, namely the splendor and worth of divine wisdom (6, 22—11, 1), the glorious events of the Exodus (11, 2—16; 12, 23—27; 15, 18—19, 22), God's mercy (11, 17—12, 22), the folly of idolatry (13, 1—15, 17), and the manner in which God's justice is vindicated in rewarding or punishing the individual soul (1, 1—6, 21). The first ten chapters especially form a preparation for the fuller teachings of Christ and his church. Many passages from this section of the book, notably 3, 1-8, are used by the church in her liturgy.

The principal divisions of the Book of Wisdom are:

> I: The Reward of Justice (1, 1—6, 21)
> II: Praise of Wisdom by Solomon (6, 22—11, 1)
> III: Special Providence of God during the Exodus (11, 2—16; 12, 23—27; 15, 18—19, 22) with digressions on God's mercy (11, 17—12, 22) and on the folly and shame of idolatry (13, 1—15, 17)

I: THE REWARD OF JUSTICE

Exhortation to Justice, the Key to Life

1 1*† LOVE JUSTICE, you who judge the earth;
think of the Lord in goodness,
and seek him in integrity of heart;

2* Because he is found by those who test him not,
and he manifests himself to those who do not disbelieve him.

3* For perverse counsels separate a man from God,
and his power, put to the proof, rebukes the foolhardy;

4* Because into a soul that plots evil wisdom enters not,
nor dwells she in a body under debt of sin.

5*† For the holy spirit of discipline flees deceit
and withdraws from senseless counsels;
and when injustice occurs it is rebuked.

6* For wisdom is a kindly spirit,
yet she acquits not the blasphemer of his guilty lips;
Because God is the witness of his inmost self
and the sure observer of his heart
and the listener to his tongue.

7*† For the spirit of the Lord fills the world,
is all-embracing, and knows what man says.

8* Therefore no one who utters wicked things can go unnoticed,
nor will chastising condemnation pass him by.

9 For the devices of the wicked man shall be scrutinized,
and the sound of his words shall reach the Lord,
for the chastisement of his transgressions;

10* Because a jealous ear hearkens to everything,
and discordant grumblings are no secret.

✿
1/1: 1 Chr 29, 17; Ps 2, 10; Is 26, 9.
1f: Sir 1, 25.
2: 1 Chr 28, 9.
3: Is 59, 2.
4: Sir 15, 7f; Rom 7, 14.
5: Is 63, 10.
6: Jer 17, 10.
6f: Jer 23, 24f.
7: 12, 1.
8: Prv 19, 5.
10f: Nm 14, 27f.

---

† 1, 1: *Justice:* not merely the cardinal virtue of that name (cf 8, 7), but the universal moral quality which is the application of Wisdom to moral conduct.

1, 5: *Discipline:* here and elsewhere, another name for Wisdom; *injustice:* the opposite of the virtue in 1, 1.

1, 7: This verse is applied to the Holy Spirit in the liturgy at Pentecost.

11† Therefore guard against profitless
      grumbling,
    and from calumny withhold your
      tongues;
  For a stealthy utterance does not go
      unpunished,
    and a lying mouth slays the soul.

12 Court not death by your erring way of life,
    nor draw to yourselves destruction by the
      works of your hands.

13* Because God did not make death,
    nor does he rejoice in the destruction of
      the living.

14 For he fashioned all things that they might
      have being;
    and the creatures of the world are
      wholesome,
  And there is not a destructive drug among
      them
    nor any domain of the nether world on
      earth,

15* For justice is undying.

The Wicked Reject Immortality and Justice Alike

16* It was the wicked who with hands and
      words invited death,
    considered it a friend, and pined for it,
    and made a covenant with it,
  Because they deserve to be in its possession,

2 1* they who said among themselves,
      thinking not aright:
  "Brief and troublous is our lifetime;
    neither is there any remedy for man's
      dying,
    nor is anyone known to have come back
      from the nether world.

2 For haphazard were we born,
    and hereafter we shall be as though we
      had not been;
  Because the breath in our nostrils is a
      smoke
    and reason is a spark at the beating of our
      hearts,

3* And when this is quenched, our body will
      be ashes
    and our spirit will be poured abroad like
      unresisting air.

4 Even our name will be forgotten in time,
    and no one will recall our deeds.
  So our life will pass away like the traces of
      a cloud,
    and will be dispersed like a mist
  Pursued by the sun's rays
    and overpowered by its heat.

5* For our lifetime is the passing of a shadow;
    and our dying cannot be deferred
    because it is fixed with a seal; and no one
      returns.

6* Come, therefore, let us enjoy the good
      things that are real,
    and use the freshness of creation avidly.

7 Let us have our fill of costly wine and
      perfumes,
    and let no springtime blossom pass us by;

8 let us crown ourselves with rosebuds ere
      they wither.

9*† Let no meadow be free from our
      wantonness;
    everywhere let us leave tokens of our
      rejoicing,
    for this our portion is, and this our lot.

10* Let us oppress the needy just man;
    let us neither spare the widow
    nor revere the old man for his hair grown
      white with time.

11 But let our strength be our norm of justice;
    for weakness proves itself useless.

12*† Let us beset the just one, because he is
      obnoxious to us;
    he sets himself against our doings,
  Reproaches us for transgressions of the law
    and charges us with violations of our
      training.

13* He professes to have knowledge of God
    and styles himself a child of the Lord.

14* To us he is the censure of our thoughts;
    merely to see him is a hardship for us,

15 Because his life is not like other men's,
    and different are his ways.

16* He judges us debased;
    he holds aloof from our paths as from
      things impure.
  He calls blest the destiny of the just
    and boasts that God is his Father.

17* Let us see whether his words be true;
    let us find out what will happen to him.

18* For if the just one be the son of God, he will
      defend him
    and deliver him from the hand of his foes.

13f: Ez 18, 32; 33, 11;
    2 Pt 3, 9.
15: Is 51, 6ff.
16: Is 28, 15.
2/1: Jb 14, 1; 7, 9.
3: Jb 7, 9; Jas 4, 14.
5: Ps 144, 4.
6: Is 22, 13; 1 Cor 15, 32.
9: Jer 13, 25.

10: Ex 22, 22ff; Lv 19, 32.
12: Hos 8, 1.
13: Mt 27, 43; Jn 8, 55;
    10, 36-39.
14: Mt 9, 4.
16: Jer 6, 30.
17: Gn 37, 20.
18: Ps 22, 9; Is 42, 1;
    Mt 27, 43; Jn 5, 18.

---

† 1, 11: *Calumny:* speech against God and his providence is meant.

2, 9: *Let no meadow . . . wantonness:* the extant Greek Mss have "Let none of us be without part in our wanton doings." Most Latin Mss have both forms of this line.

2, 12-20: Often applied to the Passion of our Lord; many have understood these verses as a direct prophecy. Cf Mt 27, 41-44.

2, 12: *Law:* the law of Moses; *training* has the same meaning.

19 With revilement and torture let us put him
　　to the test
　　　　that we may have proof of his gentleness
　　　　　and try his patience.

20 Let us condemn him to a shameful death;
　　　　for according to his own words, God will
　　　　　take care of him."

21 These were their thoughts, but they erred;
　　　　for their wickedness blinded them,

22 And they knew not the hidden counsels of
　　God;
　　　　neither did they count on a recompense
　　　　　of holiness
　　　　nor discern the innocent souls' reward.

23 For God formed man to be imperishable;
　　　　the image of his own nature he made him.

24 But by the envy of the devil, death entered
　　the world,
　　　　and they who are in his possession
　　　　　experience it.

The Hidden Counsels of God:

A. ON SUFFERING

3 **1*†** But the souls of the just are in the hand of
　　God,
　　　　and no torment shall touch them.

2 They seemed, in the view of the foolish, to
　　be dead;
　　　　and their passing away was thought an
　　　　　affliction

3 and their going forth from us, utter
　　destruction.
　　But they are in peace.

4 For if before men, indeed, they be
　　punished,
　　　　yet is their hope full of immortality;

5 Chastised a little, they shall be greatly
　　blessed,
　　　　because God tried them
　　　　and found them worthy of himself.

6*† As gold in the furnace, he proved them,
　　　　and as sacrificial offerings he took them
　　　　　to himself.

7*† In the time of their visitation they shall
　　shine,
　　　　and shall dart about as sparks through
　　　　　stubble;

8* They shall judge nations and rule over
　　peoples,
　　　　and the Lord shall be their King forever.

9* Those who trust in him shall understand
　　truth,
　　　　and the faithful shall abide with him in
　　　　　love:
　　　　Because grace and mercy are with his holy
　　　　　ones,
　　　　and his care is with his elect.

10† But the wicked shall receive a punishment
　　to match their thoughts,
　　　　since they neglected justice and forsook
　　　　　the Lord.

11* For he who despises wisdom and
　　instruction is doomed.
　　　　Vain is their hope, fruitless are their labors,
　　　　and worthless are their works.

12* Their wives are foolish and their children
　　wicked;
　　　　accursed is their brood.

B. ON CHILDLESSNESS

13† Yes, blessed is she who, childless and
　　undefiled,
　　　　knew not transgression of the marriage
　　　　　bed;
　　　　she shall bear fruit at the visitation of
　　　　　souls.

14*† So also the eunuch whose hand wrought no
　　misdeed,
　　　　who held no wicked thoughts against the
　　　　　Lord—
　　　　For he shall be given fidelity's choice
　　　　　reward
　　　　and a more gratifying heritage in the
　　　　　Lord's temple.

15* For the fruit of noble struggles is a glorious
　　one;
　　　　and unfailing is the root of
　　　　　understanding.

16* But the children of adulterers will remain
　　without issue,
　　　　and the progeny of an unlawful bed will
　　　　　disappear.

17 For should they attain long life, they will be
　　held in no esteem,
　　　　and dishonored will their old age be at
　　　　　last;

18 While should they die abruptly, they have
　　no hope
　　　　nor comfort in the day of scrutiny;

20: Jas 5, 6.
21: Rom 1, 21.
22: Ps 18, 24f; Prv 11, 18;
　　Mt 11, 25.
23: Gn 1, 26f;
　　Is 54, 16 LXX.
24: Gn 3, 1-24; Rom 5, 12.
3/1: Jb 12, 10; 5, 19.
3: Is 57, 2.
5: Tb 12, 13; 2 Cor 4, 17;
　　1 Pt 1, 6f.
6: Ps 51, 19; Prv 17, 3;
　　Sir 2, 5; Is 48, 10.

7: Dn 12, 3; Ob 18;
　　Mal 3, 3; Mt 13, 43.
8: 8, 14; Prv 8, 16; Dn 7,
　　22; 1 Cor 6, 2; Rv 20, 4.
9: 4, 15; Jb 10, 12;
　　Jn 15, 10.
11: Prv 1, 7.
11f: Sir 41, 8.
12: Dt 28, 18ff.
14: Is 56, 2-5.
15: Sir 1, 18.
16: 2 Sm 12, 14.

† 3, 1-8: Verses frequently applied to the martyrs.

3, 6: *Offerings:* the image is that of the holocaust, in which
the victim is completely consumed by fire.

3, 7: *Visitation:* God's loving judgment of those who have
been faithful to him; the same word is used in 14, 11 for the
punishment of the wicked at God's final judgment. Cf also 3, 13.

3, 10: *To match their thoughts:* a fate as empty as that which
they describe; cf 2, 1-5.

3, 13: *Visitation of souls:* that is, the last judgment. Cf 3, 7-9.

3, 14: *Fidelity's choice reward:* cf Is 56, 1-8. *More gratifying:*
better than sons and daughters; cf Is 56, 5.

19 for dire is the end of the wicked
generation.

4 **1** † Better is childlessness with virtue;
for immortal is its memory:
because both by God is it acknowledged,
and by men.

2 When it is present men imitate it,
and they long for it when it is gone;
And forever it marches crowned in
triumph,
victorious in unsullied deeds of valor.

3 But the numerous progeny of the wicked
shall be of no avail;
their spurious offshoots shall not strike
deep root
nor take firm hold.

4 For even though their branches flourish for
a time,
they are unsteady and shall be rocked by
the wind
and, by the violence of the winds,
uprooted;

5 Their twigs shall be broken off untimely,
and their fruit be useless, unripe for
eating,
and fit for nothing.

6 For children born of lawless unions
give evidence of the wickedness of
their parents, when they are examined.

C. ON EARLY DEATH

7 But the just man, though he die early, shall
be at rest.

8 For the age that is honorable comes not
with the passing of time,
nor can it be measured in terms of years.

9 Rather, understanding is the hoary crown
for men,
and an unsullied life, the attainment of
old age.

10 † He who pleased God was loved;
he who lived among sinners was
transported—

11 Snatched away, lest wickedness pervert his
mind
or deceit beguile his soul;

12 For the witchery of paltry things obscures
what is right
and the whirl of desire transforms the
innocent mind.

13 Having become perfect in a short while, he
reached the fullness of a long career;

14 for his soul was pleasing to the Lord,
therefore he sped him out of the midst of
wickedness.
But the people saw and did not understand,
nor did they take this into account.

16 Yes, the just man dead condemns the sinful
who live,
and youth swiftly completed
condemns the many years of the wicked
man grown old.

17 For they see the death of the wise man
and do not understand what the Lord
intended for him,
or why he made him secure.

18 They see, and hold him in contempt;
but the Lord laughs them to scorn.

19 And they shall afterward become
dishonored corpses
and an unceasing mockery among the
dead.
For he shall strike them down speechless
and prostrate
and rock them to their foundations;
They shall be utterly laid waste
and shall be in grief
and their memory shall perish.

The Final Judgment of the Wicked

20 † Fearful shall they come, at the counting up
of their sins,
and their lawless deeds shall convict
them to their face.

5 **1** Then shall the just one with great assurance
confront
his oppressors who set at nought his
labors.

2 Seeing this, they shall be shaken with
dreadful fear,
and amazed at the unlooked-for
salvation.

3 They shall say among themselves, rueful
and groaning through anguish of spirit:
"This is he whom once we held as a
laughingstock
and as a type for mockery, **4**fools that we
were!
His life we accounted madness,
and his death dishonored.

19: Ps 34, 22.
4/1: Sir 16, 1ff; Prv 3, 3f.
  3: Sir 23, 25.
  4: Sir 40, 15; Is 40, 24.
  7: 3, 3.
  8f: Jb 12, 12; 32, 9;
    Sir 25, 4ff.
10: Gn 5, 24; Sir 44, 16;
    Heb 11, 5.
11: Is 57, 1f.

12: 2, 21; Dn 13, 9.
14: Gn 19, 22. 29; 2 Pt 2, 7.
16: Mt 12, 41f.
18: Ps 37, 13.
19: Neh 1, 10 LXX;
    Ps 18, 8; Is 14, 19;
    Jer 23, 39f; 2 Mc 3, 29.
5/1f: 2 Thes 1, 6f.
  1: Col 2, 15.

† 4, 1: The Latin form of this line, "Oh, how fair is the chaste
generation in its glory!" is a later adaptation, which is applied in
the liturgy to the splendor of virginity.

4, 10f: There are allusions here to Enoch (Gn 5, 21-24), who
was young by patriarchal standards, and to Lot (Gn 19, 10f;
2 Pt 2, 7f). Cf also Is 57, 1f.

4, 15, here omitted, repeats the last two lines of 3, 9.

4, 20: *Counting up:* the last judgment.

5* See how he is accounted among the sons of
God;
　　how his lot is with the saints!

6* We, then, have strayed from the way of
truth,
　　and the light of justice did not shine for
us,
　　and the sun did not rise for us.

7 We had our fill of the ways of mischief and
of ruin;
　　we journeyed through impassable
deserts,
　　but the way of the Lord we knew not.

8* What did our pride avail us?
　　What have wealth and its boastfulness
afforded us?

9* All of them passed like a shadow
　　and like a fleeting rumor;

10 Like a ship traversing the heaving water,
　　of which, when it has passed, no trace
can be found,
　　no path of its keel in the waves.

11 Or like a bird flying through the air;
　　no evidence of its course is to be found—
But the fluid air, lashed by the beat of
pinions,
　　and cleft by the rushing force
Of speeding wings, is traversed:
　　and afterward no mark of passage can be
found in it.

12 Or as, when an arrow has been shot at a
mark,
　　the parted air straightway flows together
again
　　so that none discerns the way it went
through—

13* Even so we, once born, abruptly came to
nought
　　and held no sign of virtue to display,
　　but were consumed in our wickedness."

14* Yes, the hope of the wicked is like
thistledown borne on the wind,
　　and like fine, tempest-driven foam;
Like smoke scattered by the wind,
　　and like the passing memory of the
nomad camping for a single day.

15* But the just live forever,
　　and in the Lord is their recompense,
　　and the thought of them is with the Most
High.

16* Therefore shall they receive the splendid
crown,
　　the beauteous diadem, from the hand of
the Lord—
For he shall shelter them with his right
hand,
　　and protect them with his arm.

17* He shall take his zeal for armor
　　and he shall arm creation to requite the
enemy;

18 He shall don justice for a breastplate
　　and shall wear sure judgment for a
helmet;

19* He shall take invincible rectitude as a shield

20 　　and whet his sudden anger for a sword,
And the universe shall war with him against
the foolhardy.

21* Well-aimed shafts of lightnings shall go
forth
　　and from the clouds as from a well-drawn
bow shall leap to the mark;

22* 　　and as from his sling, wrathful hailstones
shall be hurled.
The water of the sea shall be enraged
against them
　　and the streams shall abruptly overflow;

23* A mighty wind shall confront them
　　and a tempest winnow them out;
Thus lawlessness shall lay the whole earth
waste
　　and evildoing overturn the thrones of
potentates.

Exhortation to Seek Wisdom

6 1* Hear, therefore, kings, and understand;
　　learn, you magistrates of the earth's
expanse!

2 Hearken, you who are in power over the
multitude
　　and lord it over throngs of peoples!

3* Because authority was given you by the
Lord
　　and sovereignty by the Most High,
　　who shall probe your works and
scrutinize your counsels!

4† Because, though you were ministers of his
kingdom, you judged not rightly,
　　and did not keep the law,
　　nor walk according to the will of God,

5 Terribly and swiftly shall he come against
you,
　　because judgment is stern for the
exalted—

6* For the lowly may be pardoned out of
mercy
　　but the mighty shall be mightily put to
the test.

※
5: Acts 26, 18; Col 1, 12.
6: Prv 4, 18f; Jn 12, 35.
6f: Is 59, 6-14.
8: Ps 49, 7; Prv 10, 2.
9ff: 1 Chr 20, 15; Ps 144, 4;
　　Jb 9, 25f LXX.
13: Ez 33, 10.
14: Jb 21, 18; Pss 1, 4;
　　37, 20; Is 17, 13.
15: Is 62, 11; Ez 18, 9.
16: Ex 33, 22; Is 62, 3;
　　2 Tm 4, 8; 1 Pt 5, 4.

17f: Is 59, 16.
19f: Dt 32, 40ff.
21: Hb 3, 9ff.
22: Dt 11, 4.
23: 11, 20; Sir 10, 13f.
6/1f: 1, 1; Sir 33, 19;
　　Mi 3, 1.9.
3: 2 Chr 36, 23; Prv 8,
　　15f; Jn 19, 11;
　　Rom 13, 1ff.
6ff: Lk 12, 48.

† 6, 4: *Law:* that of Moses; cf v 10; 2, 12.

7   For the Lord of all shows no partiality,
     nor does he fear greatness,
Because he himself made the great as well
     as the small,
     and he provides for all alike;

8   but for those in power a rigorous scrutiny
     impends.

9   To you, therefore, O princes, are my words
     addressed
     that you may learn wisdom and that you
     may not sin.

10†   For those who keep the holy precepts
     hallowed shall be found holy,
     and those learned in them will have
     ready a response.

11   Desire therefore my words;
     long for them and you shall be instructed.

12   Resplendent and unfading is Wisdom,
     and she is readily perceived by those who
     love her,
     and found by those who seek her.

13   She hastens to make herself known in
     anticipation of men's desire;

14   he who watches for her at dawn shall not
     be disappointed,
     for he shall find her sitting by his gate.

15   For taking thought of her is the perfection
     of prudence,
     and he who for her sake keeps vigil shall
     quickly be free from care;

16   Because she makes her own rounds, seeking
     those worthy of her,
     and graciously appears to them in the
     ways,
     and meets them with all solicitude.

17   For the first step toward discipline is a very
     earnest desire for her;
     then, care for discipline is love of her;

18   love means the keeping of her laws;
To observe her laws is the basis for
     incorruptibility;

19   and incorruptibility makes one close to
     God;

20   thus the desire for Wisdom leads up to a
     kingdom.

21   If, then, you find pleasure in throne and
     scepter, you princes of the peoples,
     honor Wisdom, that you may reign as
     kings forever.

II: PRAISE OF WISDOM BY SOLOMON

Introduction

22   NOW WHAT WISDOM IS, and how she came to
     be, I shall relate;
     and I shall hide no secrets from you,
But from the very beginning I shall search
     out
     and bring to light knowledge of her,
     nor shall I diverge from the truth.

23   Neither shall I admit consuming jealousy
     to my company,
     because that can have no fellowship with
     Wisdom.

24   A great number of wise men is the safety of
     the world,
     and a prudent king, the stability of his
     people;

25   so take instruction from my words, to
     your profit.

Solomon Is Like All Other Men

7 **1†**   I too am a mortal man, the same as all the
     rest,
     and a descendant of the first man formed
     of earth.
And in my mother's womb I was molded
     into flesh

2†   in a ten-months' period—body and blood,
     from the seed of man, and the pleasure
     that accompanies marriage.

3   And I too, when born, inhaled the common
     air,
     and fell upon the kindred earth;
     wailing, I uttered that first sound
     common to all.

4   In swaddling clothes and with constant care
     I was nurtured.

5   For no king has any different origin or birth,

6   but one is the entry into life for all; and
     in one same way they leave it.

Solomon Prayed and Wisdom and Riches Came to Him

7   Therefore I prayed, and prudence was
     given me;
     I pleaded, and the spirit of Wisdom came
     to me.

8   I preferred her to scepter and throne,
And deemed riches nothing in comparison
     with her,

✿

   7: Dt 1, 17; Prv 22, 2.
   9ff: Dt 4, 10; Ps 2, 12;
     Sir 32, 14; 1 Jn 3, 7.
   12: 7, 10; Prv 8, 17;
     Jer 29, 13.
   13ff: Prv 8, 3. 17. 34.
   16: Prv 8, 20f; Sir 15, 1ff.
   17-21: Ps 2, 10ff; Prv 4, 4-9; 7,
     1-4; 8, 15f; Dn 7, 27;
     Jn 14, 15. 21; 1 Jn 5, 3.
   22: Tb 12, 7. 11; Mt 13, 11;
     Jn 15, 15.

   23: 7, 13; Jas 3, 14f.
   24: Prv 24, 6; 29, 4;
     Sir 10, 1ff.
   7/1f: 10, 1; Gn 2, 7;
     Jb 10, 9-12; 33, 6;
     1 Cor 15, 47ff.
   6: Jb 1, 21; 1 Tm 6, 7f.
   7: 1 Kgs 3, 5-15;
     Prv 2, 3-11.
   8f: 8, 5; 1 Kgs 10, 21;
     Prv 3, 14ff; 8, 10.18f;
     Jb 28, 15-19.

---

†
  6, 10: *Response:* a suitable plea before the great Judge. Cf Prv 22, 21; Jb 31, 14; Hb 2, 1; Sir 8, 9.

  7, 1: *First man formed of earth:* Adam. The author omits throughout the book the proper names of the characters in sacred history of whom he speaks; see especially chapter 10.

  7, 2: *In a ten-months' period:* thus the ancients were accustomed to reckon the period of pregnancy.

9   nor did I liken any priceless gem to her;
     Because all gold, in view of her, is a little
       sand,
       and before her, silver is to be accounted
         mire.

10*   Beyond health and comeliness I loved her,
     And I chose to have her rather than the
       light,
       because the splendor of her never yields
         to sleep.

11*   Yet all good things together came to me in
       her company,
       and countless riches at her hands;

12*   And I rejoiced in them all, because Wisdom
       is their leader,
       though I had not known that she is the
         mother of these.

Solomon Prays for Help to Speak of Wisdom

13*   Simply I learned about her, and
       ungrudgingly do I share—
       her riches I do not hide away;

14†   For to men she is an unfailing treasure;
       those who gain this treasure win the
         friendship of God,
       to whom the gifts they have from
         discipline commend them.

15   Now God grant I speak suitably
       and value these endowments at their
         worth:
     For he is the guide of Wisdom
       and the director of the wise.

16*   For both we and our words are in his hand,
       as well as all prudence and knowledge of
         crafts.

17   For he gave me sound knowledge of
       existing things,
       that I might know the organization of the
         universe and the force of its elements,

18   The beginning and the end and the
       midpoint of times,
       the changes in the sun's course and the
         variations of the seasons.

19   Cycles of years, positions of the stars,

20   natures of animals, tempers of beasts,

.   Powers of the winds and thoughts of men,
     uses of plants and virtues of roots—

21   Such things as are hidden I learned, and
       such as are plain;

22*   for Wisdom, the artificer of all, taught
       me.

Nature and Incomparable Dignity of Wisdom

    For in her is a spirit
       intelligent, holy, unique,
   Manifold, subtle, agile,
       clear, unstained, certain,
   Not baneful, loving the good, keen,
       unhampered, beneficent, ²³kindly,
   Firm, secure, tranquil,
       all-powerful, all-seeing,
   And pervading all spirits,
       though they be intelligent, pure and very
         subtle.

24*   For Wisdom is mobile beyond all motion,
       and she penetrates and pervades all
         things by reason of her purity.

25   For she is an aura of the might of God
       and a pure effusion of the glory of the
         Almighty;
     therefore nought that is sullied enters
       into her.

26*   For she is the refulgence of eternal light,
       the spotless mirror of the power of God,
       the image of his goodness.

27*   And she, who is one, can do all things,
       and renews everything while herself
         perduring;
     And passing into holy souls from age to age,
       she produces friends of God and
         prophets.

28   For there is nought God loves, be it not one
       who dwells with Wisdom.

29*   For she is fairer than the sun
       and surpasses every constellation of the
         stars.
     Compared to light, she takes precedence;

30   for that, indeed, night supplants,
       but wickedness prevails not over
         Wisdom.

8   1*†   Indeed, she reaches from end to end
       mightily
       and governs all things well.

Solomon Sought Wisdom, the Source of Blessings

2*   Her I loved and sought after from my
       youth;
     I sought to take her for my bride
       and was enamored of her beauty.

3   She adds to nobility the splendor of
       companionship with God;
       even the Lord of all loved her.

4*   For she is instructress in the understanding
       of God,
       the selector of his works.

*   10: Prv 6, 23.
11: Prv 8, 21.
12: Prv 8, 14f.
13: 6, 23.
16: 3, 1.
22: 14, 2; Prv 8, 30.
22f: Heb 4, 12f; Jas 3, 17.
24: 8, 1.

26: 2 Cor 4, 4; Col 1, 15; Heb 1, 3.
27: Ex 33, 11; Jb 42, 2; Ps 104, 29; Jl 3, 1.
29f: Sg 6, 3.9.
8/1: 7, 24; 15, 1.
2: 1 Kgs 3, 7ff; Ps 45, 12; Prv 5, 18; 8, 17.
4: Prv 8, 27-31.

†   7, 14: *Discipline:* cf note on 1, 5.
8, 1: *End to end:* from one end of the heavens to the other.

5* And if riches be a desirable possession in
   life,
   what is more rich than Wisdom, who
   produces all things?

6* And if prudence renders service,
   who in the world is a better craftsman
   than she?

7† Or if one loves justice,
   the fruits of her works are virtues;
   For she teaches moderation and prudence,
   justice and fortitude,
   and nothing in life is more useful for men
   than these.

8* Or again, if one yearns for copious learning,
   she knows the things of old, and infers
   those yet to come.
   She understands the turns of phrases and
   the solutions of riddles;
   signs and wonders she knows in advance
   and the outcome of times and ages.

Solomon Sought Wisdom as His Counselor and Comfort

9 So I determined to take her to live with me,
   knowing that she would be my counselor
   while all was well,
   and my comfort in care and grief.

10* For her sake I should have glory among the
    masses,
    and esteem from the elders, though I be
    but a youth.

11 I should become keen in judgment,
   and should be a marvel before rulers.

12† They would abide my silence and attend
    my utterance;
    and as I spoke on further,
    they would place their hands upon their
    mouths.

13* For her sake I should have immortality
    and leave to those after me an everlasting
    memory.

14* I should govern peoples, and nations would
    be my subjects—

15 terrible princes, hearing of me, would be
   afraid;
   in the assembly I should appear noble,
   and in war courageous.

16* Within my dwelling, I should take my
    repose beside her;

For association with her involves no
   bitterness
   and living with her no grief,
   but rather joy and gladness.

Solomon Realizes that Wisdom Is a Gift of God

17* Thinking thus within myself,
    and reflecting in my heart
    That there is immortality in kinship with
    Wisdom,

18 and good pleasure in her friendship,
   and unfailing riches in the works of her
   hands,
   And that in frequenting her society there is
   prudence,
   and fair renown in sharing her discourses,
   I went about seeking to take her for my
   own.

19† Now, I was a well-favored child,
    and I came by a noble nature;

20 or rather, being noble, I attained an
   unsullied body.

21*† And knowing that I could not otherwise
     possess her except God gave it—
     and this, too, was prudence, to know
     whose is the gift—
     I went to the Lord and besought him,
     and said with all my heart:

Solomon's Prayer

9 1* God of my fathers, Lord of mercy,
     you who have made all things by your
     word

2* And in your wisdom have established man
   to rule the creatures produced by you,

3* To govern the world in holiness and justice,
   and to render judgment in integrity of
   heart:

4* Give me Wisdom, the attendant at your
   throne,
   and reject me not from among your
   children;

5* For I am your servant, the son of your
   handmaid,
   a man weak and short-lived
   and lacking in comprehension of
   judgment and of laws.

5: Prv 8, 18f.
6f: Prv 8, 14f.
8: Prv 1, 6; Sir 39, 1ff;
   42, 19f; Dn 2, 21.
10ff: 1 Kgs 3, 28;
   Jb 29, 8ff.21f.
13: Sir 15, 6; 41, 12f;
   Is 56, 5.
14: 3, 8; Pss 18, 48; 47, 4.
16: Prv 29, 6; Sir 15, 6;
   Bar 3, 38.
17: Prv 3, 18.

21: 1 Kgs 3, 9; 4, 29;
   Prv 2, 6; Jas 1, 5.
9/1: Ps 86, 15.
1f: Gn 1; Ps 33, 6;
   Prv 3, 19; Jer 10, 12;
   Jn 1, 3.10.
2: Ps 8, 7ff; Sir 17, 2ff.
3: 1 Kgs 3, 6; 9, 4f;
   Ps 9, 8f.
4: 2 Chr 1, 10.
5: 1 Kgs 3, 7; Ps 116, 16.

†
   8, 7: *Moderation . . . fortitude:* what are now known as the
cardinal virtues.
   8, 12: *Hands upon their mouths:* an oft-mentioned sign of
respect among the ancients for unanswerable wisdom; cf Jb 40,
4.
   8, 19f: Here the sacred writer mentions first bodily, then
spiritual, excellence. To make it plain that the latter is the governing factor in the harmonious development of the human person, he then reverses the order.
   8, 21: *Possess her:* in the Latin, "be continent." Though this
verse has often been cited in connection with the virtue of
chastity, the original must certainly mean "be possessed of
Wisdom."

6 Indeed, though one be perfect among the
sons of men,
> if Wisdom, who comes from you, be not
> with him,
> > he shall be held in no esteem.

7 You have chosen me king over your people
> and magistrate for your sons and
> daughters.

8 You have bid me build a temple on your
holy mountain
> and an altar in the city that is your
> dwelling place,
> > a copy of the holy tabernacle which you
> > had established from of old.

9 Now with you is Wisdom, who knows your
works
> and was present when you made the
> world;
> > Who understands what is pleasing in your
> > eyes
> > > and what is conformable with your
> > > commands.

10 Send her forth from your holy heavens
> and from your glorious throne dispatch
> her
> > That she may be with me and work with
> > me,
> > > that I may know what is your pleasure.

11 For she knows and understands all things,
> and will guide me discreetly in my affairs
> and safeguard me by her glory;

12 Thus my deeds will be acceptable,
> and I shall judge your people justly
> and be worthy of my father's throne.

13 For what man knows God's counsel,
> or who can conceive what the Lord
> intends?

14 For the deliberations of mortals are timid,
> and unsure are our plans.

15 For the corruptible body burdens the soul
> and the earthen shelter weighs down the
> mind that has many concerns.

16 And scarce do we guess the things on earth,
> and what is within our grasp we find with
> difficulty;
> > but when things are in heaven, who can
> > search them out?

17 Or who ever knew your counsel, except you
had given Wisdom
> and sent your holy spirit from on high?

18 And thus were the paths of those on earth
made straight,
> and men learned what was your pleasure,
> and were saved by Wisdom.

Wisdom Preserves Her Followers

10 **1** She preserved the first-formed father of
the world
> when he alone had been created;
> And she raised him up from his fall,
2 and gave him power to rule all things.
3 But when the unjust man withdrew from
her in his anger,
> he perished through his fratricidal
> wrath.
4 When on his account the earth was
flooded, Wisdom again saved it,
> piloting the just man on frailest wood.
5 She, when the nations were sunk in
universal wickedness,
> knew the just man, kept him blameless
> before God,
> and preserved him resolute against
> pity for his child.
6 She delivered the just man from among
the wicked who were being
destroyed,
> when he fled as fire descended upon
> Pentapolis—
7 Where as a testimony to its wickedness,
there yet remain a smoking desert,
> Plants bearing fruit that never ripens,
> and the tomb of a disbelieving soul, a
> standing pillar of salt.
8 For those who forsook Wisdom
first were bereft of knowledge of the
right,
> And then they left mankind a memorial
> of their folly—
> > so that they could not even be hidden
> > in their fall.
9 But Wisdom delivered from tribulations
those who served her.

✿
   6: 3, 17; 1 Kgs 11, 4;
      1 Cor 3, 18ff.
   7: 1 Chr 28, 5.
   8: Ex 25, 8f; 2 Sm 7, 13;
      1 Chr 28, 5; 2 Chr 6, 1f;
      7, 7; Tb 1, 4; Pss 15, 1;
      48, 2f.
   9: Dt 6, 17f; Prv 8, 22-31;
      Jn 1, 1ff. 10.
 10: 18, 15; Mt 5, 34;
      Jn 3, 17; 20, 21.
 11: 8, 8.
 12: 1 Kgs 3, 6-9.
 13: Is 40, 13; Bar 3, 31.

 15: Jb 4, 19.
 16: Sir 1, 3; Jn 3, 12.
 17: Jn 14, 26.
 18: 10, 9; Prv 28, 26.
10/1-16: Heb 11, 17-27.
  1: 7, 1.
  2: Gn 1, 28.
  3: Gn 4, 1-16.
  4: 14, 5f; Gn 6, 5-9.
  5: Gn 22, 7-10.
  6: Gn 18, 22-33; 19, 15-
      25; 2 Pt 2, 6f.
  7: Gn 19, 26; Lk 17, 32.
  9: 16, 8.

†
  10, 1-21: This chapter prepares for the following section
(11, 2—19, 22) on the history of Israel in the Exodus, by review-
ing the dealings of Wisdom with the patriarchs. It has a parallel
in Sir 44-50; cf also Wis 18, 9.

  10, 1f: Adam.

  10, 3: Cain.

  10, 4: Noah.

  10, 5: Abraham.

  10, 6: Lot. *Pentapolis:* the five cities, including Sodom; cf
Gn 14, 2.

  10, 7: *Disbelieving soul:* Lot's wife; cf Gn 19, 26.

10 † She, when the just man fled from his
brother's anger,
guided him in direct ways,
Showed him the kingdom of God
and gave him knowledge of holy
things;
She prospered him in his labors
and made abundant the fruit of his
works,

11 * Stood by him against the greed of his
defrauders,
and enriched him;

12 *† She preserved him from foes,
and secured him against ambush,
And she gave him the prize for his stern
struggle
that he might know that devotion to
God is mightier than all else.

13 *† She did not abandon the just man when
he was sold,
but delivered him from sin.

14 She went down with him into the
dungeon,
and did not desert him in his bonds,
Until she brought him the scepter of
royalty
and authority over his oppressors,
Showed those who had defamed him
false,
and gave him eternal glory.

15 * The holy people and blameless race—it
was she
who delivered them from the nation
that oppressed them.

16 *† She entered the soul of the Lord's servant,
and withstood fearsome kings with
signs and portents;

17 * she gave the holy ones the recompense
of their labors,
Conducted them by a wondrous road,
and became a shelter for them by day
and a starry flame by night.

18 She took them across the Red Sea
and brought them through the deep
waters—

19 † But their enemies she overwhelmed,
and cast them up from the bottom of
the depths.

20 * Therefore the just despoiled the wicked;
and they sang, O Lord, your holy name
and praised in unison your conquering
hand—

21 * Because Wisdom opened the mouths of
the dumb,
and gave ready speech to infants.

11 **1** * She made their affairs prosper through
the holy prophet.

III: SPECIAL PROVIDENCE OF GOD DURING THE EXODUS

Introduction

2 *† THEY JOURNEYED THROUGH the
uninhabited desert,
and in solitudes they pitched their
tents;

3 * they withstood enemies and took
vengeance on their foes.

4 When they thirsted, they called upon
you,
and water was given them from the
sheer rock,
assuagement for their thirst from the
hard stone.

5 * For by the things through which their
foes were punished
they in their need were benefited.

First Example: Water Punishes the Egyptians and Benefits the Israelites

6 *† Instead of a spring, when the perennial
river
was troubled with impure blood

7 as a rebuke to the decree for the
slaying of infants,
You gave them abundant water in an
unhoped-for way,

8 once you had shown by the thirst they
then had
how you punished their adversaries.

---

† 10, 10ff: Jacob.
10, 12: *Devotion to God:* in the Greek this signifies "piety"
or "religion," and is the equivalent of the Hebrew "fear of the
Lord"; cf Prv 1, 7.
10, 13f: Joseph.
10, 16: Moses.
10, 19: *Cast them up:* their bodies, on the shore.
11, 2ff: Few verses in these later chapters can be fully understood without consulting the passages in the Mosaic books
which are indicated in the cross references. The theme of this
part of the book is expressed in 11, 5, and is illustrated in the
following chapters by five examples drawn from Exodus events.
11, 6ff: *The perennial river:* the Nile; the contrast is between
the first plague of Egypt (Ex 7, 17-24) and the water drawn from
the rock in Horeb (Ex 17, 5-7; Nm 20, 8-11).

✣
10: Gn 27, 43ff; 28, 12-15.
11: Gn 30, 29f; 31, 5-12.
12: Gn 32, 24-29;
1 Tm 4, 8.
13f: Gn 37-45.
13: Gn 39, 7-10.
15: Ex 3, 9; 14, 30; 19, 6.
16: 1, 4; 7, 27; Ex 4, 10;
Ps 76, 13.
17ff: 14, 3; 19, 7; Ex 13, 21f;
14-15; Pss 77, 20f;
78, 13.53; Is 4, 5f.
20: Ex 12, 35f; 15, 1-21.

21: Ex 4, 10-15; Ps 8, 3;
Mt 11, 25.
11/1: Dt 2, 7; Hos 12, 14.
2ff: Ex 17, 2-6; Nm 20, 1-
13; Pss 63, 2; 107, 4-7;
Jer 2, 6.
3: Ex 17, 8-16; Nm 21,
1ff; 21-35; 31, 1-12;
Ps 118, 10ff.
5: 16, 1f.
6ff: 18, 5; Ex 1, 22;
7, 17-24.

9* For when they had been tried, though
only mildly chastised,
they recognized how the wicked,
condemned in anger, were being
tormented.

11* Both those afar off and those close by
were afflicted:

10 the latter you tested, admonishing
them as a father;
the former as a stern king you probed
and condemned.

12* For a twofold grief took hold of them
and a groaning at the remembrance of
the ones who had departed.

13 For when they heard that the cause of
their own torments
was a benefit to these others, they
recognized the Lord.

14* Him who of old had been cast out in
exposure they indeed mockingly
rejected;
but in the end of events, they marveled
at him,
since their thirst proved unlike that of
the just.

Second Example: Animals Punish the Egyptians and Benefit the Israelites

15*† And in return for their senseless, wicked
thoughts,
which misled them into worshiping
dumb serpents and worthless
insects,
You sent upon them swarms of dumb
creatures for vengeance;

16* that they might recognize that a man is
punished by the very things through
which he sins.

Digression on God's Mercy

17* For not without means was your
almighty hand,
that had fashioned the universe from
formless matter,
to send upon them a drove of bears or
fierce lions,

18 Or new-created, wrathful, unknown
beasts
to breathe forth fiery breath,
Or pour out roaring smoke,
or flash terrible sparks from their eyes.

19 Not only could these attack and
completely destroy them;
even their frightful appearance itself
could slay.

20* Even without these, they could have been
killed at a single blast,
pursued by retribution
and winnowed out by your mighty
spirit;
But you have disposed all things by
measure and number and weight.

21* For with you great strength abides
always;
who can resist the might of your arm?

22*† Indeed, before you the whole universe is
as a grain from a balance.
or a drop of morning dew come down
upon the earth.

23* But you have mercy on all, because you
can do all things;
and you overlook the sins of men that
they may repent.

24* For you love all things that are
and loathe nothing that you have
made;
for what you hated, you would not
have fashioned.

25* And how could a thing remain, unless
you willed it;
or be preserved, had it not been called
forth by you?

26* But you spare all things, because they are
yours, O Lord and lover of souls,

12 **1*** for your imperishable spirit is in all
things!

2 Therefore you rebuke offenders little by
little,
warn them, and remind them of the
sins they are committing,
that they may abandon their
wickedness and believe in you,
O Lord!

3* For, truly, the ancient inhabitants of your
holy land,

4 whom you hated for deeds most
odious—
Works of witchcraft and impious
sacrifices;

9ff: 3, 5; 16, 3f; Dt 8, 2-5;
  Ps 6, 2; Prv 3, 12;
  2 Mc 6, 12-16.
11: Ps 6, 2.
12f: 16, 8; Ex 14, 4. 18.
14: Ex 2, 3.
15: 12, 23f; 15, 18—16, 1;
  Ex 7, 26ff.
16: 12, 23.27; Ex 10, 16;
  Prv 1, 31f; 26, 27.
17ff: 12, 8f; 16, 1.5; Gn 1,
  1f; Dt 32, 24; 2 Kgs 17,
  25f; Hos 13, 4-8.
20: Jb 4, 9.

21: 12, 12; 2 Chr 20, 6.
22: Hos 13, 3.
23: 12, 10; Dt 9, 27;
  Acts 17, 30; Rom 2, 4;
  11, 32; 2 Pt 3, 9.
24: Ps 145, 9.
25: Is 41, 4.
26: 12, 16; Is 63, 9.
12/1: 1, 7.
3ff: 14, 23; Dt 18, 9-12;
  Pss 5, 6; 106, 28.34-39;
  Jer 19, 4f;
  Ez 16, 3.20f.36.

---

† 11, 15: *Dumb:* that is, irrational.

11, 22: *Grain from a balance:* a tiny particle used for weighing on sensitive scales.

5† a cannibal feast of human flesh
and of blood, from the midst of . . . —
These merciless murderers of children,
6✱ and parents who took with their own
hands defenseless lives,
You willed to destroy by the hands of our
fathers,
7✱ that the land that is dearest of all to
you
might receive a worthy colony of God's
children.
8✱ But even these, as they were men, you
spared,
and sent wasps as forerunners of your
army
that they might exterminate them by
degrees.
9✱ Not that you were without power to have
the wicked vanquished in battle by
the just,
or wiped out at once by terrible beasts
or by one decisive word;
10✱ But condemning them bit by bit, you
gave them space for repentance.
You were not unaware that their race was
wicked
and their malice ingrained,
And that their dispositions would never
change;
11✱ for they were a race accursed from the
beginning.
Neither out of fear for anyone
did you grant amnesty for their sins.
12✱ For who can say to you, "What have you
done?"
or who can oppose your decree?
Or when peoples perish, who can
challenge you, their maker;
or who can come into your presence as
vindicator of unjust men?
13✱ For neither is there any god besides you
who have the care of all,
that you need show you have not
unjustly condemned;
14✱ Nor can any king or prince confront you
on behalf of those you have
punished.
15✱ But as you are just, you govern all things
justly;

you regard it as unworthy of your
power
to punish one who has incurred no
blame.
16✱ For your might is the source of justice;
your mastery over all things makes you
lenient to all.
17✱† For you show your might when the
perfection of your power is
disbelieved;
and in those who know you, you
rebuke temerity.
18 But though you are master of might, you
judge with clemency,
and with much lenience you govern us;
for power, whenever you will, attends
you.
19✱ And you taught your people, by these
deeds,
that those who are just must be kind;
And you gave your sons good ground for
hope
that you would permit repentance for
their sins.
20 For these were enemies of your servants,
doomed to death;
yet, while you punished them with
such solicitude and pleading,
granting time and opportunity to
abandon wickedness,
21✱ With what exactitude you judged your
sons,
to whose fathers you gave the sworn
covenants of goodly promises!
22 Us, therefore, you chastise, and our
enemies with a thousand blows you
punish,
that we may think earnestly of your
goodness when we judge,
and, when being judged, may look for
mercy.

Second Example Resumed

23✱ Hence those unjust also, who lived a life
of folly,
you tormented through their own
abominations.
24✱ For they went far astray in the paths of
error,
taking for gods the worthless and
disgusting among beasts,
deceived like senseless infants.

✱
6: Nm 33, 52.
7: Dt 11, 12.
8: Ex 23, 28ff;
    Dt 7, 17-24.
9: 11, 18; 18, 15;
    Nm 16, 21.
10: 11, 23; Ps 55, 20;
    Sir 16, 9.
11: Gn 9, 25.
12: 2 Sm 16, 10; Eccl 8, 4;
    Sir 46, 19; Is 45, 9;
    Dn 4, 32; Rom 9, 19ff.

13: 6, 7; Dt 3, 24; 32, 39;
    Is 44, 6. 8.
14: Jer 49, 19; 50, 44.
15: Gn 18, 23ff; Dt 32, 4.
16: 2, 11; 11, 26;
    Ps 103, 19.
17: 15, 2f; Ex 9, 16.
19f: 11, 23; Sir 17, 24.
21: 18, 22; Gn 50, 24;
    Dt 7, 6-14; Ps 105, 8ff.
23: 11, 16; 16, 1.
24: Dt 11, 28; Jer 5, 28;
    Rom 1, 23.

---

† 12, 5: *And of blood, from the midst of . . . :* this line is obscure in the current Greek text and in all extant translations.
Either one or two words would complete it. The horrible crimes
here spoken of (cf 14, 23) were not unheard of in the ancient
pagan world.
12, 17: The brunt of God's anger and vindictive justice is
borne by those who know him and yet defy his authority and
might. Cf 1, 2; 15, 2, but also 12, 27; 18, 13.

25* Therefore as though upon unreasoning
children,
  you sent your judgment on them as a
  mockery;

26 But they who took no heed of
  punishment which was but child's
  play
  were to experience a condemnation
  worthy of God.

27* For in the things through which they
suffered distress,
  since they were tortured by the very
  things they deemed gods,
They saw and recognized the true God
  whom before they had refused to
  know;
  with this, their final condemnation
  came upon them.

Digression on False Worship

A. NATURE WORSHIP

13 1*† FOR ALL MEN WERE BY NATURE FOOLISH
  who were in ignorance of God,
  and who from the good things seen did
  not succeed in knowing him who is,
  and from studying the works did not
  discern the artisan;

2*† But either fire, or wind, or the swift air,
  or the circuit of the stars, or the mighty
  water,
  or the luminaries of heaven, the
  governors of the world, they
  considered gods.

3* Now if out of joy in their beauty they
  thought them gods,
  let them know how far more excellent
  is the Lord than these;
  for the original source of beauty
  fashioned them.

4* Or if they were struck by their might and
energy,
  let them from these things realize how
  much more powerful is he who
  made them.

5 For from the greatness and the beauty of
created things
  their original author, by analogy, is
  seen.

6† But yet, for these the blame is less;
  For they indeed have gone astray
  perhaps,
  though they seek God and wish to find
  him.

7 For they search busily among his works,
  but are distracted by what they see,
  because the things seen are fair.

8 But again, not even these are pardonable.

9 For if they so far succeeded in knowledge
  that they could speculate about the
  world,
  how did they not more quickly find its
  Lord?

B. IDOLATRY

10* But doomed are they, and in dead things
  are their hopes,
  who termed gods things made by
  human hands:
Gold and silver, the product of art, and
  likenesses of beasts,
  or useless stone, the work of an ancient
  hand.

The Carpenter and Wooden Idols

11* A carpenter may saw out a suitable tree
  and skillfully scrape off all its bark,
And deftly plying his art,
  produce something fit for daily use,

12 and use up the refuse from his
  handiwork in preparing his food,
  and have his fill;

13* Then the good-for-nothing refuse from
  these remnants,
  crooked wood grown full of knots,
  he takes and carves to occupy his spare
  time.
This wood he models with listless skill,
  and patterns it on the image of a man

14* or makes it resemble some worthless
  beast.
When he has daubed it with red and
  crimsoned its surface with red stain,
  and daubed over every blemish in it,

15* He makes a fitting shrine for it
  and puts it on the wall, fastening it
  with a nail.

16* Thus lest it fall down he provides for it,
  knowing that it cannot help itself;
  for, truly, it is an image and needs help.

25: Jer 4, 22.
27: 16, 16; Ex 14, 4. 28.
13/1: Acts 14, 17;
  Eph 4, 17ff.
2: Gn 1, 14-19; Dt 4, 19;
  Jb 31, 26ff.
3: Ps 8, 4.
4: Jer 10, 2; Bar 6, 39.

10: 3, 11; 15, 5.17; Dt 4,
  25-28; 7, 25; 27, 15;
  Ps 115, 4; Hos 14, 4;
  Acts 17, 29.
11-19: Is 44, 9-20.
11: 15, 7; Bar 6, 58.
13: Dt 4, 16.
14: Jer 10, 9.
15: Is 40, 20; 41, 7; 44, 13.
16: 1 Sm 5, 3ff; Bar 6, 57.

†
13, 1: *Him who is:* the Hebrew sacred name of God; cf Ex
3, 14.

13, 2: *Luminaries of heaven:* the Latin interprets, "sun and
moon"; *governors:* cf Gn 1, 16.

13, 6: *The blame is less:* the greater blame is incurred by those
mentioned in 13, 10 and 15, 14ff.

17* But when he prays about his goods or
marriage or children,
   he is not ashamed to address the thing
without a soul.
   And for vigor he invokes the powerless;
18   and for life he entreats the dead;
   And for aid he beseeches the wholly
incompetent,
    and about travel, something that
cannot even walk.
19   And for profit in business and success
with his hands
    he asks facility of a thing with hands
completely inert.

14 1* Again, one preparing for a voyage and
about to traverse the wild waves
   cries out to wood more unsound than
the boat that bears him.
2 For the urge for profits devised this latter,
   and Wisdom the artificer produced it.
3* But your providence, O Father! guides it,
   for you have furnished even in the sea
a road,
   and through the waves a steady path,
4* Showing that you can save from any
danger,
   so that even one without skill may
embark.
5* But you will that the products of your
Wisdom be not idle;
   therefore men trust their lives even to
frailest wood,
   and have been safe crossing the surge
on a raft.
6*† For of old, when the proud giants were
being destroyed,
   the hope of the universe, who took
refuge on a raft,
   left to the world a future for his race,
under the guidance of your hand.
7† For blest is the wood through which
justice comes about;
8* but the handmade idol is accursed, and
its maker as well:
   he for having produced it, and it,
   because though corruptible, it was
termed a god.
9 Equally odious to God are the evildoer
and his evil deed;
10 and the thing made shall be punished
with its contriver.

11* Therefore upon even the idols of the
nations shall a visitation come,
   since they have become abominable
amid God's works,
   Snares for the souls of men
   and a trap for the feet of the senseless.

The Origin and Evils of Idolatry
12* For the source of wantonness is the
devising of idols;
   and their invention was a corruption of
life.
13* For in the beginning they were not, nor
shall they continue forever;
14   for by the vanity of men they came
into the world,
   and therefore a sudden end is devised
for them.
15 For a father, afflicted with untimely
mourning,
   made an image of the child so quickly
taken from him,
   And now honored as a god what was
formerly a dead man
   and handed down to his subjects
mysteries and sacrifices.
16* Then, in time, the impious practice
gained strength and was observed
as law,
   and graven things were worshiped by
princely decrees.
17 Men who lived so far away that they
could not honor him in his presence
   copied the appearance of the distant
king
   And made a public image of him they
wished to honor,
   out of zeal to flatter him when absent,
as though present.
18 And to promote this observance among
those to whom it was strange,
   the artisan's ambition provided a
stimulus.
19* For he, mayhap in his determination to
please the ruler,
   labored over the likeness to the best of
his skill;
20* And the masses, drawn by the charm of
the workmanship,
   soon thought he should be worshiped
who shortly before was honored as
a man.
21 And this became a snare for mankind,
that men enslaved to either grief or
tyranny
   conferred the incommunicable Name
on stocks and stones.

17ff: 15, 15.
14/1: Is 46, 7.
  3: Ps 107, 23-30;
    Is 43, 16.
  4: 16, 8.
  5: 10, 4.
  6: Gn 6, 4; 17, 1ff. 21f.
  8: Rom 1, 23.

11: 3, 7; 23, 33; Nm 33, 4;
   Jos 23, 13; Ps 115, 4;
   Jer 6, 15; 10, 15;
   46, 25; Hos 9, 15.
12: Rom 1, 23ff.
13: Is 2, 18.
16: Dn 3, 4ff;
   1 Mc 1, 47-50.
19: Is 44, 12f LXX.
20: 15, 4.

---

† 14, 6: Noah.
14, 7: Often applied to the Cross of our Lord.

22 Then it was not enough for them to err in
their knowledge of God;
but even though they live in a great
war of ignorance,
they call such evils peace.
23 For while they celebrate either child-
slaying sacrifices or clandestine
mysteries,
or frenzied carousals in unheard-of
rites,
24 They no longer safeguard either lives or
pure wedlock;
but each either waylays and kills his
neighbor, or aggrieves him by
adultery.
25 And all is confusion—blood and murder,
theft and guile,
corruption, faithlessness, turmoil,
perjury,
26 Disturbance of good men, neglect of
gratitude,
besmirching of souls, unnatural lust,
disorder in marriage, adultery and
shamelessness.
27 For the worship of infamous idols
is the reason and source and extremity
of all evil.
28 For they either go mad with enjoyment,
or prophesy lies,
or live lawlessly or lightly forswear
themselves.
29 For as their trust is in soulless idols,
they expect no harm when they have
sworn falsely.
30 But on both counts shall justice overtake
them:
because they thought ill of God and
devoted themselves to idols,
and because they deliberately swore
false oaths, despising piety.
31 For not the might of those that are sworn
by
but the retribution of sinners
ever follows upon the transgression of
the wicked.

15 **1** But you, our God, are good and true,
slow to anger, and governing all with
mercy.

2 For even if we sin, we are yours, and
know your might;
but we will not sin, knowing that we
belong to you.
3 For to know you well is complete justice,
and to know your might is the root of
immortality.
4 For neither did the evil creation of men's
fancy deceive us,
nor the fruitless labor of painters,
A form smeared with varied colors,
5 the sight of which arouses yearning in
the senseless man,
till he longs for the inanimate form of a
dead image.
6 Lovers of evil things, and worthy of such
hopes
are they who make them and long for
them and worship them.

The Potter and Clay Idols

7 For truly the potter, laboriously working
the soft earth,
molds for our service each several
article:
Both the vessels that serve for clean
purposes
and their opposites, all alike;
As to what shall be the use of each vessel
of either class
the worker in clay is the judge.
8 And with misspent toil he molds a
meaningless god from the selfsame
clay;
though he himself shortly before was
made from the earth
And after a little, is to go whence he was
taken,
when the life that was lent him is
demanded back.
9 But his concern is not that he is to die
nor that his span of life is brief;
Rather, he vies with goldsmiths and
silversmiths
and emulates molders of bronze,
and takes pride in modeling
counterfeits.
10 Ashes his heart is! more worthless than
earth is his hope,
and more ignoble than clay his life;
11 Because he knew not the one who
fashioned him,
and breathed into him a quickening
soul,
and infused a vital spirit.

---

*
22-31: Jer 2, 20; 3, 1-25;
Hos 4, 1f.9-19;
Rom 1, 26-31;
Gal 5, 19ff; 1 Tm 1, 9f.
22: Jer 6, 14; Ez 13, 10.
23: 12, 4f; 14, 15; Is 57, 5.
25f: Jer 7, 8f; 22, 17.
27: Ex 23, 13.
28: Jer 5, 31; 29, 26.
30: 1, 1.8; 11, 20;
Jer 5, 2.7.

15/1: Ex 34, 6f; Pss 86, 5.15;
145, 8.9.14.
2: Jb 10, 14f LXX.
3: 3, 15; Jn 17, 3.
4: 13, 14.
6: Ps 115, 8.
7: 13, 11; Jer 18, 3f;
Rom 9, 21; 2 Tm 2, 20f.
8: Gn 3, 19; Eccl 12, 7.
9: Bar 6, 46.
10: Jb 13, 12 LXX.
11: Gn 2, 7; Zec 12, 1.

---

†
14, 30: *Piety:* the sanctity of oaths.

14, 31: Perjury is a form of deceit which calls for punishment
even though it be practiced in the name of a lifeless idol.

12* Instead, he esteemed our life a
plaything,
and our span of life a holiday for gain;
"For one must," says he, "make profit
every way, be it even out of evil."

13 For this man more than any knows that
he is sinning,
when out of earthen stuff he creates
fragile vessels and idols alike.

14* But all quite senseless, and worse than
childish in mind,
are the enemies of your people who
enslaved them.

15* For they esteemed all the idols of the
nations gods,
which have no use of the eyes for
vision,
nor nostrils to snuff the air,
Nor ears to hear,
nor fingers on their hands for feeling;
even their feet are useless to walk with.

16* For a man made them;
one whose spirit has been lent him
fashioned them.
For no man succeeds in fashioning a god
like himself;

17 being mortal, he makes a dead thing
with his lawless hands.
For he is better than the things he
worships;
he at least lives, but never they.

Second Example Resumed

18*† AND BESIDES, THEY WORSHIP the most
loathsome beasts—
for compared as to folly, these are
worse than the rest,

19* Nor for their looks are they good or
desirable beasts,
but they have escaped both the
approval of God and his blessing.

16

1*† Therefore they were fittingly punished
by similar creatures,
and were tormented by a swarm of
insects.

2* Instead of this punishment, you benefited
your people
with a novel dish, the delight they
craved,
by providing quail for their food;

3* That those others, when they desired
food,
since the creatures sent to plague them
were so loathsome,
should be turned from even the
craving of necessities,
While these, after a brief period of
privation,
partook of a novel dish.

4* For upon those oppressors, inexorable
want had to come;
but these needed only be shown how
their enemies were being tormented.

5* For when the dire venom of beasts came
upon them
and they were dying from the bite of
crooked serpents,
your anger endured not to the end.

6† But as a warning, for a short time they
were terrorized,
though they had a sign of salvation,
to remind them of the precept of
your law.

7 For he who turned toward it was saved,
not by what he saw,
but by you, the savior of all.

8* And by this also you convinced our foes
that you are he who delivers from all
evil.

9* For the bites of locusts and of flies slew
them,
and no remedy was found to save their
lives
because they deserved to be punished
by such means;

10* But not even the fangs of poisonous
reptiles overcame your sons,
for your mercy brought the antidote to
heal them.

11* For as a reminder of your injunctions,
they were stung,
and swiftly they were saved,
Lest they should fall into deep
forgetfulness
and become unresponsive to your
beneficence.

12* For indeed, neither herb nor application
cured them,
but your all-healing word, O Lord!

✱
12: Jas 4, 13f.
14: Ex 1, 13.
15: 14, 11; Dt 4, 28;
Pss 115, 4-7; 135, 15ff.
16f: 13, 10.
18: 11, 15; 12, 24.
19: Gn 1, 25; 3, 14.
16/1: 11, 15f; 12, 23.27;
Ex 7, 27; 8, 12.17.
2: 11, 13; 19, 11f;
Ex 16, 13; Nm 11, 31f;
Ps 105, 40.

3: 11, 15; Ex 8, 10; 16, 3.
4: 11, 8f.
5f: Nm 21, 4-9; Dt 32, 24;
Jer 8, 17 LXX.
8: Gn 48, 16; 2 Mc 1, 24f.
9: Ex 8, 16-28; 10, 4-19;
Pss 78, 45f; 105, 31.34;
Rv 9, 1-11.
10: Dt 32, 33.
11: Ps 78, 11.
12: Ex 15, 26.

---

†
15, 18ff: The author here returns to the main theme of chapters 11-19, which was interrupted by the digression 13, 1—15, 17.

15, 18: *For . . . rest:* this may mean that the creatures worshiped by the Egyptians (e. g., crocodiles, serpents, scarabs, etc.) were more patently lacking in intelligence than the general run of beasts; cf 11, 15; 12, 24.

16, 1: *They:* the Egyptian idolaters.

16, 6: *Sign:* the brazen serpent; cf Nm 21, 9.

13 For you have dominion over life and death;
you lead down to the gates of the nether world, and lead back.

14† Man, however, slays in his malice,
but when the spirit has come away, it does not return,
nor can he bring back the soul once it is confined.

15 But your hand none can escape.

Third Example: A Rain of Manna for Israel instead of the Plague of Storms

16 For the wicked who refused to know you were punished by the might of your arm,
Pursued by unwonted rains and hailstorms and unremitting downpours,
and consumed by fire.

17 For against all expectation, in water which quenches anything,
the fire grew more active;
For the universe fights on behalf of the just.

18 For now the flame was tempered
so that the beasts might not be burnt up that were sent upon the wicked,
but that these might see and know they were struck by the judgment of God;

19 And again, even in the water, fire blazed beyond its strength
so as to consume the produce of the wicked land.

20 Instead of this, you nourished your people with food of angels
and furnished them bread from heaven, ready to hand, untoiled-for,
endowed with all delights and conforming to every taste.

21 For this substance of yours revealed your sweetness toward your children,
and serving the desire of him who received it,
was blended to whatever flavor each one wished.

22† Yet snow and ice withstood fire and were not melted,
that they might know that their enemies' fruits

Were consumed by a fire that blazed in the hail
and flashed lightning in the rain.

23 But this fire, again, that the just might be nourished,
forgot even its proper strength;

24 For your creation, serving you, its maker,
grows tense for punishment against the wicked,
but is relaxed in benefit for those who trust in you.

25 Therefore at that very time, transformed in all sorts of ways,
it was serving your all-nourishing bounty
according to what they needed and desired;

26 That your sons whom you loved might learn, O Lord,
that it is not the various kinds of fruits that nourish man,
but it is your word that preserves those who believe you!

27 For what was not destroyed by fire,
when merely warmed by a momentary sunbeam, melted;

28 So that men might know that one must give you thanks before the sunrise,
and turn to you at daybreak.

29 For the hope of the ingrate melts like a wintry frost
and runs off like useless water.

Fourth Example: Darkness Afflicts the Egyptians, While the Israelites Have Light

17 **1** For great are your judgments, and hardly to be described;
therefore the unruly souls were wrong.

2 For when the lawless thought to enslave the holy nation,
shackled with darkness, fettered by the long night,
they lay confined beneath their own roofs as exiles from the eternal providence.

3 For they who supposed their secret sins were hid
under the dark veil of oblivion
Were scattered in fearful trembling, terrified by apparitions.

4 For not even their inner chambers kept them fearless,
for crashing sounds on all sides terrified them,
and mute phantoms with somber looks appeared.

13ff: Dt 32, 39; 1 Sm 2, 6; Tb 13, 2; Ps 78, 34.39; Eccl 8, 8; Dn 5, 19; 2 Mc 6, 26; 7, 23.
16: 11, 21; 12, 27; Ex 5, 2; 9, 29-34.
17: 10, 20; 19, 20; Ex 9, 23-28; 2 Mc 8, 36; 14, 34.
18f: 19, 20f.
20: Ex 16, 4; Nm 11, 8; Ps 78, 24f; Jn 6, 31.
21: Ps 34, 9.
22: Ex 9, 25-31; 10, 12; Ps 148, 8.
23: 19, 21.
24: 5, 17.20; 19, 6; Sir 39, 25ff.
26: Dt 8, 3; Mt 4, 4.
27: Ex 16, 21.
28: Pss 57, 9f; 92, 3.
29: 5, 14; 2 Sm 14, 14.
17/1: Ex 6, 6 LXX.
2: 18, 4; Ex 1, 13f; 19, 6. 10, 21ff.
3f: 1, 7f; 10, 8; 18, 17.

16, 14: *Confined:* in the nether world, in limbo.
16, 22: *Snow and ice:* the manna; cf 16, 27; 19, 21.

5* No force, even of fire, was able to give
    light,
       nor did the flaming brilliance of the
         stars
       succeed in lighting up that gloomy
         night.

6*† But only intermittent, fearful fires
    flashed through upon them;
    And in their terror they thought
       beholding these was worse
       than the times when that sight was no
         longer to be seen.

7* And mockeries of the magic art were in
    readiness,
       and a jeering reproof of their vaunted
        shrewdness.

8 For they who undertook to banish fears
    and terrors from the sick soul
       themselves sickened with a ridiculous
        fear.

9* For even though no monstrous thing
    frightened them,
       they shook at the passing of insects and
        the hissing of reptiles,

10 And perished trembling,
    reluctant to face even the air that they
       could nowhere escape.

11* For wickedness, of its nature cowardly,
    testifies in its own condemnation,
    and because of a distressed conscience,
       always magnifies misfortunes.

12 For fear is nought but the surrender of
    the helps that come from reason;

13 and the more one's expectation is of
    itself uncertain,
    the more one makes of not knowing the
       cause that brings on torment.

14† So they, during that night, powerless
    though it was,
    that had come upon them from the
       recesses of a powerless nether world,
    while all sleeping the same sleep,

15* Were partly smitten by fearsome
    apparitions
    and partly stricken by their soul's
       surrender;
    for fear came upon them, sudden and
       unexpected.

16* Thus, then, whoever was there fell
    into that unbarred prison and was kept
       confined.

17 For whether one was a farmer, or a
    shepherd,
       or a worker at tasks in the wasteland,
    Taken unawares, he served out the
       inescapable sentence;

18* for all were bound by the one bond of
    darkness.
    And were it only the whistling wind,
       or the melodious song of birds in the
        spreading branches,
    Or the steady sound of rushing water,

19 or the rude crash of overthrown rocks,
    Or the unseen gallop of bounding
       animals,
       or the roaring cry of the fiercest beasts,
    Or an echo resounding from the hollow
       of the hills
    these sounds, inspiring terror,
       paralyzed them.

20* For the whole world shone with brilliant
    light
    and continued its works without
       interruption;

21 Over them alone was spread oppressive
    night,
    an image of the darkness that next
       should come upon them;
    yet they were to themselves more
       burdensome than the darkness.

18 **1** But your holy ones had very great light;
    And those others, who heard their voices
       but did not see their forms,
       since now they themselves had
        suffered, called them blest;

2† And because they who formerly had been
    wronged did not harm them, they
       thanked them,
    and pleaded with them, for the sake of
       the difference between them.

3* Instead of this, you furnished the flaming
    pillar
    which was a guide on the unknown
       way,
    and the mild sun for an honorable
       migration.

4* For those deserved to be deprived of
    light and imprisoned by darkness,
    who had kept your sons confined
    through whom the imperishable light
       of the law was to be given to the
       world.

✿

5: 10, 17; Jer 23, 24 LXX.   16: 18, 4; Ex 10, 23.
6: Ex 9, 23f.   18f: Lv 26, 36.
7: 12, 25f; Ex 7, 11f.22;   20f: Ex 10, 23; Is 9, 1;
    8, 3; 9, 11; 10, 2.   60, 1ff; 2 Pt 2, 17.
9: 16, 1; Jer 26, 22 LXX.   18/3: Ex 13, 21.
11: 4, 6; 10, 7; Rom 2, 15.   4: 17, 2; Ps 119, 105;
15: Ex 11, 9f.   Is 2, 3.5.

---

†

17, 6: *Fires:* that is, lightnings.

17, 14: *Powerless:* the nether world, the home of darkness, has no power against God, nor even against such men as do not submit to it of themselves; cf 1, 14ff.

18, 2: *The difference between them:* God's distinctive manner of treating the Israelites and the Egyptians according to their respective merits.

Fifth Example: Death of the Egyptian Firstborn; the Israelites Are Spared

5*† When they determined to put to death
    the infants of the holy ones,
and when a single boy had been cast
    forth but saved,
As a reproof you carried off their
    multitude of sons
and made them perish all at once in
    the mighty water.

6* That night was known beforehand to our
    fathers,
that, with sure knowledge of the oaths
    in which they put their faith, they
    might have courage.

7* Your people awaited
    the salvation of the just and the
    destruction of their foes.

8* For when you punished our adversaries,
    in this you glorified us whom you had
    summoned.

9*† For in secret the holy children of the
    good were offering sacrifice
and putting into effect with one accord
    the divine institution,
That your holy ones should share alike
    the same good things and dangers,
having previously sung the praises of
    the fathers.

10* But the discordant cry of their enemies
    responded,
and the piteous wail of mourning for
    children was borne to them.

11* And the slave was smitten with the same
    retribution as his master;
even the plebeian suffered the same as
    the king.

12* And all alike by a single death
    had countless dead;
For the living were not even sufficient
    for the burial,
since at a single instant their nobler
    offspring were destroyed.

13*† For though they disbelieved at every
    turn on account of sorceries,
at the destruction of the firstborn they
    acknowledged that the people was
    God's son.

14 For when peaceful stillness compassed
    everything
and the night in its swift course was
    half spent,

15* Your all-powerful word from heaven's
    royal throne
bounded, a fierce warrior, into the
    doomed land,

16* bearing the sharp sword of your
    inexorable decree.
And as he alighted, he filled every place
    with death;
he still reached to heaven, while he
    stood upon the earth.

17* Then, forthwith, visions in horrible
    dreams perturbed them
and unexpected fears assailed them;

18 And cast half-dead, one here, another
    there,
each was revealing the reason for his
    dying.

19 For the dreams that disturbed them had
    proclaimed this beforehand,
lest they perish unaware of why they
    suffered ill.

20* But the trial of death touched at one time
    even the just,
and in the desert a plague struck the
    multitude;
Yet not for long did the anger last.

21*† For the blameless man hastened to be
    their champion,
bearing the weapon of his special
    office,
prayer and the propitiation of incense;
He withstood the wrath and put a stop to
    the calamity,
showing that he was your servant.

22*† And he overcame the bitterness
    not by bodily strength, not by force
    of arms;
But by word he overcame the smiter,
    recalling the sworn covenants with
    their fathers.

23* For when corpses had already fallen one
    on another in heaps,
he stood in the midst and checked the
    anger,
and cut off the way to the living.

24*† For on his full-length robe was the whole
    world,

✿
5: 11, 7.14; Ex 1, 16.22;
   2, 3.6-10; 15, 10;
   Neh 9, 11.
6: 12, 21; Ex 6, 8; 13, 5.
7: Ex 14, 13.
8: 19, 22; Ex 3, 18;
   Is 43, 3f.
9: Ex 12, 21-28; Sir 44-50.
10: Ex 12, 30; Jer 9, 17. 19.
11: Ex 11, 5; 12, 29.
12: Nm 33, 4.
13: 17, 7; Ex 4, 22f;
    12, 12.29; 13, 2.13.15.

15: 9, 10; Ex 15, 3.
16: 1 Chr 21, 16;
    Heb 4, 12; Rv 1, 16.
17ff: 17, 3f.
20: 16, 5; Nm 17, 9-15.
21: Nm 16, 7ff.
22: 12, 21; Ex 32, 12f;
    Ps 20, 8.
23: Nm 14, 29f.
24: Ex 28, 15-21.31-38;
    Sir 45, 8-12; 50, 11.

†
18, 5: *Single boy:* Moses.
18, 9: *Praises of the fathers:* cf Sir 44-50; Wis 10.
18, 13: *People:* the Hebrews.
18, 21: *Blameless man:* Aaron, acting according to his office
of high priest and intercessor.
18, 22: *Smiter:* the destroying angel: cf v 25.
18, 24: *Glories . . . grandeur:* the name of God and the names
of the tribes were inscribed on the high priest's apparel.

and the glories of the fathers were
　　carved in four rows upon the stones,
　　and your grandeur was on the crown
　　upon his head.
25* To these names the destroyer yielded,
　　and these he feared;
　　for the mere trial of anger was enough.

19 1*† But the wicked, merciless wrath assailed
　　until the end.
　　For he knew beforehand what they
　　were yet to do:
2*† That though they themselves had agreed
　　to the departure
　　and had anxiously sent them on their
　　way,
　　they would regret it and pursue them.
3*† For while they were still engaged in
　　funeral rites
　　and were mourning at the burials of
　　the dead,
　　They adopted another senseless plan;
　　and those whom they had sent away
　　with entreaty,
　　they pursued as fugitives.
4 For a compulsion suited to this ending
　　drew them on,
　　and made them forgetful of what had
　　befallen them,
　　That they might fill out the torments of
　　their punishment,
5† and your people might experience a
　　glorious journey
　　while those others met an
　　extraordinary death.
6* For all creation, in its several kinds, was
　　being made over anew,
　　serving its natural laws,
　　that your children might be preserved
　　unharmed.
7* The cloud overshadowed their camp;
　　and out of what had before been
　　water, dry land was seen emerging:
　　Out of the Red Sea an unimpeded road,
　　and a grassy plain out of the mighty
　　flood.
8 Over this crossed the whole nation
　　sheltered by your hand,
　　after they beheld stupendous wonders.
9* For they ranged about like horses,
　　and bounded about like lambs,
　　praising you, O Lord! their deliverer.

10* For they were still mindful of what had
　　happened in their sojourn:
　　how instead of the young of animals
　　the land brought forth gnats,
　　and instead of fishes the river swarmed
　　with countless frogs.
11* And later they saw also a new kind of
　　bird
　　when, prompted by desire, they asked
　　for pleasant foods;
12 For to appease them quail came to them
　　from the sea.
13*† And the punishments came upon the
　　sinners
　　only after forewarnings from the
　　violence of the thunderbolts.
　　For they justly suffered for their own
　　misdeeds,
　　since indeed they treated their guests
　　with the more grievous hatred.
14* For those others did not receive
　　unfamiliar visitors,
　　but these were enslaving beneficent
　　guests.
15† And not that only; but what punishment
　　was to be theirs
　　since they received strangers
　　unwillingly!
16* Yet these, after welcoming them with
　　festivities,
　　oppressed with awful toils
　　those who now shared with them the
　　same rights.
17* And they were struck with blindness,
　　as those others had been at the portals
　　of the just—
　　When, surrounded by yawning darkness,
　　each sought the entrance of his own
　　gate.
18 For the elements, in variable harmony
　　among themselves,
　　like strings of the harp, produce new
　　melody,
　　while the flow of music steadily
　　persists.
　　And this can be perceived exactly from a
　　review of what took place.
19 For land creatures were changed into
　　water creatures,
　　and those that swam went over on to
　　the land.

---

*
　　25: 1 Chr 21, 15.
19/1: Ex 14, 4.
　　2: Ex 12, 33; 14, 5, 8.
　　3: 18,·10. 12; Ex 12, 30ff.
　　6: 5, 17; 16, 24.
　　7: Ex 14, 21-29.
　　9: 10, 20; 16, 8; Ex 15, 1-
　　18; Ps 114, 4.6.
　　10: Ex 7, 27ff; 8, 12-15;
　　Ps 105, 30f.
　　11f: 16, 2; Ps 78, 18.
　　13: 2 Mc 7, 18. 32.
　　14f: Gn 15, 13; Ex 2, 22.
　　16: Gn 45, 17-20; 47, 4ff;
　　Ex 1, 11.
　　17: 17, 2; Gn 19, 11.

†
　　19, 1: *He:* i. e., God.
　　19, 2: *Them:* the Hebrews.
　　19, 3: *They:* the Egyptians.
　　19, 5: *Glorious:* more precisely, "wondrous," but the word
reflects *glorified* in 18, 8 and 19, 22.
　　19, 13: *More grievous:* than that of the people of Sodom;
cf Gn 19.
　　19, 15: *Theirs:* the people of Sodom.

20*   Fire in water maintained its own
strength,
and water forgot its quenching nature;
21   Flames, by contrast, neither consumed
the flesh

of the perishable animals that went
about in them,
nor melted the icelike, quick-melting
kind of ambrosial food.
22* For every way, O Lord! you magnified
and glorified your people;
unfailing, you stood by them in every
time and circumstance.

---

*

20f: 16, 17ff.22f.27.   22: 18, 8; Lv 26, 44;
                                        Ps 126, 3.

The Book of Sirach

(Ecclesiasticus)

Introduction

The Book of Sirach derives its name from the author, *Jesus, son of Eleazar, son of Sirach* (50, 27). Its earliest title seems to have been "Wisdom of the Son of Sirach." The designation "Liber Ecclesiasticus," meaning "Church Book," appended to some Greek and Latin manuscripts was due to the extensive use which the church made of this book in presenting moral teaching to catechumens and to the faithful.

The author, a sage who lived in Jerusalem, was thoroughly imbued with love for the law, the priesthood, the temple, and divine worship. As a wise and experienced observer of life he addressed himself to his contemporaries with the motive of helping them to maintain religious faith and integrity through study of the holy books, and through tradition.

The book contains numerous maxims formulated with care, grouped by affinity, and dealing with a variety of subjects such as the individual, the family, and the community in their relations with one another and with God. It treats of friendship, education, poverty and wealth, the law, religious worship, and many other matters which reflect the religious and social customs of the time.

Written in Hebrew between 200 and 175 B.C., the text was translated into Greek sometime after 132 B.C. by the author's grandson, who also wrote a Foreword which contains information about the book, the author, and the translator himself. Until the close of the nineteenth century Sirach was known only in translations, of which this Greek rendering was the most important. From it the Latin version was made. Between 1896 and 1900, again in 1931, and several times since 1956, manuscripts were discovered containing in all about two thirds of the Hebrew text, which agrees substantially with the Greek. One such text, from Masada, is pre-Christian in date.

Though not included in the Hebrew Bible after the first century A.D., nor accepted by Protestants, the Book of Sirach has always been recognized by the Catholic Church as divinely inspired and canonical. The Foreword, though not inspired, is placed in the Bible because of its antiquity and importance.

The contents of Sirach are of a discursive nature, not easily divided into separate parts. Chapters 1—43 deal largely with moral instruction; chapters 44, 1—50, 24 contain a eulogy of the heroes of Israel and some of the patriarchs. There are two appendices in which the author expresses his gratitude to God, and appeals to the unlearned to acquire true wisdom.

The church uses the Book of Sirach extensively in her liturgy.

Foreword

MANY IMPORTANT TRUTHS have been handed down to us through the law,* the prophets, and the later authors; and for these the instruction and wisdom of Israel merit praise. Now, those who are familiar with these truths must not only understand them themselves but, as lovers of wisdom, be able, in speech and in writing, to help others less familiar. Such a one was my grandfather, Jesus, who, having devoted himself for a long time to the diligent study of the law, the prophets, and the rest of the books of our ancestors, and having developed a thorough familiarity with them, was moved to write something himself in the nature of instruction and wisdom, in order that those who love wisdom might, by acquainting themselves with what he too had written, make even greater progress in living in conformity with the divine law.

You therefore are now invited to read it in a spirit of attentive good will, with indulgence for any apparent failure on our part, despite earnest efforts, in the interpretation of particular passages. For words spoken originally in Hebrew are not as effective when they are translated into another language. That is true not only of this book but of the law itself, the prophets and the rest of the books, which differ no little when they are read in the original.

I arrived in Egypt in the thirty-eighth year of the reign of King Euergetes,† and while there, I found a reproduction‡ of our valuable teaching. I therefore considered myself in duty bound to devote some diligence and industry to the translation of this book. Many sleepless hours of close application have I devoted in the interval to finishing the book for publication, for the benefit of those living abroad who wish to acquire wisdom and are disposed to live their lives according to the standards of the law.

The law, the prophets and the rest of the books: the Sacred Scriptures of the Old Testament written before the time of Sirach, according to the threefold division of the present Hebrew Bible.

†*Thirty-eighth . . . Euergetes:* 132 B.C. The reference is to Ptolemy VII, Physkon Euergetes II (170-163; 145-117 B.C.).

‡*Reproduction . . . teaching:* may refer to the Septuagint (Greek) translation of Hebrew wisdom writings predating Sirach.

THE WISDOM OF SIRACH

Praise of Wisdom

1

1*† ALL WISDOM comes from the LORD
and with him it remains forever.

2 The sand of the seashore, the drops of rain,
the days of eternity: who can number
these?

3 Heaven's height, earth's breadth,
the depths of the abyss: who can explore
these?

4 Before all things else wisdom was created;
and prudent understanding, from
eternity.

5* To whom has wisdom's root been revealed?
Who knows her subtleties?

6 There is but one, wise and truly
awe-inspiring,
seated upon his throne:

7* It is the LORD; he created her,
has seen her and taken note of her.

8 He has poured her forth upon all his works,
upon every living thing according to
his bounty;
he has lavished her upon his friends.

9† Fear of the LORD is glory and splendor,
gladness and a festive crown.

10 Fear of the LORD warms the heart,
giving gladness and joy and length of
days.

11 He who fears the LORD will have a happy
end;
even on the day of his death he will be
blessed.

12* The beginning of wisdom is fear of the
LORD,
which is formed with the faithful in the
womb.

13 With devoted men was she created from of
old,
and with their children her beneficence
abides.

14* Fullness of wisdom is fear of the LORD;
she inebriates men with her fruits.

15 Her entire house she fills with choice foods,
her granaries with her harvest.

16* Wisdom's garland is fear of the LORD,
with blossoms of peace and perfect
health.

17 Knowledge and full understanding she
showers down;
she heightens the glory of those who
possess her.

18 The root of wisdom is fear of the LORD;
her branches are length of days.

19† One cannot justify unjust anger;
anger plunges a man to his downfall.

20 A patient man need stand firm but for a
time,
and then contentment comes back to him.

21 For a while he holds back his words,
then the lips of many herald his wisdom.

22 Among wisdom's treasures is the paragon of
prudence;
but fear of the LORD is an abomination to
the sinner.

23 If you desire wisdom, keep the
commandments,
and the LORD will bestow her upon you;

24 For fear of the LORD is wisdom and culture;
loyal humility is his delight.

25† Be not faithless to the fear of the LORD,
nor approach it with duplicity of heart.

26 Play not the hypocrite before men;
over your lips keep watch.

27 Exalt not yourself lest you fall
and bring upon you dishonor;

28 For then the LORD will reveal your secrets
and publicly cast you down,

29 Because you approached the fear of the
LORD
with your heart full of guile.

Duties toward God

2

1*† My son, when you come to serve the LORD,
prepare yourself for trials.

2 Be sincere of heart and steadfast,
undisturbed in time of adversity.

3 Cling to him, forsake him not;
thus will your future be great.

4 Accept whatever befalls you,
in crushing misfortune be patient;

---

† 1, 1-8: The Lord is the source and preserver of wisdom (1); he created her from eternity, *before all things else* (4-7); all his works reflect wisdom (2f.8).

1, 1: *Wisdom:* here the author speaks of true wisdom, namely God's external revelation of himself. Throughout the book he describes in great detail just what wisdom is; sometimes it is divine; sometimes it is a synonym for God's law; sometimes it is human. But the author makes clear that even human wisdom, properly understood, comes from God.

1, 9-18: Here are described the spiritual and temporal blessings that come during the lifetime of him who fears the Lord, i. e., practices true religion.

1, 9: *Fear of the Lord:* see note on Ps 111, 10.

1, 19-22: The disciple of wisdom shuns *unjust anger* which brings *downfall.* By patience and self-control he preserves calm, recovers *contentment,* and receives public praise. The sinner, on the contrary, despises the restraints which religion imposes.

1, 25-29: Infidelity to religion, or the use of it for any but the single purpose of serving God, is hypocrisy and self-exaltation, deserving of public disgrace.

2, 1-11: Serving God is not without its trials (1); moreover, it must be done with sincerity, steadfastness and fidelity (2f). Misfortune and humiliation merely purify man and prove his

---

❀   1/1: 1 Kgs 3, 9.   14: Eccl 12, 13.
        5: Bar 3, 15.   16: 21, 11.
        7: Jb 28, 27.   2/1: 2 Tm 3, 12.
       12: Jb 28, 28; Ps 111, 10;
           Prv 1, 7; 9, 10.

5* For in fire gold is tested,
and worthy men in the crucible of
humiliation.

6 Trust God and he will help you;
make straight your ways and hope in
him.

7 You who fear the LORD, wait for his mercy,
turn not away lest you fall.

8 You who fear the LORD, trust him,
and your reward will not be lost.

9 You who fear the LORD, hope for good
things,
for lasting joy and mercy.

10* Study the generations long past and
understand;
has anyone hoped in the LORD and been
disappointed?
Has anyone persevered in his fear and been
forsaken?
has anyone called upon him and been
rebuffed?

11 Compassionate and merciful is the LORD;
he forgives sins, he saves in time of
trouble.

12† Woe to craven hearts and drooping hands,
to the sinner who treads a double path!

13 Woe to the faint of heart who trust not,
who therefore will have no shelter!

14 Woe to you who have lost hope!
what will you do at the visitation of the
LORD?

15* Those who fear the LORD disobey not his
words;
those who love him keep his ways.

16 Those who fear the LORD seek to please
him,
those who love him are filled with his
law.

17 Those who fear the LORD prepare their
hearts
and humble themselves before him.

18* Let us fall into the hands of the LORD
and not into the hands of men,
For equal to his majesty
is the mercy that he shows.

Duties toward Parents

3 1† Children, pay heed to a father's right;
do so that you may live.

2 For the LORD sets a father in honor over his
children;
a mother's authority he confirms over her
sons.

3 He who honors his father atones for sins;

4 he stores up riches who reveres his
mother.

5 He who honors his father is gladdened by
children,
and when he prays he is heard.

6 He who reveres his father will live a long
life;
he obeys the LORD who brings comfort to
his mother.

7 He who fears the LORD honors his father,
and serves his parents as rulers.

8* In word and deed honor your father
that his blessing may come upon you;

9* For a father's blessing gives a family firm
roots,
but a mother's curse uproots the growing
plant.

10 Glory not in your father's shame,
for his shame is no glory to you!

11 His father's honor is a man's glory;
disgrace for her children, a mother's
shame.

12* My son, take care of your father when he is
old;
grieve him not as long as he lives.

13 Even if his mind fail, be considerate with
him;
revile him not in the fullness of your
strength.

14 For kindness to a father will not be
forgotten,
it will serve as a sin offering—it will take
lasting root.

15 In time of tribulation it will be recalled to
your advantage,
like warmth upon frost it will melt away
your sins.

16* A blasphemer is he who despises his father;
accursed of his Creator, he who angers
his mother.

Humility

17† My son, conduct your affairs with humility,
and you will be loved more than a giver
of gifts.

---

† worth (4f). Patience and unwavering trust in God are always rewarded with the benefits of God's mercy and of *lasting joy* (6-11).

2, 12-18: A warning to those who compromise their religion in time of affliction; they fail in courage and trust and therefore have no security (12ff). But those who fear the Lord through obedience, reverence, love and humility find his *mercy equal to his majesty* (15-18).

3, 1-16: Besides the virtues that must characterize our conduct toward God, special duties toward our neighbor are enjoined, such as honor and respect toward parents, with corresponding blessings (1-9). Even to old and infirm parents this respect is due (10-13); through it, the sins of children are pardoned (14f). Failure to render respect is blasphemy and merits a curse from God (16). Cf Ex 20, 12; Eph 6, 2f.

3, 17-27: Humility gives a true estimate of self (17ff).

5: Prv 17, 3; Wis 3, 6;
   1 Pt 1, 7.
10: Pss 31, 2; 145, 18f.
15: Jn 14, 23.
18: 18, 3.

3/8: Ex 20, 12; Dt 5, 16;
     Mt 15, 4; Mk 7, 10;
     Eph 6, 2.
9: Gn 27, 29; 49, 2-27.
12: Prv 23, 22.
16: Prv 19, 26;
     30, 11.14.17.

18 Humble yourself the more, the greater you are,
and you will find favor with God.

19 For great is the power of God;
by the humble he is glorified.

20 What is too sublime for you, seek not,
into things beyond your strength search not.

21 What is committed to you, attend to;
for what is hidden is not your concern.

22 With what is too much for you meddle not,
when shown things beyond human understanding.

23 Their own opinion has misled many,
and false reasoning unbalanced their judgment.

24 Where the pupil of the eye is missing, there is no light,
and where there is no knowledge, there is no wisdom.

25 A stubborn man will fare badly in the end,
and he who loves danger will perish in it.

26 A stubborn man will be burdened with sorrow;
a sinner will heap sin upon sin.

27 For the affliction of the proud man there is no cure;
he is the offshoot of an evil plant.

28 The mind of a sage appreciates proverbs,
and an attentive ear is the wise man's joy.

Alms for the Poor

29 Water quenches a flaming fire,
and alms atone for sins.

30 He who does a kindness is remembered afterward;
when he falls, he finds a support.

4

1 My son, rob not the poor man of his livelihood;
force not the eyes of the needy to turn away.

2 A hungry man grieve not,
a needy man anger not;

3 Do not exasperate the downtrodden;
delay not to give to the needy.

4 A beggar in distress do not reject;
avert not your face from the poor.

5 From the needy turn not your eyes,
give no man reason to curse you;

6 For if in the bitterness of his soul he curse you,
his Creator will hear his prayer.

7 Endear yourself to the assembly;
before a ruler bow your head.

8 Give a hearing to the poor man,
and return his greeting with courtesy;

9 Deliver the oppressed from the hand of the oppressor;
let not justice be repugnant to you.

10 To the fatherless be as a father,
and help their mother as a husband would;
Thus will you be like a son to the Most High,
and he will be more tender to you than a mother.

The Rewards of Wisdom

11 Wisdom instructs her children
and admonishes those who seek her.

12 He who loves her loves life;
those who seek her out win her favor.

13 He who holds her fast inherits glory;
wherever he dwells, the Lord bestows blessings.

14 Those who serve her serve the Holy One;
those who love her the Lord loves.

15 He who obeys her judges nations;
he who hearkens to her dwells in her inmost chambers.

16 If one trusts her, he will possess her;
his descendants too will inherit her.

17 She walks with him as a stranger,
and at first she puts him to the test;
Fear and dread she brings upon him
and tries him with her discipline;
With her precepts she puts him to the proof,
until his heart is fully with her.

18 Then she comes back to bring him happiness
and reveal her secrets to him.

19 But if he fails her, she will abandon him
and deliver him into the hands of despoilers.

Sincerity and Justice

20 Use your time well; guard yourself from evil,
and bring upon yourself no shame.

---

† Through it a man performs duty, avoids what is beyond his understanding and strength (20ff). Pride, however, begets false greatness, misjudgment, stubbornness, sorrow, affliction and perdition (23-27).

3, 19: An alternate or additional line would read: "For though many have been great in the course of time, it is to the humble he reveals his secrets." Cf Mt 11, 25f; 1 Cor 1, 26-29.

3, 29—4, 10: Mercy and kindness toward those in misfortune atone for sin and endear a man to God and to his fellow men.

4, 1: *Eyes of the needy:* when they look for help; cf 18, 17.

4, 11-19: The Hebrew text presents wisdom speaking in the first person, as in ch 24. The precious fruits of wisdom: life, favor, glory, blessings, God's love, are intended to arouse desire for her (11-14). Her disciples are like priests (14) and judges (15), even partners who possess her for themselves and their descendants (16). They enjoy happiness and penetrate her profound secrets after surviving her tests (17f). Those who fail her are abandoned to destruction (19).

4, 20-31: Besides the interior trials of discipline and precept, the disciple of wisdom is warned against external dangers to his

* 18: Mt 23, 12.   29: Dn 4, 27.
20: Ps 131, 1.   4/1: Tb 4, 7-11.
27: Dt 32, 32; Wis 12, 10.   14: Wis 7, 28.

21 There is a sense of shame laden with guilt,
   and a shame that merits honor and
   respect.

22 Show no favoritism to your own discredit;
   let no one intimidate you to your own
   downfall.

23 Refrain not from speaking at the proper
   time,
   and hide not away your wisdom;

24 For it is through speech that wisdom
   becomes known,
   and knowledge through the tongue's
   rejoinder.

25 Never gainsay the truth,
   and struggle not against the rushing
   stream.

26 Be not ashamed to acknowledge your guilt,
   but of your ignorance rather be ashamed.

27 Do not abase yourself before an impious
   man,
   nor refuse to do so before rulers.

28 Even to the death fight for truth,
   and the LORD your God will battle for
   you.

29 Be not surly in your speech,
   nor lazy and slack in your deeds.

30 Be not a lion at home,
   nor sly and suspicious at work.

31 Let not your hand be open to receive
   and clenched when it is time to give.

Against Presumption

5 1*† Rely not on your wealth;
   say not: "I have the power."

2 Rely not on your strength
   in following the desires of your heart.

3 Say not: "Who can prevail against me?"
   for the LORD will exact the punishment.

4 Say not: "I have sinned, yet what has
   befallen me?"
   for the LORD bides his time.

5 Of forgiveness be not overconfident,
   adding sin upon sin.

6 Say not: "Great is his mercy;
   my many sins he will forgive."

7 For mercy and anger alike are with him;
   upon the wicked alights his wrath.

8 Delay not your conversion to the LORD,
   put it not off from day to day;

9 For suddenly his wrath flames forth;
   at the time of vengeance, you will be
   destroyed.

10* Rely not upon deceitful wealth,
   for it will be no help on the day of wrath.

Sincerity in Speech

11† Winnow not in every wind,
   and start not off in every direction.

12† Be consistent in your thoughts;
   steadfast be your words.

13* Be swift to hear,
   but slow to answer.

14 If you have the knowledge, answer your
   neighbor;
   if not, put your hand over your mouth.

15 Honor and dishonor through talking!
   A man's tongue can be his downfall.

16 Be not called a detractor;
   Use not your tongue for calumny;

17 For shame has been created for the thief,
   and the reproach of his neighbor for the
   double-tongued.

6 1† Say nothing harmful, small or great;
   be not a foe instead of a friend;
   A bad name and disgrace will you acquire:
   "That for the evil man with double
   tongue!"

2* Fall not into the grip of desire,
   lest, like fire, it consume your strength;

3 Your leaves it will eat, your fruits destroy,
   and you will be left a dry tree,

4 For contumacious desire destroys its owner
   and makes him the sport of his enemies.

True Friendship

5† A kind mouth multiplies friends,
   and gracious lips prompt friendly
   greetings.

6 Let your acquaintances be many,
   but one in a thousand your confidant.

7* When you gain a friend, first test him,
   and be not too ready to trust him.

---

† sincerity and justice, namely evil, human respect (20f), compromise of liberty in speech and action (22-25), false shame, and ignorance (26). He must fight for the truth (28), and avoid cynicism and laziness (29), and inconsistency in his conduct (30).

5, 1-10: The vices of the rich are pride and independence (1f), presumption (3), false security (4-7), and impenitence (8), which cannot escape the divine wrath (9f). Cf Prv 18, 23; 19, 1; 28, 6.

5, 11: A proverbial expression condemning inconstancy and advocating sincerity and honesty.

5, 12—6, 1: Proper use of the tongue requires constancy in speech (5, 12), prudence (13f), reserve (15), charity (6, 1), as well as the avoidance of detraction, *calumny* (16) and double talk, which bring shame and disgrace (5, 17; 6, 1).

6, 1: "*That . . . double tongue!*": people will say this against the man whose deceitful tongue has brought him to disgrace.

6, 5-17: True friends are discerned not by prosperity (11) but through the trials of adversity: distress, quarrels (9), sorrow (10) and misfortune (12). Such friends are rare and their value is beyond estimation, a gift from God (14-17).

---

* 5/1: Lk 12, 19.   6/2-3: 9, 8; 23, 17; Jb 31, 12;
  10: Prv 10, 2; 11, 4, 28.   Is 56, 3.
  13: Prv 29, 20; Jas 1, 19.   7ff: 12, 8f; 37, 1-5;
                                        Prv 19, 4.

8 For one sort of friend is a friend when it
    suits him,
      but he will not be with you in time of
      distress.

9 Another is a friend who becomes an enemy,
    and tells of the quarrel to your shame.

10 Another is a friend, a boon companion,
    who will not be with you when sorrow
    comes.

11 When things go well, he is your other self,
    and lords it over your servants;

12 But if you are brought low, he turns against
    you
    and avoids meeting you.

13 Keep away from your enemies;
    be on your guard with your friends.

14 A faithful friend is a sturdy shelter;
    he who finds one finds a treasure.

15 A faithful friend is beyond price,
    no sum can balance his worth.

16 A faithful friend is a life-saving remedy,
    such as he who fears God finds;

17 For he who fears God behaves accordingly,
    and his friend will be like himself.

Blessings of Wisdom

18† My son, from your youth embrace
    discipline;
    thus will you find wisdom with graying
    hair.

19 As though plowing and sowing, draw close
    to her;
    then await her bountiful crops.

20 For in cultivating her you will labor but
    little,
    and soon you will eat of her fruits.

21 How irksome she is to the unruly!
    The fool cannot abide her.

22 She will be like a burdensome stone to test
    him,
    and he will not delay in casting her aside.

23† For discipline is like her name,
    she is not accessible to many.

24 Listen, my son, and heed my advice;
    refuse not my counsel.

25 Put your feet into her fetters,
    and your neck under her yoke.

26 Stoop your shoulders and carry her
    and be not irked at her bonds.

27 With all your soul draw close to her;
    with all your strength keep her ways.

28 Search her out, discover her; seek her and
    you will find her.
    Then when you have her, do not let her
    go;

29 Thus will you afterward find rest in her,
    and she will become your joy.

30 Her fetters will be your throne of majesty;
    her bonds, your purple cord.

31✿† You will wear her as your robe of glory,
    bear her as your splendid crown.

32 My son, if you wish, you can be taught;
    if you apply yourself, you will be shrewd.

33 If you are willing to listen, you will learn;
    if you give heed, you will be wise.

34 Frequent the company of the elders;
    whoever is wise, stay close to him.

35✿ Be eager to hear every godly discourse;
    let no wise saying escape you.

36 If you see a man of prudence, seek him out;
    let your feet wear away his doorstep!

37✿ Reflect on the precepts of the Lord,
    let his commandments be your constant
    meditation;
    Then he will enlighten your mind,
    and the wisdom you desire he will grant.

Conduct in Public Life

7 1† Do no evil, and evil will not overtake you;
  2   avoid wickedness, and it will turn aside
    from you.

3✿ Sow not in the furrows of injustice,
    lest you harvest it sevenfold.

4 Seek not from the Lᴏʀᴅ authority,
    nor from the king a place of honor.

5✿ Parade not your justice before the Lord,
    and before the king flaunt not your
    wisdom.

6 Seek not to become a judge
    if you have not strength to root out crime,
  Or you will show favor to the ruler
    and mar your integrity.

7 Be guilty of no evil before the city's
    populace,
    nor disgrace yourself before the
    assembly.

8 Do not plot to repeat a sin;
    not even for one will you go unpunished.

9✿ Say not: "He will appreciate my many gifts;
    the Most High will accept my offerings."

10 Be not impatient in prayers,
    and neglect not the giving of alms.

---

† 6, 18-37: The various figures in each of the three strophes urge the search for wisdom through patience (19-23), docility (32-37), and perseverance in trials (25ff), promising rich rewards (28-31). Cf 4, 11-19.

6, 23: *Discipline* (*musar*, in the sense of wisdom) is a perfect homonym for *musar*, "removed, withdrawn"; thus the path of *discipline* is inaccessible to many.

6, 31: Some forms of the text speak also of the "yoke" of wisdom under the imagery of golden ornaments.

7, 1-17: In the conduct of social relations wisdom forbids *evil* and *injustice* (1ff), pride (5.15ff), ambition and human respect (4.6), public disorder (7), presumption and impatience toward God (9f), ridicule (11), *mischief* and deceit toward one's neighbor (8.12f).

✿
    31: Is 62, 3.   5: Jb 9, 2; Ps 143, 2;
    35: 8, 9.   Prv 25, 6; 1 Cor 4, 4.
    37: Ps 1, 2.   9: 34, 18; 35, 12.
    7/3: Prv 22, 8.

11† Laugh not at an embittered man;
    be mindful of him who exalts and
        humbles.

12 Plot no mischief against your brother,
    nor against your friend and companion.

13 Delight not in telling lie after lie,
    for it never results in good.

14*† Thrust not yourself into the deliberations of
        princes,
    and repeat not the words of your prayer.

15* Hate not laborious tasks,
    nor farming, which was ordained by the
        Most High.

16 Do not esteem yourself better than your
        fellows;
    remember, his wrath will not delay.

17* More and more, humble your pride;
    what awaits man is worms.

Duties of Family Life, Religion and Charity

18† Barter not a friend for money,
    nor a dear brother for the gold of Ophir.

19 Dismiss not a sensible wife;
    a gracious wife is more precious than
        corals.

20* Mistreat not a servant who faithfully serves,
    nor a laborer who devotes himself to his
        task.

21† Let a wise servant be dear to you as your
        own self;
    refuse him not his freedom.

22 If you have livestock, look after them;
    if they are dependable, keep them.

23*† If you have sons, chastise them;
    bend their necks from childhood.

24* If you have daughters, keep them chaste,
    and be not indulgent to them.

25* Giving your daughter in marriage ends a
        great task;
    but give her to a worthy man.

26 If you have a wife, let her not seem odious
        to you;
    but where there is ill-feeling, trust her
        not.

27* With your whole heart honor your father;
    your mother's birthpangs forget not.

28 Remember, of these parents you were born;
    what can you give them for all they gave
        you?

29 With all your soul, fear God,
    revere his priests.

30 With all your strength, love your Creator,
    forsake not his ministers.

31*† Honor God and respect the priest;
    give him his portion as you have been
        commanded:
    First fruits and contributions,
    due sacrifices and holy offerings.

32 To the poor man also extend your hand,
    that your blessing may be complete;

33† Be generous to all the living,
    and withhold not your kindness from the
        dead.

34* Avoid not those who weep,
    but mourn with those who mourn;

35* Neglect not to visit the sick—
    for these things you will be loved.

36 In whatever you do, remember your last
        days,
    and you will never sin.

Prudence in Dealing with Other Men

8 **1†** Contend not with an influential man,
    lest you fall into his power.

2* Quarrel not with a rich man,
    lest he pay out the price of your
        downfall;
    For gold has dazzled many,
    and perverts the character of princes.

3* Dispute not with a man of railing speech,
    heap no wood upon his fire.

4 Be not too familiar with an unruly man,
    lest he speak ill of your forebears.

---

† 7, 11: *Him who exalts and humbles:* God; cf 1 Sm 2, 7; Ps 75, 8; Lk 1, 52.

7, 14: *Repeat not . . . prayer:* brevity of speech in dealings with superiors and more especially with God is a sign of reverence and respect; cf Eccl 5, 1; Mt 6, 7.

7, 18-36: The duties of respect and appreciation, justice and kindness should characterize relations toward members of the household (18-28), and also toward God and his priests (29ff), the poor and afflicted, the living and the dead (32-36).

7, 18: *Ophir* was the port, at present unidentified, to which the ships of Solomon sailed and from which they brought back gold and silver; cf note on Ps 44 (45), 10.

7, 21: After six years of service a Hebrew slave was entitled to freedom; cf Ex 21, 2; Dt 15, 12-15.

7, 23: *Bend their necks:* keep them from rebellious pride; so with the Greek. Cf 30, 12. The present Hebrew text, which is probably not original here, reads: "Choose wives for them while they are young."

7, 31: *First fruits . . . holy offerings:* cf Ex 29, 27; Lv 7, 31-34; Nm 18, 8-20; Dt 18, 1-5.

7, 33: This seems to refer to the observances ordained toward the dead, that is, proper mourning and burial. Cf 2 Sm 21, 12ff; Tb 1, 20; 12, 12. When this verse is read in the light of later teaching, prayers for the souls of the deceased would also be recommended. Cf 2 Mc 12, 43ff.

8, 1-19: A prudent man will be circumspect, avoiding conflict with the powerful, the rich and insolent, the impious, the irascible, and with judges (1ff.10ff.14.16). He will seek friendship not with the undisciplined (4.12f) and the ruthless (15), nor with fools and strangers (17ff), but with the wise and the ancients of the people (8f).

❋
14: 32, 7ff; Mt 6, 7.   25: 1 Cor 7, 36ff.
15: Gn 2, 15; 3, 17.   27: Ex 20, 12.
17: Is 66, 24.   31: Lv 7, 31; Nm 18, 18.
20: Lv 19, 13; Dt 24, 14f;   34: Rom 12, 15.
    Jas 5, 4.   35: Mt 25, 36.
23: 30, 8-13; Prv 13, 24.   8/2: 31, 6; Dt 16, 19.
24: 42, 9ff.   3: Prv 26, 20.

5*† Shame not a repentant sinner;
    remember, we all are guilty.

6 Insult no man when he is old,
    for some of us, too, will grow old.

7 Rejoice not when a man dies;
    remember, we are all to die.

8* Spurn not the discourse of the wise,
    but acquaint yourself with their
        proverbs;
    From them you will acquire the training
        to serve in the presence of princes.

9 Reject not the tradition of old men
    which they have learned from their
        fathers;
    From it you will obtain the knowledge
        how to answer in time of need.

10 Kindle not the coals of a sinner,
    lest you be consumed to his flaming fire.

11† Let not the impious man intimidate you;
    it will set him in ambush against you.

12* Lend not to one more powerful than
        yourself;
    and whatever you lend, count it as lost.

13 Go not surety beyond your means;
    think any pledge a debt you must pay.

14 Contend not at law with a judge,
    for he will settle it according to his whim.

15 Travel not with a ruthless man,
    lest he weigh you down with calamity;
    For he will go his own way straight,
    and through his folly you will perish with
        him.

16 Provoke no quarrel with a quick-tempered
        man,
    nor ride with him through the desert,
    For bloodshed is nothing to him;
    when there is no one to help you, he will
        destroy you.

17 Take no counsel with a fool,
    for he can keep nothing to himself.

18* Before a stranger do nothing that should be
        kept secret,
    for you know not what it will engender.

19 Open your heart to no man,
    and banish not your happiness.

Advice concerning Women

9 **1**† Be not jealous of the wife of your bosom,
    lest you teach her to do evil against you.

2* Give no woman power over you
    to trample upon your dignity.

3 Be not intimate with a strange woman,
    lest you fall into her snares.

4 With a singing girl be not familiar,
    lest you be caught in her wiles.

5† Entertain no thoughts against a virgin,
    lest you be enmeshed in damages for her.

6* Give not yourself to harlots,
    lest you surrender your inheritance.

7 Gaze not about the lanes of the city
    and wander not through its squares;

8* Avert your eyes from a comely woman;
    gaze not upon the beauty of another's
        wife—
    Through woman's beauty many perish,
    for lust for it burns like fire.

9 With a married woman dine not,
    recline not at table to drink by her side,
    Lest your heart be drawn to her
    and you go down in blood to the grave.

Choice of Friends

10† Discard not an old friend,
    for the new one cannot equal him.
    A new friend is like new wine
    which you drink with pleasure only when
        it has aged.

11 Envy not a sinner's fame,
    for you know not what disaster awaits
        him.

12 Rejoice not at a proud man's success;
    remember he will not reach death
        unpunished.

13 Keep far from the man who has power to
        kill,
    and you will not be filled with the dread
        of death.
    But if you approach him, offend him not,
    lest he take away your life;
    Know that you are stepping among snares
    and walking over a net.

14 As best you can, take your neighbors'
        measure,
    and associate with the wise.

15 With the learned be intimate;
    lest all your conversation be about the
        law of the Lord.

16 Have just men for your table companions;
    in the fear of God be your glory.

---

† 8, 5: *We all are guilty:* cf 1 Kgs 8, 46; 2 Chr 6, 36; Eccl 7, 20; Rom 3, 9f; 1 Jn 1, 8.

8, 11: To give in to the wicked in one instance becomes an occasion of sin for the future.

9, 1-9: Prudence and reserve in dealing with women are the best defense of morality. To preserve the liberty and dignity of his person and the integrity of his possessions, a man must avoid jealousy toward his own wife and familiarity toward all other women. Cf 25, 12—26, 18.

9, 1: Unjust suspicions often engender hatred between husband and wife and may prompt a wife to commit those faults of which heretofore she had been innocent.

9, 5: Cf Ex 22, 15f; Dt 22, 28f; Jb 31, 1.

9, 10-16: In social relations, adherence to *the law of the Lord* should serve as a guide (15). Associate with true friends (10), with the just and the learned (14ff); avoid the company of the mighty and of sinners doomed to punishment (11ff). Cf 8, 1-19.

✿   5: 1 Kgs 8, 46; 1 Jn 1, 8.   9/2: 25, 21.
         8f: 6, 35.   6: Prv 5, 3-11; 6, 24;
         12: 29, 4-7; Prv 17, 18.   29, 3.
         18: Prv 25, 9f.   8: 25, 20; 41, 21.

Concerning Rulers

17† Skilled artisans are esteemed for their
    deftness;
    but the ruler of his people is the skilled
        sage.

18 Feared in the city is the man of railing
    speech,
    and he who talks rashly is hated.

10

1* A wise magistrate lends stability to his
    people,
    and the government of a prudent man
        is well ordered.

2* As the people's judge, so are his
    ministers;
    as the head of a city, its inhabitants.

3* A wanton king destroys his people,
    but a city grows through the wisdom
        of its princes.

4 Sovereignty over the earth is in the hand
    of God,
    who raises up on it the man of the
        hour;

5 Sovereignty over every man is in the
    hand of God,
    who imparts his majesty to the ruler.

The Sin of Pride

6*† No matter the wrong, do no violence to
    your neighbor,
    and do not walk the path of arrogance.

7 Odious to the Lord and to men is
    arrogance,
    and the sin of oppression they both
        hate.

8 Dominion is transferred from one people
    to another
    because of the violence of the arrogant.

9† When are dust and ashes proud?
    even during life man's body decays;

10 A slight illness—the doctor jests,
    a king today—tomorrow he is dead.

11* When a man dies, he inherits corruption;
    worms and gnats and maggots.

12 The beginning of pride is man's
    stubbornness
    in withdrawing his heart from his
        Maker;

13* For pride is the reservoir of sin,
    a source which runs over with vice;
    Because of it God sends unheard-of
        afflictions
    and brings men to utter ruin.

14 The thrones of the arrogant God
    overturns

and establishes the lowly in their
    stead.

15 The roots of the proud God plucks up,
    to plant the humble in their place:

16 He breaks down their stem to the level of
    the ground,
    then digs their roots from the earth.

17 The traces of the proud God sweeps away
    and effaces the memory of them from
        the earth.

18 Insolence is not allotted to a man,
    nor stubborn anger to one born of
        woman.

True Glory

19† Whose offspring can be in honor? Those
    of men.
    Which offspring are in honor? Those
        who fear God.
    Whose offspring can be in disgrace?
        Those of men.
    Which offspring are in disgrace?
        Those who transgress the
        commandments.

20 Among brethren their leader is in honor;
    he who fears God is in honor among
        his people.

21 Be it tenant or wayfarer, alien or pauper,
    his glory is the fear of the LORD.

22* It is not just to despise a man who is wise
    but poor,
    nor proper to honor any sinner.

23 The prince, the ruler, the judge are in
    honor;
    but none is greater than he who fears
        God.

24* When free men serve a prudent slave,
    the wise man does not complain.

25 Flaunt not your wisdom in managing
    your affairs,
    and boast not in your time of need.

26* Better the worker who has plenty of
    everything
    than the boaster who is without bread.

---

† 9, 17—10, 5: Public office as conducted justly or unjustly benefits or destroys the people, according to the axiom, "as the prince, so the people." Cf Is 24, 2. God, however, has sovereignty over both.

10, 6-18: Glory displayed through arrogance and pride is false and displeasing to God and men, because founded on *dust and ashes* (6-11). It is the denial of the glory due to God, and therefore the source of all sin (12f). Even the memory of the proud is destroyed and God transfers their power to the lowly (14-18).

10, 9f: The text is uncertain. Its general implication is that man deteriorates physically even while alive: a slight illness today may be followed by death tomorrow. The uncertainty of life leaves no room for pride.

10, 19—11, 6: Regardless of social barriers, genuine honor among men comes from fear of the Lord and a true estimate of self. The Lord exalts the lowly and oppressed; transgressors of the *commandments* merit dishonor and disgrace.

---

* 10/1: Wis 6, 24.
  2f: Prv 29, 12.
  3: Prv 29, 4. 8.
  6: Lv 19, 18.
  11: Jb 17, 14.
  13: Prv 18, 12.
  22: Jas 2, 1-4.
  24: Prv 17, 2.
  26: Prv 12, 9.

27 My son, with humility have self-esteem;
prize yourself as you deserve.

28 Who will acquit him who condemns
himself?
who will honor him who discredits
himself?

29 The poor man is honored for his wisdom
as the rich man is honored for his
wealth;

30 Honored in poverty, how much more so
in wealth!
Dishonored in wealth, in poverty how
much the more!

11

1 The poor man's wisdom lifts his head
high
and sets him among princes.

2 Praise not a man for his looks;
despise not a man for his appearance.

3 Least is the bee among winged things,
but she reaps the choicest of all
harvests.

4 Mock not the worn cloak
and jibe at no man's bitter day:
For strange are the works of the Lord,
hidden from men his deeds.

5† The oppressed often rise to a throne,
and some that none would consider
wear a crown.

6 The exalted often fall into utter disgrace;
the honored are given into enemy
hands.

Moderation

7† Before investigating, find no fault;
examine first, then criticize.

8* Before hearing, answer not,
and interrupt no one in the middle of
his speech.

9 Dispute not about what is not your
concern;
in the strife of the arrogant take no
part.

10 My son, why increase your cares,
since he who is avid for wealth will not
be blameless?
Even if you run after it, you will never
overtake it;
however you seek it, you will not find
it.

11* One may toil and struggle and drive,
and fall short all the more.

12 Another goes his way a weakling and a
failure,
with little strength and great misery—
Yet the eyes of the Lord look favorably
upon him;

he raises him free of the vile dust,

13 Lifts up his head and exalts him
to the amazement of the many.

14*† Good and evil, life and death,
poverty and riches, are from the Lord.

15† Wisdom and understanding and
knowledge of affairs,
love and virtuous paths are from the
Lord.

16 Error and darkness were formed with
sinners from their birth,
and evil grows old with evildoers.

17 The Lord's gift remains with the just;
his favor brings continued success.

18 A man may become rich through a
miser's life,
and this is his allotted reward:

19*† When he says: "I have found rest,
now I will feast on my possessions,"
He does not know how long it will be
till he dies and leaves them to others.

20 My son, hold fast to your duty, busy
yourself with it,
grow old while doing your task.

21 Admire not how sinners live,
but trust in the Lord and wait for his
light;
For it is easy with the Lord
suddenly, in an instant, to make a poor
man rich.

22 God's blessing is the lot of the just man,
and in due time his hopes bear fruit.

23 Say not: "What do I need?
What further pleasure can be mine?"

24 Say not: "I am independent.
What harm can come to me now?"

25* The day of prosperity makes one forget
adversity;
the day of adversity makes one forget
prosperity.

26† For its is easy with the Lord on the day
of death
to repay man according to his deeds.

27 A moment's affliction brings forgetfulness
of past delights;
when a man dies, his life is revealed.

28 Call no man happy before his death,
for by how he ends, a man is known.

---

† 11, 5: Cf 1 Sm 2, 8; Ps 105, 17-22; Lk 1, 52.

11, 7-25: Discretion regulates a man's conduct toward others and their affairs (7ff); as regards his own interests, a man should avoid solicitude for the passing external benefits of life and property (10-14.18f.21.23ff), and cultivate the lasting inward gifts of wisdom and virtue (15.17.20.22).

11, 14: Divine Providence ultimately governs the lives of men. *Evil:* misfortune and calamity sent by God either in punishment or as an incentive to repentance or to greater virtue.

11, 15f: Some ancient witnesses omit these two verses.

11, 19: Cf the parable of the rich man, Lk 12, 16-21.

11, 26ff: Sirach, writing before Christian revelation, did not go beyond the hour of death to find full divine retribution.

11/8: Prv 18, 13.
11: Ps 127, 2; Eccl 4, 8.
14: Jb 1, 21; 2, 10.
19: Eccl 4, 8; 6, 2; Lk 12, 19.
25: 18, 25.

Care in Choosing Friends

29 Bring not every man into your house,
　for many are the snares of the crafty
　　one;

30 Though he seem like a bird confined in a
　　cage,
　yet like a spy he will pick out the weak
　　spots.

31 The talebearer turns good into evil;
　with a spark he sets many coals afire.

32 The evil man lies in wait for blood,
　and plots against your choicest
　　possessions.

33 Avoid a wicked man, for he breeds only
　　evil,
　lest you incur a lasting stain.

34 Lodge a stranger with you, and he will
　　subvert your course,
　and make a stranger of you to your
　　own household.

12

1† If you do good, know for whom you are
　　doing it,
　and your kindness will have its effect.

2 Do good to the just man and reward will
　　be yours,
　if not from him, from the LORD.

3† No good comes to him who gives comfort
　　to the wicked,
　nor is it an act of mercy that he does.

4* Give to the good man, refuse the sinner;
　refresh the downtrodden, give nothing
　　to the proud man.

5 No arms for combat should you give him,
　lest he use them against yourself;

6 With twofold evil you will meet
　for every good deed you do for him.

7 The Most High himself hates sinners,
　and upon the wicked he takes
　　vengeance.

8*† In our prosperity we cannot know our
　　friends;
　in adversity an enemy will not remain
　　concealed.

9* When a man is successful even his enemy
　　is friendly;
　in adversity even his friend disappears.

10 Never trust your enemy,
　for his wickedness is like corrosion in
　　bronze.

11† Even though he acts humbly and
　　peaceably toward you,
　take care to be on your guard against
　　him.

Rub him as one polishes a brazen mirror,
　and you will find that there is still
　　corrosion.

12 Let him not stand near you,
　lest he oust you and take your place.
Let him not sit at your right hand,
　lest he then demand your seat,
And in the end you appreciate my advice,
　when you groan with regret, as I
　　warned you.

13 Who pities a snake charmer when he is
　　bitten,
　or anyone who goes near a wild beast?

14 So is it with the companion of the proud
　　man,
　who is involved in his sins:

15 While you stand firm, he makes no bold
　　move;
　but if you slip, he cannot hold back.

16 With his lips an enemy speaks sweetly,
　but in his heart he schemes to plunge
　　you into the abyss.
Though your enemy has tears in his eyes,
　if given the chance, he will never have
　　enough of your blood.

17 If evil comes upon you, you will find him
　　at hand;
　feigning to help, he will trip you up,

18 Then he will nod his head and clap his
　　hands
　and hiss repeatedly, and show his true
　　face.

Caution regarding Associates

13

1† He who touches pitch blackens his
　　hand;
　he who associates with an impious
　　man learns his ways.

2 Bear no burden too heavy for you;
　go with no one greater or wealthier
　　than yourself.
How can the earthen pot go with the
　　metal cauldron?
When they knock together, the pot will
　　be smashed:

3 The rich man does wrong and boasts of it,
　the poor man is wronged and begs
　　forgiveness.

---

† 12, 1-7: The limitations to the practice of charity here reflected were removed by Christ, who requires that good be done even to enemies and to those who hate, persecute and calumniate us (Mt 5, 43-48).
12, 3ff: The author advises against generosity to those who would abuse it.
12, 8-18: Through adversity friends are distinguished from enemies; to trust the latter or permit them intimacy is to invite disaster. Cf note on 6, 5-17.
12, 11: *Brazen mirror:* see note on Ex 38, 8.
13, 1—14, 2: By means of various figures Sirach indicates the practical impossibility of genuine and sincere companionship between the poor and the proud rich. He lays down the principle of associating with equals (13, 15).

4 As long as the rich man can use you he
will enslave you,
but when you are exhausted, he will
abandon you.

5 As long as you have anything he will
speak fair words to you,
and with smiles he will win your
confidence;

6 When he needs something from you he
will cajole you,
then without regret he will impoverish
you.

7 While it serves his purpose he will
beguile you,
then twice or three times he will terrify
you;
When later he sees you he will pass you
by,
and shake his head over you.

8 Guard against being presumptuous;
be not as those who lack sense.

9 When invited by a man of influence, keep
your distance;
then he will urge you all the more.

10 Be not bold with him lest you be
rebuffed,
but keep not too far away lest you be
forgotten.

11 Engage not freely in discussion with him,
trust not his many words;
For by prolonged talk he will test you,
and though smiling he will probe you.

12 Mercilessly he will make of you a
laughingstock,
and will not refrain from injury or
chains.

13 Be on your guard and take care
never to accompany men of violence.

14 Every living thing loves its own kind,
every man a man like himself.

15 Every being is drawn to its own kind;
with his own kind every man
associates.

16* Is a wolf ever allied with a lamb?
So it is with the sinner and the just.

17† Can there be peace between the hyena
and the dog?
Or between the rich and the poor can
there be peace?

18 Lion's prey are the wild asses of the
desert;
so too the poor are feeding grounds for
the rich.

19 A proud man abhors lowliness;
so does the rich man abhor the poor.

20 When a rich man stumbles he is
supported by a friend;
when a poor man trips he is pushed
down by a friend.

21 Many are the supporters for a rich man
when he speaks;
though what he says is odious, it wins
approval.
When a poor man speaks they make sport
of him;
he speaks wisely and no attention is
paid him.

22 A rich man speaks and all are silent,
his wisdom they extol to the clouds.
A poor man speaks and they say: "Who
is that?"
If he slips they cast him down.

23 Wealth is good when there is no sin;
but poverty is evil by the standards of
the proud.

24* The heart of a man changes his
countenance,
either for good or for evil.

25 The sign of a good heart is a cheerful
countenance;
withdrawn and perplexed is the
laborious schemer.

14 **1*** Happy the man whose mouth brings
him no grief,
who is not stung by remorse for sin.

2 Happy the man whose conscience does
not reproach him,
who has not lost hope.

The Use of Wealth

3† Wealth ill becomes the mean man;
and to the miser, of what use is gold?

4* What he denies himself he collects for
others,
and in his possessions a stranger will
revel.

5 To whom will he be generous who is
stingy with himself
and does not enjoy what is his own?

6 None is more stingy than he who is stingy
with himself;
he punishes his own miserliness.

7 If ever he is generous, it is by mistake;
and in the end he displays his greed.

8 In the miser's opinion his share is too
small;

---

† 13, 17: The hostility between the dogs which guard the flocks
at night and the rapacious hyenas is proverbial in Palestine.

14, 3-16: The miser does no good even to himself (3-10);
wealth should be wisely used during life, for it must be left
behind at death (11-16). In the light of the gospel, generosity
has a higher motivation and promise of reward than the Old
Testament writer could propose. Cf Mt 6, 19ff; Lk 12, 32ff.

*
13/16: 2 Cor 6, 14ff.   14/1: 19, 15; 25, 8; Jas 3, 2.
24: Prv 15, 13.   4: Eccl 6, 2.

9   he refuses his neighbor and brings ruin
        on himself.

10   The miser's eye is rapacious for bread,
        but on his own table he sets it stale.

11* My son, use freely whatever you have
        and enjoy it as best you can;

12   Remember that death does not tarry,
        nor have you been told the grave's
        appointed time.

13* Before you die, be good to your friend,
        and give him a share in what you
        possess.

14   Deprive not yourself of present good
        things,
        let no choice portion escape you.

15   Will you not leave your riches to others,
        and your earnings to be divided by lot?

16   Give, take, and treat yourself well,
        for in the nether world there are no
        joys to seek.

17* All flesh grows old, like a garment;
        the age-old law is: All must die.

18* As with the leaves that grow on a
        vigorous tree:
        one falls off and another sprouts—
     So with the generations of flesh and
        blood:
        one dies and another is born.

19   All man's works will perish in decay,
        and his handiwork will follow after
        him.

The Search for Wisdom and Its Blessings

20*† Happy the man who meditates on
        wisdom,
        and reflects on knowledge;

21   Who ponders her ways in his heart,
        and understands her paths;

22   Who pursues her like a scout,
        and lies in wait at her entry way;

23   Who peeps through her windows,
        and listens at her doors;

24   Who encamps near her house,
        and fastens his tent pegs next to her
        walls;

25   Who pitches his tent beside her,
        and lives as her welcome neighbor;

26   Who builds his nest in her leafage,
        and lodges in her branches;

27   Who takes shelter with her from the heat,
        and dwells in her home.

15

1   He who fears the LORD will do this;
        he who is practiced in the law will
        come to wisdom.

2   Motherlike she will meet him,
        like a young bride she will embrace
        him,

3*   Nourish him with the bread of
        understanding,
        and give him the water of learning to
        drink.

4   He will lean upon her and not fall,
        he will trust in her and not be put to
        shame.

5   She will exalt him above his fellows;
        in the assembly she will make him
        eloquent.

6*   Joy and gladness he will find,
        an everlasting name inherit.

7   Worthless men will not attain to her,
        haughty men will not behold her.

8   Far from the impious is she,
        not to be spoken of by liars.

9   Unseemly is praise on a sinner's lips,
        for it is not accorded to him by God.

10   But praise is offered by the wise man's
        tongue;
        its rightful steward will proclaim it.

Man's Free Will

11   Say not: "It was God's doing that I fell
        away";
        for what he hates he does not do.

12* Say not: "It was he who set me astray";
        for he has no need of wicked man.

13   Abominable wickedness the LORD hates,
        he does not let it befall those who fear
        him.

14* When God, in the beginning, created
        man,
        he made him subject to his own free
        choice.

15   If you choose you can keep the
        commandments;
        it is loyalty to do his will.

16   There are set before you fire and water;
        to whichever you choose, stretch forth
        your hand.

17* Before man are life and death,
        whichever he chooses shall be given
        him.

18   Immense is the wisdom of the LORD;
        he is mighty in power, and all-seeing.

---

*
11: Prv 3, 9.   15/3: Jn 4, 10; 6, 31ff.
13: 4, 1; Tb 4, 7.   6: 6, 29-32.
17: Ps 103, 14ff; Is 40, 6;   12: Jas 1, 13.
    Jas 1, 10; 1 Pt 1, 24.   14: Gn 1, 27.
18: Eccl 1, 4.   17: Dt 30, 15.
20: Ps 1, 2.

† 14, 20—15, 20: From his social teaching the sage now turns to consider individual responsibility. Happiness is to be found in the pursuit and possession of wisdom (14, 20—15, 5). Joy and honor are given, not to the sinner (7ff), but to him who fears God and observes his law (1-6.10). The sinner is fully responsible for his conduct because God, who sees all things (18f), is not the author of wickedness (11ff.20); he gives to every man the liberty to choose between good and evil (14-17).

19* The eyes of God see all he has made;
he understands man's every deed.

20 No man does he command to sin,
to none does he give strength for lies.

God's Punishment of Sinners

16

1† Desire not a brood of worthless children,
nor rejoice in wicked offspring.

2 Many though they be, exult not in them
if they have not the fear of the LORD.

3* Count not on their length of life,
have no hope in their future.
For one can be better than a thousand;
rather die childless than have godless
children!

4 Through one wise man can a city be
peopled;
through a clan of rebels it becomes
desolate.

5 Many such things has my eye seen,
even more than these has my ear
heard.

6*† Against a sinful band fire is enkindled,
upon a godless people wrath flames
out.

7*† He forgave not the leaders of old
who rebelled long ago in their might;

8*† He spared not the neighbors of Lot
whom he detested for their pride;

9† Nor did he spare the doomed people
who were uprooted because of their
sin;

10*† Nor the six hundred thousand foot
soldiers
who perished for the impiety of their
hearts.

11 And had there been but one stiffnecked
man,
it were a wonder had he gone
unpunished.
For mercy and anger alike are with him
who remits and forgives, though on the
wicked alights his wrath.

12 Great as his mercy is his punishment;
he judges men, each according to his
deeds.

13 A criminal does not escape with his
plunder;
a just man's hope God does not leave
unfulfilled.

14 Whoever does good has his reward,
which each receives according to his
deeds.

15 Say not: "I am hidden from God;
in heaven who remembers me?
Among so many people I cannot be
known;
what am I in the world of spirits?

16 Behold, the heavens, the heaven of
heavens,
the earth and the abyss tremble at his
visitation;

17 The roots of the mountains, the earth's
foundations,
at his mere glance, quiver and quake.

18 Of me, therefore, he will take no thought;
with my ways who will concern
himself?

19* If I sin, no eye will see me;
if all in secret I am disloyal, who is to
know?

20 Who tells him of just deeds
and what could I expect for doing my
duty?"

21 Such are the thoughts of senseless men,
which only the foolish knave will
think.

Divine Wisdom Seen in Creation

22† Hearken to me, my son, take my advice,
apply your mind to my words,

23 While I propose measured wisdom,
and impart accurate knowledge.

24* When at the first God created his works
and, as he made them, assigned their
tasks,

25 He ordered for all time what they were
to do
and their domains from generation to
generation.
They were not to hunger, nor grow
weary,
nor ever cease from their tasks.

26 Not one should ever crowd its neighbor,
nor should they ever disobey his word.

---

† 16, 1-21: Sinful offspring are a great misfortune (1-4), for history and experience show how God punishes sin (5-10). He judges everyone according to his deeds (11ff); no one is hidden from him or escapes retribution at his hand (15-21).

16, 6: For Korah and his *band* (6a), see Nm 16, 35; Ps 106, 18; for the disgruntled Israelites (6b), Ps 78, 21f.

16, 7: *The leaders of old:* the "mighty men of old" who were destroyed by the flood: Gn 6, 4; Wis 14, 6; Bar 3, 26ff.

16, 8: The people of Sodom and Gomorrah: Gn 19, 24f; Ez 16, 49f.

16, 9: The Canaanites: Ex 23, 23f.27-31; 33, 2; Dt 7, 1; Wis 12, 3.

16, 10: The Israelites who murmured against Moses: Nm 11, 20; 14, 12.22ff.

16, 22—17, 18: In harmony with Gn 1—2, the author describes God's wisdom in creating the universe and all things in it (22-28), endowing man with a moral nature, with wisdom and knowledge and freedom of will according to his own image (17, 1.6), so that man may govern the earth (3f), praise God's name (8), obey his law (9-12), and render to him an account of his deeds (18). Cf Pss 19; 104.

---

* 19: Pss 33, 18; 34, 16;
    Heb 4, 13.
16/3f: Wis 4, 1f.
  6: 21, 9.
  7: Gn 6, 4; Wis 14, 6;
    Bar 3, 26ff.

  8: Gn 19, 24ff.
10: Nm 14, 29.
19: 23, 18.
24: Gn 1, 4ff.

27* Then the LORD looked upon the earth,
and filled it with his blessings.

28 Its surface he covered with all manner of life
which must return into it again.

17

1* The LORD from the earth created man,
and in his own image he made him.

2* Limited days of life he gives him
and makes him return to earth again.

3 He endows man with a strength of his own,
and with power over all things else on earth.

4 He puts the fear of him in all flesh,
and gives him rule over beasts and birds.

5 He forms men's tongues and eyes and ears,
and imparts to them an understanding heart.

6 With wisdom and knowledge he fills them;
good and evil he shows them.

7 He looks with favor upon their hearts,
and shows them his glorious works,

8 That they may describe the wonders of his deeds
and praise his holy name.

9 He has set before them knowledge,
a law of life as their inheritance;

10† An everlasting covenant he has made with them,
his commandments he has revealed to them.

11 His majestic glory their eyes beheld,
his glorious voice their ears heard.

12 He says to them, "Avoid all evil";
each of them he gives precepts about his fellow men.

13 Their ways are ever known to him,
they cannot be hidden from his eyes.

14*† Over every nation he places a ruler,
but the LORD's own portion is Israel.

15 All their actions are clear as the sun to him,
his eyes are ever upon their ways.

16 Their wickedness cannot be hidden from him;
all of their sins are before the LORD.

17 A man's goodness God cherishes like a signet ring,
a man's virtue, like the apple of his eye.

18* Later he will rise up and repay them,
and requite each one of them as they deserve.

Appeal for a Return to God

19† But to the penitent he provides a way back,
he encourages those who are losing hope!

20 Return to the LORD and give up sin,
pray to him and make your offenses few.

21 Turn again to the Most High and away from sin,
hate intensely what he loathes;

22* Who in the nether world can glorify the Most High
in place of the living who offer their praise?

23 No more can the dead give praise than those who have never lived;
they glorify the LORD who are alive and well.

24 How great the mercy of the LORD,
his forgiveness of those who return to him!

25 The like cannot be found in men,
for not immortal is any son of man.

26† Is anything brighter than the sun? Yet it can be eclipsed.
How obscure then the thoughts of flesh and blood!

27 God watches over the hosts of highest heaven,
while all men are dust and ashes.

The Divine Power and Mercy

18

1† The Eternal is the judge of all things without exception;
the LORD alone is just.

2 Whom has he made equal to describing his works,
and who can probe his mighty deeds?

---

† 17, 10: *An everlasting covenant . . . his commandments:* the various covenants which God entered into with mankind, e. g., Gn 2, 15ff; 17, 1-22; especially on Mount Sinai where the people saw God's glory and heard his voice (Ex 19, 16—24, 18).

17, 14: *Ruler:* this may refer to civil authority or to angels placed over nations as guardians; see note on Dt 32, 8 and the cross references above.

17, 19-27: Exhorting the sinner to return to God (19ff.24ff), the author implies that the Lord will postpone death for a repentant sinner so that he may fulfill his destiny of praising God on earth (22f). In the light of Christian teaching, the gift of final penitence extends this divine purpose into life everlasting. See note on Ps 6, 6; cf also Ez 18, 23; 33, 11-16.

17, 26: *Obscure:* literally, evil; compare Gn 6, 5. Though moral fault is not excluded, the thought here is the inability to understand the merciful designs of God. Cf Wis 9, 14-18.

18, 1-13: Not only are God's justice and power beyond man's understanding (1-5), his mercy also is boundless and surpasses all human compassion (6-13).

27: Gn 1, 20ff.   18: Jb 19, 25; Jl 3, 4.
17/1: Gn 2, 7; 3, 19.   22f: Pss 6, 6; 115, 17;
2ff: Gn 1, 26ff; Ps 8, 4-8.   Is 38, 18.
14: Ex 19, 5; Dt 4, 19f;
     32, 8f; Dn 10, 13-21;
     12, 1; Rom 13, 1.

3 Who can measure his majestic power,
or exhaust the tale of his mercies?
4 One cannot lessen, nor increase,
nor penetrate the wonders of the
LORD.
5 When a man ends he is only beginning,
and when he stops he is still
bewildered.
6 What is man, of what worth is he?
the good, the evil in him, what are
these?
7* The sum of a man's days is great
if it reaches a hundred years:
8 Like a drop of sea water, like a grain of
sand,
so are these few years among the days
of eternity.
9 That is why the LORD is patient with men
and showers upon them his mercy.
10 He sees and understands that their death
is grievous,
and so he forgives them all the more.
11 Man may be merciful to his fellow man,
but the LORD's mercy reaches all flesh,
12* Reproving, admonishing, teaching,
as a shepherd guides his flock;
13 Merciful to those who accept his
guidance,
who are diligent in his precepts.

The Necessity of Prudence

14† My son, to your charity add no reproach,
nor spoil any gift by harsh words.
15 Like dew that abates a burning wind,
so does a word improve a gift.
16 Sometimes the word means more than
the gift;
both are offered by a kindly man.
17* Only a fool upbraids before giving;
a grudging gift wears out the expectant
eyes.
18 Be informed before speaking;
before sickness prepare the cure.
19† Before you are judged, seek merit for
yourself,
and at the time of visitation you will
have a ransom.
20 Before you have fallen, humble yourself;
when you have sinned, show
repentance.
21 Delay not to forsake sins,
neglect it not till you are in distress.
22*† Let nothing prevent the prompt payment
of your vows;

wait not to fulfill them when you are
dying.
23 Before making a vow have the means to
fulfill it;
be not one who tries the LORD.
24* Think of wrath and the day of death,
the time of vengeance when he will
hide his face.
25* Remember the time of hunger in the time
of plenty,
poverty and want in the day of wealth.
26 Between morning and evening the
weather changes;
before the LORD all things are fleeting.
27 A wise man is circumspect in all things;
when sin is rife he keeps himself from
wrongdoing.
28† Any learned man should make wisdom
known,
and he who attains to her should
declare her praise;
29 Those trained in her words must show
their wisdom,
dispensing sound proverbs like
life-giving waters.

Self-Control

30*† Go not after your lusts,
but keep your desires in check.
31 If you satisfy your lustful appetites
they will make you the sport of your
enemies.
32 Have no joy in the pleasures of a moment
which bring on poverty redoubled;
33 Become not a glutton and a winebibber
with nothing in your purse.

19   **1** He who does so grows no richer;
he who wastes the little he has will be
stripped bare.
2* Wine and women make the mind giddy,
and the companion of harlots becomes
reckless.

---

† 18, 14-27: The practice of charity is an art which avoids
every offense to the recipient (14-18). Prudence directs the
changing circumstances of daily life toward the attainment of
its reward *at the time of visitation,* i. e., the day of reckoning
(19-27).
18, 19: *Merit . . . ransom:* almsgiving is often portrayed in the
Bible as a means of approach to the forgiving mercy of God.
Cf 3, 29f; 29, 11f; Tb 12, 12f; Dn 4, 24; Lk 16, 9; Acts 10, 31.
18, 22f: The usual object of a vow in Old Testament times
was the offering of a bloody sacrifice.
18, 28f: A general statement on the teaching of wisdom,
serving either as a conclusion to the preceding section or as an
introduction to the following one. The neighbors of the wise
man are regarded as the field into which he channels the waters
of wisdom to encourage growth. Cf 24, 28-31.
18, 30—19, 4: Inordinate gratification of the senses makes a
man unreasonable, the slave of passion, *the sport of* his *enemies.*
In the end it destroys him physically and spiritually.

❋ 18/7: Ps 90, 10.   24: 7, 16.
     12: Jn 10, 11.   25: 11, 25.
     17: 20, 13.   30: Rom 6, 12; 13, 14.
     22: Nm 30, 3; Dt 23, 22;   19/2: Prv 20, 1; 23, 20ff.
         Ps 50, 14; Prv 20, 25;
         Eccl 5, 4.

4 He who lightly trusts in them has no
  sense,
   and he who strays after them sins
    against his own life.
8 Rottenness and worms will possess him,
   for contumacious desire destroys its
    owner.

The Proper Use of Speech

5† He who gloats over evil will meet with
  evil,
   and he who repeats an evil report has
    no sense.
6✿ Never repeat gossip,
   and you will not be reviled.
7✿ Tell nothing to friend or foe;
   if you have a fault, reveal it not,
8 For he who hears it will hold it against
  you,
   and in time become your enemy.
9 Let anything you hear die within you;
   be assured it will not make you burst.
10 When a fool hears something, he is in
  labor,
   like a woman giving birth to a child.
11 Like an arrow lodged in a man's thigh
   is gossip in the breast of a fool.
12✿ Admonish your friend—he may not have
  done it;
   and if he did, that he may not do it
    again.
13 Admonish your neighbor—he may not
  have said it;
   and if he did, that he may not say it
    again.
14 Admonish your friend—often it may be
  slander;
   every story you must not believe.
15✿ Then, too, a man can slip and not mean it;
   who has not sinned with his tongue?
16✿ Admonish your neighbor before you
  break with him;
   thus will you fulfill the law of the Most
    High.

How to Recognize True Wisdom

17✿† All wisdom is fear of the Lord;
   perfect wisdom is the fulfillment of the
    law.
18 The knowledge of wickedness is not
  wisdom,
   nor is there prudence in the counsel of
    sinners.

19 There is a shrewdness that is detestable,
   while the simple man may be free from
    sin.
20 There are those with little understanding
   who fear God,
   and those of great intelligence who
    violate the law.
21 There is a shrewdness keen but dishonest,
   which by duplicity wins a judgment.
22 There is the wicked man who is bowed in
  grief,
   but is full of guile within;
23 He bows his head and feigns not to hear,
   but when not observed, he will take
    advantage of you:
24 Even though his lack of strength keeps
  him from sinning,
   when he finds the opportunity, he will
    do harm.
25 One can tell a man by his appearance;
   a wise man is known as such when first
    met.
26 A man's attire, his hearty laughter and his
  gait,
   proclaim him for what he is.

Conduct of the Wise and the Foolish

20

1† An admonition can be inopportune,
   and a man may be wise to hold his
    peace.
2 It is much better to admonish than to
  lose one's temper,
   for one who admits his fault will be
    kept from disgrace.
3† Like a eunuch lusting for intimacy with a
  maiden
   is he who does right under
    compulsion.
4 One man is silent and is thought wise,
   another is talkative and is disliked.
5✿ One man is silent because he has nothing
  to say;
   another is silent, biding his time.

---

† 19, 5-16: An excellent commentary on the eighth commandment of the Decalogue, forbidding intemperance in speech through calumny, rash judgment, and detraction (5f), and inculcating discreet silence in defense of self and of neighbor (7-11). Justice requires that an accused neighbor be given a hearing, and charity urges fraternal correction; both together fulfill *the law of the Most High* (12-16); cf Mt 7, 1f; 18, 15f.

19, 17-26: True and false wisdom as here described are synonymous with virtue and vice, with *the fulfillment of the law* and the violation of it.

20, 1-7: Wisdom indicates the proper times for speech and silence, that is, the occasions when the most benefit can be gained from them.

20, 3: The sense is that violence or force against a person can prevent an external act of sin or compel a good deed without eliminating the internal sin or desire of wrongdoing. Cf 20, 20.

✿
6: Prv 25, 10.
7: 8, 18f.
12: Lv 19, 17; Mt 18, 15;
   Lk 17, 3.
15: 14, 1; Jas 3, 2.
16: Lv 19, 17.

17: 1, 1. 12. 14; Jb 28, 28;
   Ps 111, 10; Prv 1, 7;
   9, 10.
20/5: 20, 1; Prv 10, 19;
   17, 28.

6 A wise man is silent till the right time comes,
but a boasting fool ignores the proper time.

7 He who talks too much is detested;
he who pretends to authority is hated.

8† Some misfortunes bring success;
some things gained are a man's loss.

9† Some gifts do one no good,
and some must be paid back double.

10 Humiliation can follow fame,
while from obscurity a man can lift up his head.

11 A man may buy much for little,
but pay for it seven times over.

12 A wise man makes himself popular by a few words,
but fools pour forth their blandishments in vain.

13 A gift from a rogue will do you no good,
for in his eyes his one gift is equal to seven.

14 He gives little and criticizes often,
and like a crier he shouts aloud.
He lends today, he asks it back tomorrow;
hateful indeed is such a man.

15 A fool has no friends,
nor thanks for his generosity;

16 Those who eat his bread have an evil tongue.
How many times they laugh him to scorn!

17† A fall to the ground is less sudden than a slip of the tongue;
that is why the downfall of the wicked comes so quickly.

18 Insipid food is the untimely tale;
the unruly are always ready to offer it.

19 A proverb when spoken by a fool is unwelcome,
for he does not utter it at the proper time.

20 A man through want may be unable to sin,
yet in this tranquility he cannot rest.

21 One may lose his life through shame,
and perish through a fool's intimidation.

22 A man makes a promise to a friend out of shame,
and has him for his enemy needlessly.

23 A lie is a foul blot in a man,
yet it is constantly on the lips of the unruly.

24 Better a thief than an inveterate liar,
yet both will suffer disgrace;

25 A liar's way leads to dishonor,
his shame remains ever with him.

26† A wise man advances himself by his words,
a prudent man pleases the great.

27 He who works his land has abundant crops,
he who pleases the great is pardoned his faults.

28✤ Favors and gifts blind the eyes;
like a muzzle over the mouth they silence reproof.

29 Hidden wisdom and unseen treasure—
of what value is either?

30 Better the man who hides his folly
than the one who hides his wisdom.

Sin Must Be Avoided

21

1† My son, if you have sinned, do so no more,
and for your past sins pray to be forgiven.

2 Flee from sin as from a serpent
that will bite you if you go near it;
Its teeth are lion's teeth,
destroying the souls of men.

3 Every offense is a two-edged sword;
when it cuts, there can be no healing.

4 Violence and arrogance wipe out wealth;
so too a proud man's home is destroyed.

5 Prayer from a poor man's lips is heard at once,
and justice is quickly granted him.

6 He who hates correction walks the sinner's path,
but he who fears the Lord repents in his heart.

7 Widely known is the boastful speaker,
but the wise man knows his own faults.

8 He who builds his house with another's money
is collecting stones for his funeral mound.

---

† 20, 8-16: In a series of paradoxes the author indicates how much true and lasting values differ from apparent ones.

20, 9: *And some . . . double:* or perhaps, "but some are doubly precious."

20, 17-25: The ill-timed speech of *the wicked, the unruly* and *a fool* is repulsive (17ff); human respect exposes one to intimidation, rash promises and enmity (21f); lies bring dishonor and lasting disgrace (23ff).

20, 26-30: Unlike the fool who invites disaster through misuse of his tongue, the sage through prudent speech gains in honor and esteem among the great (26f). He must beware, however, of accepting bribes, lest he share in evil through silence when he should reprove (28ff).

21, 1-10: Under various figures, the consequences of sin are described as destructive of wealth, and even of bodily life, and deserving of death and a place in the depths of the nether world

✤ 28: Ex 23, 8; Dt 16, 19.

9* A band of criminals is like a bundle of
  tow;
  they will end in a flaming fire.

10† The path of sinners is smooth stones
  that end in the depths of the nether
  world.

The Wise and the Foolish Differ

11† He who keeps the law controls his
  impulses;
  he who is perfect in fear of the LORD
  has wisdom.

12 He can never be taught who is not
  shrewd,
  but one form of shrewdness is
  thoroughly bitter.

13* A wise man's knowledge wells up in a
  flood,
  and his counsel, like a living spring;

14 A fool's mind is like a broken jar—
  no knowledge at all can it hold.

15 When an intelligent man hears words of
  wisdom,
  he approves them and adds to them;
  The wanton hears them with scorn
  and casts them behind his back.

16 A fool's chatter is like a load on a journey,
  but there is charm to be found upon
  the lips of the wise.

17 The views of a prudent man are sought
  in an assembly,
  and his words are considered with
  care.

18 Like a house in ruins is wisdom to a fool;
  the stupid man knows it only as
  inscrutable words.

19 Like fetters on the legs is learning to a
  fool,
  like a manacle on his right hand.

20* A fool raises his voice in laughter,
  but a prudent man at the most smiles
  gently.

21 Like a chain of gold is learning to a wise
  man,
  like a bracelet on his right arm.

22* The fool steps boldly into a house,
  while the well-bred man remains
  outside;

23 A boor peeps through the doorway of a
  house,
  but a cultured man keeps his glance
  cast down.

24 It is rude for one to listen at a door;
  a cultured man would be
  overwhelmed by the disgrace of it.

25 The lips of the impious talk of what is not
  their concern,
  but the words of the prudent are
  carefully weighed.

26 Fools' thoughts are in their mouths,
  wise men's words are in their hearts.

27† When a godless man curses his
  adversary,
  he really curses himself.

28 A slanderer besmirches himself,
  and is hated by his neighbors.

On Laziness and Foolishness

22

1† The sluggard is like a stone in the mud;
  everyone hisses at his disgrace.

2 The sluggard is like a lump of dung;
  whoever touches him wipes his hands.

3* An unruly child is a disgrace to its father;
  if it be a daughter, she brings him to
  poverty.

4 A thoughtful daughter becomes a
  treasure to her husband,
  a shameless one is her father's grief.

5 A hussy shames her father and her
  husband;
  by both she is despised.

6† Like a song in time of mourning is
  inopportune talk,
  but lashes and discipline are at all
  times wisdom.

7* Teaching a fool is like gluing a broken
  pot,
  or like disturbing a man in the depths
  of sleep;

---

† (2ff.6a.8ff). Through prayer, forgiveness can be sought (1), and through fear of the Lord, repentance is achieved (1, 5.6b).

21, 10: *The path of sinners . . . nether world:* eternal retribution is not yet proposed in this reference. It became clearly revealed through the teaching of Christ; cf Mt 7, 13f; 25, 41-46; Lk 16, 19-31.

21, 11-28: The mind of the wise man is a fountain of knowledge (13.15); his will is trained to keep the law (11); his words are gracious, valued, carefully weighed, sincere (16f.25f); his conduct is respectful, cultured and restrained (20.22ff). The fool's mind is devoid of knowledge and impenetrable to it (12.14.18f); his will rejects it (15); his talk is burdensome (16), his laughter unrestrained (20), his conversation shallow and meddlesome (25f); his conduct is bold and rude (22ff); his abuse of others redounds on himself (27f).

21, 27: *Adversary:* this can be understood in the sense that, if a man curses one who led him into sin, he implicitly curses himself for having yielded to the sin; or in the sense that the enemy is the man's own sinful nature; or even in the sense that the enemy is the devil, since the Hebrew word used here is *satan.* Cf 1 Chr 21, 1; Zec 3, 2; 2 Pt 2, 12f; Jude 9.

22, 1-15: To Sirach, a lazy person and an unruly child are a cause of shame and disgrace; everyone wishes to be rid of them (1-5). A wicked fool is as senseless as a man asleep or dead, but the grief he causes others lasts a lifetime (7-11). He is like a brute, troublesome and intolerable (12-15).

22, 6: *Like a song . . . is . . . talk:* some understand *talk* in the sense of a rebuke unheeded by the unruly as a joyful song is out of place among mourners. Corporal punishment, however, is always effective.

---

* 21/9: Ps 21, 9.   22: Prv 25, 17.
  13: Prv 13, 14; 16, 22.   22/3: Prv 17, 21; 19, 13.
  20: Eccl 7, 6.   7-11: Prv 23, 9.

8 He talks with a slumberer who talks with a fool,
for when it is over, he will say, "What was that?"

9 Weep over the dead man, for his light has gone out;
weep over the fool, for sense has left him.

10 Weep but a little over the dead man, for he is at rest;
but worse than death is the life of a fool.

11* Seven days of mourning for the dead,
but for the wicked fool a whole lifetime.

12 Speak but seldom with the stupid man,
be not the companion of a brute;

13 Beware of him lest you have trouble
and be spattered when he shakes himself;
Turn away from him and you will find rest
and not be wearied by his lack of sense.

14 What is heavier than lead,
and what is its name but "Fool"?

15* Sand and salt and an iron mass
are easier to bear than a stupid man.

16† Masonry bonded with wooden beams
is not loosened by an earthquake;
Neither is a resolve constructed with careful deliberation
shaken in a moment of fear.

17 A resolve that is backed by prudent understanding
is like the polished surface of a smooth wall.

18 Small stones lying on an open height
will not remain when the wind blows;
Neither can a timid resolve based on foolish plans
withstand fear of any kind.

The Preservation of Friendship

19† One who jabs the eye brings tears:
he who pierces the heart bares its feelings.

20 He who throws stones at birds drives them away,
and he who insults a friend breaks up the friendship.

21 Should you draw a sword against a friend,
despair not, it can be undone.

22 Should you speak sharply to a friend,
fear not, you can be reconciled.

But a contemptuous insult, a confidence broken,
or a treacherous attack will drive away any friend.

23 Make fast friends with a man while he is poor;
thus will you enjoy his prosperity with him.
In time of trouble remain true to him,
so as to share in his inheritance when it comes.

24 Before flames burst forth an oven smokes;
so does abuse come before bloodshed.

25 From a friend in need of support
no one need hide in shame;

26 But from him who brings harm to his friend
all will stand aloof who hear of it.

Prayer

27*† Who will set a guard over my mouth,
and upon my lips an effective seal,
That I may not fail through them,
that my tongue may not destroy me?

23 **1†** LORD, Father and Master of my life,
permit me not to fall by them!

2 Who will apply the lash to my thoughts,
to my mind the rod of discipline,
That my failings may not be spared,
nor the sins of my heart overlooked;

3 Lest my failings increase,
and my sins be multiplied;
Lest I succumb to my foes,
and my enemy rejoice over me?

4 LORD, Father and God of my life,
abandon me not into their control!

5 A brazen look allow me not;
ward off passion from my heart,

6 Let not the lustful cravings of the flesh master me,
surrender me not to shameless desires.

---

† 22, 16ff: A prudent mind firmly resolved is undisturbed by violent and conflicting thoughts, whereas a foolish person is tossed about by the winds of fear, like small stones whipped about by high winds.

22, 19-26: As disputes and violence weaken friendship, and disloyalty and abuse of confidence destroy it utterly (19-22.24. 26), so kindness to a poor man in time of poverty and adversity builds up friendship and merits a share in his prosperity and inheritance (23.25).

22, 27—23, 6: The sage implores the divine assistance to preserve him through stern discipline from sins of the tongue (22, 27; 23, 1); ignorance of mind and weakness of will (2f); and inclinations of the senses and the flesh, lest he fall into the hands of his enemies, or become a prey of shameful desires (3-6).

23, 1: *Lord, Father and Master of my life:* these words express the tender personal relationship between the author's soul and God, the need of his assistance, and the truth of his providence.

The Proper Use of the Tongue

7† Give heed, my children, to the instruction
    that I pronounce,
      for he who keeps it will not be
      enslaved.

8 Through his lips is the sinner ensnared;
    the railer and the arrogant man fall
    thereby.

9✱ Let not your mouth form the habit of
    swearing,
      or becoming too familiar with the
      Holy Name.

10† Just as a slave that is constantly under
    scrutiny
      will not be without welts,
    So one who swears continually by the
    Holy Name
      will not remain free from sin.

11✱ A man who often swears heaps up
    obligations;
      the scourge will never be far from his
      house.
    If he swears in error, he incurs guilt;
      if he neglects his obligation, his sin is
      doubly great.
    If he swears without reason he cannot be
    found just,
      and all his house will suffer affliction.

12 There are words which merit death;
    may they never be heard among
    Jacob's heirs.
    For all such words are foreign to the
    devout,
      who do not wallow in sin.

13 Let not your mouth become used to
    coarse talk,
      for in it lies sinful matter.

14✱ Keep your father and mother in mind
    when you sit among the mighty,
    Lest in their presence you commit a
    blunder
      and disgrace your upbringing,
    By wishing you had never been born
      or cursing the day of your birth.

15 A man who has the habit of abusive
    language
      will never mature in character as long
      as he lives.

Sins of the Flesh

16† Two types of men multiply sins,
    a third draws down wrath;
For burning passion is a blazing fire,
    not to be quenched till it burns itself
    out:
A man given to sins of the flesh,
    who never stops until the fire breaks
    forth;

17✱ The rake to whom all bread is sweet
    and who is never through till he dies;

18✱ And the man who dishonors his marriage
    bed
      and says to himself, "Who can see me?
    Darkness surrounds me, walls hide me;
      no one sees me; why should I fear to
      sin?"
    Of the Most High he is not mindful,

19   fearing only the eyes of men;
    He does not understand that the eyes of
    the Lᴏʀᴅ,
      ten thousand times brighter than the
      sun,
    Observe every step a man takes
      and peer into hidden corners.

20 He who knows all things before they
    exist
      still knows them all after they are
      made.

21✱† Such a man will be punished in the
    streets of the city;
      when he least expects it, he will be
      apprehended.

22 So also with the woman who is
    unfaithful to her husband
      and offers as heir her son by a
      stranger.

23† First, she has disobeyed the law of the
    Most High;
    secondly, she has wronged her
    husband;
    Thirdly, in her wanton adultery
    she has borne children by another
    man.

---

†

23, 7-15: A warning against sins of the tongue through misuse of the Holy Name, thoughtless swearing which involves obligation and incurs guilt (7-11), blasphemy (12), talk that is coarse and blundersome (13f), and the incorrigible habit of *abusive language* (15).

23, 10: *As a slave . . . under scrutiny,* so is he who calls on God to witness the truth of what he says.

23, 16-27: From sins of the tongue the author proceeds to treat of sins of the flesh and their dire consequences. The passion of lust tyrannizes over its victims and, like fire, consumes and utterly destroys them (16f.22-26). The false security of the adulterer serves but to aggravate his inevitable fate (18-21). Only the fear of the Lord and observance of his commandments can assure moral safety (27).

23, 16: *Two types . . . a third:* three kinds of sins of impurity, with increasing degrees of gravity: solitary sins (16), fornication (17) and adultery (18-21).

23, 21: Cf Lv 20, 10; Dt 22, 22.

23, 23: The detailed evil of adultery includes disobedience to God's law (Ex 20, 14), injustice to a partner in marriage, and disgraceful offspring.

✱

23/9: Ex 20, 7; Lv 19, 12;
    Dt 5, 11; Mt 5, 33ff.
11: Lv 5, 4ff.
14: 7, 27; Ex 20, 13;
    Dt 5, 16.
17: Prv 9, 17.
18: Is 29, 15.
21f: Lv 20, 10; Dt 22, 21.

24† Such a woman will be dragged before
the assembly,
and her punishment will extend to her
children;

25 Her children will not take root;
her branches will not bring forth fruit.

26 She will leave an accursed memory;
her disgrace will never be blotted out.

27✱ Thus all who dwell on the earth shall
know,
and all who inhabit the world shall
understand,
That nothing is better than the fear of
the Lord,
nothing more salutary than to obey his
commandments.

Praise of Wisdom

24

1† Wisdom sings her own praises,
before her own people she proclaims
her glory;

2 In the assembly of the Most High she
opens her mouth,
in the presence of his hosts she
declares her worth:

3✱ "From the mouth of the Most High I
came forth,
and mistlike covered the earth.

4 In the highest heavens did I dwell,
my throne on a pillar of cloud.

5 The vault of heaven I compassed alone,
through the deep abyss I wandered.

6 Over waves of the sea, over all the land,
over every people and nation I held
sway.

7 Among all these I sought a resting place;
in whose inheritance should I abide?

8 "Then the Creator of all gave me his
command,
and he who formed me chose the spot
for my tent,
Saying, 'In Jacob make your dwelling,
in Israel your inheritance.'

9 Before all ages, in the beginning, he
created me,
and through all ages I shall not cease
to be.

10 In the holy tent I ministered before him,
and in Zion I fixed my abode.

11 Thus in the chosen city he has given me
rest,
in Jerusalem is my domain.

12 I have struck root among the glorious
people,
in the portion of the Lord, his
heritage.

13 "Like a cedar on Lebanon I am raised
aloft,
like a cypress on Mount Hermon,

14 Like a palm tree in Engedi,
like a rosebush in Jericho,
Like a fair olive tree in the field,
like a plane tree growing beside the
water.

15✱† Like cinnamon, or fragrant balm, or
precious myrrh,
I give forth perfume;
Like galbanum and onycha and sweet
spices,
like the odor of incense in the holy
place.

16 I spread out my branches like a
terebinth,
my branches so bright and so graceful.

17 I bud forth delights like the vine,
my blossoms become fruit fair and
rich.

18† Come to me, all you that yearn for me,
and be filled with my fruits;

19 You will remember me as sweeter than
honey,
better to have than the honeycomb.

20✱† He who eats of me will hunger still,
he who drinks of me will thirst for
more;

21 He who obeys me will not be put to
shame,
he who serves me will never fail."

22✱† All this is true of the book of the Most
High's covenant,
the law which Moses commanded us
as an inheritance for the community
of Jacob.

---

† 23, 24f: The judgment of *the assembly* determined the illegitimacy of children born of adultery or incest and excluded them from the "community of the Lord" (Dt 23, 3). Cf Wis 3, 16-19; 4, 3-6.

24, 1-27: In this chapter Wisdom speaks in the first person, describing her origin, her dwelling place in Israel, and the reward she gives her followers. As in Prv 8, Wisdom is described as a being who comes from God and is distinct from him. While we do not say with certainty that this description applies to a personal being, it does foreshadow the beautiful doctrine of the Word of God later developed in St. John's Gospel (Jn 1, 1-14). In the liturgy this chapter is applied to the Blessed Virgin because of her constant and intimate association with Christ, the Incarnate Wisdom.

24, 15: These substances were associated with worship, being mentioned in Ex 30, 22f.34 as the ingredients of the anointing oil and the sacred incense. Israel was a priestly nation.

24, 18: Compare the words of the Savior in Mt 11, 28ff.

24, 20: So pleasing is wisdom to man that, far from being satiated, he will always desire more.

24, 22: Here the author begins to speak once more, Wisdom having ended her discourse in the preceding verse. Wisdom and the law of Moses are now identified.

✱
27: 1, 10-18, 24; Prv 3, 1f.   15: Ex 30, 22-25.
24/3ff: 1, 1; Prv 2, 6; 8, 22-36;   20: Is 55, 1; Jn 6, 35.
    Wis 7, 24f.   22: Ex 24, 7.

23 It overflows, like the Pishon, with
         wisdom—
    like the Tigris in the days of the new
         fruits.
24 It runs over, like the Euphrates, with
         understanding,
    like the Jordan at harvest time.
25 It sparkles like the Nile with knowledge,
    like the Gihon at vintage time.
26 The first man never finished
         comprehending wisdom,
    nor will the last succeed in fathoming
         her.
27 For deeper than the sea are her thoughts;
    her counsels, than the great abyss.

28 Now I, like a rivulet from her stream,
    channeling the waters into a garden,
29 Said to myself, "I will water my plants,
    my flower bed I will drench";
    And suddenly this rivulet of mine
         became a river,
    then this stream of mine, a sea.
30 Thus do I send my teachings forth
         shining like the dawn,
    to become known afar off.
31 Thus do I pour out instruction like
         prophecy
    and bestow it on generations to come.

Those Who Are Worthy of Praise

25 **1** With three things I am delighted,
    for they are pleasing to the LORD and
         to men:
    Harmony among brethren, friendship
         among neighbors,
    and the mutual love of husband and
         wife.
2 Three kinds of men I hate;
    their manner of life I loathe indeed:
    A proud pauper, a rich dissembler,
    and an old man lecherous in his
         dotage.

3 What you have not saved in your youth,
    how will you acquire in your old age?
4 How becoming to the gray-haired is
         judgment,
    and a knowledge of counsel to those
         on in years!
5 How becoming to the aged is wisdom,
    understanding and prudence to the
         venerable!
6 The crown of old men is wide
         experience;
    their glory, the fear of the LORD.

7 There are nine who come to my mind as
         blessed,
    a tenth whom my tongue proclaims:
The man who finds joy in his children,
    and he who lives to see his enemies'
         downfall.
8 Happy is he who dwells with a sensible
         wife,
    and he who plows not like a donkey
         yoked with an ox.
    Happy is he who sins not with his
         tongue,
    and he who serves not his inferior.
9 Happy is he who finds a friend
    and he who speaks to attentive ears.
10 He who finds wisdom is great indeed,
    but not greater than he who fears the
         LORD.
11 Fear of the LORD surpasses all else,
    its possessor is beyond compare.

Wicked and Virtuous Women

12 Worst of all wounds is that of the heart,
    worst of all evils is that of a woman.
13 Worst of all sufferings is that from one's
         foes,
    worst of all vengeance is that of one's
         enemies:
14 No poison worse than that of a serpent,
    no venom greater than that of a
         woman.
15 With a dragon or a lion I would rather
         dwell
    than live with an evil woman.
16 Wickedness changes a woman's looks,
    and makes her sullen as a female bear.
17 When her husband sits among his
         neighbors,
    a bitter sigh escapes him unawares.

18 There is scarce any evil like that in a
         woman;
    may she fall to the lot of the sinner!

24, 25: *Gihon:* understood by some to have been a name for
the Nile; cf Gn 2, 13.

24, 28-31: Spoken by the author. He had at first drawn a
small portion of the water of wisdom for his own private benefit,
but finding it so useful, he soon began to let others share in this
boon by teaching them the lessons of wisdom.

25, 1-11: While praising brotherly love, love of neighbor, and
conjugal love, the sage condemns their opposites in the arrogant
pauper who despises his brother, the fraudulent rich man who
cheats his neighbor, and the lecherous old man unfaithful to
his wife (1f). This last, sensual from his youth, lacks the mature
blessings of judgment and wisdom in old age (3-6), and the joy
of a peaceful household, where honesty and dignity, friendship,
wisdom and fear of God prevail (7-11).

25, 8: *Like a donkey yoked with an ox:* incompatibility between husband and wife.

25, 12-25: Wickedness in a woman is most grievous, painful
and bitter to her husband. Through it she becomes vengeful,
dangerous and intolerable, jealous, talkative, intemperate and
unchaste. Even her very appearance is changed (12-17). The
worst of all evils, a source of grief, a snare and a disgrace to her
husband, she depresses his mind, saddens and breaks his heart,
destroys his strength (18-22). She must not be indulged but
made obedient or punished (24f).

23ff: Gn 2, 11-14.

19 Like a sandy hill to aged feet
   is a railing wife to a quiet man.

20 Stumble not through woman's beauty,
   nor be greedy for her wealth;

21 The man is a slave, in disgrace and
   shame,
   when a wife supports her husband.

22 Depressed mind, saddened face,
   broken heart—this from an evil wife.
   Feeble hands and quaking knees—
   from a wife who brings no happiness
   to her husband.

23† In woman was sin's beginning,
   and because of her we all die.

24 Allow water no outlet,
   and be not indulgent to an erring wife.

25 If she walks not by your side,
   cut her away from you.

26

1*† Happy the husband of a good wife,
   twice-lengthened are his days;

2† A worthy wife brings joy to her husband,
   peaceful and full is his life.

3* A good wife is a generous gift
   bestowed upon him who fears the
   LORD;

4 Be he rich or poor, his heart is content,
   and a smile is ever on his face.

5 There are three things at which my heart
   quakes,
   a fourth before which I quail:
   Though false charges in public, trial
   before all the people,
   and lying testimony are harder to
   bear than death,

6† A jealous wife is heartache and
   mourning
   and a scourging tongue like the other
   three.

7 A bad wife is a chafing yoke;
   he who marries her seizes a scorpion.

8 A drunken wife arouses great anger,
   for she does not hide her shame.

9 By her eyelids and her haughty stare
   an unchaste wife can be recognized.

10* Keep a strict watch over an unruly wife,
   lest, finding an opportunity, she make
   use of it;

11 Follow close if her eyes are bold,
   and be not surprised if she betrays
   you:

12 As a thirsty traveler with eager mouth
   drinks from any water that he finds,
   So she settles down before every tent peg
   and opens her quiver for every arrow.

13 A gracious wife delights her husband,
   her thoughtfulness puts flesh on his
   bones;

14 A gift from the LORD is her governed
   speech,
   and her firm virtue is of surpassing
   worth.

15 Choicest of blessings is a modest wife,
   priceless her chaste person.

16 Like the sun rising in the LORD's heavens,
   the beauty of a virtuous wife is the
   radiance of her home.

17† Like the light which shines above the
   holy lampstand,
   are her beauty of face and graceful
   figure.

18† Golden columns on silver bases
   are her shapely limbs and steady feet.

Dangers to Integrity and Friendship

19* These two bring grief to my heart,
   and the third arouses my horror:
   A wealthy man reduced to want;
   illustrious men held in contempt;
   And the man who passes from justice to
   sin,
   for whom the LORD makes ready the
   sword.

---

† 25, 23: According to the account in Gn 3 to which Ben Sirach refers, sin, the cause of death, originated in woman: Eve, the first human being to sin, induced Adam to follow her example. But it is through Adam, as head of the race, that original sin and its punishment of spiritual death are presented by St. Paul (Rom 5) as having entered the world, to become the occasion for the redemptive work of Christ our Lord.

26, 1-4.13-18: *A good wife* is as a gift from God, bringing *joy* and peace, happiness and contentment to her husband (1-4) through *her thoughtfulness*, reserve, modesty and chastity, *beauty*, grace and virtue (13-18).

26, 2: *Worthy*: gifted spiritually, mentally and physically. Cf Prv 31, 10.

26, 6-12: A repetition of the thought expressed in 25, 12-25.

26, 17f: *The holy lampstand* and the *golden columns* stood in the holy place of the ancient Tabernacle (Ex 25, 31-40; 26, 32).

26, 18: Among the additions found here in some manuscripts are the following lines:

"My son, take care in the prime of life
   not to surrender your strength to strangers;
Single out from the land a goodly field
   and there with confidence sow the seed of your increase;
So shall you have your offspring around you,
   and in confidence shall they grow up.

"Though a woman for hire be thought of as a trifle,
   a married woman is a deadly snare for those who embrace her. [Cf Prv 6, 26.]

"A wife's complaint should be made in meekness,
   and show itself in a slight flush;
But a loud-mouthed, scolding wife
   is a trumpet signaling for battle:
Any human being who answers that challenge
   will spend his life amid the turbulence of war."

---

* 26/1: 25, 8; Prv 18, 22;   10: 42, 11.
        31, 10ff.   19: Ez 18, 24ff.
        3: 36, 24.

20† A merchant can hardly remain upright,
nor a shopkeeper free from sin;

27 **1*** For the sake of profit many sin,
and the struggle for wealth blinds the
eyes.

2 Like a peg driven between fitted stones,
between buying and selling sin is
wedged in.

3 Unless you earnestly hold fast to the fear
of the LORD,
suddenly your house will be thrown
down.

4 When a sieve is shaken, the husks
appear;
so do a man's faults when he speaks.

5* As the test of what the potter molds is in
the furnace,
so in his conversation is the test of a
man.

6* The fruit of a tree shows the care it has
had;
so too does a man's speech disclose the
bent of his mind.

7 Praise no man before he speaks,
for it is then that men are tested.

8 If you strive after justice you will attain
it,
and put it on like a splendid robe.

9 Birds nest with their own kind,
and fidelity comes to those who live by
it.

10 As a lion crouches in wait for prey,
so do sins for evildoers.

11 Ever wise are the discourses of the
devout,
but the godless man, like the moon, is
inconstant.

12 Limit the time you spend among fools,
but frequent the company of
thoughtful men.

13 The conversation of the wicked is
offensive,
their laughter is wanton guilt.

14 Their oath-filled talk makes the hair
stand on end,
their brawls make one stop one's ears.

15* Wrangling among the haughty ends in
bloodshed,
their cursing is painful to hear.

16*† He who betrays a secret cannot be
trusted,
he will never find an intimate friend.

17 Cherish your friend, keep faith with him;
but if you betray his confidence,
follow him not;

18 For as an enemy might kill a man,
you have killed your neighbor's
friendship.

19 Like a bird released from the hand,
you have let your friend go and cannot
recapture him;

20 Follow him not, for he is far away,
he has fled like a gazelle from the trap.

21* A wound can be bound up, and an insult
forgiven,
but he who betrays secrets does
hopeless damage.

Malice, Anger and Vengeance

22 He who has shifty eyes plots mischief
and no one can ward him off;

23* In your presence he uses honeyed talk,
and admires your every word,
But later he changes his tone
and twists your words to your ruin.

24* There is nothing that I hate so much,
and the LORD hates him as well.

25* As a stone falls back on him who throws
it up,
so a blow struck in treachery injures
more than one.

26 As he who digs a pit falls into it,
and he who lays a snare is caught in it,

27 Whoever does harm will be involved in it
without knowing how it came upon
him.

28 Mockery and abuse will be the lot of the
proud,
and vengeance lies in wait for them
like a lion.

29 The trap seizes those who rejoice in
pitfalls,
and pain will consume them before
they die;

30 Wrath and anger are hateful things,
yet the sinner hugs them tight.

---

† 26, 20—27, 15: From proper conduct in family life, the author proceeds to social morality, warning especially against injustice in commerce (26, 20—27, 3), and perversity of speech in business (4-7). The pursuit of *justice* in these matters is all the more meritorious as it is difficult (8ff). The discourses of the devout are marked with wisdom, but the conversations of the wicked, with offense, swearing, *cursing*, quarrels and even *bloodshed* (11-15).

27, 16—28, 11: Betrayal of *confidence* through indiscretion destroys *friendship* and does irreparable harm (16-21); cf 22, 22. False friendship based on hypocrisy and deceit is hateful to God and man (22ff); it soon becomes a victim of its own treachery (25ff). The same fate awaits the malicious and *vengeful* (27, 28—28, 1). They can obtain mercy and forgiveness only by first forgiving their neighbor, being mindful of death and of the commandments of the Most High (28, 2-7). And they must avoid quarrels and *strife* (8-11).

✿
27/1: 7, 18; 31, 6; Prv 30, 8f.   21: 22, 20.
  5: 1 Pt 1, 7.   23: Prv 26, 24ff.
  6: Mt 7, 20.   24: Prv 6, 13. 16.
  15: 23, 9-15.   25f: Ps 7, 16f; Prv 26, 27;
  16: Prv 11, 13; 20, 19.   Eccl 10, 8.

28 1* The vengeful will suffer the LORD's vengeance,
     for he remembers their sins in detail.

2* Forgive your neighbor's injustice;
     then when you pray, your own sins will be forgiven.

3* Should a man nourish anger against his fellows
     and expect healing from the LORD?

4 Should a man refuse mercy to his fellows,
     yet seek pardon for his own sins?

5 If he who is but flesh cherishes wrath,
     who will forgive his sins?

6* Remember your last days, set enmity aside;
     remember death and decay, and cease from sin!

7 Think of the commandments, hate not your neighbor;
     of the Most High's covenant, and overlook faults.

8 Avoid strife and your sins will be fewer,
     for a quarrelsome man kindles disputes,

9* Commits the sin of disrupting friendship
     and sows discord among those at peace.

10* The more wood, the greater the fire,
     the more underlying it, the fiercer the fight;
     The greater a man's strength, the sterner his anger,
     the greater his power, the greater his wrath.

11 Pitch and resin make fires flare up,
     and insistent quarrels provoke bloodshed.

The Evil Tongue

12† If you blow upon a spark, it quickens into flame,
     if you spit on it, it dies out;
     yet both you do with your mouth!

13* Cursed be gossips and the double-tongued,
     for they destroy the peace of many.

14 A meddlesome tongue subverts many,
     and makes them refugees among the peoples;
     It destroys walled cities,
     and overthrows powerful dynasties.

15 A meddlesome tongue can drive
     virtuous women from their homes
     and rob them of the fruit of their toil;

16 Whoever heeds it has no rest,
     nor can he dwell in peace.

17 A blow from a whip raises a welt,
     but a blow from the tongue smashes bones;

18* Many have fallen by the edge of the sword,
     but not as many as by the tongue.

19 Happy he who is sheltered from it,
     and has not endured its wrath;
     Who has not borne its yoke
     nor been fettered with its chains;

20 For its yoke is a yoke of iron
     and its chains are chains of bronze!

21 Dire is the death it inflicts,
     besides which even the nether world is a gain;

22 It will not take hold among the just
     nor scorch them in its flame,

23 But those who forsake the LORD will fall victims to it,
     as it burns among them unquenchably!
     It will hurl itself against them like a lion;
     like a panther, it will tear them to pieces.

24* As you hedge round your vineyard with thorns,
     set barred doors over your mouth;

25 As you seal up your silver and gold,
     so balance and weigh your words.

26 Take care not to slip by your tongue
     and fall victim to your foe waiting in ambush.

Loans, Alms and Surety

29 1*† He does a kindness who lends to his neighbor,
     and he fulfills the precepts who holds out a helping hand.

---

† 28, 12-26: Further treatment of sins of the tongue and their havoc; cf 5, 12—6, 1; 19, 5-16; 20, 17-25; 23, 7-15. *Gossips and the double-tongued* destroy domestic peace (12-16). The *whip, the sword, chains, even the nether world,* are not so cruel as the suffering inflicted by an evil tongue (17-21). Not *the just* but *those who forsake the Lord* are *victims* of their evil tongues (22f). Therefore, guard your mouth and tongue as you would guard treasure against an enemy (24ff).

29, 1-20: Some practical maxims concerning the use of wealth. Give *to a poor man* (8f), lend to a needy neighbor, but repay *when a loan falls due* lest the lender's burden be increased (1-5) and his kindness abused (6f); through charity build up defense against evil (10-13). *Go surety for your neighbor according to your means, but take care* (20) not to fall, for the shameless play false and bring their protectors and themselves to misfortune and ruin (14-19).

---

*   28/1: Dt 32, 35; Rom 12, 19.
2: Mt 6, 14.
3: Mt 18, 23ff.
6: 7, 36; 38, 20.
9: Prv 15, 18.
10ff: Prv 26, 20f.

13: 5, 16f.
18: Jas 3, 5ff.
24: 22, 27; Ps 141, 3.
29/1: Dt 15, 8; Ps 112, 5; Prv 19, 17.

2* Lend to your neighbor in his hour of
   need,
   and pay back your neighbor when a
   loan falls due;

3 Keep your promise, be honest with him,
   and you will always come by what you
   need.

4 Many a man who asks for a loan
   adds to the burdens of those who help
   him;

5 When he borrows, he kisses the lender's
   hand
   and speaks with respect of his
   creditor's wealth;
   But when payment is due he disappoints
   him
   and says he is helpless to meet the
   claim.

6 If the lender is able to recover barely
   half,
   he considers this an achievement;
   If not, he is cheated of his wealth
   and acquires an enemy at no extra
   charge;
   With curses and insults the borrower
   pays him back,
   with abuse instead of honor.

7 Many refuse to lend, not out of
   meanness,
   but from fear of being cheated.

8 To a poor man, however, be generous;
   keep him not waiting for your alms;

9* Because of the precept, help the needy,
   and in their want, do not send them
   away empty-handed.

10 Spend your money for your brother and
   friend,
   and hide it not under a stone to perish;

11* Dispose of your treasure as the Most
   High commands,
   for that will profit you more than the
   gold.

12 Store up almsgiving in your treasure
   house,
   and it will save you from every evil;

13 Better than a stout shield and a sturdy
   spear
   it will fight for you against the foe.

14* A good man goes surety for his neighbor,
   and only the shameless would play
   him false;

15 Forget not the kindness of your backer,
   for he offers his very life for you.

16 The wicked turn a pledge on their behalf
   into misfortune,
   and the ingrate abandons his
   protector;

17* Going surety has ruined many
   prosperous men
   and tossed them about like waves of
   the sea,

18 Has exiled men of prominence
   and sent them wandering through
   foreign lands.

19 The sinner through surety comes to grief,
   and he who undertakes too much
   falls into lawsuits.

20 Go surety for your neighbor according to
   your means,
   but take care lest you fall thereby.

Frugality and Its Rewards

21*† Life's prime needs are water, bread, and
   clothing,
   a house, too, for decent privacy.

22* Better a poor man's fare under the
   shadow of one's own roof
   than sumptuous banquets among
   strangers.

23 Be it little or much, be content with what
   you have,
   and pay no heed to him who would
   disparage your home;

24 A miserable life it is to go from house to
   house,
   for as a guest you dare not open your
   mouth.

25 The visitor has no thanks for filling the
   cups;
   besides, you will hear these bitter
   words:

26 "Come here, stranger, set the table,
   give me to eat the food you have!

27 Away, stranger, for one more worthy;
   for my brother's visit I need the
   room!"

28 Painful things to a sensitive man
   are abuse at home and insults from
   his creditors.

The Training of Children

30 1*† He who loves his son chastises him
   often,
   that he may be his joy when he grows
   up.

2: Ex 22, 24ff; Lv 25, 36;
   Mt 5, 42.
9: 4, 1ff; Lv 19, 9f;
   23, 22; Dt 15, 8.
11: 17, 17; Tb 4, 7ff.
14: 8, 13.
17: Prv 6, 1f; 11, 15.
21: 39, 26.
22: 40, 29.
30/1: Prv 13, 24; 23, 13;
   29, 15; Heb 12, 7.

29, 21-28: The man who provides his own basic *needs* of
food, clothing and dwelling, and is content with what he has,
preserves his freedom and self-respect (21ff). But if he lives as
a guest, even among the rich, he exposes himself to insult and
abuse (24-28).

30, 1-13: Sound discipline and careful education of children
correct frivolity and stubbornness, prevent remorse and humiliation, and bring to parents lasting joy and delight, prestige

2 He who disciplines his son will benefit
from him,
and boast of him among his intimates.

3 He who educates his son makes his
enemy jealous,
and shows his delight in him among
his friends.

4 At the father's death, he will seem not
dead,
since he leaves after him one like
himself,

5 Whom he looks upon through life with
joy,
and even in death, without regret:

6 The avenger he leaves against his foes,
and the one to repay his friends with
kindness.

7 He who spoils his son will have wounds
to bandage,
and will quake inwardly at every
outcry.

8 A colt untamed turns out stubborn;
a son left to himself grows up unruly.

9 Pamper your child and he will be a terror
for you,
indulge him and he will bring you
grief.

10 Share not in his frivolity lest you share in
his sorrow,
when finally your teeth are clenched
in remorse.

11 Give him not his own way in his youth,
and close not your eyes to his follies.

12* Bend him to the yoke when he is young,
thrash his sides while he is still small,
Lest he become stubborn, disobey you,
and leave you disconsolate.

13 Discipline your son, make heavy his
yoke,
lest his folly humiliate you.

Health of Soul and Body

14† Better a poor man strong and robust,
than a rich man with wasted frame.

15 More precious than gold is health and
well-being,
contentment of spirit than coral.

16 No treasure greater than a healthy body;
no happiness, than a joyful heart!

17*† Preferable is death to a bitter life,
unending sleep to constant illness.

18* Dainties set before one who cannot eat
are like the offerings placed before a
tomb.

19 What good is an offering to an idol
that can neither taste nor smell?

20 So it is with the afflicted man
who groans at the good things his eyes
behold!

21* Do not give in to sadness,
torment not yourself with brooding;

22 Gladness of heart is the very life of man,
cheerfulness prolongs his days.

23* Distract yourself, renew your courage,
drive resentment far away from you;
For worry has brought death to many,
nor is there aught to be gained from
resentment.

24 Envy and anger shorten one's life,
worry brings on premature old age.

25* One who is cheerful and gay while at
table
benefits from his food.

The Proper Attitude toward Riches

31 **1†** Keeping watch over riches wastes the
flesh,
and the care of wealth drives away
rest.

2† Concern for one's livelihood banishes
slumber;
more than a serious illness it disturbs
repose.

3 The rich man labors to pile up wealth,
and his only rest is wanton pleasure;

4 The poor man toils for a meager
subsistence,
and if ever he rests, he finds himself in
want.

5 The lover of gold will not be free from
sin,
for he who pursues wealth is led
astray by it.

---

† among friends, jealousy of enemies, perpetuation and vindication of themselves through their offspring (1-6). Lack of discipline and overindulgence of children bring *sorrow* and disappointment, *terror* and *grief* (7-13).

30, 14-25: Health of mind and body and joy of heart are judged more precious than wealth (14ff); bitterness, *constant illness* and affliction, more difficult to bear than *death* (17-20). *Sadness, resentment,* anxiety, *envy and anger* shorten . . . life; they should be dispelled by *cheerfulness* and *gladness of heart,* which help to prolong one's days (21-25).

30, 17: *Preferable is death . . . constant illness:* the true value of human suffering was revealed through the passion and death of Christ. It serves as reparation for sin, and when united with Christ's suffering, as merit for eternal life.

31, 1-11: Solicitude for acquiring wealth and anxiety over preserving it disturb *repose* and easily lead to sin and ruin (1-7). Cf Mt 6, 25-34. A *rich man* who has not sinned or been seduced by wealth is worthy of praise (8-11).

31, 2: The Hebrew adds a verse that seems out of place here: "A faithful comrade drives away reproach, and the friend who keeps secrets is as dear as life."

✿
12: 7, 23.   21: 38, 20; Prv 12, 25;
17: 41, 2.   15, 13; 17, 22.
18: Tb 4, 17.   23: 38, 18f.
                 25: Prv 15, 15.

6* Many have been ensnared by gold,
    though destruction lay before their
    eyes;

7 It is a stumbling block to those who are
    avid for it,
    a snare for every fool.

8*† Happy the rich man found without fault,
    who turns not aside after gain!

9 Who is he, that we may praise him?
    he, of all his kindred, has done
    wonders,

10 For he has been tested by gold and come
    off safe,
    and this remains his glory;
    He could have sinned but did not,
    could have done evil but would not,

11* So that his possessions are secure,
    and the assembly recounts his praises.

Table Etiquette

12† If you are dining with a great man,
    bring not a greedy gullet to his table,
    Nor cry out, "How much food there is
    here!"

13* Remember that gluttony is evil.
    No creature is greedier than the eye:
    therefore it weeps for any cause.

15 Recognize that your neighbor feels as
    you do,
    and keep in mind your own dislikes:

14 Toward what he eyes, do not put out a
    hand;
    nor reach when he does for the same
    dish.

16 Behave at table like a favored guest,
    and be not greedy, lest you be
    despised.

17* Be the first to stop, as befits good
    manners;
    gorge not yourself, lest you give
    offense.

18 If there are many with you at table,
    be not the first to reach out your hand.

19* Does not a little suffice for a well-bred
    man?
    When he lies down, it is without
    discomfort.

20 Distress and anguish and loss of sleep,
    and restless tossing for the glutton!
    Moderate eating ensures sound slumber
    and a clear mind next day on rising.

21† If perforce you have eaten too much,
    once you have emptied your stomach,
    you will have relief.

22 Listen to me, my son, and scorn me not;
    later you will find my advice good.
    In whatever you do, be moderate,
    and no sickness will befall you.

23* On a man generous with food, blessings
    are invoked,
    and this testimony to his goodness is
    lasting;

24 He who is miserly with food is
    denounced in public,
    and this testimony to his stinginess is
    lasting.

25 Let not wine-drinking be the proof of
    your strength,
    for wine has been the ruin of many.

26 As the furnace probes the work of the
    smith,
    so does wine the hearts of the
    insolent.

27* Wine is very life to man
    if taken in moderation.
    Does he really live who lacks the wine
    which was created for his joy?

28 Joy of heart, good cheer and merriment
    are wine drunk freely at the proper
    time.

29 Headache, bitterness and disgrace
    is wine drunk amid anger and strife.

30 More and more wine is a snare for the
    fool;
    it lessens his strength and multiplies
    his wounds.

31 Rebuke not your neighbor when wine is
    served,
    nor put him to shame while he is
    merry;
    Use no harsh words with him
    and distress him not in the presence of
    others.

32 1 If you are chosen to preside at dinner, be
    not puffed up,
    but with the guests be as one of
    themselves;
    Take care of them first before you sit
    down;

---

† 31, 8ff: The church in her liturgy applies this passage to holy confessors of the Faith.

31, 12—32, 13: A man observing etiquette at table avoids greed and selfishness (31, 12f), is considerate of a neighbor's likes and dislikes and *generous* toward him (14f.23f), observes proper manners (16ff), is *moderate* in *eating* and drinking (19-22.25-30). A good host makes himself one with his guests, is solicitous for them (32, 1f), provides conversation and diversion (3-6), is modest in speech (7f.10), is respectful of elders (9), polite in comportment and grateful to God for his *favors* (11ff).

31, 21: *Emptied your stomach:* the practice of induced vomiting, well-known among pagan Romans, and less well-known among the Jews, seems to be referred to here.

✿
31/6: 8, 2.
8: 5, 1. 10.
13: 37, 28ff; Prv 23, 1f.
11: Prv 29, 14.
17: 37, 29.
19: Eccl 5, 11.
23: Prv 22, 9.
27: Ps 104, 15;
    1 Tm 5, 23.

2 when you have fulfilled your duty,
   then take your place,
To share in their joy
   and win praise for your hospitality.

3 Being older, you may talk; that is only
   your right,
   but temper your wisdom, not to
   disturb the singing.

4 When wine is present, do not pour out
   discourse,
   and flaunt not your wisdom at the
   wrong time.

5 Like a seal of carnelian in a setting of
   gold
   is a concert when wine is served.

6 Like a gold mounting with an emerald
   seal
   is string music with delicious wine.

7* Young man, speak only when necessary,
   when they have asked you more than
   once;

8 Be brief, but say much in those few
   words,
   be like the wise man, taciturn.

9 When among your elders be not
   forward,
   and with officials be not too insistent.

10 Like the lightning that flashes before a
   storm
   is the esteem that shines on modesty.

11 When it is time to leave, tarry not;
   be off for home! There take your ease,

12 And there enjoy doing as you wish,
   but without sin or words of pride.

13 Above all, give praise to your Creator,
   who showers his favors upon you.

The Providence of God

14*† He who would find God must accept
   discipline;
   he who seeks him obtains his request.

15* He who studies the law masters it,
   but the hypocrite finds it a trap.

16* His judgment is sound who fears the
   Lord;
   out of obscurity he draws forth a clear
   plan.

17* The sinner turns aside reproof
   and distorts the law to suit his
   purpose.

18 The thoughtful man will not neglect
   direction;
   the proud and insolent man is
   deterred by nothing.

19* Do nothing without counsel,
   and then you need have no regrets.

20 Go not on a way that is set with snares,
   and let not the same thing trip you
   twice.

21 Be not too sure even of smooth roads,

22 be careful on all your paths.

23 Whatever you do, be on your guard,
   for in this way you will keep the
   commandments.

24 He who keeps the law preserves himself;
   and he who trusts in the Lord shall not
   be put to shame.

33

1* No evil can harm the man who fears the
   Lord;
   through trials, again and again he is
   safe.

2 He who hates the law is without wisdom,
   and is tossed about like a boat in a
   storm.

3† The prudent man trusts in the word of
   the Lord,
   and the law is dependable for him as
   a divine oracle.

4 Prepare your words and you will be
   listened to;
   draw upon your training, and then
   give your answer.

5† Like the wheel of a cart is the mind of a
   fool;
   his thoughts revolve in circles.

6 A fickle friend is like the stallion
   that neighs, no matter who the rider.

7 Why is one day more important than
   another,
   when it is the sun that lights up every
   day?

8* It is due to the Lord's wisdom that they
   differ;
   it is through him the seasons and
   feasts come and go.

9* Some he dignifies and sanctifies,
   and others he lists as ordinary days.

10* So too, all men are of clay,
   for from earth man was formed;

11 Yet with his great knowledge the Lord
   makes men unlike;
   in different paths he has them walk.

---

† 32, 14—33, 4: God is shown to reveal himself through the discipline of his law, a clear and safe plan of life for the pious Jew of old. *Direction* and *counsel* are aids in following it (14ff.18-24; 33, 1.3f). Sinners and hypocrites, hating *the law* or distorting it, fail in wisdom and are devoid of security (32, 15.17f; 33, 2).

33, 3: *Oracle:* as the answer given through the Urim and Thummim to the high priest is true, so the law proves itself true to him who obeys it. Cf Ex 28, 30; Nm 27, 21.

33, 5-15: Contrasts observable in the physical universe as well as in the moral order serve the purposes of divine wisdom (5-9). All creatures are *like clay . . . in the hands of their Creator*—the fool and the wise man, the sinner, and the just (10-15). This does not imply that man is created to be a sinner: God is not the author of wickedness. Cf Jas 1, 13f.

* 32/7ff: 7, 14.   19: 37, 16; Tb 4, 18.
14: 4, 13.   33/1: Ps 91, 10.
15: 2, 16.   8: Gn 1, 14.
16: Ps 37, 6.   9: Ex 20, 11.
17: 21, 6; Prv 12, 1.   10: Gn 2, 7.

¹² Some he blesses and makes great,
    some he sanctifies and draws to
      himself.
Others he curses and brings low,
    and expels them from their place.

¹³✶ Like clay in the hands of a potter,
    to be molded according to his
      pleasure,
So are men in the hands of their Creator,
    to be assigned by him their function.

¹⁴✶ As evil contrasts with good, and death
      with life,
    so are sinners in contrast with the just;

¹⁵ See now all the works of the Most High:
    they come in pairs, the one the
      opposite of the other.

¹⁶† Now I am the last to keep vigil,
    like a gleaner after the vintage;

¹⁷ Since by the Lord's blessing I have made
      progress
    till like a vintager I have filled my
      winepress,

¹⁸ I would inform you that not for myself
    only have I toiled,
    but for every seeker after wisdom.

Property and Servants

¹⁹✶† Listen to me, O leaders of the multitude;
    O rulers of the assembly, give ear!

²⁰ Let neither son nor wife, neither brother
      nor friend,
    have power over you as long as you
      live.

²¹ While breath of life is still in you,
    let no man have dominion over you.
Give not to another your wealth,
    lest then you have to plead with him;

²² Far better that your children plead with
      you
    than that you should look to their
      generosity.

²³ Keep control over all your affairs;
    let no one tarnish your glory.

²⁴ When your few days reach their limit,
    at the time of death distribute your
      inheritance.

²⁵ Fodder and whip and loads for an ass;
    the yoke and harness and the rod of
      his master.

²⁷ Food, correction and work for a slave;
    and for a wicked slave, punishment in
      the stocks.

²⁶✶ Make a slave work and he will look for
      his rest;
    let his hands be idle and he will seek
      to be free.

²⁸ Force him to work that he be not idle,
    for idleness is an apt teacher of
      mischief.

²⁹ Put him to work, for that is what befits
      him;
    if he becomes unruly, load him with
      chains.

³⁰ But never lord it over any human being,
    and do nothing unjust.

³¹✶ If you have but one slave, treat him like
      yourself,
    for you have acquired him with your
      life's blood;

³² If you have but one slave, deal with him
    as a brother,
    for you need him as you need your
      life:

³³ If you mistreat him and he runs away,
    in what direction will you look for
      him?

Trust in the Lord and Not in Dreams

34 ¹† Empty and false are the hopes of the
      senseless,
    and fools are borne aloft by dreams.

² Like a man who catches at shadows or
    chases the wind,
    in the one who believes in dreams.

³ What is seen in dreams is to reality
    what the reflection of a face is to the
      face itself.

⁴✶ Can the unclean produce the clean?
    can the liar ever speak the truth?

⁵ Divination, omens and dreams all are
      unreal;
    what you already expect, the mind
      depicts.

⁶ Unless it be a vision specially sent by the
      Most High,
    fix not your heart on it;

⁷ For dreams have led many astray,
    and those who believed in them have
      perished.

⁸ The law is fulfilled without fail,
    and perfect wisdom is found in the
      mouth of the faithful man.

---

† 33, 16ff: Here the author refers to himself as the most recent of the writers who have endeavored to present true wisdom to their readers.

33, 19-33: Public officials should reject every influence that would restrict their freedom in the management of their affairs. They must make their own household subservient to them rather than be subservient to it (19-24). Slaves are to be given *food* and *work* and *correction* but never to be treated unjustly (25-29). Great care should be taken of good slaves (30-33).

34, 1-17: Confidence placed in *dreams*, divinations and *omens* is false because these are devoid of reality (1-8). True confidence is founded on *knowledge* and *experience* (9-12), and above all on the fear of the Lord, with its accompanying blessings of divine assistance and protection (13-17).

13: Wis 15, 7; Jer 18, 1-6;
    Rom 9, 20f.
14: 42, 25.
19: Wis 6, 1f.
26: Prv 29, 19.
31: 7, 21.
34/4: Jb 14, 4.

9 A man with training gains wide
    knowledge;
    a man of experience speaks sense.
10 One never put to the proof knows little,
    whereas with travel a man adds to his
    resourcefulness.
11 I have seen much in my travels,
    learned more than ever I could say.
12 Often I was in danger of death,
    but by these attainments I was saved.

13 Lively is the courage of those who fear
    the Lord,
    for they put their hope in their savior;
14* He who fears the Lord is never
    alarmed,
    never afraid; for the Lord is his hope.
15 Happy the soul that fears the Lord!
    In whom does he trust, and who is his
    support?
16* The eyes of the Lord are upon those who
    love him;
    he is their mighty shield and strong
    support,
    A shelter from the heat, a shade from the
    noonday sun,
    a guard against stumbling, a help
    against falling.
17 He buoys up the spirits, brings a sparkle
    to the eyes,
    gives health and life and blessing.

True Worship of God

18*† Tainted his gifts who offers in sacrifice
    ill-gotten goods!
    Mock presents from the lawless win
    not God's favor.
19 The Most High approves not the gifts of
    the godless,
    nor for their many sacrifices does he
    forgive their sins.
20 Like the man who slays a son in his
    father's presence
    is he who offers sacrifice from the
    possessions of the poor.
21* The bread of charity is life itself for the
    needy;
    he who withholds it is a man of blood.
22 He slays his neighbor who deprives him
    of his living;
    he sheds blood who denies the laborer
    his wages.

23 If one man builds up and another tears
    down,
    what do they gain but trouble?
24 If one man prays and another curses,
    whose voice will the Lord hear?
25* If a man again touches a corpse after he
    has bathed,
    what did he gain by the
    purification?
26 So with a man who fasts for his sins,
    but then goes and commits them
    again:
    Who will hear his prayer,
    and what has he gained by his
    mortification?

35 1*† To keep the law is a great oblation,
    and he who observes the
    commandments sacrifices a peace
    offering.
2† In works of charity one offers fine flour,
    and when he gives alms he presents
    his sacrifice of praise.
3 To refrain from evil pleases the Lord,
    and to avoid injustice is an atonement.
4* Appear not before the Lord
    empty-handed,
    for all that you offer is in fulfillment of
    the precepts.
5 The just man's offering enriches the altar
    and rises as a sweet odor before the
    Most High.
6 The just man's sacrifice is most pleasing,
    nor will it ever be forgotten.
7* In generous spirit pay homage to the
    Lord,
    be not sparing of freewill gifts.
8* With each contribution show a cheerful
    countenance,
    and pay your tithes in a spirit of joy.
9 Give to the Most High as he has given to
    you,
    generously, according to your means.
10* For the Lord is one who always repays,
    and he will give back to you sevenfold.

---

† 34, 18-26: To be acts of true religion, sacrifice and penance must be accompanied by the proper moral dispositions. To offer to God goods taken from the poor (18-22), or to practice penance without interior reform, is a mockery, worthless in the sight of God (23-26). Cf Mt 15, 4-7; Mk 7, 9-13.

35, 1-24: Keeping *the commandments* of the law and avoiding *injustice* constitute sacrifice pleasing and acceptable to God (1ff). Offerings also should be made to him, cheerfully and *generously;* these he *repays . . . sevenfold* (4-10). Extortion from widows and orphans is injustice, which God quickly repays (11-18). Punishing the *proud* and the *merciless* and coming to the aid of the distressed, he *requites* all *according to* their *deeds* (19-24).

35, 2: *Fine flour,* together with oil and frankincense, was a prescribed offering to God; cf Lv 2, 1ff.

✱
14: Pss 23, 4; 112, 7f;   35/1ff: 1 Sm 15, 22; Ps 51, 18f;
  Prv 3, 23ff; 28, 1.   Is 1, 11-18;
16: Pss 33, 18; 34, 16.   Hos 6, 6; Am 5, 21-24.
18: 35, 11; Prv 21, 27.   4: Ex 23, 15; 34, 20;
21f: Lv 19, 13; Dt 24, 14f;   Dt 16, 16.
  Tb 4, 14.   7: 7, 31.
25: Nm 19, 11f; Prv 26, 11;   8: 2 Cor 9, 7.
  2 Pt 2, 22.   10: Prv 19, 17.

11* But offer no bribes, these he does not
accept!
Trust not in sacrifice of the fruits of
extortion,

12* For he is a God of justice,
who knows no favorites.

13† Though not unduly partial toward the
weak,
yet he hears the cry of the oppressed.

14* He is not deaf to the wail of the orphan,
nor to the widow when she pours out
her complaint;

15 Do not the tears that stream down her
cheek
cry out against him that causes them
to fall?

16* He who serves God willingly is heard;
his petition reaches the heavens.

17 The prayer of the lowly pierces the
clouds;
it does not rest till it reaches its goal,

18 Nor will it withdraw till the Most High
responds,
judges justly and affirms the right.

19* God indeed will not delay,
and like a warrior, will not be still

20 Till he breaks the backs of the merciless
and wreaks vengeance upon the
proud;

21 Till he destroys the haughty root and
branch,
and smashes the scepter of the
wicked;

22 Till he requites mankind according to its
deeds,
and repays men according to their
thoughts;

23 Till he defends the cause of his people,
and gladdens them by his mercy.

24 Welcome is his mercy in time of distress
as rain clouds in time of drought.

A Prayer for God's People

36 1† Come to our aid, O God of the universe,
and put all the nations in dread of you!

2 Raise your hand against the heathen,
that they may realize your power.

3 As you have used us to show them your
holiness,
so now use them to show us your
glory.

4 Thus they will know, as we know,
that there is no God but you.

5 Give new signs and work new wonders;
show forth the splendor of your right
hand and arm;

6* Rouse your anger, pour out wrath,
humble the enemy, scatter the foe.

7 Hasten the day, bring on the time;

9 crush the heads of the hostile rulers.

8 Let raging fire consume the fugitive,
and your people's oppressors meet
destruction.

10 Gather all the tribes of Jacob,
that they may inherit the land as of
old.

11* Show mercy to the people called by your
name;
Israel, whom you named your
first-born.

12* Take pity on your holy city,
Jerusalem, your dwelling place.

13 Fill Zion with your majesty,
your temple with your glory.

14 Give evidence of your deeds of old;
fulfill the prophecies spoken in your
name,

15 Reward those who have hoped in you,
and let your prophets be proved true.

16 Hear the prayer of your servants,
for you are ever gracious to your
people;

17 Thus it will be known to the very ends of
the earth
that you are the eternal God.

Choice of Associates

18† The throat can swallow any food,
yet some foods are more agreeable
than others;

19 As the palate tests meat by its savor,
so does a keen mind insincere words.

20 A deceitful character causes grief,
but an experienced man can turn the
tables on him.

---

† 35, 13: Cf Lv 19, 15.

36, 1-17: Making an act of faith and hope in the supreme
Lord of the universe, the author begs God to continue manifesting his *holiness* and *mercy* through *Israel,* his people (1ff.10-13),
and his *power* and justice through the punishment of the nations
(2.5-9), that all the earth may acknowledge him *the eternal God*
(4.14-17).

36, 18—37, 15: In the choice of wife, friend or associate,
experience is a discerner of character (18-21). *Beauty* and *kindly
speech* make a woman desirable as wife (22f). The good wife
becomes *her husband's richest treasure,* his *helpmate* in establishing his household (24-27). *A true friend* fights for his comrade and shares his spoils with him (37, 5f); a false one deceives
and abandons him in time of need (1-4). A true counselor and
associate should be sought among those who keep the commandments, not among those who break them and seek their own advantage (7-12). In all things *pray to God* for light and follow
conscience (13ff).

❋
11: 34, 18f; Prv 21, 27.
12: Dt 10, 17; 2 Chr 19, 7;
    Jb 34, 19; Wis 6, 7;
    Acts 10, 34; Rom 2, 11;
    Gal 2, 6; 1 Pt 1, 17.
14f: Ex 22, 22.

19: Is 42, 13ff; 2 Pt 3, 9.
36/6: Ps 79, 6.
11: Ex 4, 22.
12: 2 Chr 6, 41;
    Ps 132, 8.14; Is 2, 1ff;
    Mi 4, 1ff.

21 Though any man may be accepted as a
    husband,
      yet one girl will be more suitable than
      another:

22* A woman's beauty makes her husband's
    face light up,
      for it surpasses all else that charms the
      eye;

23 And if, besides, her speech is kindly,
      his lot is beyond that of mortal men.

24* A wife is her husband's richest treasure,
      a helpmate, a steadying column.

25 A vineyard with no hedge will be
    overrun;
      a man with no wife becomes a
      homeless wanderer.

26 Who will trust an armed band
      that shifts from city to city?

27* Or a man who has no nest,
      but lodges where night overtakes him?

37

1* Every friend declares his friendship,
      but there are friends who are friends
      in name only.

2 Is it not a sorrow unto death
      when your bosom companion becomes
      your enemy?

3 "Alas, my companion! Why were you
    created
      to blanket the earth with deceit?"

4 A false friend will share your joys,
      but in time of trouble he stands afar
      off.

5 A true friend will fight with you against
    the foe,
      against your enemies he will be your
      shield-bearer.

6 Forget not your comrade during the
    battle,
      and neglect him not when you
      distribute your spoils.

7 Every counselor points out a way,
      but some counsel ways of their own;

8 Be on the alert when one proffers advice,
      find out first of all what he wants.
    For he may be thinking of himself alone;
      why should the profit fall to him?

9 He may tell you how good your way will
    be,
      and then stand by to watch your
      misfortune.

10 Seek no advice from one who regards
    you with hostility;
      from those who envy you, keep your
      intentions hidden.

11 Speak not to a woman about her rival,
      nor to a coward about war,
      to a merchant about business,
      to a buyer about value,
      to a miser about generosity,
      to a cruel man about mercy,
      to a lazy man about work,
      to a seasonal laborer about the
      harvest,
      to an idle slave about a great task:
      pay no attention to any advice they
      give.

12 Instead, associate with a religious man,
      who you are sure keeps the
      commandments;
    Who is like-minded with yourself
      and will feel for you if you fall.

13 Then, too, heed your own heart's
    counsel;
      for what have you that you can
      depend on more?

14 A man's conscience can tell him his
    situation
      better than seven watchmen in a
      lofty tower.

15 Most important of all, pray to God
      to set your feet in the path of truth.

Wisdom and Temperance

16*† A word is the source of every deed;
      a thought, of every act.

17 The root of all conduct is the mind;
      four branches it shoots forth:

18* Good and evil, death and life,
      their absolute mistress is the tongue.

19 A man may be wise and benefit many,
      yet be of no use to himself.

20 Though a man may be wise, if his words
    are rejected
      he will be deprived of all enjoyment.

21 When a man is wise to his own
    advantage,
      the fruits of his knowledge are seen in
      his own person;

22* When a man is wise to his people's
    advantage,
      the fruits of his knowledge are
      enduring:

23 Limited are the days of one man's life,
      but the life of Israel is days without
      number.

24 One wise for himself has full enjoyment,
      and all who see him praise him;

22: 26, 13ff.   16: 32, 19.
24: Gn 2, 18; Prv 18, 22.   18: Prv 18, 21.
27: Prv 27, 8.   22: 15, 1ff.
37/1: 6, 7ff.

† 37, 16-25: Thoughts determine action. Wisdom is the source
of *good* and *life;* folly, of *evil* and *death* (16ff). If the fruits of a
man's wisdom benefit himself, he may be praised in his own lifetime; if they benefit his people, his praise endures after him, in
their lives (19-25).

25* One wise for his people wins a heritage of glory,
    and his name endures forever.

26† My son, while you are well, govern your appetite
    so that you allow it not what is bad for you;

27* For not every food is good for everyone,
    nor is everything suited to every taste.

28* Be not drawn after every enjoyment,
    neither become a glutton for choice foods,

29 For sickness comes with overeating,
    and gluttony brings on biliousness.

30 Through lack of self-control many have died,
    but the abstemious man prolongs his life.

Sickness and Death

38 1† Hold the physician in honor, for he is essential to you,
    and God it was who established his profession.

2 From God the doctor has his wisdom,
    and the king provides for his sustenance.

3 His knowledge makes the doctor distinguished,
    and gives him access to those in authority.

4 God makes the earth yield healing herbs
    which the prudent man should not neglect;

5* Was not the water sweetened by a twig
    that men might learn his power?

6 He endows men with the knowledge
    to glory in his mighty works,

7 Through which the doctor eases pain
    and the druggist prepares his medicines;

8 Thus God's creative work continues without cease
    in its efficacy on the surface of the earth.

9* My son, when you are ill, delay not,
    but pray to God, who will heal you:

10 Flee wickedness; let your hands be just,
    cleanse your heart of every sin;

11* Offer your sweet-smelling oblation and petition,
    a rich offering according to your means.

12 Then give the doctor his place
    lest he leave; for you need him too.

13 There are times that give him an advantage,

14   and he too beseeches God
That his diagnosis may be correct
    and his treatment bring about a cure.

15 He who is a sinner toward his Maker
    will be defiant toward the doctor.

16*† My son, shed tears for one who is dead
    with wailing and bitter lament;
As is only proper, prepare the body,
    absent not yourself from his burial:

17 Weeping bitterly, mourning fully,
    pay your tribute of sorrow, as he deserves,

18 One or two days, to prevent gossip;
    then compose yourself after your grief,

19* For grief can bring on an extremity
    and heartache destroy one's health.

20* Turn not your thoughts to him again;
    cease to recall him; think rather of the end.

21* Recall him not, for there is no hope of his return;
    it will not help him, but will do you harm.

22* Remember that his fate will also be yours;
    for him it was yesterday, for you today.

23 With the departed dead, let memory fade;
    rally your courage, once the soul has left.

Vocations of the Craftsman and the Scribe

24† The scribe's profession increases his wisdom;
    whoever is free from toil can become a wise man.

25 How can he become learned who guides the plow,
    who thrills in wielding the goad like a lance,

---

* 25: 39, 9; 44, 13f.
27: 1 Cor 6, 12; 10, 23.
28f: 31, 13, 16ff.
38/5: Ex 15, 25.
9: Is 38, 2f.
11: Lv 2, 1ff.

16: 22, 9f.
19: Prv 12, 25; 15, 13; 17, 22.
20: 7, 36; 18, 24; 30, 21.
21: 2 Sm 12, 23; Wis 2, 1.
22: Jas 4, 13ff.

---

† 37, 26-30: Temperance and self-control should govern a man's appetite for food, which is intended not to destroy but to preserve life.

38, 1-15: The profession of medicine comes from *God*, who *makes the earth yield healing herbs* and gives the physician knowledge of their virtue (1-8). In illness the sick man should cleanse his soul from sin and petition God for help through an offering of sacrifice; the physician, too, does well to invoke God that he may understand the illness and apply the proper remedy (9-14). The sinner, in contrast, defies both his Maker and the doctor (15).

38, 16-23: A period of mourning for the deceased and care for their burial is becoming (16ff). But grief should not be excessive, for it neither helps the dead, who cannot return, nor fails to harm the living. The mourner's own end will quickly follow, and the time to prepare for it is now (19-23).

38, 24—39, 11: More excellent than the useful service of

Who guides the ox and urges on the
bullock,
and whose every concern is for cattle?

26 His care is for plowing furrows,
and he keeps a watch on the beasts in
the stalls.

27 So with every engraver and designer
who, laboring night and day,
Fashions carved seals,
and whose concern is to vary the
pattern.
His care is to produce a vivid impression,
and he keeps watch till he finishes his
design.

28 So with the smith standing near his anvil,
forging crude iron.
The heat from the fire sears his flesh,
yet he toils away in the furnace heat.
The clang of the hammer deafens his
ears,
His eyes are fixed on the tool he is
shaping.
His care is to finish his work,
and he keeps watch till he perfects it
in detail.

29 So with the potter sitting at his labor,
revolving the wheel with his feet.
He is always concerned for his products,
and turns them out in quantity.

30 With his hands he molds the clay,
and with his feet softens it.
His care is for proper coloring,
and he keeps watch on the fire of his
kiln.

31 All these men are skilled with their
hands,
each one an expert at his own task;

32 Without them no city could be lived in,
and wherever they stay, they need not
hunger.

33 They do not occupy the judge's bench,
nor are they prominent in the
assembly;
They set forth no decisions or judgments,
nor are they found among the rulers;

34 Yet they maintain God's ancient
handiwork,
and their concern is for exercise of
their skill.

39   1 How different the man who devotes
himself
to the study of the law of the Most
High!
He explores the wisdom of the men of
old

and occupies himself with the
prophecies;

2 He treasures the discourses of famous
men,
and goes to the heart of involved
sayings;

3 He studies obscure parables,
and is busied with the hidden
meanings of the sages.

4 He is in attendance on the great,
and has entrance to the ruler.

5 He travels among the peoples of foreign
lands
to learn what is good and evil among
men.

6 His care is to seek the LORD, his Maker,
to petition the Most High,
To open his lips in prayer,
to ask pardon for his sins.
Then, if it pleases the LORD Almighty,
he will be filled with the spirit of
understanding;
He will pour forth his words of wisdom
and in prayer give thanks to the LORD,

7 Who will direct his knowledge and his
counsel,
as he meditates upon his mysteries.

8 He will show the wisdom of what he has
learned
and glory in the law of the LORD's
covenant.

9* Many will praise his understanding;
his fame can never be effaced;
Unfading will be his memory,
through all generations his name will
live;

10 Peoples will speak of his wisdom,
and in assembly sing his praises.

11 While he lives he is one out of a
thousand,
and when he dies his renown will not
cease.

Praise of God the Creator

12† Once more I will set forth my theme
to shine like the moon in its fullness!

---

† craftsmen—farmer, engraver, smith, potter (25-34)—is the profession of the scribe (24), who studies and meditates on *the law
of the Most High*, seeks him in prayer of thanksgiving, petition
and repentance for sin (39, 1.6f), *explores the wisdom* of the
past and present, travels abroad to observe the conduct of many
peoples, and attends rulers and great men. Through the spirit of
understanding granted by God, he will show forth his wisdom
to the glory of God's law, gaining renown for generations to
come (2-5.8-11).

39, 12-35: The sage invites his disciples to join him in joyfully proclaiming his favorite theme: *The works of God are all
of them good; in its own time every need is supplied* (12-16.32-
35). He describes God's omniscience, supreme power and wisdom, whereby all created things, good in themselves, are ever
present to him, obey him, and fulfill their intended purpose (17-

13 Listen, my faithful children: open up
      your petals,
   like roses planted near running
      waters;
14 Send up the sweet odor of incense,
   break forth in blossoms like the lily.
   Send up the sweet odor of your hymn
      of praise;
   bless the Lord for all he has done!
15 Proclaim the greatness of his name,
   loudly sing his praises,
   With music on the harp and all stringed
      instruments;
   sing out with joy as you proclaim:

16* The works of God are all of them good;
   in its own time every need is
      supplied.
17* At his word the waters become still as in
      a flask;
   he had but to speak and the reservoirs
      were made.
18 He has but to command and his will is
      done;
   nothing can limit his achievement.
19* The works of all mankind are present to
      him;
   not a thing escapes his eye.
20 His gaze spans all the ages;
   to him there is nothing unexpected.
21 No cause then to say: "What is the
      purpose of this?"
   Everything is chosen to satisfy a need.
22 His blessing overflows like the Nile;
   like the Euphrates it enriches the
      surface of the earth.
23* Again, his wrath expels the nations
   and turns fertile land into a salt marsh.
24 For the virtuous his paths are level,
   to the haughty they are steep;
25 Good things for the good he provided
      from the beginning,
   but for the wicked good things and
      bad.
26* Chief of all needs for human life
   are water and fire, iron and salt,
   The heart of the wheat, milk and honey,
      the blood of the grape, and oil, and
      cloth;
27 For the good all these are good,
   but for the wicked they turn out evil.
28 There are storm winds created to punish,
   which in their fury can dislodge
      mountains;

   When destruction must be, they hurl all
      their force
   and appease the anger of their Maker.
29 In his treasury also, kept for the proper
      time,
   are fire and hail, famine, disease,
30 Ravenous beasts, scorpions, vipers,
   and the avenging sword to
      exterminate the wicked;
31 In doing his bidding they rejoice,
   in their assignments they disobey not
      his command.
32 So from the first I took my stand,
   and wrote down as my theme:
33* The works of God are all of them good;
   every need when it comes he fills.
34 No cause then to say: "This is not as good
      as that":
   for each shows its worth at the proper
      time.
35 So now with full joy of heart proclaim
   and bless the name of the Holy One.

Joys and Miseries of Life

40 1*† A great anxiety has God allotted,
      and a heavy yoke, to the sons of men;
   From the day one leaves his mother's
      womb
   to the day he returns to the mother of
      all the living,
2 His thoughts, the fear in his heart,
   and his troubled forebodings till the
      day he dies—
3 Whether he sits on a lofty throne
   or grovels in dust and ashes,
4 Whether he bears a splendid crown
   or is wrapped in the coarsest of
      cloaks—
5 Are of wrath and envy, trouble and
      dread,
   terror of death, fury and strife.
   Even when he lies on his bed to rest,
      his cares at night disturb his sleep.
6 So short is his rest it seems like none,
   till in his dreams he struggles as he did
      by day,
   Terrified by what his mind's eye sees,
      like a fugitive being pursued;

---

† 21), bringing blessing to the virtuous, but evil and punishment
to the wicked who misuse them (22-31). Cf similar hymns of
praise, 36, 1-17; 42, 15—43, 35.

   40, 1-16: The former idyllic description of the universe is contrasted with the picture of the evils afflicting humanity. Every
man, high or low, is burdened from birth to death with fears,
anxieties and troubles, by day and often by night, the time appointed for rest (1-7). For sinners, the suffering is much greater
(8ff). What they gained by violence and injustice is quickly
destroyed; but *justice endures forever* (14ff).

   40, 1: *Mother of all the living:* the earth from which man
was taken. Cf Gn 2, 7; 3, 19f; Jb 1, 21; Ps 139, 15.

---

*
   16: Gn 1, 31; Eccl 3, 11.   26: 29, 21.
   17: Gn 1, 6-10; Ex 14, 21f;   33: 39, 16; Gn 1, 31;
       Jos 3, 16.   Eccl 3, 11.
   19: 15, 19; 42, 20.   40/1: Gn 3, 17; Jb 7, 1; 14, 1;
   23: Jos 1, 2-6.   Eccl 2, 23.

7 As he reaches safety, he wakes up
    astonished that there was nothing to
    fear.

8 So it is with all flesh, with man and with
    beast,
    but for sinners seven times more.

9* Plague and bloodshed, wrath and the
    sword,
    plunder and ruin, famine and death:

10 For the wicked, these were created evil,
    and it is they who bring on
    destruction.

11† All that is of earth returns to earth,
    and what is from above returns above.

12 All that comes from bribes or injustice
    will be wiped out,
    but loyalty remains for ages.

13 Wealth out of wickedness is like a wadi
    in spate:
    like a mighty stream with lightning
    and thunder,

14* Which, in its rising, rolls along the
    stones,
    but suddenly, once and for all, comes
    to an end.

15 The offshoot of violence will not flourish,
    for the root of the godless is on sheer
    rock;

16 Or they are like reeds on the riverbank,
    withered before all other plants;

17† But goodness will never be cut off,
    and justice endures forever.

Wealth or wages can make life sweet,
    but better than either is finding a
    treasure.

18* A child or a city will preserve one's name,
    but better than either, attaining
    wisdom.

19 Sheepfolds and orchards bring
    flourishing health;
    but better than either, a devoted wife;

20* Wine and music delight the soul,
    but better than either, conjugal love.

21 The flute and the harp offer sweet
    melody,
    but better than either, a voice that is
    true.

22* Charm and beauty delight the eye,
    but better than either, the flowers of
    the field.

23 A friend, a neighbor, are timely guides,
    but better than either, a prudent wife.

24 A brother, a helper, for times of stress;
    but better than either, charity that
    rescues.

25 Gold and silver make one's way secure,
    but better than either, sound
    judgment.

26 Wealth and vigor build up confidence,
    but better than either, fear of God.
Fear of the LORD leaves nothing
    wanting;
    he who has it need seek no other
    support:

27* The fear of God is a paradise of
    blessings;
    its canopy, all that is glorious.

28† My son, live not the life of a beggar,
    better to die than to beg;

29* When one has to look to another's table,
    his life is not really a life.
His neighbor's delicacies bring revulsion
    of spirit
    to one who understands inward
    feelings:

30 In the mouth of the shameless man
    begging is sweet,
    but within him it burns like fire.

41 1† O death! how bitter the thought of you
    for the man at peace amid his
    possessions,
For the man unruffled and always
    successful,
    who still can enjoy life's pleasures.

2* O death! how welcome your sentence
    to the weak man of failing strength,
Tottering and always rebuffed,
    with no more sight, with vanished
    hope.

3* Fear not death's decree for you;
    remember, it embraces those before
    you, and those after.

4 Thus God has ordained for all flesh;
    why then should you reject the will of
    the Most High?

---

† 40, 11: *All that is of earth . . . returns above:* a reference to bodily mortality and to the divine origin of life from the Spirit of God. Cf 41, 10; Gn 2, 7; 3, 19; Jb 34, 14f; Pss 104, 29f; 146, 4; Eccl 12, 7. The Greek and the Latin render the second half of the verse: "all waters shall return to the sea."

40, 17-27: Of the many treasures making life sweet, such as *health,* children, friends, *music, vigor,* the best are called true *conjugal love, wisdom,* and, above all, *fear of God;* cf 25, 6-11.

40, 28ff: Among the Jews, beggary was considered degrading to human dignity; it was agreeable only to the shameless, who had lost their sense of honor. Cf 29, 22f.

41, 1-13: Whether *death* seems *bitter* to one who enjoys *peace,* success and pleasure, or welcome to one who is weak and in despair, it comes to all and must be accepted as the will of God (1-4). As the human body passes away (11), so do those who have sinned through the body and their offspring alike, who, needy and accursed, pass on with their parents as if they had never been (5-10). Only the good name of the virtuous endures (11ff).

* 9: 39, 28ff.
14: 23, 25; Wis 4, 3ff.
18: Prv 19, 14.
20: Ps 104, 15.
22: Mt 6, 28f.
27: Is 4, 5.
29: 29, 24.
41/2: 30, 17.
3: 38, 20ff.

Whether one has lived a thousand years,
　a hundred, or ten,
　　in the nether world he has no claim on
　　　life.

5 A reprobate line are the children of
　　sinners,
　and witless offspring are in the homes
　　of the wicked.

6 Their dominion is lost to sinners'
　　children,
　and reproach abides with their
　　descendants.

7 Children curse their wicked father,
　for they suffer disgrace through him.

8 Woe to you, O sinful men,
　who forsake the law of the Most High.

9 If you have children, calamity will seize
　　them;
　you will beget them only for groaning.
When you stumble, there is lasting joy;
　at death, you become a curse.

10 Whatever is of nought returns to nought,
　so too the godless from void to void.

11 Man's body is a fleeting thing,
　but a virtuous name will never be
　　annihilated.

12 Have a care for your name, for it will
　　stand by you
　better than precious treasures in the
　　thousands;

13 The boon of life is for limited days,
　but a good name, for days without
　　number.

True and False Shame

14 My children, heed my instruction about
　　shame;
　judge of disgrace only according to
　　my rules,
For it is not always well to be ashamed,
　nor is it always the proper thing to
　　blush:

15 Before father and mother be ashamed of
　　immorality,
　before master and mistress, of
　　falsehood;

16 Before prince and ruler, of flattery;
　before the public assembly, of crime;

17 Before friend and companion, of
　　disloyalty,
　and of breaking an oath or agreement.

18 Be ashamed of theft from the people
　　where you settle,
　and of stretching out your elbow
　　when you dine;

19 Of refusing to give when asked,
　of defrauding another of his
　　appointed share,

20 Of failing to return a greeting,
　and of rebuffing a friend;

21 Of gazing at a married woman,
　and of entertaining thoughts about
　　another's wife;
Of trifling with a servant girl you have,
　and of violating her couch;

22 Of using harsh words with friends,
　and of following up your gifts with
　　insults;

23 Of repeating what you hear,
　and of betraying secrets—

24 These are the things you should rightly
　　avoid as shameful
　if you would be looked upon by
　　everyone with favor.

42 1 But of these things be not ashamed,
　lest you sin through human respect:

2 Of the law of the Most High and his
　　precepts,
　or of the sentence to be passed upon
　　the sinful;

3 Of sharing the expenses of a business or
　　a journey,
　or of dividing an inheritance or
　　property;

4 Of accuracy of scales and balances,
　or of tested measures and weights;

5 Of acquiring much or little,
　or of bargaining in dealing with a
　　merchant;
Of constant training of children,
　or of beating the sides of a disloyal
　　servant;

6 Of a seal to keep an erring wife at home,
　or of a lock placed where there are
　　many hands;

7 Of numbering every deposit,
　or of recording all that is given or
　　received;

8 Of chastisement of the silly and the
　　foolish,
　or of the aged and infirm answering
　　for wanton conduct.
Thus you will be truly cautious
　and recognized by all men as discreet.

A Father's Care for His Daughter

9 A daughter is a treasure that keeps her
　　father wakeful,
　and worry over her drives away rest:

5ff: 3, 9ff; Wis 3, 16-19.
10: 40, 11; Wis 4, 19.
11: Prv 10, 7.
12: Prv 22, 1; Eccl 7, 1.
21: 9, 8; Mt 5, 28.
22: 18, 14; 20, 13.
23: 27, 16.
42/1: Prv 24, 23; Jas 2, 1.
4: Prv 11, 1.
5: 30, 1-13; 33, 25-33.
9: 7, 24f.

41, 13: After this verse many texts repeat 20, 29f.
41, 14—42, 8: The author illustrates the subject of true and false shame with numerous and detailed examples of sin (14-24) and virtue (41, 1-8), following the norm of the commandments.
42, 9-14: The author considers a daughter to be a source of

Lest she pass her prime unmarried,
  or when she is married, lest she be
    disliked;
10 While unmarried, lest she be seduced,
  or, as a wife, lest she prove unfaithful;
Lest she conceive in her father's home,
  or be sterile in that of her husband.
11* Keep a close watch on your daughter,
  lest she make you the sport of your
    enemies,
A byword in the city, a reproach among
  the people,
  an object of derision in public
    gatherings.
See that there is no lattice in her room,
  no place that overlooks the
    approaches to the house.
12* Let her not parade her charms before
  men,
  or spend her time with married
    women;
13 For just as moths come from garments,
  so harm to women comes from
    women:
14 Better a man's harshness than a woman's
  indulgence,
  and a frightened daughter than any
    disgrace.

The Works of God in Nature

15*† Now will I recall God's works;
  what I have seen, I will describe.
At God's word were his works brought
  into being;
  they do his will as he has ordained for
    them.
16 As the rising sun is clear to all,
  so the glory of the Lord fills all his
    works;
17 Yet even God's holy ones must fail
  in recounting the wonders of the
    Lord,
Though God has given these, his hosts,
  the strength
  to stand firm before his glory.
18 He plumbs the depths and penetrates
  the heart;
  their innermost being he understands.
The Most High possesses all knowledge,
  and sees from of old the things that are
    to come:
19 He makes known the past and the future,
  and reveals the deepest secrets.
20* No understanding does he lack;
  no single thing escapes him.

21 Perennial is his almighty wisdom;
  he is from all eternity one and the
    same,
22* With nothing added, nothing taken
  away;
  no need of a counselor for him!
23 How beautiful are all his works,
  even to the spark and the fleeting
    vision!
24 The universe lives and abides forever;
  to meet each need, each creature is
    preserved.
25* All of them differ, one from another,
  yet none of them has he made in vain,
For each in turn, as it comes, is good;
  can one ever see enough of their
    splendor?

43 1* The clear vault of the sky shines forth
  like heaven itself, a vision of glory.
2 The orb of the sun, resplendent at its
  rising:
  what a wonderful work of the Most
    High!
3 At noon it seethes the surface of the
  earth,
  and who can bear its fiery heat?
4 Like a blazing furnace of solid metal,
  it sets the mountains aflame with its
    rays;
By its fiery darts the land is consumed;
  the eyes are dazzled by its light.
5 Great indeed is the Lord who made it,
  at whose orders it urges on its steeds.
6* The moon, too, that marks the changing
  times,
  governing the seasons, their lasting
    sign,
7 By which we know the feast days and
  fixed dates,
  this light-giver which wanes in its
    course:
8 As its name says, each month it renews
  itself;
  how wondrous in this change!
9* The beauty, the glory, of the heavens are
  the stars
  that adorn with their sparkling the
    heights of God,

---

† anxiety to her father, lest she fail to marry, or *be seduced,* or lest, marrying, she *be disliked, prove unfaithful,* or find herself *sterile* (9f). He is advised to *keep a close watch* on her at home, and on her companionship while abroad, lest he suffer on her account among the people (11-14).

42, 15—43, 35: These verses comprise a new section. In them the author contemplates God's power, beauty and goodness as manifested in the mighty work of creating and preserving the universe (42, 15ff.23.25; 43, 1-27), his omniscience (42, 18ff), his perfect wisdom (21f), his eternity (24). The conclusion is a fervent hymn of praise (43, 28-35). Cf 16, 22—18, 13.

11: 26, 10.
12f: 9, 1-9.
15: Ps 77, 12f.
20: 39, 19; Wis 1, 6-10.
22: Is 40, 13; Rom 11, 34.
25: 33, 15.
43/1ff: Ps 19, 2f.
6: Lv 23, 5; Nm 28, 11-14; Ps 81, 4.
9: Ps 8, 4.

10 At whose command they keep their
        place
      and never relax in their vigils.
    A weapon against the flood waters stored
        on high,
      lighting up the firmament by its
        brilliance,

11* Behold the rainbow! Then bless its
        Maker,
      for majestic indeed is its splendor;

12 It spans the heavens with its glory,
      this bow bent by the mighty hand of
        God.

13 His rebuke marks out the path for the
        lightning,
      and speeds the arrows of his judgment
        to their goal.

14 At it, the storehouse is opened,
      and like vultures the clouds hurry
        forth.

15 In his majesty he gives the storm its
        power
      and breaks off the hailstones.

16 The thunder of his voice makes the earth
        writhe;
      before his might the mountains quake.

17 A word from him drives on the south
        wind,
      the angry north wind, the hurricane
        and the storm.

18 He sprinkles the snow like fluttering
        birds;
      it comes to settle like swarms of
        locusts.

19 Its shining whiteness blinds the eyes,
      the mind is baffled by its steady fall.

20 He scatters frost like so much salt;
      it shines like blossoms on the
        thornbush.

21 Cold northern blasts he sends
      that turn the ponds to lumps of ice.
    He freezes over every body of water,
      and clothes each pool with a coat of
        mail.

22 When the mountain growth is scorched
        with heat,
      and the flowering plains as though by
        flames,

23 The dripping clouds restore them all,
      and the scattered dew enriches the
        parched land.

24 His is the plan that calms the deep,
      and plants the islands in the sea.

25* Those who go down to the sea tell part
        of its story,
      and when we hear them we are
        thunderstruck;

26 In it are his creatures, stupendous,
        amazing,
      all kinds of life, and the monsters of
        the deep.

27* For him each messenger succeeds,
      and at his bidding accomplishes his
        will.

28† More than this we need not add;
      let the last word be, he is all in all!

29 Let us praise him the more, since we
        cannot fathom him,
      for greater is he than all his works;

30 Awful indeed is the LORD's majesty,
      and wonderful is his power.

31 Lift up your voices to glorify the LORD,
      though he is still beyond your power
        to praise;

32 Extol him with renewed strength,
      and weary not, though you cannot
        reach the end:

33* For who can see him and describe him?
      or who can praise him as he is?

34 Beyond these, many things lie hid;
      only a few of his works have we seen.

35* It is the LORD who has made all things,
      and to those who fear him he gives
        wisdom.

Praise of Israel's Great Ancestors

44 1† Now will I praise those godly men,
        our ancestors, each in his own time:

2*   The abounding glory of the Most High's
        portion,
      his own part, since the days of old.
    Subduers of the land in kingly fashion,
      men of renown for their might,

3*   Or counselors in their prudence,
      or seers of all things in prophecy;

4   Resolute princes of the folk,
      and governors with their staves;

---

† 43, 28: *All in all:* the perfections reflected in creation are
found in a transcendent way in God, who alone is their source.

44, 1—50, 24: As in the previous section God's wisdom shone
forth in the works of nature, so in these chapters it is also revealed through the history of God's people as seen in the lives of
their patriarchs, prophets, priests and rulers. The example of
these great men, whose virtues are here recalled, constitutes a
high point of the author's teaching and illustrates his belief in
the canonical Scriptures.

44, 1-15: The reader is here introduced to those men of Israel,
later mentioned by name, who through various achievements
and beneficial social activities have acquired great renown (1-
8.14f); and also to those who, though forgotten, endure through
the fruit of their *virtues* and through their families because of
God's covenant with them (9-13).

---

*
    11: Gn 9, 13.   35: Jb 28, 28.
    25: Ps 104, 25-30.   44/2: Dt 32, 8f.
    27: Ps 33, 6.   3: 39, 1.
    33: Ps 106, 2.

Authors skilled in composition,
and forgers of epigrams with their
spikes;

5 Composers of melodious psalms,
or discoursers on lyric themes;

6 Stalwart men, solidly established
and at peace in their own estates—

7 All these were glorious in their time,
each illustrious in his day.

8 Some of them have left behind a name
and men recount their praiseworthy
deeds;

9 But of others there is no memory,
for when they ceased, they ceased.
And they are as though they had not
lived,
they and their children after them.

10 Yet these also were godly men
whose virtues have not been
forgotten;

11 Their wealth remains in their families,
their heritage with their descendants;

12 Through God's covenant with them their
family endures,
their posterity, for their sake.

13 And for all time their progeny will
endure,
their glory will never be blotted out;

14* Their bodies are peacefully laid away,
but their name lives on and on.

15 At gatherings their wisdom is retold,
and the assembly proclaims their
praise.

The Early Patriarchs

16*† [ENOCH walked with the LORD and was
taken up,
that succeeding generations might
learn by his example.]

17* NOAH, found just and perfect,
renewed the race in the time of
devastation.
Because of his worth there were
survivors,
and with a sign to him the deluge
ended;

18 A lasting agreement was made with him,
that never should all flesh be
destroyed.

19* ABRAHAM, father of many peoples,
kept his glory without stain:

20*† He observed the precepts of the Most
High,
and entered into an agreement with
him;
In his own flesh he incised the ordinance,
and when tested he was found loyal.

21† For this reason, God promised him with
an oath
that in his descendants the nations
would be blessed,
That he would make him numerous as
the grains of dust,
and exalt his posterity like the stars;
That he would give them an inheritance
from sea to sea,
and from the River to the ends of the
earth.

22* And for ISAAC he renewed the same
promise
because of Abraham, his father.
The covenant with all his forebears was
confirmed,
and the blessing rested upon the head
of JACOB.

23 God acknowledged him as the first-born,
and gave him his inheritance.
He fixed the boundaries for his tribes,
and their division into twelve.

Praise of Moses, Aaron and Phinehas

45 1*† From him was to spring the man
who won the favor of all:
Dear to God and men,
MOSES, whose memory is held in
benediction.

2*† God's honor devolved upon him,
and the Lord strengthened him with
fearful powers;

3* God wrought swift miracles at his words
and sustained him in the king's
presence.

---

† 44, 16: *Enoch:* because of his friendship with God and also by reason of his unusual disappearance from the earth, this prophet's renown was great among the chosen people, particularly in the two centuries just before the coming of Christ; cf Gn 5, 21-24; Heb 11, 5. The present verse is an expansion of the original text; cf 49, 14.

44, 20: *In his own flesh . . . ordinance:* the covenant of circumcision; cf Gn 17, 10-14. *And when tested . . . loyal:* Abraham's willingness to sacrifice his son Isaac at the Lord's command; cf Gn 22, 9-12.

44, 21: *The River:* the Euphrates; cf Gn 2, 14.

45, 1-5: *Moses* manifested God's power through miracles (1ff), God's authority through the promulgation of the commandments and the law (5), and God's mercy through the intimacy granted him by the Lord for his own faithfulness and meekness (4f). The very personification of the old covenant, Moses was also a type of Christ, the Prophet and Legislator of the new; cf Dt 18, 15.

45, 2: *God's honor devolved upon him:* Moses was actually God's substitute in dealing with Pharaoh, hence God entrusted his own honor to Moses.

---

* 14: Wis 3, 3.
16: 49, 14; Gn 5, 18-24;
    Heb 11, 5.
17: Gn 6, 8-9, 29;
    Heb 11, 7.
19: Gn 12, 1-25, 10;
    Gal 3, 6; Heb 11, 8-19.
20: Gn 17, 10; 22, 1.

22: Gn 26, 3. 5. 24;
    27, 28f; 28, 14.
45/1: Ex 2, 2; 11, 3; 33, 11;
    Nm 12, 7.
2: Ex 7, 1-13, 22.
2-5: Ex 7—Dt 34.
3: Ex 4, 17; 7, 1.

He gave him the commandments for his people,
and revealed to him his glory.

4 For his trustworthiness and meekness
God selected him from all mankind;

5 He permitted him to hear his voice,
and led him into the cloud,
Where, face to face, he gave him the commandments,
the law of life and understanding,
That he might teach his precepts to Jacob,
his judgments and decrees to Israel.

6 He raised up also, like Moses in holiness,
his brother AARON, of the tribe of Levi.

7 He made him perpetual in his office
when he bestowed on him the priesthood of his people;
He established him in honor
and crowned him with lofty majesty;

8 He clothed him with splendid apparel,
and adorned him with the glorious vestments:
Breeches and tunic and robe
with pomegranates around the hem,

9 And a rustle of bells round about,
through whose pleasing sound at each step
He would be heard within the sanctuary,
and the children of his race would be remembered;

10 The sacred vestments of gold, of violet,
and of crimson, wrought with embroidery;
The breastpiece for decision, the ephod and cincture

11 with scarlet yarn, the work of the weaver;
Precious stones with seal engravings
in golden settings, the work of the jeweler,
To commemorate in incised letters
each of the tribes of Israel;

12 On his turban the diadem of gold,
its plate wrought with the insignia of holiness,
Majestic, glorious, renowned for splendor,
a delight to the eyes, beauty supreme.

13 Before him, no one was adorned with these,
nor may they ever be worn by any
Except his sons and them alone,
generation after generation, for all time.

14 His cereal offering is wholly burnt
with the established sacrifice twice each day;

15 For Moses ordained him
and anointed him with the holy oil,
In a lasting covenant with him
and with his family, as permanent as the heavens,
That he should serve God in his priesthood
and bless his people in his name.

16 He chose him from all mankind
to offer holocausts and choice offerings,
To burn sacrifices of sweet odor for a memorial,
and to atone for the people of Israel.

17 He gave to him his laws,
and authority to prescribe and to judge:
To teach the precepts to his people,
and the ritual to the descendants of Israel.

18 Men of other families were inflamed against him,
were jealous of him in the desert,
The followers of Dathan and Abiram,
and the band of Korah in their defiance.

19 But the LORD saw this and became angry,
he destroyed them in his burning wrath.
He brought down upon them a miracle,
and consumed them with his flaming fire.

20 Then he increased the glory of Aaron
and bestowed upon him his inheritance:
The sacred offerings he allotted to him,
with the showbread as his portion;

21 The oblations of the LORD are his food,
a gift to him and his descendants.

22 But he holds no land among the people
nor shares with them their heritage;
For the LORD himself is his portion,
his inheritance in the midst of Israel.

45, 5: *Face to face:* on God's intimacy with Moses, see Ex 33, 11; Nm 12, 8. St. Paul alluded to this in 1 Cor 13, 12.

45, 6-21: The author here expresses his reverence and esteem for the priesthood of the old covenant. He recalls God's choice of *Aaron* and his sons for this sublime office (6f), and describes in detail the beauty of the high priest's vestments (8-13). He relates the ordination of Aaron at the hands of Moses, his brother (15), and describes the priestly functions, of offering sacrifice to God (16), and of blessing (15), teaching, governing and judging the people (17); the *inheritance* of the high priest (20ff); the punishment of those *families* who were *jealous* of Aaron (18f); and the confirmation of the covenant of the priesthood with Aaron's descendants through *Phinehas* (23ff).

45, 7: The *priesthood* of Aaron was superseded by the priesthood of Christ; cf Heb 7, 18-28.

4: Nm 12, 3, 7.   18: Nm 16, 1ff.
6ff: Ex 28f; Wis 18, 24.   20f: Nm 18, 11-21; Dt 10, 9.

23 PHINEHAS too, the son of Eleazar,
was the courageous third of his line
When, zealous for the God of all,
he met the crisis of his people
And, at the prompting of his noble heart,
atoned for the children of Israel.

24 Therefore on him again God conferred
the right,
in a covenant of friendship, to provide
for the sanctuary,
So that he and his descendants
should possess the high priesthood
forever.

25 For even his covenant with David,
the son of Jesse of the tribe of Judah,
Was an individual heritage through one
son alone;
but the heritage of Aaron is for all his
descendants.

26 And now bless the LORD
who has crowned you with glory!
May he grant you wisdom of heart
to govern his people in justice,
Lest their welfare should ever be
forgotten,
or your authority, throughout all time.

Joshua, Caleb and the Judges

46 **1** Valiant leader was JOSHUA, son of Nun,
assistant to Moses in the prophetic
office,
Formed to be, as his name implies,
the great savior of God's chosen ones,
To punish the enemy
and to win the inheritance for Israel.

2 What glory was his when he raised his
arm,
to brandish his javelin against the city!

3 And who could withstand him
when he fought the battles of the
LORD?

4 Did he not by his power stop the sun,
so that one day became two?

5 He called upon the Most High God
when his enemies beset him on all
sides,
And God Most High gave answer to him
in hailstones of tremendous power,

6 Which he rained down upon the hostile
army
till on the slope he destroyed the foe;
That all the doomed nations might know
that the LORD was watching over his
people's battles.

And because he was a devoted follower
of God

7 and in Moses' lifetime showed himself
loyal,
He and CALEB, son of Jephunneh,
when they opposed the rebel
assembly,
Averted God's anger from the people
and suppressed the wicked
complaint—

8 Because of this, they were the only two
spared
from the six hundred thousand
infantry,
To lead the people into their inheritance,
the land flowing with milk and honey.

9 And the strength he gave to Caleb
remained with him even in his old age
Till he won his way onto the summits of
the land;
his family too received an inheritance,

10 That all the people of Jacob might know
how good it is to be a devoted follower
of the LORD.

11 The JUDGES, too, each one of them,
whose hearts were not deceived,
Who did not abandon God:
may their memory be ever blessed,

12 Their bones return to life from their
resting place,
and their names receive fresh luster in
their children!

13 Beloved of his people, dear to his Maker,
dedicated from his mother's womb,
Consecrated to the LORD as a prophet,
was SAMUEL, the judge and priest.
At God's word he established the
kingdom
and anointed princes to rule the
people.

---

† 46, 1-6: *Joshua,* whose name means "the Lord is savior" (1), was the instrument through which God delivered his people in miraculous ways (2-6) by destroying their enemies, whose land he gave to the Israelites as an *inheritance* (1).

46, 3: *The battles of the Lord:* cf Jos 6—10.

46, 7-10: *Caleb,* who with Joshua advised Moses and the people in the desert to conquer Canaan, despite the counsel of their companion scouts and the rebellion of the people, merited to lead the Israelites of the succeeding generation into the Promised Land. Caleb in his old age received as his inheritance a portion of land which he himself had previously conquered; cf Jos 15, 13f.

46, 11-20: Of the *Judges* praised and blessed for their fidelity to God in opposing idolatry, *Samuel,* a man of spotless integrity, was the greatest (11f.19). He was judge of the entire nation, and was also a prophet and priest who through his sacrificial offering obtained victory over the Philistines. He established the kingdom, anointed kings (13-18), and even after his death foretold the king's fate and *put an end to wickedness* (20).

✿
23: Nm 25, 7-13;
    Ps 106, 30f;
    1 Mc 2, 26.54.
25: 2 Sm 7, 12-16.
46/1: Ex 17, 9; Nm 27, 18;
    Dt 34, 9; Jos 1, 1-4.
  2: Jos 8, 18.

4: Jos 10, 13.
7: Nm 13, 30; 14, 6.
8: Nm 14, 22-38.
9: Jos 14, 6; 15, 13.
11: Jgs 1, 1—16, 31.
13: 1 Sm 1, 10ff; 8, 4ff;
    10, 1; 16, 13.

14 By the law of the LORD he judged the
nation,
when he visited the encampments of
Jacob.
15 As a trustworthy prophet he was sought
out
and his words proved him true as a
seer.
16* He, too, called upon God,
and offered him a suckling lamb;
17* Then the LORD thundered forth from
heaven,
and the tremendous roar of his voice
was heard.
18 He brought low the rulers of the enemy
and destroyed all the lords of the
Philistines.
19* When Samuel approached the end of his
life,
he testified before the LORD and his
anointed prince,
"No bribe or secret gift have I taken from
any man!"
and no one dared gainsay him.
20* Even when he lay buried, his guidance
was sought;
he made known to the king his fate,
And from the grave he raised his voice
as a prophet, to put an end to
wickedness.

Nathan, David and Solomon

47 **1*†** After him came NATHAN
who served in the presence of David.
2* Like the choice fat of the sacred
offerings,
so was DAVID in Israel.
3* He made sport of lions as though they
were kids,
and of bears, like lambs of the flock.
4* As a youth he slew the giant
and wiped out the people's disgrace,
When his hand let fly the slingstone
that crushed the pride of Goliath.
5 Since he called upon the Most High God,
who gave strength to his right arm
To defeat the skilled warrior
and raise up the might of his people,
6* Therefore the women sang his praises
and ascribed to him tens of thousands.
When he assumed the royal crown, he
battled

7* and subdued the enemy on every side.
He destroyed the hostile Philistines
and shattered their power till our own
day.
8 With his every deed he offered thanks
to God Most High, in words of praise.
With his whole being he loved his Maker
and daily had his praises sung;
9* He added beauty to the feasts
and solemnized the seasons of each
year
With string music before the altar,
providing sweet melody for the psalms
10 So that when the Holy Name was
praised,
before daybreak the sanctuary would
resound.
11* The LORD forgave him his sins
and exalted his strength forever;
He conferred on him the rights of royalty
and established his throne in Israel.
12*† Because of his merits he had as his
successor
a wise son, who lived in security:
13* SOLOMON reigned during an era of peace,
for God made tranquil all his borders.
He built a house to the name of God,
and established a lasting sanctuary.
14* How wise you were when you were
young,
overflowing with instruction, like the
Nile in flood!
15 Your understanding covered the whole
earth,
and, like a sea, filled it with
knowledge.
16 Your fame reached distant coasts,
and their peoples came to hear you;
17 With song and story and riddle,
and with your answers, you astounded
the nations.

† 47, 1-11: *David*, a youthful and fearless warrior, the favorite of all Israel, by defeating *Goliath*, the boastful Philistine giant, removed *the people's disgrace* and greatly strengthened their power (1-7). *With his whole being he loved* and praised God, and his devotion to divine worship led him to develop liturgical cult. David fell into sin, but repenting, received pardon from God and the promise of an everlasting kingdom (8-11).
47, 12-24: *Solomon*, son and successor of David, inherited peace through his father's conquests. He built the magnificent temple of Jerusalem (12f) and received from God the favor of unparalleled wisdom, through which he obtained great fame (14-17). Luxury and sensuality, however, brought disgrace upon him, and because of his oppressive burdens, he disposed the kingdom for division after his death (19-21.23f). Nevertheless God did not withdraw his promise of establishing his throne in the descendants of David (22).

16: 1 Sm 7, 9.
17: 12, 18.
19: 1 Sm 12, 3.
20: 1 Sm 28, 14.
47/1: 2 Sm 7, 2.
2: 1 Sm 16, 11.
3: 1 Sm 17, 35.
4: 1 Sm 17, 49.
6: 1 Sm 18, 7.
7: 2 Sm 5, 6-25.
9: 1 Chr 16, 4ff; 23, 2ff; 25, 1-7.
11: 2 Sm 12, 13; 7, 12-16.
12: 1 Kgs 2, 12.
13: 1 Kgs 5, 1.5.
14-18: 1 Kgs 5, 9-14; 10, 14-28.

18† You were called by that glorious name
which was conferred upon Israel.
Gold you gathered like so much iron,
you heaped up silver as though it were
lead;

19* But you abandoned yourself to women
and gave them dominion over your
body.

20 You brought dishonor upon your
reputation,
shame upon your marriage,
Wrath upon your descendants,
and groaning upon your domain;

21* Thus two governments came into being,
when in Ephraim kingship was
usurped.

22* But God does not withdraw his mercy,
nor permit even one of his promises to
fail.
He does not uproot the posterity of his
chosen one,
nor destroy the offspring of his friend.
So he gave to Jacob a remnant,
to David a root from his own family.

23*† Solomon finally slept with his fathers,
and left behind him one of his sons,
Expansive in folly, limited in sense,
Rehoboam, who by his policy made
the people rebel;
Until one arose who should not be
remembered,
the sinner who led Israel into sin,
Who brought ruin to Ephraim

24 and caused them to be exiled from
their land.

Elijah and Elisha

25† Their sinfulness grew more and more,
and they lent themselves to every evil,

48

1* Till like a fire there appeared the
prophet
whose words were as a flaming
furnace.

2 Their staff of bread he shattered,
in his zeal he reduced them to straits;

3* By God's word he shut up the heavens
and three times brought down fire.

4 How awesome are you, Elijah!
Whose glory is equal to yours?

5* You brought a dead man back to life
from the nether world, by the will of
the Lord.

6* You sent kings down to destruction,
and nobles, from their beds of
sickness.

7* You heard threats at Sinai,
at Horeb avenging judgments.

8* You anointed kings who should inflict
vengeance,
and a prophet as your successor.

9* You were taken aloft in a whirlwind,
in a chariot with fiery horses.

10* You are destined, it is written, in time to
come
to put an end to wrath before the day
of the Lord,
To turn back the hearts of fathers toward
their sons,
and to re-establish the tribes of Jacob.

11 Blessed is he who shall have seen you
before he dies,

12*† O Elijah, enveloped in the whirlwind!

Then Elisha, filled with a twofold
portion of his spirit,
wrought many marvels by his mere
word.
During his lifetime he feared no one,
nor was any man able to intimidate his
will.

13* Nothing was beyond his power;
beneath him flesh was brought back
into life.

14 In life he performed wonders,
and after death, marvelous deeds.

15* Despite all this the people did not
repent,
nor did they give up their sins,
Until they were rooted out of their land
and scattered all over the earth.
But Judah remained, a tiny people,
with its rulers from the house of
David.

16 Some of these did what was right,
but others were extremely sinful.

---

† 47, 18: Cf 2 Sm 12, 25, where Solomon is called Jedidiah, "beloved of the Lord." The same term is used of Israel in Jer 11, 15.

47, 23: *Expansive:* the name *Rehoboam* means "the people is expansive," that is, widespread. *The sinner: Jeroboam;* cf 1 Kgs 12, 2.20.26-32.

47, 25—48, 11: The prophetic ministry of *Elijah* amid widespread idolatry is here described as a judgment by fire (47, 25f). Through his preaching, miracles and vengeance against God's enemies within and without Israel, the prophet succeeded for a time in destroying idols and in restoring faith and the worship of the true God (48, 2-8). His miraculous departure from this life gave rise to the belief that he did not die but would return before the end of the world to *put an end to wrath* and restore the tribes of Israel (9ff). Cf Mt 17, 9-13.

48, 12-16: *Elisha* fearlessly continued the work of his predecessor by numerous miracles (12ff), but the obstinacy of the people eventually brought on the destruction of the kingdom of Israel and the dispersion of its subjects. *Judah,* however, survived under the rule of Davidic kings, both good and bad (15f).

---

* 19: 1 Kgs 11, 1ff.   6: 1 Kgs 21, 19;
21: 1 Kgs 12, 1ff.   2 Kgs 1, 17.
22: 2 Sm 7, 15; Ps 89, 34ff.   7: 1 Kgs 19, 8ff.
23: 1 Kgs 11, 43; 12, 13.21;   8: 1 Kgs 19, 15ff.
      13, 34; 2 Kgs 17, 6ff.   9: 2 Kgs 2, 11.
48/1: 1 Kgs 17, 1.   10: Mal 3, 23f; Mt 17, 10.
3: 1 Kgs 17, 1;   12: 2 Kgs 2, 9; 3, 13.
   2 Kgs 1, 9-14.   13f: 2 Kgs 13, 21.
5: 1 Kgs 17, 22.   15: 2 Kgs 15, 29; 18, 11.

Hezekiah and Isaiah

17*† HEZEKIAH fortified his city
and had water brought into it;
With iron tools he cut through the rock
and he built reservoirs for water.

18* During his reign Sennacherib led an
invasion,
and sent his adjutant;
He shook his fist at Zion
and blasphemed God in his pride.

19 The people's hearts melted within them,
and they were in anguish like that of
childbirth.

20* But they called upon the Most High God
and lifted up their hands to him;
He heard the prayer they uttered,
and saved them through ISAIAH.

21* God struck the camp of the Assyrians
and routed them with a plague.

22 For Hezekiah did what was right
and held fast to the paths of David,
As ordered by the illustrious prophet
Isaiah, who saw the truth in visions.

23* In his lifetime he turned back the sun
and prolonged the life of the king.

24* By his powerful spirit he looked into the
future
and consoled the mourners of Zion;

25 He foretold what should be till the end
of time,
hidden things yet to be fulfilled.

Josiah and the Prophets

49 **1*†** The name JOSIAH is like blended incense,
made lasting by a skilled perfumer.
Precious is his memory, like honey to the
taste,
like music at a banquet.

2 For he grieved over our betrayals
and destroyed the abominable idols.

3 He turned to God with his whole heart,
and, though times were evil, he
practiced virtue.

4 Except for David, Hezekiah and Josiah,
they all were wicked;
They abandoned the law of the Most
High,
these kings of Judah, right to the very
end.

5 So he gave over their power to others,
their glory to a foolish foreign nation

6* Who burned the holy city
and left its streets desolate,

7* As JEREMIAH had foretold; for they had
treated him badly
who even in the womb had been made
a prophet,
To root out, pull down, and destroy,
and then to build and to plant.

8* EZEKIEL beheld the vision
and described the different creatures
of the chariot;

9* He also referred to JOB,
who always persevered in the right
path.

10 Then, too, the TWELVE PROPHETS—
may their bones return to life from
their resting place!—
Gave new strength to Jacob
and saved him by their faith and hope.

The Heroes after the Exile

11*† How can we fittingly praise ZERUBBABEL,
who was like a signet ring on God's
right hand,

12 And Jeshua, Jozadak's son?
In their time they built the house of
God;
They erected the holy temple,
destined for everlasting glory.

13* Extolled be the memory of NEHEMIAH!
He rebuilt our ruined walls,
Restored our shattered defenses,
and set up gates and bars.

The Earliest Patriarchs

14*† Few on earth have been made the equal
of ENOCH,
for he was taken up bodily.

15* Was ever a man born like JOSEPH?
Even his dead body was provided for.

---

† 48, 17-25: The fidelity, trust and courage of King *Hezekiah* (17.22), the zeal of the prophet *Isaiah*, and the prayer of the people (20) availed with God. The Assyrian oppressors were routed (18f.21), the king's life was prolonged, and consolations were granted the people through Isaiah's prophecies concerning the future (23ff), especially the coming of the Messiah and the establishment of his kingdom; cf Is 7, 14; 9, 6f; 40—65.

49, 1-10: The author's praise of King *Josiah* (1-3), of the prophets *Jeremiah* and *Ezekiel* and likewise the minor prophets (7-10) derives from their spirit of fidelity to the Lord and his law amid the infidelity of kings and people (4ff.10).

49, 11ff: *Zerubbabel* and *Jeshua* in rebuilding the temple, and *Nehemiah*, the governor, in repairing the walls of the Holy City also restored what these constructions signify, namely, religious worship and civil authority as prescribed in the law.

49, 14ff: The patriarchs here mentioned were glorious because of their spirit of religion, i. e., their profound reverence for God and obedience to him. *The splendor of Adam*, moreover, was due to his direct origin from God.

✤
17: 2 Kgs 20, 20;
2 Chr 32, 3ff.30.
18: 2 Kgs 18, 13ff;
Is 36, 1ff.
20: 2 Kgs 19, 20.
21: 2 Kgs 19, 35; Is 37, 36.
23: 2 Kgs 20, 11; Is 38, 8.
24f: 2 Kgs 20, 17; Is 40, 1ff;
42, 9; 46, 10; 48, 6;
61, 2.
49/1: 2 Kgs 22, 1;
2 Chr 34, 1.

6: 2 Kgs 25, 9;
2 Chr 36, 19.
7: Jer 1, 5. 10.
8: Ez 1, 4ff.
9: Ez 14, 14. 20.
11f: Ezr 3, 2; Hg 1, 12;
Zec 3, 1.
13: Neh 1, 1; 3, 1.
14: 44, 16; Gn 5, 18-24.
15: Gn 37-50; Ex 13, 19;
Jos 24, 32.

16* Glorious, too, were SHEM and SETH and
     Enos;
     but beyond that of any living being
        was the splendor of ADAM.

Simon, Son of Jochanan

50 1† The greatest among his brethren, the
     glory of his people,
     was SIMON the priest, son of Jochanan,
    In whose time the house of God was
     renovated,
     in whose days the temple was
        reinforced.

2 In his time also the wall was built
     with powerful turrets for the temple
        precincts;

3 In his time the reservoir was dug,
     the pool with a vastness like the sea's.

4 He protected his people against brigands
     and strengthened his city against the
        enemy.

5 How splendid he was as he appeared
     from the tent,
     as he came from within the veil!

6 Like a star shining among the clouds,
     like the full moon at the holyday
        season;

7 Like the sun shining upon the temple,
     like the rainbow appearing in the
        cloudy sky;

8 Like the blossoms on the branches in
     springtime,
     like a lily on the banks of a stream;
    Like the trees of Lebanon in summer,

9   like the fire of incense at the sacrifice;
    Like a vessel of beaten gold,
     studded with precious stones;

10 Like a luxuriant olive tree thick with
     fruit,
     like a cypress standing against the
        clouds;

11* Vested in his magnificent robes,
     and wearing his garments of splendor,
    As he ascended the glorious altar
     and lent majesty to the court of the
        sanctuary.

12 When he received the sundered victims
     from the priests
     while he stood before the sacrificial
        wood,
    His brethren ringed him about like a
     garland,
     like a stand of cedars on Lebanon;

13 All the sons of Aaron in their dignity
     clustered around him like poplars,

    With the offerings to the LORD in their
     hands,
     in the presence of the whole assembly
        of Israel.

14 Once he had completed the services at
     the altar
     with the arranging of the sacrifices for
        the Most High,

15* And had stretched forth his hand for the
     cup,
     to offer blood of the grape,
    And poured it out at the foot of the altar,
     a sweet-smelling odor to the Most
        High God,

16* The sons of Aaron would sound a blast,
     the priests, on their trumpets of
        beaten metal;
    A blast to resound mightily
     as a reminder before the Most High.

17 Then all the people with one accord
     would quickly fall prostrate to the
        ground
    In adoration before the Most High,
     before the Holy One of Israel.

18 Then hymns would re-echo,
     and over the throng sweet strains of
        praise resound.

19 All the people of the land would shout
     for joy,
     praying to the Merciful One,
    As the high priest completed the services
     at the altar
     by presenting to God the sacrifice due;

20* Then coming down he would raise his
     hands
     over all the congregation of Israel.
    The blessing of the LORD would be upon
     his lips,
     the name of the LORD would be his
        glory.

21 Then again the people would lie
     prostrate
     to receive from him the blessing of the
        Most High.

---

† 50, 1-21: The *son of Jochanan* here mentioned was Simon II, *in whose time* as high priest (219-196 B. C.) great works were accomplished for the benefit of public worship and welfare (1-4). The author, a contemporary of this high priest, describes in great detail and by numerous comparisons the impression of awful majesty received, the lofty joy aroused, at sight of the high priest fully vested entering the sanctuary, ascending the altar (6-11), and, in the presence of the whole assembly of Israel, encircled by assistant priests bearing offerings, sacrificing the burnt offering on the Day of Atonement, while the trumpets blast and the people bow down in adoration of *the Most High* (12-17). The hymnody, the joyful shouts of the multitude, and finally the high priest's blessing, in which he pronounces—once only in the year, on this occasion—the holy name of Yahweh, climax the description of this most solemn Jewish liturgical function (18-21).

---

* 16: Gn 1, 27; 4, 25f.   15f: Nm 15, 5; 28, 7.
50/11: 45, 8-12; Ex 28, 2-5;   16: Nm 10, 10.
     39, 1-21.   20: Nm 6, 23-26.

22† And now, bless the God of all,
    who has done wondrous things on
      earth;
    Who fosters men's growth from their
      mother's womb,
    and fashions them according to his
      will!

23 May he grant you joy of heart
    and may peace abide among you;

24 May his goodness toward us endure in
      Israel
    as long as the heavens are above.

Epilogue and Canticles

25† My whole being loathes two nations,
    the third is not even a people:

26*† Those who live in Seir and Philistia,
    and the degenerate folk who dwell in
      Shechem.

27† Wise instruction, appropriate proverbs,
    I have written in this book,
    I, Jesus, son of Eleazar, son of Sirach,
    as they gushed forth from my heart's
      understanding.

28 Happy the man who meditates upon
    these things,
    wise the man who takes them to heart!

29 If he puts them into practice, he can
    cope with anything,
    for the fear of the Lord is his lamp.

51

1*† I give you thanks, O God of my father;
    I praise you, O God my savior!
    I will make known your name, refuge of
      my life;

2*   you have been my helper against my
      adversaries.
    You have saved me from death,
    and kept back my body from the pit,
    From the clutches of the nether world
      you have snatched my feet;

3*   you have delivered me, in your great
      mercy,
    From the scourge of a slanderous tongue,
    and from lips that went over to
      falsehood;
    From the snare of those who watched for
      my downfall,
    and from the power of those who
      sought my life;
    From many a danger you have saved me,

4*   from flames that hemmed me in on
      every side;
    From the midst of unremitting fire,

5   from the deep belly of the nether
      world;
    From deceiving lips and painters of lies,

6*   from the arrows of dishonest tongues.
    I was at the point of death,
    my soul was nearing the depths of the
      nether world;

7* I turned every way, but there was no one
    to help me,
    I looked for one to sustain me, but
      could find no one.

8 But then I remembered the mercies of
    the Lord,
    his kindness through ages past;
    For he saves those who take refuge in
      him,
    and rescues them from every evil.

9 So I raised my voice from the very earth,
    from the gates of the nether world, my
      cry.

10* I called out: O Lord, you are my father,
    you are my champion and my savior;
    Do not abandon me in time of trouble,
    in the midst of storms and dangers.

11 I will ever praise your name
    and be constant in my prayers to you.
    Thereupon the Lord heard my voice,
    he listened to my appeal;

12† He saved me from evil of every kind
    and preserved me in time of trouble.
    For this reason I thank him and I praise
      him;
    I bless the name of the Lord.

---

† 50, 22ff: Praise and thanksgiving are given to God for his wondrous works, and a blessing is invoked on man that he may enjoy peace and gladness of heart and the abiding goodness of the Most High.

50, 25f: The author's abhorrence of the pagan Edomites (Idumeans), Philistines and Samaritans can be understood in the light of Old Testament thinking, which does not always distinguish between hatred of evildoers and hatred of the evil they do.

50, 25: *Not even a people:* the Samaritans.

50, 26: *Seir:* Mount Seir in the territory of the Edomites. *Shechem:* a city in Samaria.

50, 27ff: These verses contain the subscription of the author, *Jesus, son of Eleazar, son of Sirach,* to his long and beautiful treatise on wisdom as applying to all of human life, integrating it under the direction of *the fear of the Lord.*

51, 1-12: A canticle of praise and thanks to God for delivering the author from slander, dangers, destruction, death, the nether world, and evil of every kind.

51, 12: After this verse the Hebrew text gives the litany of praise contained below. It is similar to Ps 136. Though not found in any versions, and therefore of doubtful authenticity, the litany seems from internal evidence to go back to the time of Sirach:

Give thanks to the Lord, for he is good,
    for his mercy endures forever;
Give thanks to the God of glory,
    for his mercy endures forever;
Give thanks to the guardian of Israel,
    for his mercy endures forever;
Give thanks to the creator of the universe,
    for his mercy endures forever;

---

*
26: 2 Kgs 17, 24; Jn 4, 9.
51/1: Ps 138, 1.
  2: Ps 91, 3.
  3: Pss 40, 5; 91, 3.
4: Ps 66, 12.
6: Pss 88, 4; 94, 17.
7: Pss 22, 12; 142, 5.
10: Ps 89, 27.

13 *† When I was young and innocent,
    I sought wisdom.

14 She came to me in her beauty,
    and until the end I will cultivate her.

15 As the blossoms yielded to ripening
      grapes,
    the heart's joy,

My feet kept to the level path
    because from earliest youth I was
      familiar with her.

16 In the short time I paid heed,
    I met with great instruction.

17 Since in this way I have profited,
    I will give my teacher grateful praise.

18 I became resolutely devoted to her—
    the good I persistently strove for.

19 I burned with desire for her,
    never turning back.

I became preoccupied with her,
    never weary of extolling her.

My hand opened her gate
    and I came to know her secrets.

20 * For her I purified my hands;
    in cleanness I attained to her.

At first acquaintance with her, I gained
      understanding
    such that I will never forsake her.

21 My whole being was stirred as I learned
      about her;
    therefore I have made her my prize
      possession.

22 The LORD has granted me my lips as a
      reward,
    and my tongue will declare his praises.

23 * Come aside to me, you untutored,
    and take up lodging in the house of
      instruction;

24 How long will you be deprived of
      wisdom's food,
    how long will you endure such bitter
      thirst?

25 * I open my mouth and speak of her:
    gain, at no cost, wisdom for
      yourselves.

26 * Submit your neck to her yoke,
    that your mind may accept her
      teaching.

For she is close to those who seek her,
    and the one who is in earnest finds her.

27 See for yourselves! I have labored only a
      little,
    but have found much.

28 Acquire but a little instruction;
    you will win silver and gold through
      her.

29 Let your spirits rejoice in the mercy of
      God,
    and be not ashamed to give him
      praise.

30 * Work at your tasks in due season,
    and in his own time God will give you
      your reward.

---

† Give thanks to the redeemer of Israel,
    for his mercy endures forever;
Give thanks to him who gathers the dispersed of Israel,
    for his mercy endures forever;
Give thanks to him who builds his city and his sanctuary,
    for his mercy endures forever;
Give thanks to him who makes a horn to sprout forth
    for the house of David, for his mercy endures forever;
Give thanks to him who has chosen for his priests
    the sons of Zadok, for his mercy endures forever;
Give thanks to the shield of Abraham,
    for his mercy endures forever;
Give thanks to the rock of Isaac,
    for his mercy endures forever;
Give thanks to the mighty one of Jacob,
    for his mercy endures forever;
Give thanks to him who has chosen Zion,
    for his mercy endures forever;
Give thanks to the king over kings of kings,
    for his mercy endures forever.
He has lifted up the horn of his people, be this his
    praise from all his faithful ones,
From the children of Israel, the people close to him.
    Alleluia! (Cf Ps 148, 14.)

51, 13-30: An alphabetic canticle describing: a) the approach to wisdom through prayer, persistent study and instruction (13-17), purification from sin, enlightenment and ardent desire; b) the possession of wisdom (18-22). The author concludes with an urgent invitation to men to receive *instruction* in *wisdom* from him, and to live by it, because wisdom gives herself *to those who seek her* (23-26); and for their labor, God will reward them in the end (27-30). Cf Mt 11, 28; Eccl 12, 14.

In the Greek of 13f there is an expansion introducing Solomon as the speaker. This deviates from the original author's intent. It reads: "Publicly, in my prayer, facing the temple, I asked for her."

---

* 13: 34, 11.   25: 6, 20.
    20: Prv 4, 6.   26: 6, 25.
    23: Prv 8, 5.   30: 2, 8; Jb 34, 11; Jn 9, 4.

The Prophetic Books

THE PROPHETIC BOOKS bear the names of the four major and twelve minor prophets, besides Lamentations and Baruch. The terms "major" and "minor" refer merely to the length of the respective compositions and not to any distinction in the prophetic office. Jonah is a story of the mission of the prophet rather than a collection of prophecies. Lamentations and Daniel are listed among the hagiographa in the Hebrew Bible, not among the prophetic books. The former contains a series of elegies on the fate of Jerusalem; the latter is apocalyptic in character. Daniel, who lived far removed from Palestine, was not called by God to preach; yet the book is counted as prophecy. Baruch, though excluded from the Hebrew canon, is found in the Septuagint version, and the Church has always acknowledged it to be sacred and inspired.

The prophetic books, together with the oral preaching of the prophets, were the result of the institution of prophetism, in which a succession of Israelites chosen by God and appointed by him to be prophets received communications from him and transmitted them to the people in his name (Dt 18, 15-20). The prophets were spokesmen of God, intermediaries between him and his people. The communications they received from God came through visions, dreams, and ecstasies and were transmitted to the people through sermons, writings, and symbolic actions.

The office of prophet was due to a direct call from God. It was not the result of heredity, just as it was not a permanent gift but a transient one, subject entirely to the divine will. The prophets preserved and developed revealed religion (1 Sm 12, 6-25), denounced idolatry (1 Kgs 14, 1-13), defended the moral law (2 Sm 12, 1-15), gave counsel in political matters (Is 31, 1ff), and often also in matters of private life (1 Sm 9, 6-9). At times miracles confirmed their preaching, and their predictions of the future intensified the expectation of the Messiah and of his kingdom.

The prophetic literature in this volume contains the substance of the prophets' authentic preaching, résumés, and genuine samples of such preaching. Some parts were recorded by the prophets themselves, some by persons other than the prophets who uttered them.

The prophecies express judgments of the people's moral conduct, on the basis of the Mosaic alliance between God and Israel. They teach sublime truths and lofty morals. They contain exhortations, threats, announcements of punishment, promises of deliverance, made with solemn authority and in highly imaginative language. In the affairs of men, their prime concern is the interests of God, especially in what pertains to the chosen people through whom the Messiah is to come; hence their denunciations of idolatry and of that externalism in worship which excludes the interior spirit of religion. They are concerned also with the universal nature of the moral law, with personal responsibility, with the person and office of the Messiah, and with the conduct of foreign nations.

In content, the literary genre of prophecy uses warning and threat besides exhortation and promise to declare in God's name events of the near and distant future (Is 8—9). In form, the divine source of prophetic declaration appears in: "The word (or oracle) of the Lord," or "Thus says the Lord," followed by the announcement of a coming event and its moral cause (Hos 4, 7-10). Divine exhortation and promise are introduced by such forms as: "Hear this word, O men of Israel, that the Lord pronounces over you" (Am 3, 1). Kindly and persuasive tones pervade the promises of reward and even the threats of punishment (Am 5, 14-15).

Disregard for exact chronological perspective in the prophecies is an additional characteristic. Predictions of the immediate and distant future are often interrelated, not on the basis of years separating the events but on the analogy of the pattern joining present with very distant, though similar, conditions and circumstances. This is prophetic compenetration, idealization in which persons and things of the more immediate present, in the prophet's day, fade into a wider and more perfect order of persons and things of the future; the former are figures and types of the latter. Thus, some details of what the Psalmist said of the kingdom of David and Solomon (Ps 72) went beyond what was fulfilled in these men, as St. Thomas points out, and found their realization only in the kingdom of Christ. St. Jerome before him, and still earlier the apostles themselves—Peter (Acts 2, 14-36) and Paul (Gal 4, 21-

31)—taught us that through anticipation in types we discover in Sacred Scripture the truth of things to come.

Thus the universal blessing for mankind, often promised by God through the mouths of his prophets in figures and types, was in time to become personalized and to confer its full benefit on us through the Word made flesh, who became for us the New Covenant through his life, death, and resurrection, as the prophets had foretold.

The Book of Isaiah

Introduction

The greatest of the prophets appeared at a critical moment of Israel's history. The second half of the eighth century B. C. witnessed the collapse of the northern kingdom under the hammer-like blows of Assyria (722), while Jerusalem itself saw the army of Sennacherib drawn up before its walls (701). In the year that Uzziah, king of Judah, died (742), Isaiah received his call to the prophetic office in the Temple of Jerusalem. Close attention should be given to chapter 6, where this divine summons to be the ambassador of the Most High is circumstantially described.

The vision of the Lord enthroned in glory stamps an indelible character on Isaiah's ministry and provides the key to the understanding of his message. The majesty, holiness and glory of the Lord took possession of his spirit and, conversely, he gained a new awareness of human pettiness and sinfulness. The enormous abyss between God's sovereign holiness and man's sin overwhelmed the prophet. Only the purifying coal of the seraphim could cleanse his lips and prepare him for acceptance of the call: "Here I am, send me!"

The ministry of Isaiah may be divided into three periods, covering the reigns of Jotham (742-735), Ahaz (735-715), and Hezekiah (715-687). To the first period belong, for the most part, the early oracles (1—5) which exposed the moral breakdown of Judah and its capital, Jerusalem. With the accession of Ahaz, the prophet became adviser to the king, whose throne was threatened by the Syro-Ephraimite coalition. Rejecting the plea of Isaiah for faith and courage, the weak Ahaz turned to Assyria for help. From this period came the majority of messianic oracles found in the section of Immanuel prophecies (6—12).

Hezekiah succeeded his father and undertook a religious reform which Isaiah undoubtedly supported. But the old intrigues began again, and the king was soon won over to the pro-Egyptian party. Isaiah denounced this "covenant with death" and again summoned Judah to faith in Yahweh as her only hope. But it was too late; the revolt had already begun. Assyria acted quickly and her army, after ravaging Judah, laid siege to Jerusalem (701). "I shut up Hezekiah like a bird in his cage," boasts the famous inscription of Sennacherib. But Yahweh delivered the city, as Isaiah had promised: God is the Lord of history, and Assyria but an instrument in his hands.

Little is known about the last days of this great religious leader, whose oracles, of singular poetic beauty and power, constantly reminded his wayward people of their destiny and the fidelity of Yahweh to his promises.

The complete Book of Isaiah is an anthology of poems composed chiefly by the great prophet, but also by disciples, some of whom came many years after Isaiah. In 1—39 most of the oracles come from Isaiah and faithfully reflect the situation in eighth-century Judah. To disciples deeply influenced by the prophet belong sections such as the Apocalypse of Isaiah (24—27), the oracles against Babylon (13—14), and probably the poems of 34—35.

Chapters 40—55, sometimes called the Deutero-Isaiah, are generally attributed to an anonymous poet who prophesied toward the end of the Babylonian Exile. From this section come the great messianic oracles known as the songs of the Servant, whose mysterious destiny of suffering and glorification is fulfilled in the passion and glorification of Christ. Chapters 56—66 contain oracles from a later period and were composed by disciples who inherited the spirit and continued the work of the great prophet.

The principal divisions of the Book of Isaiah are the following:

A: *The Book of Judgment*
    I: Indictment of Israel and Judah (1, 1—5, 30)
    II: Immanuel Prophecies (6, 1—12, 6)
    III: Oracles against the Pagan Nations (13, 1—23, 18)
    IV: Apocalypse of Isaiah (24, 1—27, 13)
    V: The Lord Alone, Israel's and Judah's Salvation (28, 1—33, 24)
    VI: The Lord, Zion's Avenger (34, 1—35, 10)
    VII: Historical Appendix (36, 1—39, 8)

B: *The Book of Consolation*
    I: The Lord's Glory in Israel's Liberation (40, 1—48, 21)
    II: Expiation of Sin, Spiritual Liberation of Israel (49, 1—55, 13)
    III: Return of the First Captives (56, 1—66, 24)

A: The Book of Judgment

I: INDICTMENT OF ISRAEL AND JUDAH

Israel's Sinfulness

1 ¹†THE VISION WHICH ISAIAH, SON OF AMOZ, had concerning Judah and Jerusalem in the days of Uzziah, Jotham, Ahaz and Hezekiah, kings of Judah.

²❋ Hear, O heavens, and listen, O earth,
    for the LORD speaks:
Sons have I raised and reared,
    but they have disowned me!

³† An ox knows its owner,
    and an ass, its master's manger;
But Israel does not know,
    my people has not understood.

⁴❋† Ah! sinful nation, people laden with
    wickedness,
    evil race, corrupt children!
They have forsaken the LORD,
    spurned the Holy One of Israel,
    apostatized.

⁵† Where would you yet be struck,
    you that rebel again and again?
The whole head is sick,
    the whole heart faint.

⁶ From the sole of the foot to the head
    there is no sound spot:
Wound and welt and gaping gash,
    not drained, or bandaged,
    or eased with salve.

⁷ Your country is waste,
    your cities burnt with fire;
Your land before your eyes
    strangers devour
    [a waste, like Sodom overthrown]—

⁸† And daughter Zion is left
    like a hut in a vineyard,
Like a shed in a melon patch,
    like a city blockaded.

⁹❋† Unless the LORD of hosts
    had left us a scanty remnant,
We had become as Sodom,
    we should be like Gomorrah.

¹⁰ Hear the word of the LORD,
    princes of Sodom!
Listen to the instruction of our God,
    people of Gomorrah!

¹¹❋† What care I for the number of your
    sacrifices?
    says the LORD.

I have had enough of whole-burnt rams
    and fat of fatlings;
In the blood of calves, lambs and goats
    I find no pleasure.

¹² When you come in to visit me,
    who asks these things of you?

¹³❋† Trample my courts no more!
    Bring no more worthless offerings;
    your incense is loathsome to me.
New moon and sabbath, calling of
    assemblies,
    octaves with wickedness: these I cannot
    bear.

¹⁴ Your new moons and festivals I detest;
    they weigh me down, I tire of the load.

¹⁵❋† When you spread out your hands,
    I close my eyes to you;
Though you pray the more,
    I will not listen.
Your hands are full of blood!

¹⁶   Wash yourselves clean!
Put away your misdeeds from before my
    eyes;
    cease doing evil; ¹⁷❋learn to do good.
Make justice your aim: redress the
    wronged,
    hear the orphan's plea, defend the
    widow.

¹⁸❋ Come now, let us set things right,
    says the LORD:
Though your sins be like scarlet,
    they may become white as snow;
Though they be crimson red,
    they may become white as wool.

¹⁹ If you are willing, and obey,
    you shall eat the good things of the land;

---

† 1, 1: The title of the book: an editorial addition. *Isaiah:* meaning "the salvation of the Lord," or "The Lord is salvation." *Amoz:* not the minor prophet. *Judah:* the southern kingdom of the tribes of Judah and Benjamin. *Uzziah:* also called Azariah; cf 2 Kgs 15, 1; 2 Chr 26, 1.

1, 3: *Israel:* not the northern kingdom, as in 9, 11, exclusively, which Isaiah usually calls "Ephraim" from the tribe bordering on the southern kingdom, but the entire chosen people; cf 8, 14.

1, 4: *Holy One of Israel:* a title used frequently by Isaiah, rarely by other writers.

1, 5-8: Sufferings inflicted upon God's people for their sins.

1, 8: *Daughter Zion:* Jerusalem. *Hut . . . shed:* for the shelter of watchmen and laborers.

1, 9: *Lord of hosts:* God, who is the Creator and Ruler of the heavenly armies of the angels, stars, etc. *Remnant:* St. Paul uses this text in Rom 9, 29, where he speaks of God's saving mercy toward the Jews and Gentiles. *Sodom . . . Gomorrah:* cf Gn 19.

1, 11: *The number of your sacrifices:* however numerous, they are not acceptable without the right dispositions on the part of the worshipers.

1, 13: *Octaves with wickedness:* the solemnity of the feasts marred by evil deeds.

1, 15: *Spread out your hands:* in prayer.

❋
1/2: Dt 32, 1.5f.
  4: 5, 24; Dt 32, 15.
  9: Rom 9, 29.
11: Ps 50, 8-13; Sir 34, 19;
    Mi 6, 7.
13: Prv 15, 8; Jer 6, 20.

15: Prv 1, 28; Sir 34, 21-25.
17: Ex 23, 6; Dt 24, 17;
    Sir 4, 9f; Jer 22, 3;
    Ez 22, 7; Zec 7, 9f.
18: Ps 51, 9.

20 But if you refuse and resist,
   the sword shall consume you:
   for the mouth of the LORD has spoken!

21*† How has she turned adulteress,
   the faithful city, so upright!
   Justice used to lodge within her,
   but now, murderers.

22 Your silver is turned to dross,
   your wine is mixed with water.

23* Your princes are rebels
   and comrades of thieves;
   Each one of them loves a bribe
   and looks for gifts.
   The fatherless they defend not,
   and the widow's plea does not reach
   them.

24* Now, therefore, says the Lord,
   the LORD of hosts, the Mighty One of
   Israel:
   Ah! I will take vengeance on my foes
   and fully repay my enemies!

25 I will turn my hand against you,
   and refine your dross in the furnace,
   removing all your alloy.

26* I will restore your judges as at first,
   and your counselors as in the beginning;
   After that you shall be called
   city of justice, faithful city.

27† Zion shall be redeemed by judgment,
   and her repentant ones by justice.

28 Rebels and sinners alike shall be crushed,
   those who desert the LORD shall be
   consumed.

29† You shall be ashamed of the terebinths
   which you prized,
   and blush for the groves which you
   chose.

30 You shall become like a tree with falling
   leaves,
   like a garden that has no water.

31 The strong man shall turn to tow,
   and his work shall become a spark;
   Both shall burn together,
   and there shall be none to quench the
   flames.

Zion, the Messianic Capital

2 **1†** THIS is what Isaiah, son of Amoz, saw concerning Judah and Jerusalem.

2*† In days to come,
   The mountain of the LORD's house
   shall be established as the highest
   mountain
   and raised above the hills.

All nations shall stream toward it;
   many peoples shall come and say:

3*† "Come, let us climb the LORD's mountain,
   to the house of the God of Jacob,
   That he may instruct us in his ways,
   and we may walk in his paths."
   For from Zion shall go forth instruction,
   and the word of the LORD from
   Jerusalem.

4* He shall judge between the nations,
   and impose terms on many peoples.
   They shall beat their swords into
   plowshares
   and their spears into pruning hooks;
   One nation shall not raise the sword
   against another,
   nor shall they train for war again.

5 O house of Jacob, come,
   let us walk in the light of the LORD!

The Lord's Judgment against Idols

6*† You have abandoned your people,
   the house of Jacob,
   Because they are filled with fortunetellers
   and soothsayers, like the Philistines;
   they covenant with strangers.

7 Their land is full of silver and gold,
   and there is no end to their treasures;
   Their land is full of horses,
   and there is no end to their chariots.

8* Their land is full of idols;
   they worship the works of their hands,
   that which their fingers have made.

9 But man is abased,
   each one brought low.
   [Do not pardon them!]

10* Get behind the rocks,
   hide in the dust,
   From the terror of the LORD
   and the splendor of his majesty!

---

† 1, 21: A picture of Jerusalem, once so faithful to God. Apostasy from the covenant is often likened by the prophets to unfaithfulness to the marriage vow.

1, 27: This verse is the key to the whole Book of Isaiah. Zion's defiant persistence in sin has demanded a divine *judgment*, by which her survivors will be cleansed and will return to God in *justice;* cf 40, 2.

1, 29: *Terebinths which you prized . . . groves which you chose:* as popular shrines for idolatrous worship.

2, 1: An editorial addition introducing chapters 2-5.

2, 2-4: The messianic destiny which ensures Judah's later restoration. In the messianic kingdom the prophets generally see *the Lord's house* as the seat of authority and the source of clear and certain doctrine; also, its rule willingly accepted by all peoples, maintained by spiritual sanctions, and tending to universal peace. This passage is found substantially unchanged in Mi 4, 1-3; it probably, although not certainly, has Isaiah as its author.

2, 3: *Zion . . . Jerusalem:* types of the earthly center of the messianic kingdom.

2, 6: *Fortunetellers and soothsayers:* divination was strictly forbidden; cf Dt 18, 9-14.

---

* 21: Jer 3, 8; Hos 2, 7.   3: Zec 8, 20-23.
  23: Ex 23, 8; Dt 16, 19.   4: 9, 7; 11, 4; Ps 72, 3f;
  24: Dt 32, 41.   Zec 9, 10.
  26: Jer 33, 7ff; Zec.8, 3.   6: 8, 19; 19, 3.
2/2ff: Mi 4, 1ff.   8: 31, 1ff.
  2: 56, 7.   10: 2 Thes 1, 9.

11† The haughty eyes of man will be lowered,
  the arrogance of men will be abased,
  and the Lord alone will be exalted,
   on that day.

12 For the Lord of hosts will have his day
  against all that is proud and arrogant,
  all that is high, and it will be brought
   low;

13† Yes, against all the cedars of Lebanon
  and all the oaks of Bashan,

14 Against all the lofty mountains
  and all the high hills,

15 Against every lofty tower
  and every fortified wall,

16† Against all the ships of Tarshish
  and all stately vessels.

17 Human pride will be abased,
  the arrogance of men brought low,
  And the Lord alone will be exalted,
   on that day.

18   The idols will perish forever.

19 Men will go into caves in the rocks
  and into holes in the earth,
  From the terror of the Lord
  and the splendor of his majesty,
  when he arises to overawe the earth.

20 On that day men will throw to the moles
  and the bats the idols of silver and gold
  which they made for worship.

21 They go into caverns in the rocks
  and into crevices in the cliffs,
  From the terror of the Lord
  and the splendor of his majesty,
  when he arises to overawe the earth.

22 As for you, let man alone,
  in whose nostrils is but a breath;
  for what is he worth?

Judgment of Judah and Jerusalem

3 **1*†** The Lord, the Lord of hosts,
  shall take away from Jerusalem and from
   Judah
  support and prop [all supplies of bread
   and water]:

2 Hero and warrior,
  judge and prophet, fortuneteller and
   elder,

3 The captain of fifty and the nobleman,
  counselor, skilled magician, and expert
   charmer.

4 I will make striplings their princes;
  the fickle shall govern them,

5 And the people shall oppress one another,
  yes, every man his neighbor.
  The child shall be bold toward the elder,
  and the base toward the honorable.

6 When a man seizes his brother
  in his father's house, saying,
  "You have clothes! Be our ruler,
  and take in hand this ruin!"—

7 Then shall he answer in that day:
  "I will not undertake to cure this,
  when in my own house there is no bread
   or clothing!
  You shall not make me ruler of the
   people."

8 Jerusalem is crumbling, Judah is falling;
  for their speech and their deeds are
   before the Lord,
  a provocation in the sight of his majesty.

9 Their very look bears witness against them;
  their sin like Sodom they vaunt,
  They hide it not. Woe to them!
  they deal out evil to themselves.

10 Happy the just, for it will be well with
   them,
  the fruit of their works they will eat.

11 Woe to the wicked man! All goes ill,
  with the work of his hands he will be
   repaid.

12 My people—a babe in arms will be their
   tyrant,
  and women will rule them!
  O my people, your leaders mislead,
  they destroy the paths you should follow.

13 The Lord rises to accuse,
  standing to try his people.

14 The Lord enters into judgment
  with his people's elders and princes:
  It is you who have devoured the vineyard;
  the loot wrested from the poor is in
   your houses.

15* What do you mean by crushing my people,
  and grinding down the poor when they
   look to you?
  says the Lord, the God of hosts.

16* The Lord said:
  Because the daughters of Zion are haughty,
  and walk with necks outstretched
  Ogling and mincing as they go,
  their anklets tinkling with every step,

---

† 2, 11: *That day:* the day of the Lord, a day of retribution, often referred to, especially by the minor prophets, and described in terms of natural phenomena: earthquake, fire, storm.
2, 13: *Lebanon:* Mount Lebanon in Syria, famed for its cedars. *Bashan:* the wooded uplands east of the Jordan River.
2, 16: *Tarshish:* cf note on Ps 48, 8.
3, 1-12: Anarchy will reign in Jerusalem and Judah. In the prevailing desperation, even the most unworthy and the least qualified will be sought as rulers.

3/1: Lv 26, 26; Ez 4, 16.   16ff: 32, 11f.
15: Lv 25, 42.55.

17† The Lord shall cover the scalps of Zion's
daughters with scabs,
and the LORD shall bare their heads.

18On that day the Lord will do away with the finery of
the anklets, sunbursts, and crescents; **19**the pendants,
bracelets, and veils; **20**the headdresses, bangles, cinc-
tures, perfume boxes, and amulets; **21†**the signet rings,
and the nose rings; **22**the court dresses, wraps, cloaks,
and purses; **23**the mirrors, linen tunics, turbans, and
shawls.

24 Instead of perfume there will be stench,
instead of the girdle, a rope,
And for the coiffure, baldness;
for the rich gown, a sackcloth skirt.
Then, instead of beauty:
25 Your men will fall by the sword,
and your champions, in war;
26 Her gates will lament and mourn,
as the city sits desolate on the ground.

4 **1†** Seven women will take hold of one man
on that day, saying:
"We will eat our own food
and wear our own clothing;
Only let your name be given us,
put an end to our disgrace!"

The Messianic Branch

2✻† On that day,
The branch of the LORD will be luster and
glory,
and the fruit of the earth will be honor
and splendor
for the survivors of Israel.
3✻† He who remains in Zion
and he that is left in Jerusalem
Will be called holy:
every one marked down for life in
Jerusalem.
4 When the Lord washes away
the filth of the daughters of Zion,
And purges Jerusalem's blood from her
midst
with a blast of searing judgment,
5✻ Then will the LORD create,
over the whole site of Mount Zion
and over her place of assembly,
A smoking cloud by day
and a light of flaming fire by night.
6 For over all, his glory will be shelter and
protection:
shade from the parching heat of day,
refuge and cover from storm and rain.

The Vineyard Song

5 **1†** Let me now sing of my friend,
my friend's song concerning his
vineyard.
My friend had a vineyard
on a fertile hillside;
2 He spaded it, cleared it of stones,
and planted the choicest vines;
Within it he built a watchtower,
and hewed out a wine press.
Then he looked for the crop of grapes,
but what it yielded was wild grapes.

3 Now, inhabitants of Jerusalem and men of
Judah,
judge between me and my vineyard:
4 What more was there to do for my
vineyard
that I had not done?
Why, when I looked for the crop of grapes,
did it bring forth wild grapes?
5 Now, I will let you know
what I mean to do to my vineyard:
Take away its hedge, give it to grazing,
break through its wall, let it be trampled!
6 Yes, I will make it a ruin:
it shall not be pruned or hoed,
but overgrown with thorns and briers;
I will command the clouds
not to send rain upon it.
7† The vineyard of the LORD of hosts is the
house of Israel,
and the men of Judah are his cherished
plant;
He looked for judgment, but see,
bloodshed!
for justice, but hark, the outcry!

Doom of the Unjust

8✻† Woe to you who join house to house,
who connect field with field,
Till no room remains, and you are left to
dwell
alone in the midst of the land!

---

†
  3, 17: *Bare their heads:* a mark of social disgrace; cf Nm 5,
18.
  3, 21: *Nose rings:* of gold, a feminine ornament in the East;
cf note on Gn 24, 22.
  4, 1: *Seven women . . . one man:* the disproportion of the
sexes due to war leaves the female population almost without
male partners. The women are eager to marry, not for support,
but to avoid the disgrace of being childless.
  4, 2: *Branch of the Lord:* divine blessings in general, which
later culminated in the Messiah; cf Jer 23, 5; Zec 3, 8; 6, 12.
  4, 3: *Marked down for life:* in God's list of his elect; cf Ex
32, 32.
  5, 1: *My friend had a vineyard:* the Lord and his chosen
people.
  5, 7: *Judgment . . . bloodshed . . . justice . . . outcry:* in
Hebrew, these adversative terms constitute a play on words.
  5, 8-10: Land-grabbers who unjustly acquire property will
be impoverished instead of enriched.

✻
4/2: 11, 1; Jer 23, 5; 33, 15.   5: Ex 13, 21.
3: 6, 13; 10, 20; Ob 17.   5/8: Mi 2, 2.

9* In my hearing the LORD of hosts has sworn:
  Many houses shall be in ruins,
    large ones and fine, with no one to live in
    them.
10† Ten acres of vineyard
    shall yield but one liquid measure,
  And a homer of seed
    shall yield but an ephah.
17 Lambs shall graze there at pasture,
    and kids shall eat in the ruins of the rich.

11 Woe to those who demand strong drink
    as soon as they rise in the morning,
  And linger into the night
    while wine inflames them!
12* With harp and lyre, timbrel and flute,
    they feast on wine;
  But what the LORD does, they regard not,
    the work of his hands they see not.
13 Therefore my people go into exile,
    because they do not understand;
  Their nobles die of hunger,
    and their masses are parched with thirst.
14*† Therefore the nether world enlarges its
    throat
    and opens its maw without limit;
  Down go their nobility and their masses,
    their throngs and their revelry.
15 Men shall be abased, each one brought low,
    and the eyes of the haughty lowered,
16 But the LORD of hosts shall be exalted by his
    judgment,
    and God the Holy shall be shown holy by
    his justice.

18 Woe to those who tug at guilt with cords of
    perversity,
    and at sin as if with cart ropes!
19* To those who say, "Let him make haste
    and speed his work, that we may see it;
  On with the plan of the Holy One of Israel!
    let it come to pass, that we may know it!"
20 Woe to those who call evil good, and good
    evil,
    who change darkness into light, and light
    into darkness,
    who change bitter into sweet, and sweet
    into bitter!
21* Woe to those who are wise in their own
    sight,
    and prudent in their own esteem!
22* Woe to the champions at drinking wine,
    the valiant at mixing strong drink!
23* To those who acquit the guilty for bribes,
    and deprive the just man of his rights!

24 Therefore, as the tongue of fire licks up
    stubble,
    as dry grass shrivels in the flame,
  Even so their root shall become rotten
    and their blossom scatter like dust;
  For they have spurned the law of the LORD
    of hosts,
    and scorned the word of the Holy One of
    Israel.
25 Therefore the wrath of the LORD blazes
    against his people,
    he raises his hand to strike them;
  When the mountains quake,
    their corpses shall be like refuse in the
    streets.
  For all this, his wrath is not turned back,
    and his hand is still outstretched.

Invasion

26† He will give a signal to a far-off nation,
    and whistle to them from the ends of the
    earth;
    speedily and promptly will they come.
27 None of them will stumble with weariness,
    none will slumber and none will sleep.
  None will have his waist belt loose,
    nor the thong of his sandal broken.
28 Their arrows are sharp,
    and all their bows are bent.
  The hoofs of their horses seem like flint,
    and their chariot wheels like the
    hurricane.
29 Their roar is that of the lion,
    like the lion's whelps they roar;
  They growl and seize the prey,
    they carry it off and none will rescue it.
30* [They will roar over it, on that day,
    with a roaring like that of the sea.]

II: IMMANUEL PROPHECIES

Call of Isaiah

6 1*†IN THE YEAR KING UZZIAH DIED, I saw the Lord seated on a high and lofty throne, with the train of his garment filling the temple. ²Seraphim were stationed above; each of them had six wings: with two they veiled their faces, with two they veiled their feet, and with two they hovered aloft.

9: 6, 12.
12: Am 6, 5f.
14: Hb 2, 5.
19: Jer 5, 12; 2 Pt 3, 4.
21: Prv 3, 7; Rom 12, 16.
22: Sir 31, 3.
23: Ex 23, 8; Prv 17, 15.
30: 8, 22.
6/1: Jn 12, 41.

5, 10: *Ten acres:* a field requiring ten days of plowing by a yoke of oxen. *Liquid measure:* in Hebrew, "a bath," i. e., about ten gallons. *Homer:* a dry measure of about ten bushels. *Ephah:* a dry measure of about one bushel.
5, 14: *Nether world:* cf note on Ps 6, 6.
5, 26-30: A description of the invading Assyrian army, God's instrument for punishing his people.
6, 1: *In the year King Uzziah died:* 742 B. C.
6, 1ff: *Temple:* the holy place, just in front of the holy of holies. *Seraphim:* literally "the burning ones," are celestial be-

3ᵃ"Holy, holy, holy is the LORD of hosts!" they cried one to the other. "All the earth is filled with his glory!" **4**ᵃ†At the sound of that cry, the frame of the door shook and the house was filled with smoke.

5ᵃ†Then I said, "Woe is me, I am doomed! For I am a man of unclean lips, living among a people of unclean lips; yet my eyes have seen the King, the LORD of hosts!" **6**Then one of the seraphim flew to me, holding an ember which he had taken with tongs from the altar.

7ᵃ†He touched my mouth with it. "See," he said, "now that this has touched your lips, your wickedness is removed, your sin purged."

8Then I heard the voice of the Lord saying, "Whom shall I send? Who will go for us?" "Here I am," I said; "send me!" **9**ᵃ†And he replied: Go and say to this people:

> Listen carefully, but you shall not
>   understand!
> Look intently, but you shall know
>   nothing!

10ᵃ
> You are to make the heart of this people
>   sluggish,
> to dull their ears and close their eyes;
> Else their eyes will see, their ears hear,
>   their heart understand,
> and they will turn and be healed.

> "How long, O Lord?" I asked. And he
>   replied:

> Until the cities are desolate,
>   without inhabitants,
> Houses, without a man,
>   and the earth is a desolate waste.

12†
> Until the LORD removes men far away,
>   and the land is abandoned more and
>   more.

13ᵃ
> If there be still a tenth part in it,
>   then this in turn shall be laid waste;
> As with a terebinth or an oak
>   whose trunk remains when its leaves
>   have fallen.
> [Holy offspring is the trunk.]

Birth of Immanuel

7 **1**ᵃ†IN the days of Ahaz, king of Judah, son of Jotham, son of Uzziah, Rezin, king of Aram, and Pekah, king of Israel, son of Remaliah, went up to attack Jerusalem, but they were not able to conquer it. **2**When word came to the house of David that Aram was encamped in Ephraim, the heart of the king and the heart of the people trembled, as the trees of the forest tremble in the wind.

3ᵃ†Then the LORD said to Isaiah: Go out to meet Ahaz, you and your son Shear-jashub, at the end of the conduit of the upper pool, on the highway of the fuller's field, **4**and say to him: Take care you remain tranquil and do not fear; let not your courage fail before these two stumps of smoldering brands [the blazing anger of Rezin and the Arameans, and of the son of Remaliah], **5**because of the mischief that Aram [Ephraim and the son of Remaliah] plots against you, saying, **6**"Let us go up and tear Judah asunder, make it our own by force, and appoint the son of Tabeel king there."

7
> Thus says the Lord:
>   This shall not stand, it shall not be!

8
> Damascus is the capital of Aram,
>   and Rezin the head of Damascus;
> Samaria is the capital of Ephraim,
>   and Remaliah's son the head of Samaria.

9ᵃ†
> But within sixty years and five,
>   Ephraim shall be crushed, no longer a
>   nation.
> Unless your faith is firm
>   you shall not be firm!

10Again the LORD spoke to Ahaz: **11**†Ask for a sign from the LORD, your God; let it be deep as the nether world, or high as the sky! **12**†But Ahaz answered, "I will not ask! I will not tempt the LORD!" **13**Then he said: Listen, O house of David! Is it not enough for

---

† ings who surround the throne of God. Each has six wings. Reverence for the divine majesty causes them to veil their faces with two wings; modesty, to veil their extremities in similar fashion; alacrity in God's service, to extend two wings in preparation for flight. *Holy, holy, holy:* God's perfect interior holiness whose exterior manifestation is *his glory*. These words are found in the Roman liturgy just before the Canon of the Mass.

6, 4: *Smoke:* reminiscent of the clouds which surrounded God at Mount Sinai; cf Ex 19, 16-19; Dt 4, 11f.

6, 5: *Doomed:* it was popularly believed that to see God would lead to one's death; cf Gn 32, 31; Ex 33, 20; Jg 13, 22.

6, 7: *Touched your lips:* Isaiah is thus symbolically purified to be worthy of his vocation as God's prophet. In the Roman liturgy, the celebrant at Mass makes reference to this incident just before he reads the gospel.

6, 9f: The truth that the nation will remain impenitent is vividly foretold, as if its obstinacy would be caused, instead of merely occasioned, by the prophet's warning. Cf Mt 13, 13ff; Mk 4, 12; Lk 8, 10.

6, 12: Several limited deportations in the time of Isaiah would later culminate in the Babylonian Exile.

7, 1: *Days of Ahaz:* who ruled from 735 to 715 B. C. This attack against Jerusalem by the kings of *Aram* (Syria) and *Israel* was occasioned by Ahaz' refusal to enter with them into an anti-Assyrian alliance; cf 2 Kgs 16.

7, 3: *Shear-jashub:* this name means "a remnant will return."

7, 6: *Son of Tabeel:* an adherent of Jerusalem's enemies. His appointment would interrupt the lawful succession from David.

7, 9: *Within sixty years and five:* if the text is correct, its reference is unknown.

7, 11: *Deep . . . sky:* an extraordinary or miraculous sign that would prove God's firm will to save the royal house of David from its oppressors.

7, 12: *Tempt the Lord:* Ahaz expresses in this hypocritical way his preference for depending upon the might of Assyria rather than upon God.

ᵃ
3: Rv 4, 8.
4: 1 Kgs 8, 10f; Rv 15, 8.
5: Gn 32, 3; Ex 20, 19;
    33, 20; Jgs 6, 22;
    13, 22.
7: Jer 1, 9; Dn 10, 16.
9: Mt 13, 14f; Mk 4, 12;
    Lk 8, 10; Acts 28, 26f.
10: Jer 5, 21; Jn 12, 40.
13: 10, 22.
7/1: 2 Kgs 16, 5;
    2 Chr 28, 5-15.
3: 36, 2; 2 Chr 32, 3.
9: 8. 6ff.

you to weary men, must you also weary my God? **14†**Therefore the Lord himself will give you this sign: the virgin shall be with child, and bear a son, and shall name him Immanuel. **15†**He shall be living on curds and honey by the time he learns to reject the bad and choose the good. **16**For before the child learns to reject the bad and choose the good, the land of those two kings whom you dread shall be deserted.

17The Lord shall bring upon you and your people and your father's house days worse than any since Ephraim seceded from Judah. [This means the king of Assyria.] **18**On that day

> The Lord shall whistle
> for the fly that is in the farthest streams
> of Egypt,
> and for the bee in the land of Assyria.
> **19** All of them shall come and settle
> in the steep ravines and in the rocky
> clefts,
> on all thornbushes and in all pastures.

20†On that day the Lord shall shave with the razor hired from across the River [with the king of Assyria] the head, and the hair between the legs. It shall also shave off the beard.

21On that day a man shall keep a heifer or a couple of sheep, **22**and from their abundant yield of milk he shall live on curds; curds and honey shall be the food of all who remain in the land. **23**On that day every place where there used to be a thousand vines, worth a thousand pieces of silver, shall be turned to briers and thorns. **24**Men shall go there with bow and arrows; for all the country shall be briers and thorns. **25**For fear of briers and thorns you shall not go upon any mountainside which used to be hoed with the mattock; they shall be grazing land for cattle and shall be trampled upon by sheep.

The Son of Isaiah

8 **1†**THE LORD said to me: Take a large cylinder-seal, and inscribe on it in ordinary letters: "Belonging to Maher-shalal-hash-baz." **2†**And I took reliable witnesses, Uriah the priest, and Zechariah, son of Jeberechiah. **3†**Then I went to the prophetess and she conceived and bore a son. The Lord said to me: Name him Maher-shalal-hash-baz, **4**for before the child knows how to call his father or mother by name, the wealth of Damascus and the spoil of Samaria shall be carried off by the king of Assyria.

5Again the Lord spoke to me:

> **6*†** Because this people has rejected
> the waters of Shiloah that flow gently,
> And melts with fear before the loftiness
> of Rezin and Remaliah's son,
> **7** Therefore the Lord raises against them
> the waters of the River, great and mighty
> [the king of Assyria and all his power].

> It shall rise above all its channels,
> and overflow all its banks;
> **8** It shall pass into Judah, and flood it all
> throughout:
> up to the neck it shall reach;
> It shall spread its wings
> the full width of your land, Immanuel!

> **9** Know, O peoples, and be appalled!
> Give ear, all you distant lands!
> Arm, but be crushed! Arm, but be
> crushed!
> **10†** Form a plan, and it shall be thwarted;
> make a resolve, and it shall not be carried
> out,
> for "With us is God!"

Disciples of Isaiah

11*For thus said the Lord to me, taking hold of me and warning me not to walk in the way of this people:

> **12** Call not alliance what this people calls
> alliance,
> and fear not, nor stand in awe of what
> they fear.

---

†

7, 14: The *sign* proposed by Isaiah was concerned with the preservation of Judah in the midst of distress (cf 7, 15.17), but more especially with the fulfillment of God's earlier promise to David (2 Sm 7, 12-16) in the coming of *Immanuel* (meaning, "With us is God") as the ideal king (cf 9, 5-6; 11, 1-5). The church has always followed St. Matthew in seeing the transcendent fulfillment of this verse in Christ and his Virgin Mother. The prophet need not have known the full force latent in his own words; and some Catholic writers have sought a preliminary and partial fulfillment in the conception and birth of the future King Hezekiah, whose mother, at the time Isaiah spoke, would have been a young, unmarried woman (Hebrew, *almah*). The Holy Spirit was preparing, however, for another Nativity which alone could fulfill the divinely given terms of Immanuel's mission, and in which the perpetual virginity of the Mother of God was to fulfill also the words of this prophecy in the integral sense intended by the divine Wisdom.

7, 15: *Curds and honey:* the restricted diet of those who remain after devastation has changed the once fertile fields of Judah into grazing land; cf 7, 21-25.

7, 20: God will use the Assyrians *from across the River* (the Euphrates) as his instrument (*razor*) to inflict disgrace and suffering upon his people.

8, 1: *Ordinary letters:* easily read by all. *Maher-shalah-hash-baz:* a symbolic name to be given to another son of Isaiah (v 3); it means "quick spoils; speedy plunder," and describes what the Assyrians will do.

8, 2: *Reliable witnesses:* who would testify that Isaiah had indeed prophesied the future destruction. *Uriah the priest:* cf 2 Kgs 16, 10.

8, 3: *The prophetess:* wife of Isaiah.

8, 6ff: *This people:* Judah. *Waters of Shiloah:* the stream that flows into the pool of Shiloah in Jerusalem, its slow current symbolizing the silent, divine protection which Judah has rejected. God will therefore summon the mighty Assyrian army, symbolized by *the River* (Euphrates), to devastate Judah, which, however, will not be entirely destroyed, because it is the land of *Immanuel.*

8, 10: The *plan* of Israel's enemies will be *thwarted* because, as the name "Immanuel" signifies, *With us is God.*

✻
    8/6: Jn 9, 7.11.   11: Ez 3, 14.

13   But with the LORD of hosts make your
         alliance—
         for him be your fear and your awe.
14*   Yet he shall be a snare, an obstacle and a
         stumbling stone
         to both the houses of Israel,
      A trap and a snare
         to those who dwell in Jerusalem;
15   And many among them shall stumble and
         fall,
         broken, snared, and captured.

16†The record is to be folded and the sealed instruction kept among my disciples. 17For I will trust in the
LORD, who is hiding his face from the house of Jacob;
yes, I will wait for him. 18†Look at me and the children
whom the LORD has given me: we are signs and portents in Israel from the LORD of hosts who dwells on
Mount Zion. 19*†And when they say to you, "Inquire
of mediums and fortunetellers (who chirp and mutter!); should not a people inquire of their gods, apply
to the dead on behalf of the living?" 20—then this document will furnish its instruction. That kind of thing
they will surely say.

The Prince of Peace

23†First he degraded the land of Zebulun and the
land of Naphtali; but in the end he has glorified the
seaward road, the land west of the Jordan, the District
of the Gentiles.

         Anguish has taken wing, dispelled is
            darkness:
            for there is no gloom where but now
            there was distress.

9 1*   The people who walked in darkness
            have seen a great light;
         Upon those who dwelt in the land of gloom
            a light has shone.
2   You have brought them abundant joy
            and great rejoicing,
         As they rejoice before you as at the harvest,
            as men make merry when dividing spoils.
3   For the yoke that burdened them,
            the pole on their shoulder,
         And the rod of their taskmaster
            you have smashed, as on the day of
            Midian.
4*   For every boot that tramped in battle,
            every cloak rolled in blood,
            will be burned as fuel for flames.

5*†   For a child is born to us, a son is given us;
            upon his shoulder dominion rests.
         They name him Wonder-Counselor,
            God-Hero,
            Father-Forever, Prince of Peace.

6*   His dominion is vast
            and forever peaceful,
         From David's throne, and over his
            kingdom,
            which he confirms and sustains
         By judgment and justice,
            both now and forever.
      The zeal of the LORD of hosts will do this!

Fall of the Northern Kingdom

7   The Lord has sent word against Jacob,
            it falls upon Israel;
8   And all the people know it,
            Ephraim and those who dwell in
            Samaria,
         those who say in arrogance and pride of
            heart,
9   "Bricks have fallen,
            but we will build with cut stone;
         Sycamores are felled,
            but we will replace them with cedars."
10   But the LORD raises up their foes against
            them
            and stirs up their enemies to action:
11†   Aram on the east and the Philistines on the
            west
            devour Israel with open mouth.
      For all this, his wrath is not turned back,
            and his hand is still outstretched!
12   The people do not turn to him who struck
            them,
            nor seek the LORD of hosts.
13   So the LORD severs from Israel head and
            tail,
            palm branch and reed in one day.
14   [The elder and the noble are the head,
            the prophet who teaches falsehood is the
            tail.]

---

† 8, 16: *Kept among my disciples:* for preservation and transmission.

8, 18: *Signs:* Isaiah and his sons had symbolic names.

8, 19: *Chirp and mutter:* a mocking reference to the sounds
uttered by necromancers, as if the dead were speaking; all such
practices were forbidden.

8, 21f: These verses have been transposed and placed within
14, 25, which affords the context in which they can be understood.

8, 23: *Zebulun . . . Naphtali:* northern Palestine, which
was first to be attacked by the Assyrians; God, however, redeems it, as he redeems all his people. *Seaward road:* from
Damascus, across southern Galilee to the Mediterranean Sea.
District of the Gentiles: northern Galilee, inhabited by pagans;
cf Jos 20, 7; Is 9, 1. Mt 4, 15f refers to this, since Jesus began
his public mission in Galilee.

9, 5: *A child:* the Immanuel of Is 7, 14 and 8, 8; cf 11, 1.2.9.
In Christian tradition and liturgy, this passage is used to refer
to Christ. *Upon his shoulder dominion rests:* authority. *Wonder-
Counselor:* remarkable for his wisdom and prudence. *God-
Hero:* a warrior and a defender of his people, like God himself.
Father-Forever: ever devoted to his people. *Prince of Peace:*
his reign will be characterized by peace.

9, 11: *Aram:* the Syrian kingdom, with its capital at Damascus.

    14: Rom 9, 33; 1 Pt 2, 8.   4: Ez 39, 9.
    19: Lv 19, 31; Dt 18, 10ff.   5: Ps 72, 7; Lk 2, 11.14.
    9/1f: Mt 4, 15f.   6: Jer 23, 5; Lk 1, 32f.

15* The leaders of this people mislead them
and those to be led are engulfed.
16 For this reason, the Lord does not spare
their young men,
and their orphans and widows he does
not pity;
They are wholly profaned and sinful,
and every mouth gives vent to folly.
For all this, his wrath is not turned back,
his hand is still outstretched!
17 For wickedness burns like fire,
devouring brier and thorn;
It kindles the forest thickets,
which go up in columns of smoke.
18 At the wrath of the Lord of hosts the land
quakes,
and the people are like fuel for fire;
No man spares his brother,
each devours the flesh of his neighbor.
19 Though they hack on the right, they are
hungry;
though they eat on the left, they are not
filled.
20† Manasseh devours Ephraim, and Ephraim
Manasseh;
together they turn on Judah.
For all this, his wrath is not turned back,
his hand is still outstretched!

Social Injustice

10 1* Woe to those who enact unjust statutes
and who write oppressive decrees,
2* Depriving the needy of judgment
and robbing my people's poor of their
rights,
Making widows their plunder,
and orphans their prey!
3 What will you do on the day of
punishment,
when ruin comes from afar?
To whom will you flee for help?
Where will you leave your wealth,
4 Lest it sink beneath the captive
or fall beneath the slain?
For all this, his wrath is not turned back,
his hand is still outstretched!

Assyria the Unconscious Instrument of God

5 Woe to Assyria! My rod in anger,
my staff in wrath.
6† Against an impious nation I send him,
and against a people under my wrath
I order him

To seize plunder, carry off loot,
and tread them down like the mud of
the streets.
7 But this is not what he intends,
nor does he have this in mind;
Rather, it is in his heart to destroy,
to make an end of nations not a few.
8 "Are not my commanders all kings?" he
says,
9*† "Is not Calno like Carchemish,
Or Hamath like Arpad,
or Samaria like Damascus?
10 Just as my hand reached out to
idolatrous kingdoms
that had more images than Jerusalem
and Samaria,
11* Just as I treated Samaria and her idols,
shall I not do to Jerusalem and her
graven images?"

12 [But when the Lord has brought to an
end all his work on Mount Zion and in
Jerusalem,
I will punish the utterance
of the king of Assyria's proud heart,
13 and the boastfulness of his haughty
eyes. For he says:]

"By my own power I have done it,
and by my wisdom, for I am shrewd.
I have moved the boundaries of peoples,
their treasures I have pillaged,
and, like a giant, I have put down the
enthroned.
14 My hand has seized like a nest
the riches of nations;
As one takes eggs left alone,
so I took in all the earth;
No one fluttered a wing,
or opened a mouth, or chirped!"

15 Will the axe boast against him who hews
with it?
Will the saw exalt itself above him
who wields it?
As if a rod could sway him who lifts it,
or a staff him who is not wood!
16† Therefore the Lord, the Lord of hosts,
will send among his fat ones leanness,
And instead of his glory there will be
kindling
like the kindling of fire.
17 The Light of Israel will become a fire,
Israel's Holy One a flame,

15: 28, 7; Jer 2, 8; 5, 31;   **10/1:** Jer 8, 8.
20, 6; 23, 13f; 29, 30ff;   **2:** 1, 23.
Ez 13, 1-7; 22, 28;   **9:** 36, 19; Am 6, 2.
Mi 3, 11.   **11:** 36, 20.

† **9, 20:** *Manasseh . . . Ephraim:* two of the leading tribes of the
northern kingdom.
10, 6f: *Impious nation:* Israel. It was God's intention to use
Assyria merely to punish, not to destroy, his people.
10, 9: *Calno . . . Damascus:* cities captured by the Assyrians.
10, 16: *His fat ones:* the strong men of the king of Assyria.

That burns and consumes his briers
  and his thorns in a single day.
18 His splendid forests and orchards
  will be consumed, soul and body;
19 And the remnant of the trees in his forest
  will be so few,
Like poles set up for signals,
  that any boy can record them.
20   On that day
The remnant of Israel,
  the survivors of the house of Jacob,
  will no more lean upon him who
    struck them;
But they will lean upon the Lord,
  the Holy One of Israel, in truth.
21† A remnant will return, the remnant of
    Jacob,
  to the mighty God.
22✱ For though your people, O Israel,
  were like the sand of the sea,
Only a remnant of them will return;
  their destruction is decreed
  as overwhelming justice demands.

23Yes, the destruction he has decreed, the Lord, the God of hosts, will carry out within the whole land. 24Therefore thus says the Lord, the God of hosts: O my people, who dwell in Zion, do not fear the Assyrian, though he strikes you with a rod, and raises his staff against you. 25For only a brief moment more, and my anger shall be over; but them I will destroy in wrath. 26✱Then the Lord of hosts will raise against them a scourge such as struck Midian at the rock of Oreb; and he will raise his staff over the sea as he did against Egypt. 27†On that day,

His burden shall be taken from your
    shoulder,
  and his yoke shattered from your neck.

Sennacherib's Invasion

He has come up from the direction of
    Rimmon,
28   he has reached Aiath, passed through
    Migron,
  at Michmash his supplies are stored.
29 They cross the ravine:
  "We will spend the night at Geba."
Ramah is in terror,
  Gibeah of Saul has fled.
30 Cry and shriek, O daughter of Gallim!
  Hearken, Laishah! Answer her,
    Anathoth!
31 Madmenah is in flight,
  the inhabitants of Gebim seek refuge.

32† Even today he will halt at Nob,
  he will shake his fist at the mount of
    daughter Zion,
  the hill of Jerusalem!
33 Behold, the Lord, the Lord of hosts,
  lops off the boughs with terrible
    violence;
The tall of stature are felled,
  and the lofty ones brought low;
34 The forest thickets are felled with the
    axe,
  and Lebanon in its splendor falls.

The Rule of Immanuel

11 1✱† But a shoot shall sprout from the stump
    of Jesse,
  and from his roots a bud shall
    blossom.
2✱† The spirit of the Lord shall rest upon
    him:
  a spirit of wisdom and of
    understanding,
A spirit of counsel and of strength,
  a spirit of knowledge and of fear of
    the Lord,
3   and his delight shall be the fear
    of the Lord.
Not by appearance shall he judge,
  nor by hearsay shall he decide,
4✱ But he shall judge the poor with justice,
  and decide aright for the land's
    afflicted.
He shall strike the ruthless with the rod
  of his mouth,
  and with the breath of his lips he shall
    slay the wicked.
5 Justice shall be the band around his
    waist,
  and faithfulness a belt upon his hips.
6✱† Then the wolf shall be a guest of the
    lamb,
  and the leopard shall lie down
    with the kid;
The calf and the young lion shall
    browse together,
  with a little child to guide them.

---

† 10, 21: *A remnant will return:* in Hebrew, *shear-jashub,* an allusion to the name of Isaiah's son, Shear-jashub; cf 7, 3.

10, 27-32: A poetic description of the progress of the Assyrian army, advancing from the north through Judah to the gates of Jerusalem.

10, 32ff: Just when the enemy is about to capture Jerusalem, God intervenes and destroys the hostile army.

11, 1: *Jesse:* David's father. *Shoot . . . stump:* after the Babylonian exile only a *stump* of the Davidic dynasty will remain; from it will arise the new *shoot,* the messianic King.

11, 2f: The source of the traditional names of the gifts of the Holy Spirit. The Septuagint and the Vulgate read "piety" for *fear of the Lord* in its first occurrence, thus listing seven gifts.

11, 6-9: This picture of the idyllic harmony of paradise is a

✱
22: Rom 9, 27f.   4: Pss 72, 2.4; 98, 9;
26: Jgs 7, 25.   2 Thes 2, 8.
11/1: Lk 3, 32.   6: 65, 25.
2: Mt 3, 16; Mk 1, 10.

7 The cow and the bear shall be neighbors,
together their young shall rest;
the lion shall eat hay like the ox.

8 The baby shall play by the cobra's den,
and the child lay his hand on the
adder's lair.

9* There shall be no harm or ruin on all my
holy mountain;
for the earth shall be filled with
knowledge of the Lord,
as water covers the sea.

Union of Ephraim and Judah

10* On that day,
The root of Jesse,
set up as a signal for the nations,
The Gentiles shall seek out,
for his dwelling shall be glorious.

11*† On that day,
The Lord shall again take it in hand
to reclaim the remnant of his people
that is left from Assyria and Egypt,
Pathros, Ethiopia, and Elam,
Shinar, Hamath, and the isles of the
sea.

12 He shall raise a signal to the nations
and gather the outcasts of Israel;
The dispersed of Judah he shall
assemble
from the four corners of the earth.

13* The envy of Ephraim shall pass away,
and the rivalry of Judah be removed;
Ephraim shall not be jealous of Judah,
and Judah shall not be hostile to
Ephraim;

14† But they shall swoop down on the
foothills
of the Philistines to the west,
together they shall plunder the
Kedemites;
Edom and Moab shall be their
possessions,
and the Ammonites their subjects.

15*† The Lord shall dry up the tongue of the
Sea of Egypt,
and wave his hand over the Euphrates
in his fierce anger
And shatter it into seven streamlets,
so that it can be crossed in sandals.

16 There shall be a highway for the remnant
of his people
that is left from Assyria,
As there was for Israel
when he came up from the land of
Egypt.

Song of Thanksgiving

12 1† On that day, you will say:
I give you thanks, O Lord;
though you have been angry with me,
your anger has abated, and you have
consoled me.

2* God indeed is my savior;
I am confident and unafraid.
My strength and my courage is the
Lord,
and he has been my savior.

3 With joy you will draw water
at the fountain of salvation,
and say on that day:
Give thanks to the Lord, acclaim his
name;
among the nations make known his
deeds,
proclaim how exalted is his name.

5* Sing praise to the Lord for his glorious
achievement;
let this be known throughout all
the earth.

6* Shout with exultation, O city of Zion,
for great in your midst
is the Holy One of Israel!

III: ORACLES AGAINST THE PAGAN NATIONS

Babylon

13 1 AN ORACLE CONCERNING BABYLON; a vision of Isaiah, son of Amoz.

2*† Upon the bare mountains set up a signal;
cry out to them,
Wave for them to enter
the gates of the volunteers.

3† I have commanded my dedicated
soldiers,
I have summoned my warriors,
eager and bold to carry out my anger.

---

† dramatic symbol of the universal peace and justice of messianic times.

11, 11: *Pathros . . . sea:* where God's people lived in exile. *Pathros:* upper Egypt. *Elam:* east of Babylonia. *Shinar:* Babylonia. *Hamath:* on the Orontes River in Syria. *Isles:* or coastlands, in the Mediterranean.

11, 14: *Kedemites:* tribes in the Arabian Desert.

11, 15: *Tongue . . . Egypt:* the body of water between Egypt and Palestine.

12, 1-6: Israel's thanksgiving to the Lord, expressed in language like that of the Psalms.

13, 2: *To them:* the Medes (v 17) and Persians, who would destroy Babylon. *Gates of the volunteers:* the mustering places of Babylon's enemies for war against her.

13, 3: *Dedicated soldiers:* in the sense that they will wage a "holy war" and carry out God's plan.

---

*
9: Hb 2, 14.
10: 49, 22; Rom 15, 12.
11: 27, 13; Mi 7, 12;
    Zec 10, 10.
13: Ez 37, 16-17.
15: Ex 14, 29.

12/2: Ex 15, 2;
    Ps 118, 14.
5: Ex 15, 1.
6: 41, 14.16; 54, 1;
    Zep 3, 14; Zec 2, 10.
13/2: 5, 26.

4* Listen! the rumble on the mountains:
  that of an immense throng!
Listen! the noise of kingdoms,
  nations assembled!
The Lord of hosts is mustering
  an army for battle.

5 They come from a far-off country,
  and from the end of the heavens,
The Lord and the instruments of his
  wrath,
  to destroy all the land.

6*† Howl, for the day of the Lord is near;
  as destruction from the Almighty it
  comes.

7* Therefore all hands fall helpless,
  the bows of the young men fall from
  their hands.
Every man's heart melts **8*** in terror.
  pangs and sorrows take hold of them,
  like a woman in labor they writhe;
They look aghast at each other,
  their faces aflame.

9 Lo, the day of the Lord comes
  cruel, with wrath and burning anger;
To lay waste the land
  and destroy the sinners within it!

10* The stars and constellations of the
  heavens
  send forth no light;
The sun is dark when it rises,
  and the light of the moon does not
  shine.

11* Thus I will punish the world for its evil
  and the wicked for their guilt.
I will put an end to the pride of the
  arrogant,
  the insolence of tyrants I will humble.

12† I will make mortals more rare than pure
  gold,
  men, than gold of Ophir.

13 For this I will make the heavens tremble
  and the earth shall be shaken from its
  place,
At the wrath of the Lord of hosts
  on the day of his burning anger.

14* Like a hunted gazelle,
  or a flock that no one gathers,
Every man shall turn to his kindred
  and flee to his own land.

15 Everyone who is caught shall be run
  through;
  to a man, they shall fall by the sword.

16* Their infants shall be dashed to pieces
  in their sight;
  their houses shall be plundered
  and their wives ravished.

17* I am stirring up against them the Medes,
  who think nothing of silver
  and take no delight in gold.

18 The fruit of the womb they shall not
  spare,
  nor shall they have eyes of pity for
  children.

19 And Babylon, the jewel of kingdoms,
  the glory and pride of the Chaldeans,
Shall be overthrown by God
  like Sodom and like Gomorrah.

20* She shall never be inhabited,
  nor dwelt in, from age to age;
The Arab shall not pitch his tent there,
  nor shepherds couch their flocks.

21*† But wildcats shall rest there
  and owls shall fill the houses;
There ostriches shall dwell,
  and satyrs shall dance.

22 Desert beasts shall howl in her castles,
  and jackals in her luxurious palaces.
Her time is near at hand
  and her days shall not be prolonged.

The King of Babylon

14 **1*** WHEN the Lord has pity on Jacob and again chooses Israel and settles them on their own soil, the aliens will join them and be counted with the house of Jacob. **2*** The house of Israel will take them and bring them along to its place, and possess them as male and female slaves on the Lord's soil, making captives of its captors and ruling over its oppressors. **3*** On the day the Lord relieves you of sorrow and unrest and the hard service in which you have been enslaved, **4*†** you will take up this taunt-song against the king of Babylon:

How the oppressor has reached his end!
  how the turmoil is stilled!

5 The Lord has broken the rod of the
  wicked,
  the staff of the tyrants

6 That struck the peoples in wrath
  relentless blows;
That beat down the nations in anger,
  with oppression unchecked.

4: Jer 50, 9.
6: Jer 46, 10; Jl 1, 15.
7: Ez 7, 17.
8: 21, 3; Ps 48, 7; Mi 4, 9.
10: 24, 23.
11: 2, 17; Jer 50, 32.
14: Jer 50, 16.
16: Na 3, 10.
17: 21, 2; Jer 51, 11.28.
20: Jer 51, 62.
21: 34, 13f; 35, 7.
14/1: 56, 3; 60, 4; Ps 102, 14; Jer 24, 6; Zec 1, 17.
2: 66, 20.
3: Jer 30, 10.
4: Hb 2, 6.

† 13, 6ff: *Day of the Lord:* described often in prophetical writings, it generally signified the coming of the Lord in power and majesty to destroy his enemies and inaugurate his kingdom. Here it refers to the overthrow of Babylon. The figures used convey the idea of horror and destruction. Read vv 6-8 with vv 14-16.

13, 12: *Ophir:* cf note to Ps 45, 10.

13, 21: *Satyrs:* in the popular mind, demons of goatlike form dwelling in ruins, symbols of immorality; cf Lv 17, 7.

14, 4-21: This *taunt-song*, or satire, is one of the finest in the Bible.

7 The whole earth rests peacefully,
song breaks forth;

8＊ The very cypresses rejoice over you,
and the cedars of Lebanon:
"Now that you are laid to rest,
there will be none to cut us down."

9 The nether world below is all astir
preparing for your coming;
It awakens the shades to greet you,
all the leaders of the earth;
It has the kings of all nations
rise from their thrones.

10 All of them speak out
and say to you,
"You too have become weak like us,
you are the same as we.

11＊ Down to the nether world your pomp is
brought,
the music of your harps.
The couch beneath you is the maggot,
your covering, the worm."

12† How have you fallen from the heavens,
O morning star, son of the dawn!
How are you cut down to the ground,
you who mowed down the nations!

13＊† You said in your heart:
"I will scale the heavens;
Above the stars of God
I will set up my throne;
I will take my seat on the Mount of
Assembly,
in the recesses of the North.

14＊ I will ascend above the tops of the
clouds;
I will be like the Most High!"

15 Yet down to the nether world you go
to the recesses of the pit!

16 When they see you they will stare,
pondering over you:
"Is this the man who made the earth
tremble,
and kingdoms quake?

17 Who made the world a desert,
razed its cities,
and gave his captives no release?

18 All the kings of the nations lie in glory,
each in his own tomb;

19 But you are cast forth without burial,
loathsome and corrupt,
Clothed as those slain at sword-point,
a trampled corpse.
Going down to the pavement of the pit,

20 you will never be one with them in
the grave."

For you have ruined your land,
you have slain your people!
Let him not be named forever,
that scion of an evil race!

21 Make ready to slaughter his sons
for the guilt of their fathers;
Lest they rise and possess the earth,
and fill the breadth of the world with
tyrants.

22＊I will rise up against them, says the LORD of hosts, and cut off from Babylon name and remnant, progeny and offspring, says the LORD. **23**I will make it a haunt of hoot owls and a marshland; I will sweep it with the broom of destruction, says the LORD of hosts.

Assyria

24 The LORD of hosts has sworn:
As I have resolved,
so shall it be;
As I have proposed,
so shall it stand:

25 I will break the Assyrian in my land
and trample him on my mountains;

8/21 He shall pass through it hard-pressed
and hungry,
and in his hunger he shall become
enraged,
and curse his king and his gods.
He shall look upward,
but there shall be strict darkness
without any dawn;

8/22 He shall gaze at the earth,
but there shall be distress and
darkness,
with the light blacked out by its
clouds.

(25) Then his yoke shall be removed from
them,
and his burden from their shoulder.

26 This is the plan proposed for the whole
earth,
and this the hand outstretched over
all nations.

27 The LORD of hosts has planned;
who can thwart him?
His hand is stretched out;
who can turn it back?

Philistia

28† In the year that King Ahaz died, there
came this oracle:

＊
8: Ez 31, 16.   14: Ez 28, 2.
11: Sir 10, 13.   22: Jer 51, 62.
13: Jer 51, 53; Am 9, 2.

† 14, 12: *Morning star:* the king of Babylon. The Vulgate has "Lucifer," a name applied by the church Fathers to Satan.

14, 13: *Recesses of the North:* see note on Ps 48, 3.

14, 28: *The year that King Ahaz died:* 715 B. C.

29† Rejoice not, O Philistia, not a man of
    you,
    that the rod which smote you is
    broken;
    For out of the serpent's root shall come
    an adder,
    its fruit shall be a flying saraph.
30 In my pastures the poor shall eat,
    and the needy lie down in safety;
    But I will kill your root with famine
    that shall slay even your remnant.
31 Howl, O gate; cry out, O city!
    Philistia, all of you melts away!
    For there comes a smoke from the north,
    without a straggler in the ranks.
32✶ What will one answer the messengers of
    the nation?
    "The LORD has established Zion,
    and in her the afflicted of his people
    find refuge."

Moab

15 1✶ Oracle on Moab:
    Laid waste in a night,
    Ar of Moab is destroyed;
    Laid waste in a night,
    Kir of Moab is destroyed.
2✶† Up goes daughter Dibon
    to the high places to weep;
    Over Nebo and over Medeba
    Moab wails.
    Every head is shaved,
    every beard sheared off.
3 In the streets they wear sackcloth,
    lamenting and weeping;
    On rooftops and in the squares
    everyone wails.
4✶ Heshbon and Elealeh cry out,
    they are heard as far as Jahaz.
    At this the loins of Moab tremble,
    his soul quivers within him;
5 The heart of Moab cries out,
    his fugitives reach Zoar
    [Eglath-shelishiyah].
    The ascent of Luhith
    they climb weeping;
    On the way to Horonaim
    they utter rending cries.
6 The waters of Nimrim
    have become a waste;
    The grass is withered,
    new growth is gone,
    nothing is green.

7 So now whatever they have acquired or
    stored away
    they carry across the Gorge of the
    Poplars,
8 For the cry has gone round
    the land of Moab;
    As far as Eglaim the wailing,
    and to Beer-elim, the wail.
9† The waters of Dimon are filled with
    blood,
    but I will bring still more upon
    Dimon:
    Lions for those who are fleeing from
    Moab
    and for those who remain in the land!

16 1 Send them forth, hugging the earth like
    reptiles,
    from Sela across the desert,
    to the mount of daughter Zion.
2† Like flushed birds,
    like startled nestlings,
    Are the daughters of Moab
    at the fords of the Arnon.
3✶† Offer counsel, take their part:
    at high noon let your shadow be like
    the night,
    To hide the outcasts,
    to conceal the fugitives.
4 Let the outcasts of Moab live with you,
    be their shelter from the destroyer.
    When the struggle is ended, the ruin
    complete,
    and they have done with trampling
    the land,
5✶ A throne shall be set up in mercy,
    and on it shall sit in fidelity
    [in David's tent]
    A judge upholding right
    and prompt to do justice.
6✶ We have heard of the pride of Moab,
    how very proud he is,
    With his haughty, arrogant insolence
    that his empty words do not match.
7✶† Therefore Moab wails for Moab,
    everywhere they wail;

† 14, 29: *Rod:* an Assyrian oppressor whose identity is uncertain. *Flying saraph:* a poisonous serpent, distinguished by its speedy movement; cf note on Nm 21, 6.
15, 2: *Every head . . . sheared off:* traditional signs of grief.
15, 9: There is in the Hebrew a play on words: *Dimon* and *dam,* the latter signifying "blood."
16, 2: *The Arnon:* principal river of Moab.
16, 3-5: Directed to Jerusalem, which should receive the suffering Moabites with mercy, as befits the city of David's family, who were partly descended from Ruth the Moabite.
16, 7-14: Moab had been prosperous; now it has become a desert.
16, 7: *Raisin cakes:* masses of dried compressed grapes used as food (cf 2 Sm 6, 19; 1 Chr 16, 3; Ct 2, 5), and also in pagan cult (Hos 3, 1).

✶ 32: Pss 87, 5; 102, 17f; Zep 3, 12.
15/1: 16, 7.
2: Jer 48, 38f.
4: Jer 48, 34.
5: 16, 9; Jer 48, 3.
16/5: 32, 1.
6: Jer 48, 29.
7: 15, 3.

For the raisin cakes of Kir-hareseth
    they sigh, stricken with grief.
8† The terraced slopes of Heshbon
    languish,
    the vines of Sibmah,
Whose clusters overpowered
    the lords of nations,
While they reached as far as Jazer
    and scattered over the desert,
And whose branches spread forth
    and extended over the sea.
9✣ Therefore I weep with Jazer
    for the vines of Sibmah;
I water you with tears,
    Heshbon and Elealeh;
For on your summer fruits and harvests
    the battle cry has fallen.
10✣ From the orchards are taken away
    joy and gladness,
In the vineyards there is no singing,
    no shout of joy;
In the wine presses no one treads grapes,
    the vintage shout is stilled.
11✣ Therefore for Moab
    my breast moans like a lyre,
    and my heart for Kir-hareseth.
12✣† When Moab grows weary on the high
    places,
    he shall enter his sanctuary to pray,
    but it shall avail him nothing.

13†This is the word the LORD spoke against Moab in times past. **14**But now the LORD has spoken: In three years, like those of a hireling, the glory of Moab shall be degraded despite all its great multitude; there shall be a remnant, very small and weak.

Damascus

17 **1✣†**   Oracle on Damascus:
Lo, Damascus shall cease to be a city
    and become a ruin;
2 Her cities shall be forever abandoned,
    given over to flocks to lie in
      undisturbed.
3† The fortress shall be lost to Ephraim
    and the kingdom to Damascus;
The remnant of Aram shall have the
    same glory
    as the Israelites,
    says the LORD of hosts.
4✣   On that day
The glory of Jacob shall fade,
    and his full body grow thin,
5† Like the reaper's mere armful of stalks
    when he gathers the standing grain;

Or as when one gleans the ears
    in the Valley of Rephaim.
6✣† Only a scattering of grapes shall be left!
    As when an olive tree has been beaten,
Two or three olives remain at the very
    top,
    four or five on its fruitful branches,
    says the LORD, the God of Israel.

7✣ On that day man shall look to his maker,
    his eyes turned toward the Holy One
      of Israel.
8† He shall not look to the altars, his
    handiwork,
    nor shall he regard what his fingers
      have made:
    the sacred poles or the incense stands.
9✣ On that day his strong cities shall be
    like those abandoned by the Hivites
      and Amorites
When faced with the children of Israel:
    they shall be laid waste.
10✣† For you have forgotten God, your savior,
    and remembered not the Rock, your
      strength.
Therefore, though you plant your pagan
    plants
    and set out your foreign vine slips,
11 Though you make them grow the day
    you plant them
    and make your sprouts blossom on the
      next morning,
The harvest shall disappear on the day
    of the grievous blow,
    the incurable blight.

12† Ah! the roaring of many peoples
    that roar like the roar of the seas!
The surging of nations
    that surge like the surging of mighty
      waves!

---

† 16, 8: *Desert:* to the east. *Sea:* the Dead Sea.
16, 12: In vain do the Moabites appeal to their god Chemosh.
16, 13f: A prose application of the preceding poetic oracle against Moab (15, 1—16, 12); cf Jer 4, 8. *Like those of a hireling:* who fulfills his period of service according to the shortest manner of reckoning; cf 21, 16.
17, 1: *Damascus:* capital of Syria, destroyed in 732 B. C.
17, 3: *Ephraim:* Israel, leagued with Syria against Assyria and Judah; destroyed in 721 B. C. *Aram:* Syria.
17, 5: *Valley of Rephaim:* a fertile plain to the southwest of Jerusalem; cf Jos 15, 8; 2 Sm 5, 18.
17, 6: Olives not easily picked by hand were knocked from the tree by means of a long stick; cf 24, 13.
17, 8: *Sacred poles:* see note on Ex 34, 13. *Incense stands:* small altars on which incense was burned in idolatrous worship; cf 27, 9; Lv 26, 30.
17, 10 *Pagan plants:* literally, "plants of delights," understood by some as planted in honor of the god of fertility.
17, 12f: *Many peoples:* the hordes that accompanied the invading Assyrians, whom God repels just as he vanquished the primeval waters of chaos; see notes on Jb 3, 8; 7, 12; Ps 89, 11.

✣
    9: 15, 5; Jer 48, 32.
    10: 24, 8.
    11: 15, 5; Jer 48, 36.
    12: Jer 48, 13.
    17/1: Jer 49, 23.
    4: 10, 16.
    6: 24, 13.
    7: Mi 5, 12.
    9: 27, 10.
    10: Jer 2, 32; Hos 8, 14.

13 But God shall rebuke them,
  and they shall flee far away;
Windswept, like chaff on the mountains,
  like tumbleweed in a storm.
14 In the evening, they spread terror,
  before morning, they are gone!
Such is the portion of those who despoil us,
  the lot of those who plunder us.

Ethiopia

18 **1†** Ah, land of buzzing insects,
  beyond the rivers of Ethiopia,
2*† Sending ambassadors by sea,
  in papyrus boats on the waters!
Go, swift messengers,
  to a nation tall and bronzed,
To a people dreaded near and far,
  a nation strong and conquering,
  whose land is washed by rivers.
3 All you who inhabit the world,
  who dwell on earth,
When the signal is raised on the mountain, look!
When the trumpet blows, listen!

4 For thus says the Lord to me:
  I will quietly look on from where I dwell,
Like the glowing heat of sunshine,
  like a cloud of dew at harvest time.
5 Before the vintage, when the flowering is ended,
  and the blooms are succeeded by ripening grapes,
Then comes the cutting of branches with pruning hooks
  and the discarding of the lopped-off shoots.
6 They shall all be left to the mountain birds of prey,
  and to the beasts in the land;
The birds of prey shall summer on them
  and on them all the beasts of the earth shall winter.

7*Then will gifts be brought to the Lord of hosts from a people tall and bronzed, from a people dreaded near and far, a nation strong and conquering, whose land is washed by rivers—to Mount Zion where dwells the name of the Lord of hosts.

Egypt

19 **1** Oracle on Egypt:
  See, the Lord is riding on a swift cloud
  on his way to Egypt;

The idols of Egypt tremble before him,
  the hearts of the Egyptians melt within them.
2 I will rouse Egypt against Egypt:
  brother will war against brother,
Neighbor against neighbor,
  city against city, kingdom against kingdom.
3* The courage of the Egyptians ebbs away within them,
  and I will bring to nought their counsel;
They shall consult idols and charmers,
  ghosts and spirits.
4*† I will deliver Egypt
  into the power of a cruel master,
A harsh king who shall rule over them,
  says the Lord, the Lord of hosts.
5* The waters shall be drained from the sea,
  the river shall shrivel and dry up;
6 Its streams shall become foul,
  and the canals of Egypt shall dwindle and dry up.
Reeds and rushes shall wither away,
  and bulrushes on the bank of the Nile;
7 All the sown land along the Nile
  shall dry up and blow away, and be no more.
8 The fishermen shall mourn and lament,
  all who cast hook in the Nile;
Those who spread their nets in the water
  shall pine away.
9* The linen-workers shall be disappointed,
  the combers and weavers shall turn pale;
10 The spinners shall be crushed,
  all the hired laborers shall be despondent.

11† Utter fools are the princes of Zoan!
  the wisest of Pharaoh's advisers give stupid counsel.
How can you say to Pharaoh,
  "I am a disciple of wise men, of ancient kings"?
12 Where then are your wise men?
  Let them tell you and make known
What the Lord of hosts has planned against Egypt.

18/2: 18, 7.
7: 45, 14; Zep 3, 10; Mal 1, 11.
19/3: 44, 25.
4: Ez 29, 19; 30, 10.
5: Ez 30, 12; 32, 2.
9: Ez 27, 7.

† 18, 1: *Land of buzzing insects:* the region of the upper Nile where these multiplied with great rapidity.

18, 2: *Papyrus boats:* light and serviceable vessels made of bundles of papyrus stalks and sealed with pitch. Egypt, ruled by a dynasty from *Ethiopia,* had invited Judah to join a coalition against Assyria, but Isaiah bade the *ambassadors* return to their own people.

19, 4: *Cruel master:* the king of Assyria.

19, 11.13: *Zoan,* later known as Tanis, and *Memphis* (in Hebrew *Noph*) were the key cities of the Nile Delta.

13   The princes of Zoan have become fools,
      the princes of Memphis have been
        deceived.
    The chiefs of her tribes
      have led Egypt astray.
14   The Lord has prepared among them
      a spirit of dizziness,
    And they have made Egypt stagger in
      whatever she does,
      as a drunkard staggers in his vomit.
15*†   Egypt shall have no work to do
      for head or tail, palm branch or reed.

16*On that day the Egyptians shall be like women, trembling with fear, because of the Lord of hosts shaking his fist at them. 17*And the land of Judah shall be a terror to the Egyptians. Every time they remember Judah, they shall stand in dread because of the plan which the Lord of hosts has in mind for them. 18†On that day there shall be five cities in the land of Egypt speaking the language of Canaan and swearing by the Lord of hosts; one shall be called "City of the Sun." 19On that day there shall be an altar to the Lord in the land of Egypt, and a sacred pillar to the Lord near the boundary. 20It shall be a sign and a witness to the Lord of hosts in the land of Egypt, when they cry out to the Lord against their oppressors, and he sends them a savior to defend and deliver them. 21*The Lord shall make himself known to Egypt, and the Egyptians shall know the Lord in that day; they shall offer sacrifices and oblations, and fulfill the vows they make to the Lord. 22Although the Lord shall smite Egypt severely, he shall heal them; they shall turn to the Lord and he shall be won over and heal them. 23On that day there shall be a highway from Egypt to Assyria; the Assyrians shall enter Egypt, and the Egyptians enter Assyria, and Egypt shall serve Assyria. 24*On that day Israel shall be a third party with Egypt and Assyria, a blessing in the midst of the land, 25when the Lord of hosts blesses it: "Blessed be my people Egypt, and the work of my hands Assyria, and my inheritance, Israel."

Captivity of Egypt and Ethiopia

20 1In the year the general sent by Sargon, king of Assyria, fought against Ashdod and captured it, 2†the Lord gave a warning through Isaiah, the son of Amoz: Go and take off the sackcloth from your waist, and remove the sandals from your feet. This he did, walking naked and barefoot. 3Then the Lord said: Just as my servant Isaiah has gone naked and barefoot for three years as a sign and portent against Egypt and Ethiopia, 4so shall the king of As-

syria lead away captives from Egypt, and exiles from Ethiopia, young and old, naked and barefoot, with buttocks uncovered [the shame of Egypt]. 5*They shall be dismayed and ashamed because of Ethiopia, their hope, and because of Egypt, their boast. 6*The inhabitants of this coastland shall say on that day, "Look at our hope! We have fled here for help and deliverance from the king of Assyria; where can we flee now?"

Fall of Babylon

21 1†   Oracle on the wastelands by the
      sea:
    Like whirlwinds sweeping in waves
      through the Negeb,
      there comes from the desert,
      from the fearful land,
2*†   A cruel sight, revealed to me:
      the traitor betrays,
      the despoiler spoils.
    "Go up, Elam; besiege, O Media;
      I will put an end to all groaning!"
3*   Therefore my loins are filled with
      anguish,
      pangs have seized me like those of a
        woman in labor;
    I am too bewildered to hear,
      too dismayed to look.
4   My mind reels,
      shuddering assails me;
    My yearning for twilight
      has turned into dread.
5†   They set the table,
      spread out the rugs;
      they eat, they drink.
    Rise up, O princes,
      oil the shield!

6   For thus says my Lord to me:
      Go, station a watchman,
      let him tell what he sees.
7   If he sees a chariot,
      a pair of horses,
    Someone riding an ass,
      someone riding a camel,

---

† 19, 15: *Head or tail, palm branch or reed:* the leaders or the people; cf 9, 13f.

19, 18: *Five cities:* colonies of Jews living together and speaking their languages, Hebrew and Aramaic; cf Jer, chap. 43. *City of the Sun:* the meaning is uncertain, but the reference seems to be to the city known later as Heliopolis.

20, 2-6: The symbolic act of the prophet conveyed the idea that Assyria would lead captive the Egyptians and Ethiopians. The Judeans and their allies would then realize the folly of having trusted in them.

21, 1: *Wastelands by the sea:* Babylonia. *Negeb:* the desert south of Judah.

21, 2: *Elam . . . Media:* nations which, under the leadership of Cyrus, captured Babylon in 538 B. C. *End to all groaning:* those who were captives of Babylon shall be freed.

21, 5: Babylon is destroyed while its leaders are feasting; cf Dn 5. *Oil the shield:* shields were oiled and greased so as to divert blows more easily.

---

*   15: 9, 14.   20/5: 30, 3.5.
      16: Na 3, 13.   6: 31, 3; 36, 6.
      17: Ex 14, 25.   21/2: 13, 17.
      21: Zec 14, 16.18.   3: Ps 38, 8.
      24: Gn 12, 2.

Then let him pay heed,
very close heed.

8* Then the watchman cried,
"On the watchtower, O my Lord,
I stand constantly by day;
And I stay at my post
through all the watches of the night.

9* Here he comes now:
a single chariot,
a pair of horses;
He calls out and says,
'Fallen, fallen is Babylon,
And all the images of her gods
are smashed to the ground.'"

10* O my people who have been threshed,
beaten on my threshing floor!
What I have heard
from the LORD of hosts,
The God of Israel
I have announced to you.

Edom

11† Oracle on Edom:
They call to me from Seir,
"Watchman, how much longer the
night?
Watchman, how much longer the
night?"

12 The watchman replies,
"Morning has come, and again night.
If you will ask, ask; come back again."

Arabia

13† Oracle on Arabia:
In the thicket in the nomad country
spend the night,
O caravans of Dedanites.

14 Meet the thirsty, bring them water;
you who dwell in the land of Tema,
greet the fugitives with bread.

15 They flee from the sword,
from the whetted sword;
From the taut bow,
from the fury of battle.

16†For thus says the Lord to me: In another year, like those of a hireling, all the glory of Kedar shall come to an end. **17**Few of Kedar's stalwart archers shall remain, for the LORD, the God of Israel, has spoken.

Jerusalem

22 **1†** Oracle of the Valley of Vision:
What is the matter with you now, that
you have gone up,
all of you, to the housetops,

2* O city full of noise and chaos,
O wanton town!
Your slain are not slain with the sword,
nor killed in battle.

3* All your leaders fled away together,
fled afar off;
All who were in you were captured
together,
captured without the use of a bow.

4* At this I say: Turn away from me,
let me weep bitterly;
Do not try to comfort me
for the ruin of the daughter of my
people.

5* It is a day of panic, rout and confusion,
from the Lord, the GOD of hosts, in the
Valley of Vision.
Walls crash;
they cry for help to the mountains.

6† Elam takes up the quivers,
Aram mounts the horses,
and Kir uncovers the shields.

7 Your choice valleys are filled with
chariots,
and horses are posted at the gates,

8† and shelter over Judah is removed.

On that day you looked to the weapons in the House of the Forest; **9**you saw that the breaches in the City of David were many; you collected the water of the lower pool. **10**You numbered the houses of Jerusalem, tearing some down to strengthen the wall; **11**you made a reservoir between the two walls for the water of the old pool. But you did not look to the city's Maker, nor did you consider him who built it long ago.

12* On that day the Lord,
the GOD of hosts, called on you
To weep and mourn,
to shave your head and put on
sackcloth.

---

† 21, 11f: *Seir:* another name for Edom. The Edomites ask the prophet how much longer they must suffer (*the night* of suffering); he answers ambiguously: "Liberation (*morning*) and further suffering (*night*)," but perhaps they will later receive a more encouraging answer (*ask; come back again*).

21, 13f: *Arabia:* that is, *the nomad country. Dedanites:* an Arab tribe associated with Edom and *Tema,* and living east of the Red Sea; cf Gn 10, 7; 25, 3; Jer 25, 23.

21, 16: *Year . . . of a hireling:* see note on 16, 14. *Kedar:* a nomad tribe in Arabia; cf 42, 11; 60, 7; Ps 120, 5.

22, 1-8: *Valley of Vision:* while the people live in revelry and disorder, the prophet foresees the impending doom of the city.

22, 6: *Elam, Aram, Kir:* all allies of Assyria. *Kir:* perhaps the same people referred to in Am 1, 5.

22, 8-11: Defense measures, in which the inhabitants of Jerusalem placed their trust instead of relying on God. *House of the Forest:* an armory built by Solomon; its columns of wood suggested the trees of a forest; cf 1 Kgs 7, 2; 10, 17.

* 8: Hb 2, 1.
9: 46, 1; Jer 50, 2; 51, 8; Rv 14, 8.
10: 51, 23.
22/2: 32, 13.
3: 2 Kgs 25, 4.
4: Jer 6, 26; 9, 1; 14, 17.
5: 37, 3.
12: Jl 2, 17.

13* But look! you feast and celebrate,
you slaughter oxen and butcher sheep,
You eat meat and drink wine:
"Eat and drink, for tomorrow we die!"
14 This reaches the ears of the LORD of
hosts—
You shall not be pardoned this
wickedness till you die,
says the Lord, the GOD of hosts.

Shebna and Eliakim

15† Thus says the Lord, the GOD of hosts:
Up, go to that official,
Shebna, master of the palace,
16 Who has hewn for himself a sepulcher
on a height
and carved his tomb in the rock:
"What are you doing here, and what
people have you here,
that here you have hewn for yourself a
tomb?"
17 The LORD shall hurl you down headlong,
mortal man!
He shall grip you firmly
18 And roll you up and toss you like a ball
into an open land
To perish there, you and the chariots you
glory in,
you disgrace to your master's house!
19 I will thrust you from your office
and pull you down from your station.

20*† On that day I will summon my servant
Eliakim, son of Hilkiah;
21 I will clothe him with your robe,
and gird him with your sash,
and give over to him your authority.
He shall be a father to the inhabitants of
Jerusalem,
and to the house of Judah.
22*† I will place the key of the House of
David on his shoulder;
when he opens, no one shall shut,
when he shuts, no one shall open.
23 I will fix him like a peg in a sure spot,
to be a place of honor for his family;
24† On him shall hang all the glory of his
family:
descendants and offspring,
all the little dishes, from bowls to jugs.

25On that day, says the LORD of hosts, the peg fixed
in a sure spot shall give way, break off and fall, and
the weight that hung on it shall be done away with;
for the LORD has spoken.

Tyre and Sidon

23 1† Oracle on Tyre:
Wail, O ships of Tarshish,
for your port is destroyed;
From the land of the Kittim
the news reaches them.
2 Silence! you who dwell on the coast,
you merchants of Sidon,
Whose messengers crossed the sea
over the deep waters.
3† The grain of Shihor, the harvest of the
Nile, was her revenue,
and she the merchant among nations.
4† Shame, O Sidon, fortress on the sea,
for the sea has spoken:
"I have not been in labor, nor given birth,
nor raised young men,
nor reared virgins."
5 When it is heard in Egypt
they shall be in anguish at the news of
Tyre.
6 Pass over to Tarshish, wailing,
you who dwell on the coast!
7 Is this your wanton city,
whose origin is from of old,
Whose feet have taken her
to dwell in distant lands?
8 Who has planned such a thing
against Tyre, the bestower of crowns,
Whose merchants are princes,
whose traders are the earth's honored
men?
9* The LORD of hosts has planned it,
to disgrace all pride of majesty,
to degrade all the earth's honored
men.
10 Cross to your own land,
O ship of Tarshish;
the harbor is no more.
11† His hand he stretches out over the sea,
he shakes kingdoms;
The LORD has ordered the destruction
of Canaan's strongholds.
12* You shall exult no more, he says,
you who are now oppressed,
virgin daughter Sidon.
Arise, pass over to the Kittim,
even there you shall find no rest.

---

† 22, 15: *Shebna:* referred to as the scribe in 36, 3.
22, 20: *Eliakim:* also referred to in 36, 3; he is described as
loyal to God.
22, 22: *Key:* symbol of authority; cf Mt 16, 19; Rv 3, 7.
22, 24f: If Eliakim should anger God, he and his family (compared here to dishes, bowls and jugs) will suffer disaster.
23, 1-4.12ff: these verses refer to Sidon, vv 5-11 to Tyre.
23, 1: *Kittim:* Cyprus.
23, 3: *Shihor:* a synonym for the Nile.
23, 4: *The sea* brings to distant coasts the news that Sidon
must disown her children; her people are dispersed.
23, 11: *Canaan's strongholds:* the fortresses of Phoenicia.

✿   13: 56, 12; Wis 2, 6;   22: Rv 3, 7.
       1 Cor 15, 32.   23/9: Ez 28, 7.
       20: 2 Kgs 18, 18.37.   12: Ez 28, 21f.

13*† [This people is the land of the
Chaldeans, not Assyria.]

She whom the impious founded,
   setting up towers for her,
Has had her castles destroyed,
   and has been turned into a ruin.

14 Lament, O ships of Tarshish,
   for your haven is destroyed.

15*† On that day, Tyre shall be forgotten for seventy years. With the days of another king, at the end of seventy years, it shall be for Tyre as in the song about the harlot:

16 Take a harp, go about the city,
   O forgotten harlot;
Pluck the strings skillfully,
   sing many songs,
   that they may remember you.

17* At the end of the seventy years the LORD shall visit Tyre. She shall return to her hire and deal with all the world's kingdoms on the face of the earth. **18†** But her merchandise and her hire shall be sacred to the LORD. It shall not be stored up or laid away, but from her merchandise those who dwell before the LORD shall eat their fill and clothe themselves in choice attire.

IV: APOCALYPSE OF ISAIAH

Devastation of the World: A Remnant Saved

24 **1*†** LO, THE LORD EMPTIES THE LAND and lays
   it waste;
he turns it upside down,
   scattering its inhabitants:

2 Layman and priest alike,
   servant and master,
The maid as her mistress,
   the buyer as the seller,
The lender as the borrower,
   the creditor as the debtor.

3 The earth is utterly laid waste, utterly
   stripped,
for the LORD has decreed this thing.

4 The earth mourns and fades,
   the world languishes and fades;
both heaven and earth languish.

5† The earth is polluted because of its
   inhabitants,
who have transgressed laws,
   violated statutes,
   broken the ancient covenant.

6 Therefore a curse devours the earth,
   and its inhabitants pay for their guilt;
Therefore they who dwell on earth
   turn pale,
   and few men are left.

7* The wine mourns, the vine languishes,
   all the merry-hearted groan.

8* Stilled are the cheerful timbrels,
   ended the shouts of the jubilant,
   stilled is the cheerful harp.

9 They cannot sing and drink wine;
   strong drink is bitter to those who partake of it.

10*† Broken down is the city of chaos,
   shut against entry, every house.

11* In the streets they cry out for lack of
   wine;
all joy has disappeared
   and cheer has left the land.

12 In the city nothing remains but ruin;
   its gates are battered and desolate.

13* Thus it is within the land,
   and among the peoples,
As with an olive tree after it is beaten,
   as with a gleaning when the vintage
   is done.

14† These lift up their voice in acclaim;
   from the sea they proclaim the
   majesty of the LORD:

15* "For this, in the coastlands,
   give glory to the LORD!
In the coastlands of the sea,
   to the name of the LORD, the God of
   Israel!"

16 From the end of the earth we hear songs:
   "Splendor to the Just One!"
But I said, "I am wasted, wasted away.
   Woe is me! The traitors betray:
   with treachery have the traitors
   betrayed!

17* Terror, pit, and trap
   are upon you, inhabitant of the earth;

18 He who flees at the sound of terror
   will fall into the pit;
He who climbs out of the pit
   will be caught in the trap.

---

† 23, 13: The gloss here identifies *she whom the impious founded* with *the land of the Chaldeans.*

23, 15: *Seventy years:* a conventional period of time indicating simply a long disaster; cf Jer 25, 11 and 29, 10.

23, 18: Describes the conversion of Tyre.

24, 1—27, 13: This section, probably composed at a later date, contains oracles on the day of the Lord, combined with hymns of thanksgiving and of supplication.

24, 5: *Ancient covenant:* God's commandments to all mankind.

24, 10: *City of chaos:* a symbol of godlessness as opposed to Jerusalem, the city of God.

24, 14: *These:* the saved.

13: Ez 26, 7.
15: Jer 25, 11.
17: Ez 27, 12.
24/1: 13, 9; Hos 4, 9.
7: Jl 1, 10.
8: Jer 7, 34; Hos 2, 13.
10: 25, 2.
11: Jer 48, 33; Lam 5, 14f.
13: 17, 6; Mi 7, 1.
15: 42, 10.12; Zep 2, 11.
17f: Jer 48, 43f.

For the windows on high will be opened
   and the foundations of the earth
      will shake.
19   The earth will burst asunder,
      the earth will be shaken apart,
      the earth will be convulsed.
20* The earth will reel like a drunkard,
      and it will sway like a hut;
   Its rebellion will weigh it down,
      until it falls, never to rise again."

21*† On that day the LORD will punish
      the host of the heavens in the heavens,
      and the kings of the earth on the earth.
22   They will be gathered together
      like prisoners into a pit;
   They will be shut up in a dungeon,
      and after many days they will be
         punished.
23*† Then the moon will blush
      and the sun grow pale,
   For the LORD of hosts will reign
      on Mount Zion and in Jerusalem,
      glorious in the sight of his elders.

25 1*† O LORD, you are my God,
      I will extol you and praise your name;
   For you have fulfilled your wonderful
         plans of old,
      faithful and true.
2*   For you have made the city a heap,
      the fortified city a ruin;
   The castle of the insolent is a city no
         more,
      nor ever to be rebuilt.
3   Therefore a strong people will honor
         you,
      fierce nations will fear you.
4*   For you are a refuge to the poor,
      a refuge to the needy in distress;
   Shelter from the rain,
      shade from the heat.
   As with the cold rain,
5   as with the desert heat,
      even so you quell the uproar of the
         wanton.
6†   On this mountain the LORD of hosts
      will provide for all peoples
   A feast of rich food and choice wines,
      juicy, rich food and pure, choice
         wines.

7*   On this mountain he will destroy
      the veil that veils all peoples,
   The web that is woven over all nations;
8   he will destroy death forever.
   The Lord GOD will wipe away
      the tears from all faces;
   The reproach of his people he will
         remove
      from the whole earth; for the LORD
         has spoken.

9*   On that day it will be said:
   "Behold our God, to whom we looked
         to save us!
      This is the LORD for whom we looked;
      let us rejoice and be glad that he has
         saved us!"
10*† For the hand of the LORD will rest on
         this mountain,
      but Moab will be trodden down
      as a straw is trodden down in the mire.
11* He will stretch forth his hands in Moab
      as a swimmer extends his hands to
         swim;
   He will bring low their pride
      as his hands sweep over them.
12* The high-walled fortress he will raze,
      and strike it down level with the earth,
      with the very dust.

The Divine Vindicator

26 1   On that day they will sing this song in
         the land of Judah:

   "A strong city have we;
      he sets up walls and ramparts
         to protect us.
2*   Open up the gates
      to let in a nation that is just,
      one that keeps faith.
3*   A nation of firm purpose you keep in
         peace;
      in peace, for its trust in you."

4*   Trust in the LORD forever!
      For the LORD is an eternal Rock.
5*   He humbles those in high places,
      and the lofty city he brings down;
   He tumbles it to the ground,
      levels it with the dust.
6   It is trampled underfoot by the needy,
      by the footsteps of the poor.
7*   The way of the just is smooth;
      the path of the just you make level.

---

*
   20: 9, 14.
   21: Ps 76, 13.
   23: 13, 10; Jl 3, 3f; 4, 15.
   25/1: Ex 15, 2.
   2: Jer 9, 11.
   4: 14, 32; 32, 2; Na 1, 7.
   7: 60, 1.3; 1 Cor 15, 53ff;
      Rv 7, 17; 21, 4.
   9: 30, 18f.

   10: Zep 2, 9f.
   11: 16, 6f.14.
   12: 26, 5.
   26/2: Ps 118, 19f.
   3: 32, 17f; 54, 13.
   4: 30, 29; Ps 62, 8.
   5: 25, 12; 32, 19.
   7: Ps 23, 3f; Prv 11, 3.5.

---

†
   24, 21: *Host of the heavens:* the stars, which were regarded
by the pagans as gods; cf Dt 4, 19; Jer 8, 2.
   24, 23: *His elders:* the heavenly courtiers surrounding the
throne of God.
   25, 1-8: Victory in messianic times.
   25, 6: *This mountain:* Zion, symbol of the heavenly Jerusalem.
   25, 10: *Moab:* symbol of God's enemies.

8   Yes, for your way and your judgments,
O LORD,
> we look to you;
Your name and your title
> are the desire of our souls.

9*   My soul yearns for you in the night,
> yes, my spirit within me keeps vigil
> for you;
When your judgment dawns upon the
earth,
> the world's inhabitants learn justice.

10*   The wicked man, spared, does not learn
justice;
> in an upright land he acts perversely,
> and sees not the majesty of the LORD.

11   O LORD, your hand is uplifted,
> but they behold it not;
Let them be shamed when they see
> your zeal for your people:
> let the fire prepared for your enemies
> consume them.

12*   O LORD, you mete out peace to us,
> for it is you who have accomplished
> all we have done.

13   O LORD, our God, other lords than you
have ruled us;
> it is from you only that we can call
> upon your name.

14   Dead they are, they have no life,
> shades that cannot rise;
For you have punished and destroyed
them,
> and wiped out all memory of them.

15*   You have increased the nation, O LORD,
> increased the nation to your own
> glory,
> and extended far all the borders of
> the land.

16*   O LORD, oppressed by your punishment,
> we cried out in anguish under your
> chastising.

17*   As a woman about to give birth
> writhes and cries out in her pains,
> so were we in your presence, O LORD.

18   We conceived and writhed in pain,
> giving birth to wind;
Salvation we have not achieved for
> the earth,
> the inhabitants of the world cannot
> bring it forth.

19*†   But your dead shall live, their corpses
shall rise;
> awake and sing, you who lie in the
> dust.
For your dew is a dew of light,
> and the land of shades gives birth.

Day of the Lord:
Reward and Punishment

20   Go, my people, enter your chambers,
> and close your doors behind you;
Hide yourselves for a brief moment,
> until the wrath is past.

21*   See, the LORD goes forth from his place,
> to punish the wickedness of the earth's
> inhabitants;
The earth will reveal the blood upon
her,
> and no longer conceal her slain.

27   1*†   On that day,
The LORD will punish with his sword
> that is cruel, great, and strong,
Leviathan the fleeing serpent,
> Leviathan the coiled serpent;
> and he will slay the dragon that is in
> the sea.

2*   On that day—
The pleasant vineyard, sing about it!

3*   I, the LORD, am its keeper,
> I water it every moment;
Lest anyone harm it,
> night and day I guard it.

4*   I am not angry,
> but if I were to find briers and thorns,
In battle I should march against them;
> I should burn them all.

8*   Expunging and expelling, I should strive
> against them,
> carrying them off with my cruel wind
> in time of storm.

6   In days to come Jacob shall take root,
> Israel shall sprout and blossom,
> covering all the world with fruit.

7†   Is he to be smitten as his smiter was
> smitten?
> or slain as his slayer was slain?

5*†   Or shall he cling to me for refuge?
> He must make peace with me;
> peace shall he make with me!

---

†   26, 19: This verse refers to the restoration of Israel in messianic times under the figure of the resurrection of the dead; cf Ez, chap. 37.

27, 1: *Leviathan . . . dragon:* symbols of the forces of evil which God vanquishes even as he overcame primeval chaos; cf notes on Jb 3, 8; 7, 12.

27, 5.9: Israel will *make peace with* God and destroy all signs of idolatrous worship.

27, 7: God's people will not be treated as sternly as were their enemies.

❋

9: Ps 94, 15.
10: 5, 12.
12: Jer 29, 11.
15: 54, 2f; Neh 9, 23.
16: Hos 6, 1.
17: Mi 4, 10.
19: Ez 37, 5f; Dn 12, 2;
     Hos 6, 2.

21: Mi 1, 3.
27/1: Jb 40, 25-32; Ez 32, 2.
2: 5, 1.
3: 5, 2ff; Ps 121, 4f.
4: 10, 17.
5: 37, 31; Rom 11, 12.
8: Jer 18, 17.

9   This, then, shall be the expiation of
     Jacob's guilt,
     this the whole fruit of the removal of
       his sin:
     He shall pulverize all the stones of the
       altars
       like pieces of chalk;
     no sacred poles or incense altars shall
       stand.

10*†   For the fortified city shall be desolate,
     an abandoned pasture, a forsaken
       wilderness,
     where calves shall browse and lie.
     Its boughs shall be destroyed,
11*   its branches shall wither and be
       broken off,
     and women shall come to build a fire
       with them.
     This is not an understanding people;
     therefore their maker shall not spare
       them,
     nor shall he who formed them have
       mercy on them.

12†   On that day,
     The Lord shall beat out the grain
     between the Euphrates and the Wadi
       of Egypt,
     and you shall be gleaned one by one,
       O sons of Israel.

13*†   On that day,
     A great trumpet shall blow,
     and the lost in the land of Assyria
     and the outcasts in the land of Egypt
     Shall come and worship the Lord
       on the holy mountain, in Jerusalem.

V: THE LORD ALONE, ISRAEL'S AND JUDAH'S SALVATION

The Fate of Samaria

28 1*†   WOE TO THE MAJESTIC GARLAND
     of the drunkard Ephraim,
     To the fading blooms of his glorious
       beauty,
     on the head of him who is stupefied
       with wine.
2*†   Behold, the Lord has a strong one and
     a mighty,
     who, like a downpour of
     hail, a destructive storm,
     Like a flood of water, great and
       overflowing,
     levels to the ground with violence;

3   With feet that will trample
     the majestic garland of the drunkard
       Ephraim.
4   The fading blooms of his glorius beauty
     on the head of the fertile valley
     Will be like an early fig before summer:
     when a man sees it,
     he picks and swallows it at once.

5   On that day the Lord of hosts
     will be a glorious crown
     And a brilliant diadem
     to the remnant of his people,
6   A spirit of justice
     to him who sits in judgment,
     And strength to those
     who turn back the battle at the gate.

Against Judah

7*   But these also stagger from wine
     and stumble from strong drink:
     Priest and prophet stagger from strong
       drink,
     overpowered by wine;
     Led astray by strong drink,
     staggering in their visions,
     tottering when giving judgment.
8   Yes, all the tables
     are covered with filthy vomit,
     with no place left clean.
9†   "To whom would he impart knowledge?
     To whom would he convey the
       message?
     To those just weaned from milk,
     those taken from the breast?
10   For he says,
     'Command on command, command on
       command,
     rule on rule, rule on rule,
     here a little, there a little!' "
11*†   Yes, with stammering lips and in a
     strange language
     he will speak to this people

27, 10f: *The fortified city:* symbol of the powers of evil; see note on 24, 10.

27, 12: *The Euphrates and the Wadi of Egypt:* the ideal borders of Israel; cf Gn 15, 18; 2 Kgs 24, 7.

27, 13: The triumph of God's people is described in eschatological language; they will gather in Jerusalem from *Assyria* and *Egypt.*

28, 1: *Ephraim:* the northern kingdom. Its capital, Samaria, was built upon a hill, suggestive of a *majestic garland* adorning the head of the drunken kingdom.

28, 2: *A strong one and a mighty:* Assyria.

28, 9f: The words of those who ridicule Isaiah. The Hebrew of v 10, by its very sound, conveys the idea of mocking imitation of what the prophet says, as though he spoke like a stammering child: *SAU LASAU, SAU LASAU, CAU LACAU, CAU LACAU, ZE'ER SHAM, ZE'ER SHAM.* But in v 13 God repeats these words in deadly earnest, putting them in the mouth of the victorious pagan army.

28, 11: God will answer the mockers and defend Isaiah. *Strange language:* spoken by the invading army.

❋   10: 6, 11.   2: 30, 30.
    11: Jer 4, 22.   7: 56, 10.12.
    13: Hos 11, 11.   11: Jer 5, 15; 1 Cor 14, 21;
    28/1: Hos 7, 5; Am 6, 6.   Dt 28, 49; Bar 4, 15.

12 to whom he said:
This is the resting place,
    give rest to the weary;
Here is repose—
    but they would not listen.
13 So for them the word of the Lord
      shall be:
"Command on command, command
    on command,
Rule on rule, rule on rule,
  here a little, there a little!"
So that when they walk, they stumble
    backward,
    broken, ensnared, and captured.
14 Therefore, hear the word of the Lord,
    you arrogant,
    who rule this people in Jerusalem:
15* Because you say, "We have made a
    covenant with death,
    and with the nether world we have
    made a pact;
When the overwhelming scourge passes,
    it will not reach us;
For we have made lies our refuge,
    and in falsehood we have found a
    hiding place,"—
16*†   Therefore, thus says the Lord God:
    See, I am laying a stone in Zion,
    a stone that has been tested,
A precious cornerstone as a sure
      foundation;
    he who puts his faith in it shall
      not be shaken.
17   I will make of right a measuring
      line,
      of justice a level.—
Hail shall sweep away the refuge of lies,
    and waters shall flood the hiding
      place.
18 Your covenant with death shall be
      canceled
    and your pact with the nether world
      shall not stand.
When the overwhelming scourge passes,
    you shall be trampled down by it.
19 Whenever it passes, it shall take you;
    morning after morning it shall pass,
By day and by night;
    terror alone shall convey the message.
20 For the bed shall be too short to stretch
    out in,
    and the cover too narrow to wrap in.
21*† For the Lord shall rise up as on Mount
    Perazim,
    bestir himself as in the Valley of
      Gibeon,

To carry out his work, his singular work,
    to perform his deed, his strange deed.
22* Now, be arrogant no more
    lest your bonds be tightened,
For I have heard from the Lord, the
      God of hosts,
    the destruction decreed for the whole
      earth.
23† Give ear and hear my voice,
    pay attention and listen to what I say:
24 Is the plowman forever plowing,
    always loosening and harrowing his
      land for planting?
25† When he has leveled the surface,
    does he not scatter gith and sow
      cumin,
Put in wheat and barley,
    with spelt as its border?
26 He has learned this rule,
    instructed by his God.
27 Gith is not threshed with a sledge,
    nor does a cartwheel roll over cumin.
But gith is beaten out with a staff,
    and cumin crushed for food with a
      rod.
28 No, he does not thresh it unendingly,
    nor does he crush it
    with his noisy cartwheels and horses.
29 This too comes from the Lord of hosts;
    wonderful is his counsel and great his
      wisdom.

The Fall of Jerusalem

29 **1*†** Woe to Ariel, Ariel,
    the city where David encamped!
Add year to year,
    let the feasts come round.

---

† 28, 15.18: *A covenant with death, and with the nether world:* an alliance with foreign powers, such as Egypt and Babylon, to prevent death and destruction. *Have made lies . . . a hiding place:* this confidence in human aid proves to be false and deceitful, incapable of averting the dreaded disaster. *Overwhelming scourge:* the flood of the Assyrian invasion; cf 8, 7f.

28, 16: *A stone in Zion:* the true and *sure foundation* of salvation promised by God to the Davidic dynasty (cf 7, 13-16; 9, 1-6), which the Apostles saw fulfilled in Christ the universal Savior; cf 1 Pt 2, 6-8; Rom 9, 33; 10, 9ff. *Cornerstone:* the assurance of salvation rejected by Israel in the prophet's time, is reflected by the psalmist (Ps 118, 22) and fulfilled in the Person of Christ; cf Mt 21, 42; Lk 20, 17; Acts 4, 11; Rom 9.33; 1 Pt 2, 7.

28, 21: *Mount Perazim . . . Valley of Gibeon:* where David defeated the Philistines; cf 2 Sm 5, 20, 25; 1 Chr 14, 11.16.

28, 23-29: The practical variation of the farmer's work taught him by God reflects God's dealing with his people, wisely adapted to circumstances; he does not crush their weakness altogether; cf ch 29.

28, 25: *Gith . . . cumin:* herbs used in seasoning food. *Spelt:* a variety of wheat.

29, 1f: *Ariel:* variously interpreted to mean "lion of God" or "hearth (altar) of God," a poetic name for Jerusalem; or perhaps

✿   15: Wis 1, 16; Jer 5, 12.   21: Jos 10, 10; 2 Sm 5, 20;
     16: Ps 118, 22; Mt 21, 42;   1 Chr 14, 11.
           Acts 4, 11; Rom 9, 33;   22: 10, 23.
           1 Pt 2, 6.   29/1: 2 Sm 5, 9.

2* But I will bring distress upon Ariel,
    with mourning and grief.
You shall be to me like Ariel,
3*   I will encamp like David against you;
I will encircle you with outposts
    and set up siege works against you.
4† Prostrate you shall speak from the earth,
    and from the base dust your words
    shall come.
Your voice shall be like a ghost's from
    the earth,
    and your words like chirping from the
    dust.
5* The horde of your arogant shall be like
    fine dust,
    the horde of the tyrants like flying
    chaff.
Then suddenly, in an instant,
6   you shall be visited by the LORD of
    hosts,
With thunder, earthquake, and great
    noise,
    whirlwind, storm, and the flame of
    consuming fire.
7† Then like a dream,
    a vision in the night,
Shall be the horde of all the nations
    who war against Ariel
    with all the earthworks of her
    besiegers.
8 As when a hungry man dreams he is
    eating
    and awakens with an empty stomach,
Or when a thirsty man dreams he is
    drinking
    and awakens faint and dry,
So shall the horde of all the nations be,
    who make war against Zion.

Blindness and Perversity

9*† Be irresolute, stupefied;
    blind yourselves and stay blind!
Be drunk, but not from wine,
    stagger, but not from strong drink!
10* For the LORD has poured out on you
    a spirit of deep sleep.
He has shut your eyes [the prophets]
    and covered your heads [the seers].

11* For you the revelation of all this has become like the words of a sealed scroll. When it is handed to one who can read, with the request, "Read this," he re-plies, "I cannot; it is sealed." 12When it is handed to one who cannot read, with the request, "Read this," he replies, "I cannot read."

13*   The Lord said:
Since this people draws near with words
    only
    and honors me with their lips alone,
    though their hearts are far from me,
And their reverence for me has become
    routine observance of the precepts of
    men,
14* Therefore I will again deal with this
    people
    in surprising and wondrous fashion:
The wisdom of its wise men shall perish
    and the understanding of its prudent
    men be hid.
15* Woe to those who would hide their
    plans
    too deep for the LORD!
Who work in the dark, saying,
    "Who sees us, or who knows us?"
16* Your perversity is as though the potter
    were taken to be the clay:
As though what is made should say
    of its maker,
    "He made me not!"
Or the vessel should say of the potter,
    "He does not understand."

Redemption

17*† But a very little while,
    and Lebanon shall be changed into
    an orchard,
    and the orchard be regarded as a
    forest!
18* On that day the deaf shall hear
    the words of a book;
And out of gloom and darkness,
    the eyes of the blind shall see.
19* The lowly will ever find joy in the LORD,
    and the poor rejoice in the Holy One
    of Israel.
20* For the tyrant will be no more
    and the arrogant will have gone;

---

† to be read as Uru-el, "foundation of God," an archaic name for the Jebusite city of Jerusalem; *like* that *Ariel*, against which *David encamped*, it will be besieged by God.

29, 4: *Chirping:* see note on 8, 19.

29, 7f: Just when the Assyrians think their capture of Jerusalem to be certain, the Lord will snatch victory from their hands and save his city.

29, 9-12: Jerusalem in her blindness refuses to believe God's revelation that she will be saved.

29, 17-24: The prophet presents God's plan of redemption in terms of unheard-of natural phenomena as if such changes in nature took place, e. g., the change of the cedars of Lebanon into an orchard (v 17).

* 2: 33, 7.
3: 2 Kgs 25, 1; Ez 4, 2.
5: 17, 13; Ps 18, 43;
    Jb 21, 18.
9: 19, 14; 28, 7f.
10: 6, 10; Rom 11, 8.
11: Dn 12, 4.
13: Ez 33, 31; Mt 15, 8f;
    Mk 7, 6f.
14: Jer 49, 7; 1 Cor 1, 19.
15: 30, 1; Ez 8, 12;
    Jn 3, 19f.
16: 45, 9; Jer 18, 6;
    Rom 9, 20.
17: 32, 15.
18: 35, 5; 42, 6f.
19: 61, 1.
20: 28, 22.

All who are alert to do evil will be
　　cut off,
21 those whose mere word condemns
　　a man,
Who ensnare his defender at the gate,
　　and leave the just man with an
　　empty claim.
22 Therefore thus says the LORD,
　　the God of the house of Jacob,
　　who redeemed Abraham:
　　Now Jacob shall have nothing to be
　　ashamed of,
　　nor shall his face grow pale.
23 When his children see
　　the work of my hands in his midst,
They shall keep my name holy;
　　they shall reverence the Holy One
　　of Jacob,
　　and be in awe of the God of Israel.
24 Those who err in spirit shall acquire
　　understanding,
　　and those who find fault shall receive
　　instruction.

Futile Alliance with Egypt

30 1 Woe to the rebellious children,
　　says the LORD,
Who carry out plans that are not mine,
　　who weave webs that are not inspired
　　by me,
　　adding sin upon sin.
2 They go down to Egypt,
　　but my counsel they do not seek.
They find their strength in Pharaoh's
　　protection
　　and take refuge in Egypt's shadow;
3 Pharaoh's protection shall be your
　　shame,
　　and refuge in Egypt's shadow
　　your disgrace.
4 When their princes are at Zoan
　　and their messengers reach Hanes,
5 All shall be ashamed
　　of a people that gain them nothing,
Neither help nor benefit,
　　but only shame and reproach.
6 [Oracle on the Beasts of the Negeb]

Through the distressed and troubled
　　land
　　of the lioness and roaring lion,
　　of the viper and flying saraph,

They carry their riches on the backs
　　of asses
　　and their treasures on the humps of
　　camels
To a people good for nothing,
7 to Egypt whose help is futile and vain.
Therefore I call her
　　"Rahab quelled."
8 Now come, write it on a tablet they can
　　keep,
　　inscribe it in a record;
That it may be in future days
　　an eternal witness:
9 This is a rebellious people,
　　deceitful children,
Children who refuse
　　to obey the law of the LORD.
10 They say to the seers, "Have no visions";
　　to the prophets, "Do no descry for us
　　what is right;
　　speak flatteries to us, conjure up
　　illusions.
11 Out of the way! Out of our path!
　　Let us hear no more
　　of the Holy One of Israel."
12 Therefore, thus says the Holy One
　　of Israel:
　　Because you reject this word,
And put your trust in what is crooked
　　and devious,
　　and depend on it,
13 This guilt of yours shall be
　　like a descending rift
Bulging out in a high wall
　　whose crash comes suddenly, in an
　　instant.
14 It crashes like a potter's jar
　　smashed beyond rescue,
And among its fragments cannot be
　　found
　　a sherd to scoop fire from the hearth
　　or dip water from the cistern.
15 For thus said the Lord GOD,
　　the Holy One of Israel:
By waiting and by calm you shall be
　　saved,
　　in quiet and in trust your strength lies.
But this you did not wish.

21: Am 5, 10.12.
22: 45, 17.
30/1: 1, 4.
2: 31, 1; 36, 6.
3: 20, 5; Jer 2, 36f.
4: 19, 11.
5: 36, 6.
8: 8, 1.16; Jer 36, 2; Heb 2, 2.
9: 1, 4; Jer 7, 28.
10: Jer 5, 31.
11: Jb 21, 14f.
13: Ez 13, 14.
14: Jer 19, 11.
15: 7, 4; Mi 7, 7.

29, 22: *Who redeemed Abraham:* by freeing him from the idolatry of his native land.

30, 6: *Flying saraph:* see note on Nm 21, 6.

30, 7: *Rahab:* Egypt, here as elsewhere (cf Ps 87, 4), is compared to the stormy, impetuous sea monster (cf 51, 9; Jb 26, 12; Ps 89, 11), which yet, when asked for aid by Judah, becomes silent, *quelled.*

30, 8: Isaiah will write down his condemnation of the people so that (vv 12-18) its fulfillment may afterward be admitted.

16* "No," you said,
    "Upon horses we will flee."
      —Very well, flee!
"Upon swift steeds we will ride."
      —Not so swift as your pursuers.

17 A thousand shall tremble at the threat
    of one;
    if five threaten you, you shall flee,
Until you are left like a flagstaff on the
    mountaintop,
    like a flag on the hill.

18* Yet the Lord is waiting to show you
    favor,
    and he rises to pity you;
For the Lord is a God of justice:
    blessed are all who wait for him!

19* O people of Zion, who dwell in
    Jerusalem,
    no more will you weep;
He will be gracious to you when you
    cry out,
    as soon as he hears he will answer you.

20† The Lord will give you the bread you
    need
    and the water for which you thirst.
No longer will your Teacher hide
    himself,
    but with your own eyes you shall see
    your Teacher,

21* While from behind, a voice shall sound
    in your ears:
    "This is the way; walk in it,"
    when you would turn to the right or
    or to the left.

22* And you shall consider unclean your
    silver-plated idols
    and your gold-covered images;
You shall throw them away like filthy
    rags
    to which you say, "Begone!"

Zion's Future Prosperity

23* He will give rain for the seed
    that you sow in the ground,
And the wheat that the soil produces
    will be rich and abundant.
On that day your cattle will graze
    in spacious meadows;

24 The oxen and the asses that till the
    ground
    will eat silage tossed to them
    with shovel and pitchfork.

25* Upon every high mountain and lofty hill
    there will be streams of running
    water.

On the day of the great slaughter,
    when the towers fall,

26* The light of the moon will be like that of
    the sun
    and the light of the sun will be seven
    times greater
    [like the light of seven days].
On the day the Lord binds up the
    wounds of his people,
    he will heal the bruises left by his
    blows.

Divine Judgment on Assyria

27† See the name of the Lord coming from
    afar
    in burning wrath, with lowering
    clouds!
His lips are filled with fury,
    his tongue is like a consuming fire;

28 His breath, like a flood in a ravine
    that reaches suddenly to the neck,
Will winnow the nations with a
    destructive winnowing,
    and with repeated winnowings will
    he battle against them
    [and a bridle on the jaws of the
    peoples to send them astray].

30† The Lord will make his glorious voice
    heard,
    and let it be seen how his arm
    descends
In raging fury and flame of consuming
    fire,
    in driving storm and hail.

31 When the Lord speaks, Assyria will be
    shattered,
    as he strikes with the rod;

32 While at every sweep of the rod
    which the Lord will bring down on
    him in punishment,

29 You will sing
    as on a night when a feast is observed,
And be merry of heart,
    as one marching along with a flute
Toward the mountain of the Lord,
    toward the Rock of Israel,
    accompanied by the timbrels and
    lyres.

33 For the pyre has long been ready,
    prepared for the king;

---

† 30, 20: *Teacher:* God, who in the past taught in a veiled manner through his prophets, will in future help them to understand his teaching clearly. This was eminently true when the Son of God became Man.

30, 27-33: God's punishment of Assyria. *The name of the Lord:* God himself; cf Ps 20, 2.

30, 29.33: *Pyre:* on which the corpse of the king of Assyria is burned. This is the occasion of festal rejoicing for the Israelites, who are now free from his yoke.

---

*
16: 31, 3.
18: Ps 34, 9; Jer 17, 7.
19: 58, 9.
21: Jer 31, 33f.
22: 31, 7.
23: Lv 26, 3.5.
25: Jl 4, 18.
26: Jer 30, 17.

Broad and deep it is piled
    with dry grass and wood in
      abundance,
And the breath of the Lord, like a
    stream of sulphur,
    will set it afire.

Against the Egyptian Alliance

31 **1*** Woe to those who go down to Egypt for
    help,
    who depend upon horses;
Who put their trust in chariots because
    of their number,
    and in horsemen because of their
      combined power,
But look not to the Holy One of Israel
    nor seek the Lord!

2 Yet he too is wise and will bring disaster;
    he will not turn from what he has
      threatened to do.
He will rise up against the house of the
    wicked
    and against those who help evildoers.

3* The Egyptians are men, not God,
    their horses are flesh, not spirit;
When the Lord stretches forth his hand,
    the helper shall stumble, the one
      helped shall fall,
    and both of them shall perish together.

4   Thus says the Lord to me:
As a lion or a lion cub
    growling over its prey,
With a band of shepherds
    assembled against it,
Is neither frightened by their shouts
    nor disturbed by their noise,
So shall the Lord of hosts come down
    to wage war upon the mountain and
      hill of Zion.

5* Like hovering birds, so the Lord of hosts
    shall shield Jerusalem,
To protect and deliver,
    to spare and rescue it.

6*Return, O children of Israel, to him whom you have utterly deserted. **7***On that day each one of you shall spurn his sinful idols of silver and gold, which he made with his hands.

Downfall of Assyria

8* Assyria shall fall by a sword not wielded
    by man,
      no mortal sword shall devour him;

He shall flee before the sword,
    and his young men shall be impressed
      as laborers.

9† He shall rush past his crag in panic,
    and his princes shall flee in terror from
      his standard,
Says the Lord who has a fire in Zion
    and a furnace in Jerusalem.

The Kingdom of Justice

32 **1*** See, a king will reign justly
    and princes will rule rightly.

2* Each of them will be a shelter from the
    wind,
    a retreat from the rain.
They will be like streams of water in a
    dry country,
    like the shade of a great rock in a
      parched land.

3 The eyes of those who see will not be
    closed;
    the ears of those who hear will be
      attentive.

4 The flighty will become wise and
    capable,
    and the stutterers will speak fluently
      and clearly.

5 No more will the fool be called noble,
    nor the trickster be considered
      honorable.

6* For the fool speaks foolishly,
    planning evil in his heart:
How to do wickedness,
    to speak perversely against the Lord,
To let the hungry go empty
    and the thirsty be without drink.

7 And the trickster uses wicked trickery,
    planning crimes:
How to ruin the poor with lies,
    and the needy when they plead their
      case.

8 But the noble man plans noble things,
    and by noble things he stands.

The Women of Jerusalem

9 O complacent ladies, rise up and hear
    my voice,
    overconfident women, give heed to my
      words.

10* In a little more than a year
    you overconfident ones will be shaken;
The vintage will fail,
    there will be no harvest.

11* Tremble, you who are complacent!
    Shudder, you who are overconfident!
Strip yourselves bare,
    with only a loincloth to cover you.

31/1: 30, 2; 36, 6.
   3: Ps 146, 3ff.
   5: Ps 91, 4.
   6: Jer 3, 12.
   7: 30, 22.
   8: 37, 36.

32/1: 16, 5; Ps 72, 2ff;
     Jer 23, 5.
   2: 4, 6; 25, 4.
   6: Prv 10, 32;
     Eccl 10, 12f.
  10: Zep 1, 13.
  11: Jer 4, 8.

† 31, 9: *Crag:* the king as the rallying point of the princes.

12 Beat your breasts
    for the pleasant fields, the fruitful
        vine,
13* And the soil of my people,
    overgrown with thorns and briers;
For all the joyful houses,
    the wanton city.
14*† Yes, the castle will be forsaken,
    the noisy city deserted;
19 Down it comes, as trees come down in
        the forest!
    The city will be utterly laid low.
Hill and tower will become wasteland
    forever
    for wild asses to frolic in, and flocks to
        pasture,
15*† Until the spirit from on high
    is poured out on us.

Then will the desert become an orchard
    and the orchard be regarded as a
        forest.
16 Right will dwell in the desert
    and justice abide in the orchard.
17* Justice will bring about peace;
    right will produce calm and security.
18* My people will live in peaceful country,
    in secure dwellings and quiet resting
        places.
20* Happy are you who sow beside every
        stream,
    and let the ox and the ass go freely!

Overthrow of Assyria

33 **1** Woe, O destroyer never destroyed,
    O traitor never betrayed!
When you finish destroying, you will be
    destroyed;
    when wearied with betraying, you
        will be betrayed.
2* O Lord, have pity on us, for you we wait.
    Be our strength every morning,
    our salvation in time of trouble!
3 At the roaring sound, peoples flee;
    when you rise in your majesty, nations
        are scattered.
4* Men gather spoil as caterpillars are
        gathered up;
    they rush upon it like the onrush of
        locusts.
5* The Lord is exalted, enthroned on high;
    he fills Zion with right and justice.
6* That which makes her seasons lasting,
    the riches that save her, are wisdom

and knowledge;
    the fear of the Lord is her treasure.
7† See, the men of Ariel cry out in the
        streets,
    the messengers of Shalem weep
        bitterly.
8* The highways are desolate,
    travelers have quit the paths,
Covenants are broken, their terms are
    spurned;
    yet no man gives it a thought.
9*† The country languishes in mourning,
    Lebanon withers with shame;
Sharon is like the steppe,
    Bashan and Carmel are stripped bare.

10 Now will I rise up, says the Lord,
    now will I be exalted, now be lifted
        up.
11 You conceive dry grass, bring forth
        stubble;
    my spirit shall consume you like fire.
12* The peoples shall be as in a limekiln,
    like brushwood cut down for burning
        in the fire.
13 Hear, you who are far off, what I have
        done;
    you who are near, acknowledge my
        might.
14* On Zion sinners are in dread,
    trembling grips the impious:
"Who of us can live with the consuming
        fire?
    who of us can live with the everlasting
        flames?"
15* He who practices virtue and speaks
        honestly,
    who spurns what is gained by
        oppression,
Brushing his hands free of contact with a
    bribe,
    stopping his ears lest he hear of
        bloodshed,
    closing his eyes lest he look on evil—
16 He shall dwell on the heights,
    his stronghold shall be the rocky
        fastness,
    his food and drink in steady supply.

Restoration of Zion

17† Your eyes will see a king in his splendor,
    they will look upon a vast land.

---

*   13: 7, 23; 34, 13.
     14: 27, 10.
     15: 35, 1; 44, 3.
     17: 54, 13f; Ps 72, 7;
         Jas 3, 18.
     18: Mi 4, 4.
     20: 30, 23.
     33/2: 25, 9.

     4: 2 Chr 20, 25.
     5: 1, 26.
     6: Prv 9, 10.
     8: Jgs 5, 6.
     9: Na 1, 4.
     12: 10, 17.
     14: Na 1, 6.
     15: Pss 15, 2-6; 24, 4f.

† 32, 14.19: *The castle:* the citadel of Jerusalem. *Hill and tower:* the fortified hill, in Hebrew *Ophel,* with its stronghold called "the great projecting tower" in Neh 3, 27.

32, 15-18.20: Extraordinary peace and prosperity will come to Israel under just rulers.

33, 7: *Ariel . . . Shalem:* Jerusalem; cf 29, 1; Gn 14, 18.

33, 9: *Sharon:* the fertile plain near the Mediterranean.

33, 17: *King:* the Messianic King, or God; cf v 22.

18 Your mind will dwell on the terror:
        "Where is he who counted, where is he
            who weighed?
        Where is he who counted the towers?"
19 To the people of alien tongue you will
        look no more,
        the people of obscure speech,
        stammering in a language not
            understood.
20 Look to Zion, the city of our festivals;
        let your eyes see Jerusalem
        as a quiet abode, a tent not to be
            struck,
    Whose pegs will never be pulled up,
        nor any of its ropes severed.
22 Indeed the LORD will be there with us,
        majestic;
        yes, the LORD our judge, the LORD our
            lawgiver,
        the LORD our king, he it is who will
            save us.
21† In a place of rivers and wide streams
        on which no boat is rowed,
        where no majestic ship passes,
23 The rigging hangs slack;
        it cannot hold the mast in place,
        nor keep the sail spread out.
    Then the blind will divide great spoils
        and the lame will carry off the loot.
24 No one who dwells there will say, "I am
        sick";
        the people who live there will be
            forgiven their guilt.

VI: THE LORD, ZION'S AVENGER

Judgment upon Edom

34 1° COME NEAR, O NATIONS, and hear;
            be attentive, O peoples!
        Let the earth and what fills it listen,
            the world and all it produces.
    2   The LORD is angry with all the nations
            and is wrathful against all their host;
            he has doomed them and given them
                over to slaughter.
    3° Their slain shall be cast out,
            their corpses shall send up a stench;
        The mountains shall run with their
                blood,
    4°   and all the hills shall rot;
        The heavens shall be rolled up like a
                scroll,
            and all their host shall wither away,

As the leaf wilts on the vine,
        or as the fig withers on the tree.
5° When my sword has drunk its fill in the
        heavens,
        lo, it shall come down in judgment
        upon Edom, a people I have doomed.
6° The LORD has a sword filled with blood,
        greasy with fat,
    With the blood of lambs and goats,
        with the fat of rams' kidneys;
    For the LORD has a sacrifice in Bozrah,
        a great slaughter in the land of Edom.
7   Wild oxen shall be struck down with
        fatlings,
        and bullocks with bulls;
    Their land shall be soaked with blood,
        and their earth greasy with fat.
8° For the LORD has a day of vengeance,
        a year of requital by Zion's defender.
9   Edom's streams shall be changed into
        pitch
        and her earth into sulphur,
        and her land shall become burning
            pitch;
10 Night and day it shall not be quenched,
        its smoke shall rise forever.
    From generation to generation she shall
        lie waste,
        never again shall anyone pass through
            her.
11°† But the desert owl and hoot owl shall
        possess her,
        the screech owl and raven shall dwell
            in her.
    The LORD will measure her with line and
        plummet
        to be an empty waste
        for satyrs to dwell in.
12° Her nobles shall be no more,
        nor shall kings be proclaimed there;
        all her princes are gone.
13° Her castles shall be overgrown with
        thorns,
        her fortresses with thistles and briers.
    She shall become an abode for jackals
        and a haunt for ostriches.
14† Wildcats shall meet with desert beasts,
        satyrs shall call to one another;
    There shall the lilith repose,
        and find for herself a place to rest.
15 There the hoot owl shall nest and lay
        eggs,
        hatch them out and gather them in her
            shadow;

°
34/1: Dt 32, 1.   6f: Jer 49, 12f.
    3: Ez 32, 4.6.   8: 13, 9; 63, 4.
    4: 13, 10; Ez 32, 7f; 11: 14, 23; Zep 2, 14.
    4, 15.   12: Ob 18.
    5: Jer 46, 10.   13: 13, 21; Hos 9, 6.

†
33, 21.23: Boat . . . majestic ship: of a foreign oppressor.
34, 11: Satyrs: see note on 13, 21; cf 34, 14.
34, 14: Lilith: a female demon thought to roam about the
desert.

There shall the kites assemble,
  none shall be missing its mate.
16*† Look in the book of the Lord and read:
  No one of these shall be lacking,
For the mouth of the Lord has ordered
  it,
  and his spirit shall gather them there.
17 It is he who casts the lot for them,
  and with his hand he marks off their
    shares of her;
They shall possess her forever,
  and dwell there from generation to
    generation.

Israel's Deliverance

35 **1***† The desert and the parched land will
    exult;
  the steppe will rejoice and bloom.
2* They will bloom with abundant flowers,
  and rejoice with joyful song.
The glory of Lebanon will be given to
  them,
  the splendor of Carmel and Sharon;
They will see the glory of the Lord,
  the splendor of our God.
3* Strengthen the hands that are feeble,
  make firm the knees that are weak,
4* Say to those whose hearts are
    frightened:
  Be strong, fear not!
Here is your God,
  he comes with vindication;
With divine recompense
  he comes to save you.
5* Then will the eyes of the blind be
    opened,
  the ears of the deaf be cleared;
6* Then will the lame leap like a stag,
  then the tongue of the dumb will sing.

Streams will burst forth in the desert,
  and rivers in the steppe.
7 The burning sands will become pools,
  and the thirsty ground, springs of
    water;
The abode where jackals lurk
  will be a marsh for the reed and
    papyrus.
8 A highway will be there,
  called the holy way;
No one unclean may pass over it,
  nor fools go astray on it.

9* No lion will be there,
  nor beast of prey go up to be met
    upon it.
It is for those with a journey to make,
  and on it the redeemed will walk.
10* Those whom the Lord has ransomed will
    return
  and enter Zion singing,
  crowned with everlasting joy;
They will meet with joy and gladness,
  sorrow and mourning will flee.

VII: HISTORICAL APPENDIX

Invasion of Sennacherib

36 **1***†IN THE FOURTEENTH YEAR of King Hezekiah, Sennacherib, king of Assyria, went on an expedition against all the fortified cities of Judah and captured them. **2**From Lachish the king of Assyria sent his commander with a great army to King Hezekiah in Jerusalem. When he stopped at the conduit of the upper pool, on the highway of the fuller's field, **3**there came out to him the master of the palace, Eliakim, son of Hilkiah, and Shebna the scribe, and the herald Joah, son of Asaph. **4**The commander said to them, "Tell King Hezekiah: Thus says the great king, the king of Assyria, 'On what do you base this confidence of yours? **5**Do you think mere words substitute for strategy and might in war? On whom, then, do you rely, that you rebel against me? **6***This Egypt, the staff on which you rely, is in fact a broken reed which pierces the hand of anyone who leans on it. That is what Pharaoh, king of Egypt, is to all who rely on him. **7***†But if you say to me: "We rely on the Lord, our God," is not he the one whose high places and altars Hezekiah removed, commanding Judah and Jerusalem to worship before this altar?'

8"Now, make a wager with my lord the king of Assyria: 'I will give you two thousand horses, if you can put riders on them.' **9**How then can you repulse even one of the least servants of my lord? And yet you rely on Egypt for chariots and horsemen! **10***'Was it without the Lord's will that I have come up to destroy this land? The Lord said to me, "Go up and destroy that land!"' "

---

† 34, 16: *Book of the Lord:* God's list of all his creatures; cf Ps 69, 29, "the book of the living"; Ps 139, 16, "your book."

35, 1-10: Similar to the description of the return from the Exile, as found in chaps. 40-55.

36, 1—39, 8: Except for 38, 9-20, this historical appendix describing the siege, etc., is paralleled in 2 Kgs 18, 13—20, 19, which, however, has certain details proper to itself. The events are also recorded in substantially the same way in the cuneiform inscriptions of Sennacherib.

36, 7: The Assyrians pretend that Hezekiah's removal of the *high places and altars* (illegal sanctuaries) was taken by the Lord as an insult. They declare to Jerusalem's emissaries that the city therefore no longer has a right to the Lord's protection and that they are the ones who truly carry out his will (cf v 10).

* 16: Jos 18, 10; Ps 78, 55. 35/1: 55, 12f. 2: 60, 13; Ps 96, 12. 3: Jb 4, 3f; Heb 12, 12. 4: 41, 10; Zec 8, 13. 5: 29, 18; 32, 3. 6: 41, 18; 43, 10.19. 9: 62, 10; Lv 26, 6. 10: 51, 11. 36/1: 2 Kgs 18, 13; 2 Chr 32, 1. 6: 30, 2. 7: 2 Kgs 18, 4. 10: 10, 5f.

¹¹†Then Eliakim and Shebna and Joah said to the commander, "Please speak to your servants in Aramaic; we understand it. Do not speak to us in Judean within earshot of the people who are on the wall." ¹²But the commander replied, "Was it to you and your master that my lord sent me to speak these words? Was it not rather to the men sitting on the wall, who, with you, will have to eat their own excrement and drink their own urine?" ¹³Then the commander stepped forward and cried out in a loud voice in Judean, "Listen to the words of the great king, the king of Assyria. ¹⁴Thus says the king: 'Do not let Hezekiah deceive you, since he cannot deliver you. ¹⁵Let not Hezekiah induce you to rely on the LORD, saying, "The LORD will surely save us; this city will not be handed over to the king of Assyria."' ¹⁶*Do not listen to Hezekiah, for the king of Assyria says: 'Make peace with me and surrender! Then each of you will eat of his own vine and of his own fig tree, and drink the water of his own cistern, ¹⁷until I come to take you to a land like your own, a land of grain and wine, of bread and vineyards. ¹⁸*Do not let Hezekiah seduce you by saying, "The LORD will save us." Has any of the gods of the nations ever rescued his land from the hand of the king of Assyria? ¹⁹*Where are the gods of Hamath and Arpad? Where are the gods of Sepharvaim? Where are the gods of Samaria? Have they saved Samaria from my hand? ²⁰Which of all the gods of these lands ever rescued his land from my hand? Will the LORD then save Jerusalem from my hand?'" ²¹But they remained silent and did not answer him one word, for the king had ordered them not to answer him.

²²Then the master of the palace, Eliakim, son of Hilkiah, Shebna the scribe, and the herald Joah, son of Asaph, came to Hezekiah with their garments torn, and reported to him what the commander had said.

37 ¹WHEN King Hezekiah heard this, he tore his garments, wrapped himself in sackcloth, and went into the temple of the LORD. ²He sent Eliakim, the master of the palace, and Shebna the scribe, and the elders of the priests, wrapped in sackcloth, to tell the prophet Isaiah, son of Amoz. ³†"Thus says Hezekiah: 'This is a day of distress, of rebuke, and of disgrace. Children are at the point of birth, but there is no strength to bring them forth. ⁴Perhaps the LORD, your God, will hear the words of the commander, whom his master, the king of Assyria, sent to taunt the living God, and will rebuke him for the words which the LORD, your God, has heard. Send up a prayer for the remnant that is here.'"

⁵When the servants of King Hezekiah had come to Isaiah, ⁶*he said to them: "Tell this to your master: 'Thus says the LORD: Do not be frightened by the words you have heard, with which the servants of the king of Assyria have blasphemed me. ⁷I am about to put in him such a spirit that, when he hears a certain report, he will return to his own land, and there I will cause him to fall by the sword.'"

⁸When the commander returned to Lachish and heard that the king of Assyria had left there, he found him besieging Libnah. ⁹†The king of Assyria heard a report that Tirhakah, king of Ethiopia, had come out to fight against him. Again he sent envoys to Hezekiah with this message: "Thus shall you say to Hezekiah, king of Judah: ¹⁰*'Do not let your God on whom you rely deceive you by saying that Jerusalem will not be handed over to the king of Assyria. ¹¹You yourself have heard what the kings of Assyria have done to all the countries: They doomed them! Will you, then, be saved? ¹²Did the gods of the nations whom my fathers destroyed save them? Gozen, Haran, Rezeph, and the Edenites in Telassar? ¹³Where is the king of Hamath, the king of Arpad, or a king of the cities of Sepharvaim, Hena or Ivvah?'"

¹⁴Hezekiah took the letter from the hand of the messengers and read it; then he went up to the temple of the LORD, and spreading it out before him, ¹⁵he prayed to the LORD: ¹⁶†O LORD of hosts, God of Israel, enthroned upon the cherubim! You alone are God over all the kingdoms of the earth. You have made the heavens and the earth. ¹⁷Incline your ear, O LORD, and listen! Open your eyes, O LORD, and see! Hear all the words of the letter that Sennacherib sent to taunt the living God. ¹⁸Truly, O LORD, the kings of Assyria have laid waste all the nations and their lands, ¹⁹*and cast their gods into the fire; they destroyed them because they were not gods but the work of human hands, wood and stone. ²⁰Therefore, O LORD, our God, save us from his hand, that all the kingdoms of the earth may know that you, O LORD, alone are God."

Punishment of Sennacherib

²¹Then Isaiah, son of Amoz, sent this message to Hezekiah: Thus says the LORD, the God of Israel: In answer to your prayer for help against Sennacherib, king of Assyria, ²²*this is the word the LORD has spoken concerning him:

---

† 36, 11: The Jewish emissaries ask that the conversation be carried on in *Aramaic,* not in *Judean,* for they fear the effect of the Assyrian claims upon the morale of the people.

37, 3: A proverbial expression. In the Bible the pangs of childbirth often typify extreme anguish; cf 13, 8; Jer 6, 24; Mi 4, 9f. In this instance there is reference to the desperate situation of Hezekiah from which he was scarcely able to free himself.

37, 9: *Tirhakah:* may have been general of the Egyptian army in 701 B. C.; later he became king, one of the Ethiopian dynasty of Egyptian kings (c. 690-664 B. C.). Many consider that this account in Isaiah combines features of two originally distinct sieges of Jerusalem by Sennacherib.

37, 16: In contrast to the empty boasting of the Assyrians, Hezekiah proclaims the Lord as *God over all the kingdoms of the earth.*

✿
16: 1 Kgs 4, 25; Zec 3, 10.
18: 37, 11.
19: 10, 9; 37, 13.
37/6: 41, 10-14; 51, 7.
10: 36, 14.
19: Jer 16, 20.
22: 2 Kgs 19, 21.

She despises you, laughs you to scorn,
　the virgin daughter Zion;
Behind you she wags her head,
　daughter Jerusalem.
23* Whom have you insulted and
　　blasphemed,
　　against whom have you raised your
　　　voice
And lifed up your eyes on high?
　Against the Holy One of Israel!
24 Through your servants you have insulted
　　the Lord:
　You said, "With my many chariots
　I climbed the mountain heights,
　　the recesses of Lebanon;
　I cut down its lofty cedars,
　　its choice cypresses;
　I reached the remotest heights,
　　its forest park.
25 I dug wells and drank water in foreign
　　lands;
　I dried up with the soles of my feet
　　all the rivers of Egypt.

26 Have you not heard?
　Long ago I prepared it,
From days of old I planned it,
　now I have brought it to pass:
That you should reduce fortified cities
　into heaps of ruins,
27 While their inhabitants, shorn of power,
　are dismayed and ashamed,
Becoming like the plants of the field,
　like the green growth,
　　like the scorched grass on the
　　　housetops.
28 I am aware whether you stand or sit;
　I know whether you come or go,
　　and also your rage against me.
29 Because of your rage against me
　and your fury which has reached my
　　ears,
I will put my hook in your nose
　and my bit in your mouth,
　　and make you return the way you
　　　came.

30† This shall be a sign for you:
　this year you shall eat the aftergrowth,
　next year, what grows of itself;
But in the third year, sow and reap,
　plant vineyards and eat their fruit!
31* The remaining survivors of the house of
　　Judah
　shall again strike root below
　　and bear fruit above.

32 For out of Jerusalem shall come a
　　remnant,
　and from Mount Zion, survivors.
The zeal of the Lord of hosts shall do
　this.

33Therefore, thus says the Lord concerning the king of Assyria: He shall not reach this city, nor shoot an arrow at it, nor come before it with a shield, nor cast up siegeworks against it. **34***He shall return by the same way he came, without entering the city, says the Lord. **35***I will shield and save this city for my own sake, and for the sake of my servant David.

36*†The angel of the Lord went forth and struck down one hundred and eighty-five thousand in the Assyrian camp. Early the next morning, there they were, all the corpses of the dead. **37***So Sennacherib, the king of Assyria, broke camp and went back home to Nineveh.

38†When he was worshiping in the temple of his god Nisroch, his sons Adrammelech and Sharezer slew him with the sword and fled into the land of Ararat. His son Esarhaddon reigned in his stead.

Sickness and Recovery of Hezekiah

38 **1***†IN those days, when Hezekiah was mortally ill, the prophet Isaiah, son of Amoz, came and said to him: "Thus says the Lord: Put your house in order, for you are about to die; you shall not recover." **2**Then Hezekiah turned his face to the wall and prayed to the Lord: **3***"O Lord, remember how faithfully and wholeheartedly I conducted myself in your presence, doing what was pleasing to you!" And Hezekiah wept bitterly.

4Then the word of the Lord came to Isaiah: **5**†"Go, tell Hezekiah: Thus says the Lord, the God of your father David: I have heard your prayer and seen your tears. I will heal you: in three days you shall go up to the Lord's temple; I will add fifteen years to your life. **6***I will rescue you and this city from the hand of the king of Assyria; I will be a shield to this city."

21Isaiah then ordered a poultice of figs to be taken

---

†

37, 30: *You:* Hezekiah. *A sign:* it is difficult to know the nature of this sign. Either it is merely a proverbial expression to signify that prosperity follows adversity, or it indicates that after two years the normal conditions of life will be resumed.

37, 36: The destruction of Sennacherib's army is also recorded by Herodotus, a Greek historian of the fifth century B. C. It was probably due to the bubonic plague, but the sacred author attributes it to ultimate cause, God through his angel.

37, 38: The violent death of Sennacherib (681 B. C.) is also mentioned in non-biblical sources. It occurred twenty years after his invasion of Judea.

38, 1—39, 8: The events of this section—sickness and recovery of Hezekiah, embassy of Merodach-baladan—point forward to Babylon (cc 40-66). They occurred prior to the events of 36, 1—37, 38, which point back to Assyria (1, 1—35, 10).

38, 1: *In those days:* a time prior to the siege of Jerusalem in 701 B. C.

38, 5: Since Hezekiah died in 687 B. C., this sickness of his seems to have been in 702 B. C., that is, *fifteen years* before.

---

*
23: 1, 4.
31: 27, 6.
34: 37, 29.
35: 1 Kgs 15, 4f.
36: 10, 12; 17, 14.
37: 2 Kgs 19, 35f.
38/1: 2 Kgs 20, 1.
3: 2 Kgs 18, 5f.
6: 37, 35.

and applied to the boil, that he might recover. ²²Then Hezekiah asked, "What is the sign that I shall go up to the temple of the LORD?"

⁷[Isaiah answered:] "This will be the sign for you from the LORD that he will do what he has promised: ⁸*†See, I will make the shadow cast by the sun on the stairway to the terrace of Ahaz go back the ten steps it has advanced." So the sun came back the ten steps it had advanced.

Hezekiah's Hymn of Thanksgiving

⁹The song of Hezekiah, king of Judah, after he had been sick and had recovered from his illness:

¹⁰*† Once I said,
    "In the noontime of life I must depart!
    To the gates of the nether world I shall
      be consigned
      for the rest of my years."

¹¹† I said, "I shall see the LORD no more
    in the land of the living.
    No longer shall I behold my fellow men
      among those who dwell in the world."

¹²*† My dwelling, like a shepherd's tent,
    is struck down and borne away from
      me;
    You have folded up my life, like a
      weaver
    who severs the last thread.
    Day and night you give me over to
      torment;

¹³ I cry out until the dawn.
    Like a lion he breaks all my bones;
    [day and night you give me over to
      torment].

¹⁴ Like a swallow I utter shrill cries;
    I moan like a dove.
    My eyes grow weak, gazing
      heavenward:
    O Lord, I am in straits; be my surety!

¹⁵† What am I to say or tell him?
    He has done it!
    I shall go on through all my years
      despite the bitterness of my soul.

¹⁶† Those live whom the LORD protects;
    yours . . . the life of my spirit.
    You have given me health and life;

¹⁷† thus is my bitterness transformed into
      peace.
    You have preserved my life
      from the pit of destruction,
    When you cast behind your back
      all my sins.

¹⁸*† For it is not the nether world that gives
      you thanks,
    nor death that praises you;

    Neither do those who go down into the
      pit
      await your kindness.

¹⁹ The living, the living give you thanks,
    as I do today.
    Fathers declare to their sons,
      O God, your faithfulness.

²⁰ The LORD is our savior;
    we shall sing to stringed instruments
    In the house of the LORD
    all the days of our life.

Embassy from Merodach-baladan

39 ¹*†AT that time when Merodach-baladan, son of Baladan, king of Babylon, heard that Hezekiah had recovered from his sickness, he sent letters and gifts to him. ²*Hezekiah was pleased at this, and therefore showed the messengers his treasury, the silver and gold, the spices and fine oil, his whole armory, and everything that was in his storerooms; there was nothing in his house or in his whole realm that he did not show them.

³Then Isaiah the prophet came to King Hezekiah and asked him, "What did these men say to you? Where did they come from?" Hezekiah answered, "They came to me from a distant land, from Babylon." ⁴"What did they see in your house?" he asked. Hezekiah replied, "They saw everything in my house; there is nothing in my storerooms that I did not show them."

⁵Then Isaiah said to Hezekiah, "Hear the word of the LORD of hosts: ⁶*†Behold, the days shall come

---

† 38, 8: *Stairway to the terrace of Ahaz:* this interpretation is based on a reading of the Hebrew text revised according to the Dead Sea Scroll of Isaiah; cf 2 Kgs 23, 12. Many translate the phrase as "steps of Ahaz" and understand this as referring to a sundial.

38, 10: *In the noontime of life:* long before the end of a full span of life; cf Pss 55, 24; 102, 25.

38, 11: *See the Lord:* go to the temple and take part in its service.

38, 12: These two metaphors emphasize the suddenness and finality of death.

38, 15: *What am I to say or tell him?:* a rhetorical question, as if the poet were at a loss in giving fitting expression to his gratitude; cf Ps 116, 12. *He has done it:* accomplished the cure. *Despite the bitterness:* even though the one praying was previously so dejected.

38, 16: *Yours . . . the life of my spirit:* the current Hebrew text is corrupt. The revised Latin psalter renders it: "You have revived my soul."

38, 17: *You cast behind your back all my sins:* figurative language to express the divine forgiveness of sins, as if God no longer saw or cared about them. This expression is ordinarily used of men forgetting God; cf 1 Kgs 14, 9; Ez 23, 35; Ps 50, 17.

38, 18f: See note on Ps 6, 6.

39, 1: *Merodach-baladan:* twice king of Babylon, probably from 721 to 710 B. C., and again for nine months, in 704-703. This visit of his messengers, certainly before 701, was in reality a political one. Babylon hoped to lead an anti-Assyrian confederation composed of neighboring states.

39, 6: Because Judah preferred to follow a pro-Babylonian policy, instead of trusting in God, it would later be exiled to Babylon.

✱

8: 2 Kgs 20, 9.11.   18: Pss 6, 6; 88, 11-13.
10: Jb 17, 11;   39/1-8: 2 Kgs 20, 12.
     Ps 102, 25.   2: 2 Chr 32, 25ff.
12: Jb 7, 6.   6: 2 Kgs 24, 13; 25, 13ff.

when all that is in your house, and everything that your fathers have stored up until this day, shall be carried off to Babylon; nothing shall be left, says the Lord. **7***Some of your own bodily descendants shall be taken and made servants in the palace of the king of Babylon." **8*†**Hezekiah replied to Isaiah, "The word of the Lord which you have spoken is favorable." For he thought, "There will be peace and security in my lifetime."

B: The Book of Consolation

I: THE LORD'S GLORY IN ISRAEL'S LIBERATION

Promise of Salvation

40 ¹ COMFORT, GIVE COMFORT to my people,
     says your God.
2*† Speak tenderly to Jerusalem, and
     proclaim to her
       that her service is at an end,
       her guilt is expiated;
     Indeed, she has received from the hand
       of the Lord
       double for all her sins.

3*†   A voice cries out:
     In the desert prepare the way of the
       Lord!
       Make straight in the wasteland a
       highway for our God!
4   Every valley shall be filled in,
       every mountain and hill shall be made
       low;
     The rugged land shall be made a
       plain,
       the rough country, a broad valley.
5   Then the glory of the Lord shall be
       revealed,
       and all mankind shall see it together;
       for the mouth of the Lord has spoken.

6*   A voice says, "Cry out!"
     I answer, "What shall I cry out?"
     "All mankind is grass,
       and all their glory like the flower of
       the field.
7   The grass withers, the flower wilts,
       when the breath of the Lord blows
       upon it.
       [So then, the people is the grass.]

8   Though the grass withers and the
       flower wilts,
       the word of our God stands forever."

9   Go up onto a high mountain,
       Zion, herald of glad tidings;
     Cry out at the top of your voice,
       Jerusalem, herald of good news!
     Fear not to cry out
       and say to the cities of Judah:
       Here is your God!
10 Here comes with power
       the Lord God,
       who rules by his strong arm;
     Here is his reward with him,
       his recompense before him.
11* Like a shepherd he feeds his flock;
       in his arms he gathers the lambs,
     Carrying them in his bosom,
       and leading the ewes with care.

Power of the Creator To Save His People

12† Who has cupped in his hand the waters
       of the sea,
       and marked off the heavens with a
       span?
     Who has held in a measure the dust of
       the earth,
       weighed the mountains in scales
       and the hills in a balance?
13* Who has directed the spirit of the Lord,
       or has instructed him as his counselor?
14 Whom did he consult to gain
       knowledge?
     Who taught him the path of
       judgment,
       or showed him the way of
       understanding?

15 Behold, the nations count as a drop of
       the bucket,
       as dust on the scales;
     the coastlands weigh no more than
       powder.
16† Lebanon would not suffice for fuel,
       nor its animals be enough for
       holocausts.

---

† 39, 8: *Favorable:* for the Exile would not occur in his lifetime.

40, 2: *Service:* servitude and exile.

40, 3-5: The figurative language here describes the actual return of the exiles from Babylon to Jerusalem. It is the Lord who leads them; their road is made easy for them. Mt 3, 3 and parallels see in these verses a prophecy of the Baptizer and Christ.

40, 12: *Span:* the distance between the extended little finger and the thumb. *Measure:* literally, "third"; here a small container.

40, 16: *Lebanon . . . fuel:* the famed cedars would not be enough to keep the fires of sacrifice burning.

*
7: 2 Chr 33, 11;
    Dan 1, 2f.
8: 2 Chr 32, 26.
40/2: 50, 21.
   3: Mt 3, 3; Jn 1, 23.
   6: Jb 8, 12; 14, 2;
       Ps 37, 2; Sir 14, 18;
       Jas 1, 10; 1 Pt 1, 24.
11: 49, 9f; 63, 11;
     Ez 34, 23;
     37, 24; Jn 10, 11.
13: Wis 9, 13; Rom 11, 34;
     1 Cor 2, 16; Jb 38, 1ff.

17 Before him all the nations are as nought,
    as nothing and void he accounts them.

18* To whom can you liken God?
    With what equal can you confront
      him?

19* An idol, cast by a craftsman,
    which the smith plates with gold
    and fits with silver chains?

20* Mulberry wood, the choice portion
    which a skilled craftsman picks out
      for himself,
  Choosing timber that will not rot,
    to set up an idol that will not be
      unsteady?

41/6 One man helps another,
    one says to the other, "Keep on!"

41/7 The craftsman encourages the
      goldsmith,
    the one who beats with the hammer,
      him who strikes on the anvil;
  He says the soldering is good,
    and he fastens it with nails to steady it.

21 Do you not know? Have you not heard?
    Was it not foretold you from the
      beginning?
  Have you not understood? Since the
      earth was founded

22* He sits enthroned above the vault of the
      earth,
    and its inhabitants are like
      grasshoppers;
  He stretches out the heavens like a veil,
    spreads them out like a tent to dwell
      in.

23 He brings princes to nought
    and makes the rulers of the earth as
      nothing.

24 Scarcely are they planted or sown,
    scarcely is their stem rooted in the
      earth,
  When he breathes upon them and they
      wither,
    and the stormwind carries them away
      like straw.

25 To whom can you liken me as an equal?
    says the Holy One.

26*† Lift up your eyes on high
    and see who has created these:
  He leads out their army and numbers
      them,
    calling them all by name.
  By his great might and the strength of
      his power
    not one of them is missing!

27† Why, O Jacob, do you say,
    and declare, O Israel,
"My way is hidden from the Lord,
    and my right is disregarded by my
      God"?

28 Do you not know
    or have you not heard?
  The Lord is the eternal God,
    creator of the ends of the earth.
  He does not faint nor grow weary,
    and his knowledge is beyond scrutiny.

29 He gives strength to the fainting;
    for the weak he makes vigor abound.

30 Though young men faint and grow
      weary,
    and youths stagger and fall,

31 They that hope in the Lord will renew
      their strength,
    they will soar as with eagles' wings;
  They will run and not grow weary,
    walk and not grow faint.

The Liberator of Israel

41 1† Keep silence before me, O coastlands;
    you peoples, wait for my words!
  Let them draw near and speak;
    let us come together for judgment.

2† Who has stirred up from the East the
      champion of justice,
    and summoned him to be his
      attendant?
  To him he delivers the nations
    and subdues the kings;
  With his sword he reduces them to dust,
    with his bow, to driven straw.

3 He pursues them, passing on without
      loss,
    by a path his feet do not even tread.

4* Who has performed these deeds?
    He who has called forth the
      generations since the beginning.
  I, the Lord, am the first,
    and with the last I will also be.

5 The coastlands see, and fear;
    the ends of the earth tremble:
    these things are near, they come to
      pass.

8* But you, Israel, my servant,
    Jacob, whom I have chosen,
    offspring of Abraham my friend—

---

† 40, 26: *Created:* see note on Gn 1, 1. *By name:* for he is their Creator.

40, 27f: God's people, here called *Jacob* and *Israel*, must not give way to discouragement: their *Lord is the eternal God.*

41, 1-4: It is generally agreed that these verses describe the vocation and victory of Cyrus, whom the Lord used as his instrument to redeem Israel.

41, 2: Cyrus is the *champion of justice* and God's *attendant.*

* 18f: Acts 17, 29.
19: Ps 115, 4-7.
20: 44, 13.
22: Ps 104, 2.
26: Ps 147, 4f.
41/4: 44, 7; 46, 10.
8f: 44, 1f.21; 45, 4.

9 You whom I have taken from the ends of
the earth
and summoned from its far-off places,
You whom I have called my servant,
whom I have chosen and will not
cast off—

10 Fear not, I am with you;
be not dismayed; I am your God.
I will strengthen you, and help you,
and uphold you with my right hand of
justice. ·

11 Yes, all shall be put to shame and
disgrace
who vent their anger against you;
Those shall perish and come to nought
who offer resistance.

12 You shall seek out, but shall not find,
those who strive against you;
They shall be as nothing at all
who do battle with you.

13 For I am the Lord, your God,
who grasp your right hand;
It is I who say to you, "Fear not,
I will help you."

14† Fear not, O worm Jacob,
O maggot Israel;
I will help you, says the Lord;
your redeemer is the Holy One of
Israel.

15 I will make of you a threshing sledge,
sharp, new, and double-edged,
To thresh the mountains and crush
them,
to make the hills like chaff.

16 When you winnow them, the wind shall
carry them off
and the storm shall scatter them.
But you shall rejoice in the Lord,
and glory in the Holy One of Israel.

17 The afflicted and the needy seek water in
vain,
their tongues are parched with thirst.
I, the Lord, will answer them;
I, the God of Israel, will not forsake
them.

18 I will open up rivers on the bare heights,
and fountains in the broad valleys;
I will turn the desert into a marshland,
and the dry ground into springs of
water.

19 I will plant in the desert the cedar,
acacia, myrtle, and olive;
I will set in the wasteland the cypress,
together with the plane tree and the
pine,

20 That all may see and know,
observe and understand,

That the hand of the Lord has done this,
the Holy One of Israel has created it.

21† Present your case, says the Lord;
bring forward your reasons, says the
King of Jacob.

22 Let them come near and foretell to us
what it is that shall happen!
What are the things of long ago?
Tell us, that we may reflect on them
And know their outcome;
or declare to us the things to come!

23 Foretell the things that shall come
afterward,
that we may know that you are gods!
Do something, good or evil,
that will put us in awe and in fear.

24 Why, you are nothing and your work is
nought!
To choose you is an abomination.

25† I have stirred up one from the north, and
he comes;
from the east I summon him by name;
He shall trample the rulers down like red
earth,
as the potter treads the clay.

26 Who announced this from the beginning,
that we might know;
beforehand, that we might say it is
true?
Not one of you foretold it, not one spoke;
no one heard you say,

27 "The first news for Zion: they are coming
now,"
or, "For Jerusalem I will pick out a
bearer of the glad tidings."

28 When I look, there is not one,
no one of them to give counsel,
to make an answer when I question
them.

29 Ah, all of them are nothing,
their works are nought,
their idols are empty wind!

The Servant of the Lord

42 1*† Here is my servant whom I uphold,
my chosen one with whom I am
pleased,
Upon whom I have put my spirit;

---

†
41, 14: *Redeemer:* in Hebrew, *goel,* one who frees another
from slavery and avenges his sufferings; cf Lv 25, 48; Dt 19,
6.12.
41, 21-24: An indictment of idols.
41, 25: *I summon him:* Cyrus.
42, 1-4: *Servant:* there are three other "Servant-of-the-Lord"
oracles, 49, 1-7; 50, 4-11; 52, 13—53, 12. Many identifications
have been proposed, e.g., historical Israel, ideal Israel, an Old
Testament historical character before or during the lifetime of
the prophet, the prophet himself. The New Testament and
Christian tradition, however, have seen a fulfillment of these
prophecies in Jesus Christ.

he shall bring forth justice to the
    nations,

2   Not crying out, not shouting,
    not making his voice heard in the
        street.

3†   A bruised reed he shall not break,
    and a smoldering wick he shall not
        quench,

4†   Until he establishes justice on the earth;
    the coastlands will wait for his
        teaching.

5   Thus says God, the LORD,
    who created the heavens and
        stretched them out,
    who spreads out the earth with its
        crops,
    Who gives breath to its people
    and spirit to those who walk on it:

6✻   I, the LORD, have called you for the
        victory of justice,
    I have grasped you by the hand;
    I formed you, and set you
        as a covenant of the people,
        a light for the nations,

7   To open the eyes of the blind,
    to bring out prisoners from
        confinement,
    and from the dungeon, those who live
        in darkness.

8   I am the LORD, this is my name;
    my glory I give to no other,
    nor my praise to idols.

9   See, the earlier things have come to pass,
    new ones I now foretell;
    Before they spring into being,
    I announce them to you.

The Salvation of Israel despite Its Sins

10   Sing to the LORD a new song,
    his praise from the end of the earth:
    Let the sea and what fills it resound,
    the coastlands, and those who dwell in
        them.

11†   Let the steppe and its cities cry out,
    the villages where Kedar dwells;
    Let the inhabitants of Sela exult,
    and shout from the top of the
        mountains.

12   Let them give glory to the LORD,
    and utter his praise in the coastlands.

13✻ The LORD goes forth like a hero,
    like a warrior he stirs up his ardor;
    He shouts out his battle cry,
    against his enemies he shows his
        might:

14   I have looked away, and kept silence,
    I have said nothing, holding myself in;
    But now, I cry out as a woman in labor,
        gasping and panting.

15✻ I will lay waste mountains and hills,
    all their herbage I will dry up;
    I will turn the rivers into marshes,
    and the marshes I will dry up.

16✻ I will lead the blind on their journey;
    by paths unknown I will guide them.
    I will turn darkness into light before
        them,
    and make crooked ways straight.
    These things I do for them,
    and I will not forsake them.

17   They shall be turned back in utter shame
    who trust in idols;
    Who say to molten images,
    "You are our gods."

18†   You who are deaf, listen,
    you who are blind, look and see!

19   Who is blind but my servant,
    or deaf like the messenger I send?

20   You see many things without taking
        note;
    your ears are open, but without
        hearing.

21   Though it pleased the LORD in his justice
    to make his law great and glorious,

22†   This is a people despoiled and
        plundered,
    all of them trapped in holes,
    hidden away in prisons.
    They are taken as booty, with no one to
        rescue them,
    as spoil, with no one to demand their
        return.

23   Who of you gives ear to this?
    Who listens and pays heed for the
        time to come?

24†   Who was it that gave Jacob to be
        plundered,
    Israel to the despoilers?
    Was it not the LORD, against whom we
        have sinned?
    In his ways they refused to walk,
    his law they disobeyed.

---

†
42, 3: A reference to the mercy of Christ.

42, 4: *Coastlands:* the lands of the Mediterranean. In the Old Testament the word often refers to the pagan lands of the west.

42, 11: *Kedar:* cf footnote to 21, 16. *Sela:* Petra, the capital of Edom.

42, 18-20: Because of their unbelief, the Lord rebukes his people, whom he calls his *servant,* his *messenger.*

42, 22: *A people:* Israel in exile.

42, 24: *Despoilers:* the Assyrians and Babylonians.

✻
6: 45, 13.   15: Ex 9, 25; 10, 15;
13: Ex 14, 3.   14, 21; Ps 105, 33ff.
                              16: Ex 13, 21.

25 So he poured out wrath upon them,
   his anger, and the fury of battle;
It blazed round about them, yet they did
   not realize,
   it burned them, but they took it not to
   heart.

Promises of Redemption and Restoration

43 **1** But now, thus says the LORD,
   who created you, O Jacob, and formed
   you, O Israel:
Fear not, for I have redeemed you;
   I have called you by name: you are
   mine.
2 When you pass through the water, I will
   be with you;
   in the rivers you shall not drown.
When you walk through fire, you shall
   not be burned;
   the flames shall not consume you.
3† For I am the LORD, your God,
   the Holy One of Israel, your savior.
I give Egypt as your ransom,
   Ethiopia and Seba in return for you.
4✢ Because you are precious in my eyes
   and glorious, and because I love you,
I give men in return for you
   and peoples in exchange for your life.
5 Fear not, for I am with you;
   from the east I will bring back your
   descendants,
   from the west I will gather you.
6✢ I will say to the north: Give them up!
   and to the south: Hold not back!
Bring back my sons from afar,
   and my daughters from the ends of the
   earth:
7 Everyone who is named as mine,
   whom I created for my glory,
   whom I formed and made.
8 Lead out the people who are blind
   though they have eyes,
   who are deaf though they have ears.

9† Let all the nations gather together,
   let the peoples assemble!
Who among them could have revealed
   this,
   or foretold to us the earlier things?
Let them produce witnesses to prove
   themselves right,
   that one may hear and say, "It is true!"
10 You are my witnesses, says the LORD,
   my servants whom I have chosen
To know and believe in me
   and understand that it is I.

Before me no god was formed,
   and after me there shall be none.
11 It is I, I the LORD;
   there is no savior but me.
12 It is I who foretold, I who saved;
   I made it known, not any strange god
   among you;
You are my witnesses, says the LORD.
13✢ I am God, yes, from eternity I am He;
There is none who can deliver from my
   hand:
   who can countermand what I do?
14† Thus says the LORD, your redeemer,
   the Holy One of Israel:
For your sakes I send to Babylon;
   I will lower all the bars,
   and the Chaldeans shall cry out in
   lamentation.
15 I am the LORD, your Holy One,
   the creator of Israel, your King.
16✢ Thus says the LORD,
   who opens a way in the sea
   and a path in the mighty waters,
17✢ Who leads out chariots and horsemen,
   a powerful army,
Till they lie prostrate together, never to
   rise,
   snuffed out and quenched like a wick.

18† Remember not the events of the past,
   the things of long ago consider not;
19 See, I am doing something new!
   Now it springs forth, do you not
   perceive it?
In the desert I make a way,
   in the wasteland, rivers.
20 Wild beasts honor me,
   jackals and ostriches,
For I put water in the desert
   and rivers in the wasteland
   for my chosen people to drink,
21 The people whom I formed for myself,
   that they might announce my praise.

22† Yet you did not call upon me, O Jacob,
   for you grew weary of me, O Israel.
23✢ You did not bring me sheep for your
   holocausts,
   nor honor me with your sacrifices.

---

† 43, 3f: *Egypt . . . Ethiopia and Seba:* countries which God permitted the Persians to conquer in return for having given Israel its freedom.

43, 9: Only God can know and predict future events; cf 41, 1-5.21-29.

43, 14-17: The destruction of Babylon.

43, 18: No need to think solely of the past wonders of the exodus from Egypt; equally great is the exodus from Babylon.

43, 22-28: The reason for the liberation of the Israelites is not their fidelity but rather God's mercy.

✢ 43/4: Dt 4, 37; Hos 11, 1.
   6: 49, 22; Ez 16, 20.
   13: 41, 4.
16: 51, 10f; Ex 14, 21.
17: Ex 15, 4.
23: Jer 6, 20.

I did not exact from you the service of
    offerings,
      nor weary you for frankincense.
24† You did not buy me sweet cane for
    money,
      nor fill me with the fat of your
        sacrifices;
    Instead, you burdened me with your
      sins,
      and wearied me with your crimes.
25 It is I, I, who wipe out,
    for my own sake, your offenses;
      your sins I remember no more.
26 Would you have me remember, have us
    come to trial?
      Speak up, prove your innocence!
27† Your first father sinned;
      your spokesmen rebelled against me
28 Till I repudiated the holy gates,
    put Jacob under the ban,
      and exposed Israel to scorn.

44

1 Hear then, O Jacob, my servant,
    Israel, whom I have chosen.
2† Thus says the LORD who made you,
    your help, who formed you from the
      womb:
    Fear not, O Jacob, my servant,
      the darling whom I have chosen.
3 I will pour out water upon the thirsty
    ground,
      and streams upon the dry land;
    I will pour out my spirit upon your
      offspring,
      and my blessing upon your
        descendants.
4* They shall spring up amid the verdure
    like poplars beside the flowing waters.
5*† One shall say, "I am the LORD's,"
    another shall be named after Jacob,
    And this one shall write on his hand,
      "The LORD's,"
      and Israel shall be his surname.

The True God and False Gods

6* Thus says the LORD, Israel's King
    and redeemer, the LORD of hosts:
    I am the first and I am the last;
      there is no God but me.
7 Who is like me? Let him stand up and
    speak,
      make it evident, and confront me with
      it.
    Who of old announced future events?
      Let them foretell to us the things to
      come.

8*† Fear not, be not troubled:
    did I not announce and foretell it long
      ago?
    You are my witnesses! Is there a God
      or any Rock besides me?

9*† Idol makers all amount to nothing, and their precious works are of no avail, as they themselves give witness. To their shame, they neither see nor know anything; and they are more deaf than men are. [10]Indeed, all the associates of anyone who forms a god, or casts an idol to no purpose, will be put to shame; [11]they will all assemble and stand forth, to be reduced to fear and shame.

[12]*The smith fashions an iron image, works it over the coals, shapes it with hammers, and forges it with his strong arm. He is hungry and weak, drinks no water and becomes exhausted.

[13]The carpenter stretches a line and marks with a stylus the outline of an idol. He shapes it with a plane and measures it off with a compass, making it like a man in appearance and dignity, to occupy a shrine. [14]He cuts down cedars, takes a holm or an oak, and lays hold of other trees of the forest, which the Lord had planted and the rain made grow [15]to serve man for fuel. With a part of their wood he warms himself, or makes a fire for baking bread; but with another part he makes a god which he adores, an idol which he worships. [16]Half of it he burns in the fire, and on its embers he roasts his meat; he eats what he has roasted until he is full, and then warms himself and says, "Ah! I am warm, I feel the fire." [17]Of what remains he makes a god, his idol, and prostrate before it in worship, he implores it, "Rescue me, for you are my god."

[18]The idols have neither knowledge nor reason; their eyes are coated so that they cannot see, and their hearts so that they cannot understand. [19]Yet he does not reflect, nor have the intelligence and sense to say, "Half of the wood I burned in the fire, and on its embers I baked bread and roasted meat which I ate. Shall I then make an abomination out of the rest, or worship a block of wood?" [20]†He is chasing ashes—a thing that cannot save itself when the flame consumes it; yet he does not say, "Is not this thing in my right hand a fraud?"

21   Remember this, O Jacob,
      you, O Israel, who are my servant!

---

† 43, 24: *Sweet cane:* a fragrant substance used in making incense and the sacred anointing oil; cf Ex 30, 23; Jer 6, 20.
 43, 27: *First father:* Adam or Jacob, or collectively "early ancestors." *Spokesmen:* leaders, priests, prophets.
 44, 2: *The darling:* see note on Dt 32, 15; cf also Dt 33, 5.26.
 44, 5: *Write on his hand:* an allusion to the Babylonian custom of tatooing the owner's name on the hand of his slave; cf also Rv 13, 16.
 44, 8: *Rock:* place of refuge; said of God in Dt 32, 4.18; 1 Sm 2, 2; etc.
 44, 9-20: Satire on the makers and worshipers of idols.
 44, 20: *Chasing ashes:* exerting efforts in vain; cf Hos 12, 2; Eccl 1, 14; 2, 11.17.

---

* 44/4: 54, 1ff.   8: 43, 10.12; Dt 32, 4.
   5: 43, 7; 45, 14.   9: 48, 5.7.
   6: 41, 44; 43, 15; 45, 21;   12: Wis 13, 11ff.
   48, 3.12; 51, 15; 54, 5.

I formed you to be a servant to me;
  O Israel, by me you shall never be
    forgotten:

22 I have brushed away your offenses like a
    cloud,
  your sins like a mist;
  return to me, for I have redeemed you.

23 Raise a glad cry, you heavens: the Lord
    has done this;
  shout, you depths of the earth.
  Break forth, you mountains, into song,
    you forest, with all your trees.
  For the Lord has redeemed Jacob,
    and shows his glory through Israel.

Cyrus, Anointed of the Lord, Liberator of Israel

24* Thus says the Lord, your redeemer,
  who formed you from the womb:
  I am the Lord, who made all things,
    who alone stretched out the heavens;
    when I spread out the earth, who was
      with me?

25 It is I who bring to nought the omens of
    liars,
  who make fools of diviners;
  I turn wise men back
    and make their knowledge foolish.

26 It is I who confirm the words of my
    servants,
  I carry out the plan announced by my
    messengers;
  I say to Jerusalem: Be inhabited;
    to the cities of Judah: Be rebuilt;
    I will raise up their ruins.

27* It is I who said to the deep: Be dry;
  I will dry up your wellsprings.

28*† I say of Cyrus: My shepherd,
  who fulfills my every wish;
  He shall say of Jerusalem, "Let her be
    rebuilt,"
  and of the temple, "Let its foundations
    be laid."

45 **1†** Thus says the Lord to his anointed,
    Cyrus,
  whose right hand I grasp,
  Subduing nations before him,
    and making kings run in his service,
  Opening doors before him
    and leaving the gates unbarred:

2*† I will go before you
  and level the mountains;
  Bronze doors I will shatter,
    and iron bars I will snap.

3 I will give you treasures out of the
    darkness,
  and riches that have been hidden
    away,
  That you may know that I am the Lord,
    the God of Israel, who calls you by
      your name.

4* For the sake of Jacob, my servant,
  of Israel my chosen one,
  I have called you by your name,
    giving you a title, though you knew
      me not.

5 I am the Lord and there is no other,
    there is no God besides me.
  It is I who arm you, though you know
    me not,

6† so that toward the rising and the
    setting of the sun
  men may know that there is none
    besides me.
  I am the Lord, there is no other;

7† I form the light, and create the
    darkness,
  I make well-being and create woe;
    I, the Lord, do all these things.

8*† Let justice descend, O heavens, like dew
    from above,
  like gentle rain let the skies drop it
    down.
  Let the earth open and salvation bud
    forth;
    let justice also spring up!
    I, the Lord, have created this.

9*† Woe to him who contends with his
    Maker;
  a potsherd among potsherds of the
    earth!
  Dare the clay say to its modeler, "What
    are you doing?"
    or, "What you are making has no
      hands"?

---

† 44, 28: *Cyrus:* king of Persia (559-529 B. C.) and conqueror of Babylon (538 B. C.), who liberated the Jews, permitting them to return to their native land and to rebuild Jerusalem and the temple.

45, 1: *Anointed:* in Hebrew, *meshiah,* from which the word "Messiah" is derived; from its Greek translation, *Christos,* we have the name "Christ." Applied to kings, anointed originally referred only to those of Israel, but it is here given to *Cyrus* because he is the agent of the Lord.

45, 2: *Bronze doors:* of Babylon.

45, 6: The Gentiles will come to know the true God; cf also vv 20-25.

45, 7: *Create woe:* God permits evil for the sake of a greater good.

45, 8: The Vulgate rendering gives a more precise messianic sense to this verse, using "just one" and "savior" in place of *justice* and *salvation.* The Advent liturgy uses the Vulgate form, *Rorate coeli desuper . . . ,* to express the world's longing for the coming of Christ.

45, 9: No one may challenge God's freedom of action, exemplified here by the selection of Cyrus as his anointed.

*
  24: 40, 22; Jb 9, 8.   4: 40, 26.
  27: 42, 15; 51, 10.   8: Pss 72, 6; 85, 11.
  28: Jer 3, 15; Ez 34, 23.   9: Jer 18, 6; Rom 9, 20.
  45/2: Ps 107, 16.

10 Woe to him who asks a father, "What
     are you begetting?"
   or a woman, "What are you giving
     birth to?"

11 Thus says the LORD,
   the Holy One of Israel, his maker:
You question me about my children,
   or prescribe the work of my hands
     for me!

12 It was I who made the earth
   and created mankind upon it;
It was my hands that stretched out the
     heavens;
   I gave the order to all their host.

13† It was I who stirred up one for the
     triumph of justice;
   all his ways I make level.
He shall rebuild my city
   and let my exiles go free
Without price or ransom,
   says the LORD of hosts.

14*†   Thus says the LORD:
The earnings of Egypt, the gain of
     Ethiopia,
   and the Sabeans, tall of stature,
Shall come over to you and belong to
     you;
   they shall follow you, coming in
     chains.
Before you they shall fall prostrate,
   saying in prayer:
"With you only is God, and nowhere else;
   the gods are nought.

15*† Truly with you God is hidden,
   the God of Israel, the savior!

16 Those are put to shame and disgrace
   who vent their anger against him;
Those go in disgrace
   who carve images.

17 Israel, you are saved by the LORD,
   saved forever!
You shall never be put to shame or
     disgrace
   in future ages."

18†   For thus says the LORD,
The creator of the heavens,
   who is God,
The designer and maker of the earth
   who established it,
Not creating it to be a waste,
   but designing it to be lived in:
I am the LORD, and there is no other.

19 I have not spoken from hiding
   nor from some dark place of the earth,
And I have not said to the descendants
     of Jacob,
   "Look for me in an empty waste."

I, the LORD, promise justice,
   I foretell what is right.

20† Come and assemble, gather together,
   you fugitives from among the gentiles!
They are without knowledge who bear
     wooden idols
   and pray to gods that cannot save.

21 Come here and declare
   in counsel together:
Who announced this from the beginning
   and foretold it from of old?
Was it not I, the LORD,
   besides whom there is no other God?
There is no just and saving God but
     me.

22 Turn to me and be safe,
   all you ends of the earth,
   for I am God; there is no other!

23* By myself I swear,
   uttering my just decree
   and my unalterable word:
To me every knee shall bend;
   by me every tongue shall swear,

24 Saying, "Only in the LORD
   are just deeds and power.
Before him in shame shall come
   all who vent their anger against him.

25 In the LORD shall be the vindication and
     the glory
   of all the descendants of Israel."

The Gods of Babylon

46 1† Bel bows down, Nebo stoops,
   their idols are upon beasts and cattle;
They must be borne up on shoulders,
   carried as burdens by the weary.

2 They stoop and bow down together;
   unable to save those who bear them,
   they too go into captivity.

3* Hear me, O house of Jacob,
   all who remain of the house of Israel,
My burden since your birth,
   whom I have carried from your
     infancy.

---

† 45, 13: *One:* Cyrus, called by God for the deliverance and restoration of Israel.

45, 14: *Egypt . . . Ethiopia . . . Sabeans:* the Egyptians and their allies who, when conquered by Cyrus, are seen as acknowledging the God of Israel to be the one true God; cf 43, 3.

45, 15: *God is hidden:* he dwells invisibly in the holy of holies.

45, 18: *Waste:* an allusion to the beginning of creation, when the earth was *waste and void* (Gn 1, 2), the same Hebrew word, *tohu,* being used in both passages. The further reference here is to Palestine, which God wishes again to be inhabited by the returning exiles.

45, 20: *Who bear wooden idols:* in their religious processions. The gods of the pagans have feet but cannot walk; cf Ps 115, 7; Bar 6, 25.

46, 1: *Bel . . . Nebo:* gods of Babylon; their complete helplessness is here contrasted with God's omnipotence.

---

* 14: 43, 3.
15: 55, 8; Prv 25, 2.
23: Rom 14, 11; Phil 2, 10.
46/3: 44, 2.

4 Even to your old age I am the same,
 even when your hair is gray I will bear
  you;
It is I who have done this, I who will
 continue,
 and I who will carry you to safety.

5 Whom would you compare me with, as
 an equal,
 or match me against, as though we
  were alike?
6 There are those who pour out gold from
 a purse
 and weigh out silver on the scales;
Then they hire a goldsmith to make it
 into a god
 before which they fall down in
  worship.
7 They lift it to their shoulders to carry;
 when they set it in place again, it
  stays,
 and does not move from the spot.
Although they cry out to it, it cannot
 answer;
 it delivers no one from distress.

8 Remember this and be firm,
 bear it well in mind, you rebels;
 remember the former things, those
  long ago:
9 I am God, there is no other;
 I am God, there is none like me.
10 At the beginning I foretell the outcome;
 in advance, things not yet done.
I say that my plan shall stand,
 I accomplish my every purpose.
11† I call from the east a bird of prey,
 from a distant land, one to carry out
  my plan.
Yes, I have spoken, I will accomplish it;
 I have planned it, and I will do it.
12 Listen to me, you fainthearted,
 you who seem far from the victory of
  justice:
13 I am bringing on my justice, it is not far
 off,
 my salvation shall not tarry;
I will put salvation within Zion,
 and give to Israel my glory.

The Fall of Babylon

47 **1†** Come down, sit in the dust,
 O virgin daughter Babylon;
Sit on the ground, dethroned,
 O daughter of the Chaldeans.
No longer shall you be called
 dainty and delicate.
2 Take the millstone and grind flour,
 remove your veil;

Strip off your train, bare your legs,
 pass through the streams.
3 Your nakedness shall be uncovered
 and your shame be seen;
I will take vengeance,
 I will yield to no entreaty,
 says our redeemer,
4 Whose name is the LORD of hosts,
 the Holy One of Israel.

5 Go into darkness and sit in silence,
 O daughter of the Chaldeans,
No longer shall you be called
 sovereign mistress of kingdoms.
6 Angry at my people,
 I profaned my inheritance,
And I gave them into your hand;
 but you showed them no mercy,
And upon old men
 you laid a very heavy yoke.
7* You said, "I shall remain always
 a sovereign mistress forever!"
But you did not lay these things to heart,
 you disregarded their outcome.

8* Now hear this, voluptuous one,
 enthroned securely,
Saying to yourself,
 "I, and no one else!
I shall never be a widow,
 or suffer the loss of my children"—
9† Both these things shall come to you
 suddenly, in a single day:
Complete bereavement and widowhood
 shall come upon you
For your many sorceries
 and the great number of your spells;
10 Because you felt secure in your
 wickedness,
 and said, "No one sees me."

Your wisdom and your knowledge
 led you astray,
And you said to yourself,
 "I, and no one else!"
11 But upon you shall come evil
 you will not know how to predict;
Disaster shall befall you
 which you cannot allay.
Suddenly there shall come upon you
 ruin which you will not expect.
12 Keep up, now, your spells
 and your many sorceries;
Perhaps you can make them avail,
 perhaps you can strike terror!

---

†
46, 11: *From the east a bird of prey:* Cyrus; cf 41, 2-4.

47, 1-15: A taunt-song, mocking Babylon, once queen of the nations, now made a slave girl.

47, 9.13.15: Babylon was known for its sorcery and astrology.

---

* 47/7: 14, 13f.   8: Zep 2, 15; Rv 18, 7.

13 You wearied yourself with many
     consultations,
       at which you toiled from your youth;
   Let the astrologers stand forth to save
     you,
       the stargazers who forecast at each
         new moon
       what would happen to you.

14 Lo, they are like stubble,
     fire consumes them;
   They cannot save themselves
     from the spreading flames.
   This is no warming ember,
     no fire to sit before.

15 Thus do your wizards serve you
     with whom you have toiled from your
       youth;
   Each wanders his own way,
     with none to save you.

Exhortations to the Exiles

48 1 Hear this, O house of Jacob
         called by the name Israel,
           sprung from the stock of Judah,
       You who swear by the name of the Lord
         and invoke the God of Israel
           without sincerity or justice,

     2 Though you are named after the holy
         city
       and rely on the God of Israel,
         whose name is the Lord of hosts.

     3 Things of the past I foretold long ago,
         they went forth from my mouth, I let
           you hear of them;
           then suddenly I took action and they
             came to be.

     4 Because I know that you are stubborn
         and that your neck is an iron sinew
           and your forehead bronze,

     5 I foretold them to you of old;
         before they took place I let you hear
           of them,
       That you might not say, "My idol did
         them,
         my statue, my molten image
           commanded them."

     6* Now that you have heard, look at all this;
         must you not admit it?

       From now on I announce new things to
         you,
           hidden events of which you knew not.

     7 Now, not long ago, they are brought into
         being,

   and beforetime you did not hear of
     them,
       so that you cannot claim to have
         known them;

 8* You neither heard nor knew,
     they did not reach your ears
       beforehand.
   Yes, I know you are utterly treacherous,
     a rebel you were called from birth.

 9 For the sake of my name I restrain my
     anger,
       for the sake of my renown I hold it
         back from you,
           lest I should destroy you.

10* See, I have refined you like silver,
     tested you in the furnace of affliction.

11 For my sake, for my own sake, I do this;
     why should I suffer profanation?
   My glory I will not give to another.

12* Listen to me, Jacob,
     Israel, whom I named!
   I, it is I who am the first,
     and also the last am I.

13* Yes, my hand laid the foundations of the
     earth;
       my right hand spread out the heavens.
   When I call them,
     they stand forth at once.

14† All of you assemble and listen:
     Who among you foretold these things?
   The Lord's friend shall do his will
     against Babylon and the progeny of
       Chaldea.

15 I myself have spoken, I have called him,
     I have brought him, and his way
       succeeds!

16† Come near to me and hear this!
     Not from the beginning did I speak it
       in secret;
   At the time it comes to pass, I am
     present:
       "Now the Lord God has sent me, and
         his spirit."

17 Thus says the Lord, your redeemer,
     the Holy One of Israel:
   I, the Lord, your God,
     teach you what is for your good,
       and lead you on the way you should
         go.

18 If you would hearken to my
     commandments,
       your prosperity would be like a river,
         and your vindication like the waves of
           the sea;

---

*
48/6: 42, 9.   12: 41, 4; 44, 6; 48, 12;
   8: 43, 22ff.   Rv 1, 8.17.
  10: 1, 25; Jer 6, 29f; 13: 40, 22.26; 45, 12.18.
      Zec 13, 9; Mal 3, 2.

†
  48, 14: The Lord's friend: Cyrus, who carries out God's
plans.
  48, 16: "Now the Lord . . . spirit": said by Cyrus; cf v 14.

19 Your descendants would be like the
    sand,
    and those born of your stock like its
      grains,
Their name never cut off
    or blotted out from my presence.
20 Go forth from Babylon, flee from
    Chaldea!
    With shouts of joy proclaim this, make
      it known;
Publish it to the ends of the earth, and
    say,
    "The LORD has redeemed his servant
      Jacob.
21* They did not thirst
    when he led them through dry lands;
Water from the rock he set flowing for
    them;
    he cleft the rock, and waters welled
      forth."
22 [There is no peace for the wicked,
    says the LORD.]

II: EXPIATION OF SIN
SPIRITUAL LIBERATION OF ISRAEL

The Servant of the Lord

49   1*†   HEAR ME, O coastlands,
    listen, O distant peoples.
The LORD called me from birth,
    from my mother's womb he gave me
      my name.
2† He made of me a sharp-edged sword
    and concealed me in the shadow of
      his arm.
He made me a polished arrow,
    in his quiver he hid me.
3† You are my servant, he said to me,
    Israel, through whom I show my
      glory.

4* Though I thought I had toiled in vain,
    and for nothing, uselessly, spent my
      strength,
Yet my reward is with the LORD,
    my recompense is with my God.
5 For now the LORD has spoken
    who formed me as his servant from
      the womb,
That Jacob may be brought back to him
    and Israel gathered to him;

And I am made glorious in the sight of
    the LORD,
    and my God is now my strength!
6*† It is too little, he says, for you to be my
    servant,
    to raise up the tribes of Jacob,
    and restore the survivors of Israel;
I will make you a light to the nations,
    that my salvation may reach to the
      ends of the earth.
7* Thus says the LORD,
    the redeemer and the Holy One of
      Israel,
To the one despised, whom the nations
    abhor,
    the slave of rulers:
When kings see you, they shall stand up,
    and princes shall prostrate themselves
Because of the LORD who is faithful,
    the Holy One of Israel who has
      chosen you.

The Liberation and Restoration of Zion

8*   Thus says the LORD:
In a time of favor I answer you,
    on the day of salvation I help you,
To restore the land
    and allot the desolate heritages,
9* Saying to the prisoners: Come out!
To those in darkness: Show yourselves!
Along the ways they shall find pasture,
    on every bare height shall their
      pastures be.
10* They shall not hunger or thirst,
    nor shall the scorching wind or the
      sun strike them;
For he who pities them leads them
    and guides them beside springs of
      water.
11* I will cut a road through all my
    mountains,
    and make my highways level.
12† See, some shall come from afar,
    others from the north and the west,
    and some from the land of Syene.

---

† 49, 1-7: The second of the four "Servant-of-the-Lord" oracles.

49, 1: *Gave me my name:* designated me for a special office (cf Jer 1, 5), or perhaps, made me renowned (cf Ps 45, 18).

49, 2: The Servant was made ready and fit for the preaching of God's word.

49, 3: *Israel:* the Servant is identified with the people of Israel as their ideal representative; however, since vv 5f seem to distinguish the Servant from Israel, some regard the word *Israel* here as a gloss.

49, 6: The Servant's vocation will be not only the restoration of Israel but the conversion of the world; cf Lk 2, 32.

49, 12: *Syene:* now called Aswan, at the first cataract of the Nile in southern Egypt.

---

* 21: Ex 17, 6; Nm 20, 11.   7: 49, 23; 55, 5.
49/1: 41, 9; 43, 1; 44, 2.24;   8: 2 Cor 6, 2.
    46, 3.   9: 42, 7.18ff.
  4: 40, 27.   10: 51, 14; Rv 7, 16.
  6: 42, 1-6; 44, 5; 45, 14;   11: 40, 3f.
    Lk 2, 32; Acts 13, 46f.

13   Sing out, O heavens, and rejoice, O
       earth,
      break forth into song, you mountains.
     For the LORD comforts his people
      and shows mercy to his afflicted.

14*   But Zion said, "The LORD has forsaken
       me;
      my Lord has forgotten me."

15*   Can a mother forget her infant,
      be without tenderness for the child of
       her womb?
     Even should she forget,
      I will never forget you.

16†   See, upon the palms of my hands I have
      written your name;
      your walls are ever before me.

17   Your rebuilders make haste,
      as those who tore you down and laid
       you waste
      go forth from you;

18   Look about and see,
      they are all gathering and coming to
       you.
     As I live, says the LORD,
      you shall be arrayed with them all as
       with adornments,
      like a bride you shall fasten them on
       you.

19   Though you were waste and desolate,
      a land of ruins,
     Now you shall be too small for your
      inhabitants,
      while those who swallowed you up
       will be far away.

20   The children whom you had lost
      shall yet say to you,
    "This place is too small for me,
      make room for me to live in."

21*   You shall ask yourself:
     "Who has borne me these?
    I was bereft and barren
      [exiled and repudiated];
      who has reared them?
    I was left all alone;
      where then do these come from?"

22*   Thus says the Lord GOD:
    See, I will lift up my hand to the nations,
      and raise my signal to the peoples;
    They shall bring your sons in their arms,
      and your daughters shall be carried on
       their shoulders.

23   Kings shall be your foster fathers,
      their princesses your nurses;

     Bowing to the ground, they shall
      worship you
      and lick the dust at your feet.
     Then you shall know that I am the LORD,
      and those who hope in me shall never
       be disappointed.

24   Thus says the LORD:
    Can booty be taken from a warrior?
      or captives be rescued from a tyrant?

25   Yes, captives can be taken from a
      warrior,
      and booty be rescued from a tyrant;
    Those who oppose you I will oppose,
      and your sons I will save.

26*   I will make your oppressors eat their
      own flesh,
      and they shall be drunk with their
       own blood
      as with the juice of the grape.
    All mankind shall know
      that I, the LORD, am your savior,
      your redeemer, the mighty one of
       Jacob.

Salvation Only Through the Lord's Servant

50   1*†   Thus says the LORD:
    Where is the bill of divorce
      with which I dismissed your mother?
    Or to which of my creditors
      have I sold you?
    It was for your sins that you were sold,
      for your crimes that your mother was
       dismissed.

2*†   Why was no one there when I came?
      Why did no one answer when I
       called?
    Is my hand too short to ransom?
      Have I not the strength to deliver?
    Lo, with my rebuke I dry up the sea,
      I turn rivers into a desert;
    Their fish rot for lack of water,
      and die of thirst.

3   I clothe the heavens in mourning,
      and make sackcloth their vesture.

4†   The Lord GOD has given me
      a well-trained tongue,

---

† 49, 16: *Upon the palms . . . name:* for continual remembrance; cf Ex 13, 9.16; Dt 6, 6-9.

50, 1: Responding to the people's complaint of utter abandonment by God, the prophet shows that their sins were responsible for their banishment. Since there was no bill of divorce, the bond between the Lord and his people still exists and he will ultimately save them.

50, 2: Israel's faith in God is weak; she does not answer his call, nor believe in his promises of deliverance.

50, 4-11: The third of the four "Servant-of-the-Lord" oracles; in vv 4-9 the Servant speaks; in vv 10f God reproves the people for not following the Servant.

❋
14: 40, 27.
15: 43, 4; 44, 21; 46, 3f.
21: 54, 1ff.
22: 5, 26; 13, 2.

26: 19, 2; Ez 38, 21; Zec 14, 13.
50/1: Dt 24, 1-4; Mt 19, 3; Mk 10, 2ff; Is 54, 6ff.
2: Ex 7, 18; Ps 105, 29.

That I might know how to speak to the
weary
a word that will rouse them.
Morning after morning
he opens my ear that I may hear;

5† And I have not rebelled,
have not turned back.

6*† I gave my back to those who beat me,
my cheeks to those who plucked my
beard;
My face I did not shield
from buffets and spitting.

7* The Lord God is my help,
therefore I am not disgraced;
I have set my face like flint,
knowing that I shall not be put to
shame.

8 He is near who upholds my right;
if anyone wishes to oppose me,
let us appear together.
Who disputes my right?
Let him confront me.

9* See, the Lord God is my help;
who will prove me wrong?
Lo, they will all wear out like cloth,
the moth will eat them up.

10*† Who among you fears the LORD,
heeds his servant's voice,
And walks in darkness
without any light,
Trusting in the name of the LORD
and relying on his God?

11 All of you kindle flames
and carry about you fiery darts;
Walk by the light of your own fire
and by the flares you have burnt!
This is your fate from my hand:
you shall lie down in a place of pain.

Exhortation to Trust in the Lord

51
1*† Listen to me, you who pursue justice,
who seek the LORD;
Look to the rock from which you were
hewn,
to the pit from which you were
quarried;

2* Look to Abraham, your father,
and to Sarah, who gave you birth;
When he was but one I called him,
I blessed him and made him many.

3 Yes, the LORD shall comfort Zion
and have pity on all her ruins;

Her deserts he shall make like Eden,
her wasteland like the garden of the
LORD;
Joy and gladness shall be found in her,
thanksgiving and the sound of song.

4*† Be attentive to me, my people;
my folk, give ear to me.
For law shall go forth from my presence,
and my judgment, as the light of the
peoples.

5 I will make my justice come speedily;
my salvation shall go forth
[and my arm shall judge the
nations];
In me shall the coastlands hope,
and my arm they shall await.

6† Raise your eyes to the heavens,
and look at the earth below;
Though the heavens grow thin like
smoke,
the earth wears out like a garment
and its inhabitants die like flies,
My salvation shall remain forever
and my justice shall never be
dismayed.

7 Hear me, you who know justice,
you people who have my teaching at
heart:
Fear not the reproach of men,
be not dismayed at their revilings.

8* They shall be like a garment eaten by
moths,
like wool consumed by grubs;
But my justice shall remain forever
and my salvation, for all generations.

9*† Awake, awake, put on strength,
O arm of the LORD!
Awake as in the days of old,
in ages long ago!
Was it not you who crushed Rahab,
you who pierced the dragon?

10† Was it not you who dried up the sea,
the waters of the great deep,
Who made the depths of the sea into a
way
for the redeemed to pass over?

---

† 50, 5: The Servant does not refuse the divine vocation.
50, 6: He willingly submits to insults and beatings. *Plucked my beard:* a grave insult.
50, 10f: Instead of trusting in the Lord and his Servant, the people rely on their own devices, to their own destruction.
51, 1: *Rock . . . pit:* your glorious ancestry.
51, 4f: The conversion of the Gentiles.
51, 6: God's *salvation* and *justice* are eternal, in contrast to the impermanence of *the heavens* and *the earth:* cf Mt 24, 35.
51, 9: *Rahab:* see note on 30, 7. *The dragon:* see notes on 27, 1; Ps 74, 13.
51, 10: *Great deep:* another reference to the primeval chaos of Gn 1, 2.

* 6: 2 Sm 10, 4ff;
Mt 26, 67; 27, 30.
7: Ez 3, 9.
9: 51, 6-8; Ps 102, 27.
10: 43, 1f; 44, 1f.
51/1: Rom 9, 30f.

2: Ez 33, 24; Gn 12, 2ff;
22, 17.
4: 2, 3.
8: 50, 9.
9: Ex 15, 16; Jb 9, 13;
26, 12; Pss 74, 13;
89, 11.

11   Those whom the Lord has ransomed will
         return
           and enter Zion singing,
           crowned with everlasting joy;
      They will meet with joy and gladness,
           sorrow and mourning will flee.

12   I, it is I who comfort you.
           Can you then fear mortal man,
           who is human only, to be looked upon
             as grass,
13   And forget the Lord, your maker,
           who stretched out the heavens
           and laid the foundations of the earth?
      All the day you are in constant dread
           of the fury of the oppressor;
      But when he sets himself to destroy,
           what is there of the oppressor's fury?

14   The oppressed shall soon be released;
           they shall not die and go down into
             the pit,
           nor shall they want for bread.
15*   For I am the Lord, your God,
           who stirs up the sea so that its waves
             roar;
           the Lord of hosts by name.
16   I have put my words into your mouth
           and shielded you in the shadow of
             my hand,
      I, who stretched out the heavens,
           who laid the foundations of the earth,
           who say to Zion: You are my people.

The Cup of the Lord

17*   Awake, awake!
           Arise, O Jerusalem,
      You who drank at the Lord's hand
           the cup of his wrath;
      Who drained to the dregs
           the bowl of staggering!
18   She has no one to guide her
           of all the sons she bore;
      She has no one to grasp her by the hand,
           of all the sons she reared!—
19   Your misfortunes are double;
           who is there to condole with you?
      Desolation and destruction, famine and
             sword!
           Who is there to comfort you?
20   Your sons lie helpless
           at every street corner
           like antelopes in a net.
      They are filled with the wrath of the
             Lord,
           the rebuke of your God.

21*   But now, hear this, O afflicted one,
           drunk, but not with wine,

22   Thus says the Lord, your Master,
           your God, who defends his people:
      See, I am taking from your hand
           the cup of staggering;
      The bowl of my wrath
           you shall no longer drink.
23   I will put it into the hands of your
             tormentors,
           those who ordered you
           to bow down, that they might walk
             over you,
      While you offered your back like the
             ground,
           like the street for them to walk on.

Let Zion Rejoice

52   1   Awake, awake!
           Put on your strength, O Zion;
      Put on your glorious garments,
           O Jerusalem, holy city.
      No longer shall the uncircumcised
           or the unclean enter you.
2   Shake off the dust,
           ascend to the throne, Jerusalem;
      Loose the bonds from your neck,
           O captive daughter Zion!
3   For thus says the Lord:
      You were sold for nothing,
           and without money you shall be
             redeemed.

4   Thus says the Lord God:
      To Egypt in the beginning my people
             went down,
           to sojourn there;
           Assyria, too, oppressed them for
             nought.
5   But now, what am I to do here?
           says the Lord.
      My people have been taken away
           without redress;
           their rulers make a boast of it, says the
             Lord;
           all the day my name is constantly
             reviled.
6   Therefore on that day my people shall
             know my renown,
           that it is I who have foretold it. Here
             I am!
7*† How beautiful upon the mountains
           are the feet of him who brings glad
             tidings,
      Announcing peace, bearing good news,
           announcing salvation, and saying to
             Zion,
      "Your God is King!"

---

*
15: Jer 31, 35.   21: 29, 9.
17: Jer 25, 15ff;   52/7: 40, 9; Rom 10, 15.
     Ez 23, 32ff.

† 52, 7-10: God leads his people back from Babylon to Zion, from whose ruined walls *watchmen . . . shout for joy;* cf Rom 10, 15.

8* Hark! Your watchmen raise a cry,
    together they shout for joy,
For they see directly, before their eyes,
    the Lord restoring Zion.

9 Break out together in song,
    O ruins of Jerusalem!
For the Lord comforts his people,
    he redeems Jerusalem.

10 The Lord has bared his holy arm
    in the sight of all the nations;
All the ends of the earth will behold
    the salvation of our God.

11† Depart, depart, come forth from there,
    touch nothing unclean!
Out from there! Purify yourselves,
    you who carry the vessels of the Lord.

12* Yet not in fearful haste will you come
    out,
    nor leave in headlong flight,
For the Lord comes before you,
    and your rear guard is the God of
    Israel.

Suffering and Triumph of the Servant of the Lord

13† See, my servant shall prosper,
    he shall be raised high and greatly
    exalted.

14* Even as many were amazed at him—
    so marred was his look beyond that
    of man,
    and his appearance beyond that of
    mortals—

15* So shall he startle many nations,
    because of him kings shall stand
    speechless;
For those who have not been told shall
    see,
    those who have not heard shall ponder
    it.

53

1* Who would believe what we have
    heard?
To whom has the arm of the Lord
    been revealed?

2*† He grew up like a sapling before him,
    like a shoot from the parched earth;
There was in him no stately bearing to
    make us look at him,
    nor appearance that would attract us
    to him.

3*† He was spurned and avoided by men,
    a man of suffering, accustomed to
    infirmity,

One of those from whom men hide their
    faces,
    spurned, and we held him in no
    esteem.

4*† Yet it was our infirmities that he bore,
    our sufferings that he endured,
While we thought of him as stricken,
    as one smitten by God and afflicted.

5* But he was pierced for our offenses,
    crushed for our sins;
Upon him was the chastisement that
    makes us whole,
    by his stripes we were healed.

6* We had all gone astray like sheep,
    each following his own way;
But the Lord laid upon him
    the guilt of us all.

7* Though he was harshly treated, he
    submitted
    and opened not his mouth;
Like a lamb led to the slaughter
    or a sheep before the shearers,
    he was silent and opened not his
    mouth.

8 Oppressed and condemned, he was
    taken away,
    and who would have thought any
    more of his destiny?
When he was cut off from the land of
    the living,
    and smitten for the sin of his people,

9* A grave was assigned him among the
    wicked
    and a burial place with evildoers,
Though he had done no wrong
    nor spoken any falsehood.

10† [But the Lord was pleased
    to crush him in infirmity.]

If he gives his life as an offering for sin,
    he shall see his descendants in a long
    life,
    and the will of the Lord shall be
    accomplished through him.

---

† 52, 11: *From there:* from Babylon. *Vessels of the Lord:* taken to Babylon by Nebuchadnezzar, now carried back by the exiled priests returning in procession to Zion; cf Ezr 1, 7.

52, 13—53, 12: The last of the four "Servant-of-the-Lord" oracles. An extraordinary description of the sinless Servant, who by his voluntary suffering atones for the sins of his people, and saves them from just punishment at the hands of God. Only in Jesus Christ is the prophecy perfectly fulfilled.

53, 2: Only God appreciated his Servant's true greatness.

53, 3: Because he suffered, he was regarded as a sinner and therefore as one to be *spurned.*

53, 4ff: He did indeed suffer but it was for the sins of mankind, and through his sufferings men are *healed.*

53, 10ff: Because he fulfilled the divine will by suffering for the sins of others, the Servant will be rewarded by the Lord. *See the light:* enjoy happiness. This line may originally have read, "he shall drink and eat to the full"—at the thanksgiving sacrifice at which *he shall divide the spoils* (v 12).

---

*

  8: 62, 6.
 12: Ex 12, 11.
 14: Ps 69, 8.
 15: Mi 7, 16.
53/1: 52, 10; Jn 12, 38;
    Rom 10, 16.
  2: 11, 1.

  3: Jb 19, 18; Ps 31, 11ff;
    Mk 9, 11.
  4: Jer 10, 19; Mt 8, 17.
  5: 1 Cor 15, 3; 1 Pt 2, 24.
  6: Lv 16, 21ff.
  7: Mt 26, 63; Acts 8, 32.
  9: 1 Pt 2, 22f; 1 Jn 3, 5.

11 Because of his affliction
he shall see the light in fullness of
days;
Through his suffering, my servant shall
justify many,
and their guilt he shall bear.
12 Therefore I will give him his portion
among the great,
and he shall divide the spoils with
the mighty,
Because he surrendered himself to death
and was counted among the wicked;
And he shall take away the sins of many,
and win pardon for their offenses.

The New Zion

54 **1** Raise a glad cry, you barren one who
did not bear,
break forth in jubilant song, you who
were not in labor,
For more numerous are the children of
the deserted wife
than the children of her who has a
husband,
says the LORD.
2 Enlarge the space for your tent,
spread out your tent cloths
unsparingly;
lengthen your ropes and make firm
your stakes.
3 For you shall spread abroad to the right
and to the left;
your descendants shall dispossess the
nations
and shall people the desolate cities.

4 Fear not, you shall not be put to shame;
you need not blush, for you shall not
be disgraced.
The shame of your youth you shall
forget,
the reproach of your widowhood no
longer remember.
5 For he who has become your husband is
your Maker;
his name is the LORD of hosts;
Your redeemer is the Holy One of Israel,
called God of all the earth.
6 The LORD calls you back,
like a wife forsaken and grieved in
spirit,
A wife married in youth and then cast
off,
says your God.
7 For a brief moment I abandoned you,
but with great tenderness I will take
you back.

8 In an outburst of wrath, for a moment
I hid my face from you;
But with enduring love I take pity on
you,
says the LORD, your redeemer.
9 This is for me like the days of Noah,
when I swore that the waters of Noah
should never again deluge the earth;
So I have sworn not to be angry with
you,
or to rebuke you.
10 Though the mountains leave their place
and the hills be shaken,
My love shall never leave you
nor my covenant of peace be shaken,
says the LORD, who has mercy on you.

11 O afflicted one, storm-battered and
unconsoled,
I lay your pavements in carnelians,
and your foundations in sapphires;
12 I will make your battlements of rubies,
your gates of carbuncles,
and all your walls of precious stones.
13 All your sons shall be taught by the
LORD,
and great shall be the peace of your
children.
14 In justice shall you be established,
far from the fear of oppression,
where destruction cannot come near
you.
15 Should there be any attack, it shall not
be of my making;
whoever attacks you shall fall before
you.
16 Lo, I have created the craftsman
who blows on the burning coals
and forges weapons as his work;
It is I also who have created
the destroyer to work havoc.
17 No weapon fashioned against you shall
prevail;
every tongue you shall prove false
that launches an accusation against
you.
This is the lot of the servants of the
LORD,
their vindication from me, says the
LORD.

---

† 54, 1: Jerusalem, pictured as a wife who had been *barren* and *deserted,* now suddenly finds herself with innumerable children (the returning exiles); cf Gal 4, 27 for the application of this text to the church, the New Zion.

54, 5: *Redeemer:* cf note on 41, 14.

54, 11f: Cf Rv 21. *Afflicted one:* Jerusalem; *carnelians:* reddish quartz, hard and durable; *carbuncles:* another precious stone of red color.

12: Mk 15, 28; Lk 22, 37.
54/1: Gal 4, 27.
2: 49, 20.
6: Mal 2, 14f.
9: Gn 9, 15.
10: Pss 76, 5; 46, 3.
11: Rv 21, 18-21.

An Invitation to Grace

55

1*† All you who are thirsty,
    come to the water!
You who have no money,
    come, receive grain and eat;
Come, without paying and without cost,
    drink wine and milk!

2 Why spend your money for what is not
    bread;
    your wages for what fails to satisfy?
Heed me, and you shall eat well,
    you shall delight in rich fare.

3* Come to me heedfully,
    listen, that you may have life.
I will renew with you the everlasting
    covenant,
    the benefits assured to David.

4 As I made him a witness to the peoples,
    a leader and commander of nations,

5* So shall you summon a nation you knew
    not,
    and nations that knew you not shall
    run to you,
Because of the Lord, your God,
    the Holy One of Israel, who has
    glorified you.

6 Seek the Lord while he may be found,
    call him while he is near.

7 Let the scoundrel forsake his way,
    and the wicked man his thoughts;
Let him turn to the Lord for mercy;
    to our God, who is generous in
    forgiving.

8 For my thoughts are not your thoughts,
    nor are your ways my ways, says the
    Lord.

9 As high as the heavens are above the
    earth,
    so high are my ways above your ways
    and my thoughts above your thoughts.

10 For just as from the heavens
    the rain and snow come down
And do not return there
    till they have watered the earth,
    making it fertile and fruitful,
Giving seed to him who sows
    and bread to him who eats,

11 So shall my word be
    that goes forth from my mouth;
It shall not return to me void,
    but shall do my will,
    achieving the end for which I sent it.

12 Yes, in joy you shall depart,
    in peace you shall be brought back;

Mountains and hills shall break out in
    song before you,
    and all the trees of the countryside
    shall clap their hands.

13† In place of the thornbush, the cypress
    shall grow,
    instead of nettles, the myrtle.
This shall be to the Lord's renown,
    an everlasting imperishable sign.

III: RETURN OF THE FIRST CAPTIVES

The Lord's House Open to All

56

1†   Thus says the Lord:
Observe what is right, do what is just;
    for my salvation is about to come,
    my justice, about to be revealed.

2 Happy is the man who does this,
    the son of man who holds to it;
Who keeps the sabbath free from
    profanation,
    and his hand from any evil-doing.

3† Let not the foreigner say,
    when he would join himself to the
    Lord,
    "The Lord will surely exclude me
    from his people";
Nor let the eunuch say,
    "See, I am a dry tree."

4*   For thus says the Lord:
To the eunuchs who observe my
    sabbaths
    and choose what pleases me
    and hold fast to my covenant,

5† I will give, in my house
    and within my walls, a monument and
    a name
Better than sons and daughters;
    an eternal, imperishable name will I
    give them.

6 And the foreigners who join themselves
    to the Lord,
    ministering to him,

---

† 55, 1ff: God's salvation is freely extended to his people and to all nations; through him will *the benefits assured to David* be renewed; cf 12, 3; Jn 7, 37.

55, 13: *Thornbush . . . nettles:* suggestive of the desert and therefore symbolic of suffering and hardship; *cypress, myrtle:* suggestive of fertile land and therefore symbolic of joy and strength.

56, 1-8: Participation in the future messianic salvation is offered to all who believe in the Lord and keep his commandments, regardless of origin or social condition.

56, 3: Eunuchs had originally been excluded from the community of the Lord; cf Dt 23, 2; Wis 3, 14. *Dry tree:* unable to produce the fruit of offspring.

56, 5: *A monument and a name:* a memorial inscription to prevent oblivion for one who had no children: . . . cf 2 Sm 18, 18; Neh 7, 15; 13, 14.

---

* 55/1: Jn 4, 10ff; 6, 35; 7,   5: Acts 13, 34.
  37ff; Rv 21, 6; 22, 17.   56/4: Wis 3, 14f.
  3: 2 Sm 7, 12-16.

Loving the name of the LORD,
and becoming his servants—
All who keep the sabbath free from
profanation
and hold to my covenant,

7* Them I will bring to my holy mountain
and make joyful in my house of
prayer;
Their holocausts and sacrifices
will be acceptable on my altar,
For my house shall be called
a house of prayer for all peoples.

8 Thus says the Lord GOD,
who gathers the dispersed of Israel:
Others will I gather to him
besides those already gathered.

Blind Leaders

9*† All you wild beasts of the field,
come and eat,
all you beasts in the forest!

10 My watchmen are blind,
all of them unaware;
They are all dumb dogs,
they cannot bark;
Dreaming as they lie there,
loving their sleep.

11 They are relentless dogs,
they know not when they have
enough.
These are the shepherds
who know no discretion;
Each of them goes his own way,
every one of them to his own gain:

12* "Come, I will fetch some wine;
let us carouse with strong drink,
And tomorrow will be like today,
or even greater."

57

1 The just man perishes,
but no one takes it to heart;
Devout men are swept away,
with no one giving it a thought.
Though he is taken away from the
presence of evil,

2 the just man enters into peace;
There is rest on his couch
for the sincere, straightforward man.

Faithless People

3 But you, draw near,
you sons of a sorceress,
adulterous, wanton race!

4 Of whom do you make sport,
at whom do you open wide your
mouth,
and put out your tongue?
Are you not rebellious children,
a worthless race;

5* You who are in heat among the
terebinths,
under every green tree;
You who immolate children in the
wadies,
behind the crevices in the cliffs?

6† Among the smooth stones of the wadi is
your portion,
these are your lot;
To these you poured out libations,
and brought offerings.
Should I decide not to punish these
things?

7* Upon a high and lofty mountain
you made your bed,
and there you went up to offer
sacrifice.

8 Behind the door and the doorpost
you placed your indecent symbol.
Deserting me, you spread out
your high, wide bed;
And of those whose embraces you love
you carved the symbol and gazed
upon it

9† While you approached the king with
scented oil,
and multiplied your perfumes;
While you sent your ambassadors far
away,
down even to the nether world.

10 Though worn out by your many
misdeeds,
you never said, "It is hopeless";
New strength you found,
and so you did not weaken.

11 Of whom were you afraid? Whom did
you fear,
that you became false

---

† 56, 9—57, 13: This section is apparently preexilic, written in the manner of the older prophets who condemned the pagan rites of Baal worship.

56, 9: *Wild beasts:* foreign nations, which are invited to come and ravage Israel.

57, 6: *Smooth stones:* the Hebrew word for this expression has the same consonants as the word for "portion"; instead of making the Lord their portion (cf Ps 16, 5), the people adored slabs of stone which they took from the streambeds in valleys and set up as idols; cf Jer 3, 9. Therefore, it is implied, they will be swept away as by a sudden torrent of waters carrying them down the rocky-bottomed gorge to destruction and death without burial.

57, 9: *The king:* the pagan god Moloch. *Ambassadors:* children sent to him through a sacrificial death.

---

*
7: 1 Kgs 8, 29f;
Mt 21, 13.
9: Ez 34, 5.
12: 28, 7ff; Wis 2, 7.

57/5: Jer 7, 31; 19, 5;
Ez 20, 28.31.
7: Hos 4, 13; Jer 2, 20;
Ez 6, 13.

And did not remember me
     or give me any thought?
Was I to remain silent and unseeing,
     so that you would not have me to
       fear?

12† I will expose your justice
     and your works;

13† They shall not help you when you cry
       out,
     nor save you in your distress.

All these the wind shall carry off,
     the breeze shall bear away;
But he who takes refuge in me shall
       inherit the land,
     and possess my holy mountain.

Comfort for the Afflicted

14* Build up, build up, prepare the way,
     remove the stumbling blocks from my
       people's path.

15* For thus says he who is high and exalted,
     living eternally, whose name is the
       Holy One:
On high I dwell, and in holiness,
     and with the crushed and dejected in
       spirit,
To revive the spirits of the dejected,
     to revive the hearts of the crushed.

16 I will not accuse forever,
     nor always be angry;
For their spirits would faint before me,
     the souls that I have made.

17* Because of their wicked avarice I was
       angry,
     and struck them, hiding myself in
       wrath,
     as they went their own rebellious way.

18 I saw their ways,
     but I will heal them and lead them;
I will give full comfort
     to them and to those who mourn for
       them,

19 I, the Creator, who gave them life.

Peace, peace to the far and the near,
     says the LORD; and I will heal them.

20 But the wicked are like the tossing sea
     which cannot be calmed,
And its waters cast up mud and filth.

21*   No peace for the wicked! says my God.

True Fasting

58 1† Cry out full-throated and unsparingly,
     lift up your voice like a trumpet blast;
Tell my people their wickedness,
     and the house of Jacob their sins.

2† They seek me day after day,
     and desire to know my ways,
Like a nation that has done what is just
     and not abandoned the law of their
       God;
They ask me to declare what is due
       them,
     pleased to gain access to God.

3 "Why do we fast, and you do not see it?
     afflict ourselves, and you take no note
       of it?"

Lo, on your fast day you carry out your
       own pursuits,
     and drive all your laborers.

4 Yes, your fast ends in quarreling and
       fighting,
     striking with wicked claw.
Would that today you might fast
     so as to make your voice heard on
       high!

5* Is this the manner of fasting I wish,
     of keeping a day of penance:
That a man bow his head like a reed,
     and lie in sackcloth and ashes?
Do you call this a fast,
     a day acceptable to the LORD?

6 This, rather, is the fasting that I wish:
     releasing those bound unjustly,
     untying the thongs of the yoke;
Setting free the oppressed,
     breaking every yoke;

7* Sharing your bread with the hungry,
     sheltering the oppressed and the
       homeless;
Clothing the naked when you see them,
     and not turning your back on your
       own.

8 Then your light shall break forth like the
       dawn,
     and your wound shall quickly be
       healed;
Your vindication shall go before you,
     and the glory of the LORD shall be
       your rear guard.

9 Then you shall call, and the LORD will
       answer,
     you shall cry for help, and he will say:
       Here I am!
If you remove from your midst
       oppression,
     false accusation and malicious speech;

10 If you bestow your bread on the hungry
     and satisfy the afflicted;

---

† 57, 12: *Justice:* here used ironically.
57, 13: *All these:* the wicked mentioned in 57, 3-10.
58, 1: This command is directed to the prophet.
58, 2-14: Merely external worship does not avail with God;
it must be joined to internal sincerity.

---

* 14: 40, 3f.   21: 48, 21.
15: 61, 2f.   58/5: Zec 7, 5.
17: 56, 11.   7: Ez 18, 7.16; Mt 25, 35.

Then light shall rise for you in the
    darkness,
    and the gloom shall become for you
      like midday;

11* Then the Lord will guide you always
    and give you plenty even on the
      parched land.
He will renew your strength,
    and you shall be like a watered
      garden,
    like a spring whose water never fails.

12* The ancient ruins shall be rebuilt for
    your sake,
    and the foundations from ages past
      you shall raise up;
"Repairer of the breach," they shall call
    you,
    "Restorer of ruined homesteads."

13 If you hold back your foot on the
    sabbath
    from following your own pursuits on
      my holy day;
If you call the sabbath a delight,
    and the Lord's holy day honorable;
If you honor it by not following your
    ways,
    seeking your own interests, or
      speaking with malice—

14 Then you shall delight in the Lord,
    and I will make you ride on the
      heights of the earth;
I will nourish you with the heritage of
    Jacob, your father,
    for the mouth of the Lord has spoken.

Sin and Confession

59 1* Lo, the hand of the Lord is not too short
    to save,
    nor his ear too dull to hear.

2 Rather, it is your crimes
    that separate you from your God,
It is your sins that make him hide his
    face
    so that he will not hear you.

3* For your hands are stained with blood,
    your fingers with guilt;
Your lips speak falsehood,
    and your tongue utters deceit.

4† No one brings suit justly,
    no one pleads truthfully;
They trust in emptiness and tell lies;
    they conceive mischief and bring
      forth malice.

5*† They hatch adders' eggs,
    and weave spiders' webs:

Whoever eats their eggs will die,
    if one of them is pressed, it will hatch
      as a viper;

6 Their webs cannot serve as clothing,
    nor can they cover themselves with
      their works.
Their works are evil works,
    and deeds of violence come from their
      hands.

7* Their feet run to evil,
    and they are quick to shed innocent
      blood;
Their thoughts are destructive thoughts,
    plunder and ruin are on their
      highways.

8 The way of peace they know not,
    and there is nothing that is right in
      their paths;
Their ways they have made crooked,
    whoever treads them knows no peace.

9† That is why right is far from us
    and justice does not reach us.
We look for light, and lo, darkness;
    for brightness, but we walk in gloom!

10 Like blind men we grope along the wall,
    like people without eyes we feel our
      way.
We stumble at midday as at dusk,
    in Stygian darkness, like the dead.

11* We all growl like bears,
    like doves we moan without ceasing.
We look for right, but it is not there;
    for salvation, and it is far from us.

12 For our offenses before you are many,
    our sins bear witness against us.
Yes, our offenses are present to us,
    and our crimes we know:

13 Transgressing, and denying the Lord,
    turning back from following our God,
Threatening outrage, and apostasy,
    uttering words of falsehood the heart
      has conceived.

14 Right is repelled,
    and justice stands far off;
For truth stumbles in the public square,
    uprightness cannot enter.

15 Honesty is lacking,
    and the man who turns from evil is
      despoiled.

The Redeemer in Zion

The Lord saw this, and was aggrieved
    that right did not exist.

---

† 59, 4: *Emptiness:* things having no value.
59, 5f: A proverb signifying evil works—*adders' eggs*—and useless devices—*spiders' webs;* the former do positive harm to oneself and others, the latter serve no useful purpose.
59, 9-15: Spoken by the people through the mouth of the prophet.

---

* 11: 51, 3; Ps 24.
12: 61, 4.
59/1: 50, 2; Nm 11, 23.
3: 1, 15.
5: Jb 20, 12-16.
7: Rom 3, 15.
11: 38, 14.

16 He saw that there was no one,
    and was appalled that there was none
        to intervene;
So his own arm brought about the
        victory,
    and his justice lent him its support.
17* He put on justice as his breastplate,
    salvation, as the helmet on his head;
He clothed himself with garments of
        vengeance,
    wrapped himself in a mantle of zeal.
18 He repays his enemies their deserts,
    and requites his foes with wrath.

19 Those in the west shall fear the name of
        the Lord,
    and those in the east, his glory;
For it shall come like a pent-up river
    which the breath of the Lord drives
        on.
20* He shall come to Zion a redeemer
    to those of Jacob who turn from sin,
        says the Lord.
21 This is the covenant with them
    which I myself have made, says the
        Lord:
My spirit which is upon you
    and my words that I have put into
        your mouth
Shall never leave your mouth,
    nor the mouths of your children
Nor the mouths of your children's
        children
    from now on and forever, says the
        Lord.

Glory of the New Zion

60 1† Rise up in splendor! Your light has come,
    the glory of the Lord shines upon you.
2 See, darkness covers the earth,
    and thick clouds cover the peoples;
But upon you the Lord shines,
    and over you appears his glory.
3* Nations shall walk by your light,
    and kings by your shining radiance.
4* Raise your eyes and look about;
    they all gather and come to you:
Your sons come from afar,
    and your daughters in the arms of
        their nurses.

5 Then you shall be radiant at what you
        see,
    your heart shall throb and overflow,

For the riches of the sea shall be
        emptied out before you,
    the wealth of nations shall be brought
        to you.
6 Caravans of camels shall fill you,
    dromedaries from Midian and Ephah;
All from Sheba shall come
    bearing gold and frankincense,
    and proclaiming the praises of the
        Lord.
7 All the flocks of Kedar shall be gathered
        for you,
    the rams of Nebaioth shall be your
        sacrifices;
They will be acceptable offerings on my
        altar,
    and I will enhance the splendor of my
        house.

8† What are these that fly along like clouds,
    like doves to their cotes?
9 All the vessels of the sea are assembled,
    with the ships of Tarshish in the lead,
To bring your children from afar
    with their silver and gold,
In the name of the Lord, your God,
    the Holy One of Israel, who has
        glorified you.

10 Foreigners shall rebuild your walls,
    and their kings shall be your
        attendants;
Though I struck you in my wrath,
    yet in my good will I have shown you
        mercy.
11* Your gates shall stand open constantly;
    day and night they shall not be closed
But shall admit to you the wealth of
        nations,
    and their kings, in the vanguard.
12 For the people or kingdom shall perish
    that does not serve you;
    those nations shall be utterly
        destroyed.
13*† The glory of Lebanon shall come to you:
    the cypress, the plane and the pine,
To bring beauty to my sanctuary,
    and glory to the place where I set my
        feet.
14 The children of your oppressors shall
        come,
    bowing low before you;
All those who despised you
    shall fall prostrate at your feet.

---

† 60, 1-6: The church makes use of these verses for the first reading of the Mass on the feast of Epiphany, for she sees in them symbols of her universality.

60, 8f: *Like clouds, like doves:* the white sails of *the ships of Tarshish;* cf note on Ps 48, 8.

60, 13: *Glory of Lebanon:* the cedars, together with *the cypress, the plane and the pine,* all precious, durable wood.

✿
17: Wis 5, 17ff; Eph 6, 14;
    1 Thes 5, 8.
20: Rom 11, 26f.
60/3: 42, 6; 45, 14; 49, 6.

4: 49, 18.
11: Rv 21, 25.
13: 35, 2.

They shall call you "City of the LORD,"
"Zion of the Holy One of Israel."

15 Once you were forsaken,
    hated and unvisited,
Now I will make you the pride of the
    ages,
    a joy to generation after generation.

16 You shall suck the milk of nations,
    and be nursed at royal breasts;
You shall know that I, the LORD, am your
    savior,
    your redeemer, the mighty one of
    Jacob.

17 In place of bronze I will bring gold,
    instead of iron, silver;
In place of wood, bronze,
    instead of stones, iron;
I will appoint peace your governor,
    and justice your ruler.

18 No longer shall violence be heard of in
    your land,
    or plunder and ruin within your
    boundaries.
You shall call your walls "Salvation"
    and your gates "Praise."

19 No longer shall the sun
    be your light by day,
Nor the brightness of the moon
    shine upon you at night;
The LORD shall be your light forever,
    your God shall be your glory.

20 No longer shall your sun go down,
    or your moon withdraw,
For the LORD will be your light forever,
    and the days of your mourning shall
    be at an end.

21 Your people shall all be just,
    they shall always possess the land,
They, the bud of my planting,
    my handiwork to show my glory.

22 The smallest shall become a thousand,
    the youngest, a mighty nation;
I, the LORD, will swiftly accomplish
    these things
    when their time comes.

The Mission to the Afflicted

61 **1** The spirit of the Lord GOD is upon me,
    because the LORD has anointed me;
He has sent me to bring glad tidings to
    the lowly,
    to heal the brokenhearted,
To proclaim liberty to the captives
    and release to the prisoners,

2 To announce a year of favor from the
    LORD
    and a day of vindication by our God,
    to comfort all who mourn;

3 To place on those who mourn in Zion
    a diadem instead of ashes,
To give them oil of gladness in place of
    mourning,
    a glorious mantle instead of a listless
    spirit.
They will be called oaks of justice,
    planted by the LORD to show his glory.

The Reward of Israel

4 They shall rebuild the ancient ruins,
    the former wastes they shall raise up
And restore the ruined cities,
    desolate now for generations.

5 Strangers shall stand ready to pasture
    your flocks,
    foreigners shall be your farmers and
    vinedressers.

6 You yourselves shall be named priests of
    the LORD,
    ministers of our God you shall be
    called.
You shall eat the wealth of the nations
    and boast of riches from them.

7 Since their shame was double
    and disgrace and spittle were their
    portion,
They shall have a double inheritance in
    their land,
    everlasting joy shall be theirs.

8 For I, the LORD, love what is right,
    I hate robbery and injustice;
I will give them their recompense
    faithfully,
    a lasting covenant I will make with
    them.

9 Their descendants shall be renowned
    among the nations,
    and their offspring among the peoples;
All who see them shall acknowledge
    them
    as a race the LORD has blessed.

10 I rejoice heartily in the LORD,
    in my God is the joy of my soul;
For he has clothed me with a robe of
    salvation,
    and wrapped me in a mantle of
    justice,

---

* 15: Ez 16.
19: Rv 21, 23; 22, 5.
22: Gn 12, 2; 17, 6.
61/1: 42, 1; 48, 16;
    Lk 4, 18f.

2: Mt 5, 5.
4: 58, 12.
7: 40, 2.
8: 55, 3; 59, 21.

† 61, 1f: This was spoken by the prophet in regard to the restoration of Zion, but quoted by Christ as referring to his mission; cf Lk 4, 18f. *Year of favor . . . day of vindication:* the time of God's salvation.

Like a bridegroom adorned with a
diadem,
like a bride bedecked with her jewels.

11 As the earth brings forth its plants,
and a garden makes its growth spring
up,
So will the Lord God make justice and
praise
spring up before all the nations.

Jerusalem the Lord's Bride

62 1 For Zion's sake I will not be silent,
for Jerusalem's sake I will not be
quiet,
Until her vindication shines forth like
the dawn
and her victory like a burning torch.

2*† Nations shall behold your vindication,
and all kings your glory;
You shall be called by a new name
pronounced by the mouth of the Lord.

3 You shall be a glorious crown in the
hand of the Lord,
a royal diadem held by your God.

4* No more shall men call you "Forsaken,"
or your land "Desolate,"
But you shall be called "My Delight,"
and your land "Espoused."
For the Lord delights in you,
and makes your land his spouse.

5 As a young man marries a virgin,
your Builder shall marry you;
And as a bridegroom rejoices in his bride
so shall your God rejoice in you.

Restoration of Zion

6† Upon your walls, O Jerusalem,
I have stationed watchmen;
Never, by day or by night,
shall they be silent.
O you who are to remind the Lord,
take no rest

7 And give no rest to him,
until he re-establishes Jerusalem
And makes of it
the pride of the earth.

8* The Lord has sworn by his right hand
and by his mighty arm:
No more will I give your grain
as food to your enemies;
Nor shall foreigners drink your wine,
for which you toiled.

9* But you who harvest the grain shall eat
it,
and you shall praise the Lord;

You who gather the grapes shall drink
the wine
in the courts of my sanctuary.

10*† Pass through, pass through the gates,
prepare the way for the people;
Build up, build up the highway,
clear it of stones,
raise up a standard over the nations.

11* See, the Lord proclaims
to the ends of the earth:
Say to daughter Zion,
your savior comes!
Here is his reward with him,
his recompense before him.

12* They shall be called the holy people,
the redeemed of the Lord,
And you shall be called "Frequented,"
a city that is not forsaken.

Punishment of Edom

63 1† Who is this that comes from Edom,
in crimsoned garments, from Bozrah—
This one arrayed in majesty,
marching in the greatness of his
strength?
"It is I, I who announce vindication,
I who am mighty to save."

2* Why is your apparel red,
and your garments like those of the
wine presser?

3 "The wine press I have trodden alone,
and of my people there was no one
with me.
I trod them in my anger,
and trampled them down in my
wrath;
Their blood spurted on my garments;
all my apparel I stained.

4* For the day of vengeance was in my
heart,
my year for redeeming was at hand.

5* I looked about, but there was no one to
help,
I was appalled that there was no one
to lend support;
So my own arm brought about the
victory
and my own wrath lent me its support.

---

† 62, 2: *New name:* figurative expression for a new state of happiness; cf Rv 2, 17; 3, 12.

62, 6f: *Remind the Lord . . . give no rest to him:* figuratively, as though to make certain that the Lord will remember his pledge to Jerusalem. Cf Lk 11, 7f.

62, 10: The command is given to the workmen to begin the reconstruction of the city.

63, 1-6: In a dramatic dialogue between God and the prophet, the Lord is portrayed as the sole avenger of justice against his enemies.

❋
62/2: Rv 2, 17; 3, 12.
   4: 49, 15f; 54, 1ff.
   8: 52, 10.
   9: Dt 12, 17f; 14, 23.
  10: 58, 14.
                11: 40, 10.
                12: 62, 4.
               63/2: Rv 19, 13.
                4: 34, 8; 61, 2.
                5: 59, 16.

6   I trampled down the peoples in my
        anger,
      I crushed them in my wrath,
        and I let their blood run out upon the
        ground."

Prayer for the Return of God's Favor

7*† The favors of the LORD I will recall,
        the glorious deeds of the LORD,
      Because of all he has done for us;
        for he is good to the house of Israel,
      He has favored us according to his
        mercy
        and his great kindness.

8   He said: They are indeed my people,
        children who are not disloyal;
      So he became their savior
9*   in their every affliction.
      It was not a messenger or an angel,
        but he himself who saved them.
      Because of his love and pity
        he redeemed them himself,
      Lifting them and carrying them
        all the days of old.

10   But they rebelled, and grieved
        his holy spirit;
      So he turned on them like an enemy,
        and fought against them.

11   Then they remembered the days of old
        and Moses, his servant;
      Where is he who brought up out of the
        sea
        the shepherd of his flock?
      Where is he who put his holy spirit
        in their midst;

12   Whose glorious arm
        was the guide at Moses' right;
      Who divided the waters before them,
        winning for himself eternal renown;

13   Who led them without stumbling
        through the depths
        like horses in the open country,

14   Like cattle going down into the plain,
        the spirit of the LORD guiding them?
      Thus you led your people,
        bringing glory to your name.

15* Look down from heaven and regard us
        from your holy and glorious palace!
      Where is your zealous care and your
        might,
        your surge of pity and your mercy?
      O Lord, hold not back,

16   for you are our father.
      Were Abraham not to know us,
        nor Israel to acknowledge us,

      You, LORD, are our father,
        our redeemer you are named forever.

17   Why do you let us wander, O LORD,
        from your ways,
        and harden our hearts so that we fear
        you not?
      Return for the sake of your servants,
        the tribes of your heritage.

18   Why have the wicked invaded your holy
        place,
        why have our enemies trampled your
        sanctuary?

19   Too long have we been like those you
        do not rule,
        who do not bear your name.

      Oh, that you would rend the heavens
        and come down,
        with the mountains quaking before
        you,

64 1 As when brushwood is set ablaze,
        or fire makes the water boil!
      Thus your name would be made known
        to your enemies
        and the nations would tremble before
        you,

2   While you wrought awesome deeds we
        could not hope for,
3*   such as they had not heard of from of
        old.
      No ear has ever heard, no eye ever seen,
        any God but you
        doing such deeds for those who wait
        for him.

4   Would that you might meet us doing
        right,
        that we were mindful of you in our
        ways!
      Behold, you are angry, and we are sinful;
5   all of us have become like unclean
        men,
        all our good deeds are like polluted
        rags;
      We have all withered like leaves,
        and our guilt carries us away like the
        wind.

6   There is none who calls upon your name,
        who rouses himself to cling to you;
      For you have hidden your face from us
        and have delivered us up to our guilt.

7   Yet, O LORD, you are our father;
        we are the clay and you the potter:
        we are all the work of your hands.

---

† 63, 7—64, 11: A prayer probably composed toward the end of the exile, in which the prophet, after recalling God's blessings on Israel in its past history (63, 7-10), especially at the Exodus (11-14), begs the Lord to come once more to the aid of his people (63, 15—64, 3), who now humbly confess their sins (4-11).

7: 26, 15.   15: Dt 26, 15; Bar 2, 16.
9: Dt 4, 37f.   64/3: 1 Cor 2, 9.

8 Be not so very angry, Lord,
       keep not our guilt forever in mind;
       look upon us, who are all your people.
9* Your holy cities have become a desert,
       Zion is a desert, Jerusalem a waste.
10 Our holy and glorious temple
       in which our fathers praised you
   Has been burned with fire;
       all that was dear to us is laid waste.
11 Can you hold back, O Lord, after all
       this?
       Can you remain silent, and afflict us
       so severely?

Necessity of Punishment

65 1* I was ready to respond to those who
           asked me not,
       to be found by those who sought me
           not.
       I said: Here I am! Here I am!
           To a nation that did not call upon my
           name.

2* I have stretched out my hands all the
       day
       to a rebellious people,
   Who walk in evil paths
       and follow their own thoughts,
3 People who provoke me
       continually, to my face,
   Offering sacrifices in the groves
       and burning incense on bricks,
4 Living among the graves
       and spending the night in caverns,
   Eating swine's flesh,
       with carrion broth in their dishes,
5† Crying out, "Hold back,
       do not touch me; I am too sacred for
       you!"

   These things enkindle my wrath,
       a fire that burns all the day.
6 Lo, before me it stands written;
       I will not be quiet until I have paid in
       full
7 Your crimes and the crimes of your
       fathers as well,
       says the Lord.
   Since they burned incense on the
       mountains,
       and disgraced me on the hills,
   I will at once pour out in full measure
       their recompense into their laps.

Fate of the Good and the Bad in Israel

8   Thus says the Lord:

When the juice is pressed from grapes,
       men say, "Do not discard them,
       for there is still good in them";
   Thus will I do with my servants:
       I will not discard them all;
9 From Jacob I will save offspring,
       from Judah, those who are to inherit
       my mountains;
   My chosen ones shall inherit the land,
       my servants shall dwell there.
10 Sharon shall be a pasture for the flocks
       and the valley of Achor a resting
       place for the cattle
       of my people who have sought me.

11† But you who forsake the Lord,
       forgetting my holy mountain,
   You who spread a table for Fortune
       and fill cups of blended wine for
       Destiny,
12* You I will destine for the sword;
       you shall all go down in slaughter.
   Since I called and you did not answer,
       I spoke and you did not listen,
   But did what was evil in my sight
       and preferred things which displease
       me,
13   therefore thus says the Lord God:
   Lo, my servants shall eat,
       but you shall go hungry;
   My servants shall drink,
       but you shall be thirsty;
   My servants shall rejoice,
       but you shall be put to shame;
14 My servants shall shout
       for joy of heart,
   But you shall cry out for grief of heart
       and howl for anguish of spirit.
15 The Lord God shall slay you,
       and the name you leave
   Shall be used by my chosen ones for
       cursing;
       but my servants shall be called by
       another name
16 By which he will be blessed
       on whom a blessing is invoked in the
       land.
   He who takes an oath in the land
       shall swear by the God of truth;
   For the hardships of the past shall be
       forgotten,
       and hidden from my eyes.

---

† 65, 5: *I am too sacred for you:* the uncleanness of pork, obvious to a Semite, is what these people claim has made them sacred! The prophet ridicules them. Some translate: "I will render you sacred," and understand this as referring to the concept of sacredness as something contagious.

65, 11f: *Destiny:* the Hebrew also has a play on the words: *Destiny* and *destine; meni* and *manithi.*

---

*
   9: Ps 79, 1.   12: 66, 4; Prv 1, 24;
   65/1: Rom 10, 20.   Jer 7, 13.
   2: Rom 10, 21.

The World Renewed

17* Lo, I am about to create new heavens
and a new earth;
The things of the past shall not be
remembered
or come to mind.

18 Instead, there shall always be rejoicing
and happiness
in what I create;
For I create Jerusalem to be a joy
and its people to be a delight;

19 I will rejoice in Jerusalem
and exult in my people.
No longer shall the sound of weeping be
heard there,
or the sound of crying;

20 No longer shall there be in it
an infant who lives but a few days,
or an old man who does not round out
his full lifetime;
He dies a mere youth who reaches but a
hundred years,
and he who fails of a hundred shall be
thought accursed.

21 They shall live in the houses they build,
and eat the fruit of the vineyards they
plant;

22 They shall not build houses for others to
live in,
or plant for others to eat.
As the years of a tree, so the years of my
people;
and my chosen ones shall long enjoy
the produce of their hands.

23 They shall not toil in vain,
nor beget children for sudden
destruction;
For a race blessed by the LORD
are they and their offspring.

24 Before they call, I will answer;
while they are yet speaking, I will
hearken to them.

25*† The wolf and the lamb shall graze alike,
and the lion shall eat hay like the ox
[but the serpent's food shall be dust].
None shall hurt or destroy
on all my holy mountain, says the
LORD.

True and False Worship

66 1* Thus says the LORD:
The heavens are my throne,
the earth is my footstool.

What kind of house can you build for
me;
what is to be my resting place?

2 My hand made all these things
when all of them came to be, says the
LORD.
This is the one whom I approve:
the lowly and afflicted man who
trembles at my word.

3* Merely slaughtering an ox is like slaying
a man;
sacrificing a lamb, like breaking a
dog's neck;
Bringing a cereal offering, like offering
swine's blood;
burning incense, like paying homage
to an idol.
Since these have chosen their own ways
and taken pleasure in their own
abominations,

4*† I in turn will choose ruthless treatment
for them
and bring upon them what they fear.

Because, when I called, no one
answered,
when I spoke, no one listened;
Because they did what was evil in my
sight,
and chose what gave me displeasure,

5 Hear the word of the LORD,
you who tremble at his word:
Your brethren who, because of my name,
hate and reject you, say,
"Let the LORD show his glory
that we may see your joy";
but they shall be put to shame.

6* A sound of roaring from the city,
a sound from the temple,
The sound of the LORD
repaying his enemies their deserts!

Mother Zion

7*† Before she comes to labor,
she gives birth;
Before the pains come upon her,
she safely delivers a male child.

8 Who ever heard of such a thing,
or saw the like?
Can a country be brought forth in one
day,
or a nation be born in a single
moment?

✶
17: 66, 22; Rv 21, 1.
25: 11, 6-9.
66/1: 2 Sm 7, 4ff; 1 Kgs 8,
27; Acts 7, 49; 17, 24.
3: Lv 11, 7.

4: 65, 12; Prv 1, 24;
Jer 7, 13.
6: Jl 4, 16; Am 1, 2.
7-9: 49, 18-21; 54, 1.

---

†
65, 25: See note on 11, 6-9.
66, 4f: Worship which is merely external is as evil as though
it were idolatry.
66, 7-9: The absence of labor in Zion's childbearing is a symbol of the joyful begetting of the new people of God.

Yet Zion is scarcely in labor
　　when she gives birth to her children.
9 Shall I bring a mother to the point of
　　　　birth,
　　and yet not let her child be born? says
　　　　the Lord;
　　Or shall I who allow her to conceive,
　　　　yet close her womb? says your God.

10 Rejoice with Jerusalem and be glad
　　　　because of her,
　　all you who love her;
　　Exult, exult with her,
　　　　all you who were mourning over her!
11 Oh, that you may suck fully
　　　　of the milk of her comfort,
　　That you may nurse with delight
　　　　at her abundant breasts!
12 　　For thus says the Lord:
　　Lo, I will spread prosperity over her like
　　　　a river,
　　　　and the wealth of the nations like an
　　　　　　overflowing torrent.
　　As nurslings, you shall be carried in her
　　　　arms,
　　　　and fondled in her lap;
13 As a mother comforts her son,
　　　　so will I comfort you;
　　　　in Jerusalem you shall find your
　　　　　comfort.

14 When you see this, your heart shall
　　　　rejoice,
　　　　and your bodies flourish like the grass;
　　The Lord's power shall be known to his
　　　　servants,
　　　　but to his enemies, his wrath.

15 Lo, the Lord shall come in fire,
　　　　his chariots like the whirlwind,
　　To wreak his wrath with burning heat
　　　　and his punishment with fiery flames.
16 For the Lord shall judge all mankind
　　　　by fire and sword,
　　　　and many shall be slain by the Lord.

17* They who sanctify and purify themselves to go to the groves, as followers of one who stands within, they who eat swine's flesh, loathsome things and mice, shall all perish with their deeds and their thoughts, says the Lord.

Gathering of the Nations

18† I come to gather nations of every language; they shall come and see my glory. **19** I will set a sign among them; from them I will send fugitives to the nations: to Tarshish, Put and Lud, Mosoch, Tubal and Javan, to the distant coastlands that have never heard of my fame, or seen my glory; and they shall proclaim my glory among the nations. **20** They shall bring all your brethren from all the nations as an offering to the Lord, on horses and in chariots, in carts, upon mules and dromedaries, to Jerusalem, my holy mountain, says the Lord, just as the Israelites bring their offering to the house of the Lord in clean vessels. **21** Some of these I will take as priests and Levites, says the Lord.

Lasting Reward and Punishment

22* As the new heavens and the new earth
　　　　which I will make
　　Shall endure before me, says the Lord,
　　　　so shall your race and your name
　　　　　endure.
23 From one new moon to another,
　　　　and from one sabbath to another,
　　All mankind shall come to worship
　　　　before me, says the Lord.
24*† They shall go out and see the corpses
　　　　of the men who rebelled against me;
　　Their worm shall not die,
　　　　nor their fire be extinguished,
　　　　and they shall be abhorrent to all
　　　　　mankind.

17: Lv 11, 29.　　　　　　**24:** Mk 9, 45.
22: 65, 17; Rv 21, 1.

---

† 66, 18-21: God summons the neighboring nations to Zion and from among them will send some to far distant lands to proclaim his glory. *All your brethren:* Jews in exile.

66, 24: God's enemies lie dead outside the walls of the New Jerusalem; just as in the past, corpses, filth and refuse lay in the Valley of Hinnom outside the city, where huge fires were constantly burning; cf Jos 15, 8; 2 Chr 28, 3; Mk 9, 45-48.

The Book of Jeremiah

Introduction

The Book of Jeremiah combines history, biography, and prophecy. It portrays a nation in crisis and introduces the reader to an extraordinary leader upon whom the Lord placed the heavy burden of the prophetic office. Jeremiah was born about 650 B. C. of a priestly family from the little village of Anathoth, near Jerusalem. While still very young he was called to his task in the thirteenth year of King Josiah (628), whose reform, begun with enthusiasm and hope, ended with his death on the battlefield of Megiddo (609) as he attempted to stop the northward march of the Egyptian Pharaoh Neco.

The prophet heartily supported the reform of the pious King Josiah, which began in 629 B. C. Nineveh, the capital of Assyria, fell in 612, preparing the way for the new colossus, Babylon, which was soon to put an end to Judean independence.

After the death of Josiah the old idolatry returned. Jeremiah opposed it with all his strength. Arrest, imprisonment, and public disgrace were his lot. Jeremiah saw in the nation's impenitence the sealing of its doom. Nebuchadnezzar captured Jerusalem and carried King Jehoiachin into exile (22, 24).

During the years 598-587, Jeremiah attempted to counsel Zedekiah in the face of bitter opposition. The false prophet Hananiah proclaimed that the yoke of Babylon was broken and a strong pro-Egyptian party in Jerusalem induced Zedekiah to revolt. Nebuchadnezzar took swift and terrible vengeance; Jerusalem was destroyed in 587 and its leading citizens sent into exile. About this time Jeremiah uttered the great oracle of the "New Covenant" (31, 31-34) sometimes called "The Gospel before the Gospel." This passage contains his most sublime teaching and is a landmark in Old Testament theology.

The prophet remained amidst the ruins of Jerusalem, but was later forced into Egyptian exile by a band of conspirators. There, according to an old tradition, he was murdered by his own countrymen. The influence of Jeremiah was greater after his death than before. The exiled community read and meditated the lessons of the prophet, and his influence can be seen in Ezekiel, certain of the psalms, and the second part of Isaiah. Shortly after the Exile, the Book of Jeremiah as we have it today was published in a final edition. It is divided as follows:

I: ORACLES IN THE DAYS OF JOSIAH

1 ¹†THE WORDS OF JEREMIAH, son of Hilkiah, of a priestly family in Anathoth, in the land of Benjamin. ²*The word of the LORD first came to him in the days of Josiah, son of Amon, king of Judah, in the thirteenth year of his reign, ³*†and continued through the reign of Jehoiakim, son of Josiah, king of Judah, and until the downfall and exile of Jerusalem in the fifth month of the eleventh year of Zedekiah, son of Josiah, king of Judah.

Call of Jeremiah

4   The word of the LORD came to me thus:

5*†   Before I formed you in the womb I knew
            you,
        before you were born I dedicated you,
        a prophet to the nations I appointed you.

6†   "Ah, Lord GOD!" I said,
        "I know not how to speak; I am too
            young."

---

† 1, 1: *Anathoth:* a village about three miles northeast of Jerusalem, where Solomon exiled Abiathar (1 Kgs 2, 26f); it is probable that Jeremiah belonged to the *priestly family* of Abiathar.

1, 3: *Until the downfall:* these words were originally prefixed as a title to a collection of Jeremiah's prophecies which lacked chapters 40-44. The new title in 40, 1 and the oracles that follow clearly show that Jeremiah continued to prophesy after the destruction of Jerusalem in 587 B. C.

1, 5: Jeremiah was destined to the office of prophet before his birth; cf Is 49, 1.5; Lk 1, 15; Gal 1, 15f. *I knew you:* I loved you and chose you. *I dedicated you:* I set you apart to be a prophet. Some Fathers and later theologians understand this to mean that Jeremiah was freed from original sin before his birth. The context does not justify this conclusion. *The nations:* the pagan neighbors of Judah, besides the great world powers—Assyria, Babylonia, Egypt—intimately associated with Judah's destiny.

1, 6: *I am too young:* Jeremiah's youth (he was less than thirty years old) must not be an obstacle to the responsibilities of the prophetic office; God will supply for his human defects (cf vv 7f).

❋ 1/2: 25, 3.   5: 49, 1; Gal 1, 15f.
    3: 25, 1.

7 But the LORD answered me,

Say not, "I am too young."
To whomever I send you, you shall go;
whatever I command you, you shall
speak.
8 Have no fear before them,
because I am with you to deliver you,
says the LORD.

9* Then the LORD extended his hand and
touched my mouth, saying,

See, I place my words in your mouth!
10 This day I set you
over nations and over kingdoms,
To root up and to tear down,
to destroy and to demolish,
to build and to plant.

11†The word of the LORD came to me with the
question: What do you see, Jeremiah? "I see a branch
of the watching-tree," I replied. **12**Then the LORD said
to me: Well have you seen, for I am watching to
fulfill my word. **13*†**A second time the word of the
LORD came to me with the question: What do you
see? "I see a boiling cauldron," I replied, "that appears
from the north."

14*And from the north, said the LORD to me, evil
will boil over upon all who dwell in the land.

15* Lo, I am summoning
all the kingdoms of the north, says the
LORD;
Each king shall come and set up his throne
at the gateways of Jerusalem,
Opposite her walls all around
and opposite all the cities of Judah.
16* I will pronounce my sentence against them
for all their wickedness in forsaking me,
And in burning incense to strange gods
and adoring their own handiwork.

17 But do you gird your loins;
stand up and tell them
all that I command you.
Be not crushed on their account,
as though I would leave you crushed
before them;
18* For it is I this day
who have made you a fortified city,
A pillar of iron, a wall of brass,
against the whole land:
Against Judah's kings and princes,
against its priests and people.

19 They will fight against you, but not prevail
over you,
for I am with you to deliver you, says the
LORD.

Infidelity of Israel

2 **1†**This word of the LORD came to me: **2*†**Go, cry
out this message for Jerusalem to hear!

I remember the devotion of your youth,
how you loved me as a bride,
Following me in the desert,
in a land unsown.
3*† Sacred to the LORD was Israel,
the first fruits of his harvest;
Should anyone presume to partake of them,
evil would befall him, says the LORD.

4 Listen to the word of the LORD, O house of
Jacob!
All you clans of the house of Israel,
5* thus says the LORD:
What fault did your fathers find in me
that they withdrew from me,
Went after empty idols,
and became empty themselves?
6* They did not ask, "Where is the LORD
who brought us up from the land of
Egypt,
Who led us through the desert,
through a land of wastes and gullies,
Through a land of drought and darkness,
through a land which no one crosses,
where no man dwells?"
7* When I brought you into the garden land
to eat its goodly fruits,
You entered and defiled my land,
you made my heritage loathsome.
8*† The priests asked not,
"Where is the LORD?"
Those who dealt with the law knew me not;
the shepherds rebelled against me.
The prophets prophesied by Baal,
and went after useless idols.

---

†

1, 11: *The watching-tree:* the almond tree, which is the first
to blossom in the springtime as though it had not slept. The
Hebrew name contains a play on words with "I am watching."

1, 13: *Boiling cauldron . . . the north:* symbol of an invasion
from the north; cf vv 14f.

2, 1—3, 5: These verses probably contain the earliest of
Jeremiah's preachings. The covenant relationship, symbolized
by the figure of a marriage, was frequently broken by Israel,
seen here as an unfaithful wife unworthy of reconciliation with
God (3, 1-5).

2, 2: *Devotion:* Israel's gratitude, fidelity, and love for God.

2, 3: *First fruits:* an offering to God which became his exclusive property, and could therefore not be put to profane use; cf
Lv 22, 1.

2, 8: *Those who dealt with the law:* the priests. *The shepherds:* the kings and nobles.

---

*

9: Is 6, 7.
13: Ez 11, 3.7; 24, 3.
14: 4, 6; 6, 1.
15: 6, 22.
16: Is 2, 8.
18: 6, 27; 15, 20; Ez 3, 8.
2/2: Dt 2, 7; 32, 9-12;
    Mi 6, 4.

3: 12, 14; Ex 4, 22;
    Dt 7, 6; 14, 2.
5: Is 5, 4; Mi 6, 3.
6: Ex 20, 2f; Dt 8, 14;
    Is 63, 11ff.
7: Lv 18, 24f; Dt 8, 7-10;
    32, 13f.
8: 8, 8ff; 23, 1.13.

9* Therefore will I yet accuse you, says the
LORD,
and even your children's children I will
accuse.

10† Pass over to the coasts of the Kittim and
see,
send to Kedar and carefully inquire:
Where has the like of this been done?

11* Does any other nation change its gods?—
yet they are not gods at all!
But my people have changed their glory
for useless things.

12 Be amazed at this, O heavens,
and shudder with sheer horror, says the
LORD.

13* Two evils have my people done:
they have forsaken me, the source of
living waters;
They have dug themselves cisterns,
broken cisterns, that hold no water.

14† Is Israel a slave, a bondman by birth?
Why then has he become booty?

15* Against him lions roar
full-throated cries.
They have made his land a waste;
his cities are charred ruins, without
inhabitant.

16† Yes, the people of Memphis and Tahpanhes
shave the crown of your head.

17* Has not the forsaking of the LORD, your
God,
done this to you?

18† And now, why go to Egypt,
to drink the waters of the Nile?
Why go to Assyria,
to drink the waters of the Euphrates?

19* Your own wickedness chastises you,
your own infidelities punish you.
Know then, and see, how evil and bitter
is your forsaking the LORD, your God,
And showing no fear of me,
says the Lord, the GOD of hosts.

20*† Long ago you broke your yoke,
you tore off your bonds.
"I will not serve," you said.
On every high hill, under every green tree,
you gave yourself to harlotry.

21* I had planted you, a choice vine
of fully tested stock;
How could you turn out obnoxious to me,
a spurious vine?

22* Though you scour it with soap,
and use much lye,

The stain of your guilt is still before me,
says the Lord GOD.

23† How can you say, "I am not defiled,
I have not gone after the Baals"?
Consider your conduct in the Valley,
recall what you have done:
A frenzied she-camel, coursing near and
far,

24 breaking away toward the desert,
Snuffing the wind in her ardor—
who can restrain her lust?
No beasts need tire themselves seeking her;
in her month they will meet her.

25* Stop wearing out your shoes
and parching your throat!
But you say, "No use! no!
I love these strangers,
and after them I must go."

26* As the thief is shamed when caught,
so shall the house of Israel be shamed:
They, their kings and their princes,
their priests and their prophets;

27 They who say to a piece of wood, "You are
my father,"
and to a stone, "You gave me birth."
They turn to me their backs, not their
faces;
yet, in their time of trouble they cry out,
"Rise up and save us!"

28* Where are the gods you made for
yourselves?
Let them rise up!
Will they save you in your time of
trouble?
For as numerous as your cities
are your gods, O Judah!
And as many as the streets of Jerusalem
are the altars you have set up for Baal.

29 How dare you still plead with me?
You have all rebelled against me, says
the LORD.

30* In vain I struck your children;
the correction they did not take.

---

† 2, 10: *Kittim:* a Phoenician colony in Cyprus. *Kedar:* a nomad tribe of the Syrian desert. These two names represent West
and East.

2, 14: *Bondman by birth:* a perpetual slave, different from
the debt-slave, who was to be freed after six years; cf Ex 21, 2.

2, 16: *Memphis:* the capital of Lower Egypt. *Tahpanhes:* a
frontier city of Egypt, east of the Delta. *Shave the crown of
your head:* the spoliation of Judah at the hands of the Egyptians.

2, 18: *Egypt* and *Assyria* were the protecting foreign powers
favored by rival parties within Judah. The desire for such
foreign alliances is a further desertion of the Lord, *the source of
living waters* (v 13), in favor of the above-named powers,
symbolized by *the Nile* and *the Euphrates* rivers.

2, 20: *Harlotry:* idolatry (because Israel is the bride of God).

2, 23: *The Valley:* of Ben-hinnom, south of Jerusalem, site of
the infamous sanctuary of Topheth where children were sacrificed to Molech; cf 7, 31.

---

*
9: Ex 20, 5.
11: 16, 20; Ps 106, 20.
13: 17, 13; Ps 36, 9;
Is 1, 4.
15: 9, 11.
17: 4, 18; 30, 15.
19: Prv 5, 22; Hos 5, 5.
20: 3, 6.13; Jgs 10, 6.

21: Ex 15, 17; Ps 80, 9;
Is 5, 4.
22: Jb 9, 30.
25: 18, 12.
26: 48, 27; Rom 6, 21.
28: 11, 13; Dt 32, 38;
Jgs 10, 14.
30: 5, 3; Neh 9, 26.

Your sword devoured your prophets
  like a ravening lion.
31 You, of this generation,
  take note of the word of the Lord:
Have I been a desert to Israel,
  a land of darkness?
Why do my people say, "We have moved
    on,
  we will come to you no more"?
32* Does a virgin forget her jewelry,
  a bride her sash?
Yet my people have forgotten me
  days without number.
33 How well you pick your way
  when seeking love!
You who, in your wickedness,
  have gone by ways unclean!
34 You, on whose clothing there is
  the life-blood of the innocent,
  whom you found committing no
    burglary;
35 Yet withal you say, "I am innocent;
  at least, his anger is turned away from
    me."
Behold, I will judge you
  on that word of yours, "I have not
    sinned."
36* How very base you have become
  in changing your course!
By Egypt will you be shamed,
  as you were shamed by Assyria.
37* From there also shall you go away
  with hands upon your head;
For the Lord has rejected those in whom
    you trust,
  with them you will have no success.

3 1*† If a man sends away his wife
  and, after leaving him,
  she marries another man,
Does the first husband come back to her?
  Would not the land be wholly defiled?
But you have sinned with many lovers,
  and yet you would return to me! says
    the Lord.
2*† Lift your eyes to the heights, and see,
  where have men not lain with you?
By the waysides you waited for them
  like an Arab in the desert.
You defiled the land
  by your wicked harlotry.
3* Therefore the showers were withheld,
  the spring rain failed.

But because you have a harlot's brow,
  you refused to blush.
4 Even now do you not call me, "My father,
  you who are the bridegroom of my
    youth"?
5 "Will he keep his wrath forever,
  will he hold his grudge to the end?"
This is what you say; yet you do
  all the evil you can.

Judah and Israel

6*The Lord said to me in the days of King Josiah: See now what rebellious Israel has done! She has gone up every high mountain, and under every green tree she has played the harlot. 7And I thought, after she has done all this she will return to me. But she did not return. Then, even though her traitor sister Judah saw 8*that for all the adulteries rebellious Israel had committed, I put her away and gave her a bill of divorce, nevertheless her traitor sister Judah was not frightened; she too went off and played the harlot. 9*Eager to sin, she polluted the land, committing adultery with stone and wood. 10With all this, the traitor sister Judah did not return to me wholeheartedly, but insincerely, says the Lord.

Restoration of Israel

11*Then the Lord said to me: Rebel Israel is inwardly more just than traitorous Judah. 12*Go, proclaim these words toward the north, and say:

Return, rebel Israel, says the Lord,
  I will not remain angry with you;
For I am merciful, says the Lord,
  I will not continue my wrath forever.
13* Only know your guilt:
  how you rebelled against the Lord, your
    God,
How you ran hither and yon to strangers
  [under every green tree]
  and would not listen to my voice, says
    the Lord.
14*† Return, rebellious children, says the Lord,
  for I am your Master;
I will take you, one from a city, two from
    a clan,
  and bring you to Zion.

---

† 3, 1: Such remarriage of divorced spouses was forbidden by Dt 24, 1-4. Under this figure the prophet sees the presumption of Judah, the unfaithful spouse, who thinks she can return to the Lord after uniting herself to other gods.

3, 2: *An Arab:* a marauding nomad who lay in wait for caravans.

3, 14-18: A remnant of Israel (14) will reunite with Judah (18). The elementary cult of the Lord represented by *the ark of the covenant* will now be replaced by a more deeply spiritual and universal alliance, symbolized by his throne in the ideal Jerusalem around which *all nations will be gathered together* (17).

---

* 32: 13, 25; Dt 32, 18.
36: 2 Chr 28, 16-21.
37: 2 Sm 13, 19.
3/1: Dt 24, 1-4.
2: Ez 16, 24f.
3: 6, 15; 8, 12.
6: 2, 20; Dt 12, 2.

8: 2 Kgs 17, 6.18-23; Ez 23, 11.
9: 2, 27.
11: Ez 16, 51; 23, 11.
12: Dt 4, 29ff.
13: 2, 20.25; Lv 26, 40.
14: 23, 3; Is 10, 21f.

15 I will appoint over you shepherds after my
  own heart,
  who will shepherd you wisely and
    prudently.
16 When you multiply and become fruitful in
    the land,
  says the LORD,
They will in those days no longer say,
  "The ark of the covenant of the LORD!"
They will no longer think of it, or
    remember it,
  or miss it, or make another.

17 At that time they will call Jerusalem the LORD's
throne; there all nations will be gathered together to
honor the name of the LORD at Jerusalem, and they
will walk no longer in their hardhearted wickedness.
18 In those days the house of Judah will join the house
of Israel; together they will come from the land of the
north to the land which I gave to your fathers as a
heritage.

Conditions for Forgiveness

19 I had thought:
  How I should like to treat you as sons,
And give you a pleasant land,
  a heritage most beautiful among the
    nations!
You would call me, "My Father," I thought,
  and never cease following me.
20 But like a woman faithless to her lover,
  even so have you been faithless to me,
  O house of Israel, says the LORD.
21 A cry is heard on the heights!
  the plaintive weeping of Israel's children,
Because they have perverted their ways
  and forgotten the LORD, their God.
22 Return, rebellious children,
  and I will cure you of your rebelling.
"Here we are, we now come to you
  because you are the LORD, our God.
23 Deceptive indeed are the hills,
  the thronging mountains;
In the LORD, our God, alone
  is the salvation of Israel.
24 The shame-god has devoured
  our fathers' toil from our youth,
Their sheep and their cattle,
  their sons and their daughters.
25 Let us lie down in our shame,
  let our disgrace cover us,
  for we have sinned against the LORD,
    our God,

From our youth to this day, we and our
    fathers also;
  we listened not to the voice of the LORD,
    our God."

4 **1** If you wish to return, O Israel, says the
    LORD,
  return to me.
If you put your detestable things out of my
    sight,
  and do not stray,
2 Then you can swear, "As the LORD lives,"
  in truth, in judgment, and in justice;
Then shall the nations use his name in
    blessing,
  and glory in him.

3 For to the men of Judah and to Jerusalem, thus
says the LORD:

Till your untilled ground,
  sow not among thorns.
4 For the sake of the LORD, be circumcised,
  remove the foreskins of your hearts,
  O men of Judah and citizens of
    Jerusalem;
Lest my anger break out like fire,
  and burn till none can quench it,
  because of your evil deeds.

The Invasion from the North

5 Proclaim it in Judah,
  make it heard in Jerusalem;
Blow the trumpet through the land,
  summon the recruits!
Say, "Fall in, let us march
  to the fortified cities."
6 Bear the standard to Zion,
  seek refuge without delay!
Evil I bring from the north,
  and great destruction.
7 Up comes the lion from his lair,
  the destroyer of nations has set out,
  has left his place,
To turn your land into desolation,
  till your cities lie waste and empty.
8 So gird yourselves with sackcloth,
  mourn and wail:
"The blazing wrath of the LORD
  is not turned away from us."

9 In that day, says the LORD,

---

† 3, 24: *Shame-god:* literally, shame, a term commonly substituted for Baal, the Canaanite god with many local shrines.

4, 2: *As the Lord lives:* this oath, made sincerely, implies Israel's return to God and loyal adherence to him. Thus the ancient promises are fulfilled; cf Gn 12, 3; 18, 18; 22, 18; 26, 4; Ps 72, 17.

4, 4: The mere external rite of circumcision avails nothing unless accompanied by the removal of blindness and obstinacy of heart; cf Rom 2, 25.29; 1 Cor 7, 19; Gal 5, 6; 6, 13.15.

*
15: Ez 34, 23; Jn 21, 15.   4/1: 25, 5.
17: Is 2, 2.   2: 12, 16; Dt 10, 20;
18: 30, 3; 31, 8.   Is 65, 16.
19: 31, 9.20; Is 63, 16.   3: Hos 10, 12;
20: 5, 11.   Mt 13, 7.22.
22: Hos 3, 5.   4: 9, 24.
23: 14, 8.   7: 2, 15; 5, 6.
25: 16, 11f; 22, 21.   8: 6, 26; Is 5, 25.

The king will lose heart, and the princes;
  the priests will be amazed,
  and the prophets stunned.

10*† "Alas! Lord God," they will say,
  "You only deceived us
When you said: Peace shall be yours;
  for the sword touches our very soul."

11 At that time it will be said
  of this people and of Jerusalem,
"From the glaring heights through the
    desert
  a wind comes toward the daughter of my
    people."

Not to winnow, not to cleanse,
12* does this wind from the heights come at
    my bidding;
And I myself now pronounce
  sentence upon them.

13 See! like storm clouds he advances,
  like a hurricane his chariots;
Swifter than eagles are his steeds:
  "Woe to us! we are ruined."

14 Cleanse your heart of evil, O Jerusalem,
  that you may be saved.
How long must your pernicious thoughts
  lodge within you?

15 Listen! They proclaim it from Dan,
  from Mount Ephraim they announce
    destruction:

16* "Make this known to the nations,
  announce it to Jerusalem:
The besiegers are coming from the distant
    land,
  shouting their war cry against the cities
    of Judah."

17* Like watchmen of the fields they surround
    her,
  for she has rebelled against me, says the
    Lord.

18* Your conduct, your misdeeds, have done
    this to you;
  how bitter is this disaster of yours,
  how it reaches to your very heart!

19† My breast! my breast! how I suffer!
  The walls of my heart!
My heart beats wildly,
  I cannot be still;
For I have heard the sound of the trumpet,
  the alarm of war.

20* Ruin after ruin is reported;
  the whole earth is laid waste.
In an instant my tents are ravaged;
  in a flash, my shelters.

21 How long must I see that signal,
  hear that trumpet sound!

22* Fools my people are,
  they know me not;
Senseless children they are,
  having no understanding;
They are wise in evil,
  but know not how to do good.

23* I looked at the earth, and it was waste and
    void;
  at the heavens, and their light had gone
    out!

24 I looked at the mountains, and they were
    trembling,
  and all the hills were crumbling!

25 I looked and behold, there was no man;
  even the birds of the air had flown away!

26* I looked and behold, the garden land was a
    desert,
  with all its cities destroyed
  before the Lord, before his blazing
    wrath.

27*   For thus says the Lord:
Waste shall the whole land be;
  I will [not] wholly destroy it.

28* Because of this the earth shall mourn,
  the heavens above shall darken;
I have spoken, I will not repent,
  I have resolved, I will not turn back.

29 At the shout of horseman and bowman
  each city takes to flight;
They shrink into the thickets,
  they scale the rocks:
All the cities are abandoned,
  and no one dwells in them.

30 You now who are doomed, what do you
    mean
  by putting on purple,
  bedecking yourself with gold,
Shading your eyes with cosmetics,
  beautifying yourself in vain?
Your lovers spurn you,
  they seek your life.

31* Yes, I hear the moaning, as of a woman in
    travail,
  like the anguish of a mother with her first
    child—
The cry of daughter Zion gasping,
  as she stretches forth her hands:
"Ah, woe is me! I sink exhausted
  before the slayers!"

✿
10: 6, 14.	22: Dt 32, 5f.28.
12: 1, 16.	23: Is 24, 1.3.
16: 5, 15.	26: Lv 26, 31.
17: 6, 3.	27: 5, 18.
18: 2, 17.19.	28: Is 24, 4.
20: 10, 20.	31: 6, 24.

†

4, 10: *You only deceived us:* the false prophets blame their deception on God; cf 14, 13-16.

4, 19ff: Probably the prophet's own anguish at the coming destruction of Judah.

Universal Corruption

5 1 Roam the streets of Jerusalem,
   look about and observe,
Search through her public places,
   to find even one
Who lives uprightly
   and seeks to be faithful,
   and I will pardon her!

2 Though they say, "As the LORD lives,"
   they swear falsely.

3* O LORD, do your eyes not look for
      honesty?
You struck them, but they did not cringe;
   you laid them low, but they refused
      correction;
They set their faces harder than stone,
   and refused to return to you.

4* It is only the lowly, I thought,
   who are foolish;
For they know not the way of the LORD,
   their duty to their God.

5* I will go to the great ones
   and speak with them;
For they know the way of the LORD,
   their duty to their God.
But, one and all, they had broken the yoke,
   torn off the harness.

6 Therefore lions from the forest slay them,
   wolves of the desert ravage them,
Leopards keep watch round their cities:
   all who come out are torn to pieces
For their many crimes
   and their numerous rebellions.

7 Why should I pardon you these things?
   Your sons have forsaken me,
   they swear by gods that are not.
I fed them, but they committed adultery;
   to the harlot's house they throng.

8* Lustful stallions they are,
   each neighs after another's wife.

9 Shall I not punish them for these things?
   says the LORD;
On a nation such as this shall I not take
   vengeance?

10* Climb to her terraces, and ravage them,
   destroy them [not] wholly.
Tear away her tendrils,
   they do not belong to the LORD.

11* For they have openly rebelled against me,
   both the house of Israel and the house of
      Judah,
   says the LORD.

12*† They denied the LORD,
   saying, "Not he—
No evil shall befall us,
   neither sword nor famine shall we see.

13 The prophets have become wind,
   and the word is not in them.
May their threats be carried out against
      themselves!"

14 Now, for this that you have said,
   says the LORD, the God of hosts—
Behold, I make my words
   in your mouth, a fire,
And this people is the wood
   that it shall devour!—

15* Beware, I will bring against you
   a nation from afar,
   O house of Israel, says the LORD;
A long-lived nation, an ancient nation,
   a people whose language you know not,
   whose speech you cannot understand.

16 Their quivers are like open graves;
   all of them are warriors.

17* They will devour your harvest and your
      bread,
   devour your sons and your daughters,
Devour your sheep and cattle,
   devour your vines and fig trees;
They will beat flat with the sword
   the fortified city in which you trust.

18*Yet even in those days, says the LORD, I will not wholly destroy you. 19And when they ask, "Why has the LORD done all these things to us?" say to them, "As you have forsaken me to serve strange gods in your own land, so shall you serve strangers in a land not your own."

20 Announce this to the house of Jacob,
   proclaim it in Judah:

21* Pay attention to this,
   foolish and senseless people
Who have eyes and see not,
   who have ears and hear not.

22* Should you not fear me, says the LORD,
   should you not tremble before me?
I made the sandy shore the sea's limit,
   which by eternal decree it may not
      overstep.
Toss though it may, it is to no avail;
   though its billows roar, they cannot pass.

23 But this people's heart is stubborn and
      rebellious;
   they turn and go away,

❀
5/3: 2, 30.   12: 14, 13; Is 28, 15.
  4: 8, 7.   15: Dt 28, 49.
  5: 6, 13.   17: Dt 28, 31.
  8: 13, 27.   18: 4, 27.
 10: 2, 21.   21: Is 6, 9.
 11: 3, 20.   22: Jb 38, 10f.

---

† 5, 12: *They denied the Lord:* the people act as though God does not exist and will not interfere.

24 And say not in their hearts,
    "Let us fear the Lord, our God,
Who gives us rain
    early and late, in its time;
Who watches for us
    over the appointed weeks of harvest."
25 Your crimes have prevented these things,
    your sins have turned back these
        blessings from you.
26 For there are among my people criminals;
    like fowlers they set traps,
    but it is men they catch.
27 Their houses are as full of treachery
    as a bird-cage is of birds;
Therefore they grow powerful and rich,
    fat and sleek.
28 They go their wicked way;
    justice they do not defend
By advancing the claim of the fatherless
    or judging the cause of the poor.
29 Shall I not punish these things? says the
        Lord;
    on a nation such as this shall I not take
        vengeance?
30 A shocking, horrible thing
    has happened in the land:
31 The prophets prophesy falsely,
    and the priests teach as they wish;
Yet my people will have it so;
    what will you do when the end comes?

The Enemy at the Gates

6 1 Flee, sons of Benjamin,
    out of Jerusalem!
Blow the trumpet in Tekoa,
    raise a signal over Beth-haccherem;
For evil threatens from the north,
    and mighty destruction.
2 O lovely and delicate
    daughter Zion, you are ruined!
3 Against her, shepherds come with their
        flocks;
    all around, they pitch their tents,
    each one grazes his portion.
4 "Prepare for war against her,
    Up! let us rush upon her at midday!
Alas! the day is waning,
    evening shadows lengthen;
5 Up! let us rush upon her by night,
    destroy her palaces!"

6   For thus says the Lord of hosts:

Hew down her trees,
    throw up a siege mound against
        Jerusalem.
Woe to the city marked for punishment;
    nought but oppression within her!
7 As the well gushes out its waters,
    so she gushes out her wickedness.
Violence and destruction resound in her;
    ever before me are wounds and blows.
8 Be warned, O Jerusalem,
    lest I be estranged from you;
Lest I turn you into a desert,
    a land where no man dwells.

9   Thus says the Lord of hosts:
Glean, glean like a vine
    the remnant of Israel;
Pass your hand, like a vintager,
    repeatedly over the tendrils.
10 To whom shall I speak?
    whom shall I warn, and be heard?
See! their ears are uncircumcised,
    they cannot give heed;
See, the word of the Lord has become for
        them
    an object of scorn, which they will not
        have.
11 Therefore my wrath brims up within me,
    I am weary of holding it in;
I will pour it out upon the child in the
        street,
    upon the young men gathered together.
Yes, all will be taken, husband and wife,
    graybeard with ancient.
12 Their houses will fall to strangers,
    their fields and their wives as well;
For I will stretch forth my hand
    against those who dwell in this land, says
        the Lord.
13 Small and great alike, all are greedy for
        gain;
    prophet and priest, all practice fraud.
14 They would repair, as though it were
        nought,
    the injury to my people:
"Peace, peace!" they say,
    though there is no peace.
15 They are odious; they have done
        abominable things,
    yet they are not at all ashamed,
    they know not how to blush.

---

† 5, 24: *Rain early and late:* autumn and spring rains respectively. *Appointed weeks of harvest:* the seven weeks between the Passover (Dt 16, 9f) and Pentecost, during which it ordinarily did not rain.

6, 3: *Shepherds . . . with their flocks:* foreign invaders with their armies.

6, 14: *As though it were nought:* the false assurance of well-being given by priest and prophet cannot reduce the harm which universal materialism and corruption have done to the people.

24: Gn 8, 22; Dt 11, 14.
25: 2, 17.19.
26: Prv 1, 11.
28: 12, 1; Is 1, 23.
31: 14, 14; Mi 2, 11.
6/1: 1, 14f.
3: 4, 17.
5: 2 Chr 36, 19.
6: 32, 24; Zep 3, 1-4.
7: Is 57, 20.
10: 7, 26; 20, 8.
11: Ez 9, 6.
12: 8, 10; Dt 28, 30ff.
13: 8, 10; 23, 11.
14: 8, 11.
15: 3, 3; 8, 12.

Hence they shall be among those who fall;
  in their time of punishment they shall go
    down,
  says the Lord.

16*†   Thus says the Lord:
Stand beside the earliest roads,
  ask the pathways of old
Which is the way to good, and walk it;
  thus you will find rest for your souls.
But they said, "We will not walk it."

17† When I raised up watchmen for them:
  "Hearken to the sound of the trumpet!"
  they said, "We will not hearken."

18 Therefore hear, O nations,
  and know, O earth,
  what I will do with them:

19* See, I bring evil upon this people,
  the fruit of their own schemes,
Because they heeded not my words,
  because they despised my law.

20* Of what use to me incense that comes from
    Sheba,
  or sweet cane from far-off lands?
Your holocausts find no favor with me,
  your sacrifices please me not.

21*   Therefore, thus says the Lord:
See, I will place before this people
  obstacles to bring them down;
Fathers and sons alike,
  neighbors and friends shall perish.

22*   Thus says the Lord:
See, a people comes from the land of the
    north,
  a great nation, roused from the ends of
    the earth.

23 Bow and javelin they wield;
  cruel and pitiless are they.
They sound like the roaring sea
  as they ride forth on steeds,
Each in his place, for battle
  against you, daughter Zion.

24* We hear the report of them;
  helpless fall our hands,
Anguish takes hold of us,
  throes like a mother's in childbirth.

25 Go not forth into the field,
  step not into the street,
Beware of the enemy's sword;
  terror on every side!

26* O daughter of my people, gird on
    sackcloth,
  roll in the ashes.

Mourn as for an only child
  with bitter wailing,
For sudden upon us
  comes the destroyer.

27* A tester among my people I have appointed
    you,
  to search and test their way.

28 Arch-rebels are they all,
  dealers in slander,
  all of them corrupt.

29 The bellows roars,
  the lead is consumed by the fire;
In vain has the smelter refined,
  the wicked are not drawn off.

30 "Silver rejected" they shall be called,
  for the Lord has rejected them.

II: ORACLES MOSTLY IN THE DAYS OF JEHOIAKIM

The Temple Sermon

7 **1†**THE FOLLOWING MESSAGE came to Jeremiah from the Lord: **2**Stand at the gate of the house of the Lord, and there proclaim this message: Hear the word of the Lord, all you of Judah who enter these gates to worship the Lord! **3***Thus says the Lord of hosts, the God of Israel: Reform your ways and your deeds, so that I may remain with you in this place. **4***Put not your trust in the deceitful words: "This is the temple of the Lord! The temple of the Lord! The temple of the Lord!" **5**Only if you thoroughly reform your ways and your deeds; if each of you deals justly with his neighbor; **6***†if you no longer oppress the resident alien, the orphan, and the widow; if you no longer shed innocent blood in this place, or follow strange gods to your own harm, **7***will I remain with you in this place, in the land which I gave your fathers long ago and forever.

8But here you are, putting your trust in deceitful words to your own loss! **9***Are you to steal and murder, commit adultery and perjury, burn incense to Baal, go after strange gods that you know not, **10***and yet come to stand before me in this house which bears my name, and say: "We are safe; we can commit all these abominations again"? **11***Has this house which bears my name become in your eyes a den of thieves? I too see

---

16: 7, 23f; 18, 15.   7/3: 18, 11; 26, 13.
19: Prv 1, 31.   4: Mi 3, 11.
20: Is 1, 11; 43, 24.   6: Ex 22, 21-24.
21: Is 8, 14f.   7: Dt 4, 40.
22: 1, 15; 5, 15.   9: 44, 17.
24: 4, 31.   10: 32, 34.
26: 25, 34; Am 8, 10.   11: Mt 21, 13.
27: 1, 18.

† 6, 16: *Earliest roads . . . pathways of old:* history and the lessons to be learned from it.

6, 17: *Watchmen:* the prophets who, like Jeremiah, had upheld God's moral law.

7, 1-15: *The temple of the Lord* will not serve as a place of refuge for the Jews against their enemies if they fail to reform their evil ways.

7, 6: *The resident alien:* specially protected by law; cf Ex 20, 10; Nm 9, 14; 15, 14; Dt 5, 14; 28, 43.

what is being done, says the LORD. **¹²*†**You may go to Shiloh, which I made the dwelling place of my name in the beginning. See what I did to it because of the wickedness of my people Israel. **¹³**And now, because you have committed all these misdeeds, says the LORD, because you did not listen, though I spoke to you untiringly; because you did not answer, though I called you, **¹⁴***I will do to this house named after me, in which you trust, and to this place which I gave to you and your fathers, just as I did to Shiloh. **¹⁵***I will cast you away from me, as I cast away all your brethren, all the offspring of Ephraim.

Abuses in Worship

¹⁶*You, now, do not intercede for this people; raise not in their behalf a pleading prayer! Do not urge me, for I will not listen to you. **¹⁷**Do you not see what they are doing in the cities of Judah, in the streets of Jerusalem? **¹⁸*†**The children gather wood, their fathers light the fire, and the women knead dough to make cakes for the queen of heaven, while libations are poured out to strange gods in order to hurt me. **¹⁹***Is it I whom they hurt, says the LORD; is it not rather themselves, to their own confusion? **²⁰***See now, says the Lord GOD, my anger and my wrath will pour out upon this place, upon man and beast, upon the trees of the field and the fruits of the earth; it will burn without being quenched.

²¹Thus says the LORD of hosts, the God of Israel: Heap your holocausts upon your sacrifices; eat up the flesh! **²²†**In speaking to your fathers on the day I brought them out of the land of Egypt, I gave them no command concerning holocaust or sacrifice. **²³***This rather is what I commanded them: Listen to my voice; then I will be your God and you shall be my people. Walk in all the ways that I command you, so that you may prosper. **²⁴***But they obeyed not, nor did they pay heed. They walked in the hardness of their evil hearts and turned their backs, not their faces, to me. **²⁵***From the day that your fathers left the land of Egypt even to this day, I have sent you untiringly all my servants the prophets. **²⁶***Yet they have not obeyed me nor paid heed; they have stiffened their necks and done worse than their fathers. **²⁷**When you speak all these words to them, they will not listen to you either; when you call to them, they will not answer you. **²⁸**Say to them: This is the nation which does not listen to the voice of the LORD, its God, or take correction. Faithfulness has disappeared; the word itself is banished from their speech.

²⁹*† Cut off your dedicated hair and throw it
  away!
 on the heights intone an elegy;
 For the LORD has rejected and cast off
  the generation that draws down his
  wrath.

³⁰*The people of Judah have done what is evil in my eyes, says the LORD. They have defiled the house which bears my name by setting up in it their abominable idols. **³¹**In the Valley of Ben-hinnom they have built the high place of Topheth to immolate in fire their sons and their daughters, such a thing as I never commanded or had in mind. **³²***Therefore, beware! days will come, says the LORD, when Topheth and the Valley of Ben-hinnom will no longer be called such, but rather the Valley of Slaughter. For lack of space, Topheth will be a burial place. **³³***The corpses of this people will be food for the birds of the sky and for the beasts of the field, which no one will drive away. **³⁴***In the cities of Judah and in the streets of Jerusalem I will silence the cry of joy, the cry of gladness, the voice of the bridegroom and the voice of the bride; for the land will be turned to rubble.

8 **¹***AT that time, says the LORD, the bones of the kings and princes of Judah, the bones of the priests and the prophets, and the bones of the citizens of Jerusalem will be emptied out of their graves **²*†**and spread out before the sun and the moon and the whole army of heaven, which they loved and served, which they followed, consulted, and worshiped. They will not be gathered up for burial, but will lie like dung upon the ground. **³**Death will be preferred to life by all the survivors of this wicked race who remain in any of the places to which I banish them, says the LORD of hosts.

Israel's Conduct Incomprehensible

4 Tell them: Thus says the LORD:
 When someone falls, does he not rise again?
  if he goes astray, does he not turn back?

---

† 7, 12: *Shiloh:* original place of worship from the time of Joshua to that of Samuel. The sanctuary was later rejected by God and destroyed by the Philistines; cf 1 Sm 1, 9; 4, 3f; Ps 78, 60.68f.

7, 18: *Queen of heaven:* the Assyro-Babylonian Ishtar, goddess of fertility, whose worship was introduced under King Manasseh and was revived after Josiah's death. *Cakes* shaped like stars (Ishtar was identified with the planet Venus) were offered in her honor.

7, 22: *I gave them no command:* right conduct rather than mere external cult was God's will concerning his people (v 23).

7, 29: *Dedicated hair:* the unshorn hair of the nazirite, regarded as sacred because of a vow, temporary or permanent, to abstain from cutting or shaving the hair, from contact with a corpse, and from all products of the vine; cf Nm 6, 4-8. The cutting of this hair was a sign of extreme mourning.

8, 2: *Army of heaven:* the stars, worshiped by the pagan nations and even by the inhabitants of Jerusalem during the reigns of Manasseh and Amon.

*
12: Jos 18, 1.
14: 26, 9.
15: 1 Kgs 9, 7;
 2 Kgs 17, 23.
16: 11, 14; 14, 11.
18: 44, 17.19.
19: Jb 35, 6.
20: 36, 29; 2 Kgs 22, 17.
23: 11, 4; Lv 26, 3.12.
24: 17, 23.
25: 2 Chr 36, 15f;
 Bar 1, 19.
26: 19, 15; 2 Chr 30, 8.
29: 9, 17-21.
30: 32, 34.
32: 19, 6; 32, 35.
33: 16, 4; 34, 20.
34: 16, 9.
8/1: Bar 2, 24.
2: Dt 4, 19.

5 Why do these people rebel
        with obstinate resistance?
Why do they cling to deceptive idols,
        refuse to turn back?

6 I listen closely:
        they speak what is not true;
No one repents of his wickedness,
        saying "What have I done!"
Everyone keeps on running his course,
        like a steed dashing into battle.

7 Even the stork in the air
        knows its seasons;
Turtledove, swallow and thrush
        observe their time of return,
But my people do not know
        the ordinance of the Lord.

8† How can you say, "We are wise,
        we have the law of the Lord"?
Why, that has been changed into falsehood
        by the lying pen of the scribes!

9 The wise are confounded,
        dismayed and ensnared;
Since they have rejected the word of the
        Lord,
        of what avail is their wisdom?

Shameless in Their Crimes

10 Therefore, I will give their wives to
        strangers,
        their fields to spoilers.
Small and great alike, all are greedy for
        gain,
        prophet and priest, all practice fraud.

11† They would repair, as though it were
        nought,
        the injury to the daughter of my people:
"Peace, peace!" they say,
        though there is no peace.

12 They are odious; they have done
        abominable things,
        yet they are not at all ashamed,
        they know not how to blush.
Hence they shall be among those who fall;
        in their time of punishment they shall go
        down,
        says the Lord.

Threats of Punishment

13 I will gather them all in, says the Lord:
        no grapes on the vine,
No figs on the fig trees,
        foliage withered!

14 Why do we remain here?
        Let us form ranks and enter the walled
        cities,
        to perish there;
For the Lord has wrought our destruction,
        he has given us poison to drink,
        because we have sinned against the
        Lord.

15 We wait for peace to no avail;
        for a time of healing, but terror comes
        instead.
From Dan is heard
        the snorting of his steeds;
The neighing of his stallions
        shakes the whole land.
They come devouring the land and all it
        contains,
        the city and those who dwell in it.

17 Yes, I will send against you
        poisonous snakes,
Against which no charm will work
        when they bite you, says the Lord.

The Prophet's Grief over the People's Suffering

18 My grief is incurable,
        my heart within me is faint.

19 Listen! the cry of the daughter of my
        people,
        far and wide in the land!
Is the Lord no longer in Zion,
        is her King no longer in her midst?
[Why do they provoke me with their idols,
        with their foreign nonentities?]

20 "The harvest has passed, the summer is at an
        end,
        and yet we are not safe!"

21 I am broken by the ruin of the daughter of
        my people.
I am disconsolate; horror has seized me.

22† Is there no balm in Gilead,
        no physician there?
Why grows not new flesh
        over the wound of the daughter of my
        people?

23 Oh, that my head were a spring of water,
        my eyes a fountain of tears,
That I might weep day and night
        over the slain of the daughter of my
        people!

---

*

5: 5, 3; 7, 24.26.
6: Jb 34, 31f.
7: Is 1, 3.
8: Mal 2, 8; Rom 2, 17-23.
9: 1 Cor 3, 20.
10: 6, 13; Dt 28, 30.
11: 6, 14.

12: 6, 15.
14: 9, 14; 23, 15.
15: 14, 19.
17: Dt 32, 24.
19: Dt 32, 21; Mi 4, 9.
21: 14, 17.
22: 46, 11.

†
  8, 8f: *Lying pen of the scribes:* because the interpretations and ordinances of the scribes ran counter to the *word of the Lord.*
  8, 11: *Daughter of my people:* the people itself personified as a woman.
  8, 22: *Gilead:* noted for its healing balm but unable to heal the moral wound of the people.

The Corruption of the People

9 1 Would that I had in the desert
a travelers' lodge!
That I might leave my people
and depart from them.
They are all adulterers,
a faithless band.

2 They ready their tongues like a drawn bow;
with lying, and not with truth,
they hold forth in the land.
They go from evil to evil,
but me they know not, says the LORD.

3† Be on your guard, everyone against his
neighbor;
put no trust in any brother.
Every brother apes Jacob, the supplanter,
every friend is guilty of slander.

4* Each one deceives the other,
no one speaks the truth.
They have accustomed their tongues to
lying,
and are perverse, and cannot repent.

5 Violence upon violence,
deceit upon deceit:
They refuse to recognize me,
says the LORD.

6 Therefore, thus says the LORD of hosts:
I will smelt them and test them;
how else should I deal with their
wickedness?

7* A murderous arrow is his tongue,
his mouth utters deceit;
He speaks cordially with his friends,
but in his heart he lays an ambush!

8* For these things, says the LORD,
shall I not punish them?
On a nation such as this
shall I not take vengeance?

Dirge over the Ravaged Land

9* Over the mountains, break out in cries of
lamentation,
over the pasture lands, intone a dirge:
They are scorched, and no man crosses
them,
unheard is the bleat of the flock;
Birds of the air as well as beasts,
all have fled, and are gone.

10* I will turn Jerusalem into a heap of ruins,
a haunt of jackals;
The cities of Judah I will make into a waste,
where no one dwells.

11* Who is so wise that he can understand this? Let him to whom the mouth of the LORD has spoken make it known:

Why is the land ravaged,
scorched like a wasteland untraversed?

12 The LORD answered: Because they have abandoned my law, which I set before them, and have not followed it or listened to my voice, 13* but followed rather the hardness of their hearts and the Baals, as their fathers had taught them; 14* therefore, thus says the LORD of hosts, the God of Israel: See now, I will give them wormwood to eat and poison to drink. 15* I will scatter them among nations whom neither they nor their fathers have known; I will send the sword to pursue them until I have completely destroyed them.

16 Thus says the LORD of hosts:
Attention! tell the wailing women to come,
summon the best of them;

17* Let them come quickly
and intone a dirge for us,
That our eyes may be wet with weeping,
our cheeks run with tears.

18 The dirge is heard from Zion:
Ruined we are, and greatly ashamed;
We must leave the land,
give up our homes!

19 Hear, you women, the word of the LORD,
let your ears receive his message.
Teach your daughters this dirge,
and each other this lament.

20* Death has come up through our windows,
has entered our palaces;
It cuts down the children in the street,
young people in the squares.

21 The corpses of the slain
lie like dung on a field,
Like sheaves behind the harvester,
with no one to gather them.

True Glory

22* Thus says the LORD:
Let not the wise man glory in his wisdom,
nor the strong man glory in his strength,
nor the rich man glory in his riches;

23 But rather, let him who glories, glory in
this,
that in his prudence he knows me,
Knows that I, the LORD, bring about
kindness,
justice and uprightness on the earth;
For with such am I pleased, says the LORD.

---

* 9/4: 12, 6.
    7: Pss 28, 3; 62, 4.
    8: 5, 9.29.
    9: 4, 25; 12, 4.
  10: Is 13, 22.
  11: Ps 107, 43; Hos 14, 10.
  13: 7, 24; 19, 4f.

14: 23, 15.
15: Lv 26, 33;
    Dt 28, 36.64.
17: 14, 17.
20: 14, 16.
22: Prv 21, 30.

---

† 9, 3: *Jacob, the supplanter:* in Hebrew, a play on words. Jacob, as his name indicates ("he supplants"), deprived his brother Esau of his birthright; cf Gn 25, 26.33.

Circumcision Worthless

24*See, days are coming, says the LORD, when I will demand an account of all those circumcised in their flesh: 25†Egypt and Judah, Edom and the Ammonites, Moab and the desert dwellers who shave their temples. For all these nations, like the whole house of Israel, are uncircumcised in heart.

The Folly of Idolatry

10 1HEAR the word which the LORD speaks to you, O house of Israel. 2*†Thus says the LORD:

Learn not the customs of the nations,
    and have no fear of the signs of the
        heavens,
    though the nations fear them.
3* For the cult idols of the nations are
        nothing,
    wood cut from the forest,
Wrought by craftsmen with the adze,
4*   adorned with silver and gold.
With nails and hammers they are
        fastened,
    that they may not totter.
5* Like a scarecrow in a cucumber field are
        they,
    they cannot speak;
They must be carried about,
    for they cannot walk.
Fear them not, they can do no harm,
    neither is it in their power to do good.
6* No one is like you, O LORD,
    great are you,
    great and mighty is your name.
7* Who would not fear you,
    King of the nations,
    for it is your due!
Among all the wisest of the nations,
    and in all their domain,
    there is none like you.

8 One and all they are dumb and senseless,
    these idols they teach about are
        wooden:
9 Silver strips brought from Tarshish,
    and gold from Ophir,
The work of the craftsman
    and the handiwork of the smelter,
Clothed with violet and purple—
    all of them the work of artisans.

11*Thus shall you say of them: Let the gods that did not make heaven and earth perish from the earth, and from beneath these heavens!

10* The LORD is true God,
    he is the living God, the eternal King,
    Before whose anger the earth quakes,
    whose wrath the nations cannot
        endure:
12* He who made the earth by his power,
    established the world by his wisdom,
    and stretched out the heavens by his
        skill.
13 When he thunders, the waters in the
        heavens roar,
    and he brings up clouds from the end
        of the earth;
He makes the lightning flash in the rain,
    and releases stormwinds from their
        chambers.
14* Every man is stupid, ignorant;
    every artisan is put to shame by his
        idol:
He has molded a fraud,
    without breath of life.
15 Nothingness are they, a ridiculous work;
    they will perish in their time of
        punishment.
16* Not like these is the portion of Jacob:
    he is the creator of all things;
Israel is his very own tribe,
    LORD of hosts is his name.

Abandonment of Judah

17 Lift your bundle and leave the land,
    O city living in a state of siege!
18   For thus says the LORD:
Behold, this time
    I will sling away the inhabitants of the
        land;
I will hem them in,
    that they may be taken.
19 Woe is me! I am undone,
    my wound is incurable;
Yet I had thought:
    if I make light of my wound, I can
        bear it.
20* My tent is ruined,
    all its cords are severed.
My sons have left me, they are no more:
    no one to pitch my tent,
    no one to raise its curtains.
21* Yes, the shepherds were stupid as cattle,
    the LORD they sought not;
Therefore they had no success,
    and all their flocks were scattered.
22 Listen! a noise! it comes closer,
    a great uproar from the northern land:

✿
    24: 4, 4.
  10/2: Bar 6, 6.
    3: Wis 13, 11; Is 44, 9.
    4: Is 40, 19; 41, 7.
    5: Ps 115, 4-8; Bar 6, 15.
    6: Ps 86, 8ff.
    7: 5, 22; Ps 47, 2.8.
  10: Ps 10, 16.
  11: Ps 96, 5.
  12: Ps 104, 5.
  14: Rom 1, 22f.
  16: 31, 35.
  20: 4, 20.
  21: 23, 1; Ez 34, 5f.

---

†   9, 25: *Desert dwellers . . . temples:* Arab tribesmen who cut off their hair and shaved their temples in honor of the pagan god Dushara. This was forbidden the Israelites (Lv 19, 27).

  10, 2: *Signs of the heavens:* phenomena in the sky superstitiously regarded by the pagans as dire omens.

To turn the cities of Judah
into a desert haunt of jackals.

Prayer of Jeremiah

23 You know, O Lord,
that man is not master of his way;
Man's course is not within his choice,
nor is it for him to direct his step.

24 Punish us, O Lord, but with equity,
not in anger, lest you have us dwindle
away.

25* Pour out your wrath on the nations that
know you not,
on the tribes that call not upon your
name;
For they have devoured Jacob utterly,
and laid waste his dwelling.

Plea for Fidelity to the Covenant

11 ¹THE following message came to Jeremiah
from the Lord: ²Speak to the men of Judah
and to the citizens of Jerusalem, ³*saying to them:
Thus says the Lord, the God of Israel: Cursed be the
man who does not observe the terms of this covenant,
⁴*which I enjoined upon your fathers the day I
brought them up out of the land of Egypt, that iron
foundry, saying: Listen to my voice and do all that I
command you. Then you shall be my people, and I
will be your God. ⁵Thus I will fulfill the oath which
I swore to your fathers, to give them a land flowing
with milk and honey: the one you have today. "Amen,
Lord," I answered.

⁶Then the Lord said to me: Proclaim all these words
in the cities of Judah and in the streets of Jerusalem:
Hear the words of this covenant and obey them. ⁷Ur-
gently and constantly I warned your fathers to obey
my voice, from the day I brought them up out of the
land of Egypt even to this day. ⁸*But they did not
listen or give ear. Each one followed the hardness of
his evil heart, till I brought upon them all the threats
of this covenant which they had failed to observe as
I commanded them.

⁹A conspiracy has been found, the Lord said to me,
among the men of Judah and the citizens of Jerusalem.
¹⁰*They have returned to the crimes of their forefathers who refused to obey my words. They also have
followed and served strange gods; the covenant which
I had made with their fathers, the house of Israel and
the house of Judah have broken. ¹¹*Therefore, thus
says the Lord: See, I bring upon them misfortune
which they cannot escape. Though they cry out to me,
I will not listen to them. ¹²*Then the cities of Judah
and the citizens of Jerusalem will go and cry out to
the gods to which they have been offering incense. But

these gods will give them no help whatever when misfortune strikes.

13* For as numerous as your cities
are your gods, O Judah!
And as many as the streets of Jerusalem
are the altars for offering sacrifice to
Baal.

¹⁴*Do not intercede on behalf of this people, nor
utter a plea for them. I will not listen when they call
to me at the time of their misfortune.

Sacrifices of No Avail

15 What right has my beloved in my house,
while she prepares her plots?
Can vows and sacred meat turn away
your misfortune from you?
Will you still be jubilant
16 when you hear the great invasion?
A spreading olive tree, goodly to behold,
the Lord has named you;
Now he sets fire to it,
its branches burn.

¹⁷*The Lord of hosts who planted you has decreed
misfortune for you because of the evil done by the
house of Israel and by the house of Judah, who provoked me by sacrificing to Baal.

The Plot Against Jeremiah

¹⁸I knew it because the Lord informed me; at that
time you, O Lord, showed me their doings.

12 1* You would be in the right, O Lord,
if I should dispute with you;
even so, I must discuss the case with
you.
Why does the way of the godless
prosper,
why live all the treacherous in
contentment?

2* You planted them; they have taken root,
they keep on growing and bearing
fruit.
You are upon their lips,
but far from their inmost thoughts.

3*† You, O Lord, know me, you see me,
you have found that at heart I am
with you.
Pick them out like sheep for the
slaughter,
set them apart for the day of carnage.

4 How long must the earth mourn,
the green of the whole countryside
wither?

✤
25: Ps 79, 6f.
11/3: Dt 27, 26.
4: Dt 4, 20; 1 Kgs 8, 51.
8: 2 Kgs 17, 14.
10: Dt 31, 16;
Ez 20, 21-30.
11: 14, 12; Mi 3, 4.

12: Dt 32, 37f.
13: 2, 28; Hos 10, 1.
14: 7, 16; 14, 11.
17: Is 5, 2.
12/1: Jb 21, 7; Mal 3, 15.
2: Is 29, 13.
3: 17, 18; Jb 23, 10.

† 12, 3: Jeremiah does not seek private vengeance but the
punishment of the wicked by the Lord; cf 20, 12. Nevertheless,
the prophet's reaction to persecution shows the difference between the spirit of the Old Testament and the New.

For the wickedness of those who dwell
        in it
    beasts and birds disappear,
    because they say, "God does not see
        our ways."

5 If running against men has wearied you,
        how will you race against horses?
    And if in a land of peace you fall
        headlong,
    what will you do in the thickets of the
        Jordan?

6* For even your own brothers, the members of your father's house, betray you; they have recruited a force against you. Do not believe them, even if they are friendly to you in their words.

11/**19*** Yet I, like a trusting lamb led to slaughter, had not realized that they were hatching plots against me: "Let us destroy the tree in its vigor; let us cut him off from the land of the living, so that his name will be spoken no more."

11/**20*** But, you, O Lord of hosts, O just Judge,
        searcher of mind and heart,
    Let me witness the vengeance you take
        on them,
    for to you I have entrusted my cause!

11/**21*** Therefore, thus says the Lord concerning the men of Anathoth who seek your life, saying, "Do not prophesy in the name of the Lord; else you shall die by our hand."

11/**22*** Therefore, thus says the Lord of hosts: I am going to punish them. The young men shall die by the sword; their sons and daughters shall die by famine. 11/**23*** None shall be spared among them, for I will bring misfortune upon the men of Anathoth, the year of their punishment.

The Lord's Complaint

7* I abandon my house,
        cast off my heritage;
    The beloved of my soul I deliver
        into the hand of her foes.
8* My heritage has turned on me
        like a lion in the jungle;
    Because she has roared against me,
        I treat her as an enemy.
9* My heritage is a prey for hyenas,
        is surrounded by vultures;
    Come, gather together, all you beasts of
        the field,
        come and eat!

10* Many shepherds have ravaged my
        vineyard,
        have trodden my heritage underfoot;
    The portion that delighted me they have
        turned
        into a desert waste.
11 They have made it a mournful waste,
        desolate it lies before me,
    Desolate, all the land,
        because no one takes it to heart.
12* Upon every desert height
        brigands have come up.
    The Lord has a sword which consumes
        the land, from end to end;
        no peace for all mankind.
13 They have sown wheat and reaped
        thorns,
        they have tired themselves out to no
        purpose;
    They recoil before their harvest,
        the flaming anger of the Lord.

Judah's Neighbors

14*†Thus says the Lord against all my evil neighbors who plunder the heritage which I gave my people Israel as their own: See, I will pluck them up from their land; the house of Judah I will pluck up in their midst. **15***But after plucking them up, I will pity them again and bring them back, each to his heritage, each to his land. **16***And if they carefully learn my people's custom of swearing by my name, "As the Lord lives," they who formerly taught my people to swear by Baal shall be built up in the midst of my people. **17***But if they do not obey, I will uproot and destroy that nation entirely, says the Lord.

Judah's Corruption

13 **1**†THE LORD said to me: Go buy yourself a linen loincloth; wear it on your loins, but do not put it in water. **2**I bought the loincloth as the Lord commanded, and put it on. **3**A second time the word of the Lord came to me thus: **4**Take the loincloth which you bought and are wearing, and go now to the Parath; there hide it in a cleft of the rock. **5**Obedient to the Lord's command, I went to the Parath and buried the loincloth. **6**After a long interval, he said to me: Go now to the Parath and fetch the loincloth which I told you to hide there. **7**Again I went to the Parath, sought out and took the loincloth from the place where I had hid it. But it was rotted, good for nothing! **8**Then the message came to me from the Lord:
        9*Thus says the Lord: So also I will allow the pride

* 6: 9, 4.
11/19: 18, 18; 20, 10; Wis 2, 20.
11/20: 15, 15.
11/21: Am 7, 13.16.
11/22: 18, 21f.
11/23: 23, 12.
12/7: Ps 78, 62; Lam 2, 1f.
8: Ps 106, 40.
9: 2 Kgs 24, 2; Is 56, 9.
10: 6, 3; Is 63, 18.
12: Is 42, 25; 57, 21.
14: 2 Kgs 24, 2.
15: Am 9, 14.
16: Dt 6, 13.
17: Is 60, 12.
13/9: Prv 16, 18.

† 12, 14: *My evil neighbors:* nations surrounding Israel, the land belonging to the Lord; cf Is 8, 8.
13, 1-11: This is probably a vision of the prophet symbolizing the religious corruption of Judah at the hands of the Babylonians, represented here by the river *Parath*, the Euphrates; though a spring of the same name, northeast of Anathoth, may be directly meant.

of Judah to rot, the great pride of Jerusalem. ¹⁰*This wicked people who refuse to obey my words, who walk in the stubbornness of their hearts, and follow strange gods to serve and adore them, shall be like this loincloth which is good for nothing. ¹¹*For, as close as the loincloth clings to a man's loins, so had I made the whole house of Israel and the whole house of Judah cling to me, says the Lord; to be my people, my renown, my praise, my beauty. But they did not listen.

The Broken Wineflask

¹²Now speak to them this word: Thus says the Lord, the God of Israel: Every wine flask is meant to be filled with wine. If they reply, "Do we not know that every wine flask is meant to be filled with wine?" ¹³*say to them: Thus says the Lord: Beware! I am filling with drunkenness all the inhabitants of this land, the kings who succeed to David's throne, the priests and prophets, and all the citizens of Jerusalem. ¹⁴*I will dash them against each other, fathers and sons together, says the Lord; I will show no compassion, I will not spare or pity, but will destroy them.

A Last Warning

15　Give ear, listen humbly,
　　　for the Lord speaks.
16*　Give glory to the Lord, your God,
　　　before it grows dark;
　　Before your feet stumble
　　　on darkening mountains;
　　Before the light you look for turns to
　　　　darkness,
　　　changes into black clouds.
17*　If you do not listen to this in your pride,
　　　I will weep in secret many tears;
　　My eyes will run with tears
　　　for the Lord's flock, led away to exile.

Exile

18*　Say to the king and to the queen mother:
　　　come down from your throne;
　　From your heads fall
　　　your magnificent crowns.
19　The cities of the Negeb are besieged,
　　　with no one to relieve them;
　　All Judah is banished
　　　in universal exile.

Jerusalem's Disgrace

20*　Lift up your eyes and see
　　　men coming from the north.

　　Where is the flock entrusted to you,
　　　the sheep that were your glory?
21*　What will you say when they place as
　　　　rulers over you
　　　those whom you taught to be your
　　　　lovers?
　　Will not pangs seize you
　　　like those of a woman giving birth?
22*　If you ask in your heart
　　　why these things befall you:
　　For your great guilt your skirts are
　　　　stripped away
　　　and you are violated.
23*　Can the Ethiopian change his skin?
　　　the leopard his spots?
　　As easily would you be able to do good,
　　　accustomed to evil as you are.
24*　I will scatter them like chaff that flies
　　　when the desert wind blows.
25*　This is your lot, the portion measured
　　　　out to you
　　　from me, says the Lord.
　　Because you have forgotten me,
　　　and trusted in the lying idol,
26*　I now will strip off your skirts from you,
　　　so that your shame will appear.
27*　Your adulteries, your neighings,
　　　your shameless prostitutions:
　　On the hills in the highlands
　　　I see these horrible crimes of yours.
　　Woe to you, Jerusalem, how long will it
　　　　yet be
　　　before you become clean!

The Great Drought

14 ¹*The word of the Lord that came to Jeremiah concerning the drought:

2*　Judah mourns,
　　　her gates are lifeless;
　　Her people sink down in mourning:
　　　from Jerusalem ascends a cry of
　　　　anguish.
3*　The nobles send their servants for water,
　　　but when they come to the cisterns
　　They find no water
　　　and return with empty jars.
　　Ashamed, despairing, they cover their
　　　　heads
4*　　because of the stricken soil;
　　Because there is no rain in the land
　　　the farmers are ashamed, they cover
　　　　their heads.
5　Even the hind in the field deserts her
　　　　offspring
　　　because there is no grass.
6　The wild asses stand on the bare heights,
　　　gasping for breath like jackals;
　　Their eyes grow dim,
　　　because there is no vegetation to be
　　　　seen.

＊
10: 2, 20; 7, 24; 16, 11.
11: Ex 19, 5; Dt 26, 18f.
13: 25, 15-18; Is 51, 17.
14: 19, 10f.
16: Prv 4, 18f; Is 5, 30;
　　Am 8, 9.
17: 14, 17; Ps 119, 136.
18: 22, 26;
　　2 Kgs 24, 12.15.
20: 6, 22ff.
21: 2 Kgs 16, 7.

22: Is 47, 2f.
23: Ps 55, 20.
24: Pss 1, 4; 83, 14.
25: Jb 20, 29.
26: Ez 16, 32.
27: 2, 20.
14/1: Lv 26, 19f.
2: Is 3, 26.
3: Am 4, 8.
4: Dt 28, 23.

7* Even though our crimes bear witness
    against us,
  take action, O Lord, for the honor of
    your name—
Even though our rebellions are many,
  though we have sinned against you.

8 O Hope of Israel, O Lord,
  our savior in time of need!
Why should you be a stranger in this
  land,
  like a traveler who has stopped but
    for a night?

9* Why are you like a man dumbfounded,
  a champion who cannot save?
You are in our midst, O Lord,
  your name we bear:
  do not forsake us!

10* Thus says the Lord of this people:
They so love to wander
  that they do not spare their feet.
The Lord has no pleasure in them;
  now he remembers their guilt,
  and will punish their sins.

11*Then the Lord said to me: Do not intercede for this people. **12***If they fast, I will not listen to their supplication. If they offer holocausts or cereal offerings, I will not accept them. Rather, I will destroy them with the sword, famine, and pestilence. **13***Ah! Lord God, I replied, it is the prophets who say to them, "You shall not see the sword; famine shall not befall you. Indeed, I will give you lasting peace in this place." **14***Lies these prophets utter in my name, the Lord said to me. I did not send them; I gave them no command nor did I speak to them. Lying visions, foolish divination, dreams of their own imagination, they prophesy to you. **15***Therefore, thus says the Lord: Concerning the prophets who prophesy in my name, though I did not send them; who say, "Sword and famine shall not befall this land": by the sword and famine shall these prophets meet their end. **16***The people to whom they prophesy shall be cast out into the streets of Jerusalem by famine and the sword. No one shall bury them, their wives, their sons, or their daughters, for I will pour out upon them their own wickedness. **17***Speak to them this word:

Let my eyes stream with tears
  day and night, without rest,

Over the great destruction which
  overwhelms
  the virgin daughter of my people,
  over her incurable wound.

18 If I walk out into the field,
  look! those slain by the sword;
If I enter the city,
  look! those consumed by hunger.
Even the prophet and the priest
  forage in a land they know not.

19* Have you cast Judah off completely?
  Is Zion loathsome to you?
Why have you struck us a blow
  that cannot be healed?
We wait for peace, to no avail;
  for a time of healing, but terror comes
    instead.

20* We recognize, O Lord, our wickedness,
  the guilt of our fathers;
  that we have sinned against you.

21* For your name's sake spurn us not,
  disgrace not the throne of your glory;
  remember your covenant with us, and
    break it not.

22* Among the nations' idols is there any
    that gives rain?
Or can the mere heavens send
    showers?
Is it not you alone, O Lord,
  our God, to whom we look?
You alone have done all these things.

15 **1***THE Lord said to me: Even if Moses and Samuel stood before me, my heart would not turn toward this people. Send them away from me. **2***If they ask you where they should go, tell them, Thus says the Lord: Whoever is marked for death, to death; whoever is marked for the sword, to the sword; whoever is marked for famine, to famine; whoever is marked for captivity, to captivity. **3***Four kinds of scourge I have decreed against them, says the Lord: the sword to slay them; dogs to drag them about; the birds of the sky and the beasts of the earth to devour and destroy them. **4***And I will make them an object of horror to all the kingdoms of the earth because of what Manasseh, son of Hezekiah, king of Judah, did in Jerusalem.

Scene of Tragedy

5* Who will pity you, Jerusalem,
  who will console you?
Who will stop to ask
  about your welfare?

6* You have disowned me, says the Lord,
  turned your back upon me;
And so I stretched out my hand to
    destroy you,
  I was weary of sparing you.

7* I winnowed them with the fan
  in every city gate.

❋
7: Dn 9, 4-14.
9: Is 59, 1f; 63, 19.
10: 2, 25.
11: 11, 14; Ex 32, 10.
12: 6, 20; Is 1, 11.13.
13: 4, 10; 5, 12.
14: 5, 31; 23, 16.
15: 5, 12f.
16: 7, 33; 19, 7.
17: 9, 17.
19: 8, 15; 2 Chr 36, 16.
20: Ps 106, 6; Dn 9, 5.8.

21: 14, 7; Lv 26, 44;
    Ps 25, 11.
22: 5, 24; Zec 10, 1.
15/1: Ps 99, 6;
    Ez 14, 14.16.
2: 14, 12; Ez 5, 12.
3: Ez 14, 21.
4: 24, 9; 2 Kgs 21, 11-16;
    23, 26; 24, 3f.
5: Is 51, 19.
6: Am 7, 8.
7: Is 41, 16.

I destroyed my people through
bereavement;
they returned not from their evil ways.

8 Their widows were more numerous
before me
than the sands of the sea.
I brought against the mother of youths
the spoiler at midday;
Suddenly I struck her
with anguish and terror.

9* The mother of seven swoons away,
gasping out her life;
Her sun sets in full day,
she is disgraced, despairing.
Their survivors I will give to the sword
before their enemies, says the Lord.

Jeremiah's Complaint

10* Woe to me, mother, that you gave me
birth!
a man of strife and contention to all
the land!
I neither borrow nor lend,
yet all curse me.

11* Tell me, Lord, have I not served you for
their good?
Have I not interceded with you
in the time of misfortune and anguish?

15* You know I have.
Remember me, Lord, visit me,
and avenge me on my persecutors.
Because of your long-suffering banish
me not;
know that for you I have borne insult.

16 When I found your words, I devoured
them;
they became my joy and the happiness
of my heart,
Because I bore your name,
O Lord, God of hosts.

17* I did not sit celebrating
in the circle of merrymakers;
Under the weight of your hand I sat
alone
because you filled me with
indignation.

18*† Why is my pain continuous,
my wound incurable, refusing to be
healed?
You have indeed become for me a
treacherous brook,
whose waters do not abide!

19 Thus the Lord answered me:

If you repent, so that I restore you,
in my presence you shall stand;
If you bring forth the precious without
the vile,
you shall be my mouthpiece.
Then it shall be they who turn to you,
and you shall not turn to them;

20* And I will make you toward this people
a solid wall of brass.
Though they fight against you,
they shall not prevail,
For I am with you,
to deliver and rescue you, says the
Lord.

21 I will free you from the hand of the
wicked,
and rescue you from the grasp of the
violent.

Jeremiah's Life a Warning

16 **[1]**THIS message came to me from the Lord:
[2]Do not marry any woman; you shall not have
sons or daughters in this place, **[3]**for thus says the Lord
concerning the sons and daughters who will be born
in this place, the mothers who will give them birth,
the fathers who will beget them in this land: **4***Of
deadly disease they shall die. Unlamented and unburied they will lie like dung on the ground. Sword
and famine will make an end of them, and their
corpses will become food for the birds of the sky and
the beasts of the field.

5*Go not into a house of mourning, the Lord continued: go not there to lament or offer sympathy. For
I have withdrawn my friendship from this people,
says the Lord, my kindness and my pity. **6*†**They
shall die, the great and the lowly, in this land, and
shall go unburied and unlamented. No one will gash
himself or shave his head for them. **7***They will not
break bread with the bereaved to console them in
their bereavement; they will not give them the cup
of consolation to drink over the death of father or
mother.

8Enter not a house where people are celebrating, to
sit with them eating and drinking. **9***For thus says the
Lord of hosts, the God of Israel: Before your very eyes
and during your lifetime I will silence from this place
the cry of joy and the cry of gladness, the voice of the
bridegroom and the voice of the bride.

10*When you proclaim all these words to this people
and they ask you: "Why has the Lord pronounced all
these great evils against us? What is our crime? What
sin have we committed against the Lord, our God?"—
11*you shall answer them: It is because your fathers
have forsaken me, says the Lord, and followed strange

✸

9: 1 Sm 2, 5.
10: 20, 14.
11: 39, 11-14.
15: 11, 20; 12, 3;
    Ps 69, 8.
17: Ps 25, 4.
18: 14, 19; 30, 15.
20: 1, 18; 6, 27.

16/4: 7, 33; 22, 18.
    5: Ez 24, 16f.
    6: Lv 19, 28; Dt 14, 1.
    7: Ez 24, 17.
    9: 7, 34; 25, 10.
    10: 2, 35; 5, 19; 13, 22.
    11: 22, 9; Dt 29, 25.

---

† 15, 18: *A treacherous brook:* that dries up when its waters
are needed. The prophet complains that he cannot rely on God
with unfailing assurance of his assistance.

16, 6f: These verses refer to popular mourning practices,
sometimes connected with pagan superstition; cf Dt 14, 1f.

gods, which they served and worshiped; but me they have forsaken, and my law they have not observed. [12]And you have done worse than your fathers. Here you are, every one of you, walking in the hardness of his evil heart instead of listening to me. [13]I will cast you out of this land into a land that neither you nor your fathers have known; there you can serve strange gods day and night, because I will not grant you my mercy.

Return from Exile

[14]However, days will surely come, says the LORD, when it will no longer be said, "As the LORD lives, who brought the Israelites out of Egypt"; [15]but rather, "As the LORD lives, who brought the Israelites out of the land of the north and out of all the countries to which he had banished them." I will bring them back to the land which I gave their fathers.

Double Punishment

[16]Look! I will send many fishermen, says the LORD, to catch them. After that, I will send many hunters to hunt them out from every mountain and hill and from the clefts of the rocks. [17]For my eyes are upon all their ways; they are not hidden from me, nor does their guilt escape my view. [18]I will at once repay them double for their crime and their sin of profaning my land with their detestable corpses of idols, and filling my heritage with their abominations.

Conversion of the Heathen

[19]O LORD, my strength, my fortress,
    my refuge in the day of distress!
To you will the nations come
    from the ends of the earth, and say,
"Mere frauds are the heritage of our
    fathers,
    empty idols of no use."
[20]Can man make for himself gods?
    These are not gods.
[21]Look, then: I will give them knowledge;
    this time I will leave them in no doubt
Of my strength and my power:
    they shall know that my name is LORD.

The Sin of Judah and Its Punishment

17 [1]The sin of Judah is written
    with an iron stylus,
Engraved with a diamond point
    upon the tablets of their hearts.

[And the horns of their altars, [2]when their sons remember their altars and their sacred poles, beside the green trees, on the high hills, [3]the peaks in the highland.]

Your wealth and all your treasures
    I will give as spoil.
In recompense for all your sins
    throughout your borders,
[4]You will relinquish your hold on your
    heritage
    which I have given you.
I will enslave you to your enemies
    in a land that you know not:
For a fire has been kindled by my wrath
    that will burn forever.

True Wisdom

[5]   Thus says the LORD:
Cursed is the man who trusts in human
    beings,
    who seeks his strength in flesh,
    whose heart turns away from the
    LORD.
[6]He is like a barren bush in the desert
    that enjoys no change of season,
But stands in a lava waste,
    a salt and empty earth.
[7]Blessed is the man who trusts in the
    LORD,
    whose hope is the LORD.
[8]He is like a tree planted beside the
    waters
    that stretches out its roots to the
    stream:
It fears not the heat when it comes,
    its leaves stay green;
In the year of drought it shows no
    distress,
    but still bears fruit.
[9]More tortuous than all else is the human
    heart,
    beyond remedy; who can understand
    it?
[10]I, the LORD, alone probe the mind
    and test the heart,
To reward everyone according to his
    ways,
    according to the merit of his deeds.
[11]A partridge that mothers a brood not her
    own
    is the man who acquires wealth
    unjustly:
In midlife it will desert him;
    in the end he is only a fool.

The Source of Life

[12]A throne of glory, exalted from the
    beginning,
    such is our holy place.
[13]O hope of Israel, O LORD!
    all who forsake you shall be in
    disgrace;

12: 7, 24ff.
14: 23, 7f.
15: 24, 6.
16: 2 Kgs 24, 2; Lam 4, 19.
17: 32, 19; Jb 34, 21.
18: Is 40, 2.
19: 2, 11; Is 2, 2f.
20: 2, 11; Gal 4, 8.
21: Am 5, 8.
17/1: Jb 19, 24.

4: 5, 19; Dt 32, 22.
5: Ps 146, 2f.
7: Ps 1, 3.
8: Is 58, 11.
10: 32, 19; 1 Sm 16, 7;
    Eccl 12, 14.
11: Prv 13, 11; Lk 12, 20.
12: 14, 21.
13: 2, 13.

The rebels in the land shall be put to
shame;
they have forsaken the source of
living waters
[the LORD].

Prayer for Vengeance

14 Heal me, LORD, that I may be healed;
save me, that I may be saved,
for it is you whom I praise.

15* See how they say to me,
"Where is the word of the LORD?
Let it come to pass!"

16 Yet I did not press you to send calamity;
the day without remedy I have not
desired.
You know what passed my lips;
it is present before you.

17* Do not be my ruin,
you, my refuge in the day of
misfortune.

18* Let my persecutors, not me, be
confounded;
let them, not me, be broken.
Bring upon them the day of misfortune,
crush them with repeated destruction.

Observance of the Sabbath

19*†Thus said the LORD to me: Go, stand at the
Gate of Benjamin, where the kings of Judah enter
and leave, and at the other gates of Jerusalem. 20There
say to them: Hear the word of the LORD, you kings
of Judah, and all Judah, and all you citizens of Jerusalem who enter these gates! 21*Thus says the LORD:
As you love your lives, take care not to carry burdens
on the sabbath day, to bring them in through the
gates of Jerusalem. 22*Bring no burden from your
homes on the sabbath. Do no work whatever, but
keep holy the sabbath, as I commanded your fathers,
23*though they did not listen or give ear, but stiffened
their necks so as not to hear or take correction. 24*If
you obey me wholeheartedly, says the LORD, and carry
no burden through the gates of this city on the sabbath, keeping the sabbath holy and abstaining from
all work on it, 25*then, through the gates of this city,
kings who sit upon the throne of David will continue
to enter, riding in their chariots or upon their horses,
along with their princes, and the men of Judah, and
the citizens of Jerusalem. This city will remain inhabited forever. 26*To it people will come from the
cities of Judah and the neighborhood of Jerusalem,
from the land of Benjamin and from the foothills, from

the hill country and the Negeb, to bring holocausts
and sacrifices, cereal offerings and incense and thank
offerings to the house of the LORD. 27*But if you do
not obey me and keep holy the sabbath, if you carry
burdens and come through the gates of Jerusalem on
the sabbath, I will set unquenchable fire to its gates,
which will consume the palaces of Jerusalem.

The Potter's Vessel

18 1†THIS word came to Jeremiah from the LORD:
2Rise up, be off to the potter's house; there
I will give you my message. 3I went down to the
potter's house and there he was, working at the wheel.
4*Whenever the object of clay which he was making
turned out badly in his hand, he tried again, making
of the clay another object of whatever sort he pleased.
5Then the word of the Lord came to me: 6*Can I not
do to you, house of Israel, as this potter has done?
says the LORD. Indeed, like clay in the hand of the
potter, so are you in my hand, house of Israel. 7*Sometimes I threaten to uproot and tear down and destroy
a nation or a kingdom. 8*But if that nation which I
have threatened turns from its evil, I also repent of
the evil which I threatened to do. 9Sometimes, again,
I promise to build up and plant a nation or a kingdom.
10*But if that nation does what is evil in my eyes,
refusing to obey my voice, I repent of the good with
which I promised to bless it.

11*And now, tell this to the men of Judah and the
citizens of Jerusalem: Thus says the LORD: Take care!
I am fashioning evil against you and making a plan.
Return, each of you, from his evil way; reform your
ways and your deeds. 12*But they will say, "No use!
We will follow our own devices; each one of us will
behave according to the stubbornness of his evil
heart!"

Judah's Apostasy Unnatural

13* Therefore thus says the LORD:
Ask among the nations—
who has ever heard the like?
Truly horrible things
has virgin Israel done!

14† Does the snow of Lebanon
desert the rocky heights?
Do the gushing waters dry up
that flow fresh down the mountains?

15* Yet my people have forgotten me:
they burn incense to a thing that does
not exist.

❋
15: Is 5, 19; 2 Pt 3, 4.
17: 16, 19.
18: 15, 15; 18, 20-23;
    Ps 35, 5f.
19: 7, 2.
21: Neh 13, 15-19.
22: Ex 20, 8; 23, 12.
23: 5, 3; 7, 24.
24: Is 58, 14.
25: 22, 4.
26: 32, 44.

27: Ez 22, 8.
18/4: Rom 9, 20f.
  6: Wis 15, 7; Is 45, 9.
  7: 1, 10.
  8: 26, 3; Is 55, 7;
     Ez 18, 21.27.
 10: Nm 14, 22f.
 11: 7, 3; 25, 5; 35, 15.
 12: 2, 25; 7, 24.
 13: 2, 10f; 5, 30.
 15: 2, 13.32.

---

† 17, 19: *The Gate of Benjamin:* probably the northern gate of
the temple area and city wall of Jerusalem; cf 20, 2; 37, 12;
38, 7.

18, 1-12: The lesson of the potter is not that God deals arbitrarily with his people, but that he is almighty to destroy or
restore, accordingly as they disobey him or fulfill his plans.

18, 14: *Lebanon:* here apparently including Mount Hermon,
whose snow-capped peak can be seen from parts of Palestine all
year round. The prophet contrasts the certainties of nature with
Israel's unnatural desertion of the Lord for idols (v 15).

They stumble out of their ways,
the paths of old,
To travel on bypaths,
not the beaten track.
16* Their land shall be turned into a desert,
an object of lasting ridicule:
All passers-by will be amazed,
will shake their heads.
17* Like the east wind, I will scatter them
before their enemies;
I will show them my back, not my face,
in their day of disaster.

Another Prayer for Vengeance

18*"Come," they said, "let us contrive a plot against Jeremiah. It will not mean the loss of instruction from the priests, nor of counsel from the wise, nor of messages from the prophets. And so, let us destroy him by his own tongue; let us carefully note his every word."

19 Heed me, O Lord,
and listen to what my adversaries say.
20* Must good be repaid with evil
that they should dig a pit to take my life?
Remember that I stood before you
to speak in their behalf,
to turn away your wrath from them.
21*† So now, deliver their children to famine,
do away with them by the sword.
Let their wives be made childless and widows;
let their men die of pestilence,
their young men be slain by the sword in battle.
22 May cries be heard from their homes,
when suddenly you send plunderers against them.
For they have dug a pit to capture me,
they have hid snares for my feet;
23* But you, O Lord, know
all their plans to slay me.
Forgive not their crime,
blot not out their sin in your sight!
Let them go down before you,
proceed against them in the time of your anger.

Symbol of the Potter's Flask

19 **1**THUS said the Lord: Go, buy a potter's earthen flask. Take along some of the elders of the people and of the priests, **2†**and go out toward the Valley of Ben-hinnom, at the entrance of the Potsherd Gate; there proclaim the words which I will speak to you: **3**Listen to the word of the Lord, kings of Judah and citizens of Jerusalem: Thus says the Lord of hosts, the God of Israel: I am going to bring such evil upon this place that all who hear of it will feel their ears tingle. **4***This is because they have forsaken me and alienated this place by burning in it incense to strange gods which neither they nor their fathers knew; and the kings of Judah have filled this place with the blood of the innocent. **5***They have built high places for Baal to immolate their sons in fire as holocausts to Baal: such a thing as I neither commanded nor spoke of, nor did it ever enter my mind. **6***Therefore, days will come, says the Lord, when this place will no longer be called Topheth, or the Valley of Ben-hinnom, but rather, the Valley of Slaughter. **7***In this place I will foil the plan of Judah and Jerusalem; I will make them fall by the sword before their enemies, by the hand of those that seek their lives. Their corpses I will give as food to the birds of the sky and the beasts of the field. **8**I will make this city an object of amazement and derision. Because of all its wounds, every passer-by will be amazed and will catch his breath. **9***I will have them eat the flesh of their sons and daughters; they shall eat one another's flesh during the strict siege by which their enemies and those who seek their lives will confine them.

10And you shall break the flask in the sight of the men who went with you, **11***and say to them: Thus says the Lord of hosts: Thus will I smash this people and this city, as one smashes a clay pot so that it cannot be repaired. And Topheth shall be a burial place, for lack of place to bury elsewhere. **12***Thus I will do to this place and to its inhabitants, says the Lord; I will make this city like Topheth. **13***And the houses of Jerusalem and the palaces of the kings of Judah shall be defiled like the place of Topheth, all the houses upon whose roofs they burnt incense to the whole host of heaven and poured out libations to strange gods.

14*When Jeremiah returned from Topheth, where the Lord had sent him to prophesy, he stood in the court of the house of God and said to all the people: **15***Thus says the Lord of hosts, the God of Israel: I will surely bring upon this city all the evil with which I threatened it, because they have stiffened their necks and have not obeyed my words.

20 **1*†**JEREMIAH was heard prophesying these things by the priest Pashhur, son of Immer, chief officer in the house of the Lord. **2***So he had the

16: 19, 8; Lv 26, 32;
1 Kgs 9, 8.
17: Prv 1, 24-31.
18: 11, 19; Ps 35, 15f.
20: Ps 35, 12.
21: Ps 109, 9f.
23: Neh 4, 5; Pss 35, 4;
37, 32f.
19/4: 1, 16; 2 Kgs 21, 16;
24, 4.
5: 7, 31f; 32, 35.
6: 7, 32.
7: 7, 33.
9: Lv 26, 29.
11: 7, 32.
12: 2 Kgs 23, 10.
13: 32, 29.
14: 26, 2.
15: 7, 26; Prv 29, 1.
20/1: 21, 1.
2: 29, 26.

†
18, 21: In the Old Testament a man's family was regarded as part of his personality, to be rewarded or punished along with him; cf Jos 7, 24ff.
19, 2: *Potsherd Gate:* in the south wall of Jerusalem, through which potsherds and other refuse were carried to the Valley of Ben-hinnom.
20, 1: *Chief officer in the house of the Lord:* head of the tem-

prophet scourged and placed in the stocks at the upper Gate of Benjamin in the house of the LORD. **3*†**The next morning, after Pashhur had released Jeremiah from the stocks, the prophet said to him: Instead of Pashhur, the LORD will name you "Terror on every side." **4†**For thus says the LORD: Indeed, I will deliver you to terror, you and all your friends. Your own eyes shall see them fall by the sword of their enemies. All Judah I will deliver to the king of Babylon, who shall take them captive to Babylon or slay them with the sword. **5***All the wealth of this city, all it has toiled for and holds dear, all the treasures of the kings of Judah, I will give as plunder into the hands of their foes, who shall seize it and carry it away to Babylon. **6***You, Pashhur, and all the members of your household shall go into exile. To Babylon you shall go, you and all your friends; there you shall die and be buried, because you have prophesied lies to them.

Jeremiah's Interior Crisis

7† You duped me, O LORD, and I let myself
be duped;
you were too strong for me, and you
triumphed.
All the day I am an object of laughter;
everyone mocks me.
8 Whenever I speak, I must cry out,
violence and outrage is my message;
The word of the LORD has brought me
derision and reproach all the day.
9* I say to myself, I will not mention him,
I will speak in his name no more.
But then it becomes like fire burning in
my heart,
imprisoned in my bones;
I grow weary holding it in,
I cannot endure it.
10* Yes, I hear the whisperings of many:
"Terror on every side!
Denounce! let us denounce him!"
All those who were my friends
are on the watch for any misstep of
mine.
"Perhaps he will be trapped; then we
can prevail,
and take our vengeance on him."
11* But the LORD is with me, like a mighty
champion:
my persecutors will stumble, they will
not triumph.
In their failure they will be put to utter
shame,
to lasting, unforgettable confusion.

12* O LORD of hosts, you who test the just,
who probe mind and heart,
Let me witness the vengeance you take
on them,
for to you I have entrusted my cause.
13* Sing to the LORD,
praise the LORD,
For he has rescued the life of the poor
from the power of the wicked!
14*† Cursed be the day
on which I was born!
May the day my mother gave me birth
never be blessed!
15 Cursed be the man who brought the
news
to my father, saying,
"A child, a son, has been born to you!"
filling him with great joy.
16* Let that man be like the cities
which the LORD relentlessly
overthrew;
Let him hear war cries in the morning,
battle alarms at noonday,
17* because he did not dispatch me in the
womb!
Then my mother would have been my
grave,
her womb confining me forever.
18* Why did I come forth from the womb,
to see sorrow and pain,
to end my days in shame?

III: ORACLES IN THE LAST YEARS OF JERUSALEM

Fate of Zedekiah and Jerusalem

21 **1†**THE MESSAGE WHICH CAME to Jeremiah from the LORD when King Zedekiah sent him Pashhur, son of Malchiah, and the priest Zephaniah, son of Maaseiah, with this request: **2**Inquire for us of the LORD, because Nebuchadnezzar, king of Babylon,

---

† ple police; cf 29, 26. By entering the temple court (19, 14), Jeremiah had put himself under Pashhur's jurisdiction.

20, 3: *Terror on every side:* Pashhur will share the fate of doomed Jerusalem and will experience personally all that the people as a whole have had to endure.

20, 4: *Babylon:* mentioned here for the first time as the land of exile. The prophecy probably dates from after 605 B. C., when Nebuchadnezzar defeated Egypt and made the Chaldean empire dominant in Syria and Palestine.

20, 7: *You duped me:* to be understood in the light of Jeremiah's intimate dealings with God; cf 15, 18.

20, 14-18: Deception, sorrow and terror have brought the prophet close to the point of despair; nevertheless he has expressed his utmost confidence in the triumph of God's will (vv 11ff); cf Jb 3, 3-12.

21, 1: *Zedekiah:* brother of Jehoiakim, appointed king by Nebuchadnezzar after he had carried Jehoiachin away to captivity (2 Kgs 24, 17). *Pashhur:* different from the one in 20, 1ff but also one of Jeremiah's enemies; cf 38, 1.4.

❋
3: 6, 25.
5: 2 Kgs 20, 17; 24, 12-16.
6: 14, 13f; 28, 15.
9: 6, 11; Jb 32, 18.
10: Jb 19, 19; Ps 31, 13; Lk 20, 20.
11: 1, 8; 15, 20.
12: 11, 20.
13: Pss 35, 9f; 109, 30f.
14: 15, 10; Jb 3, 1-10; 10, 18.
16: Gn 19, 25; Is 13, 19.
17: Jb 3, 10f; 10, 19.
18: Jb 14, 1.

is attacking us. Perhaps the Lord will deal with us according to all his wonderful works, so that he will withdraw from us. ³But Jeremiah answered them: This is what you shall report to Zedekiah: ⁴*Thus says the Lord, the God of Israel: I will turn back in your hands the weapons with which you intend to fight the king of Babylon and the Chaldeans who besiege you outside the walls. These weapons I will pile up in the midst of this city, ⁵*and I myself will fight against you with outstretched hand and mighty arm, in anger, and wrath, and great rage! ⁶*I will strike the inhabitants of this city, both man and beast; they shall die in a great pestilence. ⁷*After that, says the Lord, I will hand over Zedekiah, king of Judah, and his ministers and the people in this city who survive pestilence, sword, and famine, into the hand of Nebuchadnezzar, king of Babylon, into the hands of their enemies and those who seek their lives. He shall strike them with the edge of the sword, without quarter, without pity or mercy. ⁸*And to this people you shall say: Thus says the Lord: See, I am giving you a choice between life and death. ⁹*Whoever remains in this city shall die by the sword or famine or pestilence. But whoever leaves and surrenders to the besieging Chaldeans shall live and have his life as booty. ¹⁰†For I have turned against this city, for its woe and not for its good, says the Lord. It shall be given into the power of the king of Babylon who shall burn it with fire.

Oracles Regarding the Kings

11†   To the royal house of Judah:

12*   Hear the word of the Lord, O house of
         David!
         Thus says the Lord:
         Each morning dispense justice,
            rescue the oppressed from the hand of
            the oppressor,
         Lest my fury break out like fire
            which burns without being quenched,
            because of the evil of your deeds.

13†   Beware! I am against you, Valley-site,
         Rock of the Plain, says the Lord.
         You who say, "Who will attack us,
            who can penetrate our retreats?"

14*†   I will punish you, says the Lord,
         as your deeds deserve!
         I will kindle a fire in its forest
            that shall devour all its surroundings.

22 ¹THE Lord told me this: Go down to the palace of the king of Judah and there deliver this message: ²*You shall say: Listen to the word of the Lord, king of Judah, who sit on the throne of David, you, your ministers, and your people that enter by these gates! ³*Thus says the Lord: Do what is right and just. Rescue the victim from the hand of his oppressor. Do not wrong or oppress the resident alien, the orphan, or the widow, and do not shed innocent blood in this place. ⁴If you carry out these commands, kings who succeed to the throne of David will continue to enter the gates of this palace, riding in chariots or mounted on horses, with their ministers, and their people. ⁵But if you do not obey these commands, I swear by myself, says the Lord: this palace shall become rubble. ⁶†For thus says the Lord concerning the palace of the king of Judah:

     Though you be to me like Gilead,
         like the peak of Lebanon,
     I will turn you into a waste,
         a city uninhabited.

7*   Against you I will send destroyers,
         each with his axe:
     They shall cut down your choice cedars,
         and cast them into the fire.

⁸*Many people will pass by this city and ask one another: "Why has the Lord done this to so great a city?" ⁹*And the answer will be given: "Because they have deserted their covenant with the Lord, their God, by worshiping and serving strange gods."

Jehoahaz

10*†   Weep not for him who is dead,
         mourn not for him!
     Weep rather for him who is going away;
         never again will he see
         the land of his birth.

¹¹†Thus says the Lord concerning Shallum, son of Josiah, king of Judah, who succeeded his father as king. He has left this place never to return. ¹²Rather, he shall die in the place where they exiled him; this land he shall not see again.

21, 10: Jeremiah consistently pointed out the uselessness of resistance to Babylon, since the Lord had delivered Judah to Nebuchadnezzar (27, 6). Because of this the prophet was denounced and imprisoned as a traitor (37, 13f).

21, 11—23, 8: This section contains an editor's collection of Jeremiah's oracles against the kings of Judah. They are placed in the chronological order of the kings, and are prefaced by the oracles against the kings of Judah in general (21, 11—22, 9).

21, 13: *Valley-site, Rock of the Plain:* Mount Zion, surrounded by valleys, was regarded by the royal house as impregnable. Despite this natural fortification, God shows derisively that it is no more than a rock rising from the plain, undefendable against the attack of his fury.

21, 14: *Its forest:* probably the royal palace, built of cedar wood; cf 22, 14; in 1 Kgs 7, 2 the armory of Solomon's palace is called "the house of the forest of Lebanon."

22, 6: *Gilead . . . Lebanon:* both were known for their trees; cf v 7.

22, 10: *Him who is dead:* Josiah. His successor, Jehoahaz, *who is going away,* was deported by Pharaoh Neco to Egypt, where he died (2 Kgs 23, 33f).

22, 11: *Shallum:* Jehoahaz is called this only here. Presumably it was his name at birth, while Jehoahaz was his royal name.

21/4: 37, 8ff.   22/2: 17, 20.
     5: Is 63, 10; Lam 2, 4f.   3: 21, 12; Ex 22, 21-24;
     6: 16, 4.   Dt 24, 17.
     7: 24, 8ff; Dt 28, 49f.   7: 21, 14.
     8: 21, 9; Dt 30, 15.19.   8: Dt 29, 24ff.
    12: 4, 4; 22, 3; Zec 7, 9.   9: Jer 19, 4; 40, 2f.
    14: 2 Kgs 25, 9;   10: 2 Chr 35, 23ff.
       2 Chr 36, 19.

Jehoiakim

13*† Woe to him who builds his house on
wrong,
his terraces on injustice;
Who works his neighbor without pay,
and gives him no wages.

14 Who says, "I will build myself a spacious
house,
with airy rooms,"
Who cuts out windows for it,
panels it with cedar,
and paints it with vermillion.

15*† Must you prove your rank among kings
by competing with them in cedar?
Did not your father eat and drink?
He did what was right and just,
and it went well with him.

16* Because he dispensed justice to the
weak and the poor,
it went well with him.
Is this not true knowledge of me?
says the LORD.

17* But your eyes and heart are set on
nothing
except on your own gain,
On shedding innocent blood,
on practicing oppression and
extortion.

18*†Therefore, thus says the LORD concerning
Jehoiakim, son of Josiah, king of Judah:

They shall not lament him,
"Alas! my brother"; "Alas! sister."
They shall not lament him,
"Alas, Lord! alas, Majesty!"

19*† The burial of an ass shall he be given,
dragged forth and cast out
beyond the gates of Jerusalem.

Jeconiah

20*† Scale Lebanon and cry out,
in Bashan lift up your voice;
Cry out from Abarim,
for all your lovers are crushed.

21 I spoke to you when you were secure,
but you answered, "I will not listen."
This has been your way from your
youth,
not to listen to my voice.

22 The wind shall shepherd all your
shepherds,
your lovers shall go into exile.

Surely then you shall be ashamed and
confounded
because of all your wickedness.

23 You who dwell in Lebanon,
who nest in the cedars,
How you shall groan when pains come
upon you,
like the pangs of a woman in travail!

24†As I live, says the LORD, if you, Coniah, son of Jehoiakim, king of Judah, are a signet ring on my right hand, I will snatch you from it. 25*I will deliver you into the hands of those who seek your life; the hands of those whom you fear; the hands of Nebuchadnezzar, king of Babylon, and the Chaldeans. 26*†I will cast you out, you and the mother who bore you, into a different land from the one you were born in; and there you shall die. 27*Neither of them shall come back to the land for which they yearn.

28 Is this man Coniah a vessel despised, to
be broken up,
an instrument that no one wants?
Why are he and his descendants cast
out,
why thrown into a land they know
not?

29 O land, land, land,
hear the word of the LORD—

---

† 22, 13: *Without pay:* either by forced labor in public works, or inasmuch as workers were defrauded of their hire. Despite the impoverishment caused in Judah by the payment of foreign tribute, Jehoiakim embarked on a program of lavish building in Jerusalem (v 14). Social injustice is the cause of much of the prophetic condemnation of the kings (v 17).

22, 15f: Josiah, the reforming king, prospered materially without oppressing his people; he embodied all the ideals of kingship.

22, 18: *"Alas! my brother"; "Alas! sister":* customary cries of mourning.

22, 19: *The burial of an ass:* no burial at all, except to be cast outside the city as refuse. This prophecy regards the popular feeling toward Jehoiakim rather than the actual circumstances of his burial. According to 2 Kgs 24, 5 he was buried with his fathers in Jerusalem. However, his grave may have been profaned by Nebuchadnezzar.

22, 20-23: The prophet first apostrophizes Jerusalem, which is bidden to scale *Lebanon, Bashan,* and *Abarim,* i.e., the highest surrounding mountains to the north, northeast, and southeast, to gaze on the ruin of its *lovers, i.e.,* the false leaders of Judah, called its *shepherds* (22); cf 2, 8. The year is 597 B. C., after Nebuchadnezzar's deportation of Jehoiachin. Jerusalem still stands (23), apparently as secure as the heights of Lebanon, but destruction is to follow (cf v 6).

22, 24: *Coniah:* a shortened form of Jeconiah, the name which Jeremiah gives the king called elsewhere in the Bible Jehoiachin. *A signet ring:* the seal used by important men—in a sense, their most valuable possession—mounted in a ring worn constantly on the hand. The Lord says that even were Jehoiachin such a precious possession, he would reject him. The words in vv 24-30 date from the short three-month reign of Jehoiachin, before he was carried away by Nebuchadnezzar.

22, 26: *You and the mother who bore you:* the queen mother held a special position in the monarchy of Judah, and in the Books of Kings she is invariably mentioned by name along with the king (1 Kgs 15, 2; 2 Kgs 18, 2). Jehoiachin did indeed die in Babylon.

✷
13: Lv 19, 13; Dt 24, 14;
Hb 2, 9.12.
15: 2 Kgs 23, 25.
16: Prv 31, 9.
17: Ez 22, 13.27.
18: 16, 4ff; 1 Kgs 13, 30.
19: 36, 30.
20: 30, 14f; Dt 32, 49.
25: 21, 7; 34, 20.
26: 2 Kgs 24, 15.
27: 44, 14.

30*† Thus says the LORD:
Write this man down as one childless,
who will never thrive in his lifetime!
No descendant of his shall achieve
a seat on the throne of David
as ruler again over Judah.

Messianic Reign

23 **1*†**WOE to the shepherds who mislead and scatter the flock of my pasture, says the LORD. **2***Therefore, thus says the LORD, the God of Israel, against the shepherds who shepherd my people: You have scattered my sheep and driven them away. You have not cared for them, but I will take care to punish your evil deeds. **3***I myself will gather the remnant of my flock from all the lands to which I have driven them and bring them back to their meadow; there they shall increase and multiply. **4***I will appoint shepherds for them who will shepherd them so that they need no longer fear and tremble; and none shall be missing, says the LORD.

5* Behold, the days are coming, says the
LORD,
when I will raise up a righteous shoot
to David;
As king he shall reign and govern wisely,
he shall do what is just and right in
the land.
6* In his days Judah shall be saved,
Israel shall dwell in security.
This is the name they give him:
"The LORD our justice."

7*Therefore, the days will come, says the LORD, when they shall no longer say, "As the LORD lives, who brought the Israelites out of the land of Egypt"; **8**but rather, "As the LORD lives, who brought the descendants of the house of Israel up from the land of the north"—and from all the lands to which I banished them; they shall again live on their own land.

The False Prophets

9† Concerning the prophets:
My heart within me is broken,
my bones all tremble;
I am like a man who is drunk,
overcome by wine,
Because of the LORD,
because of his holy words.
10* With adulterers the land is filled;
on their account the land mourns,
the pasture ranges are seared.

Theirs is an evil course,
theirs is unjust power.
11* Both prophet and priest are godless!
In my very house I find their
wickedness,
says the LORD.
12* Hence their way shall become for them
slippery ground.
In the darkness they shall lose their
footing,
and fall headlong;
Evil I will bring upon them:
the year of their punishment, says the
LORD.
13* Among Samaria's prophets
I saw unseemly deeds:
They prophesied by Baal
and led my people Israel astray.
14* But among Jerusalem's prophets
I saw deeds still more shocking:
Adultery, living in lies,
siding with the wicked,
so that no one turns from evil;
To me they are all like Sodom,
its citizens like Gomorrah.

15* Therefore, thus says the LORD of hosts
against the prophets:
Behold, I will give them wormwood to
eat,
and poison to drink;
For from Jerusalem's prophets
ungodliness has gone forth into the
whole land.

16* Thus says the LORD of hosts:
Listen not to the words of your
prophets,
who fill you with emptiness;
Visions of their own fancy they speak,
not from the mouth of the LORD.

---

† 22, 30: *Childless:* Jehoiachin is so considered because none of his descendants will be king. From the Book of Ezekiel, who dates his oracles according to Jehoiachin's fictitious regnal years, it is evident that the people expected Jehoiachin to return. The above prophecy of Jeremiah was uttered to dispel this hope (28, 4). Of the seven sons born to Jehoiachin in exile, none became king. His grandson Zerubbabel presided for a time over the Jewish community after the return from exile, but not as king.

23, 1-8: With the false rulers who have governed his people the Lord contrasts himself, the good shepherd, who will in the times of restoration appoint worthy rulers (1-4). A messianic King will arise from the line of David who will rule over Judah and Israel with the justice of the Lord, fulfilling all the kingly ideals (5f). *"The Lord our justice"* is probably an ironic word-play on the name of the weak King Zedekiah ("The Lord is justice"); the messianic King will be in reality what Zedekiah's name falsely proclaims him. The final verses, 7-8, were probably added during the exile.

23, 9-40: After the collection of oracles against the kings, the editor of the book placed this collection of oracles against the false prophets. With them are associated the priests, for both

✱
30: 36, 30; 1 Chr 3, 16f;
　　Mt 1, 12.
23/1: 22, 22.
2: Ez 34, 4ff; Zec 11, 16f.
3: 29, 14; 32, 37.
4: 3, 15; Ez 34, 11f.
5: 33, 14ff; Is 4, 2; 9, 5f;
　　11, 1-5.
6: Dn 9, 24.
7f: 16, 14f.
10: 4, 22; 5, 7f; 9, 2, 10.
11: 6, 13.
12: Ps 35, 6.
13: 1 Kgs 18, 19.
14: 29, 21ff; Is 1, 9f.
15: 8, 14; 9, 14.
16: 14, 14.

17† They say to those who despise the word
of the Lord,
"Peace shall be yours";
And to everyone who walks in hardness
of heart,
"No evil shall overtake you."
18 Now, who has stood in the council of
the Lord,
to see him and to hear his word?
Who has heeded his word, so as to
announce it?
19 See, the storm of the Lord!
His wrath breaks forth
In a whirling storm
that bursts upon the heads of the
wicked.
20 The anger of the Lord shall not abate
until he has done and fulfilled
what he has determined in his heart.
When the time comes,
you shall fully understand.
21 I did not send these prophets,
yet they ran;
I did not speak to them,
yet they prophesied.
22 Had they stood in my council,
and did they but proclaim to my
people my words,
They would have brought them back
from evil ways
and from their wicked deeds.
23† Am I a God near at hand only, says the
Lord,
and not a God far off?
24 Can a man hide in secret
without my seeing him? says the Lord.
Do I not fill
both heaven and earth? says the Lord.

25I have heard the prophets who prophesy lies in my
name say, "I had a dream! I had a dream!" **26**How long
will this continue? Is my name in the hearts of the
prophets who prophesy lies and their own deceitful
fancies? **27**By their dreams which they recount to
each other, they think to make my people forget my
name, just as their fathers forgot my name for Baal.
28†Let the prophet who has a dream recount his
dream; let him who has my word speak my word
truthfully!

What has straw to do with the wheat?
says the Lord.
29 Is not my word like fire, says the Lord,
like a hammer shattering rocks?

30Therefore I am against the prophets, says the
Lord, who steal my words from each other. **31**Yes, I am
against the prophets, says the Lord, who borrow
speeches to pronounce oracles. **32**Yes, I am against
the prophets who prophesy lying dreams, says the
Lord, and who lead my people astray by recounting
their lies and by their empty boasting. From me they
have no mission or command, and they do this people
no good at all, says the Lord.

33†And when this people, or a prophet or a priest
asks you, "What is the burden of the Lord?" you shall
answer, "You are the burden, and I cast you off, says
the Lord." **34**If a prophet or a priest or anyone else
mentions "the burden of the Lord," I will punish that
man and his house. **35**Thus you shall ask, when speaking to one another, "What answer did the Lord give?"
or, "What did the Lord say?" **36**But the burden of the
Lord you shall mention no more. For each man his
own word becomes the burden so that you pervert the
words of the living God, the Lord of hosts, our God.
37Thus shall you ask the prophet, "What answer did
the Lord give?" or, "What did the Lord say?" **38**But if
you ask about "the burden of the Lord," then thus says
the Lord: Because you use this phrase, "the burden of
the Lord," though I forbade you to use it, **39**therefore
I will lift you on high and cast you from my presence,
you and the city which I gave to you and your fathers.
40And I will bring upon you eternal reproach, eternal,
unforgettable shame.

The Two Baskets of Figs

24 **1**†the Lord showed me two baskets of figs
placed before the temple of the Lord.—This
was after Nebuchadnezzar, king of Babylon, had exiled from Jerusalem Jeconiah, son of Jehoiakim, king
of Judah, and the princes of Judah, the artisans and
the skilled workers, and brought them to Babylon.
—**2**One basket contained excellent figs, the early-
ripening kind. But the other basket contained very bad
figs, so bad they could not be eaten. **3**Then the Lord

---

† have betrayed their trust as instructors in the religion of the
Lord; cf 2, 8; 4, 9; 6, 13f.

23, 17-20. Not only are the false prophets personally immoral, but they encourage immorality by prophesying good of
those who do evil. The true prophet, on the other hand, sees the
inevitable consequences of sin.

23, 23: *Near at hand only . . . far off:* God knows not merely
the present but also the future.

23, 28f: *Straw . . . wheat:* such is the contrast between false
and true prophecy. True prophecy is like fire (cf 5, 14; 20, 9),
producing violent results (v 29); Jeremiah's own life is a testimony of this.

23, 33-40: A wordplay on *maśśā'*, which means both oracle
(usually of woe) and burden. In 34ff it appears that the word
maśśā' itself is forbidden the people in the meaning of a divine
oracle. Doubtless this was because of some association unknown
to us. In Hos 2, 18 it is forbidden to call God "Baal" ("master"),
because of the association of this title with the Canaanite god.

24, 1-10: Jeremiah, like Ezekiel, saw that no good could be
expected from the people who had been left in Judah under
Zedekiah or who had fled into Egypt; good was to be hoped
for only from those who would pass through the purifying
experience of the exile to form the new Israel.

17: 5, 12; Ez 13, 10;
    Mi 3, 11; Zec 10, 2.
18: Jb 15, 8; Is 40, 13;
    1 Cor 2, 16.
19: 30, 23.
21: 29, 9.
23: 16, 17; Ps 139, 8.

27: Jgs 3, 7; 8, 33.
28: Nm 12, 6.
30: Dt 18, 20.
32: 28, 15ff.
40: 20, 11.
24/1: Am 8, 1f.
   3: 1, 11.

said to me: What do you see, Jeremiah? "Figs," I replied; "the good ones are very good, but the bad ones very bad, so bad they cannot be eaten." **⁴**Thereupon this word of the LORD came to me: **⁵***Thus says the LORD, the God of Israel: Like these good figs, even so will I regard with favor Judah's exiles whom I sent away from this place into the land of the Chaldeans. **⁶***I will look after them for their good, and bring them back to this land, to build them up, not to tear them down; to plant them, not to pluck them out. **⁷***I will give them a heart with which to understand that I am the LORD. They shall be my people and I will be their God, for they shall return to me with their whole heart. **⁸***And like the figs that are bad, so bad they cannot be eaten—yes, thus says the LORD—even so will I treat Zedekiah, king of Judah, and his princes, the remnant of Jerusalem remaining in this land and those who have settled in the land of Egypt. **⁹***I will make them an object of horror to all the kingdoms of the earth, a reproach and a byword, a taunt and a curse, in all the places to which I will drive them. **¹⁰***I will send upon them the sword, famine, and pestilence, until they have disappeared from the land which I gave them and their fathers.

Seventy Years of Exile

25 **¹*†**THE word that came to Jeremiah concerning all the people of Judah, in the fourth year of Jehoiakim, son of Josiah, king of Judah (the first year of Nebuchadnezzar, king of Babylon). **²**This word the prophet Jeremiah spoke to all the people of Judah and all the citizens of Jerusalem: **³***Since the thirteenth year of Josiah, son of Amon, king of Judah, to this day—these three and twenty years—the word of the LORD has come to me and I spoke to you untiringly, but you would not listen. **⁴***Though you refused to listen or pay heed, the LORD has sent you without fail all his servants the prophets **⁵**with this message: Turn back, each of you, from your evil way and from your evil deeds; then you shall remain in the land which the LORD gave you and your fathers, from of old and forever. **⁶***Do not follow strange gods to serve and adore them, lest you provoke me with your handiwork, and I bring evil upon you. **⁷***But you would not listen to me, says the LORD, and so you provoked me with your handiwork to your own harm. **⁸**Hence, thus says the LORD of hosts: Since you would not listen to my words, **⁹***lo! I will send for and fetch all the tribes of the north, says the LORD (and I will send to Nebuchadnezzar, king of Babylon, my servant); I will bring them against this land, against its inhabitants, and against all these neighboring nations. I will doom them, making them an object of horror, of ridicule, of everlasting reproach. **¹⁰**Among them I will bring to an end the song of joy and the song of gladness, the voice of the bridegroom and the voice of the bride, the sound of the millstone and the light of the lamp. **¹¹***This whole land shall be a ruin and a desert. Seventy years these nations shall be enslaved to the king of Babylon; **¹²***but when the seventy years have elapsed, I· will punish the king of Babylon and the nation and the land of the Chaldeans for their guilt, says the LORD. Their land I will turn into everlasting desert. **¹³**Against that land I will fulfill all the words I have spoken against it [all that is written in this book, which Jeremiah prophesied against all the nations]. **¹⁴***They also shall be enslaved to great nations and mighty kings, and thus I will repay them according to their own deeds and according to their own handiwork.

The Cup of Judgment on the Nations

¹⁵*†For thus said the LORD, the God of Israel, to me: Take this cup of foaming wine from my hand, and have all the nations to whom I will send you drink it. **¹⁶***They shall drink, and be convulsed, and go mad, because of the sword I will send among them. **¹⁷**I took the cup from the hand of the LORD and gave drink to all the nations to which the LORD sent me: **¹⁸**[Jerusalem, the cities of Judah, her kings and her princes, to make them a ruin and a desert, an object of ridicule and cursing, as they are today;] **¹⁹**Pharaoh, king of Egypt, and his servants, his princes, all the people under him, native **²⁰†**and foreign; all the kings of the land of Uz; all the kings of the land of the Philistines: Ashkelon, Gaza, Ekron, and the remnant of Ashdod; **²¹**Edom, Moab, and the Ammonites; **²²†**all the kings of Tyre, of Sidon, and of the shores beyond the sea; **²³†**Dedan and Tema and Buz, all the desert dwellers who shave their temples; **²⁴**[all the kings of Arabia;] **²⁵**all the kings of Zimri, of Elam, of the Medes; **²⁶†**all the kings of the north, near and far, one after the other; all the kingdoms upon the face of the earth [and after them the king of Sheshach shall drink].

25, 1-14: *The fourth year of Jehoiakim:* 605 B.C. Officially, *the first year of Nebuchadnezzar* began the following year; but as early as his victory over Egypt at Carchemish in 605, Nebuchadnezzar was the dominant power in the Near East, in whom Jeremiah now saw the fulfillment of his prophecy of the enemy to come from the north (cf 1, 13; 6, 22ff). In vv 11f occurs for the first time the prophecy of the seventy years' exile; cf 29, 10. This Jeremiah intends as a round number, to signify that the present generation must die out.

25, 15ff: Jeremiah is a prophet to the nations (cf 1, 5) as well as to his own people. All the nations mentioned here appear again in the more extensive collection of Jeremiah's oracles against the nations in chapters 46-51.

25, 20: *Uz:* the homeland of Job, in Edomite or Arabian territory.

25, 22: *The shores beyond the sea:* Phoenician commercial colonies planted throughout the Mediterranean world.

25, 23: *Dedan and Tema and Buz:* North Arabian tribes.

25, 26: *Sheshach:* Babylon. The word is formed from *bābēl* by substituting letters of the Hebrew alphabet in inverse order.

5: 29, 11; Lv 26, 44f.
6: 12, 15; Am 9, 15.
7: 30, 22; 31, 1; 32, 37; Bar 2, 31.
8: 29, 18.
9: 15, 4; Dt 28, 37.
10: 14, 12.
25/1: 36, 1.
3: 1, 2.
4: 2 Chr 36, 15.

6: 7, 6f.
7: 7, 17ff.
9: 1, 15; 43, 10.
11: Lv 26, 32-35.
12: Is 13, 20ff.
14: 27, 7; 50, 9.41f; 51, 6.24.
15: Rv 14, 10.
16: 51, 7.

27*Tell them: Thus says the LORD of hosts, the God of Israel: Drink! become drunk and vomit; fall, never to rise, before the sword that I will send among you! **28***If they refuse to take the cup from your hand and drink, say to them: Thus says the LORD of hosts: You must drink! **29**For since with this city, which is called by my name, I begin to inflict evil, how can you possibly be spared? You shall not be spared! I will call down the sword upon all who inhabit the earth, says the LORD of hosts.

30*Prophesy against them all these things and say to them:

> The LORD roars from on high,
>> from his holy dwelling he raises his voice;
> Mightily he roars over the range,
>> a shout like that of vintagers over the grapes.
> **31** To all who inhabit the earth to its very ends
>> the uproar spreads;
> For the LORD has an indictment against the nations,
>> he is to pass judgment upon all mankind:
> The godless shall be given to the sword,
>> says the LORD.
> **32**   Thus says the LORD of hosts:
> Lo! calamity stalks
>> from nation to nation;
> A great storm is unleashed
>> from the ends of the earth.

33*On that day, those whom the LORD has slain will be strewn from one end of the earth to the other. None will mourn them, none will gather them for burial; they shall lie like dung on the field.

> **34**   Howl, you shepherds, and wail!
>> roll in the dust, leaders of the flock!
> The time for your slaughter has come;
>> like choice rams you shall fall.
> **35*** There is no flight for the shepherds,
>> no escape for the leaders of the flock.
> **36** Listen! Wailing from the shepherds,
>> howling by the leaders of the flock!
> For the LORD lays waste their grazing place,
> **37**   desolate lie the peaceful pastures;
> **38*** The lion leaves his lair,
>> and their land is made desolate
> By the sweeping sword,
>> by the burning wrath of the LORD.

Jeremiah Threatened with Death

26 **1**†IN the beginning of the reign of Jehoiakim, son of Josiah, king of Judah, this message came from the LORD: **2***Thus says the LORD: Stand in the court of the house of the LORD and speak to the people of all the cities of Judah who come to worship in the house of the LORD; whatever I command you, tell them, and omit nothing. **3***Perhaps they will listen and turn back, each from his evil way, so that I may repent of the evil I have planned to inflict upon them for their evil deeds. **4**Say to them: Thus says the LORD: If you disobey me, not living according to the law I placed before you **5***and not listening to the words of my servants the prophets, whom I send you constantly though you do not obey them, **6***I will treat this house like Shiloh, and make this the city which all the nations of the earth shall refer to when cursing another.

7Now the priests, the prophets, and all the people heard Jeremiah speak these words in the house of the LORD. **8**When Jeremiah finished speaking all that the LORD bade him speak to all the people, the priests and prophets laid hold of him, crying, "You must be put to death! **9**Why do you prophesy in the name of the LORD: 'This house shall be like Shiloh,' and 'This city shall be desolate and deserted'?" And all the people gathered about Jeremiah in the house of the LORD.

10When the princes of Judah were informed of these things, they came up from the king's palace to the house of the LORD and held court at the New Gate of the house of the LORD. **11***The priests and prophets said to the princes and to all the people, "This man deserves death; he has prophesied against this city, as you have heard with your own ears." **12**Jeremiah gave this answer to the princes and all the people: "It was the LORD who sent me to prophesy against this house and city all that you have heard. **13***Now, therefore, reform your ways and your deeds; listen to the voice of the LORD your God, so that the LORD will repent of the evil with which he threatens you. **14**As for me, I am in your hands; do with me what you think good and right. **15**But mark well: if you put me to death, it is innocent blood you bring on yourselves, on this city and its citizens. For in truth it was the LORD who sent me to you, to speak all these things for you to hear."

16Thereupon the princes and all the people said to the priests and the prophets, "This man does not deserve death; it is in the name of the LORD, our God, that he speaks to us." **17**At this, some of the elders of the land came forward and said to all the people assembled, **18***†"Micah of Moresheth used to prophesy in the days of Hezekiah, king of Judah, and he told all the people of Judah: Thus says the LORD of hosts:

✿
     27: Ob 1, 16.   3: 18, 3.
     28: 49, 12.   5: 25, 4.
     30: 51, 14.   6: 7, 12.14.
     33: 8, 2; 16, 4.6.   11: 38, 4.
     35: 32, 4.   13: 7, 3.
     38: 4, 7.   18: Mi 1, 1; 3, 12.
     26/2: 7, 2.

---

†

26, 1: *The beginning of the reign:* a technical expression for the time between a king's accession to the throne and the beginning of his first official (calendar) year as king. Jehoiakim's first regnal year was 608 B. C.

26, 18: *Micah of Moresheth:* the prophet Micah, who appears among the canonical minor prophets (cf Mi 1, 1).

> Zion shall become a plowed field,
> Jerusalem a heap of ruins,
> and the temple mount a forest ridge.

19*Did Hezekiah, king of Judah, and all Judah condemn him to death? Did they not rather fear the Lord and entreat the favor of the Lord, so that he repented of the evil with which he had threatened them? But we are on the point of committing this great evil to our own undoing."

The Fate of Uriah

20There was another man who prophesied in the name of the Lord, Uriah, son of Shemaiah, from Kiriath-jearim; he prophesied the same things against this city and land as Jeremiah did. **21**When King Jehoiakim and all his officers and princes were informed of his words, the king sought to kill him. But Uriah heard of it and fled in fear to Egypt. **22**Thereupon King Jehoiakim sent Elnathan, son of Achbor, and others with him into Egypt **23**to bring Uriah back to the king, who had him slain by the sword and his corpse cast into the common grave. **24**†But Ahikam, son of Shaphan, protected Jeremiah, so that he was not handed over to the people to be put to death.

Serve Babylon or Perish

27 **1**†[In the beginning of the reign of Jehoiakim, son of Josiah, king of Judah,] . . . this message came to Jeremiah from the Lord: **2**Thus said the Lord to me: Make for yourself bands and yoke bars and put them over your shoulders. **3**Send to the kings of Edom, of Moab, of the Ammonites, of Tyre, and of Sidon, through the ambassadors who have come to Jerusalem to Zedekiah, king of Judah, **4**and charge them thus: Tell your masters: Thus says the Lord of hosts, the God of Israel: **5***It was I who made the earth, and man and beast on the face of the earth, by my great power, with my outstretched arm; and I can give them to whomever I think fit. **6***Now I have given all these lands into the hand of Nebuchadnezzar, king of Babylon, my servant; even the beasts of the field I have given him for his use. **7***All nations shall serve him and his son and his grandson, until the time of his land, too, shall come. Then it in turn shall serve great nations and mighty kings. **8***Meanwhile, if any nation or kingdom will not serve Nebuchadnezzar, king of Babylon, or will not bend its neck under the yoke of the king of Babylon, I will punish that nation with sword, famine, and pestilence, says the Lord, until I give them into his hand.

9*†You, however, must not listen to your prophets, to your diviners and dreamers, to your soothsayers and sorcerers, who say to you, "You need not serve the king of Babylon." **10***For they prophesy lies to you, in order to drive you far from your land, to make me banish you so that you will perish. **11***The people that submits its neck to the yoke of the king of Babylon to serve him I will leave in peace on its own land, says the Lord, to till it and dwell in it.

12*To Zedekiah, king of Judah, I spoke the same words: Submit your necks to the yoke of the king of Babylon; serve him and his people, so that you may live. **13***Why should you and your people die by sword, famine, and pestilence, with which the Lord has threatened the nation that will not serve the king of Babylon? **14***Do not listen to the words of those prophets who say, "You need not serve the king of Babylon," for they prophesy lies to you. **15***I did not send them, says the Lord, but they prophesy falsely in my name, with the result that I must banish you, and you will perish, you and the prophets who are prophesying to you.

16*To the priests and to all the people I spoke as follows: Thus says the Lord: Do not listen to the words of your prophets who prophesy to you: "The vessels of the house of the Lord will be brought back from Babylon soon now," for they prophesy lies to you. **17**Do not listen to them! Serve the king of Babylon that you may live; else this city will become a heap of ruins. **18**If they were prophets, if the word of the Lord were with them, they would intercede with the Lord of hosts, that the vessels which remain in the house of the Lord and in the palace of the king of Judah and in Jerusalem might not be taken to Babylon. **19**†For thus says the Lord of hosts concerning the pillars, the bronze sea, the stands, and the rest of the vessels that remain in this city, **20**which Nebuchadnezzar, king of Babylon, did not take when he exiled Jeconiah, son of Jehoiakim, king of Judah, from Jerusalem to Babylon, along with all the nobles of Judah and Jerusalem— **21***yes, thus says the Lord of hosts, the God of Israel, concerning the vessels that remain in the house of the Lord, in the palace of the king of Judah, and in Jerusalem: **22**To Babylon they shall be brought, and there they shall remain, until the day I look for them, says the Lord; then I will bring them back and restore them to this place.

---

†

26, 24: *Ahikam, son of Shaphan:* one of Josiah's officials (2 Kgs 22, 12) and father of Gedaliah, Jeremiah's friend, who was governor of Judah after Zedekiah's deportation (cf 39, 14; 40, 5ff).

27, 1–29, 32: A special collection of Jeremiah's prophecies dealing with false prophets. From stylistic peculiarities, quite evident in the Hebrew, it is plain that these three chapters once existed independently of the other prophecies of Jeremiah.

27, 1: [*In the beginning of the reign of Jehoiakim . . . Judah*]: this gloss cannot be correct because according to 28, 1 the time is the fourth year of Zedekiah, 594 B. C., the occasion of an embassy of the neighboring states (v 3), doubtless for the purpose of laying plans against Nebuchadnezzar.

27, 9: *Your prophets:* seers and diviners served the Gentile kings as the professional prophets served the kings of Judah.

27, 19-22: This prophecy was fulfilled after Zedekiah's disastrous defeat; cf 2 Kgs 25, 13ff.

✽
  19: 2 Chr 32, 26.
27/5: 32, 17.
  6: 25, 9; 43, 10;
    Ez 30, 21.25.
  7: 25, 11; 2 Chr 36, 20.
  8: 25, 9; Bar 2, 22.
  9: 29, 8.
  10: 14, 13-16.
  11: Bar 2, 21.

  12: 38, 17.
  13: 24, 8ff.
  14: 14, 14; 23, 21.
  15: 20, 6.
  16: 28, 3; 2 Chr 36,
    7.10.18.
21f: 2 Kgs 25, 13-17;
    2 Chr 36, 18.22.

The Two Yokes

28 [1]THAT same year, in [the beginning of] the reign of Zedekiah, king of Judah, in the fifth month of the fourth year, the prophet Hananiah, son of Azzur, from Gibeon, said to me in the house of the LORD in the presence of the priests and all the people: [2]"Thus says the LORD of hosts, the God of Israel: 'I will break the yoke of the king of Babylon. [3]Within two years I will restore to this place all the vessels of the temple of the LORD which Nebuchadnezzar, king of Babylon, took away from this place to Babylon. [4]And I will bring back to this place Jeconiah, son of Jehoiakim, king of Judah, and all the exiles of Judah who went to Babylon,' says the LORD, 'for I will break the yoke of the king of Babylon.'"

[5]The prophet Jeremiah answered the prophet Hananiah in the presence of the priests and all the people assembled in the house of the LORD, [6]and said: Amen! thus may the LORD do! May he fulfill the things you have prophesied by bringing the vessels of the house of the LORD and all the exiles back from Babylon to this place! [7]But now, listen to what I am about to state in your hearing and the hearing of all the people. [8]From of old, the prophets who were before you and me prophesied war, woe, and pestilence against many lands and mighty kingdoms. [9]*But the prophet who prophesies peace is recognized as truly sent by the LORD only when his prophetic prediction is fulfilled.

[10]Thereupon the prophet Hananiah took the yoke from the neck of the prophet Jeremiah, broke it, [11]and said in the presence of all the people: "Thus says the LORD: 'Even so, within two years I will break the yoke of Nebuchadnezzar, king of Babylon, from off the neck of all the nations.'" At that, the prophet Jeremiah went away.

[12]Some time after the prophet Hananiah had broken the yoke from off the neck of the prophet Jeremiah, the word of the LORD came to Jeremiah: [13]Go tell Hananiah this: Thus says the LORD: By breaking a wooden yoke, you forge an iron yoke! [14]*For thus says the LORD of hosts, the God of Israel: A yoke of iron I will place on the necks of all these nations serving Nebuchadnezzar, king of Babylon, and they shall serve him; even the beasts of the field I give him.

[15]To the prophet Hananiah the prophet Jeremiah said: Hear this, Hananiah! The LORD has not sent you, and you have raised false confidence in this people. [16]*For this, says the LORD, I will dispatch you from the face of the earth; this very year you shall die, because you have preached rebellion against the LORD. [17]That same year, in the seventh month, Hananiah the prophet died.

Letter to the Exiles in Babylon

29 [1]THIS is the contents of the letter which the prophet Jeremiah sent from Jerusalem to the remaining elders among the exiles, to the priests, the prophets, and all the people who were exiled by Nebuchadnezzar from Jerusalem to Babylon. [2]*This was after King Jeconiah and the queen mother, the courtiers, the princes of Judah and Jerusalem, the artisans and the skilled workmen had left Jerusalem. [3]†Delivered in Babylon by Elasah, son of Shaphan, and by Gemariah, son of Hilkiah, whom Zedekiah, king of Judah, sent to the king of Babylon, the letter read:

[4]Thus says the LORD of hosts, the God of Israel, to all the exiles whom I exiled from Jerusalem to Babylon: [5]Build houses to dwell in; plant gardens, and eat their fruits. [6]Take wives and beget sons and daughters; find wives for your sons and give your daughters husbands, so that they may bear sons and daughters. There you must increase in number, not decrease. [7]*Promote the welfare of the city to which I have exiled you; pray for it to the LORD, for upon its welfare depends your own.

[10]*Thus says the LORD: Only after seventy years have elapsed for Babylon will I visit you and fulfill for you my promise to bring you back to this place. [11]For I know well the plans I have in mind for you, says the LORD, plans for your welfare, not for woe! plans to give you a future full of hope. [12]*When you call me, when you go to pray to me, I will listen to you. [13]When you look for me, you will find me. Yes, when you seek me with all your heart, [14]*you will find me with you, says the LORD, and I will change your lot; I will gather you together from all the nations and all the places to which I have banished you, says the LORD, and bring you back to the place from which I have exiled you.

[16]Thus says the LORD concerning the king who sits on David's throne, and all the people who remain in this city, your brethren who did not go with you into exile; [17]thus says the LORD of hosts: I am sending against them sword, famine and pestilence. I will make them like rotten figs, too bad to be eaten. [18]*I will pursue them with sword, famine, and pestilence, and make them an object of horror to all the kingdoms of the earth, of malediction, astonishment, ridicule, and reproach to all the nations among which I will banish them. [19]*For they did not listen to my words, says the LORD, though I kept sending them my servants the prophets, only to have them go unheeded, says the LORD.

[20]You, now, listen to the word of the LORD, all you exiles whom I sent away from Jerusalem to Babylon. [15]As for your saying, "The LORD has raised up for us

---

° 28/9: Dt 18, 22.
    14: 27, 6f; Dt 28, 48.
    16: Dt 13, 6.
29/2: 2 Kgs 24, 15.
    7: 1 Tm 2, 1f.

10: 25, 11; 2 Chr 36, 21f;
    Ezr 1, 1; Dn 9, 2;
    Zec 1, 12; 7, 5.
12: 33, 3.
14: 23, 3.8.
18: 15, 4; 24, 9; 34, 17f.
19: 25, 4.

---

†
  29, 3: *Elasah:* possibly the brother of Ahikam (cf 26, 24). *Gemariah:* perhaps the son of the high priest Hilkiah; cf 2 Kgs 22, 4. Zedekiah had dispatched these men to Nebuchadnezzar for some other purpose, possibly the payment of tribute, but Jeremiah took advantage of their mission to send his letter by them.

prophets here in Babylon" —⁸*thus says the Lᴏʀᴅ of hosts, the God of Israel: Do not let yourselves be deceived by the prophets and diviners who are among you; do not listen to those among you who dream dreams. ⁹*For they prophesy lies to you in my name; I did not send them, says the Lᴏʀᴅ. ²¹*This is what the Lᴏʀᴅ of hosts, the God of Israel, has to say about those who prophesy lies to you in my name, Ahab, son of Kolaiah, and Zedekiah, son of Maaseiah: I am handing them over to Nebuchadnezzar, king of Babylon, who will slay them before your eyes. ²²All the exiles of Judah in Babylon will pattern a curse after them: "May the Lᴏʀᴅ make you like Zedekiah and Ahab, whom the king of Babylon roasted in the flames." ²³*For they are criminals in Israel, committing adultery with their neighbors' wives, and alleging in my name things I did not command. I know, I am witness, says the Lᴏʀᴅ.

The False Prophet Shemaiah

²⁴Say this to Shemaiah, the Nehelamite: ²⁵Thus says the Lᴏʀᴅ of hosts, the God of Israel: Because you sent letters on your own authority to all the people of Jerusalem, to all the priests and to Zephaniah, the priest, son of Maaseiah, with this message: ²⁶†"The Lᴏʀᴅ has appointed you priest in place of the priest Jehoiada, so that there may be police officers in the house of the Lᴏʀᴅ, to take action against all madmen and those who pose as prophets, by putting them into the stocks or the pillory. ²⁷Why, then, do you not rebuke Jeremiah of Anathoth who poses as a prophet among you? ²⁸For he sent us in Babylon this message: It will be a long time; build houses to live in; plant gardens and eat their fruits...."

²⁹When the priest Zephaniah read this letter to the prophet, ³⁰the word of the Lᴏʀᴅ came to Jeremiah: ³¹Send the message to all the exiles: Thus says the Lᴏʀᴅ concerning Shemaiah, the Nehelamite: Because Shemaiah prophesies to you without a mission from me, and raises false confidence, ³²says the Lᴏʀᴅ, I will therefore punish Shemaiah, the Nehelamite, and his offspring. None of them shall survive among this people to see the good I will do to this people, says the Lᴏʀᴅ, because he preached rebellion against the Lᴏʀᴅ.

The Restoration

30 ¹†ᴛʜᴇ following message came to Jeremiah from the Lᴏʀᴅ:

²*Thus says the Lᴏʀᴅ, the God of Israel: Write all the words I have spoken to you in a book. ³*For behold, the days will come, says the Lᴏʀᴅ, when I will change the lot of my people (of Israel and Judah, says the Lᴏʀᴅ), and bring them back to the land which I gave to their fathers; they shall have it as their possession.

⁴These are the words which the Lᴏʀᴅ spoke to Israel and to Judah: ⁵thus says the Lᴏʀᴅ:

> A cry of dismay we hear;
>   fear reigns, not peace.
> ⁶* Inquire, and see:
>   since when do men bear children?
> Why, then, do I see all these men,
>   with their hands on their loins
>   like women in childbirth?
> Why have all their faces turned
>   deathly pale?
> ⁷* How mighty is that day—
>   none like it!
> A time of distress for Jacob,
>   though he shall be saved from it.

⁸*On that day, says the Lᴏʀᴅ of hosts, "I will break his yoke from off your necks and snap your bonds." Strangers shall no longer enslave them; ⁹*†instead, they shall serve the Lᴏʀᴅ, their God, and David, their king, whom I will raise up for them.

> ¹⁰* But you, my servant Jacob, fear not, says
>   the Lᴏʀᴅ,
>   be not dismayed, O Israel!
> Behold, I will deliver you from the
>   far-off land,
>   your descendants, from their land of
>   exile;
> Jacob shall again find rest,
>   shall be tranquil and undisturbed,
> ¹¹* for I am with you, says the Lᴏʀᴅ, to
>   deliver you.
> I will make an end of all the nations
>   among which I have scattered you;
>   but of you I will not make an end.
> I will chastise you as you deserve,
>   I will not let you go unpunished.
> ¹²*   For thus says the Lᴏʀᴅ:
> Incurable is your wound,
>   grievous your bruise;

---

† 29, 26-29: The words of Jeremiah to the false prophet Shemaiah are not fully preserved in the current Hebrew text, as is seen in the incomplete sentence of this translation (vv 25-28). In his letter to Zephaniah Shemaiah reminds him of his authority, as Pashhur's successor, to imprison Jeremiah. Zephaniah, however, merely reads the letter to Jeremiah but does not imprison him.

30, 1—31, 40: These two chapters do not belong chronologically to those that precede or follow. They contain mainly oracles of salvation which Jeremiah originally uttered on behalf of the conquered remnants of the northern kingdom; then, after Judah began to share Samaria's fate, the oracles were extended to include Judah. Their composition is to be placed early in Jeremiah's ministry, probably after the fall of Nineveh (612 B. C.), when Josiah assumed power over the North; cf 2 Kgs 23, 15ff.

30, 9: David, their king: the messianic King of the Davidic line, often called David by the prophets; cf Ez 34, 23f; 37, 24f; Hos 3, 5.

---

*
8: 27, 9.14.
9: 5, 31.
21: 14, 14.
23: 23, 14.
30/2: 36, 2; Hb 2, 2;
    Rv 1, 11.
3: 29, 14; 31, 8.10.23;
    32, 37.44; Ez 39, 25;
    Am 9, 14.

6: 6, 24; 50, 43.
7: Am 5, 18; Zep 1, 14f.
8: Is 14, 5f; Ez 34, 27.
9: Ez 34, 23; 37, 24;
    Hos 3, 5; Lk 1, 69.
10: 46, 27; Is 43, 5.
11: 46, 28; Ez 11, 16f;
    Am 9, 8f.
12: 10, 19; 14, 17; 15, 18.

13 There is none to plead your cause,
no remedy for your running sore,
no healing for you.

14* All your lovers have forgotten you,
they do not seek you.
I struck you as an enemy would strike,
punished you cruelly;

15* Why cry out over your wound?
your pain is without relief.
Because of your great guilt,
your numerous sins,
I have done this to you.

16* Yet all who devour you shall be
devoured,
all your enemies shall go into exile.
All who plunder you shall be plundered,
all who pillage you I will hand over to
pillage.

17* For I will restore you to health;
of your wounds I will heal you, says
the Lord.
"The outcast" they have called you,
"with no avenger."

18* Thus says the Lord:
See! I will restore the tents of Jacob,
his dwellings I will pity;
City shall be rebuilt upon hill,
and palace restored as it was.

19* From them will resound songs of praise,
the laughter of happy men.
I will make them not few, but many;
they will not be tiny, for I will glorify
them.

20* His sons shall be as of old,
his assembly before me shall stand
firm;
I will punish all his oppressors.

21† His leader shall be one of his own,
and his rulers shall come from his kin.
When I summon him, he shall approach
me;
how else should one take the deadly
risk
of approaching me? says the Lord.

22* You shall be my people,
and I will be your God.

23* See, the storm of the Lord!
His wrath breaks forth

In a whirling storm
that bursts upon the heads of the
wicked.

24* The anger of the Lord will not abate
until he has done and fulfilled
what he has determined in his heart.
When the time comes,
you will fully understand.

Good News of the Return

31 1* At that time, says the Lord,
I will be the God of all the tribes of
Israel,
and they shall be my people.

2† Thus says the Lord:
The people that escaped the sword
have found favor in the desert.
As Israel comes forward to be given his
rest,

3* the Lord appears to him from afar:
With age-old love I have loved you;
so I have kept my mercy toward you.

4 Again I will restore you, and you shall be
rebuilt,
O virgin Israel;
Carrying your festive tambourines,
you shall go forth dancing with the
merrymakers.

5* Again you shall plant vineyards
on the mountains of Samaria;
those who plant them shall enjoy the
fruits.

6* Yes, a day will come when the
watchmen
will call out on Mount Ephraim:
"Rise up, let us go to Zion,
to the Lord, our God."

The Road of Return

7* For thus says the Lord:
Shout with joy for Jacob,
exult at the head of the nations;
proclaim your praise and say:
The Lord has delivered his people,
the remnant of Israel.

8* Behold, I will bring them back
from the land of the north;

14: 22, 22; Lam 1, 19.
15: 15, 18.
16: 2, 3.
17: 33, 6.
18: 33, 7.11; Ezr 6, 3-15;
    Ez 36, 10.
19: Is 35, 10; 51, 11.
20: Is 49, 26.
22: 24, 7; 31, 1.33; 32, 38;
    Lv 26, 12; Ez 11, 20;
    36, 28.

23: 23, 19.
24: 23, 20.
31/1: 30, 22.
  3: Dt 7, 8; 10, 15;
    Is 43, 4; 63, 9;
    Hos 11, 1.4.
  5: Is 65, 21; Am 9, 14.
  6: Is 2, 3; 27, 13; Mi 4, 2.
  7: Is 12, 6.
  8: 3, 18; 23, 3.8;
    Is 35, 5f.

---

† 30, 21: *His leader:* probably not the messianic King, but simply any one of the rulers of the restored Israel, who will no longer be foreigners, and with whom the Lord will be on terms of intimacy, as with the whole people. *The deadly risk of approaching me:* to approach God unsummoned brings death; cf Lv 16, 1f.

31, 2: *The people that escaped the sword:* the exiles who were not killed but deported; they *have found favor in the desert,* across which they were driven into captivity. The prophet alludes to the first desert wandering of Israel (Ex 16ff), in which the people found the Lord. *His rest:* the land of promise. The perfect fulfillment of this promised rest is found only in the New Testament (Heb., chapters 3 and 4).

I will gather them from the ends of the
    world,
      with the blind and the lame in their
      midst,
The mothers and those with child;
      they shall return as an immense
      throng.

9* They departed in tears,
      but I will console them and guide
      them;
I will lead them to brooks of water,
      on a level road, so that none shall
      stumble.
For I am a father to Israel,
      Ephraim is my first-born.

10 Hear the word of the LORD, O nations,
      proclaim it on distant coasts, and say:
He who scattered Israel, now gathers
      them together,
      he guards them as a shepherd his
      flock.

11* The LORD shall ransom Jacob,
      he shall redeem him from the hand of
      his conqueror.

12* Shouting, they shall mount the heights
      of Zion,
      they shall come streaming to the
      LORD's blessings:
The grain, the wine, and the oil,
      the sheep and the oxen;
They themselves shall be like watered
      gardens,
      never again shall they languish.

13 Then the virgins shall make merry and
      dance,
      and young men and old as well.
I will turn their mourning into joy,
      I will console and gladden them after
      their sorrows.

14 I will lavish choice portions upon the
      priests,
      and my people shall be filled with my
      blessings,
      says the LORD.

End of Rachel's Mourning

15*†   Thus says the LORD:
In Ramah is heard the sound of
      moaning,
      of bitter weeping!
Rachel mourns her children,
      she refuses to be consoled
      because her children are no more.

16   Thus says the LORD:
Cease your cries of mourning,
      wipe the tears from your eyes.

The sorrow you have shown shall have
      its reward,
      says the LORD,
      they shall return from the enemy's
      land.

17* There is hope for your future, says the
      LORD;
      Your sons shall return to their own
      borders.

18* I hear, I hear Ephraim pleading:
      You chastised me, and I am
      chastened;
      I was an untamed calf.
If you allow me, I will return,
      for you are the LORD, my God.

19* I turn in repentance;
      I have come to myself, I strike my
      breast;
I blush with shame,
      I bear the disgrace of my youth.

20* Is Ephraim not my favored son,
      the child in whom I delight?
Often as I threaten him,
      I still remember him with favor;
My heart stirs for him,
      I must show him mercy, says the LORD.

Summons to Return Home

21 Set up road markers,
      put up guideposts;
Turn your attention to the highway,
      the road by which you went.
Turn back, O virgin Israel,
      turn back to these your cities.

22† How long will you continue to stray,
      rebellious daughter?
The LORD has created a new thing upon
      the earth:
      the woman must encompass the man
      with devotion.

---

† 31, 15: *Ramah:* a village about five miles north of Jerusalem, where Rachel was buried (1 Sm 10, 2). *Rachel:* said to mourn for her children since she was the ancestress of Ephraim, the chief of the northern tribes. Mt 2, 18 applies this verse to the slaughter of the innocents by Herod.

31, 22: *The woman must encompass the man:* the words "with devotion," not in the Hebrew, are added for the sense. No fully satisfactory explanation has been given this text. Among the more probable are these: (a) Formerly the man (the Lord) encompassed the woman (Israel) with mercy and devotion; now in the spiritual religion of Israel which will follow on the restoration, this order will be reversed. (b) So secure will Israel be after the restoration that women will no longer need the natural protection of their husbands, but even weak women can protect men. (c) St. Jerome in his commentary on this verse understood it of Mary's virginal conception of Christ. "The Lord has created a new thing on earth; without seed of man, without carnal union and conception, 'a woman will encompass a man' within her womb—One who, though he will later appear to advance in wisdom and age through the stages of infancy and childhood, yet, while confined for the usual number of months in his mother's womb, will already be perfect man."

*   9: Ex 4, 22.   17: 29, 10-14.
11: Is 44, 23; 48, 20.   18: Lv 26, 40ff.
12: Is 58, 11.   19: Dt 30, 1ff.
15: Mt 2, 18.   20: Hos 11, 8.

²³* Thus says the LORD of hosts, the God of Israel: When I change their lot in the land of Judah and her cities, they shall again repeat this greeting: "May the LORD bless you, holy mountain, abode of justice!" **²⁴**Judah and all her cities, the farmers and those who lead the flock, shall dwell there together. **²⁵**For I will refresh the weary soul; every soul that languishes I will replenish. **²⁶**†Upon this I awoke and opened my eyes; but my sleep was sweet to me.

²⁷The days are coming, says the LORD, when I will seed the house of Israel and the house of Judah with the seed of man and the seed of beast. **²⁸***As I once watched over them to uproot and pull down, to destroy, to ruin, and to harm, so I will watch over them to build and to plant, says the LORD. **²⁹***†In those days they shall no longer say,

> "The fathers ate unripe grapes,
>   and the children's teeth are set on
>   edge,"

³⁰but through his own fault only shall anyone die: the teeth of him who eats the unripe grapes shall be set on edge.

The New Covenant

³¹*†The days are coming, says the LORD, when I will make a new covenant with the house of Israel and the house of Judah. **³²***It will not be like the covenant I made with their fathers the day I took them by the hand to lead them forth from the land of Egypt; for they broke my covenant, and I had to show myself their master, says the LORD. **³³***But this is the covenant which I will make with the house of Israel after those days, says the LORD. I will place my law within them, and write it upon their hearts; I will be their God, and they shall be my people. **³⁴***No longer will they have need to teach their friends and kinsmen how to know the LORD. All, from least to greatest, shall know me, says the LORD, for I will forgive their evildoing and remember their sin no more.

Certainty of God's Promise

³⁵*   Thus says the LORD,
    He who gives the sun to light the day,
       moon and stars to light the night;
    Who stirs up the sea till its waves roar,
       whose name is LORD of hosts:
³⁶*   If ever these natural laws give way
       in spite of me, says the LORD,
    Then shall the race of Israel cease
       as a nation before me forever.

³⁷   Thus says the LORD:
    If the heavens on high can be measured,
       or the foundations below the earth be
          sounded,
    Then will I cast off the whole race of
       Israel
    because of all they have done, says the
       LORD.

Rebuilding of Jerusalem

³⁸*†The days are coming, says the LORD, when the city shall be rebuilt as the LORD's, from the Tower of Hananel to the Corner Gate. **³⁹**The measuring line shall be stretched from there straight to the hill Gareb and then turn to Goah. **⁴⁰**†The whole valley of corpses and ashes, all the slopes toward the Kidron Valley, as far as the corner of the Horse Gate at the east, shall be holy to the LORD. Never again shall the city be rooted up or thrown down.

Pledge of Restoration

32 **¹**†THIS message came to Jeremiah from the LORD in the tenth year of Zedekiah, king of Judah, the eighteenth year of Nebuchadnezzar. **²***At that time the army of the king of Babylon was besieging Jerusalem, and the prophet Jeremiah was imprisoned in the quarters of the guard, at the king's palace. **³***Zedekiah, king of Judah, had imprisoned him there, remonstrating: "How dare you prophesy: Thus says the LORD: I am handing over this city to the king of Babylon, who will capture it. **⁴***Neither shall Zedekiah, king of Judah, escape the hands of the Chaldeans; rather shall he be handed over to the king of

---

† 31, 26: *I awoke . . . sweet to me:* probably said by the prophet himself.

31, 29: *"The fathers . . . on edge":* a proverb used in Israel, expressing the idea that children suffer for the sins of their parents (cf Ez 18, 2). The Israel of the restoration will be characterized instead by personal responsibility and retribution for one's acts (v 30; cf vv 31-34).

31, 31-34: The *new covenant* to be made with Israel is a common theme of the prophets, beginning with Hosea. According to Jeremiah, the qualities of the new covenant that make it different from the old are: (a) It will not be broken, but will last forever; (b) Its law will be written in the heart, not merely on tablets of stone; (c) The knowledge of God will be so generally shown forth in the life of the people that it will no longer be necessary to put it into words of instruction. In the fullest sense, this prophecy was fulfilled only through the work of Jesus Christ; cf Lk 22, 20; 1 Cor 11, 25.

31, 38: *From the Tower of Hananel to the Corner Gate:* from the northeast to the northwest.

31, 40: *Valley of corpses and ashes:* the Valley of Benhinnom, which joins the Kidron at the southeast of ancient Jerusalem. *The Horse Gate:* in the eastern city wall, at the southeast corner of the temple area.

32, 1: *The tenth year of Zedekiah:* 588 B. C. *The eighteenth year of Nebuchadnezzar,* dating his reign from his victory at Carchemish; see note on 25, 1-14.

32, 1-44: This chapter recounts a prophecy "in action." At the Lord's command, Jeremiah fulfills his family duty to purchase the land of his cousin, carrying out all the legal forms, including records, to testify that Judah will be restored and that the life of the past will be resumed.

✤

23: 30, 3; Ps 122, 8.
28: 1, 10; 18, 7.
29: Dt 24, 16; Ez 18, 2.
31: 32, 40; Heb 9, 15.
32: Ex 24, 7f; Dt 5, 2.
33: 32, 40; Ez 37, 26;
    Heb 10, 16.
34: Is 54, 13.
35: Gn 1, 14-18.

36: 33, 20f.
38: Neh 12, 38;
    Zec 14, 10f.
32/2: 33, 1; 37, 20; 38, 6;
    39, 14.
3: 26, 9; 34, 2; 37, 6-10.
4: 34, 3; 38, 18.23;
    39, 4-7.

Babylon. They shall meet and speak face to face, ⁵*and Zedekiah shall be taken to Babylon. There he shall remain, until I attend to him, says the LORD; in fighting the Chaldeans, you cannot win!"

⁶†This message came to me from the LORD, said Jeremiah: ⁷*†Hanamel, son of your uncle Shallum, will come to you with the offer: "Buy for yourself my field in Anathoth, since you, as nearest relative, have the first right of purchase." ⁸Then, as the LORD foretold, Hanamel, my uncle's son, came to me to the quarters of the guard and said, "Please buy my field in Anathoth, in the district of Benjamin; as nearest relative, you have the first claim to possess it; make it yours." I knew this was what the LORD meant, ⁹so I bought the field in Anathoth from my cousin Hanamel, paying him the money, seventeen silver shekels.

¹⁰When I had written and sealed the deed, called witnesses and weighed out the silver on the scales, ¹¹†I accepted the deed of purchase, both the sealed copy, containing title and conditions, and the open one. ¹²*This deed of purchase I gave to Baruch, son of Neriah, son of Mahseiah, in the presence of my cousin Hanamel and of the witnesses who had signed the deed, and before all the men of Judah who happened to be in the quarters of the guard.

¹³In their presence I gave Baruch this charge: ¹⁴†Thus says the LORD of hosts, the God of Israel: Take these deeds, both the sealed and the open deed of purchase, and put them in an earthen jar, so that they can be kept there a long time. ¹⁵For thus says the LORD of hosts, the God of Israel: Houses and fields and vineyards shall again be bought in this land.

¹⁶After giving the deed of purchase to Baruch, son of Neriah, I prayed thus to the LORD: ¹⁷*Ah, Lord GOD, you have made heaven and earth by your great might, with your outstretched arm; nothing is impossible to you. ¹⁸*You continue your kindness through a thousand generations; and you repay the fathers' guilt, even into the lap of their sons who follow them. O God, great and mighty, whose name is LORD of hosts, ¹⁹*great in counsel, mighty in deed, whose eyes are open to all the ways of men, giving to each according to his ways, according to the fruit of his deeds: ²⁰*you have wrought signs and wonders in the land of Egypt and to this day, both in Israel and among all other men, until now you have gained renown. ²¹With strong hand and outstretched arm you brought your people Israel out of the land of Egypt amid signs and wonders and great terror. ²²*This land you gave them, as you had promised their fathers under oath, a land flowing with milk and honey. ²³*They entered and

took possession of it, but they did not listen to your voice; by your law they did not live, and what you commanded they failed to do. Hence you let all these evils befall them. ²⁴*See, the siegeworks have arrived at this city to breach it; the city will be handed over to the Chaldeans who are attacking it, amid sword, famine, and pestilence. What you threatened has happened, you see it yourself; ²⁵and yet you tell me, O Lord GOD: Buy the field with money, call in witnesses. But the city has already been handed over to the Chaldeans!

²⁶Then this word of the LORD came to Jeremiah: ²⁷I am the LORD, the God of all mankind! Is anything impossible to me? ²⁸This now is what the LORD says: I will hand over this city to the Chaldeans, for Nebuchadnezzar, king of Babylon, to take. ²⁹*The Chaldeans who are attacking it shall enter this city and set fire to it, burning it and its houses, on the roofs of which incense was burned to Baal and libations were poured out to strange gods as a provocation to me. ³⁰*The Israelites and the Judeans from their youth have done only what is evil in my eyes; the Israelites did nothing but provoke me with the works of their hands, says the LORD. ³¹From the day it was built to this day, this city has excited my anger and wrath, ³²*so that I must put it out of my sight for all the wickedness the Israelites and Judeans, with their kings and their princes, their priests and their prophets, the men of Judah and the citizens of Jerusalem, have done to provoke me. ³³*They turned their backs to me, not their faces; though I kept teaching them, they would not listen to my correction. ³⁴*They defiled the house named after me by the horrid idols they set up in it. ³⁵*†They built high places to Baal in the Valley of Ben-hinnom, and immolated their sons and daughters to Molech, bringing sin upon Judah; this I never commanded them, nor did it even enter my mind that they should practice such abominations.

³⁶Now, therefore, thus says the LORD, the God of Israel, concerning this city, which as you say is handed over to the king of Babylon amid sword, famine, and pestilence: ³⁷*Behold, I will gather them together from all the lands to which in anger, wrath, and great

---

† 32, 6-9: Jeremiah's imprisonment by the weak-willed Zedekiah was a technical custody that did not deprive him of all freedom of action. The siege maintained by the Chaldeans (v 2) was only now beginning (v 24), and could be by-passed by individual persons going to and fro between Jerusalem and nearby Anathoth.

32, 7: *The first right of purchase:* the obligation of the closest relative to redeem the property of one in economic distress, so that the ancestral land might remain within the family (Lv 25, 25-28); see note on Ru 2, 20.

32, 11: *The sealed copy . . . and the open one:* the legal deed of sale was written on a scroll, which was then rolled up and sealed; about it was rolled another scroll, left unsealed, containing a copy or a summary of the first.

32, 14: *In an earthen jar:* the first of the Dead Sea Scrolls were found in such a jar.

32, 35: *Molech:* the god to whom human sacrifice was offered in the Valley of Ben-hinnom. Here, as in 19, 5, he is given the name *Baal;* see note on Lv 18, 21.

---

* 5: 39, 7; 52, 11.
7: Lv 25, 24-34; Ru 4, 4.
12: 36, 4.
17: 2 Kgs 19, 15; Jb 42, 2.
18: Ex 20, 5f; Dt 5, 9.
19: Jb 34, 21; Ps 33, 13ff.
20: Ex 6, 6; Dt 4, 34;
  Ps 135, 9.
22: 11, 5; Gn 15, 18;
  17, 8; 26, 3.
23: 7, 24ff; Dn 9, 10-14.
24: 21, 5; 33, 4.
29: 21, 10; 37, 8ff.
30: 3, 25; 44, 8.
32: 2, 26; Is 3, 8.
33: 7, 24.
34: 7, 30; 2 Kgs 21, 4f.
35: 7, 31; 19, 5;
  Ps 106, 37f.
37: 23, 3; 29, 14;
  Is 11, 12; Ez 11, 17.

rage I banish them; I will bring them back to this place and settle them here in safety. **38***They shall be my people, and I will be their God. **39**One heart and one way I will give them, that they may fear me always, to their own good and that of their children after them. **40***I will make with them an eternal covenant, never to cease doing good to them; into their hearts I will put the fear of me, that they may never depart from me. **41***I will take delight in doing good to them: I will replant them firmly in this land, with all my heart and soul.

42*For thus says the LORD: Just as I brought upon this people all this great evil, so I will bring upon them all the good I promise them. **43***Fields shall again be bought in this land, which you call a desert, without man or beast, handed over to the Chaldeans. **44***Fields shall be bought with money, deeds written and sealed, and witnesses shall be used in the land of Benjamin, in the suburbs of Jerusalem, in the cities of Judah and of the hill country, in the cities of the foothills and of the Negeb, when I change their lot, says the LORD.

Restoration of Jerusalem

33 **1**THE word of the LORD came to Jeremiah a second time while he was still imprisoned in the quarters of the guard: **2**Thus says the LORD who made the earth and gave it form and firmness, whose name is LORD: **3***Call to me, and I will answer you; I will tell to you things great beyond reach of your knowledge. **4***Thus says the LORD, the God of Israel, concerning the houses of this city and the palaces of Judah's kings, which are being destroyed in the face of siegeworks and the sword: **5***men come to battle the Chaldeans, and these houses will be filled with the corpses of those whom I slay in my anger and wrath, when I hide my face from this city for all their wickedness.

6*Behold, I will treat and assuage the city's wounds; I will heal them, and reveal to them an abundance of lasting peace. **7***I will change the lot of Judah and the lot of Israel, and rebuild them as of old. **8***I will cleanse them of all the guilt they incurred by sinning against me; all their offenses by which they sinned and rebelled against me, I will forgive. **9**Then Jerusalem shall be my joy, my praise, my glory, before all the nations of the earth, as they hear of all the good I will do among them. They shall be in fear and trembling over all the peaceful benefits I will give her.

10*Thus says the LORD: In this place of which you say, "How desolate it is, without man, without beast!" and in the cities of Judah, in the streets of Jerusalem

that are now deserted, without man, without citizen, without beast, there shall yet be heard **11***the cry of joy, the cry of gladness, the voice of the bridegroom, the voice of the bride, the sound of those who bring thank offerings to the house of the LORD, singing, "Give thanks to the LORD of hosts, for the LORD is good; his mercy endures forever." For I will restore this country as of old, says the LORD.

12Thus says the LORD of hosts: In this place, now desolate, without man or beast, and in all its cities there shall again be sheepfolds for the shepherds to couch their flocks. **13**In the cities of the hill country, of the foothills, and of the Negeb, in the land of Benjamin and the suburbs of Jerusalem, and in the cities of Judah, flocks will again pass under the hands of the one who counts them, says the LORD.

14†The days are coming, says the LORD, when I will fulfill the promise I made to the house of Israel and Judah. **15***In those days, in that time, I will raise up for David a just shoot; he shall do what is right and just in the land. **16**In those days Judah shall be safe and Jerusalem shall dwell secure; this is what they shall call her: "The LORD our justice." **17***For thus says the LORD: Never shall David lack a successor on the throne of the house of Israel, **18***nor shall priests of Levi ever be lacking, to offer holocausts before me, to burn cereal offerings, and to sacrifice victims.

19This word of the LORD also came to Jeremiah: Thus says the LORD: **20***If you can break my covenant with day, and my covenant with night, so that day and night no longer alternate in sequence, **21**then can my covenant with my servant David also be broken, so that he will not have a son to be king upon his throne, and my covenant with the priests of Levi who minister to me. **22**Like the host of heaven which cannot be numbered, and the sands of the sea which cannot be counted, I will multiply the descendants of my servant David and the Levites who minister to me.

23This word of the LORD came to Jeremiah: **24***Have you not noticed what these people are saying: "The LORD has rejected the two tribes which he had chosen"? They spurn my people as if it were no longer a nation in their eyes. **25***Thus says the LORD: When I have no covenant with day and night, and have given no laws to heaven and earth, **26**then too will I reject the descendants of Jacob and of my servant David, so as not to take from his descendants rulers for the race of Abraham, Isaac, and Jacob. For I will change their lot and show them mercy.

✿
38: 24, 7; 31, 33.	10: 32, 43.
40: 31, 31ff.	11: 1 Chr 16, 34;
41: Dt 30, 9.	Ezr 3, 11; Ps 136, 1.
42: 33, 10-14; Zec 8, 13.	15: 23, 5; Ps 72, 1-4.12ff;
43: 33, 10.	Is 11, 1.
44: 17, 26; 33, 7.	17: 2 Sm 7, 16; 1 Kgs 2, 4;
33/3: Is 48, 6.	Ps 89, 4f.29.36f.
4: 32, 24.	18: Ez 44, 15f.
5: 21, 4ff.	20f: 31, 36f; Ps 89, 37f.
6: Is 57, 18.	24: Rom 11, 1f.
7: 30, 3; 32, 44.	25f: 31, 36f; 32, 44.
8: Ez 36, 25.	

---

† 33, 14-26: This is the longest continuous passage in the Book of Jeremiah that is lacking in the Greek. It appears to be the postexilic composition of an inspired writer who used parts of the prophecies of Jeremiah—often, however, in a sense different from the prophet's. The prediction of an eternal Davidic dynasty (14-17) to fulfill the prophecy of Nathan (2 Sm 7, 11-16), and of a perpetual priesthood and sacrifice (18), was not to be realized in the restoration of the Jewish nation. It finds its fulfillment only in Jesus of Nazareth, who combined with his messianic Davidic kingship an eternal priesthood; cf Heb 6, 20; 7, 24f.

IV: FALL OF JERUSALEM

Fate of Zedekiah

34 **1**°THIS WORD CAME TO JEREMIAH from the LORD while Nebuchadnezzar, king of Babylon, and his armies and the earth's kingdoms subject to him, as well as the other peoples, were all attacking Jerusalem and all her cities: **2**°Thus says the LORD, the God of Israel: Go to Zedekiah, king of Judah, and tell him: Thus says the LORD: I am handing this city over to the king of Babylon; he will destroy it with fire. **3**°Neither shall you escape his hand; rather you will be captured and fall into his hands. You shall see the king of Babylon and speak to him face to face. Then you shall be taken to Babylon.

4But if you obey the word of the LORD, Zedekiah, king of Judah, then, says the LORD to you, you shall not die by the sword. **5**You shall die in peace, and they will lament you as their lord, and burn spices for your burial as they did for your fathers, the kings who preceded you from the first; it is I who make this promise, says the LORD.

6The prophet Jeremiah told all these things to Zedekiah, king of Judah, in Jerusalem, **7**†while the armies of the king of Babylon were attacking Jerusalem and the remaining cities of Judah, Lachish, and Azekah, since these alone were left of the fortified cities of Judah.

The Pact Broken

8†This is the word that came to Jeremiah from the LORD after King Zedekiah had made an agreement with all the people in Jerusalem to issue an edict of emancipation. **9**°Everyone was to free his Hebrew slaves, male and female, so that no one should hold a man of Judah, his brother, in slavery. **10**All the princes and the others who entered the agreement consented to set free their male and female servants, so that they should be slaves no longer. But though they agreed and freed them, **11**afterward they took back their male and female slaves whom they had set free and again forced them into service.

12Then this word of the LORD came to Jeremiah: **13**Thus says the LORD, the God of Israel: The day I brought your fathers out of the land of Egypt, out of the place where they were slaves, I made this covenant with them: **14**Every seventh year each of you shall set free his Hebrew brother who has sold himself to you; six years he shall serve you, but then you shall let him go free. Your fathers, however, did not heed me or obey me. **15**Today you indeed repented and did what is right in my eyes by proclaiming the emancipation of your brethren and making an agreement before me in the house that is named after me. **16**°But then you changed your mind and profaned my name by taking back your male and female slaves to whom you had given their freedom; you forced them once more into slavery. **17**Therefore, thus says the LORD: You did not obey me by proclaiming your neighbors and kinsmen free. I now proclaim you free, says the LORD, for the sword, famine, and pestilence. I will make you an object of horror to all the kingdoms of the earth. **18**†The men who violated my covenant and did not observe the terms of the agreement which they made before me, I will make like the calf which they cut in two, between whose two parts they passed. **19**The princes of Judah and of Jerusalem, the courtiers, the priests, and the common people, who passed between the parts of the calf, **20**°I will hand over, all of them, to their enemies, to those who seek their lives: their corpses shall be food for the birds of the air and the beasts of the field.

21°Zedekiah, too, king of Judah, and his princes, I will hand over to their enemies, to those who seek their lives, to the soldiers of the king of Babylon who have at present withdrawn from you. **22**°I will give the command, says the LORD, and bring them back to this city. They shall attack and capture it, and destroy it with fire; the cities of Judah I will turn into a desert where no man dwells.

The Faithful Rechabites

35 **1**THIS word came to Jeremiah from the LORD in the days of Jehoiakim, son of Josiah, king of Judah: **2**†Approach the Rechabites and speak to them; bring them into the house of the LORD, to one of the rooms, and give them wine to drink. **3**So I went

---

† 34, 7: *Lachish and Azekah:* fortress towns to the southwest of Jerusalem which Nebuchadnezzar besieged to prevent help coming to Jerusalem from Egypt. Between 1935 and 1938, archaeologists found at Lachish several letters written on pottery fragments which date from 598 or 588 B. C., and which mention both Lachish and Azekah.

34, 8-22: While the Chaldean siege of Jerusalem was in progress, the citizens of Jerusalem made a covenant at Zedekiah's instigation to free their brother Judeans who were in slavery. Doubtless this was both to provide additional free defenders for the city and to offer reparation for past violations of the law, according to which Hebrew slaves were to serve no longer than six years (Dt 15, 12-15). But when the siege was temporarily lifted, probably because of the help promised by Pharaoh Hophra (cf 37, 5), the inhabitants of Jerusalem broke the covenant and once more pressed their brethren into slavery (v 11).

34, 18f: As the Bible (Gn 15, 10-17) and also contemporary inscriptions make clear, agreements were sometimes ratified by walking between the divided pieces of animals while the contracting parties invoked on themselves a fate similar to that of the slaughtered beast if they should fail to keep their word. *The agreement:* that mentioned in vv 10.15.

35, 2: *The Rechabites:* reactionaries who believed that the Lord could not be well served except by maintaining the original nomadic conditions of Israel's life. Without sharing their convictions, the prophet holds up their fidelity to their ideals as an example to put to shame his faithless countrymen. *In the days of Jehoiakim:* probably in 599 or 598 B. C.

✿ 34/1: 52, 4; 2 Kgs 25, 1.
 2: 21, 10; 32, 3.28.
 3: 32, 4; 52, 11.
 9: Ex 21, 2ff;
   Lv 25, 39.46;
   Dt 15, 12-15.

16: Lv 19, 12.
20: 7, 33; 16, 4; 19, 7.
21: 37, 5.11.
22: 37, 8; 52, 7-13;
    2 Chr 36, 17.19.

and brought Jaazaniah, son of Jeremiah, son of Habazziniah, his brothers and all his sons, the whole company of the Rechabites, **4**†into the house of the LORD, to the room of the sons of Hanan, son of Igdaliah, the man of God, next to the princes' room, above the room of Maaseiah, son of Shallum, keeper of the doorway. **5**I set before these Rechabite men bowls full of wine and offered them cups to drink the wine.

6†"We do not drink wine," they said to me: "Jonadab, Rechab's son, our father, forbade us in these words: 'Neither you nor your children shall ever drink wine. **7**Build no house and sow no seed; neither plant nor own a vineyard. You shall dwell in tents all your life, so that you may live long on the earth where you are wayfarers.' **8**Now we have heeded Jonadab, Rechab's son, our father, in all his prohibitions. All our lives we have not drunk wine, neither we, nor our wives, nor our sons, nor our daughters. **9**We build no houses to live in; we own no vineyards or fields or crops, **10**and we live in tents; we obediently do everything our father Jonadab commanded us. **11**†But when Nebuchadnezzar, king of Babylon, invaded this land, we decided to come into Jerusalem to escape the army of the Chaldeans and the army of Aram; that is why we are now living in Jerusalem."

12Then this word of the LORD came to Jeremiah: **13***Thus says the LORD of hosts, the God of Israel: Go, say to the men of Judah and to the citizens of Jerusalem: Will you not take correction and obey my words? says the LORD. **14***The advice of Jonadab, Rechab's son, by which he forbade his children to drink wine, has been followed: to this day they have not drunk it; they obeyed their father's command. Me, however, you have not obeyed, although I spoke to you untiringly and insistently. **15***I kept sending you all my servants the prophets, telling you to turn back, all of you, from your evil way; to reform your conduct, and not follow strange gods or serve them, if you would remain on the land which I gave you and your fathers; but you did not heed me or obey me. **16**Yes, the children of Jonadab, Rechab's son, observed the command which their father laid on them; but this people does not obey me! **17***Now, therefore, says the LORD God of hosts, the God of Israel: I will bring upon Judah and all the citizens of Jerusalem every evil that I threatened; because when I spoke they did not obey, when I called they did not answer.

18But to the company of the Rechabites Jeremiah said: Thus says the LORD of hosts, the God of Israel: Since you have obeyed the command of Jonadab, your father, kept all his commands and done everything he commanded you, **19**thus therefore says the LORD of hosts, the God of Israel: Never shall there fail to be a descendant of Jonadab, Rechab's son, standing in my service.

Baruch Writes the Prophecies of Jeremiah

36 **1**IN the fourth year of Jehoiakim, son of Josiah, king of Judah, this word came to Jeremiah from the LORD: **2**Take a scroll and write on it all the words I have spoken to you against Israel, Judah, and all the nations, from the day I first spoke to you, in the days of Josiah, until today. **3***Perhaps, when the house of Judah hears all the evil I have in mind to do to them, they will turn back each from his evil way, so that I may forgive their wickedness and their sin. **4**So Jeremiah called Baruch, son of Neriah, who wrote down on a scroll, as Jeremiah dictated, all the words which the LORD had spoken to him.

9In the ninth month, in the fifth year of Jehoiakim, son of Josiah, king of Judah, a fast to placate the LORD was proclaimed for all the people of Jerusalem and all who came from Judah's cities to Jerusalem. **5**†Then Jeremiah charged Baruch: I cannot go to the house of the LORD; I am prevented from doing so. **6**Do you go on the fast day and read publicly in the LORD's house the LORD's words from the scroll you wrote at my dictation; read them also to all the men of Judah who come up from their cities. **7***Perhaps they will lay their supplication before the LORD and will all turn back from their evil way; for great is the fury of anger with which the LORD has threatened this people.

8Baruch, son of Neriah, did everything the prophet Jeremiah commanded; from the book-scroll he read the LORD's words in the LORD's house. **10**†It was in the room of Gemariah, son of the scribe Shaphan, in the upper court of the LORD's house, at the entrance of the New Temple-Gate, that Baruch publicly read the words of Jeremiah from his book.

11Now Micaiah, son of Gemariah, son of Shaphan, heard all the words of the LORD read from the book. **12**†So he went down to the king's palace, into the scribe's chamber, where the princes were just then in session: Elishama, the scribe, Delaiah, son of Shemaiah, Elnathan, son of Achbor, Gemariah, son of Shaphan, Zedekiah, son of Hananiah, and the other princes. **13**To them Micaiah reported all that he had heard Baruch read publicly from his book. **14**Thereupon the princes sent Jehudi, son of Nethaniah, son of Shelemiah, son of Cushi, to Baruch with the order:

---

†   35, 4: *The sons of Hanan:* probably the disciples of this *man of God* or prophet. *Maaseiah:* possibly the father of the priest Zephaniah (29, 25; 37, 3). *Keeper of the doorway:* a priestly function of responsibility; cf 52, 24.

35, 6: *Jonadab:* a contemporary of King Jehu; cf 2 Kgs 10, 15ff.

35, 11: *The army of Aram:* Nebuchadnezzar enlisted the help of Judah's foreign neighbors in his assault on Jerusalem.

36, 5: *I am prevented:* probably because of his temple sermon (7, 1-15), or because of temporary ritual uncleanness.

36, 10: *Gemariah:* member of a family friendly to Jeremiah, which had rights to a room in the fortress of the temple gateway overlooking the court of the temple; from a window in this room Baruch read Jeremiah's prophetic sermon to the people.

36, 12: *The scribe's chamber:* the office of the royal secretary.

✿   35/13: 32, 33.
      14: 7, 13; 25, 3;
        2 Chr 36, 15f.
      15: 25, 4f.7.
                          17: 11, 8f.
                          36/3: 26, 3; Is 55, 6f.
                          7: 2 Kgs 22, 13.

"Come, and bring with you the scroll you read publicly to the people." Scroll in hand, Baruch, son of Neriah, went to them. **15**"Sit down," they said to him, "and read it to us." Baruch read it to them, **16**and when they heard all its words, they were frightened and said to one another, "We must certainly tell the king all these things." **17**Then they asked Baruch: "Tell us, please, how you came to write down all these words." **18**"Jeremiah dictated all these words to me," Baruch answered them, "and I wrote them down with ink in the book." **19**At this the princes said to Baruch, "Go into hiding, you and Jeremiah; let no one know where you are."

20Leaving the scroll in safekeeping in the room of Elishama the scribe, they entered the room where the king was. When they told him everything that had happened, **21**he sent Jehudi to fetch the scroll. Jehudi brought it from the room of Elishama the scribe, and read it to the king and to all the princes who were in attendance on the king. **22**Now the king was sitting in his winter house, since it was the ninth month, and fire was burning in a brazier before him. **23**†Each time Jehudi finished reading three or four columns, the king would cut off the piece with a scribe's knife and cast it into the fire in the brazier, until the entire roll was consumed in the fire. **24**Hearing all these words did not frighten the king and his ministers or cause them to rend their garments. **25**And though Elnathan, Delaiah, and Gemariah urged the king not to burn the scroll, he would not listen to them, **26**but commanded Jerahmeel, a royal prince, and Seraiah, son of Azriel, and Shelemiah, son of Abdeel, to arrest Baruch, the secretary, and the prophet Jeremiah. But the LORD kept them concealed.

27This word of the LORD came to Jeremiah, after the king burned the scroll with the text Jeremiah had dictated to Baruch: **28**Take another scroll, and write on it everything that the first scroll contained, which Jehoiakim, king of Judah, burned up. **29**And against Jehoiakim, king of Judah, say this: Thus says the LORD: You burned that scroll, saying, "Why did you write on it: Babylon's king shall surely come and lay waste this land and empty it of man and beast?" **30***†The LORD now says of Jehoiakim, king of Judah: No descendant of his shall succeed to David's throne; his corpse shall be cast out, exposed to the heat of day, to the cold of night. **31**I will punish him and his descendants and his ministers for their wickedness; against them and the citizens of Jerusalem and the men of Judah I will fulfill all the threats of evil which went unheeded.

32Jeremiah took another scroll, and gave it to his secretary, Baruch, son of Neriah; he wrote on it at Jeremiah's dictation all the words contained in the book which Jehoiakim, king of Judah, had burned in the fire, and many others of the same kind in addition.

Jeremiah in the Dungeon

37 **1***CONIAH, son of Jehoiakim, was succeeded by King Zedekiah, son of Josiah; he was made king over the land of Judah by Nebuchadnezzar, king of Babylon. **2**Neither he, nor his ministers, nor the people of the land would listen to the words of the LORD spoken by Jeremiah the prophet. **3***Yet King Zedekiah sent Jehucal, son of Shelemiah, and Zephaniah, son of Maaseiah the priest, to the prophet Jeremiah with this request: "Pray to the LORD, our God, for us." **4**†At this time Jeremiah had not yet been put into prison; he still came and went freely among the people. **5***†Also, Pharaoh's army had set out from Egypt, and when the Chaldeans who were besieging Jerusalem heard this report they marched away from the city.

6This word of the LORD then came to the prophet Jeremiah: **7***Thus says the LORD, the God of Israel: Give this answer to the king of Judah who sent you to me to consult me: Pharaoh's army which has set out to help you will return to its own land, Egypt. **8***The Chaldeans shall return to the fight against this city; they shall capture it and destroy it with fire.

9Thus says the LORD: Do not deceive yourselves with the thought that the Chaldeans will leave you for good, because they shall not leave! **10***Even if you were to defeat the whole Chaldean army now attacking you, and only the wounded remained, each in his tent, these would rise up and destroy the city with fire.

11*When the Chaldean army lifted the siege of Jerusalem at the threat of the army of Pharaoh, **12**Jeremiah set out from Jerusalem for the district of Benjamin, to take part with his family in the division of an inheritance. **13**But when he reached the Gate of Benjamin, he met the captain of the guard, a man named Irijah, son of Shelemiah, son of Hananiah; he seized the prophet Jeremiah, saying, "You are deserting to the Chaldeans!" **14**"That is a lie!" Jeremiah answered, "I am not deserting to the Chaldeans." Without listening, Irijah kept Jeremiah in custody and brought him to the princes.

15*The princes were enraged, and had Jeremiah beaten and thrown into prison in the house of Jonathan the scribe, which they were using as a jail. **16**And so Jeremiah entered the vaulted dungeon, where he remained a long time.

---

† 36, 23: *A scribe's knife:* used to sharpen the reeds which were employed as pens.

36, 30: Jehoiakim's son Jehoiachin was named king, but reigned only three months; he was known better for his thirty-seven-year exile in Babylon. *His corpse shall be cast out:* see note on 22, 19.

37, 4: *Put into prison:* as described in 32, 1ff. Chronologically, the present episode follows 34, 1-7.

37, 5: *Pharaoh's army:* the force sent by Pharaoh Hophra which caused the Chaldeans momentarily to lift the siege of Jerusalem (cf 34, 21).

❋   30: 22, 19.   7: Ez 17, 17.
37/1: 52, 1; 2 Kgs 24, 17;   8: 34, 22.
      2 Chr 36, 10.   10: 21, 4.
      3: 21, 1.   11: Zec 14, 10.
      5: Ez 17, 15; 29, 6f.   15: 38, 6-13.

17*Once King Zedekiah had him brought to his palace and he asked him secretly whether there was any message from the LORD. Yes! Jeremiah answered: you shall be handed over to the king of Babylon. **18***Jeremiah then asked King Zedekiah: In what have I wronged you, or your ministers, or this people, that you should put me in prison? **19**And where are your own prophets now, **20**who prophesied to you that the king of Babylon would not attack you or this land? Hear now, my lord king, and grant my petition: do not send me back into the house of Jonathan the scribe, or I shall die there.

21*King Zedekiah ordered that Jeremiah be confined in the quarters of the guard, and given a loaf of bread each day from the bakers' shop until all the bread in the city was eaten up. Thus Jeremiah remained in the quarters of the guard.

Jeremiah in the Miry Cistern

38 **1**†SHEPHATIAH, son of Mattan, Gedaliah, son of Pashhur, Jucal, son of Shelemiah, and Pashhur, son of Malchiah, heard Jeremiah speaking these words to all the people: **2***Thus says the LORD: He who remains in this city shall die by sword, or famine, or pestilence; but he who goes out to the Chaldeans shall live; his life shall be spared him as booty, and he shall live. **3**Thus says the LORD: This city shall certainly be handed over to the army of the king of Babylon; he shall capture it.

4*†"This man ought to be put to death," the princes said to the king; "he demoralizes the soldiers who are left in this city, and all the people, by speaking such things to them; he is not interested in the welfare of our people, but in their ruin." **5**King Zedekiah answered: "He is in your power"; for the king could do nothing with them. **6***And so they took Jeremiah and threw him into the cistern of Prince Malchiah, which was in the quarters of the guard, letting him down with ropes. There was no water in the cistern, only mud, and Jeremiah sank into the mud.

7†Now Ebed-melech, a Cushite, a courtier in the king's palace, heard that they had put Jeremiah into the cistern. The king happened just then to be at the Gate of Benjamin, **8**and Ebed-melech went there from the palace and said to him, **9***"My lord king, these men have been at fault in all they have done to the prophet Jeremiah, casting him into the cistern. He will die of famine on the spot, for there is no more food in the city." **10**Then the king ordered Ebed-melech the Cushite to take three men along with him, and draw the prophet Jeremiah out of the cistern before he should die. **11**Ebed-melech took the men along with him, and went first to the linen closet in the palace, from which

he took some old, tattered rags; these he sent down to Jeremiah in the cistern, with ropes. **12**Then he said to Jeremiah: "Put the old, tattered rags between your armpits and the ropes." Jeremiah did so, **13**and they drew him up with the ropes out of the cistern. But Jeremiah remained in the quarters of the guard.

14*Once King Zedekiah summoned the prophet Jeremiah to come to him at the third entrance to the house of the LORD. "I have a question to ask you," the king said to Jeremiah; "hide nothing from me." Jeremiah answered Zedekiah: **15***If I tell you anything, you will have me killed, will you not? If I counsel you, you will not listen to me! **16**But King Zedekiah swore to Jeremiah secretly: "As the LORD lives who gave us the breath of life, I will not kill you; nor will I hand you over to these men who seek your life."

17*Thereupon Jeremiah said to Zedekiah: Thus says the LORD God of hosts, the God of Israel: If you surrender to the princes of Babylon's king, you shall save your life; this city shall not be destroyed with fire, and you and your family shall live. **18***But if you do not surrender to the princes of Babylon's king, this city shall fall into the hands of the Chaldeans, who shall destroy it with fire, and you shall not escape their hands.

19*King Zedekiah, however, said to Jeremiah, "I am afraid of the men of Judah who have deserted to the Chaldeans; I may be handed over to them, and they will mistreat me." **20***You will not be handed over, Jeremiah answered. Please obey the voice of the LORD and do as I tell you; then it shall go well with you, and your life will be spared. **21**But if you refuse to surrender, this is what the LORD shows me: **22***All the women left in the house of Judah's king shall be brought out to the princes of Babylon's king, and they shall taunt you thus:

> "They betrayed you, outdid you,
>   your good friends!
> Now that your feet are stuck in the mud,
>   they slink away."

23*All your wives and sons shall be led forth to the Chaldeans, and you shall not escape their hands; you shall be handed over to the king of Babylon, and this city shall be destroyed with fire.

24Then Zedekiah said to Jeremiah, "Let no one know about this conversation, or you shall die. **25**If the princes hear I spoke to you, if they come and ask you, 'Tell us what you said to the king; do not hide it from us, or we will kill you,' or 'What did the king say to you?' **26**give them this answer: 'I petitioned the king

---

*
17: 21, 7; 32, 3; 34, 21.
18: 26, 19.
21: 32, 2; 38, 28.
38/2: 21, 9f; 39, 18; 45, 5.
4: 26, 11.
6: 37, 14f.
9: 52, 6.
14: 37, 16.

15: Lk 22, 67f.
17: 27, 12f; 2 Kgs 24, 12.
18: 32, 4.
19: 1 Sm 31, 4.
20: 2 Chr 20, 20.
22: Jb 6, 15; 19, 13f.19.
23: 41, 10.

†
38, 1: Jeremiah enjoyed sufficient liberty *in the quarters of the guard* (37, 21) to speak to the people; cf 32, 6-9. *Gedaliah, son of Pashhur:* the latter is possibly the Pashhur of 20, 1. *Pashhur, son of Malchiah:* mentioned in 21, 1.

38, 4: *He demoralizes the soldiers:* literally, "he weakens their hands." One of the Lachish ostraca (see note on 34, 7) uses the same expression of the princes in Jerusalem.

38, 7: *A Cushite:* an Ethiopian. Ebed-melech evidently held a position of some authority at court.

not to send me back to Jonathan's house to die there.'"
²⁷When all the princes came to Jeremiah, they questioned him, and he answered them in the very words the king had commanded. They said no more to him, for nothing had been heard of the earlier conversation. ²⁸*Thus Jeremiah stayed in the quarters of the guard till the day Jerusalem was taken.

Jeremiah and Gedaliah

39 ¹*†WHEN Jerusalem was taken. . . . In the tenth month of the ninth year of Zedekiah, king of Judah, Nebuchadnezzar, king of Babylon, and all his army marched against Jerusalem and besieged it. ²†On the ninth day of the fourth month, in the eleventh year of Zedekiah, a breach was made in the city's defenses. ³All the princes of the king of Babylon came and occupied the middle gate: Nergal-sharezer, of Simmagir, the chief officer, Nebushazban, the high dignitary, and all the other princes of the king of Babylon. . . . ⁴*†When Zedekiah, king of Judah, saw them, he and all his warriors fled by night, leaving the city on the Royal Garden Road through the gate between the two walls. He went in the direction of the Arabah, ⁵*†but the Chaldean army pursued them, and overtook and captured Zedekiah in the desert near Jericho. He was brought to Riblah, in the land of Hamath, where Nebuchadnezzar, king of Babylon pronounced sentence upon him. ⁶*As Zedekiah looked on, his sons were slain at Riblah by order of the king of Babylon, who slew also all the nobles of Judah. ⁷*He then blinded Zedekiah and bound him in chains to bring him to Babylon.

⁸*The Chaldeans set fire to the king's palace and the houses of the people, and demolished the walls of Jerusalem. ⁹*Nebuzaradan, chief of the bodyguard, deported to Babylon the rest of the people left in the city, those who had deserted to him, and the rest of the workmen. ¹⁰*But some of the poor who had no property were left in the land of Judah by Nebuzaradan, chief of the bodyguard, and were given at the same time vineyards and farms.

¹¹Concerning Jeremiah, Nebuchadnezzar, king of Babylon, gave the following orders through Nebuzaradan, chief of the bodyguard: ¹²*"Take him and look after him; let no harm befall him, but treat him as he himself requests." ¹³Thereupon Nebuzaradan, chief of the bodyguard, and Nebushazban, the high dignitary, and Nergal-sharezer, the chief officer, and all the nobles of the king of Babylon, ¹⁴*had Jeremiah taken out of the quarters of the guard, and entrusted to Gedaliah, son of Ahikam, son of Shaphan, to be brought home. And so he remained among the people.

A Word of Comfort for Ebed-melech

¹⁵While Jeremiah was still imprisoned in the quarters of the guard, the word of the LORD came to him: ¹⁶*Go, tell this to Ebed-melech the Cushite: Thus says the LORD of hosts, the God of Israel: Behold, I am now fulfilling the words I spoke against this city, for evil and not for good; and this before your very eyes. ¹⁷But on that day I will rescue you, says the LORD; you shall not be handed over to the men of whom you are afraid. ¹⁸*I will make certain that you escape and do not fall by the sword. Your life shall be spared as booty, because you trusted in me, says the LORD.

Jeremiah Still in Judah

40 ¹*†THIS word came to Jeremiah from the LORD, after Nebuzaradan, captain of the bodyguard, had released him in Ramah, where he had found him a prisoner in chains, among the captives of Jerusalem and Judah who were being exiled to Babylon. ²When the captain of the bodyguard took charge of Jeremiah, he said to him, "The LORD, your God, foretold the ruin of this place. ³Now he has brought about in deed what he threatened; because you sinned against the LORD and did not obey his voice, this fate has befallen you. ⁴*And now, I am freeing you today from the fetters that bind your hands; if it seems good to you to come with me to Babylon, you may come: I will look after you well. But if it does not please you to come to Babylon, you need not come. See, the whole land is before you; go wherever you think good and proper"; ⁵*and then, before he left—"or go to Gedaliah, son of Ahikam, son of Shaphan, whom the king of Babylon has appointed ruler over the cities of Judah; stay with him among the people, or go wherever you please." The captain of the bodyguard gave him food and gifts and let him go. ⁶*†Jeremiah went to Gedaliah, son of Ahikam, in Mizpah, and stayed with him among the people left in the land.

⁷When the army leaders who were still in the field with all their men heard that the king of Babylon had

---

†

39, 1: *The tenth month of the ninth year:* the month Tebet (mid-December to mid-January) of the year 589/8 B.C.

39, 2: *The ninth day of the fourth month, in the eleventh year:* in July of 587 B.C.

39, 4: *The Royal Garden Road:* along the southeast side of the city; the royal garden was in the Kidron Valley. *The gate between the two walls:* the southernmost city gate, at the end of the Tyropoean Valley. *The Arabah:* the Jordan Valley. Zedekiah was attempting to escape across the Jordan when he was captured near Jericho.

39, 5: *Riblah:* Nebuchadnezzar's headquarters in Syria, which had also been used by Pharaoh Neco (2 Kgs 23, 33).

40, 1: *This word:* actually, no further word of the Lord is recorded until 42, 7ff. This is a title affixed to the following chapters after they were attached to an earlier form of the book ending with chapter 39.

40, 6: *Mizpah:* some five miles northwest of Jerusalem, where Israel chose its first king (1 Sm 10, 17-24). Presumably Jerusalem had been damaged too much by the Chaldean conquest to remain a seat of government.

*

28: 39, 14.
39/1f: 52, 4-16;
    2 Kgs 25, 1-12;
    Ez 24, 1.
4: 52, 7.
5: 32, 4f; 38, 18.
6: 34, 21.
7: 32, 4f; Ez 12, 13.
8: 21, 10; 34, 2; 52, 13.
9: 2 Kgs 25, 11.

10: 2 Kgs 25, 12.22.
12: 40, 4.
14: 26, 24; 38, 28.
16: 21, 10; Dn 9, 12.
18: 45, 5; Ps 25, 3; 36, 40.
40/1: 39, 14.
4: 39, 12.
5: 39, 14; 2 Kgs 25, 22.
6: 39, 14.

given Gedaliah, son of Ahikam, charge of the land, of men, women, and children, and of those poor who had not been led captive to Babylon, [8]†they came with their men to Gedaliah in Mizpah: Ishmael, son of Nethaniah; Johanan, son of Kareah; Seraiah, son of Tanhumeth; the sons of Ephai of Netophah; and Jezaniah of Beth-maacah. [9]*Gedaliah, son of Ahikam, son of Shaphan, adjured them and their men not to be afraid to serve the Chaldeans: to stay in the land and submit to the king of Babylon, for their own welfare; [10]saying that he himself would remain in Mizpah, as their intermediary with the Chaldeans who should come to them. They were to collect the wine, the fruit, and the oil, to store them in jars, and to settle in the cities they occupied. [11]When the people of Judah in Moab, those among the Ammonites, those in Edom, and those in all other lands heard that the king of Babylon had left a remnant in Judah, and had appointed over them Gedaliah, son of Ahikam, son of Shaphan, [12]they all returned to the land of Judah from the places to which they had scattered. They went to Gedaliah at Mizpah and had a rich harvest of wine and fruit.

Assassination of Gedaliah

[13]Now Johanan, son of Kareah, and all the leaders of the armies in the field came to Gedaliah in Mizpah [14]*†and asked him whether he did not know that Baalis, the king of the Ammonites, had sent Ishmael, son of Nethaniah, to assassinate him. [15]But Gedaliah, son of Ahikam, would not believe them. Then Johanan, son of Kareah, said secretly to Gedaliah in Mizpah: "Let me go and kill Ishmael, son of Nethaniah; no one will know it. Why should he be allowed to kill you? All the Jews who have now rallied to you will be dispersed and the remnant of Judah will perish." [16]Nevertheless, Gedaliah, son of Ahikam, answered Johanan, son of Kareah, "You shall do nothing of the kind; you have lied about Ishmael."

41 [1]*IN the seventh month Ishmael, son of Nethaniah, son of Elishama, of royal descent, one of the king's nobles, came with ten men to Gedaliah, son of Ahikam, at Mizpah. And while they were together at table in Mizpah, [2]Ishmael, son of Nethaniah, and the ten who were with him, rose up and attacked with swords Gedaliah, son of Ahikam, son of Shaphan, whom the king of Babylon had made ruler over the land; and they killed him. [3]Ishmael also slew all the men of Judah of military age who were with Gedaliah and the Chaldean soldiers who were there.

[4]The second day after the murder of Gedaliah, before anyone knew of it, [5]eighty men with beards shaved off, clothes in rags, and with gashes on their bodies came from Shechem, Shiloh, and Samaria, bringing food offerings and incense for the house of the LORD. [6]Ishmael, son of Nethaniah, went out from Mizpah to meet them, weeping as he went. "Come to Gedaliah, son of Ahikam," [7]he said as he met them. When they were once inside the city, Ishmael, son of Nethaniah, and his men slew them and threw them into the cistern. [8]But there were ten among them who pleaded with Ishmael: "Do not kill us; we have stores buried in the field: wheat and barley, oil and honey." And so he spared them and did not kill them, as he had killed their companions. [9]*The cistern into which Ishmael threw all the corpses of the men he had killed was the large one made by King Asa to defend himself against Baasha, king of Israel; this cistern Ishmael, son of Nethaniah, filled with the slain.

[10]†Ishmael, son of Nethaniah, led away the remnant of the people left in Mizpah and the princesses, whom Nebuzaradan, captain of the bodyguard, had confided to Gedaliah, son of Ahikam. With these captives, Ishmael, son of Nethaniah, set out to make his way to the Ammonites.

Flight to Egypt

[11]But when Johanan, son of Kareah, and the other army leaders with him heard of the crimes Ishmael, son of Nethaniah, had committed, [12]†they took all their men and set out to attack Ishmael, son of Nethaniah. They overtook him at the Great Waters in Gibeon. [13]At the sight of Johanan, son of Kareah, and the other army leaders, the people who were Ishmael's captives rejoiced. [14]All of those whom Ishmael had brought away from Mizpah went over to Johanan, son of Kareah. [15]But Ishmael, son of Nethaniah, escaped from Johanan and fled to the Ammonites with eight men. [16]Then Johanan, son of Kareah, and all his army leaders took charge of the remnant of the people, both the soldiers and the women and children with their guardians, whom Ishmael, son of Nethaniah, had brought away from Mizpah after he killed Gedaliah, son of Ahikam. From Gibeon, [17]they retreated to the lodging place of Chimham near Bethlehem, where they stopped, intending to flee into Egypt. [18]They were afraid of the Chaldeans, because Ishmael, son of Nethaniah, had slain Gedaliah, son of Ahikam, whom the king of Babylon had made ruler in the land of Judah.

---

† 40, 8: *Jezaniah:* the seal ring of a high official of this name was discovered in 1932 at the site usually identified with Mizpah, Tell en-Nasbe.

40, 14: *The Ammonites:* they resented the survival of their ancient enemy, Judah. *Ishmael:* their willing tool, who doubtless aspired to rule over Judah himself, as he was of the house of David; cf 41, 1.

41, 10: *The princesses:* of the royal house of Judah. They had not been deported to Babylon with the men of this house.

41, 12: *Gibeon:* today called El-Jib; it is northwest of Jerusalem. The most recent excavations have revealed the extensive dimensions of the city spring and well, called here *the Great Waters;* cf 2 Sm 2, 12ff.

---

*
    9: 27, 12f; 2 Kgs 25, 24.   9: 1 Kgs 15, 16;
    14: 41, 1ff.10.   2 Chr 16, 6.
  41/1: 40, 14ff; 2 Kgs 25, 25.

42

1THEN all the army leaders, Johanan, son of Kareah, Azariah, son of Hoshaiah, and all the people, high and low, approached the prophet Jeremiah **2**and said, "Grant our petition; pray for us to the LORD, your God, for all this remnant. We are now few who once were many, as you well see. **3**Let the LORD, your God, show us what way we should take and what we should do." **4***Very well! the prophet Jeremiah answered them: I will pray to the LORD, your God, as you desire; whatever the LORD answers you, I will tell you; I will withhold nothing from you. **5***And they said to Jeremiah, "May the LORD be our witness: we will truly and faithfully follow all the instructions the LORD, your God, will send us. **6***Whether it is pleasant or difficult, we will obey the command of the LORD, our God, to whom we are sending you, so that it will go well with us for obeying the command of the LORD, our God."

7Ten days passed before the word of the LORD came to Jeremiah. **8**Then he called Johanan, son of Kareah, his army leaders, and all the people, high and low, **9**and said to them: Thus says the LORD, the God of Israel, to whom you sent me to offer your prayer: **10***If you remain quietly in this land I will build you up, and not tear you down; I will plant you, not uproot you; for I regret the evil I have done you. **11***Do not fear the king of Babylon, before whom you are now afraid; do not fear him, says the LORD, for I am with you to save you, to rescue you from his power. **12***I will grant you mercy, so that he will be sorry for you and let you return to your land. **13**But if you disobey the voice of the LORD, your God, and decide not to remain in this land, **14***saying, "No, we will go to Egypt, where we will see no more of war, hear the trumpet alarm no longer, nor hunger for bread; there we will live"; **15**then listen to the word of the LORD, remnant of Judah: Thus says the LORD of hosts, the God of Israel: If you are determined to go to Egypt, when you arrive there to stay, **16***the sword you fear shall reach you in the land of Egypt; the hunger you dread shall cling to you no less in Egypt, and there you shall die. **17***All those men who determine to go to Egypt to stay, shall die by the sword, famine, and pestilence; not one shall survive or escape the evil that I will bring upon them. **18***For thus says the LORD of hosts, the God of Israel: Just as my furious anger was poured out upon the citizens of Jerusalem, so shall my anger be poured out on you when you reach Egypt. You shall become an example of malediction and horror, a curse and a reproach, and you shall never see this place again.

19It is the LORD who has spoken to you, remnant of Judah; do not go to Egypt! You can never say that I did not warn you this day. **20**At the cost of your lives you have deceived me, sending me to the LORD, your God, saying, "Pray for us to the LORD, our God; make known to us all that the LORD, our God, shall say, and we will do it." **21***Today I proclaim his message, but you obey the voice of the LORD, your God, in nothing that he has commissioned me to make known to you. **22***Have no doubt of this, you shall die by the sword, famine, and pestilence in the place where you wish to go and settle.

43

1WHEN Jeremiah finished speaking to the people all these words of the LORD, their God, with which the LORD had sent him to them, **2**Azariah, son of Hoshaiah, Johanan, son of Kareah, and all the insolent men shouted to Jeremiah: "You lie; it was not the LORD, our God, who sent you to tell us not to go to Egypt to settle. **3***It is Baruch, son of Neriah, who stirs you up against us, to hand us over to the Chaldeans to be killed or exiled to Babylon."

4*Johanan, son of Kareah, and the rest of the leaders and the people did not obey the LORD's command to stay in the land of Judah. **5**Instead, Johanan, son of Kareah, and all the army leaders took along the whole remnant of Judah that had been dispersed among the nations and had returned thence to dwell again in the land of Judah: **6***men, women, and children, the princesses and everyone whom Nebuzaradan, captain of the bodyguard, had entrusted to Gedaliah, son of Ahikam, son of Shaphan; also Jeremiah, the prophet, and Baruch, son of Neriah. **7***Against the LORD's command they went to Egypt, and arrived at Tahpanhes. . . .

Jeremiah in Egypt

8This word of the LORD came to Jeremiah in Tahpanhes: **9†**Take with you large stones and sink them in mortar in the brickyard at the entrance to the royal building in Tahpanhes, while the men of Judah look on, **10***and then say to them: Thus says the LORD of hosts, the God of Israel: I will send for my servant Nebuchadnezzar, king of Babylon, and bring him here. He will set his throne upon these stones which I, Jeremiah, have sunk, and stretch his canopy over them. **11***He shall come and strike the land of Egypt: with death, whoever is marked for death; with exile, everyone destined for exile; with the sword, all who are intended for the sword. **12***He shall set fire to the temples of Egypt's gods, and burn the gods or carry them off. As a shepherd delouses his cloak, he shall delouse the land of Egypt and depart victorious. **13**He shall smash the obelisks of the temple of the sun in the land of Egypt and destroy with fire the temples of the Egyptian gods.

42/4: 1 Sm 3, 18.
5: Jgs 11, 10.
6: 7, 23; Dt 5, 33; 6, 3.
10: 31, 28; 32, 41.
11: 30, 10f.
12: Ps 106, 45f; Prv 16, 7.
14: Dt 28, 68.
16: 44, 13f.27.
17: 29, 17f; 44, 14.28.
18: 44, 12.
21: Zec 7, 11f.
22: 44, 12; Hos 9, 6.
43/3: 38, 4.
4: 41, 16.
6: 41, 10.
7: 42, 13f; 44, 1.
10: 27, 6; Ez 29, 19.
11: 46, 13; Ez 30, 10.
12: 46, 25; Ez 30, 13f.

† 43, 9: *The royal building:* residence of the Egyptian governor.

44 ¹THIS word came to Jeremiah for all the people of Judah who were living in Egypt, at Migdol, Tahpanhes, and Memphis, and in Upper Egypt: ²*†Thus says the LORD of hosts, the God of Israel: You have seen all the evil I brought on Jerusalem and the other cities of Judah. Today they are ruins and uninhabited, ³*because of the evil they did to provoke me, going after strange gods, serving them and sacrificing to them, gods which neither they, nor you, nor your fathers knew. ⁴Though I kept sending to you all my servants the prophets, with the plea not to commit this horrible deed which I hate, ⁵*they would not listen or accept the warning to turn away from the evil of sacrificing to strange gods. ⁶Therefore the fury of my anger poured forth in flame over the cities of Judah and the streets of Jerusalem, so that they became the ruinous waste they are today.

⁷Now thus says the LORD God of hosts, the God of Israel: Why do you inflict so great an evil upon yourselves? Will you root out from Judah man and wife, child and nursling, and not leave yourselves even a remnant? ⁸*Will you go on provoking me by the works of your hands, by sacrificing to strange gods here in the land of Egypt where you have come to live? Will you be rooted out and become a curse and a disgrace among all the nations of the earth? ⁹*Have you forgotten the evil deeds which your fathers, and the kings of Judah and their wives, and you yourselves and your wives have done in the land of Judah and the streets of Jerusalem? ¹⁰*To this day they have not been crushed; they do not fear or follow the law and the statutes which I set before you and your fathers.

¹¹Hence, thus says the LORD of hosts, the God of Israel: I have determined evil against you; and I will uproot all Judah. ¹²*I will take away the remnant of Judah who insisted on coming to dwell in Egypt, so that they shall be wholly destroyed. In the land of Egypt they shall fall by the sword or be consumed by hunger. High and low, they shall die by the sword, or by hunger, and become an example of malediction, a horror, a curse and a reproach. ¹³*Thus will I punish those who live in Egypt, just as I punished Jerusalem with sword, hunger, and pestilence. None of the remnant of Judah that have come to settle in the land of Egypt shall escape or survive. ¹⁴None shall return to the land of Judah, though they yearn to return and live there. Only scattered refugees shall return.

¹⁵From all the men who knew that their wives were burning incense to strange gods, from all the women who were present in the immense crowd, and from all the people who lived in Lower and Upper Egypt, Jeremiah received this answer: ¹⁶*"We will not listen to what you say in the name of the LORD. ¹⁷*Rather will we continue doing what we had proposed; we will burn incense to the queen of heaven and pour out libations to her, as we and our fathers, our kings and princes have done in the cities of Judah and the streets of Jerusalem. Then we had enough food to eat and we were well off; we suffered no misfortune. ¹⁸But since we stopped burning incense to the queen of heaven and pouring out libations to her, we are in need of everything and are being destroyed by the sword and by hunger. ¹⁹*And when we burned incense to the queen of heaven and poured out libations to her, was it without our husbands' consent that we baked for her cakes in her image and poured out libations to her?"

²⁰To all the people, men and women, who gave him this answer, Jeremiah said: ²¹*Was it not this that the LORD remembered and brought to mind, that you burned incense in the cities of Judah and in the streets of Jerusalem: you, your fathers, your kings and princes, and the people generally? ²²*The LORD could no longer bear your evil deeds, the horrible things which you were doing; and so your land became a waste, a desert, a thing accursed and without inhabitants, as it is today. ²³*Because you burned incense and sinned against the LORD, not obeying the voice of the LORD, not living by his law, his statutes, and his decrees, this evil has befallen you at the present day.

²⁴Jeremiah said further to all the people, including the women: Hear the word of the LORD, all you Judeans in the land of Egypt: ²⁵Thus says the LORD of hosts, the God of Israel: You and your wives have stated your intentions, and kept them in fact: "We will continue to fulfill the vows we have made to burn incense to the queen of heaven and to pour out libations to her." Very well! keep your vows, carry out your resolutions! ²⁶But listen then to the word of the LORD, all you people of Judah who live in Egypt; I swear by my own great name, says the LORD, in the whole land of Egypt no man of Judah shall henceforth pronounce my name, saying, "As the Lord GOD lives." ²⁷*I am watching over them to do evil, not good. All the men of Judah in Egypt shall perish by the sword or famine until they are utterly destroyed. ²⁸*Those who escape the sword to return from the land of Egypt to the land of Judah shall be few in number. The whole remnant of Judah who came to settle in Egypt shall know whose word stands, mine or theirs.

²⁹That you may know how surely my threats of punishment for you shall be fulfilled, this shall be a sign to you, says the LORD, that I will punish you in this place. ³⁰*†Thus says the LORD: See! I will hand over Pharaoh Hophra, king of Egypt, to his enemies,

❋
44/2: 34, 22; Lv 26, 32f.
  3: 11, 17; Dt 32, 17.
  5: 7, 24.26; 19, 4.
  8: 25, 6f.
  9: 1 Kgs 11, 1.8.
    Ezr 9, 7.14.
 10: 7, 24.
 12: 42, 15.18.22.
 13: 43, 11.
 16: 6, 16f.

17: 5, 3; 7, 18.
19: 7, 18.
21: 11, 13.
22: 15, 6.
23: 2 Kgs 17, 15;
    Dn 9, 11f.
27: Ez 7, 3-7.
28: Dt 28, 62; Is 10, 22.
30: 39, 5ff; 46, 25f;
    Ez 29, 3f; 30, 21.

† 44, 2-30: Chronologically, this is the last of Jeremiah's prophecies to his countrymen. The narrative leaves him an old man nearing seventy, rejected by his people. According to tradition, he was murdered in Egypt by fellow Judeans.

44, 30: *Hophra:* killed by his own people. The ruler of Egypt at the time of its conquest by Nebuchadnezzar was Hophra's successor Amasis, who was also slain by his enemies.

to those who seek his life, just as I handed over Zedekiah, king of Judah, to his enemy and mortal foe, Nebuchadnezzar, king of Babylon.

A Message to Baruch

45 [1*†]THIS is the message that the prophet Jeremiah gave to Baruch, son of Neriah, when he wrote in a book the prophecies that Jeremiah dictated in the fourth year of Jehoiakim, son of Josiah, king of Judah: [2]Thus says the Lord, God of Israel, to you, Baruch, [3*]because you said, "Alas! the Lord adds grief to my pain; I am weary from groaning, and can find no rest": [4*]say this to him, says the Lord: What I have built, I am tearing down; what I have planted, I am uprooting: even the whole land. [5*]And do you seek great things for yourself? Seek them not! I am bringing evil on all mankind, says the Lord, but your life I will leave you as booty, wherever you may go.

V: ORACLES AGAINST THE NATIONS

46[†] [1]THIS IS THE WORD OF THE LORD that came to the prophet Jeremiah against the nations.

Against Egypt

[2†]Concerning Egypt. Against the army of Pharaoh Neco, king of Egypt, which was defeated at Carchemish on the Euphrates by Nebuchadnezzar, king of Babylon, in the fourth year of Jehoiakim, son of Josiah, king of Judah:

    [3] Prepare shield and buckler!
        march to battle!
    [4] Harness the horses,
        mount, charioteers!
     Fall in with your helmets;
        polish your spears, put on your
          breastplates.
    [5*] What do I see?
        With broken ranks
     They fall back;
        their heroes are routed,
     They flee headlong
        without making a stand.
     Terror on every side,
        says the Lord!
    [6] The swift cannot flee,
        nor the hero escape:
     There in the north, on the Euphrates'
        bank,
          they stumble and fall.

    [7] Who is this that surges forward like the
        Nile,
        like rivers of billowing waters?
    [8*] Egypt surges like the Nile,
        like rivers of billowing waters.
     "I will surge forward," he says, "and
        cover the earth,
        destroying the city and its people.
    [9] Forward, horses!
        drive madly, chariots!
     Set out, warriors,
        Cush and Put, bearing your shields,
        Men of Lud, stretching your bows!"
    [10*] But this is the day of the Lord GOD of
        hosts,
        a day of vengeance, vengeance on
         his foes!
     The sword devours, is sated, drunk with
        their blood:
        for the Lord GOD of hosts holds a
         slaughter feast
     in the northland, on the Euphrates.

    [11*] Go up to Gilead, and take balm,
        O virgin daughter Egypt!
     No use to multiply remedies;
        for you there is no cure.
    [12*] The nations hear of your shame,
        your cries fill the earth.
     Warrior trips over warrior,
        both fall together.

[13*†]The message which the Lord gave to the prophet Jeremiah concerning the advance of Nebuchadnezzar, king of Babylon, to attack the land of Egypt:

    [14*] Announce it in Egypt, publish it in
        Migdol,
        proclaim it in Memphis and
         Tahpanhes!

---

† 45, 1-5: At the conclusion of his narrative, Baruch appends a prophecy given him personally by Jeremiah when he first wrote down Jeremiah's words (cf chap. 36). The future revealed by the prophet had depressed Baruch; this prophecy was to assure him of his personal safety, while repeating the Lord's determination to destroy Judah.

46—51: In these chapters most of Jeremiah's oracles against the foreign nations have been gathered together and placed at the end of his book; in the Greek text they appear with the other oracles against the nations, in chap. 25. In general, they are in chronological order: 46, 1—49, 33, from the fourth year of Jehoiakim: 49, 34-39, at the beginning of Zedekiah's reign; 50, 1—51, 64, from the fourth year of Zedekiah.

46, 2: *Carchemish on the Euphrates:* the western terminus of the Mesopotamian trade route, where Nebuchadnezzar defeated Neco in 605 B. C., thus gaining undisputed control of Syria and Palestine.

46, 13: In 601 B. C. Nebuchadnezzar advanced against Egypt and even entered the country, but finally had to withdraw to Syria.

❋
45/1: 36, 4.18.32.
    3: Lam 1, 3; 5, 5.
    4: 18, 7; Is 5, 5f.
    5: 25, 26-29.
46/5: 6, 25; 49, 29.
    8: Ez 29, 3; 32, 2.
  10: Dt 32, 42; Is 13, 9;
      Ez 39, 17-20.
  11: 8, 22; 51, 8;
      Ez 30, 21f.
  12: Ez 32, 9-12.
  13: 43, 10f; 44, 30;
      Is 19, 1.
  14: 44, 1.

Say: Take your stand, prepare
yourselves,
the sword has already devoured your
neighbors.

15† Why has Apis fled,
your mighty one failed to stand?
The Lord thrust him down;

16* he stumbled repeatedly, and fell.
They said one to another,
"Up! let us return to our own people,
To the land of our birth,
away from the destroying sword."

17† Call Pharaoh, king of Egypt, by the
name
"The noise that let its time go by."

18† As I live, says the King
whose name is Lord of hosts,
Like Tabor among the mountains he
shall come,
like Carmel above the sea.

19 Pack your baggage for exile,
capital city of daughter Egypt;
Memphis shall become a desert,
an empty ruin.

20 Egypt is a pretty heifer,
from the north a horsefly lights upon
her.

21 The mercenaries in her ranks
are like fatted calves;
They too turn and flee together,
stand not their ground,
When the day of their ruin comes upon
them,
the time of their punishment.

22 She sounds like a retreating reptile!
Yes, they come in force;
like woodchoppers, they attack her
with axes.

23 They cut down her forest, says the
Lord,
impenetrable though it be;
More numerous than locusts,
they cannot be counted.

24 Disgraced is daughter Egypt,
handed over to the people of the
north.

25*†The Lord of hosts, the God of Israel, has said:
See! I will punish Amon of Thebes, and Egypt, her
gods and her kings, Pharaoh, and those who trust in
him. **26***I will hand them over to those who seek their
lives, to Nebuchadnezzar, king of Babylon, and his
ministers. But later on Egypt shall be inhabited again,
as in times past, says the Lord.

27* But you, my servant Jacob, fear not;
be not dismayed, O Israel.
Behold, I will deliver you from the
far-off land,
your descendants, from their land of
exile.
Jacob shall again find rest,
shall be tranquil and undisturbed.

28* You, my servant Jacob, never fear, says
the Lord,
for I am with you;
I will make an end of all the nations
to which I have driven you,
But of you I will not make an end:
I will chastise you as you deserve,
I will not let you go unpunished.

Against the Philistines

47 **1***THIS is the word that came from the Lord
to the prophet Jeremiah concerning the Philistines, before Pharaoh attacked Gaza: **2†**Thus says the
Lord:

Behold: waters are rising from the
north,
a torrent in flood;
It shall flood the land and all that is in it,
the cities and their people.
All the people of the land
set up a wailing cry.

3 They hear the stamping hooves of his
steeds,
the rattling chariots, the rumbling
wheels.
Fathers turn not to save their children;
their hands fall helpless

4*† Because of the day which has come
to ruin all the Philistines,
And cut off from Tyre and Sidon
the last of their allies.
Yes, the Lord is destroying the
Philistines,
the remnant from the coasts of
Caphtor.

†
46, 15: *Apis:* the chief god of Memphis, venerated in the
form of a black bull.
46, 17: *"The noise . . . go by":* in Hebrew there is wordplay
here on the name Hophra, who still made a pretense of power
though his career was at an end.
46, 18: *Tabor . . . Carmel:* outstanding mountains of
Palestine, symbols of strength, to which Nebuchadnezzar is
compared.
46, 25: *Amon:* the sun-god worshiped at Thebes, in Upper
Egypt.
47, 2-7: This prophecy was fulfilled in 605/4 B. C.
47, 4: *Tyre and Sidon:* Phoenician cities associated commercially with the Philistines, and enemies of Nebuchadnezzar; cf
27, 1-4. Nebuchadnezzar carried out a thirteen-year siege of
Tyre which was only partially successful. *Caphtor:* probably the
island of Crete, the traditional place of origin of the Philistines;
cf Am 9, 7.

❋
16: Lv 26, 37.
25: Ez 30, 15f.
26: 44, 30; Ez 30, 4;
    32, 11f.
27: 30, 10; 43, 5.
28: 30, 11.
47/1: Ez 25, 15f; Zep 2, 4.
4: 25, 22; Ez 25, 16f;
    Am 1, 8; 9, 7.

[5]*† Gaza is shaved bald,
    Ashkelon is reduced to silence;
Ashdod, the remnant of their strength,
    how long will you gash yourself?

[6]† Alas, sword of the Lord!
    how long till you find rest?
Return into your scabbard;
    stop, be still!

[7]* How can it find rest
    when the Lord has commanded it?
Against Ashkelon and the seashore
    he has appointed it.

Against Moab

48 [1]†CONCERNING Moab, thus says the Lord of hosts, the God of Israel:

Woe to Nebo, it is laid waste;
    Kiriathaim is disgraced and captured,
Disgraced and overthrown is the
      stronghold:

[2]   Moab's glory is no more.
Evil they plan against Heshbon:
    "Come, let us put an end to her as a
      people."
You, too, Madmen, shall be reduced to
      silence;
    behind you stalks the sword.

[3]* Listen! a cry from Horonaim
    of ruin and great destruction!

[4] Moab is crushed,
    their outcry is heard in Zoar.

[5] The ascent of Luhith
    they climb weeping;
On the descent to Horonaim
    the cry of destruction is heard.

[6] "Flee, save your lives,
    to survive like the wild ass in the
      desert!"

[7]*† Because you trusted in your works and
      your treasures,
    you also shall be captured.
Chemosh shall go into exile,
    his priests and princes with him.

[8] The destroyer comes upon every city,
    not a city escapes;
Ruined is the valley,
    wasted the plain, as the Lord has said.

[9] Set up a memorial for Moab,
    for it is an utter wasteland;
Its cities are turned into ruins
    where no one dwells.

[10] [Cursed be he who does the Lord's work
      remissly,
    cursed he who holds back his sword
      from blood.]

[11]* Moab has been tranquil from his youth,
    has rested upon his lees;
He was not poured from one flask to
      another,
    he went not into exile.
Thus he kept his taste,
    and his scent was not lost.

[12]Hence, the days shall come, says the Lord, when I will send him coopers to turn him over; they shall empty his flasks and break his jars. [13]*Chemosh shall disappoint Moab, as Israel was disappointed by Bethel in which they trusted.

[14]   How can you say, "We are heroes,
      men valiant in war"?

[15]   The ravager of Moab and his cities
      advances,
    the flower of his youth goes down to
      be slaughtered,
    says the King, the Lord of hosts by
      name.

[16]   Near at hand is Moab's ruin,
      his disaster hastens apace.

[17]   Mourn for him, all you his neighbors,
      all you who knew him well!
    Say: How the strong staff is broken,
      the glorious rod!

[18]*   Come down from glory, sit on the
      ground,
    you that dwell in Dibon;
    Moab's ravager has come up against
      you,
    he has ruined your strongholds.

[19]*   Stand by the wayside, watch closely,
      you that dwell in Aroer;
    Ask the man who flees, the woman who
      tries to escape:
    say to them, "What has happened?"

[20]*   Moab is disgraced, yes, destroyed,
      howl and cry out;
    Publish it at the Arnon,
      Moab is ruined!

[21]*For judgment has come on the land of the plateau: on Holon, Jahzah, and Mephaath, [22]on Dibon, Nebo, and Bethdiblathaim, [23]on Kiriathaim, Bethgamul, and Beth-meon, [24]on Kerioth and on Bozrah: on all the cities of Moab, far and near.

[25]   Moab's strength is broken,
      his might is shattered, says the Lord.

---

† 47, 5: Of the ancient Philistine cities, neither Gath nor Ekron (25, 20) is mentioned in this period of waning independence of the seacoast.

47, 6: Words of the Philistines.

48, 1-47: Moab was one of the Israelites' bitterest enemies. According to Flavius Josephus, Moab and Ammon were conquered by Nebuchadnezzar in his twenty-third year, 582 B. C., five years after the destruction of Jerusalem.

48, 7: *Chemosh:* chief god of the Moabites.

✿
5: Am 1, 7.
7: Zep 2, 5f.
48/3ff: Is 15, 5.
  7: Nm 21, 29.
 11: Zep 1, 12.

13: Is 16, 12.
18: Nm 21, 30.
19: Dt 2, 36.
20: Is 16, 7.
21: Is 15, 4.

²⁶Because he boasted against the Lord, make Moab drunk so that he retches and vomits, and he too becomes a laughingstock. ²⁷*Is Israel a laughingstock to you? Was she caught among thieves, that you shake your head whenever you speak of her?

28   Leave the cities, dwell in the crags,
      you that dwell in Moab.
     Be like a dove that nests
      out of reach on the edge of a chasm.
29*   We have heard of the pride of Moab,
      pride beyond bounds:
     His loftiness, his pride, his scorn,
      his insolence of heart.
30   I know, says the Lord, his arrogance;
      liar in boast, liar in deed.
31*   And so I wail over Moab,
      over all Moab I cry,
      over the men of Kir-heres I moan.
32*   More than for Jazer I weep over you,
      vineyard of Sibmah.
     Your tendrils trailed down to the sea,
      as far as Jazer they stretched.
     Upon your harvest, upon your vintage,
      the ravager has fallen.
33   Joy and jubilation are at an end
      in the fruit gardens of the land of
      Moab.
     I drain the wine from the wine vats,
      the treader treads no more,
      the vintage shout is stilled.

³⁴*The cry of Heshbon and Elealeh is heard as far as Jahaz; they call from Zoar to Horonaim, and to Eglath-shelishiyah, for even the waters of Nimrim turn into a desert. ³⁵I will leave no one in Moab, says the Lord, to offer a holocaust on the high place, or to burn incense to his gods. ³⁶*Hence the wail of flutes for Moab is in my heart; for the men of Kir-heres the wail of flutes is in my heart; the wealth they acquired has perished. ³⁷*Every head has been made bald, every beard shaved; every hand is gashed, and the loins of all are clothed in sackcloth. ³⁸On every roof of Moab and in all his squares there is mourning; I have shattered Moab like a pot that no one wants, says the Lord. ³⁹How terror seizes Moab, and wailing! How he turns his back in shame! Moab has become a laughingstock and a horror to all his neighbors! ⁴⁰*For thus says the Lord:

     Behold, like an eagle he soars,
      spreads his wings over Moab.
41*   Cities are taken,
      strongholds seized:

     On that day the hearts of Moab's heroes
      are like the heart of a woman in
      travail.
42*   Moab shall be destroyed, no more a
      people,
     because he boasted against the Lord.
43*   Terror, pit, and trap be upon you,
      people of Moab, says the Lord.
44   He who flees from the terror
      falls into the pit;
     He who climbs from the pit
      is caught in the trap;
     For I will bring these things upon
      Moab
      in the year of their punishment, says
      the Lord.
45*   In Heshbon's shadow stop short
      the exhausted refugees;
     For fire breaks forth from Heshbon,
      and a blaze from the house of Sihon:
     It consumes the brow of Moab,
      the skull of the noisemakers.
46   Woe to you, O Moab,
      you are ruined, O people of Chemosh!
     Your sons are taken into exile,
      your daughters into captivity.
47*   But I will change the lot of Moab
      in the days to come, says the Lord.

Thus far the judgment on Moab.

Against the Ammonites

49 ¹†CONCERNING the Ammonites, thus says the Lord:

     Has Israel no sons?
      has he no heir?
     Why then has Milcom disinherited Gad,
      why have his people settled in Gad's
      cities?
2*†   But the days are coming, says the Lord,
      when against Rabbah of the
      Ammonites
      I will sound the battle alarm;
     She shall become a mound of ruins,
      and her daughter cities shall be
      destroyed by fire.
     Israel shall inherit those who
      disinherited her,
      says the Lord.
3*   Howl, Heshbon, for the ravager
      approaches,
      shriek, daughters of Rabbah!

27: Zep 2, 8ff.
29f: Is 16, 6.
31: Is 16, 7.
32: Is 16, 8f.
34: Is 15, 4f.
36: Is 16, 11.
37: 47, 5; Is 15, 2f; Ez 7, 18.
40: 49, 22.
41: 6, 24; 30, 6.
42: Zep 2, 9f.
43: Is 24, 17f.
45: Nm 21, 28f.
47: 49, 39.
49/2: Am 1, 14.
3: Is 15, 2ff.

† 49, 1: *Milcom:* chief god of the Ammonites. The Transjordan tribe of Gad bordered on Ammon, and after the collapse of the northern kingdom the Ammonites occupied its territory.

49, 2: *Rabbah of the Ammonites:* or Rabbath-Ammon, capital of the Ammonite kingdom. The modern Amman is the capital of the kingdom of Jordan.

Put on sackcloth and mourn,
    run to and fro, gashing yourselves;
For Milcom goes into exile
    along with his priests and captains.

4 Why do you glory in your strength,
    your ebbing strength, rebellious
        daughter?
You who trust in your treasures, saying,
    "Who can come against me?"

5* I am bringing terror upon you,
    says the Lord God of hosts,
        from all round about you;
You shall be scattered, each man in
        headlong flight,
    with no one to rally the fugitives.

6 But afterward I will change the lot
    of the Ammonites, says the Lord.

Against Edom

7† Concerning Edom, thus says the Lord of hosts:

Is there no more wisdom in Teman,
    has counsel perished from the
        prudent,
    has their wisdom become corrupt?

8*† Flee, retreat, hide in deep holes,
    you who live in Dedan:
For I will bring destruction upon Esau
    when I come to punish him.

9* If vintagers came upon you,
    they would leave no gleanings;
If thieves by night,
    they would destroy as they pleased.

10* So I myself will strip Esau;
    I will uncover his retreats so that he
        cannot hide.
He is ruined: sons, and brothers,
    and neighbors, so that he is no more.

11* Leave your orphans behind, I will keep
        them alive;
    your widows, let them trust in me.

12* For thus says the Lord: Even those not sentenced to drink the cup must drink it! Shall you then go unpunished? You shall not go unpunished; you shall surely drink it. **13*†** By my own self I have sworn, says the Lord: Bozrah shall become an object of horror and a disgrace, a desolation and a curse; she and all her cities shall become ruins forever.

14 I have heard a report from the Lord,
    a herald has been sent among the
        nations:
Gather together, move against her,
    rise up for battle.

15* Small will I make you among the nations,
    despised among men!

16* The terror you spread beguiled you,
    and your presumption of heart;
You that live in rocky crags,
    that hold the heights of the hill:
Though you build your nest high as the
        eagle,
    from there I will drag you down, says
        the Lord.

17 Edom shall become an object of horror. Every passer-by shall be appalled and catch his breath at all her wounds. **18*** As when Sodom, Gomorrah, and their neighbors were overthrown, says the Lord, not a man shall dwell there: no one shall visit there.

19* As when a lion comes up from the
        thicket of Jordan
    to the permanent feeding grounds,
So I, in an instant, will drive men off;
    and whom I choose I will establish
        there!
For who is like me? who can call me to
        account?
    What shepherd can stand against me?

20 Therefore, hear the counsel of the Lord,
    which he has taken against Edom;
Hear the plans he has made
    against those that live in Teman:
They shall be dragged away, even the
        smallest sheep,
    their own pasture shall be aghast
        because of them.

21 At the noise of their fall the earth
        quakes,
    to the Red Sea the outcry is heard!

22* See! like an eagle he soars aloft,
    and spreads his wings over Bozrah;
On that day the hearts of Edom's heroes
        shall be
    like the heart of a woman in travail.

Against Damascus

Concerning Damascus:

23*† Hamath and Arpad are covered with
        shame,
    they have heard bad news;
Worried, they toss like the sea
    which cannot rest.

†
  49, 7-22: *Edom:* this implacable enemy from ancient times profited from Judah's downfall; cf Ob 11f.

  49, 7: *Teman:* a district of Edom, used here for the whole country; it was famous for its wise men; cf Jb 2, 11.

  49, 8: *Esau:* Jacob's brother, the traditional ancestor of the Edomites; cf Gn 36.

  49, 13: *Bozrah:* capital of Edom, southeast of the Dead Sea.

  49, 23: *Hamath and Arpad:* independent Aramean states to the north of Damascus; the invasion is conceived as coming from the north. The situation is of the eighth century B. C. Cf Is 10, 9ff.

✿
  5: 48, 47.
  8: Ez 25, 13.
  9: Ob 5.
  10: Mal 1, 3.
  11: Dt 10, 18; Ps 68, 6.
  12: 25, 15.28; Lam 4, 21f.
  13: Is 34, 6; Ez 35, 3-9;
      Ob 16.
  15: Ob 2.
  16: 48, 29f.
  18: 50, 40; Dt 29, 23.
  19: 12, 5; 25, 9; 50, 44f.
  22: 4, 13.
  23: Is 36, 19; 37, 13.

24 Damascus is weakened, she turns to flee,
     panic has seized her.
  Distress and pangs take hold of her,
     like those of a woman in travail.

25 How can the city of glory be forsaken,
     the town of delight!

26 But now her young men shall fall in her
     streets,
  and all her warriors shall be stilled.
     On that day, says the Lord of hosts,

27† I will set fire to the wall of Damascus,
  and it shall devour the palaces of
     Ben-hadad.

Against Arabia

28* Of Kedar and the kingdoms of Hazor, defeated by Nebuchadnezzar, king of Babylon, thus says the Lord:

     Rise up, attack Kedar,
       ravage the Easterners.

29* Their tents and herds shall be taken
     away,
     their tent curtains and all their goods;
  Their camels they shall carry off for
     themselves,
     and shout from upon them, "Terror on
     every side!"

30 Flee! leave your homes, hide in deep
     holes,
     you that live in Hazor, says the Lord;
  For counsel has been taken against you,
     a plan has been formed against you
     [Nebuchadnezzar, king of Babylon].

31 Rise up! set out against a nation that is at
     peace,
     that lives secure, says the Lord,
  That has no gates or bars,
     and dwells alone.

32* Their camels shall be your booty,
     their many herds your spoil;
  I will scatter to the winds those who
     shave their temples,
     from all sides I will bring ruin upon
     them,
     says the Lord.

33 Hazor shall become a haunt of jackals,
     a desert forever,
  Where no man lives,
     no human being stays.

Against Elam

34† The following word of the Lord against Elam came to the prophet Jeremiah at the beginning of the reign of Zedekiah, king of Judah: 35 Thus says the Lord of hosts:

     Behold I will break the bow of Elam,
      the mainstay of their might.

36 I will bring upon Elam the four winds
     from the four ends of the heavens:
  I will scatter them to all these winds, till
     there is no nation
     to which the outcasts of Elam shall
     not come.

37 I will break Elam before their foes,
     before those who seek their life;
  I will bring evil upon them,
     my burning wrath, says the Lord.
  I will send the sword to pursue them
     until I have completely made an end
     of them;

38 My throne I will set up in Elam
     and destroy from there king and
     princes,
     says the Lord.

39 But in the days to come I will change
     the lot of Elam, says the Lord.

The First Prophecy against Babylon

50 1*† THE word which the Lord spoke against Babylon, against the land of the Chaldeans, through the prophet Jeremiah:

2† Announce and publish it among the
     nations;
     publish it, hide it not, but say:
  Babylon is taken, Bel confounded,
     Merodach shattered;
     her images are put to shame, her idols
     shattered.

3* A people from the north advances
     against her
     to turn her land into a desert,
  So that no one shall live there,
     because man and beast have fled
     away.

4* In those days, at that time, says the
     Lord,
     the men of Israel and of Judah shall
     come,
  Weeping as they come, to seek the
     Lord, their God;

---

† 49, 27: *The palaces of Ben-hadad:* the royal palaces in Damascus, where at least three kings bore this name; cf 1 Kgs 15, 18; 20.

49, 34: *Elam:* the ancient kingdom to the east of Babylonia.

50, 1—51, 58: A collection of miscellaneous prophecies against Babylon which now stands as the introduction to the story in 51, 59-64. The Greek text of 50, 1 omits *through the prophet Jeremiah,* and it is in fact likely that these oracles are not Jeremiah's, but were composed by other inspired writers after the fall of Jerusalem, who may have used some of Jeremiah's texts. Babylon fell to the Persians in 538 B. C.

50, 2: *Bel:* originally the name of the god of Nippur in Mesopotamia, then identified with *Merodach* (Marduk), chief god of Babylon.

---

*
28: Is 21, 16.
29: 4, 20.
32: 9, 25.

50/1: 51, 1; Is 13, 1-14;
     21, 1-10.
3: 51, 48; Is 13, 17.
4: 3, 18; Ps 126, 6.

5 to their goal in Zion they shall ask the
      way.
   "Come, let us join ourselves to the Lord
      with covenant everlasting, never to be
      forgotten."
6 Lost sheep were my people,
      their shepherds misled them,
      straggling on the mountains;
   From mountain to hill they wandered,
      losing the way to their fold.
7 Whoever came upon them devoured
      them,
      and their enemies said, "We incur no
      guilt,
   Because they sinned against the Lord,
      the hope of their fathers, their abode
      of justice."

8 Flee from Babylon, leave the land of the
      Chaldeans,
      be like the rams at the head of the
      flock.
9 See, I am stirring up against Babylon
      a band of great nations from the north;
      from there they advance, and she shall
      be taken.
   Their arrows are arrows of the skilled
      warrior;
      none shall return without effect.
10 Chaldea shall be their plunder,
      and all her plunderers shall be
      enriched,
      says the Lord.
11 Yes, rejoice and exult,
      you that plunder my portion;
   Frisk like calves on the green,
      snort like stallions!
12 Your mother shall be sorely put to
      shame,
      she that bore you shall be abashed;
   See, the last of the nations,
      a desert, dry and waste.
13 Because of the Lord's wrath she shall be
      empty,
      and become a total desert;
   Everyone who passes by Babylon will be
      appalled
      and catch his breath, at all her
      wounds.
14 Take your posts encircling Babylon,
      you who bend the bow;
   Shoot at her, spare not your arrows,

15 raise the war cry against her on all
      sides.
   She surrenders, her bastions fall,
      her walls are torn down:
   Vengeance of the Lord is this! Take
      revenge on her,
      as she has done, do to her;
      for she sinned against the Lord.
16 Cut off from Babylon the sower
      and him who wields the sickle in
      harvest time!
   Before the destroying sword,
      each of them turns to his own people,
      everyone flees to his own land.
17 A stray sheep was Israel
      that lions pursued;
   Formerly the king of Assyria devoured
      her,
      now Nebuchadnezzar of Babylon
      gnaws her bones.

18 Therefore, thus says the Lord of hosts, the God
of Israel:

   I will punish the king of Babylon and
      his land,
      as once I punished the king of Assyria;
19 But I will bring back Israel to her fold,
      to feed on Carmel and Bashan,
   And on Mount Ephraim and Gilead,
      till she has her fill.

20 In those days, at that time, says the Lord:

   They shall seek Israel's guilt, but it shall
      be no more,
      and Judah's sins, but these shall no
      longer be found;
      for I will forgive the remnant I
      preserve.

21 Attack the land of Merathaim,
      and those who live in Pekod;
   Slaughter and doom them, says the
      Lord,
      do all I have commanded you.
22 Battle alarm in the land,
      dire destruction!
23 How has the hammer of the whole earth
      been broken and shattered!
   What an object of horror
      Babylon has become among the
      nations!
24 You ensnared yourself, and were caught,
      O Babylon, before you knew it!

5: 31, 31; 32, 40.
6: Is 53, 6; 1 Pt 2, 25.
7: 31, 23.
8: 51, 6.45; Is 48, 20.
9: 51, 27.
12: 51, 43; Is 13, 20ff.
13: 25, 12.
14: 51, 11; Is 21, 2.
15: 51, 11.44.58;
    Ps 137, 8.
16: Is 13, 14.
17: 2 Kgs 17, 24; 18, 14.
18: Is 10, 12; 14, 24f.
19: 23, 3; Ez 34, 13f.
20: 31, 34; Is 43, 25;
    Mi 7, 19.
23: 51, 20; Is 14, 6.
24: 51, 57.

† 50, 15: *Her walls are torn down:* the prophet is not predicting the details of Babylon's downfall, but describing such a
downfall in conventional language. Actually, Babylon was surrendered peaceably, without destruction.

50, 21: *Merathaim,* "twice bitter," and *Pekod,* "punishment,"
are here symbolic terms for Babylonia, though probably they
suggest also the names of regions in that country.

You were discovered and seized,
    because you challenged the Lord.
25 The Lord opens his armory
    and brings forth the weapons of his
      wrath;
For the Lord God of hosts has work to do
    in the land of the Chaldeans.

26 Come upon her from every side,
    open her granaries,
Pile up her goods in heaps and doom it,
    leave not a remnant.
27 Slay all her oxen,
    let them go down to the slaughter;
Woe to them! their day has come,
    the time of their punishment.
28 Listen! the fugitives, the escaped
    from the land of Babylon:
They announce in Zion
    the vengeance of the Lord, our God.
29 Call up against Babylon archers,
    all who bend the bow;
Encamp around her,
    let no one escape.
Repay her for her deeds;
    as she has done, do to her,
For she insulted the Lord,
    the Holy One of Israel.
30 Therefore her young men shall fall in her
    streets,
    all her warriors shall perish on that
    day,
    says the Lord.

31 I am against you, man of insolence,
    says the Lord God of hosts;
For your day has come,
    the time for me to punish you.
32 Insolence stumbles and falls;
    there is no one to raise him up.
I will kindle in his cities a fire
    that shall devour everything around
    him.
33   Thus says the Lord of hosts:
Oppressed are the men of Israel,
    and with them the men of Judah;
All their captors hold them fast
    and refuse to let them go.
34 Strong is their avenger,
    whose name is Lord of hosts;
He will defend their cause with success,
    and give rest to the earth,
    but unrest to those who live in
    Babylon.

35 A sword upon the Chaldeans, says the
    Lord,
    upon Babylon's people, her princes
    and wise men!
36 A sword upon the soothsayers,
    that they may become fools!
A sword upon her warriors,
    that they may tremble;
37 A sword upon her motley throng,
    that they may become women!
A sword upon her treasures,
    that they may be plundered;
38 A sword upon her waters,
    that they may dry up!
For it is a land of idols,
    and they shall be made frantic by
    fearful things.
39 Hence, wildcats and desert beasts shall
    dwell there,
    and ostriches shall occupy it;
Never again shall it be peopled, or lived
    in,
    from age to age.
40 As when God overturned Sodom
    and Gomorrah, with their neighbors,
    says the Lord,
Not a man shall dwell there,
    no human being shall tarry there.

41 See! a people comes from the north,
    a great nation, and mighty kings
    roused from the ends of the earth.
42 Bow and javelin they wield,
    cruel and pitiless are they;
They sound like the roaring sea,
    as they ride forth on steeds,
Each in his place for battle
    against you, daughter Babylon.
43 The king of Babylon hears news of them,
    and helpless fall his hands;
Anguish seizes him,
    throes like a mother's in childbirth.
44 As when a lion comes up from the
    Jordan's thicket
    to the permanent feeding grounds,
So I, in one instant, will drive them off,
    and whom I choose I will establish
    there;
For who is like me? who calls me to
    account?
    what shepherd can stand against me?
45 Therefore hear the counsel of the Lord
    which he has taken against Babylon;
Hear the plans he has made
    against the land of the Chaldeans:
They shall be dragged away, even the
    smallest sheep;
    their own pasture shall be aghast
    because of them.

---

*
25: 51, 11f; Is 13, 5.   39: 51, 37; Is 13, 21f.
28: 51, 10f.   40: 51, 43.
29: 51, 56.   41: 51, 27f.
30: 49, 26; 51, 4.   43: Is 13, 7.
34: 51, 36.   44: 49, 19.
37: 51, 30; Na 3, 13.   45: 51, 12.29.
38: 51, 32.36.

46 At the cry "Babylon is captured!" the
earth quakes;
the outcry is heard among the nations.

The Second Prophecy Against Babylon

51 **1**   Thus says the LORD:
See! I rouse against Babylon,
and against those who live in Chaldea,
a destroying wind.

2 Against Babylon I will send winnowers
to winnow her and lay waste her land;
They shall besiege her from all sides
on the day of affliction.

3 Let the bowman draw his bow,
and flaunt his coat of mail;
Spare not her young men,
doom her entire army.

4 The slain shall fall in the land of
Chaldea,
the transfixed, in her streets;

5 For Israel and Judah are now widowed
of their God, the LORD of hosts,
And the Chaldean land is full of guilt
to be punished by the Holy One of
Israel.

6 Flee out of Babylon;
let each one save his life,
perish not for her guilt;
This is a time of vengeance for the LORD,
he pays her her due.

7 Babylon was a golden cup in the hand of
the LORD
which made the whole earth drunk;
The nations drank its wine,
with this they have become mad.

8 Babylon suddenly falls and is crushed:
howl over her!
Bring balm for her wounds,
in case she can be healed.

9 "We have tried to heal Babylon,
but she cannot be healed.
Leave her, let us go, each to his own
land."
Her judgment reaches heaven,
it touches the clouds.

10 The LORD has brought to light our just
cause;
come, let us tell in Zion
what the LORD, our God, has done.

11 Sharpen the arrows,
fill the quivers;

The LORD has stirred up the spirit of
Media's kings;
Babylon he is resolved to destroy.
Yes, it is the vengeance of the LORD,
vengeance for his temple.

12 Against the walls of Babylon raise a
signal,
make strong the watch;
Post sentries,
arrange ambushes!
For the LORD has planned and he will
carry out
his threat against the inhabitants of
Babylon.

13 You who dwell by mighty waters,
rich in treasure,
Your end has come,
the term at which you shall be cut off!

14 The LORD of hosts has sworn by himself:
I will fill you with men as numerous
as locusts,
who shall raise over you the vintage
shout!

15 He has sworn who made the earth by his
power,
and established the world by his
wisdom,
and stretched out the heavens by his
skill.

16 When he thunders, the waters in the
heavens roar,
and he brings up clouds from the end
of the earth;
He makes the lightning flash in the rain,
and releases stormwinds from their
chambers.

17 Every man is stupid, ignorant;
every artisan is put to shame by his
idol;
He molded a fraud,
without breath of life.

18 Nothingness are they, a ridiculous work,
that will perish in their time of
punishment.

19 Not like these is the portion of Jacob,
he is the creator of all things;
Israel is his very own tribe,
LORD of hosts is his name.

20 You are my hammer,
my weapon for war;
With you I shatter nations,
with you I destroy kingdoms.

21 With you I shatter horse and rider,
with you I shatter chariot and driver.

46: 51, 29.
51/2: 15, 7; Is 41, 16.
3: 50, 14.29.
4: 50, 30.
6: 50, 8.15.29; Is 48, 20.
7: Rv 14, 8; 17, 4.
8: Rv 18, 9-18.
9: Is 13, 14; Rv 18, 5.
10: 50, 28.
11: 2 Kgs 17, 6; Is 13, 17.
13: Na 2, 1.
15: 10, 12.
21: Dn 7, 7.19.23.

51, 11: *Media's kings:* the Medes dwelt with the Persians in the land now known as Iran. At the time these words were written the Medes were the dominant people of the two, but within a short time the Persians had gained the ascendancy.

22* With you I shatter man and wife,
    with you I shatter old and young,
    with you I shatter youth and maiden.

23 With you I shatter the shepherd and his
    flock,
    with you I shatter the farmer and his
    team,
    with you I shatter satraps and
    prefects.

24* Thus will I repay Babylon,
    and all who live in Chaldea
All the evil they did to Zion,
    as you shall see with your own eyes,
    says the LORD.

25* Beware! I am against you,
    destroying mountain,
    destroyer of the entire earth, says the
    LORD;
I will stretch forth my hand against you,
    roll you down over the cliffs,
    and make you a burnt mountain:

26* They will not take from you a
    cornerstone,
    or a foundation stone;
Ruins forever shall you be,
    says the LORD.

27*† Raise a signal on the earth,
    blow the trumpet among the nations;
Dedicate peoples to war against her,
    summon against her the kingdoms,
    Ararat, Minni, and Ashkenaz;
Appoint recruiting officers against her,
    send up horses like bristling locusts.

28 Dedicate peoples to war against her:
    the king of Media,
Its governors and all its prefects,
    every land in his domain.

29 The earth quakes and writhes,
    the LORD's plan against Babylon is
    carried out,
Turning the land of Babylon
    into a desert where no one lives.

30 Babylon's warriors have ceased to fight,
    they remain in their strongholds;
Dried up is their strength,
    they have become women.
Burned are their homes,
    and broken their bars.

31* One runner meets another,
    herald meets herald,
Telling the king of Babylon
    that all his city is taken.

32 The fords have been seized,
    and the fortresses set on fire,
    while warriors are in panic.

33*For thus says the LORD of hosts, the God of
Israel:

    Daughter Babylon is like a threshing
    floor
    at the time it is trodden;
Yet a little while,
    and the harvest time will come for her.

34† He has consumed me, routed me,
    [Nebuchadnezzar, king of Babylon,]
    he has left me as an empty vessel;
He has swallowed me like a dragon:
    filled his belly with my delights, and
    cast me out.

35 My torn flesh be upon Babylon,
    says the city on Zion;
My blood upon the people of Chaldea,
    says Jerusalem.

36   But now, thus says the LORD:
Surely I will defend your cause,
    I will avenge you;
I will dry up her sea,
    and drain her fountain.

37* Babylon shall become a heap of ruins,
    a haunt of jackals;
A place of horror and ridicule,
    where no one lives.

38* They all roar like lions,
    growl like lion cubs.

39 When they are parched, I will set a drink
    before them
    to make them drunk, that they may be
    overcome
    with perpetual sleep, never to awaken,
    says the LORD.

40 I will bring them down like lambs to the
    slaughter,
    like rams and goats.

41* How has she been seized, made captive,
    the glory of the whole world!
What a horror has Babylon become
    among nations:

42   against Babylon the sea rises,
    she is overwhelmed by the roaring
    waves!

43 Her cities have become a desert,
    parched and arid land
Where no man lives,
    and no one passes through.

44 I will punish Bel in Babylon,
    and make him disgorge what he
    swallowed;
    peoples shall stream to him no more.

✿
22: Is 13, 16.18.
24: 25, 14; 50, 29;
    Ps 137, 8.
25: Rv 8, 7; 18, 8f.
26: 25, 12; Ps 118, 22.
27: Na 3, 17.

31: 2 Chr 30, 6;
    Jb 1, 14-18.
33: Rv 14, 15.
37: Is 25, 2.
38: Na 2, 11f.
41: Is 13, 19.

† 51, 27: *Ararat, Minni, and Ashkenaz:* regions or people in
what is now Armenia, subject at this time to Media.
    51, 34f: *Me, my:* refers to Jerusalem.

The wall of Babylon falls!
45   Leave her, my people, let each one
save himself
from the burning wrath of the LORD.

46* Be not discouraged for fear of rumors spread in the land; this year the rumor comes, then violence in the land, tyrant against tyrant. **47** But behold, the days are coming when I will punish the idols of Babylon; her whole land shall be put to shame, and all her slain shall lie fallen within her. **48*** Then heaven, and earth, and everything in them shall shout over Babylon with joy, when the destroyers come against her from the north, says the LORD. **49** Babylon, too, must fall, O slain of Israel, as at the hands of Babylon have fallen the slain of all the earth.

50   You who have escaped the sword,
go on, stand not still;
Remember the LORD from afar,
let Jerusalem come to your minds.
51*   We are ashamed because we have heard taunts,
confusion covers our faces; strangers have entered
the holy places of the house of the LORD.
52   But behold, the days are coming, says the LORD,
when I will punish her idols,
and in her whole land the wounded will groan.
53*   Though Babylon scale the heavens,
and make her strong heights inaccessible,
destroyers from me shall reach her, says the LORD.
54   Hear! loud cries from Babylon,
dire destruction from the land of the Chaldeans;
55   For the LORD lays Babylon waste,
stills her loud cry,
Though her waves were roaring like mighty waters,
and their clamor was heard afar.
56*   For the destroyer comes upon her, [Babylon,]
her heroes are captured, their bows broken;
The LORD is a God who requites,
he will surely repay.

57 I will make her princes and her wise men drunk, her governors, her prefects, and her warriors, so that they sleep an eternal sleep, never to awaken, says the King, whose name is the LORD of hosts. **58*** Thus says the LORD of hosts:

The walls of spacious Babylon shall be leveled utterly;
her lofty gates shall be destroyed by fire.
The toil of the nations is for nothing;
for the flames the peoples weary themselves.

The Prophecy Sent to Babylon

59† This was the errand given by the prophet Jeremiah to Seraiah, son of Neriah, son of Mahseiah, when he went to Babylon for the king in the fourth year of the reign of Zedekiah; Seraiah was chief quartermaster. **60†** Jeremiah had written all the misfortune that was to befall Babylon in a single book: all these words that were written against Babylon. **61*** And Jeremiah said to Seraiah: When you reach Babylon, see that you read aloud all these words, **62** and then say: "O LORD, you yourself threatened to destroy this place, so that neither man nor beast should dwell in it, since it would remain an everlasting desert. **63*** When you have finished reading this book, tie a stone to it and throw it in the Euphrates, **64†** and say: Thus shall Babylon sink. Never shall she rise, because of the evil I am bringing upon her. [To "weary themselves" are the words of Jeremiah.]

VI: HISTORICAL APPENDIX

Capture of Jerusalem

52 **1*†** ZEDEKIAH WAS TWENTY-ONE YEARS OLD when he became king, and he reigned eleven years in Jerusalem. His mother's name was Hamutal, daughter of Jeremiah of Libnah. **2** He did what was evil in the eyes of the LORD, just as Jehoiakim had done. **3** Indeed, what was done in Jerusalem and in Judah so angered the LORD that he cast them out from his presence.

Zedekiah rebelled against the king of Babylon. **4*†** In the tenth month of the ninth year of his reign, on the tenth day of the month, Nebuchadnezzar, king of

---

† 51, 59: *Seraiah:* the brother of Baruch; cf 32, 12. *The king:* Zedekiah. Perhaps Seraiah went to Babylon to explain away the presence of foreign ambassadors in Jerusalem that same year; cf 27, 3.

51, 60: Jeremiah prophesied against Babylon, even as he foretold Judah's release from Babylon's power (3, 14-18; 32, 15; 33, 6-9.12f); but his *book* against Babylon was thrown in the Euphrates (v 63). The preceding oracles were composed by later writers; see note on 50, 1—51, 58.

51, 64: *To "weary themselves" are the words of Jeremiah:* an editorial remark concerning the end of v 58.

52, 1-34: This supplement to the Book of Jeremiah was taken by the final editor from 2 Kgs 24, 18—25, 30 and placed here in order to show the fulfillment of Jeremiah's prophecies. In part this repeats the history given in Jer 39-41; the history of Gedaliah in 2 Kgs 25, 22-26, however, has not been reproduced here.

52, 4: *In the tenth month of the ninth year of his reign, on the tenth day of the month:* January 15, 588 B. C. Cf 39, 1.

---

*
46: Mt 24, 6f.	58: Hb 2, 13.
48: Rv 18, 20.	61: 50, 1-51.
51: Pss 44, 16f; 78, 1-4.	63: Rv 18, 21.
53: Is 14, 13.	52/1-27: 2 Kgs 24, 18—25, 21.
56: Na 1, 2.	4-16: 39, 1-10.

Babylon, and his whole army advanced against Jerusalem, encamped around it, and built siege walls on every side. **5**The siege of the city continued until the eleventh year of King Zedekiah.

6On the ninth day of the fourth month, when famine had gripped the city and the people had no more bread, **7**the city walls were breached. Then all the soldiers took to flight and left the city by night through the gate between the two walls which was near the king's garden. With the Chaldeans surrounding the city, they went in the direction of the Arabah. **8**But the Chaldean army pursued the king and overtook Zedekiah in the desert near Jericho, while his whole army fled from him.

9The king, therefore, was arrested and brought to Riblah, in the land of Hamath, to the king of Babylon, who pronounced sentence on him. **10**As Zedekiah looked on, the king of Babylon slew his sons as well as all the princes of Judah at Riblah. **11**Then he blinded Zedekiah, bound him with fetters, and had him brought to Babylon and kept in prison until the day of his death.

Destruction of Jerusalem

12†On the tenth day of the fifth month (this was in the nineteenth year of Nebuchadnezzar, king of Babylon), Nebuzaradan, captain of the bodyguard, came to Jerusalem as the representative of the king of Babylon. **13**He burned the house of the LORD, the palace of the king, and all the houses of Jerusalem; every large building he destroyed with fire. **14**And the Chaldean troops who were with the captain of the guard tore down all the walls that surrounded Jerusalem.

15Then Nebuzaradan, captain of the guard, led into exile the rest of the people left in the city, and those who had deserted to the king of Babylon, and the rest of the artisans. **16**But some of the country's poor, Nebuzaradan, captain of the guard, left behind as vinedressers and farmers.

17The bronze pillars that belonged to the house of the LORD, and the wheeled carts and the bronze sea in the house of the LORD, the Chaldeans broke into pieces; they carried away all the bronze to Babylon. **18**They took also the pots, the shovels, the snuffers, the bowls, the pans, and all the bronze vessels used for service. **19**The basins also, the fire holders, the bowls, the pots, the lampstands, the pans, the sacrificial bowls which were of gold or silver, these too the captain of the guard carried off, **20**as well as the two pillars, the one sea, and the twelve oxen of bronze under the sea, and the wheeled carts which King Solomon had made for the house of the LORD. The bronze of all these furnishings could not be weighed. **21**Each of the pillars was eighteen cubits high and

twelve cubits in diameter; each was four fingers thick, and hollow inside. **22**A bronze capital five cubits high surmounted the one pillar, and a network with pomegranates encircled the capital, all of brass; and so for the other pillar. The pomegranates . . . **23**there were ninety-six pomegranates. There were a hundred pomegranates, all around the network.

24The captain of the guard also took Seraiah, the high priest, Zephaniah, the second priest, and the three keepers of the entry. **25**And from the city he took one courtier, a commander of soldiers, and seven men in the personal service of the king who were present in the city, and the scribe of the army commander who mustered the people of the land, and sixty of the common people who were in the city. **26**The captain of the guard, Nebuzaradan, arrested these and brought them to the king of Babylon at Riblah, **27**who had them struck down and put to death in Riblah, in the land of Hamath.

Thus was Judah exiled from her land. **28**†This is the number of the people whom Nebuchadnezzar led away captive: in his seventh year, three thousand and twenty-three people of Judah; **29**in the eighteenth year of Nebuchadnezzar, eight hundred and thirty-two persons from Jerusalem; **30**in the twenty-third year of Nebuchadnezzar, Nebuzaradan, captain of the guard, exiled seven hundred and forty-five people of Judah: four thousand six hundred persons in all.

Favor Shown to Jehoiachin

31✤†In the thirty-seventh year of the exile of Jehoiachin, king of Judah, on the twenty-fifth day of the twelfth month, Evil-merodach, king of Babylon, in the inaugural year of his reign, took up the case of Jehoiachin, king of Judah, and released him from prison. **32**†He spoke kindly to him and gave him a throne higher than that of the other kings who were with him in Babylon. **33**Jehoiachin took off his prison garb and ate at the king's table as long as he lived. **34**The allowance given him by the king of Babylon was a perpetual allowance, in fixed daily amounts, all the days of his life until the day of his death.

---

† 52, 12: *On the tenth day of the fifth month . . . nineteenth year:* the tenth of Ab—July/August in 587 B. C.

52, 28-30: These verses are missing in the Greek text and have not been taken from 2 Kgs 25, but from some other source using a different system of chronology. Besides the deportations of 598 and 587 B. C., mention is made here of a final one that took place in the year 582/1, possibly as a sequel to the murder of Gedaliah, cf 41, 2.

52, 31-34: In the year 561/0 B. C., Jehoiachin was released from prison by Nebuchadnezzar's successor Awel-Marduk (Evil-merodach), who reigned only two years. Babylonian records confirm the fact that Jehoiachin and his family were supported at public expense.

52, 32: *The other kings:* who had also been brought as captives to Babylon.

✤ 31-34: 2 Kgs 25, 27-30.

The Book of Lamentations

Introduction

The sixth century B. C. was an age of crisis, a turning point in the history of Israel. With the destruction of the temple and the interruption of its ritual, the exile of the leaders and loss of national sovereignty, an era came to an end. Not long after the fall of Jerusalem (587) an eyewitness of the national humiliation composed these five laments. They combine confession of sin, grief over the suffering and humiliation of Zion, submission to merited chastisement, and strong faith in the constancy of Yahweh's love and power to restore. This union of poignant grief and unquenchable hope reflects the constant prophetic vision of the weakness of man and the strength of God's love; it also shows how Israel's faith in Yahweh could survive the shattering experience of national ruin.

As a literary work, the Book of Lamentations is carefully constructed according to a familiar structural device. The first four poems are acrostics in which the separate stanzas begin with successive letters of the Hebrew alphabet from the first to the last. Far from destroying the spontaneous pathos of the songs, this literary feature permits a symbolic and disciplined expression of the profound grief, the sinful responsibility, and the enduring hope of the suffering community. The figure of Israel as a bride of Yahweh, familiar from the prophets, appears here again; but now Zion is a desolate widow, the *Judaea Capta* of Titus' memorial coins, sustained only by the faith that God's chastisement will eventually give place to his infinite compassion.

Jerusalem Abandoned and Disgraced

1

1† How lonely she is now,
    the once crowded city!
Widowed is she
    who was mistress over nations;
The princess among the provinces
    has been made a toiling slave.

2✿ Bitterly she weeps at night,
    tears upon her cheeks,
With not one to console her
    of all her dear ones;
Her friends have all betrayed her
    and become her enemies.

3✿ Judah has fled into exile
    from oppression and cruel slavery;
Yet where she lives among the nations
    she finds no place to rest:

All her persecutors come upon her
    where she is narrowly confined.

4✿ The roads to Zion mourn
    for lack of pilgrims going to her feasts;
All her gateways are deserted,
    her priests groan,
Her virgins sigh;
    she is in bitter grief.

5 Her foes are uppermost,
    her enemies are at ease;
The LORD has punished her
    for her many sins.
Her little ones have gone away,
    captive before the foe.

6 Gone from daughter Zion
    is all her glory:
Her princes, like rams
    that find no pasture,
Have gone off without strength
    before their captors.

7 Jerusalem is mindful of the days
    of her wretched homelessness,
When her people fell into enemy hands,
    and she had no one to help her;
When her foes gloated over her,
    laughed at her ruin.

8✿ Through the sin of which she is guilty,
    Jerusalem is defiled;
All who esteemed her think her vile
    now that they see her nakedness;
She herself groans
    and turns away.

9 Her filth is on her skirt;
    she gave no thought how she would end.
Astounding is her downfall,
    with no one to console her.
Look, O LORD, upon her misery,
    for the enemy has triumphed!

10✿ The foe stretched out his hand
    to all her treasures;
She has seen those nations
    enter her sanctuary

✿
    1/2: Jer 30, 14; Ez 16, 37.   8: Is 47, 2; Jer 13, 22.26.
    3: Dt 28, 65; Jer 45, 3.   10: Jer 51, 51.
    4: Jer 14, 2.

† 1, 1-22: In this poem the poet first describes Jerusalem's miserable state after the destruction wrought by the Chaldeans (vv 1-11a); in v 11b the city itself takes up the lament.

Whom you forbade to come
  into your assembly.

11 All her people groan,
  searching for bread;
They give their treasures for food,
  to retain the breath of life.
"Look, O Lord, and see
  how worthless I have become!

12 "Come, all you who pass by the way,
  look and see
Whether there is any suffering like my
  suffering,
  which has been dealt me
When the Lord afflicted me
  on the day of his blazing wrath.

13 "From on high he sent fire
  down into my very frame;
He spread a net for my feet,
  and overthrew me.
He left me desolate,
  in pain all the day.

14† "He has kept watch over my sins;
  by his hand they have been plaited:
They have settled about my neck,
  he has brought my strength to its knees;
The Lord has delivered me into their grip,
  I am unable to rise.

15 "All the mighty ones in my midst
  the Lord has cast away;
He summoned an army against me
  to crush my young men;
The Lord has trodden in the wine press
  virgin daughter Judah.

16 "At this I weep,
  my eyes run with tears:
Far from me are all who could console me,
  any who might revive me;
My sons were reduced to silence
  when the enemy prevailed."

17 Zion stretched out her hands,
  but there was no one to console her;
The Lord gave orders against Jacob
  for his neighbors to be his foes;
Jerusalem has become in their midst
  a thing unclean.

18 "The Lord is just;
  I had defied his command.
Listen, all you peoples,
  and behold my suffering:
My maidens and my youths
  have gone into captivity.

19† "I cried out to my lovers,
  but they failed me.
My priests and my elders
  perished in the city;
Where they sought food for themselves,
  they found it not.

20 "Look, O Lord, upon my distress:
  all within me is in ferment,
My heart recoils within me
  from my monstrous rebellion.
In the streets the sword bereaves,
  at home death stalks.

21 "Give heed to my groaning;
  there is no one to console me.
All my enemies rejoice at my misfortune:
  it is you who have wrought it.
Bring on the day you have proclaimed,
  that they may be even as I.

22† "Let all their evil come before you;
  deal with them
As you have dealt with me
  for all my sins;
My groans are many,
  and I am sick at heart."

The Lord's Wrath Against Zion

2 1† How the Lord in his wrath
  has detested daughter Zion!
He has cast down from heaven to earth
  the glory of Israel,
Unmindful of his footstool
  on the day of his wrath.

2 The Lord has consumed without pity
  all the dwellings of Jacob;
He has torn down in his anger
  the fortresses of daughter Judah;
He has brought to the ground in dishonor
  her king and her princes.

3† He broke off, in fiery wrath,
  the horn that was Israel's whole strength;
He withheld the support of his right hand
  when the enemy approached;
He blazed up in Jacob like a flaming fire
  devouring all about it.

---

† 1, 14: *They have been plaited . . . my neck:* the sins of the people have been bound together and laid as a yoke on their back; cf Mt 23, 4.
1, 19: *My lovers:* Zion's foreign allies, who failed to help her, as the prophets had warned.
1, 22: Zion fully acknowledges her guilt and the justness of divine punishment; nevertheless, she pleads that her enemies also be punished for their guilt.
2, 1: *The glory of Israel:* the temple. *His footstool:* the ark of the covenant (1 Chr 28, 2; Pss 99, 5; 132, 7); or again, the temple (Ez 43, 7).
2, 3: *Horn:* symbol of power and strength; cf 2, 17; 1 Sm 2, 10; Lk 1, 69; etc.

11: Jer 52, 6.   18: Dt 28, 41.
13: Ez 12, 13.   19: Jer 30, 14.
15: Jer 8, 16.   20: 2, 11.
16: Jer 13, 17; 14, 17.   22: 3, 64.
17: Ps 74, 7.   2/3: 1, 12.

4* Like an enemy he made taut his bow;
     with his arrows in his right hand
He took his stand as a foe, and slew
     all on whom the eye doted;
Over the tent of daughter Zion
     he poured out his wrath like fire.

5 The Lord has become an enemy,
     he has consumed Israel:
Consumed all her castles
     and destroyed her fortresses;
For daughter Judah he has multiplied
     moaning and groaning.

6* He has demolished his shelter like a garden
       booth,
     he has destroyed his dwelling;
In Zion the LORD has made
     feast and sabbath to be forgotten;
He has scorned in fierce wrath
     both king and priest.

7* The Lord has disowned his altar,
     rejected his sanctuary;
The walls of her towers
     he has handed over to the enemy,
Who shout in the house of the LORD
     as on a feast day.

8*† The LORD marked for destruction
     the wall of daughter Zion:
He stretched out the measuring line;
     his hand brought ruin, yet he did not
       relent—
He brought grief on wall and rampart
     till both succumbed.

9* Sunk into the ground are her gates;
     he has removed and broken her bars.
Her king and her princes are among the
       pagans;
     priestly instruction is wanting,
And her prophets have not received
     any vision from the LORD.

10*† On the ground in silence sit
     the old men of daughter Zion;
They strew dust on their heads
     and gird themselves with sackcloth;
The maidens of Jerusalem
     bow their heads to the ground.

11*† Worn out from weeping are my eyes,
     within me all is in ferment;
My gall is poured out on the ground
     because of the downfall of the daughter
      of my people,

As child and infant faint away
     in the open spaces of the town.

12* They ask their mothers,
     "Where is the cereal?"—in vain,
As they faint away like the wounded
     in the streets of the city,
And breathe their last
     in their mothers' arms.

13* To what can I liken or compare you,
     O daughter Jerusalem?
What example can I show you for your
      comfort,
     virgin daughter Zion?
For great as the sea is your downfall;
     who can heal you?

14* Your prophets had for you
     false and specious visions;
They did not lay bare your guilt,
     to avert your fate;
They beheld for you in vision
     false and misleading portents.

15* All who pass by
     clap their hands at you;
They hiss and wag their heads
     over daughter Jerusalem:
"Is this the all-beautiful city,
     the joy of the whole earth?"

16* All your enemies
     open their mouths against you;
They hiss and gnash their teeth.
     They say, "We have devoured her.
This at last is the day we hoped for;
     we have lived to see it!"

17* The LORD has done as he decreed:
     he has fulfilled the threat
He set forth from days of old;
     he has destroyed and had no pity,
Letting the enemy gloat over you
     and exalting the horn of your foes.

18 Cry out to the Lord;
     moan, O daughter Zion!
Let your tears flow like a torrent
     day and night;
Let there be no respite for you,
     no repose for your eyes.

19 Rise up, shrill in the night,
     at the beginning of every watch;
Pour out your heart like water
     in the presence of the Lord;

✿
4: Jer 30, 14.
6: 1, 4; Is 1, 13; 5, 5.
7: Ez 24, 21.
8: Jer 52, 13.
9: Dt 28, 36.
10: Is 3, 26.
11: 3, 48.

12: 1, 11.
13: 1, 12.
14: Is 58, 1; Jer 2, 8;
    23, 16.
15: Jer 18, 16.
16: 3, 46.
17: Dt 28, 15.

†
  2, 8: *The measuring line:* used not only in building, but in deciding what must be destroyed; cf Is 34, 11; 2 Kgs 21, 13.
  2, 10: *They strew dust:* as a sign of penance; cf Jb 2, 12.
  2, 11: *My gall is poured out on the ground:* I am afflicted with bitter sorrow; cf Jb 16, 13.

Lift up your hands to him
　for the lives of your little ones
[Who faint from hunger
　at the corner of every street].

20 *† "Look, O Lord, and consider:
　whom have you ever treated thus?
Must women eat their offspring,
　their well-formed children?
Are priest and prophet to be slain
　in the sanctuary of the Lord?

21 * "Dead in the dust of the streets
　lie young and old;
My maidens and young men
　have fallen by the sword;
You have slain on the day of your wrath,
　slaughtered without pity.

22 * "You summoned as for a feast day
　terrors against me from all sides;
There was not, on the day of your wrath,
　either fugitive or survivor;
Those whom I bore and reared
　my enemy has utterly destroyed."

Sufferings of the Prophet and His People

3　1 *† I am a man who knows affliction
　from the rod of his anger,
2 One whom he has led and forced to walk
　in darkness, not in the light;
3 Against me alone he brings back his hand
　again and again all the day.
4 * He has worn away my flesh and my skin,
　he has broken my bones;
5 He has beset me round about
　with poverty and weariness;
6 * He has left me to dwell in the dark
　like those long dead.
7 He has hemmed me in with no escape
　and weighed me down with chains;
8 * Even when I cry out for help,
　he stops my prayer;
9 He has blocked my ways with fitted stones,
　and turned my paths aside.
10 * A lurking bear he has been to me,
　a lion in ambush!
11 * He deranged my ways, set me astray,
　left me desolate.
12 * He bent his bow, and set me up
　as the target for his arrow.

13 * He pierces my sides
　with shafts from his quiver.
14 * I have become a laughingstock for all nations,
　their taunt all the day long;
15 * He has sated me with bitter food,
　made me drink my fill of wormwood.
16 He has broken my teeth with gravel,
　pressed my face in the dust;
17 My soul is deprived of peace,
　I have forgotten what happiness is;
18 I tell myself my future is lost,
　all that I hoped for from the Lord.
19 The thought of my homeless poverty
　is wormwood and gall;
20 Remembering it over and over
　leaves my soul downcast within me.
21 But I will call this to mind,
　as my reason to have hope:
22 * The favors of the Lord are not exhausted,
　his mercies are not spent;
23 They are renewed each morning,
　so great is his faithfulness.
24 * My portion is the Lord, says my soul;
　therefore will I hope in him.
25 * Good is the Lord to one who waits for him,
　to the soul that seeks him;
26 It is good to hope in silence
　for the saving help of the Lord.
27 † It is good for a man to bear
　the yoke from his youth.
28 Let him sit alone and in silence,
　when it is laid upon him.
29 *† Let him put his mouth to the dust;
　there may yet be hope.
30 * Let him offer his cheek to be struck,
　let him be filled with disgrace.
31 * For the Lord's rejection
　does not last forever;
32 * Though he punishes, he takes pity,
　in the abundance of his mercies;
33 * He has no joy in afflicting
　or grieving the sons of men.
34 When anyone tramples underfoot
　all the prisoners in the land,
35 When he distorts men's rights
　in the very sight of the Most High,
36 When he presses a crooked claim,
　the Lord does not look on unconcerned.
37 Who commands, so that it comes to pass,
　except the Lord ordains it;

20: 4, 10.
21: 3, 43; 2 Chr 36, 17; Jer 6, 11.
22: Jer 42, 17.
3/1: Jer 20, 18.
4: Jb 30, 30; Is 38, 13.
6: Ps 143, 3.
8: Ps 22, 2.
10: Jb 10, 16; Hos 13, 8.
11: 1, 13.
12: 2, 4; Jb 16, 12.
13: Jb 6, 4; Ps 38, 3.
14: Jb 30, 9; Ps 69, 13.
15: Jer 9, 14; 23, 15.
22: Neh 9, 31.
24: Pss 16, 5; 73, 26.
25: Ps 130, 6; Is 30, 18.
29: Jb 42, 6.
30: Is 50, 6; Mt 5, 39.
31: Ps 103, 9.
32: Is 54, 8f.
33: Heb 12, 10f.

† 2, 20: *Must women eat their offspring:* extreme famine in a besieged city sometimes led to this form of cannibalism; cf 4, 10; 2 Kgs 6, 28f; Bar 2, 3; Ez 5, 10.
3, 1-21: The author identifies Zion's sufferings with his own.
3, 27: *To bear the yoke:* to do God's will; cf Jer 2, 20.
3, 29: *Let him put his mouth to the dust:* in humble submission; cf Ps 72, 9.

38   Except it proceeds from the mouth of the
Most High,
whether the thing be good or bad!

39   Why should any living man complain,
any mortal, in the face of his sins?

40   Let us search and examine our ways
that we may return to the Lord!

41   Let us reach out our hearts
toward God in heaven!

42   We have sinned and rebelled;
you have not forgiven us.

43   You veiled yourself in wrath and pursued
us,
you slew us and took no pity;

44   You wrapped yourself in a cloud
which prayer could not pierce.

45   You have made us offscourings and refuse
among the nations.

46   All our enemies
have opened their mouths against us;

47   Terror and the pit have been our lot,
desolation and destruction;

48   My eyes run with streams of water
over the downfall of the daughter of my
people.

49   My eyes flow without ceasing,
there is no respite,

50   Till the Lord from heaven
looks down and sees.

51   My eyes torment my soul
at the sight of all the daughters of my
city.

52   Those who were my enemies without cause
hunted me down like a bird;

53   They struck me down alive in the pit,
and sealed me in with a stone.

54   The waters flowed over my head,
and I said, "I am lost!"

55   I called upon your name, O Lord,
from the bottom of the pit;

56   You heard me call, "Let not your ear
be deaf to my cry for help!"

57   You came to my aid when I called to you;
you said, "Have no fear!"

58   You defended me in mortal danger,
you redeemed my life.

59   You see, O Lord, how I am wronged;
do me justice!

60   You see all their vindictiveness,
all their plots against me.

61   You hear their insults, O Lord,
[all their plots against me],

62   The whispered murmurings of my foes,
against me all the day;

63   Whether they sit or stand,
see, I am their taunt song.

64   Requite them as they deserve, O Lord,
according to their deeds;

65   Give them hardness of heart,
as your curse upon them;

66   Pursue them in wrath and destroy them
from under your heavens!

Miseries of the Besieged City

4

1   How tarnished is the gold,
how changed the noble metal;
How the sacred stones lie strewn
at every street corner!

2   Zion's precious sons,
fine gold their counterpart,
Now worth no more than earthen jars
made by the hands of a potter!

3 † Even the jackals bare their breasts
and suckle their young;
The daughter of my people has become as
cruel
as the ostrich in the desert.

4   The tongue of the suckling cleaves
to the roof of its mouth in thirst;
The babes cry for food,
but there is no one to give it to them.

5   Those accustomed to dainty food
perish in the streets;
Those brought up in purple
now cling to the ash heaps.

6   The punishment of the daughter of my
people
is greater than the penalty of Sodom,
Which was overthrown in an instant
without the turning of a hand.

7   Brighter than snow were her princes,
whiter than milk,
More ruddy than coral,
more precious than sapphire.

8   Now their appearance is blacker than soot,
they are unrecognized on the streets;
Their skin shrinks on their bones,
as dry as wood.

9   Better for those who perish by the sword
than for those who die of hunger,

38: Is 45, 7.
39: Prv 19, 3.
40: Jl 2, 12f.
43: 2, 21.
45: 1 Cor 4, 13.
47: Is 24, 17; Jer 48, 43.
48: Ps 119, 136.
53: Jer 37, 16, 38, 6-9.
55f: Ps 130, 1f.
59: Ps 35, 23.
65: Jer 11, 20; 2 Tm 4, 14.
4/2: Jer 19, 11.
3: Jb 39, 16.
5: Dt 28, 56.
6: Gn 19, 23-29;
2 Pt 2, 6; Jude 1, 7.
8: 3, 4.

---

† 4, 3: *Cruel as the ostrich:* see note on Jb 39, 14ff. Jerusalem, in her distress, has abandoned her children.

Who waste away, as though pierced
through,
lacking the fruits of the field!

10* The hands of compassionate women
boiled their own children,
To serve them as mourners' food
in the downfall of the daughter of my
people.

11* The LORD has spent his anger,
poured out his blazing wrath;
He has kindled a fire in Zion
that has consumed her foundations.

12 The kings of the earth did not believe,
nor any of the world's inhabitants,
That enemy or foe could enter
the gates of Jerusalem.

13*† Because of the sins of her prophets
and the crimes of her priests,
Who shed in her midst
the blood of the just!—

14* They staggered blindly in the streets,
soiled with blood,
So that people could not touch
even their garments:

15 "Away, you unclean!" they cried to them,
"Away, away, do not draw near!"
If they left and wandered among the
nations,
nowhere could they remain.

16 The LORD himself has dispersed them,
he regards them no more;
He does not receive the priests with favor,
nor show kindness to the elders.

17† Our eyes ever wasted away,
looking in vain for aid;
From our watchtower we watched
for a nation that could not save us.

18 Men dogged our steps
so that we could not walk in our streets;
Our end drew near, and came;
our time had expired.

19* Our pursuers were swifter
than eagles in the air,
They harassed us on the mountains
and waylaid us in the desert.

20*† The anointed one of the LORD, our breath of
life,
was caught in their snares,

He in whose shadow we thought
we could live on among the nations.

21*† Though you rejoice and are glad, O
daughter Edom,
you who dwell in the land of Uz,
To you also shall the cup be passed;
you shall become drunk and naked.

22* Your chastisement is completed, O
daughter Zion,
he will not prolong your exile;
But your wickedness, O daughter Edom,
he will punish,
he will lay bare your sins.

The Prophet's Lament and Supplication

5 1 Remember, O LORD, what has befallen us,
look, and see our disgrace:

2* Our inherited lands have been turned over
to strangers,
our homes to foreigners.

3 We have become orphans, fatherless;
widowed are our mothers.

4 The water we drink we must buy,
for our own wood we must pay.

5 On our necks is the yoke of those who drive
us;
we are worn out, but allowed no rest.

6† To Egypt we submitted,
and to Assyria, to fill our need of bread.

7† Our fathers, who sinned, are no more;
but we bear their guilt.

8† Slaves rule over us;
there is no one to rescue us from their
hands.

---

† 4, 13ff: The priests and the false prophets lulled the people into an illusory security (Jer 2, 8; 5, 31; 6, 13; etc.), condoning and entering into their crimes so that they themselves became unclean.

4, 17: *A nation:* Egypt, which failed to give effective aid against Babylon.

4, 20: *Our breath of life:* the king. This is a royal epithet borrowed from Egyptian usage, while *the anointed one of the Lord* is Israelite. After the disaster of 598 B. C. (2 Kgs 24, 1-17), Jerusalem could have hoped to live in peace amidst her neighbors; but they (vv 21f) as well as Babylon turned against her to ensure her total devastation in 587 B. C.

4, 21: *Uz:* see note on Jer 25, 20.

5, 6: In its state of abjection, Judah was forced to depend on its traditional enemies to the west and east for subsistence. Mesopotamia is here called by the name it had long borne, *Assyria,* though in these times the power of the Assyrians had been superseded by that of the Chaldeans.

5, 7: *Our fathers:* collective responsibility, for good and for evil, was recognized in the Old Testament; cf Jer 31, 29. But the present generation is also personally guilty of sin (v 16).

5, 8: Administrations imposed by foreign powers were notoriously corrupt and inept. The Hebrew word for "slave" is the same as that used for an official (servant of the ruler); the author doubtless intends the double meaning here.

*
10: 2, 20; Dt 28, 56f;
    2 Kgs 6, 29.
11: Jer 7, 20; Ez 5, 13.
13: Jer 6, 13.
14: Is 59, 10.

19: Jer 4, 13; Hb 1, 8.
20: 2, 9; Ez 19, 4.8.
21: 1, 21; Jer 25, 15.
22: Is 40, 2.
5/2: Ps 79, 1.

9* At the peril of our lives we bring in our
         sustenance,
      in the face of the desert heat;

10* Our skin is shriveled up, as though by a
         furnace,
      with the searing blasts of famine.

11* The wives in Zion were ravished by the
         enemy,
      the maidens in the cities of Judah;

12* Princes were gibbeted by them,
      elders shown no respect.

13 The youths carry the millstones,
      boys stagger under their loads of wood;

14† The old men have abandoned the gate,
      the young men their music.

15* The joy of our hearts has ceased,
      our dance has turned into mourning;

16 The garlands have fallen from our heads:
      woe to us, for we have sinned!

17 Over this our hearts are sick,
      at this our eyes grow dim:

18 That Mount Zion should be desolate,
      with jackals roaming there!

19* You, O Lord, are enthroned forever;
      your throne stands from age to age.

20* Why, then, should you forget us,
      abandon us so long a time?

21* Lead us back to you, O Lord, that we may
         be restored:
      give us anew such days as we had of old.

22* For now you have indeed rejected us,
      and in full measure turned your wrath
         against us.

---

* 9: Jer 6, 25.
10: 4, 8.
11: Zec 14, 2.
12: 4, 16.
15: Jer 16, 9; 25, 10;
      Am 8, 10.

19: Pss 9, 8; 45, 7;
      102, 13.27.
20: Pss 13, 1; 42, 10.
21: Ps 80, 19f.
22: Jer 14, 19.

---

† 5, 14: *The gate:* the place of assembly, where city decisions were made and judgment given by the elders and other notables; see note on Ru 4, 1.

The Book of Baruch

Introduction

The opening verses of this book ascribe it, or at least its first part, to Baruch, the well-known secretary of the prophet Jeremiah. It contains five very different compositions, the first and the last in prose, the others in poetic form. The prose sections were certainly composed in Hebrew, though the earliest known form of the book is in Greek.

An observance of the feast of Booths with a public prayer of penitence and petition (1, 15—3, 8), such as is supposed by the introduction (1, 1-14), would not have been possible during the lifetime of Baruch after the fall of Jerusalem; this indeed is suggested in the prayer itself (2, 26). The prayer is therefore to be understood as the pious reflection of a later Jewish writer upon the circumstances of the exiles in Babylon as he knew them from the Book of Jeremiah. He expresses in their name sentiments called for by the prophet, and ascribes the wording of these sentiments to the person most intimately acquainted with Jeremiah's teaching, namely, Baruch. The purpose of this literary device is to portray for his own and later generations the spirit of repentance which prompted God to bring the Exile to an end.

The lesson thus gained is followed by a hymn in praise of Wisdom (3, 9—4, 4), exalting the law of Moses as the unique gift of God to Israel; the observance of which is the way to life and peace. The ideal city of Jerusalem is then represented (4, 5-29) as the solicitous mother of all exiles, who is assured in the name of God that all her children will be restored to her (4, 30—5, 9).

The final chapter is really a separate work, with a title of its own (6, 1). It is patterned after the earlier letter of Jeremiah (Jer 29), in the spirit of the warnings against idolatry contained in Jer 10 and Is 44. Its earnestness is impressive, but in restating previous inspired teachings at a later day, it does so with no special literary grace.

Thus the principal divisions of the book are to be seen as:
  I: Prayer of the Exiles (1, 1—3, 8)
  II: Praise of Wisdom in the Law of Moses
        (3, 9—4, 4)
  III: Jerusalem Bewails and Consoles Her Captive
        Children (4, 5-29)
  IV: Jerusalem Consoled: The Captivity about To
        End (4, 30—5, 9)
  V: The Letter of Jeremiah against Idolatry (6, 1-72)

I: PRAYER OF THE EXILES

Meeting in Babylon

1 ¹*NOW THESE ARE THE WORDS of the scroll which Baruch, son of Neriah, son of Mahseiah, son of Zedekiah, son of Hasadiah, son of Hilkiah, wrote in Babylon, ²*†in the fifth year [on the seventh day of the month, at the time when the Chaldeans took Jerusalem and burnt it with fire]. ³*And Baruch read the words of this scroll for Jeconiah, son of Jehoiakim, king of Judah, to hear it, as well as all the people who came to the reading: ⁴†the nobles, the kings' sons, the elders, and the whole people, small and great alike— all who lived in Babylon by the river Sud.

⁵They wept and fasted and prayed before the Lord, ⁶*and collected such funds as each could furnish. ⁷These they sent to Jerusalem, to Jehoiakim, son of Hilkiah, son of Shallum, the priest, and to the priests and the whole people who were with him in Jerusalem. ⁸†[This was when he received the vessels of the house of the Lord that had been removed from the temple, to restore them to the land of Judah, on the tenth of Sivan. These silver vessels Zedekiah, son of Josiah, king of Judah, had had made ⁹after Nebuchadnezzar, king of Babylon, carried off Jeconiah, and the princes, and the skilled workers, and the nobles, and the people of the land from Jerusalem, as captives, and brought them to Babylon.]

¹⁰*Their message was: "We send you funds, with which you are to procure holocausts, sin offerings, and frankincense, and to prepare cereal offerings; offer

---

1, 2: *In the fifth year on the seventh day of the month:* Jerusalem fell on the seventh day of the fifth month; cf 2 Kgs 25, 8; Jer 52, 12. Either the text read originally "the fifth month," or it refers to the observance of an anniversary of the fall of Jerusalem in 587 B. C.

1, 4: *The river Sud:* one of the Babylonian canals, not otherwise identified. In ancient non-Biblical Hebrew fragments discovered in 1952, there is reference to a river "Sur" in a similar context.

1, 8f: *He:* possibly Baruch; less likely *Jehoiakim . . . the priest* (v 7), a member of the high-priestly family not mentioned elsewhere. The *silver vessels* here described are distinct from the vessels referred to in 2 Kgs 25, 14 and Ezr 1, 7ff. The author of this note may have thought of the *fifth year* (v 1) of Zedekiah, in view of Jer 28, 1; 29, 1ff. A "fifth year," again with no month mentioned, is given in Ez 1, 2 for the inaugural vision of Ezekiel's prophetic career.

1/1: Jer 32, 12; 36, 4;   51, 59-64.
    45, 1-5.   3-4: 2 Kgs 23, 1-2.
    2: 2 Kgs 25, 8ff.   6: Dt 16, 17.
    3: 2 Kgs 24, 8-17;   10: Jer 17, 26.
    Jer 22, 24-30;

these on the altar of the Lord our God, ¹¹*†and pray for the life of Nebuchadnezzar, king of Babylon, and that of Belshazzar, his son, that their lifetimes may equal the duration of the heavens above the earth; ¹²and that the Lord may give us strength, and light to our eyes, that we may live under the protective shadow of Nebuchadnezzar, king of Babylon, and that of Belshazzar, his son, and serve them long, finding favor in their sight.

Confession of Guilt

¹³"Pray for us also to the Lord, our God; for we have sinned against the Lord, our God, and the wrath and anger of the Lord have not yet been withdrawn from us at the present day. ¹⁴*And read out publicly this scroll which we send you, in the house of the Lord, on the feast day and during the days of assembly:

¹⁵*"Justice is with the Lord, our God; and we today are flushed with shame, we men of Judah and citizens of Jerusalem, ¹⁶that we, with our kings and rulers and priests and prophets, and with our fathers, ¹⁷have sinned in the Lord's sight ¹⁸and disobeyed him. We have neither heeded the voice of the Lord, our God, nor followed the precepts which the Lord set before us. ¹⁹From the time the Lord led our fathers out of the land of Egypt until the present day, we have been disobedient to the Lord, our God, and only too ready to disregard his voice. ²⁰*And the evils and the curse which the Lord enjoined upon Moses, his servant, at the time he led our fathers forth from the land of Egypt to give us the land flowing with milk and honey, cling to us even today. ²¹For we did not heed the voice of the Lord, our God, in all the words of the prophets whom he sent us, ²²but each one of us went off after the devices of our own wicked hearts, served other gods, and did evil in the sight of the Lord, our God.

2 ¹"AND the Lord fulfilled the warning he had uttered against us: against our judges, who governed Israel, against our kings and princes, and against the men of Israel and Judah. ²*He brought down upon us evils so great that there has not been done anywhere under heaven what has been done in Jerusalem, as was written in the law of Moses: ³†that one after another of us should eat the flesh of his son or of his daughter. ⁴*He has made us subject to all the kingdoms round about us, a reproach and a horror among all the nations round about to which the Lord has scattered us. ⁵We are brought low, not raised up,

because we sinned against the Lord, our God, not heeding his voice.

⁶*"Justice is with the Lord, our God; and we, like our fathers, are flushed with shame even today. ⁷All the evils of which the Lord had warned us have come upon us; ⁸and we did not plead before the Lord, or turn, each from the figments of his evil heart. ⁹*And the Lord kept watch over the evils, and brought them home to us; for the Lord is just in all the works he commanded us to do, ¹⁰but we did not heed his voice, or follow the precepts of the Lord which he set before us.

Prayer for Deliverance

¹¹*"And now, Lord, God of Israel, you who led your people out of the land of Egypt with your mighty hand, with signs and wonders and great might, and with your upraised arm, so that you have made for yourself a name till the present day: ¹²*we have sinned, been impious, and violated, O Lord, our God, all your statutes. ¹³Let your anger be withdrawn from us, for we are left few in number among the nations to which you scattered us. ¹⁴Hear, O Lord, our prayer of supplication, and deliver us for your own sake: grant us favor in the presence of our captors, ¹⁵*that the whole earth may know that you are the Lord, our God, and that Israel and his descendants bear your name. ¹⁶*O Lord, look down from your holy dwelling and take thought of us; turn, O Lord, your ear to hear us. ¹⁷*Look directly at us, and behold: it is not the dead in the nether world, whose spirits have been taken from within them, who will give glory and vindication to the Lord. ¹⁸*He whose soul is deeply grieved, who walks bowed and feeble, with failing eyes and famished soul, will declare your glory and justice, Lord!

¹⁹"Not on the just deeds of our fathers and our kings do we base our plea for mercy in your sight, O Lord, our God. ²⁰You have brought your wrath and anger down upon us, as you had warned us through your servants the prophets: ²¹*Thus says the Lord: Bend your shoulders to the service of the king of Babylon, that you may continue in the land ²²I gave your fathers: for if you do not hear the Lord's voice so as to serve the king of Babylon,

²³*   I will make to cease from the cities of Judah
         and from the streets of Jerusalem
     The sounds of joy and the sounds of
         gladness,
         the voice of the bridegroom
         and the voice of the bride;
     And all the land shall be deserted,
         without inhabitants.'

---

*
11: Dt 11, 21; Jer 29, 7;
     Dn 5, 1-2; 1 Tm 2, 1f.
14: Ex 23, 14ff; Lv 23, 35f;
     Hos 9, 5; Sir 50, 6.
15: 2, 6; 3, 8; Neh 9, 6-37;
     Ezr 9, 6-15;
     Dn 9, 4-19.
20: Lv 26, 14-39;
     Dt 28, 15-68.
2/2f: 2 Kgs 6, 28f; Jer 19, 9;
     Lam 2, 20; 4, 10;
     Ez 5, 10.

4: Jer 29, 18.
6: 1, 15.
9: Jer 1, 12; 31, 28;
     44, 27.
11: Dt 6, 21-22.
12: Ps 106, 6.
15: Sir 36, 11; Jer 14, 9.
16: Dt 26, 15.
17: Ps 6, 6; Is 38, 18.
18: Zep 2, 3.
21: Jer 27, 12.
23: Jer 7, 34.

---

† 1, 11: *Nebuchadnezzar . . . Belshazzar, his son:* as in Dn 5, 1f. Later Jewish tradition seems to have simplified the history of the past by making the last Chaldean ruler of Babylon the son of the conqueror of Jerusalem.

2, 3: *One after another of us should eat:* see note on Lam 2, 20.

24*But we did not heed your voice, or serve the king of Babylon, and you fulfilled the threats you had made through your servants the prophets, to have the bones of our kings and the bones of our fathers brought out from their burial places. **25***†And indeed, they lie exposed to the heat of day and the frost of night. They died in dire anguish, by hunger and the sword and plague. **26***†And you reduced the house which bears your name to what it is today, for the wickedness of the kingdom of Israel and the kingdom of Judah.

God's Promises Recalled

27"But with us, O Lord, our God, you have dealt in all your clemency and in all your great mercy. **28**This was your warning through your servant Moses, the day you ordered him to write down your law in the presence of the Israelites: **29**If you do not heed my voice, surely this great and numerous throng will dwindle away among the nations to which I will scatter them. **30***For I know they will not heed me, because they are a stiff-necked people. But in the land of their captivity they shall have a change of heart; **31***they shall know that I, the Lord, am their God. I will give them hearts, and heedful ears; **32***and they shall praise me in the land of their captivity, and shall invoke my name. **33***Then they shall turn back from their stiff-necked stubbornness, and from their evil deeds, because they shall remember the fate of their fathers who sinned against the Lord. **34**And I will bring them back to the land which with my oath I promised to their fathers, to Abraham, Isaac and Jacob; and they shall rule it. I will make them increase; they shall not then diminish. **35***And I will establish for them, as an eternal covenant, that I will be their God, and they shall be my people; and I will not again remove my people Israel from the land I gave them.

3 **1**"LORD Almighty, God of Israel, afflicted souls and dismayed spirits call to you. **2**Hear, O Lord, for you are a God of mercy; and have mercy on us, who have sinned against you: **3***for you are enthroned forever, while we are perishing forever. **4**Lord Almighty, God of Israel, hear the prayer of Israel's few, the sons of those who sinned against you; they did not heed the voice of the Lord, their God, and the evils cling to us. **5**Remember at this time not the misdeeds of our fathers, but your own hand and name: **6**for you are the Lord our God; and you, O Lord, we will praise! **7***For this, you put into our hearts the fear of you:

that we may call upon your name, and praise you in our captivity, when we have removed from our hearts all the wickedness of our fathers who sinned against you. **8**Behold us today in our captivity, where you scattered us, a reproach, a curse, and a requital for all the misdeeds of our fathers, who withdrew from the Lord, our God."

II: PRAISE OF WISDOM IN THE LAW OF MOSES

9*   HEAR, O ISRAEL, the commandments of life: listen, and know prudence!

10   How is it, Israel,
that you are in the land of your foes,
grown old in a foreign land,
Defiled with the dead,
11*   accounted with those destined for the nether world?

12*   You have forsaken the fountain of wisdom!
13*   Had you walked in the way of God,
you would have dwelt in enduring peace.

14*   Learn where prudence is,
where strength, where understanding;
That you may know also
where are length of days, and life,
where light of the eyes, and peace.

15*   Who has found the place of wisdom,
who has entered into her treasuries?
16*   Where are the rulers of the nations,
they who lorded it over the wild beasts of the earth,
17   and made sport of the birds of the heavens:
They who heaped up the silver
and the gold in which men trust;
of whose possessions there was no end?
18   They schemed anxiously for money,
but there is no trace of their work:
19   They have vanished down into the nether world,
and others have risen up in their stead.

20   Later generations have seen the light,
have dwelt in the land,
But the way to understanding they have not known,
21   they have not perceived her paths, or reached her;
their offspring were far from the way to her.

❋

24: Jer 8, 1f.
25: Jer 7, 34; 14, 12;
    31, 30.
26: Jer 7, 10-15.
30: Dt 30, 1f; 31, 27.
31: Jer 24, 7; Ez 36, 26;
    Ps 40, 7.
32: Tb 13, 7.
33f: Dt 30, 1-10.
35: Jer 31, 31; Lam 4, 22.

3/3: Pss 29, 10; 102, 12f.
7: Jer 31, 33.
9: Prv 4, 20ff.
11: Ps 88, 5.
12: Jer 2.13; Jn 4, 10.14.
13: Is 48, 18.
14: Prv 3, 2; 8, 14.
15ff: Jb 28, 1-28.
16: Jer 27, 6.

---

†   2, 25: *They lie exposed:* probably an allusion to Jer 36, 30; see note on Jer 22, 19.

2, 26: *The house which bears your name:* the temple of Jerusalem. *What it is today:* during the exile it lay in ruins.

22★† She has not been heard of in Canaan,
  nor seen in Teman.

23 The sons of Hagar who seek knowledge on
  earth,
  the merchants of Midian and Teman,
  the phrasemakers seeking knowledge,
 These have not known the way to wisdom,
  nor have they her paths in mind.

24† O Israel, how vast is the house of God,
  how broad the scope of his dominion:

25 Vast and endless,
  high and immeasurable!

26★ In it were born the giants,
  renowned at the first,
  stalwarts, skilled in war.

27★ Not these did God choose,
  nor did he give them the way of
   understanding;

28★ They perished for lack of prudence,
  perished through their folly.

29★ Who has gone up to the heavens and taken
  her,
  or brought her down from the clouds?

30 Who has crossed the sea and found her,
  bearing her away rather than choice
   gold?

31 None knows the way to her,
  nor has any understood her paths.

32 Yet he who knows all things knows her;
  he has probed her by his knowledge—
 He who established the earth for all time,
  and filled it with four-footed beasts;

33 He who dismisses the light, and it departs,
  calls it, and it obeys him trembling;

34 Before whom the stars at their posts
  shine and rejoice;

35★ When he calls them, they answer, "Here
  we are!"
  shining with joy for their Maker.

36 Such is our God;
  no other is to be compared to him:

37★ He has traced out all the way of
  understanding,
  and has given her to Jacob, his servant,
  to Israel, his beloved son.

38★ Since then she has appeared on earth,
  and moved among men.

4 **1**★ She is the book of the precepts of God,
  the law that endures forever;

All who cling to her will live,
  but those will die who forsake her.

2★ Turn, O Jacob, and receive her:
  walk by her light toward splendor.

3 Give not your glory to another,
  your privileges to an alien race.

4★ Blessed are we, O Israel;
  for what pleases God is known to us!

III: JERUSALEM BEWAILS AND CONSOLES HER CAPTIVE CHILDREN

---

5 FEAR NOT, my people!
  Remember, Israel,

6★ You were sold to the nations
  not for your destruction;
 It was because you angered God
  that you were handed over to your foes.

7★ For you provoked your Maker
  with sacrifices to demons, to no-gods;

8 You forsook the Eternal God who
  nourished you,
  and you grieved Jerusalem who fostered
   you.

9 She indeed saw coming upon you
  the anger of God; and she said:

"Hear, you neighbors of Zion!
  God has brought great mourning upon
   me,

10 For I have seen the captivity
  that the Eternal God has brought
  upon my sons and daughters.

11 With joy I fostered them;
  but with mourning and lament I let them
   go.

12★ Let no one gloat over me, a widow,
  bereft of many:
 For the sins of my children I am left
   desolate,
  because they turned from the law of
   God,

13 and did not acknowledge his statutes;
 In the ways of God's commandments they
  did not walk,
  nor did they tread the disciplined paths
  of his justice.

14 "Let Zion's neighbors come,
  to take note of the captivity of my sons
  and daughters,
  brought upon them by the Eternal God.

★

22: Jer 49, 7; Ez 28, 4-5;
  Zec 9, 2; Jb 2, 11.
26: Gn 6, 4; Wis 14, 6.
27: 1 Sm 16, 7-10.
28: Sir 10, 8.
29: Dt 30, 12f; Sir 24, 4;
  Rcm 10, 6f.
35: Jb 38, 7; Ps 147, 4;
  Is 40, 26.
37: Ps 147, 19;
  Sir 24, 8-12.

38: Wis 9, 18; Jn 1, 14.
4/1: Dt 4, 6-8; Prv 8, 35f;
  Sir 24, 22.
 2: Prv 4, 13.19.
 4: Dt 4, 32-37; 33, 29.
 6: Jgs 2, 14; Is 50, 1;
  52, 3.
7-8: Dt 32, 13-18;
  1 Cor 10, 20.
12: Lam 1, 1.2.7.

---

†

3, 22f: Despite the renown for wisdom of the peoples of *Canaan* or Phoenicia (Ez 28, 3f), of *Teman* (Jer 49, 7), of *the sons of Hagar* or the Arabians, they did not possess true wisdom, which is found only in the law of God.

3, 24: *The house of God:* here, the created universe.

15 He has brought against them a nation from
    afar,
    a nation ruthless and of alien speech,
That has neither reverence for age
    nor tenderness for childhood;
16 They have led away this widow's cherished
    sons,
    have left me solitary, without daughters.
17 What can I do to help you?
18 He who has brought this evil upon you
    must himself deliver you from your
    enemies' hands.
19 Farewell, my children, farewell:
    I am left desolate.
20 I have taken off the garment of peace,
    have put on sackcloth for my prayer of
    supplication,
    and while I live I will cry out to the
    Eternal God.

21 "Fear not, my children; call upon God,
    who will deliver you from oppression at
    enemy hands.
22 I have trusted in the Eternal God for your
    welfare,
    and joy has come to me from the Holy
    One
Because of the mercy that will swiftly reach
    you
    from your eternal savior.
23 With mourning and lament I sent you forth,
    but God will give you back to me
    with enduring gladness and joy.
24 As Zion's neighbors lately saw you taken
    captive,
    so shall they soon see God's salvation
    come to you,
    with great glory and the splendor of the
    Eternal God.

25 "My children, bear patiently the anger
    that has come from God upon you;
Your enemies have persecuted you,
    and you will soon see their destruction
    and trample upon their necks.
26 My pampered children have trodden rough
    roads,
    carried off by their enemies like sheep in
    a raid.
27 Fear not, my children; call out to God!
    He who brought this upon you will
    remember you.

28 As your hearts have been disposed to stray
    from God,
    turn now ten times the more to seek him;
29 For he who has brought disaster upon you
    will, in saving you, bring you back
    enduring joy."

IV: JERUSALEM CONSOLED: THE CAPTIVITY ABOUT TO END

30 FEAR NOT, Jerusalem!
    He who gave you your name is your
    encouragement.
31 Fearful are those who harmed you,
    who rejoiced at your downfall;
32 Fearful are the cities where your children
    were enslaved,
    fearful the city that took your sons.
33 As that city rejoiced at your collapse,
    and made merry at your downfall,
    so shall she grieve over her own
    desolation.
34 I will take from her the joyous throngs,
    and her exultation shall be turned to
    mourning:
35 For fire shall come upon her
    from the Eternal God, for a long time,
    and demons shall dwell in her from that
    time on.
36 Look to the east, Jerusalem!
    behold the joy that comes to you from
    God.
37 Here come your sons whom you once let go,
    gathered in from the east and from the
    west
By the word of the Holy One,
    rejoicing in the glory of God.

5 **1** Jerusalem, take off your robe of mourning
    and misery;
    put on the splendor of glory from God
    forever:
2 Wrapped in the cloak of justice from God,
    bear on your head the mitre
    that displays the glory of the eternal
    name.
3 For God will show all the earth your
    splendor:
4 you will be named by God forever
    the peace of justice, the glory of God's
    worship.

15: Dt 28, 49f; Jer 5, 15; 6, 22f.
18: Jer 32, 42.
20: Jdt 9, 1; Est 4, 16.
21: Jer 51, 5.
23: Jer 31, 12f.
24: Is 60, 1ff.
25: Is 51, 23.
26: Lam 2, 22.
27: Is 40, 1.
29: Is 35, 10.
30: Ps 46, 5; Is 60, 14.
32: Jer 51, 43.
33f: Is 13, 20ff; 47, 1-11; Jer 50, 13.
35: Is 34, 9-14.
36: Is 60, 4f.
5/1: Is 52, 1.
2: Ex 39, 30; Wis 18, 24; Is 61, 10; 62, 3.
4: Is 1, 26; 32, 17; Jer 33, 16.

4, 25: *Trample upon their necks:* love of enemies was not an Old Testament ideal. The Babylonians are considered here, however, to be God's enemies as well as Israel's.
4, 35: Deserts and desolate places were looked upon as the special habitations of *demons;* Tb 8, 3; Lk 11, 24.

5   Up, Jerusalem! stand upon the heights;
           look to the east and see your children
       Gathered from the east and the west
           at the word of the Holy One,
           rejoicing that they are remembered by
               God.

6*   Led away on foot by their enemies they
               left you:
       but God will bring them back to you
       borne aloft in glory as on royal thrones.

7*   For God has commanded
           that every lofty mountain be made low,
       And that the age-old depths and gorges
           be filled to level ground,
           that Israel may advance secure in the
               glory of God.

8*   The forests and every fragrant kind of tree
           have overshadowed Israel at God's
               command;

9   For God is leading Israel in joy
           by the light of his glory,
           with his mercy and justice for company.

V: THE LETTER OF JEREMIAH AGAINST IDOLATRY

6 **1*** A COPY OF THE LETTER WHICH JEREMIAH SENT to those who were being led captive to Babylon by the king of the Babylonians, to convey to them what God had commanded him:

For the sins you committed before God, you are being led captive to Babylon by Nebuchadnezzar, king of the Babylonians. **2†**When you reach Babylon you will be there many years, a period seven generations long; after which I will bring you back from there in peace. **3***And now in Babylon you will see borne upon men's shoulders gods of silver and gold and wood, which cast fear upon the pagans. **4**Take care that you yourselves do not imitate their alien example and stand in fear of them, **5**when you see the crowd before them and behind worshiping them. Rather, say in your hearts, "You, O Lord, are to be worshiped!"; **6***for my angel is with you, and he is the custodian of your lives.

7*Their tongues are smoothed by woodworkers; they are covered with gold and silver—but they are a fraud, and cannot speak. **8**People bring gold, as to a maiden in love with ornament, **9**and furnish crowns for the heads of their gods. Then sometimes the priests take the silver and gold from their gods and spend it on themselves, **10†**or give part of it to the harlots on the terrace. They trick them out in garments like men, these gods of silver and gold and wood; **11**but though

they are wrapped in purple clothing, they are not safe from corrosion or insects. **12**They wipe their faces clean of the house dust which is thick upon them. **13**Each has a scepter, like the human ruler of a district; but none does away with those that offend against it. **14**Each has in its right hand an axe or dagger, but it cannot save itself from war or pillage. Thus it is known they are not gods; do not fear them.

15As useless as one's broken tools **16**are their gods, set up in their houses; their eyes are full of dust from the feet of those who enter. **17**Their courtyards are walled in like those of a man brought to execution for a crime against the king; the priests reinforce their houses with gates and bars and bolts, lest they be carried off by robbers. **18**They light more lamps for them than for themselves, yet not one of these can they see. **19**They are like any beam in the house; it is said their hearts are eaten away. Though the insects out of the ground consume them and their garments, they do not feel it. **20**Their faces are blackened by the smoke of the house. **21**Bats and swallows alight on their bodies and on their heads; and cats as well as birds. **22**Know, therefore, that they are not gods, and do not fear them.

23Despite the gold that covers them for adornment, unless someone wipes away the corrosion, they do not shine; nor did they feel anything when they were molded. **24**They are bought at any price, and there is no spirit in them. **25***Having no feet, they are carried on men's shoulders, displaying their shame to all; and those who worship them are put to confusion **26**because, if they fall to the ground, the worshipers must raise them up. They neither move of themselves if one sets them upright, nor come upright if they fall; but one puts gifts beside them as beside the dead. **27***†Their priests resell their sacrifices for their own advantage. Even their wives cure parts of the meat, but do not share it with the poor and the weak; **28**the menstruous and women in childbed handle their sacrifices. Knowing from this that they are not gods, do not fear them.

29How can they be called gods? For women bring the offerings to these gods of silver and gold and wood; **30***and in their temples the priests squat with torn tunic and with shaven hair and beard, and with their heads uncovered. **31**They shout and wail before their gods as others do at a funeral banquet. **32**The priests take some of their clothing and put it on their wives and children. **33***†Whether they are treated well or ill by anyone, they cannot requite it; they can neither set

---

† **6, 2:** *Seven generations:* possibly an indication of the date of this composition by an author writing for his contemporaries for whom the conditions of the exile were still realities. He has multiplied the *seventy years* of Jer 29, 10 by three or four.

6, 10: *Harlots on the terrace:* cult prostitutes, common in the idolatrous religions of the Gentiles.

6, 27-31: From the point of view of Jewish ritual law, the practices named here were grotesque and depraved; cf Lv 12, 2ff; 15, 19-23.

6, 33-39: All that the gods cannot do, the true God does; cf 1 Sm 2, 7; Dt 23, 22; Pss 68, 6; 146, 7-9; Is 35, 4f.

---

*
6: Is 49, 22.	7: Ps 135, 16.
7: Is 40, 3f.	25: Wis 13, 16.
8: Is 41, 19.	27: Lv 12, 4; 15, 19f;
6/1: Jer 29, 1.	Dt 14, 28f.
3: Is 46, 7; Jer 10, 1-16.	30: Lv 10, 6; 21, 5.10.
6: Ex 23, 20.	33: Dn 2, 21.

up a king nor remove him. ³⁴Similarly, they cannot give anyone riches or coppers; if one fails to fulfill a vow to them, they cannot exact it of him. ³⁵*They neither save a man from death, nor deliver the weak from the strong. ³⁶To no blind man do they restore his sight, nor do they save any man in an emergency. ³⁷They neither pity the widow nor benefit the orphan. ³⁸These gilded and silvered wooden statues are like stones from the mountains; and their worshipers will be put to shame. ³⁹How then can it be thought or claimed that they are gods?

⁴⁰†Even the Chaldeans themselves have no respect for them; for when they see a deaf mute, incapable of speech, they bring forward Bel and ask the god to make noise, as though the man could understand; ⁴¹and they are themselves unable to reflect and abandon these gods, for they have no sense. ⁴²*†And their women, girt with cords, sit by the roads, burning chaff for incense; ⁴³and whenever one of them is drawn aside by some passerby who lies with her, she mocks her neighbor who has not been dignified as she has, and has not had her cord broken. ⁴⁴All that takes place around these gods is a fraud: how then can it be thought or claimed that they are gods?

⁴⁵They are produced by woodworkers and goldsmiths, and they are nothing else than what these craftsmen wish them to be. ⁴⁶Even those who produce them are not long-lived; ⁴⁷how then can what they have produced be gods? They have left frauds and opprobrium to their successors. ⁴⁸For when war or disaster comes upon them, the priests deliberate among themselves where they can hide with them. ⁴⁹How then can one not know that these are no-gods, which do not save themselves either from war or from disaster? ⁵⁰They are wooden, gilded and silvered; they will later be known for frauds. To all peoples and kings it will be clear that they are not gods, but human handiwork; and that God's work is not in them.

⁵¹Who does not know that they are not gods? ⁵²They set no king over the land, nor do they give men rain. ⁵³They neither vindicate their own rights, nor do they recover what is unjustly taken, for they are unable; ⁵⁴they are like crows between heaven and earth. For when fire breaks out in the temple of these wooden or gilded or silvered gods, though the priests flee and are safe, they themselves are burnt up in the fire like beams. ⁵⁵They cannot resist a king, or enemy forces. ⁵⁶How then can it be admitted or thought that they are gods?

They are safe from neither thieves nor bandits, these wooden and silvered and gilded gods; ⁵⁷those who seize them strip off the gold and the silver, and go away with the clothing that was on them, and they cannot help themselves. ⁵⁸*How much better to be a king displaying his valor, or a handy tool in a house, the joy of its owner, than these false gods; or the door of a house, that keeps safe those who are within, rather than these false gods; or a wooden post in a palace, rather than these false gods! ⁵⁹The sun and moon and stars are bright, and obedient in the service for which they are sent. ⁶⁰Likewise the lightning, when it flashes, is a goodly sight; and the same wind blows over all the land. ⁶¹The clouds, too, when commanded by God to proceed across the whole world, fulfill the order; ⁶²and fire, sent from on high to burn up the mountains and the forests, does what has been commanded. But these false gods are not their equal, ⁶³whether in beauty or in power; so that it is unthinkable, and cannot be claimed, that they are gods. They can neither execute judgment, nor benefit man. ⁶⁴Know, therefore, that they are not gods, and do not fear them.

⁶⁵Kings they neither curse nor bless. ⁶⁶They show the nations no signs in the heavens, nor are they brilliant like the sun, nor shining like the moon. ⁶⁷The beasts which can help themselves by fleeing to shelter are better than they are. ⁶⁸Thus in no way is it clear to us that they are gods; so do not fear them. ⁶⁹For like a scarecrow in a cucumber patch, that is no protection, are their wooden, gilded, silvered gods. ⁷⁰Just like a thornbush in a garden on which perches every kind of bird, or like a corpse hurled into darkness, are their silvered and gilded wooden gods. ⁷¹From the rotting of the purple and the linen upon them, it can be known that they are not gods; they themselves will in the end be consumed, and be a disgrace in the land. ⁷²The better for the just man who has no idols: he shall be far from disgrace!

---

* 35: Pss 68, 6; 146, 7ff.   58: Wis 13, 10-15; 15, 7ff.
42-43: Jer 3, 2.

---

† 6, 40: *Bel:* cf note on Jer 50, 2.

6, 42f: This seems to refer to the obligation of Babylonian women to serve once in their lives as cult prostitutes. The unbroken cord was a sign that this duty had not yet been fulfilled. *Chaff:* burnt as an aphrodisiac or for use in erotic rites.

The Book of Ezekiel

Introduction

Ezekiel's complex character makes him one of the most interesting figures in Israelite prophecy. In many ways he resembles the more primitive type of prophet represented by Elijah and Elisha; yet he clearly depends on all his predecessors in prophecy, and his teaching is a development of theirs. His unique contribution to the history of prophetism lies in his manifest interest in the temple and the liturgy, an interest paralleled in no other prophet—not even Jeremiah who, like Ezekiel, was also a priest. Particularly because of this interest, Ezekiel's influence on postexilic religion was enormous, and not without reason has he been called "the father of Judaism." This has resulted in his prophecies reaching us with the evident marks of editing and addition by the postexilic circles that shared his intense interest. However, we may be sure that in this book we have throughout what is in substance the prophet's own work.

Ezekiel became a prophet in Babylon—the first prophet to receive the call to prophesy outside the Holy Land. As one of the exiles deported by Nebuchadnezzar in 597, his first task was to prepare his fellow countrymen in Babylon for the final destruction of Jerusalem, which they believed to be inviolable. Accordingly, the first part of his book consists of reproaches for Israel's past and present sins and the confident prediction of yet a further devastation of the land of promise and a more general exile. In 587, when Nebuchadnezzar destroyed Jerusalem, Ezekiel was vindicated before his unbelieving compatriots.

After this time, Ezekiel's message changes. From now on his prophecy is characterized by the promise of salvation in a new covenant, and he is anxious to lay down the conditions necessary to obtain it. Even as Jeremiah had believed, Ezekiel thought that the exiles were the hope of Israel's restoration, once God's allotted time for the exile had been accomplished. His final eight chapters are a utopian vision of the Israel of the future, rid of its past evils and re-established firmly under the rule of the Lord. The famous vision of the dry bones in chapter 37 expresses his firm belief in a forthcoming restoration, Israel rising to new life from the graveyard of Babylon. But Ezekiel's new covenant, like Jeremiah's, was to see its true fulfillment only in the New Testament.

Perhaps no other prophet has stressed the absolute majesty of God as Ezekiel does. This appears not only in the tremendous vision by the river Chebar with which his prophecy opens, but throughout the book. Ultimately, says Ezekiel, whatever God does to or for man is motivated by zeal for his own holy name. The new heart and the new spirit which must exist under the new covenant cannot be the work of man; they too must be the work of God. By such teachings he helped prepare for the New Testament doctrine of salvation through grace.

The Book of Ezekiel is divided as follows:

I: CALL OF THE PROPHET

The Vision: God on the Cherubim

1 1*†IN THE THIRTIETH YEAR, on the fifth day of the fourth month, while I was among the exiles of the river Chebar, the heavens opened, and I saw divine visions. 2†—On the fifth day of the month, the fifth year, that is, of King Jehoiachin's exile, 3the word of the Lord came to the priest Ezekiel, the son of Buzi, in the land of the Chaldeans by the river Chebar.—There the hand of the Lord came upon me.

4†As I looked, a stormwind came from the North, a huge cloud with flashing fire [enveloped in brightness], from the midst of which [the midst of the fire] something gleamed like electrum. 5†Within it were figures resembling four living creatures that looked like this: their form was human, 6but each had four faces and four wings, 7and their legs went straight down; the soles of their feet were round. They sparkled with a gleam like burnished bronze.

10*†Their faces were like this: each of the four had the face of a man, but on the right side was the face of a lion, and on the left side the face of an ox, and finally each had the face of an eagle. 9Their faces [and their wings] looked out on all their four sides; they did not turn when they moved, but each went straight for-

---

† 1, 1: *The thirtieth year,* which corresponds to the fifth year of exile (v 2), has never been satisfactorily explained; possibly it refers to the prophet's age. *The river Chebar:* probably a canal near Nippur, southeast of Babylon, one of the sites on which the Jewish exiles were settled.

1, 2: *The fifth day of the* fourth *month, the fifth year:* July 31, 593 B. C.; cf v 1.

1, 4: *The North:* the abode of God; see notes on Jb 37, 22; Ps 48, 3. *Electrum:* an alloy of gold and silver, used here for some undetermined bright metal.

1, 5: *Four living creatures:* identified as cherubim in 10, 20f.

1, 10-22: Note the changed order of the verses and the omission of the textually uncertain verses 14 and 21. Such changes also occur elsewhere in this book.

ward. **¹²**[Each went straight forward; wherever the spirit wished to go, there they went; they did not turn when they moved.]

⁸Human hands were under their wings, and the wings of one touched those of another. **¹¹**Each had two wings spread out above so that they touched one another's, while the other two wings of each covered his body. **¹³**In among the living creatures something like burning coals of fire could be seen; they seemed like torches, moving to and fro among the living creatures. The fire gleamed, and from it came forth flashes of lightning.

¹⁵As I looked at the living creatures, I saw wheels on the ground, one beside each of the four living creatures. **¹⁶**The wheels had the sparkling appearance of chrysolite, and all four of them looked the same: they were constructed as though one wheel were within another. **¹⁷**They could move in any of the four directions they faced, without veering as they moved. **¹⁸***The four of them had rims, and I saw that their rims were full of eyes all around. **¹⁹**When the living creatures moved, the wheels moved with them; and when the living creatures were raised from the ground, the wheels also were raised. **²⁰**Wherever the spirit wished to go, there the wheels went, and they were raised together with the living creatures; for the spirit of the living creatures was in the wheels.

²²†Over the heads of the living creatures, something like a firmament could be seen, seeming like glittering crystal, stretched straight out above their heads. **²³**Beneath the firmament their wings were stretched out, one toward the other. [Each of them had two covering his body.] **²⁴**Then I heard the sound of their wings, like the roaring of mighty waters, like the voice of the Almighty. When they moved, the sound of the tumult was like the din of an army. [And when they stood still, they lowered their wings.]

²⁶†Above the firmament over their heads something like a throne could be seen, looking like sapphire. Upon it was seated, up above, one who had the appearance of a man. **²⁷**Upward from what resembled his waist I saw what gleamed like electrum; downward from what resembled his waist I saw what looked like fire; he was surrounded with splendor. **²⁸**Like the bow which appears in the clouds on a rainy day was the splendor that surrounded him. Such was the vision of the likeness of the glory of the Lord.

Eating of the Scroll

2 WHEN I had seen it, I fell upon my face and heard a voice that said to me: **¹**†Son of man, stand up! I wish to speak with you. **²**†As he spoke to me, spirit entered into me and set me on my feet, and I heard the one who was speaking **³**say to me: Son of man, I am sending you to the Israelites, rebels who have rebelled against me; they and their fathers have revolted against me to this very day. **⁴**Hard of face and obstinate of heart are they to whom I am sending

you. But you shall say to them: Thus says the Lord God! **⁵**And whether they heed or resist—for they are a rebellious house—they shall know that a prophet has been among them. **⁶**†But as for you, son of man, fear neither them nor their words when they contradict you and reject you, and when you sit on scorpions. Neither fear their words nor be dismayed at their looks, for they are a rebellious house. **⁷**[But speak my words to them, whether they heed or resist, for they are rebellious.] **⁸**As for you, son of man, obey me when I speak to you: be not rebellious like this house of rebellion, but open your mouth and eat what I shall give you.

⁹*It was then I saw a hand stretched out to me, in which was a written scroll **¹⁰**which he unrolled before me. It was covered with writing front and back, and written on it was: Lamentation and wailing and woe!

3 **¹**HE said to me: Son of man, eat what is before you; eat this scroll, then go, speak to the house of Israel. **²**So I opened my mouth and he gave me the scroll to eat. **³***†Son of man, he then said to me, feed your belly and fill your stomach with this scroll I am giving you. I ate it, and it was as sweet as honey in my mouth. He said: **⁴**Son of man, go now to the house of Israel, and speak my words to them.

⁵Not to a people with difficult speech and barbarous language am I sending you, **⁶**nor to the many peoples [with difficult speech and barbarous language] whose words you cannot understand. If I were to send you to these, they would listen to you; **⁷**but the house of Israel will refuse to listen to you, since they will not listen to me. For the whole house of Israel is stubborn of brow and obstinate in heart. **⁸**But I will make your face as hard as theirs, and your brow as stubborn as theirs, **⁹**like diamond, harder than flint. Fear them not, nor be dismayed at their looks, for they are a rebellious house.

¹⁰Son of man, he said to me, take into your heart all my words that I speak to you; hear them well. **¹¹**Now go to the exiles, to your countrymen, and say to them: Thus says the Lord God!—whether they heed or resist!

¹²†Then spirit lifted me up, and I heard behind me the noise of a loud rumbling as the glory of the Lord rose from its place: **¹³**the noise made by the wings of the living creatures striking one another, and by the wheels alongside them, a loud rumbling. **¹⁴**The spirit which had lifted me up seized me, and I went off

---

†

1, 22f.26: This symbolic description of God's throne is similar to that in Ex 24, 9f.

1, 26: *One who had the appearance of a man:* God appearing in human form (v 28); cf Ex 33, 18-23.

2, 1: *Son of man:* a formal way of saying simply "man"; God's habitual way of addressing the prophet throughout this book. Probably the title is used to emphasize the separation of the divine and the human.

2, 2: *Spirit:* vital power, coming from God, which enables the prophet to hear the word of God; cf 8, 3; 9, 24; 11, 1.

2, 6: *When you sit on scorpions:* the prophet must be prepared for the bitterest opposition.

3, 3: *As sweet as honey:* though the prophet must foretell terrible things, the word of God is sweet to him who receives it.

3, 12: *The glory of the Lord:* the divine presence, manifested here in visible form.

❋

   18: 10, 12; Rv 4, 6.8.   3/3: Rv 10, 9f.
   2/9: Rv 5, 1.

spiritually stirred, while the hand of the LORD rested heavily upon me. **15**†Thus I came to the exiles who lived at Tel-abib by the river Chebar, and for seven days I sat among them distraught.

The Prophet as Watchman

17°†Thus the word of the LORD came to me: Son of man, I have appointed you a watchman for the house of Israel. When you hear a word from my mouth, you shall warn them for me.

18If I say to the wicked man, You shall surely die; and you do not warn him or speak out to dissuade him from his wicked conduct so that he may live: that wicked man shall die for his sin, but I will hold you responsible for his death. **19**If, on the other hand, you have warned the wicked man, yet he has not turned away from his evil nor from his wicked conduct, then he shall die for his sin, but you shall save your life.

20If a virtuous man turns away from virtue and does wrong when I place a stumbling block before him, he shall die. He shall die for his sin, and his virtuous deeds shall not be remembered; but I will hold you responsible for his death if you did not warn him. **21**When, on the other hand, you have warned a virtuous man not to sin, and he has in fact not sinned, he shall surely live because of the warning, and you shall save your own life.

Ezekiel's Dumbness

22†The hand of the LORD came upon me, and he said to me: Get up and go out into the plain, where I will speak with you. **23**°So I got up and went out into the plain, and I saw that the glory of the LORD was in that place, like the glory I had seen by the river Chebar. I fell prone, **24**but then spirit entered into me and set me on my feet, and he spoke with me.

He said to me: Go shut yourself up in your house. **25**[As for you, son of man, they will put cords upon you and bind you with them, so that you cannot go out among them.] **26**†I will make your tongue stick to your palate so that you will be dumb and unable to rebuke them for being a rebellious house. **27**Only when I speak with you and open your mouth, shall you say to them: Thus says the Lord GOD! Let him heed who will, and let him resist who will, for they are a rebellious house.

II: BEFORE THE SIEGE OF JERUSALEM

Acts Symbolic of Siege and Exile

16†AT THE END OF seven days . . . :

4 **1**AS for you, son of man, take a clay tablet; lay it in front of you, and draw on it a city [Jerusalem]. **2**Raise a siege against it: build a tower, lay out a ramp,

pitch camps, and set up battering rams all around. **3**Then take an iron griddle and set it up as an iron wall between you and the city. Fix your gaze on it: it shall be in the state of siege, and you shall besiege it. This shall be a sign for the house of Israel. **4**Then you shall lie on your left side, while I place the sins of the house of Israel upon you. As many days as you lie thus, you shall bear their sins. **5**°For the years of their sins I allot you the same number of days, three hundred and ninety, during which you will bear the sins of the house of Israel. **6**When you finish this, you are to lie down again, but on your right side, and bear the sins of the house of Judah forty days; one day for each year I have allotted you. **7**°Fixing your gaze on the siege of Jerusalem, with bared arm you shall prophesy against it. **8**See, I will bind you with cords so that you cannot turn from one side to the other until you have completed the days of your siege.

9°Again, take wheat and barley, and beans and lentils, and millet and spelt; put them in a single vessel and make bread out of them. Eat it for as many days as you lie upon your side, three hundred and ninety. **10**The food you eat shall be twenty shekels a day by weight; each day the same. **11**And the water you drink shall be the sixth of a hin by measure; each day the same. **16**°†Then he said to me: Son of man, I am breaking the staff of bread in Jerusalem. They shall eat bread which they have weighed out anxiously, and they shall drink water which they have measured out fearfully, **17**so that, owing to the scarcity of bread and water, everyone shall be filled with terror and waste away because of his sins.

12For your food you must bake barley loaves over human excrement in their sight, said the LORD. **13**°Thus

---

†

3, 15: *Tel-abib:* one of the sites where the exiles were settled, probably near Nippur.

3, 16: *At the end of seven days . . . :* the incomplete sentence probably contained some such words as "the word of the Lord came to me." For *seven days,* see v 15.

3, 17-21: This passage refers to one of the prophet's most characteristic qualities. It was placed here by an editor, though it properly belongs to a later stage in Ezekiel's ministry; cf chapter 33.

3, 22-27: This passage also belongs to a later period, with 24, 25ff and 33, 21f, during the time of the final siege of Jerusalem, when Ezekiel's prophecies consisted mainly of symbolic actions rather than words.

3, 26: *Dumb:* unwilling to speak to the people in exile while Jerusalem was being besieged; cf 24, 27.

4, 5f: *Three hundred and ninety days . . . forty days:* symbolically representing the respective lengths of the periods of exile of northern Israelites and Judahites. Northern Israel had already fallen to Assyria in 722 B. C. The letters in the Hebrew phrase for *the days of your siege* (v 8), each of which has its own numerical value, add up to three hundred and ninety. Forty years represent one generation.

4, 7: *Bared arm:* a symbol of unrestrained power.

4, 9-17: This action represents the scarcity of food during the siege of Jerusalem, and the consequent need to eat whatever is at hand. *Twenty shekels:* about nine ounces. *The sixth of a hin:* about one quart.

4, 16: *Breaking the staff of bread:* reducing the supply of bread which sustains the life of man as the walking staff sustains the traveler on his journey; cf 5, 16; 14, 13; Lv 26, 26; Ps 105, 16; Is 3, 1.

°
   17: 33, 7.   4/13: Hos 9, 4.
   23: 1, 3; 10, 15.20.22;   16: 5, 16; 14, 13.
      43, 3.

the Israelites shall eat their food unclean among the nations where I scatter them. ¹⁴"Oh no, Lord God!" I protested. "Never have I been made unclean, and from my youth till now, never have I eaten carrion flesh or that torn by wild beasts; never has any unclean meat entered my mouth." ¹⁵Very well, he replied, I allow you cow's dung in place of human excrement; bake your bread on that.

5 ¹As for you, son of man, take a sharp sword and use it like a barber's razor, passing it over your head and beard. Then take a set of scales and divide the hair you have cut. ²†Burn a third in the fire, within the city, when the days of your siege are completed; place another third around the city and strike it with the sword; the final third strew in the wind, and pursue it with the sword. ³[But of the last take a small number and tie them in the hem of your garment. ⁴Then take some of these and throw them in the midst of the fire and burn them.]

Say to the whole house of Israel. ⁵Thus says the Lord God: This is Jerusalem! In the midst of the nations I placed her, surrounded by foreign countries. ⁶But she rebelled against my ordinances more wickedly than the nations, and against my statutes more than the foreign countries surrounding her; she has spurned my ordinances and has not lived by my statutes. ⁷Therefore thus says the Lord God: Because you have been more rebellious than the nations surrounding you, not living by my statutes nor fulfilling my ordinances, but acting according to the ordinances of the surrounding nations; ⁸†therefore thus says the Lord God: See, I am coming at you! I will inflict punishments in your midst while the nations look on. ⁹Because of all your abominations I will do with you what I have never done before, the like of which I will never do again. ¹⁰†This means that fathers within you shall eat sons, and sons shall eat fathers. I will inflict punishments upon you and scatter all that remain of your people in every direction.

¹¹Therefore, as I live, says the Lord God, because you have defiled my sanctuary with all your detestable abominations, I swear to cut you down. I will not look upon you with pity nor have mercy. ¹²A third of your people shall die of pestilence and perish of hunger within you; another third shall fall by the sword all around you; and a third I will scatter in every direction, and I will pursue them with the sword. ¹⁶*When I loose against you the cruel, destructive arrows of hunger, I will break your staff of bread; ¹⁷I will send famine against you, and wild beasts that shall rob you of your children. Pestilence and bloodshed shall stalk through you, and I will bring the sword upon you. I, the Lord, have spoken!

¹³Thus shall my anger spend itself, and I will wreak my fury upon them till I am appeased; they shall know that I, the Lord, have spoken in my jealousy when I spend my fury upon them. ¹⁴I will make you a waste

and a reproach among the nations that surround you, which every passer-by may see. ¹⁵When I execute judgment upon you in anger and fury and with furious chastisements, you shall be a reproach and an object of scorn, a terrible warning to the nations that surround you. I, the Lord, have spoken!

Against the Mountains of Israel

6 ¹Thus the word of the Lord came to me: ²Son of man, turn toward the mountains of Israel, and prophesy against them: ³*†Mountains of Israel, hear the word of the Lord God. Thus says the Lord God [to the mountains and hills, the ravines and valleys]: See, I am bringing a sword against you, and I will destroy your high places. ⁴Your altars shall be laid waste, your incense stands shall be broken, and I will cast down your slain ones before your idols; ⁵†I will scatter their bones all around your altars. ⁶In all your dwelling places cities shall be made desolate and high places laid waste, so that your altars will be made desolate and laid waste, your idols broken and removed, and your incense stands smashed to bits. ⁷[The slain shall fall in your midst, and you shall know that I am the Lord. ⁸I have warned you.]

When some of your people have escaped to other nations from the sword, and have been scattered over the foreign lands, ⁹then those who have escaped will remember me among the nations to which they have been exiled, after I have broken their adulterous hearts that turned away from me [and their eyes which lusted after idols]. They shall loathe themselves because of their evil deeds, all their abominations. ¹⁰Then they shall know that it was not in vain that I, the Lord, threatened to inflict this calamity upon them.

¹¹†Thus says the Lord God: Clap your hands, stamp your feet, and cry "Alas!" because of all the abominations of the house of Israel, for which they shall fall by the sword, by famine, and by pestilence. ¹²He that is far off shall die of pestilence, he that is near shall fall by the sword, and he that is besieged shall perish by famine; so will I spend my fury upon them. ¹³†Then shall they know that I am the Lord, when their slain shall lie amid their idols, all about their altars, on every high hill and mountaintop, beneath every green

---

† 5, 2: *The city:* the one drawn on the tablet.

5, 8: *I am coming at you:* an expression borrowed from the language of warfare in which enemies attacked one another with the sword. *You* in vv 8-17 is Jerusalem.

5, 10: *Fathers . . . shall eat sons, and sons . . . fathers:* see note on Lam 2, 20.

6, 3: *High places:* the sanctuaries on the mountaintops where illegal worship, whether of the Lord or of Canaanite deities, was performed.

6, 5: *Scatter their bones . . . altars:* dead men's bones defiled a place; cf 2 Kgs 23, 14.

6, 11: *Clap your hands, stamp your feet:* here evidently signs of mourning; in 25, 6, signs of joy.

6, 13: *Every green tree and leafy oak:* sacred groves had a long history in Palestine as places of worship; cf Dt 12, 2; note on Gn 12, 6.

tree and leafy oak, wherever they offered appeasing odors to any of their gods. [14]†I will stretch out my hand against them, and wherever they live I will make the land a desolate waste, from the desert to Riblah; thus shall they know that I am the LORD.

The End Has Come

7 [1]THUS the word of the LORD came to me: [2]Son of man, now say: Thus says the Lord GOD to the land of Israel: An end! The end has come upon the four corners of the land! [3]Now the end is upon you; I will unleash my anger against you and judge you according to your conduct and lay upon you the consequences of all your abominations. [4]I will not look upon you with pity nor have mercy; I will bring your conduct down upon you, and the consequences of your abominations shall be in your midst; then shall you know that I am the LORD.

[5]Thus says the Lord GOD: Disaster upon disaster! See it coming! [6]An end is coming, the end is coming upon you! See it coming! [7]The climax has come for you who dwell in the land! The time has come, near is the day: a time of consternation, not of rejoicing. [8]Soon now I will pour out my fury upon you and spend my anger upon you; I will judge you according to your conduct and lay upon you the consequences of all your abominations. [9]I will not look upon you with pity nor have mercy; I will deal with you according to your conduct, and the consequences of your abominations shall be in your midst; then shall you know that it is I, the LORD, who strike.

[10]See, the day of the LORD! See, the end is coming! Lawlessness is in full bloom, insolence flourishes, [11]violence has risen to support wickedness. It shall not be long in coming, nor shall it delay. [12]†The time has come, the day dawns. Let not the buyer rejoice nor the seller mourn, for wrath shall be upon all the throng. [13]The seller shall not regain what he sold as long as he lives, for wrath shall be upon all the throng. Because of his sins, no one shall preserve his life. [14]They shall sound the trumpet and make everything ready, yet no one shall go to war, for my wrath is upon all the throng.

[15]The sword is outside; pestilence and hunger are within. He that is in the country shall die by the sword; pestilence and famine shall devour those in the city. [16]Even those who escape and flee to the mountains like the doves of the valleys—I will put them all to death, each one for his own sins. [17]All their hands shall be limp, and all their knees shall run with water. [18]*†They shall put on sackcloth, and horror shall cover them; shame shall be on all their faces and baldness on all their heads. [19]*They shall fling their silver into the streets, and their gold shall be considered refuse. Their silver and gold cannot save them on the day of the LORD's wrath. They shall not be allowed to satisfy their craving or fill their bellies, for

this has been the occasion of their sin. [20]In the beauty of their ornaments they put their pride: they made of them their abominable images [their idols]. For this reason I make them refuse. [21]I will hand them over as booty to foreigners, to be spoiled and defiled by the wicked of the earth. [22]†I will turn away my face from them, and my treasure shall be profaned: robbers shall enter and profane it.

[23]They shall wreak slaughter, for the land is filled with bloodshed and the city full of violence. [24]I will bring in the worst of the nations, who shall take possession of their houses. I will put an end to their proud strength, and their sanctuaries shall be profaned. [25]When anguish comes they shall seek peace, but there will be none. [26]There shall be disaster after disaster, rumor after rumor. Prophetic vision shall fade; instruction shall be lacking to the priest, and counsel to the elders, [27]while the prince shall be enveloped in terror, and the hands of the common people shall tremble. I will deal with them according to their conduct, and according to their judgments I will judge them; thus they shall know that I am the LORD.

Vision of Abominations in the Temple

8 [3]*†SPIRIT lifted me up in the air and brought me in divine visions to Jerusalem, to the entrance of the north gate, where stood the statue of jealousy which stirs up jealousy. [5]†He said to me: Son of man, look toward the north! I looked toward the north and saw northward of the gate the altar of the statue of jealousy. [6]Son of man, he asked me, do you see what they are doing? Do you see the great abominations that the house of Israel is practicing here, so that I must depart from my sanctuary? But you shall see still greater abominations!

[7]Then he brought me to the entrance of the court, where I saw there was a hole in the wall. [8]Son of man, he ordered, dig through the wall. I dug through the wall and saw a door. [9]Enter, he said to me, and see the abominable evils which they are doing here. [10]†I entered and saw that all around upon the wall were pictured the figures of all kinds of creeping things and loathsome beasts [all the idols of the house of Israel].

---

† 6, 14: *From the desert to Riblah:* the whole land, from the far south to the far north.

7, 12f: *Mundane affairs will cease to have any meaning in view of the disaster that is to come.*

7, 18: *Baldness:* shaving the head was a sign of mourning.

7, 22: *My treasure:* the temple of Jerusalem.

8, 3: *The statue of jealousy which stirs up jealousy:* the statue which provokes the Lord's jealousy for his honor. This was probably the statue of the goddess Asherah erected by the wicked King Manasseh (cf 2 Kgs 21, 7; 2 Chr 33, 7.15). Though it had been removed by King Josiah (2 Kgs 23, 6), it had no doubt been set up again in the repaganizing of Jerusalem that followed on Josiah's death.

8, 5: *He:* an angel accompanies Ezekiel in these visions and represents the voice of the Lord; cf 40, 3f.

8, 10: *Creeping things and loathsome beasts:* probably Egyptian deities, which were represented in animal form. During the last days of Jerusalem King Zedekiah was allied with Egypt, trusting in it for protection against the Chaldeans.

❋ 7/18: Is 15, 2; Jer 48, 37.   8/3: Dn 14, 6.
    19: Prv 11, 4; Sir 5, 10; Zep 1, 18.

¹¹Before these stood seventy of the elders of the house of Israel, among whom stood Jaazaniah, son of Shaphan, each of them with his censer in his hand, and the fragrance of the incense was rising upward. ¹²Then he said to me: Do you see, son of man, what each of these elders of the house of Israel is doing in his idol room? They think: "The Lord cannot see us; the Lord has forsaken the land." ¹³He continued: You shall see still greater abominations that they are practicing.

^{14†}Then he brought me to the entrance of the north gate of the temple, and I saw sitting there the women who were weeping for Tammuz. ¹⁵Then he said to me: Do you see this, son of man? You shall see other abominations, greater than these!

^{16†}Then he brought me into the inner court of the Lord's house, and there at the door of the Lord's temple, between the vestibule and the altar, were about twenty-five men with their backs to the Lord's temple and their faces toward the east; they were bowing down to the sun. ^{17†}Do you see, son of man? he asked me. Is it such a trivial matter for the house of Judah to do the abominable things they have done here—for they have filled the land with violence, and again and again they have provoked me—that now they must also put the branch to my nose? ¹⁸Therefore I in turn will act furiously: I will not look upon them with pity nor will I show mercy.

Slaughter of the Idolaters

9 ¹THEN he cried loud for me to hear: Come, you scourges of the city! ²With that I saw six men coming from the direction of the upper gate which faces the north, each with a destroying weapon in his hand. In their midst was a man dressed in linen, with a writer's case at his waist. They entered and stood beside the bronze altar. ³Then he called to the man dressed in linen with the writer's case at his waist, ⁴*†saying to him: Pass through the city [through Jerusalem] and mark an X on the foreheads of those who moan and groan over all the abominations that are practiced within it. ⁵To the others I heard him say: Pass through the city after him and strike! Do not look on them with pity nor show any mercy! ⁶Old men, youths and maidens, women and children—wipe them out! But do not touch any marked with the X; begin at my sanctuary. So they began with the men [the elders] who were in front of the temple. ⁷Defile the temple, he said to them, and fill the courts with the slain; then go out and strike in the city.

⁸As they began to strike, I was left alone. I fell prone, crying out, "Alas, Lord God! Will you destroy all that is left of Israel when you pour out your fury on Jerusalem?" ⁹He answered me: The sins of the house of Israel are great beyond measure; the land is filled with bloodshed, the city with lawlessness. They think that the Lord has forsaken the land, that he does not see them. ¹⁰I, however, will not look upon them with pity, nor show any mercy. I will bring down their conduct upon their heads.

¹¹Then I saw the man dressed in linen with the writing case at his waist make his report: "I have done as you ordered."

^{11/24}Spirit lifted me up and brought me back to the exiles in Chaldea [in a vision, by God's spirit]. Then the vision I had seen left me, ^{11/25†}and I told the exiles everything the Lord had shown me.

God's Glory Leaves Jerusalem

^{8/1†}On the fifth day of the sixth month, in the sixth year, as I was sitting in my house, and the elders of Judah sat before me, the hand of the Lord God fell upon me there. ^{8/2†}I looked up and saw a form that looked like a man. Downward from what seemed to be his waist, there was fire; from his waist upward there seemed to be a brightness like the sheen of electrum. He stretched out what appeared to be a hand and seized me by the hair of my head. . . .

^{8/4}I saw there the glory of the God of Israel, like the vision I had seen in the plain. The cherubim were stationed to the right of the temple;

10 ²⁰*THESE were the living creatures I had seen beneath the God of Israel by the river Chebar, whom I now recognized to be cherubim. ²¹Each had four faces and four wings; something like human hands were under their wings. ²²Their faces looked just like those I had seen by the river Chebar; each one went straight forward. ¹⁴*Each had four faces: the first face was that of an ox, the second that of a man, the third that of a lion, and the fourth that of an eagle. ¹⁵Such were the living creatures I had seen by the river Chebar.

⁹*I also saw four wheels beside them, one wheel beside each cherub; the wheels appeared to have the luster of chrysolite stone. ¹⁰All four of them seemed to

---

† 8, 1-11, 25: In these chapters of the current Hebrew text, several visions involving the temple of Jerusalem were combined to form a single continuous vision. The redistribution of verses in this translation is an attempt to separate the original visions.

8, 1: *The fifth day of the sixth month, in the sixth year:* September 17, 592 B. C.

8, 2: The dots suppose the omission of some words describing the prophet's being transported in his visions to the court of the temple.

8, 14: *Weeping for Tammuz:* the withering of trees and plants in autumn was thought to be due to the descent of *Tammuz,* the Babylonian god of fertility, to the nether world of the dead; this descent was bewailed by the women.

8, 16: *Bowing down to the sun:* sun worship had been made an important part of Judahite idolatry by the impious kings; cf 2 Kgs 23, 11.

8, 17: *Put the branch to my nose:* the meaning is uncertain. Perhaps it refers to an Egyptian practice imported into Judah: the Egyptian sun god Re is pictured with a vine branch at his nose, signifying the transfer of creative power (divine breath) to living things. Such rites were abominable to the Lord.

9, 4: Ezekiel is pre-eminently the prophet of personal retribution; the innocent inhabitants of Jerusalem are to be spared when the idolatrous are punished. *An X:* literally, the Hebrew letter taw, which had the form of a cross.

---

*   9/4: Ex 12, 7; Rv 7, 3.   14: 1, 10.
     10/20: 1, 1.3.   9: 1, 15f.

be made the same, as though there were a wheel within a wheel. ¹¹When they moved, they went in any one of their four directions without veering as they moved; for in whichever direction they were faced, they went straight towards it without veering as they moved. ¹²*The rims of the four wheels were full of eyes all around. ¹³I heard the wheels given the name "wheelwork." ¹⁶*When the cherubim moved, the wheels went beside them; when the cherubim lifted their wings to rise from the earth, even then the wheels did not leave their sides. ¹⁷When they stood still, the wheels stood still; when they rose, the wheels rose with them; for the living creatures' spirit was in them.

¹I looked and saw in the firmament above the cherubim what appeared to be sapphire stone; something like a throne could be seen upon it. ²†He said to the man dressed in linen: Go within the wheelwork under the cherubim; fill both your hands with burning coals from among the cherubim, then scatter them over the city. As I looked on, he entered.

The glory of the God of Israel had gone up from the cherubim, upon which it had been, to the threshold of the temple. ³As the man entered, the cloud filled the inner court, ⁴and the glory of the LORD rose from over the cherubim to the threshold of the temple; the temple was filled with the cloud, and all the court was bright with the glory of the LORD. ⁵The noise of the wings of the cherubim could be heard as far as the outer court; it was like the voice of God the Almighty when he speaks.

⁶When he had commanded the man dressed in linen to take fire from within the wheelwork, among the cherubim, the man entered and stood by one of the wheels. ⁷Thereupon its cherub stretched out his hand toward the fire that was among the cherubim. He took up some of it and put it in the hands of the one dressed in linen, who took it and came out. ⁸[Something like human hands could be seen under the wings of the cherubim.]

¹⁸Then the glory of the LORD left the threshold of the temple and rested upon the cherubim. ¹⁹These lifted their wings, and I saw them rise from the earth, the wheels rising along with them. They stood at the entrance of the eastern gate of the LORD's house, and the glory of the God of Israel was up above them.

11 ²²THEN the cherubim lifted their wings, and the wheels went along with them, while up above them was the glory of the God of Israel. ²³And the glory of the LORD rose from the city and took a stand on the mountain which is to the east of the city.

Judgment of the Princes

¹Spirit lifted me up and brought me to the east gate of the temple. At the entrance of the gate I saw twenty-five men, among whom were Jaazaniah, son of Azzur, and Pelatiah, son of Benaiah, princes of the people. ²The LORD said to me: Son of man, these are the men who are planning evil and giving wicked counsel in this city. ³†"Shall we not," they say, "be building houses soon? The city is the kettle, and we are the meat." ⁴Therefore prophesy against them, son of man, prophesy! ⁵Then the spirit of the LORD fell upon me, and he told me to say: Thus says the LORD: This is the way you talk, house of Israel, and what you are plotting I well know. ⁶You have slain many in this city and have filled its streets with your slain. ⁷Therefore thus says the Lord GOD: Your slain whom you have placed within it, they are the meat, and the city is the kettle; but you I will take out of it. ⁸You fear the sword, but the sword I will bring upon you, says the Lord GOD. ⁹I will bring you out of the city, and hand you over to foreigners, and inflict punishments upon you. ¹⁰By the sword you shall fall; at the boundaries of Israel I will judge you; thus you shall know that I am the LORD. ¹¹The city shall not be a kettle for you, nor shall you be the meat within it. At the boundaries of Israel I will judge you, ¹²and you shall know that I am the LORD, by whose statutes you have not lived, and whose ordinances you have not kept; rather, you have acted according to the ordinances of the nations around you.

¹³While I was prophesying, Pelatiah, the son of Benaiah, died. I fell prone and cried out in a loud voice: "Alas, Lord GOD! will you utterly wipe out what remains of Israel?"

Restoration of the Exiles

¹⁴Thus the word of the LORD came to me: ¹⁵†Son of man, it is about your kinsmen, your fellow exiles, and the whole house of Israel that the inhabitants of Jerusalem say, "They are far away from the LORD; to us the land of Israel has been given as our possession." ¹⁶Therefore say: Thus says the Lord GOD: Though I have removed them far among the nations and scattered them over foreign countries—and was for a while their only sanctuary in the countries to which they had gone—¹⁷I will gather you from the nations and assemble you from the countries over which you have been scattered, and I will restore to you the land of Israel. ¹⁸They shall return to it and remove from it all its detestable abominations. ¹⁹*I will give them a new heart and put a new spirit within them; I will remove the stony heart from their bodies, and replace it with a natural heart, ²⁰so that they will live according to my statutes, and observe and carry out my ordinances;

---

† 10, 2: The *burning coals* within the wheelwork under God's throne, a sign of the divine presence (cf 28, 14; Ps 18, 13), symbolize the judgment to be visited on the city.

11, 3: These words reflect the false confidence of the inhabitants of Jerusalem in the face of the Chaldean invasion. Jerusalem, they think, is like an iron kettle protecting the meat within it from harm; but cf 24, 3-6.

11, 15-21: Like Jeremiah (cf chapter 29), Ezekiel knows that no reform is to be expected from the men of Judah who remained in Palestine; but the exiles will be the ones to form the new Israel. The new, spiritual covenant will replace the former covenant; cf Jer 24, 7.

---

thus they shall be my people and I will be their God. [21]But as for those whose hearts are devoted to their detestable abominations, I will bring down their conduct upon their heads, says the Lord God.

Acts Symbolic of the Exile

12 [1]THUS the word of the Lord came to me: Son of man, you live in the midst of a rebellious house; they have eyes to see but do not see, and ears to hear but do not hear, for they are a rebellious house. [3]Now, son of man, during the day while they are looking on, prepare your baggage as though for exile, and again while they are looking on, migrate from where you live to another place; perhaps they will see that they are a rebellious house. [4]You shall bring out your baggage like an exile in the daytime while they are looking on; in the evening, again while they are looking on, you shall go out like one of those driven into exile; [5][†]while they look on, dig a hole in the wall and pass through it; [6]while they look on, shoulder the burden and set out in the darkness; cover your face that you may not see the land, for I have made you a sign for the house of Israel.

[7]I did as I was told. During the day I brought out my baggage as though it were that of an exile, and at evening I dug a hole through the wall with my hand and, while they looked on, set out in the darkness, shouldering my burden.

[8]Then, in the morning, the word of the Lord came to me: [9]Son of man, did not the house of Israel, that rebellious house, ask you what you were doing? [10]Tell them: Thus says the Lord God: This oracle concerns Jerusalem and the whole house of Israel within it. [11]I am a sign for you: as I have done, so shall it be done to them; as captives they shall go into exile. [12]The prince who is among them shall shoulder his burden and set out in darkness, going through a hole that he has dug in the wall, and covering his face lest he be seen by anyone. [13][*][†]But I will spread my net over him, and he shall be taken in my snare. I will bring him to Babylon, into the land of the Chaldeans—but he shall not see it—and there he shall die. [14]All his retinue, his aides, and his troops I will scatter in every direction, and pursue them with the sword. [15]Then shall they know that I am the Lord, when I disperse them among the nations and scatter them over foreign lands. [16]Yet I will leave a few of them to escape the sword, famine and pestilence, so that they may tell of all their abominations among the nations to which they will come; thus they shall know that I am the Lord.

[17]Thus the word of the Lord came to me: [18]Son of man, eat your bread trembling, and drink your water shaking with anxiety. [19]Then say to the people of the land: Thus says the Lord God of the inhabitants of Jerusalem [to the land of Israel]: They shall eat their bread in anxiety and drink their water in horror, that their land may be emptied of the violence of all its inhabitants that now fills it. [20]Inhabited cities shall be in ruins, and the land shall be a waste; thus you shall know that I am the Lord.

Prophecy Ridiculed

[21]Thus the word of the Lord came to me: [22][†]Son of man, what is this proverb that you have in the land of Israel: "The days drag on, and no vision ever comes to anything"? [23]Say to them therefore: Thus says the Lord God: I will put an end to this proverb; they shall never quote it again in Israel. Rather, say to them: The days are at hand, and also the fulfillment of every vision. [25]Whatever I speak is final, and it shall be done without further delay. In your days, rebellious house, whatever I speak I will bring about, says the Lord God.

[24]There shall no longer be any false visions or deceitful divinations within the house of Israel, because it is I, the Lord, who will speak.

[26]Thus the word of the Lord came to me: [27]Son of man, listen to the house of Israel saying, "The vision he sees is a long way off; he prophesies of the distant future!" [28]Say to them therefore: Thus says the Lord God: None of my words shall be delayed any longer; whatever I speak is final, and it shall be done, says the Lord God.

Against the Prophets of Peace

13 [1]THUS the word of the Lord came to me: [2]Son of man, prophesy against the prophets of Israel, prophesy! Say to those who prophesy their own thought: Hear the word of the Lord: [3]You did not step into the breach, nor did you build a wall about the house of Israel that would stand firm against attack on the day of the Lord. [7]Was not the vision you saw false, and your divination lying? [8]Therefore thus says the Lord God: Because you have spoken falsehood and have seen lying visions, therefore see! I am coming at you, says the Lord God.

[10][†]For the very reason that they led my people astray, saying, "Peace!" when there was no peace, and that, as one built a wall, they would cover it with whitewash, [11]say then to the whitewashers: I will bring down a flooding rain; hailstones shall fall, and a stormwind shall break out. [12]And when the wall has fallen, will you not be asked: Where is the whitewash you spread on?

[13]Therefore thus says the Lord God: In my fury I will let loose stormwinds; because of my anger there shall be a flooding rain, and hailstones shall fall with destructive wrath. [14]I will tear down the wall that you

---

[†]

12, 5: *Dig a hole in the wall:* the exiles are to leave Jerusalem through the broken walls of the ruined city.

12, 13: *But he shall not see it:* Zedekiah was blinded by Nebuchadnezzar before being deported to Babylonia; cf 2 Kgs 25, 7.

12, 22.27: These words were used against Ezekiel because of the apparent failure of his prophecies; cf Jer 20, 7ff.

13, 10: To the confidence which the people had in their defenses against the Chaldeans, the false prophets contributed the illusion of security by predictions of peace, like men who whitewash a wall rather than allow its defects to be seen.

---

[*]

12/13: 17, 20; 32, 3.

have whitewashed and level it to the ground, laying bare its foundations. When it falls, you shall be crushed beneath it; thus you shall know that I am the LORD. ¹⁵When I have spent my fury on the wall and its whitewashers, I tell you there shall be no wall, nor shall there be whitewashers—¹⁶those prophets of Israel who prophesied to Jerusalem and saw for it visions of peace when there was no peace, says the Lord GOD.

Against False Prophets in Chaldea

³*Thus says the Lord GOD: Woe to those prophets who are fools, who follow their own spirit and have seen no vision. ⁴Like foxes among ruins are your prophets, O Israel! ⁶Their visions are false and their divination lying. They say, "Thus says the LORD!" though the LORD did not send them; then they wait for him to fulfill their word! ⁹But I will stretch out my hand against the prophets who have false visions and who foretell lies. They shall not belong to the community of my people, nor be recorded in the register of the house of Israel, nor enter the land of Israel; thus you shall know that I am the LORD.

Against False Prophetesses

¹⁷Now, son of man, turn toward the daughters of your people who prophesy their own thoughts; against these, prophesy: Thus says the Lord GOD: ²²Because you have disheartened the upright man with lies when I did not wish him grieved, and have encouraged the wicked man not to turn from his evil conduct and save his life; ²³therefore you shall no longer see false visions and practice divination, but I will rescue my people from your power. Thus you shall know that I am the LORD.

Against Sorceresses

¹⁸†Woe to those who sew bands for everyone's wrists and make veils for every size of head so as to entrap their owners. Do you think to entrap the lives of my people, yet keep yourselves alive? ¹⁹†You dishonor me before my people with handfuls of barley and crumbs of bread, killing those who should not die and keeping alive those who should not live, lying to my people who willingly hear lies. ²⁰Therefore thus says the Lord GOD: See! I am coming at those bands of yours in which you entrap men's lives: I will tear them from their arms and set free those you have caught. ²¹I will tear off your veils and rescue my people from your power, so that they shall no longer be prey to your hands. Thus you shall know that I am the LORD.

Prophecy Useless for Idolaters

14 ¹WHEN certain elders of Israel came and sat down before me, ²the word of the LORD came to me: ³Son of man, these men have the memory of their idols fresh in their hearts, and they keep the oc-

casion of their sin before them. Why should I allow myself to be consulted by them? ⁴Therefore speak with them, and say to them: Thus says the Lord GOD: If anyone of the house of Israel, holding the memory of his idols in his heart and keeping the occasion of his sin before him, has recourse to a prophet, I, the LORD, will be his answer in person because of his many idols. ⁵Thus would I bring back to their senses the house of Israel, who have become estranged from me through all their idols.

⁶Therefore say to the house of Israel: Thus says the Lord GOD: Return and be converted from your idols; turn yourselves away from all your abominations. ⁷For if anyone of the house of Israel or any alien resident in Israel is estranged from me, and holds the memory of his idols in his heart and keeps the occasion of his sin before him, yet asks a prophet to consult me for him, I, the LORD, will be his answer in person. ⁸I will turn against that man, and make of him an example and a byword. I will cut him off from the midst of my people. Thus you shall know that I am the LORD.

⁹*†As for the prophet, if he is beguiled into speaking a word, I, the LORD, shall have beguiled that prophet; I will stretch out my hand against him and root him out of my people Israel. ¹⁰Each shall receive punishment for his sin, the inquirer and the prophet shall be punished alike, ¹¹so that the house of Israel may no longer stray from me and may no longer be defiled by all their sins. Thus they shall be my people, and I will be their God, says the Lord GOD.

Personal Responsibility

¹²†Thus the word of the LORD came to me: ¹³*Son of man, when a land sins against me by breaking faith, I stretch out my hand against it and break its staff of bread, I let famine loose upon it and cut off from it both man and beast; ¹⁴†and even if these three men were in it, Noah, Daniel, and Job, they could save only themselves by their virtue, says the Lord GOD. ¹⁵If I were to cause wild beasts to prowl the land, depopulating it so that it became a waste, traversed by none because of the wild beasts, ¹⁶and these three men were in it, as I live, says the Lord GOD, I swear they could save neither sons nor daughters; they alone would be saved, and the land would be a waste. ¹⁷Or

---

† 13, 18: *Sew bands . . . make veils:* magical practices believed to give to the sorceresses power over those on whom they placed these objects.

13, 19: *Handfuls of barley and crumbs of bread:* used in divination and forecasting the future.

14, 9: *I, the Lord, shall have beguiled that prophet:* the ancient Israelites attributed to God every action, good or evil; cf 1 Sm 18, 10; 2 Sm 24, 1ff. We would say, rather, that God permitted this deceit.

14, 12-23: The doctrine of personal responsibility before God was not new (cf 3, 16-21; 18; 33, 1-20); but it had not been emphasized by the prophets before the exile, who mostly predicted national retribution and called for national repentance.

14, 14: *Noah, Daniel, and Job:* proverbially virtuous men. The Daniel named here may be the traditional just judge of the ancient past, celebrated in Canaanite literature, who is possibly reflected in Dn 13, but is not the hero of Dn 1-12.

13/3: 14, 9; 34, 2; Jer 23, 1.   13: 4, 16.
14/9: 1 Kgs 22, 23.

if I brought the sword upon this country, commanding the sword to pass through the land cutting off from it man and beast, **18**and these three men were in it, as I live, says the Lord God, they would be unable to save either sons or daughters; they alone would be saved. **19**Or if I were to send pestilence into this land, pouring out upon it my bloodthirsty fury, cutting off from it man and beast, **20**even if Noah, Daniel, and Job were in it, as I live, says the Lord God, I swear that they could save neither son nor daughter; they would save only themselves by their virtue.

21Thus says the Lord God: Even though I send Jerusalem my four cruel punishments, the sword, famine, wild beasts, and pestilence, to cut off from it man and beast, **22**still some survivors shall be left in it who will bring out sons and daughters; when they come out to you, you shall see their conduct and their actions and be consoled regarding the evil I have brought on Jerusalem [all that I have brought upon it]. **23**They shall console you when you see their conduct and actions, for you shall then know that it was not without reason that I did to it what I did, says the Lord God.

Parable of the Vine

15 **1**Thus the word of the Lord came to me: **2**Son of man, what makes the wood of the vine better than any other wood? That branch among the trees of the forest! **3**Can you use its wood to make anything worthwhile? Can you make even a peg from it, to hang on it any kind of vessel? **4**If you throw it on the fire as fuel and the fire devours both ends and even the middle is scorched, is it still good for anything? **5**Why, even when it was whole it was good for nothing; how much less, when the fire has devoured and scorched it, can it be used for anything! **6**Therefore, thus says the Lord God: Like the wood of the vine among the trees of the forest, which I have destined as fuel for the fire, do I make the inhabitants of Jerusalem. **7**I will set my face against them; they have escaped from the fire, but the fire shall devour them. Thus you shall know that I am the Lord, when I turn my face against them. **8**I will make the land a waste, because they have broken faith, says the Lord God.

The Faithless Spouse

16 **1**Thus the word of the Lord came to me: **2**Son of man, make known to Jerusalem her abominations: **3**†Thus says the Lord God to Jerusalem: By origin and birth you are of the land of Canaan; your father was an Amorite and your mother a Hittite. **4**As for your birth, the day you were born your navel cord was not cut; you were neither washed with water nor anointed, nor were you rubbed with salt, nor swathed in swaddling clothes. **5**No one looked on you with pity

or compassion to do any of these things for you. Rather, you were thrown out on the ground as something loathsome, the day you were born.

6Then I passed by and saw you weltering in your blood. I said to you: Live in your blood **7**and grow like a plant in the field. You grew and developed, you came to the age of puberty; your breasts were formed, your hair had grown, but you were still stark naked. **8**†Again I passed by you and saw that you were now old enough for love. So I spread the corner of my cloak over you to cover your nakedness; I swore an oath to you and entered into a covenant with you; you became mine, says the Lord God. **9**Then I bathed you with water, washed away your blood, and anointed you with oil. **10**I clothed you with an embroidered gown, put sandals of fine leather on your feet; I gave you a fine linen sash and silk robes to wear. **11**I adorned you with jewelry: I put bracelets on your arms, a necklace about your neck, **12**a ring in your nose, pendants in your ears, and a glorious diadem upon your head. **13**Thus you were adorned with gold and silver; your garments were of fine linen, silk, and embroidered cloth. Fine flour, honey, and oil were your food. You were exceedingly beautiful, with the dignity of a queen. **14** You were renowned among the nations for your beauty, perfect as it was, because of my splendor which I had bestowed on you, says the Lord God.

15But you were captivated by your own beauty, you used your renown to make yourself a harlot, and you lavished your harlotry on every passer-by, whose own you became. **16**†You took some of your gowns and made for yourself gaudy high places, where you played the harlot. . . . **17**You took the splendid gold and silver ornaments that I had given you and made for yourself male images, with which also you played the harlot. **18**You took your embroidered gowns to cover them; my oil and my incense you set before them; **19**the food that I had given you, the fine flour, the oil, and the honey with which I fed you, you set before them as an appeasing odor, says the Lord God. **20***†The sons and daughters you had borne me you took and offered as sacrifices to be devoured by them! Was it not enough that you had become a harlot? **21***You slaughtered and immolated my children to them, making them pass through fire. **22**And through all your abominations and harlotries you remembered nothing of when you were a girl, stark naked and weltering in your blood.

† 16, 3f: *By origin and birth . . . Canaan . . . Amorite . . . Hittite:* the inhabitants of Jerusalem and Judah absorbed not only pre-Israelite racial strains, but also many elements of the country's pagan cult and customs.

16, 8: *I spread the corner of my cloak over you to cover your nakedness:* and also to signify the intention of marriage; cf Ru 3, 9.

16, 16: Fine robes were used to cover a couch for harlotry; cf Prv 7, 16f. In the allegory of this chapter the viewpoint often shifts from the figure (harlotry) to the reality (idolatry).

16, 20f: Human sacrifice was introduced under Judah's impious kings; cf 2 Kgs 16, 3; 17, 17; Jer 7, 31.

✽ 16/20: 20, 26.31; 23, 37ff; Lv 18, 21; 20, 2; Dt 12, 31; 18, 10; 2 Kgs 21, 6; 23, 10;   24, 4; Jer 7, 31; 19, 5; 32, 34; Mi 6, 7. 21: 2 Kgs 16, 3; 17, 17; 21, 6; 23, 10.

²³Then after all your evildoing—woe, woe to you! says the Lord God—²⁴†you raised for yourself a platform and a dais in every public place. ²⁵*At every street corner you built a dais for yourself to use your beauty obscenely, spreading your legs for every passer-by, playing the harlot countless times. ²⁶You played the harlot with the Egyptians, your lustful neighbors, so many times that I was provoked to anger. ²⁷Therefore I stretched out my hand against you, I diminished your allowance and delivered you over to the will of your enemies, the Philistines, who revolted at your lewd conduct. ²⁸You also played the harlot with the Assyrians, because you were not satisfied; and after playing the harlot with them, you were still not satisfied. ²⁹Again and again you played the harlot, now going to Chaldea, the land of the traders; but despite this, you were still not satisfied.

³⁰How wild your lust! says the Lord God, that you did all these things, acting like a shameless prostitute, ³¹building your platform at every street corner and erecting your dais in every public place! Yet you were unlike a prostitute, since you disdained payment. ³²The adulterous wife receives, instead of her husband, payment. ³³All harlots receive gifts. But you rather bestowed your gifts on all your lovers, bribing them to come to you from all sides for your harlotry. ³⁴Thus in your harlotry you were different from all other women. No one sought you out for prostitution. Since you gave payment instead of receiving it, how different you were!

³⁵Therefore, harlot, hear the word of the Lord! ³⁶Thus says the Lord God: Because you poured out your lust and revealed your nakedness in your harlotry with your lovers and abominable idols, and because you sacrificed the life-blood of your children to them, ³⁷*I will now gather together all your lovers whom you tried to please, whether you loved them or loved them not; I will gather them against you from all sides and expose you naked for them to see. ³⁸I will inflict on you the sentence of adulteresses and murderesses; ³⁹I will wreak fury and jealousy upon you. I will hand you over to them to tear down your platform and demolish your dais; they shall strip you of your garments and take away your splendid ornaments, leaving you stark naked. ⁴⁰They shall lead an assembly against you to stone you and hack you with their swords. ⁴¹*They shall burn your apartments with fire and inflict punishments on you while many women look on. Thus I will put an end to your harlotry, and you shall never again give payment. ⁴²When I have wreaked my fury upon you I will cease to be jealous of you, I will be quiet and no longer vexed. ⁴³Because you did not remember what happened when you were a girl, but enraged me with all these things, therefore in return I am bringing down your conduct upon your head, says the Lord God. For did you not add lewdness to the rest of your abominable deeds?

⁴⁴See, everyone who is fond of proverbs will say of you, 'Like mother, like daughter.' ⁴⁵†Yes, you are the true daughter of the mother who spurned her husband and children, and you are a true sister to those who spurned their husbands and children—your mother was a Hittite and your father an Amorite. ⁴⁶†Your elder sister was Samaria with her daughters, living to the north of you; and your younger sister, living to the south of you, was Sodom with her daughters. ⁴⁷Yet not only in their ways did you walk, and act as abominably as they did; in a very short time you became more corrupt in all your ways than they. ⁴⁸As I live, says the Lord God, I swear that your sister Sodom, with her daughters, has not done as you and your daughters have done! ⁴⁹*And look at the guilt of your sister Sodom: she and her daughters were proud, sated with food, complacent in their prosperity, and they gave no help to the poor and needy. ⁵⁰Rather, they became haughty and committed abominable crimes in my presence; then, as you have seen, I removed them. ⁵¹Samaria did not commit half your sins! You have done more abominable things than they, and have even made your sisters appear just, with all the abominable deeds you have done. ⁵²You, then, bear your shame; you are an argument in favor of your sisters! In view of your sinful deeds, more abominable than theirs, they appear just in comparison with you. Blush for shame, and bear the shame of having made your sisters appear just.

⁵³I will restore their fortunes, the fortune of Sodom and her daughters and of Samaria and her daughters [and I will restore your fortune along with them], ⁵⁴that you may bear your shame and be disgraced for all the comfort you brought them. ⁵⁵Yes, your sisters, Sodom and her daughters, Samaria and her daughters, shall return to their former state [you and your daughters shall return to your former state]. ⁵⁶Was not your sister Sodom kept in bad repute by you while you felt proud of yourself, ⁵⁷before your wickedness became evident? Now you are like her, reproached by the Edomites and all your neighbors, despised on all sides by the Philistines. ⁵⁸The penalty of your lewdness and your abominations—you must bear it all, says the Lord.

⁵⁹For thus speaks the Lord God: I will deal with you according to what you have done, you who despised your oath, breaking a covenant. ⁶⁰Yet I will remember the covenant I made with you when you were a girl, and I will set up an everlasting covenant with you. ⁶¹Then you shall remember your conduct and be ashamed when I take your sisters, those older and

---

† 16, 24: *A platform and a dais:* associated with ritual prostitution, which the Israelites borrowed from Canaanite practice.

16, 45: *True daughter of the mother:* Jerusalem has followed in the footsteps of its heathen forebears; cf v 3.

16, 46: *Your elder sister was Samaria:* Samaria can be called an elder sister in view of the relatively greater importance of the northern kingdom, Israel, during most of Old Testament history. Also, the relatively insignificant Sodom of ancient history can be called *your younger sister.*

---

*
25: 23, 8; Is 57, 7;   37: 23, 10.
Jer 2, 20; 3, 2; 5, 7;   41: 2 Kgs 25, 9.
13, 27; Hos 2, 4; 4, 13.   49: Gn 19, 24.

younger than you, and give them to you as daughters, even though I am not bound by my covenant with you. ⁶²For I will re-establish my covenant with you, that you may know that I am the LORD, ⁶³that you may remember and be covered with confusion, and that you may be utterly silenced for shame when I pardon you for all you have done, says the Lord GOD.

The Eagles and the Vine

17 ¹THUS the word of the LORD came to me: ²Son of man, propose a riddle, and speak this proverb to the house of Israel: ³Thus speaks the Lord GOD:

> The great eagle, with great wings, with
> long pinions,
>   with thick plumage, many-hued,
>   came to Lebanon.
> He took the crest of the cedar,
>   tearing off its topmost branch,
> And brought it to a land of tradesmen,
>   set it in a city of merchants.
> Then he took some seed of the land,
>   and planted it in a seedbed;
> A shoot by plentiful waters,
>   like a willow he placed it,
> To sprout and grow up a vine,
>   dense and low-lying,
> Its branches turned toward him,
>   its roots lying under him.
> Thus it became a vine, produced
>   branches
>   and put forth shoots.
> But there was another great eagle,
>   great of wing, rich in plumage;
> To him this vine bent its roots,
>   sent out its branches,
> That he might water it more freely
>   than the bed where it was planted.
> In a fertile field by plentiful waters it
>   was planted,
>   to grow branches, bear fruit,
>   and become a majestic vine.

⁹Say: Thus says the Lord GOD: Can it prosper? Will he not rather tear it out by the roots and strip off its fruit, so that all its green growth will wither when he pulls it up by the roots? [No need of a mighty arm or many people to do this.] ¹⁰True, it is planted, but will it prosper? Will it not rather wither, when touched by the east wind, in the bed where it grew?

¹¹†Thus the word of the LORD came to me: ¹² Son of man, say now to the rebellious house: Do you not understand what this means? It is this: The king of Babylon came to Jerusalem and took away its king and princes with him to Babylon. ¹³Then he selected a man of the royal line with whom he made a covenant, binding him under oath, while removing the

nobles of the land, ¹⁴so that the kingdom would remain a modest one, without aspirations, and would keep his covenant and obey him. ¹⁵But this man rebelled against him, sending envoys to Egypt to obtain horses and a great army. Can he prosper? Can he who does such things escape? Can he break a covenant and still go free? ¹⁶As I live, says the Lord GOD, in the home of the king who set him up to rule, whose oath he spurned, whose covenant with him he broke, there in Babylon I swear he shall die! ¹⁷When ramps are cast up and siege towers are built for the destruction of many lives, he shall not be saved in the conflict by Pharaoh with a great army and numerous troops. ¹⁸He spurned his oath, breaking his covenant. Though he gave his hand in pledge, he did all these things. He shall not escape!

¹⁹Therefore say: Thus says the Lord GOD: As I live, my oath which he spurned, my covenant which he broke, I swear to bring down upon his head. ²⁰*I will spread my net over him, and he shall be taken in my snare. I will bring him to Babylon and enter into judgment with him there over his breaking faith with me. ²¹All the crack troops among his forces shall fall by the sword, and the survivors shall be scattered in every direction. Thus you shall know that I, the LORD, have spoken.

²²†Therefore say: Thus says the Lord GOD:

> I, too, will take from the crest of the
>   cedar,
>   from its topmost branches tear off a
>   tender shoot,
> And plant it on a high and lofty
>   mountain;
>   on the mountain heights of Israel I
>   will plant it.
> It shall put forth branches and bear
>   fruit,
>   and become a majestic cedar.
> Birds of every kind shall dwell beneath
>   it,
>   every winged thing in the shade of its
>   boughs.
> And all the trees of the field shall know
>   that I, the LORD,
> Bring low the high tree,
>   lift high the lowly tree,
> Wither up the green tree,
>   and make the withered tree bloom.

As I, the LORD, have spoken, so will I do.

---

† 17, 11-21: These verses explain the foregoing allegory. In 597 B. C. Nebuchadnezzar removed King Jehoiachin and took him into exile; in his place he set Zedekiah, Jehoiachin's uncle, on the throne and received from him the oath of loyalty. But Zedekiah was beguiled into rebellion by Pharaoh Hophra of Egypt, and thereby merited punishment; cf 2 Kgs 24, 10—25, 7.

17, 22f: *I, too, will take from the crest of the cedar . . . plant it:* the Lord will restore Israel under a Messianic king from the same Davidic dynasty.

✦ 17/20: 12, 13; 32, 3.

Personal Responsibility

18 ¹THUS the word of the LORD came to me: Son of man, ²*†what is the meaning of this proverb that you recite in the land of Israel:

> "Fathers have eaten green grapes,
> thus their children's teeth are on
> edge"?

³As I live, says the Lord GOD: I swear that there shall no longer be anyone among you who will repeat this proverb in Israel. ⁴For all lives are mine; the life of the father is like the life of the son, both are mine; only the one who sins shall die.

⁵If a man is virtuous—if he does what is right and just, ⁶†if he does not eat on the mountains, nor raise his eyes to the idols of the house of Israel; if he does not defile his neighbor's wife, nor have relations with a woman in her menstrual period; ⁷*if he oppresses no one, gives back the pledge received for a debt, commits no robbery; if he gives food to the hungry and clothes the naked; ⁸if he does not lend at interest nor exact usury; if he holds off from evil-doing, judges fairly between a man and his opponent; ⁹if he lives by my statutes and is careful to observe my ordinances, that man is virtuous—he shall surely live, says the Lord GOD.

¹⁰But if he begets a son who is a thief, a murderer, or who does any of these things ¹¹(though the father does none of them), a son who eats on the mountains, defiles the wife of his neighbor, ¹²oppresses the poor and needy, commits robbery, does not give back a pledge, raises his eyes to idols, does abominable things, ¹³lends at interest and exacts usury—this son certainly shall not live. Because he practiced all these abominations, he shall surely die; his death shall be his own fault.

¹⁴On the other hand, if a man begets a son who, seeing all the sins his father commits, yet fears and does not imitate him; ¹⁵a son who does not eat on the mountains, or raise his eyes to the idols of the house of Israel, or defile his neighbor's wife; ¹⁶who does not oppress anyone, or exact a pledge, or commit robbery; who gives his food to the hungry and clothes the naked; ¹⁷who holds off from evil-doing, accepts no interest or usury, but keeps my ordinances and lives by my statutes—this one shall not die for the sins of his father, but shall surely live. ¹⁸Only the father, since he violated rights, and robbed, and did what was not good among his people, shall in truth die for his sins. ¹⁹You ask: "Why is not the son charged with the guilt of his father?" Because the son has done what is right and just, and has been careful to observe all my statutes, he shall surely live. ²⁰*Only the one who sins shall die. The son shall not be charged

with the guilt of his father, nor shall the father be charged with the guilt of his son. The virtuous man's virtue shall be his own, as the wicked man's wickedness shall be his.

²¹But if the wicked man turns away from all the sins he committed, if he keeps all my statutes and does what is right and just, he shall surely live, he shall not die. ²²None of the crimes he committed shall be remembered against him; he shall live because of the virtue he has practiced. ²³*Do I indeed derive any pleasure from the death of the wicked? says the Lord GOD. Do I not rather rejoice when he turns from his evil way that he may live?

²⁴And if the virtuous man turns from the path of virtue to do evil, the same kind of abominable things that the wicked man does, can he do this and still live? None of his virtuous deeds shall be remembered, because he has broken faith and committed sin; because of this, he shall die. ²⁵*You say, "The LORD's way is not fair!" Hear now, house of Israel: Is it my way that is unfair, or rather, are not your ways unfair? ²⁶When a virtuous man turns away from virtue to commit iniquity, and dies, it is because of the iniquity he committed that he must die. ²⁷But if a wicked man, turning from the wickedness he has committed, does what is right and just, he shall preserve his life; ²⁸since he has turned away from all the sins which he committed, he shall surely live, he shall not die. ²⁹And yet the house of Israel says, "The LORD's way is not fair!" Is it my way that is not fair, house of Israel, or rather, is it not that your ways are not fair?

³⁰*Therefore I will judge you, house of Israel, each one according to his ways, says the Lord GOD. Turn and be converted from all your crimes, that they may be no cause of guilt for you. ³¹Cast away from you all the crimes you have committed, and make for yourselves a new heart and a new spirit. Why should you die, O house of Israel? ³²*For I have no pleasure in the death of anyone who dies, says the Lord GOD. Return and live!

19 ¹AS for you, son of man, raise a lamentation over the prince of Israel:

Allegory of the Lions

²† 　What a lioness was your mother,
　　　a lion of lions!
　　Among young lions she couched
　　　to rear her whelps.
³ 　　One whelp she raised up,
　　　a young lion he became;

---

† 18, 2: *Fathers . . . on edge:* a proverb by which the people claimed that they were being punished for their ancestors' sins rather than for their own; cf Jer 31, 29.

18, 6: *Eat on the mountains:* partake of ritual meals at the heathen high places.

19, 2-9: The meaning of this allegory is uncertain. Probably the two *young lions* are Jehoahaz and Zedekiah, sons of the same mother, who were deported to Egypt and Babylonia respectively. Cf 2 Kgs 23, 31-34; 24, 18ff.

✽
18/2: Jer 31, 29.
　7: Is 58, 7; Mt 25, 35.
　20: Dt 24, 16; 2 Kgs 14, 6;
　　　2 Chr 25, 4.
23: 33, 11; 2 Pt 3, 9.
25: 33, 20.
30: Mt 3, 2; Lk 3, 3.
32: 18, 23; 33, 11;
　　2 Pt 3, 9.

He learned to seize prey,
men he devoured.
4 Then nations raised cries against him,
in their pit he was caught;
They took him away with hooks
to the land of Egypt.
5 Then she saw that in vain she had
waited,
her hope was destroyed.
She took another of her whelps,
him she made a young lion.
6 He prowled among the lions,
a young lion he became;
He learned to seize prey,
men he devoured;
7 He ravaged their strongholds,
their cities he wasted.
The land and all in it were appalled
at the noise of his roar.
8 Nations laid out against him
snares all about him;
They spread their net to take him,
in their pit he was caught.
9 They put him in a cage and took him
away
to the king of Babylon,
So that his voice would not be heard
on the mountains of Israel.

Allegory of the Vine Branch

10† Your mother was like a vine
planted by the water;
Fruitful and branchy was she
because of the abundant water.
11 One strong branch she put out
as a royal scepter.
Stately was her height
amid the dense foliage;
Notably tall was she
with her many clusters.
12* But she was torn up in fury
and flung to the ground;
The east wind withered her up,
her fruit was torn off;
Then her strong branch withered up,
fire devoured it.
13 So now she is planted in the desert,
in a land dry and parched,
14 For fire came out of the branch
and devoured her shoots;
She is now without a strong branch,
a ruler's scepter.

This is a lamentation and serves as a lamentation.

Israel's History of Infidelity

20 ¹†IN the seventh year, on the tenth day of the fifth month, some of the elders of Israel came to consult the LORD and sat down before me. ²Then

the word of the LORD came to me: ³Son of man, speak with the elders of Israel and say to them: Thus says the Lord GOD: Have you come to consult me? As I live! I swear I will not allow myself to be consulted by you, says the Lord GOD.

⁴Will you judge them? Will you judge, son of man? Make known to them the abominations of their ancestors ⁵in these words: Thus speaks the Lord GOD: The day I chose Israel, I swore to the descendants of the house of Jacob; in the land of Egypt I revealed myself to them and swore: I am the LORD, your God. ⁶That day I swore to bring them out of the land of Egypt to the land I had scouted for them, a land flowing with milk and honey, a jewel among all lands. ⁷Then I said to them: Throw away, each of you, the detestable things that have held your eyes; do not defile yourselves with the idols of Egypt: I am the LORD, your God.

⁸But they rebelled against me and refused to listen to me; none of them threw away the detestable things that had held their eyes, they did not abandon the idols of Egypt. Then I thought of pouring out my fury on them and spending my anger on them there in the land of Egypt; ⁹but I acted for my name's sake, that it should not be profaned in the sight of the nations among whom they were, in whose presence I had made myself known to them, revealing that I would bring them out of the land of Egypt. ¹⁰Therefore I led them out of the land of Egypt and brought them into the desert. ¹¹*Then I gave them my statutes and made known to them my ordinances, which everyone must keep, to have life through them. ¹²*I also gave them my sabbaths to be a sign between me and them, to show that it was I, the LORD, who made them holy.

¹³But the house of Israel rebelled against me in the desert. They did not observe my statutes, and they despised my ordinances that bring life to those who keep them. My sabbaths, too, they desecrated grievously. Then I thought of pouring out my fury on them in the desert to put an end to them, ¹⁴but I acted for my name's sake, that it should not be profaned in the sight of the nations in whose presence I had brought them out. ¹⁵Nevertheless I swore to them in the desert not to bring them to the land I had given them, a land flowing with milk and honey, a jewel among all lands. ¹⁶So much were their hearts devoted to their idols, they had not lived by my statutes, but despised my ordinances and desecrated my sabbaths. ¹⁷But I looked on them with pity, not wanting to destroy them, so I did not put an end to them in the desert.

¹⁸Then I said to their children in the desert: Do not observe the statutes of your parents or keep their ordinances; do not defile yourselves with their idols. ¹⁹I am the LORD, your God: observe my statutes and

---

* 19/12: Hos 13, 15.   12: Ex 20, 8; 31, 13;
20, 11: Lv 18, 5; Rom 10, 5.   Dt 5, 12.

---

† 19, 10-14: *A vine:* Judah. *One strong branch:* the Davidic king.

20, 1: *The seventh year, on the tenth day of the fifth month:* August 14, 591 B. C.

be careful to keep my ordinances; **20**keep holy my sabbaths, as a sign between me and you to show that I am the Lord, your God. **21**But their children rebelled against me: they did not observe my statutes or keep my ordinances that bring life to those who observe them, and my sabbaths they desecrated. Then I thought of pouring out my fury on them, of spending my anger on them in the desert; **22**but I stayed my hand, acting for my name's sake, lest it be profaned in the sight of the nations in whose presence I brought them out. **23**Nevertheless I swore to them in the desert that I would disperse them among the nations and scatter them over foreign lands; **24**for they did not keep my ordinances, but despised my statutes and desecrated my sabbaths, with eyes only for the idols of their fathers. **25**†Therefore I gave them statutes that were not good, and ordinances through which they could not live. **26**I let them become defiled by their gifts, by their immolation of every first-born, so as to make them an object of horror.

27Therefore speak to the house of Israel, son of man, and tell them: Thus says the Lord God: In this way also your fathers blasphemed me, breaking faith with me: **28**when I had brought them to the land I had sworn to give them, and they saw all its high hills and leafy trees, there they offered their sacrifices [there they brought their offensive offerings], there they sent up appeasing odors, and there they poured out their libations. **29**I asked them: To what sort of high place do you betake yourselves?—and so they call it a high place even to the present day. **30**Therefore say to the house of Israel: Thus says the Lord God: will you defile yourselves like your fathers? Will you lust after their detestable idols? **31**By offering your gifts, by making your children pass through the fire, you defile yourselves with all your idols even to this day. Shall I let myself be consulted by you, house of Israel? As I live! says the Lord God: I swear I will not let myself be consulted by you.

32What you are thinking of shall never happen: "We shall be like the nations, like the peoples of foreign lands, serving wood and stone." **33**As I live, says the Lord God, with a mighty hand and outstretched arm, with poured-out wrath, I swear I will be king over you! **34**With a mighty hand and outstretched arm, with poured-out wrath, I will bring you out from the nations and gather you from the countries over which you are scattered; **35**†then I will lead you to the desert of the peoples, where I will enter into judgment with you face to face. **36**Just as I entered into judgment with your fathers in the desert of the land of Egypt, so will I enter into judgment with you, says the Lord God. **37**I will count you with the staff and bring back but a small number. **38**I will separate from you those who have rebelled and transgressed against me; from the land where they sojourned as aliens I will bring them out, but they shall not return to the land of Israel. Thus you shall know that I am the Lord.

39As for you, house of Israel, thus says the Lord

God: Come, each one of you, destroy your idols! Then listen to me, and never again profane my holy name with your gifts and your idols. **40**For on my holy mountain, on the mountain height of Israel, says the Lord God, there the whole house of Israel without exception shall worship me; there I will accept them, and there I will claim your tributes and the first fruits of your offerings, and all that you dedicate. **41**As a pleasing odor I will accept you, when I have brought you from among the nations and gathered you out of the countries over which you were scattered; and by means of you I will manifest my holiness in the sight of the nations. **42**Thus you shall know that I am the Lord, when I bring you back to the land of Israel, the land which I swore to give to your fathers. **43**There you shall recall your conduct and all the deeds by which you defiled yourselves; and you shall loathe yourselves because of all the evil things you did. **44**And you shall know that I am the Lord when I deal with you thus, for my name's sake, and not according to your evil conduct and corrupt actions, O house of Israel, says the Lord God.

The Sword of the Lord

21 **1**Thus the word of the Lord came to me: **2**†Son of man, look southward, preach toward the south, and prophesy against the forest of the southern land. **3**Hear the word of the Lord! you shall say to the southern forest. Thus says the Lord God: See! I am kindling a fire in you that shall devour all trees, the green as well as the dry. The blazing flame shall not be quenched, but from south to north every face shall be scorched by it. **4**Everyone shall see that I, the Lord, have kindled it, and it shall not be quenched.

5But I said, "Alas! Lord God, they say to me, 'Is not this the one who is forever spinning parables?'" **6**Then the word of the Lord came to me: **7**Son of man, look toward Jerusalem, preach against their sanctuary, and prophesy against the land of Israel, **8**†saying to the land of Israel: Thus says the Lord: See! I am coming at you; I will draw my sword from its sheath and cut off from you the virtuous and the wicked. **9**Thus my sword shall leave its sheath against everyone from south to north, **10**and everyone shall know that I, the Lord, have drawn my sword from its sheath, and it shall not be sheathed again.

---

† 20, 25f: *I gave them statutes that were not good:* the Lord permitted them to adopt pagan practices, including the abominable sacrifice of their newborn infants, which could only merit their destruction. See note on 14, 9.

20, 35-38: Exile in the pagan lands will serve the same purpose as the desert journey after the Exodus from Egypt: the rebellious will be eliminated, and only a remnant will survive.

21, 2ff: The southern kingdom, Judah, is likened to a forest about to be burned; cf Jer 21, 14.

21, 8: *Cut off from you the virtuous and the wicked:* a more complete devastation of Jerusalem than that described in 9, 6.

Act Symbolic of the City's Fall

11As for you, son of man, groan! with shattered strength groan bitterly while they look on. **12**†And when they ask you, "Why are you groaning?", you shall say: Because of a report; when it comes every heart shall fail, every hand shall fall helpless, every spirit shall be daunted, and every knee shall run with water. See, it is coming, it is here! says the Lord God.

Song of the Sword

13Thus the word of the Lord came to me: **14**Son of man, prophesy! say: Thus says the Lord:

> A sword, a sword has been sharpened,
> a sword, a sword has been burnished:
> **15** To work slaughter has it been
> sharpened,
> to flash lightning has it been
> burnished.
> Why should I now withdraw it?
> You have spurned the rod and every
> judgment!
> **16** I have given it over to the burnisher
> that he might hold it in his hand,
> A sword sharpened and burnished
> to be put in the hand of a slayer.
> **17** Cry out and wail, son of man,
> for it is destined for my people;
> It is for all the princes of Israel,
> victims of the sword with my people.

Therefore, slap your thigh, **18**†for the sword has been tested; and why should it not be so? says the Lord God, since you have spurned the rod.

> **19** As for you, son of man, prophesy,
> brushing one hand against the other:
> While the sword is doubled and tripled,
> this sword of slaughter,
> This great sword of slaughter
> which threatens all around,
> **20** That every heart may tremble;
> for many will be the fallen.
> At all their gates
> I have appointed the sword for
> slaughter,
> Fashioned to flash lightning,
> burnished for slaughter.
> **21** Cleave to the right! destroy!
> to the left! wherever your edge is
> turned.

22†Then I, too, shall brush one hand against the other and wreak my fury. I, the Lord, have spoken.

Nebuchadnezzar at the Crossroads

23Thus the word of the Lord came to me: **24**Son of man, make for yourself two roads over which the sword of the king of Babylon can come. Both roads shall lead out from the same land. Then put a signpost at the head of each road, **25**so that the sword can come to Rabbah of the Ammonites or to Judah's capital, Jerusalem. **26**†For at the fork where the two roads divide stands the king of Babylon, divining; he has shaken the arrows, inquired of the teraphim, inspected the liver. **27**†In his right hand is the divining arrow marked "Jerusalem," bidding him to give the order for slaying, to raise his voice in the battle cry, to post battering-rams at the gates, to cast up a ramp, to build a siege tower. **28**In their eyes this is but a lying oracle; yet they are bound by the oaths they have sworn, and the arrow taken in hand marks their guilt.

29Therefore thus says the Lord God: Because you have drawn attention to your guilt, with your crimes laid bare and your sinfulness in all your wicked deeds revealed (because attention has been drawn to you), you shall be taken in hand. **30**And as for you, depraved and wicked prince of Israel, whose day is coming when your life of crime will be ended, **31**thus says the Lord God: Off with the turban and away with the crown! Nothing shall be as it was! Up with the low and down with the high! **32**Twisted, twisted, twisted will I leave it; it shall not be the same until he comes who has the claim against the city; and to him I will hand it over.

Against the Ammonites

33†As for you, son of man, prophesy: Thus says the Lord God against the Ammonites and their insults: A sword, a sword is drawn for slaughter, burnished to consume and to flash lightning, **34**because you planned with false visions and lying divinations to lay it on the necks of depraved and wicked men whose day has come when their crimes are at an end. **35**Return it to its sheath! In the place where you were created, in the land of your origin, I will judge you. **36**I will pour out my indignation upon you, breathing my fiery wrath upon you; I will hand you over to ravaging men, artisans of destruction. **37**You shall be fuel for the fire, your blood shall flow throughout the land. You shall not be remembered, for I, the Lord, have spoken.

---

†

21, 12: *A report:* the news of the fall of Jerusalem; cf 33, 21f.

21, 17: *Slap your thigh:* a gesture signifying grief and dread.

21, 22: *Brush one hand against the other:* a gesture signifying the rejection of responsibility; cf 22, 13; Nm 24, 10.

21, 26: Three forms of divination are mentioned: *arrow* divination, consisting in the use of differently marked arrows extracted or shaken from a case at random; the consultation of the *teraphim* or household idols; and *liver* divination, scrutiny of the configurations of the livers of newly slaughtered animals, a common form of divination in Mesopotamia.

21, 27f: An *arrow marked "Jerusalem"* is picked out, which *marks* the guilt of the city's inhabitants for having broken their oath of allegiance to Nebuchadnezzar.

21, 33-37: In the preceding section Nebuchadnezzar is represented as deciding whether to attack Jerusalem or Rabbath-Ammon. As it happened, Jerusalem was chosen for attack; later, however, the Chaldeans also invaded Ammon. The present oracle against Ammon is inserted here, rather than in chapters 25-32, in order to complement the oracle against Jerusalem.

Crimes of Jerusalem

22 ¹ᴛʜᴜꜱ the word of the Lᴏʀᴅ came to me: ²You, son of man, would you judge, would you judge the bloody city? Then make known all her abominations, ³and say: Thus says the Lord Gᴏᴅ: Woe to the city which sheds blood within herself so that her time has come, and which has made idols for her own defilement. ⁴By the blood which you shed you have been made guilty, and with the idols you made you have become defiled; you have brought on your day, so that the end of your years has come. Therefore I make you an object of scorn to the nations and a laughingstock to all foreign lands. ⁵Those near you and those far off shall deride you because of your foul reputation and your great perversity. ⁶See! the princes of Israel, family by family, are in you only for bloodshed. ⁷Within you, father and mother are despised; in your midst, they extort from the resident alien; within you, they oppress orphans and widows. ⁸What is holy to me you have spurned, and my sabbaths you have desecrated. ⁹There are those in you who slander to cause bloodshed; within you are those who feast on the mountains; in your midst are those who do lewd things. ¹⁰In you are those who uncover the nakedness of their fathers, and in you those who coerce women in their menstrual period. ¹¹*There are those in you who do abominable things with the wives of their neighbors, men who defile their daughters-in-law by incest, men who coerce their sisters, the daughters of their own fathers. ¹²There are those in you who take bribes to shed blood. You exact interest and usury; you despoil your neighbors violently; and me you have forgotten, says the Lord Gᴏᴅ.

¹³See, I am brushing one hand against the other because of the unjust profits you have made and because of the bloodshed in your midst. ¹⁴Can your heart remain firm, will your hands be strong, in the days when I deal with you? I, the Lᴏʀᴅ, have spoken, and I will act. ¹⁵I will disperse you among the nations and scatter you over foreign lands, so that I may purge your uncleanness. ¹⁶In you I will allow myself to be profaned in the eyes of the nations; thus you shall know that I am the Lᴏʀᴅ.

¹⁷Thus the word of the Lᴏʀᴅ came to me: ¹⁸Son of man, the house of Israel has become dross for me. All of them are bronze and tin, iron and lead [in the midst of a furnace]: dross from silver have they become. ¹⁹Therefore thus says the Lord Gᴏᴅ: Because all of you have become dross, therefore I must gather you together within Jerusalem. ²⁰Just as silver, bronze, iron, lead, and tin are gathered into a furnace and smelted in the roaring flames, so I will gather you together in my furious wrath, put you in, and smelt you. ²¹When I have assembled you, I will blast you with the fire of my anger and smelt you with it. ²²You shall be smelted by it just as silver is smelted in a furnace. Thus you shall know that I, the Lᴏʀᴅ, have poured out my fury on you.

²³Thus the word of the Lᴏʀᴅ came to me: ²⁴Son of man, say to her: You are a land unrained on [that is, not rained on] at the time of my fury. ²⁵Her princes are like roaring lions that tear prey; they devour people, seizing their wealth and precious things, and make widows of many within her. ²⁶Her priests violate my law and profane what is holy to me; they do not distinguish between the sacred and the profane, nor teach the difference between the unclean and the clean; they pay no attention to my sabbaths, so that I have been profaned in their midst. ²⁷*Her nobles within her are like wolves that tear prey, shedding blood and destroying lives to get unjust gain. ²⁸Her prophets cover them with whitewash, pretending to visions that are false and performing lying divinations, saying, "Thus says the Lord Gᴏᴅ," although the Lᴏʀᴅ has not spoken. ²⁹The people of the land practice extortion and commit robbery; they afflict the poor and the needy, and oppress the resident alien without justice. ³⁰Thus I have searched among them for someone who could build a wall or stand in the breach before me to keep me from destroying the land; but I found no one. ³¹Therefore I have poured out my fury upon them; with my fiery wrath I have consumed them; I have brought down their conduct upon their heads, says the Lord Gᴏᴅ.

The Two Sisters

23 ¹ᴛʜᴜꜱ the word of the Lᴏʀᴅ came to me: ²Son of man, there were two women, daughters of the same mother, ³who even as young girls played the harlot in Egypt. There the Egyptians caressed their bosoms and fondled their virginal breasts. ⁴†Oholah was the name of the elder, and the name of her sister was Oholibah. They became mine and bore sons and daughters. [As for their names: Samaria is Oholah, and Jerusalem is Oholibah.] ⁵Oholah became a harlot faithless to me; she lusted after her lovers, the Assyrians, warriors ⁶dressed in purple, governors and officers, all of them attractive young men, knights mounted on horses. ⁷Thus she gave herself as a harlot to them, to all the elite of the Assyrians, and she defiled herself with all those for whom she lusted [with all their idols]. ⁸She did not give up the harlotry which she had begun in Egypt, when they had lain with her as a young girl, fondling her virginal breasts and pouring out their impurities on her.

⁹Therefore I handed her over to her lovers, the Assyrians for whom she had lusted. ¹⁰*They exposed her nakedness, her sons and daughters they took away,

---

*

22/11: Jer 5, 7f.   23/10: 16, 37.
   27: Mi 3, 11; Zep 3, 3.

† 23, 4: *Oholah . . . Oholibah:* symbolic names. The first, standing for Samaria, may be read to mean "her own tent"; the latter, standing for Jerusalem, means "my tent is in her." The references seem to be to the schismatic temple and cult of the Lord in Samaria, as opposed to their authentic counterpart in Jerusalem.

and herself they slew with the sword. Thus she became a byword for women, for they punished her grievously.

¹¹Though her sister Oholibah saw all this, her lust was more depraved than her sister's, and she outdid her in harlotry. ¹²She too lusted after the Assyrians, governors and officers, warriors impeccably clothed, knights mounted on horses, all of them attractive young men. ¹³I saw that she had defiled herself. Both had gone down the same path, ¹⁴yet she went further in her harlotry. When she saw men drawn on the wall, the images of Chaldeans drawn with vermillion, ¹⁵with sashes girded about their waists, flowing turbans on their heads, all looking like chariot warriors, the portraits of Babylonians, natives of Chaldea, ¹⁶she lusted for them; no sooner had she set eyes on them than she sent messengers to them in Chaldea. ¹⁷Then the Babylonians came to her, to the love couch, and defiled her with their intercourse. As soon as she was defiled by them, she became disgusted with them. ¹⁸Her harlotry was discovered and her shame was revealed, and I became disgusted with her as I had become disgusted with her sister. ¹⁹But she played the harlot all the more, recalling the days of her girlhood, when she had been a harlot in the land of Egypt. ²⁰She lusted for the lechers of Egypt, whose members are like that of an ass, and whose heat is like that of stallions.

²¹You yearned for the lewdness of your girlhood, when the Egyptians fondled your breasts, caressing your bosom. ²²Therefore, Oholibah, thus says the Lord God: I will now stir up your lovers against you, those with whom you are disgusted, and I will bring them against you from every side: ²³†the men of Babylon and all of Chaldea, Pekod, Shoa and Koa, along with all those of Assyria, attractive young men, all of them governors and officers, charioteers and warriors, all of them horsemen. ²⁴They shall come against you from the north with chariots and wagons and many peoples. Shields, bucklers, and helmets they shall array against you everywhere. ²⁵I will leave it to them to judge, and they will judge you by their own ordinances. I will let loose my jealousy against you, so that they shall deal with you in fury, cutting off your nose and ears; and what is left of you shall fall by the sword. They shall take away your sons and daughters, and what is left of you shall be devoured by fire. ²⁶They shall strip off your clothes and seize your splendid ornaments. ²⁷I will put an end to your lewdness and to the harlotry you began in Egypt; you shall no longer look toward it, nor shall you remember Egypt again.

²⁸For thus says the Lord God: I am now handing you over to those whom you hate, to those who fill you with disgust. ²⁹They shall deal with you in hatred, seizing all that you have worked for and leaving you stark naked, so that your indecent nakedness is exposed. Your lewdness and harlotry ³⁰have brought these things upon you, because you played the harlot with the nations by defiling yourself with their idols.

³¹Because you followed in the path of your sister, I will hand you her cup. ³²Thus says the Lord God:

The cup of your sister you shall drink,
so wide and deep, which holds so
much,
³³   Filled with destruction and grief,
a cup of dismay, the cup of your sister.

³⁴You shall drain it dry, and gnaw at the very sherds of the cup, and you shall tear out your breasts; for I have spoken, says the Lord God. ³⁵Therefore thus says the Lord God: Because you have forgotten me and cast me behind your back, it is for you to bear the penalty of your lewdness and harlotry.

³⁶Then the Lord said to me: Son of man, would you judge Oholah and Oholibah? Then make known to them their abominations. ³⁷For they committed adultery, and blood is on their hands. They committed adultery with their idols; to feed them they immolated the children they had borne me. ³⁸[This, too, they did to me: they defiled my sanctuary and desecrated my sabbaths. ³⁹On the very day they slew their children for their idols, they entered my sanctuary to desecrate it. Thus they acted within my house.] ⁴⁰†Moreover, they sent for men who had to come from afar, to whom messengers were sent. And so they came—and for them you bathed yourself, painted your eyes, and put on ornaments. ⁴¹You sat on a couch prepared for them, with a table spread before it, on which you had set my incense and oil. ⁴²Then was heard the shout of a carefree mob in the city, and these were men brought in from the desert, who put bracelets on the women's arms and splendid diadems on their heads. ⁴³So I said: "Oh, this woman jaded with adulteries! Now they will commit whoredom with her, and as for her. . . ." ⁴⁴And indeed they did come to her as men come to a harlot. Thus they came to Oholah and Oholibah, the lewd women. ⁴⁵But just men shall punish them with the sentence meted out to adulteresses and murderesses, for they have committed adultery, and blood is on their hands.

⁴⁶Thus says the Lord God: Summon an assembly against them, and deliver them over to terror and plunder. ⁴⁷The assembly shall stone them and hack them to pieces with their swords. They shall slay their sons and daughters, and burn their houses with fire. ⁴⁸Thus I will put an end to lewdness in the land, and all the women will be warned not to imitate your lewdness. ⁴⁹They shall inflict on you the penalty of your lewdness, and you shall pay for your sins of idolatry. Thus you shall know that I am the Lord.

---

† 23, 23: *Pekod, Shoa and Koa:* peoples living about the Tigris, part of "greater Babylonia."

23, 40: *Men who had to come from afar:* ambassadors from Assyria and Babylon. Alliances with these countries aided in the corruption of both Israel and Judah.

Allegory of the Pot

24 ¹†ON the tenth day of the tenth month, in the ninth year, the word of the LORD came to me: ²Son of man, write down this date today, for this very day the king of Babylon has invested Jerusalem. ³†Propose this parable to the rebellious house: Thus says the Lord GOD:

> Set up the pot, set it up,
>   then pour in some water.
> **4** Put in it pieces of meat,
>   all good pieces: thigh and shoulder;
> Fill it with the choicest joints
> **5**   taken from the pick of the flock.
> Then pile the wood beneath it;
>   bring to a boil these pieces
>   and the joints that are in it.
> **6*** Take out its pieces, one by one,
>   without casting lots for it.

Therefore, thus says the Lord GOD: Woe to the bloody city, a pot containing rust, whose rust has not been removed. ⁷†For the blood she shed is in her midst: she poured it on the bare rock; she did not pour it out on the earth, to be covered with dust. ⁸To work up my wrath, to excite my vengeance, she put her blood on the bare rock, not to be covered. ⁹Therefore, thus says the Lord GOD:

> I, too, will heap up a great bonfire,
> **10**   piling on wood and kindling the fire,
> Till the meat has been cooked,
>   till the broth has boiled.

¹¹Then I will set the pot empty on the coals till its metal glows red hot, till the impurities in it melt, and its rust disappears. ¹²Yet not even with fire will its great rust be removed. ¹³Because you have sullied yourself with lewdness when I would have purified you, and you refused to be purified of your uncleanness, therefore you shall not be purified until I wreak my fury on you. ¹⁴I, the LORD, have spoken; it is coming, for I will bring it about without fail. I will not have pity nor repent. By your conduct and your deeds you shall be judged, says the Lord GOD.

Symbol of the Destruction of the Temple

¹⁵Thus the word of the LORD came to me: ¹⁶Son of man, by a sudden blow I am taking away from you the delight of your eyes, but do not mourn or weep or shed any tears. ¹⁷†Groan in silence, make no lament for the dead, bind on your turban, put your sandals on your feet, do not cover your beard, and do not eat the customary bread. ¹⁸That evening my wife died, and the next morning I did as I had been commanded. ¹⁹Then the people asked me, "Will you not tell us what all these things that you are doing mean for us?" I therefore spoke to the people that morning, ²⁰saying to them: Thus the word of the LORD came to me: ²¹Say to the house of Israel: Thus says the Lord GOD: I will now desecrate my sanctuary, the stronghold of your pride, the delight of your eyes, the desire of your soul. The sons and daughters you left behind shall fall by the sword. ²⁴Ezekiel shall be a sign for you: all that he did you shall do when it happens. Thus you shall know that I am the LORD. ²²†You shall do as I have done, not covering your beards nor eating the customary bread. ²³ Your turbans shall remain on your heads, your sandals on your feet. You shall not mourn or weep, but you shall rot away because of your sins and groan one to another.

End of Ezekiel's Dumbness

²⁵*As for you, son of man, truly, on the day I take away from them their bulwark, their glorious joy, the delight of their eyes, the desire of their soul, and the pride of their hearts, their sons and daughters, ²⁶that day the fugitive will come to you, that you may hear it for yourself; ²⁷that day your mouth shall be opened and you shall be dumb no longer. Thus you shall be a sign to them, and they shall know that I am the LORD.

III: PROPHECIES AGAINST FOREIGN NATIONS

Against Ammon

25 ¹THUS THE WORD OF THE LORD came to me: ²Son of man, turn toward the Ammonites and prophesy against them. ³*Say to the Ammonites: Hear the word of the LORD! Thus says the Lord GOD: Because you cried out your joy over the desecration of my sanctuary, the devastation of the land of Israel, and the exile of the house of Judah, ⁴†therefore I will deliver you into the possession of the Easterners. They shall set up their encampments among you and pitch their tents; they shall eat your fruits and drink your milk. ⁵I will make Rabbah a pasture for camels, and the villages of the Ammonites a resting place for flocks. Thus you shall know that I am the LORD.

⁶For thus says the Lord GOD: Because you clapped your hands and stamped your feet, rejoicing most

---

† 24, 1: *The tenth day of the tenth month, in the ninth year:* January 15, 588 B. C. The same date is given in Jer 52, 4.

24, 3ff: This present comparison of the inhabitants of Jerusalem to meat boiled in a pot symbolizes their punishment rather than their supposed protection as in 11, 3.

24, 7: *Blood . . . to be covered with dust:* since blood was sacred to God, it had to be covered with earth (Lv 17, 13); the blood of a murdered man that was left uncovered cried to heaven for vengeance; cf Jb 16, 18; Gn 4, 10.

24, 17: *The customary bread:* eaten as a mourning observance; cf Jer 16, 7. The other gestures here forbidden were also popular mourning customs.

24, 22f: The fall of the city will be so sudden and final that the exiles will have no time to go into mourning.

25, 4: *The Easterners:* nomadic tribes to the east of Ammon and Moab.

❋
24/6: Na 3, 1; Hb 2, 12.   25/3: Jer 40, 14; 41, 10;
24/25ff: 3, 22-27.   49, 2; Am 1, 13ff;
                                                    Zep 2, 8ff.

maliciously in your heart over the land of Israel, [7]therefore I will stretch out my hand against you. I will make you plunder for the nations, I will cut you off from the peoples, and remove you from the lands. I will destroy you, and thus you shall know that I am the Lord.

Against Moab

[8]*Thus says the Lord God: Because Moab said, "See! the house of Judah is like all other nations," [9]†therefore I will clear the shoulder of Moab totally of its cities, the jewels of the land: Beth-jesimoth, Baalmeon, and Kiriathaim. [10]I will hand her over, along with the Ammonites, into the possession of the Easterners, that she may not be remembered among the peoples. [11]Thus I will execute judgment upon Moab, that they may know that I am the Lord.

Against Edom

[12]*Thus says the Lord God: Because Edom has taken vengeance on the house of Judah and has made itself grievously guilty by taking vengeance on them, [13]therefore thus says the Lord God: I will stretch out my hand against Edom and cut off from it man and beast. I will make it a waste from Teman to Dedan; they shall fall by the sword. [14]My vengeance upon Edom I will entrust to my people Israel, who will deal with Edom in accordance with my anger and my fury; thus they shall know my vengeance, says the Lord God.

Against the Philistines

[15]Thus says the Lord God: Because the Philistines have acted revengefully, and have taken vengeance with destructive malice in their hearts, with an undying enmity, [16]†therefore thus says the Lord God: See! I am stretching out my hand against the Philistines; I will cut off the Cherethites and wipe out the remnant on the seacoast. [17]I will execute great acts of vengeance on them, punishing them furiously. Thus they shall know that I am the Lord, when I wreak my vengeance on them.

Against the City of Tyre

26 [1]On the first day of the . . . month in the eleventh year, the word of the Lord came to me: [2]Son of man, because of what Tyre said of Jerusalem:

"Aha! it is broken, the gateway to the
    peoples;
  now that it is ruined, its wealth reverts
    to me!"

[3]*   therefore thus says the Lord God:

See! I am coming at you, Tyre;
  I will churn up against you many
    nations,
    even as the sea churns up its waves;
[4]†   They shall destroy the walls of Tyre
    and raze her towers.
  I will scrape the ground from her
    and leave her a bare rock;
[5]   She shall be a drying place for nets
    in the midst of the sea.

I have spoken, says the Lord God: and she shall be booty for the nations. [6]†And her daughters on the mainland shall be slaughtered by the sword; thus they shall know that I am the Lord.

[7]For thus says the Lord God: I am now bringing up against Tyre from the north Nebuchadnezzar the king of Babylon, the king of kings, with horses and chariots, with cavalry and a great and mighty army.

[8]   Your daughters on the mainland
    he shall slay with the sword;
  He shall place a siege tower against you,
    cast up a ramp about you,
    and raise his shields against you.
[9]   He shall pound your walls with
    battering-rams
    and break down your towers with his
    weapons.
[10]   The surge of his horses shall cover you
    with dust,
    amid the noise of steeds, of wheels
    and of chariots.
  Your walls shall shake as he enters your
    gates,
    even as one enters a city that is
    breached.
[11]   With the hoofs of his horses
    he shall trample all your streets;
  Your people he shall slay by the sword;
    your mighty pillars he shall pull to
    the ground.
[12]   Your wealth shall be plundered,
    your merchandise pillaged;
  Your walls shall be torn down,
    your precious houses demolished;
  Your stones, your timber, and your clay
    shall be cast into the sea.
[13]   I will put an end to the noise of your
    songs,
    and the sound of your lyres shall be
    heard no more.

---

† 25, 9: *The shoulder of Moab:* the edge of the Moabite plateau.

25, 16: *Cherethites:* a people forming part of the Philistine nation; cf Zep 2, 5.

26, 4f: *A bare rock:* the Tyre of Ezekiel's time was situated on a rocky island just off the Phoenician coast; it was not until the time of Alexander the Great that it was connected by a causeway to the mainland.

26, 6: *Her daughters:* tributary towns and villages on the mainland.

✿
   8: Sir 50, 26; Is 15, 1-9;   12ff: 35, 1ff; Is 34, 5;
     16, 1-14; Jer 48, 1-47;   Jer 49, 7-22; Jl 4, 19;
     Am 2, 1ff; Zep 2, 8f.   Am 1, 11f; Ob 1, 1-21.
                               26/3: Is 26, 1-21; 47, 4;
                                    Jl 4, 4f; Zec 9, 2ff.

14   I will make you a bare rock;
            a drying place for nets shall you be.

Never shall you be rebuilt, for I have spoken, says the Lord God. **15**Thus says the Lord God to Tyre: At the noise of your fall, at the groaning of the wounded, when the sword slays in your midst, shall not the isles quake? **16†**All the princes of the sea shall step down from their thrones, lay aside their robes, and strip off their embroidered garments. They shall be clothed in mourning and, sitting on the ground, they shall tremble at every moment and be horrified at you. **17**Then they shall utter a lament over you:

            How have you perished, gone from the
                seas,
                city most prized!
            Once she was mighty on the sea,
                she and her dwellers,
            Who spread terror into all
                that dwelt by the sea.
18   On this, the day of your fall,
                the islands quake!

The isles in the sea are terrified at your passing.

19For thus says the Lord God: When I make you a city desolate like cities that are no longer inhabited, when I churn up the abyss against you, and its mighty waters cover you, **20†**then I will thrust you down with those who descend into the pit, those of the bygone age; and I will make you dwell in the nether lands, in the everlasting ruins, with those who go down to the pit, so that you may never return to take your place in the land of the living. I will make you a devastation, and you shall be no more; you shall be sought, but never again found, says the Lord God.

The Ship Tyre

27 **1**Thus the word of the Lord came to me: **2**As for you, son of man, utter a lament over Tyre, **3**and say to Tyre that is situated at the approaches of the sea, that brought the trade of the peoples to many a coastland: Thus says the Lord God:

            Tyre, you said, "I am a ship,
                perfect in beauty."
4   In the midst of the sea your builders
                placed you,
                perfected your beauty.
5†   With cypress from Senir they built for
                you
                all of your decks;
            Cedar from Lebanon they took
                to make you a mast;
6†   From the highest oaks of Bashan
                they made your oars;
            Your bridge they made of cypress wood
                from the coasts of Kittim.
7†   Fine embroidered linen from Egypt
                became your sail [to serve you as a
                banner].

            Purple and scarlet from the coasts of
                Elishah
                covered your cabin.
8†   Citizens of Sidon and Arvad
                served as your oarsmen;
            Skilled men of Zemer were in you
                to be your mariners;
9   The elders and experts of Gebal were in
                you
                to caulk your seams.

Every ship and sailor on the sea came to you to carry trade. **10**Persia and Lud and Put were in your army as warriors; shield and helmet they hung upon you, increasing your splendor. **11**The men of Arvad were all about your walls, and the Gamadites were in your towers; they hung their bucklers all around on your walls, and made perfect your beauty. **12**Tarshish traded with you, so great was your wealth, exchanging silver, iron, tin, and lead for your wares. **13**Javan, Tubal, and Meshech were also traders with you, exchanging slaves and articles of bronze for your goods. **14**From Beth-togarmah horses, steeds, and mules were exchanged for your wares. **15**The Rhodanites trafficked with you; many coastlands traded with you; ivory tusks and ebony wood they gave you for payment. **16**Edom traded with you, so many were your products, exchanging garnets, purple, embroidered cloth, fine linen, coral, and rubies for your wares. **17**Judah and the land of Israel trafficked with you, exchanging Minnith wheat, figs, honey, oil, and balm for your goods. Damascus traded with you, so great was your wealth, exchanging Helbon wine and Zahar wool. **19**Javan exchanged wrought iron, cassia, and aromatic cane from Uzal for your wares. **20**Dedan traded with you for riding gear. **21**The trade of Arabia and of all the sheikhs of Kedar belonged to you; they dealt in lambs, rams, and goats. **22**The merchants of Sheba and Raamah also traded with you, exchanging for your wares the very choicest spices, all kinds of precious stones, and gold. **23**Haran, Canneh, and Eden, the merchants of Sheba, Asshur, and Chilmad **24**traded with you, marketing with you rich garments, violet mantles, embroidered cloth, varicolored carpets, and firmly woven cords. **25**Ships of Tarshish journeyed for you in your merchandising.

            You were full and heavily laden
                in the heart of the sea.

---

†
  26, 16: *The princes of the sea:* the rulers of the islands and coastal cities leagued commercially with Tyre.

  26, 20: *Those who descend into the pit:* the dead, pictured as dwelling in a place or cave of darkness.

  27, 5: *Senir:* another name for Mount Hermon; cf Dt 3, 9.

  27, 6: *Bashan:* northern Transjordan, which, like Lebanon, was noted for its great forests. *Kittim:* probably Cyprus.

  27, 7: *Elishah:* probably another term for Cyprus.

  27, 8f: *Sidon . . . Arvad . . . Zemer . . . Gebal:* Phoenician cities in Tyre's orbit of influence; the last-named is the classical Byblos.

²⁶ Through the deep waters your oarsmen
     brought you home,
But the east wind smashed you
     in the heart of the sea.
²⁷ Your wealth, your goods, your wares,
     your sailors, and your crew,

[the caulkers of your seams, those who traded for your goods, all your warriors who were in you, and all the great crowd within you]

     Sank into the heart of the sea
       on the day of your shipwreck.
²⁸ Hearing the shouts of your mariners,
     the shores begin to quake.
²⁹ Down from their ships
     come all who ply the oar;
The sailors, all the mariners of the sea,
     stand on the shore,
³⁰ Making their voice heard on your behalf,
     shouting bitter cries,
Strewing dust on their heads,
     rolling in the ashes.
³¹ For you they shave their heads
     and put on sackcloth,
For you they weep in anguish,
     with bitter lament.
³² In their mourning they utter a lament
     over you;
     thus they wail over you:
Who was ever destroyed like Tyre
     in the midst of the sea?
³³ With your goods which you drew from
     the seas
     you filled many peoples;
With your great wealth and
     merchandise
     you enriched the kings of the earth.
³⁴ Now you are wrecked in the sea,
     in the watery depths;
Your wares and all your crew
     have gone down with you.
³⁵ All who dwell on the coastlands
     are aghast over you,
Their kings are terrified,
     their faces convulsed.
³⁶ The traders among the peoples
     now hiss at you;
You have become a horror,
     and you shall be no more.

The Prince of Tyre

28 ¹THUS the word of the LORD came to me: ²Son of man, say to the prince of Tyre: Thus says the Lord GOD:

     Because you are haughty of heart,
       you say, "A god am I!
I occupy a godly throne
       in the heart of the sea!"—
And yet you are a man, and not a god,

     however you may think yourself like
       a god.
^{3†} Oh yes, you are wiser than Daniel,
     there is no secret that is beyond you.
⁴ By your wisdom and your intelligence
     you have made riches for yourself;
You have put gold and silver
     into your treasuries.
⁵ By your great wisdom applied to your
     trading
     you have heaped up your riches;
     your heart has grown haughty from
       your riches—
     therefore thus says the Lord GOD:
⁶ Because you have thought yourself
     to have the mind of a god,
⁷ Therefore I will bring against you
     foreigners, the most barbarous of
       nations.
They shall draw their swords
     against your beauteous wisdom,
     they shall run them through your
       splendid apparel.
⁸ They shall thrust you down to the pit,
     there to die
     a bloodied corpse, in the heart of the
       sea.
⁹ Will you then say, "I am a god!"
     when you face your murderers?
No, you are a man, not a god,
     handed over to those who will slay
       you.
¹⁰ You shall die the death of the
     uncircumcised
     at the hands of foreigners,
     for I have spoken,
       says the Lord GOD.

¹¹Thus the word of the LORD came to me: ^{12†}Son of man, utter a lament over the king of Tyre, saying to him: Thus says the Lord GOD:

     You were stamped with the seal of
       perfection,
     of complete wisdom and perfect
       beauty.
¹³ In Eden, the garden of God, you were,
     and every precious stone was your
       covering

[carnelian, topaz, and beryl, chrysolite, onyx, and jasper, sapphire, garnet, and emerald];

     Of gold your pendants and jewels
       were made, on the day you were
       created.

---

† 28, 3: *Wiser than Daniel:* see note on 14, 14.

28, 12-19: This picture of Tyre and its fall recalls images of the earthly paradise portraying the creation of man in perfection and his fall (Gn, chapters 2-3).

14† With the Cherub I placed you;
> you were on the holy mountain of
> God,
> walking among the fiery stones.

15 Blameless you were in your conduct
> from the day you were created,
> Until evil was found in you,

16 the result of your far-flung trade;
> violence was your business, and you
> sinned.
> Then I banned you from the mountain
> of God;
> the Cherub drove you from among
> the fiery stones.

17 You became haughty of heart because
> of your beauty;
> for the sake of splendor you debased
> your wisdom.
> I cast you to the earth, so great was your
> guilt;
> I made you a spectacle in the sight of
> kings.

18 Because of your great guilt, your sinful
> trade,
> I have profaned your sanctuaries,
> And I have brought out fire from your
> midst
> which will devour you.
> I have reduced you to dust on the earth
> in the sight of all who should see you.

19 Among the peoples, all who knew you
> stand aghast at you;
> You have become a horror,
> you shall be no more.

Against Sidon

20*Thus the word of the Lord came to me: **21***Son of man, look toward Sidon, and prophesy against it: **22***Thus says the Lord God: See! I am coming at you, Sidon; I will be glorified in your midst. Then they shall know that I am the Lord, when I inflict punishments upon it and use it to manifest my holiness.

23 Into it I will send pestilence,
> and blood shall flow in its streets.
> Within it shall fall those slain
> by the sword that comes against it
> from every side.

24Thus they shall know that I am the Lord. Sidon shall no longer be a tearing thorn for the house of Israel, a brier that scratches them more than all the others about them who despise them; thus they shall know that I am the Lord.

25Thus says the Lord God: When I gather the house of Israel from the peoples among whom they are scattered, then I will manifest my holiness through them in the sight of the nations. Then they shall live on their land which I gave to my servant Jacob; **26**they

shall live on it in security, building houses and planting vineyards. They shall dwell secure while I inflict punishments on all their neighbors who despised them; thus they shall know that I, the Lord, am their God.

Egypt the Crocodile

29 **1**†On the twelfth day of the tenth month in the tenth year, the word of the Lord came to me: **2**†Son of man, set your face against Pharaoh, king of Egypt, and prophesy against him and against all Egypt. **3**†Say this to him: Thus says the Lord God:

> See! I am coming at you, Pharaoh,
> king of Egypt,
> Great crouching monster
> amidst your Niles:
> Who say, "The Niles are mine;
> it is I who made them!"

4I will put hooks in your jaws and make the fish of your Niles stick to your scales, then draw you up from the midst of your Niles along with all the fish of your Niles sticking to your scales.

5 I will cast you into the desert,
> you and all the fish of your Niles;
> You shall fall upon the open field,
> you shall not be taken up or buried;
> To the beasts of the earth and the birds
> of the air
> I give you as food,

6* That all who dwell in Egypt may know
> that I am the Lord.
> Because you have been a reed staff
> for the house of Israel:

7 When they held you in hand, you
> splintered,
> throwing every shoulder out of joint;
> When they leaned on you, you broke,
> bringing each one of them down
> headlong;

8therefore thus says the Lord God: See! I will bring the sword against you, and cut off from you both man and beast. **9**The land of Egypt shall become a desolate waste; thus they shall know that I am the Lord.

Because you said, "The Niles are mine; it is I who made them," **10**†therefore see! I am coming at you and against your Niles; I will make the land of Egypt a

---

† 28, 14: *The holy mountain of God:* the residence of God was sometimes designated as a mountain; cf Is 14, 13. *The fiery stones:* associated with the divine presence; cf 1, 13; Ps 18, 13.

29, 1: *The twelfth day of the tenth month in the tenth year:* January 7, 587 B.C. The siege of Jerusalem had begun a year earlier; cf 24, 1.

29, 2: Egypt was allied with Judah against the Chaldeans.

29, 3: *Niles:* the many rivulets of the Nile as it branches out into the Delta.

29, 10: *From Migdol to Syene:* from the northern to the southern extremity of Egypt. *Syene* is the modern Assuan.

waste and a desolation from Migdol to Syene, and even to the frontier of Ethiopia. **11**No foot of man or beast shall pass through it; they shall not pass through it, and it will be uninhabited for forty years. **12**I will make the land of Egypt the most desolate of lands, and its cities shall be the most deserted of cities for forty years; and I will scatter the Egyptians among the nations and strew them over foreign lands. **13**Yet thus says the Lord God: At the end of forty years I will gather the Egyptians from the peoples among whom they are scattered, **14**†and I will restore Egypt's fortune, bringing them back to the land of Pathros, the land of their origin, where it will be the lowliest **15**of kingdoms, never more to set itself above the nations. I will make them few, that they may not dominate the nations. **16**No longer shall they be for the house of Israel to trust in, but the living reminder of its guilt for having turned to follow after them. Thus they shall know that I am the Lord.

The Wages of Nebuchadnezzar

17†On the first day of the first month in the twenty-seventh year, the word of the Lord came to me: **18**†Son of man, Nebuchadnezzar, the king of Babylon, has led his army in an exhausting campaign against Tyre. Their heads became bald and their shoulders were galled; but neither he nor his army received any wages from Tyre for the campaign he led against it. **19***Therefore thus says the Lord God: I am now giving the land of Egypt to Nebuchadnezzar, king of Babylon. He shall carry off its riches, plundering and pillaging it for the wages of his soldiers, who did it for me; **20**as payment for his toil I have given him the land of Egypt, says the Lord God.

21On that day I will make a horn sprout for the house of Israel, and I will cause you to speak out in their midst; thus they shall know that I am the Lord.

The Day of the Lord Against Egypt

30 **1**Thus the word of the Lord came to me: **2**Son of man, speak this prophecy: Thus says the Lord God: Cry, Oh, the day! **3**for near is the day, near is the day of the Lord; a day of clouds, doomsday for the nations shall it be. **4**Then a sword shall come upon Egypt, and anguish shall be in Ethiopia, when the slain fall in Egypt, when her riches are seized and her foundations are overthrown. **5**Ethiopia, Put, Lud, all Arabia, Libya, and people of the allied territory shall fall by the sword with them. **6**Those who support Egypt shall fall, and down shall come her proud strength; from Migdol to Syene they shall fall there by the sword, says the Lord God. **7**She shall be the most devastated of lands, and her cities shall be the most desolate of all. **8**Then they shall know that I am the Lord, when I set fire to Egypt and when all who help her are broken. **9**On that day messengers shall hasten forth at my command to terrify unsuspecting

Ethiopia; they shall be in anguish on the day of Egypt, which is surely coming.

10Thus says the Lord God: I will put an end to the throngs of Egypt by the hand of Nebuchadnezzar, king of Babylon. **11**He and his people with him, the most ruthless of nations, shall be brought in to devastate the land. They shall draw their swords against Egypt, and fill the land with the slain. **12**I will turn the Niles into dry land and sell the land over to the power of the wicked. The land and everything in it I will hand over to foreigners to devastate. I, the Lord, have spoken.

13*Thus says the Lord God: I will put an end to the great ones of Memphis and the princes of the land of Egypt, that they may be no more. I will cast fear into the land of Egypt, and devastate Pathros. **14**I will set fire to Zoan, and inflict punishments on Thebes. **15**I will pour out my wrath on Pelusium, Egypt's stronghold, and cut down the crowds in Memphis. **16**I will set fire to Egypt; Syene shall writhe in anguish; Thebes shall be breached and its walls shall be demolished. **17**The young men of On and of Pibeseth shall fall by the sword, and the cities themselves shall go into captivity. **18**In Tehaphnehes the day shall be darkened when I break the scepter of Egypt. Her haughty pride shall cease from her, clouds shall cover her, and her daughters shall go into captivity. **19**Thus will I inflict punishments on Egypt, that they may know that I am the Lord.

Pharaoh's Broken Arm

20†On the seventh day of the first month in the eleventh year, the word of the Lord came to me: **21**†Son of man, I have broken the arm of Pharaoh, the king of Egypt, and see, it has not been bound up with bandages and healing remedies that it may be strong enough to hold the sword. **22**Therefore thus says the Lord God: See! I am coming at Pharaoh, the king of Egypt. I will break his strong arm, so that the sword

---

† 29, 14: *Pathros, the land of their origin:* upper Egypt, that is, southern Egypt, where the Egyptians were thought to have originated; Is 11, 11; Jer 44, 1.15.

29, 17: *The first day of the first month in the twenty-seventh year:* April 26, 571 B. C. This is the latest date attached to any prophecy in Ezekiel.

29, 18f: The fulfillment of Ezekiel's prophecy against Tyre (chapters 26-28) was a thirteen-year siege of the city by Nebuchadnezzar (587-574 B. C.). Tyre seems to have been taken, but its resources were exhausted and the booty was small. Therefore Ezekiel now prophesies that Nebuchadnezzar will collect his *wages* as God's instrument in the punishment of Tyre, by plundering Egypt.

30, 20: *The seventh day of the first month in the eleventh year:* April 29, 587 B. C.

30, 21-26: This oracle was uttered during the siege of Jerusalem, which had now lasted more than a year (24, 1). Pharaoh Hophra went to the aid of Jerusalem, causing the Chaldeans to lift the siege temporarily; cf Jer 34, 21; 37, 6f. In the prophet's eyes, this was interfering with the divine punishment of Judah that was to be inflicted by the Chaldeans. The Egyptians were routed by the Chaldeans, and were able to offer no more help to Jerusalem; cf chapter 31.

19: Jer 46, 2. 30/13: Zec 13, 2.

drops from his hand. **23**I will scatter the Egyptians among the nations and strew them over foreign lands. **24**But I will strengthen the arms of the king of Babylon, and put my sword in his hand, which he will bring against Egypt so as to plunder and pillage it. **25**[I will make the arms of the king of Babylon strong, but the arms of Pharaoh shall drop.] Then they shall know that I am the Lord, when I put my sword in the hand of the king of Babylon for him to wield against the land of Egypt. **26**[I will scatter the Egyptians among the nations and strew them over foreign lands.] Thus they shall know that I am the Lord.

Allegory of the Cypress

31 **1**†ON the first day of the third month in the eleventh year, the word of the Lord came to me: **2**Son of man, say to Pharaoh, the king of Egypt, and to his hordes: What are you like in your greatness?

3   Behold, a cypress [cedar] in Lebanon,
        beautiful of branch, lofty of stature,
        amid the very clouds lifted its crest.
4   Waters made it grow, the abyss made it
            flourish,
        sending its rivers round where it was
            planted,
        turning its streams to all the trees of
            the field.
5   Thus it grew taller than every other tree
            of the field,
        and longer of branch because of the
            abundant water.
6   In its boughs nested all the birds of the
            air,
        under its branches all beasts of the
            field gave birth,
        in its shade dwelt numerous peoples
            of every race.
7   It became beautiful and stately in its
            spread of foliage,
        for its roots were turned toward
            abundant water.
8   The cedars in the garden of God were
            not its equal,
        nor could the fir trees match its
            boughs,
        Neither were the plane trees like it for
            branches;
        no tree in the garden of God matched
            its beauty.
9   I made it beautiful, with much foliage,
        the envy of all Eden's trees in the
            garden of God.

10Therefore thus says the Lord God: Because it became lofty in stature, raising its crest among the clouds, and because it became proud in heart at its height, **11**I have handed it over to the mightiest of the nations, which has dealt with it in keeping with its

wickedness. I humiliated it. **12**Foreigners, the most ruthless of the nations, cut it down and left it on the mountains. Its foliage was brought low in all the valleys, its branches lay broken in all the ravines of the land, and all the peoples of the land withdrew from its shade, abandoning it.

13   On its fallen trunk rested all the birds of
            the air,
        and by its branches were all the beasts
            of the field.

14Thus no tree may grow lofty in stature or raise its crest among the clouds; no tree fed by water may stand by itself in its loftiness.

        For all of them are destined for death,
            for the land below,
        For the company of mortals,
            those who go down into the pit.

15Thus says the Lord God: On the day he went down to the nether world I made the abyss close up over him; I stopped its streams so that the deep waters were held back. I cast gloom over Lebanon because of him, so that all the trees in the land drooped on his account. **16**At the crash of his fall I made the nations rock, when I cast him down to the nether world with those who go down into the pit. In the land below, all Eden's trees were consoled, Lebanon's choice and best, all that were fed by water. **17**They too have come down with him to the nether world, to those slain by the sword; those who dwelt in his shade are dispersed among the nations. **18**Which was your equal in glory or size among the trees of Eden? Yet you have been brought down with the trees of Eden to the land below. You shall lie with the uncircumcised, with those slain by the sword. Such are Pharaoh and all his hordes, says the Lord God.

Dirge over Pharaoh

32 **1**†ON the first day of the twelfth month in the twelfth year, the word of the Lord came to me: **2**Son of man, utter a lament over Pharaoh, the king of Egypt, saying to him: Lion of the nations, you are destroyed.

        You were like a monster in the sea,
            spouting in your streams,
        Stirring the water with your feet
            and churning its streams.
3*Thus says the Lord God:

        I will spread my net over you
            [with a host of many nations],
            and draw you up in my seine.
4   I will leave you on the land;
            on the open field I will cast you.

---
† 31, 1: *The first day of the third month in the eleventh year:* June 21, 587 B. C.
    32, 1: *The first day of the twelfth month in the twelfth year:* March 3, 585 B. C.

✿ 32/3: 12, 13; 17, 20.

I will have all the birds of the air alight
>   on you,
>   and all the beasts of the earth eat
>   their fill of you.

5 I will leave your flesh on the mountains,
>   and fill the valleys with your carcass.

6 I will water the land with what flows
>   from you,
>   and the river beds shall be filled with
>   your blood.

7* When I snuff you out I will cover the
>   heavens,
>   and all their stars I will darken;
>   The sun I will cover with clouds,
>   and the moon shall not give its light.

8 All the shining lights in the heavens
>   I will darken on your account,
>   And I will spread darkness over your
>   land,
>   says the Lord God.

⁹I will grieve the hearts of many peoples when I lead you captive among the nations, to lands which you do not know. ¹⁰Many peoples shall be appalled at you, and their kings shall shudder over you in horror when they see me brandish my sword, and on the day of your downfall every one of them shall continuously tremble for his own life. ¹¹For thus says the Lord God: The sword of the king of Babylon shall come upon you.

12 I will cut down your horde with the
>   blades of warriors,
>   all of them the most ruthless of the
>   nations;
>   They shall lay waste the glory of Egypt,
>   and all her hordes shall be destroyed.

13 I will have all of her animals perish
>   beside her abundant waters;
>   The foot of man shall stir them no
>   longer,
>   nor shall the hoof of beast disturb
>   them.

14 Then will I make their waters clear,
>   and their streams flow like oil,
>   says the Lord God.

¹⁵When I turn Egypt into a waste, the land shall be devastated of all that is in it; when I strike all who live there, they shall know that I am the Lord. ¹⁶This is a dirge, and it shall be sung: the daughters of the nations shall chant it; over Egypt and all its hordes shall they chant it, says the Lord God.

Dirge over Egypt

¹⁷On the fifteenth day of the first month in the twelfth year, the word of the Lord came to me: ¹⁸Son of man, lament over the throngs of Egypt, for the mighty nations have thrust them down to the bottom of the earth, with those who go down into the pit. ²⁰In the midst of those slain by the sword shall they fall, and place shall be made with them for all their hordes. Then from the midst of the nether world, the mighty warriors shall speak to Egypt: ¹⁹"Whom do you excel in beauty? ²¹Come down, you and your allies, lie with the uncircumcised, with those slain by the sword."

²²There is Assyria with all her company, all of them slain, ²³whose graves have been made in the recesses of the pit; her company is around Egypt's grave, all of them slain, fallen by the sword, who spread terror in the land of the living. ²⁴There is Elam with all her throng about Egypt's grave, all of them slain, fallen by the sword: they have gone down uncircumcised to the bottom of the earth, who spread their terror in the land of the living, and they bear their disgrace with those who go down into the pit; ²⁵in the midst of the slain they are placed. ²⁶There are Meshech and Tubal and all their throng about her grave, all of them uncircumcised, slain by the sword, for they spread their terror in the land of the living.

²⁷†They do not lie with the mighty men fallen of old, who went down to the nether world with their weapons of war, whose swords were placed under their heads and whose shields were laid over their bones, though the mighty men caused terror in the land of the living. ²⁸But in the midst of the uncircumcised shall you lie, with those slain by the sword.

²⁹There are Edom, her kings, and all her princes, who despite their might have been placed with those slain by the sword; with the uncircumcised they lie, and with those who go down into the pit. ³⁰There are all the princes of the north and all the Sidonians, who have gone down with the slain, because of the terror their might inspired; they lie uncircumcised with those slain by the sword and bear their disgrace with those who go down to the pit. ³¹When Pharaoh sees these, he shall be comforted for all his hordes slain by the sword—Pharaoh and all his army, says the Lord God. ³²Since he spread his terror in the land of the living, therefore is he laid to rest among the uncircumcised, with those slain by the sword—Pharaoh and all his hordes, says the Lord God.

IV. SALVATION FOR ISRAEL

The Prophet a Watchman

33 ¹THUS THE WORD OF THE LORD came to me: ²Son of man, speak thus to your countrymen: When I bring the sword against a country, and the people of this country select one of their number to be their watchman, ³and the watchman, seeing the sword coming against the country, blows the trumpet to warn the people, ⁴anyone hearing but not heeding the

---

7: Is 13, 10; Jl 2, 10;
4, 15; Mt 24, 29.

---

† 32, 27: *The mighty men fallen of old:* the semilegendary heroes of the prehistoric past, who were thought to have once dominated the world; cf Is 14, 9.

warning of the trumpet and therefore slain by the sword that comes against him, shall be responsible for his own death. **5**He heard the trumpet blast yet refused to take warning; he is responsible for his own death, for had he taken warning he would have escaped with his life. **6**But if the watchman sees the sword coming and fails to blow the warning trumpet, so that the sword comes and takes anyone, I will hold the watchman responsible for that person's death, even though that person is taken because of his own sin.

7*You, son of man, I have appointed watchman for the house of Israel; when you hear me say anything, you shall warn them for me. **8**If I tell the wicked man that he shall surely die, and you do not speak out to dissuade the wicked man from his way, he [the wicked man] shall die for his guilt, but I will hold you responsible for his death. **9**But if you warn the wicked man, trying to turn him from his way, and he refuses to turn from his way, he shall die for his guilt, but you shall save yourself.

Individual Retribution

10As for you, son of man, speak to the house of Israel: You people say, "Our crimes and our sins weigh us down; we are rotting away because of them. How can we survive?" **11***Answer them: As I live, says the Lord God, I swear I take no pleasure in the death of the wicked man, but rather in the wicked man's conversion, that he may live. Turn, turn from your evil ways! Why should you die, O house of Israel?

12As for you, son of man, tell your countrymen: The virtue which a man has practiced will not save him on the day that he sins; neither will the wickedness that a man has done bring about his downfall on the day that he turns from his wickedness [nor can the virtuous man, when he sins, remain alive]. **13**Though I say to the virtuous man that he shall surely live, if he then presumes on his virtue and does wrong, none of his virtuous deeds shall be remembered; because of the wrong he has done, he shall die. **14**And though I say to the wicked man that he shall surely die, if he turns away from his sin and does what is right and just, **15**giving back pledges, restoring stolen goods, living by the statutes that bring life, and doing no wrong, he shall surely live, he shall not die. **16**None of the sins he committed shall be held against him; he has done what is right and just, he shall surely live.

17Yet your countrymen say, "The way of the Lord is not fair!"; but it is their way that is not fair. **18**When a virtuous man turns away from what is right and does wrong, he shall die for it. **19**But when a wicked man turns away from wickedness and does what is right and just, because of this he shall live. **20***And still you say, "The way of the Lord is not fair!"? I will judge every one of you according to his ways, O house of Israel.

The Fugitive from Jerusalem

21†On the fifth day of the tenth month, in the twelfth year of our exile, the fugitive came to me from Jerusalem and said, "The city is taken!" **22**The hand of the Lord had come upon me the evening before the fugitive arrived, and he opened my mouth when the fugitive reached me in the morning. My mouth was opened, and I was dumb no longer.

The Survivors in Judah

23†Thus the word of the Lord came to me: **24**Son of man, they who live in the ruins on the land of Israel reason thus: "Abraham, though but a single individual, received possession of the land; we, therefore, being many, have as permanent possession the land that has been given to us." **25**Give them this answer: Thus says the Lord God: You eat on the mountains, you raise your eyes to your idols, you shed blood—yet you would keep possession of the land? **26**You rely on your sword, you do abominable things, each one of you defiles his neighbor's wife—yet you would keep possession of the land? **27**Tell them this: Thus says the Lord God: As I live, those who are in the ruins I swear shall fall by the sword; those who are in the open field I have given to the wild beasts for food; and those who are in fastnesses and in caves shall die by the plague. **28**I will make the land a desolate waste, so that its proud strength will come to an end, and the mountains of Israel shall be so desolate that no one will cross them. **29**Thus they shall know that I am the Lord, when I make the land a desolate waste because of all the abominable things they have done.

The Prophet's False Popularity

30†As for you, son of man, your countrymen are talking about you along the walls and in the doorways of houses. They say to one another, "Come and hear the latest word that comes from the Lord." **31**My people come to you as people always do; they sit down before you and hear your words, but they will not obey them, for lies are on their lips and their desires are fixed on dishonest gain. **32**For them you are only a ballad singer, with a pleasant voice and a clever touch. They listen to your words, but they will not obey them. **33**But when it comes—and it is surely com-

---

†   33, 21f: January 8, 585 B. C. According to Jeremiah (39, 2), Jerusalem was taken in July, 587. Some MSS read "eleventh" for *twelfth* year (January, 586); even so, there was ample time between the fall of Jerusalem and the arrival of the fugitive from that city to journey to Babylon. However, this is the fugitive sent to fulfill the promise of 24, 25.27, the eyewitness who would release Ezekiel from his dumbness; cf 2, 26f.

33, 23-29: News brought by the fugitive furnished the occasion of this prophecy. Like Jeremiah, Ezekiel rejects the idea that the survivors in Judah have any claim to the land. The new Israel is to be formed from the exiles.

33, 30: The fulfillment of Ezekiel's prophecies about Jerusalem was responsible for this temporary enthusiasm among the unstable people.

ing!—they shall know that there was a prophet among them.

Parable of the Shepherds

34 [1]THUS the word of the LORD came to me: [2]*†Son of man, prophesy against the shepherds of Israel, in these words prophesy to them [to the shepherds]: Thus says the Lord GOD: Woe to the shepherds of Israel who have been pasturing themselves! Should not shepherds, rather, pasture sheep? [3]You have fed off their milk, worn their wool, and slaughtered their fatlings, but the sheep you have not pastured. [4]You did not strengthen the weak nor heal the sick nor bind up the injured. You did not bring back the strayed nor seek the lost, but you lorded it over them harshly and brutally. [5]So they were scattered for lack of a shepherd, and became food for all the wild beasts. My sheep were scattered [6]and wandered over all the mountains and high hills; my sheep were scattered over the whole earth, with no one to look after them or to search for them.

[7]Therefore, shepherds, hear the word of the LORD: [8]As I live, says the Lord GOD, because my sheep have been given over to pillage, and because my sheep have become food for every wild beast, for lack of a shepherd; because my shepherds did not look after my sheep, but pastured themselves and did not pasture my sheep; [9]because of this, shepherds, hear the word of the LORD: [10]Thus says the Lord GOD: I swear I am coming against these shepherds. I will claim my sheep from them and put a stop to their shepherding my sheep so that they may no longer pasture themselves. I will save my sheep, that they may no longer be food for their mouths.

[11]For thus says the Lord GOD: I myself will look after and tend my sheep. [12]As a shepherd tends his flock when he finds himself among his scattered sheep, so will I tend my sheep. I will rescue them from every place where they were scattered when it was cloudy and dark. [13]I will lead them out from among the peoples and gather them from the foreign lands; I will bring them back to their own country and pasture them upon the mountains of Israel [in the land's ravines and all its inhabited places]. [14]In good pastures will I pasture them, and on the mountain heights of Israel shall be their grazing ground. There they shall lie down on good grazing ground, and in rich pastures shall they be pastured on the mountains of Israel. [15]I myself will pasture my sheep; I myself will give them rest, says the Lord GOD. [16]The lost I will seek out, the strayed I will bring back, the injured I will bind up, the sick I will heal [but the sleek and the strong I will destroy], shepherding them rightly.

Separation of the Sheep

[17]As for you, my sheep, says the Lord GOD, I will judge between one sheep and another, between rams and goats. [18]Was it not enough for you to graze on the best pasture, that you had to trample the rest of your pastures with your feet? Was it not enough for you to drink the clearest water, that you had to foul the remainder with your feet? [19]Thus my sheep had to graze on what your feet had trampled and drink what your feet had fouled. [20]Therefore thus says the Lord GOD: Now will I judge between the fat and the lean sheep. [21]Because you push with side and shoulder, and butt all the weak sheep with your horns until you have driven them out, [22]I will save my sheep so that they may no longer be despoiled, and I will judge between one sheep and another. [23]*†I will appoint one shepherd over them to pasture them, my servant David; he shall pasture them and be their shepherd. [24]I, the LORD, will be their God, and my servant David shall be prince among them. I, the LORD, have spoken.

[25]I will make a covenant of peace with them, and rid the country of ravenous beasts, that they may dwell securely in the desert and sleep in the forests. [26]I will place them about my hill, sending rain in due season, rains that shall be a blessing to them. [27]The trees of the field shall bear their fruits, and the land its crops, and they shall dwell securely on their own soil. Thus they shall know that I am the LORD when I break the bonds of their yoke and free them from the power of those who enslaved them. [28]They shall no longer be despoiled by the nations or devoured by beasts of the earth, but shall dwell secure, with no one to frighten them. [29]I will prepare for them peaceful fields for planting; they shall no longer be carried off by famine in the land, or bear the reproaches of the nations. [30]Thus they shall know that I, the LORD, am their God, and they are my people, the house of Israel, says the Lord GOD. [31][You, my sheep, you are the sheep of my pasture, and I am your God, says the Lord GOD.]

Against Edom

35 [1]*†THUS the word of the LORD came to me: [2]Son of man, set your face against Mount Seir, and prophesy against it. [3]Say to it: Thus says the Lord GOD: See! I am coming at you, Mount Seir. I will stretch out my hand against you and make you a desolate waste. [4]Your cities I will turn into ruins, and you shall be a waste; thus you shall know that I am the LORD.

[5]Because you never let die your hatred for the Israelites, whom you delivered over to the power of the sword at the time of their trouble, when their crimes came to an end, [6]therefore, as I live, says the Lord

---

† 34, 2: *The shepherds of Israel:* the leaders of the people.

34, 23: *One shepherd . . . my servant David:* a messianic Davidic King who will rule over the restored Israel (vv 25-31) in the name of the Lord.

35, 1-15: After the fall of Jerusalem, Edom assisted the Chaldeans in devastating the land and subduing the population, and ended by occupying part of Judah's former territory. For this reason these oracles against Edom are found in the context of the city's fall.

---

* 34/2: 13, 3; Jer 23, 1.   35/1ff: 25, 12ff.
  23: Is 40, 21; Hos 3, 5;
  Jn 10, 11.14.

God, you have been guilty of blood, and blood, I swear, shall pursue you. ⁷I will make Mount Seir a desolate waste, and cut off from it any traveler. ⁸With the slain I will fill your hills, your valleys, and all your ravines [in them the slain shall fall by the sword]: ⁹desolate will I make you forever, and leave your cities without inhabitants; thus you shall know that I am the Lord.

¹⁰†Because you said: The two nations and the two lands have become mine; we shall possess them—although the Lord was there—¹¹therefore, as I live, says the Lord God, I will deal with you according to your anger and your envy which you have exercised [in your hatred] against them. I will make myself known among you when I judge you, ¹²and you shall know that I am the Lord.

I have heard all the contemptuous things you have uttered against the mountains of Israel: "They are desolate, they have been given us to devour." ¹³I have heard the insolent and wild words you have spoken against me. ¹⁴Thus says the Lord God: Just as you rejoiced over my land because it was desolate, so will I do to you. ¹⁵In keeping with your glee over the devastation of the inheritance of the house of Israel, so will I treat you. A waste shall you be, Mount Seir, you and the whole of Edom. Thus they shall know that I am the Lord.

Regeneration of the Land

36 ¹*As for you, son of man, prophesy to the mountains of Israel: Mountains of Israel, hear the word of the Lord! ²Thus says the Lord God: Because the enemy has said of you, "Ha! the everlasting heights have become our possession" ³[therefore prophesy in these words: Thus says the Lord God:]; because you have been ridiculed and despised on all sides for having become a possession for the rest of the nations, and have become a byword and a popular jeer; ⁴therefore, mountains of Israel, hear the word of the Lord: [Thus says the Lord God to the mountains and hills, the ravines and valleys, the desolate ruins and abandoned cities, which have been given over to the pillage and mockery of the remaining nations round about; ⁵therefore thus says the Lord God:] Truly, with burning jealousy I speak against the rest of the nations [and against all of Edom] who with wholehearted joy and utter contempt have considered my land their possession to be delivered over to plunder. ⁶[Therefore, prophesy concerning the land of Israel, and say to the mountains and hills, the ravines and valleys: Thus says the Lord God:] With jealous fury I speak, because you have borne the reproach of the nations. ⁷Therefore do I solemnly swear that your neighboring nations shall bear their own reproach.

⁸As for you, mountains of Israel, you shall grow branches and bear fruit for my people Israel, for they shall soon return. ⁹See, I come to you, it is to you that I turn; you will be tilled and sown, ¹⁰and I will settle crowds of men upon you, the whole house of Israel; cities shall be repeopled, and ruins rebuilt. ¹¹I will settle crowds of men and beasts upon you, to multiply and be fruitful. I will repeople you as in the past, and be more generous to you than in the beginning; thus you shall know that I am the Lord. ¹²[My people Israel are the ones whom I will have walk upon you; they shall take possession of you, and you shall be their heritage. Never again shall you rob them of their children.]

¹³†Thus says the Lord God: Because they have said of you, "You are a land that devours men, and you rob your people of their children"; ¹⁴therefore, never again shall you devour men or rob your people of their children, says the Lord God. ¹⁵No more will I permit you to hear the reproach of nations, or bear insults from peoples, or rob your people of their children, says the Lord God.

Regeneration of the People

¹⁶Thus the word of the Lord came to me: ¹⁷Son of man, when the house of Israel lived in their land, they defiled it by their conduct and deeds. In my sight their conduct was like the defilement of a menstruous woman. ¹⁸Therefore I poured out my fury upon them [because of the blood which they poured out on the ground, and because they defiled it with idols]. ¹⁹I scattered them among the nations, dispersing them over foreign lands; according to their conduct and deeds I judged them. ²⁰*But when they came among the nations [wherever they came], they served to profane my holy name, because it was said of them: "These are the people of the Lord, yet they had to leave their land." ²¹So I have relented because of my holy name which the house of Israel profaned among the nations where they came. ²²Therefore say to the house of Israel: Thus says the Lord God: Not for your sakes do I act, house of Israel, but for the sake of my holy name which you profaned among the nations to which you came. ²³I will prove the holiness of my great name, profaned among the nations, in whose midst you have profaned it. Thus the nations shall know that I am the Lord, says the Lord God, when in their sight I prove my holiness through you. ²⁴For I will take you away from among the nations, gather you from all the foreign lands, and bring you back to your own land. ²⁵*I will sprinkle clean water upon you to cleanse you from all your impurities, and from all your idols I will cleanse you. ²⁶*I will give you a new heart and place a new spirit within you, taking from your bodies your stony hearts and giving you natural hearts. ²⁷*I will put my spirit within you and make you

---

❀
 36/1: 6, 3.
  20: Is 52, 5; Rom 2, 24.
  25: Ps 51, 4; Zec 13, 1;
   Hb 10, 22; Jn 3, 5.
  26: Jer 31, 33.
  27: 37, 14; 39, 29; Is 42, 1;
   44, 3; 59, 21; Hg 2, 5;
   Jl 3, 1f.

†
35, 10: *The two nations and the two lands:* the superseded kingdoms of Israel and Judah and their territories.

36, 13: *A land that devours men:* destroys its own population, as could be seen in its disastrous political history.

live by my statutes, careful to observe my decrees. **28**You shall live in the land I gave your fathers; you shall be my people, and I will be your God. **29**I will save you from all your impurities; I will order the grain to be abundant, and I will not send famine against you. **30**I will increase the fruit on your trees and the crops in your fields; thus you shall no longer bear among the nations the reproach of famine. **31**Then you shall remember your evil conduct, and that your deeds were not good; you shall loathe yourselves for your sins and your abominations. **32**Not for your sakes do I act, says the Lord GOD—let this be known to you! Be ashamed and abashed because of your conduct, O house of Israel.

33Thus says the Lord GOD: When I purify you from all your crimes, I will repeople the cities, and the ruins shall be rebuilt; **34**the desolate land shall be tilled, which was formerly a wasteland exposed to the gaze of every passer-by. **35**"This desolate land has been made into a garden of Eden," they shall say. "The cities that were in ruins, laid waste, and destroyed are now repeopled and fortified." **36**Thus the neighboring nations that remain shall know that I, the LORD, have rebuilt what was destroyed and replanted what was desolate. I, the LORD, have promised, and I will do it.

37Thus says the Lord GOD: This also I will be persuaded to do for the house of Israel: to multiply them like sheep. **38**As with sacrificial sheep, the sheep of Jerusalem on its feast days, the cities which were in ruins shall be filled with flocks of men; thus they shall know that I am the LORD.

Vision of the Dry Bones

37 **1†**THE hand of the LORD came upon me, and he led me out in the spirit of the LORD and set me in the center of the plain, which was now filled with bones. **2**He made me walk among them in every direction so that I saw how many they were on the surface of the plain. How dry they were! **3**He asked me: Son of man, can these bones come to life? "Lord GOD," I answered, "you alone know that." **4**Then he said to me: Prophesy over these bones, and say to them: Dry bones, hear the word of the LORD! **5**Thus says the Lord GOD to these bones: See! I will bring spirit into you, that you may come to life. **6**I will put sinews upon you, make flesh grow over you, cover you with skin, and put spirit in you so that you may come to life and know that I am the LORD. **7**I prophesied as I had been told, and even as I was prophesying I heard a noise; it was a rattling as the bones came together, bone joining bone. **8**I saw the sinews and the flesh come upon them, and the skin cover them, but there was no spirit in them. **9**Then he said to me: Prophesy to the spirit, prophesy, son of man, and say to the spirit: Thus says the Lord GOD: From the four winds come, O spirit, and breathe into these slain that

they may come to life. **10**I prophesied as he told me, and the spirit came into them; they came alive and stood upright, a vast army. **11**Then he said to me: Son of man, these bones are the whole house of Israel. They have been saying, "Our bones are dried up, our hope is lost, and we are cut off." **12**Therefore, prophesy and say to them: Thus says the Lord GOD: O my people, I will open your graves and have you rise from them, and bring you back to the land of Israel. **13**Then you shall know that I am the LORD, when I open your graves and have you rise from them, O my people! **14**I will put my spirit in you that you may live, and I will settle you upon your land; thus you shall know that I am the LORD. I have promised, and I will do it, says the LORD.

The Two Sticks

15†Thus the word of the LORD came to me: **16**Now, son of man, take a single stick, and write on it: Judah and those Israelites who are associated with him. Then take another stick and write on it: Joseph [the stick of Ephraim] and all the house of Israel associated with him. **17**Then join the two sticks together, so that they form one stick in your hand. **18**When your countrymen ask you, "Will you not tell us what you mean by all this?", **19**answer them: Thus says the Lord GOD: [I will take the stick of Joseph, which is in the hand of Ephraim, and of the tribes of Israel associated with him, and I will join to it the stick of Judah, making them a single stick; they shall be one in my hand. **20**The sticks on which you write you shall hold up before them to see. **21**Tell them: Thus speaks the Lord GOD:] I will take the Israelites from among the nations to which they have come, and gather them from all sides to bring them back to their land. **22**I will make them one nation upon the land, in the mountains of Israel, and there shall be one prince for them all. Never again shall they be two nations, and never again shall they be divided into two kingdoms.

23No longer shall they defile themselves with their idols, their abominations, and all their transgressions. I will deliver them from all their sins of apostasy, and cleanse them so that they may be my people and I may be their God. **24***My servant David shall be prince over them, and there shall be one shepherd for them all; they shall live by my statutes and carefully observe my decrees. **25**They shall live on the land which I gave to my servant Jacob, the land where their fathers lived; they shall live on it forever, they, and their children, and their children's children, with my servant David their prince forever. **26***I will make with them a covenant of peace; it shall be an everlasting covenant with them, and I will multiply them,

---

† 37, 1-14: This vision is a prediction of the restoration of Israel under the figure of a resurrection from the dead; it is not concerned with the doctrine of resurrection itself.

37, 15-22: The symbolic action of joining two sticks into one signifies the future union of Israel and Judah under one messianic King.

* 37/24: 34, 23; Jer 23, 5; 33, 15.   26: Ps 110, 4.

and put my sanctuary among them forever. **27**My dwelling shall be with them; I will be their God, and they shall be my people. **28**Thus the nations shall know that it is I, the LORD, who make Israel holy, when my sanctuary shall be set up among them forever.

First Prophecy Against Gog

38 **1**†THUS the word of the LORD came to me: **2**❋†Son of man, turn toward Gog [the land of Magog], the chief prince of Meshech and Tubal, and prophesy against him: **3**Thus says the Lord GOD: See! I am coming at you, Gog, chief prince of Meshech and Tubal. **4**I will lead you forth with all your army, horses and riders all handsomely outfitted, a great horde with bucklers and shields, all of them carrying swords: **5**Persia, Cush, and Put with them [all with shields and helmets], **6**Gomer with all its troops, Beth-togarmah from the recesses of the north with all its troops, many peoples with you. **7**Prepare yourself, be ready, you and all your horde assembled about you, and be at my disposal. **8**After many days you will be mustered [in the last years you will come] against a nation which has survived the sword, which has been assembled from many peoples [on the mountains of Israel which were long a ruin], which has been brought forth from among the peoples and all of whom now dwell in security. **9**You shall come up like a sudden storm, advancing like a cloud to cover the earth, you and all your troops and the many peoples with you.

10Thus says the Lord GOD: At that time thoughts shall arise in your mind, and you shall devise an evil scheme: **11**"I will go up against a land of open villages and attack the peaceful people who are living in security, all of them living without walls, having neither bars nor gates, **12**†to plunder and pillage, turning my hand against the ruins that were repeopled and against a people gathered from the nations, a people concerned with cattle and goods, who dwell at the navel of the earth." **13**Sheba and Dedan, the merchants of Tarshish and all her young lions shall ask you: "Is it for plunder that you have come? Is it for pillage that you have summoned your horde, to carry off silver and gold, to take away cattle and goods, to seize much plunder?"

17Thus says the Lord GOD: It is of you that I spoke in ancient times through my servants, the prophets of Israel, who prophesied in those days that I would bring you against them. **18**But on that day, the day when Gog invades the land of Israel, says the Lord GOD, my fury shall be aroused. In my anger **19**and in my jealousy, in my fiery wrath, I swear: On that day there shall be a great shaking upon the land of Israel. **20**Before me shall tremble the fish of the sea and the birds of the air, the beasts of the field and all the reptiles that crawl upon the ground, and all men who are on the land. Mountains shall be overturned, and

cliffs shall tumble, and every wall shall fall to the ground. **21**Against him I will summon every terror, says the Lord GOD, every man's sword against his brother. I will hold judgment with him in pestilence and bloodshed; **22**flooding rain and hailstones, fire and brimstone, I will rain upon him, upon his troops, and upon the many peoples with him. **23**I will prove my greatness and holiness and make myself known in the sight of many nations; thus they shall know that I am the LORD.

Second Prophecy Against Gog

14Therefore prophesy, son of man, and say to Gog: Thus says the Lord GOD: When my people Israel are dwelling in security, will you not bestir yourself **15**and come from your home in the recesses of the north, you and many peoples with you, all mounted on horses, a great horde and a mighty army? **16**You shall come up against my people Israel like a cloud covering the land. In the last days I will bring you against my land, that the nations may know of me, when in their sight I prove my holiness through you, O Gog.

Third Prophecy Against Gog

39 **1**NOW, son of man, prophesy against Gog in these words: Thus says the Lord GOD: See! I am coming at you, Gog, chief prince of Meshech and Tubal. **2**I will turn you about, I will urge you on, and I will make you come up from the recesses of the north; I will lead you against the mountains of Israel. **3**Then I will strike the bow from your left hand, and make the arrows drop from your right. **4**Upon the mountains of Israel you shall fall, you and all your troops and the peoples who are with you. To birds of prey of every kind and to the wild beasts I am giving you to be eaten. **5**On the open field you shall fall, for I have decreed it, says the Lord GOD.

6I will send fire upon Magog and upon those who live securely in the coastlands; thus they shall know that I am the LORD. **7**I will make my holy name known among my people Israel; I will no longer allow my holy name to be profaned. Thus the nations shall know that I am the LORD, the Holy One in Israel. **8**Yes, it is coming and shall be fulfilled, says the Lord GOD. This is the day I have decreed.

---

† **38, 1—39, 20:** These three oracles against Gog may refer either to a specific foreign invasion in the future, or to the apocalyptic struggle between good and evil at the end of time. By some they are ascribed to a later author than Ezekiel, who lived after the exile and the return to Palestine.

38, 2: *Gog:* the name is almost certainly a symbolic one taken from that of Gyges, king of Lydia, whether or not the prophet has a specific person in mind. The gloss *Magog* may be an Akkadian expression, *mat-Gog,* "the land of Gog." *Meshech and Tubal,* as well as *Gomer and Beth-togarmah* (v 6), were countries around the Black Sea, the northernmost countries known to the Hebrews: *the north* (cf also v 15) was the traditional direction from which invasion was expected; cf Jer 1, 13ff.

38, 12: *Who dwell at the navel of the earth:* the people of Israel (cf v 18; also 5, 5). Many ancient peoples spoke of their own homelands as "the navel," that is, the center of the earth.

⁹Then shall those who live in the cities of Israel go out and burn weapons: [shields and bucklers,] bows and arrows, clubs and lances; for seven years they shall make fires with them. ¹⁰They shall not have to bring in wood from the fields or cut it down in the forests, for they shall make fires with the weapons. Thus they shall plunder those who plundered them and pillage those who pillaged them, says the Lord God.

¹¹†On that day I will give Gog for his tomb a well-known place in Israel, the Valley of Abarim east of the sea [it is blocked to travelers]. Gog shall be buried there with all his horde, and it shall be named "Valley of Hamon-gog." ¹²To purify the land, the house of Israel shall need seven months to bury them. ¹³All the people of the land shall bury them and gain renown for it, when I reveal my glory, says the Lord God. ¹⁴Men shall be permanently employed to pass through the land burying those who lie unburied, so as to purify the land. For seven months they shall keep searching. ¹⁵When they pass through, should they see a human bone, let them put up a marker beside it, until others have buried it in the Valley of Hamon-gog. ¹⁶[Also the name of the city shall be Hamonah.] Thus the land shall be purified.

¹⁷As for you, son of man, says the Lord God, say to birds of every kind and to all the wild beasts: Come together, from all sides gather for the slaughter I am about to provide for you, a great slaughter on the mountains of Israel: you shall have flesh to eat and blood to drink. ¹⁸You shall eat the flesh of warriors and drink the blood of the princes of the land [rams, lambs, and goats, bullocks, fatlings of Bashan, all of them]. ¹⁹From the slaughter which I will provide for you, you shall eat fat until you are filled and drink blood until you are drunk. ²⁰You shall be filled at my table with horses and riders, with warriors and soldiers of every kind, says the Lord God.

Israel's Return

²¹Thus I will display my glory among the nations, and all the nations shall see the judgment I have executed and the hand I have laid upon them. ²²From that day forward the house of Israel shall know that I am the Lord, their God. ²³The nations shall know that because of its sins the house of Israel went into exile; for they transgressed against me, and I hid my face from them and handed them over to their foes, so that all of them fell by the sword. ²⁴According to their uncleanness and their transgressions I dealt with them, hiding my face from them.

²⁵Therefore, thus says the Lord God: Now I will restore the fortunes of Jacob and have pity on the whole house of Israel, and I will be jealous for my holy name. ²⁶They shall forget their disgrace and all the times they broke faith with me, when they live in security on their land with no one to frighten them. ²⁷When I bring them back from among the peoples, I will gather them from the lands of their enemies, and will prove my holiness through them in the sight of many nations. ²⁸*Thus they shall know that I, the Lord, am their God, since I who exiled them among the nations, will gather them back on their land, not leaving any of them behind. ²⁹No longer will I hide my face from them, for I have poured out my spirit upon the house of Israel, says the Lord God.

V: THE NEW ISRAEL

THE NEW TEMPLE

The Man with a Measure

40 ¹†ON THE TENTH DAY OF THE MONTH beginning the twenty-fifth year of our exile, fourteen years after the city was taken, that very day the hand of the Lord came upon me and brought me ²in divine visions to the land of Israel, where he set me down on a very high mountain. On it there seemed to be a city being built before me. ³When he had brought me there, all at once I saw a man whose appearance was that of bronze; he was standing in the gate, holding a linen cord and a measuring rod. ⁴The man said to me, "Son of man, look carefully and listen intently, and pay strict attention to all that I will show you, for you have been brought here so that I might show it to you. Tell the house of Israel all that you see." ⁵†[Then I saw an outer wall that completely surrounded the temple. The man was holding a measuring rod six cubits long, each cubit being a cubit and a handbreadth; he measured the width and the height of the structure, each of which were found to be one rod.]

The East Gate

⁶†Then he went to the gate which faced the east, climbed its steps, and measured the gate's threshold, which was found to be a rod wide. ⁷The cells were a

---

† 39, 11: *The Valley of Abarim:* in the Abarim mountains, east of the Jordan. *Hamon-gog:* means "the horde of Gog."

40, 1—48, 35: This lengthy vision of the new Israel is dated (40, 1) April 28, 573 B. C. It is largely concerned with the new temple and the prescriptions to govern it, but other details of the restored commonwealth are included, forming a kind of program for the future. The literary form of the vision has been aptly termed "utopian": it is plain that the prophet did not expect a literal fulfillment of much of what he described. The passage doubtless underwent successive additions, both from the prophet and from later inspired writers.

40, 5: *A cubit and a handbreadth:* the ordinary cubit consisted of six handbreadths; the great cubit, of seven. In measuring the temple, a rod six great cubits long was used. The ordinary cubit was about one and a half feet, or, more exactly, 17.5 inches; the large cubit, 20.4 inches.

40, 6-16: The east gate, leading into the outer court of the temple, is described more fully than the north and south gates, which, however, were of the same dimensions. On the west side of the outer court there was a large building instead of a gate (41, 12).

* 39/28: 36, 23.

rod long and a rod wide, and the pilasters between the cells measured five cubits. The threshold of the gate adjoining the vestibule of the gate toward the inside measured one rod. **8**He measured the vestibule of the gate, **9**which was eight cubits, and its pilasters, which were two cubits. The vestibule of the gate was toward the inside. **10**The cells of the east gate were three on either side, of equal size, and the pilasters on either side were also of equal size. **11**He measured the gate's entrance, which was ten cubits wide, while the width of the gate's passage itself was thirteen cubits. **12**The border before each of the cells on both sides was one cubit; the cells themselves were six cubits on either side, from opening to opening. **13**He measured the gate from the back wall of one cell to the back wall of the cell on the opposite side: the width was twenty-five cubits. **14**He measured the vestibule, which was twenty-five cubits. The pilasters adjoining the court on either side were six cubits. **15**The length of the gate from the front entrance to the front of the vestibule on the inside was fifty cubits. **16**Within the gateway on both sides there were splayed windows let into the cells [and into their pilasters]; likewise, within the vestibule on both sides there were windows. The pilasters were decorated with palms.

The Outer Court

17†Then he brought me to the outer court, where there were chambers and a pavement. The pavement was laid all around the court, and the chambers, which were on the pavement, were thirty in number. **18**The pavement lay alongside the gates, as wide as the gates were long; this was the lower pavement. **19**He measured the width of the court from the front of the lower gate to the front of the inner gate; it was one hundred cubits between them.

The North Gate

Then he proceeded north, **20**where, on the outer court, there was a gate facing north, whose length and width he measured. **21**Its cells, three on either side, its pilasters, and its vestibule had the same measurements as those of the first gate; it was fifty cubits long and twenty-five cubits wide. **22**Its windows, the windows of its vestibule, and its palm decorations were of the same proportions as those of the gate facing the east. Seven steps led up to it, and its vestibule was toward the inside. **23**The inner court had a gate opposite the north gate, just as at the east gate; he measured one hundred cubits from one gate to the other.

The South Gate

24Then he led me south, to where there was a southern gate, whose cells, pilasters, and vestibule he measured; they were the same size as the others. **25**The gate and its vestibule had windows on both sides, like the other windows. It was fifty cubits long and twenty-five cubits wide. **26**It was ascended by seven steps; its vestibule was toward the inside; and it was decorated with palms here and there on its pilasters. **27**The inner court also had a southern gate; from gate to gate he measured one hundred cubits.

Gates of the Inner Court

28†Then he brought me to the inner court by the south gate, where he measured the south gate. Its dimensions were the same as the others; **29**its cells, its pilasters, and its vestibule were the same size as the others. The gate and its vestibule had windows on both sides; and it was fifty cubits long and twenty-five cubits wide. **31**But its vestibule was toward the outer court; palms were on its pilasters, and it had a stairway of eight steps. **32**Then he brought me to the gate facing the east, where he measured the gate, whose dimensions were found to be the same. **33**Its cells, its pilasters, and its vestibule were the same size as the others; the gate and its vestibule had windows on both sides; it was fifty cubits long and twenty-five cubits wide. **34**But its vestibule was toward the outer court; palms were on its pilasters here and there, and it had a stairway of eight steps. **35**Then he brought me to the north gate, where he measured the dimensions **36**of its cells, its pilasters, and its vestibule, and found them the same. The gate and its vestibule had windows on both sides; it was fifty cubits long and twenty-five cubits wide. **37**Its vestibule was toward the outer court; palms were on its pilasters here and there, and it had a stairway of eight steps.

Side Rooms

38There was a chamber opening off the vestibule of the gate, where the holocausts were rinsed. **39**In the vestibule of the gate there were two tables on either side, on which were slaughtered the sin offerings and guilt offerings. **40**Along the wall of the vestibule, but outside, near the entrance of the north gate, were two tables, and on the other side of the vestibule of the gate there were two tables. **41**There were four tables on either side of the gate [eight tables], on which the sacrifices were slaughtered. **42**There were four tables for holocausts, made of cut stone, one and a half cubits long, one and a half cubits wide, and one cubit high. **43**The ledges, a handbreadth wide, were set on the inside all around, and on them were laid the instruments with which the holocausts were slaughtered. On the tables themselves the flesh was laid. **44**He then led me to the inner court where there were two chambers, one beside the north gate, facing south, and the other beside the south gate, facing north. **45**He said to me, "This chamber which faces south is for the priests who have charge of the temple,

---

† 40, 17: *The outer court:* the court outside the temple area proper, which had its own inner court (vv 28-37).

40, 28-37: The gates leading into the inner court of the temple area correspond to the gates leading into the outer court, with the exception that their vestibules are on the outer rather than the inner side.

[46]†and the chamber which faces north is for the priests who have charge of the altar. These are the Zadokites, the only Levites who may come near to minister to the Lord." [47]Then he measured the court, which was a hundred cubits long and a hundred cubits wide, a perfect square. The altar stood in front of the temple.

The Temple Building

[48]†Then he brought me into the vestibule of the temple and measured the pilasters on each side, which were five cubits. The width of the doorway was fourteen cubits, and the side walls on either side of the door measured three cubits. [49]†The vestibule was twenty cubits wide and twelve cubits deep; ten steps led up to it, and there were columns by the pilasters, one on either side.

41 [1]Then he brought me to the nave and measured the pilasters, which were six cubits thick on either side. [2]The width of the entrance was ten cubits, and the walls at either side of it measured five cubits each. He measured the length of the nave, which was found to be forty cubits, while its width was twenty.

[3]Then he went in beyond and measured the pilasters flanking that entrance, which were two cubits; the width of the entrance was six cubits, and the walls at either side of it extended seven cubits each. [4]He measured the space beyond the nave, twenty cubits long and twenty cubits wide, and said to me, "This is the holy of holies."

[5]Then he measured the wall of the temple, which was six cubits thick; the side chambers, which extended all the way around the temple, had a width of four cubits. [6]There were thirty side chambers built one above the other in three stories, and there were offsets in the outside wall of the temple that enclosed the side chambers; these served as supports, so that there were no supports in the temple wall proper. [7]There was a broad circular passageway that led upward to the side chambers, for the temple was enclosed all the way around and all the way upward; therefore the temple had a broad way running upward so that one could pass from the lowest to the middle and the highest story. [8]About the temple was a raised pavement completely enclosing it—the foundations of the side chambers—a full rod of six cubits in extent. [9]The width of the outside wall which enclosed the side chambers was five cubits. Between the side chambers of the temple [10]and the chambers of the court was an open space twenty cubits wide going all around the temple. [11]The side chambers had entrances to the open space, one entrance on the north and another on the south. The width of the wall surrounding the open space was five cubits. [12]†The building fronting the free area on the west side was seventy cubits front to back; the wall of the building was five cubits thick all around, and it measured ninety cubits from side to side. [13]He measured the temple, which was one hundred cubits long. The free area, together with the building and its walls, was a hundred cubits in length. [14]The façade of the temple, along with the free area, on the east side, was one hundred cubits wide. [15]He measured the building which lay the length of the free area and behind it, and together with its walls on both sides it was one hundred cubits.

Interior of the Temple

The inner nave and the outer vestibule [16]were paneled with precious wood all around, covered from the ground to the windows. There were splayed windows with trellises about them [facing the threshold]. [17]As high as the lintel of the door, even into the interior part of the temple as well as outside, on every wall on every side in both the inner and outer rooms were carved [18]the figures of cherubim and palmtrees: a palmtree between every two cherubim. Each cherub had two faces: [19]a man's face looking at a palmtree on one side, and a lion's face looking at a palmtree on the other; thus they were figured on every side throughout the whole temple. [20]From the ground to the lintel of the door the cherubim and palmtrees were carved on the walls. [21]The way into the nave was a square doorframe. In front of the holy place was something that looked like [22]†a wooden altar, three cubits in height, two cubits long, and two cubits wide. It had corners, and its base and sides were of wood. He said to me, "This is the table which is before the Lord." [23]The nave had a double door, and also the holy place had [24]a double door. Each door had two movable leaves; two leaves were on one doorjamb and two on the other. [25]Carved upon them [on the doors of the nave] were cherubim and palmtrees, like those carved on the walls. Before the vestibule outside was a wooden lattice. [26]There were splayed windows [and palmtrees] on both side walls of the vestibule, and the side chambers of the temple....

Other Structures

42 [1]Then he led me north to the outer court, bringing me to some chambers on the north that lay across the free area and which were also across from the building. [2]Their length was a hundred cubits on the north side, and they were fifty cubits wide. [3]Across the twenty cubits of the inner court and the pavement of the outer court, there were three parallel rows of them on different levels. [4]In front of the chambers, to the inside, was a walk ten cubits broad and a wall of one cubit; but the

---

† 40, 46: *The Zadokites:* descendants of the priestly line of Zadok; cf 2 Sm 15, 24-29; 1 Kgs 1, 32ff; 2, 35.

40, 48—41, 15: The description of Ezekiel's visionary temple closely follows the description of the temple of Solomon (1 Kgs 6).

40, 49—41, 4: *Vestibule . . . nave . . . holy of holies:* the three divisions of the temple building in progressing order of sanctity. The last is called "the inner sanctuary" in 1 Kgs 6.

41, 12: *The building:* the function of this structure lying behind the temple is never specified.

41, 22: *A wooden altar:* the altar of incense, standing in the nave at the entrance of the holy of holies.

entrances of the chambers were on the north. **5**†The outermost chambers were the lowest, for the system of levels set them at a level lower than the closest chambers and those in between; **6**for they were in three rows and had no foundations to conform with the foundations of the courts, therefore they were on a lower terrace of the ground than the closest and the middle chambers. **7**On the far side there was a wall running parallel to the chambers along the outer court; its length before these chambers was fifty cubits, **8**for the length of the chambers belonging to the outer court was fifty cubits, but along its entire length the wall measured one hundred cubits. **9**Below these chambers there was the way in from the east, so that one could enter from the outer court **10**where the wall of the court began.

To the south along the side of the free area and the building there were also chambers, **11**before which was a passage. These looked like the chambers to the north, just as long and just as wide, with the same exits and plan and entrances. **12**Below the chambers to the south there was an entrance at the beginning of the way which led to the back wall, by which one could enter from the east. **13**†He said to me, "The north and south chambers which border on the free area are the sanctuary chambers; here the priests who draw near to the Lord shall eat the most sacred meals, and here they shall keep the most sacred offerings: cereal offerings, sin offerings, and guilt offerings; for it is a holy place. **14**When the priests have once entered, they shall not leave the holy place for the outer court until they have left here the clothing in which they ministered, for it is holy. They shall put on other garments, and then approach the place destined for the people."

Measuring the Outer Court

15When he had finished measuring the inner temple area, he brought me out by way of the gate which faces east and measured all the limits of the court. **16**He measured the east side: five hundred cubits by his measuring rod. Then he turned **17**and measured the north side: five hundred cubits by the measuring rod. He turned **18**to the south and measured five hundred cubits by the measuring rod. **19**Then he turned to the west and measured five hundred cubits by the measuring rod. **20**Thus he measured it in the four directions, five hundred cubits long and five hundred cubits wide. It was surrounded by a wall, to separate the sacred from the profane.

RESTORATION OF THE TEMPLE

The Return of the Lord

43 **1**THEN he led me to the gate which faces the east, **2**and there I saw the glory of the God of Israel coming from the east. I heard a sound like the roaring of many waters, and the earth shone with

his glory. **3***The vision was like that which I had seen when he came to destroy the city, and like that which I had seen by the river Chebar. I fell prone **4**as the glory of the Lord entered the temple by way of the gate which faces the east, **5**but spirit lifted me up and brought me to the inner court. And I saw that the temple was filled with the glory of the Lord. **6**Then I heard someone speaking to me from the temple, while the man stood beside me. **7**The voice said to me: Son of man, this is where my throne shall be, this is where I will set the soles of my feet; here I will dwell among the Israelites forever. Never again shall they and their kings profane my holy name with their harlotries and with the corpses of their kings [their high places]. **8**†When they placed their threshold against my threshold and their doorpost next to mine, so that only a wall was between us, they profaned my holy name by their abominable deeds; therefore I consumed them in my wrath. **9**From now on they shall put far from me their harlotry and the corpses of their kings, and I will dwell in their midst forever.

The Law of the Temple

10As for you, son of man, describe the temple to the house of Israel [that they may be ashamed of their sins], both its measurements and its design; **11**[and if they are ashamed of all that they have done,] make known to them the form and design of the temple, its exits and entrances, all its statutes and laws; write these down for them to see, that they may carefully observe all its laws and statutes. **12**This is the law of the temple: its whole surrounding area on the mountain top shall be most sacred.

The Altar

13†These were the measurements of the altar in cubits of one cubit plus a handbreadth. Its base was one cubit high and one cubit deep, with a rim around its edge of one span. The height of the altar itself was as follows: **14**from its base at the bottom up to the lower ledge it was two cubits high, and this ledge was one cubit deep; from the lower to the upper ledge it was four cubits high, and this ledge also was one cubit deep; **15**the hearth of the altar was four cubits high, and extending from the top of the hearth were the four horns of the altar. **16**The hearth was a square: twelve cubits long and twelve cubits wide. **17**The

---

† 42, 5f: The three rows of identical chambers, since they rested on different ground levels, necessarily had roofs on correspondingly different levels.

42, 13: The function of these chambers is explained again in 46, 19f.

43, 8: *They placed their threshold against my threshold:* the preexilic temple and the royal palace belonged to the same complex of buildings, and this physical proximity was reflected in the use made of the temple by kings like Ahaz and Manasseh, who treated it as their private chapel for pagan rites. In the new Israel the temple is free, even physically, from civil jurisdiction; cf 45, 7f.

43, 13: *The altar:* of holocausts, standing in the inner court of the temple area; cf 40, 47.

upper ledge was also a square: fourteen cubits long and fourteen cubits wide. The lower ledge, likewise a square, was sixteen cubits long and sixteen cubits wide, with a half-cubit rim surrounding it. And there was a base of one cubit all around. The steps of the altar face the east.

¹⁸Then he said to me: Son of man, thus says the Lord God: These are the statutes for the altar when it is set up for the offering of holocausts upon it and for the sprinkling of blood against it. ¹⁹Give a young bull as a sin offering to the priests, the Levites who are of the line of Zadok, who draw near me to minister to me, says the Lord God. ²⁰Take some of its blood and put it on the four horns of the altar, and on the four corners of the ledge, and on the rim all around. Thus you shall purify it and make atonement for it. ²¹Then take the bull of the sin offering, which is to be burnt in a designated part of the temple, outside the sanctuary. ²²On the second day present an unblemished he-goat as a sin offering, to purify the altar as was done with the bull. ²³When you have finished the purification, bring an unblemished young bull and an unblemished ram from the flock, ²⁴and present them before the Lord; the priests shall strew salt on them and offer them to the Lord as holocausts. ²⁵Daily for seven days you shall offer a he-goat as a sin offering, and a young bull and a ram from the flock, all unblemished, shall be offered ²⁶for seven days. Thus atonement shall be made for the altar, and it shall be purified and dedicated. ²⁷And when these days are over, from the eighth day on, the priests shall offer your holocausts and peace offerings on the altar. Then I will accept you, says the Lord God.

The Closed Gate

44 ¹THEN he brought me back to the outer gate of the sanctuary, facing the east; but it was closed. ²He said to me: This gate is to remain closed; it is not to be opened for anyone to enter by it; since the Lord, the God of Israel, has entered by it, it shall remain closed. ³†Only the prince may sit down in it to eat his meal in the presence of the Lord. He must enter by way of the vestibule of the gate, and leave by the same way.

THE NEW LAW

Admission to the Temple

⁴Then he brought me by way of the north gate to the facade of the temple, and when I looked I saw the glory of the Lord filling the Lord's temple, and I fell prone. ⁵Then he said to me: Son of man, pay strict attention, look carefully, and listen intently to all that I will tell you about the statutes and laws of the Lord's temple; be attentive in regard to those who are to be admitted to the temple and all those who are to be excluded from the sanctuary. ⁶Say to that

rebellious house, the house of Israel: Thus says the Lord God: Enough of all these abominations of yours, O house of Israel! ⁷†You have admitted foreigners, uncircumcised both in heart and flesh, to my sanctuary to profane it when you offered me food, fat, and blood; thus you have broken my covenant by all your abominations. ⁸Instead of caring for the service of my temple, you have appointed such as these to serve me in my sanctuary in your stead. ⁹Thus says the Lord God: No foreigners, uncircumcised in heart and in flesh, shall ever enter my sanctuary; none of the foreigners who live among the Israelites.

Levites

¹⁰†But as for the Levites who departed from me when Israel strayed from me to pursue their idols, they shall bear the consequences of their sin. ¹¹They shall serve in my sanctuary as gatekeepers and temple servants; they shall slaughter the holocausts and the sacrifices for the people, and they shall stand before the people to minister for them. ¹²Because they used to minister for them before their idols, and became an occasion of sin to the house of Israel, therefore I have sworn an oath against them, says the Lord God: they shall bear the consequences of their sin. ¹³They shall no longer draw near me to serve as my priests, nor shall they touch any of my sacred things, or the most sacred things. Thus they shall bear their disgrace because of all their abominable deeds. ¹⁴But I will set them to the service of the temple, for all its work and for everything that is to be done in it.

Priests

¹⁵As for the Levitical priests, however, the Zadokites who cared for my sanctuary when the Israelites strayed from me, they shall draw near me to minister to me, and they shall stand before me to offer me fat and blood, says the Lord God. ¹⁶It is they who shall enter my sanctuary, they who shall approach my table to minister to me, and they who shall carry out my service. ¹⁷Whenever they enter the gates of the inner court, they shall wear linen garments; they shall not put on anything woolen when they minister at the gates of the inner court or within the temple. ¹⁸*They shall have linen turbans on their heads and linen drawers on their loins; they shall not gird themselves

---

† 44, 3: The prince stands at the eastern gate of the inner court while his sacrifice is offered up (46, 2); he then goes to the vestibule of the outer court, there to partake of his sacrificial meal. The closed outer gate on the eastern side signifies that the Lord has entered the temple permanently, not to depart again.

44, 7ff: In the preexilic temple various menial services had been performed by foreigners; cf Jos 9, 22-27. In the new temple the Levites will perform these services (vv 10-14).

44, 10-14: Levites other than the Zadokite priesthood of Jerusalem had performed priestly functions at the various sanctuaries and high places in Israel and Judah, where the worship of the Lord had often been corrupted with pagan elements. The demotion of the Levites to menial service in the temple was enforced in the actual restoration after the exile, and explains why relatively few Levites were willing to return; cf Ezr 8, 15ff.

with anything that causes sweat. **19***†When they are to go out to the people in the outer court, they shall take off the garments in which they ministered and leave them in the chambers of the sanctuary, putting on other garments; thus they will not transmit holiness to the people with their garments.

20*They shall not shave their heads nor let their hair hang loose, but they shall keep their hair carefully trimmed. **21***No priest shall drink wine when he is to enter the inner court. **22***They shall not take for their wives either widows or divorced women, but only virgins of the race of Israel; however, they may marry women who are the widows of priests. **23**They shall teach my people to distinguish between the sacred and the profane, and make known to them the difference between the clean and the unclean. **24***In capital cases they shall stand as judges, judging them according to my decrees. They shall observe my laws and statutes on all my festivals, and keep my sabbaths holy.

25*They shall not make themselves unclean by coming near any dead person, unless it be their father, mother, son, daughter, brother, or maiden sister; for these they may make themselves unclean. **26**After a priest has been cleansed, he must wait an additional seven days, **27**and on the day he enters the inner court to minister in the sanctuary, he shall present his sin offering, says the Lord God. **28***They shall have no inheritance, for I am their inheritance; you shall give them no property in Israel, for I am their property. **29***†They shall eat the cereal offering, the sin offering, and the guilt offering; whatever is under the ban in Israel shall be theirs. **30***All the choicest first fruits of every kind, and all the best of your offerings of every kind, shall belong to the priests; likewise the best of your dough you shall give to the priests to bring a blessing down upon your house. **31***The priests shall not eat anything, whether flesh or fowl, that has died of itself or has been killed by wild beasts.

The Sacred Tract

45 **1**WHEN you apportion the land into inheritances, you shall set apart a sacred tract of land for the Lord, twenty-five thousand cubits long and twenty thousand wide; its whole area shall be sacred. **2**Of this land a square plot, five hundred by five hundred cubits, surrounded by a free space of fifty cubits, shall be assigned to the sanctuary. **3**Also from this sector measure off a strip, twenty-five thousand cubits long and ten thousand wide, within which shall be the sanctuary, the holy of holies. **4**This shall be the sacred part of the land belonging to the priests,

the ministers of the sanctuary, who draw near to minister to the Lord; it shall be a place for their homes and pasture land for their cattle. **5**Also there shall be a strip twenty-five thousand cubits long and ten thousand wide as property for the Levites, the ministers of the temple, that they may have cities to live in. **6**As property of the City you shall designate a strip five thousand cubits wide and twenty-five thousand long, parallel to the sacred tract; this shall belong to the whole house of Israel. **7**The prince shall have a section bordering on both sides of the combined sacred tract and City property, extending westward on the western side and eastward on the eastern side, corresponding in length to one of the tribal portions from the western boundary to the eastern boundary **8**of the land. This shall be his property in Israel, so that the princes of Israel will no longer oppress my people, but will leave the land to the house of Israel according to their tribes.

Weights and Measures

9†Thus says the Lord God: Enough, you princes of Israel! Put away violence and oppression, and do what is right and just! Stop evicting my people! says the Lord God. **10***You shall have honest scales, an honest ephah, and an honest liquid measure. **11**The ephah and the liquid measure shall be of the same size: the liquid measure equal to a tenth of a homer, and the ephah equal to a tenth of a homer; by the homer they shall be determined. **12***The shekel shall be twenty gerahs. Twenty shekels, twenty-five shekels, plus fifteen shekels shall be your mina.

Offerings

13These are the offerings you shall make: one sixth of an ephah from each homer of wheat, and one sixth of an ephah from each homer of barley. **14**†The regulation for oil: for every measure of oil, a tenth of a measure, computed by the kor of ten liquid measures [or a homer, for ten liquid measures make a homer]. **15**One sheep from the flock for every two hundred

---

† 44, 19: *Thus they will not transmit holiness to the people:* holiness was thought of as something physical, as though it were communicable, and therefore not to be brought in contact with unconsecrated persons.

44, 29: *Under the ban:* dedicated to the Lord, withdrawn from profane use.

45, 9-12: Besides the land monopoly fostered by royal greed and collusion with the wealthy (Mi 2, 2; Is 3, 12-15; 5, 8-10), one grave social evil of preexilic Israel was dishonesty in business; cf Hos 12, 8; Am 8, 5. *Ephah:* a dry measure; *liquid measure:* in Hebrew "a bath," standardized according to the *homer* (a dry measure of about 10 bushels, or 80 gallons). In v 12 reference is made to the change in value of the *mina:* before the exile it was valued at 50 shekels, but afterward, in imitation of Babylonian practice, the 60-shekel mina was adopted. The shekel was a unit of weight slightly less than half an ounce. As a monetary unit, the value obviously differed greatly, depending on whether it was a gold or a silver shekel.

45, 14: *Kor:* both a liquid and a dry measure, corresponding to the homer.

---

*
19: 42, 13.14.
20: Lv 21, 5.
21: Lv 10, 9.
22: Lv 21, 7.14.
24: Dt 17, 9; 19, 17.
25: Lv 21, 1ff.11.
28: Nm 18, 20; Dt 18, 1.
29: Lv 2, 3.10; 6, 9.22; 7, 9; 10, 12; Nm 18, 9; 18, 14.

30: Ex 34, 26; Dt 18, 4.
31: Lv 22, 8.
45/10: Lv 19, 35; Dt 25, 13-16; Hos 12, 8; Am 8, 5; Mi 6, 10f.
12: Ex 30, 13; Lv 27, 25; Nm 3, 47; 18, 16.

from the pasturage of Israel, for sacrifice—holocausts and peace offerings and atonement sacrifices, says the Lord God. [16]All the people of the land shall be bound to this offering [for the prince in Israel]. [17]It shall be the duty of the prince to provide the holocausts, cereal offerings, and libations on the feasts, new moons, and sabbaths, on all the festivals of the house of Israel. He shall offer the sin offerings, cereal offerings, holocausts, and peace offerings, to make atonement on behalf of the house of Israel.

The Passover

[18]Thus says the Lord God: On the first day of the first month you shall use an unblemished young bull as a sacrifice to purify the sanctuary. [19]Then the priest shall take some of the blood from the sin offering and put it on the doorposts of the temple, on the four corners of the ledge of the altar, and on the doorposts of the gates of the inner court. [20]You shall repeat this on the first day of the seventh month for those who have sinned through inadvertence or ignorance; thus you shall make atonement for the temple. [21]*On the fourteenth day of the first month you shall observe the feast of the Passover; for seven days unleavened bread is to be eaten. [22]On that day the prince shall offer on his own behalf, and on behalf of all the people of the land, a bull as a sin offering. [23]On each of the seven days of the feast he shall offer as a holocaust to the Lord seven bulls and seven rams without blemish, and as a sin offering he shall offer one male goat each day. [24]†As a cereal offering he shall offer one ephah for each bull and one ephah for each ram; and he shall offer one hin of oil for each ephah.

The Feast of Booths

[25]On the fifteenth day of the seventh month, the feast day, and for seven days, he shall perform the same rites, making the same sin offerings, the same holocausts, the same cereal offerings and offerings of oil.

Sabbaths

46 [1]THUS says the Lord God: The gate toward the east of the inner court shall remain closed throughout the six working days, but on the sabbath and on the day of the new moon it shall be open. [2]The prince shall enter from outside by way of the vestibule of the gate and remain standing at the doorpost of the gate; then while the priests offer his holocausts and peace offerings, he shall worship at the threshold of the gate and then leave; the gate shall not be closed until evening. [3]The people of the land shall worship before the Lord at the door of this gate on the sabbaths and new moons. [4]*The holocausts which the prince presents to the Lord on the sabbath shall consist of six unblemished lambs and an unblemished ram, [5]together with a cereal offering of one ephah for the ram, whatever he pleases for the lambs, and a hin of oil for each ephah. [6]*On the day of the new moon he shall provide an unblemished young bull, also six lambs and a ram without blemish, [7]with a cereal offering of one ephah for the bull and one for the ram, for the lambs as much as he has at hand, and for each ephah a hin of oil.

Ritual Laws

[8]The prince shall always enter and depart by the vestibule of the gate. [9]*When the people of the land enter the presence of the Lord to worship on the festivals, if they enter by the north gate they shall leave by the south gate, and if they enter by the south gate they shall leave by the north gate; no one shall return by the gate through which he has entered, but he shall leave by the opposite gate. [10]The prince shall be in their midst when they enter, and he shall also leave with them. [11]On the feasts and festivals the cereal offering shall be an ephah for a bull, an ephah for a ram, but for the lambs as much as one pleases, and a hin of oil with each ephah. [12]When the prince makes a freewill offering to the Lord, whether holocausts or peace offerings, the eastern gate shall be opened for him, and he shall offer his holocausts or his peace offerings as on the sabbath; then he shall leave, and the gate shall be closed after his departure. [13]*He shall offer as a daily holocaust to the Lord an unblemished yearling lamb; this he shall offer every morning. [14]With it every morning he shall provide as a cereal offering one sixth of an ephah, with a third of a hin of oil to moisten the fine flour. This cereal offering to the Lord is mandatory with the established holocaust. [15]*The lamb, the cereal offering, and the oil are to be offered every morning as an established holocaust.

The Prince and the Land

[16]Thus says the Lord God: If the prince makes a gift of part of his inheritance to any of his sons, it shall belong to his sons; that property is theirs by inheritance. [17]†But if he makes a gift of part of his inheritance to one of his servants, it shall belong to the latter only until the year of release, when it shall revert to the prince. Only the inheritance given to his sons is permanent. [18]The prince shall not seize any part of the inheritance of the people by evicting them from their property. He shall provide an inheritance for his sons from his own property, so that none of my people will be driven from their property.

The Temple Kitchens

[19]Then he brought me by the entrance which is on the side of the gate to the chambers [of the sanctuary, reserved to the priests] which face the north.

---

*
21: Ex 12, 6; Lv 23, 5; Nm 28, 16.	9: Ex 23, 17; 34, 23; Dt 16, 16.
46/4: Nm 28, 9f.	13: Ex 29, 38-42; Nm 28, 3-8.
6: Nm 28, 11-15.	15: Ex 29, 42.

---

† 45, 24: *Hin:* a sixth part of the liquid measure called a bath.
46, 17: *The year of release:* the jubilee year; cf Lv 25, 23-55.

There, at their west end, I saw a place, **20**concerning which he said to me, "Here the priests cook the guilt offerings and the sin offerings, and bake the cereal offerings, so that they do not have to take them into the outer court at the risk of transmitting holiness to the people." **21**Then he led me into the outer court and had me pass around the four corners of the court, and I saw that in each corner there was another court: **22**in the four corners of the court, minor courts, forty cubits long and thirty wide, all four of them the same size. **23**A wall of stones surrounded each of the four, and hearths were built beneath the stones all the way around. **24**He said to me, "These are the kitchens where the temple ministers cook the sacrifices of the people."

The Wonderful Stream

47 **1*†**THEN he brought me back to the entrance of the temple, and I saw water flowing out from beneath the threshold of the temple toward the east, for the façade of the temple was toward the east; the water flowed down from the southern side of the temple, south of the altar. **2**He led me outside by the north gate, and around to the outer gate facing the east, where I saw water trickling from the southern side. **3**Then when he had walked off to the east with a measuring cord in his hand, he measured off a thousand cubits and had me wade through the water, which was ankle-deep. **4**He measured off another thousand and once more had me wade through the water, which was now knee-deep. Again he measured off a thousand and had me wade; the water was up to my waist. **5**Once more he measured off a thousand, but there was now a river through which I could not wade; for the water had risen so high it had become a river that could not be crossed except by swimming. **6**He asked me, "Have you seen this, son of man?" Then he brought me to the bank of the river, where he had me sit. **7**Along the bank of the river I saw very many trees on both sides. **8**He said to me, "This water flows into the eastern district down upon the Arabah, and empties into the sea, the salt waters, which it makes fresh. **9**Wherever the river flows, every sort of living creature that can multiply shall live, and there shall be abundant fish, for wherever this water comes the sea shall be made fresh. **10†**Fishermen shall be standing along it from En-gedi to En-eglaim, spreading their nets there. Its kinds of fish shall be like those of the Great Sea, very numerous. **11**Only its marshes and swamps shall not be made fresh; they shall be left for salt. **12**Along both banks of the river, fruit trees of every kind shall grow; their leaves shall not fade, nor their fruit fail. Every month they shall bear fresh fruit, for they shall be watered by the flow from the sanctuary. Their fruit shall serve for food, and their leaves for medicine."

Boundaries of the Land

13†Thus says the Lord GOD: These are the boundaries within which you shall apportion the land among the twelve tribes of Israel [Joseph having two portions]. **14**All of you shall have a like portion in this land which I swore to give to your fathers, that it might fall to you as your inheritance. **15***This is the boundary of the land on the north side: from the Great Sea in the direction of Hethlon, past Labo of Hamath, to Zedad, **16**Berothah, and Sibraim, along the frontiers of Hamath and Damascus, to Hazar-enon which is on the border of the Hauran. **17**Thus the border shall extend from the sea to Hazar-enon, with the frontier of Hamath and Damascus to the north. This is the northern boundary. **18**The eastern boundary: between the Hauran—toward Damascus—and Gilead on the one side, and the land of Israel on the other side, the Jordan shall form the boundary down to the eastern sea as far as Tamar. This is the eastern boundary. **19**The southern boundary: from Tamar to the waters of Meribath-kadesh, thence to the Wadi of Egypt, and on to the Great Sea. This is the southern boundary. **20**The western boundary: the Great Sea forms the boundary up to a point parallel to Labo of Hamath. This is the western boundary.

The Northern Portions

21You shall distribute this land among yourselves according to the tribes of Israel. **22***You shall allot it as inheritances for yourselves and for the aliens resident in your midst who have bred children among you. The latter shall be to you like native Israelites; along with you they shall receive inheritances among the tribes of Israel. **23**In whatever tribe the alien may be resident, there you shall assign him his inheritance, says the Lord GOD.

48 **1*†**THIS is the list of the tribes. Dan: at the northern extremity, adjoining Hamath, all along from the approaches to Hethlon through Labo of Hamath to Hazar-enon, on the northerly border with Damascus, with his possession reaching from the eastern to the western boundary. **2**Asher: on the

---

† 47, 1-12: The wonderful and superabundant stream flowing from the temple, restoring to fertility traditionally arid ground, is symbolic of the return of the conditions of primeval paradise; cf Gn 2, 10-14. Water signifies great blessings, just as dryness signifies a curse; cf 26, 5.14.

47, 10: *From En-gedi to En-eglaim:* the former was about halfway down the western shore of the Dead Sea, the latter may have been at its northern extremity.

47, 13-20: These boundaries of the restored Israel correspond to those of the Davidic kingdom at its fullest extent, the so-called "ideal boundaries" of the promised land; cf Nm 34, 3-12.

48, 1-29: This distribution of the land among the tribes does not correspond to the geographical realities of Palestine. It is a description of the ideal order, like that in 47, 1-12.

❋　47/1: Sir 24, 28f; Jl 4, 18;
　　　　Zec 13, 1; Rv 22, 1f.
　　　15: Nm 34, 7ff.
　　　　　　　　22: Ex 12, 48; Lv 19, 34;
　　　　　　　　　　24, 22; Nm 9, 14; Jos
　　　　　　　　　　8, 33.
　　　　　　　48/1: 47, 15ff.

frontier of Dan, from the eastern to the western boundary. ³Naphtali: on the frontier of Asher, from the eastern to the western boundary. ⁴Manasseh: on the frontier of Naphtali, from the eastern to the western boundary. ⁵Ephraim: on the frontier of Manasseh, from the eastern to the western boundary. ⁶Reuben: on the frontier of Ephraim, from the eastern to the western boundary. ⁷Judah: on the frontier of Reuben, from the eastern to the western boundary.

The Sacred Tract

⁸On the frontier of Judah, from the eastern to the western boundary there shall be the tract which you shall set apart, twenty-five thousand cubits from north to south, and as wide as one of the tribal portions from the eastern to the western boundary. In the center of the tract shall be the sanctuary. ⁹The tract that you set aside for the LORD shall be twenty-five thousand cubits across by twenty thousand north and south. ¹⁰In this sacred tract the priests shall have twenty-five thousand cubits on the north, ten thousand on the west, ten thousand on the east, and twenty-five thousand on the south; and the sanctuary of the LORD shall be in its center. ¹¹The consecrated priests, the Zadokites, who fulfilled my service and did not stray along with the Israelites as the Levites did, ¹²shall have within this tract of land their own most sacred domain, next to the territory of the Levites. The Levites shall have a territory corresponding to that of the priests, twenty-five thousand cubits by ten thousand. The whole tract shall be twenty-five thousand cubits across and twenty thousand north and south. ¹⁴They may not sell or exchange or alienate this, the best part of the land, for it is sacred to the LORD. ¹⁵The remaining five thousand cubits along the twenty-five-thousand-cubit line are profane land, assigned to the City for dwellings and pasture; the City shall be at their center. ¹⁶These are the dimensions of the City: the north side, forty-five hundred cubits; the south side, forty-five hundred cubits; the east side, forty-five hundred cubits; and the west side, forty-five hundred cubits. ¹⁷The pasture lands of the City shall extend north two hundred and fifty cubits, south two hundred and fifty cubits, east two hundred and fifty cubits, and west two hundred and fifty cubits. ¹⁸There shall remain an area along the sacred tract, ten thousand cubits to the east and ten thousand to the west, whose produce shall provide food for the workers of the City. ¹⁹The workers in the City shall be taken from all the tribes of Israel. ²⁰The entire tract shall be twenty-five thousand by twenty-five thousand cubits; as a perfect square you shall set apart the sacred tract together with the City property.

²¹The remainder shall belong to the prince: the land on both sides of the sacred tract and the City property, extending along the twenty-five-thousand-cubit line eastward to the eastern boundary, and westward along the twenty-five-thousand-cubit line to the western boundary, a territory parallel with the tribal portions for the prince. The sacred tract and the sanctuary of the temple shall be in the middle. ²²Thus, except for the property of the Levites and the City property, which lie in the midst of the prince's property, the territory between the portions of Judah and of Benjamin shall belong to the prince.

The Southern Portions

²³These are the remaining tribes. Benjamin: from the eastern to the western boundary. ²⁴Simeon: on the frontier of Benjamin, from the eastern to the western boundary. ²⁵Issachar: on the frontier of Simeon, from the eastern to the western boundary. ²⁶Zebulun: on the frontier of Issachar, from the eastern to the western boundary. ²⁷Gad: on the frontier of Zebulun, from the eastern to the western boundary. ²⁸Along the frontier of Gad shall be the southern boundary, which shall extend from Tamar to the waters of Meribath-kadesh, and from there to the Wadi of Egypt, and on to the Great Sea. ²⁹Such is the land which you shall apportion as inheritances among the tribes of Israel, and these are their portions, says the Lord GOD.

The Gates of the City

³⁰These are the exits of the City, the gates of which are named after the tribes of Israel. On the north side, measuring forty-five hundred cubits, ³¹there shall be three gates: the gate of Reuben, the gate of Judah, and the gate of Levi. ³²On the east side, measuring forty-five hundred cubits, there shall be three gates: the gate of Joseph, the gate of Benjamin, and the gate of Dan. ³³On the south side, measuring forty-five hundred cubits, there shall be three gates: the gate of Simeon, the gate of Issachar, and the gate of Zebulun. ³⁴On the west side, measuring forty-five hundred cubits, there shall be three gates: the gate of Gad, the gate of Asher, and the gate of Naphtali. ³⁵The perimeter of the City is eighteen thousand cubits. The name of the City shall henceforth be "The LORD is here."

The Book of Daniel

Introduction

This Book takes its name, not from the author, who is actually unknown, but from its hero, a young Jew taken early to Babylon, where he lived at least until 538 B. C. Strictly speaking, the book does not belong to the prophetic writings but rather to a distinctive type of literature known as "apocalyptic," of which it is an early specimen. Apocalyptic writing enjoyed its greatest popularity from 200 B. C. to 100 A. D., a time of distress and persecution for Jews, and later, for Christians. Though subsequent in time to the prophetic, apocalyptic literature has its roots in the teaching of the prophets, who often pointed ahead to the day of the Lord, the consummation of history. For both prophet and apocalyptist Yahweh was the Lord of history, and he would ultimately vindicate his people.

This work was composed during the bitter persecution carried on by Antiochus IV Epiphanes (167-164) and was written to strengthen and comfort the Jewish people in their ordeal.

The Book contains stories originating in and transmitted by popular traditions which tell of the trials and triumphs of the wise Daniel and his three companions. The moral is that men of faith can resist temptation and conquer adversity. The characters are not purely legendary but rest on older historical tradition. What is more important than the question of historicity, and closer to the intention of the author, is the fact that a persecuted Jew of the second century B. C. would quickly see the application of these stories to his own plight.

There follows a series of visions promising deliverance and glory to the Jews in the days to come. The great nations of the ancient world have risen in vain against Yahweh; his kingdom shall overthrow existing powers and last forever. Under this apocalyptic imagery are contained some of the best elements of prophetic teaching: the insistence on right conduct, the divine control over events, the certainty that the kingdom of God will ultimately triumph. The arrival of the kingdom is a central theme of the synoptic gospels, and Jesus, in calling himself the "Son of Man," reminds us that he fulfills the destiny of this mysterious figure in the seventh chapter of Daniel. The added episodes of Susanna, Bel, and the Dragon, found only in the Greek version, are edifying short stories with a didactic purpose.

These three sections constitute the divisions of the Book of Daniel:

I: DANIEL AND THE KINGS OF BABYLON

The Food Test

1 **1***IN THE THIRD YEAR of the reign of Jehoiakim, king of Judah, King Nebuchadnezzar of Babylon came and laid siege to Jerusalem. **2***†The Lord handed over to him Jehoiakim, king of Judah, and some of the vessels of the temple of God, which he carried off to the land of Shinar, and placed in the temple treasury of his god.

3The king told Ashpenaz, his chief chamberlain, to bring in some of the Israelites of royal blood and of the nobility, **4**young men without any defect, handsome, intelligent and wise, quick to learn, and prudent in judgment, such as could take their place in the king's palace; they were to be taught the language and literature of the Chaldeans; **5**after three years' training they were to enter the king's service. The king allotted them a daily portion of food and wine from the royal table. **6**Among these were men of Judah: Daniel, Hananiah, Mishael, and Azariah. **7**†The chief chamberlain changed their names: Daniel to Belteshazzar, Hananiah to Shadrach, Mishael to Meshach, and Azariah to Abednego.

8†But Daniel was resolved not to defile himself with the king's food or wine; so he begged the chief chamberlain to spare him this defilement. **9**Though God had given Daniel the favor and sympathy of the chief chamberlain, **10**he nevertheless said to Daniel, "I am afraid of my lord the king; it is he who allotted your food and drink. If he sees that you look wretched by comparison with the other young men of your age, you will endanger my life with the king." **11**Then Daniel said to the steward whom the chief chamber-

---

† 1, 2: *Shinar:* ancient name for Babylonia, a deliberate archaism in this text; cf Gn 10, 10; 11, 2.

1, 7: The young men are given Babylonian names as a sign of their adoption by the king.

1, 8: *This defilement:* the bread, meat, and wine of the Gentiles, which were unclean (Hos 9, 3; Tb 1, 12; Jdt 10, 5; 12, 1f) because they might have been offered to idols or prepared over firewood taken from a sacred grove. Only raw vegetables and water were safe from this danger (v 12).

❁
  1/1: 2 Kgs 24, 1;   2: 5, 2; Gn 10, 10;
    2 Chr 36, 6; Jer 25, 1.   2 Kgs 24, 2;
                         2 Chr 36, 7.

lain had put in charge of Daniel, Hananiah, Mishael, and Azariah, [12]"Please test your servants for ten days. Give us vegetables to eat and water to drink. [13]Then see how we look in comparison with the other young men who eat from the royal table, and treat your servants according to what you see." [14]He acceded to this request, and tested them for ten days; [15]after ten days they looked healthier and better fed than any of the young men who ate from the royal table. [16]So the steward continued to take away the food and wine they were to receive, and gave them vegetables.

[17]To these four young men God gave knowledge and proficiency in all literature and science, and to Daniel the understanding of all visions and dreams. [18]At the end of the time the king had specified for their preparation, the chief chamberlain brought them before Nebuchadnezzar. [19]When the king had spoken with all of them, none was found equal to Daniel, Hananiah, Mishael, and Azariah; and so they entered the king's service. [20]In any question of wisdom or prudence which the king put to them, he found them ten times better than all the magicians and enchanters in his kingdom. [21]*†Daniel remained there until the first year of King Cyrus.

The King's Dream

2 [1]†IN the second year of his reign, King Nebuchadnezzar had a dream which left his spirit no rest and robbed him of his sleep. [2]†So he ordered that the magicians, enchanters, sorcerers, and Chaldeans be summoned to interpret the dream for him. When they came and presented themselves to the king, [3]he said to them, "I had a dream which will allow my spirit no rest until I know what it means." [4]†The Chaldeans answered the king [Aramaic]: "O king, live forever! Tell your servants the dream and we will give its meaning." [5]The king answered the Chaldeans, "This is what I have decided: unless you tell me the dream and its meaning, you shall be cut to pieces and your houses destroyed. [6]But if you tell me the dream and its meaning, you shall receive from me gifts and presents and great honors. Now tell me the dream and its meaning."

[7]Again they answered, "Let the king tell his servants the dream and we will give its meaning." [8]But the king replied: "I know for certain that you are bargaining for time, since you know what I have decided. [9]If you do not tell me the dream, there can be but one decree for you. You have framed a false and deceitful interpretation to present me with till the crisis is past. Tell me the dream, therefore, that I may be sure that you can also give its correct interpretation."

[10]The Chaldeans answered the king: "There is not a man on earth who can do what you ask, O king; never has any king, however great and mighty, asked such a thing of any magician, enchanter, or Chaldean.

[11]What you demand, O king, is too difficult; there is no one who can tell it to the king except the gods who do not dwell among men." [12]At this the king became violently angry and ordered all the wise men of Babylon to be put to death. [13]When the decree was issued that the wise men should be slain, Daniel and his companions were also sought out.

[14]Then Daniel prudently took counsel with Arioch, the captain of the king's guard, who had set out to kill the wise men of Babylon: [15]"O officer of the king," he asked, "what is the reason for this harsh order from the king?" When Arioch told him, [16]Daniel went and asked for time from the king, that he might give him the interpretation.

[17]Daniel went home and informed his companions Hananiah, Mishael, and Azariah, [18]that they might implore the mercy of the God of heaven in regard to this mystery, so that Daniel and his companions might not perish with the rest of the wise men of Babylon. [19]During the night the mystery was revealed to Daniel in a vision, and he blessed the God of heaven:

[20]   "Blessed be the name of God forever and ever,
       for wisdom and power are his.
[21]   He causes the changes of the times and seasons,
       makes kings and unmakes them.
     He gives wisdom to the wise
       and knowledge to those who understand.
[22]*   He reveals deep and hidden things
       and knows what is in the darkness,
       for the light dwells with him.
[23]   To you, O God of my fathers,
       I give thanks and praise,
       because you have given me wisdom and power.
     Now you have shown me what we asked of you,
       you have made known to us the king's dream."

[24]So Daniel went to Arioch, whom the king had appointed to destroy the wise men of Babylon, and said to him, "Do not put the wise men of Babylon to death. Bring me before the king, and I will tell him the interpretation of the dream." Arioch quickly brought Daniel to the king and said, [25]"I have found a man among the Judean captives who can give the interpre-

---

† 1, 21: *The first year of King Cyrus:* the year of this Persian king's conquest of Babylon, 539/8 B. C.

2, 1-49: The chronology of v 1 is in conflict with that of 1, 5.18, and in v 25 Daniel appears to be introduced to the king for the first time. It seems that the story of this chapter was originally entirely independent of chapter 1, and later retouched slightly to fit its present setting.

2, 2: *Chaldeans:* here probably astrologers, who were so associated with the Chaldeans in the Hebrew mind that in the later language they are sometimes simply called by the name of that people.

2, 4: *Aramaic:* from 2, 4 to 7, 28 the text of Daniel is in Aramaic, not Hebrew, as indicated by this gloss.

---

* 21: 6, 28.   2/22: Jn 1, 9; 8, 12; 1 Cor 4, 5; 1 Jn 1, 6.

tation to the king." ²⁶The king asked Daniel, whose name was Belteshazzar, "Can you tell me the dream that I had, and its meaning?" ²⁷In the king's presence Daniel made this reply:

"The mystery about which the king has inquired, the wise men, enchanters, magicians, and astrologers could not explain to the king. ²⁸But there is a God in heaven who reveals mysteries, and he has shown King Nebuchadnezzar what is to happen in days to come; this was the dream you saw as you lay in bed. ²⁹To you in your bed there came thoughts about what should happen in the future, and he who reveals mysteries showed you what is to be. ³⁰To me also this mystery has been revealed; not that I am wiser than any other living person, but in order that its meaning may be made known to the king, that you may understand the thoughts in your own mind.

³¹"In your vision, O king, you saw a statue, very large and exceedingly bright, terrifying in appearance as it stood before you. ³²The head of the statue was pure gold, its chest and arms were silver, its belly and thighs bronze, ³³†the legs iron, its feet partly iron and partly tile. ³⁴While you looked at the statue, a stone which was hewn from a mountain without a hand being put to it, struck its iron and tile feet, breaking them in pieces. ³⁵The iron, tile, bronze, silver, and gold all crumbled at once, fine as the chaff on the threshing floor in summer, and the wind blew them away without leaving a trace. But the stone that struck the statue became a great mountain and filled the whole earth.

³⁶†"This was the dream; the interpretation we shall also give in the king's presence. ³⁷You, O king, are the king of kings; to you the God of heaven has given dominion and strength, power and glory; ³⁸men, wild beasts, and birds of the air, wherever they may dwell, he has handed over to you, making you ruler over them all; you are the head of gold. ³⁹Another kingdom shall take your place, inferior to yours, then a third kingdom, of bronze, which shall rule over the whole earth. ⁴⁰There shall be a fourth kingdom, strong as iron; it shall break in pieces and subdue all these others, just as iron breaks in pieces and crushes everything else. ⁴¹The feet and toes you saw, partly of potter's tile and partly of iron, mean that it shall be a divided kingdom, but yet have some of the hardness of iron. As you saw the iron mixed with clay tile, ⁴²and the toes partly iron and partly tile, the kingdom shall be partly strong and partly fragile. ⁴³The iron mixed with clay tile means that they shall seal their alliances by intermarriage, but they shall not stay united, any more than iron mixes with clay. ⁴⁴*In the lifetime of those kings the God of heaven will set up a kingdom that shall never be destroyed or delivered up to another people; rather, it shall break in pieces all these kingdoms and put an end to them, and it shall stand forever. ⁴⁵That is the meaning of the stone you saw hewn from the mountain without a hand being put to

it, which broke in pieces the tile, iron, bronze, silver, and gold. The great God has revealed to the king what shall be in the future; this is exactly what you dreamed, and its meaning is sure."

⁴⁶Then King Nebuchadnezzar fell down and worshiped Daniel and ordered sacrifice and incense offered to him. ⁴⁷To Daniel the king said, "Truly your God is the God of gods and Lord of kings and a revealer of mysteries; that is why you were able to reveal this mystery." ⁴⁸He advanced Daniel to a high post, gave him many generous presents, made him ruler of the whole province of Babylon and chief prefect over all the wise men of Babylon. ⁴⁹At Daniel's request the king made Shadrach, Meshach, and Abednego administrators of the province of Babylon, while Daniel himself remained at the king's court.

The Fiery Furnace

3 ¹†KING Nebuchadnezzar had a golden statue made, sixty cubits high and six cubits wide, which he set up in the plain of Dura in the province of Babylon. ²†He then ordered the satraps, prefects, and governors, the counselors, treasurers, judges, magistrates and all the officials of the provinces to be summoned to the dedication of the statue which he had set up. ³The satraps, prefects, and governors, the counselors, treasurers, judges, and magistrates and all the officials of the provinces, all these came together for the dedication and stood before the statue which King Nebuchadnezzar had set up. ⁴†A herald cried out: "Nations and peoples of every language, when you hear the sound of the trumpet, flute, lyre, harp, psaltery, bagpipe, and all the other musical instruments, ⁵you are ordered to fall down and worship the golden statue which King Nebuchadnezzar has set up. ⁶†Whoever does not fall down and worship shall be instantly cast into a white-hot furnace." ⁷Therefore, as soon as they heard the sound of the trumpet, flute, lyre, harp, psaltery, bagpipe, and all the other musical instruments, the nations and peoples of every language all fell down and worshiped the golden statue which King Nebuchadnezzar had set up.

---

† 2, 33: *Partly tile:* terra cotta tile was much in use among the Babylonians for decoration and for actual construction.

2, 36-45: The four successive kingdoms in this apocalyptic perspective are the Babylonian (gold), the Median (silver), the Persian (bronze), and the Hellenistic (iron). The last, after Alexander's death, was divided among his generals (vv 41f). The two resulting kingdoms, which most affected the Jews, were the dynasty of the Ptolemies in Egypt and that of the Seleucids in Syria, who tried in vain, by war and through intermarriage, to restore the unity of Alexander's empire (v 43). The stone hewn from the mountain is the messianic kingdom awaited by the Jews (vv 44f). Our Lord made this image personal to himself; cf Lk 20, 17f.

3, 1: *Dura:* several places in Babylonia bore this name. Probably the present reference is to one a few miles south of Babylon. Colossi of the type mentioned here were not uncommon in antiquity; a cubit was seventeen and a half inches.

3, 2: *Satraps:* the Persian major governors.

3, 4: *Psaltery:* a harplike instrument.

3, 6: Death by fire was not unknown as a punishment in Babylonia; cf Jer 29, 22.

---

* 44: Mt 21, 44; Lk 20, 18.

8At that point, some of the Chaldeans came and accused the Jews **9**to King Nebuchadnezzar: "O king, live forever! **10**O king, you issued a decree that everyone who heard the sound of the trumpet, flute, lyre, harp, psaltery, bagpipe, and all the other musical instruments should fall down and worship the golden statue; **11**whoever did not was to be cast into a white-hot furnace. **12**There are certain Jews whom you have made administrators of the province of Babylon: Shadrach, Meshach, Abednego; these men, O king, have paid no attention to you; they will not serve your god or worship the golden statue which you set up."

13Nebuchadnezzar flew into a rage and sent for Shadrach, Meshach, and Abednego, who were promptly brought before the king. **14**King Nebuchadnezzar questioned them: "Is it true, Shadrach, Meshach, and Abednego, that you will not serve my god, or worship the golden statue that I set up? **15**Be ready now to fall down and worship the statue I had made, whenever you hear the sound of the trumpet, flute, lyre, harp, psaltery, bagpipe, and all the other musical instruments; otherwise, you shall be instantly cast into the white-hot furnace; and who is the God that can deliver you out of my hands?" **16**Shadrach, Meshach, and Abednego answered King Nebuchadnezzar, "There is no need for us to defend ourselves before you in this matter. **17†**If our God, whom we serve, can save us from the white-hot furnace and from your hands, **18**O king, may he save us! But even if he will not, know, O king, that we will not serve your god or worship the golden statue which you set up."

19Nebuchadnezzar's face became livid with utter rage against Shadrach, Meshach, and Abednego. He ordered the furnace to be heated seven times more than usual **20**and had some of the strongest men in his army bind Shadrach, Meshach, and Abednego and cast them into the white-hot furnace. **21**They were bound and cast into the white-hot furnace with their coats, hats, shoes and other garments, **22**for the king's order was urgent. So huge a fire was kindled in the furnace that the flames devoured the men who threw Shadrach, Meshach, and Abednego into it. **23**But these three fell, bound, into the midst of the white-hot furnace.

24†They walked about in the flames, singing to God and blessing the Lord. **25**In the fire Azariah stood up and prayed aloud:

26   "Blessed are you, and praiseworthy,
      O Lord, the God of our fathers,
      and glorious forever is your name.

27   For you are just in all you have done;
      all your deeds are faultless, all your ways
        right,
      and all your judgments proper.

28   You have executed proper judgments
      in all that you have brought upon us
      and upon Jerusalem, the holy city of our
        fathers.

      By a proper judgment you have done all
        this
      because of our sins;

29   For we have sinned and transgressed
      by departing from you,
      and we have done every kind of evil.

30   Your commandments we have not heeded
        or observed,
      nor have we done as you ordered us for
        our good.

31   Therefore all you have brought upon us,
      all you have done to us,
      you have done by a proper judgment.

32   You have handed us over to our enemies,
      lawless and hateful rebels;
      to an unjust king, the worst in all the
        world.

33   Now we cannot open our mouths;
      we, your servants, who revere you,
      have become a shame and a reproach.

34   For your name's sake, do not deliver us up
        forever,
      or make void your covenant.

35   Do not take away your mercy from us,
      for the sake of Abraham, your beloved,
      Isaac your servant, and Israel your holy
        one,

36   To whom you promised to multiply their
        offspring
      like the stars of heaven,
      or the sand on the shore of the sea.

37   For we are reduced, O Lord, beyond any
        other nation,
      brought low everywhere in the world
        this day
      because of our sins.

38   We have in our day no prince, prophet, or
        leader,
      no holocaust, sacrifice, oblation, or
        incense,
      no place to offer first fruits, to find favor
        with you.

39   But with contrite heart and humble spirit
      let us be received;

40   As though it were holocausts of rams and
        bullocks,
      or thousands of fat lambs,
      So let our sacrifice be in your presence
        today
      as we follow you unreservedly;
      for those who trust in you cannot be put
        to shame.

---

† 3, 17: *If our God . . . can save us:* the youths do not question the efficacy of the divine power, but whether it will be exercised (v 18).

  3, 24-90: These verses are inspired additions to the Aramaic text of Daniel, translated from the Greek form of the book. They were originally composed in Hebrew or Aramaic, which has not been preserved. The church has always regarded them as part of the canonical Scriptures.

41 And now we follow you with our whole
heart,
     we fear you and we pray to you.
42 Do not let us be put to shame,
     but deal with us in your kindness and
     great mercy.
43 Deliver us by your wonders,
     and bring glory to your name, O Lord:
44 Let all those be routed
     who inflict evils on your servants;
     Let them be shamed and powerless,
     and their strength broken;
45 Let them know that you alone are the
     Lord God,
     glorious over the whole world."

46Now the king's men who had thrown them in continued to stoke the furnace with brimstone, pitch, tow, and faggots. 47The flames rose forty-nine cubits above the furnace, 48and spread out, burning the Chaldeans nearby. 49But the angel of the Lord went down into the furnace with Azariah and his companions, drove the fiery flames out of the furnace, 50and made the inside of the furnace as though a dew-laden breeze were blowing through it. The fire in no way touched them or caused them pain or harm. 51Then these three in the furnace with one voice sang, glorifying and blessing God:

52 "Blessed are you, O Lord, the God of our
fathers,
     praiseworthy and exalted above all
     forever;
     And blessed is your holy and glorious
     name,
     praiseworthy and exalted above all for
     all ages.
53 Blessed are you in the temple of your holy
glory,
     praiseworthy and glorious above all
     forever.
54 Blessed are you on the throne of your
kingdom,
     praiseworthy and exalted above all
     forever.
55 Blessed are you who look into the depths
     from your throne upon the cherubim,
     praiseworthy and exalted above all
     forever.
56 Blessed are you in the firmament of
heaven,
     praiseworthy and glorious forever.
57 Bless the Lord, all you works of the Lord,
     praise and exalt him above all forever.
58 Angels of the Lord, bless the Lord,
     praise and exalt him above all forever.
59* You heavens, bless the Lord,
     praise and exalt him above all forever.

60 All you waters above the heavens, bless the
Lord,
     praise and exalt him above all forever.
61 All you hosts of the Lord, bless the Lord;
     praise and exalt him above all forever.
62 Sun and moon, bless the Lord;
     praise and exalt him above all forever.
63 Stars of heaven, bless the Lord;
     praise and exalt him above all forever.
64 Every shower and dew, bless the Lord;
     praise and exalt him above all forever.
65 All you winds, bless the Lord;
     praise and exalt him above all forever.
66 Fire and heat, bless the Lord;
     praise and exalt him above all forever.
67 [Cold and chill, bless the Lord;
     praise and exalt him above all forever.
68 Dew and rain, bless the Lord;
     praise and exalt him above all forever.]
69 Frost and chill, bless the Lord;
     praise and exalt him above all forever.
70 Ice and snow, bless the Lord;
     praise and exalt him above all forever.
71 Nights and days, bless the Lord;
     praise and exalt him above all forever.
72 Light and darkness, bless the Lord;
     praise and exalt him above all forever.
73 Lightnings and clouds, bless the Lord;
     praise and exalt him above all forever.
74 Let the earth bless the Lord,
     praise and exalt him above all forever.
75 Mountains and hills, bless the Lord;
     praise and exalt him above all forever.
76 Everything growing from the earth, bless
     the Lord;
     praise and exalt him above all forever.
77 You springs, bless the Lord;
     praise and exalt him above all forever.
78 Seas and rivers, bless the Lord;
     praise and exalt him above all forever.
79 You dolphins and all water creatures, bless
     the Lord;
     praise and exalt him above all forever.
80 All you birds of the air, bless the Lord;
     praise and exalt him above all forever.
81 All you beasts, wild and tame, bless the
     Lord;
     praise and exalt him above all forever.
82 You sons of men, bless the Lord;
     praise and exalt him above all forever.
83 O Israel, bless the Lord;
     praise and exalt him above all forever.
84 Priests of the Lord, bless the Lord;
     praise and exalt him above all forever.
85 Servants of the Lord, bless the Lord;
     praise and exalt him above all forever.
86 Spirits and souls of the just, bless the Lord;
     praise and exalt him above all forever.
87 Holy men of humble heart, bless the Lord;
     praise and exalt him above all forever.

3/59f: Ps 148, 4.

⁸⁸ Hananiah, Azariah, Mishael, bless the Lord;
> praise and exalt him above all forever.
> For he has delivered us from the nether world,
> and saved us from the power of death;
> He has freed us from the raging flame
> and delivered us from the fire.

⁸⁹ Give thanks to the Lord, for he is good,
> for his mercy endures forever.

⁹⁰ Bless the God of gods, all you who fear the Lord;
> praise him and give him thanks,
> because his mercy endures forever."

Hearing them sing, and astonished at seeing them alive, ⁹¹King Nebuchadnezzar rose in haste and asked his nobles, "Did we not cast three men bound into the fire?" "Assuredly, O king," they answered. ⁹²†"But," he replied, "I see four men unfettered and unhurt, walking in the fire, and the fourth looks like a son of God." ⁹³Then Nebuchadnezzar came to the opening of the white-hot furnace and called to Shadrach, Meshach, and Abednego: "Servants of the most high God, come out." Thereupon Shadrach, Meshach, and Abednego came out of the fire. ⁹⁴When the satraps, prefects, governors, and nobles of the king came together, they saw that the fire had had no power over the bodies of these men; not a hair of their heads had been singed, nor were their garments altered; there was not even a smell of fire about them. ⁹⁵Nebuchadnezzar exclaimed, "Blessed be the God of Shadrach, Meshach, and Abednego, who sent his angel to deliver the servants that trusted in him; they disobeyed the royal command and yielded their bodies rather than serve or worship any god except their own God. ⁹⁶Therefore I decree for nations and peoples of every language that whoever blasphemes the God of Shadrach, Meshach, and Abednego shall be cut to pieces and his house destroyed. For there is no other God who can rescue like this." ⁹⁷Then the king promoted Shadrach, Meshach, and Abednego in the province of Babylon.

Vision of the Great Tree

⁹⁸†King Nebuchadnezzar to the nations and peoples of every language, wherever they dwell on earth: abundant peace! ⁹⁹†It has seemed good to me to publish the signs and wonders which the most high God has accomplished in my regard.

¹⁰⁰* How great are his signs, how mighty his wonders;
> his kingdom is an everlasting kingdom,
> and his dominion endures through all generations.

⁴ ¹I, Nebuchadnezzar, was at home in my palace, content and prosperous. ²I had a terrifying dream as I lay in bed, and the images and the visions of my mind frightened me. ³So I issued a decree that all the wise men of Babylon should be brought before me to give the interpretation of the dream. ⁴When the magicians, enchanters, Chaldeans, and astrologers had come in, I related the dream before them; but none of them could tell me its meaning. ⁵*†Finally there came before me Daniel, whose name is Belteshazzar after the name of my god, and in whom is the spirit of the holy God. I repeated the dream to him: ⁶"Belteshazzar, chief of the magicians, I know that the spirit of the holy God is in you and no mystery is too difficult for you; tell me the meaning of the visions that I saw in my dream.

⁷"These were the visions I saw while in bed: I saw a tree of great height at the center of the world. ⁸It was large and strong, with its top touching the heavens, and it could be seen to the ends of the earth. ⁹Its leaves were beautiful and its fruit abundant, providing food for all. Under it the wild beasts found shade, in its branches the birds of the air nested; all men ate of it. ¹⁰†In the vision I saw while in bed, a holy sentinel came down from heaven, ¹¹†and cried out:

> "'Cut down the tree and lop off its branches,
> strip off its leaves and scatter its fruit;
> let the beasts flee its shade, and the birds its branches.

¹² But leave in the earth its stump and roots,
> fettered with iron and bronze, in the grass of the field.
> Let him be bathed with the dew of heaven;
> his lot be to eat, among beasts, the grass of the earth.

¹³ Let his mind be changed from the human;
> let him be given the sense of a beast,
> till seven years pass over him.

¹⁴* By decree of the sentinels is this decided,
> by order of the holy ones, this sentence;

---

† 3, 92: *A son of God:* an angel; cf Jb 1, 6.

3, 98—4, 34: This section has the form of a letter written by Nebuchadnezzar to his subjects.

3, 99: *The most high God:* the Jews, especially in the diaspora, used this title to distinguish their God from those of the pagans. On the lips of a polytheist (so also in v 93) it was merely the title of another god. It was an ancient divine name used in Canaan; cf Gn 14, 18.

4, 5: *After the name of my god:* Belteshazzar, the Babylonian name given to Daniel at the king's orders (1, 7), is Balatsu-ussur, "protect his life." In the king's intention, this would be an abbreviation for *Bel-balatsu-ussur.* It would thus include an appeal to the god Bel, originally the name of the city god of Nippur, and later identified with Marduk, the chief god of Babylon. Daniel's use of the name would refer the prayer rather to the true God.

4, 10: *A holy sentinel:* an angel. This term is found in the Bible only in this chapter of Daniel, but it is common in later Jewish literature.

4, 11ff: As the tree is Nebuchadnezzar (v 19), the description passes from metaphor to the reality.

100: 4, 31; 7, 14.   14: 1 Sm 2, 8; 16, 11;
4/5: Gn 41, 38.   Is 62, 6.

That all who live may know
   that the Most High rules over the
      kingdom of men:
He can give it to whom he will,
   or set over it the lowliest of men.'

15"This is the dream that I, King Nebuchadnezzar, had. Now, Belteshazzar, tell me its meaning. Although none of the wise men in my kingdom can tell me the meaning, you can, because the spirit of the holy God is in you."

16Then Daniel, whose name was Belteshazzar, was appalled for a while, terrified by his thoughts. "Belteshazzar," the king said to him, "let not the dream or its meaning terrify you." **17**†"My lord," Belteshazzar replied, "this dream should be for your enemies, and its meaning for your foes. The large, strong tree that you saw, with its top touching the heavens, that could be seen by the whole earth, **18**which had beautiful foliage and abundant fruit, providing food for all, under which the wild beasts lived, and in whose branches the birds of the air dwelt—**19**you are that tree, O king, large and strong! Your majesty has become so great as to touch the heavens, and your rule extends over the whole earth. **20**As for the king's vision of a holy sentinel that came down from heaven and proclaimed: 'Cut down the tree and destroy it, but leave in the earth its stump and roots, fettered with iron and bronze in the grass of the field; let him be bathed with the dew of heaven, and let his lot be among wild beasts till seven years pass over him'—**21**this is its meaning, O king; this is the sentence which the Most High has passed upon my lord king: **22***†You shall be cast out from among men and dwell with wild beasts; you shall be given grass to eat like an ox and be bathed with the dew of heaven; seven years shall pass over you, until you know that the Most High rules over the kingdom of men and gives it to whom he will. **23**The command that the stump and roots of the tree are to be left means that your kingdom shall be preserved for you, once you have learned it is heaven that rules. **24***†Therefore, O king, take my advice; atone for your sins by good deeds, and for your misdeeds by kindness to the poor; then your prosperity will be long."

25All this happened to King Nebuchadnezzar. **26**Twelve months later, as he was walking on the roof of the royal palace in Babylon, **27**†the king said, "Babylon the great! Was it not I, with my great strength, who built it as a royal residence for my splendor and majesty?" **28**While these words were still on the king's lips, a voice spoke from heaven, "It has been decreed for you, King Nebuchadnezzar, that your kingdom is taken from you! **29**You shall be cast out from among men, and shall dwell with wild beasts; you shall be given grass to eat like an ox, and seven years shall pass over you, until you learn that the Most High rules over the kingdom of men and

gives it to whom he will." **30**†At once this was fulfilled. Nebuchadnezzar was cast out from among men, he ate grass like an ox, and his body was bathed with the dew of heaven, until his hair grew like the feathers of an eagle, and his nails like the claws of a bird. **31***When this period was over, I, Nebuchadnezzar, raised my eyes to heaven; my reason was restored to me, and I blessed the Most High, I praised and glorified him who lives forever:

His dominion is an everlasting dominion,
   and his kingdom endures through all
      generations.
32   All who live on the earth are counted as
      nothing;
he does as he pleases with the powers of
      heaven
as well as with those who live on the
      earth.
There is no one who can stay his hand
   or say to him, "What have you done?"

33At the same time my reason returned to me, and for the glory of my kingdom, my majesty and my splendor returned to me. My nobles and lords sought me out; I was restored to my kingdom, and became much greater than before. **34**Therefore, I, Nebuchadnezzar, now praise and exalt and glorify the King of heaven, because all his works are right and his ways just; and those who walk in pride he is able to humble.

The Writing on the Wall

5   **1**†KING Belshazzar gave a great banquet for a thousand of his lords, with whom he drank. **2**†Under the influence of the wine, he ordered the gold and silver vessels which Nebuchadnezzar, his father, had taken from the temple, in Jerusalem, to be brought in so that the king, his lords, his wives and his entertainers might drink from them. **3**When the gold and silver vessels taken from the house of God

---

†
4, 17: *"This dream . . . for your foes":* Daniel speaks as a courtier.
4, 22: The description is of a form of insanity called lycanthropy, in which the patient acts like a wolf.
4, 24: A classic Scriptural text for the efficacy of good works.
4, 27: The words attributed to the king are similar to the boastings in the royal inscriptions by which the Mesopotamian kings testified to their mighty works.
4, 30ff: There is no certainty of any such thing happening to Nebuchadnezzar as is described here. Some scholars think that the Nebuchadnezzar of this chapter is actually Nabonidus, the father of Belshazzar, who was mysteriously absent from Babylon for a number of years. The Biblical author's chief interest was not in the historicity of this popular tale, but in the object lesson it contained for the proud "divine" kings of the Seleucid dynasty.
5, 1: *King Belshazzar:* Belshazzar was actually the crown prince, but he had been given royal authority in Babylon by his father Nabonidus.
5, 2: *Nebuchadnezzar, his father:* several kings of Babylon intervened between Nebuchadnezzar and Belshazzar. Either the term *father* is used here in the broad sense of "remote predecessor," or the name *Nebuchadnezzar* is used for "Nabonidus."

*
22: 5, 21.   31: 3, 100; 7, 14.
24: Sir 3, 30; 4, 8.

in Jerusalem had been brought in, and while the king, his lords, his wives and his entertainers were drinking [4]wine from them, they praised their gods of gold and silver, bronze and iron, wood and stone.

[5]Suddenly, opposite the lampstand, the fingers of a human hand appeared, writing on the plaster of the wall in the king's palace. When the king saw the wrist and hand that wrote, [6]his face blanched; his thoughts terrified him, his hip joints shook, and his knees knocked. [7]The king shouted for the enchanters, Chaldeans, and astrologers to be brought in. "Whoever reads this writing and tells me what it means," he said to the wise men of Babylon, "shall be clothed in purple, wear a golden collar about his neck, and be third in the government of the kingdom." [8]But though all the king's wise men came in, none of them could either read the writing or tell the king what it meant. [9]Then King Belshazzar was greatly terrified; his face went ashen, and his lords were thrown into confusion.

[10]When the queen heard of the discussion between the king and his lords, she entered the banquet hall and said, "O king, live forever! Be not troubled in mind, nor look so pale! [11]There is a man in your kingdom in whom is the spirit of the holy God; during the lifetime of your father he was seen to have brilliant knowledge and god-like wisdom. In fact, King Nebuchadnezzar, your father, made him chief of the magicians, enchanters, Chaldeans, and astrologers, [12]because of the extraordinary mind possessed by this Daniel, whom the king named Belteshazzar. He knew and understood how to interpret dreams, explain enigmas, and solve difficulties. Now therefore, summon Daniel to tell you what this means."

[13]Then Daniel was brought into the presence of the king. The king asked him, "Are you the Daniel, the Jewish exile, whom my father, the king, brought from Judah? [14]I have heard that the spirit of God is in you, that you possess brilliant knowledge and extraordinary wisdom. [15]Now, the wise men and enchanters were brought in to me to read this writing and tell me its meaning, but they could not say what the words meant. [16]But I have heard that you can interpret dreams and solve difficulties; if you are able to read the writing and tell me what it means, you shall be clothed in purple, wear a gold collar about your neck, and be third in the government of the kingdom."

[17]Daniel answered the king: "You may keep your gifts, or give your presents to someone else; but the writing I will read for you, O king, and tell you what it means. [18]The Most High God gave your father Nebuchadnezzar a great kingdom and glorious majesty. [19]Because he made him so great, the nations and peoples of every language dreaded and feared him. Whomever he wished, he killed or let live; whomever he wished, he exalted or humbled. [20]But when his heart became proud and his spirit hardened by insolence, he was put down from his royal throne and deprived of his glory; [21]*he was cast out from among

men and was made insensate as a beast; he lived with wild asses, and ate grass like an ox; his body was bathed with the dew of heaven, until he learned that the Most High God rules over the kingdom of men and appoints over it whom he will. [22]You, his son, Belshazzar, have not humbled your heart, though you knew all this; [23]you have rebelled against the Lord of heaven. You had the vessels of his temple brought before you, so that you and your nobles, your wives and your entertainers, might drink wine from them; and you praised the gods of silver and gold, bronze and iron, wood and stone, that neither see nor hear nor have intelligence. But the God in whose hand is your life breath and the whole course of your life, you did not glorify. [24]By him were the wrist and hand sent, and the writing set down.

[25]†"This is the writing that was inscribed: MENE, TEKEL, and PERES. These words mean: [26]†MENE, God has numbered your kingdom and put an end to it; [27]TEKEL, you have been weighed on the scales and found wanting; [28]PERES, your kingdom has been divided and given to the Medes and Persians."

[29]Then by order of Belshazzar they clothed Daniel in purple, with a gold collar about his neck, and proclaimed him third in the government of the kingdom. [30]The same night Belshazzar, the Chaldean king, was slain;

6   [1]†AND Darius the Mede succeeded to the kingdom at the age of sixty-two.

In the Lions' Den

[2]Darius decided to appoint over his entire kingdom one hundred and twenty satraps, to safeguard his interests; [3]these were accountable to three supervisors, one of whom was Daniel. [4]Daniel outshone all the supervisors and satraps because an extraordinary spirit was in him, and the king thought of giving him authority over the entire kingdom. [5]Therefore the supervisors and satraps tried to find grounds for accusation against Daniel as regards the administration. But they could accuse him of no wrongdoing; because he was trustworthy, no fault of neglect or misconduct was to be found in him. [6]Then these men said

---

† 5, 25: *Mene, Tekel, and Peres:* these seem to be the Aramaic names of weights and monetary values: the mina, the shekel (the sixtieth part of a mina), and the parsu (a half-mina).

5, 26ff: Daniel interprets these three terms by a play on the words: *Mene,* connected with the verb meaning to number; *Tekel,* with the verb meaning to weigh; *Peres,* with the verb meaning to divide. There is also a play on the last term with the word for Persians.

6, 1: *Darius the Mede:* unknown in profane history. The Median kingdom had already been conquered by Cyrus the Persian, and it was Cyrus who captured Babylon. Evidently the author of Daniel has deliberately adopted an apocalyptic view of history, derived from prophecy (cf Is 13, 17ff; Jer 51, 11.28ff), according to which the Medes formed the second of four world kingdoms preceding the Messianic times; see note on 2, 36-45. The character of Darius the Mede has probably been modeled on that of the Persian King Darius the Great (522-486 B. C.), the second successor of Cyrus.

❈   5/21: 4, 22.

to themselves, "We shall find no grounds for accusation against this Daniel unless by way of the law of his God." **7**So these supervisors and satraps went thronging to the king and said to him, "King Darius, live forever! **8***All the supervisors of the kingdom, the prefects, satraps, nobles, and governors are agreed that the following prohibition ought to be put in force by royal decree: no one is to address any petition to god or man for thirty days, except to you, O king; otherwise he shall be cast into a den of lions. **9**†Now, O king, issue the prohibition over your signature, immutable and irrevocable under Mede and Persian law." **10**So King Darius signed the prohibition and made it law.

11Even after Daniel heard that this law had been signed, he continued his custom of going home to kneel in prayer and give thanks to his God in the upper chamber three times a day, with the windows open toward Jerusalem. **12**So these men rushed in and found Daniel praying and pleading before his God. **13**Then they went to remind the king about the prohibition: "Did you not decree, O king, that no one is to address a petition to god or man for thirty days, except to you, O king; otherwise he shall be cast into a den of lions?" The king answered them, "The decree is absolute, irrevocable under the Mede and Persian law." **14**To this they replied, "Daniel, the Jewish exile, has paid no attention to you, O king, or to the decree you issued; three times a day he offers his prayer." **15**The king was deeply grieved at this news and he made up his mind to save Daniel; he worked till sunset to rescue him. **16**But these men insisted. "Keep in mind, O king," they said, "that under the Mede and Persian law every royal prohibition or decree is irrevocable." **17**†So the king ordered Daniel to be brought and cast into the lions' den. To Daniel he said, "May your God, whom you serve so constantly, save you." **18**To forestall any tampering, the king sealed with his own ring and the rings of the lords the stone that had been brought to block the opening of the den.

19Then the king returned to his palace for the night; he refused to eat and he dismissed the entertainers. Since sleep was impossible for him, **20**the king rose very early the next morning and hastened to the lions' den. **21**As he drew near, he cried out to Daniel sorrowfully, "O Daniel, servant of the living God, has the God whom you serve so constantly been able to save you from the lions?" **22***Daniel answered the king: "O king, live forever! **23**My God has sent his angel and closed the lions' mouths so that they have not hurt me. For I have been found innocent before him; neither to you have I done any harm, O king!" **24**This gave the king great joy. At his order Daniel was removed from the den, unhurt because he trusted in his God. **25**The king then ordered the men who had accused Daniel, along with their children and their wives, to be cast into the lions' den. Before they reached the bottom of the den, the lions overpowered them and crushed all their bones.

26Then King Darius wrote to the nations and peoples of every language, wherever they dwell on the earth: "All peace to you! **27**I decree that throughout my royal domain the God of Daniel is to be reverenced and feared:

> "For he is the living God, enduring forever;
> his kingdom shall not be destroyed,
> and his dominion shall be without end.
> **28*** He is a deliverer and savior,
> working signs and wonders in heaven
> and on earth,
> and he delivered Daniel from the lions'
> power."

29So Daniel fared well during the reign of Darius and the reign of Cyrus the Persian.

II: DANIEL'S VISIONS

Vision of the Four Beasts

7 **1**†IN THE FIRST YEAR of King Belshazzar of Babylon, Daniel had a dream as he lay in bed, and was terrified by the visions of his mind. Then he wrote down the dream; the account began: **2**†In the vision I saw during the night, suddenly the four winds of heaven stirred up the great sea, **3**from which emerged four immense beasts, each different from the others. **4**†The first was like a lion, but with eagle's wings. While I watched, the wings were plucked; it was raised from the ground to stand on two feet like a man, and given a human mind. **5**†The second was

---

† 6, 9: *Immutable and irrevocable:* the passages in Est 1, 19 and 8, 8 also refer to the immutability of Medo-Persian laws. The historian Diodorus Siculus indicates that such a concept existed in the time of Darius III (335-331 B. C.), the last of the Persian kings. Cf vv 13.16.

6, 17: *The lions' den:* a pit too deep to be easily scaled; its opening was blocked with a stone (v 18).

7, 1-27: The significance of this vision is the same as that of Nebuchadnezzar's dream in chapter 2; see note on 2, 36-45. To the four succeeding world kingdoms, Babylonian, Median, Persian, and Greek, is opposed the messianic kingdom of the people of God. The imagery of this chapter has been used extensively in the Revelation of St. John, where it is applied to the Roman empire, the persecutor of the church.

7, 2: *The great sea:* the primordial ocean beneath the earth, according to primitive cosmology (Gn 7, 11; 49, 25). This was thought to contain various monsters (Is 27, 1; Jb 7, 12), and in particular mythological monsters symbolizing the chaos which God had vanquished in ancient times (Jb 9, 13; 26, 13; etc.).

7, 4: The representation of the Babylonian empire as a winged lion, a common motif in Babylonian art, symbolizes the bestial power hostile to God. The two wings that *were plucked* represent Nebuchadnezzar and Belshazzar. *On two feet like a man . . . a human mind:* contrasts with what is said in 4, 13.30.

7, 5: *A bear:* represents the Median empire, its *three tusks* symbolizing its destructive nature; hence, the command: "*Up, devour much flesh.*"

like a bear; it was raised up on one side, and among the teeth in its mouth were three tusks. It was given the order, "Up, devour much flesh." [6†]After this I looked and saw another beast, like a leopard; on its back were four wings like those of a bird, and it had four heads. To this beast dominion was given. [7†]After this, in the visions of the night I saw the fourth beast, different from all the others, terrifying, horrible, and of extraordinary strength; it had great iron teeth with which it devoured and crushed, and what was left it trampled with its feet. [8]I was considering the ten horns it had, when suddenly another, a little horn, sprang out of their midst, and three of the previous horns were torn away to make room for it. This horn had eyes like a man, and a mouth that spoke arrogantly. [9†]As I watched,

Thrones were set up
   and the Ancient One took his throne.
His clothing was snow bright,
   and the hair on his head as white as
      wool;
His throne was flames of fire,
   with wheels of burning fire.
[10*] A surging stream of fire
   flowed out from where he sat;
Thousands upon thousands were
   ministering to him,
      and myriads upon myriads attended him.

The court was convened, and the books were opened. [11]I watched, then, from the first of the arrogant words which the horn spoke, until the beast was slain and its body thrown into the fire to be burnt up. [12]The other beasts, which also lost their dominion, were granted a prolongation of life for a time and a season. [13†]As the visions during the night continued, I saw

One like a son of man coming,
   on the clouds of heaven;
When he reached the Ancient One
   and was presented before him,
[14*] He received dominion, glory, and kingship;
   nations and peoples of every language
      serve him.
His dominion is an everlasting dominion
   that shall not be taken away,
      his kingship shall not be destroyed.

[15]I, Daniel, found my spirit anguished within its sheath of flesh, and I was terrified by the visions of my mind. [16]I approached one of those present and asked him what all this meant in truth; in answer, he made known to me the meaning of the things: [17]"These four great beasts stand for four kingdoms which shall arise on the earth. [18]But the holy ones of the Most High shall receive the kingship, to possess it forever and ever."

[19]But I wished to make certain about the fourth beast, so very terrible and different from the others, devouring and crushing with its iron teeth and bronze claws, and trampling with its feet what was left; [20]about the ten horns on its head, and the other one that sprang up, before which three horns fell; about the horn with the eyes and the mouth that spoke arrogantly, which appeared greater than its fellows. [21]For, as I watched, that horn made war against the holy ones and was victorious [22]until the Ancient One arrived; judgment was pronounced in favor of the holy ones of the Most High, and the time came when the holy ones possessed the kingdom. [23]He answered me thus:

"The fourth beast shall be a fourth
      kingdom on earth,
   different from all the others;
It shall devour the whole earth,
   beat it down, and crush it.
[24] The ten horns shall be ten kings
   rising out of that kingdom;
      another shall rise up after them,
Different from those before him,
   who shall lay low three kings.
[25†] He shall speak against the Most High
   and oppress the holy ones of the Most
      High,
      thinking to change the feast days and the
         law.
They shall be handed over to him
   for a year, two years, and a half-year.
[26] But when the court is convened,
   and his power is taken away
      by final and absolute destruction,

---

† 7, 6: *A leopard:* used to symbolize the swiftness with which Cyrus the Persian established his kingdom. *Four heads:* corresponding to the four Persian kings of 11, 2.

7, 7f: Alexander's empire was *different from all the others* in that it was Western rather than Oriental in inspiration. The *ten horns* represent the kings of the Seleucid dynasty, the only part of the Hellenistic empire that concerned the author. The *little horn* is Antiochus IV Epiphanes (175-163 B. C.), the worst of the Seleucid kings, who usurped the throne.

7, 9f: A vision of the heavenly throne of God (*the Ancient One*), who sits in judgment (symbolized by *fire*) over the nations. Some of the details of the vision, depicting the divine majesty and omnipotence, are to be found in Ez 1.

7, 13f: *One like a son of man:* in contrast to the worldly kingdoms opposed to God, which appear as beasts, the glorified people of God that will form his kingdom on earth is represented in human form (v 18). Just as our Lord applied the figure of the stone hewn from the mountain to himself (2, 36-45), he also made the title "Son of Man" his most characteristic way of referring to himself, as the One in whom and through whom the salvation of God's people came to be realized.

7, 25: The reference is to the persecutions of Antiochus IV and his attempt to force the Jews to give up their customs and to adopt Hellenistic ways (1 Mc 1, 33f). *A year, two years, and a half-year:* an indefinite, evil period of time. As seven is the Jewish "perfect" number, half of it signifies great imperfection. Actually, this corresponds fairly accurately to the duration of Antiochus' persecution.

---

* 7/10: Rv 5, 11.   14: 3, 100; 4, 31; Mi 4, 7;
                                            Lk 1, 32.

27 Then the kingship and dominion and
majesty
of all the kingdoms under the heavens
shall be given to the holy people of the
Most High,
Whose kingdom shall be everlasting:
all dominions shall serve and obey him."

28†The report concluded: I, Daniel, was greatly terrified by my thoughts, and my face blanched, but I kept the matter to myself.

Vision of the Ram and He-goat

8 **1**†AFTER this first vision, I, Daniel, had another, in the third year of the reign of King Belshazzar. **2**†In my vision I saw myself in the fortress of Susa in the province of Elam; I was beside the river Ulai. **3**I looked up and saw standing by the river a ram with two great horns, the one larger and newer than the other. **4**I saw the ram butting toward the west, north, and south. No beast could withstand it or be rescued from its power; it did what it pleased and became very powerful.

5As I was reflecting, a he-goat with a prominent horn on its forehead suddenly came from the west across the whole earth without touching the ground. **6**It approached the two-horned ram I had seen standing by the river, and rushed toward it with savage force. **7**I saw it attack the ram with furious blows when they met, and break both its horns. It threw the ram, which had not the force to withstand it, to the ground, and trampled upon it; and no one could rescue it from its power.

8The he-goat became very powerful, but at the height of its power the great horn was shattered, and in its place came up four others, facing the four winds of heaven. **9**†Out of one of them came a little horn which kept growing toward the south, the east, and the glorious country. **10**†Its power extended to the host of heaven, so that it cast down to earth some of the host and some of the stars and trampled on them. **11**It boasted even against the prince of the host, from whom it removed the daily sacrifice, and whose sanctuary it cast down, **12**as well as the host, while sin replaced the daily sacrifice. It cast truth to the ground, and was succeeding in its undertaking.

13†I heard a holy one speaking, and another said to whichever one it was that spoke, "How long shall the events of this vision last concerning the daily sacrifice, the desolating sin which is placed there, the sanctuary, and the trampled host?" **14**He answered him, "For two thousand three hundred evenings and mornings; then the sanctuary shall be purified."

15While I, Daniel, sought the meaning of the vision I had seen, a manlike figure stood before me, **16**†and on the Ulai I heard a human voice that cried out, "Gabriel, explain the vision to this man." **17**†When he came near where I was standing, I fell prostrate in terror. But he said to me, "Understand, son of man, that the vision refers to the end time." **18**As he spoke to me, I fell forward in a faint; he touched me and made me stand up. **19**"I will show you," he said, "what is to happen later in the period of wrath; for at the appointed time, there will be an end.

20"The two-horned ram you saw represents the kings of the Medes and Persians. **21**The he-goat is the king of the Greeks, and the great horn on its forehead is the first king. **22**The four that rose in its place when it was broken are four kingdoms that will issue from his nation, but without his strength.

23 "After their reign,
when sinners have reached their
measure,
There shall arise a king, impudent
and skilled in intrigue.
24 He shall be strong and powerful,
bring about fearful ruin,
and succeed in his undertaking.
He shall destroy powerful peoples;
25 his cunning shall be against the holy
ones,
his treacherous conduct shall succeed.
He shall be proud of heart
and destroy many by stealth.
But when he rises against the prince of
princes,
he shall be broken without a hand being
raised.
26 The vision of the evenings and the
mornings
is true, as spoken;
Do you, however, keep this vision
undisclosed,
because the days are to be many."

27I, Daniel, was weak and ill for some days; then I

---

† 7, 28: This verse ends the Aramaic part of the Book of Daniel.

8, 1-27: This vision repeats the major part of the preceding one, though in a more explicit fashion. As explained in vv 20ff, *the two-horned ram* represents the combined kingdom of the Medes and Persians, destroyed by Alexander's Hellenistic empire originating in the west. Once again the author is interested only in the Seleucid dynasty, which emerged from the dissolution of Alexander's empire after his death in 323 B. C.

8, 2: *The fortress of Susa:* the royal palace of the Persian kings in the ancient territory of Elam, east of Babylonia. *The river Ulai:* a canal along the northern side of Susa.

8, 9: *A little horn,* as in chapter 7, is Antiochus IV. *The glorious country:* Palestine.

8, 10ff: *The host of heaven:* ordinarily meaning the stars, here refers to the people of God; cf 12, 3. *The prince of the host:* God himself, with whose holy religion Antiochus interfered (1 Mc 1, 45).

8, 13: *The desolating sin:* the Hebrew contains a wordplay (*shomem*) on the name Baal Shamem ("lord of the heavens," the Greek Zeus Olympios), referring to the statue with which Antiochus profaned the temple of Jerusalem (2 Mc 6, 2).

8, 16: The angel Gabriel is mentioned here for the first time in the Bible. There is wordplay in the preceding verse on *geber*—manlike figure.

8, 17: *The end time:* the day of the Lord, when God sits in judgment on his enemies (v 19).

arose and took care of the king's affairs. But I was appalled at the vision, which I could not understand.

Gabriel and the Seventy Weeks

9 [1][†]IT was the first year that Darius, son of Ahasuerus, of the race of the Medes, reigned over the kingdom of the Chaldeans; [2][*][†]in the first year of his reign I, Daniel, tried to understand in the Scriptures the counting of the years of which the LORD spoke to the prophet Jeremiah: that for the ruins of Jerusalem seventy years must be fulfilled.

[3]I turned to the Lord God, pleading in earnest prayer, with fasting, sackcloth, and ashes. [4][*]I prayed to the LORD, my God, and confessed, "Ah, Lord, great and awesome God, you who keep your merciful covenant toward those who love you and observe your commandments! [5][*]We have sinned, been wicked and done evil; we have rebelled and departed from your commandments and your laws. [6]We have not obeyed your servants the prophets, who spoke in your name to our kings, our princes, our fathers, and all the people of the land. [7]Justice, O Lord, is on your side; we are shamefaced even to this day: the men of Judah, the residents of Jerusalem, and all Israel, near and far, in all the countries to which you have scattered them because of their treachery toward you. [8]O LORD, we are shamefaced, like our kings, our princes, and our fathers, for having sinned against you. [9]But yours, O Lord, our God, are compassion and forgiveness! Yet we rebelled against you [10]and paid no heed to your command, O LORD, our God, to live by the law you gave us through your servants the prophets. [11][*]Because all Israel transgressed your law and went astray, not heeding your voice, the sworn malediction, recorded in the law of Moses, the servant of God, was poured out over us for our sins. [12]You carried out the threats you spoke against us and against those who governed us, by bringing upon us in Jerusalem the greatest calamity that has ever occurred under heaven. [13][†]As it is written in the law of Moses, this calamity came full upon us. As we did not appease the LORD, our God, by turning back from our wickedness and recognizing his constancy, [14]so the LORD kept watch over the calamity and brought it upon us. You, O LORD, our God, are just in all that you have done, for we did not listen to your voice.

[15][*]"Now, O Lord, our God, who led your people out of the land of Egypt with a strong hand, and made a name for yourself even to this day, we have sinned, we are guilty. [16]O Lord, in keeping with all your just deeds, let your anger and your wrath be turned away from your city Jerusalem, your holy mountain. On account of our sins and the crimes of our fathers, Jerusalem and your people have become the reproach of all our neighbors. [17]Hear, therefore, O God, the prayer

and petition of your servant; and for your own sake, O Lord, let your face shine upon your desolate sanctuary. [18][*]Give ear, O my God, and listen; open your eyes and see our ruins and the city which bears your name. When we present our petition before you, we rely not on our just deeds, but on your great mercy. [19]O Lord, hear! O Lord, pardon! O Lord, be attentive and act without delay, for your own sake, O my God, because this city and your people bear your name!"

[20]I was still occupied with my prayer, confessing my sin and the sin of my people Israel, presenting my petition to the LORD, my God, on behalf of his holy mountain—[21][*][†]I was still occupied with this prayer, when Gabriel, the one whom I had seen before in vision, came to me in rapid flight at the time of the evening sacrifice. [22]He instructed me in these words: "Daniel, I have now come to give you understanding. [23]When you began your petition, an answer was given which I have come to announce, because you are beloved. Therefore, mark the answer and understand the vision.

[24][†]   "Seventy weeks are decreed
      for your people and for your holy city:
   Then transgression will stop and sin will
      end,
      guilt will be expiated,
   Everlasting justice will be introduced,
      vision and prophecy ratified,
      and a most holy will be anointed.

[†] 9, 1: *Darius:* see the note on 6, 1.

9, 2: *Seventy years:* the prophet Jeremiah (25, 11; 29, 10) prophesied a Babylonian captivity of seventy years, a round number signifying the complete passing away of the existing generation. Jeremiah's prophecy was fulfilled in the capture of Babylon by Cyrus and the subsequent return of the Jews to Palestine. However, the author of Daniel, living during the persecution of Antiochus, sees the conditions of the exile still existing; therefore in his meditation he extends Jeremiah's number to seventy weeks of years (v 24), i. e., seven times seventy years, to characterize the Jewish victory over the Seleucids as the ultimate fulfillment of the prophecy.

9, 13: *As it is written:* the first time that this formula of Scriptural citation is used in the Bible. The reference (v 11) is to the sanctions of Lv 26, 14ff; Dt 28, 15ff.

9, 21: *At the time of the evening sacrifice:* between three and four in the afternoon.

9, 24: *Seventy weeks:* i. e., of years. Just as Jeremiah's seventy years was an approximation (see note on v 2), the four hundred and ninety years here is not to be taken literally. Similarly, the distribution of the "weeks" in the following verses indicates only relative proportions of the total figure. *A most holy:* an expression used almost always of an object, the altar or the temple, but once (1 Chr 23, 13) of Aaron the high priest. The author sees the definitive establishment of the kingdom of God, realized in the reconsecration of the temple after Antiochus' desecration, or personified in the holy community (like the Son of Man of chapter 7). The Fathers of the church almost unanimously understood the reference to be to Christ, the final realization of the prophecy.

9/2f: Jer 25, 11; 29, 10.   15: Bar 2, 11; Ex 14, 22.
    4: Neh 1, 5.   18: Jer 25, 29.
    5: Bar 1, 17.   21: Dn 8, 16.
  11: Dt 27, 15.

^{25†} Know and understand this:
From the utterance of the word
   that Jerusalem was to be rebuilt
Until one who is anointed and a leader,
   there shall be seven weeks.
During sixty-two weeks
   it shall be rebuilt,
With streets and trenches,
   in time of affliction.

^{26†} After the sixty-two weeks
   an anointed shall be cut down
   when he does not possess the city;
And the people of a leader who will come
   shall destroy the sanctuary.
Then the end shall come like a torrent;
   until the end there shall be war,
   the desolation that is decreed.

^{27*†} For one week he shall make
   a firm compact with the many;
Half the week
   he shall abolish sacrifice and oblation;
On the temple wing shall be the horrible
   abomination
   until the ruin that is decreed
   is poured out upon the horror."

Vision of the Hellenistic Wars

10 ^{1†}IN the third year of Cyrus, king of Persia, a revelation was given to Daniel, who had been named Belteshazzar. The revelation was certain: a great war; he understood it from the vision. ^{2†}In those days, I, Daniel, mourned three full weeks. ³I ate no savory food, I took no meat or wine, and I did not anoint myself at all until the end of the three weeks.

^{4†}On the twenty-fourth day of the first month I was on the bank of the great river, the Tigris. ^{5†}As I looked up, I saw a man dressed in linen with a belt of fine gold around his waist. ⁶His body was like chrysolite, his face shone like lightning, his eyes were like fiery torches, his arms and feet looked like burnished bronze, and his voice sounded like the roar of a multitude. ⁷I alone, Daniel, saw the vision; but great fear seized the men who were with me; they fled and hid themselves, although they did not see the vision. ⁸So I was left alone, seeing this great vision. No strength remained in me; I turned the color of death and was powerless. ⁹When I heard the sound of his voice, I fell face forward in a faint.

¹⁰But then a hand touched me, raising me to my hands and knees. ¹¹"Daniel, beloved," he said to me, "understand the words which I am speaking to you; stand up, for my mission now is to you." When he said this to me, I stood up trembling. ¹²"Fear not, Daniel," he continued; "from the first day you made up your mind to acquire understanding and humble yourself before God, your prayer was heard. Because of it I started out, ^{13†}but the prince of the kingdom

of Persia stood in my way for twenty-one days, until finally Michael, one of the chief princes, came to help me. I left him there with the prince of the kings of Persia, ¹⁴and came to make you understand what shall happen to your people in the days to come; for there is yet a vision concerning those days."

¹⁵While he was speaking thus to me, I fell forward and kept silent. ¹⁶Then something like a man's hand touched my lips; I opened my mouth and said to the one facing me, "My lord, I was seized with pangs at the vision and I was powerless. ¹⁷How can my lord's servant speak with you, my lord? For now no strength or even breath is left in me." ¹⁸The one who looked like a man touched me again and strengthened me, saying, ¹⁹"Fear not, beloved, you are safe; take courage and be strong." ²⁰When he spoke to me, I grew strong and said, "Speak, my lord, for you have strengthened me." "Do you know," he asked, "why I have come to you? Soon I must fight the prince of Persia again. When I leave, the prince of Greece will come; ^{21*}but I shall tell you what is written in the truthful book. No one supports me against all these except Michael, your prince,

---

† 9, 25: *From the utterance . . . to be rebuilt:* from the time of Jeremiah's prophecy. *One . . . anointed and a leader:* either Cyrus, who was called the anointed of the LORD to end the exile (Is 45, 1), or the high priest Joshua who presided over the rebuilding of the altar of sacrifice after the Exile (Ezr 3, 2). *Seven weeks:* forty-nine years, an approximation of the time of the exile. *During sixty-two weeks . . . rebuilt:* a period of 434 years, roughly approximating the interval between the rebuilding of Jerusalem after the exile and the beginning of the Seleucid persecution.

9, 26: *An anointed:* doubtless the high priest Onias III, murdered in 171 B. C., from which the author dates the beginning of the persecution. Onias was in exile when he was killed. *A leader:* Antiochus IV.

9, 27: *One week:* the final phase of the period in view, the time of Antiochus' persecution; *he* is Antiochus himself. *The many:* the faithless Jews who allied themselves with the heathen; cf 1 Mc 1, 11ff. *Half the week:* three and a half years; see note on 7, 25. The temple was desecrated by Antiochus from 167 to 165 B. C. *The temple wing:* probably the main portal. *The horrible abomination:* see note on 8, 13. Perhaps an inscription was placed on the portal of the temple dedicating it to the Olympian Zeus. Our Lord referred to this passage in his own prediction of the destruction of Jerusalem (Mt 24, 15).

10, 1—12, 13: This final vision repeats some of the material contained in the others. It is concerned with history of the worldly kingdoms from the time of Cyrus to the defeat of the tyrant Antiochus.

10, 2: *Mourned:* perhaps the author intends to recall the interruption in the rebuilding of the temple, which occurred during this time (Ezr 4, 1-4).

10, 4: *The first month:* the month Nisan (mid-March to mid-April).

10, 5f: The heavenly person of the vision is probably the angel Gabriel, as in 9, 21. *Chrysolite:* or topaz, a yellowish precious stone.

10, 13: *The prince of the kingdom of Persia:* the guardian angel of Persia. The later Judaism ascribed protecting angels to various groups of human society, often as little more than personifications. *Michael:* the angel who is the protector of God's people (v 21).

27: Mt 24, 15; 2 Mc 6, 2.   10/21: Rv 12, 7.

11 [1]STANDING as a reinforcement and a bulwark for me. [2]†Now I shall tell you the truth.

"Three kings of Persia are yet to come; and a fourth shall acquire the greatest riches of all. Strengthened by his riches, he shall rouse all the kingdom of Greece. [3]But a powerful king shall appear and rule with great might, doing as he pleases. [4]No sooner shall he appear than his kingdom shall be broken and divided in the four directions under heaven; but not among his descendants or in keeping with his mighty rule, for his kingdom shall be torn to pieces and belong to others than they.

[5]†"The king of the south shall grow strong, but one of his princes shall grow stronger still and govern a domain greater than his. [6]After some years they shall become allies: the daughter of the king of the south shall come to the king of the north in the interest of peace. But her bid for power shall fail: and her line shall not be recognized, and she shall be given up, together with those who brought her, her son and her husband. But later [7]a descendant of her line shall succeed to his rank, and shall come against the rampart and enter the stronghold of the king of the north, and conquer them. [8]Even their gods, with their molten images and their precious vessels of silver and gold, he shall carry away as booty into Egypt. For years he shall have nothing to do with the king of the north. [9]Then the latter shall invade the land of the king of the south, and return to his own country.

[10]"But his sons shall prepare and assemble a great armed host, which shall advance like a flood, then withdraw. When it returns and surges around the stronghold, [11]the king of the south, provoked, shall go out to fight against the king of the north, whose great host shall make a stand but shall be given into his hand [12]and be carried off. In the pride of his heart, he shall lay low tens of thousands, but he shall not triumph. [13]For the king of the north shall raise another army, greater than before; after some years he shall attack with this large army and great resources. [14]*In those times many shall resist the king of the south, and outlaws of your people shall rise up in fulfillment of vision, but they shall fail. [15]When the king of the north comes, he shall set up siegeworks and take the fortified city by storm. The power of the south shall not withstand him, and not even his picked troops shall have the strength to resist. [16]He shall attack him and do as he pleases, with no one to withstand him. He shall stop in the glorious land, dealing destruction. [17]He shall set himself to penetrate the entire strength of his kingdom. He shall conclude an agreement with him and give him a daughter in marriage in order to destroy the kingdom, but this shall not succeed in his favor. [18]He shall turn to the coastland and take many, but a leader shall put an end to his shameful conduct, so that he cannot renew it against him. [19]He shall turn to the strongholds of his own land, but shall stumble and fall, to be found no more. [20]In his stead one shall arise who will send a tax collector through the glorious kingdom, but he shall soon be destroyed, though not in conflict or in battle.

[21]"There shall rise in his place a despicable person, to whom the royal insignia shall not be given. By stealth and fraud he shall seize the kingdom. [22]Armed might shall be completely overwhelmed by him and crushed, and even the prince of the covenant. [23]After allying with him, he shall treacherously rise to power with a small party. [24]By stealth he shall enter prosperous provinces and do that which his fathers or grandfathers never did; he shall distribute spoil, booty, and riches among them and devise plots against their strongholds; but only for a time. [25]He shall call on his strength and cleverness to meet the king of the south with a great army; the king of the south shall prepare for battle with a very large and strong army, but he shall not succeed because of the plots devised against him. [26]Even his table companions shall seek to destroy him, his army shall be overwhelmed, and many shall fall slain. [27]The two kings, resolved on evil, shall sit at table together and exchange lies, but they shall have no success, because the appointed end is not yet.

[28]"He shall turn back toward his land with great riches, his mind set against the holy covenant; he shall arrange matters and return to his land. [29]At the time appointed he shall come again to the south, but this time it shall not be as before. [30]†When ships of the Kittim confront him, he shall lose heart and retreat. Then he shall direct his rage and energy against the holy covenant; those who forsake it he shall once more single out. [31]Armed forces shall move at his command and defile the sanctuary stronghold, abolishing the daily sacrifice and setting up the horrible abomination. [32]By his deceit he shall make some who were disloyal to the covenant apostatize; but those who remain loyal to their God shall take strong action. [33]The nation's wise men shall instruct the many; though for a time they will become victims of the sword, of flames, exile, and plunder. [34]When they fall, few people shall help them, but many shall join them

---

out of treachery. ³⁵Of the wise men, some shall fall, so that the rest may be tested, refined, and purified, until the end time which is still appointed to come.

³⁶"The king shall do as he pleases, exalting himself and making himself greater than any god; he shall utter dreadful blasphemies against the God of gods. He shall prosper only till divine wrath is ready, for what is determined must take place. ³⁷He shall have no regard for the gods of his ancestors or for the one in whom women delight; for no god shall he have regard, because he shall make himself greater than all. ³⁸Instead, he shall give glory to the god of strongholds; a god unknown to his fathers he shall glorify with gold, silver, precious stones, and other treasures. ³⁹To defend the strongholds he shall station a people of a foreign god. Whoever acknowledges him he shall provide with abundant honor; he shall make them rule over the many and distribute the land as a reward.

⁴⁰"At the appointed time the king of the south shall come to grips with him, but the king of the north shall overwhelm him with chariots and horsemen and a great fleet, passing through the countries like a flood. ⁴¹He shall enter the glorious land and many shall fall, except Edom, Moab, and the chief part of Ammon, which shall escape from his power. ⁴²He shall extend his power over the countries, and not even the land of Egypt shall escape. ⁴³He shall control the riches of gold and silver and all the treasures of Egypt; Libya and Ethiopia shall be in his train. ⁴⁴When news from the east and the north terrifies him, he shall set out with great fury to slay and to doom many. ⁴⁵He shall pitch the tents of his royal pavilion between the sea and the glorious holy mountain, but he shall come to his end with none to help him.

12 ¹*† "At that time there shall arise
       Michael, the great prince,
       guardian of your people;
It shall be a time unsurpassed in distress
       since nations began until that time.
At that time your people shall escape,
       everyone who is found written in the
       book.

²*† Many of those who sleep
       in the dust of the earth shall awake;
Some shall live forever,
       others shall be an everlasting horror
       and disgrace.

³* But the wise shall shine brightly
       like the splendor of the firmament,
And those who lead the many to justice
       shall be like the stars forever.

⁴"As for you, Daniel, keep secret the message and seal the book until the end time; many shall fall away and evil shall increase."

⁵I, Daniel, looked and saw two others, one standing on either bank of the river. ⁶One of them said to the man clothed in linen, who was upstream, "How long shall it be to the end of these appalling things?" ⁷*†The man clothed in linen, who was upstream, lifted his right and left hands to heaven; and I heard him swear by him who lives forever that it should be for a year, two years, a half-year; and that, when the power of the destroyer of the holy people was brought to an end, all these things should end. ⁸I heard, but I did not understand; so I asked "My lord, what follows this?" ⁹"Go, Daniel," he said, "because the words are to be kept secret and sealed until the end time. ¹⁰Many shall be refined, purified, and tested, but the wicked shall prove wicked; none of them shall have understanding, but the wise shall have it. ¹¹From the time that the daily sacrifice is abolished and the horrible abomination is set up, there shall be one thousand two hundred and ninety days. ¹²Blessed is the man who has patience and perseveres until the one thousand three hundred and thirty-five days. ¹³Go, take your rest, you shall rise for your reward at the end of days."

III: APPENDIX

Susanna's Virtue

13 ¹†IN BABYLON THERE LIVED A MAN named Joakim, ²who married a very beautiful and God-fearing woman, Susanna, the daughter of Hilkiah; ³her pious parents had trained their daughter according to the law of Moses. ⁴Joakim was very rich; he had a garden near his house, and the Jews had recourse to him often because he was the most respected of them all.

⁵That year, two elders of the people were appointed judges, of whom the Lord said, "Wickedness has come out of Babylon: from the elders who were to govern the people as judges." ⁶These men, to whom all brought their cases, frequented the house of Joakim. ⁷When the people left at noon, Susanna used to enter

---

†

11, 36-39: Instead of venerating Apollo, one of *the gods of his ancestors*, Antiochus venerated, and even identified himself with, Zeus Olympios, whom the Romans equated with the god of their fortress in Rome, Jupiter Capitolinus, *the god of strongholds*.

12, 1: *Written in the book:* the book of God's predestination.

12, 2: The first Israelites who have fallen (11, 33ff) *shall awake,* that is, rise to *live forever*. A resurrection of the wicked as in later, Christian teaching (Jn 5, 28f) is implied here if the *others* are included in the *many;* but cf Is 66, 24.

12, 7: *A year, two years, a half year:* see note on 7, 25. The author's perspective is the end of Antiochus, and beyond, the final consummation of all things.

13, 1—14, 42: The short stories in these two chapters may have originally been about some other Daniel or Daniels than the hero of the main part of the book. They exist now only in Greek, but probably were first composed in Hebrew or Aramaic. They are excluded from the Jewish canon of Scripture, but the Church has always included them among the inspired writings.

---

*
   12/1: Rv 12, 7.   3: Wis 3, 7.
       2: Mt 25, 46; Jn 5, 29.   7: Rv 10, 5f.

her husband's garden for a walk. [8]When the old men saw her enter every day for her walk, they began to lust for her. [9]They suppressed their consciences; they would not allow their eyes to look to heaven, and did not keep in mind just judgments. [10]Though both were enamored of her, they did not tell each other their trouble, [11]for they were ashamed to reveal their lustful desire to have her. [12]Day by day they watched eagerly for her. [13]One day they said to each other, "Let us be off for home, it is time for lunch." So they went out and parted; [14]but both turned back, and when they met again, they asked each other the reason. They admitted their lust, and then they agreed to look for an occasion when they could meet her alone.

[15]One day, while they were waiting for the right moment, she entered the garden as usual, with two maids only. She decided to bathe, for the weather was warm. [16]Nobody else was there except the two elders, who had hidden themselves and were watching her. [17]"Bring me oil and soap," she said to the maids, "and shut the garden doors while I bathe." [18]They did as she said: they shut the garden doors and left by the side gate to fetch what she had ordered, unaware that the elders were hidden inside.

[19]As soon as the maids had left, the two old men got up and hurried to her. [20]"Look," they said, "the garden doors are shut, and no one can see us; give in to our desire, and lie with us. [21]If you refuse, we will testify against you that you dismissed your maids because a young man was here with you."

[22]"I am completely trapped," Susanna groaned. "If I yield, it will be my death; if I refuse, I cannot escape your power. [23]Yet it is better for me to fall into your power without guilt than to sin before the Lord." [24]Then Susanna shrieked, and the old men also shouted at her, [25]as one of them ran to open the garden doors. [26]When the people in the house heard the cries from the garden, they rushed in by the side gate to see what had happened to her. [27]At the accusations by the old men, the servants felt very much ashamed, for never had any such thing been said about Susanna.

[28]When the people came to her husband Joakim the next day, the two wicked elders also came, fully determined to put Susanna to death. Before all the people they ordered: [29]"Send for Susanna, the daughter of Hilkiah, the wife of Joakim." When she was sent for, [30]she came with her parents, children and all her relatives. [31]Susanna, very delicate and beautiful, [32]was veiled; but those wicked men ordered her to uncover her face so as to sate themselves with her beauty. [33]All her relatives and the onlookers were weeping.

[34]In the midst of the people the two elders rose up and laid their hands on her head. [35]Through her tears she looked up to heaven, for she trusted in the Lord wholeheartedly. [36]The elders made this accusation:

"As we were walking in the garden alone, this woman entered with two girls and shut the doors of the garden, dismissing the girls. [37]A young man, who was hidden there, came and lay with her. [38]When we, in a corner of the garden, saw this crime, we ran toward them. [39]We saw them lying together, but the man we could not hold, because he was stronger than we; he opened the doors and ran off. [40]Then we seized this one and asked who the young man was, [41]but she refused to tell us. We testify to this." The assembly believed them, since they were elders and judges of the people, and they condemned her to death.

[42]But Susanna cried aloud: "O eternal God, you know what is hidden and are aware of all things before they come to be: [43]you know that they have testified falsely against me. Here I am about to die, though I have done none of the things with which these wicked men have charged me."

[44]The Lord heard her prayer. [45]As she was being led to execution, God stirred up the holy spirit of a young boy named Daniel, [46]and he cried aloud: "I will have no part in the death of this woman." [47]All the people turned and asked him, "What is this you are saying?" [48]He stood in their midst and continued, "Are you such fools, O Israelites! To condemn a woman of Israel without examination and without clear evidence? [49]Return to court, for they have testified falsely against her."

[50]Then all the people returned in haste. To Daniel the elders said, "Come, sit with us and inform us, since God has given you the prestige of old age." [51]But he replied, "Separate these two far from one another that I may examine them."

[52]After they were separated one from the other, he called one of them and said: "How you have grown evil with age! Now have your past sins come to term: [53]*passing unjust sentences, condemning the innocent, and freeing the guilty, although the Lord says, 'The innocent and the just you shall not put to death.' [54]Now, then, if you were a witness, tell me under what tree you saw them together." [55]†"Under a mastic tree," he answered. "Your fine lie has cost you your head," said Daniel; "for the angel of God shall receive the sentence from him and split you in two." [56]Putting him to one side, he ordered the other one to be brought. "Offspring of Canaan, not of Judah," Daniel said to him, "beauty has seduced you, lust has subverted your conscience. [57]†This is how you acted with the daughters of Israel, and in their fear they yielded to you; but a daughter of Judah did not tolerate your wickedness. [58]Now, then, tell me under what tree you

---

† 13, 55-59: The contrast between the *mastic tree,* which is small, and the majestic *oak* emphasizes the contradiction between the statements of the two elders. In the Greek text there is a play on words between the names of these two trees and the mortal punishment decreed by Daniel for the elders.

13, 57: Besides the evident moral intent of this story, it appears to have served the purpose of contrasting the northern and the southern kingdoms, Israel and Judah, in favor of the latter.

surprised them together." ⁵⁹"Under an oak," he said. "Your fine lie has cost you also your head," said Daniel; "for the angel of God waits with a sword to cut you in two so as to make an end of you both."

⁶⁰The whole assembly cried aloud, blessing God who saves those that hope in him. ⁶¹They rose up against the two elders, for by their own words Daniel had convicted them of perjury. According to the law of Moses, they inflicted on them the penalty they had plotted to impose on their neighbor: ⁶²they put them to death. Thus was innocent blood spared that day.

⁶³Hilkiah and his wife praised God for their daughter Susanna, as did Joakim her husband and all her relatives, because she was found innocent of any shameful deed. ⁶⁴And from that day onward Daniel was greatly esteemed by the people.

Bel and the Dragon

14 ¹AFTER King Astyages was laid with his fathers, Cyrus the Persian succeeded to his kingdom. ^{2†}Daniel was the king's favorite and was held in higher esteem than any of the friends of the king. ^{3†}The Babylonians had an idol called Bel, and every day they provided for it six barrels of fine flour, forty sheep, and six measures of wine. ⁴The king worshiped it and went every day to adore it; but Daniel adored only his God. ⁵When the king asked him, "Why do you not adore Bel?" Daniel replied, "Because I worship not idols made with hands, but only the living God who made heaven and earth and has dominion over all mankind." ⁶Then the king continued, "You do not think Bel is a living god? Do you not see how much he eats and drinks every day?" ⁷Daniel began to laugh. "Do not be deceived, O king," he said; "it is only clay inside and bronze outside; it has never taken any food or drink." ⁸Enraged, the king called his priests and said to them, "Unless you tell me who it is that consumes these provisions, you shall die. ⁹But if you can show that Bel consumes them, Daniel shall die for blaspheming Bel." Daniel said to the king, "Let it be as you say!" ¹⁰There were seventy priests of Bel, besides their wives and children.

When the king went with Daniel into the temple of Bel, ¹¹the priests of Bel said, "See, we are going to leave. Do you, O king, set out the food and prepare the wine; then shut the door and seal it with your ring. ¹²If you do not find that Bel has eaten it all when you return in the morning, we are to die; otherwise Daniel shall die for his lies against us." ¹³They were not perturbed, because under the table they had made a secret entrance through which they always came in to consume the food. ¹⁴After they departed the king set the food before Bel, while Daniel ordered his servants to bring some ashes, which they scattered through the whole temple; the king alone was present. Then they went outside, sealed the closed door with

the king's ring, and departed. ¹⁵The priests entered that night as usual, with their wives and children, and they ate and drank everything.

¹⁶Early the next morning, the king came with Daniel. ¹⁷"Are the seals unbroken, Daniel?" he asked. And Daniel answered, "They are unbroken, O king." ¹⁸As soon as he had opened the door, the king looked at the table and cried aloud, "Great you are, O Bel; there is no trickery in you." ¹⁹But Daniel laughed and kept the king from entering. "Look at the floor," he said; "whose footprints are these?" ²⁰"I see the footprints of men, women, and children!" said the king. ²¹The angry king arrested the priests, their wives, and their children. They showed him the secret door by which they used to enter to consume what was on the table. ²²He put them to death, and handed Bel over to Daniel, who destroyed it and its temple.

²³There was a great dragon which the Babylonians worshiped. "Look!" ²⁴said the king to Daniel, "you cannot deny that this is a living god, so adore it." ²⁵But Daniel answered, "I adore the Lord, my God, for he is the living God. ²⁶Give me permission, O king, and I will kill this dragon without sword or club." "I give you permission," the king said. ²⁷Then Daniel took some pitch, fat, and hair; these he boiled together and made into cakes. He put them into the mouth of the dragon, and when the dragon ate them, he burst asunder. "This," he said, "is what you worshiped."

²⁸When the Babylonians heard this, they were angry and turned against the king. "The king has become a Jew," they said; "he has destroyed Bel, killed the dragon, and put the priests to death." ²⁹They went to the king and demanded: "Hand Daniel over to us, or we will kill you and your family." ³⁰When he saw himself threatened with violence the king was forced to hand Daniel over to them. ³¹They threw Daniel into a lions' den, where he remained six days. ³²In the den were seven lions, and two carcasses and two sheep had been given to them daily. But now they were given nothing, so that they would devour Daniel.

³³In Judea there was a prophet, Habakkuk; he mixed some bread in a bowl with the stew he had boiled, and was going to bring it to the reapers in the field, ³⁴when an angel of the Lord told him, "Take the lunch you have to Daniel in the lions' den at Babylon." ³⁵But Habakkuk answered, "Babylon, sir, I have never seen, and I do not know the den!" ³⁶*The angel of the Lord seized him by the crown of his head and carried him by the hair; with the speed of the wind, he set him down in Babylon above the den. ³⁷"Daniel,

---

[†] **14, 1:** *King Astyages:* the last of the Median kings, defeated by Cyrus in 550 B. C. This story preserves the fiction of a successive Median and Persian rule of Babylon.

14, 2: This verse in the Septuagint Greek text reads: "There was once a priest, Daniel by name, the son of Abal, a favorite of the king of Babylon." This may represent an earlier form of the story, before it was attached to the Book of Daniel.

14, 3: *Bel:* see the note on 4, 5.

Daniel," cried Habakkuk, "take the lunch God has sent you." 38"You have remembered me, O God," said Daniel; "you have not forsaken those who love you." 39While Daniel began to eat, the angel of the Lord at once brought Habakkuk back to his own place.

40On the seventh day the king came to mourn for Daniel. As he came to the den and looked in, there was Daniel, sitting there! 41The king cried aloud, "You are great, O Lord, the God of Daniel, and there is no other besides you!" 42Daniel he took out, but those who had tried to destroy him he threw into the den, and they were devoured in a moment before his eyes.

The Book of Hosea

Introduction

Hosea belonged to the northern kingdom and began his prophetic career in the last years of Jeroboam II (786-746 B. C.). Some believe that he was a priest, others that he was a cult prophet; the prophecy, our only source of information concerning his life, gives us no certain answer in the matter. The collected oracles reveal a very sensitive, emotional man who could pass quickly from violent anger to the deepest tenderness. The prophecy pivots around his own unfortunate marriage to Gomer, a personal tragedy which profoundly influenced his teaching. In fact, his own prophetic vocation and message were immeasurably deepened by the painful experience he underwent in his married life.

Gomer, the adulteress, symbolized faithless Israel. And just as Hosea could not give up his wife forever even when she played the harlot, so Yahweh could not renounce Israel, who had been betrothed to him. God would chastise, but it would be the chastisement of the jealous lover, longing to bring back the beloved to the fresh and pure joy of their first love.

Israel's infidelity took the form of idolatry and ruthless oppression of the poor. No amount of mechanically offered sacrifices could atone for her serious sins. Chastisement alone remained; God would have to strip her of the rich ornaments bestowed by her false lovers and thus bring her back to the true lover. A humiliated Israel would again seek Yahweh. The eleventh chapter of Hosea is one of the summits of Old Testament theology; God's love for his people has never been expressed more tenderly. Hosea began the tradition of describing the relation between Yahweh and Israel in terms of marriage. This symbolism appears later on in the Old Testament; and, in the New, both St. John and St. Paul express in the same imagery the union between Christ and his church.

The Book of Hosea is divided as follows:
- I: The Prophet's Marriage and Its Lesson (1, 1—3, 5)
- II: Israel's Guilt and Punishment (4, 1—14, 10)

I: THE PROPHET'S MARRIAGE AND ITS LESSON

Marriage with an Unfaithful Wife

1 ¹†THE WORD OF THE LORD that came to Hosea, the son of Beeri, in the days of Uzziah, Jotham, Ahaz, Hezekiah, kings of Judah, and in the days of Jeroboam, son of Joash, king of Israel. ²†In the beginning of the LORD's speaking to Hosea, the LORD said to Hosea:

> Go, take a harlot wife and harlot's children,
>   for the land gives itself to harlotry,
>   turning away from the LORD.

³So he went and took Gomer, the daughter of Diblaim; and she conceived and bore him a son. ⁴†Then the LORD said to him:

> Give him the name Jezreel,
>   for in a little while
> I will punish the house of Jehu
>   for the bloodshed at Jezreel
> And bring to an end the kingdom
>   of the house of Israel;
> ⁵ On that day I will break the bow of Israel
>   in the valley of Jezreel.

⁶†When she conceived again and bore a daughter, the LORD said to him:

> Give her the name Lo-ruhama;
> I no longer feel pity for the house of Israel:
>   rather, I abhor them utterly.

> ⁷† Yet for the house of Judah I feel pity;
>   I will save them by the LORD, their God;

---

† 1—3: This section is ordinarily thought to be biographical, the prophet's personal tragedy figuring as the relation of God to his people Israel. Hosea's marriage to a harlot wife represents Israel's infidelity to her Lord; hence the symbolic names of the children (1, 4-9). In 2, 4-25 the Lord protests this infidelity and decrees its consequences, but promises restoration in return for amendment; his punishments are medicinal. In chapter 3 Hosea once more takes back his wife, but only conditionally, signifying God's long-suffering love for Israel and hope for her return.

1, 2: A harlot wife: this does not necessarily mean that Gomer was a harlot when Hosea married her; the verse describes the event in its final consequences.

1, 4: Jezreel: the strategic valley in northern Israel where Jehu brought the dynasty of Omri to an end through bloodshed (2 Kgs 9-10). Jeroboam II was the last king but one of the house of Jehu; the prophecy in this verse was fulfilled by the murder of his son, who reigned only six months (2 Kgs 15, 8-10).

1, 6: Lo-ruhama: "she is not pitied." The "pity" that is here withheld from Israel is God's gratuitous love which inspires his beneficent acts.

1, 7: The terrible punishments announced by the prophets were so fully realized that later generations made a point of recalling the same prophets' messages of consolation also, even though it meant taking these from another context. Thus, an editor placed the words of 2, 1ff after the repudiation of Israel in 1, 9; here the more natural order has been restored. The present verse is another example of the same thing. In addition, it may be the work of a later hand, dating from a time when the prophecies of Hosea were circulated in the south,

But I will not save them by war,
by sword or bow, by horses or horsemen.

⁸After she weaned Lo-ruhama, she conceived and bore a son. ⁹†Then the LORD said:

Give him the name Lo-ammi,
for you are not my people,
and I will not be your God.

Israel's Punishment and Restoration

2 ⁴† Protest against your mother, protest!
for she is not my wife,
and I am not her husband.
Let her remove her harlotry from before
her,
her adultery from between her breasts,

⁵† Or I will strip her naked,
leaving her as on the day of her birth;
I will make her like the desert,
reduce her to an arid land,
and slay her with thirst.

⁶ I will have no pity on her children,
for they are the children of harlotry.

⁷† Yes, their mother has played the harlot;
she that conceived them has acted
shamefully.
"I will go after my lovers," she said,
"who give me my bread and my water,
my wool and my flax, my oil and my
drink."

¹⁰ Since she has not known
that it was I who gave her
the grain, the wine, and the oil,
And her abundance of silver,
and of gold, which they used for Baal,

¹¹ Therefore I will take back my grain in its
time,
and my wine in its season;
I will snatch away my wool and my flax,
with which she covers her nakedness.

¹² So now I will lay bare her shame
before the eyes of her lovers,
and no one can deliver her out of my
hand.

¹³ I will bring an end to all her joy,
her feasts, her new moons, her sabbaths,
and all her solemnities.

¹⁴ I will lay waste her vines and fig trees,
of which she said, "These are the hire
my lovers have given me";
I will turn them into rank growth
and wild beasts shall devour them.

¹⁵† I will punish her for the days of the Baals,
for whom she burnt incense
While she decked herself out with her
rings and her jewels,
and, in going after her lovers,
forgot me, says the LORD.

⁸† Therefore, I will hedge in her way with
thorns
and erect a wall against her,
so that she cannot find her paths.

⁹ If she runs after her lovers, she shall not
overtake them;
if she looks for them she shall not find
them.
Then she shall say,
"I will go back to my first husband,
for it was better with me then than now."

¹⁶† So I will allure her;
I will lead her into the desert
and speak to her heart.

¹⁷ From there I will give her the vineyards
she had,
and the valley of Achor as a door of
hope.
She shall respond there as in the days of
her youth,
when she came up from the land of
Egypt.

¹⁸†   On that day, says the LORD,
She shall call me "My husband,"
and never again "My baal."

¹⁹ Then will I remove from her mouth the
names of the Baals,
so that they shall no longer be invoked.

²⁰ I will make a covenant for them on that
day,
with the beasts of the field,
With the birds of the air,
and with the things that crawl on the
ground.

---

† after the dissolution of the northern kingdom that he had prophesied. The second part of the verse emphasizes the power of the Lord, who needs no human agents to fulfill his will. It may refer to the deliverance of Jerusalem from the siege of Sennacherib (2 Kgs 19, 35ff).

1, 9: *Lo-ammi:* "not my people."

2, 4: The Lord speaks of Israel, still using the example of Hosea's wife.

2, 5: *I will strip her naked:* contemporary documents indicate that this was a conventional punishment for adultery.

2, 7: *My lovers:* the local fertility deities to whom, rather than to the Lord (v 10), the unfaithful Israelites attributed the produce of the land.

2, 8f: The crop failures, blight, etc., sent by the Lord (vv 11-14) have as their purpose to make Israel see the folly of her ways.

2, 15: *The days of the Baals:* ritual observances held in various local shrines in honor of Baal.

2, 16f: Israel's journey in the desert represents for Hosea the time of Israel's fidelity, before it was corrupted by the ways of Canaan; cf Jer 2, 2-7; Am 5, 25. Thus, he pictures a restoration in terms of a new entry into the promised land.

2, 18: *My baal:* the word means "lord, master." It was commonly used by women of their husbands, but it is to be shunned as a title for the Lord because of its association with the pagan god Baal. Probably it had been so used by many Israelites, who saw little if any difference between the worship of the Lord and the worship of Baal.

Bow and sword and war
   I will destroy from the land,
   and I will let them take their rest in
      security.

21† I will espouse you to me forever:
   I will espouse you in right and in justice,
      in love and in mercy;

22 I will espouse you in fidelity,
   and you shall know the LORD.

23 On that day I will respond, says the LORD;
   I will respond to the heavens,
      and they shall respond to the earth;

24 The earth shall respond to the grain, and
      wine, and oil,
   and these shall respond to Jezreel.

25✶ I will sow him for myself in the land,
   and I will have pity on Lo-ruhama.
   I will say to Lo-ammi, "You are my people,"
      and he shall say, "My God!"

Triumph of Love

3 **1†** Again the LORD said to me:
   Give your love to a woman
      beloved of a paramour, an adulteress;
   Even as the LORD loves the people of Israel,
      though they turn to other gods
      and are fond of raisin cakes.

2†So I bought her for fifteen pieces of silver and a homer and a lethech of barley. **3**Then I said to her:

   "Many days you shall wait for me;
      you shall not play the harlot
   Or belong to any man;
      I in turn will wait for you."

4† For the people of Israel shall remain many
      days
   without king or prince,
   Without sacrifice or sacred pillar,
      without ephod or household idols.

5✶† Then the people of Israel shall turn back
      and seek the LORD, their God,
      and David, their king;
   They shall come trembling to the LORD
      and to his bounty, in the last days.

2/1✶† The number of the Israelites
      shall be like the sand of the sea,
      which can be neither measured nor
         counted.
   Whereas they were called,
      "Lo-ammi,"
   They shall be called,
      "Children of the living God."

2/2 Then the people of Judah and of Israel
      shall be gathered together;

They shall appoint for themselves one head
   and come up from other lands,
   for great shall be the day of Jezreel.

2/3 Say to your brothers, "Ammi,"
   and to your sisters, "Ruhama."

II: ISRAEL'S GUILT AND PUNISHMENT

Crimes of Israel

4 **1** Hear the word of the LORD, O people of
      Israel,
   for the LORD has a grievance
      against the inhabitants of the land:
   There is no fidelity, no mercy,
      no knowledge of God in the land.

2✶ False swearing, lying, murder, stealing and
      adultery!
   in their lawlessness, bloodshed follows
      bloodshed.

3 Therefore the land mourns,
   and everything that dwells in it
      languishes:
   The beasts of the field,
      the birds of the air,
      and even the fish of the sea perish.

---

† 2, 1-3: These verses continue the conditional promise of restoration made in 3, 1-5, reversing the dire predictions of chapter 1; the symbolic names now become names of honor: *Jezreel,* "God sows"; *Ammi,* "my people"; *Ruhama,* "she is pitied."

2, 21f: The Lord will once more espouse Israel; the qualities ascribed to the renewed people are the bridal gift (cf Gn 24, 53) with which he will endow it. *In right and in justice:* two terms dear to Hosea, used by him especially to condemn the popular social injustice and corruption of the legal processes. Here they mean right conduct in general. *Love:* one of the most characteristic words of Hosea's prophecy. It means a dutiful love, based on a social relation; here it refers to the covenant between God and his people. It is a love fulfilled by the performance of mutual obligations. *Mercy:* from the same root as the word translated *pity* in 1, 6; cf v. 25. *And you shall know the Lord:* another characteristic expression of Hosea; cf 4, 1; 5, 4; 6, 3.6. It means not an abstract but a practical knowledge, i. e., acknowledgment of his will, obedience to his law.

3, 1-5: Hosea is instructed to take Gomer back, redeeming her from her paramours. On condition of her amendment, she will be restored to her former position of wife. This in turn signifies God's enduring love for his people. He will put the people through a period of trial—the dissolution of the kingdom—in order that they may return to him wholeheartedly.

3, 1: *Raisin cakes:* offerings to the fertility goddess Ashera, the female counterpart of Baal; cf Jer 7, 18; 44, 19.

3, 2: *Homer:* about ten bushels. *Lethech:* a half-homer.

3, 4: *Sacred pillar:* the stone massebah, originally perhaps a phallic symbol, representing Baal. These were also used, with another signification, in Israelite worship; see notes on Gn 28, 18; Ex 34, 13. *Ephod:* an instrument used in consulting the deity; cf 1 Sm 23, 6-12; 30, 7; see notes on Ex 28, 6.15-30. *Household idols:* images regarded as the tutelary deities of the household; cf Gn 31, 19; Jgs 17, 5; 18, 14.17f.

3, 5: *David, their king:* the messianic King of the Davidic line who will restore the kingdom of God's people; cf Jer 23, 5; Ez 34, 23f. *The last days:* the messianic age.

✶ 2/1: Rom 9, 26.   3/5: Ez 34, 23.
   2/25: Rom 9, 25; 1 Pt 2, 10.   4/2: Ex 20, 13-17.

Guilt of the Priests

4† But let no one protest, let no one complain;
    with you is my grievance, O priests!

5 You shall stumble in the day,
    and the prophets shall stumble with you
       at night;
    I will destroy your mother.

6 My people perish for want of knowledge!
    Since you have rejected knowledge,
    I will reject you from my priesthood;
    Since you have ignored the law of your
       God,
    I will also ignore your sons.

7 One and all they sin against me,
    exchanging their glory for shame.

8 They feed on the sin of my people,
    and are greedy for their guilt.

9* The priests shall fare no better than the
       people:
    I will punish them for their ways,
    and repay them for their deeds.

10 They shall eat but not be satisfied,
    they shall play the harlot but not
       increase,
    Because they have abandoned the Lord
11   to practice harlotry.

Old wine and new
    deprive my people of understanding.

12† They consult their piece of wood,
    and their wand makes pronouncements
       for them,
    For the spirit of harlotry has led them
       astray;
    they commit harlotry, forsaking their
       God.

13 On the mountaintops they offer sacrifice
    and on the hills they burn incense,
    Beneath oak and poplar and terebinth,
       because of their pleasant shade.
    That is why your daughters play the harlot,
    and your daughters-in-law are
       adulteresses.

14† Am I then to punish your daughters for
       their harlotry,
    your daughters-in-law for their adultery?
    You yourselves consort with harlots,
    and with prostitutes you offer sacrifice!
    So must a people without understanding
       come to ruin.

15† Though you play the harlot, O Israel,
    let not Judah become guilty!
    Come not to Gilgal,
       nor up to Beth-aven,
       to swear, "As the Lord lives!"

16 For Israel is as stubborn as a heifer;
    will the Lord now give them broad
       pastures
    as though they were lambs?

17† Ephraim is an associate of idols,
    let him alone!

18 When their carousing is over,
    they give themselves to harlotry;
    in their arrogance they love shame.

19† The wind has bound them up in its pinions;
    they shall have only shame from their
       altars.

Guilt of the Leaders

5 **1*†** Hear this, O priests,
    Pay attention, O house of Israel,
    O household of the king, give ear!
    It is you who are called to judgment.
    For you have become a snare at Mizpah,
    and a net spread upon Tabor.

2 In their perversity they have sunk into
       wickedness,
    and I am rejected by them all.

3 I know Ephraim,
    and Israel is not hidden from me;
    Now Ephraim has played the harlot,
    Israel is defiled.

4 Their deeds do not allow them
    to return to their God;
    For the spirit of harlotry is in them,
    and they do not recognize the Lord.

5 The arrogance of Israel bears witness
    against him;
    Ephraim stumbles in his guilt,
    and Judah stumbles with them.

---

†

4, 4ff: Hosea is particularly severe with the *priests* in the northern kingdom, who had led the way in the general apostasy from God's law. The *prophets* here associated with the priests (v 5) were doubtless cult prophets, who were often unworthy of their pretended calling; cf Jer 2, 8; 4, 9f; 6, 13f; 23, 9-40.

4, 12: *Wood . . . wand:* an idol used in divination.

4, 14: *With prostitutes you offer sacrifice:* the ritual prostitution practiced at the Canaanite shrines was introduced even into sanctuaries dedicated to the Lord. In comparison, the adultery that had become common in Israel was a far less reprehensible crime.

4, 15: *Gilgal:* not the Gilgal of the south (Jos 4, 19f), but a sanctuary north of Bethel where there was an association of cult prophets (2 Kgs 2, 1ff; 4, 38). *Beth-aven:* literally, "house of iniquity," Hosea's nickname for Bethel, or a scribal substitute for Bethel, "house of god," in this context. Bethel was one of the royal shrines of Israel, where there was a schismatic public worship of the Lord; cf 1 Kgs 12, 26-30.

4, 17: *Ephraim:* the heartland of the northern kingdom. During the latter part of Hosea's prophetic career, Ephraim was all that remained of Israel after the Assyrians had overrun Transjordan and Galilee.

4, 19: The Israelites shall be carried from their country as by a whirlwind. To this their idolatry has brought them.

5, 1: *Mizpah:* probably the Mizpah in Transjordan is meant; cf Jos 11, 8. *Tabor:* the mountain that dominates the valley of Jezreel.

---

6 With their flocks and their herds they shall go
    to seek the LORD, but they shall not find him;
    he has withdrawn himself from them.

7 They have been untrue to the LORD,
    for they have begotten illegitimate children;
    Now shall the new moon devour them
    together with their fields.

Political Upheavals

8† Blow the horn in Gibeah,
    the trumpet in Ramah!
    Sound the alarm in Beth-aven:
    "Look behind you, O Benjamin!"

9 Ephraim shall become a waste
    on the day of chastisement:
    Against the tribes of Israel
    I announce what is sure to be.

10*† The princes of Judah have become
    like those that move a boundary line;
    Upon them I will pour out
    my wrath like water.

11† Is Ephraim maltreated, his rights violated?
    No, he has willingly gone after filth!

12† I am like a moth for Ephraim,
    like maggots for the house of Judah.

13† When Ephraim saw his infirmity,
    and Judah his sore,
    Ephraim went to Assyria,
    and Judah sent to the great king.
    But he cannot heal you
    nor take away your sore.

14 For I am like a lion to Ephraim,
    like a young lion to the house of Judah;
    It is I who rend the prey and depart,
    I carry it away and no one can save it from me.

Insincere Conversion

15† I will go back to my place
    until they pay for their guilt
    and seek my presence.

    In their affliction, they shall look for me:

6 **1** "Come, let us return to the LORD,
    For it is he who has rent, but he will heal us;
    he has struck us, but he will bind our wounds.

2*† He will revive us after two days;
    on the third day he will raise us up,
    to live in his presence.

3 Let us know, let us strive to know the LORD;
    as certain as the dawn is his coming,
    and his judgment shines forth like the light of day!
    He will come to us like the rain,
    like spring rain that waters the earth."

4† What can I do with you, Ephraim?
    What can I do with you, Judah?
    Your piety is like a morning cloud,
    like the dew that early passes away.

5 For this reason I smote them through the prophets,
    I slew them by the words of my mouth;

6* For it is love that I desire, not sacrifice,
    and knowledge of God rather than holocausts.

7 But they, in their land, violated the covenant;
    there they were untrue to me.

8 Gilead is a city of evildoers,
    tracked with blood.

9 As brigands ambush a man,
    a band of priests slay on the way to Shechem,
    committing monstrous crime.

10 In the house of Israel I have seen a horrible thing:
    there harlotry is found in Ephraim,
    Israel is defiled.

11† For you also, O Judah,
    a harvest has been appointed.

---

† 5, 8-14: This passage refers to the Syro-Ephraimite war of 735-734 B. C., when a coalition of Arameans and Israelites attempted to dethrone the king of Judah. Judah repulsed the attempt with the aid of Assyria, and the latter devastated both Aram and Israel; cf 2 Kgs 16, 5-9. Hosea condemns both Israel and Judah for the war.

5, 8: A vision of invasion, from *Gibeah* and *Ramah* in northern Judah, into Israel.

5, 10: *Like those that move a boundary line:* comparison of the invaders to a classic case of social injustice; cf Dt 19, 14; 27, 17; Prv 23, 10f.

5, 11: *Gone after filth:* by allying himself with Aram.

5, 12: *Moth . . . maggots:* internal corruption will work the Lord's punishment on both Israel and Judah.

5, 13: *Ephraim went . . . the great king:* in 738 B. C. the Israelite King Manahem had to pay tribute to the Assyrian king Tiglath-pileser III, whose vassal he became (2 Kgs 15, 19f). Under the threat of the Syro-Ephraimite invasion King Ahaz of Judah also submitted himself and his country to Tiglath-pileser (2 Kgs 16, 7-9). "The great king" was the title used by the Assyrian kings.

5, 15: The Lord withdraws himself from Israel, hoping for its repentance.

6, 2: *After two days; on the third day:* after a short lapse of time.

6, 4: *Piety:* the word is translated "love" in 2, 21 and in v 6 below.

6, 11: *Harvest:* when the land will reap the consequences of its sins.

---

* 10: Dt 19, 14; 27, 17.   6: 1 Sm 15, 22; Eccl 4, 17;
6/2: 1 Cor 15, 4.   Mt 9, 13; 12, 7.

7

1 When I would bring about the restoration
of my people,
when I would heal Israel,
The guilt of Ephraim stands out,
the wickedness of Samaria;
They practice falsehood,
thieves break in, bandits plunder abroad.

2 Yet they do not remind themselves
that I remember all their wickedness.
Even now their crimes surround them,
present to my sight.

Failure of the Monarchy

3† In their wickedness they regale the king,
the princes too, with their deceits.

4 They are all kindled to wrath
like a blazing oven,
Whose fire the baker desists from stirring
once the dough is kneaded until it has
risen.

5 On the day of our king,
the princes are overcome with the heat
of wine.
He extends his hand among dissemblers;

6 the plotters approach with hearts like
ovens.
All the night their anger sleeps;
in the morning it flares like a blazing fire.

7 They are all heated like ovens,
and consume their rulers.
All their kings have fallen;
none of them calls upon me.

Foreign Alliances

8† Ephraim mingles with the nations,
Ephraim is a hearth cake unturned.

9 Strangers have sapped his strength,
but he takes no notice of it;
Of gray hairs, too, there is a sprinkling,
but he takes no notice of it.

10 The arrogance of Israel bears witness
against him;
yet they do not return to the Lord, their
God,
nor seek him, for all that.

11 Ephraim is like a dove,
silly and senseless;
They call upon Egypt,
they go to Assyria.

12 Even as they go I will spread my net
around them,
like birds in the air I will bring them
down.
In an instant I will send them captive
from their land.

Perversity of Israel

13 Woe to them, they have strayed from me!
Ruin to them, they have sinned against
me!
Though I wished to redeem them,
they spoke lies against me.

14† They have not cried to me from their hearts
when they wailed upon their beds;
For wheat and wine they lacerated
themselves,
while they rebelled against me.

15 Though I trained and strengthened their
arms,
yet they devised evil against me.

16 They have again become useless,
like a treacherous bow.
Their princes shall fall by the sword
because of the insolence of their tongues;
thus they shall be mocked in the land of
Egypt.

8

1 A trumpet to your lips,
You who watch over the house of the
Lord!
Since they have violated my covenant,
and sinned against my law,

2 While to me they cry out,
"O God of Israel, we know you!"

3 The men of Israel have thrown away what
is good;
the enemy shall pursue them.

4† They made kings, but not by my authority;
they established princes, but without my
approval.
With their silver and gold they made
idols for themselves, to their own
destruction.

5 Cast away your calf, O Samaria!
my wrath is kindled against them;
How long will they be unable to attain
innocence in Israel?

---

† **7, 3-7:** This passage refers to the dynastic upheavals of Israel's declining days. Between the death of Jeroboam II and the fall of Samaria to the Assyrians, a matter of some twenty-five years, there were four separate dynasties on the throne and as many murdered kings. The prophet compares the Israelite nobles who were inflamed with passion to an overheated oven that consumes what it is supposed to bake; thus the land consumes its kings. *Regale:* with wine (v 3). Like fire smoldering through the night and blazing up in the morning, the sleeping anger of plotters soon breaks out in open rebellion; the succession of night and morning suggests the short reigns of the various kings of this troubled period.

7, 8: *A hearth cake unturned:* burnt on one side, half baked on the other, and therefore useless. Israel's decline in power is ascribed to its disastrous meddling in the power politics of the neighboring nations.

7, 14: *They lacerated themselves:* a common oriental practice in prayers of earnest impetation (1 Kgs 18, 28); the practice was forbidden in Israelite religion (Lv 19, 28; Dt 14, 1).

8, 4-6: Israel's monarchy and separate sanctuary are here associated, as in 1 Kgs 12, 20-33; both were the result of rebellion against the divinely approved Davidic dynasty and the Jerusalem temple with the ark of the covenant. The calf image set up by Jeroboam I in the royal shrines prevented Israel from attaining *innocence* (vv 5f).

6   The work of an artisan,
      no god at all,
Destined for the flames—
      such is the calf of Samaria!

7   When they sow the wind,
      they shall reap the whirlwind;
The stalk of grain that forms no ear
      can yield no flour;
Even if it could,
      strangers would swallow it.

8   Israel is swallowed up;
      he is now among the nations
      a thing of no value.

9   They went up to Assyria—
      a wild ass off on its own—
Ephraim bargained for lovers.

10   Even though they bargain with the nations,
      I will now gather an army;
King and princes shall shortly
      succumb under the burden.

11†   When Ephraim made many altars to
           expiate sin,
      his altars became occasions of sin.

12   Though I write for him my many
           ordinances,
      they are considered as a stranger's.

13   Though they offer sacrifice,
      immolate flesh and eat it,
      the Lord is not pleased with them.
He shall still remember their guilt
      and punish their sins;
      they shall return to Egypt.

14✻   Israel has forgotten his maker
      and built palaces.
Judah, too, has fortified many cities;
      but I will send fire upon his cities,
      to devour their castles.

Exile without Worship

9   1†   Rejoice not, O Israel,
      exult not like the nations!
For you have been unfaithful to your God,
      loving a harlot's hire
      upon every threshing floor.

2   Threshing floor and wine press shall not
           nourish them,
      the new wine shall fail them.

3   They shall not dwell in the Lord's land;
      Ephraim shall return to Egypt,
      and in Assyria they shall eat unclean
           food.

4†   They shall not pour libations of wine to
           the Lord,
      or proffer their sacrifices before him.
Theirs will be like mourners' bread,
      that makes unclean all who eat of it;

Such food as they have shall be for
      themselves;
      it cannot enter the house of the Lord.

5†   What will you do on the festival day,
      the day of the Lord's feast?

6   When they go from the ruins,
      Egypt shall gather them in, Memphis
           shall bury them.
Weeds shall overgrow their silver
      treasures,
      and thorns invade their tents.

The Prophet Ridiculed

7   They have come, the days of punishment!
      they have come, the days of recompense!
Let Israel know it!
      "The prophet is a fool,
      the man of the spirit is mad!"
Because your iniquity is great,
      great, too, is your hostility.

8   A prophet is Ephraim's watchman with
           God,
      yet a fowler's snare is on all his ways,
      hostility in the house of his God.

9†   They have sunk to the depths of corruption,
      as in the days of Gibeah;
He shall remember their iniquity
      and punish their sins.

Crime of Baal-peor

10†   Like grapes in the desert,
      I found Israel;
Like the first fruits of the fig tree in its
      prime,
      I considered your fathers.
When they came to Baal-peor
      and consecrated themselves to the
           Shame,
      they became as abhorrent as the thing
      they loved.

---

† 8, 11: The very multiplicity of sanctuaries throughout the land was a danger to the purity of worship. The local shrines were speedily assimilated to the cult places used by the Canaanites, and the Lord was identified with the god Baal worshiped there. Thus the Deuteronomic writers, influenced by prophetic ideas, ended by restricting sacrificial worship to the one temple in Jerusalem.

9, 1f: *Upon every threshing floor:* an allusion to harvest festivals in honor of Baal, to whom the Israelites had attributed the fertility of the land; cf 2, 7.

9, 4: *Mourners' bread:* bread eaten at funeral rites; cf Dt 26, 13f. Contact with a corpse made a person ritually unclean, together with everything he touched. Such bread could not be offered to the Lord.

9, 5: *The Lord's feast:* doubtless the autumn feast of Booths, the most important of the Israelite public celebrations; cf Lv 23, 34.

9, 9: *The days of Gibeah:* a reference to the outrage committed at Gibeah in the days of the Judges (Jgs 19, 22-30).

9, 10: At *Baal-peor* (Nm 25, 1-5) the Israelites consecrated themselves to Baal, here called *the Shame*.

✻ 8/14: Am 2, 5.

11 The glory of Ephraim flies away like a
      bird:
   no birth, no carrying in the womb, no
      conception.
   Were they to bear children,
      I would slay the darlings of their
      womb.

12 Even though they bring up their
      children,
   I will make them childless, till not one
      is left.
   Woe to them
      when I turn away from them!

13 Ephraim, as I saw, was like Tyre,
      planted in a beauteous spot;
   But Ephraim shall bring out
      his children to the slayer.

14† Give them, O Lord!
      give them what?
   Give them an unfruitful womb,
      and dry breasts!

Crime of Gilgal

15*† All their wickedness is in Gilgal;
      yes, there they incurred my hatred.
   Because of their wicked deeds
      I will drive them out of my house.
   I will love them no longer;
      all their princes are rebels.

16 Ephraim is stricken,
      their root is dried up;
      they shall bear no fruit.

17 My God will disown them
      because they have not listened to him;
      they shall be wanderers among the
      nations.

Punishment of Idolatry

10

1† Israel is a luxuriant vine
      whose fruit matches its growth.
   The more abundant his fruit,
      the more altars he built;
   The more productive his land,
      the more sacred pillars he set up.

2 Their heart is false,
      now they pay for their guilt;
   God shall break down their altars
      and destroy their sacred pillars.

3 If they would say,
   "We have no king"—
   Since they do not fear the Lord,
      what can the king do for them?

4† Nothing but make promises,
      swear false oaths, and make alliances,
   While justice grows wild
      like wormwood in a plowed field!

5† The inhabitants of Samaria fear
      for the calf of Beth-aven;
   The people mourn for it
      and its priests wail over it,
      because the glory has departed from
      it.

6 It too shall be carried to Assyria,
      as an offering to the great king.
   Ephraim shall be taken into captivity,
      Israel be shamed by his schemes.

7 The king of Samaria shall disappear,
      like foam upon the waters.

8* The high places of Aven shall be
      destroyed,
      the sin of Israel;
   thorns and thistles shall overgrow
      their altars.
   Then they shall cry out to the
      mountains, "Cover us!"
      and to the hills, "Fall upon us!"

9* Since the days of Gibeah
      you have sinned, O Israel.
   There they took their stand;
      war was not to reach them in Gibeah.

10*† Against the wanton people I came
      and I chastised them;
   I gathered troops against them
      when I chastised them for their two
      crimes.

Time to Seek the Lord

11 Ephraim was a trained heifer,
      willing to thresh;
   I myself laid a yoke
      upon her fair neck;
   Ephraim was to be harnessed, Judah
      was to plow,
      Jacob was to break his furrows:

12* "Sow for yourselves justice,
      reap the fruit of piety;
   Break up for yourselves a new field,
      for it is time to seek the Lord,
      till he come and rain down justice
      upon you."

---

†
9, 14: *An unfruitful womb:* this appears to be a reversal of the ancient blessing of Joseph contained in Gn 49, 25f, in which the increase, hence fruitfulness, promised to the patriarch is even signified by the name of his son Ephraim, on whose descendants the prophet now invokes the curse of extinction.

9, 15: *Gilgal:* see note on 4, 15.

10, 1: *Sacred pillars:* see note on 3, 4.

10, 4: *Justice . . . like wormwood:* the administration of justice, which should have been the mainstay of the people, has in corrupt hands become another instrument of oppression; cf Am 6, 13.

10, 5: *The calf of Beth-aven:* see notes on 4, 15; 8, 4ff.

10, 10: *Their two crimes:* possibly the outrage described in Jgs 19 is conceived as a double crime, of adultery and murder. Or the prophet regards the proclamation of the monarchy (cf 1 Sm 10, 23f) as a crime.

❋
15: 1 Sm 8, 5.   9: Jgs 20, 1.
10/8: Is 2, 19; Lk 23, 30;   10: Jer 4, 3.
      Rv 6, 16.   12: Is 45, 8.

13 But you have cultivated wickedness,
    reaped perversity,
    and eaten the fruit of falsehood.

Because you have trusted in your
    chariots,
    and in your many warriors,
14*† Turmoil shall break out among your
    tribes
    and all your fortresses shall be
    ravaged
As Salman ravaged Beth-arbel in time
    of war,
    smashing mothers and their children.
15 So shall it be done to you, Bethel,
    because of your utter wickedness:
At dawn the king of Israel
    shall perish utterly.

When Israel Was a Child

11 **1*†** When Israel was a child I loved him,
    out of Egypt I called my son.
2 The more I called them,
    the farther they went from me,
Sacrificing to the Baals
    and burning incense to idols.
3 Yet it was I who taught Ephraim to
    walk,
    who took them in my arms;
4† I drew them with human cords,
    with bands of love;
I fostered them like one
    who raises an infant to his cheeks;
Yet, though I stooped to feed my child,
    they did not know that I was their
    healer.

5 He shall return to the land of Egypt,
    and Assyria shall be his king;
6 The sword shall begin with his cities
    and end by consuming his solitudes.
Because they refused to repent,
    their own counsels shall devour them.
7 His people are in suspense about
    returning to him;
    and God, though in unison they cry
    out to him,
    shall not raise them up.

End of the Exile

8*† How could I give you up, O Ephraim,
    or deliver you up, O Israel?
How could I treat you as Admah,
    or make you like Zeboiim?
My heart is overwhelmed,
    my pity is stirred.
9 I will not give vent to my blazing anger,
    I will not destroy Ephraim again;

For I am God and not man,
    the Holy One present among you;
    I will not let the flames consume you.
10 They shall follow the LORD,
    who roars like a lion;
When he roars,
    his sons shall come frightened from
    the west,
11 Out of Egypt they shall come trembling,
    like sparrows,
    from the land of Assyria, like doves;
And I will resettle them in their homes,
    says the LORD.

Infidelity of Israel

12 **1** Ephraim has surrounded me with lies,
    the house of Israel, with deceit;
Judah is still rebellious against God,
    against the Holy One, who is faithful.
2† Ephraim chases the wind,
    ever pursuing the gale.
His lies and falsehoods are many:
    he comes to terms with Assyria,
    and carries oil to Egypt.
3† The LORD has a grievance against Israel:
    he shall punish Jacob for his conduct,
    for his deeds he shall repay him.
4* In the womb he supplanted his brother,
    and as a man he contended with God;
5 He contended with the angel and
    triumphed,
    entreating him with tears.
At Bethel he met God
    and there he spoke with him:
6 The LORD, the God of hosts,
    the LORD is his name!
7 You shall return by the help of your God,
    if you remain loyal and do right
    and always hope in your God.

---

† **10, 14:** *As Salman ravaged Beth-arbel:* allusion to an invasion not otherwise mentioned in the Bible. Salman may have been the Moabite king of this name mentioned in an inscription of Tiglath-pileser III. There were several Beth-arbels in Palestine; this one was probably in Transjordan.

11, 1: *Out of Egypt:* Hosea, like most of the prophets, dates the real beginning of Israel from the time of Moses and the Exodus. Mt 2, 15 applies this text to the return of the Christ Child from Egypt.

11, 4: *I drew them . . . with bands of love:* not forcing them like draft animals, but drawing them with kindness and affection.

11, 8: *Admah . . . Zeboiim:* cities destroyed with Sodom and Gomorrah (Dt 29, 22).

12, 2: *He comes . . . Egypt:* allusion to the commercial and military pacts with the great powers, consistently condemned by the prophets as derogatory of the Lord's claim on his people.

12, 3-7: Contemporary Israel and the Israel represented by its ancestor Jacob (Israel) are here alternated, a splendid example of the Hebrew concept of "corporate personality" or easy transition from the individual to the community of which he is part. Hosea recalls the history of Jacob as it now appears in Genesis, but with some differences of detail and order.

---

*
14: Jgs 8, 10ff.   8: Gn 19, 24f.
11/1: Mt 2, 15.   12/4: Gn 25, 26; 32, 25.

8   A merchant who holds a false balance,
        who loves to defraud!
9   Though Ephraim says,
        "How rich I have become;
            I have made a fortune!"
    All his gain shall not suffice him
        for the guilt of his sin.
10   I am the Lord, your God,
        since the land of Egypt;
    I will again have you live in tents,
        as in that appointed time.
11   I granted many visions
        and spoke to the prophets,
            through whom I set forth examples.
12   In Gilead is falsehood, they have come
            to nought,
        in Gilgal they sacrifice to bullocks;
    Their altars are like heaps of stones
        in the furrows of the field.

13* When Jacob fled to the land of Aram,
        he served for a wife;
            for a wife Israel tended sheep.
14*† By a prophet the Lord brought Israel
            out of Egypt,
        and by a prophet they were protected.
15   Ephraim has exasperated his Lord;
        therefore he shall cast his blood-guilt
            upon him
        and repay him for his outrage.

13

1   Ephraim's word caused fear,
        for he was exalted in Israel;
            but he sinned through Baal and died.

Punishment for Ingratitude

2   Now they continue to sin,
        making for themselves molten images,
    Silver idols according to their fancy,
        all of them the work of artisans.
    "To these," they say, "offer sacrifice."
        Men kiss calves!
3   Therefore, they shall be like a morning
            cloud
        or like the dew that early passes away,
    Like chaff storm-driven from the
            threshing floor
        or like smoke out of the window.
4*   I am the Lord, your God,
        since the land of Egypt;
    You know no God besides me,
        and there is no savior but me.
5   I fed you in the desert,
        in the torrid land.

6   They ate their fill;
        when filled, they became proud of
            heart
        and forgot me.
7   Therefore, I will be like a lion to them,
        like a panther by the road I will keep
            watch.
8   I will attack them like a bear robbed of
            its young,
        and tear their hearts from their
            breasts;
    I will devour them on the spot like a
            lion,
        as though a wild beast were to rend
            them.
9   Your destruction, O Israel!
        who is there to help you?
10* Where now is your king,
        that he may rescue you in all your
            cities?
    And your rulers, of whom you said,
        "Give me a king and princes"?
11† I give you a king in my anger,
        and I take him away in my wrath.
12   The guilt of Israel is wrapped up,
        his sin is stored away.
13† The birth pangs shall come for him,
        but he shall be an unwise child;
    For when it is time he shall not present
            himself
        where children break forth.
14*† Shall I deliver them from the power of
            the nether world?
        shall I redeem them from death?
    Where are your plagues, O death!
        where is your sting, O nether world!
    My eyes are closed to compassion.

15* Though he be fruitful among his fellows,
        an east wind shall come, a wind from
            the Lord,
        rising from the desert,
    That shall dry up his spring,
        and leave his fountain dry.
    It shall loot his land
        of every precious thing.

---

†
    12, 14: *A prophet:* Moses.
    13, 11: *I give you a king . . . in my wrath:* the Lord punishes
the people of the northern kingdom by giving them incompetent kings who are soon deposed.
    13, 13: Israel's sin is such as to warrant its destruction (v 12),
because it refuses to do penance. It will therefore perish as
surely as the unborn child which dies in its mother's body because it does not properly employ the only way to safety.
    13, 14: *Shall . . . nether world:* a vigorous affirmation of the
Lord's determination to destroy Israel. St. Paul cites these
words in a different sense (1 Cor 15, 54f), that of the ultimate
victory of life over death in the resurrection of the body on
the last day, wrought through the merits of Christ's passion and
resurrection.

✿
    13: Gn 28, 5; 29, 20.   10: 1 Sm 8, 5.
    14: Ex 14, 21f.   14: 1 Cor 15, 54.
    13/4: Is 43, 11.   15: Ez 19, 12.

14 ¹ Samaria shall expiate her guilt,
   for she has rebelled against her God.
   They shall fall by the sword,
      their little ones shall be dashed to
         pieces,
      their expectant mothers shall be
         ripped open.

Sincere Conversion

² Return, O Israel, to the Lord, your God;
   you have collapsed through your guilt.
³ Take with you words,
      and return to the Lord;
   Say to him, "Forgive all iniquity,
      and receive what is good, that we
         may render
      as offerings the bullocks from our
         stalls.
⁴ Assyria will not save us,
      nor shall we have horses to mount;
   We shall say no more, 'Our god,'
      to the work of our hands;
      for in you the orphan finds
         compassion."

⁵ I will heal their defection,
   I will love them freely;
      for my wrath is turned away from
         them.

⁶ I will be like the dew for Israel:
   he shall blossom like the lily;
   He shall strike root like the Lebanon
      cedar,
⁷   and put forth his shoots.
   His splendor shall be like the olive tree
      and his fragrance like the Lebanon
         cedar.
⁸ Again they shall dwell in his shade
      and raise grain;
   They shall blossom like the vine,
      and his fame shall be like the wine of
         Lebanon.

⁹ Ephraim! What more has he to do with
      idols?
   I have humbled him, but I will
      prosper him.
   "I am like a verdant cypress tree"—
      Because of me you bear fruit!

                    *   *   *

10† Let him who is wise understand these
      things;
   let him who is prudent know them.
   Straight are the paths of the Lord,
      in them the just walk,
      but sinners stumble in them.

---

† 14, 10: A later addition in the style of the wisdom literature.

The Book of Joel

Introduction

This prophecy is rich in apocalyptic imagery and strongly eschatological in tone. It was composed about 400 B. C. Its prevailing theme is the day of the Lord.

A terrible invasion of locusts ravaged Judah. So frightful was the scourge that the prophet visualized it as a symbol of the coming day of the Lord. In the face of this threatening catastrophe, the prophet summoned the people to repent, to turn to the Lord with fasting and weeping. They were ordered to convoke a solemn assembly in which the priests would pray for deliverance. The Lord answered their prayer and promised to drive away the locusts and bless the land with peace and prosperity. To these material blessings would be added an outpouring of the spirit on all flesh. St. Peter, in his first discourse before the people at Pentecost (Acts 2, 16-21), sees in the coming of the Holy Spirit the fulfillment of this promise (1, 1-3, 5).

The concluding poem pictures the nations gathered in the Valley of Jehoshaphat, where the Lord is about to pass judgment. Israel's enemies are summoned to hear the solemn indictment; their evil deeds are at last requited. The tumultuous throng assembled in the valley of decision is made up of the enemies of God and they face inevitable destruction. The oracle changes abruptly from the terrifying image of judgment to a vision of Israel restored and forever secure from her enemies. God is both the vindicator of his people and the source of their blessings (4, 1-21).

The Land Invaded

1 ¹THE WORD OF THE LORD which came to Joel, the son of Pethuel.

2   Hear this, you elders!
        Pay attention, all you who dwell in the
           land!
    Has the like of this happened in your days,
        or in the days of your fathers?

3   Tell it to your children,
        and your children to their children,
        and their children to the next generation.

4†   What the cutter left,
        the locust swarm has eaten;
    What the locust swarm left,
        the grasshopper has eaten;
    And what the grasshopper left,
        the devourer has eaten.

5   Wake up, you drunkards, and weep;
        wail, all you drinkers of wine,

    Because the juice of the grape
        will be withheld from your mouths.

6†   For a people has invaded my land,
        mighty and without number;
    His teeth are the teeth of a lion,
        and his molars those of a lioness.

7   He has laid waste my vine,
        and blighted my fig tree;
    He has stripped it, sheared off its bark;
        its branches are made white.

8   Lament like a virgin girt with sackcloth
        for the spouse of her youth.

9   Abolished are offering and libation
        from the house of the LORD;
    In mourning are the priests,
        the ministers of the LORD.

10   The field is ravaged,
        the earth mourns,
    Because the grain is ravaged,
        the must has failed,
        the oil languishes.

11   Be appalled, you husbandmen!
        wail, you vinedressers!
    Over the wheat and the barley,
        because the harvest of the field has
           perished.

12   The vine has dried up,
        the fig tree is withered;
    The pomegranate, the date palm also, and
        the apple,
        all the trees of the field are dried up;
    Yes, joy has withered away
        from among mankind.

Call to Penance

13   Gird yourselves and weep, O priests!
        wail, O ministers of the altar!
    Come, spend the night in sackcloth,
        O ministers of my God!
    The house of your God is deprived
        of offering and libation.

14✱   Proclaim a fast,
        call an assembly;
    Gather the elders,
        all who dwell in the land,

✱ 1/14: 2, 15.

---

† 1, 4: *Cutter . . . locust . . . grasshopper . . . devourer*: these names refer to various species of locusts: they can only be approximate.

1, 6: *A people*: the locusts compared to an invading army.

Into the house of the LORD, your God,
   and cry to the LORD!

15   Alas, the day!
   for near is the day of the LORD,
   and it comes as ruin from the Almighty.

16   From before our very eyes
   has not the food been cut off;
  And from the house of our God,
   joy and gladness?

17   The seed lies shriveled under its clods;
   the stores are destroyed,
  The barns are broken down,
   for the grain has failed.

18   How the beasts groan!
   The herds of cattle are bewildered!
  Because they have no pasturage,
   even the flocks of sheep have perished.

19   To you, O LORD, I cry!
   for fire has devoured the pastures of the
     plain,
   and flame has enkindled all the trees of
     the field.

20   Even the beasts of the field
   cry out to you;
  For the streams of water are dried up,
   and fire has devoured the pastures of the
     plain.

The Day of the Lord

2 1   Blow the trumpet in Zion,
   sound the alarm on my holy mountain!
  Let all who dwell in the land tremble,
   for the day of the LORD is coming;

2   Yes, it is near, a day of darkness and of
     gloom,
   a day of clouds and somberness!
  Like dawn spreading over the mountains,
   a people numerous and mighty!
  Their like has not been from of old,
   nor will it be after them,
   even to the years of distant generations.

3   Before them a fire devours,
   and after them a flame enkindles;
  Like the garden of Eden is the land before
     them,
   and after them a desert waste;
   from them there is no escape.

4   Their appearance is that of horses;
   like steeds they run.

5   As with the rumble of chariots
   they leap on the mountaintops;
  As with the crackling of a fiery flame
   devouring stubble;

Like a mighty people
   arrayed for battle.

6   Before them peoples are in torment,
   every face blanches.

7   Like warriors they run,
   like soldiers they scale the wall;
  They advance, each in his own lane,
   without swerving from their paths.

8   No one crowds another,
   each advances in his own track;
  Though they fall into the ditches,
   they are not checked.

9   They assault the city,
   they run upon the wall,
   they climb into the houses;
  In at the windows
   they come like thieves.

10*   Before them the earth trembles,
   the heavens shake;
  The sun and the moon are darkened,
   and the stars withhold their brightness.

11*   The LORD raises his voice
   at the head of his army;
  For immense indeed is his camp,
   yes, mighty, and it does his bidding.
  For great is the day of the LORD,
   and exceedingly terrible; who can bear
     it?

12   Yet even now, says the LORD,
   return to me with your whole heart,
   with fasting, and weeping, and
     mourning;

13*   Rend your hearts, not your garments,
   and return to the LORD, your God.
  For gracious and merciful is he,
   slow to anger, rich in kindness,
   and relenting in punishment.

14*   Perhaps he will again relent
   and leave behind him a blessing,
  Offerings and libations
   for the LORD, your God.

15*   Blow the trumpet in Zion!
   proclaim a fast,
   call an assembly;

16   Gather the people,
   notify the congregation;
  Assemble the elders,
   gather the children
   and the infants at the breast;
  Let the bridegroom quit his room,
   and the bride her chamber.

17†   Between the porch and the altar
   let the priests, the ministers of the LORD,
     weep,

---

* 2/10: 4, 15; Is 13, 10;
    Ez 32, 7f; Mt 24, 29;
    Mk 13, 24; Lk 21, 25f.
11: Jer 30, 7; Am 5, 18;
    Zep 1, 15.

13: Ps 86, 5;
    Jon 4, 2.
14: Jon 3, 9.
15: 1, 14.

---

† 2, 17: The priests stood in the open space between the out-door altar of holocausts and the temple building, facing the latter in order thereby to look toward God present in the holy of holies.

And say, "Spare, O Lord, your people,
and make not your heritage a reproach,
with the nations ruling over them!
Why should they say among the peoples,
'Where is their God?' "

Blessings for God's People

¹⁸Then the Lord was stirred to concern for his land and took pity on his people. ¹⁹The Lord answered and said to his people:

See, I will send you
grain, and wine, and oil,
and you shall be filled with them;
No more will I make you
a reproach among the nations.

20† No, the northerner I will remove far from you,
and drive him out into a land arid and waste,
With his van toward the eastern sea,
and his rear toward the western sea;
And his foulness shall go up,
and his stench shall go up.

21 Fear not, O land!
exult and rejoice!
for the Lord has done great things.

22 Fear not, beasts of the field!
for the pastures of the plain are green;
The tree bears its fruit,
the fig tree and the vine give their yield.

23*† And do you, O children of Zion, exult
and rejoice in the Lord, your God!
He has given you the teacher of justice:
he has made the rain come down for you,
the early and the late rain as before.

24 The threshing floors shall be full of grain
and the vats shall overflow with wine and oil.

25 And I will repay you for the years
which the locust has eaten,
The grasshopper, the devourer, and the cutter,
my great army which I sent among you.

26 You shall eat and be filled,
and shall praise the name of the Lord,
your God,
Because he has dealt wondrously with you;
my people shall nevermore be put to shame.

27 And you shall know that I am in the midst of Israel;
I am the Lord, your God, and there is no other;

my people shall nevermore be put to shame.

3 **1*†** Then afterward I will pour out
my spirit upon all mankind.
Your sons and daughters shall prophesy,
your old men shall dream dreams,
your young men shall see visions;

2 Even upon the servants and the handmaids,
in those days, I will pour out my spirit.

3 And I will work wonders in the heavens
and on the earth,
blood, fire, and columns of smoke;

4* The sun will be turned to darkness,
and the moon to blood,
At the coming of the day of the Lord,
the great and terrible day.

5* Then everyone shall be rescued
who calls on the name of the Lord;
For on Mount Zion there shall be a remnant,
as the Lord has said,
And in Jerusalem survivors
whom the Lord shall call.

Judgment upon the Nations

4 **1** Yes, in those days, and at that time,
when I would restore the fortunes
of Judah and Jerusalem,

2† I will assemble all the nations
and bring them down to the Valley of Jehoshaphat,
And I will enter into judgment with them there
on behalf of my people and my inheritance, Israel;
Because they have scattered them among the nations,
and divided my land.

---

† 2, 20: *The northerner:* the locusts, that are compared to an invading army, which in Palestine came from the north; cf Jer 1, 14f; 4, 6; Ez 26, 7; 38, 6.15.

2, 23: *The teacher of justice:* the rain sent by God to show his fidelity to his promises, and to teach his people to be faithful to his commandments; cf Dt 11, 14. There is also a play on words here between the Hebrew word *moreh* (teacher) and the Hebrew word *yoreh* (the early rain). The expression likewise has a messianic connotation; cf Is 30, 20. The founder of the Essene sect of Qumran (second century B. C.) was known as "The Teacher of Justice."

3, 1f: *I will pour out my spirit:* in the Old Testament the spirit is the gift of God bestowed on those acting as his agents. The promise of the spirit is quoted by St. Peter in Acts 2, 17-21 as fulfilled in an eminent way by the gift of the Holy Spirit, the Third Person of the Blessed Trinity, bestowed on the Apostles.

4, 2: *Valley of Jehoshaphat:* a symbolic name of the place of final judgment (v 14). The name Jehoshaphat signifies "Yahweh judges." This place has been popularly identified with the Kidron Valley.

✿
23: Hos 10, 12.   4: 2, 10.
3/1-5: Is 44, 3; Acts 2, 17-21.   5: Rom 10, 13.

3 Over my people they have cast lots;
    they gave a boy for a harlot,
    and sold a girl for the wine they drank.

4Moreover, what are you to me, Tyre and Sidon, and all the regions of Philistia? Would you take vengeance upon me by some action? But if you do take action against me, swiftly, speedily, I will return your deed upon your own head. **5**You took my silver and my gold, and brought my precious treasures into your temples! **6**You sold the people of Judah and Jerusalem to the Greeks, removing them far from their own country! **7**See, I will rouse them from the place into which you have sold them, and I will return your deed upon your own head. **8†**I will sell your sons and your daughters to the people of Judah, who shall sell them to the Sabeans, a nation far off. Indeed, the Lord has spoken.

9 Declare this among the nations:
    proclaim a war,
      rouse the warriors to arms!
  Let all the soldiers
    report and march!

10† Beat your plowshares into swords,
    and your pruning hooks into spears;
    let the weak man say, "I am a warrior!"

11† Hasten and come, all you neighboring
      peoples,
    assemble there!
  [Bring down, O Lord, your warriors!]

12 Let the nations bestir themselves and
      come up
    to the Valley of Jehoshaphat;
  For there will I sit in judgment
    upon all the neighboring nations.

13*† Apply the sickle,
    for the harvest is ripe;
  Come and tread,
    for the wine press is full;
  The vats overflow,
    for great is their malice.

14 Crowd upon crowd
    in the valley of decision;
  For near is the day of the Lord
    in the valley of decision.

15* Sun and moon are darkened,
    and the stars withhold their brightness.

16* The Lord roars from Zion,
    and from Jerusalem raises his voice;
  The heavens and the earth quake,
    but the Lord is a refuge to his people,
    a stronghold to the men of Israel.

Salvation for God's Elect

17 Then shall you know that I, the Lord, am
      your God,
    dwelling on Zion, my holy mountain;
  Jerusalem shall be holy,
    and strangers shall pass through her no
      more.

18*† And then, on that day,
    the mountains shall drip new wine,
    and the hills shall flow with milk;
  And the channels of Judah
    shall flow with water:
  A fountain shall issue from the house of
      the Lord,
    to water the Valley of Shittim.

19 Egypt shall be a waste,
    and Edom a desert waste,
  Because of violence done to the people of
      Judah,
    because they shed innocent blood in
      their land.

20 But Judah shall abide forever,
    and Jerusalem for all generations.

21 I will avenge their blood,
    and not leave it unpunished.
    The Lord dwells in Zion.

---

† 4, 8: *Sabeans:* a south Arabian people known for their commerce.

4, 10: This imagery is used in the reverse sense in Is 2, 4; Mi 4, 3. Here the warlike weapons are made in response to God's summons to armies which he selected to expel forever the unlawful invaders from the land of his chosen people.

4, 11: *Warriors:* the angels; cf Zec 14, 5.

4, 13: Because of their numerous crimes, the nations are ripe for punishment. The use of warlike weapons against them is likened to the onslaught on the fields and vines at harvest time.

4, 18: *The Valley of Shittim,* or "the ravine of the acacia trees": perhaps a part of the Kidron Valley southeast of Jerusalem; the prophetic picture of a stream of water flowing from a fountain in the temple of Jerusalem is to be found in Ez 47, 1. The Shittim east of the Jordan (see note on Nm 25, 1) is hardly referred to here.

❋
4/13: Rv 14, 15.
  15: 2, 10; 3, 4.
  16: Jer 25, 30; Am 1, 2.
                          18: Am 9, 13; Ez 47, 1-12;
                                Zec 14, 8.

The Book of Amos

Introduction

Amos was a shepherd of Tekoa in Judah, who exercised his ministry during the prosperous reign of Jeroboam II (786-746 B. C.). He prophesied in Israel at the great cult center of Bethel, from which he was finally expelled by the priest in charge of this royal sanctuary. The poetry of Amos, who denounces the hollow prosperity of the northern kingdom, is filled with imagery and language taken from his own pastoral background. The book is an anthology of his oracles and was compiled either by the prophet or by some of his disciples.

The prophecy begins with a sweeping indictment of Damascus, Philistia, Tyre, and Edom; but the forthright herdsman saves his climactic denunciation for Israel, whose injustice and idolatry are sins against the light granted to her. Israel could indeed expect the day of Yahweh, but it would be a day of darkness and not light. When Amos prophesied the overthrow of the sanctuary, the fall of the royal house, and the captivity of the people, it was more than Israelite officialdom could bear. The priest of Bethel drove Amos from the shrine—but not before hearing a terrible sentence pronounced upon himself.

Amos is a prophet of divine judgment, and the sovereignty of Yahweh in nature and history dominates his thought. But he was no innovator; his conservatism was in keeping with the whole prophetic tradition calling the people back to the high moral and religious demands of Yahweh's revelation. In common with the other prophets, Amos knew that divine punishment is never completely destructive; it is part of the hidden plan of God to bring salvation to men. The perversity of the human will may retard, but it cannot totally frustrate, this design of a loving God. The last oracle opens up a perspective of restoration under a Davidic king.

The Book of Amos may be divided as follows:
    I: Judgment of the Nations (1, 1—2, 16)
    II: Words and Woes for Israel (3, 1—6, 14)
    III: Symbolic Visions: Threats and Promises
        (7, 1—9, 8b)
    Epilogue: Messianic Perspective (9, 8c-15)

I: JUDGMENT OF THE NATIONS

1 ¹* † THE WORDS OF AMOS, a shepherd from Tekoa, which he received in vision concerning Israel, in the days of Uzziah, king of Judah, and in the days of Jeroboam, son of Joash, king of Israel, two years before the earthquake:

2*   The LORD will roar from Zion,
        and from Jerusalem raise his voice:
    The pastures of the shepherds will
        languish,
        and the summit of Carmel wither.

Aram

3†   Thus says the LORD:
    For three crimes of Damascus, and for
        four,
        I will not revoke my word;
    Because they threshed Gilead
        with sledges of iron,
4†   I will send fire upon the house of Hazael,
        to devour the castles of Ben-hadad.
5†   I will break the bar of Damascus;
        I will root out those who live in the
        Valley of Aven,
    And the sceptered ruler of Beth-eden;
        the people of Aram shall be exiled to
        Kir,
        says the LORD.

Philistia

6   Thus says the LORD:
    For three crimes of Gaza, and for four,
        I will not revoke my word;
    Because they took captive whole groups
        to hand over to Edom,
7   I will send fire upon the wall of Gaza,
        to devour her castles;

---

† 1, 1: *The earthquake:* which according to Hebrew tradition marked the crime of Uzziah when he attempted to offer incense in the temple (2 Chr 26, 16-21). Zechariah mentions it several centuries later (Zec 14, 5).

1, 3: *For three crimes . . . four:* crime after crime, an indefinite number; cf 1, 6. The series of judgments on the foreign nations shows that the Lord demands the observance of the moral order everywhere; Israel and Judah, despite their privileged position, are no exception. *I will not revoke my word:* God will not withdraw his threat of punishment against each of these nations. *They threshed Gilead:* the people of Aram under King Hazael had devastated Gilead; cf 2 Kgs 10, 32f.

1, 4: *Fire:* devastation caused by the Assyrians (1, 7.10.12.14; 2, 2.5); cf 1 Sm 15, 18. *Hazael* and *Ben-hadad:* kings of the Arameans whose capital was *Damascus* (v 5); they fought against Israel (2 Kgs 13, 3), and had long occupied the region of Gilead (v 3) in Transjordan.

1, 5: *Bar of Damascus:* the beam securing the main gate of the city against invaders, symbol of its defenses. *Valley of Aven* ("vale of wickedness") and *Beth-eden* ("house of pleasure"): Aramean territory from southwest to northeast.

✱   1/1: Zec 14, 5.   2: Jer 25, 30; Jl 3, 16.

8   I will root out those who live in Ashdod,
       and the sceptered ruler of Ashkelon;
    I will turn my hand against Ekron,
       and the last of the Philistines shall
         perish,
      says the Lord GOD.

Tyre

9†   Thus says the LORD:
    For three crimes of Tyre, and for four,
      I will not revoke my word;
    Because they delivered whole groups
        captive to Edom,
      and did not remember the pact of
        brotherhood,
10   I will send fire upon the wall of Tyre,
      to devour her castles.

Edom

11†   Thus says the LORD:
    For three crimes of Edom, and for four,
      I will not revoke my word;
    Because he pursued his brother with the
        sword,
      choking up all pity;
    Because he persisted in his anger
      and kept his wrath to the end,
12†   I will send fire upon Teman,
      and it will devour the castles of Bozrah.

Ammon

13   Thus says the LORD:
    For three crimes of the Ammonites, and
        for four,
      I will not revoke my word;
    Because they ripped open expectant
        mothers in Gilead,
      while extending their territory,
14†   I will kindle a fire upon the wall of
        Rabbah,
      and it will devour her castles
    Amid clamor on the day of battle
      and stormwind in a time of tempest.
15   Their king shall go into captivity,
      he and his princes with him, says the
        LORD.

Moab

2 1†   Thus says the LORD:
    For three crimes of Moab, and for four,
      I will not revoke my word;
    Because he burned to ashes
      the bones of Edom's king,
2   I will send fire upon Moab,
      to devour the castles of Kerioth;
    Moab shall meet death amid uproar
      and shouts and trumpet blasts.

3   I will root out the judge from her midst,
      and her princes I will slay with him, says
        the LORD.

Judah

4†   Thus says the LORD:
    For three crimes of Judah, and for four,
      I will not revoke my word;
    Because they spurned the law of the LORD,
      and did not keep his statutes;
    Because the lies which their fathers
        followed
      have led them astray,
5   I will send fire upon Judah,
      to devour the castles of Jerusalem.

Israel

6†   Thus says the LORD:
    For three crimes of Israel, and for four,
      I will not revoke my word;
    Because they sell the just man for silver,
      and the poor man for a pair of sandals.
7   They trample the heads of the weak
      into the dust of the earth,
      and force the lowly out of the way.
    Son and father go to the same prostitute,
      profaning my holy name.
8†   Upon garments taken in pledge
      they recline beside any altar;
    And the wine of those who have been fined
      they drink in the house of their god.

9✶   Yet it was I who destroyed the Amorites
        before them,
      who were as tall as the cedars,
      and as strong as the oak trees.

---

† 1, 9: *Pact of brotherhood:* Hiram of Tyre had made a pact with Solomon and called him brother (1 Kgs 5, 12; 9, 13).

1, 11: *Pursued his brother:* the Edomites were descended from Esau, the brother of Jacob (Gn 25-27); nevertheless they constantly nourished enmity against Jacob's descendants, the Israelites.

1, 12: *Teman* and *Bozrah:* two of the chief cities in Edom; cf Jer 49, 20.

1, 14: *Rabbah:* now called Amman, the modern capital of the Hashemite Kingdom of Jordan.

2, 1: Here the prophet stresses the gravity of Moab's violation of the Semitic custom of providing honorable burial for the dead.

2, 4: *The lies:* false gods, who exist only in the minds of their worshipers. The crimes of Judah are infidelity and idolatry, in contrast to the sins for which the surrounding nations are judged.

2, 6: *A pair of sandals:* indicating how cheaply the rich regarded the poor.

2, 6-13: The detailed crimes of Israel are placed in strong contrast with the benefits with which the Lord favored his people.

2, 8: *Upon garments . . . any altar:* usurers kept the garments taken as pledges from the poor; but instead of restoring them to their owners before nightfall (Ex 22, 25; Dt 24, 12), they used them in idolatrous worship. *Wine . . . their god:* under the guise of a religious ceremony they drink the wine obtained through unjust fines.

I destroyed their fruit above,
and their roots beneath.

10* It was I who brought you up from the land
of Egypt,
and who led you through the desert for
forty years,
to occupy the land of the Amorites:

11† I who raised up prophets among your sons,
and nazirites among your young men.
Is this not so, O men of Israel?
says the Lord.

12 But you gave the nazirites wine to drink,
and commanded the prophets not to
prophesy.

13 Beware, I will crush you into the ground
as a wagon crushes when laden with
sheaves.

14 Flight shall perish from the swift,
and the strong man shall not retain his
strength;
The warrior shall not save his life,
nor the bowman stand his ground;

15 The swift of foot shall not escape,
nor the horseman save his life.

16 And the most stouthearted of warriors
shall flee naked on that day, says the
Lord.

II: WORDS AND WOES FOR ISRAEL

First Word

3 ¹HEAR THIS WORD, O men of Israel, that the LORD
pronounces over you, over the whole family that
I brought up from the land of Egypt:

2† You alone have I favored,
more than all the families of the earth;
Therefore I will punish you
for all your crimes.

3 Do two walk together
unless they have agreed?

4 Does a lion roar in the forest
when it has no prey?
Does a young lion cry out from its den
unless it has seized something?

5 Is a bird brought to earth by a snare
when there is no lure for it?
Does a snare spring up from the ground
without catching anything?

6† If the trumpet sounds in a city,
will the people not be frightened?
If evil befalls a city,
has not the LORD caused it?

7 Indeed, the Lord GOD does nothing
without revealing his plan
to his servants, the prophets.

8 The lion roars—
who will not be afraid!
The Lord GOD speaks—
who will not prophesy!

9† Proclaim this in the castles of Ashdod,
in the castles of the land of Egypt:
"Gather about the mountain of Samaria,
and see the great disorders within her,
the oppression in her midst."

10 For they know not how to do what is right,
says the LORD,
Storing up in their castles
what they have extorted and robbed.

11 Therefore, thus says the Lord GOD:
An enemy shall surround the land,
and strip you of your strength,
and pillage your castles.

12 Thus says the LORD:
As the shepherd snatches from the mouth
of the lion
a pair of legs or the tip of an ear of his
sheep,
So the Israelites who dwell in Samaria
shall escape
with the corner of a couch or a piece of
a cot.

¹³Hear and bear witness against the house of Jacob,
says the Lord GOD, the God of hosts:

14 On the day when I punish Israel for his
crimes,
I will visit also the altars of Bethel:
The horns of the altar shall be broken off
and fall to the ground.

15† Then will I strike the winter house
and the summer house;
The ivory apartments shall be ruined,
and their many rooms shall be no more,
says the LORD.

Second Word

4 1† Hear this word, women of the mountain of
Samaria,
you cows of Bashan,
You who oppress the weak
and abuse the needy;

---

† 2, 11: *Nazirites:* see note on Nm 6, 1ff.
3, 2: God's choice of Israel brought its own responsibility.
3, 6: The sufferings which sinful man experiences through the permissive will of God are presented here, as elsewhere in the Old Testament, simply as caused by the Lord.
3, 9: Israel's southern neighbors, beyond Judah, are invited by the prophetic orator to witness the moral disorders of God's people.
3, 15: *Ivory apartments:* rooms containing furniture inlaid in ivory, similar to the pieces discovered in the excavations at Samaria.
4, 1: *Bashan:* the region east of the Sea of Galilee, famous for its rich pasture and fattened herds, to which Amos likens the indolent women of Samaria.

* 10: Ex 14, 21; Dt 8, 2.14.

Who say to your lords,
 "Bring drink for us!"
2 The Lord God has sworn by his holiness:
 Truly the days are coming upon you
When they shall drag you away with
  hooks,
 the last of you with fishhooks;
3 You shall go out through the breached
  walls
 each by the most direct way,
And you shall be cast into the mire,
 says the Lord.

4† Come to Bethel and sin,
 to Gilgal, and sin the more;
Each morning bring your sacrifices,
 every third day, your tithes;
5 Burn leavened food as a thanksgiving
  sacrifice,
 proclaim publicly your freewill
  offerings,
For so you love to do, O men of Israel,
 says the Lord God.

6 Though I have made your teeth
 clean of food in all your cities,
  and have made bread scarce in all your
   dwellings,
Yet you returned not to me,
 says the Lord.

7 Though I also withheld the rain from you
 when the harvest was still three months
  away;
I sent rain upon one city
 but not upon another;
One field was watered by rain,
 but another without rain dried up;
8 Though two or three cities staggered to
  one city
 for water that did not quench their
  thirst;
Yet you returned not to me,
 says the Lord.

9✱ I struck you with blight and searing wind;
 your many gardens and vineyards,
 your fig trees and olive trees the locust
  devoured;
Yet you returned not to me,
 says the Lord.

10† I sent upon you a pestilence like that of
  Egypt,
 and with the sword I slew your young
  men;
Your horses I let be captured,
 to your nostrils I brought the stench of
  your camps;

Yet you returned not to me,
 says the Lord.
11✱ I brought upon you such upheaval
 as when God overthrew Sodom and
  Gomorrah:
 you were like a brand plucked from the
  fire;
Yet you returned not to me,
 says the Lord.
12 So now I will deal with you in my own
  way, O Israel!
 and since I will deal thus with you,
 prepare to meet your God, O Israel:
13 Him who formed the mountains, and
  created the wind,
 and declares to man his thoughts;
Who made the dawn and the darkness,
 and strides upon the heights of the
  earth:
 The Lord, the God of hosts by name.

Third Word

5 **1** Hear this word which I utter over you,
 a lament, O house of Israel:
2 She is fallen, to rise no more,
 the virgin Israel;
She lies abandoned upon her land,
 with no one to raise her up.

3   For thus says the Lord God:
The city that marched out with a thousand
 shall be left with a hundred,
Another that marched out with a hundred
 shall be left with ten,
 of the house of Israel.

4 For thus says the Lord
 to the house of Israel:
Seek me, that you may live,
 but do not seek Bethel;
5 Do not come to Gilgal,
 and do not cross to Beer-sheba.
For Gilgal shall be led into exile,
 and Bethel shall become nought.
6† Seek the Lord, that you may live,
 lest he come upon the house of Joseph
  like a fire
That shall consume, with none to quench it
 for the house of Israel:

---

† 4, 4f: This invitation to the sanctuaries of the northern kingdom is ironical. Pilgrimages to the shrines of *Bethel* and
Gilgal were the more displeasing to God because they were
contrary to his will and ineffective toward improvement of
morals.

4, 10: *Pestilence like that of Egypt:* plagues were well
known in Egypt; cf Dt 7, 15; 28, 27.60. *Stench of your camps:*
caused by the unburied bodies.

5, 6: *House of Joseph:* the kingdom of Israel or northern
kingdom, the chief tribes of which were descended from
Ephraim and Manasseh, the sons of Joseph; cf 5, 15; 6, 6.

8* He who made the Pleiades and Orion,
> who turns darkness into dawn,
> and darkens day into night;
Who summons the waters of the sea,
> and pours them out upon the surface of
> the earth;

9 Who flashes destruction upon the strong,
> and brings ruin upon the fortress;
> whose name is LORD.

First Woe

7 Woe to those who turn judgment to
> wormwood
> and cast justice to the ground!

10† They hate him who reproves at the gate
> and abhor him who speaks the truth.

11* Therefore, because you have trampled
> upon the weak
> and exacted of them levies of grain,
Though you have built houses of hewn
> stone,
> you shall not live in them!
Though you have planted choice
> vineyards,
> you shall not drink their wine!

12 Yes, I know how many are your crimes,
> how grievous your sins:
Oppressing the just, accepting bribes,
> repelling the needy at the gate!

13 Therefore the prudent man is silent at this
> time,
> for it is an evil time.

14 Seek good and not evil,
> that you may live;
Then truly will the LORD, the God of hosts,
> be with you as you claim!

15* Hate evil and love good,
> and let justice prevail at the gate;
Then it may be that the LORD, the God of
> hosts,
> will have pity on the remnant of Joseph.

16 Therefore, thus says the LORD,
> the God of hosts, the Lord:
In every square there shall be lamentation,
> and in every street they shall cry, Alas!
> Alas!
They shall summon the farmers to wail
> and professional mourners to lament,

17 And in every vineyard there shall be
> lamentation
> when I pass through your midst, says
> the LORD.

Second Woe

18*† Woe to those who yearn for the day of the
> LORD!
> What will this day of the LORD mean for
> you?
> Darkness and not light!

19 As if a man were to flee from a lion,
> and a bear should meet him;
Or as if on entering his house
> he were to rest his hand against the wall,
> and a snake should bite him.

20 Will not the day of the LORD be darkness
> and not light,
> gloom without any brightness?

21*† I hate, I spurn your feasts,
> I take no pleasure in your solemnities;

22 Your cereal offerings I will not accept,
> nor consider your stall-fed peace
> offerings.

23 Away with your noisy songs!
> I will not listen to the melodies of your
> harps.
But if you would offer me holocausts,

24 then let justice surge like water,
> and goodness like an unfailing stream.

25*† Did you bring me sacrifices and offerings
> for forty years in the desert, O house of
> Israel?

26† You will carry away Sakkuth, your king,
> and Kaiwan, your star god,
> the images that you have made for
> yourselves;

---

† 5, 10: *At the gate:* see note on Ps 127, 5.

5, 18: *Day of the Lord:* a technical expression which in earliest times referred to God's special intervention in human affairs. Through it his power and justice triumphed in his people. The present passage is the first instance in which it means a day of punishment of sinners. During the exile it assumed the meaning of a time when God would avenge Israel against her oppressors and bring about her restoration (Jer 50, 27; Ez 30, 3ff). Still later it came to mean the day of final judgment of the world when the good will be rewarded and the wicked punished (Mal 3, 19ff; Jl 2, 1ff; Zep 1, 14ff).

5, 21-27: The Lord condemns, not ritual worship in itself, but the cult whose exterior rites and solemnity have no relation to interior morality and justice. The Israelites falsely worshiped him as neighboring nations adored Baal or Chamos, deities which were thought to protect their respective peoples against their enemies in return for ritual observances, without any relation to right conduct.

5, 25: The meaning is not certain; according to some, the idea is that during the forty years' wandering in the desert the simple, rudimentary worship of God was accompanied by the practice of justice, in contrast to the elaborate ritual unaccompanied by works of justice in the prophet's time.

5, 26: *Sakkuth . . . star god:* although the text is uncertain, it seems quite probable that reference is made to the Assyrian deities, Sakkuth, god of war and light, and Kaiwan, the planet Saturn. The people will go into exile, from which these gods have been unable to save them.

---

*   5/8: Am 9, 6.   21: Is 1, 11; Jer 6, 20;
     11: Zep 1, 13.   Mal 1, 12.
     15: Ps 97, 10; Rcm 12, 9.   25: Acts 7, 42.
     18: Jer 30, 7; Jl 2, 11;
           Zep 1, 15.

27 For I will exile you beyond Damascus,
     say I, the LORD, the God of hosts by
     name.

Third Woe

6 ¹*† Woe to the complacent in Zion,
     to the overconfident on the mount of
       Samaria,
     Leaders of a nation favored from the first,
       to whom the people of Israel have
       recourse!
² Pass over to Calneh and see,
     go from there to Hamath the great,
     and down to Gath of the Philistines!
   Are you better than these kingdoms,
     or is your territory wider than theirs?
³ You would put off the evil day,
     yet you hasten the reign of violence!

⁴ Lying upon beds of ivory,
     stretched comfortably on their couches,
   They eat lambs taken from the flock,
     and calves from the stall!
⁵ Improvising to the music of the harp,
     like David, they devise their own
       accompaniment.
⁶ They drink wine from bowls
     and anoint themselves with the best
       oils;
     yet they are not made ill by the collapse
       of Joseph!

⁷ Therefore, now they shall be the first to go
       into exile,
     and their wanton revelry shall be done
       away with.
⁸* The Lord GOD has sworn by his very self,
     say I, the LORD, the God of hosts:
   I abhor the pride of Jacob,
     I hate his castles,
     and I give over the city with everything
       in it;
⁹ Should there remain ten men
     in a single house, these shall die.
¹⁰ Only a few shall be left
     to carry the dead out of the houses;
   If one says to a man inside a house,
     "Is anyone with you?" and he answers,
       "No one,"
   Then he shall say, "Silence!"
     for no one must mention the name of the
       LORD.
¹¹ Indeed, the LORD has given the command
     to shatter the great house to bits,
     and reduce the small house to rubble.

¹²† Can horses run across a cliff?
     or can one plow the sea with oxen?
   Yet you have turned judgment into gall,
     and the fruit of justice into wormwood.

¹³† You rejoice in Lodebar,
     and say, "Have we not, by our own
       strength,
     seized for ourselves Karnaim?"
¹⁴† Beware, I am raising up against you, O
       house of Israel,
     say I, the LORD, the God of hosts,
   A nation that shall oppress you
     from Labo of Hamath even to the Wadi
       Arabah.

III: SYMBOLIC VISIONS:
THREATS AND PROMISES

Vision of Locusts

7 ¹†THIS IS WHAT THE LORD GOD showed me: He
was forming a locust swarm when the late
growth began to come up (the late growth after the
king's mowing). ²While they were eating all the grass
in the land, I said:

     Forgive, O Lord GOD!
       How can Jacob stand?
       He is so small!

³And the LORD repented of this. "It shall not be,"
said the Lord GOD.

Vision of Fire

⁴†Then the Lord GOD showed me this: he called for
a judgment by fire. It had devoured the great abyss,
and was consuming the land, ⁵when I said:

     Cease, O Lord GOD!
       How can Jacob stand?
       He is so small!

⁶The LORD repented of this. "This also shall not be,"
said the Lord GOD.

Vision of the Plummet

⁷†Then the Lord GOD showed me this: he was
standing by a wall, plummet in hand. ⁸The LORD

---

† **6, 1-7:** The luxury of the people in Samaria will be punished
by exile. They failed to learn the lesson from *Calneh, Hamath*
and *Gath* at the approach of the powerful and warlike Assyrians.

6, 1: *The complacent in Zion . . . the overconfident . . . of
Samaria:* the proud and self-interested rulers of Judah and
Israel.

6, 12: *Can horses . . . oxen?:* one cannot change the course
of nature, as the Israelites attempted to do by their sins of
injustice.

6, 13: *Lodebar . . . Karnaim:* in Transjordan; they had been
captured by the Israelites. Perhaps it is in irony that reference
is made to these two cities, for the root of the first suggests
"nothing" and that of the second, "horns" or "strength."

6, 14: *A nation:* Assyria.

7, 1: *The king's mowing:* the first mowing, a portion of
which was payable to the king as a tax.

7, 4: *Fire:* understood by many as a burning drought.

7, 7: *Plummet in hand:* signifying that God is about to with-

---

asked me, "What do you see, Amos?" And when I answered, "A plummet," the LORD said:

> See, I will lay the plummet
>   in the midst of my people Israel;
>   I will forgive them no longer.
> 9 The high places of Isaac shall be laid
>   waste,
>   and the sanctuaries of Israel made
>   desolate;
>   I will attack the house of Jeroboam with
>   the sword.

Amos and Amaziah

¹⁰Amaziah, the priest of Bethel, sent word to Jeroboam, king of Israel: "Amos has conspired against you here within Israel; the country cannot endure all his words. ¹¹For this is what Amos says:

> Jeroboam shall die by the sword,
>   and Israel shall surely be exiled from its
>   land."

¹²To Amos, Amaziah said: "Off with you, visionary, flee to the land of Judah! There earn your bread by prophesying, ¹³but never again prophesy in Bethel; for it is the king's sanctuary and a royal temple." ¹⁴†Amos answered Amaziah, "I was no prophet, nor have I belonged to a company of prophets; I was a shepherd and a dresser of sycamores. ¹⁵The LORD took me from following the flock, and said to me, Go, prophesy to my people Israel. ¹⁶Now hear the word of the LORD!"

> You say: prophesy not against Israel,
>   preach not against the house of Isaac.
> 17   Now thus says the LORD:
> Your wife shall be made a harlot in the
>   city,
>   and your sons and daughters shall fall
>   by the sword;
> Your land shall be divided by measuring
>   line,
>   and you yourself shall die in an unclean
>   land;
> Israel shall be exiled far from its land.

Vision of the Fruit Basket

8 ¹THIS is what the Lord GOD showed me: a basket of ripe fruit. ²"What do you see, Amos?" he asked. I answered, "A basket of ripe fruit." Then the LORD said to me:

> The time is ripe to have done with my
>   people Israel;
>   I will forgive them no longer.
> 3 The temple songs shall become wailings
>   on that day,
>   says the Lord GOD.

> Many shall be the corpses,
>   strewn everywhere.—Silence!

Against Greed

> 4 Hear this, you who trample upon the
>   needy
>   and destroy the poor of the land!
> 5† "When will the new moon be over," you ask,
>   "that we may sell our grain,
>   and the sabbath, that we may display
>   the wheat?
> We will diminish the ephah,
>   add to the shekel,
>   and fix our scales for cheating!
> 6 We will buy the lowly man for silver,
>   and the poor man for a pair of sandals;
>   even the refuse of the wheat we will
>   sell!"
> 7† The LORD has sworn by the pride of Jacob:
>   Never will I forget a thing they have
>   done!
> 8† Shall not the land tremble because of this,
>   and all who dwell in it mourn,
> While it rises up and tosses like the Nile,
>   and settles back like the river of Egypt?

> 9 On that day, says the Lord GOD,
>   I will make the sun set at midday
>   and cover the earth with darkness in
>   broad daylight.
> 10* I will turn your feasts into mourning
>   and all your songs into lamentations.
> I will cover the loins of all with sackcloth
>   and make every head bald.
> I will make them mourn as for an only son,
>   and bring their day to a bitter end.

> 11 Yes, days are coming, says the Lord GOD,
>   when I will send famine upon the land:
> Not a famine of bread, or thirst for water,
>   but for hearing the word of the LORD.
> 12 Then shall they wander from sea to sea
>   and rove from the north to the east
> In search of the word of the LORD,
>   but they shall not find it.

> 13 On that day, fair virgins and young men
>   shall faint from thirst;

---

† draw his mercy from his people and that the nation is to be measured for destruction.

7, 14f: Amos denies that he belonged to the class of professional prophets; his vocation is due to the personal intervention of the Lord.

8, 5: *Ephah:* a standard of measure; a little more than a bushel.

8, 7: *The pride of Jacob:* the sinful pride detested by God (6, 8), in contrast to God himself, who is the true Pride of Jacob.

8, 8: The figure is based on the annual flooding of the river Nile.

8/10: Tb 2, 6; 1 Mc 1, 41.

14†   Those who swear by the shameful idol of
           Samaria,
           "By the life of your god, O Dan!"
       "By the life of your love, O Beer-sheba!"
           those shall fall, never to rise again.

Vision of the Altar

9 ¹†I saw the Lord standing beside the altar, and
he said:

           Strike the bases, so that the doorjambs
               totter
           till you break them off on the heads of
               them all!
           Those who are left I will slay with the
               sword;
           not one shall flee,
           no survivor shall escape.
2*   Though they break through to the nether
               world,
           even from there my hand shall bring
               them out;
           Though they climb to the heavens,
           I will bring them down;
3†   Though they hide on the summit of Carmel,
           there too I will hunt them out and take
               them away;
           Though they hide from my gaze
           in the bottom of the sea,
           I will command the serpent there·to bite
               them;
4*   Though they are led into captivity by their
               enemies,
           there will I command the sword to slay
               them.
           I will fix my gaze upon them
           for evil, and not for good,
5   I, the Lord GOD of hosts.
           I melt the earth with my touch,
           so that all who dwell on it mourn,
           While it all rises up like the Nile,
           and settles back like the river of Egypt;
6*   I have built heaven, my upper chamber,
           and established my vault over the earth;
           I summon the waters of the sea
           and pour them out upon the surface of
               the earth,
           I, the LORD by name.

7*†   Are you not like the Ethiopians to me,
           O men of Israel, says the LORD?
           Did I not bring the Israelites from the land
               of Egypt
           As I brought the Philistines from
               Caphtor
           and the Arameans from Kir?
8   The eyes of the Lord GOD are on this sinful
           kingdom:

           I will destroy it from off the face of the
           earth.

Epilogue: Messianic Perspective

           But I will not destroy the house of Jacob
               completely,
           says the LORD.
9   For see, I have given the command
           to sift the house of Israel among all the
               nations,
           As one sifts with a sieve,
           letting no pebble fall to the ground.
10   By the sword shall all sinners among my
               people die,
           those who say, "Evil will not reach or
               overtake us."
11*†   On that day I will raise up
           the fallen hut of David;
           I will wall up its breaches,
           raise up its ruins,
           and rebuild it as in the days of old,
12   That they may conquer what is left of
               Edom
           and all the nations that shall bear my
               name,
           say I, the LORD, who will do this.
13*   Yes, days are coming,
           says the LORD,
           When the plowman shall overtake the
               reaper,
           and the vintager, him who sows the seed;
           The juice of grapes shall drip down the
               mountains,
           and all the hills shall run with it.
14   I will bring about the restoration of my
               people Israel;
           they shall rebuild and inhabit their
               ruined cities,
           Plant vineyards and drink the wine,
           set out gardens and eat the fruits.
15   I will plant them upon their own ground;
           never again shall they be plucked
           From the land I have given them,
           say I, the LORD, your God.

---

† 8, 14: *Dan* and *Beer-sheba*, the extreme northern and southern limits of the country, where idolatrous worship was offered.
9, 1-8: There will be no escape from God's punishment, symbolized here by the destruction of a building, probably the schismatic temple at Bethel.
9, 3: *Serpent:* the sea monster of familiar legend, subdued by God at the time of creation and lurking still in the ocean depths; cf Ps 89, 10f.
9, 7: *The Ethiopians . . . the Philistines . . . the Arameans:* by nature Israel is not different from any other nation. It was not because of any merit on Israel's part that God delivered them from Egypt. *Caphtor:* the island of Crete.
9, 11f: In Acts 15, 15ff St. James interprets this passage in a messianic sense. *Fallen hut:* the kingdom. *The nations that shall bear my name:* the Gentile peoples who shall be converted to the Lord, that is, conquered by him, and therefore shall bear his name.

9/2: Ps 139, 8.   7: Dt 2, 23; Jer 47, 4.
4: Jer 44, 11.   11: Acts 15, 16.
6: Am 5, 8.   13: Jl 3, 18.

The Book of Obadiah

Introduction

The twenty-one verses of this book contain the shortest and sternest prophecy in the Old Testament. Nothing is known of the author, although his oracle against Edom, a long-standing enemy of Israel, indicates a date of composition sometime in the fifth century B. C. During this period the Edomites had been forced to abandon their ancient home near the Gulf of Aqaba and had settled in southern Judah, where they appear among the adversaries of the Jews returning from exile.

The prophecy is a bitter cry for vengeance against Edom for its heinous crimes. The mountain of Esau will be occupied and ravaged by the enemy but Zion shall remain inviolate. Judah and Israel shall again form one nation; and that triumphant refrain of Israelite eschatology will be heard once more: "The Kingdom is the Lord's!" Many of the verses in this prophecy can be paralleled in Jer 49, 7-22, but it is difficult to determine the precise relationship between these similar passages.

Title and Theme

1*   THE VISION OF OBADIAH.
[Thus says the Lord GOD:]

Of Edom we have heard a message from
     the LORD,
    and a herald has been sent among the
     nations:
    "Up! let us go to war against him!"

Edom Shall Perish

2*   See, I make you small among the nations;
    you are held in dire contempt.
3   The pride of your heart has deceived you:
    you who dwell in the clefts of the rock,
     whose abode is in the heights,
  Who say in your heart,
    "Who will bring me down to earth?"
4   Though you go as high as the eagle,
    and your nest be set among the stars,
  From there will I bring you down,
    says the LORD.
5*†   If thieves came to you, if robbers by night,
    how could you be thus destroyed:
     would they not steal merely till they had
     enough?
  If vintagers came to you,
    would they not leave some gleanings?

6   How they search Esau,
    seek out his hiding places!
7†   To the border they drive you—
    all your allies;
  They deceive you, they overpower you—
    those at peace with you;
  Those who eat your bread
    lay snares beneath you:
    There is no understanding in him!
8*†   Shall I not, says the LORD, on that day
    make the wise men disappear from
     Edom,
    and understanding from the mount of
     Esau?
9†   Your warriors, O Teman, shall be crushed,
    till all on Mount Esau are destroyed.

The Cause

10*†   Because of violence to your brother Jacob,
    disgrace shall cover you
    and you shall be destroyed forever.
11†   On the day when you stood by,
    on the day when aliens carried off his
     possessions,
  And strangers entered his gates
    and cast lots over Jerusalem,
    you too were one of them.
12   Gaze not upon the day of your brother,
    the day of his disaster;
  Exult not over the children of Judah
    on the day of their ruin;
  Speak not haughtily
    on the day of distress!

---

†   5: Something of value may escape the robber, and the vintager always leaves something for the gleaners, but God's devastation of Edom will be complete.

7: *There is no understanding in him:* Edom's faithless allies assure one another that he does not have sense enough to be able to defend himself.

8: *The wise men:* Edom was proverbial for its wise men; cf Jer 49, 7.

9: *Teman:* one of the names used for the land southeast of Palestine, here synonymous with Edom. *Esau:* here used as the name of the land.

10: *Your brother Jacob:* Esau, also called Edom, and Jacob, the father of Judah, were the sons of Isaac (Gn 25, 24ff).

11: After the devastation of Judah, Edom occupied the southern part of its territory. Edomites also joined the invading Chaldean forces (13) and assisted them in capturing the people of Judah (14).

✿
  1/1: Jer 49, 14.   8: Is 29, 14; 1 Cor 1, 19.
  2ff: Jer 49, 15f.   10: Gn 27, 41f.
  5: Jer 49, 9.

13   Enter not the gate of my people
       on the day of their calamity;
   Gaze not, you at least, upon his misfortune
       on the day of his calamity;
   Lay not hands upon his possessions
       on the day of his calamity!

14   Stand not at the crossroads
       to slay his refugees;
   Betray not his fugitives
       on the day of distress!

Judgment upon the Nations

15*   For near is the day of the LORD
       for all the nations!
   As you have done, so shall it be done to you,
       your deed shall come back upon your
       own head;

16†   As you have drunk upon my holy
       mountain,
       so shall all the nations drink continually.
   Yes, they shall drink and swallow,
       and shall become as though they had not
       been.

Judah Shall Be Restored

17†   But on Mount Zion there shall be a portion
       saved;
       the mountain shall be holy,
   And the house of Jacob shall take
       possession
       of those that dispossessed them.

18   The house of Jacob shall be a fire,
       and the house of Joseph a flame;

---

*   15f: Ps 137, 7ff.

The house of Esau shall be stubble,
   and they shall set them ablaze and
     devour them;
Then none shall survive of the house of
   Esau,
   for the LORD has spoken.

19   They shall occupy the Negeb, the mount of
      Esau,
      and the foothills of the Philistines;
   And they shall occupy the lands of
      Ephraim
      and the lands of Samaria,
      And Benjamin shall occupy Gilead.

20†   The captives of this host of the children of
      Israel
      shall occupy the Canaanite land as far as
      Zarephath,
   And the captives of Jerusalem who are in
      Sepharad
      shall occupy the cities of the Negeb.

21†   And saviors shall ascend Mount Zion
      to rule the mount of Esau,
      and the kingship shall be the LORD's.

---

†   16: *As you have drunk:* the Lord addresses the people of Judah. As the people of Jerusalem have drunk the cup of retribution, so shall the nations, and especially Edom (18), suffer punishment. This metaphorical use of drinking the cup of God's wrath is common in the Bible; cf Jb 21, 20; Is 19, 14; Jer 25, 15f.

17ff. The Israelites shall be restored and shall occupy the lands of those who oppressed them. The survivors of Judah shall be rejoined by the returned exiles from northern Israel.

20: *Zarephath:* a town in Phoenicia, north of Tyre; cf 1 Kgs 17, 10. Ezekiel's ideal boundaries of the new Israel (47, 13ff) extend farther north. *Sepharad:* probably Sardis in western Asia Minor. The later rabbis thought it to be Spain.

21: *Saviors:* the victorious Israelites who will rule over their enemies after the fashion of the ancient Judges; cf Jgs 3, 9.15.31; 10, 1.

The Book of Jonah

Introduction

Written in the postexilic era, probably in the fifth century B. C., this book is a didactic story with an important theological message. It concerns a disobedient prophet who attempted to run away from his divine commission, was cast overboard and swallowed by a great fish, rescued in a marvelous manner, and sent on his way to Nineveh, the traditional enemy of Israel. To the surprise of Jonah, the wicked city listened to his message of doom and repented immediately. All, from king to lowliest subject, humbled themselves in sackcloth and ashes. Seeing their repentance, God did not carry out the punishment he had planned for them. Whereupon Jonah complained to God about the unexpected success of his mission; he was bitter because Yahweh, instead of destroying, had led the people to repentance and then spared them.

From this partly humorous story, a very sublime lesson may be drawn. Jonah stands for a narrow and vindictive mentality, all too common among the Jews of that period. Because they were the chosen people, a good many of them cultivated an intolerant nationalism which limited the mercy of God to their nation. It was abhorrent to their way of thinking that nations as wicked as Assyria should escape his wrath.

The prophecy, which is both instructive and entertaining, strikes directly at this viewpoint. It is a parable of mercy, showing that God's threatened punishments are but the expression of a merciful will which moves all men to repent and seek forgiveness. The universality of the story contrasts sharply with the particularistic spirit of many in the postexilic community. The book has also prepared the way for the gospel with its message of redemption for all, both Jew and Gentile.

The First Mission

1 ¹*†THIS IS THE WORD OF THE LORD that came to Jonah, son of Amittai: ²*"Set out for the great city of Nineveh, and preach against it; their wickedness has come up before me." ³†But Jonah made ready to flee to Tarshish away from the LORD. He went down to Joppa, found a ship going to Tarshish, paid the fare, and went aboard to journey with them to Tarshish, away from the LORD.

⁴The LORD, however, hurled a violent wind upon the sea, and in the furious tempest that arose the ship was on the point of breaking up. ⁵Then the mariners became frightened and each one cried to his god. To lighten the ship for themselves, they threw its cargo into the sea. Meanwhile, Jonah had gone down into the hold of the ship, and lay there fast asleep. ⁶The captain came to him and said, "What are you doing asleep? Rise up, call upon your God! Perhaps God will be mindful of us so that we may not perish."

⁷Then they said to one another, "Come, let us cast lots to find out on whose account we have met with this misfortune." So they cast lots, and thus singled out Jonah. ⁸"Tell us," they said, "what is your business? Where do you come from? What is your country, and to what people do you belong?" ⁹"I am a Hebrew," Jonah answered them; "I worship the LORD, the God of heaven, who made the sea and the dry land."

¹⁰Now the men were seized with great fear and said to him, "How could you do such a thing!"—They knew that he was fleeing from the LORD, because he had told them.— ¹¹"What shall we do with you," they asked, "that the sea may quiet down for us?" For the sea was growing more and more turbulent. ¹²Jonah said to them, "Pick me up and throw me into the sea, that it may quiet down for you; since I know it is because of me that this violent storm has come upon you."

¹³Still the men rowed hard to regain the land, but they could not, for the sea grew ever more turbulent. ¹⁴†Then they cried to the LORD: "We beseech you, O LORD, let us not perish for taking this man's life; do not charge us with shedding innocent blood, for you, LORD, have done as you saw fit." ¹⁵Then they took Jonah and threw him into the sea, and the sea's raging abated. ¹⁶Struck with great fear of the LORD, the men offered sacrifice and made vows to him.

2 ¹*But the LORD sent a large fish, that swallowed Jonah; and he remained in the belly of the fish three days and three nights. ²From the belly of the fish Jonah said this prayer to the LORD, his God:

Psalm of Thanksgiving

³*   Out of my distress I called to the LORD,
                and he answered me;

---
† 1, 1: *Jonah, son of Amittai:* a prophet of this name lived at the time of Jeroboam II (786-746 B. C.).

1, 3: *Tarshish:* identified by many with Tartessus, an ancient Phoenician colony in southwest Spain; precise identification with any particular Phoenician center in the western Mediterranean is uncertain. To the Hebrews it stood for the far west.

1, 14: Since it has pleased the Lord to punish Jonah, the mariners ask that in ridding themselves of him they be not charged with the crime of murder.

✻
1/1: 2 Kgs 14, 25.   2/1: Mt 12, 40; 16, 4;
2: 3, 3; 4, 11.   Lk 11, 30; 1 Cor 15, 4.
                                3: Pss 18, 7; 120, 1.

From the midst of the nether world I cried
for help,
and you heard my voice.

4 For you cast me into the deep, into the
heart of the sea,
and the flood enveloped me;
All your breakers and your billows
passed over me.

5 Then I said, "I am banished from your
sight!
yet would I again look upon your holy
temple."

6 The waters swirled about me, threatening
my life;
the abyss enveloped me;
seaweed clung about my head.

7 Down I went to the roots of the mountains;
the bars of the nether world
were closing behind me forever,
But you brought up my life from the pit,
O Lord, my God.

8 When my soul fainted within me,
I remembered the Lord;
My prayer reached you
in your holy temple.

9 Those who worship vain idols
forsake their source of mercy.

10 But I, with resounding praise,
will sacrifice to you;
What I have vowed I will pay:
deliverance is from the Lord.

11 Then the Lord commanded the fish to spew Jonah upon the shore.

Conversion of Nineveh

3 ¹The word of the Lord came to Jonah a second time: ²"Set out for the great city of Nineveh, and announce to it the message that I will tell you." ³So Jonah made ready and went to Nineveh, according to the Lord's bidding. Now Nineveh was an enormously large city; it took three days to go through it. ⁴Jonah began his journey through the city, and had gone but a single day's walk announcing, "Forty days more and Nineveh shall be destroyed," ⁵when the people of Nineveh believed God; they proclaimed a fast and all of them, great and small, put on sackcloth.

⁶When the news reached the king of Nineveh, he rose from his throne, laid aside his robe, covered himself with sackcloth, and sat in the ashes. ⁷Then he had this proclaimed throughout Nineveh, by decree of the king and his nobles: "Neither man nor beast, neither cattle nor sheep, shall taste anything; they shall not eat, nor shall they drink water. ⁸Man and

beast shall be covered with sackcloth and call loudly to God; every man shall turn from his evil way and from the violence he has in hand. ⁹Who knows, God may relent and forgive, and withhold his blazing wrath, so that we shall not perish." ¹⁰When God saw by their actions how they turned from their evil way, he repented of the evil that he had threatened to do to them; he did not carry it out.

Jonah's Anger: God's Reproof

4 ¹But this was greatly displeasing to Jonah, and he became angry. ²"I beseech you, Lord," he prayed, "is not this what I said while I was still in my own country? This is why I fled at first to Tarshish. I knew that you are a gracious and merciful God, slow to anger, rich in clemency, loathe to punish. ³And now, Lord, please take my life from me; for it is better for me to die than to live." ⁴But the Lord asked, "Have you reason to be angry?"

⁵Jonah then left the city for a place to the east of it, where he built himself a hut and waited under it in the shade, to see what would happen to the city. ⁶And when the Lord God provided a gourd plant, that grew up over Jonah's head, giving shade that relieved him of any discomfort, Jonah was very happy over the plant. ⁷But the next morning at dawn God sent a worm which attacked the plant, so that it withered. ⁸And when the sun arose, God sent a burning east wind; and the sun beat upon Jonah's head till he became faint. Then he asked for death, saying, "I would be better off dead than alive."

⁹But God said to Jonah, "Have you reason to be angry over the plant?" "I have reason to be angry," Jonah answered, "angry enough to die." ¹⁰Then the Lord said, "You are concerned over the plant which cost you no labor and which you did not raise; it came up in one night and in one night it perished. ¹¹And should I not be concerned over Nineveh, the great city, in which there are more than a hundred and twenty thousand persons who cannot distinguish their right hand from their left, not to mention the many cattle?"

3, 4: *Shall be destroyed:* the Hebrew expression reminds the reader of the "overthrowing" of the wicked cities, Sodom and Gomorrah, by a special act of God.

3, 8: *Beast . . . sackcloth:* the animals carried the signs of this repentance, as on occasions of joy they bore garlands.

4, 1: *He became angry:* because of his narrowly nationalistic vindictiveness, Jonah did not wish the Lord to forgive the Ninevites.

4, 6: *Gourd plant:* the Hebrew word, *kikayon* means here a wide-leafed plant of the cucumber or castor-bean variety.

4, 10f: Jonah is selfish in bemoaning his personal loss of a shady gourd plant without any concern over the threat of loss of life to the Ninevites through the destruction of their city. If God in his kindness provided the plant for his prophet without the latter's effort or merit, how much more is he disposed to show love and mercy toward all men, Jew and Gentile, when they repent of their sins and implore his pardon! God's providence is also shown here to extend even to animals.

4: Ps 42, 8.
5: Ps 31, 23; Is 38, 11.
6: Pss 18, 5; 69, 2.
7: Pss 16, 10; 30, 4.
8: Pss 5, 8; 18, 7; 88, 3.
9: Ps 31, 7.
10: Ps 50, 14.
3/5: Mt 12, 41; Lk 11, 32.
9: Jl 2, 14.
4/2: Ps 86, 5; Jl 2, 13.
3: 1 Kgs 19, 4.

The Book of Micah

Introduction

Micah was a contemporary of Isaiah. Of his personal life and call we know nothing except that he came from the obscure village of Moresheth in the foothills. His were the broad vistas of the Judean lowland and the distant sea on the western horizon. With burning eloquence he attacked the rich exploiters of the poor, fraudulent merchants, venal judges, corrupt priests and prophets. To the man of the countryside the vices of the nation seemed centered in its capitals, for both Samaria and Jerusalem are singled out for judgment. An interesting notice in Jer 26, 17f informs us that the reform of Hezekiah was influenced by the preaching of Micah.

The prophecy may be divided into three parts:

I: The impending judgment of the Lord, followed by an exposition of its causes, Israel's sins. Censure of Judah's leaders for betrayal of their responsibility (1, 1—3, 12).

II: The glory of the restored Zion. A prince of David's house will rule over a reunited Israel. (St. Matthew's Nativity narrative points to Christ's birth in Bethlehem as the fulfillment of this prophecy.) A remnant shall survive the chastisement of Judah and her adversaries shall be destroyed (4, 1—5, 14).

III: The case against Israel, in which the Lord is portrayed as the plaintiff who has maintained fidelity to the covenant. The somber picture closes with a prayer for national restoration and a beautiful expression of trust in God's pardoning mercy (6, 1—7, 20).

It should be noted that each of these three divisions begins with reproach and the threat of punishment, and ends on a note of hope and promise.

I: PUNISHMENT OF ISRAEL'S SINS

Divine Judgment

1 [1]THE WORD OF THE LORD which came to Micah of Moresheth in the days of Jotham, Ahaz, and Hezekiah, kings of Judah: that is, the vision he received concerning Samaria and Jerusalem.

[2]*† HEAR, O PEOPLES, all of you,
give heed, O earth, and all that fills you!
Let the Lord GOD be witness against you,
the Lord from his holy temple!

[3]* For see, the LORD comes forth from his place,
he descends and treads upon the heights of the earth.

[4] The mountains melt under him
and the valleys split open,
Like wax before the fire,
like water poured down a slope.

[5] For the crime of Jacob all this comes to pass,
and for the sins of the house of Israel.
What is the crime of Jacob?
Is it not Samaria?
And what is the sin of the house of Judah?
Is it not Jerusalem?

[6] I will make Samaria a stone heap in the field,
a place to plant for vineyards;
I will throw down into the valley her stones,
and lay bare her foundations.

[7]*† All her idols shall be broken to pieces,
all her wages shall be burned in the fire,
and all her statues I will destroy.
As the wages of a harlot they were gathered,
and to the wages of a harlot shall they return.

[8]* For this reason I lament and wail,
I go barefoot and naked;
I utter lamentation like the jackals,
and mourning like the ostriches.

[9] There is no remedy for the blow she has been struck;
rather, it has come even to Judah,
It reaches to the gate of my people,
even to Jerusalem.

[10]*† Publish it not in Gath,
weep not at all;
In Beth-leaphrah
roll in the dust.

1/2: Dt 32, 1; Is 1, 2.
3f: Is 26, 21; Na 1, 5; Hb 3, 10.
7: Hos 9, 1.
8: Jb 30, 29.
10: 2 Sm 1, 20.

† 1, 2: *His holy temple:* God's heavenly temple; the prophet pictures a theophany (3f).

1, 7: The comparison of the unfaithful people with a prostitute, first found in Hosea, is frequent with the prophets; probably ritual prostitution is meant; cf Am 2, 7f; Hos 4, 14.

1, 10-15: The Judean cities here named were in the vicinity of Moresheth, the region with which Micah was most familiar.

11 Pass by,
       you who dwell in Shaphir!
   The inhabitants of Zaanan
       come not forth from their city.
   The lamentation of Beth-ezel
       finds in you its grounds.

12 How can the inhabitants of Maroth
       hope for good?
   For evil has come down from the Lord
       to the gate of Jerusalem.

13 Harness steeds to the chariots,
       O inhabitants of Lachish;
   Lachish, the beginning of sin
       for daughter Zion,
   Because there were in you
       the crimes of Israel.

14 Therefore you shall give parting gifts
       to Moresheth-gath;
   Beth-achzib is a deception
       to the kings of Israel.

15 Yet must I bring to you the conqueror,
       O inhabitants of Mareshah;
   Even to Adullam shall go
       the glory of Israel.

16† Make yourself bald, pluck out your hair,
       for the children whom you cherish;
   Let your baldness be as the eagle's,
       because they are exiled from you.

Social Evils

2 1 Woe to those who plan iniquity,
       and work out evil on their couches;
   In the morning light they accomplish it
       when it lies within their power.

2† They covet fields, and seize them;
       houses, and they take them;
   They cheat an owner of his house,
       a man of his inheritance.

3   Therefore thus says the Lord:
   Behold, I am planning against this race an
       evil
       from which you shall not withdraw your
           necks;
   Nor shall you walk with head high,
       for it will be a time of evil.

4 On that day a satire shall be sung over you,
       and there shall be a plaintive chant:
   "Our ruin is complete,
       our fields are portioned out among our
           captors,
   The fields of my people are measured out,
       and no one can get them back!"

5† Thus you shall have no one
       to mark out boundaries by lot
       in the assembly of the Lord.

6† "Preach not," they preach,
       "let them not preach of these things!"
   The shame will not withdraw.

7 How can it be said, O house of Jacob,
       "Is the Lord short of patience,
           or are such his deeds?"
   Do not my words promise good
       to him who walks uprightly?

8 But of late my people has risen up as an
       enemy:
       you have stripped off the mantle covering
           the tunic
   Of those who go their way in confidence,
       as though it were spoils of war.

9† The women of my people you drive out
       from their pleasant houses;
   From their children you take away
       forever the honor I gave them.

10† "Up! Be off,
       this is no place to rest";
   For any trifle you exact
       a crippling pledge.

11 If one, acting on impulse, should make the
       futile claim:
       "I pour you wine and strong drink as my
           prophecy,"
       then he would be the prophet of this
           people.

12† I will gather you, O Jacob, each and every
       one,
       I will assemble all the remnant of Israel;
   I will group them like a flock in the fold,
       like a herd in the midst of its corral;
       they shall not be thrown into panic by
           men.

13 With a leader to break the path
       they shall burst open the gate and go out
           through it;
   Their king shall go through before them,
       and the Lord at their head.

---

† They were to experience divine chastisement. In the Hebrew, wordplays on the names of these cities abound. The text is partly obscure.

1, 16: Shaving the head was a sign of mourning; cf Is 3, 24; Am 8, 10.

2, 2: Land monopoly, also denounced by Isaiah, was a chronic vice in Judah. To protect the poor against it, a man's *inheritance*, his ancestral property, was supposed to be inviolate; cf 1 Kgs 21, 1-4; but the wealthy in their greed were enslaving men for their debts and depriving them of their land.

2, 5: *To mark out boundaries by lot*: an allusion to the initial distribution of the land of Palestine among the Israelites; cf Jos 13-21. The appropriate punishment of those greedy for land will be the loss of their land to their enemies (v 4), a loss that will be irrevocable.

2, 6f: The words in quotation marks are the protestations of the people against the prophet's predictions of doom.

2, 9: *The honor I gave them*: their dignity as free Israelites.

2, 10: *A crippling pledge*: Israelite law forbade exacting pledges for loans that would work hardship on the borrower (Ex 22, 25f; Dt 24, 6.10-13.17); but the law was habitually violated.

2, 12f: This messianic passage concerning the restoration after the Babylonian exile seems out of place here and is probably a later addition.

Downfall of Present Leaders

3 ¹ And I said:
Hear, you leaders of Jacob,
rulers of the house of Israel!
Is it not your duty to know what is right,
²* you who hate what is good, and love
evil?
You who tear their skin from them,
and their flesh from their bones!
³ They eat the flesh of my people,
and flay their skin from them,
and break their bones.
They chop them in pieces like flesh in a
kettle,
and like meat in a caldron.
⁴ When they cry to the Lord,
he shall not answer them;
Rather shall he hide his face from them at
that time,
because of the evil they have done.

⁵*† Thus says the Lord regarding the prophets
who lead my people astray;
Who, when their teeth have something to
bite,
announce peace,
But when one fails to put something in
their mouth,
proclaim war against him.
⁶* Therefore you shall have night, not vision,
darkness, not divination;
The sun shall go down upon the prophets,
and the day shall be dark for them.
⁷ Then shall the seers be put to shame,
and the diviners confounded;
They shall cover their lips, all of them,
because there is no answer from God.
⁸ But as for me, I am filled with power,
with the spirit of the Lord,
with authority and with might;
To declare to Jacob his crimes
and to Israel his sins.
⁹ Hear this, you leaders of the house of Jacob,
you rulers of the house of Israel!
You who abhor what is just,
and pervert all that is right;
¹⁰ Who build up Zion with bloodshed,
and Jerusalem with wickedness!
¹¹* Her leaders render judgment for a bribe,
her priests give decisions for a salary,
her prophets divine for money,
While they rely on the Lord, saying,
"Is not the Lord in the midst of us?
No evil can come upon us!"

¹²* Therefore, because of you,
Zion shall be plowed like a field,
and Jerusalem reduced to rubble,
And the mount of the temple
to a forest ridge.

II: THE NEW ISRAEL

The People to Be Restored

4 ¹*† IN DAYS TO COME
the mount of the Lord's house
Shall be established higher than the
mountains;
it shall rise high above the hills,
And peoples shall stream to it:
² Many nations shall come, and say,
"Come, let us climb the mount of the Lord,
to the house of the God of Jacob,
That he may instruct us in his ways,
that we may walk in his paths."
For from Zion shall go forth instruction,
and the word of the Lord from
Jerusalem.
³ He shall judge between many peoples
and impose terms on strong and distant
nations;
They shall beat their swords into
plowshares,
and their spears into pruning hooks;
One nation shall not raise the sword against
another,
nor shall they train for war again.
⁴* Every man shall sit under his own vine
or under his own fig tree, undisturbed;
for the mouth of the Lord of hosts has
spoken.
⁵ For all the peoples walk
each in the name of its god,
But we will walk in the name of the Lord,
our God, forever and ever.

⁶ On that day, says the Lord,
I will gather the lame,
And I will assemble the outcasts,
and those whom I have afflicted.
⁷* I will make of the lame a remnant,
and of those driven far off a strong
nation;
And the Lord shall be king over them on
Mount Zion,
from now on forever.

* 3/2: Am 2, 7.
5: Ez 13, 10.
6: Jer 15, 9; Am 8, 9; Zec 13, 3.
11: Ez 22, 27; Zep 3, 3.
12: Jer 26, 18.
4/1ff: Is 2, 2ff.
4: Hos 14, 8; Am 9, 14.
7: Is 6, 13; Dn 7, 14; Zep 3, 19; Lk 1, 32.

† 3, 5-8: Almost all the prophetic books contain oracles against the false prophets. Here Micah accuses them of prophesying for venal motives and determining the prophecy by the price that is paid them; he contrasts his own disinterested preaching of the word of God.
4, 1ff: See note on Is 2, 2ff.

8† And you, O Magdal-eder,
    hillock of daughter Zion!
Unto you shall it come:
    the former dominion shall be restored,
    the kingdom of daughter Jerusalem.

9 Now why do you cry out so?
    Are you without a king?
    Or has your counselor perished,
That you are seized with pains
    like a woman in travail?

10† Writhe in pain, grow faint,
    O daughter Zion,
    like a woman in travail;
For now shall you go forth from the city
    and dwell in the fields;
To Babylon shall you go,
    there shall you be rescued.
There shall the Lord redeem you
    from the hand of your enemies.

11 How many nations are gathered against
        you!
    They say, "Let her be profaned,
    let our eyes see Zion's downfall!"

12 But they know not the thoughts of the
        Lord,
    nor understand his counsel,
When he has gathered them
    like sheaves on the threshing floor.

13* Arise and thresh, O daughter Zion;
    your horn I will make iron
And your hoofs bronze,
    that you may crush many peoples;
You shall devote their spoils to the Lord,
    and their riches to the Lord of the whole
        earth.

Restoration through the Messiah

14† Now fence yourself in, Bat-gader!
    "They have laid siege against us!"
With the rod they strike on the cheek
    the ruler of Israel.

5 **1*†** But you, Bethlehem-Ephrathah,
    too small to be among the clans of Judah,
From you shall come forth for me
    one who is to be ruler in Israel;
Whose origin is from of old,
    from ancient times.

2*† (Therefore the Lord will give them up,
        until the time
    when she who is to give birth has borne,
And the rest of his brethren shall return
    to the children of Israel.)

3 He shall stand firm and shepherd his flock
    by the strength of the Lord,
    in the majestic name of the Lord, his
        God;
And they shall remain, for now his
        greatness
    shall reach to the ends of the earth;
    he shall be peace.

4† If Assyria invades our country
    and treads upon our land,
We shall raise against it seven shepherds,
    eight men of royal rank;

5† And they shall tend the land of Assyria with
        the sword,
    and the land of Nimrod with the drawn
        sword;
And we shall be delivered from Assyria,
    if it invades our land
    and treads upon our borders.

6 The remnant of Jacob shall be
    in the midst of many peoples,
Like dew coming from the Lord,
    like raindrops on the grass,
Which wait for no man,
    nor tarry for the sons of men.

7 And the remnant of Jacob shall be among
        the nations,
    in the midst of many peoples,
Like a lion among beasts of the forest,
    like a young lion among flocks of sheep;
When it passes through, it tramples
    and tears, and there is none to deliver.

8 Your hand shall be lifted above your foes,
    and all your enemies shall be destroyed.

---

† 4, 8: *Magdal-eder:* "tower of the flock," an ancient place name (cf Gn 35, 21), here used symbolically of Jerusalem.

4, 10: *For now . . . your enemies:* probably a later addition to the text, when the prediction of exile had been fulfilled in the Babylonian captivity. The prophet sees the exile as the means whereby God will purify and restore his people.

4, 14: *Bat-gader:* "fenced-in maiden," another symbolic name for Jerusalem, then under siege from the Assyrians.

5, 1: In contrast to Bat-gader (4, 14), where *the ruler of Israel,* the reigning king, is in peril of his life from the Assyrians, is the tiny city and clan of *Bethlehem-Ephrathah,* from which comes the ancient Davidic dynasty (*whose origin is from of old, from ancient times*) with its messianic King, *one who is to be ruler in Israel.*

5, 2: *She who is to give birth:* the mother of the Messiah: cf Is 7, 14.

5, 4f: This passage, expressing confidence in Judah's ability to deliver itself from Assyria, is in contrast with the preceding messianic oracle, which ascribes deliverance to the Lord and his agent. Some believe that here the prophet is quoting the words of the defiant men of Judah. The *shepherds* and *men of royal rank* are one and the same: warriors capable of routing Assyria. The same kind of numerical progression is used by Amos (1, 3), and elsewhere in the Bible.

5, 5: *Nimrod:* the legendary ancestor of the Mesopotamians; cf Gn 10, 10ff.

---

* 13: Is 41, 15; Hos 10, 11.   2f: Is 7, 14; 11, 1f.
5/1: Ru 1, 2; 1 Sm 17, 12;
    Mt 2, 6; Jn 7, 42.

9† On that day, says the LORD,
　　I will destroy the horses from your midst
　　　and ruin your chariots;

10 I will demolish the cities of your land
　　and tear down all your fortresses.

11 I will abolish the means of divination from
　　　your use,
　　and there shall no longer be soothsayers
　　　among you.

12*† I will abolish your carved images
　　and the sacred pillars from your midst;
　　And you shall no longer adore
　　　the works of your hands.

13 I will tear out the sacred poles from your
　　　midst,
　　and destroy your cities.

14 I will wreak vengeance in anger and wrath
　　upon the nations that have not
　　　hearkened.

III: ADMONITION

Accusation and Answer

6 1* 　　HEAR, THEN, what the LORD says:
Arise, present your plea before the
　　mountains,
　　and let the hills hear your voice!

2 Hear, O mountains, the plea of the LORD,
　　pay attention, O foundations of the earth!
For the LORD has a plea against his people,
　　and he enters into trial with Israel.

3* O my people, what have I done to you,
　　or how have I wearied you? Answer me!

4* For I brought you up from the land of
　　　Egypt,
　　from the place of slavery I released you;
And I sent before you Moses,
　　Aaron, and Miriam.

5*† My people, remember what Moab's King
　　　Balak planned,
　　and how Balaam, the son of Beor,
　　　answered him
　　. . . from Shittim to Gilgal,
　　that you may know the just deeds of the
　　　LORD.

6*† With what shall I come before the LORD,
　　and bow before God most high?
Shall I come before him with holocausts,
　　with calves a year old?

7† Will the LORD be pleased with thousands of
　　　rams,
　　with myriad streams of oil?

Shall I give my first-born for my crime,
　　the fruit of my body for the sin of my
　　　soul?

8* You have been told, O man, what is good,
　　and what the LORD requires of you:
Only to do the right and to love goodness,
　　and to walk humbly with your God.

9† Hark! the LORD cries to the city.
　　[It is wisdom to fear your name!]
　　Hear, O tribe and city council,

12 You whose rich men are full of violence,
　　whose inhabitants speak falsehood
　　with deceitful tongues in their heads!

10 Am I to bear any longer criminal
　　　hoarding
　　and the meager ephah that is accursed?

11 Shall I acquit criminal balances,
　　bags of false weights?

13 Rather I will begin to strike you
　　with devastation because of your sins.

15* You shall sow, yet not reap,
　　tread out the olive, yet pour no oil,
　　and the grapes, yet drink no wine.

14* You shall eat, without being satisfied,
　　food that will leave you empty;
What you acquire, you cannot save;
　　what you do save, I will deliver up to
　　　the sword.

16† You have kept the decrees of Omri,
　　and all the works of the house of Ahab,
　　and you have walked in their counsels;
Therefore I will deliver you up to ruin,
　　and your citizens to derision;
　　and you shall bear the reproach of the
　　　nations.

---

† 5, 9-13: Part of the messianic restoration will consist in the removal of everything that has drawn Israel away from the Lord; this includes not only the objects of false worship, but also the armaments in which the idolators had trusted.

5, 12f: *Sacred pillars . . . sacred poles:* see note on Ex 34, 13.

6, 5: *From Shittim to Gilgal:* from the east to the west side of the Jordan; the events described in Jos 3-5 are meant. The text is defective; however, it is evident that this verse continues the remembrance of God's deeds of mercy to Israel, beginning with the Exodus (v 4) and extending to the conquest, deeds which have provoked so little response from his people.

6, 6ff: The people ask how they shall worship the Lord, proposing the various forms of sacrifice. The prophet replies that sacrifice avails nothing without the true spirit of religion. This is one of the best expressions of the prophetic teaching on religion, the preparation for such New Testament passages as Jas 1, 27.

6, 7: *Shall I give my first-born:* through Canaanite influence the abominable practice of human sacrifice had been introduced under impious kings (cf 2 Kgs 16, 3; 21, 6).

6, 9: *The city:* Jerusalem as the embodiment of the crimes of the entire land.

6, 16: Judah has followed the example of the northern kingdom epitomized in the semipaganism of Omri and his son Ahab (1 Kgs 16, 25-34), copying both the corrupted worship and the social injustice of their reigns.

---

*
12: Hos 3, 4; 10, 1f.
6/1: Is 6, 2; Ob 1.
3: Jer 2, 5.
4: Ex 15, 20.
5: Nm 22, 23.
6f: Hos 6, 6; 8, 13;
　　Am 5, 21.

8: Dt 26, 16; Zec 7, 9;
　　Mt 23, 23.
14: Hos 4, 10.
15: Dt 28, 38; Am 5, 11;
　　Hg 1, 6.

Condemnation and Prayer

7 ¹ Alas! I am as when the fruit is gathered,
       as when the vines have been gleaned;
    There is no cluster to eat,
       no early fig that I crave.

²* The faithful are gone from the earth,
       among men the upright are no more!
    They all lie in wait to shed blood,
       each one ensnares the other.

³* Their hands succeed at evil;
       the prince makes demands,
    The judge is had for a price,
       The great man speaks as he pleases,

⁴ The best of them is like a brier,
       the most upright like a thorn hedge.
    The day announced by your watchmen!
       your punishment has come;
       now is the time of your confusion.

⁵*† Put no trust in a friend,
       have no confidence in a companion;
    Against her who lies in your bosom
       guard the portals of your mouth.

⁶* For the son dishonors his father,
       the daughter rises up against her mother,
    The daughter-in-law against her
          mother-in-law,
       and a man's enemies are those of his
          household.

⁷* But as for me, I will look to the Lord,
       I will put my trust in God my savior;
       my God will hear me!

⁸† Rejoice not over me, O my enemy!
       though I have fallen, I will arise;
       though I sit in darkness, the Lord is my
          light.

⁹ The wrath of the Lord I will endure
       because I have sinned against him,
    Until he takes up my cause,
       and establishes my right.
    He will bring me forth to the light;
       I will see his justice.

¹⁰ When my enemy sees this,
       shame shall cover her:
    She who said to me,
       "Where is the Lord, thy God?"
    My eyes shall see her downfall;
       now shall she be trampled underfoot,
       like the mire in the streets.

¹¹† It is the day for building your walls;
       on that day the boundary shall be taken
          away.

¹²* It is the day; and they shall come to you
       from Assyria and from Egypt,
    From Tyre even to the River,
       from sea to sea, and from mountain to
          mountain;

¹³ And the land shall be a waste
       because of its citizens,
       as a result of their deeds.

¹⁴† Shepherd your people with your staff,
       the flock of your inheritance,
    That dwells apart in a woodland,
       in the midst of Carmel.
    Let them feed in Bashan and Gilead,
       as in the days of old;

¹⁵ As in the days when you came from the
          land of Egypt,
       show us wonderful signs.

¹⁶ The nations shall behold and be put to
          shame,
       in spite of all their strength;
    They shall put their hands over their
          mouths;
       their ears shall become deaf.

¹⁷ They shall lick the dust like the serpent,
       like reptiles on the ground;
    They shall come quaking from their
          fastnesses,
       trembling in fear of you [the Lord, our
          God].

¹⁸* Who is there like you, the God who
          removes guilt
       and pardons sin for the remnant of his
          inheritance;
    Who does not persist in anger forever,
       but delights rather in clemency,

¹⁹ And will again have compassion on us,
       treading underfoot our guilt?
    You will cast into the depths of the sea
       all our sins;

²⁰* You will show faithfulness to Jacob,
       and grace to Abraham,
    As you have sworn to our fathers
       from days of old.

---

† 7, 5f: Corresponding to the widespread civil corruption and apostasy from religion is the breakdown of normal human and family relations.

7, 8ff: The unnamed enemy of Judah mentioned in these verses may be Assyria or one of the neighboring countries, such as Edom, which stood by to profit at Judah's downfall.

7, 11ff: This prophecy of restoration and repopulation of the promised land by the Jews now in exile appears to be from the period after the destruction of Jerusalem by the Chaldeans (587 B. C.).

7, 14-17: This prayer appears to be from the time after the return from exile (537 B. C.), when the people, few in number, possessed only a fragment of their former land, and were surrounded by hostile nations.

---

* 7/2: Is 1, 21; Hos 4, 2.
  3: Is 1, 23.
  5: Jer 9, 3.
  6: Mt 10, 35f.
  7: Is 8, 17.

12: Zec 14, 16.
18: Jer 10, 6; Acts 10, 43.
20: Ps 105, 6;
    Is 41, 8; 63, 16.

The Book of Nahum

Introduction

Shortly before the fall of Nineveh in 612 B. C., Nahum uttered his prophecy against the hated city. To understand the prophet's exultant outburst of joy over the impending destruction it is necessary to recall the savage cruelty of Assyria, which had made it the scourge of the ancient Near East for almost three centuries. The royal inscriptions of Assyria afford the best commentary on the burning denunciation of "the bloody city." In the wake of their conquests, mounds of heads, impaled bodies, enslaved citizens, and avaricious looters testified to the ruthlessness of the Assyrians. Little wonder that Judah joined in the general outburst of joy over the destruction of Nineveh!

But Nahum is not a prophet of unrestrained revenge. God's moral government of the world is asserted. Yahweh is the avenger but he is also merciful, a citadel in the day of distress. Nineveh's doom was a judgment on the wicked city. Before many years passed, Jerusalem too was to learn the meaning of such a judgment.

The book is divided as follows:
The Lord's Coming in Judgment (1, 2—2, 2.3)
The Fall of Nineveh (2, 2—3, 19)

1 ¹ORACLE ABOUT NINEVEH. The book of the vision of Nahum of Elkosh.

The Lord's Coming in Judgment

2† A jealous and avenging God is the LORD,
an avenger is the LORD, and angry;
The LORD brings vengeance on his adversaries,
and lays up wrath for his enemies;
3❋ The LORD is slow to anger, yet great in power,
and the LORD never leaves the guilty unpunished.
In hurricane and tempest is his path,
and clouds are the dust at his feet;
4❋† He rebukes the sea and leaves it dry,
and all the rivers he dries up.
Withered are Bashan and Carmel,
and the bloom of Lebanon fades;
5 The mountains quake before him,
and the hills dissolve;
The earth is laid waste before him,
the world and all who dwell in it.
6❋† Before his wrath, who can stand firm,
and who can face his blazing anger?

His fury is poured out like fire,
and the rocks are rent asunder before him.
7 The LORD is good,
a refuge on the day of distress;
He takes care of those who have recourse to him,
when the flood rages;
8 He makes an end of his opponents,
and his enemies he pursues with darkness.

9† What are you imputing to the LORD?
It is he who will make an end!
The enemy shall not rise a second time;
10 As when a tangle of thornbushes is set aflame,
like dry stubble, they shall be utterly consumed.
12† For, says the LORD,
be they ever so many and so vigorous,
still they shall be mown down and disappear.
Though I have humbled you,
I will humble you no more.
13❋ Now will I break his yoke from off you,
and burst asunder your bonds.
11† From you he came
who devised evil against the LORD,
the scoundrel planner.

14† The LORD has commanded regarding you:
no descendant shall come to bear your name;

---

† 1, 2-8: A poem written in the style of the alphabetic psalms; cf Pss 9A; 25; 111; 119. Here, however, most of the verses beginning with the letters of the second half of the alphabet are not preserved.

1, 2: *A jealous . . . God:* see note on Ex 20, 5.

1, 4: *Bashan, Carmel* and *Lebanon* were famous for their forests.

1, 6f: The coming of God in judgment has two aspects: to those who oppose him it will be unbearable; to *those who have recourse to him* it will bring strength and consolation.

1, 9: *What are you imputing to the Lord?:* the people of Judah are asked what they think God has in mind.

1, 11: *From you . . . the scoundrel planner:* addressed to Nineveh, the capital city of Sennacherib, king of Assyria, who besieged Jerusalem c. 700 B. C.

1, 12f: *They:* the enemies of Judah. *You:* Judah. *His yoke:* the dominion of the Assyrian king over Judah.

1, 14: *You:* the king of Assyria.

❋
1/3: Ex 19, 16ff.   6: Zep 1, 15; 2, 3.
4: Is 33, 9; Hb 3, 6ff.   13: Is 9, 4; 10, 27.

From your temple I will abolish
    the carved and the molten image;
    I will make your grave a mockery.

2   **1*** See, upon the mountains there advances
    the bearer of good news, announcing
      peace!
Celebrate your feasts, O Judah,
    fulfill your vows!
For nevermore shall you be invaded
    by the scoundrel; he is completely
      destroyed.
3 The LORD will restore the vine of Jacob,
    the pride of Israel,
Though ravagers have ravaged them
    and ruined the tendrils.

The Fall of Nineveh

2† The hammer comes up against you;
    guard the rampart,
Keep watch on the road, gird your loins,
    marshal all your strength!
4 The shields of his warriors are crimsoned,
    the soldiers colored in scarlet;
Fiery steel are the chariots
    on the day of his mustering.
The horses are frenzied;
5   the chariots dash madly through the
      streets
And wheel in the squares,
    looking like firebrands,
    flashing like lightning bolts.
6† His picked troops are called,
    ranks break at their charge;
To the wall they rush,
    the mantelet is set up.
7 The river gates are opened,
    the palace shudders,
8† Its mistress is led forth captive,
    and her handmaids, under guard,
Moaning like doves,
    beating their breasts.
9 Nineveh is like a pool
    whose waters escape;
"Stop! Stop!"
    but none turns back.
10 "Plunder the silver, plunder the gold!"
    There is no end to the treasure,
    to their wealth in precious things of
      every kind!

11* Emptiness, desolation, waste;
    melting hearts and trembling knees,
Writhing in every frame,
    every face blanched!

12† Where is the lions' cave,
    the young lions' den,
Where the lion went in and out,
    and the cub, with no one to disturb
      them?
13 The lion snatched enough for his cubs,
    and strangled for his lionesses;
He filled his dens with prey,
    and his caves with plunder.
14 I come against you,
    says the LORD of hosts;
I will consume in smoke your chariots,
    and the sword shall devour your young
      lions;
Your preying on the land I will bring to an
      end,
    the cry of your lionesses shall be heard
      no more.

Ruin Imminent and Inevitable

3   **1*** Woe to the bloody city, all lies,
    full of plunder, whose looting never
      stops!
2 The crack of the whip, the rumbling sound
    of wheels;
    horses a-gallop, chariots bounding,
3 Cavalry charging,
The flame of the sword, the flash of the
    spear,
    the many slain, the heaping corpses,
    the endless bodies to stumble upon!
4* For the many debaucheries of the harlot,
    fair and charming, a mistress of
      witchcraft,
Who enslaved nations with her harlotries,
    and peoples by her witchcraft:
5*† I am come against you,
    and I will strip your skirt from you;
I will show your nakedness to the nations,
    to the kingdoms your shame!
6 I will cast filth upon you,
    disgrace you and put you to shame;
7 Till everyone who sees you runs from you,
    saying,
    "Nineveh is destroyed; who can pity her?
    Where can one find any to console her?"

8*† Are you better than No-amon
    that was set among the streams,

---

†
  2, 2: *The hammer comes up against you:* the enemy is about to crush Nineveh.
  2, 6: *Mantelet:* a movable shelter protecting the besiegers.
  2, 8: *Mistress . . . and her handmaids:* either the queen of Nineveh with the ladies of her court, or the statue of Ishtar, Nineveh's chief goddess, with her temple prostitutes.
  2, 12: *The lion:* the king of Assyria.
  3, 5f: The punishment of adulteresses.
  3, 8: *No-amon:* No was the Egyptian name of the capital of Upper Egypt, called Thebes by the Greeks; its tutelary deity was Amon. This great city was destroyed by the Assyrians in 663 B. C.

---

*
2/1: Is 52, 7; Rom 10, 15.   5: Is 47, 3; Jer 13, 26;
  11: Jl 2, 6.   Hos 2, 12.
3/1: Hb 2, 12.   8: Jer 46, 25.
  4: Mi 1, 7; Rv 17, 1f.

Surrounded by waters,
with the flood for her rampart
and water her wall?

9 Ethiopia was her strength, and Egypt,
and others without end;
Put and the Libyans were her auxiliaries.

10 Yet even she went captive into exile,
even her little ones were dashed to pieces
at the corner of every street;
For her nobles they cast lots,
and all her great men were put into
chains.

11✿ You, too, shall drink of this till you faint
away;
you, too, shall seek a refuge from the foe.

12 All your fortresses are but fig trees,
bearing early figs
That fall, when shaken,
into the hungry mouth.

13✿ See, the troops are women in your midst;
to your foes the gates of your land are
open wide,
fire has consumed their bars.

14† Draw water for the siege,
strengthen your fortresses;
Go down into the mud and tread the clay,
take hold of the brick mold!

15 There the fire shall consume you,
the sword shall cut you down.

Multiply like the grasshoppers,
multiply like the locusts!

16 Make your couriers more numerous than
the stars,

17 your garrisons as many as grasshoppers,
And your scribes as locust swarms
gathered on the rubble fences on a cold
day!
Yet when the sun warms them,
the grasshoppers will spread their wings
and fly,
and vanish, no one knows where.

18 Alas! how your shepherds slumber, O king
of Assyria,
your nobles have gone to rest;
Your people are scattered upon the
mountains,
with none to gather them.

19 There is no healing for your hurt,
your wound is mortal.
All who hear this news of you
clap their hands over you;
For who has not been overwhelmed,
steadily, by your malice?

✿

11: Mi 2, 11.　　　　13: Jer 51, 30.

---

†

3, 14: An ironic exhortation to prepare the city for a futile
defense. *Go down . . . brick mold:* make bricks for the city walls.

The Book of Habakkuk

Introduction

This prophecy dates from the years 605-597 B. C., or between the great Babylonian victory at Carchemish and Nebuchadnezzar's invasion of Judah which culminated in the capture of Jerusalem. The situation of Judah was desperate at this time, with political intrigue and idolatry widespread in the small kingdom. The first two chapters consist of a dialogue between the prophet and the Lord. For what may be the first time in Israelite literature, a man questions the ways of God, as Habakkuk calls him to account for his government of the world. To this question God replies that he has prepared a chastising rod, Babylon, which will be the avenging instrument in his hand. There is added the divine assurance that the just Israelite will not perish in the calamities about to be visited on the nation.

The third chapter is a magnificent religious lyric, filled with reminiscences of Israel's past and rich in literary borrowings from the poetry of ancient Canaan, though still expressing authentic Israelite faith. God appears in all his majestic splendor and executes vengeance on Judah's enemies. The prophecy ends with a joyous profession of confidence in the Lord, the Savior.

1 ¹THE ORACLE WHICH HABAKKUK THE PROPHET received in vision.

The Prophet's Complaint and Its Answer

2† How long, O Lord? I cry for help
    but you do not listen!
I cry out to you, "Violence!"
    but you do not intervene.

3 Why do you let me see ruin;
    why must I look at misery?
Destruction and violence are before me;
    there is strife, and clamorous discord.

4 This is why the law is benumbed,
    and judgment is never rendered:
Because the wicked circumvent the just;
    this is why judgment comes forth
        perverted.

5*† Look over the nations and see,
    and be utterly amazed!
For a work is being done in your days
    that you would not have believed, were
        it told.

6 For see, I am raising up Chaldea,
    that bitter and unruly people,
That marches the breadth of the land
    to take dwellings not his own.

7 Terrible and dreadful is he,
    from himself derive his law and his
        majesty.

8† Swifter than leopards are his horses,
    and keener than wolves at evening.
His horses prance,
    his horsemen come from afar:
They fly like the eagle hastening to devour;
    each comes for the rapine,

9 Their combined onset is that of a
        stormwind
    that heaps up captives like sand.

10 He scoffs at kings,
    and princes are his laughingstock;
He laughs at any fortress,
    heaps up a ramp, and conquers it.

11† Then he veers like the wind and is gone—
    this culprit who makes his own strength
        his god!

12† Are you not from eternity, O Lord,
    my holy God, immortal?

---

† 1, 2-4: Traditionally, these verses have been taken as the prophet's complaint against the internal evils of Judah; the language used is that employed by Amos, Isaiah, and Jeremiah to condemn the social abuses of their day. In vv 5ff the Lord answers this complaint by indicating the Chaldean empire as his instrument for punishing his people for these sins.

1, 5: *Look over the nations and see:* after Nebuchadnezzar's defeat of Egypt in 605 B. C., there could be little doubt that it was the Chaldean ambition to dominate the entire Near East.

1, 8: *Wolves at evening:* the wolf is apparently thought of as more rabid and vicious in the evening when setting out for prey (Jer 5, 6; Zep 3, 3).

1, 11: *Veers like the wind:* the conquests of the ancient Near East were mainly raiding expeditions to collect tribute. As far as administration of conquered territories was concerned, both the Assyrians and Chaldeans were usually content to install friendly rulers and then depart. *This culprit:* though the Chaldeans were used by God as the agents of his punishment, this did not diminish their own guilt as ruthless marauders.

1, 12—2, 1: It is generally thought that this complaint is directed against the Chaldeans and their terrible destruction. But it may well be a continuation of 1, 2-4, against the wicked Judahites who have merited God's punishment.

1, 12: *O Rock:* an ancient title celebrating the Lord's power; cf Ps 18, 32.

O LORD, you have marked him for
judgment,
  O Rock, you have readied him for
  punishment!

13 Too pure are your eyes to look upon evil,
  and the sight of misery you cannot
  endure.
Why, then, do you gaze on the faithless in
silence
  while the wicked man devours
  one more just than himself?

14 You have made man like the fish of the sea,
  like creeping things without a ruler.

15† He brings them all up with his hook,
  he hauls them away with his net,
He gathers them in his seine;
  and so he rejoices and exults.

16† Therefore he sacrifices to his net,
  and burns incense to his seine;
For thanks to them his portion is generous,
  and his repast sumptuous.

17 Shall he, then, keep on brandishing his
sword
  to slay peoples without mercy?

2 **1** I will stand at my guard post,
  and station myself upon the rampart,
And keep watch to see what he will say to
me,
  and what answer he will give to my
  complaint.

2✱ Then the LORD answered me and said:
  Write down the vision
Clearly upon the tablets,
  so that one can read it readily.

3 For the vision still has its time,
  presses on to fulfillment, and will not
  disappoint;
If it delays, wait for it,
  it will surely come, it will not be late.

4✱† The rash man has no integrity;
  but the just man, because of his faith,
  shall live.
Wealth, too, is treacherous:
  the proud, unstable man—

5 He who opens wide his throat like the
nether world,
  and is insatiable as death,
Who gathers to himself all the nations,
  and rallies to himself all the peoples—

6 Shall not all these take up a taunt against
him,
  satire and epigrams about him, to say:

Woe to him who stores up what is not his:
  how long can it last!
  he loads himself down with debts.

7 Shall not your creditors rise suddenly?
  Shall not they who make you tremble
  awake?
  You shall become their spoil!

8 Because you despoiled many peoples
  all the rest of the nations shall despoil
  you;
Because of men's blood shed,
  and violence done to the land,
  to the city and to all who dwell in it.

9 Woe to him who pursues evil gain for his
household,
  setting his nest on high
  to escape the reach of misfortune!

10 You have devised shame for your
household,
  cutting off many peoples, forfeiting your
  own life:

11† For the stone in the wall shall cry out,
  and the beam in the woodwork shall
  answer it!

12✱ Woe to him who builds a city by bloodshed,
  and establishes a town by wickedness!

13✱† Is not this from the LORD of hosts:
  peoples toil for the flames,
  and nations grow weary for nought!

14✱ But the earth shall be filled
  with the knowledge of the LORD's glory
  as water covers the sea.

15 Woe to you who give your neighbors
  a flood of your wrath to drink,
  and make them drunk, till their
  nakedness is seen!

16 You are filled with shame instead of glory;
  drink, you too, and stagger!
On you shall revert the cup from the LORD's
  right hand,
  and utter shame on your glory.

---

†

1, 15: The *he* of this and the following verses, to whom is
attributed such extensive evil and the destruction of many
peoples, may be the wicked of Judah embodied in King Jehoiakim, ally of the powerful Pharaoh Neco of Egypt; the devastation wrought by Jehoiakim and Neco together is condemned.

1, 16: *He sacrifices to his net:* in v 15 the wicked ruler in
question is represented as catching men in a net. This verse
alludes to some rite involving the sacrificial veneration of the
weapons of war.

2, 4: *The just man, because of his faith, shall live:* the faith
which here enables the virtuous man to survive the impending
doom is both a confident belief in God's justice, and patience in
awaiting its execution. St. Paul quotes these words (Rom 1, 17;
Gal 3, 11; Heb 10, 38) to confirm his teaching that man receives
justification and supernatural life through faith in Christ.

2, 11f: The palaces, built at the expense of gross injustice
(vv 6-10), call down vengeance on their builders. This is typical
prophetic language for the condemnation of social crimes
within Israel and Judah.

2, 13: *Peoples toil for the flames:* they build only to have fire
consume their work, when they build contrary to God's will.

✱

2/1: Ps 85, 9.   12: Ez 24, 9; Na 3, 1.
   4: Rom 1, 17; Gal 3, 11;   13: Jer 51, 58.
      Heb 10, 38.   14: Is 11, 9.

17† For the violence done to Lebanon shall
cover you,
     and the destruction of the beasts shall
terrify you;
Because of men's blood shed,
     and violence done to the land,
     to the city and to all who dwell in it.

19 Woe to him who says to wood, "Awake!"
     to dumb stone, "Arise!"
     Can such a thing give oracles?
See, it is overlaid with gold and silver,
     but there is no life breath in it.

18† Of what avail is the carved image,
     that its maker should carve it?
Or the molten image and lying oracle,
     that its very maker should trust in it,
     and make dumb idols?

20❋ But the Lord is in his holy temple;
     silence before him, all the earth!

Canticle

3 **1†**Prayer of Habakkuk, the prophet. To a plaintive tune.

2† O Lord, I have heard your renown,
     and feared, O Lord, your work.
In the course of the years revive it,
     in the course of the years make it known;
     in your wrath remember compassion!

3† God comes from Teman,
     the Holy One from Mount Paran.
Covered are the heavens with his glory,
     and with his praise the earth is filled.

4 His splendor spreads like the light;
     rays shine forth from beside him,
     where his power is concealed.

5 Before him goes pestilence,
     and the plague follows in his steps.

6 He pauses to survey the earth;
     his look makes the nations tremble.
The eternal mountains are shattered,
     the age-old hills bow low
     along his ancient ways.

7 I see the tents of Cushan collapse;
     trembling are the pavilions of the land of
Midian.

8 Is your anger against the streams, O Lord?
Is your wrath against the streams,
     your rage against the sea,
That you drive the steeds
     of your victorious chariot?

9 Bared and ready is your bow,
     filled with arrows is your quiver.
Into streams you split the earth;

10   at sight of you the mountains tremble.

A torrent of rain descends;
     the ocean gives forth its roar.
The sun forgets to rise,

11❋   the moon remains in its shelter,
At the light of your flying arrows,
     at the gleam of your flashing spear.

12 In wrath you bestride the earth,
     in fury you trample the nations.

13❋† You come forth to save your people,
     to save your anointed one.
You crush the heads of the wicked,
     you lay bare their bases at the neck.

14 You pierce with your shafts the heads of
     their princes
     whose boast would be of devouring
     the wretched in their lair.

15 You tread the sea with your steeds
     amid the churning of the deep waters.

16 I hear, and my body trembles;
     at the sound, my lips quiver.
Decay invades my bones,
     my legs tremble beneath me.
I await the day of distress
     that will come upon the people who
     attack us.

17 For though the fig tree blossom not
     nor fruit be on the vines,
Though the yield of the olive fail
     and the terraces produce no
     nourishment,
Though the flocks disappear from the fold
     and there be no herd in the stalls,

18❋ Yet will I rejoice in the Lord
     and exult in my saving God.

19 God, my Lord, is my strength;
     he makes my feet swift as those of hinds
     and enables me to go upon the heights.

For the leader; with stringed instruments.

---

† 2, 17: *The violence done to Lebanon:* the spoliation of the cedar forests of Lebanon, used in lavish building projects by the great conquerors; cf Is 14, 8; 37, 24. *The destruction of the beasts:* the killing off of the wild animals through excessive hunting by the same conquerors; cf Bar 3, 16.

2, 18-20: Idolatrous worship is here shown to be folly by contrasting man-made idols with the majesty of the one true God.

3, 1: A later liturgical rubric. So also the end of v 19.

3, 2: *In the course of the years revive it:* renew today your wondrous deeds of the past.

3, 3: *Teman:* a region in Edom. *Mount Paran:* in the territory of Edom, or the northern part of the Sinaitic peninsula. The Lord is represented as coming from Sinai, where he had appeared to Moses and given Israel the covenant and the law.

3, 3-15: Cf the theophanies in Dt 33, 2f; Jgs 5, 4f; Pss 18, 8-16; 68, 8f; 77, 17-21; 97, 1-5; Na 1, 3-6, etc. Conventional language is employed to describe the appearance of the Lord, as in Ex 19, 16-19.

3, 13: *Your anointed one:* the theocratic king, the head of God's people.

❋

20: Ps 11, 4.   13: Is 51, 9ff.
3/11: Jos 10, 12.   18f: Ps 18, 32f; Mi 7, 7.

The Book of Zephaniah

Introduction

The title of the prophecy informs us that the ministry of Zephaniah took place during the reign of Josiah (640-609 B. C.). The protest against the worship of false gods, and the condemnation of the pro-Assyrian court ministers who served as regents during Josiah's minority, allow us to place the work in the first decade of the reign. Accordingly, the prophecy of Zephaniah comes rightly before that of Jeremiah, who was probably influenced by it in both language and ideas.

The age of Zephaniah was a time of religious degradation, when the old idolatries reappeared and men worshiped sun, moon, and stars. Rites completely alien to the pure monotheism taught by Moses flourished in Jerusalem. To the corrupt city Zephaniah announced the impending judgment, the day of the Lord. The prophecy may be divided into three sections, corresponding to the three chapters of the book:

The Day of the Lord: A day of doom. The last few verses of this oracle give the classic description of the Day of the Lord as an overwhelming disaster. The Christian hymn *Dies Irae* is based on this passage (1, 2-18).

The Day of the Lord: A day of judgment of the nations, traditional enemies of God's people (2, 1-15).

Reproach and Promise for Jerusalem: Despite Judah's infidelities, the Lord in his mercy will spare a holy remnant, which will finally enjoy peace. The prophecy closes with a hymn of joy sung by the remnant restored to Zion (3, 1-20).

1 ¹THE WORD OF THE LORD which came to Zephaniah, the son of Cushi, the son of Gedaliah, the son of Amariah, the son of Hezekiah, in the days of Josiah, the son of Amon, king of Judah.

The Day of the Lord: A Day of Doom

2 I will completely sweep away all things
   from the face of the earth, says the LORD.
3* I will sweep away man and beast,
   I will sweep away the birds of the sky,
   and the fishes of the sea.
   I will overthrow the wicked;
   I will destroy mankind
   from the face of the earth, says the LORD.
4 I will stretch out my hand against Judah,
   and against all the inhabitants of
   Jerusalem;

I will destroy from this place the last
   vestige of Baal,
   the very names of his priests,
5*† And those who adore the host of heaven on
   the roofs,
   with those who adore the LORD
   but swear by Milcom;
6 And those who have fallen away from the
   LORD,
   and those who do not seek the LORD.

7† Silence in the presence of the Lord GOD!
   for near is the day of the LORD,
   Yes, the LORD has prepared a slaughter
   feast,
   he has consecrated his guests.
8 On the day of the LORD's slaughter
   feast
   I will punish the princes, and the king's
   sons,
   and all that dress in foreign apparel.
9† I will punish, on that day,
   all who leap over the threshold,
   Who fill the house of their master
   with violence and deceit.
10† On that day, says the LORD,
   A cry will be heard from the Fish Gate,
   a wail from the New Quarter,
   loud crashing from the hills.
11 Wail, O inhabitants of the Mortar!
   for all the merchants will be destroyed,
   all who weigh out silver, done away
   with.
12† At that time I will explore Jerusalem with
   lamps;

---

† 1, 5: *The host of heaven:* the stars, the worship of which was introduced into Judah by the Assyrians. *Milcom:* the god of the Ammonites; cf 1 Kgs 11, 5.7.33; 2 Kgs 23, 13.

1, 7: *He has consecrated his guests:* God has prepared those whom he has invited to share as soldiers in the booty, or as beast and bird scavengers of carrion, on the day of slaughter. Cf Jer 46, 10; Ez 39, 17.

1, 9: *Leap over the threshold:* the reference is to a superstitious custom of the pagans, witnessed to at least in regard to the worship of Dagon (1 Sm 5, 5).

1, 10f: *The New Quarter . . . the Mortar:* sections of Jerusalem (cf 2 Kgs 22, 14).

1, 12: *The men who thicken on their lees:* those who are overconfident because, like bottles of wine in which the sediment has settled to the bottom, they have remained at peace and undisturbed for a long time.

I will punish the men who thicken on
    their lees,
Who say in their hearts,
    "Neither good nor evil can the Lord do."
13 Their wealth shall be given to pillage
    and their houses to devastation;
They will build houses, but shall not dwell
    in them,
    plant vineyards, but not drink their wine.
14 Near is the great day of the Lord,
    near and very swiftly coming;
Hark, the day of the Lord!
    bitter, then, the warrior's cry.
15 A day of wrath is that day
    a day of anguish and distress,
A day of destruction and desolation,
    a day of darkness and gloom,
A day of thick black clouds,
16   a day of trumpet blasts and battle alarm
Against fortified cities,
    against battlements on high.
17 I will hem men in
    till they walk like the blind,
    because they have sinned against the
      Lord;
And their blood shall be poured out like
    dust,
    and their brains like dung.
18 Neither their silver nor their gold
    shall be able to save them
    on the day of the Lord's wrath,
When in the fire of his jealousy
    all the earth shall be consumed.
For he shall make an end, yes, a sudden
    end,
    of all who live on the earth.

The Day of the Lord: A Day of Judgment

2 1 Gather, gather yourselves together,
    O nation without shame!
2 Before you are driven away,
    like chaff that passes on;
Before there comes upon you
    the blazing anger of the Lord;
Before there comes upon you
    the day of the Lord's anger.
3 Seek the Lord, all you humble of the earth,
    who have observed his law;
Seek justice, seek humility;
    perhaps you may be sheltered
    on the day of the Lord's anger.
4 For Gaza shall be forsaken,
    and Ashkelon shall be a waste,
Ashdod they shall drive out at midday,
    and Ekron shall be uprooted.

5 Woe to you who dwell by the seacoast,
    to the Cretan folk!
The word of the Lord is against you,
    I will humble you, land of the Philistines,
    and leave you to perish without an
      inhabitant!
6 The coastland of the Cretans shall become
    fields for shepherds, and folds for flocks.
7 The coast shall belong
    to the remnant of the house of Judah;
    by the sea they shall pasture.
In the houses of Ashkelon at evening
    they shall couch their flocks,
For the Lord their God shall visit them,
    and bring about their restoration.
8 I have heard the revilings uttered by Moab,
    and the insults of the Ammonites,
When they reviled my people
    and made boasts against their territory.
9 Therefore, as I live, says the Lord of hosts,
    the God of Israel,
Moab shall become like Sodom,
    the land of Ammon like Gomorrah:
A field of nettles and a salt pit
    and a waste forever.
The remnant of my people shall plunder
    them,
    the survivors of my nation dispossess
    them.
10 Such shall be the requital of their pride,
    because they reviled and boasted against
    the people of the Lord of hosts.
11 The Lord shall inspire them with fear
    when he makes all the gods of earth to
      waste away;
Then, each from its own place,
    all the coastlands of the nations shall
      adore him.
12 You too, O Cushites,
    shall be slain by the sword of the Lord.
13 He will stretch out his hand against the
    north,
    to destroy Assyria;
He will make Nineveh a waste,
    dry as the desert.
14 In her midst shall settle in droves
    all the wild life of the hollows;
The screech owl and the desert owl
    shall roost in her columns;
Their call shall resound from the window,
    the raven's croak from the doorway.

---

† 2, 1: *Nation without shame:* Judah.
  2, 4: *Gaza . . . Ashkelon . . . Ashdod . . . Ekron:* four of the five cities of the Philistine confederation. The fifth city, Gath is not mentioned, perhaps because it was already destroyed.
  2, 5: *Cretan folk:* the Philistines, who came from Crete; see note on Dt 2, 23.
  2, 12: *Cushites:* the Egyptians, at this time under a Cushite or Ethiopian dynasty.

13: Am 5, 11.
15: Jer 30, 7; Jl 2, 11; Am 5, 18.
16: Am 2, 2.
18: 3, 8; Ez 7, 19.
2/4: Am 1, 6ff; Zec 9, 5.
14: Is 34, 11.

15† Is this the exultant city
   that dwelt secure;
That told herself,
   "There is no other than I!"
How has she become a waste,
   a lair for wild beasts?
Whoever passes by her
   hisses, and shakes his fist!

Reproach and Promise for Jerusalem

3 **1** Woe to the city, rebellious and polluted,
   to the tyrannical city!
2* She hears no voice,
   accepts no correction;
In the Lord she has not trusted,
   to her God she has not drawn near.
3* Her princes in her midst
   are roaring lions;
Her judges are wolves of the night
   that have had no bones to gnaw by
     morning.
4* Her prophets are insolent,
   treacherous men;
Her priests profane what is holy,
   and do violence to the law.
5 The Lord within her is just,
   who does no wrong;
Morning after morning he renders
    judgment
   unfailingly, at dawn.

6* I have destroyed nations,
   their battlements are laid waste;
I have made their streets deserted,
   with no one passing through;
Their cities are devastated,
   with no man dwelling in them.
7 I said, "Surely now you will fear me,
   you will accept correction";
She should not fail to see
   all I have visited upon her.
Yet all the more eagerly have they done
   all their corrupt deeds.
8* Therefore, wait for me, says the Lord,
   against the day when I arise as accuser;
For it is my decision to gather together the
    nations,
   to assemble the kingdoms,
In order to pour out upon them my wrath,
   all my blazing anger;
For in the fire of my jealousy
   shall all the earth be consumed.

9 For then I will change and purify
   the lips of the peoples,
That they all may call upon the name of the
    Lord,
   to serve him with one accord;

10 From beyond the rivers of Ethiopia
   and as far as the recesses of the North,
   they shall bring me offerings.

11   On that day
You need not be ashamed
   of all your deeds,
   your rebellious actions against me;
For then will I remove from your midst
   the proud braggarts,
And you shall no longer exalt yourself
   on my holy mountain.
12* But I will leave as a remnant in your midst
   a people humble and lowly,
Who shall take refuge in the name of the
    Lord:
13*   the remnant of Israel.
They shall do no wrong
   and speak no lies;
Nor shall there be found in their mouths
   a deceitful tongue;
They shall pasture and couch their flocks
   with none to disturb them.

14* Shout for joy, O daughter Zion!
   sing joyfully, O Israel!
Be glad and exult with all your heart,
   O daughter Jerusalem!
15 The Lord has removed the judgment
    against you,
   he has turned away your enemies;
The King of Israel, the Lord, is in your
    midst,
   you have no further misfortune to fear.
16* On that day, it shall be said to Jerusalem:
   Fear not, O Zion, be not discouraged!
17 The Lord, your God, is in your midst,
   a mighty savior;
He will rejoice over you with gladness,
   and renew you in his love,
He will sing joyfully because of you,
18   as one sings at festivals.

I will remove disaster from among you,
   so that none may recount your disgrace.
19* Yes, at that time I will deal
   with all who oppress you:
I will save the lame,
   and assemble the outcasts;
I will give them praise and renown
   in all the earth, when I bring about their
    restoration.
20 At that time I will bring you home,
   and at that time I will gather you;
For I will give you renown and praise,
   among all the peoples of the earth,
When I bring about your restoration
   before your very eyes, says the Lord.

3/2: Jer 2, 30; 7, 28.   12: Hos 14, 4.
   3: Ez 22, 27; Mi 3, 11.   13: Mi 4, 4.
   4: Jer 23, 32.   14: Zec 9, 9.
   6: Jer 2, 15.   16: Mt 14, 27.
   8: 1, 18.   19: Mi 4, 6.

† 2, 15: *The exultant city:* Nineveh.

The Book of Haggai

Introduction

Postexilic prophecy begins with Haggai, who received the word of the Lord in the second year of Darius (520 B. C.). The Jews who returned from the Exile in Babylonia had encountered formidable obstacles in their efforts to re-establish Jewish life in Judah. The Samaritans had succeeded in blocking the rebuilding of the temple; but after Darius acceded to the throne (522), permission was given to resume the work. At this critical moment, when defeatism and a certain lethargy had overtaken his repatriated countrymen, Haggai came forward with his exhortations to them to complete the great task. The first oracle, an appeal to the Jews, is contained in chapter 1. To this appeal Haggai added a short oracle of encouragement (2, 1-9) for the sake of those who gloomily contrasted the former magnificence of Sólomon's temple with the second temple: the Lord would be present in this new abode, and its glory, enhanced by the offerings of the Gentiles, would surpass the ancient splendor.

The prophecy may be divided into five oracles:

The call to rebuild the temple. The economic distress so apparent in Judah is due to the Jews' neglect of the Lord while they provide for their own needs (1, 1-15).

The future glory of the new temple, surpassing that of the old (2, 1-9).

Unworthiness of a people, who may be the Samaritans, to offer sacrifice at the newly restored altar. This oracle is cast in the literary form of a *torah*, an instruction given the people by a priest (2, 10-14).

A promise of immediate blessings, which follows upon the undertaking (chapter 1) to rebuild the temple (2, 15-19).

A pledge to Zerubbabel, descendant of David, repository of the messianic hopes (2, 20-23).

Exhortation To Rebuild the Temple of the Lord

1 1*†ON THE FIRST DAY OF THE SIXTH MONTH in the second year of King Darius, the word of the LORD came through the prophet Haggai to the governor of Judah, Zerubbabel, son of Shealtiel, and to the high priest Joshua, son of Jehozadak: ²Thus says the LORD of hosts: This people says: "Not now has the time come to rebuild the house of the LORD." ³(Then this word of the LORD came through Haggai, the prophet:) 4*†Is it time for you to dwell in your own paneled houses, while this house lies in ruins?

5   Now thus says the LORD of hosts:
        Consider your ways!
6*   You have sown much, but have brought in little;
        you have eaten, but have not been satisfied;
    You have drunk, but have not been exhilarated;
        have clothed yourselves, but not been warmed;
    And he who earned wages
        earned them for a bag with holes in it.

7   Thus says the LORD of hosts:
    Consider your ways!
8   Go up into the hill country;
        bring timber, and build the house
    That I may take pleasure in it
        and receive my glory, says the LORD.
9*   You expected much, but it came to little;
        and what you brought home, I blew away.
    For what cause? says the LORD of hosts.
        Because my house lies in ruins,
        while each of you hurries to his own house.
10* Therefore the heavens withheld from you their dew,
        and the earth her crops.
11 And I called for a drought
        upon the land and upon the mountains;
    Upon the grain, and upon the wine, and upon the oil,
        and upon all that the ground brings forth;
    Upon men and upon beasts,
        and upon all that is produced by hand.

¹²†Then Zerubbabel, son of Shealtiel, and the high priest Joshua, son of Jehozadak, and all the remnant of the people listened to the voice of the LORD, their God, and to the words of the prophet Haggai, because the LORD, their God, had sent him, and the people feared because of the LORD. ¹³And the LORD's messenger,

---

1, 1: *The sixth month in the second year:* August/September in 520 B. C.

1, 4: The luxury of the homes of the wealthy with their *paneled houses* contrasts sadly with the ruined state of the Lord's *house.*

1, 12: *The remnant of the people:* a technical term in Haggai and Zechariah for the returned exiles.

1/1: Ezr 4, 24; 5, 1; 6, 14.
4: 2 Sm 7, 2.
6: Dt 28. 38ff; Mi 6, 15.

9: 2 Kgs 25, 9.
10: Gn 27, 28; Am 4, 6-9.

Haggai, proclaimed to the people as the message of the Lord: I am with you, says the Lord.

14Then the Lord stirred up the spirit of the governor of Judah, Zerubbabel, son of Shealtiel, and the spirit of the high priest Joshua, son of Jehozadak, and the spirit of all the remnant of the people, so that they came and set to work on the house of the Lord of hosts, their God, **15**on the twenty-fourth day of the sixth month.

Future Glory of the New Temple

2 IN the second year of King Darius, **1**on the twenty-first day of the seventh month, the word of the Lord came through the prophet Haggai: **2**Tell this to the governor of Judah, Zerubbabel, son of Shealtiel, and to the high priest Joshua, son of Jehozadak, and to the remnant of the people:

3　　Who is left among you
　　　　that saw this house in its former glory?
　　And how do you see it now?
　　　　Does it not seem like nothing in your
　　　　　　eyes?
4*　But now take courage, Zerubbabel, says
　　　　the Lord,
　　and take courage, Joshua, high priest,
　　　　son of Jehozadak,
　　And take courage, all you people of the
　　　　land,
　　　　says the Lord, and work!
　　For I am with you, says the Lord of hosts.
5*　This is the pact that I made with you
　　　　when you came out of Egypt,
　　And my spirit continues in your midst;
　　　　do not fear!

6*†　　For thus says the Lord of hosts:
　　One moment yet, a little while,
　　　　and I will shake the heavens and the
　　　　　　earth,
　　　　the sea and the dry land.
7*　I will shake all the nations,
　　　　and the treasures of all the nations will
　　　　　　come in,
　　And I will fill this house with glory,
　　　　says the Lord of hosts.
8　Mine is the silver and mine the gold,
　　　　says the Lord of hosts.
9*　Greater will be the future glory of this
　　　　house
　　　　than the former, says the Lord of hosts;
　　And in this place I will give peace,
　　　　says the Lord of hosts!

Offerings of the Unclean Rejected

10On the twenty-fourth day of the ninth month, in the second year of King Darius, the word of the Lord

came to the prophet Haggai: **11***Thus says the Lord of hosts: Ask the priests for a decision: **12†**If a man carries sanctified flesh in the fold of his garment and the fold touches bread, or pottage, or wine, or oil, or any other food, do they become sanctified? "No," the priests answered. **13***Then Haggai said: If a person unclean from contact with a corpse touches any of these, do they become unclean? The priests answered, "They become unclean." **14**Then Haggai continued:

　　So is this people, and so is this nation
　　　　in my sight, says the Lord:
　　And so are all the works of their hands;
　　　　and what they offer there is unclean.

Promise of Immediate Blessings

15†But now, consider from this day forward. Before there was a stone laid upon a stone in the temple of the Lord, **16***how did you fare?

　　When one went to a heap of grain for
　　　　twenty measures,
　　　　it would yield but ten;
　　When another went to the vat to draw
　　　　fifty measures,
　　　　there would be but twenty.
17　I struck you in all the works of your hands
　　　　with blight, searing wind, and hail,
　　　　yet you did not return to me, says the
　　　　　　Lord.

18†[Consider from this day forward: from the twenty-fourth day of the ninth month. From the day on which the temple of the Lord was founded, consider!]

19　Indeed, the seed has not sprouted,
　　　　nor have the vine, the fig, the
　　　　　　pomegranate
　　　　and the olive tree yet borne.
　　From this day, I will bless!

Pledge to Zerubbabel

20†The message of the Lord came a second time to Haggai on the twenty-fourth day of the month: **21**Tell this to Zerubbabel, the governor of Judah:

---

†

2, 6-9: From the later period of Ezekiel's preaching onward, the temple became, as here, one of the dominant messianic themes. *Greater will be the future glory of this house than the former:* because Christ will enter it.

2, 12ff: According to the ritual concepts of the Jews, uncleanness was more contagious than sacredness. Inasmuch as the people were unclean, their offerings became unclean (Nm 19, 22).

2, 15-19: This prophecy is intimately linked with chapter 1, and should be read with it.

2, 18: *The ninth month:* the ordinal *ninth* has been copied incorrectly from 2, 10. This note clearly concerns the *twenty-fourth day of the sixth month*, on which the temple of the Lord *was founded* (1, 15).

2, 20: *The month:* probably again the sixth month, as in 1, 15 and 2, 18; see note on the latter.

---

*

2/4: Zec 8, 9.
5: Ex 29, 45; Lv 26, 45.
6: Heb 12, 26.
7: Gn 49, 10;
Is 60, 5.9.11;

Mal 3, 1; Rv 21, 26.
9: Is 2, 2ff; Zec 6, 13.
11: Dt 17, 8-13; Zec 7, 3.
13: Nm 19, 11.13.22.
16: Is 5, 10.

I will shake the heavens and the earth;
22*   I will overthrow the thrones of kingdoms,
        destroy the power of the kingdoms of the
        nations.
    I will overthrow the chariots and their
        riders,
    and the riders with their horses
        shall go down by one another's sword.

23* †   On that day, says the Lord of hosts,
    I will take you, Zerubbabel,
        son of Shealtiel, my servant, says the
        Lord,
    And I will set you as a signet ring;
        for I have chosen you, says the Lord of
        hosts.

---

*

22: Ez 38, 21; Dn 2, 44;   23: Sg 8, 6; Sir 49, 11;
    Zec 14, 13; Lk 1, 52.   Is 42, 1; 44, 1f.

---

† 2, 23: This promise to Zerubbabel, reversing the punishment of his grandfather (Jer 22, 24), is a continuation of the messianic hope; cf Zec 6, 11f.

The Book of Zechariah

Introduction

Zechariah's initial prophecy is dated to 520 B. C., the same year as that in which Haggai received the prophetic call. The first eight chapters of the Book of Zechariah contain oracles which certainly belong to him while the last six (sometimes called "Deutero-Zechariah") represent the work of one or more unknown authors. In the prophecies proper to Zechariah eight symbolic visions are recorded, all meant to promote the work of rebuilding the temple and to encourage the returned exiles, especially their leaders, Joshua and Zerubbabel. In the final chapter of this first division Zechariah portrays the messianic future under the figure of a prosperous land to which the nations come in pilgrimage, eager to follow the God of Israel.

The second part of Zechariah is divided into two sections, each with its own introductory title. The first (9-11) consists of oracles whose historical background, date and authorship are extremely difficult to determine. With 9, 9 begins the messianic vision of the coming of the Prince of Peace. The verses describing the triumphant appearance of the humble king are taken up by the four Evangelists to describe the entry of Christ into Jerusalem on Palm Sunday. Chapter 12 is introduced by an oracle proclaiming the victory of God's people over the heathen. The prophecy closes by describing, in apocalyptic imagery, the final assault of the enemy on Jerusalem, after which the messianic age begins.

Necessity of Conversion

1 ¹*†IN THE SECOND YEAR OF DARIUS, in the eighth month, the word of the LORD came to the prophet Zechariah, son of Berechiah, son of Iddo: ²The LORD was indeed angry with your fathers. . . . ³and say to them: Thus says the LORD of hosts: Return to me, says the LORD of hosts, and I will return to you, says the LORD of hosts. ⁴*Be not like your fathers whom the former prophets warned: Thus says the LORD of hosts: Turn from your evil ways and from your wicked deeds. But they would not listen or pay attention to me, says the LORD. ⁵Your fathers, where are they? And the prophets, can they live forever? ⁶*But my words and my decrees, which I entrusted to my servants the prophets, did not these overtake your fathers? Then they repented and admitted: "The LORD of hosts has

treated us according to our ways and deeds, just as he had determined he would."

The Four Horsemen

⁷†In the second year of Darius, on the twenty-fourth day of Shebat, the eleventh month, the word of the LORD came to the prophet Zechariah, son of Berechiah, son of Iddo, in the following way: ⁸*†I had a vision during the night. There appeared the driver of a red horse, standing among myrtle trees in a shady place, and behind him were red, sorrel, and white horses. ⁹Then I asked, "What are these, my lord?"; and the angel who spoke with me answered me, "I will show you what these are." ¹⁰*The man who was standing among the myrtle trees spoke up and said, "These are they whom the LORD has sent to patrol the earth." ¹¹And they answered the angel of the LORD who was standing among the myrtle trees and said, "We have patrolled the earth; see, the whole earth is tranquil and at rest!"

¹²*†Then the angel of the LORD spoke out and said, "O LORD of hosts, how long will you be without mercy for Jerusalem and the cities of Judah that have felt your anger these seventy years?" ¹³*To the angel who spoke with me, the LORD replied with comforting words.

¹⁴*And the angel who spoke with me said to me, Proclaim: Thus says the LORD of hosts: I am deeply moved for the sake of Jerusalem and Zion, ¹⁵*†and I am exceedingly angry with the complacent nations; whereas I was but a little angry, they added to the harm. ¹⁶*†Therefore, says the LORD: I will turn to Jerusalem in mercy; my house shall be built in it, says the LORD of hosts, and a measuring line shall be stretched over Jerusalem. ¹⁷*Proclaim further: Thus says the LORD of hosts: My cities shall again overflow

---

† 1, 1: *The second year . . . eighth month:* October/November, 520 B. C.

1, 7: *The second year . . . eleventh month:* January/February, 519 B. C.

1, 8-11: *The driver of a red horse:* apparently distinct from *the man,* or *angel of the Lord . . . standing among the myrtle trees,* who spoke with the prophet. The four horsemen are sent by God to the four corners of the earth (2, 10), to see if the whole earth is at peace.

1, 12: *These seventy years:* see note on Jer 25, 1-14.

1, 15: *The complacent nations:* the neighbors of Judah, especially Edom, which enjoyed their present prosperity and security at Judah's expense.

1, 16: *Measuring line:* not for devastation, as in Is 34, 11, but for reconstruction.

---

* 1/1: Ezr 4, 24; 5, 1; 6, 14.
4: Jer 25, 5; 35, 15;
  Mal 3, 7.
6: Lam 2, 17;
  Lv 26, 14ff; Dt 28, 15.
8: Rv 6, 4.
10: 6, 7.

12: 7, 5; Jer 25, 11;
  Dn 9, 2.
13: Jer 29, 10.
14: 8, 2; Jl 2, 18.
15: Is 47, 6; Ob 10-14.
16: 8, 3; Ezr 6, 14.
17: Is 51, 3.

with prosperity; the LORD will again comfort Zion, and again choose Jerusalem.

Four Horns and Four Blacksmiths

2 [1]†I raised my eyes and looked: there were four horns. [2]Then I asked the angel who spoke with me what these were. He answered me, "These are the horns that scattered Judah and Israel and Jerusalem." [3]Then the LORD showed me four blacksmiths. And I asked, "What are these coming to do?" [4]And he said, "Here are the horns that scattered Judah, so that no man raised his head any more; but these have come to terrify them: to cast down the horns of the nations that raised their horns to scatter the land of Judah."

The New Jerusalem

[5]*Again I raised my eyes and looked: there was a man with a measuring line in his hand. [6]*"Where are you going?" I asked. "To measure Jerusalem," he answered; "to see how great is its width and how great its length." [7]Then the angel who spoke with me advanced, and another angel came out to meet him [8]*†and said to him, "Run, tell this to that young man: People will live in Jerusalem as though in open country, because of the multitude of men and beasts in her midst. [9]But I will be for her an encircling wall of fire, says the LORD, and I will be the glory in her midst."

[10]†Up, up! Flee from the land of the north, says the LORD; for I scatter you to the four winds of heaven, says the LORD. [11]Up, escape to Zion! you who dwell in daughter Babylon. [12]*For thus said the LORD of hosts (after he had already sent me) concerning the nations that have plundered you: Whoever touches you touches the apple of my eye. [13]See, I wave my hand over them; they become plunder for their slaves. Thus you shall know that the LORD of hosts has sent me.

[14]*Sing and rejoice, O daughter Zion! See, I am coming to dwell among you, says the LORD. [15]Many nations shall join themselves to the LORD on that day, and they shall be his people, and he will dwell among you, and you shall know that the LORD of hosts has sent me to you. [16]The LORD will possess Judah as his portion in the holy land, and he will again choose Jerusalem. [17]Silence, all mankind, in the presence of the LORD! for he stirs forth from his holy dwelling.

Joshua the High Priest

3 [1]*THEN he showed me Joshua the high priest standing before the angel of the LORD, while Satan stood at his right hand to accuse him. [2]*And the angel of the LORD said to Satan, "May the LORD rebuke you, Satan; may the LORD who has chosen Jerusalem

rebuke you! Is not this man a brand snatched from the fire?"

[3]†Now Joshua was standing before the angel, clad in filthy garments. [4]*He spoke and said to those who were standing before him, "Take off his filthy garments, and clothe him in festal garments." [5]He also said, "Put a clean miter on his head." And they put a clean miter on his head and clothed him with the garments. Then the angel of the LORD, standing, said, "See, I have taken away your guilt."

[6]The angel of the LORD then gave Joshua this assurance: [7]"Thus says the LORD of hosts: If you walk in my ways and heed my charge, you shall judge my house and keep my courts, and I will give you access among these standing here. [8]*†Listen, O Joshua, high priest! You and your associates who sit before you are men of good omen. Yes, I will bring my servant the Shoot. [9]*†Look at the stone that I have placed before Joshua, one stone with seven facets. I will engrave its inscription, says the LORD of hosts, and I will take away the guilt of the land in one day. [10]*On that day, says the LORD of hosts, you will invite one another under your vines and fig trees."

4 [4]THEN I said to the angel who spoke with me, "What are these things, my lord?" [5]And the angel who spoke with me replied, "Do you not know what these things are?" "No, my lord," I answered. [6]Then he said to me, "This is the LORD's message to Zerubbabel: Not by an army, nor by might, but by my spirit, says the LORD of hosts. [7]*†What are you, O great mountain? Before Zerubbabel you are but a plain. He shall bring out the capstone amid exclamations of 'Hail, Hail' to it."

[8]This word of the LORD then came to me: [9]*The hands of Zerubbabel have laid the foundations of this house, and his hands shall finish it; then you shall

---

† 2, 1-4: *Four horns:* symbolic of the hostile forces which, from the four corners of the earth, invaded and devastated *the land of Judah. Four blacksmiths:* the powers used by God to destroy these enemies of his people.

2, 8: *That young man:* the angel or *man with a measuring line* of v 5.

2, 10: *The land of the north:* Babylonia (v 11).

3, 3: *Filthy garments:* symbolic of mourning for the dead, or of national catastrophe, and implying acknowledgement of guilt (v 5).

3, 8: *Men of good omen:* the restoration of the priesthood is a sign of the coming of the messianic times. *My servant the Shoot:* identified, in the earliest form of 6, 11f as the prophet composed it, with Zerubbabel, direct descendant of King David and rebuilder of the temple; and, as such, a type of the Messiah; cf Jer 23, 5.

3, 9: *One stone with seven facets:* apparently the same as *the select stone* of 4, 10, which seems to be a precious gem. The *seven facets* are explained in 4, 10 as signifying the Lord's vigilance over the world. *I will engrave its inscription:* the same Hebrew verb for *engrave* is used in Ex 28, 9.11 in regard to the inscriptions on the twelve precious stones of the priestly breast-piece.

4, 7: *Great mountain:* figure of the obstacles confronting Zerubbabel in building the temple. *A plain:* figure of the ease with which he will overcome these obstacles.

* 2/5: Rv 11, 1.
  6: Dt 28, 64.
  8: Ez 36, 11.
  12: Dt 32, 10; Ps 17, 8.
  14: Ez 37, 26.
3/1: Hg 1, 1; 1 Chr 21, 1.
  2: Rom 8, 33; Jude 9.
  4: Lk 15, 22.
  8: Is 4, 2; 11, 1; Jer 23, 5; 33, 15.
  9: 4, 10.
  10: 1 Kgs 4, 25.
4/7: Ezr 3, 11ff; Ps 118, 22.
  9: Ezr 6, 14ff.

know that the Lord of hosts has sent me to you. **10***For even they who were scornful on that day of small beginnings shall rejoice to see the select stone in the hands of Zerubbabel. These seven facets are the eyes of the Lord that range over the whole earth.

The Lampstand

1Then the angel who spoke with me returned and awakened me, like a man awakened from his sleep. **2***"What do you see?" he asked me. "I see a lampstand all of gold, with a bowl at the top," I replied; "on it are seven lamps with their tubes, **3***and beside it are two olive trees, one on the right and the other on the left." **11**†I then asked him, "What are these two olive trees at each side of the lampstand?" **12**And again I asked, "What are the two olive tufts which freely pour out fresh oil through the two golden channels?" **13**"Do you not know what these are?" he said to me. "No, my lord," I answered him. **14**He said, "These are the two anointed who stand by the Lord of the whole earth."

The Flying Scroll

5 **1***†THEN I raised my eyes again and saw a scroll flying. **2**"What do you see?" he asked me. I answered, "I see a scroll flying; it is twenty cubits long and ten cubits wide." **3**Then he said to me: "This is the curse which is to go forth over the whole earth; in accordance with it shall every thief be swept away, and in accordance with it shall every perjurer be expelled from here. **4***I will send it forth, says the Lord of hosts, and it shall come into the house of the thief, or into the house of him who perjures himself with my name; it shall lodge within his house, consuming it, timber and stones."

The Flying Bushel

5†Then the angel who spoke with me came forward and said to me, "Raise your eyes and see what this is that comes forth." **6**"What is it?" I asked. And he answered, "This is a bushel container coming. This is their guilt in all the land." **7**Then a leaden cover was lifted, and there was a woman sitting inside the bushel. **8**"This is Wickedness," he said; and he thrust her inside the bushel, pushing the leaden cover into the opening. **9**Then I raised my eyes and saw two women coming forth with a wind ruffling their wings, for they had wings like the wings of a stork. As they lifted up the bushel into the air, **10**I said to the angel who spoke with me, "Where are they taking the bushel?" **11***He replied, "To build a temple for it in the land of Shinar; when the temple is ready, they will deposit it there in its place."

Four Chariots

6 **1**†AGAIN I raised my eyes and saw four chariots coming out from between two mountains; and the mountains were of bronze. **2***The first chariot had red horses, the second chariot black horses, **3**the third chariot white horses, and the fourth chariot spotted horses—all of them strong horses. **4**I asked the angel who spoke with me, "What are these, my lord?" **5***The angel said to me in reply, "These are the four winds of the heavens, which are coming forth after being reviewed by the Lord of all the earth." **6**The chariot with the black horses was turning toward the land of the north, the red and the white horses went after them, and the spotted ones went toward the land of the south. **7**As these strong horses emerged, eager to set about patrolling the earth, he said, "Go, patrol the earth!" Then, as they patrolled the earth, **8**he called out to me and said, "See, they that go forth to the land of the north will make my spirit rest in the land of the north."

The Coronation

9This word of the Lord then came to me: **10**Take from the returned captives Heldai, Tobijah, Jedaiah; and go the same day to the house of Josiah, son of Zephaniah (these had come from Babylon). **11**†Silver and gold you shall take, and make a crown; place it on the head of [Joshua, son of Jehozadak, the high priest] Zerubbabel. **12***And say to him: Thus says the Lord of hosts: Here is a man whose name is Shoot, and where he is he shall sprout, and he shall build the temple of the Lord. **13***Yes, he shall build the temple of the Lord, and taking up the royal insignia, he shall sit as ruler upon his throne. The priest shall be at his right hand, and between the two of them there shall

---

† 4, 1ff.11-14: *The two anointed:* literally, "the two sons of oil," Joshua, the anointed high priest, and Zerubbabel, the anointed prince. Just as the two olive trees in this imagery supply the sacred seven-branched lampstand (Ex 25, 31-40) with oil (v 12), so these two men, in ministering to the community, *stand by* (serve) *the Lord.*

5, 1-4: The enormous scroll, thirty feet by fifteen (the dimensions in length and breadth of the portico of Solomon's temple, 1 Kgs 6, 3), contains a list of maledictions on sinners, similar to that in Dt 27, 15-26. The *thief* and the *perjurer* represent all sinners, who are expelled from the holy community.

5, 5-11: The *woman* sealed in the *bushel container* is a figure of the general corruption of the people of Judah. She is removed from the Holy Land and transported to *Shinar:* that is, Babylonia, where a dwelling is being prepared for her; this is a symbol of the reign of *Wickedness* in pagan lands, contrasted with the reign of holiness in the Lord's dwelling on Mount Zion.

6, 1-8: The *four chariots* represent the angelic hosts sent by the Lord to the four ends of the earth. The chariot with the *black horses* brings the *spirit,* i. e., anger of the Lord against the land of the north, Babylonia.

6, 11: *Make a crown; place it on the head of [Joshua, son of Jehozadak, the high priest] Zerubbabel:* according to the current Hebrew text, Joshua the high priest is to be crowned. However, since the crown is a sign of royalty, the original text must have had the name of Zerubbabel here, not that of Joshua. In 3, 8 Joshua is a different man from the one called *the Shoot,* and in v 12 it is upon the *Shoot* that the crown is to be placed.

✱
4/2: Rv 1, 12.
  3: Rv 11, 4.
 10: 3, 9.
5/1: Ez 2, 9.
  4: Lv 19, 12.
 11: Gn 11, 2ff.

6/2: 1, 8; Rv 6, 4.
  5: Ps 104, 4.
 12: 3, 8; Eph 2, 20;
     Heb 3, 3.
 13: Ps 110, 4;
     Heb 3, 1.

be friendly understanding. [14]The crown itself shall be a memorial offering in the temple of the LORD in favor of Heldai, Tobijah, Jedaiah, and the son of Zephaniah. [15]*And they who are from afar shall come and build the temple of the LORD, and you shall know that the LORD of hosts has sent me to you. And if you heed carefully the voice of the LORD your God. . . .

True Fasting

7 [1]†IN the fourth year of Darius the king [the word of the LORD came to Zechariah], on the fourth day of Chislev, the ninth month, [2]Bethelsarezer sent Regemmelech and his men to implore in favor of the LORD [3]*and to ask the priests of the house of the LORD of hosts, and the prophets, "Must I mourn and abstain in the fifth month as I have been doing these many years?" [4]Thereupon this word of the LORD of hosts came to me: [5]*Say to all the people of the land and to the priests: When you fasted and mourned in the fifth and in the seventh month these seventy years, was it really for me that you fasted? [6]And when you were eating and drinking, was it not for yourselves that you ate, and for yourselves that you drank? [7]*Were not these the words which the LORD spoke through the former prophets, when Jerusalem and the surrounding cities were inhabited and at peace, when the Negeb and the foothills were inhabited? [8][This word of the LORD came to Zechariah: [9]*Thus says the LORD of hosts:] Render true judgment, and show kindness and compassion toward each other. [10]*Do not oppress the widow or the orphan, the ailen or the poor; do not plot evil against one another in your hearts. [11]*But they refused to listen; they stubbornly turned their backs and stopped their ears so as not to hear. [12]*And they made their hearts diamond-hard so as not to hear the teaching and the message that the LORD of hosts had sent by his spirit through the former prophets. [13]*Then the LORD of hosts in his great anger said that, as they had not listened when he called, so he would not listen when they called, [14]*but would scatter them with a whirlwind among all the nations that they did not know. Thus the land was left desolate after them with no one traveling to and fro; they made the pleasant land into a desert.

In the Days of the Messiah

8 [1]THIS word of the LORD of hosts came: [2]*Thus says the LORD of hosts:

I am intensely jealous for Zion,
    stirred to jealous wrath for her.

[3]*   Thus says the LORD:
    I will return to Zion,
        and I will dwell within Jerusalem;
    Jerusalem shall be called the faithful city,
        and the mountain of the LORD of hosts,
        the holy mountain.

[4]Thus says the LORD of hosts: Old men and old women, each with staff in hand because of old age, shall again sit in the streets of Jerusalem. [5]The city shall be filled with boys and girls playing in her streets. [6]Thus says the LORD of hosts: Even if this should seem impossible in the eyes of the remnant of this people, shall it in those days be impossible in my eyes also, says the LORD of hosts? [7]*Thus says the LORD of hosts: Lo, I will rescue my people from the land of the rising sun, and from the land of the setting sun. [8]*I will bring them back to dwell within Jerusalem. They shall be my people, and I will be their God, with faithfulness and justice.

[9]*Thus says the LORD of hosts: Let your hands be strong, you who in these days hear these words spoken by the prophets on the day when the foundation of the house of the LORD of hosts was laid for the building of the temple. [10]For before those days there were no wages for men, or hire for beasts; those who came and went had no security from the enemy, for I set every man against his neighbor. [11]But now I will not deal with the remnant of this people as in former days, says the LORD of hosts. [12]for it is the seed-time of peace: the vine shall yield its fruit, the land shall bear its crops, and the heavens shall give their dew; all these things I will have the remnant of the people possess. [13]*Just as you were a curse among the nations, O house of Judah and house of Israel, so will I save you that you may be a blessing; do not fear, but let your hands be strong.

[14]*Thus says the LORD of hosts: As I determined to harm you when your fathers provoked me to wrath, says the LORD of hosts, and I did not relent, [15]so again in these days I have determined to favor Jerusalem and the house of Judah; do not fear! [16]*These then are the things you should do: Speak the truth to one another; let there be honesty and peace in the judgments at your gates, [17]*and let none of you plot evil against another in his heart, nor love a false oath. For all these things I hate, says the LORD.

[18]This word of the LORD of hosts came to me: [19]†Thus says the LORD of hosts: The fast days of the fourth, the fifth, the seventh, and the tenth months shall become occasions of joy and gladness, cheerful

---

❋
15: Eph 2, 19f.
7/3: 8, 19.
  5: Is 58, 5; Rom 14, 6.
  7: Jer 17, 26.
  9: Is 58, 6.
 10: Ex 22, 21-24;
     Dt 24, 17; Is 1, 17;
     Jer 5, 28.
 11: Neh 9, 29; Hos 4, 16.
 12: Ez 11, 19; 36, 26;
     Neh 9, 29.
 13: Is 1, 15; Mi 3, 4.

14: Dt 4, 27.
8/2: Na 1, 2.
  3: Is 2, 2; Jer 31, 23.
  7: Is 11, 11; Jer 30, 18.
  8: Jer 4, 2.
  9: Ezr 5, 1; Hg 2, 18.
 13: Is 19, 24; Jer 42, 18;
     Hg 2, 19; Zep 3, 20.
 14: Jer 31, 28.
 16: 7, 9.
 17: 7, 10.

---

† 7, 1: *The fourth year of Darius . . . the fourth day of Chislev, the ninth month:* November, 518 B. C.

8, 19: The fast day of *the fourth* month recalled the fall of Jerusalem in June, 587 B. C. (2 Kgs 25, 3f); that of *the fifth* month, the burning of the temple by Nebuzaradan in July of the same year (2 Kgs 25, 8f); that of *the seventh* month, the murder of Gedaliah in September of the same year (Jer 41, 1f); that of *the tenth* month, the beginning of the final siege of Jerusalem in January, 588 B. C. (2 Kgs 25, 1).

festivals for the house of Judah; only love faithfulness and peace. **20**Thus says the Lord of hosts: There shall yet come peoples, the inhabitants of many cities; **21**＊and the inhabitants of one city shall approach those of another, and say, "Come! let us go to implore the favor of the Lord"; and, "I too will go to seek the Lord." **22**＊Many peoples and strong nations shall come to seek the Lord of hosts in Jerusalem and to implore the favor of the Lord. **23**＊Thus says the Lord of hosts: In those days ten men of every nationality, speaking different tongues, shall take hold, yes, take hold of every Jew by the edge of his garment and say, "Let us go with you, for we have heard that God is with you."

Invasion by the Lord

9 **1**†   An oracle:
The word of the Lord is upon the land of Hadrach,
    and Damascus is its resting place,
For the cities of Aram are the Lord's,
    as are all the tribes of Israel,
2＊   Hamath also, on its border,
    Tyre too, and Sidon, however wise they
    be.
3   Tyre built herself a stronghold,
    and heaped up silver like dust,
    and gold like the mire of the streets.
4＊   Lo, the Lord will strip her of her
    possessions,
    and smite her power on the sea,
    and she shall be devoured by fire.
5   Ashkelon shall see it and be afraid;
    Gaza also: she shall be in great anguish;
    Ekron, too, for her hope shall come to
    nought.
The king shall disappear from Gaza,
    and Ashkelon shall not be inhabited,
6＊†   and the baseborn shall occupy Ashdod.
I will destroy the pride of the Philistine
7†   and take from his mouth his bloody
    meat,
    and his abominations from between his
    teeth:
He also shall become a remnant for our
    God,
    and shall be like a family in Judah,
    and Ekron shall be like the Jebusites.
8†   I will encamp by my house as a guard
    that none may pass to and fro;
No oppressor shall pass over them again,
    for now I have regard for their affliction.

Restoration under the Messiah

9＊†   Rejoice heartily, O daughter Zion,
    shout for joy, O daughter Jerusalem!

See, your king shall come to you;
    a just savior is he,
Meek, and riding on an ass,
    on a colt, the foal of an ass.
10＊†   He shall banish the chariot from Ephraim,
    and the horse from Jerusalem;
The warrior's bow shall be banished,
    and he shall proclaim peace to the
    nations.
His dominion shall be from sea to sea,
    and from the River to the ends of the
    earth.
11＊†   As for you, for the blood of your covenant
    with me,
    I will bring forth your prisoners from
    the dungeon.
12＊†   In the return to the fortress
    of the waiting prisoners,
This very day, I will return you
    double for your exile.
13   For I will bend Judah as my bow,
    I will arm myself with Ephraim;
I will arouse your sons, O Zion,
    [against your sons, O Yavan,]
    and I will use you as a warrior's sword.

14   The Lord shall appear over them,
    and his arrow shall shoot forth as
    lightning;
The Lord God shall sound the trumpet,
    and come in a storm from the south.
15   The Lord of hosts shall be a shield over
    them,
    they shall overcome sling stones
    and trample them underfoot;
They shall drink blood like wine,
    till they are filled with it like libation
    bowls,
    like the corners of the altar.

---

† 9, 1-8: Divine judgment is about to fall on the surrounding hostile peoples: *Aram* (Syria), including the cities of *Hadrach* and *Damascus;* Phoenicia, with its cities of *Tyre* and *Sidon;* Philistia, with its cities of *Ashkelon, Gaza, Ekron,* and *Ashdod.*
9, 6: *The baseborn:* people of mixed ancestry.
9, 7: *Remnant:* see note on Hg 1, 12. *The Jebusites:* the pre-Israelite inhabitants of Jerusalem, conquered by David and incorporated in Israel.
9, 8: *My house:* the Holy Land; cf Hos 8, 1; 9, 15; Jer 12, 7.
9, 9: The Messiah will come, not as a conquering warrior, but in lowliness and peace. Not like the last kings of Judah, who rode in chariots and on horses (Jer 17, 25; 22, 4), but like the princes of old (Gn 49, 11; Jgs 5, 10; 10, 4), the Messiah will ride on an ass. The Evangelists see a literal fulfillment of this prophecy in the Savior's triumphant entry into Jerusalem (Mt 21, 4f; Jn 12, 14f).
9, 10: *The River:* the Euphrates; see note on Ps 72, 8.
9, 11: *The blood of your covenant with me:* the covenant between the Lord and Israel sealed with sacrificial blood (Ex 24, 8).
9, 12: *The waiting prisoners:* the exiles awaiting the return to their country, where they will receive a double compensation for the double punishment they had suffered; cf Is 40, 2; 61, 7.

＊
   21: Is 2, 3.
   22: Is 60, 3.
   23: Is 66, 23.
9/2: Jer 49, 23.
   4: Is 23, 1-18;
      Ez 26, 1-28, 26.

   6: Am 1, 8.
   9: Is 62, 11; Jer 23, 5;
     Mt 21, 5; Jn 12, 15.
  10: Hos 1, 7.
  11: Is 42, 7; Ex 24, 8.
  12: Is 61, 7.

16 And the Lord, their God, shall save them
　　on that day,
　　his people, like a flock.
　For they are the jewels in a crown
　　raised aloft over his land.
17 For what wealth is theirs, and what
　　beauty!
　grain that makes the youths flourish,
　　and new wine, the maidens!

The New Order of Things

10
1 Ask of the Lord rain in the spring season!
　It is the Lord who makes the storm
　　clouds.
　And sends men the pouring rain;
　　for everyone, grassy fields.
2 For the teraphim speak nonsense,
　　the diviners have false visions:
　Deceitful dreams they tell,
　　empty comfort they offer.
　This is why they wander like sheep,
　　wretched: they have no shepherd.
3 My wrath is kindled against the
　　shepherds,
　and I will punish the leaders;
　For the Lord of hosts will visit his flock,
　　the house of Judah,
　and make them his stately war horse.
4 From him shall come leader and chief,
　　from him warrior's bow and every
　　officer.
5 They shall all be warriors,
　　trampling the mire of the streets in
　　battle;
　They shall wage war because the Lord
　　is with them,
　　and shall put the horsemen to rout.
6 I will strengthen the house of Judah,
　　the house of Joseph I will save;
　I will bring them back, because I have
　　mercy on them,
　　they shall be as though I had never
　　cast them off,
　　for I am the Lord, their God, and I
　　will hear them.
7 Then Ephraim shall be valiant men,
　　and their hearts shall be cheered as by
　　wine.
　Their children shall see it and be glad,
　　their hearts shall rejoice in the Lord.
8 I will whistle for them to come together,
　　and when I redeem them
　　they will be as numerous as before.

9 I sowed them among the nations,
　　yet in distant lands they remember
　　me;
　they shall rear their children and
　　return.
10 I will bring them back from the land of
　　Egypt,
　　and gather them from Assyria.
　I will bring them into Gilead and into
　　Lebanon,
　　but these shall not suffice them;
11 I will cross over to Egypt
　　and smite the waves of the sea
　　and all the depths of the Nile shall be
　　dried up.
　The pride of Assyria shall be cast down,
　　and the scepter of Egypt taken away.
12 I will strengthen them in the Lord,
　　and they shall walk in his name, says
　　the Lord.

11
1 Open your doors, O Lebanon,
　　that the fire may devour your cedars!
2 Wail, you cypress trees,
　　for the cedars are fallen,
　　the mighty have been despoiled.
　Wail, you oaks of Bashan,
　　for the impenetrable forest is cut
　　down!
3 Hark! the wailing of the shepherds,
　　their glory has been ruined.
　Hark! the roaring of the young lions,
　　the jungle of the Jordan is laid waste.

Allegory of the Shepherds

4 Thus said the Lord, my God: Shepherd the flock to be slaughtered. 5 For they who buy them slay them with impunity; while those who sell them say, "Blessed be the Lord, I have become rich!" Even their own shepherds do not feel for them. 6 (Nor shall I spare the inhabitants of the earth any more, says the Lord. Yes, I will deliver each of them into the power of his neighbor, or into the power of his king; they shall crush the earth, and I will not deliver it out of their power.)
7 So I became the shepherd of the flock to be

---

† 10, 2: *Teraphim:* household idols, used for divination; cf Gn 31, 19.34f; Jgs 17, 5; 18, 17f.20; Ez 21, 26; Hos 3, 4.

11, 4-17: In this allegory the prophet becomes the good shepherd of God's flock, which is being slaughtered; he is the defender of the people exploited by bad rulers. *The three shepherds,* rulers in general, are to destroy one another in a short time (*a single month*). The service of the good shepherd is contemptuously valued at *thirty pieces of silver,* the legal indemnity (Ex 21, 32) for a gored slave. The prophet is thus a type of Christ, whose mission of salvation to his people was appraised by the Sanhedrists, the false shepherds, at the same base price (Mt 26, 14ff). In the case of the prophet as well as of Christ (Mt 27, 5), the money is thrown into the temple treasury, i. e., paid to God, showing thereby how shamefully his divine love and care are requited.

16: Is 62, 3.
10/1: Dt 11, 14; Jer 14, 22.
2: Jer 10, 8; Ez 34, 5.
8: Ez 36, 37.
10: Is 11, 11; 49, 20; Hos 11, 11.
11: Is 11, 15; Ez 30, 13.
12: Mi 4, 5.
11/5: Jer 50, 7.
7: Hos 5, 6.

slaughtered for the sheep merchants. I took two staffs, one of which I called "Favor," and the other, "Bonds," and I fed the flock. [8]In a single month I did away with the three shepherds. I wearied of them, and they behaved badly toward me. [9]*"I will not feed you," I said. "What is to die, let it die; what is to perish, let it perish, and let those that are left devour one another's flesh."

[10]Then I took my staff "Favor" and snapped it asunder, breaking off the covenant which I had made with all peoples; [11]that day it was broken off. The sheep merchants who were watching me understood that this was the word of the Lord. [12]*I said to them, "If it seems good to you, give me my wages; but if not, let it go." And they counted out my wages, thirty pieces of silver. [13]*But the Lord said to me, "Throw it in the treasury, the handsome price at which they valued me." So I took the thirty pieces of silver and threw them into the treasury in the house of the Lord.

[14]Then I snapped asunder my other staff, "Bonds," breaking off the brotherhood between Judah and Israel. [15]The Lord said to me: This time take the gear of a foolish shepherd. [16]*For I will raise up a shepherd in the land who will take no note of those that perish, nor seek the strays, nor heal the injured, nor feed what survives—he will eat the flesh of the fat ones and tear off their hoofs!

> [17]* Woe to my foolish shepherd
> who forsakes the flock!
> May the sword fall upon his arm
> and upon his right eye;
> Let his arm wither away entirely,
> and his right eye be blind forever!

Jerusalem God's Instrument

12 [1]*†AN oracle: the word of the Lord concerning Israel. Thus says the Lord, who spreads out the heavens, lays the foundations of the earth, and forms the spirit of man within him: [2]*See, I will make Jerusalem a bowl to stupefy all peoples round about. [Judah will be besieged, even Jerusalem.] [3]*On that day I will make Jerusalem a weighty stone for all peoples. All who attempt to lift it shall injure themselves badly, and all the nations of the earth shall be gathered against her. [4]On that day, says the Lord, I will strike every horse with fright, and its rider with madness. I will strike blind all the horses of the peoples, but upon the house of Judah I will open my eyes, [5]and the princes of Judah shall say to themselves, "The inhabitants of Jerusalem have their strength in the Lord of hosts, their God." [6]*On that day I will make the princes of Judah like a brazier of fire in the wood-

land, and like a burning torch among sheaves, and they shall devour right and left all the surrounding peoples; but Jerusalem shall still abide on its own site. [7]The Lord shall save the tents of Judah first, that the glory of the house of David and the glory of the inhabitants of Jerusalem may not be exalted over Judah. [8]*On that day, the Lord will shield the inhabitants of Jerusalem, and the weakling among them shall be like David on that day, and the house of David godlike, like an angel of the Lord before them. [9]On that day I will seek the destruction of all nations that come against Jerusalem.

Messianic Jerusalem

[10]*†I will pour out on the house of David and on the inhabitants of Jerusalem a spirit of grace and petition; and they shall look on him whom they have thrust through, and they shall mourn for him as one mourns for an only son, and they shall grieve over him as one grieves over a first-born.

[11]*†On that day the mourning in Jerusalem shall be as great as the mourning of Hadadrimmon in the plain of Megiddo. [12]And the land shall mourn, each family apart: the family of the house of David, and their wives; the family of the house of Nathan, and their wives; [13]the family of the house of Levi, and their wives; the family of Shimei, and their wives; [14]and all the rest of the families, each family apart, and the wives apart.

The End of Falsehood

13 [1]*†ON that day there shall be open to the house of David and to the inhabitants of Jerusalem, a fountain to purify from sin and uncleanness. [2]*On that day, says the Lord of hosts, I will destroy the names of the idols from the land, so that they shall be mentioned no more; I will also take away the prophets and the spirit of uncleanness from the land. [3]*If a man still prophesies, his parents, father and

---

† 12, 1-9: Under the image of the deliverance of Judah and Jerusalem from invading enemies, the prophet foretells the ultimate victory of God's people in the messianic age.

12, 10: The divine blessings (*a spirit of grace and petition*) will be poured out on God's people through the intervention of an unnamed sufferer (*him whom they have thrust through*), similar to the Servant of the Lord in Is 52, 13—53, 12. In Jn 19, 37 the Evangelist sees in this passage a prophecy fulfilled in the piercing of Christ's side.

12, 11: The mourning for the pierced victim in Jerusalem is compared to a lamentation *in the plain of Megiddo* apparently over a certain personage called *Hadadrimmon*. The reference is no longer clear. Both *Hadad* and *Rimmon* were names of the Semitic storm god, often identified with the god Baal. Some see here a reference to the annual mourning by the pagans over the death of the fertility god. According to others, *Hadadrimmon* is the name of a place near Megiddo, and the reference would then be to the mourning over the death of King Josiah, who was killed in battle there; cf 2 Chr 35, 22-25.

13, 1: *A fountain to purify from sin:* in contrast to the lustral water used in ritual purification; cf Nm 19, 9.13.20; 31, 23. The Lord himself is the *fountain* of living water (Jer 2, 13); cf Is 12, 2ff.

❋
   9: Jer 15, 2.
  12: Ex 21, 32; Mt 26, 15.
  13: Mt 27, 9f.
  16: Ez 34, 2ff.
  17: Jn 10, 12.
12/1: Is 42, 5.
  2: Is 51, 17; Jer 51, 7.
  3: Mt 21, 44.
  6: Ob 18.

  8: Ex 32, 34.
 10: Jer 6, 26; Jn 19, 34; Rv 1, 7.
 11: 2 Chr 35, 22-25.
13/1: Heb 9, 14; 1 Pt 1, 18f; Rv 1, 5.
  2: Mi 5, 12; 2 Pt 2, 1.
  3: Dt 18, 20; Mi 3, 5ff.

mother, shall say to him, "You shall not live, because you have spoken a lie in the name of the LORD." When he prophesies, his parents, father and mother, shall thrust him through.

4†On that day, every prophet shall be ashamed to prophesy his vision, neither shall he assume the hairy mantle to mislead, **5***but he shall say, "I am no prophet, I am a tiller of the soil, for I have owned land since my youth." **6**†And if anyone asks him, "What are these wounds on your chest?" he shall answer, "With these I was wounded in the house of my dear ones."

The Song of the Sword

7*† Awake, O sword, against my shepherd,
       against the man who is my associate,
       says the LORD of hosts.
    Strike the shepherd
       that the sheep may be dispersed,
       and I will turn my hand against the
          little ones.
8 In all the land, says the LORD,
       two thirds of them shall be cut off and
          perish,
       and one third shall be left.
9* I will bring the one third through fire,
       and I will refine them as silver is
          refined,
       and I will test them as gold is tested.
    They shall call upon my name,
       and I will hear them.
    I will say, "They are my people,"
       and they shall say, "The LORD is my
          God."

The Fight for Jerusalem

14 **1**†LO, a day shall come for the LORD when the spoils shall be divided in your midst. **2**And I will gather all the nations against Jerusalem for battle: the city shall be taken, houses plundered, women ravished; half of the city shall go into exile, but the rest of the people shall not be removed from the city. **3**Then the LORD shall go forth and fight against those nations, fighting as on a day of battle. **4**That day his feet shall rest upon the Mount of Olives, which is opposite Jerusalem to the east. The Mount of Olives shall be cleft in two from east to west by a very deep valley, and half of the mountain shall move to the north and half of it to the south. **5**And the valley of the LORD's mountain shall be filled up when the valley of those two mountains reaches its edge; it shall be filled up as it was filled up by the earthquake in the days of King Uzziah of Judah. Then the LORD, my God, shall come, and all his holy ones with him.

6On that day there shall no longer be cold or frost. **7***There shall be one continuous day, known to the LORD, not day and night, for in the evening time there shall be light.

8*On that day, living waters shall flow from Jerusalem, half to the eastern sea, and half to the western sea, and it shall be so in summer and in winter. **9***The LORD shall become king over the whole earth; on that day the LORD shall be the only one, and his name the only one.

10*And from Geba to Rimmon in the Negeb, all the land shall turn into a plain; but Jerusalem shall remain exalted in its place. From the Gate of Benjamin to the place of the First Gate, to the Corner Gate; and from the Tower of Hananel to the king's wine presses, **11***they shall occupy her. Never again shall she be doomed; Jerusalem shall abide in security.

12And this shall be the plague with which the LORD shall strike all the nations that have fought against Jerusalem: their flesh shall rot while they stand upon their feet, and their eyes shall rot in their sockets, and their tongues shall rot in their mouths.

13On that day there shall be among them a great tumult from the LORD: every man shall seize the hand of his neighbor, and the hand of each shall be raised against that of his neighbor. **14**Judah also shall fight against Jerusalem. The riches of all the surrounding nations shall be gathered together, gold, silver, and garments, in great abundance.

15Similar to this plague shall be the plague upon the horses, mules, camels, asses, and upon all the beasts that are in those camps.

16*All who are left of all the nations that came against Jerusalem shall come up year after year to worship the King, the LORD of hosts, and to celebrate the feast of Booths. **17**If any of the families of the earth does not come up to Jerusalem to worship the King, the LORD of hosts, no rain shall fall upon them. **18**And if the family of Egypt does not come up, or enter, upon them shall fall the plague which the LORD will inflict upon all the nations that do not come up to celebrate the feast of Booths. **19**This shall be the punishment of

---

† 13, 4: *Hairy mantle:* worn by prophets as a mark of their calling; cf 2 Kgs 1, 8; Mt 3, 4.

13, 6: *Wounds on your chest:* literally, "wounds between your hands." The false prophets, like the prophet of Baal (1 Kgs 18, 28), apparently inflicted wounds on themselves; to defend himself against the accusation of being a false prophet, a man will deny having inflicted wounds on himself and say instead that he received them at home, *"in the house of my dear ones."* In the liturgy this text is applied to Christ in an accommodated sense.

13, 7: When the shepherd is killed, the sheep are scattered. In Mt 26, 31 the Evangelist quotes from this verse, in somewhat different form, the words, *I will smite the shepherd, and the sheep of the flock will be scattered,* as said by Christ shortly before his arrest in the Garden of Olives and the flight of the Apostles.

14, 1-21: An apocalyptic description of the day of the Lord, in which Jerusalem, the figure of God's elect, after much suffering (siege: vv 1ff; riot: v 13; plague: vv 12.15), is rescued by the Lord (vv 4f) and given great blessings (vv 6-11.14.16-21).

5: Am 7, 14.
7: Mt 26, 31.
9: Jer 30, 22;
   Ps 66, 10.
14/7: Rv 21, 23.
8: 13, 1; Ez 47, 1-8;
   Jl 3, 18.
9: Dt 6, 4; Eph 4, 5f;
   Rv 11, 15.
10: 12, 6; Neh 3, 6; 12, 38.
11: Jer 31, 40; Rv 22, 3.
16: Lv 23, 34.43;
    Neh 8, 14; Is 60, 6.9.

Egypt, and the punishment of all the nations that do not come up to celebrate the feast of Booths.

20On that day there shall be upon the bells of the horses, "Holy to the Lord." The pots in the house of the Lord shall be as the libation bowls before the altar. **21***And every pot in Jerusalem and in Judah shall be holy to the Lord of hosts; and all who come to sacrifice shall take them and cook in them. On that day there shall no longer be any merchant in the house of the Lord of hosts.

---

*

21: Mt 21, 12; Jn 2, 13-16.

the Lord shall be as the libation bowls before the
altar. And every pot... 'Jerusalem and in Judah
...shall be holy to the Lord of hosts; and all who come to
...sacrifice...shall...them. On that day
...more...in the house of

Egypt and the land have in all the nations that do
not come up to celebrate... Feast of Booths.
...On that day there shall be upon the bells of the
horses, "Holy to the Lord," and the pots in the house of

The Book of Malachi

Introduction

This work was composed by an anonymous writer shortly
before Nehemiah's arrival in Jerusalem (445 B. C.).
Because of the sharp reproaches he was leveling against
the priests and rulers of the people, the author probably
wished to conceal his identity. To do this he made a
proper name out of the Hebrew expression for "My
Messenger" (Malachi), which occurs in 1, 1 and 3, 1.
The historical value of the prophecy is considerable in
that it gives us a picture of life in the Jewish community
returned from Babylon, between the period of Haggai
and the reform measures of Ezra and Nehemiah. It is
likely that the author's trenchant criticism of abuses and
religious indifference in the community prepared the way
for these necessary reforms.

The chosen people had made a sorry return for divine
love. The priests, who should have been leaders, had
dishonored God by their blemished sacrifices. In his first
chapter, the writer foresees the time when all nations will
offer a pure oblation (1, 11)—a prophecy whose fulfillment
the church sees in the Sacrifice of the Mass. The author
then turns from priests to people, denouncing their
marriages with pagans and their callous repudiation of
Israelite wives. Imbued with the rationalist and critical
spirit of the times, many had wearied God with the
question, "Where is the God of justice?" To this question
the prophet replies that the day of the Lord is coming.
But first the forerunner must come, who will prepare the
soil for repentance and true worship. The gospel writers
point to John the Baptizer as the forerunner ushering in
the messianic age, the true day of the Lord. When the
ground is prepared God will appear, measuring out
rewards and punishments and purifying the nation in
the furnace of judgment. He will create a new order in
which the ultimate triumph of good is inevitable.

1 ¹AN ORACLE. THE WORD OF THE LORD to Israel
through Malachi.

Israel Preferred to Edom

2* I have loved you, says the LORD;
    but you say, "How have you loved us?"
3*† Was not Esau Jacob's brother? says the
    LORD:
    yet I loved Jacob, but hated Esau;
    I made his mountains a waste,
      his heritage a desert for jackals.

4* If Edom says, "We have been crushed
    but we will rebuild the ruins,"
Thus says the LORD of hosts:
    They indeed may build, but I will tear
      down,
And they shall be called the land of guilt,
    the people with whom the LORD is angry
      forever.
5* Your own eyes shall see it, and you will say,
    "Great is the LORD, even beyond the land
      of Israel."

Sins of the Priests and Levites

6 A son honors his father,
    and a servant fears his master;
If then I am a father,
    where is the honor due to me?
And if I am a master,
    where is the reverence due to me?—
So says the LORD of hosts to you, O priests,
    who despise his name.
But you ask, "How have we despised your
      name?"
7   By offering polluted food on my altar!
Then you ask, "How have we polluted it?"
    By saying the table of the LORD may be
      slighted!
8*† When you offer a blind animal for sacrifice,
    is this not evil?
When you offer the lame or the sick,
    is it not evil?
Present it to your governor; see if he will
      accept it,
    or welcome you, says the LORD of hosts.
9 So now if you implore God for mercy on us,
    when you have done the like
Will he welcome any of you?
    says the LORD of hosts.

---

† 1, 3ff. The thought passes from the person *Esau* to his descendants, *Edom,* and from the person *Jacob* to his descendants,
Israel. Loved: preferred; *hated:* rejected; cf Gn 25, 21ff. St.
Paul uses this passage as an example of God's freedom of choice
in calling the Gentiles to the faith (Rom 9, 13).

1, 8: The offering in sacrifice of a *lame, sick* or *blind animal*
was forbidden in the law (Lv 22, 17-25; Dt 17, 1).

* 1/2: Dt 7, 6ff; Ez 16;
    Am 1, 11.
  3: Gn 25, 23; Rom 9, 13.
  4: Is 34, 5f; 63, 1-6;
    Jer 49, 7-22; Ob 21.
  5: Is 60.
  8: Lv 22, 19-25;
    Dt 15, 21.

10† Oh, that one among you would shut the
temple gates
    to keep you from kindling fire on my
altar in vain!
I have no pleasure in you, says the LORD of
hosts;
    neither will I accept any sacrifice from
your hands,

11* For from the rising of the sun, even to its
setting,
    my name is great among the nations;
And everywhere they bring sacrifice to my
name,
    and a pure offering;
For great is my name among the nations,
    says the LORD of hosts.

12 But you behave profanely toward me by
thinking
    the LORD's table and its offering may be
polluted,
    and its food slighted.

13 You also say, "What a burden!"
    and you scorn it, says the LORD of hosts;
You bring in what you seize, or the lame,
or the sick;
    yes, you bring it as a sacrifice.
Shall I accept it from your hands?
    says the LORD.

14 Cursed is the deceiver, who has in his flock
a male,
    but under his vow sacrifices to the LORD
a gelding;
For a great King am I, says the LORD of
hosts,
    and my name will be feared among the
nations.

2 1 And now, O priests, this commandment is
for you:
    If you do not listen,

2* And if you do not lay it to heart,
    to give glory to my name, says the LORD
of hosts,
I will send a curse upon you
    and of your blessing I will make a curse.
Yes, I have already cursed it,
    because you do not lay it to heart.

3† Lo, I will deprive you of the shoulder
    and I will strew dung in your faces,
The dung of your feasts,
    and you will be carried off with it.

4* Then you will know that I sent you this
commandment
    because I have a covenant with Levi,
says the LORD of hosts.

5* My covenant with him was one of life and
peace;
    fear I put in him, and he feared me,
    and stood in awe of my name.

6* True doctrine was in his mouth,
    and no dishonesty was found upon his
lips;
He walked with me in integrity and
uprightness,
    and turned many away from evil.

7* For the lips of the priest are to keep
knowledge,
    and instruction is to be sought from his
mouth,
    because he is the messenger of the LORD
of hosts.

8 But you have turned aside from the way,
    and have caused many to falter by your
instruction;
You have made void the covenant of Levi,
    says the LORD of hosts.

9 I, therefore, have made you contemptible
    and base before all the people,
Since you do not keep my ways,
    but show partiality in your decisions.

Sins of the People

10*† Have we not all the one Father?
    Has not the one God created us?
Why then do we break faith with each
other,
    violating the covenant of our fathers?

11* Judah has broken faith; an abominable
thing
    has been done in Israel and in Jerusalem.
Judah has profaned the temple which the
LORD loves,
    and has married an idolatrous woman.

---

† 1, 10f: The imperfect sacrifices offered without sincerity by
the people of Judah are displeasing to the Lord. He will rather
be pleased with the offerings of the Gentile nations throughout
the world (*from the rising of the sun, even to its setting*), which
anticipate the *pure offering* to be sacrificed in messianic times,
the universal Sacrifice of the Mass, as we are told by the Council of Trent.

2, 3: *I will deprive you of the shoulder:* this part of a sacrificial animal, allotted by the law (Dt 18, 3) to the priests, will
be withheld from them.

2, 10-16: Intermarriage of Israelites with foreigners was forbidden according to Dt 7, 1-4. After the exile this law was
strictly enforced (Ezr 9-10). Foreign marriages are here portrayed as a violation of the covenant (v 10), which made the
sacrifices offered by the offenders unacceptable to God (v 13).
They were all the more reprehensible when accompanied by
the divorce of Israelite wives (vv 14ff). This gradual return to
the primitive ideal of the indissolubility of marriage was fully
realized in New Testament times through the teaching of
Christ; cf Mt 19, 3-12.

❋
   11: Ps 113, 3; Is 59, 19.
   2/2: Lv 26, 14-45;
      Dt 28, 15-68.
    4: Nm 25, 12f.
    5: Nm 25, 12; Ez 37, 26ff.
    6: Dt 33, 8-11.

    7: Lv 10, 10f; Dt 17, 9f;
      Jer 18, 18; Hg 2, 12.
   10: Mt 23, 9; Jb 31, 15;
      Eph 4, 6.
   11: Ezr 9, 2; Neh 13, 25.

12   May the Lord cut off from the man who
      does this
      both witness and advocate out of the
      tents of Jacob,
      and anyone to offer sacrifice to the Lord
      of hosts!

13   This also you do: the altar of the Lord you
      cover
      with tears, weeping and groaning,
      Because he no longer regards your sacrifice
      nor accepts it favorably from your hand;

14*   And you say, "Why is it?"—
      Because the Lord is witness
      between you and the wife of your youth,
      With whom you have broken faith
      though she is your companion, your
      betrothed wife.

15*   Did he not make one being, with flesh and
      spirit:
      and what does that one require but
      godly offspring?
      You must then safeguard life that is your
      own,
      and not break faith with the wife of your
      youth.

16   For I hate divorce,
      says the Lord, the God of Israel,
      And covering one's garment with injustice,
      says the Lord of hosts;
      You must then safeguard life that is your
      own,
      and not break faith.

17   You have wearied the Lord with your
      words,
      yet you say, "How have we wearied
      him?"
      By your saying, "Every evildoer
      is good in the sight of the Lord,
      And he is pleased with him";
      or else, "Where is the just God?"

The Messenger of the Covenant

3   1*†   Lo, I am sending my messenger
      to prepare the way before me;
      And suddenly there will come to the temple
      the Lord whom you seek,
      And the messenger of the covenant whom
      you desire.
      Yes, he is coming, says the Lord of hosts.

2   But who will endure the day of his coming?
      And who can stand when he appears?
      For he is like the refiner's fire,
      or like the fuller's lye.

3*   He will sit refining and purifying [silver],
      and he will purify the sons of Levi,
      Refining them like gold or like silver
      that they may offer due sacrifice to the
      Lord.

4   Then the sacrifice of Judah and Jerusalem
      will please the Lord,
      as in the days of old, as in years gone by.

5   I will draw near to you for judgment,
      and I will be swift to bear witness
      Against the sorcerers, adulterers, and
      perjurers,
      those who defraud the hired man of his
      wages,
      Against those who defraud widows and
      orphans;
      those who turn aside the stranger,
      and those who do not fear me,
      says the Lord of hosts.

6†   Surely I, the Lord, do not change,
      nor do you cease to be sons of Jacob.

7*   Since the days of your fathers you have
      turned aside
      from my statutes, and have not kept
      them.
      Return to me, and I will return to you,
      says the Lord of hosts.
      Yet you say, "How must we return?"

8*   Dare a man rob God? Yet you are
      robbing me!
      And you say, "How do we rob you?"
      In tithes and in offerings!

9   You are indeed accursed,
      for you, the whole nation, rob me.

10*†   Bring the whole tithe
      into the storehouse,
      That there may be food in my house,
      and try me in this, says the Lord of hosts:
      Shall I not open for you the floodgates of
      heaven,
      to pour down blessing upon you without
      measure?

11   For your sake I will forbid the locust
      to destroy your crops;
      And the vine in the field will not be barren,
      says the Lord of hosts.

12   Then all nations will call you blessed,
      for you will be a delightful land,
      says the Lord of hosts.

14: Gn 31, 49f; Prv 5, 18ff.
15: Gn 2, 7.22ff.
3/1: Is 40, 3; Mt 11, 10; Mk 1, 2; Lk 1, 17; 7, 27.
3: Is 1, 25; Zec 13, 9.
7: Zec 1, 3f; Acts 7, 51.
8: Neh 13, 10-14.
10: 2 Chr 31, 10f; Neh 10, 38; 13, 12; Prv 3, 9f.

---

† 3, 1: *My messenger . . . before me:* in v 23 this messenger is called Elijah. In Mt 11, 10 these words are quoted by Christ as referring to John the Baptizer, who prepared the way for the coming of the Savior; cf Mt 3, 1ff.11f; 17, 11ff; Mk 1, 2-8; Lk 3, 2-18; Jn 1, 31-34.

3, 6f: God is faithful to his promises. He will not abandon the Israelites, who are still his people.

3, 10: *Storehouse:* the temple treasury.

13 You have defied me in word, says the LORD,
    yet you ask, "What have we spoken
        against you?"
14* You have said, "It is vain to serve God,
    and what do we profit by keeping his
        command,
    And going about in penitential dress
        in awe of the LORD of hosts?
15 Rather must we call the proud blessed;
    for indeed evildoers prosper,
        and even tempt God with impunity."
16*† Then they who fear the LORD spoke with
        one another,
    and the LORD listened attentively;
    And a record book was written before him
        of those who fear the LORD and trust in
        his name.
17* And they shall be mine, says the LORD of
        hosts,
    my own special possession, on the day I
        take action.
    And I will have compassion on them,
        as a man has compassion on his son who
        serves him.
18 Then you will again see the distinction
    between the just and the wicked;
    Between him who serves God,
        and him who does not serve him.
19* For lo, the day is coming, blazing like an
        oven,
    when all the proud and all evildoers will
        be stubble,

And the day that is coming will set them on
    fire,
    leaving them neither root nor branch,
        says the LORD of hosts.
20* But for you who fear my name, there will
        arise
    the sun of justice with its healing rays;
    And you will gambol like calves out of the
        stall
21   and tread down the wicked;
    They will become ashes under the soles of
        your feet,
    on the day I take action, says the LORD of
        hosts.

22* Remember the law of Moses my servant,
    which I enjoined upon him on Horeb,
    The statutes and ordinances
        for all Israel.
23*† Lo, I will send you
    Elijah, the prophet,
    Before the day of the LORD comes,
        the great and terrible day,
24† To turn the hearts of the fathers to their
        children,
    and the hearts of the children to their
        fathers,
    Lest I come and strike
        the land with doom.

Lo, I will send you
    Elijah, the prophet,
Before the day of the LORD comes,
    the great and terrible day.

---

† 3, 16: *Record book:* see note on Ex 32, 32.

3, 23: *Elijah:* described in 2 Kgs 2, 11 as taken heavenward in a fiery chariot. Here his return to earth seems to be foretold. Jewish tradition has interpreted this literally; Christ declares it to be fulfilled in the coming of John the Baptizer (Mt 17, 10-13).

3, 24: The words in fine print, a repitition of v 23a-d, have been added by the scribes so that the collection of the twelve minor prophets will not end with the threat of doom.

*
14: Jb 21, 14f; 22, 17;
    Ps 73, 11f.
16: Rv 20, 12.
17: Ex 19, 5; Dt 7, 6;
    Pss 103, 13; 135, 4.
19: Is 13, 9; 34, 8; Jl 3, 3;
    Zep 1, 18; 2 Pt 3, 7.

20: Lk 1, 78f.
22: Ex 20; Lv 26;
    Dt 4, 1.5f.
23: Mt 11, 14; 17, 10;
    Mk 9, 10ff; Lk 1, 17.

Our Family Record

HOLY MATRIMONY

GROOM_____

and

BRIDE_____

were united in Holy Matrimony

on_____ at_____

DATE   CHURCH

The ceremony was witnessed by

_____

OFFICIATING PRIEST

OTHER MEMBERS OF THE WEDDING PARTY

_____   _____

BEST MAN   MAID OF HONOR

_____   _____

_____   _____

PARENTS

_____   _____

GROOM'S FATHER   BRIDE'S FATHER

_____   _____

GROOM'S MOTHER   BRIDE'S MOTHER

FAMILY TREE · Husband's Genealogy

NAME_____

BIRTH_____
              PLACE   DATE

BAPTISM_____
              CHURCH   OFFICIATING PRIEST   DATE

              GODPARENT   GODPARENT

FIRST COMMUNION_____
              CHURCH   OFFICIATING PRIEST   DATE

CONFIRMATION_____
              CHURCH   OFFICIATING BISHOP

              SPONSOR   DATE

MILITARY SERVICE_____
              BRANCH   ENTERED   DISCHARGED

PARENTS

Father   Mother

NAME   NAME

PLACE AND DATE OF BIRTH   PLACE AND DATE OF BIRTH

GRANDPARENTS

Paternal   Maternal

GRANDFATHER   GRANDFATHER

PLACE AND DATE OF BIRTH   PLACE AND DATE OF BIRTH

GRANDMOTHER   GRANDMOTHER

PLACE AND DATE OF BIRTH   PLACE AND DATE OF BIRTH

GREAT GRANDPARENTS

Paternal   Maternal

GRANDFATHER'S FATHER   GRANDFATHER'S FATHER

PLACE AND DATE OF BIRTH   PLACE AND DATE OF BIRTH

GRANDFATHER'S MOTHER   GRANDFATHER'S MOTHER

PLACE AND DATE OF BIRTH   PLACE AND DATE OF BIRTH

GRANDMOTHER'S FATHER   GRANDMOTHER'S FATHER

PLACE AND DATE OF BIRTH   PLACE AND DATE OF BIRTH

GRANDMOTHER'S MOTHER   GRANDMOTHER'S MOTHER

PLACE AND DATE OF BIRTH   PLACE AND DATE OF BIRTH

FAMILY TREE · Wife's Genealogy

NAME_____

BIRTH_____
                PLACE   DATE

BAPTISM_____
                CHURCH   OFFICIATING PRIEST   DATE

_____
                GODPARENT   GODPARENT

FIRST COMMUNION_____
                CHURCH   OFFICIATING PRIEST   DATE

CONFIRMATION_____
                CHURCH   OFFICIATING BISHOP

_____
                SPONSOR   DATE

MILITARY SERVICE_____
                BRANCH   ENTERED   DISCHARGED

Father   PARENTS   Mother

NAME	NAME
PLACE AND DATE OF BIRTH	PLACE AND DATE OF BIRTH

Paternal   GRANDPARENTS   Maternal

GRANDFATHER	GRANDFATHER
PLACE AND DATE OF BIRTH	PLACE AND DATE OF BIRTH
GRANDMOTHER	GRANDMOTHER
PLACE AND DATE OF BIRTH	PLACE AND DATE OF BIRTH

Paternal   GREAT GRANDPARENTS   Maternal

GRANDFATHER'S FATHER	GRANDFATHER'S FATHER
PLACE AND DATE OF BIRTH	PLACE AND DATE OF BIRTH
GRANDFATHER'S MOTHER	GRANDFATHER'S MOTHER
PLACE AND DATE OF BIRTH	PLACE AND DATE OF BIRTH
GRANDMOTHER'S FATHER	GRANDMOTHER'S FATHER
PLACE AND DATE OF BIRTH	PLACE AND DATE OF BIRTH
GRANDMOTHER'S MOTHER	GRANDMOTHER'S MOTHER
PLACE AND DATE OF BIRTH	PLACE AND DATE OF BIRTH

Children

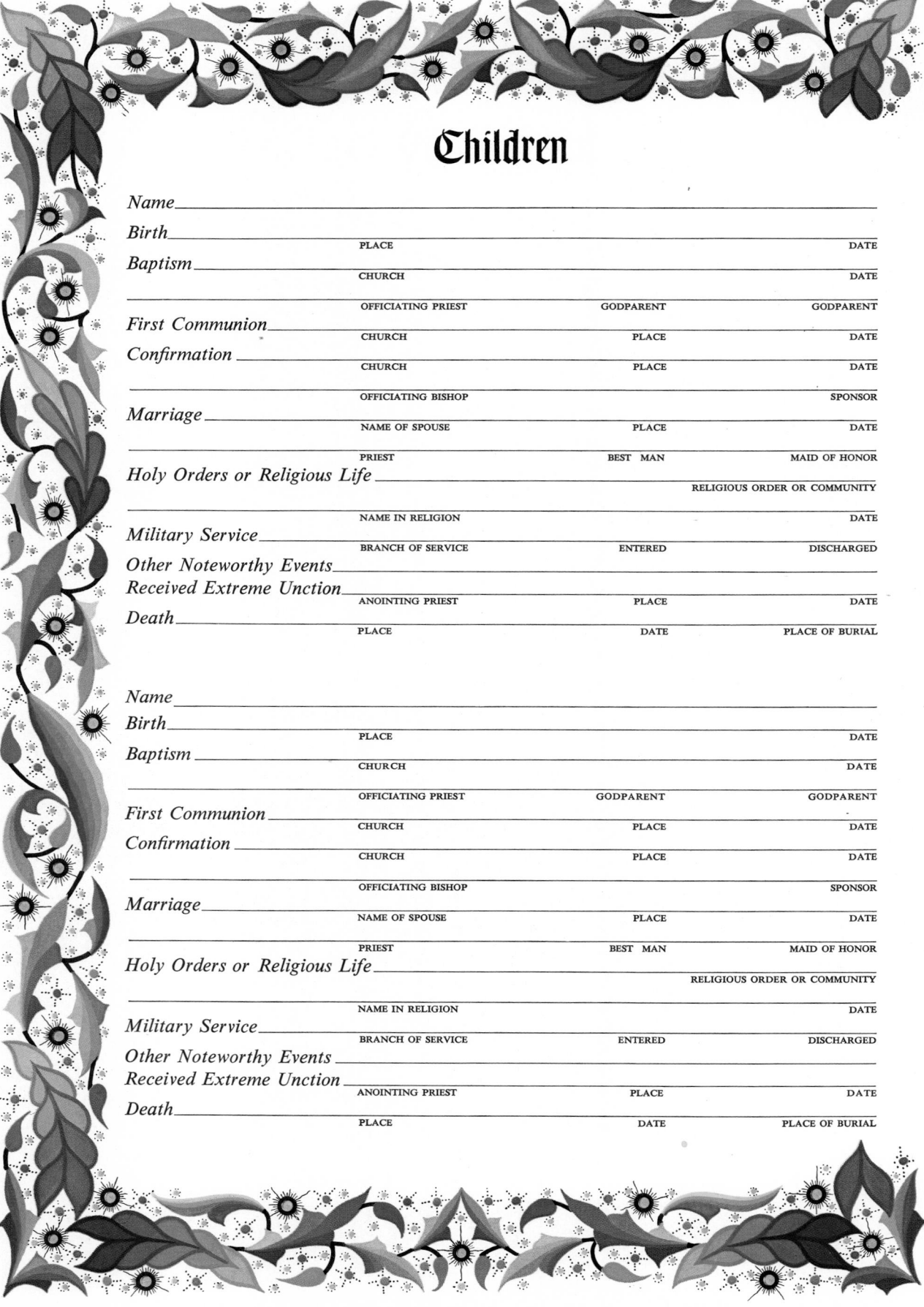

Name _____

Birth _____
                  PLACE   DATE

Baptism _____
                  CHURCH   DATE

_____
    OFFICIATING PRIEST   GODPARENT   GODPARENT

First Communion _____
         CHURCH   PLACE   DATE

Confirmation _____
         CHURCH   PLACE   DATE

_____
    OFFICIATING BISHOP   SPONSOR

Marriage _____
      NAME OF SPOUSE   PLACE   DATE

_____
    PRIEST   BEST MAN   MAID OF HONOR

Holy Orders or Religious Life _____
                                  RELIGIOUS ORDER OR COMMUNITY

_____
    NAME IN RELIGION   DATE

Military Service _____
      BRANCH OF SERVICE   ENTERED   DISCHARGED

Other Noteworthy Events _____

Received Extreme Unction _____
      ANOINTING PRIEST   PLACE   DATE

Death _____
        PLACE   DATE   PLACE OF BURIAL

Name _____

Birth _____
                  PLACE   DATE

Baptism _____
                  CHURCH   DATE

_____
    OFFICIATING PRIEST   GODPARENT   GODPARENT

First Communion _____
         CHURCH   PLACE   DATE

Confirmation _____
         CHURCH   PLACE   DATE

_____
    OFFICIATING BISHOP   SPONSOR

Marriage _____
      NAME OF SPOUSE   PLACE   DATE

_____
    PRIEST   BEST MAN   MAID OF HONOR

Holy Orders or Religious Life _____
                                  RELIGIOUS ORDER OR COMMUNITY

_____
    NAME IN RELIGION   DATE

Military Service _____
      BRANCH OF SERVICE   ENTERED   DISCHARGED

Other Noteworthy Events _____

Received Extreme Unction _____
      ANOINTING PRIEST   PLACE   DATE

Death _____
        PLACE   DATE   PLACE OF BURIAL

Children

Name _____

Birth _____
　　　　　　　PLACE　　　　　　　　　　　　　　　　　　　　　　　DATE

Baptism _____
　　　　　　　CHURCH　　　　　　　　　　　　　　　　　　　　　　DATE

_____
OFFICIATING PRIEST　　　　　　GODPARENT　　　　　　　GODPARENT

First Communion _____
　　　　　　　　　CHURCH　　　　　　　　　PLACE　　　　　　　　DATE

Confirmation _____
　　　　　　　CHURCH　　　　　　　　　　PLACE　　　　　　　　DATE

_____
OFFICIATING BISHOP　　　　　　　　　　　　　　　　　　　　SPONSOR

Marriage _____
　　　　　　　NAME OF SPOUSE　　　　　　　PLACE　　　　　　　DATE

_____
PRIEST　　　　　　　　　BEST MAN　　　　　　MAID OF HONOR

Holy Orders or Religious Life _____
　　　　　　　　　　　　　　　　　　RELIGIOUS ORDER OR COMMUNITY

_____
NAME IN RELIGION　　　　　　　　　　　　　　　　　　　　　DATE

Military Service _____
　　　　　　　　BRANCH OF SERVICE　　　　ENTERED　　　　DISCHARGED

Other Noteworthy Events _____

Received Extreme Unction _____
　　　　　　　　　　ANOINTING PRIEST　　　　　　PLACE　　　　　　　DATE

Death _____
　　　　　　PLACE　　　　　　　　　　　DATE　　　　　PLACE OF BURIAL

Name _____

Birth _____
　　　　　　　PLACE　　　　　　　　　　　　　　　　　　　　　　　DATE

Baptism _____
　　　　　　　CHURCH　　　　　　　　　　　　　　　　　　　　　　DATE

_____
OFFICIATING PRIEST　　　　　　GODPARENT　　　　　　　GODPARENT

First Communion _____
　　　　　　　　　CHURCH　　　　　　　　　PLACE　　　　　　　　DATE

Confirmation _____
　　　　　　　CHURCH　　　　　　　　　　PLACE　　　　　　　　DATE

_____
OFFICIATING BISHOP　　　　　　　　　　　　　　　　　　　　SPONSOR

Marriage _____
　　　　　　　NAME OF SPOUSE　　　　　　　PLACE　　　　　　　DATE

_____
PRIEST　　　　　　　　　BEST MAN　　　　　　MAID OF HONOR

Holy Orders or Religious Life _____
　　　　　　　　　　　　　　　　　　RELIGIOUS ORDER OR COMMUNITY

_____
NAME IN RELIGION　　　　　　　　　　　　　　　　　　　　　DATE

Military Service _____
　　　　　　　　BRANCH OF SERVICE　　　　ENTERED　　　　DISCHARGED

Other Noteworthy Events _____

Received Extreme Unction _____
　　　　　　　　　　ANOINTING PRIEST　　　　　　PLACE　　　　　　　DATE

Death _____
　　　　　　PLACE　　　　　　　　　　　DATE　　　　　PLACE OF BURIAL

Children

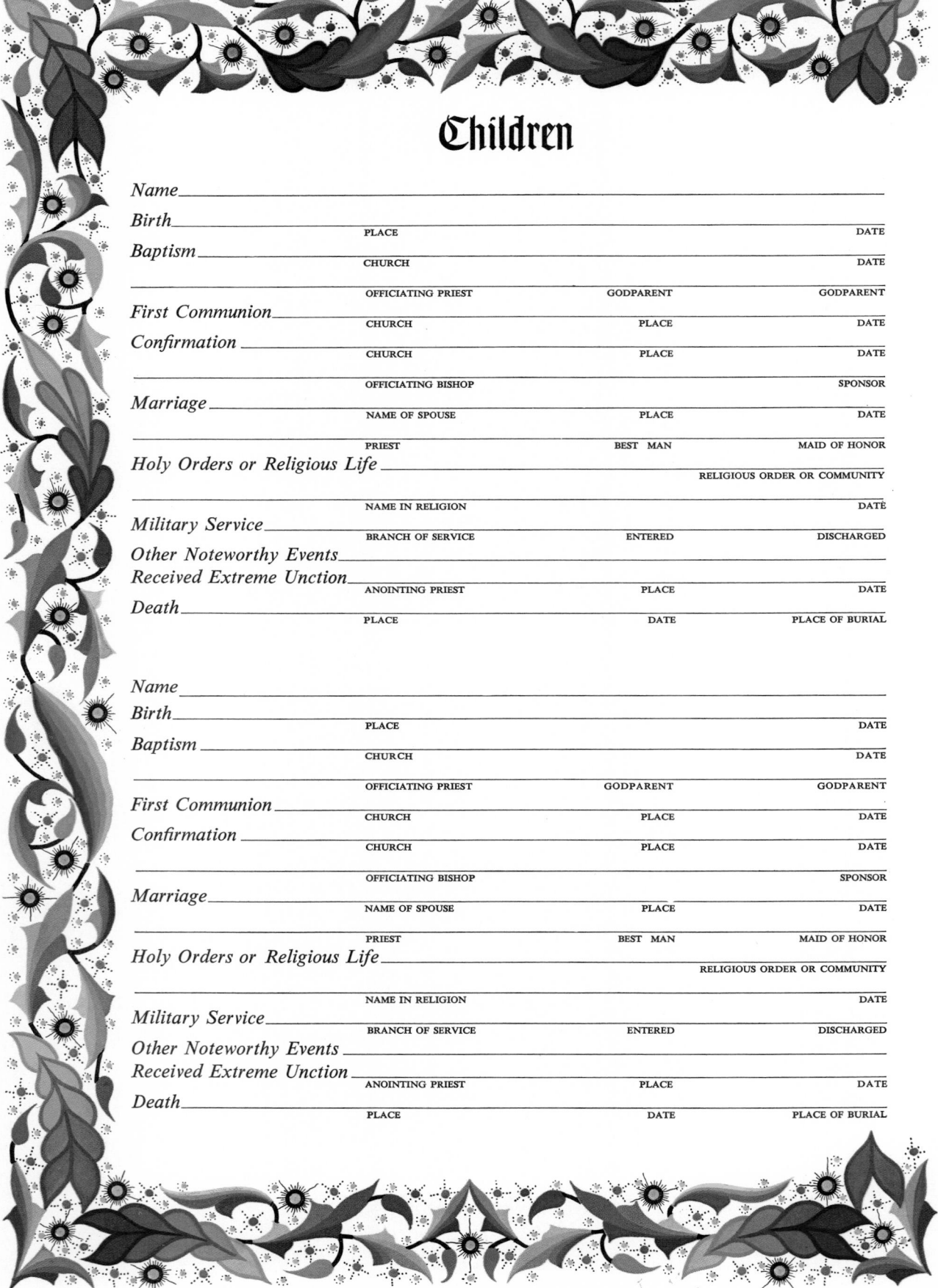

Name _____

Birth _____
                PLACE   DATE

Baptism _____
                CHURCH   DATE

_____
                OFFICIATING PRIEST   GODPARENT   GODPARENT

First Communion _____
                CHURCH   PLACE   DATE

Confirmation _____
                CHURCH   PLACE   DATE

_____
                OFFICIATING BISHOP   SPONSOR

Marriage _____
                NAME OF SPOUSE   PLACE   DATE

_____
                PRIEST   BEST MAN   MAID OF HONOR

Holy Orders or Religious Life _____
                                       RELIGIOUS ORDER OR COMMUNITY

_____
                NAME IN RELIGION   DATE

Military Service _____
                BRANCH OF SERVICE   ENTERED   DISCHARGED

Other Noteworthy Events _____

Received Extreme Unction _____
                ANOINTING PRIEST   PLACE   DATE

Death _____
                PLACE   DATE   PLACE OF BURIAL

Name _____

Birth _____
                PLACE   DATE

Baptism _____
                CHURCH   DATE

_____
                OFFICIATING PRIEST   GODPARENT   GODPARENT

First Communion _____
                CHURCH   PLACE   DATE

Confirmation _____
                CHURCH   PLACE   DATE

_____
                OFFICIATING BISHOP   SPONSOR

Marriage _____
                NAME OF SPOUSE   PLACE   DATE

_____
                PRIEST   BEST MAN   MAID OF HONOR

Holy Orders or Religious Life _____
                                       RELIGIOUS ORDER OR COMMUNITY

_____
                NAME IN RELIGION   DATE

Military Service _____
                BRANCH OF SERVICE   ENTERED   DISCHARGED

Other Noteworthy Events _____

Received Extreme Unction _____
                ANOINTING PRIEST   PLACE   DATE

Death _____
                PLACE   DATE   PLACE OF BURIAL

Children

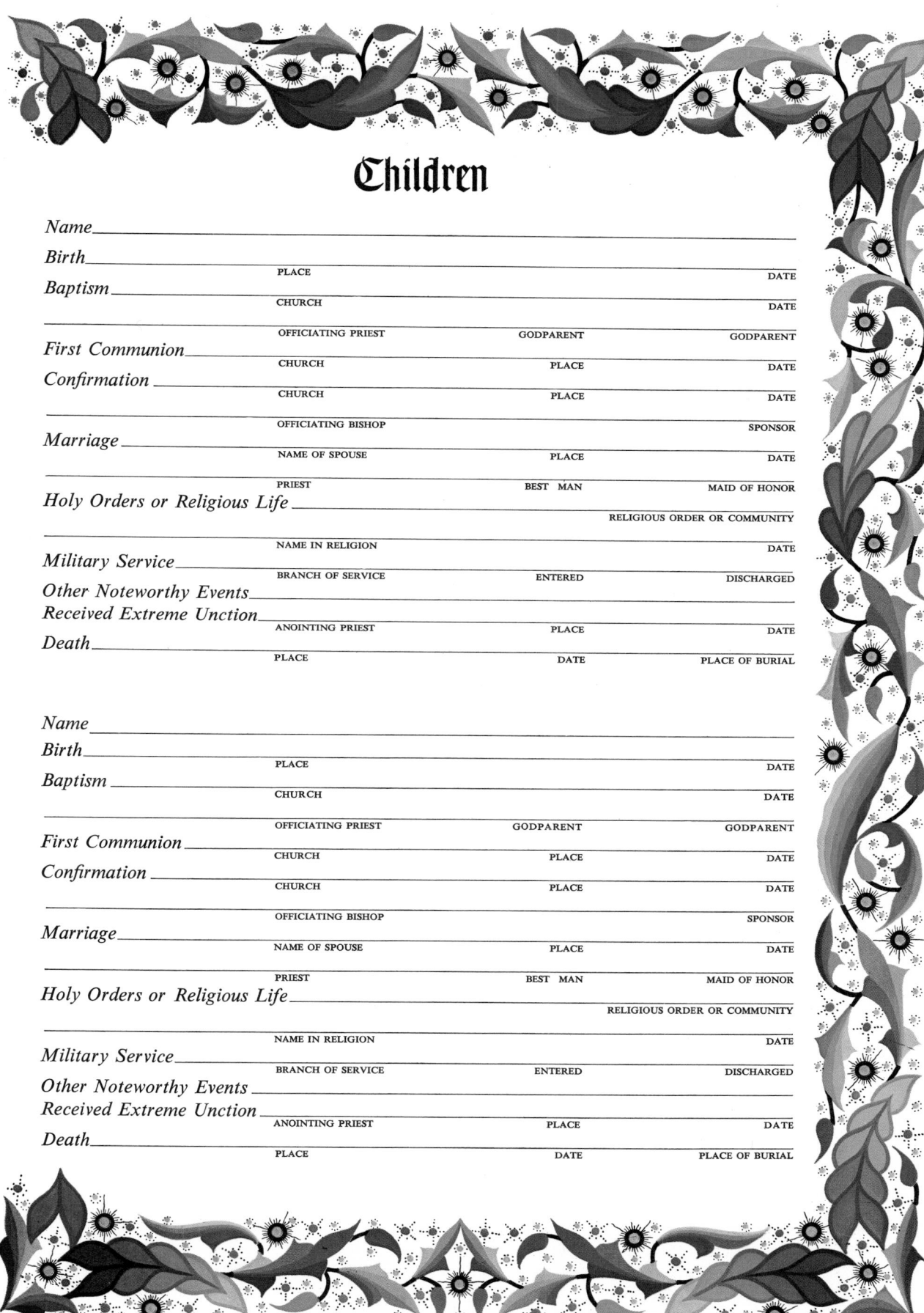

Name _____

Birth _____
               PLACE   DATE

Baptism _____
               CHURCH   DATE

           OFFICIATING PRIEST   GODPARENT   GODPARENT

First Communion _____
               CHURCH   PLACE   DATE

Confirmation _____
               CHURCH   PLACE   DATE

           OFFICIATING BISHOP   SPONSOR

Marriage _____
               NAME OF SPOUSE   PLACE   DATE

           PRIEST   BEST MAN   MAID OF HONOR

Holy Orders or Religious Life _____
                                     RELIGIOUS ORDER OR COMMUNITY

           NAME IN RELIGION   DATE

Military Service _____
           BRANCH OF SERVICE   ENTERED   DISCHARGED

Other Noteworthy Events _____

Received Extreme Unction _____
           ANOINTING PRIEST   PLACE   DATE

Death _____
           PLACE   DATE   PLACE OF BURIAL

Name _____

Birth _____
           PLACE   DATE

Baptism _____
           CHURCH   DATE

          OFFICIATING PRIEST   GODPARENT   GODPARENT

First Communion _____
           CHURCH   PLACE   DATE

Confirmation _____
          CHURCH   PLACE   DATE

         OFFICIATING BISHOP   SPONSOR

Marriage _____
          NAME OF SPOUSE   PLACE   DATE

         PRIEST   BEST MAN   MAID OF HONOR

Holy Orders or Religious Life _____
                                     RELIGIOUS ORDER OR COMMUNITY

         NAME IN RELIGION   DATE

Military Service _____
         BRANCH OF SERVICE   ENTERED   DISCHARGED

Other Noteworthy Events _____

Received Extreme Unction _____
         ANOINTING PRIEST   PLACE   DATE

Death _____
        PLACE   DATE   PLACE OF BURIAL

MEMORABLE EVENTS

Pilgrimages   SHRINE OR PLACE VISITED   DATE

NAME_____   _____   _____

_____   _____   _____

_____   _____   _____

Audiences with Religious and Other Dignitaries   WITH WHOM   DATE

NAME_____   _____   _____

_____   _____   _____

_____   _____   _____

Religious and Other Honors Received   HONOR   DATE

NAME_____   _____   _____

_____   _____   _____

_____   _____   _____

Member of the Following Organizations   ORGANIZATION   DATE JOINED

NAME_____   _____   _____

_____   _____   _____

_____   _____   _____

Deaths of Beloved Relatives and Friends   PLACE OF BURIAL   DATE

NAME_____   _____   _____

_____   _____   _____

_____   _____   _____

Other Noteworthy Events   EVENT   DATE

_____   _____   _____

_____   _____   _____

_____   _____   _____

_____   _____   _____

The New Testament

The Gospel According to Matthew

Introduction

Matthew's gospel in its present form was written in a Jewish milieu, probably after the destruction of Jerusalem in 70 A. D. There are evidences of the fulfillment of the Mosaic law (1, 19; 5, 18), and also references to violence (21, 38-41), to the burning of a city (22, 7), and to punishment in the wake of Jesus' death (27, 25).

There is also the anti-Pharisee and anti-scribe polemic in Matthew which indicates a fairly complete rift between Christians and official Judaism. By the year 85 A. D. Christians were unwelcome in Jewish synagogues—called *their synagogues* by Matthew to distinguish Jewish from Christian worship (4, 23; 9, 35; 12, 9; 13, 54).

There is thus an ambivalence between Matthew's earlier Jewishness, reflected in the elements of the gospel as they were in the process of formation, and his alienation from Jewish tradition even before these elements were incorporated into the finished gospel.

Ignatius, bishop of Antioch (†110), in his letters to certain churches of Asia Minor, uses several sayings of Jesus found only in this gospel (12, 35; 15, 13; 19, 12). Papias, bishop of Hierapolis in Phrygia, wrote (c 135) that Matthew had compiled a collection of sayings of the Lord "in the Hebrew tongue" (most likely Aramaic), "and each person translated them as he was able." This seems to indicate that various Greek versions of the early collection attributed to Matthew were in existence; one of them may have been the apocryphal gospel of the Hebrews.

Besides the sayings of the Lord, it is certain that the author of Matthew had access to the present Gospel of Mark because of the Marcan verses he uses in chapters 3, 8f, 12-17, 19-22, 24, 26ff. Matthew is obviously an expanded version of Mark, considered the first gospel form to be written. Very few scholars hold that Mark is a condensed version of Matthew.

Both Matthew and Luke, neither of whom can be proved to have copied from the other, seem to have had, besides the Gospel of Mark, another source of some 240 verses which Mark does not include. This source, not found but deduced, is designated simply as Q from Quelle, the German term for "source."

Beginning with a series of reflections relating Jesus and his parentage to the messianism of the Old Testament (1, 1-25), the gospel places his birth in the hostile political environment of the time (2, 1-23). Like the other gospels, Matthew introduces the public ministry of Jesus with a summary of the mission of John the Baptizer (3, 1-17). After the account of the temptation of Jesus (4, 1-11), the gospel reports his teaching and miracles, locating all these in Galilee and its vicinity, exclusive of Jerusalem (4, 12–20, 34). It concludes with the final events and teaching of Jesus, locating them in Jerusalem, and centering them around his passion, death and resurrection (21, 1–28, 20). For this general outline of a gospel, see Acts 1, 21f; 10, 37-41.

The Gospel of Matthew is distinctive for its practice of citing the Old Testament in connection with Jesus' activity and teaching, and for a structured presentation of his doctrine in the form of sermons or discourses (5, 1-7, 29; 10, 5-42; 13, 1-52; 18, 1-35; 24, 1–25, 46). The discourses are followed by collections of miracle-accounts and incidents which reflect Jesus' doctrinal teaching. They are presented by the evangelist in such a way as to be meaningful to the Christian communities of his time.

The gospel as a whole revolves around the concept, no doubt originally developed in Judaeo-Christian circles, that Jesus is the expected Messiah-king of Israel, mysteriously unacceptable to his own people, but no less mysteriously acceptable to many Gentiles.

The universal importance of Christ in this gospel does not derive from the notion of messianic kingship alone, but more especially from his divinity (1, 23; 16, 16; 28, 18). This makes possible his presence in Christian communities in word and sacrament (18, 19; 26, 29) and constitutes him the divine teacher of all nations (28, 19). The bond in Matthew between christology and ecclesiology portrays the mediating mission of the Christian community, that of giving witness to Christ in the world. In the judgment of modern scholars this mission is a theological development within the gospel tradition that requires a date for the Gospel of Matthew later than that of Mark and Luke. Current and more common opinion dates the composition of the Gospel of Matthew between 80-100 A. D., or roughly, 85 A. D. There is also the compelling evidence for the dependence of Matthew on Mark: namely, the 600 of Mark's 661 verses found in Matthew, as well as the relationship of language and order in these two gospels.

The principal divisions of the Gospel of Matthew are as follows:

    I: Prologue: The Coming of the Savior
         (1, 1–2, 23)
   II: Promulgation of the Reign of God (3, 1–7, 29)
  III: Preaching the Reign of God (8, 1–11, 1)
   IV: Mystery of the Kingdom of Heaven
         (11, 2–13, 53)
    V: The Reign Become Church (13, 54–19, 2)
   VI: First Steps in Establishing God's Reign
         (19, 3–26, 2)
  VII: The Passion and Resurrection (26, 3–28, 20)

I: PROLOGUE: THE COMING OF THE SAVIOR

Genealogy of Jesus

1 ¹*†A FAMILY RECORD OF JESUS CHRIST, son of David, son of Abraham. ²*†Abraham was the father of Isaac, Isaac the father of Jacob, Jacob the father of Judah and his brothers.

³*Judah was the father of Perez and Zerah, whose mother was Tamar.
Perez was the father of Hezron,
Hezron the father of Ram.

⁴*Ram was the father of Amminadab,
Amminadab the father of Nahshon,
Nahshon the father of Salmon.

⁵*Salmon was the father of Boaz, whose mother was Rahab,
Boaz was the father of Obed, whose mother was Ruth.
Obed was the father of Jesse,

⁶*Jesse the father of King David.
David was the father of Solomon, whose mother had been the wife of Uriah.

⁷*Solomon was the father of Rehoboam,
Rehoboam the father of Abijah,
Abijah the father of Asa.

⁸*Asa was the father of Jehoshaphat,
Jehoshaphat the father of Joram,
Joram the father of Uzziah.

⁹*Uzziah was the father of Jotham,
Jotham the father of Ahaz,
Ahaz the father of Hezekiah.

¹⁰*Hezekiah was the father of Manasseh,
Manasseh the father of Amos,
Amos the father of Josiah.

¹¹*Josiah became the father of Jechoniah and his brothers at the time of the Babylonian exile.

¹² After the Babylonian exile
Jechoniah was the father of Shealtiel,
Shealtiel the father of Zerubbabel.

¹³ Zerubbabel was the father of Abiud,
Abiud the father of Eliakim,
Eliakim the father of Azor.

¹⁴ Azor was the father of Zadok,
Zadok the father of Achim,
Achim the father of Eliud.

¹⁵ Eliud was the father of Eleazar,
Eleazar the father of Matthan,
Matthan the father of Jacob.

¹⁶ Jacob was the father of Joseph the husband of Mary.

It was of her that Jesus who is called the Messiah was born.

¹⁷†Thus the total number of generations is:
from Abraham to David, fourteen generations;
from David to the Babylonian captivity, fourteen generations;
from the Babylonian captivity to the Messiah, fourteen generations.

The Birth of Jesus

¹⁸*†Now this is how the birth of Jesus Christ came about. When his mother Mary was engaged to Joseph, but before they lived together, she was found with child through the power of the Holy Spirit. ¹⁹†Joseph her husband, an upright man unwilling to expose her to the law, decided to divorce her quietly. ²⁰*†Such was his intention when suddenly the angel of the Lord appeared in a dream and said to him: "Joseph, son of David, have no fear about taking Mary as your wife.

---

† 1, 1: *A family record of Jesus Christ:* the Greek may also be taken to mean "book of the history of the origin of Jesus Christ." In this sense the opening verse is a title for the whole gospel, which then begins with the genealogy of Christ; cf Gn 2, 4. *Jesus:* the Greek and Latin form of the late Hebrew and Aramaic name *Jeshua,* meaning "The Lord is salvation." *Christ:* in v 17 and elsewhere, a title from the Greek *Christos,* which translates the Hebrew *Mashiah,* "Anointed One," applied to the expected representative of God on earth. Matthew in v 1 uses "Jesus Christ" as a proper name, as was customary in later Christian circles; cf Jn 1, 17; Phil 2, 11.

1, 2-17: The genealogy points out Jesus' Davidic lineage through Joseph who, however, is called "the husband of Mary" (1, 16), not the father of Jesus. In 1, 18-25, the evangelist explains the reason for the foster paternity of Joseph. The genealogy recalls the messianic hope of Israel by alluding to the divine promises to the patriarchs (2) and to David (6); cf 2 Sm 7, 12-16. It places this hope in the context of Israel's sinfulness by allusion to David's murder of Uriah (6), and also to the Babylonian captivity (11). The constant repetition of the term "was the father of," literally "begot," implies the continuous presence of God in Israel sustaining the faith and hope of the people. For the implication of the divine presence in the Greek term, cf 1 Cor 4, 15; Gal 4, 24.

1, 17: The genealogy is artificially constructed out of three groups of fourteen names each, taken principally from Genesis, Ruth, 1 Chronicles and 2 Kings. The list of names beginning with Abiud in 1, 13 is unknown to the Old Testament. The number 14 is undoubtedly a mnemonic device, perhaps chosen because the numerical value of the three letters of David's name (DVD) yields in Hebrew the sum of 14.

1, 18-25: The evangelist shows that Jesus was introduced into the Davidic line through the divine choice of Joseph as his legal father. Throughout the public ministry of Jesus it was understandably the common opinion that Joseph was the natural father of Jesus; cf Mt 13, 55; Jn 6, 42.

1, 18: *Mary was engaged to Joseph:* they were living in a state of espousal which usually lasted one year in Galilee.

1, 19: A common opinion from the time of the Church Fathers ascribes to Joseph the fear that Mary's child was a consequence of adultery. The evangelist depicts Joseph in a dilemma: he feels it would not be honorable for him to assume the paternity of the child in view of the requirements of "justice" under Mosaic law; but at the same time he realizes that even a private divorce in the presence of only a few witnesses would eventually expose Mary to the popular suspicion of adultery.

1, 20f: To what extent the angelic visitation of Joseph through a dream is reality or popular description surrounding

---

* 1/1-17: Lk 3, 23-38.
  1: 9, 27; Gal 3, 16.
  2: Gn 21, 3; 25, 26; 29, 35; Heb 7, 14.
  3: Gn 38, 29f; Ru 4, 18; 1 Chr 2, 4f.
  4: Nm 7, 12; Ru 4, 20.
  5: Ru 4, 21.
  6: 2 Sm 12, 24.
  7: 1 Kgs 11, 43; 14, 31; 15, 8.
  8: 2 Kgs 8, 16.
  9: 2 Chr 26, 23; 27, 9; 28, 27.
  10: 2 Chr 32, 33; 33, 20.25.
  11: 2 Chr 36, 9ff.20f.
  18: Lk 1, 27; 2, 5.
  20: 2, 13.19; Lk 1, 31.35.

It is by the Holy Spirit that she has conceived this child. [21]She is to have a son and you are to name him Jesus because he will save his people from their sins." [22†]All this happened to fulfill what the Lord had said through the prophet:

> [23*]"The virgin shall be with child
>   and give birth to a son,
>   and they shall call him Emmanuel,"

a name which means "God is with us." [24]When Joseph awoke he did as the angel of the Lord had directed him and received her into his home as his wife. [25*†]He had no relations with her at any time before she bore a son, whom he named Jesus.

The Astrologers

2 [1†]AFTER Jesus' birth in Bethlehem of Judea during the reign of King Herod, astrologers from the east arrived one day in Jerusalem [2*]inquiring, "Where is the newborn king of the Jews? We observed his star at its rising and have come to pay him homage." [3]At this news King Herod became greatly disturbed, and with him all Jerusalem. [4]Summoning all of the chief priests and scribes of the people, he inquired of them where the Messiah was to be born. [5*†]"In Bethlehem of Judea," they informed him. "Here is what the prophet has written:

> [6*]'And you, Bethlehem, land of Judah,
>   are by no means least among the princes of Judah,
>   since from you shall come a ruler
>   who is to shepherd my people Israel.'"

[7]Herod called the astrologers aside and found out from them the exact time of the star's appearance. [8]Then he sent them to Bethlehem, after having instructed them: "Go and get detailed information about the child. When you have found him, report it to me so that I may go and offer him homage too." [9†]After their audience with the king, they set out. The star which they had observed at its rising went ahead of them until it came to a standstill over the place where the child was. [10]They were overjoyed at seeing the star, [11*†]and on entering the house, found the child with Mary his mother. They prostrated themselves and did him homage. Then they opened their coffers and presented him with gifts of gold, frankincense, and myrrh.

[12]They received a message in a dream not to return to Herod, so they went back to their own country by another route.

The Flight into Egypt

[13†]After they had left, the angel of the Lord suddenly appeared in a dream to Joseph with the command: "Get up, take the child and his mother, and flee to Egypt. Stay there until I tell you otherwise. Herod is searching for the child to destroy him." [14]Joseph got up and took the child and his mother and

---

† the divine message to him is subject to discussion. In either case the evangelist makes it abundantly clear to his readers that Joseph accepted Mary as his wife, together with the child, because he saw the will of God expressed in the circumstances. *He will save his people from their sins:* the child will not be a warrior-king overcoming the enemies of Israel, but will free the people from sin.

1, 22f: This is a prophetic reinterpretation of Is 7, 14, in the light of the facts Matthew has outlined: the virginal conception of Jesus, his Davidic messianic role in a spiritual sense, Joseph's legal paternity, and the unique presence of God in Jesus, which the church of the evangelist's time had to come to understand as his divinity. All these things about Jesus that were faintly traced in Is 7, 14 are now seen by Matthew to be fully brought to light as God's plan.

1, 25: *He had no relations with her at any time before:* the evangelist emphasizes the virginity of the mother of Jesus from the moment of his conception to his birth. He does not concern himself here with the period that followed the birth of Jesus, but merely wishes to show that Joseph fully respected the legal character of the paternity imposed on him by the divine will. Moreover the New Testament makes no mention anywhere of children of Joseph and Mary.

2, 1-25: The episodes which follow the explanation of Jesus' Davidic origin through the legal paternity of Joseph raise the question: Do we have here a historical composition with theological overtones or a theological composition resting on a broad historical basis? The latter supposition finds support in the typology of the second chapter of Matthew, which parallels Jesus with Israel and Moses in a way that suggests an influence of extra-biblical Jewish religious traditions.

2, 1: *King Herod:* called "the Great" because of his political astuteness and his achievements in building, which included the temple in Jerusalem. In 40 B. C. the Roman senate appointed him king of Judea. From then on Herod succeeded in extending his rule to other parts of Palestine. Since Herod is known to have died in 4 B. C., scholars assign 7 or 6 B. C. as the actual date of the birth of Jesus; cf Mt 2, 16. *Astrologers from the east:* the various personages designated by the Greek term *magoi* did not include kings. Many think that the allusion is to learned men from Babylon who had contact with Jewish messianism; cf Dn 2, 2.

2, 5f: The citation combines Mi 5, 1 and 2 Sm 5, 2. It emphasizes the fulfillment of Old Testament prophecy concerning Bethlehem, the birthplace of Jesus. For the expression of a current opinion that the Messiah was to come from Bethlehem, cf Jn 7, 42.

2, 9f: The action of the star implies that in the evangelist's thought it is a supernatural phenomenon. It is a symbol of faith leading the Gentiles to the discovery of Jesus as their king and savior; cf 2 Pt 1, 19.

2, 11: *The house:* Matthew's tradition of the astrologers' visit to a *house* is unrelated to the place of Jesus' birth as reported in Luke 2, 12. *Gold, frankincense and myrrh:* such gifts were customary in the Orient as signs of homage. The association of 2, 11 with Ps 72, 10f occasioned the mistaken supposition that the astrologers were kings. For the Old Testament oracles concerning the Gentiles' homage to Yahweh, cf Nm 24, 17; Is 49, 23; 60, 5f.

2, 13: *Flee to Egypt:* from the time of the Maccabees, Egypt had been a customary place of refuge. An earlier example is Jeroboam's flight to Egypt (1 Kgs 11, 40).

---

*

23: Is 7, 14.   5: Jn 7, 42.
25: Lk 2, 7.   6: Mi 5, 1.
2/2: Nm 24, 17.   11: Ps 72, 10f; Is 60, 5f.

left that night for Egypt. **15*****†**He stayed there until the death of Herod, to fulfill what the Lord had said through the prophet:

> "Out of Egypt I have called my son."

The Innocents

16Once Herod realized that he had been deceived by the astrologers, he became furious. He ordered the massacre of all the boys two years old and under in Bethlehem and its environs, making his calculations on the basis of the date he had learned from the astrologers. **17**†What was said through Jeremiah the prophet was then fulfilled:

> **18***"A cry was heard at Ramah,
>   sobbing and loud lamentation:
> Rachel bewailing her children;
>   no comfort for her, since they are no more."

The Return to Nazareth

19But after Herod's death, the angel of the Lord appeared in a dream to Joseph in Egypt **20***with the command: "Get up, take the child and his mother, and set out for the land of Israel. Those who had designs on the life of the child are dead." **21**He got up, took the child and his mother, and returned to the land of Israel. **22**†He heard, however, that Archelaus had succeeded his father Herod as king of Judea, and he was afraid to go back there. Instead, because of a warning received in a dream, Joseph went to the region of Galilee. **23***†There he settled in a town called Nazareth. In this way what was said through the prophets was fulfilled:

> "He shall be called a Nazorean."

II: PROMULGATION OF THE REIGN OF GOD

John the Baptizer

3 **1***†WHEN JOHN THE BAPTIZER made his appearance as a preacher in the desert of Judea, **2***†this was his theme: "Reform your lives! The reign of God is at hand." **3***It was of him that the prophet Isaiah had spoken when he said:

> "A herald's voice in the desert:
>   'Prepare the way of the Lord,
>   make straight his paths.'"

4*†John was clothed in a garment of camel's hair, and wore a leather belt around his waist. Grasshoppers and wild honey were his food. **5**At that time Jerusalem, all Judea, and the whole region around the Jordan were going out to him. **6***They were being baptized by him in the Jordan River as they confessed their sins.

7*†When he saw that many of the Pharisees and Sadducees were stepping forward for this bath, he said to them: "You brood of vipers! Who told you to flee from the wrath to come? **8**Give some evidence that you mean to reform. **9***Do not pride yourselves on the claim, 'Abraham is our father.' I tell you, God can raise up children to Abraham from these very stones. **10**Even now the ax is laid to the root of the tree. Every tree that is not fruitful will be cut down and thrown into the fire. **11***†I baptize you in water for the sake of reform, but the one who will follow me is more powerful than I. I am not even fit to carry his sandals. He it is who will baptize you in the Holy Spirit and fire. **12***His winnowing-fan is in his hand. He will clear the

---

† 2, 15: The citation of Hos 11, 1, relates Jesus to Israel. Just as God called Israel out of Egypt to create a people peculiarly his own, so he called Jesus out of Egypt into the land of Israel to accomplish his purpose of creating the new Israel or people of God. The story of the flight into Egypt illustrates the divine concealment of the child so that he might fulfill his role as head of the new Israel.

2, 17f: The plaint over the massacre is not ascribed to the people of Bethlehem but figuratively to Rachel bewailing Israel's exile (Jer 31, 15f). She is comforted by a promise of restoration. A note of consolation seems implied in Matthew's citation, which views the massacre of infants as a guarantee of God's action to create the new people of God through Jesus; cf Rv 6, 9ff.

2, 22: *Archelaus:* i. e., "leader of the people," a son of Herod the Great and brother of Herod Antipas; see note on Acts 4, 27. He ruled as ethnarch of Judea, Samaria and Idumea from 4 B. C. to 6 A. D., when he was deposed by the Emperor Augustus.

2, 23: *He shall be called a Nazorean:* unidentifiable in any Old Testament passage. Jesus' residence in Galilee amid a mixed population of Jews and Gentiles is viewed as a providential indication of his messianic mission to the Gentiles; cf Is 66, 18f; Am 9, 11f.

3, 1-17: This narrative is concerned with the prophetic message and person of John (1-5), his baptism (6), his critique of the Pharisees and Sadducees (7-10), his message concerning Jesus (11f), and his baptism of Jesus, with its theological significance (13-17).

3, 2: *Reform your lives!:* on the notion of repentance, see note on Acts 2, 38. *The reign of God is at hand:* literally, "the kingdom of heaven." "Heaven" is a conventional expression which avoids using the divine name. The term invokes God's sovereign authority over the human race. It announces that a new intervention of God is beginning in history which invites Israel to accept the prophetic manifestation of his will through the Baptizer.

3, 4: The Baptizer's garb recalls that of Elijah in 2 Kgs 1, 8: Jesus speaks of the Baptizer as Elijah who *has already come* (Mt 17, 10ff; Mk 9, 10ff); cf Mal 3, 24.

3, 7-10: John's criticism of the Pharisees and Sadducees implies that they have come to receive baptism for the purpose of gaining popular favor rather than to exercise their religious leadership in a national program of true reform. Matthew sees the Christian community to be the true *children* of *Abraham* who fulfill the Baptizer's prophetic words (v 10).

3, 11f: The baptism of John prepares for the purifying action *in the Holy Spirit and fire* which Jesus will effect; cf Is 1, 25; Zec 13, 9; Mal 3, 2. Refusal of this baptism of Jesus leads to a final judgment of condemnation *in unquenchable fire;* cf Is 34, 8ff; Jer 7, 20.

✿
  15: Hos 11, 1.
  18: Jer 31, 15.
  20: Ex 4, 19.
  23: 13, 54; Lk 2, 39;
      4, 34; Jn 19, 19.
3/1-12: Mk 1, 2-8; Lk 3, 2-17.
  2: 4, 17; 10, 7; Acts 2, 38.
  3: Is 40, 3.
  4: 11, 7f; Zec 13, 4.

  6: 21, 25.
  7: 12, 34; 23, 33; Is 59, 5.
  9: Jn 8, 33.39; Rom 9, 7f;
     Gal 4, 21-31.
  11: Jn 1, 15.24-27.33;
      Acts 1, 5.
  12: 13, 42.50; Is 41, 16;
      Jer 15, 7.

threshing floor and gather his grain into the barn, but the chaff he will burn in unquenchable fire."

The Baptism of Jesus

13***†**Later Jesus, coming from Galilee, appeared before John at the Jordan to be baptized by him. **14**John tried to refuse him with the protest, "I should be baptized by you, yet you come to me!" **15**Jesus answered: "Give in for now. We must do this if we would fulfill all of God's demands." So John gave in. **16***After Jesus was baptized, he came directly out of the water. Suddenly the sky opened and he saw the Spirit of God descend like a dove and hover over him. **17***With that, a voice from the heavens said, "This is my beloved Son. My favor rests on him."

The Temptation

4 **1*****†**THEN Jesus was led into the desert by the Spirit to be tempted by the devil. **2***He fasted forty days and forty nights, and afterward was hungry. **3**†The tempter approached and said to him, "If you are the Son of God, command these stones to turn into bread." **4***†Jesus replied, "Scripture has it:

> 'Not on bread alone is man to live
> but on every utterance that comes from the
> mouth of God.'"

5Next the devil took him to the holy city, set him on the parapet of the temple, **6***†and said, "If you are the Son of God, throw yourself down. Scripture has it:

> 'He will bid his angels take care of you;
> with their hands they will support you
> that you may never stumble on a stone.'"

7*Jesus answered him, "Scripture also has it:

> 'You shall not put the Lord your God to the
> test.'"

8The devil then took him up a very high mountain and displayed before him all the kingdoms of the world in their magnificence, **9***promising, "All these will I bestow on you if you prostrate yourself in homage before me." **10***†At this, Jesus said to him, "Away with you, Satan! Scripture has it:

> 'You shall do homage to the Lord your God;
> him alone shall you adore.'"

11At that the devil left him, and angels came and waited on him.

Jesus in Capernaum

12*†When Jesus heard that John had been arrested, he withdrew to Galilee. **13***He left Nazareth and went down to live in Capernaum by the sea near the territory of Zebulun and Naphtali, **14**to fulfill what had been said through Isaiah the prophet:

15*"Land of Zebulun, land of Naphtali
along the sea beyond the Jordan,
heathen Galilee:
16*a people living in darkness
has seen a great light.
On those who inhabit a land overshadowed by
death,
light has arisen."

17*†From that time on Jesus began to proclaim this theme: "Reform your lives! The kingdom of heaven is at hand."

The First Disciples Called

18*As he was walking along the Sea of Galilee he watched two brothers, Simon now known as Peter, and his brother Andrew, casting a net into the sea. They were fishermen. **19**†He said to them, "Come after me and I will make you fishers of men." **20**They immediately abandoned their nets and became his followers. **21**He walked along farther and caught sight of two other brothers, James, Zebedee's son, and his brother John. They too were in their boat, getting their nets in order with their father, Zebedee. **22**He called them, and immediately they abandoned boat and father to follow him.

---

† 3, 13-17: For the theological significance of this account of Jesus' baptism, see note on Mk 1, 9ff.

4, 1-11: An introduction to the gospel proper; see note on Mk 1, 12f. Some regard the account as a Christian reflection on Jesus' messianic role: he refuses to use his miraculous power simply to relieve human need (3f), or to satisfy requests of unbelievers (5ff); he disdains a messianic role (8ff) that would be purely political in its implications. The central theme is the obedience of Jesus to God as he is known through the Old Testament.

4, 3: *If you are the Son of God:* in the sense of the messianic king of Ps 2.

4, 4: A citation of Dt 8, 3, signifying that the miracles of the Exodus were signs of God's religious, rather than physical, care of Israel.

4, 6f: The tempter here applies to the Messiah verse 11 of Psalm 91 dealing with God's protection of the just. Jesus' reply (Dt 6, 16) teaches that miracles are not to be demanded of God as evidence of his care of man.

4, 10: The citation expresses the basic attitude of worship which every man should have toward God.

4, 12-17: The gospel proper begins here with a summary introduction to the Galilean ministry: the Baptizer is arrested by Herod Antipas (12); Jesus makes Capernaum the center of his activity (13) and preaching (17). The citation from Is 9, 1f identifies the ministry of Jesus as fulfilling the prophecy of the restoration of the northern kingdom, destroyed by the Assyrians in 721 B. C.

4, 17: See note on 3, 2.

4, 19: To be *fishers of men* requires abandonment of former means of livelihood in order to preach the kingdom of God and testify to its arrival in the name of Jesus; cf 10, 1f. It may be assumed that this complete dedication was accomplished only gradually.

---

*
13-17: Mk 1, 9-11; Lk 3, 21f; Jn 1, 31-34.	7: Dt 6, 16.
16: Is 11, 2.	9: 16, 23.
17: 12, 18; 17, 5; Is 42, 1; 49, 3.	10: Dt 6, 13.
4/1-11: Mk 1, 12f; Lk 4, 1-13.	12f: Mk 1, 14f; Lk 4, 14.31.
1: Heb 2, 18.	13: Jn 2, 12.
2: Ex 24, 18; 34, 28.	15f: Is 9, 1f.
4: Dt 8, 3.	16: Jn 8, 12.
6: Ps 91, 11f.	17: 3, 2; Lk 17, 20.
	18-22: Mk 1, 16-20; Lk 5, 1-11.

The Mission of Preaching

23* Jesus toured all of Galilee. He taught in their synagogues, proclaimed the good news of the kingdom, and cured the people of every disease and illness. **24** As a consequence of this, his reputation traveled the length of Syria. They carried to him all those afflicted with various diseases and racked with pain: the possessed, the lunatics, the paralyzed. He cured them all. **25*** The great crowds that followed him came from Galilee, the Ten Cities, Jerusalem and Judea, and from across the Jordan.

5 ¹WHEN he saw the crowds he went up on the mountain-side. After he had sat down his disciples gathered around him, ²and he began to teach them:

The Beatitudes

3* "How blest are the poor in spirit: the reign of God is theirs.

4* Blest too are the sorrowing; they shall be consoled.

5* [Blest are the lowly; they shall inherit the land.]

6* Blest are they who hunger and thirst for holiness;
they shall have their fill.

7† Blest are they who show mercy; mercy shall be theirs.

8*† Blest are the single-hearted for they shall see God.

9† Blest too the peacemakers; they shall be called sons of God.

10*† Blest are those persecuted for holiness' sake; the reign of God is theirs.

11* Blest are you when they insult you and persecute you and utter every kind of slander against you because of me.

12* Be glad and rejoice, for your reward is great in heaven;
they persecuted the prophets before you in the very same way.

The Disciples

13*† "You are the salt of the earth. But what if salt goes flat? How can you restore its flavor? Then it is good for nothing but to be thrown out and trampled underfoot.

14* "You are the light of the world. A city set on a hill cannot be hidden. **15*** Men do not light a lamp and then put it under a bushel basket. They set it on a stand where it gives light to all in the house. **16*** In the same way, your light must shine before men so that they may see goodness in your acts and give praise to your heavenly Father.

The Old Law and the New

17*† "Do not think that I have come to abolish the law and the prophets. I have come, not to abolish them, but to fulfill them. **18*** Of this much I assure you: until heaven and earth pass away, not the smallest letter of the law, not the smallest part of a letter, shall be done away with until it all comes true. **19*** That is why whoever breaks the least significant of these commands and teaches others to do so shall be called least in the kingdom of God. Whoever fulfills and teaches these commands shall be great in the kingdom of God. **20*** I tell you, unless your holiness surpasses that of the scribes and Pharisees you shall not enter the kingdom of God.

Against Anger

21* "You have heard the commandment imposed on your forefathers, 'You shall not commit murder; every

---

† 5, 3-12: The beatitudes announce religious happiness for the *anawim*, i. e., those who lack material goods and stand in need of the spiritual blessings promised by God; cf Dt 24, 14; Ps 37, 14; 40, 18; Is 61, 1. This happiness is to reach its fulfillment through Christ. Recognition of the *anawim* contrasts with the religious thought of the time which regarded human affliction and sorrow as the punishment of personal sin. For the Christian attitude toward the poor and afflicted, cf Mt 25, 34-46; Jas 2, 15f; 1 Jn 4, 20.

5, 7: Matthew fashions the Sermon on the Mount from the sayings of Jesus concerning Moses and the law. Luke's corresponding Sermon on the Plain (6, 17-49) is differently arranged. A key factor is that Jesus came not to abolish but to fulfill the law and the prophets. Jesus makes greater demands on men than did the law of Moses; but he bestows the justice needed for meeting these demands (Rom 8, 1-11), and his disciples are bound to respond to the divine gift (5, 20; 7, 21.24-27). Though concerned with the relationship between God and the individual, the social implications of the Sermon on the Mount are evident.

5, 8: *The single-hearted:* those who serve God loyally for his own sake and not primarily out of self-interest.

5, 9: *The peacemakers:* those whose lives promote harmony within the human community (1 Thes 5, 14) as contrasted with those who foster strife through violence for personal advantage.

5, 10: *For holiness' sake:* fidelity to the divine precepts through which holiness is attained is deepened by the test of persecution.

5, 13-16: The disciples of Jesus, despite reproach and persecution (11f), make the human community valuable in God's eyes (*salt of the earth*) and enlighten the world with *the light* of God's prophetic word, which they preach by word and example (16).

5, 17-20: Jesus' teaching does not reject the old law and the prophets; instead, it illumines the meaning God intended the Old Testament ultimately to have (17). Disregard of even the slightest detail of the law means failure to secure that fullness of the kingdom of God (19) which those achieve who both teach and fulfill the law. In contrast, the false justice of the Pharisees, their lack of true interior holiness, will exclude them from the kingdom (20).

✻
23: 9, 35; Mk 1, 39; Lk 4, 15.44.
25: Mk 3, 7; Lk 6, 17-19.
5/3-12: Lk 6, 20-23.
3: 19, 21.29; 2, Cor 3, 9.
4: Ps 126, 5; Is 61, 2f; Rv 21, 4.
5: Gn 13, 15; Ps 37, 11; Prv 2, 21.
6: Prv 21, 21.
8: Pss 24, 4f; 73, 1; Prv 22, 11.
10: 1 Pt 2, 20; 3, 14; 4, 14.
11: Acts 5, 41.
12: Phil 1, 29; Col 1, 24; Jas 1, 2.
13: Mk 9, 49; Lk 14, 34f.
14: Jn 8, 12.
15: Mk 4, 21; Lk 8, 16; 11, 33.
16: Jn 3, 21.
17: Rom 3, 31.
18: Lk 16, 17.
19: Jas 2, 10.
20: Rom 10, 3.
21: Ex 20, 13; Dt 5, 17.

murderer shall be liable to judgment.' **22*** What I say to you is: everyone who grows angry with his brother shall be liable to judgment; any man who uses abusive language toward his brother shall be answerable to the Sanhedrin, and if he holds him in contempt he risks the fires of Gehenna. **23*** If you bring your gift to the altar and there recall that your brother has anything against you, **24** leave your gift at the altar, go first to be reconciled with your brother, and then come and offer your gift. **25*** Lose no time; settle with your opponent while on your way to court with him. Otherwise your opponent may hand you over to the judge, who will hand you over to the guard, who will throw you into prison. **26** I warn you, you will not be released until you have paid the last penny.

Occasions of Impurity

27*† "You have heard the commandment, 'You shall not commit adultery.'" **28*** What I say to you is: anyone who looks lustfully at a woman has already committed adultery with her in his thoughts. **29*** If your right eye is your trouble, gouge it out and throw it away! Better to lose part of your body than to have it all cast into Gehenna. **30** Again, if your right hand is your trouble, cut it off and throw it away! Better to lose part of your body than to have it all cast into Gehenna.

Divorce

31* "It was also said, 'Whenever a man divorces his wife, he must give her a decree of divorce.'" **32*** What I say to you is: everyone who divorces his wife—lewd conduct is a separate case—forces her to commit adultery. The man who marries a divorced woman likewise commits adultery.

On Oaths

33*† "You have heard the commandment imposed on your forefathers, 'Do not take a false oath; rather, make good to the Lord all your pledges.' **34*** What I tell you is: do not swear at all. Do not swear by heaven (it is God's throne), **35*** nor by the earth (it is his footstool), nor by Jerusalem (it is the city of the great King); **36** do not swear by your head (you cannot make a single hair white or black). **37*** Say, 'Yes' when you mean 'Yes' and 'No' when you mean 'No.' Anything beyond that is from the evil one.

New Law of Retaliation

38* "You have heard the commandment, 'An eye for an eye; a tooth for a tooth.' **39*** But what I say to you is:

offer no resistance to injury. When a person strikes you on the right cheek, turn and offer him the other. **40** If anyone wants to go to law over your shirt, hand him your coat as well. **41*** Should anyone press you into service for one mile, go with him two miles. **42*** Give to the man who begs from you. Do not turn your back on the borrower.

Love of Enemies

43*† "You have heard the commandment, 'You shall love your countryman but hate your enemy.' **44** My command to you is: love your enemies, pray for your persecutors. **45** This will prove that you are sons of your heavenly Father, for his sun rises on the bad and the good, he rains on the just and the unjust. **46*** If you love those who love you, what merit is there in that? Do not tax collectors do as much? **47** And if you greet your brothers only, what is so praiseworthy about that? Do not pagans do as much? **48***† In a word, you must be made perfect as your heavenly Father is perfect.

Purity of Intention

6 **1***† "BE on guard against performing religious acts for people to see. Otherwise expect no recompense from your heavenly Father. **2*** When you give alms, for example, do not blow a horn before you in synagogues and streets like hypocrites looking for applause. You can be sure of this much, they are already repaid. **3** In giving alms you are not to let your left hand know what your right hand is doing. **4** Keep your deeds of mercy secret, and your Father who sees in secret will repay you.

Prayer

5 "When you are praying, do not behave like the hypocrites who love to stand and pray in synagogues or on street corners in order to be noticed. I give you my word, they are already repaid. **6*** Whenever you pray, go to your room, close your door, and pray to your Father in private. Then your Father, who sees what no man sees, will repay you. **7** In your prayer do

---

† 5, 27-32: Women are to be accorded the respect due to their persons as children of the same God as men. The deeper implications of the divine law are seen to prohibit, not merely indecent actions against the religious dignity of the human person, but impure thoughts and desires as well. Jesus here repudiates the norm contained in Dt 24, 1 which allows a husband to dismiss his wife with a written decree of divorce for the purpose of remarriage. See note on Mt 19, 3-8.

5, 33-37: In the ordinary conduct of human affairs, personal trustworthiness should be such that the invocation of the divine name as evidence of truth is altogether unnecessary.

5, 43-48: As God invites the unjust to respond to him through the evidence of his love, so the disciples of Jesus must be the bearers of the same love toward their enemies.

5, 48: The perfection of the Father is revealed in his redemptive love of mankind, cf Jn 3, 16; 1 Jn 4, 9ff. For an application of the principle, cf 1 Cor 8, 7-11.

6, 1-6.16ff: To be of value in the eyes of God, religious duties, public and private, must be performed for the single-hearted purpose of serving God, and not for human esteem.

*
22: Jas 1, 19f; 3, 6.	38: Ex 21, 24; Lv 24, 19f.
23: Sir 28, 2; Mk 11, 25.	39-48: Lk 6, 27-36.
25: Prv 17, 14; Lk 12, 58f.	41: Lam 3, 30;
27: Ex 20, 14; Dt 5, 18.	Rom 12, 19ff.
28: Sir 9, 5.	42: Dt 15, 7f.
29: 18, 8f; Mk 9, 42.46.	43: Lv 19, 18.
31: 19, 3-9; Dt 24, 1;	46: Lk 6, 32.
Mal 2, 14ff.	48: Lv 11, 44; 19, 2;
32: Lk 16, 18; 1 Cor 7, 10.	Jas 1, 4; 1 Pt 1, 16;
33: Lv 19, 12; Nm 30, 3.	1 Jn 3, 3.
34: Ps 11, 4; Sir 23, 9.	6/1: 23, 5; Lk 16, 15.
35: Is 66, 1.	2: Jn 12, 43.
37: Jas 5, 12.	6: Tb 3, 10f; Dn 6, 11.

not rattle on like the pagans. They think they will win a hearing by the sheer multiplication of words. [8]Do not imitate them. Your Father knows what you need before you ask him. [9]*This is how you are to pray:

'Our Father in heaven,
    hallowed be your name,
[10]*your kingdom come,
    your will be done
    on earth as it is in heaven.
[11]*Give us today our daily bread,
[12]*and forgive us the wrong we have done
    as we forgive those who wrong us.
[13]*Subject us not to the trial
    but deliver us from the evil one.'

[14]*"If you forgive the faults of others, your heavenly Father will forgive you yours. [15]*If you do not forgive others, neither will your Father forgive you.

Fasting

[16]"When you fast, you are not to look glum as the hypocrites do. They change the appearance of their faces so that others may see they are fasting. I assure you, they are already repaid. [17]When you fast, see to it that you groom your hair and wash your face. [18]In that way no one can see you are fasting but your Father who is hidden; and your Father who sees what is hidden will repay you.

True Riches

[19]*†"Do not lay up for yourselves an earthly treasure. Moths and rust corrode; thieves break in and steal. [20]*Make it your practice instead to store up heavenly treasure, which neither moths nor rust corrode nor thieves break in and steal. [21]Remember, where your treasure is, there your heart is also. [22]*†The eye is the body's lamp. If your eyes are good, your body will be filled with light; [23]if your eyes are bad, your body will be in darkness. And if your light is darkness, how deep will the darkness be! [24]*No man can serve two masters. He will either hate one and love the other or be attentive to one and despise the other. You cannot give yourself to God and money. [25]*I warn you, then: do not worry about your livelihood, what you are to eat or drink or use for clothing. Is not life more than food? Is not the body more valuable than clothes?

[26]*"Look at the birds in the sky. They do not sow or reap, they gather nothing into barns; yet your heavenly Father feeds them. Are not you more im-

portant than they? [27]Which of you by worrying can add a moment to his life-span? [28]As for clothes, why be concerned? Learn a lesson from the way the wild flowers grow. They do not work; they do not spin. [29]Yet I assure you, not even Solomon in all his splendor was arrayed like one of these. [30]If God can clothe in such splendor the grass of the field, which blooms today and is thrown on the fire tomorrow, will he not provide much more for you, O weak in faith! [31]Stop worrying, then, over questions like, 'What are we to eat, or what are we to drink, or what are we to wear?' [32]The unbelievers are always running after these things. Your heavenly Father knows all that you need. [33]*Seek first his kingship over you, his way of holiness, and all these things will be given you besides. [34]Enough, then, of worrying about tomorrow. Let tomorrow take care of itself. Today has troubles enough of its own.

Avoiding Judgment

7 [1]*†"IF you want to avoid judgment, stop passing judgment. [2]*Your verdict on others will be the verdict passed on you. The measure with which you measure will be used to measure you. [3]Why look at the speck in your brother's eye when you miss the plank in your own? [4]How can you say to your brother, 'Let me take that speck out of your eye,' while all the time the plank remains in your own? [5]You hypocrite! Remove the plank from your own eye first; then you will see clearly to take the speck from your brother's eye.

[6]*†"Do not give what is holy to dogs or toss your pearls before swine. They will trample them under foot, at best, and perhaps even tear you to shreds.

The Power of Prayer

[7]*†"Ask, and you will receive. Seek, and you will find. Knock, and it will be opened to you. [8]*For the one who asks, receives. The one who seeks, finds. The one who knocks, enters. [9]Would one of you hand his son a stone when he asks for a loaf, [10]or a poisonous snake when he asks for a fish? [11]*If you, with all your sins, know how to give your children what is good, how much more will your heavenly Father give good things to anyone who asks him!

---

†

6, 19ff: A concluding parable to confirm Jesus' teaching on the true service of God; recompense for good works is to be expected from him alone.

6, 22f: A person with proper vision can easily direct the movements of his body. In a similar way, one who makes use of the prophetic vision of Christ can direct his way to God.

7, 1-5: Judgments of condemnation upon one's neighbor and refusal to pardon him entail loss of God's pardon for one's own sins.

7, 6: The teaching of the gospel will be rejected by some precisely because it is holy, and those who teach it will themselves be subjected to attack.

7, 7-11: The persevering prayer of sinful humanity receives a divine response because of the generosity of God.

✱
9: Lk 11, 2ff; Jn 17, 26.   24: Lk 16, 13.
10: Mt 26, 42.   25-33: Lk 12, 22-31.
11: Prv 30, 8f;   26: Pss 145, 15f; 147, 9.
    Jn 6, 32.35.   33: Wis 1, 1.
12: 18, 21f; Sir 28, 2.   7/1: Rom 2, 1f; 1 Cor 4, 5.
13: Jn 17, 15;   2: Wis 12, 22; Mk 4, 24.
    2 Thes 3, 3.   4: Jn 8, 7.
14: 18, 35; Sir 28, 1-5;   6: Prv 23, 9.
    Mk 11, 25.   7-11: Mk 11, 24;
15: Jas 2, 13.   Lk 11, 9-13.
19: Lk 12, 33.   7: 18, 19.
20: Jas 5, 2f.   8: Lk 18, 1-8; Jn 14, 13.
22f: Lk 11, 34ff.   11: 1 Jn 5, 14f.

The Golden Rule

12✱†"Treat others the way you would have them treat you: this sums up the law and the prophets.

13✱†"Enter through the narrow gate. The gate that leads to damnation is wide, the road is clear, and many choose to travel it. **14**But how narrow is the gate that leads to life, how rough the road, and how few there are who find it!

15✱"Be on your guard against false prophets, who come to you in sheep's clothing but underneath are wolves on the prowl. **16**✱You will know them by their deeds. Do you ever pick grapes from thornbushes, or figs from prickly plants? Never! **17**Any sound tree bears good fruit, while a decayed tree bears bad fruit. **18**✱A sound tree cannot bear bad fruit any more than a decayed tree can bear good fruit. **19**✱Every tree that does not bear good fruit is cut down and thrown into the fire. **20**You can tell a tree by its fruit. **21**✱None of those who cry out, 'Lord, Lord,' will enter the kingdom of God but only the one who does the will of my Father in heaven. **22**✱When that day comes, many will plead with me, 'Lord, Lord, have we not prophesied in your name? Have we not exorcised demons by its power? Did we not do many miracles in your name as well?' **23**✱Then I will declare to them solemnly, 'I never knew you. Out of my sight, you evildoers!'

Conclusion of the Sermon

24✱"Anyone who hears my words and puts them into practice is like the wise man who built his house on rock. **25**✱When the rainy season set in, the torrents came and the winds blew and buffeted his house. It did not collapse; it had been solidly set on rock. **26**Anyone who hears my words but does not put them into practice is like the foolish man who built his house on sandy ground. **27**The rains fell, the torrents came, the winds blew and lashed against his house. It collapsed under all this and was completely ruined."

28†Jesus finished this discourse and left the crowds spellbound at his teaching. **29**✱†The reason was that he taught with authority and not like their scribes.

III: PREACHING THE REIGN OF GOD

The Leper

8 **1**✱WHEN HE CAME DOWN from the mountain, great crowds followed him. **2**Suddenly a leper came forward and did him homage, saying to him,

"Sir, if you will to do so, you can cure me." **3**Jesus stretched out his hand and touched him and said, "I do will it. Be cured." Immediately the man's leprosy disappeared. **4**✱†Then Jesus said to him: "See to it that you tell no one. Go and show yourself to the priest and offer the gift Moses prescribed. That should be the proof they need."

The Centurion's Servant

5✱As Jesus entered Capernaum, a centurion approached him with this request: **6**"Sir, my serving boy is at home in bed paralyzed, suffering painfully." **7**He said to him, "I will come and cure him." **8**"Sir," the centurion said in reply, "I am not worthy to have you under my roof. Just give an order and my boy will get better. **9**I am a man under authority myself and I have troops assigned to me. If I give one man the order, 'Dismissed,' off he goes. If I say to another, 'Come here,' he comes. If I tell my slave, 'Do this,' he does it." **10**†Jesus showed amazement on hearing this and remarked to his followers, "I assure you, I have never found this much faith in Israel. **11**✱Mark what I say! Many will come from the east and the west and will find a place at the banquet in the kingdom of God with Abraham, Isaac, and Jacob, **12**while the natural heirs of the kingdom will be driven out into the dark. Wailing will be heard there, and the grinding of teeth." **13**To the centurion Jesus said, "Go home. It shall be done because you trusted." That very moment the boy got better.

Peter's Mother-in-law

14✱Jesus entered Peter's house and found Peter's mother-in-law in bed with a fever. **15**✱He took her by the hand and the fever left her. She got up at once and began to wait on him.

Other Miracles

16As evening drew on, they brought him many who were possessed. He expelled the spirits by a simple

---

† 7, 12: An isolated saying introduced to show that the moral teaching concerning neighbor in the reign of God is the golden rule of true fraternal charity.

7, 13-27: A series of parables warning that only through the good works outlined in the Sermon does man find the way of life that leads to the happiness God has in store for him.

7, 28: A general formula used in Matthew at the conclusion of the five collections of the sayings of Jesus (11, 1; 13, 53; 19, 1; 26, 1).

7, 29—9, 38: By means of miracle narratives and other events, Matthew portrays Jesus' unique power in word and action. Jesus uses the twofold charism of miracles and prophecy in behalf of the people to invite them to accept the new sovereign rule of God which he proclaims (8, 16-22; 9, 13.36). The miracle accounts appear in groups of three (8, 1-15; 8, 23—9, 8; 9, 18-34). Other incidents and comments are interspersed between these groupings.

8, 4: See note on Mk 1, 40-45.

8, 10ff: The great trust of the centurion consisted in his honest acceptance of the religious authority of Jesus, displayed in curing the sick. Jesus' comment invites his contemporaries to match the centurion's trust.

✱
12: Lk 6, 31; Rom 13, 8.
13: Sir 21, 10; Lk 13, 24.
15: 2 Pt 2, 1.
16f: 12, 33; Sir 27, 6; Lk 6, 43f.
18: Jn 15, 6.
19: 3, 10.
21: Is 29, 13.
22: 25, 11f; Jas 2, 14-17.
23: Ps 5, 5.
24-27: Lk 6, 47ff.
25: Prv 10, 25.
29: Mk 1, 22; Lk 4, 32; Jn 7, 15ff.
8/1-4: Mk 1, 40-44; Lk 5, 12ff.
4: Lv 14, 2f; Lk 17, 14.
5-13: Lk 7, 1-10.
11f: 22, 13; 24, 51; 25, 30; Lk 13, 28f.
14ff: Mk 1, 29-34; Lk 4, 38-41.
15: 9, 25.

command and cured all who were afflicted, **17**⚹†thereby fulfilling what had been said through Isaiah the prophet:

> "It was our infirmities he bore,
> our sufferings he endured."

Conditions for Following Jesus

18Seeing the people crowd around him, Jesus gave orders to cross to the other shore. **19**⚹A scribe approached him and said, "Teacher, wherever you go I will come after you." **20**†Jesus said to him, "The foxes have lairs, the birds in the sky have nests, but the Son of Man has nowhere to lay his head." **21**Another, a disciple, said to him, "Lord, let me go and bury my father first." **22**†But Jesus told him, "Follow me, and let the dead bury their dead."

Storm on the Lake

23⚹He got into the boat and his disciples followed him. **24**Without warning a violent storm came up on the lake, and the boat began to be swamped by the waves. **25**Jesus was sleeping soundly, so they made their way toward him and woke him: "Lord, save us! We are lost!" **26**⚹He said to them: "Where is your courage? How little faith you have!" Then he stood up and took the winds and the sea to task. Complete calm ensued; **27**the men were dumbfounded. "What sort of man is this," they said, "that even the winds and the sea obey him?"

Expulsion of the Demons in Gadara

28⚹As he approached the Gadarene boundary, he encountered two men coming out of the tombs. They were possessed by demons and were so savage that no one could travel along that road. **29**†With a sudden shriek they cried: "Why meddle with us, Son of God? Have you come to torture us before the appointed time?" **30**Some distance away a large herd of swine was feeding. **31**⚹The demons kept appealing to him, "If you expel us, send us into the herd of swine." **32**He answered, "Out with you!" At that they came forth and entered the swine. The whole herd went rushing down the bluff into the sea and were drowned.

33The swineherds took to their heels, and upon their arrival in the town related everything that had happened, including the story about the two possessed men. **34**The upshot was that the entire town came out to meet Jesus. When they caught sight of him, they begged him to leave their neighborhood.

A Paralytic at Capernaum

9 **1**⚹THEN he reentered the boat, made the crossing, and came back to his own town. **2**⚹There the people at once brought to him a paralyzed man lying on a mat. When Jesus saw their faith he said to the paralytic, "Have courage, son, your sins are forgiven." **3**At that some of the scribes said to themselves, "The man blasphemes." **4**Jesus was aware of what they were thinking and said: "Why do you harbor evil thoughts? **5**Which is less trouble to say, 'Your sins are forgiven' or 'Stand up and walk'? **6**⚹To help you realize that the Son of Man has authority on earth to forgive sins"—he then said to the paralyzed man—"Stand up! Roll up your mat, and go home." **7**⚹The man stood up and went toward his home. **8**†At the sight, a feeling of awe came over the crowd, and they praised God for giving such authority to men.

Call of Matthew

9⚹As he moved on, Jesus saw a man named Matthew at his post where taxes were collected. He said to him,

---

†

8, 17: Matthew sees in Jesus the true servant of Yahweh (Is 53, 4), whose miraculous healings are the external sign of the redemption which Jesus was now accomplishing as *he bore,* i. e., "took upon himself," *our infirmities,* i. e., "our sins," to free us from them.

8, 20: *Son of Man:* an enigmatic title of Christ used in the gospels and in Acts 7, 56. Jesus is reported as using it frequently of himself; it was well adapted to his purpose of both veiling and revealing his person and mission. On the one hand, it simply meant "man" (Ez 2, 1) and emphasized the lowliness of the human condition (Mt 8, 20; 11, 19; 20, 28), especially in Christ's humiliation and death (17, 22). On the other hand, it expressed the triumph of Jesus' resurrection (17, 9), his return to glory (24, 30; Dn 7, 13), and his second coming as judge of the world (25, 31).

At his trial before the Sanhedrin, Jesus is described as using the title *Son of Man* in a well-defined religious sense (26, 64). Though he stood before his accusers an innocent victim, charged with blasphemy and condemned to die, he prophesied his vindication and future glory, *seated at the right hand of the Power,* i. e., God, not merely as man but as Lord (Dn 7, 13; Mk 14, 62).

Jewish apocalyptic literature (1 Enoch, 2 Ezra, 2 Baruch) employed the title to describe a unique religious personage endowed with extraordinary spiritual power, who would receive the kingdom from God at the end of time. Early Christian communities held this title in reverence because it reminded them of Jesus' awareness of his double destiny, of humiliation and of glory, in which the Christian community also shares (Mt 24, 30f).

8, 22: Jesus has subordinated family ties to the needs of his mission of salvation (8, 20). He requires the same sacrifice of those called to share this mission with him, when other members of the family can perform the deeds of filial piety. These latter are *dead* only in the sense that they have not received the divine call to separate themselves from family responsibility in order to preach the gospel of the kingdom. They can, however, be Jesus' disciples in another sense.

8, 29: *Son of God:* see note on Mk 3, 12. *Before the appointed time:* a phrase peculiar to Matthew in this account. Even in pagan territory the demons already feel the threat of Jesus before the destruction of Satan's power at the end of the world (1 Cor 15, 24f).

9, 8: *Such authority to men:* the principal issue of Jesus' authority here is the power to forgive sins. Matthew's use of the

---

⚹

17: Is 53, 4.
19-22: Lk 9, 57-60.
23-27: Mk 4, 35-40;
      Lk 8, 22-25.
26: Ps 107, 29.
28-34: Mk 5, 1-17;
      Lk 8, 26-37.
31: Lk 4, 34ff;
      Acts 10, 38.

9/1-8: Mk 2, 3-12;
      Lk 5, 18-26.
2: Lk 7, 48.
6: Jn 5, 27.
7: Jn 5, 8f.
9-13: Mk 2, 14-17;
      Lk 5, 27-32.

"Follow me." Matthew got up and followed him. **10***Now it happened that, while Jesus was at table in Matthew's home, many tax collectors and those known as sinners came to join Jesus and his disciples at dinner. **11**The Pharisees saw this and complained to his disciples, "What reason can the Teacher have for eating with tax collectors and those who disregard the law?" **12**Overhearing the remark, he said: "People who are in good health do not need a doctor; sick people do. **13***†Go and learn the meaning of the words, 'It is mercy I desire and not sacrifice.' I have come to call, not the self-righteous, but sinners."

The Question of Fasting

14*†Later on, John's disciples came to him with the objection, "Why is it that while we and the Pharisees fast, your disciples do not?" **15**Jesus said to them: "How can wedding guests go in mourning so long as the groom is with them? When the day comes that the groom is taken away, then they will fast. **16*** Nobody sews a piece of unshrunken cloth on an old cloak; the very thing he has used to cover the hole will pull, and the rip only get worse. **17**People do not pour new wine into old wineskins. If they do, the skins burst, the wine spills out, and the skins are ruined. No, they pour new wine into new wineskins, and in that way both are preserved."

A Dead Girl; a Woman with a Hemorrhage

18*†Before Jesus had finished speaking to them, a synagogue leader came up, did him reverence, and said: "My daughter has just died. Please come and lay your hand on her and she will come back to life." **19**Jesus stood up and followed him, and his disciples did the same. **20**As they were going, a woman who had suffered from hemorrhages for twelve years came up behind him and touched the tassel on his cloak. **21***"If only I can touch his cloak," she thought, "I shall get well." **22**Jesus turned around and saw her and said, "Courage, daughter! Your faith has restored you to health." That very moment the woman got well.

23When Jesus arrived at the synagogue leader's house and saw the flute players and the crowd who were making a din, he said, **24**"Leave, all of you! The little girl is not dead. She is asleep." At this they began to ridicule him. **25**When the crowd had been put out he entered and took her by the hand, and the little girl got up. **26**News of this circulated throughout the district.

Two Blind Men

27*†As Jesus moved on from there, two blind men came after him crying out, "Son of David, have pity on us!" **28**When he got to the house, the blind men caught up with him. Jesus said to them, "Are you confident I can do this?" "Yes, Lord," they told him. **29**At that he touched their eyes and said, "Because of your faith it shall be done to you"; **30**and they recovered their sight. Then Jesus warned them sternly, "See to it that no one knows of this." **31**But they went off and spread word of him through the whole area.

A Possessed Mute

32*As they were leaving, suddenly some people brought him a mute who was possessed by a demon. **33***Once the demon was expelled the mute began to speak, to the great surprise of the crowds. "Nothing like this has ever been seen in Israel!" they exclaimed. **34***But the Pharisees were saying, "He casts out demons through the prince of demons."

Mission of the Twelve

35*†Jesus continued his tour of all the towns and villages. He taught in their synagogues, he proclaimed the good news of God's reign, and he cured every sickness and disease. **36***At the sight of the crowds, his heart was moved with pity. They were lying prostrate from exhaustion, like sheep without a shepherd. **37***He said to his disciples: "The harvest is good but laborers are scarce. **38**Beg the harvest master to send out laborers to gather his harvest."

10 ¹THEN he summoned his twelve disciples and gave them authority to expel unclean spirits and to cure sickness and disease of every kind.

2*†The names of the twelve apostles are these: first Simon, now known as Peter, and his brother Andrew; James, Zebedee's son, and his brother John; **3**Philip and Bartholomew, Thomas and Matthew the tax collector; James, son of Alphaeus, and Thaddaeus; **4**Simon the Zealot Party member, and Judas Iscariot, who be-

---

† plural *men* suggests the power of the Christian community to forgive sins in Jesus' name; cf Acts 2, 38; Jas 5, 16.

9, 13: Jesus' association with tax collectors and violators of the law is conformable to his teaching about the need of repentance (4, 17). He cites Hos 6, 6 to show that love of neighbor gives value to sacrifices offered as evidence of love of God.

9, 14-17: Jesus' presence among men during his public ministry is comparable to that of a bridegroom during the marriage feast. The time of fasting is temporarily set aside until after Jesus' death to bring about those changes in the human person required for assimilating the new doctrinal ideas.

9, 18-26: See note on Mk 5, 21-43.

9, 27-31: See note on Mk 10, 46-52.

9, 35—10, 1: Having preached and ministered widely in Galilee, Jesus sees the people's need for prophetic leadership; cf Nm 27, 17. He therefore expands his missionary activity by conferring his own powers on certain of his disciples.

10, 2-33: These verses, which conserve Jesus' instructions to his disciples for their missionary activity, constitute a norm for all Christian missioners. Certain of his prophecies are incorporated into the discourse because they reflected the church's experience (10, 17-21); cf 2 Cor 11, 23ff; Acts 5, 40; 24, 1-23.

---

*

10: 19, 1-10.	32ff: 12, 22ff; Lk 11, 14f.
13: 12, 7; Hos 6, 6.	33: Mk 7, 37.
14-17: Mk 2, 18-22;	34: 10, 25.
Lk 5, 33-39.	35: Lk 8, 1.
16: Rom 7, 6; 2 Cor 5, 17.	36: Jer 50, 6; Ez 34, 5;
18-26: Mk 5, 22-43;	Mk 6, 34.
Lk 8, 41-56.	37f: Lk 10, 2; Jn 4, 35.
21: 14, 36; Nm 15, 37;	10/2-5: Mk 3, 16-19;
Acts 19, 12.	Lk 6, 13-16; Acts 1, 13.
27: 15, 22.	

trayed him. ⁵Jesus sent these men on mission as the Twelve, after giving them the following instructions:

"Do not visit pagan territory and do not enter a Samaritan town. ⁶*Go instead after the lost sheep of the house of Israel. ⁷*As you go, make this announcement: 'The reign of God is at hand!' ⁸Cure the sick, raise the dead, heal the leprous, expel demons. The gift you have received, give as a gift. ⁹*Provide yourselves with neither gold nor silver nor copper in your belts; ¹⁰*no traveling bag, no change of shirt, no sandals, no walking staff. The workman, after all, is worth his keep.

¹¹*"Look for a worthy person in every town or village you come to and stay with him until you leave. ¹²†As you enter his home bless it. ¹³If the home is deserving, your blessing will descend on it. If it is not, your blessing will return to you. ¹⁴*If anyone does not receive you or listen to what you have to say, leave that house or town, and once outside it shake its dust from your feet. ¹⁵*I assure you, it will go easier for the region of Sodom and Gomorrah on the day of judgment than it will for that town.

¹⁶*"What I am doing is sending you out like sheep among wolves. You must be clever as snakes and innocent as doves. ¹⁷*Be on your guard with respect to others. They will hale you into court, they will flog you in their synagogues. ¹⁸*You will be brought to trial before rulers and kings, to give witness before them and before the Gentiles on my account. ¹⁹*When they hand you over, do not worry about what you will say or how you will say it. When the hour comes, you will be given what you are to say. ²⁰You yourselves will not be the speakers; the Spirit of your Father will be speaking in you.

²¹*"Brother will hand over brother to death, and the father his child; children will turn against parents and have them put to death. ²²You will be hated by all on account of me. But whoever holds out till the end will escape death. ²³†When they persecute you in one town, flee to the next. I solemnly assure you, you will not have covered the towns of Israel before the Son of Man comes.

²⁴*"No pupil outranks his teacher, no slave his master. ²⁵The pupil should be glad to become like his teacher, the slave like his master. If they call the head of the house Beelzebul, how much more the members of his household! ²⁶*Do not let them intimidate you.

Nothing is concealed that will not be revealed, and nothing hidden that will not become known. ²⁷What I tell you in darkness, speak in the light. What you hear in private, proclaim from the housetops.

²⁸*"Do not fear those who deprive the body of life but cannot destroy the soul. Rather, fear him who can destroy both body and soul in Gehenna. ²⁹Are not two sparrows sold for next to nothing? Yet not a single sparrow falls to the ground without your Father's consent. ³⁰As for you, every hair of your head has been counted; ³¹so do not be afraid of anything. You are worth more than an entire flock of sparrows. ³²*Whoever acknowledges me before men I will acknowledge before my Father in heaven. ³³*Whoever disowns me before men I will disown before my Father in heaven.

³⁴*"Do not suppose that my mission on earth is to spread peace. My mission is to spread, not peace, but division. ³⁵I have come to set a man at odds with his father, a daughter with her mother, a daughter-in-law with her mother-in-law: ³⁶in short, to make a man's enemies those of his own household. ³⁷*Whoever loves father or mother, son or daughter, more than me is not worthy of me. ³⁸He who will not take up his cross and come after me is not worthy of me. ³⁹*He who seeks only himself brings himself to ruin, whereas he who brings himself to nought for me discovers who he is.

⁴⁰*"He who welcomes you welcomes me, and he who welcomes me welcomes him who sent me. ⁴¹He who welcomes a prophet because he bears the name of prophet receives a prophet's reward; he who welcomes a holy man because he is known to be holy receives a holy man's reward. ⁴²*And I promise you that whoever gives a cup of cold water to one of these lowly ones because he is a disciple will not want for his reward."

11 ¹WHEN Jesus had finished instructing his twelve disciples, he left that locality to teach and preach in their towns.

IV: MYSTERY OF THE REIGN OF GOD

The Baptizer's Deputation

²*†NOW JOHN IN PRISON heard about the works Christ was performing, and sent a message by his

---

6: 15, 24.
7: 3, 2; 4, 17.
9: Mk 6, 8f; Lk 9, 3; 10, 4.
10: Lk 10, 7; 1 Cor 9, 14; 3 Jn 8.
11-15: Mk 6, 10f; Lk 9, 4f; 10, 5-12.
14: Acts 13, 51; 18, 6.
15: 11, 24; Jude 7.
16: Lk 10, 3; 1 Cor 14, 20.
17-22: Mk 13, 9-13; Lk 21, 12-19; Jn 16, 1-4.
17: Acts 5, 40.
18: Jn 15, 27.
19: Ex 4, 11f; Jer 1, 6-10; Lk 12, 11f.

21f: 24, 9.13.
24f: Lk 6, 40; Jn 13, 16; 15, 20.
26-33: Lk 12, 2-9.
26: Mk 4, 22; Lk 8, 17; 1 Tm 5, 25.
28: 1 Pt 3, 14; Rv 2, 10.
32: Lk 12, 8f.
33: Mk 8, 38; Lk 9, 26; 2 Tm 2, 12; Rv 3, 5.
34f: Lk 2, 34; 12, 51ff.
37ff: 16, 24f; Lk 14, 26f.
39: Mk 8, 35; Lk 9, 24; Lk 12, 25.
40: Lk 10, 16; Jn 12, 44; 13, 20.
42: 25, 40; Mk 9, 41.
11/2-11: Lk 7, 18-28.

---

† 10, 12f: The blessing referred to is a wish of peace. The blessing, once invoked, is considered to continue to exist. An undeserving household will not receive it; therefore it returns and benefits the one who uttered it.

10, 23: The missioners are not to risk their lives unnecessarily. *You will not have covered . . . the Son of Man comes:* Jesus implies, not that he expects the parousia (see note on 1 Thes 4, 13-18) and God's final judgment before the termination of his disciples' mission, but rather that the divine plan of Israel's salvation will not be completed before the parousia because of hostility.

11, 2—12, 50: Jesus' messianic role is questioned and rejected. John sends a query to Jesus about his role (11, 2-6).

disciples to ask him, ^{3†}"Are you 'He who is to come' or do we look for another?" ⁴In reply, Jesus said to them: "Go back and report to John what you hear and see: ^{5*}the blind recover their sight, cripples walk, lepers are curéd, the deaf hear, dead men are raised to life, and the poor have the good news preached to them. ⁶Blest is the man who finds no stumbling block in me."

Christ's Witness to John

^{7*†}As the messengers set off, Jesus began to speak to the crowds about John: "What did you go out to the wasteland to see—a reed swaying in the wind? ⁸Tell me, what did you go out to see—someone luxuriously dressed? Remember, those who dress luxuriously are to be found in royal palaces. ⁹Why then did you go out—to see a prophet? A prophet indeed, and something more! ^{10*}It is about this man that Scripture says,

'I send my messenger ahead of you
to prepare your way before you.'

^{11†}"I solemnly assure you, history has not known a man born of woman greater than John the Baptizer. Yet the least born into the kingdom of God is greater than he. ^{12*†}From John the Baptizer's time until now the kingdom of God has suffered violence, and the violent take it by force. ¹³All the prophets as well as the law spoke prophetically until John. ^{14*}If you are prepared to accept it, he is Elijah, the one who was certain to come. ¹⁵Heed carefully what you hear!

The Wayward Children

^{16*}"What comparison can I use to describe this breed? They are like children squatting in the town squares, calling to their playmates:

¹⁷'We piped you a tune but you did not dance!
We sang you a dirge but you did not wail!'

^{18*}In other words, John appeared neither eating nor drinking, and people say, 'He is mad!' ^{19*†}The Son of Man appeared eating and drinking, and they say, 'This one is a glutton and drunkard, a lover of tax collectors and those outside the law!' Yet time will prove where wisdom lies."

The Impenitent Towns

^{20*†}He began to reproach the towns where most of his miracles had been worked, with their failure to reform: ²¹It will go ill with you, Chorazin! And just as ill with you, Bethsaida! If the miracles worked in you had taken place in Tyre and Sidon, they would have reformed in sackcloth and ashes long ago. ²²I assure you, it will go easier for Tyre and Sidon than for you on the day of judgment. ^{23*}As for you, Capernaum,

'Are you to be exalted to the skies?
You shall go down to the realm of death!'

If the miracles worked in you had taken place in Sodom, it would be standing today. ^{24*}I assure you, it will go easier for Sodom than for you on the day of judgment."

Jesus and His Father

^{25*}On one occasion Jesus spoke thus: "Father, Lord of heaven and earth, to you I offer praise; for what you have hidden from the learned and the clever you have revealed to the merest children. ²⁶Father, it is true. You have graciously willed it so. ^{27*†}Everything has been given over to me by my Father. No one knows the Son but the Father, and no one knows the Father but the Son—and anyone to whom the Son wishes to reveal him.

^{28*†}"Come to me, all you who are weary and find life burdensome, and I will refresh you. ^{29†}Take my yoke upon your shoulders and learn from me, for I am

---

† Jesus himself comments on the resistance to his message in certain key cities of Galilee (11, 20-24). The scribes and Pharisees, and even Jesus' relatives, are hostile to him (12, 1-50).

11, 3: John is puzzled because Jesus continues to appeal for repentance rather than inflict final divine punishment on the unrepentant; cf Mt 3, 12.

11, 7-15: In this collection of sayings Jesus eulogizes the strength of John the Baptizer's religious convictions, the austerity of his life (7f), and his unique prophetic role as the messianic precursor (9-15).

11, 11: *Greater than he:* the disciples benefit from Jesus' prophetic light, which surpasses that of John.

11, 12: A highly enigmatic saying—probably so because of isolation from its original historical context. It contrasts Jesus' message of renewal through repentance and the faith that leads to admission into God's kingdom, with the false messianism of the "holy war" advocated, e. g., by the Zealots and the sectaries of Qumran.

11, 19: *Time will prove where wisdom lies:* neither the austere preaching and penance of John the Baptizer nor the gentle persuasion of Jesus elicits the good will of unbelievers. God's wisdom triumphs over them in the end.

11, 20-24: Sayings of Jesus, uttered perhaps during his preaching in these cities, and summarized here. They are directed against those who fail to recognize the presence of God in Jesus so as to avoid repentance.

11, 27: This verse has a Johannine ring in thought and style (Jn 3, 16f; 5, 19-23) and uses as introduction a saying of the risen Christ (Mt 28, 18). Only God the Father fully comprehends Jesus' mission, and only Jesus fully understands God's saving plan which he gradually unveils to men. This saying may have originated in the instruction of the risen Lord; cf Acts 1, 3.

11, 28: *Who are weary . . . burdensome:* a probable allusion to the moral and legal prescriptions of rabbinic Judaism, which needed to be balanced by prophetic vision in order to give joy and peaceful expectancy to the Mosaic tradition.

11, 29: *Your souls will find rest:* through acceptance of the gospel teaching which satisfies the longings of those who are wearied by the burdens of life.

✿

5: 8, 3f; Is 26, 19; 29, 18f; 35, 5f.	18: Lk 1, 15.
7: 3, 3f.	19: 9, 10f.
10: Mal 3, 1; Mk 1, 2; Lk 1, 76f.	20-24: Lk 10, 12-15. 23: Is 14, 13ff. 24: 10, 15.
12: Lk 16, 16.	25ff: Lk 10, 21f; 1 Cor 1, 26-29.
14: 16, 14; 17, 10-13; Mal 3, 23; Lk 1, 17.	27: Jn 3, 35; 6, 46; 7, 28.
16-19: Lk 7, 31-35.	28: Sir 24, 18.

gentle and humble of heart. Your souls will find rest, **30**for my yoke is easy and my burden light."

The Disciples and the Sabbath

12 **1***ONCE on a sabbath Jesus walked through the standing grain. His disciples felt hungry, so they began to pull off the heads of grain and eat them. **2**When the Pharisees spied this, they protested: "See here! Your disciples are doing what is not permitted on the sabbath." **3*†**He replied: "Have you not read what David did when he and his men were hungry, **4***how he entered God's house and ate the holy bread, a thing forbidden to him and his men or anyone other than priests? **5**Have you not read in the law how the priests on temple duty can break the sabbath rest without incurring guilt? **6**I assure you, there is something greater than the temple here. **7***If you understood the meaning of the text, 'It is mercy I desire and not sacrifice,' you would not have condemned these innocent men. **8*†**The Son of Man is indeed Lord of the sabbath."

A Man with a Shriveled Hand

9*He left that place and went into their synagogue. **10*†**A man with a shriveled hand happened to be there, and they put this question to Jesus, hoping to bring an accusation against him: "Is it lawful to work a cure on the sabbath?" **11***He said in response: "Suppose one of you has a sheep and it falls into a pit on the sabbath. Will he not take hold of it and pull it out? **12**Well, think how much more precious a human being is than a sheep. Clearly, good deeds may be performed on the sabbath."

13To the man he said, "Stretch out your hand." He did so, and it was perfectly restored; it became as sound as the other. **14***When the Pharisees were outside they began to plot against him to find a way to destroy him. **15†**Jesus was aware of this, and so he withdrew from that place.

The Mercy of Jesus

Many people followed him and he cured them all, **16**though he sternly ordered them not to make public what he had done. **17**This was to fulfill what had been said through Isaiah the prophet:

18*"Here is my servant whom I have chosen,
    my loved one in whom I delight.
    I will endow him with my spirit
    and he will proclaim justice to the Gentiles.
  19He will not contend or cry out,
    nor will his voice be heard in the streets.

20The bruised reed he will not crush;
    The smoldering wick he will not quench
    until judgment is made victorious.
  21In his name, the Gentiles will find hope."

Blasphemy of the Pharisees

22*A possessed man who was brought to him was blind and mute. He cured the man so that he could speak and see. **23***All in the crowd were astonished. "Might this not be David's son?" they asked. **24*†**When the Pharisees heard this, they charged, "This man can expel demons only with the help of Beelzebul, the prince of demons." **25***Knowing their thoughts, he said to them: "A kingdom torn by strife is headed for its downfall. A town or household split into factions cannot last for long. **26**If Satan is expelling Satan, he must be torn by dissension. How, then, can his dominion last? **27**If I expel demons with Beelzebul's help, by whose help do your people expel them? Let them be the ones to judge you. **28***But if it is by the Spirit of God that I expel demons, then the reign of God has overtaken you.

29"How can anyone enter a strong man's house and make off with his property unless he first ties him securely? Only then can he rob his house. **30***He who is not with me is against me, and he who does not gather with me scatters.

---

†

12, 3-6: Jesus responds to the objection of the Pharisees: if they hold so rigidly to their interpretation of the law, they should be critical of David's action (1 Sm 21, 1-6), and also that of the priests who on the sabbath prepare the offerings of the lambs (Nm 28, 9f). If these violations of the law in the temple, God's dwelling, are above criticism, neither should Jesus be criticized, for God is present in him as is manifested through his miracles; cf Jn 10, 38.

12, 8: See note on Mk 2, 28.

12, 10: *Is it lawful to work a cure on the sabbath:* curing on the sabbath was a frequent issue against Jesus in the gospels and one of considerable tension between him and the religious authorities (Jn 7, 23f). The basis of this altercation is not entirely clear. The sabbath healings did not accord with the teaching of the rabbis on the limited degree of aid to be given the sick or injured on that day. It seems, however, from the complete gospel that the issue was more complex than one of mere legalism. The healings produced clamorous crowds and processions of other sick persons (Lk 13, 14), which greatly disturbed the sabbath rest. At times Jesus overrode the sabbath restrictions (Jn 5, 18), challenged the authority of the scribes and Pharisees, and thoroughly involved them in his message. They had no choice but to take a stand, whether favorable or hostile, to Jesus.

12, 15-21: Jesus shows no inclination to counteract the hostility of the Pharisees by any action on his part, such as enlisting popular support against them. Instead he withdraws *from that place,* even orders those cured *not to make public what had done.* The free citation of Is 42, 1-4 is a reflection of the meekness of Jesus, the harbinger of the divine mercy to Jews and Gentiles.

12, 24-29: To the Pharisees' charge that Jesus performs exorcisms by a pact with Satan, he replies by showing that the objection lacks common sense (25f), overlooks the tradition of exorcistic power in Israel (27), and refuses to acknowledge, in the person and teaching of Christ, the new reign of God, capable of destroying Satan's power (28f).

✿

12/1-8: Ex 20, 8; Mk 2, 23-28;
    Lk 6, 1-5.
    3: 1 Sm 21, 6.
    4: Lv 24, 5-9.
    7: 1 Sm 15, 22; Hos 6, 6.
    8: Jn 5, 16f.
  9-15: Mk 3, 1-7.
   10: Lk 20, 20.
   11: Dt 22, 4.

   14: Jn 5, 18; 11, 53.
18-21: Is 42, 1-4.
 22ff: Lk 9, 32ff; 11, 14f.
  23: 9, 27.
  24: 10, 25; Mk 3, 22.
25-29: Mk 3, 23-27;
    Lk 11, 17-22.
  28: Lk 8, 29.
  30: Mk 9, 40; Lk 11, 23.

31*† "That, I assure you, is why every sin, every blasphemy, will be forgiven men, but blasphemy against the Spirit will not be forgiven. **32** Whoever says anything against the Son of Man will be forgiven, but whoever says anything against the Holy Spirit will not be forgiven, either in this age or in the age to come. **33***† Declare a tree good and its fruit good or declare a tree rotten and its fruit rotten, one or the other, for you can tell a tree by its fruit. **34*** How can you utter anything good, you brood of vipers, when you are so evil? The mouth speaks whatever fills the mind. **35** A good man produces good from his store of goodness; an evil man produces evil from his evil store. **36*** I assure you, on judgment day people will be held accountable for every unguarded word they speak. **37** By your words you will be acquitted, and by your words you will be condemned."

The Sign of Jonah

38† Some of the scribes and Pharisees then spoke up, saying, "Teacher, we want to see you work some signs." **39*** He answered: "An evil and unfaithful age is eager for a sign! No sign will be given it but that of the prophet Jonah. **40** Just as Jonah spent three days and three nights in the belly of the whale, so will the Son of Man spend three days and three nights in the bowels of the earth. **41**† At the judgment, the citizens of Nineveh will rise with the present generation and be the ones to condemn it. At the preaching of Jonah they reformed their lives; but you have a greater than Jonah here. **42*** At the judgment, the queen of the South will rise with the present generation and be the one to condemn it. She came from the farthest corner of the earth to listen to the wisdom of Solomon; but you have a greater than Solomon here.

43*† "When the unclean spirit departs from a man, it roams through arid wastes searching for a place of rest and finding none. **44** Then it says, 'I will go back where I came from,' and returns to find the dwelling unoccupied, though swept and tidied now. **45** Off it goes again to bring back with it this time seven spirits more evil than itself. They move in and settle there. Thus the last state of that man becomes worse than the first. And that is how it will be with this evil generation."

Jesus and His Family

46*† He was still addressing the crowds when his mother and his brothers appeared outside to speak with him. **47** Someone said to him, "Your mother and your brothers are standing out there and they wish to speak to you." **48** He said to the one who had told him, "Who is my mother? Who are my brothers?" **49** Then, extending his hand toward his disciples, he said, "There are my mother and my brothers. **50** Whoever does the will of my heavenly Father is brother and sister and mother to me."

13 **1***† THAT same day, on leaving the house, Jesus sat down by the lakeshore. **2** Such great crowds gathered around him that he went and took his seat in a boat while the crowd stood along the shore. **3** He addressed them at length in parables, speaking in this fashion:

"One day a farmer went out sowing. **4** Part of what he sowed landed on a footpath, where birds came and ate it up. **5** Part of it fell on rocky ground, where it had little soil. It sprouted at once since the soil had no depth, **6** but when the sun rose and scorched it, it began to wither for lack of roots. **7** Again, part of the seed fell among thorns, which grew up and choked it. **8** Part of it, finally, landed on good soil and yielded grain a hundred- or sixty- or thirtyfold. **9** Let everyone heed what he hears!"

10† When the disciples got near him, they asked him, "Why do you speak to them in parables?" **11** He answered: "To you has been given a knowledge of the mysteries of the reign of God, but it has not been given

---

† 12, 31f: The Pharisees are said to attribute Jesus' exorcisms to satanic power and thus to deny the unique presence of God in Jesus. They thereby assign his entire work and teaching to an evil principle, making it anti-God. This is the *blasphemy against the Spirit* that *will not be forgiven,* because it negates the evidence of God's saving action in history. However, misunderstandings of Jesus' teaching and misconceptions of his Person due to human error or prejudice will be forgiven (Acts 9, 4f; 1 Tm 1, 13).

12, 33-37: Those who charge that Jesus is in league with Satan reflect a basic evil in themselves that can be cured only by a radical renewal of faith and love.

12, 38ff: A current opinion in Judaism (Jn 7, 31) was that the Messiah would perform a unique kind of miracle. This view was not supported by the Old Testament but was apparently adhered to in circles of apocalyptic thought. The only additional sign to be given the faithless is that of Jesus' death and resurrection, typified by the story of Jonah in the belly of the fish. The allusion to Jesus' resurrection could not have been grasped by his audience at the time.

12, 41f: The sayings insist that Jesus' message of repentance has been more forcefully presented than in the preaching of Jonah and that his teaching shows greater divine wisdom than the perceptions of Solomon.

12, 43ff: The religious history of man is a repetitious interchange of good and evil. The sayings warn that the option for evil can reach the point of taking full possession of a man.

12, 46-50: See note on Mk 3, 20-35.

13, 1-53: The main theme of this collection of parables is the mystery of the reign or kingship of God, a plan hidden in God and only incompletely manifested to men (10-17.34f); cf Eph 3, 4ff. The teaching of Jesus reveals that it is God who introduces his reign into history (3-9), intangibly brings it to fruition among men through his power (31ff), and will perfect it in his own good time (24-30). A secondary theme encourages adherence to Jesus' teaching despite hardships (18-23), and acceptance of God's toleration of evil (36-43.47-50). It places the reign proclaimed by Jesus above all the things in human existence which men hold dear (44ff).

13, 10-15: Precisely because the prophetic message is understandable, it can be, and frequently is, rejected (cf Is 6, 9f).

---

*

31f: Mk 3, 28ff; Lk 12, 10.	42: 1 Kgs 10, 1-6.
33: Lk 6, 43ff.	43ff: Lk 11, 24ff.
34: 3, 7; 23, 33; 15, 11f.	46-50: Mk 3, 31-35;
36f: Jas 3, 1f.	Lk 8, 19ff.
39-42: 16, 4; Jon 2, 1; 3, 5;	13/1-14: Mk 4, 1-12; Lk 8, 4-10.
Lk 11, 29-32.	

to the others. **12***To the man who has, more will be given until he grows rich; the man who has not, will lose what little he has.

13*"I use parables when I speak to them because they look but do not see, they listen but do not hear or understand. **14***Isaiah's prophecy is fulfilled in them which says:

'Listen as you will, you shall not understand,
　look intently as you will, you shall not see.
15Sluggish indeed is this people's heart.
They have scarcely heard with their ears,
they have firmly closed their eyes;
otherwise they might see with their eyes,
and hear with their ears,
and understand with their hearts,
and turn back to me,
and I should heal them.'

16*"But blest are your eyes because they see and blest are your ears because they hear. **17**I assure you, many a prophet and many a saint longed to see what you see but did not see it, to hear what you hear but did not hear it.

18*"Mark well, then, the parable of the sower. **19**The seed along the path is the man who hears the message about God's reign without understanding it. The evil one approaches him to steal away what was sown in his mind. **20**The seed that fell on patches of rock is the man who hears the message and at first receives it with joy. **21**But he has no roots, so he lasts only for a time. When some setback or persecution involving the message occurs, he soon falters. **22**What was sown among briers is the man who hears the message, but then worldly anxiety and the lure of money choke it off. Such a one produces no yield. **23***But what was sown on good soil is the man who hears the message and takes it in. He it is who bears a yield of a hundred- or sixty- or thirtyfold."

The Weeds

24*He proposed to them another parable: "The reign of God may be likened to a man who sowed good seed in his field. **25**While everyone was asleep, his enemy came and sowed weeds through his wheat, and then made off. **26**When the crop began to mature and yield grain, the weeds made their appearance as well. **27**The owner's slaves came to him and said, 'Sir, did you not sow good seed in your field? Where are the weeds coming from?' **28**He answered, 'I see an enemy's hand in this.' His slaves said to him, 'Do you want us to go out and pull them up?' **29**No,' he replied, 'pull

up the weeds and you might take the wheat along with them. **30***Let them grow together until harvest; then at harvest time I will order the harvesters, First collect the weeds and bundle them up to burn, then gather the wheat into my barn.'"

The Mustard Seed and the Leaven

31*He proposed still another parable: "The reign of God is like a mustard seed which someone took and sowed in his field. **32**It is the smallest seed of all, yet when full-grown it is the largest of plants. It becomes so big a shrub that the birds of the sky come and build their nests in its branches."

33*He offered them still another image: "The reign of God is like yeast which a woman took and kneaded into three measures of flour. Eventually the whole mass of dough began to rise." **34***All these lessons Jesus taught the crowds in the form of parables. He spoke to them in parables only, **35***to fulfill what had been said through the prophet:

"I will open my mouth in parables,
　I will announce what has lain hidden since the
　　creation of the world."

36Then, dismissing the crowds, he went home. His disciples came to him with the request, "Explain to us the parable of the weeds in the field." **37**He said in answer: "The farmer sowing good seed is the Son of Man; **38**the field is the world, the good seed the citizens of the kingdom. The weeds are the followers of the evil one **39***and the enemy who sowed them is the devil. The harvest is the end of the world, while the harvesters are the angels. **40**Just as weeds are collected and burned, so will it be at the end of the world. **41***The Son of Man will dispatch his angels to collect from his kingdom all who draw others to apostasy, and all evildoers. **42***The angels will hurl them into the fiery furnace where they will wail and grind their teeth. **43***Then the saints will shine like the sun in their Father's kingdom. Let everyone heed what he hears!

The Treasure and the Pearl

44*"The reign of God is like a buried treasure which a man found in a field. He hid it again, and rejoicing at his find went and sold all he had and bought that field. **45**Or again, the kingdom of heaven is like a merchant's search for fine pearls. **46**When he found one really valuable pearl, he went back and put up for sale all that he had and bought it.

Parable of the Net

47"The reign of God is also like a dragnet thrown into the lake, which collected all sorts of things. **48**When it was full they hauled it ashore and sat down to put what was worthwhile into containers. What was useless they threw away. **49**That is how it will be at the end of the world. Angels will go out and separate the wicked from the just **50**and hurl the wicked into the fiery furnace, where they will wail and grind their teeth.

✿

12: 25, 29; Mk 4, 25;
　Lk 8, 18; 19, 26.
13: Jn 9, 39.
14f: Is 6, 9f; Jn 12, 40;
　Acts 28, 26; Rom 11, 8.
16f: Lk 10, 23f; Acts 22, 15.
18-23: Mk 4, 13-20;
　Lk 8, 11-15.
23: Jn 15, 8.16.
24: Mk 4, 26.

30: 3, 12; Jn 15, 6.
31f: Mk 4, 30ff; Lk 13, 18f.
33: Lk 13, 20f.
34: Jn 16, 25.
35: Ps 78, 2.
39: Rv 14, 15.
41: Zep 1, 3.
42: 8, 12; Rv 21, 8.
43: Wis 3, 7; Dn 12, 3.
44: J9, 21; Prv 4, 7.

[51]†"Have you understood all this?" "Yes," they answered; [52]to which he replied, "Every scribe who is learned in the reign of God is like the head of a household who can bring from his storeroom both the new and the old."

[53]†When Jesus had finished these parables, he moved on from that district.

V: THE REIGN BECOME CHURCH

Jesus at Nazareth

[54]*JESUS NEXT WENT TO his native place and spent his time teaching them in their synagogue. They were filled with amazement, and said to one another, "Where did this man get such wisdom and miraculous powers? [55]*†Isn't this the carpenter's son? Isn't Mary known to be his mother and James, Joseph, Simon, and Judas his brothers? [56]Aren't his sisters our neighbors? Where did he get all this?" [57]*They found him altogether too much for them. Jesus said to them, "No prophet is without honor except in his native place, indeed in his own house." [58]And he did not work many miracles there because of their lack of faith.

Death of the Baptizer

14 [1]*ON one occasion Herod the tetrarch, having heard of Jesus' reputation, [2]exclaimed to his courtiers, "This man is John the Baptizer—it is he in person, raised from the dead; that is why such miraculous powers are at work in him!" [3]*Recall that Herod had had John arrested, put in chains, and imprisoned on account of Herodias, the wife of his brother Philip. [4]*That was because John had told him, "It is not right for you to live with her." [5]*Herod wanted to kill John but was afraid of the people, who regarded him as a prophet. [6]Then on Herod's birthday Herodias' daughter performed a dance before the court which delighted Herod so much [7]that he swore he would grant her anything she asked for. [8]Prompted by her mother she said, "Bring me the head of John the Baptizer on a platter." [9]The king immediately had his misgivings, but because of his oath and the guests who were present he gave orders that the request be granted. [10]He sent the order to have John beheaded in prison. [11]John's head was brought in on a platter and given to the girl, who took it to her mother. [12]Later his disciples presented themselves to carry his body away and bury it. Afterward, they came and informed Jesus.

Jesus Feeds Five Thousand

[13]*When Jesus heard this, he withdrew by boat from there to a deserted place by himself. The crowds heard of it and followed him on foot from the towns. [14]When he disembarked and saw the vast throng, his heart was moved with pity, and he cured their sick. [15]As evening drew on, his disciples came to him with the suggestion: "This is a deserted place and it is already late. Dismiss the crowds so that they may go to the villages and buy some food for themselves." [16]Jesus said to them: "There is no need for them to disperse. Give them something to eat yourselves." [17]"We have nothing here," they replied, "but five loaves and a couple of fish." [18]"Bring them here," he said. [19]†Then he ordered the crowds to sit down on the grass. He took the five loaves and two fish, looked up to heaven, blessed and broke them and gave the loaves to the disciples, who in turn gave them to the people. [20]All those present ate their fill. The fragments remaining, when gathered up, filled twelve baskets. [21]Those who ate were about five thousand, not counting women and children.

Jesus Walks on the Water

[22]*†Immediately afterward, while dismissing the crowds, Jesus insisted that his disciples get into the boat and precede him to the other side. [23]*When he had sent them away, he went up on the mountain by himself to pray, [24]remaining there alone as evening drew on. Meanwhile the boat, already several hundred yards out from shore, was being tossed about in the waves raised by strong head winds. [25]At about three in the morning, he came walking toward them

---

† 13, 51f: Jesus' teaching on the mystery of the kingdom of God is a prophetic development of the doctrine of the Old Testament requiring spiritual discernment for its acceptance; cf 1 Cor 2, 10-16.

13, 53—19, 1: The main purpose in this section of the gospel is to place the Person of Jesus at the very center of the mystery of the reign of God. Beginning with the rejection of Jesus at Nazareth and the execution of John (13, 53—14, 12), the evangelist alludes to the eucharistic mystery in the accounts of the multiplication of the loaves (14, 19; 15, 36), and of the walking on the water (14, 22-33); reports the doctrinal conflict between Jesus and the religious authorities (15, 1-20); raises again the question of the sign of Jonah (16, 1-4; see note on 12, 38ff), later explained to mean the passion, death and resurrection of Jesus (16, 21ff) which must occur before the reign of God reaches a new stage (16, 28). This is the message of the transfiguration (17, 5). A second purpose of the evangelist is to pattern the life of the Christian community after the model-life of Jesus (18, 1-35). This discourse takes its cue from Jesus' role as Servant of Yahweh (Is 42, 1) alluded to in 17, 5. Under the imagery of children, Jesus' disciples are identified with the *anawim*, who are so profoundly changed that they place the service of God entirely above personal gain; cf 2 Cor 11, 7. These members of the Christian community enjoy the divine favor, which will pursue them should they fall as a result of the entrapments set out for them by others (18, 5-14). This is to be borne in mind if the discipline of the gospel is to be enforced on those members who have deviated from it (18, 15f). If completely recalcitrant, they are to be cut off from the community; if repentant, they may be reinstated because of the limitless forgiveness within the community (18, 17-34).

13, 55: See note on Mk 6, 1-6.

14, 19: The rite of blessing and distribution anticipates the Last Supper.

14, 22-33: See note on Mk 6, 45-52.

✻
54-58: Mk 6, 1-6.　　　　　　　　4: Lv 18, 16; 20, 21.
54: 2, 23; Jn 1, 46.　　　　　　　5: 21, 26.
55: 12, 46; 27, 56; Jn 6, 42.　　13-21: 15, 32-38; Mk 6, 32-44;
57: Jn 4, 44.　　　　　　　　　　　　　Lk 9, 10-17; Jn 6, 1-13.
14/1-12: Mk 6, 14-29; Lk 9, 7ff.　22-32: Mk 6, 45-51;
1: Lk 3, 1.　　　　　　　　　　　　　　　Jn 6, 16-21.
3f: Mk 6, 17f; Lk 3, 19f.　　　　23: Mk 1, 35.

on the lake. **26**When the disciples saw him walking on the water, they were terrified. "It is a ghost!" they said, and in their fear they began to cry out. **27**Jesus hastened to reassure them: "Get hold of yourselves! It is I. Do not be afraid!" **28**†Peter spoke up and said, "Lord, if it is really you, tell me to come to you across the water." **29**"Come!" he said. So Peter got out of the boat and began to walk on the water, moving toward Jesus. **30**But when he perceived how strong the wind was, becoming frightened, he began to sink and cried out, "Lord, save me!" **31**°Jesus at once stretched out his hand and caught him. "How little faith you have!" he exclaimed. "Why did you falter?" **32**Once they had climbed into the boat, the wind died down. **33**°†Those who were in the boat showed him reverence, declaring, "Beyond doubt you are the Son of God!"

Other Miracles

34After making the crossing they reached the shore at Gennesaret; **35**and when the men of that place recognized him they spread the word throughout the region. People brought him all the afflicted, **36**°with the plea that he let them do no more than touch the tassel of his cloak. As many as touched it were fully restored to health.

Jesus and the Pharisees

15 **1**°PHARISEES and scribes from Jerusalem approached Jesus with the question: **2**°"Why do your disciples act contrary to the tradition of our ancestors? They do not wash their hands, for example, before eating a meal." **3**In reply he said to them: "Why do you for your part act contrary to the commandment of God for the sake of your 'tradition'? **4**°For instance, God has said, 'Honor your father and your mother,' and, 'Whoever curses father or mother shall be put to death.' **5**†Yet you declare, 'Whoever says to his father or his mother, Any support you might have had from me is dedicated to God, **6**need not honor his father or his mother.' This means that for the sake of your tradition you have nullified God's word.

7"You hypocrites! How accurately did Isaiah prophesy about you when he said:

8°"This people pays me lip service
   but their heart is far from me.
9°They do me empty reverence,
   making dogmas out of human precepts.' "

10°†He summoned the crowd and said to them: "Give ear and try to understand. **11**It is not what goes into a man's mouth that makes him impure; it is what comes out of his mouth." **12**His disciples approached

him and said, "Do you realize the Pharisees were scandalized when they heard your pronouncement?" **13**"Every planting not put down by my heavenly Father will be uprooted," he replied. **14**°"Let them go their way; they are blind leaders of the blind. If one blind man leads another, both will end in a pit." **15**Then Peter spoke up to say, "Explain the parable to us." **16**"Are you, too, still incapable of understanding?" he asked. **17**"Do you not see that everything that enters the mouth passes into the stomach and is discharged into the latrine, **18**°but what comes out of the mouth originates in the mind? It is things like these that make a man impure. **19**From the mind stem evil designs—murder, adulterous conduct, fornication, stealing, false witness, blasphemy. **20**These are the things that make a man impure. As for eating with unwashed hands—that makes no man impure."

The Canaanite Woman

21°†Then Jesus left that place and withdrew to the district of Tyre and Sidon. **22**It happened that a Canaanite woman living in that locality presented herself, crying out to him, "Lord, Son of David, have pity on me! My daughter is terribly troubled by a demon." **23**He gave her no word of response. His disciples came up and began to entreat him, "Get rid of her. She keeps shouting after us." **24**"My mission is only to the lost sheep of the house of Israel," Jesus replied. **25**°She came forward then and did him homage with the plea, "Help me, Lord!" **26**But he answered, "It is not right to take the food of sons and daughters and throw it to the dogs." **27**"Please, Lord," she insisted, "even the dogs eat the leavings that fall from their masters' tables." **28**°Jesus then said in reply, "Woman, you have great faith! Your wish will come to pass." That very moment her daughter got better.

Jesus Heals the Suffering

29Jesus left that place and passed along the Sea of Galilee. He went up onto the mountainside and sat

---

† 14, 28-31: These verses are proper to Matthew. Peter, who exercised the leading role among the Twelve through the decision of Christ (16, 18; Acts 1, 15), had also to find his salvation in Jesus.

14, 33: *Beyond doubt you are the Son of God:* during the mortal life of Jesus, his divine nature was concealed. The confession therefore cannot be taken as evidence that the disciples comprehended Jesus' divine status at this time (Phil 2, 5-8). In the Old Testament the term "son" of God is applied to those who enjoy God's favor (Ex 4, 23; Ps 2, 7). However, the confession may be the evangelist's retrojection of the post-Easter faith into the time of Jesus' ministry; cf Mt 16, 16.

15, 5f: Property dedicated by vow was considered sacred, and therefore not to be claimed by parents for their support. But since ownership of the property was still retained, the vow and its effect became a mere figment of law and a means of escape from the duty of filial piety. However, rabbinic evidence suggests that such was not the ordinary teaching of the rabbis.

15, 10f: Before God, human guilt or innocence stems from deliberate human decision, not from any (presumed) evil in material creation. How difficult it was to change this mentality of Jesus' contemporaries is evident from Acts 10, 9-16.

15, 21-28: See note on Mk 7, 24-30.

° 31: 8, 25f.
33-36: Mk 6, 53-56.
33: 16, 16.
36: 9, 20ff.
15/1-20: Mk 7, 1-23.
2: Lk 11, 38.
4: Ex 20, 12; 21, 17;
   Lv 20, 9; Dt 5, 16;
   Prv 20, 20;
   Sir 3, 12; Eph 6, 2.

8: Ps 78, 36f;
   Is 29, 13.
9: Col 2, 23.
10: Mk 7, 14.
14: 23, 16.19; Lk 6, 39;
   Jn 9, 40.
18: 12, 34; Ti 1, 15.
21-28: Mk 7, 24-30.
25: 10, 6; Rom 15, 8.
28: 8, 10.

down there. **30***Large crowds of people came to him bringing with them cripples, the deformed, the blind, the mute, and many others besides. They laid them at his feet and he cured them. **31***The result was great astonishment in the crowds as they beheld the mute speaking, the deformed made sound, cripples walking about, and the blind seeing. They glorified the God of Israel.

Jesus Feeds Four Thousand

32*†Jesus called his disciples to him and said: "My heart is moved with pity for the crowd. By now they have been with me three days, and have nothing to eat. I do not wish to send them away hungry, for fear they may collapse on the way." **33**His disciples said to him, "How could we ever get enough bread in this deserted spot to satisfy such a crowd?" **34**But Jesus asked them, "How many loaves of bread do you have?" "Seven," they replied, "and a few small fish." **35**Then he directed the crowd to seat themselves on the ground. **36**He took the seven loaves and the fish, and after giving thanks he broke them and gave them to the disciples, who in turn gave them to the crowds. **37***All ate until they were full. When they gathered up the fragments left over, these filled seven hampers. **38**The people who were fed numbered four thousand, apart from women and children.

39Then, after he had dismissed the crowds, he got into the boat and went to the district of Magadan.

The Pharisees and Sadducees

16 **1***THE Pharisees and Sadducees came along, and as a test asked him to show them some sign in the sky. **2**He gave them this reply: ["In the evening you say, 'Red sky at night, the day will be bright'; **3***but in the morning, 'Sky red and gloomy, the day will be stormy.' If you know how to interpret the look of the sky, can you not read the signs of the times?] **4***An evil, faithless age is eager for a sign, but no sign will be given it except that of Jonah." With that he left them abruptly.

The Leaven of the Pharisees

5*The disciples discovered when they arrived at the other side that they had forgotten to bring any bread along. **6***When Jesus said to them, "Be on the lookout against the yeast of the Pharisees and Sadducees," **7**they could think only, "This is because we have brought no bread." **8**Jesus knew their thoughts and said, "Why do you suppose it is because you have no bread? How weak your faith is! **9***Do you still not understand? Do you not remember the five loaves among five thousand and how many baskets-full you

picked up? **10***Or the seven loaves among four thousand and how many hampers-full you retrieved? **11**Why is it you do not see that I was not speaking about bread at all but warning you against the yeast of the Pharisees?" **12**They finally realized he was not issuing a warning against yeast [used for bread] but against the Pharisees' and Sadducees' teaching.

Peter the Rock

13*When Jesus came to the neighborhood of Caesarea Philippi, he asked his disciples this question: "Who do people say that the Son of Man is?" **14***They replied, "Some say John the Baptizer, others Elijah, still others Jeremiah or one of the prophets." **15**"And you," he said to them, "who do you say that I am?" **16***†"You are the Messiah," Simon Peter answered, "the Son of the living God!" **17**†Jesus replied, "Blest are you, Simon son of Jonah! No mere man has revealed this to you, but my heavenly Father. **18***†I for my part declare to you, you are 'Rock,' and on this rock I will build my church, and the jaws of death shall not prevail against it. **19***†I will entrust to you the keys of the kingdom of heaven. Whatever you declare bound on earth

†   15, 32-38: See note on Mk 8, 1-9.

16, 16-20: To the tradition of Peter's confession at Caesarea Philippi (Mk 8, 27-30), Matthew adds the doctrine of the divinity of Christ, together with Jesus' prophecy that he will successfully build a new Israel, i. e., the church, upon Peter. Considering the unresolved dispute among the Twelve as to who was the greatest (Mt 20, 20-24), it is probable that this prophecy as a whole was made by the risen Christ (Jn 21, 15ff). The importance of the prophecy is seen from the fact that Matthew conserves it three decades after Peter's martyrdom, when his leadership of the Jerusalem community is already a thing of the past. In Matthew, the building of the new Israel on Peter pertains to Jesus' own role in the mystery of the reign of God that has appeared in history; see notes on 13, 1-53; 13, 53—19, 1. Jesus cannot begin to build his church upon Peter until after his death and resurrection (16, 21ff). For Matthew, Jesus' building of the new people of God upon Peter is a continuing reality for the Christian community of his time.

16, 17: Jesus' messianic identity and divinity cannot be truly known from human reason, but only from God's revelation (1 Cor 12, 3).

16, 18: You are "Rock": the Greek petros and its Aramaic equivalent kepha, "rock" is here conferred on Simon as a personal name to indicate his role as the firm foundation on which Jesus builds his church. The jaws of death: literally, "the gates of Sheol" (Nm 16, 33), i. e., death's realm, here used to signify the power or force of evil responsible first for physical then for spiritual death. The new people of God will overcome both forms of death to achieve the glorious entrance into the final kingdom (Rv 20, 4ff).

16, 19: I will entrust . . . kingdom of heaven: i. e., spiritual power to be exercised over the life of God's people, in contrast to the previously mentioned "gates," i. e., the evil power of death that would not prevail against the church. Simon Peter is the keeper of the keys, the one who has power to open and to close, to "bind" and to "loose," to allow and to forbid; cf Is 22, 22. The exercise of this responsibility is here compared to the disciplinary and doctrinal authority of the rabbis who in Jesus' time interpreted the Old Testament for the faith and life of the people. The exact nature of the extraordinary power here conferred became clear through the historical development of the Christian community in terms of the primacy of Peter, i. e., his supreme authority in teaching, governing and sanctifying the people of God.

✿
30: Is 35, 5f.
31: 8, 3.
32-39: Mk 8, 1-10.
37: 16, 10.
16/1-10: Mk 8, 11-21.
3: Lk 12, 54.
4: 12, 39; Jon 2, 1.
5: Mk 8, 14.

6: Lk 12, 1.
9: 14, 17.21; Jn 6, 9.
10: 15, 34.38.
13-16: Mk 8, 27ff; Lk 9, 18ff.
14: 14, 2.
16: Jn 6, 69f.
18: Jn 1, 42.
19: Is 22, 22; Rv 3, 7.

shall be bound in heaven; whatever you declare loosed on earth shall be loosed in heaven." **20**Then he strictly ordered his disciples not to tell anyone that he was the Messiah.

First Prophecy of Passion and Resurrection

21*From then on Jesus [the Messiah] started to indicate to his disciples that he must go to Jerusalem and suffer greatly there at the hands of the elders, the chief priests, and the scribes, and to be put to death, and raised up on the third day. **22**At this, Peter took him aside and began to remonstrate with him. "May you be spared, Master! God forbid that any such thing ever happen to you!" **23**Jesus turned on Peter and said, "Get out of my sight, you satan! You are trying to make me trip and fall. You are not judging by God's standards but by man's."

Doctrine of the Cross

24*†Jesus then said to his disciples: "If a man wishes to come after me, he must deny his very self, take up his cross, and begin to follow in my footsteps. **25***Whoever would save his life will lose it, but whoever loses his life for my sake will find it. **26**What profit would a man show if he were to gain the whole world and destroy himself in the process? What can a man offer in exchange for his very self? **27*†**The Son of Man will come with his Father's glory accompanied by his angels. When he does, he will repay each man according to his conduct. **28***I assure you, among those standing here there are some who will not experience death before they see the Son of Man come in his kingship."

Jesus Transfigured

17 **1*†**SIX days later Jesus took Peter, James, and his brother John and led them up on a high mountain by themselves. **2**He was transfigured before their eyes. His face became as dazzling as the sun, his clothes as radiant as light. **3***Suddenly Moses and Elijah appeared to them conversing with him. **4**Then Peter said to Jesus, "Lord, how good that we are here! With your permission I will erect three booths here, one for you, one for Moses, and one for Elijah." **5***He was still speaking when suddenly a bright cloud overshadowed them. Out of the cloud came a voice which said, "This is my beloved Son on whom my favor rests. Listen to him." **6**When they heard this the disciples fell forward on the ground, overcome with fear. **7**Jesus came toward them and laying his hand on them, said, "Get up! Do not be afraid."

8When they looked up they did not see anyone but Jesus.

The Coming of Elijah

9*†As they were coming down the mountainside Jesus commanded them, "Do not tell anyone of the vision until the Son of Man rises from the dead." **10***The disciples put this question to him: "Why do the scribes claim that Elijah must come first?" **11***In reply he said: "Elijah is indeed coming, and he will restore everything. **12***I assure you, though, that Elijah has already come, but they did not recognize him and they did as they pleased with him. The Son of Man will suffer at their hands in the same way." **13**The disciples then realized that he had been speaking to them about John the Baptizer.

The Possessed Boy

14*†As they approached the crowd, a man came up to him and knelt before him. **15**"Lord," he said, "take pity on my son, who is demented and in a serious condition. For example, he often falls into the fire and frequently into the water. **16**I have brought him to your disciples but they could not cure him." **17**In reply Jesus said: "What an unbelieving and perverse lot you are! How long must I remain with you? How long can I endure you? Bring him here to me!" **18***Then Jesus reprimanded him, and the demon came out of him. That very moment the boy was cured.

19*The disciples approached Jesus at that point and asked him privately, "Why could we not expel it?" **20***"Because you have so little trust," he told them. "I assure you, if you had faith the size of a mustard seed, you would be able to say to this mountain, 'Move from here to there,' and it would move. Nothing would be impossible for you. **21**[This kind does not leave but by prayer and fasting.]"

Second Prophecy of the Passion

22*When they met again in Galilee, Jesus said to them, "The Son of Man is going to be delivered into the hands of men **23**who will put him to death, and he will be raised up on the third day." At these words they were overwhelmed with grief.

Paying the Temple Tax

24*When they entered Capernaum, the collectors of the temple tax approached Peter and said, "Does your master not pay the temple tax?" **25**"Of course he does," Peter replied. Then Jesus on entering the house asked,

---

❋
21-28: Mk 8, 31—9, 1;
    Lk 9, 22-27.
  21: 17, 22f; 20, 17ff;
    13, 33; Acts 10, 40.
  24: Lk 14, 27.
  25: Lk 17, 33; Jn 12, 25.
  27: 25, 31f; Jb 34, 11;
    Ps 62, 13; Jer 17, 10;
    2 Thes 1, 7f.
  28: 24, 30; 26, 64.
17/1-8: Mk 9, 1-7; Lk 9, 28-36.
   3: 28, 2.

     5: 3, 17; 2 Pt 1, 17.
 9-13: Mk 9, 9f.
  10: Mal 3, 23f.
  11: Lk 1, 17.
  12: 11, 14; 16, 21; 17, 22f.
14-21: Mk 9, 14-29;
    Lk 9, 37-43.
  18: 8, 29.
  19: 21, 21; Lk 17, 6.
  20: 1 Cor 13, 2.
 22f: 16, 21.
  24: Ex 30, 15.

---

†
16, 24ff: See note on Mk 8, 34—9, 1.

16, 27f: These two sayings seem to refer to distinct phases of the kingdom of God: the reign of Christ in and through the new Christian community, with its orientation through faith to the second coming of Christ (27); and the eschatological kingdom of the Father, to be inaugurated when the Son of Man comes in glory at the end of time (28). See note on Mk 9, 1; Acts 1, 11.

17, 1-8: See note on Mk 9, 2-8.

17, 9: Misunderstanding the necessity of the passion, they are not to reveal the vision until after Jesus' resurrection.

17, 14-20: See note on Mk 9, 14-29.

without giving him time to speak: "What is your opinion, Simon? Do the kings of the world take tax or toll from their sons, or from foreigners?" **26**When he replied, "From foreigners," Jesus observed: "Then their sons are exempt. **27**But for fear of disedifying them go to the lake, throw in a line, and take out the first fish you catch. Open its mouth and you will discover there a coin worth twice the temple tax. Take it and give it to them for you and me."

Against Ambition

18 **1***JUST then the disciples came up to Jesus with the question, "Who is of greatest importance in the kingdom of God?" **2**He called a little child over and stood him in their midst **3***and said: "I assure you, unless you change and become like little children, you will not enter the kingdom of God. **4***Whoever makes himself lowly, becoming like this child, is of greatest importance in that heavenly reign.

Avoiding Scandal

5"Whoever welcomes one such child for my sake welcomes me. **6***On the other hand, it would be better for anyone who leads astray one of these little ones who believe in me, to be drowned by a millstone around his neck, in the depths of the sea. **7**What terrible things will come on the world through scandal! It is inevitable that scandal should occur. Nonetheless, woe to that man through whom scandal comes! **8***If your hand or foot is your undoing, cut it off and throw it from you! Better to enter life maimed or crippled than be thrown with two hands or two feet into endless fire. **9**If your eye is your downfall, gouge it out and cast it from you! Better to enter life with one eye than be thrown with both into fiery Gehenna.

The Straying Sheep

10"See that you never despise one of these little ones. I assure you, their angels in heaven constantly behold my heavenly Father's face. **12***What is your thought on this: A man owns a hundred sheep and one of them wanders away; will he not leave the ninety-nine out on the hills and go in search of the stray? **13**If he succeeds in finding it, believe me he is happier about this one than about the ninety-nine that did not wander away. **14**Just so, it is no part of your heavenly Father's plan that a single one of these little ones shall ever come to grief.

Fraternal Correction

15* "If your brother should commit some wrong against you, go and point out his fault, but keep it between the two of you. If he listens to you, you have won your brother over. **16***If he does not listen, summon another, so that every case may stand on the word of two or three witnesses. **17***If he ignores them, refer it to the church. If he ignores even the church, then treat him as you would a Gentile or a tax collector. **18***I assure you, whatever you declare bound on earth shall be held bound in heaven, and whatever you declare loosed on earth shall be held loosed in heaven.

The Power of United Prayer

19*"Again I tell you, if two of you join your voices on earth to pray for anything whatever, it shall be granted you by my Father in heaven. **20***Where two or three are gathered in my name, there am I in their midst."

The Merciless Official

21*Then Peter came up and asked him, "Lord, when my brother wrongs me, how often must I forgive him? Seven times?" **22**"No," Jesus replied, "not seven times; I say, seventy times seven times. **23***That is why the reign of God may be said to be like a king who decided to settle accounts with his officials. **24**When he began his auditing, one was brought in who owed him a huge amount. **25**As he had no way of paying it, his master ordered him to be sold, along with his wife, his children, and all his property, in payment of the debt. **26**At that the official prostrated himself in homage and said, 'My lord, be patient with me and I will pay you back in full.' **27**Moved with pity, the master let the official go and wrote off the debt. **28**But when that same official went out he met a fellow servant who owed him a mere fraction of what he himself owed. He seized him and throttled him. 'Pay back what you owe,' he demanded. **29**His fellow servant dropped to his knees and began to plead with him, 'Just give me time and I will pay you back in full.' **30**But he would hear none of it. Instead, he had him put in jail until he paid back what he owed. **31**When his fellow servants saw what had happened they were badly shaken, and went to their master to report the whole incident. **32**His master sent for him and said, 'You worthless wretch! I canceled your entire debt when you pleaded with me. **33***Should you not have dealt mercifully with your fellow servant, as I dealt with you?' **34**Then in anger the master handed him over to the torturers until he paid back all that he owed. **35***My heavenly Father will treat you in exactly the same way unless each of you forgives his brother from his heart."

❀

18/1-5:	Mk 9, 36f; Lk 9, 46ff.
3:	19, 14; 1 Cor 14, 20.
4:	23, 12; Mk 10, 15; Lk 18, 17.
6:	Mk 9, 42; Lk 17, 1f.
8f:	5, 30; Mk 9, 43-47.
12ff:	Ez 34, 1ff.16; Lk 15, 3-7.
15:	Lv 19, 17; Sir 19, 13; Gal 6, 1.
16:	Dt 19, 15; Jn 8, 17; 1 Tm 5, 19f.
17:	1 Cor 5, 9-13.
18:	Jn 20, 23.
19:	7, 7f; Jn 15, 7.
20:	1 Cor 5, 4.
21:	6, 12; Lk 17, 4.
23:	25, 19; Sir 28, 4.
33:	1 Jn 4, 11.
35:	6, 12; Jas 2, 13.

†

18, 11: Omitted here with many MSS.

18, 15-18: Note the transition from fraternal correction to the further action (17) of delivering the obstinate sinner to the authority of the church. Exclusion and readmission of such a one is a function of the power of binding and loosing which belongs to the Christian community. There is no concrete evidence as to how the communities of New Testament times exercised this power.

19

¹*WHEN Jesus had finished this discourse, he left Galilee and came to the district of Judea across the Jordan. ²Great crowds followed him and he cured them there.

VI: FIRST STEPS IN ESTABLISHING GOD'S REIGN

The Question of Divorce

³†SOME PHARISEES CAME UP TO HIM and said, to test him, "May a man divorce his wife for any reason whatever?" ⁴*He replied, "Have you not read that at the beginning the Creator made them male and female ⁵*and declared, 'For this reason a man shall leave his father and mother and cling to his wife, and the two shall become as one'? ⁶Thus they are no longer two but one flesh. Therefore, let no man separate what God has joined." ⁷*They said to him, "Then why did Moses command divorce and the promulgation of a divorce decree?" ⁸"Because of your stubbornness Moses let you divorce your wives," he replied; "but at the beginning it was not that way. ⁹*†I now say to you, whoever divorces his wife (lewd conduct is a separate case) and marries another commits adultery, and the man who marries a divorced woman commits adultery."

¹⁰His disciples said to him, "If that is the case between man and wife, it is better not to marry." ¹¹He said, "Not everyone can accept this teaching, only those to whom it is given to do so. ¹²†Some men are incapable of sexual activity from birth; some have been deliberately made so; and some there are who have freely renounced sex for the sake of God's reign. Let him accept this teaching who can."

Jesus Blesses the Children

¹³*†At one point, children were brought to him so that he could place his hands on them in prayer. The disciples began to scold them, ¹⁴*but Jesus said, "Let the children come to me. Do not hinder them. The kingdom of God belongs to such as these." ¹⁵And he laid his hands on their heads before he left that place.

The Danger of Riches

¹⁶*†Another time a man came up to him and said, "Teacher, what good must I do to possess everlasting life?" ¹⁷*He answered, "Why do you question me about what is good? There is One who is good. If you wish to enter into life, keep the commandments." ¹⁸*"Which ones?" he asked. Jesus replied, " 'You shall not kill'; 'You shall not commit adultery'; 'You shall not

steal'; 'You shall not bear false witness'; ¹⁹*'Honor your father and your mother'; and 'Love your neighbor as yourself.' " ²⁰The young man said to him, "I have kept all these; what do I need to do further?" ²¹*†Jesus told him, "If you seek perfection, go, sell your possessions, and give to the poor. You will then have treasure in heaven. Afterward come back and follow me." ²²Hearing these words, the young man went away sad, for his possessions were many.

²³*†Jesus said to his disciples: "I assure you, only with difficulty will a rich man enter the kingdom of God. ²⁴*I repeat what I said: it is easier for a camel to pass through a needle's eye than for a rich man to enter the kingdom of God." ²⁵When the disciples heard this they were completely overwhelmed, and exclaimed, "Then who can be saved?" ²⁶Jesus looked at them and said, "For man it is impossible; but for

---

† 19, 3-8: The Pharisees wish to force Jesus to take sides on the question of divorce for the purpose of remarriage. (The stringent position at the time was that of the school of Shammai, while leniency was advocated by the school of Hillel.) In reply, Jesus proclaims the indissolubility of marriage, citing Gn 1, 27 and 2, 24. He declares this scriptural doctrine to be God's ultimate intent for marriage in human society, explaining that the divorce granted in the Old Testament was due to the stubbornness of the Jews, i. e., to their cultural *mores*, which God in his wisdom chose to leave unenlightened. *Let no man separate what God has joined:* not by mere legislation, for neither civil law, nor social custom, nor mutual consent forges the unbreakable bond, but rather the divine involvement in the union of marriage. The citation of Gn 2, 24 indicates that in the divine "joining together," God ratifies the mutual love of persons; their sexual union serves as a pledge of exclusive fidelity to each other; cf Mk 10, 2-12; Lk 16, 18; 1 Cor 7, 10f. For reflection on the theological implications of the Lord's new teaching, cf Eph 5, 21-33.

19, 9: *Lewd conduct is a separate case:* literally "except for porneia," i. e., immorality, fornication, even incest. A growing number of scholars consider this to refer to Christians who, prior to their conversion, had married within the prohibited degree of blood relationship as stated in Lv 18, 6-18. The same position seems to be taken in Acts 15, 20. As it stands, however, this Matthean clause of exception and that of 5, 32 cannot easily be reconciled with the absolute prohibition of divorce repeated in Mk 10, 11f and Lk 16, 18. Whatever may have been the situation prevailing among the Christians for whom Matthew wrote, the more stringent understanding of Jesus' words prevailed throughout the church.

19, 12: This verse is proper to Matthew. While there is no consensus on its meaning, some exegetes understand it to refer to voluntary and perpetual celibacy for members of the Christian community who wish to dedicate themselves completely to the kingdom of God; cf Mt 13, 44ff; 19, 29.

19, 13ff: Children were the symbol Jesus used for the *anawim*, the poor in spirit or the lowly, within the Christian community; see note on 5, 3-12. Like the apostles, these have surrendered personal possessions (16-30) for total dedication to his ministry.

19, 16: See note on Mk 10, 17f.

19, 21: The young man is invited to join the *anawim*.

19, 23-26: Jesus' contemporaries consider wealth a sign of divine favor. When he denies this and shows that wealth can even obstruct the spiritual perception of his message, the disciples conclude that virtually no one can be saved. Jesus replies that the rich as well as the poor are dependent on God for their salvation.

❋ 19/1-9: Mk 10, 1-12.
     4: Gn 1, 27.
     5: Gn 2, 24;
        1 Cor 6, 16;
        7, 10; Eph 5, 31.
     7: Dt 24, 1-4.
     9: 5, 32;
        Lk 16, 18;
        1 Cor 7, 11.
13ff: Mk 10, 13-16.

     14: 18, 3.
16-29: Mk 10, 17-30;
        Lk 18, 18-30.
17-20: Lk 10, 25-28.
     18: Ex 20, 12-16;
        Dt 5, 16-20.
     19: Jn 13, 34.
     21: 6, 20; 13, 44ff.
23-26: Mk 10, 23-27.
     24: 7, 14.

God all things are possible." **27***†Then it was Peter's turn to say to him: "Here we have put everything aside to follow you. What can we expect from it?" **28***Jesus said to them: "I give you my solemn word, in the new age when the Son of Man takes his seat upon a throne befitting his glory, you who have followed me shall likewise take your places on twelve thrones to judge the twelve tribes of Israel. **29**Moreover, everyone who has given up home, brothers or sisters, father or mother, wife or children or property for my sake will receive many times as much and inherit everlasting life. **30***Many who are first shall come last, and the last shall come first.

The Laborers in the Vineyard

20 **1**†"THE reign of God is like the case of the owner of an estate who went out at dawn to hire workmen for his vineyard. **2**After reaching an agreement with them for the usual daily wage, he sent them out to his vineyard. **3**He came out about midmorning and saw other men standing around the marketplace without work, **4**so he said to them, 'You too go along to my vineyard and I will pay you whatever is fair.' **5**At that they went away. He came out again around noon and midafternoon and did the same. **6**Finally, going out in late afternoon he found still others standing around. To these he said, 'Why have you been standing here idle all day?' **7**No one has hired us,' they told him. He said, 'You go to the vineyard too.' **8**When evening came the owner of the vineyard said to his foreman, 'Call the workmen and give them their pay, but begin with the last group and end with the first.' **9**When those hired late in the afternoon came up they received a full day's pay, **10**and when the first group appeared they supposed they would get more; **11**yet they received the same daily wage. Thereupon they complained to the owner, **12**This last group did only an hour's work, but you have put them on the same basis as us who have worked a full day in the scorching heat.' **13**My friend,' he said to one in reply, 'I do you no injustice. You agreed on the usual wage, did you not? **14**Take your pay and go home. I intend to give this man who was hired last the same pay as you. **15**I am free to do as I please with my money, am I not? Or are you envious because I am generous?' **16***Thus the last shall be first and the first shall be last."

Third Prophecy: Passion and Resurrection

17*As Jesus was starting to go up to Jerusalem, he took the Twelve aside on the road and said to them: **18**"We are going up to Jerusalem now. There the Son of Man will be handed over to the chief priests and scribes, who will condemn him to death. **19***They will turn him over to the Gentiles, to be made sport of and flogged and crucified. But on the third day he will be raised up."

The Mother of James and John

20*The mother of Zebedee's sons came up to him accompanied by her sons, to do him homage and ask of him a favor. **21**"What is it you want?" he said. She answered, "Promise me that these sons of mine will sit, one at your right hand and the other at your left, in your kingdom." **22**In reply Jesus said, "You do not know what you are asking. Can you drink of the cup I am to drink of?" "We can," they said. **23**He told them, "From the cup I drink of, you shall drink. But sitting at my right hand or my left is not mine to give. That is for those to whom it has been reserved by my Father." **24***The other ten, on hearing this, became indignant at the two brothers. **25**Jesus then called them together and said: "You know how those who exercise authority among the Gentiles lord it over them; their great ones make their importance felt. **26**It cannot be like that with you. Anyone among you who aspires to greatness must serve the rest, **27***and whoever wants to rank first among you must serve the needs of all. **28***Such is the case with the Son of Man who has come, not to be served by others, but to serve, to give his own life as a ransom for the many."

The Two Blind Men at Jericho

29*As they were leaving Jericho a large crowd followed him, **30***and suddenly two blind men sitting by the roadside, who heard that Jesus was passing by, began to shout, "Lord, Son of David, have pity on us!" **31**The crowd began to scold them in an effort to reduce them to silence, but they only shouted the louder, "Lord, Son of David, have pity on us!" **32**Jesus then stopped and called out to them, "What do you want me to do for you?" **33**"Lord," they told him, "open our eyes!" **34**Moved with compassion, Jesus touched their eyes, and immediately they could see; and they became his followers.

Triumphal Entry into Jerusalem

21 **1***†As they drew near Jerusalem, entering Bethphage on the Mount of Olives, Jesus sent off two disciples **2**with the instructions: "Go into the village straight ahead of you and you will im-

† 19, 27-30: Voluntary renunciation of home, property and relatives for the sake of Christ will evoke the divine generosity in this life and in the next.

20, 1-34: A development of the thought of 19, 30: God requires service of his followers while reserving to himself the modes and occasions of his generosity (1-16). He makes the same requirement of Jesus himself (17ff) and his apostles (20-28), without indicating what will be the nature of God's generous return. The cure of the blind men (29-34) shows that Jesus is still the servant of men as he proceeds to his death in Jerusalem.

21, 1-11: See note on Mk 11, 1-11.

*
27-30: Mk 10, 28-31;
    Lk 18, 28ff.
  27: 4, 20.22.
  28: Dn 7, 22; Rv 3, 21;
    20, 4.
  30: 19, 30; 20, 16;
    Mk 10, 31; Lk 13, 30.
20/16: 19, 30.
  17f: 16, 21; 17, 22f;
    Mk 10, 32f;
    Lk 18, 31ff.
  19: Acts 10, 40.

20-28: Mk 10, 35-45.
24-28: Lk 22, 25ff.
  27: Mk 9, 35; Jn 13, 14.
  28: 26, 28; Rom 5, 6;
    1 Tm 2, 6.
29-34: Mk 10, 46-52;
    Lk 18, 35-43.
  30: 9, 27.
21/1-9: Mk 11, 1-9;
    Lk 19, 28-38;
    Jn 12, 12-15.

mediately find an ass tethered and her colt with her. Untie them and lead them back to me. [3]If anyone says a word to you, say, 'The Master needs them.' Then he will let them go at once." [4]This came about to fulfill what was said through the prophet:

[5]*†"Tell the daughter of Zion,
Your king comes to you without display
astride an ass, astride a colt,
the foal of a beast of burden."

[6]So the disciples went off and did what Jesus had ordered; [7]they brought the ass and the colt and laid their cloaks on them, and he mounted. [8]*The huge crowd spread their cloaks on the road, while some began to cut branches from the trees and lay them along his path. [9]*†The groups preceding him as well as those following kept crying out:

"Hosanna to the Son of David!
Blessed is he who comes in the name of the Lord!
Hosanna in the highest!"

[10]As he entered Jerusalem the whole city was stirred to its depths, demanding, "Who is this?" [11]And the crowd kept answering, "This is the prophet Jesus from Nazareth in Galilee."

Cleaning Out the Temple

[12]*†Jesus entered the temple precincts and drove out all those engaged there in buying and selling. He overturned the money changers' tables and the stalls of the dove-sellers, [13]*saying to them: "Scripture has it,

'My house shall be called a house of prayer,'

but you are turning it into a den of thieves." [14]The blind and the lame came to him inside the temple area and he cured them. [15]The chief priests and the scribes became indignant when they observed the wonders he worked, and how the children were shouting out in the temple precincts, "Hosanna to the Son of David!" [16]*"Do you hear what they are saying?" they asked him. Jesus said to them, "Of course I do! Did you never read this:

'From the speech of infants and children
you have framed a hymn of praise'?"

[17]With that he left them and went out of the city to Bethany, where he spent the night.

Jesus Curses a Fig Tree

[18]*At dawn, as Jesus was returning to the city, he felt hungry. [19]*Seeing a fig tree by the roadside he went over to it, but found nothing there except leaves.

He said to it, "Never again shall you produce fruit!"; and it withered up instantly. [20]*The disciples were dumbfounded when they saw this. They asked, "Why did the fig tree wither up so quickly?" [21]*Jesus said: "Believe me, if you trust and do not falter, not only will you do what I did to the fig tree, but if you say to this mountain, 'Be lifted up and thrown into the sea,' even that will happen. [22]*You will receive all that you pray for, provided you have faith."

The Authority of Jesus

[23]*After Jesus had entered the temple precincts, and while he was teaching, the chief priests and elders of the people came up to him and said: "On what authority are you doing these things? Who has given you this power?" [24]Jesus answered: "I too will ask a question. If you answer it for me, then I will tell you on what authority I do the things I do. [25]*What was the origin of John's baptism? Was it divine or merely human?" They thought to themselves, "If we say 'divine,' he will ask us, 'Then why did you not put faith in it?'; [26]*while if we say, 'merely human,' we shall have reason to fear the people, who all regard John as a prophet." [27]So their answer to Jesus was, "We do not know." He said in turn, "Then neither will I tell you on what authority I do the things I do.

Parable of the Two Sons

[28]"What do you think of this case? There was a man who had two sons. He approached the elder and said, 'Son, go out and work in the vineyard today.' [29]The son replied, 'I am on my way, sir'; but he never went. [30]Then the man came to his second son and said the same thing. This son said in reply, 'No, I will not'; but afterward he regretted it and went. [31]*Which of the two did what the father wanted?" They said, "The second." Jesus said to them, "I assure you that tax collectors and prostitutes are entering the kingdom of God before you. [32]When John came preaching a way of holiness, you put no faith in him; but the tax collectors and the prostitutes did believe in him. Yet even when you saw that, you did not repent and believe in him.

Parable of the Tenants

[33]*"Listen to another parable. There was a property owner who planted a vineyard, put a hedge around it, dug out a vat, and erected a tower. Then he leased it out to tenant farmers and went on a journey. [34]When

---

*
5: Is 62, 11; Zec 9, 9.	21: 17, 20; Lk 17, 6.
8: 2 Kgs 9, 13.	22: 7, 7; 1 Jn 3, 22.
9: Ps 118, 25f.	23-27: Mk 11, 27-33;
12-16: Mk 11, 15-18;	Lk 20, 1-8.
Lk 19, 45ff; Jn 2, 14ff.	23: 28, 18; Jn 2, 18.
12: Neh 13, 8.	25: Jn 3, 27.
13: Is 56, 7; Jer 7, 11.	26: 14, 5; 21, 32.
16: Ps 8, 2; Wis 10, 21.	31: Lk 7, 29f.
18-22: Mk 11, 12ff.20-24.	33-46: Is 5, 1-7; Mk 12, 1-12;
19: Jer 8, 13; Lk 13, 6-9.	Lk 20, 9-19.
20: Hos 9, 16.	

---

† 21, 5: A free citation of Is 62, 11 and Zec 9, 9 indicating that Jesus entered Jerusalem as king of peace, riding, not the horse, symbol of the conqueror (Jer 22, 4), but the ass, the work beast of the poor.

21, 9: A citation of Ps 118, 25f used for the purpose of acknowledging Jesus to be the Messiah and son of David. See note on Mk 11, 1-11. *God save* (the Hebrew *Hōsĭ'ah-nnā*, literally "Do save!"): meant here as an acclamation or shout of praise honoring Jesus as the Savior.

21, 12-22: See notes on Mk 11, 15-19 and on 11, 12ff, in that order.

vintage time arrived he dispatched his slaves to the tenants to obtain his share of the grapes. **35**The tenants responded by seizing the slaves. They beat one, killed another, and stoned a third. **36**A second time he dispatched even more slaves than before, but they treated them the same way. **37**Finally he sent his son to them, thinking, 'They will respect my son.' **38***When they saw the son, the tenants said to one another, 'Here is the one who will inherit everything. Let us kill him and then we shall have his inheritance!' **39***With that they seized him, dragged him outside the vineyard, and killed him. **40**What do you suppose the owner of the vineyard will do to those tenants when he comes?" **41**They replied, "He will bring that wicked crowd to a bad end and lease his vineyard out to others who will see to it that he has grapes at vintage time." **42***Jesus said to them, "Did you never read in the Scriptures,

'The stone which the builders rejected
has become the keystone of the structure.
It was the Lord who did this
and we find it marvelous to behold'?

43*For this reason, I tell you, the kingdom of God will be taken away from you and given to a nation that will yield a rich harvest. **44**[The man who falls upon that stone will be smashed to bits; and he on whom it falls will be crushed.]"

45When the chief priests and the Pharisees heard these parables, they realized he was speaking about them. **46**Although they sought to arrest him, they had reason to fear the crowds who regarded him as a prophet.

The Wedding Banquet

22 **1**JESUS began to address them, once more using parables. **2***"The reign of God may be likened to a king who gave a wedding banquet for his son. **3**He dispatched his servants to summon the invited guests to the wedding, but they refused to come. **4**A second time he sent other servants, saying: 'Tell those who were invited, See, I have my dinner prepared! My bullocks and corn-fed cattle are killed; everything is ready. Come to the feast.' **5**Some ignored the invitation and went their way, one to his farm, another to his business. **6***The rest laid hold of his servants, insulted them, and killed them. **7**At this the king grew furious and sent his army to destroy those murderers and burn their city. **8**Then he said to his servants: 'The banquet is ready, but those who were invited were unfit to come. **9**That is why you must go out into the byroads and invite to the wedding anyone you come upon.' **10**The servants then went out into the byroads and rounded up everyone they met, bad as well as good. This filled the wedding hall with banqueters.

11"When the king came in to meet the guests, however, he caught sight of a man not properly dressed for a wedding feast. **12**'My friend,' he said, 'how is it you came in here not properly dressed?' The man had nothing to say. **13***The king then said to the attendants, 'Bind him hand and foot and throw him out into the night to wail and grind his teeth.' **14**†The invited are many, the elect are few."

Paying Tax to the Emperor

15*Then the Pharisees went off and began to plot how they might trap Jesus in speech. **16**They sent their disciples to him, accompanied by Herodian sympathizers, who said: "Teacher, we know you are a truthful man and teach God's way sincerely. You court no one's favor and do not act out of human respect. **17**Give us your opinion, then, in this case. Is it lawful to pay tax to the emperor or not?" **18**Jesus recognized their bad faith and said to them, "Why are you trying to trip me up, you hypocrites? **19**Show me the coin used for the tax." When they handed him a small Roman coin **20**he asked them, "Whose head is this, and whose inscription?" **21***"Caesar's," they replied. At that he said to them, "Then give to Caesar what is Caesar's, but give to God what is God's." **22**Taken aback by this reply, they went off and left him.

The Sadducees and the Resurrection

23*That same day some Sadducees, who hold there is no resurrection, came to him with a question: **24***"Teacher, Moses declared, 'If a man dies without children, his brother must take the wife and produce offspring for his brother.' **25**Once there were seven brothers. The eldest died after marrying, and since he had no children, left his wife to his brother. **26**The same thing happened to the second, the third, and so on, down to the seventh. **27**Last of all the woman died too. **28**At the resurrection, whose wife will she be, since all seven of them married her?" **29**Jesus replied: "You are badly misled because you fail to understand the Scriptures and the power of God. **30**When people rise from the dead, they neither marry nor are given in marriage but live like angels in heaven. **31**As to the fact that the dead are raised, have you not read what God said to you,

32*'I am the God of Abraham, the God of Isaac, the God of Jacob'?

He is the God of the living, not of the dead." **33**The crowds who listened were spellbound by his teaching.

---

* 38: 26, 4; 27, 1; Jn 3, 16; 11, 53.
39: Heb 13, 12.
42: Dn 2, 45; Ps 118, 22; Is 28, 16; Acts 4, 11; Rom 9, 33; 1 Pt 2, 4-7.
43: Rom 11, 11.
22/2: Prv 9, 1-6; Rv 19, 9.
2-9: Lk 14, 16-24.
6: 21, 35.
13: 8, 12; 25, 30.
15-22: Mk 12, 13-17; Lk 20, 20-26.
15: Lk 11, 54.
21: Rom 13, 7.
23-33: Mk 12, 18-27; Lk 20, 27-38; Acts 23, 8.
23: Jn 11, 25.
24: Gn 38, 8; Dt 25, 5.
32: Ex 3, 6.

† 22, 14: The failure of Israel to accept Jesus' prophetic message deserved the punishment of deprivation—a warning of divine judgment against Christians who fail to live according to their faith.

The Great Commandment

34*When the Pharisees heard that he had silenced the Sadducees, they assembled in a body; **35**and one of them, a lawyer, in an attempt to trip him up, asked him, **36***"Teacher, which commandment of the law is the greatest?" **37***Jesus said to him:

" 'You shall love the Lord your God
    with your whole heart,
    with your whole soul,
    and with all your mind.'

38This is the greatest and first commandment. **39***The second is like it:

    'You shall love your neighbor as yourself.'

40*On these two commandments the whole law is based, and the prophets as well."

The Son of David

41*In turn Jesus put a question to the assembled Pharisees, **42***"What is your opinion about the Messiah? Whose son is he?" "David's," they answered. **43**He said to them, "Then how is it that David under the Spirit's influence calls him 'lord,' as he does:

44*"The Lord said to my lord, Sit at my right hand,
    until I humble your enemies beneath your feet'?

45If David calls him 'lord,' how can he be his son?" **46***No one could give him an answer; therefore no one dared, from that day on, to ask him any questions.

Hypocrisy of the Scribes and Pharisees

23 **1***†THEN Jesus told the crowds and his disciples: **2**"The scribes and the Pharisees have succeeded Moses as teachers; **3***therefore, do everything and observe everything they tell you. But do not follow their example. **4***Their words are bold but their deeds are few. They bind up heavy loads, hard to carry, to lay on other men's shoulders, while they themselves will not lift a finger to budge them. **5***All their works are performed to be seen. They widen their phylacteries and wear huge tassels. **6***They are fond of places of honor at banquets and the front seats in synagogues, **7***of marks of respect in public and of being called 'Rabbi.' **8**†As to you, avoid the title 'Rabbi.' One among you is your teacher, the rest are learners. **9**Do not call anyone on earth your father. Only one is your father, the One in heaven. **10**Avoid being called teachers. Only one is your teacher, the Messiah. **11***The greatest among you will be the one who serves the rest. **12***Whoever exalts himself shall be humbled, but whoever humbles himself shall be exalted.

13*"Woe to you scribes and Pharisees, you frauds! You shut the doors of the kingdom of God in men's faces, neither entering yourselves nor admitting those who are trying to enter. **15**Woe to you scribes and Pharisees, you frauds! You travel over sea and land to make a single convert, but once he is converted you make a devil of him twice as wicked as yourselves. **16***It is an evil day for you, blind guides! You declare, 'If a man swears by the temple it means nothing, but if he swears by the gold of the temple he is obligated.' **17**Blind fools! Which is more important, the gold or the temple which makes it sacred? **18**Again you declare, 'If a man swears by the altar it means nothing, but if he swears by the gift on the altar he is obligated.' **19***How blind you are! Which is more important, the offering or the altar which makes the offering sacred? **20***The man who swears by the altar is swearing by it and by everything on it. **21**The man who swears by the temple is swearing by it and by him who dwells there. **22**The man who swears by heaven is swearing by God's throne and by him who is seated on that throne. **23***Woe to you scribes and Pharisees, you frauds! You pay tithes on mint and herbs and seeds while neglecting the weightier matters of the law, justice and mercy and good faith. It is these you should have practiced, without neglecting the others. **24**"Blind guides! You strain out the gnat and swallow the camel! **25***Woe to you scribes and Pharisees, you frauds! You cleanse the outside of cup and dish, and leave the inside filled with loot and lust! **26**Blind Pharisee! First cleanse the inside of the cup so that its outside may be clean. **27***Woe to you scribes and Pharisees, you frauds! You are like white-washed tombs, beautiful to look at on the outside but inside full of filth and dead men's bones. **28***Thus you present to view a holy exterior while hypocrisy and evil fill you within. **29**Woe to you scribes and Pharisees, you frauds! You erect tombs for the prophets and decorate the monuments of the saints. **30***You say, 'Had we lived in our forefathers' time we would not have joined them in shedding the prophets' blood.' **31***Thus you show that you are the sons of the prophets' murderers. **32**Now it is your turn: fill up the vessel measured out by

*
34-40: Mk 12, 28-34;
    Lk 10, 25-28.
  34: Jn 13, 34f.
  36: 1 Jn 4, 21.
  37: Dt 6, 5.
  39: Lv 19, 18; Jas 2, 8.
  40: Rom 13, 8ff; Gal 5, 14.
41-46: Mk 12, 35ff.
  42: 9, 27.
  44: Ps 110, 1; Acts 2, 35;
    Heb 1, 13.
  46: Lk 20, 40.
23/1: Rom 2, 22f.
  3: Rom 2, 23f.
  4: Lk 11, 46.
  5: 6, 1-6; Ex 13, 9;
    Nm 15, 38; Dt 6, 8.

  6: Mk 12, 38f; Lk 11, 43.
  7: Lk 20, 46.
 11: 20, 26.
 12: 18, 4; Lk 1, 52f;
    14, 11; 18, 14.
 13: Jer 8, 8.
 16: 15, 14; Jn 9, 38-41.
 19: 15, 14.
 20: 5, 33-37; Sir 23, 9.
 23: Dt 14, 22; Lk 11, 42.
 25: Mk 7, 4f; Lk 11, 39f;
    Ti 1, 15.
 27: Acts 23, 3.
 28: Lk 16, 15; 18, 9.
 30: Lk 11, 47.
 31: Acts 7, 52.

†
23, 1-36: These strong criticisms of the scribes and Pharisees are found also in Mk 12, 38ff: The collection of them in Matthew is probably explained by a hostility that had developed between Judaism and Christianity. See note on Acts 8, 3. It may also be that some members of the Judaeo-Christian communities still adhered to certain ideas and practices of the Pharisees which are here reprobated.

23, 8ff: Typical hyperbolic speech of the time. It does not reject authority in principle, but authoritarianism; not the use of titles, but the failure to acknowledge that authority exists to serve God, his anointed One, and one's neighbor.

23, 14: Omitted here with many MSS.

your forefathers. **33***Vipers' nest! Brood of serpents! How can you escape condemnation to Gehenna? **34***For this reason I shall send you prophets and wise men and scribes. Some you will kill and crucify, others you will flog in your synagogues and hunt down from city to city; **35**until retribution overtakes you for all the blood of the just ones shed on earth, from the blood of holy Abel to the blood of Zechariah son of Barachiah, whom you murdered between the temple building and the altar. **36**All this, I assure you, will be the fate of the present generation. **37***O Jerusalem, Jerusalem, murderess of prophets and stoner of those who were sent to you! How often have I yearned to gather your children, as a mother bird gathers her young under her wings, but you refused me. **38***Recall the saying, 'You will find your temple deserted.' **39**I tell you, you will not see me from this time on until you declare, 'Blessed is he who comes in the name of the Lord!' "

Beginning of Calamities

24 **1*†**JESUS left the temple precincts then, and his disciples came up and pointed out to him the buildings of the temple area. **2***His comment was: "Do you see all these buildings? I assure you, not one stone will be left on another—it will all be torn down." **3**While he was seated on the Mount of Olives, his disciples came up to him privately and said: "Tell us, when will all this occur? What will be the sign of your coming and the end of the world?" **4***In reply Jesus said to them: "Be on guard! Let no one mislead you. **5**Many will come attempting to impersonate me. 'I am the Messiah!' they will claim, and they will deceive many. **6***You will hear of wars and rumors of wars. Do not be alarmed. Such things are bound to happen, but that is not yet the end. **7**Nation will rise against nation, one kingdom against another. There will be famine and pestilence and earthquakes in many places. **8**These are the early stages of the birth pangs. **9***They will hand you over to torture and kill you. **10***Indeed, you will be hated by all nations on my account. Many will falter then, betraying and hating one another. **11**False prophets will rise in great numbers to mislead many. **12**Because of the increase of evil, the love of most will grow cold. **13***The man who holds out to the end, however, is the one who will see salvation. **14***This good news of the kingdom will be

proclaimed throughout the world as a witness to all the nations. Only after that will the end come.

The Final Test

15*""When you see the abominable and destructive thing which the prophet Daniel foretold standing on holy ground (let the reader take note!), **16***those in Judea must flee to the mountains. **17***If a man is on the roof terrace, he must not come down to get anything out of his house. **18**If a man is in the field, he must not turn back to pick up his cloak. **19**It will be hard on pregnant or nursing mothers in those days. **20**Keep praying that you will not have to flee in winter or on a sabbath, **21***for those days will be more filled with anguish than any from the beginning of the world until now or in all ages to come. **22**Indeed, if the period had not been shortened, not a human being would be saved. For the sake of the chosen, however, the days will be shortened. **23***If anyone tells you at that time, 'Look, the Messiah is here,' or 'He is there,' do not believe it. **24***False messiahs and false prophets will appear, performing signs and wonders so great as to mislead even the chosen if that were possible. **25**Remember, I have told you all about it beforehand; **26**so if they tell you, 'Look, he is in the desert,' do not go out there; or 'He is in the innermost rooms,' do not believe it. **27**As the lightning from the east flashes to the west, so will the coming of the Son of Man be. **28***Where the carcass lies, there the vultures gather.

Coming of the Son of Man

29*""Immediately after the stress of that period, 'the sun will be darkened, the moon will not shed her light, the stars will fall from the sky, and the hosts of heaven will be shaken loose.' **30***Then the sign of the Son of Man will appear in the sky, and 'all the clans of earth will strike their breasts' as they see 'the Son of Man coming on the clouds of heaven' with power and great glory. **31***He will dispatch his angels 'with a mighty trumpet blast, and they will assemble his chosen from the four winds, from one end of the heavens to the other.' **32***From the fig tree learn a lesson. When its branch grows tender and sprouts leaves, you realize that summer is near. **33**Likewise, when you see all these things happening, you will know that he is near, standing at your door. **34**I assure you, the present generation will not pass away until all this takes place. **35***The heavens and the earth will pass away but my words will not pass.

The Need for Watchfulness

36*""As for the exact day or hour, no one knows it, neither the angels in heaven nor the Son, but the Father only. **37**The coming of the Son of Man will repeat what happened in Noah's time. **38**In the days before the flood people were eating and drinking, marrying and being married, right up to the day Noah entered the ark. **39***They were totally unconcerned

---

✿

33: 3, 7; 12, 34.	16: Lk 21, 20.
34f: 5, 12; 2 Chr 24, 21f;	17: Lk 17, 31.
36, 16; Lk 11, 49ff;	21: Dn 12, 1.
Rv 18, 24.	23: Lk 17, 23;
37ff: Lk 13, 34f; 19, 41-44.	2 Thes 2, 3ff.
37: 21, 35; 22, 6.	24: 2 Pt 2, 1ff; 1 Jn 4, 1.
38: 26, 5f.	28: Lk 17, 37.
24/1-51: Mk 13, 1-37;	29: Is 13, 10; Ez 32, 7;
Lk 21, 5-36.	Am 8, 9; Lk 21, 25.
2: Lk 19, 44.	30: Dn 7, 13; 1 Thes 4, 16;
4f: Lk 21, 8.	Rv 1, 7.
6: Jer 51, 46.	31: 1 Cor 15, 52.
9: 10, 17.	32: Mk 13, 28; Lk 21, 29.
10: 10, 21.	35: Is 40, 8; 51, 6;
13: 10, 22.	Heb 12, 27.
14: Rom 10, 18.	36: Acts 1, 7.
15: Dn 11, 31; 12, 11;	39: Gn 7, 11-23; 2 Pt 3, 6.
Mk 13, 14.	

---

†   24, 1-51: See note on Mk 13, 1-37.

until the flood came and destroyed them. So it will be at the coming of the Son of Man. **40** Two men will be out in the field; one will be taken and one will be left. **41** Two women will be grinding meal; one will be taken and one will be left. **42*** Stay awake, therefore! You cannot know the day your Lord is coming.

43* "Be sure of this: if the owner of the house knew when the thief was coming he would keep a watchful eye and not allow his house to be broken into. **44** You must be prepared in the same way. The Son of Man is coming at the time you least expect. **45** Who is the faithful, farsighted servant whom the master has put in charge of his household to dispense food at need? **46** Happy that servant whom his master discovers at work on his return! **47** I assure you, he will put him in charge of all his property. **48** But if the servant is worthless and tells himself, 'My master is a long time in coming,' **49** and begins to beat his fellow servants, to eat and drink with drunkards, **50** that man's master will return when he is not ready and least expects him. **51*** He will punish him severely and settle with him as is done with hypocrites. There will be wailing then and grinding of teeth.

Parable of the Ten Virgins

25 **1†** "THE reign of God can be likened to ten bridesmaids who took their torches and went out to welcome the groom. **2** Five of them were foolish, while the other five were sensible. **3** The foolish ones, in taking their torches, brought no oil along, **4** but the sensible ones took flasks of oil as well as their torches. **5** The groom delayed his coming, so they all began to nod, then to fall asleep. **6** At midnight someone shouted, 'The groom is here! Come out and greet him!' **7** At the outcry all the virgins woke up and got their torches ready. **8** The foolish ones said to the sensible, 'Give us some of your oil. Our torches are going out.' **9** But the sensible ones replied, 'No, there may not be enough for you and us. You had better go to the dealers and buy yourselves some.' **10** While they went off to buy it the groom arrived, and the ones who were ready went in to the wedding with him. Then the door was barred. **11*** Later the other bridesmaids came back. 'Master, master!' they cried. 'Open the door for us.' **12** But he answered, 'I tell you, I do not know you.' **13*** The moral is: keep your eyes open, for you know not the day or the hour.

Parable of the Silver Pieces

14* "The case of a man who was going on a journey is similar. He called in his servants and handed his funds over to them according to each man's abilities. **15** To one he disbursed five thousand silver pieces, to a second two thousand, and to a third a thousand.

Then he went away. **16** Immediately the man who received the five thousand went to invest it and made another five. **17** In the same way, the man who received the two thousand doubled his figure. **18** The man who received the thousand went off instead and dug a hole in the ground, where he buried his master's money. **19** After a long absence, the master of those servants came home and settled accounts with them. **20** The man who had received the five thousand came forward bringing the additional five. 'My lord,' he said, 'you let me have five thousand. See, I have made five thousand more.' **21*** His master said to him, 'Well done! You are an industrious and reliable servant. Since you were dependable in a small matter I will put you in charge of larger affairs. Come, share your master's joy!' **22** The man who had received the two thousand then stepped forward. 'My lord,' he said, 'you entrusted me with two thousand and I have made two thousand more.' **23** His master said to him, 'Cleverly done! You too are an industrious and reliable servant. Since you were dependable in a small matter I will put you in charge of larger affairs. Come, share your master's joy!'

24 "Finally the man who had received the thousand stepped forward. 'My lord,' he said, 'I knew you were a hard man. You reap where you did not sow and gather where you did not scatter, **25** so out of fear I went off and buried your thousand silver pieces in the ground. Here is your money back.' **26** His master exclaimed: 'You worthless, lazy lout! You know I reap where I did not sow and gather where I did not scatter. **27** All the more reason to deposit my money with the bankers, so that on my return I could have had it back with interest. **28** You, there! Take the thousand away from him and give it to the man with the ten thousand. **29*** Those who have will get more until they grow rich, while those who have not will lose even the little they have. **30** Throw this worthless servant into the darkness outside, where he can wail and grind his teeth.

The Last Judgment

31* "When the Son of Man comes in his glory, escorted by all the angels of heaven, he will sit upon his royal throne, **32*** and all the nations will be assembled before him. Then he will separate them into two groups, as a shepherd separates sheep from goats. **33** The sheep he will place on his right hand, the goats on his left. **34** The king will say to those on his right: 'Come. You have my Father's blessing! Inherit the kingdom prepared for you from the creation of the world. **35*** For I was hungry and you gave me food, I was thirsty and you gave me drink. I was a stranger and you welcomed me, **36*** naked and you clothed me. I was ill and you comforted me, in prison and you

---

*

42: 25, 13; Rv 3, 3.
43-51: Lk 12, 39-46.
  43: 1 Thes 5, 6.
  51: 13, 42; 25, 30.
25/11: Lk 13, 25.
  13: 24, 42; Mk 13, 33.
14-30: Lk 19, 12-27.

21: Lk 16, 10.
29: 13, 12; Mk 4, 25;
     Lk 8, 18; 19, 26.
31: 16, 27.
32: 2 Cor 5, 10.
35: Is 58, 7.
36: Ez 18, 7ff; Heb 13, 3.

25, 1-46. The parables teach that the Christian community is to be ever ready to meet the Lord at his second coming (1-13); to function with a sense of personal responsibility for divine gifts received (14-30); and to be constantly aware of the primacy of love of neighbor (31-46).

came to visit me.' **37**Then the just will ask him: 'Lord, when did we see you hungry and feed you or see you thirsty and give you drink? **38**When did we welcome you away from home or clothe you in your nakedness? **39**When did we visit you when you were ill or in prison?' **40***The king will answer them: 'I assure you, as often as you did it for one of my least brothers, you did it for me.'

41*"Then he will say to those on his left: 'Out of my sight, you condemned, into that everlasting fire prepared for the devil and his angels! **42***I was hungry and you gave me no food, I was thirsty and you gave me no drink. **43**I was away from home and you gave me no welcome, naked and you gave me no clothing. I was ill and in prison and you did not come to comfort me.' **44**Then they in turn will ask: 'Lord, when did we see you hungry or thirsty or away from home or naked or ill or in prison and not attend you in your needs?' **45**He will answer them: 'I assure you, as often as you neglected to do it to one of these least ones, you neglected to do it to me.' **46***These will go off to eternal punishment and the just to eternal life."

Epilogue

26 **1**†NOW when Jesus had finished all these discourses, he declared to his disciples, **2***"You know that in two days' time it will be Passover, and that the Son of Man is to be handed over to be crucified."

VII: THE PASSION AND RESURRECTION

The Conspiracy

3AT THAT TIME the chief priests and elders of the people were assembled in the palace of the high priest, whose name was Caiaphas. **4***They plotted to arrest Jesus by some trick and kill him; **5**but they said, "Not during the festival, for fear of a riot among the people."

The Anointing at Bethany

6*While Jesus was in Bethany at the house of Simon the leper, **7**a woman carrying a jar of costly perfume came up to him at table and began to pour it on his head. **8**When the disciples saw this they grew indignant, protesting: "What is the point of such extravagance? **9**This could have been sold for a good price and the money given to the poor." **10**Jesus became aware of this and said to them: "Why do you criticize the woman? It is a good deed she has done for me.

11*The poor you will always have with you but you will not always have me. **12**By pouring this perfume on my body, she has contributed toward my burial preparation. **13**I assure you, wherever the good news is proclaimed throughout the world, what she did will be spoken of as her memorial."

14*Then one of the Twelve whose name was Judas Iscariot went off to the chief priests **15**and said, "What are you willing to give me if I hand him over to you?" They paid him thirty pieces of silver, **16***and from that time on he kept looking for an opportunity to hand him over.

Passover Preparation

17*On the first day of the feast of Unleavened Bread, the disciples came up to Jesus and said, "Where do you wish us to prepare the Passover supper for you?" **18**He said, "Go to this man in the city and tell him, 'The Teacher says, My appointed time draws near. I am to celebrate the Passover with my disciples in your house.' "

19The disciples then did as Jesus had ordered, and prepared the Passover supper.

The Betrayer

20*When it grew dark he reclined at table with the Twelve. **21**In the course of the meal he said, "I assure you, one of you is about to betray me." **22**Distressed at this, they began to say to him one after another, "Surely it is not I, Lord?" **23***He replied: "The man who has dipped his hand into the dish with me is the one who will hand me over. **24***The Son of Man is departing, as Scripture says of him, but woe to that man by whom the Son of Man is betrayed. Better for him if he had never been born."

25Then Judas, his betrayer, spoke: "Surely it is not I, Rabbi?" Jesus answered, "It is you who have said it."

The Holy Eucharist

26*During the meal Jesus took bread, blessed it, broke it, and gave it to his disciples. "Take this and eat it," he said, "this is my body." **27***Then he took a cup, gave thanks, and gave it to them. "All of you must drink from it," he said, **28***"for this is my blood, the blood of the covenant, to be poured out in behalf of many for the forgiveness of sins. **29**I tell you, I will not drink this fruit of the vine from now until the day when I drink it new with you in my Father's reign." **30***Then, after singing songs of praise, they walked out to the Mount of Olives.

Peter's Denial Foretold

31*Jesus then said to them, "Tonight your faith in me will be shaken, for Scripture has it:

> 'I will strike the shepherd
> and the sheep of the flock will be
> dispersed.'

✿
40: 10, 40.
41: 7, 23; Lk 13, 27.
42: Jb 22, 7; Jas 2, 14-17.
46: Dn 12, 2.
26/2-5: Mk 14, 1f; Lk 22, 1f.
4: Jn 11, 47-53.
6-13: Mk 14, 3-9; Jn 12, 1-8.
11: Dt 15, 11.
14ff: Mk 14, 10f; Lk 22, 3-6.
16: 27, 3f; Gn 37, 28.
17-24: Mk 14, 21;
Lk 22, 7-14.21ff.
20f: Jn 13, 21-26.
23: Jn 13, 18.
24: Jn 17, 12.
26-29: Mk 14, 22-25;
Lk 22, 18ff;
1 Cor 11, 23ff.
26: Jn 6, 51-58.
27: 1 Cor 10, 16.
28: Is 53, 12.
30-35: Mk 14, 26-31.
31: Zec 13, 7; Jn 16, 32.

---

†   26, 1-75: See note on Mk 14, 1—15, 57.

32⁕But after I am raised up, I will go to Galilee ahead of you." **33**Peter responded, "Though all may have their faith in you shaken, mine will never be shaken!" **34**⁕Jesus said to him, "I give you my word, before the cock crows tonight you will deny me three times." **35**⁕Peter replied, "Even though I have to die with you, I will never disown you." And all the other disciples said the same.

The Agony in the Garden

36⁕Then Jesus went with them to a place called Gethsemani. He said to his disciples, "Stay here while I go over there and pray." **37**He took along Peter and Zebedee's two sons, and began to experience sorrow and distress. Then he said to them, **38**"My heart is nearly broken with sorrow. Remain here and stay awake with me." **39**⁕He advanced a little and fell prostrate in prayer. "My Father, if it is possible, let this cup pass me by. Still, let it be as you would have it, not as I." **40**⁕When he returned to his disciples, he found them asleep. He said to Peter, "So you could not stay awake with me for even an hour? **41**Be on guard, and pray that you may not undergo the test. The spirit is willing but nature is weak." **42**⁕Withdrawing a second time, he began to pray: "My Father, if this cannot pass me by without my drinking it, your will be done!" **43**Once more, on his return, he found them asleep; they could not keep their eyes open. **44**He left them again, withdrew somewhat, and began to pray a third time, saying the same words as before. **45**Finally he returned to his disciples and said to them: "Sleep on now. Enjoy your rest! The hour is on us when the Son of Man is to be handed over to the power of evil men. **46**⁕Get up! Let us be on our way! See, my betrayer is here."

Jesus Arrested

47⁕While he was still speaking, Judas, one of the Twelve, arrived accompanied by a great crowd with swords and clubs. They had been sent by the chief priests and elders of the people. **48**His betrayer had arranged to give them a signal, saying. "The man I shall embrace is the one; take hold of him." **49**⁕He immediately went over to Jesus, said to him, "Peace, Rabbi," and embraced him. **50**Jesus answered, "Friend, do what you are here for!" At that moment they stepped forward to lay hands on Jesus, and arrested him. **51**Suddenly one of those who accompanied Jesus put his hand to his sword, drew it, and slashed at the high priest's servant, cutting off his ear. **52**Jesus said to him: "Put back your sword where it belongs. Those who use the sword are sooner or later destroyed by it. **53**Do you not suppose I can call on my Father to provide at a moment's notice more than twelve legions of angels? **54**But then how would the Scriptures be fulfilled which say it must happen this way?"

55At that very time Jesus said to the crowd: "Am I a brigand, that you have come armed with swords and clubs to arrest me? From day to day I sat teaching in the temple precincts, yet you never arrested me. **56**Nonetheless, all this has happened in fulfillment of the writings of the prophets." Then all the disciples deserted him and fled.

Jesus before the Sanhedrin

57⁕Those who had apprehended Jesus led him off to Caiaphas the high priest, where the scribes and elders were convened. **58**Peter kept following him at a distance as far as the high priest's residence. Going inside, he sat down with the guards to see the outcome. **59**The chief priests, with the whole Sanhedrin, were busy trying to obtain false testimony against Jesus so that they might put him to death. **60**They discovered none, despite the many false witnesses who took the stand. Finally two came forward **61**⁕who stated: "This man has declared, 'I can destroy God's sanctuary and rebuild it in three days.'" **62**The high priest rose to his feet and addressed him: "Have you no answer to the testimony leveled against you?" **63**⁕But Jesus remained silent. The high priest then said to him: "I order you to tell us under oath before the living God whether you are the Messiah, the Son of God." **64**⁕Jesus answered: "It is you who say it. But I tell you this: Soon you will see the Son of Man seated at the right hand of the Power and coming on the clouds of heaven." **65**At this the high priest tore his robes: "He has blasphemed! What further need have we of witnesses? **66**Remember, you heard the blasphemy. What is your verdict?" They answered, "He deserves death!" **67**⁕Then they began to spit in his face and hit him. Others slapped him, saying: **68**"Play the prophet for us, Messiah! Who struck you?"

Peter's Denial

69⁕Peter was sitting in the courtyard when one of the serving girls came over to him and said, "You too were with Jesus the Galilean." **70**He denied it in front of everyone: "I don't know what you are talking about!" **71**When he went out to the gate another girl saw him and said to those nearby, "This man was with Jesus the Nazorean." **72**Again he denied it with an oath: "I do not know the man!" **73**A little while later some bystanders came over to Peter and said, "You are certainly one of them! Even your accent gives you away!" **74**At that he began cursing, and swore, "I do not even know the man!" Just then a cock began to crow **75**⁕and Peter remembered the prediction Jesus had made. "Before the cock crows, you will deny me three times." He went out and began to weep bitterly.

⁕
32: Mk 16, 7.	57-68: Mk 14, 53-65;
34: Lk 22, 33f; Jn 13, 37f.	Lk 22, 54;
35: 26, 69-75.	Jn 18, 12-24.
36-46: Mk 14, 32-42;	61: Jn 2, 19.
Lk 22, 40-46.	63-66: Lk 22, 67-71.
36: Jn 18, 1; Heb 5, 7ff.	63: Is 53, 7.
39: 6, 10.	64: 16, 27; Dn 7, 13.
40: Jn 4, 34; 6, 38;	67: Wis 2, 19; Is 50, 6;
Phil 2, 8.	52, 14; Mk 14, 65;
42: Heb 10, 9.	Lk 22, 63f.
46: Jn 14, 31.	69-75: Mk 14, 66-72;
47-56: Mk 14, 43-49;	Lk 22, 55-62;
Lk 22, 47-53;	Jn 18, 17f.
Jn 18, 3-11.	75: 26, 34.
49: Prv 27, 6.	

27

1* AT daybreak all the chief priests and the elders of the people took formal action against Jesus to put him to death. **2** They bound him and led him away to be handed over to the procurator Pilate.

The End of Judas

3*† Then Judas, who had handed him over, seeing that Jesus had been condemned, began to regret his action deeply. He took the thirty pieces of silver back to the chief priests and elders **4** and said, "I did wrong to deliver up an innocent man!" They retorted, "What is that to us? It is your affair!" **5** So Judas flung the money into the temple and left. He went off and hanged himself. **6** The chief priests picked up the silver, observing, "It is not right to deposit this in the temple treasury since it is blood money." **7** After consultation, they used it to buy the potter's field as a cemetery for foreigners. **8** That is why that field, even today, is called Blood Field. **9** On that occasion, what was said through Jeremiah the prophet was fulfilled:

"They took the thirty pieces of silver, the value of a man with a price on his head, a price set by the Israelites, **10** and they paid it out for the potter's field just as the Lord had commanded me."

Jesus before Pilate

11* Jesus was arraigned before the procurator, who questioned him: "Are you the king of the Jews?" Jesus responded, "As you say." **12*** Yet when he was accused by the chief priests and elders, he had made no reply. **13** Then Pilate said to him, "Surely you hear how many charges they bring against you?" **14** He did not answer him on a single count, much to the procurator's surprise.

15* Now on the occasion of a festival the procurator was accustomed to release one prisoner, whom the crowd would designate. **16** They had at the time a notorious prisoner named Barabbas. **17** Since they were already assembled, Pilate said to them, "Which one do you wish me to release for you, Barabbas or Jesus the so-called Messiah?" **18** He knew, of course, that it was out of jealousy that they had handed him over.

19† While he was still presiding on the bench, his wife sent him a message: "Do not interfere in the case of that holy man. I had a dream about him today which has greatly upset me.

20* Meanwhile, the chief priests and elders convinced the crowds that they should ask for Barabbas and have Jesus put to death. **21** So when the procurator asked them, "Which one do you wish me to release for you?" they said, "Barabbas." **22** Pilate said to them,

"Then what am I to do with Jesus, the so-called Messiah?" "Crucify him!" they all cried. **23** He said, "Why, what crime has he committed?" But they only shouted the louder, "Crucify him!" **24** Pilate finally realized that he was making no impression and that a riot was breaking out instead. He called for water and washed his hands in front of the crowd, declaring as he did so, "I am innocent of the blood of this just man. The responsibility is yours." **25***† The whole people said in reply, "Let his blood be on us and on our children." **26** At that, he released Barabbas to them. Jesus, however, he first had scourged; then he handed him over to be crucified.

The Crowning with Thorns

27* The procurator's soldiers took Jesus inside the praetorium and collected the whole cohort around him. **28** They stripped off his clothes and wrapped him in a scarlet military cloak. **29*** Weaving a crown out of thorns they fixed it on his head, and stuck a reed in his right hand. Then they began to mock him by dropping to their knees before him, saying, "All hail, king of the Jews!" **30*** They also spat at him. Afterward they took hold of the reed and kept striking him on the head. **31** Finally, when they had finished making a fool of him, they stripped him of the cloak, dressed him in his own clothes, and led him off to crucifixion.

The Way of the Cross

32* On their way out they met a Cyrenian named Simon. This man they pressed into service to carry the cross. **33*** Upon arriving at a site called Golgotha (a name which means Skull Place), **34** they gave him a drink of wine flavored with gall, which he tasted but refused to drink.

The Crucifixion

35* When they had crucified him, they divided his clothes among them by casting lots; **36** then they sat down there and kept watch over him. **37** Above his head they had put the charge against him in writing: "THIS IS JESUS, KING OF THE JEWS." **38*** Two insurgents were crucified along with him, one at his right and one at his left. **39*** People going by kept insulting him, toss-

27/1f: Mk 15, 1; Lk 22, 66; 23, 1; Jn 18, 28.
3: 26, 15.
11-14: Mk 15, 2-5; Lk 23, 2f; Jn 18, 29-38.
12: Wis 2, 19.
15-26: Mk 15, 6-15; Lk 23, 17-25; Jn 18, 39f.
20: Acts 3, 14.
25: Acts 18, 6.
27-31: Mk 15, 16-20; Jn 19, 2f.
29: 27, 11.
30: Is 50, 6.
32: Mk 15, 21; Lk 23, 36.
33-50: Mk 15, 22-34; Lk 23, 32-38; 44ff; Jn 19, 17ff.23f.28ff.
35: Ps 22, 19.
38: Lk 22, 37.
39: Ps 22, 8.

† 27, 3-10: The tragic death of Judas is elsewhere related only in Acts 1, 18; see note. Despite differences in accounts, there is agreement in essentials: a plot of land near Jerusalem, popularly called the "Field of Blood," was purchased with the money Judas received for betraying Jesus, and the traitor died an infamous death. Matthew's free citation of Jer 18, 2f; 19, 1f; 32, 6-15 and Zec 11, 13 shows that he regards Judas' death as a divine judgment.

27, 19f: This passage is proper to Matthew. The episode concerning Pilate's wife accords with evidence that women sometimes intervened in the political affairs of the Roman world. Her concern is for the welfare of her husband rather than of Jesus; for this reason she does not wish Pilate to become involved in the religious affairs of the Jews.

27, 25: *Let his blood be on us and on our children:* probably the evangelist's commentary on the responsibility for Jesus' death; cf Jer 51, 35.

ing their heads **40*** and saying: "So you are the one who was going to destroy the temple and rebuild it in three days! Save yourself, why don't you? Come down off that cross if you are God's Son!" **41**The chief priests, the scribes, and the elders also joined in the jeering: **42**"He saved others but he cannot save himself! So he is the king of Israel! Let's see him come down from that cross and then we will believe in him. **43***He relied on God; let God rescue him now if he wants to. After all, he claimed, 'I am God's Son.' " **44**The insurgents who had been crucified with him kept taunting him in the same way.

The Death of Jesus

45From noon onward, there was darkness over the whole land until midafternoon. **46***Then toward midafternoon Jesus cried out in a loud tone, *"Eli, Eli, lema sabachthani?"*, that is, "My God, my God, why have you forsaken me?" **47**This made some of the bystanders who heard it remark, "He is invoking Elijah!" **48***Immediately one of them ran off and got a sponge. He soaked it in cheap wine, and sticking it on a reed, tried to make him drink. **49***Meanwhile the rest said, "Leave him alone. Let's see whether Elijah comes to his rescue." **50**Once again Jesus cried out in a loud voice, and then gave up his spirit.

51*†Suddenly the curtain of the sanctuary was torn in two from top to bottom. **52***The earth quaked, boulders split, tombs opened. **53**Many bodies of saints who had fallen asleep were raised. After Jesus' resurrection they came forth from their tombs and entered the holy city and appeared to many. **54***The centurion and his men who were keeping watch over Jesus were terror-stricken at seeing the earthquake and all that was happening, and said, "Clearly this was the Son of God!"

55*Many women were present looking on from a distance. They had followed Jesus from Galilee to attend to his needs. **56***Among them were Mary Magdalene, and Mary the mother of James and Joseph, and the mother of Zebedee's sons.

The Burial

57*When evening fell, a wealthy man from Arimathea arrived, Joseph by name. He was another of Jesus' disciples, **58**and had gone to request the body of Jesus. Thereupon Pilate issued an order for its release. **59**Taking the body, Joseph wrapped it in fresh linen **60***and laid it in his own new tomb which had been hewn from a formation of rock. Then he rolled a huge stone across the entrance of the tomb and went away.

61But Mary Magdalene and the other Mary remained sitting there, facing the tomb.

Precautions of the Chief Priests

62†The next day, the one following the Day of Preparation, the chief priests and the Pharisees called at Pilate's residence. **63**"Sir," they said, "we have recalled that that impostor while he was still alive made the claim, 'After three days I will rise.' **64***You should issue an order having the tomb kept under surveillance until the third day. Otherwise his disciples may go and steal him and tell the people, 'He has been raised from the dead!' This final imposture would be worse than the first." **65**Pilate told them, "You have a guard. Go and secure the tomb as best you can." **66**So they went and kept it under surveillance of the guard, after fixing a seal to the stone.

The Women at the Tomb

28 **1*†**AFTER the sabbath, as the first day of the week was dawning, Mary Magdalene came with the other Mary to inspect the tomb. **2**Suddenly there was a mighty earthquake, as the angel of the Lord descended from heaven. He came to the stone, rolled it back, and sat on it. **3***In appearance he resembled a flash of lightning while his garments were as dazzling as snow. **4**The guards grew paralyzed with fear of him and fell down like dead men. **5**Then the angel spoke, addressing the women: "Do not be frightened. I know you are looking for Jesus the crucified, **6**but he is not here. He has been raised, exactly as he promised. Come and see the place where he was laid. **7***Then go quickly and tell his disciples: 'He has been raised from the dead and now goes ahead of you to Galilee, where you will see him.' That is the message I have for you."

8They hurried away from the tomb half-overjoyed, half-fearful, and ran to carry the good news to his disciples. **9**Suddenly, without warning, Jesus stood before them and said, "Peace!" The women came up and embraced his feet and did him homage. **10***At this Jesus said to them, "Do not be afraid! Go and carry the news to my brothers that they are to go to Galilee, where they will see me."

Tale of the Guards and Chief Priests

11†As the women were returning, some of the guard went into the city and reported to the chief priests all

---

† 27, 51ff: The tearing of the sanctuary veil between the holy place and the holy of holies symbolizes a break with the past; the other phenomena portend the resurrection of all men, the final cosmic event of human history; cf Is 13, 9f; 34, 4; Dn 12, 2; Jl 2, 10.

27, 62-66: This account is proper to Matthew. It is thought to have originated among Judaeo-Christians in response to a Jewish allegation that Jesus' disciples had stolen the body. Matthew wishes to emphasize the supernatural character of Jesus' departure from the tomb, to which there was no human witness; cf 28, 2ff.

28, 1-20: See note on Lk 24, 1-53.

28, 11-15: The chief priests and elders are not concerned with

✿
40: Jn 2, 19.	57-61: Mk 15, 42-47;
43: Ps 22, 9.	Lk 23, 50ff;
46: Ps 22, 2.	Jn 19, 38-42.
48: Lk 23, 36; Jn 19, 29.	60: Is 53, 9.
49: Ps 69, 21.	64: Acts 10, 40.
51: Heb 6, 19.	28/1-8: Mk 16, 1-8;
52: 1 Pt 3, 18.	Lk 24, 1-10.
54ff: Mk 15, 39ff;	3: 17, 2.
Lk 23, 47ff.	7: 26, 32.
55: Jn 19, 25.	10: Acts 1, 3.
56: 13, 55.	

that had happened. **12**They, in turn, convened with the elders and worked out their strategy, giving the soldiers a large bribe **13**with the instructions: "You are to say, 'His disciples came during the night and stole him while we were asleep.' **14**If any word of this gets to the procurator, we will straighten it out with him and keep you out of trouble." **15**The soldiers pocketed the money and did as they had been instructed. This is the story that circulates among the Jews to this very day.

Commission of the Apostles

16†The eleven disciples made their way to Galilee, to the mountain to which Jesus had summoned them. **17**†At the sight of him, those who had entertained doubts fell down in homage. **18**Jesus came forward and addressed them in these words:

"Full authority has been given to me
both in heaven and on earth;
19❋†go, therefore, and make disciples of all the nations.
Baptize them in the name
'of the Father,
and of the Son,
and of the Holy Spirit.'

❋

19: Mk 16, 15f; Lk 24, 47.　　　　20: Jn 14, 18-21.

20❋†Teach them to carry out everything I have commanded you.
And know that I am with you always, until the end of the world!"

---

† the resurrection itself, which they simply deem impossible, but with the repercussions on the people of the apostolic preaching concerning the resurrection.

28, 16: The tradition of Jesus' appearance to his disciples in Galilee is also reflected in Jn 21, 1-23.

28, 17: *Those who had entertained doubts:* literally, "but some doubted"; probably a summary allusion to the initial doubts of the disciples over the reality of the resurrection; cf Lk 24, 22ff.38; Jn 20, 27. The resurrection narratives are characterized by a condensed description of events.

28, 19: *Go, therefore, and make . . . the nations:* some regard these words as an interpretation of Jesus' final instructions in the light of the church's early change from a mission to the Jews to one in behalf of the Gentiles; see Introduction to Acts. *Baptize them . . . Holy Spirit:* The baptismal formula reflects the church's gradual understanding of God as three Persons (Acts 2, 38; 2 Cor 13, 13).

28, 20: The apostles are to teach the world not merely the doctrine of the resurrection but the historical teaching of Jesus. This the evangelist Matthew obviously considers to be contained in the gospel he has written. *I am with you always:* The power of the risen Christ (18) will ever sustain those whom he has commissioned to preach the "good news" of salvation to the world.

The Gospel According to Mark

Introduction

The gospel of Mark has contributed much to other gospels for the Christian understanding of Jesus and his ministry. The gospels of Matthew and Luke are better understood in the light of the data provided by Mark because of their direct dependence on him. Like the other evangelists, Mark, in addressing himself to Christian readers, places his gospel within the framework of Christian tradition on the identity of Jesus which developed during the course of the apostolic teaching. In Mark's day, the title "Christ" had already become part of Jesus' proper name; for the Gentile Christian it had the religious implication of "savior" or "redeemer" rather than "Messiah," which would be meaningless to all but Jews; cf Rom 9, 5. The title "Son of God" had become the most characteristic name of Jesus, designating him as the God-man; cf Rom 1, 1-4.

The gospel of Mark revolves around the two titles "Christ" and "Son of God." The evangelist shows how the Christian community's faith in Jesus as Savior harmonized with his own knowledge of his divine destiny to suffer, die, and rise again. The miraculous powers of Jesus which so mystified his contemporaries find their satisfactory explanation in the doctrine of Jesus' divinity, which the Christian community grasped only after his resurrection. Although the gospel of Mark is developed in connection with Christian faith in Jesus as redeemer and Son of God, its contents indicate the historical reality of the person and ministry of Jesus in a manner less refined by theological reflection than the accounts of the other evangelists. In Mark, the person of Jesus is depicted with an unaffected naturalness. He reacts to events with authentic human emotion: apprehension (1, 44), anger (3, 5), triumph (4, 40), sympathy (5, 36; 6, 34), surprise (5, 30; 6, 6), admiration (7, 29), sadness (14, 33f), indignation (14, 48f). His disciples take positions toward him that are critical (4, 38; 5, 31; 6, 37; 8, 4.32) or inattentive (7, 16f). He acknowledges that there are things he does not know, e. g., the appointed time for the end of the world, known only to the Father (13, 32); cf also 5, 30; 6, 38.

From a literary standpoint this gospel is divided into clearly distinguishable parts: the title (1, 1), the prologue (1, 2-13), the ministry of Jesus (1, 14—13, 37), his passion, death, and burial (14, 1—15, 47), his resurrection, the commission of the apostles, and his ascension (16, 1-20).

The account of the ministry is doctrinal rather than chronological or geographical. The reader's attention is fixed on the mystery of Jesus' person. The average man recognizes in the teaching of Jesus something authentically new (1, 22), and he is thoroughly impressed by Jesus' curative powers (1, 37f; 3, 8-11). The religious leaders are disconcerted when Jesus challenges them on their own ground (2, 16—3, 6). The relatives of Jesus fear for his

safety (3, 20f), and his disciples discover that their understanding of him is deficient (4, 36-40; 6, 47-52). Jesus accepts the title of prophet, but he lays no explicit claim to the role of Messiah; he even imposes silence concerning his miracles (1, 44; 5, 43; 7, 36; 8, 26).

At Caesarea Philippi Jesus departs from this reticence and elicits two admissions from his disciples: one is that popular opinion concedes him the role of prophet; the other is that the disciples themselves consider him to be the Messiah (8, 27-30). At this point Mark's gospel reaches its first climax concerning the identity of Jesus, to which it has been building up. Jesus proceeds beyond the messianic confession of his disciples to state clearly his own prophetic understanding of his role: it is the divine will that he should suffer and die at the hands of the Sanhedrin. The mystery of the crucified Messiah, which is a stumbling block to the Jews (1 Cor 1, 23), is traced by Mark to Jesus' self-awareness throughout his ministry. Though the remainder of the gospel incorporates an occasional miracle story (9, 17-27; 10, 46-52; 11, 12ff.20f), and much of Jesus' teaching, it is dominated by his self-revelation as the chosen instrument who is to suffer, die, and rise again (9, 9f.31f; 10, 32ff; 12, 1-12; 14, 1—16, 8). Within the passion narrative, the second and chief climax of Jesus' self-revelation occurs when, in the inquest before the high priest, he is shown by Mark to express the church's faith that he is both Messiah and Son of God (14, 62).

Mark's geographical framework places the ministry of Jesus not only in the Galilean area (1, 14—6, 13), but outside it as well (6, 30—10, 31). The journey to Jerusalem begins in 10, 32 and ends in 11, 1 near that city, where the final days of the ministry are to be spent (11, 1—15, 37).

According to Papias (†135 A. D.), the author of the second gospel was Mark who served as Peter's "interpreter" (editor of Petrine material?). Irenaeus (c 202), Clement of Alexandria (c 215), Tertullian (c 220), and Origen (c 254) attest a similar relationship. There is no need to reject the identification of the author with that John Mark whom the New Testament associates with St. Paul (Acts 12, 25; 15, 37.39; Col 4, 10; 2 Tm 4, 11; Phlm 24), and with St. Peter (Acts 12, 12; 1 Pt 5, 13).

The Petrine influence on Mark should not be exaggerated. Modern scholarship has shown quite clearly that Mark's sources cannot be explained solely in terms of Peter's preaching. On the basis of manuscript and stylistic evidence, Mk 16, 9-20 derives from a hand other than Mark's. The gospel originally ended at 16, 8. The so-called longer ending (vv 9-20), which the Council of Trent declared to be inspired and canonical, was known to Justin Martyr (c 165), Tatian (c 170), and Irenaeus (c 202).

Data in the gospel clearly indicate that it was intended for Gentile Christian readers (7, 3f.11), or at least readers unfamiliar with Jewish customs; nonetheless, the place of composition is uncertain. Following the suggestion of Clement of Alexandria and Origen, the majority of modern scholars consider the gospel to have been written in Rome. The date of composition is c 70 A. D.

It is true that the gospel of Mark is used less than the others in liturgical worship; nevertheless it has contributed much to these gospels for the Christian understanding of Jesus and his ministry.

The principal divisions of the Gospel of Mark are as follows:

I: Prologue: Preparation for the Ministry of Jesus (1, 1-13)
II: The Mystery of Jesus (1, 14—8, 26)
III: The Mystery Begins To Be Revealed (8, 27—9, 32)
IV: The Full Revelation of the Mystery (9, 33—16, 20)

I: PROLOGUE: PREPARATION FOR THE MINISTRY OF JESUS

1 ¹†HERE BEGINS THE GOSPEL of Jesus Christ, the Son of God. ²*†In Isaiah the prophet it is written:

John the Baptizer

"I send my messenger before you
    to prepare your way:
³*†a herald's voice in the desert, crying,
'Make ready the way of the Lord,
    clear him a straight path.' "

⁴Thus it was that John the Baptizer appeared in the desert, proclaiming a baptism of repentance which led to the forgiveness of sins. ⁵†All the Judean countryside and the people of Jerusalem went out to him in great numbers. They were being baptized by him in the Jordan River as they confessed their sins. ⁶†John was clothed in camel's hair, and wore a leather belt around his waist. His food was grasshoppers and wild honey. ⁷†The theme of his preaching was: "One more powerful than I is to come after me. I am not fit to stoop and untie his sandal straps. ⁸*I have baptized you in water; he will baptize you in the Holy Spirit."

The Baptism of Jesus

⁹*†During that time, Jesus came from Nazareth in Galilee and was baptized in the Jordan by John. ¹⁰Immediately on coming up out of the water he saw the sky rent in two and the Spirit descending on him like a dove. ¹¹*Then a voice came from the heavens: "You are my beloved Son. On you my favor rests."

✻
1/2-8: Mt 3, 1-11; Lk 3, 2-16.	9ff: Mt 3, 13-17; Lk 3, 21f;
2: Mal 3, 1.	Jn 1, 32f.
3: Is 40, 3; Jn 1, 23.	11: Ps 2, 7.
8: Jn 1, 27; Acts 1, 5;	12: Mt 4, 1-11; Lk 4, 1-13.
11, 16.	14: Mt 4, 12-17.
	15: Mt 3, 2.

The Temptation

¹²*†At that point the Spirit sent him out toward the desert. ¹³He stayed in the wasteland forty days, put to the test there by Satan. He was with the wild beasts, and angels waited on him.

II: THE MYSTERY OF JESUS

Call of the First Disciples

¹⁴*†AFTER JOHN'S ARREST, Jesus appeared in Galilee proclaiming the good news of God: ¹⁵*"This is the time of fulfillment. The reign of God is at hand! Reform your lives and believe in the gospel!"

---

†
1, 1: This verse is probably the title of the entire gospel, which Mark regards as the account of Jesus' ministry of redemption. Several important early manuscripts lack the phrase *Son of God;* its authenticity, however, is accepted by most modern scholars.

1, 2f: Portions of Exodus (23, 20), Malachi (3, 1) and Isaiah (40, 3) are combined here; cf Mt 11, 10; Lk 7, 26. Mark mentions only Isaiah.

1, 3f: The historical concept of God's fulfillment of prophecy is the same as in Matthew. See note on Mt 3, 1. On repentance, see note on Acts 2, 38.

1, 5: See note on Mt 3, 11f. *They confessed their sins:* whether the confession was explicit and individual or general and collective is not determinable from the text.

1, 6: *Clothed in camel's hair . . . waist:* see note on Mt 3, 4.

1, 7f: Here the figure of Jesus is kept foremost in the Baptizer's preaching. He is the *One more powerful* who *is to come.* Matthew (3, 7-10) and Luke (3, 7-14) add elements of warning against those who hear the invitation to repentance and fail to heed it.

1, 9ff: The synoptic gospels concentrate on the baptism of Jesus, while the fourth gospel (Jn 1, 24-37) is concerned with the role of the Baptizer in identifying Jesus as the One who is to come. The synoptics ascribe directly to God the Father the identification of Jesus as "Servant of Yahweh." The dove is the symbol of the Holy Spirit (Mk 1, 10), derived perhaps from the image of the creative spirit of God hovering over the waters (Gn 1, 2). The intimation is that Jesus, possessor of the Spirit, is the creator of the new people of God. The occasion of Jesus' baptism is the response to the prayer in Is 64, 1 for the heavens to open and rain down messianic salvation (1, 10). The designation of Jesus as God's Son reflects the early Christian usage of Ps 2, 7, which sees the sonship there spoken of as prophetically fulfilled in Jesus' resurrection.

1, 12f: Jesus, possessor of the Spirit, is directed irresistibly to a confrontation with Satan over the course of forty days. Both angels and wild beasts are present. Though the sense of the imagery is uncertain, some evidence in New Testament times shows demons symbolized by wild beasts. Following the extrabiblical Jewish literary tradition of holy men subjected to temptation, Mark depicts Jesus as the faithful servant of Yahweh, loyal to God in his time of trial (Heb 2, 14-18). The temptation narrative expresses, in terms of a drama, Jesus' ministry, passion and death as a conflict with satanic power.

1, 14f: *Jesus appeared . . . the good news of God:* a summary statement concerning Jesus' preaching, to introduce his public ministry. *This is the time of fulfillment:* the period in human history appointed by God for making good his messianic promises. *The reign of God is at hand:* see note on Mt 3, 1. Though some scholars maintain that Jesus proclaimed the kingdom as imminent but not yet arrived, it is more probable that he announced it as actually arrived yet awaiting future development. *Reform your lives:* see note on Acts 2, 38.

[16]*†As he made his way along the Sea of Galilee, he observed Simon and his brother Andrew casting their nets into the sea; they were fishermen. [17]Jesus said to them, "Come after me; I will make you fishers of men." [18]They immediately abandoned their nets and became his followers. [19]Proceeding a little farther along, he caught sight of James, Zebedee's son, and his brother John. They too were in their boat putting their nets in order. He summoned them on the spot. [20]They abandoned their father Zebedee, who was in the boat with the hired men, and went off in his company. [21]*†Shortly afterward they came to Capernaum, and on the sabbath he entered the synagogue and began to teach. [22]*The people were spellbound by his teaching because he taught with authority, and not like the scribes.

Cure of a Demoniac

[23]†There appeared in their synagogue a man with an unclean spirit that shrieked: [24]"What do you want of us, Jesus of Nazareth? Have you come to destroy us? I know who you are—the holy One of God!" [25]Jesus rebuked him sharply: "Be quiet! Come out of the man!" [26]At that the unclean spirit convulsed the man violently and with a loud shriek came out of him. [27]All who looked on were amazed. They began to ask one another: "What does this mean? A completely new teaching in a spirit of authority! He gives orders to unclean spirits and they obey!" [28]From that point on his reputation spread throughout the surrounding region of Galilee.

Peter's Mother-in-law

[29]*Immediately upon leaving the synagogue, he entered the house of Simon and Andrew with James and John. [30]Simon's mother-in-law lay ill with a fever, and the first thing they did was to tell him about her. [31]He went over to her and grasped her hand and helped her up, and the fever left her. She immediately began to wait on them.

Other Miracles

[32]After sunset, as evening drew on, they brought him all who were ill, and those possessed by demons. [33]Before long the whole town was gathered outside the door. [34]†Those whom he cured, who were variously afflicted, were many, and so were the demons he expelled. But he would not permit the demons to speak, because they knew him. [35]*Rising early the next morning, he went off to a lonely place in the desert; there he was absorbed in prayer. [36]Simon and his companions managed to track him down, and [37]when they found him, they told him, "Everybody is looking for you!" [38]He said to them: "Let us move on to the neighboring villages so that I may proclaim the good news

there also. That is what I have come to do." [39]So he went into their synagogues preaching the good news and expelling demons throughout the whole of Galilee.

A Leper

[40]*†A leper approached him with a request, kneeling down as he addressed him: "If you will to do so, you can cure me." [41]*Moved with pity, Jesus stretched out his hand, touched him, and said: "I do will it. Be cured." [42]*The leprosy left him then and there, and he was cured. [43]Jesus gave him a stern warning and sent him on his way. [44]*"Not a word to anyone, now,"

"Go off and present yourself to the priest and offer for your cure what Moses prescribed. That should be a proof for them." [45]The man went off and began to proclaim the whole matter freely, making the story public. As a result of this, it was no longer possible for Jesus to enter a town openly. He stayed in desert places; yet people kept coming to him from all sides.

A Paralytic at Capernaum

2 [1]*†HE came back to Capernaum after a lapse of several days and word got around that he was at home. [2]At that they began to gather in great numbers. There was no longer any room for them, even around the door. [3]While he was delivering God's word to them, some people arrived bringing a paralyzed man to him. The four who carried him [4]were unable to bring him to Jesus because of the crowd, so they began to open up the roof over the spot where

---

† 1, 16-20: See note on Mt 4, 19.

1, 21f: The people realize that Jesus presents himself as a prophet who does not depend on rabbinic tradition for his teaching.

1, 23-28: This account of exorcism is the first of four such narratives in Mark (5, 1-20; 7, 24-30; 9, 14-27). The gospel also contains several allusions to Jesus' numerous exorcisms (1, 34.39; 3, 11f), and records a debate between Jesus and the scribes over their meaning (3, 22-30). Matthew and Luke present some of the same traditional accounts as Mark but add no new ones. Note that Jesus neither declares diabolical "possession" to be a phenomenon in Israel nor contests any affirmation of the presence of diabolic beings. When the scribes accuse Jesus of performing exorcisms by the power of Satan, they imply that there are diabolic manifestations among the sick brought to Jesus. Apart from the case of the Syro-Phoenician woman's daughter (see note on 7, 24-30), nowhere is Jesus asked precisely to perform an exorcism.

1, 34: *Because they knew him:* probably the knowledge which the demons had about Jesus is to be understood in the broad sense, i. e., they are reported as having recognized Jesus as their enemy without having specific knowledge of his actual identity.

1, 40-45: For the various forms of skin disease, cf Lv 13, 1-50 and the note on Lv 13, 2ff. Jesus shows concern for the proper interpretation of his miracles. He assumes that the priests will perceive the messianic significance of the miracle. On the "messianic secret" involved in this narrative, see note on 8, 27-30.

2, 1-12: Besides his power over demonic spirits and physical illness, Jesus manifests his power to forgive sins. This miracle story constitutes a transition to the conflict narratives which follow. Once Christians believed in the divinity of Jesus after his resurrection, they realized that he forgave sins through the power he had conferred on the community; cf Mt 9, 8.

❖ 16-20: Mt 4, 18-22; Lk 5, 2-11.
21-28: Lk 4, 31-37.
22: Mt 7, 28f.
29-34: Mt 8, 14ff; Lk 4, 38-41.
35-39: Lk 4, 42ff.

40-44: Mt 8, 2ff; Lk 5, 12ff.
41: 5, 30.
42: Lk 17, 14.
44: Lv 14, 2-32.
2/1-12: Mt 9, 2-8; Lk 5, 18-26.

Jesus was. When they had made a hole, they let down the mat on which the paralytic was lying. **5**When Jesus saw their faith, he said to the paralyzed man, "My son, your sins are forgiven." **6**Now some of the scribes were sitting there asking themselves: **7**"Why does the man talk in that way? He commits blasphemy! Who can forgive sins except God alone?" **8**Jesus was immediately aware of their reasoning, though they kept it to themselves, and he said to them: "Why do you harbor these thoughts? **9**Which is easier, to say to the paralytic, 'Your sins are forgiven,' or to say, 'Stand up, pick up your mat, and walk again'? **10**That you may know that the Son of Man has authority on earth to forgive sins" (he said to the paralyzed man), **11**"I command you: Stand up! Pick up your mat and go home." **12**The man stood and picked up his mat and went outside in the sight of everyone. They were awestruck; all gave praise to God, saying, "We have never seen anything like this!"

The Call of Levi

13Another time, while he went walking along the lakeshore, people kept coming to him in crowds and he taught them. **14**As he moved on he saw Levi the son of Alphaeus at his tax collector's post, and said to him, "Follow me." Levi got up and became his follower. **15**While Jesus was reclining to eat in Levi's house, many tax collectors and those known as sinners joined him and his disciples at dinner. The number of those who followed him was large. **16**When the scribes who belonged to the Pharisee party saw that he was eating with tax collectors and offenders against the law, they complained to his disciples, "Why does he eat with such as these?" **17**Overhearing the remark, Jesus said to them, "People who are healthy do not need a doctor; sick people do. I have come to call sinners, not the self-righteous."

The Question of Fasting

18Now John's disciples and the Pharisees were accustomed to fast. People came to Jesus with the objection, "Why do John's disciples and those of the Pharisees fast while yours do not?" **19**Jesus replied: "How can the guests at a wedding fast as long as the groom is still among them? So long as the groom stays with them, they cannot fast. **20**The day will come, however, when the groom will be taken away from them; on that day they will fast. **21**No one sews a patch of unshrunken cloth on an old cloak. If he should do so, the very thing he has used to cover the hole would pull away—the new from the old—and the tear would get worse. **22**Similarly, no man pours new wine into old wineskins. If he does so, the wine will burst the skins and both wine and skins will be lost. No, new wine is poured into new skins."

The Disciples and the Sabbath

23It happened that he was walking through standing grain on the sabbath, and his disciples began to pull off heads of grain as they went along. **24**At this the Pharisees protested: "Look! Why do they do a thing not permitted on the sabbath?" **25**He said to them: "Have you never read what David did when he was in need and he and his men were hungry? **26**How he entered God's house in the days of Abiathar the high priest and ate the holy bread which only the priests were permitted to eat? He even gave it to his men." **27**Then he said to them: "The sabbath was made for man, not man for the sabbath. **28**That is why the Son of Man is lord even of the sabbath."

A Man with a Withered Hand

3 **1**HE returned to the synagogue where there was a man whose hand was shriveled up. **2**They kept an eye on Jesus to see whether he would heal him on the sabbath, hoping to be able to bring an accusation against him. **3**He addressed the man with the shriveled hand: "Stand up here in front!" **4**Then he said to them: "Is it permitted to do a good deed on the sabbath—or an evil one? To preserve life—or to destroy it?" At this they remained silent. **5**He looked around at them with anger, for he was deeply grieved that they had closed their minds against him. Then he said to the man, "Stretch out your hand." The man did so and his hand was perfectly restored. **6**When the Pharisees went outside, they immediately began to plot with the Herodians how they might destroy him.

The Mercy of Jesus

7Jesus withdrew toward the lake with his disciples. A great crowd followed him from Galilee, **8**and an equally great multitude came to him from Judea, Jerusalem, Idumea, Transjordan, and the neighborhood of Tyre and Sidon, because they had heard what he had done. **9**In view of their numbers, he told his disciples to have a fishing boat ready for him so that he could avoid the press of the crowd against him. **10**Because he had cured many, all who had afflictions kept pushing toward him to touch him. **11**Unclean spirits would catch sight of him, fling themselves down at his feet, and shout, "You are the Son of God!", **12**while he kept ordering them sternly not to reveal who he was.

  7: Is 43, 25.
  13: 4, 1.
  14-17: Mt 9, 9-13;
      Lk 5, 27-32.
  23-28: Mt 12, 1-8; Lk 6, 1-5.
  24: Dt 23, 25.
  26: 1 Sm 21, 2-7;
      Lv 24, 5-9.

  27: 2 Mc 5, 19.
  3/1-6: Mt 12, 9-14;
      Lk 6, 6-11.
  5: Lk 14, 4.
  7-12: Mt 4, 23ff; Lk 6, 17ff.
  10: 5, 30.
  11: 1, 34; Lk 4, 41.

†
  2, 15ff: See note on Mt 9, 13.
  2, 18-22: See note on Mt 9, 14-17.
  2, 23-27: See note on Mt 12, 3-6.
  2, 28: This statement seems to be an editorial addition to teach that the early Christian community's freedom from Jewish sabbath regulations relies on the authority of Jesus, now fully vindicated by his resurrection and ascension. On the title *Son of Man*, see note on 8, 31ff.
  3, 1-6: See note on Mt 12, 10.
  3, 12: Jesus refuses to receive witness concerning his identity

Choice of the Twelve

13*†He then went up the mountain and summoned the men he himself had decided on, who came and joined him. **14***He named twelve as his companions whom he would send to preach the good news; **15**they were likewise to have authority to expel demons. **16**He appointed the Twelve as follows: **17***Simon to whom he gave the name Peter; James, son of Zebedee; and John, the brother of James (he gave these two the name Boanerges, or "sons of thunder"); **18**Andrew, Philip, Bartholomew, Matthew, Thomas, James, son of Alphaeus; Thaddaeus, Simon of the Zealot party, **19**and Judas Iscariot, who betrayed him.

Blasphemy of the Scribes

20*†He returned to the house with them and again the crowd assembled, making it impossible for them to get any food whatever. **21***When his family heard of this they came to take charge of him, saying, "He is out of his mind"; **22***while the scribes who arrived from Jerusalem asserted, "He is possessed by Beelzebul," and "He expels demons with the help of the prince of demons." **23**Summoning them, he then began to speak to them by way of examples: "How can Satan expel Satan? **24**If a kingdom is torn by civil strife, that kingdom cannot last. **25**If a household is divided according to loyalties, that household will not survive. **26**Similarly, if Satan has suffered mutiny in his ranks and is torn by dissension, he cannot endure; he is finished. **27**No one can enter a strong man's house and despoil his property unless he has first put him under restraint. Only then can he plunder his house.

28*"I give you my word, every sin will be forgiven mankind and all the blasphemies men utter, **29**but whoever blasphemes against the Holy Spirit will never be forgiven. He carries the guilt of his sin without end." **30**He spoke thus because they had said, "He is possessed by an unclean spirit."

Jesus and His Family

31*His mother and his brothers arrived, and as they stood outside they sent word to him to come out. **32**The crowd seated around him told him, "Your mother and your brothers and sisters are outside asking for you." **33**He said in reply, "Who are my mother and my brothers?" **34**And gazing around him at those seated in the circle he continued, "These are my mother and my brothers. **35**Whoever does the will of God is brother and sister and mother to me."

Parable of the Seed

4 **1***†ON another occasion he began to teach beside the lake. Such a huge crowd gathered around him that he went and sat in a boat on the water, while the crowd remained on the shore nearby. **2**He began to instruct them at great length, by the use of parables, and in the course of his teaching said: **3**"Listen carefully to this. A farmer went out sowing. **4**Some of what he sowed landed on the footpath, where the birds came along and ate it. **5**Some of the seed landed on rocky ground where it had little soil; it sprouted immediately because the soil had no depth. **6**Then, when the sun rose and scorched it, it began to wither for lack of roots. **7**Again, some landed among thorns, which grew up and choked it off, and there was no yield of grain. **8**Some seed, finally, landed on good soil and yielded grain that sprang up to produce at a rate of thirty- and sixty- and a hundredfold." **9**Having spoken this parable, he added: "Let him who has ears to hear me, hear!"

10†Now when he was away from the crowd, those present with the Twelve questioned him about the parables. **11**He told them: "To you the mystery of the reign of God has been confided. To the others outside it is all presented in parables, **12***so that they will look intently and not see, listen carefully and not understand, lest perhaps they repent and be forgiven."

13*He said to them: "You do not understand this parable? How then are you going to understand other figures like it? **14**What the sower is sowing is the word. **15**Those on the path are the ones to whom, as soon as they hear the word, Satan comes to carry off what was sown in them. **16**Similarly, those sown on rocky ground are people who on listening to the word accept it joy-

† from evil spirits. Since this identity can be known only from divine revelation, Mark does not ascribe true knowledge of Jesus to evil spirits. See note on Mt 16, 17.

3, 13-19: Within the circle of Jesus' disciples, the Twelve were given a privileged position. They alone were present with Jesus at the Last Supper (14, 17). Later they exercised leadership over the primitive community in Jerusalem (Acts 1, 26; 2, 14; 5, 20f), and were responsible for the information about Jesus that developed into the gospel tradition (Acts 6, 2.4).

3, 20-35: Reactions to the person and teaching of Jesus are varied: the crowds are favorable to him (1, 27.37.45; 2, 15; 3, 8); the scribes and Pharisees are increasingly hostile (2, 13—3, 6); his relatives are unbelieving (3, 20f). Faith in Jesus' prophetic word creates a relationship superior to that between himself and his relatives.

4, 1-34: See note on Mt 13, 1-53 for the sense of the parables of the sower, the mustard seed, and the leaven.

4, 10ff: In Mt 13, 10, attention centers on the method of teaching in parables. Jesus gives the same response here as he gave there. The light shed by the parables on the reign of God, though real, is far from complete. For the disciples, well-disposed to accept the teaching, questions are answered; not so for the crowds, ill-prepared at this time to abandon their false preconceptions. Thus Mark indicates a gradual unveiling of the mystery, beginning with the parables and continuing as a slow realization on the part of hearers that the traditional conceptions about God's reign were false and contrary to his plan; cf Mt 13, 33. Divine wisdom is described as justified in this procedure in terms of Is 6, 9f.

13-19: Mt 10, 1-4; Lk 6, 12-16.
14: 6, 7.
17: Mt 16, 18; Jn 1, 42.
20: 2, 2.
21: Jn 10, 20.
22-30: Mt 12, 24-32; Lk 11, 15-22.
28: Lk 12, 10.
31-35: Mt 12, 46-50; Lk 8, 19ff.
4/1-12: Mt 13, 18-23; Lk 8, 4-10.
1: 2, 13; Lk 5, 1.
12: Is 6, 9; Jn 12, 40; Acts 28, 26; Rom 11, 8.
13-20: Mt 13, 18-23; Lk 8, 11-15.

fully at the outset. **17**Being rootless, they last only a while. When some pressure or persecution overtakes them because of the word, they falter. **18**Those sown among thorns are another class. They have listened to the word, **19**but anxieties over life's demands, and the desire for wealth, and cravings of other sorts come to choke it off; it bears no yield. **20**But those sown on good soil are the ones who listen to the word, take it to heart, and yield at thirty- and sixty- and a hundred-fold."

Purpose of This Teaching

21*†He said to them: "Is a lamp acquired to be put under a bushel basket or hidden under a bed? Is it not meant to be put on a stand? **22***Things are hidden only to be revealed at a later time; they are covered so as to be brought out into the open. **23**Let him who has ears to hear me, hear!" **24***He said to them another time: "Listen carefully to what you hear. In the measure you give you shall receive, and more besides. **25***To those who have, more will be given; from those who have not, what little they have will be taken away."

Seed Grows of Itself

26*†He also said: "This is how it is with the reign of God. A man scatters seed on the ground. **27**He goes to bed and gets up day after day. Through it all the seed sprouts and grows without his knowing how it happens. **28**The soil produces of itself first the blade, then the ear, finally the ripe wheat in the ear. **29**When the crop is ready he 'wields the sickle, for the time is ripe for harvest.'"

The Mustard Seed

30*He went on to say: "What comparison shall we use for the reign of God? What image will help to present it? **31**It is like mustard seed which, when planted in the soil, is the smallest of all the earth's seeds, **32**yet once it is sown, springs up to become the largest of shrubs, with branches big enough for the birds of the sky to build nests in its shade." **33†**By means of many such parables he taught them the message in a way they could understand. **34**To them he spoke only by way of parable, while he kept explaining things privately to his disciples.

The Storm on the Sea

35*†That day as evening drew on he said to them, "Let us cross over to the farther shore." **36**Leaving the crowd, they took him away in the boat in which he was sitting, while the other boats accompanied him. **37**It happened that a bad squall blew up. The waves were breaking over the boat and it began to ship water badly. **38**Jesus was in the stern through it all, sound

asleep on a cushion. They finally woke him and said to him, "Teacher, does it not matter to you that we are going to drown?" **39**He awoke and rebuked the wind and said to the sea: "Quiet! Be still!" The wind fell off and everything grew calm. **40**Then he said to them, "Why are you so terrified? Why are you lacking in faith?" **41***A great awe overcame them at this. They kept saying to one another, "Who can this be that the wind and the sea obey him?"

Expulsion of the Devils in Gerasa

5 **1***THEY came to Gerasene territory on the other side of the lake. **2**As he got out of the boat, he was immediately met by a man from the tombs who had an unclean spirit. **3**The man had taken refuge among the tombs; he could no longer be restrained even with a chain. **4**In fact, he had frequently been secured with handcuffs and chains, but had pulled the chains apart and smashed the fetters. No one had proved strong enough to tame him. **5**Uninterruptedly night and day, amid the tombs and on the hillsides, he screamed and gashed himself with stones. **6**Catching sight of Jesus at a distance, he ran up and did him homage, **7**shrieking in a loud voice, "Why meddle with me, Jesus, Son of God Most High? I implore you in God's name, do not torture me!" **8**(Jesus had been saying to him, "Unclean spirit, come out of the man!") **9***"What is your name?" Jesus asked him. "Legion is my name," he answered. "There are hundreds of us." **10**He pleaded hard with Jesus not to drive them away from that neighborhood.

11It happened that a large herd of swine was feeding there on the slope of the mountain. **12**"Send us into the swine," they begged him. "Let us enter them." **13**He gave the word, and with it the unclean spirits came out and entered the swine. The herd of about two thousand went rushing down the bluff into the lake, where they began to drown. **14**The swineherds ran off and brought the news to field and village, and the people came to see what had happened. **15**As they approached Jesus, they caught sight of the man who had been possessed by Legion sitting fully clothed and perfectly sane, and they were seized with fear. **16**The spectators explained what had happened to the possessed man,

---

† 4, 21-25: These sayings, found in other contexts as well (Mt 5, 15; 7, 2; 10, 26; 13, 12), are here presented as commentary on the revelation of the reign of God. Jesus' teaching in parables begins this revelation (21); time and events will make it more clear (22). Acceptance of the original light gives promise of more in the future (24). Conversely, rejection of that light results in greater obscurity and misunderstanding (25).

4, 26-29: This parable is found only in Mark. Through the ministry of Jesus, God's sovereign rule over men is made manifest. It comes without warning; it is destined to spread throughout the world and to continue for the length of time set by God.

4, 33f: See note on 4, 10ff.

4, 35-41: The sequence of action in this event is rearranged in Mt 8, 23-27 to teach the Christian community what great trust in Jesus it must have in time of peril. In Mark, the disciples' panic is reflected in their reproachful question to Jesus. He in return interprets the event for them as showing the need for absolute confidence in him.

✻
21-25: Lk 8, 16ff.
  21: Mt 5, 15; Lk 11, 33.
  22: Mt 10, 26; Lk 12, 2.
  24: Mt 7, 2; Lk 6, 38.
  25: Mt 13, 12; Lk 19, 26.
26-29: Jas 5, 7.
30-32: Mt 13, 31f; Lk 13, 18f.

35-40: Mt 8, 18.23-27; Lk 8, 22-25.
  41: 1, 27.
5/1-17: Mt 8, 28-34; Lk 8, 26-37.
  9: Mt 12, 45; Lk 8, 2; 11, 26.

and told them about the swine. [17]Before long they were begging him to go away from their district. [18]As Jesus was getting into the boat, the man who had been possessed was pressing to accompany him. [19]Jesus did not grant his request, but told him instead: "Go home to your family and make it clear to them how much the Lord in his mercy has done for you." [20]At that the man went off and began to proclaim throughout the Ten Cities what Jesus had done for him. They were all amazed at what they heard.

The Daughter of Jairus; the Woman with a Hemorrhage

[21]*†Now when Jesus had crossed back to the other side again in the boat, a large crowd gathered around him and he stayed close to the lake. [22]*One of the officials of the synagogue, a man named Jairus, came near. Seeing Jesus, he fell at his feet [23]and made this earnest appeal: "My little daughter is critically ill. Please come and lay your hands on her so that she may get well and live." [24]The two went off together and a large crowd followed, pushing against Jesus.

[25]There was a woman in the area who had been afflicted with a hemorrhage for a dozen years. [26]She had received treatment at the hands of doctors of every sort and exhausted her savings in the process, yet she got no relief; on the contrary, she only grew worse. [27]She had heard about Jesus and came up behind him in the crowd and put her hand to his cloak. [28]"If I just touch his clothing," she thought, "I shall get well." [29]Immediately her flow of blood dried up and the feeling that she was cured of her affliction ran through her whole body. [30]Jesus was conscious at once that healing power had gone out from him. Wheeling about in the crowd, he began to ask, "Who touched my clothing?" [31]His disciples said to him, "You can see how this crowd hems you in, yet you ask, 'Who touched me?'" [32]Despite this, he kept looking around to see the woman who had done it. [33]Fearful and beginning to tremble now as she realized what had happened, the woman came and fell in front of him and told him the whole truth. [34]*He said to her, "Daughter, it is your faith that has cured you. Go in peace and be free of this illness."

[35]He had not finished speaking when people from the official's house arrived saying, "Your daughter is dead. Why bother the Teacher further?" [36]Jesus disregarded the report that had been brought and said to the official: "Fear is useless. What is needed is trust." [37]He would not permit anyone to follow him except Peter, James, and James's brother John. [38]As they approached the house of the synagogue leader, Jesus was struck by the noise of people wailing and crying loudly on all sides. [39]*He entered and said to them: "Why do you make this din with your wailing? The child is not dead. She is asleep." [40]At this they began to ridicule him. Then he put them all out.

Jesus took the child's father and mother and his own companions and entered the room where the child lay. [41]Taking her hand he said to her, *"Talitha, koum,"* which means, "Little girl, get up." [42]The girl, a child of twelve, stood up immediately and began to walk around. At this the family's astonishment knew no bounds. [43]He enjoined them strictly not to let anyone know about it, and told them to give her something to eat.

Jesus at Nazareth

6 [1]*†HE departed from there and returned to his own part of the country followed by his disciples. [2]When the sabbath came he began to teach in the synagogue in a way that kept his large audience amazed. They said: "Where did he get all this? What kind of wisdom is he endowed with? How is it that such miraculous deeds are accomplished by his hands? [3]*Is this not the carpenter, the son of Mary, a brother of James and Joses and Judas and Simon? Are not his sisters our neighbors here?" They found him too much for them. [4]*Jesus' response to all this was: "No prophet is without honor except in his native place, among his own kindred, and in his own house." [5]He could work no miracle there, apart from curing a few who were sick by laying hands on them, [6]so much did their lack of faith distress him. He made the rounds of the neighboring villages instead, and spent his time teaching.

Mission of the Twelve

[7]*Jesus summoned the Twelve and began to send them out two by two, giving them authority over unclean spirits. [8]He instructed them to take nothing on the journey but a walking stick—no food, no traveling bag, not a coin in the purses in their belts. [9]They were, however, to wear sandals. "Do not bring a second tunic," he said, [10]and added: "Whatever house you

---

† 5, 21-43: This narrative is significant for Christology. Jesus knows that a cure has occurred in favor of someone who touched him; he does not know the person's identity (30). Informed of the death of Jairus' daughter, he decides his course of action from the development of events; he recognizes in them the divine will to raise the girl to life (35f). His assertion, *The child is not dead. She is asleep,* leaves the girl's condition unclear (38), so that he can more easily prohibit the witnesses from speaking of the event as an unmistakable manifestation of his power to raise the dead (43).

6, 1-6: The townsmen of Jesus were not disposed to believe in him because he had not first exercised his power of miracles in their midst (2f). *"Is this not the carpenter . . . our neighbors here?":* some manuscripts have, "Is this not the carpenter's son?" The question about the *brothers* of Jesus and his *sisters* (v 3) cannot easily be decided on linguistic grounds. Greek-speaking Semites used the terms *adelphos* and *adelphē,* not only in the ordinary sense of blood brother and sister, but also for nephew, niece, half-brother, half-sister, and cousin. The question of meaning here would not have arisen but for the faith of the church in Mary's perpetual virginity.

---

* 21: 2, 13.
22-43: Mt 9, 18-26;
      Lk 8, 41-56.
34: Lk 7, 50.
39f: Acts 9, 40.
6/1-6: Mt 13, 54-58;
      Lk 4, 16-30.

3: 15, 40; Mt 12, 46;
    Jn 6, 42.
4: Jn 4, 44.
7-11: Mt 10, 1.9-14; Lk 9, 1;
     10, 4-11.

find yourself in, stay there until you leave the locality. ¹¹If any place will not receive you or hear you, shake its dust from your feet in testimony against them as you leave." ¹²With that they went off, preaching the need of repentance. ¹³*They expelled many demons, anointed the sick with oil, and worked many cures.

Death of the Baptizer

¹⁴*King Herod came to hear of Jesus, for his reputation had become widespread and people were saying, "John the Baptizer has been raised from the dead; that is why such miraculous powers are at work after him." ¹⁵*Others were saying, "He is Elijah"; still others, "He is a prophet equal to any of the prophets." ¹⁶On hearing of Jesus, Herod exclaimed, "John, whose head I had cut off, has been raised up!" ¹⁷*Herod was the one who had ordered John arrested, chained, and imprisoned on account of Herodias, the wife of his brother Philip, whom he had married. ¹⁸*That was because John had told Herod, "It is not right for you to live with your brother's wife." ¹⁹Herodias harbored a grudge against him for this and wanted to kill him but was unable to do so. ²⁰Herod feared John, knowing him to be an upright and holy man, and kept him in custody. When he heard him speak he was very much disturbed; yet he felt the attraction of his words. ²¹Herodias had her chance one day when Herod held a birthday dinner for his court circle, military officers, and the leading men of Galilee. ²²Herodias' own daughter came in at one point and performed a dance which delighted Herod and his guests. The king told the girl, "Ask for anything you want and I will give it to you." ²³*He went so far as to swear to her: "I will grant you whatever you ask, even to half my 'kingdom!" ²⁴She went out and said to her mother, "What shall I ask for?" The mother answered, "The head of John the Baptizer." ²⁵At that the girl hurried back to the king's presence and made her request: "I want you to give me, at once, the head of John the Baptizer on a platter." ²⁶The king bitterly regretted the request; yet because of his oath and the presence of the guests, he did not want to refuse her. ²⁷*He promptly dispatched an executioner, ordering him to bring back the Baptizer's head. ²⁸The man went and beheaded John in the prison. He brought in the head on a platter and gave it to the girl, and the girl gave it to her mother. ²⁹Later, when his disciples heard about this, they came and carried his body away and laid it in a tomb.

Return of the Disciples

³⁰The apostles returned to Jesus and reported to him all that they had done and what they had taught. ³¹*He said to them, "Come by yourselves to an out-of-the-way place and rest a little." People were coming and going in great numbers, making it impossible for them to so much as eat. ³²*So Jesus and the apostles went off in the boat by themselves to a deserted place. ³³People saw them leaving, and many got to know about it. People from all the towns hastened on foot to the place, arriving ahead of them.

Jesus Feeds Five Thousand

³⁴Upon disembarking Jesus saw a vast crowd. He pitied them, for they were like sheep without a shepherd; and he began to teach them at great length. ³⁵It was now getting late and his disciples came to him with a suggestion: "This is a deserted place and it is already late. ³⁶Why do you not dismiss them so that they can go to the crossroads and villages around here and buy themselves something to eat?" ³⁷"You give them something to eat," Jesus replied. At that they said, "Are we to go and spend two hundred days' wages for bread to feed them?" ³⁸"How many loaves have you?" Jesus asked. "Go and see." When they learned the number they answered, "Five, and two fish." ³⁹He told them to make the people sit down on the green grass in groups or parties. ⁴⁰The people took their places in hundreds and fifties, neatly arranged like flower beds. ⁴¹Then, taking the five loaves and the two fish, Jesus raised his eyes to heaven, pronounced a blessing, broke the loaves, and gave them to the disciples to distribute. He divided the two fish among all of them ⁴²and they ate until they had their fill. ⁴³They gathered up enough leftovers to fill twelve baskets, besides what remained of the fish. ⁴⁴Those who had eaten the loaves numbered five thousand men.

Jesus Walks on the Water

⁴⁵*†Immediately afterward he insisted that his disciples get into the boat and precede him to the other side toward Bethsaida, while he dismissed the crowd. ⁴⁶When he had taken leave of them, he went off to the mountain to pray. ⁴⁷As evening drew on, the boat was far out on the lake while he was alone on the land. ⁴⁸Then, seeing them tossed about as they tried to row with the wind against them, he came walking toward them on the water; the time was between three and six in the morning. He meant to pass them by. ⁴⁹When they saw him walking on the lake, they thought it was a ghost and they began to cry out. ⁵⁰They had all seen him and were terrified. He hastened to reassure them: "Get hold of yourselves! It is I. Do not be afraid!" ⁵¹He got into the boat with them and the wind died down. They were taken aback by these happenings, ⁵²*for they had not understood about the loaves. On the contrary, their minds were completely closed to the meaning of the events.

❋

13: Jas 5, 14.
14f: Lk 9, 7f.
14-29: Mt 14, 1-12.
15: Mt 16, 14.
17: Lk 3, 19f.
18: Lv 18, 16.
23: Est 5, 3.
27f: Lk 9, 9.

31: 3, 20; Mt 14, 13; Lk 9, 10.
32-44: Mt 14, 13-21; Lk 9, 10-17; Jn 6, 1-13.
45-51: Mt 14, 22-32; Jn 6, 15-21
52: 4, 13.

---

† 6, 45-52: Mt 14, 22-33 and Jn 6, 15-21, as well as Mark, place the event of Jesus' walking on the sea after the miracle of the loaves and fish. The disciples would not have been so astonished at it had they understood the meaning of the multiplication of the loaves (51f). But contrast Matthew's conclusion in 14, 33.

Other Miracles

53†After making the crossing they came ashore at Gennesaret, and tied up there. **54**As they were leaving the boat people immediately recognized him. **55**The crowds scurried about the adjacent area and began to bring in the sick on bedrolls to the place where they heard he was. **56***Wherever he put in an appearance, in villages, in towns, or at crossroads, they laid the sick in the market places and begged him to let them touch just the tassel of his cloak. All who touched him got well.

Jesus and the Pharisees

7 **1***†THE Pharisees and some of the experts in the law who had come from Jerusalem gathered around him. **2**They had observed a few of his disciples eating meals without having purified—that is to say, washed—their hands. **3**The Pharisees, and in fact all Jews, cling to the custom of their ancestors and never eat without scrupulously washing their hands. **4**Moreover, they never eat anything from the market without first sprinkling it. There are many other traditions they observe—for example, the washing of cups and jugs and kettles. **5**So the Pharisees and the scribes questioned him: "Why do your disciples not follow the tradition of our ancestors, but instead take food without purifying their hands?" **6***He said to them: "How accurately Isaiah prophesied about you hypocrites when he wrote,

> 'This people pays me lip service
>> but their heart is far from me.
> **7**Empty is the reverence they do me
>> because they teach as dogmas
>> mere human precepts.'

8You disregard God's commandment and cling to what is human tradition."

9He went on to say: "You have made a fine art of setting aside God's commandment in the interests of keeping your traditions! **10***For example, Moses said, 'Honor your father and your mother'; and in another place, 'Whoever curses father or mother shall be put to death.' **11**Yet you declare, 'If a person says to his father or mother, Any support you might have had from me is *korban*' (that is, dedicated to God), **12**you allow him to do nothing more for his father or mother. **13**That is the way you nullify God's word in favor of the traditions you have handed on. And you have many other such practices besides." **14***He summoned the crowd again and said to them: "Hear me, all of you, and try to understand. **15**Nothing that enters a man from outside can make him impure; that which comes out of him, and only that, constitutes impurity. **16**Let everyone heed what he hears!"

17*When he got home, away from the crowd, his disciples questioned him about the proverb. **18**"Are you, too, incapable of understanding?" he asked them. "Do you not see that nothing that enters a man from outside can make him impure? **19***It does not penetrate his being, but enters his stomach only and passes into the latrine." Thus did he render all foods clean. **20**He went on: "What emerges from within a man, that and nothing else is what makes him impure. **21***Wicked designs come from the deep recesses of the heart: acts of fornication, theft, murder, **22**adulterous conduct, greed, maliciousness, deceit, sensuality, envy, blasphemy, arrogance, an obtuse spirit. **23**All these evils come from within and render a man impure."

A Canaanite Woman

24*†From that place he went off to the territory of Tyre and Sidon. He retired to a certain house and wanted no one to recognize him; however, he could not escape notice. **25**Soon a woman, whose small daughter had an unclean spirit, heard about him. She approached him and crouched at his feet. **26***The woman who was Greek—a Syro-Phoenician by birth—began to beg him to expel the demon from her daughter. **27**He told her: "Let the sons of the household satisfy themselves at table first. It is not right to take the food of the children and throw it to the dogs." **28**"Please, Lord," she replied, "even the dogs under the table eat the family's leavings." **29**Then he said to her, "For such a reply, be off now! The demon has already left your daughter." **30**When she got home, she found the child lying in bed and the demon gone.

Healing of a Deaf-mute

31*†He then left Tyrian territory and returned by way of Sidon to the Sea of Galilee, into the district of

---

† 6, 53-56: This summary statement conveys the popular faith in Jesus. *Came ashore at Gennesaret:* in Jn 6, 24 the name of the place is Capernaum, an apparent indication of two traditions underlying the account.

7, 1-23: The reference to ceremonial washings (2ff) reflects, no doubt, the opposition of the early Christian communities to them. Jesus is described as criticizing the overconcern of the scribes and Pharisees for their traditions to the neglect of the commandments enunciated in the Scriptures (6ff); see note on Mt 15, 5f. Even among Gentile Christians scruples existed concerning the moral implications supposedly inherent in the eating of certain foods (Rom 14, 2f.6), a fact that accounts for the editorial observation in Mk 7, 19.

7, 24-30: The Syro-Phoenician woman ascribes her daughter's illness to an evil spirit. The mind of the time was inclined to attribute the more baffling sicknesses to satanic power. Without contesting the woman's assertion, Jesus pronounces the curing word in the same terms: *The demon has already left your daughter.*

Jewish authors sometimes used the term "dogs" of Gentiles to express their scorn of paganism. Because the woman's subtle response acknowledges her dependence on the God of Israel, whom Jesus represents, he cures her daughter.

7, 31-37: The actions attributed to Jesus (33f) were used by healers of the time, who considered them effective in themselves. With Jesus, however, they have a sacramental purpose inasmuch as they are effective by his power through his relation to the Father; cf Jn 11, 41; 17, 1.

✿
56: 5, 27f; Acts 5, 15.	17: 4, 10.13.
7/1-30: Mt 15, 1-28.	19: Acts 10, 15.
6: Is 29, 13.	21: Jer 17, 9.
10: Ex 21, 17; Lv 20, 9;	24-30: Mt 15, 21-28.
Dt 5, 16; Eph 6, 2.	26: Mt 8, 29.
14-23: Mt 15, 10-20.	31-37: Mt 15, 29ff.

the Ten Cities. **32**Some people brought him a deaf man who had a speech impediment and begged him to lay his hand on him. **33**Jesus took him off by himself away from the crowd. He put his fingers into the man's ears and, spitting, touched his tongue; **34**then he looked up to heaven and emitted a groan. He said to him, *"Ephphatha!"* (that is, "'Be opened!'") **35**At once the man's ears were opened; he was freed from the impediment, and began to speak plainly. **36**Then he enjoined them strictly not to tell anyone; but the more he ordered them not to, the more they proclaimed it. **37***Their amazement went beyond all bounds: "He has done everything well! He makes the deaf hear and the mute speak!"

Jesus Feeds Four Thousand

8 **1***†AT about that time another large crowd assembled, and they were without anything to eat. He called the disciples over to him and said: **2**"My heart is moved with pity for the crowd. By now they have been with me three days and have nothing to eat. **3**If I send them home hungry, they will collapse on the way. Some of them have come a great distance." **4**His disciples replied, "How can anyone give these people sufficient bread in this deserted spot?" **5**Still he asked them, "How many loaves do you have?" "Seven," they replied. **6**Then he directed the crowd to take their places on the ground. Taking the seven loaves he gave thanks, broke them, and gave them to his disciples to distribute, and they handed them out to the crowd. **7**They also had a few small fish; asking a blessing on the fish, he told them to distribute these also. **8**The people in the crowd ate until they had their fill; then they gathered up seven wicker baskets of leftovers. **9**Those who had eaten numbered about four thousand.

10He dismissed them and got into the boat with his disciples to go to the neighborhood of Dalmanutha.

The Pharisees Ask a Sign

11*†The Pharisees came forward and began to argue with him. They were looking for some heavenly sign from him as a test. **12**With a sigh from the depths of his spirit he said, "Why does this age seek a sign? I assure you, no such sign will be given it!" **13**Then he left them, got into the boat again, and went off to the other shore.

The Leaven of the Pharisees

14*They had forgotten to bring any bread along; except for one loaf they had none with them in the boat. **15**†So when he instructed them, "Keep your eyes open! Be on your guard against the yeast of the Pharisees and the yeast of Herod," **16**they concluded among themselves that it was because they had no bread. **17***Aware of this he said to them, "Why do you

suppose that it is because you have no bread? Do you still not see or comprehend? Are your minds completely blinded? **18***Have you eyes but no sight? Ears but no hearing? **19**Do you remember when I broke the five loaves for the five thousand, how many baskets of fragments you gathered up?" They answered, "Twelve." **20**"When I broke the seven loaves for the four thousand, how many full hampers of fragments did you collect?" They answered, "Seven." **21**He said to them again, "Do you still not understand?"

A Blind Man at Bethsaida

22†When they arrived at Bethsaida, some people brought him a blind man and begged him to touch him. **23***Jesus took the blind man's hand and led him outside the village. Putting spittle on his eyes he laid his hands on him and asked, "Can you see anything?" **24**The man opened his eyes and said, "I can see people but they look like walking trees!" **25**Then a second time Jesus laid hands on his eyes, and he saw perfectly; his sight was restored and he could see everything clearly. **26**Jesus sent him home with the admonition, "Do not even go into the village."

III: THE MYSTERY BEGINS TO BE REVEALED

The Messiah

27*†THEN JESUS AND HIS DISCIPLES set out for the villages around Caesarea Philippi. On the way he asked his disciples this question: "Who do people say that I am?" **28**They replied, "Some, John the Baptizer, others, Elijah, still others, one of the prophets." **29**"And you,"

---

† 8, 1-9: Many scholars regard this as a second version of the one multiplication of loaves, set in a Gentile context because of the eucharistic significance which the early Christian communities saw in it. Note that in this account Jesus' initiative in feeding the crowd is emphasized; the disciples appear helpless except in dependence on him (2ff.)

8, 11f: The Pharisees object that the miracles wrought by Jesus are unsatisfactory as proof of the arrival of God's reign. This is comparable to the complaint in Jn 6, 30f. Jesus replies that a request for a sign which originates in human distrust will not be provided.

8, 15: *Be on your guard against the yeast . . . of Herod:* Mt 16, 12 explains the leaven as the teaching of the religious authorities; Lk 12, 1 takes it to symbolize their hypocrisy. In the light of Mk 8, 11f, the reference here is to their deep-seated hostility toward Jesus, which for different reasons Herod also shares.

8, 22-26: Jesus' actions and the gradual cure of the blind man probably have the same purpose as in the case of the deaf man; see note on 7, 31-37. Some authors regard the cure as an intended symbol of the gradual enlightenment of the disciples concerning the difference between Jesus' teaching and the views of the authorities.

8, 27-30: This episode marks a turning point in Mark's portrait of Jesus in his public ministry. Varieties of popular opinion concerning him concur in regarding him as a prophet. The disciples, by contrast, believe him to be the Messiah. He is described as acknowledging this identification, but prohibits them from making his messianic office known.

37: Mt 15, 31.
8/1-10: Mt 15, 32-39; 6, 34-44.
11ff: Mt 12, 38f; 16, 1-4.
11: Lk 11, 16.
14f: Mt 16, 5f; Lk 12, 1.
17: 4, 13.
18: Jer 5, 21; Ez 12, 2.
23: 7, 33; Jn 9, 6.
27ff: Mt 16, 13-16; Lk 9, 18ff.

he went on to ask, "who do you say that I am?" Peter answered him, "You are the Messiah!" **30**Then he gave them strict orders not to tell anyone about him.

First Teaching of the Paschal Event

31*†He began to teach them that the Son of Man had to suffer much, be rejected by the elders, the chief priests, and the scribes, be put to death, and rise three days later. **32**He said these things quite openly. Peter then took him aside and began to remonstrate with him. **33**At this he turned around and, eyeing the disciples, reprimanded Peter: "Get out of my sight, you satan! You are not judging by God's standards but by man's!"

The Doctrine of the Cross

34*†He summoned the crowd with his disciples and said to them: "If a man wishes to come after me, he must deny his very self, take up his cross, and follow in my steps. **35***Whoever would preserve his life will lose it, but whoever loses his life for my sake and the gospel's will preserve it. **36**What profit does a man show who gains the whole world and destroys himself in the process? **37**What can a man offer in exchange for his life? **38***If anyone in this faithless and corrupt age is ashamed of me and my doctrine, the Son of Man will be ashamed of him when he comes with the holy angels in his Father's glory."

9 **1**HE also said to them: "I assure you, among those standing here there are some who will not taste death until they see the reign of God established in power."

Jesus Transfigured

2*†Six days later, Jesus took Peter, James, and John off by themselves with him and led them up a high mountain. He was transfigured before their eyes **3**and his clothes became dazzlingly white—whiter than the work of any bleacher could make them. **4**Elijah appeared to them along with Moses; the two were in conversation with Jesus. **5**Then Peter spoke to Jesus: "Rabbi, how good it is for us to be here! Let us erect three booths on this site, one for you, one for Moses, and one for Elijah." **6**He hardly knew what to say, for they were all overcome with awe. **7**A cloud came, overshadowing them, and out of the cloud a voice: "This is my Son, my beloved. Listen to him." **8**Suddenly looking around they no longer saw anyone with them—only Jesus.

On the Coming of Elijah

9*As they were coming down the mountain, he strictly enjoined them not to tell anyone what they had

seen, before the Son of Man had risen from the dead. **10**They kept this word of his to themselves, though they continued to discuss what "to rise from the dead" meant. **11***Finally they put to him this question: "Why do the scribes claim that Elijah must come first?" **12**He told them: "Elijah will indeed come first and restore everything. Yet why does Scripture say of the Son of Man that he must suffer much and be despised? **13***Let me assure you, Elijah has already come. They did entirely as they pleased with him, as the Scriptures say of him."

A Possessed Boy

14*†As they approached the disciples, they saw a large crowd standing around, and scribes in lively discussion with them. **15**Immediately on catching sight of Jesus, the whole crowd was overcome with awe. They ran up to greet him. **16**He asked them, "What are you discussing among yourselves?" **17**"Teacher," a man in the crowd replied, "I have brought my son to you because he is possessed by a mute spirit. **18**Whenever it seizes him it throws him down; he foams at the mouth and grinds his teeth and becomes rigid. Just now I asked your disciples to expel him, but they were unable to do so." **19**He replied by saying to the crowd, "What an unbelieving lot you are! How long must I remain with you? How long can I endure you? Bring him to me." **20**When they did so the spirit caught sight of Jesus and immediately threw the boy into convul-

---

† 8, 31ff: *Son of Man:* an enigmatic title. Jewish apocryphal tradition (1 Enoch, 2 Ezra, 2 Baruch) uses it to describe a unique religious personage, a messiah with extraordinary spiritual endowments. Jesus' use of it seems to derive from Ez 2, where it is a title of humility, and Dn 7, 13f, where it indicates a clearly messianic figure. It expresses for him his twofold destiny, of suffering (8, 31; 9, 11.31; 10, 33; 12, 31; 14, 21) and of glory (8, 38; 12, 36; 14, 62). Peter, along with the other disciples, fails (despite his confession) to grasp the association of suffering and death with the office of Messiah.

8, 34—9, 1: Mt 16, 24-28 and Lk 9, 23-27 place these sayings in the same context as Mark, namely, Peter's messianic confession and Jesus' rebuke to Peter and the disciples in the prophecy of the passion. Mark and Luke apply the doctrine of the cross to Christians in general. The disciples are instructed to sacrifice even life itself to follow Jesus (34). To strengthen their waning confidence, Jesus foretells that some of them will live to see the arrival of the reign of God in power (9, 1).

9, 2-8: The synoptic gospels place the transfiguration of Jesus six days after the first prediction of his passion and death and his instruction to the disciples on the doctrine of the cross (Mt 17, 1-8; Lk 9, 28-36). Thus it counterbalances the prediction of the passion by affording certain of the disciples' insight into the divine glory which he possessed. His glory will overcome his death and that of his disciples; cf 2 Pt 1, 16ff; 2 Cor 3, 18. The heavenly voice (6) prepares the disciples to understand that in the divine plan Jesus must die ignominiously before his messianic glory is made manifest; cf Lk 24, 25ff. The appearance of Moses and Elijah indicates that the purpose of both the law and the prophets was to prepare for Christ.

9, 14-29: The disciples' failure to effect a cure seems to reflect unfavorably on Jesus (14-18). In response, he exposes their lack of trust in God (19) and scores their neglect of prayer, i. e., of the conscious reliance on God's power when acting in Jesus' name. Mark and Matthew (17, 14-18) concur on this point; Luke (9, 37-43) centers attention on Jesus' sovereign power.

❖

31-38: Mt 16, 21-27;   9/2-13: Mt 17, 1-13;
     Lk 9, 22-26.   Lk 9, 28-36.
34: Mt 10, 38f; 16, 24-27;   9: 8, 31.
     Lk 14, 26f.   11f: Is 53, 3; Mal 3, 23.
35: Jn 12, 25.   13: 1 Kgs 19, 2-10.
38: Mt 10, 33; Lk 12, 8.   14-29: Mt 17, 14-21;
                           Lk 9, 37-44.

sions. As he fell to the ground he began to roll around and foam at the mouth. **21**Then Jesus questioned the father: "How long has this been happening to him?" "From childhood," the father replied. **22**"Often it throws him into fire and into water. You would think it would kill him. If out of the kindness of your heart you can do anything to help us, please do!" **23**Jesus said, " 'If you can'? Everything is possible to a man who trusts." **24**The boy's father immediately exclaimed, "Believe I do! Help my lack of trust!" **25**Jesus, on seeing a crowd rapidly gathering, reprimanded the unclean spirit by saying to him, "Mute and deaf spirit, I command you: Get out of him and never enter him again!" **26**Shouting, and throwing the boy into convulsions, it came out of him; the boy became like a corpse, which caused many to say, "He is dead." **27**But Jesus took him by the hand and helped him to his feet. **28**When Jesus arrived at the house his disciples began to ask him privately, "Why is it that we could not expel it?" **29**He told them, "This kind you can drive out only by prayer."

Second Teaching: Passion and Resurrection

30*†They left that district and began a journey through Galilee, but he did not want anyone to know about it. **31***He was teaching his disciples in this vein: "The Son of Man is going to be delivered into the hands of men who will put him to death; three days after his death he will rise." **32***Though they failed to understand his words, they were afraid to question him.

IV: THE FULL REVELATION OF THE MYSTERY

Against Ambition and Envy

33*†THEY RETURNED TO CAPERNAUM and Jesus, once inside the house, began to ask them, "What were you discussing on the way home?" **34**At this they fell silent, for on the way they had been arguing about who was the most important. **35***So he sat down and called the Twelve around him and said, "If anyone wishes to rank first, he must remain the last one of all and the servant of all." **36**Then he took a little child, stood him in their midst, and putting his arms around him, said to them, **37***"Whoever welcomes a child such as this for my sake welcomes me. And whoever welcomes me welcomes, not me, but him who sent me."

38*†John said to him, "Teacher, we saw a man using your name to expel demons and we tried to stop him

because he is not of our company." **39**Jesus said in reply: "Do not try to stop him. No man who performs a miracle using my name can at the same time speak ill of me. **40***Anyone who is not against us is with us. **41***Any man who gives you a drink of water because you belong to Christ will not, I assure you, go without his reward. **42*†**But it would be better if anyone who leads astray one of these simple believers were to be plunged in the sea with a great millstone fastened around his neck.

43"If your hand is your difficulty, cut it off! Better for you to enter life maimed than to keep both hands and enter Gehenna with its unquenchable fire. **45**If your foot is your undoing, cut it off! Better for you to enter life crippled than to be thrown into Gehenna with both feet. **47**If your eye is your downfall, tear it out! Better for you to enter the kingdom of God with one eye than to be thrown with both eyes into Gehenna, **48***where 'the worm dies not and the fire is never extinguished.' **49**Everyone will be salted with fire. **50***Salt is excellent in its place; but if salt becomes tasteless, how can you season it? Keep salt in your hearts and you will be at peace with one another."

10 **1†**FROM there he moved on to the districts of Judea and across the Jordan. Once more crowds gathered around him, and as usual he began to teach them.

The Question of Divorce

2*Then some Pharisees came up and as a test began to ask him whether it was permissible for a husband to divorce his wife. **3**In reply he said, "What command did Moses give you?" **4***They answered, "Moses permitted divorce and the writing of a decree of divorce." **5**But Jesus told them: "He wrote that commandment for you because of your stubbornness. **6***At the beginning of creation God made them male and female; **7***for this reason a man shall leave his father and mother **8**and the two shall become as one. They are no longer two but one flesh. **9**Therefore let no man separate what God has joined." **10**Back in the house

---

† 9, 30ff: Although the disciples heard Jesus' new prediction concerning his passion, they failed to accept its truth because they did not understand his messianic role.

9, 33-37: The evangelist probably intends this incident and the sayings that follow as a commentary on the disciples' lack of understanding (9, 32). Their role in Jesus' work is one of service, especially to the poor and lowly. For this concept of the child, see note on Mt 19, 13ff.

9, 38-41: Jesus warns against jealousy and intolerance toward good works, such as exorcism, performed in his name by those whose faith is imperfect. The saying in 9, 40 is a broad principle of the divine tolerance: God repays men for the smallest courtesies they show to those who teach in Jesus' name.

9, 42-50: A collection of Jesus' sayings, rather loosely connected. Vv 44 and 46 are omitted here as additions to the text taken from v 48 and a modified citation of Is 66, 24. The concluding sayings in vv 49f probably allude to the sacrifices required for loyal adherence to the teaching of Jesus. For the imagery of salt, cf Lv 2, 13 and note.

9, 44.46: Not found in many manuscripts.

10, 1-12: See notes on Mt 19, 3-8 and 19, 9.

✿

30: Jn 7, 1.
31: 8, 31; Mt 17, 22; Lk 9, 44.
32: Lk 9, 45.
33-37: Mt 18, 1-5; Lk 9, 46ff.
35: Mt 20, 27.
37: Mt 10, 40; 18, 5; Jn 13, 20.
38-41: Nm 11, 28; 1 Cor 12, 3; Lk 9, 49f.
40: Mt 12, 30.

41: Mt 10, 42; 1 Cor 3, 23.
42-47: Mt 5, 29f; Mt 18, 6-9.
42: Lk 17, 2.
48: Is 66, 24.
50: Lv 2, 13; Mt 5, 13; Lk 14, 34f; Col 4, 6.
10/2-12: Mt 19, 3-9.
4: Dt 24, 1-4.
6: Gn 1, 27.
7f: Gn 2, 24; 1 Cor 6, 16; Eph 5, 31.

again, the disciples began to question him about this. **11***He told them, "Whoever divorces his wife and marries another commits adultery against her; **12**and the woman who divorces her husband and marries another commits adultery."

Jesus Blesses the Children

13*†People were bringing their little children to him to have him touch them, but the disciples were scolding them for this. **14**Jesus became indignant when he noticed it and said to them: "Let the children come to me and do not hinder them. It is to just such as these that the kingdom of God belongs. **15***I assure you that whoever does not accept the reign of God like a little child shall not take part in it." **16**Then he embraced them and blessed them, placing his hands on them.

The Danger of Riches

17*†As he was setting out on a journey a man came running up, knelt down before him and asked, "Good Teacher, what must I do to share in everlasting life?" **18**Jesus answered, "Why do you call me good? No one is good but God alone. **19***You know the commandments:

> 'You shall not kill;
> You shall not commit adultery;
> You shall not steal;
> You shall not bear false witness;
> You shall not defraud;
> Honor your father and your mother.' "

20He replied, "Teacher, I have kept all these since my childhood." **21**Then Jesus looked at him with love and told him, "There is one thing more you must do. Go and sell what you have and give to the poor; you will then have treasure in heaven. After that, come and follow me." **22**At these words the man's face fell. He went away sad, for he had many possessions. **23***†Jesus looked around and said to his disciples, "How hard it is for the rich to enter the kingdom of God!" **24**The disciples could only marvel at his words. So Jesus repeated what he had said: "My sons, how hard it is to enter the kingdom of God! **25**It is easier for a camel to pass through a needle's eye than for a rich man to enter the kingdom of God."

26They were completely overwhelmed at this, and exclaimed to one another, "Then who can be saved?" **27**Jesus fixed his gaze on them and said, "For man it is impossible but not for God. With God all things are possible."

28†Peter was moved to say to him: "We have put aside everything to follow you!" **29**Jesus answered: "I give you my word, there is no one who has given up home, brothers or sisters, mother or father, children or property, for me and for the gospel **30**who will not receive in this present age a hundred times as many homes, brothers and sisters, mothers, children and property—and persecution besides—and in the age to come, everlasting life. **31***Many who are first shall come last, and the last shall come first."

Third Teaching: Passion and Resurrection

32*†The disciples were on the road going up to Jerusalem, with Jesus walking in the lead. Their mood was one of wonderment, while that of those who followed was fear. Taking the Twelve aside once more, he began to tell them what was going to happen to him. **33**"We are on our way up to Jerusalem, where the Son of Man will be handed over to the chief priests and the scribes. **34**They will condemn him to death and hand him over to the Gentiles, who will mock him and spit at him, flog him, and finally kill him. But three days later he will rise."

Ambition of James and John

35*†Zebedee's sons, James and John, approached him. "Teacher," they said, "we want you to grant our request." **36**"What is it?" he asked. **37**They replied, "See to it that we sit, one at your right and the other at your left, when you come into your glory." **38***Jesus told "You do not know what you are asking. Can you drink the cup I shall drink or be baptized in the same bath of pain as I?" **39**"We can," they told him. Jesus said in response, "From the cup I drink of you shall drink; the bath I am immersed in you shall share. **40**But as for sitting at my right or my left, that is not mine to give; it is for those to whom it has been reserved." **41**The other ten, on hearing this, became in-

---

† 10, 13-16: See note on Mt 19, 13ff.

10, 17f: Jesus' repudiation of the term "good" is probably in response to the man's implication that Jesus will reveal to him the secret of eternal life. What Jesus requires of the man is not necessarily congenial to his ideas. The remainder of the story in vv 19-22 bears out the point.

10, 23-27: See note on Mt 19, 23-26.

10, 28-31: See note on Mt 19, 27-30.

10, 32ff: The disciples are apprehensive because Jesus, after prophesying his execution in Jerusalem, now proceeds deliberately to confront it (Lk 9, 51; Jn 11, 16). No doubt the prophecies in the synoptic tradition about the passion of Christ have been schematized through the influence of the event of the crucifixion. There seems to be no question, however, that frequent repetition of a passion prophecy by Jesus was part of the original tradition.

10, 35-45: If Mark has placed this narrative in its actual historical context (cf Mt 20, 20), the petition of James and John becomes dramatic: they declare themselves ready to risk death with Jesus provided he will guarantee to them the highest positions in the kingdom. While accepting their pledge to suffer with him, Jesus observes that it lies beyond his personal authority to make such concessions (35-40). If not in its actual historical context, the petition of James and John has been placed here by the evangelist to align the sacrifices required of disciples with the personal sacrifice made by Jesus. Whatever authority the disciples exercise is to be viewed, like the authority of Jesus (v 45), in terms of service to others rather than as a sign of personal eminence (42ff).

---

*

11f: Mt 5, 32; Lk 16, 18;
    1 Ccr 7, 10f.
13-16: Mt 19, 13ff;
    Lk 18, 15ff.
13: Lk 9, 47.
15: Mt 18, 3.
17-31: Mt 19, 16-30;
    Lk 18, 18-30.

19: Ex 20, 12-16;
    Dt 5, 16-21.
23: Prv 11, 28.
31: Mt 19, 30; Lk 13, 30.
32ff: 8, 31; Mt 20, 17ff;
    Lk 18, 31ff.
35-45: Mt 20, 20-28.
38: Lk 12, 50.

dignant at James and John. **⁴²***Jesus called them together and said to them: "You know how among the Gentiles those who seem to exercise authority lord it over them; their great ones make their importance felt. **⁴³**It cannot be like that with you. Anyone among you who aspires to greatness must serve the rest; **⁴⁴**whoever wants to rank first among you must serve the needs of all. **⁴⁵**The Son of Man has not come to be served but to serve—to give his life in ransom for the many."

The Blind Bartimaeus

⁴⁶*†They came to Jericho next, and as he was leaving that place with his disciples and a sizable crowd, there was a blind beggar Bartimaeus ("son of Timaeus") sitting by the roadside. **⁴⁷**On hearing that it was Jesus of Nazareth, he began to call out, "Jesus, Son of David, have pity on me!" **⁴⁸**Many people were scolding him to make him keep quiet, but he shouted all the louder, "Son of David, have pity on me!" **⁴⁹**Then Jesus stopped and said, "Call him over." So they called the blind man over, telling him as they did so, "You have nothing to fear from him! Get up! He is calling you!" **⁵⁰**He threw aside his cloak, jumped up and came to Jesus. **⁵¹**Jesus asked him, "What do you want me to do for you?" "Rabboni," the blind man said, "I want to see." **⁵²**Jesus said in reply, "Be on your way. Your faith has healed you." Immediately he received his sight and started to follow him up the road.

Triumphal Entry into Jerusalem

11 **¹*†**THEN, as they neared Bethphage and Bethany on the Mount of Olives, close to Jerusalem, he sent off two of his disciples **²**with the instruction: "Go to the village straight ahead of you, and as soon as you enter it you will find tethered there a colt on which no one has ridden. Untie it and bring it back. **³**If anyone says to you, 'Why are you doing that?' say, 'The Master needs it but he will send it back here at once.' " **⁴**So they went off, and finding a colt tethered out on the street near a gate, they untied it. **⁵**Some of the bystanders said to them, "What do you mean by untying that colt?" **⁶**They answered as Jesus had told them to, and the men let them take it. **⁷**They brought the colt to Jesus and threw their cloaks across its back, and he sat on it. **⁸**Many people spread their cloaks on the road, while others spread reeds which they had cut in the fields. **⁹***Those preceding him as well as those who followed cried out:

> "Hosanna!
> Blessed is he who comes in the name of the Lord!

> **¹⁰**Blessed is the reign of our father David to come!
> Hosanna in the highest!"

¹¹*†He entered Jerusalem and went into the temple precincts. He inspected everything there, but since it was already late in the afternoon, he went out to Bethany accompanied by the Twelve.

Jesus Curses a Fig Tree

¹²*†The next day when they were leaving Bethany he felt hungry. **¹³**Observing a fig tree some distance off, covered with foliage, he went over to see if he could find anything on it. When he reached it he found nothing but leaves; it was not the time for figs. **¹⁴**Then addressing it he said, "Never again shall anyone eat of your fruit!" His disciples heard all this.

Cleansing of the Temple

¹⁵*†When they reached Jerusalem he entered the temple precincts and began to drive out those who were engaged in buying and selling. He overturned the money-changers' tables and the stalls of the men selling doves; **¹⁶**moreover, he would not permit anyone to carry things through the temple area. **¹⁷***Then he began to teach them: "Does not Scripture have it,

> 'My house shall be called a house of prayer for all peoples'—?

but you have turned it into a den of thieves." **¹⁸**The chief priests and the scribes heard of this and began to look for a way to destroy him. They were at the same time afraid of him because the whole crowd was under the spell of his teaching. **¹⁹***When evening drew

---

✿ 10, 46-52: The synoptic gospels locate this event at Jericho on Jesus' last journey to Jerusalem (Mt 20, 29-34; Lk 18, 35-43). The blind man, unaffected by what he heard of Jesus' lowly condition, accords him the messianic title, "Son of David." He requests a cure in order that he may see Jesus. On this basis his sight is restored.

11, 1-11: The nature of Jesus' entry into Jerusalem is not entirely clear in the synoptic tradition. In Jn 12, 12f the popular excitement upon his arrival in the city is associated with his raising of Lazarus to life (Jn 12, 18). This explains the acclaim Jesus receives on entering the city. In Mk 11, 9f the greeting Jesus receives stops short of proclaiming him Messiah. He is greeted rather as the prophet of the coming messianic kingdom; cf Mt 21, 11. Matthew introduces the notion of fulfillment of Old Testament prophecy (Zec 9, 9).

11, 12ff: Jesus' search for fruit on the fig tree recalls the prophets' earlier use of this image to designate Israel; cf Jer 8, 13; Ez 17, 24; Jl 1, 7; Hos 9, 10. Cursing the fig tree is a parable in action representing Christ's judgment on barren Israel for failing to receive his teaching.

11, 15-19: The expulsion of the buyers and sellers from the temple does not seem to be properly understood if regarded simply as an objection to the practice within the temple precincts, for its was fairly well controlled by the religious authorities. The key to an understanding of the incident is the citation of Is 56, 7 and Jer 7, 11. Both prophets objected that the worship in the temple was not consistent with true conversion. Jesus' action is a symbol of God's judgment against the abuses of his temple, due to the priests' failure to instruct the people in the meaning of temple worship.

✿
42-45: Lk 22, 25ff.
46-52: Mt 20, 29-34;
      Lk 18, 35-43.
11/1-10: Mt 21, 1-9;
      Lk 19, 29-38;
      Jn 12, 12-15.
9f: 2 Sm 7, 16; Ps 118, 26.

11: Mt 21, 10.17.
12ff: Mt 21, 18ff;
      Lk 13, 6-9.
15-18: Mt 21, 12f; Lk 19, 45f;
      Jn 2, 14ff.
17: Is 56, 7; Jer 7, 11.
19: Lk 21, 37.

on, Jesus and his disciples went out of the city. **20***Early next morning, as they were walking along, they saw the fig tree withered to its roots. **21**Peter remembered and said to him, "Rabbi, look! The fig tree you cursed has withered up." **22**In reply Jesus told them: "Put your trust in God. **23***I solemnly assure you, whoever says to this mountain, 'Be lifted up and thrown into the sea,' and has no inner doubts but believes that what he says will happen, shall have it done for him. **24***I give you my word, if you are ready to believe that you will receive whatever you ask for in prayer, it shall be done for you. **25***When you stand to pray, forgive anyone against whom you have a grievance so that your heavenly Father may in turn forgive you your faults."

The Authority of Jesus

27*†They returned once more to Jerusalem. As he was walking in the temple precincts the chief priests, the scribes, and the elders approached him **28**and said to him, "On what authority are you doing these things? Who has given you the power to do them?" **29**Jesus said to them, "I will ask you a question. If you give me an answer, I will tell you on what authority I do the things I do. **30**Tell me, was John's baptism of divine origin or merely from men?" **31**They thought to themselves, "If we say 'divine,' he will ask, 'Then why did you not put faith in it?' **32**But can we say, 'merely human'?" (They had reason to fear the people, who all regarded John as a true prophet.) **33**So their answer to Jesus was, "We do not know." In turn, Jesus said to them, "Then neither will I tell you on what authority I do the things I do."

Parable of the Tenants

12 **1***HE began to address them once more in parables: "A man planted a vineyard, put a hedge around it, dug out a vat, and erected a tower. Then he leased it to tenant farmers and went on a journey. **2**In due time he dispatched a man in his service to the tenants to obtain from them his share of produce from the vineyard. **3**But they seized him, beat him, and sent him off empty-handed. **4**The second time he sent them another servant; him too they beat over the head and treated shamefully. **5**He sent yet another and they killed him. So too with many others: some they beat; some they killed. **6**He still had one to send—the son whom he loved. He sent him to them as a last resort, thinking, 'They will have to respect my son.' **7**But those tenants said to one another, 'Here is the one who will inherit everything. Come, let us kill him, and the inheritance will be ours.' **8**Then they

seized and killed him and dragged him outside the vineyard. **9**What do you suppose the owner of the vineyard will do? He will come and destroy those tenants and turn his vineyard over to others. **10***Are you not familiar with this passage of Scripture:

'The stone rejected by the builders
   has become the keystone of the structure.
11It was the Lord who did it
   and we find it marvelous to behold'?"

12They wanted to arrest him at this, yet they had reason to fear the crowd. (They knew well enough that he meant the parable for them.) Finally they left him and went off.

Tribute to the Emperor

13*They next sent some Pharisees and Herodians after him to catch him in his speech. **14**The two groups came and said to him: "Teacher, we know you are a truthful man, unconcerned about anyone's opinion. It is evident you do not act out of human respect but teach God's way of life sincerely. Is it lawful to pay the tax to the emperor or not? Are we to pay or not to pay?" **15**Knowing their hypocrisy he said to them, "Why are you trying to trip me up? Bring me a coin and let me see it." **16**When they brought one, he said to them, "Whose head is this and whose inscription is it?" "Caesar's," they told him. **17***At that Jesus said to them, "Give to Caesar what is Caesar's but give to God what is God's." Their amazement at him knew no bounds.

The Sadducees and the Resurrection

18Then some Sadducees who hold there is no resurrection came to him with a question: **19***"Teacher, we were left this in writing by Moses: 'If anyone's brother dies leaving a wife but no child, his brother must take the wife and produce offspring for his brother.' **20**There were these seven brothers. The eldest took a wife and died, leaving no children. **21**The second took the woman, and he too died childless. The same thing happened to the third; **22**in fact none of the seven left any children behind. Last of all, the woman also died. **23**At the resurrection, when they all come back to life, whose wife will she be? All seven married her." **24**Jesus said: "You are badly misled, because you fail to understand the Scriptures or the power of God. **25**When people rise from the dead, they neither marry nor are given in marriage but live like angels in heaven. **26***As to the raising of the dead, have you not

---

† 11, 26: Omitted with many MSS.

† 11, 26: Omitted with many MSS.

11, 27—12, 27: For a similar series of conflicts see Mk 2, 1—3, 6. The parable of the vineyard tenants (Mt 21, 33-46; Lk 20, 9-19) indicates Jesus' self-awareness of his unique divine sonship (12, 1-12). His superior wisdom sees no conflict between Roman taxation and Israel's worship of God (12, 13-17). His prophetic insight exposes the specious arguments against resurrection of the dead adduced by the Sadducees, who fail to understand that the messianic promises benefit here and hereafter all who have hoped in God (12, 18-27).

✤
20-24: Mt 21, 20ff.
23: Mt 17, 20f; Lk 17, 6.
24: Mt 7, 7; Jn 11, 22; 14, 13.
25: Mt 6, 14; 18, 35.
27-33: Mt 21, 23-27; Lk 20, 1-8.
12/1-12: Mt 21, 33-46; Lk 20, 9-19.

1: Is 5, 1-7; Jer 2, 21.
10f: Ps 118, 22f; Is 28; 16.
13-27: Mt 22, 15-33; Lk 20, 20-39.
13: Mk 3, 6.
17: Rom 13, 7.
19: Dt 25, 5.
26: Ex 3, 6.

read in the book of Moses, in the passage about the burning bush, how God told him,

> 'I am the God of Abraham, the God of Isaac, the God of Jacob'?

27He is the God of the living, not of the dead. You are very much mistaken."

The Great Commandment

28*One of the scribes came up, and when he heard them arguing he realized how skillfully Jesus answered them. He decided to ask him, "Which is the first of all the commandments?" **29**Jesus replied: "This is the first:

> 'Hear, O Israel! The Lord our God is Lord alone!
> **30***Therefore you shall love the Lord your God
> with all your heart,
> with all your soul,
> with all your mind,
> and with all your strength.'

31*This is the second,

> 'You shall love your neighbor as yourself.'

There is no other commandment greater than these." **32**The scribe said to him: "Excellent, Teacher! You are right in saying, 'He is the One, there is no other than he.' **33***Yes, 'to love him with all our heart, with all our thoughts and with all our strength, and to love our neighbor as ourselves' is worth more than any burnt offering or sacrifice." **34***Jesus approved the insight of this answer and told him, "You are not far from the reign of God." And no one had the courage to ask him any more questions.

The Son of David

35*†As Jesus was teaching in the temple precincts he went on to say: "How can the scribes claim, 'The Messiah is David's son'? **36***David himself, inspired by the Holy Spirit, said.

> 'The Lord said to my Lord: Sit at my right hand
> until I make your enemies your footstool.'

37If David himself addresses him as 'Lord,' in what sense can he be his son?" The majority of the crowd heard this with delight.

Hypocrisy of the Opponents of Jesus

38*In the course of his teaching he said: "Be on guard against the scribes, who like to parade around in their robes and accept marks of respect in public, **39**front seats in the synagogues, and places of honor at banquets. **40**These men devour the savings of widows

and recite long prayers for appearance' sake; it is they who will receive the severest sentence."

The Widow's Mite

41*Taking a seat opposite the treasury, he observed the crowd putting money into the collection box. Many of the wealthy put in sizable amounts; **42**but one poor widow came and put in two small copper coins worth a few cents. **43**He called his disciples over and told them: "I want you to observe that this poor widow contributed more than all the others who donated to the treasury. **44**They gave from their surplus wealth, but she gave from her want, all that she had to live on."

Questions about the Temple

13   **1***†As he was making his way out of the temple area, one of his disciples said to him, "Teacher, look at the huge blocks of stone and the enormous buildings!" **2**Jesus said to him, "You see these great buildings? Not one stone will be left upon another—all will be torn down." **3**While he was seated on the Mount of Olives facing the temple, Peter, James, John, and Andrew began to question him privately. **4**"Tell us, when will this occur? What will be the sign that all this is coming to an end?"

Beginning of Calamities

5*Jesus began his discourse: "Be on your guard. Let no one mislead you. **6**Any number will come attempting to impersonate me. 'I am he,' they will claim, and will lead many astray. **7**When you hear about wars and threats of war, do not yield to panic. Such things are bound to happen, but this is not yet the end. **8**Nation will rise against nation, one kingdom against another. There will be earthquakes in various places and there will be famine. This is but the onset of the

---

† 12, 35-44: Jesus questions the claim of the scribes about the Davidic descent of the Messiah, not to deny it (Mt 1, 1; Acts 2, 20.34; Rom 1, 3; 2 Tm 2, 8), but to imply that he is more than this. His superiority derives from his transcendent origin (35ff), to which David himself attested when he addressed the Messiah with the name reserved for Yahweh (Ps 110, 1).

Jesus was pained by the scribes' abuse of religious position (38ff). At the same time he was deeply sympathetic toward the religious generosity of the poor (41-44).

13, 1-37: This chapter and its parallels (Mt 24, 1-44; Lk 21, 5-36) express the principal New Testament thought on the second coming of Christ; cf 1 Thes 4, 13-18 and note. Each of the three evangelists in his own way relates the second coming to Jesus' prophecy of the destruction of Jerusalem. The *abominable and destructive presence* (Dn 9, 27), i. e., the profanation of the temple by the Roman power, will be the sign of imminent destruction. Jesus urges flight from Jerusalem rather than defense of the city through misguided messianic hope (14-23). Intervention will only occur after the destruction (24-27), which itself is to occur before the end of the first Christian generation (28-31). No one but the Father knows the precise time, nor that of Jesus' second coming (32), hence the necessity of constant vigilance (33-37). The chronological proximity of the second coming and the destruction of the temple is not determined (2-27). Luke sets the second coming at a later date, in *the times of the Gentiles* (Lk 21, 24).

---

*
28-34: Mt 22, 34-40.   36: Ps 110, 1.
  30: Dt 6, 4f.   38ff: Mt 23, 1-7; Lk 11, 43;
  31: Lv 19, 18; Rom 13, 9;   20, 45ff.
      Gal 5, 14; Jas 2, 8.   41-44: Lk 21, 1-4.
  33: Dt 6, 4; Ps 40, 7ff.   13/1-37: Mt 24, 1-51;
  34: Mt 22, 46; Lk 20, 40.   Lk 21, 5-36.
  35ff: Mt 22, 41-45;   5: Eph 5, 6; 2 Thes 2, 3.
      Lk 20, 41-44.

pains of labor. ⁹Be constantly on your guard. They will hand you over to the courts. You will be beaten in synagogues. You will be arraigned before governors and kings on my account and have to testify to your faith before them. ¹⁰But the good news must first be proclaimed to all the Gentiles. ¹¹*When men take you off into custody, do not worry beforehand about what to say. In that hour, say what you are inspired to say. It will not be yourselves speaking but the Holy Spirit. ¹²Brother will hand over brother for execution and likewise the father his child; children will turn against their parents and have them put to death. ¹³Because of my name, you will be hated by everyone. Nonetheless, the man who holds out till the end is the one who will come through safe.

The Supreme Tribulation

¹⁴*"When you see the abominable and destructive presence standing where it should not be—let the reader take note!—those in Judea must flee to the mountains. ¹⁵*If a man is on the roof terrace, he must not come down or enter his house to get anything out of it. ¹⁶If a man is in the field, he must not turn back to pick up his cloak. ¹⁷It will go badly with pregnant and nursing women in those days. ¹⁸Keep praying that none of this happens in winter. ¹⁹*Those times will be more distressful than any between God's work of creation and now, and for all time to come. ²⁰Indeed, had the Lord not shortened the period, not a person would be saved. But for the sake of those he has chosen, he has shortened the days. ²¹If anyone tells you at that time, 'Look, the Messiah is here!' 'Look, he is there!'—do not believe it. ²²False messiahs and false prophets will appear performing signs and wonders to mislead, if it were possible, even the chosen. ²³So be constantly on guard! I have told you about it beforehand.

Last Act of the Drama

²⁴*"During that period after trials of every sort the sun will be darkened, the moon will not shed its light, ²⁵stars will fall out of the skies, and the heavenly hosts will be shaken. ²⁶*Then men will see the Son of Man coming in the clouds with great power and glory. ²⁷He will dispatch his angels and assemble his chosen from the four winds, from the farthest bounds of earth and sky. ²⁸*Learn a lesson from the fig tree. Once the sap of its branches runs high and it begins to sprout leaves, you know that summer is near. ²⁹ In the same way, when you see these things happening, you will know that he is near, even at the door. ³⁰I assure you, this generation will not pass away until all these things take place. ³¹The heavens and the earth will pass away but my words will not pass.

Need for Watchfulness

³²"As to the exact day or hour, no one knows it, neither the angels in heaven nor even the Son, but only the Father. ³³*Be constantly on the watch! Stay awake! You do not know when the appointed time will come. ³⁴*It is like a man traveling abroad. He leaves home and places his servants in charge, each with his own task; and he orders the man at the gate to watch with a sharp eye. ³⁵Look around you! You do not know when the master of the house is coming, whether at dusk, at midnight, when the cock crows, or at early dawn. ³⁶Do not let him come suddenly and catch you asleep. ³⁷What I say to you, I say to all: Be on guard!"

The Official Decision

14 ¹*†THE feasts of Passover and Unleavened Bread were to be observed in two days' time, and therefore the chief priests and scribes began to look for a way to arrest him by some trick and kill him. ²Yet they pointed out, "Not during the festival, or the people may riot."

The Anointing at Bethany

³*When Jesus was in Bethany reclining at table in the house of Simon the leper, a woman entered carrying an alabaster jar of perfume made from expensive aromatic nard. Breaking the jar, she began to pour the perfume on his head. ⁴Some were saying to themselves indignantly: "What is the point of this extravagant waste of perfume? ⁵It could have been sold for

---

† 14, 1–15, 47: In this solemn narrative the principal facts of the sufferings and death of Jesus are interwoven with implications of their religious significance. The facts include: a plan to arrest Jesus secretly and thus prevent tumult (1ff); facilitation of the plan through Judas' betrayal (10f); the arrest of Jesus (43-47); inquest before the Sanhedrin and indictment for blasphemy (55-64); transfer to Pilate's court and the insinuation of political sedition (15, 1-5); official and popular demand for Jesus' condemnation and crucifixion; Pilate's consent under pressure (15, 6-15); the mockery, scourging and crucifixion (15, 15-27); death on the cross (15, 29-39); and burial by Joseph of Arimathea (15, 42-47).

Jesus is described as interpreting the events of his passion as follows: the anointing at Bethany as a preparation for his death (14, 3-9); his celebration of the Passover (12-16) as the inauguration of a new and lasting covenant in which his body and blood are to be shared in the form of bread and wine, symbols of his passion and death (22ff). He prophesies Peter's denial and the apostles' desertion and subsequent reunion (26ff). Jesus declares his acceptance of the passion to be in conformity with his Father's will (32-42), and confesses his awareness of what was foretold by the Scriptures concerning him (48f). He refuses to throw himself on the mercy of Pilate (15, 2-5) and rejects the drug that would cloud his mind to the reality of the crucifixion (36). He prays Psalm 22 from the cross (34). The Roman centurion's tribute to Jesus' courage (39) is actually a concluding Marcan confession of faith, put on Gentile lips.

The religious cast of the Marcan passion narrative derives from the consistent theme of fulfillment of prophecy, even concerning the conduct of Jesus' disciples. Though complete in itself, this narrative is closely joined to the account of Jesus' ministry. One single item remains to be fulfilled: the prophecy of his future vindication (14, 62).

* 11ff: Mt 10, 19-22; Lk 12, 11f.
14: Dn 9, 27; Mt 24, 15.
15: Lk 17, 31.
19: Dn 12, 1.
24-27: Mt 24, 29ff; Lk 21, 25ff.
24: Is 13, 10; Ez 32, 7; Jl 2, 10.
26: 14, 62; Dn 7, 13f.
28-32: Mt 24, 32-36; Lk 21, 29-33.
33-37: Mt 24, 42; 25, 13ff.
34: Mt 25, 14-30; Lk 19, 12-27.
14/1f: Mt 26, 2-5; Lk 22, 1f.
3-9: Mt 26, 6-13; Jn 12, 1-8.

over three hundred silver pieces and the money given to the poor." They were infuriated at her. ⁶But Jesus said: "Let her alone. Why do you criticize her? She has done me a kindness. ⁷The poor you will always have with you and you can be generous to them whenever you wish, but you will not always have me. ⁸She has done what she could. By perfuming my body she is anticipating its preparation for burial. ⁹I assure you, wherever the good news is proclaimed throughout the world, what she has done will be told in her memory."

The Betrayal

¹⁰*Then Judas Iscariot, one of the Twelve, went off to the chief priests to hand Jesus over to them. ¹¹Hearing what he had to say, they were jubilant and promised to give him money. He for his part kept looking for an opportune way to hand him over.

Passover Preparation

¹²*On the first day of Unleavened Bread, when it was customary to sacrifice the paschal lamb, his disciples said to him, "Where do you wish us to go to prepare the Passover supper for you?" ¹³He sent two of his disciples with these instructions: "Go into the city and you will come upon a man carrying a water jar. Follow him. ¹⁴Whatever house he enters, say to the owner, 'The Teacher asks, Where is my guest room where I may eat the Passover with my disciples?' ¹⁵Then he will show you an upstairs room, spacious, furnished, and all in order. That is the place you are to get ready for us." ¹⁶The disciples went off. When they reached the city they found it just as he had told them, and they prepared the Passover supper.

The Betrayer

¹⁷*As it grew dark he arrived with the Twelve. ¹⁸They reclined at table, and in the course of the meal Jesus said, "I give you my word, one of you is about to betray me, yes, one who is eating with me." ¹⁹They began to say to him sorrowfully, one by one, "Surely not I!" ²⁰He said, "It is one of the Twelve—a man who dips into the dish with me. ²¹The Son of Man is going the way the Scripture tells of him. Still, accursed be that man by whom the Son of Man is betrayed. It were better for him had he never been born."

The Holy Eucharist

²²*During the meal he took bread, blessed and broke it, and gave it to them. "Take this," he said, "this is my body." ²³He likewise took a cup, gave thanks and passed it to them, and they all drank from it. ²⁴He said to them: "This is my blood, the blood of the cove-

nant, to be poured out on behalf of many. ²⁵I solemnly assure you, I will never again drink of the fruit of the vine until the day when I drink it new in the reign of God."

²⁶After singing songs of praise, they walked out to the Mount of Olives.

Peter's Denial Foretold

²⁷*Jesus then said to them: "Your faith in me shall be shaken, for Scripture has it,

> 'I will strike the shepherd
> and the sheep will be dispersed.'

²⁸But after I am raised up, I will go to Galilee ahead of you." ²⁹Peter said to him, "Even though all are shaken in faith, it will not be that way with me." ³⁰Jesus answered, "I give you my assurance, this very night before the cock crows twice, you will deny me three times." ³¹But Peter kept reasserting vehemently, "Even if I have to die with you, I will not deny you." They all said the same.

The Agony in the Garden

³²*They went then to a place named Gethsemani. "Sit down here while I pray," he said to his disciples; ³³at the same time he took along with him Peter, James, and John. ³⁴Then he began to be filled with fear and distress. He said to them, "My heart is filled with sorrow to the point of death. Remain here and stay awake." ³⁵He advanced a little and fell to the ground, praying that if it were possible this hour might pass him by. ³⁶He kept saying, "Abba (O Father), you have the power to do all things. Take this cup away from me. But let it be as you would have it, not as I." ³⁷When he returned he found them asleep. He said to Peter, "Asleep, Simon? You could not stay awake for even an hour? ³⁸*Be on guard and pray that you may not be put to the test. The spirit is willing but nature is weak." ³⁹Going back again he began to pray in the same words. ⁴⁰Once again he found them asleep on his return. They could not keep their eyes open, nor did they know what to say to him. ⁴¹He returned a third time and said to them, "Still sleeping? Still taking your ease? It will have to do. The hour is on us. You will see that the Son of Man is to be handed over to the clutches of evil men. ⁴²Rouse yourselves and come along. See! My betrayer is near."

Jesus Arrested

⁴³*Even while he was still speaking, Judas, one of the Twelve, made his appearance accompanied by a crowd with swords and clubs; these people had been sent by the chief priests, the scribes, and the elders. ⁴⁴The betrayer had arranged a signal for them, saying, "The man I shall embrace is the one; arrest him and lead him away, taking every precaution." ⁴⁵He then went directly over to him and said, "Rabbi!" and embraced him. ⁴⁶At this, they laid hands on him and arrested him. ⁴⁷One of the bystanders drew his sword and struck the high priest's slave, cutting off his ear.

✸

10f: Mt 26, 14ff.	27-31: Mt 26, 31-35;
12-16: Mt 26, 17ff;	Lk 22, 31-34:
Lk 22, 7-11.	Jn 13, 36ff.
17-21: Mt 26, 20-24;	27: Zec 13, 7; Jn 16, 32.
Lk 22, 21ff;	32-42: Mt 26, 36-46;
Jn 13, 21-26.	Lk 22, 40-46.
22-25: Mt 26, 26-30;	32: Jn 18, 1.
Lk 22, 19f;	38: Rom 7, 5.
1 Cor 11, 23ff.	43-50: Mt 26, 47-56;
	Lk 22, 47-53;
	Jn 18, 3-11.

[48]Addressing himself to them, Jesus said: "You have come out to arrest me armed with swords and clubs as if against a brigand. [49]I was within your reach daily, teaching in the temple precincts, yet you never arrested me. But now, so that the Scriptures may be fulfilled . . ." [50]With that, all deserted him and fled. [51]There was a young man following him who was covered by nothing but a linen cloth. As they seized him [52]he left the cloth behind and ran off naked.

Jesus before the Sanhedrin

[53*]Then they led Jesus off to the high priest, and all the chief priests, the elders and the scribes came together. [54]Peter followed him at a distance right into the high priest's courtyard, where he found a seat with the temple guard and began to warm himself at the fire. [55]The chief priests with the whole Sanhedrin were busy soliciting testimony against Jesus that would lead to his death, but they could not find any. [56]Many spoke against him falsely under oath but their testimony did not agree. [57]Some, for instance, on taking the stand, testified falsely by alleging, [58*]"We heard him declare, 'I will destroy this temple made by human hands,' and 'In three days I will construct another not made by human hands.'" [59]Even so, their testimony did not agree.

[60]The high priest rose to his feet before the court and began to interrogate Jesus: "Have you no answer to what these men testify against you?" [61]But Jesus remained silent; he made no reply. Once again the high priest interrogated him: "Are you the Messiah, the Son of the Blessed One?" [62*]Then Jesus answered: "I am; and you will see the Son of Man seated at the right hand of the Power and coming with the clouds of heaven." [63]At that the high priest tore his robes and said: "What further need do we have of witnesses? [64]You have heard the blasphemy. What is your verdict?" They all concurred in the verdict "guilty," with its sentence of death. [65*]Some of them then began to spit on him. They blindfolded him and hit him, saying, "Play the prophet!" while the officers manhandled him.

Peter's Denial

[66*]While Peter was down in the courtyard, one of the servant girls of the high priest came along. [67]When she noticed Peter warming himself, she looked at him more closely and said, "You too were with Jesus of Nazareth." [68]But he denied it: "I do not know what you are talking about! What are you getting at?" Then he went out into the gateway. (At that moment a cock crowed.) [69]The servant girl, keeping an eye on him, started again to tell the bystanders, "This man is one of them." [70]Once again he denied it. A little later the bystanders said to Peter once more, "You are certainly one of them! You are a Galilean, are you not?" [71]He began to curse, and to swear, "I do not even know the man you are talking about!" [72*]Just then a second cockcrow was heard and Peter recalled the prediction Jesus had made to him, "Before the cock crows twice you will deny me three times." He broke down and began to cry.

Jesus before Pilate

15 [1*]As soon as it was daybreak the chief priests, with the elders and scribes (that is, the whole Sanhedrin), reached a decision. They bound Jesus, led him away, and handed him over to Pilate. [2]Pilate interrogated him: "Are you the king of the Jews?" "You are the one who is saying it," Jesus replied. [3]The chief priests, meanwhile, brought many accusations against him. [4]Pilate interrogated him again: "Surely you have some answer? See how many accusations they are leveling against you." [5]But greatly to Pilate's surprise, Jesus made no further response.

[6*]Now on the occasion of a festival he would release for them one prisoner—any man they asked for. [7]There was a prisoner named Barabbas jailed along with the rebels who had committed murder in the uprising. [8]When the crowd came up to press their demand that he honor the custom, [9]Pilate rejoined, "Do you want me to release the king of the Jews for you?" [10]He was aware, of course, that it was out of jealousy that the chief priests had handed him over. [11]Meanwhile, the chief priests incited the crowd to have him release Barabbas instead. [12]Pilate again asked them, "What am I to do with the man you call the king of the Jews?" [13]They shouted back, "Crucify him!" [14]Pilate protested, "Why? What crime has he committed?" They only shouted the louder, "Crucify him!" [15]So Pilate, who wished to satisfy the crowd, released Barabbas to them; and after he had had Jesus scourged, he handed him over to be crucified.

The Crowning with Thorns

[16*]The soldiers now led Jesus away into the hall known as the praetorium; at the same time they assembled the whole cohort. [17]They dressed him in royal purple, then wove a crown of thorns and put it on him, [18]and began to salute him, "All hail! King of the Jews!" [19]Continually striking Jesus on the head with a reed and spitting at him, they genuflected before him and pretended to pay him homage. [20]When they had finished mocking him, they stripped him of the purple, dressed him in his own clothes, and led him out to crucify him.

The Way of the Cross: the Crucifixion

[21*]A man named Simon of Cyrene, the father of Alexander and Rufus, was coming in from the fields, and they pressed him into service to carry the cross. [22*]When they brought Jesus to the site of Golgotha

53-65: Mt 26, 57-68;
      Lk 22, 54-63ff;
      Jn 18, 12f.
58: 15, 29: 2 Cor 5, 1.
62: 13, 26; Ps 110, 1;
    Dn 7, 13; Mt 24, 30.
65: Lk 22, 63ff.
66-72: Mt 26, 69-75;
      Lk 22, 55-62;
      Jn 18, 16ff.25ff.
72: Jn 13, 38.

15/1-5: Mt 27, 11-14;
       Lk 23, 1ff.
1: Jn 18, 28.
6-15: Mt 27, 15-26;
      Lk 23, 17-25;
      Jn 18, 39f.
16-20: Mt 27, 27-31; Jn 19, 2f.
21: Mt 27, 32; Lk 23, 26.
22-38: Mt 27, 33-51;
      Lk 23, 32-46;
      Jn 19, 17ff.

(which means "Skull Place"), **23**they tried to give him wine drugged with myrrh, but he would not take it. **24***Then they crucified him and divided up his garments by rolling dice for them to see what each should take. **25**It was about nine in the morning when they crucified him. **26**The inscription proclaiming his offense read, "THE KING OF THE JEWS."

27*With him they crucified two insurgents, one at his right and one at his left. **29***People going by kept insulting him, tossing their heads and saying, "Ha, ha! So you were going to destroy the temple and rebuild it in three days! **30**Save yourself now by coming down from that cross!" **31**The chief priests and the scribes also joined in and jeered: "He saved others but he cannot save himself! **32***Let the 'Messiah,' the 'king of Israel,' come down from that cross here and now so that we can see it and believe in him!" The men who had been crucified with him likewise kept taunting him.

Death of Jesus

33When noon came, darkness fell on the whole countryside and lasted until mid-afternoon. **34***At that time Jesus cried in a loud voice, *"Eloi, Eloi, lama sabachthani?"* which means, "My God, my God, why have you forsaken me?" **35**A few of the bystanders who heard it remarked, "Listen! He is calling on Elijah!" **36**Someone ran off, and soaking a sponge in sour wine, stuck it on a reed to try to make him drink. The man said, "Now let's see whether Elijah comes to take him down."

37Then Jesus, uttering a loud cry, breathed his last. **38**At that moment the curtain in the sanctuary was torn in two from top to bottom. **39***The centurion who stood guard over him, on seeing the manner of his death, declared, "Clearly this man was the Son of God!" **40***There were also women present looking on from a distance. Among them were Mary Magdalene, Mary the mother of James the younger and Joses, and Salome. **41**These women had followed Jesus when he was in Galilee and attended to his needs. There were also many others who had come up with him to Jerusalem.

The Burial

42*As it grew dark (it was Preparation Day, that is, the eve of the sabbath), **43**Joseph from Arimathea arrived—a distinguished member of the Sanhedrin. He was another who looked forward to the reign of God. He was bold enough to seek an audience with Pilate and urgently requested the body of Jesus. **44**Pilate was surprised that Jesus should have died so soon. He sum-

moned the centurion and inquired whether Jesus was already dead. **45**Learning from him that he was dead, Pilate released the corpse to Joseph. **46**Then, having bought a linen shroud, Joseph took him down, wrapped him in the linen, and laid him in a tomb which had been cut out of rock. Finally he rolled a stone across the entrance of the tomb. **47**Meanwhile, Mary Magdalene and Mary the mother of Joses observed where he had been laid.

The Women at the Tomb

16 **1***†WHEN the sabbath was over, Mary Magdalene, Mary the mother of James, and Salome bought perfumed oils with which they intended to go and anoint Jesus. **2**Very early, just after sunrise, on the first day of the week they came to the tomb. **3**They were saying to one another, "Who will roll back the stone for us from the entrance to the tomb?" **4**When they looked, they found that the stone had been rolled back. (It was a huge one.) **5***On entering the tomb they saw a young man sitting at the right, dressed in a white robe. **6**This frightened them thoroughly, but he reassured them: "You need not be amazed! You are looking for Jesus of Nazareth, the one who was crucified. He has been raised up; he is not here. See the place where they laid him. **7***Go now and tell his disciples and Peter, 'He is going ahead of you to Galilee, where you will see him just as he told you.' " **8**They made their way out and fled from the tomb bewildered and trembling; and because of their great fear, they said nothing to anyone.

The Longer Ending: 16, 9-20

9*†Jesus rose from the dead early on the first day of the week. He first appeared to Mary Magdalene, out of whom he had cast seven demons. **10***She went to announce the good news to his followers, who were now grieving and weeping. **11**But when they heard that he was alive and had been seen by her, they refused to believe it. **12***Later on, as two of them were walking along their way to the country, he was re-

---

† 15, 28: Omitted with many MSS.

16, 1-8: The purpose of this narrative is to show, in the mystery of Jesus' resurrection, the fulfillment of Jesus' prophecy before the Sanhedrin. The women find the tomb empty and an angel stationed there announces to them what has happened: *He has been raised up; he is not here.* They are told to proclaim the news to Peter and the disciples in order to prepare them for a reunion with him. Mark's composition of the gospel ends at 16, 8 with the women silenced by mystery. This abrupt termination causes many to believe that the original ending of this gospel may have been lost. See note on vv 9-20.

16, 9-20: This passage, termed "the longer ending" to the Marcan gospel by comparison with a much briefer conclusion found in some less important manuscripts, has traditionally been accepted as an inspired part of the gospel. Early citations of it by the Fathers indicate that it was composed in the first century, although vocabulary and style argue strongly that it was written by someone other than Mark. It is a general résumé of the material concerning the appearances of the risen Jesus, reflecting, in particular, traditions found in Luke (24) and John (20).

✿

24: Ps 22, 18.
27: Lk 23, 33.
29: Jn 2, 19.
32: Lk 23, 39.
34: Ps 22, 2.
39ff: Mt 27, 54ff;
    Lk 23, 47ff.
40: 6, 3; Lk 8, 2f.
42-47: Mt 27, 57-61;
    Lk 23, 50-56;
    Jn 19, 38-42.

16/1-8: Mt 28, 1-8;
    Lk 24, 1-10;
    Jn 20, 1-10.
1f: Mt 28, 1; Lk 23, 56.
5: Jn 20, 12.
7: 14, 28.
9-20: Mt 28, 1-10;
    Jn 20, 11-18.
10f: Lk 24, 10f; Jn 20, 18.
12ff: Lk 24, 13-35.

vealed to them completely changed in appearance. [13]These men retraced their steps and announced the good news to the others; but the others put no more faith in them than in Mary Magdalene. [14]*Finally, as they were at table, Jesus was revealed to the Eleven. He took them to task for their disbelief and their stubbornness, since they had put no faith in those who had seen him after he had been raised.

[15]*Then he told them: "Go into the whole world and proclaim the good news to all creation. [16]The man who believes in it and accepts baptism will be saved; the man who refuses to believe in it will be condemned. [17]Signs like these will accompany those who have professed their faith: they will use my name to expel demons, they will speak entirely new languages, [18]*they will be able to handle serpents, they will be able to drink deadly poison without harm, and the sick upon whom they lay their hands will recover." [19]*Then, after speaking to them, the Lord Jesus was taken up into heaven and took his seat at God's right hand. [20]*The Eleven went forth and preached everywhere. The Lord continued to work with them throughout and

confirm the message through the signs which accompanied them.

The Shorter Ending*

They promptly reported to Peter and his companions all that had been announced to them. Later on it was through them that Jesus himself sent out from east to west the sacred and immortal proclamation of eternal salvation.

The Freer Logion**

They offered this excuse: "This lawless and faithless age is under Satan, who does not allow what is unclean and dominated by spirits to grasp the true power of God. Therefore," they said to Christ, "reveal your just authority now." Christ replied: "The measure of the years of Satan's power has been fulfilled, but other terrible things are imminent. Yet it was for the sake of sinners that I was handed over to death, that they might return to the truth and sin no more, and inherit the spiritual and immortal glory of justification in heaven."

----

†

*Found after Mark 16, 8 before the Longer Ending, in some late Greek manuscripts as well as some ancient versions.

**Found after Mark 16, 14 in a fourth-fifth century manuscript preserved in the Freer Gallery of Art, Washington, D. C. This ending was known to St. Jerome.

14: Lk 24, 36-49;   18: Mt 10, 1; Lk 10, 19;
     1 Cor 15, 5.   Acts 28, 3-6.
15f: 13, 10; Mt 28, 18ff;   19: Lk 24, 50-53.
     Lk 24, 47; Jn 20, 21.   20: 1 Tm 3, 16.

The Gospel According to Luke

Introduction

In accordance with the custom of Greek writers of the time, Luke introduces his gospel narrative with a brief preface (1, 1-4) probably intended to cover the Acts of the Apostles as well. Luke here alludes to his predecessors and stresses the care with which he has collected and judged his material. He regards those who wrote the gospel message before him as comprising two groups: "eyewitnesses and ministers of the word," i. e., the Twelve, who were the fundamental source of the gospel tradition (1, 2; Acts 1, 21f; 10, 39); and the "many," who attempted to arrange the preaching and teaching of the Twelve in narrative form (1, 1). Luke places himself in the latter group (1, 3)—not eyewitnesses like the Twelve, but catechists and writers who had familiarized themselves with the traditions about Jesus (the gospel) and the experiences of the Christian communities (Acts of the Apostles).

Luke dedicates his two books to a certain Theophilus (1, 3; Acts 1, 1)—a common name in the Greek world meaning "God's friend." This personage, whether a literary figure signifying Gentiles as such, or a historical individual with some degree of political importance, has received information on Christian teaching. Luke sees him either as a person of influence favorably disposed toward Christian teaching and worthy of more information, or as a Christian seeking more knowledge concerning the practical implications of his faith (1, 4). Perhaps this ambiguity concerning the religious status of Theophilus is deliberate; compare Lk 1, 4 with Acts 18, 25; 21, 21.24.

Many scholars discern in the Lucan gospel and Acts an apologetic strain presumably directed against unfounded criticisms of Christian teaching. Written after the persecution of Nero that began in 64 A. D. and caused hostility toward Christians throughout the empire, Luke-Acts reveal that Jesus himself was accounted innocent by the Roman governor Pontius Pilate (Lk 23, 4.15.22), and that St. Paul, founder of many Christian communities in the empire, was often acquitted by the Roman magistrates of charges against him (Acts 16, 36; 18, 12-17; 25, 26; 26, 32).

The evangelist portrays Christianity, not as a political movement, nor as a sect organized for an initiated few, but as a religious faith open to all men. His portrait of Jesus, drawn from the gospel tradition, manifests the Savior's concern for humanity (10, 25-37; 13, 10-16; 14, 12ff; 15, 11-32), and his identification with the poor (9, 57f; 12, 13-21), the outcast (15, 1f; 17, 11-19), and the criminal (19, 1-10; 23, 39-43). Although the apologetic thought in Luke's writings must be acknowledged, it was nevertheless not his chief purpose to produce an apology for Christianity.

Unlike the other evangelists, Luke presents no main thesis. He is content to let the material of the gospel narrative speak for itself without any argumentative intrusion of his own. The correct understanding of the importance of the Christian gospel is delicately introduced into the traditional material. By aligning Jesus' birth (2, 1ff) and the preaching of John the Baptizer (3, 1f) with the facts of secular history, the evangelist indicates that the gospel tradition did not originate in a myth about gods, but was lived out by Jesus of Nazareth in the real world wherein all men are born, struggle over the meaning of their existence, and die. He depicts Jesus as resolutely facing the reality which that world had in store for him (9, 51). Luke also, in harmony with the growing realization of the Christian communities of his time, removes the concept of the proximate parousia so prominent in Mark 13. But neither these concepts nor any particular aspects of Jesus' teaching that Luke chooses to emphasize are presented in any but a serene fashion. His reverence extends, not only to Jesus as God's Son (1, 35), and to the invisible persons of the Father (11, 2) and the Holy Spirit (11, 13), but also to humanity itself as the fruitful recipient of God's word.

No other evangelist has placed such emphasis on the prophetic word of Jesus; no other is so optimistic over the favorable response it is destined to receive. Nothing that the divine word enacts in history can fail (1, 37). The word of Jesus on love of enemies (6, 27-42) is seen as the only weapon which the small Christian communities of Luke's time possess to combat the forces of persecution. The word of God is the teaching of Jesus, to be planted in the hearts of men (8, 11). And it is the function of the Christian community (24, 27) to confront humanity with this word, which undergoes vicissitudes but inevitably finds out those who will hear, believe, and act (8, 15.21; 11, 28).

Most scholars agree that Luke made use of Mark's gospel as one of his sources; some even consider it to be Luke's principal source, to which he added other material (Lk 1-2; 6, 20—8, 3; 9, 51–18, 14) including an independently derived passion-narrative (22, 1–24, 53). In the view of others, Luke used Mark only as a supplementary source for rounding out the material he took from other traditions. Certainly, Luke's aim was not to improve upon Mark's account of the public ministry of Jesus, but rather to provide material for those like Theophilus, God's friends, desirous of living out the message of Jesus in the world.

Early Christian tradition ascribes the companion volumes of the Lucan gospel and Acts of the Apostles to approximately 75 A. D., and identifies the author with Luke the physician, friend of St. Paul, mentioned in Col 4, 14; Phlm 24; and 2 Tm 4, 11.

The Gospel of Luke is divided as follows:

Preface

1 **1***MANY HAVE UNDERTAKEN to compile a narrative of the events which have been fulfilled in our midst, **2**precisely as those events were transmitted to us by the original eyewitnesses and ministers of the word. **3**I too have carefully traced the whole sequence of events from the beginning, and have decided to set it in writing for you, Theophilus, **4**so that Your Excellency may see how reliable the instruction was that you received.

I: THE INFANCY NARRATIVE

Announcement of the Birth of John

5*†IN THE DAYS OF HEROD, king of Judea, there was a priest named Zechariah of the priestly class of Abijah; his wife was a descendant of Aaron named Elizabeth. **6**Both were just in the eyes of God, blamelessly following all the commandments and ordinances of the Lord. **7***They were childless, for Elizabeth was sterile; moreover, both were advanced in years.

8Once, when it was the turn of Zechariah's class and he was fulfilling his functions as a priest before God, **9**it fell to him by lot according to priestly usage to enter the sanctuary of the Lord and offer incense. **10**While the full assembly of people was praying outside at the incense hour, **11**an angel of the Lord appeared to him, standing at the right of the altar of incense. Zechariah was deeply disturbed upon seeing him, and overcome by fear.

13*The angel said to him: "Do not be frightened, Zechariah; your prayer has been heard. Your wife Elizabeth shall bear a son whom you shall name John. **14**Joy and gladness will be yours, and many will rejoice at his birth; **15***for he will be great in the eyes of the Lord. He will never drink wine or strong drink, and he will be filled with the Holy Spirit from his mother's womb. **16***Many of the sons of Israel will he bring back to the Lord their God. **17***God himself will go before him, in the spirit and power of Elijah, to turn the hearts of fathers to their children and the rebellious to the wisdom of the just, and to prepare for the Lord a people well-disposed."

18Zechariah said to the angel: "How am I to know this? I am an old man; my wife too is advanced in age."

✻
  1/1-4: Acts 1, 1; 1 Cor 15, 3.
     5: 1 Chr 24, 10.
     7: Gn 18, 11; Jgs 13, 2-5;
       1 Sm 1, 5f.
     9: Ex 30, 7.
   13: 1, 57.60.63; Mt 1, 20.
    15: Nm 6, 2f.
    16: 1, 76.
    17: Sir 48, 10; Mal 3, 23f;
       Mt 17, 10-13.
    27: Mt 1, 18.
    28: Ru 2, 4; Jdt 13, 18.

19The angel replied: "I am Gabriel, who stand in attendance before God. I was sent to speak to you and bring you this good news. **20**†But now you will be mute —unable to speak—until the day these things take place, because you have not trusted my words. They will all come true in due season." **21**Meanwhile, the people were waiting for Zechariah, wondering at his delay in the temple. **22**When he finally came out he was unable to speak to them, and they realized that he had seen a vision inside. He kept making signs to them, for he remained speechless.

23Then, when his time of priestly service was over, he went home.

24Afterward, his wife Elizabeth conceived. She went into seclusion for five months, saying: **25**"In these days the Lord is acting on my behalf; he has seen fit to remove my reproach among men."

Announcement of the Birth of Jesus

26In the sixth month, the angel Gabriel was sent from God to a town of Galilee named Nazareth, **27***to a virgin betrothed to a man named Joseph, of the house of David. The virgin's name was Mary. **28***†Upon arriving, the angel said to her: "Rejoice, O highly favored daughter! The Lord is with you. Blessed are you among women." **29**She was deeply troubled by his words, and wondered what his greeting meant. **30**†The angel went on to say to her: "Do not

---

† 1, 5—2, 52: Beneath the simple beauty of Luke's infancy narrative there lies a remarkable depth of theological reflection. It centers about the similarity and the contrast between the religious mission of John the Baptizer and that of Jesus. By presenting the parallel announcements of their conception and birth (1, 5-25; 1, 26-38; 1, 57f; 2, 1-20) and the parallel narratives of their circumcision (1, 59-63; 2, 21), to which are added prophecies concerning the unique religious importance of Jesus (2, 22-40), the evangelist brings into sharp focus the transcendence of Jesus' person and mission over John's.

This parallelism in literary structure, along with the pervading use of Old Testament passages and ideas, conveys the basically theological character of the infancy gospel.

Mary is presented as the virgin divinely chosen in Israel to be the mother of Jesus and to experience the mystery and the spiritual benefits of his redemptive mission (1, 34-38.42.45-55; 2, 19.35.51). She is the prefiguration of the life and destiny of the Christian community.

1, 20: Though Zechariah's punishment is usually thought to have been due to unbelief in the angelic message concerning the child's conception, the sign he was asking for (1, 18) may have been some proof within his own lifetime of the child's future prophetic role.

1, 28: *Highly favored daughter:* Mary is to be the recipient of the divine favor, i. e., of the sanctifying power of God, in view of her office of mother of the Messiah, which the angel announces to her.

1, 30-34: The angel's message to Mary (30f) shows a certain similarity to the announcements made to some sterile women of the Old Testament who by God's intervention became the mothers of personages illustrious in salvation history: Sarah, mother of Isaac (Gn 17, 16.19); Samson's mother (Jgs 13, 2f); Hannah, mother of Samuel (1 Sm 1, 9-20). Mary, however, who is betrothed but not yet married (27), cannot be called sterile. Her question, then, directs itself precisely to the issue of divine favor in her case (30-33). How is she to know that the child she is now to conceive will be the Son of the Most High?

fear, Mary. You have found favor with God. [31]You shall conceive and bear a son and give him the name Jesus. [32]*Great will be his dignity and he will be called Son of the Most High. The Lord God will give him the throne of David his father. He will rule over the house of Jacob forever [33]*and his reign will be without end."

[34]†Mary said to the angel, "How can this be since I do not know man?" [35]*†The angel answered her: "The Holy Spirit will come upon you and the power of the Most High will overshadow you; hence, the holy offspring to be born will be called Son of God. [36]Know that Elizabeth your kinswoman has conceived a son in her old age; she who was thought to be sterile is now in her sixth month, [37]*for nothing is impossible with God."

[38]Mary said: "I am the servant of the Lord. Let it be done to me as you say." With that the angel left her.

The Visit

[39]Thereupon Mary set out, proceeding in haste into the hill country to a town of Judah, [40]where she entered Zechariah's house and greeted Elizabeth. [41]When Elizabeth heard Mary's greeting, the baby leapt in her womb. Elizabeth was filled with the Holy Spirit [42]*and cried out in a loud voice: "Blest are you among women and blest is the fruit of your womb. [43]But who am I that the mother of my Lord should come to me? [44]The moment your greeting sounded in my ears, the baby leapt in my womb for joy. [45]Blest is she who trusted that the Lord's words to her would be fulfilled."

Mary's Canticle

[46]*Then Mary said:

"My being proclaims the greatness of the Lord,
  [47]my spirit finds joy in God my savior,
[48]*For he has looked upon his servant in her
    lowliness;
  all ages to come shall call me blessed.
[49]God who is mighty has done great things for me,
  holy is his name;
[50]*His mercy is from age to age
  on those who fear him.
[51]*"He has shown might with his arm;
  he has confused the proud in their inmost
    thoughts.
[52]*He has deposed the mighty from their thrones
  and raised the lowly to high places.

[53]*The hungry he has given every good thing,
  while the rich he has sent empty away.
[54]*He has upheld Israel his servant,
  ever mindful of his mercy;
[55]*Even as he promised our fathers,
  promised Abraham and his descendants
    forever."

[56]Mary remained with Elizabeth about three months and then returned home.

[57]When Elizabeth's time for delivery arrived, she gave birth to a son. [58]Her neighbors and relatives, upon hearing that the Lord had extended his mercy to her, rejoiced with her. [59]*When they assembled for the circumcision of the child on the eighth day, they intended to name him after his father Zechariah. [60]At this his mother intervened, saying, "No, he is to be called John."

[61]They pointed out to her, "None of your relatives has this name." [62]Then, using signs, they asked the father what he wished him to be called.

[63]*He signaled for a writing tablet and wrote the words, "His name is John." This astonished them all. [64]*At that moment his mouth was opened and his tongue loosed, and he began to speak in praise of God.

[65]Fear descended on all in the neighborhood; throughout the hill country of Judea these happenings began to be recounted to the last detail. [66]All who heard stored these things up in their hearts, saying, "What will this child be?" and, "Was not the hand of the Lord upon him?"

Zechariah's Canticle

[67]Then Zechariah his father, filled with the Holy Spirit, uttered this prophecy:

[68]*"Blessed be the Lord the God of Israel
  because he has visited and ransomed his people.
[69]He has raised a horn of saving strength for us
  in the house of David his servant,
[70]*As he promised through the mouths of his holy
    ones,
  the prophets of ancient times:
[71]*Salvation from our enemies
  and from the hands of all our foes.
[72]*He has dealt mercifully with our fathers
  and remembered the holy covenant he made,
[73]The oath he swore to Abraham our father he
    would grant us:
    [74]that, rid of fear and delivered from the enemy,

---

† 1, 34: *I do now know man:* i. e., as husband. Scholars generally explain this verse as a literary form emphasizing the faith of the first-century church in the virginal conception and birth of the Messiah.

1, 35ff: The overshadowing of Mary recalls the cloud that covered with glory the Meeting Tent (Ex 40, 34f) and the temple of the Lord (1 Kgs 8, 10; Hg 2, 7). The descent of the Holy Spirit upon her, the designation of her child as Son of God, are further signs of God's favor. As a divine pledge of this, she is informed of the approaching maternity of her aged and hitherto sterile cousin Elizabeth.

*
32: Is 9, 6; Mi 4, 7.
33: Dn 2, 44; 7, 14.
35: Mt 1, 20.
37: Gn 18, 14; Jer 32, 27; Mt 19, 26.
42: Jgs 5, 24; Jdt 13, 18.
46: Is 61, 10.
48: 11, 27; Ps 113, 7.
50: Ps 103, 17.
51: Ps 138, 6; Jb 5, 12.
52: Ps 75, 8.
53: Ps 107, 9.
54: Ps 98, 3; Is 41, 9.
55: Gn 13, 15; 22, 18.
59: Gn 17, 10; Lv 12, 3.
63: 1, 13.
64: 1, 20.
68: Pss 74, 12; 111, 9.
70: Jer 30, 10.
71: Ps 106, 10.
72f: Lv 26, 42; Mi 7, 20.

75We should serve him devoutly and through all
our days
be holy in his sight.
76*And you, O child, shall be called
prophet of the Most High;
For you shall go before the Lord
to prepare straight paths for him,
77Giving his people a knowledge of salvation
in freedom from their sins.
78*All this is the work of the kindness of our God;
he, the Dayspring, shall visit us in his mercy
79To shine on those who sit in darkness and in the
shadow of death,
to guide our feet into the way of peace."

80The child grew up and matured in spirit. He lived in the desert until the day when he made his public appearance in Israel.

Birth of Jesus

2 **1†**IN those days Caesar Augustus published a decree ordering a census of the whole world. **2**This first census took place while Quirinius was governor of Syria. **3**Everyone went to register, each to his own town. **4***And so Joseph went from the town of Nazareth in Galilee to Judea, to David's town of Bethlehem—because he was of the house and lineage of David—**5***to register with Mary, his espoused wife, who was with child.

6While they were there the days of her confinement were completed. **7†**She gave birth to her first-born son and wrapped him in swaddling clothes and laid him in a manger, because there was no room for them in the place where travelers lodged.

The Shepherds

8There were shepherds in the region, living in the fields and keeping night watch by turns over their flocks. **9**The angel of the Lord appeared to them as the glory of the Lord shone around them, and they were very much afraid. **10**The angel said to them: "You have nothing to fear! I come to proclaim good news to you—tidings of great joy to be shared by the whole people. **11***This day in David's city a savior has been born to you, the Messiah and Lord. **12***Let this be a sign to you: in a manger you will find an infant wrapped in swaddling clothes." **13**Suddenly, there was with the angel a multitude of the heavenly host, praising God and saying,

14*†"Glory to God in high heaven,
peace on earth to those on whom his favor
rests."

15When the angels had returned to heaven, the shepherds said to one another: "Let us go over to Bethlehem and see this event which the Lord has made known to us." **16**They went in haste and found Mary and Joseph, and the baby lying in the manger; **17**once they saw, they understood what had been told them concerning this child. **18**All who heard of it were astonished at the report given them by the shepherds.

19Mary treasured all these things and reflected on them in her heart. **20***The shepherds returned, glorifying and praising God for all they had heard and seen, in accord with what had been told them.

Circumcision of Jesus

21*When the eighth day arrived for his circumcision, the name Jesus was given the child, the name the angel had given him before he was conceived.

Presentation in the Temple

22*When the day came to purify them according to the law of Moses, the couple brought him up to Jerusalem so that he could be presented to the Lord, **23***for it is written in the law of the Lord, "Every first-born male shall be consecrated to the Lord." **24**They came to offer in sacrifice "a pair of turtledoves or two young pigeons," in accord with the dictate in the law of the Lord.

25There lived in Jerusalem at the time a certain man named Simeon. He was just and pious, and awaited the consolation of Israel, and the Holy Spirit was upon him. **26**It was revealed to him by the Holy Spirit that he would not experience death until he had seen the Anointed of the Lord. **27**He came to the temple now, inspired by the Spirit; and when the parents brought in the child Jesus to perform for him the customary ritual of the law, **28**he took him in his arms and blessed God in these words:

29"Now, Master, you can dismiss your servant in
peace;
you have fulfilled your word.
30*For my eyes have witnessed your saving deed
31displayed for all the peoples to see:

---

† 2, 1-5: Luke introduces the census to explain the time of Jesus' birth at Bethlehem. Scholars interpret inscriptions found near Tivoli in 1764, and at Antioch in Pisidia in 1912, to point to Cyrinus as governor of Syria between the years 10 and 8 B. C. The census may well have been inaugurated by him and hence named after him, even if continued and completed under Saturninus, his successor (8-6 B. C.).

2, 7: *Her first-born son:* a reference to the preferential status of the eldest son rather than an implication of subsequent offspring. In Israel the rights of primogeniture—authority, responsibility, succession—accrued to the first-born. He was considered holy; he belonged to God (Ex 13, 1f.14f; 22, 28; 34, 19f) and had to be redeemed, i. e., ransomed by an offering of five shekels made to the sanctuary (Nm 3, 47f; 18, 5f).

2, 14: *Those on whom his favor rests:* an allusion to the mystery of divine election that bestows the gift of faith upon people of divine choice. To these, the messianic mission of Jesus also brings a special gift of peace, the restored friendship between God and man.

76f: 1, 16; Is 40, 3; Mal 3, 1; Mt 11, 10.
78f: Is 42, 7; Jn 8, 12; 2 Pt 1, 19.
2/4: Mi 5, 2; Mt 2, 6.
5: Mt 1, 18.
11: Mt 1, 21.
12: Is 9, 5f.
14: 19, 38.
20: 5, 26; 7, 16.
21: 1, 31; Gn 17, 12; Mt 1, 21.
22: Lv 12, 2-6.
23f: Ex 13, 2; Lv 12, 8.
30ff: Is 46, 13; 49, 6; 52, 10; Jn 8, 12.

³²A revealing light to the Gentiles,
> the glory of your people Israel."

³³The child's father and mother were marveling at what was being said about him. ³⁴*Simeon blessed them and said to Mary his mother: "This child is destined to be the downfall and the rise of many in Israel, a sign that will be opposed—³⁵*and you yourself shall be pierced with a sword—so that the thoughts of many hearts may be laid bare."

The Prophetess

³⁶There was also a certain prophetess, Anna by name, daughter of Phanuel of the tribe of Asher. She had seen many days, having lived seven years with her husband after her marriage ³⁷and then as a widow until she was eighty-four. She was constantly in the temple, worshiping day and night in fasting and prayer. ³⁸Coming on the scene at this moment, she gave thanks to God and talked about the child to all who looked forward to the deliverance of Jerusalem.

³⁹*When the pair had fulfilled all the prescriptions of the law of the Lord, they returned to Galilee and their own town of Nazareth. ⁴⁰The child grew in size and strength, filled with wisdom, and the grace of God was upon him.

The Finding in the Temple

⁴¹*His parents used to go every year to Jerusalem for the feast of the Passover, ⁴²and when he was twelve they went up for the celebration as was their custom. ⁴³As they were returning at the end of the feast, the child Jesus remained behind unknown to his parents. ⁴⁴Thinking he was in the party, they continued their journey for a day, looking for him among their relatives and acquaintances.

⁴⁵Not finding him, they returned to Jerusalem in search of him. ⁴⁶On the third day they came upon him in the temple sitting in the midst of the teachers, listening to them and asking them questions. ⁴⁷*All who heard him were amazed at his intelligence and his answers.

⁴⁸When his parents saw him they were astonished, and his mother said to him: "Son, why have you done this to us? You see that your father and I have been searching for you in sorrow." ⁴⁹He said to them: "Why did you search for me? Did you not know I had to be in my Father's house?" ⁵⁰But they did not grasp what he said to them.

⁵¹He went down with them then, and came to Nazareth, and was obedient to them. His mother meanwhile kept all these things in memory. ⁵²*Jesus, for his part, progressed steadily in wisdom and age and grace before God and men.

II: PREPARATION FOR THE PUBLIC MINISTRY

John the Baptizer

3 ¹†IN THE FIFTEENTH YEAR of the rule of Tiberius Caesar, when Pontius Pilate was procurator of Judea, Herod tetrarch of Galilee, Philip his brother tetrarch of the region of Ituraea and Trachonitis, and Lysanias tetrarch of Abilene, ²†during the high-priesthood of Annas and Caiaphas, the word of God was spoken to John son of Zechariah in the desert. ³*He went about the entire region of the Jordan proclaiming a baptism of repentance which led to the forgiveness of sins, ⁴*as is written in the book of the words of Isaiah the prophet:

"A herald's voice in the desert, crying,
> 'Make ready the way of the Lord,
> Clear him a straight path.
⁵Every valley shall be filled
> And every mountain and hill shall be leveled.
The windings shall be made straight
> And the rough ways smooth,
⁶And all mankind shall see the salvation of God.'"

⁷He would say to the crowds that came out to be baptized by him: "You brood of vipers! Who told you to flee from the wrath to come? ⁸Give some evidence that you mean to reform. Do not begin by saying to yourselves, 'Abraham is our father.' I tell you, God can raise up children to Abraham from these stones. ⁹Even now the ax is laid to the root of the tree. Every tree that is not fruitful will be cut down and thrown into the fire."

¹⁰*The crowds asked him, "What ought we to do?" ¹¹In reply he said, "Let the man with two coats give to him who has none. The man who has food should do the same."

¹²Tax collectors also came to be baptized, and they said to him, "Teacher, what are we to do?" ¹³He answered them, "Exact nothing over and above your fixed amount."

¹⁴Soldiers likewise asked him, "What about us?" He told them, "Don't bully anyone. Denounce no one falsely. Be content with your pay."

¹⁵*†The people were full of anticipation, wondering in their hearts whether John might be the Messiah. ¹⁶*John answered them all by saying: "I am baptizing you in water, but there is one to come who is mightier than I. I am not fit to loosen his sandal strap. He will baptize you in the Holy Spirit and in fire. ¹⁷*His win-

---

† 3, 1: *In the fifteenth year . . . Caesar:* this chronological datum enables scholars to calculate that John the Baptizer began his mission sometime between 27 and 29 A. D.

3, 2-18: See notes on the verses in Mt 3, 1-17. The Lucan account of the Baptizer's mission gives examples which clarify the meaning of repentance (3, 10-14).

3, 15: This popular conception concerning John the Baptizer closely resembles that in John 1, 20.25.

* 34: 12, 51ff.
35: Jn 9, 39; 19, 25ff; Rom 9, 33; 1 Pt 2, 7.
39: Mt 2, 23.
41: Ex 23, 15.
47: 4, 22.
52: 2, 19.
3/3-10: Mt 3, 1-10; Mk 1, 2-6.

4: Is 40, 3ff; Jn 1, 23.
10f: Acts 2, 37; Jas 2, 15; 1 Jn 3, 17.
15-18: Mt 3, 11f; Mk 1, 7f; Acts 13, 25.
16: Jn 1, 27; Acts 1, 5; 11, 16.
17: Mt 3, 12.

nowing-fan is in his hand to clear his threshing floor and gather the wheat into his barn; but the chaff he will burn in unquenchable fire." ¹⁸Using exhortations of this sort, he preached the good news to the people.

¹⁹*Herod the tetrarch was censured by John on the subject of Herodias, his brother's wife, and for all his other crimes. ²⁰He added to his guilt by shutting John up in prison.

Baptism of Jesus

²¹*†When all the people were baptized, and Jesus was at prayer after likewise being baptized, the skies opened ²²*and the Holy Spirit descended on him in visible form like a dove. A voice from heaven was heard to say: "You are my beloved Son. On you my favor rests."

Genealogy of Jesus

²³*†When Jesus began his work he was about thirty years of age, being—so it was supposed—the son of Joseph, son of Heli, ²⁴son of Matthat, son of Levi, son of Melchi, son of Jannai, son of Joseph, ²⁵son of Mattathias, son of Amos, son of Nahum, son of Esli, son of Naggai, ²⁶son of Maath, son of Mattathias, son of Semein, son of Josech, son of Joda, ²⁷*son of Joanan, son of Rhesa, son of Zerubbabel, son of Shealtiel, son of Neri, ²⁸son of Melchi, son of Addi, son of Cosam, son of Elmadam, son of Er, ²⁹son of Joshua, son of Eliezer, son of Jorim, son of Matthat, son of Levi, ³⁰son of Simeon, son of Judah, son of Joseph, son of Jonam, son of Eliakim, ³¹son of Melea, son of Menna, son of Mattatha, son of Nathan, son of David, ³²son of Jesse, son of Obed, son of Boaz, son of Sala, son of Nahshon, ³³*son of Amminadab, son of Admin, son of Arni, son of Hezron, son of Perez, son of Judah, ³⁴son of Jacob, son of Isaac, son of Abraham, son of Terah, son of Nahor, ³⁵son of Serug, son of Reu, son of Peleg, son of Eber, son of Shelah, ³⁶son of Cainan, son of Arphaxad, son of Shem, son of Noah, son of Lamech, ³⁷son of Methuselah, son of Enoch, son of Jared, son of Mahalaleel, son of Cainan, ³⁸son of Enos, son of Seth, son of Adam, son of God.

Temptation in the Desert

4 ¹*†JESUS, full of the Holy Spirit, then returned from the Jordan and was conducted by the Spirit into the desert ²for forty days, where he was tempted by the devil. During that time he ate nothing, and at the end of it he was hungry. ³The devil said to him, "If you are the Son of God, command this stone to turn into bread." ⁴*Jesus answered him, "Scripture has it, 'Not on bread alone shall man live.'"

⁵Then the devil took him up higher and showed him all the kingdoms of the world in a single instant. ⁶*He said to him, "I will give you all this power and the glory of these kingdoms; the power has been given to me and I give it to whomever I wish. ⁷Prostrate yourself in homage before me, and it shall all be yours." ⁸*In reply, Jesus said to him, "Scripture has it,

'You shall do homage to the Lord your God;
    him alone shall you adore.'"

⁹Then the devil led him to Jerusalem, set him on the parapet of the temple, and said to him, "If you are the Son of God, throw yourself down from here, ¹⁰*for Scripture has it,

'He will bid his angels watch over you';

¹¹and again,

'With their hands they will support you,
    that you may never stumble on a stone.'"

¹²*Jesus said to him in reply, "It also says, 'You shall not put the Lord your God to the test.'"

¹³*When the devil had finished all the tempting he left him, to await another opportunity.

III: THE MINISTRY IN GALILEE

Beginning of Preaching

¹⁴*†JESUS RETURNED IN THE POWER of the Spirit to Galilee, and his reputation spread throughout the region. ¹⁵He was teaching in their synagogues, and all were loud in his praise.

¹⁶*He came to Nazareth where he had been reared, and entering the synagogue on the sabbath as he was in the habit of doing, he stood up to do the reading. ¹⁷When the book of the prophet Isaiah was handed him, he unrolled the scroll and found the passage where it was written:

¹⁸*"The spirit of the Lord is upon me;
    therefore he has anointed me.
He has sent me to bring glad tidings to the poor,
    to proclaim liberty to captives,
Recovery of sight to the blind
    and release to prisoners,
¹⁹To announce a year of favor from the Lord."

---

† 3, 21f: See note on Mk 1, 9ff.

3, 23-38: Luke traces the genealogy of Jesus to Adam in order to identify Jesus with all humanity; Matthew (1, 1-16) traces it to Abraham to identify Jesus with Israel.

4, 1-13: See note on Mt 4, 1-11.

4, 14-30: After noting Jesus' initial popularity throughout Galilee, Luke combines, into a single scene laid at Nazareth, the favorable reception given his announcement of the arrival of the messianic era (16-22), the objections to him which Jesus senses in the attitude of his townsmen (23-27; see note on Mk 6, 1-6), and their personal attack on him for refusing to work many miracles for them because of their lack of faith (28ff). Luke intends the entire scene to be prophetic of the ultimate rejection of Jesus by his contemporaries.

✽
19f: Mt 14, 3; Mk 6, 17f.
21f: Mt 3, 13-17; Jn 1, 32ff.
22: 2 Pt 1, 17.
23-38: Mt 1, 1-17.
23: Mt 13, 55.
27: 1 Chr 3, 17.
33: Gn 38, 29; Ru 4, 18.
4/1-13: Mt 4, 1-11; Mk 1, 12f.
4: Dt 8, 3.

6: Jer 27, 5; Rv 13, 2ff.
8: Dt 6, 13.
10: Ps 91, 11f.
12: Dt 6, 16.
13: Jn 13, 2.27.
14: 5, 15; Mt 3, 16.
16-30: Mt 13, 53-58;
    Mk 6, 1-6.
18: Is 61, 1f; Mt 3, 16.

20Rolling up the scroll he gave it back to the assistant and sat down. All in the synagogue had their eyes fixed on him. **21**Then he began by saying to them, "Today this Scripture passage is fulfilled in your hearing." **22**All who were present spoke favorably of him; they marveled at the appealing discourse which came from his lips. They also asked, "Is not this Joseph's son?"

23He said to them, "You will doubtless quote me the proverb, 'Physician, heal yourself,' and say, 'Do here in your own country the things we have heard you have done in Capernaum.' **24**But in fact," he went on, "no prophet gains acceptance in his native place. **25**Indeed, let me remind you, there were many widows in Israel in the days of Elijah when the heavens remained closed for three and a half years and a great famine spread over the land. **26**It was to none of these that Elijah was sent, but to a widow of Zarephath near Sidon. **27**Recall, too, the many lepers in Israel in the time of Elisha the prophet; yet not one was cured except Naaman the Syrian."

28At these words the whole audience in the synagogue was filled with indignation. **29**They rose up and expelled him from the town, leading him to the brow of the hill on which it was built **30**and intending to hurl him over the edge. But he went straight through their midst and walked away.

Jesus Teaches in Capernaum

31He then went down to Capernaum, a town of Galilee, where he began instructing them on the sabbath day. **32**They were spellbound by his teaching, for his words had authority.

Cure of a Demoniac

33In the synagogue there was a man with an unclean spirit, who shrieked in a loud voice: **34**"Leave us alone! What do you want of us, Jesus of Nazareth? Have you come to destroy us? I know who you are: the Holy One of God." **35**Jesus said to him sharply, "Be quiet! Come out of him." At that, the demon threw him to the ground before everyone's eyes and came out of him without doing him any harm. **36**All were struck with astonishment, and they began saying to one another: "What is there about his speech? He commands the unclean spirits with authority and power, and they leave." **37**His renown kept spreading through the surrounding country.

38Leaving the synagogue, he entered the house of Simon. Simon's mother-in-law was in the grip of a severe fever, and they interceded with him for her. **39**He stood over her and addressed himself to the fever, and it left her. She got up immediately and waited on them.

40At sunset, all who had people sick with a variety of diseases took them to him, and he laid hands on each of them and cured them. **41**Demons departed from many, crying out as they did so, "You are the son of God!" He rebuked them and did not allow them to speak because they knew that he was the Messiah.

42The next morning he left the town and set out into the open country. The crowds went in search of him, and when they found him they tried to keep him from leaving them. **43**But he said to them, "To other towns I must announce the good news of the reign of God, because that is why I was sent." **44**And he continued to preach in the synagogues of Judea.

Call of the First Disciples

5 **1**As he stood by the Lake of Gennesaret, and the crowd pressed in on him to hear the word of God, **2**he saw two boats moored by the side of the lake; the fishermen had disembarked and were washing their nets. **3**He got into one of the boats, the one belonging to Simon, and asked him to pull out a short distance from the shore; then, remaining seated, he continued to teach the crowds from the boat. **4**When he had finished speaking he said to Simon, "Put out into deep water and lower your nets for a catch." **5**Simon answered, "Master, we have been hard at it all night long and have caught nothing; but if you say so, I will lower the nets." **6**Upon doing this they caught such a great number of fish that their nets were at the breaking point. **7**They signaled to their mates in the other boat to come and help them. These came, and together they filled the two boats until they nearly sank.

8At the sight of this, Simon Peter fell at the knees of Jesus saying, "Leave me, Lord. I am a sinful man." **9**For indeed, amazement at the catch they had made siezed him and all his shipmates, **10**as well as James and John, Zebedee's sons, who were partners with Simon. Jesus said to Simon, "Do not be afraid. From now on you will be catching men." **11**With that they brought their boats to land, left everything, and became his followers.

Cure of a Leper

12On one occasion in a certain town, a man full of leprosy came to him. Seeing Jesus, he bowed down to the ground and said to him, "Lord, if you will to do so, you can cure me." **13**Jesus stretched out his hand to touch him and said, "I do will it. Be cured." Immediately the leprosy left him. **14**Jesus then instructed the man: "Tell no one, but go and show yourself to the

27: 2 Kgs 5, 14.
29: Jn 7, 30.
30: Jn 8, 59.
31-37: Mt 4, 13; Mk 1, 21-28.
32: Mt 7, 28f.
38f: Mt 8, 14ff; Mk 1, 29ff.
40f: Mt 8, 16; Mk 1, 32ff.
42f: Mk 1, 35-38.
5/1-11: Mt 4, 18-22; Mk 1, 16-20.
4: Jn 21, 6.
12ff: Mt 8, 2ff; Mk 1, 40-44.
14: Lv 14, 2-32.

† 4, 33-37: See note on Mk 1, 23-28.

5, 1-11: This scene of the miraculous catch of fish parallels the call of the disciples in Mt 4, 18-22; Mk 1, 16-20. Probably it is related to the miraculous catch after the resurrection, mentioned in Jn 21, 1-8, to which it bears a certain affinity. The final mandate which the risen Christ gave Simon Peter and the other disciples is here anticipated by Luke in an account which portrays Simon's leadership of the disciples and their role of continuing the spiritual mission of Jesus.

5, 12ff: See note on Mk 1, 40-45.

priest. Offer for your healing what Moses prescribed; that should be a proof for them." **15**His reputation spread more and more, and great crowds gathered to hear him and to be cured of their maladies. **16**He often retired to deserted places and prayed.

A Paralyzed Man Cured

17*†One day Jesus was teaching, and the power of the Lord made him heal. Sitting close by were Pharisees and teachers of the law who had come from every village of Galilee and from Judea and Jerusalem. **18**Some men came along carrying a paralytic on a mat. They were trying to bring him in and lay him before Jesus; **19**but they found no way of getting him through because of the crowd, so they went up on the roof. There they let him down with his mat through the tiles into the middle of the crowd before Jesus. **20**Seeing their faith, Jesus said, "My friend, your sins are forgiven you."

21The scribes and the Pharisees began a discussion, saying: "Who is this man who utters blasphemies? Who can forgive sins but God alone?" **22**Jesus, however, knew their reasoning and answered them by saying: "Why do you harbor these thoughts? **23**Which is easier: to say, 'Your sins are forgiven you,' or to say, 'Get up and walk'? **24**In any case, to make it clear to you that the Son of Man has authority on earth to forgive sins"—he then addressed the paralyzed man: "I say to you, get up! Take your mat with you, and return to your house."

25At once the man stood erect before them. He picked up the mat that he had been lying on and went home praising God. **26**At this they were all seized with astonishment. Full of awe, they gave praise to God, saying, "We have seen incredible things today!"

The Call of Levi

27*Afterward he went out and saw a tax collector named Levi sitting at his customs post. He said to him, "Follow me." **28**Leaving everything behind, Levi stood up and became his follower. **29***After that Levi gave a great reception for Jesus in his house, in which he was joined by a large crowd of tax collectors and others at dinner. **30**The Pharisees and the scribes of their party said to his disciples, "Why do you eat and drink with tax collectors and non-observers of the law?" **31**Jesus said to them, "The healthy do not need a doctor; sick people do. **32**I have not come to invite the self-righteous to a change of heart, but sinners."

The Question of Fasting

33*†They said to him: "John's disciples fast frequently and offer prayers; the disciples of the Phari-

sees do the same. Yours, on the contrary, eat and drink freely." **34**Jesus replied: "Can you make guests of the groom fast while the groom is still with them? **35**But when the days come that the groom is removed from their midst, they will surely fast in those days."

36He then proposed to them this figure: "No one tears a piece from a new coat to patch an old one. If he does, he will only tear the new coat, and the piece taken from it will not match the old. **37**Moreover, no one pours new wine into old wineskins. Should he do so, the new wine will burst the old skins, the wine will spill out, and the skins will be lost. **38**New wine should be poured into fresh skins. **39**No one, after drinking old wine, wants new. He says, 'I find the old wine better.' "

The Disciples and the Sabbath

6 **1***†ONCE on a sabbath Jesus was walking through the standing grain. His disciples were pulling off grain-heads, shelling them with their hands, and eating them. **2**Some of the Pharisees asked, "Why are you doing what is prohibited on the sabbath?" **3**Jesus said to them: "Have you not read what David did when he and his men were hungry—**4***how he entered God's house and took and ate the holy bread and gave it to his men, even though only priests are allowed to eat it?" **5**Then he said to them, "The Son of Man is Lord even of the sabbath."

6*†On another sabbath he came to teach in a synagogue where there was a man whose right hand was withered. **7**The scribes and Pharisees were on the watch to see if he would perform a cure on the sabbath so that they could find a charge against him. **8**He knew their thoughts, however, and said to the man whose hand was withered, "Get up and stand here in front." The man rose and remained standing. **9**Jesus said to them, "I ask you, is it lawful to do good on the sabbath—or evil? To preserve life—or destroy it?" **10**He looked around at them all and said to the man, "Stretch out your hand." The man did so and his hand was perfectly restored.

11At this they became frenzied and began asking one another what could be done to Jesus.

Choice of the Twelve

12*†Then he went out to the mountain to pray, spending the night in communion with God. **13**At daybreak he called his disciples and selected twelve of them to be his apostles: **14**Simon, to whom he gave the name Peter, and Andrew his brother, James and John, Philip and Bartholomew, **15**Matthew and Thomas, James son of Alphaeus, and Simon called the Zealot, **16**Judas son of James, and Judas Iscariot, who turned traitor.

❋

17-26: Mt 9, 1-8;
      Mk 2, 1-12.
27-38: Mt 9, 9-17;
      Mk 2, 14-22.
29-32: Mt 9, 10-13;
      Mk 2, 15ff.
33-39: Mt 9, 14-17;
      Mk 2, 18-22.

6/1-5: Mt 12, 1-8;
      Mk 2, 23-28.
    4: 1 Sm 21, 7.
6-11: 14, 1-6; Mt 12, 9-14;
      Mk 3, 1-6.
12-16: Mt 10, 1-4;
      Mk 3, 13-19.

---

†

5, 17-26: See note on Mk 2, 1-12.
5, 33-39: See note on Mt 9, 14-17.
6, 1-5: See note on Mt 12, 3-6.
6, 6-11: See note on Mt 12, 10.
6, 12-16: See note on Mk 3, 13-19.

The Great Discourse

17*Coming down the mountain with them, he stopped at a level stretch where there were many of his disciples; a large crowd of people was with them from all Judea and Jerusalem and the coast of Tyre and Sidon, **18**people who came to hear him and be healed of their diseases. Those who were troubled with unclean spirits were cured; **19**indeed, the whole crowd was trying to touch him because power went out from him which cured all. **20*†**Then, raising his eyes to his disciples, he said:

"Blest are you poor; the reign of God is yours.
Blest are you who hunger; **21**you shall be filled.
Blest are you who are weeping; you shall laugh.

22"Blest shall you be when men hate you, when they ostracize you and insult you and proscribe your name as evil because of the Son of Man. **23**On the day they do so, rejoice and exult, for your reward shall be great in heaven. Thus it was that their fathers treated the prophets.

24*"But woe to you rich, for your consolation is now. **25***Woe to you who are full; you shall go hungry.
Woe to you who laugh now; you shall weep in your grief.

26"Woe to you when all speak well of you. Their fathers treated the false prophets in just this way.

Love of One's Enemy

27*"To you who hear me, I say: Love your enemies, do good to those who hate you; **28***bless those who curse you and pray for those who maltreat you. **29***When someone slaps you on one cheek, turn and give him the other; when someone takes your coat, let him have your shirt as well. **30**Give to all who beg from you. When a man takes what is yours, do not demand it back. **31***Do to others what you would have them do to you. **32***If you love those who love you, what credit is that to you? Even sinners love those who love them. **33**If you do good to those who do good to you, how can you claim any credit? Sinners do as much. **34***If you lend to those from whom you expect repayment, what merit is there in it for you? Even sinners lend to sinners, expecting to be repaid in full.

35"Love your enemy and do good; lend without expecting repayment. Then will your recompense be great. You will rightly be called sons of the Most High, since he himself is good to the ungrateful and the wicked.

36"Be compassionate, as your Father is compassion-ate. **37***Do not judge, and you will not be judged. Do not condemn, and you will not be condemned. Pardon, and you shall be pardoned. **38***Give, and it shall be given to you. Good measure pressed down, shaken together, running over, will they pour into the fold of your garment. For the measure you measure with will be measured back to you."

39*He also used images in speaking to them: "Can a blind man act as guide to a blind man? Will they not both fall into a ditch? **40***A student is not above his teacher; but every student when he has finished his studies will be on a par with his teacher.

41*"Why look at the speck in your brother's eye when you miss the plank in your own? **42**How can you say to your brother, 'Brother, let me remove the speck from your eye,' yet fail yourself to see the plank lodged in your own? Hypocrite, remove the plank from your own eye first; then you will see clearly enough to remove the speck from your brother's eye.

43*"A good tree does not produce decayed fruit any more than a decayed tree produces good fruit. **44**Each tree is known by its yield. Figs are not taken from thornbushes, nor grapes picked from brambles. **45**A good man produces goodness from the good in his heart; an evil man produces evil out of his store of evil. Each man speaks from his heart's abundance. **46***Why do you call me 'Lord, Lord,' and not put into practice what I teach you? **47***Any man who desires to come to me will hear my words and put them into practice. I will show you with whom he is to be compared. **48**He may be likened to the man who, in building a house, dug deeply and laid the foundation on a rock. When the floods came the torrent rushed in on that house, but failed to shake it because of its solid foundation. **49**On the other hand, anyone who has heard my words but not put them into practice is like the man who built his house on the ground without any foundation. When the torrent rushed upon it, it immediately fell in and was completely destroyed."

Cure of the Centurion's Servant

7 **1*†**WHEN he had finished this discourse in the hearing of the people, he entered Capernaum. **2**A centurion had a servant he held in high re-

---

† 6, 20-49: The Lucan Sermon on the Plain characterizes the Christian as distinctive for his poverty (20-23), cautious against the dangers of wealth (24f), loving toward his enemy (27-38), critical of himself (39-45), and obedient to the teaching of Jesus (46-49). It is reasonable to assume that this Lucan arrangement of Jesus' teaching was addressed to the economically deprived and politically threatened Christian communities of Asia Minor and Greece. It thus possesses a special poignancy, born of Luke's faith in the inevitable victory of the Christian message in a hostile environment, provided Christians accept their poverty in the spirit of Christ and endeavor to conquer their persecutors by the love they show them. The sermon seems to intimate a relevance between the actual situation of the Christian communities it addresses and the teaching of Jesus.

7, 1-10: The placement of this event after the Sermon on the Plain (6, 46-49) serves as an example of that practical acknowledgment of Jesus' authority which is recommended at the conclusion of the sermon.

❋

17ff: Mt 4, 24f; Mk 3, 7-12.
20-23: Mt 5, 1-12.
  24: Is 5, 8-12; Am 6, 1.
  25: Prv 14, 13; Is 65, 13f; Jas 5, 1.
  27: Mt 5, 44.
  28: 1 Pt 3, 9.
29f: Mt 5, 39-42.
  31: Mt 7, 12.
  32: Mt 5, 46.
  34: Dt 15, 8; Mt 5, 42.

  37: Mt 7, 1; Jas 2, 13.
  38: Mt 4, 24.
  39: Mt 15, 14.
  40: Mt 10, 24; Jn 13, 16.
41f: Mt 7, 3ff.
43ff: Mt 7, 16ff; 12, 33ff.
  46: Mt 7, 21; Rom 2, 13; Jas 1, 22.
47ff: Mt 7, 24-27.
7/1-10: Mt 8, 5-13.

gard, who was at that moment sick to the point of death. **3**When he heard about Jesus he sent some Jewish elders to him, asking him to come and save the life of his servant. **4**Upon approaching Jesus they petitioned him earnestly. **5**"He deserves this favor from you," they said, "because he loves our people, and even built our synagogue for us." **6**Jesus set out with them. When he was only a short distance from the house, the centurion sent friends to tell him: "Sir, do not trouble yourself, for I am not worthy to have you enter my house. **7**That is why I did not presume to come to you myself. Just give the order and my servant will be cured. **8**I too am a man who knows the meaning of an order, having soldiers under my command. I say to one, 'On your way,' and off he goes; to another, 'Come here,' and he comes; to my slave, 'Do this,' and he does it." **9***Jesus showed amazement on hearing this, and turned to the crowd which was following him to say, "I tell you, I have never found so much faith among the Israelites." **10**When the deputation returned to the house, they found the servant in perfect health.

The Widow's Son

11†Soon afterward he went to a town called Naim, and his disciples and a large crowd accompanied him. **12**As he approached the gate of the town a dead man was being carried out, the only son of a widowed mother. A considerable crowd of townsfolk were with her. **13**The Lord was moved with pity upon seeing her and said to her, "Do not cry." **14**Then he stepped forward and touched the litter; at this, the bearers halted. He said, "Young man, I bid you get up." **15**The dead man sat up and began to speak. Then Jesus gave him back to his mother. **16***Fear seized them all and they began to praise God. "A great prophet has risen among us," they said; and, "God has visited his people." **17***This was the report that spread about him throughout Judea and the surrounding country.

Jesus' Testimony

18*†The disciples of John brought their teacher word of all these happenings. Summoning two of them, **19**John sent them to ask the Lord, "Are you 'He who is to come' or are we to expect someone else?" **20**When the men came to him they said, "John the Baptizer sends us to you with this question: 'Are you "He who is to come" or do we look for someone else?'" **21**(At that time he was curing many of their diseases, afflictions, and evil spirits; he also restored sight to many who were blind.) **22***Jesus gave this response: "Go and report to John what you have seen and heard. The blind recover their sight, cripples walk, lepers are cured, the deaf hear, dead men are raised to life, and

the poor have the good news preached to them. **23**Blest is that man who finds no stumbling block in me."

24†When the messengers of John had set off, Jesus began to speak about him to the crowds. "What did you go out to see in the desert—a reed swayed by the wind? **25**What, really, did you go out to see—someone dressed luxuriously? Remember, those who dress in luxury and eat in splendor are to be found in royal palaces. **26**Then what did you go out to see—a prophet? He is that, I assure you, and something more. **27***This is the man of whom Scripture says,

> 'I send my messenger ahead of you
> to prepare your way before you.'

28I assure you, there is no man born of woman greater than John. Yet the least born into the kingdom of God is greater than he."

John's Baptism

29*The entire populace that had heard Jesus, even the tax collectors, gave praise to God, for they had received from John the baptismal bath he administered. **30**The Pharisees and the lawyers, on the other hand, by failing to receive his baptism defeated God's plan in their regard.

Christ's Verdict

31*"What comparison can I use for the men of today? What are they like? **32**They are like children squatting in the city squares and calling to their playmates,

> 'We piped you a tune but you did not dance,
> We sang you a dirge but you did not wail.'

33I mean that John the Baptizer came neither eating bread nor drinking wine, and you say, 'He is mad!' **34**The Son of Man came and he both ate and drank, and you say, 'Here is a glutton and a drunkard, a friend of tax collectors and sinners!' **35**God's wisdom is vindicated by all who accept it."

The Penitent Woman

36*†There was a certain Pharisee who invited Jesus to dine with him. Jesus went to the Pharisee's home and reclined to eat. **37***A woman known in the town to be a sinner learned that he was dining in the Pharisee's home. She brought in a vase of perfumed oil **38**and stood behind him at his feet, weeping so that her tears fell upon his feet. Then she wiped them with her

---

† 7, 11-17: This account of the raising to life of the widow's son prepares for Jesus' response about his ministry, made to the inquiring disciples of John the Baptizer (20.22). The observation in 7, 15, *Jesus gave him back to his mother* relates the mission of Jesus to that of Elijah (1 Kgs 17, 23).

7, 18-23: See note on Mt 11, 3.

7, 24-35: See notes on Mt 11, 7-15; 11, 11; 11, 19.

7, 36-50: Jesus admits both the gravity of the woman's sins and the relative justice of Simon. But he points out her superiority to the Pharisee, for she expresses the love that stems from repentance, whereas Simon's pride prevents him from acknowledging his real, though lesser, sinfulness.

✿
    9: Mt 8, 10.   29: Mt 21, 32.
   16: 1 Kgs 17, 23;   31-35: Mt 11, 16-19.
        Mt 16, 14; Jn 4, 19.   36: 11, 37; 14, 1.
   17: 4, 14.   37ff: Mt 26, 6-13;
18-27: Mt 11, 2-11.   Mk 14, 3-9; Jn 12, 1-8.
   22: Is 35, 5f.   37: Mt 21, 32.
   27: Is 40, 3; Mal 3, 1.

hair, kissing them and perfuming them with the oil. [39]When his host, the Pharisee, saw this, he said to himself, "If this man were a prophet, he would know who and what sort of woman this is that touches him —that she is a sinner." [40]In answer to his thoughts, Jesus said to him, "Simon, I have something to propose to you." "Teacher," he said, "speak."

[41]"Two men owed money to a certain money-lender; one owed a total of five hundred coins, the other fifty. [42]Since neither was able to repay, he wrote off both debts. Which of them was more grateful to him?" [43]Simon answered, "He, I presume, to whom he remitted the larger sum." Jesus said to him, "You are right."

[44]Turning then to the woman, he said to Simon: "You see this woman? I came to your home and you provided me with no water for my feet. She has washed my feet with her tears and wiped them with hair. [45]You gave me no kiss, but she has not ceased kissing my feet since I entered. [46]You did not anoint my head with oil, but she has anointed my feet with perfume. [47]I tell you, that is why her many sins are forgiven—because of her great love. Little is forgiven the one whose love is small."

[48]*He said to her then, "Your sins are forgiven"; [49]at which his fellow guests began to ask among themselves, "Who is this that he even forgives sins?" [50]Meanwhile he said to the woman, "Your faith has been your salvation. Now go in peace."

The Women Who Served

8 [1]*†AFTER this he journeyed through towns and villages preaching and proclaiming the good news of the kingdom of God. The Twelve accompanied him, [2]*and also some women who had been cured of evil spirits and maladies: Mary called the Magdalene, from whom seven devils had gone out, [3]Joanna, the wife of Herod's steward Chuza, Susanna, and many others who were assisting them out of their means.

Parable of the Sower

[4]†A large crowd was gathering, with people resorting to him from one town after another. He spoke to them in a parable: [5]"A farmer went out to sow some seed. In the sowing, some fell on the footpath where it was walked on and the birds of the air ate it up. [6]Some fell on rocky ground, sprouted up, then withered through lack of moisture. [7]Some fell among briers, and the thorns growing up with it stifled it. [8]But some fell on good soil, grew up, and yielded grain a hundredfold."

As he said this he exclaimed: "Let everyone who has ears attend to what he has heard." [9]*His disciples began asking him what the meaning of this parable might be. [10]*He replied, "To you the mysteries of the reign of God have been confided, but to the rest in parables that,

> 'Seeing they may not perceive,
> and hearing they may not understand.'

[11]This is the meaning of the parable. The seed is the word of God. [12]Those on the footpath are people who hear, but the devil comes and takes the word out of their hearts lest they believe and be saved. [13]Those on the rocky ground are the ones who, when they hear the word, receive it with joy. They have no root; they believe for a while, but fall away in time of temptation. [14]The seed fallen among briers are those who hear, but their progress is stifled by the cares and riches and pleasures of life and they do not mature. [15]The seed on good ground are those who hear the word in a spirit of openness, retain it, and bear fruit through perseverance.

Parable of the Lamp

[16]*"No one lights a lamp and puts it under a bushel basket or under a bed; he puts it on a lampstand so that whoever comes in can see it [17]*There is nothing hidden that will not be exposed, nothing concealed that will not be known and brought to light. [18]*Take heed, therefore, how you hear: to the man who has, more will be given; and he who has not, will lose even the little he thinks he has."

True Kindred of Jesus

[19]*†His mother and brothers came to be with him, but they could not reach him because of the crowd. [20]He was told, "Your mother and your brothers are standing outside and they wish to see you." [21]*He told them in reply, "My mother and my brothers are those who hear the word of God and act upon it."

Calming of the Tempest

[22]*†One day he got into a boat with his disciples and said to them, "Let us cross over to the far side of the lake." So they set out, [23]and as they sailed he slept. A windstorm descended on the lake, and they began to ship water and to be in danger. [24]They came to awaken him, saying, "Master, master, we are lost!" He awoke and rebuked the wind and the tumultuous waves. The waves subsided and it grew calm. [25]Then

---

48: Mt 9, 2.
8/1: 4, 43; Mk 1, 39.
2: 24, 10; Mt 27, 55f; Mk 15, 40f; 16, 9; Jn 19, 25.
9-15: Mt 13, 10-23; Mk 4, 10-20.
10: Is 6, 9; Jn 12, 40; Acts 28, 26.
16ff: Mk 4, 21-25.
16: 11, 33; Mt 5, 15.
17: 12, 2; Mt 10, 26.
18: 19, 26; Mt 13, 12; 25, 29.
19ff: Mt 12, 46-50; Mk 3, 31-35.
21: 11, 27f.
22-25: Mt 8, 23-27; Mk 4, 35-41.

† 8, 1ff: Luke notes Jesus' acceptance of the aid of women during his ministry. The evangelist probably also has in mind their contributions to the early Christian communities.

8, 4-15: On the meaning of the parable of the sower and its explanation, see the note on Mt 13, 1-53.

8, 19ff: This passage is to be understood in the light of Luke's theological conception of the mother of Jesus as the figure or type of the Christian community. She acquiesces fully, as the Christian should, to the mystery of God's word; cf 1, 38.

8, 22-25: See note on Mk 4, 35-41.

he asked them, "Where is your faith?" Filled with fear and admiration, they said to one another, "What sort of man can this be who commands even the winds and the sea and they obey him?"

The Gerasene Demoniac

26*†They sailed to the country of the Gerasenes, which is opposite Galilee. **27** When he came to land, he was met by a man from the town who was possessed by demons. For a long time he had not worn any clothes; he did not live in a house, but among the tombstones. **28***On seeing Jesus he began to shriek; then he fell at his feet and exclaimed at the top of his voice, "Jesus, Son of God Most High, why do you meddle with me? Do not torment me, I beg you." **29**By now Jesus was ordering the unclean spirit to come out of the man. This spirit had taken hold of him many a time. The man used to be tied with chains and fetters, but he would break his bonds and the demon would drive him into places of solitude. **30**"What is your name?" Jesus demanded. "Legion," he answered, because the demons who had entered him were many. **31**They pleaded with him not to order them back to the abyss. **32**It happened that a large herd of swine was feeding nearby on the hillside, and the demons asked him to permit them to enter the swine. This he granted. **33**The demons then came out of the man and entered the swine, and the herd charged down the bluff into the lake, where they drowned.

34When the swineherds saw what had happened, they took to their heels and brought the news to the town and country roundabout. **35**The people went out to see for themselves what had happened. Coming on Jesus, they found the man from whom the devils had departed sitting at his feet dressed and in his full senses; this sight terrified them. **36**They were told by witnesses how the possessed man had been cured. **37**Shortly afterward, the entire population of the Gerasene territory asked Jesus to leave their neighborhood, for a great fear had seized them; so he got into the boat and went back across the lake.

38The man from whom the devils had departed asked to come with him, **39**but he sent him away with the words, "Go back home and recount all that God has done for you." The man went all through the town making public what Jesus had done for him.

Jairus' Child; a Hemorrhage Victim

40*†On his return, Jesus was welcomed by the crowd; indeed, they were all waiting for him. **41**A man named Jairus, who was chief of the synagogue, came up and fell at Jesus' feet, begging that he come to his home **42**because his only daughter, a girl of about twelve, was dying. As Jesus went, the crowds almost crushed him. **43**A woman with a hemorrhage of twelve years' duration, incurable at any doctor's hands, **44**came up behind him and touched the tassel on his cloak. Immediately her bleeding stopped. **45**Jesus asked, "Who touched me?" Everyone disclaimed doing it, while Peter said, "Lord, the crowds are milling and pressing around you!" **46**Jesus insisted, "Someone touched me; I know that power has gone forth from me." **47**When the woman saw that her act had not gone unnoticed, she came forward trembling. Falling at his feet, she related before the whole assemblage why she had touched him and how she had been instantly cured. **48**Jesus said to her, "Daughter, it is your faith that has cured you. Now go in peace."

49He was still speaking when a man came from the ruler's house with the announcement, "Your daughter is dead; do not bother the Teacher further." **50**Jesus heard this, and his response was: "Fear is useless; what is needed is trust and her life will be spared." **51**Once he had arrived at the house, he permitted no one to enter with him except Peter, John, James, and the child's parents. **52**While everyone wept and lamented her, he said, "Stop crying for she is not dead but asleep." **53**They laughed at him, being certain she was dead. **54**He took her by the hand and spoke these words: "Get up, child." **55**The breath of life returned to her and she got up immediately; whereupon he told them to give her something to eat. **56**Her parents were astounded, but he ordered them not to tell anyone what had happened.

Mission of the Twelve

9 **1***JESUS now called the Twelve together and gave them power and authority to overcome all demons and to cure diseases. **2**He sent them forth to proclaim the reign of God and heal the afflicted. **3**Jesus advised them: "Take nothing for the journey, neither walking staff nor traveling bag; no bread, no money. No one is to have two coats. **4***Stay at whatever house you enter and proceed from there. **5***When people will not receive you, leave that town and shake its dust from your feet as a testimony against them." **6**So they set out and went from village to village, spreading the good news everywhere and curing diseases.

Herod Learns of Jesus

7*Herod the tetrarch heard of all that was happening and was perplexed, for some were saying, "John has been raised from the dead"; **8**others, "Elijah has appeared"; and still others, "One of the prophets of old has risen." **9**But Herod said, "John I beheaded. Who is this man about whom I hear all these reports?" He was very curious to see him.

26-39: Mt 8, 28-34; Mk 5, 1-20.
28: 4, 34; Mt 4, 3.
40-56: Mt 9, 18-26; Mk 5, 21-43.
46: 6, 19.
9/1-6: Mt 10, 1.8-14; Mk 3, 13-16; 6, 7-13.
4: 10, 7.
5: Acts 13, 51.
7ff: Mt 14, 1f; Mk 6, 14ff.

† 8, 26-39: See note on Mk 1, 23-28 concerning the exorcisms performed by Jesus.
8, 40-56: See note on Mk 5, 21-43.

Multiplication of the Loaves

10*The apostles on their return related to Jesus all they had accomplished. Taking them with him, he retired to a town called Bethsaida, **11**but the crowds found this out and followed him. He received them and spoke to them of the reign of God, and he healed all who were in need of healing.

12As sunset approached the Twelve came and said to him, "Dismiss the crowd so that they can go into the villages and farms in the neighborhood and find themselves lodging and food, for this is certainly an out-of-the-way place." **13**He answered them, "Why do you not give them something to eat yourselves?" They replied, "We have nothing but five loaves and two fish. Or shall we ourselves go and buy food for all these people?" **14**(There were about five thousand men.) Jesus said to his disciples, "Have them sit down in groups of fifty or so." **15**They followed his instructions and got them all seated. **16**Then, taking the five loaves and the two fish, Jesus raised his eyes to heaven, pronounced a blessing over them, broke them, and gave them to his disciples for distribution to the crowd. **17**They all ate until they had enough. What they had left, over and above, filled twelve baskets.

Peter's Profession of Faith

18*†One day when Jesus was praying in seclusion and his disciples were with him, he put the question to them, "Who do the crowds say that I am?" **19**"John the Baptizer," they replied, "and some say Elijah, while others claim that one of the prophets of old has returned from the dead." **20**"But you—who do you say that I am?" he asked them. Peter said in reply, "The Messiah of God." **21**He strictly forbade them to tell this to anyone. **22***"The Son of Man," he said, "must first endure many sufferings, be rejected by the elders, the high priests and the scribes, and be put to death, and then be raised up on the third day."

Conditions of Discipleship

23*†Jesus said to all: "Whoever wishes to be my follower must deny his very self, take up his cross each day, and follow in my steps. **24***Whoever would save his life will lose it, and whoever loses his life for my sake will save it. **25**What profit does he show who gains the whole world and destroys himself in the process? **26***If a man is ashamed of me and my doctrine, the Son of Man will be ashamed of him when he comes in his glory and that of his Father and his holy angels. **27***I assure you, there are some standing here who will not taste death until they see the reign of God."

Jesus Transfigured

28*†About eight days after saying this he took Peter, John and James, and went up onto a mountain to pray. **29**While he was praying, his face changed in appearance and his clothes became dazzlingly white. **30**Suddenly two men were talking with him—Moses and Elijah. **31**They appeared in glory and spoke of his passage, which he was about to fulfill in Jerusalem. **32**Peter and those with him had fallen into a deep sleep; but awakening, they saw his glory and likewise saw the two men who were standing with him. **33**When these were leaving, Peter said to Jesus: "Master, how good it is for us to be here. Let us set up three booths, one for you, one for Moses, and one for Elijah." (He did not really know what he was saying.) **34**While he was speaking, a cloud came and overshadowed them, and the disciples grew fearful as the others entered it. **35***Then from the cloud came a voice which said, "This is my Son, my Chosen One. Listen to him." **36**When the voice fell silent, Jesus was there alone. The disciples kept quiet, telling nothing of what they had seen at that time to anyone.

A Possessed Boy

37*†The following day they came down from the mountain and a large crowd met them. **38**Suddenly a man from the crowd exclaimed: "Teacher, I beg you to look at my son; he is my only child. **39**A spirit takes possession of him and with a sudden cry throws him into a convulsion and makes him foam at the mouth, then abandons him in his shattered condition. **40**I asked your disciples to cast out the spirit but they could not." **41**Jesus said in reply: "What an unbelieving and perverse lot you are! How long must I remain with you? How long can I endure you? Bring your son here to me." **42**As he was being brought, the spirit threw him into convulsions on the ground. Jesus then rebuked the unclean spirit, cured the boy, and restored him to his father. **43**And all who saw it marveled at the greatness of God.

Second Prediction of the Passion

In the midst of their amazement at all that he was doing, Jesus said to his disciples: **44***†"Pay close attention to what I tell you: the Son of Man must be delivered into the hands of men." **45**They failed, however, to understand this warning; its meaning was so concealed from them they did not grasp it at all, and they were afraid to question him about the matter.

❋

10-17: Mt 14, 13-21;	24: 17, 33; Mt 10, 39;
Mk 6, 30-44;	Jn 12, 25f.
Jn 6, 1-13.	26: 12, 9; Mt 10, 33.
18-21: Mt 16, 13-20;	27: Mt 16, 28; Mk 9, 1.
Mk 8, 27-30.	28-36: Mt 17, 1-9; Mk 9, 2-10.
22: 24, 7.26; Mt 16, 21;	35: 2 Pt 1, 17.
Mk 8, 31.	37-43: Mt 17, 14-18;
23-26: Mt 16, 24-28;	Mk 9, 14-27.
Mk 8, 34-38; 9, 1.	44f: Mt 17, 22f; Mk 9, 30ff.
23: 14, 27; Mt 10, 38.	

---

† 9, 18-22: Luke omits reference to Caesarea Philippi (Mt 16, 13; Mk 8, 27) as the locale of Peter's confession. This is because his chief interest in the event centers upon Jesus' awareness of his messianic identity in his onward movement toward Jerusalem (not away from it) to achieve the climax of his mission through the passion and resurrection.

9, 23-27: See note on Mk 8, 34—9, 1.

9, 28-36: See note on Mk 9, 2-8. Lk 9, 31 explicitly associates the transfiguration with Jesus' passion and resurrection.

9, 37-43: See note on Mk 9, 14-29.

9, 44f: See note on Mk 9, 30ff.

Against Ambition

46***†**A discussion arose among them as to which of them was the greatest. **47**Jesus, who knew their thoughts, took a little child and placed it beside him, **48***after which he said to them, "Whoever welcomes this little child on my account welcomes me, and whoever welcomes me welcomes him who sent me; for the least one among you is the greatest."

49†It was John who said, "Master, we saw a man using your name to expel demons, and we tried to stop him because he is not of our company." **50**Jesus told him in reply, "Do not stop him, for any man who is not against you is on your side."

IV: THE JOURNEY THROUGH PEREA

Samaritan Inhospitality

51*†AS THE TIME APPROACHED when he was to be taken from this world, he firmly resolved to proceed toward Jerusalem, and sent messengers on ahead of him. **52**These entered a Samaritan town to prepare for his passing through, **53**but the Samaritans would not welcome him because he was on his way to Jerusalem. **54**When his disciples James and John saw this, they said, "Lord, would you not have us call down fire from heaven to destroy them?" **55**He turned toward them only to reprimand them. **56**Then they set off for another town.

The Apostles' Requirements

57*As they were making their way along, someone said to him, "I will be your follower wherever you go." **58**Jesus said to him, "The foxes have lairs, the birds of the sky have nests, but the Son of Man has nowhere to lay his head." **59**To another he said, "Come after me." The man replied, "Let me bury my father first." **60**Jesus said to him, "Let the dead bury their dead; come away and proclaim the kingdom of God." **61***Yet another said to him, "I will be your follower, Lord, but first let me take leave of my people at home." **62**Jesus answered him, "Whoever puts his hand to the plow but keeps looking back is unfit for the reign of God."

Mission of the Seventy-two

10 **1**AFTER this, the Lord appointed a further seventy-two and sent them in pairs before him to every town and place he intended to visit. **2***He said to them: "The harvest is rich but the workers are few; therefore ask the harvest-master to send workers to his harvest. **3***Be on your way, and remember: I am sending you as lambs in the midst of wolves. **4***Do not carry a walking staff or traveling bag; wear no sandals and greet no one along the way. **5**On entering any house, first say, 'Peace to this house.' **6**If there is a peaceable man there, your peace will rest on him; if not, it will come back to you. **7***Stay in the one house eating and drinking what they have, for the laborer is worth his wage. Do not move from house to house.

8"Into whatever city you go, after they welcome you, eat what they set before you, **9***and cure the sick there. Say to them, 'The reign of God is at hand.' **10***If the people of any town you enter do not welcome you, go into its streets and say, **11***'We shake the dust of this town from our feet as testimony against you. But know that the reign of God is near.' **12**I assure you, on that day the fate of Sodom will be less severe than that of such a town. **13***It will go ill with you, Chorazin! And just as ill with you, Bethsaida! If the miracles worked in your midst had occurred in Tyre and Sidon, they would long ago have reformed in sackcloth and ashes. **14**It will go easier on the day of judgment for Tyre and Sidon than for you. **15***And as for you, Capernaum, 'Are you to be exalted to the skies? You shall be hurled down to the realm of death!'

16*"He who hears you, hears me. He who rejects you, rejects me. And he who rejects me, rejects him who sent me."

17The seventy-two returned in jubilation saying, "Master, even the demons are subject to us in your name." **18***He said in reply: "I watched Satan fall from the sky like lightning. **19***See what I have done; I have given you power to tread on snakes and scorpions and all the forces of the enemy, and nothing shall ever injure you. **20***Nevertheless, do not rejoice so much in the fact that the devils are subject to you as that your names are inscribed in heaven."

---

† 9, 46ff: See note on Mk 9, 33-37.
9, 49f: See note on Mk 9, 38-41.
9, 51—18, 14: This section, composed mainly of sayings, parables and incidents found only in Luke, is derived from special sources at Luke's disposal and has come to be called "the great insertion." The evangelist presents these things within the framework of a geographical theme of Jesus' last journey to Jerusalem (9, 53.57; 10, 1; 13, 22.33; 17, 11). The several incidents recounted show the superior wisdom of Jesus, e. g., his response to the lawyer concerning the way to eternal life (10, 25-28), and his defense of healing on the sabbath (13, 10-17; 14, 1-6).

The principal themes of Jesus' teaching in this section concern the sacrifices required for discipleship (9, 57-62); God's action in history directing the gospel message to the simple ones (10, 21); reliance on persevering prayer (11, 1-13; 18, 1-8); the supreme value of man's response to God's word (10, 38-42; 11, 27f); the gravity of the refusal to repent (11, 29-32; 13, 1-5); the sinfulness of hypocrisy (11, 37—12, 3); the threat to salvation presented by material wealth (12, 13-34; 16, 1-15.19-31); constant readiness for divine judgment (12, 35-48.54-59; 13, 6-9.22-30; 14, 16-24; 17, 20-37); and the bestowal of the divine mercy upon sinners (15, 3-32).

  46ff: Mt 18, 1-5;   4-7: 9, 3ff.
        Mk 9, 33-37.   7: Mt 10, 10; 1 Tm 5, 18.
  46: 22, 24.   9: Mt 3, 2; 4, 17.
  48: Mt 10, 40; 18, 5;   10: Mt 10, 7.
        Jn 13, 20.   11: Acts 13, 51.
  51: 13, 22; 17, 11; 18, 31;   13: Mt 11, 21-24.
      19, 28; 24, 51.   15: Is 14, 13ff.
  57-60: Mt 8, 19-22.   16: Mt 10, 40; Jn 13, 20.
  61: 1 Kgs 19, 19ff.   18: Is 14, 12.
  10/2: Mt 9, 37; Jn 4, 35.   19: Ps 91, 13; Rv 12, 9.
  3: Mt 10, 16.   20: Rv 20, 12.

Hymn of Praise

21*At that moment Jesus rejoiced in the Holy Spirit and said: "I offer you praise, O Father, Lord of heaven and earth, because what you have hidden from the learned and the clever you have revealed to the merest children.

"Yes, Father, you have graciously willed it so. **22**Everything has been given over to me by my Father. No one knows the Son except the Father and no one knows the Father except the Son—and anyone to whom the Son wishes to reveal him."

Privilege of the Disciples

23*Turning to his disciples he said to them privately: "Blest are the eyes that see what you see. **24**I tell you, many prophets and kings wished to see what you see but did not see it, and to hear what you hear but did not hear it."

The Good Samaritan

25*On one occasion a lawyer stood up to pose him this problem: "Teacher, what must I do to inherit everlasting life?" **26**Jesus answered him: "What is written in the law? How do you read it?" **27***He replied:

"You shall love the Lord your God
with all your heart,
with all your soul,
with all your strength,
and with all your mind;
and your neighbor as yourself."

28*Jesus said, "You have answered correctly. Do this and you shall live. **29**But because he wished to justify himself he said to Jesus, "And who is my neighbor?" **30**Jesus replied: "There was a man going down from Jerusalem to Jericho who fell prey to robbers. They stripped him, beat him, and then went off leaving him half-dead. **31**A priest happened to be going down the same road; he saw him but continued on. **32**Likewise there was a Levite who came the same way; he saw him and went on. **33**But a Samaritan who was journeying along came on him and was moved to pity at the sight. **34**He approached him and dressed his wounds, pouring in oil and wine. He then hoisted him on his own beast and brought him to an inn, where he cared for him. **35**The next day he took out two silver pieces and gave them to the innkeeper with the request: 'Look after him, and if there is any further expense I will repay you on my way back.'

36"Which of these three, in your opinion, was neighbor to the man who fell in with the robbers?" **37**The answer came, "The one who treated him with compassion." Jesus said to him, "Then go and do the same."

Martha and Mary

38*On their journey Jesus entered a village where a woman named Martha welcomed him to her home. **39**She had a sister named Mary, who seated herself at the Lord's feet and listened to his words. **40**Martha, who was busy with all the details of hospitality, came to him and said, "Lord, are you not concerned that my sister has left me to do the household tasks all alone? Tell her to help me."

41The Lord in reply said to her: "Martha, Martha, you are anxious and upset about many things; **42**one thing only is required. Mary has chosen the better portion and she shall not be deprived of it."

The Our Father

11 **1**ONE day he was praying in a certain place. When he had finished, one of his disciples asked him, "Lord, teach us to pray, as John taught his disciples." **2***He said to them, "When you pray, say:

"Father,
hallowed be your name,
your kingdom come.
3Give us each our daily bread.
4Forgive us our sins
for we too forgive all who do us wrong;
and subject us not to the trial."

Two Parables on Prayer

5Jesus said to them: "If one of you knows someone who comes to him in the middle of the night and says to him, 'Friend, lend me three loaves, **6**for a friend of mine has come in from a journey and I have nothing to offer him'; **7**and he from inside should reply, 'Leave me alone. The door is shut now and my children and I are in bed. I cannot get up to look after your needs'— **8**I tell you, even though he does not get up and take care of the man because of friendship, he will do so because of his persistence, and give him as much as he needs.

9*"So I say to you, 'Ask and you shall receive; seek and you shall find; knock and it shall be opened to you.'

10"For whoever asks, receives; whoever seeks, finds; whoever knocks, is admitted. **11**What father among you will give his son a snake if he asks for a fish, **12**or hand him a scorpion if he asks for an egg? **13**If you, with all your sins, know how to give your children good things, how much more will the heavenly Father give the Holy Spirit to those who ask him."

Jesus and Beelzebul

14*Jesus was casting out a devil which was mute, and when the devil was cast out the dumb man spoke. The crowds were amazed at this. **15**Some of them said, "It is by Beelzebul, the prince of devils, that he casts out devils." **16***Others, to test him, were demanding of him a sign from heaven.

17Because he knew their thoughts, he said to them:

21f: Mt 11, 25ff.
23f: Mt 13, 16f.
25-28: Mt 22, 34-39; Mk 12, 28-31.
25: Mt 19, 16.
27: Lv 19, 18; Dt 6, 5.
28: Lv 18, 5; Prv 19, 16.
38: Jn 11, 1f.
11/2ff: Mt 6, 9-13.
9-13: Mt 7, 7-11.
9: Mk 11, 24.
14-22: Mt 12, 22-29; Mk 3, 22-27.
16: Mt 16, 1; Mk 8, 11.

"Every kingdom divided against itself is laid waste. Any house torn by dissension falls. ¹⁸If Satan is divided against himself, how can his kingdom last?—since you say it is by Beelzebul that I cast out devils. ¹⁹If I cast out devils by Beelzebul, by whom do your people cast them out? In such case, let them act as your judges. ^{20*}But if it is by the finger of God that I cast out devils, then the reign of God is upon you.

²¹"When a strong man fully armed guards his courtyard, his possessions go undisturbed. ²²But when someone stronger than he comes and overpowers him, such a one carries off the arms on which he was relying and divides the spoils. ^{23*}He who is not with me is against me, and he who does not gather with me scatters.

^{24*}"When an unclean spirit has gone out of a man, it wanders through arid wastes searching for a resting-place; failing to find one, it says, 'I will go back to where I came from.' ²⁵It then returns, to find the house swept and tidied. ²⁶Next it goes out and returns with seven other spirits far worse than itself, who enter in and dwell there. The result is that the last state of the man is worse than the first."

True Happiness

²⁷While he was saying this a woman from the crowd called out, "Blest is the womb that bore you and the breasts that nursed you!" ^{28*}"Rather," he replied, "blest are they who hear the word of God and keep it."

The Sign of Jonah

^{29*}While the crowds pressed around him he began to speak to them in these words: "This is an evil age. It seeks a sign. But no sign will be given it except the sign of Jonah. ³⁰Just as Jonah was a sign for the Ninevites, so will the Son of Man be a sign for the present age. ^{31*}The queen of the South will rise at the judgment along with the men of this generation, and she will condemn them. She came from the farthest corner of the world to listen to the wisdom of Solomon, but you have a greater than Solomon here. ^{32*}At the judgment, the citizens of Nineveh will rise along with the present generation, and they will condemn it. For at the preaching of Jonah they reformed, but you have a greater than Jonah here.

Parable of the Lamp

^{33*}"One who lights a lamp does not put it in the cellar or under a bushel basket, but rather on a lamp-

stand, so that they who come in may see the light. ³⁴The eye is the lamp of your body. When your eyesight is sound, your whole body is lighted up, but when your eyesight is bad, your body is in darkness. ³⁵Take care, then, that your light is not darkness. ³⁶If your whole body is lighted up and not partly in darkness, it will be as fully illumined as when a lamp shines brightly for you."

Hypocrisy of Pharisees and Lawyers

^{37*}As he was speaking, a Pharisee invited him to dine at his house. He entered and reclined at table. ^{38*}Seeing this, the Pharisee was surprised that he had not first performed the ablutions prescribed before eating. ^{39*}The Lord said to him: "You Pharisees! You cleanse the outside of cup and dish, but within you are filled with rapaciousness and evil. ⁴⁰Fools! Did not he who made the outside make the inside too? ⁴¹But if you give what you have as alms, all will be wiped clean for you. ^{42*}Woe to you Pharisees! You pay tithes on mint and rue and all the garden plants, while neglecting justice and the love of God. These are the things you should practice, without omitting the others. ^{43*}Woe to you Pharisees! You love the front seats in synagogues and marks of respect in public. ^{44*}Woe to you! You are like hidden tombs over which men walk unawares."

⁴⁵In reply one of the lawyers said to him, "Teacher, in speaking this way you insult us too." ^{46*}Jesus answered: "Woe to you lawyers also! You lay impossible burdens on men but will not lift a finger to lighten them. ^{47*}Woe to you! You build the tombs of the prophets, but it was your fathers who murdered them. ⁴⁸You show that you stand behind the deeds of your fathers: they committed the murders and you erect the tombs. ^{49*}That is why the wisdom of God has said, 'I will send them prophets and apostles, and some of these they will persecute and kill'; ⁵⁰so that this generation will have to account for the blood of all the prophets shed since the foundation of the world. ^{51*}Their guilt stretches from the blood of Abel to the blood of Zechariah, who met his death between the altar and the sanctuary! Yes, I tell you, this generation will have to account for it. ^{52*}Woe to you lawyers! You have taken away the key of knowledge. You yourselves have not gained access, yet you have stopped those who wished to enter!"

^{53*}After he had left this gathering, the scribes and Pharisees began to manifest fierce hostility to him and to make him speak on a multitude of questions, ⁵⁴setting traps to catch him in his speech.

Courage under Persecution

12 ^{1*}MEANWHILE a crowd of thousands had gathered, so dense that they were treading on one another. He began to speak first to his disciples: "Be on guard against the yeast of the Pharisees, which is hypocrisy. ^{2*}There is nothing concealed that will not be revealed, nothing hidden that will not be made known. ^{3*}Everything you have said in the dark

---

20: Mt 12, 28.
23: Mt 12, 30.
24ff: Mt 12, 43ff.
28: Rv 1, 3.
29-32: Mt 12, 38-42.
29: Mt 16, 1; Mk 9, 11f;
     Jn 6, 30f.
31: 1 Kgs 10, 1-10.
32: Jon 3, 5.
33: 8, 16; Mt 5, 15;
     Mk 4, 21.
37: 7, 36; 14, 1.
38: Mt 15, 2; Mk 7, 2.5.
39: Mt 23, 25f.

42: Mt 23, 23.
43: 20, 46; Mt 23, 6f;
     Mk 12, 38f.
44: Mt 23, 27.
46: Mt 23, 4.
47f: Mt 23, 29ff.
49ff: Mt 23, 34ff.
51: Gn 4, 8; 2 Chr 24, 20ff.
52: Mt 23, 13.
53: 6, 11; Mt 22, 15f.
12/1: Mt 16, 6.12; Mk 8, 15.
2: 8, 17.
2-9: Mt 10, 26-33.
3: Mk 4, 22.

will be heard in the daylight; what you have whispered in locked rooms will be proclaimed from the rooftops.

⁴"I say to you who are my friends: Do not be afraid of those who kill the body and can do no more. ⁵I will show you whom you ought to fear. Fear him who has power to cast into Gehenna after he has killed. Yes, I tell you, fear him. ⁶Are not five sparrows sold for a few pennies? Yet not one of them is neglected by God. ⁷In very truth, even the hairs of your head are counted! Fear nothing, then. You are worth more than a flock of sparrows.

⁸"I tell you, whoever acknowledges me before men —the Son of Man will acknowledge him before the angels of God. ⁹*But the man who has disowned me in the presence of men will be disowned in the presence of the angels of God. ¹⁰*Anyone who speaks against the Son of Man will be forgiven, but whoever blasphemes the Holy Spirit will never be forgiven. ¹¹*When they bring you before synagogues, rulers and authorities, do not worry about how to defend yourselves or what to say. ¹²The Holy Spirit will teach you at that moment all that should be said."

Trust in God, Not in Possessions

¹³Someone in the crowd said to him, "Teacher, tell my brother to give me my share of our inheritance." ¹⁴He replied, "Friend, who has set me up as your judge or arbiter?" ¹⁵Then he said to the crowd, "Avoid greed in all its forms. A man may be wealthy, but his possessions do not guarantee him life."

¹⁶He told them a parable in these words: "There was a rich man who had a good harvest. ¹⁷'What shall I do?' he asked himself. 'I have no place to store my harvest. ¹⁸I know!' he said. 'I will pull down my grain bins and build larger ones. All my grain and my goods will go there. ¹⁹*Then I will say to myself: You have blessings in reserve for years to come. Relax! Eat heartily, drink well. Enjoy yourself.' ²⁰But God said to him, 'You fool! This very night your life shall be required of you. To whom will all this piled-up wealth of yours go?' ²¹*That is the way it works with the man who grows rich for himself instead of growing rich in the sight of God."

Dependence on Providence

²²*He said to his disciples: "That is why I warn you, Do not be concerned for your life, what you are to eat, or for your body, what you are to wear. ²³Life is more important than food and the body more than clothing. ²⁴Consider the ravens: they do not sow, they do not reap, they have neither cellar nor barn—yet God feeds them. How much more important you are

than the birds! ²⁵Which of you by worrying can add a moment to his life-span? ²⁶If the smallest things are beyond your power, why be anxious about the rest? ²⁷"Or take the lilies: they do not spin, they do not weave; but I tell you, Solomon in all his splendor was not arrayed like any one of them. ²⁸If God clothes in such splendor the grass of the field, which grows today and is thrown on the fire tomorrow, how much more will he provide for you, O weak in faith! ²⁹It is not for you to be in search of what you are to eat or drink. Stop worrying. ³⁰The unbelievers of this world are always running after these things. Your Father knows that you need such things. ³¹Seek out instead his kingship over you, and the rest will follow in turn.

The Heart's Treasure

³²"Do not live in fear, little flock. It has pleased your Father to give you the kingdom. ³³*Sell what you have and give alms. Get purses for yourselves that do not wear out, a never-failing treasure with the Lord which no thief comes near nor any moth destroys. ³⁴Wherever your treasure lies, there your heart will be.

Preparedness for the Master's Return

³⁵"Let your belts be fastened around your waists and your lamps be burning ready. ³⁶*Be like men awaiting their master's return from a wedding, so that when he arrives and knocks, you will open for him without delay. ³⁷It will go well with those servants whom the master finds wide-awake on his return. I tell you, he will put on an apron, seat them at table, and proceed to wait on them. ³⁸Should he happen to come at midnight or before sunrise and find them prepared, it will go well with them. ³⁹*You know as well as I that if the head of the house knew when the thief was coming he would not let him break into his house. ⁴⁰Be on guard, therefore. The Son of Man will come when you least expect him."

⁴¹Peter said, "Do you intend this parable for us, Lord, or do you mean it for everyone?" ⁴²*The Lord said, "Who in your opinion is that faithful, farsighted steward whom the master will set over his servants to dispense their ration of grain in season? ⁴³That servant is fortunate whom his master finds busy when he returns. ⁴⁴Assuredly, his master will put him in charge of all his property. ⁴⁵But if the servant says to himself, 'My master is taking his time about coming,' and begins to abuse the housemen and servant girls, to eat and drink and get drunk, ⁴⁶that servant's master will come back on a day when he does not expect him, at a time he does not know. He will punish him severely and rank him among those undeserving of trust. ⁴⁷The slave who knew his master's wishes but did not prepare to fulfill them will get a severe beating, ⁴⁸whereas the one who did not know them and who nonetheless deserved to be flogged will get off with fewer stripes. When much has been given a man, much will be required of him. More will be asked of a man to whom more has been entrusted.

⁴⁹"I have come to light a fire on the earth. How I

❋

9: 9, 26; Mk 8, 38;   21: Mt 6, 19ff.
2 Tm 2, 12.   22-31: Mt 6, 25-33.
10: Mt 12, 31f; Mk 3, 28f.   22: Ps 55, 23; 1 Pt 5, 7.
11f: 21, 12-15;   33: Mt 6, 20f; 19, 21.
Mt 10, 17-20;   36: Mt 25, 1-13.
Mk 13, 11.   36ff: Mk 13, 34f.
19: Prv 27, 1; Sir 11, 24;   39f: Mt 24, 43f.
1 Tm 6, 17.   42-46: Mt 24, 45-51.

wish the blaze were ignited! **50***I have a baptism to receive. What anguish I feel till it is over! **51***Do you think I have come to establish peace on the earth? I assure you, the contrary is true; I have come for division. **52**From now on, a household of five will be divided three against two and two against three; **53***father will be split against son and son against father, mother against daughter and daughter against mother, mother-in-law against daughter-in-law, daughter-in-law against mother-in-law."

Signs of the Times

54*He said to the crowds: "When you see a cloud rising in the west, you say immediately that rain is coming—and so it does. **55**When the wind blows from the south, you say it is going to be hot—and so it is. **56**You hypocrites! If you can interpret the portents of earth and sky, why can you not interpret the present time! **57**Tell me, why do you not judge for yourselves what is just? **58***When you are going with your opponent to appear before a magistrate, try to settle with him on the way lest he turn you over to the judge, and the judge deliver you up to the jailer, and the jailer throw you into prison. **59**I warn you, you will not be released from there until you have paid the last penny."

Providential Calls to Penance

13 **1**AT that time, some were present who told him about the Galileans whose blood Pilate had mixed with their sacrifices. **2**He said in reply: "Do you think that these Galileans were the greatest sinners in Galilee just because they suffered this? **3**By no means! But I tell you, you will all come to the same end unless you reform. **4**Or take those eighteen who were killed by a falling tower in Siloam. Do you think they were more guilty than anyone else who lived in Jerusalem? **5***Certainly not! But I tell you, you will all come to the same end unless you reform."

The Barren Fig Tree

6Jesus spoke this parable: "A man had a fig tree growing in his vineyard, and he came out looking for fruit on it but did not find any. **7**He said to the vinedresser, 'Look here! For three years now I have come in search of fruit on this fig tree and found none. Cut it down. Why should it clutter up the ground?' **8**In answer, the man said, 'Sir, leave it another year, while I hoe around it and manure it; **9**then perhaps it will bear fruit. If not, it shall be cut down.'"

A Sabbath Cure

10*On a sabbath day he was teaching in one of the synagogues. **11**There was a woman there who for eighteen years had been possessed by a spirit which drained her strength. She was badly stooped—quite incapable of standing erect. **12**When Jesus saw her, he called her to him and said, "Woman, you are free of your infirmity." **13**He laid his hand on her, and immediately she stood up straight and began thanking God. **14***The chief of the synagogue, indignant that Jesus should have healed on the sabbath, said to the congregation, "There are six days for working. Come on those days to be cured, not on the sabbath." **15***The Lord said in reply, "O you hypocrites! Which of you does not let his ox or ass out of the stall on the sabbath to water it? **16**Should not this daughter of Abraham here who has been in the bondage of Satan for eighteen years have been released from her shackles on the sabbath?" **17**At these words, his opponents were covered with confusion; meanwhile, everyone else rejoiced at the marvels Jesus was accomplishing.

Parable of the Mustard Seed

18*Then he said: "What does the reign of God resemble? To what shall I liken it? **19**It is like a mustard seed which a man took and planted in his garden. It grew and became a large shrub and the birds of the air nested in its branches."

Parable of the Yeast

20*He went on: "To what shall I compare the reign of God? **21**It is like yeast which a woman took to knead into three measures of flour until the whole mass of dough began to rise."

The Narrow Door

22He went through cities and towns teaching—all the while making his way toward Jerusalem. **23**Someone asked him, "Lord, are they few in number who are to be saved?" **24***He replied: "Try to come in through the narrow door. Many, I tell you, will try to enter and be unable. **25***When once the master of the house has risen to lock the door and you stand outside knocking and saying, 'Sir, open for us,' he will say in reply, 'I do not know where you come from.' **26**Then you will begin to say, 'We ate and drank in your company. You taught in our streets.' **27***But he will answer, 'I tell you, I do not know where you come from. Away from me, you evildoers!'

28*"There will be wailing and grinding of teeth when you see Abraham, Isaac, Jacob, and all the prophets safe in the kingdom of God, and you yourselves rejected. **29**People will come from the east and the west, from the north and the south, and will take their place at the feast in the kingdom of God. **30***Some who are last will be first and some who are first will be last."

Herod the Fox

31It was then that certain Pharisees came to him. "Go on your way!" they said. "Leave this place! Herod is trying to kill you." **32**His answer was: "Go tell that

---

❋

50: 9, 22.
51ff: Mt 10, 34ff.
51: 2, 34.
53: Mi 7, 6.
54: Mt 16, 2f.
58: Mt 5, 25.
13/5: Jn 8, 24.
10-17: 14, 1-6.
14: Ex 20, 8f.

15: 14, 5; Mt 12, 11.
18f: Mt 13, 31f; Mk 4, 30ff.
20f: Mt 13, 33.
24: Mt 7, 13f.
25: Mt 25, 10ff.
27: Mt 7, 23; 25, 41.
28: Mt 8, 11f.
30: Mt 19, 30; 20, 16; Mk 10, 31.

fox, 'Today and tomorrow I cast out devils and perform cures, and on the third day my purpose is accomplished. **33**For all that, I must proceed on course today, tomorrow, and the day after, since no prophet can be allowed to die anywhere except in Jerusalem.'

Apostrophe to Jerusalem

34* "O Jerusalem, Jerusalem, you slay the prophets and stone those who are sent to you! How often have I wanted to gather your children together as a mother bird collects her young under her wings, and you refused me! **35***Your temple will be abandoned. I say to you, you shall not see me until the time comes when you say, 'Blessed is he who comes in the name of the Lord.' "

Cure and a Lesson in Humility

14 **1***WHEN Jesus came on a sabbath to eat a meal in the house of one of the leading Pharisees, they observed him closely. **2**Directly in front of him was a man who suffered from dropsy. **3***Jesus asked the lawyers and the Pharisees, "Is it lawful to cure on the sabbath or not?" **4**At this they kept silent. He took the man, healed him, and sent him on his way. **5***Then he addressed himself to them: "If one of you has a son or an ox and he falls into a pit, will he not immediately rescue him on the sabbath day?" **6**This they could not answer.

7He went on to address a parable to the guests, noticing how they were trying to get the places of honor at the table: **8***"When you are invited by someone to a wedding party, do not sit in the place of honor in case some greater dignitary has been invited. **9**Then the host might come and say to you, 'Make room for this man,' and you would have to proceed shamefacedly to the lowest place. **10**What you should do when you have been invited is go and sit in the lowest place, so that when your host approaches you he will say, 'My friend, come up higher.' This will win you the esteem of your fellow guests. **11***For everyone who exalts himself shall be humbled and he who humbles himself shall be exalted."

The Poor

12*He said to the one who had invited him: "Whenever you give a lunch or dinner, do not invite your friends or brothers or relatives or wealthy neighbors. They might invite you in return and thus repay you. **13**No, when you have a reception, invite beggars and the crippled, the lame and the blind. **14**You should be pleased that they cannot repay you, for you will be repaid in the resurrection of the just." **15**At these words one in the party said to him, "Happy is he who eats

bread in the kingdom of God." **16***Jesus responded: "A man was giving a large dinner and he invited many. **17**At dinner time he sent his servant to say to those invited, 'Come along, everything is ready now.' **18**But they began to excuse themselves, one and all. The first one said to the servant, 'I have bought some land and must go out and inspect it. Please excuse me.' **19**Another said, 'I have bought five yoke of oxen and I am going out to test them. Please excuse me.' **20**A third said, 'I am newly married and so I cannot come.' **21**The servant returning reported all this to his master. The master of the house grew angry at the account. He said to his servant, 'Go out quickly into the streets and alleys of the town and bring in the poor and the crippled, the blind and the lame.' **22**The servant reported, after some time, 'Your orders have been carried out, my lord, and there is still room.' **23**The master then said to the servant, 'Go out into the highways and along the hedgerows and force them to come in. I want my house to be full, **24**but I tell you that not one of those invited shall taste a morsel of my dinner.' "

25On one occasion when a great crowd was with him, he turned to them and said, **26*** "If anyone comes to me without turning his back on his father and mother, his wife and his children, his brothers and sisters, indeed his very self, he cannot be my follower. **27*** Anyone who does not take up his cross and follow me cannot be my disciple. **28**If one of you decides to build a tower, will he not first sit down and calculate the outlay to see if he has enough money to complete the project? **29**He will do that for fear of laying the foundation and then not being able to complete the work; for all who saw it would jeer at him, **30**saying, 'That man began to build what he could not finish.'

31"Or if a king is about to march on another king to do battle with him, will he not sit down first and consider whether, with ten thousand men, he can withstand an enemy coming against him with twenty thousand? **32**If he cannot, he will send a delegation while the enemy is still at a distance, asking for terms of peace. **33**In the same way, none of you can be my disciple if he does not renounce all his possessions. **34***Salt is good, but if salt loses its flavor what good is it for seasoning? **35**It is fit for neither the soil nor the manure heap; it has to be thrown away. Let him who hears this, heed it."

Parable of Divine Mercy

15 **1**THE tax collectors and sinners were all gathering around to hear him, **2***at which the Pharisees and the scribes murmured, "This man welcomes sinners and eats with them." **3**Then he addressed this parable to them: **4***"Who among you, if he has a hundred sheep and loses one of them, does not leave the ninety-nine in the wasteland and follow the lost one until he finds it? **5**And when he finds it, he puts it on his shoulders in jubilation. **6***Once arrived home, he invites friends and neighbors in and says to them, 'Rejoice with me because I have found my lost sheep.' **7***I tell you, there will likewise be more joy in

---

34f: 19, 41-44; Mt 23, 37ff.	26: Mt 10, 37.
35: Ps 118, 26.	27: 9, 23; Mt 10, 38;
14/1-6: 6, 6-11; 13, 10-17.	16, 24; Mk 8, 34.
3: Mk 3, 4.	34: Mt 5, 13; Mk 9, 50.
5: Mt 12, 11.	15/2-7: Mt 9, 10-13.
8f: Prv 25, 6f.	2: 19, 7.
11: 18, 14; Mt 23, 12.	4f: Mt 18, 12ff.
12: 6, 32-35.	6: 19, 10.
16-23: Mt 22, 2-10.	7: Ez 18, 23; 33, 11.

heaven over one repentant sinner than over ninety-nine righteous people who have no need to repent.

8"What woman, if she has ten silver pieces and loses one, does not light a lamp and sweep the house in a diligent search until she has retrieved what she lost? 9And when she finds it, she calls in her friends and neighbors to say, 'Rejoice with me! I have found the silver piece I lost.' 10I tell you, there will be the same kind of joy before the angels of God over one repentant sinner."

The Prodigal Son

11Jesus said to them: "A man had two sons. 12The younger of them said to his father, 'Father, give me the share of the estate that is coming to me.' So the father divided up the property. 13Some days later this younger son collected all his belongings and went off to a distant land, where he squandered his money on dissolute living. 14After he had spent everything, a great famine broke out in that country and he was in dire need. 15So he attached himself to one of the propertied class of the place, who sent him to his farm to take care of the pigs. 16He longed to fill his belly with the husks that were fodder for the pigs, but no one made a move to give him anything. 17Coming to his senses at last, he said: 'How many hired hands at my father's place have more than enough to eat, while here I am starving! 18I will break away and return to my father, and say to him, Father, I have sinned against God and against you; I no longer deserve to be called your son. 19Treat me like one of your hired hands.' 20With that he set off for his father's house. While he was still a long way off, his father caught sight of him and was deeply moved. He ran out to meet him, threw his arms around his neck, and kissed him. 21The son said to him, 'Father, I have sinned against God and against you; I no longer deserve to be called your son.' 22The father said to his servants: 'Quick! bring out the finest robe and put it on him; put a ring on his finger and shoes on his feet. 23Take the fatted calf and kill it. Let us eat and celebrate 24because this son of mine was dead and has come back to life. He was lost and is found.' Then the celebration began.

25"Meanwhile the elder son was out on the land. As he neared the house on his way home, he heard the sound of music and dancing. 26He called one of the servants and asked him the reason for the dancing and the music. 27The servant answered, 'Your brother is home, and your father has killed the fatted calf because he has him back in good health.' 28The son grew angry at this and would not go in; but his father came out and began to plead with him.

29"He said to his father in reply: 'For years now I have slaved for you. I never disobeyed one of your orders, yet you never gave me so much as a kid

goat to celebrate with my friends. 30Then, when this son of yours returns after having gone through your property with loose women, you kill the fatted calf for him.' 31" 'My son,' replied the father, 'you are with me always, and everything I have is yours. 32But we had to celebrate and rejoice! This brother of yours was dead, and has come back to life. He was lost, and is found.' "

The Wily Manager

16 1ANOTHER time he said to his disciples: "A rich man had a manager who was reported to him for dissipating his property. 2He summoned him and said, 'What is this I hear about you? Give me an account of your service, for it is about to come to an end.' 3The manager thought to himself, 'What shall I do next? My employer is sure to dismiss me. I cannot dig ditches. I am ashamed to go begging. 4I have it! Here is a way to make sure that people will take me into their homes when I am let go.'

5"So he called in each of his master's debtors, and said to the first, 'How much do you owe my master?' 6The man replied, 'A hundred jars of oil.' The manager said, 'Take your invoice, sit down quickly, and make it fifty.' 7Then he said to a second, 'How much do you owe?' The answer came, 'A hundred measures of wheat,' and the manager said, 'Take your invoice and make it eighty.'

8"The owner then gave his devious employee credit for being enterprising! Why? Because the worldly take more initiative than the other-worldly when it comes to dealing with their own kind.

Right Use of Money

9*"What I say to you is this: Make friends for yourselves through your use of this world's goods, so that when they fail you, a lasting reception will be yours. 10*If you can trust a man in little things, you can also trust him in greater; while anyone unjust in a slight matter is also unjust in greater. 11If you cannot be trusted with elusive wealth, who will trust you with lasting? 12And if you have not been trustworthy with someone else's money, who will give you what is your own?

13"No servant can serve two masters. Either he will hate the one and love the other or be attentive to the one and despise the other. You cannot give yourself to God and money." 14The Pharisees, who were avaricious men, heard all this and began to deride him. 15*He said to them: "You justify yourselves in the eyes of men, but God reads your hearts. What man thinks important, God holds in contempt.

The Law

16*"The law and the prophets were in force until John. From his time on, the good news of God's kingdom has been proclaimed, and people of every sort are forcing their way in. 17*It is easier for the heavens and the earth to pass away than for a single stroke of a letter of the law to pass. 18*Everyone who divorces his

16/9: 12, 33; Sir 29, 12.
10: 19, 17; Mt 25, 21.
15: 18, 9-14.
16: Mt 11, 12.
17: Mt 5, 18.
18: Mt 5, 32; 19, 9;
Mk 10, 11f;
1 Cor 7, 10f.

wife and marries another commits adultery. The man who marries a woman divorced from her husband likewise commits adultery.

The Rich Man and Lazarus

19"Once there was a rich man who dressed in purple and linen and feasted splendidly every day. **20**At his gate lay a beggar named Lazarus who was covered with sores. **21**Lazarus longed to eat the scraps that fell from the rich man's table. The dogs even came and licked his sores. **22**Eventually the beggar died. He was carried by angels to the bosom of Abraham. The rich man likewise died and was buried. **23**From the abode of the dead where he was in torment, he raised his eyes and saw Abraham afar off, and Lazarus resting in his bosom.

24"He called out, 'Father Abraham, have pity on me. Send Lazarus to dip the tip of his finger in water to refresh my tongue, for I am tortured in these flames.' **25***'My child,' replied Abraham, 'remember that you were well off in your lifetime, while Lazarus was in misery. Now he has found consolation here, but you have found torment. **26**And that is not all. Between you and us there is fixed a great abyss, so that those who might wish to cross from here to you cannot do so, nor can anyone cross from your side to us.'

27"'Father, I ask you, then,' the rich man said, 'send him to my father's house **28**where I have five brothers. Let him be a warning to them so that they may not end in this place of torment.' **29**Abraham answered, 'They have Moses and the prophets. Let them hear them.' **30**'No, Father Abraham,' replied the rich man. 'But if someone would only go to them from the dead, then they would repent.' **31***Abraham said to him, 'If they do not listen to Moses and the prophets, they will not be convinced even if one should rise from the dead.'"

Four Sayings of Jesus

17 **1***HE said to his disciples: "Scandals will inevitably arise, but woe to him through whom they come. **2**He would be better off thrown into the sea with a millstone around his neck than giving scandal to one of these little ones.

3"Be on your guard. If your brother does wrong, correct him; if he repents, forgive him. **4***If he sins against you seven times a day, and seven times a day turns back to you saying, 'I am sorry,' forgive him."

5The apostles said to the Lord, "Increase our faith," **6***and he answered: "If you had faith the size of a mustard seed, you could say to this sycamore, 'Be uprooted and transplanted into the sea,' and it would obey you.

7"If one of you had a servant plowing or herding sheep and he came in from the fields, would you say to him, 'Come and sit down at table'? **8**Would you not rather say, 'Prepare my supper. Put on your apron and wait on me while I eat and drink. You can eat and drink afterward'? **9**Would he be grateful to the servant who was only carrying out his orders? **10**It is quite the same with you who hear me. When you have done all you have been commanded to do, say, 'We are useless servants. We have done no more than our duty.'"

Ten Lepers

11On his journey to Jerusalem he passed along the borders of Samaria and Galilee. **12**As he was entering a village, ten lepers met him. Keeping their distance, **13**they raised their voices and said, "Jesus, Master, have pity on us!" **14***When he saw them, he responded, "Go and show yourselves to the priests." On their way there they were cured. **15**One of them, realizing that he had been cured, came back praising God in a loud voice. **16**He threw himself on his face at the feet of Jesus and spoke his praises. This man was a Samaritan.

17Jesus took the occasion to say, "Were not all ten made whole? Where are the other nine? **18**Was there no one to return and give thanks to God except this foreigner?" **19**He said to the man, "Stand up and go your way; your faith has been your salvation."

Coming of the Reign of God

20Once, on being asked by the Pharisees when the reign of God would come, he replied: "You cannot tell by careful watching when the reign of God will come. **21**Neither is it a matter of reporting that it is 'here' or 'there.' The reign of God is already in your midst."

Day of the Son of Man

22He said to the disciples: "A time will come when you will long to see one day of the Son of Man but will not see it. **23***They will tell you he is to be found in this place or that. Do not go running about excitedly. **24**The Son of Man in his day will be like the lightning that flashes from one end of the sky to the other. **25**First, however, he must suffer much and be rejected by the present age. **26***As it was in the days of Noah, so will it be in the days of the Son of Man. **27**They ate and drank, they took husbands and wives, right up to the day Noah entered the ark—and when the flood came, it destroyed them all. **28***It was much the same in the days of Lot: they ate and drank, they bought and sold, they built and planted. **29**But on the day Lot left Sodom, fire and brimstone rained down from heaven and destroyed them all.

30"It will be like that on the day the Son of Man is revealed. **31***On that day, if a man is on the rooftop and his belongings are in the house, he should not go down to get them; neither should the man in the field return home. **32***Remember Lot's wife. **33***Whoever tries to preserve his life will lose it; whoever loses it will keep it. **34**I tell you, on that night there will be two

---

*

25: 6, 24f.
31: Jn 5, 46f.
17/1f: Mt 18, 6f.
  4: Mt 18, 21f.
  6: Mt 21, 21; Mk 11, 23.
 14: 5, 14; Lv 13, 9-34;
    Mt 8, 4; Mk 1, 44.
23f: Mt 24, 23.26f;
    Mk 13, 21.

26f: Gn 6—8; Mt 24, 37ff.
28f: Gn 19, 1-29.
31: 21, 21; Mt 24, 17f;
    Mk 13, 15f.
32: Gn 19, 26.
33: 9, 24; Mt 10, 39;
    Mk 8, 35; Jn 12, 25.

men in one bed; one will be taken and the other left. **35***Two women will be grinding grain together; one will be taken and the other left." **37***"Where, Lord?" they asked him, and he answered, "Wherever the carcass is, there will the vultures gather."

The Corrupt Judge

18 **1**HE told them a parable on the necessity of praying always and not losing heart: **2***"Once there was a judge in a certain city who respected neither God nor man. **3**A widow in that city kept coming to him saying, 'Give me my rights against my opponent.' **4**For a time he refused, but finally he thought, 'I care little for God or man, **5**but this widow is wearing me out. I am going to settle in her favor or she will end by doing me violence.'" **6**The Lord said, "Listen to what the corrupt judge has to say. **7**Will not God then do justice to his chosen who call out to him day and night? Will he delay long over them, do you suppose? **8**I tell you, he will give them swift justice. But when the Son of Man comes, will he find any faith on the earth?"

The Pharisee and the Tax Collector

9*He then spoke this parable addressed to those who believed in their own self-righteousness while holding everyone else in contempt: **10**"Two men went up to the temple to pray; one was a Pharisee, the other a tax collector. **11**The Pharisee with head unbowed prayed in this fashion: 'I give you thanks, O God, that I am not like the rest of men—grasping, crooked, adulterous—or even like this tax collector. **12**I fast twice a week. I pay tithes on all I possess.' **13**The other man, however, kept his distance, not even daring to raise his eyes to heaven. All he did was beat his breast and say, 'O God, be merciful to me, a sinner.' **14***Believe me, this man went home from the temple justified but the other did not. For everyone who exalts himself shall be humbled while he who humbles himself shall be exalted."

Jesus and the Children; a Rich Man

15*†They even brought babies to be touched by him. When the disciples saw this, they scolded them roundly; **16**but Jesus called for the children, saying: "Let the little children come to me. Do not shut them off. The reign of God belongs to such as these. **17**Trust me when I tell you that whoever does not accept the kingdom of God as a child will not enter into it."

18*†One of the ruling class asked him then, "Good teacher, what must I do to share in everlasting life?"

19Jesus said to him, "Why call me 'good'? None is good but God alone **20***You know the commandments:

> 'You shall not commit adultery.
> You shall not kill.
> You shall not steal.
> You shall not bear dishonest witness.
> Honor your father and your mother.'"

21He replied, "I have kept all these since I was a boy." **22***When Jesus heard this he said to him: "There is one thing further you must do. Sell all you have and give to the poor. You will have treasure in heaven. Then come and follow me." **23**On hearing this he grew melancholy, for he was a very rich man. **24†**When Jesus observed this he said: "How hard it will be for the rich to go into the kingdom of God! **25**Indeed, it is easier for a camel to go through a needle's eye than for a rich man to enter the kingdom of heaven."

26His listeners asked him, "Who, then, can be saved?" **27**to which he replied, "Things that are impossible for men are possible for God." **28†**Peter said, "We have left all we own to become your followers." **29***His answer was, "I solemnly assure you, there is no one who has left home or wife or brothers, parents or children, for the sake of the kingdom of God **30**who will not receive a plentiful return in this age and life everlasting in the age to come."

31*†Taking the Twelve aside, he said to them: "We must now go up to Jerusalem so that all that was written by the prophets concerning the Son of Man may be accomplished. **32**He will be delivered up to the Gentiles. He will be mocked and outraged and spat upon. **33***They will scourge him and put him to death, and on the third day he will rise again."

34They understood nothing of this. His utterance remained obscure to them, and they did not grasp his meaning.

35*†As he drew near Jericho a blind man sat at the side of the road begging. **36**Hearing a crowd go by the man asked, "What is that?" **37**The answer came that Jesus of Nazareth was passing by. **38**He shouted out, "Jesus, Son of David, have pity on me!" **39***Those in the lead sternly ordered him to be quiet, but he cried out all the more, "Son of David, have pity on me!" **40**Jesus halted and ordered that he be brought to him. When he had come close, Jesus asked him, **41**"What do you want me to do for you?" "Lord," he answered, "I want to see." **42**Jesus said to him, "Receive your sight. Your faith has healed you." **43**At that very moment he was given his sight and began to follow him, giving God the glory. All the people witnessed it and they too gave praise to God.

✸
35: Mt 24, 40f.
37: Mt 24, 28.
18/9: 16, 15; Mt 23, 28.
14: 14, 11; Mt 23, 12.
15ff: Mt 19, 13ff.
18-30: Mt 19, 16-29; Mk 10, 17-30.
20: Ex 20, 12-16; Dt 5, 16-20.
22: 12, 33.
29: 14, 26.
31ff: 9, 22; Mt 20, 17ff; Mk 10, 32ff.
33: Acts 3, 18.
35-43: Mt 20, 29-34; Mk 10, 46-52.
39: Mt 9, 27.

†
17, 36: Omitted here with many MSS.
18, 15ff: See note on Mt 19, 13ff.
18, 18-21: See note on Mk 10, 17f.
18, 24-27: See note on Mt 19, 23-26.
18, 28ff: See note on Mt 19, 27-30.
18, 31-34: See note on Mk 10, 32ff.
18, 35-43: See note on Mk 10, 46-52.

Zacchaeus the Tax Collector

19 ¹ENTERING Jericho, he passed through the city. ²There was a man there named Zacchaeus, the chief tax collector and a wealthy man. ³He was trying to see what Jesus was like, but being small of stature, was unable to do so because of the crowd. ⁴He first ran on in front, then climbed a sycamore tree which was along Jesus' route, in order to see him. ⁵When Jesus came to the spot he looked up and said, "Zacchaeus, hurry down. I mean to stay at your house today." ⁶He quickly descended, and welcomed him with delight. ⁷When this was observed, everyone began to murmur, "He has gone to a sinner's house as a guest." ⁸Zacchaeus stood his ground and said to the Lord: "I give half my belongings, Lord, to the poor. If I have defrauded anyone in the least, I pay him back fourfold." ⁹*Jesus said to him: "Today salvation has come to this house, for this is what it means to be a son of Abraham. ¹⁰*The Son of Man has come to search out and save what was lost."

Parable of the Sums of Money

¹¹*†While they were listening to these things he went on to tell a parable, because he was near Jerusalem where they thought that the reign of God was about to appear. ¹²He said: "A man of noble birth went to a faraway country to become its king, and then return. ¹³He summoned ten of his servants and gave them sums of ten units each, saying to them, 'Invest this until I get back.' ¹⁴But his fellow citizens despised him, and they immediately sent a deputation after him with instructions to say, 'We will not have this man rule over us.' ¹⁵He returned, however, crowned as king. Then he sent for the servants to whom he had given the money, to learn what profit each had made. ¹⁶The first presented himself and said, 'Lord, the sum you gave me has earned you another ten.' ¹⁷*'Good man!' he replied. 'You showed yourself capable in a small matter. For that you can take over ten villages.' ¹⁸The second came and said, 'Your investment, my lord, has netted you five.' ¹⁹His word to him was, 'Take over five villages.' ²⁰The third came in and said: 'Here is your money, my lord, which I hid for safekeeping. ²¹You see, I was afraid of you because you are a hard man. You withdraw what you never deposited. You reap what you never sowed.' ²²To him the king said: 'You worthless lout! I intend to judge you on your own evidence. You knew I was a hard man, withdrawing what I never deposited, reaping what I never sowed! ²³Why, then, did you not put my money out on loan, so that on my return I could get it back with interest?' ²⁴He said to those standing around, 'Take from him what he has, and give it to the man with the ten.' ²⁵'Yes, but he already has ten,' they said. ²⁶*He re-

sponded with, 'The moral is: whoever has will be given more, but the one who has not will lose the little he has. ²⁷Now about those enemies of mine who do not want me to be king, bring them in and slay them in my presence.' "

V: THE JERUSALEM MINISTRY

Messianic Entry into Jerusalem

²⁸*†HAVING SPOKEN THUS he went ahead with his ascent to Jerusalem. ²⁹As he approached Bethphage and Bethany on the mount called Olivet, he sent two of the disciples ³⁰with these instructions: "Go into the village straight ahead of you. Upon entering it you will find an ass tied there which no one has yet ridden. Untie it and lead it back. ³¹If anyone should ask you, 'Why are you untying the beast?' say, 'The Master has need of it.' "

³²They departed on their errand and found things just as he had said. ³³As they untied the ass, its owners said to them, "Why are you doing that?" ³⁴They explained that the Master needed it. ³⁵Then they led the animal to Jesus, and laying their cloaks on it, helped him mount. ³⁶They spread their cloaks on the roadway as he moved along; ³⁷and on his approach to the descent from Mount Olivet, the entire crowd of disciples began to rejoice and praise God loudly for the display of power they had seen, ³⁸*saying:

"Blessed is he who comes as king
    in the name of the Lord!
Peace in heaven
    and glory in the highest!"

³⁹*Some of the Pharisees in the crowd said to him, "Teacher, rebuke your disciples." ⁴⁰He replied, "If they were to keep silence, I tell you the very stones would cry out."

Lamentation for Jerusalem

⁴¹*†Coming within sight of the city, he wept over it and said: ⁴²"If only you had known the path to peace

---

† 19, 11-27: The parable of the sums of money presents two principal ideas: 1) Jesus is the Messiah-king; he understands this office to be a religious one despite the opposition of his contemporaries (19, 12-15). The reign of God is actually present in his person and teaching. 2) In exercising his messianic kingship Jesus demands the response of men to the gifts of God. The kingdom will appear in its permanent form when Christ renders the final judgment on humanity's response to him (19, 15-27).

19, 28-38: See note on Mk 11, 1-11.

19, 41-44: This lamentation over Jerusalem implies that Jesus has previously visited the city in his public ministry, a fact that is brought out only in John (2, 13; 5, 1; 7, 10.14; 10, 22; 12, 12).

Here the thought of the impending destruction of Jerusalem because of its refusal to accept the Messiah is contrasted with the city's potentiality as the principal center of the Christian message. Jerusalem became that center for only a short time, as the Acts attest (9, 31; 12, 1-5); the city was destroyed in 70 A. D. The allusions here are drawn from Jeremiah: v 42 (Jer 6, 8.10.14); v 43 (Jer 6, 6); v 44 (Jer 6, 2.11.17.21).

✻
19/9: Mt 21, 31.
   10: 15, 6.9; Mt 18, 11.
   11-27: Mt 25, 14-30.
   17: 16, 10.
   26: 8, 18; Mt 13, 12;
     Mk 4, 25.

28-38: Mt 21, 1-9;
     Mk 11, 1-10;
     Jn 12, 12-15.
   38: Ps 118, 26.
   39f: Mt 21, 15f.
   41-44: 13, 34f.

this day; but you have completely lost it from view! **43***Days will come upon you when your enemies encircle you with a rampart, hem you in, and press you hard from every side. **44***They will wipe you out, you and your children within your walls, and leave not a stone on a stone within you, because you failed to recognize the time of your visitation."

The Traders Expelled

45*†Then he entered the temple and began ejecting the traders **46***saying: "Scripture has it,

'My house is meant for a house of prayer'

but you have made it 'a den of thieves.'"

47He was teaching in the temple area from day to day. The chief priests and scribes meanwhile were looking for a way to destroy him, as were the leaders of the people, **48**but they had no idea how to achieve it, for indeed the entire populace was listening to him and hanging on his words.

The Authority of Jesus

20 **1***†ONE day when he was teaching the people in the temple and proclaiming the good news, the high priests and Pharisees, accompanied by the elders, approached him **2***with the question, "Tell us, by what authority do you do these things? In other words, who has authorized you?" **3**He replied, "Let me put a question for you to answer: **4**Did the baptism of John come from God or from men?" **5**They held a brief conference during which someone said, "If we answer, 'From God,' he will say, 'Then why do you not believe in it?'; **6**whereas if we say, 'From men,' the people will stone us, so convinced are they that John was a prophet." **7**They ended by replying they did not know where it came from. **8**Jesus said to them, "In that case, neither will I tell you by whose authority I act."

Parable of the Tenants

9*He then began to tell the people the following parable: "A man planted a vineyard, leased it to tenant farmers, and went away for a long time. **10**At vintage time he sent a servant to the tenant farmers to receive his share of the crop from them; but they beat him and sent him away empty-handed. **11**He sent a second servant whom they also beat. Him too they sent away empty-handed, after treating him shamefully. **12**He sent still a third, whom they likewise maltreated before driving him away. **13**The owner of the vineyard asked himself, 'What am I to do now? Perhaps if I send the son I love, they will respect him.'

14"But when the tenant farmers saw the son, they reflected, 'This is the heir. Let us kill him so that the inheritance will be ours.' **15**With that, they dragged him outside the vineyard and killed him. What fate do you suppose the owner of the vineyard has in store for them? **16**I will tell you. He will make an end to those tenant farmers and give the vineyard to others."

When they heard this they said, "God forbid!" **17***He looked directly at them and said, "What do the Scriptures mean when they say,

'The stone which the builders rejected
has become the keystone of the structure'?

18The man who falls on that stone will be smashed to pieces. It will make dust of anyone on whom it falls." **19**At these words the scribes and high priests tried to get their hands on him, but they were afraid of the people. They were well aware that he had told the parable with them in mind.

Tribute to the Emperor

20*Waiting their chance, they sent spies to him in the guise of honest men to trap him in speech, so that they might then hand him over to the office and authority of the procurator. **21**They put to him this problem: "Teacher, we know that your words and your doctrine are completely forthright, that you are no respecter of persons but teach the way of God in truth. **22**May we pay tax to the emperor or not?" **23**Realizing their duplicity he said, **24**"Show me a coin. Whose head is this? Whose inscription do you read?" "Caesar's," they replied, **25***to which he said, "Then give to Caesar what is Caesar's, but give to God what is God's." **26**They were unable to trap him publicly in speech. His answer completely disconcerted them and reduced them to silence.

Resurrection of the Dead

27*Some Sadducees came forward (the ones who claim there is no resurrection) **28***to pose this problem to him: "Master, Moses prescribed that if a man's brother dies leaving a wife and no child, the brother should marry the widow and raise posterity to his brother. **29**Now there were seven brothers. **30**The first one married and died childless. **31**Next, the second brother married the widow, then the third, and so on. All seven died without leaving her any children. **32**Finally the widow herself died. **33**At the resurrection, whose wife will she be? Remember, seven married her."

34Jesus said to them: "The children of this age marry and are given in marriage, **35**but those judged worthy of a place in the age to come and of resurrection from the dead do not. **36**They become like angels and are no longer liable to death. Sons of the resurrection, they are sons of God. **37***Moses in the passage about the bush showed that the dead rise again when he called

✿

43: Is 29, 3.
44: 21, 6; Mt 24, 2; Mk 13, 2.
45f: Mt 21, 12f; Mk 11, 15ff; Jn 2, 14ff.
46: Is 56, 7; Jer 7, 11.
20/1-8: Mt 21, 23-27; Mk 11, 27-33.
2: Acts 4, 7.

9-19: Mt 21, 33-46; Mk 12, 1-12.
17: Ps 118, 22; Is 28, 16.
20-26: Mt 22, 15-22; Mk 12, 13-17.
25: Rom 13, 7.
27-38: Mt 22, 23-33; Mk 12, 18-27.
28: Dt 25, 5.
37: Ex 3, 6.15f.

†
19, 45f: See note on Mk 11, 15-19.
20, 1-40: See note on Mk 11, 27—12, 27.

the Lord the God of Abraham, and the God of Isaac, and the God of Jacob. **38**God is not the God of the dead but of the living. All are alive for him."

39Some of the scribes responded, "Well said, Teacher." **40**They did not dare ask him anything else.

Jesus, Son and Lord of David

41*†Jesus then said to them: "How can they say that the Messiah is the son of David? **42***Does not David himself say in the psalms,

'The Lord said to my lord: Sit at my right hand

43while I make your enemies your footstool'?

44Now if David accords him the title 'lord,' how can he be his son?"

The Scribes Condemned

45In the hearing of all the people, Jesus said to his disciples: **46***"Beware of the scribes, who like to parade around in their robes, and love marks of respect in public, front seats in synagogues, and places of honor at banquets. **47**These men are going through the savings of widows while they recite long prayers to keep up appearances. The heavier sentence will be theirs."

The Widow's Mite

21 **1***HE glanced up and saw the rich putting their offerings into the treasury, **2**and also a poor widow putting in two copper coins. At that he said: **3**"I assure you, this poor widow has put in more than all the rest. **4**They make contributions out of their surplus, but she from her want has given what she could not afford—every penny she had to live on."

The Cataclysm To Come

5*†Some were speaking of how the temple was adorned with precious stones and votive offerings. **6**He said, "These things you are contemplating—the day will come when not one stone will be left on another, but it will all be torn down." **7**They asked him, "When will this be, Teacher? And what will be the sign that it is going to happen?" **8**He said, "Take care not to be misled. Many will come in my name saying, 'I am he' and 'The time is at hand.' Do not follow them. **9**Neither must you be perturbed when you hear of wars and insurrections. These things are bound to happen first, but the end does not follow immediately."

10He said to them further: "Nation will rise against nation and kingdom against kingdom. **11**There will be great earthquakes, plagues and famines in various places—and in the sky fearful omens and great signs. **12***But before any of this, they will manhandle and persecute you, summoning you to synagogues and prisons, bringing you to trial before kings and governors, all because of my name. **13**You will be brought to give witness on account of it. **14**I bid you resolve not to worry about your defense beforehand, **15***for I will give you words and a wisdom which none of your adversaries can take exception to or contradict. **16**You will be delivered up even by your parents, brothers, relatives and friends, and some of you will be put to death. **17**All will hate you because of me, **18**yet not a hair of your head will be harmed. **19**By patient endurance you will save your lives.

Siege and Fall of Jerusalem

20*"When you see Jerusalem encircled by soldiers, know that its devastation is near. **21***Those in Judea at the time must flee to the mountains; those in the heart of the city must escape it; those in the country must not return. **22**These indeed will be days of retribution, when all that is written must be fulfilled.

23"The women who are pregnant or nursing at the breast will fare badly in those days! The distress in the land and the wrath against this people will be great. **24**The people will fall before the sword; they will be led captive in the midst of the Gentiles. Jerusalem will be trampled by the Gentiles, until the times of the Gentiles are fulfilled.

Coming of the Son of Man

25*"There will be signs in the sun, the moon and the stars. On the earth, nations will be in anguish, distraught at the roaring of the sea and the waves. **26**Men will die of fright in anticipation of what is coming upon the earth. The powers in the heavens will be shaken. **27***After that, men will see the Son of Man coming on a cloud with great power and glory. **28**When these things begin to happen, stand erect and hold your heads high, for your deliverance is near at hand."

Parable of the Fig Tree

29*Then he told them a parable: "Notice the fig tree, or any other tree. **30**You observe them when they are budding, and know for yourselves that summer is near. **31**Likewise when you see all the things happening of which I speak, know that the reign of God is near. **32***Let me tell you this: the present generation will not pass away until all this takes place. **33**The heavens and the earth will pass away, but my words will not pass.

34*"Be on guard lest your spirits become bloated with indulgence and drunkenness and worldly cares. The great day will suddenly close in on you like a trap. **35**The day I speak of will come upon all who dwell on

---

✿

41-44: Mt 22, 41-45;
    Mk 12, 35ff.
  42: Ps 110, 1.
  46: 11, 43; Mt 23, 6f;
    Mk 12, 38ff.
21/1-4: Mk 12, 41-44.
  5-19: Mt 24, 1-14;
    Mk 13, 1-13.
12-15: 12, 11f; Mt 10, 17-20.
  15: Acts 6, 10.
20-23: Mt 24, 15-20;
    Mk 13, 14-18.

  21: 17, 31.
25ff: Mt 24, 29f;
    Mk 13, 24ff.
  25: Is 13, 10; Ez 32, 7;
    Jl 4, 15.
  27: Dn 7, 13.
29-33: Mt 24, 32-35;
    Mk 13, 28-31.
  32: 9, 27; Mt 16, 28.
  34: 1 Thes 5, 3.

---

†   20, 41—21, 4: See note on Mk 12, 35-44.
    21, 5-36: See note on Mk 13, 1-37.

the face of the earth. **36**So be on the watch. Pray constantly for the strength to escape whatever is in prospect, and to stand secure before the Son of Man."

Last Days of Jesus

37He would teach in the temple by day, and leave the city to spend the night on the Mount of Olives. **38**At daybreak all the people came to hear him in the temple.

VI: THE PASSION OF JESUS

1. THE PASCHAL MEAL

The Council and the Betrayal

22 **1***†THE FEAST OF UNLEAVENED BREAD known as the Passover was drawing near, **2**and the high priests and scribes began to look for some way to dispose of him; but they were afraid of the people. **3***Then Satan took possession of Judas, the one called Iscariot, a member of the Twelve. **4***He went off to confer with the chief priests and officers about a way to hand him over to them. **5**They were delighted, and agreed to give him money. **6**He accepted, then kept looking for an opportunity to hand him over without creating a disturbance.

The Passover Preparation

7*The day of Unleavened Bread arrived on which it was appointed to sacrifice the paschal lamb. **8**Accordingly, Jesus sent Peter and John off with the instruction, "Go and prepare our Passover supper for us." **9**They asked him, "Where do you want us to get it ready?" **10**He explained to them: "Just as you enter the city, you will come upon a man carrying a water jar. Follow him into the house he enters, and say to the owner, **11**'The Teacher asks you: Do you have a guest room where I may eat the Passover with my disciples?' **12**That man will show you an upstairs room, spacious and furnished. It is there you are to prepare." **13**They went off and found everything just as he had said; and accordingly they prepared the Passover supper.

The Holy Eucharist

14When the hour arrived, he took his place at table, and the apostles with him. **15**He said to them: "I have greatly desired to eat this Passover with you before I suffer. **16**I tell you, I will not eat again until it is fulfilled in the kingdom of God."

17Then taking a cup he offered a blessing in thanks and said: "Take this and divide it among you; **18***I tell you, from now on I will not drink of the fruit of the vine until the coming of the reign of God." **19***Then, taking bread and giving thanks, he broke it and gave it to them, saying: "This is my body to be given for you. Do this as a remembrance of me." **20**He did the same with the cup after eating, saying as he did so: "This cup is the new covenant in my blood, which will be shed for you.

The Betrayer

21*"And yet the hand of my betrayer is with me at this table. **22**The Son of Man is following out his appointed course, but woe to that man by whom he is betrayed." **23**Then they began to argue among themselves as to which of them would do such a deed.

Who Is Greatest?

24A dispute arose among them about who should be regarded as the greatest. **25***He said: "Earthly kings lord it over their people. Those who exercise authority over them are called their benefactors. **26**Yet it cannot be that way with you. Let the greater among you be as the junior, the leader as the servant. **27***Who, in fact, is the greater—he who reclines at table or he who serves the meal? Is it not the one who reclines at table? Yet I am in your midst as the one who serves you. **28**†You are the ones who have stood loyally by me in my temptations. **29**I for my part assign to you the dominion my Father has assigned to me. **30***In my kingdom you will eat and drink at my table, and you will sit on thrones judging the twelve tribes of Israel.

Peter's Denials Foretold

31"Simon, Simon! Remember that Satan has asked for you, to sift you all like wheat. **32**But I have prayed for you that your faith may never fail. You in turn must strengthen your brothers." **33**"Lord," he said to him, "at your side I am prepared to face imprisonment and death itself." **34***Jesus replied, "I tell you, Peter, the

---

† 22, 1—23, 56: Certain features of this narrative of the passion of Jesus are distinctive of Luke. There are omissions: the flight of the disciples at the arrest of Jesus (Mk 14, 50ff), the false witnesses (Mk 14, 55-59), which many consider a Marcan insertion into traditional materials, the mistreatment at the hands of the Roman soldiery (Mk 15, 16-20), the offering of a narcotic to Jesus before the crucifixion (Mk 15, 23), and the praying of Psalm 22 from the cross (Mk 15, 34ff).

Additions found in Luke include: the elements of Jesus' farewell address at the Last Supper (22, 15.25-30.35-38); reference to the angel at the agony, which heightens the religious solemnity of the scene (22, 43); Jesus' look at Peter after his denial (22, 61); the appearance of Jesus before Herod (23, 6-11); his conversation with the women of Jerusalem (23, 27-31); and his words from the cross (23, 34.43.46).

Luke depicts Jesus throughout his passion as the innocent victim (23, 4.14.22.47) of satanic activity (22, 3), who forgives his enemies (22, 51; 23, 34) and accepts his suffering and death as the will of his Father (23, 46).

22, 28: *My temptations:* both from Satan (4, 13) and from the enemies of Jesus who served the purposes of Satan.

❀ 22/1f: Mt 26, 2.5; Mk 14, 1f.
    3: Jn 13, 2.27.
    4f: Mt 26, 14ff;
       Mk 14, 10f.
  7-13: Mt 26, 17ff;
       Mk 14, 12-16.
    18: Mt 26, 29; Mk 14, 25.
  19f: Mt 26, 26ff;
       Mk 14, 22ff;
       1 Cor 11, 23ff.

  21ff: Mt 26, 20-25;
       Mk 14, 17-21;
       Jn 13, 21-30.
  25ff: Mt 20, 25-28;
       Mk 10, 42ff.
    27: Jn 13, 4-15.
    30: Mt 19, 28.
    34: 22, 61; Mt 26, 33ff;
       Mk 14, 29ff; Jn 13, 36ff.

cock will not crow today until you have three times denied that you know me."

35°He asked them, "When I sent you on mission without purse or traveling bag or sandals, were you in need of anything?" "Not a thing," they replied. **36**He said to them: "Now, however, the man who has a purse must carry it; the same with the traveling bag. And the man without a sword must sell his coat and buy one. **37**°It is written in Scripture,

'He was counted among the wicked,'

and this, I tell you, must come to be fulfilled in me. All that has to do with me approaches its climax." **38**They said, "Lord, here are two swords!" He answered, "Enough."

2. THE PASSION, DEATH AND BURIAL

The Agony in the Garden

39°THEN HE WENT OUT and made his way, as was his custom, to the Mount of Olives; his disciples accompanied him. **40**On reaching the place he said to them, "Pray that you may not be put to the test." **41**He withdrew from them about a stone's throw, then went down on his knees and prayed in these words: **42**"Father, if it is your will, take this cup from me; yet not my will but yours be done." **43**An angel then appeared to him from heaven to strengthen him. **44**In his anguish he prayed with all the greater intensity, and his sweat became like drops of blood falling to the ground. **45**Then he rose from prayer and came to his disciples, only to find them asleep, exhausted with grief. **46**He said to them, "Why are you sleeping? Wake up, and pray that you may not be subjected to the trial."

Jesus Arrested

47°While he was still speaking a crowd came, led by the man named Judas, one of the Twelve. He approached Jesus to embrace him. **48**Jesus said to him, "Judas, would you betray the Son of Man with a kiss?" **49**When the companions of Jesus saw what was going to happen, they said, "Lord, shall we use the sword?" **50**One of them went so far as to strike the high priest's servant and cut off his right ear. **51**Jesus said in answer to their question, "Enough!" Then he touched the ear and healed the man. **52**But to those who had come out against him—the chief priests, the chiefs of the temple guard, and the ancients—Jesus said, "Am I a criminal

that you come out after me armed with swords and clubs? **53**When I was with you day after day in the temple you never raised a hand against me. But this is your hour—the triumph of darkness!"

Peter's Denial

54°They led him away under arrest and brought him to the house of the high priest, while Peter followed at a distance. **55**Later they lighted a fire in the middle of the courtyard and were sitting beside it, and Peter sat among them. **56**A servant girl saw him sitting in the light of the fire. She gazed at him intently, then said, "This man was with him." **57**He denied it, saying, "Woman, I do not know him." **58**A little while later someone else saw him and said, "You are one of them too." But Peter said, "No, sir, not I!" **59**About an hour after that another spoke more insistently: "This man was certainly with him, for he is a Galilean." **60**Peter responded, "My friend, I do not know what you are talking about." At the very moment he was saying this, a cock crowed. **61**°The Lord turned around and looked at Peter, and Peter remembered the word that the Lord had spoken to him, "Before the cock crows today you will deny me three times." **62**He went out and wept bitterly.

Jesus before the Sanhedrin

63°Meanwhile the men guarding Jesus amused themselves at his expense. **64**They blindfolded him first, slapped him, and then taunted him: "Play the prophet; which one struck you?" **65**And they directed many other insulting words at him.

66°At daybreak, the elders of the people, the chief priests, and the scribes assembled again. Once they had brought him before their council, they said, "Tell us, are you the Messiah?" **67**He replied, "If I tell you, you will not believe me, **68**and if I question you, you will not answer. **69**This much only will I say: 'From now on, the Son of Man will have his seat at the right hand of the Power of God.' " **70**°"So you are the Son of God?" they asked in chorus. He answered, "It is you who say I am." **71**They said, "What need have we of witnesses? We have heard it from his own mouth."

Jesus before Pilate

23 **1**°THEN the entire assembly rose up and led him before Pilate. **2**°They started his prosecution by saying, "We found this man subverting our nation, opposing the payment of taxes to Caesar, and calling himself the Messiah, a king." **3**°Pilate asked him, "Are you the king of the Jews?" He answered, "That is your term." **4**Pilate reported to the chief priests and the crowds, "I do not find a case against this man." **5**But they insisted, "He stirs up the people by his teaching throughout the whole of Judea, from Galilee, where he began, to this very place." **6**On hearing this Pilate asked if the man was a Galilean; **7**and when he learned that he was under Herod's jurisdiction, he sent him to Herod, who also happened to be in Jerusalem at the time.

°
35: 10, 4; Mt 10, 9.
37: 23, 32; Is 53, 12.
39-46: Mt 26, 30.36-46;
   Mk 14, 26.32-42.
47-53: Mt 26, 47-56;
   Mk 14, 43-50;
   Jn 18, 3-11.
54-62: Mt 26, 58.69-75;
   Mk 14, 54.66-72;
   Jn 18, 15-18.25ff.
61: 22, 34;
   Mt 26, 34;
   Mk 14, 30;
   Jn 13, 38.

63f: Mt 26, 67ff; Mk 14, 65.
66-71: Mt 26, 59-66;
   Mk 14, 55-64.
66: Mt 27, 1; Mk 15, 1.
70: Wis 2, 13; Jn 10, 30.
23/1: Mt 27, 1f; Jn 18, 28.
2-6: Mt 27, 11-14;
   Mk 15, 2-5;
   Jn 18, 29-38.
2: 20, 22-25; Acts 17, 7;
   24, 5.
3: Mt 27, 11; Mk 15, 2;
   Jn 18, 33.

8Herod was extremely pleased to see Jesus. From the reports about him he had wanted for a long time to see him, and he was hoping to see him work some miracle. **9**He questioned Jesus at considerable length, but Jesus made no answer. **10**The chief priests and scribes were at hand to accuse him vehemently. **11**Herod and his guards then treated him with contempt and insult, after which they put a magnificent robe on him and sent him back to Pilate. **12**Herod and Pilate, who had previously been set against each other, became friends from that day.

Jesus Again before Pilate

13Pilate then called together the chief priests, the ruling class, and the people, **14***and said to them: "You have brought this man before me as one who subverts the people. I have examined him in your presence and have no charge against him arising from your allegations. **15**Neither has Herod, who therefore has sent him back to us; obviously this man has done nothing that calls for death. **16**Therefore I mean to release him, once I have taught him a lesson." **18***The whole crowd cried out, "Away with this man; release Barabbas for us!" **19**This Barabbas had been thrown in prison for causing an uprising in the city, and for murder. **20**Pilate addressed them again, for he wanted Jesus to be the one he released.

21But they shouted back, "Crucify him, crucify him!" **22**He said to them for the third time, "What wrong is this man guilty of? I have not discovered anything about him that calls for the death penalty. I will therefore chastise him and release him." **23**But they demanded with loud cries that he be crucified, and their shouts increased in violence. **24***Pilate then decreed that what they demanded should be done. **25**He released the one they asked for, who had been thrown in prison for insurrection and murder, and delivered Jesus up to their wishes.

The Way of the Cross

26*As they led him away, they laid hold of one Simon the Cyrenean who was coming in from the fields. They put a crossbeam on Simon's shoulder for him to carry along behind Jesus. **27**A great crowd of people followed him, including women who beat their breasts and lamented over him. **28**Jesus turned to them and said: "Daughters of Jerusalem, do not weep for me. Weep for yourselves and for your children. **29**The days are coming when they will say, "Happy are the sterile, the wombs that never bore and the breasts that never

nursed.' **30***Then they will begin saying to the mountains, 'Fall on us,' and to the hills, 'Cover us.' **31**If they do these things in the green wood, what will happen in the dry?"

The Crucifixion

32*Two others who were criminals were led along with him to be crucified. **33***When they came to Skull Place, as it was called, they crucified him there and the criminals as well, one on his right and the other on his left. **34***[Jesus said, "Father forgive them; they do not know what they are doing."] They divided his garments, rolling dice for them.

35*The people stood there watching, and the leaders kept jeering at him, saying, "He saved others; let him save himself if he is the Messiah of God, the chosen one." **36***The soldiers also made fun of him, coming forward to offer him their sour wine **37**and saying, "If you are the king of the Jews, save yourself." **38***There was an inscription over his head:

THIS IS THE KING OF THE JEWS.

39*One of the criminals hanging in crucifixion blasphemed him: "Aren't you the Messiah? Then save yourself and us." **40**But the other one rebuked him: "Have you no fear of God, seeing you are under the same sentence? **41**We deserve it, after all. We are only paying the price for what we've done, but this man has done nothing wrong." **42**He then said, "Jesus, remember me when you enter upon your reign." **43**And Jesus replied, "I assure you: this day you will be with me in paradise."

Jesus Dies on the Cross

44*It was now around midday, and darkness came over the whole land until midafternoon with an eclipse of the sun. **45**The curtain in the sanctuary was torn in two. **46***Jesus uttered a loud cry and said,

"Father, into your hands I commend my spirit."

After he said this, he expired. **47***The centurion, upon seeing what had happened, gave glory to God by saying, "Surely this was an innocent man." **48**When the crowd which had assembled for this spectacle saw what had happened, they went home beating their breasts. **49***All his friends and the women who had accompanied him from Galilee were standing at a distance watching everything.

The Burial

50*There was a man named Joseph, an upright and holy member of the Sanhedrin, **51**who had not been associated with their plan or their action. He was from Arimathea, a Jewish town, and he looked expectantly for the reign of God. **52**This man approached Pilate with a request for Jesus' body. **53**He took it down,

14: Jn 19, 4.
18-25: Mt 27, 15-26; Mk 15, 7-15; Jn 18, 39—19, 16.
24f: Acts 3, 14f.
26: Mt 27, 31f; Mk 15, 20f.
30: Hos 10, 8; Rv 6, 16.
32: 22, 37; Is 53, 12.
33f: Mt 27, 33; Mk 15, 22ff; Jn 19, 17.
34: Ps 22, 19; Acts 7, 60.
35-38: Mt 27, 39-43; Mk 15, 29-32.
36: Mt 27, 48.
38: Jn 19, 19.
39: Mt 27, 44; Mk 15, 32.
44ff: Mt 27, 45-50; Mk 15, 33-37.
46: Ps 31, 6; Jn 19, 30; Acts 7, 60.
47: Mt 27, 54; Mk 15, 39.
49: 24, 10.
50-55: Mt 27, 57-61; Mk 15, 42-47; Jn 19, 38-41.

† 23, 17: Omit with some MSS. Others read: "At the festival time he had to release a prisoner to them."

wrapped it in fine linen, and laid it in a tomb hewn out of the rock, in which no one had yet been buried.

⁵⁴That was the Day of Preparation, and the sabbath was about to begin. ⁵⁵The women who had come with him from Galilee followed along behind. They saw the tomb and how his body was buried. ⁵⁶*Then they went home to prepare spices and perfumes. They observed the sabbath as a day of rest, in accordance with the law.

VII: APPEARANCES AFTER THE RESURRECTION

The Women at the Tomb

24 ¹*†ON THE FIRST DAY OF THE WEEK, at dawn, the women came to the tomb bringing the spices they had prepared. ²They found the stone rolled back from the tomb; ³but when they entered the tomb, they did not find the body of the Lord Jesus. ⁴While they were still at a loss over what to think of this, two men in dazzling garments stood beside them. ⁵Terrified, the women bowed to the ground. The men said to them: "Why do you search for the Living One among the dead? ⁶He is not here; he has been raised up. Remember what he said to you while he was still in Galilee—⁷*that the Son of Man must be delivered into the hands of sinful men, and be crucified, and on the third day rise again." ⁸With this reminder, his words came back to them.

⁹*On their return from the tomb, they told all these things to the Eleven and the others. ¹⁰*The women were Mary of Magdala, Joanna, and Mary the mother of James. The other women with them also told the apostles, ¹¹but the story seemed like nonsense and they refused to believe them. ¹²*Peter, however, got up and ran to the tomb. He stooped down but could see nothing but the wrappings. So he went away full of amazement at what had occurred.

Emmaus

¹³*Two of them that same day were making their way to a village named Emmaus seven miles distant from Jerusalem, ¹⁴discussing as they went all that had happened. ¹⁵In the course of their lively exchange, Jesus approached and began to walk with them. ¹⁶*However, they were restrained from recognizing him. ¹⁷He said to them, "What are you discussing as you go your way?" ¹⁸They halted, in distress, and one of them, Cleopas by name, asked him, "Are you the only resident of Jerusalem who does not know the things that went on there these past few days?" ¹⁹*He said to them, "What things?" They said: "All those that

had to do with Jesus of Nazareth, a prophet powerful in word and deed in the eyes of God and all the people; ²⁰how our chief priests and leaders delivered him up to be condemned to death, and crucified him. ²¹*We were hoping that he was the one who would set Israel free. Besides all this, today, the third day since these things happened, ²²some women of our group have just brought us some astonishing news. They were at the tomb before dawn ²³and failed to find his body, but returned with the tale that they had seen a vision of angels who declared he was alive. ²⁴Some of our number went to the tomb and found it to be just as the women said; but him they did not see."

²⁵*Then he said to them, "What little sense you have! How slow you are to believe all that the prophets have announced! ²⁶Did not the Messiah have to undergo all this so as to enter into his glory?" ²⁷*Beginning, then, with Moses and all the prophets, he interpreted for them every passage of Scripture which referred to him. ²⁸By now they were near the village to which they were going, and he acted as if he were going farther. ²⁹But they pressed him: "Stay with us. It is nearly evening—the day is practically over." So he went in to stay with them.

³⁰When he had seated himself with them to eat, he took bread, pronounced the blessing, then broke the bread and began to distribute it to them. ³¹With that

---

† 24, 1-53: The resurrection narratives in the gospels do not derive directly from the primitive stage when the apostolic testimony was as yet unchallenged by the unbeliever. They reflect a somewhat later period, when the average Christian was aware of the unbeliever's principal counter-arguments against the doctrine of the resurrection; namely, that Jesus' disciples had removed his body from the tomb, or that they were victims of visionary or other objectively unreal experiences. The gospels and the tradition that preceded them carefully interwove the data of the resurrection with the replies to these arguments, so that Christians might remain in peaceful possession of their faith.

The narratives, then, begin with the account of the women's visit to the tomb—no doubt to make clear that up to this point the male disciples of Jesus had not come near the tomb (1-8). The reaction of the disciples to the women's report reveals that they did not anticipate Jesus' immediate resurrection (10f), much less think of creating a resurrection myth by removal of the body. The stress on the incredulity of the disciples (11.25.41; cf 28, 17; Jn 20, 24-29) depicts them as men not easily convinced of the resurrection event: *They thought they were seeing a ghost* (37). But their experience of his presence for the duration of meals (42f; cf Jn 20, 9-13), and their conversation with him in which they recognized that his earlier teaching actually culminated in these new circumstances (44; cf Jn 20, 21; 21, 15ff), required the acceptance of the one before them as Jesus of Nazareth, who had returned to life after undergoing the reality of death.

The greater problem of the disciples in accepting the fact of the resurrection was, no doubt, its messianic implications. These new and unanticipated concepts presented an extraordinary challenge to the faith of Israel, a point that Luke's resurrection narrative is careful to make (25ff.44-47). In addition to the apologetic response to the denials of the resurrection, Luke (44-49), like Matthew (28, 19f) and John (20, 21ff), incorporates into his gospel the instructions of the risen Jesus concerning the mission of the disciples and of the Christian community.

✸ 56: Mk 16, 1.
24/1-8: Mt 28, 1-8; Mk 16, 1-8.
1ff: Jn 20, 1ff.
7: 9, 22; Mt 16, 21; 17, 22f; Mk 9, 31.
9ff: Mk 16, 10f.
10: 8, 2f.
12: Jn 20, 3-7.
13: Mk 16, 12f.
16: Jn 20, 14; 21, 4.
19: Mt 2, 23; Acts 2, 22.
21: 1, 54; 2, 38.
25f: 18, 31; Acts 3, 24.
27: 1 Pt 1, 10f.

their eyes were opened and they recognized him; whereupon he vanished from their sight. [32]They said to one another, "Were not our hearts burning inside us as he talked to us on the road and explained the Scriptures to us?" [33]They got up immediately and returned to Jerusalem, where they found the Eleven and the rest of the company assembled. They were greeted with, [34]"The Lord has been raised! It is true! He has appeared to Simon." [35]Then they recounted what had happened on the road and how they had come to know him in the breaking of bread.

Jesus Appears to the Eleven

[36]*While they were still speaking about all this, he himself stood in their midst [and said to them, "Peace to you."]. [37]In their panic and fright they thought they were seeing a ghost. [38]He said to them, "Why are you disturbed? Why do such ideas cross your mind? [39]Look at my hands and my feet; it is really I. Touch me, and see that a ghost does not have flesh and bones

as I do." [40]*As he said this he showed them his hands and feet. [41]They were still incredulous for sheer joy and wonder, so he said to them, "Have you anything here to eat?" [42]They gave him a piece of cooked fish, [43]which he took and ate in their presence. [44]Then he said to them, "Recall those words I spoke to you when I was still with you: everything written about me in the law of Moses and the prophets and psalms had to be fulfilled." [45]Then he opened their minds to the understanding of the Scriptures.

[46]*He said to them: "Thus it is written that the Messiah must suffer and rise from the dead on the third day. [47]*In his name, penance for the remission of sins is to be preached to all the nations, beginning at Jerusalem. [48]You are witnesses of this. See, [49]*I send down upon you the promise of my Father. Remain here in the city until you are clothed with power from on high."

The Ascension

[50]*Then he led them out near Bethany, and with hands upraised, blessed them. [51]As he blessed, he left them, and was taken up to heaven. [52]They fell down to do him reverence, then returned to Jerusalem filled with joy. [53]There they were to be found in the temple constantly, speaking the praises of God.

✿

36: Jn 20, 19f.
40f: Jn 21, 9f.13.
46: 9, 22.
47: Mt 3, 2; 28, 19f;
    Mk 16, 15f; Acts 10, 41.

49: Jn 14, 26; Acts 1, 4;
    2, 3f.
50f: Mk 16, 19; Acts 1, 9ff.

The Gospel According to John

Introduction

The reputed author of the fourth gospel was John, son of Zebedee, who published it at Ephesus in the last years of his life. Within the Christian community, this is the only important tradition that has come down from antiquity concerning this gospel. In its essentials the tradition is found in Irenaeus ("Adversus Haereses," 3:1, 1) toward the close of the second century. He claims to have had it from Polycarp of Smyrna, who knew John. Thus "the beloved disciple" himself becomes identified as the source of the tradition (19, 35; 21, 24); cf 19, 26f.

While the attestation of this tradition is impressive, it should be remembered that for the ancients authorship was a much broader concept than it is today. In their time a man could be called the "author" of a work if he was the authority behind it, even though he did not write it. Modern critical analysis makes it difficult to accept the idea that the gospel as it now stands was written by one man. Chapter 21 seems to have been added after the gospel was completed (20, 30f); it exhibits a Greek style somewhat different from the rest of the work. The Prologue (1, 1-18) was apparently an independent hymn, subsequently adapted to serve as a preface to the gospel. Within the gospel itself there are signs of some disorder; e. g., there are two endings to Jesus' discourse at the Last Supper (14, 31; 18, 1).

To solve these problems, scholars have proposed various rearrangements that would produce a smoother order. However, more and more students of this gospel are coming to believe that the inconsistencies were probably produced by subsequent editing in which homogeneous materials were added to a shorter original. Other difficulties for the theory of eyewitness authorship are presented by the gospel's highly developed theology, and by certain elements of its literary style. For instance, some of the miracles of Jesus have been worked into highly effective dramatic scenes (ch 9); there has been a careful attempt to have the miracles followed by discourses which explain them (chs 5 and 6); the sayings of Jesus have been woven into long discourses of a quasi-poetic form resembling the speeches of personified Wisdom in the Old Testament.

How can the ancient tradition about the authorship of the fourth gospel be reconciled with modern biblical scholarship? Many scholars, Protestant and Catholic, are coming to accept a theory which tries to do justice to both. This proposes that behind the fourth gospel there was an ancient tradition of the words and deeds of Jesus, a tradition of real historical value, similar in general to, but independent of, the traditions that underlie the synoptic gospels. Thus, just as the name "Peter" has been associated with one of the traditions behind the synoptic gospels, so the name "John, son of Zebedee," may well be attached to the tradition behind the fourth gospel. John, as one of the three privileged disciples who were closest to Jesus, may have preserved and preached this basic tradition about Jesus.

The theory further proposes that it was one of John's disciples who actually developed the tradition into the pattern of the gospel as we know it. Perhaps, under John's guidance, this disciple was the real evangelist: an artistic and theological genius, who gave to the tradition the distinctive literary features which we call "Johannine," and who used the gospel message to respond to the pressing theological needs of his time. All of this would have required the selection and reworking of details from the tradition, and would probably have been based on a long history of Johannine preaching.

Later, the theory continues, still another disciple of John was responsible for the editing of the evangelist's original gospel. He is often called the disciple-redactor, or editor, to distinguish him from the disciple-evangelist. This man added other material which had come down from the wide circle of Johannine disciples (the Prologue and chapter 21), and seems to have included a large body of material from the disciple-evangelist which had not been incorporated into the original edition of the gospel. For instance, if the Last Discourse of Jesus in the original edition came to an end at 14, 31, the redactor added three more chapters of Last Discourse material (15–17), quite like the material in chapter 14 and even duplicating it. But since he did not wish to tamper with the original gospel, he let the original conclusion of 14, 31 stand.

Such a theory respects the ancient tradition that John the Apostle was the authority behind the gospel. It also explains, on the basis of critical analysis, that a disciple of John, here called the disciple-evangelist, was not an eyewitness, and that more than one hand was involved in the writing of the gospel. Moreover it teaches us how to evaluate what we find therein. This gospel contains many valid historical details about Jesus not found in the synoptic gospels: e. g., that after his baptism by John, Jesus was engaged in a baptizing ministry before he changed exclusively to preaching (3, 22); that Jesus' public ministry lasted for several years (see note on 2, 13); that he traveled to Jerusalem on various feasts and met serious opposition long before his death (2, 14ff; chs 5 and 7-10); that he was put to death on the day before Passover (18, 28). These events are not always in order, however, because of the development and editing that ensued.

The fourth gospel is not simply history; the narrative has been organized and adapted to serve the evangelist's theological purposes as well. Among them are: opposition to the synagogue and to such of John the Baptizer's sectarians as tried to exalt their master at Jesus' expense; desire to show that Jesus was the Messiah; desire to convince Christians that their religious belief and practice must be rooted in Jesus. Such theological purposes have caused the evangelist to bring to the fore motifs which, as can be seen by comparison with the synoptic gospels, were not so clear in the synoptic account of Jesus' ministry, e. g., the explicit emphasis on his divinity.

The polemic between the synagogue and the church influenced Johannine language toward harshness especially by reason of the hostility toward Jesus manifested by the authorities—Pharisees and Sadducees—who are referred to frequently as "the Jews" (see note on Jn 1, 19). Such opponents are even described in Jn 8, 44 as springing from their father the devil, whose conduct they imitate in opposing God by rejecting the One whom God has sent. Today, there is a very real effort by Christians and Jews to understand and respect one another and thus to eliminate all embittered criticism.

The final editing of the gospel and arrangement in its present form probably dates between A. D. 90 and 100. Ephesus is still favored by most scholars as the place of composition, though some have proposed the Syrian city of Antioch.

The chief divisions of the Gospel of John are as follows:

    I: Prologue 1, 1-18
    II: The Book of Signs (1, 19—12, 50)
    III: The Book of Glory (13, 1—20, 31)
    IV: Appendix: The Resurrection Appearance in Galilee (21, 1-25)

I: PROLOGUE

1   **1***† IN THE BEGINNING was the Word;
    the Word was in God's presence,
    and the Word was God.
2   He was present to God in the beginning.
3*† Through him all things came into being,
    and apart from him nothing came to be.
4*   Whatever came to be in him, found life,
    life for the light of men.
5*† The light shines on in darkness,
    a darkness that did not overcome it.

6*† There was a man named John sent by God, **7*** who came as a witness to testify to the light, so that through him all men might believe—**8** but only to testify to the light, for he himself was not the light. **9***† The real light which gives light to every man was coming into the world.

10   He was in the world,
    and through him the world was made,
    yet the world did not know who he was.
11† To his own he came,
    yet his own did not accept him.

12*† Any who did accept him
    he empowered to become children of God.

These are they who believe in his name—**13***† who were begotten not by blood, nor by carnal desire, nor by man's willing it, but by God.

14*† The Word became flesh
    and made his dwelling among us,

---

† 1, 1-18: The Prologue is a hymn, formally poetic in style—perhaps originally an independent composition and only later adapted and edited to serve as an overture to the gospel. Its closest parallel is found in the christological hymns in Col 1, 15-20; Phil 2, 6-11; 1 Tm 3, 16. The Roman writer Pliny (A. D. 111) mentions the Christians of Asia Minor as singing hymns to Christ as a god. Commentators are divided on whether the initial reference to the earthly ministry of Jesus Christ is in 1, 9 or 1, 14.

1, 1: *In the beginning:* these, the first words of Gn 1, 1, serve as the Hebrew title of that book. Here, however, they introduce the two verses describing the situation before creation. *Was:* three times in the first verse this verb is used of the Word. First, it indicates timeless existence; next, relationship to the Father; finally, identity with God.

1, 3f: In the Clementine Vulgate, the words *whatever came to be* are put at the end of v 3: "*Apart from him*, nothing came into being which came to be. In him was life, etc." The best evidence favors the division given above. *Found life:* literally "was life."

1, 3: The creation was through the Word and in the Word; cf Col 1, 16.

1, 5: *Overcome:* if this translation is accepted, hostility between darkness and light is indicated, perhaps a reference to the sin of Gn 3. Other possible translations—"grasp," "comprehend," "receive"—are preferred by those who regard the verse as referring to the ministry of Jesus.

1, 6ff: These are more prosaic than the other verses of the Prologue, and their content is intrusive, separating 5 from 9 or 10. Vv 6ff, perhaps including 9, are to be regarded as a parenthetical addition by the Johannine editor of the hymn. For him, the reference to the ministry of Jesus came after 6ff.

1, 9: The earlier versions make *every man* (instead of *the light*) the subject of *coming into the world.*

1, 11: *His own:* in 11a, a neuter expression, probably meaning his own country, the Holy Land; in 11b, *his own* is masculine, and refers to Israel or to the Jews.

1, 12f: *Empowered:* or "gave authority." *These are they who believe in his name,* etc.: many regard these verses as part of the final edition rather than of the original hymn.

1, 13: *Who were begotten:* some minor textual witnesses and some early Fathers read "he who was begotten"—a reference to Jesus. This is probably a free adaptation of the text to illustrate the virgin birth. *Not by blood . . . desire:* no human agency, male or female, begets God's children. That is done through baptism and the Holy Spirit; cf 3, 5.

1, 14: *Made his dwelling:* literally, "set up his tent, or tabernacle." In the Exodus the tabernacle or tent of meeting was the site of God's dwelling among men (Ex 25, 8f); now that site is the Word-made-flesh. *Glory:* the glory of God (the visible manifestation of his majesty in power), which once filled the tabernacle (Ex 40, 34) and the temple (1 Kgs 8, 10f.27), is now centered in Jesus. *Filled with enduring love:* It is not clear whether *filled* modifies *glory* or *Word* or *only Son.* The two words *love* and *enduring* (often translated "grace and truth") represent two Old Testament terms used to describe the dealings of the God of the covenant with Israel (Ex 34, 6): *love* signifying God's love in choosing Israel and his steadfast expression of that love in the covenant; *enduring* signifying his faithfulness to his covenant promises. Jesus is a new manifestation of God's covenant, *enduring love,* replacing the old; cf v 16.

---

*
1/1: 10, 30; Gn 1, 1-5;
    Prv 8, 22-25; 1 Jn 1, 1f;
    Rv 19, 14.
3: Ps 33, 9; 1 Cor 8, 6;
    Col. 1, 15; Heb 1, 2.
4: 5, 26.
5: 3, 19; 8, 12; 1 Jn 2, 8.

6: Mt 3, 1; Mk 1, 4;
    Lk 3, 2f.
7: 1, 19-34.
9: 8, 12; 12, 46.
12: Gal 3, 26; 4, 6f;
    1 Jn 3, 2.
13: 3, 5f.
14: 1 Jn 1, 2.

and we have seen his glory:
the glory of an only Son coming from the Father,
filled with enduring love.

15*†John testified to him by proclaiming: "This is he of whom I said, 'The one who comes after me ranks ahead of me, for he was before me.' "

16†Of his fullness
we have all had a share—
love following upon love.

17*†For while the law was given through Moses, this enduring love came through Jesus Christ. **18***No one has ever seen God. It is God the only Son, ever at the Father's side, who has revealed him.

II: THE BOOK OF SIGNS

Testimony of John to the Envoys

19†THE TESTIMONY JOHN GAVE when the Jews sent priests and Levites from Jerusalem to ask, "Who are you?" **20***was the direct statement, "I am not the Messiah." **21**†They questioned him further, "Who, then? Elijah?" "I am not Elijah," he answered. "Are you the Prophet?" "No," he replied.

22Finally they said to him: "Tell us who you are, so that we can give some answer to those who sent us. What do you have to say for yourself?" **23***He said, quoting the prophet Isaiah, "I am

'a voice in the desert, crying out:
Make straight the way of the Lord!' "

24†Those whom the Pharisees had sent **25**proceeded to question him further: "If you are not the Messiah, nor Elijah, nor the Prophet, why do you baptize?" **26***John answered them: "I baptize with water. There is one among you whom you do not recognize—**27**the one who is to come after me—the strap of whose sandal I am not worthy to unfasten."

28†This happened in Bethany, across the Jordan, where John was baptizing.

His Testimony to Jesus

29†The next day, when John caught sight of Jesus coming toward him, he exclaimed:

"Look! There is the Lamb of God
who takes away the sin of the world!

30*†It is he of whom I said:

'After me is to come a man

who ranks ahead of me,
because he was before me.'

31I confess I did not recognize him, though the very reason I came baptizing with water was that he might be revealed to Israel."

32*†John gave this testimony also:

"I saw the Spirit descend
like a dove from the sky,
and it came to rest on him.

33*But I did not recognize him. The one who sent me to baptize with water told me, 'When you see the Spirit descend and rest on someone, it is he who is to baptize with the Holy Spirit.' **34***†Now I have seen for

---

† 1, 15: This verse, of the same nature as 6ff, seems to be drawn from v 30; it interrupts vv 14 and 16, which belong together.

1, 16: *Love following upon love:* the endless accumulation of God's goodness in Jesus. Other possible translations are: "love in place of love"—the love manifested in Jesus replacing the love manifested in Moses (cf. 1, 17)—and "love for love"—our love corresponding to Jesus' love.

1, 17f: Many commentators regard these verses as explanation rather than part of the pre-Prologue hymn. *God the only Son:* other MSS read "the Son, the only one" or "the only Son." *Ever at the Father's side:* literally, "in [to] the bosom of the Father."

1, 19: *The Jews:* throughout most of the gospel, with the notable exception of chapters 11 and 12, the "Jews" are not the Jewish people as such. They are the hostile authorities, the Pharisees and Sadducees, particularly those in Jerusalem, who refuse to believe in Jesus. The use of the term reflects the atmosphere at the end of the first century, when polemics expressed the hostility between the synagogue and the church.

1, 21: *"Elijah?" "I am not":* the Baptizer himself did not claim to be Elijah returned to earth; with greater insight, Jesus (Mt 11, 14) explained the Baptizer's career as fulfilling the role Malachi (4, 5) attributed to Elijah. *The Prophet:* probably the prophet like Moses of Dt 18, 15; cf Acts 3, 22.

1, 24: *Those whom the Pharisees had sent:* it would be very unusual for the priestly and levitical envoys of v 19 to have been of the Pharisees' party rather than that of the Sadducees. Some would translate: "There were some Pharisees sent," or "Some of the Pharisees' party were sent." If the latter translation is correct, the evangelist has simplified party distinctions, since the Sadducees were no longer important in the late first century.

1, 28: *Bethany, across the Jordan:* this is not the Bethany near Jerusalem (11, 18); the actual site is unknown. "Bethabara" ("place of crossing over") is read by the Old Syriac, and Origen accepted it as the correct reading.

1, 29: *The Lamb of God:* perhaps, for the Baptizer this meant the great apocalyptic lamb who would destroy evil in the world (Rv 17, 14). The evangelist may see a reference to the paschal lamb, and/or to the suffering servant led like a lamb to the slaughter as an offering for sin (Is 53, 7.10).

1, 30: *He was before me:* preexistence is a Johannine theme (1, 1; 8, 58; 17, 5).

1, 32: John the Evangelist does not actually describe the baptism of Jesus, but the occasion of the vision narrated here is almost certainly to be understood as the baptism.

1, 34: *God's chosen One:* the better Greek MSS have "God's Son." The heavenly voice in the synoptic gospels proclaims: "This is my beloved Son" (Mt 3, 17; Mk 1, 11; Lk 3, 22). It is difficult to see why scribes would change "God's Son" to "God's chosen One," and easy to see why for harmonizing and theological purposes a change in the opposite direction would be made. *Chosen One* is probably a reference to the Servant of Yahweh (Is 42, 1).

---

* 15: 1, 30; 3, 27-30.   30: 1, 15; Mt 3, 11;
17: Dt 33, 4.   Mk 1, 7; Lk 3, 16.
18: 6, 46; Ex 33, 20;   32: Is 11, 2; Mt 3, 16;
      1 Jn 4, 12.   Mk 1, 10; Lk 3, 21f.
20: 3, 28; Acts 13, 25.   33: Mt 3, 11; Mk 1, 8;
23: Is 40, 3; Mt 3, 3;   Lk 3, 16.
      Mk 1, 2; Lk 3, 4.   34: Is 42, 1; Mt 3, 17;
26: Mt 3, 11; Mk 1, 8;   Mk 1, 11; Lk 9, 35.
      Lk 3, 16.

myself and have testified, 'This is God's chosen One.' "

The First Disciples

35The next day John was there again with two of his disciples. **36**As he watched Jesus walk by he said, "Look! There is the Lamb of God!" **37**†The two disciples heard what he said, and followed Jesus. **38**When Jesus turned around and noticed them following him, he asked them, "What are you looking for?" They said to him, "Rabbi (which means Teacher), where do you stay?" **39**†"Come and see," he answered. So they went to see where he was lodged, and stayed with him that day. (It was about four in the afternoon.)

40One of the two who had followed him after hearing John was Simon Peter's brother Andrew. **41***†The first thing he did was seek out his brother Simon and tell him, "We have found the Messiah!" (This term means the Anointed.) **42***He brought him to Jesus, who looked at him and said, "You are Simon, son of John; your name shall be Cephas" (which is rendered Peter).

43†The next day he wanted to set out for Galilee, but first he came upon Philip. "Follow me," Jesus said to him. **44**Now Philip was from Bethsaida, the same town as Andrew and Peter. **45**Philip sought out Nathanael and told him, "We have found the one Moses spoke of in the law—the prophets too—Jesus, son of Joseph, from Nazareth." **46**Nathanael's response to that was, "Can anything good come from Nazareth?" and Philip replied, "Come, see for yourself." **47**†When Jesus saw Nathanael coming toward him, he remarked: "This man is a true Israelite. There is no guile in him." **48**"How do you know me?" Nathanael asked him. "Before Philip called you," Jesus answered, "I saw you under the fig tree." **49***"Rabbi," said Nathanael, "you are the Son of God; you are the king of Israel." **50**†Jesus responded: "Do you believe just because I told you I saw you under the fig tree? You will see much greater things than that."

51He went on to tell them, "I solemnly assure you, you shall see the sky opened and the angels of God ascending and descending on the Son of Man."

The Wedding at Cana

2 **1***ON the third day there was a wedding at Cana in Galilee, and the mother of Jesus was there. **2**Jesus and his disciples had likewise been invited to the celebration. **3**At a certain point the wine ran out, and Jesus' mother told him, "They have no more wine." **4***†Jesus replied, "Woman, how does this concern of yours involve me? My hour has not yet come." **5**His mother instructed those waiting on table, "Do whatever he tells you." **6**†As prescribed for Jewish ceremonial washings, there were at hand six stone water jars, each one holding fifteen to twenty-five

gallons. **7**"Fill those jars with water," Jesus ordered, at which they filled them to the brim. **8**†"Now," he said, "draw some out and take it to the waiter in charge." They did as he instructed them. **9**The waiter in charge tasted the water made wine, without knowing where it had come from; only the waiters knew, since they had drawn the water. Then the waiter in charge called the groom over **10**and remarked to him: "People usually serve the choice wine first; then when the guests have been drinking awhile, a lesser vintage. What you have done is keep the choice wine until now." **11***Jesus performed this first of his signs at Cana in Galilee. Thus did he reveal his glory, and his disciples believed in him.

12†After this he went down to Capernaum, along with his mother and brothers [and his disciples] but they stayed there only a few days.

---

†

1, 37: *Two disciples:* one is Andrew (v 40); the other, unnamed here, is traditionally identified as John, son of Zebedee. See note on 13, 23.

1, 39: *Four in the afternoon:* literally, the tenth hour. The evangelists seem to use the Roman method of reckoning time; the hours from sunrise (6 A. M.) are counted as the daylight hours. Some suggest that it was a Friday afternoon; the next day, beginning at sunset, would be the sabbath, which was why they *stayed with him.*

1, 41: The reading of *first* is uncertain: our interpretation follows the best MSS, including the early papyri. *The Messiah:* the actual Aramaic word *meshiha*—"anointed one"—appears in the Greek as the transliterated *messias* here and in 4, 25. Elsewhere the Greek translation *christos* is used.

1, 43: The subject of the first two verbs is not clear: grammatically it could be Peter, but logically it is probably Jesus.

1, 47: *A true Israelite:* Jacob was the first to bear the name "Israel" (Gn 22, 28ff), but Jacob was a man of guile (Gn 27, 35).

1, 50f: *You will see . . . :* these verses may be a play on the name "Israel," which was popularly interpreted as "a man who sees God." There may be a reference in v 51 to Jacob's ladder (Gn 28, 12). *I solemnly assure you:* literally, "Amen, amen." The double "amen" is characteristic of John.

2, 4: *Woman:* this form of address, normally given by Jesus to the women he encountered during his ministry (Mt 15, 28; Lk 13, 12) is entirely courteous. However, there is no attestation of a son's use of "woman," without any qualification, to address his mother; and so some commentators suggest a symbolic meaning. Mary is again called "woman" in 19, 26, and the mother of the Messiah in Rv 12, 1-5 is described as "a woman clothed with the sun." Is there symbolic reference to Eve, "the woman" of Genesis? *How does this concern of yours involve me?:* literally, "What is this to me and to you?"—a Hebrew expression; e. g., 2 Kgs 3, 13, where it denies the speaker's involvement in a project proposed by another. *My hour has not yet come:* the translation of this as a question ("Has not my hour now come?") is quite unlikely from a comparison with 7, 6.30. The *hour* is the hour of Jesus' passion, death, resurrection and ascension (13, 1).

2, 6: *Fifteen to twenty-five gallons:* literally, "two or three measures"; the measure in question was of eight or nine gallons.

2, 8: *Waiter in charge:* it is not clear if the official is a major-domo, or a friend of the family who acted as master of ceremonies; see Sir 32, 1.

2, 12: This transitional verse may be a harmonization with the synoptic tradition in Lk 4, 31 and Mt 4, 13. There are many textual variants.

❋

41: 4, 25.   4: 7, 30; 8, 20; 12, 23;
42: Mt 16, 18; Mk 3, 16.   13, 1.
49: 12, 13.   11: 4, 54.
2/1: 4, 46.

Cleansing of the Temple

13***†**As the Jewish Passover was near, Jesus went up to Jerusalem. **14†**In the temple precincts he came upon people engaged in selling oxen, sheep and doves, and others seated changing coins. **15†**He made a [kind of] whip of cords and drove sheep and oxen alike out of the temple area, and knocked over the money-changers' tables, spilling their coins. **16**He told those who were selling doves: "Get them out of here! Stop turning my Father's house into a marketplace!" **17***His disciples recalled the words of Scripture: "Zeal for your house consumes me."

18*At this the Jews responded, "What sign can you show us authorizing you to do these things?" **19*****†**"Destroy this temple," was Jesus' answer, "and in three days I will raise it up." **20**They retorted, "This temple took forty-six years to build, and you are going to 'raise it up in three days'!" **21**Actually he was talking about the temple of his body. **22***Only after Jesus had been raised from the dead did his disciples recall that he had said this, and come to believe the Scripture and the word he had spoken.

23*While he was in Jerusalem during the Passover festival, many believed in his name, for they could see the signs he was performing. **24**For his part, Jesus would not trust himself to them because he knew them all. **25**He needed no one to give him testimony about human nature. He was well aware of what was in man's heart.

Nicodemus

3 **1***A certain Pharisee named Nicodemus, a member of the Jewish Sanhedrin, **2***came to him at night. "Rabbi," he said, "we know you are a teacher come from God, for no man can perform signs and wonders such as you perform unless God is with him." **3†**Jesus gave him this answer:

"I solemnly assure you,
no one can see the reign of God
unless he is begotten from above."

4*"How can a man be born again once he is old?" retorted Nicodemus. "Can he return to his mother's womb and be born over again?" **5†**Jesus replied:

"I solemnly assure you,
no one can enter into God's kingdom
without being begotten of water and Spirit.
6*Flesh begets flesh,
Spirit begets spirit.
7 Do not be surprised that I tell you
you must all be begotten from above.

8***†**The wind blows where it will.
You hear the sound it makes
but you do not know where it comes from,
or where it goes.
So it is with everyone begotten of the Spirit."

9"How can such a thing happen?" asked Nicodemus. **10**Jesus responded: "You hold the office of teacher of Israel and still you do not understand these matters?

11*"I solemnly assure you,
we are talking about what we know,
we are testifying to what we have seen,
but you do not accept our testimony.
12* If you do not believe
when I tell you about earthly things,
how are you to believe
when I tell you about those of heaven?
13***†**No one has gone up to heaven
except the One who came down from there—
the Son of Man [who is in heaven].
14***†**Just as Moses lifted up the serpent in the desert,
so must the Son of Man be lifted up,

---

† **2, 13:** *Passover:* this is the first Passover mentioned in John; a second is mentioned in 6, 4, a third in 13, 1. If these chronological indications are to be taken literally, they point to a ministry of at least two years.

2, 14ff: This is almost certainly the same cleansing the other gospels place in the last days of Jesus' life (Mt, on the day Jesus entered Jerusalem; Mk, on the next day). The order of events in the gospel narratives is often determined by theological motives rather than by chronological data.

2, 15: *Sheep and oxen:* in John the cleansing is a more violent attack on the temple, because the animals necessary for sacrifice are expelled.

2, 19: This saying is reported by the false witnesses in the synoptic account of Jesus' trial before Caiaphas (Mk 14, 58; Mt 26, 61); see also Mk 15, 29; Acts 6, 14. According to John, Jesus says that it is the Jewish authorities themselves who will destroy the temple; the false witnesses say that Jesus threatened to destroy it.

3, 3: *Begotten:* the Greek verb can mean "born" from a female principle, or "begotten" by a male principle. As in 1, 13, John primarily means it as "begotten," though many early versions translate as "born" or even, with heightened baptismal symbolism, "reborn." *From above:* the Greek term *anothen* means both "again" and "from above." V 31 below shows that Jesus means it as "from above," but Nicodemus misunderstands. (A misunderstanding that brings out Jesus' teaching is a common literary device in John.)

3, 5: The Council of Trent declared that *water* here is not a metaphor but means real water. This passage has had an important role in baptismal theology.

3, 8: *Wind:* the Greek word *pneuma* means both "wind" and "spirit." We can see from the context that John is playing on the double meaning, with wind as the primary comparison.

3, 13: *Has gone up to heaven:* the seeming reference to the ascension in the past tense is difficult, but tenses in John seem to be somewhat timeless; see 8, 58. *Who is in heaven:* if this is a true reading, it may be compared to 1, 18.

3, 14: *Lifted up:* the first of three references (8, 28; 12, 32) to the "lifting up" of Jesus the Son of Man: i. e., in crucifixion, resurrection, and ascension. These are comparable to the three references to the passion and resurrection in the synoptics (Mk 8, 31; 9, 30; 10, 31).

---

* 13-22: Mt 21, 12f; 2: 9, 16.33; 10, 21.
  Mk 11, 15ff. 4: 1, 13.
  Lk 19, 45f. 6: 6, 63; 1 Cor 15, 44-50.
  17: Ps 69, 10. 8: Acts 2, 2ff.
  18: 6, 30. 11: 3, 32.34; 8, 14;
  19: Mt 26, 61. Mt 11, 27.
  22: 5, 39. 12: 6, 62ff; Wis 9, 16f.
  23: 4, 45. 13: 1, 18.
  3/1: 7, 50f; 19, 39. 14: Nm 21, 9; Wis 16, 5ff.

15† that all who believe
     may have eternal life in him.

16*†Yes, God so loved the world
     that he gave his only Son,
     that whoever believes in him may not die
     but may have eternal life.

17*†God did not send the Son into the world
     to condemn the world,
     but that the world might be saved through him.

18 Whoever believes in him avoids condemnation,
     but whoever does not believe is already
         condemned
     for not believing in the name of God's only Son.

19*†The judgment of condemnation is this:
     the light came into the world,
     but men loved darkness rather than light
     because their deeds were wicked.

20* Everyone who practices evil
     hates the light;
     he does not come near it
     for fear his deeds will be exposed.

21* But he who acts in truth
     comes into the light,
     to make clear
     that his deeds are done in God."

Final Witness of the Baptizer

22*†Later on, Jesus and his disciples came into Judean territory, and he spent some time with them there baptizing. 23†John too was baptizing at Aenon near Salim where water was plentiful, and people kept coming to be baptized. 24(John, of course, had not yet been thrown into prison.) 25†A controversy about purification arose between John's disciples and a certain Jew. 26So they came to John, saying, "Rabbi, the man who was with you across the Jordan—the one about whom you have been testifying—is baptizing now, and everyone is flocking to him." 27*†John answered:

     "No one can lay hold on anything
         unless it is given him from on high.

28* You yourselves are witnesses to the fact that I said: 'I am not the Messiah; I am sent before him.'

29*†"It is the groom who has the bride.
     The groom's best man
     waits there listening for him
     and is overjoyed to hear his voice.
     That is my joy, and it is complete.

30 He must increase,
     while I must decrease.

Discourse Concluded

31†"The One who comes from above is above all;
     the one who is of the earth is earthly,
     and he speaks on an earthly plane.
     The One who comes from heaven [who is above
         all]

32* testifies to what he has seen and heard,
     but no one accepts his testimony.

33* Whoever does accept this testimony
     certifies that God is truthful.

34 For the One whom God has sent
     speaks the words of God;
     he does not ration his gift of the Spirit.

35* The Father loves the Son
     and has given everything over to him.

36 Whoever believes in the Son
     has life eternal.
     Whoever disobeys the Son
     will not see life,
     but must endure the wrath of God."

4 ¹NOW when Jesus learned that the Pharisees had heard that he was winning over and baptizing more disciples than John ²†(in fact, however, it was not Jesus himself who baptized, but his disciples), ³he left Judea and started back for Galilee again.

The Samaritan Woman

⁴He had to pass through Samaria, ⁵*†and his journey brought him to a Samaritan town named Shechem

---

† 3, 15: This might be translated "that everyone who believes in him may have eternal life." *Eternal life,* used here for the first time in John, stresses the quality of the life rather than its duration.

3, 16: *Gave:* a reference to both the incarnation and the death of Jesus; cf Rom 8, 32.

3, 17ff: *Condemn . . . judgment:* the same Greek root is involved, and it has both shades of meaning. Jesus' coming provokes judgment; his purpose is to save, but some condemn themselves by turning from the light.

3, 19: John stresses that judgment is not only a matter of the future but is partially realized here and now.

3, 22: *Baptizing:* that after his baptism Jesus conducted a baptizing ministry is not mentioned by the synoptics; cf 4, 2.

3, 23: *Aenon near Salim:* uncertain site, either in the upper Jordan valley or in Samaria.

3, 25: *Controversy:* perhaps this dispute concerned the relative value of the two baptisms or the value of baptism vs. Jewish purifications (2, 6).

3, 27: *No one:* it is more likely that this refers to Jesus than to the Baptizer.

3, 29: *Groom's best man:* the one who arranged the wedding and acted as go-between for groom and bride.

3, 31-36: It is uncertain whether these words are spoken by the Baptizer, by Jesus, or by the evangelist. Perhaps an originally independent discourse of Jesus has been brought here by way of comment on the two preceding scenes of ch 3. *His gift:* it is uncertain to whom the "his" refers: to God or to Jesus.

4, 2: An editorial refinement on 3, 22, perhaps against followers of the Baptizer in the late first century who exalted the Baptizer above Jesus.

4, 5f: *Shechem:* most MSS have Sychar which St. Jerome identifies with Shechem. He may be correct in saying that copyists mistakenly put "Sychar" for "Shechem." *Jacob's well* (un-

*   16: 1 Jn 4, 9.   28: Lk 3, 15.
     17: 12, 47.   29: Mt 9, 15.
     19: 8, 12.   32: 3, 11.
     20: Jb 24, 13-17.   33f: 8, 26; 1 Jn 5, 10.
     21: Mt 5, 14ff.   35: Mt 28, 18.
     22f: 4, 1f.   4/5: Gn 33, 18f.
     27: 19, 11; 2 Cor 3, 5;
         Heb 5, 4.

near the plot of land which Jacob had given to his son Joseph. **⁶**This was the site of Jacob's well. Jesus, tired from his journey, sat down at the well.

The hour was about noon. **⁷**When a Samaritan woman came to draw water, Jesus said to her, "Give me a drink." **⁸**(His disciples had gone off to the town to buy provisions.) **⁹**✻†The Samaritan woman said to him, "You are a Jew. How can you ask me, a Samaritan and a woman, for a drink?" (Recall that Jews have nothing to do with Samaritans.) **¹⁰**†Jesus replied:

"If only you recognized God's gift,
and who it is that is asking you for a drink,
you would have asked him instead,
and he would have given you living water."

¹¹"Sir," she challenged him, "you do not have a bucket and this well is deep. Where do you expect to get this flowing water? **¹²**Surely you do not pretend to be greater than our ancestor Jacob, who gave us this well and drank from it with his sons and his flocks?" **¹³**Jesus replied:

"Everyone who drinks this water
will be thirsty again.
¹⁴✻But whoever drinks the water I give him
will never be thirsty;
no, the water I give
shall become a fountain within him,
leaping up to provide eternal life."

¹⁵The woman said to him, "Give me this water, sir, so that I shall not grow thirsty and have to keep coming here to draw water."

¹⁶He said to her, "Go, call your husband, and then come back here." **¹⁷**"I have no husband," replied the woman. "You are right in saying you have no husband!" Jesus exclaimed. **¹⁸**"The fact is, you have had five, and the man you are living with now is not your husband. What you said is true."

¹⁹†"Sir," answered the woman, "I can see you are a prophet. **²⁰**†Our ancestors worshiped on this mountain, but you people claim that Jerusalem is the place where men ought to worship God." **²¹**Jesus told her:

"Believe me, woman,
an hour is coming
when you will worship the Father
neither on this mountain
nor in Jerusalem.
²²✻You people worship what you do not understand,
while we understand what we worship;
after all, salvation is from the Jews.
²³†Yet an hour is coming, and is already here,
when authentic worshipers
will worship the Father in Spirit and truth.
Indeed, it is just such worshipers
the Father seeks.

²⁴God is Spirit,
and those who worship him
must worship in Spirit and truth."

²⁵†The woman said to him: "I know there is a Messiah coming." (This term means Anointed.) "When he comes, he will tell us everything." **²⁶**✻Jesus replied, "I who speak to you am he."

²⁷His disciples, returning at this point, were surprised that Jesus was speaking with a woman. No one put a question, however, such as "What do you want of him?" or "Why are you talking with her?" **²⁸**The woman then left her water jar and went off into the town. She said to the people: **²⁹**"Come and see someone who told me everything I ever did! Could this not be the Messiah?" **³⁰**At that they set out from the town to meet him.

³¹Meanwhile the disciples were urging him, "Rabbi, eat something." **³²**But he told them:

"I have food to eat
of which you do not know."

³³At this the disciples said to one another. "Do you suppose that someone has brought him something to eat?" **³⁴**✻Jesus explained to them:

"Doing the will of him who sent me
and bringing his work to completion
is my food.
³⁵✻†Do you not have a saying:
'Four months more
and it will be harvest!'?
Listen to what I say:
Open your eyes and see!
The fields are shining for harvest!

---

† mentioned in the Old Testament) is the well of Shechem. The town is situated in the valley between Mounts Gerizim and Ebal; cf Dt 27; Jos 3, 30.

4, 9: Samaritan women were regarded as ritually impure, and therefore Jews were forbidden to drink from any vessel they had handled.

4, 10f: *Living water:* Jesus is speaking of the water of life; the woman thinks of *flowing water,* so much more desirable than stale cistern water. This is a typical example of Johannine use of a hearer's misunderstanding; cf note on 3, 3.

4, 19: *Sir:* the original word (used also in v 11) means either "Sir" or "Lord"; here the latter term may be more appropriate if the woman is moving toward faith.

4, 20: The Samaritans included among the ten commandments the obligation to worship on Mount Gerizim. It was an ancient holy place. "Ebal" is probably an anti-Samaritan Jewish emendation of "Gerizim"; cf Dt 27, 4.

4, 23: *In Spirit and truth:* this is not a reference to an interior worship within man's spirit. The Spirit is the Spirit of truth (14, 16f), the Spirit given by God which reveals truth and raises up man to worship God on the appropriate level. This idea presupposes the "begetting by Spirit" in 3, 5.

4, 25: The expectations of the Samaritans are expressed here in more familiar Jewish terminology. They did not expect a messianic king of the house of David but a prophet like Moses (Dt 18, 15).

4, 35: This is probably a proverb rather than a real time indication; cf Mt 9, 37f.

✻
9: Sir 50, 25f; Mt 10, 5.   26: 9, 37.
14: 6, 35; 7, 37ff; Jl 4, 18.   34: 6, 38; 17, 4.
22: 2 Kgs 17, 27.   35: Mt 9, 37f; Lk 10, 2.

36*†The reaper already collects his wages
   and gathers a yield for eternal life,
   that sower and reaper may rejoice together.
37 Here we have the saying verified:
   'One man sows; another reaps.'
38 I sent you to reap
   what you had not worked for.
   Others have done the labor,
   and you have come into their gain.''

39Many Samaritans from that town believed in him on the strength of the woman's word of testimony: "He told me everything I ever did." **40**The result was that, when these Samaritans came to him, they begged him to stay with them awhile. So he stayed there two days, **41**and through his own spoken word many more came to faith. **42**As they told the woman: "No longer does our faith depend on your story. We have heard for ourselves, and we know that this really is the Savior of the world."

Return to Galilee

43When the two days were over, he left for Galilee. **44*†**(Jesus himself had testified that no one esteems a prophet in his own country.) **45**When he arrived in Galilee, the people there welcomed him. They themselves had been at the feast and had seen all that he had done in Jerusalem on that occasion.

Second Sign at Cana

46†He went to Cana in Galilee once more, where he had made the water wine. At Capernaum there happened to be a royal official whose son was ill. **47**When he heard that Jesus had come back from Judea to Galilee, he went to him and begged him to come down and restore health to his son, who was near death. **48***Jesus replied, "Unless you people see signs and wonders, you do not believe." **49**"Sir," the royal official pleaded with him, "come down before my child dies." **50†**Jesus told him, "Return home. Your son will live." The man put his trust in the word Jesus spoke to him, and started for home.

51He was on his way there when his servants met him with the news that his boy was going to live. **52**When he asked them at what time the boy had shown improvement, they told him, "The fever left him yesterday afternoon about one." **53†**It was at that very hour, the father realized, that Jesus had told him, "Your son is going to live." He and his whole household thereupon became believers. **54***This was the second sign that Jesus performed on returning from Judea to Galilee.

Cure on a Sabbath Feast

5 **1*†**LATER, on the occasion of a Jewish feast, Jesus went up to Jerusalem. **2†**Now in Jerusalem by the Sheep Pool there is a place with the Hebrew name Bethesda. Its five porticoes **3†**were crowded with sick people lying there blind, lame or disabled **[4]†** [waiting for the movement of the waters]. **5**There was one man who had been sick for thirty-eight years. **6**Jesus, who knew he had been sick a long time, said when he saw him lying there, "Do you want to be healed?" **7**"Sir," the sick man answered, "I do not have anyone to plunge me into the pool once the water has been stirred up. By the time I get there, someone else has gone in ahead of me." **8**Jesus said to him, "Stand up! Pick up your mat and walk!" **9**The man was immediately cured; he picked up his mat and began to walk.

The day was a sabbath. **10*†**Consequently, some of the Jews began telling the man who had been cured, "It is the sabbath, and you are not allowed to carry that mat around." **11**He explained: "It was the man who cured me who told me, 'Pick up your mat and walk.'" **12**"This person who told you to pick it up and walk," they asked, "who is he?" **13**The man who had been restored to health had no idea who it was. The crowd in that place was so great that Jesus had been able to slip away.

---

†

4, 36: *Already:* it is possible that this word belongs at the end of v 35.

4, 44: The parenthetical verse is probably the reminiscence of a tradition similar to that in Mk 6, 4.

4, 46-52: The story of the royal official's son is probably a third version of the story of the centurion's boy (Mt 8, 5-13) or servant (Lk 7, 1-10) found in slightly different forms in the synoptic tradition. The variants are inconsequential details, of the sort that could arise in oral tradition.

4, 50f.53: *Live:* this theme of life will be commented on by Jesus in 5, 21ff.

4, 53: The author ends a section by referring back to its beginning (2, 11).

5, 1: This was probably not a winter feast or the people would not have been in open porticoes. The reference later in the discourse to Moses (5, 45f) leads some scholars to think that the feast was Pentecost (fifty days after Passover; the feast of the giving of the law to Moses on Sinai). Another suggestion is Passover. All that John emphasizes is that it was a sabbath.

5, 2: Another possible translation is "Now in Jerusalem, by the Sheep [Gate], there is a pool with the Hebrew name Bethesda." The name of the region was given to the pool as well. Variants of *Bethesda* are "Bethsaida" and "Be(t)zatha." This pool with its five porticoes has been excavated in recent years in the area northeast of the temple.

5, 3: Some good Western MSS, including St. Jerome's Vulgate, have the additional phrase [waiting for the movement of the wafer]. We may conclude from v 7 that there was an intermittent spring in the pool that bubbled up occasionally. People attributed a curative value to the turbulence produced by the spring.

5, 4: Toward the end of the second century in the West, and among the fourth-century Greek Fathers, there is knowledge of an additional verse: "For [from time to time] an angel of the Lord used to come down into the pool; and the water was stirred up, so the first one to get in [after the bubbling of the water] was healed of whatever sickness he had had." The appearance of the angel is probably a popular explanation of the turbulence and the healing powers attributed to it. This verse is missing in our best early Greek witnesses, and the earliest versions; it is not to be found in St. Jerome's original Vulgate. The vocabulary of the verse is markedly non-Johannine.

5, 10: Carrying a sleeping mat on the sabbath was specifically forbidden in rabbinic law.

✱
36: Ps 126, 5f.   54: 2, 11.
44: Mt 13, 57.   5/1: 6, 4.
48: Mt 12, 38.   10: Ex 20, 8; Jer 17, 21-27.

14†Later on, Jesus found him in the temple precincts and said to him: "Remember, now, you have been cured. Give up your sins so that something worse may not overtake you." **15**The man went off and informed the Jews that Jesus was the one who had cured him.

Discourse on His Sabbath Work

16*It was because Jesus did things such as this on the sabbath that they began to persecute him. **17**†But he had an answer for them:

> "My Father is at work until now,
> and I am at work as well."

18The reason why the Jews were even more determined to kill him was that he not only was breaking the sabbath but, worse still, was speaking of God as his own Father, thereby making himself God's equal.

The Work of the Son

19This was Jesus' answer:

> "I solemnly assure you,
> the Son cannot do anything by himself—
> he can do only what he sees the Father doing.
> For whatever the Father does,
> the Son does likewise.
> **20***For the Father loves the Son
> and everything the Father does he shows him.
> Yes, to your great wonderment,
> he will show him even greater works than these.
> **21***Indeed, just as the Father raises the dead and grants life,
> so the Son grants life to those to whom he wishes.
> **22***The Father himself judges no one,
> but has assigned all judgment to the Son,
> **23** so that all men may honor the Son
> just as they honor the Father.
> He who refuses to honor the Son
> refuses to honor the Father who sent him.
> **24***I solemnly assure you,
> the man who hears my word
> and has faith in him who sent me
> possesses eternal life.
> He does not come under condemnation,
> but has passed from death to life.
> **25***I solemnly assure you,
> an hour is coming, has indeed come,
> when the dead shall hear the voice of the Son of God,
> and those who have heeded it shall live.
> **26***Indeed, just as the Father possesses life in himself,
> so has he granted it to the Son to have life in himself.

27*The Father has given over to him power to pass judgment
> because he is Son of Man;
> **28***no need for you to be surprised at this,
> for an hour is coming
> in which all those in their tombs
> shall hear his voice and come forth.
> **29***Those who have done right shall rise to live;
> the evildoers shall rise to be damned.
> **30***I cannot do anything of myself.
> I judge as I hear,
> and my judgment is honest
> because I am not seeking my own will
> but the will of him who sent me.

Witnesses to Jesus

31*"If I witness on my own behalf,
> you cannot verify my testimony;
> **32**† but there is another who is testifying on my behalf,
> and the testimony he renders me
> I know can be verified.
> **33*** You have sent to John,
> who has testified to the truth.
> **34** (Not that I myself accept such human testimony—
> I refer to these things only for your salvation.)
> **35***†He was the lamp, set aflame and burning bright,
> and for a while you exulted willingly in his light.
> **36*** Yet I have testimony greater than John's,
> namely, the works the Father has given me to accomplish.
> These very works which I perform
> testify on my behalf
> that the Father has sent me.
> **37*** Moreover, the Father who sent me
> has himself given testimony on my behalf.
> His voice you have never heard,
> his form you have never seen,
> **38** neither do you have his word abiding in your hearts
> because you do not believe
> the One he has sent.

---

*

16: 7, 23; Mt 12, 8.	29: Mt 16, 27; Acts 24, 15;
20: 3, 35.	2 Cor 5, 10.
21: Dt 32, 29; 2 Kgs 5, 7;	30: 6, 38.
Wis 16, 13.	31f: 8, 13f.18.
22: Acts 10, 42.	33: 1, 19-27; Mt 11, 10f.
24: 3, 18.	35: 1, 8; Sir 48, 1.
25: 8, 51; 11, 25f.	36: 10, 25.
26: 3, 35; 1 Jn 5, 11.	37: 8, 18; Dt 4, 12.15;
27: 5, 22; Dn 7, 13.	1 Jn 5, 9.
28: 11, 43.	

---

†

5, 14: *Give up your sins:* Jesus never draws a one-to-one connection between sin and sickness or misfortune; cf Jn 9, 3; Lk 12, 1-5. Nevertheless he regards sickness as part of the evil introduced into the world by sin, and his mission is to destroy the kingdom of evil in all its forms (Mk 2, 8-11).

5, 17: The sabbath observance was based on God's resting after the six days of creation, but the Jewish theologians were perfectly aware that divine providence remained active on the sabbath, keeping all things in existence. It was obvious that on the sabbath God gave life in birth and took it away in death. Jesus is claiming the same right to work as the Father, and, in the discourse that follows, the same power over life and death.

5, 32: *Another:* this is generally understood to be the Father who in four different ways gives testimony to Jesus, as indicated in the verse groupings 33f; 36; 37f; 39f.

5, 35: *Lamp:* this may reflect the description of Elijah in Sir 48, 1.

39*†Search the Scriptures
    in which you think you have eternal life—
    they also testify on my behalf.
40   Yet you are unwilling to come to me
    to possess that life.

Unbelief of Jesus' Hearers

41†"It is not that I accept human praise—
42* it is simply that I know you,
    and you do not have the love of God in your
       hearts.
43* I have come in my Father's name,
    yet you do not accept me.
    But let someone come in his own name
    and him you will accept.
44* How can people like you believe,
    when you accept praise from one another
    yet do not seek the glory that comes from the One
       [God]?
45   Do not imagine that I will be your accuser before
       the Father;
    the one to accuse you is Moses
    on whom you have set your hopes.
46* If you believed Moses
    you would then believe me,
    for it was about me that he wrote.
47   But if you do not believe what he wrote,
    how can you believe what I say?"

Multiplication of the Loaves at Passover

6 **1***†LATER on, Jesus crossed the Sea of Galilee [to the shore] of Tiberias; **2**a vast crowd kept following him because they saw the signs he was performing for the sick. **3**Jesus then went up the mountain and sat down there with his disciples. **4***The Jewish feast of Passover was near; **5**†when Jesus looked up and caught sight of a vast crowd coming toward him, he said to Philip, "Where shall we buy bread for these people to eat?" **6**(He knew well what he intended to do but he asked this to test Philip's response.) **7**Philip replied, "Not even with two hundred days' wages could we buy loaves enough to give each of them a mouthful!"

8One of Jesus' disciples, Andrew, Simon Peter's brother, remarked to him, **9**"There is a lad here who has five barley loaves and a couple of dried fish, but what good is that for so many?" **10**Jesus said, "Get the people to recline." Even though the men numbered about five thousand, there was plenty of grass for them to find a place on the ground. **11***Jesus then took the loaves of bread, gave thanks, and passed them around to those reclining there; he did the same with the

dried fish, as much as they wanted. **12**When they had had enough, he told his disciples, "Gather up the crusts that are left over so that nothing will go to waste." **13***At this, they gathered twelve baskets full of pieces left over by those who had been fed with the five barley loaves.

14†When the people saw the sign he had performed they began to say, "This is undoubtedly the Prophet who is to come into the world." **15***At that, Jesus realized that they would come and carry him off to make him king, so he fled back to the mountain alone.

Walking on the Sea

16*As evening drew on, his disciples came down to the lake. **17**They embarked, intending to cross the lake toward Capernaum. By this time it was dark, and Jesus had still not joined them; **18**moreover, with a strong wind blowing, the sea was becoming rough. **19**†Finally, when they had rowed three or four miles, they sighted Jesus approaching the boat, walking on the water. They were frightened, **20**†but he told them, "It is I; do not be afraid." **21**†They wanted to take him into the boat, but suddenly it came aground on the shore they had been approaching.

22†The crowd remained on the other side of the lake. The next day they realized that there had been only one boat there and that Jesus had not left in it with his disciples; rather, they had set out by themselves. **23**†Then some boats came out from Tiberias near the place where they had eaten the bread after the Lord had given thanks. **24**Once the crowd saw that neither

---

† 5, 39: *Search:* this may be a statement: "You search the Scriptures because you think [them] to have eternal life."

5, 41: *Praise:* the same Greek word means "praise" (from men) and "glory" (from God). There will be a play on this in v 44.

6, 1: *Of Tiberias:* if the bracketed clause is omitted, "Tiberias" stands in awkward apposition as another name of the lake. It was only considerably later than Jesus' time that this name was given to the lake, since the city of Tiberias was completed only just before Jesus' ministry. If the clause is left in, then the multiplication took place near Tiberias.

6, 5ff: The Gospels of John and Luke have only one account of a multiplication of loaves and fish; Mark and Matthew have two accounts.

6, 14: *The Prophet:* probably the prophet like Moses (see note on 1, 21). Jesus, like Moses, had fed the people miraculously.

6, 19: *Walking on the water:* the Greek would permit a translation "on the seashore" or "by the sea." This would eliminate the miraculous from the story and leave it pointless. In Mt 14, 24-25, it is quite clear that Jesus walked upon the sea.

6, 20: *It is I:* literally, "I am"—perhaps the expression intended to connote divinity; see note on 8, 24.

6, 21: It is not clear whether Jesus got into the boat, or whether the sudden arrival at the shore is presented as miraculous. Possibly both are intended.

6, 22ff: These verses have many variants in the manuscripts and are awkward and somewhat illogical. Were all five thousand transported? There may be several forms of the account combined in our present readings.

6, 23: *From Tiberias near the place:* it is not clear whether Tiberias is near the place or the boats came near to the place; cf v 1 and the note there.

---

*
39: 12, 16; 19, 28; 20, 9.   4: 2, 13; 11, 55.
42: 1 Jn 2, 15.   11: 21, 13.
43: Mt 24, 24.   13: 2 Kgs 4, 42ff.
44: 12, 43.   15: 18, 36.
46: 5, 39; Dt 18, 15;   16-21: Mt 14, 22-33;
    Lk 16, 31; 24, 44.   Mk 6, 45-52.
6/1-13: Mt 14, 13-21;
    Mk 6, 32-44;
    Lk 9, 10-17.

Jesus nor his disciples were there, they too embarked in the boats and went to Capernaum looking for Jesus.

Discourse on the Bread of Life

25When they found him on the other side of the lake, they said to him, "Rabbi, when did you come here?" **26**Jesus answered them:

"I assure you,
   you are not looking for me because you have seen signs
   but because you have eaten your fill of the loaves.
27You should not be working for perishable food
   but for food that remains unto life eternal,
   food which the Son of Man will give you;
   it is on him that God the Father has set his seal."

28At this they said to him, "What must we do to perform the works of God?" **29**Jesus replied:

   "This is the work of God:
     have faith in the One whom he sent."

30*"So that we can put faith in you," they asked him, "what sign are you going to perform for us to see? What is the 'work' you do? **31*†**Our ancestors had manna to eat in the desert; according to Scripture, 'He gave them bread from the heavens to eat.'" **32***Jesus said to them:

   "I solemnly assure you,
   it was not Moses who gave you bread from the heavens;
   it is my Father who gives you the real heavenly bread.
33†God's bread comes down from heaven
   and gives life to the world."

34"Sir, give us this bread always," they besought him.

35*†Jesus explained to them:

"I myself am the bread of life.
   No one who comes to me shall ever be hungry,
   no one who believes in me shall ever thirst.
36 But as I told you—
   though you have seen me, you still do not believe.
37† All that the Father gives me shall come to me;
   no one who comes will I ever reject,
38*because it is not to do my own will
   that I have come down from heaven,
   but to do the will of him who sent me.
39*It is the will of him who sent me
   that I should lose nothing of what he has given me;
   rather, that I should raise it up on the last day.

40*Indeed, this is the will of my Father,
   that everyone who looks upon the Son
   and believes in him
   shall have eternal life.
   Him I will raise up on the last day."

41At this the Jews started to murmur in protest because he claimed, "I am the bread that came down from heaven." **42***They kept saying: "Is this not Jesus, the son of Joseph? Do we not know his father and mother? How can he claim to have come down from heaven?"

43"Stop your murmuring," Jesus told them.

44 "No one can come to me
   unless the Father who sent me draws him;
   I will raise him up on the last day.
45* It is written in the prophets:
   'They shall all be taught by God.'
   Everyone who has heard the Father
   and learned from him
   comes to me.
46* Not that anyone has seen the Father—
   only the one who is from God
   has seen the Father.
47 Let me firmly assure you,
   he who believes has eternal life.
48 I am the bread of life.
49 Your ancestors ate manna in the desert, but they died.
50 This is the bread that comes down from heaven
   for a man to eat and never die.

51*†I myself am the living bread
   come down from heaven.
   If anyone eats this bread
   he shall live forever;
   the bread I will give
   is my flesh, for the life of the world."

52At this the Jews quarreled among themselves, saying, "How can he give us his flesh to eat?" **53**Thereupon Jesus said to them:

---

†

6, 31: There is evidence that the Jews believed the miracle of the manna would be repeated in the last days; hence their challenge to discover whether these were the last days.

6, 33: *God's bread comes down:* the Greek is ambiguous for it literally reads, "God's bread is that which [or he who] comes down," etc.

6, 35: What does Jesus mean by "the bread of life"? Because of the emphasis on believing and teaching in vv 35-50, most scholars today think of the bread in these verses as primarily a figurative reference to Jesus' revelation or teaching. There may well be a secondary reference to the Eucharist. In vv 51-58, however, the eucharistic theme comes to the fore. Many, then, place a break in the discourse between vv 50 and 51.

6, 37.39: *All that . . . nothing:* for a reason not totally clear, the evangelist uses the neuter in these verses. Some think it is a grammatical peculiarity with no special significance; others see it as a reading indicative of universality.

6, 51: The last two lines of 51 may be compared to the Lucan eucharistic formula (22, 19): "This [bread] is my body which is given for you."

✤

30: Mt 16, 1-4; Lk 11, 29f.
31: Ex 16, 4f; Ps 78, 24.
32: Mt 6, 11.
35: Is 55, 1ff.
38: 4, 34; Mt 26, 39; Heb 10, 9.
39: 10, 28f; 17, 12; 18, 9.
40: 1 Jn 2, 25.
42: Mt 13, 54-57; Mk 6, 1-4.
45: Is 54, 13.
46: 7, 29; Ex 33, 20.
51: Mt 26, 26f; Lk 22, 19.

"Let me solemnly assure you,
  if you do not eat the flesh of the Son of Man
  and drink his blood,
  you have no life in you.
54† He who feeds on my flesh
  and drinks my blood
  has life eternal,
  and I will raise him up on the last day.
55 For my flesh is real food
  and my blood real drink.
56 The man who feeds on my flesh
  and drinks my blood
  remains in me, and I in him.
57*† Just as the Father who has life sent me
  and I have life because of the Father,
  so the man who feeds on me
  will have life because of me.
58 This is the bread that came down from heaven.
  Unlike your ancestors who ate and died
    nonetheless,
  the man who feeds on this bread shall live
    forever."
59 He said this in a synagogue instruction at Capernaum.

Effect of the Discourse

60† After hearing his words, many of his disciples remarked, "This sort of talk is hard to endure! How can anyone take it seriously?" **61** Jesus was fully aware that his disciples were murmuring in protest at what he had said. "Does it shake your faith?" he asked them.

62† "What, then, if you were to see the Son of Man
  ascend to where he was before . . . ?
63† It is the spirit that gives life;
  the flesh is useless.
  The words I spoke to you
  are spirit and life.
64 Yet among you there are some who do not
    believe."

(Jesus knew from the start, of course, the ones who refused to believe, and the one who would hand him over.) **65†** He went on to say:

  "This is why I have told you
    that no one can come to me
    unless it is granted him by the Father."

66 From this time on, many of his disciples broke away and would not remain in his company any longer. **67** Jesus then said to the Twelve, "Do you want to leave me too?" **68** Simon Peter answered him, "Lord, to whom shall we go? You have the words of eternal life. **69*** We have come to believe; we are convinced that you are God's holy one."

70 Jesus replied, "Did I not choose the Twelve of you myself? Yet one of you is a devil." **71*†** (He was talking

57: 5, 26.
69: 11, 27; Mt 16, 16.
71: 13, 2.27.

7/2: Lv 23, 34; Nm 29, 12; Zec 14, 16-19.

about Judas, son of Simon the Iscariot, who, though one of the Twelve, was going to hand Jesus over.)

Feast of Booths

7 **1** AFTER this, Jesus moved about within Galilee. He had decided not to travel in Judea because some of the Jews were looking for a chance to kill him. **2*†** However, as the Jewish feast of Booths drew near, **3†** his brothers had this to say: "You ought to leave here and go to Judea so that your disciples there may see the works you are performing. **4** No one who wishes to be known publicly keeps his actions hidden. If you are going to do things like these, you may as well display yourself to the world at large." **5** (As a matter of fact, not even his brothers had much confidence in him.) **6†** Jesus answered them:

  "It is not yet the right time for me,
    whereas the time is always right for you.
7 The world is incapable of hating you,
  but it does hate me
  because of the evidence I bring against it
  that what it does is evil.

8† Go up yourselves to the festival. I am not going up to this festival because the time is not yet ripe for me." **9** Having said this, he stayed on in Galilee. **10** However, once his brothers had gone up to the festival he too went up, but as if in secret and not for all to see.

† 6, 54-58: *Feeds:* the verb that John uses in these verses is not the regular verb "to eat," but a very realistic verb with a rather crude connotation of "munch, gnaw." This may be part of John's emphasis on the reality of the flesh and blood of Jesus; cf v 55.

6, 57: *Because of me:* this can mean either "from me" (as the source) or "for my sake" (as the reason).

6, 60ff: These verses seem to refer more to the themes of vv 35-50, than to those of vv 51-58.

6, 62: This unfinished conditional sentence is obscure. Probably there is a reference to vv 49-51. Jesus claims to be *the bread that comes down from heaven;* this claim provokes incredulity (v 60); and so Jesus asks what will be said when he goes up to heaven.

6, 63: *Spirit . . . flesh:* probably not a reference to the eucharistic flesh of Jesus but to the supernatural and the natural, as in 3, 6.

6, 65: *I have told:* presumably, this is a reference to v 44 combined with v 37.

6, 71: Here and in 13, 2.26, it is not entirely clear whether Iscariot (man from Kerioth?) modifies *Judas* or *Simon.*

7, 2: *Booths:* the autumn harvest feast lasting eight days, during which the people lived in huts. This was looked on as a reminiscence of their ancestors' life in tents in the desert after the Exodus. The Hebrew name for this festival and its booths is Sukkoth.

7, 3: *Brothers:* these relatives are never portrayed as disciples until after the resurrection (Acts 1, 14). Mt 13, 55 and Mk 6, 3 give the names of four of them.

7, 6: *Time:* a synonym for "hour" (see 2, 4), the period of Jesus' death and resurrection. The Christian reader of the gospel understands the theological play on words: this feast does not yet mark the time of Jesus' glorification; he will not die at this time.

7, 8: *I am not going up:* another play on words. "Go up" refers to his elevation in crucifixion, resurrection, and ascension; cf 20, 17.

[11]During the festival, naturally, the Jews were looking for him, asking, "Where is that troublemaker?" [12]Among the crowds there was much guarded debate about him. Some maintained, "He is a good man," while others kept saying, "Not at all—he is only misleading the crowd!" [13]*No one dared talk openly about him, however, for fear of the Jews.

First Episode

[14]The feast was half over by the time Jesus went into the temple area and began to teach. [15]*†The Jews were filled with amazement and said, "How did this man get his education when he had no teacher?" [16]This was Jesus' answer:

"My doctrine is not my own;
    it comes from him who sent me.
[17]Any man who chooses to do his will
    will know about this doctrine—
namely, whether it comes from God
    or is simply spoken on my own.
[18]Whoever speaks on his own
    is bent on self-glorification.
The man who seeks glory for him who sent him is
    truthful;
there is no dishonesty in his heart.
[19]Moses has given you the law, has he not?
Yet not one of you keeps it.
Why do you look for a chance to kill me?"

[20]*†"You are mad!" the crowd retorted. "Who wants to kill you?" [21]Jesus answered:

"I have performed a single work
    and you profess astonishment over it.
[22]*Moses gave you circumcision
    (though it did not originate with Moses but with
    the patriarchs).
And so, even on a sabbath you circumcise a man.
[23]*If a man can be circumcised on the sabbath
    to prevent a violation of Mosaic law,
how is it you are angry with me
    for curing a whole man on the sabbath?
[24] Stop judging by appearances
    and make an honest judgment."

[25]This led some of the people of Jerusalem to remark: "Is this not the one they want to kill? [26]†Here he is speaking in public and they don't say a word to him! Perhaps even the authorities have decided that this is the Messiah. [27]*Still, we know where this man is from. When the Messiah comes, no one is supposed to know his origins." [28]*At this, Jesus, who was teaching in the temple area, cried out:

"So you know me,
    and you know my origins?
The truth is, I have not come of myself.
I was sent by One who has the right to send,
    and him you do not know.
[29]*I know him
    because it is from him I come:
    he sent me."

[30]*At this they tried to seize him, but no one laid a finger on him because his hour had not yet come. [31]*Many in the crowd came to believe in him. They kept saying, "When the Messiah comes, can he be expected to perform more signs than this man?" [32]The Pharisees overheard this debate about him among the crowd, and the chief priests and Pharisees together sent temple guards to arrest him.

[33]*Jesus then said to them:

"Only a little while longer am I to be with you,
    then I am going away to him who sent me.
[34]*You will look for me, but you will not find me;
    where I am you cannot come."

[35]†This caused the Jews to exclaim among themselves: "Where does he intend to go that we will not find him? Surely he is not going off to the Diaspora among the Greeks, to teach them? [36]What does he mean by saying, 'You will look for me, but you will not find me,' and, 'Where I am you cannot come'?"

Second Episode

[37]†On the last and greatest day of the festival, Jesus stood up and cried out:

"If anyone thirsts, let him come to me;
    let him drink [38]*who believes in me.
    Scripture has it:
'From within him rivers of living water shall flow.'"

---

† 7, 15: *Education:* literally, "How does he know letters . . . ?" Children were taught to read and write by means of the Scriptures. But here more than Jesus' literacy is being discussed; the people are wondering how he can teach like a rabbi. Rabbis were trained by other rabbis and loved to quote their teachers.

7, 20: *Mad:* literally, "You have a demon." The insane were thought to possess or be possessed by a demonical spirit. One has to determine from the context whether the charge in our terms is one of insanity or of possession.

7, 26: *Authorities:* the Sanhedrin members; the same term is used to describe Nicodemus (3, 1).

7, 35: *Diaspora:* the Jews living outside Palestine. *Greeks:* probably refers to the Gentiles in the Mediterranean area; cf 12, 20.

7, 37f: *Last and greatest day:* probably the seventh day, since the eighth was a day of rest after the feast. There is some MS evidence for the omission of *greatest* as a copyist's clarification.

The translation given makes Christ the source of the living water. Another reading is possible which makes the believer himself the source; in that case a period is placed after *drink* and what remains becomes an independent sentence. "He who believes in me," etc. *Scripture has it* is not an exact citation of any passage. Perhaps the reference is to the rock that Moses tapped during the Exodus. *From within him:* literally, "from his belly."

13: 9, 22; 12, 42.
15: Lk 2, 47.
20: 10, 20.
22: Gn 17, 10.
23: 5, 2-9.16; Mt 12, 11f;
    Lk 14, 5.
27: Heb 7, 3.
28: 8, 19.
29: 6, 46; 8, 55.
30: 7, 44; 8, 20; Lk 4, 29f.
31: 2, 11; 10, 42; 11, 45.
33: 13, 33; 16, 16.
34: 8, 21; Prv 1, 28.
38: 4, 10.14; 19, 34;
    Is 12, 3.

39*†(Here he was referring to the Spirit, whom those that came to believe in him were to receive. There was, of course, no Spirit as yet, since Jesus had not yet been glorified.)

40Some in the crowd who heard these words began to say, "This must be the Prophet." **41**Others were claiming, "He is the Messiah." But an objection was raised: "Surely the Messiah is not to come from Galilee? **42***Does not Scripture say that the Messiah, being of David's family, is to come from Bethlehem, the village where David lived?" **43**In this fashion the crowd was sharply divided over him. **44**Some of them even wanted to apprehend him. However, no one laid hands on him.

45When the temple guards came back, the chief priests and Pharisees asked them, "Why did you not bring him in?" **46**"No man ever spoke like that before," the guards replied. **47**"Do not tell us you too have been taken in!" the Pharisees retorted. **48**"You do not see any of the Sanhedrin believing in him, do you? Or the Pharisees? **49**Only this lot, that knows nothing about the law—and they are lost anyway!" **50***One of their own number, Nicodemus (the man who had come to him), spoke up to say, **51***"Since when does our law condemn any man without first hearing him and knowing the facts?" **52**"Do not tell us you are a Galilean too," they taunted him. "Look it up. You will not find the Prophet coming from Galilee."

The Adulteress

53†[Then each went off to his own house,

8 **1***WHILE Jesus went out to the Mount of Olives. **2**At daybreak he reappeared in the temple area; and when the people started coming to him, he sat down and began to teach them. **3**The scribes and the Pharisees led a woman forward who had been caught in adultery. They made her stand there in front of everyone. **4**"Teacher," they said to him, "this woman has been caught in the act of adultery. **5***In the law, Moses ordered such women to be stoned. What do you have to say about the case?" **6†**(They were posing this question to trap him, so that they could have something to accuse him of.) Jesus bent down and started tracing on the ground with his finger. **7***When they persisted in their questioning, he straightened up and said to them, "Let the man among you who has no sin be the first to cast a stone at her." **8**A second time he bent down and wrote on the ground. **9**Then the audience drifted away one by one, beginning with the elders. This left him alone with the

woman, who continued to stand there before him. **10***Jesus finally straighted up and said to her, "Woman, where did they all disappear to? Has no one condemned you?" **11***"No one, sir," she answered. Jesus said, "Nor do I condemn you. You may go. But from now on, avoid this sin."]

Third Episode

12*Jesus spoke to them once again:

"I am the light of the world.
No follower of mine shall ever walk in darkness;
no, he shall possess the light of life."

13This caused the Pharisees to break in with: "You are your own witness. Such testimony cannot be valid." **14***Jesus answered:

"What if I am my own witness?
My testimony is valid nonetheless,
because I know where I came from
and where I am going;
you know neither the one nor the other.
15*†You pass judgment according to appearances
but I pass judgment on no man.
16*†Even if I do judge,
that judgment of mine is valid
because I am not alone:
I have at my side the One who sent me [the
    Father].
17*It is laid down in your law
that evidence given by two persons is valid.
18*I am one of those testifying in my behalf,
the Father who sent me is the other."

19*They pressed him: "And where is this 'Father' of yours?" Jesus replied:

"You know neither me nor my Father.
If you knew me, you would know my Father too."

20*He spoke these words while teaching at the temple treasury. Still, he went unapprehended, because his hour had not yet come.

---

†

7, 39: *No Spirit as yet:* in relation to the Christian, the sending of the Spirit was not to take place until Jesus' death, resurrection, and ascension; cf 20, 22.

7, 53ff: The story of the adulteress is missing from the best early Greek MSS. Where it does appear, it is found in different places in different MSS: here; or after 7, 36; or at the end of this gospel; or after Lk 21, 38. It seems to have been preserved largely in Western and Latin circles. There are many non-Johannine features in the language, and there are also many doubtful readings. It appears in Jerome's Vulgate. However, it is certainly out of place here; it fits better with the general situation in Lk 21, 38. The Catholic Church accepts it as inspired Scripture.

8, 6: *Tracing:* or "writing" or "recording"; whether Jesus was writing something meaningful is not clear.

8, 15: *Appearances:* literally, "according to the flesh."

8, 16: The last line is literally, "but I and the One who sent me [the Father]."

✻

39: 16, 7.
42: 2 Sm 7, 12; Ps 89, 4f;
    Mi 5, 1; Mt 2, 5f.
50: 3, 1; 19, 39.
51: Dt 1, 16f.
8/1f: Lk 2, 37f.
  5: Lv 20, 10; Dt 22, 22ff.
  7: Mt 7, 1-5.
10: Ez 33, 11.
11: 5, 14.

12: 1, 5.9; 12, 46;
    Ex 13, 22; Is 42, 6.
14: 5, 31.
15: 12, 47.
16: 5, 30.
17: Dt 17, 6; 19, 15;
    Nm 35, 30.
18: 5, 23.37.
19: 7, 28; 14, 7; 15, 21.
20: 7, 30.

Warning to Unbelievers

21* Again he said to them:

> "I am going away. You will look for me
> but you will die in your sins.
> Where I am going you cannot come."

22 At this some of the Jews began to ask, "Does he mean he will kill himself when he claims, 'Where I am going you cannot come'? **23*** He went on:

> "You belong to what is below;
> I belong to what is above.
> You belong to this world—
> a world which cannot hold me.
> **24†** That is why I said you would die in your sins.
> You will surely die in your sins
> unless you come to believe that I AM."

25*† "Who are you, then?" they asked him. Jesus answered:

> "What I have been telling you from the beginning.
> **26*** I could say much about you in condemnation,
> but no, I only tell the world
> what I have heard from him,
> the truthful One who sent me."

27 They did not grasp that he was speaking to them of the Father. **28*** Jesus continued:

> "When you lift up the Son of Man,
> you will come to realize that I AM
> and that I do nothing by myself.
> I say only what the Father has taught me.
> **29** The One who sent me is with me.
> He has not deserted me
> since I always do what pleases him."

30 Because he spoke this way, many came to believe in him.

Jesus and Abraham

31 Jesus then went on to say to those Jews who believed in him:

> "If you live according to my teaching,
> you are truly my disciples;
> **32*** then you will know the truth,
> and the truth will set you free."

33* "We are descendants of Abraham," was their answer. "Never have we been slaves to anyone. What do you mean by saying, 'You will be free'?" **34** Jesus answered them:

> "I give you my assurance,
> everyone who lives in sin
> is the slave of sin.

35* (No slave has a permanent place in the family,
> but the son has a place there forever.)
> **36** That is why, if the son frees you,
> you will really be free.
> **37†** I realize you are of Abraham's stock.
> Nonetheless, you are trying to kill me
> because my word finds no hearing among you.
> **38†** I tell what I have seen in the Father's presence;
> you do what you have heard from your father."

39 They retorted, "Our father is Abraham." Jesus told them:

> "If you were Abraham's children,
> you would be following Abraham's example.
> **40†** The fact is, you are trying to kill me,
> a man who has told you the truth
> which I have heard from God.
> Abraham did nothing like that.
> **41†** Indeed you are doing your father's works!"

They cried, "We are no illegitimate breed! We have but one father and that is God himself." **42*** Jesus answered:

> "Were God your father
> you would love me,
> for I came forth from God, and am here.
> I did not come of my own will;
> it was he who sent me.
> **43** Why do you not understand what I say?
> It is because you cannot bear to hear my word.
> **44*†** The father you spring from is the devil,
> and willingly you carry out his wishes.
> He brought death to man from the begining,
> and has never based himself on truth;
> the truth is not in him.
> Lying speech
> is his native tongue;
> he is a liar and the father of lies.
> **45** But because I deal in the truth,
> you give me no credence.

---

† 8, 24.28: *I AM*, an expression which late Jewish tradition understands as a name for God; cf 8, 58.

8, 25: *What I have been telling you from the beginning:* this is a very unclear verse and several other translations are possible: (I am) "what I say to you; How is it that I speak to you at all?" The earliest attested reading (Bodmer Papyrus P⁶⁶) has, "I told you at the beginning what I am also telling you (now)."

8, 37: *Finds no hearing:* or "finds no place in you; does not continue in you"; "takes no hold in you."

8, 38: The translation given in the text understands the second part of the verse to be a sarcastic reference to the descent of the Jews from their father, the devil. There are good grounds, however, for another translation in which (as in the first part of the verse) "father" means God: "You should do what you have heard from the Father."

8, 40: Nowhere else in the New Testament is Jesus described as *a man* in this broad sense. Probably the phrase is a Semitic expression for "someone."

8, 41: *Illegitimate:* literally, "of fornication"; in the Old Testament, fornication signifies the worship of false gods.

8, 44: *The father of lies:* literally, "of him [i. e., the liar]" or "of it [i. e., the lie]."

---

* 21: 7, 34; 13, 33.
23: 3, 31; 17, 14; 18, 36.
25: 10, 24.
26: 12, 50.
28: 3, 14; 12, 34.
32: Is 42, 7; Gal 4, 31.

33: Mt 3, 9.
35: Gn 21, 10; Gal 4, 30.
42: 1 Jn 5, 1.
44: 3, 1f; Wis 1, 13; 2, 24;
Acts 13, 10;
1 Jn 3, 8-15.

46*Can any one of you convict me of sin?
If I am telling the truth,
why do you not believe me?
47*Whoever is of God
hears every word God speaks.
The reason you do not hear
is that you are not of God."

48†The Jews answered, "Are we not right, after all, in saying you are a Samaritan, and possessed besides?" **49**Jesus replied:

"I am not possessed.
However, I revere my Father,
while you fail to respect me.
50*I seek no glory for myself;
there is one who seeks it, and it is he who judges.
51*I solemnly assure you,
if a man is true to my word
he shall never see death."

52"Now we are sure you are possessed," the Jews retorted. "Abraham is dead. The prophets are dead. Yet you claim, 'A man shall never know death if he keeps my word.' **53***Surely you do not pretend to be greater than our father Abraham, who died! Or the prophets, who died! Whom do you make yourself out to be?" **54**Jesus answered:

"If I glorify myself,
that glory comes to nothing.
He who gives me glory is the Father,
the very one you claim for your God,
55*even though you do not know him.
But I know him.
Were I to say I do not know him,
I would be no better than you—a liar!
Yes, I know him well,
and I keep his word.
56*†Your father Abraham rejoiced
that he might see my day.
He saw it and was glad."

57†At this the Jews objected: "You are not yet fifty! How can you have seen Abraham?" **58***Jesus answered them:

"I solemnly declare it:
before Abraham came to be, I AM."

59*At that they picked up rocks to throw at Jesus, but he hid himself and slipped out of the temple precincts.

The Man Born Blind

9 **1***†As he walked along, he saw a man who had been blind from birth. **2**His disciples asked him, "Rabbi, was it his sin or that of his parents that caused him to be born blind?" **3***"Neither," answered Jesus:

"It was no sin, either of this man
or of his parents.
Rather, it was to let God's works show forth in him.
4*We must do the deeds of him who sent me
while it is day.
The night comes on
when no one can work.
5*While I am in the world
I am the light of the world."

6*With that Jesus spat on the ground, made mud with his saliva, and smeared the man's eyes with the mud. **7**†Then he told him, "Go, wash in the pool of Siloam." (This name means "One who has been sent.") So the man went off and washed, and came back able to see.

8His neighbors and the people who had been accustomed to see him begging began to ask, "Isn't this the fellow who used to sit and beg?" **9**Some were claiming it was he; others maintained it was not but someone who looked like him. The man himself said, "I am the one." **10**They said to him then, "How were your eyes opened?" **11**He answered: "That man they call Jesus made mud and smeared it on my eyes, telling me to go to Siloam and wash. When I did go and wash, I was able to see." **12**"Where is he?" they asked. He replied, "I have no idea."

13Next, they took the man who had been born blind to the Pharisees. **14**†(Note that it was on a sabbath that Jesus had made the mud paste and opened his eyes.) **15**The Pharisees, in turn, began to inquire how he had recovered his sight. He told them, "He put mud on my eyes. I washed it off, and now I can see." **16***This prompted some of the Pharisees to assert, "This man cannot be from God because he does not keep the sabbath." Others objected, "If a man is a sinner, how

---

† 8, 48: *Samaritan:* the Samaritans were noted for an interest in magical powers; see Simon Magus in Acts 7, 14-24.

8, 56: *He saw it:* presumably this is a reference to the birth of Jacob (Israel), which was the beginning of the fulfillment of the promises concerning Abraham's seed; see Gn 17, 7 and 21, 6. But there may also be a reference to a popular Jewish tradition that Abraham saw all of his descendants.

8, 57: There is equally good evidence for reading: "How can Abraham have seen you?"

9, 1: It is difficult to be certain where or when this scene took place. The similarity of 9, 5 and 8, 12 may indicate that the scene is also part of the "Booths" setting. The next time indication is in 10, 22, three months after the feast of Booths. The evangelist may have given to this story a secondary baptismal symbolism by stressing that the man was born blind and was healed by the waters of the pool (v 7).

9, 7: *One who has been sent:* a reference to Jesus, sent by the Father.

9, 14: In using spittle, and in kneading mud, Jesus had broken the sabbath rules laid down by the scribes.

---

*

46: Heb 4, 15; 1 Pt 2, 22.
47: 10, 26; 1 Jn 4, 6.
50: 7, 18.
51: 5, 24-29; 6, 40.47;
   11, 25f.
53: 4, 12.
55: 7, 28f.
56: Mt 13, 17; Lk 17, 22.
58: 1, 30; 17, 5.

59: 10, 31.39; 11, 8;
   Lk 4, 29f.
9/1f: Is 42, 7.
  3: 11, 4.
  4: 11, 9f; 12, 35f.
  5: 8, 12.
  6: 5, 11; Mk 7, 33; 8, 23.
16: 3, 2; Mt 12, 10f;
  Lk 13, 10f; 14, 1-4.

THE NEW TESTAMENT IN PICTURES

THE LIFE OF CHRIST

as illustrated by

the great masters of religious art

together with

interesting historical facts

about the artists

and their paintings

Celebrated paintings in museums, churches,
and private collections throughout the world, reproduced
in full color

Betrothal of Mary

(MATTHEW 1, 18)

■ *Jacopo Amigoni (1675–1752) was a Venetian painter and etcher, noted for his historical paintings and portraits. For many years Amigoni lived in England, where his work was very popular. He also painted in Germany and Spain.*

According to Jewish custom, the betrothal of Mary to Joseph was arranged by Joseph's parents. The betrothal usually took place about a year prior to the marriage. Under Jewish law, betrothal was sacred and holy, and the bride legally belonged to the bridegroom, although they did not live together until after the marriage was formally celebrated. Jewish maidens were regarded to be of marriageable age when they were twelve or thirteen years old and a man was betrothed between the ages of eighteen and twenty-four. These were probably the ages of Mary and Joseph at the time of their betrothal.

The Annunciation

(LUKE 1, 26-38)

■ *Roger van der Weyden (1400–1464) was a Flemish painter of portraits and religious themes in the manner of Van Eyck. A man of deeply religious feeling, his devotional paintings are noted for their tone of sadness and pathos.*

Six months after the conception of John the Baptizer, the angel Gabriel was sent by God to the town of Nazareth to a virgin named Mary who was betrothed to the carpenter, Joseph. The angel greeted Mary in a courtly manner and announced that God had chosen her to be the mother of the Messiah. Since Mary had vowed her virginity to God, the angel reassured her that the conception of Jesus would be miraculous and her Son would have no father but God. Humbly Mary gave her consent and at that moment the Son of God became Man.

The Visit between Mary and Elizabeth

(LUKE 1, 39-56)

■ *Johann David Passavant (1787–1861) was a German painter, art scholar, and author of books on painting. He is best known for his book on Raphael.*

Immediately after the Annunciation, Mary set out from Nazareth for Judea to visit her kinswoman Elizabeth and rejoice with her over the coming birth of John the Baptizer. The trip from Nazareth to the hill country of Judea was long and tiresome, but Mary made the journey apparently alone and entered Zechariah's house.

At the meeting of the two mothers, special divine illumination was given Elizabeth and the infant Baptizer leaped in her womb. Filled with the Holy Spirit, she recognized Mary as the Mother of God. Mary, at this moment of great joy, sang her heart out in her canticle, the beautiful Magnificat. In it she contrasts her own lowliness with the greatness of God and foresees that all generations shall call her blessed.

Mary remained with Elizabeth for three months and then returned to Nazareth.

Betrothal of Mary *by Jacopo Amigoni*
ARCHBISHOP'S GALLERY : ZAGREB

The Annunciation *by Roger van der Weyden*
THE LOUVRE : PARIS

The Visit between Mary and Elizabeth *by Johann David Passavant*
NATIONAL GALLERY : BERLIN

Adoration
of the Shepherds

(LUKE 2, 8-20)

■ *Bartolome Esteban Murillo (1617–1682) was a Spanish painter of religious subjects, portraits, and themes from everyday life. One of the most beloved of all painters, he drew his inspiration entirely from his own native land. His paintings are known for their individuality, sincerity, and charm. He died from injuries suffered when he fell from scaffolding while painting the unfinished "Marriage of St. Catherine" in the church at Cadiz.*

During the night on which Jesus was born, shepherds were guarding their flocks out on the plains bordering Bethlehem. Suddenly an angel of the Lord appeared to them and announced the birth of the Messiah. As a sign, they were told they would find the Child wrapped in swaddling clothes and lying in a manger. Joyfully, the shepherds hurried to the cave where they found the Infant with Mary and Joseph. They adored the newborn Messiah and then, glorifying God, carried the good news to others in the vicinity.

Massacre of the Innocents

(MATTHEW 2, 16-18)

■ *Peter Paul Rubens (1577–1640) was a prolific Flemish painter, the most eminent of his school. His outstanding characteristics were his vigor of composition, beauty of coloring, and fine decorative sense. From 1600 to 1608 he painted in Rome on commission of the Duke of Mantua. Later he returned to Antwerp where he was appointed court painter. He gained great wealth and popularity and his studio became the training school for students from all over Europe. His influence dominated artistic taste in Europe for almost a century.*

When the Magi failed to return to Jerusalem after worshiping the newborn Messiah, Herod was filled with rage. To make sure that his throne was in no danger from this Infant King, he ordered that all male children under two years of age in Bethlehem and the surrounding territory be slain. He allowed a generous margin in the age limit, so that the Child could not possibly escape him. But the Child did escape him, for by the time Herod's henchmen reached Bethlehem, Joseph and his family were already on their way to Egypt.

The probable number of little victims massacred was between twenty and twenty-five. This inhuman slaughter was in keeping with the character of Herod, who had murdered two of his own sons and was about to murder a third. Yet only a few months after the massacre in Bethlehem, Herod himself died after an illness attended by the cruelest suffering.

Adoration of the Shepherds *by Bartolome Esteban Murillo*
THE PRADO : MADRID

Massacre of the Innocents *by Peter Paul Rubens*
PINAKOTHEK : MUNICH

Sermon on the Mount

(MATTHEW 5, 1—7, 29)

■ *Carl Heinrich Bloch (1834–1890) was a Danish painter of historical and religious subjects. He studied at the Copenhagen Academy and in Rome and was one of the most popular religious painters of his day.*

Although Jesus' Apostles and disciples loved Him with all their hearts, as yet they knew very little of His teaching. They, and also the increasing crowds of people gathering to hear Him, needed a complete and precise exposition of His doctrines. Thus Jesus gave His sublime discourse which is known as the "Sermon on the Mount," the mount being one of the hills of Galilee.

Jesus opened the sermon with the Beatitudes, described the dignity and duties of the Apostles, and explained how the New Law completed and perfected the Old. He spoke of the general duties of Christians one to another and gave commands regarding the nature and sanctity of marriage. He decried the vanities of life and the folly of gathering riches on earth. Jesus condemned religious hypocrisy and taught the people how to pray the beautiful "Lord's Prayer."

This Discourse was really more than a mere sermon, for it stands alone as the grand charter of Principles of the kingdom of heaven. When the sermon was ended, the people were astonished at Christ's words, for He spoke to them, not as did the Scribes and Pharisees, but with divine authority.

Christ Healing the Sick

(MATTHEW 4, 23-25)

■ *Christian Dietrich (1712–1774) was a German painter and engraver. He became director of painting at the world famous Meissen porcelain factory. His historical paintings and landscapes were in the style of the Dutch masters.*

The healing ministry of Jesus Christ was far more extensive than is indicated by the numerous specific cures recorded in the gospels. "Jesus toured all of Galilee.- - -, and cured the people of every disease and illness, - - - They carried to Him all those afflicted with various diseases and raked with pain: the possessed, the lunatics, the paralyzed. He cured them all."

Jesus was indeed the universal Friend of suffering humanity. He was free of Jewish prejudices and therefore receptive to the unfortunate and suffering of every nationality and race. His ministry of teaching and healing drew vast throngs from such alien countries as Edom, Tyre, Sidon, the Decapolis, and other neighboring provinces, even as it was attended by multitudes from all Galilee, Judea, and Jerusalem.

The primary mission of Jesus Christ in the world was the redemption of the souls of men, but He illustrated and enforced His power to heal the sin-sick soul by miraculously healing the maladies of the body. In showing His compassion for those diseased in body, He set forth His deeper compassion for those who are spiritually sick.

Sermon on the Mount [Detail] *by Carl Heinrich Bloch*
FREDERIKSBORG CASTLE : COPENHAGEN

Christ Healing the Sick *by Christian Dietrich*
METROPOLITAN MUSEUM OF ART : NEW YORK

The Raising of Jairus' Daughter

(MARK 5, 21-24 and 35-43)

Johann Friedrich Overbeck (1789–1869) was a German painter whose entire career was devoted to Christian art. He was one of the founders of the Nazarenes, the aim of the movement being the revival of the religious in German painting. This group worked in Rome and attracted many outstanding artists.

Jesus was preaching in Caphernaum when a prominent Jew, named Jairus, approached and fell at His feet. Jairus' twelve year old daughter was at the point of death and he begged the Master to come and heal her. Jesus set out immediately with the anguished father, but on the way the news came that the child was already dead. Nevertheless, He continued on to Jairus' house.

Entering the child's room, Jesus took the little girl's cold hand in His and spoke only two words, "Talitha, Koum," which means "Little girl, get up." At once the girl was restored to life and she arose and began to walk about the room, to the amazement of all those present. He then ordered that food be brought to the girl. This was done, and the girl at once consumed it.

The Good Samaritan

(LUKE 10, 25-37)

Juan Manchola was probably a Mexican painter of Spanish descent. Details of his life are unknown, but his painting is done in the style of Spanish art which flourished in the period between 1850 and 1900 A.D.

In reply to the question, "Who is my neighbor?" Jesus told the following parable: A man was en route from Jerusalem to Jericho when he was waylaid by robbers who, stripping and beating him, left him half dead. A priest coming along the road saw the man, but passed by. So also did a Levite. Then a third traveler, a Samaritan, came along. Moved with pity, he dressed the man's wounds and took him to an inn where he paid the innkeeper to care for the unfortunate victim.

Jesus then asked His questioner which of the three travelers proved himself a neighbor to the wounded man. The reply was, "The one who treated him with compassion." Then Jesus said, "Then go and do the same."

Christ and the Children

(MARK 10, 13-16)

Pietro Benvenuti (1769–1844) was an Italian painter. He studied the works of Andrea del Sarto in Florence and the works of Raphael in Rome. His style is noble and elevated, his design is pure and correct, and his color is often brilliant. He was considered one of the leading painters of the Tuscan school.

When His disciples tried to prevent children coming to him and bothering him, Christ rebuked them, saying "Let the children come to Me, and do not hinder them. It is to just such as these that the kingdom of God belongs." By this He meant that to attain heaven his disciples must become like children in their humility and simplicity, and in their belief and trust in God. After the children had gathered around Him, He lovingly laid His hands upon them, and blessed them.

The Raising of Jairus' Daughter *by Johann Friedrich Overbeck*
MUSEUM AT STUTTGART : GERMANY

The Good Samaritan *by Juan Manchola*
MUSEO REGIONAL OF CITY OF QUERETARO : MEXICO

Christ and the Children *by Pietro Benvenuti*
UFFIZI PALACE : FLORENCE

The Rich Young Man

(MARK 10, 17-27)

■ *Heinrich Hofmann (1824–1911) was a German portraitist and painter of historical and mythological subjects. He is best known for his representations of the life of Christ. His biblical paintings are distinguished for their ideality, refined beauty, and harmonious color.*

A certain rich young ruler saw Jesus, and he fell down on his knees before him, saying: "Good teacher, what must I do to share in everlasting life?" and Jesus told him to keep His commandments, and then He recited them. But the ruler replied that all these commands he had kept faithfully from his youth. Looking lovingly upon him, Jesus answered that to be perfect, "There is one thing more you must do. Go and sell what you have and give to the poor; you will then have treasure in heaven. After that, come and follow me." But the ruler's face became sad at these words, and he went away sorrowful, for he had great possessions.

When the man had left, Christ told His watching disciples that the possessor of riches would have difficulty attaining heaven, and they were astounded at this teaching. However, Jesus did not imply that the possession of riches was necessarily evil, but that riches are often unjustly acquired and therefore unjustly retained, they easily lead a man to commit sins of self-indulgence, and, what is probably the most important point in Christ's teaching, the pursuit of the things of this world keeps a man from the whole-hearted service of God and induces a certain self-confidence that is opposed to the humble trust that we must have in God's providence.

Christ's Triumphal Entry into Jerusalem

(MATTHEW 21, 1-11)

■ *Bernhard Plockhorst (1825–1907) was a German artist, but his religious paintings received acclaim in many countries. He was a professor of art at Weimar, and was a distinguished designer and lithographer as well as a historical painter.*

On Saturday, six days before the Passover, and on His journey from Jericho to Jerusalem, Jesus rested overnight in Bethany, in the house of Simon the leper. While dining there, a woman anointed Him with very expensive ointments. The others present criticized her "waste," but Jesus defended her good deed.

The next day, Jesus resumed His journey. Arriving at Bethphage near the Mount of Olives, He instructed two disciples to go into the nearby village and bring Him back a colt which they would find tethered there. The disciples did as directed, and when they brought the colt to Jesus they placed their cloaks upon the animal for Him to sit on.

The group then set forth for Jerusalem, with Jesus riding the colt. As they entered the city, word of His impending arrival had already reached the great throngs of people who had assembled for the feast of the Passover. Cutting themselves palms, they went forth to meet Him. As Jesus approached, they spread their cloaks on the ground before Him and strewed palms in His path. All that witnessed this event were filled with great joy and ecstasy, and in loud voices they sang His praises, saying: "Hosanna to the Son of David! Blessed is He who comes in the name of the Lord! Hosanna in the highest!"

The Rich Young Man *by Heinrich Hofmann*
RIVERSIDE CHURCH : NEW YORK

Christ's Triumphal Entry into Jerusalem *by Bernhard Plockhorst*
SYRACUSE MUSEUM OF FINE ARTS : SYRACUSE, NEW YORK

The Last Supper

(MATTHEW 26, 20-29)

Philippe de Champaigne (1602–1674) was a Flemish painter of many religious and historical works in the churches and palaces of France. Flemish realism combined with intense religious feeling and a masterly technique make him a painter of extraordinary power.

One of the most solemn and meaningful events in the entire life of our Blessed Saviour is the Last Supper. The evening preceding His betrayal by Judas Iscariot was crowded with the festive events of the celebration of the Passover or Paschal Supper. During the meal Jesus reclined at the table with his twelve Apostles, and spoke of His approaching betrayal by one of those present. He further indicated that the events of his betrayal, arrest, conviction, and execution had been the subject of divinely inspired prophecies, and all that which was to follow was in fulfillment of the will of God.

After the Paschal Supper, Jesus instituted the Holy Eucharist, the sacrament and sacrifice of His Body and Blood. Taking a loaf of unleavened bread and breaking it into portions for each of those present, he blessed it and gave it to his Apostles, saying: "Take this and eat it," he said, "this is my body." Then he took a cup, gave thanks, and gave it to them. "All of you must drink from it," he said, "for this is my blood, the blood of the covenant, to be poured out in behalf of many for the forgiveness of sins." He then asked those present to continue to carry out this same ordinance of bread and wine in commemoration of His own bloody sacrifice on the cross for the sins of all mankind which was soon to transpire.

Christ in the Garden of Gethsemani

(MATTHEW 26, 36-46)

Heinrich Hofmann. For biographical details see "The Rich Young Man" in this section.

After the Last Supper, Christ took Peter, James, and John along with Him into the Garden of Gethsemani. Inside He knelt down a short distance apart from the others and began to pray. Jesus was sad and sorely troubled, having a divine knowledge of His suffering and crucifixion to come. Sweating drops of blood in His agony, He pleaded with His heavenly Father that He be spared this ordeal, yet He was resigned to accept His Father's will, saying: "My Father, if it is possible, let this cup pass me by. Still, let it be as you would have it, not as I."

Going back to the three Apostles, he found them asleep, and he asked: "So you could not stay awake with me for even an hour?" Twice more He knelt apart and prayed that His heavenly Father would spare Him, and twice more He returned to find the three sleeping. On the last time He said to them: "Sleep on now. Enjoy your rest! The hour is on us when the Son of Man is to be handed over to the power of evil men. Get up! Let us be on our way! See, my betrayer is here."

Apprehension of Christ

(LUKE 22, 54–62)

Dierick Bouts the Elder (1410–1475) was one of the earliest of Netherland painters. In landscape effects and in the use of rich and subtle color harmonies he was unsurpassed in his day. He excelled in the portrayal of facial expression and character.

Knowing that Jesus would most likely go to the Garden of Gethsemani to pray after the momentous events of the Last Supper, Judas led a band of armed officers from the Jewish Sanhedrin to apprehend Him there.

The Last Supper *by Philippe de Champaigne*
DETROIT INSTITUTE OF ART : DETROIT

Christ in the Garden of Gethsemani *by Heinrich Hofmann*
RIVERSIDE CHURCH : NEW YORK

Apprehension of Christ *by Dierick Bouts the Elder*
PINAKOTHEK : MUNICH

The Crucifixion

(MATTHEW 27, 33-56)

Diego Velasquez (1599–1660) was the most eminent painter of the Spanish school. He painted genre and religious subjects in the manner of the Spanish naturalists, with strong outlines and bold brushwork. Velasquez is probably the most naturalistic and objective of all painters, and has rarely been equaled as a technician. His portraits are masterpieces of realistic thinking and penetrating psychology.

Jesus was found guilty of blasphemy by the Jewish Sanhedrin, and His punishment of death was demanded by the clamoring crowd. After prolonged efforts to evade rendering judgment, Pilate finally yielded to the Jewish authorities and the demands of the mob and issued orders that Jesus was to be crucified.

After being scourged, beaten, and crowned with thorns, the cross on which He was to be hung was placed on His shoulder and He was forced to carry it to Calvary where His execution was to take place. He was there stripped of His garments, nailed to the cross, and hanged. Two other men, criminals, were crucified at the same time. At the top of Jesus' cross an inscription was placed, reading, "This is Jesus, King of the Jews."

After three hours of agony on the cross, the Spirit of Jesus left Him and He died—and at that very moment the sky darkened, the veil of the Temple was torn asunder, graves were opened, and the earth quaked violently. And the awe-struck watchers said one to another, "Clearly this was the Son of God."

The Mourning of Christ

(MARK 15, 42-47)

Pompeo Girolamo Batoni (1708–1787) was an Italian painter, one of the foremost of his day. His works are largely of a religious nature, but he is also renowned for his many fine portraits of sovereigns and other dignitaries of the period.

When Christ expired on the cross, there was great mourning among the people who had followed Him on the road to Calvary to minister to Him. Among these were Mary Magdalene and Mary the mother of James and Joseph. They were joined by Joseph of Arimathea, who was also a disciple of Christ. He had gone to Pilate to get permission to take down and bury the body of Christ, and Pilate had assented. With the help of Nicodemus, another disciple, Joseph lovingly and tenderly took down the body of Christ from the cross. They then wrapped the body in a clean linen cloth, together with spices, and laid it in a new tomb hewn out of the rock in a nearby garden. Rolling a stone over the tomb, they departed. But the two Mary's stayed awhile by the sepulchre in mourning.

In this beautiful and symbolic picture showing a heartbroken woman standing at the entrance to the sepulchre with a child at her feet, the artist has pictured the sorrow of all people over the terrible events which culminated in Christ's death. However, the look of this woman heavenward and the expression of submissiveness and hope on her face clearly suggests that she is not among those who "mourn without hope."

The Crucifixion
by Diego Velasquez
THE PRADO : MADRID

The Mourning of Christ
by Pompeo Girolamo Batoni
KUNSTHALLE : HAMBURG

The Ascension *by Henrik Krock*
HELLIGAANDSHUSET CHURCH : COPENHAGEN

The Ascension

(LUKE 24, 36-51)

Henrik Krock (1671–1738) was a Danish painter, born in Flensburg. He studied in Copenhagen, and in Italy under Carlo Marotti. He decorated many buildings in Copenhagen.

In His last appearance after the Resurrection, Jesus ate with His Apostles, and then led them to the Mount of Olives, where He continued to talk to them. Finally He lifted up His hands and blessed them. As He did this, He was lifted up to heaven before their very eyes, and a cloud took him out of their sight. Enraptured, the Apostles fell down and worshiped Him; then they returned to Jerusalem with great joy in their hearts.

can he perform signs like these?" They were sharply divided over him. **17**Then they addressed the blind man again: "Since it was your eyes he opened, what do you have to say about him?" "He is a prophet," he replied.

18The Jews refused to believe that he had really been born blind and had begun to see, until they summoned the parents of this man who now could see. **19**"Is this your son?" they asked, "and if so, do you attest that he was blind at birth? How do you account for the fact that now he can see?" **20**The parents answered: "We know this is our son, and we know he was blind at birth. **21**But how he can see now, or who opened his eyes, we have no idea. Ask him. He is old enough to speak for himself." **22***†(His parents answered in this fashion because they were afraid of the Jews, who had already agreed among themselves that anyone who acknowledged Jesus as the Messiah would be put out of the synagogue. **23***That was why his parents said, "He is of age—ask him.")

24†A second time they summoned the man who had been born blind and said to him, "Give glory to God! First of all, we know this man is a sinner." **25**"I do not know whether he is a sinner or not," he answered. "I know this much: I was blind before; now I can see." **26**They persisted: "Just what did he do to you? How did he open your eyes?" **27**"I have told you once, but you would not listen to me," he answered them. "Why do you want to hear it all over again? Do not tell me you want to become his disciples too?" **28**They retorted scornfully: "You are the one who is that man's disciple. We are disciples of Moses. **29**We know that God spoke to Moses, but we have no idea where this man comes from." **30**He came back at them: "Well, this is news! You do not know where he comes from, yet he opened my eyes. **31***We know that God does not hear sinners, but that if someone is devout and obeys his will, he listens to him. **32**It is unheard of that anyone ever gave sight to a person blind from birth. **33**If this man were not from God, he could never have done such a thing." **34**"What!" they exclaimed, "You are steeped in sin from your birth, and you are giving us lectures?" With that they threw him out bodily.

35When Jesus heard of his expulsion, he sought him out and asked him, "Do you believe in the Son of Man?" **36**He answered, "Who is he, sir, that I may believe in him?" **37***"You have seen him," Jesus replied. "He is speaking to you now." **[38]**†["I do believe, Lord," he said, and bowed down to worship him. **39***Then Jesus said:]

> "I came into this world to divide it,
>   to make the sightless see
>   and the seeing blind."

40*Some of the Pharisees around him picked this up,

saying, "You are not calling us blind, are you?" **41**To which Jesus replied:

> "If you were blind
>   there would be no sin in that.
> 'But we see,' you say,
>   and your sin remains."

The Good Shepherd

10 **1***†"Truly I assure you:
>   Whoever does not enter the sheepfold
>   through the gate
>   but climbs in some other way
>   is a thief and a marauder.
> **2**The one who enters through the gate
>   is shepherd of the sheep;
> **3**the keeper opens the gate for him.
>   The sheep hear his voice
>   as he calls his own by name
>   and leads them out.
> **4***When he has brought out [all] those that
>   are his,
>   he walks in front of them,
>   and the sheep follow him
>   because they recognize his voice.
> **5**They will not follow a stranger;
>   such a one they will flee,
>   because they do not recognize a
>   stranger's voice."

6†Even though Jesus used this figure with them, they did not grasp what he was trying to tell them. **7**†He therefore said [to them again]:

> "My solemn word is this:
>   I am the sheepgate.
> **8**All who came before me
>   were thieves and marauders
>   whom the sheep did not heed.
> **9***I am the gate.
>   Whoever enters through me
>   will be safe.
>   He will go in and out,
>   and find pasture.

---

†

9, 22f: This parenthetical explanation seems to envisage a situation during the writer's lifetime after Jesus' ministry. Rejection from the synagogue of those Jews who confessed Jesus as the Messiah seems to have begun in the late eighties, when the curse against the *minim* or heretics was introduced.

9, 24: *Give glory to God:* this oath formula before taking testimony is attested in Jos 7, 19.

9, 38: This verse, omitted in important MSS, may be an addition from a baptismal liturgy.

10, 1: The exact time when these parables were spoken is difficult to determine—whether at the feast of Booths, as in chapters 7—9, or at the feast of the Dedication, as in 10, 22; but they continue the theme of attack on the Pharisees that ends chapter 9.

10, 6: *Figure:* John uses a different word for illustrative speech than the "parable" of the synoptics, but the idea is the same.

10, 7-10: In 7f, the figure is of a gate for the shepherd to come to the sheep; in 9f, of a gate for the sheep to *go in and out.*

*

22: 7, 13.
23: 12, 42.
31: 10, 21.
37: 4, 26.
39: Mt 13, 13ff.

40: Mt 15, 14; 23, 26; Rom 2, 19.
10/1-5: Jer 23, 1ff; Ez 34, 1-31.
4: Mi 2, 12f.
9: Ps 23, 1ff; Is 49, 9f.

10 The thief comes
only to steal and slaughter and destroy.
I came that they might have life
and have it to the full.

11*†I am the good shepherd;
the good shepherd lays down his life for the sheep.

12* The hired hand—who is no shepherd
nor owner of the sheep—
catches sight of the wolf coming
and runs away, leaving the sheep
to be snatched and scattered by the wolf.

13 That is because he works for pay;
he has no concern for the sheep.

14 "I am the good shepherd.
I know my sheep
and my sheep know me

15 in the same way that the Father knows me
and I know the Father;
for these sheep I will give my life.

16*†I have other sheep
that do not belong to this fold.
I must lead them, too,
and they shall hear my voice.
There shall be one flock then, one shepherd.

17* The Father loves me for this:
that I lay down my life
to take it up again.

18* No one takes it from me;
I lay it down freely.
I have power to lay it down,
and I have power to take it up again.
This command I received from my Father."

19Because of these words, the Jews were sharply divided once more. **20***Many were claiming: "He is possessed by a devil—out of his mind! Why pay any attention to him?" **21***Others maintained: "These are not the words of a madman. Surely a devil cannot open the eyes of the blind!"

Feast of the Dedication

22*†It was winter, and the time came for the feast of the Dedication in Jerusalem. **23***Jesus was walking in the temple area, in Solomon's Portico, **24*†**when the Jews gathered around him and said, "How long are you going to keep us in suspense? If you really are the Messiah, tell us so in plain words." **25***Jesus answered:

"I did tell you, but you do not believe.
The works I do in my Father's name
give witness in my favor,
26*but you refuse to believe
because you are not my sheep.

27 My sheep hear my voice.
I know them,
and they follow me.

28* I give them eternal life,
and they shall never perish.
No one shall snatch them out of my hand.

29*†My Father is greater than all, in what he has given me,
and there is no snatching out of his hand.

30* The Father and I are one."

31*When some of the Jews again reached for rocks to stone him, **32**Jesus protested to them, "Many good deeds have I shown you from the Father. For which of these do you stone me?" **33***"It is not for any 'good deed' that we are stoning you," the Jews retorted, "but for blaspheming. You who are only a man are making yourself God." **34*†**Jesus answered:

"Is it not written in your law,
'I have said, You are gods'?
35 If it calls those men gods
to whom God's word was addressed—
and Scripture cannot lose its force—
36*†do you claim that I blasphemed
when, as he whom the Father consecrated
and sent into the world,
I said, 'I am God's Son'?

37 If I do not perform my Father's works,
put no faith in me.
38* But if I do perform them,
even though you put no faith in me,
put faith in these works,

---

† 10, 11.14: The normal Greek word for *good* does not occur here. Were not the expression *good shepherd* traditional, it might be preferable to translate "model" or "noble" shepherd.

10, 16: *Other sheep:* the Gentiles, God's dispersed children destined to be gathered into one (11, 52). *One flock:* St. Jerome in the Vulgate translates "one fold," but there is no evidence in Greek or Latin to support this reading. Translating the Greek word as "sheep-herd" would bring out the wordplay involved as the Greek terms for "flock" and "shepherd" are as much alike as "sheep-herd" and "shepherd."

10, 22: *Feast of the Dedication:* held in December, three months after the feast of Booths (7, 2), to celebrate the Maccabees' rededication of the altar and reconsecration of the temple in 164 B. C., after their desecration by the Syrians (1 Mc 4, 36.59). Under its Hebrew name, Hanukkah, this feast is still a regular part of Jewish religious observance.

10, 23: *Solomon's Portico* was on the east side of the temple area and would offer protection from the cold winds sweeping in from the desert.

10, 24: *Keep us in suspense:* the literal translation of the words is "How long will you take away our life?" Cf 11, 48ff.

10, 29: The textual evidence for the first clause is very divided; it may also be translated: "As for the Father, what he has given me is greater than all."

10, 34: This is a reference to the judges who, since they exercised the divine prerogative to judge (Dt 1, 17), were called "gods"; cf Ex 21, 6, besides Ps 82, 6 from which the quotation comes.

10, 36: *Consecrated:* may be a reference to the theme of the Hanukkah feast; see note on 10, 22. In place of the rededicated temple altar, Jesus is consecrated by the Father.

---

*
11: Heb 13, 20.
12: Zec 11, 17.
16: Jer 23, 3; Eph 2, 14f.
17: Heb 10, 10.
18: 19, 11.
20: 7, 20; 8, 48.
21: 3, 2.
22: 1 Mc 4, 54.59.
24: Lk 22, 67.
25: 5, 36.

26: 8, 47.
28: Dt 32, 39.
29: Wis 3, 1; Is 43, 13.
30: 1, 1; 12, 45; 14, 9.
31: 8, 59.
33: 5, 18; 19, 7.
34: Ps 82, 6.
36: 5, 18.
38: 14, 10f.20.

so as to realize what it means
that the Father is in me
and I in him.”

39At these words they again tried to arrest him, but he eluded their grasp.

Return to the Jordan

40*Then he went back across the Jordan to the place where John had been baptizing earlier, and while he stayed there **41**many people came to him. “John may never have performed a sign,” they commented, “but whatever John said about this man was true.” **42**In that place, many came to believe in him.

The Raising of Lazarus

11 **1*†**THERE was a certain man named Lazarus who was sick. He was from Bethany, the village of Mary and her sister Martha. **2**(This Mary whose brother Lazarus was sick was the one who anointed the Lord with perfume and dried his feet with her hair.) **3**The sisters sent word to Jesus to inform him, “Lord, the one you love is sick.” **4**Upon hearing this, Jesus said:

“This sickness is not to end in death;
rather it is for God’s glory,
that through it the Son of God may be glorified.”

5Jesus loved Martha and her sister and Lazarus very much. **6**Yet, after hearing that Lazarus was sick, he stayed on where he was for two days more. **7**Finally he said to his disciples, “Let us go back to Judea.” **8***“Rabbi,” protested the disciples, “with the Jews only recently trying to stone you, you are going back up there again?” **9***Jesus answered:

“Are there not twelve hours of daylight?
If a man goes walking by day he does not stumble
because he sees the world bathed in light.
10†But if he goes walking at night he will stumble
since there is no light in him.”

11After uttering these words, he added, “Our beloved Lazarus has fallen asleep, but I am going there to wake him.” **12**At this the disciples objected, “Lord, if he is asleep his life will be saved.” **13***Jesus had been speaking about his death, but they thought he meant sleep in the sense of slumber. **14**Finally Jesus said plainly: “Lazarus is dead. **15**For your sakes I am glad I was not there, that you may come to believe. In any event, let us go to him.” **16†**Then Thomas (the name means “Twin”) said to his fellow disciples, “Let us go along, to die with him.”

17When Jesus arrived at Bethany, he found that Lazarus had already been in the tomb four days. **18**The village was not far from Jerusalem—just under two miles—**19***and many Jewish people had come out to console Martha and Mary over their brother. **20**When Martha heard that Jesus was coming she went to meet him, while Mary sat at home. **21***Martha said to Jesus, “Lord, if you had been here, my brother would never have died. **22**Even now, I am sure that God will give you whatever you ask of him.” **23**“Your brother will rise again,” Jesus assured her. **24***“I know he will rise again,” Martha replied, “in the resurrection on the last day.” **25***Jesus told her:

“I am the resurrection and the life:
26whoever believes in me,
though he should die, will come to life;
and whoever is alive and believes in me
will never die.

Do you believe this?” **27***“Yes, Lord,” she replied. “I have come to believe that you are the Messiah, the Son of God: he who is to come into the world.”

28When she had said this she went back and called her sister Mary. “The Teacher is here, asking for you,” she whispered. **29**As soon as Mary heard this, she got up and started out in his direction. **30**(Actually Jesus had not yet come into the village but was still at the spot where Martha had met him.) **31**The Jews who were in the house with Mary consoling her saw her get up quickly and go out, so they followed her, thinking she was going to the tomb to weep there. **32**When Mary came to the place where Jesus was, seeing him, she fell at his feet and said to him, “Lord, if you had been here my brother would never have died.” **33†**When Jesus saw her weeping, and the Jews who had accompanied her also weeping, he was troubled in spirit, moved by the deepest emotions. **34**“Where have you laid him?” he asked. “Lord, come and see,” they said. **35***Jesus began to weep, **36**which caused the Jews to remark, “See how much he loved him!” **37**But some said, “He opened the eyes of that blind man. Why could he not have done something to stop this man from dying?” **38**Once again troubled in spirit, Jesus approached the tomb.

It was a cave with a stone laid across it. **39**“Take away the stone,” Jesus directed. Martha, the dead man’s sister, said to him, “Lord, it has been four days now; surely there will be a stench!” **40**Jesus replied, “Did I not assure you that if you believed you would

---

† 11, 1: *Bethany:* a town near Jerusalem (v 18), distinct from Bethany in the Transjordan (1, 28). Among the synoptics, only Luke (10, 38) writes of Mary and Martha, but he locates the scene involving them in the journey from Galilee toward Jerusalem.

11, 10: *No light in him:* the ancient Palestinians apparently did not grasp clearly the entry of light *through* the eye, but seem to have thought of it as being *in* the eye; cf Lk 11, 34; Mt 6, 23.

11, 16: *The name means “Twin”:* or “Thomas, the one called Didymus.” “Thomas” is derived from the Hebrew word for twin; “Didymus,” a Greek personal name of the time, from the Greek word for twin.

11, 33: *He was troubled in spirit . . . deepest emotions:* probably signifies that Jesus was angry, perhaps at the lack of faith or at the presence of evil (death).

---

*
40: 1, 28.	19: 12, 9.17f.
11/1f: 12, 1-8; Lk 10, 38f.	21: 11, 32.
8: 8, 59; 10, 31.	24: 5, 29.
9: 8, 12; 9, 4.	25: 5, 24; 8, 51.
9f: 12, 35; 1 Jn 2, 10.	27: 1, 9; 6, 69.
13: Mt 9, 24.	35: Lk 19, 41.

see the glory of God displayed?" **41**They then took away the stone and Jesus looked upward and said:

"Father, I thank you for having heard me.
42* I know that you always hear me
but I have said this for the sake of the crowd,
that they may believe that you sent me."

43Having said this, he called loudly, "Lazarus, come out!" **44**The dead man came out, bound hand and foot with linen strips, his face wrapped in a cloth. "Untie him," Jesus told them, "and let him go free."

Session of the Sanhedrin

45This caused many of the Jews who had come to visit Mary, and had seen what Jesus did, to put their faith in him. **46**Some others, however, went to the Pharisees and reported what Jesus had done. **47*†**The result was that the chief priests and the Pharisees called a meeting of the Sanhedrin. "What are we to do," they said, "with this man performing all sorts of signs? **48**If we let him go on like this, the whole world will believe in him. Then the Romans will come in and sweep away our sanctuary and our nation." **49*†**One of their number named Caiaphas, who was high priest that year, addressed them at this point: "You have no understanding whatever! **50†**Can you not see that it is better for you to have one man die [for the people] than to have the whole nation destroyed?" **51**(He did not say this on his own. It was rather as high priest for that year that he prophesied that Jesus would die for the nation—**52**and not for this nation only, but to gather into one all the dispersed children of God.) **53***From that day onward there was a plan afoot to kill him. **54†**In consequence, Jesus no longer moved about freely in Jewish circles. He withdrew instead to a town called Ephraim in the region near the desert, where he stayed with his disciples.

The Last Passover

55*The Jewish Passover was near, which meant that many people from the country went up to Jerusalem for Passover purification. **56**They were on the lookout for Jesus, various people in the temple vicinity saying to each other, "What do you think? Is he likely to come for the feast?" **57**(The chief priests and the Pharisees had given orders that anyone who knew where he was should report it, so that they could apprehend him.)

Anointing at Bethany

12 **1*†**six days before Passover Jesus came to Bethany, the village of Lazarus whom Jesus had raised from the dead. **2***There they gave him a banquet, at which Martha served. Lazarus was one of those at table with him. **3*†**Mary brought a pound of costly perfume made from genuine aromatic nard, with which she anointed Jesus' feet. Then she dried his feet with her hair, and the house was filled with the ointment's fragrance. **4**Judas Iscariot, one of his disciples (the one about to hand him over), protested: **5†**"Why was not this perfume sold? It could have brought three hundred silver pieces, and the money have been given to the poor." **6***(He did not say this out of concern for the poor, but because he was a thief. He held the purse, and used to help himself to what was deposited there.) **7†**To this Jesus replied: "Leave her alone. Let her keep it against the day they prepare me for burial. **8**The poor you always have with you, but me you will not always have."

9*†The great crowd of Jews discovered he was there and came out, not only because of Jesus but also to see Lazarus, whom he had raised from the dead. **10**The fact was, the chief priests planned to kill Lazarus too, **11***because many Jews were going over to Jesus and believing in him on account of Lazarus.

Entry into Jerusalem

12*The next day the great crowd that had come for the feast heard that Jesus was to enter Jerusalem, **13*†**so they got palm branches and came out to meet him. They kept shouting:

---

† 11, 47: *What are we to do?*: could be the rhetorical "Why are we doing nothing?"

11, 49: *That year*: emphasizes the conjunction of the office and the year. The Jews attributed a gift of prophecy, sometimes unconscious, to the high priest.

11, 50: *For the people*: this phrase is omitted in some impressive patristic witnesses, and may be a gloss. If it is original, Caiaphas meant "in place of the people"; but in v 51, John takes it to mean "on behalf of."

11, 54: Ephraim is usually located about twelve miles northeast of Jerusalem, as the mountains descend into the Jordan valley.

12, 1ff: This is probably the same scene of anointing that we find in Mk 14, 3-9. The anointing reported in Lk 7, 36-38 is part of a different scene. Details from these various episodes may have become interchanged.

12, 3: *Perfume made from genuine aromatic nard*: this phrase, found also in Mk 14, 3, is of uncertain meaning.

12, 5: *Silver pieces*: literally, "denarii." A denarius is a day's wage in Mt 20, 2.

12, 7: An obscure verse. It could be taken to mean that Mary was to keep the perfume for Jesus' future burial, though Mk 14, 8 and Jn 19, 39 seem to rule out a future reference. The present scene probably represents Jesus' embalming in a figurative sense.

12, 9: The expression *the great crowd*, here and in v 12, is even more awkward in Greek than in English; many textual witnesses have smoothed it out by omitting the article. It seems to have the function of uniting the crowd of the entry scene with the witnesses of the Lazarus miracle.

12, 13: See Psalm 118, 25f, and the note there on *Hosanna*.

✱
42: 12, 30.   3: 11, 2.
47: 12, 19; Mt 26, 3ff;   6: 13, 29.
    Lk 22, 2; Acts 4, 16.   9: 11, 19.
49f: 18, 13f.   11: 11, 45.
53: 5, 18; 7, 1; Mt 12, 14.   12-19: Mt 21, 1-16;
55: 2, 13; 5, 1; 6, 4; 18, 28.   Mk 11, 1-10;
12/1-11: Mt 26, 6-13;   Lk 19, 28-40.
    Mk 14, 3-9.   13: 1, 49; Ps 118, 26;
1f: 11, 1.   Rv 7, 9.
2: Lk 10, 38ff.

"Hosanna!
Blessed is he who comes in the name of the Lord!
Blessed is the King of Israel!"

14Jesus found a donkey and mounted it, in accord with Scripture:

15*"Fear not, O daughter of Zion!
Your king approaches you
on a donkey's colt."

16*(At first, the disciples did not understand all this, but after Jesus was glorified they recalled that the people had done to him precisely what had been written about him.)

17†The crowd that was present when he called Lazarus out of the tomb and raised him from the dead kept testifying to it. **18**The crowd came out to meet him because they heard he had performed this sign. **19***†The Pharisees remarked to one another, "See, there is nothing you can do! The whole world has run after him."

The Coming of Jesus' Hour

20†Among those who had come up to worship at the feast were some Greeks. **21***They approached Philip, who was from Bethsaida in Galilee, and put this request to him: "Sir, we should like to see Jesus." **22***Philip went to tell Andrew; Philip and Andrew in turn came to inform Jesus. **23***Jesus answered them:

"The hour has come
for the Son of Man to be glorified.
24*†I solemnly assure you,
unless the grain of wheat falls to the earth and
dies,
it remains just a grain of wheat.
But if it dies,
it produces much fruit.
25*†The man who loves his life
loses it,
while the man who hates his life in this world
preserves it to life eternal.
26If anyone would serve me,
let him follow me;
where I am,
there will my servant be.
If anyone serves me,
him the Father will honor.
27*My soul is troubled now,
yet what should I say—
Father, save me from this hour?
But it was for this that I came to this hour.
28*Father, glorify your name!"

Then a voice came from the sky:

"I have glorified it,
and will glorify it again."

29When the crowd of bystanders heard the voice, they said it was thunder. Others maintained, "An angel was speaking to him." **30***Jesus answered, "That voice did not come for my sake, but for yours.

31*"Now has judgment come upon this world,
now will this world's prince be driven out,
32*and I—once I am lifted up from earth—
will draw all men to myself."

33(This statement indicated the sort of death he had to die.) **34***†The crowd objected to his words: "We have heard it said in the law that the Messiah is to remain forever. How can you claim that the Son of Man must be lifted up? Just who is this 'Son of Man'?" **35***Jesus answered:

"The light is among you only a little longer.
Walk while you still have it
or darkness will come over you.
The man who walks in the dark
does not know where he is going.
36While you have the light,
keep faith in the light;
thus you will become sons of light."

After this utterance, Jesus left them and went into hiding.

Evaluation of the Ministry

37Despite his many signs performed in their presence, they refused to believe in him. **38***†This was to fulfill the word of the prophet Isaiah:

"Lord, who has believed what has reached our ears?
To whom has the might of the Lord been revealed?"

39The reason they could not believe was that, as Isaiah says elsewhere:

† 12, 17f: There seem to be two different crowds in these verses. There are good witnesses to the text which have another reading for v 17: "Then the crowd that was with him began to testify that he had called Lazarus out of the tomb and raised him from the dead."

12, 19: *The whole world:* the sense is that everyone is following Jesus, but John has an ironic play on *world;* he alludes to the universality of salvation (3, 17; 4, 42).

12, 20: *Greeks:* not used here in a nationalistic sense. These are Gentile proselytes to Judaism; cf 7, 35.

12, 24: *It remains just a grain of wheat:* literally, "it remains alone."

12, 25: *His life:* the Greek word *psyche* refers to a man's natural life. It does not mean "soul," for Hebrew anthropology did not postulate body/soul dualism in the way that is familiar to us.

12, 34: There is no passage in the Old Testament that states precisely that *the Messiah is to remain forever.* Perhaps the closest is Ps 89, 37.

12, 38ff: John gives a historical explanation of Jewish disbelief, not a psychological one. The Old Testament had to be fulfilled in the New; the disbelief that met Isaiah's message

*
15: Zec 9, 9.
16: 2, 22.
19: 11, 47f; Mt 21, 16.
21: 1, 43.
22: 1, 40.
23: 2, 4.
24: Is 53, 10ff;
1 Cor 15, 36.
25: Mt 16, 25; Mk 8, 35;
Lk 9, 24.
26: 14, 3; 17, 24;
27: 6, 38; 18, 11;
Lk 22, 42; Heb 5, 7f.
28: 2, 11; 17, 5.
30: 11, 42; 16, 11.
31: Lk 10, 18; Rv 12, 9.
32: 3, 14; 8, 28.
34: Ps 89, 5; Is 9, 6;
Dn 7, 14.
35: 9, 4; Jb 5, 14.
38: Is 53, 1; Rom 10, 16.
Mt 16, 24.

⁴⁰*"He has blinded their eyes,
and numbed their hearts,
lest they see
or comprehend,
or have a change of heart—
and I should heal them."

⁴¹*Isaiah uttered these words because he had seen Jesus' glory, and it was of him he spoke.

⁴²*There were many, even among the Sanhedrin, who believed in him; but they refused to admit it because of the Pharisees, for fear they might be ejected from the synagogue. ⁴³*They preferred the praise of men to the glory of God.

Summary Proclamation

⁴⁴*Jesus proclaimed aloud:

"Whoever puts faith in me
believes not so much in me
as in him who sent me;
⁴⁵*and whoever looks on me
is seeing him who sent me.
⁴⁶*I have come to the world as its light,
to keep anyone who believes in me
from remaining in the dark.
⁴⁷*If anyone hears my words and does not keep them,
I am not the one to condemn him,
for I did not come to condemn the world
but to save it.
⁴⁸*Whoever rejects me and does not accept my words
already has his judge,
namely, the word I have spoken—
it is that which will condemn him on the last day.
⁴⁹*For I have not spoken on my own;
no, the Father who sent me
has commanded me
what to say and how to speak.
⁵⁰ Since I know that his commandment means eternal life,
whatever I say
is spoken just as he instructed me."

III: THE BOOK OF GLORY

The Washing of the Feet

13 ¹*BEFORE THE FEAST OF PASSOVER, Jesus realized that the hour had come for him to pass from this world to the Father. He had loved his own in this world, and would show his love for them to the end. ²*†The devil had already induced Judas, son of Simon Iscariot, to hand him over; and so, during the supper, ³*Jesus—fully aware that he had come from God and was going to God, the Father who had handed everything over to him—⁴rose from the meal and took off his cloak. He picked up a towel and tied it around himself. ⁵†Then he poured water into a basin and began to wash his disciples' feet and dry them with the towel he had around him. ⁶Thus he came to Simon Peter, who said to him, "Lord, are you going to wash my feet?" ⁷Jesus answered, "You may not realize now what I am doing, but later you will understand." ⁸Peter replied, "You shall never wash my feet!" "If I do not wash you," Jesus answered, "you will have no share in my heritage." ⁹"Lord," Simon Peter said to him, "then not only my feet, but my hands and head as well." ¹⁰*†Jesus told him, "The man who has bathed has no need to wash [except for his feet]; he is entirely cleansed, just as you are; though not all." ¹¹*(The reason he said, "Not all are washed clean," was that he knew his betrayer.)

¹²After he had washed their feet, he put his cloak back on and reclined at table once more. He said to them:

"Do you understand what I just did for you?
¹³ You address me as 'Teacher' and 'Lord,'
and fittingly enough,
for that is what I am.
¹⁴ But if I washed your feet—
I who am Teacher and Lord—
then you must wash each other's feet.
¹⁵* What I just did was to give you an example:
as I have done, so you must do.
¹⁶*†I solemnly assure you,
no slave is greater than his master;
no messenger outranks the one who sent him.
¹⁷ Once you know all these things,
blest will you be if you put them into practice.

Role of Judas

¹⁸*"What I say is not said of all,
for I know the kind of men I chose.
My purpose here is the fulfillment of Scripture:
'He who partook of bread with me
has raised his heel against me.'

---

† was a foreshadowing of the disbelief that Jesus encountered. In 12, 42 and also in 3, 20, we see that there is no negation of freedom.

13, 2: *Induced:* literally, "The devil put into the heart that Judas should hand him over." It is uncertain into whose heart, Judas' or devil's.

13, 5: *Basin:* the exact vessel is not certain, but it was used for washing, perhaps by pouring, in which case the translation should be "pitcher."

13, 10: *Bathed:* many have suggested that this passage is a symbolic reference to baptism. The Greek root involved is used in baptismal contexts in 1 Cor 6, 11; Eph 5, 26; Ti 3, 5; Heb 10, 22. The washing of the feet was connected with baptism in early Christian liturgy.

13, 16: *Messenger:* the Greek has *apostolos,* the only occurrence of the term in John. It is not used in the technical sense here.

✽
40: Mt 13, 13f; Is 6, 9f.
41: 5, 39; Is 6, 1.4.
42: 9, 22.
43: 5, 44.
44: 13, 20; 14, 1.
45: 14, 7ff.
46: 1, 9; 8, 12.
47: 3, 17.
48: Lk 10, 16.
49: 14, 10.31; Dt 18, 18f.

13/1: 2, 4; 7, 30; 8, 20;
    Mt 26, 17.
2: 6, 71; 17, 12;
    Mt 26, 20; Lk 22, 3.
3: 3, 35.
10: 15, 3.
11: 6, 70.
15: Lk 22, 27.
16: 15, 20; Mt 10, 24;
    Lk 6, 40.
18: Ps 41, 10.

¹⁹I tell you this now, before it takes place,
so that when it takes place you may believe
that I AM.
²⁰⸎I solemnly assure you,
he who accepts anyone I send
accepts me,
and in accepting me
accepts him who sent me."

²¹⸎After saying this, Jesus grew deeply troubled.
He went on to give this testimony:

"I tell you solemnly,
one of you will betray me."

²²The disciples looked at one another, puzzled as to whom he could mean. **²³**⸎†One of them, the disciple whom Jesus loved, reclined close to him as they ate. **²⁴**Simon Peter signaled him to ask Jesus whom he meant. **²⁵**He leaned back against Jesus' chest and said to him, "Lord, who is he?" **²⁶**Jesus answered, "The one to whom I give the bit of food I dip in the dish." He dipped the morsel, then took it and gave it to Judas, son of Simon Iscariot. **²⁷**⸎Immediately after, Satan entered his heart. Jesus addressed himself to him: "Be quick about what you are to do." **²⁸**(Naturally, none of those reclining at table understood why Jesus had said this to him. **²⁹**⸎A few had the idea that, since Judas held the common purse, Jesus was telling him to buy what was needed for the feast, or to give something to the poor.) **³⁰**No sooner had Judas eaten the morsel than he went out. It was night.

³¹†Once Judas had left, Jesus said:

"Now is the Son of Man glorified
and God is glorified in him.
³²⸎†[If God has been glorified in him,]
God will, in turn, glorify him in himself,
and will glorify him soon.
³³⸎ My children, I am not to be with you much longer.
You will look for me,
but I say to you now
what I once said to the Jews:
'Where I am going, you cannot come.'
³⁴⸎ I give you a new commandment:
Love one another.
Such as my love has been for you,
so must your love be for each other.
³⁵ This is how all will know you for my disciples:
your love for one another."

Peter's Denial Predicted

³⁶⸎"Lord," Simon Peter said to him, "Where do you mean to go?" Jesus answered:

"I am going where you cannot follow me now;
later on you shall come after me."

³⁷"Lord," Peter said to him, "why can I not follow you now? I will lay down my life for you!" **³⁸**⸎"You will lay down your life for me, will you?" Jesus answered. "I tell you truly, the cock will not crow before you have three times disowned me!

Last Discourse

14 **¹**"Do not let your hearts be troubled.
Have faith in God
and faith in me.
²†In my Father's house there are many dwelling places;
otherwise, how could I have told you
that I was going to prepare a place for you?
³⸎I am indeed going to prepare a place for you,
and then I shall come back to take you with me,
that where I am you also may be.
⁴ You know the way that leads where I go."

⁵"Lord," said Thomas, "we do not know where you are going. How can we know the way?" **⁶**Jesus told him:

"I am the way, and the truth, and the life;
no one comes to the Father but through me.
⁷⸎†If you really knew me, you would know my Father also.
From this point on you know him; you have seen him."

⁸"Lord," Philip said to him, "show us the Father and that will be enough for us." **⁹**⸎"Philip," Jesus replied, "after I have been with you all this time, you still do not know me?

"Whoever has seen me has seen the Father.
How can you say, 'Show us the Father'?

¹⁰⸎Do you not believe that I am in the Father
and the Father is in me?

⸎
20: Mt 10, 40; Mk 9, 37; Lk 9, 48.
21-30: Mt 26, 21-25; Mk 14, 18-21; Lk 22, 21ff.
23: 19, 26; 20, 2; 21, 7.20.
27: 13, 2; Lk 22, 3.
29: 12, 5f.
32: 17, 1-5.
33: 7, 33; 8, 21.
34: 15, 12f.17; Lv 19, 18.
36: Mk 14, 27; Lk 22, 33.
38: 18, 27; Mt 26, 33ff; Mk 14, 29ff; Lk 22, 33f.
14/3: 12, 26; 17, 24.
7: 8, 19; 12, 45.
9: 1, 18; 10, 30; 12, 45.
10: 1, 1; 12, 49.

† 13, 23: *The disciple whom Jesus loved* is mentioned in 19, 26; 20, 2; 21, 7. A disciple, called *another disciple* or *the other disciple*, is mentioned in 18, 15 and 20, 2; and in the latter reference he is identified with the disciple whom Jesus loved. There is also an unnamed disciple in 1, 35-40. It has been traditional to identify the disciple thus variously referred to as St. John.

13, 31-38: These verses form an introduction to the last discourse of Jesus, which runs through chapters 14—17. In it John has collected Jesus' words to *his own* (cf 13, 1). There are indications that several speeches have been fused together, e. g., in 14, 31 and 17, 1.

13, 32: *God will . . . glorify him in himself:* the concluding word probably refers to the Father rather than to Jesus; cf 17, 5.21.

14, 2: A number of MSS omit *that* in this sentence, thus giving different inflections of meaning to the verse, with three distinct statements in it.

14, 7: An alternative reading is: "If you know me, then you know my Father also." The form in the text above is a rebuke akin to 8, 19.

The words I speak are not spoken of myself;
it is the Father who lives in me accomplishing his
    works.

11* Believe me that I am in the Father
and the Father is in me,
or else, believe because of the works I do.

12 I solemnly assure you,
the man who has faith in me
will do the works I do,
and greater far than these.
Why? Because I go to the Father,

13* and whatever you ask in my name
I will do,
so as to glorify the Father in the Son.

14 Anything you ask me in my name
I will do.

15*† If you love me
and obey the commands I give you,

16*† I will ask the Father
and he will give you another Paraclete—
to be with you always:

17*† the Spirit of truth,
whom the world cannot accept,
since it neither sees him nor recognizes him;
but you can recognize him
because he remains with you
and will be within you.

18 I will not leave you orphaned;
I will come back to you.

19*† A little while now and the world will see me no
    more;
but you see me
as one who has life, and you will have life.

20 On that day you will know
that I am in my Father,
and you in me, and I in you.

21* He who obeys the commandments he has from
    me
is the man who loves me;
and he who loves me will be loved by my Father.
I too will love him
and reveal myself to him."

22† Judas (not Judas Iscariot) said to him, "Lord, why
is it that you will reveal yourself to us and not to the
world?" **23*** Jesus answered:

"Anyone who loves me
will be true to my word,
and my Father will love him;
we will come to him
and make our dwelling place with him.
24 He who does not love me does not keep my
    words.

Yet the word you hear is not mine;
it comes from the Father who sent me.

25 This much have I told you while I was still with
    you;

26* the Paraclete, the Holy Spirit
whom the Father will send in my name,
will instruct you in everything,
and remind you of all that I told you.

27*† 'Peace' is my farewell to you,
my peace is my gift to you;
I do not give it to you as the world gives peace.
Do not be distressed or fearful.

28 You have heard me say,
'I go away for a while, and I come back to you.'
If you truly loved me
you would rejoice to have me go to the Father,
for the Father is greater than I.

29* I tell you this now, before it takes place,
so that when it takes place you may believe.

30 I shall not go on speaking to you longer;
the Prince of this world is at hand.
He has no hold on me,

31* but the world must know that I love the Father
and do as the Father has commanded me.
Come, then! Let us be on our way.

The Vine and the Branches

15 **1*†** "I am the true vine
and my Father is the vinegrower.
2† He prunes away
every barren branch,
but the fruitful ones
he trims clean
to increase their yield.

---

† 14, 15: There is attestation for several other readings of this verse: "If you love me, keep my commandments" or "If you love me, you will keep my commandments."

14, 16: *Another Paraclete:* evidently Jesus is the first Paraclete; see 1 Jn 2, 2, where Jesus is a Paraclete in the sense of heavenly intercessor. However, this verse could be translated: "another, a Paraclete." The Johannine term *paraclete* derived from Greek legal terminology is used secularly for a defense attorney, a spokesman, an intercessor, although none of these terms fits precisely in John. The Paraclete in John is a teacher, a witness to Jesus, and a prosecutor of the world. He represents the continued presence on earth of the Jesus who has returned to the Father.

14, 17: The Greek word for "Spirit" is neuter, and while we use personal pronouns in English ("he," "his," "him"), most Greek MSS employ "it."

14, 19: The last part can be made a separate sentence: "Because I have life, you also will have life."

14, 22: *Not Judas Iscariot:* other readings are "Judas the Cananean" and "Judas Thomas." Perhaps the original had simply "Judas." There is a Judas, son of James in the Lucan lists of the Twelve (Lk 6, 16; Acts 1, 13), but there is no corresponding name in the Matthean or Marcan lists.

14, 27: *Peace:* Jesus gives to his disciples the traditional Hebrew salutation "Shalom"; but his *shalom* is a gift of salvation and not a conventional word of farewell, as it is among other men.

15, 1: In the Bible Israel is spoken of as a vineyard (Is 5, 1-7; Mt 21, 33-46) and as a vine (Jer 2, 21). The identification of the vine as the son of man in Ps 80, 16, and Wisdom's description

---

*
11: 10, 38.
13: 15, 7.16; 16, 23f;
    Mt 7, 7-11.
15: 15, 10; Wis 6, 18;
    1 Jn 2, 3.
16: 15, 26.
17: 16, 13; Mt 28, 20;
    2 Jn 1f.
19: 16, 16.

21: Jn 16, 27; 1 Jn 2, 5;
    3, 24.
23: Rv 3, 20.
26: 15, 26; 16, 13f.
27: Eph 2, 14-18.
29: 13, 19; 16, 4.
31: 6, 38.
15/1: Is 5, 1.

3＊ You are clean already,
     thanks to the word I have spoken to you.
4† Live on in me, as I do in you.
     No more than a branch can bear fruit of itself
     apart from the vine,
     can you bear fruit
     apart from me.
5＊ I am the vine, you are the branches.
     He who lives in me and I in him,
     will produce abundantly,
     for apart from me you can do nothing.
6＊ A man who does not live in me
     is like a withered, rejected branch,
     picked up to be thrown in the fire and burnt.
7＊ If you live in me,
     and my words stay part of you,
     you may ask what you will—
     it will be done for you.
8＊ My Father has been glorified
     in your bearing much fruit
     and becoming my disciples.

A Disciple's Love

9＊ "As the Father has loved me,
     so I have loved you.
     Live on in my love.
10＊ You will live in my love
     if you keep my commandments,
     even as I have kept my Father's commandments,
     and live in his love.
11＊ All this I tell you
     that my joy may be yours
     and your joy may be complete.
12＊ This is my commandment:
     love one another
     as I have loved you.
13＊† There is no greater love than this:
     to lay down one's life for one's friends.
14 You are my friends
     if you do what I command you.
15＊ I no longer speak of you as slaves,
     for a slave does not know what his master is
       about.
     Instead, I call you friends,
     since I have made known to you all that I heard
       from my Father.
16＊ It was not you who chose me,
     it was I who chose you
     to go forth and bear fruit.
     Your fruit must endure,
     so that all you ask the Father in my name
     he will give you.

17＊ The command I give you is this,
     that you love one another.

The World's Hate

18＊†"If you find that the world hates you,
     know it has hated me before you.
19＊ If you belonged to the world,
     it would love you as its own;
     the reason it hates you
     is that you do not belong to the world.
     But I chose you out of the world.
20＊† Remember what I told you:
     no slave is greater than his master.
     They will harry you
     as they harried me.
     They will respect your words
     as much as they respected mine.
21＊† All this they will do to you because of my name,
     for they know nothing of him who sent me.
22＊† If I had not come to them and spoken to them,
     they would not be guilty of sin;
     now, however, their sin cannot be excused.
23＊ To hate me is to hate my Father.
24＊ Had I not performed such works among them
     as no one has ever done before,
     they would not be guilty of sin;
     but as it is, they have seen,
     and they go on hating me and my Father.
25† However, this only fulfills the text in their law:
     'They hated me without cause.'

＊
3: 13, 10.	15: Rom 8, 15; Gal 4, 7.
5: Ps 127, 1.	16: 14, 13; Dt 7, 6.
6: Ez 15, 6f; 19, 10ff;	17: 13, 34; 1 Jn 3, 23;
3, 10.	4, 21.
7: 14, 13; 1 Jn 5, 14.	18: 7, 7; 1 Jn 3, 13.
8: Mt 5, 16.	19: 17, 14ff; 1 Jn 4, 5.
9: 17, 23.	20: 13, 16; Mt 10, 24.
10: 8, 29; 14, 15.	21: 8, 19; 16, 3.
11: 16, 22; 17, 13.	22: 8, 21.24.
12: 13, 34.	23: 5, 23; 1 Jn 2, 23.
13: Rom 5, 6ff; 1 Jn 3, 16.	24: 3, 2; 9, 32.

†
of herself as a vine in Sir 24, 17, are important background for Jesus' use of this figure as a self-description. In the synoptic account of the institution of the Eucharist at the Last Supper, we hear of "the fruit of the vine" (Mk 12, 25). The Didache refers to the eucharistic cup as "the holy vine of David your servant revealed through Jesus Christ." Consequently there may be secondary eucharistic symbolism here.

15, 2: *Prunes away . . . trims clean:* in Greek there is a play on two related verbs, *airein* and *kathairein.*

15, 4-7: *Live on in . . . live in . . . stay part of:* these all represent the same Greek expression for "remain in."

15, 13: *For one's friends:* in 9-13a, the words for love are related to the Greek *agapan.* In 13b-15, the words for love are related to the Greek *philein.* For John, the two roots are synonymous and mean "to love." The word *philos* in vv 13ff, is here translated "friend."

15, 18: The section 15, 18—16, 4 has numerous parallels with predictions of persecution made by Jesus in the synoptic gospels —especially with Mt 10, 17-25.

15, 20: *What I told you:* a reference to 13, 16.

15, 21: *Because of my name:* the idea of persecution because of Jesus' name is frequent in the New Testament (Mt 10, 22; 24, 9; Acts 9, 14). For John, association with Jesus' name implies union with Jesus.

15, 22.24: Jesus' words (*spoken*) and deeds (*works performed*) are the great motives of credibility. *They have seen . . . go on hating:* probably means they have seen his works and still have hated; but the Greek can be read: "have seen both me and my Father and still have hated both me and my Father."

15, 25: *Law:* a larger concept than the Pentateuch, for the reference is to Ps 35, 19 or 69, 5. See notes on 10, 34; 12, 34.

26✥† When the Paraclete comes,
     the Spirit of truth who comes from the Father—
     and whom I myself will send from the Father—
     he will bear witness on my behalf.
27✥† You must bear witness as well,
     for you have been with me from the beginning.

16

1 "I have told you all this
     to keep your faith from being shaken.
2✥† Not only will they expel you from
         synagogues;
a time will come
when anyone who puts you to death
will claim to be serving God!
3✥ All this they will do to [you]
     because they knew neither the Father nor me.
4✥ But I have told you these things
     that when their hour comes
     you may remember my telling you of them.

Jesus' Departure; Coming of the Paraclete

"I did not speak of this with you from the
     beginning
     because I was with you.
5† Now that I go back to him who sent me,
     not one of you asks me, 'Where are you going?'
6 Because I have had all this to say to you,
     you are overcome with grief.
7✥ Yet I tell you the sober truth:
     It is much better for you that I go.
     If I fail to go,
     the Paraclete will never come to you,
     whereas if I go,
     I will send him to you.
8† When he comes,
     he will prove the world wrong
     about sin,
     about justice,
     about condemnation.
9✥ About sin—
     in that they refuse to believe in me;
10 about justice—
     from the fact that I go to the Father
     and you can see me no more;
11✥ about condemnation—
     for the prince of this world has been condemned.
12 I have much more to tell you,
     but you cannot bear it now.
13✥† When he comes, however,
     being the Spirit of truth
     he will guide you to all truth.
     He will not speak on his own,
     but will speak only what he hears,
     and will announce to you the things to come.

14 In doing this he will give glory to me,
     because he will have received from me
     what he will announce to you.
15 All that the Father has belongs to me.
     That is why I said that what he will announce to
         you
     he will have from me.
16✥ Within a short time you will lose sight of me,
     but soon after that you shall see me again."

The Return of Jesus

17† At this, some of his disciples asked one another: "What can he mean, 'Within a short time you will lose sight of me, but soon after that you will see me'? And did he not say that he is going back to the Father'? 18 They kept asking: "What does he mean by this 'short time'? We do not know what he is talking about." 19 Since Jesus was aware that they wanted to question him, he said: "You are asking one another about my saying, 'Within a short time you will lose sight of me, but soon after that you will see me.'

20✥† "I tell you truly:
     you will weep and mourn
     while the world rejoices;
     you will grieve for a time,
     but your grief will be turned to joy.

---

†

15, 26: *Comes from the Father:* refers to the mission of the Spirit to men, not to the eternal procession of the Spirit. Compare 14, 26, where the Father, not Jesus, is said to send the Spirit.

15, 27: *You . . . as well:* this witness of the disciples is not different or distinct from that of the Paraclete; rather, it exteriorizes the Paraclete's internal witness.

16, 2: *Time* is literally "hour"—not "the hour" of Jesus but the period of persecution.

16, 5: *Not one of you asks me:* the difficulty of reconciling this with Simon Peter's question in 13, 36 and Thomas' words in 14, 5 strengthens the supposition that the last discourse has been made up of several collections of Johannine material.

16, 8-11: These verses illustrate the forensic character of the Paraclete's role: in the forum of the disciples' conscience he prosecutes the world. He leads believers to see (a) that the basic sin of men was and is their refusal to believe in Jesus; (b) that, although Jesus was found guilty and apparently died in disgrace, in reality justice has triumphed, for Jesus has returned to his Father; (c) finally, that it is the prince of this world, Satan, who has been condemned through Jesus' death (12, 32).

16, 13: *Announce to you the things to come:* this is not necessarily a reference to new future predictions; the Greek verb is used in Daniel for interpretation, in relation to the present and the future, of what has already happened. The Paraclete makes Jesus' message continually relevant for each generation.

16, 17: The disciples are puzzled by the contrast between their seeing Jesus soon again (v 16) and his return to the Father (v 10), presumably to stay.

16, 20: Jesus does not discuss the *short time* mentioned in v 18, but the contrast between sorrow and joy implicit in v 16. The *grief* of this verse and the *pain* of the next are the same Greek word as the *grief* of v 6. The promise of joy will be fulfilled in 20, 20.

✥

26: 14, 26.
27: Lk 1, 2; Acts 1, 8.
16/2: 9, 22; 12, 42;
     Mt 10, 17; Lk 21, 12;
     Acts 26, 11.
3. 15, 21.
4: 13, 19; 14, 29.

7: 14, 16.26.
9: 8, 21-24; 15, 22.
11: 12, 31.
13: 14, 26.
16: 7, 33; 14, 19.
20: Ps 126, 6.

21* When a woman is in labor
  she is sad that her time has come.
  When she has borne her child,
  she no longer remembers her pain
  for joy that a man has been born into the world.
22* In the same way, you are sad for a time,
  but I shall see you again;
  then your hearts will rejoice
  with a joy no one can take from you.
23*†On that day you will have no questions to ask me.
  I give you my assurance,
  whatever you ask the Father,
  he will give you in my name.
24 Until now you have not asked for anything in my
    name.
  Ask and you shall receive,
  that your joy may be full.
25*†I have spoken these things to you in veiled
    language.
  A time will come when I shall no longer do so,
  but shall tell you about the Father in plain
    speech.
26* On that day you will ask in my name
  and I do not say that I will petition the Father for
    you.
27 The Father already loves you,
  because you have loved me
  and have believed that I came from God.
28 [I did indeed come from the Father;]
  I came into the world.
  Now I am leaving the world
  to go to the Father."

29"At last you are speaking plainly," his disciples exclaimed, "without talking in veiled language! 30†We
are convinced that you know everything. There is no
need for anyone to ask you questions. We do indeed
believe you came from God." 31Jesus answered them:

  "Do you really believe?
32*An hour is coming—has indeed already come—
  when you will be scattered and each will go his
    way,
  leaving me quite alone.
  (Yet I can never be alone;
  the Father is with me.)
33*I tell you all this
  that in me you may find peace.
  You will suffer in the world.
  But take courage!
  I have overcome the world."

Completion of Jesus' Work

17 ¹*†AFTER he had spoken these words, Jesus
looked up to heaven and said:

  "Father, the hour has come!
  Give glory to your Son
  that your Son may give glory to you,
2*†inasmuch as you have given him authority over
    all mankind,
  that he may bestow eternal life on those you gave
    him.
3*†(Eternal life is this:
  to know you, the only true God,
  and him whom you have sent, Jesus Christ.)
4 I have given you glory on earth
  by finishing the work you gave me to do.
5* Do you now, Father, give me glory at your side,
  a glory I had with you before the world began.
6† I have made your name known
  to those you gave me out of the world.
  These men you gave me were yours;
  they have kept your word.
7 Now they realize
  that all that you gave me comes from you.
8 I entrusted to them
  the message you entrusted to me,
  and they received it.
  They have known that in truth I came from you,
  they have believed it was you who sent me.

---

† 16, 23: Having no questions to ask is a matter of seeking or
not seeking understanding. "Ask and you shall receive" is a
matter of petitioning.

16, 25: *In veiled language:* may be a reference to the para-
bolic comparisons of the vine and the branches (15, 1-16) and
the woman in labor (16, 21).

16, 30: The reference is seemingly to the fact that Jesus
could anticipate their question in v 19. The disciples naively
think they have the full understanding that is the climax of
"the hour" of Jesus' death, resurrection and ascension (v 25),
but the only part of the hour that is at hand for them is their
share in the passion (v 32).

17, 1-26: Since the sixteenth century this part of the last discourse has been called the "high priestly prayer" of Jesus. Here
his words are addressed directly to the Father rather than to
the disciples, who only overhear. Although still in the world
(v 13), Jesus looks on his earthly ministry as a thing of the past
(vv 4.12). Whereas Jesus has hitherto stated that the disciples
could not follow him (13, 33.36), now he wishes them to be
with him in union with the Father (vv 12ff). He is crossing the
threshold of eternity.

17, 1: The action of looking up to heaven and the address
Father are typical of Jesus at prayer; cf 11, 41.

17, 2: Another possible interpretation is to treat the first
line of the verse as parenthetical and the second as an apposi-
tive to the clause that ends v 1: *that your Son may give glory
to you (inasmuch . . . mankind), that he may bestow eternal
life. . . .*

17, 3: This verse was clearly added in the editing of the
gospel, for Jesus would hardly have referred to himself as
Jesus Christ.

17, 6: *I have made your name known:* perhaps the name is
I AM; cf 8, 24.28.58; 13, 19.

---

* 21: Is 26, 17f; Jer 31, 13.
  22: 14, 19; 15, 11; 20, 20.
  23: 14, 13.
  25: Mt 13, 34f.
  26: 14, 13.
  28: 1, 1.
  32: 8, 29; Zec 13, 7;
     Mt 26, 31.
  33: 14, 27.
  17/1: 13, 31.
  2: 3, 35; Mt 28, 18.
  3: Wis 14, 7; 1 Jn 5, 20.
  5: 12, 28; Phil 2, 6.9ff.

Prayer for the Disciples

9 "For these I pray—
not for the world
but for these you have given me,
for they are really yours.

10* (Just as all that belongs to me is yours,
so all that belongs to you is mine.)
It is in them that I have been glorified.

11† I am in the world no more,
but these are in the world
as I come to you.
O Father most holy,
protect them with your name which you have
   given me
[that they may be one, even as we are one].

12*† As long as I was with them,
I guarded them with your name which you gave
   me.
I kept careful watch,
and not one of them was lost,
none but him who was destined to be lost—
in fulfillment of Scripture.

13* Now, however, I come to you;
I say all this while I am still in the world
that they may share my joy completely.

14* I gave them your word
and the world has hated them for it;
they do not belong to the world
[any more than I belong to the world].

15*† I do not ask you to take them out of the world,
but to guard them from the evil one.

16 They are not of the world,
any more than I belong to the world.

17*† Consecrate them by means of truth—
'Your word is truth.'

18 As you have sent me into the world,
so I have sent them into the world;

19 I consecrate myself for their sakes now,
that they may be consecrated in truth.

Prayer for All Believers

20 "I do not pray for them alone.
I pray also for those who will believe in me
   through their word,

21*† that all may be one
as you, Father, are in me, and I in you;
I pray that they may be [one] in us,
that the world may believe that you sent me.

22 I have given them the glory you gave me
that they may be one, as we are one—

23 I living in them, you living in me—
that their unity may be complete.
So shall the world know that you sent me,
and that you loved them as you loved me.

24*† Father,
all those you gave me
I would have in my company
where I am,
to see this glory of mine
which is your gift to me,
because of the love you bore me before the world
   began.

25* Just Father,
the world has not known you,
but I have known you;
and these men have known that you sent me.

26† To them I have revealed your name,
and I will continue to reveal it
so that your love for me may live in them,
and I may live in them."

Jesus Arrested

18 1*† AFTER this discourse, Jesus went out with his disciples across the Kedron Valley. There was a garden there, and he and his disciples entered it. 2The place was familiar to Judas as well (the one who was to hand him over) because Jesus had often met there with his disciples. 3*†Judas took the cohort as well as guards supplied by the chief priests and the Pharisees, and came there with lanterns, torches and weapons. 4Jesus, aware of all that would happen to him, stepped forward and said to them, "Who is it you want?" 5†"Jesus the Nazorean,"

---

† 17, 11: *Protect them with your name which you have given me:* here and in the next verse, some witnesses read: "Protect with your name those whom you have given to me."

17, 12: *Scripture:* Jn 13, 18 cites Ps 41, 10.

17, 15: Note the resemblance to the petition of the Our Father, "deliver us from the evil one." Both probably refer to the devil rather than to abstract evil.

17, 17: *'Your word is truth':* seemingly a citation from the Greek form of Ps 119, 142, as found in Codex Sinaiticus.

17, 21: For other Johannine passages on unity, see 10, 16; 11, 52. The world (21.23) is once more to be challenged by the mission of the disciples and given the opportunity of self-judgment inasmuch as it will either accept or reject Jesus.

17, 24: *Where I am:* Jesus prays for the believers ultimately to join him in heaven. Then they will not see his glory as in a mirror but clearly (2 Cor 3, 18; 1 Jn 3, 2).

17, 26: *Will continue to reveal:* through the Paraclete.

18, 1-13: John does not mention the agony in the garden and the kiss of Judas, nor does he identify the place as Gethsemani or the Mount of Olives.

18, 1: *Jesus went out:* see 14, 31, where it seems he is leaving the supper room. *Kedron Valley:* literally, "the winter-flowing Kedron"; this wadi has water only during the winter rains.

18, 3: *Cohort:* seems to refer to Roman troops, the full cohort of 600 soldiers or the maniple of 200 under their tribune (v 12). In this case John is hinting at Roman collusion in the action against Jesus before he was brought to Pilate.

18, 5: *Nazorean:* The form found in Matthew is here used in preference to the *Nazarene* of Mark. *I am he:* this *Ego eimi* may

---

* 10: 16, 15; 2 Thes 1, 10.12.
12: 13, 18; 18, 9; Ps 41, 10;
   Mt 26, 24; Acts 1, 16.
13: 15, 11.
14: 15, 19.
15: Mt 6, 13; 1 Jn 5, 18.
17: 1 Pt 1, 22.
21: 10, 30; 14, 10ff.20.

24: 14, 3; 1 Thes 4, 17.
25: 1, 10.
18/1: Mt 26, 30.36;
   Mk 14, 26.32;
   Lk 22, 39.
3: Mt 26, 47-51;
   Mk 14, 43f; Lk 22, 47.

they replied. "I am he," he answered. (Now Judas, the one who was to hand him over, was there with them.) [6]As Jesus said to them, "I am he," they retreated slightly and fell to the ground. [7]Jesus put the question to them again, "Who is it you want?" "Jesus the Nazorean," they repeated. [8]"I have told you, I am he," Jesus said. "If I am the one you want, let these men go." [9]*†(This was to fulfill what he had said, "I have not lost one of those you gave me.")

[10]†Then Simon Peter, who had a sword, drew it and struck the slave of the high priest, severing his right ear. (The slave's name was Malchus.) [11]†At that Jesus said to Peter, "Put your sword back in its sheath. Am I not to drink the cup the Father has given me?"

[12]Then the soldiers of the cohort, their tribune, and the Jewish guards arrested Jesus and bound him. [13]*†They led him first to Annas, the father-in-law of Caiaphas who was high priest that year. [14]*(It was Caiaphas who had proposed to the Jews the advantage of having one man die for the people.)

Peter's First Denial

[15]*†Simon Peter, in company with another disciple, kept following Jesus closely. This disciple, who was known to the high priest, stayed with Jesus as far as the high priest's courtyard, [16]while Peter was left standing at the gate. The disciple known to the high priest came out and spoke to the woman at the gate, and then brought Peter in. [17]This servant girl who kept the gate said to Peter, "Are you not one of this man's followers?" "Not I," he replied.

[18]Now the night was cold, and the servants and the guards who were standing around had made a charcoal fire to warm themselves by. Peter joined them and stood there warming himself.

The Inquiry before Annas

[19]The high priest questioned Jesus, first about his disciples, then about his teaching. [20]*†Jesus answered by saying:

"I have spoken publicly to any who would listen.
I always taught in a synagogue or in the temple
    area
where all the Jews could come together.
There was nothing secret about anything I said.

[21]Why do you question me? Question those who heard me when I spoke. It should be obvious that they will know what I said." [22]*At this reply, one of the guards who was standing nearby gave Jesus a sharp blow on the face. "Is that the way to answer the high priest?" he said. [23]Jesus replied, "If I said anything wrong produce the evidence, but if I spoke the truth why hit

me?" [24]*†Annas next sent him, bound, to the high priest Caiaphas.

The Further Denials

[25]*All through this, Simon Peter had been standing there warming himself. They said to him, "Are you not a disciple of his?" He denied it and said, "I am not!" [26]"But did I not see you with him in the garden?" insisted one of the high priest's slaves—as it happened, a relative of the man whose ear Peter had severed. [27]†Peter denied it again. At that moment a cock began to crow.

The Trial before Pilate

[28]*†At daybreak they brought Jesus from Caiaphas to the praetorium. They did not enter the praetorium themselves, for they had to avoid ritual impurity if they were to eat the Passover supper. [29]Pilate came out to them. "What accusation do you bring against this man?" he demanded. [30]"If he were not a criminal," they retorted, "we would certainly not have handed

---

† be intended by the evangelist as an expression of divinity; see note on 8, 24. John sets the confusion of the arresting party against the background of Jesus' divine majesty.

18, 9: The citation may refer to 17, 12; 6, 39; or 10, 28.

18, 10: Only John gives the names of the two antagonists; both John and Luke mention the right ear.

18, 11: The theme of the cup is found in the synoptic account of the agony (Mk 14, 36) and parallels.

18, 13: Annas: only John mentions an inquiry before Annas, who is presumably the high priest of vv 16 and 19. Patriarch of a family of high priests, he had been deposed by the Romans in 15 A.D.; but since, according to Jewish law, the office was for life, Annas may still have been the legitimate high priest in the eyes of many. Luke (3, 2) and Acts (4, 6) mention him in terms of high priesthood. There have been many attempts by scribes and commentators to rearrange or interpret the verses of John so that Caiaphas does the interrogating. It may be said with reasonable certainty that this night time interrogation before Annas is not the same as the trial before Caiaphas placed by Matthew and Mark at night and by Luke in the morning.

18, 15: Courtyard: the Greek word can mean this or "palace."

18, 15f: Another disciple: many scholars identify him with the other disciple of 20, 2, who is the beloved disciple; see note on 13, 23. But how would a Galilean fisherman be known to the high priest? An early (but unlikely) tradition has it that John was himself a priest. See note on 19, 25 for John's possible relation to Mary, who had priestly relatives.

18, 20: I always taught . . . in the temple area: in the synoptics a similar statement appears in the garden scene (Mk 14, 49).

18, 24: Caiaphas: John may leave room here for the trial before Caiaphas not narrated by him but dealt with in the synoptic gospels. Details paralleling those of the synoptic trial are scattered throughout John.

18, 27: Cockcrow was the third Roman division of the night lasting from 12 to 3 A. M.

18, 28: Daybreak: literally, "the early hour," or fourth Roman division of the night, 3 to 6 A. M.; here presumably about 6 A. M. Praetorium: the residence of the Roman governor in Jerusalem was either the Herodian palace on the western hill or the fortress Antonia near the temple. The Passover supper: the synoptic gospels give the impression that the Thursday night supper was the Passover meal (Mk 14, 12); for John that meal is still to be eaten Friday night.

9: 6, 39; 17, 12.
13: Lk 3, 2.
14: 11, 49f.
15ff: Mt 26, 58.69f;
    Mk 14, 54.66f;
    Lk 22, 54.
20: 7, 26; Is 48, 16;
    Lk 19, 47; 22, 53.
22: Acts 23, 2.
24: Mt 26, 57.
25ff: Mt 26, 69-75;
    Lk 22, 55-62;
    Mk 14, 66-72.
28-40: Mt 27, 11-25;
    Mk 15, 1-15;
    Lk 23, 1-4.13-25.

him over to you." **31**†At this Pilate said, "Why do you not take him and pass judgment on him according to your law?" "We may not put anyone to death," the Jews answered. **32***†(This was to fulfill what Jesus had said indicating the sort of death he had to die.)

33Pilate went back into the praetorium and summoned Jesus. "Are you the King of the Jews?" he asked him. **34**Jesus answered, "Are you saying this on your own, or have others been telling you about me?" **35**"I am no Jew!" Pilate retorted. "It is your own people and the chief priests who have handed you over to me. What have you done?" **36***Jesus answered:

"My kingdom does not belong to this world.
If my kingdom were of this world,
my subjects would be fighting
to save me from being handed over to the Jews.
As it is, my kingdom is not here."

37*†At this Pilate said to him, "So, then, you are a king?" Jesus replied:

"It is you who say I am king.
The reason I was born,
the reason why I came into the world,
is to testify to the truth.
Anyone committed to the truth hears my voice."

38"Truth!" said Pilate, "What does that mean?"

After this remark, Pilate went out again to the Jews and said to them: "Speaking for myself, I find no case against this man. **39***†Recall your custom whereby I release someone to you at Passover time. Do you want me to release to you the king of the Jews?" **40**†They shouted back, "We want Barabbas, not this one!" (Barabbas was an insurrectionist.)

19 **1***†PILATE's next move was to take Jesus and have him scourged. **2**The soldiers then wove a crown of thorns and fixed it on his head, throwing around his shoulders a cloak of royal purple. **3**Repeatedly they came up to him and said, "All hail, king of the Jews!", slapping his face as they did so.

4*Pilate went out a second time and said to the crowd: "Observe what I do. I am going to bring him out to you to make you realize that I find no case [against him]." **5***When Jesus came out wearing the crown of thorns and the purple cloak, Pilate said to them, "Look at the man!" **6***As soon as the chief priests and the temple guards saw him they shouted, "Crucify him! Crucify him!" Pilate said, "Take him and crucify him yourselves; I find no case against him." **7***†"We have our law," the Jews responded, "and according to that law he must die because he made himself God's

Son." **8**When Pilate heard this kind of talk, he was more afraid than ever.

9*Going back into the praetorium, he said to Jesus, "Where do you come from?" Jesus would not give him any answer. **10**"Do you refuse to speak to me?" Pilate asked him. "Do you not know that I have the power to release you and the power to crucify you?" **11***Jesus answered:

"You would have no power over me whatever
unless it were given you from above.
That is why he who handed me over to you
is guilty of the greater sin."

12*†After this, Pilate was eager to release him, but the Jews shouted, "If you free this man you are no 'Friend of Caesar.' Anyone who makes himself a king becomes Caesar's rival." **13**†Pilate heard what they were saying, then brought Jesus outside and took a seat on a judge's bench at the place called the Stone Pavement—*Gabbatha* in Hebrew. **14**†(It was the Preparation Day for Passover, and the hour was about noon.) He said to the Jews, "Look at your king!" **15**At this they shouted, "Away with him! Away with him! Crucify him!" "What!" Pilate exclaimed. "Shall I crucify your king?" The chief priests replied, "We have

---

†

18, 31: *We may not put anyone to death:* only John gives this reason for their bringing Jesus to Pilate. Jewish sources are not clear on the competence of the Sanhedrin at this period to sentence and to execute for political crimes.

18, 32: The Jewish punishment for blasphemy was stoning (Lv 24, 16). In coming to the Romans to ensure that Jesus would be crucified, the Jewish authorities fulfilled his prophecy that he would be *lifted up;* cf 12, 32f.

18, 37: *It is you who say I am a king:* see Mt 26, 64 for a similar response to the high priest. It is a reluctant affirmative, equaling "Yes, but the terminology is yours."

18, 39: This privilege connected with *Passover* is not clearly attested outside the gospels.

18, 40: *Insurrectionist:* a guerrilla warrior fighting both for nationalistic aims and for gain, Barabbas had been arrested for murder in a recent insurrection (Mk 15, 7).

19, 1: Luke places the mockery of Jesus at the midpoint in the trial when Jesus was sent to Herod. Mark and Matthew place the scourging and mockery at the end of the trial after the sentence of death. Scourging was an integral part of the crucifixion penalty.

19, 7: *Made himself God's Son:* this question was not raised in John's account of the Jewish interrogations of Jesus as it was in the synoptic account. Nevertheless, see 5, 18; 8, 53; 10, 36.

19, 12: *'Friend of Caesar':* a technical Roman term of honor.

19, 13: *Took a seat:* many scholars think this should be translated transitively, "sat him down." In John's thought, Jesus is the real judge of men, and they suggest that John portrays him seated on the judgment bench. We find this tradition in the second century. *Stone Pavement:* under the fortress Antonia, one of the conjectured locations of the praetorium, a tremendous stone pavement has been uncovered. The Aramaic word *Gabbatha* probably means "ridge, elevation."

19, 14: *Preparation Day for Passover:* the synoptics describe this as Friday (Mk 15, 42). *Noon:* Mk 15, 25 has Jesus crucified "at the third hour," which means either 9 A. M. or the period from 9 to 12. Noon, the time when, according to John, Jesus was sentenced to death, was the hour at which the priests began to slaughter Passover lambs in the temple; see Jn 1, 29.

✿
32: 3, 14; 8, 28; 12, 32f.
36: 1, 10; 8, 23.
37: 8, 47.
39f: Mt 27, 15; Lk 23, 20.
19/1-16: Mt 27, 27-31;
      Mk 15, 16-21;
      Lk 23, 13-25.
4: 18, 38.
5: Is 52, 14.
6: 18, 31; 19, 15.
7: 10, 33-36; Lv 24, 16.
9: 7, 28.
11: 3, 27; 10, 18.
12: Acts 17, 7.

no king but Caesar." [16]†In the end, Pilate handed Jesus over to be crucified.

Crucifixion and Death

Jesus was led away, and [17]*†carrying the cross by himself, went out to what is called the Place of the Skull (in Hebrew, *Golgotha*). [18]There they crucified him, and two others with him: one on either side, Jesus in the middle. [19]†Pilate had an inscription placed on the cross which read,

JESUS THE NAZOREAN
THE KING OF THE JEWS

[20]This inscription, in Hebrew, Latin, and Greek, was read by many of the Jews, since the place where Jesus was crucified was near the city. [21]*The chief priests of the Jews tried to tell Pilate, "You should not have written, 'The King of the Jews.' Write instead, 'This man claimed to be King of the Jews.' " [22]Pilate answered, "What I have written, I have written."

[23]*†After the soldiers had crucified Jesus they took his garments and divided them four ways, one for each soldier. There was also his tunic, but this tunic was woven in one piece from top to bottom and had no seam. [24]They said to each other, "We should not tear it. Let us throw dice to see who gets it." (The purpose of this was to have the Scripture fulfilled:

> "They divided my garments among them;
> for my clothing they cast lots.")

And this was what the soldiers did.

[25]*†Near the cross of Jesus there stood his mother, his mother's sister, Mary the wife of Clopas, and Mary Magdalene. [26]†Seeing his mother there with the disciple whom he loved, Jesus said to his mother, "Woman, there is your son." [27]In turn he said to the disciple, "There is your mother." From that hour onward, the disciple took her into his care.

[28]*†After that, Jesus, realizing that everything was now finished, said to fulfill the scripture, "I am thirsty." [29]†There was a jar there, full of common wine. They stuck a sponge soaked in this wine on some hyssop and raised it to his lips. [30]*†When Jesus took the wine, he said, "Now it is finished." Then he bowed his head, and delivered over his spirit.

The Blood and Water

[31]*Since it was the Preparation Day the Jews did not want to have the bodies left on the cross during the sabbath, for that sabbath was a solemn feast day. They asked Pilate that the legs be broken and the bodies be taken away. [32]Accordingly, the soldiers came and broke the legs of the men crucified with Jesus, first of the one, then of the other. [33]When they came to Jesus and saw that he was already dead, they did not break his legs. [34]*†One of the soldiers thrust a lance into his side, and immediately blood and water flowed out. [35]*†(This testimony has been given by an eyewitness, and his testimony is true. He tells what he knows is true, so that you may believe.) [36]*†These events took place for the fulfillment of Scripture:

---

† 19, 16: *In the end, Pilate handed Jesus over to be crucified:* according to the sequence this would seem to mean "handed him over to the chief priests." Lk 23, 25 has a similar ambiguity. There is a polemic tendency in the later gospels to place the guilt of the crucifixion solely on the Jewish authorities and to excuse the Romans from blame. Actually, John later mentions the Roman soldiers, and it was to these soldiers that Pilate handed Jesus over.

19, 17: *Carrying the cross by himself:* this is a different picture from that of the synoptics, especially Lk 23, 26, where Simon of Cyrene is made to bear the cross, walking behind Jesus. In John's theology Jesus remained master of his destiny (10, 18). *Place of the Skull:* the Latin word for skull is *Calvaria;* hence "Calvary." *Golgotha* is actually an Aramaic rather than a Hebrew word.

19, 19: The inscription or "title," found here in its technical form appears with slightly different words in each of the four gospels. Only John mentions its polyglot character and Pilate's role in keeping the title unchanged.

19, 23: Perhaps this seamless tunic is meant to recall the tunic of the high priest which Josephus (*Antiquities* III, 8, 4) says was without seam. Rv 1, 13 shows Jesus in priestly robes. The synoptics do not have the details about Jesus' garments.

19, 25: It is not clear whether three or four women are meant (i. e., whether *Mary the wife of Clopas* is or is not in apposition with *his mother's sister*); the Syriac tradition has four women. Only John mentions the mother of Jesus. The synoptics have a group of women *at a distance* from the cross (Mk 15, 40). If *his mother's sister* is not *Mary the wife of Clopas,* is she to be identified with *Salome* of the synoptic account? Salome was the mother of James and John, the sons of Zebedee; and thus these two disciples would have been Jesus' cousins.

19, 26f: This scene is to be read in the light of the Cana story in Chapter 2. The presence of the mother of Jesus, the use of *woman,* and the mention of the *hour,* are elements of both scenes. Now that the hour has come, Mary (a symbol of the church?) is given a role as the mother of Christians (personified by the beloved disciple).

19, 28: *The Scripture:* it is not certain whether the fulfillment is in the scene of 25-27, or in the *I am thirsty* of 28. If the latter, Pss 69, 22 and 22, 16 deserve consideration.

19, 29: *Common wine:* John does not mention the drugged wine, a narcotic which Jesus refused as the crucifixion began (Mk 15, 25), but only this final gesture of kindness at the end (Mk 15, 36). Hyssop, a small plant, is scarcely suitable for carrying a sponge (Mark mentions a reed) and may be a symbolic reference to the hyssop used to put the blood of the paschal lamb on the doorpost of the Hebrews (Ex 12, 22).

19, 30: *Delivered over his spirit:* it is awkward in English to preserve the possible double nuance of dying (giving up the last breath or spirit) and that of passing on the Holy Spirit; see 7, 39, which connects the giving of the Spirit with Jesus' glorious return to the Father.

19, 34f: John probably emphasizes these verses to show the reality of Jesus' death, against the Docetic heretics. In the blood and water there may also be a symbolic reference to the Eucharist and Baptism.

19, 35: *He tells:* it is not certain from the Greek that this *he* is the *eyewitness* of the first part of the sentence.

19, 36: The scriptural reference is probably to Ex 12, 46 (Nm 9, 12), which has directions for dealing with the Passover lamb.

---

*

17-22: Mt 27, 32-37;	28: Ps 22, 16; 69, 22.
Mk 15, 21-26;	30: 4, 34; 10, 18; 17, 4;
Lk 23, 26.33.	Lk 23, 46.
21: 18, 33; Lk 19, 14.	31: Ex 12, 16; Dt 21, 23.
23f: Ps 22, 19; Mt 27, 35;	34: Nm 20, 11; 1 Jn 5, 6.
Mk 15, 24.	35: 7, 37ff; 21, 24.
25: Mt 27, 55; Mk 15, 40f;	36: Ex 12, 46; Nm 9, 12;
Lk 8, 2; 23, 49.	Ps 34, 21.
28ff: Mt 27, 48ff;	
Mk 15, 36f.	

"Break none of his bones."

37*†There is still another Scripture passage which says:

"They shall look on him whom they have pierced."

Burial

38*†Afterward, Joseph of Arimathea, a disciple of Jesus (although a secret one for fear of the Jews), asked Pilate's permission to remove Jesus' body. Pilate granted it, so they came and took the body away. **39***Nicodemus (the man who had first come to Jesus at night) likewise came, bringing a mixture of myrrh and aloes which weighed about a hundred pounds. **40**They took Jesus' body, and in accordance with Jewish burial custom bound it up in wrappings of cloth with perfumed oils. **41**In the place where he had been crucified there was a garden, and in the garden a new tomb in which no one had ever been buried. **42**Because of the Jewish Preparation Day they buried Jesus there, for the tomb was close at hand.

Peter and the Disciple

20 **1***†EARLY in the morning on the first day of the week, while it was still dark, Mary Magdalene came to the tomb. She saw that the stone had been moved away, **2**so she ran off to Simon Peter and the other disciple (the one Jesus loved) and told them, "The Lord has been taken from the tomb! We don't know where they have put him!" **3**†At that, Peter and the other disciple started out on their way toward the tomb. **4**They were running side by side, but then the other disciple outran Peter and reached the tomb first. **5**He did not enter but bent down to peer in, and saw the wrappings lying on the ground. **6***†Presently, Simon Peter came along behind him and entered the tomb. He observed the wrappings on the ground **7***and saw the piece of cloth which had covered the head not lying with the wrappings, but rolled up in a place by itself. **8**Then the disciple who had arrived first at the tomb went in. He saw and believed. **9***†(Remember, as yet they did not understand the Scripture that Jesus had to rise from the dead.) **10**With this, the disciples went back home.

Mary Magdalene

11Meanwhile, Mary stood weeping beside the tomb. Even as she wept, she stooped to peer inside, **12**and there she saw two angels in dazzling robes. One was seated at the head and the other at the foot of the place where Jesus' body had lain. **13**"Woman," they asked her, "why are you weeping?" She answered them, "Because the Lord has been taken away, and I do not know where they have put him." **14***She had no sooner said this than she turned around and caught sight of Jesus standing there. But she did not know him. **15***"Woman," he asked her, "why are you weeping? Who is it you are looking for?" She supposed he was the gardener, so she said, "Sir, if you are the one who carried him off, tell me where you have laid him and I will take him away." **16**Jesus said to her, "Mary!" She turned to him and said [in Hebrew], "*Rabbouni!*" (meaning "Teacher"). **17***†Jesus then said: "Do not cling to me, for I have not yet ascended to the Father. Rather, go to my brothers and tell them, 'I am ascending to my Father and your Father, to my God and your God!'" **18**Mary Magdalene went to the disciples. "I have seen the Lord!" she announced. Then she reported what he had said to her.

Appearance to the Disciples

19†On the evening of that first day of the week, even though the disciples had locked the doors of the place

---

†
That Jesus is the Paschal Lamb is a Johannine theme, and thus at the end of the gospel we are called back to 1, 29. There may also be a reference to Ps 34, 21, describing God's safeguarding of an innocent man.

19, 37: John cites Zec 12, 10 (also cited in Rv 1, 7), but not exactly according to either the standard Hebrew reading or the Greek Old Testament. There was a Jewish tradition of uncertain date that this text referred to the Messiah.

19, 38-42: In the first three gospels there is no embalming on Friday. In Matthew and Luke the women come to the tomb on Sunday morning precisely to anoint Jesus.

20, 1: *Still dark:* according to Mark the sun had risen, and Matthew speaks of the first rays of light.

20, 3-10: The basic narrative is told of Peter alone in Lk 24, 12, a verse missing in important MSS and which may be borrowed from tradition similar to John. Lk 24, 24 also generally reflects this story.

20, 6-8: There was some special feature about the state of the burial wrappings that caused the beloved disciple to believe. Some suggest that Jesus had passed through them without their being unrolled.

20, 9: Probably a general reference to the Scriptures is intended, as in Lk 24, 26 and 1 Cor 15, 4. Some individual Old Testament passages suggested are Ps 16, 10; Hos 6, 2; Jon 1, 17; 2, 1.

20, 17: *Do not cling to me:* literally "Don't keep touching me." See Mt 28, 9, where the women take hold of his feet. *I have not yet ascended:* for John and many of the New Testament writers, the ascension in the theological sense of going to the Father to be glorified took place with the resurrection as one action. This scene in John dramatizes such an understanding, for by Easter night Jesus is glorified and can give the Spirit. Therefore his ascension takes place immediately after he has talked to Mary. In such a view, the ascension after forty days described in Acts 1, 1-11 would be simply the termination of earthly appearances. *My Father and your Father:* this echoes Ru 1, 16, *Your people shall be my people, and your God my God.* The Father of Jesus will now become the Father of the disciples because, once ascended, Jesus can give them the Spirit that comes from the Father and beget them as God's children (3, 5). That is why he calls them *my brothers.*

20, 19: *The disciples:* by implication from v 24, this means ten of the Twelve. Lk 24, 33 mentions a larger group; Mk 16, 14 refers to the Eleven. Presumably they are in Jerusalem; see Lk 24, 33. The "upper room" is first mentioned in Acts 1, 13, as the place to which the Eleven came forty days later, after Jesus' final departure. *Peace be with you:* although this

---

❋
37: Nm 21, 9; Zec 12, 10; Rv 1, 7.
38-42: Mt 27, 57-60; Mk 15, 42-46; Lk 23, 50-54.
39: 3, 1f; 7, 50.
20/1-18: Mt 28, 1-10; Mk 16, 1-11; Lk 24, 1-11.

1: 19, 25.
6: Lk 24, 12.
7: 11, 44; 19, 40.
9: Acts 2, 26f; 1 Cor 15, 4.
14: 21, 4; Lk 24, 16.
15ff: Mt 28, 9f.
17: Acts 1, 9.

where they were for fear of the Jews, Jesus came and stood before them. "Peace be with you," he said. **20***†When he had said this, he showed them his hands and his side. At the sight of the Lord the disciples rejoiced. **21***†"Peace be with you," he said again.

> "As the Father has sent me,
> so I send you."

22†Then he breathed on them and said:

> "Receive the Holy Spirit.
> **23***†If you forgive men's sins,
> they are forgiven them;
> if you hold them bound,
> they are held bound."

Thomas

24It happened that one of the Twelve, Thomas (the name means "Twin"), was absent when Jesus came. **25***The other disciples kept telling him: "We have seen the Lord!" His answer was, "I will never believe it without probing the nailprints in his hands, without putting my finger in the nailmarks and my hand into his side."
26*A week later, the disciples were once more in the room, and this time Thomas was with them. Despite the locked doors, Jesus came and stood before them. "Peace be with you," he said; **27**then, to Thomas: "Take your finger and examine my hands. Put your hand into my side. Do not persist in your unbelief, but believe!" **28**†Thomas said in response, "My Lord and my God!" **29***Jesus then said to him:

"You became a believer because you saw me.
Blest are they who have not seen and have believed."

Conclusion

30†Jesus performed many other signs as well—signs not recorded here—in the presence of his disciples. **31***†But these have been recorded to help you believe that Jesus is the Messiah, the Son of God, so that through this faith you may have life in his name.

IV: APPENDIX

THE RESURRECTION APPEARANCE IN GALILEE

The Fishermen

21 **1***†LATER, AT THE SEA OF TIBERIAS, Jesus showed himself to the disciples [once again]. This is how the appearance took place. **2**†Assembled were Simon Peter, Thomas ("the Twin"), Nathanael (from Cana in Galilee), Zebedee's sons, and two other disciples. **3***†Simon Peter said to them, "I

am going out to fish." "We will join you," they replied, and went off to get into their boat. All through the night they caught nothing. **4**Just after daybreak Jesus was standing on the shore, though none of the disciples knew it was Jesus. **5***He said to them, "Children, have you caught anything to eat?" "Not a thing," they answered. **6** Cast your net off to the starboard side," he suggested, "and you will find something." So they made a cast, and took so many fish they could not haul the net in. **7**Then the disciple Jesus loved cried out to Peter, "It is the Lord!" On hearing it was the Lord, Simon Peter threw on some clothes—he was stripped—and jumped into the water.

8Meanwhile the other disciples came in the boat, towing the net full of fish. Actually they were not far from land—no more than a hundred yards.

9*†When they landed, they saw a charcoal fire there with a fish laid on it and some bread. **10**"Bring some of

---

† could be an ordinary greeting, John intends here to echo 14, 27. The theme of rejoicing in v 20 echoes 16, 22.

20, 20: *Hands and . . . side:* Lk 24, 39f mentions "hands and feet"; cf Ps 22, 17.

20, 21: By means of this sending, the Eleven were made *apostles,* that is, "those sent"; cf 17, 18. A solemn mission or "sending" is also the subject of the post-resurrection appearances to the Eleven in Mt 28, 19; Lk 24, 47; Mk 16, 15.

20, 22: According to the Second Council of Constantinople, the Spirit was truly given here and the breathing on the disciples was not merely symbolic. This action recalls Gn 2, 7, where God breathed on man and gave him the natural spirit or life-force; in John it is the life-source for supernatural life that is given. The apostles are recreated as new men, sons of God. The further giving of the Spirit in chapter 2 of Acts is a more public charism for the church.

20, 23: The Council of Trent defined that the power to forgive sins given here is the same power exercised in the Sacrament of Penance. See Mt 16, 19 and 18, 18. *If you hold them bound, they are held bound:* the reference of *they, them,* not wholly clear in the Greek, is more probably to *sins* than to *men.*

20, 28: The Second Council of Constantinople defined that this confession of Thomas referred to Christ and was not simply an expression of glory to God the Father. *Lord* and *God* are two Old Testament titles of God (Ps 35, 23).

20, 30f: These verses are clearly a conclusion to the gospel.

20, 31: See 1 Jn 5, 13: *To help you believe:* it is difficult to determine whether the Greek should be read "that you may continue to believe" (i. e., the readers are Christians) or "that you may come to believe" (i. e., perhaps the readers are non-Christians).

21, 1-23: There are many non-Johannine peculiarities in this chapter, some suggesting Lucan Greek style; yet there are many Johannine features as well. Perhaps the tradition was ultimately derived from John but preserved by some disciple other than the writer of the rest of the gospel. The appearances narrated seem to be independent of those in chapter 20. Even if a later addition, the chapter was added before publication of the gospel, for it appears in all MSS.

21, 2: *Zebedee's sons:* the only mention by name of James and John in this gospel. Perhaps the phrase was inserted to identify the *two other disciples.* The anonymity of the latter phrase is more Johannine (1, 35).

21, 3-6: This may be a variant of Luke's account of the catch of fish (5, 1-11), which he joined with the call of the first disciples.

21, 9.12f: It is strange that Jesus already has fish since none have yet been brought ashore. This meal may have had eucharistic significance for early Christians since v 13 recalls John

---

✿

20: 14, 27.
21: 17, 18; Mt 28, 19; Mk 16, 15; Lk 24, 47f.
23: Mt 16, 19; 18, 18.
25: 1 Jn 1, 1.
26: 21, 14.

29: 4, 48; Lk 1, 45.
31: 1 Jn 5, 13.
21/1: Mt 26, 32; 28, 7.
3: Mt 4, 18; Lk 5, 4-10.
5: Lk 24, 41.
9: Lk 24, 41ff.

the fish you just caught," Jesus told them. **11†**Simon Peter went aboard and hauled ashore the net loaded with sizable fish—one hundred fifty-three of them! In spite of the great number, the net was not torn.

12†"Come and eat your meal," Jesus told them. Not one of the disciples presumed to inquire, "Who are you?" for they knew it was the Lord. **13***Jesus came over, took the bread and gave it to them, and did the same with the fish. **14†**This marked the third time that Jesus appeared to the disciples after being raised from the dead.

Peter the Shepherd

15*†When they had eaten their meal, Jesus said to Simon Peter, "Simon, son of John, do you love me more than these?" "Yes, Lord," he said, "you know that I love you." At which Jesus said, "Feed my lambs."

16A second time he put his question, "Simon, son of John, do you love me?" "Yes, Lord," Peter said, "you know that I love you." Jesus replied, "Tend my sheep."

17*A third time Jesus asked him, "Simon, son of John, do you love me?" Peter was hurt because he had asked a third time, "Do you love me?" So he said to him: "Lord, you know everything. You know well that I love you." Jesus said to him, "Feed my sheep."

18*†"I tell you solemnly:
as a young man
you fastened your belt
and went about as you pleased;
but when you are older
you will stretch out your hands,
and another will tie you fast
and carry you off against your will."

19*(What he said indicated the sort of death by which Peter was to glorify God.) When Jesus had finished speaking he said to him, "Follow me."

The Beloved Disciple

20*Peter turned around at that, and noticed that the disciple whom Jesus loved was following (the one who

had leaned against Jesus' chest during the supper and said, "Lord, which one will hand you over?"). **21**Seeing him, Peter was prompted to ask Jesus, "But Lord, what about him?" **22**"Suppose I want him to stay until I come," Jesus replied, "how does that concern you? Your business is to follow me." **23†**This is how the report spread among the brothers that this disciple was not going to die. Jesus never told him, as a matter of fact, that the disciple was not going to die; all he said was, "Suppose I want him to stay until I come [how does that concern you]?"

Conclusion

24*†It is this same disciple who is the witness to these things; it is he who wrote them down and his testimony, we know, is true. **25***There are still many other things that Jesus did, yet if they were written about in detail, I doubt there would be room enough in the entire world to hold the books to record them.

---

†
6, 11, which uses the vocabulary of Jesus' action at the Last Supper.

21, 11: The exact number, 153, is probably meant to have a symbolic meaning, perhaps in relation to the apostles' mission to catch men. The net which was not torn *may* represent the church.

21, 12: *Not one . . . presumed:* is Jesus' appearance strange to them? See Lk 24, 16; Mk 16, 12; Jn 20, 14.

21, 14: This verse connects chapters 20 and 21.

21, 15ff: In these three verses there is a remarkable variety of synonyms: two different Greek verbs for *love;* two verbs for *feed/tend;* two or three nouns for *sheep;* two verbs for *know.* Apparently there is no difference of meaning. The First Vatican Council cited this verse in defining that the risen Jesus gave Peter the jurisdiction of supreme shepherd and ruler over the whole flock.

21, 15: *More than these:* probably "more than these disciples do" rather than "more than you love these things [fishing, etc.]."

21, 18: A figurative reference to the crucifixion of Peter.

21, 23: This whole scene takes on more significance if the disciple is already dead. The death of the apostolic generation caused problems in the church because of a belief that Jesus was to have returned first. Loss of faith sometimes resulted; cf 2 Pt 3, 4.

21, 24: *Who wrote them down:* this does not necessarily mean he wrote them with his own hand. The same expression is used in 19, 9 of Pilate, who certainly did not write the inscription himself. *We know:* it is probably not the beloved disciple of v 7 who speaks here as *we.*

❋
13: Lk 24, 42.	19: 13, 36.
15: Lk 5, 10; Acts 20, 28.	20: 13, 25.
17: 13, 37f; 18, 17.25ff;	24: 15, 27; 19, 35.
Mt 16, 17ff; Lk 22, 31f.	25: 20, 30.
18: 2 Pt 1, 14.	

The Acts of the Apostles

Introduction

Luke is the only one of the evangelists who supplements his gospel with a second volume describing the origin and spread of the Christian communities in New Testament times. He attributes the establishment of these churches to the action of the Holy Spirit, specifically upon Peter (2, 14-18; 4, 8; 15, 8) and Paul (13, 2ff; 16, 6; 20, 22f). Peter was the leading member of the Twelve (1, 13.26) and the recognized authority over the Judaeo-Christian communities (12, 17; 15, 6-12). Paul eventually joined the church at Antioch (11, 25f), which subsequently commissioned him and Barnabas to undertake the spread of the gospel to Asia Minor. This missionary venture generally failed to win the Jews of the diaspora to the gospel, but enjoyed a measure of success among the Gentiles (13, 14—14, 27). Paul's refusal to impose the Mosaic law upon his Gentile converts provoked very strong objection among the Judaeo-Christians of Jerusalem (15, 1), but both Peter and James supported his position (15, 6-21). Paul's second and third missionary journeys (16, 36—21, 16) resulted in the same pattern: of failure among the Jews generally but of some success among the Gentiles.

In Acts, Luke has provided a broad survey of the church's development from the resurrection of Jesus to Paul's first Roman imprisonment, the point at which the book ends. Originally a Judaeo-Christian community in Jerusalem, the church was placed in circumstances impelling it to include within its membership people of other cultures: the Samaritans (8, 4-25), at first an occasional Gentile (8, 26-40; 10, 1-48), and finally the Gentiles on principle (11, 20f). Fear on the part of the Jewish people that Christian messianism, particularly as preached to the Gentiles, threatened their own cultural heritage caused them to be suspicious of Paul's gospel (15, 1-5; 13, 42-45; 28, 17-24). The inability of Christian missioners to allay this apprehension inevitably created a situation wherein the gospel was preached more and more to the Gentiles. Toward the end of Paul's career, the Christian communities, with the exception of those in Palestine itself (9, 31), were mainly of Gentile membership.

In the development of the church from a Judaeo-Christian origin in Jerusalem, with its roots in Jewish religious tradition, to a series of Christian communities among the Gentiles of the Roman Empire, Luke perceives the action of God in history laying open the hearts of all mankind to the divine message of salvation. His approach to the history of the church is predominantly theological. He conceives of the church as a mystery of God introduced into history through the apostolic preaching (1, 21f), which was forced to adapt itself to circumstances and so to carry forward the predestined spread of God's word among men, again in history. His preoccupation with the mystery of the church as the bearer of the word of salvation rules out of his book detailed histories of the various members of the Twelve as well as of the churches founded by Paul. Only the main lines of the roles of Peter and Paul serve Luke's interest. Nonetheless, the historical data he utilizes are of value for the understanding of the church's early life and development and as general background to the Pauline epistles. In the interpretation of Acts, care must be exercised to determine Luke's theological aims and interests and to evaluate his historical data without either exaggerating their literal accuracy or underestimating their factual worth. Concerning the date of Acts, see Introduction of the Gospel according to Luke.

The book of The Acts of the Apostles is divided as follows:

I: PROLOGUE

Jesus' Final Instructions and Ascension

1 **1*** †IN MY FIRST ACCOUNT, THEOPHILUS, I dealt with all that Jesus did and taught **2***until the day he was taken up to heaven, having first instructed the apostles he had chosen through the Holy Spirit. **3**†In the time after his suffering he showed them in

---

---

† 1, 1-26: This introductory material connects Acts with Luke's gospel (1, 1f); shows that the apostles were instructed by the risen Jesus (1, 3ff); points out that the parousia or renewed presence of Jesus will occur as certainly as his resurrection occurred (1, 6-11); and lists the members of the Twelve, stressing their role as a body of divinely mandated witnesses to his life, teaching, and resurrection (1, 12-26).

1, 3: *In many convincing ways:* the meaning of the Greek is that the apostles received evidence of Jesus' resurrection decisive enough to eliminate doubt from their minds (Lk 24, 36-49). This divinely offered proof, however, entailed more than an appeal to human reason. It included prophetic illumination many convincing ways that he was alive, appearing to them over the course of forty days and speaking to them about the reign of God. **4*****†**On one occasion when he met with them, he told them not to leave Jerusalem: "Wait, rather, for the fulfillment of my Father's promise, of which you have heard me speak. **5***John baptized with water, but within a few days you will be baptized with the Holy Spirit."

6While they were with him they asked, "Lord, are you going to restore the rule to Israel now?" **7*****†**His answer was: "The exact time it is not yours to know. The Father has reserved that to himself. **8***You will receive power when the Holy Spirit comes down on you; then you are to be my witnesses in Jerusalem, throughout Judea and Samaria, yes, even to the ends of the earth." **9*****†**No sooner had he said this than he was lifted up before their eyes in a cloud which took him from their sight.

10*They were still gazing up into the heavens when two men dressed in white stood beside them. **11***"Men of Galilee," they said, "why do you stand here looking up at the skies? This Jesus who has been taken from you will return, just as you saw him go up into the heavens."

12*After that they returned to Jerusalem from the mount called Olivet near Jerusalem—a mere sabbath's journey away. **13**Entering the city, they went to the upstairs room where they were staying: Peter and John and James and Andrew; Philip and Thomas, Bartholomew and Matthew; James son of Alpheus; Simon, the Zealot party member, and Judas son of James. **14**Together they devoted themselves to constant prayer. There were some women in their company, and Mary the mother of Jesus, and his brothers.

II: THE COMMUNITY IN JERUSALEM FINDS MATURITY IN THE SPIRIT

Matthias Chosen

15AT ONE POINT DURING THOSE DAYS, Peter stood up in the center of the brothers; there must have been a hundred and twenty gathered together. **16***"Brothers," he said, "the saying in Scripture uttered long ago by the Holy Spirit through the mouth of David was destined to be fulfilled in Judas, the one who guided those that arrested Jesus. **17**He was one of our number and he had been given a share in this ministry of ours.

18†"That individual bought a piece of land with his unjust gains, and fell headlong upon it. His body burst wide open, all his entrails spilling out. **19**This event came to be known by the inhabitants of Jerusalem,

who named the property Field of Blood—'Akeldama' in their own language.

20*"It is written in the Book of Psalms,

'Let his encampment be desolate.
May no one dwell on it.'

And again,

'May another take his office.'

21It is entirely fitting, therefore, that one of those who was of our company while the Lord Jesus moved among us, **22***from the baptism of John until the day he was taken up from us, should be named as witness with us to his resurrection." **23**At that they nominated two, Joseph (called Barsabbas, also known as Justus) and Matthias. **24**Then they prayed: "O Lord, you read the hearts of men. Make known to us which of these two you choose **25**for this apostolic ministry, replacing Judas, who deserted the cause and went the way he was destined to go." **26†**They then drew lots between the two men. The choice fell to Matthias, who was added to the eleven apostles.

---

†
which rendered the apostles certain that the appearances of the risen Christ were actions of God manifesting himself to their human experience. *Appearing to them over the course of forty days:* Christian tradition considered especially sacred the interval in which the appearances and instructions of the risen Jesus occurred, and expressed it therefore in terms of the sacred number forty; cf Dt 8, 2.

According to John (20, 17), the ascension of Jesus to the kingdom of his Father took place on the day of his resurrection. Luke writes from a different perspective and speaks of a visible ascension of Jesus after forty days. For John, the ascension means primarily the risen Jesus' new existence with the Father, and the appearances are those of the risen and ascended One. For Luke, the ascension marks the end of the appearances of Jesus except for the extraordinary appearance to Paul.

1, 4: *My Father's promise:* the Holy Spirit, as is clear from 1, 5. This gift of the Spirit formed part of the instructions of the risen Jesus on the kingdom of God, of which Luke speaks in 1, 3. Probably this instruction is the source of the material on the Holy Spirit in Jn 15, 26f and 16, 7-15.

1, 7: This verse echoes the tradition that the precise time of the parousia is not revealed to men; cf Mk 13, 32; 1 Thes 5, 1ff.

1, 9: Comparison of this verse with Lk 24, 51 suggests that there were several visible ascensions of the risen Christ. Mt 28, 16-20 raises the possibility of a similar visible ascension of Christ in Galilee. The visible ascension accorded with the cosmological conception of the time that held the sky to be a solid vault above which was God's throne. On other occasions, Jesus simply vanished; cf Lk 24, 31. A visible ascension is not described in Jn 20, 17.

1, 18: Luke records a popular tradition on the death of Judas that seems to differ from that in Mt 27, 5, according to which Judas hanged himself. Here, though the text is not entirely clear, Judas is depicted as purchasing a piece of property with the betrayal money and being killed on it in a fall.

1, 26: The need for replacing Judas so as to restore the apostolic college to the number of twelve was probably dictated by the symbolism of the number. It recalled the twelve tribes from which all Israelites were thought to be descended, and indicated that the messianic teaching about Jesus was to be directed first to the whole of Israel.

*
4: Jn 14, 26.
5: 11, 16; Mt 3, 11; Mk 1, 8; Lk 3, 16; Jn 1, 26; Eph 1, 13.
7: Mt 24, 36; 1 Thes 5, 1f.
8: 2, 2; Is 43, 10; Mt 28, 19.
9: 2 Kgs 2, 11; Mk 16, 19.
10: Jn 20, 17.
11: Lk 24, 51; Eph 4, 8ff; 1 Pt 3, 22.
12ff: Lk 6, 14ff.
16: Lk 22, 47.
20: Pss 69, 26; 109, 8; Jn 17, 12.
22: 1, 8; 10, 39.

Descent of the Holy Spirit

2 ¹*†WHEN the day of Pentecost came it found them gathered in one place. ²*†Suddenly from up in the sky there came a noise like a strong, driving wind which was heard all through the house where they were seated. ³†Tongues as of fire appeared, which parted and came to rest on each of them. ⁴*†All were filled with the Holy Spirit. They began to express themselves in foreign tongues and make bold proclamation as the Spirit prompted them.

⁵*Staying in Jerusalem at the time were devout Jews of every nation under heaven. ⁶†These heard the sound, and assembled in a large crowd. They were much confused because each one heard these men speaking his own language. ⁷The whole occurrence astonished them. They asked in utter amazement, "Are not all of these men who are speaking Galileans? ⁸How is it that each of us hears them in his native tongue? ⁹We are Parthians, Medes, and Elamites. We live in Mesopotamia, Judea and Cappadocia, Pontus, the province of Asia, ¹⁰Phrygia and Pamphylia, Egypt, and the regions of Libya around Cyrene. There are even visitors from Rome—all Jews, ¹¹*or those who have come over to Judaism; Cretans and Arabs too. Yet each of us hears them speaking in his own tongue about the marvels God has accomplished." ¹²They were dumbfounded, and could make nothing at all of what had happened.

"What does this mean?" they asked one another, while a few remarked with a sneer, ¹³*"They have had too much new wine!"

Peter's Discourse

¹⁴†Peter stood up with the Eleven, raised his voice, and addressed them: "You who are Jews, indeed all of you staying in Jerusalem! Listen to what I have to say. ¹⁵You must realize that these men are not drunk, as you seem to think. It is only nine in the morning! ¹⁶No, it is what Joel the prophet spoke of:

¹⁷*'It shall come to pass in the last days, says God,
    that I will pour out a portion of my spirit on all mankind:
Your sons and daughters shall prophesy,
    your young men shall see visions
    and your old men shall dream dreams.
¹⁸Yes, even on my servants and handmaids
    I will pour out a portion of my spirit in those days,
    and they shall prophesy.
¹⁹I will work wonders in the heavens above
    and signs on the earth below:
    blood, fire, and a cloud of smoke.

²⁰The sun shall be turned to darkness and the moon to blood
    before the coming of that great and glorious day of the Lord.

---

† 2, 1-41: Luke's pentecostal narrative consists of an introduction (2, 1-13), a speech ascribed to Peter declaring the resurrection of Jesus and its messianic significance (2, 14-36), and a favorable response from the audience (2, 39ff). It is likely that the narrative telescopes events that took place over a period of time and on a less dramatic scale. The Twelve were not originally in a position to proclaim publicly the messianic office of Jesus without incurring immediate reprisal from those religious authorities in Jerusalem who had encompassed Jesus' death precisely to stem the rising tide in his favor; cf Jn 11, 47f. Once the "new covenant" had acquired many adherents, public teaching could more easily be undertaken. In any case, these reflections point up Luke's emphasis on the Holy Spirit. He is at pains to show that Christianity cannot be accounted a mere religious sect within Judaism that developed its own brand of messianism. On the contrary, it declared itself from the beginning as originating in the inspiration and under the impulsion of God.

2, 2: *From up in the sky there came a noise like a strong, driving wind:* the wind and the Holy Spirit are associated in Jn 3, 8. The sound of a great rush of wind would aptly presage a new action of God in the history of salvation.

2, 3: *Tongues as of fire:* see Ex 19, 18, where fire symbolizes the presence of God to initiate the covenant on Sinai. Here the Holy Spirit acts upon the apostles, preparing them to proclaim the new covenant with its unique gift of the Spirit (2, 38).

2, 4: *To express themselves in foreign tongues:* ecstatic prayer in praise of God; cf 2, 11.

2, 6-13: The multitude receives the charism of interpretation of tongues (1 Cor 12, 10). The question of the meaning of this charism is raised. To some of the hearers, however, the language is unintelligible, and they conclude the apostles are drunk. Luke may have in mind here the varying reactions to the gift in the early Christian communities; cf 1 Cor 14, 22-25.

2, 14-36: The first of six discourses in Acts (see 3, 12-26; 4, 8-12; 5, 29-32; 10, 34-43; 13, 16-41) dealing with the substance of Christian messianism, the resurrection of Jesus and its messianic import. Five of these are attributed to Peter, the final one to Paul. In 1 Cor 15, 11 Paul refers to the apostolic teaching on the death and resurrection of Jesus as "the preaching" or "proclamation." Hence modern scholars term these discourses in Acts the "kerygma," the Greek word for proclamation.

In the present discourse, Peter appeals to the religious faith of the audience and presents himself as one in possession of certain religious information given him by God together with the ability to interpret it. This is called a prophetic announcement. The following chief points are made:

(1) The ecstatic prayer is due to the influence of the Spirit, which the prophet Joel foretold would be especially active in messianic times (16-21); (2) the crucifixion of Jesus of Nazareth, a man publicly known in Jerusalem because of his miracle-working, was an integral part of God's saving plan, as God has indicated by raising him from the dead (22ff); (3) the prophetic understanding of the Old Testament reveals that the resurrection and ascension of the Messiah was God's actual saving plan (25-35); (4) the true meaning of the death, resurrection and ascension of Jesus is that he is the divinely enthroned messianic King of Israel (36), bestowing the gift of the Spirit upon all who accept him as Savior (38).

The prophetic character of the kerygmatic discourses in Acts explains why they do not include accounts of the appearances of Jesus. Only to one who accepts the prophetic announcement of Jesus' resurrection will accounts of his subsequent appearances convey any meaning.

✿
    2/1: Ex 23, 14.
    2f: Jn 3, 8.
    4: 1, 5; 4, 31; 11, 16;
       19, 6; Ps 104, 30;
       Jn 20, 33.
                5: Wis 1, 7.
                11: 10, 46.
                13: 1 Cor 14, 23.
                17: Is 2, 2; 44, 3; Jl 3, 1-5.

21*Then shall everyone be saved who calls on the name of the Lord.'

22*"Men of Israel, listen to me! Jesus the Nazorean was a man whom God sent to you with miracles, wonders, and signs as his credentials. These God worked through him in your midst, as you well know. **23***He was delivered up by the set purpose and plan of God; you even made use of pagans to crucify and kill him. **24***God freed him from death's bitter pangs, however, and raised him up again, for it was impossible that death should keep its hold on him. **25***David says of him:

'I have set the Lord ever before me,
     with him at my right hand I shall not be disturbed.
26My heart has been glad and my tongue has rejoiced,
     my body will live on in hope,
27*for you will not abandon my soul to the nether world,
     nor will you suffer your faithful one to undergo corruption.
28You have shown me the paths of life;
     you will fill me with joy in your presence.'

29"Brothers, I can speak confidently to you about our father David. He died and was buried, and his grave is in our midst to this day. **30***He was a prophet and knew that God had sworn to him that one of his descendants would sit upon his throne. **31***He said that he was not abandoned to the nether world, nor did his body undergo corruption, thus proclaiming beforehand the resurrection of the Messiah. **32**This is the Jesus God has raised up, and we are his witnesses. **33***Exalted at God's right hand, he first received the promised Holy Spirit from the Father, then poured this Spirit out on us. This is what you now see and hear. **34***David did not go up to heaven, yet David says,

'The Lord said to my Lord,
     Sit at my right hand
35until I make your enemies your footstool.'

36*Therefore let the whole house of Israel know beyond any doubt that God has made both Lord and Messiah this Jesus whom you crucified."

37When they heard this, they were deeply shaken. They asked Peter and the other apostles, "What are we to do, brothers?" **38***†Peter answered: "You must reform and be baptized, each one of you, in the name of Jesus Christ, that your sins may be forgiven; then you will receive the gift of the Holy Spirit. **39**It was to you and your children that the promise was made, and to all those still far off whom the Lord our God calls."

40*In support of his testimony he used many other arguments, and kept urging, "Save yourselves from this generation which has gone astray." **41***Those who accepted his message were baptized; some three thousand were added that day.

Communal Life

42*†They devoted themselves to the apostles' instruction and the communal life, to the breaking of bread and the prayers. **43***A reverent fear overtook them all, for many wonders and signs were performed by the apostles. **44***Those who believed shared all things in common; **45**they would sell their property and goods, dividing everything on the basis of each one's need. **46**They went to the temple area together every day, while in their homes they broke bread. With exultant and sincere hearts they took their meals in common, **47**†praising God and winning the approval of all the people. Day by day the Lord added to their number those who were being saved.

Cure of a Cripple

3 **1**†ONCE, when Peter and John were going up to the temple for prayer at the three o'clock hour, **2**a man crippled from birth was being carried in. They would bring him every day and put him at the temple gate called "the Beautiful" to beg from the

---

† 2, 38: *You must reform and be baptized:* repentance is a positive concept, a change of heart toward God reflected in the actual goodness of one's own life. It is in accord with the apostolic teaching derived from Jesus (2, 42) and ultimately recorded in the four gospels. Jesus made use of baptism at the beginning of his ministry (Jn 3, 22; 4, 2), but according to the synoptic evangelists abandoned the practice after the arrest of the Baptizer. Matthew tells us (28, 19) that the sacramental usage of baptism was an instruction given to the apostles by the risen Christ. Jesus spoke of this new baptism to Nicodemus (Jn 3, 5).

2, 42-47: The first of three summary passages (see 4, 32-37 and 5, 12-16) which outline, somewhat ideally, the chief characteristics of the Jerusalem community: adherence to the teachings of the Twelve concerning repentance; the centering of its religious life in the eucharistic liturgy (42); a system of distribution of goods that led wealthier Christians to sell their possessions when the needs of the community's poor required it (44 and note on 4, 32—5, 11); continued attendance at the Temple, since in this initial stage there was little or no thought of dividing lines between Judaism and Christianity.

2, 47: *Those who were being saved:* not that Christians are absolutely saved, but rather that to those who believe in Christ God directly reveals his saving action in their behalf. If Christians are not saved, it is because of their failure to respond to God's saving action; cf Rom 8, 1.

3, 1—4, 31: This section presents a series of related events: the dramatic cure of a lame beggar (3, 1-10) produces a large audience for the kerygmatic discourse of Peter (3, 11-26). The Sadducees, taking exception to the doctrine of resurrection, have Peter, John, and apparently the beggar as well arrested (4, 1-4) and brought to trial before the Sanhedrin. The issue concerns the authority on which Peter and John publicly teach religious doctrine in the temple (5ff). Peter replies with a brief summary of the kerygma, implying that his authority is pro-

---

   21: Rom 10, 13.
   22: 10, 38; Lk 24, 19.
   23: 1 Thes 2, 15.
   24: 13, 34.
25-28: Ps 16, 8-11.
   27: 13, 35.
   30: 2 Sm 7, 12; Ps 132, 11.
   31: 13, 35; Ps 16, 10.
   33: 1, 4f.
   34: Ps 110, 1.

   36: 9, 22; Rom 10, 9; Phil 2, 11.
   38: 2, 33; 16, 31.
   40: Lk 9, 41.
   41: 1, 5.
42-47: 4, 32-35.
   42: 1, 14; 6, 4.
   43: 5, 12-16.
   44: 4, 32.34f.

people as they entered. ³When he saw Peter and John on their way in, he begged them for an alms. ⁴Peter fixed his gaze on the man; so did John. "Look at us!" Peter said. ⁵The cripple gave them his whole attention, hoping to get something. ⁶†Then Peter said: "I have neither silver nor gold, but what I have I give you! In the name of Jesus Christ the Nazorean, walk!" ⁷*Then Peter took him by the right hand and pulled him up. Immediately the beggar's feet and ankles became strong; ⁸*he jumped up, stood for a moment, then began to walk around. He went into the temple with them—walking, jumping about, and praising God. ⁹When the people saw him moving and giving praise to God, ¹⁰they recognized him as that beggar who used to sit at the Beautiful Gate of the temple. They were struck with astonishment—utterly stupefied at what had happened to him.

Peter's Discourse

¹¹As the man stood there clinging to Peter and John, the whole crowd rushed over to them excitedly in Solomon's Portico. ¹²*When Peter saw this, he addressed the people as follows: "Fellow Israelites, why does this surprise you? Why do you stare at us as if we had made this man walk by some power or holiness of our own? ¹³†The God of Abraham, of Isaac, and of Jacob, the God of our fathers, has glorified his Servant Jesus, whom you handed over and disowned in Pilate's presence when Pilate was ready to release him. ¹⁴*†You disowned the Holy and Just One and preferred instead to be granted the release of a murderer. ¹⁵†You put to death the Author of life. But God raised him from the dead, and we are his witnesses. ¹⁶*It is his name, and trust in this name, that has strengthened the limbs of this man whom you see and know well. Such faith has given him perfect health, as all of you can observe.

¹⁷*†"Yet I know, my brothers, that you acted out of ignorance, just as your leaders did. ¹⁸*†God has brought to fulfillment by this means what he announced long ago through all the prophets: that his Messiah would suffer. ¹⁹Therefore, reform your lives! Turn to God, that your sins may be wiped away! ²⁰†Thus may a season of refreshment be granted you by the Lord when he sends you Jesus, already designated as your Messiah. ²¹Jesus must remain in heaven until the time of universal restoration which God spoke of long ago through his holy prophets. ²²*†For Moses said:

" 'The Lord God will raise up for you a prophet like me from among your own kinsmen: you shall listen to him in everything he says to you. ²³Anyone who does not listen to that prophet shall be ruthlessly cut off from the people.'

²⁴"Moreover, all the prophets who have spoken, from Samuel onward, have announced the events of these days. ²⁵*You are the children of those prophets, you are the heirs of the covenant God made with your fathers when he said to Abraham, 'In your offspring, all the families of the earth shall be blessed.' ²⁶*When God raised up his servant, he sent him to you first to bless you by turning you from your evil ways."

4 ¹†WHILE Peter and John were still addressing the crowd, the priests, the captain of the temple guard, and the Sadducees came up to them, ²*angry because they were teaching the people and proclaiming the resurrection of the dead in the person

---

† phetic (8-12). The court warns the apostles to abandon their practice of invoking prophetic authority in the name of Jesus (13-18). When Peter and John reply that the prophetic role cannot be abandoned to satisfy the objections of men, the court nevertheless releases them, afraid to do otherwise since the beggar, lame from birth and over forty years old, is a well-known figure in Jerusalem and the facts of his cure are common property (19-22). The narrative concludes with a prayer of the Christian community imploring divine aid against threats of persecution (23-31).

3, 1: *Prayer at the three o'clock hour:* when the evening sacrifice was offered in the temple; cf Ex 29, 38f.

3, 6-10: The miracle has a dramatic cast; it symbolizes the saving power of Christ and leads the beggar to enter the temple, where he hears Peter's proclamation of salvation through Jesus.

3, 13: *Servant:* the Greek word can be rendered "son" or even "child" here and also in 3, 26; 4, 25 (applied to David); 4, 27-30. Scholars are of the opinion, however, that the original concept reflected in the word identified Jesus in the early apostolic preaching with the suffering Servant of the Lord of Is 52, 13—53, 12. *Has glorified:* through the resurrection and ascension of Jesus, God reversed the judgment against him on the occasion of his trial.

3, 14: *The Holy and Just One:* a characterization of Jesus as Messiah, emphasizing his sinlessness and extraordinary religious dignity, which are placed in sharp contrast with the guilt of those who rejected him in favor of Barabbas; Mt 27, 15-23.

3, 15: *The Author of life:* the source of the messianic benefits for Israel.

3, 17: *You acted out of ignorance, just as your leaders did:* even those actually responsible for the execution of Jesus were unaware of his messianic dignity.

3, 18: *Through all the prophets:* Christian prophetic insight into the Old Testament saw the crucifixion and death of Jesus as the main burden of messianic prophecy. The Jews themselves did not anticipate a suffering Messiah; they usually understood the Servant Song in Is 52, 13—53, 12 to signify their own suffering as a people (as most Jews still do to the present day).

3, 20: *Thus may a season of refreshment be granted you:* an allusion to the parousia or second coming of Christ, judged to be imminent in the apostolic age. This reference to its nearness is the only explicit one in Acts; see note on 5, 1-11.

3, 22: A loose citation of Dt 18, 15, which teaches that the Israelites are to learn the will of Yahweh from no one but their prophets. At the time of Jesus the Jews expected a unique prophet to come in fulfillment of this text (Jn 1, 21; 6, 14; 7, 40). Early Christianity understood this tradition and text as applying to Jesus, and used them especially in defense of the divergence of Christian teaching from traditional Judaism.

4, 1: *The priests, the captain of the temple guard, and the Sadducees:* the priests performed the temple liturgy. The officer of the temple, a Levite, was in charge of the temple guard. The

---

❋
3/7: 4, 10.
   8: Is 35, 6; Lk 7, 22.
  12: 14, 15.
  14: Mt 27, 20; Mk 15, 11;
     Lk 23, 18; Jn 18, 40.
  16: 4, 10.
  17: 13, 27; 1 Cor 2, 8.

18: Lk 18, 31.
22: 7, 37; Dt 18, 15.18.
25: Gn 12, 3; 22, 18;
    Sir 44, 19ff.
26: Gal 3, 8f.
4/2: 23, 6ff; 24, 21.

of Jesus. ³It was evening by now, so they arrested them and put them in jail for the night. ⁴Despite this, many of those who had heard the speech believed; the number of the men came to about five thousand.

Before the Sanhedrin

⁵When the leaders, the elders, and the scribes assembled the next day in Jerusalem, ⁶Annas the high priest, Caiaphas, John, Alexander, and all who were of the high-priestly class were there. ⁷They brought Peter and John before them and began the interrogation in this fashion: "By what power or in whose name have men of your stripe done this?"

⁸*Then Peter, filled with the Holy Spirit, spoke up: "Leaders of the people! Elders! ⁹If we must answer today for a good deed done to a cripple and explain how he was restored to health, ¹⁰then you and all the people of Israel must realize that it was done in the name of Jesus Christ the Nazorean whom you crucified and whom God raised from the dead. In the power of that name this man stands before you perfectly sound. ¹¹*†This Jesus is 'the stone rejected by you the builders which has become the cornerstone.' ¹²There is no salvation in anyone else, for there is no other name in the whole world given to men by which we are to be saved."

¹³Observing the self-assurance of Peter and John, and realizing that the speakers were uneducated men of no standing, the questioners were amazed. Then they recognized these men as having been with Jesus. ¹⁴When they saw the man who had been cured standing there with them, they could think of nothing to say, ¹⁵so they ordered them out of the court while they held a consultation. "What shall we do with these men? ¹⁶Everyone who lives in Jerusalem knows what a remarkable show of power took place through them. We cannot deny it. ¹⁷To stop this from spreading further among the people we must give them a stern warning never to mention that man's name to anyone again." ¹⁸So they called them back and made it clear that under no circumstances were they to speak the name of Jesus or teach about him. ¹⁹Peter and John answered, "Judge for yourselves whether it is right in God's sight for us to obey you rather than God. ²⁰Surely we cannot help speaking of what we have heard and seen." ²¹At that point they were dismissed with further warnings. The court could find no way to punish them because of the people, all of whom were praising God for what had happened. ²²The fact was, the man thus miraculously cured was more than forty years of age.

Thanksgiving

²³After being released, the two went back to their own people and told them what the priests and elders

had said. ²⁴†All raised their voices in prayer to God on hearing the story: "Sovereign Lord, who made heaven and earth and sea and all that is in them, ²⁵*you have said by the Holy Spirit through the lips of our father David your servant:

'Why did the Gentiles rage,
   the peoples conspire in folly?
²⁶The kings of the earth were aligned,
   the princes gathered together
      against the Lord and against his anointed.'

²⁷*†Indeed, they gathered in this very city against your holy Servant, Jesus, whom you anointed—Herod and Pontius Pilate in league with the Gentiles and the peoples of Israel. ²⁸They have brought about the very things which in your powerful providence you planned long ago. ²⁹But now, O Lord, look at the threats they are leveling against us. Grant to your servants, even as they speak your words, complete assurance ³⁰by stretching forth your hand in cures and signs and wonders to be worked in the name of Jesus, your holy Servant."

³¹†The place where they were gathered shook as they prayed. They were filled with the Holy Spirit and continued to speak God's word with confidence.

Life of the Christians

³²†The community of believers were of one heart and one mind. None of them ever claimed anything as

---

† Sadducees, a party within Judaism at this time, rejected those doctrines (among them bodily resurrection) which they believed alien to the ancient Mosaic religion. The Sadducees were drawn from priestly families and the lay aristocracy.

4, 11: Early Christianity applied this citation from Ps 118, 22 to Jesus; cf Mk 12, 10; 1 Pt 2, 7.

4, 24-30: An example of the type of prayer common in the early Christian community. After invoking God as Creator (4, 24) it cites the messianic Psalm 2, 1f, much favored in early Christianity, to recall men's impotence against God's designs (4, 25f), as exemplified by the resurrection of Jesus, which frustrated the actions of Herod and Pilate against him (4, 27f). It then appeals to the members of the community for courage to proclaim the Christian kerygma in a hostile world and pleads for divine aid through the bestowal of the charism to perform physical cures (4, 29f).

4, 27: *Herod:* Herod Antipas, ruler of Galilee and Perea from 4 B. C. to 39 A. D., who executed John the Baptizer, and before whom Jesus was arraigned; cf Lk 23, 6-12.

4, 31: *The place . . . shook:* the earthquake is used as a sign of the divine presence in Ex 19, 18; Is 6, 4. Here the shaking of the building symbolizes God's favorable response to prayer. Luke may have had as an additional reason for using the symbol in this sense the fact that it was familiar to the Hellenistic world. Ovid and Virgil also employ it.

4, 32-37: This is a second summary characterization of the Jerusalem community (see note on 2, 42-47). It highlights the system of the distribution of goods, and introduces Barnabas, who figures later in Acts as the friend and companion of Paul, and who, as noted here (v 37), endeared himself to the community by a donation of money through the sale of property. Careful examination of Luke's statements on *everything in common* indicates that: (1) members of the community were free to dispose of their property or to retain it as they saw fit; (2) donation of property or of money accruing from its sale was not a condition of membership in the community; and (3) the

---

* 8: Mt 10, 20.
11: Ps 118, 22; Is 28, 16; Mt 21, 42; Mk 12, 10; Lk 20, 17; Rom 9, 33; 1 Pt 2, 7.
25: Ps 2, 1f.
27: Lk 23, 12.

his own; rather, everything was held in common. [33]With power the apostles bore witness to the resurrection of the Lord Jesus, and great respect was paid to them all; [34]nor was there anyone needy among them, for all who owned property or houses sold them and donated the proceeds. [35]They used to lay them at the feet of the apostles to be distributed to everyone according to his need.

[36*]There was a certain Levite from Cyprus named Joseph, to whom the apostles gave the name Barnabas (meaning "son of encouragement"). [37]He sold a farm that he owned and made a donation of the money, laying it at the apostles' feet.

Ananias and Sapphira

5 [1†]ANOTHER man named Ananias and his wife Sapphira likewise sold a piece of property. [2]With the connivance of his wife he put aside a part of the proceeds for himself; the rest he took and laid at the feet of the apostles. [3]Peter exclaimed: "Ananias, why have you let Satan fill your heart so as to make you lie to the Holy Spirit and keep for yourself some of the proceeds from that field? [4]Was it not yours so long as it remained unsold? Even when you sold it, was not the money still yours? How could you ever concoct such a scheme? You have lied not to men but to God!" [5]At the sound of these words, Ananias fell dead. Great fear came upon all who later heard of it. [6]Some of the young men came forward, wrapped up the body, and carried it out for burial. [7]Three hours later Ananias' wife came in, unaware of what had happened. [8]Peter said to her, "Tell me, did you sell that piece of property for such and such an amount?" She answered, "Yes, that was the sum." [9]Peter replied, "How could you two scheme to put the Spirit of the Lord to the test? The footsteps of the men who have just buried your husband can be heard at the door. They stand ready to carry you out too." [10]With that, she fell dead at his feet. The young men came in, found her dead, and carried her out for burial beside her husband. [11]Great fear came on the whole church and on all who heard of it.

Signs and Wonders

[12†]Through the hands of the apostles, many signs and wonders occurred among the people. By mutual agreement they used to meet in Solomon's Portico. [13]No one else dared to join them, despite the fact that the people held them in great esteem. [14]Nevertheless more and more believers, men and women in great numbers, were continually added to the Lord. [15]The people carried the sick into the streets and laid them on cots and mattresses, so that when Peter passed by at least his shadow might fall on one or another of them. [16]Crowds from the towns around Jerusalem would gather, too, bringing their sick and those who

were troubled by unclean spirits, all of whom were cured.

Second Trial before the Sanhedrin

[17†]The high priest and all his supporters (that is, the party of the Sadducees), filled with jealousy, [18]arrested the apostles and threw them into the public jail. [19*]During the night, however, an angel of the Lord opened the gates of the jail, led them forth, and said, [20]"Go out now and take your place in the temple precincts and preach to the people all about this new life." [21]Accordingly they went into the temple at dawn and resumed their teaching.

When the high priest and his supporters arrived they convoked the Sanhedrin, the full council of the elders of Israel. They sent word to the jail that the prisoners were to be brought in. [22]But when the temple guard got to the jail they could not find them, [23]and hurried back with the report, "We found the jail securely locked and the guards at their posts outside the gates, but when we opened it we found no one inside."

[†] holding of property *in common* meant that the poor of the community were cared for through the substantial donations of the wealthier members.

5, 1-11: The peculiarities latent in this narrative afford the basis of its proper interpretation. The harsh treatment meted out to Ananias (3f) does not accord with Luke's portrait of the love operative within the community; cf 2, 44-47. This harshness becomes even more painfully evident when Sapphira is not informed of her husband's death, or of the fact that their deceit has been discovered (7f); neither of them is given that opportunity for repentance which lies at the heart of the teaching of the Christian community (2, 38).

Their sin did not consist in the withholding of part of the money, even deceitfully, but in their deception of the community. The true nature of this deceit is revealed in the light of the early Christian expectation of the parousia; cf Acts 3, 20; 1 Thes 4, 13-17. Their gift supposedly symbolized their complete confidence in the proximity of Christ's final coming, which rendered earthly possessions unimportant. (For a similar line of thought, cf 1 Cor 7, 29ff.) Their deaths are ascribed to a lie to the Holy Spirit (3-9), i. e., they accepted the honor accorded them by the community for their apparent faith in the proximate parousia, but in reality they were not deserving of it.

5, 12-16: This, the third summary portrait of the Jerusalem community, underscores the Twelve as its bulwark, especially because of their charismatic power to heal the sick; cf 2, 42-47; 4, 32-37.

5, 17-42: A second action against the community is taken by the Sanhedrin in the arrest and trial of the Twelve; cf 4, 1ff. The motive is the jealousy of the religious authorities over the popularity of the apostles (17), who are now charged with defiance of the Sanhedrin's previous order to them to abandon their prophetic role (28; cf 4, 18). In this crisis the apostles are favored by a miraculous release from prison (18-24). (For similar incidents involving Peter and Paul, cf 12, 6-11; 16, 25-29.) The real significance of such an event, however, would be manifest only to men of faith, not to unbelievers; since the Sanhedrin had already judged the Twelve to be unauthentic prophets, it could disregard reports of their miracles. When the Twelve immediately resumed public teaching, the Sanhedrin determined to invoke upon them the penalty of death (5, 33) prescribed in Dt 13, 6-10. Gamaliel's advice against this course finally prevailed, but it did not save the Twelve from the punishment of scourging (5, 40f), in a last endeavor to shake their conviction of their prophetic mission.

²⁴On hearing this report, the captain of the temple guard and the high priests did not know what to make of the affair. ²⁵Someone then came up to them, pointing out, "Look, there! Those men you put in jail are standing over there in the temple, teaching the people." ²⁶At that, the captain went off with the guard and brought them in, but without any show of force, for fear of being stoned by the crowd. ²⁷When they had led them in and made them stand before the Sanhedrin, the high priest began the interrogation in this way: ²⁸*"We gave you strict orders not to teach about that name, yet you have filled Jerusalem with your teaching and are determined to make us responsible for that man's blood." ²⁹To this, Peter and the apostles replied: "Better for us to obey God than men! ³⁰The God of our fathers has raised up Jesus whom you put to death, hanging him on a tree. ³¹He whom God has exalted at his right hand as ruler and savior is to bring repentance to Israel and forgiveness of sins. ³²We testify to this. So too does the Holy Spirit, whom God has given to those that obey him."

³³When the Sanhedrin heard this, they were stung to fury and wanted to kill them. ³⁴*Then a member of the Sanhedrin stood up, a Pharisee named Gamaliel, a teacher of the law highly regarded by all the people. He had the accused ordered out of court for a few minutes, ³⁵and then said to the assembly, "Fellow Israelites, think twice about what you are going to do with these men. ³⁶Not long ago a certain Theudas came on the scene and tried to pass himself off as someone of importance. About four hundred men joined him. However he was killed, and all those who had been so easily convinced by him were disbanded. In the end it came to nothing. ³⁷Next came Judas the Galilean at the time of the census. He too built up quite a following, but likewise died, and all his followers were dispersed. ³⁸The present case is similar. My advice is that you have nothing to do with these men. Let them alone. If their purpose or activity is human in its origins, it will destroy itself. ³⁹If, on the other hand, it comes from God, you will not be able to destroy them without fighting God himself."

This speech persuaded them. ⁴⁰*In spite of it, however, the Sanhedrin called in the apostles and had them whipped. They ordered them not to speak again about the name of Jesus, and afterward dismissed them. ⁴¹*The apostles for their part left the Sanhedrin full of joy that they had been judged worthy of ill-treatment for the sake of the Name. ⁴²Day after day, both in the temple and at home, they never stopped teaching and proclaiming the good news of Jesus the Messiah.

III: SPREAD OF THE CHURCH THROUGH PERSECUTION IN JERUSALEM

The Need of Assistants

6 ¹†IN THOSE DAYS, AS THE NUMBER of disciples grew, the ones who spoke Greek complained that their widows were being neglected in the daily distribution of food, as compared with the widows of those who spoke Hebrew. ²†The Twelve assembled the community of the disciples and said. "It is not right for us to neglect the word of God in order to wait on tables. ³Look around among your own number, brothers, for seven men acknowledged to be deeply spiritual and prudent, and we shall appoint them to this task. ⁴This will permit us to concentrate on prayer and the ministry of the word." ⁵The proposal was unanimously accepted by the community. Following this they selected Stephen, a man filled with faith and the Holy Spirit; Philip, Prochorus, Nicanor, Timon, Parmenas, and Nicolaus of Antioch, who had been a convert to Judaism. ⁶†They presented these men to the apostles, who first prayed over them and then imposed hands on them.

⁷The word of God continued to spread, while at the same time the number of the disciples in Jerusalem enormously increased. There were many priests among those who embraced the faith.

Stephen Accused

⁸†The Stephen already spoken of was a man filled with grace and power, who worked great wonders

---

† 6, 1-11: An example of the solution of conflicts within the Christian community. It is probable that the seven men assigned to this duty from among the Hellenist Christians, i. e., Jews from the diaspora, already possessed standing in the community as catechists, a role later ascribed to Stephen (8ff) and Philip (8, 5).

6, 2.4: The essential function of the Twelve is the "service of the word," i. e., development of the kerygma by formulation of the teachings of Jesus. This became the material that went into the formation of the gospels.

6, 6: They . . . imposed hands on them: the customary Jewish way of designating a person for a task and invoking upon him the divine blessing and power to perform it.

6, 8—8, 1: The summary statement (6, 7) on the progress of the Jerusalem community, illustrated by the conversion of the priests, is followed by a lengthy narrative regarding Stephen. Stephen's defense is not a response to the charges made against him, but takes the form of a discourse that reviews the fortunes of God's word to Israel and leads to a prophetic declaration: a plea for the hearing of that word as announced by Christ and now possessed by the Christian community.

The charges that Stephen depreciated the importance of the temple and the Mosaic law and elevated Jesus to a stature above Moses (6, 13f) were in fact true. Before a non-Christian audience such as the Sanhedrin, no defense against them was possible. With Stephen, who thus perceived the fuller implications of the teaching of Jesus, the differences between Judaism and Christianity began to appear. Luke's account of Stephen's martyrdom and its aftermath shows how the major impetus behind the Christian movement passed from Jerusalem, where temple

---

28: Mt 27, 25.   40: Mt 10, 17.
34: 22, 3.   41: Mt 5, 10f.

and signs among the people. **9**Certain members of the so-called "Synagogue of Roman Freedmen" (that is, the Jews from Cyrene, Alexandria, Cilicia and Asia) would undertake to engage Stephen in debate, **10**but they proved no match for the wisdom and spirit with which he spoke. **11***They persuaded some men to make the charge that they had heard him speaking blasphemies against Moses and God, **12**and in this way they incited the people, the elders, and the scribes. All together they confronted him, seized him, and led him off to the Sanhedrin. **13†**There they brought in false witnesses, who said: "This man never stops making statements against the holy place and the law. **14*†**We have heard him claim that Jesus the Nazorean will destroy this place and change the customs which Moses handed down to us." **15**The members of the Sanhedrin who sat there stared at him intently. Throughout, Stephen's face seemed like that of an angel.

Stephen's Discourse

7 **1**THE high priest asked whether the charges were true. **2†**To this Stephen replied: "My brothers! Fathers! Listen to me. The God of glory appeared to our father Abraham when he was still in Mesopotamia and before he settled in Haran. **3***God said to him, Leave your country and your kinsfolk, and go to the land I will show you. **4**So he left the land of the Chaldeans and settled in Haran. After his father died, God made him move from there to this land where you now dwell. **5***God did not give him any of it as his heritage, not even a foot of land, but he promised to give it to him and his descendants after him as a possession—although he had no child. **6***These are the words God used: Abraham's posterity will be strangers in a foreign land, and they will be subject to slavery and oppressed four hundred years. **7**But I will judge that nation which they serve, God said, and after that they will worship me in this place.

8*"God then made a covenant of circumcision with him, and Abraham, who had become the father of Isaac, circumcised him on the eighth day. Isaac did the same for Jacob, and Jacob for the twelve patriarchs. **9***Out of envy, the patriarchs sold Joseph into slavery in Egypt, **10***but God was with him and rescued him from all his tribulations. He granted him favor and wisdom in the court of the Pharaoh, king of Egypt, and made him the governor of Egypt and of the Pharaoh's entire household. **11**When famine and great trial came upon Egypt and Canaan, our fathers could find no sustenance. **12***Hearing that there was grain in Egypt, Jacob sent our fathers there on a first mission. **13***The second time, Joseph made himself known to his brothers, and his family ties became

known to the Pharaoh. **14**Then Joseph sent for his father Jacob, inviting him and all his kinsfolk—seventy-five persons in all. **15***Jacob went down to Egypt and died there, as did our fathers. **16***Their remains were transferred to Shechem and placed in the tomb which Abraham had bought with silver from the sons of Hamor at Shechem.

17*"When the time drew near for the fulfillment of the promise made by God to Abraham, our people in Egypt grew more and more numerous, **18**until a new king came to power in Egypt, who knew not Joseph. **19**This one dealt craftily with our people and oppressed them. He forced our fathers to abandon their infants to exposure so that the people would not survive.

20*"It was at this time that Moses was born. He proved to be an exceedingly handsome child. For the first three months he was reared in his father's house, **21**but afterward he was abandoned, and Pharaoh's daughter adopted him and brought him up as her own son. **22**Moses was educated in all the lore of Egypt. He was a man powerful in word and deed. **23**When he was forty, he decided to visit his kinsmen, the Israelites. **24***Upon seeing one of them maltreated, he went to his aid and avenged the victim by slaying the Egyptian. **25**He assumed that his kinsmen would understand that God was using him to bring them deliverance; but they did not. **26***He appeared the next day while some of them were fighting, and tried to reconcile them by saying: 'Friends, you are blood brothers. Why are you trying to hurt each other?' **27**At that, the man who was wronging his neighbor pushed Moses aside. 'And who has appointed you ruler and judge over us?' he said. **28**'Are you thinking of killing me as you killed the Egyptian yesterday?' **29**On hearing this, Moses fled. He took up his residence as an alien in the land of Midian, where he became the father of two sons.

30*"Forty years later an angel appeared to him in the desert near Mount Sinai in the flame of a burning

---

†
and law prevailed, to Antioch in Syria, where these influences were less pressing.

6, 13: *False witnesses:* here and in his account of Stephen's execution (7, 54-60), Luke parallels the martyrdom of Stephen with the death of Jesus.

6, 14: *Will destroy this place and change the customs:* a possible indication that Stephen and other members of the community had begun to reflect upon the religious significance of Christ's prophecy concerning the destruction of the temple (Mk 13, 1f) and upon his attitude toward the law; cf Mk 2, 18—3, 6.

7, 2: *God . . . appeared to . . . Abraham . . . in Mesopotamia:* the first of a number of minor discrepancies between the data of the Old Testament and the data of Stephen's discourse. According to Gn 12, 1 God first spoke to Abraham in Haran. The main discrepancies are these: In 7, 16 it is said that Jacob was buried in Shechem, whereas Gn 50, 13 says he was buried at Hebron; in the same verse it is said that the tomb was purchased by Abraham, but in Gn 33, 19 and Jos 24, 32 the purchase is attributed to Jacob himself. The exactitude of detail achievable by modern scholarship was not a concern of ancient writers—who in any case were dealing with a variety of biblical and extra-biblical traditions.

✱

6/11: 21, 21.	13: Gn 45, 3.
14: Mt 26, 59ff.	15: Gn 49, 32.
7/3: Gn 12, 1.	16: Gn 23, 15f; 50, 13;
5: Gn 12, 7; 15, 2.	Jos 24, 32.
6f: Gn 15, 13f.	17: Ex 1, 7.
8: Gn 17, 10; 21, 2ff.	20: Ex 2, 2f; Heb 11, 23.
9: Gn 37, 28.	24: Ex 2, 12.
10: Gn 41, 37; Ps 105, 21.	26: Ex 2, 13.
12: Gn 42, 2.	30-34: Ex 3, 2-10.

thornbush. **31**When Moses saw it, he marveled at the sight. As he drew near to observe it carefully, the voice of the Lord was heard: **32**'I am the God of your fathers, the God of Abraham, of Isaac, and of Jacob.' Moses began to tremble and dared look no more. **33**The Lord said to him: 'Remove the sandals from your feet, for the place where you stand is holy ground. **34**I have witnessed the affliction of my people in Egypt and have heard their groaning, and I have come down to rescue them. Come now, I will send you into Egypt.'

35"This very Moses whom they had rejected with the words, 'Who has appointed you ruler and judge?', was the one whom God, through the angel appearing to him in the thornbush, sent to be their ruler and deliverer. **36**It was he who led them forth, all the while performing wonders and signs in the land of Egypt, in the Red Sea, and for forty years in the desert. **37**This Moses is the one who said to the Israelites, 'God will raise up for you from among your kinsmen a prophet like me.' **38**In that desert assembly, it was he who was in conversation with the angel on Mount Sinai and with our fathers; he too received the oracles of life to pass on to you. **39**He it was whom our fathers would not obey; rather, they thrust him aside and longed to return to Egypt. **40**'Make us gods that will be our leaders,' they said to Aaron. 'As for that Moses who brought us out of the land of Egypt, we have no idea what has happened to him.' **41**It was then that they fashioned the calf and offered sacrifice to the idol, and had a festive celebration over the product of their own hands. **42**But God turned away from them and abandoned them to the worship of the galaxies in the heavens. So we find it written in the Book of the Prophets:

'Did you bring me sacrifices and offerings
   for forty years in the desert, O house of Israel?
43Not at all! You took along the tent of Moloch
   and the star of the god Rephan,
   the images you had made for your cult.
For that I will exile you beyond Babylon.'

44"Our fathers in the desert had the meeting tent as God prescribed it when he spoke to Moses, ordering him to make it according to the pattern he had seen. **45**The next generation of our fathers inherited it. Under Joshua, they brought it into the land during the conquest of those peoples whom God drove out to make room for our fathers. So it was until the time of David, **46**who found favor with God and begged that he might find a dwelling place for the house of Jacob. **47**It was Solomon, however, who constructed the building for that house. **48**Yet the Most High does not dwell in buildings made by human hands, for as the prophet says:

49'The heavens are my throne,
   the earth is my footstool;
What kind of house can you build me?
   asks the Lord.
What is my resting-place to be like?
50Did not my hand make all these things?'

Conclusion

51"You stiff-necked people, uncircumcised in heart and ears, you are always opposing the Holy Spirit just as your fathers did before you. **52**Was there ever any prophet whom your fathers did not persecute? In their day, they put to death those who foretold the coming of the Just One; now you in your turn have become his betrayers and murderers. **53**You who received the law through the ministry of angels have not observed it."

Stephen's Martyrdom

54Those who listened to his words were stung to the heart; they ground their teeth in anger at him. **55**Stephen meanwhile, filled with the Holy Spirit, looked to the sky above and saw the glory of God, and Jesus standing at God's right hand. **56**"Look!" he exclaimed, "I see an opening in the sky, and the Son of Man standing at God's right hand." **57**The onlookers were shouting aloud, holding their hands over their ears as they did so. Then they rushed at him as one man, **58**dragged him out of the city, and began to stone him. The witnesses meanwhile were piling their cloaks at the feet of a young man named Saul. **59**As Stephen was being stoned he could be heard praying, "Lord Jesus, receive my spirit." **60**He fell to his knees and cried out in a loud voice, "Lord, do not hold this sin against them." And with that he died.

The Church Persecuted

8 **1**SAUL, for his part, concurred in the act of killing. That day saw the beginning of a great persecution of the church in Jerusalem. All except the apostles scattered throughout the countryside of Judea

---

7, 55: *Stephen . . . saw . . . Jesus standing at God's right hand:* whether this statement is intended to introduce the description of a vision, or is a dramatized version of Stephen's expression of faith in Christ, is of less importance than the meaning Luke attaches to it for his Christian reader. Stephen affirms to the Sanhedrin that the prophecy Jesus made before them has been fulfilled (Mk 14, 62).

7, 57: *Holding their hands over their ears:* Stephen's declaration, like that of Jesus, is a scandal to the court, which regards it as blasphemy.

7, 59f: Compare Lk 23, 34.46.

8, 1-40: Some idea of the severity of the persecution that now breaks out against the Jerusalem community can be gathered from Acts 22, 4 and 26, 9ff. Luke, however, concentrates on the fortunes of the word of God among men, indicating how the dispersal of the Jerusalem community resulted in the conversion of the Samaritans (8, 4-17.25). His narrative is further expanded to include the account of Philip's acceptance of a Gentile from Ethiopia (8, 26-39).

8, 1: *All except the apostles scattered:* this observation leads some modern scholars to conclude that the persecution was limited to the Hellenist Christians, and that the Judaeo-Chris-

---

37: Dt 18, 15.
38: Ex 19, 3.
40: Ex 32, 1.
42: Am 5, 25.
44: Ex 25, 40.
45: Jos 3, 14.
46: Ps 132, 5.
47: 1 Kgs 6, 1; 1 Chr 17, 12.
48: 17, 24.
49: Is 66, 1.

and Samaria. ²Devout men buried Stephen, bewailing him loudly as they did so. ³*†After that, Saul began to harass the church. He entered house after house, dragged men and women out, and threw them into jail.

IV: THE COMMUNITY CARRIES THE MESSAGE TO SAMARIA, SYRIA AND CYPRUS

Philip in Samaria

⁴*THE MEMBERS OF THE CHURCH who had been dispersed went about preaching the word. ⁵*Philip, for example, went down to the town of Samaria and there proclaimed the Messiah. ⁶Without exception, the crowds that heard Philip and saw the miracles he performed attended closely to what he had to say. ⁷There were many who had unclean spirits, which came out shrieking loudly. Many others were paralytics or cripples, and these were cured. ⁸The rejoicing in that town rose to fever pitch.

Simon Magus

⁹†A certain man named Simon had been practicing magic in the town and holding the Samaritans spellbound. He passed himself off as someone of great importance. ¹⁰People from every rank of society were paying attention to him. "He is the power of the great God," they said. ¹¹Those who followed him had been under the spell of his magic over a long period; ¹²but once they began to believe in the good news that Philip preached about the kingdom of God and the name of Jesus Christ, men and women alike accepted baptism. ¹³Even Simon believed. He was baptized like the rest and became a devoted follower of Philip. He watched the signs and the great miracles as they occurred, and was quite carried away.

¹⁴When the apostles in Jerusalem heard that Samaria had accepted the word of God, they sent Peter and John to them. ¹⁵The two went down to these people and prayed that they might receive the Holy Spirit. ¹⁶It had not as yet come down upon any of them since they had only been baptized in the name of the Lord Jesus. ¹⁷The pair upon arriving imposed hands on them and they received the Holy Spirit. ¹⁸Simon observed that it was through the laying on of hands that the apostles conferred the Spirit, and he made them an offer of money ¹⁹with the request, "Give me that power too, so that if I place my hands on anyone he will receive the Holy Spirit."

²⁰*Peter said in answer: "May you and your money rot—thinking that God's gift can be bought! ²¹You can have no portion or lot in this affair. Your heart is not steadfastly set on God. ²²Reform your evil ways. Pray

that the Lord may pardon you for thinking the way you have. ²³I see you poisoned with gall and caught in the grip of sin." ²⁴Simon responded, "I need the prayers of all of you to the Lord, so that what you have just said may never happen to me."

²⁵†After giving their testimony and proclaiming the word of the Lord, they went back to Jerusalem bringing the good news to many villages of Samaria on the way.

Philip and the Ethiopian

²⁶†An angel of the Lord then addressed himself to Philip: "Head south toward the road which goes from Jerusalem to Gaza, the desert route." Philip began the journey. ²⁷*It happened that an Ethiopian eunuch, a court official in charge of the entire treasury of Candace (a name meaning queen) of the Ethiopians, had come on a pilgrimage to Jerusalem and was returning home. ²⁸He was sitting in his carriage reading the prophet Isaiah. ²⁹The Spirit said to Philip, "Go and catch up with that carriage." ³⁰†Philip ran ahead and heard the man reading the prophet Isaiah. He said to him, "Do you really grasp what you are reading?" ³¹"How can I," the man replied, "unless someone explains it to me?" With that, he invited Philip to get in and sit down beside him. ³²*This was the passage of Scripture he was reading:

---

† tians were not molested. Whatever the facts, it appears that the Twelve took no public stand regarding Stephen's position, choosing, instead, to await the development of events.

8, 3: *Saul began to harass the church:* like Stephen, Saul was able to perceive that the Christian movement contained the seeds of serious doctrinal divergence from Judaism. A pupil of Gamaliel (22, 3), and totally dedicated to the law as the way of salvation (Gal 1, 13f), Saul accepted the task of crushing the Christian movement, at least insofar as it detracted from the importance of the temple and the law. His vehement opposition to Christianity reveals how difficult it was for a Jew of his time to accept a messianism that differed so greatly from the general expectation.

8, 9-13; 18-24: Sorcerers were well known in the ancient world. Probably the incident involving Simon and his altercation with Peter is introduced to show that the miraculous charisms possessed by members of the Christian community (8, 6f) were not to be confused with the magic of sorcerers.

8, 25: Stephen's insistence that the presence of God was not confined to the temple in Jerusalem (7, 48f) is now fully accepted by the apostles as a result of the success of Philip in Samaria.

8, 26-40: In the account of the conversion of the Ethiopian eunuch, Luke adduces additional evidence to show that the spread of Christianity outside the confines of Judaism itself was in accord with the plan of God. He does not make clear whether the Ethiopian was originally a convert to Judaism or, as is more probable, a "God-fearer" (10, 1), i. e., one who accepted Jewish monotheism and ethic and attended the synagogue but did not consider himself bound by other regulations. The story of his conversion to Christianity is given a strong supernatural cast by the introduction of an angel (8, 26), instruction from the Holy Spirit (8, 29), and the strange removal of Philip from the scene (8, 38).

8, 30-34: Philip is brought alongside the carriage at the very moment when the Ethiopian is pondering the meaning of Is 53, 7f, a passage which Christianity, from its earliest origins, has understood of Jesus; cf note on 3, 13.

---

*
8/3: 9, 1f.	20: 13, 10.
4: 11, 19.	27: Is 56, 3ff.
5: 6, 5; 21, 8.	32f: Is 53, 7f.

"Like a sheep he was led to the slaughter,
      like a lamb before its shearer he was silent
      and opened not his mouth.
33In his humiliation he was deprived of justice.
      Who will ever speak of his posterity,
      for he is deprived of his life on earth?"

34The eunuch said to Philip, "Tell me, if you will, of whom the prophet says this—himself or someone else?" **35**Philip launched out with this Scripture passage as his starting point, telling him the good news of Jesus. **36***As they moved along the road they came to some water, and the eunuch said, **37**"Look, there is some water right there. What is to keep me from being baptized?" **38**He ordered the carriage stopped, and Philip went down into the water with the eunuch and baptized him. **39**When they came out of the water, the Spirit of the Lord snatched Philip away and the eunuch saw him no more. Nevertheless the man went on his way rejoicing. **40**Philip found himself at Azotus next, and he went about announcing the good news in all the towns until he reached Caesarea.

The Vocation of Saul

9 **1***†SAUL, still breathing murderous threats against the Lord's disciples, went to the high priest **2**†and asked him for letters to the synagogues in Damascus which would empower him to arrest and bring to Jerusalem anyone he might find, man or woman, living according to the new way. **3***As he traveled along and was approaching Damascus, a light from the sky suddenly flashed about him. **4**He fell to the ground and at the same time heard a voice saying, "Saul, Saul, why do you persecute me?" **5***"Who are you, sir?" he asked. The voice answered, "I am Jesus, the one you are persecuting. **6**Get up and go into the city, where you will be told what to do." **7**The men who were traveling with him stood there speechless. They had heard the voice but could see no one. **8**†Saul got up from the ground unable to see, even though his eyes were open. They had to take him by the hand and lead him into Damascus. **9**For three days he continued blind, during which time he neither ate nor drank.

Saul's Baptism

10There was a disciple in Damascus named Ananias to whom the Lord had appeared in a vision. "Ananias!" he said. "Here I am, Lord," came the answer. **11**The Lord said to him, "Go at once to Straight Street, and at the house of Judas ask for a certain Saul of Tarsus. **12**He is there praying." (Saul saw in a vision a man named Ananias coming to him and placing his hands on him so that he might recover his sight.) **13**But Ananias protested: "Lord, I have heard from many sources about this man and all the harm he has done to your holy people in Jerusalem. **14**He is here now with au-thorization from the chief priests to arrest any who invoke your name." **15**†The Lord said to him: "You must go! This man is the instrument I have chosen to bring my name to the Gentiles and their kings and to the people of Israel. **16**I myself shall indicate to him how much he will have to suffer for my name." **17**With that Ananias left. When he entered the house he laid his hands on Saul and said, "Saul, my brother, I have been sent by the Lord Jesus who appeared to you on the way here, to help you recover your sight and be filled with the Holy Spirit." **18***Immediately something like scales fell from his eyes and he regained his sight. He got up and was baptized, **19**†and his strength returned to him after he had taken food.

Saul Preaches in Damascus

Saul stayed some time with the disciples in Damascus, **20**†and soon began to proclaim in the synagogues that Jesus was the Son of God. **21**Any who heard it were greatly taken aback. They kept saying: "Isn't this the man who worked such havoc in Jerusalem among those who invoke this name? Did he not come here purposely to apprehend such people and bring them before the chief priests?"

22Saul for his part grew steadily more powerful, and reduced the Jewish community of Damascus to silence with his proofs that this Jesus was the Messiah.

---

† 9, 1-19: This is the first of three accounts of Paul's conversion (see 22, 3-16 and 26, 2-18), with some differences of detail. Paul's experience was not visionary but was precipitated by the actual appearance of Jesus, as he insists in 1 Cor 15, 8. The words of Jesus, *"Saul, Saul, why do you persecute me?",* related by Luke with no variation in all three accounts, exerted a profound and lasting influence on the thought of Paul. Under the impulsion of this experience he gradually developed his understanding of justification by faith (see Epistles to Galatians and Romans), and of the identification of the Christian community with Jesus Christ; cf Col 1, 18.

9, 2: *The new way:* an early name for Christian discipleship; cf 16, 17; 18, 26; 19, 9.23; 24, 14.22. The term, no doubt Christian in origin, expresses the idea that Christian discipleship is the culmination of God's revelation to men and of men's relationship to God.

9, 8: *Unable to see:* a temporary blindness (9, 18), miraculous in origin, symbolizing the religious blindness of Saul as persecutor.

9, 15: *To bring my name to the Gentiles:* only gradually was the significance of this prophecy realized by Paul as the church was compelled to turn its attention more and more to the Gentiles.

9, 19-30: This is a brief résumé of Paul's initial experience as an apostolic preacher, though that aspect of his career did not begin immediately upon his conversion (Gal 1, 17). At first he found himself in the position of being both a turncoat to the Jews and an enigma to the Christian community of Jerusalem. His acceptance by the latter was finally brought about through his friendship with Barnabas.

9, 20: *The Son of God:* to be understood in the sense of "the Christ" in 9, 22; cf Acts 13, 33 citing Ps 2, 7 in this sense. Perhaps Luke chooses this expression here because, for Paul and Christians generally, the title "Son of God" soon became the one most expressive of Jesus' true dignity; cf 1 Thes 1, 10; Rom 1, 2ff.

✿
  36: 10, 47.   5: Mt 25, 40.
9/1: Gal 1, 13f.   18: Tb 11, 12ff.
  3: 22, 6; 1 Cor 15, 8.

Saul Visits Jerusalem

23After quite some time had passed, certain Jews conspired to kill Saul, **24***but their plot came to his attention. They went so far as to keep close watch on the city gates day and night in an attempt to do away with him. **25**Some of his disciples, therefore, took him along the wall one night and lowered him to the ground, using ropes and a hamper. **26**When he arrived back in Jerusalem he tried to join the disciples there; but it turned out that they were all afraid of him. They even refused to believe that he was a disciple. **27**Then Barnabas took him in charge and introduced him to the apostles. He explained to them how on his journey Saul had seen the Lord, who had conversed with him, and how Saul had been speaking out fearlessly in the name of Jesus at Damascus. **28**Saul stayed on with them, moving freely about Jerusalem and expressing himself quite openly in the name of the Lord. **29**He even addressed the Greek-speaking Jews and debated with them. They for their part responded by trying to kill him. **30**When the brothers learned of this, some of them took him down to Caesarea and sent him off to Tarsus.

The Church at Peace

31†Meanwhile throughout all Judea, Galilee, and Samaria the church was at peace. It was being built up and was making steady progress in the fear of the Lord; at the same time it enjoyed the increased consolation of the Holy Spirit.

Peter Visits Lydda and Joppa

32Once when Peter was making numerous journeys, he went—among other places—to God's holy people living in Lydda. **33**There he found a man named Aeneas, a paralytic who had been bedridden for eight years. **34**Peter said to him, "Aeneas, Jesus Christ cures you! Get up and make your bed." The man got up at once. **35**All the inhabitants of Lydda and Sharon, upon seeing him, were converted to the Lord.

36Now in Joppa there was a certain woman convert named Tabitha (in Greek Dorcas, meaning a gazelle). Her life was marked by constant good deeds and acts of charity. **37**At about that time she fell ill and died. They washed her body and laid it out in an upstairs room. **38**Since Lydda was near Joppa, the disciples who had heard that Peter was there sent two men to him with the urgent request, "Please come over to us without delay." **39**Peter set out with them as they asked. Upon his arrival they took him upstairs to the room. All the widows came to him in tears and showed him the various garments Dorcas had made when she was still with them. **40**Peter first made everyone go outside; then he knelt down and prayed. Turning to the dead body, he said, "Tabitha, stand up." She opened her eyes, then looked at Peter and sat up. **41**He gave her his hand and helped her to her feet. The next thing he did was to call in those who were believers and the widows to show them that she was alive. **42**This became known all over Joppa, and because of it, many came to believe in the Lord. **43**†Thus it happened that Peter stayed on in Joppa for a considerable time at the house of Simon, a tanner of leather.

The Vision of Cornelius

10 **1**†NOW in Caesarea there was a centurion named Cornelius, of the Roman cohort Italica, who was religious and God-fearing. The same was true of his whole household. **2**He was in the habit of giving generously to the people and he constantly prayed to God. **3**One afternoon at about three he had a vision in which he clearly saw a messenger of God coming toward him and calling, "Cornelius!" **4**He stared at the sight and said in fear, "What is it, sir?" The answer came: "Your prayers and your generosity have risen in God's sight, and because of them he has remembered you. **5**Send some men to Joppa and summon a certain Simon, known as Peter. **6**He is a guest of Simon the leather-tanner whose house stands by the sea." **7**When the messenger who spoke these words had disappeared, he called two servants and a devout soldier from among those whom he could trust. **8**He explained everything to them and dispatched them to Joppa.

Peter's Vision

9†About noontime the next day, as the men were traveling along and approaching the city, Peter went

---

† 9, 31-43: In the context of the period of peace enjoyed by the community through the cessation of Paul's activities against it, Luke introduces two traditions concerning the miraculous powers of Peter. The towns of Lydda, Sharon and Joppa were populated by both Jews and Gentiles, and their Christian communities may well have been mixed. No particular motive for the cure of Aeneas is assigned, though it is not said that he was a Christian prior to the cure. The actual motive for the raising of Tabitha may have been the expectation of the parousia; in view of her unique charity, the community apparently found it hard to understand her death before this event had occurred.

9, 43: The fact that Peter lodged with a tanner would have been significant to both Gentile and Judaeo-Christians, for Judaism considered the tanning occupation unclean.

10, 1-48: The narrative centers on the conversion of Cornelius, a Gentile and a "God-fearer" (see note on 8, 26-40). Luke considers the event of great importance, as is evident from his long treatment of it. The incident is again related in 11, 1-18 and alluded to in 15, 7ff. The narrative divides itself easily into a series of distinct episodes, concluding with Peter's presentation of the Christian kerygma (34-43), and a pentecostal experience undergone by Cornelius' household preceding their reception of baptism (44-48).

10, 7: A *devout soldier*: by using this adjective Luke probably intends to classify him as a "God-fearer." The point is that Cornelius is careful to select a soldier who will respect his account of the apparition.

10, 9-16: The vision is intended to prepare Peter to share the food of Cornelius' household without qualms of conscience (10, 48). The necessity of such instruction to Peter reveals that at first not even the apostles fully grasped the implications of Jesus' teaching on the law. The initial insight belongs to Stephen.

❈   24f: 2 Cor 11, 32f.

up to the roof terrace to pray. **10**He became hungry and asked for some food, and while it was being prepared he fell into a trance. **11**He saw the sky open and an object come down that looked like a big canvas. It was lowered to the ground by its four corners. **12**Inside it were all the earth's four-legged creatures and reptiles and birds of the sky. **13**A voice said to him: "Get up, Peter! Slaughter, then eat." **14**He answered: "Sir, it is unthinkable! I have never eaten anything unclean or impure in my life." **15***The voice was heard a second time: "What God has purified you are not to call unclean." **16**This happened three times; then the object was snatched up into the sky. **17**†While Peter was trying to make out the meaning of the vision he had had, the men sent by Cornelius arrived at the gate asking for the house of Simon. **18**They called out to inquire whether Simon Peter was a guest there. **19**Peter was still pondering the vision when the Spirit said to him: "There are two men in search of you. **20**Go downstairs and set out with them unhesitatingly, for it is I who sent them." **21**Peter went down to the men and said, "I am the man you are looking for. What brought you here?" **22***They answered: "The centurion Cornelius, who is an upright and God-fearing man, well thought of in the whole Jewish community, has been instructed by a holy messenger to summon you to his house. There he is to hear what you have to say." **23**With that, Peter invited them in and treated them as guests.

Peter in Caesarea

The next day he went off with them, accompanied by some of the brothers from Joppa. **24**†The following day, he arrived in Caesarea. Cornelius, who was expecting them, had called in his relatives and close friends. **25**As Peter entered, Cornelius went to meet him, dropped to his knees before him and bowed low. **26**Peter said as he helped him to his feet, "Get up! I am only a man myself." **27**Peter then went in, talking with him all the while. He found many people assembled there, and **28***†he began speaking to them thus: "You must know that it is not proper for a Jew to associate with a Gentile or to have dealings with him. But God has made it clear to me that no one should call any man unclean or impure. **29**That is why I have come in response to your summons without raising any objection. I should, of course, like to know why you summoned me." **30**Cornelius replied: "Just three days ago at this very hour, namely three o'clock, I was praying at home when a man in dazzling robes stood before me. **31**'Cornelius,' he said, 'your prayer has been heard and your generosity remembered in God's presence. **32**Send someone to Joppa to invite Simon known as Peter to come here. He is a guest in the house of Simon the leather-tanner, by the sea.' **33**I sent for you im-

mediately, and you have been kind enough to come. All of us stand before God at this moment to hear whatever directives the Lord has given you."

Peter's Discourse

34*†Peter proceeded to address them in these words: "I begin to see how true it is that God shows no partiality. **35**Rather, the man of any nation who fears God and acts uprightly is acceptable to him. **36**This is the message he has sent to the sons of Israel, the good news of peace proclaimed through Jesus Christ who is Lord of all. **37***†I take it you know what has been reported all over Judea about Jesus of Nazareth, beginning in Galilee with the baptism John preached; **38**of the way God anointed him with the Holy Spirit and power. He went about doing good works and healing all who were in the grip of the devil, and God was with him. **39**†We are witnesses to all that he did in the land of the Jews and in Jerusalem. **40**They killed him, finally, hanging him on a tree, only to have God raise him up on the third day and grant that he be seen, **41***not by all, but only by such witnesses as had been chosen beforehand by God—by us who ate and drank with him after he rose from the dead. **42**†He commissioned us to preach to the people and to bear witness that he is the one set apart by God as judge of the living and the dead. **43**To him all the prophets testify, saying that everyone who believes in him has forgiveness of sins through his name."

---

† 10, 17-23: The arrival of the Gentile emissaries with their account of the angelic apparition illuminates Peter's vision: he is to be prepared to admit Gentiles into the Christian community.

10, 24ff: So impressed is Cornelius with the apparition that he invites close personal friends to support him in his confrontation with Peter. But his understanding of the personage he is about to meet is not devoid of superstition. For a similar experience of Paul and Barnabas, see 14, 10-17.

10, 28: Peter now fully understands the meaning of his vision; see note on 10, 17-23.

10, 34f: *God shows no partiality:* the revelation of his choice of Israel to be the people of God did not mean he withheld the divine favor from other men.

10, 37: *You know what has been reported all over Judea about Jesus of Nazareth:* God's revelation of his plan for the destiny of mankind through Israel culminated in Jesus of Nazareth. Consequently, the ministry of Jesus is an integral part of God's revelation. This viewpoint explains why the early Christian communities were interested in conserving the historical substance of the ministry of Jesus, a tradition leading to the production of the four gospels.

10, 39: *We are witnesses:* the apostolic testimony was not restricted to the resurrection of Jesus but also included his historical ministry. This witness, however, was theological in character: the Twelve, divinely mandated as prophets, were empowered to interpret his sayings and deeds in the light of his redemptive death and resurrection. The meaning of these words and deeds was to be made clear to the developing Christian community as the bearer of the word of salvation; cf 1, 21-26.

10, 42: *As judge of the living and the dead:* the apostolic preaching to the Jews appealed to their messianic hope, while the appeal to the Gentiles stressed the coming divine judgment; cf 1 Thes 1, 10.

❋
10/15: Lv 11, 1-42.
22: Lk 7, 4f.
28: Gal 2, 12.15f.
34: Dt 10, 17; 2 Chr 19, 7; Jb 34, 19; Wis 6, 8;
Rom 2, 11; Gal 2, 6; Eph 6, 9; 1 Pt 1, 17.
37: Lk 4, 14.
41: Lk 24, 41ff.

Baptism of Cornelius

44*Peter had not finished these words when the Holy Spirit descended upon all who were listening to Peter's message. **45**The circumcised believers who had accompanied Peter were surprised that the gift of the Holy Spirit should have been poured out on the Gentiles also, **46**whom they could hear speaking in tongues and glorifying God. Peter put the question at that point: **47**"What can stop these people who have received the Holy Spirit, even as we have, from being baptized with water?" **48**So he gave orders that they be baptized in the name of Jesus Christ. After this was done, they asked him to stay with them for a few days.

The Call of the Gentiles Explained

11 **1**†ALL through Judea the apostles and the brothers heard that Gentiles, too, had accepted the word of God. **2**As a result, when Peter went up to Jerusalem some among the circumcised took issue with him, saying, **3**"You entered the house of uncircumcised men and ate with them." **4**Peter then explained the whole affair to them step by step from the beginning: **5**"I was at prayer in the city of Joppa when, in a trance, I saw a vision. An object like a big canvas came down; it was lowered down to me from the sky by its four corners. **6**As I stared at it I could make out four-legged creatures of the earth, wild beasts and reptiles, and birds of the sky. **7**I listened as a voice said to me, 'Get up, Peter! Slaughter, then eat.' **8**I replied: 'Not for a moment, sir! Nothing unclean or impure has ever entered my mouth!' **9**A second time the voice from the heavens spoke out: 'What God has purified you are not to call unclean.' **10**This happened three times; then the canvas with everything in it was drawn up again into the sky.

11"Immediately after that, the three men who had been sent to me from Caesarea came to the house where we were staying. **12**†The Spirit instructed me to accompany them without hesitation. These six brothers came along with me, and we entered the man's house. **13**He informed us that he had seen an angel standing in his house and that the angel had said: 'Send someone to Joppa and fetch Simon, known also as Peter. **14**In the light of what he will tell you, you shall be saved, and all your household.' **15**As I began to address them the Holy Spirit came upon them, just as it had upon us at the beginning. **16***Then I remembered what the Lord had said: 'John baptized with water but you will be baptized with the Holy Spirit.' **17***If God was giving them the same gift he gave us when we first believed in the Lord Jesus Christ, who was I to interfere with him?" **18**When they heard this they stopped objecting, and instead began to glorify God in these words: "If this be so, then God has granted life-giving repentance even to the Gentiles."

The Church Established at Antioch

19†Those in the community who had been dispersed by the persecution that arose because of Stephen went as far as Phoenicia, Cyprus and Antioch, making the message known to none but Jews. **20**However, some men of Cyprus and Cyrene among them who had come to Antioch began to talk even to the Greeks, announcing the good news of the Lord Jesus to them. **21**The hand of the Lord was with them and a great number of them believed and were converted to the Lord. **22**News of this eventually reached the ears of the church in Jerusalem, resulting in Barnabas' being sent to Antioch. **23**On his arrival he rejoiced to see the evidence of God's favor. He encouraged them all to remain firm in their commitment to the Lord, **24**since he himself was a good man filled with the Holy Spirit and faith. Thereby large numbers were added to the Lord. **25**Then Barnabas went off to Tarsus to look for Saul; **26**once he had found him, he brought him back to Antioch. For a whole year they met with the church and instructed great numbers. It was in Antioch that the disciples were called Christians for the first time.

Prediction of Agabus

27†At about that time, certain prophets came down from Jerusalem to Antioch. **28**One of them named Agabus was inspired to stand up and proclaim that there was going to be a severe famine all over the world. (It did in fact occur while Claudius was emperor.) **29**This made the disciples determine to set something aside,

---

† 11, 1-18: Scholars differ regarding the historical realities behind this narrative and Luke's purpose in utilizing them. Simply understood, the narrative indicates the following: (1) The Judaeo-Christians of Jerusalem were scandalized to learn of Peter's sojourn in the house of the Gentile Cornelius; (2) nonetheless they had to accept the divine directions given to both Peter and Cornelius; (3) they concluded that the setting aside of the legal barriers between Jew and Gentile was an exceptional ordinance of God in this one case to indicate that the apostolic kerygma was also to be directed to the Gentiles. As yet, the Jerusalem Christians were unwilling to accept mixed communities.

11, 12: *These six brothers:* companions from the Christian community of Joppa; cf 10, 23.

11, 19-26: The Judaeo-Christian antipathy to the mixed community was reflected by the early missioners generally. The few among them who entertained a different view succeeded in introducing Gentiles into the community at Antioch (in Syria). When the disconcerted Jerusalem community sent Barnabas to investigate, he was so favorably impressed by what he observed that he persuaded his friend Saul to participate in the Antioch experiment. The venture was successful; within a year, members of the mixed community in Antioch had acquired the new name of "Christians."

11, 27-30: It is not clear whether the prophets from Jerusalem came to Antioch to request help in view of the coming famine or whether they received this insight during their visit there. The former supposition seems more likely. Suetonius and Tacitus speak of famines during the reign of Claudius (A. D. 41-54), while the Jewish historian Josephus records a famine in Judea in A. D. 46-48. Luke is interested, rather, in showing the charity of the Antiochean community toward the Judaeo-Christians of Jerusalem despite their differences on mixed communities.

✿
   44f: 15, 8.   17: 15, 8f.
   11/16: 1, 5; 19, 4; Mt 3, 11.

each according to his means, and send it to the relief of the brothers who lived in Judea. ³⁰They did this, dispatching it to the presbyters in the care of Barnabas and Saul.

Herod Persecutes the Church

12 ¹†DURING that period, King Herod started to harass some of the members of the church. ²He beheaded James the brother of John, ³and when he saw that this pleased certain of the Jews, he took Peter into custody too. During the feast of Unleavened Bread ⁴he had him arrested and thrown into prison, with four squads of soldiers to guard him. Herod intended to bring him before the people after the Passover. ⁵Peter was thus detained in prison, while the church prayed fervently to God on his behalf. ⁶During the night before Herod was to bring him to trial, Peter was sleeping between two soldiers, fastened with double chains, while guards kept watch at the door. ⁷Suddenly an angel of the Lord stood nearby and light shone in the cell. He tapped Peter on the side and woke him. "Hurry, get up!" he said. With that, the chains dropped from Peter's wrists. ⁸The angel said, "Put on your belt and your sandals!" This he did. Then the angel told him, "Now put on your cloak and follow me."

⁹Peter followed him out, but with no clear realization that this was taking place through the angel's help. The whole thing seemed to him a mirage. ¹⁰They passed the first guard, then the second, and finally came to the iron gate leading out to the city, which opened for them of itself. They emerged and made their way down a narrow alley, when suddenly the angel left him. ¹¹Peter had recovered his senses by this time, and said, "Now I know for certain that the Lord has sent his angel to rescue me from Herod's clutches and from all that the Jews hoped for."

¹²After coming to realize this, he went to the house of Mary the mother of John (also known as Mark), where many others were gathered in prayer. ¹³Peter knocked at the door and a maid named Rhoda came to answer it. ¹⁴On recognizing his voice she was so overjoyed that she did not stop to open the door, but ran in and announced that Peter was outside. ¹⁵"You're out of your wits," they said to her, but she insisted it was true. All they could say was, "It must be his angel." ¹⁶Through all this, Peter kept on knocking. They finally opened the door and were astonished to see him. ¹⁷†He motioned to them to be quiet, and explained how the Lord had brought him out of prison. "Report this to James and the brothers," he said, then left them to go off to another place. ¹⁸At daybreak confusion broke out among the soldiers, who did not know what had happened to Peter. ¹⁹Herod then initiated a search for him. When it proved unsuccessful, he had the guards tried and executed. Shortly after this, Herod left Judea to spend some time in Caesarea.

Herod's Death

²⁰†Herod had long been infuriated by the people of Tyre and Sidon, who now by common consent came before him in his court. They won over his royal chamberlain Blastus and attempted to placate him, because their country was supplied with food from the king's territory. ²¹On an appointed day Herod, arrayed in royal robes, took his seat on the rostrum and publicly addressed them. ²²The assembled crowd shouted back, "This is the voice of a god, not a man!" ²³The angel of the Lord struck Herod down at once because he did not ascribe the honor to God, and he died eaten by worms.

²⁴Meanwhile the word of the Lord continued to spread and increase.

V: MISSION OF BARNABAS AND SAUL

²⁵BARNABAS AND SAUL RETURNED to Jerusalem upon completing the relief mission, taking with them John Mark.

13 ¹†THERE were in the church at Antioch certain prophets and teachers: Barnabas, Symeon known as Niger, Lucius of Cyrene, Manaen (who had been brought up with Herod the tetrarch), and Saul. ²On one occasion, while they were engaged in the liturgy of the Lord and were fasting, the Holy Spirit spoke to them: "Set apart Barnabas and Saul for me to do the work for which I have called them." ³Then, after they had fasted and prayed, they imposed hands on them and sent them off.

---

† 12, 1-19: Herod Agrippa ruled Judea A. D. 41-44. While Luke does not assign a motive for his execution of James and his intended execution of Peter, the broad background lies in Herod's policy of conciliating his Jewish subjects. The Judaeo-Christians had lost the popularity they had had in Jerusalem (2, 47), perhaps because of suspicions against them traceable to the teaching of Stephen. The account of Peter's escape derives from his subjective visionary experience, making him aware essentially of what was happening to him. Exactly how divine power effected the release is not possible to determine. The events related in this narrative are probably to be dated before the occurrence of the famine mentioned in 11, 27-30.

12, 17: He . . . left them to go off to another place: the conjecture that Peter left for Rome at this time has nothing to recommend it. His chief responsibility was still the leadership of the Judaeo-Christian communities in Palestine: Gal 2, 7. The concept of the great missionary effort of the church was yet to come; cf 13, 1ff.

12, 20-23: Josephus gives a similar account of Herod's death. Early Christian tradition considered the manner of it to be a divine punishment upon his evil life. See 2 Kgs 19, 35 for the figure of the angel of the Lord in such a context.

13, 1ff: The impulse for the first missionary effort in Asia Minor is ascribed to the prophets of the Antiochean community, under the inspiration of the Holy Spirit. The thinking behind the mission was perhaps that if the Jews of the diaspora could be converted as successfully as had been the case at Antioch, the Jews of Palestine would eventually lose their hostility toward Christian messianism.

First Mission Begins in Cyprus

4†These two, sent forth by the Holy Spirit, went down to the port of Seleucia and set sail from there for Cyprus. **5**On their arrival in Salamis they proclaimed the word of God in the Jewish synagogues, John accompanying them as an assistant. **6**†They traveled over the whole island as far as Paphos, where they came across a Jewish magician named Bar-Jesus who posed as a prophet. **7**He was attached to the court of the proconsular governor Sergius Paulus, a man of intelligence who had summoned Barnabas and Saul and was anxious to hear the word of God. **8**But Elymas —"the magician," for that is what his name means— opposed them and sought to turn the governor away from the faith. **9**Saul (also known as Paul) was filled with the Holy Spirit; he stared at him **10**and exclaimed: "You are an impostor and a thoroughgoing fraud, you son of Satan and enemy of all that is right! Will you never stop trying to make crooked the straight paths of the Lord? **11**†The Lord's hand is upon you even now! For a time you shall be blind, unable so much as to see the sun." At once a misty darkness came over him, and he groped about for someone to lead him by the hand. **12**When the governor saw what had happened, he believed, so impressed was he by the teaching about the Lord.

Arrival at Antioch in Pisidia

13†From Paphos, Paul and his companions put out to sea and sailed to Perga in Pamphylia. There John left them and returned to Jerusalem. **14**They continued to travel on from Perga and came to Antioch in Pisidia. On the sabbath day they entered the synagogue and sat down. **15**After the reading of the law and of the prophets, the leading men of the synagogue sent this message to them: "Brothers, if you have any exhortation to address to the people, please speak up."

Preaching in the Synagogue

16So Paul arose, motioned to them for silence, and began: "Fellow Israelites and you others who reverence our God, listen to what I have to say! **17***The God of the people Israel once chose our fathers. He made this people great during their sojourn in the land of Egypt, and with an outstretched arm he led them out of it. **18***For forty years he put up with them in the desert; **19***then he destroyed seven nations in the land of Canaan to give them that country as their heritage **20***at the end of some four hundred and fifty years. Later on he set up judges to rule them until the time of

the prophet Samuel. **21***When they asked for a king, God gave them Saul son of Kish, of the tribe of Benjamin, who ruled for forty years. **22***Then God removed him and raised up David as their king; on his behalf God testified, 'I have found David son of Jesse to be a man after my own heart who will fulfill my every wish.'

23*"According to his promise, God has brought forth from this man's descendants Jesus, a savior for Israel. **24***John heralded the coming of Jesus by proclaiming a baptism of repentance to all the people of Israel. **25***As John's career was coming to an end, he would say, 'What you suppose me to be I am not. Rather, look for the one who comes after me. I am not worthy to unfasten the sandals on his feet.' **26**My brothers, children of the family of Abraham and you others who reverence our God, it was to us that this message of salvation was sent forth. **27**The inhabitants of Jerusalem and their rulers failed to recognize him, and in condemning him they fulfilled the words of the prophets which we read sabbath after sabbath. **28***Even though they found no charge against him which deserved death, they begged Pilate to have him executed. **29**Once they had thus brought about all that had been written of him, they took him down from the tree and laid him in a tomb. **30***Yet God raised him from the dead, **31**†and for many days thereafter Jesus appeared to those who had come up with him from Galilee to Jerusalem. These are his witnesses now before the people.

32"We ourselves announce to you the good news that what God promised our fathers **33***he has fulfilled for us, their children, in raising up Jesus, according to what is written in the second psalm, 'You are my son;

---

† 13, 4—14, 27: The key event in Luke's account of the first missionary journey is the experience of Paul and Barnabas at Pisidian Antioch (14-52). The Christian kerygma proclaimed by Paul in the synagogue was favorably received. Some Jews and "God-fearers" were effectively converted (42f—see note on 8, 26-40), and the congregation at large asked the missionaries to speak again on the following sabbath. By that time, however, the appearance of a large number of Gentiles from the city had so disconcerted the Jews that they became hostile toward the apostles (44f). Thus the Jews of Pisidian Antioch proved no less opposed to the mixed community than the Judaeo-Christians of Jerusalem. As long as Paul refused to incorporate the Gentiles into Judaism as the condition for their acceptance of Christ, the Jews continued to regard Christian messianism as destructive of their religious traditions and their culture. This fear of theirs appears in all three accounts of Paul's missionary journeys in Acts, the Jews of Iconium (14, 1f) and Beroea (17, 11) being notable exceptions.

13, 6: A Jewish magician named Bar-Jesus who posed as a prophet: again Luke takes the opportunity to dissociate Christianity from the magical arts of the time (7-11); cf 8, 18-24.

13, 11f: The temporary blindness symbolized the falsity of the man's teaching.

13, 13: There John left them: it has been conjectured that John Mark objected to Paul's ascendancy over his cousin Barnabas, but it is more likely that the rugged country and alien culture had made Mark homesick for Jerusalem; cf 12, 12.

13, 31: These are his witnesses now before the people: the prophetic rule of the Twelve concerning Jesus; see note on 10, 39.

❋
13/17: Ex 1, 1.
  18: Ex 16, 3.
  19: Jos 14, 2.
  20: Jgs 3, 9.
  21: 1 Sm 8, 5; 9, 16; 10, 1.
  22: 1 Sm 13, 14; 16, 13;
     Ps 89, 21.
  23: Is 11, 1.
  24: Mt 3, 1; Mk 1, 4;
     Lk 3, 2f.

  25: Mt 3, 11; Mk 1, 7;
     Jn 1, 20.
  28: Mt 27, 20.23;
     Mk 15, 13;
     Lk 23, 21.23;
     Jn 19, 15.
  30: Mt 28, 8ff.16-20;
     Mk 16, 9.12-20;
     Lk 24, 15-53;
     Jn 20, 14-29.
  33: Ps 2, 7.

this day I have begotten you.' **34***As a proof that the one whom he raised from the dead would never again see the decay of death, God declared, 'I will give you the benefits assured to David under the covenant.' **35***That is why he said in still another place, 'You will not suffer your faithful one to undergo corruption.' **36***Now David, after he had spent a lifetime in carrying out God's will, fell asleep and joined his fathers, thereby undergoing corruption. **37**But the one whom God has raised up did not undergo corruption. **38†**You must realize, my brothers, that it is through him that the forgiveness of sins is being proclaimed to you, including the remission of all those charges you could never be acquitted of under the law of Moses. **39***In him, every believer is acquitted. **40**Have a care, then, lest what was said by the prophets be realized in you: **41***'Look on in amazement, you cynics, then disappear! For I am doing a deed in your days which you never would have believed even if you had been told.'"

42As they were leaving, the people invited them to speak on this subject again on the following sabbath. **43**When the congregation finally broke up, many Jews and devout Jewish converts followed Paul and Barnabas, who spoke to them and urged them to hold fast to the grace of God.

Address to the Gentiles

44The following sabbath, almost the entire city gathered to hear the word of God. **45**When the Jews saw the crowds, they became very jealous and countered with violent abuse whatever Paul said. **46†**Paul and Barnabas spoke out fearlessly, nonetheless: "The word of God has to be declared to you first of all; but since you reject it and thus convict yourselves as unworthy of everlasting life, we now turn to the Gentiles. **47**For thus were we instructed by the Lord: 'I have made you a light to the nations, a means of salvation to the ends of the earth.'" **48**The Gentiles were delighted when they heard this and responded to the word of the Lord with praise. All who were destined for life everlasting believed in it. **49**Thus the word of the Lord was carried throughout that area.

50But some of the Jews stirred up their influential women sympathizers and the leading men of the town, and in that way got a persecution started against Paul and Barnabas. The Jews finally expelled them from their territory. **51***So the two shook the dust from their feet in protest and went on to Iconium. **52**The disciples could not but be filled with joy and the Holy Spirit.

Preaching at Iconium

14 **1**IN Iconium likewise, they entered the Jewish synagogue and spoke in such a way as to convince a good number of Jews and Greeks.

2But the Jews who remained unconvinced stirred up the Gentiles and poisoned their minds against the brothers. **3***Paul and Barnabas spent considerable time there and spoke out fearlessly, in complete reliance on the Lord. He for his part confirmed the message with his grace and caused signs and wonders to be done at their hands. **4**Most of the townspeople were divided over them, some siding with the Jews and others with the apostles. **5***A move was made by Gentiles and Jews, together with their leaders, to abuse and stone them. **6**When Paul and Barnabas learned of this, they fled to the Lycaonian towns of Lystra and Derbe and to the surrounding country, **7**where they continued to proclaim the good news.

A Cure in Lystra

8†At Lystra there was a man who was lame from birth; he used to sit crippled, never having walked in his life. **9**On one occasion he was listening to Paul preaching, and Paul looked directly at him and saw that he had the faith to be saved. **10**He called out to him in a loud voice, "Stand up! On your feet!" The man jumped up and began to walk around. **11***When the crowds saw what Paul had done, they cried out in Lycaonian, "Gods have come to us in the form of men!" **12**They named Barnabas Zeus; Paul they called Hermes, since he was the spokesman. **13**Even the priest of the temple of Zeus, which stood outside the town, brought oxen and garlands to the gates because he wished to offer sacrifice to them with the crowds.

14When the apostles Barnabas and Paul heard of this, they tore their garments and rushed out into the crowd. **15***"Friends, why do you do this?" they shouted frantically. "We are only men, human like you. We are bringing you the good news that will convert you from just such follies as these to the living God, 'the one who made heaven and earth and the sea and all that is in them.' **16**In past ages he let the Gentiles go their way. **17***Yet in bestowing his benefits, he has not hidden himself completely, without a clue. From the heavens he sends down rain and rich harvests; your spirits he fills with food and delight." **18**Yet even with a speech such as this, they could scarcely stop the crowds from offering sacrifice to them.

End of the First Mission

19*Just at that point, some Jews from Antioch and Iconium arrived and won the people over. They stoned

---

† 13, 38: *Including the remission of all those charges you could never be acquitted of under the law of Moses:* a doctrinal statement of justification by faith, particularly appropriate to Paul; see note on 9, 1-19.

13, 46: *Unworthy of everlasting life:* the refusal to believe frustrates God's plan for his chosen people; however no adverse judgment is made here concerning their ultimate destiny.

14, 8-17: In an effort to convince his hearers that the divine power works through his word, Paul cures the cripple. However, the pagan tradition of the occasional appearance of gods among men leads the people astray in interpreting the miracle. The incident reveals the cultural difficulties with which the church had to cope.

❋
34: Is 55, 3.	14/3: Mk 16, 17-20.
35: Ps 16, 10.	5: 2 Tm 3, 11.
36: 1 Kgs 2, 10.	11: 28, 6.
39: Rom 3, 20.	15: 3, 12; 10, 26.
41: Heb 1, 5.	17: Wis 13, 1.
51: Mt 10, 14; Mk 6, 11;	19f: 2 Cor 11, 25;
Lk 9, 5.	2 Tm 3, 11.

Paul and dragged him out of the town, leaving him there for dead. **20**His disciples quickly formed a circle about him, and before long he got up and went back into the town. The next day he left with Barnabas for Derbe. **21**After they had proclaimed the good news in that town and made numerous disciples, they retraced their steps to Lystra and Iconium first, then to Antioch. **22**They gave their disciples reassurances, and encouraged them to persevere in the faith with this instruction: "We must undergo many trials if we are to enter into the reign of God." **23**†In each church they installed presbyters and, with prayer and fasting, commended them to the Lord in whom they had put their faith.

Return to Antioch

24Then they passed through Pisidia and came to Pamphylia. **25***After preaching the message in Perga, they went down to Attalia. **26**†From there they sailed back to Antioch, where they had first been commended to the favor of God for the task they had now completed. **27**On their arrival, they called the congregation together and related all that God had helped them accomplish, and how he had opened the door of faith to the Gentiles. **28**Then they spent some time there with the disciples.

Council of Jerusalem

15 **1***†SOME men came down to Antioch from Judea and began to teach the brothers: "Unless you are circumcised according to Mosaic practice, you cannot be saved." **2**This created dissension and much controversy between them and Paul and Barnabas. Finally it was decided that Paul, Barnabas, and some others should go up to see the apostles and presbyters in Jerusalem about this question. **3**The church saw them off and they made their way through Phoenicia and Samaria, telling everyone about the conversion of the Gentiles as they went. Their story caused great joy among the brothers. **4**When they arrived in Jerusalem they were welcomed by that church, as well as by the apostles and the presbyters, to whom they reported all that God had helped them accomplish. **5**Some of the converted Pharisees then got up and demanded that such Gentiles be circumcised and told to keep the Mosaic law.

6†The apostles and the presbyters accordingly convened to look into the matter. **7***†After much discussion, Peter took the floor and said to them: "Brothers, you know well enough that from the early days God selected me from your number to be the one from whose lips the Gentiles would hear the message of the gospel and believe. **8***God, who reads the hearts of men, showed his approval by granting the Holy Spirit to them just as he did to us. **9**He made no distinction between them and us, but purified their hearts by means of faith also. **10***†Why, then, do you put God to

the test by trying to place on the shoulders of these converts a yoke which neither we nor our fathers were able to bear? **11***†Our belief is rather that we are saved by the favor of the Lord Jesus and so are they." **12**At that the whole assembly fell silent. They listened to Barnabas and Paul as the two described all the signs and wonders God had worked among the Gentiles through them.

James on Dietary Law

13†When they concluded their presentation, James spoke up: "Brothers, listen to me. **14**†Symeon has told you how God first concerned himself with taking from among the Gentiles a people to bear his name. **15**The words of the prophets agree with this, where it says in Scripture, **16***'Hereafter I will return and rebuild the

---

† 14, 23: *In each church they installed presbyters:* the communities are given their own religious leaders. Seemingly (cf Jas 5, 14), a part of their task is the performance of liturgical rites, especially the liturgy of the Eucharist; cf 2, 42. Paul's caution in organizing the communities is shown by the fact that they receive presbyters only after a period of testing.

14, 26: The report of the missioners to the church at Antioch was not wholly encouraging. The attempt to create mixed communities after the Antiochean model had been essentially a failure; cf 13, 46.50f; 14, 2.4f.19. On the other hand, the receptivity among the Gentiles offered hope for the future.

15, 1-5: When some of the converted Pharisees of Jerusalem discover the results of the first missionary journey of Paul, they conclude that their worst fears over the Antiochean experiment of the mixed community have been realized. They urge that the lesson to be learned from Paul's failure to convert the Jews of the diaspora is that the Gentiles must be taught to adopt the religious traditions of Judaism, for only in this way will it be possible for the Jews of the diaspora to form a common church with the Gentiles.

15, 6-12: This gathering is probably the same as that recalled by Paul in Gal 2, 1-10. Note that in 15, 2 it is only the apostles and presbyters, a small group, with whom Paul and Barnabas are to meet. Here Luke gives the meeting a public character because he wishes to emphasize its doctrinal significance for the entire world; cf v 22.

15, 7ff: Paul's refusal to impose the Mosaic law on the Gentile Christians is supported by Peter on the ground that within his own experience God bestowed the Holy Spirit upon Cornelius and his household without preconditions concerning the adoption of the Mosaic law; cf 10, 44-47.

15, 10: A devout Jew considered the law a blessing. For the Christian, however, who understood that in his regard its observance was not a condition for receiving the divine benefits, such observance could be only a burden; cf Gal 4, 31.

15, 11: In support of Paul, Peter formulates the fundamental meaning of the gospel: that all mankind is invited to be saved through faith in the salvific power of Christ; personal observance of the divine law is man's necessary response to God's saving action, though not the cause of it.

15, 13-35: Some scholars think that this apostolic decree requested by James, the immediate leader of the Jerusalem community, derives from another historical occasion than the meeting in question. This seems to be the case if the meeting is the same as the one related in Galatians 2, 1-10. According to that account, nothing was imposed upon Gentile Christians in respect to Mosaic law; whereas the decree instructs Gentile Christians of mixed communities to abstain from meats offered to idols and from blood-meats, and to avoid marriage within forbidden degrees of kindred (Lv 18), all of which practices were especially abhorrent to Jews.

15, 14: *Symeon:* Simon Peter; cf 15, 7.

✤   25: 13, 1ff.   8: 10, 44-47.
15/1-4: Gal 2, 1-9.   10: Mt 23, 4; Gal 5, 1.
       1: Gal 5, 2.   11: Gal 3, 11.
       7: 10, 20.   16: Am 9, 11f.

fallen hut of David: from its ruins I will rebuild it and set it up again, **¹⁷**so that all the rest of mankind and all the nations that bear my name may seek out the Lord. **¹⁸**Thus says the Lord who accomplishes these things known to him from of old.' **¹⁹***It is my judgment, therefore, that we ought not to cause God's Gentile converts any difficulties. **²⁰**We should merely write to them to abstain from anything contaminated by idols, from illicit sexual union, from the meat of strangled animals, and from eating blood. **²¹**After all, for generations now Moses has been proclaimed in every town and has been read aloud in the synagogues on every sabbath."

Letter of the Apostles

²²It was resolved by the apostles and the presbyters, in agreement with the whole Jerusalem church, that representatives be chosen from among their number and sent to Antioch along with Paul and Barnabas. Those chosen were leading men of the community, Judas, known as Barsabbas, and Silas. **²³**They were to deliver this letter:

"The apostles and the presbyters, your brothers, send greetings to the brothers of Gentile origin in Antioch, Syria, and Cilicia. **²⁴**We have heard that some of our number without any instructions from us have upset you with their discussions and disturbed your peace of mind. **²⁵**Therefore we have unanimously resolved to choose representatives and send them to you, along with our beloved Barnabas and Paul, **²⁶**who have dedicated themselves to the cause of our Lord Jesus Christ. **²⁷**Those whom we are sending you are Judas and Silas, who will convey this message by word of mouth: **²⁸**'It is the decision of the Holy Spirit, and ours too, not to lay on you any burden beyond that which is strictly necessary, **²⁹**namely, to abstain from meat sacrificed to idols, from blood, from the meat of strangled animals, and from illicit sexual union. You will be well advised to avoid these things. Farewell.'"

Delegates to Antioch

³⁰Thus were the representatives sent on their way to Antioch; and upon their arrival there they called the assembly together to deliver the letter. **³¹**When it was read there was great delight at the encouragement it gave. **³²**Judas and Silas, who were themselves prophets, strengthened the community and gave them reassurance in a long discourse. **³³**After passing some time there, they were sent back with greetings from the brothers to those who had commissioned them. **³⁵***Paul and Barnabas continued in Antioch, along with many others, teaching and preaching the word of the Lord.

VI: PAUL'S MISSION TO THE GENTILES

Paul and Barnabas Separate

³⁶†AFTER A CERTAIN TIME Paul said to Barnabas, "Let us go back now and see how the brothers are getting on in each of the towns where we proclaimed the word of the Lord." **³⁷**Barnabas wanted to take along John, called Mark. **³⁸***But Paul insisted that, as he had deserted them at Pamphylia, refusing to join them on that mission, he was not fit to be taken along now. **³⁹**The disagreement which ensued was so sharp that the two separated. Barnabas took Mark along with him and sailed for Cyprus.

⁴⁰Paul, for his part, chose Silas to accompany him on his journey, and in this he was commended by the brothers to the favor of the Lord. **⁴¹**He traveled throughout Syria and Cilicia, giving the churches there renewed assurance.

In Lycaonia: Timothy

16 **¹***PAUL arrived first at Derbe; next he came to Lystra, where there was a disciple named. Timothy, whose mother was Jewish and a believer, and whose father was a Greek. **²***Since the brothers in Lystra and Iconium spoke highly of him, **³**†Paul was anxious to have him come along on the journey. Paul had him circumcised because of the Jews of that region, for they all knew that it was only his father who was Greek. **⁴**As they made their way from town to town, they transmitted to the people for observance the decisions which the apostles and presbyters had made in Jerusalem.

⁵Through all this, the congregations grew stronger in faith and daily increased in numbers.

---

† 15, 34: Certain codices add: "But Silas decided to remain there"; however, the verse is omitted in the Greek manuscripts.

15, 36—18, 22: This continuous narrative recounts Paul's second missionary journey. On the internal evidence of the Lucan account it lasted about three years. Paul first visited the communities he had established on his first journey (16, 1-5), then pushed on into Macedonia, where he established communities at Philippi, Thessalonica and Beroea (16, 6—17, 15). To escape the hostility of the Jews of Thessalonica he left for Greece, and while resident in Athens attempted, without success, to establish an effective Christian community there. From Athens he proceeded to Corinth, and after a stay of a year and a half, returned to Antioch by way of Ephesus and Jerusalem (17, 16—18, 22). Luke's narrative is colorful and lively. He does not concern himself with the structure or statistics of the communities but aims to show the general progress of the gospel in the Gentile world, as well as its continued failure to take root in the Jewish community.

16, 3: *Paul had him circumcised:* in order that Timothy might be able to socialize with the Jews and so perform a ministry among them. Paul did not object to the Judaeo-Christians' adherence to the law out of custom, as was the case in Palestine. But he insisted that the law could not be imposed on the Gentiles. Paul himself lived in accordance with the law, or as exempt from the law, according to particular circumstances; cf. 1 Cor 9, 19-23.

✿

19: 21, 25.   16/1: 1 Tm 1, 2; 2 Tm 1, 5.
35: 14, 28.   2: Heb 13, 23.
38: 13, 13.

Through Asia Minor

6†They next traveled through Phrygia and Galatian territory because they had been prevented by the Holy Spirit from preaching the message in the province of Asia. **7**When they came to Mysia they tried to go on into Bithynia, but again the Spirit of Jesus would not allow them. **8**Crossing through Mysia instead, they came down to Troas. **9**There one night Paul had a vision. A man of Macedonia stood before him and invited him, "Come over to Macedonia and help us."

10†After this vision, we immediately made efforts to get across to Macedonia, concluding that God had summoned us to proclaim the good news there.

Into Europe

11†We put out to sea from Troas and set a course straight for Samothrace, and the next day on to Neapolis; **12**from there we went to Philippi, a leading city in the district of Macedonia and a Roman colony. **13**We spent some time in that city. Once, on the sabbath, we went outside the city gate to the bank of the river, where we thought there would be a place of prayer. We sat down and spoke to the women who were gathered there. **14**One who listened was a woman named Lydia, a dealer in purple goods from the town of Thyatira. She already reverenced God, and the Lord opened her heart to accept what Paul was saying. **15**After she and her household had been baptized, she extended us an invitation: "If you are convinced that I believe in the Lord, come and stay at my house." She managed to prevail on us.

Philippi: Imprisonment

16It was while we were on our way out to the place of prayer that we met a slave girl who had a clairvoyant spirit. She used to bring substantial profit to her masters by fortune-telling. **17***The girl began to follow Paul and the rest of us shouting, "These men are servants of the Most High God; they will make known to you a way of salvation." **18***She did this for several days until finally Paul became annoyed, turned around, and said to the spirit, "In the name of Jesus Christ I command you, come out of her!" Then and there the spirit left her.

19*When her masters saw that their source of profit was gone, they seized Paul and Silas and dragged them into the main square before the local authorities. **20**They turned them over to the magistrates with this complaint: "These men are agitators disturbing the peace of our city! Furthermore, they are Jews, **21**which means they advocate customs which are not lawful for us Romans to adopt or practice." **22***†The crowd joined in the attack on them, and the magistrates stripped them and ordered them to be flogged. **23**After receiv-

ing many lashes they were thrown into prison, and the jailer was given instructions to guard them well. **24**Upon receipt of these instructions he put them in maximum security, going so far as to chain their feet to a stake.

The Earthquake

25†About midnight, while Paul and Silas were praying and singing hymns to God as their fellow prisoners listened, **26***a severe earthquake suddenly shook the place, rocking the prison to its foundations. Immediately all the doors flew open and everyone's chains were pulled loose. **27***The jailer woke up to see the prison gates wide open. Thinking that the prisoners had escaped, he drew his sword to kill himself; **28**but Paul shouted to him: "Do not harm yourself! We are all still here." **29**The jailer called for a light, then rushed in and fell trembling at the feet of Paul and Silas. **30**After a brief interval he led them out and said, "Men, what must I do to be saved?" **31**Their answer was, "Believe in the Lord Jesus and you will be saved, and all your household." **32**They proceeded to announce the word of God to him and to everyone in his house. **33**At that late hour of the night he took them in and bathed their wounds; then he and his whole household were baptized. **34**He led them up into his house, spread a table before them, and joyfully celebrated with his whole family his newfound faith in God.

Release from Prison

35When it was day, the magistrates dispatched officers with orders to let these men go. **36**The jailer conveyed this information to Paul: "The magistrates have sent orders that you are to be released. Get started, now. On your way!" **37***Paul's response to this was, "They flogged us in public without even a trial, then they threw us into jail, although we are Roman citizens! Now they want to smuggle us out in secret. Not a bit of it! Let them come into the prison and escort

---

† 16, 6: The prohibition may have come through one of Paul's companions endowed with a prophetic charism; cf 11, 27f.

16, 10-17: This is the first of the so-called "we-sections" in Acts, where Luke writes as one of Paul's companions. The other passages are 20, 5-15; 21, 1-18; 27, 1—28, 16. Scholars debate whether Luke may not have used the first person plural simply as a literary device to lend color to the narrative. It is more probable, however, that the "we" includes Luke or another companion of Paul whose data Luke used as a source.

16, 11-40: The church at Philippi became a sufficiently flourishing community for Paul to honor it with one of his letters. Judging, however, from Luke's account of Paul's vicissitudes in the city, his personal success was minimal. Evidently the community grew considerably after his departure and, as is clear from Paul's letter to them, he reserved his greatest affection for the Christians of Philippi.

16, 22: Apparently the attack on Paul and Silas was so violent that they were unable to invoke their Roman citizenship to avoid the scourging; cf 16, 37f.

16, 25f: The earthquake seems to have been a visionary experience that accompanied the opening of the doors and the unfastening of the chains. It is otherwise difficult to see why the jailer was so impressed; cf 16, 27-34.

❋　17: Mt 8, 29.　　　　　26: 12, 6-11.
　　18: Mk 1, 25f.　　　　27: 12, 18f; 27, 42.
　　19: 19, 24-27.　　　　37: 22, 25.
　　22: 2 Cor 11, 25;
　　　　1 Thes 2, 2.

us out." **38***The officers reported this to the magistrates, who were immediately alarmed at hearing they were Roman citizens. **39**They came along and tried to quiet them; then they escorted them out with the request that they leave the city. **40**Once outside the prison, however, the two first made their way to Lydia's house, where they saw and encouraged the brothers; afterward they departed.

Problems at Thessalonica

17 **1**PAUL and Silas took the road through Amphipolis and Apollonia and came to Thessalonica, where there was a Jewish synagogue. **2**Following his usual custom, Paul joined the people there and conducted discussions with them about the Scriptures for three sabbaths. **3***He explained many things, showing that the Messiah had to suffer and rise from the dead: "This Jesus I am telling you about is the Messiah!" **4**Some of the Jews were convinced and threw in their lot with Paul and Silas. So, too, did a great number of Greeks sympathetic to Judaism, and numerous prominent women.

5*This only aroused the resentment of the Jews, however, who engaged loafers from the public square to form a mob and start a riot in the town. They marched on the house of Jason in an attempt to bring Paul and Silas before the people's assembly. **6**When they could not find them there, they dragged Jason himself and some of the brothers to the town magistrates, shouting: "These men have been creating a disturbance all over the place. Now they come here **7***†and Jason has taken them in. To a man, they disregard the Emperor's decrees and claim instead that a certain Jesus is king." **8**In this way they stirred up the crowd. When the town's magistrates heard the whole story, they released Jason and the others on bail.

Paul in Beroea

10As soon as it was night, the brothers sent Paul and Silas off to Beroea. On their arrival, they went to the Jewish synagogue. **11***Its members were better disposed than those in Thessalonica, and welcomed the message with great enthusiasm. Each day they studied the Scriptures to see whether these things were so. **12**Many of them came to believe, as did numerous influential Greek women and men. **13**But when the Jews of Thessalonica learned that the word of God had been proclaimed by Paul in Beroea also, they hurried there to cause a commotion and stir up the crowds. **14***The brothers sent Paul off directly on his way to the sea, while Silas and Timothy stayed behind. **15**Paul was taken as far as Athens by his escort, who then returned with instructions for Silas and Timothy to join him as soon as possible.

Paul at Athens

16While Paul was waiting for them in Athens, he grew exasperated at the sight of idols everywhere in the city. **17**In the synagogue he used to hold discussions with the Jews and those sympathetic to Judaism, as well as daily debates in the public square with ordinary passersby. **18**Epicurean and Stoic philosophers disputed with him, some of them asking, "What is this magpie trying to say to us?" Others commented, "He sounds like a promoter of foreign gods," because he was heard to speak of "Jesus" and "the resurrection." **19***They then led him off to the Areopagus, saying, "We are curious to know what this new teaching is that you propose. **20**†You are introducing subjects unfamiliar to us and we should like to know what it is all about." **21**(Indeed, all Athenian citizens, as well as the foreigners who live there, love nothing more than to tell about or listen to something new.)

Paul's Discourse

22†Then Paul stood up in the Areopagus and delivered this address: "Men of Athens, I note that in every respect you are scrupulously religious. **23**As I walked around looking at your shrines, I even discovered an altar inscribed, 'To a God Unknown.' Now, what you are thus worshiping in ignorance I intend to make known to you. **24***For the God who made the world and all that is in it, the Lord of heaven and earth, does not dwell in sanctuaries made by human hands; **25**nor does he receive man's service as if he were in need of it. Rather, it is he who gives to all life and breath and everything else. **26**From one stock he made every nation of mankind to dwell on the face of the earth. It is he who set limits to their epochs and fixed the boundaries of their regions. **27***They were to seek God, yes to grope for him and perhaps eventually to find him—though he is not really far from any one of us. **28**'In him we live and move and have our being,' as some of your own poets have put it, 'for we too are his offspring.' **29***If we are in fact God's offspring, we ought not to think of divinity as something like a

---

† 17, 7: *A certain Jesus is king:* a distortion into a political sense of the apostolic proclamation of Jesus' religious kingship.

17, 20f: According to ancient writers the Athenians' interest in novel ideas was proverbial.

17, 22-31: Paul's discourse appeals to the Greek world's belief in divinity as responsible for the origin and existence of the universe. It contests the common belief in a multiplicity of gods supposedly exerting their powers through their images (idolworship). It acknowledges (17, 27) that mankind's attempt to understand God is one of the most anxious of all its endeavors. It declares, further, that the divine being is the judge of mankind, and concludes by hinting that the apostle has information on the latter subject concerning a man whom God raised from the dead and who is to be judge of all men. The speech reflects sympathy with pagan religiosity, handles the subject of idolworship gently, and appeals for a new examination of divinity, not from the standpoint of creation but from the standpoint of judgment. It is possible that Luke intends to show in the whole incident the difficulties of the learned men of the time in accepting the Christian message; cf 17, 32ff; 1 Cor 1, 26f.

*

38: 22, 29.
17/3: Lk 24, 25ff.46.
  5: Rom 16, 21.
  7: Lk 23, 2; Jn 19, 12-15.
 11: Jn 5, 39.
 14: 1 Thes 3, 2.

19: 1 Cor 1, 22.
24: 7, 48ff; Gn 1, 1;
    Is 42, 5.
27: Wis 13, 6; Rom 1, 19.
29: 19, 26; Is 40, 18f;
    Rom 1, 22f.

statue of gold or silver or stone, a product of man's genius and his art. **30**God may well have overlooked bygone periods when men did not know him; but now he calls on all men everywhere to reform their lives. **31**He has set the day on which he is going to 'judge the world with justice' through a man he has appointed—one whom he has endorsed in the sight of all by raising him from the dead."

32When they heard about the raising of the dead, some sneered, while others said, "We must hear you on this topic some other time." **33**At that point, Paul left them. **34**A few did join him, however, to become believers. Among these were Dionysius, a member of the court of the Areopagus, a woman named Damaris, and a few others.

Paul Founds the Church in Corinth

18 **1***AFTER that, Paul left Athens and went to Corinth. **2†**There he found a Jew named Aquila, a native of Pontus recently arrived from Italy with his wife Priscilla. An edict of Claudius had ordered all Jews to leave Rome. Paul went to visit the pair, **3**whose trade he had in common with them. He took up lodgings with them and they worked together as tentmakers. **4**Every sabbath, in the synagogue, Paul led discussions in which he persuaded certain Jews and Greeks.

5When Silas and Timothy came down from Macedonia, Paul was absorbed in preaching and giving evidence to the Jews that Jesus was the Messiah. **6***When they opposed him and insulted him, he would shake out his garments in protest and say to them: "Your blood be on your own heads. I am not to blame! From now on, I will turn to the Gentiles."

7*Later, Paul withdrew and went to the house of a Gentile named Titus Justus, who reverenced God; his house was next door to the synagogue. **8***A leading man of the synagogue, Crispus, along with his whole household, put his faith in the Lord. Many of the Corinthians, too, who heard Paul believed and were baptized. **9**One night in a vision the Lord said to Paul: "Do not be afraid. Go on speaking and do not be silenced, **10***for I am with you. No one will attack you or harm you. There are many of my people in this city." **11**Paul ended by settling there for a year and a half, teaching them the word of God.

Paul Accused before Gallio

12During Gallio's proconsulship in Achaia, the Jews rose in a body against Paul and brought him before the bench. **13**"This fellow," they charged, "is influencing people to worship God in ways that are against the law." **14**Paul was about to speak in self-defense when Gallio said to the Jews: "If it were a crime or a serious fraud, I would give you Jews a patient and reasonable hearing. **15**But since this is a dispute about terminology and titles and your own law, you must see to it yourselves. I refuse to judge such matters." **16**With that, he dismissed them from the court. **17**Then they all pounced on Sosthenes, a leading man of the synagogue, and beat him in full view of the bench; but Gallio paid no attention to it.

Return to Antioch

18*Paul stayed on in Corinth for quite a while; but eventually he took leave of the brothers and sailed for Syria, in the company of Priscilla and Aquila. At the port of Cenchreae he shaved his head because of a vow he had taken. **19**When they landed at Ephesus, he left Priscilla and Aquila behind and entered the synagogue to hold discussions with the Jews. **20**They asked him to stay on longer but he declined. **21**As he said goodbye he gave them his promise, "God willing, I will come back to you again." Then he set sail from Ephesus. **22**On landing at Caesarea, he went up and paid his respects to the congregation, and then went down to Antioch.

23†After spending some time there he set out again, traveling systematically through the Galatian country and Phrygia to reassure all his disciples.

The Orator Apollos

24*†A Jew named Apollos, a native of Alexandria and a man of eloquence, arrived by ship at Ephesus. He was both an authority on Scripture **25**and instructed in the new way of the Lord. Apollos was a man full of spiritual fervor. He spoke and taught accurately about Jesus, although he knew only of John's baptism. **26**He too began to express himself fearlessly in the synagogue. When Priscilla and Aquila heard him, they took him home and explained to him God's new way in greater detail. **27**He wanted to go on to Achaia, and so the brothers encouraged him by writing the disciples there to welcome him. When he arrived, he greatly strengthened those who through God's favor had become believers. **28**He was vigorous

---

† 18, 2: *Aquila . . . with his wife Priscilla:* if this couple were not already Christians they soon became such; cf 18, 26. According to 1 Cor 16, 19 their home became a Christian meeting place.

18, 23—21, 16: Luke's account of Paul's third missionary journey devotes itself mainly to his work at Ephesus (19, 1—20, 1) and to his farewell address to the elders of this community (20, 17-35). Throughout the narrative runs a theme reflecting a certain restlessness and uneasiness on Paul's part. He has a growing conviction that the Spirit bids him return to Jerusalem and prepare to go to Rome (19, 21). He senses that imprisonment and suffering will be his lot in Jerusalem (20, 22f) and that he has paid his last visit to the Ephesian community (20, 25). Arriving at Tyre, on the Phoenician coast, he is warned by Christian prophets not to proceed to Jerusalem (21, 4). When he reaches Caesarea on the way to Jerusalem, another Christian prophet utters the same warning (21, 10f).

18, 24f: Apollos became a celebrated Christian preacher in the Corinthian community; 1 Cor 1, 12; 3, 5. He made use of the teaching of Jesus but placed it in the context of John's baptism of repentance. Since the teaching of Jesus was already known in an oral form to Apollos, it seems evident that the Christian communities likewise possessed this teaching.

---

*
   18/1: Rom 16, 3.   10: Jer 1, 8.
       6: Mt 27, 24f.   18: Nm 6, 18.
       7: 13, 46f.51; 28, 28. 24: 1 Cor 1, 12.
       8: 1 Cor 1, 14.

in his public refutation of the Jewish party as he went about establishing from the Scriptures that Jesus is the Messiah.

Paul in Ephesus

19 [1†]WHILE Apollos was in Corinth, Paul passed through the interior of the country and came to Ephesus. There he found some disciples [2]to whom he put the question, "Did you receive the Holy Spirit when you became believers?" They answered, "We have not so much as heard that there is a Holy Spirit." [3]"Well, how were you baptized?" he persisted. They replied, "With the baptism of John." [4*]Paul then explained, "John's baptism was a baptism of repentance. He used to tell the people about the one who would come after him in whom they were to believe—that is, Jesus." [5]When they heard this, they were baptized in the name of the Lord Jesus. [6*†]As Paul laid his hands on them, the Holy Spirit came down on them and they began to speak in tongues and to utter prophecies. [7]There were in the company about twelve men in all.

[8]Paul entered the synagogue, and over a period of three months debated fearlessly, with persuasive arguments, about the kingdom of God. [9]When some in their obstinacy would not believe, but chose to speak ill of the new way in the presence of the assembly, Paul simply left them. He took his disciples with him, and after that held his discussions from day to day in the lecture hall of Tyrannus. [10]This continued for two years, with the result that all the inhabitants of the province of Asia, Jews and Greeks alike, heard the word of the Lord. [11]Meanwhile God worked extraordinary miracles at the hands of Paul. [12*]When handkerchiefs or cloths which had touched his skin were applied to the sick, their diseases were cured and evil spirits departed from them.

The Jewish Exorcists

[13]Some itinerant Jewish exorcists once tried to invoke the name of the Lord Jesus over those who were possessed by evil spirits, saying, "I adjure you by the Jesus whom Paul preaches." [14]Another time, when the seven sons of Sceva, a Jewish high priest, were doing this, [15]the evil spirit answered, "Jesus I recognize, Paul I know; but who are you?" [16]Then the man with the evil spirit sprang at them and overpowered them all. He dealt with them so violently that they fled from his house naked and bruised. [17]When this became known to the Jews and Greeks living in Ephesus, fear fell upon all, and the name of the Lord Jesus came to be held in great reverence. [18]Many who had become believers came forward and openly confessed their former practices. [19]A number who had been dealing in magic even collected their books and burned them

in public. When the value of these was assessed, it came to fifty thousand silver pieces.

[20]Thus did the word of the Lord continue to spread with influence and power.

Future Plans

[21*]When all this was concluded, Paul made up his mind to travel through Macedonia and Achaia again, and then go on to Jerusalem. "Once I have been there," he said, "I must visit Rome too." [22]So he sent two of his assistants, Timothy and Erastus, into Macedonia ahead of him, while he himself stayed on for a time in Asia.

Riot of the Silversmiths

[23]At about that time a serious disturbance broke out concerning the new way. [24]There was a silversmith named Demetrius who made miniature shrines of Artemis and brought in no little work for his craftsmen. [25]He called a meeting of these men and other workers in the same craft. "Men," he said, "you know that our prosperity depends on this work. [26]But as you can see and hear for yourselves, not only at Ephesus but throughout most of the province of Asia, this Paul has persuaded great numbers of people to change their religion. He tells them that manmade gods are no gods at all. [27*]The danger grows, not only that our trade will be discredited, but even that the temple of the great goddess Artemis will count for nothing. In fact, she whom Asia and all the world revere may soon be stripped of her magnificence."

[28]When they heard this speech, they were overcome with fury and began to shout, "Long live Artemis of Ephesus!" [29*]Before long, confusion spread throughout the city. People rushed together to the theater and dragged in Gaius and Aristarchus, Paul's traveling companions from Macedonia. [30]Paul wanted to go before this gathering but his disciples would not let him. [31]Even some of the Asiarchs who were friends of Paul sent word to him advising him not to venture into the theater. [32]Meanwhile, various people were shouting all sorts of things, with the whole assembly in chaos and the majority not even knowing why they had come together. [33]Some brought out of the crowd Alexander, as the Jews pushed him forward. He motioned for silence, indicating that he wanted to explain something to the gathering. [34]But when they recognized that he was a Jew, they started to chant in unison, "Long live Artemis of Ephesus!" and kept shouting for about two hours.

[35]Finally the town clerk quieted the mob. "Citizens of Ephesus," he said, "what man is there who does not know that Ephesus is the custodian of the temple of

---

✿
19/4: 1, 5; 11, 16; 13, 24f;
       Mt 3, 11.
6: 8, 15ff.
12: Lk 8, 44-47.

21: Rom 15, 22-32.
27: 17, 29.
29: Col 4, 10.

†
  19, 1-4: Upon his arrival in Ephesus Paul discovers other men at the same religious stage as Apollos, though they seem to have considered themselves followers of Christ, not of the Baptizer.
  19, 6: A pentecostal experience at Ephesus.

the great Artemis, and of her image which fell from the sky? **36**Since this is beyond question, you must calm yourselves and not do anything rash. **37**These men whom you have brought here are not temple-robbers. They have not insulted our goddess. **38**If Demetrius and his fellow craftsmen want to bring charges against anyone, there are courts in session for that. There are proconsuls. Let the parties argue their case. **39**If there is any further matter you want to investigate, it ought to be settled in the lawful assembly. **40**As it is, we run the risk of being accused of rioting because of today's conduct. We have no valid excuse for this wild demonstration." These words of his broke up the meeting.

Paul Departs for Greece

20 **1*** WHEN the disturbance was over, Paul brought his disciples together to encourage them. Then he said goodbye and set out on his journey to Macedonia. **2**He traveled throughout its regions, providing as he went many words of encouragement for the Christians there. Finally he arrived in Greece, **3**where he stayed for three months. As he was on the point of embarking for Syria, a plot was hatched against him by certain Jews; so he decided to return by way of Macedonia.

Return to Troas

4*Accompanying him were Sopater, son of Pyrrhus, from Beroea; Aristarchus and Secundus from Thessalonica; Gaius from Derbe; Timothy; Tychicus and Trophimus from Asia. **5***These companions went on ahead and waited for us in Troas. **6**We ourselves set sail from Philippi as soon as the festival of Unleavened Bread was over. Five days later we joined them in Troas, where we spent a week.

Eutychus Restored to Life

7†On the first day of the week when we gathered for the breaking of bread, Paul preached to them. Because he intended to leave the next day, he kept on speaking until midnight. **8**As it happened, there were many lamps in the upstairs room where we were assembled. Paul talked on and on, and **9**a certain young lad named Eutychus who was sitting on the window-sill became drowsier and drowsier. He finally went sound asleep, and fell from the third story to the ground. When they picked him up he was dead. **10***Paul hurried down immediately and threw himself on him, clutching the boy to himself. "Don't be alarmed!" he said to them. "There is life in him." **11**Afterward Paul went upstairs again, broke bread, and ate. Then he talked for a long while—until his departure at dawn. **12**To the great comfort of the people, they were able to take the boy away alive.

Journey to Miletus

13We ourselves went on ahead to the ship and set sail for Assos, where we were to pick Paul up. This was the arrangement he had made, since his plan was to travel overland. **14**When he met us at Assos we took him aboard and sailed to Mitylene. **15**From there we took off the next day, and reached a point opposite Chios; on the second day we crossed to Samos, and on the day after that we put in at Miletus. **16†**Paul had decided to sail past Ephesus so as not to lose time in Asia, for he was eager to get to Jerusalem by the feast of Pentecost if at all possible.

Address to the Miletus Presbyters

17Paul sent word from Miletus to Ephesus, summoning the presbyters of that church. **18**When they came to him he delivered this address: "You know how I lived among you from the first day I set foot in the province of Asia—**19**how I served the Lord in humility through the sorrows and trials that came my way from the plottings of certain Jews. **20**Never did I shrink from telling you what was for your own good, or from teaching you in public or in private. **21**With Jews and Greeks alike I insisted solemnly on repentance before God and on faith in our Lord Jesus. **22**But now, as you see, I am on my way to Jerusalem, compelled by the Spirit and not knowing what will happen to me there —**23**except that the Holy Spirit has been warning me from city to city that chains and hardships await me. **24**I put no value on my life if only I can finish my race and complete the service to which I have been assigned by the Lord Jesus, bearing witness to the gospel of God's grace. **25**I know as I speak these words that none of you among whom I went about preaching the kingdom will ever see my face again. **26**Therefore I solemnly declare this day that I take the blame for no man's conscience, **27**for I have never shrunk from announcing to you God's design in its entirety.

28*"Keep watch over yourselves, and over the whole

---

† 20, 7: *The first day of the week:* the day after the sabbath, apparently chosen originally by the Jerusalem community for the celebration of the liturgy of the Eucharist in order to relate it to the resurrection of Christ. Thus, in view of the sacramental presence of Christ in the Eucharist, the liturgy of the Eucharist was an anticipated parousia; cf 1 Cor 10, 16.

20, 16-35: Apparently Paul was aware of difficulties in the Christian communities at Ephesus and neighboring areas, and felt that he would be long detained if he undertook to deal with them himself. He determined to remind the presbyters of the communities of their responsibility, calling them together for this purpose at Miletus, about thirty miles from Ephesus. Paul's moving discourse reminds them of his apostolic activity in their area and stresses his total dedication to the gospel (18-21); it describes his reaction to his presentiment that he is about to suffer for the gospel (22-27), and admonishes them to guard their communities against the teaching of false prophets, who he feels sure will arise upon his departure (20ff). He concludes by citing a saying of Jesus (35) not recorded in the gospel tradition but known to them. To the extent that Luke may be responsible for the discourse in this form, he portrays Paul as the model leader of the Christian community.

❊ 20/1: 1 Cor 16, 5.
   4: Rom 16, 21.
   5: 21, 29; 2 Tm 4, 20.

10: 1 Kgs 17, 17-24;
    2 Kgs 4, 30-37;
    Mk 5, 39.
28: Jn 21, 15ff.

flock the Holy Spirit has given you to guard. Shepherd the church of God, which he has acquired at the price of his own blood. **29***I know that when I am gone, savage wolves will come among you who will not spare the flock. **30***From your own number, men will present themselves distorting the truth and leading astray any who follow them. **31**Be on guard, therefore. Do not forget that for three years, night and day, I never ceased warning you individually even to the point of tears. **32**I commend you now to the Lord, and to that gracious word of his which can enlarge you, and give you a share among all who are consecrated to him. **33**Never did I set my heart on anyone's silver or gold or envy the way he dressed. **34***You yourselves know that these hands of mine have served both my needs and those of my companions. **35***I have always pointed out to you that it is by such hard work that you must help the weak. You need to recall the words of the Lord Jesus himself, who said, 'There is more happiness in giving than receiving.' "

36After this discourse, Paul knelt down with them all and prayed. **37**They began to weep without restraint, throwing their arms around him and kissing him, **38**for they were deeply distressed to hear that they would never see his face again. Then they escorted him to the ship.

Arrival in Tyre

21 **1**WHEN we had finally taken leave of them, we put out to sea and sailed straight to Cos. On the following day we came to Rhodes and went on from there to Patara. **2**When we found a ship bound for Phoenicia, we boarded it and sailed off. **3**We caught sight of Cyprus but passed it by on our left as we continued on toward Syria. Finally we put in at Tyre, where the ship had to unload cargo.

4We looked for the disciples there and stayed with them for a week. Under the Spirit's prompting, they tried to tell Paul that he should not go up to Jerusalem; **5**but to no purpose. Then, when our time was up, we continued our journey. All of them—wives and children included—came out of the city to see us off, and we knelt down on the beach and prayed. After we had said goodbye to one another, **6**we boarded the ship and they returned home.

At Ptolemais and Caesarea

7Continuing our voyage from Tyre we put in at Ptolemais, where we greeted the brothers and spent the day with them. **8***†The next day we pushed on and came to Caesarea. There we entered the home of Philip the evangelist, one of the Seven, with whom we stayed. **9**This man had four unmarried daughters gifted with prophecy. **10**During our few days' stay, a prophet named Agabus arrived from Judea. **11***He

came up to us, and taking Paul's belt, tied his own hands and feet with it. Then he said, "Thus says the Holy Spirit: 'This is how the Jews in Jerusalem will bind the owner of this belt and hand him over to the Gentiles.' " **12**Upon hearing this, both we ourselves and the people of Caesarea urged Paul not to proceed to Jerusalem. **13***He answered with a question: "Why are you crying and breaking my heart in this way? For the name of the Lord Jesus I am prepared, not only for imprisonment, but for death, in Jerusalem." **14***Since he would not be dissuaded, we said nothing further except, "The Lord's will be done."

VII: PAUL THE PRISONER BEARS WITNESS TO THE RESURRECTION

Paul and James in Jerusalem

15AT THE CONCLUSION OF OUR STAY, we got ready and started up toward Jerusalem. **16**Some of the disciples from Caesarea came along to escort us to the house of Mnason, a Cypriot and an early disciple, with whom we were to stay. **17**†On our arrival in Jerusalem, the brothers there gave us a warm welcome. **18**The next day, Paul and the rest of us paid a visit to James in the presence of all the presbyters. **19**Paul first greeted them, and then described in detail all that God had accomplished among the Gentiles through his ministry. **20**When they heard it they praised God, and said to Paul:

"You see, brother, how many thousands of Jews have come to believe, all of them staunch defenders of the law. **21**Yet they have been informed that you teach the Jews who live among the Gentiles to abandon Moses, to give up the circumcision of their children, and to renounce their customs. **22**What are we to do about your coming, of which they are sure to hear? **23**†Please do as we tell you. There are four men among us who have made a vow. **24***Take them along with you and join with them in their rite of purification; pay the fee for the shaving of their heads. In that way, everyone will know that there is nothing in what they have been told about you, but that you follow the law

---

† 21, 8: *One of the Seven:* see note on 6, 1-11.

21, 17-26: The leaders of the Judaeo-Christians of Jerusalem inform Paul that the Jews there believe he has encouraged the Jews of the diaspora to abandon the Mosaic law. In reality, Paul had no objection to the retention of the law, according to custom, by the Judaeo-Christians of Jerusalem, and left the Jews of the diaspora who accepted Christian messianism free to follow the same practice. Perhaps this misunderstanding of Paul's position was supported by the fact that some Judaeo-Christians of the diaspora had abandoned the law.

21, 23f: The leaders of the community suggest that Paul, on behalf of four members of the Jerusalem community, make the customary payment for the sacrifices offered at the termination of the nazirite vow; cf Nm 6, 1-21. Since Paul himself had once made this vow (18, 18), his respect for the law would be on public record.

❀
29: 1 Pt 5, 1ff.
30: Mt 7, 15; 2 Pt 2, 1f.
34: 1 Cor 4, 12;
    2 Thes 3, 8.
35: Sir 4, 31.

21/8: 6, 5; 8, 4f.
11: 11, 27; 20, 23.
13: 9, 15f.
14: Mt 6, 10; Lk 22, 42.
24: 18, 18; Nm 6, 18.

yourself with due observance. **25***†As for the Gentile converts, we sent them a letter with our decision that they were merely to avoid meat sacrificed to idols, blood, the flesh of strangled animals, and illicit sexual union."

26Accordingly, Paul gathered the men together and went through the rite of purification with them the next day. Then he entered the temple precincts to give notice of the day when the period of purification would be over, at which time the offering was to be made for each of them.

Riot in the Temple

27The seven-day period was nearing completion when some Jews from the province of Asia recognized Paul in the temple precincts and began to stir up the whole crowd there. They seized him, **28***shouting: "Fellow Israelites, help us! This is the man who is spreading his teaching everywhere against our people, our law, and this sanctuary. He has even brought Greeks into the temple area and thus profaned this sacred place." **29**They had seen Trophimus, an Ephesian, with him in the city earlier, so they now assumed that Paul had brought him into the temple.

30Before long the whole city was in turmoil. People came running from all sides. They seized Paul, dragged him outside the temple, and immediately closed its gates. **31**Attempts were being made on his life when a report reached the commander of the cohort that all Jerusalem was rioting. **32**Immediately the commander took his soldiers and centurions and charged down on the rioters. As soon as the crowd caught sight of him and the soldiers, they stopped assaulting Paul. **33**Then, when the commander arrived on the scene, he arrested Paul and had him bound with double irons. He tried to find out who he was and what he had been doing, **34**but different people in the crowd shouted out different answers.

The commander could not get at the truth because of the uproar, so he ordered Paul to be led away to headquarters. **35**When Paul reached the steps, he actually had to be carried up by the soldiers because of the violence of the mob. **36**A crowd of people was following along shouting, "Kill him! Kill him!" **37**Just as Paul was about to be led into the headquarters, he said to the commander, "May I say something to you?" "So you know Greek!" the commander exclaimed. **38**"Aren't you that Egyptian who caused the riot some time ago and led a band of four thousand cutthroats out into the desert?" **39**Paul replied, "I am a Jew, a citizen of Tarsus in Cilicia—no mean city; I beg you, let me address these people." **40**†With his permission Paul then stood on the steps and motioned the people to silence. A great hush fell on them as he began to speak to them in Hebrew.

Discourse to the Crowd

22 **1**"MY brothers and fathers, listen to what I have to say to you in my defense." **2**When they heard him addressing them in Hebrew, they grew quieter still. He went on: **3***"I am a Jew, born in Tarsus in Cilicia, but I was brought up in this city. Here I sat at the feet of Gamaliel and was educated strictly in the law of our fathers. I was a staunch defender of God, just as all of you are today. **4***Furthermore I persecuted this new way to the point of death. I arrested and imprisoned both men and women.

5"On this point the high priest and the whole council of elders can bear me witness, for it was from them that I received letters to our brother Jews in Damascus. I set out with the intention of bringing the prisoners I would arrest back to Jerusalem for punishment. **6**†As I was traveling along, approaching Damascus around noon, a great light from the sky suddenly flashed all about me. **7**I fell to the ground and heard a voice say to me, 'Saul, Saul, why do you persecute me?' **8**I answered, 'Who are you, sir?' He said to me, 'I am Jesus the Nazorean whom you are persecuting.' **9**My companions saw the light but did not hear the voice speaking to me. **10**'What is it I must do, sir?' I asked, and the Lord replied, 'Get up and go into Damascus. There you will be told about everything you are destined to do.' **11**But since I could not see because of the brilliance of the light, I had to be taken by the hand and led into Damascus by my companions.

12"A certain Ananias, a devout observer of the law and well spoken of by all the Jews who lived there, **13**came and stood by me. 'Saul, my brother,' he said, 'recover your sight.' In that instant I regained my sight and looked at him. **14**The next thing he said was, 'The God of our fathers long ago designated you to know his will, to look upon the Just One, and to hear the sound of his voice; **15**before all men you are to be his witness to what you have seen and heard. **16**Why delay, then? Be baptized at once and wash away your sins as you call upon his name.'

17"Upon my return to Jerusalem I was praying in the court of the temple, where I fell into a trance **18**and saw Jesus speaking to me. 'You must make haste,' he said 'Leave Jerusalem at once because they will not accept your testimony about me.' **19**I answered: 'Lord, it is because they know that I imprisoned those who believed in you and flogged them in every synagogue. **20***While the blood of your witness Stephen was being

---

† 21, 25: The allusion to the apostolic decree (15, 13-29) was probably introduced here by Luke to remind his readers that the Gentile Christians themselves were asked to respect certain Jewish practices deriving from the law. Paul was not being asked to violate his conscience.

21, 40: *In Hebrew:* more precisely, "Aramaic," which at this time was the Semitic tongue in common use. This indicates that Paul's audience was principally composed of native-born Palestinian Jews.

22, 6-16: See note on 9, 1-19.

✢
     25: 15, 19f.28f.   4: 8, 3; 9, 2.
     28: Rcm 15, 31.   20: 7, 58.
  22/3: 5, 34; 26, 4f;
        2 Cor 11, 22;
        Gal 1, 13f; Phil 3, 5f.

shed, I stood by and approved it. I even guarded the cloaks of those who killed him!' **21***†With that he said to me: 'Be on your way. I mean to send you far from here, among the Gentiles.' "

Paul Imprisoned

22†Up to this point in his speech the crowd had been listening to Paul, but now they began to shout, "Kill him! Rid the earth of the likes of him! He isn't worthy to live!" **23**They yelled and waved their cloaks and flung dirt through the air. **24**At that display, the commander directed Paul to be brought inside the headquarters. He issued orders that he be examined under the lash to find out why they made such an outcry against him. **25***†No sooner had they bound Paul than he said to the centurion who was standing by, "Is it legal to flog a Roman citizen without a trial?" **26**On hearing this, the centurion ran to the commander and demanded, "Do you realize what you are doing? This man is a Roman citizen!" **27**The commander rushed in and asked Paul, "Is it true? Are you a Roman citizen?" "I am," Paul answered. **28**The commander then observed, "It cost me quite a sum to get my citizenship." "Ah," said Paul, "but I am a citizen by birth!" **29**At these words, those who were about to interrogate him backed away. The commander became alarmed because he realized that in restraining Paul he had restrained a citizen of Rome.

Paul before the Sanhedrin

30The next day the commander released Paul from prison, intending to look carefully into the charge which the Jews were bringing against him. He summoned the chief priests and the whole Sanhedrin to a meeting; then he brought Paul down and made him stand before them.

23 **1***PAUL gazed intently at the Sanhedrin. Then he said, "Brothers, to this day I have lived my life with a clear conscience before God." **2**At that, the high priest Ananias ordered his attendants to strike Paul on the mouth. **3***Paul said to him in rebuttal: "You are the one God will strike, you whitewashed wall! You sit there judging men according to the law, yet you violate the law yourself by ordering me to be struck!" **4**At this, the attendants protested, "How dare you insult God's high priest?" **5**†Paul answered: "My brothers, I did not know that he was the high priest. Indeed, Scripture has it, 'You shall not curse a prince of your people!' "

6*Paul, it should be noted, was aware that some of them were Sadducees and some Pharisees. Consequently he spoke out before the Sanhedrin: "Brothers, I am a Pharisee and was born a Pharisee. I find myself on trial now because of my hope in the resurrection of the dead." **7**At these words, a dispute arose between Pharisees and Sadducees which divided the whole assembly. **8***(The Sadducees, of course, maintain that there is no resurrection and that there are neither angels nor spirits, while the Pharisees believe in all these things.) **9**A loud uproar ensued. Finally, some scribes of the Pharisee party arose and declared emphatically: "We do not find this man guilty of any crime. If a spirit or an angel has spoken to him. . . ." **10**At this, the dispute grew worse and the commander feared they would tear Paul to pieces. He therefore ordered his troops to go down and rescue Paul from their midst and take him back to headquarters. **11**†That night the Lord appeared at Paul's side and said: "Keep up your courage! Just as you have given testimony to me here in Jerusalem, so must you do in Rome."

Transfer to Caesarea

12When it was day, certain Jews formed a conspiracy in which they bound themselves by oath not to eat or drink until they had killed Paul. **13**(There were more than forty of them who took the oath together.) **14**They then went to the chief priests and the elders and said: "We have bound ourselves by oath to touch no food until we kill Paul. **15**Now, together with the Sanhedrin, you must suggest to the commander that he have Paul brought down to you on the pretext that you would like to examine his case more carefully. We are prepared to kill him before he gets there." **16**The son of Paul's sister heard about the plot, and when he did so he came to headquarters. They allowed him to enter, and he told Paul about it. **17**Paul then called for one of the centurions, to whom he said, "Take this young man to the commander; he has something to report to him." **18**The centurion took him in charge and led him to the commander, with the explanation, "The prisoner Paul called me and asked me to bring you this boy, who has something to tell you." **19**The commander took him by the hand and drew him aside to ask privately, "What do you have to report?" **20**The boy replied: "The Jews have agreed among themselves to ask you tomorrow to have Paul brought down to the Sanhedrin, on the pretext that they want to question him more carefully. **21**But don't be fooled by them. More than forty of them are lying in wait;

---

†

22, 21: Paul endeavors to explain that his position on the law has not been identical with that of his audience because it has been his prophetic mission to preach to the Gentiles, to whom the law was not addressed and who had no faith in it as a way of salvation.

22, 22: Paul's suggestion that his prophetic mission to the Gentiles did not involve his imposing the law on them provokes the same opposition as occurred in Pisidian Antioch (13, 45f).

22, 25: A Roman citizen could not be punished unless legally condemned. The tribune considers it his duty to be assured that Paul is not a seditionist.

23, 5: This was probably not said in sarcasm. Paul withdraws the epithet *whitewashed wall* when he is reminded of the rule in Ex 22, 27.

23, 11: The occurrence of the vision of Christ suggests that Paul's experiences may have placed him in a state of depression.

*
21: 9, 15.
25: 16, 37.
23/1: 24, 16.
3: Ez 13, 10-15; Mt 23, 27.
6: Phil 3, 5.
8: Mt 22, 23.

they have bound themselves by oath not to eat or drink until they kill him. They are all ready now, waiting only for your consent." **22**The commander sent the boy away with the order, "Don't tell anyone that you gave me this information."

23Then the commander summoned two of his centurions and said to them, "Get ready to leave for Caesarea by nine o'clock tonight, with two hundred infantrymen, seventy cavalrymen, and two hundred spearmen. **24**Also provide horses for Paul's journey, so that you may give him safe conduct to Felix the governor." **25**He then wrote the governor a letter to this effect:

26†"Claudius Lysias sends greetings to His Excellency Felix, Governor. **27***Here is a man whom the Jews seized and were about to murder. When I learned that he was a Roman citizen, I intervened with my troops and rescued him. I then had him brought before the Sanhedrin, **28**hoping to determine what their charge against him was. **29***I subsequently discovered that he was accused in matters of their own law and was in no way guilty of anything deserving death or imprisonment. **30**When I later came to be informed of a plot against this man's life, I decided at once to send him to you. I have also instructed his accusers to take the matter up with you."

31According to their orders, the infantry took Paul and escorted him that night as far as Antipatris. **32**The next day they returned to headquarters, leaving it to the cavalry to go on with him. **33**When the cavalrymen arrived in Caesarea, they delivered the letter to the governor and brought Paul before him. **34**The governor, upon reading the letter, asked Paul what province he came from, only to learn he was from Cilicia. **35**"I shall hear your case," he said, "when your accusers arrive." Then he ordered Paul to be kept under guard in Herod's praetorium.

Trial before Felix

24 **1**FIVE days later, the high priest Ananias came down to Caesarea with some of the elders and an attorney named Tertullus. They presented their case against Paul to the governor. **2**Following Paul's summons to the bar, Tertullus began his prosecution by addressing Felix: "Your Excellency, through your efforts we enjoy great peace. Many improvements have been made in this nation through your provident care. **3**Therefore we must always and everywhere acknowledge our deep gratitude to you. **4**But now, lest I impose on your time unduly, I beg your indulgence for a brief hearing of our case. **5***†We have found that this man is a troublemaker who stirs up sedition among the Jews all over the world. He is a ringleader of the sect of Nazoreans. **6**†He even tried to desecrate our temple, but we apprehended

him in time. **8**Feel free now to question him about all this and learn for yourself why we are accusing him." **9**The Jews supported this indictment and maintained that these were the facts.

10The governor then gestured to Paul, who replied as follows: "I know that you have been a judge over this nation for many years. I am thus encouraged to make my defense before you, **11**†since you are in a position to understand. Not more than twelve days have passed since I went to Jerusalem to worship there. **12**Neither in the temple area, nor in the synagogue, nor anywhere else in the city, did my accusers find me debating with anyone or inciting a mob. **13**They cannot substantiate the charges they are making against me. **14**I admit to you that it is according to the new way—which they call a sect—that I worship the God of our fathers. At the same time, I believe all that is written in the law and the prophets, **15***and I have the same hope in God as these men have that there is to be a resurrection of the good and the wicked alike. **16**In this regard I too always strive to keep my conscience clear before God and man.

17"After several years' absence, I had come to bring alms to my own people and to make my offerings. **18***That is what I was doing when they found me in the temple court completing the rites of purification without any crowd around me or any disturbance. **19**Certain Jews from the province of Asia are the ones who found me. These are the men who should be here before you to make whatever charge they have against me. **20**Let those who are here declare what crime they found me guilty of when I stood before the Sanhedrin, **21***unless it was what I called out as I stood in their presence: 'I am on trial before you today because of the resurrection of the dead.' "

Captivity at Caesarea

22†Felix was rather well informed about the new way, and when he heard these words he adjourned the trial, saying merely, "I will decide the case when Lysias the commander arrives." **23**He gave orders to the centurion that Paul was to be kept in custody but allowed some freedom, and that no one was to prevent his friends from seeing to his wants.

---

† 23, 26-30: The letter emphasizes the fact that Paul is a Roman citizen and asserts the lack of evidence that he is guilty of a crime against the empire. The tone of the letter implies that the commander became initially involved in Paul's case because of his Roman citizenship, but this is not an exact description of what really happened; cf 21, 31-33; 22, 25ff.

24, 5f: The charges leveled against Paul accurately reflect the portrait formed of him among the Jews.

24, 6b-7: This portion is not found in the best Greek MSS.

24, 11ff: Whereas the lawyer Tertullus referred to Paul's activities on his missionary journeys, the apostle narrowed the charges down to the riot connected with the incident in the temple; cf 21, 27-30; 24, 17-20.

24, 22: *Rather well informed about the new way:* he probably had learned from talking to Christians that Christianity posed no threat to the empire. He may have kept Paul in custody simply to forestall fresh trouble in Jerusalem.

---

*   27: 21, 31ff.   15: Jn 5, 29.
      29: 18, 15; 25, 18f.   18: 21, 26.
      24/5: Lk 23, 2.   21: 23, 6.

[24]†A few days later Felix came with his Jewish wife Drusilla, and sent for Paul to hear him speak about faith in Christ Jesus. [25]As Paul talked on about uprightness, continence, and the coming judgment, Felix became frightened. Before long he exclaimed: "That's enough for now! You can go. I'll send for you again when I find the time." [26]†At the same time, he hoped he would be offered a bribe by Paul, so he used to send for him frequently to converse with him.

[27]Two years passed, following which Felix was succeeded by Porcius Festus. The latter wanted to ingratiate himself with the Jews, so he left Paul in prison.

Appeal to the Emperor

25 [1]THREE days after Festus had arrived in the province, he went up from Caesarea to Jerusalem. [2]†There the Jewish chief priests and the leaders presented him with their case against Paul, [3]requesting that he favor them rather than Paul, and urging Festus to send him to Jerusalem. Their plot was to kill him on the way. [4]But Festus answered that Paul was being kept in custody at Caesarea, and that he himself would be returning there soon. [5]"Your leading men can come down with me," he said, "and if this man is at fault, they can prosecute him there."

[6]After spending eight or ten days in Jerusalem, Festus went down to Caesarea. On the following day he took his seat on the bench and ordered Paul to be brought in. [7]When Paul appeared, the Jews who had come down from Jerusalem surrounded him and leveled many serious charges against him, none of which they were able to prove. [8]Paul's defense was, "I have committed no crime either against the law of the Jews or against the temple or against the emperor." [9]But Festus, wishing to please the Jewish people, asked Paul, "Are you willing to go up to Jerusalem and stand trial before me there on these charges?" [10]Paul answered: "I stand before the imperial bench; that is where I must be tried. I have done the Jews no wrong, as you yourself realize. [11]†If I am guilty, if I have committed a crime deserving death, I do not seek to escape that penalty. But if there is nothing to the charges these men bring against me, no one has a right to hand me over to them. I appeal to the emperor!" [12]Thereupon Festus conferred with his council and finally declared: "You have appealed to the emperor. To the emperor you shall go."

Agrippa Invited To Hear Paul

[13]†A few days later King Agrippa and Bernice arrived in Caesarea and paid Festus a courtesy call. [14]Since they were to spend several days there, Festus referred Paul's case to the king. "There is a prisoner here," he said, "whom Felix left behind in custody. [15]While I was in Jerusalem the chief priests and the elders of the Jews presented their case against this man and demanded his condemnation. [16]I replied that it was not the Roman practice to hand an accused man over before he had been confronted with his accusers and given a chance to defend himself against their

charges. [17]When they came here with me, I did not delay the matter. The very next day I took my seat on the bench and ordered the man brought in. [18]His accusers surrounded him but they did not charge him with any of the crimes I expected. [19]Instead they differed with him over issues in their own religion, and about a certain Jesus who had died but who Paul claimed is alive. [20]Not knowing how to decide the case, I asked whether the prisoner was willing to go to Jerusalem and stand trial there on these charges. [21]Paul appealed to be kept here until there could be an imperial investigation of his case, so I issued orders that he be kept in custody until I could send him to the emperor."

[22]Agrippa said to Festus, "I too should like to hear this man." "Tomorrow you shall hear him," replied Festus. [23]So the next day Agrippa and Bernice came with great pomp and entered the audience chamber in the company of military officers and prominent men of the city. At Festus' command Paul was brought in. [24]The governor began to speak: "King Agrippa and all you who are here present with us, look at this man! The whole Jewish community, both here and in Jerusalem, has appealed to me about him, clamoring that he should live no more. [25]But I did not find that he had done anything deserving of death, so when he appealed to His Majesty the Emperor, I determined to send him on. [26]The trouble is, I have nothing definite to write about him to our sovereign. That is why I have brought him before all of you, and in particular before you, King Agrippa, that from this investigation I may have something to set down in his regard. [27]†It seems to me a senseless procedure to send on a prisoner without indicating the charges against him."

Agrippa Hears Paul

26 [1]AGRIPPA now spoke to Paul: "You have permission to state your case." So Paul stretched out his hand and began his defense.
[2]"Many charges have been leveled against me by the Jews, King Agrippa. I count myself fortunate to be

---

†

24, 24f: The way of Christian discipleship greatly disquiets Felix, who has entered into an adulterous marriage with Drusilla, daughter of Herod Agrippa I.

24, 26: As time passed Felix began to hope that Paul would be willing to leave the country under Roman protection, which he would be prepared to arrange in exchange for a bribe.

25, 2: Even after two years the animosity toward Paul in Jerusalem has not subsided; cf 24, 27.

25, 11f: Paul uses his right as a Roman citizen to appeal his case to the jurisdiction of the emperor (Nero, c 60 A. D.). This move broke the deadlock between Roman protective custody of Paul and the plan of his enemies to kill him; cf 25, 3.

25, 13: *King Agrippa and Bernice:* brother and sister, children of Herod Agrippa I whose activities against the Jerusalem community are mentioned in 12, 1-19. Agrippa was a petty ruler over small areas in northern Palestine and some villages in Perea.

25, 27: Festus' difficulty of lacking a charge against Paul from the Roman jurisdiction is not solved by Agrippa; cf 26, 31f. One solution open to the governor would have been a statement similar to Lysias's letter (23, 26-30) with the addition of Paul's appeal to the emperor.

able to make my defense today in your presence, ³especially since you are expert in all the various Jewish customs and disputes. I beg you to listen to me patiently.

⁴"The way I have lived since my youth, and the life I have led among my own people from the beginning and later at Jerusalem, is well known to all Jews. ⁵*They have been acquainted with me for a long time and can testify, if they wish, to my life lived as a Pharisee, the strictest sect of our religion. ⁶But today I stand trial because of my hope in the promise made by God to our fathers. ⁷The twelve tribes of our people fervently worship God day and night in the hope that they will see that promise fulfilled. It is because of this hope, Your Majesty, that I stand accused by the Jews. ⁸Let me ask why you, above all, who are Jews, should find it hard to believe that God raises dead men to life.

⁹†"For my part, I once thought it my duty to oppose the name of Jesus the Nazorean in every way possible. ¹⁰That is just what I did in Jerusalem. With the authority I received from the chief priests, I sent many of God's holy people to prison. When they were to be put to death I cast my vote against them. ¹¹Many a time, in synagogue after synagogue, I compelled them by force to blaspheme. Indeed, so wild was my fury against them that I pursued them even to foreign cities.

¹²"On one such occasion I was traveling toward Damascus armed with the authority and commission of the chief priests. ¹³On this journey, Your Majesty, I saw a light more brilliant than the sun shining in the sky at midday. It surrounded me and those who were traveling with me. ¹⁴All of us fell to the ground and I heard a voice saying to me in Hebrew, 'Saul, Saul, why do you persecute me? It is hard for you to kick against the goad.' ¹⁵I said, at that, 'Who are you, sir?' and the Lord answered: 'I am that Jesus whom you are persecuting. ¹⁶Get up now and stand on your feet. I have appeared to you to designate you as my servant and as a witness to what you have seen of me and what you will see of me. ¹⁷I have delivered you from this people and from the nations, ¹⁸to open the eyes of those to whom I am sending you, to turn them from darkness to light and from the dominion of Satan to God; that through their faith in me they may obtain the forgiveness of their sins and a portion among God's people.'

¹⁹"King Agrippa, I could not disobey that heavenly vision. ²⁰I preached a message of reform and of conversion to God, first to the people of Damascus, then to the people of Jerusalem and all the country of Judea; yes, even to the Gentiles. I urged them to act in conformity with their change of heart. ²¹*That is why the Jews seized me in the temple court and tried to murder me. ²²But I have had God's help to this very day, and so I stand here to testify to great and small alike. Nothing that I say differs from what the prophets and Moses foretold: ²³*namely, that the Messiah must suffer, and that, as the first to rise from the dead, he will proclaim light to our people and to the Gentiles."

Reactions to Paul's Speech

²⁴As Paul went on defending himself in this way, Festus interrupted with a shout, "Paul, you are mad! And your great learning is driving me mad!" ²⁵"No, Your Excellency," answered Paul, "I am not mad. The message I proclaim is the sober truth. ²⁶The king here is well acquainted with these matters. Before him I can speak freely. I am convinced that none of this escapes him—after all, it did not take place in a dark corner! ²⁷Do you believe the prophets, King Agrippa? I am sure you do." ²⁸At this, Agrippa said, "A little more, Paul, and you will make a Christian out of me!" ²⁹*Paul replied, "Whether little more or much more, I would to God that not only you but all who listen to me today might become what I am—without these chains!"

³⁰Then the king rose, and with him the governor and Bernice and the rest of the company. ³¹†After they had left the chamber, they talked matters over among themselves and admitted, "This man is doing nothing that deserves death or imprisonment." ³²Agrippa further remarked to Festus, "He could have been set at liberty if he had not appealed to the emperor!"

Departure for Rome

27 ¹†WHEN it was decided that we were to sail for Italy, Paul and some other prisoners were handed over to a centurion named Julius from the cohort known as Augusta. ²*We boarded a ship from Adramyttium bound for ports in the province of Asia, and set sail. With us was a Macedonian, Aristarchus of Thessalonica. ³The following day we put in at Sidon, where Julius kindly allowed Paul to visit some friends who cared for his needs. ⁴Then, putting out from Sidon, we sailed around the sheltered side of Cyprus because of strong headwinds. ⁵We crossed the open sea off the coast of Cilicia and Pamphylia, and came to Myra in Lycia.

Storm and Shipwreck

⁶There the centurion discovered an Alexandrian vessel bound for Italy, and he ordered us aboard. ⁷For

---

* 26/5: Gal 1, 14.   29: 28, 20.
21: 21, 31.   27/2: 2 Cor 11, 25.
23: 1 Cor 15, 20-23.

† 26, 9-18: See note on 9, 1-19.

26, 31: In recording the episode of Paul's appearance before Agrippa, Luke wishes to show that when Paul's case was judged impartially, no grounds for legal action against him were found.

27, 1–28, 15: Here Luke has written a stirring account of adventure on the high seas, incidentally to his main purpose of showing how well Paul got along with his captors and how his prophetic influence ultimately saved the lives of all on board. The recital also establishes the existence of Christian communities in Puteoli and Rome.

many days we made little headway, arriving at Cnidus only with difficulty. Since the winds would not permit us to continue our course, we sailed for Salmone and the shelter of Crete. **8**Again with difficulty we moved along the coast to a place called Fair Havens, near the town of Lasea.

9*Much time had now gone by. The autumn fast was over, and with the lateness of the year sailing had become hazardous. It was then that Paul uttered this warning: **10**"Men, I can see that this voyage is bound to meet with disaster and heavy loss, not only to ship and cargo, but to our own lives as well." **11**However, the centurion preferred listening to the pilot and the shipowner to listening to Paul.

12Since the harbor was not fit to pass the winter in, the majority preferred to put out to sea in the hope of making Phoenix and spending the winter there. This was a Cretan port exposed on the southwest and the northwest. **13**When a gentle south wind began to blow, they thought they had what they were looking for, so they weighed anchor and proceeded, hugging the coast of Crete. **14**It was not long before a hurricane struck, the kind called a "northeaster." **15**Since the ship was caught up in it and could not head into the wind, we yielded and ran before it. **16**We passed under the lee of a small island named Cauda and only with difficulty were we able to gain control of the ship's boat. **17**They hoisted it aboard and then made use of cables to brace the ship itself. Because of their fear that they would be driven on the reef of Syrtis, they lowered the small anchor used for moving the ship and the ship was carried along. **18**We were being pounded by the storm so violently that the next day some of the cargo was thrown over the side. **19**On the third day they deliberately threw even the ship's gear overboard. **20**For many days neither the sun nor the stars were to be seen, so savagely did the storm rage. Toward the end, we abandoned any hope of survival.

21All hands had gone without food for a long time when Paul stood up among them and said: "Men, you should have taken my advice and not set sail from Crete. Then you would not have incurred this disastrous loss. **22**I urge you now to keep up your courage. None among you will be lost—only the ship. **23**Last night a messenger of the God whose man I am and whom I serve, stood by me. **24**'Do not be afraid, Paul,' he said. 'You are destined to appear before the emperor. Therefore, as a favor to you, God has granted safety to all who are sailing with you.' **25**So keep up your courage, men. I trust in God that it will all work out just as I have been told, **26**though we still have to face shipwreck on some island."

27It was the fourteenth night of the storm, and we were still being driven across the Ionian Sea, when toward midnight the sailors began to suspect that land was near. **28**They took a sounding and found a depth of twenty fathoms; after sailing on a short distance

they again took a sounding and found it to be fifteen. **29**For fear that we should be dashed against some rocky coast, they dropped four anchors from the stern and prayed for daylight. **30**Then the sailors tried to abandon ship. Pretending that they were going to run out anchors from the bow of the ship, they let the ship's boat down into the sea. **31**Paul alerted the centurion and the soldiers to this: "If these men do not stay with the ship, you have no chance to survive." **32**At this, the soldiers cut the ropes and let the boat drift.

33At dawn Paul urged all on board to take some food: "For fourteen days you have been in constant suspense; you have gone hungry—eaten nothing. **34**Now I urge you to take some food, which will give you strength to survive. Not one of you shall lose a hair of his head." **35**When he had said this he took some bread, gave thanks to God before all of them, broke it, and began to eat. **36**This gave them new courage, and they too had something to eat. **37**(In all, there were two hundred and seventy-six of us on board.) **38**When they had had enough to eat, they lightened the ship further by throwing the wheat overboard.

39With the coming of daylight, they did not recognize the land they saw. They could make out a bay with a sandy beach, however, so they planned to run the ship aground on it if possible. **40**They cut loose the anchors and abandoned them to the sea. At the same time they untied the guy-ropes of the rudders, hoisted the foresail into the wind, and made for the beach; **41**but the ship hit a sandbar and ran aground. The bow stuck fast and could not be budged, while the stern was shattered by the pounding of the sea. **42***The soldiers thought at first of killing the prisoners so that none might swim away and escape; **43**but because the centurion was anxious to save Paul, he opposed their plan. Instead, he ordered those who could swim to jump overboard first and make for land. **44**The rest were to follow, on planks, or on other debris from the ship. In this way all came safely ashore.

Winter in Malta

28 **1**ONCE on shore, we learned that the island was called Malta. **2**The natives showed us extraordinary kindness by lighting a fire and gathering us all around it, for it had begun to rain and was growing cold. **3**Paul had just fed the fire with a bundle of brushwood he had collected, when a poisonous snake, escaping from the heat, fastened itself on his hand. **4**At the sight of the snake hanging from his hand, the natives said to one another, "This man must really be a murderer if, after his escape from the sea, Justice will not let him live." **5**But Paul shook the snake off into the fire and suffered no ill effects from the bite. **6***They expected to see him swell up or suddenly fall dead. After waiting for quite some time, however, and seeing nothing unusual happen to him, they changed their minds and began to say that he was a god.

7In the vicinity of that place was the estate of Pub-

9-44: Jon 1, 4-16.   28/6: 14, 11.
42: 16, 27.

lius, the chief figure on the island. He took us in and gave us kind hospitality for three days. **8**It happened that Publius' father was sick in bed, laid up with chronic fever and dysentery. Paul went in to see the man and, praying, laid his hands on him and cured him. **9**After this happened, the rest of the sick on the island began to come to Paul and they too were healed. **10**They paid us much honor, and when we eventually set sail they brought us provisions for our needs.

Arrival in Rome

11Three months later we set sail in a ship which had passed the winter at the island. It was an Alexandrian vessel with the "Heavenly Twins" as its figurehead. **12**We put in at Syracuse and spent three days there. **13**Then we sailed around the toe and arrived at Rhegium. A day later a south wind began to blow which enabled us to reach Puteoli in two days. **14**Here we found some of the brothers, who urged us to stay on with them for a week.

This is how we finally came to Rome. **15**Certain brothers from Rome who heard about us came out as far as the Forum of Appius and the Three Taverns to meet us. When Paul saw them, he thanked God and took fresh courage. **16†**Upon our entry into Rome Paul was allowed to take a lodging of his own, although a soldier was assigned to keep guard over him.

Testimony to Roman Jews

17†Three days later Paul invited the prominent men of the Jewish community to visit him. When they had gathered he said: "My brothers, I have done nothing against our people or our ancestral customs; yet in Jerusalem I was handed over to the Romans as a prisoner. **18**The Romans tried my case and wanted to release me because they found nothing against me deserving of death. **19***When the Jews objected, I was forced to appeal to the emperor, though I had no cause to make accusations against my own people. **20**This is the reason, then, why I have asked to see you and speak with you. I wear these chains solely because I share the hope of Israel."

21They replied: "We have had no letters from Judea about you, nor have any of the brothers arrived with a report or rumor to your discredit. **22***For our part, we are anxious to hear you present your views. We know very well that this sect is denounced everywhere."

23*†With that, they arranged a day with him and came to his lodgings in great numbers. From morning to evening he laid the case before them, bearing witness to the reign of God among men. He sought to

convince them about Jesus by appealing to the law of Moses and the prophets. **24**Some, indeed, were convinced by what he said; others would not believe.

25Without reaching any agreement among themselves, they began to leave. Then Paul added one final word: "The Holy Spirit stated it well when he said to your fathers through the prophet Isaiah:

26*'Go to this people and say:
You may listen carefully yet you will never understand;
   you may look intently yet you will never see.
27The mind of this people has grown sluggish.
They have scarcely used their ears to listen;
   their eyes they have closed,
Lest they should see with their eyes,
   hear with their ears,
   understand with their minds,
And repent;
   and I should have to heal them.'

28Now you must realize that this salvation of God has been transmitted to the Gentiles—who will heed it!"

Summary

30†For two full years Paul stayed on in his rented lodgings, welcoming all who came to him. **31**With full assurance, and without any hindrance whatever, he preached the reign of God and taught about the Lord Jesus Christ.

---

† 28, 16: The mild form of custody in which Paul is detained reflects, perhaps, the arrangements made for him by Festus; cf 25, 27.

28, 17-22: Paul's first act in Rome is to learn from the leaders of the Jewish community whether the Jews of Jerusalem plan to pursue their case against him before the Roman jurisdiction. He is informed that no such plan is afoot, but that the Jews of Rome have heard the Christian teaching denounced. Paul's offer to explain it to them is readily accepted.

28, 23-28: Some critics of Acts have expressed doubt that these meetings between Paul and the leading Jews of Rome took place; they incline to the view that Luke here created ideal scenes to show the final separation between Judaism and Christianity. The scenes, however, are historically plausible: Paul would naturally have been concerned that the Christian community of Rome be not embarrassed by charges against it if he were brought to trial; while the Jews of Rome stood to gain from an explanation of the new doctrines by a trained rabbi. The citation from Isaiah is probably introduced by Luke, who uses the unbelief of Israel as typical of the difficulty men meet when confronted with the prophetic word of God.

28, 29: This verse is not found in the Greek manuscripts.

28, 30f: Many attempts have been made to explain what seems to be the abrupt ending of Luke's Acts of the Apostles. The author has Paul still in detention, though he intimates a bright outcome for his case. Perhaps the most satisfactory explanation is that Luke does not regard the subsequent missionary activity of Paul or his martyrdom as necessary for his account of the origin and development of the church.

✿ 19: 25, 11.   22: 24, 5.14.   23: 13, 15-41.   26: Is 6, 9; Mt 13, 14; Mk 4, 12; Lk 8, 10; Jn 12, 40; Rom 11, 8.

The Epistle of Paul to the Romans

Introduction

Christians in Rome seem to have become numerous first among the Jewish population of the city. The Roman historian Suetonius mentions an edict of the Emperor Claudius (died c 49 A. D.) ordering the expulsion of Jews from Rome in connection with a certain "Chrestus," probably an error for "Christus." According to Acts 18, 2, Aquila and Priscilla (or Prisca, as in this epistle) were affected by this edict; cf Rom 16, 3. Since neither early Christian tradition nor Paul's letter to the Romans mentions a founder of the Christian community in Rome, it may be concluded that the Christian faith came to that city through members of the Jewish community of Jerusalem who were Christian converts. About 57 A. D., when Paul wrote the letter, most probably from Corinth, Christians in Rome were predominantly Gentile, with a Judaeo-Christian minority, a circumstance which the majority of scholars see reflected in the letter itself.

At this time Paul was considering a missionary journey to Spain and desired to make Rome his headquarters for the project (15, 22f.28). He was informed about the Roman community (14, 1-11), perhaps by Aquila and Prisca, and it may be assumed that he in turn was known to the Christians there. It would be difficult to explain why he should have written this lengthy letter to them unless they were aware of his apostolic role and his whole remarkable history, and would receive his reflections with corresponding interest.

The principal theme of the letter is the relationship between Judaism and Christianity, a topic which Paul judged to be much in the minds of the Roman Christians. Each of these religious faiths claimed to be the way of salvation which established a covenant between God and man and made man the beneficiary of divine gifts. But Christianity regarded itself as the prophetic development and fulfillment of the faith of the Old Testament, declaring that the preparatory Mosaic covenant must now give way to the new and more perfect covenant in Jesus Christ. Paul himself had been the implacable advocate of freedom from the laws of the Mosaic covenant, and he refused to impose them on Gentile converts to Christianity. He had witnessed the personal hostilities that developed between the adherents of the two faiths, and had written his strongly worded letter to the Galatians against those Judaeo-Christians who were persuading Gentile Christian communities to adopt the religious practices of Judaism. For him, the purity of the religious understanding of Jesus as the source of salvation would be seriously impaired if Gentile Christians were obliged to amalgamate the two religious faiths.

Although Paul expressed his grief over Israel's failure to accept Christian messianism (9, 1-8), he remained unsympathetic toward both Jewish and Gentile unbelievers (2 Thes 1, 8ff). This need not seem startling if Paul in fact considered the parousia or second coming of Christ to be a distinct possibility in his own lifetime. His attitude would thus reflect the urgency of conversion and the imminence of the judgment of the world. See notes on 1 Thessalonians 4, 13-18, and on Mark 13, 1-37.

The implication of Paul's exposition of justification by faith rather than by the law is that the divine plan of salvation works itself out on a broad theological plane to include the whole of humanity despite the differences in the content of the given religious system to which a human culture is heir.

The Epistle to the Romans contains a powerful exposition of the doctrine of the supremacy of Christ and of faith in him as the source of salvation. It is an implicit plea to the Christians of Rome to hold fast to that faith. They are to resist any pressure put on them to accept a doctrine of salvation through works of the law. At the same time they are not to exaggerate Christian freedom through repudiation of law itself.

Romans is a well-constructed epistle. It is divided as follows:

- I: Introduction (1, 1-17)
- II: Humanity without Christ (1, 18—3, 20)
- III: Salvation through Faith in Christ (3, 21—5, 21)
- IV: Justification and the Christian Life (6, 1—8, 39)
- V: Israel's Present Rejection (9, 1—11, 36)
- VI: The Duties of Christians (12, 1—15, 13)
- VII: Conclusion (15, 14—16, 27)

I: INTRODUCTION

Greetings

1 1*†GREETINGS FROM PAUL, a servant of Christ Jesus, called to be an apostle and set apart to proclaim the gospel of God **2**which he promised long ago through his prophets, as the holy Scriptures record—**3***the gospel concerning his Son, who was descended from David according to the flesh **4***†but

---

1/1: Gal 1, 15.
3: Rv 22, 16.
4: 10, 9.

---

† 1, 1-7: The address follows the epistolary style of Paul's time, naming the sender and the addressees and extending good wishes (1.7). Paul proclaims the Christian faith in the humanity of Jesus (v 3) and in his divine sanctifying power (v 4).

1, 4: *Was made Son of God in power:* other possible translations are "was declared" or "proclaimed the powerful Son of God." *By his resurrection from the dead:* the resurrection made was made Son of God in power according to the spirit of holiness, by his resurrection from the dead: Jesus Christ our Lord. **5†**Through him we have been favored with apostleship, that we may spread his name and bring to obedient faith all the Gentiles, **6**among whom are you who have been called to belong to Jesus Christ.

7To all in Rome, beloved of God and called to holiness, grace and peace from God our Father and the Lord Jesus Christ.

Paul and the Romans

8*First of all, I give thanks to my God through Jesus Christ for all of you because your faith is heralded throughout the world. **9**The God I worship in the spirit by preaching the gospel of his Son will bear witness that I constantly mention you in prayer, **10***always pleading that somehow by God's will I may at last find my way clear to visit you. **11**For I long to see you and share with you some spiritual gift to strengthen you— **12**rather, what I wish is that we may be mutually encouraged by our common faith. **13***My brothers, I want you to know that I have often planned to visit you (though up to now I have been kept from it) in order to do some fruitful work among you, as I have among the other Gentiles. **14**I am under obligation to Greeks and non-Greeks, to learned and unintelligent alike. **15**That is why I am eager to preach the gospel to you Romans as well.

God's Power for Salvation

16†I am not ashamed of the gospel. It is the power of God leading everyone who believes in it to salvation, the Jew first, then the Greek. **17*†**For in the gospel is revealed the justice of God which begins and ends with faith; as Scripture says, "The just man shall live by faith."

II: HUMANITY WITHOUT CHRIST

Punishment of Idolatry

18†THE WRATH OF GOD is being revealed from heaven against the irreligious and perverse spirit of men who, in this perversity of theirs, hinder the truth. **19**In fact, whatever can be known about God is clear to them; he himself made it so. **20***Since the creation of the world, invisible realities, God's eternal power and divinity, have become visible, recognized through the things he has made. Therefore these men are inexcusable. **21***They certainly had knowledge of God, yet they did not glorify him as God or give him thanks; they stultified themselves through speculating to no purpose,

and their senseless hearts were darkened. **22**They claimed to be wise, but turned into fools instead; **23***they exchanged the glory of the immortal God for images representing mortal man, birds, beasts, and snakes. **24***In consequence, God delivered them up in their lusts to unclean practices; they engaged in the mutual degradation of their bodies, **25**these men who exchanged the truth of God for a lie and worshiped and served the creature rather than the Creator— blessed be he forever, amen! **26**God therefore delivered them up to disgraceful passions. Their women exchanged natural intercourse for unnatural, **27**and the men gave up natural intercourse with women and burned with lust for one another. Men did shameful things with men, and thus received in their own persons the penalty for their perversity. **28**They did not see fit to acknowledge God, so God delivered them up to their own depraved sense to do what is unseemly. **29**They are filled with every kind of wickedness: maliciousness, greed, ill will, envy, murder, bickering, deceit, craftiness. They are gossips **30**and slanderers, they hate God, are insolent, haughty, boastful, ingenious in their wrongdoing and rebellious toward their parents. **31**One sees in them men without conscience, without loyalty, without affection, without pity. **32**They know God's just decree that all who do such things deserve death; yet they not only do them but approve them in others.

---

† Jesus a "life-giving spirit" (1 Cor 15, 45), able to communicate the Spirit to those who believe in him. This is the power which he now exercises as exalted Son of God.

1, 5: Paul recalls his apostolic office, implying that the Romans know something of his history.

1, 16f: The principal theme of the letter is salvation through faith. *I am not ashamed of the gospel:* a reminder of the criticism which Jews and Gentiles leveled against the doctrine of the crucified Savior; cf 1 Cor 1, 23f. Paul affirms, however, that it is precisely through the crucifixion and resurrection of Jesus that God chose to manifest his saving will and power. The apostle appeals through Jesus and his teaching for a faith to be held by all the world.

1, 17: *In the gospel is revealed the justice of God which begins and ends with faith:* the gospel is concerned with Jesus, in whom God has made known his saving presence and justice in history. Through Jesus, God offers the gift of faith, which makes his saving action effective in man. It manifests God's supremacy over man and his destiny, and likewise moves man to respond to the divine generosity. Faith makes clear the purpose and meaning of the Old Testament, revealing through the history of Israel the inability of man to effect his salvation in terms of covenant law.

1, 18-32: The conversion of the Gentiles through the gospel preaching constituted the divine indictment against paganism, which error had benighted and moral depravity had corrupted. It was the evil will of the pagan world that provoked the divine anger and abandonment (v 18). Contrary to nature itself which provides evidence of God's existence, power, and divinity through creation (19f), pagan society misread the evidence, fashioned gods of its own that could not exert any moral restraint, and freely indulged its perverse desires through every kind of wickedness (21-32; cf Wis 13, 1—14, 31).

*   8: 16, 19; 1 Thes 1, 8.   20: Wis 13, 1-9;
     10: 1 Thes 2, 17.   Acts 17, 24-29;
     13: Acts 19, 21.   1 Cor 1, 21.
     17: Hb 2, 4; Gal 3, 11;   21: Is 5, 21; 1 Cor 1, 19f.
          Heb 10, 38.   23: Jer 2, 11.
                                   24: Wis 12, 24; 13, 10f;
                                   Eph 4, 19.

God's Just Judgment

2 **1*****†**THAT is why every one of you who judges another is inexcusable. By your judgment you convict yourself, since you do the very same things. **2**"We know that God's judgment on men who do such things is just." **3**Do you suppose, then, that you will escape his judgment, you who condemn these things in others yet do them yourself? **4**Or do you presume on his kindness and forbearance? Do you not know that God's kindness is an invitation to you to repent? **5***In spite of this, your hard and impenitent heart is storing up retribution for that day of wrath when the just judgment of God will be revealed, **6**when he will repay every man for what he has done: **7**eternal life to those who strive for glory, honor, and immortality by patiently doing right; **8**wrath and fury to those who selfishly disobey the truth and obey wickedness. **9**Yes, affliction and anguish will come upon every man who has done evil, the Jew first, then the Greek. **10**But there will be glory, honor, and peace for everyone who has done good, likewise the Jew first, then the Greek. **11***With God there is no favoritism.

Judgment by the Interior Law

12Sinners who do not have the law will perish without reference to it; sinners bound by the law will be judged in accordance with it. **13***For it is not those who hear the law who are just in the sight of God; it is those who keep it who will be declared just. **14**When Gentiles who do not have the law keep it as by instinct, these men although without the law serve as a law for themselves. **15**They show that the demands of the law are written in their hearts. Their conscience bears witness together with that law, and their thoughts will accuse or defend them **16**on the day when, in accordance with the gospel I preach, God will pass judgment on the secrets of men through Christ Jesus.

Judgment by the Mosaic Law

17Let us suppose you bear the name of "Jew" and rely firmly on the law and pride yourself on God. **18**Instructed by the law, you know his will and are able to make sound judgments on disputed points. **19**You feel certain that you can guide the blind and enlighten those in darkness, **20**that you can discipline the foolish and teach the simple, because in the law you have at hand a clear pattern of knowledge and truth. **21***Now then, teacher of others, are you failing to teach yourself? You who preach against stealing, do you steal? **22**You who forbid adultery, do you commit adultery? You who abhor idols, do you rob temples? **23**You who pride yourself on the law, do you dishonor God by

breaking the law? **24***As Scripture says, "On your account the name of God is held in contempt among the Gentiles."

25*Circumcision, to be sure, has value if you observe the law, but if you break it you might as well be uncircumcised! **26***Again, if an uncircumcised person keeps the precepts of the law, will he not be considered circumcised? **27**If a man who is uncircumcised keeps the law, he will pass judgment on you who, with your written law and circumcision, break it. **28**Appearance does not make a Jew. True circumcision is not a sign in the flesh. **29***He is a real Jew who is one inwardly, and true circumcision is of the heart; its source is the spirit, not the letter. Such a one receives his praise, not from men, but from God.

Answers to Objections

3 **1**WHAT is the advantage, then, of being a Jew, and what value is there in circumcision? **2**The answer is, much in every respect. First of all, the Jews were entrusted with the words of God. **3***You may ask, what if some of them have not believed? Will not their unbelief put an end to God's faithfulness? **4***Of course not! God must be proved true even though every man be proved a liar, so that, as Scripture says,

"You shall be vindicated in what you say,
   and win out when you are judged."

5*But if our wrongdoing provides proof of God's justice, what are we to say? "Is not God unjust when he inflicts punishment?" (I speak in a merely human way.) **6**Assuredly not! If that were so, how could God judge the world? **7**Another question: If my falsehood brings to light God's truth and thus promotes his glory, why must I be condemned as a sinner? **8***Or why may we not do evil that good may come of it? This is the very thing that some slanderously accuse us of teaching; but they will get what they deserve.

Universal Bondage of Sin

9*Well, then, do we find ourselves in a position of superiority? Not entirely. We have already brought the charge against Jews and Greeks alike that they

---

† 2, 1—3, 9: The key to this passage is in the final verse: *We have already brought the charge against Jews and Greeks alike that they are under the domination of sin.* This judgment is based on the doctrine of universal salvation through the redemptive death of Christ. The Jew cannot condemn the sins of Gentiles without implicitly condemning himself (2, 1-11). He cannot reasonably demand from them the standard of conduct inculcated in the Old Testament since God did not address its revelation to them. Rather, God gave the Gentile the law of reason and conscience by which he was to be judged (2, 12-16). Not mere possession of the law by Jew or Gentile, but observance of it, is evidence of virtue (2, 17-29). Paul responds to the objection that his teaching on the sinfulness of all humanity detracts from the religious privileges of Israel, by stressing that the Jew always remained the vehicle of God's revelation despite his sins. His privileges depend, not on his own attainments, but on the fidelity of God (3, 1-4).

❉
2/1: Mt 7, 1.
  5: Acts 7, 51.
 11: Dt 10, 17; Acts 10, 34.
 13: Lk 8, 21; Jas 1, 22-25.
 21: Ps 50, 16-21; Mt 23, 3f.
 24: Is 52, 5; Ez 36, 20.
 25: 1 Cor 7, 19; Gal 5, 3.
 26: Jer 9, 24f.
 29: Jer 4, 4.
3/3: Ps 89, 30-37;
   2 Tm 2, 13.
 4: Ps 116, 11.
 5: Jb 34, 12-17.
 8: 6, 1.15.
 9: Sir 8, 5.

are under the domination of sin. [10]It is as Scripture says:

> "There is no just man, not even one;
> [11]*there is no one who understands,
>   no one in search of God.
> [12]All have taken the wrong course,
>   all alike have become worthless;
>   not one of them acts uprightly, no, not one.
> [13]*Their throats are open tombs;
>   they use their tongues to deceive;
>   The venom of asps lies behind their lips.
> [14]*Their mouths are full of curses and bitterness.
> [15]*Swiftly run their feet to shed blood;
>   [16]ruin and misery strew their course.
> [17]The path of peace is unknown to them;
>   [18]*the fear of God is not before their eyes."

[19]We know that everything the law says is addressed to those who are under its authority. This means that every mouth is silenced and the whole world stands convicted before God, [20]*since no one will be justified in God's sight through observance of the law; the law does nothing but point out what is sinful.

III: SALVATION THROUGH FAITH IN CHRIST

Justice apart from the Law

[21]†BUT NOW THE JUSTICE OF GOD has been manifested apart from the law, even though both law and prophets bear witness to it—[22]that justice of God which works through faith in Jesus Christ for all who believe. [23]All men have sinned and are deprived of the glory of God. [24]*All men are now undeservedly justified by the gift of God, through the redemption wrought in Christ Jesus. [25]*Through his blood, God made him the means of expiation for all who believe. He did so to manifest his own justice, for the sake of remitting sins committed in the past—[26]to manifest his justice in the present, by way of forbearance, so that he might be just and might justify those who believe in Jesus.

[27]*What occasion is there then for boasting? It is ruled out. By what law, the law of works? Not at all! By the law of faith. [28]*For we hold that a man is justified by faith apart from observance of the law. [29]Does God belong to the Jews alone? Is he not also the God of the Gentiles? Yes, of the Gentiles, too. [30]It is the same God who justifies the circumcised and the uncircumcised on the basis of faith. [31]*†Are we then abolishing the law by means of faith? Not at all! On the contrary, we are confirming the law.

Abraham Justified by Faith

4 [1]*†WHAT, then, shall we say of Abraham, our ancestor according to the flesh? [2]Certainly if Abraham was justified by his deeds he has grounds for boasting, but not in God's view; [3]*for what does Scripture say? "Abraham believed God, and it was credited to him as justice." [4]Now, when a man works, his wages are not regarded as a favor but as his due. [5]But when a man does nothing, yet believes in him who justifies the sinful, his faith is credited as justice. [6]Thus David congratulates the man to whom God credits justice without requiring deeds:

> [7]*"Blest are they whose iniquities are forgiven,
>   whose sins are covered over.
> [8]Blest is the man to whom the Lord
>   imputes no guilt."

[9]Does this blessedness apply only to the circumcised, or to the uncircumcised as well? For we say that Abraham's faith was "credited as justice." [10]What were the circumstances in which it was credited? Was it after he was circumcised or before? It was before. [11]*In fact, he received the sign of circumcision as a seal attesting to the justice received through faith while he was still uncircumcised. Thus he was to be the father of all the uncircumcised who believe, so that for them too faith might be credited as justice, [12]as well as the father of those circumcised who are not merely so but who follow the path of faith which Abraham walked while still uncircumcised.

Inheritance through Faith

[13]*Certainly the promise made to Abraham and his descendants that they would inherit the world did not depend on the law; it was made in view of the justice that comes from faith. [14]If only those who observe the law are heirs, then faith becomes an empty word and the promise loses its meaning. [15]*Indeed, the law serves only to bring down wrath, for where there is no law there is no transgression. [16]Hence, all depends on faith, everything is a grace. Thus the promise holds true for all Abraham's descendants, not only for those

---

† 3, 21-31: *The justice of God* is his mercy whereby he declares guilty man innocent and makes him so. He does this, not as a result of the law, but *apart from it* (v 21); not because of any merit of man, but through forgiveness of his sins (v 24), in virtue of *the redemption wrought in Christ Jesus* for all who believe (22.24f). No man can boast of his own holiness, since it is God's free gift (v 27), both to the Jew who practices circumcision out of faith, and to the Gentile who accepts faith without the Old Testament religious culture symbolized by circumcision (29f).

3, 31: *We are confirming the law:* placing it in its proper perspective. The Old Testament law, unable to effect salvation, was observed out of the motive of faith. Now, through the revelation of Christ, the importance of faith is manifest.

4, 1-25: This is an expanded treatment of the significance of Abraham's faith, which Paul discusses in Gal 3, 6-18; see notes there.

---

*   11: Ps 14, 1ff.   28: 5, 1.
13: Pss 5, 10; 140, 4.   31: Mt 5, 17.
14: Ps 10, 7.   4/1: Gal 3, 6-9.
15: Is 59, 7; Prv 1, 16.   3: Gn 15, 6;
18: Ps 36, 2.   Jas 2, 14.20-24.
20: 7, 7.   7: Ps 32, 1f.
24: 5, 2.   11: Gn 17, 10f.
25: Acts 17, 30; 1 Jn 4, 10.   13: Gal 3, 16ff.
27: 1 Cor 1, 29.   15: 5, 13.

who have the law but for all who have his faith. He is father of us all, [17]*which is why Scripture says, "I have made you father of many nations." Yes, he is our father in the sight of God in whom he believed, the God who restores the dead to life and calls into being those things which had not been. [18]*Hoping against hope, Abraham believed and so became the father of many nations, just as it was once told him, "Numerous as this shall your descendants be." [19]Without growing weak in faith he thought of his own body, which was as good as dead (for he was nearly a hundred years old), and of the dead womb of Sarah. [20]*Yet he never questioned or doubted God's promise; rather, he was strengthened in faith and gave glory to God, [21]fully persuaded that God could do whatever he had promised. [22]Thus his faith was credited to him as justice.

[23]The words, "It was credited to him," were not written with him alone in view; [24]they were intended for us too. For our faith will be credited to us also if we believe in him who raised Jesus our Lord from the dead, [25]*the Jesus who was handed over to death for our sins and raised up for our justification.

Faith, Hope and Love

5 [1]*†NOW that we have been justified by faith, we are at peace with God through our Lord Jesus Christ. [2]Through him we have gained access by faith to the grace in which we now stand, and we boast of our hope for the glory of God. [3]But not only that— we even boast of our afflictions! We know that affliction makes for endurance, [4]*and endurance for tested virtue, and tested virtue for hope. [5]*And this hope will not leave us disappointed, because the love of God has been poured out in our hearts through the Holy Spirit who has been given to us. [6]At the appointed time, when we were still powerless, Christ died for us godless men. [7]It is rare that anyone should lay down his life for a just man, though it is barely possible that for a good man someone may have the courage to die. [8]*It is precisely in this that God proves his love for us: that while we were still sinners, Christ died for us. [9]*Now that we have been justified by his blood, it is all the more certain that we shall be saved by him from God's wrath. [10]*For if, when we were God's enemies, we were reconciled to him by the death of his Son, it is all the more certain that we who have been reconciled will be saved by his life. [11]Not only that; we go so far as to make God our boast through our Lord Jesus Christ, through whom we have now received reconciliation.

Mankind's Sin through Adam

[12]*†Therefore, just as through one man sin entered the world and with sin death, death thus coming to all men inasmuch as all sinned—[13]before the law there was sin in the world, even though sin is not imputed when there is no law—[14]I say, from Adam to Moses death reigned, even over those who had not sinned by breaking a precept as did Adam, that type of the man to come.

Grace and Life through Christ

[15]But the gift is not like the offense. For if by the offense of the one man all died, much more did the grace of God and the gracious gift of one man, Jesus Christ, abound for all. [16]The gift is entirely different from the sin committed by the one man. In the first case, the sentence followed upon one offense and brought condemnation, but in the second, the gift came after many offenses and brought acquittal. [17]If death began its reign through one man because of his offense, much more shall those who receive the overflowing grace and gift of justice live and reign through the one man, Jesus Christ.

[18]To sum up, then: just as a single offense brought condemnation to all men, a single righteous act brought all men acquittal and life. [19]*Just as through one man's disobedience all became sinners, so through one man's obedience all shall become just.

Purpose of the Law

[20]*The law came in order to increase offenses; but despite the increase of sin, grace has far surpassed it, [21]so that, as sin reigned through death, grace may reign by way of justice leading to eternal life, through Jesus Christ our Lord.

IV: JUSTIFICATION AND THE CHRISTIAN LIFE

Death to Sin, Life in God

6 [1]*†WHAT, THEN, ARE WE TO SAY? "Let us continue in sin that grace may abound"? [2]Certainly not! How can we who died to sin go on living in it?

---

† 5, 1-5: A development of the doctrine of justification by faith. It is God who effects man's justification through Christ. This gives the believer a firm confidence in his salvation (5, 1f). The hardships of life should merely teach him patience and strengthen his hope (3f), which will not disappoint him because the Holy Spirit dwells in his heart and infuses into it God's love (v 5).

5, 12-21: Paul reflects on the sin of Adam (Gn 3, 1-13) in the light of the redemptive mystery of Christ. Sin, i. e., man's guilt before God which merited the punishment of death and loss of grace, began with Adam and infected the entire human race (v 12). Through the Old Testament law the sinfulness of mankind, operative from the beginning (v 13), became abundantly manifest (v 20). The judgments in 5, 12ff are based on the mystery of man's redemption through the death of Christ. Paul contrasts the divergent effects of Adam and of Christ on the human race (15-21) to show the culmination in Christ of what is revealed concerning man's condition and destiny.

6, 1-11: Paul denies that sin calls forth the grace of God; it is rather the divine generosity that is the source of the gift of

---

❋

    17: Gn 17, 50.
    18: Gn 15, 5.
    20: Heb 11, 11.
    25: Is 53, 6.11;
        1 Cor 15, 17; 1 Pt 1, 3.
  5/1: Eph 3, 12.
     4: 2 Cor 12, 9f; Jas 1, 2ff;
        1 Pt 4, 13f.

     5: 8, 14ff.
     8: 1 Jn 4, 10.19.
     9: 8, 32.
   10: 2 Cor 5, 18.
   12: Wis 2, 24.
   19: Is 53, 11; Phil 2, 8f.
   20: 7, 7f.
 6/1: 3, 8.

³*Are you not aware that we who were baptized into Christ Jesus were baptized into his death? ⁴Through baptism into his death we were buried with him, so that, just as Christ was raised from the dead by the glory of the Father, we too might live a new life. ⁵*If we have been united with him through likeness to his death, so shall we be through a like resurrection. ⁶This we know: our old self was crucified with him so that the sinful body might be destroyed and we might be slaves to sin no longer. ⁷A man who is dead has been freed from sin. ⁸*If we have died with Christ, we believe that we are also to live with him. ⁹*We know that Christ, once raised from the dead, will never die again; death has no more power over him. ¹⁰His death was death to sin, once for all; his life is life for God. ¹¹In the same way, you must consider yourselves dead to sin but alive for God in Christ Jesus.

¹²†Do not, therefore, let sin rule your mortal body and make you obey its lusts; ¹³*no more shall you offer the members of your body to sin as weapons for evil. Rather, offer yourselves to God as men who have come back from the dead to life, and your bodies to God as weapons for justice. ¹⁴Sin will no longer have power over you; you are now under grace, not under the law.

¹⁵What does all this lead to? Just because we are not under the law but under grace, are we free to sin? By no means! ¹⁶*You must realize that, when you offer yourselves to someone as obedient slaves, you are the slaves of the one you obey, whether yours is the slavery of sin, which leads to death, or of obedience, which leads to justice. ¹⁷Thanks be to God, though once you were slaves of sin, you sincerely obeyed that rule of teaching which was imparted to you; ¹⁸freed from your sin, you became slaves of justice. ¹⁹(I use the following example from human affairs because of your weak human nature.) Just as formerly you enslaved your bodies to impurity and licentiousness for their degradation, make them now the servants of justice for their sanctification. ²⁰†When you were slaves of sin, you had freedom from justice. ²¹*What benefit did you then enjoy? Things you are now ashamed of, all of them tending toward death. ²²But now that you are freed from sin and have become slaves of God, your benefit is sanctification as you tend toward eternal life. ²³*The wages of sin is death, but the gift of God is eternal life in Christ Jesus our Lord.

Freedom from the Law

7 ¹†ARE you not aware, my brothers (I am speaking to men who know what law is), that the law has power over a man only so long as he lives? ²*For example, a married woman is bound to her husband by law while he lives, but if he dies she is released from the law regarding husbands. ³She will be called an adulteress if, while her husband is still alive, she gives herself to another. But if her husband dies she is freed from that law, and does not commit adultery by consorting with another man. ⁴In the same way, my brothers, you died to the law through the body of Christ, that you might belong to that Other who was raised from the dead, so that we might bear fruit for God. ⁵When we were in the flesh, the sinful passions roused by the law worked in our members and we bore fruit for death. ⁶*Now we have been released from the law—for we have died to what bound us—and we serve in the new spirit, not the antiquated letter.

Knowledge of Sin through the Law

⁷*†What follows from what I have said? That the law is the same as sin? Certainly not! Yet it was only through the law that I came to know sin. I should never have known what evil desire was unless the law had said, "You shall not covet." ⁸*Sin seized that opportunity; it used the commandment to rouse in me every kind of evil desire. Without law sin is dead, ⁹and at first I lived without law. Then the commandment came; with it sin came to life, ¹⁰and I died. The commandment that should have led to life brought me death. ¹¹*Sin found its opportunity and used the commandment: first to deceive me, then to kill me. ¹²*Yet the law is holy and the commandment is holy and just and good.

Sin and Death

¹³*†Did this good thing then become death for me? Not that either! Rather, sin, in order to be seen clearly

---

† grace (3, 22; cf note on Mk 1, 9ff). Grace is bestowed at baptism and produces a true renewal. It makes the baptized person capable of responding effectively to the dictates of his conscience concerning faith and life. This renewal is the prelude to the Christian's bodily resurrection and admission to eternal life (5, 21).

6, 12-19: While the Christian remains in this mortal life, the power of sin in him is not fully overcome; his personal effort under the influence of grace is required to surmount the weakness remaining in him.

6, 20-23: The two ways of life, intrinsically opposed, produce opposite results: false *freedom from justice* brings enslavement by sin and the punishment of death; freedom from sin begets sanctification and *eternal life in Christ Jesus.*

7, 1-6: Paul reflects upon the fact that the Christian has a different understanding of the law because of his faith in Christ. Law binds the living, not the dead, as exemplified in marriage, which binds in life but is dissolved through death. Similarly the Christian, who through baptism has died with Christ to sin, is freed from the law that occasioned sin and its punishment of death. Having risen with Christ, he is joined to him in newness of life so as to *bear fruit for God.*

7, 7-12: The apostle defends himself against the charge of identifying law with sin. Sin does not exist in law but rather in man, whose sinful inclinations are not overcome by the mere proclamation of law.

7, 13-25: The man who does not experience the justifying grace of God recognizes a rift between his reasoned desire for the goodness of the law and his actual performance contrary to

✻

3: Gal 3, 27; Col 2, 12; 1 Pt 3, 21f.	23: Gn 2, 17; Gal 6, 7ff; Jas 1, 15.
5: Phil 3, 10f.	7/2: 1 Cor 7, 39.
8: Acts 13, 34.	6: 2 Cor 3, 6.
9: 1 Cor 15, 26; 2 Tm 1, 10; Rv 1, 18.	7: 3, 20; Ex 20, 17; Dt 5, 21.
13: Col 3, 5.	8: 1 Cor 15, 56.
16: Jn 8, 31; 2 Pt 2, 19.	11: Gn 3, 13.
21: 8, 6; Prv 12, 28.	12: 1 Tm 1, 8.
	13: 5, 20.

as sin, used what was good to bring about my death. It did so that, by misusing the commandment, sin might go to the limit of sinfulness. [14]We know that the law is spiritual, whereas I am weak flesh sold into the slavery of sin. [15]I cannot even understand my own actions. I do not do what I want to do but what I hate. [16]When I act against my own will, by that very fact I agree that the law is good. [17]This indicates that it is not I who do it but sin which resides in me. [18]I know that no good dwells in me, that is, in my flesh; the desire to do right is there but not the power. [19]What happens is that I do, not the good I will to do, but the evil I do not intend. [20]But if I do what is against my will, it is not I who do it, but sin which dwells in me. [21]This means that even though I want to do what is right, a law that leads to wrongdoing is always ready at hand. [22]My inner self agrees with the law of God, [23]but I see in my body's members another law at war with the law of my mind; this makes me the prisoner of the law of sin in my members. [24]What a wretched man I am! Who can free me from this body under the power of death? [25]All praise to God, through Jesus Christ our Lord! So with my mind I serve the law of God but with my flesh the law of sin.

The Flesh and the Spirit

8 [1†]THERE is no condemnation now for those who are in Christ Jesus. [2]The law of the spirit, the spirit of life in Christ Jesus, has freed you from the law of sin and death. [3*]The law was powerless because of its weakening by the flesh. Then God sent his Son in the likeness of sinful flesh as a sin offering, thereby condemning sin in the flesh, [4]so that the just demands of the law might be fulfilled in us who live, not according to the flesh, but according to the spirit. [5]Those who live according to the flesh are intent on the things of the flesh, those who live according to the spirit, on those of the spirit. [6]The tendency of the flesh is toward death but that of the spirit toward life and peace. [7]The flesh in its tendency is at enmity with God; it is not subject to God's law. Indeed it cannot be; [8*]those who are in the flesh cannot please God. [9*]But you are not in the flesh; you are in the spirit, since the Spirit of God dwells in you. If anyone does not have the Spirit of Christ, he does not belong to Christ. [10]If Christ is in you, the body is dead because of sin, while the spirit lives because of justice. [11]If the Spirit of him who raised Jesus from the dead dwells in you, then he who raised Christ from the dead will bring your mortal bodies to life also, through his Spirit dwelling in you.

[12]We are debtors, then, my brothers—but not to the flesh, so that we should live according to the flesh. [13]If you live according to the flesh, you will die; but if by the spirit you put to death the evil deeds of the body, you will live.

Sons of God through Adoption

[14†]All who are led by the Spirit of God are sons of God. [15*]You did not receive a spirit of slavery leading you back into fear, but a spirit of adoption through which we cry out, "Abba!" (that is, "Father"). [16*]The Spirit himself gives witness with our spirit that we are children of God. [17]But if we are children, we are heirs as well: heirs of God, heirs with Christ, if only we suffer with him so as to be glorified with him.

Destiny of Glory

[18†]I consider the sufferings of the present to be as nothing compared with the glory to be revealed in us. [19]Indeed, the whole created world eagerly awaits the revelation of the sons of God. [20]Creation was made subject to futility, not of its own accord but by him who once subjected it; yet not without hope, [21*]because the world itself will be freed from its slavery to corruption and share in the glorious freedom of the children of God. [22*]Yes, we know that all creation groans and is in agony even until now. [23]Not only that, but we ourselves, although we have the Spirit as first fruits, groan inwardly while we await the redemption of our bodies. [24]In hope we were saved. But hope is not hope if its object is seen; how is it possible for one to hope for what he sees? [25]And hoping for what we cannot see means awaiting it with patient endurance.

[26]The Spirit too helps us in our weakness, for we do not know how to pray as we ought; but the Spirit himself makes intercession for us with groanings that cannot be expressed in speech. [27]He who searches hearts knows what the Spirit means, for the Spirit intercedes for the saints as God himself wills.

God's Love for Man

[28*†]We know that God makes all things work together for the good of those who have been called ac-

---

† the law. These two are found to be basically opposed. Unable to free himself from the slavery of sin and the power of death, he can only be rescued from defeat in the conflict by the power of God's grace working through Jesus Christ.

8, 1-13: This is a reflection on the redemptive work of Christ mentioned in 7, 25. The Christian is freed from God's judgment of condemnation by reason of Christ's death for the sins of humanity (1-4). With *the just demands of the law* thus fulfilled, he must live now, not *according to the flesh, . . . at enmity with God*, threatened with death, but *according to the spirit* which dwells in him and leads to *life and peace* (5-17).

8, 14-17: The Christian, by reason of the Spirit's presence within him, enjoys not only new life but also a new relationship to God, that of adopted son and heir through Christ, whose sufferings and glory he shares.

8, 18-27: The glory which the believer is destined to share with Christ far exceeds the sufferings of the present life. Paul considers the created world to be linked to human destiny through its solidarity with man. As it shares in man's penalty of corruption through sin, so also it will share in his benefits of redemption and future glory (19ff). At present both must suffer until they achieve through hope and patient endurance the full harvest of the Spirit's presence, of which they now possess the first fruits or guarantee.

8, 28ff: These verses outline the Christian vocation as it was designed by God: *to share the image of his Son, that the Son*

❋
8/3: 2 Cor 5, 21; Gal 3, 13.
    8: 1 Jn 2, 16.
    9: 1 Cor 3, 16.
   15: Jn 1, 12; Gal 4, 6.

16: Gal 3, 26-29.
21: 2 Pt 3, 12f; Rv 21, 1.
22: 2 Cor 5, 2-5.
28f: Eph 1, 4-14.

cording to his decree. [29]Those whom he foreknew he predestined to share the image of his Son, that the Son might be the first-born of many brothers. [30]Those he predestined he likewise called; those he called he also justified; and those he justified he in turn glorified. [31]†What shall we say after that? If God is for us, who can be against us? [32]*Is it possible that he who did not spare his own Son but handed him over for the sake of us all will not grant us all things besides? [33]*Who shall bring a charge against God's chosen ones? God, who justifies? [34]*Who shall condemn them? Christ Jesus, who died or rather was raised up, who is at the right hand of God and who intercedes for us?

Indomitable Love for Christ

[35]Who will separate us from the love of Christ? Trial, or distress, or persecution, or hunger, or nakedness, or danger, or the sword? [36]*As Scripture says: "For your sake we are being slain all the day long; we are looked upon as sheep to be slaughtered." [37]Yet in all this we are more than conquerors because of him who has loved us. [38]For I am certain that neither death nor life, neither angels nor principalities, neither the present nor the future, nor powers, [39]neither height nor depth nor any other creature, will be able to separate us from the love of God that comes to us in Christ Jesus, our Lord.

V: ISRAEL'S PRESENT REJECTION

Grief for the Jews

9 [1]†I SPEAK THE TRUTH IN CHRIST: I do not lie. My conscience bears me witness in the Holy Spirit [2]that their is great grief and constant pain in my heart. [3]Indeed, I could even wish to be separated from Christ for the sake of my brothers, my kinsmen [4]the Israelites. Theirs were the adoption, the glory, the covenants, the law-giving, the worship, and the promises; [5]theirs were the patriarchs, and from them came the Messiah (I speak of his human origins). Blessed forever be God who is over all! Amen.

God's Free Choice

[6]*†Not that God's word has failed. For not all Israelites are true Israelites [7]nor are all Abraham's descendants his children, but as Scripture says, "Through Isaac shall your descendants be called." [8]That means that it is not the children of the flesh who are the children of God; it is the children of the promise who are to be considered descendants. [9]*And this was the promise: "I will return at this time, and Sarah shall have a son." [10]Not only that; for when Rebecca had conceived twin children by one man, our father Isaac— [11]while they were yet unborn and had done neither good nor evil, in order that God's decree might stand fast [12]*"not by works but by the favor of him who calls"—God said to her, "The older shall serve the younger." [13]*It is just as Scripture says, "I have loved Jacob and hated Esau." [14]†What are we to say, then? That God is unjust? Not at all! [15]He says to Moses, "I will show mercy to whomever I choose; I will have pity on whomever I wish." [16]*So it is not a question of man's willing or doing but of God's mercy. [17]*Scripture says to Pharaoh, "This is why I raised you up: that through you I might show my power, and my name might be proclaimed throughout all the earth." [18]*In other words, God has mercy on whom he wishes, and whom he wishes he makes obdurate.

[19]*†You will say to me, "Why, then, does he find fault? For who can oppose his will?" [20]*Friend, who are you to answer God back? Does something molded say to its molder, "Why did you make me like this?" [21]Does not a potter have the right to make from the same lump of clay one vessel for a lofty purpose and

---

† *might be the first-born of many brothers.* In terms of God's initiative, the call in its totality consists in the exercise of the divine foreknowledge, God's predetermination, God's gift of the call, his sanctification and glorification of the Christian. Thus all that happens to one who loves God is directed by God toward the achievement of that *good* which is likeness to God's Son through grace and glory.

8, 31-39: The all-conquering power of God's love has overcome every obstacle to man's salvation and every threat of his separation from God. That power manifested itself fully when God delivered up to death even his own Son for our salvation. Through him, the Christian can overcome all his afflictions and trials.

9, 1—11, 36: Israel's unbelief and its rejection of Jesus as Savior astonished and puzzled Christians. It constituted a serious theological problem for them in view of God's specific preparation of Israel for the advent of the Messiah. Paul addresses himself here to the essential question of how the divine plan could be frustrated by Israel's unbelief.

9, 1-5: The apostle speaks in strong terms of the depth of his grief over the unbelief of his own people. He would willingly undergo a curse himself for the sake of their coming to the knowledge of Christ (v 3; cf Lv 27, 28f). His love of them derives from God's choice of them and the spiritual benefits he bestowed on them (4f).

9, 6-13: Israel's unbelief reflects the mystery of the divine election that was always operative within it. Mere natural descent from Abraham did not ensure the full possession of the divine gifts; it was God's sovereign prerogative to bestow this fullness upon, or to withhold it from, whomsoever he wished; cf Mt 3, 9; Jn 3, 3f. The choice of Jacob over Esau is a case in point.

9, 14-18: The principle of divine election does not mean that God is unfair in his dealings with men. Rather, he reveals in this way that the gift of faith is the enactment of his mercy (v 16). God raised up Moses to display his mercy and Pharaoh to display his severity in punishing those who obstinately oppose him.

9, 19-29: The apostle responds to the objection that if God rules over faith through the principle of divine election, he cannot then accuse the unbelieving man of sin (v 19). For Paul, this objection is in the last analysis a manifestation of human insolence, and his "answer" is less an explanation of God's ways than the rejection of an argument which places man on the level of God.

✿
32: Jn 3, 16.	13: Mal 1, 3.
33f: Is 50, 8f.	16: Ex 33, 19.
34: Heb 7, 25.	17: Ex 9, 16.
36: Ps 44, 23; 2 Tm 3, 12.	18: Ex 7, 3.
9/6f: Gn 21, 12; Mt 3, 9.	19: 3, 7; Wis 12, 12.
9: Gn 18, 10.	20f: Wis 15, 7; Is 29, 16;
12: 11, 5f; Gn 25, 23f.	45, 9; Jer 18, 6.

another for a humble one? **22***What if God, wishing to show his wrath and make known his power, has endured with much patience vessels fit for wrath, ready to be destroyed, **23**in order to make known the riches of his glory toward the vessels for mercy which he prepared for glory—**24**I am speaking about us whom he called, not only from the Jews, but from among the Gentiles.

Witness of the Old Testament

25*As it says in the Book of Hosea: "Those who were not my people I will call 'my people,' and those who were not loved I will call 'Beloved'; **26***in the very place where it was said to them, 'You are not my people,' they shall be called sons of the living God." **27***Isaiah cries out, referring to Israel, "Though the number of the Israelites should be as the sands of the sea, only the remnant will be saved, **28**for quickly and decisively will the Lord execute sentence upon the earth." **29***It is just as Isaiah predicted: "Unless the Lord of hosts had left us a remnant, we should have become as Sodom, we should be like Gomorrah."

Israel's Unbelief

30*†How, then, shall we put it? That the Gentiles, who were not seeking justice, attained it—the justice which comes from faith—**31**while Israel, seeking a law from which justice would come, did not arrive at that law? **32***And why did it not? Because justice comes from faith, not from works. They stumbled over the stumbling stone, **33***as Scripture says: "Behold, I am placing in Zion a stone to make men stumble and a rock to make them fall; but he who believes in him will not be put to shame."

10 **1**†BROTHERS, my heart's desire, my prayer to God for the Israelites, is that they may be saved. **2**Indeed, I can testify that they are zealous for God though their zeal is unenlightened. **3**Unaware of God's justice and seeking to establish their own, they did not subject themselves to the justice of God. **4***Christ is the end of the law. Through him, justice comes to everyone who believes. **5***†Moses writes of the justice that comes from the law, "The one who observes the law shall live by it." **6***But of the justice that comes from faith he says, "Do not say in your heart, 'Who shall go up into heaven?' (that is, to bring Christ down), **7***or 'Who shall go down into the abyss?' (that is, to bring Christ up from the dead)." **8***What is it he does say? "The word is near you, on your lips and in your heart" (that is, the word of faith

which we preach). **9***For if you confess with your lips that Jesus is Lord, and believe in your heart that God raised him from the dead, you will be saved. **10**Faith in the heart leads to justification, confession on the lips to salvation. **11***Scripture says, "No one who believes in him will be put to shame." **12**Here there is no difference between Jew and Greek; all have the same Lord, rich in mercy toward all who call upon him. **13***"Everyone who calls on the name of the Lord will be saved."

14*†But how shall they call on him in whom they have not believed? And how can they believe unless they have heard of him? And how can they hear unless there is someone to preach? **15***And how can men preach unless they are sent? Scripture says, "How beautiful are the feet of those who announce good news!" **16***But not all have believed the gospel. Isaiah asks, "Lord, who has believed what he has heard from us?" **17**Faith, then, comes through hearing, and what is heard is the word of Christ. **18***I ask you, have they not heard? Certainly they have, for "their voice has sounded over the whole earth, and their words to the limits of the world." **19***I put the question again, did Israel really not understand? First of all, Moses says, "I will make you jealous of those who are not even a nation; with a senseless nation I will make you angry." **20***Then Isaiah says boldly, "I was found by those who were not seeking me; to those who were not looking for me I revealed myself." **21**But of Israel he says, "All day long I stretched out my hands to an unbelieving and contentious people."

Partial Rejection of Israel

11 **1***†I ask, then, has God rejected his people? Of course not! I myself am an Israelite, descended from Abraham, of the tribe of Benjamin. **2**No, God has not rejected his people whom he foreknew. Do you not know what Scripture says about Elijah,

---

† 9, 30-33: In the conversion of the Gentiles, and by contrast, of relatively few Jews, the Old Testament prophecies are seen to be fulfilled; cf 9, 25-29. Israel placed an unbalanced overemphasis on the literal observance of the law and was thus unwilling to accept the doctrine of justification by faith; the Gentiles were more open to this doctrine because to them the very idea of justification was new.

10, 1-4: Despite Israel's unbelief in Christ, Paul does not abandon hope for its salvation (v 1). Israel misunderstood the true nature of salvation (v 3), but retained its faith in God (v 4).

10, 5-13: In the past, Israel was promised particular benefits for observance of the law (v 5), but in Christ the law has been fulfilled (4f). It is faith in Jesus which is the source of God's saving action for Jew and Gentile alike (6-13).

10, 14-21: The gospel has been sufficiently proclaimed to Israel, which has adequately understood it, but, as in the past, has not accepted the prophetic message; cf Acts 7, 51ff.

11, 1-10: Though Israel has been unfaithful to the prophetic message of the gospel (10, 14-21), God remains faithful to Israel. Proof of the divine fidelity lies in the existence of the Judaeo-Christians like Paul himself. The unbelieving Jews have been blinded by the Christian teaching concerning the Messiah.

*

22: Wis 12, 20f.
25: Hos 2, 25.
26: 11, 5.
27: Is 10, 22f; Hos 2, 1.
29: Is 1, 9.
30: 10, 4.
32: Is 8, 14.
33: Is 28, 16; 1 Pt 2, 6ff.
10/4: 2 Cor 3, 14.
5: Gal 3, 12.
6: Dt 30, 12.
7: 1 Pt 3, 19.

8: Dt 30, 14.
9: 1 Cor 12, 3.
11: 9, 33; Is 28, 16.
13: Jl 3, 5; Acts 2, 21.
14: Acts 8, 31.
15: Is 52, 7.
16: Is 53, 1.
18: Ps 19, 5; Mt 24, 14.
19: 11, 1; Dt 32, 21.
20f: 9, 30; Is 65, 1f.
11/1f: 1 Sm 12, 22; Ps 94, 14.

how he pleaded with God against Israel? **3***"Lord, they have killed your prophets, they have torn down your altars; I alone am left and they are seeking my life." **4***How does God answer him? "I have left for myself seven thousand men who have not bowed the knee to Baal." **5**Just so, in the present time there is a remnant chosen by the grace of God. **6**But if the choice is by grace, it is not because of their works—otherwise grace would not be grace. **7**What then are we to say? Just this: Israel did not obtain what she was seeking, but those who were chosen did. The rest became blind, **8***as Scripture says: "God gave them a spirit of stupor; blind eyes and deaf ears, and it is so to this day." **9***David says: "Let their table become a snare and a trap, a stumbling stone and a retribution; **10**let their eyes be darkened so that they may not see. Bow down their back forever."

Israel's Fall the Gentiles' Salvation

11†I further ask, does their stumbling mean that they are forever fallen? Not at all! Rather, by their transgression salvation has come to the Gentiles to stir Israel to envy. **12**But if their transgression and their diminishing have meant riches for the Gentile world, how much more their full number!

13I say this now to you Gentiles: Inasmuch as I am the apostle of the Gentiles, I glory in my ministry, **14**trying to rouse my fellow Jews to envy and save some of them. **15**For if their rejection has meant reconciliation for the world, what will their acceptance mean? Nothing less than life from the dead! **16**†If the first fruits are consecrated, so too is the whole mass of dough, and if the root is consecrated, so too are the branches. **17**If some of the branches were cut off and you, a branch of the wild olive tree, have been grafted in among the others and have come to share in the rich root of the olive, do not boast against the branches. **18***If you do boast, remember that you do not support the root; the root supports you. **19**You will say, "Branches were cut off that I might be grafted in." **20**Well and good. They were cut off because of unbelief and you are there because of faith. Do not be haughty on that account, but fearful. **21**If God did not spare the natural branches, he will certainly not spare you.

22Consider the kindness and the severity of God—severity toward those who fell, kindness toward you, provided you remain in his kindness; if you do not, you too will be cut off. **23**And if the Jews do not remain in their unbelief they will be grafted back on, for God is able to do this. **24**If you were cut off from the natural wild olive and, contrary to nature, were grafted into the cultivated olive, so much the more will they who belong to it by nature be grafted into their own olive tree.

Israel's Final Conversion

25†Brothers, I do not want you to be ignorant of this mystery lest you be conceited: blindness has come upon part of Israel until the full number of Gentiles enter in, and then all Israel will be saved. **26***As Scripture says: "Out of Zion will come the deliverer who shall remove all impiety from Jacob; **27***and this is the covenant I will make with them when I take away their sins." **28**In respect to the gospel, the Jews are enemies of God for your sake; in respect to the election, they are beloved by him because of the patriarchs. **29***God's gifts and his call are irrevocable.

Triumph of God's Mercy

30Just as you were once disobedient to God and now have received mercy through their disobedience, **31**so they have become disobedient—since God wished to show you mercy—that they too may receive mercy. **32***God has imprisoned all in disobedience that he might have mercy on all.

33*†How deep are the riches and the wisdom and the knowledge of God! How inscrutable his judgments, how unsearchable his ways! **34***For "who has known the mind of the Lord? Or who has been his counselor? **35**Who has given him anything so as to deserve return?" **36***For from him and through him and for him all things are. To him be glory forever. Amen.

VI: THE DUTIES OF CHRISTIANS

Sacrifice of Body and Mind

12 **1**†AND NOW, BROTHERS, I BEG YOU through the mercy of God to offer your bodies as a living sacrifice holy and acceptable to God, your spiritual worship. **2**Do not conform yourselves to this age but be transformed by the renewal of your

---

† 11, 11-15: The unbelief of Israel has paved the way for the preaching of the gospel to the Gentiles and for their easier acceptance of it outside the context of Jewish culture. In God's design it should follow that Israel's ultimate acceptance of the gospel message will benefit the world even more than its original unbelief.

11, 16-24: Israel remains holy in the eyes of God and stands as a witness to the faith of the Old Testament because of the *first fruits* which *are consecrated,* i. e., the converted remnant, and the *root* which *is consecrated,* i. e., the patriarchs (v 16). The Jews' failure to believe in Christ is a warning to Gentile Christians to be on guard lest they themselves fail through loss of faith.

11, 25-32: In God's design, Israel's unbelief is being utilized to grant the light of faith to the Gentiles. Meanwhile, Israel remains dear to God, still the object of his special providence, the mystery of which will one day be revealed.

11, 33-36: This final reflection celebrates the wisdom of God's plan of salvation. As Paul has indicated throughout these chapters, both Jew and Gentile, despite the religious recalcitrance of each, have received the gift of faith. Thus the divine plan of salvation has become open and comprehensible to the whole human race.

12, 1—13, 14: This moral teaching expresses the necessary

✸
3: 1 Kgs 19, 10.14.	27: Jer 31, 33.
4: 1 Kgs 19, 18.	29: Nm 23, 19; Is 54, 10.
8: Dt 29, 3; Is 29, 10;	32: Gal 3, 22.
Mt 13, 14.	33: Ps 139, 6.17f.
9f: Ps 69, 23f.	34f: Wis 9, 13; Is 40, 13;
18: 1 Cor 1, 31.	1 Cor 2, 11.
26f: Is 59, 20f.	36: 1 Cor 8, 6; Col 1, 16f.

mind, so that you may judge what is God's will, what is good, pleasing and perfect.

Many Members in One Body

3*Thus, in virtue of the favor given to me, I warn each of you not to think more highly of himself than he ought. Let him estimate himself soberly, in keeping with the measure of faith that God has apportioned him. **4***Just as each of us has one body with many members, and not all the members have the same function, **5***so too we, though many, are one body in Christ and individually members one of another. **6***We have gifts that differ according to the favor bestowed on each of us. One's gift may be prophecy; its use should be in proportion to his faith. **7**It may be the gift of ministry; it should be used for service. One who is a teacher should use his gift for teaching; **8**one with the power of exhortation should exhort. He who gives alms should do so generously; he who rules should exercise his authority with care; he who performs works of mercy should do so cheerfully.

Fraternal Charity

9*Your love must be sincere. Detest what is evil, cling to what is good. **10***Love one another with the affection of brothers. Anticipate each other in showing respect. **11**Do not grow slack but be fervent in spirit; he whom you serve is the Lord. **12**Rejoice in hope, be patient under trial, persevere in prayer. **13**Look on the needs of the saints as your own; be generous in offering hospitality. **14***Bless your persecutors; bless and do not curse them. **15***Rejoice with those who rejoice, weep with those who weep. **16***Have the same attitude toward all. Put away ambitious thoughts and associate with those who are lowly. Do not be wise in your own estimation. **17***Never repay injury with injury. See that your conduct is honorable in the eyes of all. **18**If possible, live peaceably with everyone. **19***Beloved, do not avenge yourselves; leave that to God's wrath, for it is written: "'Vengeance is mine; I will repay,' says the Lord." **20***But "if your enemy is hungry, feed him; if he is thirsty, give him something to drink; by doing this you will heap burning coals upon his head." **21**Do not be conquered by evil but conquer evil with good.

Obedience to Authority

13 **1***LET everyone obey the authorities that are over him, for there is no authority except from God, and all authority that exists is established by God. **2***As a consequence, the man who op-

poses authority rebels against the ordinance of God; those who resist thus shall draw condemnation down upon themselves. **3**Rulers cause no fear when a man does what is right but only when his conduct is evil. Do you wish to be free from the fear of authority? Do what is right and you will gain its approval, **4**for the ruler is God's servant to work for your good. Only if you do wrong ought you to be afraid. It is not without purpose that the ruler carries the sword; he is God's servant, to inflict his avenging wrath upon the wrongdoer. **5**You must obey, then, not only to escape punishment but also for conscience' sake. You pay taxes for the same reason, **6**magistrates being God's ministers who devote themselves to his service with unremitting care. **7***Pay each one his due: taxes to whom taxes are due; toll to whom toll is due; respect and honor to everyone who deserves them.

Love Fulfills the Law

8Owe no debt to anyone except the debt that binds us to love one another. He who loves his neighbor has fulfilled the law. **9***The commandments, "You shall not commit adultery; you shall not murder; you shall not steal; you shall not covet," and any other commandment there may be are all summed up in this, "You shall love your neighbor as yourself." **10***Love never wrongs the neighbor, hence love is the fulfillment of the law.

Christian Use of Time

11*Take care to do all these things, for you know the time in which we are living. It is now the hour for you to wake from sleep, for our salvation is closer than when we first accepted the faith. **12***The night is far spent; the day draws near. Let us cast off deeds of darkness and put on the armor of light. **13**Let us live honorably as in daylight; not in carousing and drunkenness, not in sexual excess and lust, not in quarreling and jealousy. **14***Rather, put on the Lord Jesus Christ and make no provision for the desires of the flesh.

To Live and Die for Christ

14 **1†**EXTEND a kind welcome to those who are weak in faith. Do not enter into disputes with them. **2***A man of sound faith knows he can eat anything, while one who is weak in faith eats only

---

*

12/3: Phil 2, 3.
4: 1 Cor 12, 9.
5: 1 Cor 12, 12.
6f: 1 Cor 12, 8ff.28ff;
   Eph 4, 7-12;
   1 Pt 4, 10.
9: Am 5, 15.
10: Jn 13, 34.
14-21: Mt 5, 38-48.
15: Sir 7, 34.
16: Prv 3, 7.
17: 1 Thes 5, 15.
19: Lv 19, 18; Dt 32, 35;
   1 Cor 6, 6f.

20: Prv 25, 21f.
13/1: Ti 3, 1.
2: Prv 8, 15.
7: Mt 22, 21.
9: Ex 20, 13-17;
   Dt 5, 17-21.
10: 1 Cor 13, 4-7.
11: Eph 5, 8-16.
12: Jn 8, 12; 1 Thes 5, 4-8;
   1 Jn 2, 8.
14: Gal 3, 27; 5, 16;
   Eph 6, 11.
14/2: 1 Cor 8, 1-13;
   10, 14-33.

---

† response to the gift of justification through faith. It is the Christian's personal sacrificial way of serving God (12, 1f). It consists in the humble use of one's gifts for the benefit of the community (12, 3-13); it is marked by love of enemies (12, 14-21), and by the acceptance of legitimate civil authority (13, 1-7). The commandments of the Mosaic covenant (Ex 20, 13-17) remain its norm, and the hope of salvation in Christ its incentive (13, 11-14).

14, 1—15, 6: Paul applies the principle of love of neighbor to a certain conflict existing within the Roman community over clean and unclean foods. Although he acknowledges that in principle no food is a source of moral contamination (14, 14), he recommends that the consciences of Christians who are scrupulous in this regard be respected by other Christians (14, 21).

vegetables. **³***The man who will eat anything must not ridicule him who abstains from certain foods; the man who abstains must not sit in judgment on him who eats. After all, God himself has made him welcome. **⁴***Who are you to pass judgment on another's servant? His master alone can judge whether he stands or falls. And stand he will, for the Lord is able to make him stand. **⁵**One man regards this day as better than that; someone else considers all days alike. Each should be certain of his own conscience. **⁶**The man who observes the day does so to honor the Lord. The man who eats does so to honor the Lord, and he gives thanks to God. The man who does not eat abstains to honor the Lord, and he too gives thanks to God. **⁷**None of us lives as his own master and none of us dies as his own master. **⁸**While we live we are responsible to the Lord, and when we die we die as his servants. Both in life and in death we are the Lord's. **⁹***That is why Christ died and came to life again, that he might be Lord of both the dead and the living. **¹⁰**But you, how can you sit in judgment on your brother? Or you, how can you look down on your brother? We shall all have to appear before the judgment seat of God. **¹¹***It is written, "As surely as I live, says the Lord, every knee shall bend before me and every tongue shall give praise to God."

Peace and Joy in the Holy Spirit

¹²Every one of us will have to give an account of himself before God. **¹³**Therefore we must no longer pass judgment on one another. Instead you should resolve to put no stumbling block or hindrance in your brother's way. **¹⁴***I know with certainty on the authority of the Lord Jesus that nothing is unclean in itself; it is only when a man thinks something unclean that it becomes so for him. **¹⁵**If, then, your brother feels remorse for the food he has eaten, you have ceased to follow the rule of love. You must not let the food you eat bring to ruin him for whom Christ died; **¹⁶**neither may you allow your privilege to become an occasion for blasphemy. **¹⁷***The kingdom of God is not a matter of eating or drinking, but of justice, peace, and the joy that is given by the Holy Spirit. **¹⁸**Whoever serves Christ in this way pleases God and wins the esteem of men. **¹⁹**Let us, then, make it our aim to work for peace and to strengthen one another.

²⁰*Take care not to destroy God's work for the sake of something to eat. True, all foods are clean; but it is wrong for a man to eat when the food offends his conscience. **²¹**You would be acting nobly if you abstained from eating meat, or drinking wine, or anything else that offers your brother an occasion for stumbling or scandal, or that weakens him in any way. **²²**Use the faith you have as your rule of life in the sight of God. Happy the man whose conscience does

not condemn what he has chosen to do! **²³**But if a man eats when his conscience has misgivings about eating, he is already condemned, because he is not acting in accordance with what he believes. Whatever does not accord with one's belief is sinful.

Patience and Self-denial

15 **¹**WE who are strong in faith should be patient with the scruples of those whose faith is weak; we must not be selfish. **²**Each should please his neighbor so as to do him good by building up his spirit. **³***Thus, in accord with Scripture, Christ did not please himself: "The reproaches they uttered against you fell on me." **⁴***Everything written before our time was written for our instruction, that we might derive hope from the lessons of patience and the words of encouragement in the Scriptures. **⁵**May God, the source of all patience and encouragement, enable you to live in perfect harmony with one another according to the spirit of Christ Jesus, **⁶**so that with one heart and voice you may glorify God, the Father of our Lord Jesus Christ.

God's Fidelity and Mercy

⁷Accept one another, then, as Christ accepted you, for the glory of God. **⁸***Yes, I affirm that Christ became the servant of the Jews because of God's faithfulness in fulfilling the promises to the patriarchs, **⁹***whereas the Gentiles glorify God because of his mercy. As Scripture has it, "Therefore I will praise you among the Gentiles and I will sing to your name." **¹⁰**Again, "Rejoice, O Gentiles, with his people." **¹¹***And, "Praise the Lord, all you Gentiles and sing his glory, all you peoples." **¹²***Once more, Isaiah says, "The root of Jesse will appear, he who will rise up to rule the Gentiles; in him the Gentiles will find hope." **¹³**So may God, the source of hope, fill you with all joy and peace in believing so that through the power of the Holy Spirit you may have hope in abundance.

VII: CONCLUSION

Apostle of the Gentiles

¹⁴I AM CONVINCED, MY BROTHERS, that you are filled with goodness, that you have complete knowledge, and that you are able to give advice to one another. **¹⁵**Yet I have written to you rather boldly in parts of this letter by way of reminder. I take this liberty because God has given me the grace **¹⁶**to be a minister of Christ Jesus among the Gentiles, with the priestly duty of preaching the gospel of God so that the Gentiles may be offered up as a pleasing sacrifice, consecrated by the Holy Spirit. **¹⁷**This means I can take glory in Christ Jesus for the work I have done for God. **¹⁸**I will not dare to speak of anything except what Christ has done through me to win the Gentiles to obedience by word and deed, **¹⁹**with mighty signs and marvels, by the power of God's Spirit. As a result, I have completed preaching the gospel of Christ from Jerusalem

❋

  3: Col 2, 16.
  4: Jas 4, 12.
  9: Acts 10, 42.
  11: Is 45, 23f; Phil 2, 10f.
  14: Acts 10, 15; 1 Tm 4, 4.
  17: 1 Cor 8, 8.
20f: 1 Cor 8, 11ff; 10, 28f;
     Ti 1, 15.

15/3: Ps 69, 10.
  4: 2 Tm 3, 16.
  8: Mt 15, 24; Acts 3, 25.
  9: Ps 18, 50.
  11: Ps 117, 1.
  12: Is 11, 1.10.

all the way around to Illyria. **20**It has been a point of honor with me never to preach in places where Christ's name was already known, for I did not want to build on a foundation laid by another **21***but rather to fulfill the words of Scripture, "They who received no word of him will see him, and they who have never heard will understand."

Paul's Plans; Need for Prayers

22That is why I have so often been hindered from visiting you. **23***Now I have no more work to do in these regions, and I continue to cherish the desire to visit you which I have had for many years. **24**As soon as I can set out for Spain, I hope to see you in passing; I trust that you will send me on my journey only after I have had the joy of being with you for a little while. **25**Just now I am leaving for Jerusalem to bring assistance to the saints. **26***Macedonia and Achaia have kindly decided to make a contribution for those in need among the saints in Jerusalem. **27**They did so of their own accord, yet they are also under obligation. For if the Gentiles have shared in the spiritual blessings of the Jews, they ought to contribute to their temporal needs in return. **28**When I have finished my task and have safely handed over this contribution to them, I shall set out for Spain, passing through your midst on the way. **29**I am certain that when I do visit you, I shall come with Christ's full blessing.

30I beg you, brothers, for the sake of our Lord Jesus Christ and the love of the Spirit, join me in the struggle by your prayers to God on my behalf. **31**Pray that I may be kept safe from the unbelievers in Judea, and that the offerings I bring to Jerusalem may be well received by the saints there; **32**so that, God willing, I may come to you with joy and be refreshed in spirit by your company. **33**May the God of peace be with you all. Amen.

Phoebe Commended

16 **1**†I commend to you our sister Phoebe, who is a deaconess of the church of Cenchrae. **2**Please welcome her in the Lord, as saints should. If she needs help in anything, give it to her, for she herself has been of help to many, including myself.

Paul's Greetings

3*Give my greetings to Prisca and Aquila; they were my fellow workers in the service of Christ Jesus **4**and even risked their lives for the sake of mine. Not only I but all the churches of the Gentiles are grateful to them. **5**Remember me also to the congregation that meets in their house. Greetings to my beloved Epaenetus; he is the first offering that Asia made to Christ. **6**My greetings to Mary, who has worked hard for you, **7**and to Andronicus and Junias, my kinsmen and fellow prisoners; they are outstanding apostles, and they were in Christ even before I was. **8**Greetings to Ampliatus, who is dear to me in the Lord; **9**to Urbanus, our fellow worker in the service of Christ; and to my beloved Stachys. **10**Greetings to Apelles, who proved himself in Christ's service, and to all who belong to the household of Aristobulus. **11**Greetings to my kinsman Herodion and to the members of the household of Narcissus who are in the Lord. **12**Greetings, too, to Tryphaena and Tryphosa, who have worked hard for the Lord; and also to dear Persis, who has labored long in the Lord's service. **13**Greetings to Rufus, a chosen servant of the Lord, and to his mother, who has been a mother to me as well. **14**Greetings to Asyncritus, Phlegon, Hermes, Patrobas, Hermas, and the brothers who are with them; **15**to Philologus and Julia, to Nereus and his sister, to Olympas, and all the saints who are with them. **16**Greet one another with a holy kiss. All the churches of Christ send you greetings.

Against Dissenters

17Brothers, I beg you to be on the watch against those who cause dissension and scandal, contrary to the teaching you have received. Avoid their company. **18***Such men serve, not Christ our Lord, but their own bellies, and they deceive the simpleminded with smooth and flattering speech. **19***Your obedience is known to all, and so I am delighted with you. I want you to be wise in regard to what is good and innocent of all evil. **20***Then the God of peace will quickly crush Satan under your feet. May the grace of our Lord Jesus Christ be with you.

Greetings from Corinth

21Timothy, my fellow worker, sends you his greetings; so, too, do my kinsmen Lucius, Jason, and Sosipater. **22**I, Tertius, who have written this letter, send you my greetings in the Lord. **23**Greetings also from Gaius, who is host to me and to the whole church. **24**Erastus, the city treasurer, and our brother Quartus wish to be remembered to you.

Doxology

25*†Now to him who is able to strengthen you in the gospel which I proclaim when I preach Jesus Christ, the gospel which reveals the mystery hidden for many ages **26**but now manifested through the writings of the prophets, and, at the command of the eternal God, made known to all the Gentiles that they may believe and obey—**27***to him, the God who alone is wise, may glory be given through Jesus Christ unto endless ages. Amen.

---

† 16, 1-23: Some authorities regard these verses as a later addition to Paul's letter, but in general the evidence favors the view that they were included in the original.

16, 25: *The gospel which reveals the mystery hidden for many ages:* justification and salvation through faith, with all the implications for Jew and Gentile that Paul has developed in this letter.

21: Is 52, 15.
23: Acts 19, 21f.
26: 1 Cor 16, 1.
16/3: Acts 18, 2.26.
18: Phil 3, 19.
19: Mt 10, 16; 1 Cor 14, 20.
20: Gn 3, 15.
25: Eph 3, 3; Col 1, 26.
27: Gal 1, 5; Eph 3, 21; Phil 4, 20; 1 Tm 1, 17.

The First Epistle of Paul to the Corinthians

Introduction

St. Paul established a Christian community in Corinth about the year 50, on his second missionary journey. According to his own testimony in this epistle (written c 56), he began his work in Corinth in "fear and trepidation" (2, 3) because of the city's extreme moral depravity and its pagan cult, which included the practice of religious prostitution. Moderate success attended his efforts among the Jewish Corinthians at first, but they soon turned against him (Acts 18, 1-8). More fruitful was his year-and-a-half mission among the Gentiles (Acts 18, 11), which won to the faith many of the city's poor and unprivileged (1, 26). After his departure, the eloquent and fervent Apollos, an Alexandrian Judaeo-Christian, rendered great service to the Corinthian community. He expounded "from the Scriptures that Jesus is the Messiah" (Acts 18, 27f).

While Paul was in Ephesus on his third missionary journey (16, 8; Acts 19, 1-20), he received disquieting news about Corinth. The community there was displaying open factionalism, certain members identifying themselves with, respectively, the teaching of Paul, of Apollos, of Cephas and others apparently claiming a relationship with Jesus peculiar to themselves alone (1, 12). Christian teaching was being interpreted as a superior wisdom for the initiated few, rather than as the divine means for the humble opening of all hearts to the prophetic word of God in Christ (1, 10—4, 21). The community lacked the moral power to take appropriate action against one of its members who was living publicly in an incestuous union (5, 1-13). Other members engaged in legal conflicts, presenting in pagan courts of law a disedifying portrait of their fellows (6, 1-11); still others had even revived the old practice of religious prostitution (6, 13-20) and participated in sacrifices in the temples of the gods (10, 14-22). Some in the community questioned Paul's apostolic authority and pressed the point that, unlike the other apostles, he did not use the rights of apostleship since he did not accept financial support from the community (9, 15-18). Women appeared at the liturgical assembly without the customary head-covering (11, 2-16), and quarreled over their right to address the assembly (14, 34f).

The community's ills were reflected in the celebration of the eucharistic liturgy itself, when some members behaved clannishly, drank too freely at the agape, and denied Christian social courtesies to the poor among the membership (11, 17-22). Charisms, such as ecstatic prayer and messages, attributed freely to the impulse of the Holy Spirit, were more highly prized than works of charity (13, 1f.8), and were used at times in a disordered and even ridiculous way (14, 1-40). There were also members who, despite their belief in the resurrection of Christ, had accepted the opinion of certain peripatetic philosophers against the possibility of general bodily resurrection (15, 1-57).

The lesser problems Paul had to deal with in this epistle concerned matters of conscience discussed among the faithful members of the community: the eating of meats that had been offered to idols (8, 1-13); the use of sex in marriage (7, 1-7); and the attitude to be taken by the unmarried toward marriage in view of the possible nearness of Christ's second coming (7, 8-40). The introductory section of the epistle shows that this general group was in the majority (1, 19), and that it was actually on its behalf that Paul wrote against the threat posed to the community by the views and conduct of the minority.

The epistle illustrates well the mind and character of Paul. He does not stigmatize people by mentioning names. He always treats the questions at issue on the level of the purity of Christian teaching and conduct. Though impelled to insist on his God-given office as founder of the community, and generously including Apollos in this labor, he nevertheless evaluates his own leading role as that of a servant of God (3, 5-8). On the other hand, he does not hesitate to exercise his authority accordingly as his judgment dictates in every situation, even going so far as to promise a direct confrontation with the recalcitrant should the abuses he scores remain uncorrected (4, 18-21).

Paul writes with confidence in the authority of his apostolic mission. He presumes that the Corinthians will recognize and accept it, despite the deficiencies of their faith. Certain passages in the epistle are of the greatest importance for an understanding of the early Christian teaching on the Eucharist (10, 14-22; 11, 17-34) and on the resurrection of the body (15, 1-57).

The First Epistle to the Corinthians is divided as follows:

I: INTRODUCTION

Greeting to the Church

1 **1*****†**PAUL, CALLED BY GOD'S WILL to be an apostle of Christ Jesus, and Sosthenes our brother, **2**send greetings to the church of God which is in Corinth; to you who have been consecrated in Christ Jesus and called to be a holy people, as to all those who, wherever they may be, call on the name of our Lord Jesus Christ, their Lord and ours. **3**Grace and peace from God our Father and the Lord Jesus Christ.

Thanksgiving

4I continually thank my God for you because of the favor he has bestowed on you in Christ Jesus, **5**in whom you have been richly endowed with every gift of speech and knowledge. **6**Likewise, the witness I bore to Christ has been so confirmed among you **7***that you lack no spiritual gift as you wait for the revelation of our Lord Jesus Christ. **8***He will strengthen you to the end, so that you will be blameless on the day of our Lord Jesus [Christ]. **9***God is faithful, and it was he who called you to fellowship with his Son, Jesus Christ our Lord.

II: CONDEMNATION OF DISORDERS IN THE CORINTHIAN CHURCH

Factions

10*†I BEG YOU, BROTHERS, in the name of our Lord Jesus Christ, to agree in what you say. Let there be no factions; rather, be united in mind and judgment. **11**I have been informed, my brothers, by certain members of Chloe's household that you are quarreling among yourselves. **12***This is what I mean: One of you will say, "I belong to Paul," another, "I belong to Apollos," still another, "Cephas has my allegiance," and the fourth, "I belong to Christ." **13**Has Christ, then, been divided into parts? Was it Paul who was crucified for you? Was it in Paul's name that you were baptized? **14***Thank God, I baptized none of you except Crispus and Gaius, **15**so there are none who can say that you were baptized in my name. **16***Oh, and I baptized the household of Stephanas. Beyond that, I am not aware of having baptized anyone else. **17***†For Christ did not send me to baptize, but to preach the gospel—not with wordy "wisdom," however, lest the cross of Christ be rendered void of its meaning!

The Wisdom and Folly of the Cross

18*The message of the cross is complete absurdity to those who are headed for ruin, but to us who are experiencing salvation it is the power of God. **19***Scripture says,

"I will destroy the wisdom of the wise,
        and thwart the cleverness of the clever."

20*Where is the wise man to be found? Where the scribe? Where is the master of worldly argument? Has not God turned the wisdom of this world into folly? **21**Since in God's wisdom the world did not come to know him through "wisdom," it pleased God to save those who believe through the absurdity of the preaching of the gospel. **22***Yes, Jews demand "signs" and Greeks look for "wisdom," **23**but we preach Christ crucified—a stumbling block to Jews, and an absurdity to Gentiles; **24**but to those who are called, Jews and Greeks alike, Christ the power of God and the wisdom of God. **25**For God's folly is wiser than men, and his weakness more powerful than men.

The Case of the Corinthians

26†Brothers, you are among those called. Consider your situation. Not many of you are wise, as men account wisdom; not many are influential; and surely not many are wellborn. **27**God chose those whom the world considers absurd to shame the wise; he singled out the weak of this world to shame the strong. **28***He chose the world's lowborn and despised, those who count for nothing, to reduce to nothing those who were something; **29**so that mankind can do no boasting before God. **30***God it is who has given you life in Christ Jesus. He has made him our wisdom and also our justice, our sanctification, and our redemption. **31***This is just as you find it written, "Let him who would boast, boast in the Lord."

---

† 1, 1-9: After the customary salutation (1ff), Paul commends the Christian community of Corinth (4-7), and reminds its members of their expectation of Christ's second coming (8f; cf note on 1 Thes 4, 13-18).

1, 10-16: The presence in the community of factions due to particular attachments to Paul, Apollos, and Cephas (the reference to Christ may well be ironically intended) is an indication both of the enthusiasm for the newfound faith and the imperfect understanding of it among some of the Corinthians. We can merely conjecture about the divisions and the groups to which the apostle refers.

1, 17-25: From the allusions here to *wisdom* (17) and the *wise* (19), it seems the Christians mentioned in v 12 were attempting unsuccessfully to align their faith with the philosophies of the day. Paul points out that the Christian message of redemption through the crucifixion of Christ (17f) lies outside the ken of philosophical speculation. It is God, not man, who controls human destiny beyond this life.

1, 26-31: God's choice of the foolish, the weak, the lowborn and the despised among the Corinthians to bestow on them the gift of faith in Christ, while shaming the wise and the strong of this world and reducing to nothing those who were something, is a sign that man receives life and attains to God in Christ Jesus, not by his own effort, but by God's act.

✿	
1/1: Rom 1, 1.	18: 2, 14.
7: Ti 2, 13.	19: Is 29, 14.
8: Phil 1, 6.	20: Is 19, 12.
9: 1 Jn 1, 3.	22: Mt 12, 38; 16, 1;
10: Phil 2, 2.	Acts 17, 18.
12: 3, 4.22; Acts 18, 24.	28: Jas 2, 5.
14: Acts 18, 8.	30: Eph 2, 9.
16: 16, 15ff.	31: Jer 9, 23f;
17: 2, 4.	2 Cor 10, 17.

Paul's Preaching

2 [1]*†As for myself, brothers, when I came to you I did not come proclaiming God's testimony with any particular eloquence or "wisdom." [2]*No, I determined that while I was with you I would speak of nothing but Jesus Christ and him crucified. [3]When I came among you it was in weakness and fear, and with much trepidation. [4]*My message and my preaching had none of the persuasive force of "wise" argumentation, but the convincing power of the Spirit. [5]As a consequence, your faith rests not on the wisdom of men but on the power of God.

True Wisdom

[6]†There is, to be sure, a certain wisdom which we express among the spiritually mature. It is not a wisdom of this age, however, nor of the rulers of this age, who are men headed for destruction. [7]*No, what we utter is God's wisdom: a mysterious, a hidden wisdom. God planned it before all ages for our glory. [8]None of the rulers of this age knew the mystery; if they had known it, they would never have crucified the Lord of glory. [9]*Of this wisdom it is written:

"Eye has not seen, ear has not heard,
    nor has it so much as dawned on man
      what God has prepared for those who love him."

[10]*†Yet God has revealed this wisdom to us through the Spirit. The Spirit scrutinizes all matters, even the deep things of God. [11]Who, for example, knows a man's innermost self but the man's own spirit within him? Similarly, no one knows what lies at the depths of God but the spirit of God. [12]The Spirit we have received is not the world's spirit but God's Spirit, helping us to recognize the gifts he has given us. [13]We speak of these, not in words of human wisdom but in words taught by the Spirit, thus interpreting spiritual things in spiritual terms. [14]The natural man does not accept what is taught by the Spirit of God. For him, that is absurdity. He cannot come to know such teaching because it must be appraised in a spiritual way. [15]The spiritual man, on the other hand, can appraise everything, though he himself can be appraised by no one. [16]*For, "Who has known the mind of the Lord so as to instruct him?" But we have the mind of Christ.

Immaturity of the Corinthians

3 [1]†BROTHERS, the trouble was that I could not talk to you as spiritual men but only as men of flesh, as infants in Christ. [2]I fed you with milk, and did not give you solid food because you were not ready for it. You are not ready for it even now, [3]*being still very much in a natural condition. For as long as there are jealousy and quarrels among you, are you not of the flesh? And is not your behavior that of ordinary men? [4]When someone says, "I belong to Paul," and someone else, "I belong to Apollos," is it not clear that you are still at the human level?

The Office of God's Ministers

[5]After all, who is Apollos? And who is Paul? Simply ministers through whom you became believers, each of them doing only what the Lord assigned him. [6]*I planted the seed and Apollos watered it, but God made it grow. [7]This means that neither he who plants nor he who waters is of any special account, only God, who gives the growth. [8]He who plants and he who waters work to the same end. Each will receive his wages in proportion to his toil. [9]*We are God's co-workers, while you are his cultivation, his building.

The Work of God's Ministers

[10]†Thanks to the favor God showed me I laid a foundation as a wise master-builder might do, and now someone else is building upon it. Everyone, however, must be careful how he builds. [11]No one can lay a foundation other than the one that has been laid, namely Jesus Christ. [12]If different ones build on this foundation with gold, silver, precious stones, wood, hay or straw, [13]*the work of each will be made clear. The day will disclose it. That day will make its appearance with fire, and fire will test the quality of each man's work. [14]If the building a man has raised on this foundation still stands, he will receive his recompense; [15]if a man's building burns, he will suffer loss. He himself will be saved, but only as one fleeing through fire.

---

†
  2, 1-5: In Paul's preaching at Corinth, he proclaimed the crucified Jesus as God's message of salvation to mankind. He is not denying here that he employed human eloquence, but rather pointing out that he presented himself as a man commissioned by God; cf Gal 4, 14. Thus the Corinthians believed in the gospel message on God's authority rather than on its intrinsic appeal to human reason.

  2, 6-9: The Christian message is rightly termed a "wisdom," but a God-given wisdom pertaining to man's ultimate destiny through God's power. It is completely unknown to the rulers and great minds of the world (v 8).

  2, 10-16: Just as the individual is the only one cognizant of his own thoughts, which he alone can reveal, so it is with God and his plans for the salvation of humanity (10f). The Christian message expresses the secret thoughts, not of men, but of God (12f). It applies those thoughts to the innermost recesses of the mind and soul of man. By his acceptance or rejection of the gospel, a person shows himself to be affected or unaffected by the presence of God in the gospel (14ff).

  3, 1-9: Here Paul seems to address himself to those who were more impressed by Apollos' preaching than by his own. His teaching had to be elementary, since it was the Corinthians' first confrontation with the demands of the Christian message. However, comparison between Apollos and himself is irrelevant, for they performed different tasks for the community, whose actual success was due to the presence of God.

  3, 10-15: Paul's work was to found the community on Christ (10f). The work of others for the spiritual good of the community is to be evaluated in terms of enhancing faith in Christ, and of this, God is ultimately the judge (12-15).

2/1: 1, 17.	16: Wis 9, 13; Is 40, 13;
2: Gal 6, 14.	Rom 11, 34.
4: 1 Thes 1, 5.	3/3: 1, 10ff; Jas 3, 16.
7: Rom 16, 25f.	6: Acts 18, 8.11.24.
9: Is 64, 3.	9: Eph 2, 20; 1 Pt 2, 4ff.
10: Jn 14, 26; 16, 13.	13: Mt 3, 11f.

16*†Are you not aware that you are the temple of God, and that the spirit of God dwells in you? **17**If anyone destroys God's temple, God will destroy him. For the temple of God is holy, and you are that temple.

18†Let no one delude himself. If any one of you thinks he is wise in a worldly way, he had better become a fool. In that way he will really be wise, **19***for the wisdom of this world is absurdity with God. Scripture says, "He catches the wise in their craftiness"; **20**and again, "The Lord knows how empty are the thoughts of the wise." **21**Let there be no boasting about men. All things are yours, **22**whether it be Paul, Apollos, or Cephas, or the world, or life, or death, or the present, or the future: all these are yours, **23**and you are Christ's, and Christ is God's.

Christ Judges His Ministers

4 **1***†MEN should regard us as servants of Christ and administrators of the mysteries of God. **2**The first requirement of an administrator is that he prove trustworthy. **3**It matters little to me whether you or any human court pass judgment on me. I do not even pass judgment on myself. **4***Mind you, I have nothing on my conscience. But that does not mean that I am declaring myself innocent. The Lord is the one to judge me, **5***so stop passing judgment before the time of his return. He will bring to light what is hidden in darkness and manifest the intentions of hearts. At that time, everyone will receive his praise from God.

Corinthians Contrasted with Apostles

6*†Brothers, I have applied all this to myself and Apollos by way of example for your benefit. May you learn from us not to go beyond what is set down, so that none of you will grow self-important by reason of his association with one person rather than another. **7**Who confers any distinction on you? Name something you have that you have not received. If, then, you have received it, why are you boasting as if it were your own? **8**At the moment you are completely satisfied. You have grown rich! You have launched upon your reign with no help from us. Would that you had really begun to reign, that we might be reigning with you!

9*As I see it, God has put us apostles at the end of the line, like men doomed to die in the arena. We have become a spectacle to the universe, to angels and men alike. **10***We are fools on Christ's account. Ah, but in Christ you are wise! We are the weak ones, you the strong! They honor you, while they sneer at us! **11***Up to this very hour we go hungry and thirsty, poorly clad, roughly treated, wandering about homeless. **12***We work hard at manual labor. When we are insulted we respond with a blessing. Persecution comes our way; we bear it patiently. **13**We are slandered, and we try conciliation. We have become the world's refuse, the scum of all; that is the present state of affairs.

14†I am writing you in this way not to shame you but to admonish you as my beloved children. **15**Granted you have ten thousand guardians in Christ, you have only one father. It was I who begot you in Christ Jesus through my preaching of the gospel. **16***I beg you, then, be imitators of me. **17***This is why I have sent you Timothy, my beloved and faithful son in the Lord. He will remind you of my ways in Christ, just as I teach them in all the churches.

18Some have grown full of self-importance, thinking that I will not come to you. **19**But I shall come to you soon, the Lord willing, and find out, not what they say, but what they can do. **20***The kingdom of God does not consist in talk but in power. **21***Which do you prefer, that I come to you with a rod, or with love and a gentle spirit?

III: MORAL DISORDERS

An Incestuous Man

5 **1***†IT IS ACTUALLY REPORTED that there is lewd conduct among you of a kind not even found among the pagans—a man living with his father's wife. **2**Still you continue to be self-satisfied, in-

---

† 3, 16f: *You are the temple of God . . . dwells in you:* God's Spirit sanctifies the Christian community, making it a fit abode for God. *If anyone destroys . . . God will destroy him:* the sudden vehemence seems strange in the context. Some scholars believe Paul has in mind those guilty of corrupting the community morally; cf 5, 1-13; 6, 12-20. However, he may now wish to stress the importance of the Christian teacher's work (10-15), since he previously subordinated this role (5-19) to the effective action of God.

3, 18-23: The Corinthians will prove themselves fools, no better than "the wise" of this world, if they continue *boasting about men.* But since through their faith they belong to Christ, and through him to God, all things, *life* and *death* themselves, can assist them in attaining their end.

4, 1-5: Paul and his associates are to be regarded as assistants and managers in God's household, charged with administering the mysteries in complete dependence upon him. It is his truth which they preach and his interests which they serve. Therefore they are accountable only to him, not to the judgments of men.

4, 6-13: The example of Paul and Apollos is offered as a norm or pattern of conduct for the Corinthians. The sufferings of the apostles, their humiliations and lowly condition, contrast sharply with the self-satisfaction and boastfulness of the Corinthians. And yet all the benefits the latter enjoy are gifts from God, and, as such, should preclude their boasting as if they had not received them.

4, 14-21: Paul tempers his severity by reminding them that, as the founder of their community, he has a certain right to display his feelings. Moreover, he reserves the further right to confront personally in the future those who may remain recalcitrant.

5, 1-13: Two deviations of the community are considered

---

*
16: 6, 19; 2 Cor 6, 16; Eph 2, 20ff.	10: 2 Cor 13, 9.
19: Jb 5, 13; Ps 94, 11.	11: 2 Cor 11, 23-27.
4/1: Ti 1, 7.	12: Acts 18, 3; 20, 34; 1 Thes 2, 9.
4: 2 Cor 5, 10.	16: 11, 1; 2 Thes 3, 7.
5: 3, 13.	17: Acts 16, 1.
6: Rom 12, 13.	20: 2, 4; 1 Thes 1, 5.
9: Rom 8, 36; 2 Cor 4, 8-12.	21: 2 Cor 10, 2.
	5/1: Lv 18, 7f; Dt 23, 10.

stead of grieving, and getting rid of the offender! **3***As for me, though absent in body I am present in spirit, and have already passed sentence in the name of our Lord Jesus Christ on the man who did this deed. **4**United in spirit with you and empowered by our Lord Jesus, **5***I hand him over to Satan for the destruction of his flesh, so that his spirit may be saved on the day of the Lord.

6This boasting of yours is an ugly thing. Do you not know that a little yeast has its effect all through the dough? **7***Get rid of the old yeast to make of yourselves fresh dough, unleavened loaves, as it were; Christ our Passover has been sacrificed. **8**Let us celebrate the feast not with the old yeast, that of corruption and wickedness, but with the unleavened bread of sincerity and truth.

9*I wrote you in my letter not to associate with immoral persons. **10***I was not speaking of association with immoral people in this world, or the covetous or thieves or idolaters. To avoid them, you would have to leave the world! **11***What I really wrote about was your not associating with anyone who bears the title "brother" if he is immoral, covetous, an idolater, an abusive person, a drunkard, or a thief. It is clear that you must not eat with such a man. **12**What business is it of mine to judge outsiders? Is it not those inside the community you must judge? **13***God will judge the others. "Expel the wicked man from your midst."

Lawsuits before Pagans

6 **1†**HOW can anyone with a case against another dare bring it for judgment to the wicked and not to God's holy people? **2**Do you not know that the believers will judge the world? If the judgment of the world is to be yours, are you to be thought unworthy of judging in minor matters? **3***Do you not know that we are to judge angels? Surely, then, we are up to deciding everyday affairs. **4**If you have such matters to decide, do you accept as judges those who have no standing in the church? **5**I say this in an attempt to shame you. Can it be that there is no one among you wise enough to settle a case between one member of the church and another? **6**Must brother drag brother into court, and before unbelievers at that? **7***Why, the very fact that you have lawsuits against one another is disastrous for you. Why not put up with injustice, and let yourselves be cheated? **8**Instead, you yourselves injure and cheat your very own brothers. **9*†**Can you not realize that the unholy will not fall heir to the kingdom of God? Do not deceive yourselves: no fornicators, idolaters, or adulterers, no sod-

omites, **10***thieves, misers, or drunkards, no slanderers or robbers will inherit God's kingdom. **11***And such were some of you; but you have been washed, consecrated, justified in the name of our Lord Jesus Christ and in the Spirit of our God.

Against Sexual Immorality

· **12**"Everything is lawful for me"—but that does not mean that everything is good for me. "Everything is lawful for me"—but I will not let myself be enslaved by anything. **13**"Food is for the stomach and the stomach for food, and God will do away with them both in the end"—but the body is not for immorality; it is for the Lord, and the Lord is for the body. **14***God, who raised up the Lord, will raise us also by his power.

15*Do you not see that your bodies are members of Christ? Would you have me take Christ's members and make them the members of a prostitute? God forbid! **16***Can you not see that the man who is joined to a prostitute becomes one body with her? Scripture says, "The two shall become one flesh." **17***But whoever is joined to the Lord becomes one spirit with him. **18**Shun lewd conduct. Every other sin a man commits is outside his body, but the fornicator sins against his own body. **19***You must know that your body is a temple of the Holy Spirit, who is within—the Spirit you have received from God. You are not your own. **20***You have been purchased, and at a price! So glorify God in your body.

Advice to the Married

7 **1†**NOW for the matters you wrote about. A man is better off having no relations with a woman. **2**But to avoid immorality, every man should have his own wife and every woman her own husband. **3**The husband should fulfill his conjugal obliga-

---

† here: the toleration of the incestuous union of a man with his stepmother (1-8); and the misunderstanding of Paul's admonition against associating with fellow Christians guilty of sexual immorality (9-13). In the first case, Paul (impelled perhaps by his belief in the imminence of the parousia) recommends the ecclesial penalty of separating the offender from the unity of the faithful and handing him over to Satan, i. e., for medicinal punishment through bodily affliction, even death (1 Tm 1, 20), so that the incestuous relationship may be destroyed and the path to repentance and reunion laid open.

6, 1-8: The apostle expresses his dismay that the image of mutual charity among Christians is being tarnished by their lawsuits in Roman courts. This is all the more deplorable since Christians are to share with Christ the judgment of the world, and ought therefore to be capable of settling one another's minor cases within the society of believers; cf Dn 7, 22.27.

6, 9-20: Paul insists that the Christian give evidence of the reality of his faith in Christ by living according to a high moral standard. The gravity of the sins mentioned in vv 9f can be gauged from the fact that they exclude the offender from inheriting the kingdom of God. In 6, 12-20 the fornication referred to is probably that of religious prostitution, an accepted part of pagan culture in Rome.

7, 1-11: Paul's teaching concerning marriage and the celibate state is placed in the framework of the second coming of Christ (26.28f); see note on 1 Thes 4, 13-18. The apostle commends

❋

3: Col 2, 5.	7: Mt 5, 38-42;
5: 1 Tm 1, 20.	Rom 12, 17ff;
7: 1 Pt 1, 19.	1 Thes 5, 15.
9: 2 Thes 3, 14.	9: Gal 5, 19ff; Eph 5, 5.
10: Jn 17, 15.	10: 15, 50.
11: Mt 18, 17; 2 Thes 3, 6;	11: Ti 3, 3-7; 1 Jn 2, 12.
2 Jn 10.	14: Rom 8, 11; 2 Cor 4, 14.
13: Dt 13, 6.	15: Rom 6, 12f.
6/3: Wis 3, 8; Mt 19, 28;	16: Gn 2, 24; Eph 5, 30.
Rv 20, 4.	17: Rom 8, 9f; 2 Cor 3, 17.
	19: 3, 16f; Rom 5, 5.
	20: 3, 23; Phil 1, 20.

tions toward his wife, the wife hers toward her husband. **⁴**A wife does not belong to herself but to her husband; equally, a husband does not belong to himself but to his wife. **⁵**Do not deprive one another, unless perhaps by mutual consent for a time, to devote yourselves to prayer. Then return to one another, that Satan may not tempt you through your lack of self-control. **⁶**I say this by way of concession, not as a command. **⁷***Given my preference, I should like you to be as I am. Still, each one has his own gift from God, one this and another that.

Advice to the Unmarried

⁸To those not married and to widows I have this to say: It would be well if they remain as they are, even as I do myself; **⁹***but if they cannot exercise self-control, they should marry. It is better to marry than to be on fire. **¹⁰***To those now married, however, I give this command (though it is not mine; it is the Lord's): a wife must not separate from her husband. **¹¹**If she does separate, she must either remain single or become reconciled to him again. Similarly, a husband must not divorce his wife.

Obligations of the Believing Partner

¹²*†As for the other matters, although I know of nothing the Lord has said, I say: If any brother has a wife who is an unbeliever but is willing to live with him, he must not divorce her. **¹³**And if any woman has a husband who is an unbeliever but is willing to live with her, she must not divorce him. **¹⁴***The unbelieving husband is consecrated by his believing wife; the unbelieving wife is consecrated by her believing husband. If it were otherwise, your children should be unclean; but as it is, they are holy.

¹⁵If the unbeliever wishes to separate, however, let him do so. The believing husband or wife is not bound in such cases. God has called you to live in peace. **¹⁶**Wife, how do you know that you will not save your husband; or you, husband, that you will not save your wife?

No Change To Be Sought

¹⁷†The general rule is that each one should lead the life the Lord has assigned him, continuing as he was when the Lord called him. This is the rule I give in all the churches. **¹⁸**Was someone called after he had been circumcised? He should not try to hide his circumcision. Did the call come to another who had never been circumcised? He is not to be circumcised. **¹⁹***Circumcision counts for nothing, and its lack makes no difference either. What matters is keeping God's commandments. **²⁰**Everyone ought to continue as he was when he was called. **²¹**Were you a slave when your call came? Give it no thought. Even supposing you

could go free, you would be better off making the most of your slavery. **²²***The slave called in the Lord is a freedman of the Lord, just as the freeman who has been called is a slave of Christ. **²³***You have been bought at a price! Do not enslave yourselves to men. **²⁴**Brothers, each of you should continue before God in the condition of life that was his when he was called.

The State of Virginity

²⁵†With respect to virgins, I have not received any commandment from the Lord, but I give my opinion as one who is trustworthy, thanks to the Lord's mercy. **²⁶**It is this: In the present time of stress it seems good to me for a person to continue as he is. **²⁷**Are you bound to a wife? Then do not seek your freedom. Are you free of a wife? If so, do not go in search of one. **²⁸**Should you marry, however, you will not be committing sin. Neither does a virgin commit a sin if she marries. But such people will have trials in this life, and these I should like to spare you.

²⁹I tell you, brothers, the time is short. From now on those with wives should live as though they had none; **³⁰**those who weep should live as though they were not weeping, and those who rejoice as though they were not rejoicing; buyers should conduct themselves as though they owned nothing, **³¹**and those who make use of the world as though they were not using it, for the world as we know it is passing away.

³²†I should like you to be free of all worries. The unmarried man is busy with the Lord's affairs, concerned with pleasing the Lord; **³³***but the married

---

† sexual asceticism in marriage provided it is agreed to by both parties, spiritually motivated, and not carried beyond either party's limits of control (1-7). The existing practice within the community of widows and widowers remaining unmarried is also commended, without, however, any implication against the freedom to remarry should sexual attraction prove irresistible. Christ's teaching against divorce and remarriage must be strictly adhered to in marriages between Christians; cf Mk 10, 9.

7, 12-16: In the case of marriage between Christians and non-Christians, there must be no divorce as long as the unbelieving partner is willing to live peacefully with the Christian spouse (12f). But if the non-believer wishes to separate, or refuses to live peacefully with the Christian, the latter is no longer bound (15f).

7, 17-24: A degree of importance is attached to the circumstances that basically condition one's life at the time of conversion. Normally, everyone, whether Jew or Gentile, slave or free, should expect to retain his particular state.

7, 25-31: The above principle of retention of one's state applies also to both the unmarried and the married because, in the light of the second coming of Christ, it is not the state that is important but rather the use of it in a spirit of sacrifice, i. e., as though not using it. In this way all things are made subservient to the supreme end of preparedness for Christ's coming in judgment.

7, 32-35: Those who were unmarried at the time of conversion should realize that their celibate state relieves them of the responsibilities of marriage and family, and the resulting involvement in worldly affairs. They are more free to engage directly in the service of the Lord (32ff). This does not, however, contradict the individual's freedom to marry (v 35; cf 7, 8f.28).

*
7/7: Mt 19, 12.
9: 1 Tm 5, 11-14.
10: Mt 5, 32; 19, 9.
12: 1 Pt 3, 1.
14: Rom 11, 16.
19: Rom 2, 25; Gal 5, 6.
22: Eph 6, 5-9; Phlm 16.
23: 6, 20.
33: Lk 14, 20.

man is busy with this world's demands and occupied with pleasing his wife. This means he is divided. **34**The virgin—indeed, any unmarried woman—is concerned with things of the Lord, in pursuit of holiness in body and spirit. The married woman, on the other hand, has the cares of this world to absorb her and is concerned with pleasing her husband. **35***I am going into this with you for your own good. I have no desire to place restrictions on you, but I do want to promote what is good, what will help you to devote yourselves entirely to the Lord.

A Question of Marriage

36†If anyone thinks he is behaving dishonorably toward his virgin because a critical moment has come and it seems that something should be done, let him do as he wishes. He commits no sin if there is a marriage. **37**The man, however, who stands firm in his resolve, who while without constraint and free to carry out his will makes up his mind to keep his virgin, also acts rightly. **38**To sum up: the man who marries his virgin, acts fittingly; the one who does not, will do better.

Widows

39*†A wife is bound to her husband as long as he lives. If her husband dies she is free to marry, but on one condition, that it be in the Lord. **40**She will be happier, though, in my opinion, if she stays unmarried. I am persuaded that in this I have the Spirit of God.

Meats Offered to Idols

8 **1†**NOW about meats that have been offered to idols. Of course we all "know" about that. But whereas "knowledge" inflates, love upbuilds. **2***If a man thinks he knows something, that means he has never really known it as he ought. **3**But if anyone loves God, that man is known by him. **4***So then, about this matter of eating meats that have been offered to idols: we know that an idol is really nothing, and that there is no God but one. **5**Even though there are so-called gods in the heavens and on the earth—there are, to be sure, many such "gods" and "lords"—**6***for us there is one God, the Father, from whom all things come and for whom we live; and one Lord Jesus Christ, through whom everything was made and through whom we live.

Practical Rules

7*Not all, of course, possess this "knowledge." Because some were so recently devoted to idols, they eat meat, fully aware that it has been sacrificed, and because their conscience is weak, it is defiled by the eating. **8***Now food does not bring us closer to God. We suffer no loss through failing to eat, and we gain no favor by eating. **9***Take care, however, lest in exercising your right you become an occasion of sin to the weak. **10**If someone sees you, with your "knowledge," reclining at table in the temple of an idol, may not his conscience in its weak state be influenced to the point that he eats the idol-offering? **11***Because of your "knowledge" the weak one perishes, that brother for whom Christ died. **12***When you sin thus against your brothers and wound their weak consciences, you are sinning against Christ. **13***Therefore, if food causes my brother to sin I will never eat meat again, so that I may not be an occasion of sin to him.

Paul's Rights as an Apostle

9 **1*†**AM I not free? Am I not an apostle? Have I not seen Jesus our Lord? And are you not my work in the Lord? **2**Although I may not be an apostle for others, I certainly am one for you. You are the very seal of my apostolate in the Lord.

3My defense against those who criticize me is this: **4**Do we not have the right to eat and drink? **5**Do we not have the right to marry a believing woman like the rest of the apostles and the brothers of the Lord and Cephas? **6**Is it only myself and Barnabas who are forced to work for a living? What soldier in the field pays for his rations? **7**Who plants a vineyard and does not eat of its yield? What shepherd does not nourish himself with the milk of his flock? **8**You may think the reasons I am giving are merely human ones, but does not the law itself speak of these things? It is written in the law of Moses, "You shall not muzzle an ox while it treads out grain." **9***Is God concerned here for oxen, **10**or does he not rather say this for our sakes? You can be sure it was written for us, for the plowman should plow in hope and the harvester expect a share in the grain. **11***If we have sown for you in the spirit, is it

---

† 7, 36ff: These verses may mean either that a) a man living chastely with a virgin may marry her; or b) a father may give his daughter in marriage, or a guardian his ward. However, dedicated celibacy and virginity anticipate the life of glory after the resurrection, when marriage will no longer exist; cf Mt 22, 30.

7, 39f: Widows who choose to remarry should prefer Christian husbands.

8, 1-13: See note on Romans 14, 1—15, 6.

9, 1-23: Behind this passage lies some objection within the Corinthian community to Paul's apostolic role. Since he does not accept material support from the community or make use of a woman servant, like the other apostles, he is apparently not to be considered their equal. Paul replies that he is quite aware of his right to do these things, but that he has made a free, personal decision not to exercise this right. He feels that his preaching of the gospel is a duty laid upon him by God, which he must fulfill by presenting the gospel to men as gratuitously as God gave it to him (15-18). He cannot be accused of pride, for his apostolic life is proof that he has conquered his pride; he adapts himself to the customary observances of the law when residing among Judaeo-Christians, and to its non-observance when he shares the life of Gentile Christians (19-23).

✱
35: Lk 10, 39.42.
39: Rom 7, 2.
8/2: Gal 6, 3.
4: 10, 19.
6: Mal 2, 10; Jn 1, 3; Col 1, 16.
7: 10, 28; Rom 14, 23.
8: Rom 14, 17; Col 2, 21f.

9: Rom 14, 20.
11: Rom 14, 15.
12: Acts 9, 5.
13: Rom 14, 21.
9/1: Acts 26, 16.
9: Dt 25, 4; 1 Tm 5, 18.
11: Rom 15, 27.

too much to expect a material harvest from you? **12***If others have this right over you, is not our right even greater? But we have not used this right. On the contrary, we put up with all sorts of hardships so as not to place any obstacle in the way of the gospel of Christ. **13***Do you not realize that those who work in the temple are supported by the temple, and those who minister at the altar share the offerings of the altar? **14***Likewise the Lord himself ordered that those who preach the gospel should live by the gospel.

Reason for Not Using Rights

15*As for me, I have not used any of these rights, nor do I write this now to see to it that anything should be done for me. I would rather die than let anyone rob me of my boast! **16***Yet preaching the gospel is not the subject of a boast; I am under compulsion and have no choice. I am ruined if I do not preach it! **17**If I do it willingly, I have my recompense; if unwillingly, I am nonetheless entrusted with a charge. **18***And this recompense of mine? It is simply this, that when preaching I offer the gospel free of charge and do not make full use of the authority the gospel gives me.

All Things to All Men

19*Although I am not bound to anyone, I made myself the slave of all so as to win over as many as possible. **20**I became like a Jew to the Jews in order to win the Jews. To those bound by the law I became like one who is bound (although in fact I am not bound by it), that I might win those bound by the law. **21**To those not subject to the law I became like one not subject to it (not that I am free from the law of God, for I am subject to the law of Christ), that I might win those not subject to the law. **22***To the weak I became a weak person with a view to winning the weak. I have made myself all things to all men in order to save at least some of them. **23**In fact, I do all that I do for the sake of the gospel in the hope of having a share in its blessings.

24*You know that while all the runners in the stadium take part in the race, the award goes to one man. In that case, run so as to win! **25***Athletes deny themselves all sorts of things. They do this to win a crown of leaves that withers, but we a crown that is imperishable.

26I do not run like a man who loses sight of the finish line. I do not fight as if I were shadowboxing. **27***What I do is discipline my own body and master

it, for fear that after having preached to others I myself should be rejected.

Against Overconfidence

10 **1***†BROTHERS, I want you to remember this: our fathers were all under the cloud and all passed through the sea; **2**by the cloud and the sea all of them were baptized into Moses. **3***All ate the same spiritual food. **4***All drank the same spiritual drink (they drank from the spiritual rock that was following them, and the rock was Christ), **5***yet we know that God was not pleased with most of them, for "they were struck down in the desert."

6These things happened as an example to keep us from wicked desires such as theirs. **7***Do not become idolaters, as some of them did. Scripture says, "The people sat down to eat and drink, and arose to take their pleasure." **8***Let us not indulge in lewdness as some of them did, so that in one day twenty-three thousand perished. **9***Let us not test the Lord as some of them did, only to be destroyed by snakes. **10***Nor are you to grumble as some of them did, to be killed by the destroying angel. **11**The things that happened to them serve as an example. They have been written as a warning to us, upon whom the end of the ages has come. **12**For all these reasons, let anyone who thinks he is standing upright watch out lest he fall! **13***No test has been sent you that does not come to all men. Besides, God keeps his promise. He will not let you be tested beyond your strength. Along with the test he will give you a way out of it so that you may be able to endure it.

The Eucharist versus Pagan Sacrifices

14†I am telling you, whom I love, to shun the worship of idols, **15**and I address you as one addresses sensible people. You may judge for yourselves what I am saying. **16***Is not the cup of blessing we bless a sharing in the blood of Christ? And is not the bread we break a sharing in the body of Christ? **17***Because the loaf of bread is one, we, many though we are, are one body, for we all partake of the one loaf.

18Look at Israel according to the flesh and see if those who eat the sacrifices do not share in the altar! **19**What am I saying—that meat offered to an idol is really offered to that idol, or that an idol is a reality? **20***No, I mean that the Gentiles sacrifice to demons and not to God, and I do not want you to become sharers with demons. **21**You cannot drink the cup of

---

❋

12: 2 Cor 11, 9.
13: Nm 18, 8.31; Dt 18, 1ff.
14: Lk 10, 7.
15: 2 Cor 11, 9.
16: Acts 4, 20; 22, 14f.
18: 2 Cor 11, 7.
19: Mt 20, 26.
22: 2 Cor 11, 29.
24: 2 Tm 4, 7f.
25: Jas 1, 12.
27: Rom 8, 13.
10/1: Ex 13, 21; 14, 19-22.
3: Ex 16, 4-35.

4: Ex 17, 6; Nm 20, 7-11.
5: Nm 14, 16; Jude 5.
7: Ex 32, 6.
8: Nm 25, 1-9.
9: Nm 21, 5f.
10: Nm 14, 2.36.
13: Mt 6, 13; Jas 1, 13f.
16: Mt 26, 26f; Acts 2, 42.
17: 12, 7; Rom 12, 5;
        Eph 4, 4.
20: Dt 32, 17;
        2 Cor 6, 14ff.

---

†

10, 1-13: Paul approaches the question of participation in the sacrificial worship of pagan temples (14-22) by invoking Old Testament traditions from the history of Israel in the desert, especially Israel's forbidden worship of the golden calf (Ex 32, 1-29). Christians, in their turn, possess the spiritual gifts of God but this does not free them from the danger of yielding to temptation.

10, 14-22: Paul repudiates idol-worship on the ground of the meaning of the Eucharist: it is the Christian sacrifice that effects union with the living Christ. Although the pagan sacrifices aim at a union with the gods, in the light of Christian teaching they are seen to serve only the cause of evil.

the Lord and also the cup of demons. You cannot partake of the table of the Lord and likewise the table of demons. **²²**Do we mean to provoke the Lord to jealous anger? Surely we are not stronger than he!

Concerning Idol Offerings

²³*†"All things are lawful," but not all are advantageous. "All things are lawful"—which does not mean that everything is constructive. **²⁴***No man should seek his own interest but rather that of his neighbor. **²⁵**Eat whatever is sold in the market without raising any question of conscience. **²⁶***"The earth and its fullness are the Lord's." **²⁷**If an unbeliever invites you to his table and you want to go, eat whatever is placed before you, without raising any question of conscience. **²⁸**But if someone should say to you, "This was offered in idol worship," do not eat it, both for the sake of the one who called attention to it and on account of the conscience issue—**²⁹**not your own conscience but your neighbor's. You may ask, Why should my liberty be restricted by another man's conscience? **³⁰***And why is it, if I partake thankfully, that I should be blamed for the food over which I gave thanks?

Conclusion

³¹The fact is that whether you eat or drink—whatever you do—you should do all for the glory of God. **³²**Give no offense to Jew or Greek or to the church of God, **³³**just as I try to please all in any way I can by seeking, not my own advantage, but that of the many, that they may be saved.

11 **¹***IMITATE me as I imitate Christ.

IV: CONDUCT AT PUBLIC WORSHIP

Headdress of Women

²†I PRAISE YOU BECAUSE you always remember me and are holding fast to the traditions just as I handed them on to you. **³***I want you to know that the head of every man is Christ; the head of a woman is her husband; and the head of Christ is the Father. **⁴**Any man who prays or prophesies with his head covered brings shame upon his head. **⁵**Similarly, any woman who prays or prophesies with her head uncovered brings shame upon her head. It is as if she had had her head shaved. **⁶**Indeed, if a woman will not wear a veil, she ought to cut off her hair. If it is shameful for a woman to have her hair cut off or her head shaved, it is clear that she ought to wear a veil. **⁷***A

man, on the other hand, ought not to cover his head, because he is the image of God and the reflection of his glory. Woman, in turn, is the reflection of man's glory. **⁸**Man was not made from woman but woman from man. **⁹***Neither was man created for woman but woman for man. **¹⁰***For this reason a woman ought to have a sign of submission on her head, because of the angels. **¹¹**Yet, in the Lord, woman is not independent of man nor man independent of woman. **¹²**In the same way that woman was made from man, so man is born of woman; and all is from God. **¹³**I will let you judge for yourselves. Is it proper for a woman to pray to God unveiled? **¹⁴**Does not nature itself teach you that it is dishonorable for a man to wear his hair long, while the long hair of a woman is her glory? **¹⁵**Her hair has been given her for a covering. **¹⁶**If anyone wants to argue about this, remember that neither we nor the churches of God recognize any other usage.

The Lord's Supper

¹⁷†What I now have to say is not said in praise, because your meetings are not profitable but harmful. **¹⁸***First of all, I hear that when you gather for a meeting there are divisions among you, and I am inclined to believe it. **¹⁹**There may even have to be factions among you for the tried and true to stand out clearly. **²⁰**When you assemble it is not to eat the Lord's Supper, **²¹**for everyone is in haste to eat his own supper. One person goes hungry while another gets drunk. **²²***Do you not have homes where you can eat and drink? Would you show contempt for the church of God, and embarrass those who have nothing? What can I say to you? Shall I praise you? Certainly not in this matter!

²³*I received from the Lord what I handed on to you, namely, that the Lord Jesus on the night in which he was betrayed took bread, **²⁴**and after he had given thanks, broke it and said, "This is my body, which is for you. Do this in remembrance of me." **²⁵***In the same way, after the supper, he took the cup, saying, "This cup is the new covenant in my blood. Do this, whenever you drink it, in remembrance of me." **²⁶**Every time, then, you eat this bread and drink this cup, you proclaim the death of the Lord until he

---

† 10, 23—11, 1: See note on Romans 14, 1–15, 6.

11, 2-16: The apostle regards the independence of the Corinthian women who participate in worship with unveiled heads as a lack of humility, since a woman's veil is regarded as a sign of dependence on the authority of her husband. Paul's argument is based on his view of nature and on propriety, i. e., the custom of the earliest Christian communities.

11, 17-34: Paul concerns himself with the proper celebration of the eucharistic liturgy (33f). He has become aware that at the agape preceding the celebration of the Eucharist, the mutual charity of sharing food and companionship is being violated through discrimination against the needy (21f). Moreover, even drunkenness has not been unknown (21). In this earliest written account of the Lord's Supper Paul emphasizes its sacrificial aspect, i. e., the proclamation of Jesus' death in atonement for sin (23-26). Participation in this mystery requires a clean conscience (27ff). Abuse of the mystery on the part of some is the cause of their punishment through illness and death (30ff).

✱
23: 6, 12.
24: Rom 15, 2; Phil 2, 4.
26: Ps 24, 1.
30: Rom 14, 6; 1 Tm 4, 3f.
11/1: 4, 16; Phil 3, 17.
3: Eph 5, 23.
7: Gn 1, 27; 5, 1.
9: Gn 2, 21ff.
10: 14, 34.
18: 1, 10ff.
22: Jas 2, 5ff.
23: 10, 16f; Mt 26, 26-29; Mk 14, 22-25; Lk 22, 14-20.
25: Ex 24, 8; Heb 8, 6-13.

comes! **27**This means that whoever eats the bread or drinks the cup of the Lord unworthily sins against the body and blood of the Lord. **28**A man should examine himself first; only then should he eat of the bread and drink of the cup. **29**He who eats and drinks without recognizing the body eats and drinks a judgment on himself. **30**That is why many among you are sick and infirm, and why so many are dying. **31**If we were to examine ourselves, we would not be falling under judgment in this way; **32**＊but since it is the Lord who judges us, he chastens us to keep us from being condemned with the rest of the world. **33**Therefore, my brothers, when you assemble for the meal, wait for one another. **34**If anyone is hungry let him eat at home, so that your assembly may not deserve condemnation. As for other matters, I shall give instructions when I come.

V: SPIRITUAL GIFTS

Variety and Unity

12 **1**†NOW BROTHERS, I DO NOT WANT to leave you in ignorance about spiritual gifts. **2**＊You know that when you were pagans you were led astray to mute idols, as impulse drove you. **3**＊That is why I tell you that nobody who speaks in the Spirit of God ever says, "Cursed be Jesus." And no one can say: "Jesus is Lord," except in the Holy Spirit.

4＊There are different gifts but the same Spirit; **5**＊there are different ministries but the same Lord; **6**there are different works but the same God who accomplishes all of them in everyone. **7**To each person the manifestation of the Spirit is given for the common good. **8**To one the Spirit gives wisdom in discourse, to another the power to express knowledge. **9**Through the Spirit one receives faith; by the same Spirit another is given the gift of healing, **10**＊and still another miraculous powers. Prophecy is given to one; to another power to distinguish one spirit from another. One receives the gift of tongues, another that of interpreting the tongues. **11**＊But it is one and the same Spirit who produces all these gifts, distributing them to each as he wills.

Analogy of the Body

12＊The body is one and has many members, but all the members, many though they are, are one body; and so it is with Christ. **13**＊It was in one Spirit that all of us, whether Jew or Greek, slave or free, were baptized into one body. All of us have been given to drink of the one Spirit. **14**Now the body is not one

member, it is many. **15**If the foot should say, "Because I am not a hand I do not belong to the body," would it then no longer belong to the body? **16**If the ear should say, "Because I am not an eye I do not belong to the body," would it then no longer belong to the body? **17**If the body were all eye, what would happen to our hearing? If it were all ear, what would happen to our smelling? **18**As it is, God has set each member of the body in the place he wanted it to be. **19**If all the members were alike, where would the body be? **20**There are, indeed, many different members, but one body. **21**The eye cannot say to the hand, "I do not need you," any more than the head can say to the feet, "I do not need you." **22**Even those members of the body which seem less important are in fact indispensable. **23**We honor the members we consider less honorable by clothing them with greater care, **24**thus bestowing on the less presentable a propriety which the more presentable already have. God has so constructed the body as to give greater honor to the lowly members, **25**that there may be no dissension in the body, but that all the members may be concerned for one another. **26**If one member suffers, all the members suffer with it; if one member is honored, all the members share its joy.

The One Body of Christ

27＊You, then, are the body of Christ. Every one of you is a member of it. **28**＊Furthermore, God has set up in the church first apostles, second prophets, third teachers, then miracle workers, healers, assistants, administrators, and those who speak in tongues. **29**Are all apostles? Are all prophets? Are all teachers? Do all work miracles **30**or have the gift of healing? Do all speak in tongues, all have the gift of interpretation of tongues? **31**Set your hearts on the greater gifts.

Excellence of the Gift of Love

13 NOW I will show you the way which surpasses all the others. **1**†If I speak with human tongues and angelic as well, but do not have love, I am a noisy gong, a clanging cymbal. **2**＊If I have the gift of prophecy and, with full knowledge,

---

† 12, 1—14, 40: Here Paul speaks of special spiritual gifts (charisms) enabling individuals to exercise an office or function within the community. He provides a list of charisms in 12, 8ff (cf Rom 12, 6ff; Eph 4, 11) which he wishes to be recognized as a manifestation of the presence of the Holy Spirit (3-11), each contributing in its own way to the good of the whole community (12-30). (Paul does not value the charisms for their own sake, since Christian love is the only enduring gift of God; cf 12, 31—13, 13). Corinthians may lawfully desire to possess the charisms, but they should aspire especially to the gift of prophecy (probably, the gift of directing the community in new situations, and of revealing what could not otherwise be known; cf 14, 3.30; Acts 13, 1f). The apostle criticizes the overstressing of the gift of tongues (probably ecstatic utterances requiring an interpreter; cf 14, 1-25), and directs that this gift be employed only when an interpreter is present. At the assembly no more than three persons, not including women, are to act on the basis of a charism (26-40).

13, 1-13: See note on 1 John 4, 7—5, 5.

＊
32: Dt 8, 5; Heb 12, 5ff.
12/2: Heb 2, 18f.
3: Mk 9, 39; 1 Jn 4, 2f.
4: Rom 12, 6; Eph 4, 4.
5: 12, 28; Eph 4, 11.
10: 14, 5; Acts 2, 4.
11: 7, 7; Eph 4, 7.
12: 10, 17; Rom 12, 4f; Col 3, 15.
13: Gal 3, 28; Eph 2, 13.16; Col 3, 11.
27: Rom 12, 5-8; Eph 5, 20.
28: Eph 4, 11.
13/2: Mt 7, 22; 17, 20; Jas 2, 14-17.

comprehend all mysteries, if I have faith great enough to move mountains, but have not love, I am nothing. **³***If I give everything I have to feed the poor and hand over my body to be burned, but have not love, I gain nothing.

⁴*Love is patient; love is kind. Love is not jealous, it does not put on airs, it is not snobbish. **⁵***Love is never rude, it is not self-seeking, it is not prone to anger; neither does it brood over injuries. **⁶**Love does not rejoice in what is wrong but rejoices with the truth. **⁷***There is no limit to love's forbearance, to its trust, its hope, its power to endure.

⁸Love never fails. Prophecies will cease, tongues will be silent, knowledge will pass away. **⁹**Our knowledge is imperfect and our prophesying is imperfect. **¹⁰**When the perfect comes, the imperfect will pass away. **¹¹**When I was a child I used to talk like a child, think like a child, reason like a child. When I became a man I put childish ways aside. **¹²***Now we see indistinctly, as in a mirror; then we shall see face to face. My knowledge is imperfect now; then I shall know even as I am known. **¹³***There are in the end three things that last: faith, hope, and love, and the greatest of these is love.

Gift of Prophecy

14 **¹**SEEK eagerly after love. Set your hearts on spiritual gifts—above all, the gift of prophecy. **²**A man who speaks in a tongue is talking not to men but to God. No one understands him, because he utters mysteries in the Spirit. **³**The prophet, on the other hand, speaks to men for their upbuilding, their encouragement, their consolation. **⁴**He who speaks in a tongue builds up himself, but he who prophesies builds up the church. **⁵**I should like it if all of you spoke in tongues, but I much prefer that you prophesy. The prophet is greater than one who speaks in tongues, unless the speaker can also interpret for the upbuilding of the church.

Interpretation of Tongues

⁶Just suppose, brothers, that I should come to you speaking in tongues. What good will I do you if my speech does not have some revelation, or knowledge, or prophecy, or instruction for you? **⁷**Even in the case of lifeless things which produce a sound, such as a flute or a harp, how will anyone know what is being played if there is no distinction among the notes? **⁸**If the bugle's sound is uncertain, who will get ready for battle? **⁹**Similarly, if you do not utter intelligible speech because you are speaking in a tongue, how will anyone know what you are saying? You will be talking to the air. **¹⁰**There are many different languages in the world and all are marked by sound; **¹¹**but if I do not know the meaning, I shall be a foreigner to

the speaker and he a foreigner to me. **¹²**Since you have set your hearts on spiritual gifts, try to be rich in those that build up the church.

¹³This means that the man who speaks in a tongue should pray for the gift of interpretation. **¹⁴**If I pray in a tongue my spirit is at prayer but my mind contributes nothing. **¹⁵***What is my point here? I want to pray with my spirit, and also to pray with my mind. I want to sing with my spirit and with my mind as well. **¹⁶**If your praise of God is solely with the spirit, how will the one who does not comprehend be able to say "Amen" to your thanksgiving? He will not know what you are saying. **¹⁷**You will be uttering praise very well indeed, but the other man will not be helped. **¹⁸**Thank God, I speak in tongues more than any of you, **¹⁹**but in the church I would rather say five intelligible words to instruct others than ten thousand words in a tongue.

Function of These Gifts

²⁰*Brothers, do not be childish in your outlook. Be like children as far as evil is concerned, but in mind be mature. **²¹**It is written in the law, "In strange tongues and in alien speech I will speak to this people, and even so they will not heed me, says the Lord." **²²**The gift of tongues is a sign, not for those who believe but for those who do not believe, while prophecy is not for those who are without faith but for those who have faith. **²³***If the uninitiated or unbelievers should come in when the whole church is assembled and everyone is speaking in tongues, would they not say that you are out of your minds? **²⁴**But if an unbeliever or an uninitiate enters while all are uttering prophecy, he will be taken to task by all and called to account by all, **²⁵***and the secret of his heart will be laid bare. Falling prostrate, he will worship God, crying out, "God is truly among you."

Rules of Order

²⁶What do we propose, brothers? When you assemble, one has a psalm, another some instruction to give, still another a revelation to share; one speaks in a tongue, another interprets. All well and good, so long as everything is done with a constructive purpose. **²⁷**If any are going to talk in tongues let it be at most two or three, each in turn, with another to interpret what they are saying. **²⁸**But if there is no one to interpret, there should be silence in the assembly, each one speaking only to himself and to God. **²⁹**Let no more than two or three prophets speak, and let the rest judge the worth of what they say. **³⁰**If another, sitting by, should happen to receive a revelation, the first ones should then keep quiet. **³¹**You can all speak your prophecies, but one by one, so that all may be instructed and encouraged. **³²**The spirits of the prophets are under the prophets' control, **³³**since God is a God, not of confusion, but of peace.

³⁴*According to the rule observed in all the assemblies of believers, women should keep silent in such gatherings. They may not speak. Rather, as the law

---

⬧
3: Mt 6, 2.	14/15: Eph 5, 19.
4: Rom 13, 8ff.	20: Mt 10, 16; Rom 16, 19;
5: Rom 12, 9f.	Eph 4, 14.
7: Prv 10, 12; Gal 6, 2.	23: Acts 2, 6.13.
12: 2 Cor 5, 7; 1 Jn 3, 2.	25: Is 45, 14; Zec 8, 23.
13: 1 Thes 1, 3.	34: 1 Tm 2, 11f.

states, submissiveness is indicated for them. [35]If they want to learn anything, they should ask their husbands at home. It is a disgrace when a woman speaks in the assembly. [36]Did the preaching of God's word originate with you? Are you the only ones to whom it has come?

[37]If anyone thinks he is a prophet or a man of the Spirit, he should know that what I have written you is the Lord's commandment. [38]If anyone ignores it, he in turn should be ignored. [39]Set your hearts on prophecy, my brothers, and do not forbid those who speak in tongues, [40]but make sure that everything is done properly and in order.

VI: THE RESURRECTION

Christ's Resurrection

15 [1†]BROTHERS, I WANT TO REMIND YOU of the gospel I preached to you, which you received and in which you stand firm. [2]You are being saved by it at this very moment if you hold fast to it as I preached it to you. Otherwise you have believed in vain. [3]I handed on to you first of all what I myself received, that Christ died for our sins in accordance with the Scriptures; [4*]that he was buried and, in accordance with the Scriptures, rose on the third day; [5*]that he was seen by Cephas, then by the Twelve. [6]After that he was seen by five hundred brothers at once, most of whom are still alive, although some have fallen asleep. [7]Next he was seen by James; then by all the apostles. [8]Last of all he was seen by me, as one born out of the normal course. [9*]I am the least of the apostles; in fact, because I persecuted the church of God, I do not even deserve the name. [10]But by God's favor I am what I am. This favor of his to me has not proved fruitless. Indeed, I have worked harder than all the others, not on my own but through the favor of God. [11]In any case, whether it be I or they, this is what we preach and this is what you believed.

The Resurrection and Faith

[12]Tell me, if Christ is preached as raised from the dead, how is it that some of you say there is no resurrection of the dead? [13]If there is no resurrection of the dead, Christ himself has not been raised. [14]And if Christ has not been raised, our preaching is void of content and your faith is empty too. [15*]Indeed, we should then be exposed as false witnesses of God, for we have borne witness before him that he raised up

Christ; but he certainly did not raise him up if the dead are not raised. [16]Why? Because if the dead are not raised, then Christ was not raised; [17]and if Christ was not raised, your faith is worthless. You are still in your sins, [18*]and those who have fallen asleep in Christ are the deadest of the dead. [19]If our hopes in Christ are limited to this life only, we are the most pitiable of men.

Christ, the First Fruits

[20*]But as it is, Christ is now raised from the dead, the first fruits of those who have fallen asleep. [21*]Death came through a man; hence the resurrection of the dead comes through a man also. [22]Just as in Adam all die, so in Christ all will come to life again, [23*]but each one in proper order: Christ the first fruits and then, at his coming, all those who belong to him. [24*]After that will come the end, when, after having destroyed every sovereignty, authority, and power, he will hand over the kingdom to God the Father. [25*]Christ must reign until God has put all enemies under his feet, [26*]and the last enemy to be destroyed is death. [27*]Scripture reads that God "has placed all things under his feet." But when it says that everything has been made subject, it is clear that he who has made everything subject to Christ is excluded. [28*]When, finally, all has been subjected to the Son, he will then subject himself to the One who made all things subject to him, so that God may be all in all.

Practical Faith

[29]If the dead are not raised, what about those who have themselves baptized on behalf of the dead? If the raising of the dead is not a reality, why be baptized on their behalf? [30*]And why are we continually putting ourselves in danger? [31*]I swear to you, brothers, by the very pride you take in me, which I cherish in Christ Jesus our Lord, that I face death every day. [32*]If I fought those beasts at Ephesus for purely human motives, what profit was there for me? If the dead are not raised, "Let us eat and drink, for tomorrow we die!" [33]Do not be led astray any longer.

---

† 15, 1-58: This exposition of the Christian doctrine of the resurrection of the dead in Christ was prompted by the belief among some of the Corinthians that the resurrection of the body was impossible (12, 35), though apparently they did not deny the resurrection of Christ (v 12). Paul takes up the issue by listing the divinely appointed witnesses to the resurrection (1-11). He develops its significance as revealing God's plan to raise the dead (12-28), belief in which has been a basic Christian incentive. It encourages the apostles in the face of the hardships of their ministry, and has even occasioned the practice in Corinth of baptism on behalf of the dead (29-34). Those who reject the doctrine of resurrection because of the fact of bodily corruption fail to understand the mystery of God's creative activity, which provides the kind of body suited to the new life after death (35-49). The risen body of man will be a body so changed by the power of God as to be immortal (50-53). Christ died for sin, which is the cause of man's death (Gn 3, 19); he rose from the dead to be the cause of man's resurrection (54-58).

❋ 15/4: Acts 2, 23.
5: Mk 16, 14; Lk 24, 34-43.
9: Eph 3, 8; 1 Tm 1, 15.
15: Acts 5, 32.
18: Rom 10, 9.
20: Rom 8, 11; Col 1, 18; 1 Thes 4, 14.
21: Gn 3, 17f; Rom 5, 12-18.
23: 1 Thes 4, 16.
24: Eph 1, 22.
25: Ps 110, 1.
26: Rom 6, 9; 2 Tm 1, 10; Rv 20, 14.
27: Ps 8, 7; Phil 3, 21.
28: Eph 4, 6; Col 3, 11.
30: 2 Cor 4, 10ff.
31: Rom 8, 36.
32: Is 22, 13; 1 Cor 4, 9; 2 Cor 1, 8.

"Bad company corrupts good morals." Return to reason, as you ought, and stop sinning. [34]Some of you are quite ignorant of God; I say it to your shame.

Manner of the Resurrection

[35]Perhaps someone will say, "How are the dead to be raised up? What kind of body will they have?" [36*]A nonsensical question! The seed you sow does not germinate unless it dies. [37]When you sow, you do not sow the full-blown plant, but a kernel of wheat or some other grain. [38*]God gives body to it as he pleases —to each seed its own fruition. [39]Not all bodily nature is the same. Men have one kind of body, animals another. Birds are of their kind, fish are of theirs. [40]There are heavenly bodies and there are earthly bodies. The splendor of the heavenly bodies is one thing, that of the earthly another. [41]The sun has a splendor of its own, so has the moon, and the stars have theirs. Even among the stars, one differs from another in brightness. [42]So is it with the resurrection of the dead. What is sown in the earth is subject to decay, what rises is incorruptible. [43*]What is sown is ignoble, what rises is glorious. Weakness is sown, strength rises up. [44]A natural body is put down and a spiritual body comes up.

The Natural and the Spiritual Body

If there is a natural body, be sure there is also a spiritual body. [45*]Scripture has it that Adam, the first man, became a living soul; the last Adam has become a life-giving spirit. [46]Take note, the spiritual was not first; first came the natural and after that the spiritual. [47]The first man was of earth, formed from dust, the second is from heaven. [48*]Earthly men are like the man of earth, heavenly men are like the man of heaven. [49*]Just as we resemble the man from earth, so shall we bear the likeness of the man from heaven.

Glorification of the Body

[50*]This is what I mean, brothers: flesh and blood cannot inherit the kingdom of God; no more can corruption inherit incorruption. [51*]Now I am going to tell you a mystery. Not all of us shall fall asleep, but all of us are to be changed—[52*]in an instant, in the twinkling of an eye, at the sound of the last trumpet. The trumpet will sound and the dead will be raised incorruptible, and we shall be changed. [53*]This corruptible body must be clothed with incorruptibility, this mortal body with immortality. [54]When the corruptible frame takes on incorruptibility and the mortal immortality, then will the saying of Scripture be fulfilled: "Death is swallowed up in victory." [55*]"O death, where is your victory? O death, where is your sting?" [56*]The sting of death is sin, and sin gets its power from the law. [57*]But thanks be to God who has given us the victory through our Lord Jesus Christ. [58]Be steadfast and persevering, my beloved brothers, fully engaged in the work of the Lord. You know that your toil is not in vain when it is done in the Lord.

VII: CONCLUSION

The Collection

16 [1*][†]ABOUT THE COLLECTION FOR THE SAINTS, follow the instructions I gave the churches of Galatia. [2]On the first day of each week everyone should put aside whatever he has been able to save, so that the collection will not have to be taken up after I arrive. [3]When I come I shall give letters of introduction to those whom you have chosen to take your gift to Jerusalem. [4]If it seems fitting that I should go myself, they will accompany me.

Paul's Plans

[5*]I shall come to you after I have passed through Macedonia. [6]If it is at all possible, I should like to remain with you for some time—even to spend the winter with you—that you may provide me with what I need for the rest of my journey. [7*]I do not want to see you just in passing. I hope to spend some time with you, if the Lord permits. [8*]I intend to stay in Ephesus until Pentecost. [9*]A door has been opened wide for my work, but at the same time there are many opposed. [10*]If Timothy should come, be sure to put him at ease among you. He does the Lord's work just as I do, [11]so let no one treat him disdainfully. Rather, help him come to me by sending him on his way in peace. I am expecting him with the brothers. [12*]As for our brother Apollos, I urged him strongly to go to you with the brothers, but he did not wish to go at this time. He will go when circumstances are more favorable.

Directions and Greetings

[13]Be on your guard, stand firm in the faith, and act like men. In a word, be strong. [14]Do everything with love. [15*]You know that the household of Stephanas is the first fruits of Achaia and is devoted to the service of the saints. [16]I urge you to serve under such men and under everyone who cooperates and toils with them. [17]I was very happy at the arrival of Stephanas, Fortunatus, and Achaicus, because they made up for your

---

36: Jn 12, 24.
38: Gn 1, 11.
43: Phil 3, 20.
45: Gn 2, 7; Jn 5, 21;
　2 Cor 3, 6f.
48: Rom 8, 29; Phil 3, 21.
49: Gn 5, 3.
50: Jn 3, 3-6.
51: 1 Thes 4, 14.
52: Jl 2, 1; Zec 9, 14;
　Mt 24, 31.
53: 2 Cor 5, 4.

55: Is 25, 8; Hos 13, 14.
56: Rom 4, 15; 7, 7.13.
57: Jn 16, 33.
16/1: Gal 2, 10.
5: Acts 19, 21.
7: Acts 18, 21.
8: Acts 19, 1.10.
9: Acts 14, 27.
10: 4, 17; Acts 19, 22;
　Phil 2, 20ff.
12: Acts 18, 24.
15: 1, 16.

[†] 16, 1: This collection taken up for the poor Christians of Jerusalem is elsewhere referred to (Acts 24, 17; Rom 15, 26ff; 2 Cor 8, 1–9, 15; Gal 2, 10). Paul is especially interested in it as an opportunity to break down the barriers between Jew and Gentile.

absence. **18***They have refreshed my spirit as they did yours. You should recognize the worth of such men.

19*The churches of Asia send you greetings. Aquila and Prisca, together with the assembly that meets in their house, send you cordial greetings in the Lord. **20***All the brothers greet you. Greet one another with a holy kiss.

21*It is I, Paul, who send you this greeting in my own hand. **22*†**If anyone does not love the Lord, let a curse be upon him. O Lord, come! **23**The favor of the Lord Jesus be with you. **24**My love to all of you in Christ Jesus.

---

*
18: 1 Thes 5, 12.
19: Acts 18, 2.18.26;
    Rom 16, 3.5.
20: Rom 16, 16;
    2 Cor 13, 12;
    1 Pt 5, 14.
21: Col 4, 18; 2 Thes 3, 17.
22: Gal 1, 8f.

---

† 16, 22: *O Lord, come!: Maranatha:* an Aramaic expression, reflected also in Rv 22, 20, probably used in the Christian liturgy of the time. It may be read as a prayer for the arrival of the second coming of Christ: *Marana tha,* "Lord, come"; or as an expression of hope in the proximity of the parousia, *Maran atha,* "The Lord is coming." See note on 1 Thes 4, 13-18.

The Second Epistle of Paul to the Corinthians

Introduction

This epistle contains Paul's reflections on events that occurred after his first letter had been sent to the Corinthians. He had changed his plan to stay with that community, an intention he had previously announced (1 Cor 16, 5ff), and was criticized by the Corinthian Christians for this; one of them had even publicly reviled him (2, 5). Their attitude caused Paul much anxiety (2, 3f) and greatly strained the relationship between himself and the community he had founded and knew so well (6, 11f; Acts 18, 11). It indirectly impeded his work of ministry at Troas, where he was to be joined by Titus (2, 12f) to receive his personal report on the state of the church at Corinth. Not finding him there, Paul left Troas for Macedonia in search of him. When they finally met, he was greatly relieved, for the letter of reproof Titus had carried to the Corinthians from Paul had won the day at Corinth (7, 5-9). Accordingly, Paul wrote the present letter to confirm the Corinthians' renewed acceptance of his apostolic authority and to prepare them for his coming visit (12, 14; 13, 1).

Although these data do not constitute a complete reconstruction of events in Corinth between the writing of the two Corinthian letters, they are adequate to account for the nature of this second letter, the most subjective of all the Pauline epistles.

The themes of the epistle must be understood in terms of this general background: Paul's suffering and consolation (1, 3-11); his sincerity (1, 12ff); his honesty (1, 15—2, 4); his forgiveness of the offender (2, 5-11); his past anxiety and present relief (2, 12-17); his confidence in the apostolic office despite its hardships (3, 1—6, 10); his plea for frankness (6, 11ff; 7, 2ff); Titus' report upon the effect of the reproachful letter he had brought to the community from Paul (7, 5-16); the appeal concerning the collection for the poor Christians of Jerusalem, delayed because of the troubles within the community (8, 1—9, 15); the reaffirmation of Paul's apostolic authority (10, 1—13, 10).

Many scholars have felt that the lack of continuity in the Second Epistle to the Corinthians and the repetition of material on the same topic (e. g., 2, 14—6, 3 and 10, 1—13, 8, 1-24 and 9, 1-15) are evidence that the epistle was formed from several Pauline letters, including perhaps the letter to the Corinthians written before First Corinthians (1, Cor 5, 9), and the second, severe letter which preceded Second Corinthians (2 Cor 7, 8).

However, no theory fragmenting Second Corthinians into several letters has proved entirely convincing. A partial explanation of the degree of discontinuity and repetition in the letter would be Paul's own state of mind when he composed it. As new thoughts on the themes of his letter occurred to him, he recorded them in the hope that the outpouring of his own heart (6, 11) would ensure the community's faithfulness to him.

The Second Epistle to the Corinthians was written in Macedonia (2 Cor 2, 12f; 7, 5f; 8, 1-4; 9, 2ff), probably in the autumn of 57 A. D., during the course of Paul's third missionary journey (Acts 20, 1f).

Greeting to the Church

1 [1]†PAUL, BY GOD'S WILL AN APOSTLE of Jesus Christ, and Timothy his brother, to the church of God that is at Corinth and to all the holy ones of the church who live in Achaia. [2]Grace and peace from God our Father and the Lord Jesus Christ.

Thanksgiving after Affliction

[3]*†Praised be God, the Father of our Lord Jesus Christ, the Father of mercies, and the God of all consolation! [4]He comforts us in all our afflictions and thus enables us to comfort those who are in any trouble, with the same consolation we have received from him. [5]†As we have shared much in the suffering of Christ, so through Christ do we share abundantly in his consolation. [6]If we are afflicted it is for your encouragement and salvation, and when we are consoled it is for your consolation, so that you may endure patiently the same sufferings we endure. [7]Our hope for you is firm because we know that just as you share in the sufferings, so you will share in the consolation.

[8]*Brothers, we do not wish to leave you in the dark about the trouble we had in Asia; we were crushed beyond our strength, even to the point of despairing of

---

† 1, 1f: See note on Rom 1, 1-7.

1, 3-11: Paul gives thanks to God, as he informs the Corinthians that he has been relieved of the serious troubles he experienced in the province of Asia Minor, and is now at peace. The community was evidently aware of the apostle's difficulties, but their nature is now unknown.

1, 5: The sufferings of Paul are identified with those of Christ, for whom they are endured; the consolation he receives is shared with the Christians at Corinth.

* 1/3: Eph 1, 3; 1 Pt 1, 3.   8: Acts 20, 19.

life. **9***We were left to feel like men condemned to death so that we might trust, not in ourselves, but in God who raises the dead. **10**He rescued us from that danger of death and will continue to do so. We have put our hope in him who will never cease to deliver us. **11***But you must help us with your prayers, so that on our behalf God may be thanked for the gift granted us through the prayers of so many.

Paul's Sincerity

12†Conscience gives testimony to the boast that in our behavior toward all and especially toward you we have always acted from God-given holiness and candor; this has been prompted, not by debased human wisdom, but by God's goodness. **13**We never write anything that you cannot read and understand. I hope that, just as you know us to a certain degree already, you will in time come to know us well, **14**and will recognize that we shall be your boast, and you ours, on the day of our Lord Jesus.

15*Confident as I am about this, I wanted to visit you first so that a double grace might be yours. **16**I planned to visit you, both on my way to Macedonia and on my return, that I might receive your help on my journey to Judea. **17***Do you suppose that in making those plans I was acting insincerely? Or that my plans are so determined by self-interest that I change my mind from one minute to the next? **18**As God keeps his word, I declare that my word to you is not "yes" one minute and "no" the next. **19**Jesus Christ, whom Silvanus, Timothy, and I preached to you as Son of God, was not alternately "yes" and "no"; he was never anything but "yes." **20**Whatever promises God has made have been fulfilled in him; therefore it is through him that we address our Amen to God when we worship together. **21**God is the one who firmly establishes us along with you in Christ; it is he who anointed us **22*†**and has sealed us, thereby depositing the first payment, the Spirit, in our hearts.

23I call on God as my witness that it was out of consideration for you that I did not come to Corinth again. **24**Domineering over your faith is not my purpose. I prefer to work with you toward your happiness. As regards faith, you are standing firm.

2 **1**I did decide, however, not to visit you again in painful circumstances. **2**For if I cause you pain, who can make me happy again but the ones I grieved? **3**I wrote as I did so that when I come I may not be saddened by those who should rejoice my heart. I know you all well enough to be convinced that my happiness is yours. **4**That is why I wrote you in great sorrow and anguish, with copious tears—not to make you sad but to help you realize the great love I bear you.

Forgiveness for the Offender

5†If anyone has given offense he has hurt not only me, but in some measure, to say no more, every one of you. **6**The punishment already inflicted by the majority on such a one is enough; **7***you should now relent and support him so that he may not be crushed by too great a weight of sorrow. **8**I therefore beg you to reaffirm your love for him. **9**The reason I wrote you was to test you and learn whether you are obedient in all matters. **10**If you forgive a man anything, so do I. Any forgiving I have done has been for your sakes and, before Christ, **11***to prevent Satan—whose guile we know too well—from outwitting us.

Paul's Anxiety and Relief

12When I came to Troas to preach the gospel of Christ, the door of opportunity was opened wide for me by the Lord. **13***Yet I was inwardly troubled because I did not find my brother Titus there. So I said good-bye to them and went off to Macedonia. **14†**Thanks be to God, who unfailingly leads us on in Christ's triumphal train, and employs us to diffuse the fragrance of his knowledge everywhere! **15**We are an aroma of Christ for God's sake, both among those who are being saved and those on the way to destruction; **16***to the latter an odor dealing death, to the former a breath bringing life. For such a mission as this, is anyone really qualified? **17**We at least are not like so many who trade on the word of God. We speak in Christ's name, pure in motivation, conscious of having been sent by God and of standing in his presence.

Ministers of the New Covenant

3 **1**AM I beginning to speak well of myself again? Or do I need letters of recommendation to you or from you as others might? **2**You are my letter, known and read by all men, written on your hearts. **3***Clearly you are a letter of Christ which I have de-

---

† 1, 12—2, 4: Paul answers the criticism leveled against him for having twice planned and twice failed to visit the Corinthians (1, 15f). He denies that his original plan failed for any but apostolic reasons (1, 17-22), namely, lack of favorable circumstances to discharge his office peaceably. Instead of visiting the Corinthians he sent them a severe letter which caused them distress (2, 3; cf 7, 8), for it was weighted with his own anguish over the situation in their community (2, 4).

1, 22: *First payment:* on full messianic benefits; cf Eph 1, 13f.

2, 5-11: Some scholars believe that the person alluded to here rejected Paul's authority, thereby scandalizing many in the community. It is clear that these latter took action against him, and the apostle now recommends that the punishment be terminated.

2, 14—4, 18: Paul wishes to convince the Corinthians that his actions toward them were motivated, not by selfish reasons, but by apostolic concern. This leads him to a series of reflections on the apostolic office: his effectiveness as an apostle derives from Christ (2, 14-17); his achievements are supported by the Holy Spirit (3, 1ff); his qualifications for the apostolate are gifts of God; and his ministry of the justifying power of God is superior to that of the Mosaic covenant (3, 4-11). The

9: 4, 7; Rom 4, 17.
11: 4, 15; 9, 12.
15: Phil 2, 16;
    1 Thes 2, 19f.
17: Mt 5, 37.
22: Rom 5, 5; Eph 1, 13f;
    1 Jn 2, 20.

2/7: Col 3, 13.
11: Eph 4, 27.
13: 7, 6; Ti 1, 3.
16: 1 Cor 1, 18.
3/3: Ex 24, 12; Jer 31, 33;
    Ez 11, 19; 36, 26.

livered, a letter written not with ink but by the Spirit of the living God, not on tablets of stone but on tablets of flesh in the heart.

4This great confidence in God is ours, through Christ. **5***It is not that we are entitled of ourselves to take credit for anything. Our sole credit is from God, **6***who has made us qualified ministers of a new covenant, a covenant not of a written law but of spirit. The written law kills, but the Spirit gives life.

7*If the ministry of death, carved in writing on stone, was inaugurated with such glory that the Israelites could not look on Moses' face because of the glory that shone on it (even though it was a fading glory), **8**how much greater will be the glory of the ministry of the Spirit? **9**If the ministry of the covenant that condemned had glory, greater by far is the glory of the ministry that justifies. **10**Indeed, when you compare that limited glory with this surpassing glory, the former should be declared no glory at all. **11**If what was destined to pass away was given in glory, greater by far is the glory that endures.

12Our hope being such, we speak with full confidence. **13**We are not like Moses, who used to hide his face with a veil so that the Israelites could not see the final fading of that glory. **14**Their minds, of course, were dulled. To this very day, when the old covenant is read the veil remains unlifted; it is only in Christ that it is taken away. **15***Even now, when Moses is read a veil covers their understanding. **16**"But whenever he turns to the Lord, the veil will be removed." **17**The Lord is the Spirit, and where the Spirit of the Lord is, there is freedom. **18***All of us, gazing on the Lord's glory with unveiled faces, are being transformed from glory to glory into his very image by the Lord who is the Spirit.

Treasure in Earthen Vessels

4 **1†**BECAUSE we possess this ministry through God's mercy, we do not give in to discouragement. **2***Rather, we repudiate shameful, underhanded practices. We do not resort to trickery or falsify the word of God. We proclaim the truth openly and commend ourselves to every man's conscience before God. **3**If our gospel can be called "veiled" in any sense, it is such only for those who are headed toward destruction. **4***Their unbelieving minds have been blinded by the god of the present age so that they do not see the splendor of the gospel showing forth the glory of Christ, the image of God. **5**It is not ourselves we preach but Christ Jesus as Lord, and ourselves as your servants for Jesus' sake. **6***For God, who said, "Let light

shine out of darkness," has shone in our hearts, that we in turn might make known the glory of God shining on the face of Christ. **7†**This treasure we possess in earthen vessels to make it clear that its surpassing power comes from God and not from us. **8***We are afflicted in every way possible, but we are not crushed; full of doubts, we never despair. **9**We are persecuted but never abandoned; we are struck down but never destroyed. **10***Continually we carry about in our bodies the dying of Jesus, so that in our bodies the life of Jesus may also be revealed. **11***While we live we are constantly being delivered to death for Jesus' sake, so that the life of Jesus may be revealed in our mortal flesh. **12**Death is at work in us, but life in you. **13*†**We have that spirit of faith of which the Scripture says, "Because I believed, I spoke out." We believe and so we speak, **14***knowing that he who raised up the Lord Jesus will raise us up along with Jesus and place both us and you in his presence. **15**Indeed, everything is ordered to your benefit, so that the grace bestowed in abundance may bring greater glory to God because they who give thanks are many.

Living by Faith

16†We do not lose heart, because our inner being is renewed each day even though our body is being destroyed at the same time. **17***The present burden of our trial is light enough, and earns for us an eternal weight of glory beyond all comparison. **18***We do not fix our gaze on what is seen but on what is unseen. What is seen is transitory; what is not seen lasts forever.

5 **1***INDEED, we know that when the earthly tent in which we dwell is destroyed we have a dwelling provided for us by God, a dwelling in the heavens, not made by hands but to last forever. **2***We groan while we are here, even as we yearn to have our heavenly habitation envelop us. **3***This it will, provided we are found clothed and not naked. **4**While we live in our present tent we groan; we are weighed down because we do not wish to be stripped naked but rather to have the heavenly dwelling envelop us,

---

† apostle knows that his work is to result in the permanent presence of Christ among men through the power of the Holy Spirit (3, 13-18).

4, 1-6: The power of the gospel is divine; the apostle, therefore, has no need to modify it to make it acceptable to men (1f). It is men who blind themselves to the light of Christ (3-6).

4, 7-12: The apostle's sufferings reenact the life of Jesus, both as a sign and as an instrument of the divine life he ministers to men.

4, 13f: Paul lives through faith in his own future resurrection and that of his fellow Christians. *He . . . will raise us up:* this may imply that Paul did not expect to be alive at the parousia; cf 1 Cor 15, 51-55.

4, 16ff: Though the apostle's physical forces are being spent, his soul is renewed daily through living the Christ life and meriting that transformation of soul and body after death in which transitory realities are exchanged for those that are eternal; cf 1 Cor 15, 42ff.

✿
5: Jn 3, 27.	8: 6, 4-10; 1 Cor 4, 9-13.
6: Eph 3, 7.	10: Col 1, 24.
7: Ex 32, 15f; 34, 29-35.	11: 1 Cor 15, 31.
15: Rom 11, 7-10.	13: Ps 116, 10.
18: 4, 6; Rom 8, 29;	14: Rom 8, 11.
1 Jn 3, 2.	17: Mt 5, 11f; Rom 8, 18.
4/2: 1 Thes 2, 4f.	18: Rom 8, 24f; Heb 11, 1.
4: 2 Thes 2, 10;	5/1: Is 38, 12.
1 Tm 1, 11.	2: Rom 8, 23; Col 3, 3f.
6: Gn 1, 3; Jn 8, 12;	3: 1 Cor 15, 51ff;
Heb 1, 3.	1 Thes 4, 15.

so that what is mortal may be absorbed by life. **5***God has fashioned us for this very thing and has given us the Spirit as a pledge of it.

6†Therefore we continue to be confident. We know that while we dwell in the body we are away from the Lord. **7**We walk by faith, not by sight. **8***I repeat, we are full of confidence and would much rather be away from the body and at home with the Lord. **9***This being so, we make it our aim to please him whether we are with him or away from him. **10***The lives of all of us are to be revealed before the tribunal of Christ so that each one may receive his recompense, good or bad, according to his life in the body.

Ministry of Reconciliation

11†Standing in awe of the Lord we try to persuade men, but what we are is known to God. I hope that it is also known to you in your consciences. **12***We shall not begin to recommend ourselves to you again, but we are giving you an opportunity to boast about us so that you may have something to say to those who take pride in external appearances, and not in what lies in the heart. **13**Indeed, if we are ever caught up out of ourselves, God is the reason; and when we are brought back to our senses, it is for your sakes. **14**The love of Christ impels us who have reached the conviction that since one died for all, all died. **15***He died for all so that those who live might live no longer for themselves, but for him who for their sakes died and was raised up.

16Because of this we no longer look on anyone in terms of mere human judgment. If at one time we so regarded Christ, we no longer know him by this standard. **17***This means that if anyone is in Christ, he is a new creation. The old order has passed away; now all is new! **18**All this has been done by God, who has reconciled us to himself through Christ and has given us the ministry of reconciliation. **19***I mean that God, in Christ, was reconciling the world to himself, not counting men's transgressions against them, and that he has entrusted the message of reconciliation to us. **20**This makes us ambassadors for Christ, God as it were appealing through us. We implore you, in Christ's name: be reconciled to God! **21***For our sakes God made him who did not know sin to be sin, so that in him we might become the very holiness of God.

6 **1**As your fellow workers we beg you not to receive the grace of God in vain. **2***For he says, "In an acceptable time I have heard you; on a day of salvation I have helped you." Now is the acceptable time! Now is the day of salvation! **3***We avoid giving anyone offense, so that our ministry may not be blamed. **4***On the contrary, in all that we do we strive to present ourselves as ministers of God, acting with patient endurance amid trials, difficulties, distresses, **5**beatings, imprisonments, and riots; as men familiar with hard work, sleepless nights, and fastings; **6***conducting ourselves with innocence, knowledge, and patience, in the Holy Spirit, in sincere love; **7***as men with the message of truth and the power of God; wielding the weapons of righteousness with right hand and left, **8**whether honored or dishonored, spoken of well or ill. We are called imposters, yet we are truthful; **9***nobodies who in fact are well known; dead, yet here we are, alive; punished, but not put to death; **10**sorrowful, though we are always rejoicing; poor, yet we enrich many. We seem to have nothing, yet everything is ours!

11*Men of Corinth, we have spoken to you frankly, opening our hearts wide to you. **12**There is no lack of room for you in us; the narrowness is in you. **13***In fair exchange, then (I speak as a father to his children), open wide your hearts!

The Temple of the Living God

14†Do not yoke yourselves in a mismatch with unbelievers. After all, what do righteousness and lawlessness have in common, or what fellowship can light have with darkness? **15**What accord is there between Christ and Belial, what common lot between believer and unbeliever? **16***Tell me what agreement there is between the temple of God and idols. You are the temple of the living God, just as God has said:

> "I will dwell with them and walk among them.
> I will be their God
> and they shall be my people.

17*Therefore, 'Come out from among them
> and separate yourselves from them,' says the Lord;
> 'and touch nothing unclean.

---

† 5, 6-9: Paul comforts himself with the thought that his present existence is in a sense an exile from Christ, whereas death brings life with Christ through the possession of heavenly glory.

5, 11—6, 14: Paul trusts that his dispositions, known to God, may also be recognized by the Corinthians whom he serves, so that they in turn can answer his critics (5, 11f). In his dealings with people, he is motivated by love for Christ (5, 14). To delve into his past might reveal that he once entertained mistaken ideas about the Savior (5, 16). This may be the meaning of looking upon Christ *in terms of mere human judgment*. But the apostle, like other Christians, is also a new man; reconciled to God through Christ, he is given the special mission of serving as Christ's ambassador, the essential purpose of his own personal renewal by God (5, 17-21). His mission is to appeal to men to accept God's salvation in Christ (6, 1f), a task he tries to perform with the greatest possible discretion. The attempt nevertheless produces personal hardships and social upheavals, even though all that he strives to offer is God's word and power (6, 3-10). In conclusion, Paul asks of the Corinthians that they be as open to him in acceptance of his ministry as he has been frank and loving toward them (6, 11ff; cf 7, 2).

6, 14—7, 1: It is difficult to account for this passage in the present context. It has similarities with the Qumran literature, and may be an excerpt of a lost Pauline epistle.

✿

  5: 1, 22.
  8: Rom 8, 24; Phil 1, 21ff.
  9: Mt 25, 31f.
10: Rom 14, 10.
12: Phil 1, 26.
15: Rom 6, 4-11; 14, 9.
17: Is 43, 19; Eph 2, 10;
    Rv 21, 5.
19: Jn 3, 17.
21: Is 53, 6-9; Gal 3, 13;
    1 Pt 2, 24; 1 Jn 3, 5.

6/2: Is 49, 8.
  3: 8, 21.
  4: 4, 8ff; Cor 4, 9-13.
  6: Gal 5, 22.
  7: Eph 6, 11.
  9: 4, 11.
11: 7, 3.
13: Gal 4, 19.
16: Lv 26, 12; Ez 37, 27;
    1 Cor 3, 17; 6, 19.
17: Is 52, 11.

I will welcome you [18*]and be a father to you
and you will be my sons and daughters,'
says the Lord Almighty."

7 [1]SINCE we have these promises, beloved, let us
purify ourselves from every defilement of flesh
and spirit, and in the fear of God strive to fulfill
our consecration perfectly.

Joy over Repentance

[2]Make room for us in your hearts! We have injured
no one, we have corrupted no one, we have cheated
no one. [3*]I do not condemn you. I have already said
that you are in our hearts, even to the sharing of death
and life together. [4]I speak to you with utter frankness
and boast much about you. I am filled with consolation, and despite my many afflictions my joy knows no
bounds.

[5†]When I arrived in Macedonia I was restless and
exhausted. I was under all kinds of stress—quarrels
with others and fears within myself. [6]But God, who
gives heart to those who are low in spirit, gave me
strength with the arrival of Titus. [7]This he did, not
only by his arrival but by the reinforcement Titus had
already received from you; for he reported your longing, your grief, and your ardent concern for me, so
that my joy is greater still. [8*]If I saddened you by my
letter I have no regrets. Or if I did feel some regret
(because I understand that the letter caused you grief
for a time), [9]I am happy once again; not because you
were saddened, but because your sadness led to repentance. You were filled with a sorrow that came
from God; thus you did not suffer any loss from us.
[10]Indeed, sorrow for God's sake produces a repentance
without regrets, leading to salvation, whereas worldly
sorrow brings death. [11]Just look at the fruit of this sorrow which stems from God. What a measure of holy
zeal it has brought you, not to speak of readiness to
defend yourselves! What indignation, fear, and longing! What ardent desire to restore the balance of justice! In every way you have displayed your innocence
in this matter. [12]Therefore, my writing to you was not
intended for the man who had given the offense or for
the one offended, but to make plain in the sight of God
the devotion you have for us. [13]This done, we are comforted.

Beyond this consolation, we have rejoiced even
more at the joy of Titus because his mind has been set
at rest by all of you. [14]For though I had boasted to
him about you, I was not put to shame. Rather, just
as everything I ever said to you was true, so my boasting to Titus has been proved equally true. [15]His heart
embraces you with an expanding love as he recalls the
obedience you showed to God when you received him
in fear and trembling. [16]I rejoice because I trust you
utterly.

Liberal Giving

8 [1*†]BROTHERS, I should like you to know of the
grace of God conferred on the churches of Macedonia. [2]In the midst of severe trial their overflowing joy and deep poverty have produced an abundant generosity. [3]According to their means—indeed I
can testify even beyond their means—and voluntarily,
[4]they begged us insistently for the favor of sharing in
this service to members of the church. [5]Beyond our
hopes they first gave themselves to God and then to
us by the will of God. [6]That is why I have exhorted
Titus, who had already begun this work of charity
among you, to bring it to successful completion:
[7*]that just as you are rich in every respect, in faith and
discourse, in knowledge, in total concern, and in the
love we bear you, so may you abound in this charity.

[8]I am not giving an order but simply testing your
generous love against the concern which others show.
[9*]You are well acquainted with the favor shown you
by our Lord Jesus Christ: how for your sake he made
himself poor though he was rich, so that you might
become rich by his poverty. [10]I am about to give you
some advice on this matter of rich and poor. It will
help you who began this good work last year, not only
to carry it through, but to do so willingly. [11]Carry it
through now to a successful completion, so that your
ready resolve may be matched by giving according to
your means. [12]The willingness to give should accord
with one's means, not go beyond them. [13]The relief of
others ought not to impoverish you; there should be a
certain equality. [14]Your plenty at the present time
should supply their need so that their surplus may
one day supply your need, with equality as the result.
[15*]It is written, "He who gathered much had no excess
and he who gathered little had no lack."

Titus and His Companions

[16]Thanks be to God, who has put an equal zeal for
you in the heart of Titus! [17]Not only did he welcome
our appeal, but being very eager he has gone to you
freely. [18*]We have sent along with him that brother

---

† 7, 5-16: Paul resumes the thought from which he had di-
gressed in 2, 13, completing the account of his meeting with
Titus to discuss the community's reaction to his severe letter;
see note on 1, 12—2, 4. He expresses genuine satisfaction over
the steps they have taken to correct what he had found objec-
tionable in their conduct. The joy of Titus over their response
to the apostle's admonitions pleases Paul all the more and justifies his complete trust in them.

 8, 1—9, 15: See note on 1 Corinthians 16, 1 concerning the
collection spoken of here. No doubt the conflicts in Corinth to
which this letter alludes were responsible for delaying this collection (8, 10). Paul here presents certain motives to the community for completing it: they are to emulate the generosity
of the Macedonians (8, 1-5) and imitate the poverty of Christ
(8, 9); they too may at some time need the charity of others
(8, 14). Paul plans to visit them and convey the generous fruit
of their charity to the community in Jerusalem. Not only will
it supply the needs of that church; it will be the cause of their
giving thanks and glory to God and of obtaining God's favor
for themselves (9, 6-15).

✽
  18: Jer 31, 9.   7: 1 Cor 1, 5.
  7/3: 6, 11-13.   9: Mt 8, 20; Phil 2, 6f.
    8: Heb 12, 11.   15: Ex 16, 18.
    8/1: 11, 8f.   18: 12, 18.

whom all the churches praise for his preaching of the gospel. ¹⁹He has been appointed our traveling companion by the churches, as we willingly carry on this work of charity for the glory of the Lord. ²⁰There is one thing I wish to avoid, namely any blame over my handling of this generous collection. ²¹*We are concerned not only for God's approval but also for the good esteem of men. ²²We have sent along that brother whose eagerness has been proved to us in many ways. He is now more eager than ever for this work because of his great trust in you. ²³As for Titus, he is my companion and fellow worker in your behalf; our brothers too are apostles of the churches, the glory of Christ. ²⁴Therefore, show these men the proof of your love, and why we boast about you, for all the churches to see.

The Offering for the Saints

9 ¹THERE is really no need for me to write you about this collection for the members of the church. ²I already know your willingness, and boast about you to the Macedonians with respect to it, saying that Achaia has been ready since last year. Your zeal has stirred up most of them. ³I nonetheless send the brothers so that our claims for you in this regard may not be shown empty. I do so that you may be ready, as I have been saying you are, ⁴lest any Macedonians come with me and find you unready; then I should be put to shame—to say nothing of you—for having had this trust. ⁵I have thought it necessary to exhort the brothers to go to you and arrange in advance for the bountiful gift you have already promised. It should be ready as a gracious gift, not as an exaction.

⁶*Let me say this much: He who sows sparingly will reap sparingly, and he who sows bountifully will reap bountifully. ⁷Everyone must give according to what he has inwardly decided; not sadly, not grudgingly, for God loves a cheerful giver. ⁸God can multiply his favors among you so that you may always have enough of everything and even a surplus for good works, ⁹*as it is written:

> "He scattered abroad and gave to the poor,
>   his justice endures forever."

¹⁰He who supplies seed for the sower and bread for the eater will provide in abundance; he will multiply the seed you sow and increase your generous yield. ¹¹In every way your liberality is enriched; through us it results in thanks offered to God. ¹²The administering of this public benefit not only supplies the needs of the members of the church but also overflows in much gratitude to God. ¹³Because of your praiseworthy service they are glorifying God for your obedient faith in the gospel of Christ, and for your generosity in sharing with them and with all. ¹⁴They pray for you longingly because of the surpassing grace God has given you. ¹⁵Thanks be to God for his indescribable gift!

Paul Defends His Ministry

10 ¹†I, Paul, exhort you by the meekness and kindness of Christ, I who (you say) when present in your midst am lowly, but when absent am bold toward you. ²*I beg you that when I am there, I may not have to act boldly, with that assurance I might dare to use courageously against certain ones who accuse us of weak human behavior. ³We do indeed live in the body but we do not wage war with human resources. ⁴*The weapons of our warfare are not merely human. They possess God's power for the destruction of strongholds. We demolish sophistries ⁵and every proud pretension that raises itself against the knowledge of God; we likewise bring every thought into captivity to make it obedient to Christ. ⁶We are ready to punish disobedience in anyone else once your own obedience is perfect.

⁷You view things superficially. If anyone is convinced that he belongs to Christ, let him reflect on this: he may belong to Christ but just as much do we. ⁸*If I find I must make a few further claims about the power the Lord has given us for your upbuilding and not for your destruction, this will not embarrass me in the least. ⁹At the same time, I do not wish to intimidate you with my letters. ¹⁰His letters, they say, are severe and forceful, but when he is here in person he is unimpressive and his word makes no great impact. ¹¹Well, let such people give this some thought, that what we are by word, in the letters during our absence, that we mean to be in action when we are present.

¹²*We are not so bold, of course, as to classify or compare ourselves with certain people who recommend themselves. Since people like that are their own appraisers, comparing themselves with one another, they only demonstrate their ignorance. ¹³When we make claims we will not go over the mark but will stay within the bounds the God of moderation has set for us—leading us to you. ¹⁴We are not overreaching ourselves, as we should be doing if we had not bothered to come to you. But indeed we did get as far as you with the gospel of Christ. ¹⁵We do not boast immoderately of the work of others; we hope that as your faith grows our influence may also grow among you and overflow. ¹⁶Following the rule laid down for us, we hope to preach the gospel even beyond your borders without having to boast of work already done by

---

† 10, 1-18: Since Paul's previous tone of gentleness changes in chapters 10 through 13 to one of aggressive criticism, some scholars conclude that these chapters belong to a lost Pauline epistle, probably the severe letter; see note on 2 Corinthians 7, 5-16. The background to these chapters is the criticism directed against Paul by people whom he names *super-apostles* (11, 5; 12, 11). He appeals to the community to take the proper steps to safeguard his authority; otherwise he will exercise it personally and fully (10, 1-11). He observes that the disturbers of the community are self-praisers, boasting of work which not they, but others, have accomplished. To be approved requires recommendation by God, not by oneself (10, 12-18).

21: Rom 12, 17.
9/6: Prv 11, 24f.
9: Ps 112, 9.
10/2: 1 Cor 4, 21.
4: 1 Cor 1, 25; Eph 6, 11.
8: 13, 10.
12: 3, 1.

another in his allotted territory. [17]*"Let him who would boast, boast in the Lord." [18]It is not the man who recommends himself who is approved but the man whom the Lord recommends.

Paul and the False Apostles

11 [1]†YOU must endure a little of my folly. Put up with me, I beg you! [2]*I am jealous of you with the jealousy of God himself, since I have given you in marriage to one husband, presenting you as a chaste virgin to Christ. [3]*My fear is that, just as the serpent seduced Eve by his cunning, your thoughts may be corrupted and you may fall away from your sincere and complete devotion to Christ. [4]*I say this because, when someone comes preaching another Jesus than the one we preached, or when you receive a different spirit than the one you have received, or a gospel other than the gospel you accepted, you seem to endure it quite well. [5]*I consider myself inferior to the "super-apostles" in nothing. [6]*I may be unskilled in speech but I know that I am not lacking in knowledge. We have made this evident to you in every conceivable way.

[7]*Could I have done wrong when I preached the gospel of God to you free of charge, humbling myself with a view to exalting you? [8]*I robbed other churches, I accepted support from them in order to minister to you. [9]When I was with you and in want I was a burden to none of you, for the brothers who came from Macedonia supplied my needs. In every way possible I kept myself from being burdensome to you, and I shall continue to do so. [10]I swear by the Christ who is in me that this boast of mine will not cease in the regions of Achaia! [11]Why? Because I do not love you? God knows I do. [12]What I am doing I shall continue to do, depriving at every turn those who look for a chance to say that in their much-vaunted ministry they work on the same terms as we do. [13]Such men are false apostles. They practice deceit in their disguise as apostles of Christ. [14]And little wonder! For even Satan disguises himself as an angel of light. [15]It comes as no surprise that his ministers disguise themselves as ministers of the justice of God. But their end will correspond to their deeds.

Paul's Sufferings as an Apostle

[16]†I repeat: let no one think me foolish. But if you do, then accept me as a fool all the way and let me do a little boasting. [17]What I am about to say in this self-assured boasting, I speak not as the Lord desires but after the manner of a fool. [18]Since many are bragging about their human distinctions, I too will boast. [19]*Being wise yourselves, you gladly put up with fools.

[20]You even put up with those who exploit you, who impose upon you and put on airs, with those who slap your face. [21]To my shame I must confess that we have been too weak to do such things. But what anyone else dares to claim—I speak with absolute foolishness now —I, too, will dare. [22]*Are they Hebrews? So am I! Are they Israelites? So am I! Are they the seed of Abraham? So am I! [23]Are they ministers of Christ? Now I am really talking like a fool—I am more: with my many more labors and imprisonments, with far worse beatings and frequent brushes with death. [24]*Five times at the hands of the Jews I received forty lashes less one; [25]*three times I was beaten with rods; I was stoned once, shipwrecked three times; I passed a day and a night on the sea. [26]I traveled continually, endangered by floods, robbers, my own people, the Gentiles; imperiled in the city, in the desert, at sea, by false brothers; [27]*enduring labor, hardship, many sleepless nights; in hunger and thirst and frequent fastings, in cold and nakedness. [28]Leaving other sufferings unmentioned, there is that daily tension pressing on me, my anxiety for all the churches. [29]*Who is weak that I am not affected by it? Who is scandalized that I am not aflame with indignation? [30]If I must boast, I will make a point of my weaknesses. [31]The God and Father of the Lord Jesus knows—blessed be he forever—that I do not lie. [32]*In Damascus the ethnarch of King Aretas was keeping a close watch on the city in order to arrest me, [33]but I was lowered in a basket through a window in the wall and escaped his hands.

Visions and Revelations

12 [1]I must go on boasting, however useless it may be, and speak of visions and revelations of the Lord. [2]*I know a man in Christ who, fourteen years ago, whether he was in or outside his body I cannot say, only God can say—a man who was snatched up to the third heaven. [3]I know that this man —whether in or outside his body I do not know, God knows—[4]was snatched up to Paradise to hear words which cannot be uttered, words which no man may speak. [5]About this man I will boast; but I will do no boasting about myself unless it be about my weaknesses. [6]And even if I were to boast it would not be folly in me because I would only be telling the truth.

---

† 11, 1-15: Paul sees in the work of the *super-apostles* a threat to the purity of the gospel as he preached it to Corinthians (1-6). He regards his own selflessness in the ministry as worthy of a hearing against the conduct of those whom he now designates as false apostles (7-15).

11, 16—12, 10: Since the false apostles have thrilled the community with accounts of their achievements, Paul will boast of his sufferings and humiliations (16-33). If they seek from Paul evidence of unique religious experiences, his have been so extraordinary as to be incapable of expression in words (12, 1-5). To keep him humble despite his unique visions, God gave Paul a special affliction, *a thorn in the flesh* (12, 7)—whether a disease or a spiritual affliction is not certain (12, 7-10). If this phrase is an echo of Nm 33, 55 or Ez 28, 24, the thorn is the "super-apostles."

17: 1 Cor 1, 31.
11/2: Eph 5, 27.
3: Gn 3, 4.
4: Gal 1, 6-9.
5: 12, 11.
6: 1 Cor 2, 1-5.
7: Acts 18, 3; 1 Cor 9, 18.
8: 1 Cor 9, 15.
19: 3, 1.
22: Acts 22, 3; Rom 11, 1.
24: Dt 25, 2f; Acts 16, 22.
25: Acts 14, 19.
27: 1 Cor 4, 11.
29: 1 Cor 9, 22.
32: Acts 9, 24.
12/2: Acts 9, 3.

7*But I refrain, lest anyone think more of me than what he sees in me or hears from my lips. As to the extraordinary revelations, in order that I might not become conceited I was given a thorn in the flesh, an angel of Satan to beat me and keep me from getting proud. **8***Three times I begged the Lord that this might leave me. **9**He said to me, "My grace is enough for you, for in weakness power reaches perfection." And so I willingly boast of my weaknesses instead, that the power of Christ may rest upon me.

10*Therefore I am content with weakness, with mistreatment, with distress, with persecutions and difficulties for the sake of Christ; for when I am powerless, it is then that I am strong.

Concern for the Corinthian Church

11†What a fool I have become! You have driven me to it. You are the ones who should have been commending me. Even though I am nothing, I am in no way inferior to the "super-apostles." **12***Indeed, I have performed among you with great patience the signs that show the apostle, signs and wonders and deeds of power. **13**In what way are you inferior to the other churches except in this, that I was no burden to you? Forgive me this injustice! **14**This is the third time that I am about to visit you, and I am not going to burden you; for I do not want what you have, I only want you. Children should not save up for their parents, but parents for children. **15**I will gladly spend myself and be spent for your sakes. If I love you too much, will I be loved the less for that? **16**Granted that I did not burden you—but being crafty, you say, I caught you by guile. **17**Did I ever take advantage of you through any of the men I sent to you? **18**I urged Titus to go to you, and I sent the other brother with him. Did Titus take advantage of you in any way? Did we not act in the one spirit, walk in the same footsteps?

19Do you think throughout this recital that I am defending myself to you? Before God I tell you, in Christ, I have done everything to build you up, my dear ones. **20**I fear that when I come I may not find you to my liking, nor may you find me to yours. I fear I may find discord, jealousy, outbursts of anger, selfish ambitions, slander and gossip, self-importance, disorder. **21**I fear that when I come again my God may humiliate me before you, and I may have to mourn over the many who sinned earlier and have not repented of the uncleanness, fornication, and sensuality they practiced.

Final Warnings

13 **1***†THIS is the third time I shall be coming to you. "A judicial fact shall be established only on the testimony of two or three witnesses." **2**I said before when I was there the second time—and I repeat it now in my absence—to those who sinned before and to all the rest, that if I come again I shall not spare you. **3**You are, after all, looking for a proof of the Christ who speaks in me. He is not weak in dealing with you, but is powerful in you. **4***It is true he was crucified out of weakness, but he lives by the power of God. We too are weak in him, but we live with him by God's power in us. **5**Test yourselves to see whether you are living in faith; examine yourselves. Perhaps you yourselves do not realize that Christ Jesus is in you—unless, of course, you have failed the challenge. **6**I hope you will understand that we have not failed. **7**We pray God that you may do no evil—not in order that we may appear approved but simply that you may do what is good, even though we may seem to have failed. **8**We cannot do anything against the truth, but only for the sake of the truth. **9**We even rejoice when we are weak and you are strong. Our prayer is that you may be built up to completion.

Farewell

10*I am writing in this way while away from you, so that when I am with you I may not have to exercise with severity the authority the Lord has given me—authority to build up rather than to destroy. **11**And now, brothers, I must say good-bye. Mend your ways. Encourage one another. Live in harmony and peace, and the God of love and peace will be with you. **12***Greet one another with a holy kiss. All the holy ones send greetings to you. **13**The grace of the Lord Jesus Christ, and the love of God, and the fellowship of the Holy Spirit be with you all!

---

† 12, 11-21: Paul recalls to the minds of the Corinthians the kind of apostle he showed himself in their midst (11-15). He indicates the absurdity of the false apostles' suggestion that he and Titus took no support from the community in order to gain control of it more easily (16ff). His aim has been, not to defend himself, but to keep the community faithful to the teaching of Christ (19ff).

13, 1-10: The apostle's final appeal is that the community correct the evils within it through an examination of its own conscience. This will preclude the disagreeable necessity of his taking severe action against them.

❋
7: Nm 33, 35; Ez 28, 24; Mt 26, 39.42.44.
8: 4, 7.
10: Phil 4, 13.
12: Rom 15, 19; 1 Thes 1, 5.

13/1: Dt 19, 15; Mt 18, 16; Jn 8, 17; Heb 10, 28.
4: Rom 8, 11.
10: 10, 8.
12: 1 Cor 16, 20.

The Epistle of Paul to the Galatians

Introduction

Until the nineteenth century it was assumed that the Epistle to the Galatians was addressed to Christian communities which Paul founded in the interior of Asia Minor on his second missionary journey (Acts 16, 6) and visited on his third (Acts 18, 23). The epistle would then have been written at some time during these journeys between the years 52 and 57. Since the last century, however, many scholars have advanced what is called the South Galatian theory, contending that the epistle was actually written to the communities founded on Paul's first missionary journey in the area of Asia Minor extending from the seacoast inland (Acts 13, 13—14, 27). This premise has also been adopted here. If valid, it places the epistle among Paul's earliest writings, possibly in 48 A. D., or even before, but more probably after the Council of Jerusalem, 49 or 50 A. D. The meeting with James, Cephas, and John on which Paul reports in 2, 1-10 would then be the meeting described by Luke in Acts 15 as the Council itself.

The background facts regarding the Epistle to the Galatians provide a needed explanation of the complex data relative to it in the epistle itself and in Acts. They help to account for the passionate intensity with which Galatians is written.

Paul shows no knowledge of any limitation of the freedom of Gentile Christians in respect to Mosaic law (2, 9). This suggests that Luke's account of the Council of Jerusalem in which that freedom is limited by the provisions of the apostolic decree (Acts 15, 23-29) is a theological construct. After Paul had left Galatia, Judaeo-Christians from Jerusalem came there, and urged the Galatian communities to adopt the practices of the Mosaic law. The "false claimants to the title of brother" (2, 4), as Paul names these preachers who followed him, did not reject Christ as Savior in favor of the law. But, holding to the Christian doctrine of his central role, they nevertheless advocated the law as a highly beneficial addition to Christian living, and appealed for precedent to the actual practice in Palestine under Cephas (2, 1-10). They made light of Paul's apostolic role, holding him to be less informed than the Twelve (1, 11-24) because he had not been a disciple of Jesus during the ministry. They succeeded in disturbing and confusing the consciences of the Galatians, who were tending more and more to follow their teaching as a surer way of salvation (3, 1).

This subtle form of religiosity evoked from Paul a resounding declaration of the true nature of justification by faith in Christ, which frees the conscience from the Mosaic law as a principle of man's justice before God. The process thus begun in Galatians, of reflecting intensively on the meaning of the Christian gospel, eventually led Paul to his more far-reaching and profound exposition in the Epistle to the Romans.

The Epistle to the Galatians is divided as follows:

I: INTRODUCTION

Greetings

1 **1*** †PAUL, AN APOSTLE SENT not by men or by any man, but by Jesus Christ and God his Father who raised him from the dead—**2**I and my brothers who are with me send greetings to the churches in Galatia. **3**We wish you the favor and peace of God our Father and of the Lord Jesus Christ, **4***who gave himself for our sins, to rescue us from the present evil age, as our God and Father willed—**5**to him be glory for endless ages. Amen.

Reproof for Disloyalty

6* †I am amazed that you are so soon deserting him who called you in accord with his gracious design in

---

† 1, 1-5: Together with his customary greeting (see note on Rom 1, 1-7), Paul abruptly introduces the two main topics of the epistle: the authenticity of his apostolic office (1ff) and the doctrine of justification through faith rather than through observance of the law. Alluding to the Judaizers, i. e., Judaeo-Christians who have attempted to introduce traditional Jewish observances into the Galatian churches (cf 2, 4), he reminds the Galatians of his direct appointment to the office of apostle by Christ (v 1). He reaffirms what he had previously preached to them, that Christ's sacrificial death alone saves from sin (v 4).

1, 6-10: To impress upon the Galatians the doctrinal seriousness of their inclination to combine the practices of Judaism as saving acts with their faith in Christ, Paul calls this teaching *another gospel*, i. e., a doctrine of salvation substantially different from authentic Christian teaching (v 6), and declares that the Judaeo-Christians responsible for introducing it into the Galatian communities are to be condemned (v 9). The Judaizers have alleged that Paul originally refrained from teaching the Galatians the practices of Judaism in order to win them over more easily; the charge is now refuted, for he has made it clear that he will not compromise even with his fellow Jewish-Christians (v 10).

  1/1: 1, 11f.   6: 2 Cor 11, 4.
    4: 2, 20; 1 Tm 2, 6.

Christ, and are going over to another gospel. **7**But there is no other. Some who wish to alter the gospel of Christ must have confused you. **8**For even if we, or an angel from heaven, should preach to you a gospel not in accord with the one we delivered to you, let a curse be upon him! **9**I repeat what I have just said: if anyone preaches a gospel to you other than the one you received, let a curse be upon him!

10*Whom would you say I am trying to please at this point—men or God? Is this how I seek to ingratiate myself with men? If I were trying to win man's approval, I would surely not be serving Christ!

II: PAUL'S DEFENSE OF HIS AUTHORITY AND DOCTRINE

Called by Christ

11*I ASSURE YOU, BROTHERS, the gospel I proclaimed to you is no mere human invention. **12***I did not receive it from any man, nor was I schooled in it. It came by revelation from Jesus Christ. **13***You have heard, I know, the story of my former way of life in Judaism. You know that I went to extremes in persecuting the church of God and tried to destroy it; **14***I made progress in Jewish observance far beyond most of my contemporaries, in my excess of zeal to live out all the traditions of my ancestors.

15*But the time came when he who had set me apart before I was born and called me by his favor **16***chose to reveal his Son to me, that I might spread among the Gentiles the good tidings concerning him. Immediately, without seeking human advisers **17**or even going to Jerusalem to see those who were apostles before me, I went off to Arabia; later I returned to Damascus. **18***Three years after that I went up to Jerusalem to get to know Cephas, with whom I stayed fifteen days. **19**I did not meet any other apostles except James, the brother of the Lord. **20**I declare before God that what I have just written is true.

21Thereafter I entered the regions of Syria and Cilicia. **22**The communities of Christ in Judea had no idea what I looked like; **23**they had only heard that "he who was formerly persecuting us is now preaching the faith he tried to destroy," **24**and they gave glory to God on my account.

The Council of Jerusalem

2 **1†**THEN, after fourteen years, I went up to Jerusalem again with Barnabas, this time taking Titus with me. **2**I went prompted by a revelation, and I laid out for their scrutiny the gospel as I present it to the Gentiles—all this in private confer-

ence with the leaders, to make sure the course I was pursuing, or had pursued, was not useless. **3**Not even Titus, who was with me, was ordered to undergo circumcision, despite his being a Greek. **4**Certain false claimants to the title of brother were smuggled in; they wormed their way into the group to spy on the freedom we enjoy in Christ Jesus and thereby to make slaves of us, but **5***we did not submit to them for a moment. We resisted so that the truth of the gospel might survive intact for your benefit.

6*Those who were regarded as important, however (and it makes no difference to me how prominent they were—God plays no favorites), made me add nothing.

7On the contrary, recognizing that I had been entrusted with the gospel for the uncircumcised, just as Peter was for the circumcised **8**(for he worked through Peter as his apostle among the Jews had been at work in me for the Gentiles), **9***and recognizing, too, the favor bestowed on me, those who were the acknowledged pillars, James, Cephas, and John, gave Barnabas and me the handclasp of fellowship, signifying that we should go to the Gentiles as they to the Jews. **10**The only stipulation was that we should be mindful of the poor—the one thing I was making every effort to do.

† 1, 11-24: *The gospel I proclaimed:* this is shown to be the common possession of all the apostles including himself (see note on v 4). It was an understanding of the meaning of Christ's death in the order of salvation, divinely granted to Paul (11f), which led him to surrender his early career in Judaism (13f). Once he received this understanding of Christ and the apostolic office, he deemed it unnecessary to confer with the other apostles. Instead he went into retirement for a time (15ff). When, three years later, he spent two weeks with Peter in Jerusalem, he did not compare his understanding of Christ with that of the other apostles (18f). He is speaking truthfully, for the Judaeo-Christian churches near Jerusalem also recognized that he had abandoned Judaism for Christ as the way of salvation (20-24).

2, 1-10: The *private conference with the leaders* is probably the same described by Luke in Acts 15; see note on Acts 15, 6-12. The first time Paul discussed the nature of the Christian gospel with other apostles was some fourteen years after his conversion (v 1), and then in consequence of a prophetic inspiration (v 2). The misgivings about Paul entertained at that time did not pertain to his doctrine, but probably to his persistence in establishing Christian communities among the Gentiles despite Jewish opposition (v 2; cf Acts 13, 13f.27). When it was suggested by Judaeo-Christians who opposed him that the Gentile Christian Titus be circumcised so as to display Paul's respect for Judaism, he refused to comply lest such a concession be turned against him (2, 3ff). James, Cephas, and John, far from objecting to his stand, even conceded that he possessed a God-given mission to the Gentiles, just as Peter was founder and leader of the Judaeo-Christian communities of Palestine. It was agreed then that Gentile Christians would not adopt the practices of Judaism, even though the Judaeo-Christian communities continued to retain them for cultural reasons (6-9). Paul readily acceded to the idea of organizing a collection among the Gentile communities for the poor Christians of Jerusalem (v 10), for he saw in it an occasion to develop unity of faith despite the prevailing diversity of culture; cf 2 Cor 9, 13.

❋
10: 1 Thes 2, 4.
11: 1, 1.
12: Eph 3, 3.
13: Acts 8, 1ff.
14: Acts 26, 4f.
15: Is 49, 1; Lk 1, 15.
16: 2, 7; Acts 9, 3-19.
18: Acts 9, 23-30.
2/5: 3, 1.
6: Dt 10, 17; Rom 2, 11; Eph 6, 9.
9: Eph 3, 8.

Peter and the Judaizers

11*†When Cephas came to Antioch I directly withstood him, because he was clearly in the wrong. **12**He had been taking his meals with the Gentiles before others came who were from James. But when they arrived he drew back to avoid trouble with those who were circumcised. **13**The rest of the Jews joined in his dissembling, till even Barnabas was swept away by their pretense. **14**As soon as I observed that they were not being straightforward about the truth of the gospel, I had this to say to Cephas in the presence of all: "If you who are a Jew are living according to Gentile ways rather than Jewish, by what logic do you force the Gentiles to adopt Jewish ways?"

Paul's Basic Teaching

15†We are Jews by birth, not sinners of Gentile origin. **16***Nevertheless, knowing that a man is not justified by legal observance but by faith in Jesus Christ, we too have believed in him in order to be justified by faith in Christ, not by observance of the law; for by works of the law no one will be justified. **17**But if, in seeking to be justified in Christ, we are shown to be sinners, does that mean that Christ is encouraging sin? Unthinkable! **18**If, however, I were to build up the very things I had demolished, I should then indeed be a transgressor. **19**It was through the law that I died to the law, to live for God. I have been crucified with Christ, **20***and the life I live now is not my own; Christ is living in me. I still live my human life, but it is a life of faith in the Son of God, who loved me and gave himself for me. **21***I will not treat God's gracious gift as pointless. If justice is available through the law, then Christ died to no purpose!

III: CHRISTIAN FAITH AND LIBERTY

Justification through Faith

3 **1**†YOU SENSELESS GALATIANS! Who has cast a spell over you—you before whose eyes Jesus Christ was displayed to view upon his cross? **2**I want to learn only one thing from you: how did you receive the Spirit? Was it through observance of the law or through faith in what you heard? **3**How could you be so stupid? After beginning in the spirit, are you now to end in the flesh? **4**Have you had such remarkable experiences all to no purpose—if indeed they were to no purpose? **5**Is it because you observe the law or because you have faith in what you heard that God lavishes the Spirit on you and works wonders in your midst? **6***†Consider the case of Abraham: he "believed God, and it was credited to him as justice."

7*This means that those who believe are sons of Abraham. **8***Because Scripture saw in advance that God's way of justifying the Gentiles would be through faith, it foretold this good news to Abraham: "All nations shall be blessed in you." **9**Thus it is that all who believe are blessed along with Abraham, the man of faith.

No Justification from the Law

10*†All who depend on observance of the law, on the other hand, are under a curse. It is written, "Cursed is he who does not abide by everything written in the book of the law and carry it out." **11***It should be obvious that no one is justified in God's sight by the law, for "the just man shall live by faith." **12***But the law does not depend on faith. Its terms are: "Whoever does these things shall live by them." **13***Christ has delivered us from the power of the law's curse by himself becoming a curse for us, as it is writ-

---

† 2, 11-14: This incident, which probably occurred after the meeting of 2, 1-10, is more understandable if the policy then arrived at was not publicly promulgated to the Judaeo-Christians of Jerusalem (see note on Acts 15, 6-12). When Peter realized that sharing the agape-meal (see note on 1 Cor 11, 17-34) with Gentile Christians wounded the sensibilities of Judaeo-Christians, he abandoned the practice out of deference to their presence (11f). Other Judaeo-Christians in Antioch followed suit, thereby placing in jeopardy the unity of the Antiochean church (v 13). Paul publicly criticized Peter's conduct because it implied that, although in theory the Judaeo-Christian could eat with Gentile Christians, in practice the Gentile Christian should not eat with Judaeo-Christians (v 14).

2, 15-21: Although the Judaeo-Christian enjoys a certain religious privilege by birth (v 15), he knows that he is not justified by the Mosaic law but by faith in Christ (v 16). If he insists on his privilege as a Jew (v 11-14), he implies that Christ has misled him (a probable sense of v 17), and that he has sinned in abandoning his privilege by accepting Christ (v 18). The Judaeo-Christian, like Paul, knows that his privileged position occasioned his transgression of the law and revealed him to be a sinner in need of the redemptive death of Christ (v 19). Therefore, disregarding his privileged status as Jew, he values only the new condition received from Christ, the source of his holiness (v 20). He seeks no privileged status in the Christian community—*I will not treat God's gracious gift as pointless* (v 21)—lest his justification seem to come from the law and not from the sacrifice of Christ.

3, 1-5: Paul suggests that the Galatians must be under an evil spell to have forgotten the redemptive meaning of Jesus' crucifixion (v 1). He asks them to recall the reason for their conversion: the reception of the Spirit, not the works of the law (2-5).

3, 6-9: Probably in response to the argument of the Judaizers that if a Christian wishes to benefit fully from the promises made to Abraham he should embrace Judaism, Paul cites Gn 15, 6 to the effect that Abraham won God's favor because of his faith. Christians too have already won God's favor through their faith in Christ; cf 3, 2-5. They therefore may expect the fullness of the benefits promised Abraham for the Gentile nations (7-9).

3, 10-14: To seek salvation through observance of the law is to subject oneself to divine retribution (v 10), for the law is not the source of justification (v 11). It is associated with justification only if it is observed through faith (v 12). Christ removed the threat of divine retribution which came with non-observance of the law (v 13) in order that the Gentiles might receive through faith the blessings promised to Abraham on their behalf. Thus they are freed of the continual threat of divine punishment (v 14).

11ff: Acts 15, 1.
16: Rom 3, 20.22; Phil 3, 9.
20: Rom 8, 10f; Col 3, 3f.
21: 5, 2.
3/6: Gn 15, 6; Rom 4, 3; Jas 2, 23.
7: Sir 44, 19ff.
8: Gn 12, 3.
10: Dt 27, 26; Rom 7, 7.
11: Hb 2, 4; Rom 1, 17.
12: Lv 18, 5.
13: Dt 21, 23.

ten: "Accursed is anyone who is hanged on a tree." [14]This has happened so that through Christ Jesus the blessing bestowed on Abraham might descend on the Gentiles in Christ Jesus, thereby making it possible for us to receive the promised Spirit through faith.

Promise Not Nullified by the Law

[15]* †Brothers, let me give you an everyday example. You cannot add anything to a man's will or set it aside once it is legally validated. [16]*There were promises spoken to Abraham and to his "descendant." Scripture does not say "and to your descendants," as if it applied to many, but as if it applied only to one, "and to your descendant"; that is, to Christ. [17]My point is this: a covenant formally ratified by God is not set aside as invalid by any law that came into being four hundred and thirty years later, nor is its promise nullified. [18]Clearly, if one's inheritance comes through the law, it is no longer conferred in virtue of the promise. Yet it was by way of promise that God granted Abraham his privilege.

True Function of the Law

[19]* †What is the relevance of the law, in such case? It was given in view of transgressions and promulgated by angels, at the hands of a mediator; it was to be valid only until that descendant or offspring came to whom the promise had been given. [20]Now, there can be no mediator when only one person is involved; and God is one. [21]Does this mean that the law is opposed to the promises [of God]? Again, unthinkable! If the law that was given was such that it could impart life, then justice would be a consequence of the law. [22]*In fact, however, Scripture has locked all things in under the constraint of sin. Why? So that the promise might be fulfilled in those who believe, in consequence of faith in Jesus Christ.

The Benefit of Faith

[23]†Before faith came we were under the constraint of the law, locked in until the faith that was coming should be revealed. [24]In other words, the law was our monitor until Christ came to bring about our justification through faith. [25]But now that faith is here, we are no longer in the monitor's charge. [26]*Each one of you is a son of God because of your faith in Christ Jesus. [27]*All of you who have been baptized into Christ have clothed yourselves with him. [28]*There does not exist among you Jew or Greek, slave or freeman, male or female. All are one in Christ Jesus. [29]*Furthermore, if you belong to Christ you are the descendants of Abraham, which means you inherit all that was promised.

Free Sons of God in Christ

4 [1]†BROTHERS: as long as a designated heir is not of age his condition is no different from that of a slave, even though in name he is master of all his possessions; [2]for he is under the supervision of guardians and administrators until the time set by his father. [3]*In the same way, while we were not yet of age we were like slaves subordinated to the elements of the world; [4]but when the designated time had come, God sent forth his Son born of a woman, born under the law, [5]*to deliver from the law those who were subjected to it, so that we might receive our status as adopted sons. [6]*The proof that you are sons is the fact that God has sent forth into our hearts the spirit of his Son which cries out "Abba!" ("Father!") [7]You are no longer a slave but a son! And the fact that you are a son makes you an heir, by God's design.

---

† 3, 15-18: The example of the promise to Abraham derives its force from a certain continuity in the divine plan of salvation. Abraham, on whom the law that came only centuries later was not imposed, is the type or figure of God's gift of salvation to the Gentiles as well as to Israel. Hence to impose the law upon men as a means of salvation would be to deface the image of Abraham in Genesis as the spiritual father of all nations; cf Gn 12, 3.

3, 19-22: Though not the source of justification and salvation (3, 11), the Mosaic law fulfilled the purpose of revealing through Israel's history, illumined by the sacrifice of Christ, the sinfulness of all humanity; (v 19; cf Rom 3, 9-20). Through the coming of Christ, this divine revelation is now fully grasped by those who believe in him (v 22). The fact that the law was delivered through Moses as mediator indicates that the law is not the fulfillment of the promise to Abraham concerning the Gentiles (v 19; cf Gn 12, 3). It is God alone who fulfills this promise of his for their salvation (v 20; cf Rom 3, 24). He could have imposed a law upon man that would justify him through its observance (v 21); instead he used the Mosaic law to reveal the sinfulness of man, and thus prepare him for salvation from sin through faith in Christ (v 22).

3, 23-29: Paul here summarizes his previous thought. The purpose of the Mosaic law was to keep man aware of his own sinfulness—*locked in*—that he might realize his need of justification through an act of God accepted in faith (v 23). The value of the law lay in its role leading to an understanding of the absolute necessity of faith in Christ (v 24). This having been accomplished, its function is fulfilled (v 25). The Galatian Christians, whether Jew or Gentile, slave or free, men or women, all walk the same path of salvation through faith in Christ. In this they are the true descendants of Abraham, the man of faith (23-29).

4, 1-7: Paul draws on the culture of the time to indicate to the Galatians their status in the history of salvation. They have reached a point in the religious history of humanity comparable to the state of a child in a Roman family who has attained his majority. From that moment he enjoys the goods, rights and privileges of an adult (1-3). The Galatians have been freed through Christ from the tutelage of the law, which kept humanity conscious of its slavery to sin. As a result they have experienced the power of the Holy Spirit, who has recreated them as God's sons and enabled them to live their lives according to the sense and spirit of this new relationship (4-7).

❊
15: Heb 9, 17.
16: Gn 12, 7; Mt 1, 1.
19: Rom 5, 20.
22: Rom 3, 9-20.23.
26: 4, 5ff; Jn 1, 12;
    Rom 8, 14f.
27: Rom 6, 4; Eph 4, 24.

28: Rom 10, 12;
    1 Cor 12, 13; Col 3, 11.
29: Heb 6, 12; Jas 2, 5.
4/3: 3, 23.
5: 3, 13.26.
6: Rom 8, 15ff.

No Return to Slavery

8*†In the past, when you did not acknowledge God, you served as slaves to gods who are not really divine. **9**Now that you have come to know God—or rather, have been known by him—how can you return to those powerless, worthless, natural elements to which you seem willing to enslave yourselves once more? **10***You even go so far as to keep the ceremonial observance of days and months, seasons and years! **11**I fear for you; all my efforts with you may have been wasted.

Former Devotion of the Galatians

12†I beg you, brothers, to become like me as I became like you. (Understand, you have not done me any wrong.) **13**You are aware that it was a bodily ailment that first occasioned my bringing you the gospel. **14**My physical condition was a challenge which you did not despise or brush aside in disgust. On the contrary, you took me to yourselves as an angel of God, even as if I had been Christ Jesus! **15**What has happened to your openhearted spirit? I can testify on your behalf that if it were possible you would have plucked out your eyes and given them to me. **16**Have I become your enemy just because I tell you the truth?

17*The people I have referred to are not courting your favor in any generous spirit. What they really want is to exclude you so that you may court their favor. **18**It would be well for you to be courted for the right reasons at all times, and not only when I happen to be with you. **19***You are my children, and you put me back in labor pains until Christ is formed in you. **20**If only I could be with you now and speak to you differently! You have me at a complete loss!

Allegory on Freedom

21†You who want to be subject to the law, tell me: do you know what the law has to say? **22***There it is written that Abraham had two sons, one by the slave girl, the other by his freeborn wife. **23***The son of the slave girl had been begotten in the course of nature, but the son of the free woman was the fruit of the promise. **24***All this is an allegory: the two women stand for the two covenants. One is from Mount Sinai, and brought forth children to slavery: this is Hagar. **25**The mountain Sinai [Hagar] is in Arabia and corresponds to the Jerusalem of our time, which is likewise in slavery with her children. **26**But the Jerusalem on high is freeborn, and it is she who is our mother. **27***That is why Scripture says:

"Rejoice, you barren one who bear no children;
break into song, you stranger to the pains of childbirth!
For many are the children of the wife deserted
—far more than of her who has a husband!"

28*You, my brothers, are children of the promise, as Isaac was. **29**But just as in those days the son born in nature's course persecuted the one whose birth was in the realm of spirit, so do we find it now. **30***What does Scripture say on the point? "Cast out slave girl and son together; for the slave girl's son shall never be an heir on equal terms with the son" of the one born free. **31***Therefore, my brothers, we are not children of a slave girl but of a mother who is free.

IV: EXHORTATION TO CHRISTIAN LIVING

Basic Import of Faith

5 **1**IT WAS FOR LIBERTY that Christ freed us. So stand firm, and do not take on yourselves the yoke of slavery a second time! **2***Pay close attention to me, Paul, when I tell you that if you have yourselves circumcised, Christ will be of no use to you! **3**I point out once more to all who receive circumcision that they are bound to the law in its entirety. **4**Any of you who seek your justification in the law have severed yourselves from Christ and fallen from God's favor! **5**It is in the spirit that we eagerly await the justification we hope for, and only faith can yield it. **6***In Christ Jesus neither circumcision nor the lack of it counts for anything; only faith, which expresses itself through love.

Against Being Misled

7†You were progressing so very well; who diverted you from the path of truth? **8***Such enticement does not come from him who calls you. **9***"A little yeast can

---

8: 1 Cor 12, 2.
10: Col 2, 16-20.
17: 1, 7.
19: 1 Cor 4, 14f;
    2 Cor 6, 13;
    1 Thes 2, 7f.
22: Gn 16, 15; 21, 2.
23: Gn 17, 16.
24: 5, 1.

27: Is 54, 1.
28: Rom 9, 8.
30: Gn 21, 10.
31: 3, 29; Jn 8, 35.
5/2: 2; 21; Acts 15, 1ff.
6: 6, 15; 1 Cor 7, 19.
8: 1, 6.
9: 1 Cor 5, 6.

†

4, 8-11: Referring to the conversion of the Galatians, Paul presses his argument against their adoption of practices of the law by showing that, if they were to accept Judaism as a partial principle of salvation, it would be no less futile than to return to polytheism.

4, 12-20: The apostle appeals to their personal loyalty to him through whom Christ was formed in them.

4, 21-31: Paul creates an allegory out of the story of Sarah and Hagar (Gn 21, 8-21; cf Gn 16, 1-16). The two women represent two covenants: Hagar, the slave girl, represents the covenant of Sinai. The children of this covenant are sons of Abraham *begotten in the course of nature*. By the covenant of Sinai they were enslaved to the law like Hagar's offspring, who were born into slavery. Sarah, the freewoman, represents the covenant made by God with Abraham. The children of this covenant, also sons of Abraham, are *the fruit of the promise*. Like the offspring of Sarah, born to freedom, these are free from the slavery of the Mosaic law.

5, 7-12: A strongly worded appeal that they will reject the teachers who are misleading them.

affect the entire dough." [10]I trust that, in the Lord, you will not adopt a different view. May condemnation fall on whoever it is that is unsettling you! [11]*As for me, brothers, if I am still preaching circumcision, why do the attacks on me continue? If I were, the cross would be a stumbling block no more. [12]Would that those who are troubling you might go the whole way, and castrate themselves!

Proper Use of Freedom

[13]*†My brothers, remember that you have been called to live in freedom—but not a freedom that gives free rein to the flesh. Out of love, place yourselves at one another's service. [14]*The whole law has found its fulfillment in this one saying: "You shall love your neighbor as yourself." [15]If you go on biting and tearing one another to pieces, take care! You will end up in mutual destruction!

[16]*My point is that you should live in accord with the spirit and you will not yield to the cravings of the flesh. [17]The flesh lusts against the spirit and the spirit against the flesh; the two are directly opposed. This is why you do not do what your will intends. [18]If you are guided by the spirit, you are not under the law. [19]It is obvious what proceeds from the flesh: lewd conduct, impurity, licentiousness, [20]idolatry, sorcery, hostilities, bickering, jealousy, outbursts of rage, selfish rivalries, dissensions, factions, [21]envy, drunkenness, orgies, and the like. I warn you, as I have warned you before: those who do such things will not inherit the kingdom of God!

[22]*In contrast, the fruit of the spirit is love, joy, peace, patient endurance, kindness, generosity, faith, [23]mildness, and chastity. Against such there is no law! [24]*Those who belong to Christ Jesus have crucified their flesh with its passions and desires. [25]Since we live by the spirit, let us follow the spirit's lead. [26]Let us never be boastful, or challenging, or jealous toward one another.

The Demands of Conscience

6 [1]*MY brothers, if someone is detected in sin, you who live by the spirit should gently set him right, each of you trying to avoid falling into temptation himself. [2]Help carry one another's burdens; in that way you will fulfill the law of Christ.

[3]*If anyone thinks he amounts to something, when in fact he is nothing, he is only deceiving himself. [4]Each man should look to his conduct; if he has reason to boast of anything, it will be because the achievement is his and not another's. [5]Everyone should bear his own responsibility.

[6]The man instructed in the word should share all he has with his instructor. [7]*Make no mistake about it, no one makes a fool of God! A man will reap only what he sows. [8]*If he sows in the field of the flesh, he will reap a harvest of corruption; but if his seedground is the spirit, he will reap everlasting life. [9]*Let us not grow weary of doing good; if we do not relax our efforts, in due time we shall reap our harvest. [10]*While we have the opportunity, let us do good to all men—but especially those of the household of the faith.

V: CONCLUSION

The Cross, Our True Boast

[11]*†SEE, I WRITE TO YOU in my own large handwriting! [12]*Those who are trying to force you to be circumcised are making a play for human approval—with an eye to escaping persecution for the cross of Christ. [13]The very ones who accept circumcision do not follow the law themselves. They want you to be circumcised only that they may boast about your bodily observance.

[14]May I never boast of anything but the cross of our Lord Jesus Christ! Through it, the world has been crucified to me and I to the world. [15]*It means nothing whether one is circumcised or not. All that matters is that one is created anew. [16]Peace and mercy on all who follow this rule of life, and on the Israel of God.

[17]Henceforth, let no man trouble me, for I bear the brand marks of Jesus in my body.

[18]Brothers, may the favor of our Lord Jesus Christ be with your spirit. Amen.

---

*
11: 1 Cor 1, 23.
13: Rom 6, 15; 1 Pt 2, 16.
14: Lv 19, 18; Mt 22, 39;
    Rom 13, 9.
16: 1 Pt 2, 11.
21: 1 Cor 6, 10.
22: 1 Cor 13, 4-7;
    1 Tm 4, 12.
24: Rom 6, 6; Col 3, 5.

6/1: Mt 18, 15; 2 Tm 2, 25.
3: 1 Cor 3, 18.
7: Hos 8, 7.
8: Prv 11, 18.
9: 2 Thes 3, 13.
10: 1 Thes 5, 15.
11: 1 Cor 16, 21.
12: 5, 11.
15: 5, 6; 2 Cor 5, 17.

† 5, 13-26: Since the teaching of the Judaizers has apparently provoked dissension within the community, Paul urges upon all the Christian law of love of neighbor (13ff). He forestalls the accusation that his doctrine of justification by faith opens the way to a life of moral irresponsibility (16-26).

6, 11-18: Paul asserts that the Judaizers wish the Gentile Christians to observe the laws of Judaism only in order that they themselves may escape persecution by the Jews. He observes that he already bears the scars of such persecution, but this has not prevented him from reaffirming the true doctrine in the present epistle.

The Epistle of Paul to The Ephesians

Introduction

Early Christian tradition, beginning with Irenaeus and Clement of Alexandria in the late second century, unhesitatingly ascribed this epistle to St. Paul. Since the early nineteenth century, however, critical scholarship has considered the word-usage, style, comparison with Colossians, the epistle's concept of the church, as well as the doctrine put forward by the writer, to be the basis for strong doubts about its Pauline authorship. This divergence between the two capital sources of opinion on the origin of Ephesians makes it impossible to give a categorical pronouncement for or against authorship by Paul. He was probably not the author of Ephesians in the same sense as of other epistles such as Romans, Galatians, 1 and 2 Corinthians. Whatever the epistle's literary origin, however, the author considered its teachings to be in the Pauline tradition (1, 1; 3, 1); and for purposes of interpreting the text itself, it is practical to adopt the clear implication therein that Paul is its author. If Ephesians is analyzed within the context of Pauline writings, the question of its relationship to the thought of Colossians and other letters of Paul may be fruitfully studied.

It seems certain that this epistle was not specifically addressed to the Christians of Ephesus. Paul had labored there for well over two years (Acts 19, 10), and would hardly have written so impersonally to a community with which he was intimately acquainted. Important early manuscripts (Vaticanus and Sinaiticus) omit the words *at Ephesus* in 1, 1. If Ephesians is the letter referred to in Colossians 4, 16, it may well have been addressed to a number of Christian communities, a possibility that would account for its impersonal character. What is called the letter to the Ephesians is traditionally regarded as having been written by Paul from prison—Colossians, Philippians, Philemon, and Ephesians are in fact known as the "captivity epistles." If the letter is authentically Pauline, it was probably written, as tradition has held, during Paul's first(?) Roman imprisonment, 61-63 A. D.

Ephesians consists of a greeting (1,1f); a doxology of the greatest importance for the cosmic significance it attaches to Christ (1, 3-14); reflections on the Christian mystery of salvation (1, 15-22) as well as the mystery of the church (2, 22–3, 13); a prayer for the Christian community (3, 14-21); a discussion of the practical implications of the Christian mysteries (4, 1–6, 20), with special attention to family life and a famous reflection on the theology of Christian marriage (5, 22-23); and a friendly conclusion (6, 21-24).

Greeting

1 **1***PAUL, BY THE WILL OF GOD an apostle of Jesus Christ, to the holy ones [at Ephesus], believers in Christ Jesus. **2***Grace and peace to you from God our Father and the Lord Jesus Christ.

The Father's Plan of Salvation

3*†Praised be the God and Father of our Lord Jesus Christ, who has bestowed on us in Christ every spiritual blessing in the heavens! **4***God chose us in him before the world began, to be holy and blameless in his sight, to be full of love; **5***he likewise predestined us through Christ Jesus to be his adopted sons—such was his will and pleasure—**6***that all might praise the glorious favor he has bestowed on us in his beloved.

Fulfillment through Christ

7*It is in Christ and through his blood that we have been redeemed and our sins forgiven, **8***so immeasurably generous is God's favor to us. **9***God has given us the wisdom to understand fully the mystery, the plan he was pleased to decree in Christ, **10**to be carried out in the fullness of time: namely, to bring all things in the heavens and on earth into one under Christ's headship.

✿
1/1: Rom 1, 7; 1 Cor 1, 2; Col 1, 1.
2: Col 1, 2.
3: 2, 6.
4: 5, 27; Jn 15, 16; 17, 24; Rom 8, 29.
5: Jn 1, 12; 1 Jn 3, 1.
6: Mt 3, 17.
7: 2, 7; Rom 3, 24; Col 1, 14.20.
8: Col 1, 9.
9: 3, 9; Rom 16, 25.

† 1, 3-14: This prayer of thanksgiving, similar in its opening words to Colossians 1, 12, is better understood if the later verses also (Col 1, 15-20) are taken into consideration. The exalted Christology of the second passage of Colossians is at one with this prayer which reflects upon the divine plan of salvation centering in Christ and revealed to Christians as fully at work in themselves. The spiritual blessings the Christian communities have received through Christ (v 3) are gratefully enumerated: the call to faith and holiness (v 4; cf Rom 3, 30); the gift of divine adoptive sonship establishing a unique spiritual relationship with God the Father through Christ (v 5; cf Rom 8, 14-17); the liberation from sin through Christ's sacrificial death (v 7); the revelation of God's plan of salvation in Christ (v 9; cf Rom 16, 25; Eph 3; 3f); the gift of faith in Christ bestowed upon Jews (11f); and finally, the same gift granted to Gentiles (v 13). In the christological faith of the Christian communities the apostle sees the predetermined plan of God (4.11) to bring all creation under the final rule of Christ (v 10). The Christian community has the initial understanding of the gifts God has so freely given to men for the sake of Christ (6.8f), which all humanity will eventually possess.

Blessing for Jew and Gentile

11*In him we were chosen; for in the decree of God, who administers everything according to his will and counsel, we were predestined **12**to praise his glory by being the first to hope in Christ. **13***In him you too were chosen; when you heard the glad tidings of salvation, the word of truth, and believed in it, you were sealed with the Holy Spirit who had been promised. **14***He is the pledge of our inheritance, the first payment against the full redemption of a people God has made his own, to praise his glory.

Fulfillment in the Church

15*†For my part, from the time I first heard of your faith in the Lord Jesus and your love for all the members of the church, **16**I have never stopped thanking God for you and recommending you in my prayers. **17***May the God of our Lord Jesus Christ, the Father of glory, grant you a spirit of wisdom and insight to know him clearly. **18**May he enlighten your innermost vision that you may know the great hope to which he has called you, the wealth of his glorious heritage to be distributed among the members of the church, **19***and the immeasurable scope of his power in us who believe. It is like the strength **20***he showed in raising Christ from the dead and seating him at his right hand in heaven, **21***high above every principality, power, virtue, and domination, and every name that can be given in this age or in the age to come.

22*He has put all things under Christ's feet and has made him, thus exalted, head of the church. **23***which is his body: the fullness of him who fills the universe in all its parts.

Generosity of God's Plan

2 **1***†YOU were dead because of your sins and offenses, **2***as you gave allegiance to the present age and to the prince of the air, that spirit who is even now at work among the rebellious. **3*** All of us were once of their company; we lived at the level of the flesh, following every whim and fancy, and so by nature deserved God's wrath like the rest. **4**But God is rich in mercy; because of his great love for us **5***he brought us to life with Christ when we were dead in sin. By this favor you were saved. **6***Both with and in Christ Jesus he raised us up and gave us a place

in the heavens, **7**that in the ages to come he might display the great wealth of his favor, manifested by his kindness to us in Christ Jesus. **8***I repeat, it is owing to his favor that salvation is yours through faith. This is not your own doing, it is God's gift; **9***neither is it a reward for anything you have accomplished, so let no one pride himself on it. **10***We are truly his handiwork, created in Christ Jesus to lead the life of good deeds which God prepared for us in advance.

All United in Christ

11†You men of Gentile stock—called "uncircumcised" by those who, in virtue of a hand-executed rite on their flesh, call themselves "circumcised"—remember **12***that, in former times, you had no part in Christ and were excluded from the community of Israel. You were strangers to the covenant and its promise; you were without hope and without God in the world. **13***But now in Christ Jesus you who once were far off have been brought near through the blood of Christ. **14***It is he who is our peace, and who made the two of us one by breaking down the barrier of hostility that kept us apart. **15***In his own flesh he abolished the law with its commands and precepts, to create in himself one new man from us who had been two and to make peace, **16***reconciling both of us to God in one body through his cross, which put that enmity to death. **17***He came and "announced the good news of peace to you who were far off, and to those who were near"; **18***through him we both have access in one Spirit to the Father.

19*This means that you are strangers and aliens no longer. No, you are fellow citizens of the saints and

---

† 1, 15-23: Paul prays that the blessings of the faith imparted by God the Father (v 3) to the Ephesians will be strengthened in them through the message of the gospel (1, 17ff). Those blessings are to be measured by his power in establishing the sovereignty of Christ over all other creatures (1, 20f) and in appointing him head of the church (1, 22f). For the allusion to angelic spirits, see the note on Colossians 1, 15.20.

2, 1-10: The recipients of Paul's letter have experienced, in their redemption from sin, the effect of Christ's supremacy (1f), the power of which overcame the evil force of demons. (In Jewish thought these were considered to dwell in the air.) Both Jew and Gentile have experienced, through Christ, God's generosity, his free gift of salvation which already marks them for a heavenly destiny (3-6). In Christ, God reveals the wealth of his kindness (v 7), saving men through faith and not by any works of their own (8f). Christians are a newly created people in Christ, fashioned by God for a new life of goodness (v 10).

2, 11-22: The Gentiles were without Israel's messianic expectation, without the various covenants God made with Israel, without hope of salvation and knowledge of the true God (11f); but through Christ, all these religious barriers between Jew and Gentile have been transcended (13f) by the abolition of the Mosaic covenant-law (v 15) for the sake of uniting Jew and Gentile into a single religious community (15ff), imbued with the same Holy Spirit and worshiping the same Father (v 18). The Gentiles are now within the pale of God's revelation (v 19) as it derives from the apostles, assisted by those endowed with the prophetic charism, the preachers of Christ (v 20; cf Acts 8, 4f; 1 Cor 12, 28). With Christ as the capstone (v 20), they are being built into the holy temple of God's people where the divine presence dwells (21f).

✿

11: Is 46, 10; Rom 8, 28; Col 1, 12; Rv 4, 11.
13: 4, 30; Col 1, 5f; Acts 2, 33.
14: 2 Cor 1, 22; 5, 5.
15: Col 1, 3f; Phlm 4f.
17: 3, 14.16; 1 Jn 5, 20.
19: 2 Cor 13, 4; Col 1, 11.
20: Ps 110, 1.
21: Phil 2, 9; 1 Pt 3, 22.
22: Ps 8, 6; Mt 28, 18; Col 1, 18.
23: 4, 10; Rom 12, 5; 1 Cor 12, 27; Col 1, 19.
2/1: Col 1, 21; 2, 13.
2: 6, 12; Jn 12, 31; Col 1, 13.

3: Col 3, 6.
5: Rom 5, 8; 6, 13; Col 2, 13.
6: Rom 8, 10f; Phil 3, 20; Col 2, 12.
8: Gal 2, 16.
9: 1 Cor 1, 29.
10: 2 Cor 5, 17.
12: Rom 9, 4; Col 1, 21.27.
13: Is 57, 19; Col 1, 20.
14: Gal 3, 28.
15: 2 Cor 5, 17; Col 2, 14.
16: Col 1, 20.22.
17: Is 57, 19; Zec 9, 10.
18: 3, 12.
19: Heb 12, 22f.

members of the household of God. **20***You form a building which rises on the foundation of the apostles and prophets, with Christ Jesus himself as the capstone. **21***Through him the whole structure is fitted together and takes shape as a holy temple in the Lord; **22***in him you are being built into this temple, to become a dwelling place for God in the Spirit.

Commission to Preach God's Plan

3 **2**I am sure you have heard of the ministry which God in his goodness gave me in your regard. **1*†**That is why to me, Paul, a prisoner for Christ Jesus on behalf of you Gentiles, **3**God's secret plan as I have briefly described it was revealed. **4**When you read what I have said, you will realize that I know what I am talking about in speaking of the mystery of Christ, **5***unknown to men in former ages but now revealed by the Spirit to the holy apostles and prophets. **6**It is no less than this: in Christ Jesus the Gentiles are now co-heirs with the Jews, members of the same body and sharers of the promise through the preaching of the gospel.

Mission to the Gentiles

7*Through the gift God in his goodness bestowed on me by the exercise of his power, I became a minister of the gospel. **8***To me, the least of all believers, was given the grace to preach to the Gentiles the unfathomable riches of Christ **9***and to enlighten all men on the mysterious design which for ages was hidden in God, the Creator of all. **10***Now, therefore, through the church, God's manifold wisdom is made known to the principalities and powers of heaven, **11**in accord with his age-old purpose, carried out in Christ Jesus our Lord. **12***In Christ and through faith in him we can speak freely to God, drawing near him with confidence. **13***Hence, I beg you not to be disheartened by the trials I endure for you; they are your glory.

Prayer for the Readers

14†That is why I kneel before the Father **15**from whom every family in heaven and on earth takes its name; **16***and I pray that he will bestow on you gifts in keeping with the riches of his glory. May he strengthen you inwardly through the working of his Spirit. **17***May Christ dwell in your hearts through faith, and may charity be the root and foundation of

your life. **18***Thus you will be able to grasp fully, with all the holy ones, the breadth and length and height and depth of Christ's love, **19***and experience this love which surpasses all knowledge, so that you may attain to the fullness of God himself.

20*To him whose power now at work in us can do immeasurably more than we ask or imagine—**21**to him be glory in the church and in Christ Jesus through all generations, world without end. Amen.

Unity in the Mystical Body

4 **1*†**I plead with you, then, as a prisoner for the Lord, to live a life worthy of the calling you have received, **2***with perfect humility, meekness, and patience, bearing with one another lovingly. **3***Make every effort to preserve the unity which has the Spirit as its origin and peace as its binding force. **4***There is but one body and one Spirit, just as there is but one hope given all of you by your call. **5***There is one Lord, one faith, one baptism; **6***one God and Father of all, who is over all, and works through all, and is in all.

---

† 3, 1: *A prisoner for Christ Jesus:* see the Introduction.

3, 1-13: Paul reflects on his mission to the Gentiles. He alludes to his conversion and appointment to the apostolic office (2f) and observes that his own apostolic experience, as well as that of the other apostles and charismatic prophets in the church (4f), has deepened his understanding of God's plan of salvation in Christ. Paul is the special herald (v 7) of a new revelation to the world (v 6): that the divine plan includes the Gentiles in the spiritual benefits promised to Israel. Not only does he enjoy this unique apostolic role, but he also has been given the task of explaining to all men the divine plan of salvation (8f). Through the church, God's plan of salvation in Christ becomes manifest to angelic beings (v 10), a plan which God had kept hidden from all creatures (v 11). The fulfillment of the plan in Christ gives the whole church more confidence in God (v 12). The readers of this epistle are also encouraged to greater confidence despite Paul's imprisonment (v 13).

3, 14-21: The apostle prays that those he is addressing may, like the rest of the church, deepen their understanding of God's plan of salvation in Christ. It is a plan which affects the whole universe: this is the sense of *the breadth and length and height and depth* (v 18). The apostle prays further that they may perceive the redemptive love of Christ for them and be completely immersed in the mystery of Christ in God (14-19). The prayer concludes with a doxology to God the Father (20f).

4, 1-16: A general plea for unity in the churches. Christians have been fashioned through the Spirit into a single harmonious religious community (*one body*), distinguished by a single Lord in contrast to the many gods of the pagan world, and by one way of salvation through faith, brought out especially by the significance of baptism (1-6; cf Rom 6, 1-11). But Christian unity is more than adherence to a common belief. It works itself out functionally through Christ's gifts to individuals to rule and teach so as to make the community ever more Christ-like (11-16). This teaching on Christ as the source of the charisms is introduced by a citation of Psalm 68, 18 which depicts Yahweh triumphantly leading Israel to salvation in Jerusalem. It is here understood of Christ, the God-man, head of the church; through his redemptive death, resurrection and ascension he has become the source of the church's spiritual gifts. The "descent" of Christ (9f) refers more probably to the incarnation than to Christ's presence after his death in the abode of the dead.

20: Is 28, 16; Rv 21, 14.
21: Col 2, 19; 1 Cor 3, 16.
22: 1 Pt 2, 5.
3/1: Phil 1, 7.13; Col 1, 24-29; 2 Tm 2, 9.
5: Col 1, 26.
7: Col 1, 25.29; 1 Thes 2, 4.
8: 1 Cor 15, 8f; Gal 1, 16; 2, 8.
9: Rom 16, 25; Col 1, 26f.
10: 1 Pt 1, 12.
12: Rom 5, 1f; Heb 4, 16.
13: Col 1, 22.24; 2 Tm 1, 8.
16: 6, 10; Col 1, 11; 2 Pt 1, 3.
17: Jn 14, 23; Rom 7, 22; Col 1, 23; 2, 7.
18: Col 2, 2.
19: Col 2, 3.9.
20: Rom 16, 25f; Col 1, 29.
4/1: Col 1, 10.
2: Col 3, 12.
3: Col 3, 14f.
4: Rom 12, 15; 1 Cor 10, 17.
5: 1 Cor 8, 6.
6: 1 Cor 12, 6.

Diversity of Graces

7* Each of us has received God's favor in the measure in which Christ bestows it. **8*** Thus you find Scripture saying:

> "When he ascended on high, he took
> a host of captives
> and gave gifts to men."

"He ascended"—**9** what does this mean but that he had first descended into the lower regions of the earth? **10** He who descended is the very one who ascended high above the heavens, that he might fill all men with his gifts.

11* It is he who gave apostles, prophets, evangelists, pastors and teachers **12** in roles of service for the faithful to build up the body of Christ, **13*** till we become one in faith and in the knowledge of God's Son, and form that perfect man who is Christ come to full stature.

14* Let us, then, be children no longer, tossed here and there, carried about by every wind of doctrine that originates in human trickery and skill in proposing error. **15*** Rather, let us profess the truth in love and grow to the full maturity of Christ the head. **16** Through him the whole body grows, and with the proper functioning of the members joined firmly together by each supporting ligament, builds itself up in love.

Renewal in Christ

17*† I declare and solemnly attest in the Lord that you must no longer live as the pagans do—their minds empty, **18*** their understanding darkened. They are estranged from a life in God because of their ignorance and their resistance; **19*** without remorse they have abandoned themselves to lust and the indulgence of every sort of lewd conduct. **20** That is not what you learned when you learned Christ! **21** I am supposing, of course, that he has been preached and taught to you in accord with the truth that is in Jesus: **22*** namely, that you must lay aside your former way of life and the old self which deteriorates through illusion and desire, **23*** and acquire a fresh, spiritual way of thinking. **24*** You must put on that new man created in God's image, whose justice and holiness are born of truth.

Vices to Be Avoided

25* See to it, then, that you put an end to lying; let everyone speak the truth to his neighbor, for we are members of one another. **26*** If you are angry, let it be without sin. The sun must not go down on your wrath; **27*** do not give the devil a chance to work on you. **28*** The man who has been stealing must steal no longer; rather, let him work with his hands at honest labor so that he will have something to share with those in need. **29*** Never let evil talk pass your lips; say only the good things men need to hear, things that will really help them. **30** Do nothing to sadden the Holy Spirit with whom you were sealed against the day of redemption. **31*** Get rid of all bitterness, all passion and anger, harsh words, slander, and malice of every kind. **32** In place of these, be kind to one another, compassionate, and mutually forgiving, just as God has forgiven you in Christ.

5 **1*** BE imitators of God as his dear children. **2*** Follow the way of love, even as Christ loved you. He gave himself for us as an offering to God, a gift of pleasing fragrance.

3* As for lewd conduct or promiscuousness or lust of any sort, let them not even be mentioned among you; your holiness forbids this. **4** Nor should there be any obscene, silly, or suggestive talk; all that is out of place. Instead, give thanks. **5*** Make no mistake about this: no fornicator, no unclean or lustful person—in effect an idolator—has any inheritance in the kingdom of Christ and of God. **6*** Let no one deceive you with worthless arguments. These are sins that bring God's wrath down on the disobedient; **7** therefore have nothing to do with them.

Duty to Live in the Light

8* There was a time when you were darkness, but now you are light in the Lord. Well, then, live as children of light. **9** Light produces every kind of goodness and justice and truth. **10** Be correct in your judgment of what pleases the Lord. **11*** Take no part in vain deeds done in darkness; rather, condemn them. **12** It is shameful even to mention the things these people do in secret; **13*** but when such deeds are condemned they are seen in the light of day, and all that then appears is light. **14*** That is why we read:

> "Awake, O sleeper,
> arise from the dead,
> and Christ will give you light."

15* Keep careful watch over your conduct. Do not act like fools, but like thoughtful men. **16** Make the most of the present opportunity, for these are evil days. **17** Do not continue in ignorance, but try to discern the

---

✿

7: Rom 12, 6;
   1 Cor 12, 28.
8: Ps 68, 19; Col 2, 15.
11: 1 Cor 12, 28.
13: Col 1, 28.
14: 1 Cor 14, 20;
   Col 2, 4.8; Heb 13, 9.
15: Col 1, 18; 2, 19.
17: Rom 1, 21.
18: Col 1, 21; 1 Pt 1, 14.
19: Col 3, 5.
22: Rom 8, 13; Col 3, 9.
23: Rom 12, 2.
24: Col 3, 10.
25: Zec 8, 16.
26: Mt 5, 22.
27: 2 Cor 2, 11.
28: 1 Thes 4, 11.

29: 5, 4; Col 3, 16; 4, 6.
31: Col 3, 8.
32: Mt 6, 14; Col 3, 12f.
5/1: Mt 5, 48.
2: 1 Jn 3, 16.
3: Gal 5, 19;
   Col 3, 5.
5: 1 Cor 6, 9f;
   Gal 5, 21.
6: Rom 1, 18;
   Col 2, 4.8.
8: 4, 18; Jn 12, 36;
   Col 1, 12f.
11: 1 Thes 5, 4-8.
13: Jn 3, 20f.
14: Is 60, 1.
15: Col 4, 5.

---

† 4, 17—5, 20: For similar exhortations to a morally good life in response to God's gift of faith, see notes on Romans 12, 1-13, 14 and Galatians 5, 13-26.

THE LIFE OF THE

Blessed Virgin

WITH THE STORY OF

THE ROSARY

AND OTHER

BEAUTIFUL MARIAN PRAYERS

◆

The Life of the Blessed Virgin

FROM ALL ETERNITY, God knew that Mary would be the Mother of His Son. Since she was to be the Mother of Him who is God, in view of the redemption which Her Son would bring by His sacrificial death and resurrection, God formed her to His purpose and honored her at the very first moment of her existence by filling her with the fullness of His grace. She alone of all mere human beings was preserved free from all sin, original and actual. This privilege is known as the Immaculate Conception.

Nothing at all is known of the life or parentage of Mary except the few scant verses that are given us in Scripture. Legends coming from apocryphal books of the third and fourth century say that Mary's parents were Joachim and Anne, both of the house of David. They say that she lived as an ordinary Jewish girl and that her parents looked for a husband for her when she was about twelve years old, the usual age for marriage (so these legends say). The legends say that Mary had a vow of virginity. Although this does not seem to fit in with the official Jewish culture we know, nevertheless, vows of virginity were common among a group of Jews called Essenes—the same people who are responsible for the Dead Sea Scrolls. The vow of virginity also fits in with what St. Luke describes in his Gospel (1:34). We would have to state, however, that we know as much about Mary's childhood as we know about the childhood of her Son, and that is nothing.

Shortly thereafter, Mary and Joseph were betrothed. This was the ceremony in which the actual marriage took place, although husband and wife usually remained in their respective homes for about a year in preparation for their life together. A short time after her betrothal, Mary was alone in her room when the Angel Gabriel appeared and announced that she was to become the Mother of God. Disturbed, she asked the Angel: "How shall this happen, since I do not know man?" for she did not understand how this could come about in view of her vow of virginity. When the Angel told her that she was to conceive through the power of the Holy Spirit, and that Joseph would be the Child's foster-father, she consented without hesitation.

Shortly after this event, Mary visited her elderly kinswoman, Elizabeth, in another village. Elizabeth, too, after years of barrenness, was with child through the grace of God. When Mary greeted her on arrival, the child in Elizabeth's womb stirred, and Elizabeth was filled with the Holy Spirit. Prophetically she cried out, "Blessed are you among women!" Now for the first time, Mary and Elizabeth saw clearly God's plans for them. In this hour of exultation, Mary spoke her inmost thoughts in her beautiful *Magnificat,* exclaiming on the honor God had paid her and foretelling that henceforth all generations would call her blessed.

After a 3-month stay with Elizabeth, Mary returned home. By this time her condition had become obvious. Joseph was confused and troubled, but when an angel assured him that Mary had conceived only by the power of God, he took her into his home. Some months later a census was ordered taken, and Joseph was required to register at Bethlehem. He and Mary made the journey and upon arrival could find no lodging. They sought shelter in a stable, and here Mary gave birth to Jesus.

Forty days after the birth, Mary took Jesus to the Temple for her own Purification and for the Presentation of Christ. Here they met a holy man named Simeon. Seeing Jesus, he proclaimed Him to be the promised Messiah, and at the same time predicted that Mary would undergo great suffering. Soon after the Presentation, there came

The Immaculate Conception
by Bartolomé Esteban Murillo

Magi from the East to Jerusalem on their way to worship the newborn "King of the Jews." Now when Herod, the local governor, heard this, he was troubled. He sent for the Magi and after questioning them, asked them to report to him all that they learned, on their return. The Magi proceeded to Bethlehem where they found the Holy Family, and they worshipped Jesus and offered Him precious gifts. Then being warned in a dream not to return to Herod, they went back to their own country by a different route.

When the Magi did not return, Herod became enraged and ordered that all male children under two years of age in the Bethlehem area be slain. Before Herod's assassins arrived, an angel warned Joseph and told him to take Mary and Jesus and flee into Egypt. They immediately set out, and thus Jesus was saved from the slaughter. After a few months in Egypt, Herod died, and once more the angel appeared to Joseph and told him to return. Joseph obeyed, and all three returned to Israel and settled in Nazareth. Jesus was about two years old at this time.

We next hear of Mary when Jesus was 12 years old. He went with Joseph and Mary to Jerusalem for the annual celebration of the Passover. When the festival was over, they left for home. Jesus was not with Mary and Joseph, but they assumed He was with another part of the caravan. However, when the groups gathered for the first night stop, Jesus was missing. Alarmed, Mary and Joseph returned to the city, and after three days search found Jesus in the Temple surrounded by Doctors of the Law, listening and asking them questions. Jesus returned with His parents to Nazareth, and this is the last we hear of the Holy Family until the beginning of Christ's public ministry. During these years of Jesus' "hidden life" He was subject to Mary and Joseph in all things, helping Mary with the household chores as a boy and later learning the trade of a carpenter from Joseph.

The next mention of Mary is at the wedding feast of Cana, 18 years later, by which time Joseph had already died. Mary seems to have been more than just a guest, perhaps a relative, and this would account for her concern when she saw the wine running short, as a lack of wine would have considerably dampened the spirits of the feast. Mary mentioned this fact to her Son, who ordered some jars filled with water and worked His first public miracle by changing the water into wine.

From this time on we know little about Mary, but she undoubtedly shared intimately in the three years of Christ's public ministry by accompanying Him on many occasions, especially when He suffered His passion. We know that Mary was present at the Crucifixion, as was the Apostle John. Shortly before He expired, Christ looked down on His sorrowing mother at the foot of the cross and said: "Woman, there is your son." And then to John He said: "There is your mother." In this, the dying Jesus consigned Mary to John's care and declared her the spiritual mother of all the members of the Mystical Body of Christ. After His death, Mary helped prepare the body for burial. When this was accomplished, John took the Mother of Jesus home with him to care for her as her adopted son.

After His resurrection three days later, Jesus appeared to many of His disciples, and it is most reasonable to assume that He also appeared to His beloved mother. It is quite likely that she was also present at Christ's Ascension and later on she was present at the gathering of the Apostles in Jerusalem when the Holy Spirit descended upon them.

Because Mary had been preserved free from sin, it was not fitting that her body should undergo corruption. It was also fitting that she should be the first of the redeemed to share completely in the victory of her Son over sin and death. At her death, then, she was taken body and soul to heaven. She is the first human to share in the resurrection of Christ. This privilege is called the "Assumption."

Since Mary has been taken to heaven, there have been in history numerous reports

The Marriage of the Virgin
by Raphael Santi

of her appearances to individuals on earth. Some of these reports the Church has sanctioned by establishing liturgical feast days, and by using the practices which have been recommended. It is a pious custom to believe in these appearances which the Church has sanctioned. However, this must never be confused with faith. We could be perfectly good and devout Catholics and still have hesitations and doubts about these appearances. We should not be so rash, however, as to scoff at the good which has been accomplished by these apparitions. Some of the most outstanding of these reported apparitions are as follows:

OUR LADY OF GUADALUPE. On Dec. 12, 1531, the Blessed Virgin appeared to Juan Diego, an Indian, on Tepeyac Hill, near Mexico City. She requested that a church be built on the spot, and when Bishop Zumárraga later asked Juan for proof of her presence, she had Juan pick some roses which miraculously bloomed in the middle of winter. She arranged these in his cloak, and then impressed her portrait on the coarse fabric. This portrait is preserved now in the famous Shrine of Guadalupe which was subsequently built on the site, and where innumerable miraculous cures have been effected.

OUR LADY OF THE MIRACULOUS MEDAL. Our Lady appeared to St. Catherine Labouré in Paris on three occasions in 1830. Our Lady instructed her to have a medal made in her honor, bearing on one side an image of herself, with the words, "O Mary, conceived without sin, pray for us who have recourse to thee." The other side of the medal was to have, surrounded by twelve stars, the first letter of the name Mary in the center, a cross above it, and the heart of Jesus crowned with thorns and the heart of Mary pierced with a sword, engraved beneath it. The Blessed Virgin promised her that persons who wore the medal would gain much grace. Several years later, a few medals were made and distributed, and at once miraculous cures, conversions, and favors were attributed to it. Quickly the news spread and the devotion to the Medal became world-wide. So many wonderful blessings were wrought through its use that it has come to be known as the "Miraculous Medal."

OUR LADY OF LOURDES. In 1858 Our Lady appeared to Bernadette Soubirous, a young peasant girl, near Lourdes in southern France. Each time Our Lady had a Rosary draped over her arm. She revealed herself as the Immaculate Conception, asked that a chapel be built on the site of the apparition, and told her to drink from a fountain in the grotto. No fountain was to be seen, but when Bernadette dug on the dry ground at a spot designated by Our Lady, a spring began to flow. The water from this still-flowing spring has shown miraculous healing power, though it contains no special curative properties that science can identify.

OUR LADY OF FATIMA. In 1917, Our Lady appeared several times to three children at Fatima in Portugal, and identified herself as the Lady of the Rosary. Through these children, the Mother of God made known to the entire world certain heavenly requests. the recitation of the Rosary, the return of men to a life of repentance for sin and sanctifying grace, reparation for sinners, and reverence for the Immaculate Heart of Mary.

◆　◆　◆

The Annunciation
by Bartolomé Esteban Murillo

Beautiful Marian Prayers

G OD THE FATHER, God the Son, and God the Holy Spirit alone, do we adore. But next to the triune God, of all the saints, we venerate most the Mother of God. Inestimably honored by God while on earth, she has been exalted in Heaven. It is no wonder then that more holy songs, more pious devotions, and more prayers have been dedicated to her honor than to any other person; it is no wonder that many great nations, including the United States, Canada, and Mexico, have been consecrated to her and have placed themselves under her protection. Below are just a few of the most popular Marian devotions.

THE LITANY OF LORETO

Lord, have mercy on us.
Christ, have mercy on us.
Lord, have mercy on us.
Christ, hear us.
Christ, graciously hear us.
God, the Father of Heaven, have mercy on us.
God the Son, Redeemer of the world, have mercy on us.
God the Holy Spirit, have mercy on us.
Holy Trinity, one God, have mercy on us.

Holy Mary,	pray for us
Holy Mother of God,	pray for us
Holy Virgin of virgins,	pray for us
Mother of Christ,	pray for us
Mother of divine grace,	pray for us
Mother most pure,	pray for us
Mother most chaste,	pray for us
Mother inviolate,	pray for us
Mother undefiled,	pray for us
Mother most amiable,	pray for us
Mother most admirable,	pray for us
Mother of good counsel,	pray for us
Mother of our Creator,	pray for us
Mother of our Savior,	pray for us
Virgin most prudent,	pray for us
Virgin most venerable,	pray for us
Virgin most renowned,	pray for us
Virgin most powerful,	pray for us
Virgin most merciful,	pray for us
Virgin most faithful,	pray for us
Mirror of justice,	pray for us
Seat of wisdom,	pray for us
Cause of our joy	pray for us
Spiritual vessel,	pray for us
Vessel of honor,	pray for us
Singular vessel of devotion,	pray for us
Mystical rose,	pray for us
Tower of David,	pray for us
Tower of ivory,	pray for us
House of gold,	pray for us
Ark of the Covenant,	pray for us
Gate of heaven,	pray for us

Morning star,	pray for us
Health of the sick,	pray for us
Refuge of sinners,	pray for us
Comforter of the afflicted,	pray for us
Help of Christians,	pray for us
Queen of Angels,	pray for us
Queen of Patriarchs,	pray for us
Queen of Prophets,	pray for us
Queen of Apostles,	pray for us
Queen of Martyrs,	pray for us
Queen of Confessors,	pray for us
Queen of Virgins,	pray for us
Queen of all Saints,	pray for us
Queen conceived without original sin,	pray for us
Queen assumed into heaven,	pray for us
Queen of the most holy Rosary,	pray for us
Queen of peace,	pray for us

Lamb of God, who takes away the sins of the world, spare us, O Lord.

Lamb of God, who takes away the sins of the world, graciously hear us, O Lord.

Lamb of God, who takes away the sins of the world, have mercy on us.

℣ Pray for us, O holy Mother of God.

℟ That we may be made worthy of the promises of Christ.

Let us pray.

Grant, we beseech You, O Lord God, unto us Your servants, that we may rejoice in continual health of mind and body; and, by the glorious intercession of blessed Mary ever Virgin, may be delivered from present sadness, and enter into the joy of Your eternal gladness. Through Christ our Lord. Amen.

The Nativity
by Federigo Barocci

TO MARY IMMACULATE

You are all fair, O Mary, the original stain is not in You. You are the glory of Jerusalem, You, the joy of Israel, You, the great honor of our people You, the advocate of sinners. O Mary, O Mary, Virgin most prudent, Mother most merciful, pray for us, intercede for us with our Lord Jesus Christ.

CONSECRATION TO MARY

Hail Mary, *etc.*

My Queen! my Mother! I give you all myself, and, to show my devotion to you, I consecrate to you my eyes, my ears, my mouth, my heart, my entire self. Wherefore, O loving Mother, as I am your own, keep me, defend me, as your property and possession.

ACT OF CONSECRATION OF THE UNITED STATES TO OUR BLESSED MOTHER

MOST HOLY TRINITY: Our Father in Heaven, who chose Mary as the fairest of your daughters; Holy Spirit who chose Mary as your spouse; God the Son, who chose Mary as your Mother; in union with Mary, we adore your majesty and acknowledge your supreme, eternal dominion and authority.

MOST HOLY TRINITY, we put the United States of America into the hands of Mary Immaculate in order that she may present the country to you. Through her we wish to thank you for the great resources of this land and for the freedom which has been its heritage. Through the intercession of Mary, have mercy on the Catholic Church in America. Grant us peace. Have mercy on our President and on all the officers of our government. Grant us a fruitful economy born in justice and charity. Have mercy on capital and industry and labor. Protect the family life of the nation. Guard the innocence of our children. Grant the precious gift of many religious vocations. Through the intercession of our Mother, have mercy on the sick, the poor, the tempted, sinners—on all who are in need.

MARY, IMMACULATE VIRGIN, Our Mother, Patroness of our land, we praise you and honor you and give ourselves to you. Protect us from every harm. Pray for us, that acting always according to your will and the Will of your Divine Son, we may live and die pleasing to God.

HAIL MARY

Hail Mary, full of grace! the Lord is with you; blessed are you among women and blessed is the fruit of your womb, Jesus. Holy Mary, Mother of God, pray for us sinners, now and at the hour of our death. Amen.

MARY'S CANTICLE

"My being proclaims the greatness of the Lord, my spirit finds joy in God my savior,

For he has looked upon his servant in her lowliness: all ages to come shall call me blessed.

God who is mighty has done great things for me, holy is his name;

His mercy is from age to age on those who fear him.

He has shown might with his arm; he has confused the proud in their inmost thoughts.

He has deposed the mighty from their thrones and raised the lowly to high places.

The hungry he has given every good thing, while the rich he has sent empty away.

He has upheld Israel his servant, ever mind of his mercy.

Even as he promised our fathers, promised Abraham and his descendants forever," Amen.

THE MEMORARE

Remember, O most gracious Virgin Mary, that never was it known that any one who fled to your protection, implored your help, or sought your intercession, was left unaided. Inspired with this confidence, I fly unto you, O Virgin of virgins and mother; to you do I come; before you I stand, sinful and sorrowful; O Mother of the World Incarnate, despise not my petitions, but in your mercy hear and answer me. Amen.

HAIL, HOLY QUEEN

(For the words of this prayer turn to the last page of this section.)

The Crucifixion
by Paolo Veronese

The Story of the Rosary

T HE ROSARY is one of the Church's greatest treasures, and over the years since the Blessed Virgin herself gave it to us in the early 13th Century, it has proved itself to be one of the most popular forms of prayer in honor of Our Lady. Every day of the year, throughout the world, millions of people recite the Rosary in obedience to the Blessed Virgin's many requests that they do so as a most effective means for overcoming the evils of modern society, for restoring peace to the world and to men's souls, and in helping man gain his eternal reward in heaven. Saints have acclaimed its effectiveness and Popes in all ages have recognized it as a rich source of divine blessing.

The complete Rosary consists essentially of 15 Our Fathers and 150 Hail Marys; however, the Church has divided the original Rosary into three equal parts, each consisting of 5 Our Fathers and 50 Hail Marys, and these groups are called the Joyful, Sorrowful, and Glorious Mysteries. They are so named because the meditations in each group correspond to either joyful, sorrowful, or glorious events in the lives of Jesus and Mary. Nowadays, when we speak of the Rosary, we usually refer to only one of the groups, that is, to one-third of the Rosary, which is the ordinary and more convenient length for recitation, and the Rosary beads are arranged accordingly. The *Apostles' Creed*, the *Glory Be to the Father*, and the *Hail, Holy Queen* are also recited in the Rosary.

The Rosary originated about the year 1208, during the period when St. Dominic was preaching against the Albigensian heresy in southern France. Dominic had preached for years to members of this sect without much success. One night, while praying in the chapel of Notre Dame at Prouille, Our Lady appeared to him, holding a Rosary in her hand. According to tradition, she taught him how to say it, and bade him teach it to the world, promising that it would convert sinners and obtain graces for the just.

Armed with this weapon, St. Dominic's preaching among the Albigenses began to show effect, and many of them returned to the faith. In the military crusade carried on against these people by Simon de Montfort, the Rosary scored another triumph. The Christian army, instructed by St. Dominic, recited the Rosary before the crucial battle of Muret in 1213 and De Montfort ascribed his victory, under God, to those prayers.

Perhaps the mightiest of victories attributed to the Rosary was the naval battle of Lepanto. The Saracens threatened to overrun Christian Europe. In this extremity, Pope Pius V formed a league against them, with a Christian fleet furnished by Venice, Genoa, and Spain. As early as September, 1569, Pope Pius V ordered all the churches in Christendom to hold the Forty Hours Devotion, with public processions and recitation of the Rosary, for the success of the Christian arms. In the year 1627, when King Louis XIII moved against the rebellious Huguenots, he ordered the public recitation of the Rosary, and fifteen thousand Rosaries were distributed among the soldiers and at appointed hours were recited night and day. As a result, victory was won and France was saved for the Catholic faith.

The defeat at Lepanto broke the sea power of the Saracens, but they still possessed a mighty land army. Invading the Balkan area, they laid siege to the key city of Vienna in 1683. In these dire circumstances, King Leopold put his hope in Our Lady of the Rosary, and the city was miraculously saved by a rescuing army under John Sobieski, King of Poland.

The Assumption of the Blessed Virgin
by Peter Paul Rubens

In more modern times, the Blessed Virgin appeared to Bernadette Soubirous in 1858 at Lourdes in France on eighteen occasions, each time with a Rosary draped over her arm, and at Lourdes today the Church of the Rosary has been built and marvelous cures and conversions are wrought there. Our Lady also appeared at Pompeii, Italy, in 1884, to Fortuna Agrelli and indicated her pleasure at the recitation of the Rosary and told her that whoever desires to obtain heavenly favors should make three novenas of the prayers of the Rosary in petition and three novenas in thanksgiving. Again, during the first World War, in 1917, the Blessed Virgin appeared to three shepherd children at Fatima, in Portugal. The most important of the Blessed Mother's instructions, repeated on several occasions, was "To say the Rosary every day" in order to obtain peace for the world and to save souls that would otherwise be lost.

On many occasions the Popes have urged the faithful to recite the Rosary, and it will suffice to quote just one, the saintly Pius X: "The Rosary, of all prayers, is the most beautiful, the most rich in grace, the one which most touches the heart of the Mother of God. If you want peace to reign in your home, say the beads there, every day, with your family."

To get the most benefits, we should "pray" the Rosary, rather than just recite the prayers. To each decade is attached a meditation, and while reciting the whole Rosary decade, we should raise our mind and hearts to God by meditating on the important event in the lives of Christ and His Blessed Mother indicated by the Rosary Mystery. By custom, the following schedule for saying the Mysteries of the Rosary is observed. The Joyful Mysteries are recited on Mondays and Thursdays, the Sorrowful on Tuesdays and Fridays, and the Glorious on Wednesdays, Saturdays, and Sundays. Exceptions to these are the recitation of the Joyful Mysteries on Sundays in Advent and the Sorrowful Mysteries on Sundays in Lent.

The five Joyful Mysteries are: 1. The Annunciation, 2. The Visitation, 3. The Nativity of Christ, 4. The Presentation, and 5. The Finding of the Christ Child in the Temple. The five Sorrowful Mysteries are: 1. The Agony in the Garden, 2. The Scourging at the Pillar, 3. The Crowning with Thorns, 4. The Carrying of the Cross, and 5. The Crucifixion. The five Glorious Mysteries are: 1. The Resurrection, 2. The Ascension, 3. The Descent of the Holy Spirit on the Apostles, 4. The Assumption, and 5. The Coronation of Mary as Queen of Heaven.

The Coronation of Mary in Heaven
by Diego Velásquez

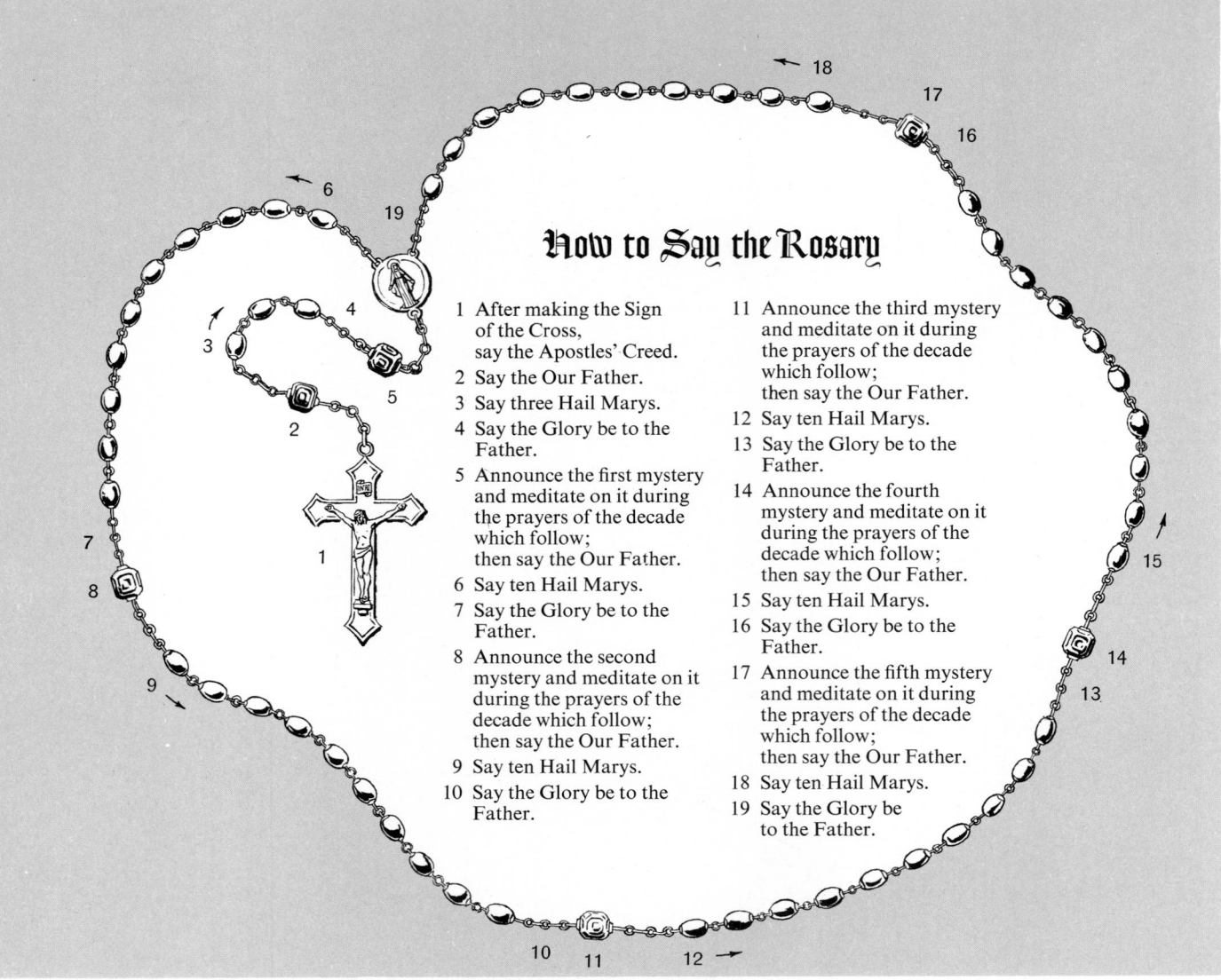

How to Say the Rosary

1 After making the Sign of the Cross, say the Apostles' Creed.
2 Say the Our Father.
3 Say three Hail Marys.
4 Say the Glory be to the Father.
5 Announce the first mystery and meditate on it during the prayers of the decade which follow; then say the Our Father.
6 Say ten Hail Marys.
7 Say the Glory be to the Father.
8 Announce the second mystery and meditate on it during the prayers of the decade which follow; then say the Our Father.
9 Say ten Hail Marys.
10 Say the Glory be to the Father.
11 Announce the third mystery and meditate on it during the prayers of the decade which follow; then say the Our Father.
12 Say ten Hail Marys.
13 Say the Glory be to the Father.
14 Announce the fourth mystery and meditate on it during the prayers of the decade which follow; then say the Our Father.
15 Say ten Hail Marys.
16 Say the Glory be to the Father.
17 Announce the fifth mystery and meditate on it during the prayers of the decade which follow; then say the Our Father.
18 Say ten Hail Marys.
19 Say the Glory be to the Father.

ADDITIONAL PRAYERS

While not an essential part of the Rosary, the following prayers are a fitting conclusion. On finishing these, it is a pious custom to kiss the cross on the Rosary and to end the devotion with the Sign of the Cross.

HAIL, HOLY QUEEN

Hail, Holy Queen, Mother of Mercy, hail, our life, our sweetness, and our hope. To you do we cry, poor banished children of Eve: to you we send up our sighs, mourning and weeping in this vale of tears. Turn, then, most gracious Advocate, your eyes of mercy towards us, and after this our exile, show unto us the blessed fruit of your womb, Jesus. O clement, O pious, O sweet Virgin Mary!

℣ Queen of the most Holy Rosary, pray for us:

℟ That we may be made worthy of the promises of Christ.

LET US PRAY

O God, whose only-begotten Son, by His life, death and resurrection, has purchased for us the rewards of eternal life, grant, we beseech You, that meditating upon these mysteries of the Holy Rosary of the Blessed Virgin Mary, we may imitate what they contain, and obtain what they promise, through the same Christ, our Lord. Amen.

will of the Lord. **18***Avoid getting drunk on wine; that leads to debauchery. Be filled with the Spirit, **19***addressing one another in psalms and hymns and inspired songs. Sing praise to the Lord with all your hearts. **20***Give thanks to God the Father always and for everything in the name of our Lord Jesus Christ. **21**†Defer to one another out of reverence for Christ.

Christian Wives and Husbands

22*Wives should be submissive to their husbands as if to the Lord. **23***because the husband is head of his wife just as Christ is head of his body the church, as well as its savior. **24**As the church submits to Christ, so wives should submit to their husbands in everything.

25*Husbands, love your wives, as Christ loved the church. He gave himself up for her **26***to make her holy, purifying her in the bath of water by the power of the word, **27***to present to himself a glorious church, holy and immaculate, without stain or wrinkle or anything of that sort. **28**Husbands should love their wives as they do their own bodies. He who loves his wife loves himself. **29**Observe that no one ever hates his own flesh; no, he nourishes it and takes care of it as Christ cares for the church—**30***for we are members of his body.

> **31***"For this reason a man shall leave his father
>   and mother,
> and shall cling to his wife,
> and the two shall be made into one."

32This is a great foreshadowing; I mean that it refers to Christ and the church. **33**In any case, each one should love his wife as he loves himself, the wife for her part showing respect for her husband.

Children and Parents

6 **1***†CHILDREN, obey your parents in the Lord, for that is what is expected of you. **2***"Honor your father and mother" is the first commandment to carry a promise with it—**3**"that it may go well with you, and that you may have long life on the earth."

4*Fathers, do not anger your children. Bring them up with the training and instruction befitting the Lord.

Slaves and Masters

5*Slaves, obey your human masters with the reverence, the awe, and the sincerity you owe to Christ. **6***Do not render service for appearance only and to please men, but do God's will with your whole heart as slaves of Christ. **7**Give your service willingly, doing it for the Lord rather than men. **8**You know that each one, whether slave or free, will be repaid by the Lord for whatever good he does.

9*Masters, act in a similar way toward your slaves. Stop threatening them. Remember that you and they have a Master in heaven who plays no favorites.

Christian Warfare

10†Finally, draw your strength from the Lord and his mighty power. **11***Put on the armor of God so that you may be able to stand firm against the tactics of the devil. **12***Our battle is not against human forces but against the principalities and powers, the rulers of this world of darkness, the evil spirits in regions above. **13**You must put on the armor of God if you are to resist on the evil day; do all that your duty requires, and hold your ground. **14***Stand fast, with the truth as the belt around your waist, justice as your breastplate, **15***and zeal to propagate the gospel of peace as your footgear. **16***In all circumstances hold faith up before you as your shield; it will help you extinguish the fiery darts of the evil one. **17***Take the helmet of salvation and the sword of the spirit, the word of God.

Assiduous Prayer

18*At every opportunity pray in the Spirit, using prayers and petitions of every sort. Pray constantly and attentively for all in the holy company. **19***Pray for me that God may put his word on my lips, that I may courageously make known the mystery of the gospel—**20***that mystery for which I am an ambassador in chains. Pray that I may have courage to proclaim it as I ought.

---

† 5, 21-33: The apostle exhorts married Christians to a strong mutual love. Holding with Genesis 2, 24 that marriage is a divine institution (v 31), he sees Christian marriage as taking on a new meaning symbolic of the intimate relationship of love between Christ and the church. The wife should serve her husband in the same spirit as that of the church's service to Christ (22ff), and the husband should care for his wife with the devotion of Christ to the church (25-30). In his conclusion Paul gives to the Genesis passage its highest meaning in the light of the union of Christ and the church, of which Christlike loyalty and devotion in Christian marriage is a clear reflection (31ff).

6, 1-9: See note on Colossians 3, 18—4, 1.

6, 10-20: A general exhortation to courage and prayer. Drawing upon the imagery and ideas of Isaiah 11, 5; 59, 16ff and Wisdom 5, 17-23, Paul describes the Christian in terms of the dress and equipment of the Roman soldier. He observes, however, that the Christian's readiness for combat is not directed against men but against the spiritual powers of evil (10-17). Observe the unique importance he places on prayer (18ff).

---

*

18: Lk 21, 34.	6: 1 Pt 2, 18.
19: Col 3, 16.	9: Col 4, 1.
20: Col 3, 17.	11: 2 Cor 6, 7; 10, 4;
22: Col 3, 18—4, 1;	Jas 4, 7.
1 Pt 3, 1-7.	12: Col 1, 13.
23: 1 Cor 11, 3;	14: Wis 5, 17-20; Is 11, 5;
Col 1, 18.	Lk 12, 35;
25: Col 3, 19.	1 Thes 5, 8.
26: Rom 6, 4; Ti 3, 5ff.	15: Is 52, 7.
27: 2 Cor 11, 2;	16: 1 Pt 5, 9.
Col 1, 22.	17: Is 59, 17;
30: 1 Cor 6, 15.	1 Thes 5, 8.
31: Gn 2, 24; Mt 19, 5;	18: Mt 26, 41;
Mk 10, 7f.	Col 4, 2f.
6/1: Prv 6, 20; Sir 3, 1-6;	19: Acts 4, 29;
Col 3, 20.	Col 4, 3;
2: Ex 20, 12.	2 Thes 3, 1.
4: Col 3, 21f.	20: 2 Cor 5, 20.
5: Col 3, 22-25;	
Ti 2, 9f.	

Conclusion

21 * †Tychicus, my dear brother and faithful minister in the Lord, will keep you informed as to how I am and what I am doing. **22**I have sent him to you for the very purpose of giving you news about me for your hearts' consolation.

23May God the Father and the Lord Jesus Christ grant the brothers peace and love and faith. **24**Grace be with all who love our Lord Jesus Christ with unfailing love.

---

*

    21: Acts 20, 4; Col 4, 7;
       2 Tm 4, 12.

† 6, 21-24: Tychicus is the bearer of the letter. On the assumption that Ephesians was addressed to several Christian communities (see the Introduction), it is understandable that no greetings to individual members of these communities should have been included in it.

The Epistle of Paul to The Philippians

Introduction

The Christian community at Philippi dates from about 50 A. D., when Paul, apparently in the company of Luke (Acts 16, 10-40), visited the city on his second missionary journey. On his third journey he again visited Philippi (Acts 20, 1f). The city had a proud history. It was founded by Philip of Macedonia, father of Alexander the Great, and was the scene of the defeat of Mark Antony by Octavian in 42 B. C. After this event it became a Roman colony, and its citizens were granted the right of Roman citizenship. Their esteem for this privilege is reflected in Luke's account of Paul's treatment in Philippi (Acts 16, 35-40).

Describing himself in the present epistle as a prisoner (1, 7.17) facing a possibly unfavorable outcome to his trial (1, 19-26), he three times warns the Philippians against the enemies of their faith (1, 28; 3, 2.18f). He also gives them news of Epaphroditus, one of their number, who had become extremely ill while attending to Paul's needs (2, 25-30). He expresses his own deep affection for the Philippians (1, 3-11), and thanks them warmly for the donations they have sent him (4, 11-20). He exhorts them to be faithful to their vocation (2, 12-18), and to maintain their present unity of belief (2, 1f; 3, 15f; 4, 1), mentioning only one instance of disharmony (4, 2). He ponders the favorable effect his imprisonment has had on the spread of the gospel (1, 12-26), and points to the disinterested sacrifice of Christ as the transcendent formative rule for every Christian action (2, 1-11); proposing his own complete abnegation for the sake of Christ as the example to be followed against the false teaching of the Judaizers (3, 3-18).

The somewhat rambling quality of the epistle has led certain scholars to suggest that several brief letters of Paul to the Philippians were formed into this single composition. The alternative view is that the apostle dictated portions of the letter on separate occasions. Traditionally, Philippians has been assigned to the period of Paul's first Roman imprisonment (61-63 A. D.). In recent years Ephesus has been proposed by a growing number of scholars as the place of composition. It is known to have had a praetorian guard (alluded to in Philippians 4, 22), and therefore probably a judicial authority. It can readily be assumed that Luke did not record all of Paul's imprisonments in Acts; cf 2 Cor 6, 5. Others, however, consider the prison at Caesarea to have been the place (Acts 23, 23.31ff). If the epistle was written in Ephesus, it is to be dated about the year 53; if in Caesarea, about five years later; if in Rome, about 62. Its famous passage on the *kenosis* or emptying of Christ (2, 5-11), probably taken from a Christian hymn,

was of inestimable value for the early Christian understanding of the mystery of the incarnation.

The Epistle to the Philippians is divided as follows:
Greeting (1, 1f)
I: The Example of Paul (1, 3-26)
II: Pleas for Christian Heroism (1, 27–2, 18)
III: Paul's Assistants and Plans (2, 19-30)
IV: Christian Dedication (3, 1-21)
V: Exhortations to Virtue (4, 1-23)

Greeting

1 [1]†PAUL and Timothy, servants of Christ Jesus, to all the holy ones at Philippi, with their bishops and deacons in Christ Jesus. [2]Grace and peace be yours from God our Father and from the Lord Jesus Christ!

I: THE EXAMPLE OF PAUL

Gratitude and Hope

[3]*†I GIVE THANKS TO MY GOD every time I think of you— [4]which is constantly, in every prayer I utter—rejoicing, as I plead on your behalf, [5]at the way you have all continually helped promote the gospel from the very first day.

[6]*I am sure of this much: that he who has begun the good work in you will carry it through to completion, right up to the day of Christ Jesus. [7]It is only right that I should entertain such expectations in your regard since I hold all of you dear—you who, to a man, are sharers of my gracious lot when I lie in prison or am summoned to defend the solid grounds on which the gospel rests. [8]God himself can testify how much I long for each of you with the affection of Christ Jesus! [9]*My prayer is that your love may more and more

---

† 1, 1f: See note on Romans 1, 1-7. *Bishops and deacons:* literally, "overseers and assistants." This structure of the Christian community is similar to that found in the Pastoral Epistles.

1, 3-11: The Philippians' devotion to their faith and to Paul made them his pride and joy. Here he is possibly alluding to their monetary gifts (5f; cf 4, 14ff), and surely to their sufferings for the faith (1, 29f), and he expresses his conviction that the characteristics thus manifested are evidence of the community's preparation for the Lord's parousia (5f). He feels keenly (v 8) their concern for his apostolic work, which has created a special relationship between them and himself (v 7). He prays that the love they have shown for him may also affect other phases of their lives so as to prepare them perfectly for the parousia (9ff; see note on 1 Thes 4, 13-18).

❋
    1/3: 1 Thes 1, 2.   9: Col 1, 9f; Phlm 6.
    6: 1 Cor 1, 6ff.

abound, both in understanding and wealth of experience, [10]*so that with a clear conscience and blameless conduct you may learn to value the things that really matter, up to the very day of Christ. [11]*It is my wish that you may be found rich in the harvest of justice which Jesus Christ has ripened in you, to the glory and praise of God.

The Spreading Gospel

[12]*†My brothers, I want you to know that my situation has worked out to the furtherance of the gospel. [13]My imprisonment in Christ's cause has become well known throughout the praetorium here, and to others as well; [14]most of my brothers in Christ, taking courage from my chains, have been further emboldened to speak the word of God fearlessly. [15]It is true, some preach Christ from motives of envy and rivalry, but others do so out of good will. [16]Some act from unaffected love, aware that my circumstances provide an opportunity to defend the gospel's cause; [17]others promote Christ, not from pure motives but as an intrigue against me, thinking that it will make my imprisonment even harsher.

[18]What of it? All that matters is that in any and every way, whether from specious motives or genuine ones, Christ is being proclaimed! That is what brings me joy: Indeed, I shall continue to rejoice, [19]*in the conviction that this will turn out to my salvation, thanks to your prayers and the support I receive from the Spirit of Jesus Christ. [20]*I firmly trust and anticipate that I shall never be put to shame for my hopes; I have full confidence that now as always Christ will be exalted through me, whether I live or die. [21]*For, to me, "life" means Christ; hence dying is so much gain. [22]If, on the other hand, I am to go on living in the flesh, that means productive toil for me—and I do not know which to prefer. [23]*I am strongly attracted by both: I long to be freed from this life and to be with Christ, for that is the far better thing; [24]yet it is more urgent that I remain alive for your sakes. [25]This fills me with confidence that I will stay with you, and persevere with you all, for your joy and your progress in the faith. [26]My being with you once again should make you even prouder of me in Christ.

II: PLEAS FOR CHRISTIAN HEROISM

Courage in Professing the Faith

[27]*†CONDUCT YOURSELVES, THEN, in a way worthy of the gospel of Christ. If you do, whether I come and see you myself or hear about your behavior from a distance, it will be clear that you are standing firm in unity of spirit and exerting yourselves with one accord for the faith of the gospel. [28]Do not be intimidated by your opponents in any situation. Their opposition foreshadows downfall for them, but salvation for you. All this is as God intends, [29]*for it is your special privilege to take Christ's part—not only to believe in him but also to suffer for him. [30]Yours is the same struggle as mine, the one in which you formerly saw me engaged and now hear that I am caught up.

Imitating Christ's Humility

2 [1]†IN the name of the encouragement you owe me in Christ, in the name of the solace that love can give, of fellowship in spirit, compassion, and pity, I beg you: [2]*make my joy complete by your unanimity, possessing the one love, united in spirit and ideals. [3]*Never act out of rivalry or conceit; rather, let all parties think humbly of others as superior to themselves, [4]*each of you looking to others' interests rather than his own.

[5]Your attitude must be that of Christ:

> [6]*Though he was in the form of God,
> he did not deem equality with God
> something to be grasped at.

---

† 1, 12-26: Knowing their concern for his apostolate, Paul informs the Philippians of the positive effect his imprisonment has had upon the spread of the gospel (12ff). He notes, however, that some Christian preachers have been hostile to him personally (15f), a fact that pains him until he recalls that in any case Christ is being made known (v 18) and that his own pain will contribute to his salvation (v 19). Facing the possibility of a death sentence, he reflects that for him both life and death take their meaning from Christ (20f). In life he can bear witness to him (v 22), in death, which he prefers as the outcome of his imprisonment, he will be finally united to him (v 23). But the Philippians' need of him makes him confident that he will be released from his imprisonment (24ff).

1, 27-30: He encourages them to hold fast, in the face of opposition, to their faith in the gospel.

2, 1-11: This passage is composed of two parts: introductory exhortations pleading for unity in the Philippian church and for the elimination of differences that are harmful to the community (1-4); and a panegyric hymn (6-11) which reflects the self-effacement of Christ, the model for Christian service (v 5). The hymn begins by invoking Christian faith in Jesus' divinity (*Though he was in the form of God*), and by recalling that, paradoxically, his divinity was concealed throughout his mortal life (v 6). Divesting himself of his divine prerogatives, not indeed of the divinity itself but of the state of glory rightfully his, and assuming the role of a servant, he presented himself simply as a man (v 7; cf Is 52, 13-53; 42, 1). Having fully accepted the human condition, he followed it in obedience to the Father even to death on a cross (v 8). The Father responded by raising him from the dead and placing him at his right hand. The resurrection and ascension are the theological sense of *hypsoun*, the Greek verb used; cf also Acts 2, 33. God endowed him with his own name (v 9), so that the name JESUS (Savior) would be identified in the knowledge of every creature with the very same name (*kyrios*, "Lord") that is addressed to God the Father (2, 10f).

❋
10: Rom 2, 18.
11: Jn 15, 8.
12f: Eph 3, 1; 6, 20f;
　　2 Tm 2, 9.
19: Jb 13, 16.
20: 1 Cor 6, 20; 1 Pt 4, 16.
21: Gal 2, 20.
23: 2 Cor 5, 8.
27: Col 1, 10; 1 Thes 2, 12.
29: Mt 5, 10ff; Acts 5, 41.
2/2: Rom 15, 5.
3: Rom 12, 3;
　　1 Cor 1, 10f;
　　Gal 5, 26.
4: 1 Cor 10, 33; 13, 5.
6: Jn 1, 1f; 17, 5;
　　Heb 1, 3.

⁷*Rather, he emptied himself
and took the form of a slave,
being born in the likeness of men.

He was known to be of human estate,
⁸* and it was thus that he humbled himself,
obediently accepting even death,
death on a cross!

⁹*Because of this,
God highly exalted him
and bestowed on him the name
above every other name,

¹⁰*So that at Jesus' name
every knee must bend
in the heavens, on the earth,
and under the earth,
¹¹* and every tongue proclaim
to the glory of God the Father:
Jesus Christ Is Lord! ·

Innocence of the Children of God

¹²†So then, my dearly beloved, obedient as always to my urging, work with anxious concern to achieve your salvation, not only when I happen to be with you but all the more now that I am absent. ¹³It is God who, in his good will toward you, begets in you any measure of desire or achievement. ¹⁴In everything you do, act without grumbling or arguing; ¹⁵*prove yourselves innocent and straightforward, children of God beyond reproach in the midst of a twisted and depraved generation—among whom you shine like the stars in the sky ¹⁶*while holding fast to the word of life. As I look to the day of Christ, you give me cause to boast that I did not run the race in vain or work to no purpose. ¹⁷*Even if my life is to be poured out as a libation over the sacrificial service of your faith, I am glad of it and rejoice with all of you. ¹⁸May you be glad on the same score, and rejoice with me!

III: PAUL'S ASSISTANTS AND PLANS

Timothy

¹⁹*†I hope, in the lord Jesus, to send Timothy to you very soon, that I may derive courage from learning how things go with you. ²⁰I have no one quite like him for genuine interest in whatever concerns you. ²¹*Everyone is busy seeking his own interests rather than those of Christ Jesus. ²²You know from experience what Timothy's qualities are, how he was like a son at his father's side serving the gospel along with me. ²³I

hope to send him as soon as I see how things go with me. ²⁴In fact, I am confident in the Lord that I myself will be coming soon.

Epaphroditus

²⁵*I have decided, too, that I must send you Epaphroditus, my brother, co-worker, and comrade in arms, whom you sent to take care of my needs. ²⁶He has been longing for all of you, and was distressed that you heard about his illness. ²⁷He was, in fact, sick to the point of death, but God took pity on him; not just on him, I should say, but on me, too, so as to spare me one sorrow after another. ²⁸I have been especially eager to send him so that you may renew your joy on seeing him, and my own anxieties may be lessened. ²⁹Welcome him joyously in the Lord and hold men like him in esteem, ³⁰for he came near to death for the sake of Christ's work. He risked his life in an effort to render me those services you could not render.

IV: CHRISTIAN DEDICATION

Breaking with the Past

3 ¹For the rest, my brothers, rejoice in the Lord. I find writing you these things no burden, and for you it is a safeguard.

²*†Beware of unbelieving dogs. Watch out for

---

†
2, 12-18: Paul exhorts his readers further through a reminder that the goal of their endeavors within the community is their salvation (v 12); this is the whole purpose of the divine activity within them (v 13). Consequently, all complaints and disputes harmful to the community should be avoided so that the Philippians may be a shining light to pagans everywhere (14f). They should transmit to the world the life of the gospel and thus become a source of pride for him at the parousia (v 16). If they achieve this, he can rejoice in the sufferings of his imprisonment and they in turn can be happy because of his joy (17f).

2, 19—3, 1: To show his concern for the Philippians, Paul announces his intention of sending them his most trusted assistant in his apostolate—Timothy, whom they already know (cf Acts 16, 1-15). If Paul is released, as he anticipates, he himself plans a visit to them (19-24). He commends Epaphroditus, whom they had sent to aid him in his imprisonment. He is relieved that Epaphroditus' recovery from a critical illness spares him, Paul, the sorrow of a death in the midst of this display of the Philippians' charity; indicating that as soon as Epaphroditus is well enough to make the journey, he will return to them (25-30). 3, 1 seems to be the beginning of a conclusion to the letter, interrupted by Paul's second thought of adding a strong warning against the teaching of the Judaizers (see notes on Gal 1, 1-5 and 1, 6-10). Some scholars think the verse implies a previous letter to the Philippians, now lost.

3, 2—4, 1: The Judaizers are called *unbelieving dogs* (the customary Jewish term at the time for Gentiles, here applied ironically) and *workers of evil*. Their urging of the religious rite of circumcision upon Christians is regarded as mutilation (v 2). The apostle declares that Christians, who possess the true worship prefigured by circumcision, have no need of this religious rite (v 3). He offers himself an example of one reared in the Jewish tradition of circumcision and the law, which he thought it his duty to defend by persecuting the Christian com-

---

*
7: Is 53, 3; 2 Cor 8, 9;   11: Acts 2, 36; Rom 10, 9.
    Gal 4, 4;   15: Mt 10, 16.
    Heb 2, 14.17.   16: Is 49, 4.
8: Mt 26, 39; Heb 5, 8;   17: Rom 15, 16.
    12, 2.   19: 1 Cor 4, 17; 16, 10.
9: Is 52, 12; Mt 23, 12;   21: 1 Cor 13, 5.
    Eph 1, 20-23.   25: Phil 4, 18.
10: Is 45, 23f; Jn 5, 23;   3/2: 2 Cor 11, 13;
    Rom 14, 11; Rv 5, 13.   Rv 22, 15.

workers of evil. Be on guard against those who mutilate. ³*It is we who are the circumcision, who worship in the spirit of God and glory in Christ Jesus rather than putting our trust in the flesh—⁴*though I can be confident even there. If anyone thinks he has a right to put his trust in external evidence, all the more can I! ⁵*I was circumcised on the eighth day, being of the stock of Israel and the tribe of Benjamin, a Hebrew of Hebrew origins; in legal observance I was a Pharisee, ⁶*and so zealous that I persecuted the church. I was above reproach when it came to justice based on the law.

⁷But those things I used to consider gain I have now reappraised as loss in the light of Christ. ⁸I have come to rate all as loss in the light of the surpassing knowledge of my Lord Jesus Christ. For his sake I have forfeited everything; I have accounted all else rubbish so that Christ may be my wealth ⁹*and I may be in him, not having any justice of my own based on observance of the law. The justice I possess is that which comes through faith in Christ. It has its origin in God and is based on faith. ¹⁰*I wish to know Christ and the power flowing from his resurrection; likewise to know how to share in his sufferings by being formed into the pattern of his death. ¹¹*Thus do I hope that I may arrive at resurrection from the dead.

¹²*It is not that I have reached it yet, or have already finished my course; but I am racing to grasp the prize if possible, since I have been grasped by Christ [Jesus]. ¹³Brothers, I do not think of myself as having reached the finish line. I give no thought to what lies behind but push on to what is ahead. ¹⁴*My entire attention is on the finish line as I run toward the prize to which God calls me—life on high in Christ Jesus. ¹⁵All of us who are spiritually mature must have this attitude. If you see it another way, God will clarify the difficulty for you. ¹⁶It is important that we continue on our course, no matter what stage we have reached.

Christ Our Goal

¹⁷*Be imitators of me, my brothers. Take as your guide those who follow the example that we set. ¹⁸*Unfortunately, many go about in a way which shows them to be enemies of the cross of Christ. I have often said this to you before; this time I say it with tears. ¹⁹*Such as these will end in disaster! Their god is their belly and their glory is in their shame. I am talking about those who are set upon the things of this world. ²⁰*As you well know, we have our citizenship in heaven; it is from there that we eagerly await the coming of our Savior, the Lord Jesus Christ. ²¹*He will give a new form to this lowly body of ours and remake it according to the pattern of his glorified body, by his power to subject everything to himself.

V: EXHORTATIONS TO VIRTUE

Christian Concord

4 ¹*FOR THESE REASONS, MY BROTHERS, you whom I so love and long for, you who are my joy and my crown, continue, my dear ones, to stand firm in the Lord. ²†I plead with Euodia just as I do with Syntyche: come to some mutual understanding in the Lord. ³*Yes, and I ask you, too, my dependable fellow worker, to go to their aid; they have struggled at my side in promoting the gospel, along with Clement and the others who have labored with me, whose names are in the book of life.

Joy and Peace

⁴Rejoice in the Lord always! I say it again. Rejoice! ⁵*Everyone should see how unselfish you are. The Lord is near. ⁶*Dismiss all anxiety from your minds. Present your needs to God in every form of prayer and in petitions full of gratitude. ⁷Then God's own peace, which is beyond all understanding, will stand guard over your hearts and minds, in Christ Jesus.

---

† munities (4ff). Because of his faith in Christ he has now abandoned this religious tradition of salvation (7f). He relies solely on Christ for his justice before God, not on his own efforts to observe the law (v 9). He conforms his life to the sufferings of Christ, that he may know him alone, and experience bodily resurrection through him (10f). This adherence to Christ in faith does not mean that Paul has already ensured his own salvation by arriving at perfect spiritual maturity (v 12). He strives for still greater perfection, mindful of the meaning of God's call in Christ (13f).

Paul's prayer is that God may correct the Philippians if their attitude in this regard is different, though he sincerely believes they have no need except to make still greater progress (15f). His way and that of his followers are the model for their study (v 17). He mourns for those in the Christian community who fail to perceive that salvation lies in the cross of Christ, not in food regulations or circumcision (18f). Salvation does not lie in the body but in Christ, who at his second coming, will transform the body (20f). Paul begs the Philippians, in terms of great affection, to adhere firmly to what he has taught (4, 1).

4, 2-9: The apostle appeals personally to these two women to reconcile their differences (v 2) and adds an appeal to his *syzgos* to aid them in achieving a reconciliation. This word means "comrade, yoke-fellow," and may be a proper name, though no evidence has been found of its use as such (v 3). Paul wishes the Philippians to be a model community, marked by a joy that will have its effect also upon non-Christians (4f). Mindful of the possible nearness of the parousia (see note on 1 Thes 4, 13-18), the Philippians are not to be overly concerned about their troubles but instead are to resolve them in prayer (5f). Thus they will always be at peace (v 7). Their thoughts and lives should reflect only what is true, pure, admirable, virtuous or worthy of praise, as exemplified by his own life among them (8f).

3: Rom 2, 29.
4: 2 Cor 11, 18.21f; Col 2, 11.
5: Acts 22, 3; 26, 5.
6: Acts 23, 6.
9: Rom 3, 21f.
10: Rom 6, 3ff; 8, 17; Gal 6, 17.
11: Rv 20, 4-6.
12: 1 Tm 6, 12.
14: 1 Cor 9, 24f; 2 Tm 4, 7.
17: 1 Cor 11, 1; 1 Pt 5, 3.

18: 1 Cor 1, 17.23; Gal 6, 12.
19: Rom 16, 18.
20: Eph 2, 6; Col 3, 1f; Heb 12, 22.
21: Rom 8, 23.29; 2 Cor 15, 43ff.
4/1: 2 Cor 1, 14; 1 Thes 2, 19f.
3: Ex 32, 32; Ps 69, 29; Lk 10, 20; Rv 3, 5.
5: Ti 3, 2.
6: Mt 6, 25-34; 1 Pt 5, 7.

[8]*Finally, my brothers, your thoughts should be wholly directed to all that is true, all that deserves respect, all that is honest, pure, admirable, decent, virtuous, or worthy of praise. [9]*Live according to what you have learned and accepted, what you have heard me say and seen me do. Then will the God of peace be with you.

Generosity

[10]†It gave me great joy in the Lord that your concern for me bore fruit once more. You had been concerned all along, of course, but lacked the opportunity to show it. [11]*I do not say this because I am in want, for whatever the situation I find myself in I have learned to be self-sufficient. [12]*I am experienced in being brought low, yet I know what it is to have an abundance. I have learned how to cope with every circumstance—how to eat well or go hungry, to be well provided for or do without. [13]*In him who is the source of my strength I have strength for everything.

[14]Nonetheless, it was kind of you to want to share in my hardships. [15]You yourselves know, my dear Philippians, that at the start of my evangelizing, when I left Macedonia, not a single congregation except yourselves shared with me by giving me something for what it had received. [16]Even when I was at Thessalonica you sent something for my needs, not once but twice. [17]*It is not that I am eager for the gift; rather, my concern is for the ever-growing balance in your account. [18]*Herewith is my receipt, which says that I have been fully paid and more. I am well supplied because of what I received from you through Epaphroditus, a fragrant offering, a sacrifice acceptable and pleasing to God.

[19]My God in turn will supply your needs fully, in a way worthy of his magnificent riches in Christ Jesus. [20]All glory to our God and Father for unending ages! Amen.

Farewell

[21]†Give my greetings in Christ Jesus to every member of the church. My brothers here send you theirs, [22]as do all those who believe, particularly those in Caesar's service. [23]May the favor of the Lord Jesus Christ be with your spirit. Amen.

---

*   8: Rom 12, 17.   13: 2 Cor 12, 10;
    9: 1 Thes 4, 1.   2 Tm 4, 17.
   11: 2 Cor 11, 9; 1 Tm 6, 6.   17: 1 Tm 6, 19.
   12: 1 Cor 4, 11;   18: Eph 5, 2; Heb 13, 16.
       2 Cor 6, 10; 11, 27;
       12, 9f; Col 1, 29.

† 4, 10-20: Paul thanks the Philippians for their monetary contribution, brought by Epaphroditus (v 18). He accepts it gratefully, though not because he needs the money, for with God's help he always manages to provide for his wants (10-13); rather, he appreciates their sharing with him, noting that they are the only community from which he has taken such a gift (14ff). His joy in accepting the gift, more than he actually needed, comes from his certainty that God will reward their charity by fulfilling all their needs in turn (17-20).

4, 21ff: The final greetings, extended to all the members of the Philippian community individually, come not only from Paul but also from the Christians of the place where the letter originated (see Introduction).

The Epistle of Paul to The Colossians

Introduction

The Christian community at Colossae was not established by Paul, who had never visited there (1, 4; 2, 1), but by Epaphras (1, 7; 4, 12; Phlm 23), to whom Paul refers as a member of the Colossian group. He was probably one of Paul's Ephesian converts. A second likely inference is that he had requested the apostle's aid in the matter of certain religious tenets of non-Christian origin which were influencing the Colossian community. The epistle's two christological passages (1, 15-20; 2, 9-15) are set in contexts suggesting that certain doctrines having to do with angelic spirits (1, 16) and ascetical practices (2, 16) were being advocated at Colossae in a way that detracted from the person of Christ (1, 17.20) and distorted the nature of the Christian life (2, 16-23).

Without entering into debate over the existence of angelic spirits or their function, Paul simply affirms that Christ possesses the sum total of redemptive power (1, 19) and that the spiritual renewal of the human person occurs through contact in baptism with the person of Christ, who died and rose again for man's justification (2, 9-14). It is unnecessary for the Christian to be concerned about placating spirits (2, 15) or avoiding imagined defilement through ascetical practices in regard to food and drink (2, 20-23). True Christian asceticism consists in the conquering of personal sins (3, 5-10) and the practice of love of neighbor in accordance with the standard set by Christ (3, 12-16).

Paul commends the community as a whole (1, 3-8), which seems to indicate that, though the Colossians have been under a certain pressure to adopt the false doctrines, they have not yet succumbed. The apostle expresses his prayerful concern for them (1, 9-14). His preaching has cost him persecution, suffering, and imprisonment, but he regards these as the completion of the sufferings of Christ (i.e., the church?), a required discipline for the sake of the gospel (1, 24—2, 4). His instructions to the Christian family and to slaves and masters require a new spirit of reflection and action. Love, obedience, and service are to be rendered *in the Lord* (3, 18—4, 1).

Paul wrote the letter to the Colossians while in prison, but his several imprisonments leave the specific place and date of composition uncertain. On this point the same problem of determination exists as with Ephesians and Philippians (see the Introductions to these epistles). The highly developed Christology of Colossians would seem to indicate a later imprisonment, most likely the traditional Roman house arrest in which he enjoyed a certain restricted freedom in preaching (61-63 A. D.).

I: INTRODUCTION

Greeting

1 ¹†PAUL, AN APOSTLE OF CHRIST JESUS by the will of God, and Timothy our brother, ²to the holy ones at Colossae, faithful brothers in Christ. May God our Father give you grace and peace.

Thanksgiving

³*†We always give thanks to God, the Father of our Lord Jesus Christ, in our prayers for you ⁴because we have heard of your faith in Christ Jesus and the love you bear toward all the saints—moved as you are by the hope held in store for you in heaven. ⁵*You heard of this hope through the message of truth, the gospel, ⁶which has come to you, has borne fruit, and has continued to grow in your midst, as it has everywhere in the world. This has been the case from the day you first heard it and comprehended God's gracious ⁷intention through the instructions of Epaphras, our dear fellow slave, who represents us as a faithful minister of Christ. ⁸He it was who told us of your love in the Spirit.

---

† 1, 1f: For the epistolary form used by Paul at the beginning of his letters, see note on Romans 1, 1-7. The apostle frequently designates the members of the Christian community as *holy ones* (literally, "saints"), a term that includes the Old Testament idea of the people of God, and now expresses a relation to Christ. They have been called by God to union with Christ and have experienced the spiritual benefits of this union. The awareness of it helps them to be *faithful brothers in Christ,* i. e., dedicated to the tasks implied in their calling.

1, 3-8: Recalling his prayers for them and the deeply satisfying account of them he has received, the apostle congratulates the Colossians upon their acceptance of Christ and their faithful efforts to live his gospel (3ff). For their encouragement he mentions the success of the gospel elsewhere (v 6), and assures them that his knowledge of their community is accurate since he has been in personal contact with Epaphras, their presumed founder (7f).

Prayer for Continued Progress

⁹*†Ever since we heard this we have been praying for you unceasingly and asking that you may attain full knowledge of his will through perfect wisdom and spiritual insight. ¹⁰Then you will lead a life worthy of the Lord and pleasing to him in every way. You will multiply good works of every sort and grow in the knowledge of God. ¹¹By the might of his glory you will be endowed with the strength needed to stand fast, even to endure joyfully whatever may come, ¹²*giving thanks to the Father for having made you worthy to share the lot of the saints in light. ¹³He rescued us from the power of darkness and brought us into the kingdom of his beloved Son. ¹⁴Through him we have redemption, the forgiveness of our sins.

II: THE PREEMINENCE OF CHRIST

Fullness and Reconciliation

¹⁵*†HE IS THE IMAGE OF THE INVISIBLE GOD, the first-born of all creatures. ¹⁶*In him everything in heaven and on earth was created, things visible and invisible, whether thrones or dominations, principalities or powers; all were created through him, and for him. ¹⁷He is before all else that is. In him everything continues in being. ¹⁸*It is he who is head of the body, the church; he who is the beginning, the first-born of the dead, so that primacy may be his in everything. ¹⁹It pleased God to make absolute fullness reside in him ²⁰*and, by means of him, to reconcile everything in his person, both on earth and in the heavens, making peace through the blood of his cross.

²¹†You yourselves were once alienated from him; you nourished hostility in your hearts because of your evil deeds. ²²But now Christ has achieved reconciliation for you in his mortal body by dying, so as to present you to God holy, free of reproach and blame. ²³But you must hold fast to faith, be firmly grounded and steadfast in it, unshaken in the hope promised you by the gospel you have heard. It is the gospel which has been announced to every creature under heaven, and I, Paul, am its servant.

The Mystery: Christ in Us

²⁴†Even now I find my joy in the suffering I endure for you. In my own flesh I fill up what is lacking in the sufferings of Christ for the sake of his body, the church. ²⁵I became a minister of this church through the commission God gave me to preach among you his word in its fullness, ²⁶*that mystery hidden from ages and generations past but now revealed to his holy ones. ²⁷*God has willed to make known to them the glory beyond price which this mystery brings to the Gentiles—the mystery of Christ in you, your hope of glory. ²⁸This is the Christ we proclaim while we admonish all men and teach them in the full measure of wisdom, hoping to make every man complete in Christ. ²⁹*For this I work and struggle, impelled by that energy of his which is so powerful a force within me.

---

† 1, 9-14: Moved by Epaphras' account, the apostle has prayed fervently for the Colossians that their· response to the gospel may bring the fullest knowledge of God's will, *through perfect wisdom and spiritual insight* (v 9; cf 3, 10). He expects a mutual interaction between their life according to the gospel and this knowledge (v 10), which will reveal the power of God's presence among them, inspire them to courage and calm determination (v 11), and result in grateful love of the Father for his saving gifts (v 12). For he conquers the power of evil over men by offering them the power of his Son, who is his love in person (v 13) and has already forgiven their sins (v 14).

1, 15-20: Scholars raise the question whether Paul may not have adapted these verses from a Christian hymn or a Hellenistic wisdom poem. Whatever the case, the passage with all its lyricism is probably Paul's. Its exalted Christology synthesizes the growing awareness in New Testament times of Christ as man, Son of God, king and judge of the world, endowed with divine redemptive power, and containing in himself the fullness of that effective presence of God among men which was first manifested in the Old Testament (cf Jn 1, 1-18). Whereas man is patterned after the image of God, being given a certain likeness to him (Gn 1, 26f), Christ is the actual likeness of God. Through faith, the remote reality of the Deity is rendered discernibly present in him and comprehensible to men. *He is the image of the invisible God* (v 15), in the sense that as a person he is supreme in every way over all creation. Christ's supremacy requires not only that nothing appear in creation except in relation to him but also that he himself share in the creation of all things (v 16). Such is his supremacy that he existed before creation came into being. It is to him that creation owes all that it has been, is, and will be (v 17).·

Christ cannot be anything but supreme over the church, which in any case is unthinkable and unrealizable without him (his *body*). Furthermore, because of his supremacy he was the first to be raised by God from the dead; and his resurrection placed him in full possession of headship over the community which he brought into being (v 18). Since, as is clear from Christ's role in creation (v 16), the cosmos is dependent on him (v 19), his death upon the cross has its effect on the whole of creation without exception, pacifying it and uniting it to God (v 20). Paul's clear exposition of the supremacy of Christ was occasioned by the Colossians' difficulties concerning the relationship of angelic spirits to the world (see Introduction).

1, 21ff: Paul reminds them that they have experienced the reconciling effect of Christ's death, and appeals to them to adhere firmly to him as their only conciliator with God.

1, 24f–2.5: As the community at Colossae is not personally known to Paul (see Introduction), he here invests his recommendations with greater authority by presenting a brief sketch of his apostolic ministry and sufferings as they reflect those of Christ in behalf of the church (v 24). The preaching of God's word (v 25) manifests the divine will to sanctify the Gentiles (v 26) by revealing God's saving presence among them in Christ (v 27). It teaches men the God-given wisdom about Christ (v 28), whose power works mightily in· the apostle (v 29). Even in those communities which do not know him personally (2, 1), he can increase the perception of God in Christ, unite the faithful more firmly in love, and so bring spiritual comfort to them (v 2). He hopes that his apostolic authority will make the Colossians perceive more readily the defects in the teaching of others who have sought to delude them (4f).

---

*

9: Eph 5, 17; Phil 1, 9.
12: Jn 8, 12; Acts 26, 18; 1 Pt 2, 9.
15: Ps 89, 28; Jn 1, 3.18.
16: 1 Cor 8, 6; Eph 1, 10.21.

18: 1 Cor 15, 20; Eph 1, 22f; Rv 1, 5.
20: Eph 2, 14.16.
26: Rom 16, 25.
27: 3, 4.
29: Phil 4, 13.

2 ¹I want you to know how hard I am struggling for you and for the Laodiceans and the many others who have never seen me in the flesh. ²*I wish their hearts to be strengthened and themselves to be closely united in love, enriched with full assurance by their knowledge of the mystery of God— namely Christ—³*in whom every treasure of wisdom and knowledge is hidden.

III: WARNINGS AGAINST FALSE TEACHERS

A General Admonition

⁴*I TELL YOU ALL THIS so that no one may delude you with specious arguments. ⁵*I may be absent in body but I am with you in spirit, happy to see good order among you and the firmness of your faith in Christ. ⁶†Continue, therefore, to live in Christ Jesus the Lord, in the spirit in which you received him. ⁷*Be rooted in him and built up in him, growing ever stronger in faith, as you were taught, and overflowing with gratitude. ⁸*See to it that no one deceives you through any empty, seductive philosophy that follows mere human traditions, a philosophy based on cosmic powers rather than on Christ.

Sovereign Role of Christ

⁹*In Christ the fullness of Deity resides in bodily form. Yours is a share of this fullness, in him ¹⁰who is the head of every principality and power. ¹¹*You were also circumcised in him, not with the circumcision administered by hand but with Christ's circumcision which strips off the carnal body completely. ¹²*In baptism you were not only buried with him but also raised to life with him because you believed in the power of God who raised him from the dead. ¹³*Even when you were dead in sin and your flesh was uncircumcised, God gave you new life in company with Christ. He pardoned all our sins. ¹⁴*He canceled the bond that stood against us with all its claims, snatching it up and nailing it to the cross. ¹⁵*Thus did God disarm the principalities and powers. He made a public show of them and, leading them off captive, triumphed in the person of Christ.

Practices contrary to Faith

¹⁶*No one is free, therefore, to pass judgment on you in terms of what you eat or drink or what you do on yearly or monthly feasts, or on the sabbath. ¹⁷*All these were but a shadow of things to come; the reality is the body of Christ. ¹⁸*Let no one rob you of your prize by insisting on servility in the worship of angels. Such a one takes his stand on his own experience; he is inflated with empty pride by his human reflections ¹⁹when he should be in close touch with the head. The whole body, mutually supported and upheld by joints and sinews, achieves a growth from this source which comes from God.

²⁰If with Christ you have died to cosmic forces, why should you be bound by rules that say, ²¹"Do not handle! Do not taste! Do not touch!" as though you were still living a life bounded by this world? ²²Such prescriptions deal with things that perish in their use. They are based on merely human precepts and doctrines. ²³While these make a certain show of wisdom in their affected piety, humility, and bodily austerity, their chief effect is that they indulge men's pride.

IV: THE IDEAL CHRISTIAN LIFE IN THE WORLD

Mystical Death and Resurrection

3 ¹*SINCE YOU HAVE BEEN RAISED UP in company with Christ, set your heart on what pertains to higher realms where Christ is seated at God's right hand. ²Be intent on things above rather than on things of earth. ³After all, you have died! Your life is hidden now with Christ in God. ⁴When Christ our life appears, then you shall appear with him in glory.

---

† 2, 6—3, 4: The Colossians are admonished to adhere to the gospel as it was first preached to them (v 6), steeping themselves in it with grateful hearts (v 7). They must reject religious teachings originating in any source except the gospel (v 8) because in Christ alone will they have access to the divinity (v 9). So fully has he enlightened them that they need no other source of religious knowledge or virtue (v 10). They do not require circumcision (v 11), for in baptism their whole being has been affected by Christ (v 12) through forgiveness of sin and restoration to a new life (v 13; cf Rom 6, 1-11).

On the cross Christ canceled the bond that stood against us, with all its claims; i. e., he eliminated the law (cf Eph 2, 15), which men could not observe—and which could not save them. He forgave sins against the law (v 14), and exposed as false and misleading (v 15) all other powers which offer salvation to men. Therefore the Colossians are not to judge food and drink or the keeping of religious festivals according to the rule of other religious powers, including angelic spirits (16ff), for they thereby risk severing themselves from Christ (v 19). If, when they accepted the gospel, they believed in Christ as their Savior, they must be convinced that their salvation cannot be achieved by appeasing ruling spirits through dietary practices, or through a wisdom gained simply in virtue of harsh asceticism (20-23). By retaining the message of the gospel that the risen, living Christ is the source of their salvation, they will be free from false religious evaluations of the things of the world (3, 1f). The Colossians, it is true, will not have the personal satisfaction that material religious practices offer. They have died to these; but one day they will live with Christ in the presence of God (3f).

✿
2/2: Eph 3, 18f.
3: Prv 2, 4f.
4: Eph 4, 14.
5: Phil 1, 27.
7: Eph 3, 17.
8: Gal 4, 3.
9: Eph 3, 19.
11: Jer 4, 4; Rom 2, 25-29; Phil 3, 3.

12: Rom 6, 3f.
13: Eph 2, 1.
14: Eph 2, 15.
15: 2 Cor 2, 14.
16: Rom 14, 3f; 1 Tm 4, 3.
17: Heb 10, 1.
18: Mt 24, 4.
3/1: Phil 3, 20.

Renunciation of Vices

5*†Put to death whatever in your nature is rooted in earth: fornication, uncleanness, passion, evil desires, and that lust which is idolatry. **6***These are the sins which provoke God's wrath. **7**Your own conduct was once of this sort, when these sins were your very life. **8***You must put that aside now: all the anger and quick temper, the malice, the insults, the foul language. **9***Stop lying to one another. What you have done is put aside your old self with its past deeds **10**and put on a new man, one who grows in knowledge as he is formed anew in the image of his Creator. **11***There is no Greek or Jew here, circumcised or uncircumcised, foreigner, Scythian, slave, or freeman. Rather, Christ is everything in all of you.

The Practice of Virtues

12*Because you are God's chosen ones, holy and beloved, clothe yourselves with heartfelt mercy, with kindness, humility, meekness, and patience. **13***Bear with one another; forgive whatever grievances you have against one another. Forgive as the Lord has forgiven you. **14***Over all these virtues put on love, which binds the rest together and makes them perfect. **15***Christ's peace must reign in your hearts, since as members of the one body you have been called to that peace. Dedicate yourselves to thankfulness. **16***Let the word of Christ, rich as it is, dwell in you. In wisdom made perfect, instruct and admonish one another. Sing gratefully to God from your hearts in psalms, hymns, and inspired songs. **17***Whatever you do, whether in speech or in action, do it in the name of the Lord Jesus. Give thanks to God the Father through him.

The Christian Family

18*†You who are wives, be submissive to your husbands. This is your duty in the Lord. **19**Husbands, love your wives. Avoid any bitterness toward them. **20***You children, obey your parents in everything as the acceptable way in the Lord. **21***And fathers, do not nag your children lest they lose heart.

Slaves and Masters

22*To slaves I say, obey your human masters perfectly, not with the purpose of attracting attention and pleasing men but in all sincerity and out of reverence for the Lord. **23**Whatever you do, work at it with your whole being. Do it for the Lord rather than for men, **24**since you know full well you will receive an inheritance from him as your reward. Be slaves of Christ the Lord. **25***Whoever acts unjustly will be repaid for the wrong he has done. No favoritism will be shown.

4   **1**YOU slaveowners, deal justly and fairly with your slaves, realizing that you too have a master in heaven.

Prayer and Apostolic Spirit

2*Pray perseveringly, be attentive to prayer, and pray in a spirit of thanksgiving. **3***Pray for us, too, that God may provide us with an opening to proclaim the mystery of Christ, for which I am a prisoner. **4**Pray that I may speak it clearly, as I must. **5***Be prudent in dealing with outsiders; make the most of every opportunity. **6**Let your speech be always gracious and in good taste, and strive to respond properly to all who address you.

V: CONCLUSION

Tychicus and Onesimus

7*TYCHICUS, OUR DEAR BROTHER, our faithful minister and fellow slave in the Lord, will give you all the news about me. **8**I am sending him to you for this purpose, and to comfort your hearts. **9***With him is Onesimus, our dear and faithful brother, who is one of you. They will tell you all that has happened here.

From Paul's Co-workers

10*Aristarchus, who is a prisoner along with me, sends you greetings. So does Mark, the cousin of Barnabas. You have received instructions about him: if he comes to you, make him welcome. **11**Jesus known also as Justus sends greetings. These are the only circumcised ones among those who are working with me for the kingdom of God. They have been a great comfort to me. **12***Epaphras, who is one of you, sends greetings. He is a servant of Christ Jesus who is always pleading earnestly in prayer that you stand firm, that you be perfect and have full conviction

---

❋

5: Eph 5, 3.
6: Rom 1, 18.
8: Eph 4, 31.
9: Rom 6, 4.6;
    Eph 4, 22-25;
    Heb 12, 1; 1 Pt 2, 1;
    4, 2.
11: 1 Cor 12, 13;
     Gal 3, 27f.
12: Eph 4, 1f.32;
     1 Thes 5, 15.
13: Mt 6, 14; 18, 21-35;
     Eph 4, 32.
14: Rom 13, 8ff.
15: 1 Cor 12, 12;
     Eph 2, 16; 4, 3f.
16: Eph 5, 19f.
17: 1 Cor 10, 31.

18: Eph 5, 22; Ti 2, 5;
     1 Pt 3, 1.
20: Eph 6, 1.
21: Eph 6, 4.
22: Eph 6, 5; 1 Tm 6, 1;
     Ti 2, 9f; 1 Pt 2, 18.
25: Rom 2, 5.
4/2: Lk 18, 1; Rom 12, 12;
     Eph 6, 18-20;
     1 Thes 5, 17.
3: Rom 15, 30; Eph 6, 19;
    2 Thes 3, 1.
5: Eph 5, 15f.
7: Acts 20, 4; Eph 6, 21.
9: Phlm 10f.
10: Acts 19, 29.
12: Rom 15, 30.

---

† 3, 5-17: In lieu of false asceticism and superstitious festivals, the apostle reminds the Colossians of the moral life that is to characterize their response to God through Christ. He urges their participation in the liturgical hymns and prayers that center upon God's plan of salvation in Christ (16f).

3, 18—4, 18: After general recommendations which connect family life and the social condition of slavery with the service of Christ (3, 18—4, 1), Paul requests prayers for himself, especially in view of his imprisonment (2f), and recommends friendly relations and meaningful discussions of Christian teaching with non-Christians (5f). He concludes with greetings and information concerning various Christians known to the Colossians (7-18).

about whatever pertains to God's will. [13]I can certainly testify how solicitous he is for you and for those at Laodicea and Hierapolis. [14]*Luke, our dear physician, sends you greetings. So does Demas.

A Message for the Laodiceans

[15]Give our best wishes to the brothers at Laodicea and to Nymphas and the assembly that meets at his house. [16]†Once this letter has been read to you, see that it is read in the assembly of the Laodiceans as well, and that you yourselves read the letter that is coming from Laodicea. [17]To Archippus say, "Take care to discharge the ministry you have received in the Lord."

[18]*This greeting is from Paul—in my own hand! Remember my chains. Grace be with you.

---

* 14: 2 Tm 4, 11.

18: 1 Cor 16, 21; 2 Thes 3, 17.

---

† 4, 16: The reference is perhaps to a letter Paul wrote to be read in a number of Christian communities in the area of the Lycus Valley, that eventually became known as the letter to the Ephesians (see Ephesians Introduction).

The First Epistle of Paul
to the Thessalonians

Introduction

Paul's formation of a Christian community at Thessalonica on his second missionary journey (Acts 17, 1-9) produced a considerable disturbance among the Jews residing there. To prevent further disorder he and his companion, Silas, agreed to leave the city (Acts 17, 10). However, he revisited the community on his third journey (Acts 20, 1f). Indications from 1 Thessalonians itself and from Acts permit the almost certain conclusion that the epistle was written only a short time after Paul's departure from Thessalonica (1 Thes 2, 17). In that interval he had been in Athens (3, 1; Acts 17, 16), and from there had sent Timothy to the Thessalonians (3, 2). He now writes to them from Corinth (1, 7; Acts 18, 1-18). Gallio is mentioned as proconsul of Achaia (Acts 18, 12-17) during Paul's Corinthian sojourn of more than a year; and since Gallio assumed the office in 51 or 52 A. D., the letter is to be dated at that time.

Paul writes after receiving Timothy's report on the Thessalonian community (3, 6). Deeply grateful for the information it conveys (1, 2f), he is also moved to declare how valuable to his own work the news of their conversion has been (1, 4-10). Probably to offset slanders uttered against him from outside the community after his departure from Thessalonica, he recalls his undemanding manner of life among them (2, 1-12). He reminds them of the prophetic character of the Christian message and relates it to the harassment they continue to suffer at the hands of the Jews (2, 14ff). He is satisfied of their firm adherence to the gospel, and prays that he may be able to visit them soon (3, 6-10). He exhorts them to greater care in carrying out the gospel precepts, particularly those pertaining to right sexual conduct (4, 1-8). He urges them to live peaceably and to avoid idleness (4, 11f).

Paul next turns his attention to the most serious problem which Timothy's visit to the community has brought to light: their excessive sorrow over the death of members of the community, who are thought to be deprived thereby of the joy of the second coming of Christ. Paul appeals to his own knowledge of Christ's teaching to affirm that the resurrection of the dead is to occur before the parousia, so that Christians living at the time are to have no advantage over those who have died (4, 13-18). He reminds them of Christ's words on the suddenness of the parousia and on the need of constant spiritual readiness for it (5, 1-11). He concludes with a request that they esteem those who occupy positions of authority in the community (5, 12f), and show the proper attitude toward one another in the Christian spirit (5, 14f). His final words are a prayer that they may be ready at the glorious coming of Christ (5, 23f).

The epistle is of great doctrinal value, revealing as it does the faith of the community. It also manifests the care and labor which were expended in instructing the Christian communities in New Testament times.

The principal divisions of 1 Thessalonians are as follows:
    I: Introduction (1, 1-10)
    II: Relations with the Thessalonians (2, 1—4, 12)
    III: The Lord's Second Coming (4, 13—5, 28)

I: INTRODUCTION

Greeting

1 1*†PAUL, SILVANUS, AND TIMOTHY, to the church of the Thessalonians who belong to God the Father and the Lord Jesus Christ. Grace and peace be yours.

A Model for Believers

2*†We keep thanking God for all of you and we remember you in our prayers, 3for we constantly are mindful before our God and Father of the way you are proving your faith, and laboring in love, and show-

---

*1/1: Acts 15, 40; 16, 19;
2 Thes 1, 1f.
    2: 2 Thes 1, 3.

---

† 1, 1: For Paul's use of the conventional epistolary form, see note on Romans 1, 1-7.

1, 2-10: The apostle expresses his satisfaction that the three principal Christian characteristics, faith, hope and love, are at work in the Thessalonian community (2f). Unhesitatingly he places its members among those specially beloved and chosen by God (v 4); recalling that his preaching of the gospel to them was not received as a mere intellectual exercise but had made a strong actual impact on their lives (v 5) which not even the opposition of unbelievers could dispel (v 6). Their faith has been an inspiration to Christians elsewhere (7f), who have been impressed especially by the Thessalonians' complete abandonment of idolatry for the worship of the true God, and by their profound orientation toward the second coming of Jesus (9f).

ing constancy of hope in our Lord Jesus Christ. **4**We know, too, brothers beloved of God, how you were chosen. **5**Our preaching of the gospel proved not a mere matter of words for you but one of power; it was carried on in the Holy Spirit and out of complete conviction. You know as well as we do what we proved to be like when, while still among you, we acted on your behalf. **6***You, in turn, became imitators of us and of the Lord, receiving the word despite great trials, with the joy that comes from the Holy Spirit. **7***Thus you became a model for all the believers of Macedonia and Achaia. **8**The word of the Lord has echoed forth from you resoundingly. This is true not only in Macedonia and Achaia; throughout every region your faith in God is celebrated, which makes it needless for us to say anything more. **9***The people of those parts are reporting what kind of reception we had from you, and how you turned to God from idols, to serve him who is the living and true God **10***and to await from heaven the Son he raised from the dead—Jesus, who delivers us from the wrath to come.

II: RELATIONS WITH THE THESSALONIANS

Paul's Sincerity

2 **1†**YOU KNOW WELL ENOUGH, BROTHERS, that our coming among you was not without effect. **2***Fresh from the humiliation we had suffered at Philippi—about which you know—we drew courage from our God to preach his good tidings to you in the face of great opposition. **3**The exhortation we deliver does not spring from deceit or impure motives or any sort of trickery; **4***rather, having met the test imposed on us by God, as men entrusted with the good tidings, we speak like those who strive to please God, "the tester of our hearts," rather than men.

5We were not guilty, as you well know, of flattering words or greed under any pretext, as God is our witness! **6***Neither did we seek glory from men, you or any others, **7**even though we could have insisted on our own importance as apostles of Christ.

On the contrary, while we were among you we were as gentle as any nursing mother fondling her little ones. **8**So well disposed were we to you, in fact, that we wanted to share with you not only God's tidings but our very lives, so dear had you become to us. **9***You must recall, brothers, our efforts and our toil: how we worked day and night all the time we preached God's good tidings to you in order not to impose on you in any way. **10**You are witnesses, as is God himself, of how upright, just, and irreproachable our conduct was toward you who are believers. **11***You likewise know how we exhorted every one of you, as a father does his children—**12***how we encouraged and pleaded with you to make your lives worthy of the God who calls you to his kingship and glory. **13†**That is why we thank God constantly that in receiving his message from us you took it, not as the word of men, but as it truly is, the word of God at work within you who believe.

Partnership in Suffering

14Brothers, you have been made like the churches of God in Judea which are in Christ Jesus. You suffered the same treatment from your fellow countrymen as they did from the Jews **15***who killed the Lord Jesus and the prophets, and persecuted us. Displeasing to God and hostile to all mankind, **16***they try to keep us from preaching salvation to the Gentiles. All this time they have been "filling up their quota of sins," but the wrath has descended upon them at last.

17*†Brothers, when we were orphaned by separation from you for a time—in sight, not in mind—we were seized with the greatest longing to see you. **18**So we tried to come to you—I, Paul, tried more than once—but Satan blocked the way. **19***Who, after all, if not you, will be our hope or joy, or the crown we exult in, before our Lord Jesus Christ at his coming? **20**You are our boast and our delight.

Mission of Timothy

3 **1*†**THAT is why, when we could endure it no longer, we decided to remain alone at Athens **2***and send you Timothy. He is our brother and God's fellow worker in preaching the gospel of Christ, and so we sent him to strengthen and encourage you in regard to your faith **3**lest any one of you be shaken by these trials. You know well enough that such trials

---

*
6: Acts 13, 52; 17, 1-9.
7: 2 Thes 1, 4.
9: Acts 14, 15; Gal 4, 8.
10: Acts 17, 31; Rom 5, 9.
2/2: Acts 16, 19-40.
4: Gal 1, 10.
6: Jn 5, 41.44.
9: Acts 20, 34;
    2 Thes 3, 7-9.

11: Acts 20, 31.
12: Phil 1, 27; 1 Pt 5, 10.
15: Acts 2, 23; 7, 52.
16: 2 Mc 6, 14.
17: 3, 10; Rom 1, 10f.
19: 2 Cor 1, 14.
3/1: Acts 17, 14f.
2: Acts 16, 1f.

---

†

2, 1-12: Paul had experienced such great opposition in Thessalonica that he had to be secretly escorted from the city (Acts 17, 1-10). It is probably the memory of this which underlies the present words recalling his selflessness in preaching the gospel to them (1-7), his affection for them (8f), and the pleasant relationships he established with them (10ff).

2, 13-16: The apostle is grateful because the Thessalonians accepted his preaching as a message from God and not as a mere human communication (v 13). This perception has enabled them, as well as the Judaeo-Christians of Jerusalem, to be steadfast in the face of persecution (v 14). Paul condemns the active Jewish opposition to the gospel, branding it as sinful and worthy of divine punishment (15f).

2, 17-20: Twice had Paul made an effort to visit the community at Thessalonica, only to be "blocked by Satan"—an expression which probably refers to the situation in Thessalonica itself; cf 3, 5.

3, 1-10: Troubled by the lack of news concerning the Thessalonians, Paul had sent Timothy to them as his representative. Timothy's report was reassuring (6ff) except as regards certain possible *shortcomings* in their faith (v 10). Paul is probably dealing with these defects concretely in chapters 4 and 5 of the epistle.

are our common lot. **⁴*** When we were still with you, we used to warn you that we would undergo trial; now it has happened, and you know what we meant. **⁵** That is why I sent to find out about your faith when I could stand the suspense no longer, fearing that the tempter had put you to the test and all our labor might have gone for nothing. **⁶** But now, brothers, since Timothy has returned to us from you reporting the good news of your faith and love, and telling us that you constantly remember us and are as desirous to see us as we are to see you, **⁷** we have been much consoled by your faith throughout our distress and trial— **⁸** so much so that we shall continue to flourish only if you stand firm in the Lord!

Plea for Growth in Holiness

⁹ What thanks can we give to God for all the joy we feel in his presence because of you, **¹⁰** as we ask him fervently night and day that we may see you face to face and remedy any shortcomings in your faith? **¹¹†** May God himself, who is our Father, and our Lord Jesus make our path to you a straight one! **¹²*** And may the Lord increase you and make you overflow with love for one another and for all, even as our love does for you. **¹³*** May he strengthen your hearts, making them blameless and holy before our God and Father at the coming of our Lord Jesus with all his holy ones.

Chastity and Charity

4 **¹†** NOW, my brothers, we beg and exhort you in the Lord Jesus that, even as you learned from us how to conduct yourselves in a way pleasing to God—which you are indeed doing—so you must learn to make still greater progress. **²** You know the instructions we gave you in the Lord Jesus. **³** It is God's will that you grow in holiness: that you abstain from immorality, **⁴** each of you guarding his member in sanctity and honor, **⁵** not in passionate desire as do the Gentiles who know not God; **⁶** and that each refrain from overreaching or cheating his brother in the matter at hand; for the Lord is an avenger of all such things, as we once indicated to you by our testimony. **⁷** God has not called us to immorality but to holiness; **⁸** hence, whoever rejects these instructions rejects, not man, but God who sends his Holy Spirit upon you.

⁹* As regards brotherly love, there is no need for me to write you. God himself has taught you to love one another, **¹⁰** and this you are doing with respect to all the brothers throughout Macedonia. Yet we exhort you to even greater progress, brothers. **¹¹*** Make it a point of honor to remain at peace and attend to your own affairs. Work with your hands as we directed you to do, **¹²** so that you will give good example to outsiders and want for nothing.

III: THE LORD'S SECOND COMING

Witnessed by the Dead

¹³† WE WOULD HAVE YOU BE CLEAR about those who sleep in death, brothers; otherwise you might yield to grief, like those who have no hope. **¹⁴*** For if we believe that Jesus died and rose, God will bring forth with him from the dead those also who have fallen asleep believing in him. **¹⁵*** We say to you, as if the Lord himself had said it, that we who live, who survive until his coming, will in no way have an advantage over those who have fallen asleep. **¹⁶*** No, the Lord himself will come down from heaven at the word of command, at the sound of the archangel's voice and God's trumpet; and those who have died in Christ will rise first. **¹⁷** Then we, the living, the survivors, will be caught up with them in the clouds to meet the Lord in the air. Thenceforth we shall be with the Lord unceasingly. **¹⁸** Console one another with this message.

---

† 3, 11ff: The theme of this prayer is solidarity: between Paul and the Thessalonian Christians (his prospective visit); among themselves; between them and all men (Christian love); and between them and God (holiness).

4, 1-12: To conserve their holiness they are to recall what the apostle taught them in the name of Christ at the time of their conversion (1f). Fornication and all sexual misconduct are to be avoided (3-6), in consideration of the truth that God sanctifies his faithful by the presence of the Holy Spirit (7f). They have heeded Christ's message of love of neighbor and should improve it within the community (9f). He urges that they concern themselves with their own affairs, each laboring faithfully to earn his own living and all presenting a good example to the outside world (11f; cf 5, 14; 2 Thes 3, 10ff).

4, 13-18: Here Paul takes up the practice among the Thessalonians of mourning excessively for their dead (v 13), a reaction deriving from the stress placed by the community on the proximity of the parousia; cf 1, 10. The apostle reminds them of the Christian doctrine of the resurrection of the dead in Christ (v 14). On the basis of Christ's teaching, he affirms that the resurrection of the dead is to precede the second coming. Those who are alive at the time of the latter will not have the advantage over the dead of being the first witnesses to it (v 15), for the Lord will first command the dead to rise (v 16); the living will then join them and both groups will be witnesses of the parousia (v 17; this and the preceding verse reflect the traditional apocalyptic imagery for an act of God).

The doctrine spoken of here is to be recalled when future bereavements overtake the community (v 18). Since Paul does not know the time of the parousia (5, 2; Mt 24, 43) he aligns himself with the Thessalonians (*we . . . who survive*, v 15) in the hope of living until that day, i.e., within the first Christian generation. In his mind such a possibility seems not to have been excluded by the teaching of Jesus himself.

❊
4: Acts 14, 22;	11: 2 Thes 3, 6-12.
2 Tm 3, 12.	14: 1 Cor 15, 3f.12.20.
12: 2 Thes 1, 3.	15: 1 Cor 15, 51.
13: 5, 23; 1 Cor 1, 8.	16: Mt 24, 31;
4/9: Jn 6, 45; 13, 34;	1 Cor 15, 23.52.
1 Jn 4, 7.	

The Need for Preparation

5 **1***†As regards specific times and moments, brothers, we do not need to write you; **2***you know very well that the day of the Lord is coming like a thief in the night. **3**Just when people are saying, "Peace and security," ruin will fall on them with the suddenness of pains overtaking a woman in labor, and there will be no escape. **4***You are not in the dark, brothers, that the day should catch you off guard, like a thief. **5***No, all of you are children of light and of the day. We belong neither to darkness nor to night; **6***therefore let us not be asleep like the rest, but awake and sober! **7**Sleepers sleep by night and drunkards drink by night. **8***We who live by day must be alert, putting on faith and love as a breastplate and the hope of salvation as a helmet. **9**God has not destined us for wrath but for acquiring salvation through our Lord Jesus Christ. **10**He died for us, that all of us, whether awake or asleep, together might live with him. **11**Therefore, comfort and upbuild one another, as indeed you are doing.

Christian Conduct

12†We beg you, brothers, respect those among you whose task it is to exercise authority in the Lord and admonish you; **13**esteem them with the greatest love because of their work. Remain at peace with one another. **14**We exhort you to admonish the unruly; cheer the fainthearted; support the weak; be patient toward all. **15***See that no one returns evil to any other; always seek one another's good and, for that matter, the good of all.

16Rejoice always, **17**never cease praying, **18***render constant thanks; such is God's will for you in Christ Jesus.

19Do not stifle the Spirit. **20**Do not despise prophecies. **21**Test everything; retain what is good. **22**Avoid any semblance of evil.

Blessing and Greeting

23*†May the God of peace make you perfect in holiness. May he preserve you whole and entire, spirit, soul, and body, irreproachable at the coming of our Lord Jesus Christ. **24**He who calls us is trustworthy, therefore he will do it.

25Brothers, pray for us too.

26Greet all the brothers with a holy embrace. **27**†I adjure you by the Lord that this letter be read to them all.

28May the grace of our Lord Jesus Christ be with you.

---

†

5, 1-11: Paul does not wish his criticism of the Thessalonians' grief over their dead to de-emphasize the doctrine of the parousia itself; he commends the importance they accord it and its influence over their lives. They know how unexpected, sudden, and certain it will be (1ff); therefore they are to live in constant anticipation of it, for it will determine their salvation (4-11).

5, 12-22: Respect and love are due to those who hold positions of authority in the community (12f); possibly the presbyters are meant; cf Acts 14, 23. It is the duty of all to reprove and strengthen those who fail in their Christian duty and to show patience toward non-believers, especially by quenching the spirit of revenge (14f). The spirit of joy, prayer, and thanksgiving must prevail (16ff). Due respect is to be shown to the charism of prophecy, but its authentic presence is not to be admitted uncritically (19ff), as evil may make its entrance even by this door (v 22).

5, 23ff: The burden of the apostle's prayer is the sanctification of the community (cf 3, 13—4, 12) in preparation for the second coming of Christ.

5, 27: The public reading of the Pauline letters is the method to be employed for insuring their acceptance by the Christian assembly as the word of God.

---

*

5/1-3: Mt 24, 36-45.	8: Eph 6, 11.14-17;
2: 2 Pt 3, 10.	Is 59, 17.
4: Eph 5, 8f.	15: Prv 20, 22; Mt 5, 38;
5: Jn 8, 12.	Rom 12, 17.
6: Mt 24, 42;	18: Eph 5, 20.
Rom 13, 12f; 1 Pt 5, 8.	23: 2 Thes 3, 16.

The Second Epistle of Paul to the Thessalonians

Introduction

Most scholars accept the authenticity of the second letter to the Thessalonians, as being written in Paul's characteristic language and style. Both letters were written from Corinth, and within a short time of each other, since they show that the apostle is still accompanied by his companions of the second missionary journey, Silas and Timothy (2 Thes 1, 1; Acts 18, 5).

Despite the remarkable literary similarities in the letters, however, the second is the more impersonal, its approach to the subject being somewhat set and formal in tone. The explanation may well lie in the apostle's own less serene circumstances and state of mind, as well as in the disturbing news he had received from Thessalonica after the first letter was written.

He himself is experiencing the difficulties caused by *confused and evil men* (2 Thes 3, 1ff). Meanwhile, persecution against the Thessalonian Christians has intensified (2 Thes 1, 3-10), and the situation among them is worsened by idleness due to the spreading expectation of the parousia (2 Thes 3, 6-12), despite Paul's admonitions in his first letter. He now repeats that the community's life is not to be guided by the false belief that the second coming is imminent, i. e., a day-to-day possibility, whether the source of the belief be the oracular utterance of a self-styled prophet or a letter supposedly written by himself (2 Thes 2, 1ff). He originally taught the Thessalonians, he reminds them, that certain religious events must occur before the parousia can be expected (2 Thes 2, 3-12). Finally, he knows that the community has its refractory members from whom he cannot anticipate simple acquiescence to his teaching, and he gives directions regarding them (2 Thes 3, 14).

The letters to the Thessalonians present incontrovertible evidence that the expectation of the parousia played a capital role in the development of New Testament thought. There is no evidence that this expectation attained in other communities the strength it came to exert in Thessalonica; but the data of 1 and 2 Thessalonians compel its recognition as a conditioning element in the presentation of doctrine while the literature of the New Testament developed.

The principal divisions of 2 Thessalonians are as follows:

I: INTRODUCTION

Greeting

1 1*†PAUL, SILVANUS, AND TIMOTHY, to the church of the Thessalonians who belong to God our Father and the Lord Jesus Christ. ²Grace and peace be yours from God the Father and the Lord Jesus Christ.

Praise for the Church at Thessalonica

³*†It is no more than right that we thank God unceasingly for you, brothers, because your faith grows apace and your mutual love increases; ⁴so much so that in God's communities we can boast of your constancy and your faith in persecution and trial. You endure these ⁵*as an expression of God's just judgment, in order to be found worthy of his kingdom—it is for his kingdom you suffer—⁶even if strict justice would require that God visit hardships on those who visit them on you. ⁷He will provide relief to you who are sorely tried, as well as to us, when the Lord Jesus is revealed from heaven with his mighty angels; ⁸*when "with flaming power he will inflict punishment on those who do not acknowledge God nor heed" the good news of our Lord Jesus. ⁹Such as these will suffer the penalty of eternal ruin apart from the presence of the Lord and the glory of his might ¹⁰*on the Day when he comes, to be glorified in his holy

---

† 1, 1f: On the address and greeting, see note on Romans 1, 1-7.

1, 3-12: The Thessalonian community is encouraged to stand fast under the severe trial they are experiencing (3ff). *God's just judgment* will bring relief to the afflicted as well as punishment to the persecutors (6-10). The harassment of the community seems to have intensified during the interval between the writing of 1 and 2 Thessalonians; cf 1 Thes 2, 14ff. This plight may well have contributed to the notion that the parousia was near. Paul considers this question in 2, 1-12.

❋
  1/1: 1 Thes 1, 1.
     3: 1 Thes 1, 2.
     5: 1 Thes 3, 4.
       8: Ps 79, 6; Is 66, 15; Jer 10, 25.
    10: Ps 89, 8.

ones and adored by all who have believed—for you already have our witness to you.

Prayer for Their Progress

11*We pray for you always that our God may make you worthy of his call, and fulfill by his power every honest intention and work of faith. **12**In this way the name of our Lord Jesus may be glorified in you and you in him, in accord with the gracious gift of our God and of the Lord Jesus Christ.

II: THE LORD'S SECOND COMING

Adversary Restrained

2 **1*†**ON THE QUESTION OF THE COMING of our Lord Jesus Christ and our being gathered to him, we beg you, brothers, **2**not to be so easily agitated or terrified, whether by an oracular utterance, or rumor, or a letter alleged to be ours, into believing that the day of the Lord is here.

3Let no one seduce you, no matter how. Since the mass apostasy has not yet occurred nor the man of lawlessness been revealed—that son of perdition **4**and adversary who exalts himself above every so-called god proposed for worship, he who seats himself in God's temple and even declares himself to be God— **5**do you not remember how I used to tell you about these things when I was still with you? **6**You know what restrains him until he shall be revealed in his own time. **7***The secret force of lawlessness is already at work, mind you, but there is one who holds him back until that restrainer shall be taken from the scene. **8***Thereupon the lawless one will be revealed, and the Lord Jesus will destroy him with the breath of his mouth and annihilate him by manifesting his own presence. **9***This lawless one will appear as part of the workings of Satan, accompanied by all the power and signs and wonders at the disposal of falsehood— **10**by every seduction the wicked can devise for those destined to ruin because they have not opened their hearts to the truth in order to be saved. **11**Therefore God is sending upon them a perverse spirit which leads them to give credence to falsehood, **12**so that all who have not believed the truth but have delighted in evildoing will be condemned.

Encouraging Words

13*†We are bound to thank God for you always, beloved brothers in the Lord, because you are the first fruits of those whom God has chosen for salvation, in holiness of spirit and fidelity to truth. **14***He called you through our preaching of the good news so that you might achieve the glory of our Lord Jesus Christ.

15Therefore, brothers, stand firm. Hold fast to the traditions you received from us, either by our word or by letter. **16**May our Lord Jesus Christ himself, may God our Father who loved us and in his mercy gave us eternal consolation and hope, **17**console your hearts and strengthen them for every good work and word.

III: EXHORTATION

Request for Prayers

3 **1*†**FOR THE REST, BROTHERS, pray for us that the word of the Lord may make progress and be hailed by many others, even as it has been by you. **2**Pray that we may be delivered from confused and evil men. For not every man has faith, but **3***the Lord keeps faith; he it is who will strengthen you and guard you against the evil one. **4***In the Lord we are confident that you are doing and will continue to do whatever we enjoin. **5**May the Lord rule your hearts in the love of God and the constancy of Christ.

† 2, 1-12: Though the parousia is certain (v 1), the Thessalonians are not to expect it to occur at almost any time in the immediate future. No appeal to an utterance of a self-styled prophet, or to any supposed letter of Paul justifies such an expectation (v 2). They should not allow themselves to be duped into this way of thinking, for a religious apostasy is destined to precede the Lord's second coming. It will be embodied in *the man of lawlessness,* a personage totally dedicated to evil, *that son of perdition* marked for eternal doom (vv 3f); cf Jn 17, 12. In the epistles of John he is usually identified with the antichrist (1 Jn 2, 18.22; 4, 3; 2 Jn 7). He will be anti-God and will himself lay claim to divine honors (v 4).

During Paul's stay at Thessalonica (Acts 17, 1-9) he instructed the people on this subject (v 5). Now he wishes to add that there is a restraining power which prevents *the lawless one* from coming into his own (v 6). *The secret force of lawlessness,* though *already at work,* is held down now by a restraining power (v 7), the nature of which Paul does not explain. While the restraint continues, the parousia cannot occur; but when it is removed, *the man of lawlessness* will make his appearance accompanied by all the panoply of satanic power (vv 8f). He will bring some to ruin (v 10), but is destined to be destroyed by Jesus' coming (v 8). God acts toward the impious in such a way as to allow them to become confirmed in evil (v 11; cf Rom 1, 24f) through their deliberate rejection of the truth (v 12).

2, 13-17: The Christian faithful are on the path of salvation. They have received, through the medium of Paul's preaching, the divine gift of sanctification that flows from faith in the gospel (v 13); it is the first step toward ultimate participation in Christ's glory (v 14). They are not to depart from the instructions given them at the time of their conversion (cf Acts 17, 1-9) nor from those contained in Paul's previous letter (1 Thes 2, 15). The apostle's prayer is that God may comfort and strengthen them as they strive to live out the gospel in their own lives (16f).

3, 1-5: Paul requests prayers that his preaching of the gospel may continue to be successful (v 1), and he himself may be free from hindrance by the wicked (v 2). He is confident that the Lord will preserve the faith of the community (v 3) and help them to carry out faithfully all that has been enjoined upon them (v 4). A second prayer reminds them that the goal of their efforts is to love God through patient acceptance of trials, inspired by the example of Christ (v 5).

11: Phil 2, 13.
2/1: 1 Thes 4, 13-17.
7: Acts 20, 29.
8: Is 11, 4; Rv 19, 15.
9: Mt 24, 24.
13: 1 Thes 2, 13; 1 Pt 1, 2.
14: 1 Thes 4, 7; 5, 9.
3/1: Eph 6, 19; Col 4, 3.
3: Mt 6, 13; 1 Thes 5, 34.
4: 2 Cor 7, 16.

Dealing with the Idle

6†We command you, brothers, in the name of the Lord Jesus Christ, to avoid any brother who wanders from the straight path and does not follow the tradition you received from us. **7**You know how you ought to imitate us. We did not live lives of disorder when we were among you, **8***nor depend on anyone for food. Rather, we worked day and night, laboring to the point of exhaustion so as not to impose on any of you. **9***Not that we had no claim on you, but that we might present ourselves as an example for you to imitate. **10***Indeed, when we were with you we used to lay down the rule that anyone who would not work should not eat.

11*We hear that some of you are unruly, not keeping busy but acting like busybodies. **12**We enjoin all such, and we urge them strongly in the Lord Jesus Christ, to earn the food they eat by working quietly.

13You must never grow weary of doing what is right, brothers.

14If anyone will not obey our injunction, delivered through this letter, single him out to be ostracized that he may be ashamed of his conduct. **15***But do not treat him like an enemy; rather, correct him as you would a brother.

Final Blessing and Greeting

16*May he who is the Lord of peace give you continued peace in every possible way. The Lord be with you all.

17*†This greeting is in my own hand—Paul's. I append this signature to every letter I write.

18May the grace of our Lord Jesus Christ be with you all.

✿

8: 1 Thes 2, 9.	15: 2 Cor 2, 7; Gal 6, 1.
9: Mt 10, 10.	16: Jn 14, 27.
10: 1 Thes 4, 11.	17: Gal 6, 11.
11: 1 Thes 5, 14.	

---

†

3, 6-15: Some members of the community, whether in good or bad faith, have ceased to work for a living; they claim to regard money as useless in view of the imminence of the parousia (cf 2, 1-12), and consequently depend upon others for sustenance (8.10). This result of their false expectation has posed a perplexing problem to the charitable of the community. Stringent measures are to be taken against them: avoidance of voluntary association with them (v 6); refusal to support them gratuitously (v 10); and a gradual but firm exclusion of them from the community (v 14).

3, 17: The apostle takes up the pen himself, evidence that he normally engaged a secretary in the composition of his epistles. Out of fear of possible forgeries composed in his name (2 Thes 2, 2), he points to the unusually large Greek letters that characterize his handwriting.

The First Epistle of Paul to Timothy

Introduction

The three letters, 1 and 2 Timothy, and Titus, were first named "pastoral epistles" in the eighteenth century. From the late second century to the nineteenth, their Pauline authorship went unchallenged. Since then, discussion of that question has reached an impasse. Some scholars are convinced that Paul could not have been responsible for the vocabulary and style of the letters, their concept of church organization, or the theological expressions found in them. Others believe just as firmly that, on the basis of statistical evidence, the vocabulary and style are Pauline, even if at first sight the contrary appears to be the case; that the concept of church organization in these epistles is not as advanced as the opponents of Pauline authorship make it out to be, the notion of a hierarchical order in a religious community having existed among the Jews even before the time of Christ, as the scrolls of Qumran indicate; and, finally, that there are affinities between the theological thought of the pastorals and that of unquestionably genuine letters of Paul. A third group, while conceding a degree of validity to the position of the other two, suggests that either the apostle made use of a secretary (possibly Luke; see 2 Tm 4, 11) who was responsible for the composition of the letters, or that they are the work of an anonymous writer compiling traditions about Paul in his later years.

The problem of the literary authorship of the pastorals has not disproved the authenticity of their content. If Paul is considered their more immediate author, they are to be dated between the end of his first Roman imprisonment (Acts 28, 16) and his execution under Nero (63-67 A. D.); if they are regarded as only more remotely Pauline, their date may be as late as the early second century.

The first of the pastorals, 1 Timothy, is presented as having been written from Macedonia. Timothy, whom Paul converted, was of mixed Jewish and Gentile parentage (Acts 16, 1ff). He was the apostle's companion on both the second and third missionary journeys (Acts 16, 3; 19, 22), and was often sent by him on special missions (1 Thes 3, 2; 1 Cor 4, 17; Acts 19, 22). In 1 Timothy (1, 3) he is described as the administrator of the entire Ephesian community. The epistle instructs him on his duty to restrain false and useless teaching (1, 3-11; 4, 1-5; 6, 3-16); proposes principles pertaining to his relationship to the older members of the community (5, 1f) and to the presbyters (5, 17-25); gives rules for aid to widows (5, 3-8), and their selection for charitable ministrations (5, 9-16); deals with liturgical celebrations (2, 1-15); the selection of men for the offices of bishop and deacon (3, 1-13), the relations of slaves and their masters (6, 1f), and the obligations of the wealthier members of the community (6, 17ff). It also reminds Timothy of the prophetic character of his office (1, 12-18), and encourages him in his exercise of it (4, 6-16). The central passage of the letter (3, 14ff) expresses the chief motive that should guide the conduct of Timothy—preservation of the purity of the church's doctrine. On this same note the epistle concludes (6, 20-21).

1 ¹†PAUL, AN APOSTLE OF CHRIST JESUS by command of God our savior and Christ Jesus our hope, ²*to Timothy, my own true child in faith. May grace, mercy, and peace be yours from God the Father and Christ Jesus our Lord.

On Holding Fast to Sound Doctrine

³†I repeat the directions I gave you when I was on my way to Macedonia: stay on in Ephesus in order to warn certain people there against teaching false doctrines ⁴*and busying themselves with interminable myths and genealogies, which promote idle speculations rather than that training in faith which God requires.

⁵What we are aiming at in this warning is the love that springs from a pure heart, a good conscience, and sincere faith. ⁶Some people have neglected these and instead have turned to meaningless talk, ⁷wanting to be teachers of the law but actually not understanding the words they are using, much less the matters they discuss with such assurance.

⁸*†We know that the law is good, provided one uses it in the way law is supposed to be used—⁹that is, with the understanding that it is aimed, not at good men but at the lawless and unruly, the irreligious and the sinful, the wicked and the godless, men who kill their fathers or mothers, murderers, ¹⁰fornicators, sexual perverts, kidnapers, liars, perjurers, and those who in

---

† 1, 1f: For Pauline use of the conventional epistolary form, see note on Romans 1, 1-7.

1, 3-7: Here Timothy's initial task in Ephesus (cf Acts 20, 17-35) is outlined: to suppress the idle religious speculations, probably about Old Testament figures (3f), which do not contribute to the development of love within the community (v 5) but rather encourage others to similar useless conjectures (1, 6f).

1, 8-11: Those responsible for the empty surmises which are to be suppressed by Timothy do not present the Old Testament from the Christian viewpoint. The Christian values the Old Testament, not as a system of law, but as the first stage in God's revelation of his saving plan, which is brought to fulfillment in the good news of salvation through faith in Jesus Christ.

❋ 1/2: Acts 16, 1.   8: Rom 7, 12.
   4: 6, 4.20; 2 Tm 2, 14.16;
   Ti 3, 9.

other ways flout the sound teaching **11**that pertains to the glorious gospel of God—blessed be he—with which I have been entrusted.

12†I thank Christ Jesus our Lord, who has strengthened me, that he has made me his servant and judged me faithful. **13***I was once a blasphemer, a persecutor, a man filled with arrogance; but because I did not know what I was doing in my unbelief, I have been treated mercifully, **14**and the grace of our Lord has been granted me in overflowing measure, along with the faith and love which are in Christ Jesus. **15***You can depend on this as worthy of full acceptance: that Christ Jesus came into the world to save sinners. Of these I myself am the worst. **16**But on that very account I was dealt with mercifully, so that in me, as an extreme case, Jesus Christ might display all his patience, and that I might become an example to those who would later have faith in him and gain everlasting life.**17***To the King of ages, the immortal, the invisible, the only God, be honor and glory forever and ever! Amen.

18*†I have a solemn charge to give you, Timothy, my child. This charge is in accordance with the prophecies made in your regard, and I give it to you so that under the inspiration of these prophecies you may fight the good fight **19**and hold fast to faith and a good conscience. Some men, by rejecting the guidance of conscience, have made shipwreck of their faith, **20***among them Hymenaeus and Alexander; these I have turned over to Satan so that they may learn not to blaspheme.

Conduct of Men and Women

2 **1**†FIRST of all, I urge that petitions, prayers, intercessions, and thanksgivings be offered for all men, **2***especially for kings and those in authority, that we may be able to lead undisturbed and tranquil lives in perfect piety and dignity. **3**Prayer of this kind is good, and God our savior is pleased with it, **4**for he wants all men to be saved and come to know the truth. **5***And the truth is this:

> "God is one.
> One also is the mediator between God and men,
> the man Christ Jesus,
> **6***who gave himself as a ransom for all."

This truth was attested at the fitting time. **7***I have been made its herald and apostle (believe me, I am not lying but speak the truth), the teacher of the nations in the true faith.

8It is my wish, then, that in every place the men shall offer prayers with blameless hands held aloft, and be free from anger and dissension. **9***†Similarly, the women must deport themselves properly. They should dress modestly and quietly, and not be decked out in fancy hair styles, gold ornaments, pearls, or costly clothing; **10**rather, as becomes women who profess to be religious, their adornment should be good deeds. **11**A woman must learn in silence and be completely submissive. **12***I do not permit a woman to act as teacher, or in any way to have authority over a man; she must be quiet. **13***For Adam was created first, Eve afterward; **14***moreover, it was not Adam who was deceived but the woman. It was she who was led astray and fell into sin. **15**She will be saved through childbearing, provided she continues in faith and love and holiness—her chastity of course being taken for granted.

Qualifications of Various Ministers

3 **1***†YOU can depend on this: whoever wants to be a bishop aspires to a noble task. **2***A bishop must be irreproachable, married only once, of even temper, self-controlled, modest, and hospitable. He should be a good teacher. **3**He must not be addicted to

† 1, 12-17: Present gratitude for the Christian apostleship leads to a recalling of the earlier time when "Paul" was a fierce persecutor of the Christian communities (cf Acts 26, 9ff), until his conversion by intervention of the divine mercy. This and his subsequent apostolic experience testify to the saving purpose of Jesus' incarnation. The fact of his former ignorance of the truth has not kept the apostle from regarding himself as having been the worst of sinners (v 15). Yet he was chosen to be an apostle, that God might manifest his firm will to save sinful humanity through Jesus Christ (v 16). The recounting of so great a mystery of mercy leads to a spontaneous outpouring of adoration (v 17).

1, 18ff: Timothy is to be mindful of his calling, which is here compared to that of Barnabas and Saul; cf Acts 13, 1ff. Such is probably the sense of the allusion to *the prophecies* that committed him to holding firmly to the traditional Christian teaching (v 18). His task is not to yield, whether in doctrine or in conduct, to erroneous opinions, taking warning from what has already happened at Ephesus in the case of Hymenaeus and Alexander (19f). For the error of Hymenaeus, cf 2 Tm 2, 17f.

2, 1-8: This marked insistence that the liturgical prayer of the community concern itself with the needs of all men, whether Christian or not, and especially of those in authority, may imply that a disposition existed at Ephesus to refuse prayer for pagans. In actuality, such prayer aids the community to achieve peaceful relationships with non-Christians (v 2) and contributes to their salvation, since it derives its value from the presence within the community of Christ who is the one and only Savior of all men (3-6). The vital apostolic mission to the Gentiles concerning Christ's purpose of the universal salvation should be reflected in the prayer of the community (v 7), which should be unmarred by internal dissension (v 8); cf Mt 5, 23ff.

2, 9-13: At the liturgical assembly the dress of women should be appropriate to the occasion (v 9); their chief adornment is to be their reputation for good works (v 10). Women are not to take part in the charismatic activity of the assembly (11f; cf 1 Cor 14, 34); their conduct there should not reflect authority but the role of man's helpmate (v 13; cf Gn 2, 18), thus reversing the relationship of Eve to Adam (v 14; cf Gn 3, 6f). As long as women perform their role as wives and mothers in faith and love, their salvation is assured (v 15).

3, 1-7: The passage begins by commending those who aspire to the office of bishop within the community (v 1), and proceeds to list the qualifications required: personal stability and graciousness; talent for teaching (v 2); moderation in habits and temperament (v 3); managerial ability (v 4), and experience in

*
13: Acts 8, 3.
15: 3, 1; 4, 9; Mt 9, 13;
   Mk 2, 17.
17: Ps 145, 13.
18: 4, 14.
20: 2 Tm 2, 17; 4, 14.
2/5: Heb 8, 6.
  6: Mt 20, 28; Gal 1, 4.

7: Gal 2, 7; 2 Tm 1, 11.
9: 1 Pt 3, 3.
12: 1 Cor 14, 34.
13: Gn 1, 27.
14: Gn 3, 6.
3/1: 1, 15.
2: Ti 1, 7.

drink. He ought not to be contentious but, rather, gentle, a man of peace. Nor can he be someone who loves money. **4**He must be a good manager of his own household, keeping his children under control without sacrificing his dignity; **5**for if a man does not know how to manage his own house, how can he take care of the church of God? **6**He should not be a new convert, lest he become conceited and thus incur the punishment once meted out to the devil. **7**He must also be well thought of by those outside the church, to ensure that he does not fall into disgrace and the devil's trap. **8***†In the same way, deacons must be serious, straightforward, and truthful. They may not overindulge in drink or give in to greed. **9**They must hold fast to the divinely revealed faith with a clear conscience. **10**They should be put on probation first; then, if there is nothing against them, they may serve as deacons. **11**The women, similarly, should be serious, not slanderous gossips. They should be temperate and entirely trustworthy. **12**Deacons may be married but once and must be good managers of their children and their households. **13**Those who serve well as deacons gain a worthy place for themselves and much assurance in their faith in Christ Jesus.

14†Although I hope to visit you soon, I am writing you about these matters **15**so that if I should be delayed you will know what kind of conduct befits a member of God's household, the church of the living God, the pillar and bulwark of truth. **16***Wonderful, indeed, is the mystery of our faith, as we say in professing it:

> "He was manifested in the flesh,
> vindicated in the Spirit;
> Seen by the angels;
> preached among the Gentiles,
> Believed in throughout the world,
> taken up into glory."

False Asceticism

4 **1***†THE Spirit distinctly says that in later times some will turn away from the faith and will heed deceitful spirits and things taught by demons **2**through plausible liars—men with seared consciences **3***who forbid marriage and require abstinence from foods which God created to be received with thanksgiving by believers who know the truth. **4***Everything God created is good; nothing is to be rejected when it is received with thanksgiving, **5**for it is made holy by God's word and by prayer.

Counsel to Timothy

6If you put these instructions before the brotherhood you will be a good servant of Christ Jesus, reared in the words of faith and the sound doctrine you have

faithfully followed. **7***Have nothing to do with profane myths or old wives' tales. Train yourself for the life of piety, **8**for while physical training is to some extent valuable, the discipline of religion is incalculably more so, with its promise of life here and hereafter. **9**You can depend on this as worthy of complete acceptance.

10This explains why we work and struggle as we do; our hopes are fixed on the living God who is the savior of all men, but especially of those who believe.

11Such are the things you must urge and teach. **12***†Let no one look down on you because of your youth, but be a continuing example of love, faith, and purity to believers. **13**Until I arrive, devote yourself to the reading of Scripture, to preaching and teaching. **14***Do not neglect the gift you received when, as a result of prophecy, the presbyters laid their hands on you. **15**Attend to your duties; let them absorb you, so that everyone may see your progress. **16**Watch yourself and watch your teaching. Persevere at both tasks. By doing so you will bring to salvation yourself and all who hear you.

5 **1***†NEVER censure an older man, but appeal to him as to a father. You should treat younger men as brothers, **2**older women as mothers, and younger women as sisters, with absolute purity.

---

†Christian living (3, 5f). Moreover the candidate's life before his conversion should provide no grounds for the charge that he did not previously practice what he now preaches.

3, 8-13: Deacons, besides possessing the virtue of moderation (v 8), are to be outstanding for their faith (v 9) and well respected within the community (v 10). Women in this same role (cf Rom 16, 1) must be of serious mien, temperate, and dedicated, and not given to malicious talebearing (v 11). Deacons must have shown stability in marriage and have a good record as family men (v 12), for such experience prepares them well for the exercise of their ministry in behalf of the community (v 13).

3, 14ff: Lest there be some delay in the visit planned for the near future to Timothy at Ephesus, the present letter is being sent on ahead to arm and enlighten him in his task of preserving sound Christian conduct in the Ephesian church (14f). The care he must exercise over this community is required by the profound nature of Christianity. It centers in Christ, preexistent but appearing in human flesh; the goodness of his mortal existence was verified by the Holy Spirit; the mystery of his Person was revealed to the angels, announced to the Gentiles, and accepted by them in faith. He himself was returned (through his resurrection and ascension) to the divine glory that is properly his (v 16). This passage apparently includes part of a liturgical hymn used among the Christian communities in and around Ephesus, and directed against the cult of Artemis.

4, 1-11: Doctrinal deviations within the church from the true Christian message have been prophesied, though the origin of the prophecy is not specified (1f); cf Acts 20, 29f. The letter warns against a false asceticism which prohibits marriage and regards certain foodstuffs as morally contaminating (v 3). Timothy is urged to reiterate the Christian teaching that neither salvation nor damnation is to be found in material creation (4-8). Man is saved only by the action of God (9ff).

4, 12-16: Timothy is urged to preach and teach with confidence, relying on the gifts and the mission that God has bestowed on him.

5, 1-16: After a few words of general advice based on common sense (1f), the letter takes up, in its several aspects, the

*
8: Acts 6, 1-6.
16: Mk 16, 19; Jn 1, 14; Acts 1, 2.
4/1: Acts 20, 29f; 2 Tm 3, 1; 2 Pt 3, 3.
3: Gn 9, 3; Col 2, 16-23.
4: Gn 1, 31; 1 Cor 10, 25.30.
7: 1, 4; 2 Tm 2, 23; Ti 3, 9.
12: 1 Cor 16, 11.
14: 1, 18.
5/1: Ti 2, 2.

Rules for Widows

3Honor the claims of widows who are real widows—that is, who are alone and bereft. **4**If a widow has any children or grandchildren, let these learn that piety begins at home and that they should fittingly support their parents and grandparents; this is the way God wants it to be. **5**The real widow, left destitute, is one who has set her hope on God and continues night and day in supplications and prayers. **6**A widow who gives herself up to selfish indulgence, however, leads a life of living death.

7Make the following rules about widows, so that no one may incur blame. **8**If anyone does not provide for his own relatives and especially for members of his immediate family, he has denied the faith; he is worse than an unbeliever. **9**To be on the church's roll of widows, a widow should be not less than sixty years of age. She must have been married only once. **10***Her good character will be attested to by her good deeds. Has she brought up children? Has she been hospitable to strangers? Has she washed the feet of Christian visitors? Has she given help to those in distress? In a word, has she been eager to do every possible good work?

11*Refuse to enroll the younger widows, for when their passions estrange them from Christ they will want to marry. **12**This will bring them condemnation for breaking their first pledge. **13**Besides, they learn to be ladies of leisure, who go about from house to house —becoming not only timewasters but gossips and busybodies as well, talking about things they ought not. **14**That is why I should like to see the younger ones marry, have children, keep house, and in general give our enemies no occasion to speak ill of us. **15**Already, some have turned away to follow Satan. **16**If a woman church member has relatives who are widows, she must assist them. She should not let them become a burden to the church, which ought to be free to give help to the widows who are really in need.

17*†Presbyters who do well as leaders deserve to be paid double, especially those whose work is preaching and teaching. **18***The Scripture says, "You shall not put a muzzle on an ox when he is threshing the grain," and also, "The worker deserves his wages."

19*Pay no attention to an accusation against a presbyter unless it is supported by two or three witnesses. **20**The ones who do commit sin, however, are to be publicly reprimanded, so that the rest may fear to offend. **21**I charge you before God, Christ Jesus, and the chosen angels: apply these rules without prejudice, act with complete impartiality! **22**Never lay hands hastily on anyone, or you may be sharing in the misdeeds of others. Keep yourself pure.

23Stop drinking water only. Take a little wine for the good of your stomach, and because of your frequent illnesses.

24Some men's sins are flagrant and cry out for judgment now, while other men's sins will appear only later. **25**Similarly, some good deeds stand out clearly as such; even inconspicuous ones cannot be hidden forever.

6 **1*†**ALL under the yoke of slavery must regard their masters as worthy of full respect; otherwise the name of God and the church's teaching suffer abuse. **2**Those slaves whose masters are brothers in the faith must not take liberties with them on that account. They must perform their tasks even more faithfully, since those who will profit from their work are believers and beloved brothers. These are the things you must teach and preach. **3†**Whoever teaches in any other way, not holding to the sound doctrines of our Lord Jesus Christ and the teaching proper to true religion, **4**should be recognized as both conceited and ignorant, a sick man in his passion for polemics and controversy. From these come envy, dissension, slander, evil suspicions—**5**in a word, the bickering of men with twisted minds who have lost all sense of truth. Such men value religion only as a means of personal gain. **6**There is, of course, great gain in religion—provided one is content with a sufficiency. **7***We brought

---

† subject of widows. The first responsibility for their care belongs to the family circle, not to the Christian community as such (3f.16). The widow left without the aid of relatives may benefit the community by her prayer, and the community should consider her material sustenance its responsibility (5f). Widows who wish to work directly for the Christian community should not be accepted unless they are well beyond the probability of marriage, i. e., sixty years of age, married only once, and with a reputation for good works (9f). Younger widows are apt to be troublesome and should be encouraged to remarry (11-15).

5, 17-25: The function of *presbyters* is not exactly the same as that of the "episkopos," *bishop* (3, 1); in fact, the relation of the two at the time of this epistle is obscure. The pastorals seem to reflect a transitional stage that developed into the monarchical episcopate of the second century (v 17). The presbyters possess the responsibility of preaching and teaching, for which functions they are supported by the community (5, 17f). The realization that their position subjects them to adverse criticism is implied in the direction to Timothy (19f) to make sure of the truth of any accusation against them before public reproof is given. He must be as objective as possible in weighing charges against presbyters (v 21), learning from his experience both to take care in selecting them (v 22) and to judge prudently any criticism of them. The letter now sounds an informal note of personal concern in its advice to Timothy not to take his task so strenuously that he even avoids table wine (v 23).

Judgment concerning the fitness of candidates to serve as presbyters is easy with persons of open conduct, more difficult and prolonged with those of greater reserve (24f).

6, 1f: Domestic relationships derive supernatural value from the Christian faith.

6, 3-10: Timothy is exhorted to maintain steadfastly the position outlined in this letter, not allowing himself to be pressured into any other course. He must realize that false teachers can be discerned by their pride, envy, quarrelsomeness, and their greed for material gain.

✿

    10: Jn 13, 14.
11-16: 1 Cor 7, 8f.39f.
    17: 1 Thes 5, 12.
    18: Dt 25, 4; Lk 10, 17;
        1 Cor 9, 9.

    19: Dt 19, 15; Mt 18, 16.
6/1: 1 Cor 7, 21f;
        Eph 6, 5-8;
        Col 3, 22-25.
     7: Jb 1, 21; Ps 49, 17.

nothing into this world, nor have we the power to take anything out. ⁸If we have food and clothing we have all that we need. ⁹Those who want to be rich are falling into temptation and a trap. They are letting themselves be captured by foolish and harmful desires which drag men down to ruin and destruction. ¹⁰The love of money is the root of all evil. Some men in their passion for it have strayed from the faith, and have come to grief amid great pain.

¹¹*†Man of God that you are, flee from all this. Instead, seek after integrity, piety, faith, love, steadfastness, and a gentle spirit. ¹²*Fight the good fight of faith. Take firm hold on the everlasting life to which you were called when, in the presence of many witnesses, you made your noble profession of faith. ¹³*Before God, who gives life to all, and before Christ Jesus, who in bearing witness made his noble profession before Pontius Pilate, ¹⁴I charge you to keep God's command without blame or reproach until our Lord Jesus Christ shall appear. ¹⁵*This appearance God will bring to pass at his chosen time. He is the blessed and only ruler, the King of kings and Lord of lords ¹⁶*who alone has immortality and who dwells in unapproachable light, whom no human being has ever seen or can see. To him be honor and everlasting rule! Amen.

¹⁷*†Tell those who are rich in this world's goods not to be proud, and not to rely on so uncertain a thing as wealth. Let them trust in the God who provides us richly with all things for our use. ¹⁸Charge them to do good, to be rich in good works and generous, sharing what they have. ¹⁹*Thus will they build a secure foundation for the future, for receiving that life which is life indeed.

²⁰*†O Timothy, guard what has been committed to you. Stay clear of worldly, idle talk and the contradictions of what is falsely called knowledge. ²¹In laying claim to such knowledge, some men have missed the goal of faith. Grace be with you.

---

*

11: 2 Tm 2, 22; 4, 1f.	16: Jn 1, 18; 1 Jn 4, 12.
12: 2 Tm 4, 7.	17: Lk 12, 17-21.
13: Mt 27, 11;	19: Mt 6, 20.
Jn 18, 33.37.	20: 2 Tm 1, 14.
15: Dt 10, 17; Rv 17, 14;	
19, 16.	

---

†

6, 11-16: Timothy's position demands total dedication to God and faultless witness to Christ (11-14) operating from an awareness, through faith, of the coming revelation of Jesus as King, Lord, and God (15f).

6, 17ff: Timothy is directed to instruct the rich, advising them to make good use of their wealth by aiding the poor.

6, 20f: The final words reflect the chief concern of this letter: that Timothy take every means to preserve the traditional Christian faith.

The Second Epistle of Paul to Timothy

Introduction

The authorship and date of this epistle are discussed in the Introduction to the First Epistle of Paul to Timothy.
The letter portrays Paul as a prisoner (1, 8.16; 2, 9) in Rome (1, 17), and indicates that Timothy is in Ephesus (4, 12). It reveals that, with rare exceptions, Christians have not rallied to Paul's support (1, 15-18), and takes a pessimistic view of the outcome of his case (4, 16).
It describes Paul as fully aware of what impends, looking to God, not to men, for his deliverance (4, 3-8.18).
It recalls with affectionate remembrance his mission days with Timothy (1, 3ff; cf Acts 16, 1-4). It points to his preaching of the gospel as the reason for his imprisonment and offers Timothy as a motive of steadfastness his own example of firmness in faith despite adverse circumstances (1, 6-14). The epistle suggests that Timothy should prepare others to replace himself as Paul has prepared him for his own replacement (2, 1f), urging him not to desist out of fear from preserving and spreading the Christian message (2, 3-7). It presents the resurrection of Jesus and his messianic role as the heart of the gospel for which Paul has been ready to lay down his life (2, 8f), not only to express fully his own conviction but to support the conviction of others (2, 10-13).

This letter, like the preceding one, urges Timothy to protect the community from the inevitable impact of false teaching (2, 14—3, 9), without fear of the personal attacks which may result (3, 10-14). It recommends that he rely on the power of the Scriptures and on the positive proposal of doctrine (3, 15—4, 2) without being troubled by those who do not accept him (4, 3ff). The epistle observes in passing that Paul has need of his reading materials and his cloak (4, 13), and what will be best of all, a visit from Timothy.

1 ¹†PAUL, BY THE WILL OF GOD an apostle of Christ Jesus sent to proclaim the promise of life in him, ²to Timothy, my child whom I love. May grace, mercy, and peace from God the Father and from Christ Jesus our Lord be with you.

Thanksgiving and Prayer

³I thank God, the God of my forefathers whom I worship with a clear conscience, whenever I remember you in my prayers—as indeed I do constantly, night and day. ⁴†Recalling your tears when we parted, I yearn to see you again. That would make my happiness complete. ⁵*I find myself thinking of your sincere faith—faith which first belonged to your grandmother Lois and to your mother Eunice, and which (I am confident) you also have.

Exhortation to Faithfulness

⁶†For this reason, I remind you to stir into flame the gift of God bestowed when my hands were laid on you. ⁷*The Spirit God has given us is no cowardly spirit, but rather one that makes us strong, loving, and wise. ⁸*†Therefore, never be ashamed of your testimony to our Lord, nor of me, a prisoner for his sake; but with the strength which comes from God bear your share of the hardship which the gospel entails.

⁹*†God has saved us and has called us to a holy life, not because of any merit of ours but according to his own design—the grace held out to us in Christ Jesus before the world began ¹⁰*but now made manifest through the appearance of our Savior. He has robbed death of its power and has brought life and immortality into clear light through the gospel. ¹¹*In the service of this gospel I have been appointed preacher and apostle and teacher, ¹²†and for its sake I undergo present hardships. But I am not ashamed, for I know him in whom I have believed, and I am confident that he is able to guard what has been entrusted to me until that day. ¹³Take as a model of sound teaching what you have heard me say, in faith and love in Christ Jesus. ¹⁴Guard the rich deposit of faith with the help of the Holy Spirit who dwells within us.

¹⁵†You know that all in Asia, including even Phygelus and Hermogenes, have turned their backs on

---

† 1, 1f: For the formula of address and greeting, see note on Romans 1, 1-7. *The promise of life in him:* which God grants to men through union with Christ in faith and love; cf Col 3, 4; 1 Tm 4, 8.

1, 4f: Purportedly written from prison in Rome (1, 8; 4, 6ff) shortly before the writer's death, the letter recalls the earlier sorrowful parting from Timothy, commending him for his faith and expressing the longing to see him again.

1, 6: *The gift of God bestowed when my hands were laid on you:* the grace of ordination, signified by the laying on of hands; cf 1 Tm 4, 14.

1, 8: *Never be ashamed of your testimony to our Lord:* i. e., of preaching and suffering for the sake of the gospel.

1, 9f: Redemption from sin and the call to holiness of life are not won by personal deeds but gratuitously bestowed through the incarnation according to God's eternal plan; cf Eph 1, 4.

1, 12: *He is able to guard . . . until that day:* the deposit of faith (or, less likely, the reward of Christian ministry) until the second coming of Christ.

1, 15: Keen disappointment is expressed, here and later (4, 16), that the Christians of the province of Asia, especially

---

1/5: 3, 14f; Acts 16, 1.
7: Rom 8, 15.
8: Lk 9, 26; Rom 5, 3.
9: Mt 10, 10; Lk 10, 7; Ti 3, 5.
10: Rom 6, 9.
11: 1 Tm 2, 7.

me. **16**†May the Lord have mercy on the family of Onesiphorus, because he has often given me new heart and has not been ashamed of me, even in my chains. **17**When he was in Rome, he sought me out earnestly and found me. **18**When he stands before the Lord on the great day, may the Lord grant him mercy! And the many services he has performed for Christ in Ephesus you know even better than I.

The Gospel versus Empty Fables

2 **1**†so you, my son, must be strong in the grace which is ours in Christ Jesus. **2**The things which you have heard from me through many witnesses you must hand on to trustworthy men who will be able to teach others. **3**Bear hardship along with me as a good soldier of Christ Jesus. **4**No soldier becomes entangled in the affairs of civilian life; he avoids this in order to please his commanding officer. **5***Similarly, if one takes part in an athletic contest, he cannot receive the winner's crown unless he has kept the rules. **6**The hardworking farmer is the one who should have the first share of the crop. **7**Reflect on what I am saying, for the Lord will make my meaning fully clear.

8*†Remember that Jesus Christ, a descendant of David was raised from the dead. This is the gospel I preach; **9***in preaching it I suffer as a criminal, even to to the point of being thrown into chains—but there is no chaining the word of God! **10***Therefore I bear with all of this for the sake of those whom God has chosen, in order that they may obtain the salvation to be found in Christ Jesus and with it eternal glory.

11*You can depend on this:

> If we have died with him
> we shall also live with him;
> **12***If we hold out to the end
> we shall also reign with him.

But if we deny him he will deny us. **13***If we are unfaithful he will still remain faithful, for he cannot deny himself.

14†Keep reminding people of these things and charge them before God to stop disputing about mere words. This does no good and can be the ruin of those who listen. **15***Try hard to make yourself worthy of God's approval, a workman who has no cause to be ashamed, following a straight course in preaching the truth. **16**Avoid worldly, idle talk, for those who indulge in it become more and more godless, **17**and the influence of their talk will spread like the plague. This is the case with Hymenaeus and Philetus, **18***who have gone far wide of the truth in saying that the resurrection has already taken place. They are upsetting some people's faith. **19***But the foundation God has laid

stands firm. It bears this inscription: "The Lord knows those who are his"; and, "Let everyone who professes the name of the Lord abandon evil."

20In every large household there are vessels not only of gold and silver but also of wood and clay, some for distinguished and others for common use. **21**The lesson is that if a person will but cleanse himself of evil things he may be a distinguished vessel, dedicated and useful to the master of the house and ready for every noble service. **22***†So, turn from youthful passions and pursue integrity, faith, love, and peace, along with those who call on the Lord in purity of heart. **23***Have nothing to do with senseless, ignorant disputations. As you well know, they only breed quarrels, **24***and the servant of the Lord must not be quarrelsome but must be kindly toward all. He must be an apt teacher, patiently **25***and gently correcting those who contradict him, in the hope always that God will enable them to repent and know the truth. **26**Thus, taken captive by God to do his will, they shall escape the devil's trap.

Against False Teachers

3 **1***†DO not forget this: there will be terrible times in the last days. **2***Men will be lovers of self and of money, proud, arrogant, abusive, disobedient to their parents, ungrateful, profane, **3**inhuman, im-

---

† Phygelus and Hermogenes, should have *abandoned* the writer and done nothing to defend his *case in court.*

1, 16ff: *The family of Onesiphorus, because he . . . even in my chains:* Onesiphorus seems to have died before this letter was written. His family is mentioned twice (v 16 and 4, 19), though it was Onesiphorus himself who was helpful to Paul in prison and rendered much service to the community of Ephesus (16ff). Because the apostle complains of abandonment by *all in Asia* during his second imprisonment and trial, the assistance of Onesiphorus is understood as having been given to Paul during his first Roman imprisonment (61-63 A. D.).

2, 1-7: This passage manifests a characteristic deep concern for safeguarding the deposit of faith and faithfully transmitting it through *trustworthy men* (1f; cf 1, 14; 1 Tm 6, 20; Ti 1, 9). Comparisons to the soldier's loyalty, the athlete's fidelity, and the farmer's arduous work as the price of reward (4ff) emphasize the need of singleness of purpose in preaching the word, even at the cost of hardship, for the sake of Christ (v 3).

2, 8-13: Through baptism, Christians die spiritually with Christ and *live with him* in the hope of reigning with him forever, but not without giving witness to him through suffering in the present life, even as the apostle has been imprisoned for preaching the gospel (v 9). His sufferings are helpful to the elect in attaining salvation and glory in Christ (v 10), who will reward the faithful and disown the unfaithful (12f).

2, 14-19: For those who dispute about mere words (cf 2, 23f) and indulge in irreligious talk to the detriment of their listeners (14.16-19), see note on 1 Tm 1, 3f. *Hymenaeus and Philetus* (v 17), while accepting the Christian's mystical death and resurrection in Christ through baptism, deny the resurrection of the body and eternal glory.

2, 22: *Those who call on the Lord:* those who believe in Christ and worship him as Lord, i. e., Christians (Acts 9, 14ff.20f; Rom 10, 12f).

3, 1-9: The moral depravity and false teachings of men that will prevail in the last days are already at work (1-5). Frivolous and superficial women too, devoid of the true spirit of religion, will be easy victims of those who pervert them by falsifying the truth (6ff), just as Jannes and Jambres, the magicians of Egypt (Ex 7, 11f.22), discredited the truth in Moses' time.

2/5: 1 Cor 9, 25.
8: Acts 13, 22f; Rom 1, 3f.
9: Phil 1, 13-18.
10: Col 1, 24.
11: Rom 6, 5.
12: Mt 10, 33; Mk 8, 38; Rom 8, 17.
13: Rom 3, 3.
15: 1 Tm 4, 6f.
18: 1 Tm 1, 20.
19: Nm 16, 5; Eph 2, 20.
22: 1 Tm 6, 11.
23: 1 Tm 1, 4; Ti 3, 9.
24: 1 Tm 3, 2; Ti 1, 7.
25: Mt 12, 20; Gal 6, 1.
3/1: 1 Tm 4, 1; 2 Pt 3, 3; Jude 18.
2: Rom 1, 29.

placable, slanderous, licentious, brutal, hating the good. **⁴**They will be treacherous, reckless, pompous, lovers of pleasure rather than of God **⁵**as they make a pretense of religion but negate its power. Stay clear of them. **⁶**It is such as these who worm their way into homes and make captives of silly women burdened with sins and driven by desires of many kinds, **⁷**always learning but never able to reach a knowledge of the truth. **⁸***Just as Jannes and Jambres opposed Moses, so these men also oppose the truth; with perverted minds they falsify the faith. **⁹**But they will not get very far; as with those two men, the stupidity of these will be plain for all to see.

Paul's Example and Teaching

¹⁰You have followed closely my teaching and my conduct. You have observed my resolution, fidelity, patience, love, and endurance, **¹¹***through persecutions and sufferings in Antioch, Iconium, and Lystra. You know what persecutions I have had to bear, and you know how the Lord saved me from them all. **¹²**Anyone who wants to live a godly life in Christ Jesus can expect to be persecuted. **¹³***But all the while evil men and charlatans will go from bad to worse, deceiving others, themselves deceived. **¹⁴**You, for your part, must remain faithful to what you have learned and believed, because you know who your teachers were. **¹⁵***†Likewise, from your infancy you have known the sacred Scriptures, the source of the wisdom which through faith in Jesus Christ leads to salvation. **¹⁶***All Scripture is inspired of God and is useful for teaching—for reproof, correction, and training in holiness **¹⁷**so that the man of God may be fully competent and equipped for every good work.

Apostolic Charge

4 **¹***†IN the presence of God and of Christ Jesus, who is coming to judge the living and the dead, and by his appearing and his kingly power, **²**I charge you to preach the word, to stay with this task whether convenient or inconvenient—correcting, reproving, appealing—constantly teaching and never losing patience. **³**For the time will come when people will not tolerate sound doctrine, but, following their own desires, will surround themselves with teachers who tickle their ears. **⁴***They will stop listening to the truth and will wander off to fables. **⁵**As for you, be steady and self-possessed; put up with hardship, perform your work as an evangelist, fulfill your ministry.

Reward for Fidelity

⁶*†I for my part am already being poured out like a libation. The time of my dissolution is near. **⁷***†I have

fought the good fight, I have finished the race, I have kept the faith. **⁸**†From now on a merited crown awaits me; on that day the Lord, just judge that he is, will award it to me—and not only to me, but to all who have looked for his appearing with eager longing.

Paul's Loneliness

⁹Do your best to join me soon, **¹⁰***†for Demas, enamored of the present world, has left me and gone to Thessalonica. Crescens has gone to Galatia and Titus to Dalmatia. **¹¹***I have no one with me but Luke. Get Mark and bring him with you, for he can be of great service to me. **¹²**Tychicus I have sent to Ephesus. **¹³***When you come, bring the cloak I left in Troas with Carpus, and the books, especially the parchments.

Comfort in Trial

¹⁴*†Alexander the coppersmith did me a great deal of harm; the Lord will repay him according to his deeds. **¹⁵**Meanwhile, you too had better be on guard, for he has strongly resisted our preaching. **¹⁶**At the first hearing of my case in court, no one took my part. In fact, everyone abandoned me. May it not be held

---

† 3, 15ff: The Scriptures are the source of wisdom, i. e., of belief in and loving fulfillment of God's word revealed in Christ, through whom man finds salvation. *All Scripture is inspired of God:* has God as its principal author, with the writer as the human collaborator. Thus the Scriptures are the word of God in human language. *Useful for teaching . . . every good work:* because as God's word the Scriptures share his divine authority. It is exercised through those who are ministers of the word.

4, 1-5: The gravity of the obligation incumbent on Timothy to preach the word can be gauged from the solemn adjuration: *in the presence of God,* and of Christ coming as universal judge *and by his appearing and his kingly power* (v 1). Patience, courage, constancy, and endurance are required despite the opposition, hostility, indifference, and defection of many to whom the truth has been preached (2-5).

4, 6: The apostle recognizes his death through martyrdom to be imminent. He regards it, like the death of Christ, as an act of worship in which his blood will be poured out in sacrifice; cf Ex 29, 40.

4, 7: *I have fought the good fight, I have finished the race:* at the close of his life Paul could testify to the accomplishment of what Christ himself had foretold concerning him at the time of his conversion: *I myself shall indicate to him how much he will have to suffer for my name* (Acts 9, 16). *I have kept the faith:* preserved the true teaching concerning Christ, both in his personal adherence to it, and in his ministry.

4, 8: When the world is judged at the parousia all who have eagerly *looked for his appearing,* i. e., lived according to his teaching, will be rewarded. *A merited crown:* a reference to the laurel wreath placed on the heads of conquerors and winners of various contests; cf 2, 5; 1 Cor 9, 25.

4, 10-13: *Demas* either abandoned the work of the ministry for worldly affairs or, perhaps, gave up the faith itself (v 10). *Luke* may have accompanied Paul on part of his second and third missionary journeys (Acts 16, 10-18; 20, 5–21, 19). *Mark,* once rejected by Paul (Acts 13, 13; 15, 39-40), is now to render him *great service* (v 11); cf Col 4, 10; Phlm 24. *Tychicus I have sent to Ephesus:* see Eph 6, 21; cf also Acts 20, 4; Col 4, 7 (12f).

4, 14-18: *Alexander:* an opponent of Paul's preaching (14f), perhaps the same who is mentioned in 1 Tm 1, 20. Despite Paul's abandonment by his friends in the province of Asia

---

✳
    8: Ex 7, 11; Jn 8, 32.
    11: Acts 14, 1-5.22.
    13: 1 Thes 3, 4f.
    15: 1, 5.
    16: Rom 15, 4; 1 Cor 10, 6;
        2 Pt 1, 20f.
    4/1: Acts 10, 42;
        1 Tm 6, 14.
    4: 1 Tm 1, 4.

    6: Phil 2, 17.
    7: Acts 20, 24;
        1 Tm 1, 18.
    10: Phlm 4, 14.
    11: Col 4, 10.
    13: Ti 3, 10.
    14: Pss 28, 4; 62, 13;
        Prv 24, 12; 1 Tm 1, 20.

against them! **17***But the Lord stood by my side and gave me strength, so that through me the preaching task might be completed and all the nations might hear the gospel. That is how I was saved from the lion's jaws. **18***The Lord will continue to rescue me from all attempts to do me harm and will bring me safe to his heavenly kingdom. To him be glory forever and ever. Amen.

Greetings

19*†Greet Prisca and Aquila and the family of Onesiphorus. **20***Erastus has stayed in Corinth, while Trophimus I had to leave ill at Miletus. **21**Get here before winter if you can. Eubulus, Pudens, Linus, Claudia, and all the brothers send greetings.

22The Lord be with your spirit. Grace be with you.

---

† (cf 1, 15f), the divine assistance brought this first trial to a successful issue—even to the point of making the gospel message known to those who participated in or witnessed the trial (16f). Though Paul was not released from prison, he was made ready for the *heavenly kingdom* (v 18).

4, 19-22: *Prisca and Aquila* assisted Paul in his ministry in Corinth (Acts 18, 2f) and Ephesus (Acts 18, 19.26; 1 Cor 16, 19). They risked death to save his life, and all the Gentile communities are indebted to them (Rom 16, 3ff), (v 19). *Erastus:* treasurer of the city of Corinth (Rom 16, 23); cf also Acts 19, 22. *Trophimus:* from the province of Asia, who accompanied Paul from Greece to Troas (Acts 20, 4f). *Linus:* possibly to be identified with Linus, the supposed successor of Peter as Bishop of Rome. *Claudia:* in the Constitutio Apostolica 7.46, 17:19, she is called mother of Linus, Bishop of Rome.

---

*
17: Ps 22, 22; Mt 10, 19.
18: Rom 16, 27.
19: 1, 16.
20: Acts 18, 2; 19, 22; Rom 16, 23.

The Epistle of Paul to Titus

Introduction

The authorship and date of the Epistle to Titus are discussed in the Introduction to 1 Timothy. Titus was a Gentile Christian, apparently from Antioch (Gal. 2, 1). According to 2 Corinthians (2, 13; 7, 6.13f), he was with Paul on his third missionary journey; there is, however, no mention of him in Acts. Besides being the bearer of Paul's severe letter to the Corinthians (2 Cor 7, 6ff), he had the responsibility of taking up the collection in Corinth for the Christian community of Jerusalem (2 Cor 8, 6.16.23). In the present letter (1, 5), he is mentioned as the administrator of the Christian community in Crete, charged with the task of organizing it through the appointment of presbyters and bishops (1, 5-9; here the two terms refer to the same personages).

The letter instructs Titus about the character of the men he is to choose in view of the pastoral difficulties peculiar to Crete (1, 5-16). It suggests the special individual and social virtues which the various age groups and classes in the Christian community should be encouraged to acquire (2, 1-10). The motives for improving one's personal character are to be found preeminently in the mysteries of the incarnation and the second coming of Christ (2, 11-15; 3, 5ff). The community is to be fashioned into a leaven for Christianizing the social world about it (3, 1ff). Good works are to be the evidence of their faith in God (3, 8); those who engage in religious controversy are, after suitable warning, to be ignored (3, 9ff).

The material in Titus is similar to that in 1 Timothy; it is, however, differently oriented.

The principal divisions of the Epistle to Titus are as follows:

    I: Introduction (1, 1-4)
    II: Pastoral Charge (1, 5-16)
    III: Teaching the Christian Life (2, 1—3, 15)

I: INTRODUCTION

Greeting

1 **1**†PAUL, A SERVANT OF GOD, sent as an apostle of Jesus Christ for the sake of the faith of those whom God has chosen, and to promote their knowledge of the truth as our religion embodies it, **2***in the hope of that eternal life which God, who cannot lie, promised in endless ages past. **3***This he has now manifested in his own good time as his word, in the preaching entrusted to me by the command of God our Savior. **4**Paul to Titus, my own true child in our common faith: May grace and peace from God our Father, and Christ Jesus our Savior, be with you.

II: PASTORAL CHARGE

Qualities of a Presbyter

5†MY PURPOSE IN LEAVING YOU in Crete was that you might accomplish what had been left undone, especially the appointment of presbyters in every town. As I instructed you, **6***a presbyter must be irreproachable, married only once, the father of children who are believers and are known not to be wild and insubordinate. **7***The bishop as God's steward must be blameless. He may not be self-willed or arrogant, a drunkard, a violent or greedy man. **8**He should, on the contrary, be hospitable and a lover of goodness; steady, just, holy, and self-controlled. **9**In his teaching he must hold fast to the authentic message, so that he will be able both to encourage men to follow sound doctrine and to refute those who contradict it. **10**†There are many irresponsible teachers, especially from among the Jewish converts—men who are empty talkers and deceivers. **11***These must be si-

---

*

1/2: Nm 23, 19.
3: 1 Tm 1, 1.
6: Rom 12, 8; 1 Tm 3, 2.

7: 1 Pt 5, 2.
11: 1 Tm 6, 10.

---

†

1, 1-4: On the epistolary form, see note on Romans 1, 1-7. The apostolate is the divinely appointed mission to lead others to the true faith, and through it to eternal salvation (1ff).

1, 5-9: This instruction on the selection and appointment of presbyters, substantially identical in 1 Timothy 3, 1-7 (see note), was aimed at strengthening the authority of Titus by apostolic mandate; cf 2, 15. In Titus 1, 6f and Acts 20, 17.28 the terms *episkopos* and *presbyteros* ("bishop" and "presbyter") refer to the same persons. As they did not exercise the functions reserved to the apostle Paul and his legates, such as Timothy and Titus, they were not bishops in the later sense familiar to us.

1, 10-16: This adverse criticism of the defects within the community is directed especially against certain Judaeo-Christians, who busy themselves with useless speculations over persons mentioned in the Old Testament and insist on the observance of Jewish ritual purity regulations, thereby *upsetting whole families by teaching things they have no right to teach;* cf 3, 9; 1 Tm 1, 3-10; 4, 1-10; 6, 3-10. One of Titus' main tasks in Crete is to become acquainted with the national character of the Cretans and thereby learn to cope with its deficiencies (cf 1, 12, the citation from the sixth-century B. C. Cretan poet Epimenides).

lenced. They are upsetting whole families by teaching things they have no right to teach—and all for sordid gain! [12]A man of Crete, one of their own prophets, has testified,

> "Cretans have ever been liars, beasts, and lazy gluttons,"

[13]and that is the simple truth!

Admonish them sharply, in an attempt to keep them close to sound faith, [14]*and unaffected by Jewish myths or rules invented by men who have swerved from the truth. [15]*To the clean all things are clean, but to those defiled unbelievers nothing is clean. Their very minds and consciences are tainted. [16]They claim to "know God," but by their actions they deny that he exists. They are disgusting—intractable and thoroughly incapable of any decent action.

III: TEACHING THE CHRISTIAN LIFE

Various Counsels

2 [1]As for yourself, let your speech be consistent with sound doctrine. [2]Tell the older men that they must be temperate, serious-minded, and self-controlled; likewise sound in the faith, loving, and steadfast. [3]Similarly, the older women must behave in ways that befit those who belong to God. They must not be slanderous gossips or slaves to drink. [4]By their good example they must teach the younger women to love their husbands and children, [5]*to be sensible, chaste, busy at home, kindly, submissive to their husbands. Thus the word of God will not fall into disrepute. [6]Tell the young men to keep themselves completely under control—[7]*nor may you yourself fail to set them good example. [8]Your teaching must have the integrity of serious, sound words to which no one can take exception. If it does, no opponent will be able to find anything bad to say about us, and hostility will yield to shame.

[9]*Slaves are to be submissive to their masters. They should try to please them in every way, not contradicting them [10]nor stealing from them, but expressing a constant fidelity by their conduct, so as to adorn in every way possible the doctrine of God our Savior.

Transforming of Life

[11]*†The grace of God has appeared, offering salvation to all men. [12]It trains us to reject godless ways and worldly desires, and live temperately, justly, and

devoutly in this age [13]as we await our blessed hope, the appearing of the glory of the great God and of our Savior Christ Jesus. [14]*It was he who sacrificed himself for us, to redeem us from all unrighteousness and to cleanse for himself a people of his own, eager to do what is right.

[15]*These are the things you are to say. Make our appeals and corrections with the authority of command. Let no one look down on you.

3 [1]*†Remind people to be loyally subject to the government and its officials, to obey the laws, to be ready to take on any honest employment. [2]Tell them not to speak evil of anyone or be quarrelsome. They must be forbearing and display a perfect courtesy toward all men. [3]*We ourselves were once foolish, disobedient, and far from true faith; we were the slaves of our passions and of pleasures of various kinds. We went our way in malice and envy, hateful ourselves and hating one another. [4]*But when the kindness and love of God our savior appeared, [5]*he saved us; not because of any righteous deeds we had done, but because of his mercy. He saved us through the baptism of new birth and renewal by the Holy Spirit. [6]This Spirit he lavished on us through Jesus Christ our Savior, [7]*that we might be justified by his grace and become heirs, in hope, of eternal life. [8]†You can depend on this to be true.

Advice to Titus

I want you to lay great weight on the things I have been saying, so that those who have committed themselves to God may be careful to do what is right. This is what is good and advantageous for men. [9]*See to it that you abstain from stupid arguments and genealogies, and from all controversies and quarrels about the law. They are useless and have no point. [10]Warn a heretic once and then a second time; after that, have nothing to do with him. [11]You must recognize such a person as perverted and sinful; he stands self-condemned.

Directives, Greetings and Blessing

[12]*†When I send Artemas to you, or perhaps Tychicus, hurry to me at Nicopolis; I have decided to spend

14: 1 Tm 1, 4.
15: Rom 14, 14-20.
2/5: Eph 5, 22; Col 3, 18.
7: 1 Tm 4, 12.
9: Eph 6, 5; Col 3, 22; 1 Pt 2, 18.
11: 3, 4.
14: Ex 19, 5; Ps 130, 8; 1 Tm 2, 6.
15: 1 Tm 4, 12.
3/1: Rom 13, 1-7; 1 Pt 2, 13f.
3: Eph 2, 3-10; Col 3, 7; 1 Pt 1, 3.
4: 2, 11.
5: Jn 3, 5; Rom 5, 5; 6, 4; Eph 5, 26; 2 Tm 1, 9.
7: Rom 3, 24.
9: 1 Tm 4, 7; 2 Tm 2, 23.
12: Acts 20, 4.

† 2, 11-15: The moving force in the moral improvement outlined in 2, 1-10 is to be the constant appeal to God's revelation of salvation in Christ, with its demand for transformation of life.

3, 1-7: The spiritual renewal of the Cretans, signified in God's merciful gift of baptism (4-7), should be reflected in their improved attitude toward civil authority and in their Christian relationship with all (1ff).

3, 8-11: In matters of good conduct and religious doctrine Titus is to show himself uncompromising.

3, 12-15: Artemas or Tychicus (2 Tm 4, 12) is to replace Titus, who will join Paul in his winter sojourn at Nicopolis in Epirus, on the western coast of Greece. Titus will no doubt report on his efforts in Crete, and perhaps also assist in preaching the gospel.

the winter there. ¹³*Speed Zenas the lawyer and Apollos on their journey, having first seen to it that they have everything they need. ¹⁴Let our people devote themselves to honest work in order to take care of their needs, so that they may be in position to live fruitful lives.

¹⁵All who are with me send their greetings. Greet those who love us in the faith.

May grace be with you all!

13: Acts 18, 24.

The Epistle of Paul to Philemon

Introduction

The date of this epistle is discussed in the Introduction to Ephesians. Its Pauline authorship is considered to be incontestable. The interesting fact is that this very personal and undoubtedly private letter was conserved and made public by the second century in a society in which human slavery was an accepted part of the culture.

The letter concerns Onesimus, slave of Philemon, a well-to-do Christian of Colossae (Col 4, 9). Onesimus escaped Philemon's service (v 15), and was guilty of theft in the process (v 18). Paul converted Onesimus to the gospel (v 10) and persuaded him to return to his former condition (v 12); this had been his teaching concerning slaves from the first; cf 1 Cor 7, 21. Evidently Onesimus was fearful of the possible punishment that would be meted out to him, but Paul was confident both of Philemon's understanding of Christian teaching (15f) and of his own influence over Philemon (19f). The apostle promised to visit Philemon, meanwhile placing him under a telling kind of moral pressure to accede to his request and receive back his slave with nothing but kindness.

The delicate tone of this letter reflects, against the legal fact of slavery at the time, the incipient Christian insight into its injustice. Paul does not attack the institution, for the small Christian communities were in no position to raise such an issue in a dictatorial political structure. Also, the fact that they regarded the second coming of Christ as an occurrence possible within their lifetime lessened the impulse to any abrupt and widespread change. That Onesimus the slave was "brother" to Philemon, his legal master (v 16), was a revolutionary idea in the context of the times.

Greeting

[1]†PAUL, A PRISONER OF CHRIST JESUS, and Timothy our brother, to our beloved friend and fellow worker Philemon, [2]*to Apphia our sister, to our fellow soldier Archippus, and to the church that meets in your house. [3]Grace to you and peace from God our Father and from the Lord Jesus Christ.

Philemon's Faith and Charity

[4]*†I thank God always, my brother, as I commend you in my prayers, [5]for I keep hearing of your love and faith toward the Lord Jesus and all God's people. [6]*And my prayer is that your sharing of the faith with others may enable you to know all the good which is ours in Christ. [7]I find great joy and comfort in your love, because through you the hearts of God's people have been refreshed.

Plea for Onesimus

[8]Therefore, although I feel that I have every right to command you to do what ought to be done, [9]*I prefer to appeal in the name of love. Yes, I, Paul, ambassador of Christ and now a prisoner for him, [10]*†appeal to you for my child, whom I have begotten during my imprisonment. [11]He has become in truth Onesimus [Useful], for he who was formerly useless to you is now useful indeed both to you and to me. [12]It is he I am sending back to you—and that means I am sending my heart!

[13]I had wanted to keep him with me, that he might serve me in your place while I am in prison for the gospel; [14]but I did not want to do anything without your consent, that kindness might not be forced on you but might be freely bestowed. [15]Perhaps he was separated from you for a while for this reason: that you might possess him forever, [16]no longer as a slave but as more than a slave, a beloved brother, especially dear to me; and how much more to you, since now you will know him both as a man and in the Lord.

[17]If then you regard me as a partner, welcome him as you would me. [18]If he has done you an injury or

---

† 1ff: It is the prisoner and friend appealing, rather than the apostle commanding with authority, who greets Philemon, Apphia, Archippus, and the assembly that meets in Philemon's house.

4-7: Philemon's faith in and love for the Lord and the people of God whom he refreshes have urged him to share these blessings with others (5.7). Paul prays that as a result Philemon himself will benefit by a deepening knowledge and appreciation of the endless good they possess in common in possessing Christ (4.6).

10-22: *Appeal to you for my child:* Onesimus, Philemon's runaway slave, whom Paul the prisoner converted to the Christian faith (v 10), and whom he now asks Philemon to receive back as *a beloved brother* (16f), rather than as a slave liable to punishment for theft and damage and for escape (18). The name Onesimus means "useful" or profitable. Paul realizes that his convert has shown himself "useless" by his previous conduct; but he is confident that Onesimus will now live up to his name and be useful both to Philemon and to Paul himself (11.20). He would even prefer to have the service of Onesimus for the work of the ministry, but recognizes Philemon's prior right (13ff).

❖
2: Col 4, 17.
4: Eph 1, 15f.
6: Col 1, 9ff.

9: Eph 3, 1.
10: Gal 4, 19; Col 4, 9.

owes you anything, charge it to me. [19]I, Paul, write this in my own hand: I agree to pay—not to mention that you owe me your very self! [20]You see, brother, I want to make you "useful" to me in the Lord. Refresh this heart of mine in Christ.

Farewell Blessing

[21]Confident of your compliance, I write you, knowing that you will do more than I say. [22]*And get a room ready for me; I hope that through your prayers I shall be restored to you.

[23]†Epaphras, my fellow prisoner in Christ Jesus, greets you, [24]*as do Mark, Aristarchus, Demas, and Luke, my fellow workers.

[25]The grace of our Lord Jesus Christ be with your spirit.

---

*   22: Heb 13, 19.   24: Col 4, 10.

†   23f: *Epaphras:* a Colossian who founded the church in Colossae (Col 1, 7) and perhaps also in Laodicea and Hierapolis (Col 2, 1; 4, 12f). *Aristarchus:* a native of Thessalonica and fellow worker of Paul (Acts 19, 29; 20, 4; 27, 2). For Mark, Demas, and Luke, see 2 Timothy 4, 10-13 and note.

The Epistle to the Hebrews

Introduction

There are numerous features of this epistle that indicate authorship other than that of St. Paul the apostle. There is the high quality of its style, which makes Hebrews one of the distinguished works of the New Testament. Its literary structure intermingles doctrinal teaching and moral exhortation. The manner of citing the Old Testament is different, and the system of exegesis it follows reflects Hellenistic rather than Palestinian Judaism.

As early as the end of the second century the Eastern churches had accepted Hebrews as an inspired work composed by Paul, but until the second half of the fourth century the churches of the West questioned its Pauline authorship. Since the letter of Clement of Rome to the Corinthians, written about 96 A. D., cites the Epistle to the Hebrews, it is necessary to date the letter before that time. The identity of its author is a matter of pure speculation. Among those considered, Apollos seems more likely than Luke and Barnabas (cf Acts 18, 24), although nothing is known of his history beyond his activity in Corinth (1 Cor 1, 12; 3, 5). The data of the epistle indicate that its author wrote to a specific Christian community, or at least to communities in a particular area (13, 23; 6, 11f; 10, 19-25), but the allusions are insufficient to permit a judgment on their location. Commentators today are sharply divided on whether the addressees of the epistle were Judaeo-Christian or predominantly Gentile Christian, although the latter view is regarded with slightly more favor. The title "To the Hebrews" may merely represent an inference of the late second century: that the epistle's extensive use of the Old Testament points to its having been addressed to Judaeo-Christians.

The letter seeks to strengthen the practical faith of its recipients, and appeals to them for perseverance (6, 11f) despite harassment (12, 7-13) from forces outside the community (13, 3). Their knowledge and love of Christ hardly support the opinion of those who, on the basis of 6, 4-8, consider them to have been Judaeo-Christians on the point of reversion to Judaism.

The author begins with a reminder of the mysteries of the incarnation and exaltation of Jesus (1, 3), which proclaimed him the culminator of God's word to humanity (1, 1ff). He dwells upon the dignity of the Person of Christ, superior to the angels, who according to Old Testament tradition appeared in order to make God's plans known to men (1, 4—2, 2). Christ is God's final word of salvation communicated (in association with accredited witnesses to his teaching: 2, 3f; cf Acts 1, 21ff) not merely by word but through the suffering humanity common to Jesus and to the rest of men (2, 5-16). This enactment of salvation went beyond the pattern known to Moses, faithful prophet though he was of God's word; for Jesus as high priest personally expiated sin and was faithful to God with the fidelity of God's own Son (2, 17—3, 6).

Just as the infidelity of the people thwarted Moses' effort to save them all, so the infidelity of any Christian thwarts God's plan in Christ (3, 6—4, 13). Christians are to reflect that it is their humanity which Jesus assumed, with all its defects except its sinfulness, and that he bore the burden of it to his death out of obedience to God. This work of his Son God declared to be the cause of salvation for all (4, 14—5, 10). Although Christians recognize this fundamental doctrine, they may grow weary of its repetition and therefore require other reflections to stimulate their faith (5, 11—6, 20).

The author of Hebrews presents to his Christian readers for their reflection the everlasting priesthood of Christ (7, 1-28), a priesthood which fulfills the promise of the Old Testament (8, 1-13). It also provides the meaning God ultimately intended in the sacrifices of the Old Testament (9, 1-28): these were symbols of the unique sacrifice of Christ which alone obtains forgiveness of the sins of mankind (10, 1-18). Any trial of faith the readers of the epistle may have should resolve itself through consideration of the reality of Jesus' actual existence in the heavenly sanctuary, his foreordained parousia, and the fruits they have already enjoyed through their faith (11, 19-39). It is in the nature of faith to trust the intangible (11, 1ff) which in God's providence one day becomes reality, as the Old Testament itself demonstrates (11, 4-40). This truth shines forth throughout the life of Christ. Despite the afflictions of his ministry, he remained confident of God's final intervention to ensure his resurrection and triumph (12, 1ff). Life's difficulties have meaning when they are accepted as God's discipline (12, 4-13). The message of the gospel is the word of Christ (12, 18-29), advocating peace among men (12, 14-17) and reverence toward all (13, 1-4), respect for authority (13, 7f), and complete reliance upon Christ for holiness of life (13, 9-17).

The principal divisions of the Epistle to the Hebrews are as follows:

I: Introduction (1, 1-4)
II: The Son Higher than the Angels (1, 5—2, 18)
III: Jesus, Faithful and Compassionate High Priest (3, 1—5, 10)
IV: Jesus' Eternal Priesthood and Eternal Sacrifice (5, 11—10, 39)

I: INTRODUCTION

1 ¹†IN TIMES PAST, GOD SPOKE in fragmentary and varied ways to our fathers through the prophets; ²*in this, the final age, he has spoken to us through his Son, whom he has made heir of all things and through whom he first created the universe. ³*This Son is the reflection of the Father's glory, the exact representation of the Father's being, and he sustains all things by his powerful word. When he had cleansed us from our sins, he took his seat at the right hand of the Majesty in heaven, ⁴*as far superior to the angels as the name he has inherited is superior to theirs.

II: THE SON HIGHER THAN THE ANGELS

Messianic Enthronement

⁵*†TO WHICH OF THE ANGELS did God ever say,

"You are my son; today I have begotten you"?

Or again,

"I will be his father, and he shall be my son"?

⁶*And again, when he leads his first-born into the world, he says,

"Let all the angels of God worship him."

⁷*Of the angels he says,

"He makes his angels winds, and his ministers flaming fire";

⁸*but of the Son,

"Your throne, O God, stands forever and ever;
a righteous scepter is the scepter of your kingdom.
⁹You have loved justice and hated wickedness,
therefore God, your God, has anointed you
with the oil of gladness above your fellow kings."

¹⁰*And,

"Lord, of old you established the earth,
and the heavens are the work of your hands.

¹¹They will perish, but you remain;
all of them will grow old like a garment.
¹²You will roll them up like a cloak;
like a garment they will be changed.
But you are the same, and your years will have no
end."

¹³*To which of the angels has God ever said,

"Sit at my right hand till I make your enemies your footstool"?

¹⁴*Are they not all ministering spirits, sent to serve those who are to inherit salvation?

Exhortation to Faithfulness

2 ¹*†IN view of this, we must attend all the more to what we have heard, lest we drift away. ²*For if the word spoken through angels stood unchanged, and all transgression and disobedience received its due punishment, ³how shall we escape if we ignore a salvation as great as ours? Announced first by the Lord, it was confirmed to us by those who had heard him. ⁴*God then gave witness to it by signs, miracles, varied acts of power, and distribution of the gifts of the Holy Spirit as he willed.

Exaltation through Abasement

⁵†For he did not make the world to come—that world of which we speak—subject to angels. ⁶*Somewhere this is testified to, in the passage that says:

---

† 1, 1-4: The letter opens with a reflection on the climax of God's revelation to mankind in his Son (v 3). The divine communication with men was initiated and maintained during Old Testament times through chosen men, the prophets (v 1). But now in messianic times, the final period of man's religious history, God the Son, creator and end of all things, is the communicator with men (v 2). He is the perfect and *exact representation of the Father's being*—even to the divine creative power—who entered human existence to destroy the power of sin. After accomplishing this he returned, through his resurrection and ascension, to his natural place with the Father (v 3). No creature, not even angels, can match the unique dignity of his Person (v 4).

1, 5-14: The citations from the psalms in v 5 (Ps 2, 7) and v 13 (Ps 110, 1) were traditionally used of Jesus' messianic sonship (cf Acts 13, 33) through his resurrection and ascension (cf Acts 2, 33ff); those in v 8 (Ps 45, 6f) and vv 10ff (Ps 102, 25ff) are concerned with his divine kingship and his creative function. The author states that, in the Christian understanding of Christ, the Old Testament elevates him above the angels. At best the angels can only be servants at the disposal of the creator (v 7, citing Ps 104, 4) and consequently they are *sent to serve those who are to inherit salvation* (v 14).

2, 1-4: The absolute supremacy of Christ should greatly strengthen Christians against abandoning their faith (v 1). If, according to Jewish tradition (Gal 3, 19), angels played the role of intermediaries for the Mosaic covenant, the violation of which was divinely punished (v 2), an even severer punishment awaits those who knowingly neglect the salvation offered in Christ's own word, proclaimed by witnesses whom God appointed (Lk 1, 1f; Acts 1, 21f) and confirmed by divine power through *signs* and *miracles* (3f).

2, 5-18: The humanity and the suffering of Jesus do not constitute a valid reason for relinquishing the Christian faith. The thought of the psalmist (Ps 8, 4ff in the Septuagint) concerning

---

✿
1/2: Jn 1, 3; Gal 4, 4.
3: Ps 110, 1; Wis 7, 26;
Mk 16, 19; Col 1, 15.
4: Phil 2, 9ff; Col 1, 14.
5: 2 Sm 7, 14; Ps 2, 7;
Acts 13, 33.
6: Rv 1, 5.
7: Ps 104, 4.
8: Ps 45, 7f.

10ff: Ps 102, 26ff.
13: Ps 110, 1.
14: Ps 91, 11; Dn 7, 10.
2/1: 2 Pt 3, 17.
2: Acts 7, 53; Gal 3, 19.
4: Mk 16, 20; Acts 14, 3;
19, 11.
6: Ps 8, 5ff.

"What is man that you should be mindful of him,
  or the son of man that you should care for him?
[7]You made him for a little while lower than the
    angels;
  you crowned him with glory and honor,
[8*]and put all things under his feet."

In subjecting all things to him, God left nothing unsubjected. At present we do not see all things thus subject, [9*]but we do see Jesus crowned with glory and honor because he suffered death: Jesus, who was made for a little while lower than the angels, that through God's gracious will he might taste death for the sake of all men. [10*]Indeed, it was fitting that when bringing many sons to glory God, for whom and through whom all things exist, should make their leader in the work of salvation perfect through suffering. [11]He who consecrates and those who are consecrated have one and the same Father. Therefore he is not ashamed to call them brothers, [12*]saying,

"I will announce your name to my brothers,
  I will sing your praise in the midst of the assembly";

[13*]and,

      "I will put my trust in him";

and again,

  "Here am I, and the children God has given me!"

[14*]Now, since the children are men of blood and flesh, Jesus likewise had a full share in ours, that by his death he might rob the devil, the prince of death, of his power, [15*]and free those who through fear of death had been slaves their whole life long. [16]Surely he did not come to help angels, but rather the children of Abraham; [17*]therefore he had to become like his brothers in every way, that he might be a merciful and faithful high priest before God on their behalf, to expiate the sins of the people. [18]Since he was himself tested through what he suffered, he is able to help those who are tempted.

III: JESUS, FAITHFUL AND COMPASSIONATE HIGH PRIEST

Jesus, Superior to Moses

3 [1†]THEREFORE, HOLY BROTHERS who share a heavenly calling, fix your eyes on Jesus, the apostle and high priest whom we acknowledge in faith, [2*]who was faithful to him who appointed him. Moses, too, "was faithful in all God's household," [3*]but Jesus is more worthy of honor than he, as the founder of a house is more honorable than the house itself. [4]Every house is founded by someone, but God is the founder of all. [5*]Moses "was faithful in all God's household" as a servant charged with the task of witnessing to what would be spoken; [6*]but Christ was faithful as the Son placed over God's house. It is we who are that house if we hold fast to our confidence and the hope of which we boast.

Israel's Infidelity, a Warning

[7*†]Wherefore, as the Holy Spirit says:

"Today, if you should hear his voice,
  [8]harden not your hearts as at the revolt
  in the day of testing in the desert,
[9]When your fathers tested and tried me,
  and saw my works [10]for forty years.
Because of this I was angered with that generation
  and I said, 'They have always been of erring
    heart,
  and have never known my ways.'
[11]"Thus I swore in my anger,
  'They shall never enter into my rest.'"

[12]Take care, my brothers, lest any of you have an evil and unfaithful spirit and fall away from the living God. [13]Encourage one another daily while it is still "today," so that no one grows hardened by the deceit of sin. [14*]We have become partners of Christ if only we maintain to the end that confidence with which we began. [15]When Scripture says,

---

† man's glory and splendor despite his subordination to the angels (6f) is perfectly reflected in the history of Jesus, who lived a truly human existence during his mortal life but is now in full possession of the divine kingly glory (v 9). It was altogether fitting that God should direct him along the path of suffering (v 10), since in the spirit of the Old Testament (Ps 22, 22; Is 8, 17f) he identified himself entirely with those for whom he obtained sanctification (11-15). He deliberately allied himself with the descendants of Abraham (v 16) in order to function as an authentic high priest, expiating the sins of the people (v 17) as one who experienced the same tests as they (v 18).

3, 1-6: Christians must have full confidence in Jesus, whom their faith recognizes as the one sent by God (*the apostle*) to be the high priest of the Christian community (v 1). Like Moses, the leader of the people of Israel, Jesus was faithful to the task assigned to him (v 2). Moses, however, was faithful *in* the house of God, i. e., he was himself but a member of God's chosen people (3ff), whereas Jesus possesses the fidelity of God's Son *over* the new people of God (v 6).

3, 7-4, 11: The author appeals for steadfastness of faith in Jesus. Citing the Old Testament warning (Ps 95, 7-11) against hardness of heart, i. e., practical disregard of the divine message (7-11), he urges the community to watchfulness and mutual encouragement (12ff). They are to remember the example of Israel's revolt in the desert which cost a whole generation the loss of the promised land (15-19; cf Nm 14, 20-29). The promised land, designated here under the concept of *rest*, is the author's symbol for final union with Christ. He concludes his appeal, developing the idea that his Christian audience is experiencing a test of faith similar to that of Israel in the desert, and one which could have the same unfortunate results (4, 1-11).

8: Mt 28, 18;	15: Rom 8, 15.
1 Cor 15, 25-28;	17: 4, 15; Phil 2, 7.
Eph 1, 20-23;	3/2: 10, 23; Nm 12, 7.
Phil 3, 21.	3: Mt 12, 41f; 16, 18;
9: Phil 2, 6-11.	2 Cor 3, 7.
10: 12, 2; Is 53, 4;	5: Dt 18, 18.
Rom 11, 36; 1 Cor 8, 6.	6: 10, 21; Eph 2, 19-22;
12: Ps 22, 23.	1 Tm 3, 15.
13: 2 Sm 22, 3; Is 8, 17f.	7: Nm 14, 21ff;
14: Is 25, 8; Hos 13, 14;	Ps 95, 8-11.
Jn 12, 31; Rom 6, 9;	14: Rom 8, 17.
1 Cor 15, 54.	

"Today, if you should hear his voice,
harden not your hearts as at the revolt,"

[16]who were those that revolted when they heard that voice? Was it not all whom Moses had led out of Egypt? [17]With whom was God angry for forty years? Was it not those who had sinned, whose corpses fell in the desert? [18]To whom but to the disobedient did he swear that they would not enter into his rest? [19]We see, moreover, that it was their unbelief that kept them from entering.

4 [1]THEREFORE, while the promise of entrance into his rest still holds, we ought to be fearful of disobeying lest any one of you be judged to have lost his chance of entering. [2]We have indeed heard the good news, as they did. But the word which they heard did not profit them, for they did not receive it in faith. [3]It is we who have believed who enter into that rest, just as God said:

"Thus I swore in my anger,
'They shall never enter into my rest.'"

Yet God's work was finished when he created the world, [4]for in reference to the seventh day Scripture somewhere says, "And God rested from all his work on the seventh day"; [5]and again, in the place we have referred to, God says, "They shall never enter into my rest." [6]Therefore, since it remains for some to enter, and those to whom it was first announced did not because of unbelief, [7]God once more set a day, "today," when long afterward he spoke through David the words we have quoted:

"Today, if you should hear his voice,
harden not your hearts."

[8]Now if Joshua had led them into the place of rest, God would not have spoken afterward of another day. [9]Therefore a sabbath rest still remains for the people of God. [10]And he who enters into God's rest, rests from his own work as God did from his. [11]Let us strive to enter into that rest, so that no one may fall, in imitation of the example of Israel's unbelief.

[12][†]Indeed, God's word is living and effective, sharper than any two-edged sword. It penetrates and divides soul and spirit, joints and marrow; it judges the reflections and thoughts of the heart. [13]Nothing is concealed from him; all lies bare and exposed to the eyes of him to whom we must render an account.

Jesus, Compassionate High Priest

[14]Since, then, we have a great high priest who has passed through the heavens, Jesus, the Son of God, let us hold fast to our profession of faith. [15]For we do not have a high priest who is unable to sympathize with our weakness, but one who was tempted in every way that we are, yet never sinned. [16]So let us confidently approach the throne of grace to receive mercy and favor and to find help in time of need.

5 [1][†]EVERY high priest is taken from among men and made their representative before God, to offer gifts and sacrifices for sins. [2]He is able to deal patiently with erring sinners, for he himself is beset by weakness [3]and so must make sin offerings for himself as well as for the people. [4]One does not take this honor on his own initiative, but only when called by God as Aaron was. [5]Even Christ did not glorify himself with the office of high priest; he received it from the One who said to him,

"You are my son;
today I have begotten you";

[6]just as he says in another place,

"You are a priest forever,
according to the order of Melchizedek."

[7]In the days when he was in the flesh, he offered prayers and supplications with loud cries and tears to God, who was able to save him from death, and he was heard because of his reverence. [8]Son though he was, he learned obedience from what he suffered; [9]and when perfected, he became the source of eternal salvation for all who obey him, [10]designated by God as high priest according to the order of Melchizedek.

[†] 4, 12-15: The word of God, i. e., the divine message of salvation in Jesus, lays open to God man's real intentions and purposes in this life (v 12) so that there is no escaping the manifestation of his conscience (v 13). But the Christian who holds fast to his faith in Jesus as high priest (v 14; 2, 17) need have no fear even of his own weakness (16), for his appeal is to a high priest who understands the human condition from his own experience of suffering and temptation, sin excepted (v 15).

5, 1-10: The true humanity of Jesus (see note on 2, 5-18) makes him a more rather than a less effective high priest to the Christian community. In Old Testament tradition the high priest was identified with the people, guilty of personal sin just as they were (1ff). Even so, the office was of divine appointment (v 4), as was also the case with the sinless (4, 15) Christ (v 5). For v 6, see note on Ps 110, 4. Although Jesus was Son of God, he was destined as man to learn obedience by accepting the suffering he had to endure (v 8). Because of his perfection through this experience of human suffering he is the cause of salvation for all (v 9), a *high priest according to the order of Melchizedek* (v 10; cf 7, 3).

✳

17: Nm 14, 29.
18: Nm 14, 23; Dt 1, 35.
4/3: Ps 95, 11.
4: Gn 2, 2.
7: 3, 7f; Ps 95, 7f.
8: Dt 31, 7.
12: Jos 22, 4; Wis 18, 15f;
     Is 49, 2; Eph 6, 17;
     Rv 1, 16; 19, 15.
13: Jb 34, 21f; Pss 90, 8;
     139, 2f.

14: 9, 11.24.
15: 2, 17f; 5, 7.
16: 10, 19; Eph 3, 12.
5/3: Lv 9, 7; 16, 17.
4: Ex 28, 1.
5: Ps 2, 7; Jn 8, 54.
6: Ps 110, 4.
7: Mt 26, 38ff.
8: Phil 2, 8.
9: 7, 28.
10: 6, 20.

IV: JESUS' ETERNAL PRIESTHOOD AND ETERNAL SACRIFICE

Exhortation to Spiritual Renewal

[11]†ABOUT THIS WE HAVE MUCH TO SAY, and it is difficult to explain, for you have become deaf. [12]*Although by this time you should be teaching others, you need to have someone teach you again the basic elements of the oracles of God; you need milk, not solid food. [13]Everyone whose food is milk alone is ignorant of the word that sanctifies, for he is a child. [14]Solid food is for the mature, for those whose faculties are trained by practice to distinguish good from evil.

[6] [1]*†LET us, then, go beyond the initial teaching about Christ and advance to maturity, not laying the foundation all over again: repentance from dead works, faith in God, [2]instruction about baptisms and laying-on of hands, resurrection of the dead, and eternal judgment. [3]And, God permitting, we shall advance!

[4]*For when men have once been enlightened and have tasted the heavenly gift and become sharers in the Holy Spirit, [5]when they have tasted the good word of God and the powers of the age to come, [6]*and then have fallen away, it is impossible to make them repent again, since they are crucifying the Son of God for themselves and holding him up to contempt. [7]Ground which drinks in the rain falling on it again and again, and brings forth vegetation useful to those for whom it is cultivated, receives the blessing of God. [8]*But if it bears thorns and thistles, it is worthless; it is soon cursed, and finally is burned.

[9]†Beloved, even though we speak in this way, we are persuaded of better things in your regard, things pointing to your salvation. [10]God is not unjust; he will not forget your work and the love you have shown him by your service, past and present, to his holy people. [11]*Our desire is that each of you show the same zeal till the end, fully assured of that for which you hope. [12]*Do not grow lazy, but imitate those who, through faith and patience, are inheriting the promises.

[13]When God made his promise to Abraham, he swore by himself, having no one greater to swear by, [14]*and said, "I will indeed bless you, and multiply you." [15]*And so, after patient waiting, Abraham obtained what God had promised. [16]Men swear by someone greater than themselves; an oath gives firmness to a promise and puts an end to all argument. [17]God, wishing to give the heirs of his promise even clearer evidence that his purpose would not change, guaranteed it by oath, [18]*so that, by two things that are unchangeable, in which he could not lie, we who have taken refuge in him might be strongly encouraged to seize the hope which is placed before us. [19]*Like a sure and firm anchor, that hope extends beyond the veil [20]*through which Jesus, our forerunner, has entered on our behalf, being made high priest forever according to the order of Melchizedek.

Melchizedek a Type of Christ

[7] [1]*†THIS Melchizedek, king of Salem and priest of the Most High God, met Abraham returning from his defeat of the kings and blessed him. [2]And Abraham apportioned to him one tenth of all his booty. His name means "king of justice"; he was also king of Salem, that is, "king of peace." [3]Without father, mother or ancestry, without beginning of days or end of life, like the Son of God he remains a priest forever.

[4]†See the greatness of this man to whom Abraham the patriarch gave one tenth of his booty! [5]*The law provides that the priests of the tribe of Levi should receive tithes from the people, their brother Israelites, even though all of them are descendants of Abraham; [6]but Melchizedek, who was not of their ancestry, received tithes of Abraham and blessed him who had received God's promises. [7]It is indisputable that a

---

† 5, 11-14: By way of preparation for his reflections on the priesthood of Christ, in chapter 7, the author deliberately arouses his audience by provocation, observing that they are not really prepared to assimilate advanced theological reflection.

6, 1-8: The author judges that the community's faith will benefit more from profound theological reflection than from a repetition of traditional catechesis (1ff). He will make no effort to address himself to apostates, for their very hostility to the Christian message cuts them off completely from Christ (4-8).

6, 9-20: To balance his criticism of the community (1ff.9), the author expresses his confidence that its members are living truly Christian lives, and that God will justly reward their efforts (v 10). He is concerned especially about their persevering (11f), and cites in this regard the achievement of Abraham, who relied on God's promise and on God's oath (13-18; cf Gn 22, 16). The author proposes to point out to them a firm anchor of Christian hope, the high priesthood of Christ now living with God (19f).

7, 1ff: Recalling the meeting between Melchizedek and Abraham described in Genesis 14, 17-20, the author enhances the significance of this priest by providing the etymological meaning of his name and that of the city over which he ruled (v 2). Since Genesis gives no information on the parentage or the death of Melchizedek, he is seen here as a type of Christ, representing a priesthood that is unique and eternal (v 3).

7, 4-10: The tithe which Abraham gave to Melchizedek (v 4), a practice later followed by the levitical priesthood (v 5), was a gift (v 6) acknowledging a certain superiority in Melchizedek, the foreign priest (v 7). This is further indicated by the fact that the institution of the levitical priesthood was sustained by hereditary succession in the tribe of Levi, whereas the absence of any mention of Melchizedek's death in Genesis implies that his personal priesthood is permanent (v 8). The levitical priesthood itself, through Abraham, its ancestor, paid tithes to Melchizedek, thus acknowledging the superiority of his priesthood over its own (9f).

* 12: 1 Cor 3, 1ff.
6/1: 9, 14.
4: 10, 26; Mt 12, 45; 2 Pt 2, 20.
6: 1 Jn 5, 16.
8: Gn 3, 17f.
11: 3, 14.
12: Gal 3, 14; Eph 1, 13f.

14: Gn 22, 16.
15: Rom 4, 20.
18: Nm 23, 19; 2 Tm 2, 13.
19: 10, 20; Lv 16, 2; Jn 14, 3.
20: 5, 10; Ps 110, 4.
7/1: Gn 14, 17-20.
5: Nm 18, 21.

lesser person is blessed by a greater. [8]And whereas men subject to death receive tithes, Scripture testifies that this man lives on. [9]Levi, who receives tithes, was, so to speak, tithed in the person of his father, [10]for he was still in his father's loins when Melchizedek met Abraham.

[11]*†If, then, perfection had been achieved through the levitical priesthood (on the basis of which the people received the law), what need would there have been to appoint a priest according to the order of Melchizedek, instead of choosing a priest according to the order of Aaron? [12]When there is a change of priesthood, there is necessarily a change of law. [13]Now he of whom these things are said was of a different tribe, none of whose members ever officiated at the altar. [14]*It is clear that our Lord rose from the tribe of Judah, regarding which Moses said nothing about priests. [15]†The matter is clearer still if another priest is appointed according to the likeness of Melchizedek: [16]one who has become a priest, not in virtue of a law expressed in a commandment concerning physical descent, but in virtue of the power of a life which cannot be destroyed. [17]*Scripture testifies: "You are a priest forever according to the order of Melchizedek."

[18]*The former commandment has been annulled because of its weakness and uselessness, [19]for the law brought nothing to perfection. But a better hope has supervened, and through it we draw near to God. [20]†This has been confirmed by an oath. The priests of the old covenant became priests without an oath, [21]*unlike Jesus to whom God said:

"The Lord has sworn, and he will not repent:
'You are a priest forever, according to the
order of Melchizedek.'"

[22]Thus has Jesus become the guarantee of a better covenant. [23]Under the old covenant there were many priests because they were prevented by death from remaining in office; [24]but Jesus, because he remains forever, has a priesthood which does not pass away. [25]*Therefore he is always able to save those who approach God through him, since he forever lives to make intercession for them.

[26]†It was fitting that we should have such a high priest: holy, innocent, undefiled, separated from sinners, higher than the heavens. [27]*Unlike the other high priests, he has no need to offer sacrifice day after day, first for his own sins and then for those of the people; he did that once for all when he offered himself. [28]*For the law sets up as high priests men who are weak, but the word of the oath which came after the law appoints as priest the Son, made perfect forever.

The Heavenly Priesthood of Jesus

8 [1]†THE main point in what we are saying is this: we have such a high priest, who has taken his seat at the right hand of the throne of the Majesty in heaven, [2]*minister of the sanctuary and of that true tabernacle set up, not by man, but by the Lord. [3]Now every high priest is appointed to offer gifts and sacrifices; hence the necessity for this one to have something to offer. [4]*If he were on earth he would not be a priest, for there are priests already offering the gifts which the law prescribes. [5]*They offer worship in a sanctuary which is only a copy and shadow of the heavenly one, for Moses, when about to erect the tabernacle, was warned, "See that you make everything according to the pattern shown you on the mountain." [6]*†Jesus has obtained a more excellent ministry now, just as he is mediator of a better covenant, founded on better promises.

---

† 7, 11-14: The levitical priesthood was not typified by the priesthood of Melchizedek, for Psalm 110, 4 speaks of a priesthood of a new order, the order of Melchizedek, to arise in messianic times (v 11). Since the levitical priesthood served the Mosaic law, a new priesthood (v 12) would not come into being without a change in the law itself. Thus Jesus was not associated with the Old Testament priesthood, for he was a descendant of the tribe of Judah, which had never exercised the priesthood (13f).

7, 15-19: Jesus does not exercise a priesthood through family lineage but through his immortal existence (15f), fulfilling Psalm 110, 4 (v 17; cf 7, 3). Thus he abolishes forever both the levitical priesthood and the law it serves, because neither could effectively sanctify men (v 18) by leading them into direct communication with God (v 19).

7, 20-25: As was the case with the promise to Abraham (6, 13)—but not with the levitical priesthood—the eternal priesthood of the order of Melchizedek was confirmed by God's oath (20f); cf Ps 110, 4. Thus Jesus becomes the guarantee of a permanent covenant (v 22) that does not require a succession of priests as did the levitical priesthood (v 23), because his high priesthood is eternal and unchangeable (v 24). Jesus, therefore, is able to save all who draw near to God through him since he is their everliving intercessor (v 25).

7, 26-28: Jesus is precisely the high priest whom mankind requires, holy and sinless, installed far above humanity (v 26); one having no need to offer his sacrifice daily for the sins of men, but making a single offering of himself (v 27) once and for all. The law could only appoint high priests with human limitations, but the fulfillment of God's oath regarding the priesthood of Melchizedek (Ps 110, 4) makes the Son of God the perfect priest forever (v 28).

8, 1-5: The Christian community has in Jesus the kind of high priest described in 7, 26ff. In virtue of his ascension Jesus has taken his place at God's right hand in accordance with Psalm 110, 1 (v 1), where he presides over the heavenly sanctuary established by God himself (v 2). Like every high priest, he has his offering to make (v 3; cf 9, 12.14), but it differs from that of the levitical priesthood in which he had no share (v 4), and which was in any case but a shadowy reflection of the true offering in the heavenly sanctuary (v 5).

8, 6-13: Jesus' ministry in the heavenly sanctuary is that of mediator of a superior covenant which accomplishes what it signifies (v 6). Since the first covenant was deficient in this respect, it had to be replaced (v 7), as Jeremiah (31, 31-34) had prophesied (8-12). Even in the time of Jeremiah, the first covenant was antiquated (v 13).

❊
    11: Ps 110, 4.   27: 5, 3; 9, 12.25-28;
    14: Gn 49, 10; Is 11, 1;   10, 11-14; Lv 16, 6.17;
        Mt 1, 1f; 2, 6;   Rom 6, 10.
        Rom 1, 3; Rv 5, 5.   28: 5, 9.
    17: Ps 110, 4.   8/2: Ex 33, 7.
    18: 10, 1.   4: 7, 13.
    21: Ps 110, 4.   5: 9, 23; Ex 25, 40;
    25: Rom 8, 34; 1 Jn 2, 1.   Acts 7, 44; Col 2, 17.
                                6: 7, 22.

The Old and the New Covenants

7If that first covenant had been faultless, there would have been no place for a second one. **8***But God, finding fault with them, says:

"Days are coming, says the Lord,
when I will make a new covenant with the house
of Israel
and with the house of Judah.
9It will not be like the covenant I made with their
fathers
the day I took them by the hand
to lead them forth from the land of Egypt;
For they broke my covenant
and I grew weary of them, says the Lord.
10*But this is the covenant I will make with the house
of Israel
after those days, says the Lord:
I will place my laws in their minds
and I will write them upon their hearts;
I will be their God
and they shall be my people.
11And they shall not teach their fellow citizens
or their brothers, saying, 'Know the Lord,'
for all shall know me, from least to greatest.
12I will forgive their evildoing,
and their sins I will remember no more."

13When he says, "a new covenant," he declares the first one obsolete. And what has become obsolete and has grown old is close to disappearing.

The Worship of the Old Covenant

9 **1**†THE first covenant had regulations for worship and an earthly sanctuary. **2***For a tabernacle was constructed, the outer one, in which were the lampstand, the table, and the showbread; this was called the holy place. **3***Behind the second veil was the tabernacle called the holy of holies, **4***in which were the golden altar of incense and the ark of the covenant entirely covered with gold. In the ark were the golden jar containing the manna, the rod of Aaron which had blossomed, and the tablets of the covenant. **5***Above the ark were the cherubim of glory overshadowing the place of expiation. We cannot speak now of each of these in detail. **6**These were the arrangements for worship. In performing their service the priests used to go into the outer tabernacle constantly, **7***but only the high priest went into the inner one, and that but once a year, with the blood which he offered for himself and for the sins of the people. **8**The Holy Spirit was showing thereby that while the first tabernacle was still standing, the way into the sanc-

tuary had not yet been revealed. **9**This is a symbol of the present time, in which gifts and sacrifices are offered that can never make perfect the conscience of the worshiper, **10***but can only cleanse in matters of food and drink and various ritual washings: regulations concerning the flesh, imposed until the time of the new order.

The Sacrifice of Jesus

11But when Christ came as high priest of the good things which have come to be, he entered once for all into the sanctuary, passing through the greater and more perfect tabernacle not made by hands, that is, not belonging to this creation. **12***He entered, not with the blood of goats and calves, but with his own blood, and achieved eternal redemption. **13***For if the blood of goats and bulls and the sprinkling of a heifer's ashes can sanctify those who are defiled so that their flesh is cleansed, **14***how much more will the blood of Christ, who through the eternal spirit offered himself up unblemished to God, cleanse our consciences from dead works to worship the living God!

15*†This is why he is mediator of a new covenant: since his death has taken place for deliverance from transgressions committed under the first covenant, those who are called may receive the promised eternal

---

† 9, 1-14: The regulations for worship under the old covenant permitted all the priests to enter the holy place (2, 6), but only the high priest to enter the holy of holies and then only once a year (3ff.7). The description of the sanctuary and its furnishing is taken essentially from Exodus 25-26. This exclusion of the people from the holy of holies signified that they were not allowed to stand in God's presence (v 8) because their offerings and sacrifices, which were merely symbols of their need of spiritual renewal (v 10), could not obtain forgiveness of their sins (v 9). But Christ, the high priest of the spiritual blessings foreshadowed in the Old Testament sanctuary, has actually entered the true sanctuary of heaven that is not of man's making (v 11). His place there is permanent, and his offering is his own blood which won man's eternal redemption (v 12). If the sacrifice of animals could bestow legal purification (v 13), how much more effective is the blood of the sinless, divine Christ who spontaneously offered himself to purge man of his sins and to render him fit for the service of God (v 14)!

9, 15-28: Jesus' role as mediator of the new covenant resulted in his death, which freed men from the sins committed under the Mosaic covenant and made them instead inheritors of the benefits of the new covenant (v 15). This effect of his work follows the human pattern whereby a last will and testament becomes effective only with the death of the testator (16f). The Mosaic covenant was also associated with death, for Moses made use of blood to seal the pact between God and the people (18-21). In Old Testament tradition guilt could normally not be remitted without the use of blood (v 22; cf Lv 17, 11). Since inevitably the blood of animals became a cleansing symbol among Old Testament prefigurements, it was necessary that the realities foreshadowed be brought into being by a shedding of blood that was infinitely more effective by reason of its worth (v 23). Christ did not simply prefigure the heavenly realities (v 24) by performing an annual sacrifice with a blood not his own (v 25), but offered the single sacrifice of himself as the final annulment of sin (v 26). Just as death is the unrepeatable act which ends man's life, so Christ's offering of himself for all men is the unrepeatable sacrifice which has once and for all achieved redemption (27f).

8: Jer 31, 31-34;
   Mt 26, 28.
10: 10, 16f.
9/2: Ex 25, 23-30.
3: Ex 26, 31ff.
4: Lv 16, 12f; Ex 16, 33;
   25, 10; Nm 17, 2-7.
5: Ex 25, 16-22; 26, 34.
7: Ex 30, 10.
10: Col 2, 16.
12: 7, 27; Mt 26, 28.
13: 10, 4; Lv 16, 6:16;
   Nm 19, 17-18.
14: 10, 10; Ti 2, 14;
   1 Pt 1, 18f; 1 Jn 1, 7;
   Rv 1, 5.
15: 1 Tm 2, 5.

inheritance. [16]Where there is a testament, it is necessary that the death of the testator be confirmed. [17]For a testament comes into force only in the case of death; it has no force while the testator is alive. [18]Hence, not even the first covenant was inaugurated without blood. [19]When Moses had read all the commandments of the law to the people, he took the blood of goats and calves, together with water and crimson wool and hyssop, and sprinkled the book and all the people, [20]*saying, "This is the blood of the covenant which God has enjoined upon you." [21]He also sprinkled the tabernacle and all the vessels of worship with blood. [22]*According to the law almost everything is purified by blood, and without the shedding of blood there is no forgiveness.

[23]It was necessary that the copies of the heavenly models be purified in this way, but the heavenly realities themselves called for better sacrifices. [24]*For Christ did not enter into a sanctuary made by hands, a mere copy of the true one; he entered heaven itself that he might appear before God now on our behalf. [25]Not that he might offer himself there again and again, as the high priest enters year after year into the sanctuary with blood that is not his own; [26]*if that were so, he would have had to suffer death over and over from the creation of the world. But now he has appeared at the end of the ages to take away sins once for all by his sacrifice. [27]*Just as it is appointed that men die once, and after death be judged, [28]*so Christ was offered up once to take away the sins of many; he will appear a second time not to take away sin but to bring salvation to those who eagerly await him.

One Sacrifice instead of Many

10 [1]*†SINCE the law had only a shadow of the good things to come, and no real image of them, it was never able to perfect the worshipers by the same sacrifices offered continually year after year. [2]Were matters otherwise, the priests would have stopped offering them, for the worshipers, once cleansed, would have had no sin on their conscience. [3]*But through those sacrifices there came only a yearly recalling of sins, [4]*because it is impossible for the blood of bulls and goats to take sins away. [5]*Wherefore, on coming into the world, Jesus said:

"Sacrifice and offering you did not desire,
    but a body you have prepared for me;
[6]Holocausts and sin offerings you took no delight in.
[7]Then I said, 'As is written of me in the book,
    I have come to do your will, O God.' "

[8]*First he says,

"Sacrifices and offerings, holocausts and sin offerings,
    you neither desired nor delighted in."

(These are offered according to the prescriptions of the law.) [9]*Then he says,

"I have come to do your will."

In other words, he takes away the first covenant to establish the second.

[10]*By this "will," we have been sanctified through the offering of the body of Jesus Christ once for all. [11]†Every other priest stands ministering day by day, and offering again and again those same sacrifices which can never take away sins. [12]*But Jesus offered one sacrifice for sins and took his seat forever at the right hand of God; [13]now he waits until his enemies are placed beneath his feet. [14]By one offering he has forever perfected those who are being sanctified. [15]The Holy Spirit attests this to us, for after saying,

[16]*"This is the covenant I will make with them
    after those days, says the Lord:
I will put my laws in their hearts
    and I will write them on their minds,"

[17]he also says,

"Their sins and their transgressions
    I will remember no more."

[18]Once these have been forgiven, there is no further offering for sin.

Recalling the Past

[19]*†Brothers, since the blood of Jesus assures our entrance into the sanctuary [20]*by the new and living

---

20: Ex 24, 6ff; Mt 26, 28.
22: Lv 17, 11.
24: 1 Jn 2, 1f.
26: 7, 27; Jn 1, 29;
    Gal 4, 4.
27: Gn 3, 19.
28: 10, 10; Is 53, 12.
10/1: 8, 5; Col 2, 17.
3: Lv 16, 21.

4: Mi 6, 6ff.
5: Ps 40, 7f.
8: 1 Sm 15, 22.
9: Mt 26, 38; Jn 6, 38.
10: 9, 14.
12f: Ps 110, 1.
16: 8, 8.10; Jer 31, 33f.
19: 4, 16.
20: 6, 19f; 9, 8.11f.

† 10, 1-10: Christian faith now realizes that the Old Testament sacrifices did not effect the spiritual benefits to come, but only prefigured them (v 1). For if the sacrifices actually effected the forgiveness of sin, there would have been no reason for their constant repetition (v 2). They were rather a continual reminder of the people's sins (v 3). It is not reasonable to suppose that human sins could be removed by the blood of animal sacrifices (v 4). Christ, therefore, is here shown to understand his mission in terms of Psalm 40, 6ff, cited according to the Septuagint (5-7). Jesus acknowledged that the Old Testament sacrifices did not remit the sins of the people and so, perceiving the will of God, offered his own body for this purpose (8ff).

10, 11-18: Whereas the levitical priesthood offered daily sacrifices that were ineffectual in remitting sin (v 11), Jesus offered a single sacrifice which won him a permanent place at God's right hand. There he has only to await the final outcome of his work (12f; cf Ps 110, 1). Thus he has brought into being in his own person the new covenant prophesied by Jeremiah (31, 33f) which has rendered meaningless all other offerings for sin (14-18).

10, 19-39: Practical consequences from these reflections on the priesthood and the sacrifice of Christ should make it clear that Christians may now have direct and confident access to God through the person of Jesus (19f), who rules God's house as high priest (v 21). They should approach God with sincerity and faith, in the knowledge that through baptism their sins have been remitted (v 22), reminding themselves of the hope they expressed in Christ at that event (v 23). They are to encourage one another to Christian love and activity (v 24), not refusing, no matter what the reason, to participate in the compath he has opened up for us through the veil (the "veil" meaning his flesh), [21]and since we have a great priest who is over the house of God, [22]*let us draw near in utter sincerity and absolute confidence, our hearts sprinkled clean from the evil which lay on our conscience and our bodies washed in pure water. [23]Let us hold unswervingly to our profession which gives us hope, for he who made the promise deserves our trust. [24]We must consider how to rouse each other to love and good deeds. [25]We should not absent ourselves from the assembly, as some do, but encourage one another; and this all the more because you see that the day draws near.

[26]*If we sin willfully after receiving the truth, there remains for us no further sacrifice for sin—[27]*only a fearful expectation of judgment and a flaming fire to consume the adversaries of God. [28]*Anyone who rejects the law of Moses is put to death without mercy on the testimony of two or three witnesses. [29]*Do you not suppose that a much worse punishment is due the man who disdains the Son of God, thinks the covenant-blood by which he was sanctified to be ordinary, and insults the Spirit of grace? [30]*We know who said,

> "Vengeance is mine; I will repay,"

and

> "The Lord will judge his people."

[31]It is a fearful thing to fall into the hands of the living God.

[32]Recall the days gone by when, after you had been enlightened, you endured a great contest of suffering. [33]*At times you were publicly exposed to insult and trial; at other times you associated yourselves with those who were being so dealt with. [34]*You even joined in the sufferings of those who were in prison and joyfully assented to the confiscation of your goods, knowing that you had better and more permanent possessions. [35]Do not, then, surrender your confidence; it will have great reward. [36]*You need patience to do God's will and receive what he has promised.

[37]*For, just a brief moment,
> and he who is to come will come; he will not
>   delay.
[38]*My just man will live by faith,
> and if he draws back
> I take no pleasure in him.

[39]We are not among those who draw back and perish, but among those who have faith and live.

V: EXAMPLES, DISCIPLINE, DISOBEDIENCE

Faith of the Ancients

11 [1]*†FAITH IS CONFIDENT ASSURANCE concerning what we hope for, and conviction about things we do not see. [2]Because of faith the men of old were approved by God. [3]*Through faith we perceive that the worlds were created by the word of God, and that what is visible came into being through the invisible. [4]*By faith Abel offered God a sacrifice greater than Cain's. Because of this he was attested to be just, God himself having borne witness to him on account of his gifts; therefore, although Abel is dead, he still speaks. [5]*By faith Enoch was taken away without dying, and "he was seen no more because God took him." Scripture testifies that, before he was taken up, he was pleasing to God—[6]but without faith, it is impossible to please him. Anyone who comes to God must believe that he exists, and that he rewards those who seek him. [7]*By faith Noah, warned about things not yet seen, revered God and built an ark that his household might be saved. He thereby condemned the world and inherited the justice which comes through faith. [8]*By faith Abraham obeyed when he

---

† munity's assembly especially in view of the parousia (v 25; cf 1 Thes 4, 13-18). If refusal to participate in the assembly indicates rejection of Christ, no sacrifice exists to obtain forgiveness for so great a sin (v 26); only the dreadful judgment of God remains (v 27). For if violation of the Mosaic law could be punished by death, how much worse will be the punishment of those who have turned their backs on Christ by despising his sacrifice and disregarding the gifts of the Holy Spirit (28f)! Judgment belongs to the Lord, and he enacts it by his living presence (30f). There was a time when the spirit of their community caused them to welcome and share their sufferings (32ff). To revitalize that spirit is to share in the courage of the Old Testament prophets (cf Is 26, 20; Hab 2, 3f), the kind of courage that must distinguish the faith of the Christian (35-39).

11, 1-40: This chapter draws upon the people and events of the Old Testament to paint an inspiring portrait of religious faith, firm and unyielding in the face of any obstacles that confront it. In the opinion of some authorities, these pages rank among the most eloquent and lofty to be found in the Bible. They expand the author's theme, broached in 6, 12, to which he now returns (10, 39).

The material of the chapter is consistently developed. Verses 3-7 draw upon the first nine chapters of Genesis; 8-22, upon the period of the patriarchs; 23-31, upon the time of Moses; 32-38, upon the history of the judges, the prophets and the Maccabean martyrs. The author gives the most extensive description of faith provided in the New Testament, though his interest does not lie in a technical, theological definition. In view of the needs of his audience he describes what authentic faith does, not what it is in itself. Through faith God guarantees the blessings to be hoped for from him, providing evidence in the gift of faith that what he promises will eventually come to pass (v 1). Because they accepted in faith God's guarantee of the future, the biblical personages discussed in 3-38 were themselves commended by God (v 2). Christians have even greater reason to remain firm in faith, since they, unlike the Old Testament men of faith, have perceived the beginning of God's fulfillment of his messianic promises (39f).

22: Ez 36, 25; 1 Pt 3, 21.	11/1: Rom 4, 20; 2 Cor 4, 18.
26: 6, 4.	3: Gn 1, 3; Jn 1, 3.
27: Zep 1, 18.	4: 12, 24; Gn 4, 4.
28: Dt 17, 6.	5: Gn 5, 24.
29: 6, 6.	7: Gn 6, 8-22; Sir 44, 17;
30: Dt 32, 35f; Rom 12, 19.	Mt 24, 37ff; 1 Pt 3, 20.
33: 1 Cor 4, 9.	8: Gn 12, 1-4;
34: Mt 6, 20.	Sir 44, 19-23;
36: Lk 21, 19.	Acts 7, 2-8;
37: Hb 2, 3.	Rom 4, 16-22.
38: Hb 2, 4; Rom 1, 17.	

was called, and went forth to the place he was to receive as a heritage; he went forth, moreover, not knowing where he was going. **9***By faith he sojourned in the promised land as in a foreign country, dwelling in tents with Isaac and Jacob, heirs of the same promise; **10***for he was looking forward to the city with foundations, whose designer and maker is God. **11***By faith Sarah received power to conceive though she was past the age, for she thought that the One who had made the promise was worthy of trust. **12***As a result of this faith, there came forth from one man, who was himself as good as dead, descendants as numerous as the stars in the sky and the sands of the seashore.

13All of these died in faith. They did not obtain what had been promised but saw and saluted it from afar. By acknowledging themselves to be strangers and foreigners on the earth, **14***they showed that they were seeking a homeland. **15**If they had been thinking back to the place from which they had come, they would have had the opportunity of returning there. **16***But they were searching for a better, a heavenly home. Wherefore God is not ashamed to be called their God, for he has prepared a city for them. **17***By faith Abraham, when put to the test, offered up Isaac; he who had received the promises was ready to sacrifice his only son, **18***of whom it was said, "Through Isaac shall your descendants be called." **19***He reasoned that God was able to raise from the dead, and so he received Isaac back as a symbol. **20***By faith Isaac invoked for Jacob and Esau blessings that were still to be.

21*By faith Jacob, when dying, blessed each of the sons of Joseph, and worshiped God, leaning on the head of his staff. **22***By faith Joseph, near the end of his life, spoke of the Exodus of the Israelites, and gave instructions about his burial. **23***By faith Moses' parents hid him for three months after his birth, thereby disregarding the king's edict, because they saw that he was a beautiful child.

24*By faith Moses, when he had grown up, refused to be known as the son of Pharaoh's daughter; **25**he wished to be ill-treated along with God's people rather than enjoy the fleeting rewards of sin. **26**Moses considered the reproach borne by God's Anointed greater riches than the treasures of Egypt, for he was looking to the reward. **27***By faith he left Egypt, not fearing the king's wrath, for he persevered as if he were looking on the invisible God. **28***By faith he kept the Passover and sprinkled the lamb's blood, that the destroying angel might not touch the first-born of Israel. **29***By faith the Israelites crossed the Red Sea as if it were dry land, but when the Egyptians attempted the same thing they were drowned. **30***Because of Israel's faith, the walls of Jericho fell after being encircled for seven days. **31***By faith Rahab the harlot escaped from being destroyed with the unbelievers, for she had peacefully received the spies.

32*What more shall I recount? I have no time to tell of Gideon, Barak, Samson, Jephthah, of David and Samuel and the prophets, **33***who by faith conquered kingdoms, did what was just, obtained the promises; they broke the jaws of lions, **34***put out raging fires, escaped the devouring sword; though weak they were made powerful, became strong in battle, and turned back foreign invaders. **35***Women received back their dead through resurrection. Others were tortured and would not receive deliverance, in order to obtain a better resurrection. **36***Still others endured mockery, scourging, even chains and imprisonment. **37**They were stoned, sawed in two, put to death at sword's point; they went about garbed in the skins of sheep or goats, needy, afflicted, tormented. **38***The world was not worthy of them. They wandered about in deserts and on mountains, they dwelt in caves and in holes of the earth. **39**Yet despite the fact that all of these were approved because of their faith, they did not obtain what had been promised. **40**God had made a better plan, a plan which included us. Without us, they were not to be made perfect.

God's Treatment of His Sons

12 **1†**THEREFORE, since we for our part are surrounded by this cloud of witnesses, let us lay aside every encumbrance of sin which clings to us and persevere in running the race which lies ahead; **2***let us keep our eyes fixed on Jesus, who inspires and perfects our faith. For the sake of the joy which lay before him he endured the cross, heedless of its shame. He has taken his seat at the right of the throne of God. **3**Remember how he endured the opposition of sinners; hence do not grow despondent or abandon the struggle. **4**In your fight against sin you have not yet resisted to the point of shedding blood. **5*†**Moreover, you have forgotten the encouraging words addressed to you as sons:

"My sons, do not disdain the discipline of the Lord
    nor lose heart when he reproves you;
6For whom the Lord loves, he disciplines;
    he scourges every son he receives."

❊

9: Gn 23, 4; 26, 3.
10: 13, 14; Rv 21, 10-22.
11: Gn 17, 19; 21, 2;
    Rom 4, 19-21.
12: Gn 15, 5; 22, 17;
    32, 12; Ex 32, 13.
14: Ps 39, 13.
16: 13, 14; Ex 3, 6;
    Phil 3, 20.
17: Gn 22, 1-10;
    1 Mc 2, 52; Jas 2, 21.
18: Gn 21, 12; Rom 9, 7.
19: Rom 4, 17-21.
20: Gn 27, 27-40.
21: Gn 48, 15.
22: Gn 50, 23ff.
23: Ex 2, 2; Acts 7, 20.
24: Ex 2, 10-15.

27: Ex 2, 15.
28: Ex 12, 21ff.
29: Ex 14, 22ff.
30: Jos 6, 12-21.
31: Jos 2, 1-21; 6, 22-25;
    Jas 2, 25.
32: Jgs 4, 6; 6, 11; 11, 1.
33: Dn 6, 22.
34: Dn 3, 22-25.
35: 1 Kgs 17, 23;
    2 Mc 6, 18—7, 42.
36: Jer 20, 2; 37, 15.
38: 1 Mc 2, 28ff.
12/2: 2, 10; Ps 110, 1;
    Phil 2, 6ff.
5: Prv 3, 11f.

---

† 12, 1-4: Christian life is to be inspired not only by the Old Testament men of faith (v 1), but above all by Jesus. As the architect of Christian faith, he had himself to endure the cross before receiving the glory of his triumph (v 2). Reflection on his sufferings should give his followers courage to continue the struggle, if necessary even to the shedding of blood (3f).

12, 5-13: Christians should regard their own sufferings as the affectionate correction of the Lord, who loves them as a father loves his children.

7*Endure your trials as the discipline of God, who deals with you as sons. For what son is there whom his father does not discipline? **8**If you do not know the discipline of sons, you are not sons but bastards. **9**If we respected our earthly fathers who corrected us, should we not all the more submit to the Father of spirits, and live? **10**They disciplined us as seemed right to them, to prepare us for the short span of mortal life; but God does so for our true profit, that we may share his holiness. **11**At the time it is administered, all discipline seems a cause for grief and not for joy, but later it brings forth the fruit of peace and justice to those who are trained in its school. **12***So strengthen your drooping hands and your weak knees. **13***Make straight the paths you walk on, that your halting limbs may not be dislocated but healed.

Penalties of Disobedience

14*†Strive for peace with all men, and for that holiness without which no one can see the Lord. **15***See to it that no man falls away from the grace of God; that no bitter root springs up through which many may become defiled; **16***that there be among you no fornicator or godless person like Esau, who sold his birthright for a meal. **17***You know that afterward he wanted to inherit his father's blessing, but he was rejected because he had no opportunity to alter his choice, even though he sought the blessing with tears.

18*†You have not drawn near to an untouchable mountain and a blazing fire, nor gloomy darkness and storm **19***and trumpet blast, nor a voice speaking words such that those who heard begged that they be not addressed to them, **20***for they could not bear to hear the command: "If even an animal touches the mountain, it must be stoned to death." **21***Indeed, so fearful was the spectacle that Moses said, "I am terrified and trembling." **22**No, you have drawn near to Mount Zion and the city of the living God, the heavenly Jerusalem, to myriads of angels in festal gathering, **23***to the assembly of the first-born enrolled in heaven, to God the judge of all, to the spirits of just men made perfect, **24***to Jesus, the mediator of a new covenant, and to the sprinkled blood which speaks more eloquently than that of Abel.

25Do not refuse to hear him who speaks. For if the Israelites did not escape punishment when they refused to listen as God spoke to them on earth, how much greater punishment will be ours if we turn away from him who speaks from heaven! **26***His voice then shook the earth, but now he has promised, "I will once more shake not only earth but heaven!" **27***And that "once more" shows that shaken, created things will pass away, so that only what is unshaken may remain. **28**Wherefore, we who are receiving the unshakable kingdom should hold fast to God's grace, through which we may offer worship acceptable to him in reverence and awe. **29***For our God is a consuming fire.

VI: FINAL EXHORTATION, BLESSING, GREETINGS

13 **1**LOVE YOUR FELLOW CHRISTIANS ALWAYS. **2***Do not neglect to show hospitality, for by that means some have entertained angels without knowing it. **3***Be as mindful of prisoners as if you were sharing their imprisonment, and of the ill-treated as of yourselves, for you may yet suffer as they do. **4**Let marriage be honored in every way and the marriage bed be kept undefiled, for God will judge fornicators and adulterers. **5***Do not love money but be content with what you have, for God has said, "I will never desert you, nor will I forsake you." **6***Thus we may say with confidence:

> "The Lord is my helper,
> I will not be afraid;
> What can man do to me?"

7Remember your leaders who spoke the word of God to you; consider how their lives ended, and imitate their faith. **8**Jesus Christ is the same yesterday, today, and forever.

9*Do not be carried away by all kinds of strange teaching. It is good to have our hearts strengthened by the grace of God and not by foods which are useless to those who take them as a standard for living.

---

† 12, 14-17: The example of Esau's conduct should warn the community against apostasy from Christ.

12, 18-29: As a final appeal for adherence to Christian teaching, the two covenants, of Moses and of Christ, are compared. The Mosaic covenant is shown to have originated in fear of God and threats of divine punishment (18-21). The covenant in Christ gives men direct access to God (v 22), makes them members of the Christian community, God's sons, a sanctified people (v 23) who have Jesus as mediator to speak for them (v 24). Not to heed the voice of the risen Christ is a sin more grave by far than the rejection of the word of Moses (25ff). Though men fall away, God's kingdom in Christ will remain, and his justice will punish those guilty of deserting it (28f).

13, 1-16: After recommendations on social and moral matters (1-6), the letter turns to doctrinal issues. The fact that the original leaders are dead should not cause the recipients of this letter to lose their faith (v 7), for Christ still lives and he remains always the same (v 8). They must not rely for their personal sanctification on regulations concerning foods (v 9), nor should they entertain the notion that Judaism and Christianity can be intermingled (v 10; cf note on Gal 2, 11-14; 15-21). As Jesus died separated from his own people, so must the Christian community remain apart from the religious doctrines of Judaism (11-14). Christ must be the heart and center of the community (15-16).

7: Prv 13, 24; Sir 30, 1.	24: 8, 6; Gn 4, 10.
12: Is 35, 3.	26: Ex 19, 18; Jgs 5, 4f;
13: Prv 4, 26.	Ps 68, 9; Hg 2, 6.
14: Rom 12, 18.	27: Mt 24, 35.
15: Dt 29, 18.	29: Dt 4, 24; Is 33, 14.
16: Gn 25, 33.	13/2: Gn 18, 3; 19, 2f;
17: Gn 27, 38.	Jgs 6, 11-22; Tb 5, 4.
18: Ex 19, 12.	3: Mt 25, 36.
19: Ex 19, 16.19; 20, 19.	5: Dt 31, 6; Jos 1, 5.
20: Ex 19, 13.	6: Pss 27, 1ff; 118, 6.
21: Dt 9, 19.	9: Rom 14, 17; 1 Cor 8, 8;
23: Lk 10, 20.	Eph 4, 14.

¹⁰We have an altar from which those who serve the tabernacle have no right to eat. ¹¹*The bodies of the animals whose blood is brought into the sanctuary by the high priest as a sin offering are burned outside the camp. ¹²Therefore Jesus died outside the gate, to sanctify the people by his own blood. ¹³Let us go to him outside the camp, bearing the insult which he bore. ¹⁴*For here we have no lasting city; we are seeking one which is to come. ¹⁵*Through him let us continually offer God a sacrifice of praise, that is, the fruit of lips which acknowledge his name.

¹⁶Do not neglect good deeds and generosity; God is pleased by sacrifices of that kind. ¹⁷†Obey your leaders and submit to them, for they keep watch over you as men who must render an account. So act that they may fulfill their task with joy, not with sorrow, for that would be harmful to you. ¹⁸Pray for us; we are confident that we have a good conscience, wishing, as we do, to act rightly in every respect. ¹⁹I especially ask your prayers that I may be restored to you very soon.

²⁰*†May the God of peace, who brought up from the dead the great Shepherd of the sheep by the blood of the eternal covenant, Jesus our Lord, ²¹furnish you with all that is good, that you may do his will. Through Jesus Christ may he carry out in you all that is pleasing to him. To Christ be glory forever! Amen.

²²My brothers, I beg you to bear with this word of encouragement, for I have written to you rather briefly. ²³I must let you know that our brother Timothy has been set free. If he is able to join me soon, he will be with me when I see you. ²⁴Greetings to all your leaders, and to all the people of God. ²⁵Grace be with you all.

11: Ex 29, 14; Lv 16, 27.
12: Mt 21, 39; Jn 19, 17.
14: 11, 10.
15: Is 57, 19; Hos 14, 2.
20: Is 63, 11; Zec 9, 11; Jn 10, 11; Acts 2, 24; Rom 15, 33.

† 13, 17ff: Recommending obedience to the leaders of the community, the author observes that he has done his best not to give cause for objection to himself.

13, 20-25: The letter concludes with a prayer (20f); a final request for the acceptance of its message (v 22); casual information regarding Timothy; and general greetings (23ff).

The Epistle of James

Introduction

The title "catholic" gradually came into use to designate seven New Testament epistles: JAMES; 1, 2 and 3 JOHN; 1 and 2 PETER; and JUDE. It first appears in reference to 1 John in the writings of Apollonius about 197 A. D., and later in reference to all these epistles in the church historian Eusebius (260-340 A.D.). The title supposes the epistles in question to lack specific addressees and therefore to be directed to the whole church. This, however, is not the case for 2 and 3 John. With the exception of 1 Peter and 1 John, the inspired character of these catholic epistles was disputed in the early church, and finally settled in their favor only at the beginning of the fifth century.

The Epistle of James has a general addressee: *To the twelve tribes in the dispersion* (1, 1). Its content, however, affords no evidence that the author wrote to non-Christian Jews outside Palestine. Scholarly opinion concerning addressees is undecided between Judaeo-Christian communities outside Palestine and Christians generally. The author concerns himself entirely with Christian conduct. He writes in the spirit of Old Testament wisdom literature (Proverbs, Sirach, Wisdom) and of the moral teaching of Tobit. He is influenced by the tradition of moral exhortation within Judaism, as is indicated by similarities between his letter and extracanonical Jewish literature, e. g., *The Testament of the Twelve Patriarchs; 1 Enoch; The Manual of Discipline* discovered at Qumran.

Some forty-eight verses in James reveal the influence of sayings of Jesus, especially those in Matthew's Sermon on the Mount. However, except for two allusions to Jesus (1, 1; 2, 1) and one to the parousia (5, 7), the epistle does not relate its moral exhortation to Christology or to the authoritative teaching of Jesus. The force of its teaching is made to rest on the reputation of its author, *James, a servant of God and of the Lord Jesus Christ* (1, 1). The author is a known figure and possesses a standing enabling him to speak with authority.

Of the various personages in the New Testament bearing this name, the James mentioned by Paul in Galatians 2, 9 as one of the pillars of the church in Palestine well meets the requirements for the authorship of this epistle. He is designated by Paul, not as one of the Twelve, but as *the brother of the Lord* (Gal 1, 19). The risen Christ made a significant appearance to him (1 Cor 15, 7). James was the administrator of the Jerusalem community (Acts 12, 17), and for this reason played a leading role in the apostolic Council (Acts 15, 13-21). He was the adviser of Paul on the latter's arrival in Jerusalem after the third missionary journey (Acts 21, 17-25). He is probably to be identified as one of the relatives of Jesus who did not believe in him during the ministry; cf Mk 6, 13; Jn 7, 2-5.

Though not all scholars are satisfied that James, leader of the Jerusalem community, is the author, it must be conceded that the epistle is datable before 62 A. D., when, according to Josephus, James was executed in Jerusalem. Nevertheless, scholars who do not admit James of Jerusalem as the author of the epistle select a date for it toward the end of the first century.

The Epistle of James has acquired special prominence in Christendom because of Martin Luther's claim that its emphasis on good works does not agree with St. Paul's doctrine of justification by faith, and because the Council of Trent declared that James 5, 14f pertains to the promulgation of the sacrament of the Anointing of the Sick.

Endurance

1 ¹*†TO THE TWELVE TRIBES IN THE DISPERSION, James, a servant of God and of the Lord Jesus Christ, sends greeting. ²*†My brothers, count it pure joy when you are involved in every sort of trial. ³†Realize that when your faith is tested this makes for endurance. ⁴Let endurance come to its perfection so that you may be fully mature and lacking in nothing.

Prayer for Wisdom

⁵*If any of you is without wisdom, let him ask it from the God who gives generously and ungrudgingly to all, and it will be given him. ⁶*Yet he must ask in faith, never doubting, for the doubter is like the surf tossed and driven by the wind. ⁸A man of this sort, devious and erratic in all that he does, ⁷must not expect to receive anything from the Lord.

---

† 1, 1: *James, a servant of God and of the Lord Jesus Christ:* a declaration of authority for instructing the Christian communities; cf Rom 1, 1. Regarding the identity of the author, see the Introduction.

1, 2: *Count it pure joy . . . every sort of trial:* a frequent teaching of the New Testament derived from the words and sufferings of Christ (Mt 5, 10ff; Jn 10, 11; 15, 12f; Acts 5, 41).

1, 3-8: The gradation of testing, endurance, and perfection indicates the manner of achieving spiritual maturity and full preparedness for the coming of Christ (3f; cf Rom 5, 3ff; 1 Pt 1, 6f). To sustain trials, to achieve endurance and perfection, require wisdom which God readily grants to believing petitioners but withholds from those who doubt (5-8; cf Sir 4, 7).

* 1/1: Acts 26, 7; Jn 7, 35.
  2: Rom 5, 3ff; 1 Pt 1, 6; 4, 13f.
5: Prv 2, 3-6; Wis 8, 21.
6: Mt 21, 21; Mk 11, 24.

Humility

9*†Let the brother in humble circumstances take pride in his eminence **10***and the rich man be proud of his lowliness, for he will disappear "like the flower of the field." **11**When the sun comes up with its scorching heat it parches the meadow, the field flowers droop, and with that the meadow's loveliness is gone. Just so will the rich man wither away amid his many projects.

Temptation

12*†Happy the man who holds out to the end through trial! Once he has been proved, he will receive the crown of life the Lord has promised to those who love him. **13***†No one who is tempted is free to say, "I am being tempted by God." Surely God, who is beyond the grasp of evil, tempts no one. **14**Rather, the tug and lure of his own passion tempt every man. **15**Once passion has conceived, it gives birth to sin, and when sin reaches maturity it begets death.

Response to God's Gift

16Make no mistake about this, my dear brothers. **17***Every worthwhile gift, every genuine benefit comes from above, descending from the Father of the heavenly luminaries, who cannot change and who is never shadowed over. **18***†He wills to bring us to birth with a word spoken in truth so that we may be a kind of first fruits of his creatures. **19***†Keep this in mind, dear brothers.

Let every man be quick to hear, slow to speak, slow to anger; **20***for a man's anger does not fulfill God's justice. **21***Strip away all that is filthy, every vicious excess. Humbly welcome the word that has taken root in you, with its power to save you. **22***Act on this word. If all you do is listen to it, you are deceiving yourselves.

23A man who listens to God's word but does not put it into practice is like a man who looks into a mirror at the face he was born with; **24**he looks at himself, then goes off and promptly forgets what he looked like. **25***There is, on the other hand, the man who peers into freedom's ideal law and abides by it. He is no forgetful listener, but one who carries out the law in practice. Blest will this man be in whatever he does.

26*†If a man who does not control his tongue imagines that he is devout, he is self-deceived; his worship is pointless. **27***†Looking after orphans and widows in their distress and keeping oneself unspotted by the world make for pure worship without stain before our God and Father.

Against Favoritism

2 **1**†MY brothers, your faith in our glorious Lord Jesus Christ must not allow of favoritism. **2**Suppose there should come into your assembly a man fashionably dressed, with gold rings on his fingers, and at the same time a poor man in shabby clothes. **3**Suppose further that you were to take notice of the well-dressed man and say, "Sit right here, please," whereas you were to say to the poor man, "You can stand!" or "Sit over there by my footrest." **4**Have you not in a case like this discriminated in your hearts? Have you not set yourselves up as judges handing down corrupt decisions?

5*Listen, dear brothers. Did not God choose those who are poor in the eyes of the world to be rich in faith and heirs of the kingdom he promised to those who love him? **6**Yet you treated the poor man shamefully. Are not the rich exploiting you? They are the ones who hale you into the courts **7***and who blaspheme that noble name which has made you God's own.

8*You are acting rightly, however, if you fulfill the law of the kingdom. Scripture has it, "You shall love your neighbor as yourself." **9***But if you show favoritism, you commit sin and are convicted by the law as transgressors. **10***Whoever falls into sin on one point of the law, even though he keeps the entire remainder,

---

† 1, 9ff: From the religious standpoint, the lot of the poor and the lowly as opposed to that of the proud rich is, here and elsewhere in the epistle, found to have value in inverse ratio to circumstance (2, 5.13; 4, 10.13-16; 5, 1-6).

1, 12: *The crown of life:* the ultimate and eternal reward for fidelity and perseverance in following the law of Christ; cf Rom 8, 28; 2 Tm 4, 8; 1 Pt 5, 4; Rv 2, 10.

1, 13ff: It is contrary to the nature of God for him to be the author of man's temptation (v 13). In the genesis of sin, man is first beguiled by passion (v 14), then gives his consent, which in turn begets the act of sin. As sin grows, it incurs the ultimate penalty of death (v 15).

1, 18: *He wills to bring us to birth . . . truth:* acceptance of the gospel message constitutes a new birth and makes the recipient the first fruits of a new creation; cf Jn 3, 5f; Rom 8, 23.

1, 19-25: To *be quick to hear* the gospel is to accept it readily and to act in conformity with it, removing from one's soul whatever opposes it so that it may take root and effect salvation (19-22). To listen to and not practice the gospel message is to misunderstand religion (23f). Only conformity of life to the ideal law of true freedom brings happiness (v 25).

1, 26: For control of the tongue, see note on 3, 1-12.

1, 27: *Orphans and widows:* the defenseless and oppressed; cf Acts 6, 1ff.

2, 1-13: In the Christian community there must be no discrimination against the poor, or favoritism toward the rich based on a mistaken exaltation of status or wealth (2ff); cf Mt 23, 6. Divine favor rather consists in God's promises, his election, and his rewards elicited by man's faith and response to his love (v 5); cf Mt 5, 3; 11, 5; 1 Cor 1, 17-29. The impious rich who oppress the poor dishonor the name of Christ. By violating the law of love of neighbor, they offend against the whole law (6f.9ff). On the other hand, abiding consciousness of the final judgment helps the faithful to fulfill the whole law (v 12).

✼

9: 2, 5.
10: Is 40, 6ff.
12: Wis 5, 15f; 1 Cor 9, 25;
   2 Tm 4, 8; 1 Pt 5, 4;
   Rv 2, 10.
13: Sir 15, 11-20;
   1 Cor 10, 13.
17: 1 Jn 1, 5.
18: 1 Pt 1, 23; 1 Jn 1, 12f.
19: Prv 14, 17; Sir 5, 13.
20: Eph 4, 26.
21: Col 3, 8.

22: Mt 7, 24-27; Rom 2, 13.
25: Ps 19, 8; Jn 13, 17.
26: 3, 2f; Ps 33, 14.
27: Ex 22, 21.
2/5: 1, 12; 1 Cor 1, 26-29;
   Rv 2, 9.
7: 1 Pt 4, 14.
8: Lv 19, 18; Mt 22, 39;
   Rom 13, 9.
9: Dt 1, 17.
10: Mt 5, 19; Gal 3, 10.

has become guilty on all counts. **11***For he who said, "You shall not commit adultery," also said, "You shall not kill." If therefore you do not commit adultery but do commit murder, you have become a transgressor of the law.

12*Always speak and act as men destined for judgment under the law of freedom. **13***Merciless is the judgment on the man who has not shown mercy; but mercy triumphs over judgment.

Faith and Good Works

14*†My brothers, what good is it to profess faith without practicing it? Such faith has no power to save one, has it? **15***If a brother or sister has nothing to wear and no food for the day, **16***and you say to them, "Goodbye and good luck! Keep warm and well fed," but do not meet their bodily needs, what good is that? **17**So it is with the faith that does nothing in practice. It is thoroughly lifeless.

18To such a person one might say, "You have faith and I have works—is that it?" Show me your faith without works, and I will show you the faith that underlies my works! **19**Do you believe that God is one? You are quite right. The demons believe that, and shudder. **20**Do you want proof, you ignoramus, that without works faith is idle? **21***Was not our father Abraham justified by his works when he offered his son Isaac on the altar? **22**There you see proof that faith was both assisting his works and implemented by his works. **23***You also see how the Scripture was fulfilled which says, "Abraham believed God, and it was credited to him as justice"; for this he received the title "God's friend."

24You must perceive that a person is justified by his works and not by faith alone. **25***Rahab the harlot will illustrate the point. Was she not justified by her works when she harbored the messengers and sent them out by a different route? **26**Be assured, then, that faith without works is as dead as a body without breath.

Restraining the Tongue

3 **1**†NOT many of you should become teachers, my brothers; you should realize that those of us who do so will be called to the stricter account. **2***All of us fall short in many respects. If a person is without fault in speech he is a man in the fullest sense, because he can control his entire body. **3**When we put bits into the mouths of horses to make them obey us, we guide the rest of their bodies. **4**It is the same with ships: how-

ever large they are, and despite the fact that they are driven by fierce winds, they are directed by very small rudders on whatever course the steersman's impulse may select. **5**The tongue is something like that. It is a small member, yet it makes great pretensions.

See how tiny the spark is that sets a huge forest ablaze! **6***The tongue is such a flame. It exists among our members as a whole universe of malice. The tongue defiles the entire body. Its flames encircle our course from birth, and its fire is kindled by hell. **7**Every form of life, four-footed or winged, crawling or swimming, can be tamed, and has been tamed, by mankind; **8***the tongue no man can tame. It is a restless evil, full of deadly poison. **9**We use it to say "Praised be the Lord and Father"; then we use it to curse men, though they are made in the likeness of God. **10**Blessing and curse come out of the same mouth. This ought not to be, my brothers! **11**Does a spring gush forth fresh water and foul from the same outlet? **12***A fig tree, brothers, cannot produce olives, or a grapevine figs; no more can a brackish source yield fresh water.

True Wisdom

13*†If one of you is wise and understanding, let him show this in practice through a humility filled with good sense. **14**Should you instead nurse bitter jealousy and selfish ambition in your hearts, at least refrain from arrogant and false claims against the truth. **15***Wisdom like this does not come from above. It is earthbound, a kind of animal, even devilish, cunning. **16**Where there are jealousy and strife, there also are inconstancy and all kinds of vile behavior. **17***Wisdom from above, by contrast, is first of all innocent. It is also peaceable, lenient, docile, rich in sympathy and the kindly deeds that are its fruits, impartial and sincere. **18***The harvest of justice is sown in peace for those who cultivate peace.

†

2, 14-26: The theme of these verses is the relationship of faith and good works. Neither can merit salvation without the other, as even the demons, who believe that God exists (v 19), can testify (14-20). The faith that justified Abraham was accompanied by his willingness, at the divine behest, to sacrifice his son Isaac (21ff). A living faith works through love, as opposed to a dead faith that lacks good works (24.26).

3, 1-12: The use and abuse of the important role of teaching in the church are here (v 1) related to the good or bad use of the tongue (9-12), the instrument through which teaching was chiefly conveyed; cf Sir 5, 13—6, 1; 28, 12-26. The bit and the rudder are figures of the tongue's control (2ff), just as the spark and destroying flames portray the evils of unbridled speech. The tongue is *a whole universe of malice*, a defiler of the body (v 6), *a restless evil, full of deadly poison* (5-8).

3, 13-18: This discussion on true wisdom is related to the previous reflection on the role of the teacher as one who is in control of his speech. The qualities of the wise man endowed from above (17f) are: innocence, peace, docility, sincerity, impartiality, sympathy and kindly deeds (cf Gal 5, 22f): all this in contrast to earthbound wisdom with its cunning, jealousy, strife, inconstancy, arrogance and endless variety of vile behavior (14ff); cf 2 Cor 12, 20.

*

11: Ex 20, 13f; Dt 5, 17f.
12: 1, 25.
13: Mt 5, 7; 6, 14f; 18, 29-34.
14: Gal 5, 6.
15: Mt 25, 41-44.
16: 1 Jn 3, 17.
21: Gn 22, 9-12; Rom 4, 1; Heb 11, 17.
23: Gn 15, 6; Rom 4, 3; Gal 3, 6.
25: Jos 2, 4-16; 6, 17; Heb 11, 31.
3/2: 1, 26; Prv 10, 19; 13, 3; Sir 14, 1; 28, 13-26.
6: Prv 26, 18ff.
8: Ps 140, 4.
12: Mt 7, 16ff.
13: Eph 4, 1f.
15: 1, 5.17.
17: Wis 7, 22.
18: Mt 5, 9.

Worldly Desires

4 [1]*†WHERE do the conflicts and disputes among you originate? Is it not your inner cravings that make war within your members? [2]What you desire you do not obtain, and so you resort to murder. You envy and you cannot acquire, so you quarrel and fight. You do not obtain because you do not ask. [3]*You ask and you do not receive because you ask wrongly, with a view to squandering what you receive on your pleasures. [4]*O you unfaithful ones, are you not aware that love of the world is enmity to God? A man is marked out as God's enemy if he chooses to be the world's friend. [5]Do you suppose it is to no purpose that Scripture says, "The spirit he has implanted in us tends toward jealousy"? [6]*Yet he bestows a greater gift, for the sake of which it is written,

> "God resists the proud
> but bestows his favor on the lowly."

[7]*Therefore submit to God; resist the devil and he will take flight. [8]*Draw close to God, and he will draw close to you. Cleanse your hands, you sinners; purify your hearts, you backsliders. [9]Begin to lament, to mourn, and to weep; let your laughter be turned into mourning and your joy into sorrow. [10]*Be humbled in the sight of the Lord and he will raise you on high.

Judging One's Fellows

[11]Do not, my brothers, speak ill of one another. The one who speaks ill of his brother or judges his brother is speaking against the law. It is the law he judges. If, however, you judge the law you are no observer of the law, you are its judge. [12]*There is but one Lawgiver and Judge, one who can save and destroy. Who then are you to judge your neighbor?

Against Presumption

[13]*†Come now, you who say, "Today or tomorrow we shall go to such and such a town, spend a year there, trade, and come off with a profit!" [14]*You have no idea what kind of life will be yours tomorrow. You are a vapor that appears briefly and vanishes. [15]Instead of saying, "If the Lord wills it, we shall live to do this or that," [16]all you can do is make arrogant and pretentious claims. All such boasting is reprehensible. [17]*When a man knows the right thing to do and does not do it, he sins.

Warning to the Rich

5 [1]*†As for you, you rich, weep and wail over your impending miseries. [2]*Your wealth has rotted, your fine wardrobe has grown moth-eaten, [3]*your gold and silver have corroded, and their corrosion shall be a testimony against you; it will devour your flesh like a fire. See what you have stored up for yourselves against the last days. [4]*Here, crying aloud, are the wages you withheld from the farmhands who harvested your fields. The cries of the harvesters have reached the ears of the Lord of hosts. [5]*You lived in wanton luxury on the earth; you fattened yourselves for the day of slaughter. [6]*You condemned, even killed, the just man; he does not resist you.

Patience

[7]*†Be patient, therefore, my brothers, until the coming of the Lord. See how the farmer awaits the precious yield of the soil. He looks forward to it patiently while the soil receives the winter and the spring rains. [8]You, too, must be patient. Steady your hearts, because the coming of the Lord is at hand. [9]Do not grumble against one another, my brothers, lest you be condemned. See! The judge stands at the gate. [10]*As your models in suffering hardship and in patience, brothers, take the prophets who spoke in the name of the Lord. [11]*Those who have endured we call blessed. You have heard of the steadfastness of Job, and have seen what the Lord, who is compassionate and merciful, did in the end.

[12]*†Above all else, my brothers, you must not swear an oath, any oath at all, either "by heaven" or "by

---

† 4, 1-12: The concern here is with the origin of conflicts in the Christian community. These are occasioned by misuse of the tongue (cf 3, 2-16), and false wisdom shown by *love of the world* which *is enmity to God* (v 4). Further, the conflicts are bound up with failure to pray properly (cf Mt 7, 7-11; Jn 6, 33) —that is, not petitioning God at all or using his kindness only for the petitioner's pleasure (2f). In contrast, the proper dispositions are submission to God, repentance, humility, and resistance to evil (7-10).

4, 13-17: The uncertainty of life (v 14), its complete dependence on God, the necessity of submitting to his will (v 15), all help man to know and to do *the right* (v 17). To disregard this standard is to live arrogantly and presumptuously (v 16), i. e., without God. This is sin (v 17).

5, 1-6: Continuing with the theme of the transitory character of life on earth, the epistle traces the impending ruin of the godless. It denounces the unjust rich, whose victims cry to heaven for judgment on their exploiters (4ff). The decay and corrosion of the costly garments and metals, which here signalize *wealth*, prove them worthless and portend the destruction of their possessors (2f).

5, 7-11: Those oppressed by the unjust rich are reminded of the need for patience, both in bearing the sufferings of human life (v 9) and in their expectation of the coming of the Lord. It is then that they will receive their reward (7f.10f; cf Heb 10, 25; 1 Jn 2, 18).

5, 12: This is a threat of condemnation for the abuse of an oath; cf Mt 5, 33-37. *By heaven* and *by earth* were substitutes for the original form of an oath, to circumvent its binding force, and to avoid pronouncing the holy name of Yahweh; cf Ex 22, 10.

4/1: Rom 7, 23.
3: Mt 6, 5-13; Rom 8, 26.
4: Mt 6, 24; 1 Jn 2, 15ff.
6: Jb 22, 29; Prv 3, 34; Mt 23, 12; 1 Pt 5, 5.
7: Eph 6, 12; 1 Pt 5, 8f.
8: Is 1, 16; Zec 1, 13.
10: Mt 23, 12; Lk 14, 11; 18, 14; 1 Pt 5, 6.
12: Mt 7, 1; Rom 2, 1.
13: Prv 27, 1; Lk 12, 19f.
14: Ps 39, 6f.
17: Lk 12, 47.

5/1: Lk 6, 24.
2: Sir 29, 10ff; Mt 6, 19.
3: Prv 11, 4.28.
4: Ex 22, 22; Lv 19, 13; Dt 24, 14f; Mal 3, 5.
5: Lk 16, 19.25.
6: Wis 2, 10-20.
7: Dt 11, 14; Lk 21, 19; Heb 10, 36.
10: Mt 5, 12.
11: Jb 1, 21f; Ps 103, 8.
12: Mt 5, 34ff.

earth." Rather, let it be "yes" if you mean yes and "no" if you mean no. In this way you will not incur condemnation.

Anointing and Prayer

13If anyone among you is suffering hardship, he must pray. If a person is in good spirits, he should sing a hymn of praise. **14***†Is there anyone sick among you? He should ask for the presbyters of the church. They in turn are to pray over him, anointing him with oil in the Name [of the Lord]. **15**†This prayer uttered in faith will reclaim the one who is ill, and the Lord will restore him to health. If he has committed any sins, forgiveness will be his. **16***†Hence, declare your sins to one another, and pray for one another, that you may find healing.

The fervent petition of a holy man is powerful indeed. **17***Elijah was only a man like us, yet he prayed earnestly that it would not rain and no rain fell on the land for three years and six months. **18***When he prayed again, the sky burst forth with rain and the land produced its crop.

19*†My brothers, the case may arise among you of someone straying from the truth, and of another bringing him back. **20***†Remember this: the person who brings a sinner back from his way will save his soul from death and cancel a multitude of sins.

---

† **5, 14:** *Is there anyone sick . . . Lord:* in case of the serious, even if not extreme, illness of a member of the community, *he should ask for the presbyters,* i. e., those who have authority in the church (Acts 15, 2.22f; 1 Tm 5, 17; Ti 1, 5). *They . . . are to pray over him* (cf Sir 38, 9), *anointing him with oil:* oil was used for medicinal purposes in Oriental medicine (cf Is 1, 6; Lk 10, 34). In Mark 6, 13 it is also the medium through which miraculous healing is effected *in the name* [*of the Lord*]; i. e., by the power of Jesus Christ.

5, 15: *This prayer uttered in faith . . . to health:* though other passages in James speak of saving or salvation in reference to the soul (1, 21; 2, 14; 4, 12; 5, 20), here the reference is to bodily health: *the Lord will restore him to health,* literally "raise him up" (Mk 1, 31; 9, 27). *If he has committed any sins, forgiveness will be his:* in the public ministry of Jesus, bodily cures and forgiveness of sins are often closely related (Mt 9, 1-8; Mk 2, 1-12; Jn 5, 14). The Council of Trent (Sess. 14) declared the Anointing of the Sick to be a sacrament "instituted by Christ our Lord and promulgated by blessed James the apostle."

5, 16ff: *Declare . . . sins:* as a sign of repentance (cf Lv 5, 5; Ps 31, 5; Ezr 9, 6-15; Mt 3, 6; Acts 19, 18); *to one another:* probably in connection with liturgical prayer to make the public confession more efficacious, as witness the *Didache. Pray for one another:* cf Col 3, 4; 1 Thes 5, 25; Heb 13, 18.

5, 19f: This passage is reminiscent of the parable of the Good Shepherd (Lk 15, 3-7).

5, 20: *Will save his soul from death:* the soul of the sinner will be saved from eternal condemnation.

14: Mk 6, 13.
16: Prv 28, 13.
17: 1 Kgs 17, 1; Lk 4, 25.
18: 1 Kgs 18, 42.
19: Mt 18, 15; Gal 6, 1.
20: Prv 10, 12.

The First Epistle of Peter

Introduction

There is abundant evidence in this epistle that *scattered strangers* in 1, 1 refers to Gentile Christian communities (1, 14.18; 2, 9f; 4, 3f; cf Introduction to James). They are envisioned as the new people of God, aliens in the pagan world. The place-names in 1, 1 indicate that the epistle was intended for Christian communities in Asia Minor, but it is uncertain whether those founded by Paul are also included.

Early Christian tradition, starting with Irenaeus at the beginning of the third century, unhesitatingly ascribed the epistle to Peter. Since the early nineteenth century, however, many scholars have considered it a pseudonymous work. Those who defend its Petrine authorship hold that certain data in the epistle favor the traditional view: its allusions to the sufferings of Jesus (2, 21-24; 3, 18; 4, 1); its recollections of his sayings (1, 6-12; Jn 1, 10f; 16, 20; Mt 5, 10; 13, 17); and its relationship to the kerygmatic speeches attributed to Peter in Acts (1, 16-22; 2, 14-36; 3, 12-26; 4, 8-12). Such evidence, though valuable, is not conclusive for Petrine authorship since other Christians of the first century familiar with the church's teachings could have been responsible for these formulations. For those who believe Peter wrote the epistle, it must be dated before 64-67 A. D., the period within which his execution under Nero took place. Those who regard it as a pseudonymous work date it at 90-95 A. D. It is generally conceded that its place of composition was Rome—the *Babylon* referred to in 5, 13.

Unlike the Epistle of James, this letter presents the moral exhortation which is its dominant feature in close relationship to Christian doctrine: the Trinity of persons in God (1, 2f.12; 4, 14); the redemptive value of Jesus' death and resurrection (1, 3; 3, 21f); the sinfulness of man (1, 18; 2, 24), whom God destined to be holy (1, 15f). Some scholars are of the opinion that 1 Peter 1, 3—2, 10 is taken substantially from an early Christian baptismal liturgy. Whether this view is correct or not, the passages in question are among the clearest expositions on the meaning of Christian baptism to be found in the New Testament.

Greeting

1 1*†PETER, AN APOSTLE OF JESUS CHRIST, to those who live as strangers scattered throughout Pontus, Galatia, Cappadocia, Asia, and Bithynia; to men chosen 2*according to the foreknowledge of God

the Father, consecrated by the Spirit to a life of obedience to Jesus Christ and purification with his blood. Favor and peace be yours in abundance.

Thanksgiving

3*†Praised be the God and Father
of our Lord Jesus Christ,
he who in his great mercy
gave us new birth;
a birth unto hope which draws its life
from the resurrection of Jesus Christ from the dead;
4* a birth to an imperishable inheritance,
incapable of fading or defilement,
which is kept in heaven for you
5 who are guarded with God's power through faith;
a birth to a salvation which stands ready
to be revealed in the last days.

6*†There is cause for rejoicing here. You may for a time have to suffer the distress of many trials; 7*but this is so that your faith, which is more precious than the passing splendor of fire-tried gold, may by its genuineness lead to praise, glory, and honor when Jesus Christ appears. 8*Although you have never seen him, you love him, and without seeing you now believe in him, and rejoice with inexpressible joy touched with glory 9because you are achieving faith's goal, your salvation. 10†This is the salvation which the prophets carefully searched out and examined. They prophesied

---

† 1, 1f: The introductory formula names Peter as the writer (see Introduction). He is Simon, son of John (Mt 16, 18; Jn 21, 15ff), whom Christ called Cephas, meaning Peter, "rock" (Jn 1, 42): an apostle (Mt 10, 2) and fellow elder (1 Pt 5, 1). In his office of apostle he addresses himself to the Gentile converts of Asia Minor. Their privileged status of a *chosen, consecrated,* and purified people makes them worthy of God's peace and favor. In contrast is their actual existence as pilgrims and strangers, scattered among pagans, far from their true country.

1, 3ff: A prayer of praise and thanksgiving to God who bestows the gift of new life and hope that derive from the resurrection of his Son. It contains the promise, not of an earthly land, but of *an imperishable inheritance . . . in heaven,* for those *guarded with God's power through faith,* and it is *to be revealed in the last days.*

1, 6-9: As the glory of Christ's resurrection was preceded by his sufferings and death, the new life of faith which it bestows is to be subjected to *many trials* (v 6) while achieving its goal: the glory of the fullness of salvation (v 9) at the coming of Christ (v 8).

1, 10ff: *The Spirit of Christ* (v 11) is here shown to have been present in both the prophets and the apostles: in the prophets moving them to search out, examine, investigate, and predict the divine favor of salvation that was to come (v 10); in

---

1/1: Jas 1, 1.
2: Rom 8, 29.
3: Jn 3, 5; 1 Jn 2, 29.
4: Mt 6, 19f; Col 1, 5.
6: Jas 1, 2f.
7: Prv 17, 3; 1 Cor 3, 13.
8: 2 Cor 5, 7.

the divine favor that was destined to be yours. **11***They investigated the times and the circumstances which the Spirit of Christ within them was pointing to, for he predicted the sufferings destined for Christ and the glories that would follow. **12**They knew by revelation that they were providing, not for themselves but for you, what has now been proclaimed to you by those who preach the gospel to you, in the power of the Holy Spirit sent from heaven. Into these matters angels long to search.

Filial Obedience and Fear

13†So gird the loins of your understanding; live soberly; set all your hope on the gift to be conferred on you when Jesus Christ appears. **14**†As obedient sons, do not yield to the desires that once shaped you in your ignorance. **15***Rather, become holy yourselves in every aspect of your conduct, after the likeness of the holy One who called you; **16***remember, Scripture says, "Be holy, for I am holy." **17***In prayer you call upon a Father who judges each one justly on the basis of his actions. Since this is so, conduct yourselves reverently during your sojourn in a strange land. **18***† Realize that you were delivered from the futile way of life your fathers handed on to you, not by any diminishable sum of silver or gold, **19***but by Christ's blood beyond all price: the blood of a spotless, unblemished lamb **20**chosen before the world's foundation and revealed for your sake in these last days. **21**It is through him that you are believers in God, the God who raised him from the dead and gave him glory. Your faith and hope, then, are centered in God.

Brotherly Love

22*By obedience to the truth you have purified yourselves for a genuine love of your brothers; therefore, love one another constantly from the heart. **23***†Your rebirth has come, not from a destructible but from an indestructible seed, through the living and enduring word of God. **24***For,

"All mankind is grass
  and the glory of men is like the flower of the field.
  The grass withers, the flower wilts,
  but the word of the Lord endures forever."

25Now this "word" is the gospel which was preached to you.

Growth in Holiness

2 **1***†so strip away everything vicious, everything deceitful; pretenses, jealousies, and disparaging remarks of any kind. **2**Be as eager for milk as newborn babies—pure milk of the spirit to make you grow unto salvation, **3***now that you have tasted that the Lord is good.

4*†Come to him, a living stone, rejected by men but approved, nonetheless, and precious in God's eyes. **5***You too are living stones, built as an edifice of spirit, into a holy priesthood, offering spiritual sacrifices acceptable to God through Jesus Christ. **6***For Scripture has it:

"See, I am laying a cornerstone in Zion,
  an approved stone, and precious.
  He who puts his faith in it shall not be shaken."

7*The stone is of value for you who have faith. For those without faith, it is rather,

"A stone which the builders rejected
  that became a cornerstone."

8*It is likewise "an obstacle and a stumbling stone." Those who stumble and fall are the disbelievers in God's word; it belongs to their destiny to do so.

9*†You, however, are "a chosen race, a royal priesthood, a holy nation, a people he claims for his own to proclaim the glorious works" of the One who called

---

† the apostles impelling them to preach the fulfillment of salvation in the mystery of Christ's sufferings and glory (v 12).

1, 13-25: These verses are concerned with the call of God's people to holiness and to fraternal love by reason of their relationship with him, a covenant sealed with the blood of his Son.

1, 13: *Gird the loins of your understanding:* a figure reminiscent of the rite of Passover when the Israelites were in flight from their oppressors (Ex 12, 11), and suggesting also the vigilance of the Christian people in expectation of the second coming of Christ (Lk 12, 35f).

1, 14-17: The *ignorance* here referred to (v 14) was their former lack of knowledge of God, leading inevitably to godless conduct; holiness (15f), on the contrary, is the result of their call to the knowledge and love of God as the *Father who judges each one justly* (v 17).

1, 18f: The deliverance or ransom of Israel foretold by Isaiah (52, 3) is here fulfilled in behalf of the Christian people at the cost of the blood (i. e., the life) of the spotless lamb (Is 53, 7.10; Rom 3, 24f; 1 Cor 6, 20; cf Ex 12, 5).

1, 23ff: The rebirth of Christians (v 23) derives from Christ, the *indestructible seed* effecting a new and lasting existence in those who accept the gospel (24f), and making them brothers with the duty of loving one another (v 22).

2, 1ff: Growth *unto salvation* (v 2) is here considered negatively, as a stripping away of all that is contrary to the new life received from Christ; and positively, as the taking of the *pure milk,* i. e., the nourishment which the newly baptized *have tasted* and found *good* (1f).

2, 4-8: *Come to him:* to Christ, *a living stone, rejected by men but approved* by God because of his death and resurrection (v 4). Believers joined by the Spirit (1 Cor 3, 16) to Christ the *cornerstone* (v 7) themselves become *living stones* and constitute the spiritual edifice of the Christian community. They are *a holy priesthood* whose function is to offer *spiritual sacrifices acceptable to God through Jesus Christ* (5f). To unbelievers, Christ is *an obstacle and a stumbling stone* on which they are destined to fall (v 8); cf. Rom 11, 11.

2, 9: The prerogatives of ancient Israel here mentioned are now more fully and fittingly applied to the Christian people: *a chosen race* (cf Is 44, 1ff) indicates their divine election (Eph 1, 4ff); *a royal priesthood* (cf *a kingdom of priests,* Ex 19, 6) to serve and worship God in Christ, thus continuing the priestly

---

❋
11: Is 52, 13; 53, 12.
15: Mt 5, 48; 1 Jn 3, 3.
16: Lv 19, 2.
17: Dt 10, 17; Mal 1, 6; Rom 2, 11.
18: Is 52, 3; 1 Cor 6, 20.
19: Jn 1, 29; Heb 9, 14.
22: Rom 12, 9.
23: 1 Jn 3, 9.

24: Is 40, 6ff.
2/1: Jas 1, 21.
3: Ps 34, 9.
4: Mt 21, 42; Acts 4, 11.
5: Eph 2, 21f.
6: Is 28, 16; Rom 9, 33.
7: Ps 118, 22; Mt 21, 42.
8: Is 8, 14.
9: Ex 19, 6.

you from darkness into his marvelous light. **10***Once you were no people, but now you are God's people; once there was no mercy for you, but now you have found mercy.

Good Example

11*†Beloved, you are strangers and in exile; hence I urge you not to indulge your carnal desires. By their nature they wage war on the soul. **12**Though the pagans may slander you as troublemakers, conduct yourselves blamelessly among them. By observing your good works they may give glory to God on the day of visitation.

For the Citizen

13*†Because of the Lord, be obedient to every human institution, whether to the emperor as sovereign **14**or to the governors he commissions for the punishment of criminals and the recognition of the upright. **15**Such obedience is the will of God. You must silence the ignorant talk of foolish men by your good behavior. **16*†**Live as free men, but do not use your freedom as a cloak for vice. In a word, live as servants of God. **17***You must esteem the person of every man. Foster love for the brothers, reverence for God, respect for the emperor.

For the Slave

18*†You household slaves, obey your masters with all deference, not only the good and reasonable ones but even those who are harsh. **19**When a man can suffer injustice and endure hardship through his awareness of God's presence, this is the work of grace in him. **20**If you do wrong and get beaten for it, what credit can you claim? But if you put up with suffering for doing what is right, this is acceptable in God's eyes. **21***It was for this you were called, since Christ suffered for you in just this way and left you an example, to have you follow in his footsteps. **22***He did no wrong; no deceit was found in his mouth. **23**When he was insulted, he returned no insult. When he was made to suffer, he did not counter with threats. Instead, he delivered himself up to the One who judges justly. **24***In his own body he brought your sins to the cross, so that all of us, dead to sin, could live in accord with God's will. By his wounds you were healed. **25†**At one time you were straying like sheep, but now you have returned to the Shepherd, the Guardian of your souls.

For Wife and Husband

3 **1*†**YOU married women must obey your husbands, so that any of them who do not believe in the word of the gospel may be won over apart

from preaching, through their wives' conduct. **2**They have only to observe the reverent purity of your way of life. **3***The affectation of an elaborate hairdress, the wearing of golden jewelry or the donning of rich robes is not for you. **4**Your adornment is rather the hidden character of the heart, expressed in the unfading beauty of a calm and gentle disposition. This is precious in God's eyes. **5**The holy women of past ages used to adorn themselves in this way, reliant on God and obedient to their husbands—**6**for example, Sarah, who was subject to Abraham and called him her master. You are her children when you do what is right and let no fears alarm you.

---

†

functions of his life, passion, and resurrection; *a holy nation* (Ex 19, 6) reserved for God; *a people he claims for his own* (cf Mal 3, 17) in virtue of their baptism into his death and resurrection. This transcends all natural and national divisions, and unites the people into one community to glorify him who led them from the darkness of paganism to the light of faith in Christ. From being "no people, deprived of all mercy, they have become the very people of God, the chosen recipients of his mercy; cf Hos 1, 9; 2, 25.

2, 11—3, 12: After explaining the doctrinal basis for the Christian community, the letter traces practical applications in terms of the virtues that should prevail in all the social relationships of the members of the community: good example to pagan neighbors (2, 11f); respect for human authority (2, 13-17); obedience, patience, and endurance of hardship in domestic relations (2, 18-25); Christian behavior of husbands and wives (3, 1-7); mutual charity (3, 8-12).

2, 11: *You are strangers and in exile:* no longer signifying absence from one's native land (Gn 23, 4), this denotes rather their estrangement from this world during their earthly pilgrimage in search of the city *which is to come* (Heb 13, 14).

2, 13: *Be obedient to every human institution:* the text could also mean, though less probably, "every human creature." This obedience is enjoined *because of the Lord,* i. e., because it conforms to his will (v 15).

2, 16f: *Live as free men . . . vice:* the freedom of the Christian is that which derives from right order, i. e., service of God and *reverence* toward him, besides *esteem* for *every man* (v 17).

2, 18-25: The author's concern for *household slaves* was not aimed at overthrowing the institution of slavery, but was meant rather to indicate how those in servitude should accept it through the power of grace as a means of imitating the suffering Christ. They are reminded that his willing endurance of insult, suffering, and death delivered men from the bondage of sin and won for them the freedom of living according to God's will; cf Is 53, 1-12; Gal 3, 13.

2, 25: *The Shepherd, the Guardian of your souls:* the familiar shepherd-and-flock figures express the care, vigilance, and love of God for his people in the Old Testament (Ps 23; Is 23, 3f; 40, 11; Ez 34, 11-16), and of Christ for all men in the New (Mt 18, 10-14; Lk 15, 3-6; Jn 10, 11; Heb 13, 20). In Acts (20, 28), St. Paul calls the elders of the church of Ephesus, shepherds and guardians of the flock.

3, 1-7: This passage outlines, on the one hand, the marital duties of wives: reverence, chaste conduct, and obedience to their husbands; and on the other, the love and consideration husbands owe their wives (cf Eph 5, 21-28). At the same time, attention is called to the opportunity of wives for winning over their pagan husbands to belief in the gospel by their own Christian conduct. In imitation of the pious women of the past, they are to cultivate the virtues of the interior life instead of indulging in the display of robes and jewelry. The fulfillment of these duties by husbands and wives is the surest guarantee of God's response to their prayers.

✿

10: Hos 1, 6.9; 2, 3.
11: Gal 5, 24.
13: Rom 13, 1-7.
16: Gal 5, 13.
17: Jude 4; Prv 24, 21; Mt 22, 21.
18: Eph 6, 5.

21: Mt 16, 24.
22: Is 53, 9; Mt 5, 39.
24: Is 53, 5f; Rom 6, 11.
3/1: 1 Cor 7, 12-16; Eph 5, 22-24; Col 3, 18.
3: 1 Tm 2, 9-15.

7*You husbands, too, must show consideration for those who share your lives. Treat women with respect as the weaker sex, heirs just as much as you to the gracious gift of life. If you do so, nothing will keep your prayers from being answered.

In Christian Charity

8†In summary, then, all of you should be like-minded, sympathetic, loving toward one another, kindly disposed, and humble. **9***Do not return evil for evil or insult for insult. Return a blessing instead. This you have been called to do, that you may receive a blessing as your inheritance.

10*"He who cares for life
and wants to see prosperous days
must keep his tongue from evil
and his lips from uttering deceit.
11 He must turn from evil and do good,
seek peace and follow after it,
12 because the Lord has eyes for the just
and ears for their cry;
but against evildoers the Lord sets his face."

In Christian Suffering

13†Who indeed can harm you if you are committed deeply to doing what is right? **14***Even if you should have to suffer for justice' sake, happy will you be. "Fear not and do not stand in awe of what this people fears." **15**Venerate the Lord, that is, Christ, in your hearts. Should anyone ask you the reason for this hope of yours, be ever ready to reply, **16**but speak gently and respectfully. Keep your conscience clear, so that, whenever you are defamed, those who libel your way of life in Christ may be shamed. **17**If it should be God's will that you suffer, it is better to do so for good deeds than for evil ones.

18*The reason why Christ . . . for all, a just man for the sake of the unjust, so that he might lead you to God. He was put to death insofar as fleshly existence goes, but was given life in the realm of the spirit. **19**†It was in the spirit also that he went to preach to the spirits in prison. **20***They had disobeyed as long ago as Noah's day, while God patiently waited until the ark was built. At that time, a few persons, eight in all, escaped in the ark through the water. **21***You are now saved by a baptismal bath which corresponds to this exactly. This baptism is no removal of physical stain, but the pledge to God of an irreproachable conscience through the resurrection of Jesus Christ. **22***He went to heaven and is at God's right hand, with angelic rulers and powers subjected to him.

In Christian Faithfulness

4 **1**†CHRIST suffered in the flesh; therefore arm yourselves with his same mentality. He who has suffered in the flesh has broken with sin. **2**You are not to spend what remains of your earthly life on human desires but on the will of God. **3***Already you have devoted enough time to what the pagans enjoy, living lives of debauchery, evil desires, drunkenness, orgies, carousing, and wanton idolatry. **4**It is no wonder that those blasphemers are surprised when you do not plunge into the same swamp of profligacy as they. **5***They shall give an accounting to him who stands ready to judge the living and the dead. **6**†The reason the gospel was preached even to the dead was that, although condemned in the flesh in the eyes of men, they might live in the spirit in the eyes of God.

Mutual Charity

7†The consummation of all is close at hand. Therefore do not be perturbed; remain calm so that you will be able to pray. **8***†Above all, let your love for one another be constant, for love covers a multitude of sins. **9***Be mutually hospitable without complaining. **10***As generous distributors of God's manifold grace, put your gifts at the service of one another, each in the measure he has received. **11***†The one who speaks is

---

† 3, 8-12: To the proper ordering of Christian life in its various aspects as described in 2, 11—3, 9 there is promised the blessing expressed in Psalm 34, 13-17. In the Old Testament, this referred to the temporal benefits of longevity and prosperity; in the New, it refers to eternal life.

3, 13-22: This exposition, centering on verse 17, runs as follows: By his suffering and death Christ the just One saved the unjust (v 18); by his resurrection he acquired new life in the spirit, which he communicates to believers through the baptismal bath that cleanses their consciences from sin. As the ark saved Noah's family, so baptism saves sinners from the flood waters that would destroy them (19-22). Hence they need not share the fear of sinners; they should rather rejoice in suffering because of their hope in Christ. Thus their innocence disappoints their accusers (13-16; Mt 10, 28; Rom 8, 35-39).

3, 19: There are various interpretations of this verse. It probably refers to the risen Christ making known to imprisoned souls his victory over sin and death.

4, 1-6: Willingness to suffer with Christ equips the Christian with the power to conquer sin. Christ is here portrayed as the judge to whom those guilty of pagan vices must render an account; cf Jn 5, 22-27; Acts 10, 42; 2 Tm 4, 1.

4, 6: The gospel was preached even to the dead: this may refer to bringing the benefits of salvation to the "spirits" in prison (cf 3, 19), or to the preaching of the gospel to Christians who have since died.

4, 7-11: The author outlines the means to be used in preparing for the consummation of all at the parousia (7): calmness, prayer, and constant love for one another through unfeigned hospitality and the generous use of one's gifts for the glory of God and of Christ (8-11); cf Lk 21, 34ff; 1 Cor 7, 29ff; Jas 5, 7-12.

4, 8: Love covers a multitude of sins: a favorite maxim of the apostles, based on Proverbs 10, 12. Fraternal love will overcome such evils as occur (cf Lk 7, 47; Jas 5, 20).

4, 11: God is to be glorified . . . throughout the ages. Amen: this doxology concludes the portion of 1 Peter begun in 1, 3.

7: Eph 5, 25.
9: Mt 5, 44; Lk 6, 28; Rom 12, 14.
10-12: Ps 34, 13-17.
14: Is 8, 12.
18: Rom 5, 6.
20: Gn 7, 7.17; 2 Pt 2, 5.
21: Eph 5, 26.
22: Eph 1, 20f.
4/3: Eph 4, 17f.
5: Acts 10, 42; Rom 14, 9f; 1 Tm 4, 1.
8: Prv 10, 12.
9: Heb 13, 2.
10: Rom 12, 6ff; 1 Cor 12, 4-11.
11: Rom 12, 7.

to deliver God's message. The one who serves is to do it with the strength provided by God. Thus, in all of you God is to be glorified through Jesus Christ: to him be glory and dominion throughout the ages. Amen.

Blessings of Persecution

¹²*†Do not be surprised, beloved, that a trial by fire is occurring in your midst. It is a test for you, but it should not catch you off guard. **¹³***Rejoice instead, in the measure that you share Christ's sufferings. When his glory is revealed, you will rejoice exultantly. **¹⁴*†**Happy are you when you are insulted for the sake of Christ, for then God's Spirit in its glory has come to rest on you. **¹⁵**See to it that none of you suffers for being a murderer, a thief, a malefactor, or a destroyer of another's rights. **¹⁶**If anyone suffers for being a Christian, however, he ought not to be ashamed. He should rather glorify God in virtue of that name. **¹⁷***The season of judgment has begun, and begun with God's own household. If it begins this way with us, what must be the end for those who refuse obedience to the gospel of God? **¹⁸***And if the just man is saved only with difficulty, what is to become of the godless and the sinner? **¹⁹**Accordingly, let those who suffer as God's will requires continue in good deeds, and entrust their lives to a faithful Creator.

For the Ministry

5 **¹*†**To the elders among you I, a fellow elder, a witness of Christ's sufferings and sharer in the glory that is to be revealed, make this appeal. **²*†**God's flock is in your midst; give it a shepherd's care. Watch over it willingly as God would have you do, not under constraint; and not for shameful profit either, but generously. **³**Be examples to the flock, not lording it over those assigned to you, **⁴***so that when the chief Shepherd appears you will win for yourselves the unfading crown of glory.

Counsel to the Laity

⁵*†In the same way, you younger men must be obedient to the elders. In your relations with one another, clothe yourselves with humility, because God "is stern with the arrogant but to the humble he shows kindness." **⁶***Bow humbly under God's mighty hand, so that in due time he may lift you high. **⁷***Cast all your cares on him because he cares for you. **⁸*†**Stay sober and alert. Your opponent the devil is prowling like a roaring lion looking for someone to devour. **⁹***Resist him, solid in your faith, realizing that the brotherhood of believers is undergoing the same sufferings through-

out the world. **¹⁰***The God of all grace, who called you to his everlasting glory in Christ, will himself restore, confirm, strengthen, and establish those who have suffered a little while. **¹¹**Dominion be his throughout the ages! Amen.

Farewell

¹²†I am writing briefly through Sislvanus, whom I take to be a faithful brother to you. Herewith are expressed my encouragement and my testimony that this is the true grace of God. Be steadfast in it. **¹³***The church that is in Babylon, chosen together with you, sends you greeting, as does Mark my son. **¹⁴***Greet one another with the embrace of true love. Peace to all of you who are in Christ.

---

† The source of the letter here used seems to have been a sermon of exhortation on the sacrament of baptism, to which numerous references are made.

4, 12-19: A trial of suffering faces the followers of Christ (12). If it is inflicted on them for the sake of his name, i. e., because of their being Christians (16), they are to rejoice in thus sharing the sufferings of the Christ whose glorification they will also share (13f; cf Rom 8, 17). If the trial is inflicted because of sins and misdeeds (v 15), the present judgment, though severe even for those of *God's own household*, is but the beginning of punishment for those *who refuse obedience to the gospel of God* (17f). The watchword is perseverance in the good and trust in God's fidelity (19).

4, 12: *A trial by fire*: severe affliction—in the form of slander (2, 12), insult (4, 14), and persecution from pagan neighbors; cf 3, 14.17.

4, 14: *God's Spirit in its glory has come to rest on you*: the Spirit both strengthens Christians to endure suffering and then glorifies them because they suffer for Christ; even as the glorification of Christ consisted, not only in his resurrection and ascension, but in his passion as well (Jn 13, 31f).

5, 1: *Elders*: "presbyteroi"—those to whom the task, both of governing the faithful and of conducting worship for them, was entrusted; cf 1 Tm 5, 17f; Ti 1, 5.7f; Jas 5, 14. Peter, here called *a fellow elder*, nevertheless admonishes the others as one exercising authority over them.

5, 2ff: In imitation of Christ, *the chief Shepherd*, those charged with the pastoral office are to shepherd the flock by their care, by their solicitude for what pertains to doctrine and discipline, and by their example. They are to render this service, *not under constraint, and not for shameful profit*, nor to lord it over the flock, but out of generosity and kindness, as God would have them do, thus meriting *the unfading crown of glory*; cf Acts 20, 17-31 and note on 2, 25.

5, 5-11: The laity are to be obedient toward the elders, and to show humility toward one another and complete trust in God's loving care (5ff). By sobriety, alertness, and firm faith, they must ward off the evil one who seeks to destroy their souls. Their sufferings are shared with Christians everywhere (8ff). As a reward for their faith and trust in God, they will be strengthened and attain to *everlasting glory in Christ* (10).

5, 8: *Your opponent the devil . . . someone to devour*: the synonymous Greek terms "antidikos" (*opponent*) and "diabolos" (*accuser*) are used to designate those who persecute Christians. In the manner of Satan they prowl about *like a roaring lion* seeking to destroy their victims (Ps 22, 14).

5, 12ff: *Sislvanus*: Paul's companion (2 Cor 1, 19; 1 Thes 1, 1; 2 Thes 1, 1). *This is the true grace of God*: a possible reference to the trials which the Christians were enduring, regarded from the standpoint of their salutary effects. *Babylon*: Rome which, like ancient Babylon, conquered Jerusalem and destroyed its temple. *Mark my son*: cf Acts 12, 25; 13, 5; Col 4, 10.

✿
12: 1, 6f; 3, 14.	5: Prv 3, 34; Mt 23, 12.
13: Rom 5, 3-5; 8, 17;	6: Jb 22, 29; Jas 4, 10.
2 Tm 2, 12.	7: Ps 54, 23; Mt 6, 25;
14: Is 11, 2; Acts 5, 41;	Phil 4, 6.
Col 3, 4.	8: 1 Thes 5, 6.
17: Lk 23, 31; 2 Thes 1, 8.	9: Eph 6, 11ff.
18: Prv 11, 31.	10: Rom 8, 18; 2 Cor 4, 17;
5/1: Rv 1, 9.	1 Thes 5, 24.
2: Acts 20, 28;	13: Acts 12, 12.25;
1 Tm 3, 2-7; Ti 1, 7.	2 Tm 4, 11.
4: 2 Tm 4, 8.	14: 1 Cor 16, 20.

The Second Epistle of Peter

Introduction

Early Christian tradition was not so impressed by the claim of Petrine authorship of this epistle (1, 1.14.16ff; 3, 1.15f) as to concede its authenticity without question. Both Origen (185-254) and St. Jerome (342-420) found it debatable. In the early fifth century the epistle was accepted into the canon of the Scriptures.

The chief reason for concluding that 2 Peter was not composed by the chief of the apostles is its discussion of the parousia (3, 1-13). The main purpose of the epistle was to meet the difficulty caused in many minds by the non-fulfillment of the expectation of Christ's second coming. This difficulty could not have arisen in the lifetime of Peter, who died between the years 64 and 67 A. D. Only after the destruction of Jerusalem, in 70 A. D., did Christians begin slowly to realize that the parousia was reserved for a date in the more remote future. The epistle was written at a time when Christian teaching was placing less emphasis on the proximity of the parousia, and therefore not while Peter was still living. Scholars add other arguments against Petrine authorship from the epistle's vocabulary and theology, and from its clear relationship to Jude—without, however, removing all doubt on the question.

It is not unreasonable to conclude that 2 Peter was written by an unknown author who followed the pseudonymous convention of the time in order to attract readers to his work. The date of composition is conjectural. Some think that the author was close enough to the tradition of Petrine teaching to assume the important name Peter, but it is probable that he was a third- or fourth-generation Christian who wrote in the period between 100 and 125. The letter is addressed to Christians generally (1, 1), without giving any indication of its place of composition.

The epistle is well composed, leading gradually to its discussion of the parousia. It reminds its readers of the divine authenticity of Christ's teaching (1, 3f), continues reflections on Christian conduct (1, 5-15), then returns to the exalted dignity of Jesus by incorporating in the text the apostolic witness to his transfiguration (1, 16ff). It takes up the question of the interpretation of Scripture by pointing out that it is possible to misunderstand the sacred writings (1, 19—2, 1) and that divine punishment will be visited upon false teachers (2, 2-22). It explains that the parousia is the doctrine of Jesus and of the apostles and is therefore an eventual certainty (3, 1-13); at the same time it warns that the meaning of St.

Paul's writing on this question should not be distorted (3, 14-18).

Greeting

1 [1]†SIMEON PETER, SERVANT AND APOSTLE of Jesus Christ, to those who have been given a faith like ours in the justifying power of our God and Savior Jesus Christ: [2]may grace be yours and peace in abundance through your knowledge of God and of Jesus, our Lord.

Christian Virtue

[3]*†That divine power of his has freely bestowed on us everything necessary for a life of genuine piety, through knowledge of him who called us by his own glory and power. [4]*By virtue of them he has bestowed on us the great and precious things he promised, so that through these you who have fled a world corrupted by lust might become sharers of the divine nature. [5]*†This is reason enough for you to make every effort to undergird your virtue with faith, your discernment with virtue, [6]and your self-control with discernment; this self-control, in turn, should lead to perseverance, and perseverance to piety, [7]*and piety to care for your brother, and care for your brother, to love.

[8]Qualities like these, made increasingly your own, are by no means ineffectual; they bear fruit in true knowledge of our Lord Jesus Christ. [9]*Any man who lacks these qualities is shortsighted to the point of blindness. He forgets the cleansing of his long-past sins. [10]†Be solicitous to make your call and election

---

† 1, 1: *Simeon Peter, servant and apostle of Jesus Christ:* on the question of authorship of 2 Peter, see the Introduction. *To those who have been given a faith . . . Jesus Christ:* it is *the justifying power* of Jesus, *God and Savior,* which causes the faith of the apostles and of succeeding believers to be one and the same.

1, 3f: Christian life in its fullness is a gift of divine power to those who are called. This power effects in them a knowledge of Christ and fulfills the divine promises in their regard, making them sharers of the divine nature, safe from a *world corrupted by lust;* cf 1, 2.8; 3, 18; Jn 17, 22; Rom 8, 14-17; 1 Jn 3, 2.

1, 5-9: Note the climactic gradation of qualities, beginning with faith and leading to the fullness of Christian life which is love (5-7); cf Rom 5, 3ff; 10, 14f. Their fruit is the knowledge of Christ (v 8) referred to in 1, 3; their absence is spiritual blindness (v 9).

1, 10f: Perseverance in the Christian vocation is the best preventative against losing it and the safest provision for attaining its goal, entrance *into the everlasting kingdom,* identified here as the *kingdom of our Lord and Savior Jesus Christ.*

1/3: 2 Cor 4, 6; 1 Pt 2, 9.
4: 2 Cor 7, 1; 1 Jn 2, 15.
5: Gal 5, 22f.
7: Gal 6, 10.
9: 1 Jn 2, 9.11.

permanent, brothers; surely those who do so will never be lost. [11]On the contrary, your entry into the everlasting kingdom of our Lord and Savior Jesus Christ will be richly provided for.

Witness to Christ

[12†]I intend to recall these things to you constantly, even though you already understand and are firmly rooted in the truth you possess. [13]I consider it my duty, as long as I live, to prompt you with this reminder. [14*]I know, by the indications our Lord Jesus Christ has given me, how close is the day when I must fold my tent. [15]I shall press to have you recall these things frequently after my departure. [16*]It was not by way of cleverly concocted myths that we taught you about the coming in power of our Lord Jesus Christ, [17*]for we were eyewitnesses of his sovereign majesty. He received glory and praise from God the Father when that unique declaration came to him out of the majestic splendor: "This is my beloved Son, on whom my favor rests." [18]We ourselves heard this said from heaven while we were in his company on the holy mountain. [19*]Besides, we possess the prophetic message as something altogether reliable. Keep your attention closely fixed on it, as you would on a lamp shining in a dark place until the first streaks of dawn appear and the morning star rises in your hearts.

The Nature of Prophecy

[20]First you must understand this: there is no prophecy contained in Scripture which is a personal interpretation. [21]Prophecy has never been put forward by man's willing it. It is rather that men impelled by the Holy Spirit have spoken under God's influence.

False Teachers

2 [1*†]IN times past there were false prophets among God's people, and among you also there will be false teachers who will smuggle in pernicious heresies. They will go so far as to deny the Master who acquired them for his own, thereby bringing on themselves swift disaster. [2*]Their lustful ways will lure many away. Through them, the true way will be made subject to contempt.

Warning from the Past

[3*†]They will deceive you with fabricated tales, in a spirit of greed. Their condemnation has not lain idle all this time, however; their destruction is not asleep. [4*†]Did God spare even the angels who sinned? He did not! He held them captive in Tartarus—consigned them to pits of darkness, to be guarded until judgment. [5*†]Nor did he spare the ancient world—even

though he preserved Noah as a preacher of holiness, with seven others, when he brought down the flood on that godless earth. [6*†]He blanketed the cities of Sodom and Gomorrah in ashes and condemned them to destruction, thereby showing what would happen in the future to the godless. [7]He did deliver Lot, however, a just man oppressed by the conduct of men unprincipled in their lusts. [8](Day after day that just one, good as he was, felt himself tormented by seeing and hearing about the lawless deeds of those among whom he lived.) [9*]The Lord, indeed, knows how to rescue devout men from trial, and how to continue the punishment of the wicked up to the day of judgment.

Punishment of Evildoers

[10*†]He knows, especially, how to treat those who live for the flesh in their desire for whatever corrupts,

---

† 1, 12-19: Alive to his responsibility even when faced with the proximity of death, the apostle bequeaths to his readers a perpetual reminder of the teachings of the faith (12-15) and of the certainty of Christ's coming in power (v 16). As motives for belief in the parousia, he offers the prophetic message of Scripture and also his own testimony as eyewitness to the transfiguration of Christ in glory and majesty, confirmed by the voice of God the Father (18-22). These serve as a shining light amid the darkness to those preparing for the parousia. The value of continual reminders and repeated instructions, for preserving the truths of the faith and the historic facts surrounding them, is insisted on in the New Testament (12f.15; 3, 1f; 1 Cor 11, 2; 15, 1).

2, 1-22: This account of the false teachers and evildoers and the dire punishments which threaten them finds a parallel in Jude 4-13. The present passage is generally considered by scholars to be dependent on Jude, despite modifications and omissions.

2, 1ff: the pattern of false teaching in the Old Testament recurs in apostolic times among the people of the New, and will be repeated (10-22) before the final cataclysm at the end of the world (Mt 24, 11). It is accompanied by denial of faith in Christ, immorality, scandal, and contempt for the way of salvation.

2, 3-9: *Their condemnation . . . ; their destruction is not asleep:* the interventions of the divine chastisement are exemplified in the case of the rebellious angels (v 4; Jude 6), the deluge (v 6; Jude 7), and the destruction of Sodom and Gomorrah.

2, 4: *Tartarus:* a term borrowed from Greek mythology to indicate the infernal regions, *pits of darkness* where sinners, especially fallen angels, are punished.

2, 5: The deluge is described as marking the end of *the ancient world* and the beginning of the new. Noah, the preacher of holiness, is the type of new life initiated through Christian baptism and made conformable to God's sanctity (1 Pt 3, 20f).

2, 6: The destruction of the cities of Sodom and Gomorrah stands for all time as a warning of punishment of sin. The association of this catastrophe with that of the deluge is also found in Wisdom 10, 4ff and in Christ's prediction concerning the signs of the coming of the kingdom of God (Lk 17, 26-29).

2, 10-22: These verses portray in detail the conduct of the false teachers. They are slaves of the flesh and its passions; they despise true sovereignty, that of Christ and his church (v 10); they even revile the *celestial beings* considered to be fallen angels (cf 2, 4) in comparison to the angels in 2, 11. Abusive in their ignorance, imitating brute animals in their irrationality, decadent in their instincts, they deserve, like animals, *to be caught and destroyed* (v 12). In their day-long revelries they seduce others (v 13), even those who *have just come free of a life of errors* (v 18), making their new condition of return to corruption and rejection of Christ worse than the first (18-22). In

---

✱
14: Is 38, 12; Jn 21, 18f.
16: Jn 1, 14.
17: Ps 2, 7; Mt 17, 4-6.
19: Lk 1, 78; Rv 2, 28.
2/1: Mt 24, 11; 1 Tm 4, 1; Jude 4.
2: Is 52, 5.

3: Rom 16, 18; 1 Thes 2, 5.
4: Jude 6.
5: Gn 8, 18; Heb 11, 7.
6: Gn 19, 25; Jude 7.
9: 1 Cor 10, 13; Rv 3, 10.
10: Jude 8.

and who despise authority. These bold and arrogant men have no qualms whatever about reviling celestial beings, **11*** on whom angels, though greater than men in strength and power, pass no opprobrious sentence in the Lord's presence. **12*** These men pour abuse on things of which they are ignorant. They act like creatures of instinct, brute animals born to be caught and destroyed. Because of their decadence they too will be destroyed, suffering the reward of their wickedness. **13*** Thinking daytime revelry a delight, they are stain and defilement as they share your feasts in a spirit of seduction. **14** Constantly on the lookout for a woman, theirs is a never-ending search for sin. They lure the weaker types. Their hearts are trained in greed. An accursed lot are they! **15*** They have abandoned the straight road and wander off on the path taken by Balaam, son of Beor. He was a man attracted to dishonest gain, **16*** but he was rebuked for his evil-doing. A mute beast spoke with a human voice to restrain the prophet's madness.

17* These men are waterless springs, mists whipped by the gale. The darkest gloom has been reserved for them. **18*** They talk empty bombast while baiting their hooks with passion, with the lustful ways of the flesh, to catch those who have just come free of a life of errors. **19*** They promise them freedom though they themselves are slaves of corruption—for surely anyone is the slave of that by which he has been overcome. **20*** When men have fled a polluted world by recognizing the Lord and Savior Jesus Christ, and then are caught up and overcome in pollution once more, their last condition is worse than their first. **21*** It would have been better for them not to have recognized the road to holiness than to have turned their backs on the holy law handed on to them, once they had known it. **22*** How well the proverb fits them: "The dog returns to its vomit," and, "A sow bathes by wallowing in the mire."

Christt Will Come in Judgment

3 **1†** I am writing you this second letter, dear friends, intending them both as reminders urging you to sincerity of outlook. **2*** Recall the teaching delivered long ago by the holy prophets, as well as the new command of the Lord and Savior preached to you by the apostles.

3* Note this first of all: in the last days, mocking, sneering men who are ruled by their passions will arrive on the scene. **4*†** They will ask: "Where is that promised coming of his? Our forefathers have been

laid to rest, but everything stays just as it was when the world was created." **5*†** In believing this, they do not take into account that of old there were heavens and an earth drawn out of the waters and standing between the waters, all brought into being by the word of God. **6*** By water that world was then destroyed; it was overwhelmed by the deluge. **7*** The present heavens and earth are reserved by God's word for fire; they are kept for the day of judgment, the day when godless men will be destroyed.

8* This point must not be overlooked, dear friends. In the Lord's eyes, one day is as a thousand years and a thousand years are as a day. **9*†** The Lord does not delay in keeping his promise—though some consider it "delay." Rather, he shows you generous patience, since he wants none to perish but all to come to repentance. **10*** The day of the Lord will come like a thief, and on that day the heavens will vanish with a roar; the elements will be destroyed by fire, and the earth and all its deeds will be made manifest.

11*† Since everything is to be destroyed in this way, what sort of men must you not be! How holy in your conduct and devotion, **12*†** looking for the coming of the day of God and trying to hasten it! Because of it, the heavens will be destroyed in flames and the ele-

---

†
their greed they abandon righteousness, like Balaam of old, for the sake of material gain (14ff).

3, 1-4: The false teachers not only flout Christian morality (cf Jude 18f), they also deny the second coming of Christ and eternal retribution. They seek to justify their licentiousness, arguing that the promised return of Christ has not been realized and the world is the same, no better than it was before (3f). The author wishes to strengthen the faithful against this pernicious error by reminding them of the instruction in his letters (1 and 2 Peter), and of the teaching of the prophets and of Christ, conveyed through the apostles (1f;) cf 1 Pt 1, 10ff, 16-21; Eph 2, 20.

3, 4: *Our forefathers have been laid to rest:* the death of the apostolic fathers indicates a date after that time for the composition of 2 Peter.

3, 5-10: The scoffers' objection (v 4) is refuted by showing that the power of God's word, which called the world into being, also destroyed it by the waters of a flood, and will destroy it again by fire on the day of judgment (5ff). The delay of the Lord is not an indication of failure to fulfill his word but rather of his *generous patience* in giving time for repentance before the final judgment (8ff; 1 Thes 5, 2). The new Testament writers used the deluge as a figure of eschatological events; cf Mt 24, 37ff; Lk 17, 26f. The effect of Christian baptism is compared to the radical action of fire which purifies metal of dross. For Old Testament examples of God's judgment described by the imagery of fire see Is 66, 15f; Mi 1, 4; Dn 7, 9ff; Zep 1, 18; 3, 8; Ps 97, 3. Acceptance of the truths of faith does not require acceptance of the popular imagery used to describe them.

3, 9: *He shows you generous patience:* the longsuffering of God is a sign of his mercy toward man, who is so slow to change. God wills all men to be saved and to come to the knowledge of the truth; cf Wis 11, 23-26; Ez 18, 23; 33, 11; Rom 11, 32; 1 Tm 2, 4.

3, 11-15: The coming of Christ and the judgment of the world are the doctrinal bases here and elsewhere in the New Testament for the moral exhortation to preparedness through vigilance and a virtuous life (Mt 24, 42.51; Lk 12, 40; 1 Thes 5, 1-11; Jude 20f).

3, 12: *Trying to hasten it:* i. e., the day of God, by advancing his kingdom through holiness of life; cf v 9.

---

*

11: Jude 9.
12: Ps 49, 13-15; Jude 10.
13: Jude 12.
15: Nm 22, 2; Jude 4.
16: Nm 22, 28-33.
17: Jude 12f.
18: Jude 16.
19: Jn 8, 34; Rom 6, 16f.
20: Mt 12, 45.
21: Ez 3, 20.
22: Prv 26, 11.
3/2: Jude 17.

3: 1 Tm 4, 1; Jude 18.
4: Is 5, 19.
5: Gn 1, 2.6.8; Ps 24, 2.
6: Gn 7, 21.
7: Is 51, 6; Mt 3, 12.
8: Ps 90, 4.
9: Ez 18, 23; 1 Tm 2, 4.
10: Is 66, 15f;
    Mt 24, 29.43;
    1 Thes 5, 2f.
11: Acts 3, 19f.
12: Is 34, 4; Heb 12, 27.

ments will melt away in a blaze. [13]†What we await are new heavens and a new earth where, according to his promise, the justice of God will reside.

Preparation for the Coming

[14]So, beloved, while waiting for this, make every effort to be found without stain or defilement, and at peace in his sight. [15]*†Consider that our Lord's patience is directed toward salvation. Paul, our beloved brother, wrote you this in the spirit of wisdom that is his, [16]dealing with these matters as he does in all his letters. There are certain passages in them hard to understand. The ignorant and the unstable distort them (just as they do the rest of Scripture) to their own ruin.

[17]*†You are forewarned, beloved brothers. Be on your guard lest you be led astray by the error of the wicked, and forfeit the security you enjoy. [18]*Grow rather in grace, and in the knowledge of our Lord and Savior Jesus Christ. Glory be to him now and to the day of eternity! Amen.

---

† 3, 13: *New heavens and a new earth:* the fulfillment of the divine promises after the day of judgment will have passed and the universe will be transformed by the reign of perfect justice; cf Is 65, 17; 66, 22; Acts 3, 21; Rom 8, 19ff; Rv 21, 1.

3, 15f: The teachings of this epistle—the Lord's salvific will toward mankind (Rom 2, 4; 9, 22f; 1 Cor 1, 7f); preparedness for the judgment (Eph 1, 4-14; 4, 30; 5, 5.14ff; Col 1, 22f); the coming of Christ (1 Thes 4, 16f; 1 Cor 15, 23.52)—are further confirmed by the letters of Paul. He is called here *our beloved brother,* i. e., a fellow apostle of Peter, after whom this letter is named.

The rest of Scripture: the sacred writings inspired by the Holy Spirit to regulate the religious life of the people. The writings of Paul are thus recognized as having the same quality and authority as the books of the Old Testament.

3, 17f: To avoid the danger of error and loss of security, the faithful are exhorted to persevere in the principles of the Christian life through growth *in the knowledge* of Christ. The final doxology recalls that of 1 Pt 4, 11.

---

* 13: Is 65, 17; 66, 22,   17: Mk 13, 5; Heb 2, 1.
      Rom 8, 21; Rv 21, 1.27.   18: Rom 16, 27.
   15: Rom 8, 19; Jude 24.

The First Epistle of John

Introduction

Early Christian tradition attributed this letter to John the apostle. Subsequently, the majority of scholars have concluded, from its resemblance to the fourth gospel in style, vocabulary, and ideas, that one author actually was responsible for both works. These resemblances are not so compelling as absolutely to exclude the possibility of separate authors, as some critics have shown. But it is very probable that the person who composed the fourth gospel also wrote 1 John. On the identity of this author, see the Introduction to the gospel itself.

The opening of the epistle does not state to whom it is addressed, but the data indicate that it was written to specific Christian communities some of whose members were advocating false doctrines (2, 18f.26; 3, 7). These errors are here recognized and rejected (4, 4); although their advocates have left the community (2, 19), the threat posed by them remains (3, 11). They have refused to acknowledge that Jesus is the Christ (2, 22) the Son of God (2, 23) who came into the world as true man (4, 2). They are difficult people to deal with, claiming special knowledge of God but disregarding the divine commandments (2, 4), particularly the commandment of love of neighbor (4, 8), and refusing to accept faith in Christ as the source of sanctification (1, 6; 2, 6.9). Thus they are denying the redemptive value of Jesus' death (5, 6). Scholars generally agree that the group so stigmatized had adopted some form of Gnosticism, but as yet it has not been identified with any specific body of heretical teaching.

The epistle is of particular value for its declaration of the humanity and divinity of Christ as apostolic teaching (1, 1-4), and for its development of the intrinsic connection between Christian moral conduct and Christian doctrine. Although the author recognizes that Christian doctrine presents intangible mysteries of faith about Christ, he insists that the concrete Christian life brings to light the deeper realities of the gospel. The epistle is generally held to date at the same time as the fourth gospel, c 90-100 A. D.

Prologue

1 1*† THIS IS WHAT we proclaim to you:
what was from the beginning,
what we have heard,
what we have seen with our eyes,
what we have looked upon
and our hands have touched—
we speak of the word of life.
2* (This life became visible;
we have seen and bear witness to it,
and we proclaim to you the eternal life
that was present to the Father
and became visible to us.)
3* What we have seen and heard
we proclaim in turn to you
so that you may share life with us.
This fellowship of ours is with the Father
and with his Son, Jesus Christ.
4* Indeed, our purpose in writing you this
is that our joy may be complete.

The Light of God

5† Here, then, is the message
we have heard from him
and announce to you:
that God is light;
in him there is no darkness.

Claims of False Teachers

6* If we say, "We have fellowship with him,"
while continuing to walk in darkness,
we are liars and do not act in truth.
7* But if we walk in light,
as he is in the light,
we have fellowship with one another,
and the blood of his Son Jesus cleanses us
from all sin.

---

† 1, 1-4: There is a striking parallel between this prologue and that of the gospel of John (1, 1-16). The substance of the apostles' teaching is their experience of the historic Christ and the witness they bear to him (v 1; cf Jn 1, 7f.15). He is *the word of life* (v 1; cf Jn 1, 4), *eternal life that was present to the Father and became visible* to the apostles (v 2; cf Jn 1, 1.14). The purpose of their teaching is to share that *life,* called *fellowship . . . with the Father and with his Son Jesus Christ,* with those who receive their witness (v 3; Jn 1, 14.16), and thus to make the joy of the apostles complete (v 4).

1, 5ff: *Light* is to be understood here as truth and goodness; *darkness,* as error and depravity; cf Jn 3, 19ff; 17, 17; Eph 5, 8f; 1 Thes 5, 5. To walk in light or darkness is to live according to truth or error, not merely intellectual but moral as well; that is, in accordance with, or contrary to, God's will. Thus, fellowship with God (v 6) and with one another (v 7) consists in a life according to truth and goodness as found in God and in Christ, their source. This is made possible through the redemptive work of Christ, who cleanses us from our sins; cf Jn 8, 12; 12, 35f.

❀
1/1: 2, 13; Jn 1, 1.14;
　　 20, 20.25.27.
　2: Jn 15, 27; 17, 5.
　3: Jn 17, 21; Acts 4, 20.
　4: Jn 15, 11; 2 Jn 12.

6: Jn 12, 35.
7: Mt 26, 28; Rom 3, 24f;
　 Heb 9, 14; 1 Pt 1, 19;
　 Rv 1, 5.

8*† If we say, "We are free of the guilt of sin,"
we deceive ourselves; the truth is not to be
    found in us.

9* But if we acknowledge our sins,
he who is just can be trusted
to forgive our sins
and cleanse us from every wrong.

10* If we say, "We have never sinned,"
we make him a liar
and his word finds no place in us.

2   **1***† MY LITTLE ONES,
I am writing this to keep you from sin.
But if anyone should sin,
we have, in the presence of the Father,
Jesus Christ, an intercessor who is just.

2* He is an offering for our sins,
and not for our sins only,
but for those of the whole world.

Keeping the Commandments

3*† The way we can be sure of our knowledge
    of him
is to keep his commandments.

4* The man who claims, "I have known him,"
without keeping his commandments,
is a liar; in such a one there is no truth.

5* But whoever keeps his word,
truly has the love of God been made perfect
    in him.
The way we can be sure we are in union
    with him

6 is for the man who claims to abide in him
to conduct himself just as he did.

7*† Dearly beloved,
it is no new commandment that I write to
    you,
but an old one which you had from the
    start.
The commandment, now old, is the word
    you have already heard.

8* On second thought, the commandment that
    I write you is new,
as it is realized in him and you,
for the darkness is over
and the real light begins to shine.

9* The man who claims to be in light,
hating his brother all the while,
is in darkness even now.

10* The man who continues in the light
    is the one who loves his brother;
there is nothing in him to cause a fall.

11 But the man who hates his brother is in
    darkness.
He walks in shadows,
not knowing where he is going,
since the dark has blinded his eyes.

Members of the Community

12*† Little ones, I address you,
for through his Name your sins have been
    forgiven.

13* Fathers, I address you,
for you have known him who is from the
    beginning.
Young men, I address you,
for you have conquered the evil one.

14 I address you, children,
for you have known the Father.
I address you, fathers,
for you have known him who is from the
    beginning.
I address you, young men,
for you are strong,
and the word of God remains in you,
and you have conquered the evil one.

---

† 1, 8ff: One is never entirely free from sin. To claim the contrary would be self-deception and would even contradict divine revelation (v 10; cf 1 Kgs 8, 46; Prv 24, 16). There is the continual possibility of sin's recurrence. Forgiveness and deliverance from sin through Christ are assured provided the sin is acknowledged through repentance. Such acknowledgment refers probably to a rite of confession; cf Mt 16, 19; 18, 18; Jn 20, 23; Jas 5, 16.

2, 1f: Believers are here addressed as *little ones* (v 1), elsewhere as *children* (2, 18) or *dearly beloved* (2, 7), to express the pastoral love and devotion of the apostles toward those entrusted to their care; cf Jn 13, 33; 21, 5; 1 Cor 4, 15; Gal 4, 19. After exhorting Christians to keep free from sin, the author returns to the thought of 1, 9: the assurance of forgiveness of sin through the power of Christ's intercession. *He is an offering for our sins:* literally, "propitiation," i. e., a permanent office exercised by Christ on behalf of sinners.

2, 3-6: *The way we can be sure of our knowledge . . . commandments:* not mere intellectual knowledge of Christ but a life conformable to the divine will revealed to mankind through his teaching and example (v 6; cf Jn 14, 21-24; 17, 3). Thus *love of God is made perfect* (v 5) and those who live in this manner abide in Christ (v 6) and achieve union with him; cf 3, 2f. Disparity between moral life and doctrinal teaching was the error of the Gnostics.

2, 7-11: The law of fraternal charity is based on human nature itself and is confirmed by the divine positive command to the Israelites (Lv 19, 18). Through Christ, however, a new and higher relationship with neighbor (vv 8.10) is achieved as a result of the new relationship with the Father: that of sons of God (cf Jn 1, 12) and brothers of Christ (Lk 8.21). Note here and elsewhere the characteristic Johannine polemic in which a positive assertion is further emphasized by the negative statement of its opposite (9ff).

2, 12-17: The Christian community, which has experienced the grace of God through forgiveness of sin and knowledge of Christ, i. e., practice of the faith, is thereby armed against *the evil one* and protected from the world with its allurements; cf 3, 7-10; 5, 18f.

---

*
   8: 2 Chr 6, 36; Prv 20, 9.   7: 3, 11; Dt 6, 5;
   9: Prv 28, 13; Jas 5, 16.   Mt 22, 37-40.
   10: Jn 5, 38.   8: Jn 1, 5; 13, 34;
   2/1: Jn 14, 16; Heb 7, 25.   Rom 13, 12.
     2: 4, 10.   9: Jn 8, 12.
     3: Jn 14, 15; 15, 10.   10: Eccl 2, 14; Jn 11, 10.
     4: 4, 20.   12: 1 Cor 6, 11.
     5: Jn 14, 23.   13: 1, 1; Jn 1, 1.

Against the World

15✻† Have no love for the world,
nor the things that the world affords.
If anyone loves the world,
the Father's love has no place in him,

16† for nothing that the world affords
comes from the Father.
Carnal allurements,
enticements for the eye,
the life of empty show—
all these are from the world.

17✻ And the world with its seductions is passing
away
but the man who does God's will
endures forever.

Against Antichrists

18✻† Children, it is the final hour;
just as you heard that the antichrist was
coming,
so now many such antichrists have
appeared.
This makes us certain that it is the final
hour.

19† It was from our ranks that they took their
leave—
not that they really belonged to us;
for if they had belonged to us,
they would have stayed with us.
It only served to show that none of them
was ours.

20✻† But you have the anointing that comes from
the Holy One,
so that all knowledge is yours.

21✻ My reason for having written you
is not that you do not know the truth
but that you do,
and that no lie has anything in common
with the truth.

22✻† Who is the liar?
He who denies that Jesus is the Christ.
He is the antichrist,
denying the Father and the Son.

23✻ Anyone who denies the Son
has no claim on the Father,
but he who acknowledges the Son
can claim the Father as well.

Life for God's Anointed

24✻ As for you,
let what you heard from the beginning
remain in your hearts.

If what you heard from the beginning
does remain in your hearts,
then you in turn will remain in the Son and
in the Father.

25✻† He himself made us a promise
and the promise is no less than this:
eternal life.

26 I have written you these things
about those who try to deceive you.

27 As for you,
the anointing you received from him
remains in your hearts.
This means you have no need
for anyone to teach you.
Rather, as his anointing teaches you about
all things
and is true—free from any lie—
remain in him
as that anointing taught you.

Children of God

28† Remain in him now, little ones,
so that, when he reveals himself,

---

† 2, 15: *The world:* men subject to sin and therefore hostile toward God. Love of the world and love of God are mutually exclusive; cf Jas 4, 4.

2, 16: *Carnal allurements:* inordinate desire for sensuality (cf Eph 2, 3; 1 Pt 2, 11; 2 Pt 2, 10.18); *enticements for the eye:* avarice; the eyes are regarded as the windows of the soul (cf Jb 31, 1; Ez 23, 12-17; Mt 5, 27ff); *the life of empty show:* ostentation, pride and arrogance, independence of God, in the temporal existence of man.

2, 18: *The final hour:* the time between the first and second coming of Christ. *The antichrist:* the opponent or adversary of Christ; one who denies *the Father and the Son* (v 22). The term is found in 1 and 2 John; cf Mt 24, 23f; Mk 3, 21f. Paul calls him *the man of lawlessness, that son of perdition and adversary* (2 Thes 2, 3.8; cf Rv 13; 17, 7-14). Matthew, Mark, and Revelation seem to refer to a collectivity of persons. *Many such antichrists have appeared:* the reference is to all the false teachers who afflict the church in *the final hour.* The early Christian community was familiar with this doctrine and expected an early return or second coming of Christ.

2, 19: *If they had belonged to us, . . . stayed with us:* the antichrists, apostate teachers, have always lacked the true spirit of the community of God's people.

2, 20f.27: *The anointing that comes from the Holy One:* the Spirit of God which the faithful received. It preserves them against the errors of the antichrists. The *Holy One* may refer to Christ, whose name (*Christos*, "anointed one") and mission are in a real sense shared by his followers. *All knowledge is yours:* one of the gifts of the Holy Spirit (Is 11, 2) by which the faithful could distinguish truth from falsehood (Jn 16, 13ff). The author's purpose is to reassure rather than instruct (v 21), because his readers have already received knowledge through their anointing (v 27).

2, 22f: To deny the Son is to deny the Father since only in and through the Son has God fully revealed his fatherhood; cf Mt 11, 27; Lk 10, 22; Jn 5, 23; 10, 30; Jn 14, 7.9.

2, 25: *The promise is no less than this: eternal life:* the only passage of the Johannine writings in which *eternal life* has the exclusively eschatological sense of the life of glory, the object of Christian hope and striving. Elsewhere the term is invariably used of the present life of grace leading to glory.

2, 28f: A renewed exhortation to Christians to *remain* in Christ, i. e., to live the Christ-life and thus enjoy the assur-

---

✻

15: Rom 8, 7f; Jas 4, 4;
    2 Pt 1, 4.
17: Is 40, 8; Mt 7, 21;
    1 Cor 7, 31; 1 Pt 4, 2.
18: 1 Tm 4, 1.
20: Jn 14, 26.

21: 3, 19; 2 Pt 1, 12.
22: 2 Thes 2, 4.
23: Jn 14, 7-9.
24: Jn 14, 23.
25: Jn 5, 24; 10, 28; 17, 2.

we may be fully confident
and not retreat in shame at his coming.

29 If you consider the holiness that is his,
you can be sure that everyone who acts in holiness
has been begotten by him.

3 **1***† SEE WHAT LOVE the Father has bestowed on us
in letting us be called children of God!
Yet that is what we are.
The reason the world does not recognize us
is that it never recognized the Son.

2* Dearly beloved,
we are God's children now;
what we shall later be has not yet come to light.
We know that when it comes to light
we shall be like him,
for we shall see him as he is.

3* Everyone who has this hope based on him
keeps himself pure, as he is pure.

Avoiding Sin

4† Everyone who sins acts lawlessly,
for sin is lawlessness.

5* You know well that the reason he revealed himself
was to take away sins;
in him there is nothing sinful.

6 The man who remains in him does not sin.
The man who sins has not seen him
or known him.

7 Little ones,
let no one deceive you;
the man who acts in holiness is holy indeed,
even as the Son is holy.

8* The man who sins belongs to the devil,
because the devil is a sinner from the beginning.
It was to destroy the devil's works
that the Son of God revealed himself.

9 No one begotten of God acts sinfully
because he remains of God's stock;
he cannot sin
because he is begotten of God.

10 That is the way to see who are God's children,
and who are the devil's.
No one whose actions are unholy belongs to God,
nor anyone who fails to love his brother.

Keeping the Commandments

11*† This, remember, is the message
you heard from the beginning:
we should love one another.

12* We should not follow the example of Cain
who belonged to the evil one
and killed his brother.
Why did he kill him?
Because his own deeds were wicked
while his brother's were just.

13* No need, then, brothers, to be surprised
if the world hates you.

14* That we have passed from death to life we know
because we love the brothers.
The man who does not love is among the living dead.

15* Anyone who hates his brother is a murderer,
and you know that eternal life
abides in no murderer's heart.

16* The way we came to understand love
was that he laid down his life for us;
we too must lay down our lives for our brothers.

17* I ask you, how can God's love survive in a man
who has enough of this world's goods
yet closes his heart to his brother
when he sees him in need?

18* Little children,
let us love in deed and in truth
and not merely talk about it.

19 This is our way of knowing we are committed to the truth
and are at peace before him

❋ 3/1: Jn 1, 12; 15, 21; 17, 25; Eph 1, 5.
2: Phil 3, 21.
3: 2, 6.
5: Is 53, 9; Jn 1, 29; 8, 46; 1 Pt 2, 22.
8: Jn 8, 44; 12, 31f.
11: 2, 7; Jn 13, 34; 15, 12.17.
12: Gn 4, 8; Jude 11.
13: Mt 24, 9; Jn 15, 18; 17, 14.
14: Lv 19, 17; Jn 5, 24.
15: Jn 8, 44.
16: 2, 6; Mt 20, 28; Jn 10, 11; 15, 13.
17: Dt 15, 7.11; Jas 2, 15f.
18: Jas 1, 22.

---

† ance of acceptance by him at his second coming. The verses prepare them for the transition to the theme of their divine sonship and the duties flowing from it: *Everyone who acts in holiness has been begotten by him.*

3, 1ff: The greatest proof of God's love for men is the gift of his Son, through whom they are not only called, but are in reality, God's sons; cf Jn 3, 16. This condition is true of their present life and, in the fullest sense, of the life to come when the divine filiation will result in their being like God and in seeing him *as he is*. They prepare for it by leading a life like that of God's Son, keeping themselves *pure, as he is pure* (v 3). Since the world never recognized the Father in the Son, neither will it recognize those who are children of the Father.

3, 4-10: The two contrary states, of sin and of holiness, are shown here in their intrinsic opposition. Release from sin establishes union and fellowship with Christ; adherence to sin, fellowship with the devil, who is *a sinner from the beginning*. Thus virtue and sin are the two opposite characteristics for distinguishing the children of God from the children of the devil.

3, 4: *Lawlessness:* hostility toward God and rejection of Christ, the standard of holiness.

3, 11-24: The virtue of charity, even to the point of giving up one's life for his neighbor as Christ did (v 16), is the fulfillment of the commandments (22ff), the guarantee of life and union with God through the presence of the Spirit (21.24).

20 no matter what our consciences may charge
     us with;
for God is greater than our hearts
and all is known to him.

21 Beloved,
if our consciences have nothing to charge
     us with,
we can be sure that God is with us

22* and that we will receive at his hands
     whatever we ask.
Why? Because we are keeping his
     commandments
and doing what is pleasing in his sight.

23* His commandment is this:
we are to believe in the name of his Son,
     Jesus Christ,
and are to love one another as he
     commanded us.

24* Those who keep his commandments
     remain in him
and he in them.
And this is how we know that he remains
     in us:
from the Spirit that he gave us.

Testing the Spirits

4 **1***† BELOVED,
do not trust every spirit,
but put the spirits to a test
to see if they belong to God,
because many false prophets have
     appeared in the world.

2* This is how you can recognize God's Spirit:
every spirit that acknowledges Jesus Christ
     come in the flesh
belongs to God,

3* while every spirit that fails to acknowledge
     him
does not belong to God.
Such is the spirit of the antichrist
which, as you have heard, is to come;
in fact, it is in the world already.

4 You are of God, you little ones,
and thus you have conquered the false
     prophets.
For there is One greater in you
than there is in the world.

5* Those others belong to the world;
that is why theirs is the language of the
     world
and why the world listens to them.

6* We belong to God
and anyone who has knowledge of God
     gives us a hearing,

while anyone who is not of God refuses to
     hear us.
Thus do we distinguish the spirit of truth
from the spirit of deception.

God's Love and Ours

7† Beloved,
let us love one another
because love is of God;
everyone who loves is begotten of God
and has knowledge of God.

8 The man without love has known nothing
     of God,
for God is love.

9*† God's love was revealed in our midst in this
     way:
he sent his only Son to the world
that we might have life through him.

10*† Love, then, consists in this:
not that we have loved God,
but that he has loved us
and has sent his Son as an offering for our
     sins.

11† Beloved,
if God has loved us so,
we must have the same love for one
     another.

12* No one has ever seen God.
Yet if we love one another
God dwells in us,
and his love is brought to perfection in us.

13 The way we know we remain in him
and he in us
is that he has given us of his Spirit.

---

† 4, 1-6: Delusion and deception are invariably possible in matters of spiritual phenomena. Discernment between a true and false spirit of prophecy depends on acceptance or rejection of sound doctrine; cf 1 Cor 12, 3.10. Thus, acknowledgment or denial of the central truth of Christianity, the incarnation of Jesus Christ, the Son of God, is proof of whether one belongs to God or to antichrist (1ff). A power greater than that of the world abides in those who belong to God and who heed the teaching of the apostles (2.6). It conquers the false prophets (v 4) who belong to the world, speak its language and receive its attention (v 5; cf 2, 12-17.22-27).

4, 7-21: These verses explain the nature of love as revealed by God and accepted by man through faith.

4, 7f: *Love is of God:* therefore one who loves shows that he is begotten of God. *God is love:* love is his very being. To love God is to know him and to share his life.

4, 9: *God's love . . . in this way:* the revelation of God's being consists in sending the Son of his love *to the world* as our Savior (cf v 14) that *we might have life through him;* cf Jn 3, 16.

4, 10: *Love . . . consists in this: not that we have loved God but that he has loved us:* man has not merited God's love. It has been given freely and its value consists in sharing and continuing that love which is in God; cf v 19. *He . . . has sent his Son as an offering for our sins:* an act of his mercy and forgiveness manifested through the death of Christ; cf 2, 2. This is the motive of our love for one another.

4, 11f: Through love for one another we can be certain that *God dwells in us* and brings *his love . . . to perfection* in us. Thus we are able to "see," i. e., to know, the invisible God.

---

*
22: 5, 15; Mt 7, 7-11;   3: 2, 22.
    21, 22; Jn 14, 13f.   5: Jn 15, 19.
23: Jn 13, 34; 15, 17.   6: Jn 8, 47; 10, 16.
24: 4, 13; Jn 14, 21-23.   9: Jn 3, 16.
4/1: 2, 18; Mt 24, 24.   10: Rom 5, 8.
  2: 1 Cor 12, 3;   12: Jn 1, 18; 1 Tm 6, 16.
     1 Thes 5, 21.

14 We have seen for ourselves, and can testify,
that the Father has sent the Son as savior
of the world.

15 When anyone acknowledges that Jesus is
the Son of God,
God dwells in him
and he in God.

16 We have come to know and to believe
in the love God has for us.

God is love,
and he who abides in love
abides in God,
and God in him.

17* Our love is brought to perfection in this,
that we should have confidence on the day
of judgment;
for our relation to this world is just like his.

18 Love has no room for fear;
rather, perfect love casts out all fear.
And since fear has to do with punishment,
love is not yet perfect in one who is afraid.

19 We, for our part, love
because he first loved us.

20* If anyone says, "My love is fixed on God,"
yet hates his brother,
he is a liar.
One who has no love for the brother he has
seen
cannot love the God he has not seen.

21* The commandment we have from him is
this:
whoever loves God must also love his
brother.

5 1*† EVERYONE WHO BELIEVES that Jesus is the
Christ
has been begotten of God.
Now, everyone who loves the father
loves the child he has begotten.

2 We can be sure that we love God's children
when we love God
and do what he has commanded.

3* The love of God consists in this:
that we keep his commandments—
and his commandments are not
burdensome.

4* Everyone begotten of God conquers the
world,
and the power that has conquered the
world
is this faith of ours.

5* Who, then, is conqueror of the world?
The one who believes that Jesus is the Son
of God.

6*† Jesus Christ it is who came through water
and blood—
not in water only,
but in water and in blood.
It is the Spirit who testifies to this,
and the Spirit is truth.

7*† Thus there are three that testify,
8 the Spirit and the water and the blood—
and these three are of one accord.

9* Do we not accept human testimony?
The testimony of God is much greater:
it is the testimony God has given
on his own Son's behalf.

10*† Whoever believes in the Son of God
possesses that testimony within his heart.
Whoever does not believe God
has made God a liar
by refusing to believe in the testimony
he has given on his own Son's behalf.

11*† The testimony is this:
God gave us eternal life,
and this life is in his Son.

12 Whoever possesses the Son
possesses life;
whoever does not possess the Son of God
does not possess life.

13*†I have written this to you to make you realize
that you possess eternal life—you who believe in the
name of the Son of God.

---

† 5, 1-5: To become a child of God it is necessary to believe in
the divine sonship of Jesus Christ, the only-begotten Son of
the Father. It is through him that we receive our sonship. The
proof of love for God consists in keeping his commandments
(cf 2, 3-6; 3, 24), the greatest of which, after love for God, is
love of the brethren, i. e., those begotten of God; cf 4, 21; Mt
22, 37-40; Mk 12, 30f; Lk 10, 27f. Practical faith of this kind
confers a power that conquers the world of evil, even as Christ
overcame the world (Jn 16, 33).

5, 6: *Jesus Christ it is who came through water and blood:*
references to the Father's testimony: *This is my beloved Son*
(Mt 3, 17) when Jesus was baptized in the waters of the Jordan,
and to Jesus' office of Savior through the shedding of his blood
on the cross (Jn 19, 34).

5, 7ff: The testimony to Christ, the Son of God and Savior
(v 5), is confirmed by divine witness, greater by far than the two
legally required human witnesses (Dt 17, 6) to substantiate
truth; cf Jn 8, 17f. There is probably a symbolic reference
here to baptism and the Eucharist whose existence and efficacy,
like that of all the sacraments, derive from the death of Christ;
cf Jn 19, 34.

5, 10: Through man's belief in the divine sonship of Christ,
God dwells in man through Christ. Thus he becomes the witness to this truth. Unbelief in the divine sonship of Jesus means
rejecting the divine testimony, thereby making God the author
of a lie.

5, 11f: By accepting Christ as Son of God through faith, we
receive Christ himself who becomes in us the source of eternal
life.

5, 13: This summary of the epistle recalls the epilogue of
the gospel of John (20, 30f).

✱
17: 2, 28.
20: 2, 4.
21: Jn 13, 34; 14, 15.21;
　　15, 17.
5/1: Jn 8, 42; 1 Pt 1, 23.
3: Jn 14, 15.
4: Jn 16, 33.
5: 1 Cor 15, 57.

6: Jn 15, 26; 19, 34.
7: Jn 5, 32.36; 15, 26.
9: Jn 5, 32.37.
10: Jn 3, 33.
11: 1, 2; Jn 1, 4; 5, 21.26;
　　17, 3.
13: Jn 1, 12; 20. 31.

Prayer for Sinners

14*†We have this confidence in God: that he hears us whenever we ask for anything according to his will. **15**And since we know that he hears us whenever we ask, we know that what we have asked him for is ours. **16***†Anyone who sees his brother sinning, if the sin is not deadly, should petition God, and thus life will be given to the sinner. This is only for those whose sin is not deadly. There is such a thing as a deadly sin; I do not say that one should pray about that. **17**True, all wrongdoing is sin, but not all sin is deadly.

18†We know that no one begotten of God commits sin; rather, God protects the one begotten by him, and so the evil one cannot touch him. **19**We know that we belong to God, while the whole world is under the evil one. **20***We know, too, that the Son of God has come and has given us discernment to recognize the One

who is true. And we are in the One who is true, for we are in his Son Jesus Christ. He is the true God and eternal life.

21My little children, be on your guard against idols.

---

*

14: 3, 22; Mt 7, 7; Jn 14, 13f.
16: Mt 12, 31.
20: Jer 24, 7; Jn 17, 3; Eph 1, 17.

---

†

5, 14f: The intimate relationship between God and those begotten of him creates in his children conformity to the divine will which gives them confident assurance of receiving what they ask for; cf 2, 28; 4, 17; 3, 21f.

5, 16f: The prayer of Christians for their erring brethren is in conformity to the will of God, who in turn will restore life to the sinners. *Deadly sin:* probably apostasy or final impenitence.

5, 18-21: The epistle concludes with the solemn reaffirmation and summary of the great truths contained therein as well as the false doctrines which these truths condemn. There is again the sharp antithesis between, on the one hand, God, his Son, and those begotten of God through faith, and on the other, the evil one and the world of those enslaved by him. The Son reveals the God of truth in himself and in those who accept him. He conquers the evil one, and by dwelling in his followers and giving them eternal life, preserves them from the sin of the world and from the *idols* of false teachings that threaten the Christian community.

The Second Epistle of John

Introduction

The Second and Third Epistles of John are of the same length (probably determined by the practical consideration of the writing space on one piece of papyrus). Each is in the usual letter format, and treats a specific problem. In each, the writer calls himself "the elder"; and their common authorship is further evidenced internally by similarities in style and wording, especially in the introductions and conclusions. The mention in each of an impending visit by the elder to the respective community (2 Jn 12; 3 Jn 14) has led to the suggestion that they were written about the same time and perhaps carried by the same messenger to the two localities, both on the elder's proposed route of travel. The traditionally assigned place and date of composition, Ephesus in the 90's, are plausible.

The identity of the elder is a problem. Certainly, more than age is implied in the use of the title. If the man was simply one of the group of elders or presbyters who were officials in Christian churches by the latter part of the first century (Jas 5, 14; 1 Pt 5, 1; 1 Tm 5, 17), the absence of a proper name that would distinguish him from the other elders is curious. Seemingly, the title "elder" was also applicable to an apostle (1 Pt 1, 5); and it was certainly applicable to the disciple of an apostle, as we learn from Papias and Irenaeus. It is doubtful that the elder who wrote 3 John was an apostle, for he admits that the leader of the community involved in the letter ignores his authority. One can scarcely believe that a member of the Christian community, even a leader, could resist an apostle, especially at this time toward the close of the century, when the Twelve were venerated as the foundation of the church (Rv 21, 14).

On the other hand, the elder is important enough to exercise a certain authority over communities other than his own, to teach authoritatively and brand others as heretical, to send out missionary preachers, etc. The most probable supposition is that the elder was the disciple of an apostle, with a claim to some of the apostolic prestige and authority—a claim not, however, accepted by all. The traditional association with John, son of Zebedee, may mean that the elder was one of John's prominent disciples. Whether or not he is the same disciple who was the fourth evangelist is disputed; see the Introduction to the Gospel according to John.

The Second Epistle is addressed to "a Lady who is elect and to her children." Since the contents of the letter are scarcely appropriate to an individual, scholars assume that the elder was using an accepted literary device by personifying a Christian community as a woman.

Love and truth are the great themes of the letter. The elder encourages the Christians of this community to let their Christianity show forth in their daily lives in two ways: first, by truly adhering to the great commandment of mutual love; and second, by adhering to the truth about Jesus. There is critical need for this admonition because heretical missionaries are about to descend upon the community. The heresy in question is apparently the one referred to in 1 Jn 4, 2—a denial of the reality of the incarnation of Jesus. The elder urgently insists that no hospitality be shown to these false teachers lest they use the opportunity to infiltrate the community.

¹*†THE ELDER TO A LADY who is elect and to her children.

In truth I love each of you—and not only I but also all those who have come to know the truth. ²This love is based on the truth that abides in us and will be with us forever. ³†In truth and love, then, we shall have grace, mercy, and peace from God the Father and from Jesus Christ, the Father's Son.

⁴*†It has given me great joy to find some of your children walking in the path of truth, just as we were commanded by the Father. ⁵*But now, my Lady, I would make this request of you (not as if I were writ-

---

†

1: *A lady who is elect:* the adjective *elect* ("chosen by God") is applied to Christians at the beginning of some other New Testament epistles (1 Pt 1, 1f; Ti 1, 1). In 1 Peter 5, 13, a Christian community (in Rome under the name *Babylon*) is referred to as *chosen together with you* (the Christians of the dispersion; 1 Pt 1, 1). *The truth:* the revelation of God in Jesus, which Christians accept through faith.

3: *Grace, mercy, and peace:* like 1 and 2 Tm, this letter adds *mercy* to the *grace and peace* salutation that is common in the Pauline letters. *The Father's Son:* this title embodies the substance of the entire New Testament, and close variations of it occur; cf, e. g., Jn 1, 14.18; 3, 35; 5, 20. However, the precise wording used here is not found elsewhere in the New Testament. It is echoed in the hymn "Glory to God" of the Roman Mass.

4: *To find some of your children:* those whom he met. There is no necessary indication that others were not *walking in the path* of truth, literally "walking in truth": a Semitic expression used in Johannine writing to describe a way of living in which the Christian faith comes to expression. *Commanded:* either the commandment of brotherly love is meant (Jn 13, 34; 15, 12; 1 Jn 2, 7-11; 4, 21), or the twofold commandment of love and of orthodox belief about Jesus Christ (1 Jn 3, 23). Love is stressed in 2 Jn 4ff, belief in 7ff.

❊

1: Jn 8, 32.   5: Jn 13, 34; 15, 12.
4: 3 Jn 3.

ing you some new commandment; rather, it is a commandment we have had from the start): let us love one another. **6***This love involves our walking according to the commandments, and as you have heard from the beginning, the commandment is the way in which you should walk.

7*†Many deceitful men have gone out into the world, men who do not acknowledge Jesus Christ as coming in the flesh. Such is the deceitful one! This is the antichrist! **8**†Look out that you yourselves do not lose what you have worked for; you must receive your reward in full. **9***†Anyone who is so "progressive" that he does not remain rooted in the teaching of Christ does not possess God, while anyone who remains rooted in the teaching possesses both the Father and the Son. **10**†If anyone comes to you who does not bring this teaching, do not receive him into your house; do not even greet him, **11**for whoever greets him shares in the evil he does.

12*†While there is much more that I could write you, I do not intend to put it down on paper; instead, I hope to visit you and talk with you face to face, so that our joy may be full.

13†The children of your elect sister send you their greetings.

❈

6: Jn 14, 15; 1 Jn 5, 3.
7: 1 Jn 2, 22; 4, 2f.
9: Jn 8, 31; 1 Jn 2, 24.

12: Jn 15, 11; 17, 13; 1 Jn 1, 4.

---

†

7: *Such is the deceitful one:* another title of antichrist and of those associated with antichrist; cf 1 Jn 2, 18f.22; 4, 2f.

8: *We:* it is not certain whether this means the elder (3 Jn 9f.12) or the Christians as above in vv 2-4. Many MSS have "you."

9: *Anyone who is so "progressive":* literally "Everyone who moves ahead." The elder does not condemn all theological development but only that which departs from Jesus' teaching.

10f: The attitude inculcated here reflects the life-and-death struggle between Christianity and Docetism at the end of the first century. To imitate this attitude in the changed circumstances of our own times would be to misuse Scripture and to fail to understand its time-conditioned aspect. The love that the elder inculcates above (5f) requires in our times that we extend kindness to one another in a divided Christianity.

12: *Our joy:* other textual witnesses read "your joy."

13: *Your elect sister:* the community where the elder resides.

The Third Epistle of John

Introduction

General questions concerning format and authorship are adverted to in the Introduction to 2 John. The main purpose of the letter is to secure hospitality and support for missionaries approved by the elder and perhaps sent out by him. Although the missionaries preach to the pagans, it is possible also that they embody the elder's influence and doctrinal authority over communities. Perhaps this is why Diotrephes, the ambitious leader of the community who rejects the elder's authority, refuses to receive the missionaries and tries to force others within the community to follow the same policy. The exact position of Diotrephes himself is not clear; for example, is he a monarchical bishop, as we might conceive the office nowadays, or one of the elders who by force of personality has taken over leadership?

To gain his purpose despite Diotrephes' opposition, the elder writes to Gaius, seemingly a man of position and wealth within the community. The elder praises Gaius' past hospitality, emphasizing that this attitude represents the true exercise of Christianity—"walking in the path of truth." He urges Gaius to continue to extend hospitality and to help outfit the missionaries for further travels. He recommends Demetrius to Gaius, perhaps for the double reason that Demetrius is the head of the missionary band and yet is unknown to Gaius. The elder also mentions a forthcoming visit of his own. This visit, during which he will also rebuke Diotrephes, may be meant to assure Gaius of support if Diotrephes seeks to expel Gaius from the church for granting the hospitality the elder requests. Despite its brevity and the inadequacy of its details, 3 John furnishes an extremely important insight into the problem of authority and influence in Christianity at the end of the first century.

¹†THE ELDER TO THE BELOVED GAIUS, whom indeed I love.

²*Beloved, I hope you are in good health—may you thrive in all other ways as you do in the spirit. ³†For it has given me great joy to have the brothers bear witness to how truly you walk in the path of truth. ⁴Nothing delights me more than to hear that my children are walking in this path.

⁵†Beloved, you demonstrate fidelity by all that you do for the brothers even though they are strangers; ⁶†indeed, they have testified to your love before the church. And you will do a good thing if, in a way that pleases God, you help them to continue their journey. ⁷†It was for the sake of the Name that they set out, and they are accepting nothing from the pagans. ⁸Therefore, we owe it to such men to support them and thus to have our share in the work of truth.

⁹†I did write to the church; but Diotrephes, who enjoys being their leader, ignores us. ¹⁰†Therefore, if I come I will speak publicly of what he is doing in spreading evil nonsense about us. And that is not all. Not only does he refuse to welcome the brothers himself but he even hinders those who wish to do so and expels them from the church!

¹¹†Beloved, do not imitate what is evil but what is good. Whoever does what is good belongs to God; whoever does what is evil has never seen God. ¹²*†De-

---

† 1: *Gaius:* although influential, he does not seem to have had an office in the community. He is referred to as one of the elder's spiritual children (v 4); whether this means he was converted by the elder, or simply that he accepted the elder's leadership, is uncertain. Gaius is called *beloved,* a frequent form of address for fellow Christians in New Testament epistolary literature.

3: *The brothers:* a designation of fellow Christians; cf Jn 21, 23. In this letter it refers to Christians who have been on a missionary enterprise, visiting Gaius and receiving hospitality from him, even though they had been previously unknown to him (v 5).

5: *Demonstrate fidelity by all that you do:* literally, "Whatever work you do for the brothers, you are doing something faithful." Gaius' hospitality is a manifestation of his true Christian faith.

6: *Help them to continue:* besides asking for maintenance for the missionaries while they are in Gaius' community, the elder asks him to equip them for their further travels.

7: *The Name:* Jesus, referred to in this manner in the New Testament (Acts 5, 41) and in later Christian works. *Accepting nothing:* not expecting support from the pagans to whom they preach the gospel, in contrast to some of the devotees of pagan gods who were constantly begging money.

9: *I did write:* a letter probably destroyed by Diotrephes. *Enjoys being their leader:* the elder does not deny that Diotrephes is the leader of the community but implicitly criticizes his ambition to be independent of the elder's influence.

10: *Spreading evil nonsense:* probably Diotrephes is accusing the elder of dictatorial interference in the community on account of his sending the missionaries.

11: *What is evil:* Gaius should not be influenced by Diotrephes but should maintain his previous policy of hospitality.

12: *Testimonial:* because of the danger of heretical teachers (2 Jn), strange missionaries needed recommendation from someone who could vouch for them; cf 2 Cor 3, 1; Rom 16, 1f; Col 4, 7f. *From truth itself:* refers probably to the way Demetrius lived this external witness to the truth that was in him (2 Jn 2).

3: 2 Jn 4.   12: Jn 19, 35; 21, 24.

metrius is one who gets a good testimonial from all, even from truth itself. We give our testimonial as well, and you know that our testimony is true.

13There is much more that I had in mind to write you, but I do not wish to write it out with pen and ink. **14**Rather, I hope to see you soon, when we can talk face to face.

15†Peace be with you. The beloved here send you their greetings; greet the beloved there, each by name.

---

† 15: *Beloved:* The Greek word *philos* in the Johannine vocabulary is probably a synonym for *agapetos,* "beloved," which appears in vv 1, 2, 5 and 11. Every Christian was a *philos* of Jesus and of every other Christian: "I no longer speak of you as slaves, . . . Instead I call you friends (*philous*)," i. e., beloved (Jn 15, 15). See note on Jn 15, 13.

The Epistle of Jude

Introduction

The epistle purports to have been written by *Jude, a servant of Jesus Christ and brother of James* (see Introduction to James). Since this claimant is not identified as one of the Twelve, he is presumably not Jude the apostle (Lk 6, 16), but that relative of Jesus who doubted him during the ministry (Mk 6, 3). Nearly all scholars agree on this point of identification. However, some hold that the epistle itself cannot be dated early enough to make the superscription anything but pseudonymous. They instance the allusion to the apostles as men of a past time (v 17; cf v 3), and assert, in addition, that the characterization of the false teachers (v 18) and the use of a Greek translation of 1 Enoch (14f) point to the date of approximately 100 A. D.

These arguments, however, should be viewed with caution. Though the allusion to the apostles cited above does indicate that the author of Jude was thinking of a second-generation Christian community, the reference point need not have been the end of that generation; it could equally well have been its beginning, therefore not long after 70 A. D. Moreover, the author of Jude might have so described false teachers about 80 A. D., and might also have had access to a Greek translation of 1 Enoch. The date of about 80 A. D. for the epistle remains entirely possible. For this reason many other scholars accept Jude, the relative of Jesus and brother of James of Jerusalem, as its author. Nothing is known of this Jude's history, nor does his epistle provide information on the location of the Christians to whom it is addressed. Since he invokes the name of James by way of introducing himself, he seems not to have been very well known among the Christians to whom he wrote.

The epistle warns its recipients against the false brethren who have infiltrated their community (v 4). These persons are to be identified by their exaggerated doctrine of Christian freedom, for they encourage sensuality (v 4) and reject authority (v 8). The community must be alert to this threat in its midst, mindful of the divine judgments against those who fail to live according to faith or to Christian standards of conduct (5ff.11; 14ff).

On the foundation of faith, supported by prayer, the Christian is preserved in the love of God, and awaits a merciful judgment and eternal life (20f). This common faith delivered to the saints is the criterion of right belief (v 3). What is contrary to it is *destined for condemnation* because it turns the grace of God into wantonness and denies Jesus Christ, the *only Master and Lord* (v 4).

The energetic and picturesque style of this epistle is reminiscent of that of the early prophets. St. Jerome acknowledges that some rejected the epistle because of its citation of the apocryphal Book of Enoch, but states that the ancient authority it enjoyed and its use in the churches assured its place in the canon of inspired writings.

Scholars agree that the author of 2 Peter drew upon the Epistle of Jude.

Greeting

1*†JUDE, A SERVANT OF JESUS CHRIST and brother of James, to those who have been called by God; who have found love in God the Father and have been guarded safely in Jesus Christ. **²**May mercy, peace, and love be yours in ever greater measure.

Exhortation to Steadfastness

3*†I was already fully intent on writing you, beloved, about the salvation we share. But now I feel obliged to write and encourage you to fight hard for the faith delivered once for all to the saints. **4***Certain individuals have recently wormed their way into your midst, godless types, long ago destined for the condemnation I shall describe. They pervert the gracious gift of our God to sexual excess and deny Jesus Christ, our only master and Lord.

Against False Teachers

5*†I wish to remind you of certain things, even though you may already be very well aware of them.

---
†

1f: *Jude, . . . brother of James:* for the identity of the author of this letter, see the Introduction. *To those who have been called by God:* the vocation to the Christian faith is God's free gift to those whom he loves and whom he safely protects in Christ until the Lord's second coming.

3f: *The salvation we share:* the teachings of the Christian faith *delivered once for all to the saints:* i. e., handed down in their entirety and accepted by the Christian community. They are not to be perverted by heterodoxy; cf 1 Cor 3, 11; 15, 1; Gal 1, 6-19; 1 Tm 1, 3; 6, 3. *Certain individuals . . . destined for the condemnation:* false teachers within the community who deny Christ as Lord and Savior and seduce the people by advocating sexual lawlessness. Their punishment is already foreshadowed in Old Testament examples of unfaithful ones among the angels and among God's people (5ff). There is also reference here to the apocryphal Book of Enoch (14f), which was highly regarded in the early centuries of the Christian era.

5: *Destroyed those who refused to believe:* see note on Nm 14, 28f.

❋

1: Mt 13, 55.
3: 2 Pt 2, 1.
4: 2 Jn 10.

5: Nm 14, 35; 1 Cor 6, 3; 10, 5.

The Lord first rescued his people from the land of Egypt but later destroyed those who refused to believe. [6]*†There were angels, too, who did not keep to their own domain, who deserted their dwelling place. These the Lord has kept in perpetual bondage, shrouded in murky darkness against the judgment of the great day. [7]†Sodom, Gomorrah, and the towns thereabout indulged in lust, just as those angels did; they practiced unnatural vice. They are set before us to dissuade us, as they undergo a punishment of eternal fire.

[8]†Similarly, these visionaries pollute the flesh; they spurn God's dominion and revile the angelic beings. [9]*†Even the archangel Michael, when his case with the devil was being judged—a dispute over Moses' body—did not venture to charge him with blasphemy. He simply said, "May the Lord punish you." [10]These people, however, not only revile what they have no knowledge of but are corrupted through the very things they know by instinct, like brute animals. [11]*†So much the worse for them! They have taken the road Cain took. They have abandoned themselves to Balaam's error for pay, and like Korah they perish in rebellion. [12]*†These men are blotches on your Christian banquets. They join your solemn feasts without shame and only look after themselves. They are blown on the wind like clouds that bring no rain. Like trees at the year's end they bear no fruit, being dead and uprooted. [13]*They are wild ocean waves, splashing their shameless deeds abroad like foam, or shooting stars for whom the thick gloom of darkness has been reserved forever. [14]*†It was about these that Enoch, who was of the seventh generation descended from Adam, prophesied when he said, "See, the Lord has come with his countless holy ones about him [15]*to pass judgment on all men, indicting the godless for every evil deed they have done, and convicting those godless sinners of every harsh word they have uttered against him."

[16]These men are grumblers and whiners. They live by their passions, uttering bombast. Whenever it is expedient, they resort to flattery. [17]*†Remember, beloved, all of you, the prophetic words of the apostles of our Lord Jesus Christ; [18]†how they kept telling you, "In the last days there will be impostors living by their godless passions." [19]These sensualists, devoid of the Spirit, are causing divisions among you.

Christian Admonitions

[20]*†But you, beloved, grow strong in your holy faith through prayer in the Holy Spirit. [21]Persevere in God's love, and welcome the mercy of our Lord Jesus Christ which leads to life eternal. [22]Correct those who are confused; the others you must rescue, snatching them from the fire. [23]*Even with those you pity, be on your guard; abhor so much as their flesh-stained clothing.

Doxology

[24]*†There is One who can protect you from a fall and make you stand unblemished and exultant in the presence of his glory. [25]Glory be to this only God our savior, through Jesus Christ our Lord. Majesty, too, be his, might and power from ages past, now and for ages to come. Amen.

---

† 6: See note on Gn 6, 1-4; cf also 2 Pt 2, 4-6.

7: *Sodom, Gomorrah:* frequently used in the Scriptures as examples of sin and punishment; cf Is 1, 9; Jer 50, 40; Lam 4, 6; Ez 16, 56; Mt 10, 15; 11, 24; Lk 17, 29. See note on Gn 19, 25.

8: *Visionaries:* victims of hallucination, or self-authorized prophets of revelation (cf 2 Pt 2, 10.18) who distort and debase Christian revelation to the detriment of the community.

Revile the angelic beings: i. e., probably by attributing their own disorders to the angels whom they invoke as their patrons.

9: *The archangel Michael . . . blasphemy:* an apparent reference to the story concerning the dispute between Michael and the devil over Moses' body, as described in the apocryphal *Assumption of Moses.* If Michael did not accuse even the devil but left the judgment of him to God, how much less should men presume to revile the angels! Michael was regarded as the protector of ancient Israel and of the new Israel, the church; cf Rv 12, 7; Dan 10, 13.20f; 13, 1ff.

11: *Cain . . . Balaam . . . Korah:* examples of rebellious leaders and of the punishments their conduct incurred; cf Gn 4, 8-16; Nm 16, 1-35; 31, 16.

12f: *Blotches on your Christian banquets:* scandalous conduct in connection with the eucharistic celebrations (cf 2 Pt 2, 13) which in apostolic times were associated with a community meal; cf Acts 2, 46; 1 Cor 11, 20-34.

Clouds that bring no rain; trees . . . dead and uprooted; wild ocean waves; shooting stars: empty display of force and beauty and splendor devoid of any genuine source to sustain them. Shooting stars were considered by the ancients to forebode catastrophe. Here they symbolize Christians who have withdrawn far from God as they plunge into exterior darkness; cf Enoch 18-21.

14f: A reference to Enoch (1, 9). For the description of Christ the universal judge of mankind, surrounded by his angels, cf Dn 7, 10; Mt 25, 21; Heb 12, 22.

17ff: The prophetic utterances of the apostles concerning the last days are repeated here to help Christians prepare themselves for the struggle against the enemies of their faith.

18: *In the last days . . . godless passions:* the substance rather than the direct quotation of the many New Testament passages, such as Mk 13, 22; Acts 20, 30; 1 Tm 4, 1ff; 2 Pt 3, 3. *The last* refers not to the imminent proximity of the second coming of Christ, as thought by many in the early Christian community, but to various stages in messianic times.

20f: These verses contain the trinitarian doctrine: God (the Father) who loves us, *the Holy Spirit* who prays in us, and *our Lord Jesus Christ* who *leads* us to *life eternal.* They also sum up the Christian life in terms of the theological virtues (faith, hope, charity) and the practice of prayer.

24f: *There is One who can protect you:* God through Jesus Christ. The purpose of the epistle is brought back into focus at its conclusion: perseverance of Christians in the faith amid the many evils that threaten to destroy it; cf 1 Pt 3, 17f. Verse 25 contains an illustrious New Testament doxology; cf also Rom 16, 27; Eph 3, 20; 1 Pt 4, 11; 2 Pt 3, 18.

✱

6: 2 Pt 2, 4.
9: Zec 3, 2.
11: Gn 4, 8; Nm 16, 22; 31, 16.
12: Prv 25, 14.
13: Is 57, 20.
14: Gn 5, 21; Dt 33, 24.

15: Mal 3, 13.
17: 2 Pt 3, 2f.
20: 1 Cor 3, 9-17.
23: Am 4, 11; Zec 3, 2; Jas 5, 19f.
24: 2 Pt 3, 14.

The Book of Revelation

Introduction

The Book of Revelation, or the Apocalypse, is the last book of the Bible, and perhaps the least read. It is also one of the most difficult to understand because it abounds in unfamiliar and extravagant symbolism, which at best appears unusual to the modern reader. Symbolic language, however, is one of the chief characteristics of apocalyptic literature, of which this book is an outstanding example. Such literature enjoyed wide popularity in both Jewish and Christian circles from 200 B. C. to 200 A. D.

This book contains an account of visions in symbolic and allegorical language borrowed in part from the Old Testament, especially Ezekiel, Zechariah, and the apocalyptic Book of Daniel. Whether these visions were real experiences of the author or simply literary conventions employed by him is an open question, the solution of which in no way adds to, or detracts from, the divine inspiration of the book.

Symbolic descriptions are not to be taken as literal descriptions, nor is the symbolism capable of being pictured realistically. One would find it both difficult and repulsive to visualize a lamb with seven horns and seven eyes; yet Christ our Lord is described in precisely such words (5, 6). The author used these images to suggest Christ's universal power (seven horns) and knowledge (seven eyes). Another significant feature of apocalyptic writing is the use of symbolic colors (1, 13-16; 3, 18; 4, 4; 6, 1-8; 17, 4; 19, 8) and numbers (*four* signifies the world; *six*, imperfection; *seven*, totality or perfection; *twelve*, Israel's tribes or the Apostles; *thousand*, immensity). Finally, the vindictive language in the book (6, 9f; 18, 1—19, 4) is also to be understood symbolically, and not literally. The cries for vengeance that sound so harsh on the lips of Christian martyrs are in fact literary devices the author employed to evoke in the reader and hearer a feeling of horror for apostasy and rebellion, which will be severely punished by God.

The Book of Revelation cannot be adequately comprehended except against the historical background which occasioned its writing. Like the Book of Daniel and other apocalypses, it was composed as resistance literature to meet a crisis. The book itself suggests that the crisis was ruthless persecution of the early Church by the Roman authorities; the harlot Babylon symbolizes pagan Rome, the city on seven hills (17, 9). The book is, then, an exhortation and admonition to the Christian to stand firm in the faith and to avoid compromise with paganism, despite the threat of adversity and martyrdom; he is to await patiently the fulfillment of God's mighty promises. The triumph of God in the world of men remains a mystery, to be accepted in faith and longed for in hope. It is a triumph that unfolded in the history of Jesus of Nazareth, and continues to unfold in the history of the individual Christian who follows the way of the cross, even, if necessary, to a martyr's death.

Though the perspective is eschatological—ultimate salvation and victory are said to take place at the end of the present age when Christ will come in glory at the Parousia—the book presents the decisive struggle of Christ and his followers against Satan and his cohorts as already over. Christ's overwhelming defeat of the kingdom of Satan has ushered in the everlasting reign of God (11, 15; 12, 10). Even the forces of evil unwittingly carry out the divine plan (17, 17), for God is the sovereign Lord of history.

The Book of Revelation had its origin in a time of crisis, but it remains valid for Christians of all time. In the face of evils from within and without, the Christian can confidently trust in God's promise to be with the church forever.

The author of the book calls himself John (1, 1.4.9; 22, 8), who because of his Christian faith had been exiled to the rocky island of Patmos. Although he never claims to be the apostle of the same name, many of the early church Fathers so identified him. This identification is not altogether certain. Vocabulary, grammar and style make it doubtful that the book could have been put into its present form by the person(s) responsible for the fourth gospel. Nevertheless, there are definite linguistic and theological affinities between the two books. The tone of the letters to the seven churches (1, 4—3, 22) is indicative of the great authority the writer enjoyed over the Christian communities in Asia. It is quite likely, therefore, that he was at least a disciple of the apostle John, who also lived in that part of the world. The date of composition is probably near the end of the reign of Domitian (81-96 A. D.), a fierce persecutor of the Christians.

The principal divisions of the Book of Revelation are the following:

I: PROLOGUE

1 ¹THIS IS THE REVELATION GOD GAVE to Jesus Christ, that he might show his servants what must happen very soon. He made it known by sending his angel to his servant John, ²who in reporting all he saw bears witness to the word of God and the testimony of Jesus Christ. ³†Happy is the man who reads this prophetic message, and happy are those who hear it and heed what is written in it, for the appointed time is near!

II: LETTERS TO THE CHURCHES OF ASIA

Greeting

⁴†TO THE SEVEN CHURCHES in the province of Asia: John wishes you grace and peace—from him who is and who was and who is to come, and from the seven spirits before his throne, ⁵*†and from Jesus Christ the faithful witness, the first-born from the dead and ruler of the kings of earth. To him who loves us and freed us from our sins by his own blood, ⁶who has made us a royal nation of priests in the service of his God and Father—to him be glory and power forever and ever! Amen.

⁷*See, he comes amid the clouds!
Every eye shall see him,
even of those who pierced him.
All the peoples of the earth
shall lament him bitterly.
So it is to be! Amen!

⁸*†The Lord God says, "I am the Alpha and the Omega, the One who is and who was and who is to come, the Almighty!"

First Vision

⁹†I, John, your brother, who share with you the distress and the kingly reign and the endurance we have in Jesus, found myself on the island called Patmos because I proclaimed God's word and bore witness to Jesus. ¹⁰†On the Lord's day I was caught up in ecstasy, and I heard behind me a piercing voice like the sound of a trumpet, ¹¹which said, "Write on a scroll what you now see and send it to the seven churches: to Ephesus, Smyrna, Pergamum, Thyatira, Sardis, Philadelphia, and Laodicea." ¹²†I turned around to see whose voice it was that spoke to me. When I did so I saw seven lampstands of gold, ¹³*†and among the lampstands One like a Son of Man wearing an ankle-length robe, with a sash of gold about his breast. ¹⁴†The hair of his head was as white as snow-white wool and his eyes blazed like fire. ¹⁵†His feet gleamed like polished brass refined in a furnace, and his voice sounded like the roar of rushing waters. ¹⁶*†In his right hand he held seven stars. A sharp, two-edged sword came out of his mouth, and his face shone like the sun at its brightest.

¹⁷*†When I caught sight of him I fell down at his feet as though dead. He touched me with his right hand and said: "There is nothing to fear. I am the First and the Last ¹⁸†and the One who lives. Once I was dead but now I live—forever and ever. I hold the keys of death and the nether world. ¹⁹*Write down, therefore, whatever you see in visions—what you see now and will see in time to come. ²⁰†This is the secret meaning of the seven stars you saw in my right hand, and of the seven lampstands of gold: the seven stars are the presiding spirits of the seven churches, and the seven lampstands are the seven churches.

---

† 1, 3: *Happy is the man:* the first of seven beatitudes in this book; the others are in 14, 13; 16, 15; 19, 9; 20, 6; 22, 7.14. *Those who hear it:* in the liturgical assembly. *The appointed time:* when Jesus will return in glory; cf 1, 7; 3, 11; 22, 7.10.12.20.

1, 4: *Seven churches . . . Asia:* in western Asia Minor (modern Turkey). These representative churches are mentioned by name in 1, 11; each is the recipient of a message (2, 1–3, 22). *Seven* is the biblical number suggesting fullness and completeness; thus John is writing for the whole church.

1, 5: *Freed us:* other ancient MSS read "washed us."

1, 8: *The Alpha and the Omega:* the first and last letters of the Greek alphabet. In 22, 13 the same words occur, together with the expressions *the First and the Last, the Beginning and the End;* cf 1, 17; 2, 8; 21, 6; Is 44, 6.

1, 9: *Island called Patmos:* in the Aegean Sea, southwest of Ephesus.

1, 10: *The Lord's day:* Sunday.

1, 12-16: A symbolic description of Christ in glory; cf Introduction.

1, 13: *Son of Man:* see note on Mt 8, 20. *Ankle-length robe:* Christ is priest; cf Ex 28, 4; 29, 5. *Sash of gold:* Christ is king; cf 1 Mc 10, 89; 11, 58.

1, 14: *Hair . . . white as snow-white wool:* Christ is eternal (v 18; Dn 7, 9). *His eyes blazed like fire:* Christ is omniscient; cf 2, 23; Ps 7, 10; Jer 17, 10.

1, 15: *His feet . . . furnace:* Christ is immutable; cf Ez 1, 27; Dn 10, 6. *His voice . . . waters:* Christ speaks with divine authority; cf Ez 1, 24.

1, 16: *A sharp, two-edged sword:* the word of God (Eph 6, 17; Heb 4, 12), which will destroy unrepentant sinners (2, 16; 19, 15). *His face . . . brightest:* the divine majesty of Christ; cf 21, 23; Is 60, 19.

1, 17: It was an Old Testament belief that for sinful man to see God was to die (Ex 19, 21; 33, 20; Is 6, 5).

1, 18: *Nether world:* the abode of the dead (20, 13).

1, 20: *Presiding spirits:* literally, angels. Angels were thought to be in charge of the physical world (7, 1; 16, 5), as well as of nations (Dn 10, 13; 12, 1), communities (the seven churches), and individuals (Mt 18, 10; Acts 12, 15).

---

* 1/5: 1 Cor 15, 20; Col 1, 18; Heb 9, 14; 1 Pt 1, 19; 1 Jn 1, 7.
7: Zec 12, 10; Mt 24, 30; Jn 19, 37.
8: 21, 6; 22, 13; Is 44, 6.
13: Dn 7, 13; 10, 5.
16: Ez 43, 2; Heb 4, 12.
17: Is 41, 4; Dn 8, 18.
19: Is 44, 6; 48, 12.

To Ephesus

2 ¹†"To the presiding spirit of the church in Ephesus, write this:

"'The One who holds the seven stars in his right hand and walks among the seven lampstands of gold has this to say: ²†I know your deeds, your labors, and your patient endurance. I know you cannot tolerate wicked men; you have tested those self-styled apostles who are nothing of the sort, and discovered that they are impostors. ³You are patient and endure hardship for my cause. Moreover, you do not become discouraged. ⁴I hold this against you, though: you have turned aside from your early love. ⁵Keep firmly in mind the heights from which you have fallen. Repent, and return to your former deeds. If you do not repent I will come to you and remove your lampstand from its place. ⁶†But you have this much in your favor: you detest the practices of the Nicolaitans, just as I do.

⁷*†"'Let him who has ears heed the Spirit's word to the churches! I will see to it that the victor eats from the tree of life which grows in the garden of God.'

To Smyrna

⁸†"To the presiding spirit of the church in Smyrna, write this:

"'The First and the Last who once died but now lives has this to say: ⁹*†I know of your tribulation and your poverty, even though you are rich. I know the slander you endure from self-styled Jews who are nothing other than members of Satan's assembly. ¹⁰Have no fear of the sufferings to come. The devil will indeed cast some of you into prison to put you to the test; you will be tried over a period of ten days. Remain faithful until death and I will give you the crown of life.

¹¹*†"'Let him who has ears heed the Spirit's word to the churches! The victor shall never be harmed by the second death.'

To Pergamum

¹²†"To the presiding spirit of the church in Pergamum, write this:

"'The One with the sharp, two-edged sword has this to say: ¹³†I know you live in the very place where Satan's throne is erected; and I know you hold fast to my name and have not denied the faith you have in me, not even at the time when Antipas, my faithful witness, was martyred in your city where Satan has his home. ¹⁴*†Nevertheless I hold a few matters against you: there are some among you who follow the teaching of Balaam, who instructed Balak to throw a stum-

bling block in the way of the Israelites by tempting them to eat food sacrificed to idols and to practice fornication. ¹⁵Yes, you too have those among you who hold to the teaching of the Nicolaitans. ¹⁶Therefore repent! If you do not, I will come to you soon and fight against them with the sword of my mouth.

¹⁷*†"'Let him who has ears heed the Spirit's word to the churches! To the victor I will give the hidden manna; I will also give him a white stone upon which is inscribed a new name, to be known only by him who receives it.'

To Thyatira

¹⁸†"To the presiding spirit of the church in Thyatira, write this:

"'The Son of God, whose eyes blaze like fire and whose feet gleam like polished brass, has this to say: ¹⁹I know your deeds—your love and faith and service—as well as your patient endurance; I know also that your efforts of recent times are greater than ever. ²⁰†Nevertheless I hold this against you: you tolerate a Jezebel—that self-styled prophetess who seduces my servants by teaching them to practice lewdness and to eat food sacrificed to idols. ²¹I have given her a chance to repent but she refuses to turn from her lewdness. ²²I mean to cast her down on a bed of pain; her companions in sin I will plunge into intense suffering unless they repent of their sins with her, ²³*and her chil-

---

† 2, 1—3, 22: Each of the seven letters follows the same pattern: address; description of the exalted Christ; blame and/or praise for the church addressed; threat and/or admonition; final exhortation and promise to all Christians.

2, 1: *Ephesus:* capital of the Roman province of Asia. *Walks among the seven lampstands:* Christ is always present in the church; see note on 1, 4.

2, 2: *Self-styled apostles . . . impostors:* unauthorized and perverse missionaries; cf Acts 20, 29f.

2, 6: *Nicolaitans:* perhaps the impostors of v 2; see note on vv 14f.

2, 7: *The tree of life . . . garden of God:* reference to the tree in the primeval paradise (Gn 2, 9); cf 22, 2.14.19.

2, 8: *Smyrna:* modern Izmir, north of Ephesus.

2, 9f: The church in Smyrna was materially poor but spiritually rich. Accusations made by Jews occasioned the persecution of Christians; cf Acts 14, 2.19; 17, 5.13.

2, 11: *The second death:* when sinners will receive their final punishment (20, 6.14f; 21, 8).

2, 12: *Pergamum:* modern Bergama, north of Smyrna.

2, 13: *Satan's throne:* reference to emperor worship and other pagan practices that flourished in the city.

2, 14f: Like Balaam, the biblical prototype of religious compromisers (Nm 25, 1ff; 31, 16; 2 Pt 2, 15; Jude 11), the Nicolaitans in Pergamum and Ephesus (v 6) accommodated their Christian faith to paganism. They misused the law of liberty enunciated by St. Paul (1 Cor 9, 19-23).

2, 17: *The hidden manna:* the food of life; cf Ps 78, 24f. *White stone:* symbol of victory and joy; cf 3, 4f. *New name:* reference to the Christian's rebirth in Christ; cf 3, 12; 19, 12; Is 62, 2; 65, 15.

2, 18: *Thyatira:* modern Akhisar, southeast of Pergamum.

2, 20: The scheming and treacherous Jezebel of old (1 Kgs 21, 1-14; 2 Kgs 9, 22.30-34) introduced pagan customs into the religion of Israel; this new Jezebel was doing the same to Christianity.

---

* 2/7: 13, 9; 22, 2; Gn 2, 9.
9: Jas 2, 5.
11: 20, 6.14; 21, 8; 1 Cor 9, 25.
14: Nm 24, 3; 25, 2.
17: Is 62, 2; 65, 15.
23: 1 Sm 16, 7; Ps 7, 10; Jer 17, 10.

dren I will put to death. Thus shall all the churches come to know that I am the searcher of hearts and minds, and that I will give each of you what your conduct deserves. [24]†And now I address myself to you others in Thyatira who do not uphold this teaching and know nothing of the so-called "deep secrets" of Satan; on you I place no further burden. [25]In any case, hold fast to what you have until I come.

[26]*†"To the one who wins the victory, who keeps to my ways till the end, I will give authority over the nations—the same authority I received from my Father. [27]He shall rule them with a rod of iron and shatter them like crockery; [28]and I will give him the morning star.

[29]*"'Let him who has ears heed the Spirit's word to the churches!'

To Sardis

3 [1]†"ᴛo the presiding spirit of the church in Sardis, write this:

"'The One who holds the seven spirits of God, the seven stars, has this to say: I know your conduct; I know the reputation you have of being alive, when in fact you are dead! [2]Wake up, and strengthen what remains before it dies. I find that the sum of your deeds is less than complete in the sight of my God. [3]*Call to mind how you accepted what you heard; keep to it, and repent. If you do not rouse yourselves I will come upon you like a thief, at a time you cannot know. [4]*†I realize that you have in Sardis a few persons who have not soiled their garments; these shall walk with me in white because they are worthy.

[5]"The victor shall go clothed in white. I will never erase his name from the book of the living, but will acknowledge him in the presence of my Father and his angels.

[6]*"'Let him who has ears heed the Spirit's word to the churches!'

To Philadelphia

[7]*†"To the presiding spirit of the church in Philadelphia, write this:

"'The holy One, the true,
    who wields David's key,
who opens and no one can close,
who closes and no one can open,

has this to say:

[8]†"'I know your deeds; that is why I have left an open door before you which no one can close. I know that your strength is limited; yet you have held fast to my word and have not denied my name. [9]*I mean to

make some of Satan's assembly, those self-styled Jews who are not really Jews but frauds, come and fall down at your feet; they will learn of my love for you in that way. [10]Because you have kept my plea to stand fast, I will keep you safe in the time of trial which is coming on the whole world, to test all men on earth. [11]I am coming soon. Hold fast to what you have lest someone rob you of your crown.

[12]*†"'I will make the victor a pillar in the temple of my God and he shall never leave it. I will inscribe on him the name of my God and the name of the city of my God, the new Jerusalem which he will send down from heaven, and my own name which is new.

[13]"'Let him who has ears heed the Spirit's word to the churches!'

To Laodicea

[14]*†"To the presiding spirit of the church in Laodicea, write this:

"'The Amen, the faithful Witness and true, the Source of God's creation, has this to say: [15]†I know your deeds; I know you are neither hot nor cold. How I wish you were one or the other—hot or cold! [16]But because you are lukewarm, neither hot nor cold, I will spew you out of my mouth! [17]†You keep saying, "I am so rich and secure that I want for nothing." Little do you realize how wretched you are, how pitiable and poor, how blind and naked! [18]†Take my advice. Buy from me gold refined by fire if you would be truly rich.

---

† 2, 24: *The so-called "deep secrets" of Satan:* a scathing reference to the perverse teaching of the Nicolaitans (v 15).

2, 26ff: The Christian who perseveres in faith will share in Christ's messianic authority and victory over death, symbolized by *the morning star* (22, 16); cf Ps 2, 8f.

3, 1f: *Sardis,* south and east of Thyatira, is reproached for the feverish activity of its Christians (*the reputation you have of being alive*), since such activity could not substitute for a living faith.

3, 4f: *In white:* the sign of victory and joy; see note on 2, 17. *The book of the living:* where the names of the redeemed are kept (21, 27); cf 13, 8; 17, 8; 20, 12.15; Phil 4, 3; Dn 12, 1. They will be acknowledged by Christ in heaven (Mt 10, 32).

3, 7: *Philadelphia,* modern Alasehir, southeast of Sardis. Destroyed by earthquake in 17 A. D. and rebuilt with money from the Emperor Tiberius, the city was renamed Neocaesarea, "New Caesar City." *David's key:* to the heavenly City of David, the new Jerusalem (v 12), over which Christ has supreme authority; cf Is 22, 22.

3, 8: *An open door:* opportunities for sharing and proclaiming the faith; cf 1 Cor 16, 19; 2 Cor 2, 12.

3, 12: *A pillar:* allusion to the rebuilding of the city; see note on v 7. *New Jerusalem:* described in 21, 10—22, 5.

3, 14: *Laodicea,* southeast of Philadelphia, was a wealthy commercial center. *The Amen:* a divine title applied to Christ; cf Is 65, 16; 2 Cor 1, 20. *Source of God's creation:* a concept found also in Jn 1, 3; Col 1, 16f; Heb 1, 2; cf Wis 9, 1f.

3, 15f: Halfhearted commitment to the faith is nauseating to Christ.

3, 17: Material well-being occasioned spiritual bankruptcy.

3, 18: *Gold . . . fire:* God's grace. *White garments:* symbol of an upright life (the city was noted for its black woolen cloth). *Ointment . . . eyes:* to remove spiritual blindness (one of the city's exports was eye ointment).

✻
26: Ps 2, 8f.
29: 2 Pt 1, 19.
3/3: Mt 24, 42-44;
    Mk 13, 33; 1 Thes 5, 2;
    2 Pt 3, 10.
4: 1 Thes 5, 2.

6: Ps 69, 29; Mt 10, 32.
7: Is 22, 22; Mt 16, 19.
9: Is 45, 14; 60, 14.
12: Ez 48, 35.
14: 1, 5; Jn 1, 3.

Buy white garments in which to be clothed, if the shame of your nakedness is to be covered. Buy ointment to smear on your eyes, if you would see once more. **19***Whoever is dear to me I reprove and chastise. Be earnest about it, therefore. Repent!

20†"Here I stand, knocking at the door. If anyone hears me calling and opens the door, I will enter his house and have supper with him, and he with me. **21**I will give the victor the right to sit with me on my throne, as I myself won the victory and took my seat beside my Father on his throne.

22"Let him who has ears heed the Spirit's word to the churches.'"

III: PREPARATION FOR THE DAY OF THE LORD

Vision of Heavenly Worship

4 **1**†AFTER THIS I HAD ANOTHER VISION: above me there was an open door to heaven, and I heard the trumpetlike voice which had spoken to me before. It said, "Come up here and I will show you what must take place in time to come." **2***†At once I was caught up in ecstasy. A throne was standing there in heaven, and on the throne was seated One **3***whose appearance had a gemlike sparkle as of jasper and carnelian. Around the throne was a rainbow as brilliant as emerald. **4**†Surrounding this throne were twenty-four other thrones upon which were seated twenty-four elders; they were clothed in white garments and had crowns of gold on their heads. **5**†From the throne came flashes of lightning and peals of thunder; before it burned seven flaming torches, the seven spirits of God. **6***†The floor around the throne was like a sea of glass that was crystal-clear.

At the very center, around the throne itself, stood four living creatures covered with eyes front and back. **7**The first creature resembled a lion, the second an ox; the third had the face of a man, while the fourth looked like an eagle in flight. **8***Each of the four living creatures had six wings and eyes all over, inside and out.

Day and night, without pause, they sing:

"Holy, holy, holy, is the Lord God Almighty,
    He who was, and who is, and who is to come!"

9Whenever these creatures give glory and honor and praise to the One seated on the throne, who lives forever and ever, **10**the twenty-four elders fall down before the One seated on the throne, and worship him who lives forever and ever. They throw down their crowns before the throne and sing:

11"O Lord our God, you are worthy
    to receive glory and honor and power!
For you have created all things;
    by your will they came to be and were made!"

The Scroll and the Lamb

5 **1***†IN the right hand of the One who sat on the throne I saw a scroll. It had writing on both sides and was sealed with seven seals. **2**Then I saw a mighty angel who proclaimed in a loud voice: "Who is worthy to open the scroll and break its seals?" **3**But no one in heaven or on earth or under the earth could be found to open the scroll or examine its contents. **4**I wept bitterly because no one could be found worthy to open or examine the scroll. **5***†One of the elders said to me: "Do not weep. The Lion of the tribe of Judah, the Root of David, has won the right by his victory to open the scroll with the seven seals."

6*†Then, between the throne with the four living creatures and the elders, I saw a Lamb standing, a Lamb that had been slain. He had seven horns and seven eyes; these eyes are the seven spirits of God, sent to all parts of the world. **7**The Lamb came and received the scroll from the right hand of the One who sat on the throne. **8**When he had taken the scroll, the four living creatures and the twenty-four elders fell down before the Lamb. Along with their harps, the elders were holding vessels of gold filled with aromatic spices, which were the prayers of God's holy people. **9**This is the new hymn they sang:

"Worthy are you to receive the scroll
    and break open its seals,
    for you were slain.
With your blood you purchased for God
    men of every race and tongue,
    of every people and nation.

---

† 3, 20: Christ invites all men to the messianic banquet in heaven (Lk 14, 15; 22, 30); cf Is 25, 6.

4, 1: The ancients viewed heaven as a solid vault, entered by way of actual doors.

4, 2-8: Much of the imagery here is taken from Ez 1 and 10.

4, 4: *Twenty-four elders:* representing the twelve tribes of Israel and the twelve apostles; cf 21, 12ff.

4, 5: *Flashes of lightning and peals of thunder:* as in other descriptions of God's appearances or activity (8, 5; 11, 19; 16, 18; Ex 19, 16; Ez 1, 13).

4, 6ff: *A sea of glass . . . crystal-clear:* image adapted from Ez 1, 22-26. *Four living creatures:* symbols taken from Ez 1, 5-21; they are identified as cherubim in Ez 10, 20. *Covered with eyes:* suggesting God's knowledge and concern. *Six wings:* like the seraphim of Is 6, 2.

5, 1: *A scroll:* containing the list of afflictions reserved for sinful men; cf Ez 2, 9f. *Sealed with seven seals:* totally hidden from all but God. Only the Lamb (vv 7ff) has the right to carry out the divine plan.

5, 5: *The Lion of the tribe of Judah, the Root of David:* messianic titles applied to Christ (22, 16; Gn 49, 9; Is 11, 1.10).

5, 6: Christ is the Paschal Lamb without blemish, whose blood saved the new Israel from sin and death (Jn 1, 29.36; 1 Pt 1, 18f; Acts 8, 32); cf Ex 12; Is 53, 7. *Seven horns and seven eyes:* Christ has the fullness (see note on 1, 4) of power and knowledge. *Seven spirits:* as in 1, 4 and 4, 5.

❋
    19: Prv 3, 12; Heb 12, 6.
    4/2: Dn 2, 28.
    3: Ex 24, 10; Ez 1, 26-28.
    6: Ex 24, 10; Ez 1, 5-21; 10, 14.
    8: 1, 4; Is 6, 3; Ez 1, 5-21.
    5/1: Is 29, 11.
    5: Is 11, 1.10.
    6: Jn 1, 29.

¹⁰*You made of them a kingdom,
  and priests to serve our God,
  and they shall reign on the earth."

¹¹*As my vision continued, I heard the voices of many angels who surrounded the throne and the living creatures and the elders. They were countless in number, thousands and tens of thousands, ¹²and they all cried out:

"Worthy is the Lamb that was slain
  to receive power and riches, wisdom and strength,
  honor and glory and praise!"

¹³*Then I heard the voices of every creature in heaven and on earth and under the earth and in the sea; everything in the universe cried aloud:

"To the One seated on the throne, and to the Lamb,
  be praise and honor, glory and might,
  forever and ever!"

¹⁴The four living creatures answered, "Amen," and the elders fell down and worshiped.

The First Six Seals

6 ¹†THEN I watched while the Lamb broke open the first of the seven seals, and I heard one of the four living creatures cry out in a voice like thunder, "Come forward!" ²*†To my surprise I saw a white horse; its rider had a bow, and he was given a crown. He rode forth victorious, to conquer yet again.

³When the Lamb broke open the second seal, I heard the second living creature cry out, "Come forward!" ⁴*†Another horse came forth, a red one. Its rider was given power to rob the earth of peace by allowing men to slaughter one another. For this he was given a huge sword.

⁵†When the Lamb broke open the third seal, I heard the third living creature cry out, "Come forward!" This time I saw a black horse, the rider of which held a pair of scales in his hand. ⁶*†I heard what seemed to be a voice coming from in among the four living creatures. It said: "A day's pay for a ration of wheat and the same for three of barley! But spare the olive oil and the wine!"

⁷When the Lamb broke open the fourth seal, I heard the voice of the fourth living creature cry out, "Come forward!" ⁸*†Now I saw a horse sickly green in color. Its rider was named Death, and the nether world was in his train. These four were given authority over one quarter of the earth, to kill with sword and famine and plague and the wild beasts of the earth.

⁹When the Lamb broke open the fifth seal, I saw under the altar the spirits of those who had been martyred because of the witness they bore to the word of God. ¹⁰They cried out at the top of their voices: "How long will it be, O Master, holy and true, before you judge our cause and avenge our blood among the inhabitants of the earth?" ¹¹Each of the martyrs was given a long white robe, and they were told to be patient a little while longer until the quota was filled of their fellow servants and brothers to be slain, as they had been.

¹²*†When I saw the Lamb break open the sixth seal, there was a violent earthquake; the sun turned black as a goat's-hair tentcloth and the moon grew red as blood. ¹³*The stars in the sky fell crashing to earth like figs shaken loose by a mighty wind. ¹⁴Then the sky disappeared as if it were a scroll being rolled up; every mountain and island was uprooted from its base. ¹⁵*The kings of the earth, the nobles and those in command, the wealthy and powerful, the slave and the free—all hid themselves in caves and mountain crags. ¹⁶They cried out to the mountains and rocks, "Fall on us! Hide us from the face of the One who sits on the throne and from the wrath of the Lamb! ¹⁷The great day of their vengeance has come. Who can withstand it?"

Sealing of the Thousands

7 ¹*†AFTER this I saw four angels standing at the four corners of the earth; they held in check the earth's four winds so that no wind blew on land or sea or through any tree. ²I saw another angel come up from the east holding the seal of the living God. He cried out at the top of his voice to the four angels who were given power to ravage the land and the sea, ³*"Do no harm to the land or the sea or the trees until we imprint this seal on the foreheads of the servants of our God." ⁴†I heard the number of those who were so marked—one hundred and forty-four thousand from every tribe of Israel: ⁵twelve thousand from the tribe of Judah, twelve thousand from the

---

† 6, 1-8: Each of the four horsemen symbolizes a particular woe connected with war and destruction. The imagery is adapted from Zec 1, 8ff; 6, 1-8.

6, 2: *White horse . . . bow:* symbolizing the Parthians on the eastern border of the Roman empire. Expert in the use of the bow, they constantly harassed the Romans.

6, 4: *Huge sword:* symbol of war and violence.

6, 5: *Black horse:* symbol of famine, the usual accompaniment of war in antiquity.

6, 6: *A day's pay:* literally, "denarius," a silver coin. Famine brought about the rationing of supplies, and the prices were exorbitant. *Barley:* food of the poor.

6, 8: *Sickly green:* symbol of death.

6, 12ff: Symbolic rather than literal description of the cosmic upheavals attending the day of the Lord, when the martyrs' prayer for vindication (v 10) would be answered; cf Mt 24, 29; Am 8, 8f; Is 34, 4; Jl 2, 10; 3, 3f.

7, 1-17: Two scenes precede the breaking of the seventh seal. In the first (vv 1-8), the elect receive *the seal of the living God;* cf Ez 9, 4ff. The second scene (vv 9-17) portrays the victorious martyrs before God's throne.

7, 4-8: *One hundred and forty-four thousand:* the square of twelve (the number of Israel's tribes) multiplied by a thousand, symbolic of the new Israel that embraces men *from every nation and race, people and tongue* (v 9); cf Gal 6, 16; Jas 1, 1.

---

*
10: Ex 19, 6.
11: Dn 7, 10.
13: Ps 150, 6.
6/2: Zec 1, 8-10; 6, 1-3.
4: Ez 21, 14-16.
6: Lv 26, 26; Ez 4, 16f.
8: Ez 14, 21.
12: Jl 3, 4; Mt 24, 29.
13: Is 34, 4.
15f: Is 2, 19; Hos 10, 8; Lk 23, 30.
7/1: Jer 49, 36; Zec 6, 5.
3: 14, 1f; Ez 9, 4.

tribe of Reuben, twelve thousand from the tribe of Gad, **6**twelve thousand from the tribe of Asher, twelve thousand from the tribe of Naphtali, twelve thousand from the tribe of Manasseh, **7**twelve thousand from the tribe of Simeon, twelve thousand from the tribe of Levi, twelve thousand from the tribe of Issachar, **8**twelve thousand from the tribe of Zebulun, twelve thousand from the tribe of Joseph, and twelve thousand from the tribe of Benjamin.

Triumph of the Elect

9†After this I saw before me a huge crowd which no one could count from every nation and race, people and tongue. They stood before the throne and the Lamb, dressed in long white robes and holding palm branches in their hands. **10**They cried out in a loud voice, "Salvation is from our God, who is seated on the throne, and from the Lamb!" **11**All the angels who were standing around the throne and the elders and the four living creatures fell down before the throne to worship God. They said: **12**"Amen! Praise and glory, wisdom and thanksgiving and honor, power and might, to our God forever and ever. Amen!"

13Then one of the elders asked me, "Who are these people all dressed in white? And where have they come from?" **14**†I said to him, "Sir, you should know better than I." He then told me, "These are the ones who have survived the great period of trial; they have washed their robes and made them white in the blood of the Lamb.

15"It was this that brought them before God's throne:
　　day and night they minister to him in his temple;
　　he who sits on the throne will give them shelter.
16*Never again shall they know hunger or thirst,
　　nor shall the sun or its heat beat down on them,
17*†for the Lamb on the throne will shepherd them.
　　He will lead them to springs of life-giving water,
　　and God will wipe every tear from their eyes."

The Seven Trumpets

8 **1***†WHEN the Lamb broke open the seventh seal, there was silence in heaven for about half an hour. **2**†Then, as I watched, the seven angels who minister in God's presence were given seven trumpets.

The Gold Censer

3Another angel came in holding a censer of gold. He took his place at the altar of incense and was given large amounts of incense to deposit on the altar of gold in front of the throne, together with the prayers of all God's holy ones. **4***From the angel's hand the smoke of the incense went up before God, and with it the prayers of God's people. **5***Then the angel took the

censer, filled it with live coals from the altar, and hurled it down to the earth. Peals of thunder and flashes of lightning followed, and the earth trembled.

First Four Trumpets

6*The seven angels with the seven trumpets made ready to blow them.

7†When the first angel blew his trumpet, there came hail and then fire mixed with blood, which was hurled down to the earth. A third of the land was scorched, along with a third of the trees and every green plant.

8†When the second angel blew his trumpet, something like a huge mountain all in flames was cast into the sea. A third of the sea turned to blood, **9***a third of the creatures living in the sea died, and a third of the ships were wrecked.

10*When the third angel blew his trumpet, a huge star burning like a torch crashed down from the sky. It fell on a third of the rivers and the springs. **11**The star's name was "Wormwood" because a third part of all the water turned to wormwood. Many people died from this polluted water.

12When the fourth angel blew his trumpet, a third of the sun, a third of the moon, and a third of the stars were hit hard enough to be plunged into darkness. The day lost a third of its light, as did the night.

13†As my vision continued, I heard an eagle flying in midheaven cry out in a loud voice, "Woe, woe, and again woe to the inhabitants of earth from the trumpet blasts the other three angels are about to blow!"

The Fifth Trumpet

9 **1**†THEN the fifth angel blew his trumpet, and I saw a star fall from the sky to the earth. The star was given the key to the shaft of the abyss; **2***†he opened it and smoke poured out of the shaft like

---

† 7, 9: *Long white robes . . . palm branches:* symbols of joy and victory; see note on 3, 4f.

7, 14: *Great period of trial:* fierce persecution by the Romans; cf Introduction.

7, 17: *Life-giving water:* God's grace, which flows from Christ (21, 6; 22, 1.17; Jn 4, 10.14).

8, 1: *Silence in heaven:* as in Zep 1, 7, a prelude to the eschatological woes that are to follow.

8, 2: The breaking of the seventh seal brings not one, but seven, symbolic disasters, each to be announced by the blowing of a trumpet (8, 6ff); see note on 6, 12ff.

8, 7: This woe resembles the seventh plague of Egypt (Ex 9, 23f); cf Jl 3, 3.

8, 8-11: The background of these two woes is the first plague of Egypt (Ex 7, 20f).

8, 11: *Wormwood:* a bitter plant symbolizing the punishment God inflicts on the ungodly; cf Jer 9, 12ff; 23, 15.

8, 13: *Woe, woe, and again woe:* each of the three woes pronounced by the angel·represents a separate disaster; cf 9, 12; 11, 14. The final woe, released by the seventh trumpet blast, includes the plagues of chapter 16.

9, 1: *A star:* an angel. *The abyss:* where Satan and the fallen angels are kept for a thousand years, to be cast afterward into the pool of fire (20, 7-10).

9, 2-6: This woe combines elements from the eighth and ninth plagues of Egypt (Ex 10, 12-15.21ff); cf Jl 1, 4—2, 10.

---

*
16: 49, 10.
17: 21, 4; Is 25, 8.
8/1: Hb 2, 20; Zec 2, 17.
4: Ps 141, 2.
5: Lv 16, 12; Ps 11, 6; Ez 10, 2.

6: 16, 1-9.
9: Ex 7, 20.
10: Is 14, 12; Jer 9, 14.
9/2: Gn 19, 28.

smoke from an enormous furnace. The sun and the air were darkened by the smoke from the shaft. **3***Out of the smoke, onto the land, came locusts as powerful as scorpions in their sting. **4**The locusts were commanded to do no harm to the grass in the land or to any plant or tree but only to those men who had not the seal of God on their foreheads. **5**The locusts were not allowed to kill them but only to torture them for five months; the pain they inflicted was like that of a scorpion's sting. **6***During that time these men will seek death but will not find it; they will yearn to die but death will escape them.

7*In appearance the locusts were like horses equipped for battle. On their heads they wore something like gold crowns; their faces were like men's faces **8**but they had hair like women's hair. Their teeth were the teeth of lions, **9**their chests like iron breastplates. Their wings made a sound like the roar of many chariots and horses charging into battle. **10**They had tails with stingers like scorpions; in their tails was enough venom to harm men for five months. **11†**Acting as their king was the angel in charge of the abyss, whose name in Hebrew is Abaddon and in Greek Apollyon.

The Sixth Trumpet

12The first woe is past, but beware! There are two more to come. **13†**Then the sixth angel blew his trumpet, and I heard a voice coming from between the horns of the altar of gold in God's presence. **14**It said to the sixth angel, who was still holding his trumpet, "Release the four angels who are tied up on the banks of the great river Euphrates!" **15**So the four angels were released; this was precisely the hour, the day, the month, and the year for which they had been prepared, to kill a third of mankind. **16**Their cavalry troops, whose count I heard, were two hundred million in number—a number I heard myself. **17**Now, in my vision, this is how I saw the horses and their riders. The breastplates they wore were fiery red, deep blue, and pale yellow. The horses' heads were like heads of lions, and out of their mouths came fire and sulphur and smoke. **18**By these three plagues—the smoke and sulphur and fire which shot out of their mouths—a third of mankind was slain. **19**The deadly power of the horses was not only in their mouths but in their tails; for their tails were like snakes with heads poised to strike.

20*†That part of mankind which escaped the plagues did not repent of the idols they had made. They did not give up the worship of demons, or of gods made from gold and silver, from bronze and stone and wood, which cannot see or hear or walk.

21Neither did they repent of their murders or their sorcery, their fornication or their thefts.

Angel with the Scroll

10 **1†**THEN I saw another mighty angel come down from heaven wrapped in a cloud, with a rainbow about his head; his face shone like the sun and his legs like pillars of fire. **2**In his hand he held a little scroll which had been opened. He placed his right foot on the sea and his left foot on the land, **3*†**and then gave a loud cry like the roar of a lion. When he cried out, the seven thunders raised their voices too. **4**I was about to start writing when the seven thunders spoke, but I heard a voice from heaven say, "Seal up what the seven thunders have spoken and do not write it down!" **5**Then the angel whom I saw standing on the sea and on the land raised his right hand to heaven **6*†**and took an oath by the One who lives forever and ever, who created heaven and earth and sea along with everything in them: "There shall be no more delay. **7*†**When the time comes for the seventh angel to blow his trumpet, the mysterious plan of God, which he announced to his servants the prophets, shall be accomplished in full."

8Then the voice which I heard from heaven spoke to me again and said, "Go, take the open scroll from the hand of the angel standing on the sea and on the land." **9†**I went up to the angel and said to him, "Give me the little scroll." He said to me, "Here, take it and eat it! It will be sour in your stomach, but in your mouth it will taste as sweet as honey." **10***I took the little scroll from the angel's hand and ate it. In my mouth it tasted as sweet as honey, but when I swallowed it my stomach turned sour. **11†**Then someone said to me, "You must prophesy again for many peoples and nations, languages and kings."

---

† 9, 11: *Abaddon:* destruction or ruin. *Apollyon:* destroyer.

9, 13-19: The sixth woe is a symbolic invasion by the Parthians living east of the Euphrates; see note on 6, 2. At the appointed time (v 15), the frightful horses act as God's agents of judgment. The imaginative details are not to be taken literally; see Introduction and note on 6, 12ff.

9, 20: *The idols they had made:* literally, the works of their hands.

10, 1—11, 14: An interlude in two scenes (10, 1-11 and 11, 1-14) precedes the sounding of the seventh trumpet; cf 7, 1-17.

10, 3f: *The seven thunders:* God's voice announcing judgment and doom; cf Ps 29, 3-9.

10, 6: *Heaven and earth and sea:* the three parts of the universe.

10, 7: *The mysterious plan of God:* the end of the present age, when the forces of evil will be put down (17, 1—19, 4.11-21; 20, 7-10; cf 2 Thes 2, 6-12; Rom 16, 25f), and the establishment of the reign of God, when all creation will be made anew (21, 1—22, 5).

10, 9f: The little scroll was sweet because it predicted the final victory of God's holy people; it was sour because it also announced the sufferings they are to endure; cf Ez 3, 1ff.

10, 11: This further prophecy is contained in chapters 12—22.

✿

    3: Ex 10, 12.15;   10/3: Am 3, 8.
        Wis 16, 9.   6: Dn 12, 7; Dt 32, 40;
    6: Jb 3, 21.   Ez 12, 28.
    7: Wis 16, 9.   7: Am 3, 7.
    20: Ps 135, 15-17.   10: Ez 3, 1-3.

The Two Witnesses

11 **1*****†**SOMEONE gave me a measuring rod and said: "Come and take the measurements of God's temple and altar, and count those who worship there. **2**†Exclude the outer court of the temple, however; do not measure it, for it has been handed over to the Gentiles, who will crush the holy city for forty-two months. **3**†I will commission my two witnesses to prophesy for those twelve hundred and sixty days, dressed in sackcloth."

4*These are the two olive trees and the two lampstands which stand in the presence of the Lord of the earth. **5**†If anyone tries to harm them, fire will come out of the mouths of these witnesses to devour their enemies. Anyone attempting to harm them will surely be slain in this way. **6***These witnesses have power to close up the sky so that no rain will fall during the time of their mission. They also have power to turn water into blood and to afflict the earth at will with any kind of plague.

7†When they have finished giving their testimony, the wild beast that comes up from the abyss will wage war against them and conquer and kill them. **8***†Their corpses will lie in the streets of the great city, which has the symbolic name "Sodom" or "Egypt," where also their Lord was crucified. **9**†Men from every people and race, language and nation, stare at their corpses for three and a half days but refuse to bury them. **10**The earth's inhabitants gloat over them and in their merriment exchange gifts, because these two prophets harassed everyone on earth. **11***But after the three and a half days, the breath of life which comes from God returned to them. When they stood on their feet sheer terror gripped those who saw them. **12**The two prophets heard a loud voice from heaven say to them, "Come up here!" So they went up to heaven in a cloud as their enemies looked on. **13**At that moment there was a violent earthquake and a tenth of the city fell in ruins. Seven thousand persons were killed during the earthquake; the rest were so terrified that they worshiped the God of heaven.

14The second woe is past, but beware! The third is coming very soon.

The Seventh Trumpet

15†Then the seventh angel blew his trumpet. Loud voices in heaven cried out, "The kingdom of the world now belongs to our Lord and to his Anointed One, and he shall reign forever and ever." **16**The twenty-four elders who were enthroned in God's presence fell down to worship God **17**and said:

"We praise you, the Lord God Almighty
    who is and who was.

You have assumed your great power,
    you have begun your reign.
18*The nations have raged in anger,
    but then came your day of wrath
    and the moment to judge the dead:
The time to reward your servants the prophets
    and the holy ones who revere you,
    the great and the small alike;
The time to destroy those who lay the earth waste."

19Then God's temple in heaven opened and in the temple could be seen the ark of his covenant. There were flashes of lightning and peals of thunder, an earthquake, and a violent hailstorm.

The Woman and the Dragon

12 **1***†A great sign appeared in the sky, a woman clothed with the sun, with the moon under her feet, and on her head a crown of twelve stars. **2**†Because she was with child, she wailed aloud in pain as she labored to give birth. **3***†Then another sign appeared in the sky: it was a huge dragon, flam-

---

† 11, 1: The temple and altar symbolize the new Israel; see note on 7, 4-8. The worshipers represent Christians; cf Ez 40, 3–42, 20; 47, 1-12; Zec 2, 5f. The measuring of the temple suggests that God will preserve the faithful remnant who continue true to Christ (14, 1-5); cf Is 4, 2f.

11, 2: *the outer court:* the court of the Gentiles. *Crush . . . forty-two months:* the duration of the vicious persecution of the Jews by Antiochus IV Epiphanes (Dn 7, 25; 12, 7). This persecution of three and a half years (1260 days: v 3; 12, 6) became the prototype of periods of trial for God's people; cf Lk 4, 25; Jas 5, 17. The reference here is to the persecution by the Romans; cf Introduction.

11, 3f: The two witnesses who are *dressed in sackcloth,* symbolizing lamentation and repentance, are perhaps the apostles Peter and Paul, who represent all Christian martyrs. *The two olive trees and the two lampstands:* the martyrs who stand *in the presence of the Lord.* The imagery is taken from Zec 4, 1-3.11-14, where the olive trees refer to Joshua and Zerubbabel.

11, 5f: These details are derived from stories of Moses, who turned *water into blood* (Ex 7, 17-20), and of Elijah, who called down fire from heaven (1 Kgs 18, 36-40; 2 Kgs 1, 10) and closed up the sky (1 Kgs 17, 1).

11, 7: *The wild beast . . . from the abyss:* the Roman emperor Nero, who symbolizes the forces of evil, or the antichrist (13, 1.8; 17, 8); cf Introduction; Dn 7, 2-8.11f.19-22.

11, 8: *"Sodom" or "Egypt":* symbols of immorality and oppression of God's people; cf Ex 1, 11-14; Is 1, 10. *Where also their Lord was crucified:* not the geographical, but the symbolic Jerusalem which rejects God and his witnesses—Rome, called Babylon in chapters 16—19; see note on 17, 9 and Introduction.

11, 9-12: Over the martyrdom (v 7) of the two witnesses, now called prophets, the ungodly rejoice *for three and a half days,* a symbolic period of time; see note on v 2. Afterward they go in triumph to heaven, as did Elijah (2 Kgs 2, 11).

11, 15-19: The seventh trumpet proclaims the coming of God's reign; see note on 10, 7.

12, 1f.4-6: The woman adorned with the sun, the moon, and the stars symbolizes God's people in the Old and the New Testament; cf Gn 37, 9f. The Israel of old gave birth to the Messiah (v 5) and then became the new Israel, the church, which suffers persecution by the dragon (vv 6.13-17).

12, 2: Because of Eve's sin, the woman gives birth in distress and pain (Gn 3, 16).

12, 3: *Huge dragon:* symbol of the forces of evil (v 9).

❊
    11/1: Zec 2, 5-9.   11: Ez 37, 10.
       4: Zec 4, 3.14.   18: Ps 2, 1.5.
       6: Ex 7, 17.   12/1: Gn 37, 9.
       8: Dn 7, 21.   3: Dn 7, 7.

ing red, with seven heads and ten horns; on his heads were seven diadems. **4*** His tail swept a third of the stars from the sky and hurled them down to the earth. Then the dragon stood before the woman about to give birth, ready to devour her child when it should be born. **5*†** She gave birth to a son—a boy destined to shepherd all the nations with an iron rod. Her child was caught up to God and to his throne. **6†** The woman herself fled into the desert, where a special place had been prepared for her by God; there she was taken care of for twelve hundred and sixty days.

7*† Then war broke out in heaven; Michael and his angels battled against the dragon. Although the dragon and his angels fought back, **8** they were overpowered and lost their place in heaven. **9†** The huge dragon, the ancient serpent known as the devil or Satan, the seducer of the whole world, was driven out; he was hurled down to earth and his minions with him.

10† Then I heard a loud voice in heaven say:

"Now have salvation and power come,
     the reign of our God and the authority
         of his Anointed One.
For the accuser of our brothers is cast out,
     who night and day accused them before our God.
11 They defeated him by the blood of the Lamb
     and by the word of their testimony;
     love for life did not deter them from death.
12 So rejoice, you heavens,
     and you that dwell therein!
But woe to you, earth and sea,
     for the devil has come down upon you!
His fury knows no limits,
     for he knows his time is short."

13 When the dragon saw that he had been cast down to the earth, he pursued the woman who had given birth to the boy. **14*†** But the woman was given the wings of a gigantic eagle so that she could fly off to her place in the desert, where, far from the serpent, she could be taken care of for a year and for two and a half years more. **15†** The serpent, however, spewed a torrent of water out of his mouth to search out the woman and sweep her away. **16** The earth then came to the woman's rescue by opening its mouth and swallowing the flood which the dragon spewed out of his mouth. **17*†** Enraged at her escape, the dragon went off to make war on the rest of her offspring, on those who keep God's commandments and give witness to Jesus. He took up his position by the shore of the sea.

The First Beast

13 **1†** THEN I saw a wild beast come out of the sea with ten horns and seven heads; on its horns were ten diadems and on its heads blasphemous names. **2*†** The beast I saw was like a leopard, but it had paws like a bear and the mouth of a lion. The dragon gave it his own power and throne, together with great authority. **3†** I noticed that one of the beast's heads seemed to have been mortally wounded, but this mortal wound was healed. In wonderment, the whole world followed after the beast. **4†** Men worshiped the dragon for giving his authority to the beast; they also worshiped the beast and said, "Who can compare with the beast, or come forward to fight against it?"

5*† The beast was given a mouth for uttering proud boasts and blasphemies, but the authority it received was to last only forty-two months. **6** It began to hurl blasphemies against God, reviling him and the members of his heavenly household as well. **7** The beast was allowed to wage war against God's people and conquer them. It was likewise granted authority over every race and people, language and nation. **8** The beast will be worshiped by all those inhabitants of earth who did not have their names written at the world's beginning in the book of the living, which belongs to the Lamb who was slain.

9 Let him who has ears heed these words! **10*** If one is destined for captivity, into captivity he goes! If one is destined to be slain by the sword, by the sword he will be slain! Such is the faithful endurance that distinguishes God's holy people.

The Second Beast

11† Then I saw another wild beast come up out of the earth; it had two horns like a ram and it spoke like

†

12, 5: *Shepherd . . . iron rod:* fulfilled in 19, 15; cf Ps 2, 9. *Was caught up to God:* a reference to Christ's ascension.

12, 6: God protects the persecuted church; see note on 11, 2.

12, 7: *Michael:* the archangel, guardian and champion of Israel; cf Dn 10, 13.21; 12, 1; Jude 9.

12, 9: *The ancient serpent who seduced Eve* (Gn 3, 1-6), mother of mankind; cf 20, 2; Eph 6, 12.

12, 10: *The accuser:* the meaning of the Hebrew word "Satan," who seduced Eve, found in v 9; Jb 1—2; Zec 3, 1; and 1 Chr 21, 1.

12, 14: *Gigantic eagle:* symbol of the power and swiftness of divine help; cf Ex 19, 4; Dt 32, 11; Is 40, 13.

12, 15: The serpent is depicted as the sea monster; cf 13, 1; Is 27, 1; Ez 32, 2; Ps 74, 13.

12, 17: Though the church is protected by God's special providence (v 16), the individual Christian is to expect persecution and suffering.

13, 1-8: This wild beast, combining features of the four beasts in Dn 7, 2-28, symbolizes the Roman empire; the seven heads represent the emperors; see notes on 17, 9f.12ff.

13, 2: Satan (12, 9), the prince of this world (Jn 12, 31), commissioned the beast to persecute the church (vv 5ff).

13, 3: This is perhaps a reference to the popular legend that Nero would come back to life and rule again after his death (which occurred in 68 A. D. from a self-inflicted wound in the throat); cf v 14; 17, 8. Domitian (81-96 A. D.) embodied all the cruelty and impiety of Nero; cf Introduction.

13, 4: *Worshiped the dragon:* allusion to emperor worship, which Domitian insisted upon and ruthlessly enforced.

13, 5f: Domitian, like Antiochus IV (Dn 7, 8.11.25), demanded that he be called by divine titles as "our lord and god" and "Jupiter"; see note on 11, 2.

13, 11-17: The second beast is described in terms of the false prophets; cf 16, 13; 19, 20; 20, 10; they accompany the false

❋
4: Dn 8, 10.
5: Ps 2, 9; Is 66, 7.
7: Dn 10, 13.
14: Gn 3, 15; Ex 19, 4.
17: 2 Thes 2, 3-12.
13/2: Dn 7, 3-6.
5: Dn 11, 36.
10: Jer 15, 2; Mt 13, 9.

a dragon. [12]It used the authority of the first beast to promote its interests by making the world and all its inhabitants worship the first beast, whose mortal wound had been healed. [13]*It performed great prodigies; it could even make fire come down from heaven to earth as men looked on. [14]Because of the prodigies it was allowed to perform by authority of the first beast, it led astray the earth's inhabitants, telling them to make an idol in honor of the beast that had been wounded by the sword and yet lived. [15]The second wild beast was then permitted to give life to the beast's image, so that the image had the power of speech and of putting to death anyone who refused to worship it. [16]It forced all men, small and great, rich and poor, slave and free, to accept a stamped image on their right hand or their forehead. [17]Moreover, it did not allow a man to buy or sell anything unless he was first marked with the name of the beast or with the number that stood for its name.

[18]†A certain wisdom is needed here; with a little ingenuity anyone can calculate the number of the beast, for it is a number that stands for a certain man. The man's number is six hundred sixty-six.

Companions of the Lamb

14 [1]*†THEN the Lamb appeared in my vision. He was standing on Mount Zion, and with him were the hundred and forty-four thousand who had his name and the name of his Father written on their foreheads. [2]I heard a sound from heaven which resembled the roaring of the deep, or loud peals of thunder; the sound I heard was like the melody of harpists playing on their harps. [3]*They were singing a new hymn before the throne, in the presence of the four living creatures and the elders. This hymn no one could learn except the hundred and forty-four thousand who had been ransomed from the world. [4]†These are men who have never been defiled by immorality with women. They are pure and follow the Lamb wherever he goes. They have been ransomed as the first fruits of mankind for God and the Lamb. [5]*†On their lips no deceit has been found; they are indeed without flaw.

The Three Angels

[6]†Then I saw another angel flying in midheaven, the herald of everlasting good news to the whole world, to every nation and race, language and people. [7]He said in a loud voice: "Honor God and give him glory, for his time has come to sit in judgment. Worship the Creator of heaven and earth, the Creator of the sea and the springs."

[8]*†A second angel followed and cried out:

"Fallen, fallen is Babylon the great,
which made all the nations drink
the poisoned wine of her lewdness!"

[9]A third angel followed the others and said in a loud voice: "If anyone worships the beast or its image, or accepts its mark on his forehead or hand, [10]†he too will drink the wine of God's wrath, poured full strength into the cup of his anger. He will be tormented in burning sulphur before the holy angels and before the Lamb, [11]and the smoke of their torment shall rise forever and ever. There shall be no relief day or night for those who worship the beast or its image or accept the mark of its name." [12]†This is what sustains the holy ones, who keep the commandments of God and their faith in Jesus.

[13]*I heard a voice from heaven say to me: "Write this down: Happy now are the dead who die in the Lord!" The Spirit added, "Yes, they shall find rest from their labors, for their good works accompany them."

The Harvest of the Earth

[14]*†Then, as I watched, a white cloud appeared, and on the cloud sat One like a Son of Man wearing a gold crown on his head and holding a sharp sickle in his hand. [15]*Another angel came out of the temple and in a loud voice cried out to him who sat on the

---

† messiahs (the first beast) foretold by Jesus (Mt 24, 24; Mk 13, 22; 2 Thes 2, 9); cf Dt 13, 2ff. Christians had either to worship the emperor and his image or to suffer martyrdom.

13, 18: Each of the letters of the alphabet in Hebrew as well as in Greek has a numerical value. Many possible combinations of letters will add up to the total *six hundred sixty-six*, and many candidates have been nominated for this infamous number. The most likely, however, is the emperor Caesar Nero (see note on v 3), whose name in Hebrew letters gives the required sum. Nero personifies the emperors who viciously persecuted the church.

14, 1: *Mount Zion:* Jerusalem, the traditional place where the true remnant, the Israel of faith, is to be gathered together in the messianic reign of Christ; cf 2 Kgs 19, 30f; Mi 4, 6ff; Ob 17; Jl 3, 5; Zep 3, 12-20. *His name . . . foreheads:* in contrast to the pagans who were marked with the name or number of the beast (13, 17); cf note on 7, 4-8.

14, 4: *Pure:* literally, virgins, because they never indulged in any idolatrous practices, which are considered to be adultery and fornication (2, 14f.20ff; 17, 1-7; cf Ez 16, 1-58; ch 23).

14, 5: *No deceit:* because they did not deny Christ or do homage to the beast.

14, 6: *Everlasting good news:* that God's eternal reign is about to begin; see note on 10, 7.

14, 8: This verse anticipates the lengthy dirge over Babylon (Rome) in chapter 18.

14, 10f: *The wine of God's wrath:* image taken from Is 51, 17; Jer 25, 15f; 49, 12; 51, 7; Ez 23, 31-34. Eternal punishment in the fiery pool of burning sulphur is also reserved for the devil, the beast, and the false prophet (19, 20; 20, 10; 21, 8).

14, 12f: In addition to *faith in Jesus* John insists upon the necessity and value of *good works*, as in 2, 23; 20, 12f; 22, 12; see note on 1, 3.

14, 14-20: The cutting down of the harvest as well as the gathering and treading of the grapes symbolize the doom of the ungodly which will come (19, 11-21); cf Jl 4, 12f; Is 63, 1-6.

---

* 13: Dt 13, 2-4; Mt 24, 24; 2 Thes 2, 9f.
14/1: Jl 3, 5; Ob 17; Acts 2, 21.
3: Ps 33, 3; Is 42, 10.
5: Zep 3, 13.
8: 18, 2f; Is 21, 9; Jer 25, 15; 51, 8.
13: Heb 4, 10.
14: Dn 7, 13.
15: Mt 13, 36-43; Jl 4, 13.

cloud, "Use your sickle and cut down the harvest, for now is the time to reap; the earth's harvest is fully ripe." ¹⁶So the one sitting on the cloud wielded his sickle over all the earth and reaped the earth's harvest.

¹⁷Then out of the temple in heaven came another angel, who likewise held a sharp sickle. ¹⁸A second angel, who was in charge of the fire at the altar of incense, cried out in a loud voice to the one who held the sharp sickle, "Use your sharp sickle and gather the grapes from the vines of the earth, for the clusters are ripe." ¹⁹*So the angel wielded his sickle over the earth and gathered the grapes of the earth. He threw them into the huge winepress of God's wrath. ²⁰†The winepress was trodden outside the city, and so much blood poured out of the winepress that for two hundred miles around, it reached as high as a horse's bridle.

The Seven Last Plagues

15 ¹†I saw in heaven another sign, great and awe-inspiring: seven angels holding the seven final plagues which would bring God's wrath to a climax.

²*I then saw something like a sea of glass mingled with fire. On the sea of glass were standing those who had won the victory over the beast and its image, and also the number that signified its name. They were holding the harps used in worshiping God, ³*†and they sang the song of Moses, the servant of God, and the song of the Lamb:

"Mighty and wonderful are your works,
        Lord God Almighty!
Righteous and true are your ways,
        O King of the nations!
⁴*Who would dare refuse you honor,
        or the glory due your name, O Lord?
Since you alone are holy,
        all nations shall come
        and worship in your presence.
Your mighty deeds are clearly seen."

⁵†After this I had another vision. The heavenly sanctuary which is the tent of witness opened up, ⁶and out of it came the seven angels holding the seven plagues. The angels were dressed in pure white linen, each with a sash of gold about his breast. ⁷One of the four living creatures gave to the seven angels seven golden bowls filled with the wrath of the God who lives forever and ever. ⁸*Then the sanctuary became so filled with the smoke which arose from God's glory and might that no one could enter it until the seven plagues of the seven angels had come to an end.

The Seven Bowls

16 ¹†I heard a mighty voice from the sanctuary say to the seven angels, "Go and pour out upon the earth the seven bowls of God's wrath!"

²†The first angel went out, and when he poured out his bowl on the earth, severe and festering boils broke out on the men who had accepted the mark of the beast or worshiped its image.

³†The second angel poured out his bowl on the sea. The sea turned to blood like that of a corpse, and every creature living in the sea died.

⁴*The third angel poured out his bowl on the rivers and springs. These also turned to blood. ⁵Then I heard the angel in charge of the waters cry out:

"You are just, O holy One
        who is and who was,
        in passing this sentence!
⁶*To those who shed the blood of saints and prophets,
        you have given blood to drink;
        they deserve it."

⁷*Then I heard the altar cry out:

"Yes, Lord God Almighty,
        your judgments are true and just!"

⁸The fourth angel poured out his bowl on the sun. He was commissioned to burn men with fire. ⁹Those who were scorched by the intense heat blasphemed the name of God who had power to send these plagues, but they did not repent or give him due honor.

¹⁰*†The fifth angel poured out his bowl on the throne of the beast. Its kingdom was plunged into darkness; men bit their tongues in pain ¹¹*and blasphemed the God of heaven because of their suffering and their boils. But they did not turn away from their wicked deeds.

¹²†The sixth angel poured out his bowl on the great river Euphrates. Its water was dried up to prepare the way for the kings of the East. ¹³I saw three unclean

---

† 14, 20: *Two hundred miles:* literally, 1600 stadia. The stadion, a Greek unit of measurement, was about 607 feet in length.

15, 1-4: A vision of the victorious martyrs precedes the vision of woe in 15, 5—16, 21; cf 7, 9-12.

15, 3: *The song of Moses:* which Moses and the Israelites sang after their escape from the oppression of Egypt (Ex 15, 1-19). The martyrs have escaped from the oppression of the devil.

15, 5: *The tent of witness:* the name of the meeting tent in the Greek text of Ex 40.

16, 1-21: These seven bowls, like the seven seals (6, 1-17; 8, 1) and the seven trumpets (8, 2—9, 21; 11, 15-19), bring on a succession of disasters modeled in part on the plagues of Egypt (Ex 7—12); see note on 6, 12ff.

16, 2: Like the sixth Egyptian plague (Ex 9, 8-11).

16, 3f: Like the first Egyptian plague (Ex 7, 20f). The same woe followed the blowing of the second trumpet (8, 8f).

16, 10: *The throne of the beast:* symbol of the forces of evil. *Darkness:* like the ninth Egyptian plague (Ex 10, 21ff); cf 9, 2.

16, 12: *The kings of the East:* Parthians; see notes on 6, 2 and 17, 12ff.

❋
    19: Is 63, 1-6.
15/2: 7, 9.14; 13, 15-18.
    3: Pss 92, 5; 98, 1;
        145, 17.
    4: Jer 10, 7.
    8: Is 6, 4.
16/4: Ex 7, 14-24.
    6: Ez 35, 6; Mt 23, 35.
    7: Dn 3, 27.
    10: Ex 10, 21-23.
    11: Ex 9, 8-11; Jer 5, 3.

spirits like frogs come from the mouth of the dragon, from the mouth of the beast, and from the mouth of the false prophet; **14**these spirits were devils who worked prodigies. They went out to assemble all the kings of the earth for battle on the great day of God the Almighty. **15***†(Be on your guard! I come like a thief. Happy the man who stays wide awake and fully clothed for fear of going naked and exposed for all to see!) **16**†The devils then assembled the kings in a place called in Hebrew "Armageddon."

17Finally, the seventh angel poured out his bowl upon the empty air. From the throne in the sanctuary came a loud voice which said, "It is finished!" **18**There followed lightning flashes and peals of thunder, then a violent earthquake. Such was its violence that there has never been one like it in all the time men have lived on the earth. **19**†The great city was split into three parts, and the other Gentile cities also fell. God remembered Babylon the great, giving her the cup filled with the blazing wine of his wrath. **20**†Every island fled and mountains disappeared. **21***Giant hailstones like huge weights came crashing down on mankind from the sky, and men blasphemed God for the plague of hailstones, because this plague was so severe.

IV: PUNISHMENT OF BABYLON

Babylon the Great

17 **1***†THEN ONE OF THE SEVEN ANGELS who were holding the seven bowls came to me and said: "Come, I will show you the judgment in store for the great harlot who sits by the waters of the deep. **2**†The kings of the earth have committed fornication with her, and the earth's inhabitants have grown drunk on the wine of her lewdness." **3***†The angel then carried me away in spirit to a desolate place where I saw a woman seated on a scarlet beast which was covered with blasphemous names. This beast had seven heads and ten horns. **4**†The woman was dressed in purple and scarlet and adorned with gold and pearls and other jewels. In her hand she held a gold cup that was filled with the abominable and sordid deeds of her lewdness. **5**On her forehead was written a symbolic name, "Babylon the great, mother of harlots and all the world's abominations." **6**I saw that the woman was drunk with the blood of God's holy ones and the blood of those martyred for their faith in Jesus.

The Meaning of Beast and Harlot

When I saw her I was greatly astonished. **7**The angel said to me: "Why are you so taken aback? I will explain to you the symbolism of the woman and of the seven-headed and ten-horned beast carrying her. **8**†The beast you saw existed once but now exists no longer. It will come up from the abyss once more before going to final ruin. All the men of the earth whose names have not been written in the book of the living from the creation of the world shall be amazed when they see the beast, for it existed once and now exists no longer, and yet it will exist again. **9**†Here is the clue for one who possesses wisdom! The seven heads are seven hills on which the woman sits enthroned. They are also seven kings: **10**†five have already fallen, one lives now, and the last has not yet come; but when he does come he will remain only a short while. **11**†The beast which existed once but now exists no longer, even though it is an eighth king, is really one of the seven and is on its way to ruin. **12***†The ten horns you saw represent ten kings who have not yet been crowned; they will possess royal authority along with the beast, but only for an hour. **13**Then they will come to agreement and bestow their power and authority on the beast. **14***They will fight against the Lamb but the Lamb will conquer them, for he is the Lord of lords and the King of kings; victorious, too, will be his followers—the ones who were called: the chosen and the faithful."

15The angel then said to me: "The waters on which you saw the harlot enthroned are large numbers of peoples and nations and tongues. **16**†The ten horns you saw on the beast will turn against the harlot with hatred; they will strip off her finery and leave her naked; they will devour her flesh and set her on fire. **17**For God has put it into their minds to carry out his plan, by making them agree to bestow their sov-

---

† 16, 15: *Like a thief:* as in 3, 3; cf Mt 24, 42ff; 1 Thes 5, 2. *Happy:* see note on 1, 3. *Fully clothed:* see note on 3, 18.

16, 16: *Armageddon:* "Mountain of Megiddo." Since Megiddo was the scene of many decisive battles in antiquity (Jgs 5, 19f; 2 Kgs 9, 27; 2 Chr 35, 20-24), the town became the symbol of the final disastrous rout of the forces of evil; see note on v 19.

16, 19: *The great city:* Rome and the empire.

16, 20f: See note on 6, 12ff. *Hailstones:* as in the seventh Egyptian plague (Ex 9, 23f); cf 8, 7.

17, 1-6: Babylon, *a symbolic name* (v 5) of Rome, is graphically described as *the great harlot.*

17, 2: *Fornication . . . . lewdness:* see note on 14, 4. The pagan kings subject to Rome adopted the cult of the emperor.

17, 3: *Scarlet beast:* see note on 13, 1-8. *Blasphemous names:* divine titles assumed by the Roman emperors; see note on 13, 5f.

17, 4: Reference to the great wealth of Rome.

17, 8: Allusion to the belief that the dead Nero would return to power (v 11); see note on 13, 3.

17, 9: *Seven hills:* of Rome.

17, 10: There is little agreement as to the identity of the Roman emperors alluded to here. The number *seven* (v 9) suggests that all the emperors are meant; see note on 1, 4.

17, 11: *The beast:* Nero; see note on v 8.

17, 12ff: *Ten kings . . . not yet . . . crowned:* perhaps Parthian satraps who are to accompany the revived Nero (*the beast*) in his march on Rome to regain power; see note on 13, 3. In 19, 11ff. *the Lamb* and *his followers* will conquer them.

17, 16ff: The ten pagan kings (v 12) unwittingly fulfill God's will against *the harlot* Rome, *the great city;* cf Ez 16, 37.

✼   15: 3, 3; Mt 24, 43;   3: Jer 51, 7.
       Lk 12, 39.   12: Dn 7, 24.
      21: Ex 9, 22-26.   14: 19, 16; Rom 6, 15;
      17/1: Jer 51, 13.   1 Tm 6, 15.

ereignty on the beast until his will is accomplished. [18]The woman you saw is the great city which has sovereignty over the kings of the earth."

The Fall of Babylon

18 [1]*†AFTER this I saw another angel coming down from heaven. His authority was so great that all the earth was lighted up by his glory. [2]*He cried out in a strong voice:

"Fallen, fallen is Babylon the great!
  She has become a dwelling place for demons.
She is a cage for every unclean spirit,
  a cage for every filthy and disgusting bird;
[3]†For she has made all the nations drink
  the poisoned wine of her lewdness.
The kings of the earth committed fornication with her,
  and the world's merchants grew rich from her wealth and wantonness."

[4]*Then I heard another voice from heaven say:

"Depart from her, my people,
  for fear of sinning with her
  and sharing the plagues inflicted on her!
[5]*For her sins have piled up as high as heaven,
  and God keeps count of her crimes.
[6] Pay her back as she has paid others;
  pay her double for her deeds!
Pour into her cup twice the amount she concocted!
[7]* In proportion to her boasting and sensuality,
  repay her in torment and grief!
For she said to herself,
  'I sit enthroned as a queen.
No widow am I,
  and never will I go into mourning!'
[8] Therefore her plagues will come all at once,
  death and mourning and famine.
She shall be consumed by fire,
  for mighty is the Lord God who condemns her."

[9]The kings of the earth who committed fornication with her and wallowed in her sensuality will weep and lament over her when they see the smoke arise as she burns. [10]They will keep their distance for fear of the punishment inflicted on her, and will say:

"Alas, alas, great city that you are,
  Babylon the mighty!
In a single hour your doom has come!"

[11]†The merchants of the world will weep and mourn over her too, for there will be no more market for their imports—[12]their cargoes of gold and silver, precious stones and pearls; fine linen and purple garments, silk and scarlet cloth; fragrant wood of every kind, all

sorts of ivory pieces and expensive wooden furniture; bronze, iron and marble; [13]cinnamon and amomum, perfumes, myrrh and frankincense; wine and olive oil, fine flour and grain; cattle and sheep, horses and carriages; slaves and human lives.

[14]*"The fruit your appetite craved
  has deserted you.
All your luxury and splendor are gone;
  you shall never find them again!"

[15]The merchants who deal in these goods, who grew rich from business with the city, will keep their distance for fear of the punishment inflicted on her. Weeping and mourning, [16]*they cry out:

"Alas, alas, the great city,
  dressed in fine linen
  and purple and scarlet,
Adorned all in gold
  and jewels and pearls!
[17]In a single hour
  this great wealth has been destroyed!"

Every captain and navigator, all sailors and seafaring men, then stood at a distance [18]and cried out when they saw the smoke go up as the city burned to the ground: "What city could have compared with this great one!" [19]They poured dust on their heads and cried out, weeping and mourning:

"Alas, alas, the great city,
  in which all shipowners grew rich
  from their profitable trade with her!
In a single hour
  her destruction has come about!"

[20]*Rejoice over her, you heavens, you saints, apostles and prophets! For God has exacted punishment from her on your account.
[21]*A powerful angel picked up a stone like a huge millstone and hurled it into the sea and said:

"Babylon the great city
  shall be cast down like this, with violence,
  and nevermore be found!
[22]*No tunes of harpists and minstrels,
  of flutists and trumpeters,
  shall ever again be heard in you!
No craftsmen in any trade
  shall ever again be found in you!
No sound of the millstone
  shall ever again be heard in you!

---

† 18, 1—19, 4: A stirring dirge over the fall of Babylon-Rome. The perspective is prophetic—as if the fall of Rome had already taken place. The imagery here, as elsewhere in this book, is not to be taken literally. The vindictiveness of some of the language is meant to portray symbolically the inexorable demands of God's holiness and justice.

18, 3.24: Rome is condemned for *her lewdness*, symbol of idolatry (see note on 14, 4), and for persecuting the church; cf 19, 2.

18, 11: Ironically, the merchants weep not for Babylon-Rome, but for their lost markets; cf Ez 27, 36.

18/1: Jer 50, 39.
2: 14, 8; Is 21, 9; Jer 51, 8.
4: Jer 50, 8.
5: Jer 51, 9.
7: Is 47, 8.
14: Hos 10, 5.
16: 17, 4; Ez 27, 27-29.
20: Jer 51, 48.
21: Jer 51, 63f.
22: Is 24, 8; Ez 26, 13.

23No light from a burning lamp
    shall ever again shine out in you!
No voices of bride and groom
    shall ever again be heard in you!
Because your merchants were the world's nobility,
    you led all nations astray by your sorcery.

24*"In her was found the blood of prophets and saints and of all who were slain on the earth."

19   **1**AFTER this I heard what sounded like the loud song of a great assembly in heaven. They were singing:

    "Alleluia!
Salvation, glory and might belong to our God,
  2*for his judgments are true and just!
He has condemned the great harlot
    who corrupted the earth with her harlotry.
He has avenged the blood of his servants
    which was shed by her hand."

3Once more they sang "Alleluia!" And as the smoke began to rise from her forever and ever, **4***the four and twenty elders and the four living creatures fell down and worshiped God seated on the throne and sang, "Amen! Alleluia!"

Song of Victory

5A voice coming from the throne cried out:

    "Praise our God, all you his servants,
    the small and the great, who revere him!"

6Then I heard what sounded like the shouts of a great crowd, or the roaring of the deep, or mighty peals of thunder, as they cried:

    "Alleluia!
The Lord is king,
    our God, the Almighty!
7*†Let us rejoice and be glad,
    and give him glory!
For this is the wedding day of the Lamb;
    his bride has prepared herself for the wedding.
8*†She has been given a dress to wear
    made of finest linen, brilliant white."

(The linen dress is the virtuous deeds of God's saints.)
9*†The angel then said to me: "Write this down: Happy are they who have been invited to the wedding feast of the Lamb." The angel continued, "These words are true; they come from God." **10**†I fell at his feet to worship him, but he said to me, "No, get up! I am merely a fellow servant with you and your brothers who give witness to Jesus. Worship God alone. The prophetic spirit proves itself by witnessing to Jesus."

V: DESTRUCTION OF PAGAN NATIONS

The King of Kings

11†THE HEAVENS WERE OPENED, and as I looked on, a white horse appeared; its rider was called "The Faithful and True." Justice is his standard in passing judgment and in waging war. **12**†His eyes blazed like fire, and on his head were many diadems. Inscribed on his person was a name known to no one but himself. **13***†He wore a cloak that had been dipped in blood, and his name was the Word of God. **14***The armies of heaven were behind him riding white horses and dressed in fine linen, pure and white. **15***†Out of his mouth came a sharp sword for striking down the nations. He will shepherd them with an iron rod; it is he who will tread out in the winepress the blazing wrath of God the Almighty. **16***A name was written on the part of the cloak that covered his thigh: "King of kings and Lord of lords."

17*†Next I saw an angel standing on the sun. He cried out in a loud voice to all the birds flying in midheaven: "Come! Gather together for the great feast God has prepared for you! **18**You are to eat the flesh of kings, of commanders and warriors, of horses and their riders; the flesh of all men, the free and the slave, the small and the great." **19**Then I saw the beast and the kings of the earth, and the armies they had mustered to do battle with the One riding the horse, and with his army. **20***†The beast was captured along with the false prophet who performed in its presence the prodigies that led men astray, making them accept the mark

---

†   19, 7: *The wedding day of the Lamb:* symbol of God's reign about to begin (21, 1-22, 5); see note on 10, 7. *His bride:* the church (2 Cor 11, 2; Eph 5, 22-27). Marriage is one of the biblical metaphors used to describe the covenant relationship between God and his people (Hos 2, 16-22; Is 54, 5f; 62, 5; Ez 16, 6-14). Hence, idolatry and apostasy are viewed as adultery and prostitution (Hos 2, 4-15; Ez 16, 15-63); see note on 14, 4.
   19, 8: See note on 14, 12f.
   19, 9: *Happy:* see note on 1, 3.
   19, 10: *The prophetic spirit . . . Jesus:* As the prophets were inspired to proclaim God's word, so the Christian is called to give witness to the Word of God (v 13) made flesh; cf 1, 2; 6, 9; 12, 17.
   19, 11-16: Symbolic description of the exalted Christ (1, 13-16), who, together with the armies of heaven, overcomes the beast and its followers (17, 14).
   19, 12: *A name . . . no one but himself:* in Semitic thought, the name conveyed the reality of the person; cf Mt 11, 27; Lk 10, 22.
   19, 13: *Had been dipped in:* other ancient MSS read "had been sprinkled with"; cf v 15. *The Word of God:* Christ is the revelation of the Father (Jn 1, 1.14; 1 Jn 2, 14).
   19, 15: The treading of *the winepress* is a prophetic symbol used to describe the destruction of God's enemies (Is 63, 1-6; Jl 4, 13).
   19, 17f.21: Gruesome imagery borrowed from Ez 39, 4.17-20.
   19, 20: *Beast . . . false prophet:* see notes on chapter 13. *The fiery pool . . . sulphur:* symbol of hell (14, 10; 20, 10.14f), different from the abyss; see note on 9, 1.

✽

    24: Mt 23, 35-37.   13: Is 63, 1.
 19/2: Dn 3, 27.   14: Jn 1, 1.
     4: Is 34, 10.   15: Ps 2, 9.
     7: Mt 22, 9; Eph 5, 27.   16: 17, 14; Is 63, 3;
     8: Is 61, 10.   1 Tm 6, 15.
     9: Mt 22, 2; Lk 14, 16.   17: Ez 39, 17.

of the beast and worship its image. Both were hurled down alive into the fiery pool of burning sulphur. ²¹The rest were slain by the sword which came out of the mouth of the One who rode the horse, and all the birds gorged themselves on the flesh of the slain.

Thousand-Year Reign

20 ¹†THEN I saw an angel come down from heaven, holding the key to the abyss and a huge chain in his hand. ²*†He seized the dragon, the ancient serpent, who is the devil or Satan, and chained him up for a thousand years. ³The angel hurled him into the abyss, which he closed and sealed over him. He did this so that the dragon might not lead the nations astray until the thousand years are over. After this, the dragon is to be released for a short time.

⁴*†Then I saw some thrones. Those who were sitting on them were empowered to pass judgment. I also saw the spirits of those who had been beheaded for their witness to Jesus and the word of God, those who had never worshiped the beast or its image nor accepted its mark on their foreheads or their hands. They came to life again and reigned with Christ for a thousand years. ⁵The others who were dead did not come to life till the thousand years were over. This is the first resurrection; ⁶†happy and holy are they who share in the first resurrection! The second death will have no claim on them; they shall serve God and Christ as priests, and shall reign with him for a thousand years.

⁷†When the thousand years are over, Satan will be released from his prison. ⁸*†He will go out to seduce the nations in all four corners of the earth, and muster for war the troops of Gog and Magog, numerous as the sands of the sea. ⁹*†They invaded the whole country and surrounded the beloved city where God's people were encamped; but fire came down from heaven and devoured them. ¹⁰The devil who led them astray was hurled into the pool of burning sulphur, where the beast and the false prophet had also been thrown. There they will be tortured day and night, forever and ever.

The Last Judgment

¹¹*Next I saw a large white throne and the One who sat on it. The earth and the sky fled from his presence until they could no longer be seen. ¹²†I saw the dead, the great and the lowly, standing before the throne. Lastly, among the scrolls, the book of the living was opened. The dead were judged according to their conduct as recorded on the scrolls. ¹³†The sea gave up its dead; then death and the nether world gave up their dead. Each person was judged according to his

conduct. ¹⁴†Then death and the nether world were hurled into the pool of fire, which is the second death; ¹⁵anyone whose name was not found inscribed in the book of the living was hurled into this pool of fire.

VI: NEW CREATION

New Heavens and New Earth

21 ¹*†THEN I SAW NEW HEAVENS and a new earth. The former heavens and the former earth had passed away, and the sea was no longer. ²†I also saw a new Jerusalem, the holy city, coming down out of heaven from God, beautiful as a bride prepared to meet her husband. ³*†I heard a loud voice from the throne cry out: "This is God's dwelling among men. He shall dwell with them and they shall be his people and he shall be their God who is always with them. ⁴*He shall wipe every tear from their eyes, and there shall be no more death or mourning, crying out or pain, for the former world has passed away."

⁵*†The One who sat on the throne said to me, "See, I make all things new!" Then he said, "Write these matters down, for the words are trustworthy and true!" ⁶*†He went on to say: "These words are already fulfilled! I am the Alpha and the Omega, the Beginning and the End. To anyone who thirsts I will

---

†   20, 1-6: Like the other numerical values in this book, *the thousand years* are not to be taken literally; they symbolize the long period of time between the chaining up of Satan (a symbol for Christ's resurrection-victory over death and the forces of evil) and the end of the world. During this time God's people share in the glorious reign of God which is present to them in virtue of their baptism-victory over death and sin (Rom 6, 1-8; Jn 5, 24f; 16, 33; 1 Jn 3, 14; Eph 2, 1).

20, 1: *Abyss:* see note on 9, 1.

20, 2: *Dragon . . . serpent . . . Satan:* see notes on 12, 3.9f.15.

20, 4: *Beast . . . mark:* see chapter 13 and its notes.

20, 6: *Happy:* see note on 1, 3. *Second death:* see note on 2, 11. *Priests:* as in 1, 6; 5, 10; 22, 3; cf 1 Pt 2, 9.

20, 7-10: A description of the symbolic battle to take place when Satan is released at the end of time, *when the thousand years are over;* see note on vv 1-6.

20, 8: *Gog and Magog:* symbols of all pagan nations; the names are taken from Ez 38, 1—39, 20.

20, 9: *The whole country:* Palestine. *The beloved city:* Jerusalem; see note on 14, 1.

20, 12: *The book of the living:* see note on 3, 4f. *Judged . . . scrolls:* see note on 14, 12f.

20, 13: *The nether world:* see note on 1, 18.

20, 14: *Second death:* see note on 2, 11.

21, 1—22, 5: A description of God's eternal kingdom in heaven under the symbols of new heavens and a new earth (Is 65, 17-25; 66, 22).

21, 2: *New Jerusalem . . . bride:* symbol of the church (Gal 4, 26); see note on 19, 7.

21, 3f: Language taken from Ez 37, 27; Is 8, 8; 25, 8; 35, 10; cf 7, 17.

21, 5: *The One . . . on the throne:* God himself; cf 4, 1-11.

21, 6: *These words . . . fulfilled:* God's reign has already begun; see note on 20, 1-6. *Alpha and . . . Omega:* see note on 1, 8. *Life-giving water:* see note on 7, 17.

❋   20/2: Gn 3, 1.   21/1: Is 65, 17; 66, 22;
       4: Mt 19, 28.   2 Pt 3, 13.
       8: Ez 38, 2.9; 39, 2.   3: Ez 37, 27.
       9: Ez 38, 22.   4: 7, 17; Is 25, 8; 35, 10.
     11: Rom 2, 6.   5: Is 43, 19; 2 Cor 5, 17.
                                     6: 22, 17; Is 55, 1.

give to drink without cost from the spring of life-giving water. **7***†He who wins the victory shall inherit these gifts; I will be his God and he shall be my son. **8**†As for the cowards and traitors to the faith, the depraved and murderers, the fornicators and sorcerers, the idol-worshipers and deceivers of every sort—their lot is the fiery pool of burning sulphur, the second death!"

The New Jerusalem

9†One of the seven angels who held the seven bowls filled with the seven last plagues came and said to me, "Come, I will show you the woman who is the bride of the Lamb." **10***He carried me away in spirit to the top of a very high mountain and showed me the holy city Jerusalem coming down out of heaven from God. **11***It gleamed with the splendor of God. The city had the radiance of a precious jewel that sparkled like a diamond. **12**Its wall, massive and high, had twelve gates at which twelve angels were stationed. Twelve names were written on the gates, the names of the twelve tribes of Israel. **13***There were three gates facing east, three north, three south, and three west. **14***†The wall of the city had twelve courses of stones as its foundation, on which were written the names of the twelve apostles of the Lamb.

15†The one who spoke to me held a rod of gold for measuring the city, its gates, and its wall. **16**The city is perfectly square, its length and its width being the same. He measured the city with the rod and found it twelve thousand furlongs in length, in width, and in height. **17**Its wall measured a hundred and forty-four cubits in height by the unit of measurement the angel used. **18***†The wall was constructed of jasper; the city was of pure gold, crystal-clear. **19**The foundation of the city wall was ornate with precious stones of every sort: the first course of stones was jasper, the second sapphire, the third chalcedony, the fourth emerald, **20**the fifth sardonyx, the sixth carnelian, the seventh chrysolite, the eighth beryl, the ninth topaz, the tenth chrysoprase, the eleventh hyacinth, and the twelfth amethyst. **21**The twelve gates were twelve pearls, each made of a single pearl; and the streets of the city were of pure gold, transparent as glass.

22†I saw no temple in the city. The Lord, God the Almighty, is its temple—he and the Lamb. **23***†The city had no need of sun or moon, for the glory of God gave it light, and its lamp was the Lamb. **24***†The nations shall walk by its light; to it the kings of the earth shall bring their treasures. **25***During the day its gates shall never be shut, and there shall be no night. **26**The treasures and wealth of the nations shall be brought there, **27***but nothing profane shall enter it, nor anyone who is a liar or has done a detestable

act. Only those shall enter whose names are inscribed in the book of the living kept by the Lamb.

22 **1***†THE angel then showed me the river of life-giving water, clear as crystal, which issued from the throne of God and of the Lamb **2**†and flowed down the middle of the streets. On either side of the river grew the trees of life which produce fruit twelve times a year, once each month; their leaves serve as medicine for the nations. **3**Nothing deserving a curse shall be found there. The throne of God and of the Lamb shall be there, and his servants shall serve him faithfully. **4***†They shall see him face to face and bear his name on their foreheads. **5***The night shall be no more. They will need no light from lamps or the sun, for the Lord God shall give them light, and they shall reign forever.

VII: EPILOGUE

6THE ANGEL SAID TO ME: "These words are trustworthy and true; the Lord, the God of prophetic spirits, has sent his angel to show his servants what must happen very soon."

7†"Remember, I am coming soon! Happy the man who heeds the prophetic message of this book!"

8It is I, John, who heard and saw all these things, and when I heard and saw them I fell down to wor-

† 21, 7: *The victory:* over the forces of evil; see the conclusions of the seven letters (2, 7.11.17.26; 3, 5.12.21). *He shall be my son:* the victorious Christian enjoys divine sonship by adoption (Gal 4, 4-7; Rom 8, 14-17); see note on 2, 26ff.
21, 8: *Cowards:* their conviction is so weak that they deny Christ in time of trial and become *traitors. Second death:* see note on 2, 11.
21, 9—22, 5: Symbolic description of the new Jerusalem, the church. Most of the images are borrowed from Ez 40—48.
21, 9: *The woman . . . bride of the Lamb:* the church (v 2), the new Jerusalem (v 10).
21, 14: *Courses of stones . . . apostles:* cf Eph 2, 19f.
21, 15ff: The city is shaped like a gigantic cube, a symbol of perfection (cf 1 Kgs 6, 19f). The measurements of the city and its wall are multiples of the symbolic number twelve; see note on 7, 4-8. *Twelve thousand furlongs:* literally, 12,000 stadia, about 1500 miles; see note on 14, 20. The *cubit* was about 18 inches.
21, 18-21: The gold and precious gems symbolize the beauty and excellence of the church; cf Ex 28, 15-21; Is 54, 11f; Tb 13, 16f.
21, 22: Christ is present throughout the church; hence, no temple is needed as an earthly dwelling for God; cf Mt 18, 20; 28, 20; Jn 4, 21.
21, 23: *Lamp . . . Lamb:* cf Jn 8, 12.
21, 24-27: All men of good will are welcome in the church; cf Is 60, 1.3.5.11. *The book of the living:* see note on 3, 4f.
22, 1.17: *Life-giving water:* see note on 7, 17.
22, 2: *The tree of life:* cf v 14; see note on 2, 7. *Fruit . . . medicine:* cf Ez 47, 12.
22, 4: *See him face to face:* cf Mt 5, 8; 1 Cor 13, 12; 1 Jn 3, 2.
22, 7.12.20: *I am coming soon:* Christ is the speaker; see note on 1, 3.
22, 7.14: *Happy:* see note on 1, 3.

✱
7: 2 Sm 7, 14.
10: Heb 11, 10.
11: Is 60, 1f.
13: Ez 48, 31-35.
14: Eph 2, 20.
18: Is 54, 11f.
23: Is 60, 19f; Jn 2, 19-21; 2 Cor 3, 18.
24: Is 60, 3.
25: Is 60, 11.
27: Is 35, 8; 52, 1; 2 Pt 3, 13.
22/1: Ez 47, 1-12.
4: 1 Cor 13, 12; 1 Jn 3, 2.
5: Is 60, 20.

ship at the feet of the angel who showed them to me. ⁹But he said to me: "No, get up! I am merely a fellow servant with you and your brothers the prophets and those who heed the message of this book. Worship God alone!"

¹⁰*†Then someone said to me: "Do not seal up the prophetic words of this book, for the appointed time is near! ¹¹Let the wicked continue in their wicked ways, the depraved in their depravity! The virtuous must live on in their virtue and the holy ones in their holiness!"

¹²*"Remember, I am coming soon! I bring with me the reward that will be given to each man as his conduct deserves. ¹³*†I am the Alpha and the Omega, the First and the Last, the Beginning and the End! ¹⁴†Happy are they who wash their robes so as to have free access to the tree of life and enter the city through its gates! ¹⁵Outside are the dogs and sorcerers, the fornicators and murderers, the idol-worshipers and all who love falsehood.

¹⁶†"It is I, Jesus, who have sent my angel to give you this testimony about the churches. I am the Root and Offspring of David, the Morning Star shining bright."

¹⁷*†The Spirit and the Bride say, "Come!" Let him who hears answer, "Come!" Let him who is thirsty come forward; let all who desire it accept the gift of life-giving water.

¹⁸*I myself give witness to all who hear the prophetic words of this book. If anyone adds to these words, God will visit him with all the plagues described herein! ¹⁹If anyone takes from the words of this prophetic book, God will take away his share in the tree of life and the holy city described here!

²⁰†The One who gives this testimony says, "Yes, I am coming soon!" Amen! Come, Lord Jesus!

²¹The grace of the Lord Jesus be with you all. Amen!

---

*
10: 10, 4.
12: Is 40, 10; 62, 13.
13: 1, 8; Is 41, 4; 44, 6.
17: Is 55, 1.
18: Dt 4, 2.

†
22, 10: *The appointed time:* see note on 1, 3.
22, 13: Christ applies to himself the words used by God in 1, 8.
22, 14: *The city:* heavenly Jerusalem; see note on 21, 2.
22, 16: *The Root . . . of David:* see note on 5, 5. *Morning Star:* see note on 2, 26ff.
22, 17: *Bride:* the church; see note on 21, 2.
22, 20: *Come, Lord Jesus:* a liturgical refrain, similar to the Aramaic expression *Marana tha,* "Our Lord, come!" in 1 Cor 16, 22. It was a prayer for the coming of Christ in glory at the parousia; see note on 1, 3.

A Catholic

ENCYCLOPEDIC DICTIONARY

And Biblical Reference Guide

THIS UNIQUE combination Catholic Encyclopedic Dictionary and Biblical Reference Guide has been created to provide maximum benefit to Bible students and general readers alike. There is an article on many important biblical subjects accompanied by textual references whenever possible. Thus it combines the best features of a biblical encyclopedia, dictionary, and concordance, making it a useful and efficient research aid. In addition to the biblical articles, many other subjects of interest to Catholics are discussed.

The articles on biblical subjects cover nearly everything the Bible scholar wishes to know. There are commentaries on individual men and women, tribes, towns, and events. Animals and plants of Bible times are discussed. There are articles on various facets of the Hebrew and other biblical civilizations. After each subject is thoroughly explained, every important textual reference is cited by subject, book, chapter, verse, and page number, providing complete data. Combined in one article, here is information which otherwise could be obtained only from several different volumes.

The articles on subjects not found in the Bible cover a wide range of topics and answer everyday questions and problems of the Catholic family. This section is written in nontechnical language so everyone can understand the Church's teachings, the reasoning behind these teachings, and their importance in the daily life of the practical Catholic.

SUBJECT	BOOK	CHAP.	VERSE	PAGE

A

AARON. The great-grandson of Levi, son of Amram and Jochebed, brother of Moses and his associate in leading the Jews out of Egypt. Although Aaron was a subordinate to Moses and derived all his authority from him, his individual responsibilities and duties were of equal importance to those of his younger brother. Most important in the history of Aaron is his divine appointment as the first high priest of Israel, resulting in the setting apart of Levi as the priestly tribe and the promulgation of the levitical system of sacrifices and offerings.

SUBJECT	BOOK	CHAP.	VERSE	PAGE
Son of Amram, brother of Moses and Miriam of the tribe of Levi	*Ex	6	16-20	51
	Ex	7	1, 7	52
	Nm	26	59	131
Married Elisheba, daughter of Amminadab of the tribe of Judah, father of four sons	*Ex	6	23	51
	Nm	3	2	108
Death of two eldest sons; priesthood perpetuated by other two, Eleazar and Ithamar	*Lv	10	1-2	88
	1 Chr	24	2-3	328
Divinely chosen as assistant to Moses	*Ex	4	14-16, 27	49
	Ex	4	29-31	49
	Ex	7	1	52
Spokesman for Moses before Pharaoh joined in bringing upon Egypt ten plagues	*Ex	5-12		50-55

SUBJECT	BOOK	CHAP.	VERSE	PAGE
Accompanies Moses part way up Sinai; sees symbol of Divine presence	*Ex	24	1-11	66
Appointed first high priest of Israel; tribe of Levi set apart to priestly caste	*Ex	28	1	69
	Ex	29	29-30	70
	Ex	40	12-14	80
	Nm	18	1-7	123
	Ps	133	2	589
	Heb	5	4	1197
Yielded to Israel's demands to make a calf of gold	*Ex	32	1-6, 21-24	73
	Dt	9	16	150
	Neh	9	18	376
	Ps	106	19	569
	Acts	7	41	1091
He and his sons anointed for the priesthood	*Ex	40	12-14	80
	Lv	8	1-13	86
	Nm	25	11-13	130
His famous benediction	*Nm	6	22-27	111
Vindicated with Moses in destruction of conspirators	*Nm	16	12-35	121
	Dt	11	6	151
	Ps	106	16-17	569
His priesthood confirmed by "budding of rod"	*Nm	17	21-26	122
	Heb	9	4	1200
Aaron not permitted to enter Promised Land	*Nm	20	7-13, 22-24	125
	Nm	27	14	132
	Dt	1	37	142
	Dt	32	51-52	169
Aaron dies on Mt. Hor; buried at Moserah	*Nm	20	25-29	125
	Nm	33	38-39	138
	Dt	32	50	169
	Dt	10	6	150
His descendants blessed; numbered among priest and Levites	*Ps	115	12	576
	Nm	4	5	109
	Jos	21	1-4	188
	1 Chr	12	27	320

---

*The first entry of a multiple reference will be indicated with an asterisk. Succeeding entries of the multiple references will not show asterisks. Single entries carry asterisks.

SUBJECT	BOOK	CHAP.	VERSE	PAGE

AARONITES. The Levites of the family of Aaron were sometimes designated by this title, particularly the priests who served in the sanctuary.

3700 supported David as "fighting men"	*1 Chr	12	27	320
Zadok, a chief of	1 Chr	27	17	330

ABADDON. *destruction.* A Hebrew word sometimes used to signify destruction or the place of destruction. It is never used of a personal being in the Old Testament, but only as synonymous with Sheol, the abode of the dead.

Reference made by John	*Rv	9	10-11	1239

ABARIM, MOUNT. *regions beyond.* A chain, or group of mountains which belong to the mountainous district east of the Dead Sea and the lower Jordan River. Mt. Nebo was one of the highest of this range; Mt. Pisgah was the most commanding peak.

Israel encamped in the midst of	*Nm	33	47-48	138
	Nm	27	12-13	132
Scene of Moses' death	*Dt	32	49-50	169
	Dt	34	1-3	172

ABBA. This is the emphatic form of the Aramaic word for father, and is employed in addressing God as *The Father,* the one and only spiritual Father.

Jesus so addressed God	*Mk	14	36	1014
Christians may so address	*Rom	8	15	1122
God in the Holy Spirit	Gal	4	6	1154

ABBESS. The superior of an abbey of nuns in those orders of which the male members are governed by abbots. This office has existed from the 6th century, and during the middle ages abbesses possessed almost all the temporal powers exercised by abbots. Now, however, the manner of election, rights, limits of power, and privileges are decreed by Canon Law. The local bishop confers the office which is symbolized by a ring, pastoral staff, and pectoral cross. An abbess assumes full domestic authority, but unlike the abbots, she has absolutely no spiritual jurisdiction.

ABBEY. An independent monastery usually built around a quadrangle. An abbey must be canonically erected, and is governed by an abbot or abbess. Each community must contain not less than twelve monks or nuns.

ABBOT. The superior of a community of men dwelling in monastic institutions. He must be a priest at least thirty years of age who is elected to the office for life. After election he is blessed by the local bishop. This blessing is necessary only for the conferring of minor orders, since it grants no further powers or grace. An abbot has complete domestic authority over the community he heads and whatever spiritual authority Canon Law permits. His duties are to administer the abbey's properties, to enforce the community rule, to confer Tonsure and Minor Orders. He also is permitted the limited use of the Pontificals and may, at times, pontificate at Mass. As an indication of his office he wears a ring and is given the use of the mitre and crosier.

ABDUCTION. The carrying off or keeping of a woman against her will; it is a diriment impediment to marriage. However, the impediment ceases if the woman obtains her freedom and, of her own volition, chooses to marry her abductor.

ABEDNEGO

Chaldean name given Azariah, one of Daniel's companions in captivity	*Dn	1	7	888
	Dn	3	13-30	890
Canticle they sang was recorded	*Dn	3	52-94	890
Attendants of King Nebuchadnezzar	*Dn	1	3-7	888

ABEL. 1. The second son of Adam and Eve, a shepherd, who sought to honor God by a sacrifice of the best lamb of his flock. Abel's brother, Cain, also made an offering, but it was rejected by the Lord. When Abel's offering, made humbly in a penitent spirit, was received by God, Cain murdered his brother, Abel, in a state of melancholy, envy, and anger. Abel is a type of Christ through his innocence, his charity, and pleasing sacrifice.

Offering accepted by God	*Gn	4	4	4
Murdered by Cain	*Gn	4	8	4
St. Paul compared his blood to Blood of Jesus	*Hb	12	24	1203

SUBJECT	BOOK	CHAP.	VERSE	PAGE
First of martyrs	*Mt	23	35	990
	Lk	11	51	1033

2. Name of several villages in Israel, with additions in the case of the more important, to distinguish them from one another. The places so named were evidently in particularly verdant locations.

ABIATHAR, *father of abundance.* A descendant of Ithamar, one of Aaron's two sons, and of Eli upon whose house divine judgment had been pronounced; and a son of the high priest Ahimelech. When King Saul ordered the slaying of all the priests of Nob because of their friendly attitude toward David, only Abiathar escaped. He joined the refugee David and served as priest for him and his followers during their long period of wanderings. In the meantime, King Saul had appointed Zadok of the lineage of Eleazar to be high priest. When David came to the throne he made Abiathar high priest, and since there was no justifiable reason for deposing Zadok, the two served as joint high priests. Abiathar's support of Adonijah's claims to the throne afforded an opportunity for Eli's priestly house to be brought to an end; Abiathar was deposed and Zadok was given exclusive rank as high priest by Solomon.

Son of Ahimelech who escaped when Saul slew priest at Nob	*1 Sm	22	2-23	235
	1 Sm	23	6	235
Acted as priest for David	*1 Sm	23	9	235
	1 Sm	30	7	240
Abiathar and Zadok joint high priests under David	*2 Sm	8	17	248
	1 Chr	18	16	324
	1 Chr	24	6	328
Abiathar and Zadok loyal to David in Absalom's rebellion	*2 Sm	15	24-29, 35	254
	2 Sm	17	15-17	255
Supported Adonijah in his conspiracy against Solomon	*1 Kgs	1	7, 19, 25	264
Deposed by Solomon; judgment on Eli's house accomplished	*1 Kgs	2	26-27, 35	266
	1 Sm	2	27-36	217
Spoken of by Christ	*Mk	2	26	1000

ABIGAIL. *the father is happy.* 1. Wife of Nabal, and later wife of David, famed for beauty and for her efforts to avert the wrath of David toward her evil-designing husband. She is a striking example of prudent remonstrance and wise management. After becoming the wife of David she shared in his misfortunes and in his successes.

Her noble service to David; becomes wife of David	*1 Sm	25	3, 14-42	237
Accompanies David to Gath and Ziklag; taken captive by Amalekites and recovered	*1 Sm	27	3	239
	1 Sm	30	5, 18	240
Mother of Chileab or Daniel	*2 Sm	3	3	244
	1 Chr	3	1	312
2. Daughter of Jesse, step-sister of David, mother of Amasa	*2 Sm	17	25	255
	1 Chr	2	16-17	311

ABIHAIL. *father of splendor.*

1. A chief Gadite residing in Bashan	*1 Chr	5	14	314
2. Esther's father, uncle of Mordecai	*Est	2	15	410
	Est	9	29	416
3. Wife of Abishur of tribe of Judah	*1 Chr	2	29	311
4. Mother of Rehoboam's wife, Mahalath, daughter or descendant of David's brother Eliab	*2 Chr	11	18	341

ABIHU.

The second of four sons of Aaron born to Elisheba; all of them dedicated to the priesthood	*1 Chr	6	3	315
	Ex	6	23	51
	Nm	26	60	131
	Ex	28	1	69
Neglected the original fire sent from heaven and destroyed with his brother, Nadab, for employing strange fire	*Lv	10	1-2	88
	Nm	3	2-4	108
	Nm	26	61	131
	1 Chr	24	2	328

ABIJAH, ABIAM, ABIJAM. *my father is Jehovah.*

SUBJECT	BOOK	CHAP.	VERSE	PAGE
1. Son and successor of Rehoboam reigned in	*1 Chr	3	10	312
	1 Kgs	14	31	278
Judah for three years	1 Kgs	15	1-8	279
Makes superior claims in obedience to God over Jeroboam; is victorious in war against Northern Kingdom	*2 Chr	13	1-20	342
Has 14 wives; 22 sons, 16 daughters	*2 Chr	13	21	342
His mother's name Maacah, daughter of Abishalom	*1 Kgs	15	2, 10	279
Correct name of his mother, Michaiah, daughter of Uriel	*2 Chr	13	2	342
2. Son of Jeroboam who died in childhood	*1 Kgs	14	1-18	278
3. Second son of Samuel; both sons perverted judgment as judges and brought shame upon their father	*1Sm	8	1-5	221
	1 Chr	6	28	315
4. Descendant of Eleazar; priest head of eighth course in David's organization, to which father of John the Baptist belonged	*1 Chr	24	10	328
	Lk	1	5	1020
5. A postexilic priest; covenant signer; father of Zichri	*Neh	12	4, 17	379
	Neh	10	7	378
6. A Benjamite, son of Becher	*1 Chr	7	8	316
7. Wife of Ahaz, mother of Hezekiah, also called Abi	*2 Chr	29	1	353
	2 Kgs	18	2	302
8. Wife of Hezron	*1 Chr	2	24	311

ABILENE.

This small district took its name from the chief town, Abila. Its exact borders are not known, but it was one of the four parts into which the kingdom of the Itureans had been divided. It probably reached above the Upper Barrada northward and southward to Mount Hermon.

SUBJECT	BOOK	CHAP.	VERSE	PAGE
Province of Syria	*Lk	3	1	1023

ABIMELECH.

SUBJECT	BOOK	CHAP.	VERSE	PAGE
1. A son of Gideon by a Canaanite concubine of a prominent family of Shechem	*Jgs	8	31	199
	Jgs	9	18	200
Supported by his kinsmen in Shechem, he slew his 70 brothers and made himself king	*Jgs	9	1-6	200
Rebuked by Jotham, a brother who escaped murder	*Jgs	9	7-21	200
Waged civil war in which he was slain by a woman	*Jgs	9	22-55	200
	2 Sm	11	21	250
2. A titular name for kings of Philistine Gerar, Abraham's dealings with the first mentioned	*Gn	20	1-18	17
Isaac's dealings with the second one mentioned	*Gn	26	1-33	22

ABINADAB. *father of generosity.*

SUBJECT	BOOK	CHAP.	VERSE	PAGE
1. One of eight sons of Jesse and older brother of David; soldier in Saul's army	*1 Chr	2	13	311
	1 Sm	16	8	229
	1 Sm	17	13	230
2. A son of King Saul; slain in battle at Mt. Gilboa	*1 Sm	31	2	241
	1 Chr	10	2	319

SUBJECT	BOOK	CHAP.	VERSE	PAGE
3. A Levite of Kiriath-jearim in whose house the Ark was placed when it was returned by Philistines; it remained here until removed to Jerusalem by David, 70 years later	*1 Sm	7	1-2	221
	2 Sm	6	1-5	247
	1 Chr	13	5-8	321
4. Father of one of Solomon's purveyors Abinadab	*1 Kgs	4	11	268

ABINOAM. *the father is pleasant.*

SUBJECT	BOOK	CHAP.	VERSE	PAGE
Father of Barak, army commander under Deborah	*Jgs	4	6, 12	196
	Jgs	5	1, 12	196

ABIRAM. *the father is exalted.*

SUBJECT	BOOK	CHAP.	VERSE	PAGE
1. A Rubenite who joined Dathan in conspiracy against Moses and Aaron; died under curse with all others	*Nm	16	1-34	121
	Dt	11	6	151
	Ps	106	17	569
2. The first-born son of Hiel who perished with his father in efforts to rebuild Jericho	*1 Kgs	16	34	279
	Jos.	6	26	176

ABISHAG.

the father has strayed. A young woman of Shunam purported to be very beautiful. She was taken into David's harem in his last illness for the special purpose of ministering to him. After David's death, his fourth son, Adonijah, sought to make Abishag his wife as a part of his scheme to seize the throne. For this action, Solomon ordered the death of Adonijah.

SUBJECT	BOOK	CHAP.	VERSE	PAGE
Abishag ministers to David	*1 Kgs	1	3-4	264
Solomon orders Adonijah's death	*1 Kgs	2	17-25	266

ABISHAI.

my father is Jesse. This nephew of David and his brothers Joab and Asahel devoted themselves zealously to their uncle during his fugitive years as Saul sought to have him slain. Abishai appears to have been especially attached to David's person; he was a man of impulsive and sometimes rash action, fearless in his defense of his king.

SUBJECT	BOOK	CHAP.	VERSE	PAGE
Saved David's life	*2 Sm	21	17	259
David prevented him from killing Saul	*1 Sm	26	5-9	238
David also saved Shimei from Abishai	*2 Sm	16	9-12	255
Aided in overthrow of Ishbaal	*2 Sm	2	18-24	243
Defeated the Edomites	*2 Sm	8	13-14	248
	1 Chr	18	12-13	324
Sent against Ammonites	*2 Sm	10	10	249
Commanded David's army against Absalom	*2 Sm	18	2	256
Sent against Sheba	*2 Sm	20	6	258
	2 Sm	23	18-19	262

ABLUTION.

That part of the Mass after the Communion when the priest purifies the chalice with wine. The priest then consumes the wine and water and dries his lips and the chalice with the purificator.

ABLUTION CUP.

The small container of water kept at the side of the tabernacle. It is used to wash the priest's fingers after touching the Blessed Sacrament whenever he is not celebrating Mass.

ABNER.

the father is a lamp. A cousin of King Saul who was commander-in-chief of the nation's army during Saul's reign. Following the death of Saul, Abner aspired to be king of Israel, even though he knew that David had been divinely chosen for this position. He sought to accomplish this ambition by making Ishbaal, an imbecile surviving son of Saul, the ruling monarch, thus setting up a rival ruler to David. When he realized his scheme was doomed to failure and after a quarrel with Ishbaal, he proposed to join David with the hope of supplanting Joab as commander. Joab, however, sensed Abner's motives, and as an act of avenging the blood of his brother Asahel who had been slain by Abner, Joab assassinated this scheming opportunist.

SUBJECT	BOOK	CHAP.	VERSE	PAGE
Son of Ner, a brother of Saul's father, Kish	*1 Sm	14	50-51	226
	1 Chr	9	36	318

SUBJECT	BOOK	CHAP.	VERSE	PAGE
Commander of Saul's armies	*1 Sm	17	55	230
	1 Sm	26	7	238
Intimately associated with Saul	*1 Sm	20	25	233
	1 Chr	26	28	330
Sets up Ishbaal as rival king to David; slays Asahel	*2 Sm	2	8-32	243
Seeks alliance with David	*2 Sm	3	6-21	244
Joab accuses Abner of treachery and slays him	*2 Sm	3	22-27	244
David's lamentation	*2 Sm	3	28-39	244

ABOMINATION OF DESOLATION. A forewarning as prophesied by Our Lord whereby the fall of Jerusalem would be known. The nature of this sign, however, was not definitely indicated, although Christ used the phrase as it is used in the Book of Daniel where it refers to the introduction of idolatrous worship into the Temple of Jerusalem, thus presaging its destruction. The erection of a statue to Zeus in the Temple by Antiochus Epiphanes in 168 B.C. is one example; St. Jerome suggested the statue of Caesar which Pilate placed in the Temple representing an abomination to the Jews and bringing desolation to the Temple.

Predicted by Daniel	*Dn	9	27	899
	Dn	12	11	902
Of Jerusalem	*Mt	24	15	991

ABORTION. The intentional removal of the fetus from the womb before it is capable of living outside of the uterus. Direct abortion is a grievous sin comparable to homicide, since a fetus is considered a living human being. According to Canon Law, all who participate in obtaining an abortion, whether such action is physical or moral, incur an automatic excommunication from the Catholic Church. Accidental or unintentional abortion is known as miscarriage.

ABRAHAM. *father of a multitude.* Abraham's original name, Abram, was changed by the Lord as a token of the covenant that he should become the "father of many nations." He was born at Ur of the Chaldees, a descendant of Shem and son of Terah and an uncle of Lot. There he married Sarai, his half sister, and migrated to Haran with Terah and Lot. Abraham was then called by God to leave his home and relatives and go to the land which the Lord would show him. This divine call marks the period in the history of salvation when Israel would be the bearer of religious truths. According to the divine plan, Abraham was to be the father of a great nation; he was to acquire a great name and was to be the instrument by which God's special blessings would be conferred upon all mankind, since the future Messiah would descend from him. Some time later the Lord appeared to Abraham and declared that he would have numerous descendants, although his wife had been barren, and that his heir would be a son called Isaac.

Before his death Abraham underwent a most difficult trial. The divine promise of numerous descendants was intimately linked with his son Isaac; yet, when God called upon him to sacrifice Isaac, Abraham showed his perfect obedience to the divine will. On this occasion Isaac even carried the wood for the human sacrifice to Mount Moriah and thus became a type of Jesus Christ carrying His cross to Calvary. Abraham was saved from sacrificing his son, however, when a ram was substituted. Having manifested his faith, hope, and love of God in such an heroic manner, Abraham was blessed with renewed promises of offspring. In every detail of his career, Abraham stands out as the "father of the faithful" and thus occupies a very prominent position in the Christian liturgy. His feast is named in the Martyrology for October 9, and his sacrifice is mentioned in the Canon of the Mass.

Early history:

SUBJECT	BOOK	CHAP.	VERSE	PAGE
Abram, originally	*Gn	11	27	10
Son of Terah	*Gn	11	26	10
A descendant of Shem	*1 Chr	1	24-27	310
Lived in Ur	*Gn	11	31	10
Married Sarai, his half sister	*Gn	11	29	10
	Gn	20	8-13	17

Called of God:

First call in Ur	*Acts	7	2-4	1091
Received second call	*Gn	12	1-3	11
Journeyed to Canaan	*Gn	12	5	11
Went into Egypt	*Gn	12	10	11
Reproved by Pharaoh	*Gn	12	18-20	11
Returned to Canaan	*Gn	13	1	11

Second period in Canaan:

SUBJECT	BOOK	CHAP.	VERSE	PAGE
Separated from Lot	*Gn	13	8-12	11
Rescued Lot	*Gn	14	14-16	12
Blessed by Melchizedek	*Gn	14	18-20	12
Promised a son	*Gn	15	1-6	13
Takes Hagar as concubine	*Gn	16	1-4	13
Birth of Ishmael	*Gn	16	15	13

Third period; covenant established:

Name changed	*Gn	17	5	14
Sarah promised a son	*Gn	17	19	14
Interceded for Sodom	*Gn	18	20-33	15
Dealings with Abimelech	*Gn	20	1-18	17
Birth of Isaac	*Gn	21	1-3	17
Banishes Hagar	*Gn	21	12-21	17

Fourth period:

Offered Isaac	*Gn	22	1-13	18
Made covenant with Abimelech	*Gn	21	27-34	17
Death of Sarah	*Gn	23	1-2	19
Provided Isaac a wife	*Gn	24	1-67	19
Died, age 175 years	*Gn	25	7	21
Buried beside Sarah	*Gn	25	8-10	21

ABSALOM. *the father is peace.* This third son of David was also of royal blood on his mother's side, Maacah being the daughter of Talmai, king of Geshur. Since Absalom's two older brothers were dead at the time of his conspiracy to seize the throne, he doubtless claimed justification for his ambition. It may be that he also condoned his bloody act of vengeance against his half brother Amnon on the grounds that in countries where polygamy is allowed, the honor of a sister is in the guardianship of her full brother, even more than in that of her father. Absalom was, however, a man of many faults: his plots and scheming, his conjuring of hatred and revenge, his disregard for the Divine will in the choice of Solomon as successor to his father, all disqualified him for the throne of Israel.

Third son of David	*2 Sm	3	3	244
Noted for his beauty	*2 Sm	14	25	253
Slew Amnon	*2 Sm	13	28-29	251
Fled to Geshur	*2 Sm	13	37-38	251
Returned by Joab	*2 Sm	14	23	253
Forgiven by David	*2 Sm	14	33	253
Won hearts of people	*2 Sm	15	6	254
Plotted against David	*2 Sm	15	10-12	254
Rebelled against David	*2 Sm	17	1-14	255
Defeated by David	*2 Sm	18	7	256
Caught in a tree	*2 Sm	18	9	256
Slain by Joab's men	*2 Sm	18	15	256
Buried in pit	*2 Sm	18	17	256
Wept for by David	*2 Sm	18	33	256

ABSOLUTION. 1. The power of a priest to forgive sins through the Sacrament of Penance. Christ gave this power to the Apostles when He said, "If you forgive men's sins, they are forgiven them; if you hold them bound, they are held bound." (Jn 20, 23.) All rightfully ordained ecclesiastics can remit the sins of penitents who confess their sins, express sorrow for having committed them, resolve not to offend God again, and perform the penances given them.

2. Conditional absolution is granted when the priest is not sure the penitent has fulfilled all the requirements necessary for complete absolution, but where the refusal to absolve might result in the individual's spiritual loss, or where the Sacrament is in danger of nullity.

3. Absolution of the dead is the blessing given and the prayers said for the deceased after a Requiem Mass. This ceremony is part of the funeral rite and is given either over the body of the deceased or over the catafalque.

4. General absolution is the simultaneous forgiveness of the sins of a group when individual private confession is not possible. Soldiers going into battle receive general absolution. However, those who do receive it are obliged to state those forgiven sins when they next are able to confess privately.

Christ gives power to absolve	*Jn	20	22-23	1080
	Mt	9	2, 6	974
	Lk	5	21	1025
Secured through faith	*Acts	10	43	1095
	Rom	3	24-26	1118
Complete, irrevocable	*Jn	8	36	1062
	Rom	6	18	1120

ABYSS. *bottomless.* This term in the Scriptures refers, generally, to deep uncertainty, or the fathomless deep—the abode of the devil and his helpers. The reference in the New Testament is to the resting place of the dead in limbo—a state of perfect natural happiness for the just who died before Christ's Ascension, or for those deprived of Baptism.

SUBJECT	BOOK	CHAP.	VERSE	PAGE
The abode of the devil	*Lk	8	31	1029
"Abraham's bosom," limbo	*Lk	16	19-25	1038
Abaddon, king of	*Rv	9	1-2, 11	1239
Abode of evil spirits	*Rv	20	1, 3	1248

ACACIA WOOD. The wood of the setim tree used in the building of the tabernacle. It may be the same as acacia of which the Mosaic tabernacle was made. The wood is exceedingly hard and repels insects.

SUBJECT	BOOK	CHAP.	VERSE	PAGE
Used for tabernacle	*Ex.	25	5	67
Ark made of	*Dt	10	3	150

ACCO. *hot sand.* One of the most important seaports on the coast of Palestine. It was assigned to the tribe of Asher but never conquered by the Israelites. It was also known as Acca, or Ace. It was besieged many times, but in the 3rd century it was given the name of Ptolemais in honor of the Egyptian ruler. Jonathan was killed in this seaport, and Paul spent a day in the Christian area which had developed in this community.

SUBJECT	BOOK	CHAP.	VERSE	PAGE
Assigned to tribe of Asher	*Jgs	1	31	193
Important during days of Maccabees	*1 Mc	5	15	425
Jonathan Apphus murdered here	*1 Mc	12	45-48	437
Paul visited seaport	*Acts	21	7	1108

ACHAIA. This name was originally applied to a strip of land on the north coast of the Peloponnesus; but when the Romans annexed this territory, the province of Achaia included that part of Greece south of Macedonia with its capital at Corinth. Paul preached at Rome, and his enemies appealed to the proconsul, Gallio, but the case was dismissed. Paul again visited Achaia on his third missionary journey.

SUBJECT	BOOK	CHAP.	VERSE	PAGE
Senatorial province under Gallio	*Acts	18	12	1105
Visited by Apollos	*Acts	18	27	1105
People opposed Paul	*Acts	18	12-17	1105
Visited again by Paul	*Acts	19	21	1106

ACHAICUS. A member of the church at Corinth and one of a group who "refreshed Paul" while he was at Ephesus. He was a companion of Stephanas and Fortunatus in their missionary work.

SUBJECT	BOOK	CHAP.	VERSE	PAGE
Visited Paul at Ephesus	*1 Cor	16	6-8, 17-18	1141

ACHAN. *troubler.* A son of Carmi of Judah. Because he disobeyed Joshua and took spoils from Jericho, the Israelites were unable to capture Ai. As a consequence, when his sin was revealed by lot, Achan was stoned to death.

SUBJECT	BOOK	CHAP.	VERSE	PAGE
Kept some of spoils of Jericho	*Jos	7	1	177
Stoned to death and possessions burned	*Jos	7	24-26	177

ACOLYTE. 1. A cleric in the highest of the four minor orders received by those who aspire to the priesthood. His duties are to light the altar candles, to carry them in procession, to serve the priest at Mass by offering him the cruets of wine and water, and to assist the priests in other services of the Church.

2. A layman or boy, commonly referred to as an altar boy or server, who performs the duties of an ordained acolyte at any ritualistic ceremony.

ACTA APOSTOLICAE SEDIS. *The Acts of the Apostolic See.* The official magazine of the Holy See which publishes its decrees, decisions, encyclical letters, pronouncements, ecclesiastical appointments, etc. In addition, all legislative acts of the Holy See are first promulgated in the Acta Apostolicae Sedis.

ACTION, CATHOLIC. "The participation of the Catholic laity in the apostolate of the hierarchy" (Pope Pius XI). While Catholic Action has existed from the time of Christ who sent forth His twelve Apostles to win all souls for Him, our complex modern way of life with its attendant paganistic tendencies has made it extremely difficult for our priests to reach all people. Therefore, the objective of Catholic Action is the winning or bringing back of souls to God. This is accomplished by authorized, organized groups doing apostolic work in accordance with the forms shown in the teachings of Pope Pius XI.

Catholic Action groups operate in a very orderly manner. Their work is closely supervised by the clergy; a Bishop's man-date is essential for their founding in each diocese. The members must be true, practicing Catholics who have a knowledge of the eternal truths and who lead good Christian lives. Each group "specializes" in its own environment. Thus a laborer endeavors to win fellow laborers; a clerk, his associates; professional people, the men, women, and children with whom they come in contact. If each individual wins his own associates, it must follow that the whole world will be won for Christ.

Pope Pius XI described the aims and methods of Catholic Action in his two great encyclicals, "Quadragesimo anno" and "Non abbiamo bisogno." The work has been given additional impetus by the interest and encouragement of Pope Pius XII.

Not all Catholic societies are to be construed as Catholic Action groups. Cardinal Pizzardo, the Papal Secretary, explains the difference in these words: "(1) Catholic Action is rigidly hierarchic, its organization being grafted upon the hierarchic economy of the Church. (2) Catholic Action gives its members a complete shaping or structure, not only religious and moral, but social and specialized in accordance with their professions. It trains consciences to be more sensitive and more courageous in meeting and solving the problems of life in a Christian way. (3) Catholic Action embraces in its program *every* form of apostolate, while the auxiliary societies and associations are engaged solely in a work of religious development or in some *particular* apostolic work."

ACTIVE CONGREGATIONS. Those religious congregations of men and women whose daily labors are the works of active charity, whether spiritual or temporal, are usually designated as active congregations. Thus they are in contrast to the strictly contemplative orders. The active congregation may preach, teach, give retreats, hear confessions, or care for the sick and the orphans, etc. Among men there are the Passionists, Christian Brothers, Redemptorists, etc. Some of the Religious Orders are also dedicated to some of these works of active charity. A few of the active religious Congregations for women are the Benedictines, Sisters of Providence, Franciscans, Dominicans, Carmelites, Sisters of Charity, Little Sisters of the Poor, Ursulines, etc.

ACT OF CHARITY. An act of the will by which we attest our love of God above all things because He is infinitely good, and our neighbors as ourselves for His sake. If an individual makes a sincere, perfect act of charity, any stain of mortal sin is immediately removed from his soul, although the obligation of confessing it still remains. An Act of Charity may be expressed as follows:

"Oh my God, I love Thee above all things, with my whole heart and soul, because Thou art all good and worthy of all love. I love my neighbor as myself for the love of Thee. I forgive all who have injured me, and ask pardon of all whom I have injured."

ACT OF CONTRITION. An act of the will by which we express sorrow for having offended God, declare our hatred for our sins, and sincerely and firmly resolve to avoid sin in the future. There are two kinds of contrition, perfect and imperfect. Perfect contrition is motivated by the love of God because He *is* God; imperfect contrition is sorrow for one's sins because of the fear of God's punishment or the despicable nature of the sins themselves. An Act of Perfect Contrition also removes any stain of mortal sin, but here again the obligation to confess the sin still remains. The most common Act of Contrition is:

"Oh my God, I am heartily sorry for having offended Thee, and I detest all my sins because of Thy just punishments, but most of all because they have offended Thee, my God, who art all good and deserving of all my love. I firmly resolve, with the help of Thy grace, to sin no more and to avoid the near occasions of sin."

ACT OF FAITH. An act of the intellect by which we affirm certain truths revealed by God solely because they were revealed by Him. The following is the most common version:

"Oh my God, I firmly believe that Thou art One God in three Divine Persons, Father, Son, and Holy Ghost; I believe that Thy Divine Son became man, and died for our sins, and that He will come to judge the living and the dead. I believe these and all the truths which the Holy Catholic Church teaches, because Thou hast revealed them, who canst neither deceive nor be deceived."

ACT OF HOPE. A fervent trust in God's promises of mercy, justice, and eternal salvation for the penitent sinners.

"Oh my God, relying on Thy almighty power and infinite

SUBJECT	BOOK	CHAP.	VERSE	PAGE

mercy and promises, I hope to obtain pardon of my sins, the help of Thy grace, and life everlasting, through the merits of Jesus Christ, my Lord and Redeemer."

ACTS OF THE MARTYRS. Written accounts of the confessions of faith and martyrdoms of the saints. During Diocletian's purge in the 4th century, many eyewitness accounts of the trials and deaths of martyrs of that period were destroyed. However, there still remain many accurate records of martyrdoms written by those who actually viewed the occurrences.

ACTUAL GRACE. That supernatural help from God which enlightens the mind and enables our will to resist temptation, thus avoiding evil, and to do good.

ACTUAL SINS. Any thought, word, or deed contrary to the Law of God. They may be venial or mortal sins against God, our neighbors, or ourselves.

ADAM. God created Adam out of the dust of the ground and infused into his body a spiritual soul. Thus, the first human being was preeminently distinguished from the animal kingdom. He was not only endowed with an immortal soul, with an intellect and free will, but with bodily immortality and original integrity. God endowed Adam further by showing him in a vision the creation of Eve from one of his own ribs and gave her to him as his wife. Although both Adam and Eve had the all-embracing knowledge to attain eternal happiness in their home, Paradise, they permitted temptation to prevail and disobeyed God by eating of the forbidden fruit. For this they were condemned to toil for their livelihood, the earth was cursed, and all women were to endure the pains of childbirth. They were consoled, however, by the promise of a future Redeemer and the opportunity to save their souls.

After their expulsion from Paradise, Adam and Eve had two sons, Cain and Abel, and after the death of Abel, Seth was born when Adam was 130 years old. Adam died at the age of 930 years.

SUBJECT	BOOK	CHAP.	VERSE	PAGE
Created by God	*Gn	1	26-27	2
	Gn	2	7-9	2
Eve given to him as a wife	*Gn	2	21-25	2
Ate forbidden fruit	*Gn	3	4-13	3
Cast out of Paradise	*Gn	3	21-24	3
Birth of Cain and Abel	*Gn	4	1-2	4
The birth of Seth	*Gn	5	3	5
Lived to 930 years	*Gn	5	5	5

ADESTE FIDELES. "O come all ye faithful." A Latin Christmas hymn of unknown date and authorship inviting the faithful to come to Bethlehem to worship the newborn Savior.

ADJURATION. A command or earnest request made in the name of God that something be done, or that He will refrain from doing something. During Baptism ritual adjuration is made over the salt and over the child three times; during the rite of Exorcism, many times.

AD LIMINA VISITS. *Ad Limina Apostolorum.* To the thresholds of SS. Peter and Paul, visits all bishops must make at specified times prescribed by Canon Law. During each visit the bishop must submit to the pope a written account of the state of his diocese.

ADMAH. A city of Pentapolis that was destroyed together with Sodom and Gomorrah. It is believed that these cities were in the region south of the Dead Sea and now part of this body of water.

SUBJECT	BOOK	CHAP.	VERSE	PAGE
Destroyed for wickedness	*Dt	29	22	166
	Hos	11	8	914
Now covered with water	*Gn	14	2-3	12

ADONAI. *my lord.* A Hebrew word meaning "my lord" or "my commander." God had revealed to Moses the Tetragrammaton, YHWH, His divine proper name, but because of a misunderstanding the Jews dared not pronounce the holy name, and in synagogues it was always read as if it were Adonai.

SUBJECT	BOOK	CHAP.	VERSE	PAGE
One of the holy names of God	*Jdt	16	16	406

ADONIBEZEK. *lord of Bezek.* King of the Canaanites city of Bezek, about seventeen miles from Sechem. He also ruled seventy other cities which he had captured, having inflicted upon conquered kings the cruelty of cutting off their thumbs. His army was defeated and he was captured by the men of Judah and Simeon, after the death of Joshua and in retribution his hands and feet were mutilated.

SUBJECT	BOOK	CHAP.	VERSE	PAGE
His hands and feet mutilated	*Jgs	1	5-8	193

ADONIJAH. 1. The fourth son of David and Haggith. He tried to seize the throne even though his father solemnly proclaimed Solomon king. When his conspiracy failed, Adonijah received his father's forgiveness, but Solomon felt there might be further designs on the throne and ordered Adonijah to be put to death.

SUBJECT	BOOK	CHAP.	VERSE	PAGE
Son of David and Haggith	*2 Sm	3	4	244
	1 Chr	3	2	312
Tried to seize the throne	*1 Kgs	1	5-25	264
Received reprieve from Solomon	*1 Kgs	1	50-52	264
Put to death by Solomon	*1 Kgs	2	13-25	266
2. A Levite who was sent by Jehoshaphat to persuade the people to give up their idols. Sent to instruct people	*2 Chr	17	8	344

ADONIZEDEK. *the lord is righteousness.* The Canaanites king of Jerusalem at the time of the conquest of Canaan by Joshua. He led in the confederation of five Amorite kings, after having been defeated in his attack upon the Gibeonites who had aligned themselves with Israel. After a prolonged war in which Joshua was supported by supernatural interventions, this confederated army was defeated and the five kings slain.

SUBJECT	BOOK	CHAP.	VERSE	PAGE
Defeated by Joshua	*Jos	10	1-27	180

ADOPTION. 1. The legal action whereby one person takes the child of another as his own. Those who, by virtue of adoption, are considered by civil law as being incapable of valid marriage due to legal affinity resulting from that adoption, are also forbidden by Canon Law to contract such marriages. If civil law regards such marriages as illicit, but not invalid, Canon Law also considers them illicit, but not invalid. In other words, where civil law recognizes a legal relationship which is the result of an adoption, the Church also recognizes that relationship and attributes to it particular ecclesiastical effects or rules (c. 1080).

2. The result of supernatural grace whereby we forego the status of strangers in sin, whether original or otherwise, and become, in effect, adopted children of God. This necessitates an internal change in our souls which is due to the grace of God working in us.

SUBJECT	BOOK	CHAP.	VERSE	PAGE
Spiritual adoption by God	*Rom	8	15, 23	1122
	Gal	4	4-5	1154

ADRUMYTTIUM. A seaport town in the province of Mysia in Asia Minor; it is said to have been a Lydian colony. It flourished under Roman rule, and Paul began his voyage to Rome on one of its ships.

SUBJECT	BOOK	CHAP.	VERSE	PAGE
Paul on ship of	*Acts	27	2	1113

ADULLAM. *refuge.* A Canaanite city between Jarmuth and Socoh. Joshua allotted the territory to the tribe of Judah. It was also called Adullam.

SUBJECT	BOOK	CHAP.	VERSE	PAGE
Alloted to tribe of Judah	*Jos	15	35	184

ADULT BAPTISM. The Roman Ritual describes the special ceremony followed for baptizing adults. It is considerably longer than the procedure used in the baptism of infants. However, in the United States most bishops have authorized their priests to use the shorter form for the adults.

ADULTERY. Sexual intercourse of a married person with another who is not his lawful spouse. It is a sin against both chastity and justice, and Canon Law permits the injured partner to separate from the offender, provided the guilt be certain. However, the Catholic Church holds that no valid marriage can be completely dissolved because of the adultery of either party. For Catholics there is no absolute divorce for any reason. If two married people, each unfaithful to his spouse, commit this sin of adultery with each other and agree to marry in the future, they incur a diriment impediment which prevents them from marrying each other even though their respective spouses should die. Neither can one married person consent to the adultery of his spouse with another party; marriage rights are inalienable.

ADVENT. *on arrival.* Advent is the penitential season which precedes Christmas and also marks the beginning of the liturgical year of the Church. It starts on the Sunday nearest the Feast of St. Andrew the Apostle (Nov. 30) and ends on Christmas. During Advent we commemorate the thousands of years

SUBJECT	BOOK	CHAP.	VERSE	PAGE

of waiting for the coming of the promised Messiah. During these four weeks the Gloria is omitted from the Mass; the Te Deum is omitted from Matins. However, the laws of compulsory fast and abstinence are not applicable at this time.

ADVOCATE. A lawyer, either clerical or lay, who pleads a case in an ecclesiastical court. Whatever the result of a case may be, he is given a fixed sum as a fee, and a poor person obtains his services without charge.

ADVOCATUS DIABOLI. *the devil's advocate.* The vernacular or slang name given to the Promoter of the Faith who deals juridically with processes of beatification and canonization. As the name indicates, his duties are to set forth all the arguments against the beatification or canonization under discussion. He must examine all claims of miracles, and the Church must answer fully all objections he raises. The Catholic Church insists upon this procedure to insure her against honoring someone unworthy of such esteem.

AFFINITY. The relationship which exists between a man and his wife's blood relatives, and between a wife and her husband's blood relatives. This affinity exists in any valid Christian marriage, whether consummated or not. According to Canon Law affinity in the direct line constitutes a diriment impediment to marriage in all degrees; in the collateral line, to the second degree inclusive.

AGABUS. A prophet, probably of Judah, and thought by many to have been one of the seventy-two disciples appointed by Jesus. He visited Antioch and there foretold a famine which took place during the reign of Claudius. Agabus made another prediction when Paul was in Caesarea; this time he foretold Paul's imprisonment in Jerusalem, which also came true.

Foretold great famine	°Acts	11	27-30	1097
Predicted Paul's imprisonment	°Acts	21	10-13	1108

AGE OF REASON. The age (normally seven years) at which a child begins to be morally responsible and becomes subject to the laws of the Church. From this time on each Catholic child incurs the obligation of hearing Mass, of abstaining from flesh meat on the prescribed days (but not of fasting), of annual confession, etc.

AGNUS DEI. 1. The three invocations, each beginning with the words, "Lamb of God," which precede the Communion of the Mass.
2. A sacramental consisting of discs of wax on which are imprinted the figure of a lamb, and which are blessed by the pope at prescribed seasons. During the prayers of blessing, the dangers of fire, flood and storm, childbirth, and plague are referred to. The discs may vary in size and shape, but usually are covered with cloth and most often worn suspended from the neck.

AGONY OF CHRIST. The phrase used to designate the anguish of Our Lord in the Garden of Gethsemane on the night before His death. After the Last Supper, Christ exhorted His disciples to beware of temptation, then led them across the torrent Kidron and into Gethsemane. Leaving some of his disciples near the entrance, He took Peter, James, and John further into the garden. After asking them to "Sit down here while I pray." Christ knelt and begged His Father, "Father, if it is your will, take this cup from me; yet not my will but yours be done" (Matt. 26, 36-39; Mark 14, 32-36; Luke 22, 39-42; John 18, 1). This proves Christ's perfect humanity did not doubt God. As a man, He dreaded the impending suffering and death He (as God) knew He would experience. Luke tells us that an angel appeared from heaven to strengthen Him, and His sweat became as drops of blood running down upon the ground. After He had finished praying and had returned to His sleeping disciples, Judas, the betrayer, appeared.

AGRARIAN LAWS. Prior to their settlement in Palestine the Israelites had been largely a pastoral people, with limited agricultural pursuits in Egypt. Once they occupied Canaan as a national home, their attention was directed more and more to the cultivation of the soil and regulations governing its use.

An equal distribution of land	°Nm	26	53-54	131
	Jos	11	23	181
Ownership protected by restrictive laws	°Lv	25	35-38	101
	Dt	15	7-11	154
Agrarian life protected in the military	°Dt	20	5-9	158

SUBJECT	BOOK	CHAP.	VERSE	PAGE

ALB. A long, white, linen vestment reaching to the ankles. When celebrating Mass, the priest wears this garment which symbolizes purity of heart.

ALBIGENSIANISM. A Manichaeism heresy, named from the town of Albi in southern France, and which flourished there during the 12th and 13th centuries. It taught there are two opposing principles, one good (the spirit) and the other evil (the flesh); that all spirit is in itself good; all flesh is in itself evil. Their followers believed that Christ as God (and a spirit, necessarily good) could not have had a real human body (necessarily evil), and consequently there could be no resurrection of the body. Christ's presence on earth was considered merely an "appearance." Among other heretical practices, they encouraged suicide and rejected the sacraments, particularly marriage.

ALCIMUS. A wicked Jew who was appointed high priest by Antiochus V Eupator (164–162 B.C.). His position was secured by the king's murderer and successor, Demetrius I Soter (162–150 B.C.). Alcimus was successful in ruling in the name of Demetrius with the help of Bacchides, a Syrian general. Judas Maccabeus however, was successful in driving Alcimus from the city; but he returned in a short time and destroyed the inner wall of the temple. His sudden death due to paralysis was regarded by the Jews as divine retribution.

Received priesthood from Antiochus	°1 Mc	7	20-21	429
Opposed Maccabees	°1 Mc	7	22-25	429
	2 Mc	14	26	460
Defeated and killed Judas Maccabeus	°1 Mc	9	1-18	431
Died in great agony	°1 Mc	9	54-56	431

ALIENATION OF CHURCH PROPERTY. The transfer of title or right over Church property to another by sale, mortgage, exchange, lease, gift, or otherwise. Such alienation is forbidden except for just reason, such as urgent necessity or expedient usefulness. Permission for alienation must be granted by the pope or the local bishop, and a proper appraisal of the property by at least two experts must be made.

ALLELUIA. A Hebrew liturgical interjection meaning "Praise the Lord." Many of the Psalms begin or end with this expression, and it appears in the Apocalypse as being heard in heaven. Throughout the Latin liturgies, it frequently appears, and is used repeatedly throughout the Paschal season. Since it is a joyful ejaculation, it never is used during times of penance or during Masses of the dead.
The section of the mass called the "Alleluia" has now been replaced. See article "Gradual" for full description.

ALLOCUTION. A solemn address by the pope delivered to the cardinals in a secret consistory. This pronouncement of policy may concern either ecclesiastical or civil affairs; if the subject is one of general interest or concern, the allocution is later published.

ALL SAINTS DAY. The feast in honor of all the saints, whether canonized or not, celebrated on November 1. It is a Holy Day of Obligation and has both a vigil and an octave.

ALL SOULS' DAY. The solemn commemoration of all the souls in purgatory. A day set apart, November 2, to pray for all the faithful departed who still are suffering for their sins. On this day each priest is permitted to offer three Requiem Masses, a privilege granted by Pope Benedict XV in 1915.

ALMS, ALMSGIVING. The giving of alms is different from tithe contributions, the latter being a regular contribution to one's church. An alm is something freely given, in money or its kind, to the needy, prompted by love and pity for the recipient. Almsgiving may be practiced in a general consideration for the needy as one has opportunity, or it may be done through organized charities. It should be remembered, however, that support of organized charities should not be allowed to become a substitute for personal aid to those in distress.

Almsgiving, a distinct duty	°Lv	25	35	101
	Ps	112	9	575
	Prv	14	21	611
	Job	29	12-13	482
	2 Cor	9	5-7	1148
Christ urges almsgiving in his name	°Mt	6	1-4	971
	Mt	25	35-46	992
	Mk	9	40-41	1008
	Acts	20	35	1107
	Lk	12	33	1034

SUBJECT	BOOK	CHAP.	VERSE	PAGE
Special provision in early	°Acts	4	32-34	1087
Church	Acts	6	1-4	1090
	1 Cor	16	1-4	1141
Special charge to the rich	°1 Tm	6	17-19	1183
A striking exception	°2 Thess	3	10	1178

ALOES. A product of the aromatic eaglewood tree which produces a valuable oil used for perfume. It was worth its weight in gold and was probably one of the spices brought by Nicodemus to anoint the Body of Jesus.

Figurative of the graces of	°Ps	45	9	524
the Church	Sg	4	14	640
Used in embalming	°Jn	19	39	1078

ALPHA AND OMEGA. The first and last letters of the Greek alphabet. Our Lord said He was the first and the last, the beginning and the end. This assertion of His divinity is a fulfillment of the Old Testament statement that God is the first and the last, the Creator of all, knowing all that was and all that shall be.

Expresses eternity of God	°Rv	1	8	1234
	Rv	22	13	1249
Fulfillment of Old	°Is	41	4	752
Testament				

ALTAR BREADS. The round wafers made of pure wheaten flour, unleavened, which are used for Mass.

ALTAR CARDS. Printed or hand painted cards, usually three in number, which are placed in the center and at each side of the altar at Mass. These contain certain prayers which are constant parts of the Mass and serve to aid the celebrant who refers to these cards instead of to the Missal.

ALTAR CLOTHS. Linens or other cloths used to cover the altar.

ALTAR COVER. The covering placed on the altar when it is not in use to protect the altar cloths from dust and grime. No color or material is prescribed, although red or green are most commonly used.

ALTAR LINENS. The corporal, pall, and purificator used in the Mass.

ALTAR OF REPOSE. See *Repository.*

ALTAR, PAPAL. The special altar used only by the pope or his particular representative for the celebration of Mass. Each of the greater basilicas of Rome has a papal altar.

ALTAR PIECE. A painting or fresco above the altar. This may be either a part of the reredos or a separate part of the altar.

ALTAR, STRIPPING OF. A ceremony commemorative of the stripping of Christ's garments on Calvary. After Mass on Holy Thursday the priest removes everything from the altar while reciting Psalm 22 and leaves the tabernacle door open.

AMBO. A raised platform approached by steps which was placed in the nave of early Christian churches. From this platform, or pulpit, the Epistle and Gospel were sung, sermons were read, and pronouncements made. Later there were two, one for the Epistle side, the other for the Gospel. Today, however, the ambo has been superseded by the lectern or pulpit, although it may still be seen in Rome in the Church of San Clemente.

AMBROSIAN RITE. The ancient liturgy of the Church and Province of Milan which today is used in a few places in Italy, including Milan. Believed to be of Gallican origin, it differs considerably from the Roman Rite. Pope Pius XI belonged to the Ambrosian Rite.

AMBRY. The chest or case in which the holy oils are kept. It usually is found on the sanctuary wall.

AMEN. An adverb derived from the Hebrew verb *'aman,* meaning to confirm, support. In the Old Testament the term is found at the end of curses, and also at the close of public prayers and benedictions. It also occurs at the end of the first four books of the Psalter. In the New Testament, it is often placed at the beginning of a discourse, where it means "truly," or it may be found at the end of a statement where it means "so be it." The Jewish people used "Amen" as the response to prayers, and the Christians adopted the word as indicated in the Gospels.

SUBJECT	BOOK	CHAP.	VERSE	PAGE
Confirming various	°Nm	5	22	110
maledictions	Dt	27	15-26	163
At the close of public	°1 Chr	16	36	323
prayers	Neh	8	6	375
	Tb	13	23	392
At conclusion of first four	°Ps	41	14	521
books of Psalter	Ps	72	19	542
	Ps	89	53	555
	Ps	106	48	569
Also means "truly"	°Mt	5	18	970
	Mk	3	28	1001
	Lk	4	24	1024
Used as "so be it"	°Rom	1	25	1116
	Gal	1	5	1151
	Eph	3	21	1159

AMENDMENT, FIRM PURPOSE OF. An explicit and real determination to avoid sin. It is a necessary part of true contrition and requires a firm resolve to avoid all occasions of sin. Even though we have broken this resolution, we should make it again, sincerely. God is just and forgiving and realizes the frailties of human nature; thus He does not require a guarantee, but a firm desire to lead a good Catholic life and to try to avoid the pitfalls of sin.

AMICE. A rectangular white linen garb with two long strings at the top corners. It is worn under the alb around the neck and the shoulders of the priest at Mass. Symbolically it represents the "helmet of salvation" and "discipline of the tongue."

ANABAPTISM. A 16th century heresy started by two Lutherans: Thomas Münzer, a Lutheran preacher, and Nicholas Storch, a weaver. They taught that baptism of infants was invalid, and rebaptism when grown (by immersion) was necessary. Luther strongly opposed their beliefs, which included the sharing of all material goods. However, their baptismal theory was adopted by certain Baptist sects of England and Wales and is practiced by the Mennonites here in the United States.

ANATHEMA. The basic meaning of this term is accursed, and in a number of New Testament passages the original Greek term is so rendered. In the Greek Old Testament "anathema" is used to translate a Hebrew root meaning not accursed, but "dedicated to destruction," and therefore untouchable. In the Old Testament anyone who made use of an anathematized thing was punished by death. In the New Testament Paul is willing to endure this punishment if thereby he could bring salvation to his people. This term was adopted by the Church to express the exclusion of a sinner, especially a heretic, from the Sacraments. Since the Council of Nicaea (325) dogmatic canons are usually worded: "If anyone says . . . let him be *anathema.*"

ANGEL. *messenger,* that is, of God. A pure spirit created by God. The Old Testament theology included the belief in angels, the name applied to certain spiritual beings or intelligences of heavenly residence, employed by God as the ministers of His will. The Scriptures give no indication of the precise time of the creation of angels; their existence is taken for granted from the earliest times.

Cherubim at entrance to	°Gn	3	24	3
Garden of Eden				
Angels appeared to	°Gn	18	1-33	15
Abraham				
Saved Lot and his family	°Gn	19	1-22	16
Angel intervened at	°Gn	22	11-18	18
sacrifice of Isaac				
Heavenly ladder of angels	°Gn	28	12	25
in Jacob's vision				
Angel accompanied Israel	°Ex	23	20	65
through desert	Nm	20	16	125
Angels aided the prophets:				
Isaiah	°Is	6	2-7	721
Ezekiel	°Ez	1	4-28	848
Daniel	°Dn	7	9-10	896
Zechariah	°Zec	1	9-19	951

Our Lord often speaks of angels; according to the New Testament angels are exceedingly numerous, and seven classes of angels are mentioned: Angels, Powers, Virtues, Principalities, Dominations, Thrones, and Archangels. (In addition, the Old Testament mentions Cherubim and Seraphim.) God bestowed

SUBJECT	BOOK	CHAP.	VERSE	PAGE

upon angels great wisdom, freedom, and power, and their many appearances in the New Testament are ample indication of the leading role God has assigned to them.

SUBJECT	BOOK	CHAP.	VERSE	PAGE
Appeared in connection	°Mt	1	20	966
with the birth of Christ	Lk	1	26-38	1020
Appear to:				
Paul	°Acts	27	23	1113
Peter	°Acts	12	7-11	1098
Cornelius	°Acts	10	3-6	1095
Only Sadducees did not believe in angels	°Acts	23	8	1110
Twelve legions of angels	°Mt	26	53	993
Three angels mentioned by name:				
Raphael	°Tb	12	15	391
Michael	°Dn	10	13	900
	Rv	12	7	1241
Gabriel	°Dn	8	16	898
	Lk	1	19	1020

Both the New and Old Testaments refer to the fall of many angels. The temptation of Adam and Eve presupposes the existence of bad spirits or demons who were cast into hell from which they have no hope of redemption.

	BOOK	CHAP.	VERSE	PAGE
Fall of the angels	°Dt	32	17	169
	2 Pt	2	4	1217
	Jude	1	6	1231
	Rv	12	7-9	1241

ANGELIC DOCTOR. A title given to St. Thomas Aquinas (1225–1274) who was one of the greatest theologians and philosophers of the Catholic Church. He was so named because of the quality and sanctity of his mind, life, and teachings.

ANGELUS. A short prayer said in the morning, at midday, and in the evening in honor of the Incarnation of Jesus Christ and in veneration of the Blessed Virgin Mary. During Paschal time the Regina Coeli is said instead. The text of the Angelus is as follows:

The Angelus

V. The Angel of the Lord declared unto Mary.
R. And she conceived of the Holy Spirit.
   Hail Mary, etc.
V. Behold the handmaid of the Lord.
R. Be it done to me according to your Word.
   Hail Mary, etc.
V. And the Word was made flesh.
R. And dwelt among us. Hail Mary, etc.
V. Pray for us, O Holy Mother of God.
R. That we may be made worthy of the promises of Christ.

Let us Pray.

Pour forth, we beseech Thee, O Lord, Thy grace into our hearts, that we to whom the Incarnation of Christ, Thy Son, was made known by the message of an angel, may by His passion and cross be brought to the glory of His resurrection, through the same Christ Our Lord, Amen.

ANGER. An unjust outburst of emotion combined with a great desire for revenge. Anger is a sin against justice and charity and is one of the seven capital sins. It is often the cause of such special sins as indignation, the swelling of passion, disorder, blasphemy, contumely, murder, etc.

ANGLICANISM. The schismatic teachings adopted as the official religion of England. When Henry VIII was denied a divorce, he severed all connections with Rome and was declared head of the English Church by Parliament (1534). Today in the Anglican Church there are many so-called divisions, with accompanying differences in beliefs, but the primary teachings follow the "39 articles" adopted in 1563. According to these articles, the Anglican Church and its followers accept the Trinity, Incarnation, and Redemption, but reject Purgatory; maintain only Baptism and the Lord's Supper as sacraments established by Christ; and still do not recognize the authority of the Pope in England. In the United States the Protestant Episcopal Church is a member of the Anglican Church.

ANIMA CHRISTI. *soul of Christ.* The opening words of a prayer to Christ in His Passion. Its author is unknown. The prayer is as follows:

Anima Christi

"Soul of Christ, sanctify me.
Body of Christ, save me.
Blood of Christ, inebriate me.
Water from the side of Christ, wash me.
Passion of Christ, strengthen me.
O good Jesus, hear me.
Within Your Wounds, hide me.
Permit me not to be separated from You.
From the malignant enemy defend me.
In the hour of my death call me,
And bid me come to You.
That, with Your saints, I may praise You.
Forever and ever, Amen."

ANNE DE BEAUPRÉ, SAINTE. The devotion to Ste Anne, mother of the Blessed Virgin, under the title of Ste Anne de Beaupré goes back to the beginning of New France, in what is now Canada. The French had always had a particular devotion to her, and in 1658 Father Vignal came to Beaupré to select a site for a chapel in her honor. Sieur Etienne Lessard offered to pay for the selected land. Louis Guimont, who was suffering severely from rheumatism of the loins, placed three stones in the foundation, imploring the aid of Ste Anne to relieve him of his affliction. Miraculously, he was cured. Thus was begun the series of cures which could be explained only as miracles of God, through the intercession of Ste Anne. The old church was completed in 1676. The present building was opened in 1926 following two disastrous fires. The church is a minor basilica.

ANNULMENT OF MARRIAGE. A civil or ecclesiastical declaration that in a particular case there was no valid marriage by reason of a known or hidden impediment. There is no such thing as an annulment of a valid marriage.

ANNUNCIATION OF THE BLESSED VIRGIN MARY. The exact moment of the Incarnation, when the Angel Gabriel told the Blessed Virgin Mary she had been chosen to be the Mother of God, the Son. The Feast of the Annunciation is celebrated March 25th.

	BOOK	CHAP.	VERSE	PAGE
The Annunciation	°Lk	1	26-38	1020

ANOINT. *to pour oil upon.* Anointings spoken of in the Scriptures are of two kinds: material and spiritual. Material anointings were of ordinary or official kinds. Ordinary anointing of the head or body was a common practice in ancient times among all Orientals, and was performed for a variety of purposes: as a mark of respect, as a token of prosperity and happiness, and in preparation of bodies for burial.

Official anointing formed a part of the rites of inauguration in all three of the typical offices of the commonwealth of ancient Israel: for priest, for prophets, for kings. It appears to have been practiced for all priests at first, but later for high priests only. The practice was not generally followed in the case of prophets, but only in special instances. In the inauguration of kings, the Israelites had observed this practice by other nations before they became a monarchy, and appear to have made it a universal practice under divine directions. The anointings of New Testament times were generally confined to acts of respect and to treatments of the sick. Anointing of objects associated with the Tabernacle was of a distinct religious nature and formed an element of the act of consecration for holy purposes.

	BOOK	CHAP.	VERSE	PAGE
Olive oil ordinarily used	°Dt	28	40	164
Oil mixed with aromatic spices	°1 Sm	8	13	221
Jacob poured oil, over stone	°Gn	28	18	25
Aaron anointed by Moses	°Ex	28	41	69
Anointing of early kings:				
Saul	°1 Sm	10	1	223
Solomon	°1 Kgs	1	34-39	264
David	°1 Sm	16	13	229
Preparation of body for burial	°Mk	16	1	1017
Act of courtesy to honored guest	°Mt	26	6-13	993
A symbol of consecration and pouring out of the Holy Spirit	°Lk	4	18-21	1024

ANOINTING OF THE SICK. See Sacrament of the Sick.

SUBJECT	BOOK	CHAP.	VERSE	PAGE

ANTIMENSION. A piece of linen or silk, eighteen inches square and doubled, used in the Byzantine Rite in place of an altar stone, or sometimes even on a consecrated altar. The instruments of Christ's passion and entombment are embroidered or painted on it, and relics of martyrs are sewn onto it. A bishop consecrates it with a rite very much like that used for an altar.

ANTIPHON. 1. A piece sung by two sides of a choir, each chanting separate verses. In the public recitations of the Divine Office, the Psalms are sung antiphonally.

2. The words or verses prefixed to and following Psalms or Canticles. Depending upon the rank of the feast, only part or all of the antiphon preceding the Psalms may be sung. In the Mass, the prayers of the entrance hymn, Offering, and Communion are called antiphons.

ANTIPHONARY. A liturgical book which contains the antiphons and musical notes of the Divine Office.

ANTIPHON OF OUR LADY. Four prayers in honor of the Blessed Virgin Mary which are sung in the Divine Office according to the seasons of the year. They are *Alma Redemptoris Mater, Ave Regina Coelorum, Regina Coeli,* and *Salve Regina.*

APOCALYPSE. (THE REVELATIONS) *to uncover, reveal.* A style of writing common in Jewish circles in the centuries immediately preceding and following the life of Christ. Written at a time of persecution, in the style of a revelation made to a prophet, it is marked by the use of *symbolic* numbers, animals, and other creatures. Written to those people familiar with the Bible and its symbols (i.e. Christians and Jews) its meaning is decipherable to its readers but not to outsiders. This, of course, is most useful during persecution since the code is known by the faithful but not by the persecutor. A prominent feature is its telescoping of past, present, and future events so that all three may be interpreted in the light of each other to give hope that God's saving acts will always endure.

Personal revelation made to	°Gal	1	12	1151
Paul	Eph	3	3	1159
	2 Cor	12	1	1149
Mysteries of God revealed	°Rom	16	25	1128
by Christ	Lk	2	32	1022
The Last Day	°Rom	2	5	1118
	1 Cor	1	7	1130
	2 Thes	1	7	1177

APOCRYPHAL BOOKS. *hidden.* Scripture-like books spuriously claimed to be inspired and not entitled to a place in the Canon of Scripture. For the most part, these books attempt to fill in historical vacancies of the accepted writings, but many of them are definitely heretical. Since their authenticity is either doubtful or obviously false, the Catholic Church has rejected these writings which are not included in the Catholic Bible. A few of the books classified unacceptable are III and IV Ezra, III and IV Maccabees, Prayer of Manasses, and the Gospel of James.

The Protestant Apocrypha differs from that of the Catholic Church. They erroneously refuse to accept Tobit, Judith, Sirach, Baruch, I and II Maccabees, and parts of Esther and Daniel; all of which are part of the Catholic Bible.

APOLOGETICS. The theological science which establishes, defends, and explains the Christian religion and Catholic doctrine through arguments from reason.

APOSTASY. 1. The complete renunciation of the Catholic Faith by a baptized person who had professed it. An apostate incurs excommunication, ipso facto, from the Church, and is refused Christian burial unless he repents. In 2 Thes 2, 3 St. Paul warns that a great apostasy will be a prelude to the Second Coming of Christ.

2. Apostasy from the religious life occurs when a professed male or female religious who had taken perpetual vows unlawfully deserts his or her community with the intention of making the separation permanent.

APOSTLE. *one sent forth, a messenger or delegate.* In the New Testament the word is used in a wide sense to a messenger, and in a special sense to the Twelve chosen by Christ to be a witness to His life and Resurrection and then preach His Gospel. According to the order of the First Gospel, which deviates somewhat from the three other lists, the Apostles are as follows:

SUBJECT	BOOK	CHAP.	VERSE	PAGE
(1) Simon, called Cephas (Peter) and Bar Jona (son of John)	°Jn	1	40-42	1050
(2) Andrew, brother of Peter	°Jn	1	40	1050
(3) James the Greater, the son of Zebedee and Salome, the brother of John, a fisherman	°Mt	4	21	969
(4) John, the brother of James the Greater, among first disciples	°Jn	1	35-40	1050
(5) Philip of Bethsaida, the town of Andrew and Peter, among the first followers	°Jn	1	43-44	1050
(6) Bartholomew, son of Tolmai, identified with Nathanael, among the first disciples	°Jn	1	45-49	1050
(7) Thomas, also called in Greek Didymus (a twin)	°Lk	6	13-15	1026
(8) Matthew or Levi, a publican, son of Alpheus, called at start of first Galilean ministry	°Lk / Mt / Mk	5 / 9 / 2	27-32 / 9-13 / 13-17	1025 / 974 / 1000
(9) James the Less, son of Alpheus (Cleophas) and Mary, who was the brother of Jude, close relative of Our Lord	°Lk / Mt	6 / 10	15 / 3	1026 / 975
(10) Jude, also called Thaddeus, the brother of James the Less	°Jude	1	1	1231
(11) Simon the Zealot or Cananean	°Lk / Matt	6 / 10	15 / 4	1026 / 975
(12) Judas Iscariot, the betrayer	°Lk	6	16	1026
Chosen after death of Judas:				
(13) Matthias, one of seventy disciples of Our Lord	°Acts / Lk	1 / 10	23-26 / 1	1083 / 1032
Divinely chosen:				
(14) Paul of Tarsus, Cilicia, converted to Christianity after the Ascension of Jesus	°Acts	22	6-15	1109
(15) Barnabas of Cyprus, one of the seventy disciples of Our Lord	°Acts / Lk	13 / 10	2 / 1	1098 / 1032

Of the original twelve Apostles, all except Judas came from Galilee; Peter and Philip were married. Most of the Apostles died through martyrdom for their faith in Christ, Our Lord.

APOSTLES' CREED. A prayer containing the fundamental Christian beliefs which summarize the doctrine taught by the Apostles. Catholics are bound to the articles of this creed under pain of heresy. The text follows:

Apostles' Creed

"I believe in God, the Father Almighty, Creator of Heaven and earth; and in Jesus Christ, His only Son, Our Lord; who was conceived by the Holy Spirit, born of the Virgin Mary, suffered under Pontius Pilate, was crucified, died, and was buried. He descended into hell; the third day He arose again from the dead; He ascended into heaven, sitteth at the right hand of God, the Father Almighty; from thence He shall come to judge the living and the dead. I believe in the Holy Spirit, the Holy Catholic Church, the communion of saints, the forgiveness of sins, the resurrection of the body, and life everlasting. Amen."

APOSTOLIC DELEGATE. An ecclesiastical appointee who represents the pope in a country whose government does not maintain diplomatic relations with the Holy See; for example, the United States. His duties are religious in nature, and he reports to the pope on the state of the Church in the country he represents. In a country which does maintain diplomatic relations with the Vatican, the representative is called a papal nuncio or internuncio, and his duties automatically become primarily diplomatic, not religious.

APOSTOLIC FATHERS. Those early Christian writers who lived near enough to apostolic times either to have had personal contact with the Apostles or to have come under their influence. A few of their works are the "Didache," the "Letter of Clement," and the letters of St. Ignatius of Antioch and the "Shepher" of Hermas.

APOSTOLIC SEE. The episcopal see of Rome founded by St. Peter, the first pope. Although Alexandria, Antioch, and Jerusalem were also sees of apostolic origin, they were not founded by St. Peter, who alone had the authority to establish the papal diocese.

APOSTOLIC SUCCESSION. The continuous and authoritative succession of the Church from the time of Jesus Christ to the present day. Our Lord selected Peter and the other Apostles, conferring upon them various powers, and ordaining them to carry on the work of His Church. These powers and the mission have been lawfully passed on to the present day pope and bishops by the valid consecration of bishops and the conferring of holy orders.

APPARITIONS. Supernatural manifestations made either bodily or in luminous form. Two striking examples within two centuries are the visible appearances of Our Blessed Lady to Ste Bernadette Soubirous at Lourdes, France, in 1858; and to the three children at Fatima, Portugal, in 1917.

Both the Old and the New Testaments contain many accounts of angels appearing to various people and of the risen Christ Himself manifested to His followers. A few of the better known apparitions are listed:

SUBJECT	BOOK	CHAP.	VERSE	PAGE
Angel visits Abraham	°Gn	18	1-33	15
Angel visits Jacob	°Gn	32	24-30	29
Mary Magdalene sees	°Mk	16	9	1017
Christ	Jn	20	11-18	1080
Christ appears to Apostles	°Mk	16	14-18	1017
	Jn	20	19-23	1080
	Acts	1	1-5	1083
Thomas believes	°Jn	20	24-29	1080
Saul (Paul) receives vision	°Acts	26	12-18	1112

ARCHANGELS. Spiritual beings who belong to the eighth group of the nine orders or choirs of angels. The word *angel* means messenger; an archangel is a messenger sent by God on an assignment of greater importance. The only three archangels mentioned in the Bible are Michael, captain of the heavenly host; Gabriel, who announced to Mary that she was to become the Mother of God; and Raphael who guided Tobiah. The apocryphal book of Enoch lists four more.

SUBJECT	BOOK	CHAP.	VERSE	PAGE
Michael	°Dn	10	13-21	900
	Jude	1	9	1231
	Rv	12	7-8	1241
Gabriel	°Dn	8	15-26	898
	Dn	9	21-27	899
	Lk	1	26-38	1020
	Lk	1	11-20	1020
Raphael	°Tb	3	24-25	384
	Tb	5-		386
		12		391

ARCHBISHOP. The bishop of an archdiocese who has certain authority, decreed by Canon Law, over the other bishops in his ecclesiastical province. The bishops who head dioceses under him are known as "suffragans"; he then is called a "metropolitan" and obtains the right to wear the pallium. If there are no bishops under him he is known only as an archbishop. A metropolitan's jurisdiction over the affairs of other dioceses is strictly limited and clearly defined. There are twenty-three archdioceses in the United States. Only one, that of Washington, D.C., is headed by an archbishop who is not also a metropolitan.

ARCHBISHOP, TITULAR. One who is entitled to the rank and title of archbishop but who is not the ruling head of an archdiocese. This honorary title is most commonly given to retired archbishops or to apostolic delegates.

ARCHDEACON. The name given to the office of chief assistant of the bishop in the early days of the Church. The Council of Trent in 1553 revoked most of the jurisdictional powers this office once held. Today, in the United States the position is held by the Vicar General, and the title, archdeacon, is merely honorary.

ARCHDIOCESE. An ecclesiastical province, usually composed of several dioceses, which is governed by an archbishop.

ARCHPRIEST. In early times, the special representative of a bishop in performing liturgical duties. Today the title is an honorary one.

ARIANISM. The heresy of Arius (256–326), an Alexandrian priest, who denied the divinity of Christ. He claimed Our Lord was a superior creature born of a human and used by God for creative purposes. He taught that because Christ was human He was liable to sin and limited in intelligence, and thus He differed from God—both in substance and intellect. St. Athanasius attacked this heresy which spread through the Christian world with amazing rapidity; the Council of Nicaea denounced it in 325. However, for many years it still flourished, declining in the East from about the year 361. History records Arianism as the strongest heresy which confronted the early Church.

ARISTOTELIANISM. The system of philosophy originated by Aristotle (384–322 B.C.), who is universally considered to be one of the greatest original thinkers of all time. He is known as the *Stagirite*, from the place of his birth, Stagira, a Greek colony on the northwestern shore of the Aegean Sea. He studied under Plato, tutored Alexander the Great, and later founded his own school called the Lyceum. Aristotle is particularly important to Catholics, because the Scholastics of the Middle Ages—especially St. Thomas Aquinas—developed their philosophy largely on his system.

To Aristotle, the object of philosophy is first principles and essences. It is not possible to prove or to demonstrate the existence of these first principles or essences, but reasoning makes their existence self-evident. On this basis Aristotle develops the idea that these universal truths are in every individual substance which make up the universe. These individuals, however, are not immediately evident, but through a form of reasoning called the syllogism, the mind is able to abstract the essence of the substance from the individual form. With this as a basis, Aristotle then applies his theory to the fields of logic, metaphysics, natural science, ethics, politics, rhetoric, and poetics.

ARTICLE OF FAITH. An expression which refers principally to the truths contained in the Apostles' Creed. But an article of faith also includes other truths explicitly laid down by the Catholic Church for Christian belief. The "Catechism of the Council of Trent" in speaking of the Apostles' Creed reads, "as the members of the body are divided by joints, so also we properly and appropriately call an article whatever in the profession of faith is to be believed by us distinctly and severally from anything else." Each article of faith must be accepted equally because each is equally true.

ASCENSION OF CHRIST. The Ascension of Christ before His disciples took place forty days after the Resurrection. The Body of Christ, locally and visibly, with suddeness, swiftness, and triumphant glory, rose into the heavens and passed from the sight of those who beheld Him. In His Ascension, Christ fulfilled many prophecies. He opened the way to heaven for His people and assured the saints of their ascension into heaven after their resurrection.

SUBJECT	BOOK	CHAP.	VERSE	PAGE
Witnessed by disciples	°Lk	24	50-51	1047
	Acts	1	9-10	1083
Testified by angels	°Acts	1	11	1083

ASCETICISM. Self-discipline and mortification in pursuit of perfection sought out of love for God. Asceticism is an integral part of Christian life; its aim is to make us more Christ-like. We strive toward the perfection Christ, by His own example, revealed to us during His life here on earth, and desire it as a means of personal sanctification and not as an end in itself. There are two types of self-discipline, external and internal, and some of each is essential to Christian lives. Externally it may be sought by practicing various forms of bodily mortification such as fasting, chastity, obedience, etc., but our efforts must always be made with the intention of renouncing for the sake of pleasing God. In its internal form our minds, hearts, and wills seek spiritual perfection.

ASH WEDNESDAY. The first day of Lent, and the seventh Wednesday before Easter. On this day blessed ashes of burnt

SUBJECT	BOOK	CHAP.	VERSE	PAGE

palms are placed on the foreheads of the people to remind them that physically they are but dust and that penance is necessary for the salvation of their souls.

ASHDOD. One of the five principal Philistine cities on the road between Egypt and Aram and about midway between Gaza and Joppe. The Israelites could not seize this fortified city, but it was assigned to the tribe of Judah nonetheless. The city was conquered by Uzziah, king of Judah (789–740 B.C.), who demolished its walls. Then in 711 B.C. it was captured by the commander-in-chief under Sargon II. After the return of the Jews from exile, the people of Ashdod were hostile and tried to deter them from rebuilding the walls of Jerusalem. During the Maccabean Wars, Ashdod was captured by Judas, and after the defeat of Apollonius it was destroyed together with its temple of Dagon by Jonathan.

Occupied by some Anakim during time of Joshua	°Jos	11	22	181
Assigned to Judah	°Jos	15	47	184
Philistines capture Ark of Covenant and place it in temple of Dagon	°1 Sm	4	10-11	219

ASPERSION. 1. The sprinkling of any person or object with holy water.
2. One of the three methods of baptism (immersion and infusion are the other two), accomplished by sprinkling the head with holy water. This method is forbidden, although it is a valid form of baptism.

ASPIRATION. A short prayer consisting of a few words which can be repeated easily, and to which an indulgence is usually attached.

ASSOCIATIONS, PIOUS. Societies which are organized: (1) to nurture the desire of its members for religious perfection, and (2) to accomplish various works of charity, piety, and public worship. These organizations are not to be confused with religious orders, although they do exist under direct ecclesiastical supervision. All Catholics are urged to become members of some of these societies which Church Law divides into four general classifications: Confraternities and Arch-confraternities, Pious Unions, Sodalities, and Third Orders.

ASSUMPTION OF THE BLESSED VIRGIN. 1. The taking up to heaven of the body of the Blessed Virgin Mary after her death and burial, and the reuniting of her uncorrupt body with her soul. While her assumption has been a common Catholic belief for at least 1500 years, it was not declared an article of faith until 1950. On November 1, 1950, Pope Pius XII defined the Assumption of the Blessed Virgin Mary as a dogma of the faith.
2. The Feast of the Assumption which is celebrated on August 15th. Known as the oldest feast of Mary, it is a Holy Day of Obligation.

ASTROLOGY. The false science which claims human affairs are influenced by the stars and their positions in the heavens. That this pseudo-science existed in Old Testament times is revealed in the Book of Isaiah 47, 13-15, where Isaiah tells the people of Babylon to seek aid from their astrologists, but that it will avail them nothing since God had doomed them because of their unrepented sins. Astrology becomes popular periodically, but each re-appearance is followed by the inevitable decline, since its initial appeal cannot be sustained by facts.

ATHANASIAN CREED. The official declaration of Christian doctrine regarding the Holy Trinity and the Incarnation. It was written during the life of St. Athanasius (296–373), but not composed by him, to refute the Arian heresy. It explains very clearly and definitely the fact that there are three persons, the Father, the Son, and the Holy Ghost in the one divine nature of God. It testifies that in Christ there is one divine person but two natures, one divine and one human. The Athanasian Creed often is called the *Quicumque* from its opening word.

ATHEIST. One who denies the existence of God or theism. To an atheist a material source is responsible for all being, and God, the Supreme Creator, is denied.

ATONEMENT. The action by which satisfaction is made in accordance with justice. In a religious sense, atonement means a reparation for an offense to God so that guilt is forgiven. The Bible mentions almsgiving, fasting, suffering, and especially expiatory sacrifices as means of atonement. The acceptance of

SUBJECT	BOOK	CHAP.	VERSE	PAGE

atonement is an act of divine mercy and God alone can formulate the conditions necessary for expiation.

Reparation for an offense	°Ex	29	33	70
to God	Lv	1	4	81
Means of atonement:				
Almsgiving	°Tb	12	9	391
	Dn	4	24	893
Fasting	°Jl	2	12	918
Suffering	°Jb	33	19-29	486

ATTRITION. Imperfect contrition for sin arising from supernatural motives inferior to the love of God. The penitent is sorry for his sins because he fears the punishment of hell and the loss of Heaven, or because of the detestable nature of the sin itself. Thus attrition is opposed to perfect contrition whereby the penitent's sorrow for his sin is motivated by his unselfish love for God. Imperfect contrition is sufficient to obtain forgiveness in the Sacrament of Penance.

AUDIENCES, PAPAL. Any reception accorded by the pope to an individual or to groups of individuals. Travelers who wish an audience should present themselves to the rector of the college of their nation in Rome. A letter of introduction is helpful. The rector then refers the request to the Maestro di Camera, head of the papal chamberlains, and arrangements for the papal audience are made. Group or public audiences are easily obtained; private audiences, for the obvious reason of a lack of time and the pope's busy schedule, are rarely given.

AUGUSTINE, HERMITS OF ST. (O.S.A.). Popularly known as Augustinians, this order follows the Rule of St. Augustine, of which the present Constitutions were compiled in 1278 A.D. This order was canonically established as a mendicant order by Pope Alexander IV in 1256 when several monasteries following the Rule of St. Augustine were reunited. The order is dedicated to educational, missionary, and parochial activities, and is found throughout the United States. Its general motherhouse is in Rome, Italy.
Another order, the Augustinian Recollects (O.R.S.A.), was established in 1574 by a reform for a stricter observance of the Rule of St. Augustine.

AUREOLE. 1. A symbolic halo of light placed over the heads of saints in Christian art to symbolize their special honor in heaven.
2. In theology, an additional reward given in Heaven to those who have most bravely withstood their trials and tribulations here on earth, for example, virgins and martyrs.

AVE MARIA. The title and first two words of the Hail Mary in Latin. This prayer is said very frequently to honor Our Lady and to recall to mind the Incarnation of God the Son. The words of the Angel Gabriel and St. Elizabeth comprise the first portion; the Catholic Church added the second part under the inspiration of the Holy Spirit. The Latin version has been set to music by many composers, among them Franz Schubert and Charles Gounod.

AVE REGINA COELORUM. *Hail Queen of the Heavens.* The first words of an antiphon of Our Blessed Mother.

AVIGNON POPES. The seven French popes, legitimately elected, from Clement V (1305) to Gregory XI (1370), who ruled the Church from Avignon instead of Rome. The appellation also refers to the Clementine Pontiffs who lived in Avignon during the Western Schism.

B

BABEL. *to confuse,* also *gate of god.* This was the name given to the tower built in the Plain of Shinar. It was never completed, as the purpose of those responsible for the building of the Tower of Babel was to provide a man-made access to God. In the vain hope of ascending to heaven this tower was begun. The builders were rebuked and stopped in their presumptuous scheme by the "confusion" of languages, resulting in utter inability to continue with understanding and cooperative labors. Identification of the exact place where the building of this tower was undertaken cannot be made; but it is of more importance to understand that the story of the Tower of Babel teaches us that the sin of pride and self-sufficiency cannot prevail.

Built by ancients	°Gn	11	1-9	10

BAGOAS. A eunuch of Holofernes, the cruel general of Nebuchadnezzar. It was during the siege of Bethulia that Holofernes

SUBJECT	BOOK	CHAP.	VERSE	PAGE
Bagoas instructed to invite	°Jdt	12	10-12	403
Judith to banquet	Jdt	13	1	404
Discovers body of Holofernes	°Jdt	14	13-18	404

instructed Bagoas to invite Judith to attend a banquet which resulted in the death of Holofernes and the liberation of Bethulia from the Assyrians.

BALTIMORE, COUNCILS OF. The assemblies of prelates which meet to establish the decrees and laws for the conduct of ecclesiastical affairs in the United States. By right of priority of the See, the Archbishop of Baltimore presides over these Plenary Councils, which are under the presidency of the Papal Legate. These meetings are attended by archbishops, bishops, mitred abbots, vicars apostolic, rectors of major seminaries, religious order provincials, experts in Canon Law and in sacred theology, and administrators. All decisions made by the councils must be approved by the Holy See, whereupon they become binding in the entire United States. To date there have been three Plenary Councils of Baltimore. The first was held in May, 1852, and professed allegiance to the pope, belief in the doctrines of the Catholic Church, regulated parish life, the teaching of Christian doctrine, Church ceremonies, and the administration of Church funds.

The Second Plenary Council was called in October, 1866. Its principal decrees concerned the condemnation of the heresies then prevalent, the regulation of the organization of new dioceses, the education and conduct of the clergy, handling of Church property, and general education. In November, 1884, the Third Plenary Council was called. A commission for the creation of a Catholic University was appointed, elementary and higher education was discussed, and six Holy Days of Obligation in the United States were decreed. Another commission was delegated to prepare a catechism of Christian Doctrine. A petition to promote the cause of beatification of the Jesuit Martyrs was signed.

BANNS. A public proclamation of the names of two people and their intention to marry, in order to discover if any impediment exists. According to Church Law, these banns must be proclaimed during sacred services on three successive Sundays or Holy Days of Obligation. If the marriage does not occur within six months of the final announcement of the banns, they must be published again. The faithful are obliged to reveal any knowledge of impediments which would make the marriage unlawful or invalid. No banns are announced for a mixed marriage. If there is a good and just reason, a dispensation from the banns can be obtained from the local bishop.

BAPTISM. The sacrament instituted by Christ by which the soul is cleansed from sin through the pouring of water and the invocation of the Holy Trinity, and is infused with sanctifying grace, making it an heir of heaven, a child of God, and a member of the Catholic Church. Baptism removes both original and actual sin (in the case of adults), and remits any punishment due to those sins. There are three types of Baptism: Baptism of water, Baptism of blood, and Baptism of desire. Only Baptism of water is a sacrament which indelibly marks the soul with the sacramental character.

Baptism of water is administered by the pouring of water on the head of the person to be baptized while invoking the Blessed Trinity. However, there are two other forms of Baptism of water: *immersion*, practiced primarily by the Eastern Churches; and *aspersion*, a valid form which is forbidden.

The priest is the ordinary minister of Baptism. In cases of necessity, however, any lay person may baptize, provided he has the right intention and follows the simple rules. While pouring water on the head of the person to be baptized, he must pronounce these words, "I baptize thee in the name of the Father, and of the Son, and of the Holy Spirit."

In the formal rite of Baptism administered by a priest, the Church has added exorcisms; the placing of salt in the candidate's mouth (symbolic of purification and preservation); anointing with oil and chrism; holding of a lighted candle and a profession of faith (performed by a sponsor if an infant is being baptized).

BAPTISM OF BLOOD. Martyrdom for Christ or His Church which removes original sin from the soul and imparts sanctifying grace, because it is a perfect act of charity. Any actual sins also are forgiven by the Baptism of Blood if the individual has imperfect or perfect contrition for them. It must be remembered that Baptism of Blood is not a sacrament.

BAPTISM OF DESIRE. A perfect act of love of God made by an unbaptized person who expresses true contrition for his sins and declares his intention of doing everything God has ordained for our salvation, including the desire to receive the Sacrament of Baptism. Baptism of Desire is not a sacrament, and therefore does not entitle one to receive the other sacraments. However, it does remove both original and actual sins, and through it sanctifying grace is infused into the soul.

BAPTISMAL NAME. The Christian or saint's name given to an individual at the time of Baptism, and signifying that he has become a new person in Christ. Ordinarily the parents select the baptismal name. It is not unlawful, according to Church laws, for one to change the name given at Baptism.

BAPTISMAL VOWS. A promise to renounce Satan and all his pomps and his works, which either the person baptized makes, or which his sponsors make for him.

BAPTISMAL WATER. Water blessed on Holy Saturday and on the Vigil of Pentecost and to which oil of catechumens and chrism are added. The priest blesses this water in the baptismal font, and it is used in administering solemn baptism.

BAPTISTRY. In the early days of the Church this was a separate building or part of a church which was used solely for administering the Sacrament of Baptism. Today, however, it usually is a special room within the Church walls which contains the baptismal font.

BEADS. A string or chain with bead variations to aid the memory in specific devotions. The most commonly known are the rosary beads, which consist of a crucifix, large beads on which the "Our Father" is said, and smaller ones on which the "Hail Mary" is prayed. Besides the rosary, chaplets are made of beads.

BEATIFIC VISION. The vision of God face to face which forms the essential happiness of angels and men in Heaven. The souls of the faithful departed see God directly. The human intellect is incapable of this vision. Our limited knowledge of the supreme magnificence of God stems from the things He created, from revealed images, and from the teachings of the Church. The vision of God in Heaven is called beatific because the sight of Him, the Divine Essence, completely fulfills all the soul's desires.

BEATIFICATION. The permission granted by the Holy See to publicly venerate a deceased person whose life on earth was extremely virtuous or who died a heroic death for Christ or His Church. It is, in effect, a statement by the Church that the deceased is regarded as dwelling in heaven. Before beatification takes place, the Church judicial authories must examine thoroughly the life, virtues, and writings of the candidate; and must establish definitely the occurrence of at least two authentic miracles performed through the candidate's intercession with God. If the findings are favorable, the person is declared "blessed," and limited public devotion can be held in his honor. Beatification is the second preliminary action to actual canonization.

BEATITUDES. *blessed, happy.* The eight blessings proclaimed by Christ at the beginning of the Sermon on the Mount. They contain a compendium of religious perfection and the basic laws of the Messianic Kingdom. St. Matthew gives them as follows:

1. "How blest are the poor in spirit; the reign of God is theirs.
2. Blest too are the sorrowing; they shall be consoled.
3. Blest are the lowly; they shall inherit the land.
4. Blest are they who hunger and thirst for holiness; they shall have their fill.
5. Blest are they who show mercy; mercy shall be theirs.
6. Blest are the single-hearted for they shall see God.
7. Blest too are the peacemakers; they shall be called sons of God.
8. Blest are those persecuted for holiness' sake; the reign of God is theirs."

BEATUS. *blessed one.* The official title which is given to one who has been beatified.

BEGHARDS. Associations of laymen who lived together in a community under a specific rule, but who took no vows. During the 13th and 14th centuries they were common in Flanders and the Netherlands. Unfortunately, they fell into Pantheistic errors,

SUBJECT	BOOK	CHAP.	VERSE	PAGE

for which they were condemned several times. The Beghards are remembered chiefly for their influence on the religious thinking of the peoples in the countries in which they lived and worked.

BEGUINES. Associations of lay women who live in communities without taking perpetual vows. Bound only by temporary vows of obedience and chastity, they are able to leave the life at will. They retain possession of their own property and usually teach to support themselves. In earlier days they became involved in the Pantheistic errors of the Beghards, and were almost suppressed. Today, the principal beguinage is located in Ghent.

BENEDICTINES. Monks and nuns of the order of St. Benedict which was founded in 529 A.D. At the age of 17, St. Benedict, son of a wealthy family of Umbria, became a hermit in a cave at Subiaco. Many followers wished to lead similar contemplative lives for God. Many persecutors haunted his life also, and, finally, in 529, he left Subiaco, went to Monte Cassino and founded the famous monastery there. He is considered the founder of Western monasticism, and his Benedictine Rule has become the pattern and inspiration of religious orders today.

St. Benedict did not intend that all Benedictines belong to a single group. Rather, it was his intention that each abbey be independent, each ruled by an abbot. Primarily, Benedictines engaged in manual labor and study, and celebrated the Divine Office in choir. Their work contributed greatly to the advancement of culture in the Western world.

Benedictine nuns regard St. Scholastica, St. Benedict's twin sister, as their foundress. Originally established as a community near the Monte Cassino Abbey, the Benedictine way of life spread rapidly and many other communities of women were established. There are over 30 separate communities of Benedictine nuns in the United States today. Benedictine monks have established 21 abbeys in the United States, each one largely autonomous. Both the monks and the nuns are distinguished by the initials O.S.B. (Order of St. Benedict) after their names.

BENEDICTION, APOSTOLIC. A solemn public blessing with plenary indulgence given by the pope, and, since 1870, by bishops and priests on special occasions. In addition, all priests must give this blessing to a person in danger of death. Also called the "Last Blessing," it must be given according to the formula of Pope Benedict XIV. The clergy are forbidden to impart this blessing to the excommunicated or the impenitent. The sick person receiving this Apostolic Benediction should pronounce the Holy Name and make an act of contrition and submission to the Will of God. This may be done aloud or inwardly.

BENEDICTION OF THE BLESSED SACRAMENT. A short religious service which originated in the 14th century for the purpose of adoring the Sacred Host. During this service the Blessed Sacrament may be exposed in the monstrance or ostensorium, or it may be enclosed in the ciborium and placed in the doorway of the tabernacle. The consecrated Host is incensed while the choir or congregation sings *O Solutaris Hostia* and *Tantum Ergo*. The priest sings a prayer and then blesses the congregation with the Sacred Host. Following the blessing the Divine Praises are recited. The Host is finally replaced inside the tabernacle.

BENEDICTUS. 1. The Canticle of Zechariah spoken by him upon the birth of his son, St. John the Baptizer. Beginning with "Blessed be the Lord God of Israel," this canticle is recited daily in the Divine Office of Lauds.

2. In the Mass, at the end of the Preface the priest recites, "Blessed [*benedictus*] be he who comes in the name of the Lord!"

Spoken by Zechariah	°Lk	1	68-79	1020
Christ greeted with	°Mt	21	9	987

BENEFICE. A permanently constituted church foundation comprised of a religious responsibility and the right to any income from it. In the Middle Ages much abuse resulted from these when those who held the benefice would subcontract the responsibility while keeping the revenue from them. More recently the tendency is towards salaried employees (pastors usually are).

BERENGARIUS, HERESY OF. The heresy taught by Berengarius, a French archdeacon, in the 11th century. He claimed Christ was present only spiritually in the Holy Eucharist; that

true transubstantiation did not take place. Several Synods, and finally, in 1079, the Council of Rome condemned this theory. A few years before his death in 1088, Berengarius made a full and final retraction of his heresy.

BIBLE READING. The Church has always encouraged the reading of the Bible, and many indulgences have been granted the faithful in all ages for such reading. A list of the present indulgences attached to reading the Bible will be found in this dictionary under "Indulgences." The Church, however, as the true shepherd of its members, has always insisted that only versions approved by the Holy See through the hierarchy be read. An approved version can be determined by the word "Imprimatur" (It may be printed) given by the local bishop of the place where the Bible is published. The word Imprimatur and the name of the bishop giving it is generally printed in the first few pages of the Bible and is usually accompanied by the words "Nihil Obstat" (No objection) and the name of the censor who reviewed the text at the behest of the bishop granting the Imprimatur, to see that no theological errors were introduced into the text.

Reading of a version of the Bible not approved by the hierarchy is forbidden. It can be readily understood why this is necessary, because the Bible, indeed, is not always easy to understand, even by the learned. For this reason Catholic versions are not permitted to be published without adequate footnotes to explain difficult passages of the text, so error may be avoided. Since none of the original manuscripts have withstood the ravages of time, there is also the problem of determining which of the many copies and translations of the originals which have survived are correct. The Church, as the guardian of the Bible, has definitely established which Bible books and which translations of these Bible books are in substantial agreement with the originals, and has so proclaimed them so that none of the faithful can be misled.

While Bible reading is and always has been encouraged as an adjunct to the preachings and teachings of the living Church, there have been times and places in the history of the Church where such reading was temporarily and rightly enjoined. It must be remembered that until the invention of printing in the 15th Century, Bible texts could only be reproduced by hand copying—usually the work of monks—and that very few Bibles existed. A Bible, therefore, in these early days was an extremely valuable book, and it is no wonder that a Bible might be chained to its stand or that not everyone would be given access to it. Again, from time to time in the early history of the Church, various heretics denied the authority of the Church to interpret infallibly the Bible, and they made and circulated erroneous and unauthorized translations. To combat these errors, local bishops on occasion temporarily forbade the faithful from reading the Bible to stop the transmission of these errors. However, the faithful were never without the guidance of their priests who, in their regular instruction, brought the true biblical message to the people. In late years when more and more approved translations have become available, modern Popes have encouraged Bible reading with the publication of such encyclicals as *Providentissimus Deus, Spiritus Paraclitus,* and *Divino Afflante Spiritu.* In the United States, Bible reading has been strongly encouraged by the local bishops who also have sponsored a modern translation called the Confraternity of Christian Doctrine Translation. The Confraternity translation is the one used in this Bible.

BINATION. The celebration of two Masses by the same priest on the same day. Ordinarily each priest is allowed to say only one Mass each day with the exception of All Souls Day (Nov. 2) and Christmas, when three Masses each may be offered. However, in certain areas where large groups would be unable to attend Mass at a given hour on Sundays and Holy Days of Obligation, the local bishop will give his priest permission to say two Masses (that is, to binate). Many priests now have the privilege of celebrating two masses whenever there is a funeral or wedding in a parish or, indeed, whenever the needs of the faithful demand it. Moreover, the privilege of trination (three masses in one day) on Holy Days and Sundays is enjoyed by many priests at this time.

BIRTH CONTROL. Any voluntary act which deliberately frustrates conception, the primary purpose of marriage. It includes the use of any chemical or mechanical device before, during, or after the marriage act, or the withdrawal during the act so that the male seed cannot fertilize the female ovum.

The practice of birth control is a mortal sin against the natural law of God. Pope Pius XI said, "Since the conjugal act is destined primarily by nature for the begetting of children, those who in exercising it deliberately frustrate its natural power and purpose, sin against nature and commit a deed which is shameful and intrinsically vicious."

The Church cannot and will not modify or change her stand on the interpretation of God's own natural law. Pope Pius XI expressed the stand of Holy Mother Church thusly, "No reason, however great, may be put forward by which anything intrinsically against nature may become conformable to nature and morally good."

It must be made clear that while the Church condemns the artificial methods of birth control, she does not denounce natural control, called rhythm, where its use is justified. Rhythm is the practice of limiting the marital act to the period of the wife's menstrual cycle when conception is least likely to take place. For urgent reasons of health, or where the family's economic situation would be seriously aggravated by the addition of another child, the use of rhythm may be permitted after consultation.

BISHOP. A successor of the Apostles, an ecclesiastic who has received the highest of the sacred orders. Bishops are appointed by the Holy See and are consecrated by another bishop who is assisted by two other Catholic bishops. Over and above his priest powers, a consecrated bishop receives the power to confer the Sacraments of Confirmation and Holy Orders. A bishop may be an auxiliary, coadjutor, suffragan, or titular.

BISHOP, AUXILIARY. One consecrated a bishop and named a titular bishop, but who is appointed to assist a ruling bishop on account of the latter's age, ill health, or huge volume of work. He receives his jurisdiction from the ruling bishop, and usually confers the Sacraments of Confirmation and Holy Orders in place of the diocesan head. Very often he also may be a pastor or a vicar general.

BISHOP, COADJUTOR. A bishop appointed to govern a diocese in which the residential bishop is unable to perform all his duties. He assumes the full authority of his office, and usually is given the right of succession.

BISHOP, SUFFRAGAN. The local bishop of a diocese which is part of the ecclesiastical province of an archbishop or metropolitan. A suffragan bishop is the ruling head of his own diocese. His immediate superior is the pope, except for a very few instances in which the archbishop could exercise a limited authority.

BISHOP, TITULAR. A bishop consecrated for a see which no longer exists or has lapsed generally through a decrease or a shift in Catholic population. Since auxiliary bishops have no see of their own, they are named titular bishops, meanwhile performing their duties as assistants to the diocesan bishops, acting as vicar generals, etc.

BLACK. A liturgical color introduced in the late middle ages and used for masses for the dead and on Good Friday. Recently the trend has been towards allowing such colors as purple and white (the latter symbolic of the Resurrection) to replace the somewhat somber and morbid black (symbolic of death).

BLACK FAST. A fast day in the early Church in which only one full meal was allowed. Not only was the quantity of food limited, it had to be eaten only in the evening. Abstinence from flesh meat, milk, eggs, butter, and cheese was required. During Lent only bread, water, salt, and vegetables were permitted.

BLESSING. A rite dedicating persons, places, or things to a sacred office. The most common blessings applied to persons are: to bride and bridegroom at a nuptial Mass; to dying persons; to women before and after childbirth; to children; to people in general on various occasions. The Church has a special blessing for homes, churches, and cemeteries. Objects which may be blessed are baptismal and holy water, holy oils, bells, vestments, candles, incense, palms on Palm Sunday, rosaries, medals, and other religious objects. A blessing is valid only if the prescribed formula is followed by a properly authorized ecclesiastic.

BLOOD. The Hebrews considered blood the seat of life, because when it is permitted to run out of the body, life is extinguished. Meat could be eaten only after the blood had been fully drained out, and violation of this law meant expulsion from the community. Because blood was considered the essence

of life, it was used as a sacrificial means of atoning for sins.

In the New Testament, the Blood of Christ is the true sacrificial blood shed to ratify the New Covenant. The specific character of Christ's Blood is taught by Christ Himself: "This is My Blood, the blood of the covenant, to be poured out on behalf of many." As a reward for the blood which Jesus shed, His Father raised Him from the dead, and thus His bloody death merited for Him and for us a glorious resurrection.

SUBJECT	BOOK	CHAP.	VERSE	PAGE
Blood, the seat of life	°Gn	9	4	8
	Lv	17	14	95
Blood as food forbidden	°Gn	9	4	8
Blood must be drained from food	°Lv	19	26	96
Used as sacrificial means of atonement	°Lv	17	11	95
Hebrews to smear blood on doorposts in Egypt	°Ex	12	7	55
Blood of Christ true sacrificial blood	°Ex	24	8	66

BOOKS, LITURGICAL. The books containing the prayers and rites used by the Church. Each liturgical celebration must be conducted in a manner according to the methods set forth in the official liturgical books.

BREVIARY. A book containing the scriptural readings and other prayers which are of obligation for those members of the clergy who are at least of subdiaconate rank. The traditional hours were matins, lauds, prime, terce, sext, none, vespers, and compline. There has been much revision both in the composition of these and the number of them which must be said in recent times. The prayers in the breviary and the breviary itself are sometimes referred to as the "Divine Office" or "Office" (duty).

BRIEF. A papal letter written on fine parchment, signed by the pope's secretary of briefs, and sealed with the pope's signet ring, the Seal of the Fisherman.

BROAD STOLE. The vestment which the deacon wears at a solemn Mass during Advent or Lent, from the Epistle to the Communion of the Mass. It is a long piece of cloth, about ten inches wide. The deacon wears it diagonally across the chest and back, over the left shoulder and under the right arm.

BUGIA. A candlestick with a short handle. At a Mass offered by a prelate, an assistant holds the bugia to illuminate the Missal for the reading of the Epistle or Gospel. It also is called a palmatoria or scotula.

BULL, PAPAL. The most formal official document issued by the pope. It is written on strong parchment and bears the signatures of the pope and certain members of the papal chancery. It receives its name from the lead or gold seal, called the *bulla*, which bears a representative of SS. Peter and Paul on one side and the reigning pope on the other. This seal is attached to the document by a silken cord if the bull is one of grace, and by a hempen cord if it is a bull of justice.

BULLARIUM. A compilation of papal bulls.

BURSE. 1. Formerly the square case in which the corporal was carried for mass or benediction. It is no longer obligatory.

2. The leather pocket in which the pyx is carried.

3. A fund for the support and education of poor students studying for the priesthood.

BUSKINS. The ceremonial stockings of silk and gold thread worn by a bishop over his purple stockings at Pontifical Mass.

BYZANTINE RITE. One of the five principal rites used by the Eastern Churches. Originally it was proper to the Church of Istanbul (Byzantium). Based on the Rite of St. James of Jerusalem, it was reformed by St. Basil, and later by St. John Chrysostom. Now the whole Orthodox Eastern Church, as well as some Eastern Catholics, use this rite.

C

CALENDAR, ECCLESIASTICAL. The days of the year set apart for religious veneration. A liturgical calendar gives the day by day list of feasts as followed by the Church in her liturgy. This begins with the first Sunday of Advent and continues in the cycle until the first Sunday of Advent in the next year. Since many of the feasts of the Church are determined by Easter, the calendar changes from year to year.

CALVARY. *skull.* A rocky hill north of Jerusalem where Christ was crucified. There was an old popular belief that Adam's head was buried there; then, too, it was a mound-like eminence. For these reasons it was called the *Skull* (Latin, *Calvaria*; Aramaic, *Golgotha*).

SUBJECT	BOOK	CHAP.	VERSE	PAGE
Place where Jesus was	°Lk	23	33	1045
crucified	Mt	27	33-35	995
	Mk	15	22-25	1016
	Jn	19	17-18	1078

CALVINISM. This is the heretical theological system or religion founded by John Calvin (1509–1564), who was born in Noyon, France, but lived most of his life in Switzerland. The essence of Calvinism is predestination, by which God, through a direct act of His Will, preordains the salvation of some and the damnation of others, without regard to the merit of the individual. In this view man is completely corrupt as the result of Original Sin, and justification or salvation must come from an outside source or an extrinsic principle.

Calvin borrowed many of his ideas from Luther and Zwingli, especially with regard to the private interpretation of Scripture, the sufficiency of good works alone for salvation, and the consequences of Original Sin. The Presbyterian Church adopted many of the Calvinistic doctrines on predestination, but in recent years these doctrines have undergone some modification. Calvinism was condemned by the Council of Trent (1545–1563).

CAMPANILE. 1. A bell tower developed by Lombardian architects, still used in Italy. It is usually a slender tower detached from the church building and crowned with a turret containing bells.

2. The name is also applied to an open construction on top of a roof in which the bell is constructed.

CANA CONFERENCE. The Cana Conference movement started in Chicago in 1944, and since has spread throughout the United States and into many foreign countries. Cana is a biblical name, taken after the wedding feast at Cana, where Christ worked His first miracle in changing water into wine. The purpose of the Cana Conferences is to build happier, healthier, and holier marriages by taking married couples away from the everyday hustle and bustle to re-evaluate and enrich the vocation and sacrament they are living together. Cana Conferences are open to married couples of all faiths.

Husband-Wife Conferences deal with all the important things that concern couples in their physical, psychological, and spiritual union. *Parent-Child Conferences* treat the vital questions of parents of young children. *Parent-Teenage Conferences* provide parents with realistic help for guiding adolescents through the difficult years to maturity. *Christian Attitudes in the Home Conferences* are designed to foster and enrich the basic family virtues in the home.

Each conference consists of talks on its respective subject matter in terms of practical, down-to-earth, living experiences; short periods for personal discussion and meditation; lively question-answering sessions; and refreshments. The afternoon is climaxed by a renewal of marriage vows. The conferences are conducted by specially trained priests who draw from their own invaluable experience in counselling married couples, plus the work of doctors, theologians, sociologists, and other professional authorities.

The Cana movement also sponsors Pre-Cana Conferences for engaged couples. The purpose is to help engaged couples to understand themselves better in their courtship and to prepare themselves for the vocation of marriage and its responsibilities.

CANDELABRUM. The name applied to a chandelier for lamps, but now it is also applied to a candlestick, usually holding five or seven branches.

CANDLEMASS. The medieval term for the mass at which candles were blessed (as Christmas, Michaelmas, etc. referred to the feast days in question). Formerly called the "Feast of the Purification of the Blessed Mother" it is more recently (and accurately) called the "Feast of the Presentation of Christ in the Temple."

CANDLES, LITURGICAL. These candles are cylindrical wax sticks or tapers with a wick in the center used for illumination. These candles used for liturgical purposes are of pure wax, for the greater portion, and white in color, except in Masses for the Dead when they may be of yellow wax. A specified number of candles, prescribed in the rubrics, must be used lighted during various ceremonies.

CANON. *a reed or rule for measuring.* Originally this meant a rule or measure. In the Church it has come to mean a rule of belief or conduct.

1. *The Old Testament,* which the Catholic Church has declared to be divinely inspired, and a partial rule of faith and morals. Since the 16th century there has been an acknowledged distinction between the Books of the Bible which are declared to be divinely inspired and those denied or doubted by some. The first class are termed *protocanonical* and the latter *deuterocanonical.* Among the deuterocanonical books are Tobit, Judith, Wisdom, Sirach, Baruch, 1 and 2 Maccabees, the last six chapters of Esther and three passages in Daniel. Catholics believe both classes of these canonical books were inspired. These deuterocanonical books are called *apocrypha* by Protestants and Jews.

In the history of the Church there have been various movements to question the inspiration of the deuterocanonical books and passages. These movements were not successful: the Canons of Bishop Melito of Sardis c. 170; the Council of Laodicea c. 360. Some Fathers followed the Palestinian Canon in theory: this included only the protocanonical books distributed in a tripartite division; but they used the Alexandrian Canon in practice: this included also the deuterocanonical books and passages, known as the Septuagint (250–100 B.C.). These opinions never required an outright decision on the part of the Church, since the preferences were isolated; but with the advent of Protestantism, the Council of Trent (1545–63) made a formal decision, namely, the authenticity of the Latin Vulgate and the canonicity of all books contained therein and of them only.

2. *The New Testament Canon* was a slow process because of the difficulties of communication in the early Church. Final cognizance came about however in the following periods in which the Catholic Church declared twenty-seven books to be divinely inspired; twenty are protocanonical and seven are deuterocanonical. The latter are: Hebrews, James, 2 Peter, 2 and 3 John, Jude, Book of Revelation.

(1) First period: up to A.D. 150—accepted the writings of the Apostles and apostolic writers Mark and Luke.

(2) Second period: covering A.D. 150–210—excluded all books which were not of Apostolic origin.

(3) Third period: A.D. 210–350—established the New Testament Canon as we have it today.

(4) Fourth period: A.D. 350–504—brought about the absolute stabilization of the Canon with twenty-seven books, finally declared *de fide* by the Council of Trent in its Decree *Sacrosancta* on April 8, 1546.

3. *Canon Law.* This is the body of rules for the faithful in matters of faith, morals and discipline.

4. *Canon of Saints.* This is a list of all those who have been canonized by the Church, thus officially recognizing their holiness and the honor due to them.

5. *Canon of the Mass.* Name given formerly to the prayers immediately adjacent to the consecration prayers. Now called Eucharistic Prayer. In the old rite (post Trent) there was only one version of it but with the translation into the vernacular variety was added to blunt the dullness of repetition.

CANONICAL HOURS. The hours or offices of the daily recitation of the breviary or Divine Office.

CANONIZATION. The decree of judgment by the Church, given in a Papal bull, that one already beatified is to be regarded as a saint and to be venerated everywhere. Proof of two miracles through intercession must first be accepted as having occurred after beatification. The celebration of canonization is held at St. Peter's in Rome.

CANTICLE. *a little song.* This term refers to a spiritual song in praise of God or Jesus Christ. There are many canticles in the Scriptures, some of which are used in the Divine Office. A few famous examples of canticles are:

The canticle of Moses	°Ex	15	1-18	58
The canticle of David	°1 Chr	29	10-19	332
The canticle of Judith	°Jdt	16	1-21	406
The canticle of Isaiah	°Is	12	1-6	727
The canticle of Jeremiah	°Jer	31	10-14	809
The canticle of the Blessed Virgin Mary	°Lk	1	46-55	1020
The canticle of Zechariah	°Lk	1	68-79	1020
The canticle of Simeon	°Lk	2	29-32	1022

SUBJECT	BOOK	CHAP.	VERSE	PAGE

CAPITAL SINS. Grave offenses, often called "deadly sins," seven in number, and also called *capital* because they are the source of most other sins which, if habitual, can easily lead to mortal sins. They are: pride, covetousness, lust, anger, gluttony, envy, and sloth. They need not be distinct acts but can exist as habits or vices.

CAPUCHIN. A religious order following the Franciscan Rule. The name is derived from the cowl worn on the habit. The order was begun by Matteo da Bassi in 1525 as a return to the original observance of the Rule of St. Francis. Their abbreviation is: O.F.M.Cap.

CARDINAL. The name given to the members of the Sacred College designated by the Pope, the number of which did not exceed seventy, until Pope John XXIII increased the number to 85 in 1960. They advise the Holy Father and govern in the Church, and it is their function to gather at the death of the pope and elect a successor.

CARDINAL VIRTUES. The four great moral virtues of prudence, justice, fortitude, and temperance, so named because of their importance, since all other moral virtues are connected with one or another of these. *Prudence* enables men to form right judgments; *justice* inclines the will to give to others their due; *fortitude* disposes man to pursue good in spite of difficulties; and *temperance* aids man to control his desires of the senses.

CARMELITE. An order of monks founded in the 12th century and deriving their name from Mount Carmel, the place of their first monastery. Carmelite nuns were instituted in the 15th century. The order claims Elijah as its founder, and it is devoted to education and charitable works. The General Motherhouse is in Rome, Italy, and the order is found throughout the United States.

CARMELITES, ORDER OF DISCALCED: O.C.D. This is a reform of the Order of Our Lady of Mt. Carmel founded in 1562. The Motherhouse is in Rome, Italy, and the order is found throughout the United States.

CARNAL, CARNAL-MINDED. There are many references to this term in the Scriptures. The entire atmosphere of the ancient world stressed the nature of the flesh as opposed to the nature of the Spirit of God.

The fruit of sin	*Rom	7	14	1121
At enmity with God	*Rom	8	5-11	1122
Produces envy, strife	*1 Cor	3	1-3	1131
Material needs classified	*1 Cor	9	11	1135
Faith above reason	*2 Cor	10	3-6	1148

CASPIN, CASBON, CASPHOR. A fortified city in Gilead captured by Judas Maccabeus. It is identified by many scholars with the modern Khisfin, to the east of the Sea of Galilee.

A fortified city	*2 Mc	12	13-16	457

CASSOCK. A tunic-like garment reaching from the neck to the heels. It is worn as an outside garment by priests or clerics. It is called a soutane in French.

CASTEL GANDOLFO. The summer residence of the Pope; it is an estate in the Alban Hills near Rome. The Treaty of Lateran confirmed its possession by the Holy See. The neighboring Villa Barberini was added to the estate.

CASUISTRY. The science which treats of matters of conscience. It is the study of moral principles applied to concrete cases. Though casuistry is sometimes used in a somewhat negative way, abuses in the use of it do not justify a general condemnation of a useful and necessary science.

CATACOMBS. The ancient underground cemeteries, the most famous of which were in Rome. The walls were lined with niches where the dead were buried during the early persecutions of the Church. There were sections where these tunnels widened out, and it was in these places where people could be accommodated for Mass, which was celebrated upon altars of stone. As time went on there were three or four stories to these catacombs, each hollowed out beneath the preceding one. During the first two centuries these chambers were decorated with sculpture and painting; but in the 3rd century the catacombs could no longer be used in safety and many of the Christians were martyred. Following the 3rd century they became pilgrimage sites; but during the 7th and 8th centuries they were desecrated by the Lombard invaders. After this most of the catacombs were closed and neglected, but in the 16th century interest was renewed.

CATAFALQUE. 1. A frame shaped like a bier covered with a black cloth and used during Masses for the Dead when the corpse is not present. It is over the catafalque that absolution for the dead is given.

2. A stand on which the coffin, or casket when the body is absent, is placed during funeral service.

CATECHISM. Instructions in Christian Doctrine. This is usually in question and answer form by which the elements of faith or belief are taught to children and converts. The Third Plenary Council of Baltimore (1884) ordered the preparation of a catechism for the United States. This came to be known as The Baltimore Catechism, a revised edition of which appeared in 1949.

The Baltimore Catechism was an outline of instruction based upon the Catechism of the Council of Trent. Since the Second World War and especially after the II Vatican Council many new catechisms based on varying catechetical methods have been published with ecclesiastical approval. However, as yet none have had the universal acceptance that the Baltimore Catechism received and it, in turn, has been revised and brought up to date.

CATECHIST. One who teaches those preparing to receive Baptism, namely, one giving instruction in catechism.

CATECHUMEN. One who is preparing to receive Baptism. A period of two years or more was required in the early Church for this preliminary instruction.

CATHEDRA. 1. The chair in which the bishop sits; it is now called a throne.

2. It is a symbol of the authority of the bishop and a symbol of authoritative teaching.

3. *Ex cathedra*, a term used to denote the Pope's supreme authority when he teaches the faithful concerning matters of faith and morals.

CATHEDRAL. The home church of the bishop in his diocese. This is the church in which the chair of the bishop is located and from which it derives its name.

CATHEDRATICUM. A small, determined tax, which is payable to the bishop by all churches and benefices of a diocese. It is a token of subjection. The tax due from each parish church for the support of the bishop in the United States is called cathedraticum rather than synodaticum.

CATHOLIC. 1. The term means universal and was applied from very early ages to the true Church. Today, it is recognized as the name of the Church.

2. A member of the Roman Catholic Church, one who practices his religion to the best of his ability.

CATHOLIC ACTION. "The participation of the laity in the apostolate of the hierarchy" by the pursuit of personal Christian perfection. This work is done upon approval and under the direction of the bishop. The work advances the cause of Christ in temporal and spiritual matters; this must be done first in ourselves, second in our families, and third in the associations of our social life. See Action, Catholic.

CATHOLICITY. One of the four marks of the Catholic Church according to which the Church extends to all times and peoples, and teaches all the truths necessary for salvation.

CELEBRET. A testimonial letter by a bishop or major superior of an exempt clerical institute to one of his clergy. In it is stated that the priest bearing the letter has been duly ordained and is free of canonical censure. The purpose is to allow the priest to celebrate Mass in other dioceses.

CELIBACY. State of being unmarried. This law in the Western Church forbids under pain of nullity the marriage of men in Holy Orders, beginning with the subdiaconate, and prohibiting a married man who has received Holy Orders from cohabiting with his wife.

Recommended under	*Mt	19	10-12	986
certain circumstances	1 Cor	7	1-38	1133

CHALICE. The cup-shaped vessel used in the Mass in which the wine is consecrated. It should be of gold or silver; or the cup may be of silver, but gold lined. The bishop consecrates the chalice with chrism, and it may not be touched except by those in Holy Orders or those given special permission.

CHALICE VEIL. A square silk veil used to cover the paten and chalice. It is also called the *peplum*.

SUBJECT	BOOK	CHAP.	VERSE	PAGE
Aid them	*Is	1	17	717
	Jer	7	6	786
Punishment for ungrateful:				
The stubborn	*Dt	21	18-21	159
The scorners	*Prv	30	17	627
The embezzlers	*Prv	28	24	625
Parental cursers	*Lv	20	9	97
Parental smiters	*Ex	21	15	63
God's special care of:				
When forsaken	*Ps	27	10	510
When in need	*Is	40	11	751

CHOIR. 1. The persons who sing certain parts of the liturgy. It also refers to the place or gallery from which they sing.

2. An innumerable host of angels or one of the nine divisions of angels.

3. In cathedra, collegiate, and conventual churches, that part of the building raised up and closed off from the nave where the canons, monks, or nuns have their stalls.

CHRISM, THE HOLY. A mixture of olive oil and balsam blessed by the bishop and used in the administration of the Sacraments of Baptism and Confirmation. It is not used in the ordination of priests. It is used, however, in the consecration of bishops, the consecration of churches, altar stones, and in the solemn blessing of bells and baptismal water. It is blessed on Maundy Thursday.

CHRIST. This is the Greek title corresponding to the Hebrew and Aramaic Messias or Messiah. In its more general use in the New Testament, it is joined with the given name, Jesus. The name Jesus alone is sometimes used.

His coming prophesied	*Ps	2	2	495
	Dn	9	25-27	899
	Is	9	6-7	724
He is the promised	*Mt	16	16, 20	983
Messiah	Mt	26	63-64	993
Pre-existent with the	*Mi	5	2	936
Father	Jn	1	1	1050
One with God	*Jn	17	5, 24	1075
	Rv	22	13	1249
Equal with God	*Phlm	2	5-8	1164
Came from Heaven	*Jn	6	38	1058
Omnipotent	*Mt	28	18	996
Omniscient	*Jn	2	24	1052
Divinity declared	*Mt	3	16-17	968
Divinity acclaimed	*Mt	16	16	983
Divinity acknowledged	*Mk	1	24	999
by devils	Lk	4	41	1024
Endured deep humilia-	*2 Cor	8	9	1147
tion	Phlm	2	5-11	1164
Hated by the world	*Jn	7	7	1060
Mocked and reviled	*Mt	27	26-30	995
Called:				
Jesus	*Mt	1	21	966
Son of God	*Lk	1	35	1020
Son of Man	*Mt	9	6	974
Emmanuel	*Mt	1	23	966
Savior	*Lk	2	11	1022
Lamb of God	*Jn	1	29, 36	1050

CHRISTIAN. *follower of Christ.* The word Christian was first applied to the faithful of Antioch. It was not used by the Jews, but perhaps by pagan Gentiles to differentiate the followers of Christ from the Jews in the public eye. The followers of Christ usually applied to themselves such terms as disciples, brethren, saints, faithful, and believers.

Applied to faithful of Antioch	*Acts	11	26	1097
Used by Herod Agrippa	*Acts	26	28	1112
Used by Peter	*1 Pt	4	16	1214
Christian Attributes:				
Abhorrence of evil	*Rom	12	9	1125
A forgiving spirit	*Lk	17	3-4	1039
Benevolence	*Acts	4	34-37	1087
Burden-bearing	*Gal	6	2	1156
Charitableness	*1 Pt	4	8	1214
Consideration for others	*Mt	7	12	972
Contentment	*Heb	13	5-6	1204
	1 Tm	6	6-10	1183
Devotion to duty	*Acts	5	27-32	1089
Diligence	*2 Pt	1	10	1216
Discernment of good	*Heb	5	14	1197

SUBJECT	BOOK	CHAP.	VERSE	PAGE
Faith in God	*Mk	11	22	1011
Faithfulness	*Mt	25	14-30	992
Fervency of spirit	*Ti	2	11-14	1190
	Rom	12	11	1125
Gentleness	*2 Tm	2	24	1186
Godliness	*2 Pt	1	5-7	1216
Growing in grace	*2 Pt	3	18	1218
Guilelessness	*Phlm	2	15	1164
Holiness	*1 Pt	1	14-16	1211
Honesty	*Rom	12	17	1125
Hopefulness	*Rom	15	4, 13	1127
Hospitable	*Heb	13	2	1204
Humility	*Phlm	2	1-9	1164
	1 Pt	5	5-6	1215
Kindness	*Eph	4	32	1159
Love for enemies	*Mt	5	44	970
Love for God	*Mt	22	36-37	989
Love for another	*Jn	15	12-13	1072
Meekness	*Mt	5	4	970
Mercifulness	*Mt	5	7	970
Militancy in faith	*1 Tm	6	12	1183
Mutual edification	*1 Thes	5	11, 15	1176
Obedience	*Mt	7	21	972
Patience	*Rom	12	12	1125
	Jas	5	7-8	1209
Peaceableness	*Heb	12	14	1203
	Mt	5	9	970
Perseverance	*Gal	6	9	1156
Prayerfulness	*1 Thes	5	17	1176
Purity of heart	*Mt	5	5, 8	970
Ready for good works	*Ti	3	1	1190
Rejoicing in persecution	*Mt	5	11-12	970
Reliance upon God	*1 Pt	5	6-7	1215
	Phlm	4	6-7	1166
Respect for rulers	*Rom	13	1-7	1126
Righteousness	*1 Tm	6	11	1183
Scripture reading	*2 Tm	3	15-17	1186
Self-denial	*Mt	16	24	983
Steadfastness	*1 Cor	15	58	1140
Sympathy	*Rom	12	15	1125
Temperate	*Eph	5	18	1160
Thankfulness	*Eph	5	20	1160
Truthfulness	*Eph	4	25	1159
Unity in Mystical Body	*Eph	4	1-6	1159
Unity with Christ	*Jn	15	1-6	1072

CHRISTMAS. The twenty-fifth day of December; the day celebrating the birth of Christ; the Feast of the Nativity. The name means Christ's Mass.

CHRONISTA. The cleric who sings the narrative parts of the Gospel of the Passion when it is sung solemnly by chanters.

CHURCH. 1. A place where Christians assemble; a building devoted to divine worship. It is from the Greek *Kyriakon* meaning the "Lord's house," used to designate the House of God from the beginning of the 4th century. When Constantine in the Edict of Milan, 313 A.D., extended universal toleration to the church, the buildings became works of art. In the early churches, the sanctuary was in the east end, facing the rising sun, and it was divided into parts for men and women, different classes of the faithful; and another section, the presbyterium, for bishops and priests.

2. The *Catholic Church.* The body of Christians who profess the faith of Christ and believe in all the teachings of Jesus Christ. They are united under one visible head, the Pope, who is the vicar of Christ on earth. The Church has as its marks oneness, apostolicity, holiness, and universality.

Founded by Christ	*Mt	16	18	983
Unity in Mystical Body	*Eph	4	1-6	1159
Loved by Christ	*Eph	5	25-29	1160
Christ the Head of	*Col	1	18	1168
	Eph	5	23	1160
Persecuted	*Acts	8	1-3	1092
	Acts	12	1-25	1098
	Mk	13	9	1013
	Lk	21	12	1043
Christ always present	*Mt	28	20	996

CIBORIUM. The vessel, chalicelike in shape and having a cover, in which Communion hosts are kept. It is kept in the tabernacle. The early meaning was that of a canopy over the altar.

CIRCUMCISION. *a cutting around.* God commanded Abraham and his male descendants to be circumcised as the sign of His covenant with them. Though circumcision was practiced at times by the Samaritans, Arabians, and Egyptians for hygienic reasons, among the Hebrews it was always considered as something religious, as a commandment coming directly from God.

SUBJECT	BOOK	CHAP.	VERSE	PAGE
Instituted by God	°Gn	17	10-14	14
	Acts	7	8	1091
Abraham obeys God	°Gn	17	23-27	14
Enacted in the Mosaic Law	°Lv	12	3	90
	Jn	7	22-23	1060
Observed in Canaan	°Jos	5	2-8	175
Jews so called	°Gal	2	7-8	1152
	Col	4	11	1171
Unnecessary now	°Acts	15	1-12	1101
	Gal	2	3-10	1152
	Gal	5	2-6	1155

CIRCUMCISION, FEAST OF. Celebrated on January 1, this feast is a Holy Day of Obligation. It commemorates Our Lord's submission to the old Jewish rite eight days after His birth, and marks the first time His blood was shed. Under the New Law, circumcision is not necessary.

Jesus submits	°Lk	2	21	1022

CISTERCIANS. This religious order is a reform of the Benedictines, officially known as the Monks of the Order of Citeaux. It was founded in 1098 by St. Stephen Harding, St. Alberic, and St. Robert of Molesme. Its two divisions are those of the Common and the Strict Observance, popularly known as Trappists. Except under certain serious circumstances (emergencies, health, etc.), members of the Strict Observance maintain complete silence and abstain from many of the usual foods such as meat, fish, eggs, etc. They are principally farmers, and their days are devoted to manual labor and prayer. St. Bernard of Clairvaux is probably the best known member of this order. Cistercian nuns are enclosed and contemplative in both observances, and their rules are similar to those followed by the monks.

CLOISTER. 1. The canonically enclosed living quarters of a convent or monastery.

2. An enclosed space with covered passages around the outer wall and pillars on the inner side. Such a covered passageway around an inner square or garden is often found in monasteries.

COLLEGE. 1. A corporation of persons joined in a common pursuit.

2. The collective name used for the cardinals who form the advisory body of the pope: the College of Cardinals. In 1586, the number of this Sacred College was fixed at 70. In 1960, however, Pope John XXIII increased the number to 85.

COLORS, LITURGICAL. According to the Roman Rite five colors are ordinarily used for vestments and other insignia, with three colors permitted as substitutes.

Color	Symbolism	Worn
White	Joy and Purity	Feasts of Our Lord, Blessed Virgin, angels, Saints not martyrs, Sundays after Easter.
Red	Love	Feasts of the Holy Cross, Martyrs, and at Pentecost.
Green	Hope	Sundays after Epiphany, and Pentecost.
Violet	Penance	During Advent, Lent, vigils outside Easter season, and the Rogation Days.
Black	Mourning or death	Masses of the Dead, and Good Friday.

The three substitutes are:

Cloth of silver, substitute for white.
Cloth of gold,   ”   ” white, red, or green.
Cloth of Rose,   ”   ” violet on Gaudete and Laetare Sundays.

Other colors cannot be used except by indult. Blue vestments are permitted by indult in Spain and Spanish America on the Feast of the Immaculate Conception. Varicolored vestments in which no one color predominates are forbidden. However, the rules do not specify particular shades of the accepted colors, nor do they apply to the linings or decorations of the vestments.

Recently, violet has been permitted for funerals to diminish any note of despair and white is now widely used as a symbol of the Resurrection in the same kinds of masses formerly limited to black alone.

COLORS, SCRIPTURAL. It appears quite certain that the art of coloring cloth attained excellent perfections among the ancient Hebrews, though it did not originate with them, but with the Egyptians and Phoenicians. The following colors are frequently mentioned in the Bible: white, red, blue, purple, green, black, yellow, vermillion. White, scarlet, blue, and purple were the four liturgical colors used for the sanctuary veils and priestly garments.

Some of the colors have a symbolic quality: *white* is the symbol of joy, purity, and holiness; *red* typifies blood, sin, war, and carnage; *purple* was an emblem of royalty and affluence; *blue,* the color of the sky was in the dress of the high priest; *black* was the symbol of mourning.

Purple indicative of wealth	°Jgs	8	26	199
	Est	8	15	414
	Lk	16	19	1038
	Rv	17	4	1245
Various colors in tabernacle	°Ex	25	3-5	67
Colors used in king's palaces	°Est	1	6	409

COMING, SECOND. The New Testament clearly differentiates between two comings of Christ. The First Coming is His incarnation, life, and death on the cross for our redemption. The Second Coming refers to the time when Our Lord will appear at the end of the world to judge the living and the dead. This is one of the fundamental doctrines of our faith, and the petition in the Our Father, "Thy kingdom come," became a petition among early Christians for this coming of Christ.

Christ explicitly taught that only God the Father knew the day of the Last Judgment. The certainty of Christ's Coming, however, and the hope of the future resurrection of the just are a powerful incentive to good Christian conduct.

Second Coming called:

SUBJECT	BOOK	CHAP.	VERSE	PAGE
Coming	°Mt	24	3	991
	1 Cor	15	23	1140
	1 Thes	2	19	1174
Brightness	°2 Thes	2	8	1178
Coming of Our Lord	°1 Tm	6	14	1183
Glorious	°Ti	2	13	1190
Day of Wrath	°Rom	2	5	1118
Appearance	°1 Cor	1	7	1130
Day of the Coming	°1 Cor	1	8	1130
Day of the Lord	°2 Cor	1	14	1143
Day of Jesus Christ	°Phil	1	6	1163
The (or that) Day	°Mt	7	22	972
	1 Cor	3	13	1131
The Last Day	°Jn	6	39	1058

Preparatory signs to be fulfilled:

Gospel must be preached in the whole world	°Mt	24	14	991
	Mk	13	10	1013
	Lk	18	8	1040
Jews as a nation will be converted	°Rom	11	25-26	1124
Elias will come to restore all things	°Mt	17	11	984
Before Christ's Coming, great apostasy will exist	°Mt	24	10-12	991
	Lk	18	8	1040
	2 Thes	2	3	1178
The Antichrist will appear	°2 Thes	2	3-12	1178
	1 Jn	2	18	1221
Physical transformation of the universe	°Mt	24	29	991
	Mk	13	24-25	1013
	Lk	21	25-26	1043
World will be purified by fire	°2 Pt	3	5-7	1218
Sign of the Son of Man will appear in heaven	°Mt	24	30	991
	Mk	13	26	1013
	Lk	21	27	1043

COMMANDMENTS OF THE CHURCH. The laws of the Church as distinguished from the laws of God. The six laws which concern all of the faithful all the time are:

1. To assist at Mass on all Sundays and Holy Days of Obligation.
2. To fast and to abstain on the days appointed.
3. To confess our sins at least once a year.

SUBJECT		BOOK	CHAP.	VERSE	PAGE

4. To receive Holy Communion during the Easter time.
5. To contribute to the support of the Church.
6. To observe the laws of the Church concerning marriage.

COMMEMORATION. *act of remembrance.* On certain days when two feasts coincide the mass of one will be said and the other will be "commemorated" only in the opening prayer (formerly the "collect"), the prayer over the gifts (formerly the "secret"), and in the prayer after communion (postcommunion). In the older liturgies such commemorations were frequent and sometimes multiple but they seldom occur now and the two prayers are combined into one now with only one conclusion. The tendency is to transfer feasts in such cases instead of multiple commemorations.

COMMENDATION OF A SOUL. A prayer for the dying, found in the Roman ritual.

COMMENDATORY LETTERS. Letters given by the bishop to members of the Church who travel to a foreign country and wish to be identified as being in communion with the Church. Such letters are also given to clerics who go from one diocese to another; these testify that they are duly ordained and free of canonical censure.

COMMUNION, HOLY. Another name for the Body and Blood of Our Lord in the Holy Eucharist. It also is the act of receiving the Eucharist. The priest at Mass receives the Eucharist under the forms of both bread and wine. The people receive it as bread alone. Christ instituted the Holy Eucharist at the Last Supper and commanded His Apostles and their successors to perpetuate the act.

Instituted by Christ	*Mt	26	26-29	993
	Mk	14	22-25	1014
	Lk	22	14-20	1044
	1 Cor	11	23-34	1137

COMMUNION OF SAINTS, THE. The union of the faithful in heaven, on earth, and in purgatory. The ninth article of the Apostles' Creed expresses belief in the Communion of Saints. The preceding article, "I believe in the Holy Catholic Church," embraces the Church Triumphant, the Church Militant, and the Church Suffering. We are in communion with the elect in heaven when we ask them to intercede to God in our behalf by praying to them, imitating them, and honoring them.

COMMUNISM. An extreme theory of government in which all material goods are owned by an organization or state. It can be voluntary or involuntary. *Voluntary Communism* exists where the individual member of the organization willingly gives up his natural right to private property for the good of the organization or when the rules of the organization which he joined of his own free will require it. A religious order where its members voluntarily take the vows of obedience, poverty, and chastity would be an example of a voluntary communistic society. *Compulsory Communism*, on the other hand—and as we know it in the world today—is an erroneous philosophy of government which is based on class warfare, atheistic materialism, and the denial of personal property and personal rights. It is an extreme form of socialism, but it differs from socialism in two important aspects. It holds revolution to be both necessary and inevitable, and it calls for complete abolition of private property in productive goods. Communism preys particularly on backward and poverty-ridden states by promising great material rewards to its followers.

Compulsory state communism had its beginning in the dialectical materialism of Karl Marx, in the middle of the 19th Century. Seeking a radical cure for the obvious economic ills of his time, he rejected any form of legislation which would merely correct the abuses of the current economic system of Capitalism, and he thought that State Socialism, as a substitute for Capitalism, was too weak to solve the pressing problems of the masses of people. Marx brought out his new theory of government in his book, *Das Kapital*, published in 1867. In this theory Marx held that the only true source of economic value was labor, which created material goods or wealth. Capitalism took part of the profits of labor and gave labor only a minimum subsistence return. Joining this theory of materialism with the dialectical philosophy of Hegel, he concluded that society is determined by material or economic forces and that the state exists merely to protect property for the masses. He held that eventually all exploited peoples would organize to overthrow their capitalistic rulers, and there would be a Dictatorship of the Proletariat, which would, in turn, organize production for the interests of all. Each person in this ideal Communistic State would produce according to his ability, and each person, would, in turn, be given those things according to his needs. Thus a classless society would be formed which would have no need for dictatorship or the state. In such an ideal setting, religion has no place, since the Church condones private property and its philosophy is heaven-centric, wherein the sufferings of this world are willingly undergone for the greater reward of heaven. To communists, therefore, religion is the opiate of the people. It diverts them from the materialistic, social problems, and hence must be eradicated, by force, if necessary.

Communism as practiced today in Russia, China, etc., has for expediency toned down some of its more radical doctrines from time to time, but the leaders of Communism have never denied or denounced its basic revolutionary and atheistic character.

COMPLINE. The last hour of the Divine Office. Compline is the final prayer in the hours of the Breviary and is concerned with sleep and waking, life and death, sin and grace.

CONCLAVE. The closed hall where the cardinals assemble for the election of a pope and the assembly itself. In order to be canonical, one more vote than two-thirds should be cast for the successful candidate. The election is to begin the fifteenth or the eighteenth day after the death. On the day of the conclave, a solemn Mass of the Holy Spirit is said in the Pauline Chapel, and after that the cardinals form a procession and proceed to the Sistine Chapel where the voting takes place. In the morning and in the evening, the cardinals meet in chapel, and a secret count is made to ascertain whether any candidate has the required majority of one more than two-thirds. There are three modes of election: (1) *Scrutiny* is the ordinary mode and elections have been concluded with reasonable dispatch; (2) *Compromise* is an agreement by all the cardinals to entrust the election to a small committee; (3) *Quasi-inspiration* consists in the electors unanimously proclaiming one name without proceeding to a vote.

CONCOMITANCE. Since Christ, "having risen from the dead, dies now no more," His Body and Blood can no longer be separated. Thus the whole Christ is present under the Host alone or under the species of the consecrated wine. The past emphasis on communion under one kind (only) for laymen was to emphasize this truth. Recently, since the danger of denial of this doctrine seemed remote, and in order to allow the faithful to more perfectly fulfill the injunction Christ gave *His Apostles* (alone) at the Last Supper, the laity have been permitted more frequent use of the privilege of communion under both kinds in the Western Church. In the East the custom of communion under both kinds remains a constant tradition.

CONCORDANCE. An alphabetical index to the Bible arranged according to the principal words in each text.

CONCORDAT. A treaty drawn up between the Holy See and a secular state or government concerning the interests of the faith in that particular country.

CONCUPISCENCE. The natural tendency in man to sensuous pleasure or evil which is the result of the fall of our first parents. It presents a struggle between the flesh and reason. In man there are two opposing forces: one which is carnal and a part of our lower nature; and another force which is essentially good and allied with our superior or rational nature. Of these two opposing tendencies in the one man, the former leads to sin, while the latter inclines to the Law of God.

The depravity of human nature	*Jas	1	14-16	1206
Actual inclinations to sinful conduct	*Rom	7	18	1121
Exhortation to chastity	*Col	3	5	1170
	1 Thes	4	3-5	1175

CONFESSION. The voluntary accounting of one's sins to a priest. Confession is one of the necessary elements of the Sacrament of Penance.

Power of absolution given to Apostles	*Mt	16	19	983
	Mt	18	18	985
	Jn	20	21-23	1080

CONFIRMATION. A Sacrament instituted by Jesus Christ through which grace is bestowed on a baptized person to strengthen him in his faith. It increases sanctifying grace and imprints a lasting mark on the soul. Through the anointing with chrism on the forehead of the person, the Holy Spirit is received to make one a strong and perfect Christian and soldier of Christ. The bishop is the ordinary minister of this Sacrament.

SUBJECT	BOOK	CHAP.	VERSE	PAGE
Promised by Our Lord	°Acts	1	4-8	1083
Descent of Holy Spirit	°Acts	2	1-4	1085

CONFIRMATION NAME. The name which an individual selects and which the bishop confers at the time of confirmation. This is in addition to the baptismal name, although such a new name may not be required.

CONFITEOR. *I confess.* The first two Latin words of a form of prayer which includes a general confession of sin. In the unrevised Latin mass it was said in the "prayers at the foot of the altar" while a revised version is one of the options now available at the beginning of mass.

CONFRATERNITY. A corporate fraternal group of the faithful devoted to the furtherance of special works of charity or piety for the increase of divine worship. These ecclesiastically authorized associations, such as Confraternities of the Blessed Sacrament and of Christian Doctrine, are to be erected in every parish church. In this way the layman can acquaint himself with their functions as part of his parish life. An association of confraternities is called an archconfraternity.

CONGREGATION. 1. This term designates the body of people in a church, as distinguished from the clergy.

2. When referring to priests or religious, it means a community or order bound together by a common rule, either without vows, or without solemn vows.

3. Roman Congregations. Bodies composed of Cardinals and Church officials for the transaction, under the superintendence of the Pope, of the business of the Church. Such are the Congregations: of the Consistory, of the Holy Office of the Inquisition, of the Index, of Rites, of Bishops and Regulars, of Propaganda, of Indulgences, etc. *See* Curia, Roman.

CONSCIENCE. A judgment of the practical reason on the moral goodness or sinfulness of an action. The judgment which is passed before the action whereby a person realizes his obligations in relation to the norm of morality is called *antecedent* conscience; whereas the judgment passed after something is done and is accompanied by a feeling of satisfaction or remorse is called *consequent* conscience.

Man has the obligation of following the authority or voice of conscience. This judgment on the moral goodness or sinfulness of an action is linked with man's scope of religious knowledge and his union with God.

SUBJECT	BOOK	CHAP.	VERSE	PAGE
All that is not done with clear conscience is sinful	°Rom	14	23	1126
God remains final judge	°1 Cor	4	4	1132
Pure conscience a safeguard of faith	°1 Tm	1	19	1180

CONSECRATION. Dedication. The act whereby a person or thing is separated from general use and dedicated to service of God. This included the ordination of priests of the Old Testament, the anointing of the altar of holocausts, the dedication of the temple of Solomon.

SUBJECT	BOOK	CHAP.	VERSE	PAGE
Ordination of priests in Old Testament	°Ex	29	1-35	70
Anointing of altar of holocausts	°Ex	29	36-42	70
Temple of Solomon dedicated	°1 Kgs	8	62-66	271
	2 Chr	5	1-9	337

CONSECRATION AT MASS. The climax of the Mass where the priest, acting for Christ, changes the bread and wine into the Body and Blood of Our Lord with these words, "This is My Body" and "This is My Blood."

SUBJECT	BOOK	CHAP.	VERSE	PAGE
Holy Eucharist promised	°Jn	6	26-60	1058
Established by Christ	°Mt	26	26-28	993
	Mk	14	22-24	1014
	Lk	22	17-20	1044

CONSISTORY. A meeting of official persons, or their meeting place, where business is transacted. In the Catholic Church the term is now seldom used except with reference to the papal consistory. This is the ecclesiastical senate in which the pope in session with the College of Cardinals deliberates upon matters of ecclesiastical importance.

CONSUBSTANTIATION. The Lutheran doctrine which holds that the substance of the bread and wine merely exists together with the substance of the Body and Blood of Our Lord after consecration in the Eucharist.

CONTEMPLATION. A sublime state of interior union with God. The term is also applied to the manner of life of religious who devote themselves to meditation and prayer rather than active works such as teaching.

CONTRITION. Sorrow of heart and detestation for sin committed, with the resolution not to sin again. A contrite heart is one that is severely pained by the sense of guilt and deeply affected by the realization of the pain suffered by God as a result of sin. This contrition leads the sinner to repentance, confession of guilt, and trust in God for forgiveness and deliverance through Christ.

Examples of:

SUBJECT	BOOK	CHAP.	VERSE	PAGE
The prodigal son	°Lk	15	18-19	1037
The publican	°Lk	18	13	1040
The sinner in the city	°Lk	7	37	1027
Peter	°Mt	26	75	993

CONVERSION. The change from the state of being detached from God to union with His Church. Conversion is the result of the action of divine grace and the response of man to this grace. The true conversion of a sinner includes the recognition of his sinful state together with repentance, and the resolution to follow the Will of God.

SUBJECT	BOOK	CHAP.	VERSE	PAGE
A turning from sin to God	°1 Kgs	8	35-36	271
	Acts	11	21	1097

Examples of:

SUBJECT	BOOK	CHAP.	VERSE	PAGE
Implored by Peter	°Acts	3	19	1086
Of Gentiles foretold	°Is	60	3	771
Of Manasseh	°2 Chr	33	1-16	357
Of Good Thief	°Lk	23	40-43	1045
Of 3,000 at Pentecost	°Acts	2	41	1085
Of 5,000 by Peter and John	°Acts	4	4	1087
Of Cornelius	°Acts	10	1-48	1095
Of Saul (Paul)	°Acts	9	1-22	1094
Of Paul's jailer	°Acts	16	25-34	1102
A superficial	°Mt	13	20-21	979
Of erring Christians	°Jas	5	19-20	1209

CONVERT. A person who has not been baptized or one baptized as a non-Catholic who becomes a Catholic by reception of Baptism. This is done by a profession of faith and abjuration of errors.

COPE. A cape-like vestment reaching from the shoulders to the feet. It is usually of silk, fastened with a clasp in front, called the morse; it usually has a smaller cape resting on the shoulders. It is worn for liturgical services as Exposition or processions and the absolution of the dead. It is not limited to the use of priests alone; it may be worn by a cantor even if a layman.

CORONATION. 1. The Coronation of Mary, the mother of God, is the 5th of the Glorious Mysteries of the Rosary. This refers to her crowning in heaven, as the Queen of Heaven, after her Assumption. 2. After a Pope is elected, he is crowned after a Mass, and a tiara is placed on his head by the senior cardinal deacon. 3. When a Catholic king is crowned or blessed, a special religious rite or service is performed.

CORPORAL. The square linen cloth which is carried to the altar in the burse and placed on the table of the altar before the tabernacle. It symbolizes the winding sheet in which the body of Christ was wrapped inasmuch as the chalice is placed upon it.

CORPORAL WORKS OF MERCY. Seven forms of charity or mercy directed to the physical well-being of a needy person. The seven works of mercy are: to feed the hungry, to clothe the naked, to give drink to the thirsty, to visit the sick, to visit prisoners, to give shelter to strangers, and to bury the dead.

CORPUS CHRISTI. *the body of Christ.* The name of the Feast of the Blessed Sacrament celebrated on the Sunday following the first Sunday of Pentecost.

COUNSEL. 1. Mutual advising.

SUBJECT	BOOK	CHAP.	VERSE	PAGE
To heed, is wise	°Prv	12	15	610
Benefits of	°Prv	11	14	609
Of God, neglected	°Jos	9	14	179
	Prv	1	25-30	600

SUBJECT	BOOK	CHAP.	VERSE	PAGE
Of God, to be sought	°Jgs	20	18	209
	Jb	12	13	470
	Prv	8	14	606
Of David	°1 Kgs	2	1-9	266
Evangelical for Religious	°Mt	19	12-29	986

2. One of the Gifts of the Holy Spirit which enables one to decide by a sort of supernatural intuition what is to be done in a particular case. It differs from prudence in that the decision is made promptly and without reflection.

Gift of Holy Spirit	°Is	11	2	726

COUNTER-REFORMATION. The movement within the Church to combat the errors of the Reformation of the 16th Century, and to bring back the people into its fold. At the height of the Reformation against the Church, the Pope convened the Council of Trent (1546–1563). From this Council arose many reforms of clerical discipline which effectively combated the defects of the time and which have proved extremely effective down to the present. In addition, the Council defined, dealt in detail with, and refuted the theological errors of the Reformation. As a result, the entire Church was filled with new life and vigor. Saints appeared everywhere, especially such notable ones as St. Francis de Sales, St. Philip Neri, St. Ignatius Loyola and St. Vincent de Paul, among many others. New, aggressive orders, such as the Society of Jesus, were formed and aided the older orders in spreading the Counter-Reformation. The order of the Sisters of Charity, the first of hundreds of orders devoted to charitable works, was founded. While much of what the Church lost to the Reformation was re-won, the Church never fully regained her spiritual authority over the nations and the Christian world still remains divided.

COWL. A hood usually attached to the upper part of a monk's habit. It is so designed that it may be pulled up to cover the head.

CREDENCE. The table placed in the sanctuary near the Epistle side of the altar on which the cruets containing wine and water are kept. During a Solemn High Mass the chalice and burse and humeral veil for the subdeacon are placed upon the credence when they are not in use at the altar.

CREMATION. The act of burning the mortal remains of a person. This is not in keeping with the rite of Christian burial which reverences the body that in life was the temple of the Holy Spirit. This practice was originated by unbelievers in an attempt to deny the resurrection of the body. Catholics may not carry out the wish of an individual to have his body cremated; nor may they receive ecclesiastical burial if they leave instructions for their own bodies to be cremated.

CRIB. A representation of the manger wherein Jesus is said to have been laid after His birth at Bethlehem. It consists of a stable, together with Jesus, the Blessed Virgin, and St. Joseph erected at Christmas time in churches and is also called a crèche.

The custom of erecting cribs dates back to the time of St. Francis of Assisi in 1223, who obtained from Pope Honorius III permission to represent the mystery of Christmas in the form of a crib.

CRUCIFIX. A representation of the cross of the Crucifixion together with the figure of Christ. It differs from the cross because it has affixed to it the body or corpus of a representation of Christ. It is a sacramental representing the death of Christ.

CRUET. A vessel with a long neck and a handle in which the wine or water to be used in Mass is stored. It has a stopper to prevent evaporation and preserve purity.

CURATE. An antiquated term for an assistant priest. The term is still in use in Ireland where "C.C." following a priest's name means "Catholic Curate" or the equivalent of an assistant priest or associate pastor in this country.

CURIA, ROMAN. The bureaus which assist the Pope in the government of the universal church.

D

DALMATIC. The outer vestment worn by the deacon or subdeacon at Mass. It was part of the clothing of the higher classes adapted for ecclesiastical use, and was introduced from Dal-

matia to Rome from whence it received its name. In the ordination service, it is called "the garment of salvation, the vesture of gladness and the dalmatic of righteousness."

DEACON. The Greek term of which deacon is the English equivalent signifies a servant, a ministrant, a waiting man. It appears, however, that the term became identified with a distinct order or office in the ministry of the primitive church. This is indicated in the specific qualifications outlined for deacons, just as they were for bishops, elders, or pastors. It has been contended that they were not appointed to an office, but to a service; but the fact that they were formally ordained points to an official position and to official duties. In some of the Epistles deacons are addressed or referred to as officers just as are bishops. Following the Apostolic era in the history of the early church, the office of deacon became fully established. He performed certain distinct functions as assistant to the bishop or pastor, such as assisting in the ordinances, instructing the laity, receiving the offerings, and caring for the poor. Thus, the ordination of a deacon is a sacrament, identified with Holy Orders.

Today the function of a deacon is being revived as an active role in the Western Church. For centuries in the West it had become a mere stepping stone to the priesthood. Now those studying to be priests may use the year they are ordained deacons as a sort of internship and fulfill the traditional roles of a deacon in a parish (preach, baptize, distribute communion, etc.).

Moreover, a permanent diaconate (men ordained to be deacons but without the intention of going on for the priesthood) is being established. These men may be married. They may administer the parish property (a traditional role they fulfilled in service to the Popes for centuries) or they may administer certain parish organizations as, for example, those that care for the poor (another traditional Roman role). In mission territories, they can provide permanent on-the-spot assistance in those missions which lack the services (habitual or permanent) of a priest. In such places the pace was often killing in the past, for the missionary might arrive to find hundreds awaiting, baptism, confession, marriage, and the distribution of communion. The permanent deacon can baptize, catechize, witness marriage, and help prepare the negligent penitent for confession. He cannot, of course, hear the confession or absolve.

Selection and ordination of seven "helpers" in the church at Jerusalem	°Acts	6	1-8	1090
Deacons in the church at Philippi	°Phil	1	1	1163
Qualifications and duties defined	°1 Tm	3	8-10	1181

DEACONESS. This term does not appear in the Bible. It is contended, however, that the reference to Phoebe in Romans 16, 1 signifies that she held a distinct office in the church at Cenchrae and that she was not merely a servant in the general sense. Among the more important duties of the deaconess were those of assisting in the baptism of women, instructing converted women for baptism, serving at the entrance of church edifices, and visiting the sick and prisoners.

DEAD, MASS FOR THE. Any Mass can be offered for the dead to aid the souls detained in Purgatory. The special liturgy of the Mass for the Dead, is particularly appropriate. It also has a proper preface, summarizing the Christian's resignation concerning death.

DEAN. 1. The title for the chief dignitary of a collegiate chapter as founded particularly in Europe. He is appointed by the Holy See, but he has no greater powers, generally, than the other canons.

2. In the United States the term "Dean" may indicate the equivalent of the Vicar Forane (q.v.).

DEAN OF THE SACRED COLLEGE. The senior of the six cardinal bishops of the suburban sees of Rome who is also head of the College of Cardinals. He is always bishop of Ostia; and has no jurisdiction over the other cardinals. He acts as president of the electors of the cardinal, consecrates the pope if he is only a priest, and presides at his coronation.

DECRETALS. Decisions of the popes given on matters of discipline. The Decretals usually refers to the collection of laws

SUBJECT	BOOK	CHAP.	VERSE	PAGE

made by St. Raymund of Penafort in 1320–34 by order of Pope Gregory IX. These were supplanted, however, by the new *Codex Iuris Canonici* which came into force in 1918.

DEDICATION, FEAST OF. 1. The feast referred to by this name in the Gospel of St. John was an annual celebration held for eight days throughout Palestine, commencing on the 25th day of Kislev, a Jewish month corresponding to our December. It was in commemoration of the cleansing of the temple and rededication of the altar by Judas Maccabeus in 165 B.C., after the desecration by Antiochus IV Epiphanes.

SUBJECT	BOOK	CHAP.	VERSE	PAGE
Established by Judas	°1 Mc	4	56	424
Maccabeus	2 Mc	10	6-7	455
Attended by Jesus	°Jn	10	22	1065

2. Also, the anniversary of the dedication of a consecrated church. The dedication of a cathedral church is always celebrated separately. The feasts of the dedication of the major Roman basilicas, St. John Lateran, St. Peter's, St. Paul's, and St. Mary Major are celebrated by the entire Latin Church.

DEFENDER OF THE BOND. An authority appointed in every diocese to sustain the validity of a marriage or an ordination if either is under attack. This official must appeal to the higher court in case a marriage is declared null. The defender may consent to a declaration of nullity without appeal if the reputed marriage took place before a Justice of the Peace and the parties were Catholic.

DEFENDER OF THE FAITH. The title conferred on King Henry VIII of England by Pope Leo X in 1521. It was bestowed in acknowledgement of the king's defense of the Seven Sacraments and the Mass against the writings of Luther. The title is still used today by the sovereigns of England.

DELEGATE, APOSTOLIC. A papal representative to a country which has no official diplomatic relations with the Holy See. He reports the state of the Church in the country and performs ecclesiastical duties. He also gives final decisions upon diocesan appeal, although the appellants may elect to appeal directly to Rome.

DEPOSIT OF FAITH. This term was consecrated by the first Vatican Council. "And the doctrine of faith which God revealed is proposed, not as a mere philosophical discovery to be elaborated by human minds, but as the divine deposit delivered by Christ to his spouse, to be by her faithfully guarded and infallibly declared."

It consists of that body of revelation given by Christ to the Apostles to be preserved by them and their successors. The word is found in I Tim. 6, 20, *Depositum custodi*, "Keep safe what has been entrusted to thee."

DE PROFUNDIS. The opening words, "Out of the depths," of Psalm 130, which is used as a prayer for the dead and to beg forgiveness of sin.

DETACHMENT. Detachment emphasizes the direction of one's affection toward God rather than things of the world. It may be exercised in regard to wealth, success, and worldly possessions. The detached individual places himself in God's hands and acknowledges "not as I will but as thou wilt."

DETRACTION. Detraction is the depriving of another of his good name unjustly by revealing a truth. Despite the fact that the information disclosed is true, no one has the right to ruin another's reputation as long as it has been maintained. The degree of the seriousness of the sin of detraction, of course, depends on the harm done to the person detracted and the intent of the speaker. Restitution as far as possible must always be made. There are a few exceptions, however, to the sin of detraction: if the disclosure is necessary to the common good; if a third party must be protected; if it is for the correction of the guilty party.

DEUTEROCANONICAL BOOKS. Those Books of the Bible whose place in the canon was established after that of the other books are generally known among Catholic critics as Deuterocanonical. Sometimes this term is used to refer to these books in the Old Testament. The Deuterocanonical Books of the Old Testament are: Tobit, Judith, Wisdom, Sirach (Ecclesiasticus), Baruch, First and Second Books of Maccabees, and parts of Esther (10, 4–16, 24) and Daniel (3, 24–80; 13; 14). The Deuterocanonical books of the New Testament are: The Epistle of St. James, The Second Epistle of St. Peter, The Second and Third Epistles of St. John, The Epistle to the Hebrews, The

Epistle of St. Jude, and the Revelation. Their authority is not inferior to that of the other Books of the Bible.

DEVOTION. Prayers and practices of a pious nature in honor of Our Lord, Our Blessed Mother, the angels, or the saints. The Sacred Scriptures give many instances of devotion, ardent affection, and religious fervor:

SUBJECT	BOOK	CHAP.	VERSE	PAGE
A boastful	°Jn	13	36-38	1070
A benevolent	°Mk	12	41-44	1012
An excessive	°Phil	2	25-30	1164
A fraternal	°Rom	16	3-4	1128
Of Paul and Silas	°Acts	16	25	1102
Morning devotions:				
Jacob	°Gn	28	16, 18	25
Samuel's parents	°1 Sm	1	19	216
Hezekiah	°2 Chr	29	20	353
Job	°Jb	1	5	463
Jesus	°Mk	1	35	999

DEVOTIONS, PRIVATE. Prayers and acts of piety approved by the Church which are not required of the individual, but are certainly encouraged: Stations of the Cross; the Rosary; the *Tre Ore;* the *Angelus; Compline;* and many others.

DIOCESE. That area, together with its population which are under the jurisdiction of a bishop.

DIPTYCH. *twice folded.* Two tablets, joined by a hinge, having on one the names of the living to be commemorated at Mass, and on the other the names of the dead. The names of the pope, bishop, emperor, and benefactors were always found on the diptychs of the living, and the lists were read aloud during the Mass. This practice is no longer followed. The references are made simply in silence by the priest.

DISCALCED. *without shoe.* Those branches of religious orders who observe the rule of wearing sandals. Among those adhering to this practice are certain orders of the Carmelites, Franciscans, and Augustinians.

DISPENSATION. The relaxing of a law under special circumstances. Just cause must be present when petitioning for a dispensation, and the interpretation of the case must be very strict. Impediments of the natural law, however, can never be dispensed. Examples of dispensations are: attendance at Mass on Sundays and holidays; fast and abstinence days; mixed marriages; etc.

DIVINE PRAISES. A series of ejaculations of praise which are said aloud by the priest and repeated by the people after the Benediction of the Blessed Sacrament, before the Host is replaced in the tabernacle. They are as follows:
"Blessed be God;
Blessed be His Holy Name;
Blessed be Jesus Christ, true God and true Man;
Blessed be the name of Jesus;
Blessed be His most Sacred Heart;
Blessed be His most precious blood;
Blessed be Jesus in the Holy Sacrament of the altar;
Blessed be the great Mother of God, Mary most holy;
Blessed be her holy and Immaculate Conception;
Blessed be her Glorious Assumption;
Blessed be the name of Mary, virgin and mother;
Blessed be Saint Joseph, her most chaste spouse;
Blessed be God in His angels and in His saints."

DIVINE RIGHT OF KINGS. An interpretation of sovereignty which holds that monarchy is a divinely instituted form of government and, as a result, gives kings complete jurisdiction over their subjects. The theory, however, has no true basis. The idea was apparently appropriated by monarchs to exalt their position and suppress any question of their power.

DIVINI REDEMPTORIS. An encyclical letter written by Pope Pius XI in 1937 condemning communism and pointing out its errors. The Pope concluded that Catholics may not become associated with communism under any pretext without committing sin.

DIVORCE. Although there is only one passage in the Mosaic legislation that deals directly with the subject of divorce, and only a few passages in the entire Old Testament that relate to the subject indirectly, it appears quite certain that the annulment of the marriage bond was common throughout the history of the Hebrew nation.

SUBJECT	BOOK	CHAP.	VERSE	PAGE

The one specific reference in the writings of Moses which makes the putting away of a wife by the husband *allowable* is if she is found guilty of "some uncleanness"; but it does not make it *obligatory*. Two distinct schools of thought prevailed among the Jews as to the meaning of the Hebrew words giving the basis for allowable divorcement. One interpretation, that of Shammai, made the words signify "unchastity" or "adultery"; whereas the other, that of Hillel, placed emphasis on the conditional clause "if she find no favor in his eyes" and broadened the grounds to a long list of reasons, some both ridiculous and ludicrous. This liberal interpretation was the one most generally followed, and this made the putting away of a wife by a dissatisfied or discontented husband easy and common.

It is worthy of special note that the Mosaic direction in this matter was not in the form of a command, but an enactment of expediency for the regulation of a practice altogether too common and an effort to prevent husbands from putting away their wives for insufficient cause. No provision was made for a wife to put away a husband for any reason whatsoever. Under the marriage laws and practices of the Hebrews, it was very difficult, if not impossible, for a wife to divorce her husband.

Christ recognized the Mosaic provision as an *expediency* to meet a laxity in this matter, and then affirmed the original principles whereby marriage was established by God as a permanent monogamous relationship until concluded by the death of one of the parties.

SUBJECT	BOOK	CHAP.	VERSE	PAGE
Mosaic regulation of expediency	°Dt	24	1-4	161
	Mt	19	8	986
The explicit teachings of Christ	°Mt	19	3-9	986
	Mk	10	2-12	1009
	Lk	16	18	1038
	Mt	5	31-32	970

The Catholic Church, of course, does not recognize divorce as such. If a marriage has been declared null by Canon Law, however, the parties may apply for a civil divorce after obtaining permission to do so. In all these instances, the civil action is simply a legal procedure and in itself does not affect the marriage bond.

DOCTRINE. In the Old Testament the usual meaning of this term is *instruction,* something *heard* or *received,* or a pronouncement. Christian doctrine, however, comprehends that body of revealed and defined truth which a Catholic must hold, but frequently it extends to those teachings which are not of faith, but are held and acted upon.

DOGMA. A truth revealed by God and, therefore, an article of faith. It is thus proposed by the Church to be believed by all Catholics. Some of the dogmas of the Church are the Incarnation, Redemption, and Assumption.

DOM. A title given to the religious of the Benedictine, Carthusian, and Cistercian orders, as well as some canons regular. It is contracted from the Latin, *dominus,* which means master.

DOMICILE. A permanent place of residence in the eyes of Canon Law. It is acquired by residence begun in a parish or diocese with the intention of remaining there permanently, or by actual residence for ten years. An intention to remain for six months, or an actual six months stay in a fixed place is termed a *quasi-domicile.* These are important because they determine one's pastor or local bishop with reference to the administration of baptism, the granting of dispensations, marriage, etc.

DOMINE NON SUM DIGNUS. *Lord, I am not worthy.* . . .

In the old Latin rite a triple recitation of a prayer based on the prayer of the centurion, changing ". . . that my servant shall be healed" to ". . . that my soul will be healed." It has been much modified. Moreover, the new version, whether in the vernacular or Latin, is said but once.

The words of the centurion	°Mt	8	8	973

DOMINICANS, THE. The title of the religious order, more specifically, "The Order of Preachers" (O.P.) founded by St. Dominic in the beginning of the 13th Century and approved in 1216 by Honorius III. The Dominicans are mendicant friars whose chief work is defense of the faith through preaching, teaching, and writing. The order is especially noted for its learned men in the fields of scholastic theology and philosophy. St. Thomas Aquinas was a Dominican, and his writings have been studied widely; indeed, his "Summa Theologiae" has been commended to the respect of all Christians and to the study, especially, of all seminarians and the clergy by unique papal pronouncements. The habit of the Dominicans is white with a black outer cloak. Thus, they have become more popularly known as the Black Friars.

An order of women, known as the Second Order of Saint Dominic, was also founded by St. Dominic. They are cloistered and follow a rule very similar to the First Order. Another order known as the Third Order of St. Dominic grew out of the "Militia of Jesus Christ" founded by St. Dominic, and its nature, life, and scope was approved by Honorius IV in 1286. It is now divided into Third Order Secular and Third Order Conventional, which includes many congregations of nuns. The Third Order Secular includes laymen and laywomen who live in accordance with the Rule of St. Dominic.

DOMINUS VOBISCUM. This is the salutation formerly used in the Mass and Office. "The Lord be with you" is the translation, which was a general greeting among the Jews in early times.

DOXOLOGY. The utterance or the singing of succinct expressions of praise and honor to God in ritualistic forms has formed a part of public worship from very early times. Doxologies are frequently found in the Psalms and among the writers of the New Testament. Those used in the early Church usually consisted of one sentence, such as, *Glory be to the Father, to the Son, and to the Holy Spirit.* This is known as the minor or lesser doxology. The *Gloria in excelsis Deo* of the Mass is referred to as the greater doxology.

For of him and through him and unto him are all things. To him be the glory forever. Amen	°Rom	11	36	1124
To him be glory in the Church and in Christ Jesus down through all the ages of time without end. Amen.	°Eph	3	21	1159
To the King of the ages, who is immortal, invisible, the one only God, be honor and glory forever and ever. Amen	°1 Tm	1	17	1180

DUEL. A prearranged encounter between two persons with deadly weapons for the purpose of settling a personal disagreement. Unless a duel is considered a part of an actual war, it is always sinful. If one of the participants is killed in a personal duel, he is refused Christian burial. Further, everyone connected with the duel, directly or indirectly, is subject to excommunication.

DULIA. The special reverence paid to the saints and angels because of their distinctive relationship with God. This is to be distinguished from the adoration of God which is termed *latria* and the special honor paid the Blessed Mother, *hyperdulia.*

E

EASTER DUTY. The obligation to receive Holy Communion during the Easter time, which is generally from Palm Sunday to the first Sunday after Easter. The time, however, varies in different parts of the world according to custom. In the United States the period is calculated from the first Sunday of Lent to Trinity Sunday, during which time Catholics are urged to receive Communion in their own parish church, although the requirement may be fulfilled elsewhere.

EASTER WATER. This is the water which is blessed before Mass on Holy Saturday, and it is then distributed to the faithful. In early times, water was blessed only on the vigils of Easter and Pentecost. Later, however, the custom of blessing water before Mass on every Sunday prevailed. The present custom of the distribution of Easter water continues, nonetheless, and is a vestige of the earlier ceremonies when water was blessed only twice a year.

EASTERN CHURCH. The title given to the Christian Church which originally was a part of the eastern division of the Roman Empire. This was simply a geographical division corresponding with the separation of the Roman Empire into two parts, with Rome as the capital of the western division and Constantinople as the capital of the eastern part. These terms, however, have now lost much of their geographical significance as Western Churches are found all over the world, and in the same manner Eastern Churches are found in many parts of the western world.

The important differences, however, are the rites and laws of the two parts of the Church which have developed since the 3rd century when this division took place. Further, the Eastern Church must be divided into two parts, those which have cut themselves off from the authority of the Pope and those which are united to the Pope and have remained Catholic.

The Catholic Eastern Church comprehends many groups, called *rites,* due to the differences in their laws, language, and ceremonies Five general categories cover the various divisions:

The *Alexandrian Rite,* sometimes called the *Egyptian* or the *Coptic Rite,* arose in Alexandria, Egypt. The Catholic Copts in Egypt and the Catholic Ethiopians comprise this group today.

The *Armenian Rite* developed in Armenia. The liturgical language is Old Armenian and the Eucharistic liturgy is practically that of the Greek St. Basil translated, with Syrian and peculiar variations and with additions from the Latin Mass.

The *Byzantine Rite* takes its name from the city of Byzantium, now known as Istanbul. In this rite there are many Catholic groups, differing principally in the liturgical language. Among the languages used are the Albanian, Arabic, Georgian, Greek, Hungarian, Old Slavonic, and Rumanian. The name is sometimes extended to include the entire Orthodox Eastern Church, which includes many dissident groups.

The *Eastern Syrian* or the *Chaldean Rite* took its form in Chaldea, the ancient name of Mesopotamia. The Chaldeans in the Near East, and the Malabarese in India comprise this group, both of which use the Syrian language in their liturgy.

The *Western Syrian Rite,* often called the *Antiochene,* arose in the city of Antioch and then spread to other parts of the Near East. It has three forms: Pure Syrian, Maronite, and Malankar. The liturgical language is Syrian, but Arabic, Turkish, and, in India, Malayalam are also used.

ECUMENISM. ECUMENICAL. *world wide.* The name given to a movement to find common ground between different faiths and among all faiths. False ecumenism would attempt to water down real differences between us by ignoring principles, doctrines, and real issues of difference. Real ecumenism attempts to find those areas of agreement where cooperation can exist and to gain a greater understanding of and tolerance for the beliefs of others. Even when error exists good intentions should be presumed until the contrary is proved.

1. Nicaea I 323
2. Constantinople I 381
3. Ephesus 431
4. Chalcedon 451
5. Constantinople II 553
6. Constantinople III 680–1
7. Nicaea II 787
8. Constantinople IV 869–70
9. Lateran I 1123
10. Lateran II 1139
11. Lateran III 1179
12. Lateran IV 1215
13. Lyons I 1245
14. Lyons II 1274
15. Vienne (France) 1311–12
16. Constance 1414–18
               (in part only)
17. Basle-Ferrara-Florence 1431–45
18. Lateran V 1512–17
19. Trent 1545–63
20. Vatican 1869–70
     (adjourned 1870; formally closed by Pope John 23rd 1962)
21. Vatican II 1962–65

EDIFICATION. Used in a religious or spiritual sense, the word edification signifies advancing, improving, and perfecting the Christian mind and character. The means for promoting edification are prayer, self-examination, mediations, reading of the Holy Scriptures, devout attendance at Mass, and frequent reception of the sacraments.

SUBJECT	BOOK	CHAP.	VERSE	PAGE
Individual edification to be sought	°1 Thes	5	11	1176
	2 Cor	12	19	1149

EDUCATION. It is quite evident that moral, ethical, and religious discipline and training for children was incumbent upon parents in the times of the ancient patriarchs of biblical history. With the formation of the Hebrew nation these responsibilities and duties were incorporated into law. It appears also that secular education was not lacking in the most ancient times. Evidence abounds that Abraham, the founder of the Hebrew people, was well versed in secular training; Moses was highly educated in Egyptian knowledge and wisdom. There were those who were capable in the process or art of measuring; some were skilled in writing; some understood and spoke foreign languages; some were capable of keeping accounts; and others were highly gifted in composing poetry and proverbs. The Babylonian Captivity resulted in distinctive advantages to the Jews in creating greater and more advanced processes of education. After their return from captivity, synagogues were established in all the communities of Palestine and the rabbis maintained regular schools in these synagogues.

SUBJECT	BOOK	CHAP.	VERSE	PAGE
Men trained in the art of measuring	°Jos	18	8-9	186
Men skilled in foreign languages	°2 Kgs	18	26	302
Trained scribes; keepers of accounts	°2 Sm	8	16-17	248
	2 Kgs	18	37	302
	Jer	52	25	832
Special duty of Levites to teach the people	°Lv	10	11	88

Catholic parents must make every effort to send their children to Catholic schools, and a pastor must do everything possible to provide Catholic education for the children of his parish. An exception to this rule may be made only with the permission of the local bishop. In that event, religious instruction must be provided for the child and every precaution must be taken to prevent the loss of the child's faith.

EJACULATIONS. A prayer consisting of only a few words which can be repeated easily and frequently. A few examples are: "Most Sacred Heart of Jesus, have mercy on us." "My Lord and My God!" "Our Mother of Perpetual Help, pray for us."

ELEVATION. That part of the Mass just after the Consecration when the Host and the chalice containing the Precious Blood are raised by the priest for adoration by the faithful. As the Host and then the chalice are elevated, the people look and adore the Body and Blood of Christ. This is a relatively recent custom first observed at the end of the 12th century, although veneration of the Body and Blood of Christ always took place in some form during the Mass.

ELEVATION, THE LITTLE. This elevation occurs at the end of the Canon of the Mass at which time the priest lifts the chalice and the Host a few inches above the altar. It may originally have been a sign to the faithful to adore, as the gesture was known at least 300 years before the Elevation at the Consecration.

EMBER DAYS. Days formerly designated by the church at the beginning of each season of the year as times of fast and abstinence. The Ember Days are the Wednesday, Friday, and Saturday which follow the third Sunday in Advent, the first Sunday of Lent, Pentecost, and September 14. These days of fasting were not only for the special sanctification of the four seasons, but also for obtaining God's blessing on the clergy, for whose ordination the Ember Saturdays were specially set apart.

EMBOLISM. This word is applied particularly to the prayer inserted immediately after the last phrase of the Our Father, elaborating upon this last petition. During the Mass of the Presanctified on Good Friday the priest recites it aloud, but during other times of the year it is said in a low tone of voice.

ENCYCLICAL. An encyclical letter is one addressed by the pope to the episcopate throughout the world or to the bishops of a particular country or region. In recent years the popes have more and more given expression on various subjects in this form of utterance. Encyclicals are not necessarily infallible documents, but Catholics must accept the doctrinal content. Some encyclicals have not received wide publicity, but some have become renowned: Leo XIII in *Aeterni Patris,* on the philosophy of St. Thomas; *Rerum Novarum,* on the condition of the working classes; *Providentissimus Deus,* on the study of the Bible; Pius XII in *Mystici Corporis Christi,* on the Mystical Body of Christ.

In 1943 Pope Pius XII issued his encyclical, *Divino Afflante Spiritu,* on Bible study, emphasizing the need for a new trans-

SUBJECT   BOOK   CHAP.   VERSE   PAGE

lation of the Bible directly from the original languages of the sacred authors. Recent important encyclicals include that of John XXIII, *Mater et Magistra*, which dealt with the obligation of wealthy nations to help undeveloped ones, and Pope Paul VI' *Humani Generis*, reaffirming the traditional teaching against artificial contraception.

ENVY. One of the seven capital sins. There is no temper or passion of the human mind and heart more self-destructive than that of looking with displeasure upon the prosperity of another. This may be a mortal sin if one's neighbors good fortune is of significant importance to him. The warnings in Holy Scriptures against this evil are both specific and comprehensive; examples of its folly abound:

EPHESUS, COUNCIL OF. The Third Ecumenical Council which declared Mary to be the Mother of God. This council was held at Ephesus, Asia Minor, in 431, and condemned the Nestorian heresy which taught that there were two persons in Christ.

EPIKLESIS. *invocation.* A prayer to God the Father, or to the Son, or to both, imploring them to send down the Holy Spirit on the bread and wine at Mass and to change them into the Body and Blood of Christ. The dissident, or non-Catholic Eastern churches, teach the doctrine that the Body and Blood of Christ are not present until the *epiklesis* has been said. The Catholic doctrine, however, teaches that the words of institution, "This is my body; this is my blood." effect the change. The epiklesis then follows and may be termed a delayed invocation.

EPIPHANY. *appearance, manifestation.* The feast of the Magi or wise men formerly celebrated on January 6 in the Western Rite and on January 5 in the Eastern Rite. It is now celebrated on the Sunday nearest January 6. Although a Holy Day of Obligation for the universal church it had not been of obligation (by dispensation) in the United States and had fallen into disuse; thus, the change. The term itself means an appearance of a divine being. It is also used for the manifestation of Christ through the testimony of the Father (and descent of the Holy Spirit) at Christ's baptism in the Jordan, and more rarely used in connection with the wedding at Cana.

The First Advent of Christ	°2 Tm	1	10	1185
through His Incarnation				
The Second Advent of	°2 Thes	2	8	1178
Christ for the Last	1 Tm	6	14	1183
Judgment	2 Tm	4	8	1187
	Ti	2	13	1190

EPISCOPACY. 1. The bishops of the Church, as a body.
2. One of the holy orders whereby a priest becomes a bishop. It is the special duty of bishops to govern their flocks, consecrate churches, ordain and consecrate other priests and bishops, and to administer confirmation. Generally, a bishop also rules a part of the Church.

EUCHARIST, HOLY. The sacrament known as Holy Communion in which, under the appearances of bread and wine, the Body and Blood of Christ are truly and substantially present, thus enabling man to receive supernatural grace so very necessary for the saving of his soul and ultimate union with Our Lord Jesus Christ. The origin of the word "eucharist" comes from Our Lord giving "thanks" at the Last Supper. Only a priest or bishop may say Mass, at which time the Eucharist is consecrated. In many respects, the Holy Eucharist may be termed the greatest of sacraments, and Catholics should take advantage of the sublime opportunity to receive Holy Communion frequently and devoutly.

The Last Supper	°Mt	26	27	993

EUCHARISTIC CONGRESS. An international gathering which gives honor to the Holy Eucharist and increases devotion to the Blessed Sacrament. It is presided over by a papal delegate and carries on religious exercises, discussions, and addresses to further love and honor to Our Lord at the altar. The first Eucharistic Congress was held at Lille, France, in 1881, and other congresses have been held in Paris, Jerusalem, Lourdes, Rome, London, Quebec, Chicago, Dublin, and Sydney.

EX CATHEDRA. *from the throne.* This phrase is used figuratively with reference to certain pronouncements made by

the pope. When "exercising his office as the shepherd and teacher of all Christians, he, in virtue of his supreme apostolic authority, defines a doctrine concerning faith or mortals to be held by the whole Church," the pope is said to speak *ex cathedra.* Such utterances are of the most solemn kind and must be accepted as infallible.

EXAMINATION OF CONSCIENCE. The serious contemplation of one's actions for the purpose of determining what sins have been committed prior to confession. Genuine sorrow for the sins committed and a firm resolution not to commit these sins again must also be uppermost in the penitent's mind. A great deal of care should be exercised when examining one's conscience since all mortal sins and as many venial sins as one can remember must be confessed in order to gain absolution. Sins which are forgotten are also forgiven, but they must be confessed if they are recalled the next time one goes to confession. If the exact number of times a sin has been committed cannot be remembered, the approximate number is satisfactory. Recalling the commandments of God and of the Church in relation to one's calling in life aids considerably in a thorough examination of conscience.

EXAMPLE. It is incumbent upon all to give good example to others, particularly to children. Conversely, it is the obligation of Catholics to observe the good example of others and to benefit by it. Many excellent references to this subject are found in the Holy Scriptures, particularly the eminent example of Our Lord Himself:

Given by Jesus	°Jn	13	15	1070
As warnings	°1 Cor	10	1-11	1136
A ministerial	°1 Tm	4	12	1182
Evil, to be avoided	°Lv	20	23	97
In public life	°Est	1	9-22	409
Of the prophets	°Jas	5	10	1209
In prayer	°Lk	11	1-4	1033
Observation of	°Phil	4	9	1166
Encouragement by	°Acts	27	33-36	1113

EXCOMMUNICATION. Under the laws of Jewish ecclesiasticism, individuals were deprived of the privileges of the congregation of Israel for certain notorious crimes, or removed from membership for the violation of fundamental regulations. Similarly the Church excludes a Catholic from the communion of the faithful, with consequent deprivations. There are two kinds of excommunicates: *vitandi,* those excommunicated by name and publicly denounced, whom the faithful are bound to shun; and *tolerati,* whom the faithful do not have to shun. Rarely is an excommunicated person declared *vitandus.* Excommunicates lose the right of assisting at divine services, lose all privileges of indulgences, and are excluded from the sacraments, etc.

Before a sinner can be termed an excommunicate, he must have been baptized; his sin must have comprehended an external act; he must have recognized the sin as being mortal; and he must have some knowledge of the possibilities of excommunication. Some of the sins for which a Catholic may be excommunicated are: treating the Host with irreverence; molesting a religious; violation of the seal of confession; impersonating a priest; forging papal documents; granting indulgences for a monetary return; becoming associated with the Freemasons or other forbidden societies; dueling; distributing false relics; publishing the Holy Scriptures without proper permission; agreeing before marriage that the children shall be deprived of the Catholic faith; attempting to be married outside the Church, etc.

The absolution from an excommunication, *as well as the sin itself,* depends upon the nature of the act. Some excommunications are within the province of the pope; some are reserved to the bishop; and lesser sins to the priest. Thus, one's confessor must be consulted in grave circumstances of this kind.

EXHORTATION. *to incite and encourage.*

To repentance	°Acts	2	38	1085
To faith	°Heb	11	1-6	1202
To constancy	°Col	2	1-7	1170
To fear God	°Prv	1	7-9	600
To holiness	°2 Cor	7	1	1147
To patience	°Heb	12	1-13	1203
To steadfastness	°1 Cor	15	58	1140

EXORCISM. The power to expel demons in case of demoniacal possession. The practice of exorcism among the Jews was more or less general; adjurations, invocations, ceremonies, the use of

SUBJECT	BOOK	CHAP.	VERSE	PAGE

magical formulae, and other forms of divination varied, and it was even claimed by some that the power of the exorcist had a divine source. Certain exorcists encountered by Paul sought to exercise this power in the name of the Lord Jesus. All occult magics, divinations, exorcisms, and heathen superstitions were condemned by the Holy Scriptures from the beginning; such claims and practices have no place in the life of a Catholic.

Christ, however, gave to his disciples the real power of driving out demons or devils. In the earliest times this power was exercised by those persons who had received this special grace. Later it was ordained that only priests could exercise privately or in church. The order of Exorcists is the third of the minor orders. Power is given to drive out demons, but today, and for some time past, this power is restricted.

SUBJECT	BOOK	CHAP.	VERSE	PAGE
Jesus accused of exorcism	°Mt	12	22-24	978
Casting demons by Christ's	°Mk	9	37-40	1008
followers not exorcism	Lk	9	49-50	1030
The power promised	°Mt	10	8	975
Christ's followers not of	Mk	16	17	1017
the character of exorcism				
False pretensions of exor-	°Acts	19	13-16	1106
cists encountered by Paul				

EXPIATION. *atonement.* The act of making atonement or propitiation for sin. Christ's death on the cross is the greatest example of expiation the world has known, and the Sacrifice of the Mass is an opportunity for all Catholics to share in this act of atonement. Thus, frequent attendance at the Sacrifice of the Mass is urged.

One of the solemn feasts of the Jews, on the tenth day of the seventh month, was called the Feast of the Expiation or the Day of Atonement. This was the only day during the year on which the high priest could enter the Holy of Holies with the blood of a bullock. This was one class of Old Testament sacrifices, also called sin or guilt offerings.

The Day of Atonement	°Lv	16	29-34	94
Expiation for the sins of	°Heb	2	17	1195
the people	Heb	9	10	1200

EXPOSITION OF THE BLESSED SACRAMENT. The displaying of the Blessed Sacrament so that it may be seen by the people and honored and adored by them. For this purpose the Sacred Host is placed in a monstrance, although in private exposition the tabernacle is opened so that the ciborium containing the Host may be seen. The latter may be held at any time without consent of the bishop. Public exposition, however, requires an important reason and must follow certain rules laid down to insure proper solemnity. At the beginning of the exposition the *O Salutaris* is sung, the Host incensed, and then the hymn *Tantum Ergo* follows. Finally, the priest blesses the people by making the Sign of the Cross over their heads with the monstrance.

Recently permission has been granted to sing the *O Salutaris* in the vernacular version, *O Saving Victim.* The same is true for the *Tantum Ergo*, the English version of which is called *Falling Down in Adoration.*

EXTREME UNCTION. The anointing in danger. See Sacrament of the Sick.

EXULTET. Latin version of the "Paschal Praise" sung or recited at the Easter Vigil Service. Composed in the musical and liturgical form of a preface, it recounts the saving acts of God in Old and New Testament and explains the symbolism of the candle which recalls the Pillar of Fire of Exodus and the Light of the World, Christ.

F

FAITH, AN ACT OF. An act of faith implies the free assent of man's intellect to accept the testimony of God. Divine grace is, therefore, required because of the supernatural aspects of the act. St. Thomas defines an act of divine supernatural faith as "the act of the intellect assenting to a divine truth owing to the movement of the will, which is itself moved by the grace of God" (St. Thomas, II-II, Q. iv. art. 2). The above title is also used when referring to the prayer, "An Act of Faith," expressing this act.

FAITH, DEPOSIT OF. This is the title given to the sum of all the truths contained in tradition as revealed by God. When St. John, the last Apostle died, the deposit of faith was closed since no new public revelation have been made by God since

then. Those revelations which have been reported are deemed to be private.

The Bible is the Inspired Word of God containing Tradition in written form.

FAITH, RULE OF. The Church teaches that the rule by which one determines the truths which God wishes us to accept and believe covers the source of revelation: tradition. Tradition is defined as the living teaching of the Church. Thus, the ultimate rule of our belief is the teaching authority of the Church.

St. Paul stresses both tradi-	°2 Thes	2	15	1178
tion and his preaching	2 Tm	1	13	1185
	2 Tm	2	2	1186

FAITH AND WORKS. St. James in his Epistle states, "So it is with the faith that does nothing in practice. It is thoroughly lifeless" (James 2, 17). The Catholic Church has thus always taught that faith without good works is useless. It is true that faith is a prerequisite, but it is by good works also that man obtains an increase of grace and merits eternal life. The doctrinal differences between Martin Luther and the Catholic Church were based on this problem. Luther held that faith alone was sufficient for the salvation of one's soul and that works of charity, love of neighbor, mortification, and others were of no additional merit in gaining heaven.

FAITHFUL, THE. The title applied to those who have been baptized, and profess the truths of the Catholic Church. This term is often used loosely when referring to the congregation in general. At other times it is employed strictly and does not include the catechumens who are receiving religious instructions preparatory to Baptism.

FALDSTOOL. A chair with arms but no back which is used in certain ceremonies by the local bishop. The rubrics require the use of the faldstool instead of the bishop's throne when he is confirming or ordaining. The faldstool is always used by an auxiliary bishop in the diocese to which he is appointed.

FALSE WITNESS. The Eighth Commandment warns us against the harm that may be done to another by our words. This may involve perjury: the making upon oath a statement known to be untrue. Should this cause harm to another, the sin of injustice would also result and the obligation of reparation would fall upon the offender.

FAST, LAW OF THE EUCHARIST. The faithful are obliged to abstain from anything except water or medicine for one hour before communion. For the sick who need a special diet, food can be considered to be a form of medicine and even the one hour law is not imposed.

FATHERS OF THE CHURCH. Generally, this title was applied to those writers of the first eight centuries whose writings concerning the Church were held in esteem.

More specifically, the Church at the present time limits this title to those writers who possess the following attributes: *antiquity, orthodoxy, sanctity,* and *approbation* of the Church. Further, the writer must have been a Catholic and died in the Church to qualify. The scope of the characteristic *antiquity* covers to approximately the 8th century so that many prominent writers thereafter would not qualify strictly. *Orthodoxy* and *sanctity,* of course, imply absolute truth, although minor errors are reconciled. *Approbation* of the Church may be explicit or implied depending upon the nature of the writing. Thus, the authority of the Fathers is great but not unlimited. If a certain group of writers, however, concur unanimously on a point of doctrine, it is accepted as infallibly true.

FATIMA, OUR LADY OF. This is the title given to our Blessed Lady after her appearance to three shepherd children near Fatima, Portugal, in 1917. The children were Lucy dos Santos, aged ten, and her two cousins, Jacinta, aged seven, and Francis Martos, aged nine. The children lived in a little hamlet of Aljustrel, in the parish of Fatima, but they had taken their sheep to the Cova da Iria, and it was here that the first apparition took place on May 13, 1917. Our Blessed Mother asked for prayers, especially the daily recitation of the rosary, and for other acts of sanctity for the conversion of sinners. On the 13th day of six consecutive months from May to October of that year, our Blessed Mother repeated the same request to the children, and on the last occasion in October, 70,000 people gathered and witnessed the Miracle of the Sun. This has been described as an unnatural rotation of the sun for about ten minutes.

Since there has been so much interest in the appearance of Our Lady at Fatima, the Bishop of Leiria began an investigation of the apparitions at the Cova da Iria. In 1930, after meticulous research, the *Pastoral Letter on Devotion to Our Lady of Fatima* was published which set forth that the apparitions are worthy of belief and authorized devotion to Our Lady of Fatima.

FEASTS, CHRISTIAN. Special days set apart for commemoration of some event in the life of Our Lord, the Blessed Mother, or the Saints; or to honor God or celebrate an important religious event. Feast days are often classified as *immovable*, those which occur on fixed days such as the feast days of the saints; and those known as *movable*, which depend on the date of Easter, such as Pentecost. Some feast days are celebrated universally, whereas others are only local or proper to religious orders, countries, dioceses, or other places. The following set forth the principal feasts of Our Lord and the Blessed Mother:

Feasts of Our Lord

Christmas	Dec. 25
Circumcision	Jan. 1
Epiphany Sunday nearest	Jan. 6
Presentation	Feb. 2
Finding of the Holy Cross	May 3
Precious Blood	July 1
Transfiguration	Aug. 6
Exaltation of the Holy Cross	Sept. 14
Easter	Sunday following the first full moon on or after March 21
Ascension	40 days after Easter
Corpus Christi	Sunday after Trinity Sunday
Sacred Heart of Jesus	Friday after Corpus Christi
Christ the King	the last Sunday in October
Holy Name of Jesus	Sunday between Jan. 1 and 6 (or Jan. 2)

Feasts of Our Blessed Mother

The Immaculate Conception	Dec. 8
The Annunciation	Mar. 25
The Visitation	July 2
Our Lady of Mount Carmel	July 16
Our Lady of the Snow	Aug. 5
The Assumption	Aug. 15
Immaculate Heart of Mary	Aug. 22
The Nativity of Mary	Sept. 8
The Seven Sorrows	Sept. 15
Feast of the Holy Rosary	Oct. 7
The Maternity	Oct. 11
The Presentation of Mary	Nov. 21

FERIA. The liturgical name for all days of the week, except Sunday and Saturday. Thus, Monday, *feria Secunda;* Tuesday, *feria Tertia;* Wednesday, *feria Quarta;* Thursday, *feria Quinta;* Friday, *feria Sexta.* In Portugal, these names are still used for the names of the week, but in most other countries the pagan names have replaced them, such as our Monday, Tuesday, etc.

At the present time, most days of the year commemorate the feast day of some saint and the day takes its liturgical name from that feast. On those days on which no saint's feast is celebrated, the term *ferial day* is used, and the Mass said on such a day is called a *ferial Mass.*

The word Feria itself means a holiday. It refers to the fact that days which are not the feasts of Christ, the Blessed Mother, or saints, is a "day off" or "holiday" in the liturgical calendar. Since the recent revisions the number of such days has increased. This was done to emphasize the Season of the Church year more (Advent, Lent, Pentecost), for on Feria days the mass of the previous Sunday is repeated.

FERMENTUM. *leaven.* The second of the three portions into which the Host was broken in the primitive Mass. This was then carried by the deacons to other churches of the city and dropped into the chalice at the breaking of the bread at this church's Mass. In Rome, it was sent from the pope's Mass to those of the cardinal priests, and in this way the unity of the Holy Sacrifice of the Mass was symbolized.

FIELD MASS. A Mass celebrated out of doors as in the case of chaplains during time of war where a chapel is not available. Special permission must be secured from the local bishop for such a practice.

FILIOQUE. *and from the son.* A phrase occurring in the Nicene Creed affirming that the Holy Spirit proceeds from the Father *and from the son.* The word *filioque* was not in the original Creed formulated in 325, but began to appear in Spain in the 4th and 5th centuries. It was subsequently accepted by the Western Church, but it was not adopted by the Eastern Church. Although this implied no change in doctrine, it became a disciplinary matter and developed into one of the disputes that has separated the Eastern and Western Churches.

The Catholic Church teaches that the Holy Spirit proceeds from the Father and from the Son, whereas, most of the non-Catholic Eastern churches teach that the Holy Spirit proceeds only from the Father. The Catholic Eastern churches, on the other hand, accept the *filioque* although they do not all incorporate the phrase in their creeds.

FIRST FRIDAYS. The First Fridays, or the *Nine Fridays,* are the names given to the devotion which has arisen as a result of the appearance of Our Lord to St. Margaret Mary Alacoque. In a series of apparitions between 1672 and 1690, at the Visitation Convent at Paray-le-Monial in France, Our Lord promised the grace of a happy death to those who receive Holy Communion on the First Fridays of nine consecutive months. Catholics are not bound to believe in these revelations, but they have been approved by the Church and have been acted upon to the good of many.

FIRST VESPERS. That part of the Divine Office said on the eve of a feast, particularly if the feast is of such high rank that the celebration begins the day before. The Vespers said on the feast itself, then, are called Second Vespers.

FISHERMAN'S RING. A ring with which the pope is invested at his election. It is used only for sealing papal documents, and its device is that of St. Peter fishing from a boat. At the death of the pope the ring is officially broken up by the Chamberlain of the Vatican.

FISTULA. *tube.* A tube of gold used by the pope when he receives the Precious Blood, standing at his throne, at a Solemn Papal Mass.

FLAG, PAPAL. The gold and white standard of the Vatican is known as the papal flag. Its insignia is a triple crown with two keys. According to the words of the pope's coronation, the crown makes him "the father of princes and of kings, guide of the world, and vicar upon earth of Christ Jesus Our Savior." The two keys symbolize the power to bind and the power to loose which were bestowed by Our Lord. The papal flag is carried on the left of a national flag in processions.

FLAGELLANTS. *scourgers.* Groups of fanatical persons who performed exaggerated physical penances in medieval times. Although individuals such as St. Vincent Ferrer used beating as a form of mortification, the Church generally did not encourage it and definitely condemns excesses.

FLECTAMUS GENUA. *Let us genuflect.* This Latin phrase was chanted by the deacon at Solemn Mass immediately before the orations. "Let us kneel" is still said on certain days of Lent. The priest says *Levate* (rise), the words in both cases being accompanied by the appropriate movements.

FLOOD. See *Deluge.*

FLOWERS, LITURGICAL USE. The use of flowers in the Church has always been condoned if moderation is followed. During funeral services, however, and during Lent or Advent whenever the Sunday or ferial Mass is said, the use of flowers is forbidden. Exceptions are Gaudete Sunday in Advent and Laetare Sunday in Lent, Holy Thursday, and Holy Saturday.

FONT. A large bowl of a permanent nature for baptismal water at which Baptism is administered. There should also be a receptacle to receive the surplus water from the person's head, both bowls having drains which run into the earth. The base of the font should be below the level of the floor, and it should be surmounted by a ciborium. The term is sometimes applied to the receptacles for Holy Water used at the entrances of churches and at the doorways in monasteries, convents, homes, etc.

FORGIVENESS. Forgiveness of sin is an act of God toward man because to forgive sin is an exclusive prerogative of God, of whose law sin is the transgression and against whose Person sin is an offense. Our Lord, Jesus Christ, by virtue of His Divine Person, assumed the prerogative and exercised the power to forgive sin which is a further proof of His Divinity. Through the sacrament of Penance, Our Lord extended the power to forgive sin to His Apostles and their successors. Thus, man is given every opportunity to avail himself of the fruits of salvation.

SUBJECT	BOOK	CHAP.	VERSE	PAGE
Forgiveness by God made	°Lv	4	13-21	82
possible only through	Lv	17	11	95
blood atonement	Heb	9	22	1200
By Our Lord's death full	°Mt	26	28	993
atonement for the sins of	Rom	3	23-26	1118
all men is made	Eph	1	7	1157
	Col	1	14, 20	1168
Forgiveness is offered to all	°Acts	13	38-39	1098
who accept Christ	1 Jn	2	12	1221
Penitence and confession	°Acts	3	19	1086
required	1 Jn	1	9	1220
To be petitioned in prayer	°Mt	6	12	971

FORGIVING ONE ANOTHER. The continuous and consistent practice of the forgiving spirit toward those who may offend us is obligatory upon all Catholics; the extent and measure of this forgiveness, further, is to be similar to that expected and received of God. The actual act of forgiveness should be preceded by repentance on the part of the offender; it is only by the mutual understanding of both that right relations may be restored.

SUBJECT	BOOK	CHAP.	VERSE	PAGE
Forgiveness of others com-	°Mt	6	14	971
manded by Our Lord	Lk	17	3-4	1039
"Even as God forgave us"	°Eph	4	32	1159
	Mk	11	25-26	1011
Extent: seventy times seven	°Mt	18	21-22	985
Enemies to be loved	°Lk	6	27, 35	1026
	Mt	5	44	970
	Rom	12	14, 20	1125

FORTITUDE. A cardinal virtue and one of the gifts of the Holy Spirit, fortitude assists man in facing evil and contolling his fears. Fortitude also enables us to pursue good and to resist recklessness, which distorts a sense of values. Patience and perseverance are closely identified with fortitude and should be practiced to strengthen fortitude.

FORTY HOURS. The solemn exposition of the Blessed Sacrament in the monstrance for 40 hours, the time of Our Lord's entombment, for the purpose of continuous adoration. This devotion was held at least once a year in every Church where the Blessed Sacrament was reserved. The devotion began after a Mass of Exposition, and the Host is placed in the monstrance on the throne above the altar. On the second day, a Mass for peace was celebrated, and on the third day the Host was replaced in the tabernacle at the end of the Mass of Reposition. Both the first and third Masses were accompanied by processions and specific prayers. Originally, this devotion was an intercession for peace, and as such it is particularly appropriate today; it is also regarded as an act of reparation for the sins of men.

Modified forms of this devotion are permitted in some churches, depending upon the circumstances. Although this is an act of extra-liturgical worship, it is an admirable opportunity for grace, as a plenary indulgence may be gained by a visit to a church during the time of Forty Hours. Confession, Holy Communion, and a prayer for the Holy Father are further conditions.

FOUR LAST THINGS. Death, judgment, heaven, and hell. That branch of theology which deals with these is known as eschatology.

FRANCISCANS. The religious order founded by St. Francis of Assisi in 1209. This is divided into the First, Second, and Third Orders of Franciscans. The *First Order* is that of the men, which is further split into three groups: 1. The Order of Friars Minor (O.F.M.); 2. The Order of Friars Minor and Conventual (O.F.M. Conv.); and 3. The Order of Friars Minor Capuchin (O.F.M. Cap.). The distinguishing characteristic of the above three groups is the degree of poverty practiced by each.

The *Second Order* is for women founded in 1212 by St. Clare of Assisi under the direction of St. Francis; thus, the order is better known as the Poor Clares. This is a cloistered order practicing the contemplative life.

The *Third Order* includes both lay and religious, the latter being known as the Third Orders Regular. The lay persons carry on religious work in the world after the Franciscan spirit. The religious engage in active works of charity, teaching, hospital work, and other activities.

FREEDOM OF CONSCIENCE. The right and obligation of every man to form his conscience correctly and to follow it when it has been formed. A member of the Catholic Church recognizes that formation of conscience includes using the help of those more competent to make decisions in delicate areas; that is, the Church. The Church has, in her official teaching, always recognized the obligation and right of every man to follow his conscience without coercion (provided he did not violate the rights of others in doing so). In practice, however, many cases can be presented in history where this principle was violated. The definition of the Church, it must be noted, does not make the conscience absolute in itself. See the decrees of the II Vatican Council for a full treatment of this.

FREEDOM OF THOUGHT. The unrestricted process of thought. Although the complete freedom of thought is contradicted by many, essentially, the mind can function without external restrictions. More specifically, freedom of thought is closely associated with laws, circumstances, and the influences created by training. Thus it may be said that thought is molded and is not entirely free. However, it is incumbent upon all to seek for truth. particularly from an infallible authority such as the church. Once these truths have been determined, they cannot be rejected.

G

GALLICANISM. A political belief maintaining that a local or national church should have powers over and above the authority of the Holy See, thus resulting in the dominance of the State over the Church. The teaching is set forth in "The Gallican Liberties" drawn up by the clergy of the Church in France in 1628. Gallicanism first appeared at the beginning of the 15th century and was widely followed in France and Flanders during the 17th and 18th. At the present time, it is professed only by the heretical Old Catholics. These theories were condemned by the Vatican Council and Pope Alexander VIII in 1693.

GAMBLING. Gambling or betting is essentially lawful if the basis of the bet is not sinful and that both or all parties have the same understanding of the bet. Further, cheating or fraud must be absent and the payment of the bet must not result in family hardships. Artificial devices used to cause rapid rise or fall of stock prices is fraudulent and sinful.

GATE OF HEAVEN. This is a title given to the Blessed Mother in the litany of Loreto. This was first expressed by St. Peter Damian in which he likens Our Lady to the gate whereby Christ came to open Heaven to mankind. Further, at her intercession the gates of Heaven are opened to the souls in Purgatory.

GAUDETE SUNDAY. The third Sunday of Advent, so named because of the first word of the old Latin Introit which is the Latin of the verb "Rejoice." Although it occurs during a penitential season, it is a day of liturgical rejoicing, and rose vestments may be worn, the altar adorned with flowers, and the organ may be played.

GENERAL ABSOLUTION. In times where it is not possible for a confessor to hear individual confessions (to members of the armed services before going into battle) a confessor may absolve the sins of a group simultaneously, provided certain conditions are carried out. First, the individuals involved must express sorrow for their sins by some outward sign; secondly, those absolved are obligated to confess their sins in their next confession, even though those sins had been forgiven by the general absolution.

GENERAL CONFESSION. The repeating, in confession, of all sins committed by the penitent since baptism or the last general confession, to the best of his memory. It is customary to make a general confession before First Communion, ordination, or the taking of religious vows. It may be necessary to make a general confession if the penitent wilfully concealed

SUBJECT   BOOK   CHAP.   VERSE   PAGE

a mortal sin in a previous confession, if he were lacking in honest penitence, or if there is grave doubt about the validity of a previous confession.

Sometimes people wish to make general confessions for reasons other than those stated above. While this practice may be desirable in certain specific cases, and only for good reason, moral theologians agree it should be discouraged generally, because of the grave dangers of leading to or promoting scrupulosity.

GENERAL OF AN ORDER. The head, or superior, of a religious order who has certain spiritual jurisdiction over his community as well as administrative authority. These generals are elected, either for a fixed term or for life, depending upon their orders. The title, general, usually is suffixed to a noun, giving us the Augustinian and Carmelite "prior general," the Dominican "master general," or the Franciscan "minister general."

GENUFLECTION. The act of bending the right knee to the floor as a sign of reverence for and adoration of God. The faithful always genuflect when they pass the tabernacle in which the Blessed Sacrament is kept. At Mass, the priest genuflects a number of times in adoration of the Holy Eucharist. The priest and the congregation genuflect at the mention of the Incarnation in the Creed and at the end of the Last Gospel at Mass. It also is customary to genuflect as a sign of homage before the Pope, cardinals, or a bishop in his own diocese. The faithful execute a double genuflection upon entering or leaving a church where the Blessed Sacrament is exposed. This is done by bending both knees, the right one first, to the floor and bending the head slightly while kneeling in this position.

GIFTS OF THE HOLY SPIRIT. The seven gifts bestowed upon the faithful by the Holy Spirit. They are: Wisdom, Understanding, Counsel, Fortitude, Knowledge, Piety, and Fear of the Lord. These are supernatural gifts which dispose the intellect or the will to act upon the assistance and light of the Holy Spirit, and reside with the confirmed soul as long as he remains in the state of grace. The prophecy of Isaiah (11, 2-3) mentions six of these gifts; the seventh comes from the Latin Vulgate.

GLORIA IN EXCELSIS DEO. "Glory be to God in the highest." The first words of the prayer said in the old Latin Mass after the Kyrie Eleison. A hymn of joy it never is said during Masses for the Dead, during Advent, or between Septuagesima Sunday and Holy Thursday. The choir sings this hymn at Solemn or sung Masses.

The Gloria also is called the "Angelic Hymn" because its opening words are those said by the angels at Christ's birth, "Glory to God in high heaven, peace on earth to those on whom his favor rests."

Spoken by angels   *Lk   2   13-14   1022

GLORIA PATRI, Et Filio, Et Spiritui Sancto. "Glory be to the Father, and to the Son, and to the Holy Spirit. As it was in the beginning, is now, and ever shall be, world without end. Amen."

GLORIOUS MYSTERIES OF THE ROSARY. The five glorious subjects for meditation while praying the Rosary are: 1. the Resurrection of Christ from the tomb; 2. the Ascension of Christ into Heaven; 3. the Descent of the Holy Spirit upon the Apostles; 4. the Assumption of the Blessed Virgin into Heaven; 5. the Crowning of the Blessed Virgin Mary as Queen of Heaven. Sunday, Wednesday, and Saturday are the days on which the glorious mysteries usually are used.

GOD. "The one absolutely and infinitely perfect Spirit Who is the Creator of all" is the definition of God given by the Fourth Lateran Council and the Vatican Council. God owes His existence to no other; He always was and always will be. Infinitely perfect, He has created all things and is the Ruler of the entire universe. There are Three Persons in One God, the Father, the Son, and the Holy Spirit. God, the Father, is the first Person of the Blessed Trinity; God, the Son, is the Second; and God, the Holy Spirit, is the Third. St. Thomas, in his *Summa*, sets forth five arguments from reason which prove the existence of a Supreme Being. Briefly, his reasoning in the fifth argument is as follows: In the mechanism of created things there are clear marks which prove their creation by a most intelligent being who has immense power as well as the highest degree of wisdom. Obviously, this intelligence is not a part of the things themselves, because a thing cannot

SUBJECT   BOOK   CHAP.   VERSE   PAGE

be its own cause and effect. Therefore, one must concede that "things that are" were created by a superior Being, God.

GODPARENTS. Baptismal sponsors of a child who make the promises for the child and assume a responsibility for the spiritual guidance and education of the child if the parents die or neglect it. There exists a spiritual relationship between the child baptized and his sponsors.

GOLDEN ROSE. An ornament fashioned of gold which the Pope blesses every year on Laetare Sunday (fourth Sunday in Lent.) Sometimes the golden rose is sent by the Pope to Catholic sovereigns or others, to churches, or to Catholic cities as an award for distinguished services to the Church.

GOOD FRIDAY. The Friday in Holy Week on which the Catholic Church commemorates the passion and death of Our Lord, Jesus Christ. It is a day of fasting and abstinence, and the Church services of the day fully reflect the sorrow and solemnity of the occasion. There is no regular Mass, in the strict sense of the word, on Good Friday. The principal parts of the Good Friday Liturgy are the reading or chanting of the Passion; prayers said for various individuals and groups; the adoration of the cross; and a short communion service.

GRACE AT MEALS. Before meals, the blessings asked of God by those who are about to eat; after meals the "thank you" prayer. Catholics customarily pray before and after meals. However, the omission of these prayers is not sinful. Following are the usual prayers said at mealtime:

BLESSING BEFORE MEALS

"Bless us, O Lord, and these Thy gifts, which we are about to receive from Thy bounty, through Christ Our Lord. Amen."

GRACE AFTER MEALS

"We give Thee thanks for all Thy benefits, O Almighty God, who livest and reignest forever; and may the souls of the faithful departed, through the mercy of God, rest in peace. Amen."

GRACE, BAPTISMAL. Through the Sacrament of Baptism the soul becomes the recipient of sanctifying grace, the Gifts of the Holy Spirit, and the infused virtues. At the moment of baptism the recipient receives a certain aspect of sanctifying grace so that original sin, any actual sins, and the punishment due therefrom are remitted. Along with the infused virtues, the Gifts of the Holy Spirit are bestowed to help the spiritually regenerated recipient to lead a good Christian life. It opens the door to the actual graces which are necessary to help keep the Baptismal vows and to remain in God's favor.

GRACE, SACRAMENTAL. The interior grace received through a sacrament, and which is proper to that sacrament and cannot be received in any other way. It commonly is held to be a special type of sanctifying grace, fitted to the sacrament and intended to aid the recipient in fulfilling the obligations and purpose of the sacrament more perfectly. Thus we see that in Baptism, sacramental grace helps one to start a new, supernatural life and to carry out the Baptismal vows. In Confirmation it helps to strengthen one's faith and, when necessary, to stand up and defend it. In the Holy Eucharist, through sacramental grace our souls are nourished and united with God. In Penance, with its help, we can expiate our sins and make a sincere effort to amend our lives and to abstain from future sins. In the Sacrament of the Sick (the anointing in danger), the soul is prepared for immediate entrance into everlasting life. In Holy Orders it helps one to properly carry out his duties and to administer the sacraments. In Matrimony the spouses are given the graces necessary to remain faithful to each other and to perform the duties of the married state.

GRACE, STATE OF. A person who possesses sanctifying grace is said to be in the state of grace. This condition is essential at the moment of death if one is to be saved.

GRADINE. A raised shelf or shelves at the back of an altar used to hold flower vases, candles, crucifix, etc. According to strict liturgical principles the gradine is not an essential part of an altar, since an altar is defined as a flat table. For many years gradines were very popular; now, however, there seems to be a tendency toward the return of the flat table-like altars.

GRADUAL. Selected verses of Scripture (usually two verses from a psalm) which were said immediately after the Epistle in the old Latin Mass. The name comes from the Latin "gradus" (step). On Good Friday the Gradual is replaced by the Tract; from the Saturday after Easter to Trinity Sunday the greater Alleluia is said instead.

This "Gradual" together with the Tract (in penitential seasons) and the "Alleluia" (in joyful seasons) has been replaced by the "Scriptural Response" and the "Gospel Acclamation" in the revised Liturgy. The Scriptural Response and Gospel Acclamation are said or sung in that order between the two scriptural lessons in masses having only two. If there are three scriptural readings, the Scriptural Response occurs between the first and second and the Gospel Acclamation between the second and third.

GRADUAL PSALMS. Fifteen psalms (Pss 120-134) sometimes called "songs of ascents" which seem to have been selected because of their similarity in theme, namely, that of joy and trust in God's providence. Various explanations of their name have been offered by scholars, but no official decision has ever been made. It is quite possible that the title refers to their being sung on steps of the Temple, or to their use on pilgrimages up to Jerusalem.

GRAIL, HOLY. According to legend, the sacred vessel which Christ used at the Last Supper. Numerous quests for the cup have been made throughout the centuries, and various claims of authenticity have been offered for certain containers; but the Church does not recognize any known relic as the original cup Our Lord used.

GREEN. A liturgical color of vestments which are worn from the Epiphany until Lent and from the 2nd Sunday after Pentecost until the first Sunday of Advent. The color green symbolizes our hope for eternal life.

GREGORIAN CHANT. Another name for Gregorian music, or plain chant, a liturgical music approved by the Church. Its name is derived from St. Gregory the Great (d. 604) who improved and finally arranged it.

GREGORIAN MASSES. Thirty Masses read on successive days by the same celebrant for the repose of a specified soul after death. The hope for and belief in the special merit of these Masses stems from St. Gregory the Great's (d. 604) report of a deceased monk who had been released from purgatory after the completion of this series of Masses.

GRILLE. 1. The screen or grating which separates the priest and the penitent in the confessional.

2. The screen which separates a cloister of nuns from visitors in the reception parlor. Cloistered nuns can speak to visitors only through this screen.

GUADALUPE, OUR LADY OF. The title given to the Blessed Virgin Mary after she appeared to a Mexican peon, Juan Diego, in 1531. She became visible to Juan, a convert, on Tepeyac Hill and asked that a church in her honor be built on that spot. When the bishop requested proof of her presence, she told Juan to pick some roses which were blooming miraculously though it was winter. She arranged them in his cloak and then imprinted her likeness on the inside of the garment. This cloak still is preserved in the Shrine of Guadalupe which was built as the Blessed Mother requested. Our Lady of Guadalupe was named patroness of Mexico and December 12 declared her feast and a holy day of obligation for Mexico by Pope Benedict XIV.

GUARDIAN ANGELS. The angels commissioned by God to protect and guide each individual soul throughout life on earth. This teaching is accepted by theologians, but has not been defined as an article of faith by the Church. However, Christ Himself said, "See that you never despise one of these little ones." That the Church approves the devotion to guardian angels is evidenced by the fact that Pope Clement X named October 2 as the feast of the guardian angels.

SUBJECT	BOOK	CHAP.	VERSE	PAGE
Angels guard us	°Ps	91	11	558
Christ's words concerning	°Mt	18	10	985

H

HABIT. 1. The external garb worn by members of religious orders, particularly nuns and monks. Some congregations have their own distinctive garments, which usually are either black, brown, or white in color. These habits constitute an outward and visible sign of the dedication and consecration of the wearer to the religious life.

2. Habits of a good nature, as well as bad, become steadfast by repetition of the same acts. Thus, an aptitude or inclination for some action is acquired, showing itself in facility of performance or in decreased power of resistance. Habit implies a settled disposition or tendency; consequently, the acts are performed with ease and enjoyment. Mother Church is especially interested in Catholics acquiring good habits because once perfected they are not readily lost.

HAIL HOLY QUEEN. The first three words of a popular prayer and antiphon addressed to the Blessed Virgin Mary. In Latin it is called the *Salve Regina*. As an antiphon it is recited from Whitsuntide to Advent. It also is one of the Leonine Prayers said after low Mass as ordered by Pope Leo XIII. In this prayer we salute Mary as Our Heavenly Mother and beseech her protection and help during our earthly life. The text follows:

Hail Holy Queen

"Hail, Holy Queen, Mother of mercy, our life, our sweetness, and our hope! To thee do we cry, poor banished children of Eve! To thee do we send up our sighs, mourning and weeping in this vale of tears! Turn then, most gracious advocate, thine eyes of mercy towards us; and after this, our exile, show unto us the blessed fruit of thy womb, Jesus! Oh clement, Oh loving, Oh sweet Virgin Mary!"

HAIL MARY. The first words of the most popular prayer to Our Blessed Mother. It also is called the Angelic Salutation or, in Latin, the *Ave Maria*. The Hail Mary consists of three parts; the first two are taken from the New Testament, and the third was added by the Church. According to St. Luke, 1, 28, when the Angel Gabriel came to tell Mary she was to become the mother of God, he greeted her thusly, "Hail, (Mary) Rejoice, O highly favored daughter! The Lord is with you. Blessed are you among women." Luke 1, 42 tells St. Elizabeth's greeting to Mary when she came to visit her "Blessed are you among women and blessed is the fruit of your womb." The Catholic Church added the final petition, "Holy Mary, mother of God," pray for us sinners now, and at the hour of our death. Amen."

The Hail Mary is an essential part of the Rosary; is used extensively in various devotions and novenas; and also is said three consecutive times as part of the Leonine prayers said after low Mass.

HALLOWEEN. The eve of All Saints. The old English word for saint is *hallow*, and what used to be known as All Hallow's Eve has evolved into the present day Halloween.

HALO. The nimbus, or ring of light, which encircles the heads of pictorial or sculptured representations of Our Lord, the saints, or other holy persons to denote their sanctity, virtue, and grace.

HEART OF JESUS (Sacred Heart). The physical heart of Jesus Christ, divine in essence, which is the symbol of His infinite love for man. Our devotion to the Sacred Heart actually is the adoration of the whole Christ, the second Person of the Blessed Trinity, and the acknowledgement of His Divine Nature in human form. Devotion to the Sacred Heart of Jesus, as we know it, began after the revelations of St. Margaret Mary Alacoque at the Visitation Convent of Paray-le-Monial, France, from 1673–75. Christ appeared to St. Margaret Mary and complained, "Behold the Heart which has so loved men that it has spared nothing, exhausting and consuming itself in testimony of its love. Instead of gratitude I receive from most only indifference, by irreverence and sacrilege and the coldness and scorn that men have for Me in the Sacrament of Love." He asked that the Friday after the Octave of Corpus Christi be made a feast of reparation, and, in return, made the following twelve promises to all who pay homage to His Sacred Heart:

1. I will give them all the graces necessary in their state of life.

2. I will establish peace in their homes.

3. I will comfort them in all their afflictions.

4. I will be their secure refuge during life and above all in death.

5. I will bestow abundant blessings upon all their undertakings.

6. Sinners shall find in My Heart the source and the infinite ocean of mercy.

7. By devotion to My Heart tepid souls shall grow fervent.

8. Fervent souls shall quickly mount to high perfection.

9. I will bless every place where a picture of My Heart shall be set up and honored.

10. I will give to priests the gift of touching the most hardened hearts.

SUBJECT	BOOK	CHAP.	VERSE	PAGE

11. Those who promote this devotion shall have their names written in My Heart, never to be blotted out.

12. I will grant the grace of final penitence to those who communicate on the First Friday of nine consecutive months.

In 1929 the Feast of the Sacred Heart was raised to the rank of a double of the first class with a privileged octave of the third class. In all churches on the feast day, an act of reparation is recited.

In the most recent revisions of the church calendar the feast was retained as a "Solemnity" (First Class) and now occurs on the Friday following Corpus Christi (the second Sunday after Pentecost).

HERESY. The rejection of one or more truths revealed by God and infallibly defined by the Catholic Church, or the false interpretation of an infallibly defined doctrine, by one who has been baptized and who has professed the Christian religion. Heresy is either *formal* or *material. Formal* heresy, a serious sin, is committed when a baptized Christian knowingly and willingly denies or doubts one or more truths. *Material* heresy is the result of ignorance of the truth and is not accompanied by a rejection of the will. Material heresy is not sinful unless the individual suspects the truth and either neglects seeking the correct interpretations, or refuses to submit willingly to the rulings of the Church on the matter in question. A few of the principal heresies are as follows: Adoptionism; Albigensianism; Anabaptism; Anglicanism; Arianism; Berengarius, Heresy of; Calvinism; Catharism; Congregationalism; Gnosticism; Iconoclasm; Jansenism; Lutheranism; Macedonianism; Methodism; Millenarianism; Modernism; Monophysitism; Monothelitism; Montanism; Mormonism; Pelagianism; Quakerism; Rosicrucianism; Swedenborgianism; Unitarianism; Universalism; and Waldensianism.

SUBJECT	BOOK	CHAP.	VERSE	PAGE
To be avoided	°Ti	3	10-11	1190
Among the Corinthians	°1 Cor	11	19	1137

HERETIC. A baptized person who deliberately and with full consent of his will, rejects one or more infallibly defined doctrines of the Catholic Church. The Church automatically excommunicates those guilty of formal heresy.

HIERARCHY. The orderly gradation of the Catholic clergy according to their rank or grade of power. There is both a hierarchy of jurisdiction and a hierarchy of orders. In the hierarchy of jurisdiction the primacy of the Holy See and the power of the bishops is considered to be of divine origin. The Supreme Pontiff, by divine right, has jurisdiction over the entire Catholic Church. Diocesan bishops have complete authority in their own dioceses. The other members of the clergy receive their power and authority according to the positions they hold; thus theirs is considered to be of ecclesiastical origin rather than divine. The hierarchy of orders pertains to the graded priestly powers which are exercised in saying Mass, administering the Sacraments, etc. Therefore, the powers of bishops, priests, and deacons, by virtue of the divine conferring of orders, are considered to be of divine origin; those of the subdeacon and the minor orders are of ecclesiastical origin. Popularly, the term hierarchy refers to the bishops of a country as a group.

HOLOFERNES. In the Judith story a pagan general who is conquered by an intrepid Jewess. Since Holofernes name is a Persian one and the country and monarch he serves are Assyrian (!) too many historical incongruities exist that are unreconcilable for this to be accepted as straight history. It remains a great religious parable teaching trust in God and not "tempting" Him through time limits on His mercy.

SUBJECT	BOOK	CHAP.	VERSE	PAGE
Holofernes commissioned by the king of Assyria	°Jdt	2	4-6	396
Judith taken to Holofernes	°Jdt	10	17	402
Judith kills Holofernes	°Jdt	12-13		403
				404

HOLY DAYS OF OBLIGATION. Days on which Catholics are obliged under pain of mortal sin to attend Mass and to abstain from all unnecessary servile work. Every Sunday in the year is a Holy Day of Obligation. In addition, Church Law has declared certain other great feast days as holy days. These may vary between countries according to the rulings of the Holy See. In the United States the holy days of obligation are as follows:

Circumcision	January 1
Ascension	Forty days after Easter
Assumption	August 15
All Saints	November 1
Immaculate Conception	December 8
Christmas	December 25

Canada's holy days of obligation are:

Circumcision	January 1
Epiphany	January 6
Ascension	Forty days after Easter
All Saints	November 1
Immaculate Conception	December 8
Christmas	December 25

Permission to fulfill mass obligations on the eve of holy days (including Sunday) have been given more frequently in recent times and is a return to the ancient Hebrew custom of reckoning time from sundown to sundown (one day) instead of midnight to midnight.

HOLY FAMILY. The family consisting of Our Lord, Jesus Christ, His Blessed Mother, and His foster father, St. Joseph. Since their household was one of perfect harmony and unity, it should be the model for every Christian home. The Church honors the Holy Family with a special feast day, the Sunday within the Octave of Epiphany.

HOLY FATHER. One of the titles of honor and respect given to the pope, i.e., Our Holy Father, the Pope.

HOLY HOUR. An hour spent in devotion to the Blessed Sacrament. Our Lord Himself taught this practice to St. Margaret Mary Alocoque. The hour may be made publicly or privately, and it may be divided into prayer and meditation or singing. No rigid formula has been declared.

HOLY NAME OF JESUS. The title of Our Lord. In Hebrew the name means "The Lord is Salvation." It is customary for Catholics to bow their heads whenever they hear His name. The Catholic Church celebrates the Feast of the Holy Name on the second Sunday after Epiphany.

HOLY NAME SOCIETY. A confraternity of Catholic men which endeavors "to teach men and to nourish their souls through reverence for Jesus and His Holy Name." It had its origin in the Council of Lyons, 1274, and Gregory X directed the Dominicans to preach the devotion. St. Pius V, 1571, restricted the canonical erection of the society to the Dominicans. Besides receiving Holy Communion in a body once a month, and endeavoring to advance themselves spiritually, the members also participate in various external works suggested by their bishops or pastors. The society is divided into units or parish groups, each organized with the approval of the local bishop.

HOLY OF HOLIES. The inner sanctuary of the Tabernacle or Temple which, originally, contained the Ark of the Covenant. This inner room was considered the most sacred of places because the Ark, which contained principally the Tables of the Law, was the guarantee of God's abiding help.

HOLY OILS. The oil of catechumens, the oil of the sick, and chrism are the three holy oils consecrated by the bishop at Holy Thursday services and given to the parish priests. The oil of catechumens is used in blessing fonts, consecrating churches, ordaining priests, etc. The oil of the sick is used in the Sacrament of Extreme Unction. Holy chrism is used in the Sacraments of Baptism, Confirmation, and Holy Orders, and also for other blessings and consecrations.

HOLY ORDERS. The Sacrament instituted by Jesus Christ by which priests, bishops, etc. are ordained. Through Holy Orders they receive the power of the priesthood and are conferred with the grace necessary to carry out the sacred duties of that state. A seminarian must advance through seven steps in attaining priesthood. The first four, called Minor Orders, are: Ostiarius (Porter), Exorcist, Lector, and Acolyte. The last three, called Major Orders are: Subdeacon, Deacon, and, finally, Priest.

HOLY PLACES. All those places in the Holy Land which were sanctified by Our Lord's presence during His tenure on earth. Primarily, these are the Church of the Annunciation, Grotto of the Nativity, Church of the Visitation, the River Jordan, the Sea of Galilee, the Upper Room, Gethsemani, Via Dolorosa, Calvary, and the Holy Sepulchre. The claims for the authenticity of some of these Holy Places are substantiated by historical and archaeological facts; for others there is some doubt; a few can be considered just guesses. The Friars Minor have cared for some of these places for the Western Church since

SUBJECT	BOOK	CHAP.	VERSE	PAGE

the 13th century; others are in the custody of the Eastern schismatic Churches.

HOLY SATURDAY. The day before Easter Sunday.

HOLY SCRIPTURE. Another name for the Bible. The title includes both the Old and the New Testaments.

HOLY SEE. The episcopal see of Rome. The title more commonly refers to the pope and all the Roman Congregations, Tribunals, and offices which comprise the government of the whole Catholic Church.

HOLY SHROUD. The relic of the linen cloth in which it is claimed Our Lord was wrapped when He was placed in the tomb. Although many claims have been made for shrouds in various cities, the one preserved in Turin bears the imprint of a body, with the face particularly clear. This shroud which measures 13½ feet by 4¼ feet has been accepted as the authentic holy shroud by many scholars.

HOLY SOULS. The souls of the faithful departed who, as members of the Church Suffering, are detained in purgatory until they are freed from all punishment due to sin. This punishment may be the result of sins for which satisfaction has not yet been made, even though they had been forgiven. The suffering of a soul in purgatory is proportionate to his guilt. The Catholic Church teaches that the Holy Souls are helped by our prayers and good works, and the Council of Trent decreed they are aided primarily by the Holy Sacrifice of the Mass. Since they cannot help themselves while in purgatory, we here on earth most certainly should help them. The Catholic Church earnestly beseeches us to pray in their behalf, and has set aside the entire month of November for additional aid for the Holy Souls. The commemoration of Holy Souls Day is November 2nd. Although it is not a Holy Day of Obligation, the cause is so essential that all should attend Mass on that day.

HOLY SPIRIT. The third Divine Person of the Blessed Trinity who proceeds from the Father and the Son, yet is equal to Them in every respect. To Him are attributed the works of love, regeneration, revelation, and sanctification. Holy Scripture records four instances where the Holy Spirit appeared with a visible sign. They are:

Dove at Jesus' baptism	°Mt.	3	16	968
	Mk	1	10	999
Cloud at Transfiguration	°Mt	17	5	984
	Mk	9	6	1008
Breath when given power to forgive sins	°Jn	20	22-23	1080
Tongues of fire at Pentecost	°Acts	2	1-4	1085

HOLY SPIRIT, FRUITS OF. Those supernatural works that are done joyfully and with peace of soul. This is the definition set forth by St. Thomas for this term and is the sense most writers attribute to St. Paul when he mentions the list, "But the fruit of the Spirit is, charity, joy, peace, patience, benignity, goodness, longanimity, mildness, faith, modesty, continency, chastity." The charity, patience, mildness, etc. mentioned by the Apostle are not the virtues themselves, but rather, their acts or operations. In addition, these acts must belong to that category which are performed with ease and pleasure in order to come under this heading of *fruits*. In fact, St. Thomas extends this title to "Every virtuous act which man performs with pleasure. . . ." In other words, delight and satisfaction must replace any difficulty involved in performing these acts.

List mentioned by St. Paul	°Gal.	5	22-23	1155

HOLY SPIRIT, GIFTS OF. The gifts of the Holy Spirit are of two kinds: the first are specially intended for the sanctification of the person who receives them; the second, also called *charismata*, are extraordinary favors granted for the help of another, which do not necessarily sanctify by themselves, and may be separated from sanctifying grace. Those of the first class are the gifts of understanding, wisdom, counsel, fortitude, knowledge, piety, and fear of the Lord. The gifts of the second class are the gift of speaking with wisdom, the gift of speaking with knowledge, faith, the grace of healing, the gift of miracles, the gift of prophecy, the gift of discerning spirits, the gift of tongues, the gift of interpreting speeches, the gift of government, and the gift of helps. Some writers look upon these gifts as perfections of a higher order than the virtues, because they render the will obedient and docile to the inspirations of the Holy Spirit. The "Spirit of God" mentioned in Old Testament passages was not recognized as a distinct person until after His coming at Pentecost. "Spirit" meant power.

SUBJECT	BOOK	CHAP.	VERSE	PAGE
Enumerated by Isaiah	°Is	11	2-3	726
The diversity of spiritual gifts	°1 Cor	12	4-11	1138
	1 Cor	12	28-31	1138
	Rom	12	6-8	1125

HOLY THURSDAY. The Thursday in Holy Week on which the Church commemorates the institution of the Holy Eucharist of Jesus Christ at the Last Supper. Sometimes it is called Maundy Thursday, after the ceremony of the washing of the feet, or the *Mandatum* in Latin. At the Last Supper Christ washed the Apostles' feet as a symbol of His humility and love for mankind.

In Cathedral churches, following solemn procession, the bishops of each diocese bless the Holy Oils which then are distributed to all the churches of each diocese. Next comes the reading of Psalm 21, the story of the agony, followed by the stripping of the altars. Only the crucifix and candlesticks remain. This altar stripping is symbolic of the stripping of Christ of His garments before His crucifixion. The washing of the feet, the next step, usually is not performed in all churches in these times. However, in Rome, the pope washes the feet of thirteen priests; the bishops of some dioceses may continue the traditional ceremonies and may wash the feet of thirteen poor or thirteen members of the clergy.

The washing of the feet is now within the Mass of the Lord's Supper itself and no longer after mass as previously.

HOLY WATER. A sacramental which consists of water mixed with a little salt and which is blessed by the Church. On Holy Saturday (or before the principal Mass on Sundays if more is needed) the priest exorcizes water and salt, removing them from Satan's power. He then prays that the water may aid and promote the spiritual health of the user and drive away any of the devil's cohorts. Finally the water and salt are mixed in the name of the Blessed Trinity.

Holy water is used very extensively in the Western Church. The faithful bless themselves with it upon entering or leaving a church. It is used extensively to bless people or things. The devout use of holy water can remove venial sin. The washing with water is a natural symbol of spiritual purification; the salt symbolizes preservation from evil.

More importantly, Holy Water reminds us of the new life of grace received in Baptism. Thus every use of it reminds us of our Christian vocation.

HOLY WEEK. This is the week preceding Easter, during which the Church commemorates the sufferings and death of Christ and the principal mysteries of man's redemption. The Holy Week liturgy now closely resembles the practices of the early Church, these practices having been restored to the liturgy by Pope Pius XII as a universal observance with the decree "Maxima Redemptionis Nostrae Mysteria" (Nov. 16, 1955).

Holy Week begins with Palm Sunday, the most important event of the day being the solemn Church procession. This day commemorates Christ's triumphal entry into Jerusalem, and derives its name from the fact that the people that Christ met along the way threw palms at His feet. Holy Thursday commemorates the institution of the Holy Eucharist by Christ at the Last Supper. The principal Mass is celebrated between 4 and 9 P.M. On Good Friday the solemn liturgical action takes place at some time between 12 noon and 9 P.M. All other observances are secondary to this. Under the restored services, Holy Communion may now be received by all on Good Friday. The ceremonies of the Easter Vigil can be kept on Holy Saturday. Lent ends with the vigil service.

HOLY YEAR. One during which the Holy Father grants the Jubilee Indulgence to all the faithful who: 1. worthily receive the Sacraments of Penance and the Holy Eucharist; 2. devoutly visit the basilicas of St. John Lateran, St. Peter, St. Paul-outside-the-walls, and St. Mary Major in Rome; 3. in each basilica, recite three times the *Our Father, Hail Mary,* and *Glory be to the Father,* and one *Creed,* plus an additional *Our Father, Hail Mary,* and *Glory Be to the Father,* for the intention of the Holy Father. Usually during the Holy Year all other indulgences, with a few exceptions, are suspended, when applied to the living. However, they still are applicable to the souls in purgatory.

Customarily, at the end of a Holy Year, the pope extends the Jubilee Indulgence to the whole world. Instead of visiting the basilicas in Rome, the faithful can visit designated churches in their dioceses.

SUBJECT	BOOK	CHAP.	VERSE	PAGE

The first Holy Year was decreed in 1300 by Pope Boniface VIII, who intended they should be celebrated every 100 years. His successors shortened the periods to 50, then 33, and finally to 25 years. A regular Holy Year was declared in 1950 by Pope Pius XII. Traditionally, a Holy Year begins on December 24, and ends a year later on the same date. The beginning and ending are marked with special ceremonies, including the symbolic opening and closing of the Holy Door in each apostolic basilica in Rome.

HOMILY. The oldest form of preaching, which consists of an informal talk on some passage in Sacred Scripture. The speaker endeavors to explain the lesson and to exhort the listener to apply the teachings to his daily life. The Fathers of the Church first employed this type of sermon.

HOPE, ACT OF. A prayer expressing our hope in God:
"O my God, relying on Thy almighty power and infinite mercy and promises, I hope to obtain pardon of my sins, the help of Thy grace, and life everlasting, through the merits of Jesus Christ, my Lord and Redeemer."

HOSANNAH. A Hebrew word taken from Psalm 25, verse 117, which means, "O Lord, save us, we pray." The Jews uttered this phrase on joyful occasions, and thus Our Lord was greeted as He entered Jerusalem triumphantly on Palm Sunday. The church uses the expression as part of the Sanctus in the Mass. "Hosannah in the highest. Blessed be He who comes in the name of the Lord! Hosannah in the highest."

SUBJECT	BOOK	CHAP.	VERSE	PAGE
An acclamation of honor,	°Mt	21	9, 15	987
praise, and glory to	Mk	11	9-10	1011
Christ as Lord and King	Jn	12	13	1068

HOST. 1. The presence of Christ under the appearance of bread after the Consecration in the Holy Sacrifice of the Mass.
2. Word used to denote the unleavened bread before it has been consecrated.

HOUSE, BLESSING OF. This blessing may take place at any time according to the form prescribed in the "Rituale Romanum." There is a special blessing given to new houses.

HUMERAL VEIL. An oblong cloth about eight feet by three feet which is worn by the priest when he elevates the Blessed Sacrament and at Benediction; by the priest when he carries the Blessed Sacrament in procession, or when moving the Sacred Host from one place to another. It is worn over the shoulders with the ends covering the hands. Made of silk, it usually is white in color. A red humeral veil is worn when a relic of the True Cross is carried.

HYPERDULIA. The special veneration paid to the Blessed Virgin because she is the Mother of God. The reverence and devotion due her is greater than that accorded the angels and saints, but less than that given to God. The veneration of the saints and angels is called *Dulia*. The higher form of homage paid Mary is called *Hyperdulia*. *Latria* is the kind of adoration and worship we owe only to God, the Supreme Being. Thus Mary, as the Mother of God, and consequently nearer to Him, is deserving of greater reverence than are the saints and angels. We recognize that she is a creature but are confident of her power, holiness, and benevolence.

I

ICON. *an image.* An image or representation, but in the Eastern Church it refers to an image of Christ, the Blessed Virgin, or a saint. These were usually in the form of flat paintings often protected by a metal covering stamped with the outline of the picture. This outline was then cut so as to show the face and hands of the figure. Icons are venerated in place of statues in the East; but some Catholic churches of Eastern rites now have statues as well as icons, and some have eliminated icons altogether, adopting statues as we know them.

IHS. The first three letters of the name, Jesus, in Greek. The abbreviation should be written without the period after each letter, since IHS is the abbreviation of one word.

ILLEGITIMACY. Condition of one who is born out of wedlock. Canon Law decrees that an illegitimate child can become legitimized by the subsequent marriage of its parents, if they were free to marry each other at the time of conception or birth of the child, or at any time in between. In certain other cases a special dispensation by "ordinary power" or edict of the Holy See may declare a child legitimate.

ILLICIT. That which is unlawful or forbidden, and consequently sinful. However an action which is illicit is not necessarily invalid. Illicit means sinful. Invalid means that the thing was not, in fact, done. To receive communion while in the state of mortal sin would be illicity (sinful) but the consecration of the host would not be invalid.

IMAGES. Representations of Christ, likenesses of the Blessed Virgin Mary, the Saints, or others which may be sculptured, painted, or formed in any other way. Images are never adored. The honor and veneration given them is referred to the person they represent. Thus, in praying before a statue of the Blessed Virgin Mary, our prayers actually are directed to Our Lady in Heaven, and not to the inanimate likeness. Public veneration of sacred images, long a Church tradition, can be made with the permission of the local bishop. He decides which images shall receive public honor.

IMAGES, THE VEILING OF. The custom of the Church to cover all the crosses, pictures, and statues with plain purple or violet veils before the first vespers on Passion Sunday. These veils remain until Good Friday when they are removed from the crucifixes. On Holy Saturday morning at the *Gloria in excelsis* of the Mass they are taken off the statues and pictures. This practice is an obvious indication of mourning, although its true origin is in doubt.

IMMACULATE CONCEPTION. The preservation and exemption of the Blessed Virgin Mary from every stain of original sin from the first moment of her conception. On December 8, 1854, Pope Pius IX issued the bull, "Ineffabilis Deus" which defined the Immaculate Conception as an article of faith and truth contained in the original teachings of the Apostles. The dogma is defined, "We declare, pronounce, and define that the Most Blessed Virgin Mary, at the first instant of her conception was preserved immaculate from all stain of original sin, by the singular grace and privilege of the omnipotent God, in virtue of the merits of Jesus Christ, the Saviour of mankind, and that this doctrine was revealed by God, and therefore, must be believed firmly and constantly by all the faithful."

Mary's birth should not be confused with Christ's Virgin Birth. That is, the actions of her parents caused her body to be formed. It is God, however, Who breathes the rational soul into man. Since the fall of Adam and Eve, each of us comes into the world bearing the stain of original sin on our souls. But Mary was to become the mother of the Divine Son, the Saviour of the world, Who was to come down on earth, suffer, and die that all the faithful might live eternally in heaven. To her God poured forth special graces at the moment of her conception, and thus she was conceived without original sin. The Church celebrates this feast on December 8th. It is a Holy Day of Obligation in the United States, Canada, and many other countries. The patroness of the United States of America is the Blessed Virgin under the title of the Immaculate Conception.

IMMOVABLE FEASTS. Those feasts which are celebrated on a prescribed day of a month. For example, December 8th is always the Feast of the Immaculate Conception; and Christmas, Christ's birthday, always is celebrated the 25th of December, regardless of what week day these dates fall. Generally speaking, the feast days of the different saints are considered immovable feasts.

In contrast, a movable feast is one which falls on a different date each year. Easter, perhaps, is the most commonly known movable feast. In 325 the Council of Nicaea decreed the Feast of Easter was to be celebrated the first Sunday after the first full moon on or after March 21st. Each year, therefore, the Easter date is different. When a movable and an immovable feast occur on the same date, the feast of greater importance is celebrated. The secondary feast may be celebrated on another date or may be eliminated entirely that year.

IMMUNITY. The right the Church possesses to remain free from secular interference of its sacred places, property, and persons. Included in this immunity is the exemption of religious from military duty or civil duties such as jurors. Most governments recognize this right.

IMPECCABILITY. Sinlessness; the impossibility of committing sin. Christ was impeccable because He was divine, and a Divine Person cannot sin. In assuming a human nature, Christ did not lose His divinity. Thus, whether as God or as Man, He never could sin. Mary, too, was impeccable, although her sinlessness was due to special graces granted by God. God bestowed upon her a "fullness of grace," because she was to become the mother of God; it would not be suitable for an ordinary human, capable of sin, to bear an impeccable Being.

IMPEDIMENTS TO MARRIAGE. Circumstances which prevent people from marrying lawfully either because they are contrary to the divine laws of God or to the decrees of the Church.

IMPENITENCE. The lack of, or absence of, contrition in a sinner. Impenitence is considered to be one of the sins against the Holy Ghost when the refusal to admit sorrow for one's sins is deliberate and absolute.

IMPRIMATUR. Latin word meaning "let it be printed." Before a book pertaining to Catholic teachings or morals can be printed for the use of the faithful, the contents must be examined by a censor, and approved by the bishop of the diocese. Such approbation is indicated by the stamps, *Nihil Obstat* and *Imprimatur*, which usually appear on the back of the title page of a publication.

IMPROPERIA. The reproaches which Christ addressed to all men in the person of the Jews. These are contained in the Divine Office of Good Friday, are sung by the choir and recited by the celebrant during the veneration of the crucifix on that day.

INCARDINATION. The formal and permanent admission of a cleric into a particular diocese; the opposite of excardination. If letters of excardination are granted by his diocesan bishop, a cleric may transfer into another diocese.

INCARNATION. The Mystery of the Incarnation means that God the Son assumed a human nature so that the divine nature and the human nature were personally united in the one Person of the Word and Jesus Christ was true God and true man. In order to redeem all mankind, the Son came down upon earth in human form. As a man He was able to suffer and die. The fact that He also was God made His sacrifice infinitely more valuable and acceptable to the Father. Christmas is the commemoration of this truth of the Incarnation.

SUBJECT	BOOK	CHAP.	VERSE	PAGE
And the Word was made flesh	°Jn	1	14	1050
	Lk	1	26-38	1020
	Lk	2	1-7	1022
	Mt	1	18-25	966
	Mt	2	1-15	967
Inspired revelation and testimonies of the Incarnation	°Gal	4	4-5	1154
	Heb	2	16	1195
	Rom	8	3	1122
	Phil	2	5-8	1164

INCENSATION. The act of incensing; the motion performed with the thurible whereby the thurible is raised to the breast and thrust outward, so the aromatic smoke is wafted toward the object or person to be incensed.

INCENSE. As used by the Catholic Church, powdered or granulated resin or vegetable gums which are burned over charcoal in a censer or thurible during various liturgical services, such as Benediction and Solemn Masses. The burning of incense is symbolic of the zeal with which we Christians should be consumed; the sweet fragrance emitted symbolizes a pure and virtuous life; the smoke which ensues reminds us of the ascent of our prayers to the throne of God. Incense is a sacramental blessed by the Church. It was one of the three gifts which the Magi offered to Christ.

SUBJECT	BOOK	CHAP.	VERSE	PAGE
Use of and directions for making	°Ex	30	1-10	71
	Ex	30	34-38	71
	Ex	37	29	77
Burned in making sacrifices	°Lv	2	1-2, 15-16	81
	Lv	6	15	84
Offered with the showbread	°Lv	24	7-9	101
Used in idolatrous worship	°2 Kgs	18	4	302
Burned by Zechariah	°Lk	1	5-11	1020
Offered by angel	°Rv	8	3-4	1239
Smoke rises like prayer	°Ps	141	2	593

INCEST. Sexual intercourse between two people closely related either by blood or by marriage, and whose relationship prevents them from marrying. It is a sin against both chastity and piety, and it gravely violates the natural reverence due those drawn together by family ties.

SUBJECT	BOOK	CHAP.	VERSE	PAGE
Severely condemned	°Lv	18	6-18	96

INDEX OF FORBIDDEN BOOKS. Books harmful to faith and morals, the reading of which is expressly forbidden by the Holy See. Any book or publication whose material constitutes a danger to the faith or morals of the reader is prohibited. Forbidden books would include: 1. Any non-Catholic edition or translation of the Holy Bible (for example, the King James Version); 2. any book advocating or defending any heresy or schism or attempting to undermine any basic principle of the Church; 3. any book dealing with religion which does not have ecclesiastical approval to insure the reader the material within conforms to the fundamental truths of the Church; 4. any book attacking or ridiculing any phase of Catholicity, whether it concerns matters of faith and morals, Catholic liturgical services, the hierarchy, or the religious communities, etc.; 5. any book supporting or teaching superstitious practices; 6. any lewd or obscene book; 7. any book which advocates secret societies or declares them harmless and useful.

In special cases, and for sufficient reason, the Bishop may grant permission to Catholics to read forbidden books. However, even this special permission is prohibited when the reading of the book in question actually would endanger the faith or morals of a Catholic.

INDIFFERENTISM. The false theory which maintains that one religion is as good as another. Christ founded only one Church which has come down through the centuries, with His protection, as the Catholic Church.

The dangers of differentism are obvious. When some law or rule becomes personally obnoxious, the indifferent follower is inclined to follow the line of least resistance and to forget God's claims on His immortal soul. He lulls himself into a state of self-conviction, and either deteriorates to the level whereby he feels "it makes no difference what you believe so long as you do good," or he may even reject God altogether, as an atheist does. Sometimes this indifferentism has, as its beginning, a dangerous tolerance which causes one to believe a man must only follow his conscience, instead of the additional fact that his conscience first must be developed according to God's laws on truth and morality. Then, and then only, can he safely "follow his conscience."

Unfortunately, during this modern age in which we live, this false theory of indifferentism has been so widely proclaimed through the printed and the spoken word that even well-meaning Catholics have become confused. The Catholic Church, however, remains firm; it cannot and will not change its doctrines which have been laid down by God Himself.

INDISSOLUBILITY OF MARRIAGE. A valid marriage which has been consummated by two baptized persons cannot be dissolved except by death. Even separation is not permitted except by ecclesiastical permission for very serious reasons.

INDULGENCES. The remission granted by the Church of the temporal punishment due to sin after its guilt has been forgiven. Through the sacrament of Penance the guilt of sin is removed. However, there still may be a debt of temporal punishment, the result of the injustice done to God through each sin. It is this temporal punishment which may be removed, partially or entirely, by indulgences as well as by sufferings or good works offered to God as atonements. Any temporal punishment due and not atoned for in this world will have to be atoned for in purgatory after death. However, no indulgence can remove the temporal punishment due to unforgiven sin.

We can gain indulgences for ourselves, or for any soul in purgatory, but we cannot apply indulgences to other living persons. The living should earn their own. In praying for the dead we actually are beseeching God, in His mercy, to apply the merits of the indulgence to that particular soul.

There are two types of indulgences, *partial* and *plenary*. By *partial* indulgence we mean a portion of the temporal punishment due is remitted. However, to obtain any indulgence it is essential that one be in the state of grace, at least when the prescribed work or prayer is finished. A *plenary* indulgence remits all temporal punishment due to sin. To gain a plenary indulgence one must comply fully with all the conditions required: 1. one must have the intention of avoiding even venial sin; 2. confession; 3. Communion; 4. a visit to a church; 5. prayers for the intention of the Holy Father (usually one Our Father, one Hail Mary, and one Gloria, except an indulgence *toties quoties*, then the prayers are six Our Fathers, six Hail Marys, and six Glorias. Other prayers may be assigned. See Ench. p. XV, n. 1 and 2). One may go to confession at any time within the eight days preceding or eight days following the time set

SUBJECT	BOOK	CHAP.	VERSE	PAGE

for gaining the indulgence. One may receive Holy Communion on the day the plenary indulgence is gained or within the following eight days.

INDULGENCES, APOSTOLIC. Partial or plenary indulgences attached to crucifixes, rosaries, medals, or other images which have been blessed by the pope personally or by his delegate. One condition attached to such blessed objects is that they must be kept on one's person, or at least in one's home. Any article so blessed must be made of durable material and not of something easily broken or destroyed. The amount of the indulgence and the conditions to be fulfilled are determined by each pope at the beginning of his pontificate.

INDULGENCES FOR READING THE BIBLE. The Church consistently encourages Catholics to read Sacred Scripture, providing the Bible used is an approved translation and not a Protestant version. In addition, the Church has richly endowed Bible reading with various indulgences: 1. To the faithful who read the Bible for at least 15 minutes an indulgence of three years is granted. 2. To the faithful who read at least some verses of the Gospel and in addition, while kissing the Gospel Book, devoutly recite one of the following invocations: "May our sins be blotted out by virtue of the words of the Gospel," "May Christ teach us the words of the Holy Gospel," "May the reading of the Gospel be our salvation and protection," a partial indulgence is given; a plenary indulgence is granted, under the usual conditions, to those who daily for a whole month do the above; a plenary indulgence is granted at the hour of death to those who often during life perform this pious exercise, as long as, having confessed and received communion, or at least having sorrow for their sins, they invoke the most holy name of Jesus on their lips, if possible, or at least in their hearts, and accept death from the hand of God as the price of sin.

INDULT. Permission granted by the pope or local cardinal, archbishop, or bishop to do something not allowed by the common law of the Church.

INDWELLING OF THE HOLY SPIRIT. The inhabitation of a soul by the Holy Spirit and by the Blessed Trinity as a whole so long as that soul remains in the state of sanctifying grace.

INFALLIBILITY. In theological usage, the supernatural prerogative by which the Church of Christ is, by a special divine assistance, preserved from liability to error in her faith and morals. This was expressed by the Vatican Council (sess. iii, cap. 4), "The doctrine of faith which God has revealed has not been proposed as a philosophical discovery to be improved by human talent, but has been committed as a divine deposit to the Bride of Christ (the Church) to be faithfully guarded and infallibly interpreted by her." This infallibility resided (a) in the pope personally and alone; (b) in an ecumenical council subject to papal confirmation (these infallibilities are distinct but correlative); (c) in the bishops of the Church, dispersed throughout the world, teaching definitively in union with the pope. This is not a different infallibility from (b) but is the ordinary exercise of a prerogative (hence called the "ordinary *magisterium*") which is manifested in a striking manner in an ecumenical council. This ordinary *magisterium* is exercised by pastoral letters, preaching, catechisms, the censorship of publications dealing with faith and morals, the reprobation of doctrines and books; it is thus in continuous function and embraces the whole deposit of faith. Infallibility does not involve inspiration or a fresh revelation; the Church can teach no *new* dogma but only "religiously guard and faithfully expound" the original deposit of faith with all its truths, explicit and implicit; nevertheless, infallibility extends to indirect and secondary doctrines and facts whose connection with revealed truths is so intimate as to bring them within its scope.

INFALLIBILITY, PAPAL. The truth that the pope who is vested with the authority of the Vicar of Christ is divinely preserved from error whenever he defines a doctrine concerning faith or morals. That this special prerogative exists has always been the teaching of the Catholic Church. In 1870 the Vatican Council declared "it to be a dogma of divine revelation that when the Roman Pontiff speaks *Ex Cathedra*, that is, when he, using his office as shepherd and teacher of all Christians, in virtue of his apostolic authority, defines a doctrine of faith or morals to be held by the whole Church he, by the divine assistance promised him in blessed Peter, possesses that infallibility with which the divine Redeemer was pleased

to invest His Church in the definition of doctrine on faith and morals, and, that therefore, such definitions of the Roman Pontiff are irreformable in their own nature and not because of the consent of the Church."

This prerogative does not pertain to the personal moral life of any pope. He is a human being subject to the same pitfalls as any other human. The power of infallibility is his, however, whenever he pronounces officially, by virtue of his office, any specific teaching concerning faith or morals. While he is acting as the teacher of the Church, the Holy Spirit guides his pronouncements, so there is no error or possibility of error.

INFANTICIDE. The killing of an infant before or after birth. Unfortunately, economic reasons more than any others have led to the murder of infants before or after birth. Christianity first opposed the generally accepted customs of infanticide when the Emperor Constantine enacted two laws (about A.D. 320) directed against child-murder. In order to remove the temptation, parents overburdened with children were assisted by the imperial treasury; and second, all the rights of property of exposed infants were accorded to those who had had the charity to save and nurture them. The church, of course, does not consider economics, or any other reason, as valid for the deprivation of life from the moment of conception.

SUBJECT	BOOK	CHAP.	VERSE	PAGE
By Pharaoh	°Ex	1	16	47
By Herod the Great	°Mt	2	16	967

INFIDEL. One who has not been baptized; one who rejects Christianity. Popularly, one who has never heard of Christianity is called a heathen, rather than an infidel.

INFINITY OF GOD. That which has no end, limit, or boundary. The infinity of God is Catholic dogma in every respect. The Vatican Council at its Third Session declared God to be almighty, eternal, immense, incomprehensible, infinite in intellect and will and every perfection, really and essentially distinct from the world, infinitely blessed in Himself and through Himself, and inexpressibly above all things that can exist and be thought of besides Him. Thus, God is the self-existing, uncreated Being, whose entire explanation must be in Himself, in Whom there can be no trace of chance.

SUBJECT	BOOK	CHAP.	VERSE	PAGE
Infinite in understanding	°Ps	147A	5	597
Infinite in knowledge and wisdom	°Ps	36	6	517
	Rom	11	33	1124
Infinite in power and might	°Rom	1	20	1116
	Heb	11	3	1202
Infinite in goodness	°Ps	16	2	502

INNOCENCE, ORIGINAL. The state of man before his Fall whereby he possessed the supernatural gift of sanctifying grace.

INQUISITION. An ecclesiastical tribunal for the discovery and prevention of heresy. In the 13th century the Holy See set up an inquisition for the trial of persons accused of the heresy of Albigensianism. This tribunal generally was administered by Dominicans.

The Spanish Inquisition was founded in 1478 by King Ferdinand and Queen Isabella to test the Christian convictions of Moor and Jewish converts who were suspected of having lapsed back into heresy. Although it was intended to be of a religious nature it became, at times, a political tool used to get rid of unwanted foes, and often was guilty of what we would term inhuman cruelties.

Before passing judgment on either of the above inquisitions it must be remembered they were instituted to defend the Church from what she considered a mortal danger. The injustices and cruelties sometimes attached to such tribunals are not in line with the teachings of the Catholic Church, nor were they validated by the fact that the courts were ruled by clerics. In all fairness it must be stated that there were some injustices, but not as many as some prejudiced historians have claimed.

In 1542 Paul III founded an inquisition to combat heresy, which was progressing rapidly on the waves of Protestantism then sweeping the world. This inquisition, which was made the supreme doctrinal tribunal for the Church, has its authority vested in a congregation of twelve cardinals, over which the pope presides. Today this tribunal is known as the Holy Office. Its chief duties are to guard faith and morals, prohibit dangerous books, and issue dispensations for mixed marriages.

INSPIRATION OF SCRIPTURE. The supernatural guidance of the Holy Spirit whereby the writers of the books of the Bible were supernaturally moved to write what God wished to be written. Thus, God is the principal author of the Bible. Because of this divine influence on the writers, they were unable to write anything except what God had predetermined would be written. Therefore, there are no errors in the divine revelations. Today, because of the many translations we may find a few copyist's errors, but there has been no serious corruption of the Scriptures.

SUBJECT	BOOK	CHAP.	VERSE	PAGE
Divine inspiration asserted	°2 Tm	3	16	1186
	2 Pt	1	17-18	1216
	Mi	3	8	935
	Ez	11	5	854
Prophets aided by divine	°Is	6	1-13	721
visions	Jer.	1	4-10	778
Scriptures spoken through	°Acts	1	16	1083
divinely chosen men	Acts	4	24-25	1087
	Heb	3	7-11	1196
	Heb	10	15-17	1201
Christ's promise of divine	°Jn	14	26	1071
inspiration	Jn	16	13	1074

INTERDICT. An ecclesiastical censure inflicted by the pope or local bishop upon a group or an individual or both, barring them from the use of the sacraments, religious services, and Christian burial. It may be used to correct the faithful, or as a punishment. When imposed upon a place it is known as a *local* interdict; when inflicted upon an individual, it is a *personal* interdict.

IRREGULARITY. Canonical impediment preventing a person from becoming a cleric, from attaining a higher office, or from exercising his office. It is a permanent obstruction instituted to protect the dignity of the clerical state. It can be imposed because of the defect of an individual, such as bodily defects. Irregularities also may be invoked because of crimes such as apostasy, heresy, schism, bigamy, attempted suicide, etc.

ITINERARY. A prayer found at the end of the breviary and said by clerics before setting out on a journey. It consists of the *Benedictus*, the *Our Father*, a number of versicles and responses, and four orations.

J

J. A. C. Abbreviation for the French name, *Jeunesse Agricole Chrétienne*, the Young Christian Farmer. This organization is extremely active in Catholic Action work, particularly in France and Canada, and is composed chiefly of agricultural workers.

JESUITS. Members of the Society of Jesus founded in 1534–40 by St. Ignatius Loyola. At first the order was called the Company of Jesus and was dedicated to missionary work. Later they expanded their talents and became equally distinguished as educators, scholars, and parish priests. St. Ignatius Loyola himself drew up the constitution, "Institutum Societatis Jesu," which calls for a long, strenuous training period during which the Jesuit spirit of versatility, obedience, zeal, and efficiency is developed. The Jesuit also makes a special vow of obedience to the pope in addition to the usual religious vows. A primary purpose of the Society is to be always at the beck and call of the pope for whatever he may ask of them.

Jesuit schools are famous. Their standards are high and the training given is strenuous and complete. Some of the best known Jesuit institutions of higher learning are Fordham University in New York; Marquette at Milwaukee, Wisconsin; Loyola at Chicago, Illinois; Loyola in New Orleans; and Georgetown University in Washington, District of Columbia.

JOYFUL MYSTERIES, THE. Subjects of the first cycle of meditations of the Rosary, consisting of five joyful events in the lives of Our Lord and the Blessed Virgin. The five meditations which are contemplated on Mondays and Thursdays are: 1. The Annunciation; 2. The Visitation; 3. The Nativity; 4. The Presentation in the Temple; 5. The Finding of the Child Jesus in the Temple. The other two cycles of meditations of the Rosary are the Sorrowful Mysteries and the Glorious Mysteries.

JOYS OF THE BLESSED VIRGIN. The Joys of the Blessed Virgin are generally summarized as follows: 1. The annunciation of the Angel Gabriel to Mary that she was to become the mother of God; 2. The visitation of the Blessed Virgin to St. Elizabeth; 3. The birth of Our Lord; 4. The adoration of the Magi (Epiphany); 5. The finding of the Child Jesus in the Temple; 6. The resurrection of Our Lord; 7. The ascension.

JUBILEE INDULGENCE. The extraordinary plenary indulgence granted by the Pope during a Holy Year and usually

SUBJECT	BOOK	CHAP.	VERSE	PAGE

during the year following. By special grant this indulgence may be given at other times also.

JURISDICTION. The legislative, judicial, and executive powers of the church over her members for the purpose of guiding them toward their supernatural goal, eternal salvation. There are several divisions of this power which are set forth in the Code of Canon Law, the church's law books. Probably the two most commonly known phases of ecclesiastical jurisdiction are: 1. the power of authorized members of the church to ordain bishops and priests; 2. the jurisdiction given a priest to absolve sins validly through the Sacrament of Penance.

JUSTIFICATION. The sanctification of the soul by God's graces and the gifts and virtues of the Holy Spirit, through which it leaves its status as a sinful enemy of God and becomes just and a friend of God. This initial justification is a gift of God at Baptism when He infuses the newly-baptized soul with sanctifying grace. If lost through mortal sin, it can be recovered in the Sacrament of Penance. Once sanctifying grace has been restored, it can be increased by good works.

Obtained only through God's grace	°Rom	3	20, 24	1118

K

KISSING THE ALTAR. From very earliest times a kiss was not only a token of love, but also a symbol of respect. In accordance with this symbolism, the Church enjoins kissing many holy objects, such as relics, the cross, blessed palms, candles, and nearly all the utensils and vestments connected with the liturgy. The altar is also kissed by the celebrant in the course of the Mass. Earliest records mention it twice, and then it is spoken of three times; but in the days of Durandus nine such salutations were in use. The altar has been regarded from a very early period as typical of Christ, abiding permanently with His Church in the Sacrifice of the Mass. Thus, the appropriateness of kissing the altar implies that the greeting comes not only from the priest but from Christ Himself.

KNIGHT, PAPAL. A member of one of the six pontifical orders of knighthood which have been established by the Church: (1) The Supreme Order of Christ, (2) The Order of the Golden Spur, (3) Order of Pius IX, (4) Order of St. Gregory the Great, (5) Order of St. Sylvester, and (6) Order of the Holy Sepulcher. The sixth of these orders may be given to women and clerics; and the second and third may be conferred on non-Catholics. The others are reserved for Catholic laymen.

KNIGHTS OF COLUMBUS. A fraternal benefit society of men founded in New Haven, Connecticut, in 1882, the purpose of which is: 1. To render pecuniary aid to its members and beneficiaries of members. 2. To render assistance to sick and disabled members. 3. To promote social and intellectual intercourse among its members. 4. To promote and conduct educational, charitable, religious, social, and relief work. This organization also publishes an excellent monthly magazine, *Columbia*. Besides its great contribution in the fields of boy guidance and university endowments and other numerous social service activities, the Knights, in 1948, inaugurated the advertising of Catholic doctrine and practice in paid space in secular publishings of large circulation. Through these advertisements they offer free booklets explaining Catholicity and invite inquiry. The response to these ads has been most encouraging.

KU KLUX KLAN. A secret society which developed in the lawless and bigoted group after the Civil War. When the Klan realized the terror it struck into the Negro after the war, it developed a program of violence designed to "protect the constitutional rights of the whites." During the days of the Reconstruction of the South its crusade became so infamous that President Grant was forced to suppress it. In 1915 it was revived with a platform of bigotry and racism with particular hatred for Catholics, Jews, Negroes, and all foreign born. During the early 1920's it wielded considerable political influence, but in 1926 scandals and lawlessness caused its decline. It was revived, however, during the Smith presidential campaign in 1928; but it was officially deorganized in 1944.

It has undergone a minor local revival in certain areas, notably in the South.

KYRIALE, THE. A liturgical book containing the chants for the ordinary of the Mass. It contains eighteen different plainchants for as many Masses, each of which is assigned to a particular rank of season or feast.

KYRIE ELEISON. The Greek words meaning, "Lord have mercy on us," occurring the Mass immediately after the Introit. The Kyrie consists of nine invocations, three Kyrie Eleisons (addressed to God, the Father), three Christe Eleisons (addressed to Christ, the Son), and again three Kyrie Eleisons. At low Masses the priest and server alternate in saying these invocations. At a Solemn or a sung Mass the choir sings the nine invocations.

L

LAETARE SUNDAY. The fourth Sunday of Lent, named from the first word of the Introit of the Mass for that day, *Laetare*, meaning "rejoice." This day also is known as Rose Sunday because rose vestments may be worn in place of the usual purple vestments of Lent. On this day flowers may decorate the altar, the organ can be played, and, in general, the somber spirit of Lent is lifted and a spirit of joy prevails.

LAICIZATION. 1. The appropriation, secularization, or compulsory administration by civil authorities of ecclesiastical property contrary to the rights of the Church. This would include civil administration of Church enterprises such as hospitals, schools, and institutions as well as maintenance of churches and convents.

2. The changing or reduction of an ecclesiastical person or thing to a lay state by the authority of the Church. This may include the turning over of a Church building for a secular use.

LAMENTABILI. The decree issued in 1907 by Pope Pius X (now St. Pius) which condemned Modernism as the "synthesis of all heresies." It takes its name from the first word of the Latin version, "Lamentabili."

LAMENTATIONS. This word signifies mourning or giving expression to grief; it is used in elegies and in mournful speeches or compositions. It is in this last sense that the name is applied to one of the poetical books of the Bible.

SUBJECT	BOOK	CHAP.	VERSE	PAGE
For Jacob at his burial	*Gn	50	10	45
For Jonathan and Saul	*2 Sm	1	17-27	243
Of Jeremiah at the death of	*2 Chr	35	25	359
King Josiah	Lam	1-5		834
				839
Of Christians over martyrdom of Stephen	*Acts	8	2	1092
For Christ	*Lk	23	26-28	1045
For Israel	*Am	5	1-4	924

LAMP, SANCTUARY. The light which, by Church Law, is kept burning wherever the Blessed Sacrament is as a reminder that Jesus Christ is truly present there. According to Church Law, olive oil or beeswax candle should be burned. However, in extraordinary circumstances the local bishop may grant permission for the use of another kind of oil, or even an electric light.

LANGUAGES OF THE CHURCH. The official language of the liturgy of the Western Roman Catholic Church is Latin. Latin also is the diplomatic language of the Church. The Eastern Churches, with the permission of the Church authorities, use the following languages in their liturgies: Greek, Arabic, Armenian, Coptic, Rumanian, Gheez, Slavonic, and Syriac.

LA SALETTE. In southeastern France there is a mountain called La Salette. In mid-afternoon on September 19, 1846, a fifteen year old shepherdess, Melanie (Calvat) Matthien, and an eleven year old shepherd, Maximin Giraud, beheld a beautiful lady seated there and bitterly weeping. She asked the children to warn the people they would suffer severe punishment unless they amended their ways and avoided evil. To the children she confided a message which was sent to Pope Pius IX in 1851 and has since been designated as the "secret" of La Salette.

The day following the apparition the children told the parish priest about Our Lady. A visit to the scene revealed the presence of a miraculous fountain at the spot where Our Lady sat. In 1851 the authenticity of the vision was declared and devotions to Our Lady of La Salette were approved. Pilgrimages to the site were made, and several miraculous cures occurred.

LAST BLESSING, THE. A blessing given to one who is dying, with a plenary indulgence attached. The sick person must of course make an Act of Contrition and at least interiorly pronounce the Holy Name. The formula of Pope Benedict XIV must be used; and the blessing may not be given to a person who has been excommunicated, to one who is impenitent, or anyone dying in mortal sin.

LAST DAY, THE. The day of the general judgment when the present world will come to an end.

LAST SACRAMENTS, THE. The sacraments which are administered to those sick who are in danger of death. These are Extreme Unction and Holy Viaticum.

LAST SUPPER. The meal Our Lord took with the Apostles the night before His passion and death. At that time He instituted the Mass and commanded the Apostles to perpetuate the rite.

SUBJECT	BOOK	CHAP.	VERSE	PAGE
The Holy Eucharist instituted	*Mt	26	26-29	993
	Mk	14	22-25	1014
	Lk	22	19-20	1044
	1 Cor.	11	23-26	1137

LAST THINGS, FOUR. Death, judgment, heaven, and hell are the four last things.

LATERAN, THE. The name applied to a group of buildings of southeast Rome on land once belonging to the family of the Laterani. The properties were confiscated by Nero and later presented to the Church by Constantine. The Lateran basilica is the cathedral of Rome, the pope's church, and is the first-ranking church of the Catholic Church. Over the entrance is inscribed, "The Mother and Head of all churches of the City and of the World." It was officially named The Basilica of the Savior, but it is familiarly called St. John Lateran, from the monastery of St. John formerly near by. It was built perhaps before 311 and has been altered many times.

Another very ancient building is the Lateran baptistery, built probably in the 4th century. It is a fine example of early baptisteries, although it has been much restored.

The Lateran palace, the papal residence until the removal to Avignon in the 14th century, survived although greatly changed until the 16th century when it was demolished to make way for the present palace, considerably smaller than the old one. It now contains the Pontifical Museum of Christian Antiquities. The older palace was the scene of the five Lateran Councils, and the newer one of the signing of the Lateran Treaty.

LATERAN TREATY. On February 11, 1929, the Italian government and the Holy See signed a contract which recognized the sovereignty of the Holy See and guaranteed full rights as an independent territory to the Vatican State. Besides those buildings within the Vatican boundaries, the agreement gave the Holy See certain other properties outside the limits. These include the Basilicas of St. John Lateran, St. Paul-outside-the-walls, St. Mary Major, the summer palace of Castel Gandolfo, and several other churches and sites. The signing of this treaty ended the voluntary imprisonment of the Popes within the Vatican walls. With the end of World War II a free Italian republic was formed. Incorporated in its constitution is the Lateran Treaty.

LATIN. The official diplomatic language of the Church and the official language of the Roman Rite of the Church. Since Rome was the seat of the Church and the center of missionary activities, the language of the Romans was adopted and, subsequently, carried to the Western nations by missionaries. Most official documents are composed in Latin. It differs considerably from the classical Latin of the early Romans.

LATRIA. The supreme homage and highest form of worship which is due to God alone. The principal act of latria is the sacrifice of the Mass. Homage paid to images of the Sacred Heart, to crucifixes, and other religious objects connected with a divine person is referred to as *relative latria*. The symbol itself, of course, is not venerated, but the person for whom the symbol stands is the object of the homage paid.

LAUDA SION. The title and opening words, "Praise, O Sion," of the sequence in the Mass of Corpus Christi, composed by St. Thomas Aquinas.

LAUDS. The second hour of the Divine Office or breviary. Literally, it means praises and is so named because many of the Psalms used begin either with *Lauda or Laudete*.

LAY BROTHERS. Members of religious communities whose duties consist of taking care of the secular affairs of monasteries,

SUBJECT	BOOK	CHAP.	VERSE	PAGE

tending farms, maintaining the households, taking care of the sacristies, etc. They do not receive Holy Orders nor are they bound to say the breviary.

LAYMAN. Any person who is not a member of the clergy or any religious order; a member of the laity.

LECTIONARY. Any liturgical volume containing passages to be read aloud in the services of the Church. In practice, the term *lectionary* is more commonly used to denote one of two things: (1) the book containing the collection of Scriptural readings which are chanted by the deacon, subdeacon, or a lector during Mass; (2) any book from which the readings were taken which are read aloud in the Office of Matins, after each nocturn or group of psalms.

LEGATE, PAPAL. An envoy of the pope sent by him to represent the Holy See on a special mission to a government or to a sovereign. There are three classes of papal legates: the *legatus a latere* (always cardinals) who are sent on confidential missions or matters of international importance and are the highest form; nuncios and internuncios who represent the Vatican as diplomats in countries recognizing the Vatican State; apostolic delegates who represent the Vatican in countries not maintaining diplomatic relations with the Holy See.

LEGION OF MARY. This association of Catholic laity was founded in 1921 in Dublin, Ireland, for the purpose of sanctifying its members, intensifying Catholic life, reclaiming fallen away Catholics, and seeking converts. It is not concerned with material relief, but concentrates only on spiritual aims. Realizing Our Blessed Mother is the divinely appointed Mediatrix of All Graces, the Legion strives to accomplish its works under her sponsorship. Now a world-wide organization, it constitutes one answer to Pope Pius XI's appeal for Catholic action.

LENT. Forty days of fast and penance before Easter in preparation for the glorious feast. It begins on Ash Wednesday and ends at noon on Easter Saturday. The forty days, excluding Sundays, remind us of Our Lord's forty-day fast in the desert. During this period the Gloria and Alleluia are omitted from the Church liturgy, special Lenten services are held, nuptial blessings are forbidden because of the solemnity of the season, and the use of the organ is restricted. The faithful are encouraged to concentrate on Our Lord's passion and death. The name, "Lent," is taken from the Anglo-Saxon *lencten* meaning spring, and refers to the time in which the Lenten season occurs.

As early as the 5th century, some of the Fathers, St. Leo for example, exhorted the faithful to abstain that they may "fulfill with their fasts the Apostolic institution of the forty days." Later, however, scholars were almost unanimous in recognizing that there was considerable diversity of practice regarding the fast before Easter as well as the number of days covering the preliminary fast. In determining the period of forty days the example of Moses, Elijah, and Christ must have exercised a great influence.

Examples of 40 day fasts:

SUBJECT	BOOK	CHAP.	VERSE	PAGE
By Moses	*Ex	24	18	66
	Ex	34	28	74
By Elijah	*1 Kgs	19	8	282
By Christ	*Mt	4	1-2	969

LICENTIATE. An academic degree which follows the degree of bachelor and precedes that of doctor. It is conferred upon the satisfactory completion of studies in theology, philosophy, Scripture, and Canon Law, and would be comparable to a master's degree in a secular school.

LIMBO. 1. The place where the souls of the faithful who died before Christ redeemed mankind were detained. After Our Lord's Ascension the gates of Heaven were open to them and they attained the Beatific Vision.
2. The place where the souls of unbaptized infants live in a state of natural happiness after death. Since an infant is incapable of committing mortal sin which would condemn him to hell, and since the stain of original sin still remains on an unbaptized soul which prevents it from reaching Heaven, theologians teach the truth that such souls are placed in Limbo. Souls in Limbo enjoy eternal happiness but are deprived of the vision of God.

Also called:

SUBJECT	BOOK	CHAP.	VERSE	PAGE
Abraham's bosom	*Lk	16	22	1038
Paradise	*Lk	23	43	1045

LITANY. A prayer consisting of a series of invocations with responsive petitions. Five litanies have been approved for public devotions: Litanies of Loreto, the Holy Name, All Saints, the Sacred Heart, and St. Joseph. Other litanies may be said privately.

LITTLE FLOWER, THE. A title by which Saint Teresa-of-the-Child-Jesus is known. This recalls her mystical saying that she would let fall a shower of roses from heaven. Her unusual holiness and the many miracles attributed to her intercession caused her canonization only 28 years after her death. Her feast is October 3, and her shrine at Lisieux has become a major place of prayer and pilgrimage.

LITTLE OFFICE OF THE BLESSED VIRGIN MARY. A short form of breviary divided into seven hours and consisting of psalms, lessons, and hymns recited in honor of the Blessed Virgin Mary. During Lent the *Alleluia* is omitted, and from Advent to the Purification a change is made in the office; otherwise it is not changed according to the liturgical season. It is believed to have been written about the middle of the 8th century and is recited today by many religious orders for women, lay persons, members of third orders, and sodalists.

LITURGY. The official public worship of God by the Church, as opposed to private devotion. Consisting of the Holy Sacrifice of the Mass, all public rites, ceremonies, and prayers of the Church, it includes the sacraments, sacramentals, and the Divine Office.

In the Eastern Church the name liturgy applies exclusively to the Sacrifice of the Mass which is, after all, the highest form of worship.

LORD'S PRAYER. The prayer Jesus Christ taught His disciples. In Latin it is called the *Pater Noster.* In English it is commonly known as the *Our Father.*

SUBJECT	BOOK	CHAP.	VERSE	PAGE
Taught by Our Lord	*Mt	6	9-13	971
	Lk	11	2-4	1033

LOST BOOKS. Those books mentioned in the Bible which have never been transmitted to us. There is no evidence that these books were inspired, and, thus, they have never belonged to the Canon of the Bible.

SUBJECT	BOOK	CHAP.	VERSE	PAGE
Book of the Wars	*Nm	21	14	126
Book of Jashar	*Jos	10	13	180
Book of Nathan the Prophet	*1 Chr	29	29	332

LOURDES, OUR LADY OF. One of the titles under which Our Blessed Lady is honored. In 1858 in the grotto of Massabielle, near Lourdes, France, the Blessed Virgin appeared eighteen times to a poor fourteen year old peasant girl, St. Bernadette Soubirous. Her declaration that she had seen Our Blessed Lady brought forth a demand for proof. On February 25, the Virgin appeared to St. Bernadette again and told her to drink the water and to wash in the spring which gushed forth miraculously when the peasant girl scratched the dry earth. On March 25 the vision reappeared and revealed her identity, "I am the Immaculate Conception." She asked that a chapel be built at the grotto.

After four years of rigid examination the Church finally approved devotion to Our Lady of Lourdes, and a chapel in her honor was built in 1862, and a feast instituted on February 11, the date of the first apparition. In 1870 the Church of Notre Dame was raised to the rank of a minor basilica. The water from the spring has proved effective in healing although analysis has shown it contains no curative properties. The miraculous cures at Lourdes cannot be explained on any natural basis. A great number of the cures occur when the afflicted are blessed with the Sacred Host after the traditional procession of the Blessed Sacrament.

Many pilgrimages are made to Lourdes each year. In order to accommodate the vast throngs, the famed Church of the Rosary was built. Countless faithful who visit Lourdes each year are moved by devotion alone; it is not only the sick and infirm who make their way to the grotto.

LUNA, LUNETTE, LUNULA. A small, usually circular, case which is the receptacle for the Sacred Host. At the time of Benediction the luna is placed in the ostensorium or monstrance. After Benediction the luna is placed in the tabernacle in a capsula or custodial.

M

MADONNA. An Italian word meaning "My Lady"; a title applied to the Blessed Virgin, to pictures and statues of her, and also used in certain devotions to her.

MAGNIFICAT, THE. First Latin word and title of the Song or Canticle of Mary, the Blessed Virgin. The theme is the Mercy, Providence, and Fidelity of God and was most fittingly pronounced by our Blessed Mother in her joyful response to the salutation of her cousin, Elizabeth, whom she had come to visit. The Magnificat is said daily at Vespers and is the last of the Old and first of the New Testament songs.

SUBJECT	BOOK	CHAP.	VERSE	PAGE
Mary's canticle	°Lk	1	46-55	1020
God's mercy	°Lk	1	46-50	1020
His might	°Lk	1	51-53	1020
His fidelity	°Lk	1	54-55	1020

MAJOR ORDERS. The name applied to the three orders of subdeaconship, deaconship, and priesthood. Deaconship and the priesthood are sacraments instituted by Christ. Subdeaconship was classed as a major order during the 12th century. In the Western Church the obligations of daily recitation of the Divine Office and of clerical celibacy are imposed upon all those ordained from subdeacon up.

MANDATUM, THE. A ceremony held in cathedral churches on Holy Thursday, taken from the first word of the initial antiphon in Latin, *Mandatum novum do vobis* (A new commandment I give you). The ceremony consists of the deacon singing the Gospel of the Mass and the prelate washing and kissing the feet of thirteen poor men or others (in monastic churches, the superior washes the feet of thirteen monks). After the choir sings certain antiphons, and the prelate says the Our Father silently and certain versicles, the concluding prayer is: "that as here the outward stains are washed away for us and by us, so the inward sins of us all may be washed away by Thee."

MARIOLOGY. A branch of theology which deals with the life of the Blessed Virgin. It emphasizes her prerogatives as the Mother of God; her importance as a mediatrix; her aid toward our sanctification and salvation; and her relationship with the Incarnation and Redemption.

MARKS OF THE CHURCH. The four distinguishing characteristics of the holy Catholic Church which declare it to be the one true Church founded by Christ. They are its unity, holiness, catholicity, and apostolicity. It has unity, that is, it is one Church because all its members profess the same faith, worship in the same manner, are united with the pope as head, following the will of Christ. It is holy because its purpose is the sanctification of man, again according to Christ's Holy Will. It is universal (catholic) because it is for all men, for all times. It is apostolic because Christ Himself founded it on the Apostles. "I for my part declare to you, you are "Rock," and on this rock I will build my church, and the jaws of death shall not prevail against it." Mt. 16: 18-983

MARTYROLOGY. A liturgical catalogue of martyrs and saints listed according to the calendar and containing a brief resume of their lives and deaths. Pope Gregory XIII issued the first official Roman Martyrology in 1584. Since that time various revisions have been made by his successors.

MARY, FEAST DAYS OF. The Catholic Church honors Mary, the Mother of God in its liturgy many times a year. The principal feasts include the following:

Dec. 8	The Immaculate Conception
Feb. 2	The Purification
Feb. 11	Our Lady of Lourdes
Mar. 25	The Annunciation
Friday of Passion Week	The Seven Sorrows
May 31	The Queenship of Mary
July 2	The Visitation
July 16	Our Lady of Mount Carmel
Aug. 5	Our Lady of the Snow
Aug. 15	The Assumption
Aug. 22	Immaculate Heart of Mary
Sept. 8	The Nativity of Mary
Sept. 12	The Holy Name of Mary
Sept. 15	The Seven Sorrows
Sept. 24	Our Lady of Ransom
Oct. 7	Feast of the Holy Rosary
Oct. 11	The Maternity
Nov. 21	The Presentation of Mary

MARY, SEVEN SORROWS OF. There are seven sorrows which Mary suffered as the Mother of God. They are: (1) the prophecy of Simeon; (2) the flight into Egypt; (3) the loss of Jesus in the Temple at Jerusalem; (4) the meeting of Mary and Jesus on His way to Calvary; (5) Mary standing at the foot of the cross; (6) the removal of Christ's Body from the cross; (7) the burial of Jesus.

In 1817 the devotion to the Seven Sorrows was approved for the Roman Catholic Church. Here in the United States the *Via Dolorosa*, incorporated into the Novena to the Sorrowful Mother, has attained considerable popularity. In addition, the Sorrows of Mary are mediated upon in a Rosary.

MASONRY. The teachings and practices of the secret fraternal order of Free and Accepted Masons, also referred to as Freemasonry. Although its claims to ancient origins are not generally accepted, yet organizations of builders in stone, or "operative masons," existed in the Middle Ages, with rites and symbols very similar to those of modern "speculative masonry," which does not work in stone but retains the rites and spirit of the medieval guilds. The teachings of the order include obedience to the law of the land, and the organization of each country is independent of all others. All higher masonic degrees are based on the three degrees of the Blue Lodge: Entered Apprentice, Fellowcraft, and Master Mason. Higher degrees include those of the Royal Arch Masons, the Knights Templar, and the Scottish Rite Masons. Affiliated organizations include the Order of the Mystic Shrine, to which only those with masonic degrees are eligible; the Order of the Eastern Star, to which women are admitted; and Acacia, for Masons who are college students.

Catholics are forbidden to belong to the Masons. The ultimate aim of Masonry is to establish a society and culture in which God and the supernatural have no part whatsoever. In fact, it is diametrically opposed to Christianity, and professes to represent a naturalistic religion that accepts nothing of what God has revealed in Scripture and tradition. Since Freemasonry has been hostile to the Church ever since the fraternity was founded, the organization was condemned in 1738 by Pope Clement XII. The majority of American Masons advance no higher than the third degree and do not understand the real aims and purposes of the organization.

MASS. The unbloody sacrifice of the Body and Blood of Christ, the renewal of Our Lord's sacrifice upon the cross at Calvary. The priest, as the representative of Christ, takes His place and offers to God bread and wine which he then changes into the Body and Blood of Christ at the Consecration. The sacrifice is brought to completion with the consumption of the Sacred Species in accordance with Christ's instructions.

The Mass is the highest act of worship in the Catholic Church. Certain ceremonies and prayers are prescribed by the Church and are followed universally, varying slightly only in Rite. The name is derived from the Latin word, *missa* (dismissal), as first used by the priest in dismissing the catechumens and today in the *Ite missa est* which is said before the Last Gospel.

According to present Church Law, no priest may say more than one Mass a day except on All Soul's Day and Christmas, unless he has received special permission from his bishop (see *Bination*) or an apostolic indult. Although priests are not obliged to say Mass daily, it has become the custom to do so. According to Canon Law, each priest must offer the Holy Sacrifice several times a year. Whenever the faithful must hear Mass (Sundays and Holy Days of Obligation), a parish priest is under obligation to say it.

Ordinarily, Mass must be said on a consecrated altar, or altar stone, in a church or public oratory. However, under extraordinary conditions, ecclesiastical permission may be given to say Mass in another decent place. For instance, when a new parish is being formed, permission may be granted to say Mass in a hall or other auditorium until a church can be erected. Military chaplains may say Mass on portable altars in any decent place. At sea, however, Mass may be celebrated only by cardinals or bishops or by a priest who has received special permission to do so.

Since the 3rd century the official language of the Roman Rite has been Latin. Before that time Greek was used. It still is found in the *Kyrie*, the *Improperia*, and the Epistle and Gospel of a Papal Mass. In the Eastern Rites the liturgical languages include Arabic, Armenian, Coptic, Ethiopian, Greek, Georgian, Hungarian, Rumanian, and Syriac.

The Holy Sacrifice of the Mass is offered for four purposes: (1) to worship and to give glory to God; (2) to give thanks to

SUBJECT	BOOK	CHAP.	VERSE	PAGE

Him for all His benefits; (3) to seek and to obtain pardon for our sins; (4) through Christ the Son to obtain countless other graces.

MASS, OBLIGATION OF HEARING. All Catholics who have reached their seventh birthday and have the use of reason are obliged, under pain of mortal sin, to hear Mass on all Sundays and Holy Days of Obligation. They must be: (1) present bodily (2) at the entire Mass (3) paying sufficient attention to the Holy Sacrifice and (4) must have the correct intention. To be present bodily means they must either be inside the church or a member of the group outside (if the church is crowded and some of the congregation are forced to remain outside). The obligation to hear Mass is not fulfilled by listening to it over the radio or watching it on television. Each Catholic is obliged to hear the entire Mass, from the prayers at the foot of the altar, to the end. A venial sin is committed if a small part of the Mass is missed through one's own fault. If a large part of the Mass is missed (including any or all of the three principal parts, Offertory, Consecration, or Communion) through one's own fault, a mortal sin is committed. Adequate attention means the individual should be conscious of the fact he is attending Mass and should not be asleep. The purpose of the Mass is to worship God; therefore each individual should attend with the intention of paying homage to Him.

Any Catholic who is confined by illness is excused from attending Mass. Likewise, those who attend the sick or small children may be excused if their presence at Mass means their charges would be left unattended.

MASS, TYPES OF.
Pontifical Mass: A Solemn High Mass celebrated by a bishop assisted by a priest, a deacon (one or more), and a subdeacon. The celebrant remains at his throne from the Introit to the Offertory. At the end of the Mass he says the Last Gospel while returning to his throne or to the sacristy.
Papal Mass: A Pontifical High Mass celebrated by the Pope. A few differences between a Pontifical and Papal Mass are: (1) The Epistle and Gospel are sung both in Greek and Latin; (2) At the Consecration, the elevated Host and Chalice are moved in a half circle, instead of being raised only; (3) the deacon and subdeacon receive under both species.
Conventual: A Mass celebrated daily at a time and in a manner prescribed by Church Law in cathedral and college churches, and in the churches of those religious who are obliged to recite the canonical hours in choir.
Parochial: The *missa pro populo.* The Mass which all pastors and certain other ecclesiastics must offer for the members of their parishes and souls under their care every Sunday of the year and certain other days. If the pastor is unable to offer the Mass, someone else must do it for him.
Nuptial: A special Mass celebrated for marriages. The special Nuptial Blessing is given after the *Pater Noster* and before the last blessing of the Mass. No nuptial Masses can be celebrated during Advent and Lent.
Red Mass: The Votive Mass of the Holy Spirit which is offered each year in some dioceses for the special benefit of Catholic judges and lawyers.
Requiem: One offered at a funeral or in commemoration of a deceased person.
Votive: A Mass which does not conform to the office of the day, but which is said according to the wishes (*votum*) of the celebrant or of the person for whose intention it is being offered.

MASS OF THE CATECHUMENS. That part of the Mass from the beginning up to the Offertory. In the early days of the Church the catechumens were permitted to hear that part only. Not until they were baptized and had made their First Communion could they assist at the entire Mass.

MASS OF THE FAITHFUL. The Mass from the Offertory to the end, including the Consecration and the Communion. During the early days of Christianity and the Church, only the baptized were permitted to assist at the entire Mass. The catechumens were dismissed before the Offertory.

MASTER OF NOVICES. One who trains novices of a religious order or congregation. He must be a highly qualified person at least thirty-five years of age and a religious for at least ten years. He must be pious, charitable, and faithfully observant of his society's rules.

SUBJECT	BOOK	CHAP.	VERSE	PAGE

MATINS. The name given the first and longest part of the Divine Office. Derived from the Latin word *matutinum,* meaning "morning," it consists of psalms and readings which formerly were recited very early in the morning and are still recited very early by some monastic groups.

MATRIMONY. Matrimony is the sacrament instituted by Christ by which a Christian man and a Christian woman are united as husband and wife and are given sufficient grace to fulfill the duties of the married state. The word matrimony means motherhood, the prime purpose of marriage being the conception, birth, and rearing of children. The second purpose of marriage is the mutual help and affection of the married couple and the satisfaction of their legitimate desires.

Obligations of: A husband and wife are bound to each other under pain of mortal sin in the following ways: (1) a husband is bound to suitably support his wife. If he is rich, she should share his wealth; if he is poor, she should be willing to share his poverty; (2) a wife must submit to her husband as head of the household. St. Paul, in the Epistle to the Ephesians, says, "Wives should be submissive to their husbands as if to the Lord because the husband is head of his wife just as Christ is head of his body the church, as well as its savior. As the church submits to Christ, so wives should submit to their husbands in everything." In the same Epistle husbands are commanded, "Husbands, love your wives, as Christ loved the church."

The actual graces bestowed upon the subjects enable them to properly discharge their duties, giving them constant help to lead holy lives and ultimately to save their souls.

Wives subject to husbands	°Eph	5	22-24	1160
Husbands love wives	°Eph	5	25	1160

Duties to Children: As parents, both husband and wife are strictly bound to provide for the physical and spiritual needs of their children. The home should be a haven of peace and holiness, not just a place to eat and sleep. Parents have a serious obligation to bring up their children in the fear and love of God, giving them a Catholic education: in short, helping their children to save their souls. God, in His goodness, gives parents the aid they need to carry this heavy responsibility. Through fervent and constant prayer He will increase His graces and help.

Unity and Dissolubility: By unity of marriage we mean there can be but one man and one woman as partners in each contract. Both polygamy (having two or more wives at the same time) and polyandry (having two or more husbands at the same time) are forbidden. Most pagans regarded polyandry as an abomination. While polygamy was tolerated under the imperfect Mosaic Law, it was abolished by Christ when He told the Pharisees, "I now say to you, whoever divorces his wife (lude conduct is a separate case) and marries another commits adultery, and the man who marries a divorced woman commits adultery."

The bonds of valid marriage cannot be broken either by the contracting parties themselves or by any other human being. Christ Himself explicitly commanded, "Have you not read that at the beginning the Creator made them male and female and declared, 'For this reason a man shall leave his father and mother and cling to his wife, and the two shall become as one'? . . . "Therefore, let no man separate what God has joined." They said to him, "Then why did Moses command divorce' . . . "Because of your stubbornness Moses let you divorce your wives," He replied; "but at the beginning it was not that way." With those words Our Lord abolished the permission for divorce given under the old Mosaic Law.

The church, as the representative of Christ, does not have the power to dissolve any valid marriage, if the parties have lived together as man and wife. For certain very serious reasons she can grant a separation of husband and wife, but this separation does not give either party permission to remarry within the lifetime of the other. A few causes which would justify the seeking of a separation are: living a criminal or ignominious life; causing grave danger to soul or body of the partner; habitual drunkenness; adultery. Pope Eugene IV (1421–47) in his *Decretum Pro Armenis* said, "Though it be allowed, because of fornication, to obtain a separation, it is not permissible to contract a new marriage, because the bond of lawful wedlock is perpetual."

Occasionally the Holy See may decide, after extremely careful and detailed examination, that a supposedly valid marriage actually was not so. In such cases the Church issues a declaration of invalidity; that is, a declaration that, from the beginning, because of the absence of some condition essential to validity, there never was a valid marriage in that particular case.

Pauline Privilege: A marriage between unbaptized persons is not a sacrament. However, if one of the parties becomes a Catholic, he or she then is free, under certain conditions, to contract a sacramental marriage with a Catholic, and the non-sacramental marriage is dissolved. It must be noted that it is more fitting that the convert marry a Catholic and not just a Christian, but it is possible by dispensation to marry a non-Catholic. Before this privilege can be invoked, the Catholic party must inquire of the other (1) whether he or she would be willing to become a Catholic too, and, if not, (2) whether he or she would promise to live in harmonious wedlock without insulting the Catholic religion or interfering with the other party's practice of it. Only when the unbaptized partner replies negatively to *both* questions can the Pauline Privilege be invoked.

This is called the Pauline Privilege because St. Paul wrote about it to the Corinthians, explaining that he was not quoting the direct words of Christ but was speaking as an Apostle of Christ with His authority. Thus, under the Pauline Privilege, it is God who dissolves the non-sacramental marriage, and not man.

SUBJECT	BOOK	CHAP.	VERSE	PAGE
Polygamy abolished	°Mk	10	11-12	1009
	Lk	16	18	1038
Divorce forbidden	°Mt	19	6-8	986
Pauline Privilege	°1 Cor	7	12-16	1133
Instituted by God	°Gn	2	18-25	2
	Mt	19	3-6	986
Purpose to propagate race	°Gn	1	27-28	2
	Ps.	127	3	586
A life-time union	°Prv	5	15-20	604
	Eccl	9	9	635
	Eph	5	21-24	1160
Faithfulness and purity	°Ex	20	14, 17	62
required	Dt	22	22	159
	1 Cor	7	1-5	1133
Rules governing marriage:				
Preceded by betrothal	°Gn	29	18-20	25
	Lk	1	26-27	1020
Parent's consent required	°Gn	24	50-51	19
Binding for life	°Rom	7	2-3	1121

MAUNDY THURSDAY. Another name given to Holy Thursday of Holy Week. A part of the liturgy of that day consists of the ceremony of the washing of the feet. Maundy is derived from *mandatum* (commandment), the first word of the first antiphon sung during this ceremony.

MEDAL. A piece of metal or plastic on which has been impressed a representation of Our Lord, the Blessed Virgin Mary, or of the saints. Medals are sacramentals of the Church and serve to remind us of those they represent and inspire us to invoke their protection or aid. We must remember that the primary purpose of a blessed medal is the spiritual welfare of the wearer. Sometimes this best can be attained by physical suffering or through trial.

MEDAL, MIRACULOUS. The medal struck in obedience to the Blessed Virgin Mary when she appeared to St. Catherine Laboure, a novice of the Daughters of Charity of St. Vincent de Paul in 1830 in Paris, France. In one apparition the Blessed Virgin appeared, standing on a globe while dazzling rays of light were emitted from her hands. These rays were a "symbol of the graces I send upon those who ask for them." An oval frame appeared around the figure and bore the following inscription in gold lettering. "O Mary, conceived without sin, pray for us who have recourse to thee." As the vision reversed, there was shown the letter M surmounted by a cross and twelve stars. The Sacred Hearts of Jesus and Mary appeared below. Our Lady commanded that a medal be fashioned like the apparition and promised great favors to all who would wear it.

In 1832, with ecclesiastical approval, the first medal was made. Devotion to it spread rapidly, and various indulgences have been attached to it. The Feast of the Miraculous Medal is observed on November 27 and novenas and other devotions in its honor are held throughout the world.

MEDIATOR DEI. *Mediator of God.* Title of an encyclical issued by Pope Pius XII in 1947 on the sacred liturgy. It defines and regulates the sacred liturgy of the Church, explains at length the true purpose of the Mass and the Holy Eucharist,

emphasizes the method in which the laity should assist at Mass, and encourages the people to frequent reception of the Holy Eucharist in order to partake more fully in the fruits of the Mass. The Divine Office is defined, and the laity encouraged to recite the same prayers as a means of fostering piety. Pope Pius XII explains the purpose and meaning of the Liturgical Cycle and the Liturgical Apostolate, and deals at length with the importance of private devotions, suggesting approved ones and cautioning against pitfalls to be avoided.

MEDIATRIX OF ALL GRACES. The title given to the Blessed Virgin Mary because she, as the Mother of God, acts as the intercessor between Christ and man and becomes the channel through which all graces given to man are dispensed. Christ is the only true Mediator between God and man. Mary's role is that of secondary or intercessory mediatrix, but theologians teach that she intercedes for each grace given to us by Christ.

MEMORARE, THE. The prayer to the Blessed Virgin Mary, beginning with the Latin word, *Memorare.* Attributed to St. Bernard by tradition, this prayer expresses complete trust in the Blessed Mother.

The Memorare

"Remember, O most gracious Virgin Mary, that never was it known that any one who fled to thy protection, implored thy help, or sought thy intercession, was left unaided. Inspired by this confidence, I fly unto thee, O Virgin of virgins, my Mother; to thee I come, before thee I stand, sinful and sorrowful; O Mother of the Word Incarnate, despise not my petitions, but in thy mercy hear and answer me. Amen."

MENDICANTS. Friars of the Augustinian, Carmelite, Dominican, and Franciscan Orders who depended upon begging for their main support. Their members as individuals were bound by the vow of poverty; in addition, the orders as such also renounced ownership of property. The Council of Trent changed the rules of these orders and now, in common they may possess property. The Friars Minor and Capuchins are two exceptions to this rule. However, the name *mendicant* still is applied to all of the above-named orders.

METHODISM. This movement started originally in England in 1739 by John Wesley (1703-1791) to induce members of the Anglican Church to seek a higher spiritual life. His teachings were aimed at greater personal holiness of his followers, and with his brother, Charles, he organized into groups for that purpose. However, before his death these groups broke away from the Church of England and developed into several denominations. Today there are 21 bodies of Methodism which follow modified forms of episcopal, congregational, and presbyterian systems, and serve about 12,000,000 members.

The principal doctrines of Methodism are: (1) the belief that the Bible is the sole rule of faith; (2) salvation is assured those who have faith and cooperate with God's graces; (3) baptism (one of the two sacraments retained) does not produce sanctifying grace but only increases faith; (4) the Eucharist (the second sacrament observed) is retained but merely as a memorial to the passion and death of Christ; (5) the existence of purgatory is denied.

METROPOLITAN. In the Western Church, the title given an archbishop who rules not only his own archdiocese but also has jurisdiction, strictly limited by law, over the bishops of suffragan sees within his ecclesiastical province. Although a metropolitan is an archbishop, it does not follow that each archbishop is a metropolitan; the titles are not synonymous.

In the Catholic Eastern Churches archbishops often call themselves Metropolitans even though they have no suffragan sees under them.

MINISTERS OF THE SACRAMENTS. One who has the power to validity administer a Sacrament. Since sacraments are external rites, they must be administered by visible ministers who act with authority bestowed by Christ Himself. In order for a sacrament to be valid, the authorized ministers must use the correct rite and have the proper intention, expressed or implied, of administering it in accordance with the teachings of the Catholic Church. Lawfully, he should have faith and should be in the state of grace, but the validity of the sacrament is not affected by the absence of either.

The priest is the ordinary minister of Baptism, Holy Eucharist, Penance, and Extreme Unction. In cases of emergency when no priest is available, a layman can administer Baptism. Deacons are also ordinary ministers of the Eucharist in the distribution of it. Some dioceses now permit laymen and women to aid in the distribution. The bishop is the minister of Confirmation and Holy Orders. In Matrimony the priest acts as the Church's appointed and official witness; the contracting couple are the ministers and subjects, each party administering the sacrament to the other.

MINOR ORDERS. The four lower ranks which constitute preparation for major orders and ultimate priesthood. They are: porter, reader or lector, exorcist, and acolyte. In the early days of the Church these titles were conferred upon Church officials who had specific duties to perform. Today, however, they are merely steps leading toward the priesthood, and although only seminarians now can receive minor orders, even they seldom exercise the rights of their rank.

MISERERE, THE. The first word of the Vulgate text of Psalm 1: (*Miserere mei Deus, secundum magnam misericordiam tuam.*) Have mercy on me, O God, according to thy great mercy. The Miserere has a most prominent place in the Divine Office and in various ceremonies: at Lauds, at the end of Tenebrae, in the consecration of a church, at burials, in reconciling a profaned church, and at numerous other times. In some Jewish rituals the Miserere is recited on the Day of Atonement.

SUBJECT	BOOK	CHAP.	VERSE	PAGE
First word and title of	*Ps	51	1	528

MISSAL. A book containing the prayers for mass. Those containing such prayers for periods such as a day, week, or month are sometimes called MISSALLETTES.

MODERNISM. Described by Pius X as a "synthesis of all heresies," and condemned in the decree "Lamentabili" and the encyclical "Pascendi" (1907). Modernism strives to destroy the objective validity of religious belief, making it the product of the human soul, not of supernatural revelation. This heresy, which denies the divinity of Christ and rejects the authority of His Church, is particularly treacherous because it usurps Catholic terms to which it attributes new and false meanings.

MONASTERY. The permanent residence of a community of monks, canons regular, and nuns. The term is also applied to houses of friars and congregations such as the Passionists, Redemptorists, but never of the Jesuits. Generally, at least twelve religious must live in a monastery and permission of the bishop is always required. In certain countries, permission must also be secured from the Holy See. As a rule, the monastery consists of a church, cloisters, chapterhouse, refectory, dormitory, the superior's quarters, library, work rooms, guest rooms, and parlors for visitors. The medieval monastery played a most important part in the preservation of civilization during the Middle Ages. Oftentimes, the poor, the feeble, and the peace-loving found their only refuge in a monastery.

MONASTICISM. The religious life based on withdrawal from the world is the basis of monasticism. It is defined by Abbot Butler, O.S.B., as "a community of monks, bound to live together until death, under rule, in common life, in the monastery of their profession, as a religious family, leading a life not of marked austerity, but devoted to the service of God." The origin of monasticism is undetermined, but long before Christianity, religious individuals were drawn together and lived apart from the world. Monasticism is known in the great Oriental religions, especially Buddhism. One great exception, however, is Judaism.

MONKS. Members of a community of men living apart from the world in a monastery. They lead a life of contemplation in accordance with the order to which they belong under strict vows of poverty, chastity, and obedience. Generally, monks remain in the monastery, whereas friars usually work outside the friary, which is their residence. In the United States, however, many monks also work outside their monastery and carry on their activities very much like friars. The chief orders of monks are the Benedictines, Carthusians, Premonstratensians, and the Camaldolese.

MONOPHYSITISM. A heresy of the 5th and 6th centuries, so called from the belief that there was in Christ only one nature. It was condemned by the Council of Chalcedon (451), but it became very powerful in Palestine, Egypt, and Syria. Although Justinian I tried to heal the schism by calling the Second Council of Constantinople (A.D. 553), it continued to be dominant in Armenia, Ethiopia, and Mesopotamia. The title *Jacobites* is sometimes given to this sect, and is taken from the name of one of its leaders, Jacob el-Baradai. Monophysitism is still a strong factor in the Greek Church.

MONSIGNOR. *my lord.* A title used in addressing those who have received certain papal honors. In English speaking areas, the title *Monsignor* is used for those priests who have been given recognition. Thus, it is a title which carries no jurisdiction with it; it is simply honorary.

MONSTRANCE. A container in which the Blessed Sacrament is exposed to the faithful at Benediction and Exposition. It is similar to an enclosed chalice with a broad base, a stem, and a closed glass or crystal receptacle, within which the Host is fixed for visibility, and which is usually surrounded by metal rays of silver or gold, surmounted by a cross.

MORTAL SIN. A serious offense against the Law of God, and it is called *mortal* because the soul becomes "dead" to sanctifying grace and subject to the eternal punishments and death of hell. The conditions necessary for commission of a mortal sin are: serious matter, sufficient reflection, and full consent of the will. Thus, the violation must be grave, such as murder, blasphemy, or serious theft; the individual must realize the gravity of the situation; and the will must be free to choose the bad deed.

MORTIFICATION. Acts of self-denial; hardships, austerities, and penances undergone for progress in virtue.

SUBJECT	BOOK	CHAP.	VERSE	PAGE
Crucified with Christ in baptism	*Rom	6	4-6	1120
Necessary	*Mt	5	29	970
	Rom	8	12-13	1122
	Gal	5	24	1155
	Col	3	5	1170
	1 Pt	2	11	1212
	1 Cor	9	27	1135
Christ, our example	*Heb	12	1-2	1203

MOVABLE FEASTS. Those feasts whose dates depend on the paschal moon, beginning with Easter; and those feasts in turn depending on Easter, namely, the Ascension, Pentecost, the Holy Trinity, and Corpus Christi. Other kinds of movable feasts are those which fall on a certain Sunday, such as Christ the King on the last Sunday in October. Then there are those feasts which fall on a certain weekday after a Sunday has been determined by the date of Easter.

MUSIC, LITURGICAL. That which is suitable by style, composition, and manner of execution for use in the official and public services of the Church. The basis and most highly regarded standard of liturgical music is the plain vocal chant. An instrument may be used to sustain the chant, but extensive instrumental accompaniment is not desirable.

N

NAILS, HOLY. The nails with which Our Lord was fastened to the cross. According to tradition, St. Helena discovered the true Holy Cross and the nails after it had been hidden and buried by infidels for 180 years. History differs on the number of nails used. Several early writers claimed only two or three were used. Saint Gregory de Tours said four were used, each foot being nailed separately. Today relics claiming to be the original nails are venerated in various churches throughout the world, but the Catholic Church has not declared any authentic.

SUBJECT	BOOK	CHAP.	VERSE	PAGE
Nails used to crucify Christ	*Jn	20	25	1080
	Col	2	14	1170

NARBERTH MOVEMENT. In 1929 a small group of men from St. Margaret's Parish at Narberth, Pennsylvania, organized a lay apologetical movement in response to the Pope's plea for more Catholic Action. Forming a committee of seven with their pastor as censor, they were inaugurated under the title, Catholic Information Society of Narberth.

Led by Karl Rogers (d. 1942), this group sent pamphlets to non-Catholic neighbors, explaining the purpose of the Society. Each short leaflet was intended to be read in two minutes and contained information about various practices or beliefs of the Catholic Church which are most often misunderstood. No article was a condemnation of Protestant beliefs; all were friendly, courteous, always informative but never compromising. At the conclusion of each leaflet, the readers were invited to write for an explanation of any other Catholic practice or belief.

Today, the National Council of Catholic Men has taken over the promotion and extension of this service, and there are Catholic Information Societies throughout the United States. The

SUBJECT   BOOK   CHAP.   VERSE   PAGE

master leaflet copy is obtained from the National Council of Catholic Men, and each group then has its leaflets printed locally. In addition, over 300 lay groups are publishing Narberth literature in their local secular papers as free feature articles. It has been estimated this information now reaches over 2,500,000 people and has done much to promote good will and an understanding of Catholicism.

NATIONAL CATHOLIC COMMUNITY SERVICE. In November, 1940, the Catholic hierarchy in the United States established the N.C.C.S. as the Church's official agency to serve the spiritual, educational, recreational, and welfare needs of members of the armed forces, patients in Veterans' hospitals, civilians working on defense projects and their families. When the United Service Organizations (USO) was formed, the N.C.C.S. became affiliated with it; then, when the USO was discontinued in December, 1947, the N.C.C.S. not only continued but also expanded nationally. Each time the USO was re-activated, the N.C.C.S. worked with it, relying greatly upon the National Council of Catholic Women and the National Council of Catholic Men to help coordinate and to promote their interests. The N.C.C.S. functions under a Board of Trustees comprised of archbishops and bishops who are members of the Administrative Board of the National Catholic Welfare Conference, plus the Military Vicar of the Army and Navy Ordinariate and his Military Delegate. In addition there is a Governing Committee, an Executive Committee and a National Staff serving under an Executive Director.

NATIONAL CATHOLIC CONFERENCE. This is a voluntary organization of the bishops of the United States for the purpose of unifying and coordinating as well as organizing the efforts of the American Catholics in education, social welfare, immigrant aid, and various other national activities. It is not a legislative body. Its founders stated, "We have grouped together, under the N.C.C. the various agencies by which the cause of religion is furthered. Each of these, continuing its own special work in its chosen field, will now derive additional support through general cooperation."

NATIONAL CATHOLIC RURAL LIFE CONFERENCE. In order to strengthen Catholicity in rural areas and to promote the general welfare of the rural population, the late Bishop Edwin V. O'Hara led Catholic rural leaders into forming this conference. Today among its more than 10,000 members are rural pastors, teachers, sociologists, agricultural agents, and officials, farmers, and economists. Its national headquarters are in Des Moines, Iowa, and there are local directors in almost every diocese in the United States.

Since about 80 per cent of American Catholics live in cities, Catholic life in rural areas has suffered. The N.C.R.L.C., therefore, has as its aims: 1. to care for underprivileged Catholics who live on the land; 2. to keep on the land the Catholics who are there; 3. to settle more Catholics on the land; 4. to convert the non-Catholics there. To accomplish its aim, this organization sponsors rural institutes and schools, furnishes study club material, provides speakers, and supplies information on land settlement and other rural subjects. The Conference also keeps a watchful eye on proposed farm legislation, and publishes books and leaflets on subjects related to rural family life.

Each year at the bishops' meeting in Washington, D.C., an Administration Board of ten archbishops and bishops is elected. Under the members of this board function eight departments of the N.C.C. In addition, there are Bishops' Special Committees which were set up to meet particular national problems.

NATIVITY. The feast day celebrating the natural birth of Jesus. It is another name for Christmas, December 25th.

NATIVITY OF THE BLESSED VIRGIN MARY. The feast day, September 8, on which the birth of the Blessed Virgin is commemorated. This is nine months following the date of the Immaculate Conception, December 8.

NATURAL LAW. Rules for ethical moral conduct which God has implanted in the rational nature of man (as opposed to supernatural revelations by the Almighty which constitute the positive law). By obeying these laws, man naturally tends toward God as his rightful end.

NATURAL THEOLOGY. That branch of philosophy which establishes the existence of God, His main attributes, and His relations to the world by arguments from reason alone, with no references to any written revelations. Its subject matter is God

SUBJECT   BOOK   CHAP.   VERSE   PAGE

as He can be known through human reason. It does not refute revelation as a source of knowledge of the Divine; it merely makes no use of it in compiling its data. In effect, natural theology provides the rational foundation for human belief in divine revelation. If, through natural theology, the actual existence of God can be proved, then the divine revelations can be accepted as the Word of God.

NATURALISM. The tendency to look upon nature as the one original and fundamental source of all that exists, thus attempting to explain everything in terms of nature. It denies the possibility of any transitory intervention of God in nature, and of any revelation and permanent supernatural order for man. In general naturalism contradicts the most vital doctrines of the Church, which rest essentially on supernaturalism.

NAVE. That part of the church in which the faithful kneel and assist at services. The name is derived from the Latin word, *navis*, meaning "ship," and given to the church because of the usual shape of that section.

NE TEMERE. The first two words (Latin, *lest rashly*) of the papal decree issued in 1907 by Pope St. Pius X, stating that all marriages of baptized Catholics must take place before a parish priest in his own parish, or before a bishop in his own diocese, or by a priest delegated by either; must be solemnized in the presence of at least two witnesses; must be registered in the baptismal churches of the couple married. The present day Code of Canon Law which became effective in 1918 adopted the Ne Temere decree with only slight changes.

NEW FIRE, BLESSING OF. The first of the Holy Saturday ceremonies during which new fire is kindled outside the door or in the vestibule of a church. From this fire the triple candle and the paschal candle are lit. In this ceremony the new fire is symbolic of Christ who is the Light of the World.

NEWMAN CLUB. The official Catholic association in non-Catholic colleges. In 1893 five Catholic students at the University of Pennsylvania formed the first club. Similar clubs in other universities were organized and finally affiliated into the Newman Club Federation. Today this federation is a member of the National Catholic Youth Council under the N.C.W.C. Youth Department. Its purpose is to assist young Catholic men and women who are attending secular schools to apply Christian principles to their college training. Spiritually, they are aided by chaplains, and discussion groups are encouraged. A monthly letter, "Newman Newsnotes," is published along with various information bulletins and reports. The national headquarters of the Newman Club are in Washington, D. C.

NICENE COUNCILS. The two general councils held in Nicaea, the first in 325 A.D., the second in 787 A.D. The first council condemned the Arian heresy which taught that the Son, Christ, was inferior to God the Father. It also formulated the Nicene Creed. The second Council condemned the iconoclast heresy which rejected veneration of all relics and images, even those of Christ and the Blessed Mother.

NICENE CREED. The first General Council of Nicaea met in 325 A.D. to refute the heretical theories of Arius. In addition the council formulated a summary of Catholic beliefs which is known as the Nicene Creed. Originally the creed did not contain the phrase *filioque* in the passage, "I believe in the Holy Spirit, the Lord and giver of life, who proceeds from the Father *and from the son.*" In the 4th and 5th centuries this phrase, actually an established article of faith, began to appear. The Greeks refused to accept it, and it finally became one of the principal issues in the Eastern schism.

NIHIL OBSTAT. A Latin phrase which means *nothing hinders.* The phrase is printed in the front of a book which indicates it has been examined by an ecclesiastical censor who has found nothing in the publication which would be contrary to faith or morals.

NIMBUS. A circle or halo of light which surround the head of Christ or of one of the saints in pictures, etc. The use of the nimbus is restricted to those worthy of veneration, since it is symbolic of grace and virtue.

NINE FIRST FRIDAYS. A popular devotion to the Sacred Heart of Jesus which was begun in the 17th century. Christ Himself revealed this devotion to St. Margaret Mary Alacoque at the Visitation Monastery of Paray-le-Monial, France, in a

SUBJECT	BOOK	CHAP.	VERSE	PAGE

series of apparitions, during which He made twelve promises to those who would pay homage to Him in His Sacred Heart.

St. Margaret Mary quotes Our Divine Saviour in these words, "I promise thee in the excessive mercy of My Heart that my all-powerful love will grant to all those who receive Holy Communion on the First Friday of nine consecutive months the grace of final penitence; they shall not die in My disgrace nor without receiving their Sacraments; My Divine Heart shall be their safe refuge in this last moment."

The Catholic Church has approved this devotion even though the revelations were privately made. Theologians teach that the words "their Sacraments" do not necessarily mean the individual will receive the Last Sacraments at the hour of death. Rather, they teach that the Sacred Heart promises that all those who duly fulfill the specified conditions will receive whatever Sacraments may be necessary to put them in the state of grace before death. As further proof of the Church's acceptance of the promises as authentic, the complete text of the Great Promise was inserted in the Bull of Canonization of St. Margaret Mary.

NODE. On a chalice, the knob in the stem between the base and the cup is called a node. Its purpose is to enable the priest to grasp the chalice more securely.

NONE. Literally, "the ninth." The hour of the Divine Office formerly said at the ninth hour, between noon and three in the afternoon. Traditionally it commemorates the death of Christ which occurred between noon and three o'clock.

NOTRE DAME. *Our Lady.* The French words meaning *Our Lady.* It is frequently used in the name for a church dedicated to the Blessed Virgin, such as Notre Dame de Paris. In the United States, possibly, the most famous is the University of Notre Dame.

NOVATIANISM. A heresy which was begun by Novatian, a 3rd century anti-pope. Its followers believed the Church had no power to forgive sins of idolatry and sometimes sins of murder, adultery, fornication, and similar offenses. This heresy existed until about the 7th century.

NOVENA. Nine days of public or private prayer made in preparation for a feast or for special graces. This is in imitation of the Apostles who prayed for nine days from Ascension Thursday to the day of the descent of the Holy Spirit, Pentecost.

There are countless other novenas which are conducted publicly or which may be said privately in honor of the Sacred Heart, the Blessed Mother, or of various saints.

NOVICE. The name given to a candidate for a religious community during one stage of his or her probation. One who enters such a community must first spend a short period of time as a postulant. Then he or she becomes a novice for a prescribed period (at least a year). During this time the candidate is free to leave the community since no vows are taken. A modified form of a habit usually distinguishes the novice during this period. At the end of the prescribed time the candidate is professed, that is, takes either simple or solemn vows, accepting the rules of the order.

NOVITIATE. The probation period during which a candidate is a novice. It also refers to the place where a novice spends his period of probation in preparation for the profession of vows in a religious community.

NULLITY, DECREE OF. The declaration by a competent ecclesiastical court that a marriage was invalid and therefore null or non-existent. Some of the diriment or nullifying impediments which would constitute grounds for a decree of nullity are: 1. Impediment of age; 2. impediment of impotency; 3. impediment of an existing bond; 4. impediment of disparity of worship; 5. impediment of Sacred Orders; 6. impediment of religious profession; 7. impediment of abduction; 8. impediment of crime; 9. impediment of relationship; 10. impediment of public honesty.

Whenever a decree of nullity is sought, the ecclesiastical court must examine the particular facts of each individual case and proof of any impediment is essential.

NUN. Strictly, a woman who belongs to a religious order or community and who has taken solemn vows. Properly, one who has taken only simple vows is called a *sister.*

NUNC DIMITTIS. *Now do you dismiss.* These are the first two words in the Latin version of the Canticle of Simeon, the prayer he said when the Blessed Virgin presented Jesus at the Temple. It reads, "Now, Master, you can dismiss your servant

in peace; you have fulfilled your word. For my eyes have witnessed your saving deed displayed for all the peoples to see."

Daily, it is said at Compline in the Divine Office; during the distribution of blessed candles on the Feast of the Purification of the Blessed Virgin (February 2) it is sung; if the Feast of the Purification falls after Septuagesima, it is used as the tract of the Mass.

Prayer of Simeon	°Lk	2	29-32	1022

NUNCIO. An official papal legate sent by the Holy See to a foreign government as its ambassador. He handles all diplomatic affairs between the Holy See and the civil government.

NUPTIAL MASS AND BLESSING. A special Mass for marriages which may be said except during Lent and Advent. The Mass has for its theme the unity, indissolubility, and holiness of the marriage state, and appropriate readings are part of the ceremony. The Nuptial Blessing is given after the Lord's Prayer of the Mass.

Because the Nuptial Mass and Blessing bestow such essential graces upon the bride and groom, the church strongly urges all couples to take advantage of the help God offers through them.

O

OBLATES. 1. Name given some religious congregations organized for a specific purpose, such as missionary work, or congregations of secular priests who serve their local bishop in whatever capacity he assigns. Some examples are the Oblates of Mary Immaculate (priests and lay brothers), Oblates of St. Charles (priests), Oblates of St. Francis de Sales (priests), Oblates of the Immaculate Conception (sisters), and Oblates of the Sacred Heart of Jesus (sisters).

2. A lay person who follows a partial religious rule while living in the world.

OBLATION. 1. The offering of bread and wine to God in the Mass.

2. The gift of a sacrifice which is offered to God.

OBLIGATION, HOLY DAYS OF. Days on which all Catholics are bound under pain of mortal sin to hear Mass. In the United States these are: all Sundays, Christmas Day (December 25), the Circumcision (January 1), Ascension Thursday (forty days after Easter), the Assumption (August 15), All Saints' Day (November 1), the Immaculate Conception (December 8). In Canada, the Feast of the Epiphany (January 6) is observed as a Holy Day of Obligation.

OCTAVE. The continued celebration of certain major feasts such as Easter for eight days following the feast itself. The word, octave, is taken from the Latin, *octava dies,* meaning "eighth day."

OCTOBER. The tenth month of the year which is dedicated to the Holy Rosary. In all parish churches and public chapels dedicated to Our Lady, the five decades of the Rosary, Litany of the Blessed Virgin, and a prayer to St. Joseph are recited daily from October 1st to November 2nd. In an encyclical, Pope Leo XIII decreed this public devotion be held either in the morning during Mass, or at evening devotions before the exposed Blessed Sacrament. The seventh day of October is celebrated as the Feast of the Most Holy Rosary.

ODD FELLOWS. A secret society officially known as the Independent Order of Odd Fellows, membership in which is forbidden to Catholics under pain of serious sin. Established in the United States in 1819 as a fraternal organization, its religious ritual and requirement of an oath of secrecy make it one forbidden to Catholics.

OFFERTORY. That part of the Mass immediately following the Creed, and in which the priest offers plain bread and wine to God. It extends to the Preface. In the early days of the Church the faithful, at this time, would make their offerings of bread and wine for the Mass and also their donations for the support of the clergy. Today the faithful no longer bring bread and wine, but it is the custom in most churches to take up the collection at this time.

The Offertory is begun with the Offertory prayer which varies with the day or feast. Then the priest offers up the bread and wine to God as symbols of the Christ who gave up His life for our salvation. He asks God to accept this as yet unconsecrated bread, "Accept, O holy Father, almighty, everlasting

God, this stainless host. . , ." Then raising the chalice containing unconsecrated water and wine he says, "We offer unto thee, O Lord, the chalice of salvation. . . ."

Thus the Offertory (one of the three principal parts of the Mass) anticipates and becomes a preparation for the Canon of the Mass during which this same bread and wine will be changed into the Body and Blood of Our Lord.

OFFICE DIVINE. A prayer which the Catholic Church requires that all the clergy in major orders and all solemnly professed religious recite daily. A liturgical book called the Breviary contains the Divine Office which consists of hymns, prayers, psalms, readings from the Bible and from various Doctors and Fathers of the Church. These vary with the feast or the season.

Saying of the Divine Office is not restricted to those in religious orders. The laity are encouraged to recite it daily as one of the best means of fostering piety. To promote this practice, the League of the Divine Office was formed. Its members aspire to the daily recitation of at least a part each day.

OFFICE OF THE B.V.M., LITTLE. A short office honoring the Blessed Virgin Mary. Although it follows the canonical hours in form, it does not change with the church seasons, except that the Alleluia is omitted during Lent, and from Advent to the Purification a change is made. Many religious communities recite this Little Office daily.

OFFICE OF THE DEAD. A special office which is offered for the repose of a departed soul. All who are required to say the Divine Office recite this on All Souls' Day, November 2nd.

OIL OF CATECHUMENS. *Oleum sanctum* (holy oil). One of the three holy oils blessed by the bishop on Holy Thursday. It is olive oil and is used in the sacrament of Baptism, in the blessing of a baptismal font, in the ceremonies of Holy Orders, in consecrating altars and churches, and in the coronation and blessing ceremonies of Catholic kings and queens. The oil of catechumens (and the other two holy oils) must be kept in vessels of silver or alloyed metals. Oils from previous years may not be used, but when the current supply is low, a small amount of common oil may be added to extend the amount until the new supply is blessed.

OIL OF CHRISM. One of the three holy oils, but the only one which consists of olive oil mixed with balm. The olive oil signifies fullness of grace, and the balm signifies incorruption. Chrism is used in administering the sacraments of Baptism and Confirmation, in consecrating bishops, churches, altars, chalices, patens, and in blessing baptismal water and church bells.

OIL OF THE SICK. A pure olive oil, one of the three holy oils, which the bishop blesses each year on Holy Thursday. It is used in the Sacrament of the Sick.

SUBJECT	BOOK	CHAP.	VERSE	PAGE
Preparation of	*Ex	30	22-25	71
Uses	*Ex	30	26-33	71
	Ex	29	7, 21	70

OILSTOCK. A special container. This vessel is used to hold the three holy oils.

OLD CATHOLICS. In 1870 the Vatican Council issued a decree on the infallibility of the Pope in matters concerning faith and morals. A group of priests and lay people led by Dr. Dollinger and other Swiss and German theologians refused to accept this definition and broke away from the Catholic Church. Eventually their group fell into other errors, such as permitting the clergy to marry and changing marriage laws, etc.

Today in the United States there are four bodies of Old Catholic Churches, with membership of between 70,000 and 80,000. Their members still follow Roman Catholic ritual. They claim their holy orders are valid, since they originally were received from a bishop in Holland and have been passed on through schismatic divisions of the Roman Catholic Church.

OMBRELLINO. A small canopy, usually made of white silk supported by one staff, which is held over the Blessed Sacrament when it is carried in procession, or, in some places, when it is taken to a sick person.

ORANT. A likeness of a female figure, either standing or kneeling, with arms outstretched, symbolizing a saved soul in heaven interceding for the faithful on earth. This image was commonly used in the catacombs in the early days of the Church.

ORATORY. A chapel which may be private, semi-public, or public. A private chapel is one erected in a private home for the sole benefit of a family or individual. An example of a semi-public oratory would be a convent or a college chapel. A public oratory is one which was erected for a particular group of people but which the general public would have permission to enter during divine services. No one can satisfy the obligation of hearing Mass in a private oratory without special permission.

ORDERS, HOLY. The sacrament instituted by Christ through which a man receives sacramental graces and spiritual powers enabling him to worthily and validly perform the sacred duties of priests, bishops, or other ecclesiastical ministers of the Catholic Church. By virtue of his ordination a priest receives the power to consecrate the Body and Blood of Christ and to forgive sins. Only a bishop can confer Holy Orders, and a man can receive this sacrament only once.

In order to receive the sacrament of Holy Orders, a candidate must first have received the four sacramental minor orders: acolyte, exorcist, reader, and doorkeeper; followed by the reception of the major orders; subdeacon, deacon, and, ultimately, the priesthood. Although the ceremonies which make up an ordination are lengthy and beautifully impressive, the actual priestly powers are conferred by the imposition of hands and accompanying prayers.

ORDERS, RELIGIOUS. Originally each monastery and convent was completely independent and subject only to the laws of the Church. In the 10th century separate communities were formed under the Benedictine name, and orders, as we know them today, were established. Today the term religious orders refers to groups of people leading the lives of religious under a particular rule and having taken solemn vows.

ORDINARY. An ecclesiastical prelate who governs a particular territory in the name of the Church. Included under this title are the Pope; diocesan bishops; vicars general; prelates nullius; vicars apostolic; prefects apostolic; superiors general; provincials; abbots primate; and, during the vacancy of a see, vicars capitular.

ORDINATION. The sacred ceremonies by means of which worthy candidates receive the sacrament of Holy Orders. Young men who aspire to the priesthood must first advance through prescribed stages, called the minor and the major orders. The minor orders (preceded by tonsure) are acolyte, exorcist, reader, and doorkeeper. The major orders are the subdeaconship, deaconship, and the priesthood. The bishop usually confers all minor orders, although abbots are permitted to confer them on men in their own orders. Only bishops can confer major orders, since they are the logical descendants of the Apostles to whom Christ first gave the priestly powers.

The ceremonies which accompany an ordination are lengthy and beautiful. The Church follows a prescribed form from which no bishop can deviate.

The Apostles originally received the Sacrament of Holy Orders from Christ. They in turn conferred the powers upon their successors through the imposition of hands and prayer.

Examples of:

SUBJECT	BOOK	CHAP.	VERSE	PAGE
Joshua, by Moses	*Nm	27	18	132
	Dt	34	9	172
Apostles, by Christ	*Mk	3	14-15	1001
Deacons	*Acts	6	1-6	1090
	1 Tm	3	10-13	1181
Paul	*Acts	13	1-3	1098

ORDO. A book containing a daily calendar indicating which Masses should be celebrated each day. It directs the variant parts of the Mass for each day and the Divine Office to be read. The book gives directions regarding the various liturgical functions, but it does not include the text.

ORGAN. Since the 13th century the organ has been used commonly to accompany the chant or other church music. In modern times the electric organ is used most widely. A recent encyclical allows other instruments in church.

ORIENTAL CHURCH. Another name for the Eastern Church, which are Catholic Churches of the Eastern Rite. Followers of the Eastern Rite are Catholics who recognize the Pope as the Supreme Pontiff of the Catholic Church. Their teachings with regard to faith and morals are those taught by Christ Himself, and, therefore, the same as those taught by the so-called Western Church. The principal differences between the Eastern or Oriental Church and the Western or Roman are in the rites and the languages, and it is as correct for Eastern Catholics to follow their rites in their approved languages as it is proper for Roman Catholics to follow the Latin Rite.

SUBJECT	BOOK	CHAP.	VERSE	PAGE

The term "Eastern Churches" is often inaccurately applied by both Catholics and others to dissident, that is, non-Catholic, churches of the East. These dissident churches are the group which form the Orthodox Eastern Church and the Coptic, Nestorian, Armenian, Ethiopic, and Syrian Jacobite Churches.

ORIENTATION. The once-common practice of building churches so that the congregation, facing the altar, would also be facing east. Originally begun because it was believed God would come from the east to judge mankind, this practice now has become almost obsolete because of the arrangements of some city streets.

ORIGINAL JUSTICE. The state of grace and original innocence in which Adam and Eve were created by God. It is called "original" because they were created with it. Original justice consisted of sanctifying grace, and the supernatural gifts and virtues of the Holy Spirit.

ORIGINAL SIN. The sin commited originally by Adam and inherited by all mankind. We, as his descendants, are restored to sanctifying grace through the Sacrament of Baptism. Only Our Blessed Lady was exempt from the stain of original sin.

Adam's sin	°Gn	3	6	3
God's punishment	°Gn	3	16-24	3
Adam forgiven	°Wis	10	1-2	653
All born in	°Rom	5	19	1120

ORPHREY. An embroidered ornamental cross which adorns a chasuble; also the decorative band around the border of a cope. An orphrey is not a required part of a vestment, but is used merely to beautify.

ORTHODOX CHURCH. The name generally applied to certain schismatic Eastern groups which broke away from the Catholic Church around 1054. They accept only the first seven Ecumenical Councils, rejecting the others; deny the supremacy and infallibility of the pope; contend the Holy Spirit proceeded from God the Father only (and not from the Son); and refuse to accept the dogma of the Immaculate Conception.

Their Holy Orders are valid; they recognize seven sacraments; they celebrate Mass, but they believe a special invocation to God to send down the Holy Spirit to change the bread and wine into the Body and Blood of Christ is necessary for the consecration.

The Eastern Orthodox Churches consist of about twelve bodies which follow the Byzantine Rite.

O SALUTARIS. The opening words of the hymn which often is sung at Benediction of the Blessed Sacrament, although it is not essential to the ceremony as the hymn, "Tantum Ergo," is. The Latin text of the verses sung at Benediction and the English translation follow:

O Salutaris
"O Salutaris Hostia,
Quae coeli pandis ostium.
Bella premunt hostilia;
Da robur, fer auxilium.
Uni trinoque Domino,
Sit sempiterna gloria;
Qui vitam sine termino,
Nobis donet in patria. Amen."

English Translation
"O Saving Victim, opening wide
The gate of heav'n to man below!
Our foes press on from every side;
Your aid supply, Your strength bestow.
To Your great name be endless praise;
Immortal Godhead, One in Three;
Oh, grant us endless length of days,
In our true native land with You.
Amen."

OSSERVATORE ROMANO. *The Roman Observer*, a newspaper printed in Vatican City under the direction of the Papal Secretary of State. While it is not considered the official publication of the Vatican State, the Papal Secretary of State does furnish one column for each issue, and it (the paper) generally reflects the attitude of the Vatican on various matters.

OSTENSORIUM. Another name for the monstrance, a portable gold-plated vessel in which the Blessed Sacrament is exposed for veneration at Benediction, carried in procession, or placed for exposition.

OSTIARY. Another name for porter or doorkeeper, a sacramental which is the first of the minor orders which lead to the

priesthood. The recipient of this title is declared to be the custodian of the door to divine services, and his duties enumerated as: ringing the church bell; unlocking the church doors; opening the book for the speaker. In modern times, these duties are not usually performed specifically by the ostiary. In the early days of Christianity, however, it was necessary to have someone guard the doors where services were held in order to keep out enemies or those unqualified to attend.

OUR LADY. One of the best-loved appellations for Mary, the Mother of God. Very often it precedes the names of places in which she appeared, such as: Our Lady of Guadalupe; Our Lady of La Salette; Our Lady of Lourdes; Our Lady of Fatima; etc. Among countless other titles, the Blessed Virgin also is known as Our Lady of the Miraculous Medal and Our Lady of Sorrows. Many of these titles are remembered in feasts, and also appear in Litanies.

OUR LORD. One of the more commonly used titles for Jesus Christ. Actually, it is an abbreviated version of "Our Lord, Jesus Christ."

PALM SUNDAY. The Sunday before Easter on which is celebrated Christ's triumphant entry into Jerusalem. The sixth Sunday of Lent, it also marks the beginning of the Holy Week liturgical ceremonies. Palms are blessed before the principal Mass of the day. In commemoration of Christ's entry, the palms are carried in procession.

Christ's entry into Jerusalem	°Mt	21	1-11	987
	Mk	11	1-11	1011
	Lk	19	29-44	1041
	Jn	12	12-19	1068

PALMS. Palms which have been blessed are a sacramental and should be treated with reverence. When they are blessed on Palm Sunday, some are kept by the priest to be burned for ashes used on Ash Wednesday. The remainder is distributed to the faithful. The following year when new palms are blessed, the old ones should be burned. The distribution of palms commemorates the triumphant entry of Christ into Jerusalem.

PANGE LINGUA. *sing with tongue.* A Latin hymn in honor of the Blessed Sacrament composed by St. Thomas Aquinas for the Office of the Feast of Corpus Christi. The last two stanzas of this hymn, the *Tantum Ergo*, are sung at the close of all Benedictions and Expositions of the Blessed Sacrament. It is sung also on Holy Thursday during the procession to the repository.

PAPACY. Pertaining to the authority or the office of the pope; the succession of all the popes since the time of St. Peter.

PAPAL DECORATIONS. Various titles or medals may be bestowed upon laymen for distinguished services to the Catholic Church, the Holy See, or to society in general. There are seven honorary orders by which the recipients become papal knights. They are:

1. The Supreme Order of Christ (Militia of Our Lord Jesus Christ). This was instituted in 1319 by Pope John XXII as a remembrance of the Portuguese Templars and was intended to be a religious military organization dedicated to good works. In the 19th century all properties of the order were confiscated by secular officials. Today it exists only as a papal decoration.

2. Order of the Golden Spur (Golden Militia). The founder of this oldest of papal decorations is not known definitely. At one time one of the most highly sought honors, it fell into abuse when it was handed out too freely. The order then had been placed under the patronage of St. Sylvester in 1841 by Pope Gregory XVI. In 1905 Pope St. Pius X reestablished this papal order under the title, the Golden Militia, and placed it under the patronage of the Immaculate Conception. The old Order of the Golden Spur was then named the Order of St. Sylvester. To the Golden Militia are admitted only those who have performed outstanding service to the Catholic Church by feat of arms, the written word, or by some particularly notable act.

3. Order of Pius IX. This honor may be bestowed upon non-Catholics as well as Catholics. It was founded in 1847 by Pope Pius IX to reward outstanding feats of service which benefit the Catholic Church or mankind in general. Divided into three classes, the recipient may be declared: (1) Knight of the Grand Cross; (2) Commander; (3) Knight.

4. Order of St. Gregory the Great. This order was founded in 1831 by Pope Gregory XVI to show gratitude to eligible

SUBJECT   BOOK CHAP. VERSE PAGE

subjects of the Papal States for particularly noteworthy civil or military virtues. It, too, is divided into three groups: Knights of the Grand Cross, Commanders, and Knights.

5. *Order of St. Sylvester.* Originally part of the Order of the Golden Spur, this order was placed under the patronage of St. Sylvester by Pope Gregory XVI in 1841. In 1905 Pope St. Pius X divided it into two organizations, one the Golden Militia under the protection of the Immaculate Conception, and the other the Order of St. Sylvester. The three classes of the Order are: (1) Knights of the Grand Cross; (2) Commanders; (3) Knights.

6. *Orders of the Holy Sepulchre.* One of the oldest of papal decorations, this is believed to have been founded in 1099. After many changes, in 1847 Pope Pius IX bestowed the power of conferring this honor on the Patriarch of Jerusalem and his successors. In 1949 Pope Pius XII issued an apostolic brief, "Quam Romani Pontifices," establishing new and more solemn statutes for this order. In addition to the three classes of knights, there is a separate division to which women are admitted, the Dames of the Holy Sepulchre. Prospective members first are named by the bishop of the diocese in which they live. Then their qualifications are passed on by the Patriarch of Jerusalem, and finally the Holy See must approve the selection.

7. *Knights of Malta.* Originally part of the Hospitallers of St. John of Jerusalem, the Knights of Malta Order adopted that name sometime in the 16th century. The evils of the Reformation and the appointment of Czar Paul of Russia, a non-Catholic, as grand master, led to a decline of the order. In 1797 the pope refused to recognize this appointment and reserved the right to select the grand master to the Holy See. The original purpose of the order was to aid and shelter Holy Land pilgrims. Today, however, the Knights of Malta are dedicated to charitable, educational, and religious works.

In addition to the orders conferring knighthood on deserving men and women, there are three pontifical medals which are bestowed by the Holy See. The recipient of any of these may have been recommended for the honor by his local bishop, or the pope himself may decide to confer it. The three medals are:

a) *"Pro Ecclesia et Pontifice."* Originally given by Pope Leo XIII as a memento to all those men and women who helped to make the Vatican Exposition and the Pope's Jubilee successful, it has been retained by succeeding popes. Today it is given for outstanding service to the Catholic Church and the pope.

b) *"Benemerenti."* This was originated in 1832 by Pope Gregory XVI to reward particular daring and courage both in civil and in military life. Today it is given for the same reasons.

c) *Medal of the Holy Land.* Designed by Pope Pius XII, this decoration is conferred by the Custodian of the Holy Land upon pilgrims to the Holy Land whose pilgrimage is genuinely religious in purpose. Candidates for this medal also must present a certificate from their parish priest stating their moral fitness.

PAPAL LETTERS. Some of the principal letters issued by the Holy See are:

1. *Apostolic Bull.* A formal, solemn document dealing with very important matters. Beginning with the reigning pontiff's name, it continues, "Servus Servorum Dei" (Servant of the Servants of God). The subject matter follows, and it closes with the place of origin, date of issue, and year of the reign of the author pope.

2. *Apostolic Brief.* A less formal document which concerns less important matters. It is impressed with a seal representing St. Peter drawing his fisherman's net from the sea.

3. *Motu Proprio* (By one's own accord). A letter which the pope writes, signs, and issues on his own initiative.

4. *Pontifical Letters.* Letter in which the pope explains some phase of Catholic doctrine, instructs, or perhaps congratulates the recipient.

5. *Encyclicals.* Usually letters on doctrinal subjects which are addressed to bishops throughout the world or to those in certain countries.

PAPAL STATES. The term *Papal States* refers to the area of Rome and surrounding territories which once were under the jurisdiction of the Church. This territory was variously acquired as the result of political grants, wars, etc., going back to the 8th Century when the northern Lombards invaded Italy and were subsequently defeated by the Franks to whom the Pope had appealed for protection. From time to time thereafter, the Papal Sees waned and waxed in area, as the land was fought over, won, lost, added to, sacked, etc. With the rise of nationalism in Europe in the 19th Century, Italian troops

SUBJECT   BOOK CHAP. VERSE PAGE

under Victor Emmanuel invaded the Papal States in 1870, and this brought an end to the temporal power of the Pope and the Papal States as such. The Italian Law of May 13, 1871, made all the Papal States a part of Italy except the small areas surrounding the Vatican, the Lateran, and the villa of Castel Gandolfo, an estate near Rome where the Pope usually spends the hot summer months. From this date until 1929, the Popes remained "Prisoners of the Vatican" until the Holy See and the Italian Government signed the Lateran Treaty of June 7, 1929, in which the Italian Government recognized the independence of Vatican City and paid an indemnity for the former Papal States, while the Holy See, in turn, recognized that the former Papal States were now Italian territory.

PARASCEVE. The day before the Jewish Sabbath, that is, Friday. The name is derived from a Greek word meaning *preparation*, and was used by the Jews as an indication all work necessary for Sabbath celebrations had to be done on this day.

The Confraternity translation of the New Testament calls Good Friday, the day on which Christ died, "Preparation Day." In the Missal, Good Friday is called Parasceve.

| Day Christ died | *Jn | 19 | 31, 42 | 1078 |

PARENTS. A man and woman who bring forth offspring; the father and mother.

Should be honored	*Sir	7	27-28	671
	Dt	5	16	147
	Ex	20	12	62
	Eph	6	1-3	1161
	Prv	30	17	627
	Prv	20	20	617

Duties of:

Parents are obliged to care for the temporal and spiritual needs of their children. Their temporal needs are satisfied when their parents provide them with food, clothing, shelter, and any other physical necessities. Caring for their children's spiritual needs also begins with the birth of their offspring. Parents must see that each child is baptised soon after birth; that he receives the sacraments of Penance, Holy Eucharist, and Confirmation at the proper time; and the other sacraments when he is eligible. It is the duty of parents to teach their children God's ways and Laws, and to watch over their moral development, removing them from harmful influences such as bad companions, filthy publications, movies, plays, etc. It is also the duty of Catholic parents to see that their children are educated in Catholic schools whenever this is possible. Each parent, because he brings a child into the world, is obliged to direct that child toward eternal salvation.

Child training	*Sir	22	3-6	684
	Prv	22	6	619
	Sir	7	23-25	671
	Dt	6	6-7	148
	Eph	6	4	1161
	Col	3	21	1170
Chastisements	*Dt	21	18-21	159
	Prv	23	13-14	620
	Prv	13	24	610
Responsibility of	*1 Sm	3	11-14	218
Need for correction	*Sir	30	1-13	692
	Prv	29	15-17	626
	Prv	22	15	619
	1 Sm	3	13	218
Good influence of	*2 Chr	17	3	344
	2 Tm	1	5	1185

PARISH. An ecclesiastical division of a diocese by territory or other method. Each parish is directed by a parish priest called a pastor. On the pastor's shoulders rests the responsibility of caring for the spiritual (and oftentimes physical) needs of his parishioners, those who live within the boundaries of his parish. Finally, there is required a suitable church which must have the liturgical equipment necessary for Divine worship, a baptismal font, a confessional, and a cemetery, although the latter no longer pertains in modern times. Records must be kept of the baptisms, marriages, and burials in the parish; and the parish must generally furnish the parish priest with his dwelling. The strict participation in the rites of one's own parish is not enforced at the present time, but, as a general rule, baptisms, marriages, funerals, and Easter Communion should take place in the parish in which one resides.

PARTICLE. Any piece, no matter how small, which, through Consecration, becomes the Body and Blood of Christ. Also the

SUBJECT   BOOK   CHAP.   VERSE   PAGE

name given to the small Host which is distributed to the faithful at Holy Communion.

PASCHAL CANDLE. The large candle placed on the Gospel side of the altar, lighted during Holy Saturday ceremonies. Thereafter it is lit during High Masses, parochial Masses, vespers on Sunday, Monday, Tuesday, and Saturday of Easter Week, and on all Sundays until Ascension Thursday. On the vigil of Pentecost it is used in the blessing of the baptismal font. It symbolizes Christ, the Light of the World, and the five grains of incense pressed into it in the form of a cross represent His five wounds.

PASSION MUSIC. On Palm Sunday and Good Friday the Gospel account of Our Lord's Passion is sung during the liturgical services. According to Church rules, the *narrator* or *chronista*, sings the narrative; the words of Our Lord are sung by the *christus*; the *synagoga* sings the words of the Apostles and all others. However, the church choir generally sings the responses of the crowds.

PASSION PLAY. A genre of the Miracle Play depicting the sufferings and death of Our Lord. Passion plays probably first appeared as introductions added to Easter plays in the 14th century. They were especially popular among German-speaking Catholics and have survived among them, principally those at Oberammergau, Horitz (Hörice, Bohemia), and Brixlegg (Tyrol, Austria). The best known is, of course, that of Oberammergau, which is the most spectacular and has been given every ten years since approximately 1634 in fulfillment of a vow that was made if the black death should leave the town quickly. It presents the story of the Passion from the triumphal entry into Jerusalem, with scenes from the Old Testament given as prefigurations of the Passion. In the United States, *Veronica's Veil* has been a popular revival of the Passion Play as given during Lent at the Passionist monastery, Union City, New Jersey.

PASSION, RELICS OF THE. There are a number of relics purported to be part of the true cross, or connected, in some way, with the passion and death of Our Lord. Holy Mother Church permits the veneration of a few of these. In the Basilica of the Holy Cross of Jerusalem in Rome are preserved the inscription placed above the cross and two thorns from the crown of thorns. The crown of thorns itself and one of the Holy Nails are kept in Paris. Part of the lance is in Rome; the point is in Paris. The Church of Argenteuil in Paris holds the tunic; the Church of Treves preserves the holy robe; part of the winding sheet or shroud is in Turin. In Rome at the Church of St. John Lateran, the sponge is kept. Rome also possesses part of the pillar at which Our Lord was scourged; another part is preserved in Jerusalem. The linen cloth with which Veronica wiped Christ's face is at St. Peter's in Rome.

PASSION SUNDAY. Formerly the designation for the Fifth Sunday in Lent. Before the liturgical changes statues and images were covered in the churches throughout the final two weeks of Lent which was known as "Passiontide."

PASSIONISTS, THE. The full title of the Passionist institute is: The Congregation of Discalced (Barefooted) Clerks of the Most Holy Cross and Passion of Our Lord Jesus Christ. The founder was St. Paul of the Cross who began the Rules in 1720. Then in 1725 St. Paul visited Rome with his brother John Baptist and received from Benedict XIII permission to form a congregation according to these Rules. The congregation embraces both the contemplative and the active life, the idea of the founder being to unite the solitary life of the Carthusians or Trappists with the active life of the Jesuits. The end of the congregation, as stated in the rules, is the sanctification of its members and the sanctification of others. This twofold mission is accomplished by the practice and promotion of devotion to the Passion of Our Lord as the most efficacious means of withdrawing the minds of men from sin and leading them on to Christian excellence. The Passionists are also bound by the usual religious vows of poverty, chastity, and obedience, to which is added a fourth—to promote to the utmost of their power, especially by such means as their rules point out, a devotion to the Passion of Our Divine Saviour. The vows made in the congregation are *simple*, not *solemn* vows, and they are for life, meaning that no individual may leave the congregation of his own accord after profession, and no one can be dismissed except for some grave and canonical reason. Besides practicing the austerities and mortifications prescribed by Rule, the Passionists spend five hours every day in choir chanting the Divine Office or in meditation; Matins and Lauds are said at 2 a.m.;

SUBJECT   BOOK   CHAP.   VERSE   PAGE

and three fast days a week are prescribed. They wear only sandals on their feet, and their habit is a coarse woolen tunic, the mantle of which bears a heart-shaped badge of the congregation on which are inscribed the words *Jesu XPI Passio* (Passion of Jesus Christ). In the United States, a branch of the congregation was started in 1852 in Pittsburgh. The congregation increased gradually until the province became so extended that a second was founded, under the title of the Holy Cross in 1906.

PASTOR. Derived from the Latin word meaning shepherd, a pastor is the title given the priest in charge of a particular parish. His duties are to care for the spiritual needs of his parishioners and to administer the business affairs of his church properties. Some of his more commonly known duties include: administering the sacraments to his flock; offering Mass for his parishioners every Sunday of the year plus a few other designated days; arranging for the Catholic education of the children; helping the poor and others in need of aid, spiritual or otherwise; encouraging the spiritual development of his flock, bringing back prodigals and easing the way for those who are seeking the truth and who wish to become converts.

PASTORAL. A letter written by a bishop and addressed to all members of his diocese. These letters are read at Mass on Sunday. The subject matter may be anything pertaining to the spiritual welfare of Catholics.

PASTORAL STAFF. The crosier; a staff, usually ornamented, with a crook on top, bestowed upon a bishop at his consecration as a symbol of his authority.

PATEN. 1. A saucer-like dish used to hold the Host at the Offertory and after the Consecration during the celebration of Mass. The paten is consecrated with a special blessing; lay people are not permitted to handle it.
2. The communion paten, a round disk with a handle, held beneath the chin of a person receiving Holy Communion, to catch any particles of the Host which might drop.

PATER NOSTER. The Latin words for the first two words of the Lord's Prayer, meaning "Our Father." The Latin version is as follows: "Pater noster, qui es in caelis, sanctificetur nomen tuum. Adveniat regnum tuum. Fiat voluntas tua, sicut in caelo et in terra. Panem nostrum quotidianum da nobis hodie. Et dimitte nobis debita nostra, sicut et nos dimittimus debitoribus nostris. Et ne nos inducas in tentationem: sed libera nos a malo. Amen."

PATRIARCHATE. The derived word meaning a patriarch's office, see, reign, or, generally, the territory he governs. The oldest Canon Law admitted only three bishops as having what later ages called patriarchal rights: the Bishops of Rome, Alexandria, and Antioch. Jerusalem next rose to importance when pilgrims flocked to the Holy City, and the Council of Chalcedon (451) cut away Palestine and Arabia from Antioch and formed the Patriarchate of Jerusalem. Constantine having made Byzantium "New Rome," the Council of Chalcedon also raised Constantinople (Istanbul) to patriarchal rank. There are now five major patriarchates. The Pope as Bishop of Rome is Patriarch of all the Western Church. In the Eastern Church there are Patriarchs of Istanbul, Alexandria, Antioch, and Jerusalem. The Latin Patriarch of Jerusalem has jurisdiction over Palestine and Cyprus. The Coptic Patriarch of Alexandria and the Syrian, Maronite, and Melkite Patriarchs of Antioch rule over Eastern Catholics of their respective Rites. Minor Patriarchs in the East are the Patriarch of Babylon for the Chaldeans and the Patriarch of Cilicia for the Armenians. Minor Patriarchs in the West are merely titular. They bear the titles of Patriarchs of the West Indies, the East Indies, Lisbon and Venice.

In the 5th century the Nestorians broke away from the patriarchate at Antioch, and during the long Monophysite quarrels during the 5th, 6th, and 7th centuries there were continually rival or alternate Catholic and Monophysite patriarchs of Alexandria and Antioch. And so the multiplication of patriarchs grew with Cerularious's schism (1054), the Crusades, the discovery of America, and other historical developments. As a territorial division the patriarchate has practically fallen into disuse. The Western Church alone retained territorial integrity; the other Catholic patriarchates have been in part re-established in the form of organizations of Catholics of different Eastern rites wherever found.

PATRIARCHATE	RITE
Constantinople, Turkey	Latin
Alexandria, Egypt °	Coptic

SUBJECT	BOOK	CHAP.	VERSE	PAGE
Antioch, Syria	...............Syrian			
	Latin			
	Maronite			
	Melkite °			
Jerusalem, Palestine °	........Latin			
Babylon, Iraq	...............Chaldean			
Cilicia, Turkey	..............Armenian			
West Indies	................Latin			
East Indies	................Latin			
Lisbon, Portugal	...........Latin			
Venice, Italy	................Latin			

° The Melkite Patriarch of Antioch has also the personal titles of Melkite Patriarch of Alexandria and of Jerusalem.

PATRIMONY OF ST. PETER, THE. The expression "Patrimonium Sancti Petri" originally designated the landed possessions and revenues of various kinds that belonged to the Church of St. Peter at Rome. This consisted wholly of private property until the middle of the 8th century, but the term was later applied to the States of the Church, and especially to the Duchy of Rome. The Law of Constantine the Great (321) first gave a legal basis to the possessions of the Church of Rome. It was hereby declared qualified to hold and transmit property; and subsequently the possessions were rapidly increased by donations.

PATRON SAINTS. One who has been chosen by election, or assigned by a venerable tradition, as a special intercessor with God and the proper advocate of a particular locality, and is honored by clergy and people with a particular form of religious observation.

PATRON SAINTS AND THEIR FEAST DAYS. Patron saints are those saints that are particularly selected by the Church or through popular acclaim, because of their connection or association with various causes or groups of people. Some of the best known of these are as follows.

Patron Saints of Countries
Argentina. Our Lady of Lujan.
Armenia. St. Gregory Illuminator.
Australia. St. Francis Xavier.
Belgium. St. Joseph.
Bohemia. Sts. Wenceslaus, Ludmilla.
Borneo. St. Francis Xavier.
Brazil. Immaculate Conception.
Canada. St. Joseph; St. Anne.
Chile. St. James; Our Lady of Mt. Carmel.
China. St. Joseph
Colombia. St. Peter Claver; St. Louis Bertrand.
Czechoslovakia. St. Wenceslaus; St. John Nepomucene; St. Procopius.
Denmark. St. Ansgar; St. Canute.
Dominican Rep. Our Lady of High Grace; St. Dominic.
East Indies. St. Thomas, Apostle.
Ecuador. Sacred Heart.
England. St. George.
Finland. St. Henry.
France. St. Joan of Arc.
Germany. St. Boniface.
Greece. St. Nicholas of Myra.
Holland. St. Willibrord.
Hungary. St. Stephen, King.
India. Our Lady of Assumption.
Ireland. Sts. Patrick, Brigid, and Columba.
Italy. St. Francis of Assisi; St. Catherine of Siena.
Japan. St. Peter Baptist.
Lithuania. St. Casimir, Bl. Cunegunda.
Mexico. Our Lady of Guadalupe.
Norway. St. Olaf.
Paraguay. Our Lady of Assumption.
Philippines. Sacred Heart of Mary.
Poland. St. Casimir.
Portugal. Immaculate Conception; St. Francis Borgia; St. Anthony of Padua.
Russia. St. Andrew.
Scotland. St. Andrew.
Slovakia. Our Lady of Sorrows.
Spain. St. James; St. Teresa.
Sweden. St. Bridget; St. Eric.
Union of South Africa. Our Lady of Assumption.
United States. Immaculate Conception.
Uruguay. Our Lady of Lujan.

Patron Saints of Occupations, Diseases and Infirmities. Professions, and States of Life
Actors. St. Genesius, Aug. 25.
Alpinists. St. Bernard of Menthon, May 28.
Altar Boys. St. John Berchmans, Aug. 13.
Architects. St. Thomas, Apostle, Dec. 21; St. Barbara, Dec. 4.
Artillerymen. St. Barbara, Dec. 4.
Art. St. Catherine (Bologna), Mar. 9.
Artists. St. Luke, Oct. 18.
Astronomers. St. Dominic, Aug. 4.
Athletes. St. Sebastian, Jan. 20.
Authors. St. Francis de Sales, Jan. 29.
Aviators. Our Lady of Loreto, Dec. 10; St. Therese of Lisieux, Oct. 3.
Bakers. St. Elizabeth of Hungary, Nov. 19; St. Nicholas, Dec. 6.
Bankers. St. Matthew, Sept. 21.
Barbers. SS. Cosmas and Damian, Sept. 27; St. Louis, Aug. 25.
Barren Women. St. Anthony of Padua, June 13; St. Felicitas, Nov. 23.
Basket-makers. St. Anthony, Abbot, Jan. 17.
Beggars. St. Alexius, July 17.
Blacksmiths. St. Dunstan, May 19.
Blind. St. Odilia, Dec. 13; St. Raphael, Oct. 24.
Bodily Ills. Our Lady of Lourdes, Feb. 11.
Bookbinders. St. Peter Celestine, May 19.
Booksellers. St. John of God, March 8.
Boy Scouts. St. George, April 23.
Brewers. St. Augustine of Hippo, Aug. 28; St. Luke, Oct. 18; St. Nicholas of Myra, Dec. 6.
Bricklayers. St. Stephen, Dec. 26.
Brides. St. Nicholas of Myra. Dec. 6.
Builders. St. Vincent Ferrer, April 5.
Butchers. St. Anthony, Abbot, Jan. 17; St. Hadrian, Sept. 8; St. Luke, Oct. 18.
Cab-drivers. St. Fiacre, Aug. 30.
Cabinet-makers. St. Anne, July 26.
Cancer Patients. St. Peregrine, May 2.
Carpenters. St. Joseph, March 19.
Catholic Action. St. Francis of Assisi, Oct. 4.
Charitable Societies. St. Vincent de Paul, July 19.
Children. St. Nicholas of Myra, Dec. 6.
Choir Boys. Holy Innocents, Dec. 28.
Clerics. St. Gabriel of the Sorrowful Mother, Feb. 27.
Comedians. St. Vitus, June 15.
Confessors. St. Alphonsus Liguori, Aug. 2; St. John Nepomucene, May 16.
Convulsion in Children. St. Scholastica, Feb. 10.
Cooks. St. Lawrence, Aug. 10; St. Martha, July 29.
Coppersmiths. St. Maurus, Jan. 15.
Dairy Workers. St. Brigid, Feb. 1.
Deaf. St. Francis de Sales, Jan. 29.
Dentists. St. Apollonia, Feb. 9.
Desperate Situations. St. Gregory of Neocaesarea, Nov. 17; St. Jude Thaddeus, Oct. 28.
Druggists. SS. Cosmas and Damian, Sept. 27; St. James the Less, May 1.
Dying. St. Joseph, March 19; St. Barbara, Dec. 4.
Emigrants. St. Frances Xavier Cabrini, Dec. 22.
Engineers. St. Ferdinand III, May 30.
Expectant Mothers. St. Margaret, July 20; St. Raymund Nonnatus, Aug. 31; St. Gerard Majella, Oct. 16.
Eye Trouble. St. Lucy, Dec. 13.
Falsely Accused. St. Raymund Nonnatus, Aug. 31.
Farmers. St. George, April 23; St. Isidore, Mar. 22.
Firemen. St. Florian, May 4.
Fire Prevention. St. Catherine of Siena, April 30; St. Barbara, Dec. 4.
First Communicants. Bl. Imelda, May 12; St. Tarcisius, Aug. 15.
Fishermen. St. Andrew, Nov. 30.
Florists. St. Dorothy, Feb. 6; St. Therese, Oct. 3.
Forest-workers. St. John Gualbert, July 12.
Founders. St. Barbara, Dec. 4.
Foundlings. Holy Innocents, Dec. 28.
Funeral Directors. St. Joseph of Arimathea, March 17.
Gardeners. St. Dorothy, Feb. 6; St. Adalard, Jan. 2; St. Tryphon, Nov. 10; St. Fiacre, Aug. 30.
Glass-workers. St. Luke, Oct. 18.
Goldsmiths. St. Dunstan, May 19; St. Anastasius, Sept. 7.
Grave-diggers and Graveyards. St. Anthony, Abbot, Jan. 17.

SUBJECT   BOOK   CHAP.   VERSE   PAGE

Greetings. St. Valentine, Feb. 14.
Grocers. St. Michael, Sept. 29.
Gunners. St. Barbara, Dec. 4.
Hatters. St. Severus of Ravenna, Feb. 1; St. James the Less, May 1.
Haymakers. SS. Gervase and Protase, June 19.
Headaches, St. Teresa of Avila, Oct. 15.
Heart Ailments. St. John of God, Mar. 8.
Hospitals. St. Camillus de Lellis, July 18; St. John of God, March 8; St. Jude Thaddeus, Oct. 28.
Housewives. St. Anne, July 26.
Hunters. St. Hubert, Nov. 3.
Huntsmen. St. Eustachius, Sept. 20.
Inn-keepers. St. Amand, Feb. 6.
Invalids. St. Roch, Aug. 16.
Jewelers. St. Eligius, Dec. 1.
Journalists. St. Francis de Sales, Jan. 29.
Jurists. St. Catherine of Alexandria, Nov. 25; St. John Capistran, March 28.
Laborers. St. Isidore, May 10; St. James, July 25.
Lawyers. St. Ivo, June 17; St. Genesius, Aug. 25.
Learning. St. Ambrose, Dec. 7; St. Acca, Nov. 27.
Librarians. St. Jerome, Sept. 30.
Locksmiths. St. Dunstan, May 19.
Lost Articles. St. Anthony of Padua, June 13.
Lovers. St. Raphael, Oct. 24.
Marble-workers. St. Clement I, Nov. 23.
Mariners. St. Michael, Sept. 29; St. Nicholas of Tolentino, Sept. 10.
Mentally Ill. St. Dympna, May 15.
Merchants. St. Francis of Assisi, Oct. 4; St. Nicholas of Myra, Dec. 6.
Messengers. St. Gabriel, March 24.
Metalworkers. St. Eligius, Dec. 1.
Millers. St. Arnulph, Aug. 15; St. Victor, July 21.
Miners. St. Barbara, Dec. 4.
Missions. St. Francis Xavier, Dec. 3; St. Therese of Lisieux, Oct. 3; (Home), St. Leonard of Port Maurice, Nov. 26; (Negro), St. Peter Claver, Sept. 9; St. Benedict the Moor, April 4.
Mothers. St. Monica, May 4.
Motorists. St. Christopher, July 25.
Motorcyclists. Our Lady of Grace, May 31.
Mountaineers. St. Bernard of Menthon, May 28.
Musicians. St. Cecilia, Nov. 22.
Notaries. St. Luke, Oct. 18; St. Mark, April 25.
Nurses. St. Agatha, Feb. 5; St. Camillus de Lellis, July 18; St. Alexius, July 17; St. John of God, March 8; St. Raphael, Oct. 24.
Old Maids, St. Andrew, Nov. 30.
Orators. St. John Chrysostom, Jan. 27.
Orphans. St. Jerome Aemilian, July 20.
Painters. St. Luke, Oct. 18.
Pawnbrokers. St. Nicholas of Myra, Dec. 6.
Philosophers. St. Justin, Apr. 14; St. Catherine of Alex., Nov. 25.
Physicians. St. Pantaleon, July 27; SS. Cosmas and Damian, Sept. 27; St. Luke, Oct. 18; St. Raphael, Oct. 24.
Pilgrims. St. Alexius, July 17; St. James, July 25.
Plasterers. St. Bartholomew, Aug. 24.
Poets. St. David, Dec. 29; St. Cecilia, Nov. 22.
Poisoning. St. Benedict. Mar. 21.
Policemen. St. Michael, Sept. 29.
Poor. St. Lawrence, Aug. 10; St. Anthony of Padua, June 13.
Porters. St. Christopher, July 25.
Possessed. St. Bruno, Oct. 6; St. Denis, Oct. 9.
Postal Employees. St. Gabriel, March 24.
Pregnant Women. St. Margaret, July 20; St. Raymund Nonnatus, Aug. 31; St. Gerard Majella, Oct. 16.
Priests. St. Jean-Baptiste Vianney, Aug. 9.
Printers. St. John of God, March 8; St. Augustine of Hippo, Aug. 28; St. Genesius, Aug. 25.
Prisoners. St. Dismas, Mar. 25; St. Barbara, Dec. 4.
Prisons. St. Joseph Cafasso, June 23.
Protector of Crops. St. Ansovinus, Mar. 13.
Radiologists. St. Michael, Sept. 29.
Radio-workers. St. Gabriel, March 24.
Retreats. St. Ignatius Loyola, July 31.
Rheumatism. St. James the Greater, July 25.
Saddlers. SS. Crispin and Crispinian, Oct. 25.

Sailors. St. Cuthbert, March 20; St. Brendan, May 16; St. Eulalia, Feb. 12; St. Christopher, July 25; St. Peter Gonzales, April 15; St. Erasmus, June 2.
Scholars. St. Brigid, Feb. 1.
Schools. St. Thomas Aquinas, March 7.
Scientists. St. Albert, Nov. 15.
Sculptors. St. Claude, Nov. 8.
Seminarians, St. Charles Borromeo, Nov. 4.
Servants. St. Martha, July 29; St. Zita, April 27.
Shoemakers. SS. Crispin and Crispinian, Oct. 25.
Sick. St. Michael, Sept. 29; St. John of God; March 8; St. Camillus de Lellis, July 18; St. Philomena, Aug. 11.
Silversmiths. St. Andronicus, Oct. 11.
Singers. St. Gregory, March 12; St. Cecilia, Nov. 22.
Skaters. St. Lidwina, Apr. 14.
Skiers. St. Bernard of Menthon, May 28.
Soldiers. St. Hadrian, Sept. 8; St. George, April 23; St. Ignatius, July 31; St. Sebastian, Jan. 20; St. Martin of Tours, Nov. 11; St. Joan of Arc, May 30.
Sore Throat. St. Blaise, Feb. 3.
Stenographers. St. Genesius, Aug. 25; St. Cassian, Dec. 3.
Stone-cutters. St. Clement, Nov. 23.
Stone-masons. St. Stephen. Dec. 26; St. Barbara, Dec. 4.
Students. St. Thomas Aquinas, Mar. 7; St. Catherine of Alexandria, Nov. 25.
Surgeons. SS. Cosmas and Damian, Sept. 27.
Tailors, St. Homobonus, Nov. 13.
Tanners. SS. Crispin and Crispinian, Oct. 25; St. Simon, May 10.
Tax-gatherers. St. Matthew, Sept. 21.
Teachers. St. Gregory the Great, March 12; St. Catherine of Alexandria, Nov. 25; (principal patron), St. John Baptist de la Salle, May 15.
Telegraph/Telephone Workers. St. Gabriel, March 24.
Television-workers. St. Gabriel, March 24.
Tertiaries. St. Louis of France, Aug. 25; St. Elizabeth of Hungary, Nov. 19.
Theologians. St. Augustine, Aug. 28; (Moral), St. Alphonsus Liguori, Aug. 2.
Travelers. St. Anthony of Padua, June 13; St. Nicholas of Myra, Dec. 6; St. Christopher, July 25; St. Raphael, Oct. 24.
Undertakers. St. Dismas, Mar. 25.
Universal Church. St. Joseph, March 19.
Vocations. St. Alphonsus, Aug. 2.
Watchmen. St. Peter of Alcantara, Oct. 19.
Weavers. St. Paul the Hermit, Jan. 15; St. Anastasius the Fuller, Sept. 7; St. Anastasia, Dec. 25.
Wheelwrights. St. Catherine of Alexandria, Nov. 25.
Wine growers. St. Vincent, Jan. 22.
Wine-merchants. St. Amand, Feb. 6.
Women in labor. St. Anne, July 26.
Women's Army Corps. St. Genevieve, Jan. 3.
Workingmen. St. Joseph, March 19.
Writers. St. Francis de Sales, Jan. 29; St. Lucy, Dec. 13.
Yachtsmen. St. Adjutor, Sept. 1.
Young Girls. St. Agnes, Jan. 21.
Youth. St. Aloysius Gonzaga, June 21; St. John Berchmans, Aug. 13; St. Gabriel Possenti, Feb. 27.

PAX. The Latin word for peace.
(a) The kiss of peace given in Mass just before the Communion.
(b) An osculatorium, or tablet, representing Christ, given to the faithful to kiss during certain Masses.

PAX ROMANA. 1. The period during which the Roman Empire enjoyed peace: during the rule of the emperors Nerva, Trajan, Hadrian, and Antoninus Pius (96–161).
2. An international confederation of societies of Catholic university undergraduates. Their aim is the promotion of international understanding and peace.

PECTORAL CROSS. A small cross worn on the breast by the pope, cardinals, bishops, and abbots as a mark of their offices. The pectoral cross contains certain relics and is studded with precious stones. It is suspended from the neck by a chain, or, in the case of the pope's, by a cord which ends in a gold tassel.

PENANCE, SACRAMENT OF. The Sacrament by which sins committed after Baptism are forgiven by the absolution of a priest. Christ conferred upon the Apostles the power to forgive sins, and thereby raised the virtue of penance to a Sacrament. The words by which Christ conferred this power upon the Apostles and the Church were uttered after the Resurrection when He said: "Peace with you! As the Father has sent Me, so I send you. Receive the Holy Spirit. If you forgive men's sins, they are forgiven them; if you hold them bound, they are held bound." (Jn 20, 21-23).

The Sacrament is predicated upon three acts of the penitent: contrition, confession, and penance.

(1) *Contrition* is sorrow and detestation for the sin committed, with the resolution not to sin again. The resolution not to sin again must be firm and includes a resolve to avoid the occasions of sin and extends to all the mortal sins that one might commit.

SUBJECT	BOOK	CHAP.	VERSE	PAGE
Must come from the heart	°Lk	3	7-9	1023
	Jl	2	13	918
Sin to be hated as greatest of evils	°Lk	15	11-21	1037
Must extend to mortal sins one might commit in future	°Jas	2	8-11	1207

Contrition may be *perfect* or *imperfect*. Perfect contrition is sorrow for sin inspired by a perfect love of God. Thus, the sinner may be justified before the actual reception of the Sacrament. Imperfect contrition proceeds from some other motive than perfect love of God, such as the hatred of sin, or the fear of the temporal or eternal punishment that God inflicts upon sinners. The latter is sufficient for reception of the Sacrament and remission of sin.

(2) *Confession* is the telling of our sins to an authorized priest for the purpose of obtaining forgiveness. A good confession must have three qualities: it must be *humble, sincere,* and *complete*. The necessity for the confession of mortal sins in order to obtain forgiveness is clearly evident from the judicial power conferred by Christ upon the Apostles to forgive sin.

(3) *Penance* or satisfaction is necessary for a good confession in order to make reparation to God and to take away the temporal punishment due to sin.

SUBJECT	BOOK	CHAP.	VERSE	PAGE
Self-denial urged by Christ	°Mt	16	24	983
Paul practiced mortification	°1 Cor	9	27	1135
Converts to practice mortification	°Eph	4	17-24	1159
	Col	3	5	1170
	Gal	5	24	1155

PENITENTIARY, SACRED. The Sacred Apostolic Penitentiary is one of the three tribunals in the Roman Curia. A cardinal, known as the Grand Penitentiary, heads the tribunal which has jurisdiction to judge all cases of conscience, both sacramental and non-sacramental. Anyone can, without charge, submit any matter of conscience at any time and in any language. It can also handle cases pertaining to the use and concession of indulgences so long as a question of dogma reserved to the Holy Office is not involved. Questions concerning dispensation also are handled here.

PERPETUAL ADORATION. The continued adoration of the Blessed Sacrament for 24 hours a day in certain chapels in religious communities. The Blessed Sacrament is usually exposed in a monstrance, and each religious community devotes a certain period to adoration. Numerous religious congregations carry on this perpetual adoration.

PETER'S PENCE. The voluntary offering Catholics throughout the world make to His Holiness, the Pope, once each year to defray the costs of administering the properties of the Holy See and of the numerous charities of the pontiff. Originating in England during the 8th century, this collection first was a tax of a penny per house and was collected on St. Peter's feast day, hence the name.

PIETA. Any representation of Our Blessed Mother seated, holding the dead Body of Our Lord in her arms after He had been removed from the cross.

PILEOLUS. A skullcap worn by bishops and other prelates. It is also called a zucchetto.

PILGRIMAGE. The journey to a shrine or some place of religious significance. There are several organizations which sponsor pilgrimages to various shrines such as Lourdes in France, Fatima in Portugal, Guadalupe in Mexico, St. Anne de Beaupré in Canada, and the Holy Land.

PLENARY COUNCIL. National councils or meetings of the bishops of a nation or particular territory under the presidency of the pope's legate to determine matters of discipline and regulation. Their decrees are binding throughout the territory. In the United States three plenary councils have been held in Baltimore, because it was the first established see in the United States. The first was held in 1852, pledging allegiance to the faith and to the pope, and issued edicts regarding parish life, ceremonies, administration of Church funds, and the teaching of Catholic doctrine. The second, in 1866, condemned the heresies of that time, making laws concerning the organization of dioceses, the education and conduct of the clergy, among other things. The third Plenary Council, in 1884, made plans to create a Catholic University, appointed a commission to prepare a Christian Doctrine catechism, and determined six Holy Days of Obligation for the United States.

PLENARY INDULGENCE. A plenary indulgence is one which remits all the temporal punishment due because of sin. In order to gain a plenary indulgence, one must be in the state of sanctifying grace, must detest all sin and resolve to try to avoid even venial sin, must have been to confession and received Holy Communion and prayed for the intention of the Holy Father. The confession may be made within eight days before or eight days following the time one seeks the indulgence. The reception of Holy Communion must take place either on the day or within the following eight days.

PONTIFF. Any bishop. The title is used commonly in referring to the pope, who also is the bishop of Rome—that is, the Holy Pontiff.

PONTIFICAL MASS. A High Mass celebrated by bishops, abbots, and other higher prelates at which they wear their pontificals, their special vestments, and ornaments.

PONTIFICALS. Those ceremonial vestments and ornaments worn by bishops when officially pontificating.

PONTIFICATE.
1. The reign of any pope.
2. To officiate at a Pontifical Mass.

POPE. The Bishop of Rome who, as the Vicar of Christ and the legitimate successor of St. Peter, is the visible head of the Church. The title, Pope, is derived from the Greek word *papas*, meaning *father*. The pope is elected for life by the College of Cardinals. He has the privilege of resigning if he wishes, in which case a new pope would be elected. Any male Catholic, regardless of race or color, cleric or layman, could be elected. However, if a layman were selected, he would have to be ordained a priest and consecrated a prelate before he could ascend the throne of St. Peter.

Christ declared Peter the primate of His Church at Caesarea Philippi, with these words, "I for my part declare to you, you are 'Rock,' and on this rock I will build my church, and the jaws of death shall not prevail against it." From the time of Peter the pope's duties are to exercise supreme authority over the faith and morals of the faithful. He can enact laws for the Church, grant dispensations, excommunicate, create dioceses—in fact, take charge of the entire Church, hierarchy, clergy, and laymen. In matters concerning faith and morals, his decisions are infallible.

Named by Christ	°Mt	16	18-19	983

PORTABLE ALTAR. A small consecrated stone slab which contains relics of two canonized martyrs, and which is large enough to hold the altar bread and most of the chalice base. It is inserted into the flat top of an unconsecrated table.

PORTIUNCULA. The ruined chapel of St. Mary of the Angels near Assisi, Italy, which the Benedictines gave to St. Francis who repaired it and founded his order there. At his request the Portiuncula indulgence was established. To gain the plenary indulgence one must visit the chapel or any Franciscan Church at any time from noon of August 1st to midnight of August 2nd, go to confession, receive Holy Communion, and recite six Our Fathers, six Hail Marys, and six Glorias for the intention of the pope. Where there is no Franciscan Church, members of the Third Order may gain the indulgence at their parish churches.

POSSESSION, DIABOLICAL. Internal control of our actions by the devil, with the permission of God. By diabolical possession we mean the devil actually inhabits the body of a person, causing it to perform unusual acts, including blasphemy or

SUBJECT	BOOK	CHAP.	VERSE	PAGE

cursing. Although the possessed person is sorely tempted and grievously tortured he is not guilty of any of the sins committed during this state, because he is merely the medium through which the devil himself is operating. The Church casts out demons by means of the rite called exorcism. Diabolical possession is one of the three ways the devil torments man. The other two are temptation and obsession (external torment).

POSTCOMMUNION. Part of the Mass. These prayers or prayer vary with the feast and are said after Communion. In them we thank God for the privilege of the Mass, beseeching Him to grant us the fruits of the Holy Sacrifice.

POSTULANCY. The probation period of about six months which precedes the entrance of an aspirant into a novitiate. It is a time of strict religious discipline purported to help the individual decide whether or not he or she is suited for the religious life.

PRAYER, MENTAL. The wordless raising of the mind and heart to God. This may take many forms, the most common of which are meditation and contemplation.

Meditation is the reflection of the mind upon a particular truth, such as an event in the life of Christ, the mystery of the Blessed Trinity, some passage from the Bible, etc. It also can be described as prayer by reasoning.

Contemplation is the highest form of mental prayer. St. Bernard, Cant. I, describes it: "It consists not in words of the mouth, but a song of the heart; nor is it a sound with the lips, but a movement of joy. It is the harmony not of voices but of wills." Thus it can be attained only by those who are extremely virtuous. The mind mentally gazes upon God or another truth with deep, fervent love. The power for this type of prayer also may be given by God to help one get rid of sinful inclinations. In this case it is called "infused contemplation" and does not necessarily mean the possessor has attained perfection of virtue. Occasionally, God sends this grace to help the individual.

PRECEPTS OF THE CHURCH. The laws of the Church intended to promote the spiritual good of the faithful, and which are binding under sin. The six laws which pertain directly to the people are:
1. To assist at Mass on Sundays and all Holy Days of Obligation.
2. To fast and to abstain on the days appointed.
3. To go to confession at least once a year.
4. To receive Holy Communion during the Easter time.
5. To contribute to the support of the Church.
6. To observe the laws of the Church concerning marriage.

PREDESTINATION. From the beginning it was God's Holy Will that each man be given sufficient graces to enable him to attain eternal salvation. But man also was given free will, the power to accept or to reject those graces, the stepladder to the Beatific Vision. Thus, through God's foreknowledge, He knows beforehand which men, through their own actions, will accept the graces and will finally achieve eternal happiness, and which will refuse them and be condemned. God foresees our salvation or damnation, not as an end He decreed, but as the result of our own behavior, but nevertheless in His decree, by which He predestinates the number of the elect from all eternity. St. Augustine wrote, "As you, by your memory, do not cause past acts to be done, so God, by His foreknowledge, does not cause future acts to be done."

The plan of God	*Rom	8	29-30	1122
	Eph	1	4-5	1157

PREFACE OF THE MASS. A prayer of praise and thanksgiving said at the beginning of the Euchristic Prayer. There are several Prefaces which change according to the feast being celebrated or the liturgical seasons of the year. In a sung Mass the celebrant sings the Preface while the congregation stands.

PREFECT APOSTOLIC. In a missionary country where the Church hierarchy and dioceses have not been established, the Catholics are governed by a Prefect Apostolic. Although he usually is a priest, the Prefect Apostolic performs certain functions which normally are the prerogative of a resident bishop. He may confer minor orders and the Sacrament of Confirmation, and he may also consecrate portable altars and chalices which would be needed by the missionary priests in the field. Since he acts as the head of an undeveloped or partially developed territory, the Prefect Apostolic must make the regular *Ad Limina* visits to Rome.

SUBJECT	BOOK	CHAP.	VERSE	PAGE

PRELATE. The name given to a member of the clergy who has a higher rank than priest, such as Monsignor, Bishop, etc. Those who bear the title, Monsignor, wear special dress but do not have any special or extraordinary jurisdiction and are called Minor Prelates. The rank is considered a papal honor. Those who are bishops, abbots, etc., exercise ordinary jurisdiction in the external forum.

PRESBYTERS. In the early days of the Church certain authorized priests and bishops were called presbyters. Nowadays the title is sometimes applied to assistant priests.

Alms sent to	*Acts	11	29-30	1097
Met with Peter	*Acts	15	1-12	1101

PRESENTATION. The offering of the first born to God in the Temple. This was to stand as a reminder that God had slain every firstborn of the Egyptians so that Israel might go free. The Presentation of Our Lord in the Temple is the fourth Joyful Mystery of the Rosary. The Feast of the Presentation is celebrated February 2nd.

Commanded by God	*Ex	13	1-2, 11-16	57
	Nm	3	11-13	108
Of Christ	*Lk	2	22-39	1022

PRESENTATION OF THE BLESSED VIRGIN MARY. The feast commemorating the legendary presentation of the Blessed Virgin in the Temple according to the Jewish law. This event took place at the age of three, and accounts are contained in certain gospels. In 1585 Pope Sixtus V established this feast in the Western Church. It is celebrated November 21.

PRESIDENTIAL CHAIR. A chair in the sanctuary from which the presiding priest at mass leads the prayers of the first part of the mass. It should be noteworthy in design but not the equivalent of a bishop's throne.

PRIEST, PRIESTHOOD. A priest is one who is duly authorized to minister in sacred things, particularly to offer sacrifices at the altar, and who acts as mediator between God and man.

Old Testament Priesthood:

As a result of man's alienation from God through sin the requirement for mediation became universal, and sacrifices were made by Adam and his sons and by their descendants down through the annals of time. In setting up an order of priesthood in Israel, God appointed Aaron as the first high priest, directing that the high priesthood should be perpetuated in his family through each succeeding elder son, and that all males of the succeeding generations should be priests. It was later ordered that the tribe of Levi be designated as assistant priests or Levites.

The functions of the priesthood were minutely defined in the Mosaic Law; the sacredness of the office of both high priest and subordinate priests were clearly set forth in forms of ordination and in duties defined.

Heads of families:				
Noah	*Gn	8	20	7
Abraham	*Gn	22	13	18
Isaac	*Gn	26	25	22
Jacob	*Gn	33	20	30
Job	*Jb	1	5	463
Tribal chief: Melchizedek	*Gn	14	18-20	12
Aaronic priesthood directed	*Ex	28	1-43	69
by God	Ex	29	1-37	70
Duties of Levites	*Lv	1-7		81-85
	Nm	8	5-22	114
	Dt	10	8-9	150
Duties of high priest:				
Offered blood sacrifices	*Lv	1	5	81
	Heb	5	1	1197
	Heb	8	3	1199
Invoked God's aid	*Lv	9	22-24	87
	Nm	6	22-27	111
Entered Holy of Holies	*Lv	16	1-3, 12-19, 33-34	94
Offered sacrifice of expiation	*Ex	30	10	71
	Lv	16	6-11	94
	Heb	9	7	1200
Regulations governing priests:				
Forbidden wine and strong drinks	*Lv	10	8-11	88
Forbidden to shave	*Lv	21	5	98

SUBJECT	BOOK	CHAP.	VERSE	PAGE
Exempt from tax	°Ezr	7	24	366
No inheritance	°Nm	26	62	131
Supported by offerings	°Lv	2	3	81
	Dt	18	1-8	157
Rules for marriage	°Lv	21	13-15	98

Priesthood of Christ:
Christ was made High Priest of the New Covenant by His Father at the time of the Incarnation. He made atonement for the sins of the world in His own death on Calvary, and, rising triumphant over death, He entered the Holy of Holies at the right hand of God where he ever lives as our High Priest.

Christ the High Priest	°Heb	5	1-10	1197
	Heb	7	11-19	1198
	Ps	110	4	574
Instituted Holy Eucharist	°Mt	26	26-29	993
	Mk	14	22-25	1014
	Lk	22	19-20	1044
	1 Cor	11	23-26	1137
Sacrificed His life	°Heb	7	26-28	1198
Ordained His Apostles	°Mk	16	14-18	1017
	Mt	28	16-20	996

PRIESTHOOD. 1. The office of priest.

Christ's minister	°1 Cor	4	1-4	1132
	1 Pt	5	1-4	1215

2. The indelible character stamped upon the soul of a man who has validly received the Sacrament of Holy Orders. Through this sacrament those ordained have the power to say Mass, to administer the sacraments, to bless, and to preach.

"Thou art a priest forever"	°Ps	110	4	574

PRIMACY OF PETER. The supreme episcopal jurisdiction given Peter as head of the entire Church, conferred upon him and his successors by Jesus Christ. This primacy was inherited by succeeding popes.

Promised by Christ	°Mt	16	15-19	983
Given by Christ	°Jn	21	15-19	1081
Preached first sermon	°Acts	2	14-41	1085
Admitted Gentiles to	°Acts	10	1-48	1095
church	Acts	11	1-18	1097

PRIMATE. Formerly the title given to certain bishops who had authority over other bishops of a province or country. Today the title is purely honorary, carrying with it no jurisdiction, merely the right to precedence over certain other Church dignitaries in religious functions.

PRISONER OF THE VATICAN, THE. A name given to the popes from the time of the capture of Rome by the Piedmontese troops in 1870 until the Treaty of the Lateran in 1929. During this period the popes did not leave the precincts of the Vatican palace because it would mean a recognition of the *de facto* government and the pope as one of its subjects.

PRIVATE INTERPRETATION. The Protestant belief that the meaning of the Bible will be clear to anyone who reads it with the proper intention. The Catholic Church refutes this policy, and teaches instead that the Holy Spirit who gave us the Bible interprets it correctly through the Church Christ founded. Our Lord said, "the Paraclete, the Holy Spirit whom the Father will send in my name, will instruct you in everything, and remind you of all that I have told you."

Finally, the Council of the Vatican, in corroborating the decrees set down by the Council of Trent stated, "We, renewing the said decree, declare this to be its meaning: that in matters of faith and morals pertaining to the building up of Christian doctrine, that is to be held as the true sense of Sacred Scripture which Holy Mother Church has held and does hold, to whom it belongs to judge the true sense and interpretation of Holy Scripture, and therefore that it is permitted to no one to interpret the said Scriptures against this sense or, likewise, against the unanimous consent of the Fathers."

Given by God	°Jn	14	26	1071
Peter advised caution	°2 Pt	3	16	1218

PRIVILEGE. Granting a special favor which diverts from the ordinary interpretation of a law to a particular place or person. In the religious sense, Canon Law (and in certain cases, civil law, also) lists a few definite privileges granted members of the clergy in deference to their offices:

1. *Privilege of the Canon.* Anyone laying hands violently upon a member of the clergy incurs the penalty of excommunication.

2. *Privilege of the Tribunal.* In criminal and in certain other cases, the clergy may not be called before a lay court without the permission of the bishop or the pope. An ecclesiastical court ordinarily will hear their cases.

3. *Privilege of Immunity.* Members of the clergy are excused from military service and certain other civil offices, such as jury duty, magistrate, or judge.

PRIVILEGED ALTAR. 1. An altar to which the special grant of a plenary indulgence is given to a particular soul whenever Mass is celebrated at that altar. During Forty Hours devotion and on the Feast of All Souls (November 2), all altars are privileged.

2. A personal privilege of a privileged altar may be given certain priests. Thus a plenary indulgence may be gained for a particular soul whenever the priest says Mass, regardless of the altar at which it is offered.

PROBABILISM. The principle of moral theology which teaches that where there is a doubt about the righteousness and lawfulness of a particular action, and there is no reasonable way to solve the problem by the usual proper means, and there is a possibility that in the particular instance the law does not forbid that action, the individual may follow his conscience and not fulfill the law, if there is a solidly probable reason for so doing.

However, this principle does not apply in any case where the faith and morals of an individual are at stake, where the doubt would constitute a possible block to the valid reception of a sacrament, or would interfere with the inalienable rights of another individual.

PROCATHEDRAL. A church which is used as the cathedral in a diocese until the permanent cathedral can be built.

PROCESSION. A public demonstration by clergy and laity of love for God, in thanksgiving for favors received, or in supplication. The chief processions today are held during Holy Week; penitential ones on the Feast of St. Mark (April 25); on Rogation days; and festive processions on the Feast of Corpus Christi. "Procession now forms a part of the 'entrance rite' of each mass during which either a hymn is sung or the entrance antiphon is recited", (if not itself sung).

PROCESSION OF THE HOLY SPIRIT. The mode or manner of origin of the Third Person of the Blessed Trinity. The Three Persons are equal in all things; each is God. But the Son came from the Father, and the Holy Spirit from the Father and the Son. St. Thomas Aquinas explains it, "God the Father and God the Son loved one another from all eternity, for each beheld in the other the Supreme Goodness of the Divinity. Their mutual Love is their own very Substance, a Living Person, the Holy Spirit."

PROCESSIONAL CROSS. The special crucifix mounted on a staff of wood or metal which is carried at the head of processions.

PROFANITY. The use of vulgar expressions which offend good taste. They are not sinful provided they are not intended to be blasphemous, disrespectful to sacred things, or uncharitable; however, their use should be avoided.

PROFESSION OF FAITH. The oral recitation of belief in the tenets of the Catholic Church. This may be done by saying the Apostle's Creed or the Nicene Creed. A profession of faith is part of the ceremonies of the Sacrament of Baptism. However, a sponsor recites the Apostle's Creed in the case of an infant Baptism, while an adult being baptized recites it himself.

PROFESSION, RELIGIOUS. The taking of the simple or solemn vows of poverty, chastity, and obedience by a person entering a religious order after having completed the postulancy and novitiate.

PROHIBITING IMPEDIMENTS. Some barrier which renders a marriage unlawful but not invalid.

PROMOTER OF THE FAITH. An ecclesiastical official of the Sacred Congregation of Rites whose duty it is to thoroughly examine all causes for beatification and canonization in order to ascertain the truth and to avoid any possible error in determining the worth of each cause. He commonly is called the Devil's Advocate.

PROMULGATION. The official declaration of a law issued by the Holy Mother Church. This is usually done by publication in the *Acta Apostolicae Sedis*, but the pope is at liberty to announce it in any other manner.

PROPAGATION OF THE FAITH, SOCIETY FOR THE. A pontifical society founded for the purpose of soliciting prayers and alms for the support of missions throughout the world. The only requirements for membership are a daily prayer for the missions and a dollar yearly contribution for their support. This international organization is an auxiliary of the Sacred Congregation for the Propagation of the Faith.

PROPER OF THE MASS. Those parts of the Mass which vary according to the liturgical season or feast being celebrated.

PROTOCANONICAL BOOKS. Those books of the Bible which always have been accepted as genuine Sacred Scripture, and about which there never was any controversy over their authenticity. The disputed books are called deuterocanonical books. The Catholic Church accepts both the protocanonical and the deuterocanonical books as genuine; for various reasons most Protestant sects reject the deuterocanonical texts.

PROTONOTARY APOSTOLIC. Also called *Prothonotary*. Members of the chief order of prelates in the Roman Curia; they are divided into four groups or classes:

1. *Protonotaries Apostolic de Numero Participantium:* As part of their duties, they sign papal bills, aid in the examination of candidates for canonization, and help in the actual canonization proceedings. They enjoy the use of the pontificals.

2. *Protonotaries Apostolic Supernumary:* Domestic prelates in charge of the Basilicas of St. Peter, St. Mary Major, the Lateran, and certain other European cathedrals.

3. *Protonotaries Apostolic ad instar Participantium:* Prelates appointed by the pope and who are entitled to the use of pontificals as are the Protonotaries Apostolic de numero participantium.

4. *Protonotaries Apostolic Titular (or Honorary):* The honorary title bestowed upon certain priests outside of Rome. This privilege carries the title of Monsignor and entitles the designated ecclesiastic to a certain distinctive dress and certain other privileges.

PROVINCIAL COUNCIL. A meeting of all the bishops of one province. According to Canon Law each province must hold a council at least every twenty years. The Metropolitan calls the meeting and presides over it. Measures for increasing the faith, regulating morals, correcting abuses, and establishing uniformity may be discussed. Any act or decree must receive the approbation of the Sacred Congregation of the Council in Rome before it can be put into effect in the province.

PUBERTY. The age at which one attains sexual maturity, generally conceded to be fourteen years of age for boys and twelve for girls. Church Law prohibits legal and valid marriage before the individuals are at least two years beyond those ages.

PURGATORY. That place or state of punishment where the souls of those who have died in the state of grace, but who still may have some unrepented venial sins or may have to make satisfaction for forgiven mortal sins, suffer until admitted into heaven. The Church proves the Doctrine of Purgatory. Sacred Scripture, in the Old Testament, relates how Judas Maccabeus sent 12,000 drachmas of silver to Jerusalem for sacrifice to be offered for the sins of the dead. Through the inspiration of the Holy Spirit, the writer of the book wrote, "It is therefore a holy and a wholesome thought to pray for the dead that they may be loosed from their sins." Christ Himself inferred there are sins which can be forgiven after death: "Whoever says anything against the Holy Spirit will not be forgiven, either in this age or in the age to come." That complete satisfaction must be made is noted by Christ, "I warn you, you will not be released until you have paid the last penny."

Holy Scripture also tells us that "there shall not enter anything defiled" into heaven. Therefore, it is logical to reason that a soul in the state of grace but with venial sin staining it must be cleansed of that venial sin before entering heaven.

In Purgatory the poor souls primarily suffer a pain of loss, because, while there, they cannot see the Beatific Vision. The realization that their sins alone prevent this happiness causes dreadful suffering. Too, knowing that the soul did not take advantage of any opportunities of purging it of sin while still living adds to the torture.

SUBJECT	BOOK	CHAP.	VERSE	PAGE
Belief in prayers for dead	*2 Mc	12	38-46	457
Christ's words	*Mt	12	32	978
Nothing defiled in heaven	*Rv	21	27	1248

PURIFICATION OF THE BLESSED VIRGIN MARY. According to Mosaic Law, a Jewish mother had to go to the tem-

ple forty days after the birth of a male child and eighty days after the birth of a female to undergo a legal cleansing. An offering of a lamb and a turtle dove were made, or, in the case of the poor, two pigeons or two turtle doves were given. The priest sprinkled the mother with holy water and prayed over her. Our Blessed Mother conformed to this custom, even though she was a virgin both before and after Christ's birth. The feast celebrated February 2nd also commemorates the first time Our Lord was brought into the temple. It is also called Candlemas Day because candles are blessed on that day, and it is also known as the Presentation.

SUBJECT	BOOK	CHAP.	VERSE	PAGE
Mosaic rite	*Lv	12	1-8	90
Mary submitted to	*Lk	2	21-24	1022

PURIFICATOR. A linen or hemp cloth, anywhere from twelve to eighteen inches long and nine or ten inches wide. A small cross is embroidered in the center. It is placed between the chalice and the paten at the beginning of the Mass. The priest uses the purificator to cleanse the chalice before it is used at the Offertory, to cleanse the paten before the Host is placed on it, to dry the chalice and his lips after his Communion, and to purify his fingers. A lay person cannot touch a used purificator until it first has been washed by an ordained cleric.

PUTATIVE MARRIAGE. A marriage contracted in good faith but which is declared invalid because of the existence of a prohibiting impediment which had not been known by at least one of the parties. Children of such a marriage, however, are legitimate.

Q

QUADRAGESIMO ANNO. A famous encyclical letter on the social order published in 1931 by Pope Pius XI. The title is derived from the fact that it was issued on the fortieth anniversary of Pope Leo XIII's labor encyclical, "Rerum Novarum."

Since the supreme purpose of life on earth is to attain eternal happiness in the Almighty Presence, proper physical resources also are essential to help reach the spiritual end. This encyclical explains the problems associated with modern economic situations and offers solutions based on reason, social justice, and strict justice. It defends the rights and responsibilities of private ownership and the right to inheritance. It demands a living wage; deplores the existence of "working mothers" and child labor; condemns excessive taxation, etc. It proposes a just distribution of industry's income through balanced prices, maximum wages, etc. It deplores the individualism and economic dictatorship which have brought about the injustices of modern economic life, thus also incurring great spiritual loss.

The encyclical offers a solution to the problem based on a return to Christian principles and partial economic organization aided, but not controlled, by government action.

QUADRAGESIMO ANNO MEDAL. The medal annually awarded by the Association of Catholic Trade Unionists to the individual who has made an outstanding contribution to the Christian solution of industrial problems. In 1948, the first year of its existence, John Quincy Adams, head of a refrigeration company, received the medal. In 1949, the Labor-Management head of Manhattan College, Brother Justin, F.S.C., was the recipient. Joseph Beirne, president of the Communications Workers of America, and an official of the C.I.O., received it in 1950. Other recipients include Senator Robert Wagner and Labor leaders George Meany and Philip Murray.

QUASI DOMICILE. The residence of an individual within the limits of a diocese or parish, acquired by the intention of remaining there at least six months but not indefinitely. Such residence grants the full rights and duties of a member of the diocese or parish. It ceases with the individual's departure and intention of not returning.

QUEEN OF HEAVEN. 1. Popular title for the Blessed Virgin, in litanies and other prayers.

R

RACCOLTA. *a collection.* A book that contains all the prayers, religious devotions, and ejaculations which have been indulgenced. In 1938 the Vatican Press published the "Preces et Pia Opera," Prayers and Acts of Devotion, which now is the official replacement for the Raccolta.

SUBJECT	BOOK	CHAP.	VERSE	PAGE

REAL PRESENCE. The true existence of the Body and Blood of Jesus Christ together with His Soul and Divinity in the Blessed Eucharist under the physical appearance of bread and wine. Thus we believe Christ is truly present in the Blessed Sacrament by transubstantiation, and that the bread and wine are not merely symbols of His presence. Our Holy Mother Church solemnly teaches that Christ is wholly present under both species. When the consecrated bread and wine are separated, He still is wholly present in each.

REASON, AGE OF. The age at which an individual is able to distinguish correctly between good and evil, can assume moral responsibility, and can understand an obligation. Since there is no definite calendar age at which this ability takes place in each person, the Church for practical purposes presumes it to be seven. In some children this realization does come earlier.

RECOLLECTION, DAY OF. A single day set aside for religious exercises and meditation. Our Lord Himself often went by Himself to pray. His inspiration led laymen to follow His example. The best method is to attend a retreat, a series of days devoted to prayer and meditation. Since everyday duties often prevent some of the laity from devoting several consecutive days to this purpose, the Church conducts the Day of Recollection for those people. These usually are held in the parish churches or established retreat houses.

RED. 1. The papal color granted Pope John I (d. 526) by the Emperor Justin. It is also the color proper to cardinals.

2. Red is the color designated for vestments which are used on Pentecost and on all the feasts of martyrs, being a symbol of the ardent love of the Holy Spirit and of the shedding of one's blood.

RED MASS. Liturgically, any Mass celebrated in red vestments. Specifically, a Votive Mass of the Holy Spirit usually celebrated once a year for the benefit of lawyers and judges. The aid of the Holy Spirit is invoked so that they may exercise their duties with greater prudence and justice.

REDEMPTORISTS. The Congregation of the Most Holy Redeemer founded in Italy in 1732 by St. Alphonsus Mary Liguori. Primarily devoted to mission work, the Redemptorists have houses throughout the United States. The General Motherhouse is in Rome, Italy.

REFORMATION. The name given to the division of Christian unity in the 16th century which resulted in Protestantism. The Reformation is a very complicated period of history which includes not only the attacking of real abuses within the Catholic Church on all levels, but also a dispute on the fundamental teachings of the Church itself. There are many reasons for the Reformation: the corruption and materialism of the Renaissance bishops; a reaction on the part of spiritual men to the humanism of the Renaissance; decadence of theology in such a way that it appeared that man was saved by his practices and things rather than by faith and grace; rising nationalism, particularly the desire of German provinces to be free from political connections with Rome; the peculiar psychology of the great reformers, especially Dr. Martin Luther; a general low level of morality; lack of educated priests and teachers; failure of councils of the Church which had been called for reform; and many others. The Reformation spawned troubles for political and religious power on all sides. In response to the Reformation, the Council of Trent (1546–1553) reformed the Church from within and clarified Catholic teaching on justification, the Mass, the sacraments, as well as issued decrees to reform Christian life.

REGENERATION. A word used to describe a baptism. St. Paul referred to the sacrament as the "bath of regeneration." St. John quotes Jesus, "unless a man be born again of water and the Holy Spirit, he cannot enter the kingdom of God." Through regeneration, we are incorporated into the death and resurrection of Christ. We have now died to all sin and we now live the risen life of Christ; hence we are "regenerated." In the viewpoint of St. John, we are regenerated by having a new birth that Baptism gives us: we were born of our parents naturally; but through Baptism we are now born as children of God. The word regeneration itself means reborn.

SUBJECT	BOOK	CHAP.	VERSE	PAGE
Through Baptism	*Tit	3	5	1190
	Rom	6	4	1120
	1 Pt	3	21	1213
Essential	*Jn	3	3-7	1053

SUBJECT	BOOK	CHAP.	VERSE	PAGE
Result of God's love for us	*Jas	1	17-18	1206
	1 Pt	1	3-4	1211
Faith necessary	*1 Jn	5	1, 4	1225
	Jn	1	12-13	1050
Must lead new lives	*Col	3	9-10	1170
	Eph	4	20-24	1159
	Rom	6	1-7	1120
	1 Jn	2	29	1221
Brings sanctifying grace	*1 Jn	3	9	1223

REGULARS. According to Canon Law, those who belong to a religious order and are bound by solemn vows. These may be either men or women, but are distinguished from those religious who are bound only by simple vows.

RELICS. The remains of saints, either their entire physical bodies, portions of the bodies, or articles of clothing or possessions they used during their lifetimes. The Church permits veneration of relics, because the holy lives led by the saints and their consequent closeness to God could lead others to strive for that same holiness. Thus, in venerating a relic we are paying homage to God, the Supreme Being. He often works miracles through the intercession of the saint whose relics are so used.

Before veneration can be paid, relics must be authenticated. The Church must be reasonably sure the relics actually belonged to or were a part of the saint. They usually are divided into three classes. First class relics are actual parts of the saint's body. Second class relics are parts of the clothing or other possessions used by the saint during his life. Third class relics are objects which have been touched by the dead body or the tomb of the saint.

According to Church Law, the relic of at least one martyr must be enclosed in every altar or altar stone. This practice began during the Roman persecutions when the early Christians celebrated Mass in the catacombs, on the tombs of martyrs.

RELICS OF THE PASSION. There are in existence certain reputed relics of Our Lord's Passion and Death. Part of the pillar on which He was scourged is in Jerusalem, another part in Rome. The robe is in the Church of Treves; the tunic in the Church of Argenteuil near Paris. In Rome is kept the linen with which Veronica wiped Our Lord's face. At the Basilica of St. John Lateran in Rome is the sponge. The point of the lance used to pierce His side is in Paris; the remainder, in Rome. Also in Paris are the crown of thorns and one of the nails. The Basilica of the Holy Cross of Jerusalem in Rome has the inscription placed above the cross. Parts of the true cross can be found in Brussels, Ghent, Limbourg, Paris, Ragusa, Mt. Athos, Rome, and Venice. Part of the winding sheet is in Turin.

RELIGIOUS LIFE. Community life according to a specific rule. Canon Law defines it as a "stable manner of community life in which the faithful, besides observing the common precepts, bind themselves to the observance of the evangelical counsels by the vows of obedience, chastity, and poverty." There are many different religious orders of men and women. Basically, they may be divided into three groups: contemplative, active, and mixed.

Contemplative societies strive for union with God by prayer and penance and withdrawal from the world. Active groups serve God by devoting their lives to performing corporal works of mercy for mankind. Mixed groups are a combination of both, performing spiritual works of mercy which require contemplative practices as well as physical labors. Each order has a specific rule which must have the approval of Holy Mother Church before it can be established.

RELIQUARY. A vessel, sometimes shaped like a monstrance, in which relics are preserved and exposed.

REPARATION. An act performed to make amends for a material or spiritual injustice committed against God or a person. Such acts include adultery, contumely, detraction, fornication, homicide, or scandal. If the harm caused is great, the obligation to make reparation becomes very serious as justice must be rendered.

REPOSITORY. ALTAR OF REPOSITION. Name given to a place, usually temporary, set up for the Blessed Sacrament. Used usually in the Holy Thursday Liturgy.

REQUIEM. The first word (rest) in the Latin Mass for the Dead. A term formerly given to funeral masses or those said for the souls of the dead which used the funeral mass propers.

SUBJECT   BOOK   CHAP.   VERSE   PAGE

REREDOS. An ornamental screen usually made of wood or stone which is placed behind an altar. It may be either a part of the altar or separately constructed. The term also is used to define a painting placed there for the same purpose.

RERUM NOVARUM. "Of the New Things." The great social encyclical issued on May 15, 1891 by Pope Leo XIII concerning the laboring conditions of the working classes. At that time the trend was toward two divisions, the "haves" and the "have-nots." The "haves," represented by certain unscrupulous employers who controlled an increasing amount of wealth and power, were consistently subjugating the "have-nots," their workers, who were suffering ever-increasing oppressions of poverty.

Pope Leo XIII stressed the fact that the solution to this evil practice would not be found in socialism, which delegates possessions to the state. Rather, he wrote, the just solution must be reached through the combined efforts of the Church and the State, those who employ, and the employees. He advocated the organization for the mutual benefit of employer and employee. The State possesses the right to protect the rights of all concerned and to see that justice is obtained. Recognizing the right of each individual to possess property and material possessions, the church assumes the role of moral protector.

RESCRIPT. A written answer to a request or a special dispensation given by the Holy See or other proper ordinaries.

RESERVATION OF THE BLESSED SACRAMENT. The practice of keeping the consecrated Host in the tabernacle at all times to be used for the dying or present to receive the adoration of the faithful. The presence of the lighted sanctuary lamp and the tabernacle veil signifies the Holy Eucharist reposes within.

RESERVED CASES. Certain mortal, external, and consummated sins, the absolution of which is reserved to the Holy See or certain other high authorities. Only the Pope can declare such reservation for the entire Church. Bishops have the right to do so in their own territories. By special permission, or in certain emergencies, such as in danger of death, any priest can absolve a penitent from a reserved sin.

RESIDENCE. According to Canon Law, the rule which states no parish priest may be absent from his rectory and the proper discharge of his duties for more than a week without the permission of his bishop. The term is also used to designate a Catholic's proper parish when this is determined by territorial boundaries.

RESPECT OF PERSONS. A vice which implies that the judgments of men are more important than the judgment of God.

God is impartial	°Dt	10	17	150
	Rom	2	11	1118

RESTITUTION. The restoration of ill-gotten material goods, or of another's reputation and name destroyed by calumny. Any person who unjustly possesses anything belonging to another is bound to return or to restore it to its lawful owner. Anyone who deliberately destroys the reputation of another is bound to undo the harm he has done, insofar as he is able. Failure to make proper reparation, or the promise to do so, means the sin committed cannot be absolved.

RESURRECTION OF CHRIST. The reunion of Christ's immortal Soul and Body, through His own divine power, commemorated on Easter Sunday. The Resurrection of Our Lord from the sepulcher is His most important miracle, and this glorious fact is part of the very foundation of our faith. The Jews were concerned about this possibility and took every precaution by placing guards at the tomb to prevent the Apostles from carrying away the body and misleading the people into believing that He had risen. Yet, Christ rose on the third day as He had foretold. The Risen Christ was seen by numerous witnesses and, thus, proved His Divinity incontestably.

Promised by Christ	°Mt	12	38-41	978
	Jn	2	18-22	1052
Feared by His enemies	°Mt	27	62-66	995

RESURRECTION OF THE BODY. The reunion of the soul to the body of every human at the general judgment. This doctrine, an article of faith, was gradually developed in the Old Testament. One of the favorite expressions was that Yahweh kills and restores to life; He brings man to Sheol and brings him back again. Ezekiel, in his famous vision, saw dead bones being clothed with flesh and then returning to life. However, the doctrine of individual bodily resurrection was first

SUBJECT   BOOK   CHAP.   VERSE   PAGE

stated by the prophet Daniel, and it gradually became the common belief of most pious Jews. At the time of Christ, the doctrine of the resurrection was generally accepted by the Jewish people and the Pharisees, but it was rejected by the Sadducees. Christ taught the doctrine of the resurrection when He said that the children of the resurrection will be equal to the angels (Luke 20, 36). Thus, our own risen bodies, reunited with our own souls, will share their rewards or punishments for all eternity.

REVELATION. Truths revealed to mankind by God. These are divided into two classifications, *public* and *private*.

1. *Public revelation* is that contained in the Bible, both in the Old and New Testaments, and through Tradition. Since man's knowledge of God is imperfect, it follows that supernatural revelation must assist man in his quest for this knowledge. Christ said that unless human teachers are supernaturally enlightened, they can speak only of earthly truths. The divine revelations of the Old Testament were given to the individual prophets by dreams, visions, or direct instructions by God, and they explained them to others. Christ and His Apostles then brought the Old Testament revelation to completion through the assistance of the Holy Spirit. Christ made known to the Apostles everything that he had heard from His Father, even truths previously unknown. Public revelation came to an end with the death of the last Apostle, but those carrying on the faith were promised the assistance of the Holy Spirit to guide them and protect the faith that they had learned.

2. *Private revelation* is the manifestation of particular truths to individuals, even though the revealed truths apply to all people. Examples of private revelations are the appearances of the Sacred Heart in 1673–75 to St. Margaret Mary Alacoque at the Visitation Monastery of Paray-le-Monial, France; the Blessed Virgin's appearance to St. Bernadette Soubirous at Lourdes, France, in 1858; and to the three children at Fatima, Portugal, in 1917. The Catholic Church is extremely careful in expressing approval of any claims of supernatural revelation. Only after the most searching scrutiny during which every possible argument against the case in question has been disclaimed, will the Church declare a revelation authentic. While we as Catholics must believe revelations are possible, we are obliged to believe the truths of particular ones only when the Church has declared that particular one authentic, but this is by human and not divine faith, for private revelations never become part of the Catholic Faith.

REVENGE. The sin of desiring to inflict more than just punishment; to punish the wrong person; or to punish out of hatred, rather than for justice. Revenge is usually combined with human anger which is a sin against justice and charity. Christians are to put aside all bitterness, anger, and malice, and should not let the sun go down upon their wrath. Our Lord urged a spirit of forgiveness, and in the Lord's Prayer taught us: "Forgive us the wrong we have done as we forgive those who wrong us" (Matt. 6, 9-13.)

RHYTHM. The practice of limiting intercourse between husband and wife to the time of the wife's menstrual cycle when conception is least likely to occur. Although the primary purpose of marriage is the procreation of children, married people are not under obligation to have as many children as possible. Where for economic conditions or for reasons of health, additional children would cause serious hardship, couples may restrict the marriage relationship to infertile times. For clarification of the church's position on the use of rhythm in individual cases, the couples should seek the counsel of their confessors.

RIDDELS. Curtains hung at the sides of the altar. The curtains or drapes hung behind the altar are called dorsals or dossals.

RIGORISM. The moral theory principally taught by the heretical Jansenists, which stated that when one is in strict doubt about the validity of a particular act, he must adhere to a rigid interpretation of the law. Pope Alexander VIII condemned this theory in 1690. In place of heretical Rigorism, Catholic moral theology teaches probabilism, the system which declares if there is an honest, reasonable opinion that a certain law does not bind, that law need not be fulfilled, providing there is no easy access to an official decision on the facts of that particular question.

RING. A circular band of metal, usually gold or silver, generally worn on the finger, although it can be used in other ways.

SUBJECT	BOOK	CHAP.	VERSE	PAGE

1. Hebrews used rings of precious metals and stones as ornaments for the ears, nose, and fingers. Occasionally the Assyrian custom was followed whereby a ring was worn around the arm or wrist. A ring was sometimes given to a son to distinguish him from the servants. Signet rings or seal-rings were also used in early times for legal documents.

SUBJECT	BOOK	CHAP.	VERSE	PAGE
Nose rings worn by Hebrew	*Gn	24	22	19
women	Is	3	21	719
	2 Kgs	19	28	303
Assyrian custom	*2 Sm	1	10	243
On finger of right hand	*Jer	22	24	800
Given to a son as symbol	*Lk	15	22	1037
Gold ring sign of wealth	*Jas	2	2	1207

2. As part of their official insignia, bishops are entitled to wear a ring usually set with an amethyst, although any other stone except a sapphire may be used. Bishops wear their rings even when pontificating. A cardinal is entitled to wear a ring set with a sapphire. The pope wears the "ring of the fisherman," a signet ring which is used as his private seal. At his death his ring is broken. Doctors of Theology are entitled to wear plain gold rings except at liturgical functions. Abbots and abbesses wear rings as a sign of office. Some orders of nuns receive plain gold wedding bands after their profession as signs of their consecration to God and mystical betrothal to Christ. The use of rings in the Church signifies fidelity to the Holy Mother Church.

RITE. 1. The prescribed manner of performing or conducting liturgical services, such as the specific way of administering sacraments, etc.

2. The complete liturgical ceremonies, both the actions and the language, used by the particular divisions of the Western and Eastern Catholic Churches. In the Western Church the Roman Rite is most common, although there are also the Carmelite Rite, the Carthusian Rite, the Gallican Rite (almost disappeared), and the Dominican Rite. In addition, in Milan, Italy, and in the Archdiocese of Milan, the Ambrosian Rite is used. In Toledo, Spain, the Mozarabic Rite is followed. The Cathedral of Salamanca, Spain, uses the Mozarabic Rite only three days a year.

The Eastern Catholic Churches can be divided roughly as followers of the five principal Rites: Byzantine (the largest, second only to the Roman Rite of the Western Church); Alexandrian; Antiochian; Armenian; and Chaldean. A few further divisions are the Coptic, Melkite, Ethiopian, Malabarese, Marorite, Syrian, Italo-Greek, and Ruthenian.

The Church does not wish to abolish these various rites in favor of one. All are agreed on matters regarding faith and morals. Pope Benedict XIV expressed the Church's stand thusly, "Eastern Catholics should be Catholics; they have no need to become Latins."

RITES, SACRED CONGREGATION OF. That part of the Roman Curia which supervises and prescribes that which pertains to ceremonies and rites of the Latin Catholic Church. It also is in charge of everything concerning beatifications, canonizations, authenticity and dispensation of relics, etc.

RITUAL. A book containing the form for the administration of sacraments; blessings; and conduct of certain functions such as the burial rite. It was formerly called the Rituale Romanum and more recently the Collectio Rituum.

ROGATION DAYS. Traditional days of prayer in agricultural areas, the word itself means prayer. In the past, litanies honoring the saints were said on the three days prior to Ascension Thursday and special masses were offered to obtain a good harvest.

ROMAN COLLAR. The white, stiffly-starched upright collar, fastened at the back of the neck, worn by clerics and priests.

ROME. 1. Capital of the Roman Republic and Empire. It is first mentioned in the Old Testament during the time of the Maccabees when Rome agreed to a treaty of friendship with the Jews. The Romans inaugurated the gradual conquest of Asia Minor in 190 B.C. when they defeated the Syrian king, Antiochus the Great. Roman control was extended to Judea in 63 B.C. after Pompey subdued the Seleucid Kingdom. Although the Romans found the Jews notoriously difficult to govern, they respected the religious practices of the Jews, and the worship of the emperor was not introduced. The observance of the Sabbath was permitted, and local tribunals were allowed to exercise their power except in the passing of the death sentence. The Church was founded at a time when the Roman legions were completing the unification of the Mediterranean world.

SUBJECT	BOOK	CHAP.	VERSE	PAGE
Rome agrees to friendship	*1 Mc	1	11	418
with Jews	2 Mc	4	11	448

2. The Eternal City, site of the Vatican State which is the official seat of His Holiness, the Pope. Very little is known with certainty about the origin of the Church at Rome. According to tradition, St. Peter come to Rome during the second year of the Emperor Claudius (A.D. 42), which is closely connected with the time of his miraculous delivery from prison in Jerusalem during the persecution of Herod Agrippa I. St. Peter ruled the Church from Rome, was martyred on June 29, 67, and was buried there. All his successors, with the exception of the Avignon Popes, have resided at Rome. One of the titles of the Pope is Bishop of Rome.

SUBJECT	BOOK	CHAP.	VERSE	PAGE
Peter "went to another place" (Rome)	*Acts	12	17	1098
Jews expelled from city A.D. 49	*Acts	18	2	1105
Paul preached here while in prison	*Acts	28	16-31	1114

ROOD. A large crucifix, usually containing also the figures of Mary and St. John, used extensively in old English churches.

ROOD SCREEN. The wooden (sometimes iron) screen used to separate the nave from the choir or from the chancel in a church.

RORATE SUNDAY. The fourth Sunday in Advent. The name is derived from the first Latin word of the old Latin Mass in the introit for that day, "Rorate" (Let dew fall).

ROSARY. A series of prayers in honor of Our Blessed Mother. The complete rosary contains fifteen decades, each decade consisting of one Our Father, ten Hail Marys, and a Glory be to the Father, etc. The rosary itself is a circlet of beads devised to help us count and pray without distraction. An extension of the circlet contains a crucifix (on which the Apostles Creed is said); a single bead (on which the Our Father is said); three beads together (for three Hail Marys); and another single bead (for the Our Father) marking the beginning of the first decade of the rosary. Each five decades is devoted to meditating on the joyful, sorrowful, or glorious mysteries which commemorate some event in the life of Our Lord or of His Blessed Mother.

The Joyful Mysteries:

SUBJECT	BOOK	CHAP.	VERSE	PAGE
1. The Annunciation	*Lk	1	26-38	1020
2. The Visitation	*Lk	1	39-56	1020
3. The Birth of Our Lord	*Lk	2	1-7	1022
4. The Presentation	*Lk	2	21-38	1022
5. The Finding in the Temple	*Lk	2	41-50	1022

The Sorrowful Mysteries:

SUBJECT	BOOK	CHAP.	VERSE	PAGE
1. The Agony in the Garden	*Lk	22	40-46	1044
	Mt	26	36-46	993
	Mk	14	32-42	1014
2. The Scourging	*Mt	27	26	995
	Mk	15	15	1016
	Jn	19	1	1078
3. The Crowning with Thorns	*Mt	27	29	995
	Mk	15	17	1016
	Jn	19	2	1078
4. The Carrying of the Cross	*Lk	23	26-33	1045
	Mt	27	31-33	995
	Mk	15	20-22	1016
	Jn	19	16-17	1078
5. The Crucifixion	*Lk	23	33	1045
	Mt	27	34-35	995
	Mk	15	23-24	1016
	Jn	19	18	1078

The Glorious Mysteries:

SUBJECT	BOOK	CHAP.	VERSE	PAGE
1. The Resurrection	*Lk	24	1-49	1047
	Mt	28	1-20	996
	Mk	16	1-18	1017
	Jn	20	1-29	1080
	Jn	21	1-23	1081
2. The Ascension	*Lk	24	50-53	1047
	Mk	16	19	1017
	Acts	1	9-12	1083
3. The Descent of the Holy Spirit	*Acts	2	1-4	1085
4. The Assumption	*Tradition			
5. The Coronation	*Tradition			

Before the time of St. Dominic, prayer beads were used to

SUBJECT   BOOK   CHAP.   VERSE   PAGE

help concentration. Tradition tells us that during the 13th century while St. Dominic was preaching to the Albigenses, Our Lady appeared to him and confirmed the efficacy of praying to her in this manner.

The common rosary we use today consists only of five decades instead of the fifteen. The circlet is completed with a medallion bearing a likeness of the Blessed Virgin, on which a "Hail Holy Queen" is said at the completion of the decades.

ROSE. 1. A flower indigenous to Media and Persia and introduced to Mediterranean countries at an early period.

SUBJECT	BOOK	CHAP.	VERSE	PAGE
Rose wreath placed on head for festivals	°Wis	2	8	646
Wisdom compared with	°Sir	24	14	687
God's glory like	°Sir	39	13	701

2. A liturgical color, less penitential than violet, which is used on Gaudete Sunday (the third Sunday of Advent) and on Laetare Sunday (the Fourth Sunday of Lent). These two Sundays are considered joyful in the midst of penitential seasons.

ROSMINIANS. The name commonly given to the members of the congregation, Fathers of the Institute of Charity, founded at Domodossola, Italy, in 1828 by Antonio Rosmini. Its members perform external acts of charity and also strive for personal sanctification through contemplation and prayers. The General Motherhouse is in Rome; in the United States they are found in the Diocese of Peoria.

ROTA. One of the three tribunals of the Roman Curia, the others being the Sacred Apostolic Penitentiary, and the Supreme Tribunal Apostolic Signature. Appointed by the Pope, members of the Sacred Roman Rota must be doctors of theology and Canon Law. It is the ordinary court of appeals which rules on judicial cases sent from lower Church courts all over the world. It has no jurisdiction in cases reserved to the Pope himself or to the Sacred Congregation of Rites.

ROTARY CLUBS. Secular clubs founded in 1905 to "promote higher standards of business and professional practice, to encourage acquaintance and fellowship in business and professional activities, and to quicken interest in public welfare and community development." Since then the Rotary Clubs achieved international status and adopted the title, Rotary International.

By 1929 Rotary International had been accused of adopting a tendency toward religious indifferentism and secularistic ethical codes. At that time the Sacred Consistorial Congregation ruled it was not expedient for bishops to grant their priests permission to join Rotary. The Catholic laity in the United States are permitted to belong to the Rotary Clubs.

RULE OF FAITH. The actual teaching of the Church at a given time. This is expressed by the pope on special matters and by bishops and priests on matters of general instruction. The Church, founded by Christ, thus infallibly teaches through the correct interpretation of the Scriptures and Apostolic Tradition what is necessary for redemption.

RULE, RELIGIOUS. The order of life, aims, restrictions, and regulations of each religious order. Basically there are four rules which have been approved by the Church, namely those established by St. Augustine, St. Basil the Great, St. Benedict, and St. Francis of Assisi. Each religious group has its own approved constitution which follows either precisely or similarly one or another of these rules.

RUSSIAN ORTHODOX CHURCH. The official State Church permitted in the U.S.S.R. After the establishment of the Soviet Rule in 1917 all religious worship was forbidden. In 1943 the ban was lifted, the Holy Synod reconstituted, and a new patriarch of the Schismatic Orthodox Church was selected. The Russian Orthodox Church broke away from Rome during the 11th century.

RUTHENIAN CATHOLICS. Members of the Catholic Eastern Church who follow a modification of the Byzantine Rite using the Slavic language. Principally, they are Ukrainians and Carpatho-Russians. Here in the United States they constitute the majority of Eastern Rite Catholics.

S

SACRAMENT. The Council of Trent defined a sacrament as "a visible sign of invisible grace instituted for our justification." Our catechisms told us in simpler terms, a sacrament is

SUBJECT   BOOK   CHAP.   VERSE   PAGE

an outward sign instituted by Christ which produces interior grace.

There are seven sacraments: Baptism, Confirmation, Penance, Holy Eucharist, Holy Orders, Matrimony, and Anointing of the Sick. Confirmation, Holy Eucharist, Holy Orders, Matrimony, and Anointing of the Sick are called sacraments of the living since they increase sanctifying grace already present in a soul. Baptism and Penance are called sacraments of the dead, because a soul is supernaturally dead without them. However, when these sacraments are administered, sanctifying grace pours into the soul, making it supernaturally alive.

Each sacrament is conferred by an outward sign which is the rite, or ceremony. Each rite is composed of the actions prescribed (for example, pouring of water at Baptism; slap at Confirmation; etc.) and the words spoken by the priest or bishop in conferring the sacrament.

The "interior grace" is the sanctifying grace which flows to the soul through the confirmation of a sacrament.

SACRAMENT OF THE SICK. A sacrament which is administered to those in danger of death to restore the health of the soul; oftentimes, the recovery of the individual also follows. This sacrament is conferred by a priest who anoints the person with olive oil, which has been blessed by the bishop, and recites the following prayer: "Through this holy anointing, and His most tender mercy, may the Lord forgive you whatever sins you have committed by the sins of sight (hearing, smell, taste and speech, touch, and steps) Amen." Only those who have been baptized and have reached the age of reason may receive the sacrament of the sick, the grace of which wipes away sins, if any still are to be atoned for, and the remains of sins. If the sick person in the state of mortal sin has sufficient sorrow, any mortal sin not yet submitted to the Power of the Keys will be forgiven. If possible, of course, the sacrament of Penance should precede the Sacrament of the Sick.

SUBJECT	BOOK	CHAP.	VERSE	PAGE
Anointing the sick with oil	°Mk	6	13	1004
Specific direction for the sacrament	°Jas	5	14-15	1209

SACRAMENTALS. Outward signs, actions or objects blessed by the Church and intended to give temporal blessings and to increase the devotion of the people. Sacramentals were instituted by the Church; Christ instituted the Sacraments. Sacramentals do not remit sin or the temporal punishment due to sin. By them, however, we may get actual grace and obtain temporal blessings; they can provide a special protection against the power of evil. The efficacy of a sacramental depends upon the disposition of the user and the pleasure of God.

A sacramental can be a prayer; for example, the Sign of the Cross. Or it can be material, such as the ashes blessed and distributed on Ash Wednesday, a rosary, medal, scapular, holy water, etc.

SACRAMENTARY. Formerly the "holy book" contained all the ritual used in the Western Church. Later the term was applied to a book containing all the prayers of mass except the Scriptural readings which formed a separate book, the Lectionary (readings).

SACRARIUM. The piscina. A sink with a drain going directly into the ground, usually under the sacristy. Here all sacred linens are first washed, and holy water, baptismal water, blessed ashes, etc. disposed of. It is covered or enclosed to restrict its use for the purpose defined.

SACRED ORDERS. A term used to denote major officials in the church; the top ranks of the ordained clergy.

SACRIFICE. 1. An act of external worship by a qualified priest in which something is offered to God in recognition of His supremacy over all things, for the reparation of sins, and the hope of pardon and salvation. Christ offered the perfect sacrifice by His death on the cross. He was both the priest and the victim, and by His bloody sacrifice, gave His life for the redemption of sinners. Thus, His sacrifice is called the Sacrifice of Redemption, because through it man's sins were expiated, making Heaven possible for mankind.

The Sacrifice of the Mass is a Eucharistic sacrifice, a thanksgiving to God for the redemption. It is a true sacrifice; the outward sign is the ceremony; the priest offers the Victim to Almighty God; the Victim is Our Lord Himself, offered in an unbloody manner in the consecrated Host. To be a true sacrifice, the victim must be consummated; in the reception of Holy Communion the priest completes the sacrifice.

2. A voluntary act of self-denial offered for the proper intention.

SUBJECT	BOOK	CHAP.	VERSE	PAGE

SACRISTY. A special room usually just off the sanctuary in which vestments and altar linens are stored, sacred vessels, books, etc. are kept, and where the priest vests for Mass. Each sacristy must have a crucifix and also a place for the priest to wash his hands.

SAINTS. Members of the Church Triumphant, who lived their lives on earth in an exemplary manner, observing not only the essential moral laws of God but also attaining a high degree of heroic holiness for love of God. Holy Mother Church has determined, through her exhaustive processes of beatification and canonization, that these souls are now enjoying the Beatific Vision in heaven. The Council of Trent approved the practice of seeking the intercession of saints with God for us. In invoking the aid of certain saints by prayer, we do not take away homage from God. Instead, we believe our requests are made more pleasing to God if presented by a saint whose life on earth was most virtuously spent.

Mentioned in Scriptures	°1 Sm	2	9	217
	2 Chr	6	41	337
	1 Cor	6	2	1133
Intercede for us	°Rom	8	27	1122
	Eph	6	18	1161

SALVATION. The ultimate achievement of man's proper end; the attainment of the everlasting sight of the Beatific Vision, God, in heaven, after the punishment due to sin has been paid.

SALVATION ARMY. A heretical Protestant sect founded by William Booth, an ex-Wesleyan minister. He disagreed with Methodist teachings, and in 1861 left to become an independent evangelist. In 1877 he organized his followers into the Salvation Army, naming himself General. His avowed purpose was to convert the poor as well as to take care of their temporal needs. The Army has done excellent charitable work in helping the needy. Its members are noted for their sacrifices and zeal. Doctrinally, the followers believe in the Bible and say, "Believe in the Name of Christ and that you are saved by Him." But they reject Christ's teaching on the Eucharist, some reject Baptism, and in general, only part of Christ's doctrines are accepted.

SALVE REGINA. The Latin words for "Hail, Holy Queen." This prayer is part of the Divine Office said from the end of Eastertide to the beginning of Advent. The prayer is as follows:

SALVE REGINA

"Hail, Holy Queen, Mother of Mercy, our life, our sweetness, and our hope! To thee do we cry, poor banished children of Eve; to thee do we send up our sighs, mourning and weeping in this valley of tears! Turn then, most gracious advocate, thine eyes of mercy towards us; and after this, our exile, show unto us the blessed fruit of thy womb, Jesus. Oh clement, Oh loving, Oh sweet virgin Mary!"

Helps David escape	°1 Sm	19	18-24	232
Dies; buried at Ramah	°1 Sm	25	1	237
	1 Sm	28	3	239

SANATIO IN RADICE. *a healing at the root.* A special validation of an invalid marriage in certain cases where the invalidating obstacle was ecclesiastical and not due to an impediment of the natural or divine law. Only the Holy See can validate under this law. Renewal of consent is not necessary, because it is presumed in this case that the consent endures.

SANCTIFYING GRACE. A supernatural gift of God, an inward or internal gift, by which the soul is made pleasing to Him. It elevates man's nature, making it more God-like, and enables him to receive the divine virtues of faith, hope, and charity, all the moral virtues necessary to lead a Christian life, and the Gifts of the Holy Ghost. Without sanctifying grace, salvation is impossible. Sanctifying grace is lost through mortal sin, regained through the proper reception of the sacrament of Penance. All just men do not possess equal amounts of it; those who fulfill the commandments of God and the Church, and do good works, receive increased amounts according to their deeds.

SANCTUARY. *holy place.* 1. The part of a church or temple immediately adjacent to the principal altar.

2. In olden days, the refuge provided in a church for a person sought by public officials or private citizens. According to a now obsolete law, any criminal or fugitive was untouchable so long as he remained within the confines of a holy place.

SANCTUARY LAMP. The lamp or candle which is left burning in the sanctuary to indicate the presence of Our Lord in the Blessed Sacrament. If a lamp is used it must contain olive oil; otherwise a beeswax candle is required by Church Law. Besides signifying the Holy Presence, the lamp is symbolic of Christ, the light of faith.

SANCTUS. *holy.* The Latin term for the prayer or hymn which closes the Preface of a mass. The latter part of it is sometimes called the "Benedictus" which is the Latin word for "Blessed." In music the term refers to that part of a musical composition in the form of the old Latin mass which corresponds to the equivalent section of mass.

SANDALS. 1. Episcopal footwear worn by bishops and other hierarchy when celebrating Pontifical Mass. The upper part of the sandals is made of embroidered silk and usually matches the color of the vestments.

2. The footwear of certain religious orders known as discalced. Among these are the Discalced Carmelites, Capuchins, Augustinian Friars and Friars Minor.

SATISFACTION. The voluntary acceptance of the penance imposed by the priest in confession. Its object is to remove, in part, the temporal punishment due to sin. This satisfaction is an essential condition of absolution, and while the penance imposed may not relieve all the punishment due to sin, the penitent accepts it and is bound to fulfill it.

SCALA SANTA. The Holy Staircase, 28 marble steps now covered with wood, is reputed to have been brought to Rome by St. Helena, mother of Constantine, in 326 A.D. from Jerusalem. There they led to the court of Pilate, and according to legend, Jesus walked these steps on His way to the Crucifixion. As an act of penitence and faith the faithful ascend these steps on their knees. The authenticity of this relic has not been positively determined.

SCAPULAR. 1. A garment worn by many religious, symbolic of the yoke of Christ. It is made of two strips of cloth which cover the shoulders and fall partly in front and partly down the back, and is worn over the tunic. Benedictines, Cistercians, Carthusians, and Dominican lay brothers wear various forms of the scapular as part of their habits.

2. The most common scapulars today consist of two small pieces of cloth, between 2″ and 3″ long, joined by two cords so that one hangs in front and one down the back. The brown scapular of the Confraternity of Our Lady of Mt. Carmel is the best known. Scapulars are blessed and indulgenced and are worn by the faithful with the hope of God's mercy and blessings. Catholics do not believe that the material itself holds any special powers; such belief would be superstitious and sinful.

SCAPULAR MEDAL. A small medal which has a likeness of the Sacred Heart on one side and the Blessed Mother on the other. This, when properly blessed, may be worn in place of the cloth scapulars.

SCHISM. The formal refusal of a church to submit to the authority of the Vicar of Christ; the separation from communion with the Church. Schisms often lead to heresies. Schismatics are forbidden to receive the sacraments of the Catholic Church.

SCHOLASTIC. 1. A philosopher or student of Scholasticism.

2. A Jesuit who has completed his novitiate, taken simple perpetual vows, and now will either teach or study for from ten to seventeen years. During this period the scholastic is ordained a priest.

SCHOLASTICISM. The Schoolmen and Scholasticism began with the Carolingian Schools in the 8th Century and reached their peak in the 13th Century with St. Albert the Great, St. Bonaventure, and St. Thomas Aquinas. Scholasticism reduced Christian Doctrine or Theology to a scientific form, harmonizing revelation and reason, faith and science. They were the defenders of the rights of reason without encroaching on the rights of revelation; revelation cannot contradict reason nor reason contradict revelation. When Aristotle became known in Europe they began a scientific construction of philosophy based on him, but other philosophers were not neglected.

St. Thomas Aquinas was the greatest propounder of Scholasticism, based primarily on the philosophy of Aristotle. However, St. Augustine, who was not a follower of Aristotle, also was responsible for an important part of Scholasticism, as were Abelard, Peter Lombard, etc.

SCOTISM. Another school of Scholastic philosophy formulated by Duns Scotus, a Franciscan. This employs what is called a "formal distinction," which is neither mental (the distinctness

SUBJECT BOOK CHAP. VERSE PAGE

exists before the mind operates) nor real (it is not a distinction between things, only between formalities). The Scotists claim individuality exists because a formality is present in the being which is distinct from the reality of that being. Scotism differs from the Scholasticism of St. Thomas; in some aspects there is direct opposition.

SCRUPLES. Exaggerated fear about the lawfulness of an act, whether something actually permitted is forbidden, or something actually only a venial sin is mortal. Thus such a conscience leads one to unusually strict or false judgments, occasionally resulting in damage to both the physical and spiritual health of the scrupulous one. The aid of the confessor should always be sought to right an erroneous conscience.

SEAL OF CONFESSION. The solemn and inviolate obligation of the priest in the Sacrament of Penance to maintain absolute secrecy concerning anything revealed to him in the confessional. St. Thomas Aquinas wrote, "Whilst hearing confessions, the priest acts in the name of God and should behave as God Himself behaves. But God does not reveal, but keeps silent concerning sins manifested in confession." The Fourth Lateran Council clearly stated the position of the Church regarding the seal of confession: "Let the priest be most careful not to betray any penitent, by word, or sign, or in any other way. Any priest who presumes to reveal a sin manifested to him in Confession must not only be deposed from his priestly office, but must be sent to an enclosed monastery, there to do penance for the rest of his life." Secondarily, everyone who knows something by reason of the confession (one who overhears the confession) is bound to the seal.

SECRET SOCIETY. Any group whose secret format is dangerous to religion, to the state, or to one's conscience. Any Catholic who dares to join any such secret society incurs excommunication. Usually these societies conduct pagan rituals simulating Christian rites, and demand unreasonable obedience to the rules of the society, regardless of the moral beliefs of its members.

SECRETARIUM. The name formerly given the sacristy. Now the name for a small room or side chapel reserved for a cardinal, bishop, or abbot, where he may rest or recite the Divine Office.

SECULAR CLERGY. Another name for diocesan clergy. They are ordained priests who do not belong to a particular order. These diocesan priests make a promise of chastity, but are permitted to own property, and are subject to the authority of the diocesan bishop. Instructing the faithful and conducting parishes comprises their chief labors.

SECULARIZATION. 1. The permission granted to a professed religious to live permanently in the world and to leave the community or congregation. It involves a dispensation from religious vows, but not from the obligations of sacred orders. A papal indult is usually required for secularization.

2. The act by which the church, by force, relinquishes title to certain property, turning it over to secular authorities. Throughout history this has taken place, and monasteries, schools, hospitals, etc. have been taken over by civil governments, but this relinquishment cannot take place justly without the consent of the Holy See, which consent is seldom asked for or obtained.

SEDIA GESTATORIA. A portable chair. The chair attached to a small platform and fastened to two poles (one on each side) on which the pope is carried when making solemn entries into St. Peter's or other places. Twelve men (six on each side) dressed in red carry this chair.

SEDILIA. The bench or chair in the sanctuary, on which the celebrant and servers sit.

SEE. That territory presided over by a bishop. Another name for the diocese. The Holy See is literally the diocese of Rome, but common usage makes its present meaning the government of the entire Catholic Church centered at Rome.

SEMINARIAN. A young man studying for the priesthood in a seminary.

SEMINARY. *a seed bed.* The term used for an institution which trains young men for the priesthood. It may be a "preparatory" seminary for high school students; a college as such or a house connected to a regular university where students for the priesthood live and study; or a post-college school for the study of theology.

SEMI-PELAGIANISM. A 5th century Pelagianism heresy which originally claimed: (1) Original sin of Adam and Eve was not transmitted to mankind; (2) Christ came into the world to set a virtuous example, counteracting Adam's weakness and fall; (3) we can attain the eternal happiness by ourselves with no help from God via graces, etc. When St. Augustine irrefutably disclosed the errors of this heresy, the followers changed their beliefs to the claim that man can merit the first grace. They also taught a doctrine of predestination. This latter heresy of Semi-Pelagianism was condemned by the Second Council of Orange in 529.

SEPULCRUM, SEPULCHRE. The rectangular or square opening in the top of the altar (the mensa) in which are contained the relics of saints. At the beginning of Mass, when the priest ascends the steps to the altar, he kisses the place saying, "Through the merits of thy saints whose relics are here, and of all the saints, we pray thee, O Lord, that thou wilt forgive us all our sins."

SEQUENCE. A kind of hymn sung in certain Masses.

SERMON. The homily, instruction, or discourse preached in church at Mass after the gospel. According to the ruling set forth by the Third Council of Baltimore, sermons should be preached in all parishes at all Masses on Sundays and Holy Days.

SEVEN DOLORS. The seven sorrows suffered by Our Blessed Mother because she was the mother of Christ. They are: (1) the prophecy of Simeon; (2) the flight into Egypt; (3) the three day loss of Jesus; (4) the meeting with Christ on the way to Calvary; (5) the Blessed Mother standing at the foot of the Cross; (6) the descent of the Body of Christ from the Cross; (7) the burial of Jesus Christ. A Novena to the Sorrowful Mother promoted by the Servite Fathers has become nationally popular. Partially as a result of this devotion nurtured at Our Lady of Sorrows Church in Chicago, Illinois, the Holy Father raised the Church to a basilica.

The seven dolors also are commemorated in Masses on the Friday in Passion Week and the 15th of September, and also in the rosary.

SEXT. One of the day hours of the Divine Office. Literally it means sixth, and is said about midday.

SEXTON. A corruption of the word, sacristan; also another name for a church caretaker or janitor, or one who rings the outside church bells.

SHOWBREAD. The twelve thin cakes of bread that were placed in two rows on the table in the Holy Place of the temple. They had to be replaced every Sabbath, and the priests ate the stale bread. Another name for these cakes is Loaves of Proposition.

SHRINE. 1. A holy place, perhaps where the Blessed Mother or some saint has appeared and to which pilgrimages now are made.

2. A grotto or chapel containing the image of a saint erected to promote devotion or to commemorate some religious event. Usually flowers are placed by the statue and a candle burns before it.

SHRIVE. SHROVE TUESDAY. SHROVETIDE. The word shrive is an archaic term meaning "to forgive sins" (in the sacrament of confession). "Shrove Tuesday," the Tuesday before Ash Wednesday, and "Shrovetide"—the Monday and Tuesday before Ash Wednesday, were traditional times for making confession before the penitential season of Lent began. Later they became a time of carnival.

SHROUD, THE HOLY. A relic of the holy linen cloth which held the Body of Christ while He was entombed. Although there have been numerous claims of possession of the holy shroud, in the Cathedral of Turin is preserved a relic which bears the impression of the Body of Our Lord. This relic measures thirteen and a half feet by four and a quarter feet. Many religious scholars accept the authenticity of this holy shroud although officially Holy Mother Church has not ruled on it.

SICK CALL. In any cases of serious illness or accidents a priest should be called at once to administer the sacraments to the sick or hurt person. When a priest is called to a home, certain essentials should be provided: a chair near the bed for the priest; a small table covered with a white cloth (linen, if possible) placed at the foot of the bed so the patient can see it; on the

SUBJECT BOOK CHAP. VERSE PAGE

table, a crucifix and two blessed candles; holy water, a glass of water, and a teaspoon; a small white cloth which can be used as a communion cloth; a few cotton balls, if possible, with which the Holy Oil will be wiped after it has been applied. If the priest is bringing Holy Viaticum with him, he must be met at the door with a lighted, blessed candle. The priest will enter the house and say, "Peace unto this house and to all who dwell therein."

SIGN OF THE CROSS. The sacramental in which a cruciform motion is made on one's person by touching the forehead, breast, left and right shoulders with the fingers of the right hand, the while saying, "In the name of the Father and of the Son and of the Holy Spirit. Amen." By performing this act, we confess our faith in Christ crucified and ask His protection.

SIGNATURE, APOSTOLIC. The highest of the three tribunals or courts of the Roman Curia. Primarily a court of appeals, it also handles special cases.

SIN. A willful transgression of the laws of God or of the Church. The moral defilement which results when a soul deliberately rebels against the commandments. We are born with original sin. The reception of Baptism removes this stain, filling our souls with sanctifying grace. Other sins are called venial or mortal, depending upon the seriousness of the transgression and the willfulness of the act. These can be divided further into sins of omission and sins of commission.

SISTER, RELIGIOUS. A female religious who belongs to a congregation which is bound only by simple vows, in contrast with a nun who takes solemn vows.

SISTINE CHAPEL. The principal chapel of the Vatican Palace, also called the pope's chapel. Here the cardinals vote for a new pope, and here most papal observances take place. Canonizations, however, and certain other services of worldwide importance are held in St. Peter's Basilica which adjoins the Vatican Palace. The name is derived from that of Pope Sixtus IV who ordered its construction in 1473.

SOLEMNITY. Any feast celebrated with full liturgical ceremonies, either locally or universally. The title is also applied to the feast, the Solemnity of St. Joseph, which is celebrated a second time because the primary feast, March 19th, occurs during the penitential season of Lent.

SOLEMN VOWS. Those vows which render contrary acts illicit and invalid. Religious who take solemn vows cannot marry nor are they permitted to own property. No solemn vow can be taken by a person less than twenty-one years old. Women who take solemn vows are called nuns in contradistinction to sisters who belong to congregations and take simple vows.

SORROWFUL MYSTERIES OF THE ROSARY. The five sorrowful events commemorated in the second meditation cycle of the Rosary. They are: (1) the Agony in the garden; (2) the Scourging at the pillar; (3) the Crowning with thorns; (4) the Carrying of the Cross; (5) the Crucifixion.

SOUL. The intellectual principle. That which determines a man, as contrasted with an animal which has no intellectual soul. St. Thomas Aquinas in his *Summa Theologica*, I, q. 76, a.l, states:

"The nature of each thing is shown by its operation. Now the proper operation of man is to understand; because he thereby surpasses all other animals. . . . Man must therefore derive his species from that which is the principle of this operation. But the species of anything is derived from its form. It follows, therefore, that the intellectual principle is the proper form of man." A soul is a spiritual being. As such it cannot be too dependent upon matter. Since that is true, it follows that it need not be destroyed with the destruction of the body. Since it is not subject to dissolution, the soul is said to be intrinsically and naturally immortal.

SPIRITUAL BOUQUET. The offering of the spiritual benefits gained from indulgenced prayers, Masses, or other devotions which are given to another.

SPIRITUAL WORKS OF MERCY. Those acts of love performed to help our neighbor, either bodily or spiritually. They are: to instruct the ignorant, to counsel the doubtful, to comfort the sorrowful, to admonish the sinner, to forgive injuries, to bear injustices patiently, to pray for the living and the dead.

SUBJECT BOOK CHAP. VERSE PAGE

SPIRITUALISM. The belief and practices of those who claim the ability to communicate with spirits or with the souls of the dead. In most cases where spirits are supposed to have appeared, fraud can be proved. However, in a few cases the information received seems to have come from an intellectual source. Too, in some instances the interference of evil spirits can be shown. It must be noted that no spiritualistic seance ever revealed truths of general public interest. Too often they are either agnostic errors or trivial or ridiculous remarks. Two decrees of the Holy Office, one on March 30, 1898, and the other April 24, 1917, declare it is unlawful to assist, either with or without a medium, at any spiritualistic seance regardless of any outward sign of piety which might be shown. Merely watching one is sinful. God will never permit Himself to become the servant of man, to be called like a genii whenever a medium goes into a trance.

SPONSOR. One who vouches for another, assuming a spiritual relationship which carries a certain responsibility for the spiritual welfare of that person. One or two persons are required as sponsors for baptism. They act for the child in making the responses at the time of baptism. A baptismal sponsor must be a practicing Catholic over 14 years of age, unless there is a just cause to the contrary.

One sponsor only is required for Confirmation, but he must be of the same sex as the one confirmed. No marriage impediment is incurred through this sponsorship. A Confirmation sponsor must be a practicing Catholic of at least 14 years of age.

SPY WEDNESDAY. The name given to Wednesday of Holy Week because Christ was betrayed to the high priests by Judas on this day.

STABAT MATER. "Stabat Mater dolorosa." The first words of the song sequence used on the Feasts of the Seven Dolors of Our Lady. The hymn usually is sung during Stations of the Cross devotions. It is translated as "The sorrowful mother stood."

STATIONS OF THE CROSS. The Way of the Cross probably started soon after Our Lord's death. Surely His mother, Mary, and the Apostles walked over the same sorrowful route many times afterwards. Even today devout pilgrims tread the "Via Dolorosa," the sorrowful way, from Pilate's Praetorium to Calvary. Since it was impossible for most pilgrims to visit the original site, reproductions of The Way began to appear. In the 15th century Blessed Alvarez, a Dominican, erected in Spain groups of Chapels in which were painted Passion scenes. The Franciscans probably are responsible for the Way of the Cross devotion. Throughout Europe they erected the Stations in their churches, obtaining rich indulgences for them. However, a uniform number was never used, and at one time 37 stations were erected. Finally Pope Clement XII fixed the number as 14 in 1731. They are:

1. Christ is condemned to death.
2. Christ takes up His Cross.
3. Jesus falls the first time.
4. Jesus meets His Blessed Mother.
5. Simon of Cyrene helps Jesus carry His Cross.
6. Veronica wipes the face of Jesus.
7. Jesus falls the second time.
8. Jesus consoles the women of Jerusalem.
9. Jesus falls the third time.
10. Jesus is stripped of His garments.
11. The Crucifixion.
12. Jesus dies on the Cross.
13. Jesus is taken down from the Cross.
14. The Body of Jesus is placed in the tomb.

All that is necessary for the Way of the Cross devotions are fourteen blessed wooden crosses, but the faculties are obtained from the Minister General of the Franciscans. In most modern churches these are accompanied by images or paintings of the scenes commemorated. In "making the Way" we spiritually accompany Our Lord on His sorrowful journey to Calvary, meditating at each scene of His passion and death.

Those who devoutly make the Stations of the Cross may gain a plenary indulgence under the usual conditions. The sick also may gain this indulgence if they will kiss devoutly or gaze upon a crucifix especially blessed for the Way of the Cross. They also must recite, if possible, a short prayer in commemoration of the Passion and Death.

STIGMATA. The wounds of Our Lord, the pierced hands, feet and side, and the impression of the crown of thorns which ap-

63

SUBJECT	BOOK	CHAP.	VERSE	PAGE

pear in the flesh of certain persons who suffer corresponding pain. The first stigmata was suffered by St. Francis of Assisi in 1224. The Italian Padre Pio is an example of a modern day stigmatist. It seems that God selects certain souls to share the sufferings of Our Lord to help atone for the sins of all mankind.

STIPEND. The offering made to a priest by the faithful when requesting a Mass be said for their intentions. A priest, in accepting the stipend, has a moral obligation to say that Mass for that intention.

STOCK. The metal containers in which the holy oils are kept. There must be three, one for the Oil of Catechumens, one for Chrism, and one for the Oil of the Sick.

STOLE. The long (about 8 ft.) narrow silk vestment matching the chasuble in color, worn about the neck. A deacon wears it suspended from his left shoulders, crossing his chest diagonally and fastened at right side of his waist. A priest crosses the ends at the breast if worn over an alb. While hearing confessions the priest wears it hanging loosely from his neck. A bishop always wears it hanging loosely. While priests, bishops, etc. must wear it only when saying Mass or administering sacraments, the pope can wear the stole at all times. A stole symbolizes immortality of the soul and the yoke of obedience which the priest accepts.

A stole has traditionally stood for knowledge and jurisdiction. Symbolic meanings given to it include immortality of the soul and the yoke of Christ.

STOUP. The holy water font which can be placed near each entrance of a Catholic Church.

STRIKING THE BREAST. A gesture used to indicate contrition and repentance.

SUDARIUM. 1. The shroud of Our Lord. 2. The name sometimes given to the cloth Veronica used in wiping the face of Christ.

SUICIDE. The taking of one's own life deliberately. If the person were adjudged sane at the time of the deed, ecclesiastical burial is denied. If, however, temporary insanity can be assumed, Christian burial is permitted. Suicide is a mortal sin against the 5th Commandment. By taking his own life a suicide infringes upon God's authority and power over human life. Any act dangerous to human life which is performed voluntarily but unnecessarily is also sinful.

SUISSE. A soldier who belongs to the pope's Swiss Guards.

SULPICIANS. The society of priests devoted to the teaching in seminaries. In the 17th century Abbe Olier founded the Society at the Church of St. Sulpice in Paris, France. At the present time there are Sulpicians in the United States and in Canada as well as in France.

SUMMA. The name commonly given to the major work of St. Thomas Aquinas, the *Summa Theologica.* Divided into three parts, the first considers God as Himself and as the Creator; the second considers God as the intended ultimate end of man and how our actions either lead us to Him or turn us away from Him eternally; the third discusses the Incarnation, the sacraments, and the last things.

SUNDAY. The first day of the week, also called the Lord's Day. According to the laws of the Catholic Church it is to be kept holy, attendance at Mass is obligatory, and no servile work is to be done that day.

SURPLICE. The loose, white linen garment with full, wide sleeves which the priest wears over the cassock while administering certain sacraments.

SUSPENSION. The ecclesiastical censure which forbids a cleric to perform the duties of his office or to accept any financial support ordinarily due because of his office.

SWISS GUARD. The soldiers who guard Vatican City, the doors to the palaces, and the papal apartment, and who are in the attendance at all papal functions. This corps was established in 1505. All members must be Swiss Catholics. At present there are 104 guards and 6 officers. Their parade uniforms, designed by Michelangelo, consists of wide blue, yellow, and red striped tunic, breeches, and stockings, with a white ruff around the neck and a steel morion. On state occasions a steel breastplate also is worn. For fatigues and night duty they wear a blue tunic and breeches and a black beret.

SUBJECT	BOOK	CHAP.	VERSE	PAGE

SYLLABUS. 1. The list of errors condemned by Pope Pius IX. In December, 1864, this digest was compiled and released. The eighty subjects covered include pantheism, naturalism, communism, socialism, relations of church and state, and the temporal power of the pope.

2. The name also given to Pope St. Pius X's decree, "Lamentabili" issued July 3, 1907, condemning modernism.

SYMBOL. The representation or sign by which something is known. In church paintings symbolism is used frequently to describe the Holy Trinity (a triangle), the Holy Spirit (a dove), the Holy See (keys), and the Cross (the Crucifixion). The four evangelists are portrayed symbolically as follows: Matthew, a winged man; Mark, a winged lion; Luke, a winged ox; John, an eagle. In the early church a fish often was used as a symbol. The Greek letters for fish, I–Ch–Th–U–S are an abbreviation of the Greek words, "Jesus Christ, Son of God, Saviour." Thus the fish became a symbol of Jesus Christ. Again from the Greek, the familiar letters, IHS, are an abbreviation of the Greek word Iesaus, meaning Jesus.

Symbolism in the early church served another purpose, to protect the Christians from onslaughts of the pagans. Since holy things were represented by material objects whose true meanings were known only to Christians, the curiosity of the pagans was not aroused readily. The word symbol is also applied to the Apostle's Creed because it was considered to have been written as a joint effort by all the Apostles.

SYNAGOGA. The name given the singer who, in Passion music during Holy Week, chants the words of persons other than Jesus Christ.

SYNAXIS. In the early church, the gathering together of Christians for worship. Also applied to any congregation assembled to hear Mass or to pray together.

SYNDIC. The layman appointed to administer the goods and property of a religious community whose laws state no property may be held even in common. Those communities which follow the rule of St. Francis which forbids the owning of property found changing social conditions and the growth of their communities made ownership inevitable. Therefore, the Holy See assumes ownership of any property willed to them, and a syndic is appointed to manage those goods.

SYNOD, DIOCESAN. A gathering of the bishop and ordained clergy of a diocese to discuss problems and legislation pertinent to the spiritual welfare of its people. All decisions must be made by the bishop; the rest of the clergy is present as consultants or advisers. Canon Law states each diocese must conduct a Synod at least once every ten years.

SYNODAL EXAMINERS. A group of from 4 to 12 priests appointed at a diocesan synod who investigate the qualifications of candidates for parish benefices or church offices.

SYNODAL JUDGES. Four to twelve competent priests well schooled in Canon Law who are appointed to judge ecclesiastical cases in the diocesan courts.

T

TABERNACLE. The receptacle in the middle of the altar in which the Blessed Sacrament is reserved. This solidly-built enclosure must have a door which is kept locked. The priests see to it that the key is kept in a safe place. The bottom, or floor, is covered with a corporal (white linen square). No flowers, statues, etc. can be placed on top of it. Only vessels containing the Holy Eucharist can be kept within.

TABULA. The wooden clapper, used in place of a bell, in giving signals at Holy Thursday and Good Friday services.

TANTUM ERGO. *therefore.* The title and first two words of the hymn sung during Benediction. Actually it comprises only the last two stanzas of the *Pange Lingua,* written by St. Thomas Aquinas. The Latin and the English translation follow:

Tantum Ergo

"Tantum ergo sacramentum,
  Veneremur cernui;
  Et antiquum documentum
  Novo cedat ritui;
  Praestet fides supplementum
  Sensuum defectui.

Genitori, Genitoque,
Laus et jubilatio;
Salus, honor, virtus quoque
Sit et benedictio:
Procedenti ab utroque
Compar sit laudatio. Amen."

English Translation
"Down in adoration falling,
Lo! the sacred Host we hail!
Lo! o'er ancient forms departing,
Newer rites of grace prevail;
Faith for all defects supplying,
Where the feeble senses fail.

To the everlasting Father,
And the son who reigns on high,
With the Holy Spirit proceeding
Forth from each eternally,
Be salvation, honor, blessing,
Might, and endless majesty. Amen."

TE DEUM LAUDAMUS. *We praise Thee, O God.* A hymn of praise and thanksgiving sung at the close of special services of thanksgiving.

TEMPERANCE. One of the four cardinal virtues. This is the virtue which regulates, according to right and proper reason, the moderate desire and use of the senses of taste and touch, particularly with regard to eating, drinking, and sexual gratification.

TEMPORAL POWER OF THE POPE. The right of the pope to govern a territory such as Vatican State, and to be recognized by other nations of the world as the sovereign of that state.

TEN COMMANDMENTS. The Ten Words or Commandments which were spoken by God on Mount Sinai and written on two stone tablets. They appear in two forms: Ex. 20, 1-17 and Deut. 5, 6-21, which are almost identical verbally, but there is a considerable difference regarding the last commandment. The Decalogue of Roman Catholics is based upon the Deuteronomy text and is as follows:

I. I the Lord, am thy God . . . you shall not have other gods besides me.
II. You shall not take the name of the Lord your God in vain.
III. Remember to keep holy the Sabbath day.
IV. Honor your father and your mother.
V. You shall not kill.
VI. You shall not commit adultery.
VII. You shall not steal.
VIII. You shall not bear false witness against your neighbor.
IX. You shall not covet your neighbor's house.
X. You shall not covet your neighbor's wife.

SUBJECT	BOOK	CHAP.	VERSE	PAGE
Given by God	°Ex	20	1-17	62
	Dt	5	5-22	147
Written on stone tables	°Ex	24	12	66
	Ex	31	18	72
	Ex	32	15-16	73
	Dt	4	13	145
	Dt	9	10	150
Broken by Moses	°Ex	32	19	73
	Dt	9	15-17	150
Replaced by God	°Ex	34	1-4	74
	Dt	10	1-4	150
Put into Ark of Covenant	°Dt	10	5	150
	1 Kgs	8	9	271
Laws transcribed	°Dt	27	1-8	163
	Jos	8	30-32	178
Ratified by Christ and	°Mt	5	17-48	970
Apostles	Mt	22	36-40	989
	Mk	7	9-13	1006
	Mk	10	19	1009
	Rom	13	8-10	1126
	Jas	2	8	1207
Praise of God's Law	°Ps	119	1-176	579
Necessary for eternal life	°Mt	19	17	986

Catholics and Protestants differ on the manner of dividing the Commandments. What the Catholics interpret as the First Commandment, Protestants divide into two separate ones. What Catholics believe are the Ninth and Tenth Commandments, Protestants unite into one.

TENEBRAE. *night, darkness.* An evening service of Holy Week based on the unrevised Office. As Psalms are sung the lights in the church are gradually extinguished (including candles on a multi-branched candlestick). A single candlestick, usually white to distinguish it from the tallow colored others, is removed to symbolize Christ's death. A noise of thunder is made and the Christ candle brought back into church. This symbolizes the Resurrection. For "Tenebrae Hearse" see article "Hearse."

THABORSTAND. A small, movable, often highly ornamented platform on which is placed the monstrance for Exposition of the Blessed Sacrament. This special stand is not an essential, hence is not widely used.

THAUMATURGUS. *wonder-worker.* The title or name given to various saints who had performed many miracles. Perhaps the best example is St. Gregory, Bishop of Neocaesarea, known as St. Gregory Thaumaturgus.

THIRD ORDERS, LAY. Associations of the laity affiliated with certain religious orders, and organized for the personal sanctification of their members, who, though living in the world, desire a more spiritual, Catholic way of life. Third order members follow a rule similar to the dedicated religious, prescribing moderation and decency in every day living; daily office; frequent, if not daily, attendance at Mass; at least monthly confession and reception of the Holy Eucharist; exercise of spiritual and corporal works of mercy; observance of more fast days; attendance at meetings; wearing of the scapular. Members have a habit which is not worn publicly. They share spiritual benefits of their parent religious orders.

The first Third Order was founded in 1221 by St. Francis of Assisi. Today the Third Order Secular of St. Francis is the largest group of its kind. Other third orders are associated with the Augustinians, Carmelites, Dominicans, Franciscans, Minims, Premonstratensians, Servites, and Trinitarians.

Third Order members who live in convents are known as Third Order, Coventuals.

THOMISM. The teachings of St. Thomas Aquinas on philosophy and theology. Canon Law has approved his system in teaching rational philosophy and theology in Catholic schools. However, only the *system* is approved and obligatory, not every one of his teachings. In any particular teaching where noted theologians dispute his idea on a specific theory, Catholics are not bound to follow that particular teaching. Rather, the Church decrees St. Thomas' teachings be taught as norms, fundamentally indicative of the Church's official attitude.

THRONE. 1. A seat of honor occupied by a person of authority. From time immemorial sovereigns have used a decorated chair raised to an elevation for state occasions. Such a seat, or throne, was a symbol of supreme authority and power. The throne was also a figure of the power and majesty of God whose throne is in heaven.

2. An armed chair, usually mounted on a platform in the sanctuary of a cathedral, used by the bishop during solemn religious ceremonies.

3. An elevated platform, also called a thaborstand, on which is placed the monstrance during Exposition of the Blessed Sacrament.

TITULAR SEE. Dioceses in which the faith once flourished but which were overrun by pagans and now no longer are Catholic or in need of a resident bishop. Auxiliary or titular bishops are given titular sees, simply as titles, since they have other duties.

TONSURE. The ceremony in which hair from the upper part of the head is cut, as an indication the recipient has left the ranks of a layman to become a member of the clergy, either as a cleric or a religious. Part of the crown is shaved, and in five places, in front, over each ear, in the back, and on top, the hair is clipped. Tonsure is not a part of either the major or minor orders. It is administered to those students who have begun the study of theology, and as a sacramental, is considered a preparation for Holy Orders. The "shaving" is now more symbolic than real as a few strands are snipped instead.

TOTALITARIANISM. The placing of the state as a divine entity with complete control over all social, economic, religious, and educational activities of the people. The Church condemns such political philosophy, since the state should serve the basic needs of man and not usurp the God-given rights of mankind.

The position of the Church is clearly stated by Pope Pius XII in his encyclical, *Summa Pontificatus*, "To consider the State as something ultimate to which everything else should be subordinated and directed, cannot fail to harm the true and lasting prosperity of nations."

TOTIES QUOTIES. *so often as.* This expression is used with reference to plenary indulgences which may be obtained as often as one desires provided the necessary conditions are fulfilled during the specified time.

TRANSUBSTANTIATION. The change, at the Consecration of the Mass, of the whole substance of bread and wine into the Body and Blood of Christ. The physical appearance of bread and wine remains unchanged. It is defined by the Council of Trent as "the wonderful and singular conversion of the whole substance of the bread into the Body of Christ and of the whole substance of the wine into the Blood, the species of bread and wine alone remaining." It was also declared an article of faith by the Council of Trent, after the 16th century Protestants had denied it.

SUBJECT	BOOK	CHAP.	VERSE	PAGE
Christ's promise	°Mt	26	26-28	993
	Mk	14	22-24	1014
	Lk	22	19-20	1044
	Jn	6	51	1058
Taught by Paul	°1 Cor	10	16	1136
	1 Cor	11	23-29	1137

TRAPPISTS. The popular name for what is properly the Order of Cistercians of the Strict Observance. In 1098 a group of monks led by St. Robert left a Cluniac Benedictine monastery and went to Citeaux, France, to establish the Order of Citeaux, following a stricter observance of the Rule of St. Benedict. From time to time as various laxities occurred, reforms would take place. One of these occurred at LaTrappe, France, under the leadership of Abbot de Rance. In 1892 several Trappist monasteries combined under the present title, Order of Cistercians of the Strict Observance.

In the United States Trappist monasteries may be found in the Archdioceses of Dubuque, Louisville, and Santa Fe, and the Dioceses of Charleston, Kansas City, Richmond, Rochester, Salt Lake City, Savannah-Atlanta, and Worcester.

Trappists lead a strictly cloistered life, devoting their time chiefly to prayer, except for the four to six hours of manual labor they do each day. They eat no meat, fish, or eggs. They maintain silence except during prayers or on very special occasions. Communication with each other is maintained by signs.

TRIDUUM. *space of three days.* A retreat or series of devotions over a period of three days. This usually precedes the celebration of a great feast, such as the Octave of Corpus Christi, the Holy Trinity, or in preparation for First Communion.

TRINITY SUNDAY. The feast of the Blessed Trinity observed by the Western Church on the first Sunday after Pentecost. It was introduced into England by St. Thomas Becket in the Church of Canterbury, and was ordered for the whole Church a century and a half later by Pope John XXII, but it is still unknown in most Eastern Rites.

U

UNCTION. An act of anointing. This is an ancient custom and is mentioned frequently in the Books of Exodus and Leviticus. Oil is the material or liquid used in religious services. Christ signified its importance with reference to the sick when He instituted the Sacrament of the Sick. It is also used at Baptism, Confirmation, etc.

SUBJECT	BOOK	CHAP.	VERSE	PAGE
Holy oil of	°Ex	29	7, 21	70
	Ex	30	22-32	71
	Lv	8	12	86
Altar sanctified with	°Ex	30	25	71
	Ex	40	9-11	80
	Lv	8	10	86
Included in Tabernacle	°Ex	35	15	76
	Lv	8	2	86
	Nm	4	16	109
Made, cared for by priests	°Ex	31	11	72
Sacrament of the Sick	°Jas	5	14	1209

UNDERSTANDING. One of the seven gifts of the Holy Spirit. This gift of understanding enables our intellect to grasp the revealed truths the Holy Mother Church teaches. At Baptism we received these gifts in small measure; at Confirmation they are poured into the soul in fuller form.

UNIAT, UNIATE. An erroneous name given to Catholics belonging to one of the Eastern Rites which recognizes the jurisdiction of the Pope. This designation should not be used since it is held as a term of contempt among certain peoples, and thus may offend the Catholics to whom it may be applied. The Catholic Church does not use this name in any of its documents.

UNION. An association of workers organized for the purpose of improving working conditions and salaries, establishing pension funds, etc., through collective bargaining with management. In return these organizations propose to maintain high-level standards of workmanship and aim to promote loyalty from the employer's viewpoint.

Pope Leo XIII in his encyclical, *Rerum Novarum*, recognized the fact that workers have a natural right to join unions to improve their welfare, and he urged their formation according to high moral standards. In his encyclical, *Quadragesimo Anno*, Pope Pius XI encouraged the workers' associations as being necessary to bring about social and strict justice.

UNITARIANISM. A heretical sect which arose in the 16th century and which is united more through its anti-dogmatic tendency than by its uniformity of belief. Its members deny that Christ is God, considering Him merely a deified man. They reject the Trinity. Religious freedom is stressed; thus, in conformity, the local church is autonomous. Founded by an Italian priest, Laelius Socinus (1525–62), this heresy developed first on the European continent and then spread to England. In the latter part of the 18th century Unitarianism spread to the United States, primarily as a reaction to the dogmatism of the Anglican and Congregationalist sects.

UNITIVE WAY. The third and highest stage of spiritual life in which the soul enters into habitual and intimate union with God through Jesus Christ. The first two states are the *purgative* and *illuminative* ways.

UNITY. *oneness.* One of the four distinguishing marks of the Catholic Church. Christ founded one church. According to His Will, all its members profess the same faith; worship God in the same manner; receive the same sacraments; recognize the same authority, the Vicar of Christ, His Holiness, the Pope, as the head of the Church on earth. The three other marks of the Catholic Church are its *apostolicity, catholicity,* and its *holiness.*

UNIVERSALISM. This heresy arose in England in the 18th century. Its advocates taught there is no hell, no eternal punishment, and that all souls will win salvation. The present day Universalist Church also rejects the Trinity. Baptism and the Lord's Supper are administered, although the reception of the sacraments is not prescribed.

UNLEAVENED BREAD. Wheat bread made without yeast. The pure wheat flour is mixed only with water and baked in an altar bread baker. The resultant hosts are consecrated by the priest at Mass and become the Holy Eucharist. It is also another name for the Feast of the Passover, because it was forbidden to eat leavened bread on the feast and throughout its entire octave.

URBI ET ORBI. Latin words for "to the city and to the world." They refer to the solemn blessing the Pope bestows not only on his immediate audience, but on all the world following his election and at various occasions during the year.

URSULINES, THE. An order of nuns founded in 1537 by St. Angela Merici at Brescia, Italy. These teaching nuns devote their lives to the education of girls.

USUAL CONDITIONS. Conditions over and above the completion of certain prescribed works which necessarily must be fulfilled in order to obtain the indulgences. These requirements are a good confession, the reception of Holy Communion, a visit to a church or public oratory, and prayers for the intention of the Holy Father. The faithful may go to confession within eight days preceding the day on which the good work is completed, the day itself, or the seven days following. Communion may be received on the eve of the day the work is finished, the day itself, or within the following seven days. The praying of one Our Father, Hail Mary, and Glory Be to the Father for the intention of the Pope will fulfill that condition where specified prayers are not listed.

SUBJECT	BOOK	CHAP.	VERSE	PAGE

V

VALID. Based on truth or fact. In Church Law, those conditions which render a sacrament efficacious, that is, a sacrament is valid where the sign instituted or determined by Christ has its effect. These include the prescribed administration by the proper ministers, the moral fitness of the recipient, and the proper intention of both minister and receiver.

VALIDATION. The ecclesiastical process or legal action through which a marriage which has been declared invalid because of a diriment impediment is made valid. First, all requirements must be fulfilled, the necessary dispensations obtained, and the prescribed methods of validation then observed.

VATICAN CITY STATE. The independent state and the seat of the Roman Catholic Church which is located in the city of Rome, Italy. By virtue of the Lateran Treaty of 1929, the Italian government recognizes this independent and officially designated Vatican City State. The pope is the sovereign ruler of this comparatively small territory (less than one square mile in area), possessing all executive, judicial, and legislative powers. Vatican City is perpetually neutral, is bound to no nation, and possesses all sovereign rights, including diplomatic immunity. The official residence of the pope is in the palace which also houses the famed Vatican Library, the archives of the Roman Catholic Church, museums, etc. His Holiness appoints a governor and a council to handle the civil affairs of the Vatican City State and thus can direct his attention to the spiritual welfare of Catholics throughout the world.

VATICAN COUNCIL. The latest ecumenical council, convoked by Pope Pius IX on December 8, 1869, and not yet concluded. On October 20, 1870 it was adjourned because of the invasion of Rome by Italian troops who seized the Papal States. During its convention two constitutions were passed and confirmed by apostolic authority, one on the Catholic faith and its relation to reason, and the other on the primacy of the pope and his infallibility in matters dealing with faith and morals.

VEGETABLES. The principal vegetables of biblical times were cucumbers, beans, lentils, garlic, and onions. Meat was eaten only on special occasions by the masses; vegetables, bread, and wine, then, were the chief sources of food, and herbs, as vegetables were commonly termed, were often exulted.

Herbs held in respect	°Prv	15	17	612

VELUM. The humeral veil. The long vestment worn over the shoulders of the priest during Benediction of the Blessed Sacrament and by the subdeacon at High Mass.

VENERABLE. A title given to one who, by papal decree, has been declared heroically virtuous and whose sanctity has been proved. It is a preliminary step toward the beatification and ultimate canonization of the subject.

VENI CREATOR SPIRITUS. *Come, creating Spirit.* Title and first words of a prayer beseeching the Holy Spirit to enlighten our minds and to strengthen our wills. It is sung at the dedication of churches, consecration of bishops, the election of popes, as well as at certain vespers.

VENIAL SIN. An offense against God in a light matter, or without full consent of the will in a grave matter. Venial sin does not destroy sanctifying grace in the soul thus depriving it of the right to eternal happiness, but it does weaken the soul, consequently disposing it toward more serious sin.

VERONICA'S VEIL. The legendary cloth with which the holy woman in the crowd wiped the face of Jesus as He was carrying the cross on His way to Calvary. Miraculously, His sacred features were imprinted on the veil which now is preserved in St. Peter's in Rome.

It is not known whether the name Veronica is formed from the Greek name, *Berenike*, which means bearing victory; or if the distinguishing epithet, *vera icon* (true image), as applied to Christ's image on the sacred veil, is the basis for the tradition surrounding the name. The Evangelists do not record the name of the woman; yet, she is often identified as the woman with an issue of blood, as the wife of Zacchaeus in France, and as the helper of Peter and Paul in Italy.

The woman with a hem-	°Mt	9	20-22	974
orrhage	Mk	5	25-34	1003

VERSICLE. *little verse.* A short prayer which is followed by a response.

SUBJECT	BOOK	CHAP.	VERSE	PAGE

VESPERS. The evening hour or sixth canonical hour of the Breviary.

VESTMENTS. The distinctive garments worn by the clergy when celebrating Mass or conducting other divine services, such as administering the sacraments. The vestments worn today had their origin in the secular dress worn in the days of the Roman Empire.

VIATICUM. The Latin word meaning "provision for a journey." To us, Viaticum is Holy Communion given to those in probable danger of death. It may be received by the sick without fasting and can be repeated during that same illness whenever there is danger of death. In administering the Holy Viaticum, the priest says these words, "Receive, brother (or sister), the viaticum of the Body of Our Lord Jesus Christ. May He guard thee from the malignant foe, and lead thee to eternal life." The same form is also used for soldiers on the battlefield or prior to a military engagement.

VICAR APOSTOLIC. One appointed by the Holy See to govern a territory which has not yet been established as a diocese. The appointee usually is a titular bishop, although a priest can be selected. Missionary territories comprise most of the present day "vicariates apostolic" as they are called.

VICAR FORANE. A senior priest, usually a pastor, whom the bishop appoints and who is entrusted with vigilance over Church discipline in a particular section or district of his diocese. He has the power to call and preside at meetings of the clergy in that district. He has to report to the bishop on the observance of all canonical and liturgical laws in the area. In some dioceses he is called a "dean."

VICAR GENERAL. A priest appointed by the bishop to help him rule the diocese. Considered the second highest official in the diocese, he has the same powers of jurisdiction as the bishop except insofar as his bishop or Canon Law makes certain exceptions. The bishop may remove him from office at any time. At the death of the bishop, his office automatically is lost.

VICAR OF CHRIST. A title given to the Pope who, as a successor of St. Peter, is the visible head of the Church, the representative of Our Lord, and in whom is invested the spiritual leadership of Catholics throughout the world.

VICARIATE APOSTOLIC. An ecclesiastical section or district of a missionary country to which the Holy See appoints a vicar apostolic as spiritual governor.

VIGIL. A watching; a time of preparation for a feast. Originally it meant a night-long watch with prayer and fasting.

VIGIL LIGHTS OR VOTIVE CANDLES. Small candles burned before a shrine or statue in honor of Our Lord, His Blessed Mother, or the Saints as a sign of continuing devotion to them. They are a symbol of prayer and cannot be construed as prayer itself.

VINCENT DE PAUL, SOCIETY OF ST. A charitable and pious society organized in 1833 by Frederick Ozanam, a University of Paris student, to help combat the tribulations which were a direct result of the Industrial Revolution. Ozanam and his companions selected St. Vincent de Paul for their patron and began visiting the poor and the sick in their homes.

Originally intended as a local group dedicated to helping their fellow men to lead Christian lives, the fame of their good works spread and the Society expanded to Rome, Italy, England, Ireland, and, in 1845, to the United States. The works of the Society today include: spiritual and material aid to inmates of hospitals and institutions; care of poor and neglected children; religious instruction of public school students; country vacations for underprivileged; providing books for parochial students unable to buy their own; providing Christian burial for the poor and friendless; furnishing food and shelter for homeless transients; and many other corporal works of mercy.

Popes Gregory XVI, Pius IX, Leo XIII, St. Pius X, Benedict XV, Pius XI, and Pius XII have praised and encouraged the Society, heavily endowing it with indulgences. Active membership is restricted to practical Catholic men over eighteen years of age. Attendance of at least three weekly meetings of the Conference each month is compulsory, as is a weekly visit to a poor family or families assigned to them. The Society also includes honorary members whose contribution consists of monetary aid annually donated so that the work of the association may be continued.

SUBJECT	BOOK	CHAP.	VERSE	PAGE

VIOLATION. The act whereby a church, chapel, or cemetery is desecrated because one of the following crimes is committed within: homicide and suicide; any sinful shedding of blood; using the church for impious acts; burial of a sentenced and condemned excommunicant; burial of an infidel.

VIOLET. A liturgical color more commonly referred to as purple. It is a color reserved for penitential seasons and times of sadness.

VIRGIN BIRTH OF CHRIST. A dogma of the Church which states that Christ, the Son of God, was conceived of the Holy Spirit and was born of the Virgin Mary who remained a virgin before the conception, during, and after His birth. Luke repeatedly stressed that the betrothed Mary was still a virgin at the time of the Annunciation to her. The account of Matthew is in perfect agreement with that of Luke—that Mary was with child from the Holy Spirit before she lived with her betrothed, Joseph. Although the other two evangelists omit this information they do mention the Heavenly Father of Jesus, and thus presuppose His virgin birth.

SUBJECT	BOOK	CHAP.	VERSE	PAGE
Predicted by Isaiah	°Is	7	14	722
Virgin's name, Mary	°Lk	1	27	1020
By power of Holy Spirit	°Lk	1	35	1020
	Mt	1	18	966
Jesus Christ, the Son of	°Mk	1	1	999
God	Mk	1	11	999
	Jn	1	1-14	1050

VISITATION, EPISCOPAL. The obligation the bishop or his delegate has to visit each church and religious institution in his diocese every five years.

VITANDUS. The name given to an excommunicant, part of whose penalty is that he be avoided by the faithful. Only the Holy See has the authority to declare any one *vitandi.* One so condemned cannot attend any church services; any worship in progress must cease when a vitandus enters. Neither can he receive Christian burial.

VOTIVE MASS. A Mass which does not correspond with the office of the day but which is said at the discretion of the celebrant. Except on all Sundays, feast days of double rank, and certain other specified days, the priest may say the Mass of the Angels, Mass of the Trinity, Mass for the Dead, etc., instead of that prescribed for the day.

VULGATE. The official Latin version of the Holy Bible authorized by the Catholic Church as authentic. It is founded on St. Jerome's 4th century Latin translation of the Hebrew and Chaldee originals.

W

WAKE. The vigil or watch kept over a corpse before its burial. In its modern conception, a Catholic wake is a gathering of relatives and friends to pray for the soul of the deceased and to offer condolences to the bereaved family. It is not intended to be a cause for immoderate drinking and excessive eating, abuses which caused ecclesiastical disapproval in olden times. Properly observed by prayer and consolation, wakes are commendable.

A recitation of Psalms and other prayers from the Office of the Dead, Ritual, and Masses of the Dead sometimes called a "Bibil Vigil" or "Bible Wake" has recently been introduced a pious custom.

WHITE. A liturgical color symbolizing holiness, joy, and purity. White vestments are worn on Feasts of Our Lord, the Blessed Virgin Mary, angels, confessors, virgins, All Saints, the Trinity, Nativity of St. John the Baptizer, on the Sundays and ferial days of the Paschal season, and at funerals of infants.

WHITSUNDAY. The name used in England for the Feast of Pentecost; literally, White Sunday. The name is derived from the white garments worn in earlier times by those who received the Sacrament of Baptism on the eve, or vigil, of the Feast of Pentecost.

WORKS OF MERCY, CORPORAL. Those Christian deeds of charity performed to relieve the bodily needs of one's neighbor. They are: 1. to feed the hungry; 2. to give drink to the thirsty; 3. to clothe the naked; 4. to shelter the homeless; 5. to visit the sick; 6. to visit the imprisoned; 7. to bury the dead.

WORKS OF MERCY, SPIRITUAL. Those Christian deeds of spiritual charity performed to relieve the soul of one's neighbors. They are: 1. to counsel the doubtful; 2. to instruct the ignorant; 3. to admonish the sinner; 4. to comfort the sorrowful; 5. to forgive offenses; 6. to bear wrongs patiently; 7. to pray for the living and the dead.

WORLD, END OF. On many occasions Christ prophesied the end of the world—of heaven and earth—referring to its renovation and purification rather than to its destruction or annihilation.

Heaven and earth to pass	°Mt	24	35	991
away	Lk	21	33	1043

X

XANTHICUS. A Macedonian month that corresponds to the Hebrew month of Nisan (March/April).

A Macedonian month	°2 Mc	11	30	456

XEROPHAGY. A particular type of strict fast in which only bread, salt, water, and certain vegetables can be eaten. The Greek name, Xerophagy, literally translated means dry food.

XERXES I. A Persian king to be identified with Assuerus, the husband of Vashti and later of Esther. In the second year of his reign, Xerxes I (485–465) marched against Egypt and subdued this land; he invaded Greece in 480 B.C., but his army was defeated and returned to Susa. Esther was made queen in the seventh year of his reign.

Husband of Vashti	°Est	1	10-11	409
Esther becomes his wife	°Est	2	15-18	410

Y

YAHWEH. The proper name of the God of Israel. The name Yahweh was used to express the nature of God, while other names stressed His various attributes. Yahweh is called the "tetragrammaton" from the four consonants YHWH employed in the Hebrew. It was God's name as it was revealed to Moses, and was translated by the writers of the Septuagint as *Kyrios,* Lord. God's proper name was "I am who am," but Israel was to address Him, *Yahweh,* "He is." This expresses God's absolute and unchangeable Being in all His perfection.

Revealed to Moses	°Ex	3	14-15	48

YEAR. 1. The Jewish year was lunar and consisted normally of 354 days, or twelve months of alternately 29 and 30 days. The difference between the lunar and solar year was eleven days; so, a thirteenth or intercalary month, called Veadar, was added every second or third year. The insertion of this thirteenth month was determined by the growth of the barley, so that the ripe barley could be offered as first fruits during the Feast of the Passover. The religious year began with the first day of Nisan (March/April); whereas the civil new year began on the first of Tishri (September/October).

2. Jubilee Year. The 50th year, which occurred after seven times seven years, or forty-nine years, had been counted from the institution of the Jubilee, or from the last Jubilee celebration. It was proclaimed on the 10th of Tishri, that is, the Day of Atonement. During this year, the whole land rested and was not to be cultivated.

3. Sabbatical Year. Every seventh year, which meant a year's rest for the entire land. Beginning in the autumn, no field was to be cultivated or sown. This was to remind the Israelites that the land belonged to God.

Z

ZEDEKIAH. The last king of Judah (597–586 B.C.). He was the third son of King Josiah and uncle of King Jehoiachin. His name originally was Mattaniah, but it was changed to Zedekiah when Nebuchadnezzar appointed him king. He was a weak monarch, and although he could have benefited from the counsel of Jeremiah he did not take the prophet seriously.

In 589 Zedekiah revolted from the Babylonian ruler and allied himself with the Egyptians and neighboring nations. In the next year Nebuchadnezzar collected his forces and laid siege to Jerusalem. The city held out for about two years, but was finally forced to capitulate. Zedekiah was captured; his sons were slain in his presence; his own eyes were put out; and he was imprisoned in Babylon until his death.

SUBJECT	BOOK	CHAP.	VERSE	PAGE
King of Judah	°2 Kgs	24	17	308
Ruled wickedly	°2 Chr	36	10-14	360
Warned by Jeremiah	°Jer	27	12-22	806
Captured and blinded	°2 Kgs	25	1-7	308

ZENAS. A Christian lawyer who was commended by Paul to Titus as an aid in the work at Crete.

SUBJECT	BOOK	CHAP.	VERSE	PAGE
Recommended to serve at Crete	°Ti	3	13	1190

ZEPHANIAH. 1. A Minor Prophet who prophesied in the early days of Josiah (640–609 B.C.). He was a contemporary of Jeremiah and Nahum and prophesied against the idolatry and injustices of the times.

SUBJECT	BOOK	CHAP.	VERSE	PAGE
Prophecy of	°Zep	1-3		945-947

2. The son of Maaseiah and priest during the time of Zedekiah, king of Judah. He was sent twice by the king with important messages to Jeremiah, the prophet. After the destruction of the temple, he was put to death by Nebuchadnezzar.

SUBJECT	BOOK	CHAP.	VERSE	PAGE
A priest	°2 Kgs	25	18	308
Messenger to Jeremiah	°Jer	21	1	799
	Jer	37	3	816
Put to death by Nebuchadnezzar	°Jer	52	24-27	832

ZERAH. 1. The son of Reuel and grandson of Esau; an Edomean chieftain.

SUBJECT	BOOK	CHAP.	VERSE	PAGE
Son of Reuel	°Gn	36	13	32
	1 Chr	1	37	310

2. The son of Judah and Tamar; his twin brother was Pharez. Over 600 of Zerah's descendants returned to Jerusalem after the Captivity.

SUBJECT	BOOK	CHAP.	VERSE	PAGE
Son of Judah and Tamar	°Gn	38	30	34
	1 Chr	2	4	311
Mentioned in genealogy of Christ	°Mt	1	3	966
Founded Zerahites	°Nm	26	20	131
Over 600 descendants returned to Jerusalem after Captivity	°1 Chr	9	6	318

ZERESH. The wife of Haman, who was vizier at the court of Ahasuerus. Although Zeresh influenced her husband to hang Mordecai upon a gibbet, she later warned Haman that Mordecai was a Jew and could not be dispensed with so readily.

SUBJECT	BOOK	CHAP.	VERSE	PAGE
Haman prepares gibbet for Mordecai	°Est	5	14	413
Haman warned against harm to Mordecai	°Est	6	13	414

ZERUBBABEL. The grandson of Jeconiah and a descendant of David and Solomon. He with Joshua headed the list of the twelve leaders who returned to Palestine in 535 B.C. after the Babylonian Exile. In the second year of their return, Zerubbabel and Joshua began to collect material for the construction of the second temple, and after several delays due to the opposition of the Samaritans, the temple was completed and solemnly dedicated in 516 B.C. Nothing further is known of Zerubbabel's life.

SUBJECT	BOOK	CHAP.	VERSE	PAGE
Grandson of Jeconiah	°1 Chr	3	17-19	312
Descendant of David and Solomon	°1 Chr	3	1-19	312
Returned from Babylonian Exile	°Ezr	2	2	362
	Neh	7	7	374
Collected materials for second Temple	°Ezr	3	8	363
Completed second Temple 516 B.C.	°Ezr	5-6		364-365
	Hg	1-2		948-949
	Zec	4	6-10	952

ZIKLAG. A city in the southern section of Judah assigned to the tribe of Simeon. At the time of King Saul it was occupied by the Philistine king, Achish of Gath, who entrusted it to David after his flight from Saul. David resided there until the death of Saul.

SUBJECT	BOOK	CHAP.	VERSE	PAGE
Assigned to tribe of Simeon	°Jos	19	5	186
	1 Chr	4	30	313
Entrusted to David	°1 Sm	27	5-6	239
Destroyed by Amalekites	°1 Sm	30	1-20	240

ZILPAH. A maidservant of Leah, the daughter of Laban. Laban gave Zilpah to Leah at the time of her marriage to Jacob; and later Leah gave her as a concubine to Jacob. Zilpah then gave birth to Gad and Asher.

SUBJECT	BOOK	CHAP.	VERSE	PAGE
A maidservant of Leah	°Gn	29	24	25
Leah gives Zilpah to Jacob	°Gn	30	9	26
The mother of Gad and Asher	°Gn	35	26	32

ZIMRAN. The eldest of the nine sons of Abraham and Keturah whose name probably means "antelope." His descendants are not listed in the Old Testament.

SUBJECT	BOOK	CHAP.	VERSE	PAGE
Eldest son of Abraham and Ketutah	°Gn	25	2	21
	1 Chr	1	32	310

ZION. A hill located in the southeastern part of Jerusalem. It was originally a Jebusite fortification, but it was captured by David and called the City of David. After the building of the temple, the city and the temple were called Zion; thus, Jerusalem came to be known as "the daughter of Zion," and the term "Zion" was applied to all the people of Israel. In the New Testament, Zion served as a type of Messianic Kingdom.

SUBJECT	BOOK	CHAP.	VERSE	PAGE
Captured by David	°2 Sm	5	7-9	246
Ark brought here	°2 Sm	6	1-19	247
Called holy mountain	°Ps	2	6	495
Jerusalem, daughter of Zion	°Ps	9A	15	499
	Ps	73	28	543
	Sg	3	11	640
	Is	1	8	717
	Jer	4	31	782

ZIPPORAH. A daughter of Jethro or Reuel, she was the wife of Moses and mother of Gershom and Eliezer. Zipporah adopted Israelite customs and accompanied her husband to Egypt. At the time of the Exodus, Moses sent his wife and two sons to visit Jethro, but the family was later reunited in the desert.

SUBJECT	BOOK	CHAP.	VERSE	PAGE
Mother of Gershom and Eliezer	°Ex	2	16-22	48
	Ex	18	3-4	61
A Cushite	°Nm	12	1	117
Returned to Moses	°Ex	18	2-6	61

ZOAN. An ancient Egyptian town on the eastern Nile Delta. It was founded about the time of Abraham, and it is known that the miraculous interventions by which the Israelites were freed from Egyptian bondage took place near Tanis. There is nothing left of its great splendor, as five years after the Babylonians seized Jerusalem, they marched to the Delta and laid waste to the towns of the Nile.

SUBJECT	BOOK	CHAP.	VERSE	PAGE
Ancient Egyptian city	°Nm	13	23	118
Moses worked miracles at	°Ps	78	12, 43	547
Princes of, reproached	°Is	19	11-15	732
	Is	30	1-7	742

ZOAR. One of the cities of the Pentapolis; it was also called Bela. Lot interceded for Zoar and there he found a safe refuge. In a cave on a nearby hill, he and his daughters lived after the destruction of Sodom.

SUBJECT	BOOK	CHAP.	VERSE	PAGE
Also called Bela	°Gn	14	2	12
Saved by Lot	°Gn	19	20-23	16

ZOBAH. An Aramaean Kingdom in Syria between the Euphrates and the Orontes. King David (1012–972 B.C.) succeeded in defeating Hadadezer of Zobah and occupying Damascus, an ally of Zobah. About the time of Solomon, Zobah declined and leadership passed to Damascus.

SUBJECT	BOOK	CHAP.	VERSE	PAGE
Hostile to King Saul	°1 Sm	14	47	226
David defeated Zobah and occupied Damascus	°2 Sm	8	1-12	248
	2 Sm	10	1-19	249

ZOPHAR. The third friend of Job, a Naamathite. He judges Job most severely, intensifying the previous accusations of Bildad. He is, however, admonished by God just as were his two friends.

SUBJECT	BOOK	CHAP.	VERSE	PAGE
Third friend of Job	°Jb	11	1-20	470
	Jb	42	7-10	493

ZUCCHETTO. The small skull cap worn by bishops and other prelates. Originally it was designed to cover the tonsure; today, however, it has become a sign of dignity.